S0-CBU-204

Encyclopedia of Major Marketing Campaigns

VOLUME 2

Highlights

This second volume of *Encyclopedia of Major Marketing Campaigns (EMMC)* profiles 474 of the most notable advertising and marketing initiatives of the twentieth and twenty-first centuries, including:

- Aflac's "Duck"
- California Milk Processor Board's "Got Milk"
- Dell's "Dude, You're Getting a Dell"
- Geico's "Gecko"
- General Motors's "Looking for Mr. Goodwrench"
- Hewlett-Packard's "You + HP"
- Mastercard International's "Priceless"
- Old Navy's "Retro 70s"
- PepsiCo's "Generation Next"
- Taco Bell's "Think Outside the Bun"
- Unilever PLC's "Campaign for Real Beauty"
- United Parcel Service's "What Can Brown Do For You?"

EMMC covers campaigns that were important for their innovation, for their effectiveness in selling products or services, or for the significance of their companies. It also focuses on products or services that changed how we view consumer brands, had positive or negative social significance, and/or affected our lifestyles in some far-reaching way. Information in each chapter is easily accessed under the headings Historical Context, Target Market, Competition, Marketing Strategy, and Outcome.

INCLUDES PHOTOS AND DESCRIPTIVE SIDEBARS

Enhancing the text are pertinent and interesting visual elements. There are close to 150 reproductions of television and print advertisements and more than 500 sidebars. A valuable addition, the photos lend context to the data featured within the chapters while the sidebars provide anecdotal statistics and unusual incidents and facts.

ADDITIONAL FEATURES

- Companies are arranged alphabetically
- Campaigns represent a wide variety of marketing strategies, such as branding and direct mail, and were featured in various media, including television, radio, and print
- The Index organizes essays under broad subject and topic headings, as well as lists company and product names, key advertising agencies, and people
- Further Reading sections suggest avenues for continued study
- *EMMC, Volume 2* perfectly complements the first volume of *Encyclopedia of Major Marketing Campaigns*, published in 1999.

A valuable addition to Gale's business resource collection, *EMMC* is the only publication of its kind that provides detailed commentary on major marketing campaigns throughout the twentieth and twenty-first centuries.

Encyclopedia of Major Marketing Campaigns

VOLUME 2

Thomas Riggs

EDITOR

THOMSON
GALE™

Detroit • New York • San Francisco • New Haven, Conn. • Waterville, Maine • London

Encyclopedia of Major Marketing Campaigns, Volume 2

Thomas Riggs, Editor

Associate Editors
Mariko Fujinaka, Patrick Hutchins

Chief Line Editor
Robert Rauch

Line Editors
Laura Gabler, Anne Healey

Proofreaders
Kimberly Burton, Jennifer Zielinski

Thomson Gale Project Editors
Jacqueline K. Mueckenheim, Holly Selden

Thomson Gale Editorial Staff
Miranda Ferrara, Kristy A. Swartout

Technical Support
Luann Brennan, Mike Weaver

Indexing Services
Laurie Andriot

Rights and Acquisitions
Margaret Chamberlain-Gaston, Sue Rudolph

Imaging and Multimedia
Leitha Etheridge-Sims, Lezlie Light, Michael Logusz, Audrey Pettengill, Kelly Quin, Robyn Young

Composition and Electronic Prepress
Evi Seoud

Manufacturing
Wendy Blurton

© 2007 Thomson Gale, a part of The Thomson Corporation.

Thomson and Star Logo are trademarks and Gale is a registered trademark used herein under license.

For more information, contact
Thomson Gale
27500 Drake Rd.
Farmington Hills, MI 48331-3535
Or you can visit our Internet site at
http://www.gale.com

ALL RIGHTS RESERVED
No part of this work covered by the copyright hereon may be reproduced or used in any form or by any means—graphic, electronic, or mechanical, including photocopying, recording, taping, Web distribution, or information storage retrieval systems—without the written permission of the publisher.

This publication is a creative work fully protected by all applicable copyright laws, as well as by misappropriation, trade secret, unfair competition, and other applicable laws. The authors and editors of this work have added value to the underlying factual material herein through one or more of the following: unique and original selection, coordination, expression, arrangement, and classification of the information.

For permission to use material from this product, submit your request via Web at http://www.gale-edit.com/permissions, or you may download our Permissions Request form and submit your request by fax or mail to:

Permissions Department
Thomson Gale
27500 Drake Rd.
Farmington Hills, MI 48331-3535
Permissions Hotline:
248-699-8006 or 800-877-4253, ext. 8006
Fax: 248-699-8074 or 800-762-4058

Since this page cannot legibly accommodate all copyright notices, the acknowledgments constitute an extension of the copyright notice.

While every effort has been made to ensure the reliability of the information presented in this publication, Thomson Gale does not guarantee the accuracy of the data contained herein. Thomson Gale accepts no payment for listing; and inclusion in the publication of any organization, agency, institution, publication, service, or individual does not imply endorsement of the publisher. Errors brought to the attention of the publisher and verified to the satisfaction of the publisher will be corrected in future editions.

LIBRARY OF CONGRESS CATALOGING-IN-PUBLICATION DATA

Encyclopedia of major marketing campaigns, volume 2 / Thomas Riggs, editor.
p. cm.
Includes bibliographical references and index.
ISBN-13: 978-0-7876-7356-7 (hardcover)
ISBN-10: 0-7876-7356-0 (hardcover)
1. Advertising campaigns – United States – History – 20th century. I. Riggs, Thomas, 1963 – .
HF5837.E53 1999
658.1'0973 – dc21
99 – 31858

This title is also available as an e-book.
ISBN-13: 978-1-4144-0607-7, ISBN-10: 1-4144-0607-X
Contact your Thomson Gale sales representative for ordering information.

Printed in the United States of America
10 9 8 7 6 5 4 3 2 1

Contents

Advisors and Contributors XV
Foreword XVII
Introduction XXI

A

A & E Television Networks
In Case You Missed It Campaign . . . 1
ABC, Inc.
TV Is Good Campaign . . . 5
Abercrombie & Fitch
A & F Quarterly Campaign . . . 9
Accenture, Ltd.
I Am Your Idea Campaign . . . 15
adidas America, Inc.
Runners. Yeah, We're Different Campaign . . . 19
adidas-Salomon AG
Impossible Is Nothing Campaign . . . 23
Yankee Fans Campaign . . . 26
The Advertising Council, Inc.
Campaign for Freedom Campaign . . . 31
Aflac, Inc.
The Aflac Duck (2000) Campaign . . . 35
The Broken Leg Campaign . . . 38
AirTran Holdings, Inc.
Go. There's Nothing Stopping You Campaign . . . 43
Allied Domecq PLC
Loosen Up a Little Campaign . . . 47
The Allstate Corporation
Our Stand Campaign . . . 51
Altria Group Inc.
It's a Woman Thing Campaign . . . 55
Amazon.com, Inc.
Amazon Theater Campaign . . . 59
America Online, Inc.
AOL Latino Campaign . . . 63
Welcome to the World Wide Wow Campaign . . . 66
American Apparel Inc.
American Apparel Campaign . . . 71
American Civil Liberties Union
Racial Profiling Campaign . . . 75
American Express Company
Competitive Campaign . . . 79
Do More Campaign . . . 82
Seinfeld Campaign . . . 86
American Honda Motor Company
What About Now? Campaign . . . 91
American Legacy Foundation
Truth Campaign . . . 97
Americans for the Arts
Art. Ask for More Campaign . . . 101
Anheuser-Busch Companies, Inc.
Beer... or Michelob? Campaign . . . 105
Frogs Campaign . . . 108
I Love You, Man Campaign . . . 112
Louie the Lizard Campaign . . . 116
Oh, and Beware of the Penguins Campaign . . . 120
Real American Heroes/Real Men of Genius Campaign . . . 123
Whassup?! Campaign . . . 126
Apple Computer, Inc.
iMac Campaign . . . 131
Silhouette Campaign . . . 135

Switchers Campaign 138
Think Different Campaign 141

AT&T Inc.
Carrot Top Campaign 147
It's All Within Your Reach Campaign. 150
Privacy Manager Campaign 153

Audi of America, Inc.
Art of the Heist Campaign 157

B

Barclays Global Investors
New School Campaign 161

The Basketball Club of Seattle, LLC
In Your Home Campaign 165

Bayerische Motoren Werke AG
Counterfeit Campaign 169
Mini Robots Campaign 172
The Hire Campaign 175

BC Dairy Foundation
Don't Take Your Body for Granted Campaign. 181

Binney & Smith
Make Play Campaign 187

The Body Shop International PLC
Ruby Campaign 191

Borders Group, Inc.
This Season, It's the Original Thought That Counts Campaign 195

Boston Beer Company, Inc.
It's What's Inside Campaign 199

Boston Market Corp.
Eat Something Campaign 203

Brigham's, Inc.
Reverse the Curse Campaign. 207

Budget Rent A Car System, Inc.
Up Your Budget Campaign 211

Bureau of Engraving and Printing
The New Color of Money Campaign 215

Burger King Corp.
Lunch Break Campaign 219
Subservient Chicken Campaign. 222
When You Have It Your Way, It Just Tastes Better Campaign 225

Business Leaders for Sensible Priorities
Move Our Money Campaign 229

C

Cadbury Adams USA LLC
Four Out of Five Dentists Campaign 233

Cadbury Schweppes Americas Beverages
Bottles Personified Campaign 237
Go for Zero Campaign 240

California Department of Health Services, Tobacco Control Section
Antitobacco Campaign 243
Tobacco Control Section Media Campaign. 248

California Milk Advisory Board
Happy Cows Campaign 253

California Milk Processor Board
Got Milk? Campaign 257

Calvin Klein Cosmetics Company
cK be Campaign. 261

Campbell Soup Company
Goldfish Crackers Campaign 265
Make It Campbell's Instead Campaign 268

Canadian Film Centre
2004 Toronto Worldwide Short Film Festival Campaign. 273

Canon U.S.A., Inc.
85 Second Photo Lab Campaign. 277

CareerBuilder Inc.
Time to Move On Campaign 281

Cargill, Inc.
Collaborate>Create>Succeed Campaign. 285

Carl's Jr.
Six Dollar Burger Campaign. 289

Carnival Corporation
Fun Ships Campaign 293

Cellco Partnership
Can You Hear Me Now? Campaign 297

The Charles Schwab Corporation
Smarter Investor Campaign. 301

Chevron Corporation
A World of Energy Campaign 305

Church & Dwight Company, Inc.
Trojan Man Campaign 311

Church's Chicken
Full Flavor, Full Pockets, Full Life/Full Flavor, Full Pockets Campaign. 317

Cisco Systems, Inc.
The Self-Defending Network Campaign 321

Citibank
Identity Theft Solutions Campaign 325

Citigroup Inc.
Live Richly Campaign. 329

Clairol, Inc.
Totally Organic Campaign 333

CNS, Inc.
Back in the Sack Campaign 337

The Coca-Cola Company
Keep Playing Campaign 341
Obey Your Thirst Campaign (1998). 344
Obey Your Thirst Campaign (2004). 347
Real Campaign. 350
You Are What You Drink Campaign 353

Columbia Sportswear Company
Mother Boyle Campaign 359
ConAgra Foods' Feeding Children Better Foundation
Child Hunger Campaign 363
Conseco, Inc.
Protect/Create Wealth Campaign 367
Cunard Line Limited
Can You Wait? Campaign 371
CVS Corporation
Life to the Fullest Campaign. 375
Cyan Worlds Inc.
Riven Campaign 379

D

DaimlerChrysler Corp.
Employee Pricing Plan Plus Campaign 383
Engineered to Be Great Cars Campaign 386
Jeep Campaign 389
There's Only One Campaign 392
Darden Restaurants, Inc.
Life on Land Is Dry Campaign. 395
Davidson Development Inc.
Repositioning Campaign. 399
Dell Inc.
Dude, You're Getting a Dell Campaign 403
Delta Air Lines, Inc.
Let Yourself Fly Campaign 407
On Top of the World Campaign 411
The Passenger's Airline Campaign. 414
DHL Holdings (USA), Inc.
Competition. Bad for Them. Great for You. Campaign. 419
Diageo plc
Keep Walking Campaign 423
Not Everything in Black and White Makes Sense Campaign. 426
Dial-A-Mattress
Always Out There Campaign 431
The Dial Corporation
You're Not as Clean as You Think Campaign. 435
Diamond Foods, Inc.
Emerald Nuts Marketing Campaign 439
The Diamond Trading Company
Raise Your Right Hand Campaign 443
DirecTV Group, Inc.
Celebrities Read Fan Mail to DirecTV (Become a DirecTV Fan Now) Campaign 447
Discovery Communications, Inc.
Two Guys Campaign 451
Doctor's Associates Inc.
Jared Fogle Campaign. 455
Dr. Martens Airwair USA LLC
Beliefs Campaign 459
Dr Pepper/Seven Up, Inc.
This Is the Taste Campaign 463
Dreyer's Grand Ice Cream Holdings, Inc.
Unbelievable Campaign 467
drugstore.com, inc.
A Very Healthy Way to Shop Campaign 471
Dyson Ltd.
Doesn't Lose Suction Campaign 475

E

Eastman Kodak Company
Advantix Campaign 479
The Best Part of Photography Is the Prints Campaign. 482
Take Pictures. Further. Campaign. 485
Tall Tales Campaign. 488
eBay Inc.
Abbreviated Campaign 493
eBay 2004 Television Campaign. 496
Electronic Data Systems
Cat Herders Campaign .501
Eli Lilly and Company
Prozac Print Campaign. 505
Energizer Holdings, Inc.
Bunny Chasers Campaign. 509
ESPN, Inc.
The Rick Campaign 513
This Is SportsCenter Campaign 517
Without Sports Campaign 520
E*TRADE Financial Corp.
Monkey Trilogy Campaign. 525
Why Wouldn't You? Campaign 528
Euromarket Design, Inc.
Crate & Barrel 1998 Print Ads Campaign 533

F

FedEx Corp.
Be Absolutely Sure Campaign. 537
Our Office Is Your Office Campaign 541
Relax, It's Fedex Campaign. 544
The Way the World Works Campaign 547
Fila USA
Grant Hill 4 Campaign 551
Ford Motor Company
Driving American Innovation Campaign. 555
Life in Drive Campaign 558
Storytelling Campaign .561
Fortune Brands, Inc.
Sign Boy Campaign 565
Foster's Group Limited
How to Speak Australian Campaign 569

Fox Entertainment Group, Inc.
NHL on FOX Campaign 575
French Connection Group PLC
Scent to Bed Campaign 579
Frito-Lay Inc.
The Loudest Taste on Earth Campaign 583
Fuji Photo Film U.S.A., Inc.
Meet the Greens Campaign 587

G
Game Show Network
You Know You Know Campaign 591
Gap Inc.
For Every Generation Campaign 595
How Do You Wear It? Campaign 598
Khakis Campaign 601
This Is Easy Campaign 605
Gateway, Inc.
People Rule Campaign 609
GEICO
Gecko Campaign 613
Good News Campaign 616
Mini-Campaigns 618
General Electric Co.
Imagination at Work Campaign 623
General Mills, Inc.
Stories Campaign 627
General Motors Corporation
An American Revolution Campaign 631
Break Through Campaign 634
The Caddy that Zigs Campaign 638
EV1 Introduction Campaign 641
Hummer Campaign 645
Looking for Mr. Goodwrench Campaign 648
Start Something Campaign 652
Gill Foundation
Turnout Campaign 657
GlaxoSmithKline plc
Power to Quit Campaign 661
Social Anxiety Disorder Campaign 665
Global Gillette
Anything Else Would Be Uncivilized Campaign 669
Go Daddy Software, Inc.
Godaddy.Com Super Bowl Commercial Campaign 675
The Goodyear Tire & Rubber Company
On the Wings of Goodyear Campaign 679
William Grant & Sons Ltd.
Single Malt Campaign 683

H
H&R Block, Inc.
Worried about Bill Campaign 687
Hallmark Cards, Inc.
Sneak a Peek Campaign 691
Hardee's Food Systems, Inc.
Revolution Campaign 697
Harley-Davidson Motor Company
The Book of Harley-Davidson Campaign 701
Heineken USA Inc.
It's All About the Beer Campaign 705
The Hershey Company
The Crisp You Can't Resist! Campaign 709
There's No Wrong Way to Eat a Reese's Campaign 712
Hewlett-Packard Company
Built by Engineers, Used by Ordinary People Campaign 717
Expanding Possibilities Campaign 720
You + HP Campaign 723
Hilton Hotels Corporation
It Happens at the Hilton Campaign 729
Hollywood Entertainment Corporation
Welcome to Hollywood Campaign 733
Home Box Office, Inc.
It's Not T.V. It's HBO Campaign 737
Honda Motor Company
The Power of Dreams Campaign 741
Honda UK
Grrr Campaign 745

I
Iconix Brand Group, Inc.
Jenny McCarthy for Candie's Campaign 749
IKEA International A/S
Unböring Campaign 755
InBev USA
Grab a Rock Campaign 759
ING Groep N.V.
ING Launch Campaign 763
Intel Corporation
Bunny People Campaign 767
Time for a Pentium II Processor? Campaign 771
Intercontinental Hotels Group PLC
Holiday Inn Brand Rejuvenation Campaign 777
Stay Smart Campaign 780
International Business Machines Corp.
Can You See It? Campaign 785
E-Business Campaign 788
Gizmo Campaign 791
Linux Campaign 794
Solutions for a Small Planet Campaign 797
Isuzu Motors America, Inc.
The Call Campaign 803

J

J.C. Penney Company, Inc.
It's All Inside Campaign . . . 807

Jack in the Box, Inc.
Jack's Back Campaign . . . 811

Jenny Craig, Inc.
Kirstie Alley Campaign . . . 815

JetBlue Airways Corporation
JetBlue Launch Campaign . . . 819

John Hancock Financial Services Inc.
Insurance for the Unexpected. Investments for the Opportunities. Campaign (1996) . . . 823
Insurance for the Unexpected. Investments for the Opportunities. Campaign (2000) . . . 826

K

Kellogg Company
Gotta Have My Pops Campaign . . . 831
Special K Kick-Start Diet Plan Campaign . . . 834

KFC Corp.
Chicken Capital USA Campaign . . . 839

Kimberly-Clark Corporation
Kleenex Anti-Viral Campaign . . . 843

Kmart Corp.
Kmart Joe Boxer Launch Campaign . . . 847
Martha Stewart Everyday Campaign . . . 850
Rosie O'Donnell and Penny Marshall Campaign . . . 854

Kraft Foods, Inc.
It's How to Unplug Campaign . . . 859
It's Not Delivery, It's DiGiorno Campaign . . . 862

L

Labatt USA
Rolling Rock Ads Campaign . . . 867

Las Vegas Convention & Visitors Authority
Vegas Stories Campaign . . . 871

La-Z-Boy Inc.
The New Look of Comfort Campaign . . . 875

LeapFrog Enterprises, Inc.
Learn Something New Every Day! Campaign . . . 879

Levi Strauss & Co.
It's Wide Open Campaign . . . 883
Levi's Type 1 Jeans Campaign . . . 886
They Go On Campaign . . . 889

Lincoln National Corp.
Hello Future Campaign . . . 893

Little Caesar Enterprises, Inc.
Cloning Campaign . . . 897
Grand Canyon Campaign . . . 900
Safety Video Campaign . . . 903
Talking Pizzas Campaign . . . 906

Logitech International S.A.
What Will You Do with All That Freedom? Campaign . . . 911

Lycos, Inc.
Go Get It Campaign . . . 915

M

Mail Boxes Etc., Inc.
See Your Small Business on the Super Bowl Campaign . . . 919

Malden Mills Industries, Inc.
Forward Fabric Campaign . . . 923

Marriott International
Never Underestimate the Importance of a Good Night's Rest Campaign . . . 927

Mars, Inc.
The Energy You Crave Campaign . . . 931
Inner Beast Campaign . . . 934
M&M's New Millennium Campaigns . . . 937
Snickers Cruncher Campaign . . . 940

Maryland State Lottery Agency
Cash in Hand Campaign . . . 945

MasterCard International
Priceless Campaign . . . 949

Mattel, Inc.
Play. Laugh. Grow. Campaign . . . 953

McDonald's Corporation
Campaign 55 Campaign . . . 957
Did Somebody Say McDonald's? Campaign . . . 960
I'm Lovin' It Campaign . . . 964
We Love to See You Smile Campaign . . . 967

MCI LLC
1-800-Collect Campaign . . . 971
Dennis Miller Ads Campaign . . . 974

McIlhenny Company
Mosquito Campaign . . . 979

Mercedes-Benz USA, LLC
Mercedes-Benz Corporate Branding Campaign . . . 983
Passion Campaign . . . 987
Smooth Ride Campaign . . . 990
Unlike Any Other Campaign . . . 994

MetLife, Inc.
MetLife Helps You Make Sense of It All Campaign . . . 997

Microsoft Corp.
It's Good to Play Together Campaign . . . 1001
Where Do You Want to Go Today? Campaign . . . 1004

Midas, Inc.
Trust the Midas Touch Campaign . . . 1009

Mike's Hard Lemonade Company
Hard Day Campaign . . . 1013

Miller Brewing Company
Miller High Life Man Campaign . . . 1017

Miller Lite's Miller Time Campaign 1021

Minnesota Partnership for Action against Tobacco

Minnesota Partnership for Action against Tobacco Campaign. 1027

Mitsubishi Motors North America, Inc.

Wake Up and Drive Campaign. 1031

Monsanto Company

Monsanto Image Campaigns. 1035

Monster

Today's the Day Campaign. 1039

Montres Rolex SA

Celebrity Endorsement Campaign. 1043

Morgan Stanley

At Your Side Campaign 1047

It Pays to Discover Revisited Campaign 1050

Make a Statement Campaign 1053

Tow Truck Campaign 1056

Mothers Against Drunk Driving, Connecticut Chapter

Drunk Driving's a Serious Crime. Let's Treat It That Way. Campaign 1061

Motorola, Inc.

Intelligence Everywhere Campaign 1065

Moto Campaign 1068

MoveOn.org

Real People Campaign 1073

MTV Networks Company

Watch and Learn Campaign 1077

The Museum of Contemporary Art, Los Angeles

Labels Campaign 1081

N

Napster, Inc.

It's Coming Back Campaign 1085

The Nasdaq Stock Market, Inc.

Listed on Nasdaq Campaign 1089

National Association for Stock Car Auto Racing

How Bad Have You Got It? Campaign. 1093

National Football League

NFL Playoffs Campaign 1099

National Railroad Passenger Corporation

Life on Acela Campaign 1103

Negro Leagues Baseball Museum

1998 Print Campaign 1107

Nestlé Purina PetCare Co.

Incredible Dogs Campaign 1111

Multiple Strength for Multiple Cats Campaign. 1114

Nestlé S.A.

Made Like No Other Campaign 1119

New Balance Athletic Shoe, Inc.

New Balance Thunderstorm, Stairs Campaign. . . . 1123

New York State Lottery

If I Had a Million Dollars Campaign 1127

Nike, Inc.

9,000 Shots Campaign 1131

Hello World and "I Am Tiger Woods" Campaigns 1134

Meet the Lebrons Campaign 1138

Move Campaign 1141

Play Campaign 1144

Product Assault Campaign 1147

What If We Treated All Athletes the Way We Treat Skateboarders? Campaign 1150

Women's Campaign 1154

Nikon Corporation

Mass Market Initiative Campaign 1159

The Nikon School Campaign 1162

Nissan Motor Company, Ltd.

Do You Speak Micra? Campaign 1167

Nissan North America, Inc.

Enjoy the Ride Campaign 1171

Nissan Quest Minivan Launch Campaign 1174

Own One and You'll Understand Campaign. 1177

Nordstrom, Inc.

Make Room for Shoes Campaign 1181

Reinvent Yourself Campaign. 1184

Norelco Consumer Products Company

Norelco Reflex Action Razor Campaign 1189

Normark Corporation

Custom Lures Campaign 1193

North American Coffee Partnership (Starbucks Corp.)

Bring On the Day Campaign 1197

North Carolina Division of Tourism, Film and Sports Development

Heritage Campaign. 1201

Northwest Airlines Corporation

E-Ticket Campaign. 1205

Novartis AG

Tummies Campaign 1209

O

Office Depot, Inc.

What You Need. What You Need to Know. Campaign. 1213

Office of National Drug Control Policy

Early Intervention Youth Campaign 1217

OfficeMax Inc.

What's Your Thing? Campaign 1221

Old Navy, Inc.

'70s Retro TV Campaign 1225

Destination Campaign 1228

Orange S.A.
Goldspot Campaign 1233
Outward Bound USA
Oceans, Mountains, Forests, Fear. Which Do You Conquer First? Campaign 1237
Oxygen Media
Fresh Television for Women Campaign 1241

P

Pabst Brewing Company
Remember Rainier Campaign 1245
Pacific Cycle, Inc.
Fast. It's Corporate Policy. Campaign 1249
What a Ride Campaign 1252
Palace Sports & Entertainment
Goin' to Work. Every Night. Campaign 1257
Peace Corps
Life Is Calling. How Far Will You Go? Campaign. 1261
PepsiCo, Inc.
Code Red Campaign 1267
Do the Dew Campaign. 1270
Drink More Water Campaign. 1274
Generation Next Campaign 1277
The Joy of Pepsi Campaign 1280
The Not-So-Vanilla Vanilla Campaign 1283
Origins Campaign 1286
Pepsi. It's the Cola Campaign. 1289
Quaker—Warms You, Heart and Soul Campaign. 1292
Security Camera Campaign 1295
That's Brisk, Baby! Campaign. 1298
This Is Diet? Campaign 1303
Perdue Farms Inc.
Now Arriving Campaign. 1307
Pfizer Inc.
The Power of Zyrtec Campaign 1311
Schick Tracer FX Ads Campaign 1314
See You Later, Alligator Campaign 1317
Super Fans Campaign. 1322
Viagra Launch Campaign 1325
Pharmavite LLC
Trusted by the Ones You Trust Campaign 1329
Philips Electronics North America Corp.
Getting Better Campaign 1333
Piaggio USA, Inc.
Vespa Reintroduction Campaign. 1337
Piedmont Federal Savings and Loan Association
It's Your Mortgage. Keep It Here. Campaign . . . 1341
Pizza Hut, Inc.
Big New Yorker Pizza Campaign 1345
Polaris Industries, Inc.
The New American Motorcycle Campaign 1349
Ride the Best Campaign 1352
Polaroid Corporation
I-Zone/Joycam/Sticky Film Teen Campaign 1357
See What Develops Campaign 1360
Porsche Cars North America Inc.
Cayenne Launch Campaign 1365
priceline.com Incorporated
Troubadour Campaign 1369
The Procter & Gamble Company
The Best Part of Wakin' Up Is Folgers in Your Cup Campaign 1373
Cleaner Close Campaign. 1377
Got the Power Campaign 1380
Habits Campaign 1382
Ingenious Protection for Ingenious Women Campaign. 1385
Sharing and Connecting Campaign. 1388
Sink Boy Campaign 1391
Strange but True Campaign 1395
Tasting Is Believing Campaign 1398
When You're Strong, You Sparkle Campaign . . . 1401
The Prudential Insurance Company of America
Be Your Own Rock Campaign 1405
Public Broadcasting Service
Be More Campaign 1409

Q

The Quiznos Master LLC
Baby Bob Campaign. 1413

R

Reebok International Ltd.
Terry Tate, Office Linebacker Campaign 1417
The Rheingold Brewing Company
Rheingold Beer Campaign 1421
Rock the Vote
Yes/No Ballot Box Campaign 1425
Round Table Pizza
The Last Honest Pizza Campaign 1429
Royal Appliance Manufacturing Company
Darin' Campaign 1433
Fred Astaire Campaign 1437
Royal Caribbean Cruises Ltd.
Get Out There Campaign. 1441

S

Saab Cars USA, Inc.
Life Is Not a Spectator Sport Campaign 1445
SABMiller plc
Low Carb Campaign 1449
Miller High Life Campaign 1452

Sanford, L.P.
Write Out Loud Campaign 1457
Sanofi-Aventis
Spirit of Freedom Campaign 1461
Saturn Corporation
Saturn Relaunch Campaign 1465
Why Didn't Anyone Think of This Before? Campaign 1468
SBC Communications Inc.
Laurel Lane Campaign 1473
Schick-Wilkinson Sword
Shaving Made Simple Campaign 1477
Scotts Miracle-Gro Company
Neighbor to Neighbor Campaign 1481
Sears, Roebuck & Co.
Come See the Softer Side of Sears Campaign 1487
Sears. Where Else? Campaign 1491
Sega of America, Inc. & Take-Two Interactive Software, Inc.
Beta-7 Campaign 1497
Serta International
Counting Sheep Campaign 1501
Sharp Corp.
More to See Campaign 1505
Sierra Club
Hybrid Evolution Campaign 1509
Sims Sports, Inc.
Be Free Campaign 1513
Six Flags, Inc.
It's Playtime Campaign 1517
Sony Corporation
Fun, Anyone? Campaign 1523
Sony Bravia Campaign 1526
Sony Corporation of America
What's Next? Campaign 1531
Southwest Airlines Company
Must Be Football Season Campaign 1535
Specialized Bicycle Components Inc.
Specialized Campaign 1539
Sprint Nextel Corporation
Dime Zone Campaign 1543
Monday Nights Free and Clear Campaign 1546
Nextel. Done. Campaign 1550
Sprint PCS Campaign 1553
Stanley Steemer International, Inc.
Living Brings It In. We Take It Out. Campaign 1557
Staples, Inc.
That Was Easy Campaign 1563
Yeah, We've Got That Campaign 1567
State Farm Mutual Automobile Insurance Company
True Stories Campaign 1571
Steelcase, Inc.
Work Effectiveness Campaign 1575
Suburban Auto Group
Trunk Monkey Campaign 1579
Swift Boat Veterans for Truth
Swift Boat Veterans for Truth Campaign 1583
Swiss Army Brands, Inc.
Swiss Army Equipped Campaign 1587

T

Taco Bell Corp.
Think Outside the Bun Campaign 1591
Want Some? Campaign 1594
Target Corporation
New Yorker Magazine Sponsorship Campaign . . . 1599
Take Charge of Education Campaign 1603
Thomas Cook Tour Operations Ltd
Perspectives Campaign 1607
Time Warner, Inc.
Cartoon Network Promotional and Branding Campaign 1611
The World's Most Interesting Magazine Campaign 1615
TiVo Inc.
TiVo, TV Your Way Campaign 1619
T-Mobile International AG & Company KG
Get More Campaign 1623
Tommy Hilfiger U.S.A., Inc.
American Tartans Campaign 1627
Toyota Motor Sales, U.S.A., Inc.
A Car to Be Proud Of Campaign 1631
Everyday Campaign 1634
Fuel for Thought Campaign 1638
Get the Feeling Campaign 1641
Kids Rule Campaign 1643
The Road Is Calling Campaign 1646
Travelocity
Roaming Gnome Campaign 1651
Triarc Companies, Inc.
Return of the Snapple Lady Campaign 1655
Turner Broadcasting System, Inc.
31 Days of Oscar Campaign 1659
TBS Very Funny Campaign 1662
TV Guide, Inc.
On the Inside Campaign 1667
Tyson Foods, Inc.
Powered by Tyson Campaign 1671

U

UBS Financial Services Inc.
Thank You, Paine Webber Campaign 1675
Unilever PLC
Campaign for Real Beauty Campaign 1679
Do It Once. Do It Right. Campaign 1683

Unilever United States
Real Cooking Campaign 1687
Soothing Cucumber Eye Treatments Ads Campaign 1690
United Airlines Corp.
It's Time to Fly Campaign 1695
Rising Campaign 1698
Ted Launch Campaign 1701
United Distillers and Vintners of North America
Russian Art Campaign 1705
United Parcel Service, Inc.
Moving at the Speed of Business Campaign 1709
What Can Brown Do for You? Campaign 1713
United States Postal Service
Fly Like an Eagle Campaign 1717
United States Tennis Association
US Open Excitement Campaign 1721
UnitedHealth Group, Inc.
It Just Makes Sense Campaign 1725

V

V & S Vin & Sprit AB
Absolut Director Campaign 1729
Absolut Print Campaign 1733
Jesse Ventura for Governor
Retaliate in '98 Campaign 1739
VF Corporation
Cut to Be Noticed Campaign 1743
Find Your One True Fit Campaign 1746
Rugged Wear Campaign 1749
Village Voice LLC
Not America's Favorite Paper Campaign 1753
Virgin Atlantic Airways Limited
Go, Jet Set, Go! Campaign 1757
Virginia Tourism Corporation
Meet Virginia Campaign 1761
Visa U.S.A., Inc.
Visa. It's Everywhere You Want to Be Campaign 1765
Works Like a Check Campaign 1769
Volkswagen of America, Inc.
All Grown Up. Sort Of. Campaign 1773
Drivers Wanted Campaign 1776
Live Large Campaign 1780
New Beetle Campaign 1783

W

Wachovia Corporation
Financial World Campaign 1789
Uncommon Wisdom Campaign 1792
Walgreen Company
Perfect Campaign 1797
Washington Mutual, Inc.
Fear Not Campaign 1801
The Weather Channel Companies
Painted Faces Campaign 1805
Wendy's International, Inc.
Fresh Stuffed Pita Campaign 1809
Good to Be Square Campaign 1812
Wholesome & Hearty Foods Company
Eating Good Just Got Great Campaign 1817
Wm. Wrigley Jr. Company
Altoids Campaign 1821
Altoids Gone Sour Campaign 1824
Gotta Have Twisted Sweet Campaign 1827
No Matter What Campaign 1830
Working Assets Long Distance
Direct Marketing Campaign 1835
Wyeth
Liqui-Gels Campaign 1839

X

Xerox Corporation
Keep the Conversation Going, Share the Knowledge Campaign 1843

Y

Yahoo! Inc.
Do You Yahoo!? Campaign 1849
Live Billboard Dating Campaign 1854
Yard Strength, Inc.
Yard Fitness Center Campaign 1859

Index 1863

Advisors and Contributors

ADVISORS

Borders, Bill. Founding partner, Borders, Perrin & Norrander, Portland, Oregon.

Jaffe, Andrew. Former executive director, Clio Awards; president, Compass Consulting, LLC, Norwalk, Connecticut.

Zilavy, Julie. Manager, Online Services, American Association of Advertising Agencies, New York, New York.

CONTRIBUTORS

Amorosino, Chris John. Freelance writer living in Unionville, Connecticut. He creates a variety of communications materials for clients in the advertising, financial services, and medical fields.

Arrigo, Jan. Louisiana-based freelance writer focusing on travel and culture. Author of *Cemeteries of New Orleans: A Journey through the Cities of the Dead and New Orleans.*

Bailey, Rayna. Former newspaper managing editor and magazine associate editor. She is now a freelance writer living in Westcliffe, Colorado.

Baue, William B. Freelance writer who has published articles on William Faulkner and Toni Morrison, as well as on work apprenticeships. He has taught writing and literature to both college and high school students.

Benbow-Pfalzgraf, Taryn. Freelance writer living in the Chicago area.

Brady, Barbra. Freelance writer and curator based in Missoula, Montana.

Caso, Frank. Freelance writer living in Hartford, Connecticut. His work has appeared in publications in the United States, Canada, and Russia.

Coryell, Anita. Freelance writer living in Missoula, Montana.

Crow, Alden Scott. Writer based in Clements, California.

Cunningham, Guy Patrick. Freelance writer living in New York City.

Dinger, Ed. New York-based writer.

Fujinaka, Mariko. Editor and writer living in Portland, Oregon.

Hutchins, Patrick. Advertising copywriter, creative director, and journalist for more than 20 years. Formerly employed at several agencies in Los Angeles, he freelances from his home in Montana.

Kazemi, Kim. Freelance writer living in Missoula, Montana.

Knight, Judson. Author and coauthor of numerous books, including *Abbey Road to Zapple Records: A Beatles Encyclopedia* and a three-volume *Ancient Civilizations* series. He lives in Atlanta, Georgia.

Kolberg, Sharyn. New York-based freelance writer and editor. She has written or ghostwritten more than a dozen books in a variety of fields, including direct marketing, sales, self-help, and nutrition.

Kolstad, Jonathan. Freelance writer and photographer living in Portland, Oregon.

Lane, Mark. Freelance writer living in Brooklyn, New York.

Mack, Deborah. Freelance writer and researcher living in Maryland.

Mancini, Candice. Freelance writer who teaches English composition and literature to college and high school students. She lives in Missoula, Montana.

McGinniss Kerr, Bridget. Freelance writer and editor living in El Portal, California.

McNamer, Megan. Freelance writer and movie critic in Missoula, Montana. Her articles have appeared in several national publications, including *Sports Illustrated*, the *Miami Herald*, *Islands*, and *Child*.

Millstein, Sarah. Freelance writer and editor. In addition to working on projects for nonprofit organizations and corporations, she has written articles on sustainable agriculture and food. Her work has appeared in *Mother Earth News*, *Green Guide*, and *Just Food News*.

Minderovic, Christine Miner. Freelance writer who works in the field of medicine. She has written about science, medicine, dance, art, and literature.

Porter, Allison I. Writer, editor, and researcher based in Washington, D.C. She has written *The Path to Poverty: An Analysis of Women's Retirement Income*, *Your 1991/92 Guide to Social Security Benefits*, and *Porter's Guide to Congressional Roll Call Votes*.

Risland, Susan. Writer whose work has appeared in *Ferguson's Guide to Apprenticeship Programs*, *Exploring Tech Careers*, and other publications.

Salter, Susan. Writer contributing to numerous reference books, including *Contemporary Authors*, *Newsmakers*, and the *Encyclopedia of Consumer Brands*.

Samano, Simone. Freelance writer living in Ann Arbor, Michigan.

Schnakenberg, Robert E. Author of reference, biographical, and instructional materials, including *The Encyclopedia of Shatnerica*. He lives in New York City.

Stanfel, Rebecca. Freelance writer living in Helena, Montana.

Steiner, Susan M. Freelance writer, editor, and translator. She was formerly editor-in-chief, German Information Center.

Tokumitsu, Cynthia. New York-based writer focusing on business and education. She also served for four years as editorial director of Quality Resources.

Teague, Kevin. Freelance writer living in the central coast region of California. Author of the novel *The Rise of Charlie Drop*.

Wilson Peacock, Kathy. Freelance writer living in Dearborn, Michigan.

Foreword

Trying to expound on any large body of advertising work is always dangerous. Since Cro-Magnon man scratched an image onto a cave wall for others to see, the business of mass communication has been evolving. Advertising is a fluid, ever-changing craft. I hesitate to label it as art only because doing so tends to raise howls of indignation from those in the field of so-called serious art—playwrights, filmmakers, musicians, painters, sculptors, and such. I could build a strong case, however, that any well-conceived, beautifully executed ad, in any medium, differs from traditional art in only one sense: its purpose, either directly or indirectly, is to evoke a mercantile response. Regular art has merely to evoke an emotional response so that, by comparison, it gets off easy.

For the purposes of this encyclopedia, let us say that advertising falls closer to fashion. Like fashion, it is an art form with decidedly commercial ends. As with fashion, there are trendy, fleeting styles of advertising that come on strong, cause a stir, and then fade away with the next hot "ad couture." And there are sturdy classics, ads that wear well with age and that look fine and still touch people after 10, 20, or even 30 or more years. These are creations that rest upon timeless human emotions or truths rather than on a passing currency. An ad headlined "Lemon" and featuring, say, a new Lexus would be no less compelling today than it was for Volkswagen 40 years ago.

In any given year we see ads of both kinds—splashy, contemporary messages of the moment (such as iPod's "Silhouette" campaign and countless print ads flaunting jagged, beat-up typefaces) and durable works that rest on less ephemeral trends (such as John Hancock's "Insurance for the Unexpected"). Is one form "better" than the other? Not inherently. Both work or fail for other reasons, for their freshness, relevance, involvement of the viewer, execution, or memorability.

Like Hollywood, advertising is often criticized for shaping, if not lowering, cultural and social standards. The usual response from studio executives is that they merely reflect, not cause, what is already happening in our collective midst. Consider Clark Gable's 1934 appearance sans undershirt in *It Happened One Night,* which reputedly prompted the sales of men's undershirts to drop by 75 percent. (Hollywood made up for this later, in 1951, when Marlon Brando appeared in a T-shirt and jeans in the film *A Streetcar Named Desire* and the sales of T-shirts spiked to new heights.) Did Gable cause this to happen, or was he reflecting changes then under way? Was he initiating a trend or following one? The truth is usually somewhere in between.

The same can be said of much modern-day advertising, although here we have to be careful. In marketing today the pickup of information and trends is so fast that advertising may be creeping ever closer to being a cause of change. In an era in which people are wired together and in which "cool hunters" track buying patterns among young people, a budding local fad or an emerging trend can be sniffed out in its infancy and catapulted into the national consciousness, sometimes with startling speed. Indeed, many marketers pride themselves on lightning turnarounds from the time a new movement is spotted to its appearance in their advertising, thus making them appear to be at the forefront of the ever-shifting edge of change. Thus, in increasing instances contemporary advertising involves a good deal more than the passive reflection of trends. At the very least, to borrow a term from Malcolm Gladwell's 2000 book *The Tipping Point,* marketers vastly accelerate the "contagiousness" of an idea or social phenomenon. Whether it is merely a new set of words ("Got [blank]?"), a social shift like the emphasis on fitness, or an emerging technology like text messaging, advertising, probably even more so than Hollywood, can and often does play the role of an accelerator, if not an out-and-out instigator, of cultural change.

One reason for the growing potency of advertising, besides the ever-improving accuracy and penetration of research, is its sheer ubiquity. To some extent this has resulted from the splintering and proliferation of the media. Not long ago advertising was primarily limited to the big five: television, radio, print, outdoor, and direct mail. In 1984 one study revealed that in a single day the average American was exposed to 560 commercial messages via these five media. Of these messages 76 were noticed, and of these 12 could be recalled 24 hours later. Of the 12 that could be recalled, 3 were remembered negatively. This meant that only 9 messages, or 1.6 percent, were recalled in a positive sense, which is a pretty dismal figure. Today, however, cable and satellite networks offer hundreds of television channels. Added to this is the cyberworld of websites, pop-up ads, E-mail spam, blogs, podcasts, and text messaging on cell phones, in addition to the "ambient" advertising that appears on such things as shopping carts, store shelves, the handles of gas pumps, banana peels, and even urinals. It has become virtually impossible to elude the grasp of advertising, and in general such increased pervasiveness has translated into increased persuasiveness.

It also has produced increased annoyance, however. Advertising has long been labeled the uninvited guest in our homes, offices, and cars. It arrives unbeckoned, usually interrupting some form of entertainment or search for information, insinuates itself into the recipient's mind with its hand out, and then goes away momentarily, only to resurface and repeat the cycle within a few minutes. As people feel more and more victimized by the omnipresence of advertising, their shell of resistance against it hardens. This is nothing new, but as advertising grows more and more ubiquitous, the shell grows more and more impenetrable. It is a vicious cycle. Just as industrialized nations spew noxious greenhouse gasses into the atmosphere in record amounts, so marketers spew vast clouds of often obnoxious advertising.

At least some of the advertising in this encyclopedia demonstrates there is a silver lining to these dark clouds. There is an increasing appreciation for the one tactic that has proven consistently adept at penetrating the shell of resistance. This is creativity. More specifically, it is advertising that defies traditional approaches in some way and that is fresh and interesting enough and, ironically, enough unlike advertising to slip past the resistance against it. Thus, brands like adidas, Nike, Burger King, FedEx, IKEA, Altoids, Volkswagen, and BMW Mini have consistently wielded the leverage of strong creativity in their branding. Without undertaking a detailed and difficult discussion of the many facets and hurdles of producing truly original advertising today, suffice it to say that there is an encouraging awareness of its growing importance and, in turn, of its implementation. This results not so much from curiosity or desire but more from coldhearted necessity. Ordinary advertising can no longer easily be justified by the dollars thrown at it. Bland advertising is being seen for what it is, a rotten business investment. To quote one of the more visionary creative deans of the industry, Jeff Goodby of Goodby, Silverstein & Partners, "The best thing to have happened in advertising in the last 20 years is without a single doubt happening right now. This business, which for the most part has always tolerated creativity as a kind of goateed necessary evil, is now about to turn the joystick over to the creative force, big-time. It has no choice." This is good news not only for those in the business who endure the usually uphill battle of selling atypical work to clients and management but also to the vast public at the receiving end.

This brings us to another phenomenon, without which any discussion of the contemporary advertising landscape is incomplete, namely, the one new technology out of several that is most rapidly changing the ground rules. It is called, disarmingly enough, TiVo, a product that uses DVR, or digital video recording, technology. The TiVo black box already allows approximately 9 percent of U.S. television viewers merrily to fast-forward past all the uninvited advertising. Estimates are that by 2010 its penetration will reach one of every three households, which places an even greater premium and burden on creativity in advertising. As more viewers are armed with a simple button that can eradicate advertising, the advertising must become so entertaining that the viewer wants to watch it and makes a conscious decision to do so. Advertising must become so visually alluring that it compels a fast-forwarder to hit the brakes and view it, which is no small order.

Of course, another antidote to DVR technology is to embed advertising within the programming itself. This will likely move well beyond product placement, the technique that is used today, to the point that in a sitcom, for instance, an actor will not only swig on a Bud but the Bud will somehow become an integral part of the story line. Some screenwriters may well rebel at this, but others may happily pocket the increased residuals that would flow from such artful intertwining of commerce and scripting. Likewise, in printed media there may be an increasing use of advertorials, in which the lines between news about and advertising for new products become progressively fuzzier. Subliminal advertising in the twenty-first century may take this approach. Whereas the much maligned, though in fact rarely practiced, form of subliminal advertising in the 1950s supposedly relied on subconscious flashes of messages so fleetingly fast that the viewer was unaware of them, this new iteration is so subtle that it does not look or smell like advertising at all. It is woven into the entertainment in such a way that it is TiVo-proof.

But certainly the arena in which advertising and content will become the most homogenized is on the Web. While it is not possible to have a crystal ball that shows all of the twists and turns that are bound to take place over even the next few years, one thing is certain: the role of advertising on the Web will grow exponentially. We should expect the proliferation of cooperative websites like MySpace.com, on which two, three, or more advertisers join forces to allow consumers to do everything from conduct personal business and send E-mail, to share photos, play games, and post blogs that revolve around a communal topic. Think of adidas and Penn, for instance, on a tennis-centric site. In addition, television programming will make increasing use of the Web by allowing viewers to "split-watch" both, with commentary and ads on the Web related to what is happening simultaneously on the television screen. We should expect that virtually any television program will be available for instant downloading gratis, with one small string attached: the downloader must agree to accept certain commercials along with it.

BMW revealed the power of exciting minifilms with their products-in-action epics on the Web. Burger King allowed Web surfers to let a willing, kinky chicken do their bidding. And countless other brands have dabbled in experiential, if experimental, forms of "webvertising." This will surely continue to evolve into far more interactive, and far more widely watched, fare as technology ramps up connection speeds, hard drives become insatiable, wireless connections become universal, and computer displays, TVs, cell phones, PDAs, and iPods continue to converge. But all of the convergence in the world will mean little commercially unless the content of the ad messages also continues to evolve in terms of entertainment and freshness.

As one who has ranted about the effectiveness of creativity in advertising for more than a few years, I naturally find these developments encouraging. And the looming hyperfragmentation of the media, while a bit unnerving, should serve only to solidify the importance of how well each message is crafted. Dare I say how artfully? Clearly the status quo is dead meat.

So peruse the 474 campaigns discussed in this encyclopedia. It is a unique gathering. From them you will glean insights and fresh perspectives, not the least of which will be an accurate sense of how far advertising has advanced during the first years of this new century. And with a little interpolation you may also emerge with a reasonably accurate sense of how it will continue to evolve over the rest of the decade.

Bill Borders

Introduction

Thomson Gale published the first volume of the *Encyclopedia of Major Marketing Campaigns* in 1999. It included nearly 500 essays, each on an important advertising campaign of the twentieth century. The present volume serves as an update to the first, offering an additional 474 essays on campaigns that appeared between the late 1990s and 2005.

There were three main criteria for selecting a campaign: its conceptual value or innovation (sometimes represented by the winning of awards); the importance of the company or brand for which it was run; and its effectiveness in selling the advertised product or service. The campaigns covered in this book were for products or services in various categories, such as alcoholic and other beverages, automobiles, food items, footwear, insurance, public service, pharmaceuticals, and telecommunications.

CONTENT AND ARRANGEMENT

EMMC is organized alphabetically by the name of the company for which the campaign was run. Thus, the "Miller High Life" campaign is listed under SABMiller plc, which manufactures Miller High Life beer. Each entry in the encyclopedia has the same sections:

Entry Head: Lists the company's name, address, phone and fax numbers, and web page.

Overview: Provides a brief summary of the campaign.

Historical Context: Discusses historical details of the brand, the company, the industry, or general culture needed to understand the featured campaign.

Target Market: Specifies the audience toward which the campaign was directed and the reason why that audience was targeted.

Competition: Points out the brand's major competitors and, if known, their market shares. Often discusses the competitors advertising campaigns.

Marketing Strategy: Discusses how the campaign was started, who started it, and what were some of the concerns and goals.

Outcome: Discusses the campaign's success in achieving its goals, if sales increased or decreased during the campaign, and whether the campaign received any awards or other critical attention.

Further Reading: Lists articles and books that provide information on the campaign or on marketing within the category.

Sidebar: Discusses a topic often peripheral to the main discussion but important in understanding the campaign, brand, product, or company.

In addition to the entries, the encyclopedia features a comprehensive index, photographs illustrating many of the campaigns and products, and a foreword—written by Bill Borders, founding partner of Borders, Perrin & Norrander—discussing important trends in contemporary marketing.

ACKNOWLEDGMENTS

Many people were involved in putting together this book, some of whom are listed on the staff page. I would like to thank the advisers, who provided invaluable help with the selection of campaigns; Bill Borders, for the introduction; the contributors, who conducted extensive research for their entries, often with the help of the companies and advertising agencies associated with the campaigns; and the companies and agencies, without whom many of the essays could not have been written. I would also like to express my appreciation to Patrick Hutchins, whose advice at various stages of the project was essential; Mariko Fujinaka, who commissioned authors and assisted with other important tasks; Robert Rauch, Laura Gabler, and Anne Healey, for their editing; and Kimberly Burton and Jennifer Zielinski, who proofread the text. Finally, I would like to thank Holly Selden, who coordinated various in-house responsibilities.

COMMENTS AND SUGGESTIONS

Comments and suggestions, including ideas for future essays, are welcome. We invite readers to send us their thoughts to the following address:

Editor
Encyclopedia of Major Marketing Campaigns
Thomson Gale
27500 Drake Road
Farmington Hills, MI 48331-3535
Toll-free phone: 800-877-GALE

A & E Television Networks

235 East 45th Street
New York, New York 10017
USA
Telephone: (212) 210-1400
Fax: (212) 850-9370
Web site: www.aetv.com

IN CASE YOU MISSED IT CAMPAIGN

OVERVIEW

In 2001 the Concept Farm, a boutique advertising agency based in New York, launched a promotional effort for History Channel International, part of A & E Television Networks, itself a joint venture of Hearst, ABC, Inc., and NBC. History Channel International was carried alongside its older cousin, the History Channel, on many U.S. cable and satellite television systems, but it faced different challenges in reaching its target audience, men in the age range of 24 to 54. Not only did the agency have to find a way to make familiar historical footage seem fresh, but the spots also had to work in any number of cultures around the world.

Modestly budgeted, the Concept Farm's second campaign for History Channel International, called "In Case You Missed It," attempted to meet those challenges through a humorous mix of stock and contrived footage. The unfortunate heroes of the campaign's three 30-second spots were well situated to witness some of the most important moments in history, only to be accidentally distracted and miss the climax. Each ad closed with the title card, "In case you missed it the first time," and the History Channel logo.

The campaign, which began in 2001, was successful with American audiences, winning several awards and improving the status of the Concept Farm. The humor was not as well received in other countries, however, causing some overseas broadcast partners not to run the spots. As a result, more serious-minded promotional campaigns followed.

HISTORICAL CONTEXT

The Concept Farm was founded by advertising veterans frustrated by working at big agencies. According to Anthony Vagnoni, writing for *Print,* "They started the company so that they could freely pursue ideas for new kinds of advertising and explore projects that would otherwise be abandoned." Griffin Stenger, one of the firm's cofounders and creative directors, told Vagnoni, "We've all seen too many ideas get killed by account people or marketing executives at big corporate clients." Like many boutiques, the Concept Farm looked for niche opportunities, in particular in the field of broadcast promotions (ads for TV channels and their programs).

As the number of television channels increased dramatically with the rise of cable television, so, too, did the need to promote them. Although the budgets were small and the deadlines tight, the Concept Farm was attracted to the freedom afforded by broadcast clients. Television marketing departments had fewer management layers than those of other companies, and this streamlined the approval process and allowed ad agencies a better chance of seeing their work on the screen unfiltered. As Gregg

Wasiak, a cofounder of the Concept Farm, told Ann-Christine Diaz of *Advertising Age's Creativity,* "The speed at which everything has to happen really means broadcast clients have to make a lot of gut decisions. They understand their brand and they go with it." Time was not the only limited commodity. Promoting a TV channel required a great number of commercials, and so the budget for each spot was small. Wasiak put a positive spin on the problem, explaining, "It forces you to be simple and think creatively."

When the Concept Farm landed the job of promoting History Channel International, it faced hurdles beyond time and budgetary constraints. Because of language and cultural barriers related to the channel's global market, the shop had to focus on visuals. Given the limited budget, the firm knew that it would rely on stock film footage, but the task of making the overly familiar seem interesting again remained daunting. Wasiak told Diaz, "We wanted to serve up what's great about the History Channel, some of the most spectacular film you've ever seen about history, in a way you've never seen before."

The Concept Farm's first History Channel International campaign, "Go Back in Time," employed the simple technique of playing a tired film backward to make it fresh. One spot showed Jesse Owens landing in the pit on his gold-medal-winning long jump at the 1936 Berlin Olympics. He was pulled back in the air and ran in reverse, accompanied by a voiceover: "Go back in time and see the leaps we've made." Another spot reversed the infamous summary execution of a prisoner during the Vietnam War. One ad in the campaign used footage of the *Hindenburg* disaster, showing the exploding dirigible returning to its original form. Wasiak elaborated on the effect of seeing the tragedy in reverse: "You understand that those were not 'moments in history' until that instant. We wanted to work backwards from that point and understand that that's when history was made."

For its second effort for History Channel International, the Concept Farm elected to continue exploiting stock material. It found another creative way to breathe life into tired footage in the "In Case You Missed It" campaign.

TARGET MARKET

Like its cousin, the History Channel, History Channel International considered its target audience to be men between the ages of 24 and 54. Most viewers, however, tended to be closer to the upper end of that age range. The broadcaster was interested in lowering the average, but as Charlie Mayday, A & E's senior vice president of programming, explained to Michael Rose of *Video Age International,* "You have to accept that the subject appeals to an older audience." On the upside, continued Mayday, the audience existed all over the world, and "a good story" would transcend national boundaries.

A LONG COUNT

One of the subjects in History Channel International's "In Case You Missed It" ads, German boxer Max Schmeling, became the unwilling tool of the Nazis following his defeat of African-American Joe Louis in 1936. Although portrayed as the "Aryan Superman" by Nazi propagandists, Schmeling hid a pair of Jewish boys in his apartment to spare them from a Nazi mob and reportedly helped some Jewish friends avoid the death camps. When Louis in later life fell upon hard times, Schmeling quietly provided him money. Looking back on the second fight with Louis in 1938, he said that he was almost happy he lost, "Just imagine if I would have come back to Germany with a victory. I had nothing to do with the Nazis, but they would have given me a medal. After the war I might have been considered a war criminal." In February 2005 Schmeling died at the age of 99, his only regret being that he did not live to see 100.

COMPETITION

In the realm of cable television, History Channel International's main rivals were the multitude of broadcasters—such as the Discovery Channel, ESPN, and other sports programmers—that targeted the same male demographic. In a larger sense, however, History Channel International was vying with every other advertiser for the attention of its coveted audience; thus, its competitors included deep-pocketed beer companies, automakers, and Hollywood film studios.

MARKETING STRATEGY

As was the case with the initial promotional campaign for History Channel International, the Concept Farm in its second effort had to contend with a small budget, a limited number of chances to speak to its target audience, and a crowded marketplace, while finding a way to achieve global appeal and to overcome language and cultural barriers. The new campaign, titled "In Case You Missed It," centered on spectators who were distracted and missed the key moment of an important historical event. Wasiak told Diaz that the inspiration came from his own life: "I remember when Buster Douglas knocked out Mike Tyson, I was taking a pee. I missed the whole thing. When man first landed on the moon, there must have been somebody who was in the bathroom and missed all that."

The Concept Farm used the History Channel's film archives as well as two stock footage houses, Archive Films in New York and WPA in Chicago. Then the team created its own "lost footage," the shots of the commercials' protagonists. The newly filmed action, though humorous, was carefully matched in style to the real historical clips.

The three 30-second spots in the "In Case You Missed It" campaign were written by Wasiak and first appeared in the spring of 2001. The ad called "Boxing" concerned the first historic fight between Joe Louis and Max Schmeling in 1936. Intercut with actual footage of the fight were shots of a ringside photographer poised to take the climactic shot in the bout. By accident his flash went off, temporarily blinding him and causing him to miss Schmeling delivering the knockout punch to Louis. As would be the case with all the spots, a title card then faded in, reading "In case you missed it the first time," followed by the History Channel logo. The second spot, "Coronation," used footage from the coronation of England's Queen Elizabeth II in 1953. Two members of the nobility quietly watched the solemn occasion, but just as the archbishop was about to place the crown on Elizabeth's head, one of them dropped his hat. In the course of bending over to retrieve it, he inadvertently hit his neighbor in the groin with his scepter. The victim doubled over in pain and missed the crowning. The spot closed with his valiant effort to share in his comrade's joy while suffering through the pain. The final ad, called "Moon Landing," depicted astronaut Neil Armstrong's first steps on the moon. In Mission Control a NASA engineer looked on, watching the television screen and drinking coffee. He spilled the coffee on his lap and looked away just as Armstrong was about to hop onto the lunar surface. By the time he looked up again, Armstrong had already completed his historic moment. The engineer could do nothing but feign enthusiasm and mask his embarrassment.

OUTCOME

The "In Case You Missed It" campaign garnered several awards for the Concept Farm. It won a Eurobest Award in 2001, the Gold Pencil in the Consumer Television Campaign (:30/:25) category at the One Show in 2002, an American Advertising Award (ADDY) in 2002, and an Andy Award from the Advertising Club of New York in 2003. The Concept Farm's Stenger told Millie Takaki, writing for *Shoot,* about the importance of winning the Gold Pencil: "We were up against many top production companies and ad agencies, and for us it validated our whole creative philosophy." After receiving that award the Concept Farm began getting requests from other agencies to direct their commercials. In response the agency created the Production Farm, an independently operated production company that used the directorial talent of the Concept Farm.

Although the Concept Farm's work was lauded by the firm's peers, History Channel International was not completely pleased with the campaign. As the number of countries it served grew significantly, the broadcaster became increasingly worried about offending local sensitivities. Humor, in particular, played differently from country to country. The Concept Farm developed two more promotional campaigns for History Channel International that took a more serious approach, the last one relying on montages of historical footage set to music, thus eliminating the need for graphics that would have had to have been translated dozens of times.

FURTHER READING

Diaz, Ann-Christine. "Ecce Promo: The Fertile Field of Broadcast Promotions." *Advertising Age's Creativity,* October 1, 2002.

———. "Revisionism Reconsidered: New York's the Concept Farm Cultivates New Ideas from Old Events for the History Channel." *Advertising Age's Creativity,* September 1, 2001.

Diedrick, Brian. "BBDO N.Y., GSD&M Top TV ADDYs." *Shoot,* June 14, 2002, p. 1.

Kim, Hank. "The One Show." *AdAgeGlobal,* May 2002, p. 14.

Solman, Gregory. "New History Channel Ads Remember Things Past." *Adweek,* June 14, 2004, p. 15.

Takaki, Millie. "The Concept Farm Launches Product Farm." *Shoot,* September 19, 2003, p. 8.

Vagnoni, Anthony. "Look at Me." *Print,* January 2003, p. 48.

Wilcha, Kristin. "It's Hip to Be 'Square' at the ANDYs." *Shoot,* May 9, 2003, p. 1.

———. "Short Route: BMW Tops One Show." *Shoot,* May 17, 2002, p. 1.

Zammit, Deanna. "Concept Farm Touts A & E Overseas." *Adweek* (eastern ed.), May 27, 2003.

Ed Dinger

ABC, Inc.

77 W. 66th Street
New York, New York 10023-6298
USA
Telephone: (212) 456-7777
Fax: (212) 456-7777
Web site: www.abc.go.com

■■■

TV IS GOOD CAMPAIGN

OVERVIEW

Traditionally, every summer the broadcast television networks launched marketing campaigns to spotlight their program offerings for the coming season. The campaigns were often uneventful and run-of-the-mill, with viewers and the media paying little notice. In 1997, however, ABC, Inc., unveiled a different kind of campaign created by TBWA\Chiat\Day in Los Angeles. The campaign, called "TV Is Good," was designed to help ABC break out of the traditional confines of network slogans and logos, and it created a stir.

Targeting viewers aged 18 to 49 and leveraging a budget of $12 million in its first season, "TV Is Good" directly addressed the guilt associated with watching television. Commercials featured messages that verged on the cynical, such as "Don't worry, you've got billions of brain cells," and "Life Is Short. Watch TV." While many in the media criticized the campaign's apparently insincere celebration of decadent TV-watching, the resulting debate about the merits of "TV Is Good" built considerable buzz around the ABC brand. A 1998–99 modification of the campaign, budgeted at $15 million and tagged "We Love TV," further contributed to ABC's emerging personality.

Although industry observers widely credited the overall campaign with contributing a distinct brand positioning to ABC, the network continued to suffer ratings declines. Because this was a problem endemic to broadcast TV at the time, however, such statistics were not an accurate measure of the success of the marketing campaign. During the 1999–2000 TV season and beyond, ABC continued to refine the marketing style and tone first introduced in 1997.

HISTORICAL CONTEXT

While ABC and the other two main broadcast networks, CBS Broadcasting Inc. (CBS) and the NBC Television Network (NBC), had enjoyed a virtual monopoly on prime-time television for decades, the 1980s saw increasing competition from cable television networks such as the Cable News Network (CNN) and Home Box Office (HBO) as well as the Fox Broadcasting Company. Cable networks gradually eroded the big three's dominance of the market. In 1977, 93 percent of households watched one of the big three networks, but 10 years later that figure had slipped to 70 percent. By 1996 the big three commanded only 49 percent of the prime-time audience, the first time ever that the combined share of ABC, CBS, and NBC had fallen below 50 percent.

Like CBS and NBC, ABC faced tough financial times in the 1980s, and it had to enact cost-cutting measures just to stay profitable. Capital Cities purchased ABC in 1985, and in 1995 it was bought by Disney. By 1996 ABC had fallen to third place in prime-time ratings, with only 15 percent of all viewers, behind front-runners NBC (18 percent) and CBS (16 percent). The network decided that it had to seek a clear, strong image to compete with NBC and CBS and the various cable channels.

TARGET MARKET

While television networks, as mass-media businesses, wanted to attract as many viewers as possible for their advertisers, ABC's 1997 campaign targeted a narrower market. The whimsical style of the "TV Is Good" campaign was specifically aimed at a youthful audience. During the early 1990s ABC was the number one network among the 18–49 age group, the market advertisers coveted; by 1997, however, the network had slipped to a distant second in this market. All efforts were directed at winning back this audience.

This tactic did not please everyone. For example, Joseph Turow, professor of media at the University of Pennsylvania's Annenberg School for Communication, said of the "TV Is Good" campaign, "I don't think they care if it turns off people who are over the hill. Advertisers and networks are really getting manic about attracting people under 30." Alan Cohen, ABC's executive vice president for marketing, said that the network was not intentionally spurning people over 49. Cohen told the *Pittsburgh Post-Gazette* that, when ABC tested its campaign promos on viewers aged 18–54, "The campaign played universally the same... The audience is right with us on this."

COMPETITION

In addition to CBS and NBC, ABC faced competition from the increasingly robust Fox network. The many cable networks, including CNN, HBO, ESPN, Showtime, Nickelodeon, Comedy Central, the Discovery Channel, USA Network, E! Entertainment Television, and the Family Channel, also presented ABC with competition.

Before 1997 there was a difference in the way broadcast networks and cable channels used marketing campaigns. Broadcast networks relied on slogans—such as "We're still the one"—and promos to market their new seasons. Cable networks, however, used the style of marketing known as branding, in which consumers were led to identify the company or product with a specific image. For example, Nickelodeon marketed its shows as family-based entertainment that children especially would enjoy. Its marketing encouraged viewers to think of family fun whenever they saw or heard the Nickelodeon name. CNN marketed its shows as no-nonsense programs for people who enjoyed hard news, inviting viewers to identify the network as a reputable, sober source for information.

The 1997 season saw the broadcast networks attempting to use branding for the first time. While ABC was using "TV Is Good" to project a lighthearted image, NBC's marketing campaign promoted "Must-see TV," and CBS advertised "Welcome Home." The NBC campaign attempted to capitalize on its ratings successes, using stars from top-rated programs such as *Seinfeld* in on-air promos. The CBS "Welcome Home" campaign, which was also used in 1996, attempted to portray the network as the place for "comfort and dependability," according to a company executive. Fox, UPN, and the WB had similar slogans. "The name of the game now is branding, the quaint notion of imbuing a network with a personality that will give a sort of halo effect to the programs it presents," wrote Gary Levin in *Variety,*

NBC'S TAKEOFF

ABC and competitor NBC took a few shots at each other over the "TV Is Good" campaign. NBC fired the first volley when it ran a satirical spot during its prime-time megahit *Seinfeld.* The spot featured black lettering on a yellow background, just like the ABC ads. The copy read, "Right now you could be watching another network. But you're not stupid. You're watching the number-one network in America. The National Broadcasting Company." On the record ABC responded through a spokesman, who quipped, "Imitation is the sincerest form of flattery." Off the record ABC faxed a five-page memo to NBC headquarters, reportedly with one line on each page: (1) "Right now you could be writing original promos"; (2) "But you're not"; (3) "You're copying ours"; (4) "Thanks!" (5) "ABC."

The wackiness was not over, however. According to the *New York Times,* NBC employees—allegedly writers for the sitcom *3rd Rock from the Sun*—drafted mock promotions of the ABC campaign. The promos, which clearly were takeoffs on the "TV Is Good" theme, featured lines such as "Museums cause cancer; we mean it. You'll die," and "Our laziness and stupidity are good news for Japan." But ABC had the last laugh, for the hubbub surrounding the campaign only meant more publicity for a third-place network anxious for attention.

describing the networks' 1997 campaigns. "Desperate to hold viewers, ABC, CBS, NBC, and Fox are copying successful cable networks with identifiable personalities," added the *Orange County Register* 's Kinney Littlefield.

MARKETING STRATEGY

ABC's third-place position in the ratings convinced its executives that the time was right to try something completely different. As Cohen told *Broadcasting & Cable,* "When you're not number one, you have to take more chances." ABC's research had revealed that most television viewers could not distinguish between the existing network advertising slogans and that most people tended to ignore logos or stars repeating catchphrases. Cohen said, "They were all drowning out each other, and it left networks without a brand identity." The goal of the ABC campaign was clear. Cohen explained to the *Salt Lake Tribune,* "We want to establish an attitude and personality for ABC that's funny, friendly, and irreverent."

Through test and focus groups the network had further discovered that people enjoyed television more than they were willing to admit, and as Lee Clow, TBWA\Chiat\Day's chairman, explained, the agency based its creative approach on this knowledge. "As you talk to people about their lives these days and how stressed they are, TV is this period of time where they actually get to recuperate a little bit," Clow said. "Kind of just plop yourself down and let something happen to you so you don't have to use your brain and work too hard for a few minutes. So we thought, why not kind of honestly celebrate the notion that TV is a good part of our lives, and sitting down in front of it for a while isn't a bad thing."

Launching a marketing campaign that celebrated television was not without risks in 1997. At the time there was outspoken criticism of television, with many people objecting to the sexual situations, strong language, and violence found in the programming. By choosing to praise television at a time when it was popular to criticize the medium, ABC knew that it was taking a chance.

The first phase of the campaign, which did not mention specific network programs, appeared on television. These spots established the visual elements that would define the campaign throughout its run: a yellow background on which appeared the black text of witty slogans offering a variety of takes on the "TV Is Good" theme. The initial wave of spots featured messages such as "Don't worry, you've got billions of brain cells," "You can talk to your wife anytime," "The couch is your friend," and "Life is short. Watch TV." Print and billboard ads appeared next, and, finally, the network began running spots for individual shows that incorporated the campaign style. In addition to the ads, ABC initiated cross-promotions with American Airlines, McDonald's, and Toys "R" Us. In the American Airlines promotion, the monthly newsletter for AAdvantage members included trivia questions about plot twists in ABC shows. AAdvantage members could then earn frequent-flier miles by mailing in correct answers to the questions. This extensive marketing reflected the fact that ABC had increased its advertising and promotion budget by 30 percent over the previous year. The budget for "TV Is Good" was approximately $12 million in 1997–98.

The TV spots got the attention of the press even before they were first broadcast. The message was quickly picked up by newspaper writers, and ABC was thrust into the media spotlight. Under the headline "Ads that Rot Your Brain," Jonathan Foreman of the *Wall Street Journal* wrote, "The new TV season gets under way this week, amidst one of the worst ad campaigns of all time. In an apparent effort to win over the young viewers of 'Generation X,' ABC settled on irony as an advertising gimmick." Monica Collins of the *Boston Herald* said, "At ABC, they're underestimating us like mad while the network runs the snootiest ad campaign ever." Some ABC affiliates had misgivings about the advertisements, too. Complaints from several affiliates convinced the network to drop one spot that said, "Books are overrated." In addition, organizations critical of television, including the nonprofit TV-Free America, blasted the commercials. As the spots began to air and the media debate about the campaign's merits gathered steam, Cohen told Bill Carter of the *New York Times,* "The reality is the spots have already worked. People are talking about ABC." Jamie Tarses, then the entertainment president for ABC, told *Broadcasting & Cable,* "Anybody would give their left arm for this kind of attention. This is what you want if you're selling television shows or cars or whatever... It's about making noise."

For the 1998–99 TV season, TBWA\Chiat\Day offered what it called an "evolved" version of the campaign, which, according to the *New York Times,* "is adspeak for 'You don't like it? All right, already! We'll change it.'" The ironic humor was toned down, and "TV Is Good" was changed to the slightly more sincere "We Love TV." The messages continued to be delivered in the same visual style (black text on a bright yellow background), and many seemed in keeping with the brashness of the previous seasons. For instance, one spot advised viewers, "Don't just sit there. Okay, just sit there&" another offered the dubious historical interpretation "Before TV, two world wars. After TV, zero." But the campaign also began to offer less polarizing messages, such as "TV, so good they named a frozen meal after it," and "Without a TV, how would you know where to put the sofa?" The 1998–99 season likewise marked an increase in series-specific commercials using the overall campaign's visual elements, humorous tone, and tagline. The campaign budget for that season was estimated at $15 million.

OUTCOME

ABC saw its "TV Is Good" campaign as successful for a number of reasons. First, the campaign received an impressive amount of press coverage. Second, another of the big three networks added to the publicity windfall by mocking the campaign with a television spot of its own. Third, public response to the campaign was mostly favorable. Cohen said to Tom Feran of the *Cleveland Plain Dealer,* "We did talk to a lot of viewers around the country and show them this material, and I think people sort of got it. They said, 'Wow, this is funny. ABC is funny. They must have good comedies.' And that's exactly the connection we wanted them to make."

Though industry observers likewise credited the network with effectively generating consumer interest and with building an identifiable brand image for itself, 1997–98 saw ABC's ratings decline more precipitously than those of the other two major networks. The many problems confronting ABC—ratings declines, an inability to create popular new programs, and ever-increasing competition from cable networks—were, however, the problems facing its broadcast competitors as well. In this context, ratings increases were not necessarily a realistic eventuality, at least in the short term. "The story isn't so much growth anymore," Joe Mandese, editor of the industry newsletter *The Myers Report,* told the *New York Times,* "as preserving your share." The network's ratings continued to decline in the following years, but so did those of NBC and CBS.

In the 1999–2000 season ABC and TBWA\Chiat\Day further redefined the brand-building project. Although the network's promotional spots continued to employ the visual elements and a measure of the ironic humor from the previous two seasons' campaigns, the new tagline, "America's Broadcasting Company," seemed to mark a departure in tone and strategy. The network and its agency maintained that the campaign was not a reversal of the previous years' tactics but rather a further evolution. This view was supported by a recurring message in the "America's Broadcasting Company" spots: "United we watch."

FURTHER READING

Battaglio, Stephen. "ABC Enjoys the Spread of Yellow-Spotted Fever." *Hollywood Reporter,* August 18, 1997, p.1.

Carter, Bill. "ABC's 'TV Is Good' Campaign Spawns Satirical Admiration." *Arizona Republic,* August 21, 1997, p. C6.

Elliott, Stuart. "ABC Stays with Old Yellow, but It's an 'Evolved' Form." *New York Times,* June 11, 1998.

———. "In an Unconventional Campaign, ABC Labels Itself America's Broadcasting Company." *New York Times,*

Feran, Tom. "ABC's Edgy Ads Getting Sharp Reaction." *Cleveland Plain Dealer,* August 25, 1997, p. 1E.

Holston, Noel. "Dumb and Dumber: ABC Promos Embrace the Boob Tube." *Minneapolis-St. Paul Star Tribune,* August 16, 1997, p. 1E.

Levin, Gary. "Promos: No 'Slogans Heroes.'" *Variety,* June 22, 1997, p. 1.

Lippert, Barbara. "I Want My ABC." *New York Magazine,* August 18, 1997, p. 20.

Littlefield, Kinney. "'TV Is Good' Says Nothing about ABC." *Santa Ana (CA) Orange County Register,* August 24, 1997, p. F5.

Moore, Frazier. "'TV Is Good'? ABC's Ad Campaign Strives for Irony." *Salt Lake Tribune,* May 28, 1997, p. B7.

Pope, Kyle,"ABC Brings Back a New Variation of 'TV Is Good,'" *Wall Street Journal,* June 11, 1998.

Santiago, Denise-Marie. "ABC's 'Hip' Ad Campaign Is Causing Comment—Pro and Con." *Pittsburgh Post-Gazette,* August 25, 1997, p. D3.

Alden Scott Crow
Mark Lane

Abercrombie & Fitch

6301 Fitch Path
New Albany, Ohio 43054
USA
Telephone: (614) 283-6500
Fax: (614) 283-6710
Web site: www.abercrombie.com

A & F QUARTERLY CAMPAIGN

OVERVIEW

Once renowned for supplying the rich and famous of America with outdoor gear, Abercrombie & Fitch (A & F) went bankrupt in the 1970s and was reinvented in the late 1980s as an apparel retailer for college-age teens and young adults. After going public in 1996, the company began to focus on marketing itself as a lifestyle brand, selling a freewheeling collegiate image more than engaging in any sustained pitches about product quality. With the help of Sam Shahid and Bruce Weber, the creative director and photographer who had together created such sexually explicit ad campaigns as those on behalf of Calvin Klein's Obsession fragrance in the 1980s, A & F in 1997 launched a hybrid of consumer magazine and product catalog—an increasingly popular marketing tool commonly called a "magalog"—that became the focus of its branded advertising for the next six years.

The "A & F Quarterly," as the publication was called, leaned heavily on magazine-like editorial features and art photography, with much less emphasis on traditional catalog fare like product specifications and pictures in which the clothing was central. In keeping with Weber's past work, the photos were notable for their focus on male bodies and for an open attitude toward sexuality in general. Many of the features in the magazine were controversial, including one encouraging the consumption of alcohol and another focusing on group sex. Though the magalog aimed to showcase the college lifestyle in a way that appealed to A & F's target market, many believed that it had the simultaneous goal of intentionally inciting controversy.

When the "A & F Quarterly" was discontinued in 2003, opinions were mixed as to its effectiveness as a marketing tool. There was little argument about the fact that it had raised the brand's profile immeasurably, but A & F sales had been consistently underwhelming since 2000. Some commentators observed that the company had reached a point beyond which further escalation of the magalog's shock value would become virtually impossible, and the company's future marketing course was uncertain. Nevertheless, the "A & F Quarterly" was a groundbreaking entry in the emerging magalog field.

HISTORICAL CONTEXT

Abercrombie & Fitch began life as a lower-Manhattan-based purveyor of high-quality hunting, fishing, and camping gear, and in the early twentieth century the store developed a loyal customer base among wealthy outdoors enthusiasts, including numerous famous Americans. Teddy Roosevelt visited the store to prepare for his numerous big-game expeditions, and every subsequent president through Gerald Ford was said to have been an Abercrombie & Fitch patron. Aviators Charles

Abercrombie & Fitch store in Bridgewater (New Jersey) Commons Shopping Mall.
© NAJLAH FEANNY/CORBIS.

Lindbergh and Amelia Earhart were notable Abercrombie & Fitch customers, as were screen stars Greta Garbo, Katharine Hepburn, and Clark Gable. The author Ernest Hemingway regularly bought gear and guns from Abercrombie & Fitch, including the shotgun he used to commit suicide.

By the late 1960s Abercrombie & Fitch had expanded substantially, with stores across the United States, but the company's fortunes nevertheless declined through the late 1970s, when it went bankrupt and was purchased by the sporting goods chain Oshman's. Abercrombie & Fitch fared little better under its new corporate parent, and in 1988 it was sold again, this time to The Limited, Inc. (later called Limited Brands). The Limited, Inc., had experienced success with concept-store startups including the women's clothing retailers The Limited and Express as well as the lingerie emporium Victoria's Secret. During the 1990s Abercrombie & Fitch's image was drastically recast. Though still retaining hints of its rugged outfitter's roots, the company became a maker of high-end casual wear for teens and college students. Abercrombie & Fitch went public in 1996, and The Limited divested itself of equity in the company.

Abercrombie & Fitch marketing was helmed in-house by Sam Shahid, the company's creative director as well as the president and creative director of his own agency, Shahid & Co., which represented other fashion brands as well. In preparing for the introduction of "A & F Quarterly," Shahid enlisted the photographer Bruce Weber, whose arty fashion photographs were well known for their sensuality. Shahid, creative director for Calvin Klein in the 1980s, had worked with Weber on the famously controversial sexual images in ads for such products as Obsession cologne.

TARGET MARKET

Abercrombie & Fitch's official target market from the late 1990s onward was no secret. Chairman and CEO Michael S. Jeffries told the *Wall Street Journal,* "We're a life-style brand, projecting inside the store and outside the store the life style of a very specific customer, the 18-to-22-year-old American college student." Though these young people were undoubtedly the brand's core loyalists, some critics believed that the company was also intentionally targeting younger teens with the consistently controversial images and editorial content in "A & F Quarterly." Abercrombie & Fitch (A & F) acknowledged that younger teens had been won over to the brand but argued that this was a function of kids' desire to emulate elder siblings and other trendsetters. After numerous complaints that young teens were purchasing the magalog, A & F established a policy requiring identification upon its purchase.

A & F was in the business of selling casual clothes often described as having a preppy or fraternity-house look, but its marketing focused less on the clothes

THE LIMITS OF PROVOCATION

Though Abercrombie & Fitch claimed that it did not intentionally incite controversy as a means of spurring sales, many industry observers took it for granted that this was the company's overriding strategy for building its image. After crossing the line, in the opinion of numerous public-advocacy groups, with a 1998 "A & F Quarterly" issue encouraging college students to drink creatively (and, accordingly, to excess), the company's magalog (a cross between a magazine and a catalog) continued to push the bounds of decency with images that included exposed male pubic hair and that depicted Santa and Mrs. Claus in a scene of sadomasochistic sexual play. In 2002 the company's provocation moved into new territory: it released a line of T-shirts featuring images of Asians along with text that many considered overtly racist. A & F apologized, as was its practice after inciting controversy, and it saw its stock price reach a yearly high. Later that year the company unveiled a line of thong underwear for girls aged 7 to 14 and then pulled the product a month later in the face of intense criticism, apologizing for any offense it had caused.

themselves than on a brand personality. This personality was built on celebratory and irreverent evocations of the college lifestyle, including an emphasis on freewheeling behavior, alcohol consumption, and especially on sexually suggestive images. Though many provocative images of women appeared, the preponderance of nearly nude men in the magalog, many of whom were pictured in groups, led to widespread observations that the publication was homoerotic. Though A & F built a following among gay men during this time, the company denied that it was intentionally marketing to gays. In response to charges that the magalog objectified the male body, campaign creator Sam Shahid told the *Wall Street Journal,* "Fine. Let them complain. Gays love it; straights love it; girls love it . . . It's in the eye of the beholder."

Beginning with a 1998 installment said to encourage irresponsible drinking, individual issues of the magalog repeatedly courted controversy, as did A & F clothing products in the 2000s. The company denied the widespread belief that it intentionally sparked controversy even at the expense of seeming offensive, but conventional wisdom maintained that the cultivation of a spirit of rebelliousness verging on the offensive was a marketing tactic of particular usefulness among college students.

COMPETITION

One of A & F's chief competitors was the mammoth chain the Gap, which was long associated with basic casual apparel such as khakis, T-shirts, and jeans. After several years of slumping sales and an ill-conceived attempt to branch out into more ambitious fashion styles, the chain refocused its energy on its basic lines in 1998. This return to form was announced and driven by a $300 million marketing campaign. TV spots in the campaign showed young men and women in Gap khakis and shirts, dancing and riding skateboards against a soundtrack of energetic music. Gap sales began to rebound, supplementing gains in the parent company Gap Inc.'s other chains, which included Banana Republic and Old Navy.

American Eagle Outfitters was a more direct competitor, as it targeted virtually the same group of young people as A & F, and with markedly similar clothing. In fact, the resemblance was close enough that A & F filed an unsuccessful lawsuit in 1998, alleging that American Eagle had copied its styles. Though A & F was perceived as having more status among teens and college students, American Eagle clothing was less expensive. The competition between the two clothiers became especially intense during the bleak sales season following the terrorist attacks of September 11, 2001. In the months leading up to Christmas 2001, A & F fought American Eagle with large-scale discounts and coupons, forcing American Eagle to discount even further (and forcing both companies to absorb heavy losses). The holiday 2001 season also saw American Eagle run its first TV commercials ever. Though less explicit than A & F's marketing, the American Eagle campaign similarly appealed to teen and young adult sexuality with scenes of young people dancing and kissing.

MARKETING STRATEGY

Though analysts contended that magalogs were not an efficient way of generating sales, A & F was able to build a signature environment with the "A & F Quarterly" and to rival the distribution numbers of successful mainstream magazines, thereby communicating its brand message in great depth to a loyal audience. Meanwhile, the provocative photographs and editorial content had the effect of consistently generating controversy. Far from hurting the company, these successive controversies added to the word-of-mouth buzz around the brand, which extended well beyond the magalogs' distribution base. The "A & F Quarterly" showed shots of merchandise for sale, but its primary focus was on images of attractive young men and women wearing minimal amounts of A & F apparel while engaged in suggestive recreational activities. There were also editorial features geared to the college lifestyle. Each issue focused on a seasonal range of activities in the college student's life. The fall issue used variations on a back-to-school theme, whereas the winter issue featured holiday imagery and content, the spring issue focused logically on spring break, and the summer issue evoked summer vacation. The magalog initially sold for $5 a copy—the price was later increased to $6—with a yearly subscription fee of $12. At the height of its popularity the quarterly's circulation was estimated at 220,000.

This format remained consistent throughout the six years that "A & F Quarterly" was produced, but several issues were singled out by critics for their alleged objectionable content. The fall 1998 issue was the first of these. Together with images of naked young people in a feature on campus "streaking" and tongue-in-cheek sexual advice in an article called "The Rules of Attraction," A & F ran a piece called "Drinking 101," which offered recipes for drinks such as the "Brain Hemorrhage" and advised its college-age audience (many of whom were not of legal drinking age) to "indulge in some creative drinking this semester." Vocal complaints from groups such as Mothers Against Drunk Driving led A & F to recall the unsold issues and physically excise the "Drinking 101" article. Once issues were returned to stores, A & F placed a responsible-drinking message on the magalog cover.

The Christmas 1999 issue of the magalog incited further controversy. The cover featured a shirtless young man holding a teddy bear, his pubic hair exposed by the low waistline of his pants, and another image in the magalog showed Santa Claus on his knees in front of Mrs. Claus, who was wearing a leather bustier and brandishing a whip. The issue also included an interview with the pornographic-movie star Jenna Jameson and a photo of the actor and comedian Andy Dick standing naked on an urban street with a sign in front of his midsection reading, "Hot nuts." Complaints from the Michigan attorney general about the Christmas issue further stoked the A & F buzz, and the company responded by placing a warning on the issue's cover declaring that it was intended for mature audiences only. The year 1999 also saw A & F take its sensual imagery to cable TV with commercials focusing on college men's wrestling teams.

After the terrorist attacks of September 11, 2001, marketers in all sectors found themselves rethinking their advertising messages, and A & F's irreverently sexual personality was not a good fit for the historical moment. The company canceled publication of the magalog's winter 2001 issue. A significant evolution in the "A & F Quarterly" came with 2002's summer issue, in which the company sold advertising space to other marketers looking to reach a college-age audience. Products advertised in that issue included SoBe beverages and the Sony Playstation 2 video-game system. In 2002 the magalog also came under fire for the lack of racial diversity among its models, many of whom had blond hair and blue eyes. This controversy dovetailed with the uproar over A & F T-shirts featuring text and images that were widely seen as promoting an offensive caricature of Asians. The Christmas 2003 issue, the cover of which touted "group sex and more," was recalled after widespread protests, and a *60 Minutes* report alleged that the company relegated its minority employees and others who did not fit the blond-haired, blue-eyed archetype to positions in back of the store rather than in more visible jobs. Meanwhile softening sales at A & F stores nationwide led investors to question the company's relative neglect of advertising channels outside of the magalog. On December 9, 2003, the company announced that the Christmas issue then in circulation would be the last "A & F Quarterly" to see publication.

OUTCOME

Between 1997 and 1999, while A & F expanded rapidly and posted double-digit sales growth in individual stores, the "A & F Quarterly" was praised as an innovative and effective marketing tool. As disappointing 1999 sales results began to emerge, however, many in the media began to question A & F's marketing strategy. Sales figures in the years 2000–03 proved equally disappointing, and though these years corresponded with a dramatically slumping American economy, analysts also criticized A & F's approach to marketing. Richard E. Jaffe, a retail analyst with the firm UBS, told the *New York Times* that "the magalog was effective at raising visibility" but that "in terms of its racy content, it became harder and harder to outdo themselves, to provoke, to generate a reaction and create the excitement of the past." At the time of the discontinuation of "A & F Quarterly," A & F had seen declines in its key sales measurement—sales at stores open at least a year—for 39 of the preceding 46 months. Despite these criticisms, the "A & F Quarterly" was indisputably one of the most talked-about print campaigns of its time, and it was roundly acknowledged as an influential pioneer in the growing magalog movement.

FURTHER READING

Carr, David, and Tracie Rozhon. "Abercrombie & Fitch to End Its Racy Magazine." *New York Times,* December 10, 2003.

Cuneo, Alice Z. "Abercrombie & Fitch." *Advertising Age,* June 28, 1999.

———. "Abercrombie & Fitch Takes Its Ads to TV." *Advertising Age,* August 2, 1999.

Edwards, Jim. "Saving Face." *Brandweek,* October 6, 2003.

Elliott, Stuart. "After Sept. 11, Value and Price Become the Themes for Promoting Holiday Shopping." *New York Times,* November 16, 2001.

———. "Come Hither: Abercrombie & Fitch Invites Other Advertisers into Its A & F Quarterly." *New York Times,* May 3, 2002.

Gross, Daniel. "Abercrombie & Fitch's Blue Christmas." *Slate,* December 8, 2003. Available from <http://www.slate.com/id/2092175>

Lindsay, Greg. "Morphing Magalogs." *Folio: The Magazine for Magazine Management,* July 2002.

Lippert, Barbara. "Season's Meetings." *Adweek,* December 20, 1999.

Wells, Melanie. "Anticlimax." *Forbes,* March 20, 2000.

White, Erin. "Showdown in Sweaterland: A & F, American Eagle Tussle Selling Look-Alike Clothing to Same Group of Teens." *Wall Street Journal,* December 21, 2001.

Williams, Mark. "Catalog Controversy." *Marketing News,* September 14, 1998.

Mark Lane

Accenture, Ltd.

22 Victoria Street
Hamilton, HM12
Bermuda
Telephone: (441) 296-8262
Fax: (441) 296-4245
Web site: www.accenture.com

I AM YOUR IDEA CAMPAIGN

OVERVIEW

Andersen Consulting, a global technology, management, and outsourcing consultancy, was forced to change its name after splitting with its sibling company, the accounting firm Arthur Andersen, in January 2001. The rebranded company, Accenture, Ltd., publicized its new name in a high-profile marketing campaign in 2001 that was widely criticized but that was effective, according to some observers, at raising awareness of the Accenture brand among corporate executives, the ultimate target of all consulting-industry advertising. Accenture and its agency, New York–based Young & Rubicam, followed up this initial effort with "I Am Your Idea," a 2002–03 campaign designed to further heighten the company's brand image among high-level executives.

"I Am Your Idea" was a global campaign employing an estimated budget of $70 million to spread the message that Accenture had the capability to turn ideas into effective business practices. TV, print, and poster executions used the notion of ideas actually addressing their owners—corporate executives—via interior voices and written messages in public areas, among other modes of communication. In each case the ideas sought to make their presence and, accordingly, their value known to their owners. Print ads and TV spots alike employed the message "It's not how many ideas you have. It's how many you make happen," along with the tagline "Innovation Delivered."

The campaign was credited with substantially increasing global awareness of the Accenture brand and with increasing the likelihood that high-level executives would consider the consulting firm for future projects. Accenture's billings during the campaign's run far exceeded the goal of $12 billion set prior to the launch. "I Am Your Idea" won a 2004 Euro EFFIE for its success in Europe.

HISTORICAL CONTEXT

Accenture's roots went back to the 1950s, when the Chicago-based accounting firm Arthur Andersen developed a consulting division. As this division grew, its leadership became dissatisfied with the subservient position that consulting occupied in the company's hierarchy. A new corporate structure was thus created in 1989, making Arthur Andersen and Andersen Consulting separate subsidiaries of the same parent company, but a clause in the companies' contract with one another mandated that the more lucrative of the two share its annual profits with the other. This clause resulted in increasing friction between the two entities in the context of a booming consulting industry and a flat market for accountants, and Andersen Consulting's sense of the agreement's unfairness was exacerbated when Arthur Andersen launched a competing consulting division. Andersen Consulting initiated a split with Arthur Andersen in 1997, but the split was delayed by years of legal wrangling. Andersen Consulting finally won the right to sever its ties with the accounting firm in 2000, on the conditions that it pay Arthur Andersen $1 billion and rebrand itself under a new name. Andersen Consulting was renamed Accenture in late 2000, and the company was officially relaunched on January 1, 2001.

The Accenture name was widely derided by analysts and media critics, even as the company and its agency, New York's Young & Rubicam, were setting out to imbue that name with an identity via an estimated $175 million global advertising campaign. Tagged "Now It Gets Interesting," the campaign appeared in print before making its TV debut via four spots that aired during the 2001 Super Bowl. These spots were ranked among the least-recalled of all commercials that aired on that year's broadcast, and the campaign as a whole was generally maligned by ad-industry critics. *B to B* magazine, however, claimed that "Now It Gets Interesting" resonated with its ultimate target: the high-level corporate executives responsible for hiring consulting firms such as Accenture.

Because they were dependent on other corporations for their business, consulting companies' fortunes were directly linked to the state of the economy at large. A cooling global economic climate in the first few years of the twenty-first century meant slowed growth for the consulting industry. Therefore, if they hoped to grow, Accenture and its competitors had to steal market share from one another. Because many competitors offered the same suite of services as Accenture—corporations typically turned to Accenture for help with technology, management, and outsourcing issues—a particular emphasis was placed on differentiating the company through marketing.

WHAT'S AN "ACCENTURE"?

Andersen Consulting's lengthy and bitter effort to separate itself from its sibling, the accounting firm Arthur Andersen, was concluded in late summer 2000, when an international arbitrator ruled that the separation could proceed as long as Andersen Consulting paid Arthur Andersen $1 billion and changed its name by January 2001. The consulting company thus embarked on an intense search for a new name, hiring a leading identity-and-design agency to come up with ideas before settling on Accenture, the brainchild of Kim Peterson, an Andersen Consulting employee in Oslo, Norway. Peterson came up with the name by combining the words "accent" and "future." He told *Advertising Age,* "I wanted a word that had a lot of positive associations to it . . . and that would emphasize accomplishment and accelerated growth . . . as well as adventure and excitement and also the future." As compensation for his idea, Peterson was awarded a free trip to Melbourne, Australia, to attend a company-sponsored golf championship.

TARGET MARKET

"I Am Your Idea," the follow-up to "Now It Gets Interesting," again targeted corporate decision makers—senior executives with titles such as CEO, CFO, COO, CIO, and CMO—but was not saddled with the simultaneous mainstream branding challenge of its predecessor. The campaign's goal was to make Accenture one of the companies that these executives naturally thought of when considering embarking on major projects requiring outside consultants. Young & Rubicam sought to accomplish this by addressing a negative perception that the target group often brought to its dealings with consultants: the idea that consulting firms dogmatically insisted on their own ideas without taking fully their clients' needs into consideration. As with "Now It Gets Interesting," "I Am Your Idea" was a global effort, focusing on business-oriented print and TV outlets as well as signage in airports worldwide.

COMPETITION

Accenture's most direct competitor at this time was the newly strengthened consulting division of the old-line tech giant International Business Machines Corporation (IBM). It was initially known for its computer-focused consulting, but with its July 2002 acquisition of the consulting division of accounting firm PricewaterhouseCoopers, IBM Business Consulting Services (later called IBM Global Services) doubled in size and dramatically extended its range of business expertise. IBM was thus positioned to transcend its reputation as a tech firm, and this project dictated much of its consulting-focused advertising in the following years. The IBM division's first major postacquisition campaign, for instance, used the theme "Deeper" to communicate its new strength. Released in late 2002, the $90 million print campaign employed images such as that of a jungle, with copy suggesting the immensely complex nature of thoroughly assessing a business's needs. "Everything at once?" the ad's copy read, "Who would have the depth?" Another ad in the campaign used an image of the Grand

Canyon to illustrate the idea that IBM's knowledge went "deeper" than that of competitors in a long list of industries.

Another of Accenture's competitors, Electronic Data Systems (EDS), was likewise in a transitional phase that, during this time, dictated the focus and tone of its advertising. EDS broke the consulting-industry mold with an overtly zany 2000 Super Bowl commercial, via the advertising agency Fallon Worldwide, in which cowboys on horseback were shown rounding up thousands of cats, an image meant to evoke EDS's ability to impose order on a chaotic business situation. In 2001 another EDS Super Bowl spot dramatized the same idea using imagery recalling the running of the bulls in Pamplona, Spain, with a key difference: the animals chasing the frenzied participants were squirrels. The following year EDS lost market share and prestige as a result of a number of badly managed major contracts, and the company's marketing profile accordingly diminished. EDS commercials returned to TV in 2003, but the new global campaign was meant to repair the company's reputation among corporate executives and thus eschewed the attention-getting advertising concepts for which the company had become known.

MARKETING STRATEGY

The controlling idea behind the "I Am Your Idea" campaign was that Accenture could help corporate executives turn their ideas into reality. An initial set of TV spots were released at the start of the campaign in February 2002, and a second round of commercials headlined a September 2002 campaign update. Given Accenture's belief that business-oriented magazines and newspapers worldwide were the best way to reach high-level corporate executives, print executions ran throughout the campaign's cycle. Airport posters likewise were employed for the duration of the campaign, in keeping with the target group's need to travel frequently. The campaign ran through August 2003, leveraging an estimated budget of $70 million.

The TV spots all used the conceit of an idea speaking to its owner. In each case the owner of the idea was an upscale, middle-aged executive, and the idea was depicted as an admonitory voice urging the executive to act before it, the idea, disappeared. Several spots featured the idea speaking via voice-over, as though in the executive's mind. For instance, an executive was shown walking, briefcase in hand, through the deserted streets of a city at night, while his idea said, "Listen, it's me. You know, I'm your idea. You can't ignore me. I'm what keeps you up at night. I make you restless, maybe even a little nervous." Streetlights and storefront displays mysteriously lit up, as though the idea was employing supernatural force to win the executive's attention. "After all," the idea continued, proclaiming the message that ran in each of the campaign's executions, "It's not how many ideas you have. It's how many you make happen." A more humorous spot showed an idea speaking to an executive by other means. The commercial opened on the scene of a doctor entering a patient's room to explain the nature of his malady: "You seem to have one of those office sticky notes lodged in your head." The doctor displayed the incriminating X-ray, which clearly showed a yellow sticky note reading "USE ME" embedded in the man's skull. "Do something with that idea," the doctor advised, "and then it should disappear." "But what if I can't?" the patient asked. The doctor's deadpan response was, "It could develop into a notepad, a folder, possibly even a filing cabinet." Each TV spot closed with the Accenture logo and the tagline "Innovation Delivered."

Print ads used a similar concept to send the same warning about the necessity to realize the potential of one's ideas. In the ads ideas spoke through signs on airport walls, the steps of office buildings, freeway exit signs, and other backdrops typically frequented by elite businesspeople. One ad showed a rack of airport luggage carts with attached signs that read, "I am your idea. Push me." Another ad featured a close-up of a golf ball on a tee as a golfer prepared to strike it. On the ball was printed, "I am your idea. Drive me." Yet another print execution focused on a disposable coffee cup wrapped in an insulating cardboard sleeve reading, "I am your idea. I won't stay hot forever." Small copy at the bottom of each ad reiterated the message from the TV spots: "It's not how many ideas you have. It's how many you make happen. So whether it's your idea or Accenture's, we'll help you turn innovation into results." Readers were directed to the Accenture website, www.accenture.com, and the "Innovation Delivered" tagline ran underneath the Accenture logo.

The advertising was supported by a schedule of global events showcasing the Accenture brand, and dozens of case studies were made available on the corporate website, detailing the ways in which Accenture had helped prominent clients in the past.

OUTCOME

In-house research concluded that, as a result of "I Am Your Idea," unaided global awareness of the Accenture brand grew from 29 percent to 34 percent. The company also concluded that the number of target executives who might consider Accenture as a consulting partner in the future had tripled, and Accenture generated $16.1 billion in bookings during the campaign's run, well surpassing its precampaign goal of $12 billion in bookings. For its effectiveness in the European market, the campaign won a 2004 Euro EFFIE Gold Award in the corporate category as well as the inaugural Sappi Print Media Efficiency Award at that year's Euro EFFIE ceremony (the pan-European counterpart to the New York American Marketing Association's annual EFFIE Awards).

A combination of factors, however, led Accenture to recast its marketing in 2003. For one, the sustained economic downturn had made the idea of innovation, showcased so prominently in "I Am Your Idea" television and print executions, seem outdated, according to James Murphy, Accenture's global managing director of marketing and communications. Additionally, IBM's acquisition of PricewaterhouseCoopers, coming midway through the first year of the "I Am Your Idea" campaign, heightened Accenture's need to raise its corporate profile. In October 2003, accordingly, a new campaign featuring professional-golf superstar Tiger Woods was unveiled.

FURTHER READING

Callahan, Sean. "Tiger Tees Off in New Accenture Campaign." *B to B,* October 13, 2003.

Clark, Philip B. "Andersen Becomes Accenture." *B to B,* November 6, 2000.

Crain, Rance. "'Accenture' Seemed Foolish; Now It Seems a Stroke of Luck." *Advertising Age,* January 28, 2002.

Davis, Wendy. "Accenture May Finesse Effort after Criticism." *Advertising Age,* February 12, 2001.

Linnett, Richard. "Andersen's Accenture Gets $175 Mil Ad Blitz." *Advertising Age,* December 4, 2000.

Maddox, Kate. "Sawyer Awards." *B to B,* December 10, 2001.

Steinberg, Brian. "Media & Marketing—Advertising: Accenture Ads Tee Off with Tiger; Consultancy Starts Effort with Golfer in the Hopes of Taking Share from IBM." *Wall Street Journal,* October 3, 2003.

Sweeney, Jack. "The Origin of Species." *Consulting Magazine,* January 2004.

Walker, Rob. "Making a Name in Consulting." *Slate,* January 10, 2001. Available from <http://www.slate.com/?id=1006844>

Wasserman, Todd. "Accenture Accents 'Idea' Campaign." *Brandweek,* September 30, 2002.

Mark Lane

adidas America, Inc.

5055 N. Greeley Avenue
Portland, Oregon 97217
USA
Telephone: (800) 448-1796
Fax: (800) 448-1796
Web site: www.adidas.com

RUNNERS. YEAH, WE'RE DIFFERENT CAMPAIGN

OVERVIEW

German sporting-goods company adidas-Salomon AG returned from near death in the mid-1990s with a new focus and global strategy. No longer content to allow competitors, especially the seemingly invincible Nike, to dominate the sporting-goods category, adidas launched a full-scale offensive designed to increase awareness of the brand, enhance its image, and elevate sales. The company moved production facilities to Asia to cut manufacturing costs, formed high-visibility alliances with sports organizations and athletes (including a sponsorship of the New York Yankees baseball team beginning in 1997), purchased the French company Salomon SA (a manufacturer of golf, ski, and bike equipment) in 1997, and pumped additional funds into its modest marketing budget. Hoping to increase the sales of its running accessories in the United States, adidas America, Inc., the U.S. headquarters for adidas, released a provocative campaign titled "Runners. Yeah, We're Different."

The San Francisco office of advertising agency Leagas Delaney released the branding campaign with an estimated $1 million. To prove that the company understood the sport of running, the "Runners. Yeah, We're Different" campaign, which began in 1998, targeted the serious runner, a relatively small and anonymous audience. With full-page and two-page ads in specialty magazines such as *Runner's World* and *Running Times* and with some executions in the general-interest *Sports Illustrated,* the series of print ads celebrated the rather unusual but relatively common habits of dedicated runners, such as smearing Vaseline on the inner thighs and under the arms to prevent chafing. Sean Ehringer, Leagas Delaney's creative director, explained, "[adidas] wanted to do a brand focus campaign that gave them some running credentials, and the way we decided to do that was to let runners know that we understand them… Runners have their own kind of weird way of doing things, so there's a lot of things to talk about there." The campaign ended in 2000.

According to the ad-industry publication *Campaign,* "Runners. Yeah, We're Different" was the third most awarded series of print ads in the world for 2000. It helped adidas's brand awareness in the United States reach record highs and was eventually expanded globally.

HISTORICAL CONTEXT

Adolf Dassler, known as Adi, began making athletic shoes in 1920 in Germany. His shoes made their first appearance in the Olympics in 1928, and in 1936 Jesse Owens won four Olympic gold medals running in Dassler's track shoes. It was not until 1948 that Dassler founded the adidas company. The company was immensely successful, flourishing through the 1960s and 1970s. At the 1972 Olympic Games, noted *Advertising Age,* more than 80 percent of the gold-medal winners sported adidas shoes, and all of the Olympic officials were outfitted in uniforms designed by adidas. During that decade adidas gear could be found on most professional soccer players and on about 75 percent of professional basketball players. By 1978, the year of Dassler's death, the adidas brand enjoyed a global recognition rate of about 95 percent.

Although it took years for adidas to build a reputation, the company's commanding grip of the athletic-goods market deteriorated quickly. Not only did adidas miss some important athletic trends, such as the jogging craze of the late 1970s, but it also suffered from management problems. Dassler's son Horst took control of the company in 1985, but he died just two years later, and adidas was sold in 1989 to French businessman Bernard Tapie, who soon declared bankruptcy during the course of a political scandal. By the time creditors approached French businessman Robert Louis-Dreyfus to take over the failing company in 1992, adidas's share of the U.S. running-shoe market had fallen from a leading 70 percent share in the early 1970s to a dismal 1.9 percent, and the company was losing more than $100 million annually.

Louis-Dreyfus knew nothing about the athletic-shoe business, but he had succeeded in turning around other failing companies, notably the London advertising agency Saatchi & Saatchi. After taking the helm at adidas in 1993, Louis-Dreyfus downsized the staff, moved production to Asia, and nearly doubled the marketing budget, from 6 percent of sales to 11 percent, to acknowledge the importance of advertising and image. Not only did adidas manage to elude death, but it also quickly and steadily began to increase sales and boost its reputation. Between 1992 and 1996 the company's share of the $8 billion U.S. market increased from 2 percent to a small but more respectable 5 percent, and its revenues grew from $1.7 billion to $2.8 billion. In 1994 U.S. sales grew 62 percent, and a year later the company went public, the same year the rather unfit Louis-Dreyfus symbolically demonstrated his commitment to adidas by running in and completing the Boston Marathon. By the late 1990s the company's U.S. sales were growing at an annual rate of nearly 50 percent, and adidas had no intention of slowing its pace. Steve Wynne, president of adidas America, told *Fortune* in 1997, "We have huge market share to gain in the United States... We're very focused on what we need to do right now. In 1998, you're going to see some very big improvements in our sales."

TARGET MARKET

Because adidas was a multisport company, it traditionally geared its goods and its advertising toward athletes.

> ### STARS AND STRIPES
>
> Adidas's comeback was boosted by the resurgent popularity in the early 1990s of adidas gear, adorned with the trademark three-stripes design and once again considered stylish after decades of being passé. Celebrities such as Madonna, Cindy Crawford, and the band Luscious Jackson all appeared sporting adidas apparel.

The company developed equipment for numerous sports, including wrestling, weight lifting, basketball, tennis, running, and soccer. Adidas's target audience suddenly expanded in the 1990s, however, as renewed interest in the adidas brand, particularly in apparel, grew. Adidas was no longer associated solely with sports enthusiasts but with fashion-conscious youth, and the company embraced the market composed of 20- to 25-year-olds.

Despite its popularity with the youth market, adidas continued its marketing efforts in niche segments, directing advertising toward markets with specific athletic needs. For the "Runners. Yeah, We're Different" campaign, adidas narrowed its audience to pinpoint the serious runner, a group frequently overlooked by the sports media despite the popularity of running. The lack of hype surrounding running could perhaps be attributed to the individuality and solitude of the sport. As Leagas Delaney's Ehringer remarked, "Most people who run run silently on their own for their own reasons, and nobody even knows they exist." Ehringer also emphasized the importance of running and said, "It is very much a unique and individual sport, but it's a part of almost every athlete's life at some point." To lure runners, an extremely dedicated lot, adidas adopted an honest and direct approach. Ryan Erickson, a marketing executive at adidas's rival Reebok International Ltd., explained the importance of credibility when advertising to runners. Erickson said in *Footwear News,* "Runners sniff out fake stuff in a heartbeat."

COMPETITION

In the highly competitive U.S. athletic-footwear category, adidas America faced considerable competition from Nike and Reebok, the top two athletic-shoe manufacturers in the nation. Nike, which had dominated the field since the 1980s, when it wrested market share away from adidas during the running craze, boasted a 47 percent share of the U.S. athletic-footwear market in 1997, up from 45.2 percent in 1996, according to the industry newsletter *Sporting Goods Intelligence.* Reebok held a market share of 15.2 percent in 1997 and 16.5 percent in 1996. Although it was trailing Nike and Reebok considerably, adidas was becoming increasingly successful and profitable. Adidas's share of the athletic-footwear market had grown from 5.4 percent in 1996 to 6.1 percent a year later, and in 1997 adidas snagged the number three position away from Fila Sport SpA, the U.S. arm of Fila Holding SpA. Also that year, adidas's U.S. sales enjoyed a 66 percent increase over 1996.

Helping adidas was the rejuvenation of the running-shoe category in the late 1990s. Running-shoe sales in the United States increased by 11 percent in 1997, and even smaller niche players, such as New Balance Athletic Shoe, Inc., and Saucony, Inc., were doing well. By 1996 adidas had managed to move up to the number two spot in the running category, and that year its running business increased an impressive 74 percent in the United States.

Although adidas had a long way to go before it could hope to come within hitting range of Nike, the company still set its sights on taking market share away from Nike and Reebok. Adidas did not have the aggressive marketing budget of its chief rivals—adidas estimated that Nike's media budget was 10 times greater than its own—but adidas believed that its quality products and careful marketing could generate enthusiasm among consumers. Fortunately for adidas, Nike hit a rough patch in the late 1990s that helped pave the way for adidas's success. Although Nike still dominated the athletic-footwear category, its hold grew weaker. Its U.S. athletic-footwear sales dropped 18 percent in the third quarter that ended February 28, 1998. David Aaker, a professor at the University of California at Berkeley, explained in *Adweek,* "The Nike brand has grown universal and ubiquitous to the point where it is losing its core appeal as a maverick." In reaction, Nike expanded its famous "Just Do It" tagline and added the gentler "I Can" slogan in 1998, and its swoosh logo was toned down, no longer boldly emblazoned on every Nike product. Adidas, meanwhile, planned to take advantage of Nike's slump to build its brand image. Ehringer noted, "Our job here in the U.S. specifically has been to replace the notion, 'I'm buying this for what it isn't' to 'I'm buying this for what it is.' We've been trying to rebuild the brand in a sense and put its credentials out there and make sure people understand that it's a multisport brand... so when fashions come and go, in the end, [adidas is] still a legitimate sports brand for sports."

MARKETING STRATEGY

In planning the "Runners. Yeah, We're Different" branding campaign, adidas and Leagas Delaney felt that it was important to speak directly to the runner. Ehringer told Joan Voight of *Adweek,* "I am so tired of this huge trend where ads keep telling you that you are not adequate in some way. 'Be that' or 'Do this.'... What is wrong with celebrating the fun-ness of the brand?... Better to have a conversation with people, not a conversation at people." In keeping with this belief, and to make the most of adidas's marketing dollars, Leagas Delaney created a series of colorful print ads that celebrated running with a direct and unique approach only runners would likely appreciate and understand. Ehringer explained, "The unusual thing about [the campaign] was we were really very literal about it. I think it was pretty courageous to do ads that were so honest about really talking to runners that a lot of people wouldn't even know what you were talking about." To add an extra element of interest and to further suggest adidas's bond with runners, many of the ads starred adidas-sponsored runners, talented athletes with little face-recognition value.

One of the early ads was a two-page color spread featuring a male runner—an adidas-sponsored marathon runner—applying bandages to his nipples at a road race. His shirt, with pinned-on race number, was casually tucked into the waistband of his shorts as he completed the bandaging task. Skyscrapers and other runners appeared in the background. A heavyset woman in nonrunning attire, perhaps a spectator, observed the runner's ritual with a slightly bewildered look, emphasizing how odd the act must appear to nonrunners. The only text in the ad was the adidas logo in one corner and the tagline in another. A second ad showed a walking and running path in a city. A male runner blew his nose in typical runner fashion—with a finger pressed against one nostril to allow the forceful emanation of mucus from the other—as a disgusted nonrunning female looked on. The "Runners. Yeah, We're Different" slogan appeared in the middle of the ad, and the text at the bottom read, "You've never experienced a support shoe like this. The incredibly smooth ride of the Equipment Tyranny is something different too." The $1 million campaign appeared in running-specific publications such as *Runner's World* and *Running Times* and in the popular magazine *Sports Illustrated.* Another ad showed two male runners racing a cable car up a steep San Francisco hill as cable car riders looked on. The Vaseline ad featured a male and a female runner getting ready for a race by applying Vaseline to various body parts that might otherwise get rubbed raw while running. The male runner was Peter Julian, who was a four-time all-American while at the University of Portland. Similar ads continued until the campaign ended in 2000.

OUTCOME

The "Runners. Yeah, We're Different" campaign generated much interest and discussion among runners. The campaign ended in 2000, and some of the final ads were bolder than those from 1998. One 1999 ad, for example, featured a full view of the backside of a naked male runner (two-time 10,000-meter Olympian and four-time 10,000-meter U.S. champion Todd Williams) who stood by the open trunk of his car to change out of his muddy running clothes. Another ad showed a female runner squatting by a tree next to a trail, her shorts pulled down. Although these ads were quite daring, the acts featured were not out of the ordinary for runners. Adidas's director of marketing communications, Karyn Thale, told *Adweek* that the company was pleased with the advertising efforts and said, "It is time to tell our story in the U.S., and the Leagas ads are doing a great job of [expressing] our brand's young, fresh and hardworking image here."

Adidas continued to thrive and in 1998 held onto its number three ranking in the athletic-footwear industry with a 6 percent share, according to market research firm NPD Group, Inc. In comparison, Nike's retail dollar share was 34 percent and Reebok's 13 percent. Although overall spending on athletic shoes dropped 6 percent from the previous year, running shoes continued to lead the athletic-footwear category, acquiring 17.1 percent of retail sales. Adidas's U.S. net sales jumped 68 percent to $1.59 billion, and the running category grew more than 50 percent from 1997. Adidas spokesperson John Fread told the *Business Journal of Portland,* "For us, [1998] was an outstanding year, another record." Adidas was definitely back in the game, and it planned to stay there, pursuing its commitment to sports and athletes around the globe.

In the campaign's final year adidas reached its highest brand awareness in company history. The adidas sales increase during the campaign shocked sporting-goods analysts because running shoes were previously considered a slow-growth category. The print ads collected more awards than print ads released by any other competitor in 2000, and adidas eventually expanded the campaign internationally.

FURTHER READING

Cowen, Matthew. "'Surfer' Sends AMV to Top of the Gunn League." *Campaign,* November 10, 2000, p. 7.

Dill, Mallorre. "Crowned Prints." *Adweek* (eastern ed.), June 5, 2000, p. 24.

Jensen, Jeff. "Reebok Backs New Shoe with Anti-Nike Stance." *Advertising Age,* May 25, 1998, p. 4.

Levine, Joshua. "Adidas Flies Again." *Forbes,* March 25, 1995, p. 44.

Puris, Martin. "Bringing Back Adidas." *Advertising Age,* March 8, 1999, p. 14.

Voight, Joan. "Adidas American Style." *Adweek,* October 5, 1998.

Wallace, Charles P. "Adidas Back in the Game." *Fortune,* August 18, 1997, p. 176f.

Mariko Fujinaka
Kevin Teague

adidas-Salomon AG

Adi-Dassler-Strasse 1-2
Herzogenaurach, 91074
Germany
Telephone: 49 9132840
Fax: 49 9132842241
Web site: www.adidasgroup.com

IMPOSSIBLE IS NOTHING CAMPAIGN

OVERVIEW

Over the years adidas-Salomon AG has maintained an international reputation as a premier maker of sporting goods and athletic footwear. It has hired some of the sporting world's top athletes as spokespersons for its products, and the company has also owned a sponsorship deal with the New York Yankees. Despite its high profile in the industry, however, the company remained the also-ran athletic footwear company in the United States, behind Nike, Reebok, and New Balance. In addition, in 2003 the company reported that its total sales in the United States had dropped 16 percent in the first nine months of that year. Further confounding adidas, which sponsored the 2004 Olympic Summer Games, was the loss of its sponsorship rights to the 2008 Olympics to its competitor Nike.

To gain an edge over the competition and to reenergize its business in the United States, in 2004 adidas-Salomon AG introduced a $50 million brand-marketing campaign—the largest ever undertaken by the company—that included television, print, and Internet ads. Themed "Impossible Is Nothing," the yearlong global campaign was created for adidas by 180/TBWA, a partnership between 180, an agency based in Amsterdam, and the San Francisco agency TBWA/Chiat/Day. It kicked off with television spots featuring digitally altered footage of boxing legend Muhammad Ali jogging with some of the top athletes of the 1990s and 2000s, such as soccer star David Beckham. Athletes featured in subsequent ads included Ali's daughter Laila, also a boxer, NBA greats Tracy McGrady and Tim Duncan, and tennis champion Justine Henin-Hardenne.

The campaign clearly resonated with consumers and earned praise and official recognition from the advertising industry. After it began, the company reported that U.S. sales were up 11 percent compared with the same period the previous year.

HISTORICAL CONTEXT

Adidas was founded in the late 1920s in Germany by brothers Adi and Rudi Dassler. According to the company, Adi Dassler "had passion for every sport and a passion to make equipment to help every athlete perform better." In 1928 adidas began equipping Olympic athletes, and it continued to do so over the years. Runner Jesse Owens wore the company's track shoes during his Olympic competition in 1936, and it was reported that at the 1972 Olympics some 80 percent of the gold-medal-winning athletes wore adidas shoes. Adi Dassler's innovations included inventing screw-in cleats for soccer shoes and introducing a lightweight sprint spike. When the brothers ended their partnership in the late 1940s, Adi kept the business going and continued to develop

© PETER KNEFFEL/DPA/CORBIS.

sporting equipment intended to enhance the performance of athletes at all levels.

By the 1990s, however, the company was struggling. This was due in part to mismanagement by Adi's son Horst, who, after Adi died, had taken control of adidas in 1985. Horst's death in 1987 led to the sale of the company in 1989 to French businessman Bernard Tapie, who filed for bankruptcy soon after purchasing adidas. By 1992 the company's U.S. market share had taken a nosedive, dropping to 1.9 percent from a high of 70 percent 20 years earlier.

In 1992 another French businessman, Robert Louis-Dreyfus, took the helm at adidas, and by the late 1990s the company was on an upward swing, increasing its business by 74 percent in the United States. But in 2003 adidas, with a 10 percent market share, still lagged behind Nike in sales, and its North American business was again on a downward slide, dropping 16 percent in the first nine months of that year. Herbert Hainer, who had succeeded Louis-Dreyfus as adidas-Salomon president and CEO in 2001, told *Advertising Age* that the drop in U.S. sales in 2003 was not a one-year problem but rather had been ongoing for several years. Hainer blamed the problem on the fact that adidas had been "slow to adapt to a shift in demand from many of our customers."

In an effort to revitalize its U.S. business, the company refocused its marketing to attract younger consumers and shifted its global marketing functions to the company's American headquarters in Portland, Oregon. Adidas also implemented a new, more cohesive approach to its international advertising by hiring American agency TBWA/Chiat/Day as its "global agency network." For the development of the upcoming campaign, TBWA was partnered with 180, an Amsterdam-based shop that had been creating successful ads for adidas since 1998.

TARGET MARKET

The "Impossible Is Nothing" campaign was driven by adidas's efforts to shift its marketing focus to reach its target audience, 12- to 24-year-old consumers involved in sports. Based on statistics showing that men between the ages of 18 and 34 spent more time online than watching television, adidas also shifted some of its marketing to the Internet. Tara Moss, Internet business developer for adidas America, explained during an interview with *Advertising Age,* "We were trying to reach that teen audience that is dedicated to sports. Their apparel and footwear is really necessary to them in their daily lives."

Whether the new campaign would actually appeal to its target audience was questioned by some. In an interview with the *Oregonian,* Paul Swangard, managing director of the Warsaw Sports Marketing Center at the University of Oregon, said that adidas needed to make changes in its marketing to be competitive with such companies as Nike and Reebok, who were using high-profile athletes, including NBA stars LeBron James and Yao Ming, respectively, to promote their products. "The challenge here is whether young teenagers, who are really the hot market for shoes and apparel, resonate with [Muhammad] Ali," he said. "Many of these kids may never have seen him compete in their lifetime."

COMPETITION

With a 37 percent market share in the United States, Nike had a firm hold on its position as the number one sporting goods company. In 2004 it introduced one of its most extensive advertising pushes, a campaign that asked the question "What If?" Like the adidas ads that featured star athletes, Nike's commercials used a roster of top athletic performers. But rather than showing the athletes doing what they did best, the Nike ads depicted athletes participating in sports other than their specialty. For instance, tennis star Serena Williams played beach volleyball, and Tour de France champion Lance Armstrong sparred in a boxing ring. As Nancy Monsarrat, Nike's director of U.S. advertising, explained to the *Washington Times,* "What if Lance Armstrong was given a pair of boxing gloves instead of a bike as a child? Our belief is that a passionate athlete's drive to win would translate into success in any sport."

Reebok International Ltd., the number two maker of athletic shoes in the United States, had employed numerous memorable marketing campaigns, from "Because Life Is Not a Spectator Sport" in the mid-1980s to "Life Is Short, Play Hard" in 1991. In 2003 it introduced its "Outperform" campaign. According to the company, this campaign allowed Reebok "to educate consumers about our heritage in performance. The first commercial went all the way back to 1895 and the beginnings of the J.W. Foster Company, working our way up to the present day." Reebok increased its international marketing in 2004, starting a major ad campaign in China, where the market for sneakers was $500 million and Reebok's sales accounted for just $40 million of that. The company's international presence also was expanded in Europe, with French soccer star Nicolas Anelka serving as spokesman. In Latin America and the United States the brand partnered with pop singer Shakira.

MARKETING STRATEGY

The adidas "Impossible Is Nothing" campaign, created by 180/TBWA, was designed first to reach American consumers and to improve the company's market share in the United States. Adidas stressed that the campaign was aimed at a global market and that ads would eventually include athletic stars from a variety of sports and regions. "Impossible Is Nothing" was launched in February 2004 with television, print, and Internet advertising. "Wallscapes"—huge ads on the sides of buildings—were installed in New York, Los Angeles, Chicago, San Francisco, Miami, and Portland.

The first television spot featured American boxing icon Muhammad Ali as a young man setting off on one of his legendary long runs; the footage was digitally altered to show him running alongside members of a new generation of athletes, including soccer great David Beckham and NBA star Tracy McGrady, all dressed in adidas merchandise. Meanwhile, Ali's daughter Hannah narrated, "Some people listen to themselves, rather than listen to what others say . . . they remind us that once you set out on a path, even though critics may doubt you, it's okay to believe there is no 'can't,' 'won't,' or 'impossible.' They remind us it's okay to believe impossible is nothing." Another TV ad employed digital effects to depict a young Muhammad Ali sparring with his daughter Laila. In a voice-over Laila dismissed the idea that women should not box, saying, "Impossible isn't a fact; it's an opinion."

In addition to print ads and TV spots, the campaign, described by the company as a "fully integrated communication campaign," also included ads and promotions on the adidas website as part of an effort to reach consumers, especially teens, all over the world. For a limited

Boxing legend Muhammad Ali (R) and daughter, Laila at the unveiling of a billboard featuring their image as part of the launch of Adidas' campaign "Impossible is Nothing." © JEFF CHRISTENSEN/REUTERS/CORBIS.

time the "Laila" TV spot was made available on the Yahoo!, MSN, and ESPN home pages. The online aspect of the campaign also featured 20 elite athletes, each telling his or her personal "Impossible Is Nothing" story. Consumers who logged onto the site were encouraged to share their own stories of overcoming the impossible to succeed. The best stories were awarded prizes.

Additional television commercials showed past and present Olympic stars interacting with each other. One ad had sprinter Kim Collins on the track encountering the 1936 gold-medal-winner Jesse Owens. Another depicted gymnast Nastia Liukin retracing the moves of the legendary Nadia Comaneci, who in 1976 became the first gymnast to complete a perfect-10 Olympic performance. The spot starring Haile Gebrselassie, known as one of the greatest runners of all time, was digitally altered to feature him running a 10,000-meter race in the Long Beach Memorial Stadium against nine competitors: all himself.

OUTCOME

As the "Impossible Is Nothing" campaign advanced, it became evident that it was resonating with consumers, and it earned accolades within the marketing arena. The campaign received a Silver EFFIE Award and won a Gold Lion Award at the International Advertising Festival in Cannes, France, and adidas was named the 2004 Marketer of the Year by *Footwear News.* Ad critics praised the campaign as well. Speaking specifically of the

ADIDAS, PAL PARTNER IN PROGRAMS FOR KIDS

As adidas kicked off its "Impossible Is Nothing" advertising campaign, the company did not forget some of New York City's youngest athletes and perhaps its future champions. The company announced plans to partner with the city's Police Athletic League (PAL) to support boxing and basketball programs for boys and girls. Offering words of encouragement to kids and lending support for the proposed partnership, Laila Ali, who was featured in some of the "Impossible Is Nothing" ads with her father, boxing legend Muhammad Ali, said during an interview (at the program's unveiling at the PAL center in Harlem), "A lot of people told me I shouldn't go into boxing. If I had listened to them, I wouldn't be where I am now. It's very important for you to follow your dreams. You really can't let anyone decide your future for you."

commercials created for the U.S. market, Barbara Lippert of *Adweek* said that the campaign had been "incredibly successful." She continued, "Those ads really capture the viewer's imagination. They are beautifully executed and organic, effectively leveraging the brand's image. Adidas has made a lot of noise. To come that far, that quickly, is just incredible."

The Internet component of the campaign was also successful in reaching the target audience. According to Moss, there was a 125 percent increase in the use of the search term "adidas" on the Yahoo! home page the day the ad featuring Ali and Laila appeared online. The highest number of search requests was from young men aged 13 to 17. Despite the campaign's success, the NPD Group, an international market-research organization, listed adidas as the number four athletic-footwear brand in the United States—behind Nike, Reebok, and New Balance—the same position it had held in 2003. But based on dollar sales adidas made advances in 2004. According to the company, sales in 2004 were 11 percent higher than in 2003, pushing adidas closer to its proposed goal of doubling its 10 percent U.S. market share and closing the gap between itself and the top company, Nike.

FURTHER READING

"Calling the Shots: With RBK, the Company Is Putting Forth a Younger, Hipper, and Much More Aggressive Front." *Footwear News,* October 25, 2004.

Drier, Melissa. "Adidas Net Rises 41.1% in Qtr." *Women's Wear Daily,* May 6, 2004.

Fisher, Eric. "New Nike Ad Theme: 'What If?'" *Washington Times,* February 29, 2004.

Garfield, Bob. "By Mimicking Apple, Adidas Paints Itself as Second String." *Advertising Age,* February 16, 2004.

Holmes, Stanley, and Aaron Bernstein. "The New Nike." *Business Week,* September 20, 2004.

Holmes, Stanley, and Ira Sager. "Punchy New Ads from Adidas." *Business Week,* February 9, 2004.

Kletter, Melanie. "Adidas Looks to Regain Steam with New Ads." *Women's Wear Daily,* February 6, 2004.

Marcial, Gene G. "Reebok Sprints Ahead." *Business Week,* April 12, 2004.

"Mission Impossible: Armed with a New 'Brand Attitude,' adidas Amped Up Its Marketing All Year Long." *Footwear News,* December 6, 2004.

"New Nike Campaign Is a Real Change of Pace." *Milwaukee Journal Sentinel,* February 26, 2004.

Oser, Kris. "Adidas Mines Possibilities with Web Effort; Ali Spot Snags 5 Mil Views from Key Demographics." *Advertising Age,* May 3, 2004.

"The Player: Stamminger Invokes Heritage to Revive Adidas Sales in U.S." *Advertising Age,* May 3, 2004.

Russak, Brian. "Ad-ing It Up." *Footwear News,* October 25, 2004.

Sickinger, Ted. "Adidas Spends $50 Million on Ads to Get Footing in Marketplace Race." *Oregonian,* February 6, 2004.

Thomaselli, Rich. "Terry Tate Builds Buzz for Reebok, but Not Shoe Sales; Real Celebs Are Behind 70% Spike." *Advertising Age,* February 2, 2004.

Rayna Bailey

YANKEE FANS CAMPAIGN

OVERVIEW

After more than a decade of dismal performance worldwide and a 1995 company relaunch by a group of international investors, the Germany-based athletic-footwear-and-apparel brand adidas (the official company name became adidas-Salomon AG after a 1997 merger with French sports-equipment maker Salomon) set its sights on rebuilding its share of the U.S. market. It dramatically raised its marketing profile in the United States and sought partnerships and licensing agreements. One such agreement, with the New York Yankees, caused controversy among other members of the Major League Baseball association. The partnership also resulted in a modestly scaled yet successful advertising campaign focusing on the nature of that baseball team's fans.

"Yankee Fans" was developed by the San Francisco ad agency Leagas Delaney. It began during the 1997 baseball season and also ran during the following season, leveraging an estimated $1 million annual budget. The campaign was headlined by black-and-white TV and cinema spots as well as print and outdoor support, all of which revolved around five out-of-shape Yankee fans who painted letters on their bare chests so that collectively they spelled "YANKS." The TV spots ran primarily in the New York area, but they also received national exposure during postseason broadcasts of Yankees games.

The campaign was a hit with Yankee fans and New Yorkers. The five principal characters from the TV spots became local celebrities, and their fictional exploits were well received by advertising-industry critics. "Yankee Fans" won a Silver Lion at the Cannes International Advertising Festival and a silver and two bronze Clios, among other awards. Even though it was not designed to drive national adidas sales, the campaign corresponded with a period of sustained profit and market-share increases.

HISTORICAL CONTEXT

Strong in the 1970s, adidas practically disappeared in the United States in the 1980s and early '90s. The German sports-shoe company, once the category leader with a 70 percent U.S. market share, slid completely out of the top four spots, down to a 2 percent share in 1993. Name recognition was low, and it was not viewed as a high-quality product. *Fortune* magazine said that by 1993 the company was losing $100 million a year. During those same years Nike had become the dominant athletic-shoe manufacturer on the strength of its powerful, sustained marketing effort. At adidas's low point an international group of investors led by Frenchman Robert Louis-Dreyfus bought the company and revamped it. It went public in November 1995.

Louis-Dreyfus fired the German senior management staff, closed down high-cost factories, and doubled spending on marketing (the marketing budget was set at 6 percent of the sales revenue in 1993). As a result, by 1997 sales had doubled, and Louis-Dreyfus kept the marketing budget at 12.5 percent of revenue. Ad agency Leagas Delaney, which previously had been creating a single commercial per year for adidas, was by 1997 making 40 spots and spending close to $20 million in the United States on advertising.

The resurgence took adidas past Fila to number three in the U.S. athletic-footwear-and-apparel market. Much of the rebound was built on a huge increase in adidas's apparel business. To further enhance this growth, adidas bought French sports-equipment maker Salomon in September 1997. The move balanced the company's geographic reach and provided better insulation against swings in fashion and sales downturns in one region or country. "The move gives [a]didas a leg up on Nike in one of its final frontiers for growth," said Jeff Jensen of *Advertising Age.*

Another key marketing decision helped lead to the "Yankee Fans" campaign. After Nike signed a sponsorship agreement with the National Football League's Dallas Cowboys, adidas looked for similar opportunities. The company won the Yankee sponsorship by acting quickly; Nike and Reebok received calls from the Yankees about sponsorship, but adidas won by listening and moving fast, according to the Yankees' vice president for business affairs, Derek Schiller. The baseball team also accepted partial payment of the sponsorship agreement in the purchase of adidas stock. "The Yankees and Adidas personify tradition and performance. Everyone knows who the Yankees are. Around the world. It's a great relationship for both parties," explained Sam Rothman, account manager at Leagas Delaney. The sponsorship agreement, however, immediately generated controversy. Major League Baseball (MLB) maintained that the deal violated the league's licensing policy. The Yankees and adidas responded by suing all of the other MLB teams as well as some leaders of the organization, claiming that these parties had disrupted a legitimate business partnership.

TARGET MARKET

In the late 1990s the major competitors in the athletic-shoe market received the bulk of their sales from young males, many of whom bought multiple (often five to six) pairs of athletic shoes each year. Adidas's overall core market was the 14- to 18-year-old elite athlete, but the "Yankee Fans" campaign strictly targeted Yankee baseball fans. For the Yankee sponsorship to be of the most value to adidas, the company needed to build a strong association with the club in the minds of its fans. Leagas Delaney said that it was not an intensely researched campaign with focus groups, statistics, or scientific analysis. Instead the agency built the spots informally. Yankee fans were known to be passionate about their team. And the Yankee franchise had the proudest tradition in baseball, a long history, and more glory years than any other major U.S. sports team.

The agency chose the five actors who played the Yankee fans based on their abilities to project a New York attitude—an attitude that indicated, "Let's get it done with full gusto." Campaign success hinged on accurately portraying the male New York Yankee fan yet doing so in a humorous, exaggerated way.

COMPETITION

Since the 1980s Nike had dominated the athletic-footwear-and-apparel category. With its ubiquitous swoosh

YANKEE FANS LOVE "YANKEE FANS"

■

Leagas Delaney account manager Sam Rothman paraphrased the sentiments of art director Peter Nicholson and copywriter Scott Wild, the creative minds behind the "Yankee Fans" campaign. "We shot the 'Yankee Fans' ads for 1998 at Yankee Stadium. They were playing the Braves. We kept the Yankee Fans around and had them do personal appearances. We had them sitting in the stands watching the game. When they were shown on the JumboTron (the in-stadium video screen) the crowd went absolutely nuts. We showed the commercials. Then we took the guys and moved them to another part of the stadium. I've never seen a crowd go so crazy. People were jumping up and down, yelling, screaming, running over to them, taking their pictures, and asking for autographs. These guys, like Mr. 'S' signs his autograph, 'Mr. S.' That is what we wanted—acceptance from the fans. That was the best proof of how we accomplished our goal."

logo, Nike owned 47 percent of the 1997 U.S. athletic-footwear market. Nike's hold on the category was so strong it redefined advertising for the entire category, emphasizing brash confidence, endorsers, the soft sell, and cinematic savvy. In 1997 Nike overhauled its long-standing, world-famous "Just Do It" campaign as a new campaign titled "I Can."

Even with such a dominant player, because of its growth the market continued to present a strong attraction to other companies. Athletic shoes enjoyed solid demand in the United States, and a steady economy and rapid rollouts of new styles that kept capturing new sales spurred their popularity. Apparel other than footwear was another way competitors increased their sales and profits.

For several years Reebok, the number two competitor with 21 percent of the U.S. athletic-footwear market, ran ads similar to Nike's (for example, the "Reebok Lets U.B.U." campaign). Reebok tried to counter Nike's staple of star athletes, such as basketball's Michael Jordan, with its own superstars (Shaquille O'Neal). Reebok later dropped O'Neal and tried to exploit the anti-Nike sentiment.

MARKETING STRATEGY

Nike's dominance was so impressive that other product categories, such as soft drinks and telephone companies, also adopted its ad style. Eventually market research found young consumers tiring of athlete-as-God and win-at-all-costs approaches. Ads with highly paid, "perfect-body" endorsers and so-called "full-of-itself" attitude began to suffer. After years of seeing the Nike swoosh logo everywhere, some people in focus groups began referring to it as a "swooshtika." "The underlying cocky, prescriptive, hipper-than-thou tone of the ads started to get on people's nerves, as did the company's tendency to deify athletes," wrote Warren Berger in *Advertising Age*.

In this environment the "Yankee Fans" campaign gave people a low-key approach. Whereas Nike portrayed the athlete as hero and hard worker, and Reebok fought back with its own sports-celebrity endorsers, adidas focused on the fan. (This focus, however, was at least partly a result of adidas's and the Yankees' ongoing lawsuit against the rest of MLB: adidas was not allowed to use Yankees players in the campaign's spots until the lawsuit was settled.) The competition showed the athlete's muscle, but the adidas spots showed the fans' potbellies and lack of muscle tone. The spots came across as real and down to earth. Another twist was having one of the world's greatest sports franchises represented not by its stable of stars but by the people who paid to see those stars play.

Among the campaign's four initial black-and-white TV/cinema spots, two in particular resonated with New Yorkers and Yankee fans as well as with ad-industry critics. "Abandoned Mr. S" opened with a dance beat and the image of a shirtless and bald man waiting nervously on a busy street corner. Painted on his chest was an "S." Viewers pondered this man's purpose and felt his discomfort until a taxicab pulled up. His relief was palpable: inside were four other men, each shirtless and with a letter painted on his not-so-muscular chest. Together the men spelled out "YANKS." In the spot "Spelling Trouble" the five guys were again in a cab and were again shirtless, each with a letter painted on his chest. The driver sized them up and said, "Ansky? What the hell is Ansky?" The guys, realizing that they were not sitting in the correct order, started moving around in the backseat, creating a tangle of limbs and torsos before settling into position, spelling out "YANKS." Mr. "N" ended the spot by yelling "Yanks!" at the top of his lungs. Each commercial closed with the tagline "Only in New York."

When in May 1998 the adidas/Yankees lawsuit against the other MLB teams was settled, the campaign began featuring Yankees players in addition to the "ANSKY guys," as the Yankee fans in the spots had become known. For instance, the Yankees' pitching coach was shown advising pitcher David Cone to rest his arm. The ANSKY guys accordingly began doing everything in their power to help him rest his arm: they answered his cell phone for him, fed him, and even helped him relieve himself in the men's room.

The campaign's annual budget was estimated to be $1 million. The spots initially ran on the large video screen at Yankee Stadium as well as on TV during local sports programming and in movie theaters in the New York area. During postseason games involving the Yankees the spots were aired nationally. Print and outdoor ads using photographs of the ANSKY guys were also employed.

Some criticized the advertisements for not showing or talking about the product, but adidas wanted all emphasis on the audience. "It's not like [a]didas is a new brand that has burst out and needs to create a new identity," said Courtney Buechert, managing director of Leagas Delaney. "Adidas's identity was and is and has been for 70 years about love for a sport and a mission to create products to help athletes perform better."

OUTCOME

The "Yankee Fans" campaign ran during an upswing for the company. Financially the year 1997 was the best ever for adidas, especially in the United States, where its growth rates outpaced Nike's and Reebok's. Worldwide sales were $3.72 billion in 1997, up 23 percent over 1996. North American sales were up 66 percent, increasing the company's market share in the world's most important sporting-goods market to more than 6 percent. In 1998 adidas also made huge strides in its attempt to catch Reebok and Nike; that year it doubled its share of the U.S. market to 12.6 percent.

The campaign's target market seemed to love the spots. The five guys became celebrities, attracting crowds, autograph hounds (each ANSKY guy signed with his individual letter), and applause whenever they made a public appearance. The campaign also won many industry awards, including a Silver Lion at the International Advertising Festival in Cannes, France, one silver and two bronze Clio Awards, and a 1998 American Advertising Federation Award. It was also a finalist at the One Show and earned a "Best Spot of 1997" recognition from *Adweek.* The campaign's profile was heightened considerably by the Yankees' championship season of 1998, during the course of which the spots ran on national television. The ANSKY guys were featured prominently in the victory parade following the Yankees' World Series victory.

Leagas Delaney's success with the "Yankee Fans" campaign landed it the New York Yankees' own advertising duties in 1999. The agency was also entrusted with the job of crafting adidas's first umbrella branding initiative in the United States since 1993. That campaign, the high-profile "Long Live Sport," was released in 1999. The partnership between adidas and the New York Yankees was renewed in 2006, guaranteeing that adidas would remain the "Official Athletic Apparel and Footwear Company of the New York Yankees" at least through 2013.

FURTHER READING

Berger, Warren. "Advertising Age's Creativity." *Advertising Age,* March 1, 1998.

Jensen, Jeff. "Marketer of the Year: Nike." *Advertising Age,* December 1996.

Kaufman, David. "Leagas Delaney's 'Liquid Loofah' Mixes Baseball and Cosmetics." *Shoot,* August 29, 1997.

"MLB Settles Adidas/Yankees Lawsuit, Extends Deals." *Brandweek,* May 4, 1998.

Peltz, James F. "Miles to Go? Sneaker Stocks Are Still on the Fast Track." *Los Angeles Times,* March 18, 1997, p. FI4.

Sandomir, Richard,"How Does an Ad Spell Success? A-N-S-K-Y." *New York Times,* October 23, 1998.

Saporito, Bill. "Can Nike Get Unstuck?" *Time,* March 30, 1998, p. 48.

Voight, Joan. "Leagas to Unveil Adidas Image Work." *Adweek* (western ed.), April 26, 1999.

———. "Yankee Fever in California." *Adweek* (western ed.), August 24, 1998.

Wallace, Charles P. "Adidas Back in the Game." *Fortune,* August 18, 1997, p. 176.

Chris John Amorosino
Mark Lane

The Advertising Council, Inc.

261 Madison Ave., 11th Fl.
New York, New York 10016
USA
Telephone: (212) 922-1500
Fax: (212) 922-1676
E-mail: info@adcouncil.org
Web site: www.adcouncil.org

CAMPAIGN FOR FREEDOM CAMPAIGN

OVERVIEW

In the wake of the September 11, 2001, terrorist attacks on the United States, several advertising industry associations decided to join together to develop a public service advertising campaign to inspire and rally the American people. They turned to the Advertising Council, an organization that for more than a half-century had coordinated and distributed public service announcements of all types.

Several advertising agencies also donated their services to develop the television and radio spots and print ads that constituted the resulting "Campaign for Freedom." The first phase was launched to coincide with the 2002 Fourth of July celebrations; the second phase was timed for the two-year anniversary of the 9/11 attacks. There was no budget for the effort, which relied on free airtime and print space from media companies. The commercials and ads explored the theme of freedom in a number of ways: positing an America in which people could be arrested for asking about the wrong book at a public library; portraying the real-life stories of people who fled repressive countries to come to America; and celebrating America's religious and cultural inclusiveness.

Following the first two phases of the "Campaign for Freedom," the purpose shifted from inspiration to action, as the audience was urged to participate in civic activities such as voting and to volunteer time to worthwhile causes. One of the ads in the "Campaign for Freedom" won a One Show award, but while it drew praise from many quarters, the company was also criticized by others, who viewed the advertising as little more than propaganda.

HISTORICAL CONTEXT

No different than anyone else, members of the advertising industry were stunned by the September 11, 2001, terrorist attacks on the United States. And like many citizens, they gave thought to what gave strength to the country and made it unique among nations. Employees of Texas ad agency GSD&M were in Maryland in a client meeting when the attacks unfolded, and because air flights were suspended for several days, they drove home to Texas. With ample time for reflection, they decided to create a public service announcement (PSA) that celebrated America's diversity, a message with resonance given the suspicions that were laid upon people of Middle Eastern descent or mistaken for it. GSD&M broadcast producers quickly lined up pro bono help from directors, producers, and editors, and the agency's president contacted the Ad Council about being a partner in the endeavor. The organization agreed to participate and for the first time in its history became the sole signatory of a PSA. The result was the "I Am an American" spot, featuring a wide range of men and women, young and old, of different races, declaring, "I am an American."

The "I Am an American" spot aired within 10 days of the attacks. Also during this time three advertising industry associations—the American Association of Advertising Agencies (AAAA), the Association of National Advertisers (ANA), and the American Advertising Federation (AAF)—met and began to plan a full-fledged advertising campaign to help Americans reflect on the bedrock of democracy: freedom. It was also agreed that the Ad Council was the proper vehicle to lead what would become the "Campaign for Freedom." Unlike traditional Ad Council campaigns that were developed by a single agency, this effort would be the joint work, free of charge, of four agencies: Omnicom Group's Chicago office of DDB, the Los Angeles office of TBWA\Chiat\Day, DeVito/Verdi of New York, and the New York office of Lowe & Partners Worldwide, a subsidiary of Interpublic Group of Companies. Heading the effort would be Philip B. Dusenberry, who had recently retired as chairman of BBDO North America. Instead of relying on the backing of a sponsoring organization, the Ad Council, in another break from tradition, sought funding to cover production and distribution costs from a variety of sources, including ad agencies, agency employees, trade groups, advertisers, and media companies. After several months of development, the "Campaign for Freedom" was ready to launch in time for the Fourth of July holiday.

"LOOSE LIPS SINK SHIPS"

The Advertising Council, originally called the War Advertising Council, was launched in the midst of World War II in 1942. Not only did the organization develop "Buy War Bonds" advertisements, but it also coined the famous "Loose Lips Sink Ships" slogan and introduced the United States to Rosie the Riveter in an effort to recruit women into the workforce to support the war effort. Following the war the Ad Council devoted itself to peacetime endeavors, such as the work it did for the National Safety Council.

TARGET MARKET

While the "I Am an American" spot aired at a time when the emotional reaction to the September 11 events was fresh and raw, by the time the "Campaign for Freedom" broke nine months later, the mood in the country was somewhat different. "Right after 9/11 there was this upsurge of patriotism in America," Dusenberry commented in a radio interview on New York radio station WNYC in July 2002. "But over time that sense has waned a little bit because other things come into play and people let this blessing we have, which is called freedom, flip to the back of their mind." In essence every strata of America was the campaign's target audience. For those people who had grown somewhat complacent in the months since the terrorist attacks, the PSAs were a wake-up call. For people more vigilant, they offered reinforcement.

COMPETITION

The "Campaign for Freedom" lacked traditional competition. People were not being asked to choose between tyranny and freedom, to buy democracy over totalitarianism. They were not even asked to take any particular action, other than to ruminate about the nature and importance of freedom. Following the attack on Pearl Harbor that ushered in America's involvement in World War II, Ad Council ads pursued patriotic themes but with a more tangible purpose: to sell war bonds to finance the war to achieve the greater end of preserving freedom and democracy. As Dusenberry explained to WNYC, "Most advertising is designed to sell a product, a service, a brand. In this particular case, this advertising is asking people to feel something."

MARKETING STRATEGY

Peggy Conlon, president and chief executive officer of the Ad Council, told Jane L. Levere of the *New York Times* in July 2002, "According to research, Americans are looking for messages that will inform, involve and inspire them during the war on terrorism." The theme that resonated was freedom. Hence it was the concept of freedom that the alliance of advertising associations decided to focus on in the aftermath of September 11. "Freedom is our strength," Conlon explained to Levere. "However, freedom is also at risk. The 'Campaign for Freedom' recognizes that it is every American's responsibility to protect the foundation of our nation, and this is the heart of the strategy. The campaign wasn't designed to define what freedom is, but to stimulate a dialogue, to make people think about it."

To emphasize the theme of freedom, the campaign was timed to coincide with the Fourth of July. The first phase of the campaign included eight television commercials and one print ad, which the Ad Council distributed to 10,000 print and broadcast outlets. All the PSAs were run in advertising time and space donated by the media. A wide swath of network and cable TV channels—including ABC, CBS, Fox, Bravo, Discovery, Lifetime, and VH1—immediately began to carry the ads.

DeVito/Verdi produced four of the initial eight television spots and supplied the campaign's tag line: "Freedom. Appreciate it. Cherish it. Protect it." Three of the DeVito/Verdi spots asked what life would be like in America if freedoms that many people took for granted were lost: freedom to read whatever material they like, freedom of speech, and freedom of religion. In the spot called "Library," for example, a man was detained because he requested a pair of banned books. The fourth DeVito/Verdi spot was perhaps the most notable of the first wave of commercials. Called "Main Street USA," it showed a stretch of row houses in Bayonne, New Jersey, as a voice-over said, "On September 11th, terrorists tried to change America forever." After a fade to black the same street was shown again, this time adorned with a multitude of American flags, sometimes two or three to a house. "Well, they succeeded," noted the voice-over. A white title card then revealed the campaign's tagline.

The three spots produced by Lowe dealt with the concepts of freedom of choice and freedom of opportunity. The spot titled "Change" showed students in a multicultural classroom studying the civil-rights movement. Another, called "Choice," reminded Americans about the abundance of choices they enjoy at the supermarket. The lone DDB spot, "Arrest," showed the police pull over a young man, drag him out of his car, and then after finding newspapers in the back seat, handcuff and arrest him. The copy read, "Imagine America without freedom." The print ad in the first phase was developed by TBWA\Chiat\Day. The text accompanying a picture of a tattered America flag declared, "Read this ad. Or, don't. An exercise in freedom. By deciding to continue reading, you've just demonstrated a key American freedom—choice. And should you choose to turn the page, take a nap or go dye your hair blue, that's cool too."

The second phase of the "Campaign for Freedom" was launched in September 2003, more than a year after the initial wave of PSAs, this time coinciding with the second anniversary of the September 11 attacks. "Main Street USA" was brought back, and three new television and radio spots and a pair of print ads were distributed as well. Produced by Ogilvy & Mather, the three television spots were presented as documentary-style interviews. They featured three immigrants and their stories of fleeing oppression to come to America. In the spot called "Tom," Tom Tor told how he escaped the "killing fields" of Cambodia. With images of the Statue of Liberty, the Lincoln Memorial, and excerpts from the Constitution in the background, Tor explained, "If I stayed in Cambodia, I would have been dead . . . Why did I come here? Freedom." The subjects of the other spots were Eugenia Dallas, who fled the Soviet Union during the time of Stalin, and Yuri Gevorigian, who escaped torture in Armenia. The spots were cut in 30- and 60-second versions, and the audio was used to fashion radio spots. The two print ads in the second phase of the "Campaign for Freedom" were created by TBWA\Chiat\Day had also focused on the immigrant experience, reminding the audience that virtually everyone in America was the offspring of immigrants, while celebrating the country's diversity. The copy of one ad featured the headline "A Priest, a Rabbi, and an Imam Are Walking Down the Street. (There's no punch line.)" The text, accompanying a picture of three religious men on a street corner, then posed the question "What do you get when you mix Christianity, Judaism and Islam? In many parts of the world it's a recipe for disaster. Yet in America, it's a formula that's endured for over 200 years."

OUTCOME

The "Campaign for Freedom" became a long-term effort for the Ad Council and its alliance of advertising agencies. Subsequent phases were added to move beyond the initial inspirational messages and to call on people to express freedom in action through participation in everyday civic activities, such as voting. The campaign was also aided by a dedicated website, http://www.explorefreedomusa.org, where all the advertising could be found and visitors could learn more about the Constitution, American history, and homeland security, as well as access links for registering to vote or volunteering their time.

It was difficult, if not impossible, to gauge the effectiveness of the "Campaign for Freedom," given that its goal was ethereal. But it did succeed in raising money from such media companies as Knight-Ridder and the Hearst Corp. as well as major corporations like the Coca-Cola Company and Home Depot. It also received an abundance of free media time and space, worth tens of millions of dollars. Levere reported that "some advertising industry experts praised the campaign's intent and execution." TBWA\Chiat\Day Los Angeles won an award for the print ad "A Priest, a Rabbi, and an Imam Are Walking Down the Street," taking home a Bronze Pencil in the Consumer Magazine category of the 2004 One Show, sponsored by New York City-based One Club, a nonprofit organization dedicated to recognizing and promoting excellence in advertising.

The "Campaign for Freedom" was not without its share of critics, however. Levere interviewed New York University media studies professor Mark Crispin Miller, who deemed the ads unfocused and exploitative. "The campaign is inappropriate because these ads are not thought-provoking but emotionally manipulative. They are bits of rousing propaganda," he commented. "What we need now in a time of terror is more information, more truth, more clarity of mind. The Ad Council is merely giving us a kind of feel-good blather for the nation's couch potatoes." Minneapolis freelance writer and activist Jeff Nygaard offered an even more cynical view of the Ad Council's efforts in *Nygaard Notes:* "They are selling, first of all, the idea that ads are good things, sources of information and inspiration—Ads are our friends. This message is brought to you, after all, by the 'Ad Council.'" The Ad Council's Conlon answered the critics by telling Levere, "There are always critics and skeptics, no matter how well-intentioned anyone's efforts are. We're doing everything within our power to protect these people's right to say whatever they want to say about this campaign."

FURTHER READING

Bednarski, P.J. "Freedom to Disagree." *Broadcasting & Cable,* September 15, 2003, p. 37.

Champagne, Christine. "P&G and Ford among Few Advertisers on 9/11." *Shoot,* September 6, 2002, p. 1.

Garfield, Bob. "Ad Council's Latest 'Freedom' Commercials Miss the Mark." *Advertising Age,* September 15, 2003, p. 49.

Levere, Jane L. "An Ad Council Campaign Sells Freedom, but Some Call It Propaganda." *New York Times,* July 1, 2002, p. C8.

Melillo, Wendy. "Ad Council Launches Campaign to Celebrate Freedom." *Adweek,* July 1, 2002, p. 5.

———. "Ad Council Marks 9/11 with Immigrants' Tales." *Adweek,* September 8, 2003, p. 11.

Nygaard, Jeff. "Read This Ad." *Nygaard Notes,* September 13, 2002.

Pesca, Mike. "Freedom in 30 Seconds." *On the Media,* July 5, 2002. Available from <http://www.wnyc.org>

Teinowitz, Ira. "Ad Council Rolls Out New Ads in 'Campaign for America.'" *Advertising Age,* September 8, 2003, p. 8.

———. "Selling the U.S.A." *Advertising Age,* July 1, 2002, p. 3.

Ed Dinger

Aflac, Inc.

1932 Wynnton Road
Columbus, Georgia 31999
USA
Telephone: (706) 323-3431
Fax: (706) 324-6330
E-mail: advertising@aflac.com
Web site: www.aflac.com

THE AFLAC DUCK (2000) CAMPAIGN

OVERVIEW

Aflac, Inc., was a major insurance company based in Columbus, Georgia. In 2000 its top product was its cancer-expense coverage, which the company had invented in 1958. Though profitable, Aflac suffered from poor brand recognition; only 12 percent of consumers remembered the company, in part because it had such an unusual name. In response, Aflac wanted to expand its business by improving consumer's awareness of the brand. It also wanted to target 35- to 54-year-old consumers.

In 1999 the company hired a new advertising agency, the Kaplan Thaler Group, to improve its name recognition. The New York–based agency was known for its "Big Bang" approach to advertising: the belief that campaigns succeeded most when they altered consumers' views about the brand advertised. To accomplish this for Aflac, the agency created a new spokescharacter, the Aflac Duck. Voiced by comedian and actor Gilbert Gottfried, the Duck appeared in spots that featured consumers having trouble remembering the company's name. The Duck attempted to remedy this by "quacking" the answer: "Aflac." The lighthearted spots were broadcast on prime-time network TV and during broadcasts of sporting events such as Major League Baseball games. Aflac spent $35 million on the campaign.

The Duck was a major success. According to *USA Today* 's Ad Track poll, it was one of the most popular spots of 2000. Brand recognition shot up to more than 70 percent and later topped 90 percent. Sales improved 28 percent, a result in part of improved name recognition. The company's accident/disability insurance took off, outselling the company's cancer-expense plans for the first time. The Duck became a cultural icon and continued as the company's advertising focal point through 2004. That year the Duck became one of the first characters to appear on the Advertising Walk of Fame in New York City.

HISTORICAL CONTEXT

The American Family Life Assurance Company (later called Aflac) was founded as an international holding company in 1955 by brothers John, Paul, and Bill Amos. In 1958 it became one of the first companies in the world to offer insurance against cancer. It expanded its offerings significantly in the 1980s, and by the late 1990s it sold a variety of policies, from dental care to short-term disability to hospital-confinement indemnity and life insurance. In 1990 the company adopted the acronym "AFLAC" as its official name.

By 2000 Aflac was insuring more than 40 million people. The company excelled at providing policies that helped pay out-of-pocket expenses not covered by someone's primary insurer. This was also known as "supplemental insurance." Aflac was respected in the industry, and in January 2000 *Fortune* included it in its list of the 100 best companies to work for in the United States. Because of the Fortune 500 company's solid core business and steady growth, in 1999 the National Association of Investors Corporation named Aflac one of its favorite stocks. Aflac was especially adept at reaching out to small businesses. It tailored certain plans specifically for this market, with a sales force of about 60,000 that helped reach small businesses face-to-face. It was also the largest provider of guaranteed-renewable insurance in the United States. The company thrived overseas as well, becoming the largest provider of individual insurance policies in Japan. Aflac's primary business strategy revolved around expanding its product line and focusing on gaining clients through businesses.

TARGET MARKET

Aflac was especially eager to connect with consumers in the 35- to 54-year-old age group and to boost sales of accident and disability insurance. While the company's cancer-expense insurance had always been the backbone of its sales, there was not much room left for growth in that sector. In order for Aflac to grow, it needed to expand its other businesses. Because accident/liability insurance was a major part of the industry, Aflac felt that that was the area it most needed to expand. The company also wanted to sell more of its supplemental insurance.

The company especially wanted to reach consumers with families. Aflac had a good reputation, but its difficult-to-remember name impeded its efforts to attract new customers. Insurance was a buyer's market. Many companies offered similar coverage policies, and it was important to stand out. Aflac suffered from terrible brand recognition: only about 12 percent of consumers remembered the brand's name. This limited the company's new sales leads.

COMPETITION

Aflac's primary competition came from other accident- and health-insurance brands, such as Citizens Financial Corp., Conseco, Inc., and Amerisafe, Inc. All offered services comparable to Aflac's. There were a number of companies competing in the sector, making Aflac's low brand recognition a serious liability. Aflac issued 98 percent of its coverage on a payroll-deduction basis. This meant that, while the company's sales force and its reputation were able to help it sell its products to cost-conscious corporations, it had a hard time drawing sales leads outside of the corporate sphere. Aflac believed that it needed to change its image with consumers to survive in a tough industry.

ONE FUNNY DUCK

When the Kaplan Thaler Group created the Aflac Duck, it chose Gilbert Gottfried to provide the Duck's voice. Gottfried was no stranger to voice-over work, having provided the voice of the parrot Iago in the classic 1992 Disney animated film *Aladdin.* A longtime stand-up comic, Gottfried first rose to prominence in 1975 when he appeared on the NBC variety show *Saturday Night Live.* He later acted in a string of diverse films, including *Beverly Hills Cop 2, Problem Child*, and *Look Who's Talking Too.*

Never a leading man, Gottfried nonetheless drew a solid fan base with his offbeat humor and distinctive voice. As a stand-up comedian he was often known for his bawdy humor, which was perhaps most evident in his performance of an old vaudeville joke shown in the 2005 documentary *The Aristocrats.* But his nasal, high-pitched voice also resonated in children's animated films, in which he often voiced comic relief. His character Iago was one of the most popular Disney villains, and the character later popped up in other Disney projects, including the television show *House of Mouse.*

MARKETING STRATEGY

Aflac contracted the ad agency Kaplan Thaler Group (KTG), a division of Bcom3 based in New York City, to help the brand break through to consumers. This was the first major campaign conducted by KTG on Aflac's behalf. The company earmarked $35 million for the campaign. KTG was run by cofounders Linda Kaplan Thaler and Robin Koval. They had developed an approach to advertising that they called the "Big Bang." A "Big Bang" campaign altered people's perceptions of a brand or product. Aflac, which suffered from poor brand recognition, decided that this was a good approach for the company.

While trying to develop an idea for the Aflac campaign, some of the KTG personnel had trouble remembering the brand's name themselves. While repeating the name in an effort to memorize it, the ad agency employees noticed that it sounded a little like a duck quacking. That prompted the creation of Aflac's new "spokesman," the Aflac Duck. The new "Duck" campaign began on December 21, 1999. Gilbert Gottfried, a nasal-voiced comedian who was known for his work in films such as *Beverly Hills Cop 2,* performed the Duck's voice.

One key spot featured two men in a steam room talking about insurance. One man was praising his insurance company, which helped him pay his out-of-pocket expenses following a serious accident. Every time he forgot the company's name, the Aflac Duck popped up to remind him by quacking, "Aflac." As the conversation continued, the Duck grew increasingly impatient with the man, eventually shouting at him. This was the second spot in the campaign, following the Duck's debut in "Park Bench," which featured a similar conversation located on a park bench. Both commercials revolved around people's difficulty in remembering the company's name.

More spots followed. One showed a young couple discussing having their first child. They realized that they needed supplemental insurance and were trying to think of the name of a good insurer. Once again, the Duck appeared to remind them: "Aflac." All of the initial spots played on the theme of consumers' difficulty in remembering the insurer's name. The commercials turned this weakness into a strength by using it as the source of much of the campaign's humor. The Duck himself was a humorous character, especially in the way that he grew increasingly frustrated by consumers' inability to either recall Aflac's name or listen to his prompts.

The spots were mostly aired as a part of what the ad industry called a "prime-time roadblock," a strategy involving running the same commercial on many different stations at about the same time. Aflac ensured a large audience by airing spots during every major network evening news program. The spots were also aired on CNN during *Larry King Live* and *Headline News* and on the financial network CNBC throughout the day. In addition, the spots ran during major sporting events, especially college football, professional baseball, and major tennis tournaments such as Wimbledon. As the campaign took off, the company's advertising spread into prime-time programming across the three major networks, ABC, NBC, and CBS. In July 2001 the Duck made his premiere in Japan, where it was just as successful.

OUTCOME

The "Duck" campaign was an unqualified success. *USA Today* reported that, based on a poll conducted by the newspaper and market-research firm Harris Interactive, it was one of the most popular campaigns of 2000. The company's name recognition among consumers shot up from 12 percent immediately before the campaign to a resounding 71 percent after the Duck's introduction. As the campaign continued, Aflac's brand recognition soared above 90 percent. The "Duck" spots were a key reason. According to the advertising research company Ipsos ASI, the initial "Duck" campaign scored more than double the industry average in brand recall.

Aflac also saw sales improve. In the first two weeks of 2000 the company had more sales leads than in all of 1998 and 1999 combined. It also saw annualized premium sales jump 28.5 percent in the second quarter of 2000, giving the company a record $168 million in sales that quarter. For the first time accident/disability insurance replaced cancer-expense insurance as the company's number-one product. Sales for the year were up a healthy 28 percent, and recruiting was up 22 percent.

The Duck's popularity prompted the company to offer stuffed "talking" Aflac Ducks, which quacked when squeezed, for sale on its website. Proceeds were donated to the Aflac Cancer Center at Children's Healthcare of Atlanta. The company's relationship with the institution dated to 1995, when it funded construction of the cancer unit. Aflac promoted the initiative on CNBC's *Power Lunch.* Company CEO Dan Amos appeared on the program in July with the Duck. The Duck made return appearances on the program throughout the month, promoting the charity effort. By August the company had raised $75,000.

Aflac's reputation thrived. In 2001 it was named the fifth most admired company in the health and life insurance industry by *Fortune.* The magazine sighted Aflac's "bold approach to advertising" as one reason for the honor. The Aflac Duck became a cultural icon, and the company began to associate itself with the Duck mascot, placing it on the company's website. In 2004 the Duck was named one of the country's favorite advertising figures, besting such characters as Ronald McDonald to be one of the inaugural members of the Advertising Walk of Fame in New York City.

In subsequent years a number of celebrities appeared in "Duck" spots, including comedian Chevy Chase, retired baseball star Yogi Berra, and singer Wayne Newton. The Duck was also featured on the TV shows *The Tonight Show with Jay Leno* and *Saturday Night Live.* The Duck would remain the focus of Aflac's advertising for several years. In an effort to explain the company's services better, however, the company began to de-emphasize the Duck in some of its advertising in 2004.

FURTHER READING

Elliott, Stuart. "Why a Duck? Because It Sells Insurance." *New York Times,* June 24, 2002.

Fass, Allison. "Ayer, One of Madison Avenue's Oldest Names, Is Fading Away as It Is Absorbed by Kaplan Thaler." *New York Times,* April 8, 2002.

Howard, Theresa. "Kaplan Ads Shoot for 'Big Bang.'" *USA Today,* July 25, 2004.

Insana, Ron. "Insurance Business Just Ducky for Aflac." *USA Today,* July 5, 2005.

Kaplan Thaler, Linda, and Robin Koval. *Bang!: Getting Your Message Heard in a Noisy World,* New York: Doubleday, 2003.

Rose, Lacey. "America's Most Loved Spokes-Creatures." *Forbes,* January 5, 2006.

Shubin, Seymour. *The Man from Enterprise: The Story of John B. Amos, Founder of AFLAC.* Macon, GA: Mercer University Press, 1998.

Sperber, Bob. "Linda Kaplan Thaler On the Spot." *Adweek,* April 21, 2003.

Vranica, Suzanne. "New Aflac Ad Campaign Muzzles Iconic Duck." *Wall Street Journal,* December 2, 2004.

Witkoski, Michael. "The Bottle that Isn't There and the Duck that Can't Be Heard: The 'Subjective Correlative' in Commercial Messages." *Studies in Media & Information Literacy Education* 3, issue 3 (August 2003).

Guy Patrick Cunningham

THE BROKEN LEG CAMPAIGN

OVERVIEW

The primary business of Aflac, Inc., a Fortune 500 company based in Columbus, Georgia, was supplemental insurance. In an effort to make a major push to turn around its poor brand recognition among consumers, the company hired ad agency Kaplan Thaler Group (KTG) to devise a new campaign in 2000. KTG came up with a humorous set of TV commercials that introduced the Aflac Duck, which became an advertising icon. By 2004 Aflac's brand recognition stood at 90 percent, and the Duck was appearing in Hollywood films such as the 2004 hit *Lemony Snicket's A Series of Unfortunate Events.* The company even integrated the character into its logo. Surveys indicated, however, that many customers were still unsure of what Aflac actually did.

The company decided to initiate a $50 million campaign in December 2004 that would de-emphasize the Duck in favor of explaining supplemental insurance and what it provided consumers. KTG would once again mastermind all of the advertising. The new TV spots kept the Duck but moved him into the background. For example, in "The Broken Leg," the Duck busied himself writing checks to handle an accident victim's out-of-pocket expenses, while the injured man himself explained that Aflac was taking care of all of the expenses that his primary health insurance would not cover. Another new spot featured an on-screen appearance from Gilbert Gottfried, the comedian who had provided the Duck's voice since the character's initial appearance in the 2000 "Park Bench" spot.

The spots were largely successful. Aflac's revenues continued to climb, and its brand recognition held steady. A survey conducted by the Customer Respect Group (a research and consulting firm that focused on how corporations treated their customers online) indicated that the company was also hitting new highs in customer satisfaction. Aflac continued to tweak its use of the Duck in future campaigns.

HISTORICAL CONTEXT

Aflac, Inc., was founded as the American Family Life Assurance Company (also known by its acronym, AFLAC) in 1955 by three brothers, John, Paul, and Bill Amos. The company began as a small insurer and grew significantly after its 1958 creation of the first policy to cover cancer expenses. This policy remained the backbone of the company's business for decades. Until 2000 it had been Aflac's best-selling plan. Aflac grew steadily over the years since its founding, and by 2004 it was large enough to be listed among the Fortune 500. In the first few years of the twenty-first century more than 40 million people were insured by Aflac, and the insurer possessed assets worth more than $50 billion. The company adopted "Aflac" as its official name in 1990.

Aflac's business plan revolved around growing its core business. The company was especially successful in selling supplemental insurance, a type of insurance that helped pay for out-of-pocket expenses not covered by a primary health-insurance policy. These policies had been the focus of the company's most popular advertising campaign, the 2000 introduction of the Aflac Duck. The Duck, voiced by Gilbert Gottfried, first appeared in the spot "Park Bench" on December 31, 1999. The character remained the star of the company's advertising efforts for several years, appearing in more than 20 spots between 2000 and 2004.

The spots were devised by Kaplan Thaler Group (KTG), a part of Bcom3, which was in turn bought by the Publicis Groupe, Europe's largest communications company, in 2002. KTG was known for its "Big Bang" approach to advertising. The theory, which was articulated by agency founders Linda Kaplan Thaler and Robin Koval in their 2003 book *Bang!: Getting Your Message Heard in a Noisy World,* was based on the idea that advertising campaigns should strive to alter perceptions of the brand.

The Duck was a prime example of this approach in action. Other insurance companies often invoked stability or practicality in their commercials. Aflac's approach was built around humor. The original "Park Bench" spot featured two men on a park bench discussing supplemental insurance. Neither could remember the name of the carrier under discussion, so a duck appeared to "help" them by quacking the answer: "Aflac!" The spot's humor was underscored by the fact that neither man appeared to hear the Duck, who grew louder and more frustrated as the spot continued. The genesis of the character stemmed from a problem that KTG marketers shared with Aflac's pre-Duck customers: an inability to remember the company's unusual name. While trying to memorize the name, KTG members began repeating it to themselves, and one of the noticed that word "Aflac" sounded like a duck quacking. And the Aflac Duck was born.

The Duck boosted the company's profile significantly. Aflac's brand recognition exceeded 90 percent in 2004. In the first two weeks after the campaign began, Aflac garnered more sales leads than it had in all of 1998 and 1999 combined. Sales for the first year jumped about 28 percent. Increased brand recognition was a key contributor. The company began selling stuffed Aflac Ducks on its website, donating the profits from that venture to the Aflac Cancer Center at Children's Healthcare of Atlanta. Finally, in 2004 the company incorporated the Duck into the company's official logo.

The Duck became a celebrity in his own right. Soon he was parodied on television programs such as *The Tonight Show* and *Saturday Night Live.* Well-known stars, including retired New York Yankees hall-of-famer Yogi Berra and comedian Chevy Chase, made appearances in Duck spots. In 2004 the Duck made his feature-film debut in *Lemony Snicket's A Series of Unfortunate Events.* The Jim Carrey vehicle grossed more than $118 million at the box office. The Duck remained successful and popular, but Aflac was concerned that the spokes-character's fame was beginning to draw some focus away from the services that the company offered.

TARGET MARKET

The primary targets for Aflac's products were adults aged 35 to 54, especially those with children. Most of its insurance was sold via employers, because at the time, most Americans received insurance coverage through their jobs. Aflac was especially adept at reaching small-business owners. The company had several plans tailored to these kinds of companies.

Aflac's "Duck" campaign had done an incredible job of boosting the company's brand identification. While only about 13 percent of consumers recognized the brand in 1999, by 2004 that number was higher than 90 percent. The company's spokes-duck was a large reason for this. The character had become an advertising icon. In 2004 the Duck was honored with a place on the Advertising Walk of Fame in New York City. The character beat out more than two dozen other nominees in an online poll. Other characters honored included Kellogg's Tony the Tiger (associated with Frosted Flakes cereal) and Planter's Mr. Peanut.

One problem that Aflac faced was a lack of full awareness of what the company did. An October 2003 survey conducted by the market-intelligence firm the Bantam Group indicated that, while most respondents had heard of the company, 60 percent were unsure about what kind of services Aflac offered.

SO WHAT DOES AFLAC DO?

In December 2004 Aflac began a new drive to inform customers about its core business: supplemental insurance. Supplemental insurance was a form of insurance that worked as a "supplement" to traditional health insurance. It covered the kinds of expenses that traditional health insurance did not. The most obvious benefit was that it covered deductibles and other out-of-pocket expenses. But supplemental insurance also paid for treatment-related travel (if a patient needed to see a specialist in another city, for example) and the daily living expenses that could accrue during an illness, particularly when there was lost income from missed work. The key benefit of supplemental insurance was that it would come into effect immediately, whereas traditional health insurance required a patient to pay a certain initial cost (called a deductible) before covering other expenses.

Aflac's most popular policy for several decades was its cancer-expense insurance. Developed in 1958, this insurance worked as a supplement to a patient's primary health coverage, picking up the costs of deductibles on doctor's visits, hospital stays, and drug therapies. Supplemental accident and disability insurance offered similar benefits. In addition it bridged the gap in earnings until a patient was eligible for long-term disability benefits (which did not come into effect until a patient missed work for a predetermined period of time).

COMPETITION

Beginning in 2000 accident/disability insurance surpassed cancer-expense insurance as Aflac's biggest-selling plan. Unlike in the 1950s through the 1990s, when

Aflac's success depended on holding onto a business it had largely invented (cancer-expense insurance), the company now relied on a service other insurers had specialized in for a long period (accident and disability insurance). Competition was provided by companies that offered services similar to those of Aflac, including supplemental insurance and accident/disability insurance. Just a few of its main rivals on this front were Citizens Financial Corp. of Louisville, Kentucky; Conseco, based in Carmel, Indiana; and Amerisafe, a company out of DeRidder, Louisiana. The latter specialized in workers' compensation insurance for those employed in hazardous industries. Aflac offered a variety of plans and needed to make sure to differentiate its plans from those of its competitors.

MARKETING STRATEGY

In an effort to build on its newly strong brand recognition, Aflac decided to close 2004 with a new campaign that would emphasize the company's core business. It retained the Kaplan Thaler Group (KTG), with which it had established a highly successful relationship, to run the new campaign. The company earmarked $50 million for this new campaign, which would focus on television spots aired mostly on network television.

The move carried risks: the Duck was popular with consumers, and it was so identified with the company that Aflac had inserted it into the company logo. The new spots offered a chance for Aflac to explain its services to consumers. One commercial, which aired during college football's year-end bowl games, featured two men sitting down and talking. The spot was titled "The Broken Leg." The setup recalled the "Park Bench" commercial that had kicked off the initial "Duck" campaign. The difference was that in the new spot the two men had no problem remembering the company's name. One of the men was shown wearing a cast as a result of a serious leg injury. His friend was surprised by the injured man's composure. The injured man explained that he was not alarmed by the situation because he had accident insurance from Aflac. Even though the man was missing work, his bills were being paid by Aflac. Aflac's supplemental insurance covered the bills that the man's primary insurance company did not pay.

The Duck was featured in the spot, although he did not speak. He appeared in the background, writing checks to cover the injured man's bills. The Duck even produced cash to pay for the man's Chinese takeout food. While the spot did not revolve around the Duck, Aflac and KTG made sure that he appeared. The company had to move delicately, since the Duck was so intertwined with the company's identity. If the Duck did not appear at all, Aflac reasoned, customers might get confused. This way the Duck's presence reminded consumers that the injured man was praising Aflac, the company whose name sounded like a duck quacking.

Another spot, titled "Pet Store," used humor to forge an independent identity for the brand. It starred none other than comedian Gilbert Gottfried, the man who had provided the Duck's voice since the character's inception. In the spot Gottfried tried to return the Duck to the pet store, complaining that he kept saying the same thing over and over again. The Duck then refused to quack. A helpful parrot chimed in and told the pet-store owner both the company's name and its business. Again, the spot explained supplemental insurance and underscored Aflac's strong and quick performance.

OUTCOME

The campaign was largely successful. Aflac retained its high level of brand recognition. In 2005 *Fortune* named Aflac number 465 on its Global 500 list, an improvement from its previous year's ranking at 477. The company generated $13.3 billion in revenue in 2004. Customers responded to the company's new tack and named Aflac one of the best companies in customer satisfaction, according to a survey by the Customer Respect Group. This indicated that Aflac's effort to focus attention on its performance paid dividends in customer satisfaction.

In the spring of 2005 Aflac unveiled the next phase in the Duck's evolution. A new spot, titled "Experiment," featured the Duck's brain being switched with that of model Melania Trump. The Duck then proceeded to explain Aflac's business in Melania's voice. The spot brought back the "quack"—only it came from Melania. This was a careful calibration on the company's part. It did not want too many spots to pass without the "quack" for fear of losing its hard-earned gains in brand recognition. But Aflac wanted people to know about its core business, too. It continued to tweak future campaigns in an effort to strike the right balance.

By later in 2005 the Duck was back helping customers directly. In "Pitching In," the Duck watched a couple's baby and engaged in household chores. This marked a decision to go back to the late 2004 phase in which the duck was an active Aflac representative.

FURTHER READING

Auletta, Ken. "The New Pitch: Do Ads Still Work?" *New Yorker,* March, 28 2005.

Elliott, Stuart. "Why a Duck? Because It Sells Insurance. Kaplan Thaler Puts Consumers Ahead of Peer Approval." *New York Times,* June 24, 2002.

Howard, Theresa. "Kaplan Ads Shoot for 'Big Bang.'" *USA Today,* July 25, 2004.

Insana, Ron. "Insurance Business Just Ducky for Aflac." *USA Today,* July 5, 2005.

Kaplan Thaler, Linda, and Robin Koval. *Bang!: Getting Your Message Heard in a Noisy World,* New York: Doubleday, 2003.

Rose, Lacey. "America's Most Loved Spokes-Creatures." *Forbes,* January 5, 2006.

Shubin, Seymour. *The Man from Enterprise: The Story of John B. Amos, Founder of AFLAC.* Macon, GA: Mercer University Press, 1998.

Sperber, Bob. "Linda Kaplan Thaler On the Spot." *Adweek,* April 21, 2003.

Vranica, Suzanne. "New Aflac Ad Campaign Muzzles Iconic Duck." *Wall Street Journal,* December 2, 2004.

Witkoski, Michael. "The Bottle that Isn't There and the Duck that Can't Be Heard: The 'Subjective Correlative' in Commercial Messages." *Studies in Media & Information Literacy Education* 3, issue 3 (August 2003).

Guy Patrick Cunningham

AirTran Holdings, Inc.

9955 AirTran Boulevard
Orlando, Florida 32827
USA
Telephone: (407) 251-5600
Fax: (407) 251-5727
Web site: www.airtran.com

■■■

GO. THERE'S NOTHING STOPPING YOU CAMPAIGN

OVERVIEW

AirTran Airways took to the skies in 1997 following the merger of AirTran, a small carrier serving 11 cities from its base in Orlando, Florida, and ValuJet, a discount carrier struggling to rebuild after the crash of one of its planes. Within two years AirTran was emerging as a strong competitor in the discount airline market, and the trouble-plagued ValuJet was fading into memory. By 1999 AirTran served 30 cities with 280 daily flights, and plans were under way to replace its entire fleet of planes with newer aircraft. AirTran's revenues were also steadily increasing, as passengers came back to the carrier. Following the terrorist attacks on September 11, 2001, which involving the hijackings of four commercial aircraft, AirTran was one of the few U.S. airlines to report rising income, with revenues of $733 million in 2002.

To help with the transition from ValuJet to AirTran, the airline hired the Milwaukee office of Cramer-Krasselt to create a rebranding campaign. The initial effort, "It's Something Else," was launched in 1997. As the success of the rebranding effort became apparent, Cramer-Krasselt replaced "It's Something Else" in 2000 with a new campaign, "Your Airline Has Arrived." To increase consumer awareness of AirTran's low prices and services, promoted as helping to make travel easy and affordable, the $23 million "Go. There's Nothing Stopping You" campaign was launched in 2003.

The humorous ads that formed the "Go. There's Nothing Stopping You" campaign were a hit with consumers and industry watchdogs alike. Included were television and radio spots, as well as print, outdoor, and Internet ads. The campaign received a 2004 Gold EFFIE Award and in the month after its launch was recognized by *Boards Magazine* as one of the top spots.

HISTORICAL CONTEXT

In June 1993 ValuJet joined the ranks of discount airline carriers when its first flight took off, traveling between Atlanta, Georgia, and Tampa, Florida. With its low fares and reliable service, the airline quickly grew in popularity with consumers. But ValuJet was plagued with problems, including planes that slid off runways and a fire on one flight. Then, in May 1996, tragedy struck ValuJet when one of its airliners crashed into the Florida Everglades, killing all 110 people onboard. Following the crash, the Federal Aviation Administration (FAA) grounded ValuJet while the airline's maintenance and safety procedures were investigated. The airline's operating license was returned in September 1996, but travelers deserted ValuJet amid ongoing fears of safety problems. Soon after its license was restored, ValuJet announced plans to merge with AirTran, a small carrier based in Orlando. The ValuJet name was dropped, and the carrier began operation in 1997 as AirTran Airways.

The Milwaukee office of Cramer-Krasselt was hired to help reshape the airline and win back wary travelers. The agency replaced ValuJet's agency, Atlanta-based Hughes Advertising. Cramer-Krasselt's initial campaign included references to the ValuJet name. "It would have been disastrous if we had tried to cover up the connection and then had it leak out that AirTran was flying ValuJet planes," Peter Krivkovich, president of Cramer-Krasselt, told the *Milwaukee Journal Sentinel*. The initial campaign, "It's Something Else," had such taglines as "By the time we're through reinventing ValuJet, you won't even recognize it... New Management. New thinking. New airline." The effort helped put the airline back on track, but by October 1998 its flights were still taking off only slightly more than half full.

Undaunted, AirTran pushed ahead. In 2000 Cramer-Krasselt created a new campaign to replace "It's Something Else." This $8 million campaign, under the title "Your Airline Has Arrived," sent the message that AirTran could stand up against the major carriers, while offering affordable fares. Taglines included "We're the David vs. Goliath." The campaign seemed to work. Customers came back, and AirTran's revenues steadily increased, rising from $439 million in 1998 to $733 million in 2002. In 2003 Cramer-Krasselt created a campaign to replace "Your Airline Has Arrived." This new campaign, "Go. There's Nothing Stopping You," promoted AirTran's low business fares.

TARGET MARKET

Although AirTran's revenues were climbing and passengers were slowly rediscovering the carrier, the airline was still trying to convince consumers to think of AirTran first when they scheduled trips. The campaign was aimed particularly at business travelers, who were considered to make up one of the industry's most lucrative sectors. Thus, the campaign was designed to appeal both to leisure travelers planning quick getaways and to frequent business fliers. But more than anything, the campaign was aimed at any consumer looking for a low airfare. "Now more than ever consumers are looking for hassle-free, affordable travel options," said Tad Hutcheson, AirTran's director of marketing. He added that the new campaign showed how AirTran could give consumers what they wanted, including affordable ticket prices and flights to major destinations.

COMPETITION

The concept of no-frills, low-cost air travel had been introduced by Texas-based Southwest Airlines in 1971 when its first flight, between Dallas, Houston, and San Antonio, took off. Building on the innovative idea of providing passengers on-time flights at the lowest possible fares, the airline helped redefine air travel. Within three years Southwest had carried its millionth passenger, and by 2003 it had grown to become the number four carrier in the United States, with almost 2,800 daily departures that carried 65 million passengers to cities in 30 states. Besides helping to set the standard for future low-cost carriers, Southwest's innovative thinking was reflected in its marketing. In 2000 the airline launched a television campaign designed to encourage people to book flights on its website. The spots used humor to show people how they could leave uncomfortable daily situations behind by booking a quick vacation getaway on southwest.com. In an attempt to reach its target audience—25- to 54-year-old men who made frequent business trips—the airline also signed a sponsorship agreement with the National Hockey League. In 2003 Southwest took another unique approach to marketing when it partnered with the Arts & Entertainment Television Network (A&E) for a new reality show titled *Airline*. The program, which in effect starred Southwest Airlines and which debuted in early 2004, provided a behind-the-scenes look at the airline industry. It followed both passengers traveling to various U.S. locations as well as the airline staff, from ticket agents to pilots, who helped them on their way.

THE IMPACT OF AIRTRAN AND OTHER DISCOUNT AIRLINES

In 2003, according to Deutsche Bank, the international financial services provider, the top five U.S. airlines—American, Continental, Delta, Northwest, and United—reported combined losses estimated at almost $6.5 billion. As the big airlines were floundering, they also were thumbing their noses at the discount carriers. They should have been paying attention, however. The investment banking firm Lehman Brothers reported that by the end of 2002 discount airlines had captured 28 percent of the domestic market, up from 9 percent in 1991. In addition, discount airlines were affecting fares in markets that accounted for 56 percent of the larger airlines' revenue. With the promise of reliable, inexpensive flights, even without frills, airlines like AirTran, Southwest, and JetBlue were making money and attracting passengers away from the big five.

While Southwest was promoting itself with a reality television show, Delta Air Lines, one of the big five carriers in the United States, was preparing to compete with the discount carriers. In February 2003, in the hopes of winning back passengers, Delta launched Song, the airline's updated version of a discount carrier to replace its low-frills sibling, Delta Express. Described as an "airline within an airline," Song provided video screens at each seat and planned to include video games, live television programming, and music in its 36 planes. Song also announced plans to charge lower fares than the competition. As part of its marketing strategy, the airline opened Song retail shops, modeled after the inside of a airplane cabin. The first store opened in 2003 in New York's SoHo area, and a second store opened in 2004 in Boston's Prudential Center. Merchandise included video games and other entertainment options available on Song flights. For people who could not seem to get enough airline food, a selection of the items included on the Song menu could be purchased in the shops. And for those travelers anxious to book their next trip on Song, the stores had computers at the ready for customers to buy tickets. Although the airline reportedly planned to launch a television marketing campaign promoting Song, the retail shops were meant to enable consumers to enjoy the full Song experience without traveling to an airport. It was not clear, however, that the retail project was successful in selling tickets for flights on the airline, and in October 2005, as part of its restructuring plans under bankruptcy protection, Delta announced that Song would be phased out.

MARKETING STRATEGY

Cramer-Krasselt designed "Go. There's Nothing Stopping You," AirTran's new 2003 advertising campaign, to send a clear message about the carrier's low fares and the ways in which its services could help consumers avoid various travel difficulties. The $23 million campaign was launched in February 2003 with five television spots. Also included were radio, print, outdoor, and Internet advertising. The television spots were limited to the larger markets served by AirTran, including Atlanta, Baltimore, and Milwaukee. The print and outdoor portions of the campaign appeared in all of the airline's markets.

Humor was the driving force in the "Go. There's Nothing Stopping You" campaign. Television spots targeting business travelers portrayed office situations with a twist. For example, the spot titled "Shipping" showed business people sent to a meeting in packing crates. The people climbed out of the crates with packing peanuts stuck in their hair before convening in a boardroom. One unfortunate employee missed the meeting, however, when his packing crate fell off the back of the delivery truck. A voice-over asked, "Is the cost of getting there getting in the way of business?" Another spot targeting business travelers, titled "Client Dinner," showed two businessmen entertaining a new client. At the end of the meal the businessmen walked out without paying the restaurant check. The spot ended with the question "Business trips getting too expensive?"

Among the TV spots aimed at leisure travelers was "Babysitters." This commercial showed grandparents arriving at their daughter's house for a visit. The parents quickly handed their small children to the grandparents before tossing luggage into a cab and driving off, with the grandfather running after the cab as he shouted, "Don't leave us with the babies." Another spot targeting leisure travelers, titled "Mouthwash," showed a family whose members shared a bottle of mouthwash. After each person rinsed, he or she spit the mouthwash back into the bottle, before passing it on to the next person. The voice-over asked, "Does the cost of travel have you cutting back in other areas?"

Print ads followed themes similar to the television spots. For example, one ad pictured a sleeping man in a business suit stretched out on a park bench, with his suitcase stashed underneath. The lights of a big city twinkled in the background. Another showed a business meeting taking place around a boardroom table that was made of plywood supported by stacks of plastic milk crates. The text in all of the print ads asked the question "Does the cost of flying have you cutting back in other areas?"

OUTCOME

According to Hutcheson of AirTran Airways, both the consumer and industry response to the "Go. There's Nothing Stopping You" campaign was overwhelmingly positive. In the months following the campaign's launch in February 2003, the airline reported a steady increase in passenger traffic. By the end of 2003 the carrier's passenger traffic had jumped nearly 30 percent, to about 607 million travelers, compared to 466 million over the same period in 2002. In March 2003 *Boards Magazine* named the campaign one of its top spots. The campaign also received a 2004 Gold EFFIE Award for, among other things, reaching consumers, especially business travelers, and increasing ticket sales, which allowed AirTran plant to fly with full passenger loads, well above the break-even point.

In 2005, as further evidence of the campaign's success, Cramer-Krasselt introduced additional advertising under the "Go. There's Nothing Stopping You" banner. Included were five new television spots, which followed the same humorous formats that had been used in the originals. Other supporting efforts included new radio, print, outdoor, and Internet advertising.

FURTHER READING

"AirTran Ads Continue to 'Go.'" May 3, 2005. Available from <http://www.mediaweek.com>

"AirTran Airways, Formerly Value Jet, On the Move." *Bergen County (NJ) Record,* November 7, 1997.

"AirTran Airways Launches Five New Television Spots." *PR Newswire,* May 3, 2005.

"AirTran Airways Says 'Go'; New Advertising Campaign to Help Airline Break Down Travel Barriers." *Business Wire,* February 17, 2003.

Barrett, Rick. "Fledgling Airline ValuJet Nearly Collapsed Following a 1996 Crash That Killed 110 People: A Milwaukee Ad Agency Shaped Its New Image as AirTran." *Milwaukee Journal Sentinel,* May 11, 2003, p. D1.

Bynum, Russ. "ValueJet Takes Off Again as AirTran." *Los Angeles Daily News,* September 25, 1997.

Dinell, David. "AirTran Rolls Out New Marketing Effort." *Wichita Business Journal,* February 19, 2003.

Goetzl, David. "AirTran Flies in the Face of Big-Time Carriers: New $8 Million Spot TV Campaign Takes David-vs-Golilath Approach." *Advertising Age,* May 8, 2000.

Grantham, Russell. "Delta's Song All Tuned Up for Battle: Hip Discount Unit Has Made Inroads." *Atlanta Journal-Constitution,* November 9, 2003.

"It's a Bird . . . It's a Plane . . . It's Southwest Airlines in a New A&E Network Documentary Series: 'Airline' to Debut on A&E. 1st Quarter 2004." *PR Newswire,* July 28, 2003.

Serwer, Andy. "Naked Ambition in the Air: The Growing Influence of Discount Carriers Is Changing the Game for Big Airlines." *Fortune,* December 8, 2003.

"Sky Hooks." *Advertising Age's Creativity,* April 1, 2003, p. 20.

Thurston, Scott. "Not Out of the Clouds: Weakness Amid Strength; AirTran Continues to Struggle for a Comeback; While Virtually All Other Sizeable Carriers Make Money." *Atlanta Journal-Constitution,* November 12, 1998.

"Top Spots: A Look at the Month's Most Notable Work." *Boards Magazine,* March 1, 2003.

Tully, Shawn, and Paolo Hjelt. "Straighten Up and Fly Right: The U.S. Airline Industry Is Broke; Here Are Five Ways to Fix It." *Fortune,* February 17, 2003.

Rayna Bailey

Allied Domecq PLC

The Pavilions
Bridgwater Rd.
Bristol, BS13 8AR
United Kingdom
Telephone: 44 117 9785000
Fax: 44 117 9785300
Web site: www.allieddomecq.co.uk

LOOSEN UP A LITTLE CAMPAIGN

OVERVIEW

Dunkin' Donuts, the wholly owned subsidiary of the United Kingdom–based Allied Domecq PLC, reigned in 2000 as the world's largest coffee-and-baked-goods chain. With 3,500 outlets and $2 billion in annual sales, the quick-service restaurant was outperforming competitors such as Starbucks Coffee Company and Krispy Kreme Doughnuts, Inc. Even though Starbucks and Krispy Kreme were rising in popularity, executives at Dunkin' Donuts remained undaunted. They believed that Dunkin' Donuts' customers preferred the chain's low prices and rapidly prepared drinks, such as its Dunkin' Donuts Dunkaccino, an adaptation of a café mocha. After a survey conducted by the ad agency Hill, Holliday, Connors & Cosmopulos of Boston revealed that most customers considered Dunkin' Donuts a respite from their everyday anxieties, Dunkin' Donuts released its "Loosen Up a Little" campaign to brand its stores as a place to relax.

The $60 million campaign was created by Hill, Holliday, Connors & Cosmopulos (often referred to as Hill Holliday) and targeted several different demographics. It first appeared during Labor Day weekend in 2000. The campaign's television, radio, outdoor, and print advertisements suggested that its audience "Loosen Up a Little" with Dunkin' Donuts. One spot featured a woman smearing cream cheese in the shape of a smiley face on a high-strung businessman's jacket. In another spot a man removed his toupee during a coffee break, while in a different spot a businessman licked the jelly filling from his tie. Posters were hung inside elevators in office buildings throughout New England. The campaign included a fantasy-sports promotion that offered encounters with professional athletes such as the football linebacker Ted Johnson of the New England Patriots. Commercials for the campaign aired across major U.S. markets during the season premieres of the hit TV shows *ER, Friends,* and *Law & Order.*

"Loosen Up a Little" ended prematurely in August 2002 because Dunkin' Donuts executives considered the tagline "Loosen Up a Little" to be inappropriate for the advertising climate following the terrorist attacks on September 11, 2001. Nonetheless, the campaign helped Dunkin' Donuts generate more than $2.7 billion in sales for the 2001 fiscal year and record a 7 percent sales growth for 2002. It also earned a plethora of awards at the 2002 Francis W. Hatch Awards, which recognized New England's best ad campaigns.

HISTORICAL CONTEXT

Founded in 1950, Dunkin' Donuts grew to become a leading quick-service restaurant on the East Coast. One of the chain's longest-running campaigns, created by the ad agency

Ally & Gargano, New York, featured "Fred the baker," played by actor Michael Vale. The 15-year campaign used more than 200 spots, and in many Fred uttered the refrain "Time to make the doughnuts" early in the morning.

In 1989, while that campaign was underway, Dunkin' Donuts was purchased by Allied Domecq, the world's second-largest alcohol distiller. Dunkin' Donuts was not the only quick-service restaurant owned by the British enterprise. Allied Domecq had also acquired the ice-cream giant Baskin-Robbins and the sandwich chain Togo's Eateries. In 1997, when Dunkin' Donuts began expanding its offerings beyond just doughnuts and drip coffee, the chain ended its "Fred the Baker" campaign. New menu items helped Dunkin' Donuts increase sales by 10 percent in 1998. That same year Dunkin' Donuts awarded its advertising account to Hill, Holliday, Connors & Cosmopulos. The agency's copywriter Marty Donohue and art director Tim Foley successfully pitched commercial ideas to Dunkin' Donuts executives. One spot was about a police car chase that ended at Dunkin' Donuts. Another commercial depicted a construction site past which beautiful women walked unnoticed, yet when a man carrying Dunkin' Donuts Coolata drinks passed by, construction workers began whistling and hollering. Dunkin' Donuts vice president of marketing Eddie Binder praised Foley and Donohue in *Adweek* for their lighthearted, humorous approach. "They just got it. They understood the brand," he said.

Some of the agency's first work for Dunkin' Donuts included a doughnut-naming promotion in which participants were eligible for either $50,000 or a lifetime supply of Dunkin' Donuts. The promotion included the commercial "Ski Lodge," which featured a woman using her beauty to dupe men out of Dunkaccinos. The ad agency conducted a survey that revealed that many Dunkin' Donuts customers considered their shopping experience inside Dunkin' Donuts as a "break from reality." The survey results became the impetus for the upcoming "Loosen Up a Little" campaign.

COMMERCIALS AFTER TIVO

With the emergence of TiVo, a product that allowed audiences to skip unwanted television commercials, advertisers began creating new opportunities for television advertising. Coca-Cola reportedly spent $13 million to place its soft drink on the judges' table on Fox's hit reality show *American Idol.* Dunkin' Donuts, the world's largest coffee-and-baked-goods chain, paid to have its coffee placed on the reality television show *High School Reunion.* Phil Risinger, director of advertising for Dunkin' Donuts, noted in the *Boston Globe* that the Dunkin' Donuts' product placement on the show was not intrusive. "It's not in your face," he explained. "They're doing what folks do in the morning. They're drinking coffee."

TARGET MARKET

The campaign included several executions to reach three distinct target markets. First, a poster execution appeared inside the elevators of 69 office buildings on the East Coast in early 2001. The posters, along with a majority of the campaign's commercials, targeted what the ad critic David Gianatasio referred to in *Adweek* as "stressed-out urbanites." The posters suggested that in the hectic lives of most workers, Dunkin' Donuts offered a desirable place to "Loosen Up a Little." By placing the posters in elevators, in which many business professionals spent a few minutes every work day, the campaign targeted what Dunkin' Donuts field marketers called a "captive" target. Marty Donohue of Hill Holiday explained the timeliness of the campaign to the *Boston Globe*: "Dot-coms were rampant, and people were under a lot of stress. Dunkin' Donuts was seen as a safe haven."

The campaign also targeted a demographic that Hill Holliday dubbed the "regular guy." While Starbucks sold premium coffee drinks such as the café mocha for an average price of $3, Dunkin' Donuts sold its equivalent, the Dunkaccino (a mixture of coffee, milk, and chocolate), for about $1.50. Dunkin' Donuts was considered by its marketing department to be a brand for the mass market. To effectively reach this target, the campaign included "one-of-a-kind" sports-fantasy prizes. One prize allowed participants to win tickets to a Celtics basketball game and sit with Nomar Garciaparra of the Red Sox. Similar prizes included interactions with Ted Johnson of the Patriots, Paul Pierce of the Celtics, and Joey Franchino of the New England Revolution. "We're the regular guy's brand, so sports becomes a big part of getting access to our customer," Dunkin' Donuts vice president Ken Kimmel explained to the *Boston Globe.*

The campaign's third target included the East Coast's burgeoning Latino community. Select spots that were originally filmed in English were later released with Spanish voice-overs on Hispanic television networks. The Latino community of Boston, the city with the most Dunkin' Donut stores in America, had expanded from an estimated 36,000 Latinos in 1980 to 85,000 in 2000.

COMPETITION

In October 2001 Starbucks was aggressively adding new stores to its existing 3,000 locations in North America.

Advertising analysts were amazed by Starbuck's ability to expand the specialty-coffee retail industry with relatively little advertising. Executives at Starbucks firmly believed that word-of-mouth advertising was more effective than paid advertising. Therefore, instead of financing exorbitant campaigns, Starbucks spent operating costs on its enjoyable in-store environment, premium coffee-based products, and unparalleled customer service. From 2001 to 2002 alone, sales for Starbucks jumped from $2.6 billion to $3.3 billion.

When Starbucks did advertise, it was usually in partnership with other major brands. In 2000 Starbucks formed an exclusive relationship with the *New York Times.* In exchange for publishing print ads announcing new Starbucks drinks and holiday gift cards, the *New York Times* became the sole newspaper sold inside Starbucks. To compete with Dunkin' Donuts, Starbucks temporarily sold the popular Krispy Kreme doughnuts inside select Starbucks stores. The relationship ended after Krispy Kreme announced its own line of espresso beverages. In 2002 the North American Coffee Partnership, a joint venture between Starbucks and PepsiCo, released its first television advertising campaign, which promoted bottled Frappuccino and Starbucks DoubleShot drinks. The campaign included print ads, four 15-second TV spots, and one 30-second spot.

MARKETING STRATEGY

Commercials for "Loosen Up a Little" first aired during Labor Day weekend in 2000. In addition to television spots, the $60 million campaign included radio, outdoor, and print advertisements. One of the campaign's lead creatives, Marty Donohue, explained in an interview with *Adweek* that the campaign aimed to brand Dunkin' Donuts as "little comfort zones. Not a serious place, but a place people go every day" to escape the stressfulness of life. Donohue and Foley led a team of 12 copywriters and art directors for "Loosen Up a Little" and hired the acclaimed commercial director Noam Murro of Biscuit Filmworks to direct the spots.

One of the first spots featured a man who took advantage of being stuck in a traffic jam by leaving his car to fetch a Dunkin' Donuts breakfast. "The work probes a little deeper into the human condition than previous Dunkin' ads, while retaining the humor and freshness of the earlier work," Foley told *Adweek.* Storylines for the commercials were created from the agency's "honest assessment" of real-life customer experiences, he added.

In a television spot titled "Smile," two obnoxious business executives discussed a meeting that was taking place later that day. "I am stoked. Locked and loaded," the more brazen of the two exclaimed. The bus lurched, and a woman standing behind the man accidentally smeared Dunkin' Donuts cream cheese on his jacket. "Hey, why don't you watch yourself," he snapped. The woman then appeared to scrape the cream cheese off his jacket. When the man exited the bus, however, it was revealed that she had only shaped the cream cheese into a smiley face.

Later in the 2000 holiday season another spot featured Christmas carolers trying to eat doughnuts while singing. By the spot's end their words had become unintelligible. Commercials aired on network channels during the season premieres of shows such as *ER, Friends,* and *Law & Order.* The campaign targeted what advertising critics referred to as "stressed-out urbanites." Posters promoting Dunkaccinos and the chain's "Coffee by the Pound" offering were posted inside elevators of 69 East Coast office buildings. To target Boston's expanding Latino community, commercials were rereleased with Spanish voice-overs across Spanish-language television networks.

In 2001 the campaign targeted what the creatives from Hill Holliday referred to as the "regular guy." "Peel-and-win" stickers that allowed participants to win sports-fantasy prizes were placed on Dunkin' Donuts drinks. Prizes for the promotion included opportunities with athletes from six of New England's professional sports teams. One prize offered several hours of soccer coaching from Kristine Lilly of the Boston Breakers. Another prize included the ice-hockey captain Joe Thornton of the Bruins delivering coffee and doughnuts to the winner's office.

OUTCOME

Advertising critics, Hill Holliday, and executives from Dunkin' Donuts all considered "Loosen Up a Little" to be a success. Dunkin' Donuts exceeded $2.7 billion in sales for the 2001 fiscal year. It also posted a 7 percent sales increase for the beginning of 2002, outperforming the collective growth rate of 3 percent for the entire quick-service-restaurant industry. Overall sales for Allied Domecq, the owner of Dunkin' Donuts, jumped from $3.8 billion in 2000 to $5.2 billion in 2002. The campaign also collected a variety of awards at the 2002 Hatch Awards, which recognized New England's best ad campaigns. Unfortunately for Dunkin' Donuts, the campaign ended prematurely in August 2002. The company's executives deemed the tagline "Loosen Up a Little" too irreverent in the wake of the September 11th terrorist attacks.

When Dunkin' Donuts began its "Just the Thing" campaign in August 2002, creatives at Hill Holiday explained the shortcomings of the "Loosen Up a Little" campaign to the *Boston Globe.* "The problem was, though, you had to spend half your 30 seconds talking about how hectic life was. You had to explain it and set it up. That left us with only 15 seconds to talk about the product. 'Just the Thing' gets to the point quickly," Marty Donohue said. "It's wonderfully simple and you get it right off the bat. It's so perfectly Dunkin' Donuts. The new tagline is as comforting as a doughnut and a cup of coffee."

FURTHER READING

Adams, Steve. "Dunkin' Donuts Pours Effort into Courting Hispanics." *Quincy (MA) Patriot Ledger,* September 28, 2004, p. 9.

———. "Dunkin' Tests Appetite for Sandwiches." *Quincy (MA) Patriot Ledger,* July 22, 2005, p. 14.

———. "Funky Dunkin'." *Quincy (MA) Patriot Ledger,* January 25, 2005, p. 15.

Aoki, Naomi. "Where Reality TV, Commerce Meet." *Boston Globe,* March 21, 2004, p. A1.

Collins, Monica. "A War's Brewing in Cutthroat World of Coffee, Doughnuts." *Boston Herald,* August 10, 2003, p. 28.

Gatlin, Greg. "Dunkin' Approach Recasts Ads as Serious Biz." *Boston Herald,* October 11, 2004, p. 31.

———. "Product Placement Carries a Premium." *Boston Herald,* March 30, 2005, p. 27.

Goodison, Donna. "Dunkin' Taps Customers for New Ad Blitz." *Boston Herald,* November 2, 2005, p 035.

MacArthur, Kate. "BK, McD's Wake Up to Premium Coffee." *Advertising Age,* April 11, 2005, p. 14.

Noyes, Jesse. "Versatile Brown Stars in Dunkin' Ad." *Boston Herald,* August 26, 2005, p. 37.

Powell, Jennifer Heldt. "Making a Pitch for Dunkin' Donuts." *Boston Herald,* April 12, 2005, p. 38.

Slajda, Rachel. "Making It All Ad Up." *Quincy (MA) Patriot Ledger,* June 1, 2005, p. 28.

Wentz, Laurel. "Dunkin' Donuts Creates Spanish-Language Spot." *Advertising Age,* September 6, 2004, p. 15.

Kevin Teague

The Allstate Corporation

2775 Sanders Road
Northbrook, Illinois 60062-6127
USA
Telephone: (847) 402-5000
Fax: (847) 326-7519
Web site: www.allstate.com

OUR STAND CAMPAIGN

OVERVIEW

The Allstate Corporation, America's longtime number two auto insurer, faced new challenges in the 1990s when competitors such as GEICO and the Progressive Corporation blanketed television with spots playing up the low prices of their policies. Long reliant on its slogan "You're in Good Hands," Allstate found itself in need of a brand refurbishing to counteract the inroads made by these direct marketers. In November 2003 Allstate released the "Our Stand" marketing campaign, its first to feature a celebrity spokesperson, actor Dennis Haysbert, known for playing the president of the United States on the hit television series *24*.

While "Our Stand" included radio, print, and Internet elements, the core of the campaign was the television spots featuring Haysbert. The spots offered a soft sell in which Haysbert made the case that price was not everything when it came to buying car insurance—a relationship with an agent was important as well—and vouched for Allstate's integrity and commitment to take a stand for customers and promote their interests. Although the company did not reveal the advertising budget for the campaign, Allstate was reported in the press to have increased its ad budget 56 percent to more than $120 million in 2003, a level it maintained in 2004 and 2005.

"Our Stand" helped Allstate reestablish its position in the marketplace. The company reported that the number of consumers contacting Allstate through its sales agents, website, and call center had increased after the campaign began, but it did not provide any financial data to support the claim. Haysbert's contract was extended through 2006, however, indicating that the company was pleased with the campaign's effectiveness.

HISTORICAL CONTEXT

Allstate was credited with having the oldest surviving tagline in paid advertising: "You're in Good Hands with Allstate," which dated back to 1951, when a print ad first depicted a pair of hands cradling an automobile. (The oldest tagline in use was "Only You Can Prevent Forest Fires," a long-standing public-service effort produced by the Advertising Council; it had been used since 1947.) Throughout its history Allstate and its rivals produced advertising that was serious in tone, emphasizing such company virtues as trust and reliability and never mentioning price. Then, in the 1990s, GEICO, a direct marketer of car insurance ranked seventh in sales, upset the status quo by bombarding the television airways with humorous commercials that challenged the likes of number two Allstate and market leader State Farm solely on the basis of price. The Progressive Corporation soon followed suit, and Allstate came under increasing pressure to protect its market share.

To keep its slogan fresh and maintain relevance in the marketplace, Allstate offered variations on the "Good Hands" theme. The insurer also dabbled with celebrity endorsers. In 2001, for example, Allstate began a television, print, and radio advertising campaign that used the tagline "The Right Hands Make All the Difference." The advertisements featured football players Joe Montana and Jerry Rice as well as inventor Ann Lai, all of who whom relied on their hands in their professions. But the "Right Hands" campaign failed to stem a drop in Allstate policyholder growth, and after 18 months it was retired, replaced by the "Our Stand" campaign, which was the first Allstate advertising campaign to center on a celebrity spokesperson: actor Dennis Haysbert.

An African-American, Haysbert had acted in numerous films and television shows since getting his break in 1979, when he first appeared on the television series *The White Shadow.* But he achieved true celebrity status in 2001, when he was cast in the television series *24* to play Senator David Palmer, a character who would later become president. At the core of Palmer's character was moral integrity, an attribute that viewers associated with Haysbert the actor and that thus made him an ideal advocate for Allstate's message. Jill Weaver, Allstate's vice president of brand strategy, was quoted in a press release as saying that Haysbert embodied "the spirit of the Allstate brand. Experienced, honest, and understanding, with a sense of strength and conviction."

GOOD HANDS

Allstate's venerable slogan "You're in Good Hands With Allstate" was inspired by an incident in life of one of the company's general sales managers, Davis W. Ellis. In the spring of 1950 his youngest daughter was hospitalized with hepatitis. To ease his concern his wife told him not to worry: "We're in good hands with the doctor." That remark came to mind later in the year when Allstate was struggling to coin a slogan for its first national advertising campaign. Ellis shared the story about his daughter, and soon the company had settled on a slogan that endured for well over half a century.

TARGET MARKET

The "Our Stand" campaign sought to update the brand image of Allstate while appealing to a more diverse customer base. In essence, auto insurers were faced with the difficult task of reaching one of the broadest markets imaginable: anyone who drove a car, whether they were male or female, young or old, and regardless of ethnicity. In this regard Haysbert was a good choice as spokesperson; he had wide appeal, even with younger consumers, despite the fact that he was born in 1954. Allstate's main pitch was that picking an insurance company was more involved than just choosing the lowest price. More important, the company argued, was the service a policyholder could expect and the integrity of the insurance agents and of the company that stood behind them. Hence, the "Our Stand" target audience was somewhat older than the demographic targeted by GEICO and Progressive. This older market also had more money to spend on car insurance and placed greater value on a relationship with a broker and the solidity of the insurance company backing the policy.

COMPETITION

In terms of market share, State Farm was Allstate's top rival. It controlled about 18.5 percent of the market in 2004, compared with Allstate's 10 percent. Next in line were Progressive with 7.1 percent and GEICO with 5.5 percent. Rounding out the top 10 in direct premiums written were Farmers Insurance Group (4.9 percent), Nationwide Group (4.5 percent), United Services Automobile Association Group (3.5 percent), American International Group (3 percent), Liberty Mutual Group (2.8 percent), and American Family Insurance Group (2.2 percent). All insurers were boosting their marketing budgets, eager to take business from each other, a result in large measure of the increasing profitability of the auto-insurance business. Because cars had become better built, they needed less repairs and were involved in fewer accidents. Consequently, insurance companies had fewer claims to pay out. Moreover, America's population was growing older, resulting in people driving slower, again leading to a decrease in accidents, greater profits for insurers, and a heated scramble to peel away the customers of rivals.

In addition, Allstate, State Farm, and other old-guard broker-based insurers found themselves competing against the likes of GEICO and Progressive in another way. Mya Frazier reported in *Advertising Age,* "It's a battle of the business model, pitting the call-center row of headset-wearing operators taking claims and signing on new customers against neighborhood agents who know a customer's kids and may even be a neighbor. It's pitting Internet price quotes [against] in-office consultations and the yearly search for a best price [against] a lifetime relationship with an agent." It was at this fundamental level that the "Our Stand" campaign made its case with consumers.

MARKETING STRATEGY

In answer to GEICO and Progressive's blitz of advertising focusing on price, Allstate's "Our Stand" campaign made an emotional appeal to urge consumers to re-evaluate what was really important in insurance. Lisa Cochrane, the insurer's assistant vice president of marketing communications, told *American Banker* reporter Lee Ann Gjertsen, "We know that customers are looking for more than just a low price; they need good value, good protection. That's why they buy insurance or financial security products." At the same time, Cochrane noted, Allstate believed that "quality insurance should be affordable." A secondary purpose of the campaign was to promote research that, according to Allstate, revealed that 70 percent of customers who switched to Allstate saved $200. Moreover, because Allstate had in recent years become involved in banking and financial services, the "Our Stand" campaign served to build general awareness of what Allstate had to offer in addition to its core auto-insurance business.

The "Our Stand" campaign broke in November 2003. The crux of it was the television spots anchored by Haysbert, but the company also included radio spots that began airing later in the month, print ads that debuted in early 2004, and Internet executions. The first four TV spots were shot and produced by Sam Mendes, the director of the Oscar-winning film *American Beauty.* These initial spots set the serious tone of the more than 20 spots featuring Haysbert. In the spot titled "Pay Phone," Allstate took a subtle dig at GEICO and its telephone-based operation. The camera slowly zoomed in on Haysbert standing next to a pay phone on a dark, deserted stretch of road. In a low-key voice he asked, "If you needed your insurance, who would you call? Not the name of the company, but the name of the person? You got two seconds. Coming up blank? You may want to consider Allstate... You deserve a relationship with a real person. That's Allstate's stand. Are you in good hands?" A wide shot of the scene capped the commercial, with the Allstate logo and "You're in Goods Hands" tagline offering a counterpoint to Haysbert's final question.

A number of other commercials featuring Haysbert followed. In "Chop Shop" he stood in a dank garage where thieves ripped apart a stolen SUV to sell for parts, and he spoke about Allstate's 600-person fraud team. In "Guardrail" he stood next to a crumpled highway guardrail to talk about Allstate's 20 percent discount for people with good driving records. The spot called "Boiling Turkey" showed Haysbert in a backyard with a deep-fat turkey fryer, which was used to illustrate the potential of holiday mishaps, whether they were caused by fryers or car accidents on icy roads. In "Life Raft" he compared Allstate to a life raft and other insurers, such as GEICO, to little more than a circular life preserver—a zero. In addition, the spot promoted new policy features that dovetailed with the marketing campaign: Accident Forgiveness, which prevented rates from increasing in the event of an accident, and New Car Replacement, so that if a car was "totaled" the policyholder received a new car rather than a check that deducted appreciation.

Allstate built on the "Our Stand" campaign in 2004 and 2005. Haysbert appeared in television, radio, and print advertisements that were specifically aimed at African-Americans. Because research indicated that these consumers relied heavily on the referral of family and friends when buying car insurance, the advertisements centered on family reunions. Also in 2004 Allstate targeting the Hispanic market by airing four Spanish-language television spots featuring actor Esai Morales. The tagline for these executions was "Así piensa Allstate" (That's what Allstate believes). The Hispanic component of the "Our Stand" campaign also included radio, print, and outdoor elements. In addition, the "Our Stand" campaign was used in 2005 to introduce a new Allstate product: Your Choice Auto Insurance, which could be customized to suit individual needs.

OUTCOME

Allstate was pleased with the "Our Stand" campaign. The television spots polled well with consumers. According to *USA Today* 's Ad Track survey, 17 percent of consumers liked the commercials "a lot." While that number was below the Ad Track average of 21 percent, it represented a strong showing in a category that consumers generally did not like. The campaign was also recognized by advertising trade publication *Adweek,* which named "Boiling Turkey" a "Best Spot" in December 2003. Haysbert's work was also much appreciated by Allstate. In fall 2005 the company renewed his contract to serve as Allstate spokesperson through the end of 2006. The most important measure of the campaign's success, however, was to be found on Allstate's balance sheet. While the company reported no hard numbers, it did note in its 2003 annual report, "[R]eaction, as measured by increased contact with agencies, allstate.com, and 1-800-Allstate, has been positive." Allstate had pulled the plug on the previous marketing campaign after 18 months, so the fact that the company renewed its commitment to Haysbert through 2006 indicated that the "Our Stand" campaign was having an appreciable effect on Allstate's bottom line.

FURTHER READING

"Allstate Addresses Latino Marketplace." *Adweek* (midwest ed.), May 18, 2004.

"Allstate Signs Celebrity to New Ads." *Best's Review,* January 2004, p. 64.

Anderson, Mae. "53 Years Later, Still in Good Hands." *Adweek,* February 3, 2003, p. 40.

Frazier, Mya. "Progressive, Geico Prod Auto Rivals into Price War." *Advertising Age,* February 28, 2005, p. 4.

Gjertsen, Lee Ann. "Insurers Cut Marketing, but 3 Campaigns Shine." *American Banker,* March 11, 2004, p. 11.

Goch, Lynna. "Get Emotional: Reaching Out to Consumers' Feelings Is the Key to Successful Insurance Marketing." *Best's Review,* July 2005, p. 15.

Howard, Theresa. "Presidential Allstate Ads Counter the Gecko." *USA Today,* August 16, 2004, p. 6B.

Kirk, Jim. "Allstate's New Campaign Takes Stand on Old Values." *Chicago Tribune,* November 11, 2003.

Yerak, Becky. "Allstate's Ads Push Agenda." *Chicago Tribune,* November 24, 2005.

Ed Dinger

Altria Group Inc.

120 Park Ave.
New York, New York 10017
USA
Telephone: (917) 663-4000
Fax: (917) 663-2163
Web site: www.altria.com

IT'S A WOMAN THING CAMPAIGN

OVERVIEW

NOTE: Since the initial appearance of this essay in the 1998 edition of *Major Marketing Campaigns Annual,* The Philip Morris Companies changed its name to Altria Group Inc. The essay continues to refer to the company's former name, as that was the official name of the organization when the campaign was launched.

The slogan Philip Morris Companies Inc. used in 1968 to launch its Virginia Slims campaign—"You've Come a Long Way, Baby"—effectively combined the two seemingly dissimilar marketing themes of female attractiveness and women's rights. The series of ads were highly successful, however, and in 1996 the company introduced a successor campaign with the slogan "It's a Woman Thing."

The new campaign, which was directed by Leo Burnett USA of Chicago, took on what might be called a post-feminist ironic tone. For example, a photo of a beautiful blond woman on a motorcycle was accompanied by the line "I don't necessarily want to run the world, but I wouldn't mind taking it for a ride." Another ad showed a young woman who exuded beauty, happiness, and "female cool" polishing her nails a metallic blue. The accompanying line asked, "Does this look stupid on me? The correct answer to the question is 'No.'"

HISTORICAL CONTEXT

Cigarettes had been marketed directly to women since the 1880s, when the Kimball Tobacco Company tried to sell perfumed cigarettes called Satin Straight Cuts in satin drawstring purses. The effort failed because of the social climate. When in the 1920s Lucky Strike ads appeared that featured slender young women who advised, "Reach for a Lucky instead of a sweet," suggesting a correlation between smoking and thinness, sales tripled within a year, however. The image of Amelia Earhart was used in Lucky Strike ads of 1928, which implied that the aviator had smoked Luckys on her transatlantic flight. (Earhart, a nonsmoker, protested.) The following year, fashion and activism combined when debutantes and feminists marched in New York's Easter Day parade smoking "torches of freedom" in the form of Lucky Strikes.

In 1967 the American Tobacco Company failed in an attempt to market king-size cigarettes for women with the line "Cigarettes are like girls. The best ones are thin and rich." But when Philip Morris introduced Virginia Slims a year later with the slogan "You've Come a Long Way, Baby," the brand rose into the number one spot for sales to women. The strategy behind the initial marketing of Virginia Slims linked good looks and emancipation, or, in the words of Ellen Merlo, the company's group director for brand management, "Old-time fashion and fun." Sepia-tinted photographs of downtrodden "women of yesteryear" shown sneaking cigarettes and then feeling shame upon being discovered were juxtaposed with bright, glossy images of beautiful contemporary women who seemed to have arrived at full-blown independence. The ads were slightly sardonic about the lot of women in earlier times, when "a woman wasn't allowed to vote, earn, talk, think or smoke like a man," as characterized in the Virginia Slims Book of Days Engagement Calendar.

Direct advertising was never the sole promotional device used by Virginia Slims. The Book of Days Engagement Calendar, introduced in 1970 and offered free at points of sale, contained humorous historical anecdotes and memorable sexist quotes but few overt selling lines. The Virginia Slims Opinion Poll, a series of polls conducted by the Roper Center to survey the changing status of women in society, was launched in the same year. Soon after, Virginia Slims created the first professional women's tennis tour, which allowed the brand name to continue to appear on television without direct pitches for the product. In the 1980s sponsorship of the visual and performing events by parent corporation Philip Morris led the *Wall Street Journal* to call it "the art world's favorite company." And the 1990s saw the introduction of Virginia Slims V-Wear, advertised as a "fashion collection with a streetwise attitude" and available free with proofs of purchase. Critics, however, lambasted the relatively short period of time—six months—and number of proofs of purchase—980—needed to obtain a complete ensemble, calculating that a smoker would have to go through five packs of cigarettes a day to meet the goal.

TARGET MARKET

The "It's a Woman Thing" campaign targeted women smokers. The ads invoked the "feel-good solidarity of a Hollywood female buddy movie," wrote Lucy O'Brien in *The Independent.* O'Brien quoted Mandy Merck, a lecturer in media studies at Sussex University: "It's a woman thing implies that you can share this culture of smoking with your friends. Smokers adore each other—shared vices and addictions make great bonding experiences." Worldwide, women were a market of great interest because they invariably smoked less than men and in some markets did not smoke at all. In Hong Kong, for example, where only 1 percent of women smoked, tobacco companies had spent millions trying to persuade them to begin.

Despite antismoking campaigns, the *Wall Street Journal* reported that U.S. consumption of cigarettes held steady in 1996 and possibly was rising. One significant factor was the new generation of smokers in their late teens and early 20s who saw the habit as hip. From 85 to 90 percent of new smokers in the United States in 1997 were teenagers, with 3,000 minors beginning to smoke each day according to figures provided by the American Lung Association. According to reports by the association and the Robert Wood Johnson Foundation, virtually all smokers began the habit by age 18. *Consumer Reports* reported that a high proportion of young smokers were girls, who associated smoking with weight loss, social acceptance, and independence.

YOUNG SMOKERS

Of young female smokers in the early 1990s, the overwhelming majority were white. In a 1995 survey on high school smoking in the United States, the Centers for Disease Control and Prevention found that 40 percent of white females attending high school had smoked in the previous month and that 21 percent were heavy smokers. Of young African-American females attending high school, only 12 percent smoked at all, with just 1 percent being heavy smokers. Some observers suggested that the female cool of the "It's a Woman Thing" ads continued to play to the social pressure to be thin, which was more of a concern to white than to African-American teenage girls, who held different ideas of beauty.

Philip Morris and Leo Burnett were careful, however, not to pitch the Virginia Slims ads directly to underage smokers. "They didn't say it's a girl thing; it's a woman thing," observed Carol Boyd, director of the University of Michigan's Substance Abuse Research Center. "It has to do with growing up, being independent." Nevertheless, this was an enticing prospect for young girls. As quoted on CNN, teenage smoker Tiffany Walter summed up the image by saying, "[It's] like this beautiful supermodel that'll never gain weight. [She's] just gorgeous, has a lot of money, is classy, up in the business world, just like women of the '90s want to be."

COMPETITION

In 1997 Philip Morris was the largest tobacco company in the world, with 45 percent of the U.S. and 12 percent of the world market, and its Marlboro cigarettes were the world's best-selling brand. Nearly three-fourths

(72 percent) of smokers between the ages of 18 and 24 were loyal to two brands—Marlboro (59 percent) and R. J. Reynolds' Camel (13 percent). Both brands pursued advertising that incorporated female images or broadened their formerly masculine images. R. J. Reynolds announced plans to add a Josephine Camel character to its "Joe Camel" campaign, and some ads for Marlboro Lights become more androgynous, with desert scenes and tumbleweed replacing the Marlboro Man.

According to Margaretha Haglund, head of tobacco control at Stockholm's Institute of Public Health, young women smokers traditionally favored so-called light or low-tar brands. Early brands developed specifically for women included Eve, Cooper, Charm, and Kim, as well as Virginia Slims. A main competitor for Virginia Slims was Capri, whose ads retained a classic style of feminine imagery, showing a woman in an elegant gown holding a long, thin cigarette with the accompanying line "She's gone to Capri and she's not coming back." Other competitors included Dakota, aimed at "virile females with a high-school education," according to Sussex University's Merck, and Misty, a budget-priced cigarette advertised with young-looking models and the slogan "Light 'n Sassy... Light Price, Too."

Nonetheless, by 1985 the market share of Virginia Slims was double that of all other women's cigarettes combined. Among all brands Virginia Slims was number 10 in sales in 1996. Its market share was 2.4 percent, far behind Marlboro's 32.3 percent, but not far behind Camel's 4.6 percent. No other women's brand made the top 10 list. Ad spending for Virginia Slims in 1996 was $30.9 million, a $4.4 million increase over the previous year.

MARKETING STRATEGY

Some of the "It's a Woman Thing" magazine ads followed the "competent and liberated" theme put forth by previous Virginia Slims ads and placed a lit cigarette squarely in the center of the image. One ad, for example showed a well-groomed woman in a stylish straw hat who eyed the camera over her cigarette and stated, "If it slices, dices or scrubs, it's hardly ever the gift we've always wanted." Some of the ads did not depict or address smoking itself but instead showed women refusing to feel tormented by problems with boyfriends. In one a long-haired blond girl shared a denim jacket with a grinning young man, with the line saying, "It takes time to get over a breakup. Fortunately, a new boyfriend can cut that time in half." In another a short-cropped, tousle-haired girl slouched in her slip and smiled ruefully at the camera: "Making up with us is easy; admit you're wrong even if you're not."

Accompanying the ads was a new Virginia Slims promotional program—Woman Thing Music—a label for emerging female musicians. Woman Thing Music was envisioned as a series of CDs and tours promoting undiscovered women artists. It was all part of the Virginia Slims "tradition of providing opportunities for women to showcase their talents and interests," Mary Jo Gennaro, Philip Morris's manager of events marketing, told the *Wall Street Journal.* The CDs were not sold at record stores but were available free with the purchase of Virginia Slims in special packages of two at supermarkets, convenience stores, and other outlets.

Brand-name CDs had been used by other marketers. In January 1997 *Time* magazine reported that the Woman Thing Music label was just the latest in a list of brand-name labels that included those by Banana Republic, Gap, Victoria's Secret, and Pottery Barn. Most of these CDs were compilations of previously released songs by well-known musicians. In contrast, Woman Thing Music aimed to promote new and unknown female performers by underwriting their albums and sponsoring live performances. The first CD, released in the spring of 1997, was a six-song mini-album by 27-year-old Martha Byrne, who played Lily on the soap opera *As the World Turns.* Four of the songs were originals, including one titled "It's a Woman Thing," and one was a cover of John Lennon's "Imagine," which contained the line "It's a woman thing."

OUTCOME

Antismoking activists saw the "It's a Woman Thing" campaign as propaganda. The new slogan was lampooned in critical press reports as "It's a chemo thing," and the previous "You've Come a Long Way, Baby" was cynically interpreted in light of dire health statistics. *The Independent*'s O'Brien wrote, "As regulations against tobacco advertising become more stringent, it is inevitable that the dated image of the woman with the healthy grin and the skinny cigarette will fade away. Companies are already shifting their focus from magazines and posters to other areas such as sponsorship and the Internet. For the Virginia Slims woman, at last it seems her days are numbered."

According to *Time,* critics of the CD project called it "an attempt to get pop music-loving kids to smoke." The Woman Thing Music campaign met with active resistance in the form of a counter concert called Virginia Slam. Leslie Nuchow, a New York singer and songwriter, organized the event in May 1997. She had been contacted by a representative of Philip Morris to participate in the Woman Thing Music project but declined, saying that the CDs and tours exploited women for the profit of the tobacco industry. Nuchow then gained recognition for her own music through the counter event, which had the support of popular performers such as Ani Di Franco. In August 1998 *Mediascope* reported that Woman Thing Music CDs were no longer available.

FURTHER READING

Brotman, Barbara. "Why Is It a Woman Thing? Feeling Pressure to Be Thin, More Women and Girls Smoke." *Pittsburgh Post-Gazette,* August 5, 1996.

Carpi, John. "New Evidence That Cigarette Ads Targeted Teen Girls." *American Medical News,* March 14, 1994, p. 8.

Cohen, Elizabeth. "Women Targeted by Cigarette Ads, Not Health Ads." CNN, November 21, 1996.

Farley, Christopher John. "C'mon Baby, Light My Fire: Cigarette Giant Philip Morris Goes After the Youth Market by Starting Its Own Record Label." *Time,* January 27, 1997.

Guthrey, Molly. "Former Tobacco Executive Says Youths Never Targeted." *Pioneer Press,* April 23, 1998.

Hardin, Peter. "Virginia Slims Effort Slammed." *Richmond Times-Dispatch,* February 16, 1997.

Henningsen, Michael. "You've Come a Long Way, Baby!" *Weekly Alibi,* January 29–February 4, 1997.

Jones, Chip. "Philip Morris to Revamp Ad Practices: Chairman Wants Emphasis on Not Marketing to Youth." *Richmond Times-Dispatch,* June 3, 1998.

O'Brien, Lucy. "The Market: Smoking: It's a Woman Thing." *The Independent,* August 25, 1996.

Reilly, Patrick M. "Virginia Slims Gets Its Own Record Label." *Wall Street Journal,* January 15, 1997.

Robinson, William A. "Virginia Slims Comes a Long Way in 17 Years." *Advertising Age,* May 30, 1985, p. 30.

"Women and Smoking." *Mediascope,* August 15, 1998.

Megan McNamer

Amazon.com, Inc.

1200 12th Ave. South, Ste. 1200
Seattle, Washington 98144-2734
USA
Telephone: (206) 266-1000
Fax: (206) 266-1821
Web site: www.amazon.com

■■■

AMAZON THEATER CAMPAIGN

OVERVIEW

Amazon.com, Inc., entered the retail marketplace as a pioneering online bookseller in 1995, and though it had been steadily diversifying its product offerings all along, by 2004 most consumers still thought of the website only in connection with books and music. Having recently made the transition, thanks to years of capital-intensive investment, from dot-com trendsetter to actual profit maker, Amazon wanted its customers to begin thinking of its site whenever they needed anything. Unconvinced that television and other traditional forms of advertising could translate into online sales, Amazon and its founder and CEO, Jeff Bezos, enlisted Fallon Worldwide's Minneapolis office, a leader in online branded entertainment, to spread the message about Amazon's breadth of products via Amazon.com itself.

The result was "Amazon Theater," a series of five short films starring well-known Hollywood actors and integrating products available for purchase on Amazon.com. The films, sponsored by JP Morgan Chase & Co., cost approximately $2.5 million to produce. Timed to coincide with peak holiday traffic, they premiered on Amazon.com each Tuesday between November 9 and December 7, 2004, and were packaged as a free "holiday gift" to customers. Though the featured Amazon products were folded into the stories without fanfare, they were listed as starring players in an interactive credit roll at the end of each movie, allowing viewers to click and go to linked Amazon pages to make immediate purchases.

This innovative integration of entertainment and shopping attracted industry and media attention and pointed the way to future explorations of interactive advertising. Amazon continued to experiment with the inclusion of entertainment on its website by partnering with the Tribeca Film Festival in 2005 to stage a short-film competition. Candidate films were available for free viewing on the website, and Amazon customers selected the winner.

HISTORICAL CONTEXT

Inspired by a statistic claiming that Internet usage was growing at a rate of 2,300 percent a year, entrepreneur Bezos launched Amazon in July 1995 as an online bookseller. By doing away with the costs associated with the building and operation of traditional retail stores, the pioneering Web business was able to offer consumers lower prices than its physical-world counterparts while still delivering a high level of customer service. As the Web population grew exponentially in the late 1990s, so did Amazon. It went public in 1997; extended its product range to music, videos, toys, and electronics in

1998; began a concerted effort to buy up other dot-coms and to offer a wider range of online services; and increasingly established an international presence by 2000, with websites serving England, Germany, France, and Japan. In 2002 Amazon partnered with hundreds of clothing retailers. In 2003, after years of steady investment aimed at allowing it to boast "Earth's biggest selection" and to claim to be "Earth's most customer-centric company," Amazon posted its first yearly profit.

By 2004, despite the fact that Amazon's product selection rivaled that of Wal-Mart, most consumers still thought of the online retail powerhouse as a site strictly for buying books and music. Amazon wanted to change this perception, but it had almost entirely quit investing in traditional media advertising, choosing instead to keep prices low and offer free shipping. The company had, however, already experimented with branded entertainment on its site. During the 2003 holiday season Amazon had enlisted celebrities Jack Black, Bruce Springsteen, Hillary Clinton, and Tom Brokaw, among others, to offer exclusive content and gift recommendations on its site. Because Amazon represented "a hybrid between stores and a media outlet," according to branding consultant Allen Adamson, the promotion also served the interests of the celebrities, who contributed their content and recommendations free of charge.

Amazon's interest in continuing to experiment with online branded entertainment made it a logical match for Fallon Worldwide, the agency widely credited with inventing the category. In 2002 Fallon's Minneapolis office had teamed up with successful feature-film directors, including Ang Lee, John Frankenheimer, and Guy Ritchie, to create short, online action films starring BMW cars. The BMW films won several major awards and helped boost the carmaker's sales by 8 percent in 2003. Though the BMW films seemed to herald the arrival of a dynamic new outlet for marketers, the dot-com slump, together with the fact that a majority of Web surfers still did not have the high-speed Internet connections required to watch video footage efficiently, kept the category from becoming viable for most companies.

TARGET MARKET

Because it could air the "Amazon Theater" films in a prominent place on its own site, Amazon had a built-in audience that was available to few other Web advertisers. "Amazon enjoys real critical mass," Fallon's Rob Buchner told *Adweek*. "They are a network unto themselves." At the time of the campaign's launch, more than 30 million Americans were visiting Amazon.com each month, and the site had more than 44 million registered members. During the holiday season Amazon, like most retailers, saw its traffic spike significantly, so Fallon chose the 2004 holidays as the ideal time to undertake a branding effort.

The majority of Amazon's customers were affluent and college educated, and they generally felt comfortable with new technologies and media. They were accustomed to having their shopping experience include free entertainment and informational content, such as the previous holiday season's celebrity contributions, customer reviews of Amazon's products, and recommendations based on previous purchases.

The "Amazon Theater" films did not try to push products or the Amazon brand in a traditionally aggressive way; rather, they were intended to be a natural extension of the ongoing effort to improve the overall customer experience, which the company viewed as an important way of promoting loyalty. Though the films integrated products for sale on Amazon.com and offered links for purchasing those products in their credit sequences, there was no mention of or reference to Amazon at all. Amazon received no product-placement fees and did not make product names or logos easy to spot. Instead, the films were offered as a gift to customers. As founder and CEO Bezos said, "It's a great example of Amazon's relentless commitment to finding new and innovative ways to surprise and delight customers and deliver an unparalleled online experience."

COMPETITION

As an online book and music vendor, Amazon was far ahead of its competitors during this time. Its nearest bookselling competitor was barnesandnoble.com, the online complement to the category-leading bookstore Barnes and Noble. Like Barnes and Noble, barnesandnoble.com used features such as magazine subscriptions and author events to attract customers. Although Amazon

CHOOSE YOUR OWN ENDING

Although all of the "Amazon Theater" films had interactive credits, "Do Geese See God," directed by David Slade and starring Blair Underwood, took even further advantage of its medium of distribution by making the story itself interactive. The movie's title, a palindrome, mirrored the structure of the story, which circled back on itself endlessly unless viewers participated by choosing one of several alternate endings, thereby freeing Underwood's character from the story's otherwise infinite loop.

had a larger selection of book titles, barnesandnoble.com had a larger inventory on hand at any given time.

The online auction site eBay, with nearly 50 million visitors per month in the fall of 2004, generated more monthly traffic than any other Internet commerce site. Although its business model differed from Amazon's—it allowed individuals to buy and sell their own items and derived income from user fees and advertising—it rivaled Amazon as an online stop for purchasing almost anything at all. After a two-year advertising campaign that promoted its range of products and featured average people singing show tunes, eBay shifted to a "People Are Good" message in 2004. The campaign ran on TV, in magazines, and online, and, in conjunction with a newly established buyer-protection program, it endeavored to reassure consumers about the merits of doing business with strangers.

As a superstore Amazon fell far short, in sales, of the behemoth bricks-and-mortar retailer Wal-Mart, which was the world's largest company of its kind. With about 75 percent of its 5,700 stores located in the United States, Wal-Mart was, during this time, expanding its international presence while projecting sustained U.S. growth for the coming decade. Criticized for its employment practices and battling dozens of lawsuits, Wal-Mart undertook a national newspaper campaign to repair its image.

MARKETING STRATEGY

Although Bezos and Amazon wanted the emphasis to be on entertainment—the presiding idea being that the "Amazon Theater" films were meant as a gift to customers—Fallon was charged with the goal of making customers aware that the website was more than just a place to shop for books and CDs; it was a one-stop online destination for virtually any product imaginable. Fallon's creative team thus devised five film scripts loosely organized around the theme of karmic balance, each of which showcased a particular segment of products that consumers did not necessarily associate with Amazon. The agency hired the bicoastal production company RSA USA, run by Hollywood filmmaker brothers Ridley and Tony Scott, to collaborate on the project. RSA USA matched the five scripts with directors from its diverse roster, and actors Minnie Driver, Blair Underwood, Darryl Hannah, and Chris Noth were enlisted to star in the films. Each Tuesday for the five weeks between November 9 and December 7, 2004, a new film, ranging from 5 to 10 minutes, premiered on Amazon.com. The films, the budgets of which were estimated at roughly $500,000 apiece, were sponsored by JP Morgan Chase & Co. The Chase brand appeared throughout the "Amazon Theater" experience, and Chase's Amazon.com platinum Visa card was featured.

"Portrait," featuring Driver as an envious boss and focusing mainly on fashion products, told the story of an overweight female employee whose inner beauty was uncovered when a magical portraitist photographed her. "Agent Orange," directed by Tony Scott, also featured fashion products and was billed as a suspenseful, psychedelic love story in which strangers were brought together on a subway by a goldfish. "Do Geese See God," starring Underwood as a man caught in a futile race against time, highlighted home electronics, while "Tooth Fairy" integrated housewares and appliances into the story of a father (Noth) searching for a tooth hidden by his daughter. The "Amazon Theater" series concluded with "Careful What You Wish For," a tale of comeuppance featuring Hannah and a wide array of jewelry.

So that the product placement did not interfere with the stories, special care was taken to integrate the products seamlessly into each film. Instead of playing up the products' appearances in the narratives themselves, after the manner of traditional product-placement agreements, Fallon and Amazon listed products as though they were actors in the closing credits. The credits, moreover, were interactive. Viewers could click on an actor's or a director's name and go to an "artist boutique" offering gift and philanthropic recommendations and showcasing that artist's other movies, books, and CDs available for sale. Likewise, viewers of "Amazon Theater" films could click on any starring product in the credit roll and go to the appropriate Amazon page for purchasing it. After premiering on Amazon.com and running through the 2004 holiday season, the "Amazon Theater" films ran in theaters prior to featured movies.

OUTCOME

Adweek credited the campaign with offering "a glimpse at what the merger of the PC and the TV could mean: a shopping portal within programming," and *Advertising Age* placed the films at the top of their "10 Best Web Series or Films" list for 2004. But Bezos downplayed the potential of "Amazon Theater" to generate sales, maintaining that the films were meant primarily as entertainment and telling the *Wall Street Journal* that, if the films were advertising for Amazon, "they're the worst advertising in the world." Amazon was able, of course, to track traffic and purchasing activity related to "Amazon Theater," but the company was unwilling to release any numbers. Both Amazon and Fallon spokespersons claimed that the campaign was a success on all fronts, and Amazon indicated that it would continue looking for new ways to provide interactive entertainment and to incorporate short films on its website.

In March 2005 Amazon partnered with the Tribeca Film Festival and its sponsor, American Express, to announce the "Amazon Theater"/Tribeca Film Festival Short-Film Competition. Amazon invited filmmakers to submit short films of up to seven minutes, and Amazon customers could view them for free on Amazon.com and vote on their favorites. The five that received the most votes were screened at the Tribeca Film Festival, which ran from April 19 to May 1, 2005. The top-rated filmmaker, after another round of customer voting, was given a $50,000 grant for a future film in the form of a prepaid American Express card.

FURTHER READING

Arndorfer, James B., and T.L. Stanley. "Amazon Jumps on Internet-Film Trend." *Advertising Age,* September 6, 2004.

Champagne, Christine. "RSA Takes Short Route for Amazon." *Shoot,* November 19, 2004.

"Cinema Amazonia." *Creativity,* December 2004.

Cuneo, Alice Z. "EBay Effort Plays Up Public Honesty." *Advertising Age,* October 4, 2004.

Fritz, Ben. "Shorts Long on Innovation." *Variety,* November 28, 2004.

Graham, Jefferson. "At the (Amazon) Movies: E-Tailer Offers New Way to Sell." *USA Today,* November 9, 2004.

Nason, Pat. "Feature: Amazon.com Jump-Starts Short Films." *UPI,* November 24, 2004.

Parpis, Eleftheria. "American Theater." *Adweek,* November 29, 2004.

Reinan, John. "Fallon to Create Amazon Web Flicks." *Minneapolis Star Tribune,* November 20, 2004.

"Showtime at Amazon." *Newsweek,* November 29, 2004.

"10 Best Web Series or Films." *Advertising Age,* December 20, 2004.

Wingfield, Nick. "Amazon Lures Stars—Gratis—to Promote Holiday Gifts." *Wall Street Journal,* November 11, 2003.

———. "Amazon Offers Free Short Films in Holiday Push." *Wall Street Journal,* November 9, 2004.

Mark Lane

America Online, Inc.

22000 AOL Way
Dulles, Virginia 20166
USA
Telephone: (703) 265-1000
Fax: (703) 265-1101
Web site: www.corp.aol.com

AOL LATINO CAMPAIGN

OVERVIEW

America Online, Inc. (AOL) emerged in the 1990s as the largest Internet service provider (ISP) in the United States, a feat it accomplished in large measure through the mass distribution of start-up CD-ROMs and free trials. Many of its customers were families and people new to the Internet who were won over by AOL's claims that it was easy to use. By the early 2000s, however, AOL's strong growth came to an end, and it began to lose subscribers to cheaper dial-up ISPs as well more expensive but much faster broadband providers. On its rise to the top AOL had netted a great deal of Hispanic customers, and as a matter of course AOL became the leading portal for Hispanics. They were an alluring demographic—fast growing, family oriented, and cost conscious—making them an ideal source to replace the dial-up customers that AOL was losing at an alarming rate. To better attract and serve this market, AOL launched a Spanish-language portal called AOL Latino in September 2001. While AOL reached out to the Latino market with Spanish-language advertising, the commercials were merely translated versions of material developed for the general population. In 2003 AOL finally hired an Hispanic advertising agency, Casanova Pendrill Publicidad, Inc., and released an advertising campaign that was specifically developed for the Hispanic market.

The AOL Latino campaign, the budget of which was not made public, unfolded in waves and included television, radio, print, outdoor, and Internet elements. The early TV spots highlighted AOL features that were popular with Hispanics: music downloads, education support, and instant messaging. Later the campaign emphasized the theme of empowerment, stressing the idea that having the Internet in the home was important in the educational development of children.

AOL was pleased with the results of its Latino campaign. Although the company did not reveal subscriber gains, the campaign clearly solidified AOL Latino's position as the number one Spanish-language ISP. Furthermore, it helped mitigate AOL's continuing loss of general-population subscribers.

HISTORICAL CONTEXT

The precursor of AOL was Q-Link, an online service established in 1985 for owners of Commodore personal computers. The company that operated it, Quantum Computer Services, changed its name to America Online in 1991. With the advent of the World Wide Web in the 1990s, an increasing number of people bought personal computers to take advantage of the Internet. AOL vied with two other early online entrants, CompuServe and Prodigy, to become the market leader among Internet service providers (ISPs). AOL was relentless in its efforts to distribute start-up CD-ROMs and enticed new subscribers with free trials of its service. AOL was successful in selling itself to parents who wanted to maintain limits on content for their children; it also attracted customers who were simply new to the Internet and preferred more guidance than was available with other services. In 1997 AOL became America's largest online service, boasting 8 million subscribers, a number that would double just a year later.

During its rise to the top AOL attracted a large number of Hispanics. It was not until September 2001, however, that it launched AOL Latino to cater specifically to the Spanish-speaking market. In July 2002 the company established a U.S. Hispanic interactive-marketing unit. By this time AOL had merged with Time Warner, creating the largest media company in the world, and the online unit came under increasing pressure as the subscriber base, which had reached about 25 million in the United States, began to erode. AOL was losing out on one end to cheaper dial-up services and on the other end to providers of faster high-speed Internet connections. As a result it began to view the Hispanic market as an important source for replenishing its pool of customers. In January 2003 *Advertising Age* reported, "2.5 million Hispanic households [were] likely to go online for the first time in 2003, and ... those new to the Internet [were] increasingly Spanish-dominant." In January 2003 Casanova Pendrill Publicidad, an ad agency that was part of Interpublic Group and was based in Irvine, California, was awarded AOL's Hispanic advertising account. In May of that year AOL released its first-ever comprehensive campaign targeting Hispanics, both to reinforce its position as the top ISP for Spanish-speaking Americans and to attract new business. Prior efforts were simply Spanish-language versions of advertising created for mass audiences.

CORPORATE LOVE

America Online, introduced by Stephen M. Case in 1985 as a small dial-up Internet service called Q-Link, evolved into a media powerhouse 15 years later. In 1999 it acquired the companies Netscape Communications (known for its Web browser), MovieFone (a ticketing service), and two major Internet music providers: Spinner Networks and Nullsoft. A year later it added the mapping-services company MapQuest, and in 2001 it merged with Time Warner in a $183 billion deal that created the largest media company in the world. Case was named chairman of the new behemoth.

TARGET MARKET

In 2000 the Hispanic population in the United States numbered more than 40 million, or about 13 percent of the overall population. It not only was the largest minority group in the country but also was growing at a fast clip: about 5 percent each year, four times faster than the general public. Thus, according to the U.S. Census Bureau, by 2010 there were expected to be 50 million Hispanics in the United States, making them an increasingly inviting opportunity for marketers of all stripes. The AOL Latino campaign targeted bilingual and Spanish-dominant speakers who either planned to switch ISPs or intended to begin using an ISP in the next 6 to 12 months. Within that group AOL looked to appeal to families, as it did with the general population. Mary Ann Donaghy, AOL's executive director of marketing strategy and new-product development, explained to *Advertising Age,* "Hispanic Internet users tend to be younger than other users, are more likely to use instant messaging and to download music and videos, and spend more if they shop online, especially on music and DVDs." Therefore they were an ideal audience for AOL's product-enhancements pitch, which addressed these activities.

COMPETITION

In appealing to the Hispanic market AOL faced much of the same competition as it did with the general population, because many in the target demographic were bilingual and might easily choose an English-language Web interface over a Spanish-language one. Hispanics tended to be very price sensitive, so they generally opted for dial-up connections. Thus, AOL had to contend with cheaper dial-up ISPs, such as Earthlink, the NetZero and Juno brands of United Online, Yahoo!, lesser-known brands such as Copper and Toast.net, and local ISPs. In the broadband category AOL competed against telephone companies offering DSL service and cable TV operators offering cable-modem service, which was even faster than DSL. An increasing number of consumers opted for a high-speed connection, foregoing AOL's offer of premium content at an additional cost. AOL also had to contend with small Spanish-language ISPs—such as Pasito.com, which teamed up with the popular Hispanic portal Para—and a more formidable challenge from Microsoft's MSN, which in 2001 bought Yupi Internet, a Spanish-language Internet portal. Although it faced a lot of competition for the business of Hispanics, AOL was the unchallenged market leader.

MARKETING STRATEGY

The AOL Latino campaign, estimated to be budgeted at $10 million, broke in May 2003 and included television, radio, and print elements. The focus was on music downloads, education support, and instant messaging, features that Hispanic consumers used more than the general population. Writing for *Adweek Online,* Ann M. Mack reported that the two initial 30-second television spots played on "the themes of family, friends and education, and emphasize[d] AOL features that are appealing to Hispanics, such as entertainment and the ability to communicate with people domestically and abroad via the Web." The spots relied on the tagline "Get closer to your world"; one showed a boy clicking a mouse to explore a botanical garden online, and another showed a girl clicking on a link to listen to the words of Abraham Lincoln. The spots ran on the popular Spanish-language television channels Univision, Telefutura, and Galavision in several of the top-10 Spanish-speaking markets, including Chicago, Miami, New York, and Los Angeles. They were aired again in July 2003. A print component of the campaign also began in May, and radio spots were unveiled in July.

A second phase of the AOL Latino campaign began in November 2003 and included television, radio, print, and outdoor advertising. Three of the television spots featured AOL's Running Man icon. For example, the spot titled "School" depicted the character in a classroom. While writing in Spanish on a blackboard, a teacher heard a disruption and turned around to ask, "Who's passing notes?" ("Notes" in Spanish translated as "messages," thus drawing a connection to AOL's instant-messaging feature.) The children in the room then pointed to an unlikely student, the Running Man, AOL's icon for instant messaging, who looked away in an attempt to appear innocent. The spot closed with him dashing out as class was dismissed, with a voice-over commenting, "America Online learned Spanish... introducing the new AOL Latino." Writing for *Adweek,* Rebecca Flass explained, "In showing Running Man learning Spanish, AOL is hoping to convey that it now speaks the language of Latinos." The second Running Man spot, "Housekeeper," featured a mother apparently interviewing an unseen person as a housekeeper, asking how the person intended to protect the kids. The punch line of the spot was the revelation that the woman had been addressing the Running Man and talking about AOL and its parental-control features. The third spot, titled "Love," followed the same pattern, this time with a man in a cubicle talking to someone offscreen, presumably a lover. "Finally we understand each other," he said. "We're talking the same language." Once again the Running Man was revealed as the silent partner. The tagline for these spots was "Acércate a tu mundo" (Get closer to your world).

Other television spots in this phase of the campaign were 30-second vignettes that, according to company literature, were "meant to supply tips to users that address offerings like homework help, instant messaging, and parental controls." The campaign's radio spots, featured on the 66 stations of Univision Radio, focused on Hispanic families' affinity for Spanish even when communicating online. Billboard ads were placed in the top 10 Hispanic markets, print ads appeared in leading Spanish-language magazines, and Spanish advertising was run on websites. In addition, AOL began an aggressive distribution of CDs containing AOL Latino 9.0 Optimizado (the Spanish version of the new version of AOL, AOL 9.0 Optimized) through direct mail.

In June 2004 AOL began a final campaign phase that ran through the end of the year. The advertising shifted its focus to the theme of empowerment; this idea was based on market research showing that 70 percent of Hispanics believed that having an Internet connection in the home increased a child's performance in school, thus giving them a better chance to go to college and ultimately land a good job. The first television spot in this series, titled "The Talk," showed a young boy asking his parents why the family did not have Internet access at home. The spot then showcased AOL Latino's educational features, such as bilingual homework help. The father then brought home a computer with access to AOL Latino; the family began to experience the Internet, and the spot closed with the boy bringing home an excellent report card.

AOL also introduced a pair of supporting programs. One, the "Sign On a Friend" promotion, paid a $50 bounty to an existing member when he or she referred a friend to AOL Latino. The other was the introduction of the AOL Optimized PC, a personal computer priced at $299.99 with a one-year AOL membership commitment of $23.90 a month; it was available at Office Depot stores and other retailers. In addition to a computer and a printer, the system came bundled with a suite of software that included word-processing and spreadsheet applications. Although the PCs were made available to all consumers, they were especially suited to cost-conscious Hispanic families and could be purchased preloaded with AOL Latino service. Moreover, the PCs could easily switch from Spanish to English to accommodate bilingual consumers and families with members who preferred one language over the other.

OUTCOME

AOL continued to experience serious erosion in its overall number of U.S. subscribers and subscriber revenues, losing out to high-speed providers as well as less-expensive dial-up ISPs, but AOL Latino was able to make gains with the Hispanic population to offset losses in the general public. The campaign succeeded in doubling normal call volume to AOL member-services centers, as the target audience embraced the opportunity to receive more information about a free trial. The company did not reveal the exact number of Hispanics it added to its customer base other than to say that AOL Latino "significantly increased memberships." Focus groups and other research, according to the company, also showed that the campaign was well received by the target audience.

FURTHER READING

"America Online Launches $10 Million Advertising Campaign Directed at U.S. Hispanics." *Technology Advertising & Branding Report,* May 19, 2003.

"AOL Targeting Hispanic Population." *Communications Today,* May 13, 2003.

Flass, Rebecca. "AOL Begins Hispanic Push in Major Cities." *Adweek* (southeast ed.), November 10, 2003.

Mack, Ann M. "AOL Debuts Spanish-Language Effort." *Adweek Online,* May 13, 2003.

———. "AOL Introduces Hispanic Service." *Adweek Online,* October 1, 2003.

———. "AOL Promotes Its New Optimized PC." *Adweek,* August 23, 2004, p10.

Wasserman, Todd. "AOL Running Man Has Message for Hispanics." *Brandweek,* November 10, 2003, p. 6.

———. "AOL Says Hola." *Brandweek,* April 7, 2003, p. 3.

Wentz, Laurel. "Hispanics' Web World Widens." *Advertising Age,* January 26, 2004, p. 27.

———. "Online Marketing: Niche Within a Niche." *Advertising Age,* August 5, 2002, p. 33.

Ed Dinger

WELCOME TO THE WORLD WIDE WOW CAMPAIGN

OVERVIEW

America Online, Inc. (AOL) used a strategy of mass distribution of start-up CD-ROMs and free trials along with unsophisticated late-night television spots to become the largest Internet service provider (ISP) by 1997. Because it relied on dial-up service, AOL faced a major challenge with the advent of broadband (high-speed) Internet access provided by telephone and cable TV companies. Moreover, AOL joined forces with Time Warner in a celebrated 2001 merger, creating a media giant. Expectations for performance were heightened, but AOL found the business landscape shifting and began to lose subscribers, both to cheaper dial-up ISPs and faster broadband service providers. AOL, pigeonholed as a dial-up ISP in the minds of consumers, attempted to become a broadband provider but soon abandoned that strategy. Instead it decided to reposition itself as a premium-content provider—an add-on service for people acquiring broadband connections from other sources. In an effort to rebrand itself and pitch the broadband package, in January 2003 AOL hired Len Short, formerly of Charles Schwab & Co., to serve as chief of brand marketing. Short recruited a new ad agency, BBDO New York, to develop a campaign to sell AOL Broadband.

In March 2003 AOL unveiled a $35 million, two-month campaign with a new tagline, "Welcome to the World Wide Wow." Unlike previous efforts, the new AOL television spots possessed all the glitz expected from a Madison Avenue advertising agency. They aired during prime time rather than being relegated to cheap late-night slots. The campaign also included an online blitz that saturated the Web with ads touting AOL Broadband. The television spot that received the most attention featured movie star Sharon Stone in a nightgown in bed, a life-size version of the AOL running-man icon, and a bit of double entendre.

The campaign's "World Wide Wow" tagline was questioned by critics, and the Sharon Stone spot was singled out for vituperation. While Short maintained that he was pleased with the campaign and insisted that it had met its intended goals, his words were belied by his actions. He asked for new ideas from ad agencies, and a few months later AOL trotted out a new approach and a fresh tagline. Despite the changes, AOL continued to lose subscribers and failed to win many converts to its broadband service. By February 2004 Short had left the company, and AOL reverted to its previous marketing strategy.

HISTORICAL CONTEXT

America Online, an early participant in the Internet revolution, had by 1997 emerged as the leading Internet service provider (ISP), relying mostly on the mass mailing and distribution of program CD-ROMs and free trials. Beyond that, the company's marketing was a ragtag affair that included buying television time on the cheap and airing crude spots late at night; it possessed no coordination and achieved little impact. *Adweek* critic Barbara Lippert described AOL commercials as "cheap-looking, numbed-out affairs featuring an array of smiley, zomboid converts at their keyboards, spouting lines stiffer than the ubiquitous sign-up discs." The tagline was "So easy to use, no wonder it's No. 1!" Nevertheless, AOL thrived because of it ease of use and low price, both of which appealed to the millions of

Through free trials and mass distribution of CDs, America Online became the largest Internet Service Provider. © RUARIDH STEWART/ZUMA/CORBIS.

consumers who began to buy their first computers and were unsure about how to navigate the new world of the Internet.

The scattershot approach worked until the 2000s. After it merged with Time Warner in 2001, creating the largest media company in the world, AOL began to see subscriber growth slow down. The market was becoming more sophisticated about computers and the Internet, as many people opted not to pay for AOL's proprietary content and to simply subscribe to a less expensive, bare-bones Internet connection. Moreover, as a dial-up service AOL was beginning to feel pressure from broadband service providers, such as telephone companies offering DSL service and cable television companies offering even faster cable-modem service. AOL launched its own broadband service, offering a connection and AOL content while touting speed and ease of use. Given that all broadband products presented the same advantages, however, AOL struggled to differentiate itself from the competition. The company then changed course, electing instead to bundle its content with broadband carriers at an extra charge to consumers. The add-on service included more video clips, better parental controls to keep children within the confines of the AOL site, virus protection, and a block on pop-up advertising.

To support the broadband service and meet challenges in the marketplace, AOL hired a new brand marketing head, Len Short, formerly with Charles Schwab & Co. In early 2003, after just one week on the job, he fired the company's advertising agency, Gotham, which had held the account since 1997 and had not impressed Short with its approach to selling AOL Broadband. He then asked other agencies to pitch ideas for a broad $150 million campaign to rebrand AOL, but it quickly became apparent that the crux of the rebranding effort would be promoting the broadband service, and that $35 million job was given to BBDO New York. According to Julia Angwin, writing for the *Wall Street Journal* in March 2003, "The stakes are high. The AOL Time Warner unit is under fierce pressure to show results by the end of this year, or face the possibility of being spun off or sold."

TARGET MARKET

In general AOL appealed to the family market. The service was not only easy to use for all age levels but also provided parents with a measure of control, preventing children—especially AOL's large base of teenage customers—from being inadvertently exposed to the seamier side of the Internet. The company also touted the service's ease of use for people new to home computing and first-time users of the Internet, those in need of "training wheels."

The broadband campaign targeted a narrower subset of the family market: people with enough disposable income to upgrade from dial-up Internet service to a high-speed connection, costing $40 to $50 per month, and who were also willing to pay an additional premium,

COMMODORE ONLINE

America Online was launched in 1985 as Q-Link, an exclusive online service for owners of Commodore personal computers that was introduced by Quantum Computer Services, Inc. Tandy computer owners were added in 1987 and IBM-compatible computers a year later. A Macintosh version of Q-Link was introduced in 1989, the same year that Quantum Computer Services unveiled a nationwide network for personal computer owners called America Online. In 1991 Quantum assumed the America Online name.

$14.95 ($9.95 for AOL subscribers), to receive the AOL interface and content. A major part of the campaign involved Internet marketing, which would inundate the Web with advertising urging current broadband users to subscribe to AOL's content. But the campaign's top priority, according to the *Wall Street Journal* 's Angwin, was "to convince its 35 million subscribers to keep their America Online service when they upgraded to a high-speed Internet connection."

COMPETITION

Although AOL viewed itself as a step up from Internet service providers (ISPs), which merely offered a connection, it still faced stiff competition from dial-up ISPs such as Earthlink and United Online (created by the 2001 merger of ISPs NetZero and Juno). These providers offered accelerators to boost dial-up Internet speeds. To compete on this end of the market, AOL added its own speed-enhancing upgrades. The company also received competition from telephone companies offering DSL service and from cable TV operators with their cable modems. By no longer offering broadband connections and repositioning itself as an add-on service, AOL skirted direct competition and formed partnerships with many of these broadband providers, making AOL available to their customers at an extra charge.

Nevertheless, many of these broadband customers would be content with a bare high-speed connection and would therefore forego AOL's exclusive content and added features. Moreover, customers could increasingly turn to other sources for the types of services that AOL offered; as Angwin reported in the *Wall Street Journal,* "cable and phone companies . . . are adding snazzier features to their broadband services." To make the landscape even more competitive, Internet portals such as Yahoo and Microsoft's MSN also added virus protection and pop-up blockers and teamed up with telephone companies to offer high-speed Internet connections at a lower price than broadband plus AOL. In an interview with Catharine P. Taylor of *Adweek,* Short said that AOL Broadband's competition was essentially "everybody," adding, "But in some ways, we don't have competition, because our product is fundamentally compatible with all the connection providers, and we have proprietary content. However, at this early stage of broadband, some people are making a decision between us and another broadband provider, because they see us a dial-up connection. That's going to get eliminated as we go forward."

MARKETING STRATEGY

To promote AOL Broadband, in March 2003 AOL released a $35 million, two-month advertising campaign developed by ad agency BBDO. The first two commercials, using the tagline "Welcome to the World Wide Wow," were unveiled on the Academy Awards telecast. One of the spots, "Six Million Dollar Man," was a parody of the opening of the old television show about a man with artificial parts that gave him superhuman powers. Instead of actor Lee Majors the spot featured AOL's familiar Running Man icon being rebuilt "better than before," making the case that AOL Broadband was a quantum leap above the old dial-up version of the service. The second spot featured actress Sharon Stone rolling around in bed, apparently after making love, telling someone off-camera, "that was the most amazing experience I ever had. So, can you stay? Or do you have to run?" A life-size version of the Running Man was then revealed. As he rushed offscreen, an announcer said, "The new AOL for Broadband is just a little sexier than you might have imagined." Left alone, Stone muttered in disgust, "icons," as if saying, "men!" Subsequent spots in this initial phase of the campaign showed a model whose body was covered with pop-up ads that were removed by AOL's new blocking software, and monks, who had taken a vow of silence, communicating to one another through AOL's instant messaging feature.

In addition to the television spots, the campaign included a large Internet component. Some of the animated Internet ads were designed for specific types of content. On the Weather Channel's website, for example, clouds forming the Running Man floated across the home page, then the clouds dissolved into an ad with the headline "Life needs a better outlook." The goal was to reach more than 80 percent of the online population within two days.

OUTCOME

The broadband campaign met with quick criticism. The "Welcome to the World Wide Wow" tag was widely ridiculed. In a review for *Adweek,* Barbara Lippert asked, "Has anyone actually uttered the words World, Wide and Web together since, like, 1999?" Simon Dumenco wrote in *New York* magazine, "The only wow factor is roughly along the lines of, 'Wow, does Sharon Stone need money that badly?'" As much as the tagline was criticized, the Sharon Stone spot was eviscerated. Lippert wondered, "And what is the take-away here? That if you sign up for AOL Broadband, like Sharon, you'll get screwed? And unlike what you see from an ISP, why would you want a lover who is superfast?" Dumenco further commented, "The irony is that in aligning itself with a silver-screen temptress whose moment has come and gone, AOL has only reminded us all how precipitously it, too, has faded."

After two months AOL once again put up its advertising account for review in what was called a "repitch." Catharine P. Taylor, writing for *Adweek,* cited sources who said that AOL was dissatisfied with BBDO's broadband campaign. Short disputed this contention, maintaining that the campaign had met all of its objectives. "This is a two-stage game," he said. "And I'm dead serious about stage one and I'm dead serious about stage two."

Stage two was the release of AOL 9.0 Optimized, a new version of the AOL software that included a fuller package of the company's broadband capabilities as well as enhanced features for dial-up users. Despite a new series of television spots, a new tagline ("Life needs . . ."), another online advertising blitz, and partnership deals to add popular content such as professional-sports video highlights, AOL continued to lose subscribers to faster or cheaper competitors. Very few of its dial-up customers making the switch to broadband elected to pay extra for AOL's premium-content package. Media analyst Tom Wolzien explained to Ann M. Mack of *Adweek,* "You can have the greatest advertising in the world, but if the value proposition isn't appropriate to your consumers, nothing's going to work." After little more than a year on the job, Short's tenure with AOL came to an end in February 2004. The advertising budget was also slashed by about a third, and the company reverted to a more conservative marketing approach.

FURTHER READING

Angwin, Julia. "America Online Sets Revival Effort." *Wall Street Journal,* March 24, 2003, p. B6.

Consoli, John. "Leaning More on TV: AOL Inks Big Super Bowl Deal." *Adweek,* September 22, 2003, p. 7.

Dumenco, Simon. "Base Instincts." *New York,* April 7, 2003.

Lippert, Barbara. "AOL: Anti-Climactic: Better than It Was Before, but New Effort Lacks 'Wow.'" *Adweek,* March 31, 2003, p. 28.

———. "AOL's Upgrade." *Adweek,* October 13, 2003, p. 30.

Mack, Ann M. "In the End, Short's Style Fails to Connect at AOL." *Adweek,* February 23, 2004, p. 9.

McMains, Andrew, and Catharine P. Taylor. "AOL Cuts 'Short' Its Relationship with Gotham." *Adweek* (western ed.), January 13, 2003, p. 3.

Sampey, Kathleen, and David Gianatasio. "America Online Seeks Star Treatment." *Adweek,* March 10, 2003, p. 8.

Taylor, Catharine P. "A Conversation with Len Short." *Adweek,* March 3, 2003, p. S8.

———. "AOL Calls 'Repitch' for Creative." *Adweek Online,* May 22, 2003.

Ed Dinger

American Apparel Inc.

747 Warehouse Street
Los Angeles, California 90021
USA
Telephone: (213) 488-0226
Fax: (213) 488-0334
Web site: www.americanapparel.net

AMERICAN APPAREL CAMPAIGN

OVERVIEW

American Apparel Inc., founded by Dov Charney in 1997, rose to profitability as a T-shirt maker with an unconventional business model. Countering the almost universal garment-industry practice of outsourcing labor to other countries, Charney located his company headquarters and manufacturing facility in the same building in downtown Los Angeles, paying his factory workers high wages and providing comprehensive benefits. Despite the higher costs of its manufacturing process, the company was able to grow by using a "vertically integrated" structure in which all facets of business were intermingled for maximum efficiency and speed of production. After seeing sales double each year after 2000, American Apparel expanded into retail, with a widened offering of basic knitwear, in 2003. Charney himself devised the accompanying print ad campaign.

The American Apparel ads premiered in concert with the retail-store openings in 2003 and expanded geographically as more stores opened, running in lifestyle publications and alternative newsweeklies in relevant urban markets. Charney himself sometimes took the photographs for the ads, which featured sexually provocative images of company employees as well as men and women whom Charney had sought out on the street and elsewhere. The campaign openly courted comparisons with soft-core pornography while at the same time publicizing American Apparel's commitment to social justice, a combination intended to appeal to the progressive values of young, hip urbanites.

While the campaign ran, American Apparel sustained its rapid growth. Sales continued to double each year, and the number of retail stores grew from 2 in 2003 to more than 50 in 2005. The ads generated considerable controversy and resulted in public scrutiny of Charney's overlapping personal and business lives, but his marketing savvy, as demonstrated by the print campaign and the company's distinct brand image, went virtually uncontested.

HISTORICAL CONTEXT

Dov Charney started selling T-shirts on the streets of his native Montreal during high school, and he dropped out of Tufts University to start the first incarnation of his T-shirt manufacturing business, American Apparel, in South Carolina. When this effort failed, Charney moved to Los Angeles, where he relaunched American Apparel in 1997.

Despite the prevailing conventional wisdom decreeing that profitability in the garment trade required the use of cheap foreign labor in the manufacturing process, American Apparel's business headquarters and factory operations were located in a single building in downtown

Los Angeles. From the start American Apparel paid well over the minimum wage and offered comprehensive benefits and perks to its factory workers, while also making significant improvements in fabric quality and fit relative to other major American T-shirt brands. These two brand attributes—a politically attractive sweatshop-free business model and a superior product that was competitively priced—helped Charney carve out an ever-growing niche among T-shirt wholesalers. The company found particular success as a supplier of T-shirts to rock bands, who screen-printed their logos onto the shirts and sold them at concerts and online. American Apparel first became profitable in 2000, and the company nearly doubled its sales growth and employee force each year thereafter, eventually adding new products, such as tank tops and women's underwear. In explaining American Apparel's success, Charney pointed to his antiestablishment business model, arguing that it simply made more sense for his company to locate its factory operations in the United States. American Apparel's "vertically integrated" structure, the concentration and strategic intermingling of all company departments under one roof—Charney, for instance, served as head fashion designer and marketer as well as CEO—was a cost-saving, efficiency-enhancing way of doing business that allowed the company to accommodate higher manufacturing costs.

While continuing to focus on basic casual knitwear, American Apparel further enlarged its range of products and styles, and in November 2003 it began opening retail stores with an art-gallery look in fashionable urban neighborhoods. The products sold in the stores had no logos, and the company positioned itself as an alternative to the vigorously branded garments found in most other retail outlets. The American Apparel stores' selection of wall-mounted photographs (including the work of prominent photographers, Charney's own photographs, and images from 1970s and '80s pornographic magazines) and the hiring of retail employees were undertaken with an eye toward maximizing a brand image that was uniquely urban and gritty as well as overtly sexual. This image was intended to work with the company's socially conscious reputation to appeal to youthful urbanites, and the accompanying advertising campaign, chiefly developed by Charney himself, shared this mandate.

TARGET MARKET

American Apparel targeted 20-something urban hipsters with a combination of social consciousness, a lack of visible branding, quality products, and reasonable pricing—but primarily with sexual images. Charney downplayed media attempts to cast him as a do-gooder, maintaining that an appeal to the conscience alone would never result in profitability. He openly acknowledged that the American Apparel image was rooted in hedonism more than social justice but asserted that both were organic parts of youth culture. "This is a new generation of young adults," he told the *New York Times.* "They want what their parents wanted at that age, what kids always want: to have a beer, to smoke a joint, to go to a good movie, to party . . . At the same time it doesn't feel good when their happiness is based on exploitation." In his company's print ads, therefore, Charney showcased provocative images of scantily clad women (and occasionally, men) that clearly verged on pornography. Meanwhile, American Apparel's socially conscious agenda was mentioned in accompanying small print. Charney contended that an appreciation for pornography did not conflict with a social consciousness and that those who thought otherwise were out of step with the rising generation that he was targeting.

COMPETITION

Several other clothing and footwear makers were at this time pitting themselves against supposedly exploitative megacorporations. Part of Charney's inspiration for the American Apparel business model and image was the anticonsumerist magazine *Adbusters,* which sought to change the power structure and exploitative norms of twenty-first-century life. In 2004 *Adbusters* unveiled its Blackspot shoes, an "anti-brand" that was intended as part of a campaign to "unswoosh" Nike (a reference to Nike's logo, the swoosh) and "give birth to a new kind of cool in the sneaker industry," according to a Blackspot mission statement. Purchasers of Blackspots automatically became voting members of the Blackspot Anticorporation, a status that allowed them to weigh in on new designs and uses for the profits generated by sales of the sneakers. Blackspots had, logically, a black spot instead of a logo, but some critics pointed out that the black spot itself functioned as a logo.

TeamX, a company located in the same downtown Los Angeles neighborhood as American Apparel's headquarters, launched a sweatshop-free clothing brand called SweatX in 2002. Funded by an investment from a hedge fund endowed by Ben & Jerry's Ice Cream cofounder Ben Cohen, TeamX employed only union workers and paid them at least $10 an hour. The company never became profitable, however, and it folded in 2004.

Waltham, Massachusetts–based No Sweat also sold sweatshop-free, union-made garments and shoes. Unlike American Apparel, No Sweat claimed that its social-justice mission was central to its existence, rather than a mere selling point. "We're creating an opportunity for progressive customers to participate in an experiment," the company's founder and CEO, Adam Neiman, told the *Boston Phoenix.* "Call it entrepreneurial

HARASSMENT?

American Apparel founder and CEO Dov Charney was widely known for his libertarian attitudes toward sex. Not only were these attitudes embodied in the company's advertising, which he largely crafted, but Charney also publicly defended his right to have consensual relations with his employees and was said to foster an overtly sexual work environment. These personal attributes proved troublesome, as many industry observers had predicted they would, in May 2005, when three female former employees filed suit against Charney, claiming sexual harassment. Among the offensive actions the women cited were Charney's frequent off-color comments, his suggestive actions and gifts, and his policy of hiring women (sometimes strangers on the street) based on physical appearance. Charney dismissed the complaints and maintained that he had never pressured anyone into a sexual relationship. He told *BusinessWeek,* "I should tone down? So I don't get in trouble? It's fascism. You're asking me to succumb to tyranny." *BusinessWeek* interviewed seven former American Apparel workers, however, who were not involved in the controversy but claimed that they had found the sexual environment of American Apparel offensive. One said, "It was a company built on lechery." Another said, "I thought it was a male contemporary perspective on feminism, but it turns out to be just a gimmick." A third former employee stated that she intentionally stayed away from the retail store where she was employed when Charney was in town. "It's not one person," she said, "he's aiming for all women."

activism—[an experiment] to see whether a niche market can be used to reform the larger industry." American Apparel's Charney scoffed at his competitor's sincerity: "No Sweat—boring! That guy from Massachusetts—c'mon, dude, how many panties has he sold?" Charney, whose workers were not unionized (to the dismay of many union activists), also questioned the righteousness of No Sweat's commitment to hiring only unionized workers. Regarding the unionized Indonesian workers who made No Sweat sneakers, Charney told the *Phoenix,* "[Neiman] says they're making more than the minimum wage in that country. But it's like 70 cents an hour; that's not sweatshop-free to me."

American Apparel's long-term goals included challenging the likes of clothing giants the Gap and Old Navy, but American Apparel's sales, though growing rapidly (from roughly $20 million in 2001 to a projected $250 million in 2005), were still only a fraction of those larger competitors, both of which were owned by Gap Inc., whose 3,000-plus stores generated more than $16 billion in 2004. American Apparel's explosive growth during the early 2000s did recall, however, the Gap's rapid expansion in the late 1970s.

MARKETING STRATEGY

The American Apparel ads ran in alternative urban weeklies, including New York's *Village Voice* and *L.A. Weekly,* as well as in lifestyle magazines such as *Vice* and *Beautiful/Decay.* The campaign began with the opening of the first retail locations in New York and Los Angeles, and it was expanded into new markets as more stores were opened.

What distinguished American Apparel's sexuality-based approach from those of other risqué marketers, such as Victoria's Secret and Abercrombie & Fitch, was the nature of the photographs and models in its advertising. Many of the photographs were taken by Charney himself, and the subjects that were shown wearing American Apparel clothes were not professional models. Charney recruited his models personally on urban streets, at trade shows, and in his stores, among other places. Many models either became American Apparel employees after their photo shoots or were already American Apparel employees before being chosen to appear in the company's advertising. The resulting ads showcased a range of female beauty and body types and were not doctored to eliminate imperfections. The images therefore had the appearance of intimate casual snapshots or art photographs, and they were meant to look more genuine than sexual images found in conventional advertising, which, in the opinion of many consumers, presented destructively unreal images of beauty.

The early American Apparel ads established the prototype that would remain in place, with variations, throughout the campaign's run. In an ad publicizing the first American Apparel store in Los Angeles, for instance, a young woman in a bra was shown from the waist up, looking casually away from the camera. Accompanying copy read, "Come see what we're doing at our new Community Store and Gallery." The store's address appeared below, as did—in smaller print at the bottom of the page—an explanation of American Apparel's identity and commitment to social justice. Other ads showcased underwear by using cropped, close-up images of the garments on models. Some of the ads included narrative copy providing details about the model pictured, as in the following example: "Mananita Lira (aka Spring) was born in La Paz, Mexico. When she was 12 years old she and her family moved to the United States. 'My sisters and I bought some sunglasses and new clothes and tried to pass ourselves off as American girls at the Mexican/American border.' Thirteen years later Spring, age 25, is involved as a retail strategist at American Apparel."

The ads became more sexually explicit in 2004 and 2005, and many made reference to the porn aesthetic governing the campaign. Charney himself posed for an ad in which he was photographed from behind wearing an American Apparel T-shirt and no pants. Another ad showed a young man in underwear with copy reading, "Meet Glen. He's a 25-year-old New Jersey native living in New York. Glen's a bright guy and works as a tutor, but he has shown off some other features in Sweetaction Magazine, a porn mag created by ladies for ladies. Who better to test out the new Men's Brief, coming soon to our stores." One ad depicted "Melissa," the winner of "an unofficial wet T-shirt contest held at the American Apparel apartment in Montreal," and another showed a company employee, Kelley, reenacting "her favorite poses from vintage porn mags." In 2005 an actual pornographic-movie star, Lauren Phoenix, was featured in an ad wearing only American Apparel tube socks; accompanying copy instructed consumers to "look her up on Google."

OUTCOME

As the campaign ran, American Apparel's explosive growth continued. After opening its two initial retail locations in 2003, by the end of 2005 the company had 29 U.S. stores and 28 international stores, with 35 more stores slated to open. The American Apparel factory in Los Angeles became the country's largest garment-manufacturing facility, with a workforce of more than 3,000 and the capacity to produce one million T-shirts per week. Continued exponential growth was predicted.

The sexual emphasis of the American Apparel ads incited substantial negative media attention, especially as it became known that the ads' imagery was in keeping with the work environment Charney fostered at his company: he unapologetically revealed in multiple sources that he regularly engaged in sexual relations with his employees, including some of the ad models. Though many observers questioned Charney's judgment on such matters, few disputed the marketing instincts behind the print campaign and the American Apparel brand image. *Advertising Age*'s Simon Dumenco said, "[Charney's] ads are not only hot (they show his sexy employees modeling the merch) and briskly reinforce the brand message (which is all about well-constructed, no-frills, eminently wearable, sweatshop-free clothing), but are refreshingly not celebrity-obsessed." Dumenco further compared the trendsetting power of American Apparel's ads to that of what was perhaps the most lauded print campaign in history, "Absolut Vodka," and praised the innovative attention to the personal stories of the models pictured.

FURTHER READING

Baker, Linda. "The Goal: 'Sweatshop Free.' The Problem: Defining It." *New York Times,* December 14, 2003.

Dodero, Camille. "Trying Ethics On for Size: Worker-Friendly Clothing Companies Look to Break the Sweatshop Mold." *Boston Phoenix,* March 4–10, 2005.

Dumenco, Simon. "Media Guy Slips into Coma; Are Print Ads to Blame?" *Advertising Age,* August 29, 2005.

Gladwell, Malcolm. "The Young Garmentos." *New Yorker,* April 24, 2000.

La Ferla, Ruth. "Building a Brand by Not Being a Brand." *New York Times,* November 23, 2004.

Navarro, Mireya. "His Way Meets a Highway Called Court." *New York Times,* July 10, 2005.

Macklem, Katherine. "Doing the Rag Trade Right." *Maclean's,* April 14, 2003.

Palmeri, Christopher. "Living on the Edge at American Apparel." *BusinessWeek,* June 27, 2005.

Strasburg, Jenny. "Made in the U.S.A." *San Francisco Chronicle,* July 4, 2004.

Walker, Rob. "Conscience Undercover." *New York Times Magazine,* August 1, 2004.

Wright, Christian. "Mister T." *New York,* August 23, 2004.

Mark Lane

American Civil Liberties Union

125 Broad St., 18th Fl.
New York, New York 10004-2400
USA
Telephone: (212) 549-2500
Fax: (212) 549-2646
Web site: www.aclu.org

RACIAL PROFILING CAMPAIGN

OVERVIEW

In 1999 the American Civil Liberties Union (ACLU), a nonprofit corporation dedicated to the preservation and extension of constitutional liberties, hired its first advertising agency, New York City–based DeVito/Verdi. The ACLU hoped to use consumer-advertising techniques to improve the image of the organization, which in recent decades had become vilified by conservatives in the United States. In addition, the advertising was to be used to call attention to particular causes backed by the ACLU. One issue that received its own campaign within the framework of the greater effort was the racial profiling of motorists stopped by the police.

The ACLU began its racial-profiling campaign in June 1999 by releasing a report on the issue and filing a lawsuit involving one of the cases it documented. In this way the organization was able to generate a great deal of publicity, which was important given the campaign's mere $1 million budget. In late 1999 the first print ads appeared in newspapers. More advertising followed in 2000, including the ACLU's first-ever television spots, which were run in Utah to put pressure on one of the state's senators, Orrin Hatch, chairman of the Senate Judiciary Committee. The print ads succeeded in attracting attention by being provocative. One showed pictures of Martin Luther King, Jr., and Charles Manson with a headline that read: "The man on the left is 75 times more likely to be stopped by the police while driving than the man on the right."

The ACLU's racial-profiling campaign, which ran until the end of 2000, achieved its main goals. It brought a great deal of attention to the practice of racial profiling, forcing police departments to become more cautious about the way they approached traffic stops; also, many state legislatures introduced legislation to curb racial profiling. In addition, the campaign was recognized by the advertising industry, with *Advertising Age* naming it a Best of Show in its annual awards in 2001.

HISTORICAL CONTEXT

From its inception in 1920, when it supported the rights of conscientious objectors and opponents of America's entry into World War I, the ACLU never shied away from controversy. Over the decades it made news through its participation in the well-known Scopes Trial that engendered a debate about evolution (1925); fought the U.S. Customs Service ban on the sale of James Joyce's novel *Ulysses* in 1933; opposed the internment of more than 100,000 Japanese-Americans during World War II; supported school desegregation in the 1950s and the civil rights movement of the 1960s; opposed the war on drugs starting in the 1960s; supported reproduction rights in the 1970s while also defending the right of a neo-Nazi group to march through the streets of Skokie, Illinois, in 1978. While the latter issue cost the ACLU support from the left wing of the political spectrum, resulting in a dip in membership, in general the ACLU irritated conservatives. In the 1988 presidential campaign, Republican George H. Bush made Democrat Michael Dukakis's ACLU membership an issue, attempting to disparage him by calling him a "card-carrying member of the ACLU." The hatred of the ACLU among conservatives was further hardened in 1989, when the group convinced the U.S. Supreme Court to invalidate a Texas law that made flag desecration a punishable offense; likewise, it was later successful with the court when it recognized the civil rights of gays and lesbians in the 1996 case *Romer v. Evans.*

In early 1999 the ACLU began a general campaign that used the tagline "Support the ACLU." The main issue pursued within it was the practice of police employing racial profiling in stopping motorists, a problem bitterly dubbed "DWB" (driving while black), a play on the term for a real crime, DWI (driving while intoxicated). The ACLU decided to hire an ad agency to develop consumer-style advertising. In doing so, its goals were to counteract the nefarious image that conservatives had created about the organization, to present its core values to the public, and to deal with specific issues.

Four agencies vied for the account, which was awarded in June 1999 to DeVito/Verdi, a firm that was not unfamiliar with controversy. Two years earlier it had run afoul of New York City Mayor Rudolph Giuliani with a bus ad for *New York* magazine that used the tagline "Probably the only good thing in New York Rudy hasn't taken credit for." After the mayor had the ads removed, the New York chapter of the ACLU helped the magazine successfully argue to an appeals court that, in running the ad, the magazine was within its First Amendment rights. Upon winning the ACLU account, DeVito/Verdi president Ellis Verdi told the press, "We know from personal experience how effective they can be, and we look forward to communicating that message to the public."

The ACLU had never had difficulty generating publicity, but hiring a Madison Avenue ad agency represented a significant shift. "The organization has advertised in the past," wrote Patricia Winters Lauro in the *New York Times,* in 2000, "but its approach has either been event-driven—the mass arrests of antiwar protesters—or, in recent years, all-text ads about issues that ran on op-ed pages in newspapers."

DAFFY START

DeVito/Verdi, the advertising agency that produced the ACLU's provocative print ads about racial profiling, was not new to controversy. Shortly after opening shop in 1991, it created an ad for a discount clothier called Daffy's that showed a picture of a straitjacket accompanied by a headline that read: "If you're paying over $100 for a dress shirt, may we suggest a jacket to go with it?" The ad was a hit with consumers and the advertising industry, but because a mental-health advocacy group took exception to the use of a straitjacket in the ad, it led to picketing at an advertising awards show.

TARGET MARKET

In press comments issued after the hiring of DeVito/Verdi, ACLU executive director Ira Glasser said, "We want to target opinion leaders." In addition, he noted, "we also want to reach out to a broader audience: those members of the public we call 'persuadables,' that is, people who are highly likely to share the ACLU's core values even if they don't agree with everything we do." Those "persuadables" were not likely to be found among conservatives and those leaning to the political right in America. Rather, the ACLU was hoping to spur into action an audience that was "liberal, progressive, and somewhat shrinking," as described to Lauro by Victor Kamber, head of the Kamber Group, which produced advocacy advertising for such groups as labor unions.

Regarding the racial-profiling component of the general campaign, the advertising tried to influence police departments to change the way the way they stopped motorists based on race. It also reached out to state legislators, whom the ACLU hoped to pressure into passing laws to curtail the practice. The campaign was also directed at victims of racial profiling, urging them to share their stories with the ACLU and to lodge complaints. The more examples of racing profiling the ACLU could gather, the better the case that could be made that the problem was pervasive and required action.

COMPETITION

Although the ACLU prided itself on being nonpartisan—willing to take on cases regardless of political party affiliation or ideology—the organization found vigorous opposition from Republicans and conservatives, who were not reluctant to characterize the ACLU as the epitome of evil. Right-wing media pundits were especially vituperative in their denunciation of the ACLU and the causes it championed. An example of this criticism came from commentator David Horowitz, who took specific exception to an ACLU print ad concerning the subject of racial profiling. Horowitz espoused the belief that racial profiling was, in fact, good police work that targeted the types of people most likely to commit crimes. After challenging the statistics in the ad as well as asking how many of the questionable traffic stops were conducted by Hispanic or black officers, Horowitz commented, "When facts like these make no difference, it is a sure sign that we are in the presence of an ideological force, disconnected from reality." Horowitz was not alone in opposing the ACLU and in claiming that examples of abuse of police power were simply blown out of proportion by the ACLU and other forces of political correctness.

MARKETING STRATEGY

To build its campaign to combat racial profiling, the ACLU conducted extensive research to determine the depth of the problem and to create documentation. It drew upon government reports, case studies from two dozen states, traffic-stop statistics obtained from ACLU lawsuits, and news stories. A report on the phenomenon of DWB was written, concluding that it was a nationwide problem. The report was released and disseminated shortly after the ACLU undertook a high-profile lawsuit in Oklahoma involving an egregious example of DWB, in which a decorated Army sergeant and his 12-year-old son were held in a grueling two-and-a-half-hour traffic stop. The ACLU was then able to drum up widespread media interest in DWB and to begin the process of educating the public on the subject. A website was also created to serve as a clearinghouse on racial profiling and a place where people could report instances of unwarranted traffic stops, thus providing the ACLU with information and possible cases for litigation.

The next step in the campaign against racial profiling involved consumer advertising. ACLU executive director Glasser told Lauro of the *New York Times,* "We have taken to advertising for the same reason people who market products have taken to advertising in a dramatic and splashy and visible way. We want to get the message into people's consciousness without forcing them to have to read a law review article."

In December 1999 the ACLU took the unusual and attention-grabbing tactic of promoting its message by running three ads in the classified pages of major newspapers, including the *New York Times.* Each ad addressed a different example of injustice; one, which ran in the automotive ads, served as the opening salvo in the effort to fight racial profiling. The text read: "Car for Sale: 500 SL Luxury Sport Coupe. Its performance is unmatched on the highway. Unless you're black and driving on some interstates. Then you could be pulled over and searched by state troopers for fitting a drug courier profile. These humiliating and illegal searches are violations of the Constitution and must be fought. Support the ACLU."

The ACLU also ran full-page print ads, which proved controversial in their own way. One involved the death of Amadou Diallo, an unarmed man killed in a hail of gunfire outside his apartment building in New York City. According to witnesses, he was simply returning home from dinner and made the mistake of reaching into his jacket when four plainclothes policemen ordered him to show his hands. They fired 41 shots, 19 of which struck Diallo. The incident had received international press coverage, and the ACLU referenced it in a new ad, which showed 41 bullet holes and the following text: "On February 4th, 1999, the NYPD gave Amadou Diallo the right to remain silent. And they did it without ever saying a word. Firing 41 bullets in 8 seconds, the police killed an unarmed, innocent man. Also wounded was the constitutional right of every American to due process of law. Help us defend your rights. Support the ACLU."

Several months later, in May 2000, the ACLU ran another controversial print ad, which appeared first in the *New York Times* and a day later in the *New Yorker.* The ad showed a picture of Martin Luther King, Jr., on the left side of the page and notorious killer Charles Manson on the right. The headline read: "The man on the left is 75 times more likely to be stopped by the police while driving than the man on the right."

The ACLU also took its campaign to the local level in September 2000, airing its first-ever paid television spots. They targeted Utah, whose senator Orrin Hatch, a Republican, was the chairman of the Senate Judiciary Committee. In addition to ads sponsored by national organizations, local branches of the ACLU made their own contributions to the campaign. The Washington state chapter of the ACLU, for example, launched its own advertising effort to call attention to racial profiling.

OUTCOME

The ACLU's focus on racial profiling continued until the end of 2000, and then in the spring of 2001 the emphasis switched to the issue of gay civil rights laws. A few months later the terrorist attacks of September 11, 2001, took place, and the problem of DWB was pushed further aside, as the ACLU began addressing a host of civil-liberties questions that emerged with the launch of the so-called war on terror.

The ACLU was pleased with the results of its campaign. It claimed that many police departments had begun to require that officers record the race of every driver they stopped. In addition, more than 25 states introduced legislation connected to the DWB issue.

The campaign was also able to achieve the goal of drawing attention to the issue, receiving a great deal of free media concerning racial profiling. The advertising played an important role in this regard. Although it upset a large number of people, it stood out and met its purpose. The advertising industry recognized the work as well. In 2001 the campaign won an Ad Age Best of Show Award (Magazines category).

FURTHER READING

"ACLU Attacks Racial Profiling with Ad Citing Dr. King and Charles Manson." *Jet,* June 26, 2000, p. 38.

Berger, Warren. "Stirring Up Trouble, without Even Trying." *One. A Magazine,* Fall 2004.

Davilla, Florangela. "ACLU Ads to Spotlight Racial Profiling Issue." *Seattle Times,* April 20, 2000, p. B5.

Foster, Shawn. "ACLU Targets Hatch for Support of Study." *Salt Lake Tribune,* September 14, 2000, p. D1.

Horowitz, David. "Racial Profiling: The Death of the Civil Rights Movement." *FrontPageMagazine.com,* September 5, 2000. Available from <http://www.frontpagemag.com/Articles/ReadArticle.asp?ID=1078>

Johannes, Laura. "For the ACLU Head, Terrorism Battle Threatens Liberties." *Wall Street Journal,* November 19, 2001, p. B1.

Lauro, Patricia Winters. "The A.C.L.U. Is Taking a Provocative Madison Avenue Route to Raise Support for Its Causes." *New York Times,* May 30, 2000, p. C10.

Lee, Henry K. "Study Indicates Racial Profiling by Oakland Cops." *San Francisco Chronicle,* May 12, 2001, p. A13.

Sampey, Kathleen. "Taking the Liberties." *Adweek,* December 13, 1999, p. 7.

Vagnoni, Anthony. "Advertising Age Best Awards." *Advertising Age,* May 28, 2001, p. S1.

Ed Dinger

American Express Company

World Financial Ctr.
200 Vesey St.
New York, New York 10285
USA
Telephone: (212) 640-2000
Web site: www.americanexpress.com

COMPETITIVE CAMPAIGN

OVERVIEW

In June 1996 American Express Company launched a $200 million global marketing campaign to emphasize its strong brand presence and also to introduce new products and services. As competition in the credit card market intensified, American Express (AmEx) had suffered declining revenues in the early 1990s. At the same time AmEx lost market share as the company made a failed attempt at becoming a financial services supermarket by purchasing several brokerage firms, investment banking companies, and real estate businesses.

American Express hoped that its "Do More" campaign, which consisted of both print and television ads, would lure consumers with the company's historic brand image of reliability and prestige. Once interest was captured, AmEx planned to inform consumers of its wide variety of services and programs, with the belief that consumers would take advantage of the offers because they trusted and respected AmEx. John Hayes, the company's executive vice president of global advertising, explained, "Our advertising used to be about a limited number of products and services, and was often defined by the people who used them. This campaign stresses our growing number of services and what American Express can do for you."

The "Do More" campaign continued into 1997, spreading information about the American Express collection of charge cards, credit cards, investment products, travel services, and more. In January AmEx also launched the "Competitive" campaign, which was part of the "Do More" effort yet focused exclusively on addressing the faults of its competitors' services. The campaign primarily targeted longtime rival Visa International, which had a history of attacking American Express in its ad campaigns.

HISTORICAL CONTEXT

The competitive portion of the "Do More" campaign was a reaction to continual onslaughts from Visa's marketing. Since the mid-1980s Visa had deliberately pitted itself against American Express, producing numerous television commercials that pointed out AmEx's alleged shortcomings as a credit card provider. James Desrozier, vice president of MasterCard International's advertising division, said in a 1992 *Newsday* article, "Visa went against American Express without mentioning MasterCard. It was the two of them and it just knocked us out of the game. It was a brilliant strategy."

American Express generally ignored Visa's attacks, although battles occasionally arose. Prior to the 1994 Olympics in Lillehammer, Norway, agreement had been reached between the two companies to refrain from attacking one another in Olympic-related advertising.

In addition, because Visa was an official sponsor of the Olympics, AmEx was not to use images or shots from the events in its ads or to imply an affiliation with the Olympic Games. When the Olympics began, however, the agreement crumbled. Visa objected to AmEx television ads that claimed, "So if you're traveling to Norway, you'll need a passport, but you don't need a visa." The play on words could be confusing, it was charged, and Visa accused AmEx of suggesting that it was connected with the Olympics by emphasizing its history with and presence in Norway. Visa then countered with television ads using its standard anti-AmEx slogan, "And they don't take American Express."

American Express had long been marketed as a charge card that exemplified prestige and status, and its fees could pack a wallop. In 1995, for example, the standard green card commanded a $55 annual fee. An older marketing campaign embraced the tag line "Membership has its privileges," which hinted at AmEx's exclusive reputation. Its promises of privileges and perks, however, were not enough to sustain customer loyalty. *Time* magazine reported that in the early 1990s more than 2 million AmEx cardholders chose to cancel their membership. Other credit card companies such as Visa and MasterCard offered low interest rates and fee-free cards to consumers, and they garnered a lower usage fee from merchants, which made them more attractive to retailers. In 1977, for example, Visa reportedly took a 2 percent fee from purchases, whereas AmEx still took 2.74 percent, down from 3.22 percent in 1990. In 1995 H. Eugene Lockhart, MasterCard's chief executive officer at the time, told *Fortune,* "The consumer today simply doesn't see the need to pay fees for a card that gives them no greater functionality than anything we or Visa would give them." It appeared that the card of prestige had become the card of the privileged few rather than that of the masses, and, according to *Fortune,* AmEx's share of the domestic card market declined from close to 25 percent in 1990 to 16 percent in 1995.

TARGET MARKET

American Express's clientele had traditionally included those who were financially established and for whom "membership ha[d] its privileges." AmEx had long been embraced by business travelers and corporate clients, and, according to *Time,* AmEx customers were "big spenders who charged an average of $6,000 on their cards in 1996, in contrast to some $3,200 for charges per Visa card." Business charges and travel expenses accounted for the bulk of this spending, however, and customers used AmEx cards infrequently for personal purchases. To remedy this situation and to increase its market share in the competitive credit card arena, AmEx needed to appeal to a broader market. The company thus expanded its target clientele to include not only the upscale crowd but also the credit card-carrying masses. To compete with Visa and MasterCard, AmEx promoted its Optima credit card, which allowed the cardholder to pay off a percentage of the balance each month rather than the entire balance, as with the traditional AmEx charge card.

For the "Competitive" campaign American Express took aim at non-AmEx cardholders to inform them of its numerous incentive programs and premiums. While companies such as Visa and MasterCard had long offered a slew of cards and rewards to its cardholders, including discounts on purchases and free airline miles, AmEx had generally refrained from such programs and stuck with its traditional card offerings. But the company learned a lesson, reported *Time,* during a focus group session in the early 1990s when the holder of a competing card that offered free airline miles stated, "I want to go with you guys, but you guys are so stupid that you're not offering this product to me." In a company survey AmEx learned that its cardholders would use their AmEx cards for more purchases if the spending rewarded them with travel, food, and merchandise perks. AmEx thus expanded its small airline mileage program in 1995 to offer a wide-ranging rewards program. The Membership Rewards program allowed cardholders to earn points by using their AmEx cards, which could later be exchanged for travel rewards, merchandise, gift certificates, and more. AmEx also began to offer a wider variety of cards, including some with no annual fee and some co-branded with other companies, and solicited retailers to increase the number of outfits at which the card could be used. As AmEx president Kenneth Chenault told *U.S. News & World Report,* "If our customer wants to use the American Express card at a hot dog stand, we want to be there."

COMPETITION

Although American Express faced competition from credit card companies, major banks, and other financial service providers, Visa provided the most visible rivalry.

HE SAID, SHE SAID

The Better Business Bureau had dealt with American Express and Visa on numerous occasions throughout the 1990s. However, until Visa cried foul over AmEx's Visa-bashing "Paris" spot, AmEx had been doing all of the complaining.

According to RAM Research findings reported in *Advertising Age,* the ubiquitous Visa card dominated the credit card market with a share of 50.5 percent during the first half of 1996. MasterCard followed with 26.4 percent, AmEx with 15.9 percent, and Discover with 7.3 percent. Similar reports by SMR Research in *USA Today* indicated that AmEx's share dropped from 20.4 percent in 1992 to 16.4 percent in 1996. Visa's market share, on the other hand, rose from 45.1 to 49.2 percent, while MasterCard's share remained essentially steady at 27.6 percent.

American Express's market share could not match Visa's, but AmEx showed signs of improvement in 1996 when it finally reversed a decade-long decline in its share of the credit card market. *Advertising Age* reported that spending on AmEx cards went up 15.6 percent in 1996 from 1995, while Visa's purchase volume increased 15.5 percent. And according to *U.S. News & World Report,* 41.5 million AmEx cards were in circulation in 1996, an increase of 8 percent from the previous year. Carl Pascarella, CEO of Visa U.S.A., was not impressed, however, as he told *Time:* "They haven't changed much.... Over the past eight or nine years, consumers have been pulling out their Visa card significantly more often than their American Express card." AmEx indeed had a long way to go to catch Visa. There were almost 600 million Visa cards in distribution, and Visa was accepted by more than 14 million retailers globally. Although AmEx had been signing up more businesses to accept its cards and had more than 5 million merchant partners, this was still a far cry from Visa's 14 million.

MARKETING STRATEGY

The primary purpose of the American Express "Competitive" campaign was to point out the shortcomings of its competitor Visa. The "Do More" campaign of 1996 had laid the groundwork by introducing AmEx's numerous new services and programs, while also capitalizing on its image of reliability and downplaying its snobbishness. As the company's Hayes explained in *Advertising Age,* "We're reshaping the American Express brand to fit a wide variety of uses in the next century—we want to have long-term, meaningful relationships with people and we're going to build them through marketing."

The "Competitive" campaign consisted of a print effort and of three television spots that aired on the national networks during prime time. The first spot, "Paris," began airing in January of 1997 during the National Football League play-offs and implied that many of Visa's alleged services were nonexistent or unreliable. The spot featured a Visa cardholder embarking on a vacation to Paris. The cardholder had intended to use the free airline miles he had accumulated on his Visa card but discovered at the airport that his miles had expired. He then attempted to charge the plane ticket on his Visa card, only to be told that he had reached his credit limit. The cardholder was forced to pay cash for his ticket, and his troubles did not end there. Upon reaching France, the traveler encountered problems entering the country. He then contacted Visa for traveler assistance but was turned down. Other obstacles lay in wait as well, for when the traveler injured himself and also was arrested for mistakenly declaring himself a spy in French, he was unable to use his Visa's free medical or legal services. The message AmEx intended to send was that the traveler would not have had such problems had he used an AmEx card.

American Express timed its aggressive campaign to begin shortly after many airlines had cleared out a large number of free airline miles, many of which had accumulated on credit cards. An AmEx spokesperson told *Credit Card Management,* "There are a lot of inconsistencies in Visa programs because they vary from issuer to issuer.... We feel it is important to set the record straight. And with many frequent-flier miles having just expired, we felt it was a good time to remind people of the benefits of Membership Rewards." AmEx's free airline miles came with no expiration date.

The print effort, which began in February, declared, "Visa says they're everywhere, but isn't it more important to have a card that helps you with just about everything?" One of the print ads showed an American Express card next to a Visa card. The ad listed mocking descriptions of Visa's services, including "No medical referrals, but rounded corners for safety."

A second television spot, "Grand Canyon," featured another unlucky traveler. This Visa cardholder was on his way to Las Vegas to see Steve Lawrence and Eydie Gorme but en route encountered problems in the Grand Canyon. He lost his wallet, dropped his camera into the canyon, and then crashed his rental car into a billboard as Lawrence and Gorme passed by on their tour bus, uncorking a bottle of champagne. In this spot American Express challenged Visa's purchase protection plans, rental car insurance services, and lost card assistance, implying that its own services in these areas were superior.

The spot "Virtual Reality" featured a male, played by the unlucky traveler from the Grand Canyon, standing in a store and wearing a virtual reality headset. In his fantasy he danced with a beautiful woman, but just as they were about to kiss, he was jarred from his dream by a store clerk who informed him that he was over the spending limit on his Visa card and thus could not continue with his virtual reality session. A struggle over the headset ensued, and the police arrived. This ad questioned Visa's credit limits, in turn emphasizing that American Express cards had no preset spending limits.

OUTCOME

Visa obviously was not pleased with the American Express "Competitive" campaign and in July 1997 filed a complaint with the National Advertising Division (NAD) of the Better Business Bureau, hoping to put a stop to the airing of the ads. Visa claimed that the AmEx spots were misleading because the advertising implied that Visa did not offer any of the services discussed in the campaign. Visa argued that many of its cards offered various services, including medical and legal referrals, purchase protection, and airline mileage programs. David Sandor, a Visa spokesman, told *American Banker,* "Millions of Visa cards offer the enhancements AmEx claims Visa doesn't have." *Advertising Age* indicated that 85 million Visa Gold cardholders received free medical and legal services as opposed to 40 million AmEx cardholders who benefited from similar programs.

The NAD reviewed Visa's complaints and determined that American Express needed to change only a few words that could be considered confusing. AmEx was required to make it clear that some Visa classic cards did offer medical and legal services and that some cards also offered mileage programs in which the airline miles had no expiration date. AmEx spokesperson Emily Porter indicated to *American Banker,* "We are pleased that we just have to make some minor changes.... We see this as a victory." Another AmEx spokesperson downplayed Visa's complaints and explained to *Credit Card Management,* "We are not surprised Visa is uneasy with the spot.... Visa is not providing its members with products and services consumers want. We want to make it clear that we would like to provide those products to their members."

Viewers were not as unhappy as Visa about the "Competitive" campaign. The "Virtual Reality" spot was nominated for a best commercial Emmy Award for 1997, and "Paris" won an award at the 1997 Cannes International Advertising Festival. One cardholder, a victim of the purge of airline miles, said that the American Express "Paris" spot was especially effective. The cardholder told *Credit Card Management,* "Losing miles after spending years to build them is a maddening situation.... The ad also correctly points out that Visa issuers do little for their cardholders when it comes to travel services." Other viewers may also have been swayed, for, according to *Time,* AmEx saw its market share increase from 18.3 to 18.9 percent during the first half of 1997, while Visa's share dropped from 48.88 to 48.85 percent. AmEx stock shares had increased fourfold since 1993, and profits were on the rise.

FURTHER READING

"American Express Strikes Back." *Credit Card Management,* March 1, 1997, p. 6.

Fickenscher, Lisa. "BBB Endorses Most of Amex's Visa-Bashing Ads." *American Banker,* December 3, 1997, p. 14.

Fitzgerald, Kate. "AmEx Retools Ad Effort to Global Vision." *Advertising Age,* June 10, 1996, p. 4.

———. "AmEx's Ads Needle Rival: Visa Labels Them 'Unfair.'" *Advertising Age,* February 17, 1997, p. 38.

Greenwald, John. "Charge! American Express May Not Have the Cachet It Once Did, but Its Card Business Is Growing Again, Thanks to a Grittier Game Plan and No-Nonsense Management." *Time,* January 12, 1998.

Sherrid, Pamela. "A New Class Act at AMEX." *U.S. News & World Report,* June 23, 1997, p. 39.

Spencer, Peter. "Advertising Battles." *Consumers' Research Magazine,* April 1, 1998, p. 43.

Mariko Fujinaka

DO MORE CAMPAIGN

OVERVIEW

The American Express Company (AmEx) was long associated with the celebrities whose appearance in print campaigns was meant to position "membership" in its credit-card brand as the domain of a privileged few. But AmEx's elitist brand image became a serious hindrance in the 1980s and 1990s. Rivals such as Visa U.S.A. and MasterCard International had been using their own marketing to exploit the fact that their card brands were accepted more universally than AmEx, and by 1996 their gains had significantly eroded AmEx's market share. The launch of a new umbrella advertising campaign tagged "Do More" was not just the debut of new creative concepts; it marked a concerted attempt to reposition the AmEx brand.

Created by ad agency Ogilvy & Mather, "Do More" aimed to convey all the advantages AmEx could offer, ranging from its numerous charge and credit cards to travel services and financial-planning assistance. "We want consumers to see American Express as more than a charge card company," John Hayes, AmEx's head of global advertising, told *USA Today.* The company also used "Do More" to broaden its consumer base, employing celebrities, such as Tiger Woods and Jerry Seinfeld, who appealed to consumers across demographic and income boundaries. The umbrella effort had various incarnations and encompassed several individual campaigns through 2001. AmEx typically spent between $170 million and $200 million on U.S. credit-card advertising during these years.

AmEx gained market share in the first two years that "Do More" ran. Difficulties in later years were reversed by the introduction of a new card appealing to young adults, a product whose existence itself was a measure of the evolving nature of the AmEx brand. "Do More" did a great deal to bring about and to publicize this evolution, and many of the hallmarks of this repositioning campaign—including the continued participation of Tiger Woods and Jerry Seinfeld—were visible in the advertising that followed its discontinuation in 2002.

HISTORICAL CONTEXT

American Express had built its reputation as a prestigious charge card. In 1976 the company began its famed "Do You Know Me?" campaign in which celebrities ranging from dancer Mikhail Baryshnikov to puppeteer Jim Henson appeared in ads that pictured them and an AmEx Green Card bearing their names. In 1987 the "Portraits" campaign followed a similar formula. By aligning the brand with stars, AmEx cultivated the notion that carrying one of its cards was more akin to joining an elite country club than making a financial transaction. As later ads sniffed, "membership has its privileges."

In the 1980s, however, AmEx's careful positioning began to backfire. According to *Brandweek,* while AmEx "clung to its old, elite ways," the credit card industry went through monumental changes. With so many cards vying for consumers' attention, Visa and MasterCard (specifically, the member banks that comprised the Visa and MasterCard consortia) began to cross-market with various businesses so they could offer incentives to consumers. For instance, by teaming up with airlines, Visa and MasterCard could entice consumers to charge purchases with the promise of frequent-flier miles. Moreover, companies such as AT&T and GM allied themselves with the Visa and MasterCard brands and began to peddle cards that tied in to phone service or car purchases. But while the entire industry became hyper-segmented, AmEx continued to sell itself on its reputation alone and lost market share as a result. Also damaging was Visa's 1987 launch of an attack campaign that stressed Visa's global acceptance by featuring countless businesses that declined to take American Express. Further limiting AmEx's appeal was the fact that the company continued to charge its hefty $55 membership fee, while Visa and MasterCard offered fee-free cards and low interest rates. Taken together these factors weakened AmEx considerably. In fact more than 2 million AmEx cardholders canceled their memberships in the early 1990s, and the company's share of the domestic credit-card market sank from nearly 20 percent in 1990 to 16 percent in 1995, according to *Fortune.*

In 1995 AmEx began to explore new ways to stanch the flood of cardholders abandoning AmEx and to persuade existing cardholders to use AmEx more often. After negotiating an agreement with Delta Airlines, AmEx was able to offer a frequent-flier program like those of its rivals. The company also debuted its Membership Rewards program, which gave consumers points for each AmEx purchase made. These points could then be redeemed for bonuses such as gift certificates, travel vouchers, or car rentals at an array of participating businesses. AmEx also introduced the Optima card, a revolving credit account similar to Visa and MasterCard in that consumers could carry a balance on it from month to month rather than having to pay it in full at the close of each billing period (as the Green Card required). Moreover, AmEx pushed more retailers to accept its cards. This effort was punctuated by the inauguration of the "Do More" campaign in June 1996. "This company has had a great history of reinventing itself," Hayes told *American Banker.* "This is the next logical step."

TARGET MARKET

Because AmEx wanted to use "Do More" ads to gain new cardholders, the company crafted individual ads to appeal to distinct groups, especially those that it had not targeted in its previous advertising. One of the key approaches AmEx used to broaden its customer base was to employ spokespeople who counteracted the company's image as "a stodgy, premium brand that caters to older customers," according to the *Wall Street Journal.* In 1997, for instance, AmEx signed Woods, who had won the Masters Tournament that year. As a 21-year-old phenomenon of mixed race, Woods provided AmEx an opportunity to reach younger consumers as well as African-American consumers. It was essential to AmEx's future that it garner younger consumers because they "tend to stick with the first credit card they use," explained *USA Today.* Furthermore, Woods was able "to cross every demographic line...and appeal to an audience that makes $250,000 a year as well as an audience that makes $25,000," an industry analyst told *American Banker.*

Seinfeld, who pitched the Green Card in spots that aired during such high-profile events as the Super Bowl, was another figure that transcended the traditional AmEx audience. "The Seinfeld advertising has attracted a new and younger group to the franchise and has also helped promote everyday usage, which is key," Hayes told *Brandweek.* While AmEx was typically associated with the travel and leisure retail sector, the company wanted to increase the routine purchases consumers charged each month to their AmEx cards. Instead of presenting Seinfeld in the same sort of glamorous settings that permeated "Portraits" or "Do You Know Me?" AmEx showed Seinfeld wielding his Green Card at grocery stores and gas stations. One commercial paired Seinfeld with the animated figure of Superman and portrayed Seinfeld (rather than the caped hero) rescuing Lois Lane at a grocery store by pulling out his AmEx card. (She had forgotten her wallet; Superman's costume had no pockets; Seinfeld paid for the food.)

Similarly, in the 1998 series of spots for AmEx's Small Business Services division, the company focused on African-American, Latino, and female entrepreneurs. "We have represented the three groups who represent the strongest growth in new business starts," an AmEx spokesperson told *Brandweek.* In the 1998 ads that did present wealthy and prominent businesspeople, AmEx chose the likes of Jake Burton, a snowboarding pioneer, and Earvin "Magic" Johnson, a basketball hall-of-famer who had been diagnosed with HIV, both of whom Hayes classified as "people who have challenged the status quo and appreciated the service we give . . . [They are] not just those that fit the traditional view of success."

Despite AmEx's desire to broaden its consumer base, it was careful not to "move downscale," as Hayes described it in *Brandweek.* The company had considerable brand equity rooted in AmEx's reputation for superior service, and it did not want to alienate its core group of affluent card users. "Creating the balance where the brand becomes accessible, yet . . . remains special at the same time, is a real challenge," Hayes said. AmEx relied on its spokespeople's ability to walk this tightrope. Though Woods was young, he was nevertheless a golfer, a player of a sport popular among businessmen. Moreover, Woods was not a rebellious upstart. Though barely out of his teens, he was one of the best golfers in the world. Similarly, Seinfeld's hit sitcom was watched by a huge audience. Popular with many viewers, Seinfeld was not exclusively a Generation X hero, and the commercials featuring him also appealed to AmEx's older cardholders as well.

COMPETITION

Industry leader Visa had persisted in its attacks on AmEx since the 1985 launch of its "It's Everywhere You Want to Be" campaign. Although Visa's share of the domestic credit-card market fell to 48.8 percent from 49.2 percent in 1996, it continued to portray businesses, restaurants, and entertainment providers that would not accept AmEx as a way to stress the universality of its own cards. Like AmEx, Visa also addressed specific new markets in its 1998 efforts. Under the umbrella of the "Everywhere" theme, Visa targeted Generation X consumers in "The Attic," a commercial featuring a trendy used-clothing store. In "eToys," a television spot for an online merchant, Visa linked itself to the growing e-commerce sector by presenting itself as the credit card of choice for Internet purchases. With a commercial highlighting Jack Nicklaus's golf school (which only took Visa), Visa tried to reach more affluent cardholders.

A cornerstone of Visa's marketing strategy was its sponsorship of sporting events. In addition to being the official sponsor of the National Football League (NFL), horse racing's Triple Crown races (the Kentucky Derby, the Belmont Stakes, and the Preakness), and NASCAR auto racing, Visa had been an Olympic Games sponsor since 1986. Visa used the 1998 Winter Olympic Games as a platform to reinforce its message of global acceptance. As a Visa executive explained in the January 30, 1998, edition of *American Banker,* "nothing was better for a brand" than associating itself with the Olympics.

Like American Express, Visa also endeavored to expand its empire—and its name recognition—beyond credit cards. In 1998 Visa continued to promote its debit card, the Visa CheckCard, with big-budget advertisements depicting celebrities being hassled for identification when writing a check. Visa touted its small-business cards as well. According to the October 5, 1998, issue of *Advertising Age,* Visa's long-term goal was to leverage "its brand equity into different kinds of payment."

MasterCard, too, vied to be consumers' card of choice. Breaking free from a long period of mediocre advertising and negligible growth, in 1997 the company debuted "Priceless," which "bec[ame] one of the industry's most admired campaigns, creating an almost

"DO MORE" EVERYWHERE

American Express Company's "Do More" campaign truly was a global one, running in 23 different countries simultaneously. Although the same basic ads were used everywhere, the ad agency Ogilvy & Mather changed small details when appropriate. "We've created an overall platform for positioning," John Hayes, the company's head of global advertising, told *Advertising Age.* "We make modifications and customizations everywhere to make sure what we do is right." Golfer Tiger Woods proved an especially valuable global representative—particularly in Japan, where golf was a passion among a large percentage of the population.

nonstop buzz . . . [and] raising consumer awareness and consumer usage of the card," *Adweek* raved. Using the tagline "There Are Some Things Money Can't Buy. For Everything Else There's MasterCard," MasterCard's agency, McCann-Erickson, made an emotional appeal to its viewers. These print and television advertisements showed scenes of various activities, such as a father and child at a baseball game and an older couple celebrating a wedding anniversary. The voice-over announced the cost of various aspects of these endeavors, and the commercials all culminated in a "priceless" moment (such as "real conversation with 11-year-old son" at the end of the baseball spot), followed by the campaign's tagline. Buoyed by "Priceless," MasterCard's purchase volume rose 16 percent from 1997 to 1998 and its market share remained steady, increasing slightly to 27.8 percent from 27.6 percent, according to *Credit Card News.*

MARKETING STRATEGY

Because the primary goal of "Do More" was to establish the brand's relevance to diverse consumers, AmEx used a targeted strategy to pair specific messages with specific groups. For instance, the print executions portraying small-business entrepreneurs ran almost entirely in publications such as *Success, Entrepreneur,* and *Forbes.* The initial Tiger Woods ads touting American Express Financial Advisors favored major newspapers (especially the *Wall Street Journal,* the *New York Times,* and *USA Today*) and newsweeklies (including *Time* and *Newsweek*) over lifestyle publications. AmEx chose to air the Seinfeld commercials on mainstream, high-profile television programming because the company hoped the comedian could connect a mass audience of credit-card users to the Green Card. "Superman" first appeared during NFL playoff games, which reached viewers across demographic lines.

The message of "Do More" was that AmEx—not Visa or MasterCard—could improve one's ventures and that AmEx was a global solution always available to make things better (or easier). Part of the way AmEx delivered this message was by making its ads attention-getters. The spokespeople chosen to represent the various facets of the brand were not only well known but also had a certain renegade charm. Certainly Johnson was one of the greatest basketball players of all time, and his excellence was intended to mirror AmEx's reputation for service and prestige. But Johnson had also shocked the nation when he announced he was HIV-positive. Pundits had decried him, and some fellow basketball players even shunned him. Using him in the AmEx spots was a daring choice and attracted much notice.

Similarly, the "Superman" spot was designed "to break through commercial clutter," Hayes said. Instead of banking on Seinfeld's celebrity, AmEx created a commercial that juxtaposed him with a comic book character and spoofed the notion of any credit card (or personality) being able to "save the day." As he took his AmEx card out of his pocket, Seinfeld spun around in a blur. An onlooker asked, "What's with the spinning?" "He idolizes me," Superman wryly explained. "It's embarrassing." Again, the notion was to twist the genre slightly, to prompt viewers to sit up and take note that American Express was not quite what everyone assumed it to be. In 1999 AmEx extended its association with Seinfeld. One noteworthy spot showed the comedian embarking on a cross-country road trip after observing that he needed to "get some kind of real life." In keeping with his persona, his adventures were simultaneously large-scale and trivial: among other activities, he saw Mount Rushmore, held a cup of coffee that was too hot, had a conversation with an attractive blond woman, and visited the Saint Louis Arch.

American Express updated the "Do More" concept in 2000, adapting the tagline to a subcampaign dubbed "Moments of Truth," the first phase of which consisted of five TV spots featuring ordinary people. Each of these commercials focused on the fact that AmEx offered "more" services than its competitors. For instance, American Express's travel-assistance benefits were touted in one spot that showed a woman waiting fruitlessly at an airport baggage claim. Another spot emphasized American Express's partnership with the bulk-sales supermarket Costco; yet another focused on the company's online-banking offerings via the juxtaposition of a "wired" young woman with her "analog" father, who was paying bills by hand. The tagline's flexibility was further demonstrated by that year's highest-profile and most imaginative spot, which featured Tiger Woods playing an outsized game of golf on the streets of Manhattan. Woods was shown swatting a ball over the Empire State Building and then from Central Park all the way downtown to Wall Street, before sinking a putt in a paper cup positioned on the Brooklyn Bridge. In this case "do more" was intended as a suggestion that American Express could help cardholders realize their most ambitious hopes.

OUTCOME

When AmEx inaugurated "Do More" in 1996, critics predicted that the company would lose its ability to differentiate itself by shedding some of its snobbish image. Ogilvy and AmEx quickly seemed to prove the skeptics wrong, however: the company's 1996 purchase volume rose 15.6 percent, and "after years of decline," its 1997 share of the domestic credit-card market climbed to 17 percent from 16.4 percent, according to *Advertising*

Age. AmEx posted global market share declines in 1998 and 1999, but this was partly a result of the Visa and MasterCard emphasis on debit cards, a product AmEx did not offer. AmEx countered with its most successful product launch in recent memory, the Blue Card, aimed at college-age consumers and other young adults. The ranks of Blue Card holders steadily increased in 2000 and 2001, and AmEx unveiled a Blue Card designed for small-business owners. Although the Blue Card's marketing did not fall under the "Do More" umbrella, it did build on the strategy of democratizing the traditionally upscale AmEx brand image, an approach whose merits were no longer questioned at the beginning of the new century. This change in perception was perhaps a measure of the success of the brand repositioning accomplished through the "Do More" campaign.

The Seinfeld and other "Do More" spots aired through 2001, but AmEx, like many advertisers, struggled to find appropriate ways to promote itself in the somber months after the terrorist attacks of September 11, 2001. AmEx's post-9/11 difficulties were compounded by the fact that the company's headquarters were located at the World Financial Center, adjacent to the Twin Towers, which had collapsed. In early 2002 the "Do More" tagline was dropped in favor of "Make Life Rewarding." Both Seinfeld and Woods continued to be involved with the American Express brand.

FURTHER READING

Arndorfer, James. "Credit Card Industry Attempts to Build Usage in Tight Market." *Advertising Age,* October 5, 1998.

———. "Unity Becomes Watchword for Global Credit Dollars." *Advertising Age,* October 20, 1997.

Cardona, Mercedes,"With Blue, Tiger as Stars, AmEx Soars." *Advertising Age,* October 9, 2000.

Coulton, Antoinette. "At Winter Olympics, Visa Has No Competition." *American Banker,* June 30, 1998.

———. "Fore! AmEx Signs Tiger Woods as Spokesman." *American Banker,* May 20, 1997.

Frank, Stephen. "Tiger Woods Is Plugging American Express Products." *Wall Street Journal,* May 21, 1997.

Kim, Hank,"Credit Cards." *Adweek* (eastern ed.), April 23, 2001.

———. "Inside Priceless: MasterCard Moments." *Adweek,* April 12, 1999.

Meece, Mickey. "Career Tracks: AmEx Goes Well beyond Cards with New TV Spots Series." *American Banker,* June 18, 1996.

"Off-Beat Entrepreneurs." *Brandweek,* August 24, 1998.

"Tiger Practices for U.S. Open with AmEx Spot." *Bank Advertising News,* July 10, 2000.

Vranica, Suzanne,"American Express Will Launch New Ads." *Wall Street Journal,* March 15, 2002.

Wells, Melanie. "AmEx Ads Will Push the Big Picture." *USA Today,* June 14, 1996.

———. "Woods, AmEx Partner in $13 Million Deal." *USA Today,* May 20, 1997.

"Widening the Expressway." *Brandweek,* September 7, 1998.

Rebecca Stanfel
Mark Lane

SEINFELD CAMPAIGN

OVERVIEW

Although the American Express Company (AmEx) had built its brand on an idea of exclusionary "membership," its elitist image proved a weak spot in the 1980s and 1990s, when competitors such as Visa and MasterCard eroded AmEx's market share by positioning themselves as more convenient alternatives. One of the AmEx marketing moves meant to counteract the company's outdated image was enlisting the comedian Jerry Seinfeld in 1992 as a collaborator on TV commercials that reproduced the observational comedy of his stand-up routine and of his NBC sitcom *Seinfeld,* which at the time had a devoted but comparatively small viewership. As *Seinfeld* became increasingly popular, AmEx heightened Seinfeld's role in its marketing. Between 1995 and 2002 the comedian was a centerpiece of the credit-card giant's American marketing efforts.

In one spot Seinfeld was shown foiling, thanks to his AmEx card, a gas-station attendant who wanted to inconvenience him by failing to stop the pump at exactly $20. This focus on humorously trivial acts was characteristic of Seinfeld's comedy, but the tone and content of the commercials represented risky new territory for American Express. Seinfeld's intelligent and accessible persona helped the card-issuer bridge generational divisions and position itself as suitable for use in unglamorous hubs of daily life, such as grocery stores, without undermining the upscale image it had spent so many years creating. The cost of retaining Seinfeld and of running the commercials was not disclosed, but the comedian was, at the peak of his popularity, one of the highest-paid TV stars, and his AmEx spots often debuted on Super Bowl broadcasts, the most expensive of all advertising forums. American Express annually spent about $300 million advertising its credit cards.

The commercials were well received by consumers and ad-industry critics; they were consistently named among *Adweek* 's monthly Best Spots in the late 1990s, and the "Gas Station" spot won a Silver Lion at the Cannes International Advertising Festival in 1997. Seinfeld was a central part of AmEx's long-term brand repositioning, a project that paid intermittent dividends during the years of the campaign's run. Seinfeld and AmEx further collaborated on a well-received online campaign in 2004.

Comedian Jerry Seinfeld. © STEVE AZZARA/CORBIS.

HISTORICAL CONTEXT

Beginning in the 1960s American Express distinguished itself for two decades with several highly acclaimed campaigns. *Advertising Age* included two 1970s American Express campaigns ("Do You Know Me?" and "Don't Leave Home without It" featuring Karl Malden) on its list of the "50 Best Commercials." The 1988 print campaign featuring photos of famous card members by Annie Leibovitz was a finalist for the book *Advertising's Ten Best of the Decade 1980–1990.*

But in 1990 AT&T Corp. disrupted the general-purpose credit-card market by introducing its Universal Card with no annual fees. The move adversely affected American Express, which relied on annual fees for much of its revenue, for two reasons. First, American Express was not a credit card but rather a charge card that had to be paid in full monthly, and so it did not earn interest by extending credit. Second, American Express collected on average 3.22 percent of the transaction, making Visa a much more attractive card for merchants to honor, since it charged about half of this percentage. CEO James Robinson III attempted to salvage American Express by turning it into what *Time* magazine called "an unwieldy financial supermarket." In 1993 the board of directors replaced Robinson with Harvey Golub, who streamlined the company by severing the brokerage, investment-banking, and life-insurance divisions. Golub's tactics turned the company around in short order. Spending on American Express cards increased by 15.6 percent in 1996, outpacing the 13.4 percent rise for credit cards overall (exclusive of debit transactions and cash advances). And in the first half of 1997 American Express finally reversed its decade-long downward trend in market share, rising from 18.3 to 18.9 percent of the $469 billion credit-card market.

TARGET MARKET

The Seinfeld commercials were part of a larger AmEx effort to counteract a damaging perception that the brand was the elitist province of older, wealthy consumers. To broaden its card-holding base AmEx needed to reach younger consumers, who tended to remain loyal to their first credit-card brand, but it was also important that the company not alienate those who had been drawn to AmEx's long-cultivated aura of prestige. Seinfeld was a key figure in this brand repositioning beginning with his initial involvement with AmEx in 1992. The comic's ironic, urban-inflected sensibility attracted a devoted following among young consumers, but his value to the company became increasingly evident in the following years, as his eponymous sitcom achieved a level of popularity that transcended demographic divisions. Even as *Seinfeld* became universally known and appreciated, Jerry Seinfeld's hold on younger, hipper consumers remained strong. His persona was that of an intelligent yet accessible and self-effacing everyman. He thus emerged as a spokesperson who fit neatly with the AmEx imperative to broaden the brand's target market without alienating its existing cardholders.

Seinfeld's centrality to AmEx's advertising increased in concert with his celebrity. As of 1995 *Seinfeld* was well on its way to becoming perhaps the defining TV sitcom of its era, and the comic became one of the chief elements of the wider AmEx marketing effort tagged "Do More," a branding campaign that was intended to extend the ongoing redefinition of the company's image. AmEx's other primary spokesperson during this time, the young golf phenom Tiger Woods, likewise contributed a uniquely inclusive aura to the brand. As a 21-year-old of mixed ethnicity, Woods appealed to young people across ethnic lines, but his overwhelming mastery of a

KNIX TIX

In an underscoring of American Express Company's affiliation with the New York Knicks, Michael Bay of Propaganda Films directed a 30-second spot titled "Knicks Tickets," in which spokesperson Jerry Seinfeld brandished his American Express card to pursue his lost Knicks tickets from his limo to horseback to in-line skates to underwater diving. The final frames, shot outside Madison Square Garden (because it was too expensive to shoot inside), showed Seinfeld in full scuba gear telling his date, "I'd have gone to the moon for these." The spot ended on a two-shot of Seinfeld and film director and Knicks fanatic Spike Lee, in an astronaut's suit, affirming, "Tell me about it." Seinfeld performed his own stunts for the spot—mounting a horse, diving backward off a boat, and even in line skating for just the second time in his life.

sport closely linked with older, moneyed consumers likewise won him respect from many established AmEx customers.

COMPETITION

While American Express's market share was rising in the first half of 1997, to 18.9 percent, Visa's was falling slightly, from 48.88 to 48.85 percent. Visa nevertheless dominated almost half of the market, with about 600 million cards accepted at more than 14 million locations worldwide. This made American Express pale in comparison, with 42.3 million cardholders able to charge at 5 million locations worldwide. In an attempt to make its numbers more competitive, American Express lowered the average percentage of the fee it charged merchants on each transaction from 3.22 percent in 1990 to 2.74 percent in 1998. The discount increased merchant acceptance of the card. In a 1997 survey cardholders confirmed that they could use their cards at 92 percent of the locations where they wanted to shop, up from 72 percent five years earlier. These statistics substantiated the portrayals in the commercials of Seinfeld charging gas and purchasing single stamps. But Visa still charged merchants a fee of less than 2 percent, allowing the front-runner to claim, "It's everywhere you want it to be."

American Express edged out its main competition in the corporate and small-business markets, where it controlled a 65 percent share. Consistent with its image, American Express cardholders tended to be bigger spenders, charging on average $6,000 yearly in 1996, compared with Visa's per-card average of $3,200. Consumers tended to use their American Express cards for higher-priced purchases, such as travel and entertainment. They also, however, tended to rack up a much higher volume of charges on competitors' cards on day-to-day spending. The use of debit cards, which drew directly from checking accounts and thus worked well for this kind of spending, increased by 75 percent in 1996. University of Maryland economics professor Lawrence Ausubel predicted that consumer spending would bifurcate between the extremes of immediate payment (debit cards) and extended payment (credit cards), emptying the middle ground of charge cards with monthly payments in full that represented American Express's traditional arrangement. In fact, exclusive agreements with Visa and MasterCard barred major banks from joining American Express to offer debit cards and make other arrangements, a case that was contested in federal courts. Internationally, American Express established relationships with banks that benefited both.

MARKETING STRATEGY

Ogilvy & Mather creative director David Apicella had first noticed Seinfeld as a promising stand-up comic in the 1970s. In 1992, acting on a hunch, Apicella hired Seinfeld to endorse American Express, although the *Seinfeld* show was still in its infancy and not yet the pop-culture juggernaut that it eventually became. "When we started, he hadn't quite reached the spectacular levels of success," Apicella recalled. "He had kind of a cult following. But I thought he was a nice combination of being Everyman—and appealing to every man—and being insightful in his observations." At first Seinfeld's role was supplemental to the company's brand advertising, and his minimalist spots simply mimicked his stand-up routine, with his material focusing on touting American Express. By 1995 Seinfeld's role at American Express had expanded to include being the spokesperson for the general brand campaign.

The Seinfeld spots that appeared in those years imitated the plots of the eponymous sitcom that had become a part of the collective American consciousness, and like the *Seinfeld* show, they were crafted via brainstorming sessions, according to participants in the creative process. "We do it much like a sitcom is written," Apicella said. "We just sit around a room for as long as it takes to get a funny commercial… Having spent however many days it takes to get the thing right with Jerry in the room, we're usually pretty together, but we're always changing things on the set." Apicella continued, "Jerry does some ad-libbing, but things are generally scripted. Jerry's commercials are done the way Jerry's show is, which is done the way Jerry's act was—[they are] carefully constructed beforehand."

One well-known spot, "Gas Station," showed Seinfeld filling his car with gas, preparing to stop the pump at exactly $20, presumably because this amount would facilitate the cash payment he wanted to make. When the pump went slightly over $20, the gas-station attendant began to delight in the irritation the error would cause, but Seinfeld responded by giving the pump handle another gratuitous squeeze and victoriously producing his AmEx green card, which made the precise total of his purchase irrelevant. The humorously trivial nature of the comedian's triumph was in keeping with his sitcom character's personality, a necessary element of the campaign from the point of view of the TV show's loyal audience. Additionally, the fact that AmEx was being connected with the commonplace act of purchasing gas was noteworthy. Typically associated with upscale travel and leisure purchases, AmEx had not, prior to the Seinfeld campaign, been regularly promoted as a card to be used for such mundane, unglamorous tasks.

Another prominent spot in the campaign, which made its debut during the 1998 Super Bowl, showed an American Express card being put to a similarly commonplace use, while further deriving humor from the small scale of Seinfeld's personal triumphs. This time, however, the spot—set in a grocery store—literally juxtaposed the comedian's character with that of Superman, who appeared as an animated figure. When Lois Lane, having forgotten her wallet, needed help purchasing her groceries, it was Seinfeld who was able to oblige, thanks to his American Express card. Superman's costume, alas, had no pockets, limiting his ability to save the day.

Although the last episode of *Seinfeld* aired in May 1998, Seinfeld's relationship with AmEx continued; indeed, in the aftermath of the show's end the public appetite for new Seinfeld material could only be satisfied via AmEx commercials. The Seinfeld campaign was put on hold during 2000 as AmEx relied more heavily on Tiger Woods and a more aspiration-minded iteration of its ongoing "Do More" message. A new batch of Seinfeld spots began appearing on TV with the March 2001 broadcast of the Academy Awards, and the Seinfeld campaign remained an integral part of AmEx's television advertising through 2002.

OUTCOME

Adweek editors consistently included commercials from the "Seinfeld" campaign on their monthly list of the "Best Spots" breaking on broadcast and cable television, and "Gas Station" garnered a Silver Lion at the Cannes Advertising Festival in June 1997. Although AmEx began to make up ground against its rivals in 1997, it was locked out of the debit-card market by an agreement between Visa, MasterCard, and the banks that issued debit cards. Therefore, AmEx lost market share in 1998 and 1999. It reversed the trend by introducing its Blue Cards, which featured a microchip meant to store the consumer's personal information to facilitate online purchasing—a feature that was not fully functional because it required retailers to use special equipment that was not then cost-effective or readily available. The microchip nevertheless effectively positioned the card as a hip, youth-focused accessory, the only credit card of its kind. AmEx attracted millions of new cardholders in this way in 2000 and 2001. The Seinfeld commercials were not used to pitch the Blue Card, but the card's success marked an extension of the ongoing brand repositioning of which the comedian had long been an integral part.

The concept behind the 1998 Seinfeld and Superman commercial was revived in 2004 for a much-publicized pair of "webisodes," five-minute films available for viewing only online. The comedian and the superhero passed their time together in much the same way that Seinfeld and his onscreen friends Elaine, George, and Kramer typically passed their time on *Seinfeld.* In the first webisode, for instance, Seinfeld and Superman made small talk in a diner, returned a damaged DVD player (thanks to an AmEx policy of replacing faulty merchandise within 90 days of purchase), and attended a lackluster Broadway musical about the state of Wyoming. The second webisode touted, among other AmEx attributes, the company's roadside-assistance service, by showing Superman and Seinfeld stranded on a road in Death Valley. This Web campaign attracted more than 2 million visitors. Although ad-industry observers questioned its practical brand-building and product-promotion benefits, "The Adventures of Seinfeld and Superman" was widely considered one of the most innovative online campaigns of its time. Because of the campaign *Adweek* named American Express its Interactive Marketer of the Year for 2004.

FURTHER READING

DeSalvo, Kathy. "Paper Chase: American Express Advertisement Featuring Jerry Seinfeld." *Shoot,* January 19, 1996, p. 16.

Garfield, Bob. "American Express Spot Seeks Some Laughs and Hides the Sell." *Advertising Age,* October 7, 2002.

Greenwald, John. "Charge! American Express May Not Have the Cachet It Once Did, but Its Card Business Is Growing Again, Thanks to a Grittier Game Plan and No Nonsense Management." *Time,* January 12, 1998, p. 60.

Lefton, Terry. "Widening the Expressway." *Brandweek,* September 7, 1998.

Mack, Ann M., and Patricia Orsini,"Buddy Movies." *Adweek,* November 22, 2004.

Schumer, Charles E.. "Let the Credit Cards Compete." *New York Times,* August 4, 1996.

Sherrid, Pamela. "A New Class Act at AMEX." *U.S. News & World Report,* June 23, 1997, p. 39.

"Shipwreck II on Super Bowl XXIX." *Adweek,* January 30, 1995.

Wallenstein, Andy. "David Apicella: Ogilvy & Mather's Creative Director Brought Seinfeld to AmEx Ads." *Shoot,* September 12, 1997, p. 46.

William D. Baue
Mark Lane

American Honda Motor Company

1919 Torrance Blvd.
Torrance, California 90501-2722
USA
Telephone: (310) 783-2000
Fax: (310) 783-2110
Web site: www.honda.com

WHAT ABOUT NOW? CAMPAIGN

OVERVIEW

In 1998 advertising agency Rubin Postaer of Santa Monica developed a campaign for the American Honda Motor Company that was set in a corporate world from which workers yearned to escape. The ads proposed the Honda Civic both as the enticement for getting away from the responsibilities of work and as the means of escape. This approach attempted to solve a difficult targeting problem: how to appeal to the spirit of younger buyers, who were adopting the Civic as their signature car, while still acknowledging the demographic group who could better afford to buy the car, 30- and 40-something professionals as well as the baby boomer parents of the younger buyers. Rubin Postaer solved the problem by portraying the everyday situation of the older audience with the spirit of a younger attitude. The subtext of the ads suggested that a person could fulfill his responsibilities with the Civic while also managing to inject some fun into the equation.

The tag line of the campaign asked, "What about Now?," focusing attention on the present. The print as well as the television campaign juxtaposed images of work with symbols of recreation. Each print execution featured a small picture of a Civic with a roof rack holding a stereotypical piece of recreational equipment. One print ad pictured a pair of sand-covered pumps, suggesting that the owner had just visited the beach, while the roof rack on the Civic held a surfboard. Another ad showed a pinstriped suit on a hanger, with a lift pass to "Mt. Doom" affixed to its bottom button, while the Civic had skis on the roof rack. A final ad filled the page with an open briefcase revealing a fish on ice and the Civic with a fishing pole strapped on top.

The television commercial entitled "Snorkeling" similarly explored the line between work and play, investigating their odd points of convergence. This spot started with an underwater scene and then revealed a business-suited man swimming in snorkeling gear. When the camera surfaced above the water, it revealed a Honda Civic awaiting the man on the beach. The voice-over said that the businessman was supposed to be attending a symposium but that his attention had been drawn elsewhere—to his automobile, which promised more excitement than a conference. The spot "Leaving Early" created an Orwellian atmosphere of the totalitarianism of modern work, against which was set the liberation of fleeing with the assistance of a Honda Civic. A man's offhand comment about leaving work early was overheard and set in motion an elaborate series of countermeasures designed to prevent his departure. The final scene showed the man fleeing in his Civic, barely making it through the closing gate and leaving behind the helicopters and cars pursuing him.

What about now?
The Honda Civic.
1-800-33-HONDA and www.honda.com
HONDA

A print advertisement from Honda's "What About Now?" campaign. RUBIN POSTAER & ASSOCIATES. REPRODUCED BY PERMISSION.

HISTORICAL CONTEXT

The Honda Motor Company was founded by Soichiro Honda in 1948. In 1990 Nobuhiko Kawamoto, an engineer who had joined Honda's research department in 1963, became president and chief executive. Honda's success reached a peak in the 1980s, but the lean economy of the 1990s pushed the company to the verge of being bought out by rival Mitsubishi Motors. Instead, in 1992 Kawamoto restructured the company by slashing his beloved Formula One racing division and by introducing a top-down management style, with performance-based promotions replacing Honda's collegial corporate culture based on seniority. Even more important, Kawamoto divested his fellow engineers of sole decision-making power, handing over more power to those who manufactured and marketed the automobiles. The move allowed Honda to take into account consumer input and preferences when building its automobiles.

The marketing of Honda automobiles in the United States dated back to 1970, when the Los Angeles office of advertising agency Chiat Day introduced American drivers to the N600 model. In 1974, when Honda was selling a mere 43,000 cars per year, Gerry Rubin arrived at Needham Harper Steers (now DDB Needham), which had just taken the account away from Chiat Day in time to introduce Honda's newest model, the Civic. Needham responded to the new assignment by focusing attention on the car itself. An early commercial depicted a family loading groceries into a Civic hatchback, and in 1978, at the height of the oil crisis, print ads for the Civic highlighted the fact that it ran on regular as well as unleaded gasoline. In 1986 Larry Postaer joined Gerry Rubin at Needham, and later that year they broke off to establish their own agency, Rubin Postaer, to service the Honda account. Honda exhibited great confidence in the new agency by awarding it the $100 million account without a public review.

TARGET MARKET

As the young drivers who had originally favored Hondas grew older, the company struggled to maintain the interest of this aging demographic group while simultaneously generating interest from younger drivers. Fortunately for Honda, the younger generation adopted the Civic as its unofficial automobile. This demographic group,

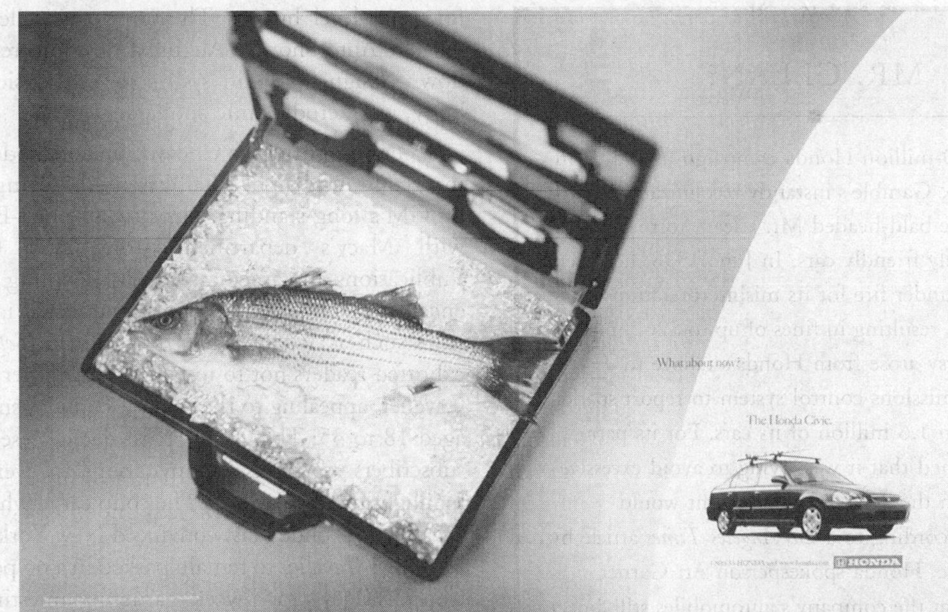
What about now?
The Honda Civic.
HONDA

A print advertisement from Honda's "What About Now?" campaign. RUBIN POSTAER & ASSOCIATES. REPRODUCED BY PERMISSION.

sometimes known as Generation Y, numbered approximately 77 million people born since 1979 and was about twice as large as its predecessor, Generation X. According to a 1999 survey of 2,000 young people conducted by Chicago-based Teenage Research Unlimited Inc., 6 percent of teenagers owned new cars, and 12 percent planned on buying a new car within the year. Rival carmaker Toyota estimated that approximately 4 million teens would reach driving age in the United States every year until 2010, when the demographic group of drivers under age 30 would number 123 million, or a third of all car buyers. Although these younger consumers could not afford the pricier cars—those with higher profit margins—they remained a key to future profits since brand preference was created early on. Companies such as Levi Strauss & Co. had already been burned by ignoring the preferences of Generation Yers when it failed to pick up on the wide-leg look in jeans.

Generation Y swelled in numbers because of the size of its parents' generation, the baby boomers. The baby boomers were responsible not only for the size of Generation Y but also, until the children left home, for its financial status. While many Generation Yers could afford to buy their own cars, many also needed assistance from their parents, and so marketers had to appeal to the sensibilities of both the younger and the older generations. In an article by Joyzelle Davis in the *Montreal Gazette,* Mark Del Russo, the leader of Toyota's Genesis Team, which was charged with the task of figuring out the purchasing preferences of Generation Y, said, "It's important to respect and not alienate the baby-boomer generation." Honda focused its "What about Now?" campaign on corporate themes as a means of connecting with the responsible side of baby boomer conscious while also appealing to the latent sense of rebellion in the group, which had come of age in the turbulent 1960s.

Honda connected with the younger generation almost by happenstance. Analysts speculated that the low price of the Civic appealed to teens and 20-somethings, but even more important was Honda's history in Formula One racing, which attracted young men especially. "You've just gotta have a Civic—it's the car," 19-year-old Luis Aguirre of Hollywood, who owned a 1996 Civic DX coupe, was quoted as saying in Davis's article. Aguirre had modified his Civic into a "slammed-down" version by boosting power to the engine and enhancing the sound system, while other young men also lowered the car body and added custom wheels, oversized exhaust pipes, and turbochargers. Auto industry analyst Eric Noble noted that these modifications, combined with Honda's racing heritage, created a "halo of hipness" for the brand. Honda picked up on this trend by introducing the Civic SI model, which came with custom wheels and side sill panels that made the body appear to be closer to the ground. Honda also installed a 160-horsepower engine to replace the 106-horsepower engine standard in most Civics.

MR. CLEAN?

In 1998 a $20-million Honda campaign used a tie-in with Procter & Gamble's instantly recognizable icon of cleanliness, the bald-headed Mr. Clean, to tout its environmentally friendly cars. In June 1998, however, Honda came under fire for its misinterpretation of the Clean Air Act, resulting in fines of up to $262 million. The controversy arose from Honda's failure to program its emissions control system to report spark plug failures in 1.6 million of its cars. For its part Honda explained that it was trying to avoid excessive instances when the "check engine" light would illuminate. According to a *Los Angeles Times* article by Denise Gellene, Honda spokesperson Art Garner maintained that the company's automobiles still "meet or exceed every requirement" of the Clean Air Act. Larry Kopald, a Los Angeles advertising executive, pointed out that Honda's decision to continue running the Mr. Clean ads might appear hypocritical to consumers. "If people see the ads right now, Honda runs the risk of being seen as a manipulator of the media," said Kopald in Gellene's article, adding that the controversy "does make them seem a little foolish." On the other hand, Clay Timon, chairman of the San Francisco image consulting firm Landor Associates, was cited in Gellene's article as doubting that the controversy would register negatively with consumers, since the ads had "created an image of Honda as fuel-efficient, with engines that don't pollute, well in advance of the settlement coming down." If anything, according to Timon, consumers would simply see the settlement as "out of character."

COMPETITION

The Honda Civic competed against other subcompacts in both the import and the domestic categories. Among imports the Honda competed against Volkswagen for the attention of the younger audience. The average age of Honda buyers in the United States was 40, while the average age of Volkswagen buyers was 38, the youngest in the industry. Volkswagen wooed younger buyers with its economically priced performance models, the Golf, Jetta, and reintroduced New Beetle. On the domestic front Honda competed primarily against Ford and General Motors (GM). Ford introduced a new model, the Focus, to augment the Escort in competing for entry-level buyers. The Focus, unveiled at the Los Angeles Auto Show in August 1998, featured a slammed-down design with stiff sports car suspension, a lowered body, and aerodynamic spoilers.

GM supported its Chevy Cavalier model with a fully integrated campaign. The "Essentials" campaign, created by GM's long-standing agency Campbell-Ewald, tied in with Macy's department stores and Conde Nast Publications to target an educated young female audience. A total of 400,000 booklets inserted in Conde Nast titles such as *Women's Sports & Fitness, Self,* and *Bride's* exhorted readers not to test-drive but rather to "try on" a Cavalier, appealing to the fashion consciousness of women aged 18 to 35. The Conde Nast database selected 30,000 subscribers as targets for invitations to events at Macy's highlighting the Cavalier. The coup came when Campbell-Ewald and Conde Nast convinced New York City officials to allow a Cavalier to remain parked in a no parking zone in front of Macy's for a week, garnering an estimated 15,000 impressions per hour. A security guard patrolled the car to ensure against vandalism, and according to Chevrolet brand advertising manager Bridget McCarvillean in an *Adweek* profile of Campbell-Ewald by Lisa Granatstein, he "turned out to be a good product ambassador."

MARKETING STRATEGY

Davis quoted 21-year-old Julia Gulia as saying, "I want something more present, very updated, because that describes me," as she was picking up her new Civic from a Honda dealership outside Chicago. Rubin Postaer recognized the fact that many prospective Civic buyers focused on the present in its many definitions. Gulia used the term to refer to the reputation of the Civic among her contemporaries as a popular car. Honda sought to support this notion of the Civic as a hip car with the irreverent tone of the "What about Now?" campaign, since irreverence was one of the defining features of youth culture in the late 1990s. Simultaneously, the "What about Now?" campaign stressed the importance of focusing on the here and now. "Carpe diem," or "seize the day," could have served as a motto for this younger generation. The tag line underscored the preoccupation with present gratification by stressing "now" as its focal point.

OUTCOME

According to statistics compiled by J. D. Powers & Associates, the Honda Civic continued to lead the subcompact category in sales in 1998. Rubin Postaer also reported that intentions to purchase the Civic were on an upward trend after the 1998 "What about Now?" campaign and that dealers were registering increasing demand for the Civic. What was more, Honda achieved this success through very efficient advertising, which cost only a little more than half as much as the advertising of its competitors. In 1997 Honda budgeted $43 million in media expenditures, while Ford and Chevrolet each spent $77 million on the second-place Escort and the fourth-place Cavalier, respectively. Saturn devoted an astronomical $185 million to media expenditures, more than four times as much as Honda.

Honda expressed its satisfaction and confidence in Rubin Postaer by awarding the agency the advertising account of its upscale Acura division. As it had done in 1986, when it awarded its main ad account to Rubin Postaer without a review, Honda forwent a review in transferring the Acura account from Suissa Miller of Los Angeles to Rubin Postaer. The victory was particularly satisfying for Rubin Postaer in light of its having lost the bid for the account in 1996, when it landed at Suissa Miller. In awarding the Acura account, Honda acknowledged that Rubin Postaer understood best how to position Honda's many models in various markets and to different target audiences.

FURTHER READING

Davis, Joyzelle. "Automakers Tune In to 'Phat' Vibrations: Reinventing Themselves in Bid to Win Loyalty of Generation Y." *Montreal Gazette,* July 17, 1999.

Gellene, Denise. "Honda Seeks to Clear the Air over Ads." *Los Angeles Times,* June 18, 1998, p. D6.

Johnson, Greg. "Agency Followed 'Simple' Equation for Honda Success." *Los Angeles Times,* July 29, 1999.

"The Trouble with Excellence." *Economist,* July 4, 1998.

William D. Baue

American Legacy Foundation

2030 M Street, NW, 6th Fl.
Washington, DC 20036
USA
Telephone: (202) 454-5555
Fax: (202) 454-5599
E-mail: info@americanlegacy.org
Web site: www.americanlegacy.org

■■■

TRUTH CAMPAIGN

OVERVIEW

In 1998, 46 state attorneys general reached a settlement with tobacco companies, which included an agreement to fund a five-year, $1.5 billion, national teen antismoking campaign under the auspices of a new nonprofit corporation, the Washington, D.C.–based American Legacy Foundation. The state of Florida also used some of the money it received from the settlement to launch a local teen antismoking campaign called "Truth." It was so successful that the foundation took it national in 2000.

"Truth," created by Miami-based advertising agency Crispin Porter + Bogusky and Boston-based Arnold Worldwide, was a multifaceted campaign heavily influenced by the input provided by annual youth summits and a youth review board, which provided feedback and suggestions. Rather than taking a "just say no" approach that would likely prove counterproductive, the marketers tried to channel youths' natural rebelliousness by directing it against the practices of the tobacco companies. The television commercials were confrontational and controversial, as well as a call to action. One spot, for example, showed teens delivering hundreds of stuffed body bags to the New York headquarters of Philip Morris, representing the deaths they said the company was responsible for. The campaign also marketed "Truth" like any other youth product, advertising in the type of magazines teens read, as well as touring the country in vans, showing up at beaches, skate parks, and other hangouts to give away free gear and "Infect Truth" viral kits so that youths could engage in their own guerrilla marketing efforts.

The "Truth" campaign was a highly successful campaign, playing a major role in a significant decrease in teen smoking. Although the loss of funding from tobacco companies after five years resulted in budget cuts, the campaign was able to carry on. "Truth" was also recognized by the advertising industry, which presented the campaign with a number of celebrated awards.

HISTORICAL CONTEXT

Although people speculated about the health risks of using tobacco, it wasn't until the twentieth century that the issue was addressed scientifically. As early as 1930 German researchers drew a statistical correlation between smoking and cancer. Despite warning about the dangers of smoking, the American Cancer Society circa World War II still relied on the disclaimer that "no definite evidence exists" to tie smoking with lung cancer. A turning point in the public debate about smoking came in 1952 when *Reader's Digest* published "Cancer by the Carton," an article that brought the dangers of smoking to a mass audience and led to other periodicals addressing the subject, as well as a decline in cigarette sales for the first time in a generation. The tobacco industry responded by forming the Tobacco Industry Research Council, little more than a public relations ploy, and also began producing "healthier" cigarettes with better filters and low-tar formulations. Sales rebounded. Then in 1964, at a time when nearly half of adult Americans smoked, U.S. Surgeon General Luther Terry issued a report, *Smoking and Health,* which concluded that cigarette smoking was causally related to lung cancer in men, and the data for women pointed "in the same direction."

From the time of Luther's report, the tobacco industry came under siege. A year later Congress passed the Federal Cigarette Labeling and Advertising Act, requiring that every cigarette package carry the surgeon general's warning. Cigarette consumption dropped as did the number of smokers, but the industry brought out a new generation of healthier cigarettes, which forced people to smoke more to receive their daily nicotine fix and as a result led to even greater sales. In the late 1960s the first national antitobacco ad campaign was launched and proved so effective that the tobacco industry was forced to take notice. Because antismoking advocates were gaining equal time from broadcasters, the companies in 1971 elected to pull all radio and television ads as a way to prevent a deluge of antismoking public service messages.

Tobacco companies continued to fight a rear-guard action against the scientific evidence that linked smoking to cancer as well as heart disease and emphysema. While enjoying some success in the political arena, where it could count on the support of senators and congressmen from tobacco-growing states, the tobacco industry was unable to fend off the assaults in the courts from state attorneys general. In 1998 the industry agreed to a settlement worth almost $250 billion with state attorneys general—this after the U.S. Senate had killed a comprehensive tobacco bill and undercut the leverage of the attorneys general.

As part of the $206 billion 1998 master settlement agreement, the tobacco companies agreed to fund a new nonprofit corporation, the Washington, D.C.–based American Legacy Foundation, in a five-year, $1.5 billion, national teen antismoking campaign. To receive the money, however, the foundation had to agree not to vilify the industry, a condition that would soon become controversial. Florida, drawing on its $11.3 billion portion of the settlement, provided $200 million to the Florida Department of Health, to become one of the first states to establish its own teen antismoking campaign. Miami-based advertising agency Crispin Porter + Bogusky landed the account and launched the "Truth" campaign, which was heavily influenced by teen input. It proved so effective that in 2000 the American Legacy Foundation decided to take "Truth" national.

TARGET MARKET

The "Truth" campaign targeted youths between the ages of 12 and 17, television's "golden demographic." It was also a pivotal time of life when people are especially susceptible to the allures of smoking. While adult smoking declined at a steady rate after the 1970s, teen smoking increased just as steadily. According to a federally funded study in 1991, more than 25 percent of high school students nationwide were smokers. By 1997 that number reached 36.4 percent. As Florida prepared to launch the original "Truth" campaign, it determined that 27.4 percent of its high school students had used tobacco in the past 30 days. Among middle school students that percentage was 18.5 percent. Marketing to this demographic was tricky, however. As Alex Bogusky of Crispin Porter + Bogusky explained to Alison Sloane Gaylin of *Shoot,* "You didn't have to do too much research to find out that typical PSAs [public service announcements], with the 'say no' approach, would actually increase the prevalence of tobacco usage among teen because it makes [smoking] more alluring. Tobacco use is tied into rebellion. It would just make it more of a rebellious act." As a result the marketers relied on teens themselves to help drive the direction of the "Truth" campaign.

COMPETITION

Although individual states and such organizations as the American Lung Association also ran teen antismoking campaigns, they were pursuing the same goal and hardly in competition with the American Legacy Foundation. Rather, all of them faced common adversaries: the tobacco companies and the media that often glamorized smoking. Big tobacco may have been barred from radio and television, but it still spent more than $5 billion each year on advertising. It also spent money on its own teen antismoking efforts. Philip Morris USA, for example, funded its own campaign at the same time the "Truth" campaign was going national. Called "Think. Don't Smoke," the $100-million-per-year effort took a more traditional approach than the confrontational "Truth" campaign. The Philip Morris ads preached to its audience, which as Bogusky had noted was more likely to make teens interested in smoking. Moreover the ads were somewhat self-congratulatory. Lyndon Haviland, chief operating officer of the American Legacy Foundation, told Lynn Porter, writing for the *Tampa Tribune,* that the "Think. Don't Smoke" campaign "makes teens more likely to feel good about Philip Morris and more likely to feel good about the tobacco industry in general." The

THE MARLBORO LADY

Marlboro, the best-selling cigarette in the world since 1972, was introduced by Philip Morris in the early 1900s as one of the first cigarettes aimed at women. It featured a red tip to hide lipstick marks but failed to catch on. It was reintroduced in 1924, still targeting women, with the slogan "Mild as May." Thirty years later Chicago ad agency Leo Burnett took over the brand, which at the time had less than 1 percent of the market. The new campaign featured Marlboro Men, which over the next decade included athletes and sailors in addition to cowboys. In 1963 Marlboro began using cowboys exclusively and a year later launched the "Marlboro Country" campaign: "Come to where the flavor is. Come to Marlboro Country." Sales began to grow at a 10 percent clip each year until Marlboro eclipsed Winston as America's top-selling brand and soon conquered the world. Dozens of men would portray the Marlboro Man in television and print ads over the decades. Two of them, Wayne McLaren and David McLean, died of lung cancer.

"Truth" campaign, on the other hand, gained much of its power by casting tobacco companies as the villains.

MARKETING STRATEGY

Crispin Porter + Bogusky had never been involved in social marketing before, so it was not surprising that the agency, as it prepared to make its pitch to Florida officials to win the account, would draw on its experience in youth marketing—to sell the product of "not smoking" in the same way it did for other clients at the time (a basketball shoe company, a fast-food restaurant, and a bicycle company). First it conducted research where members of the target market felt comfortable and likely to be uninhibited in giving their answers, such as skate parks and shopping malls. The agency also analyzed successful new product launches to the teen market by Sega, Nintendo, Mountain Dew, and youth fashion brands like Vans, Skechers, and JNCO. As a result the marketing plan would go far beyond television spots to include promotional tours and a magazine that was to be distributed in record stores and surf shops. Most importantly the agency decided to channel teens' natural rebelliousness against tobacco companies. Research indicated that a large number of teens thought that farmers made cigarettes; the campaign would seek to disabuse them of that notion, teach them how tobacco companies operated, and transform them into an army of teens demanding straight answers from big tobacco. The campaign pitched by Crispin Porter + Bogusky to Florida was initially called "Rage." The agency won the account, changed the campaign's title to "Truth," and convened a summit of 500 young people and a youth review board to provide feedback and guide the creative process. Over the course of two years the Florida program succeeded in cutting middle school cigarette consumption in half and lowering high school consumption by a fifth.

The American Legacy Foundation decided to expand the "Truth" campaign to go national in 2000. Crispin Porter + Bogusky teamed up with Boston-based Arnold Worldwide and public relations firms to form an alliance to handle the $185 million account. The first two television spots were quick to create controversy. In one a woman, in the style of confrontational filmmaker Michael Moore, entered Philip Morris's New York headquarters in an attempt to deliver a lie detector and get at the truth about nicotine addiction. The other spot featured teenagers unloading body bags outside of Philip Morris's headquarters. The company complained that the ads defied the vilification provision of the 1998 settlement agreement. Threatened with losing its funding, the foundation withdrew the ads. Four other spots portrayed common consumer products, such as soda or athletic footwear, as if they were as dangerous as tobacco. Each relied on the same voice-over, saying, "There is only one product that actually kills a third of the people who use it. Tobacco." The television networks initially refused to run the spots but soon gave in. Later in 2000 the "Truth" campaign revisited the use of body bags in a series of five new commercials developed to break during the Olympics. One of them spoofed the Marlboro Man by strapping a body bag onto a horse, which then rode off into the sunset as a teen yelled, "Go be a cowboy." Another showed youths tossing body bags out of an airplane while shouting, "Hey, tobacco! Advertise this!... Taste the adventure."

Building on the success of the first year, the marketers added an important element to the campaign in 2001, launching the Outbreak Tour, a counterpoint to how tobacco companies promoted their products. In 2000 the campaign had used an RV to tour 27 markets in six weeks to present the "Truth" message. The Outbreak Tour used 10 orange vans and three Lincoln Navigators rigged with deejay turntables, video monitors, Sega video games, Internet access, and lounge chairs. More importantly, perhaps, they were staffed with "ambassadors," including a variety of rappers, ravers, graffiti artists, skateboarders, musicians, fashion designers, and ex-smokers who could effectively carry the no-smoking message to the target audience. Over the summer the tour hit 158 cities, visiting beaches, skate parks, concerts, and anywhere else young people might congregate. The tour also attracted its own audience by staging concerts and martial-arts demonstrations and hosting graffiti-art galleries. The ambassadors handed out T-shirts, bandannas, hats, and "Infect Truth" viral kits containing stickers and stencils so teens could engage in their own guerrilla marketing efforts. In addition to the Outbreak Tour, grassroots marketing was encouraged by print ads with removable "Truth" stencils that appeared in summer editions of such magazines as *Mass Appeal, Snowboarder, Vibe,* and *Teen People.*

OUTCOME

"Truth" received immediate acclaim and was named Best Campaign of 2000 by *Adweek.* The magazine noted, "Approaching 'truth' as a brand like Marlboro or Camel, the umbrella campaign is a guerrilla-style war that attacks on multiple, psychological levels and, literally, takes its message to the streets." Some of the television spots, such as when teens piled stuffed body bags around the Philip Morris headquarters, crossed over from TV spot to live protest, providing a dynamic, energizing element to "Truth."

The "Truth" campaign received its last payment from the tobacco settlement in 2003, forcing the American Legacy Foundation to slash its budget from $160 million a year to $40 million a year. Regardless, "Truth" was a success on every level. The most important measure was the rate of teenage smoking. According to research published in the *American Journal of Public Health* in 2005, between 2000 and 2002 the number of young people between the ages of 12 and 17 who smoked decreased from 28.8 percent to 18 percent. An estimated 300,000 fewer teens took up smoking during that period. Tobacco companies also contributed to the decline by raising their prices to offset settlement costs. Without doubt the price of cigarettes was a major influencing factor on whether young people smoked or not, but the impact of the "Truth" campaign was not to be discounted. It was also recognized by the advertising industry. In addition to being named *Adweek* 's Best Campaign of 2000, "Truth" won best of show at the annual awards given to New England ad agencies, sponsored by the Boston Idea Group. In 2005 "Truth" tied for the highest honor, the Grand EFFIE, at the prestigious annual EFFIE Awards, administered by the New York chapter of the American Marketing Association.

FURTHER READING

Andrews, Helena. "Teen Smoking Declines, Truth Campaign Credited." *Capital Times* (Madison, Wisconsin), February 26, 2005, p. 2C.

Beirne, Mike. "Butt-Kicking Big Tobacco." *Brandweek,* November 12, 2001, p. 28.

———. "Gold Winner: Smoking Ain't Glam, Dude." *Brandweek,* March 18, 2002, p. R18.

"Best Campaign of the Year 2000: American Legacy Foundation." *Adweek,* February 5, 2001.

Boccella, Kathy. "Surveys Show High School Smoking Is on the Decline." *Philadelphia Inquirer,* January 15, 2002.

Gaylin, Alison Sloane. "Getting at the Truth." *Shoot,* November 23, 2001, p. 19.

Hicks, Jennifer. "The Strategy behind Florida's 'Truth' Campaign." *Tobacco Control,* March 2001.

Ives, Nat. "2 Agencies in a Tie for the Grand Effie." *New York Times,* June 5, 2003, p. C8.

McGregor, Paloma. "Teens Spread Truth about Smoking Risks." *Plain Dealer,* July 22, 2000, p. 1E.

Porter, Lynn. "The 'Truth' Gets Results." *Tampa Tribune,* July 21, 2002, p. 1.

Reidy, Chris. "Boston-Based Agency's Controversial Antismoking TV Ads to Run during Olympics." *Boston Globe,* September 19, 2000.

Teinowitz, Ira. "Foundation Yanks Two Controversial Anti-Smoking Ads." *Advertising Age,* February 21, 2000, p. 63.

Ed Dinger

Americans for the Arts

1000 Vermont Ave. NW, 12th Fl.
Washington, DC 20005
USA
Telephone: (202) 371-2830
Fax: (202) 371-0424
Web site: www.americansforthearts.org

ART. ASK FOR MORE CAMPAIGN

OVERVIEW

In 2002 the nonprofit arts-advocacy group Americans for the Arts (AFA) teamed up with the Advertising Council, the producer of a myriad of public-service advertising campaigns, to present the "Art. Ask for More" campaign. The organizers believed that the arts were a valuable component in the education of children and were concerned that, in an age of budget cuts, it was receiving short shrift. In order to make the case for increased funding for arts education in public schools, the campaign targeted parents and community leaders.

Texas-based ad agency GSD&M created the campaign, which was funded by a $1 million grant and was the recipient of approximately $30 million in donated media each year. It consisted of television and radio spots, print ads, outdoor advertisements, and Internet elements. Many of the advertisements highlighted Americans' lack of arts knowledge, claiming, for instance, that trumpet player Louis Armstrong was often confused with astronaut Neil Armstrong, the first man to walk on the moon. They also humorously illustrated the effects of too little art in a child's development. One television spot showed a child boring everyone at the dinner table by reciting a typical day at school, minus art; another depicted a child whose idea of a fun bedtime story was a volume of arcane zoning regulations.

The "Art. Ask for More" campaign, according to organizers, succeeded in raising awareness about the importance of the arts in education. It was also successful in attracting a great deal of free national media as well as participation from local arts groups. In 2003 the print campaign won three ATHENA Awards, which were given out annually to honor newspaper ads.

HISTORICAL CONTEXT

Americans for the Arts (AFA) was formed in 1996 through the merger of the National Assembly of Local Arts Agencies and the American Council for the Arts. Their combined resources allowed AFA to better advocate for greater emphasis on arts education in the United States. The state of public education in America in the final decades of the twentieth century had come under question, as it appeared that U.S. students were falling further behind their foreign counterparts in a number of areas. Because so many jobs of the future were related to information and technology, most of the remedies for fixing school systems called for a greater emphasis on reading, math, and science. Many schools had never offered much in terms of arts education, but now, because of budget cuts, schools had to make difficult choices about how to allocate funds, and in many cases art programs were slashed or eliminated altogether.

AFA and other arts advocates argued that the elimination of art programs—including the visual arts, music, dance, and drama—in public schools was shortsighted. Their position, backed by various studies, was that arts education played a vital role in the development of children and that building cultural awareness was just as important as improving math skills and an understanding of science. AFA argued that art education was important to early childhood development and was especially valuable in shaping brain and motor coordination. As children grew older, involvement in the arts helped increase self-esteem, improved problem-solving skills, instilled a sense of discipline, and promoted the concept of teamwork. A quality arts education often led to a strong overall academic performance, as reflected in College Board research that indicted that students who studied the arts for four years scored 89 points higher on the Scholastic Aptitude Test. Moreover, AFA contended that after-school arts programs were an effective way to reduce the problem of delinquency and truancy in youth.

To make its case for the arts to the general public, AFA received a $1 million grant from the Doris Duke Charitable Foundation. It then enlisted the services of Texas advertising agency GSD&M and the Ad Council to develop an ad campaign. "Art. Ask for More" was released in February 2001. Nearly 300 smaller arts organizations agreed to promote the campaign on the local level, although many more ultimately participated.

TARGET MARKET

According to research cited by AFA, 9 out of 10 parents agreed that it was important to teach art in the schools. What they failed to understand, AFA asserted, was that a cursory exposure to the arts was not sufficient and that schools needed to do more than simply fend off further budget cuts; they also needed to add more to their arts programs. Because only 7 percent of funding for public education came from the federal government, the focus of the "Art. Ask for More" campaign was on civic leaders and on parents with children in public schools. AFA wanted to impress upon this audience the value of an arts education and to urge them to put pressure on their local school boards, where a great deal of budgetary decisions were increasingly being made. In addition AFA sought to encourage parents to expose their children to the arts outside of the school by, for example, making sure that the home included an abundance of pictures and books, taking advantage of local cultural resources, enrolling in art classes as a family, encouraging children to draw at home, singing songs together, and making up stories. The campaign was also intended to encourage people with an artistic skill to share it by serving as a volunteer to help teach children.

FOCUS ON CHILDREN

The Advertising Council, the nonprofit organization responsible for distributing the "Art. Ask for More" campaign, had a long history of involvement with public-service announcements before working with Americans for the Arts, the campaign's sponsor. Over the years the Ad Council was involved in a wide range of issues, including the selling of war bonds in World War II, fighting drunk driving, and preventing forest fires. In 1995 the Ad Council decided to focus much of its resources on a single topic: children. It launched "Commitment 2000: Raising a Better Tomorrow," a 10-year effort to pursue a range of issues relating to children, including violence, education, and health care. Some of the ongoing campaigns, such as drunk driving, were recast to include children. The "Art. Ask for More" campaign was part of this new targeted strategy.

COMPETITION

While it was hard to argue that art education did not have its place in public schools, AFA was not without its share of critics, who questioned the underlying assumption of the "Art. Ask for More" campaign. Writing for *Arts Education Policy Review,* Constance Bumgarner Gee noted that AFA "does not mention what type of art is important for kids to 'get' or what desirable knowledge or experience is to be had by getting more art." Regarding the campaign's goal of generating press coverage about art education, Gee commented that "no explanation is offered of the value or purpose of getting more art for kids other than to 'gain local media attention for your organization.'"

In addition, AFA's attempt to make art programs a panacea for all manners of societal ills was also debatable. Of course, after-school programs helped to reduce problems among at-risk youths. That was a lesson learned a century prior, when Boys Clubs were established to provide an after-school alternative for disadvantaged urban youths. There the emphasis was on sports, but the clubs also offered reading rooms and art activities. It could be argued that after-school art programs were not necessarily more effective than, say, a boxing program such as the Gold Gloves, which over the decades had developed a proven track record in curbing youth problems in the inner city. Boxing could also make the claim that it instilled discipline and a sense of accomplishment.

According to Karen Libman, also writing for *Arts Education Policy Review,* arts advocates "have often garnered support for the arts through any means necessary, even unsupported advocacy claims. It is time to own up to this.... Advocacy cannot mean that we portray ourselves as all things to all people ... while art can do many things, it cannot do everything. If we promise that, or try to prove it, we will certainly fail."

Aside from questions about its premise, "Art. Ask for More" had to compete for attention with something that also assumed the mantle of art: entertainment. A study conducted by the Columbia School of Journalism revealed that coverage of the arts had in recent years been replaced by entertainment news, much of which was dominated by celebrity gossip. In fact, the largest category of arts coverage was obituaries of artists and entertainers. The blurred distinction between entertainment and art was yet another challenge facing the campaign.

MARKETING STRATEGY

"Art. Ask for More" was released in January 2002 and included television and radio spots, print ads, outdoor advertisements, and Web banners. The strategy of the advertising was to demonstrate, often in a humorous way, the effects of having too little art education. The first television spot, for example, featured a young boy who encountered a street musician playing a violin and told him, "Get a job!" Next the boy was shown at a party; when a clown made a giraffe out of balloons, the boy commented, "I don't see it."

Later TV spots showed other children affected by the lack of art in their lives. In the spot called "Dinner" a young boy was asked about his day at school. His parents were dismayed by the monotony of his routine: "I went to lunch and then I ate it, and then lunch was over ..." A voice-over by actor Alec Baldwin interrupted the boy's narrative, commenting, "The less art a kid gets, the more it shows. Are yours getting enough? Art. Ask for more." In another spot, "Girl," a young girl riding in a car with her mother changed radio stations, switching from music to financial news. Then before going to bed she asked her father to read from a thick volume titled "Zoning and Variances." Other television spots relied on celebrities such as rapper Chuck D, who stressed the role that art played in a child's development.

The campaign's radio spots took a man-in-the-street approach, as an interviewer recorded people's misidentification of famous artists. Thus, the ballet dancer Rudolph Nureyev was confused with a hockey player, jazz musician Louis Armstrong was mistaken for the first man to walk on the moon, and modern-dance pioneer Martha Graham was credited with the invention of the graham cracker. The print ads also played with the same idea using the same artists. In one ad a picture of Louis Armstrong playing his horn was accompanied by a headline that read: "No wonder people think Louis Armstrong was the first man to walk on the moon." The text of the ad offered a brief biography of Armstrong, who learned to play the trumpet at a reformatory for boys, and then commented, "the arts are dismissed as extravagant in today's schools," before making the case that the arts made better students. Other print ads focused on the sixteenth-century painter Caravaggio and the composer Peter Ilyich Tchaikovsky.

Another major facet of the "Art. Ask for More" campaign was local participation. Area arts groups contacted local media to draw attention to the resources of the campaign's website. An example of local initiatives was the commissioning of a bus in Chicago to showcase the artwork of area students by allowing them to decorate the outside of the bus, essentially turning it into a rolling mural. The idea was also taken up in Hampton Roads, Virginia. On the backs of the buses the national "Art. Ask for More" campaign was promoted.

OUTCOME

"Art. Ask for More" became a long-term campaign for AFA and the Ad Council. After two years the organizers announced that they were pleased with the results. Polling indicated a strong increase in support for arts education in U.S. schools. The campaign had also received a great deal of media support, in two years garnering $110 million in national media donations for television and radio airtime and print space. It also received time from major broadcast TV, cable, and radio networks in America's top 100 media markets as well as placement in such publications as the *New York Times, USA Today, Parade,* and *Time.* In addition, the campaign was bolstered by the support of 367 local partners across the country. In June 2005 AFA began to modify the focus of the campaign. Having made its point about the need for arts education, it began attempting to educate people about how they could effectively serve as advocates for the arts in their own communities.

The "Art. Ask for More" campaign was also well received by the advertising industry. In 2003 GSD&M was honored by the Newspaper Association of America in its annual ATHENA Awards, which recognized excellence in newspaper advertising. The agency won a gold award for the campaign as well as a gold award and silver awards for individual print ads.

FURTHER READING

"Ads Suggest the Pitfalls of Losing Art Education." *New York Times,* January 26, 2002, p. B12.

"Alec Baldwin Stars in Arts Ad Campaign." *Long Island Business News,* February 8, 2002, p. 13A.

Burck, Jodi. "Teach Aims to Ignite Art 'Spark' for All." *Grand Rapids (MI) Press,* April 8, 2002, p. D1.

Charski, Mindy. "Print Honors Go to Richards, DDB, GSD&M." *Adweek* (southwest ed.), September 25, 2003.

Gee, Constance Bumgarner. "Spirit, Mind, and Body: Arts Education the Redeemer." *Arts Education Policy Review,* March–April 2004, p. 9.

Houston, Allen. "Nonprofit Group Presents Arts to American Children." *PR Week,* February 11, 2002, p. 7.

Libman, Karen. "Some Thoughts on Arts Advocacy: Separating the Hype from the Reality." *Arts Education Policy Review,* January–February 2004, p. 31.

Messina, Debbie. "City Buses Showcase Artwork of Students to Promote Courses." *Norfolk (VA) Virginian-Pilot,* March 22, 2002, p. B4.

"Mining Arts' Value in Austin." *Back Stage,* June 16, 2005.

Riley, Kevin W. "Art: A Recreation Thing." *Parks & Recreation,* July 2002, p 22.

Ed Dinger

Anheuser-Busch Companies, Inc.

1 Busch Place
St. Louis, Missouri 63118
USA
Telephone: (314) 577-2000
Fax: (314) 577-2000
Web site: www.anheuser-busch.com

BEER... OR MICHELOB? CAMPAIGN

OVERVIEW

In 1998 Anheuser-Busch Companies, the Saint Louis, Missouri–based brewery best known for its premium Budweiser and Bud Light beers, greatly increased the advertising budget of its Michelob line of superpremium beers. After spending just over $17 million in 1996 and even less in 1997 on promoting Michelob, Anheuser-Busch devoted an estimated $30 million to the brand in 1998, primarily for a television-based campaign created by Leap Partnership of Chicago. Using the tagline "Beer... or Michelob?" the campaign sought to differentiate Michelob from a confusing plethora of superpremium, specialty, and microbrewery brands flooding the U.S. market. It placed particular emphasis on publicizing Michelob Light, which was widely seen as having more potential for sales growth than its full-calorie Michelob siblings.

The humor-based television spots broke during CBS's broadcast of the Winter Olympics from Nagano, Japan, in February 1998 and continued with little conceptual modification through 2001. One characteristic spot featured an actor unwilling to order a beer in a scene that called for him to do so; instead, he insisted on ordering a Michelob. Other prominent spots in the campaign focused on a negligent grocery-store employee whose bagging technique changed radically for the better when a customer purchased Michelob Light. The campaign began to focus more on Michelob Light, and the tagline was adjusted to "Beer... or Michelob Light?" Print gradually became a more prominent element of the increasingly robust campaign; by 2001 Anheuser-Busch had boosted its budget for the Michelob brand family's marketing to an estimated $50 million.

Michelob Light sales grew each year that "Beer... or Michelob?" ran. Although it was true that the brand had been growing since 1993, increases in sales growth closely mirrored increases in Michelob's advertising budget.

HISTORICAL CONTEXT

In 1852 George Schneider founded the Bavarian Brewery in St. Louis, but in 1860 he sold it to Eberhard Anheuser. The latter hired his son-in-law, Adolphus Busch, in 1864, and in 1872 they first used the "A and Eagle" trademark that would evolve into the logo of Anheuser-Busch. The U.S. centennial year of 1876 saw the introduction of Budweiser, a brand created to resemble beers from Bohemia in Central Europe. Twenty years later, in 1896, the company introduced Michelob as "a draft beer for connoisseurs."

The company took the name Anheuser-Busch in 1919, the same year the Eighteenth Amendment outlawed the production and sale of alcoholic beverages in the United States. For the next 14 years, as America underwent Prohibition, the company turned to a variety of enterprises such as bottling soft drinks and selling yeast. It even produced a nonalcoholic version of Budweiser. But when Prohibition was repealed in 1933, August Busch, son of Adolphus, personally delivered a case of Budweiser to President Franklin D. Roosevelt in a carriage pulled by a team of Clydesdale horses. The latter would become the Anheuser-Busch symbol, and their use would be closely tied to the Budweiser brand in coming years.

By 1957 Budweiser had become the nation's most popular brand of beer, a position it still held more than 40 years later. Anheuser-Busch diversified its holdings into a number of nonbeverage enterprises and expanded internationally during the 1970s and 1980s. In 1981, responding to the growing market for light beers, it introduced the first extension in what would become the Michelob family of beers: Michelob Light. The latter became America's first brand of superpremium light beer. Three years later, in 1984, the brand added Michelob Classic Dark, which it billed as "the ultimate in dark beers." Finally, as part of yet another industry-wide trend, in 1988 Michelob presented Michelob Ice, for which it also claimed status as the nation's first superpremium dry beer.

TARGET MARKET

Michelob's 1998 advertising placed an emphasis on Michelob Light, part of a larger light-beer category that had grown by 3 percent in the preceding year. By contrast, Anheuser-Busch's Budweiser Light—better known as Bud Light—had seen its revenues grow by more than 16 percent in the same period. And because Michelob Light had performed better than any brand in the Michelob family during the preceding year, accounting for 50 percent of Michelob revenues, Anheuser-Busch elected to divert much of its Michelob budget toward the light brand.

"Beer drinkers may be couch potatoes," a supermarket category manager told *Chain Drug Review* in March 1998, "but if they can't rouse themselves to shed their fat with exercise, at least they want to slow the weight gains. If they drink a light beer with their baked chips, they can tell themselves they're not neglecting their health." This somewhat derogatory assessment carried more than a grain of truth: light beers appealed to a category of buyer that on the surface might seem like a contradiction in terms—beer drinkers concerned about health and fitness. But of course at heart there was nothing truly contradictory about the desire to enjoy a premium beer on the one hand and the desire not to gain excess pounds on the other. Thus a large portion of the nation's top-selling brands were light beers. Furthermore, the association of beer and sports, symbolized by Michelob's launch of its campaign with the Winter Olympics in February 1998, was an old one.

What was new, however, was Michelob's thrust: along with a drastic increase in spending for the brand's advertising, spots drew attention to Michelob's traditional image in a way that many Michelob ads in recent years had not. "In 1896," Michelob brands vice president David English told *Chain Drug Review,* "Adolphus Busch created Michelob as a beer for connoisseurs—a step above the ordinary. That image has been blurred by the proliferation of micros [beers marketed by microbreweries], specialties, and imports in today's market. Our new campaign returns to Michelob's 102-year heritage as the worldwide symbol of brewing excellence."

COMPETITION

Anheuser-Busch and Michelob were not the only ones profiting from the steadily increasing interest in light beers. Miller Brewing Company's Miller Lite, as well as Coors Light, a product of the Adolph Coors Company, had also shown noticeable increases during 1997. But data presented in *Prepared Foods* in March 1998 showed that Anheuser-Busch held a formidable share of the top brands.

First, of course, was Budweiser, followed by Bud Light. Fifth and sixth places belonged to Busch and Natural Light, and Busch Light was in ninth place, bringing Anheuser-Busch's holdings to a total of 5 out of 10 slots on the top-10 list. Miller held three spots with Miller Lite, Miller Genuine Draft, and Miller High Life. The other two spots belonged to Coors Light and Milwaukee's Best. Michelob Light stood in 13th place, followed by Michelob.

As a superpremium beer, Michelob was hardly likely to make the top-10 list, which in fact included no superpremium brands. Among its prominent competitors were Heineken from Holland and Lowenbrau and Beck's from Germany. Closer to home was Samuel Adams, which used marketing tied to American heritage themes in order to establish a link between itself and the Founding Father whose name it had adopted as its own. In 1997 Anheuser-Busch ran an ad in the Boston area, drawing attention to the fact that, whereas Samuel Adams used images of Revolutionary War–era Boston in its advertising, it was Michelob that actually had a bottling plant in that city.

Michelob also competed with a number of other superpremium brands as well as specialty beers and microbrews. The latter were extremely small operations that typically sold their products only in local markets.

A 'KINDER, GENTLER' OLYMPICS

"I think you'll find a lot of kinder, gentler advertising in the Winter Olympics," *Advertising Age* sports-marketing writer Jeff Jensen told Keith J. Kelly of the *New York Daily News.* The phrase "kinder, gentler," of course, was borrowed from Vice President George Bush's successful 1988 campaign for the White House, but Jensen was referring to the 1998 Nagano Winter Olympics' emphasis on advertising geared toward women. With events that tended to be more popular among female viewers than male, the Winter Games typically drew a much larger ratio of women viewers than did the Summer Olympics. Hence advertising tended to be more specifically geared toward women.

A Michelob Light spot, part of Anheuser-Busch's "Beer... or Michelob?" campaign, was to be directed toward the female demographic group, as was a Ford Taurus commercial showing a female doctor driving a Taurus to a hospital to deliver a baby. Ford spokesman Joe Koenig said, "In years past, that might have been a man driving the car." Nike ran spots that included poetry written by female high school athletes, and other Nike commercials featured female athletes such as skier Picabo Street and hockey player Cammi Granato.

A John Hancock Mutual Life spot, while not geared specifically to female viewers, certainly carried a serious, thoughtful message. In fact, the commercial was not a pitch for John Hancock so much as a plea for viewers to donate to the Sarajevo Olympic Children's Fund. Visuals were made up of footage from the 1984 Winter Games, held in that city, which was then part of Yugoslavia. This was combined with scenes of war-torn Sarajevo, which, as the capital of independent Bosnia and Herzegovina since 1992, had been the site of bitter ethnic fighting. A voice-over by actress Sigourney Weaver stated, "The children of Sarajevo never forgot the Olympics. Please don't forget them."

MARKETING STRATEGY

In 1995 Michelob had ended a long relationship with the ad agency D'Arcy Macius Benton & Bowles and selected Glennon Company of St. Louis as its primary agency—though not necessarily its agency of record, since Anheuser-Busch had recently adopted a policy of working with several firms. Among Glennon's spots had been the "Gimme Guys," a May 1997 campaign tied to a golf-ball giveaway promotion.

Such advertising, based as it was in a raucous brand of humor more typical of Budweiser, was at odds with the strategy Michelob had employed in the 1980s, when its television spots had carried the tagline "Some things just speak for themselves." The latter campaign had stressed the image of quality associated with the brand; and for its 1998 advertising Michelob sought to use both quality and humor.

In the fall of 1997 Anheuser-Busch replaced Glennon with Leap Partnership as the lead agency on its Michelob account. It also announced, at the end of the year, a decision to raise its overall advertising budget 22 percent, or $70 million. As 1998 rolled around, Anheuser-Busch let it be known that it would invest a full $30 million on a brand-family campaign for Michelob. This represented a significant jump over previous years: in 1996 the parent company had devoted about $17 million to advertising for its superpremium beer, and during the first half of 1997 it spent only $3.7 million on Michelob. With "Beer... or Michelob?" the company presented what Anheuser-Busch vice president for brand management Bob Lachky called "situational spots" designed to emphasize the brand's quality image while using humor. Thus, James B. Arndorfer reported in *Advertising Age,* "The TV spots will be similar in spirit to those for Bud Light, but less wacky."

"Beer... or Michelob?" was launched with two commercials that first aired during the CBS broadcast of the 1998 Winter Olympics from Nagano, Japan, in February. One showed a movie actor in the middle of a scene in which his script called on him to ask for a beer; however, he could not seem to restrain himself from asking specifically for a Michelob Light—much to his director's consternation. Another spot, targeting female viewers, was entitled "Surprise." In it, a woman returned home from a shopping trip—during which she had bought a sexy item of lingerie—to find a note from her husband suggesting that she grab two Michelobs and meet him in the living room. Before doing so, however, she put on her new purchase, then tiptoed into the darkened and quiet living room. Suddenly, the lights came on, and she found herself surrounded by a crowd of family and friends shouting "Surprise!" Painfully embarrassed, she saw her parents among the group and said timidly, "Hi, Daddy." Outdoor, radio, and point-of-purchase advertisements supplemented the TV spots.

The campaign's creative strategy remained consistent throughout its three-year run, with later TV spots continuing to use situational humor reminiscent of other Anheuser-Busch brands' marketing. One well-known commercial that first ran in late 1999, for instance, showed a grocery-store bag boy handling a customer's purchases with exaggerated carelessness. After shoving a potted plant upside-down into a bag and ruining a loaf of French bread, the bag boy came to the customer's six-pack of Michelob Light and changed his behavior radically, packing the beer in bubble wrap, bagging it with care, and marking the bag "Fragile." The bag boy was used again in TV spots that aired in 2000, and the same concept was applied to commercials featuring a bartender.

The "Beer . . . or Michelob?" TV spots typically appeared during prime-time sports programming, and print ads in sports magazines became an increasingly prominent element of the campaign beginning in 1999. The campaign's emphasis on Michelob Light resulted in a gradual tagline modification to "Beer . . . or Michelob Light?" and Anheuser-Busch continued attempting to drum up interest in the brand among women, most notably through sponsorships of women's professional tennis and women's professional golf. There was also a 2000 print element that specifically targeted women. The campaign's budget consistently increased as Michelob Light experienced sales growth each year after it began. The previously unprecedented $30 million budget of the campaign's first year grew to an estimated $34 million in 1999. The next year the budget increased by an additional 20 percent, and in 2001, the campaign's final year, Anheuser-Busch spent an estimated $50 million on advertising for Michelob beers.

OUTCOME

In 1998 Michelob Light sales topped the 2.6 million barrel record that the brand had reached in 1996, up from a sales low of 2 million barrels in 1992. As *Advertising Age* noted, demographics, distributor interest, and economic factors also converged to aid the brand's resurgence, but the disparity between the brand's 1997 and 1998 sales levels corresponded clearly with the 1998 increase in the Michelob advertising budget. Indeed, sales of Michelob Light had grown every year since 1993, with the exception of 1997, when Anheuser-Busch spending on behalf of the brand was at its low ebb. Anheuser-Busch accordingly continued to ratchet spending higher in subsequent years, and sales of Michelob Light continued to grow.

In 2001 Anheuser-Busch asked the numerous advertising agencies on its roster, including Leap Partnership, to pitch new Michelob campaign ideas. The brewer eventually awarded the account to Goodby, Silverstein & Partners, the San Francisco agency that shared the primary advertising duties for Anheuser-Busch's Budweiser brand. The resulting 2002 Michelob Light campaign, "Nice Finish," marked a departure from the humor-based approach with which Leap Partnership had found success. That year also marked the introduction of Anheuser-Busch's enormously popular low-carb offering, Michelob Ultra, which overshadowed Michelob Light amid the growing consumer obsession with low-carbohydrate diets.

FURTHER READING

Arndorfer, James B.. "A-B Debuts $30 Mil Campaign for Michelob on Olympics: Brewer Concentrates on Light Brand in a Significant Switch in Ad Focus." *Advertising Age,* January 19, 1998, p. 4.

"Brewers Hop Back to Basics." *Prepared Foods,* March 1998, p. 108.

Chura, Hillary. "A-B Cranks Up Michelob Ads, Accents Light." *Advertising Age* (midwest ed.), July 17, 2000.

———. "Michelob Light Thrives as Ad Spending Rockets." *Advertising Age* (midwest ed.), November 22, 1999.

Desloge, Rick. "A-B Pouring $70 Million More into '98 Ad Budget." *St. Louis Business Journal,* December 15, 1997, p. A6.

———. "Glennon Pushed Off Michelob Job: Picked Up by Leap." *St. Louis Business Journal,* October 20, 1997, p. A8.

Kelly, Keith J.. "A Big Pitch for the Gold: Winter Games to Offer 'Kinder, Gentler' Spots." *New York Daily News,* February 9, 1998, p. 42.

Kirk, Jim. "Anheuser-Busch to Launch Frog-Free, Adult-Oriented Budweiser Ads." *Knight-Ridder Tribune Business News,* February 6, 1998.

"The Leap Partnership Named to Handle Anheuser-Busch's Michelob Advertising." *Business Wire,* September 24, 1997.

"Michelob to Tee Off." *Supermarket News,* May 5, 1997, p. 32.

Panczyk, Tania D., and Trevor Jensen. "Shops Get a Shot at Michelob." *Adweek* (eastern ed.), September 10, 2001.

Reidy, Chris. "The Pitch." *Boston Globe,* February 6, 1998, p. C4.

Sherwood, Sonja. "When It Comes to New Products, Experts Won't Throw Them a Line." *Beverage World,* November 30, 1998.

"Top Brewers Jockey for Sales." *Chain Drug Review,* March 2, 1998, p. 120.

"Twin Tracks of Heritage and Hilarity to Continue to Build Budweiser in '99." *Brandweek,* January 25, 1999, p. 12.

Judson Knight
Mark Lane

FROGS CAMPAIGN

OVERVIEW

Founded in St. Louis, Missouri, in 1860, Anheuser-Busch rose to become the largest brewing company in the world, largely because of the success of its flagship brand, Budweiser. But Budweiser's sales began to slow in the late 1980s. Indeed, the three largest beer makers in the United States—Anheuser-Busch, Miller Brewing Company, and Coors Brewing Company—realized with dismay that Americans were drinking less alcohol. Moreover, consumers aged 21 to 27—the key market for beer sales—were turning away from these three traditional breweries and were instead embracing the beers produced by smaller, often local microbreweries. In 1994 Anheuser-Busch responded to these challenges by firing its ad agency of 79 years, D'Arcy, Masius, Benton, & Bowles. Anheuser-Busch wanted to craft a new image for Budweiser that would appeal to younger consumers without alienating loyal Budweiser drinkers.

After hiring a new advertising agency, DDB Needham, Chicago, Anheuser-Busch launched its Budweiser "Frogs" campaign. The commercials featured animatronic (a form of animation) frogs who croaked out the brand's name one syllable at a time: "Bud" -"Weis" - "Er." The original frog spot debuted during the 1995 Super Bowl and showed the amphibians on lily pads. At first it sounded as if the frogs were making nonsensical noises, but eventually the three distinct syllables came together to form the brand's name. A neon Budweiser sign hung in the background. "Frogs II," the second commercial in the campaign, showed the frogs waiting by the side of a road as they croaked out the brand's name. As a Budweiser truck passed by, they latched onto the side with their tongues. "Frogs III," which was first aired on ABC's *Monday Night Football,* introduced a female frog. The commercial began with the male and female calling back and forth "Bud" and "Weis" respectively, as the male sought to hone in on the sultry female's location. The "Er" was provided in a sort of chuckle by the male as he finds the female. "Frogs IV" took the amphibians to a snowstorm, where they continued to call out "Bud" -"Weis" -"Er" undeterred by the cold that froze their tongues.

Although Anheuser-Busch took strong criticism during the "Frogs" campaign from groups such as Mothers Against Drunk Driving (MADD), who claimed the commercials were targeting children, the campaign was immensely popular. The commercials topped *USA Today*'s Ad Track, a poll that measured the popularity and effectiveness of ad campaigns. According to *Advertising Age,* the "Frogs" campaign resulted in a tripling of the younger target group's awareness of Budweiser. In 1997 Anheuser-Busch phased out the "Frogs" campaign by introducing two lizards to replace the frogs. The company did not want to overexpose the concept. "We expect our advertising to stay ahead of the curve," said August A. Busch IV, Anheuser-Busch's vice-president of marketing, in *Advertising Age.* During their run, the frogs had proved to be a great success for the company. They were able to effect a dramatic change in the way consumers, particularly the coveted young adult market, viewed Budweiser.

HISTORICAL CONTEXT

In 1860 a German immigrant named Eberhard Anheuser bought the Bavarian Brewery in St. Louis, Missouri. Four years later, his son-in-law, Adolphus Busch, began working there, and in 1876 the two introduced Budweiser Beer to the world. Renamed Anheuser-Busch in 1879, the company grew to become the largest brewer in the world. By 1986 Anheuser-Busch had brewed a billion barrels of beer.

Anheuser-Busch also had a long history of distinctive advertising. Pre-Prohibition ads sought to appeal to various ethnic groups and featured figures such as Otto Von Bismarck and the Scottish folk hero William Wallace. The famous Clydesdale horses, which became the company's symbol, were first used to sell Budweiser in 1933. At their first public appearance they delivered Budweiser to the White House. In the 1940s and 1950s brewers strove to gentrify their products; Anheuser-Busch used the slogan "Beer Belongs" in ads picturing middle-class families sipping beer from Pilsner glasses. By the 1970s, however, beer ads were omnipresent on televised sports programs, and brewers began to "celebrate the traditional values of the American male: sports, camaraderie, and hard work," according to the *Wall Street Journal.* In 1979 Anheuser-Busch's long-time ad agency, D'Arcy, Masius, Benton, & Bowles, conceived of the "This Bud's For You" campaign, which featured construction workers, lumberjacks, and laborers. These men were saluted "for being on the job and working hard all day long." The company stayed with this advertising theme throughout the 1980s, often running ads portraying manly Bud drinkers surrounded by women in various states of undress. By 1994 Budweiser maintained a market share of 21.9 percent of all beer sales, but sales growth was flattening and Anheuser-Busch realized that a new marketing approach was needed.

TARGET MARKET

As the nation's largest brewery, Anheuser-Busch was hit hard by some shifts in American drinking habits and demographics. The number of 21- to 27- year-olds, historically the group who drank the most beer, fell by about 3 million between 1990 and 1998, from 27.6 to 24.6 million. Not only did this group consume more beer than others but they also formed their beer brand loyalty during this period of their lives. For the most part, what they learned to drink during these years was what they continued to drink throughout their lives. These "entry-level drinkers" of the 1990s were media-savvy and, according to the *Sacramento Bee,* "both highly brand conscious and notoriously lacking in brand loyalty." Compounding these challenges was the fact that this segment of the population was increasingly turning to trendy microbreweries instead of the established giants such as Anheuser-Busch for their beer. These smaller breweries tended to produce darker, richer beers, sometimes with more exotic flavors that included essences of fruits and nuts.

Anheuser-Busch crafted the "Frogs" campaign specifically to appeal to this demographic group. According to the *St. Louis Business Journal,* "Budweiser needed to regain trends with 20-somethings to maintain and grow its total share. No normal Generation X campaign would work." Nor would the company's traditional marketing style. As the *Wall Street Journal* noted, "Anheuser-Busch was concerned that [its] image was getting stale, with its ads featuring scantily clad women and gritty blue-collar workers." Although D'Arcy, Masius, Benton, & Bowles first developed the concept of the beer-hawking frogs, its was DDB Needham, Chicago, that brought the idea to its full fruition.

In order to recapture this group that avoided "drinking their father's beer," Anheuser-Busch wanted the Budweiser campaign to captivate its audience. The "Frogs" commercials were meant to entertain the viewer with a more ironic sense of humor. A Manhattan analyst told the *Sacramento Bee* that the ads had a "twisted, childish humor" that appealed to the under-30 set. The ads were intended to project a fresher, more youthful image, with a sensibility that was more modern than some of the older themes commonly perceived as sexist by the younger generation.

The resulting commercials were noticeably devoid of any "hard sell" tactics. For a generation raised on sitcoms and commercials, image was often an end in itself. "They look at advertising and marketing as almost a spectator sport," a marketing analyst told the *Sacramento Bee.* The "Frogs" campaign also appealed to its target market because of its inclusiveness. Using animals as the new beer mascots allowed Anheuser-Busch to step away from earlier campaigns with their pervasive bikini-clad barflies and all-American tough guys that frequently offended women. As late as the 1970s, beer was characterized as a "20/80 product," which meant that 20 percent of the population drank 80 percent of the beer. Women were not a part of that 20 percent. As time passed, women accounted for greater percentages of beer sales. Young men, however, still comprised the core of the beer-drinking market. The quirky "Frogs" campaign allowed Anheuser-Busch to "communicate with young men without offending women," according to the *Milwaukee Journal Sentinel.* The ads could imbue Budweiser with an off-beat personality without risking going overboard. "Animals don't focus on gender. Advertisers don't have to worry if it's a man or a woman or how the man or woman is behaving," the *Journal Sentinel* noted. As the success of the amorous amphibians in "Frogs III" demonstrated, this campaign was also able to play on the traditionally sexist slant of beer advertising.

Additionally, the "Frogs" campaign enabled Anheuser-Busch to include minorities in its marketing message. Traditionally, beer advertising shunted minorities over to "malt liquor" products, such as Anheuser-Busch's own King Cobra malt liquor, Michelob Malt, and Hurricane Malt Liquor. By 1996 Anheuser-Busch had begun to dedicate separate Budweiser ad campaigns featuring rap stars and R & B music to appeal to African American and Hispanic markets. Census data in the mid-1990s predicted that the number of African Americans and Hispanics would grow at a much greater rate than the white population and that combined the two minorities would represent nearly a quarter of the U.S. population by 2000. Given this information, Anheuser-Busch recognized the advantages of a campaign that did not turn away any potential consumers.

As much as it needed to update Budweiser's image for a new generation of beer drinkers, Anheuser-Busch and DDB Needham understood that the "Frogs" campaign had to walk a fine line. In seeking out a new market, they could not alienate loyal Budweiser drinkers—those over the age of 30 for whom Budweiser was clearly the beer of choice. For this reason Anheuser-Busch continued to release other advertising targeting a more traditional audience at the same time that the "Frogs" campaign was aired. For example, August Busch III, chairman of the company, appeared in one series of commercials that stressed Anheuser-Busch's century-old heritage and its exacting standards of quality. But the *St. Louis Business Journal* found that Budweiser was such "an elite brand" and was "so well entrenched that [it could] step outside the traditional rules."

COMPETITION

Anheuser-Busch was not the only large brewery to grasp the potential impact of shifting demographics and new marketing needs. In 1995 beer sales declined 1.5 percent, a figure that reflected a decade of stagnant beer sales. Budweiser's most significant mainstream competitor, Miller Brewing Company, took note of Budweiser's success in building a brand personality through quirky advertisements such as those in the "Frogs" campaign. The advertising agency Wieden & Kennedy oversaw the marketing efforts for Miller Genuine Draft, the brand that competed most directly with Budweiser. Miller's new campaign featured grainy black and white images of young people drinking beer and dancing. The scenes presented stylized images reminiscent of the early 1970s,

KIDS AND FROGS

Anheuser-Busch's advertising blitz impressed its frogs deep into the consciousness of American consumers. In fact, a survey done by the Center for Alcohol Advertising, based in Berkeley, California, revealed that children between the ages of 9 and 11 years old could more readily identify the Bud frogs than other advertising icons such as Tony the Tiger and Smokey Bear (as well as the Mighty Morphin' Power Rangers). Only Bugs Bunny was more recognizable to this age group than the frogs. Some commentators took this survey as evidence that Anheuser-Busch was targeting underage drinkers. Others, however, attributed this result simply to Budweiser's heavy marketing. "If Tampax Tampons advertised as much as Budweiser, they'd have the same product recognition," wrote columnist Tom Jackman in the *Kansas City Star.* Anheuser-Busch firmly denied that its ads were intended to encourage underage drinking and noted that it spent over $20 million per year to discourage alcohol and drug abuse.

and in fact one commercial borrowed heavily and deliberately from the classic film *A Clockwork Orange.* Under the tag line of "It's Time to Drink Beer," the Miller ads asserted the implicit "hipness" of drinking a "good old-fashioned macro-beer" (in the words of one of the commercials).

Miller intended its campaign to reach the same demographic target as Budweiser's "Frogs" campaign. "The greatest opportunity to influence your business—the most evolving dynamic—is in the 21- to 30-year-old group," a spokesperson for Miller told *Beverage World.* Like Anheuser-Busch, Miller recognized the need to reach out to previously neglected segments of the American beer-drinking market by designing spots that did not exclude women or minorities. As Tom Dudrek, a senior vice president ad the advertising agency Leo Burnett, told *Crain's Chicago Business News,* "[Beer advertising] is not as Neanderthal. I don't think you see the Swedish Bikini Team anymore."

In addition to facing competition from other large-scale breweries, such as Coors, Stroh, Pabst, and Genesee, Budweiser was also losing business to smaller breweries that claimed to produce a higher-quality beer. These more expensive labels, including Samuel Adams and Pete's Wicked Ale, could not hope to approximate the sheer volume of Budweiser's sales. But the higher-end beers did appeal disproportionately to younger consumers, who liked the cache of these more elite brands. Even smaller regional breweries, such as Henry Weinhard of Portland, Oregon, developed strong local followings based on word-of-mouth reputation, not glitzy advertising campaigns. Anheuser-Busch was thus in danger of having its market share eroded from all sides.

MARKETING STRATEGY

Anheuser-Busch, however, could not rely on word-of-mouth to update Budweiser's image as the "King of Beers." Instead, the company pumped millions of dollars into a media blitz for its "Frogs" campaign. Although the company was unwilling to disclose how it allocated its nearly half billion dollar annual advertising budget among its various products, company publications termed the "Frogs" campaign a "total advertising effort" encompassing radio, print, and television ads. The frogs also appeared on billboards, hats, t-shirts, and other paraphernalia. In addition, their biographies were recounted on Budweiser's web site.

The most attention was devoted to the "Frogs" television commercials, however, because they could reach the greatest number of consumers. The "Frogs" spots each debuted during prime-time, "event" sports broadcasting. The first ad in the campaign premiered during the 1995 Super Bowl. The Super Bowl was generally the most-watched television program of the year, and this status has made it the launching pad for some of the highest-profile advertising campaigns in television history. In fact, the commercials have been known to eclipse the game itself in terms of stimulating viewer interest. Anheuser-Busch's goal was to use this huge stage to create a "buzz" around the unique "Frogs" spot, which would in turn generate more attention for the Budweiser brand. When this approach proved successful, Anheuser-Busch decided to continue its launch strategy. "Frogs III" was introduced during ABC-TV's popular *Monday Night Football* broadcast, while the fourth installment in the campaign debuted during the 1996 Super Bowl.

Because the campaign was designed to change the image of the tremendously well-known product rather than introduce it to consumers, the ads did not contain a great deal of specific information about Budweiser. Instead, the commercials sought to create a hip status for the brand in order "to fashion a more positive consumer attitude to [the beer]," as Anheuser-Busch executive Robert Lachky told the *Chicago Tribune.* By using humor, entertainment, and sheer exposure, Anheuser-Busch strove to forge a more emotional connection with its target audience through the "Frogs" campaign.

The company also wanted to ensure that virtually every consumer in America would be exposed to its message. To achieve this end, Anheuser-Busch saturated the market with a barrage of television and radio spots, as well as billboards, print ads, and special promotions. The frogs' ubiquity and immense popularity was a great boon to Budweiser (nearly 50 percent of consumers surveyed by *USA Today*'s Ad Track poll after the campaign's debut said they like the ads "a lot"—the highest mark recorded by the survey in 1995).

OUTCOME

Anheuser-Busch executives declared the "Frogs" campaign to be a success. Lachky told *USA Today* that "Budweiser was losing market share and the new ads helped to turn the brand around." He further emphasized that the commercials were "especially popular among core 21- to 27-year-old consumers." Industry analysts agreed with Anheuser-Busch's assessments. *Advertising Age* asserted that the campaign tripled its targets' awareness of the brand. Consumers seemed to concur. The ads topped *USA Today* 's Ad Track poll for three months straight. Other *USA Today* surveys revealed that the "Frogs" campaign appealed to viewers across income and age lines. The ads were well received in the advertising industry as well. The campaign won a slew of awards, including several Clio Awards and the prestigious Silver Lion Award at the 1995 Cannes Film Festival.

Not everyone commended the "Frogs" campaign, however. According to *USA Today,* elementary school children were quite familiar with the campaign and its famous frogs. Critics alleged that this demonstrated that these "critter" campaigns actually targeted children, thereby encouraging underage drinking (and building a future market for beer sales). Anheuser-Busch denied that the Budweiser ads were designed to draw in children. "Watching a beer ad does not cause a kid to drink," Anheuser-Busch's head of consumer awareness told the newspaper.

Eventually Anheuser-Busch did end the "Frogs" campaign—at least those ads that exclusively featured the frogs. Company officials denied that the decision was related in any way to pressure exerted by children's interest groups. Instead, Anheuser-Busch stated that it did so in order to ensure that the campaign, and thus the image of the brand it supported, remained fresh and positive in consumers' minds. In subsequent ads, two lizards with Brooklyn accents were introduced. Frank and Louie, as they were called, plotted to overthrow the frogs' successful reign as Budweiser "spokesfrogs."

FURTHER READING

Arndorfer, James. "Anheuser-Busch Sets $70 Million Hike in '98 Ad Spending." *Advertising Age,* December 1, 1998.

Beatty, Sally Goll. "Anheuser-Busch Promotes Dogs, Frogs, and Sermons on Moderate Drinking." *Wall Street Journal,* August 14, 1997.

Cahill, Joseph. "Suds City: Chicago Beer Pitchers Pour It On." *Crain's Chicago Business,* September 18, 1995.

"Campaign Clout: Budweiser's New Menagerie Hops to the Top of the Ad Charts." *Advertising Age,* March 18, 1998.

Causey, James. "Mascots With Attitude Invade a Wild Kingdom of Marketing." *Milwaukee Journal Sentinel* April 29, 1996.

Enrico, Dottie. "Budweiser Ads Up the Ante." *USA Today,* October 16, 1995.

Finnie, William. "Frogs a Breakthrough Campaign for Anheuser-Busch." *St. Louis Business Journal,* May 29, 1995.

Hays, Constance. "New Beer Drinkers Baffle Industry." *Sacramento Bee,* April 26, 1998. Examines the demographic target of the Budweiser "Frogs" campaign.

Jackman, Tom. "'Bud Frogs' Study Impaired By Leap in Logic." *Kansas City Star,* May 9, 1996.

Lazarus, George. "For Bud Lovers, This Frogs For You." *Chicago Tribune,* September 4, 1995.

Prince, Greg. "Time and Again: Miller Goes Straight to the Core and Likes the Results." *Beverage World,* February 15, 1998.

Rebecca Stanfel

I LOVE YOU, MAN CAMPAIGN

OVERVIEW

Anheuser-Busch Companies, the largest beer maker in the world, introduced Bud Light to its product line in 1982. In those days the light beer market was relatively young and was dominated by Miller Lite, a beer made by Anheuser-Busch's main competitor, the Miller Brewing Company. "Light" beers are so named because they contain fewer calories (and less alcohol) than "regular" beer. To create a market niche for its new product, Anheuser-Busch relied heavily on creative advertising campaigns to generate consumer awareness about its new brand and to alter the perception that Miller Lite was the only reduced-calorie beer available on the market. This approach proved to be quite successful, and Bud Light steadily gained in sales and market share at the expense of Miller Lite. By 1993 Bud Light had overtaken Miller Lite to become the best-selling light beer in the United States.

In the mid-1990s, however, the entire beer market had begun to slump as American alcohol consumption declined overall. Moreover, demographic trends indicated a decrease in the number of consumers between the ages of 21 and 30, the prime beer-drinking years. Bud Light was particularly affected by this decline. It lost its number-one position in the light beer market back to Miller Lite and struggled to create an advertising campaign that could reinvigorate its sales figures. To halt this decline, Anheuser-Busch turned to the DDB Needham advertising agency, the shop that had created the initial Bud Light campaign in 1982 that launched the brand to prominence.

DDB Needham sought to craft a campaign that would appeal to a generation of young men raised on sitcoms and commercials but that would also not alienate either older drinkers or women, who might prefer a light beer because of its lower calorie count. The "I Love You, Man" campaign, which debuted in 1995, was designed to serve these multiple goals. The first spot of the campaign featured "Johnny," a scruffy-looking man in his mid- to late thirties fishing off the end of a pier with his father and brother. Saucer-eyed, Johnny looks over to his father and says, in a voice redolent with emotion, "Dad. Well, you're my dad. And I love you, man." His father eyes him coolly and responds, "You're not getting my Bud Light, Johnny." Subsequent commercials showed Johnny pulling similar faux-sincere beer scams on his brother and girlfriend, always without success.

Anheuser-Busch ran the commercials heavily during major sporting events, including Major League Baseball's World Series and the Super Bowl, generally the highest-rated television broadcast of the year. Marketing surveys revealed the campaign's popularity. A poll conducted for *USA Today* by the Louis Harris Company revealed that 34 percent of those surveyed liked the "I Love You, Man" spots "a lot," which compared quite favorably with the 23 percent average for other commercials rated. As the "I Love You, Man" tag line insinuated its way into popular culture (actor Rob Fitzgerald, who played Johnny, appeared on David Letterman's latenight show), Anheuser-Busch sought to expand the campaign's appeal. Fitzgerald was featured in profiles in *People* magazine and *USA Today,* and DDB Needham strove to develop new scenarios in which Johnny could beg for Bud Light.

The fourth and final "I Love You, Man" commercial debuted during the 1996 Super Bowl and featured actor Charlton Heston. In it Johnny crashes a Hollywood party and meets the Bud Light-drinking Heston, who is perhaps best known for his roles as Moses and in the movie *Planet of the Apes.* Heston coaches Johnny on how to say the famous line but remains immune when Johnny turns the appeal on him. "Since the viewers already know the punch line, we needed to take Johnny's character someplace bigger," campaign creator David Merhar told *Life* magazine. "Everything leading up to the line had to be the funny part."

The campaign was a resounding success. Bud Light sales rose 12 percent while the "I Love You, Man" commercials ran, recapturing the number one slot in the light beer market and rising to become the second best-selling beer in the United States, behind only Anheuser-Busch's flagship brand Budweiser. Wary of overexposing the premise, Anheuser-Busch quietly ended the campaign in 1997.

HISTORICAL CONTEXT

When Anheuser-Busch brought out Bud Light in 1982, the light beer market was dominated by Anheuser-Busch's closest competitor, the Miller Brewing Company, and its Miller Lite beer. Miller's advertising campaign, featuring famous retired athletes and other well-known personalities debating whether Miller Lite was a superior beer because it tasted great or because it was less filling, established the brand as a major feature of the beer landscape. Miller Lite's success demonstrated the impact a popular advertising campaign could have on sales volume in the highly competitive beer market and the growth potential for light beers in general. Anheuser-Busch wanted to tap into this growing market with Bud Light.

Anheuser-Busch's first ad campaign in support of its new offering focused on generating name recognition for the brand and altering the consumer's assumption that light beer meant Miller Lite. This television campaign presented various people walking into bars and saying "Gimme a light." In response, they were offered items ranging from neon signs to dogs jumping through flaming hoops to blowtorches. "No," the surprised consumers would respond, "Bud Light." The humorous ads were quite successful, and Bud Light gradually began to erode Miller Lite's commanding share of the market.

Bud Light's advertising success continued with the 1987 launch of its Spuds McKenzie campaign. This series, featuring a bull terrier dubbed "the original party animal," followed the exploits of this ladies' hound as he celebrated life and Bud Light in the company of skimpily dressed women. Boosted by the popularity of this campaign (which generated an entire subindustry of Spuds paraphernalia, including tee shirts and hats), Bud Light sales continued to climb. However, the Spuds ads also drew heavy criticism from parents and anti-alcohol groups concerned that the use of the endearing canine was intended to appeal to children under the legal drinking age. Anheuser-Busch adamantly denied any intent to target people under age 21, but the company also responded by recasting Spuds as a youthful executive striving to spread a message encouraging responsible drinking. This shift did not placate the critics, and the campaign was discontinued in 1989. Anheuser-Busch rejected the notion that the Spuds ads were eliminated because of outside pressure. But as a senior executive at DDB Needham, the agency that created the ads, told the *Wall Street Journal,* "You have to pay attention to what's being said. If you don't, the heat gets hotter."

Bud Light's strong growth continued through the early 1990s. By 1993, Bud Light had overtaken Miller Lite as the best-selling light beer in the United States. Moreover, the light beer market as a whole continued to expand. "Unlike the diet segment in soft drinks," Beverage Marketing Corporation chairman Michael Bellas said in *Beverage World,* "the light category is a significant [part of the entire beer market,]" rather than just a small subcategory of its own. By 1997 three of the five best-selling beers in America were light beers: Bud Light, Miller Lite, and Coors Light.

Bud Light could not afford to rest on its laurels, however. While light beer's share of the beer industry grew, total beer sales volume flattened throughout the early and mid-1990s. According to the *Milwaukee Journal-Sentinel,* this stagnation could be attributed to "the changing tastes of baby boomers . . . and lack of enough 21 year olds to take their place." Bud Light was hit particularly hard in the mid-1990s, ceding its newly acquired primacy back to Miller Lite.

TARGET MARKET

Anheuser-Busch targeted its Bud Light advertising predominantly to the 21 to 30-year-old market. Twenty-somethings consumed more beer than people in any other age bracket. As the *Milwaukee Journal Sentinel* noted, "Beer consumption declines with age. The biggest drop occurs when a person reaches 34, [but] with a majority of the population over 30, the [beer] industry has reached a glass ceiling." Moreover, drinkers in their twenties were more liable to form their lifelong brand preferences during this decade of their lives. A spokesman for Miller Brewing Company concluded in *Beverage World* that "the most evolving dynamic is the 21- to 30-year group . . . . It would take a lot of pounding away to try to accomplish a [brand] switch [after that]."

Although not wanting to ignore older consumers, especially the increasingly health-conscious baby boomers who might be more drawn to a lower-calorie beer, the company recognized the significance of the youth market. "Marketing, and 21- to 30-year-old men's receptivity to it, is absolutely critical to a beer brand's success," Budweiser's vice president of brand management Bob Lachky told the *Dallas Morning News.* DDB Needham attempted to reach this market by crafting ads that were irreverent and entertaining. This approach was a necessary one to reach this audience. As Mark Johnson, director of brand management for Miller Lite told the *Sacramento Bee,* "This is a savvy audience. They started shopping earlier, they've had candy marketed to them, they've had Channel One in their classrooms. They've been there, they've done that, they've bought the t-shirt."

As Anheuser-Busch learned from its "Gimme a Light" campaign, humor was a very effective way of reaching its preferred audience. However, the sort of humor employed was quite significant. The company could not afford to alienate potential customers—particularly women, who were often ignored in traditional beer advertising. Jim Schumacker, a vice president of Bud Light marketing, recognized the challenge posed by creating Bud Light promotional spots in *USA Today:* "Bud Light advertising is more difficult to create than Budweiser's because Light's customers are more diverse . . . . That means ads must appeal to both sexes." Anheuser-Busch had received a great deal of criticism for the sexism implicit in the Spuds McKenzie campaign. After an outcry from women (who were drinking more beer with each passing year of the 1980s and 1990s) and even from trade such publications as *Ad Age* (which in 1993 condemned most beer ads for using women to "represent sexual imagery and nothing else"), Anheuser-Busch recognized a need for care in its selection of promotional messages. "Treating women as objects is not in tune with today's markets," Lachky told the *Milwaukee Journal Sentinel.*

The "I Love You, Man" campaign sought to appeal to its target audience by tweaking on a familiar cultural trope. The opening scenes of emotional bonding were designed "to pull people in like a Hallmark card," David Merhar, the DDB Needham creative executive who devised the "I Love You, Man" concept, explained to the *Wall Street Journal.* Media-literate 20-somethings were quick to grasp the reference and adored the concluding twist where the smarmy appeal for Bud Light was resoundingly rebuffed. In fact, the spots were so popular among their chosen demographic that "I Love You, Man" became a cultural catchphrase, being recited on talk shows, comedy routines, and even casually among beer drinkers. "I have definitely said 'I love you, man' to my friends," reported one consumer interviewed by the *Wall Street Journal.*

COMPETITION

Bud Light's main competitors in the light beer market were Coors Light, made by the Adolph Coors Company, which was the third-largest brewer in the United States, and Miller Lite. Although Coors Light's sales were good (revenue generated by the brand surpassed the Coors Company's flagship brand Original

I LOVE YOU, DAD

The inspiration for the "I Love You, Man" campaign came from the real-life experience of David Merhar, the DDB Needham associate who conceived of the ads. After a dinner at home with his 61-year-old father, Merhar hugged his dad and uttered the now-famous words, "I love you, man." As Merhar explained to *USA Today,* "This is how guys say 'I love you,' with a little disclaimer."

Coors in 1987 and increased every year for the next decade), Bud Light had its sights set squarely on surpassing Miller Lite. In 1990 Bud Light controlled 19 percent of the light beer market, while Miller Lite retained a strong 33 percent. Three years later Bud Light surpassed Miller Lite as the best-selling light beer in America, as its light beer market share rose to 30 percent while Miller Lite's dropped to 22 percent. This lead was short lived, however, as Miller Lite rebounded to first place during a period in which sales volumes for both competitors decreased. But the "I Love You, Man" campaign elevated Bud light sales and restored the Anheuser-Busch brand to primacy, frustrating the Miller Brewing Company so much that it pulled its advertising account from the Leo Burnett agency in December 1996 and gave it to the Minneapolis-based Fallon McElligot firm.

Fallon McElligot recognized the necessity of appealing to the under-30 market and devised offbeat anti-ads attributed to the fictional account executive superstar "Dick." These "Ads by Dick" had an ironic sensibility designed to reach the younger target market. Early spots in the campaign were introduced by a 1970s-style year book picture displayed on the screen, while the voice-over declared: "This is Dick. Dick is a creative superstar and the man behind the advertising you are about to witness. We gave Dick a six-pack of Miller Lite and some money and asked him to come up with a commercial for Miller Lite." This inside-jokey style continued throughout the ads. One of the first of the more than 50 "Ads by Dick" Fallon McElligot produced showed a group of Lite-drinking cowboys slowly sauntering into the men's room of their rustic bar to the strains of "Adios Amigos." Another portrayed a rancher trading a truckload of Miller Lite to a turncoat steer in exchange for information about a planned stampede. In a third spot, a group of professional wrestlers were shown faking their moves in the ring. Later, they adjourned to a bar where they poured their cans of Miller Lite right past their mouths without making contact.

Miller Brewing Company hoped the new ad campaign would reinvigorate its flagging sales and increase the favorable impression of its brand among consumers. "We wanted to redefine the brand and do it quickly," Mike Johnson, Miller Lite's brand director told *Adweek.* "We wanted something that would shake up the system to say it's not the same old Miller Lite." To ensure its message reached the widest possible distribution, Miller tripled its advertising budget to support the "Ads by Dick" campaign, spending $38.7 million dollars during the first quarter of 1997 alone, nearly 70 percent of Miller Brewing Company's total beer advertising budget. The campaign proved successful, as Miller Lite's sales in supermarkets rose 13 percent and total sales rose 1.7 percent overall in 1997. "Awareness of the brand is high, recall is high, and sales are up," Johnson said. The popularity of the campaign forced Anheuser-Busch to increase its own advertising budget to retain its lead in the market.

MARKETING STRATEGY

Anheuser-Busch employed its tried-and-true strategy of high-profile athletic event advertising for the "I Love You, Man" campaign. The commercials ran during major sporting events, such as the National Basketball Association's playoffs and telecasts and Major League Baseball's World Series. They appeared during regular-season broadcasts as well. The Charlton Heston "I Love You, Man" commercial debuted during the 1996 Super Bowl.

At least as important as placement, however, was the tone Anheuser-Busch sought to strike in the ads. By using humor and an absence of sexual messaging, the company was able to avoid alienating potential consumers who did not happen to be men between the ages of 21 and 30. But by making the commercials entertaining and ironic, Anheuser-Busch was still able to play directly to the sensibilities of its desired audience. As *Beverage World* noted, "[Generation] X-ers also appreciate marketing with a sense of humor. Bud Light's 'I love you, man' commercials offer an astute marketing approach to Generation X-ers."

Once Anheuser-Busch recognized the popularity of the "I Love You, Man" campaign, it strove to expand on it, pushing the campaign beyond traditional advertising formats. "The question became, 'How can I take an idea that's going to be on paid media and get some extra boost out of it?'" Bob Lachky, Anheuser-Busch's director of brand marketing explained to the *Wall Street Journal.* To accomplish this goal, the company arranged for profiles of Rob Fitzgerald, the actor who played Johnny, to appear in such publications as *People* and *USA Today.* Fitzgerald also made other public appearances on behalf of the brand and was twice invited onto *Late Night with David Letterman.*

OUTCOME

The "I Love You, Man" campaign was a tremendous success. Immediately prior to the campaign, Bud Light had been struggling. During its run, however, Bud Light became the fastest-growing beer in America, with its market share topping 10 percent of the total U.S. beer market. "Years from now, this will be the case study of how to turn around a dying brand," *Modern Brewery Age* editor Peter Reid told the Portland *Oregonian.* DDB Needham did not disguise its pleasure with the results. "Advertising has established the brand as hip, and that translates into sales," Bob Scarpelli, chief creative officer and vice chairman of the ad agency, told the *Dallas Morning News.*

The campaign's success was not just limited to the beer market. The "I Love You, Man" ads became a full-scale cultural phenomenon. As the *Oregonian* reported, "The line is the new mantra of the TV-watching crowd, like 'Where's the beef' before it. Signs proclaiming 'I love you, man' are all over the stands at sporting events." "I love 'I love you, man,'" concurred one 26-year-old interviewed by the *Wall Street Journal.* "It's a total manly moment." That response was exactly what Anheuser-Busch had hoped for when it launched the campaign.

FURTHER READING

Beatty, Sally Goll. "Nipped in the Bud: How the Beer Industry Uses TV Ads to Mollify Critics, Buff Its Image." *The Wall Street Journal,* August 14, 1997.

Causy, James E. "Brewers Look Ahead to a Market Upswing: More Twenty-One Year Olds Expected in Near Future." *Milwaukee Journal Sentinel,* September 23, 1996.

"I Love Your New Bud Light Ad, Man." *Dallas Morning News,* December 17, 1996.

Dutka, Elaine. "Heston Pokes Fun at Himself in Beer Ads." *Life,* April 5, 1996.

Hays, Constance, "New Beer Drinkers Baffle Industry." *Sacramento Bee,* April 26, 1998.

Horovitz, Bruce. "Bud Light Guy Ain't Loving His Job, Man." *USA Today,* January 26, 1998.

Parpis, Eleftheria. "Of Beer and Brain Candy." *Adweek,* March 16, 1998.

Prince, Greg W. "Good Old Premium Beer: Is There Still Room at the Bar for Homer Simpson's Favorite?" *Beverage World,* April 15, 1997.

Stein, Jeannine. "Johnny Savors Success While Sobbing for Beer." *Portland Oregonian,* January 27, 1996.

Tieszen, Lori. "The X Market." *Beverage World,* December 15, 1996.

Wells, Melanie. "Beermaker's Flat Results." *USA Today,* July 27, 1998.

Rebecca Stanfel

LOUIE THE LIZARD CAMPAIGN

OVERVIEW

In June 1997 Anheuser-Busch Companies introduced a multimedia national advertising campaign to bolster its Budweiser brand beer. Although Anheuser-Busch dominated the American beer market with a 45.3 percent market share and a diverse product line that included the beers Budweiser, Bud Light, Busch, Michelob, and numerous other brands, Budweiser's sales had begun to slip in the late 1980s. The company turned to its advertising agencies to seek a solution to Budweiser's problems through a revamped marketing image. After launching, in 1995, the highly successful "Frogs" campaign, which attempted to capture the 21- to 29-year-old segment of the American population, Anheuser-Busch continued to pour advertising dollars into Budweiser. A substantial portion of the estimated $150 million spent annually on Budweiser between 1997 and 2001 went to a campaign called "Louie the Lizard," developed by the ad agency Goodby, Silverstein & Partners to target younger beer drinkers.

The campaign, which had TV, radio, print, outdoor, online, and promotional components, focused on an embittered animatronic lizard named Louie who railed against the Budweiser frogs in a Brooklyn accent. Louie was galled that Budweiser had chosen the frogs as brand representatives instead of him; the frogs were each capable of uttering only a single syllable, whereas Louie was articulate and intelligent, if somewhat unstable. Over the course of the campaign Louie became increasingly jealous of the frogs, hiring a ferret to kill them during one memorable series of commercials. In 2000 he focused his resentment on a wildly popular contemporaneous Bud advertising campaign. Soon thereafter, the swamp-creatures storyline faded from prominence, to be only briefly resurrected in 2001, 2004, and 2005.

The campaign was one of the most popular in recent advertising history, and it was credited with sustaining the freshness of Budweiser's image among its target audience of young beer drinkers. It won numerous ad-industry awards, including a 1998 Silver Lion at the Cannes International Advertising Festival and an assortment of

Clio Awards in 2000. Nevertheless, Budweiser sales continued to decline during the life of the campaign. Although some observers pointed to this fact as evidence of the fruitlessness of Bud advertising, the reality of changing American beer preferences was inarguably the leading cause of Budweiser's steady sales erosion.

HISTORICAL CONTEXT

In the fiercely competitive American beer market, Anheuser-Busch had often used high-profile advertising campaigns to promote its flagship beer brand, Budweiser. Even with a history of brewing in the United States that dated back to 1852 and a solid reputation as the world's largest beer maker, Anheuser-Busch still felt the squeeze of flattening beer sales that plagued the entire beer sector in the 1990s. In 1995 American beer sales continued a decade-long trend of descent and dropped an additional 1.5 percent. Anheuser-Busch soon realized that, although Budweiser remained the beer of choice for older Americans, the brand's popularity with the highly desirable segment of younger beer drinkers, aged 21 to 29, had waned.

By 1994 Anheuser-Busch determined that Budweiser's image—carefully cultivated through visible ad campaigns—sorely needed to be energized and updated. That year Anheuser-Busch severed its long-term relationship with D'Arcy Masius Benton & Bowles, the agency that had created the iconic 1979 "This Bud's for You" campaign that featured hardworking, Budweiser-drinking blue-collar laborers. Prior to this dismissal, however, D'Arcy had produced a single TV spot that would lay the groundwork for one of Budweiser's most popular advertising platforms of all time.

That initial commercial, featuring three swamp-dwelling frogs who stared at a neon Budweiser sign and who each croaked a syllable of the brand name in turn, immediately resonated with consumers. DDB Needham Chicago (the agency later dropped "Needham" from its name), one of the group of ad agencies Anheuser-Busch chose to work with after severing its relationship with D'Arcy Masius, followed this introductory commercial with more than a dozen spots featuring the amphibians croaking out the syllables of the Budweiser brand in humorous scenarios. Over the course of the next two years the campaign almost single-handedly vaulted the Budweiser brand out of its slump. Sales of the brew among younger beer drinkers boomed; industry publications, including *Advertising Age,* lauded the campaign's creativity and wit; and polls measuring consumer response revealed that the "Frogs" campaign was one of the most popular ever.

Anheuser-Busch was under constant pressure to end the beloved "Frogs" campaign, though. Children's advocacy groups claimed that the commercials were designed to "hook" kids on the Budweiser brand by using "critters." In 1996 a survey of San Francisco–area children revealed that 9- to 11-year-olds were more likely to recall the Budweiser frogs than they were Smokey Bear or Kellogg's Frosted Flakes' Tony the Tiger. The company was also aware of the risk of taking the "Frogs" concept beyond the point of freshness and innovation.

TARGET MARKET

The lizards' saga of jealousy and murderous rage, as presented in the "Louie the Lizard" spots, was designed to capture the same audience pursued by the "Frogs" campaign. Attracting men aged 21 to 29 had long been the aim for beer advertisers. Not only did these younger drinkers consume far more beer than their over-30 counterparts, but also, they cemented their beer brand loyalty during these years of their lives. In the 1990s, however, Anheuser-Busch was plagued both by younger consumers turning to trendier microbrews and by a falling number of 20-somethings in the population at large. The smaller pool of younger drinkers was more likely to consider Budweiser as their "father's brand" and less as the choice for a younger generation.

The "Frogs" campaign did much to reinvigorate the brand's image among more youthful drinkers. *Advertising Age* correlated a near tripling of this age group's awareness of Budweiser with the release of the "Frogs" commercials. The so-called Generation X, however, was more media-savvy than its predecessors and thus more likely to lose interest in a campaign. "They look to advertising and marketing as almost a spectator sport," a specialist in targeting Generation X consumers told the *Sacramento Bee.*

The lizards, especially Louie, with his solipsistic plot to overthrow the frogs and become a commercial star, provided Anheuser-Busch with the perfect opportunity to deliver a style of tongue-in-cheek humor that often performed well with the target audience. By purposefully poking fun at the "Frogs" campaign—which was beginning to wear thin with some viewers—the "Lizards" commercials delivered a sophisticated spoof on advertising itself. *Beverage World* agreed that it was the type of consciously cultivated "self-deprecating" humor that sold well with consumers in their 20s.

COMPETITION

Anheuser-Busch's largest rivals launched their own advertising campaigns to capture the same demographic group targeted by the "Lizards" commercials. Miller Brewing Co., always a strong competitor, teamed up with Portland-based ad agency Wieden+Kennedy to create the "It's Time to Drink Beer" campaign for Miller

INVENTING REPTILIAN PERSONALITIES

In addition to constructing an elaborate plotline in the "Lizards" campaign, Goodby and Anheuser-Busch made up profiles for their new stars, Louie and Frank. On Budweiser's Web page Goodby created "Bios and Headshots" for the reptiles. Using the same cute humor that defined the commercials, these profiles listed such fictional details as Louie's "Last Book Read" (*The Work Habits of Seven Highly Effective Lizards*) and "Hobbies" ("swatting flies, tracking grasshoppers, and bowling"). Moreover, in press releases Budweiser executives spoke of the lizards as though they were real. A marketing representative was quoted as saying, "We're delighted that Louie and Frank have decided to spend their summer with us in Texas."

Genuine Draft (MGD) in 1997. With Miller facing the same stagnating sales figures as Budweiser, its campaign was intended to reposition MGD as the hip brand of the 1990s. Following the popular resurgence of 1970s fashion, the black-and-white commercials featured frolicking youths wearing bell-bottom jeans and swigging MGD to funk music. But the Miller campaign employed the same irreverent humor that marked Louie's rants. "It's time for good old macrobrew" made in "vats the size of Rhode Island," one commercial proclaimed in block type. Miller's vice president of marketing explained to *Beverage World* that the target market of the MGD campaign did not "like typical advertising."

Like Budweiser's "Lizards," MGD's campaign also sought not to exclude women and minorities—two groups noticeably absent from earlier beer commercials. Instead of avoiding the issue with "critter" ads, MGD's "It's Time to Drink Beer" sought to build a more modern image through an inclusive cast of characters. Women appeared in the commercials but danced and drank with "the boys." Their function was not that of sex symbols. African-Americans with outrageously tall afro hairstyles (again reminiscent of the 1970s) were prominently featured in the campaign as well.

Adolph Coors Brewing Co., the third-largest American brewery, relaunched its Original Coors beer in 1996 with a $10 million advertising campaign. For years Coors had dedicated most of its efforts to marketing Coors Light. The Original Coors commercials were themed "the last real beer" and centered on the notion that Original Coors was an "honest," anti-elitist brew.

MARKETING STRATEGY

Although Anheuser-Busch would not reveal the exact dollar amount it committed to the saga of Louie and Frank, the company typically spent between $300 and $350 million a year on advertising during the years that "Louie the Lizard" ran. The bulk of that figure was dedicated to Budweiser and Bud Light, and multiple campaigns for each brand tended to run simultaneously. This giant budget ensured that Anheuser-Busch was able to support Budweiser with a "total advertising effort," according to the company. In addition to a vast array of "Lizard" television commercials, the reptiles also appeared in national radio spots, on promotional clothing, in outdoor and print ads, and as the sponsors of athletes and sporting events.

Indeed, if there was one word to encapsulate Anheuser-Busch's strategy in reaching its target audience, it would be sports. The television commercials were usually aired during big-ticket athletic events watched by millions of American viewers. The campaign debuted during a National Basketball Association (NBA) game carried by NBC, made numerous Super Bowl appearances, and often ran during Major League Baseball games and the Monday Night Football series.

Radio spots were similarly broadcast during sporting events. Not only did Anheuser-Busch dole out considerable funds to ensure that Budweiser was named the "Official Beer of Major League Baseball" in 1998 but it also crafted specialized radio commercials for baseball fans. Budweiser also sought and achieved the distinction of being recognized as the "Official Beer of NASCAR," the stock-car racing circuit. In conjunction with this development, Louie the Lizard was painted on the Budweiser team's car in 1998. Michael LaBroad, director of Budweiser marketing, explained in a press release that the company was "always looking for ways to extend our advertising icons beyond television."

The "Louie the Lizard" spots starred Louie and Frank, two disaffected animatronic lizards who felt spurned because Anheuser-Busch had made stars of the earlier Bud campaign's croaking frogs instead of them. "I can't believe they went with the frogs," Louie complained to Frank in a distinct Brooklyn accent in the campaign's first commercial. "Our audition was flawless." Perhaps the best known of the commercials were those released during the 1998 Super Bowl in a sequence of four spots that related Louie's attempt to assassinate the frogs (and thus be able to take their place) by hiring a ferret hit man. The campaign continued with Louie trying out a Texas accent after he learned that one of the Bud frogs he had tried to eliminate was a Texan. "Frank, these Texans, they hold grudges," said Louie. "You know the phrase, 'Remember the Alamo?' Well now it's going to be 'Remember the frog.'" In July 1998 a commercial showed Louie being given a chance to join the croaking-frogs chorus. But he became flustered and botched the shoot, crying, "I can't work in this environment. Cut! Cut!"

As the campaign matured, the jealousy plotline escalated. Although the ferret successfully managed to electrocute the frogs with the neon sign on which they so obsessively focused, the frogs lived. The incomprehensibly gibbering ferret was well received by consumers and Anheuser-Busch executives and became a regular character in the campaign. In 2000 Louie's jealousy found a new target: the cast of another set of DDB-created Budweiser spots, the enormously popular "Whassup?!" campaign. That effort, centering on the comically ebullient "Whassup?!" greeting exchanged, with elaborate tongue-wagging, among friends, had for the moment eclipsed even the universally famous frogs and lizards. ("Whassup?!" parodies flooded the Internet, and the campaign won the Grand Prix at the 2000 International Advertising Festival in Cannes.) Louie claimed, with characteristic resentment, that the "Whassup?!" crew had stolen the protruding-tongue idea from him.

Always wary of overexposing even its most successful advertising concepts, Anheuser-Busch sent the swamp creatures into semiretirement midway through 2000, and the hiatus lasted roughly a year. In 2001 Louie and company reappeared in commercials that, surprisingly, were aimed at an over-40 audience. These spots included work that mimicked Budweiser product-quality advertising of the past as well as further ferret-related drama. The swamp-creatures storyline again faded from the airwaves, only to reappear briefly in 2004. Amid an increasingly acrimonious advertising spat between Anheuser-Busch and SABMiller (the parent company of Miller Brewing), which had been initially triggered by Miller's claims that its Miller Lite had fewer carbohydrates than Bud Light, Louie was tapped to foment the anti-Miller sentiment. Anheuser-Busch again allowed the lizards to be resurrected in 2005 at the request of JibJab, the animation team that had created a wildly popular online cartoon parodying the 2004 presidential-campaign efforts of George W. Bush and John Kerry. JibJab, given creative license to spread the Budweiser message online, showcased the lizards and frogs in a barbershop sing-along deriding drinkers of pretentious cocktails and wine.

OUTCOME

The exploits of the disgruntled reptiles quickly won popular approval. *USA Today* 's Ad Track survey of adult consumers revealed that the campaign was among the most popular in modern advertising history. Anecdotal evidence and analysts' observations indicated that the "Louie the Lizard" campaign connected with the desired audience. Janine Misdom, a Manhattan marketing- firm partner, explained to the *Sacramento Bee* why consumers under 30 responded to the Louie and Frank saga: "It's funny, it's a little bit nostalgic, and there's a little bit of the bad-boy thing." On June 22, 1998, *USA Today* reported that its most recent Ad Track indicated that the "Louie the Lizard" campaign appealed to consumers across lines of class and age. Marketing insiders heaped praise on Goodby's lizards. *Advertising Age* commended the campaign as the "Best of Show" from a pool of nationally aired commercials. The TV campaign won a Silver Lion at the Cannes International Advertising Festival in 1998. In 2000 the radio portion of the campaign was awarded a gold, two silvers, and two bronzes at the Clio Awards (one of the world's largest advertising-awards programs), while the TV campaign took home a bronze Clio Award.

Neither "Louie the Lizard" nor "Whassup?!" could arrest Budweiser's seemingly permanent sales slide, however. This led many advertising-industry observers to question the value of Budweiser's marquee image-building campaigns, but Anheuser-Busch felt that the declines were the inevitable result of changing American tastes in beer. Besides, Budweiser advertising was meant to have the ancillary effect of driving sales of other Anheuser-Busch brands, especially Bud Light, which in 2001 surpassed Budweiser to become the best-selling beer in the United States.

FURTHER READING

Arndorfer, James. "Actual People to Join Lizards in '98 Budweiser Creative." *Advertising Age,* March 16, 1998.

———. "Anheuser-Busch Sets $70 Million Hike in '98 Ad Spending." *Advertising Age,* December 1, 1997.

Cuneo, Alice Z., and Hillary Chura. "Bud's King Lizard Back." *Advertising Age,* July 23, 2001.

———. "Whassup? Bud Agencies Exchange Beer Barbs." *Advertising Age,* May 29, 2000.

Finnie, William. "Frogs a Breakthrough for Anheuser-Busch." *St. Louis Business Journal,* May 29, 1995.

Hays, Constance. "New Beer Drinkers Baffle Industry." *Sacramento Bee,* April 26, 1998.

Lippert, Barbara. "Lounge Lizards." *Adweek,* May 29, 2000.

Parpis, Eleftheria. "JibJab Takes a Stab at Budweiser." *Adweek,* July 25, 2005.

Prince, Greg W.. "Good Old Premium Beer: Is There Still Room at the Bar for Homer Simpson's Favorite?" *Beverage World,* April 15, 1997.

Tieszen, Lori. "The X Market." *Beverage World,* December 15, 1996.

Voight, Joan. "'Louie the Lizard' on the Stump." *Adweek,* February 21, 2000.

Rebecca Stanfel
Mark Lane

OH, AND BEWARE OF THE PENGUINS CAMPAIGN

OVERVIEW

Anheuser-Busch introduced two new beers to its Budweiser family in 1995. Bud Ice and Bud Ice Light were both "ice brewed" by pumping the beer through ice chambers during the brewing process. Both varieties of Bud Ice were packaged in distinctive long-necked bottles shaped to look and feel like a handful of ice cubes. To inaugurate its newest product, as well as to bolster Bud Ice in the competitive ice beer market, Anheuser-Busch selected the San Francisco-based ad agency Goodby, Silverstein, & Partners to develop an advertising campaign that would reflect the values of the fledgling brand and that would appeal to viewers through creative, memorable, and entertaining commercials. The resulting "Oh, and Beware of the Penguins" campaign, which featured slightly sinister penguins, was launched during the Super Bowl on January 28, 1996. Since that first spot garnered almost immediate positive responses from both consumers and critics, Anheuser-Busch continued with the campaign. Over the next two years, the "Penguins" campaign was expanded to include other television commercials, as well as ads on billboards and trucks. Additionally, marketing teams dressed as penguins turned up in bars handing out samples of the beverage.

The television "Penguins" spots all featured tuxedo-clad penguins that went to edgy extremes to steal people's Bud Ice. The spots, which parodied movie genres, included such commercials as "Penguin Express," in which a film-noir-type detective was frightened in his train car by a Bud Ice-seeking penguin who sang the refrain from the classic Frank Sinatra song "Strangers in the Night" in a nasal-toned "Dooby Dooby Doo." In another commercial, this time spoofing horror movies, a suburban couple was terrified by a penguin's crank calls from their upstairs bedroom. The bird, of course, wanted their ice beer. In 1997 Anheuser-Busch released an ad that portrayed the thieving penguin making off with the National Hockey League's Stanley Cup trophy. "Jungle" told the tale of jungle explorers who made the mistake of resting and drinking a Bud Ice. Spear-pointing natives captured the party, lashed them to stakes, and used the Bud Ice to summon their penguin god, which they did by chanting "Dooby Dooby Doo" and placing the beer on a shrine before a roaring fire. At the close of each ad, viewers were advised to "Drink Bud Ice… But Beware of the Penguins."

Anheuser-Busch chose the quirky and slightly-threatening penguin as its mascot for Bud Ice to target the company's professed target market—the "contemporary adult" aged 21 to 34 years old. Moreover, using a bird instead of a person to promote its beer allowed Budweiser to reach across race and gender lines to appeal to a wide audience of potential Bud Ice drinkers. The campaign and its high-visibility tie-ins, such as Bud Ice's partnership as the "official beer" of the National Hockey League, helped propel Bud Ice and Bud Ice Light to become the highest-selling ice brand in the United States.

HISTORICAL CONTEXT

Anheuser-Busch, the world's largest brewery with a history dating back to the 1860s, originally launched an ice draft brand in 1994. The beer, which was added to Anheuser-Busch's vast repertoire of beers—including Budweiser, Bud Light, Michelob, and the nonalcoholic O'Doul's—was first marketed under the more cumbersome name Ice Draft from Budweiser. This brand met with stiff competition from other brewers and did not fare as well as expected, partially because Budweiser's contribution to the ice genre contained 5 percent alcohol instead of the 5.5 percent alcohol of other ice draft brands. In addition, shortly after Ice Draft from Budweiser was released, Anheuser-Busch's competitors hurried their own versions to the shelves. Miller Brewing Company, Budweiser's chief competitor, introduced six ice beers. Although Ice Draft from Budweiser was the best-selling ice beer in 1994, its market share was eclipsed by Miller's total line of ice drafts. Anheuser-Busch expected to sell 3.5 million barrels but actually realized sales of only 2.5 million barrels in the highly competitive market.

Rather than abandon the concept, however, Anheuser-Busch chose to repackage and relaunch the brew as Bud Ice in 1995. Bud Ice Light was released the same year. The new formulation had the higher alcohol content of its rivals and was bottled to look as if the glass container were sculpted out of ice. But even more important to the brand's success was the estimated $35 million Anheuser-Busch dedicated to promoting Bud Ice.

TARGET MARKET

Bud Ice and Bud Ice Light were targeted at what Anheuser-Busch termed the "contemporary adult," who ranged in age from 21 to 34 years old. More specifically, though, the brand sought to appeal to a group "a little younger than the mainstream—to people from 21 to 27," according to *Advertising Age.* These young adults represented the pinnacle of the market for breweries. Not only were 20-somethings bigger beer consumers, they were also more liable to form their life-long brand preferences during this decade of their lives. A spokesman for one of Budweiser's competitors, Miller Brewing Company, told *Beverage World* that "the most evolving dynamic is the 21- to 30-year group . . . it would take a lot of pounding away to try to accomplish a [brand] switch [after that age]."

Budweiser knew from its experience with the wildly successful Budweiser frogs and wise-cracking lizards that humor worked well to attract this younger target audience. Bob Lachky, vice president of Budweiser brands, explained to *Advertising Age* that "the only way to appeal to [this demographic group] was with something off-beat and a little edgy." The cute but malicious singing penguins fit this bill neatly and indeed were like nothing else on television.

Budweiser was also aware that by focusing the campaign on penguin mascots it could obtain a competitive boost without offending or excluding any group, which was a risk run by ads featuring real people. Although young men by far consumed more beer than any other group, Anheuser-Busch had only recently abandoned its more sexist ads that featured scantily-clad women as barroom objects of desire for beer-guzzling men. After an outcry from women (who were drinking more beer with each passing year of the 1980s and 1990s), as well as from trade publications such as *Advertising Age* (which in 1993 condemned most beer ads for using women to "represent sexual imagery and nothing else"), Anheuser-Busch changed its strategies. "Treating women as objects is not in tune with today's markets," Lachky told the *Milwaukee Journal Sentinel.* Beer campaigns that relied on animal mascots rather than party scenes did not run the risk of excluding women from their appeal.

The penguins did provide Bud Ice and Bud Ice Light with an abundance of personality. Bud Ice brand manager, Michael La Broad, emphasized to *USA Today* that the "beauty of the [Penguins] campaign is that it's memorable." Analysts concurred that the "critter ads" had sufficient wit and entertainment value to reach both 20-something Generation Xers and aging baby boomers, an impressive sweep for a beer campaign. Moreover, by cleverly parodying standard film tropes, each commercial allowed the brand to capitalize on the popularity, image, and hip campiness of the various genres the campaign spoofed.

A LAWSUIT FOR THE BIRDS

In 1997 Bud Ice's use of the penguin resulted in a lawsuit filed by a Miami clothing maker, Supreme International, which alleged that Anheuser-Busch stole that company's signature bird trademark.

"Now I know what it's like to be kicked in the stomach by a Clydesdale," said Supreme's chairman, George Feldenkreis, referring to the mammoth horses that had served for decades as Budweiser's signature image.

COMPETITION

Bud Ice and Bud Ice Light faced stiff competition from every major brewer (as well as many minor brewers) in the United States. When Anheuser-Busch launched its Ice Draft from Budweiser, it quickly encountered nearly 40 competitors. Foremost among these was Miller Brewing Company, which released six ice beers in 1994 and 1995. Ice Draft from Budweiser was originally released to compete with cold-filtered Miller Genuine Draft. As Bud Ice, it clashed with Miller's Icehouse, which was advertised in corporate identity spots produced by BBDO Worldwide, Toronto. Miller also sought to win over the coveted 20-something target market. One of the early Icehouse spots showed two bodysurfers in a mosh pit trying unsuccessfully to swim over the crowd to get to the bar. In response, a waitress—with a tray of perfectly balanced Ice House beer—was passed over the audience to reach them. The Milwaukee-based company spent more than $26 million promoting its Lite Ice beer in 1994 alone.

Beyond its specific ice draft competitors, Bud Ice initially had to struggle to keep the entire ice draft category afloat. This new beer category saw its sales fluctuate widely, and sometimes its very existence seemed tenuous. But by 1996 the market had begun to steady, and ice beers came to account for 5 percent of the 190 million barrel U.S. beer market. But the market faced encroachment from a new source. Trendy microbreweries and smaller national breweries like Samuel Adams vied for Bud Ice's young and brand-conscious target market. Moreover, other major breweries—Miller and Coors Brewing Company, among others—always remained poised to capture any unguarded share of Budweiser's leading position in the market.

MARKETING STRATEGY

Anheuser-Busch first confined its television advertising efforts for Bud Ice to sports-oriented programming. A *USA Today* poll revealed that as of July 15, 1996, Bud Ice's "Penguin" ads were resoundingly popular, yet had been seen by only 30 percent of the viewers quizzed for the survey. The reason for this discrepancy was that Anheuser-Busch ran the commercials only during televised sporting events that "reached a young, affluent audience." "Penguins" spots did appear regularly on local and cable sports programming, including ESPN, the preeminent sports broadcasting station in the country. As the campaign caught on, however, Budweiser attempted to reach a wider audience. "Penguins" commercials ran on programs such as *Saturday Night Live,* the *Late Show with David Letterman,* and *Mad TV,* as well as on the VH-1 music video network.

As the television campaign gained momentum, Anheuser-Busch devoted more time and money to so-called on-premise activity, referring to promotions carried out at locations (most notably bars) at which alcohol is sold and consumed "on the premise." In late 1996 marketing teams dressed in tuxedos turned up in bars giving out Bud Ice-icles, which were plastic icicles that customers could use to add a bright color and a fruity taste to their bottled Bud Ice. Flavors included "Brain Freeze," "Ice-otope," and "Kiss My Face."

Anheuser-Busch also sought to draw in more of its key market with promotional tie-ins with the National Hockey League (NHL) and other regional hockey associations, such as the East Coast Hockey League and the American Hockey League. Jim Schumacker, marketing chief for Bud Light and Bud Ice, revealed to *Brandweek* that Bud Ice's marketing strategy was two-pronged. "We've got two thrusts," he said. "Equity in the penguin has been very strong in the contemporary-adult market, as has equity in the National Hockey League." Since the NHL itself targeted the same contemporary young adult male demographic, the link was natural. In one television commercial that illustrated the dual strategies of the "Penguins" campaign, a Bud Ice penguin stole the Stanley Cup, the National Hockey League's championship trophy. In addition to these national efforts, Anheuser-Busch also strove to bring the "Penguins" campaign into key regional markets. For instance, Florida—home of two NHL teams—proved to be essential to Bud Ice because of the success Miller's Icehouse had achieved in that market. The ubiquitous penguin made personal appearances throughout the state (dressed for the sunny climate in sandals and sunglasses) and was christened "Florida's Snowbird," a pun on the state's nickname for transplants from northern states. According to *Brandweek,* Bud Ice "created the most tightly-woven plan for the brand, interlacing local market activity with a raft of hockey association, and, of course, that larcenous penguin." This combination of targeted television advertising and concentrated local and regional efforts proved quite successful as Bud Ice strengthened its grip on the top slot in the ice beer market.

The company also devoted a website to the birds, providing information about how the commercials were made, tie-ins to other Budweiser websites, and biographical data on the penguins. The graphics and prose style of the site were clearly targeted to the young adult audience.

OUTCOME

Although industry analyst Jerry Steinman acknowledged to *USA Today* that "it's hard to link increased sales of Bud Ice to one specific factor," the "Penguins" campaign was remarkably well received by television viewers. This enthusiasm was borne out by *USA Today* 's Ad Track survey, which monitored the popularity and effectiveness of national advertising campaigns. The penguin spots proved to be among the 10 most popular ads measured, winning the approval of nearly a third of the polled consumers. In 1996 Bud Ice's sales rose 21 percent, compared to the 1.8 percent increase of ice draft sales in general.

The campaign did receive stiff criticism from a variety of groups who accused Anheuser-Busch of using a cute mascot to lure children to its brand (and thereby create a lifelong market for it). A former ad executive told the *Milwaukee Journal Sentinel,* "When I worked on the McDonald's account [at another ad agency], the theory was to target kids 4- to 7-years-old. We thought if we could capture them at that age, we could keep them for life." Critics believed Anheuser-Busch's "Penguins" campaign was employing a similar strategy. Company officials, however, disputed the claim that the ads targeted kids, and Anheuser-Busch refused to pull the "Penguins" campaign. A spokeswoman for the company cited Anheuser-Busch's $160 million educational campaign against underage drinking as evidence of the brewer's opposition to youth drinking and its firm commitment to deterring it.

FURTHER READING

Causey, James. "Mascots with Attitude Invade a Wild Kingdom of Marketing." *Milwaukee Journal Sentinel,* April 29, 1996.

Enrico, Dottie. "Penguin Waddles to Popularity for Bud Ice." *USA Today,* July 15, 1996.

"Penguin on a Mission." *Brandweek,* May 19, 1997.

Prince, Greg. "Time and Again: Miller Goes Straight to the Core and Likes the Results." *Beverage World,* February 15, 1997.

Pruzan, Todd. "Bud Ice Gets Humming with Musical Penguins." *Advertising Age,* March 11, 1996.

Rebecca Stanfel

REAL AMERICAN HEROES/REAL MEN OF GENIUS CAMPAIGN

OVERVIEW

Anheuser-Busch Companies, Inc., had the two best-selling beers in the United States in 2000 as well as more than double the market share of any competitor. The company's flagship brew, Budweiser, remained the country's most popular alcoholic beverage despite a decade-long decline in sales. Bud Light had meanwhile been making double-digit percentage gains in sales and was poised to overtake the "King of Beers," thanks to the growing consumer preference for reduced-calorie beer. Anheuser-Busch maintained its market dominance in part by consistently setting the standard for beer advertising.

After assuming responsibility for advertising for the Bud family of brands in 1994, August A. Busch IV (son of August A. Busch III, the company's CEO) made it a priority to update Bud's image for a new generation of beer drinkers. Anheuser-Busch advertising, under Busch and marketing executive Bob Lachky, increasingly relied on irreverent, ironic humor to appeal to younger segments of its legal-drinking-age audience. Although radio had become an afterthought for many advertisers by the late 1990s, Anheuser-Busch continued to explore the medium's possibilities. In keeping with the tone of a mid-1990s radio campaign and Bud Light's consistently popular television campaigns, Anheuser-Busch unveiled a tongue-in-cheek series of radio spots called "Real American Heroes," which parodied beer advertisements of previous decades. Anheuser-Busch spent a reported $4 million on the radio campaign in 2002.

The "Real American Heroes" campaign made a bigger splash than many believed possible for a radio effort. Renamed "Real Men of Genius" after September 11, 2001, the campaign ran successfully for years, earning dozens of awards from the advertising industry while building a dedicated base of fans. "Real Men of Genius" made the rare leap from radio to television in 2003. Though the television commercials were likewise well regarded, the campaign returned exclusively to radio the following year.

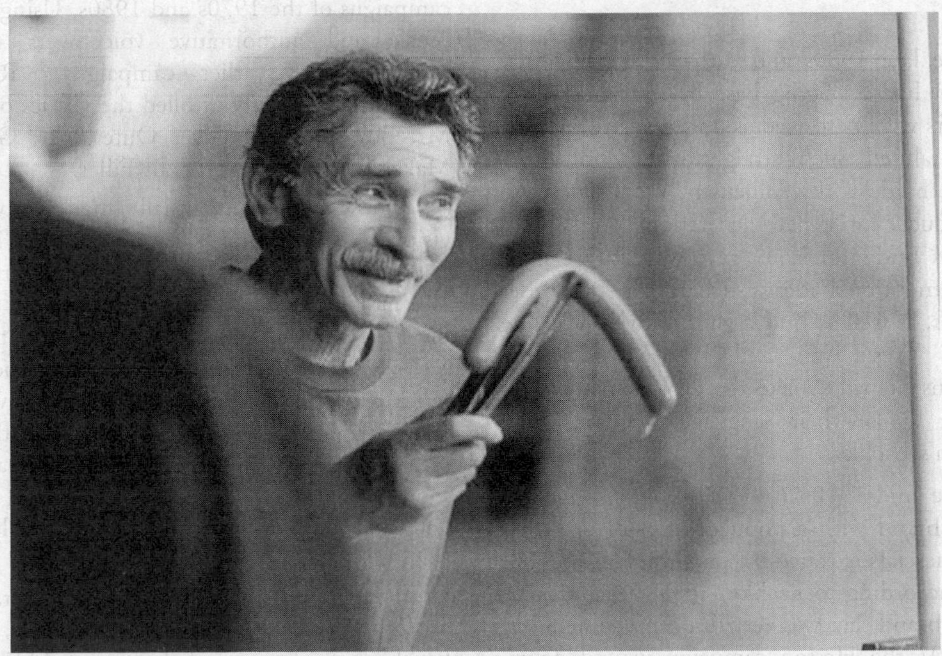

Mr. Footlong Hotdog Inventor, A Real American Hero. DDB/NEEDHAM, CHICAGO. REPRODUCED BY PERMISSION.

Mr. Really Bad Toupe Wearer, a Real American Hero. DDB/NEEDHAM, CHICAGO. REPRODUCED BY PERMISSION.

HISTORICAL CONTEXT

In the 1970s and 1980s top American brewers marketed their beers by appealing to consumers' affection for the blue-collar American workingman. Classic slogans such as "Miller Time" and "This Bud's for You" suggested that hardworking men deserved a quality beer at the end of the day and that, moreover, the "regular guy" was a hero deserving of recognition. Anthemic music and patriotic undercurrents were used to enhance the sincere, heroic tone of these commercials, and the formula proved successful until the early 1990s.

During the late 1980s and early 1990s, however, Anheuser-Busch had an aging base of consumers, and younger drinkers were perceived as unresponsive to commercials that saluted such straightforward values as patriotism and hard work. Anheuser-Busch sought to update its products for a new generation. The sincere statement "This Bud's for You" gave way, in the mid-1990s, to less traditional ideas, such as the Budweiser frogs and lizards, as well as Bud Light creative, including "Ladies Night," "Yes I Am!" and "I Love You, Man." These campaigns helped "make the 25-year-old believe that Budweiser spoke their language," according to Anheuser-Busch's Lachky.

Also in the mid-1990s Anheuser-Busch supported the Bud Light brand with a popular series of over-the-top radio commercials narrated by Charlton Heston. The Heston spots, according to Lachky, "carved out an area attached to the brand that was very fun, very young, very cut through." As the Heston campaign wound down, Anheuser-Busch commissioned Bud Light lead agency DDB Worldwide Chicago to come up with a replacement radio campaign.

TARGET MARKET

The focus of Anheuser-Busch's marketing efforts during this time was 21- to 27-year-old drinkers, a segment of the population that consumed more beer per capita than other age groups and had not yet formed strict brand allegiances. Like preceding Anheuser-Busch campaigns of the 1990s, "Real American Heroes" used ironic humor to reach its core audience. Beyond simply appealing to this audience's tastes, however, the radio spots capitalized on the younger market's wariness of traditional advertising techniques by mocking the sincere "work-reward" campaigns of the 1970s and 1980s. Using dramatic rock music and authoritative voice-overs that explicitly recalled those earlier campaigns, "Real American Heroes" sarcastically extolled the virtues of "heroes" like Mr. Bowling Shoe Giver Outer, Mr. Garden Gnome Maker, and Mr. Jelly Donut Filler.

The campaign eventually made its way onto television (after having been renamed "Real Men of Genius"), but many of the spots were particularly suited to a radio audience because they created, as Lachky told the *St. Louis Post-Dispatch,* a "theater of the mind" that activated the consumer's imagination. Though the spots mocked supposed everyday heroes, they were similar to the classic work-reward campaigns in that they were meant to reflect listeners' ordinary observations and personal experience. "Everybody has got their quirks," Lachky said, "and everybody has probably been a 'Real Man of Genius.'"

Supplementing Bud Light's brand strategy via radio campaigns became increasingly sensible, in Anheuser-Busch's view, because of the rise of cable television and the resulting fragmentation of the network viewing audience. Additionally Anheuser-Busch was able to place many of its radio spots locally as well as nationally.

MIDLER WAS NO SURVIVOR

DDB Worldwide Chicago originally envisioned using a Bette Midler song like "The Wind Beneath My Wings" for the sound track to the "Real American Heroes" commercials. But the rights to Midler's songs proved prohibitively expensive, and the Midler music did not work well in test runs. DDB's creative team began, instead, to lean toward a 1980s anthem-rock sound along the lines of Survivor's "Eye of the Tiger." The agency hired Chicago's Scandal Music to do an original parody of that sound, and it happened that Scandal's owner, Sandy Torano, was a friend of Survivor's lead singer, David Bickler. Far from being offended at the suggestion that he mock someone like himself, Bickler embraced the role. Indeed Bickler had long enjoyed a career not just as a rock star but as an ad pitchman, with singing credits that included a Kentucky Fried Chicken "Finger Lickin' Good" spot, a Frosted Flakes commercial, and work for Sprite's "Uncola" campaign. In TV versions of the "Real Men of Genius" spots, Bickler was shown wearing an unflattering wig and pumping his fists triumphantly while singing. "That's part of my role, to provide that exclamation point," he told *USA Today.* "I get into the spirit. I want it to be as good as it could be."

This benefited wholesalers, who needed to be able to respond to varying local conditions. Further, television viewing traditionally dropped off significantly during the summer months, the time of year when consumers drank the most beer. Radio allowed Anheuser-Busch to reach otherwise unreachable segments of its audience, including those who were traveling or engaging in leisure activities away from their televisions.

COMPETITION

Though Miller Brewing Company remained Anheuser-Busch's nearest rival, its market share had been decreasing for years, and its leading product, Miller Lite, was likewise losing market share when Bud Light's "Real American Heroes" campaign broke. Miller's advertising campaigns had been partially blamed for these declines. Miller Lite's "Dick" campaign, which ran on television in 1997 and 1998 and consisted of a series of absurdist vignettes supposedly dreamed up by a fictional advertising copywriter named Dick, attracted attention for its unpredictability and humor but did little to promote the beer itself. After abandoning "Dick," Miller Lite struggled to find new, compelling themes in its advertisements. In 2002, after being purchased by South Africa Breweries, Miller began using taste-test commercials claiming that Miller Lite outperformed Bud Light, and in 2004 Miller Lite began to make up ground against Bud Light and Coors Light by positioning itself, amid the low-carbohydrate diet craze, as a lower-carb alternative to its rivals.

The Adolph Coors Company, a distant third in the American beer wars, increased its market share in the late 1990s, and its leading product, Coors Light, had by 2001 surpassed Miller Lite to become the country's third most popular beer (and second most popular light beer). Coors Light's multiyear "Beer Man" television campaign, focusing on ballpark vendors, was seen by many wholesalers as a refreshing real-life contrast to campaigns like the Budweiser lizards and Miller Lite's "Dick."

MARKETING STRATEGY

Extending the tone of the Heston radio campaign and directly parodying Anheuser-Busch's own "This Bud's for You" concept, DDB's creative team singled out "regular guys" in overlooked jobs or with comical foibles, "people who just need to be called out to take a bow for whatever reason," as agency creative director John Immesoete said, and began scripting music-based mock tributes to them. For the commercials' sound track, DDB commissioned Chicago-based Scandal Music to compose a comically overblown 1980s song similar to the Survivor hit "Eye of the Tiger," and David Bickler, who had himself been Survivor's lead singer, was hired to do a bombastic parody of his own vocal work. After a lengthy search DDB hired announcer Pete Stacker, whose experience included traditional beer advertising, to do voice-over for the spots. The lyrics, sung in dramatic fashion by Bickler, worked in counterpoint to Stacker's deadpan baritone voice-over, and a portrait of each "hero" emerged against the background of soaring music. Anheuser-Busch was uncertain, in the beginning, about the extreme sarcasm of the commercials. "But we ran them past the consumer," Lachky told *Adweek,* "and they were a home run."

The initial series of 12 "Real American Heroes" spots attracted fans almost immediately. Radio personality Howard Stern lauded them on the air, and websites devoted to the jingles' lyrics began appearing. Tape recordings of the spots showed up for sale at the online auction site eBay, and "Real American Heroes," along with Budweiser's famous "Whassup?!" television commercials (also created by DDB Worldwide Chicago), began to dominate the awards circuit. The radio commercials were likewise popular with Anheuser-Busch executives and distributors, and DDB was told to "keep 'em coming," according to Immesoete. Another 17 spots followed the original 12. With the terrorist attacks of September 11, 2001, however, the premise of mocking American heroes suddenly seemed questionable, and the spots were pulled from circulation. The campaign reemerged in early 2002 as "Real Men of Genius."

The continuing success of "Real Men of Genius" led Anheuser-Busch to commission the campaign's adaptation for a 2003–04 television run. The move was seen as risky, even though similar Anheuser-Busch spots had already aired on British TV. The spots' success in the United States had depended, until then, on allowing the consumer to visualize the characters being parodied via song and voice-over. As DDB's Bob Winter told *Adweek,* "It was hard to think of how to do it visually on TV." The initial spots adapted included "Mr. Way Too Much Cologne Wearer," "Mr. Foot Long Hot Dog Inventor," and "Mr. Really Bad Toupee Wearer" and appeared on programs such as *Saturday Night Live* and *Monday Night Football.* A "Real Men of Genius" commercial likewise made it onto Anheuser-Busch's famously competitive Super Bowl roster, and the television campaign was, like its radio counterpart, a favorite on the awards circuit. Anheuser-Busch decided early on, however, to limit the number of TV adaptations. "Sometimes the best ideas are [best] left alone in the medium where they flourish," Lachky told the *St. Louis Post-Dispatch.*

The spots continued on radio. In 2004 the number of spots produced since the campaign's inception surpassed 100, and in Anheuser-Busch's view the potential to extend the idea was still endless.

OUTCOME

In addition to exceeding 100 spots, the "Real American Heroes/Real Men of Genius" campaign earned more than 100 advertising awards. The radio campaign won the top Radio-Mercury Award two years in a row, the 2003 Grand Clio, and numerous other Clio, ADDY, Kinsale, One Show, and ANDY awards. The television campaign won a Gold Lion at the International Advertising Festival in Cannes, France. Numerous websites devoted to lyrics and MP3 recordings of the commercials could be found on the Internet throughout the campaign's run. In 2003 and 2004 Anheuser-Busch released two volumes of official compact disc recordings of selected spots along with bonus tracks of unreleased spots. The campaign was credited with raising the profile of radio advertising as a whole.

In 2001 Bud Light, overtaking Budweiser in sales for the first time, became the number one beer in America. Continuing to dominate the domestic beer market, Anheuser-Busch had approached a market share of 50 percent by 2001 and held steady at that unprecedented level in following years. "We knew we had a winner with the 'Real Men of Genius' campaign early on," Lachky told *PR Newswire,* "but the popularity and longevity of the series has exceeded our expectations and provided a fantastic promotional opportunity for Bud Light."

FURTHER READING

Anderson, Mae. "'Genius' Gets Promotion." *Adweek,* December 1, 2003.

"Bud Light Roars at Cannes Lion Ad Festival as 'Real Men of Genius' Wins 'Gold Lion' for Creative Campaign." *PR Newswire,* June 28, 2004.

Cancelada, Gregory. "Bud Light Presents Radio Men of Genius." *St. Louis Post-Dispatch,* July 28, 2004.

Holt, Douglas B. "Interview with Steven Jackson." *Advertising and Society Review* 4, no. 2 (2003).

Howard, Theresa. "Anheuser-Busch's Silly 'Mr.' Ads Hit a High Note with Viewers." *USA Today,* January 12, 2004.

Jensen, Trevor. "DDB Produces 17 More 'Heroes.'" *Adweek,* July 24, 2000.

Khermouch, Gerry, and Trevor Jensen. "Least Likely to Succeed." *Brandweek,* November 9, 1998.

Lee, Thomas. "Long-Running Anheuser-Busch Radio Ad to Make It to Small Screen." *St. Louis Post-Dispatch,* November 12, 2003.

MacArthur, Kate. "A Sharp Wit and Modesty Mark Immesoete at DDB." *Advertising Age,* July 9, 2001.

McBride, Sarah. "Radio to Make Big Noise in Upfront: Advance Sales of Airtime, National Campaigns Seen as Way to Battle with TV." *Wall Street Journal,* May 18, 2004.

McCarthy, Michael. "Top Brewer Also Reigns as King of Marketing: Young, Hip Ads Help Anheuser-Busch Reach Consumers." *USA Today,* September 8, 2000.

"Survivor Singer Belts It Out for Bud Light." *USA Today,* January 12, 2004.

Wolf, Barnet D. "Anheuser-Busch Taps 'Genius.'" *Columbus (OH) Dispatch,* May 19, 2004.

Mark Lane

WHASSUP?! CAMPAIGN

OVERVIEW

In December 1999 Anheuser-Busch Companies, Inc., had the two best-selling beers in the United States and more than double the market share of any competitor. Despite a decade-long decline in sales, Budweiser, the company's flagship brew, remained the country's most popular alcoholic beverage, although, thanks largely to the growing consumer preference for reduced-calorie beer, Bud Light was poised to overtake the "King of

A still from Anheuser Busch's "Wassup?!" campaign. DDB/NEEDHAM, CHICAGO. REPRODUCED BY PERMISSION.

Beers." Anheuser-Busch already had the industry's biggest and most successful advertising presence, but the Budweiser television campaign called "Whassup?!" resonated with a new, more youthful audience and became not just an industry award winner but also a pop-culture phenomenon.

The idea behind the "Whassup?!" commercials, developed for Anheuser-Busch by DDB Worldwide Chicago, was simple. In the initial spot, called "Whassup True," four male friends, speaking over the phone, greeted one another with the slang phrase "Whassup?!" The answer—"Watching the game. Having a Bud"—elicited the response "True, true," before the conversation escalated into a chorus of "Whassups?!" delivered with mouths open, tongues protruding, and an air of intense glee. "It didn't feel like advertising," said DDB's Don Pogany. "It seemed different than anything else. And it seemed to be totally what Bud is about: camaraderie and friendship and what guys do." A second spot aired during the 2000 Super Bowl, and several more featuring the "Whassup?!" guys aired later in the winter. Each of the spots ended with the Budweiser logo against a black background and the tagline "True."

Within a few months of the campaign's introduction, unauthorized Internet parodies began to appear that featured people in the news, cartoon superheroes, and many others greeting one another with innumerable variations on "Whassup?!" Disc jockeys and late-night talk-show hosts began saying "Whassup?!" and soon it became a common greeting and a pop-culture phrase around the world, even in countries where Budweiser was not sold. The initial campaign won nearly every major industry award, and later installments continued to win awards. "Whassup?!" ran through 2001 and was then developed into a more expansive campaign called "True," in which the tagline from the original commercials was interpreted in new ways meant to show beer drinkers that Budweiser understood them and their lives.

HISTORICAL CONTEXT

In 1992 August A. Busch IV, whose father, August A. Busch III, was the CEO of Anheuser-Busch, took charge of marketing for the Budweiser family of brands. At the time imports and microbrews posed threats to the Anheuser-Busch juggernaut, and as Michael McCarthy of *USA Today* put it, "Bud was becoming your dad's beer." Though Anheuser-Busch and Budweiser had a long history of marketing prowess, as evidenced by the iconic status of their trademark Clydesdale horses and by enduring slogans like the "King of Beers" and "This

Bud's for You," Busch set out to update the Bud image for a new generation of beer drinkers.

Busch and Anheuser-Busch executive Bob Lachky oversaw a period of breakthroughs in creative work on behalf of the Budweiser brands. Between 1993 and 1995 campaigns such as "Ladies Night," "Yes I Am!" and "I Love You Man," all on behalf of Bud Light, helped, in Lachky's words, "make the 25-year-old believe that Budweiser spoke their language." Anheuser-Busch began using a combination of different advertising agencies while relying primarily on DDB and on Goodby, Silverstein & Partners, the San Francisco agency responsible for the successful "Louie the Lizard" campaign. According to Lachky, the use of multiple agencies encouraged "a healthy competition and better creative work."

By 1999 Anheuser-Busch had an estimated market share of 47.5 percent, up from 43 percent at the beginning of the decade. Budweiser, however, continued to lose ground yearly. Although this was seen as a reflection of consumer preference rather than a deficiency in the product or in marketing, Anheuser-Busch continued to allocate large amounts of advertising money and energy to Budweiser. This was intended to arrest the slide in Budweiser's market share, but also, as Hillary Chura noted in *Advertising Age,* "Advertising dedicated to Budweiser often boosts sales of other brands like Bud Light, Bud Ice, and the rest of the brand family."

TARGET MARKET

Anheuser-Busch expected the "Whassup?!" ads to resonate across demographic lines within the 21- to 27-year-old segment of the population, an essential part of Budweiser's larger target market of all legal-age drinkers. Not only did this segment of young adults account for a disproportionate percentage of beer sales relative to other adults, its brand loyalties had presumably not yet been formed. The spots featured a mostly African-American cast, and the campaign's central verbal exchange was based on slang terms used in minority communities, although the universal principles of friendship that were displayed had the power, Anheuser-Busch believed, to attract young viewers across racial, ethnic, and gender divides. Barbara Lippert argued in *Adweek* that the ads were about "feeling so connected to your best buds you can watch TV together through the phone. And that while you are supposedly 'chillin,' you are all maniacally dialing each other."

Anheuser-Busch, however, wanted to avoid alienating older customers who did not understand the significance of the characters' boisterous attitudes and protruding tongues. When a group of wholesalers expressed their disapproval of the emerging campaign, Lachky and Busch decided not to continue to air the original version but to showcase "Whassup?!" spots that relied on individual narratives and thereby helped viewers make sense of the characters. They also decided to trim the 60-second spots to 30 seconds in order to reduce the amount of time occupied by the "Whassup?!" ritual itself. Soon Internet parodies began, and the campaign attracted mainstream media attention. Once "Whassup?!" became part of the pop-culture vocabulary, the campaign had an air of widespread public validation that overcame all demographic divisions. As *Advertising Age* put it, "Any advertising that bridges generation gaps so that even our mothers are leaving 'Whassup?!' messages on our answering machines must be a good one."

THE QUESTION OF ORIGIN

After "Whassup?!" had won both the Grand Clio and the Cannes Grand Prix in 2000, there were complaints within the advertising industry. Some felt that it was inappropriate to give the industry's highest honors to a campaign that had not originally come from an advertising agency at all. The idea, of course, was Charles Stone III's, and the initial spot was similar to his independent film *True.* But Stone was not himself the sole author of the idea. "Whassup?!" was a greeting that he and his friends had been using with one another since 1984.

COMPETITION

Although Miller Brewing Company remained Anheuser-Busch's nearest rival, Miller's market share, which had been decreasing for years, dropped from 21.7 to 19.6 percent between 1999 and 2001. Advertising campaigns for the company's two top brews, Miller Lite and Miller Genuine Draft, had been blamed for failing to move the products. Miller Lite's "Dick" campaign, which ran in 1997 and 1998 and consisted of a series of absurdist vignettes dreamed up by a fictional advertising copywriter named Dick, attracted attention for its unpredictability and humor, but it did little to promote the beer itself. Miller Genuine Draft's "Never Miss a Genuine Opportunity" campaign, which relied on openly sexual themes and narratives, was derided by many for being too graphic and, like the "Dick" campaign, for failing to establish any connection between the story line and the product. After abandoning these campaigns, Miller struggled to find new, compelling themes in its advertising.

TALK VALUE

DDB Worldwide Chicago claimed to have pioneered the concept of "talk value," that elusive quality that makes advertising campaigns and phrases cultural touchstones, but the "Whassup?!" campaign far exceeded the agency's and Anheuser-Busch's expectations. The phrase appeared as a headline on the cover of *Forbes,* and the commercials were parodied on *Saturday Night Live* in addition to being mentioned countless times in the media while being spread around the world via more than 80 homemade Internet parodies. At the 2000 Grammy Awards performers Christina Aguilera and LeVar Burton imitated the "Whassup?!" commercials on the red carpet, and during that year's NBA season the Sacramento Kings gave a collective cry of "Whassup?!" after each team huddle.

The Adolph Coors Company, a distant third in the American beer wars, had increased its market share to 11.1 percent by 2001, and its leading product, Coors Light, had surpassed Miller Lite to become the country's third most popular beer. "Beer Man," a Coors Light advertising campaign that focused on ballpark vendors, was seen by many wholesalers as a refreshing, real-life contrast to campaigns like the Budweiser lizards and Miller Lite's "Dick." An effort to turn back slumping sales of the company's Original Coors beer by touting its alcohol content and rich taste met with mixed results in the declining market for full-calorie domestic beers.

MARKETING STRATEGY

"Whassup?!" had its genesis outside the advertising world in a short film called *True,* created by music-video director Charles Stone III as a means of trying to break into feature films. A DDB creative director discovered *True* and immediately recommended it to his supervisor as suitable for a Budweiser advertisement. The film, which became "Whassup True" after minor adjustments in content, featured Stone and three of his friends. Stone himself was tapped to direct and to act in the series of commercials DDB began scripting, and though roughly 80 other actors were auditioned for the parts of Stone's friends, with one exception DDB hired the real-life friends to play themselves. Stone worried that the slang response "True" might need to be scrapped in favor of a more mainstream line like "Right on," but Anheuser-Busch's Lachky recognized the trend setting potential of the original.

"Whassup True" originally aired with little fanfare on sports programming in December 1999. The 60-second commercial was a hit with the 21- to 27-year-old demographic, but for the 2000 Super Bowl Anheuser-Busch chose the shorter and less risky "Girlfriend," in which one of the "Whassup?!" friends answered the phone in characteristic fashion while trying not to let on that the "game" he was watching with his girlfriend was actually a figure-skating competition. Other spots in the original campaign included one in which a pizza deliverer was mistaken for a friend and subjected, over an apartment-building intercom, to the "Whassup?!" routine. The spots eventually ran during sports programming, as well as prime-time and late-night shows.

After Internet parodies and media attention became widespread, "Whassup?!" was at risk of becoming over-exposed, and Anheuser-Busch and DDB worked to keep the campaign fresh by running their own spoofs. In "Come Home" an alien, returning to his home planet after infiltrating Earth in the guise of a dog, was asked by his ruler what he had learned from his time among humans. After a short pause the alien declared, mouth wide and tongue lolling, "Whassup?!" In addition, DDB created a unique hybrid commercial called "Language Tape," in which a professor-like character directed viewers to Budweiser.com, where they could learn how to say "Whassup?!" in 36 different languages. Website traffic increased to 1.265 million visitors per month, compared to the previous year's average of 400,000.

Anheuser-Busch and DDB went on to run commercials featuring New Jersey men bearing a strong resemblance to characters on the hit television show *The Sopranos,* who said, "Howyoudoin," instead of "Whassup?!" After this final twist on the original idea, Budweiser's advertising agencies, along with its in-house marketing team, began producing various television spots that more broadly interpreted the tagline "True." These spots included story lines offering honest and affectionate reflections on gender differences and male behavior, commercials with a focus on product quality, and several series of vignettes, such as the well-known "Leon" commercials, which revolved around the comical exploits of an extremely self-centered professional football player.

OUTCOME

"Whassup?!" was one of the most acclaimed and popular campaigns in advertising history. It won nearly every major award in the industry, including the prestigious Grand Clio and the Grand Prix at the International

Advertising Festival in Cannes, France. During the second year of the "Whassup?!" campaign, Busch was named Advertiser of the Year at the Cannes festival. The campaign's signature phrase earned comparisons to classic advertising phrases like Wendy's "Where's the Beef?" and Nike's "Just Do It." Busch said of the "Whassup?!" campaign, "In our lifetimes, we'll never see so much value created from a single idea. It makes Budweiser a brand for every culture, every demographic and every community. It makes Budweiser a younger, hipper, more contemporary brand."

The decline in Budweiser sales could not be stopped, however. Meanwhile, sales of Bud Light continued to grow at double-digit rates, and in 2001 it surpassed Budweiser to become the best-selling beer in the United States. Anheuser-Busch continued to dominate the domestic beer market. In 2000 the company increased shipments and sales by 2.8 percent, and in 2001 it likewise outperformed the industry, approaching a market share of nearly 50 percent. Budweiser's umbrella "True" campaign, so memorably launched by the "Whassup?!" commercials, continued.

FURTHER READING

Beirne, Mike. "Can Your Beer Do This?" *Brandweek,* October 15, 2001.

Burford, Ru-El. "In Defense of 'Whassup?!': Bud Campaign Struck Chord with Minority Communities." *Advertising Age,* September 25, 2000.

Chura, Hillary. "Budweiser Loses Share While Its Siblings Grow." *Advertising Age,* November 22, 1999.

———. "Miller, Shops Prep for Ultimate Test." *Advertising Age,* April 16, 2001.

"Cybercritique: DDB Ad Pours a Pleasing Dose of 'Whassup?!'" *Advertising Age,* November 13, 2000.

Heller, Karen. "Budweiser's Whassup Ads Light Up Director's Career." *Philadelphia Inquirer,* March 17, 2000.

Khermouch, Gerry. "The Quiet Beer Man." *Brandweek,* October 12, 1998.

Khermouch, Gerry, and Trevor Jenson. "Least Likely to Succeed." *Brandweek,* November 9, 1998.

Lauro, Patricia Winters. "Whassup? America's Asking." *New York Times,* February 16, 2001.

Lippert, Barbara. "'True' Love." *Adweek* (midwest ed.), July 3, 2000.

McCarthy, Michael. "Top Brewer Also Reigns as King of Marketing: Young, Hip Ads Help Anheuser-Busch Reach Consumers." *USA Today,* September 8, 2000.

———. "'Whassup?!' Four Buddies Find Fame as Their Personal Greeting Enters the Pop Culture Lexicon in an Ad Campaign." *USA Today,* March 14, 2000.

Panczyk, Tania D. "Bud Extends 'True' Campaign." *Adweek* (midwest ed.), March 25, 2002.

Prince, Greg W. "Long Live the King." *Beverage Aisle,* May 15, 2002.

Mark Lane

Apple Computer, Inc.

1 Infinite Loop
Cupertino, California 95014
USA
Telephone: (408) 996-1010
Web site: www.apple.com

IMAC CAMPAIGN

OVERVIEW

In the late 1990s technology analysts speculated that Apple Computer, Inc.'s fate hinged on its new personal computer the iMac. Apple's share of the worldwide desktop-computer market had plummeted since 1995, the last year the company had been profitable. Ever greater numbers of consumers were buying personal computers (PCs) that ran on Microsoft's Windows operating system rather than Apple's version. Although Apple had pioneered user-friendly computers, the company had not introduced a consumer-targeted computer since 1992. Hoping that its stylish new iMac would propel Apple back into this vast segment of the market, Apple released its "iMac" campaign.

The $100 million campaign, created by the ad agency TBWA\Chiat\Day, debuted on August 16, 1998. Its advertisements featured brightly hued computers against a plain white background, thereby further emphasizing the iMac's one-of-a-kind colorful shell, and contained snappy copy that underscored either the iMac's aesthetics or its user-friendliness. The campaign, which consisted of network and national cable television commercials (as well as spot television marketing in Apple's top 10 markets), magazine, billboard, and bus ads, and radio spots, was the largest marketing effort in Apple's history. But despite the high stakes involved for the company, the "iMac" campaign delivered its message in a "fun and factual" way, an Apple spokesperson stated in the August 14, 1998, *San Francisco Chronicle.* The ads highlighted the iMac's easy Internet access, its simplicity (especially when compared to rival PCs), and its speed. Central to each ad was the iMac's unique design. "Chic, not geek," proclaimed one, while another simply said, "iCandy."

The iMac's debut was triumphant, and 1998 proved to be Apple's first profitable year since 1995. Many industry analysts credited the iMac as the primary force behind this turnaround. "A year and a half ago, Apple had no future; now it does," proclaimed *Fortune.* Consumer surveys revealed that a substantial percentage of iMac purchasers were first-time Apple buyers, which indicated that the "iMac" campaign had succeeded in its goal of winning over new computer buyers and PC converts.

HISTORICAL CONTEXT

Founded in 1977, Apple had fallen on hard times by the mid-1990s. The company had made history in 1984 when it introduced the Macintosh, a machine that revolutionized the computer world with its graphical screen displays, pull-down menus, and other user-friendly features. While International Business Machines Corp. (IBM) licensed its operating system and other technologies, thereby launching an armada of inexpensive PC clones, Apple instead honed its image as the purveyor

© LWA- JDC/CORBIS.

of "machine[s] for free-thinking, discriminating nonconformists and rebels," according to *Macworld.* Apple consistently touted the fact that its computers, unlike those of its rivals, were simple to use. The introduction of Microsoft's Windows operating system in the early 1990s undermined the force of these claims, however, as Windows provided similar graphical features and screen windows. A proliferation of similar products confused customers at the same time that Apple's image-making efforts devolved into chaos. By 1996, 25 separate Apple campaigns were running simultaneously. As the company's market share plummeted precipitously—from a high of around 14 percent in 1993 to a paltry 3 percent in 1997—software writers threatened to stop creating programs for the Apple operating system, claiming there was no profit to be made. Consumers began to doubt that Apple would survive and were reluctant to spend thousands of dollars on a machine that might quickly become a dinosaur. "This company was in a death spiral," an Apple executive told *Newsweek.*

Steve Jobs, one of Apple's founders, returned to the company as interim CEO in 1997 and quickly strove to right the troubled company. After trimming the product line to two broad categories—home and business—Jobs vowed to focus the "home" line on Apple's key markets of consumers and school users. At the same time Jobs oversaw the creation of 1997's "Think Different" advertising campaign, a high-profile effort designed to reassert that Apple, though plagued by bad press and sinking profits, was a vibrant company producing innovative products for innovative people. Jobs' strategy halted the company's free fall, and in April 1998 Apple reported its second straight profitable quarter. The company still needed to prove that it could compete for the consumer market with rival PC makers such as Hewlett-Packard, Compaq, and Dell. While Apple retained "Think Different" as an overarching branding campaign, it needed advertisements to herald the arrival of its newest machine, the iMac.

TARGET MARKET

Apple wanted to market the iMac predominantly to three groups: loyal Apple users, first-time computer buyers, and PC owners. As the company had not introduced a new consumer product since 1992, it hoped that many Apple users would choose to upgrade to the iMac. The company had long cultivated a rebellious image, with advertisements ranging from the famous "1984" commercial to the stark "Think Different" photos of maverick geniuses who had flouted conventional wisdom to make stunning contributions. As a result Apple buyers tended to be those who perceived themselves to be somewhat outside the mainstream and who valued creativity. Advertisements for the iMac were crafted to reach this group as well. The print ads used arty photos of the iMac that made the computer look less like a machine and more like a museum piece. The taglines in some of the print pieces also followed the Apple advertising formula. For instance, "I think therefore iMac," punned on Descartes' famous maxim, and understanding the reference required a degree of intellectual

© PATRICK DURAND/CORBIS/SYGMA.

literacy. Moreover, the quirky, insider-type wit was likely to appeal to the alternative audience comprising the bulk of Apple loyalists.

Reaching first-time computer buyers presented an entirely different set of challenges. An industry analyst estimated that 5 million to 10 million consumers were ready to buy their first computer. According to an Apple news release this analyst concluded that "access to the Internet is a leading reason for consumers to buy a personal computer." The technological world was often overwhelming to the uninitiated, though, with its talk of RAM, gigabytes, and modem speed. The "iMac" campaign sought to allay these consumers' fears. One print ad suggested that the most complicated aspect of buying an iMac was deciding which color to purchase. "The thrill of surfing. The agony of choosing," the piece quipped. "Buying a computer used to be a decision based on processor power, functions, and software packages," said the *Austin American-Statesman.* "iMac has changed things because it is now about choosing between strawberry and grape." Other print ads—"Yum" and "iCandy"—likened the machine to a sweet treat, further demystifying it. The television commercials, such as "Simplicity Shootout," also emphasized the iMac's user-friendliness by juxtaposing Apple's easy setup and Internet access with the hassle of trying to use a Windows-based PC for the first time. Commercials featuring the actor Jeff Goldblum validated the insecurities of the Internet "newbie." "It seems a big party is going on these days," Goldblum said to the camera, referring to the Internet. "[But] I don't have an e-mail." He then proceeded to explain how easy it was to get on the Internet with the iMac.

The third group Apple strove to target with the "iMac" campaign was consumers using other PCs. Many analysts doubted that Apple could entice an appreciable number of Windows aficionados to purchase the iMac as their next computer, according to *Tulsa World.* Apple believed it could. To do so, the company hammered home the message that the iMac was faster, simpler, and equally as affordable as comparable PCs. The "iMac" campaign conveyed that "[w]e have a better product," an Apple executive told *Advertising Age.* Apple also used the iMac's style as an important selling point. One particular print ad (that humorously declared, "Sorry, no beige" above a turquoise iMac) embodied an underlying premise of the "iMac" campaign: "people [would] be able to further express themselves through their computers," as an Apple spokesperson told the *Austin American-Statesman.*

COMPETITION

The magnitude of Apple's goal of convincing first-time computer buyers and PC owners to consider the iMac was mammoth. According to *Investor's Business Daily,* 85 percent of the desktop-computer market consisted of Windows-based PCs. The leading computer manufacturer was Compaq, which in 1994 overtook IBM to

AN INTERNATIONAL CAMPAIGN

The "iMac" campaign was truly a global marketing effort. Half of the $100 million ad budget was used in the United States, but the remaining sum brought the message of the iMac's simplicity to Europe, Japan, and other international markets. The campaign was released in these regions on August 29, 1998.

become the market leader. Compaq was no stranger to consumer-oriented advertising campaigns. In 1995 Compaq debuted "Has It Changed Your Life Yet?," which was created by the ad agency Ammirati Puris Lintas. The commercials were intended to show how Compaq PCs "change[d] . . . lives in small but important ways for the better," an Ammirati spokesperson told *Marketing Computers.* One spot showed a delighted child receiving a Compaq for Christmas. In 1998 Compaq doubled its ad spending for its Presario computer, which was its primary consumer-oriented machine. In February 1999 Compaq inaugurated a worldwide branding campaign. As of October 1998 Compaq maintained a 13.7 percent share of the worldwide computer market.

IBM devoted a massive advertising budget to reaching home-computer users. In the early 1990s IBM came under attack for being an unwieldy behemoth in the increasingly nimble computer industry. In an effort to revamp its image IBM began its "Solutions for a Small Planet" campaign in 1995. Although many of these Ogilvy & Mather spots directly addressed businesses, the overall goal of the campaign was to bolster the IBM brand. In February 1998 IBM specifically sought to reach consumers when it spent $50 million on an Olympics ad campaign. The print ads and television spots celebrated little-known athletes whose personal accomplishments embodied the spirit of the Olympic Games. As *Advertising Age* explained, IBM planned to "make viewers feel better about IBM and better about IBM technology." In addition to airing the campaign during Olympics broadcasts on CBS and TNT, print pieces appeared in *Sports Illustrated, Time,* the *Wall Street Journal,* and *USA Today.* IBM had an 8.6 percent share of the market in October 1998.

Another rival, Hewlett-Packard, teamed up with agency Goodby, Silverstein & Partners in 1997 to produce "Expanding Possibilities," a $40 million consumer campaign. Other competitors, such as Microsoft, Intel, and Dell, also engaged in brand-building campaigns during the period.

MARKETING STRATEGY

To reach the diverse audience comprising its three target markets, Apple unleashed the "iMac" campaign with a media blitz. "It is easily our most far-reaching, coordinated use of the media," a company spokesperson told the *San Francisco Chronicle.* Television commercials played a central role in communicating the campaign's message to a vast number of consumers. While many rival computer companies focused heavily on trade publications, Apple aggressively pursued consumers where they lived. "Determining the media mix was complicated," an Apple executive told *Editor & Publisher.* "iMac is targeted toward a variety of different markets, [and buyers] don't necessarily need to be technologically savvy." After the campaign's launch on *The Wonderful World of Disney,* iMac spots aired on popular network shows that garnered a mainstream audience, such as *Home Improvement, Spin City, Just Shoot Me, Friends,* and *20/20.* Apple also used national cable channels, such as Comedy Central, FX, and MSNBC. To ensure that its base of Apple users knew of the iMac and its updated features, the company also bought local air time in its top 10 markets: Boston, Los Angeles, New York, San Francisco, Chicago, Philadelphia, Washington, D.C., Seattle, Minneapolis, and Denver.

The television commercials relied on humor to convey the iMac's qualities. A spot called "Simplicity Shootout" featured "Adam Taggert, 26, Brown University graduate, Class of 1994" competing against a 7-year-old boy and his dog in a duel to set up their respective new computers. Taggert, who had selected a PC, fumbled with cables and manuals for quite a while, while the youngster had his iMac up and running in five minutes. Later television spots portrayed actor Jeff Goldblum (who had provided the voice-over on earlier iMac commercials) talking frankly and calmly about the iMac. Still others concentrated on the visual vividness of the machine. In January 1999, after Apple launched five additional iMac colors (tangerine, lime, strawberry, blueberry, and grape), TBWA\Chiat\Day created a commercial that pictured the five bright iMacs spinning artfully to the Rolling Stones' song "She's a Rainbow."

Apple used other media as well. The colorful print "iMac" pieces were published in a number of consumer magazines, including *ESPN, Time, Entertainment Weekly, Wired, Vanity Fair, Elle,* and *Metropolitan Home.* Moreover, the company engaged in a major saturation effort in its top 10 markets. Billboard versions of the ads (showing the iMac and containing a single tagline, such as "Mental Floss"), bus ads, and radio spots all played an important role. Apple also broadcast "countdown to iMac" radio pieces in these markets during the days prior to the iMac's introduction. In addition, it sponsored radio promotions in which an iMac was given away every day. The company even went so far as to install 20-foot inflatable iMacs atop some computer stores. "Apple is acting more like a package[d]-good marketer than a technology company," exclaimed *Advertising Age.* An analyst for the magazine concurred: "They're creating an environment in which an awful lot of potential consumers are paying attention to them." Maintaining such a high profile was essential not only for Apple to sell more iMacs, but also "to reestablish the company's credibility," according to the *San Francisco Chronicle.*

OUTCOME

Despite a blockbuster launch of the iMac, many commentators predicted that the quirky machine would not convert PC users or lure first-time buyers. They were wrong. In its first weekend the iMac generated $25 million in sales. "It was the best-selling computer we ever had in a single day," a representative from CompUSA proclaimed to the *New York Daily News.* Nor was this a flash in the pan. At the close of 1998 Apple announced $309 million in profits, of which "sales of the iMac accounted for a good portion," said the *San Jose Mercury News.* The company's stock prices shot up, as did its market share, which reached 5 percent in October 1998. The following month the iMac was the best-selling desktop computer in the United States. And, as the *San Jose Mercury News* noted, the iMac "wooed not only Mac faithfuls but also first-time buyers and veteran users of other systems who were new to Mac." A consumer survey reported in *Newsbytes News Network* revealed that an estimated 40 percent of iMac buyers were new Apple buyers.

Apple remained committed to growth in the consumer sector. "Apple's future is in the consumer market," an ebullient Jobs told *Fortune.* In July 1999 the company debuted the iBook, a portable computer designed for consumer use. This laptop, like the iMac, featured bright colors and a unique design. Even though the campaign's exposure waned after 2000, the "iMac" campaign did not officially end until Apple released its 2002 "Switchers" campaign, which featured real-life people whose lives were improved after they switched to Apple computers.

FURTHER READING

Emert, Carol. "The Selling of Apple's iMac." *San Francisco Chronicle,* August 19, 1998.

Ha, K. Oanh. "Apple Computer Earnings Surpass Expectations." *San Jose Mercury News,* October 15, 1998.

Hines, Matt. "iMac Launches and Continues to Sell." *Newsbytes News Network,* August 17, 1998.

"iMac Ads Top $19 Million." *Editor & Publisher,* June 26, 1999.

Johnson, Bradley. "$100 Million iMac Blitz Is Tops in Home Computer History." *Advertising Age,* August 17, 1998.

Kallenberg, Gregory. "Candy Computers." *Austin (TX) American-Statesman,* April 13, 1999.

Kirkpatrick, David. "The Second Coming of Apple." *Fortune,* November 9, 1998.

Levy, Steve. "Hello Again. A New Computer, the iMac, from Apple Computer." *Newsweek,* May 18, 1998.

Li, Steve. "iMac Sales Add Polish." *New York Daily News,* August 18, 1998.

Piller, Charles. "Macintosh Mystique" *Macworld,* February 1, 1994.

Smith, Dawn. "Portrait of a Marriage" *Marketing Computers,* June 1, 1995

Swartz, Jon. "Big Apple Ad Blitz for iMac" *San Francisco Chronicle,* August 14, 1998.

Turner, Nick. "iMac Gives Apple Spotlight, but Can It Stay Center Stage?" *Investor's Business Daily,* August 17, 1998.

Rebecca Stanfel
Kevin Teague

SILHOUETTE CAMPAIGN

OVERVIEW

Released by Apple Computer, Inc., in November 2001, the iPod rapidly grew in sales and by 2005 had become the world's top-selling MP3 player. With a 1,000-song capacity, the first iPod worked only with Apple computers and retailed at $400. From 2003 to 2005, however, Apple ferociously promoted five new Windows-compatible iPod models, along with the company's digital music store, iTunes. In an attempt to define the fun associated with the iPod brand and to steer advertising away from the Apple computer, the company released its "Silhouette" campaign.

In October 2003 ad agency TBWA\Chiat\Day (TBWA\C\D) introduced outdoor "Silhouette" ads in Los Angeles, followed by a nationwide print and television launch. All ads displayed black silhouettes of people listening to white iPods and dancing in front of radiant green, yellow, fuchsia, and pink backgrounds. The television spots were accompanied by upbeat music from bands like N.E.R.D. and the Black Eye Peas. The band U2 shocked fans and critics in 2004 by endorsing iPod through the release of a new single, "Vertigo." Shrugging off criticism, U2's front man, Bono, stated that the iPod was "the most beautiful object art in music culture since the electric guitar." Seventy-two hours after the U2 endorsement, Apple stock reached

The iPod U2 Special Edition. © KIM KULISH/CORBIS.

a 52-week high of $53.20 per share. Apple reportedly spent $49.6 million on the "Silhouette" campaign between January and August of 2004.

Not only did "Silhouette" earn TBWA\C\D a Global Effie from the New York American Marketing Association and a Kelly Award from the Magazine Publishers of America, the agency was nominated as the U.S. Agency of the Year for 2004 by *Adweek.* Even though analysts' early forecasts for iPod sales were $400 million, product improvement and the "Silhouette" campaign helped Apple reach an incredible $1.2 billion in net sales during the first quarter of 2005 alone. Despite the fact that iPod's market share had dropped from 92 percent in October 2004 to 87 percent by March 2005, demand still overshadowed supply.

HISTORICAL CONTEXT

Led by CEO Steve Jobs, Apple held a meager 2.5 percent share of the worldwide computer market in 2001. Learning from its proprietary mistakes in the 1980s, the company released Windows-compatible iPods in 2002. Apple also allowed third-party companies like BMW, Bose Corporation, and Griffin Technology to create iPod accessories, which led to more than $100 million in sales in 2004. Apple even allowed Hewlett-Packard to release the Apple iPod from HP.

The first commercial for iPod, also created by TBWA\C\D, aired in 2001. It showed a bespectacled man huddled over an Apple iBook. At first the audience heard only the man's clicking keyboard, until music from Propellerheads's "Take California" grew louder. By the end of the spot it became apparent that the man was downloading music onto his iPod. Next TBWA\C\D shifted away from computer-centric ads to develop spots with people singing out loud while wearing iPods. One commercial, which featured a young boy singing Eminem's "Lose Yourself," resulted in a lawsuit by Eminem, but it was settled amicably.

Apple needed success from the "Silhouette" campaign. By 2002 the company still had only 5 percent of the computer market. "The history of Apple is a long, complicated business story with a lot of mistakes made," Lee Clow, worldwide chairman and chief creative officer of TBWA\C\D, told *Advertising Age.* "Particularly the decision to stick with a proprietary system for PCs which resulted in Microsoft's dominance." In 2004 iPod contributed 23 percent of Apple's earnings. Jobs said that iPod sales "should also help introduce Windows users to Apple's clever and stylish designs, thus encouraging more PC users to switch to Macintosh computers." Apple hoped that the fun-oriented, carefree format of the "Silhouette" ads would appeal to a more inclusive audience than past campaigns had. Instead of pitting itself against Microsoft or PCs, Apple wanted to focus solely on the fun associated with the iPod in order to solidify its position as the top-selling MP3 player.

TARGET MARKET

According to Beth Snyder Bulik of *Advertising Age,* iPod's target market "is wide, including current iPod owners looking for a second device; Gen X parents now willing to bankroll the $100 to placate their teens; and consumers with more modest income." Experts like Seth Godin, an author of marketing books, explained to the *Dayton Daily News* that the target demographic was much larger: "It's unusual for a product like this to cross all the gender and age lines right away, but iPod is doing both." U.S. President George W. Bush, singer and songwriter Tom Petty, Queen Elizabeth II, and even the late motion-picture star Marlon Brando all owned iPods. "The new ads do a terrific job of seducing and selling, of making the target turn on and want the product, now," Marian Salzman, executive vice president and chief strategy officer of Euro RSCG Worldwide, told *USA Today.* "Interestingly, the ads also transcend nationality and age. They are about an Apple state of mind."

Ad Track, *USA Today* 's weekly consumer survey, stated that across age groups the "Silhouette" campaign was most popular with 25- to 29-year-olds. For consumers between the ages of 50 and 64, 19 percent gave "Silhouette" ads the highest possible rating. The iPod's compatibility with illegally downloadable music drew criticism from some, however. Eric Garland, president of Big Champagne (a company that tracks Internet file

iPOD KNOCKOFFS

The iPod "Silhouette" campaign drew an outpouring of knockoffs. One came from a Fuse TV outdoor ad that showed a silhouetted Iraqi war prisoner next to a bomb resembling Apple's logo and with the copy "iRaq." Apple was reportedly infuriated by the ad. Fuse TV also produced an ad with a silhouetted stripper who pole danced next to the tagline "fuse music television. watch different."

sharing), told the *Irish Times,* "If anything, the illegal MP3 user base makes up a large part of the target market."

By using contemporary pop music, the "Silhouette" campaign directly targeted fans of N.E.R.D., the Caesars, Daft Punk, Jet, the Black Eye Peas, and, most famously, U2. This last group, notorious for turning down multimillion-dollar endorsements, not only gave Apple consent to use its music but actually released its single "Vertigo" in a 30-second "Silhouette" spot.

COMPETITION

South Korea's ReignCom Ltd., trying to move into an MP3 market dominated by iPod, which had 92 percent of sales in 2004, launched an outdoor, print, and Web campaign for its iRiver player; the campaign featured porn star Jenna Jameson. The iRiver PMC 140 boasted video capabilities but was priced $200 above Apple's iPod Photo. Earlier versions of iRiver MP3 players had featured radio tuners and voice recorders that were not available on iPods. For the promotion of iRiver's H10 model, print ads showed people listening to their MP3 players and biting into apples along with the tagline "Sweeter One." In 2005 iRiver ranked second in terms of market share.

By 2002 Sony Corporation, which had dominated the portable music market during the 1980s and 1990s, had lost considerable ground to the Apple iPod. In 2004 Sony released the Network Walkman, an MP3 player resembling the iPod in price and features and that was user-friendly. Sony's U.S. advertising, lead by Young & Rubicam, featured music by Macy Gray. Advertisements in Europe, however, used edgier music by bands like Teddy Bears STHLM. One commercial featured the painter Liam Yates listening to a Sony MP3 player and working on an image resembling a "Silhouette" ad. In 2005 Sony released its PlayStation Portable (PSP), a handheld gaming device that played MP3s. Early on industry analysts had forecast that the PSP would be an "iPod killer," but its release had little effect on iPod's market share.

MARKETING STRATEGY

TBWA\C\D introduced outdoor "Silhouette" ads in Los Angeles during the second week of September 2003, immediately after Apple had announced earnings of $2.15 billion for its third fiscal quarter. On September 15 TBWA\C\D launched "Silhouette" print ads in newspapers. In October "Silhouette" ads appeared in music, sports, and men's magazines. The campaign's first television spot, with Duncan Milner and Eric Gunbaum as creative directors, featured silhouettes of people wearing iPods and dancing to the Black Eyed Peas's "Hey, Mama."

The first three commercials were directed by Dave Myers, who, Milner told *Adweek,* "was great in that he knew the best choreographers, knew the dancers and knew a lot about the music." In fact, it was Myers who had originally suggested that TBWA\C\D use "Hey, Mama." In later television spots Myers used Jet's "Are You Gonna Be My Girl" and N.E.R.D.'s "Rock Star." "Silhouette" print ads used taglines such as "Welcome to the digital music revolution" and "More than 1 million iPods have been sold."

According to *Advertising Age,* Apple's U.S. advertising budget from January to August 2004 was $49.6 million. Later in 2004 Apple spent $20 million worldwide to promote its 30-second U2 "Silhouette" spot using "Vertigo," a single from the band's new album, *How to Dismantle an Atomic Bomb.* The commercial starred U2, partially silhouetted against fuchsia, green, yellow, and blue backgrounds. In addition to the commercial, U2 cobranded with Apple by releasing the single exclusively on iTunes. Apple then released a special red and black iPod U2, with the band members' autographs engraved on the back casing.

The iPod U2 shipped with a $50 coupon toward the download of iTune's *The Complete U2,* a collection of 25 years of U2 albums. Explaining why U2 had chosen iPod for its first endorsement, Bono told the *Chicago Tribune,* "We looked at the iPod commercial as a rock video. We chose the director. We thought, how are we going to get our single off in the days when rock music is niche? When it's unlikely to get a three-minute punk-rock song on top of the radio? So we piggybacked this phenomenon to get ourselves to a new, younger audience, and we succeeded." The band was not paid for the "Vertigo" ad.

Apple continued using the "Silhouette" campaign well into 2005 to promote variations of the iPod, not only the iPod U2 but also the iPod Photo, iPod Mini,

EVEN THE PRESIDENT

Even U.S. President George W. Bush owned an iPod. A 2004 birthday gift from his daughters, Bush's 10,000-song-capacity iPod only held 250 songs when its existence became known in 2005. The president's iPod consisted of a song list predominantly made up of male artists. Busy with other things, Bush did not have time to set up the iPod himself, and he instructed an aide, Blake Gottesman, to purchase the songs from iTunes. Notable songs on the president's play list included "Fortunate Son" by Credence Clearwater Revival and "Don't Drink That Wine" by NWA. Joe Levy of *Rolling Stone* quipped, "One thing that's interesting is that the president likes artists who don't like him."

and iPod Shuffle, as well as its 99-cents-per-song online store, iTunes.

OUTCOME

Despite critics who accused Apple of overusing the campaign, "Silhouette" dramatically helped iPod move to the forefront of the market for portable music. The U2 spot alone bolstered Apple's stock to a 52-week high in 2004, which added $2 billion to Apple's overall market value. In 2004 sales of the iPod peaked, with 92 percent of the market share; this slipped to 87 percent by March 2005. Andrew Shafer, a writer for the *Iowa State Daily,* wrote, "[iPod's] popularity may be attributed, at least in part, to a simple dancing Silhouette. The Silhouette, although faceless and unidentifiable, has given an identity to the iPod." Despite losing ground to emerging MP3 players, in 2005 Apple reported its 16 millionth iPod sold, and iTunes was providing 82 percent of the world's legally downloadable songs. Accessories for the iPod alone yielded $100 million in 2004.

The "Silhouette" campaign earned TBWA\C\D a number of prizes, including the $100,000 Kelly Award, presented by Magazine Publishers of America for the best ad competition. It also helped TBWA\C\D earn *Adweek* 's honor as Agency of the Year in 2004 and a Grand Effie in 2005. "One can look at the iPod ads and easily see it's a very good campaign," Eric Einhorn, executive vice president and chief strategy officer at McCann Worldgroup, stated in the *Iowa State Daily.* "It really finds an iconic way to represent the musical freedom that the iPod delivers."

FURTHER READING

Amer, Suzie. "Moving with the Music." *Print,* May 1, 2005.

Anderson, Mae, and Parpis, Eleftheria. "The Best of '04 and the Worst." *Adweek,* January 3, 2005.

Avery, Simon. "How iPod Spawned Lucrative Spinoff Industry: 'Halo Effect' Already at $100-Million." *Toronto Globe and Mail,* January 5, 2005, p. B1.

Bulik, Beth Snyder. "Apple: Look Back; 2003 Winner." *Advertising Age,* December 13, 2004, p. S10.

Johnson, Michelle. "iPod May Be a Bit Too Minimalist." *Boston Globe,* February 7, 2005, p. D2.

Kloer, Phil. "Me, Myself & iPod Music Lovers Gush about Pocket-Size Hip, Hot Jukebox." *Atlanta Journal-Constitution,* April 1, 2004, p. NW4.

Kot, Gret. "Bono on the Band: In a Frank Interview, U2's Lead Singer Tackles Big Questions about the Nature of Rock Music and Suggestions His Iconic Group Has Sold Its Soul." *Chicago Tribune,* June 5, 2005, p. B1.

Newman, Melinda. "Bombs Away! U2 Sets Sights on Top of Charts." *Billboard,* November 27, 2004, p. 3.

Newsday, Stephen Williams. "Tinseltown Tech Celebrities Give Gadgets Star Power." *Fort Wayne Journal Gazette,* June 5, 2005, p. 2D.

Pfanner, Eric. "Sony Wages Battle of the Brands." *International Herald Tribune,* October 25, 2004, p. 13.

Piccalo, Gina. "The Marketing Pitch You Won't See Coming." *Los Angeles Times,* November 17, 2005, p. F4.

Shafer, Andrew. "Three Years after the First Release of Apple's iPod, It Still Reigns Supreme as the Top MP3 Player on the Market." *Iowa State Daily,* March 10, 2005.

Kevin Teague

SWITCHERS CAMPAIGN

OVERVIEW

By June 2002, after 18 months of new products that included the eMac, OS X operating system, G4 processor, iPod, and new flat-screen monitor, Apple Computer, Inc., still held only 5 percent of the U.S. market and between 2 and 3 percent of the worldwide market in personal computers. Apple's proprietary lock on technology in the 1980s had forced hardware manufacturers like Dell, Gateway, and Compaq to avoid Apple software and to ship their PCs with Microsoft's operating system. Apple isolated itself from the masses even more with its 1997 "Think Different" campaign, which associated the brand with revolutionary figures like Mahatma Gandhi and John Lennon. It was to attract a broader range of computer users that Apple launched its "Switchers" campaign in 2002.

With the cost estimated at $75 million, the "Switchers" campaign was executed by Apple's longtime partner and marketing firm TBWA\Chiat\Day (TBWA\C\D). Using print, television, and the company's website, the "Switchers" campaign began with Apple's requests for testimonials from its loyal customer base. After receiving more than 1,000 submissions, TBWA\C\D hired the documentary filmmaker Errol Morris to create 32 television spots that featured people ad-libbing their reasons for switching from the Windows-based PC to Apple. Hoping to connect with a wide demographic, the "Switchers" spots starred common people like a network administrator, a lawyer, an illustrator, a small-business owner, a programmer, and a DJ. The first spot aired on June 10, 2002.

Early indicators led Apple to believe that the campaign was helping to capture business from the Windows market. In the second half of 2002, for example, 4 of 10 Mac purchases in Apple stores were made by first-time owners. Despite early successes and a few impressive ad accolades, including *Adweek* 's 2002 Campaign of the Year Award, there was little improvement in Apple's market share. *Brandweek* noted that the research firms Gartner Dataquest and IDC showed Apple's worldwide market share unchanged in October 2003, after the campaign had ended.

HISTORICAL CONTEXT

In 1997 Apple launched its $100 million "Think Different" campaign, which joined images of cultural icons like Bob Dylan, Albert Einstein, and Pablo Picasso to the Apple brand. The effort backfired on Apple, however, by pigeonholing the company as part of a small community of writers, photographers, educators, and graphic designers. By 2002 the tech industry's slump was also affecting Apple, which lost money in the first fiscal quarter of that year. Despite industry trends in 2002, Apple CEO Steve Jobs said that the company planned to "innovate our way through the downturn" by developing new hardware and software, along with opening 51 Apple stores throughout the United States.

In the weeks preceding the "Switchers" campaign Jobs told *Adweek,* "We're going after the ninety-five out of 100 people not using Macs." The opening of new Apple stores also was meant to play a major role in the forthcoming campaign by giving consumers a place to purchase Apple computers. Because of contractual disagreements between Apple and retailers, many Apple products were not available at larger stores. Apple supposedly stopped allowing Best Buy to sell iMacs, for example, after the company resisted stocking the regulated range of colors that Apple insisted upon. Sears and CompUSA had similar fallouts with Apple. Increasing the number of Apple stores would allow the company to sell its own products on its own terms.

"We've been giving people a ton of compelling reasons to switch to a Mac," Jobs told *USA Today.* "We've got 10,000 people writing to us to say, 'I've switched,' but people have lots of questions. We decided that to get people over their concerns, they should hear from people just like them."

TARGET MARKET

The 1997 "Think Different" Campaign was widely criticized for excluding the average computer user by targeting what Therese Poletti of the *San Jose Mercury News* called "radical thinkers such as Albert Einstein, John Lennon and other rebellious, creative types." It was for this reason that TBWA\C\D aimed the "Switchers" campaign at Windows users, the 95 percent of computer users who fell outside Apple's market share. It was also important, Jobs emphasized to TBWA\C\D, to target the Windows user who wanted a Mac but who feared that switching to one would discombobulate his or her digital life. "There are a lot more people out there that use Windows computers than no computers, so that's a very rich target for us," Jobs told the *Wall Street Journal.* "For those thinking of switching to the Mac, we'd like to help that process along."

For the ads TBWA\C\D and director Morris used mostly ordinary consumers who were accustomed to Windows, people such as a network administrator, an illustrator, a small-business owner, and a programmer. Jobs also wanted to dispel the myth that Apple was only for consumers who had never used a computer before. When *USA Today* 's Ad Track polled consumers on their reaction to the "Switchers" campaign, the most favorable response was from 30- to 39-year-olds, 23 percent of whom liked the ads. The worst response came from 18- to 24-year-olds, with 47 percent disliking them.

COMPETITION

In 2001 Microsoft, the antagonist of the "Switchers" campaign, was the biggest threat to Apple, with a staggering 93 percent of all operating systems for personal computers. Although some analysts favored the stability of the Mac's UNIX-based operating system, others valued the wider product selection offered by Microsoft. John Torro of the *Saint Petersburg Times* wrote, "Windows XP supports about 12,000 device and software drivers. The Mac? Probably a fraction of that. What that means is you have more flexibility if you want to upgrade or change your computer. The PC world is wide open; Apple dictates the Mac world." Apple did, however, outshine Microsoft in advertising. To counter the

INTERROTRON

Errol Morris, the director of the "Switchers" television spots, also worked with Michael Williams to create *The Fog of War,* which won the 2003 Academy Award as the best documentary feature. The film consisted of Morris asking Robert S. McNamara, former U.S. secretary of defense, candid questions about his involvement with the 1945 firebombing of Tokyo, the 1962 Cuban missile crisis, and the initial U.S. deployments in Vietnam. The well-crafted documentary allowed McNamara to explain his views on the morality of war through his "Eleven lessons from the life of Robert S. McNamara." For *The Fog of War* Morris used techniques similar to those of the "Switchers" commercials, including the patented Interrotron and the shouting of questions at the interviewee during the filming.

"Switchers" campaign, Microsoft's website featured stories and photos of "real people" who had left Macintosh for Windows. When it was later revealed that the Microsoft photos were stock images and that the stories had been written by a marketing team, Microsoft's antics were widely criticized.

In PC hardware Hewlett-Packard, after merging with Compaq, was the worldwide leader, with 16.1 percent of the market in 2002. The company's share was slipping, however, to Dell, which held 15.7 percent worldwide and an even greater percentage in the United States. Dell was praised by advertising aficionados for its clear vision of the product it was advertising. Mike Dell, founder and CEO, spent his efforts solely pushing Dell PCs and the company's "just-in-time" manufacturing. By 2005 Dell, with 16.9 percent of the worldwide market for PCs, had become the leader. "Dell has a lot of momentum. It grew at rates above 24 percent, year over year," said Loren Loverde, an analyst with IDC. "HP is doing well relative to its merger issues, and it also means that we could have a pretty close race... for a number of quarters."

MARKETING STRATEGY

Jobs attended the showing of Errol Morris's short film *The Academy Awards Movie,* which played at the 2002 Academy Awards. Later, in response to the film, Jobs was quoted as saying, "This guy has to do the new Apple campaign." But Apple had considered Morris to direct the "Switchers" campaign even before the 2002 Oscars.

Before Morris began work on the "Switchers" campaign, Apple requested stories, through Apple.com, from people who had switched from Windows to Apple. After selecting 60 replies from thousands of submissions, Morris and his team spent 10 days interviewing candidates in New York, Los Angeles, and Boston. Morris set the camera behind a half-silvered mirror, on which he projected his face. He called the invention, which allowed him to make eye contact with the person being interviewed, an Interrotron.

Looking into the camera lens "is the very opposite of conversation," Morris said in *Adweek.* "Interrotron is a way of having your cake and eating it too." During the filming TBWA\C\D representatives gave Morris details about each interviewee. None of the 32 commercials that were created were scripted. "Steve [Jobs] did much of the deciding; he was the impartial jury. The ones who made it were the most believable," Lee Clow, chief creative officer at TBWA\C\D, told *Adweek.* "We also made a conscious effort to avoid choosing [those who might be perceived as] 'Apple people.'"

In addition to the ordinary people featured in the "Switchers" ads, four celebrities—actor-comedian Will Ferrell, skateboarder Tony Hawk, musician Yo-Yo Ma, and surfer Kelly Slater—made appearances. Most of the ads, however, featured people like a programmer, lawyer, disc jockey, or software projects manager. One featured a student, Ellen Feiss, who stood before a white screen while she explained her frustrations with Windows: "I was writing a paper on the PC, and it was, like, beep, beep, beep, beep, beep. And then, like, half of my paper was gone. And I was, like... heh. It devoured my paper. It was a really good paper. And then I had to do it again and I had to do it fast so it wasn't as good. It's kind of a... bummer."

The "Switchers" spot with Aaron Adams, a Windows network administrator, which *Adweek* deemed the campaign's most poignant, helped TBWA\C\D earn the publication's honor as Best Campaign of 2002. In the spot Adams said, "I'm a Windows guy who's changed to Macintosh. I deal with Windows all day and when I'm tired of fighting with that, I come home to a Macintosh that works. I haven't found anything I can do with a PC that I cannot do with my Mac."

The "Switchers" spots first aired on June 10, 2002, on cable networks such as ESPN, CNBC, and Comedy Central and then appeared on ABC and NBC. Print ads appeared during the same month in magazines like *Time* and *Newsweek.* Even though Jobs denied animosity between Apple and Microsoft, "Switchers" ads in *Newsweek, Rolling Stone,* and the *New Yorker* boasted that Windows "has made a good business out of copying the innovative Mac." Both print and television advertisements directed the audience to Apple.com/Switch, where the company posted reasons for switching to the Mac, along with positive press reports to reinforce the message.

OUTCOME

The "Switchers" campaign did little to increase Apple's market share, which was its main objective. Over the lifetime of the campaign Apple's worldwide share remained at a meager 2 to 3 percent. Sales in Apple stores did, however, increase during the campaign, bringing in $163 million during the second half of 2002. According to *USA Today,* 4 of 10 of the buyers had never owned a Mac before. The "Switchers" campaign also earned awards from the ad industry, including *Adweek*'s Campaign of the Year Award for 2002. The "Switchers" spot with Feiss was named Best Performance in *Adweek*'s 2003 Maddy Awards.

Part of the problem, according to analysts, was that, even though the "Switchers" stars were real people, their perceptions of Apple computers were false. Most "Switchers" spokespersons boasted of Mac's advantages over Windows, such as a more stable operating system and a more intuitive functionality. As Torro wrote in the *Saint Petersburg Times,* "If Mac users are going to tell you that their operating system never has problems, I have some land to sell you about 20 miles out in the gulf. I've heard many stories about Macs getting 'the bomb' (the Mac version of a Windows general protection fault)." Apple's PowerBook 5300 was earlier dubbed by some journalists as the "hindenbook" for its tendency to burst into flames.

When the "Switchers" campaign was launched in 2002, Apple still had enough capital to float through the industry slump of the decade's early years. In June 2002 Jobs stated, "Apple and Dell are the only two making money in the industry right now. It's a tough business now. But I'm an optimist. I think things will get better." By 2004 Apple had shifted its advertising priorities to the wildly successful iPod, which earned an incredible $1.2 billion during the first quarter of 2005 alone.

FURTHER READING

Azhar, Azeem. "The Fruit of Apple's Labour." *Guardian,* November 21, 2002, p. 2.

Dill, Mallorre. "Reality TV: Errol Morris Focuses His Interrotron on Apple and Cantor Fitzgerald." *Adweek,* June 24, 2002, p. 21.

Garcia, Sandra. "i-Advertising: TBWA\C\D, Morris Help Dispel the Mac Myth." *Shoot,* August 2, 2002, p. 18.

Hamm, Steve, Jay Greene, and Andy Reinhardt. "What's a Rival to Do Now? Getting Out of Microsoft's Way Becomes a Key Survival Skill." *Business Week,* November 18, 2002, p. 44.

Howard, Theresa. "Apple Ads Make Impression: Small Companies Prove Their Spots Can Rival Big Firms." *USA Today,* July 15, 2002, p. B6.

———. "PC Users Make the Switch in Mac Ads: Apple Launches $75M Campaign to Nab Some of Microsoft's Market." *USA Today,* June 11, 2002, p. B2.

Lippert, Barbara. "The Right Notes: Apple's Fun New Music Spots Are Not As Simple As They Look." *Adweek,* May 26, 2003, p. 28.

McCarthy, Michael. "Apple Takes Swipe at Partner Microsoft in Mac Ads: Spots Feature Users Who Rejected PCs." *USA Today,* December 16, 2002, p. B4.

Nudd, Tim. "The Burden of Truth: Will the Real Switchers Please Stand Up?" *Adweek* (eastern ed.), October 21, 2002, p. 9.

Poletti, Therese. "New Apple Advertising Campaign Aims to Convert PC Users." *San Jose Mercury News,* June 11, 2002.

Schwartz, John. "Apple's Quirky Ads Evoke Parodies of Themselves." *New York Times,* November 25, 2002, p. 4.

Tam, Pui-Wing. "New Apple Campaign Targets Windows User." *Wall Street Journal,* June 10, 2002, p. B1.

Wasserman, Todd. "Memo from the Front." *Brandweek,* October 13, 2003.

Kevin Teague

THINK DIFFERENT CAMPAIGN

OVERVIEW

The decision of Apple Computer, Inc., to make its technology proprietary had constricted the computer manufacturer's product growth in the 1980s and allowed computer-hardware manufacturers such as International Business Machines Corporation (IBM) and Compaq Computer Corporation to blossom by using Microsoft Corporation's operating systems. In early 1997 Apple was in danger of ending its second consecutive profitless year. In an attempt to salvage the Apple brand, Apple's board of directors invited the company's cofounder, Steve Jobs, to lead as CEO. The homecoming was bittersweet. More than a decade earlier the board of directors had asked Jobs to resign. After his return to leadership Jobs consolidated Apple's advertising account with one agency, reduced Apple's product line from 14 to 4, and hoped to build consumer confidence in the Apple brand with a campaign called "Think Different."

The $90 million "Think Different" campaign debuted on September 28, 1997, with a 60-second spot aired during the television network premiere of the animated film *A Toy Story.* The global campaign, which included television spots, print ads in newspapers and magazines, and outdoor displays on billboards, bus wraps, and wall coverings, featured stark black-and-white photographs of maverick thinkers such as Bob Dylan, Martin Luther King, Jr., Sir Richard Branson, and John Lennon. The first spot featured a voice-over by the actor Richard Dreyfuss and ended with the Apple logo and the tagline "Think Different." It was produced by the advertising agency TBWA\Chiat\Day, although the "Think Different" concept itself had emerged from a collaborative effort between the agency's worldwide creative director, Lee Clow, and Steve Jobs. The campaign ended in 2002.

"Think Different" improved Apple's bottom line. In April 1998 the company reported its second straight profitable quarter after nearly two years and $2 billion in losses. Although Apple increased its market share at the beginning of "Think Different," in early 2002 it was again posting profit losses. Some advertising analysts criticized "Think Different" for aiming Apple products at artists, writers, designers, and revolutionaries—all minorities in the computer-using community.

HISTORICAL CONTEXT

In August 1997 Jobs, who had cofounded Apple Computer in his garage 20 years earlier, returned to the company to become its interim chief executive officer. At that time Apple was in the midst of a crisis. Its share of the computer market had plummeted from a peak of 14 percent in 1993 to below 3 percent four years later. "The company was in a death spiral," its chief financial officer, Fred Anderson, told *Newsweek* in 1998. Jobs set out to address the problems. He believed that Apple's difficulties stemmed from the company's incoherent agenda, which consisted of efforts to move various products without a clearly defined purpose or method. Jobs attempted to redefine the company's strategy by concentrating on Apple's key markets: design and publishing, education, and consumers who purchased personal computers for use in the home. He also cut Apple's product line from 14 to 4.

Jobs took charge of Apple's image-making process as well. When he arrived back at the company, Apple was running more than 25 different advertising campaigns. The company's domestic and international sales offices advertised independently from, and were often not coordinated with, the campaigns conducted from Apple's headquarters in California. Apple's advertising agency during this period, BBDO, had opted to focus its advertisements on specific Apple products and the technological features of Apple computers. These efforts did nothing to allay consumers' fears that Apple's demise was imminent. "The talk of Apple going under was the worst thing for the company," said Jessica Schulman, the TBWA\Chiat\Day art director for the "Think Different" campaign. "People won't buy computer equipment that they think won't be around in the next year." Jobs replaced BBDO with TBWA\Chiat\Day and began to work with his friend Clow, the agency's creative director, on new advertising strategies. The two had collaborated in the past to forge an identity for Apple's Macintosh brand in the renowned "1984" commercial. In an effort to bring order to Apple's marketing chaos, the new campaign was to be a unified, worldwide effort overseen by TBWA\Chiat\Day's international and domestic offices.

TARGET MARKET

The "Think Different" ads reached out to what Apple termed its "installed base," those consumers who had purchased Apple computer equipment in the past. Apple consistently performed well in three core markets: designers and desktop publishers, educators and students, and home users. It was these groups that were most likely to have bought Apple products and who were keeping the company afloat during its downturn. But with the publicized record of Apple's financial troubles, many of them were not purchasing new Apple systems for fear that the company would soon fold, leaving them with obsolete machines. "Our number one priority was to make people realize that we were still here and still fighting for this brand," said Rhona Hamilton, a marketing representative for Apple.

In order to appeal to these users, the campaign stressed the creative roots of the Apple brand. The people who were selected to appear in the "Think Different" campaign were bold thinkers, men and women who were not merely great in a certain field but who were also innovative and independent and who had changed the worlds in which they moved. By aligning itself with the likes of Muhammad Ali, Bob Dylan, and Albert Einstein, Apple clearly strove to deliver a message about itself and its products. "After talking to a lot of consumers and Macintosh enthusiasts, our strategic direction was to stop acting like a computer company and start acting like a company dedicated to creative thinking," said Schulman. The "Think Different" ads stressed that Apple was an innovative company that, with its creative users, could change the world. With these images and themes, Apple hoped to appeal to its core markets, people who as artists, illustrators, designers, and students valued their own creativity and who viewed themselves as being somewhat outside the mainstream. As *Brandweek* noted, "'Think Different' [was] clear that it [was] not targeting its message to everyone."

GRAMMAR TAKES A HIT

The choice of the tagline "Think Different" rather than "Think Differently" was deliberate. Even though "Think Different" drew public flak for not being grammatically correct, Apple settled on the line because it "conveyed a total change in the whole body of what you think about," said Jessica Schulman, art director at TBWA\Chiat\Day, the agency that developed the campaign. "Instead of thinking in your everyday way, 'Think Different.'"

COMPETITION

As a manufacturer of both computers and operating systems, Apple was involved in two highly contested markets. Apple's line of computer hardware competed directly with that of other makers of personal computers, most notably Dell, Compaq, and IBM. Apple and Dell also vied for market share in the growing business of built-to-order computers. Apple, through its online Apple Store, and Dell, the fastest-growing major computer maker, both offered consumers the opportunity to customize their systems at the point of purchase.

Apple's operating system, Mac OS, faced its stiffest challenge from Microsoft's windows. The competition between Apple and Microsoft had been particularly difficult for Apple because Microsoft had succeeded in making its Windows system a near standard for business and commercial users. Particularly in light of Apple's financial difficulties and loss of consumer confidence before Jobs returned to the company, Apple was losing a great deal of ground to the Microsoft system. Apple's share of the personal computing market, which stood at 14 percent in 1993, had plummeted to 2.8 percent by 1997.

Apple was not alone in its advertising campaign. By 1998 its major competitors had all launched branding campaigns that were attempting to create favorable images of the companies rather than focus on individual products. IBM spent more than $140 million on its massive "Solutions for a Small Planet" branding campaign. In 1998 Dell set out on a $70 million "Be Direct" worldwide image campaign, which marked the first time the company had sought to target consumers outside of trade publications. Dell's TV spot, which featured a mouse blowing up a maze, rather than running through it, to obtain a chunk of cheese, aired during evening network news programs and on national cable channels such as CNN, FN, and CNBC; the print version appeared in mainstream magazines such as *Newsweek, Time,* and *Forbes.* Compaq spent an estimated $300 million annually on global campaigns and announced plans to double its U.S. consumer ad budget in 1998 to approximately $50 million. Microsoft had taken its "Where Do You Want to Go Today" campaign onto prime-time television and into national magazines. Intel, the manufacturer of the Pentium processors employed in most PCs, had also continued its ongoing and widely popular "Bunny People" campaign, which centered on disco-dancing Intel technicians.

MARKETING STRATEGY

Upon his return Jobs recognized immediately that Apple's public image needed to be reinvigorated if the company were to survive. Although Apple had long been viewed as making superior computing equipment, the company was in danger of going the way of Sony's ill-fated Betamax videotape system, for few people were willing to invest in a product from a company that was believed to be on the verge of extinction. To counter this perception, Jobs brought in TBWA\Chiat\Day and worked closely with Clow and others in the agency to develop the campaign that became "Think Different." The creators of the campaign realized that, because the company's image was so tarnished, Apple could not revitalize its brand by relying on ads touting its products. Instead the campaign sought to celebrate the creative genius of its subjects and to assert that Apple, too, had a unique role to play on the world stage by making the tools that allowed creative people to achieve extraordinary feats. "'Think Different' celebrates the soul of the Apple brand—that creative people with passion can change the world for the better," Jobs told the *Wall Street Journal Europe* in April 1998.

Apple wanted to kick off the campaign in dramatic fashion and decided that the first advertisement should run on television during the September 28, 1997, network television premiere of *A Toy Story* on ABC. Although difficulties in obtaining the rights to use and publish the photographs of the subjects of the campaign nearly caused Apple to miss its target, the 60-second spot aired as planned. The commercial consisted of the black-and-white images of the 12 visionary thinkers and the reading of a manifesto written in part by Jobs and read by actor Dreyfuss. "Here's to the crazy ones," began the voice-over. "The misfits. The rebels. The troublemakers. The round pegs in square holes. The ones who see things differently. They're not fond of rules. And they have no respect for the status quo. You can quote them, disagree with them, glorify or vilify them. About the only thing you can't do is ignore them. Because they change things. They push the human race forward. And while some may see them as the crazy ones, we see genius. Because the people who are crazy enough to think they can change the world are the ones who do." A shorter version was also produced. To reinforce the message of the television commercials, Apple conducted a brief second phase of the campaign and ran print ads in major newspapers, including the *New York Times* and the *Wall Street Journal,* that consisted of the text of the manifesto and some of the images from the television campaign.

After this initial burst Apple continued to run the television spots during such highly rated television programs as *ER, Prime Time Live, Frasier,* and *Ally McBeal* and soon followed with its first wave of magazine ads. Forgoing computer trade and industry publications, Apple instead placed its ads on the back covers of magazines such as *BusinessWeek, Time, Newsweek,* the *New Yorker, Harper's Magazine,* and the *Atlantic Monthly* and in advertising trade journals such as *Advertising Age* and *Adweek.* These ads, which incorporated new figures, such as choreographer Martha Graham and architect Frank Lloyd Wright into the campaign, consisted solely of a single black-and-white photograph of the subject. The only text was the phrase "Think Different," the Apple logo, and the address of the company's website. In hopes of piquing audience interest all the more, the ads did not identify the subject in any way.

By its final year "Think Different" had transitioned into a print and billboard campaign. For example, billboards placed on the tower of the Pine Street Inn in Boston featured black-and-white images of Martin Luther King, Jr., and Franklin and Eleanor Roosevelt. The tagline "Think Different" and an image of Rosa Parks covered buses in New York City. Parks, an African-American, had become famous when she refused to sit at the back of a segregated bus in Montgomery, Alabama, in 1955. The campaign ended in mid-2002, but it briefly resurfaced on October 24, 2005, when Parks, the woman dubbed the "Mother of the Modern-Day Civil Rights Movement," died. To pay homage to Parks, Apple placed her photo on its website's home page with the text "Think Different" in the image's upper-left corner.

OUTCOME

The "Think Different" campaign elicited an outpouring of opinions. Apple's headquarters was inundated with letters, faxes, phone calls, and E-mails commenting on the campaign. Some questioned the cast of innovative thinkers included in the ads, others were perplexed by the message, and still others were delighted with Apple's attempt to pay tribute to its heroes. People formed websites spontaneously, discussing who the individuals were, whether the phrase "Think Different" was grammatically correct, and why Apple's ad campaign would focus on a group of people who for the most part had never touched a computer. Apple and TBWA\Chiat\Day considered the attention paid to the campaign to be a sign of its impact.

At first the advertising industry praised the "Think Different" campaign. The December 15, 1997, edition of *USA Today* listed Apple's "bolder" ads as one of the year's best campaigns. As reported in the same article, ad agency creative directors ranked the campaign as the second best of the year. On May 18, 1998, *Advertising Age* also voiced its approval: "The decision to celebrate the kind of independent thinking that has always typified Mac users seems now to make total sense." In fact, the article stated, "the shots of heroes, geniuses, wildmen, and iconoclasts assembled here makes a strong emotional statement for Apple's underdog role."

Not everyone loved "Think Different," however. At first Apple had to contend with criticism for launching a "campaign of dead people." Apple marketing representative Rhona Hamilton spoke of having to educate consumers about what the campaign was attempting to convey. *CMP Techwire* reported that the company was drawing bad press for undertaking an expensive marketing effort during a period of financial losses. A *USA Today* Ad Track survey revealed that consumers preferred Intel's "Bunny People" spots, which were ranked as the most popular technology-industry commercial of 1997.

The campaign had a positive effect on Apple's bottom line. In April 1998 Apple reported its second straight profitable quarter after nearly two years and $2 billion in losses. Apple attributed the increasing sales to the "Think Different" campaign. "It let people know that we're still around and not going anywhere, so that they can feel good about buying the product," said Hamilton. Apple's market share rose to 4.1 percent. Unfortunately for Apple, the computer maker's American market share hovered at about 5 percent for the campaign's final four years. Advertising critics began discrediting "Think Different" for limiting the Apple brand to the small minority of "revolutionaries" that used computers. "For years, the Apple brand has been associated with artists, writers and designers," Sandra Garcia wrote in the August 2, 2002, issue of *Shoot,* an ad-industry magazine. "The so-called 'creative types' who seemingly belonged to this secret society of Mac users while the rest of the working public toiled in a clunky PC world." In 2002 Apple suffered with the majority of the technology industry and posted its first profit loss since 1997. In mid-2002 Apple officially replaced its "Think Different" campaign with one titled "Switchers."

FURTHER READING

"Apple Launches Brand Advertising Campaign Premiering This Sunday on Toy Story." *PR Newswire,* September 26, 1997.

Enrico, Dottie. "When Ads Get Creative, Some Click, Some Bomb." *USA Today,* December 15, 1997.

Judge, Michael. "Apple Should 'Think Different' about Asia." *Wall Street Journal Europe,* April 24, 1998.

Levy, Steven. "Hello Again: A New Computer, the iMac, from Apple Computer." *Newsweek,* May 18, 1998.

Mahoney, Jerry. "Dell Ads Tout Image Not Product." *Austin American-Statesman,* June 15, 1998.

Picarille, Lisa. "The Apple Report: Jobs in the Spotlight." *CMP Techwire,* October 17, 1997.

"Relationship Marketing." *Brandweek,* April 20, 1998.

"Slice-of-Life Truism a Bell-Ringer for Southwestern." *Advertising Age,* May 18, 1998.

Rebecca Stanfel

AT&T Inc.

175 E. Houston Street
San Antonio, Texas 78205-2233
USA
Telephone: (210) 821-4105
Fax: (210) 821-4105
Web site: www.att.com

CARROT TOP CAMPAIGN

OVERVIEW

In 1982 the U.S. government mandated the breakup of the vast network of the American Telephone and Telegraph Company (AT&T) into smaller regional companies, the so-called Baby Bells. The regional companies handled local telephone calls, while AT&T continued to offer long-distance service. One area in which the new AT&T decisively lagged behind its competitors was in collect calls. The AT&T brand, 1-800 Call ATT for Collect Calls, had an uphill battle to overtake the category leader, or at least to gain market share, in long-distance collect calls, an area that was itself dwindling.

In order to address the problem, AT&T initiated a national campaign in 2001 to win the hearts and minds of young callers. The campaign was the brainchild of AT&T's longtime advertising agency, Foote, Cone & Belding Worldwide of New York, but in October 2001 AT&T switched agencies, giving Young & Rubicam of New York all of its consumer advertising business. Young & Rubicam also inherited the latest ad campaign for 1-800 Call ATT for Collect Calls, which featured the brash young comic Carrot Top, the stage name of Scott Thompson. The integrated "Carrot Top" campaign consisted mainly of 15- and 30-second television spots, but it also included radio spots, print ads in newspapers and consumer magazines, outdoor signage, public relations work, ads shown in movie theaters, special events, and an online interactive component. The media expenditure for the campaign was in excess of $20 million.

By August 2003 the "Carrot Top" campaign had met or exceeded all of its goals, and in 2004 it received a Bronze EFFIE Award for its marketplace effectiveness. Not only did the brand become more recognizable to the target market, but market share and revenue increased over a period of more than two years.

HISTORICAL CONTEXT

The 1982 court ruling that broke up AT&T created numerous rivals in the telecommunications field. With the various regional Baby Bells providing local services, AT&T concentrated on long-distance services and ancillary businesses such as the sales of telephony hardware. At first this arrangement seemed to work well, but by the early twenty-first century the telecommunications landscape looked a lot different than it had 20 years earlier. In response, the leadership of AT&T decided to split the company into four units: AT&T Business, AT&T Wireless, AT&T Broadband, and AT&T Consumer. The consumer unit was responsible for most long-distance calling, including the 1-800 Call ATT for Collect Calls brand. "Carrot Top" was not the brand's first advertising campaign, nor was Carrot Top its first

Carrot Top (Scott Thompson), a spokesperson for AT&T. **AP IMAGES.**

spokesperson; he followed the actor David Arquette. Foote, Cone & Belding ostensibly had chosen the edgy comedian because of his appeal to young people, and Young & Rubicam seconded the choice when it took over the account.

TARGET MARKET

The majority of collect telephone calls were made by people between the ages of 16 and 24, and this was precisely the group for which Carrot Top held the highest appeal. He was well known as a comic on the college campus circuit and as someone who projected an anti-corporate image. This type of image was especially important in attracting people in the target age group, since in many cases the first instinct of such people was to question, or even reject out of hand, authority or corporate messages. Although collect calling was not something young people spent much time thinking about beforehand, Carrot Top was the type of celebrity with whom this audience could identify. A secondary target market consisted of people 25 to 34 years of age.

COMPETITION

AT&T faced a variety of competition in the collect calling marketplace. The competition ranged from store-bought calling cards to the Baby Bells, Sprint, and, most important, MCI, whose own collect calling brand, 1-800-COLLECT, was the industry leader. A different type of competition altogether was coming from cellular phone services. As more and more people within both the primary and the secondary target markets were becoming cell phone users, cell phones were cutting into the overall collect calling market. In fact, from the beginning of 1999 through the end of 2002 the collect calling market shrank approximately 68 percent. Likewise, cell phones were deemed responsible for the decline in the number of public pay telephones, obvious points of usage for collect callers.

Gaining ground on the enormous lead in market share enjoyed by MCI's 1-800-COLLECT was the priority of the "Carrot Top" campaign. MCI's 1-800-COLLECT advertising also used celebrity spokespeople, ranging from basketball superstar Michael Jordan to pop singer Britney Spears. In addition, as Young & Rubicam acknowledged in the EFFIE Awards Brief of Effectiveness, 1-800-COLLECT had become the generic name for the category, making it more or less the default number for collect callers, which presented a major obstacle to overcome. Two other obstacles acknowledged in the Brief of Effectiveness were the facts that there was no obvious benefit to callers to switch to 1-800 Call ATT for Collect Calls and that the brand was not part of a subscriber service. Thus, continual reinforcement was required to gain market share.

THE BREAKUP OF MA BELL

In 1974 the U.S. Department of Justice (DOJ) filed an antitrust suit against AT&T, seeking the breakup of the telecommunications giant popularly known as "Ma Bell." The suit did not come to trial until January 15, 1981, however. With Judge Harold Green presiding, the trial lasted until January 8, 1982, when both parties came to an agreement that called for the breakup of AT&T. The breakup took place on January 1, 1984. The regional phone companies, the "Baby Bells," took over local telephone service, while parent AT&T retained long-distance service. In effect, this was how things had stood when AT&T was formed in 1885. The nineteenth-century model, if that was what the DOJ was striving for, was turned on its head, however. Not only did AT&T have competition from other long-distance service providers, but through mergers some of the Baby Bells quickly became stronger than AT&T. In 2005 the one-time monopolistic corporation was taken over by SBC, a former Baby Bell.

MARKETING STRATEGY

Young & Rubicam identified four objectives for the "Carrot Top" campaign, with the achievement of each of the first three objectives leading to the next one. The first of the goals was to instill recall of the 1-800 Call ATT number in the target audience. It was believed that this would lead to achieving the second goal, which was to increase interest in the brand. Increased interest would, it was believed, then lead to the third goal, an increase in market share. The final goal of the campaign was to equal or exceed planned revenue.

Young & Rubicam, which took over the 1-800 Call ATT for Collect Calls account from Foote, Cone & Belding in October 2001, retained Carrot Top in the advertising. The comedian had been AT&T's collect calling spokesperson since June 2001, and Foote, Cone & Belding deemed him able to deliver on the objectives of the campaign. The decision was not without controversy, however. Outside the target market Carrot Top was seen by some people as having an obnoxious persona. Media critics in particular seemed to enjoy reviling him, with at least one writer appearing to border on the libelous. In a *Brandweek* article by Todd Wasserman, Carol Eversen, general manager for 1-800 Call ATT for Collect Calls, responded to the Carrot Top criticism. "We've noticed it," she said. "He is noticed. [There are] no questions within the market we're targeting he's been a big success."

Carrot Top's success as a comedian was explained by his irreverent attitude, his sense of humor, and his in-your-face attitude. This was exactly what appealed to the target audience. Furthermore, within the spots he used catchy phrases that reinforced directly either the product or its benefits. These included turning the brand name into a rhythm—"C-A-L-L-A-T-T"—and by making it easy and cool to use the number—"Dial down the center." This phrase referred to the fact that the letters *CALL ATT* were positioned on the center numbers—2, 5 and 8—of the telephone keypad. Another pivotal phrase was "Free for you and cheap for them," bolstering the target market's argument for dialing 1-800 Call ATT, presumably to phone their parents.

Perhaps more than for most advertising campaigns, it was important that the "Carrot Top" spots be placed where they would have the highest visibility for the target market. The obvious choices, therefore, were music, sports, and sports entertainment, including professional-wrestling television programs. By 2003 "Carrot Top" spots were seen during telecasts of MTV and MTV2, VH1, Much Music, ESPN and ESPN2, and WWE professional wrestling. Not only did these shows attract a high percentage of the target market, but they also melded readily with Carrot Top's persona.

One interesting feature of the "Carrot Top" campaign evolved from a spot that was originally scheduled for theatrical release. Young & Rubicam hired the director Billy Jayne, who shot the spot with a Sony 24p high-definition camera. As Debra Kaufman reported in *Millimeter,* "[Young & Rubicam] producer Paisley McCaffery felt confident that the AT&T commercial could be shot 24p and then easily transferred back to film for big-screen theatrical exhibition. Eventually, the theatrical commercial evolved into a 14-spot national television campaign—all shot in 24p." Kaufman also quoted McCaffery on the switch to the less expensive digital high-definition: "Originally, when we inherited the account, it was a very simple commercial. Now we're telling bigger stories with multiple setups, and making it visually a lot more active and action-packed in the way we can tell the story. Working with the HD camera allows us to capture more when we're in an ad-lib situation, and it's affordable enough to allow us to use two cameras." The "Carrot Top" campaign became one of the earliest high-profile national campaigns to be shot with a Sony 24p high-definition camera.

In September 2003 Carrot Top himself alluded to the ad-lib situations in an interview with Gregory Solman published in *Adweek:* "We shoot what's approved, and we shoot what I come up with. Then they can choose." In the interview Carrot Top also discussed what Solman termed his "love/hate persona," something Young & Rubicam had played up in the spots: "As long as I'm part of the joke, I think it's great . . . I think it's great to make fun of myself."

That attitude and the evolving tone of the spots both came through when the 1-800 Call ATT for Collect Calls brand was connected with a NASCAR promotion in which Carrot Top was teamed up with popular race car driver Rusty Wallace. Running during April 2002, the promotion used radio and print media as well as television. As Wasserman described it in *Brandweek,* "At the end of the TV spot Wallace exits with denim miniskirted model Angie Everhart . . . and gives a shove to Carrot Top, who doubles over." The object of the promotion was to encourage people to use the 1-800 Call ATT number by running a contest in which 20 randomly chosen people were matched with drivers for a specific race. The winners were those contestants whose drivers finished among the top three. Winners received two tickets to any future NASCAR race, $300 in spending money, three days in a hotel, and airfare. The hook was that the more a person used the 1-800 Call ATT for Collect Calls service the better his or her chances were of being chosen.

In addition to the NASCAR promotion, other special events were used to reinforce the "Carrot Top" campaign message. These included advertising on MTV Spring Break, the MTV Video Music Awards, the National Basketball Association All-Star Game, the ESPN X Games, and WWE Wrestlemania. There also was an interactive website allied with the campaign.

OUTCOME

The "Carrot Top" campaign for the 1-800 Call ATT for Collect Calls brand achieved all of its goals. The first goal was to increase the recall of the 1-800 Call ATT number by 7 points per year. Recall actually increased by slightly more than 28 points during the 18-month span from February 2002 to August 2003. The campaign also met its goal to increase interest in the brand by 5 points, and by August 2003, 1-800 Call ATT for Collect Calls had even exceeded rival 1-800 COLLECT. This allowed the brand to narrow the market share gap with 1-800 COLLECT from almost 16 points to 10 points by the end of 2002. Over a two-year period the AT&T brand increased its market share by 8 points, and by August 2003 revenue had exceeded the target by 12 percent. The "Carrot Top" campaign was also a success within the industry, winning a Bronze EFFIE Award in 2004.

While business was looking up for the 1-800 Call ATT for Collect Calls brand, the AT&T Consumer division as a whole did not fare as well. In the fourth quarter of 2003 AT&T had only 9 percent of all revenue in the telecommunications market, though it was still the long-distance leader, with a 28 percent share. In 2004, however, the company threw in the towel on its AT&T Consumer division to focus on business-to-business services. In a 2004 *Brandweek* article Wasserman speculated that the company's $50 million television and print business-to-business campaign "could be the swan song for the 119-year-old brand."

AT&T executives noted that approximately 80 percent of the company's revenues were linked to its business-to-business services, and most analysts felt that the decision to drop the consumer division was probably made to prepare the company for acquisition. Wasserman quoted Randy Ringer, a managing partner of the branding firm Verse Group in New York, who said, "I expect that the AT&T brand itself will disappear soon or will live on as a trademark that is licensed by others who will put it on phones, equipment and so on." This prediction of AT&T's future were correct, for in 2005 SBC acquired AT&T, and in the acquisition the AT&T name was retained. Ironically SBC had originally been Southwest Bell, one of the Baby Bells created by the breakup of AT&T in the 1980s.

FURTHER READING

"For the Record." *Advertising Age,* October 29, 2001.

Grimm, Matthew. "False Consciousness." *Brandweek,* September 3, 2001.

Kaufman, Debra. "Seeking HD Spots." *Millimeter,* March 1, 2003.

Norton, Justin M., and Andrew McMains. "AT&T Wireless Sends Feelers Out: Keeshan, Ex-Saatchi Exec, Is Overseeing $300–400 Mil. Search." *Adweek,* March 12, 2001.

"1-800 CALL ATT for Collect Calls: Carrot Top." *EFFIE Awards Brief of Effectiveness,* 2004.

Sheridan, Patricia. "Carrot Top." *Pittsburgh Post-Gazette,* March 11, 2002.

Solman, Gregory. "Carrot Top on the Spot." *Adweek,* September 8, 2003.

Wasserman, Todd. "Promotions: AT&T Redials Carrot Top, Hitches Ride with NASCAR." *Brandweek,* April 1, 2002.

———. "Strategy: AT&T: We're All About Business Now." *Brandweek,* August 9, 2004.

"Who/What/Wi-Fi." *CFO: The Magazine for Senior Financial Executives,* March, 2003.

Frank Caso

IT'S ALL WITHIN YOUR REACH CAMPAIGN

OVERVIEW

In the 1990s the telecommunications giant AT&T found itself competing against new rivals. Telecommunications companies had expanded their products and services beyond long-distance telephone service and were offering cellular phones, Internet access, and cable television. Consumers were satisfied with the new low-priced choices available to them but were often overwhelmed by the number of companies entering the telecommunications marketplace. AT&T chose to address this increasing complexity by establishing an emotional connection with consumers in an advertising campaign tagged "It's All Within Your Reach."

Introduced in early 1997, "It's All Within Your Reach" did not address the nuts and bolts of AT&T's product offerings, nor did the campaign mention the pricing of its various services. Instead the TV spots that ran through 1998 depicted scenes in which communications technologies made customers' lives better in various ways. For instance, one spot showed a working mother who was able to field a conference call while entertaining her children at the beach. Another commercial showed a son visiting Vietnam in order to understand what his father experienced there as a soldier; during his trip the son made an emotional phone call to his father using an AT&T calling card. The campaign's budget was $53.3 million in its first year and $44.6 million in its second.

The campaign was well received by consumers and advertising-industry critics, and it won numerous awards, including a Gold EFFIE in 1998. Although AT&T continued to employ the campaign tagline in 1999 and 2000, it did virtually no corporate-image advertising in these years, and its brand image came under fire for its lack of focus and relevance.

HISTORICAL CONTEXT

The company name AT&T was at one time synonymous with long-distance phone service, but during the 1990s the telecommunications industry underwent dramatic changes. Competitors such as MCI and Sprint were steadily gaining market share at AT&T's expense. In the wake of deregulation, long-distance and local phone companies began dipping into each other's markets, offering the variety of services AT&T once had a unique hold on. New, smaller, and more aggressive competitors had also surfaced, offering "dial-around" services that gave consumers the ability to punch in an access code to circumvent their long-distance carrier. In addition, emerging technologies such as Internet access, electronic commerce, and wireless phones were changing the face of telecommunications and forcing AT&T to alter its business strategy.

In this fiercely competitive marketplace AT&T's growth had stalled, and its stock value was falling. The consumer division was losing customers more rapidly than the company had anticipated. In 1996 AT&T's consumer long-distance revenues grew only 1 percent, and its business-division revenues climbed just 5 percent. AT&T claimed 54 percent of the residential long-distance market in 1996 as opposed to 60 percent just one year earlier.

TARGET MARKET

"The telecommunications market had steadily become a commodity category. It was all about price," stated Elizabeth McKee, vice president and account director at Young & Rubicam Advertising. In the early 1990s AT&T was swept up in the price wars with other long-distance providers. In 1997 it recognized that, as a leader and the company with the most to lose, it needed to step above the price fray. Although separate advertising campaigns were used to promote specific products and services, AT&T sought to generate broad emotional resonance around its brand with the "It's All Within Your Reach" campaign—and to do so in a way that portrayed it as attuned to the changing telecommunications landscape.

CONFUSING, COMPETITIVE, AND DOWNRIGHT NASTY

Telecommunications commercials historically performed poorly in consumer polls that measured campaign popularity and effectiveness. Of more than 90 spots reviewed by *USA Today*'s Ad Track since 1995, telecommunications spots consistently ranked among the least popular and most disliked campaigns. Consumers complained that the commercials were often confusing, competitive, and mean-spirited.

The intended audience for the brand campaign was, accordingly, "primary active networkers," which AT&T defined as people who were balancing family and work and who actively communicated by traditional phone, wireless phone, or the Internet. AT&T was not alone in targeting this core market. The entire telecommunications category had begun shifting its focus from long-distance callers to the active networker. Technological innovations were rapidly providing consumers with multiple ways to communicate. In order to stay competitive, telecommunications companies needed to provide a full spectrum of these products and services. Some unusual corporate alliances formed in 1997 to take advantage of synergistic technologies. For instance, the Internet giant America Online (AOL) created a joint offering with Tel-Save, a long-distance provider. According to Wendy Brown, vice president of electronic commerce at AOL, online users tended to have higher than average incomes and higher than average monthly phone bills. While the average consumer spent about $22 each month on long distance, the average online user spent about $40.

Despite its declining long-distance market share, AT&T was well positioned to compete in this new marketplace in which companies sold a bundle of services not limited to long distance. A *BusinessWeek* article in 1996 noted that AT&T had all the right ingredients for success: an expansive cellular network, plans to offer local service in every state, a stake in pay-TV service, and an Internet strategy. In order to gain and keep the business of these active networkers, AT&T recognized that it would have to fulfill active networkers' needs in fresh ways. AT&T WorldNet president Dan Schulman told *Advertising Age,* "As we look into the future, we will start transitioning our customer care from 'fix it when it's broken' to 'help people with the new technology and enable them.'"

COMPETITION

In previous years the long-distance market was AT&T's stronghold. But in the face of so many new competitors, it found itself losing ground. According to the Yankee Consulting Group, AT&T's market share for long-distance phone services was chipped from 62.7 percent in 1995 down to 60.6 percent in 1996.

The breadth of telecommunications services had expanded to such an extent that simply defining AT&T's competitors was difficult. Two years earlier the so-called "Big Three"—AT&T, MCI, and Sprint—had controlled 90 percent of the long-distance calls in the United States. Suddenly smaller, more flexible rivals such as Telco Communications, Excel Communications, and Qwest were nipping at that market share. AT&T, as the market leader, took the hardest blows. In July 1996 AT&T reported a scant 5 percent growth in long-distance call volume compared with 15 percent for MCI and 19 percent for Sprint. Local phone companies also presented a challenge to AT&T when they began providing long-distance service. A Price Waterhouse survey in 1997 showed that 40 percent of those consumers polled preferred to get their telecommunications service from a local phone company, while only 21 percent wanted it from a long-distance carrier. "Dial-around" companies also bit into AT&T's market share. These services offered callers the ability to dial into a discount service on a call-by-call basis, circumventing their long-distance carrier. Prepaid calling cards presented another assault on AT&T's core business. These cards allowed callers to pay in advance for calling time with smaller, alternative carriers.

The advertising campaigns produced by AT&T's major competitors continued to fan the flames of the price war. MCI promoted the value of its long-standing Friends & Family calling plan and 1-800-COLLECT service, and Sprint commercials featured actress Candice Bergen explaining the company's low-cost calling plans. Advertising for the smaller telecommunications companies focused almost exclusively on their inexpensive rates.

In the emerging telecommunications category of Internet services, AT&T was up against large competitors such as AOL and Microsoft as well as local Internet service providers. This market represented tremendous future potential; once the glitches in Internet-voice-communication technology were resolved, the Internet promised to be a new source of long-distance and international calling. In the expanding arena of wireless services, AT&T's strongest competition came from NexTel Communications and Sprint. In April 1997 Jeff Kagan, president of Kagan Telecom Associates, a telecommunications consultancy group, summed up the competitive environment in a *USA Today* article. "AT&T has got to move quickly," Kagan said. "A year from now, it will either be on top of the world or eating dust. It won't be the same. The world is moving too fast."

MARKETING STRATEGY

In 1997 AT&T worked with Young & Rubicam Advertising to develop a new marketing strategy. AT&T no longer wanted to compete solely on the basis of price. The new strategy would focus on building long-lasting relationships with customers, not simply selling specific services or products. "To move from being product-centered to being customer-focused is seismic, not insignificant," AT&T president John Walter told *USA Today.* "Every aspect of what we are doing is about the customer. That is a total reversal in our procedures and our strategic intent."

In order to heighten consumers' perceptions of AT&T as a brand, the commercials took what Burke Stinson, district manager of media relations at AT&T, called "an old-fashioned approach." He explained, "The approach was cinematic rather than commercial. The AT&T products on display are incidental to the central theme of people communicating." Each spot featured an emotional glimpse of life in the high-tech 1990s. Ted Bell, worldwide creative director at Young & Rubicam, told *USA Today,* "AT&T is not just a phone company. It's selling a lot of sophisticated high-tech services, and that can sometimes scare people. One of the best ways to offset the fear is to focus on the emotional needs that can be met by using AT&T's products."

The corporate branding account helmed by Young & Rubicam—one among numerous AT&T advertising assignments—was allotted $53.3 million of AT&T's nearly $1 billion total marketing budget in 1997. That year's spots included "Teen Date," in which a teenage girl came home from a date and continued her budding flirtations with the boy online. Another spot, "Beaches," depicted a working mother whose young daughters convinced her to play hooky from work and take them to the beach, where she was able to take an important conference call using her cellular phone. In a spot titled "Rocket Man" a husband traveling on business faxed his wife from the airplane, asking her to be on the porch to take his call that night. Each of the commercials featured classic pop or country songs that appealed to baby boomers' nostalgia. National print ads used the same tagline and similar imagery.

The same spots continued to run in 1998 and were supplemented by new ones, including a Super Bowl commercial that showed teenagers gossiping—via fax, E-mail, pager, and other new technologies—about a romance that was developing among their ranks. The most striking of the 1998 spots, however, had actually been filmed and slated to run in the campaign's first year. Set to the Crosby, Stills, and Nash song "Long Time Gone," the commercial recounted a young soldier's trip to contemporary Vietnam, where his father had fought a generation earlier. The journey's emotional resonance reached its dramatic peak when the son, using an AT&T calling card, phoned his father in America to tell him where he was. AT&T executives, fearful of offending people still sensitive to the unresolved issues surrounding the Vietnam War, had withheld their approval to run the spot for nearly a year before yielding to the pleas of Crosby, Stills, and Nash's David Crosby and Young & Rubicam's chairman and chief executive Edward H. Vick (a highly decorated Vietnam veteran), both of whom felt passionate about the spot. The budget for the campaign's second year was $44.6 million.

OUTCOME

In a field of telecommunications commercials that virtually shouted about low prices, AT&T's commercials were a welcome change to many television viewers. In recent years telecommunications advertising had become something that consumers endured rather than enjoyed. The AT&T campaign proved to be an exception. In fact, advertising critic Dottie Enrico of *USA Today* reported that "AT&T's latest corporate ad campaign has achieved the near-impossible in the telecommunications industry." She explained that almost one-third of the consumers questioned in an Ad Track poll conducted by the newspaper said that they liked the AT&T "All Within Your Reach" campaign. The ads were especially popular with women—41 percent of women and 19 percent of men said they liked the ads very much—and with consumers in the 18 to 24 age bracket—almost 40 percent said the campaign was effective, versus 24 percent of those polled in the 30 to 39 age range.

Advertising aficionados found plenty to like about the commercials, too. The campaign won a Gold EFFIE Award for its effectiveness in the category of corporate reputation, image, and identity. "Teen Date" was singled out by *Adweek* as one of the 50 best spots of the year. "Beaches" was a finalist for an International ANDY Award. In the American Advertising Awards (ADDYs) national competition, AT&T received an ADDY for the "Beaches," "Rocket Man," and "Teen Date" trio and also received citations for two individual commercials. At the District 2 ADDY Awards, AT&T took home three awards. A spot called "Father and Son" was a finalist in the prestigious One Show. At the New York Festival's International Television Advertising Competition, the campaign won Best of Show and Best Campaign for Telecommunications. At the same festival AT&T took home a silver for print executions of the campaign.

Despite these successes, 1999 saw AT&T virtually abandon the branding strategy introduced with "It's All Within Your Reach." The company's corporate-image advertising expenditures were slashed, accounting for a mere $8.9 million of its overall marketing budget that year. Although the "It's All Within Your Reach" tagline remained in place through 2000, AT&T focused its marketing resources on individual business segments as it continued searching for ways to update its overall brand. The most prominent AT&T campaigns in these years included one in which the actor Paul Reiser touted the company's long-distance rates and one in which the actor David Arquette pitched the dial-around service 1-800-CALL-ATT. A critical May 2000 report issued by the Boston market-research firm Yankee Group, titled "AT&T in the Brave New World of the Internet: A Brand Out of Time," suggested that AT&T had failed to create a consistent brand image and risked becoming irrelevant in the Internet age.

FURTHER READING

Comiteau, Jennifer. "New Branding Ads for AT&T." *Adweek,* March 3, 1997.

Elliott, Stuart. "AT&T Ad Filmed in Vietnam Was a Long Time Coming." *New York Times,* July 24, 1998.

Enrico, Dottie. "AT&T Makes Connection with Ad Campaign." *USA Today,* May 19, 1997, p. 06B.

Garfield, Bob. "AT&T Presses the Right High-Tech Buttons." *Advertising Age,* March 10, 1997.

Rosenbush, Steve. "Putting the Buzz Back into AT&T." *USA Today,* April 4, 1997, p. 01B.

Snyder, Beth. "Telcos, Internet Companies Team Up." *Advertising Age,* April 1998.

Verity, John W.. "AT&T Is Being Bitten on the Ankles." *BusinessWeek,* August 5, 1996.

Vranica, Suzanne,"AT&T to Use FCB, Y&R for Image Ads." *Wall Street Journal,* August 23, 2000.

Kim Kazemi
Mark Lane

PRIVACY MANAGER CAMPAIGN

OVERVIEW

NOTE: Since the initial appearance of this essay in the 1999 edition of *Major Marketing Campaigns Annual,* Ameritech became AT&T Inc. The essay continues to refer to Ameritech, as that was the official name of the organization when the campaign was launched.

The first campaign for Ameritech from its new advertising agency, Ammirati Lintas Puris of New York, was launched on October 6, 1997, in an attempt to move customers from simply recognizing the brand to preferring it over other telecommunications companies. The following year's campaign took an even more aggressive stance, with the goal of creating "active preference" in consumers—in other words, that they not only prefer the Ameritech brand but actually switch to it from other brands or expand their existing Ameritech services.

The company provided firepower for such an ambitious goal. In an article by Sally Beatty in the *Wall Street Journal,* Richard Notebaert, CEO of Ameritech, was quoted as saying, "We have never had a product test this good." He was referring to the Privacy Manager system, a service that worked in conjunction with Caller ID, whereby Ameritech intercepted calls from unidentified callers and requested that they identify themselves. In test runs 7 out of 10 calls did not make it through this first screening process and ring through to the customers, and as with collect calls, those that did offered customers the option of accepting or rejecting the calls depending on the callers' recorded identification of themselves. With the rise in unsolicited telemarketing calls flooding into homes, Privacy Manager "satisfied a need that consumers have been pleading to have resolved," said Notebaert.

The 1997 campaign personalized Ameritech by presenting a number of its employees as profiled by their own relatives—a wife, a nephew, and a father—who discussed the Ameritech workers' commitment to providing outstanding service to customers. The 1998 campaign further personalized Ameritech's services by presenting vignettes of inviolable family moments, such as reading a story to the kids at bedtime and shampooing their hair at bath time. Beneath these serene scenes Ammirati superimposed text about the Privacy Manager: "Would you interrupt this moment for an aluminum siding deal? Introducing Privacy Manager, a new service from Ameritech. It stops unwanted, unidentified calls before your phone even rings. Interested? For availability in your area, call 1-800-PRIVACY." The understated simplicity of the spots won critical praise, and the launch of the Privacy Manager system was a business success.

HISTORICAL CONTEXT

In July 1997 Ameritech awarded the creative portion of its $100 million advertising account to Ammirati Puris Lintas, which beat out contender BBDO of New York, to end a four-month account review. The move consolidated Ameritech's corporate, small business, and residential advertising, which had been split between Fallon McElligott of Minneapolis, DDB Needham of Chicago, and Leo Burnett of Chicago. According to Joan Walker, Ameritech's senior vice president of corporate communications, as cited in an *Adweek* article by Alison Fahey, Ammirati won the account on the strength of its "strategic and creative insights." Ammirati creative director Tom Nelson explained, "Everybody came together and the creative department came through. Usually, we have great strategy and [fine tune] the creative later. This time it was a total lock." In order to service the account, Ammirati established an office in Chicago, where Ameritech was headquartered.

Ammirati revamped Ameritech's existing tag line—dating back to 1993 and revised in 1995 to become "Your Link to Better Communication"—changing it to read "In a World of Technology, People Make the Difference." The 1997 advertising campaign focused on three Ameritech people: repairman Ted, customer service representative Angela, and emergency relief worker Jack. But instead of portraying them telling their own stories, Ammirati shifted the focus to family members speaking about their dedication. This displacement maintained the humility of the workers while contributing to the atmosphere of the campaign, which sought to highlight Ameritech as a company that fostered lasting familial relationships with its customers.

According to Sean Horgan, writing in the *Indianapolis Star,* the strategy arose from in-depth research suggesting that "consumers always expect technological expertise and competitive prices, but make their final decisions based on which company is the most attentive to their needs." Ameritech thus sought to present itself as user-friendly and responsive to customers' needs. Lest these claims ring false, the company backed up its statements by spending as much as $1 billion over three years on substantive changes that included consolidated billing, employee and customer service training, and expanded products and services for small businesses. Above all, Ameritech sought to present its employees as attentive to the paramount importance of the telephone in modern life. "When you're doing telecommunications, you're doing something that makes a difference to the customer. The phone can be a lifeline. That makes our employees feel very important," said Karen Sheriff, Ameritech's director of corporate marketing and branding, in an *Advertising Age* article by Beth Snyder.

TARGET MARKET

By the time Ameritech hired Ammirati, the telecommunications corporation had achieved its goal of capturing consumer awareness, increasing brand recognition in its region from 8 percent in 1994 to 95 percent in 1997, or near complete saturation. Ameritech's brand message

AMERITECH IRONS OUT THE IRONY

Numerous commentators pointed out the irony of Ameritech offering its Privacy Manager system to residential customers to block out unsolicited telemarketing calls from even ringing into the home. After all, Ameritech's business included an arm devoted to telemarketing. Bob Garfield, the most acerbic of critics, commented in his *Advertising Age* review that "Ameritech protecting you from telemarketers is like R.J. Reynolds selling nicotine gum." Commentators who picked up on this irony were quick to add, however, that Ameritech's potential conflict of interest did not negate the benefits of the Privacy Manager system for consumers. Ameritech responded that it was simply answering consumer needs. "We have a variety of customers, some of whom have asked us for an intelligent way to manage calls into their home," said Ameritech representative Dave Onak in a 1998 *Adweek* article. "So we really see no irony in this." Furthermore, Ameritech maintained that "outbound" telemarketing, or calls into the home, represented a mere fraction of its overall business.

thus had to become more sophisticated, moving consumers from merely recognizing the brand to preferring it over competitors. "People are looking beyond technology for people who can help them," said Ameritech's Walker in an *Adweek* article by Trevor Jensen. Hence the "people-centered" campaign of 1997.

Ameritech did not, however, abandon technological innovation as a means of appealing to consumers and of distinguishing itself from competitors. At the time the hot telecommunications technology was Caller ID, which displayed the name and telephone number of the incoming caller. As of September 1997, 19 percent of households in the United States had Caller ID, whereas a year later some 31 percent of the country's households were using it. The Caller ID feature was not exclusive to Ameritech, however, and so the technology did not offer a clear point of distinction between Ameritech and the competition. Ameritech shrewdly extended the Caller ID concept into a more proactive system, gaining exclusivity with Privacy Manager. Ameritech applied for two patents to maintain the exclusivity and, in fact, intended to license the service to other telecommunications companies.

COMPETITION

Because the best means for growth for each company would be to carve into the other's regional strongholds, Bell Atlantic, which had merged with Nynex Corp., represented Ameritech's major competitor. According to Competitive Media Reporting, Bell Atlantic spent $160 million on advertising in 1996, compared to Ameritech's $73 million. Both companies launched new advertising campaigns in 1997. Whereas Ameritech's campaign leveraged family values and used fairly traditional techniques, Bell Atlantic attempted a more innovative strategy by riding the popular wave of animated advertising. Bell Atlantic did not abandon the past, however, as it retained the deep, resonating sound of James Earl Jones for its voice-overs. In addition, it used characters from Maurice Sendak's popular children's book *Where the Wild Things Are,* the first time Sendak had licensed the characters since his creation of them in 1963.

Bell Atlantic's ad agency—the Lord Group of New York—applied current advertising strategies to give its campaign a fully contemporary feel. The campaign commenced with unidentified teaser ads, a contemporary advertising technique for creating interest in a campaign by capturing consumers' attention and then further peaking their interest by leaving the identity of the advertiser a mystery. The teaser campaign started with outdoor advertising, including the 300-foot billboard adjacent to Manhattan's Grand Central Station, a hub of commuter traffic and hence a highly visible site. Fifteen-second commercials, which began running on October 13, 1997, followed up on the outdoor effort by depicting the approaching footfalls of a Sendak cartoon monster, who burst through a white television screen containing the message "Wild things are happening." The monster then pulled down a new screen containing the Bell Atlantic logo, like a history teacher pulling down a political map.

Two weeks later, on October 27, 1997, 30- and 60-second spots broke, accompanied by magazine and newspaper spreads, fully unveiling the campaign by extending the tag line to read, "Wild things are happening. Bell Atlantic. We'll see you there." The ads supported the theme by portraying the Sendak monsters guiding children through mazelike jungles. Snyder pointed out in her *Advertising Age* article that, according to Ray Smith, Bell Atlantic's CEO, the campaign, which continued into 1998, was intended to "establish Bell Atlantic as the friendly, gentle giant leading customers through the communications jungle."

MARKETING STRATEGY

Ammirati hired veteran director Bob Giraldi of bicoastal Giraldi Suarez Productions—known for what *Advertising*

Age critic Bob Garfield called "bombastic '80s-era music videos" —to direct a series of five spots that introduced consumers to the Privacy Manager system. Giraldi responded with commercials that went counter to his stereotype, employing understatement instead of pushing the product with a hard sell. Giraldi easily could have resorted to presenting the problem, probably to great comic or shocking effect, by depicting the most heinous of privacy invasions by telemarketers. Instead, Giraldi and the Ammirati team—which included creative directors Jon Moore and Tim Kane, art director Sharon Dershin, copywriter Jody Finver, and producer Mary Ann Marino—chose to focus on the solution, depicting the kinds of familial and intimate scenes that would not be interrupted by unwanted telemarketing calls in those households that employed Privacy Manager.

"Rubber Ducky," one of the most memorable and effective of the spots, portrayed a father shampooing his son, who sat in a bathtub singing his ABCs. Giraldi positioned the camera to view the scene from the next room, with the bathroom door framing the shot, as if to respect the sacred space of this communal moment between father and son. Similarly, in the spot entitled "Snooze," he angled the camera from the foot of the bed so that the audience focused on the father's feet sandwiched between the two sets of his daughters' feet. Even the book, which the father held open to their nighttime story, hid their faces, maintaining privacy. No voice-over interrupted the scenes. Instead, information about Privacy Manager scrolled unobtrusively across the bottom of the screen, further supporting the sense of respect for personal space.

The advertisers were so confident of the desirability of the Privacy Manager system that they limited their sales pitch to one word: "Interested?" "Hell yes, I'm interested," Garfield responded in his review of the ads. Ameritech had succeeded in tapping into a nearly universal revulsion to telemarketers. "People don't like telemarketers," explained Fred Voit, consumer communications analyst with the Boston-based market research firm Yankee Group. While Voit stopped short of predicting the demise of telemarketing, as not all consumers annoyed by telemarketers would pay the extra monthly charges for Privacy Manager on top of the charges for the necessary Caller ID, he did, nevertheless, expect there to be a demand for the service.

OUTCOME

Garfield, the tough ad critic for *Advertising Age,* gave the Ameritech Privacy Manager campaign a rating of 3 1/2 out of a possible 4 stars. He praised the marketing technique behind the five commercials in the campaign, which "dramatize the product benefits magnificently." He complimented director Giraldi for "turn[ing] out cinematic vignettes of surpassing tenderness." Describing the atmosphere of the spots, Garfield explained that the "mood, the moments are sublime." The Advertising Women of New York joined Garfield in praising the campaign by giving Giraldi a 1999 Addy Award in the category of best direction for his work on the campaign.

It was interesting that even the contingent that stood to lose the most from the innovation applauded it. The American Telemarketing Association released a press statement maintaining that the organization had "always supported consumer choice in receiving information on goods and services over the phone." The advent of the Privacy Manager sent the message to telemarketers that they needed to modify their strategies, since households were taking measures to protect themselves from existing telemarketing techniques. "I truly believe we're at the saturation level," commented telemarketing consultant Rudy Oetting of Oetting & Co. of New York. He saw the potential benefit of the Privacy Manager system to the telemarketing field in forcing it to improve techniques of targeting and reaching consumers who were truly interested in the services or products offered. Services such as Privacy Manager "will cause marketers who use the telephone channel to become more selective and creative in their approach so that people who do receive calls will be interested in what they're being called about," stated Oetting in Beatty's *Wall Street Journal* article.

FURTHER READING

Beatty, Sally. "Ameritech's New Phone Service Aims to Keep Telemarketers at Bay." *Wall Street Journal,* September 23, 1998.

Fahey, Alison. "Ammirati Wins Ameritech's $100 Mil. Consolidated Account." *Adweek,* July 21, 1997.

Garfield, Bob. "Ameritech Connects with Its Privacy Pitch." *Advertising Age,* October 12, 1998.

Horgan, Sean. "Ameritech Launches a New Ad Campaign." *Indianapolis Star,* October 7, 1997.

Snyder, Beth. "Bell Atlantic, Ameritech Follow Different Ad Paths: Ameritech Tries Traditional, Bell Atlantic Going a Little Wild." *Advertising Age,* October 13, 1997.

William D. Baue

Audi of America, Inc.

3800 Hamlin Road
Auburn Hills, Michigan 48326
USA
Telephone: (248) 754-5000
Web site: www.audiusa.com

ART OF THE HEIST CAMPAIGN

OVERVIEW

The car maker Audi of America, Inc. (AoA), was the American arm of the German company Audi AG. The Michigan-based automaker's advertising changed drastically in fall 2004 when Stephen Berkov took control as marketing director. The first vehicle launched under Berkov's supervision was the new Audi A3, a luxury wagon that AoA planed to release in mid-2005. Berkov defined the A3's target market as 25- to 34-year-old upper-income males. Aware that this target disliked mainstream advertisements, Berkov oversaw the release of an atypical campaign titled "Art of the Heist."

Created by the ad agency McKinney & Silver and the production firm Chelsea Pictures/Campfire, "Art of the Heist" employed audience participation via the Internet and outside events to shape the campaign's narrative. Ad critics used the gaming phrase "alternate-reality game" (ARG) to describe the campaign's blend of reality, fiction, and audience participation. The $3 million to $4 million campaign began on March 31, 2005, three months before the A3 was available. The campaign first surfaced when an Audi A3 was reportedly "stolen" from the rotating display at the New York Auto Show. For the next three months McKinney & Silver used real events, along with integrated television, print, and online advertising, to tell the story of a thwarted art heist. The campaign's narrative featured the characters Nisha Roberts and Ian Yarbrough driving across America in an Audi A3 while being chased by hit men. The "Heist" actors made public appearances at the popular Coachella Music Festival and on the music TV channel VH1. Television spots and magazine ads posed as real alerts about the stolen A3 until the campaign ended in late June 2005.

Advertising critics credited "Art of the Heist" with being the auto industry's first ARG campaign. It garnered the Best in Show award at the 2005 MIXX Awards, an advertising-industry event sponsored by the Interactive Advertising Bureau and *Adweek* magazine. In 2005 sales of A3s surpassed AoA's original expectations. During May 2005 the automaker's website also registered 30 percent more visitors than it had in the previous May.

HISTORICAL CONTEXT

Audi of America was the U.S. branch of Audi AG, 99 percent of which was owned by Volkswagen AG in 1999. AoA's advertising shifted drastically when Stephen Berkov, who had previously headed advertising for the German-based Audi AG, was reassigned in 2004 as marketing director for AoA. To allocate more capital for advertising, the newly appointed director disbanded AoA's e-business team and reduced spending on the company's online infrastructure. Berkov also reduced AoA's dependency on multiple ad agencies and allocated more control to McKinney & Silver, which had done work for the company since 1993. Referring to AoA's advertising account, Berkov said to *Advertising Age,* "I wanted it integrated because it blurred the brand too much."

To advertise its all-new A4 model, in early 2005 AoA released its "Sum of All Parts Challenge" campaign. The campaign included the tagline "Never Follow," a slogan used for all AoA models. "We said, 'let's break out of just doing banners,'" said Dave Cook, group creative director at McKinney & Silver to *Adweek.* "Let's have people do something." Resembling an online scavenger hunt, the "Sum of All Parts Challenge" asked consumers to collect nine different banner ads touting A4 features. Ads were placed on websites relating to finance, lifestyle, and automotive interests. The challenge's winner was eligible for a two-year lease on a new A4. Other prizes included personal digital assistants (PDAs) and high-end stereos.

Even though the A3 would not be available until mid-2005, Berkov wanted to target 25- to 34-year-olds starting in March. He believed that traditional television spots and print ads would not appeal to the car's target, who, he explained to *Advertising Age,* did not appreciate commercials "shouting at them, telling them what to buy. They smell artificial messaging and lack of authenticity." Instead Berkov wanted McKinney & Silver to create a campaign that engaged consumers as an alternate-reality computer game would.

AUGUST'S AUDI

August Horch founded the car manufacturer Auto Union in 1932. The German-based company featured four models of cars, including a touring car called Audi, which was a Latin translation of the founder's first name. The corporation later dropped the name "Auto Union" in favor of "Audi."

TARGET MARKET

The campaign targeted an audience of video-game enthusiasts, also called gamers, who enjoyed playing alternate-reality games (ARGs) that blended fiction with reality and were ultimately controlled by the games' designers, or "puppeteers." This target market, which Berkov profiled in the *News & Observer* as 23- to 34-year-old males, typically disliked traditional advertising that told consumers what to purchase. Also, according to advertising analysts, gamers typically avoided pop-up Internet ads by installing pop-up blockers on their computers. Many skipped through television spots by using TiVo, a television accessory allowing audiences to fast-forward through commercial breaks. Instead of being told what to purchase, gamers preferred to discover products on their own. "Engaging consumers so they follow your brand is the new holy grail," Brad Brinegar, the CEO of McKinney & Silver, was quoted in *BusinessWeek Online.*

Some marketing analysts titled this tech-savvy demographic as Generation C; the *C* abbreviated the word "creative." Generation C, according to Trendwatching.com's director Reinier Evers, created most of the content of Internet forums, online blogs, and virtual bulletin boards. McKinney & Silver thus used such sites to make contact with its target market, releasing important details about the "Art of the Heist" storyline on the campaign's main website, LastResortRetrieval.com. Actors playing roles in the campaign even answered questions in Internet chat rooms. Subsequent fan sites materialized during "Art of the Heist," and the campaigns' outcome was debated in blogs and bulletin boards.

In an approach that was unusual for advertising campaigns, the target that the agency chose for the "Art of the Heist" represented a different demographic from the one that AoA executives believed would actually purchase the product advertised. The target market for the Audi A3 wagon, which carried a price tag of more than $26,000, was defined by Berkov in *BusinessWeek Online* as 25- to 34-year-old males that were college-educated and earned more than $125,000 annually. This group was somewhat older and typically more affluent than the 23- to 34-year-old gamers. Creatives at McKinney & Silver assumed that if enough trendsetting gamers approved of the "Art of the Heist," their opinions would persuade the more-affluent A3 target market.

COMPETITION

In March 2005 Volkswagen of America (VWoA,) the American branch of the German automaker Volkswagen AG, released print ads, radio spots, television spots, and other events heralding its newly designed A5 Jetta, which was larger and more expensive than its predecessors. The campaign, titled "All Grown Up. Sort Of," was created by the agency Arnold Worldwide of Boston. It targeted 20-something consumers transitioning into adulthood. The campaign's first commercial, "Airport," featured a young businessman using his A5 Jetta to shuttle an older, conservative colleague from the airport. When the tense older executive turned on the Jetta's radio to "check the scores," the speakers blared loud rock music. The spot ended with the tagline "The

AUDI VICTIMS NETWORK

In the 1980s an American Audi owner named Alice Weinstein claimed that a brake malfunction had caused her Audi 5000 to unexplainably accelerate. After suffering an injury from the reported malfunction, Weinstein sued AoA dealerships and created the Audi Victims Network. The CBS program *60 Minutes* even reported on the incident, which eventually sent AoA sales into a downward spiral. Fortunately for AoA, the New York courts favored the AoA dealerships in a 1986 settlement.

new Jetta. It's all grown up. Sort of." In addition, as part of the campaign Arnold representatives distributed wooden puzzles and coloring books depicting adults performing mundane tasks until their lives were enlivened by the new Jetta. The campaign also included a six-minute film titled *The Check Up,* which featured a man in his late 20s humorously being criticized for not behaving like an adult.

On February 14, 2005, the ad agency Crispin Porter + Bogusky released a campaign titled "Counterfeit" to increase awareness about the premium small car MINI Cooper, a brand owned by Bayerische Motoren-Werke AG (BMW). Similar to "Art of the Heist," the "Counterfeit" campaign used a nontraditional narrative that blended fiction and realty. It featured one television spot that warned of "counterfeiters" selling dilapidated cars as MINI Coopers. In addition to the one commercial, Crispin Porter + Bogusky created a fictional watchdog organization to educate the public about counterfeit MINIs. The 10-minute DVD spoof "Counterfeit MINI Cooper" could also be purchased on the website www.CounterfeitMini.org.

MARKETING STRATEGY

The "Art of the Heist" began on March 31, 2005, when AoA announced that its brand-new Audi A3 had been stolen from the New York Auto Show. To reinforce the claim, McKinney & Silver distributed handbills in 10 cities that announced the missing Audi. The A3's vehicle identification number (VIN) was listed on the handbills. People who spotted the car were asked to call a phone number or visit Audi's website. From the website visitors were led to a fictitious company called Last Resort Retrieval, which supposedly retrieved stolen art from high-profile thieves. LastResortRetrieval.com served as the hub for the campaign's narrative and introduced the characters Nisha Roberts and Ian Yarbrough. A "glitch" on the website offered a glimpse into Last Resort Retrieval's private intranet, which was loaded with clues such as tapped phone calls, surveillance videos, and puzzles.

Ian and Nisha discovered that an art thief had stolen the A3 and that memory cards with information about an art heist were hidden inside the car. Ian retrieved the A3 from a New Jersey chop shop. The act spurred the original car's thief and then the police to chase Ian from the East Coast to the West Coast. To lend further credibility to the story, phony "ads" announcing the services and contact information of Last Resort Retrieval were placed in issues of *Wired, Esquire,* and *USA Today.*

"What was certainly surprising to us was the importance and impact of good, old-fashioned traditional media in helping make ['Art of the Heist'] explode," Lee Newman, the AoA account director at McKinney & Silver, said to *Adweek.* In May 2005 a television spot featured interior and exterior images of the new A3. To relate the commercial to the campaign's narrative, copy appeared during the spot asking the public to report the missing Audi to audiusa.com. "It was like a chemistry experiment," Newman continued. "Adding a little bit of this, a little of that—you really sort of get an explosion."

Public events were also announced on LastResortRetrieval.com. The campaign changed unexpectedly for its creators after the website reported that Ian and Nisha were appearing on May 1 at the Coachella Valley Music Festival. When AoA's tent was inundated with fans earlier than expected, Chelsea Pictures, which produced the online video for the campaign, was forced to suddenly change the script. "One of our [fictional] characters was killed as a result of that," Jonathan Cude, group creative director at McKinney & Silver, said to the *News & Observer.*

Fortunately for AoA and its ad agency, fans following the campaign began creating websites that speculated about the game's outcome. Even websites such as VWVortex.com, an automotive website, tracked the story. The campaign ended in late June at E3, a video game convention held at the Los Angeles Convention Center. Attendees, unaware that they were observing a staged performance, watched Ian physically apprehend the art thief responsible for the A3 robbery.

OUTCOME

AoA partially assessed the campaign's success by measuring traffic to AoA's U.S. website and Audi AG's international website. Total traffic for both sites in April 2005 was double the amount recorded during the same month in 2004. AoA estimated that 500,000 people followed the "Art of the Heist" storyline until its completion in

June. The car company also reported that 33 percent of the website's visitors further searched for extended A3 features, such as dealer locations and lease options; this was higher than the 25 percent who further researched AoA's A4 model. The campaign was credited with preselling 500 A3s before they were even available in North America. "'The Art of the Heist' represents a true innovation in the way Audi connects with its target consumer," Berkov was quoted in the PR Newswire news service. "The power of this program comes from our deep understanding of the A3 target audience," Berkov continued.

Advertising critics praised "Art of the Heist" for being the first ARG campaign within the auto industry. It garnered the Best in Show award at the 2005 MIXX Awards, along with gold awards for online integration and product launch and a silver award within the word-of-mouth category. AoA and McKinney & Silver considered "Art of the Heist" a success when AoA posted 5,389 A3s sold at the year's end, making 2005 one of AoA's best years in its 73-year legacy.

FURTHER READING

Anderson, Mae. "Marketers Lure Consumers with Involvement, but Are They Asking Too Much?" *Adweek,* August 22, 2005.

Chon, Gina. "Advertising: Car Makers Hone Their Pitch Online." *Wall Street Journal,* October 14, 2005, p. B4.

Halliday, Jean. "Exec Uses 'Acupuncture Approach' to Craft Uniform Marketing Theme." *Advertising Age,* August 22, 2005, p. 29.

Hiawatha, Bray. "Through a Hole, and into Hidden Worlds of Fun." *Boston Globe,* April 25, 2005, p. B8.

Hoxsey, Rich, and Maggie Kinser Hohle. "Stranger than Unfiction." *Print: America's Graphic Design Magazine,* July 1, 2005.

Iezzi, Teressa. "Marketers Tapping into the Magic of an Alternate Reality." *Advertising Age,* November 21, 2005, p. 15.

Kiley, David. "Advertising Of, By, and For the People." *BusinessWeek,* July 25, 2005, p. 63.

Lazare, Lewis. "Graffiti Ad Gets Graffiti Treatment." *Chicago Sun-Times,* June 16, 2005, p. 65.

Morrissey, Brian. "Locked Out of Prime Sites, Clients Try New Avenues." *Adweek,* October 10, 2005.

———. "Maturing Industry Feels Growing Pains." *Adweek,* October 3, 2005.

———. "McKinney + Silver Takes Top MIXX Honors." *Adweek,* September 28, 2005.

Ranii, David. "Car Theft Is an Ad." *Raleigh (NC) News & Observer,* June 25, 2005, p. D1.

Shortman, Melanie. "Chelsea Gathers around Campfire." *Advertising Age's Creativity,* September 1, 2005, p. 48.

Wegert, Tessa. "Advertisers Reap Real-World Benefits from 'Alternate Realty.'" *Toronto (ON) Globe and Mail,* August 18, 2005, p. B9.

Westhead, Rick. "Web Clicks with Advertisers." *Toronto (ON) Star,* November 19, 2005, p. D01.

Kevin Teague

Barclays Global Investors

45 Fremont Street
San Francisco, California 94105
USA
Telephone: (415) 777-8389
Fax: (415) 597-2171
Web site: www.barclaysglobal.com

■■■

NEW SCHOOL CAMPAIGN

OVERVIEW

Barclays Global Investors (BGI), a subsidiary of the United Kingdom's Barclays PLC, was a little-known mutual-fund provider in the United States when in 1999 it developed a new investment product called iShares. It was essentially an index mutual fund that could be bought and sold like shares of stock. Such funds held shares of stock in every company listed on a particular index in order to enjoy the growth of the entire group, the winners more than offsetting the losers. It was not imaginative investing, but over time it proved to be a worthwhile strategy. Making the index funds tradable was an innovation, but given the abundance of mutual funds competing for investment dollars and BGI's limited marketing budget, it was difficult to bring iShares to the attention of investors. In 2004 BGI released the "New School" campaign, which targeted the top ranks of investment advisers rather than the general investing public.

The "New School" campaign consisted mostly of television spots and print ads. Airtime was limited to the high-profile financial cable channels CNBC and Bloomberg. Print ads were run in prestigious publications such as the *Wall Street Journal* and *Barron's.* The less-than-$5 million campaign ran from January 2004 through August 2004. The target of the advertising was younger financial advisers who were willing to entertain new ideas in investment. Many of the television spots depicted a financial adviser who, having decided he was ready to embrace a "new school" of thought and action, debated his mirror image, who was stuck in the past.

The "New School" campaign significantly improved awareness of iShares among financial advisers and greatly increased investments in iShares. During the course of the campaign, Barclays became the third-best-selling fund family. The campaign also won a pair of prestigious awards: a Midas and an EFFIE.

HISTORICAL CONTEXT

BGI's U.S. predecessor, a Wells Fargo Bank unit, was a pioneer of the index fund—a mutual fund that mirrored a market index such as the S&P 500 (a list of the top 500 U.S. corporations ranked by their stock value). By holding shares in all companies of an index in proportion to their worth, an index fund achieved the same growth as the entire index. It was a passive form of investing but produced steady results and became a popular investment vehicle. In 1999 BGI unveiled a new index-investment product, iShares, but instead of taking the form of a mutual fund iShares were exchange-traded funds, which could be bought or sold just like shares of stock, even though they represented a large bundle of stocks. In addition to containing stocks, iShares funds would also be developed to collect baskets of bonds, currencies, and commodities.

BGI began marketing iShares in 2000 with a $10 million campaign developed by the ad agency Saatachi & Saatchi, San Francisco; it focused on wealthier, more sophisticated investors, taking what *Adweek* magazine's Justin M. Norton called a "buttoned-down approach." As BGI struggled to establish iShares in the marketplace, Saatchi closed its San Francisco office, and BGI's advertising account was put up for review. In a surprise outcome, a new advertising agency, Venables, Bell & Partners, founded by veterans of San Francisco's well-regarded Goodby, Silverstein & Partners, won the business. The new agency took a more lighthearted approach than its predecessor, focusing on the close relationship between investors and the financial advisers who handled their iShares account. In one of the television spots, for example, a man urged his adviser to don a helmet because of nearby construction projects, while in another spot a man mistook a car backfire for gunshots and reacted by knocking down and then shielding his adviser. The tagline was "Industrial Strength Investment Tools."

BGI was experiencing only modest success with iShares in the early 2000s, a result in large measure of the depressed state of the stock market. In 2003 Venables began looking for a new approach to promoting iShares. Because it lacked the hefty ad budgets of its competitors, BGI could not hope to target the general investing public. Instead Venables and BGI decided to target financial advisers. Agency personnel spent a month meeting with financial advisers to hone the new strategy. Out of this fieldwork emerged the "New School" campaign, which was released in 2004.

TARGET MARKET

The "New School" campaign was aimed at financial advisers, the people who could urge their clients to purchase iShares. Because of a limited advertising budget BGI narrowed its target to the top 200,000 financial advisers in the United States, who were responsible for placing the lion's share of the investments made by wealthy Americans. But after devoting a month to meet with many of these advisers for lunch, dinner, or drinks, the marketers came to recognize a major difference between older and younger advisers. The former clung to tried-and-true recommendations, such as traditional mutual funds, while the younger group was more open to new ideas like iShares. It was this insight that laid a foundation for the "New School" campaign and led to the narrowing of the target audience to younger advisers—and to the older ones who would respond positively to the challenge of fresh thinking.

DEEP ROOTS

Barclays Global Investors was originally a unit of the legendary Wells Fargo, founded in the early 1850s by Henry Wells and William Fargo, who had earlier established American Express. Wells Fargo was started in San Francisco to serve the stagecoach and banking needs created by the California gold rush, and as a sister company to American Express it handled the express shipping business west of the Mississippi River. What would become Barclays Global Investors was introduced in 1973 as Wells Fargo Investment Advisors. Barclays PLC acquired the operation in 1995 and merged it with other divisions to create Barclays Global Investors, which like its famous ancestor remained based in San Francisco.

COMPETITION

BGI's main competition for iShares came from mutual funds, especially the larger ones, such as those sold by the Vanguard Group, Fidelity Investments, and T. Rowe Price Group. Together they spent about $200 million on advertising each year, cast a wide net, and as a result had developed tremendous brand recognition. Fidelity itself spent nearly $100 million a year on ads, according to *Adweek*. While BGI was preparing its new marketing effort, Fidelity was pursuing its "Personally Invested" campaign, which targeted individual investors. Vanguard was spending another $40 to $50 million promoting its multitude of funds, and the marketing efforts of T. Rowe Price were estimated by *Adweek* to cost $35 million a year. With far less money at its disposal, BGI could not hope to compete directly with the major fund providers, hence the decision to focus on investment advisers rather than the general investing public. To further complicate the task, iShares also had to compete against scores of other fund providers, many of which—such as Dreyfuss, Oppenheimer, Janus, American Century, Franklin Templeton, and Nuveen—had been around for years and had built up their own level of brand recognition. In short, iShares faced a crowded marketplace, a situation that forced the narrow focus of the "New School" campaign.

MARKETING STRATEGY

Venables set three campaign objectives. The first was to gain notice for iShares in the marketplace. Second was to drive traffic to a website where interested parties could learn more about the new product by downloading articles and accessing other information. Finally, and most importantly, the campaign wanted to drive the sale of iShares.

To reach the target audience of upper-tier financial advisers, BGI and its agency Venables concentrated their resources on select television programming and print media, including cable TV channels CNBC and Bloomberg, the *Wall Street Journal, Investor's Business Daily,* and *Barron's,* and smaller trade publications. In addition, the campaign promoted iShares in direct mailings, through online and interactive advertising, via public relations, and at tradeshows. To gain the most impact from the campaign's limited budget, television commercials were aired before and after stock-market trading hours. The campaign also involved tracking the Federal Open Market Committee Meetings, of which there were eight in 2004. At these meetings Alan Greenspan, chairman of as the Federal Reserve, announced the agency's short-term monetary policy. Believing that financial advisers were certain to pay closer attention to the media whenever Greenspan was scheduled to make a pronouncement, Venables pursued a strategy of running daytime television spots at these times. The day after each meeting, when financial advisers were likely to be reading news coverage, BGI spent money on newspaper ads promoting iShares.

The "New School" television spots first began airing in early 2004. One, titled "Clean Slate," showed a group of financial professionals trapped in a conference room by a flood. When the sun rose the next day, the spot offered the message: "Investment advisers: It's a new day. The new school of investing is here. iShares.com/newschool." Another set of commercials in the campaign featured text that read, "Say goodbye to the old you. Here's to the new smarter you." They included "Break Up," in which trick photography was used to show a financial adviser on a lunch date with himself; he explained to his chagrined former self, "This just isn't working for me... You're holding me back. I'm moving our clients in new directions with new investment strategies." In "Fired" a financial adviser called her double into her office to terminate her employment. Another spot, titled "Grave," portrayed a man digging a burial plot for his old self, while his identical image stood by and attempted to talk the man out of leaving the old ways behind: "Are you sure you want to do this? We had a pretty good run. Making trades, picking stocks..." The man cheerfully replied, "I'm sure... Get in the hole." Each spot ended with the tagline "iShares. This is the new school of investing."

The print ads of the "New School" campaign followed a similar approach to the television spots. In one ad a man stood on a sidewalk with a briefcase, a deflated version of himself at his feet, as if he had just shed his skin. In the corner appeared the text: "Eric White, Financial Adviser; 1965 born; 2005 evolved." Ironically, or not, this was also the campaign's target audience: white financial advisers around 40 years of age. Other print ads played up the simplicity of dealing in iShares. In one execution an adviser was shown drinking a cup of coffee, his feet propped up on his mahogany desk. In another a man in a cubicle environment was shown looking a little under the weather. The headline read: "Gentle Relief from Bond Ladder Discomfort Is Here." (A bond ladder was an investment strategy in which bonds or certificate of deposits were arranged to mature simultaneously).

OUTCOME

The "New School" campaign was successful on a number of levels. It increased recognition of iShares in the marketplace. According to a 2003 tracking study, 57 percent of financial advisers were aware of iShares without given any aid, and awareness of iShares among financial advisers totaled 98 percent. The campaign also drove increased traffic to the iShares website. From January until September 2004, visits increased 74 percent over the comparable period in 2003. Finally, during the campaign period, January through August 2004, iShares enjoyed a surge in cash investments (inflows), a 280 percent increase over the same period of time in 2003. Inflows increased from $6.37 billion to more than $24.25 billion. As a result, iShares became the number three fund family according to cash inflows during this period. The "New School" campaign also garnered advertising-industry awards for Venables. It won a Silver EFFIE in the Small Budgets category of the 2005 EFFIE Awards, a prestigious competition produced by the New York American Marketing Association, a trade organization for marketing professionals. In addition, the spot "Clean Slate" won a 2005 Midas Award for best special effects. The Midas Awards, produced by New York Festivals, honored marketing work in financial services.

FURTHER READING

"Barclays Launches New Funds." *Global Investor,* June 2000, p. 6.

"'Clean Slate' Spot for New Ishares Campaign from Venables, Bell and Partners." *All VF Magazine,* April 2004. Available from <http://www.allvfx.com/news/article.asp?articleid=23>

Elliott, Stuart. "TV Commercials Adjust to a Shorter Attention Span." *New York Times,* April 8, 2005, p. C6.

Garcia, Sandra. "It Only Looked Risky." *Shoot,* May 3, 2002, p. 15.

Norton, Justin M. "Barclays Eyes Venables, Eleven." *Adweek,* September 10, 2001, p. 4.

———. "Saatchi Touts Barclays iShares." *Adweek* (eastern ed.), June 5, 2000, p. 5.

———. "VB&P Lightens Up Barclays' iShares Investment." *Adweek,* May 13, 2002, p. 8.

Steinberg, Brian. "Stay Tuned for the Next Commercial." *Wall Street Journal,* March 28, 2005, p B2.

Ed Dinger

The Basketball Club of Seattle, LLC

351 Elliot Ave. W, Ste. 500
Seattle, Washington 98119
USA
Telephone: (206) 281-5800
Fax: (206) 281-5828
Web site: www.nba.com/sonics

IN YOUR HOME CAMPAIGN

OVERVIEW

The Basketball Club of Seattle, LLC, owners of both the National Basketball Association's Seattle SuperSonics and the Women's National Basketball Association's Seattle Storm, had seen the Sonics through several successful seasons in the 1990s, but the organization wanted to prepare for a future that would doubtless include down years. Increasing fan loyalty, the franchise believed, was the only way to guarantee ticket sales and TV viewership during losing seasons as well as winning seasons. The team's front office set out to achieve this through a combination of enhanced free TV offerings and marketing. After moving Sonics games from pay-per-view TV to local TV stations preparatory to the 1997–98 season, the team's executives charged Seattle advertising agency WongDoody with the task of publicizing the new schedule of TV broadcasts in a way that would strengthen the bond between fans and their team.

WongDoody, allotted less than $500,000 for the entire campaign, arrived at the concept of sending actual Sonics stars on unannounced visits to the homes of ordinary Seattle residents. The idea gave the campaign its tagline, "In Your Home," which made direct reference to the newly expanded TV schedule for the team's games. The depiction of Sonics players interacting with ordinary Seattle residents also served the important purpose of humanizing the stars, which was particularly important given the fan cynicism of the time, a result of negative stereotypes then abounding about overpaid, misbehaving, out-of-touch players. For the first two weeks after its fall 1997 release, the campaign was aired heavily on regional stations during high-profile prime-time programming; it then continued on the local stations with which the team had partnered for the new game-broadcasting arrangement.

"In Your Home" was a success, achieving goals of increasing both TV ratings and interest in the team among Seattle residents. It also became one of the most awarded regional campaigns as well as one of the most awarded sports campaigns of its time, winning top honors at almost every major advertising festival. The campaign was extended for the 1998–99 basketball season, though it was updated to show players in public locations like grocery stores and bowling alleys rather than in residents' homes.

HISTORICAL CONTEXT

The Seattle SuperSonics entered the NBA in 1967. Like many expansion teams (teams new to a professional sports league), the franchise struggled in its first few years of existence, not posting a winning record until its fifth full season of play. The late 1970s, however, saw the

Sonics become one of the league's best teams; it reached the NBA finals at the end of the 1977–78 season and won the league championship in 1978–79. After experiencing winning seasons in the early 1980s the team slumped in the middle part of the decade. Though the Sonics rallied in the late 1980s, the team did not become a consistent winner again until the 1990s. After bringing in George Karl as head coach in 1992, the Sonics averaged 60 wins a season (out of a total of 82 regular season games) for six seasons in a row. They did not win a championship during this time, but they became one of the most elite franchises in the NBA.

The Sonics, accordingly, had little trouble generating fan loyalty in Seattle. In fact, home games almost always sold out. The team's front office, however, was looking to the franchise's future and knew that the Sonics would not always be able to count on a winning record to sell seats and generate revenue. Only fan loyalty could guarantee a healthy franchise.

Nurturing fan loyalty in the NBA of the late 1990s was a more difficult task than in previous eras. The gulf between fans and players had never been so wide; this was a result of the rise of free agency, which empowered players but did not encourage them to be loyal to their teams, and the corresponding phenomenon of exponentially increasing salaries. Occasional but highly publicized scandalous behavior on the part of players—such as Latrell Sprewell of the Golden State Warriors choking his coach, P.J. Carlesimo—further fueled the disconnect between fans and players, and rising ticket prices meant that many of the die-hard NBA fans of the past could no longer see their teams in person. Though a winning team could overcome the widespread fan cynicism of the time, the perception that players were only interested in money and inhabited a distant, impossibly privileged world was common among fans in all NBA markets.

TARGET MARKET

"In Your Home" targeted exactly these formerly die-hard but now disenchanted NBA fans, many of whom could not afford to attend games in person. While such people tended to be more aware of the problems with the NBA than casual fans, they were also more likely to become enthusiastic about their team and the league if the right conditions were in place. These fans were typically males between the ages of 25 and 54.

The Sonics' larger strategy of bringing such fans back into the fold included, crucially, a change in policy regarding the local TV broadcasting of the team's games. In previous years, games had been broadcast primarily on pay-pay-view television—a situation that did not encourage those disenchanted with high ticket prices to tune in or feel loyalty toward the team—and ratings had been in decline for years. The 1997–98 season saw Sonics management address this issue to fans' benefit, reaching a new agreement with the three major local networks in Seattle that called for a substantially increased network-TV schedule. Of the 82 regular-season Sonics games in the 1997–98 season, 56 would be televised on local network stations. Fans whose loyalty had been tested by changes in the NBA would now be granted comprehensive access to the team, free of charge.

WongDoody thus had a concrete basis upon which to build the message that the Sonics were an integral part of the Seattle community. The idea of the Sonics being "In Your Home" arose directly from the new broadcasting arrangement, taking the premise to a logical extreme: players were shown arriving at the homes of ordinary Seattle residents. Not only did this concept provide a natural way of publicizing the new 56-game TV schedule, but by also showing individual players interacting with ordinary people, it suggested that the gap between players and fans was not as distinct as many fans feared.

COMPETITION

Though no NBA team produced a campaign as highly regarded as "In Your Home" during the 1990s or early 2000s, the Sonics were not the first franchise to build its

THE FOLLOW-UP

After the monumental success of "In Your Home," which ran during the 1997–98 season, ad agency WongDoody's client, the Seattle SuperSonics, had no interest in changing marketing tactics for the 1998–99 season. This presented WongDoody with a new creative challenge. The initial year's spots had made such a splash partly because of the novelty of seeing Sonics stars showing up unannounced at people's homes. Having achieved such notoriety, however, the campaign could not possibly catch viewers off-guard through simply extending this concept. WongDoody thus opted to satisfy its client's demands for more of the same by showing Sonics players in other ordinary places: Gary Payton was shown shopping for groceries, Vin Baker was pictured bowling, and Olden Polynice was shown doing his laundry at a Laundromat. The campaign was well regarded, but it achieved nowhere near the acclaim of its predecessor. Rarely had a follow-up to a hugely acclaimed advertising campaign done so.

marketing on the idea of humanizing its star players. A successful campaign touting the Indiana Pacers, for instance, began during the 1994–95 season. Attempting to leverage success on the court—the Pacers had posted their first promising season in recent memory only a year earlier, in 1993–94 –into ticket sales and enduring fan loyalty, the franchise decided to focus on player personalities. One TV spot introduced the "many faces of Dale Davis," an impassive Pacers forward who, the punch line went, showed one face to the camera despite the multiple scenarios posited in the voice-over. Another spot showed guard Reggie Miller addressing his abrasive on-the-court demeanor by arguing that he was misunderstood. Over the next two years full-season ticket sales for Pacers games grew by 25 percent, half-season sales grew by 69 percent, and 10-game ticket packages rose by 181 percent.

The Orlando Magic attempted to generate increased ticket sales via different means in a 2000–01 marketing campaign, and in the process the team's executives found a way to measure the success of emerging advertising platforms. After acquiring exciting players, including one of the league's star forwards, Grant Hill, as well as young players Tracy McGrady and Mike Miller, the team expected a bump in ticket sales. The franchise's front office attempted to generate further interest in the 2000–01 season by advertising a contest offering fans a chance to play one-on-one with Hill. Advertisements ran online and on radio and television, and those who entered the contest received a brochure promoting season-ticket sales. Half of the season-ticket brochures were sent via E-mail and half via regular mail. Season-ticket sales well outpaced those in previous years, and the Magic found that 16 percent of fans who received E-mailed brochures bought season tickets, compared with 1.5 percent of those who received print brochures.

MARKETING STRATEGY

The concept of showing real Sonics stars showing up unannounced at the homes of real Seattle residents accomplished the campaign's two primary goals at once: it humorously dramatized the news of the Sonics' increased TV presence, and it demonstrated that Sonics players, far from being prima donnas, were ordinary people when they were away from the court. To emphasize "real" behavior, the spots were unscripted, and the ordinary people whose residences the Sonics players visited were not given advance warning. This resulted in a narrative situation reminiscent of the well-known "Publishers Clearing House" commercials, in which the surprise of the individuals featured in the spots formed a major part of the story. The players' interactions with their hosts developed over time as they engaged in numerous and varied "ordinary" activities with the families and groups that they visited.

For instance, Sonics guard Gary Payton was shown entering the common room of a nursing home, to the delight and applause of residents. He was then pictured reacting to comments such as "I always thought you were awfully thin," learning how to knit, and taking a lead role in a heated game of Monopoly. Guard Nate McMillan, meanwhile, arrived unannounced at a suburban Tupperware party populated exclusively by middle-aged women; after the expected interval of surprised exclamations, he settled into the sofa and participated in the party. McMillan innocently wisecracked his way through the lead Tupperware promoter's spiel before being caught off-guard by a post-party question, "And you play quarterback, right?" Forward/center Sam Perkins showed up at the home of a family of five, whose three young boys immediately began monopolizing his attention. Perkins roughhoused with them around their backyard basketball goal, played video games with the smallest son sitting in his lap, and engaged in a pillow fight with them just before bedtime. Each of the commercials opened with text reading, "The Sonics are coming to your home." At the end of the player-fan interactions, on-screen text stated, "See them in your home," and then text appeared reading, "56 games on free TV."

WongDoody was allotted a relatively small budget of just under $500,000, though this was a workable amount of money given that regionally placed TV spots cost only a fraction of national placements on the same programs. WongDoody still sought to get the most possible mileage out of its budget by opening the campaign on prominent prime-time shows. The campaign broke during ABC's *Monday Night Football,* and for the first two weeks after its launch it ran in heavy rotation on such high-profile programs as *Seinfeld* and *Friends,* in addition to cable destinations popular with the male target, such as ESPN and Fox Sports Net. Additionally, WongDoody media planners negotiated airtime with the local networks that would be airing the Sonics games. The agency likewise informed the news teams of the three leading local TV networks, all of which ran stories on the campaign.

Print elements played a lesser role in the campaign. An initial three-page spread in regional editions of *Sports Illustrated* magazine's NBA preview issue helped publicize the new TV schedule, and small-space newspaper ads carrying the "In Your Home" theme ran adjacent to prime-time TV listings.

OUTCOME

Research conducted at the end of the 1997–98 season indicated a 51 percent jump in viewership over the previous year's pay-per-view numbers and judged community involvement with the Sonics to have substantially increased, especially compared with other NBA teams. Season-ticket renewals reached an all-time high. Harry Hutt, senior vice president of marketing for rival NBA team the Portland Trailblazers, called the "In Your Home" campaign "a brilliant example of what the right kind of campaign can do," a judgment that was echoed by his own team's adoption of a similar marketing concept a few years later.

"In Your Home" became one of the most acclaimed professional-sports campaigns of its time as well as one of the most acclaimed regional campaigns. It won the GRANDY, the top award bestowed at the ANDY Awards, in 1998, as well as both the Grand Prize (top prize among all campaigns) and the prize for best low-budget campaign at the 1998 London International Advertising Awards. It won four Clios that year, a Gold Lion at the Cannes International Advertising Festival, and a Gold EFFIE. *USA Today* placed the campaign among its top ads of the year, and *Adweek* included it in its "Best Ads of the '90s" list.

The overwhelming success of the campaign posed only one difficulty for the Sonics and WongDoody: the challenge of following up such a successful campaign the next year. After some debate, "In Your Home" was extended with a twist. Rather than showing Sonics players arriving unannounced at people's homes, the 1998–99 campaign placed the players in everyday locations, such as bowling alleys, grocery stores, and Laundromats.

FURTHER READING

"ANDY's Team." *Adweek* (western ed.), May 4, 1998.

Beatty, Sally. "There Are Award-Winning Ads that You're Unlikely to Ever See." *Wall Street Journal* (eastern ed.), June 2, 1998.

Berger, Warren. "Equal Sequels." *Advertising Age's Creativity,* May 1999.

Buyikian, Teresa. "WongDoody Tops in London." *Adweek* (western ed.), November 16, 1998.

Johnson, J. Douglas. "Ads that Worked." *Indiana Business Magazine,* April 1995.

Rauch, Maggie. "A Marketing Slam Dunk." *Sales & Marketing Management,* December 2000.

Mark Lane

Bayerische Motoren Werke AG

Petuelring 130
Munich, D-80788
Germany
Telephone: 49 8938224272
Fax: 49 8938224418
E-mail: bmwgroup.customerservice@bmwgroup.com
Web site: www.bmwgroup.com

COUNTERFEIT CAMPAIGN

OVERVIEW

After the United States mandated collapsible steering wheels in 1967, the British Mini Cooper retreated back to the United Kingdom and was not sold stateside for 35 years. Reintroduced in 2002 after being purchased and then reengineered by Bayerische Motoren-Werke AG (BMW), the MINI Cooper, as it was later capitalized, began a long series of unorthodox advertising campaigns. Whether it was being strapped to the roofs of SUVs or parked in the bleachers of sports venues, the car rapidly gained traction within the premium-small-car sector. While Volkswagen AG's New Beetle and DaimlerChrysler AG's PT Cruiser sales suffered in 2005, the MINI Cooper flourished under the brand's "Let's Motor" tagline. Hoping to not only to entertain consumers but also to immerse them deeper within the MINI Cooper brand, BMW released its "Counterfeit" campaign on February 14, 2005.

With an estimated budget of $25 million, the advertising agency Crispin Porter + Bogusky launched "Counterfeit" across television, DVD, Internet, and print mediums. Airing only on cable networks, the campaign's one TV commercial warned viewers of fictional counterfeiters who were supposedly selling counterfeit MINI Coopers on the black market. The commercial directed viewers to www.CounterfeitMini.org, a website created by the Counter Counterfeit Commission (CCC), an equally fictional watchdog organization that educated consumers about MINI Cooper counterfeits. If website visitors wanted to learn more, they could order a DVD containing the 10-minute spoof "Counterfeit MINI Cooper," which absurdly documented con artists converting junk cars into look-alike MINI Coopers.

For March 2005, MINI Cooper posted its highest sales month ever and surpassed the previous March by 44 percent. At the Cannes International Advertising Festival in 2005 the campaign garnered a Gold Lion as well as the only American-won Titanium Lion. The ceremony awarded four Titanium Lions to work that the judges considered to be innovative and that utilized several mediums.

HISTORICAL CONTEXT

Even though the British Mini Cooper was an extremely popular car throughout the United Kingdom, its American stint ended in 1967 after collapsible steering wheels were required on every new car sold. Sales of the Mini increasingly dropped after its 1960s heyday. Eventually the Mini brand and other British automobiles were managed by the Rover Group, which was purchased by BMW in 1994. At first BMW was unsure of how to reintroduce the tiny car to the United States. Even after engineers modernized the

BMW's MINI Cooper. © REUTERS/CORBIS.

interior, upgraded the car with a 115-hp Chrysler engine, and increased the length by 20 inches, it was still the smallest car in the U.S. market. By 2001 consumer trends, including the burgeoning markets for SUVs and full-size trucks, suggested a daunting forecast for the MINI Cooper. "If we'd listened to the market research, we'd have never done the MINI Cooper," Jack Pitney, general manager of Mini USA, admitted to the *Cleveland Plain Dealer*.

In 2002 Crispin Porter + Bogusky released what was the first of many innovative advertisements for the MINI Cooper. To promote the car's recreational qualities, MINI Coopers were welded onto the roofs of SUVs and driven cross-country. Crispin Porter + Bogusky parked MINI Coopers in the seating sections of sporting arenas. Supermarket tabloids warned about "mutant bat boy in MINI Cooper." *Playboy* magazine allowed a MINI Cooper to be featured as a centerfold in 2002. Worldwide sales for the MINI Cooper S skyrocketed 46 percent in 2003. As part of the "MINI Robots" campaign, in 2004 a booklet was inserted into consumer magazines such as *Motor Trend, National Geographic,* and *Rolling Stone.* The booklets were written by the fictional Roland Samuel, a journalist validating stories about robots made from MINI Cooper parts that prevented traffic accidents in Oxford, England.

Hoping to continue its string of innovative campaigns, creatives at Crispin Porter + Bogusky wanted to create a 2005 campaign with a "call to action," or advertising that motivated consumers to look someplace else for brand information. The ad agency reasoned that the more time a consumer invested with a brand, the more likely it was that he or she would tell others about it.

TARGET MARKET

"Counterfeit" targeted men 18 to 34 years old. The campaign's 60-second commercial did not air on network television, where advertising cost more, but rather across cable channels popular with men, such as ESPN, MTV, and Spike TV. "Cable offers many more opportunities than the broadcast TV networks, at lower prices," Jim Poh, media director of Crispin Porter + Bogusky, told *Automotive News.* "Cable is going to be a more effective use of your dollars. In a nutshell, the viewers of these channels have the MINI mindset."

One requirement for the "MINI mindset" was a sense of humor. The campaign's TV commercial, along with the website to which it directed viewers, www.CounterfeitMINI.org, facetiously showed junk cars painted to resemble MINI Coopers. "Mini customers appreciate the joke. They are a group that doesn't like being hit in the face with traditional advertising," Pitney told the *Wall Street Journal.* "They are very much into discovery. They like to come upon something in an interesting way and learn about it on their own terms."

COMPETITION

Volkswagen's Golf GTI and New Beetle were considered "premium small cars," the classification of high-quality, high-priced, petite cars like the MINI Cooper. To promote the 2005 Golf GTI, the ad agency DDB created a television spot that used computers to juxtapose actor Gene Kelly's face onto the body of a break-dancer. At the spot's beginning it appeared that Kelly was standing on the rainy street corner from his 1952 movie *Singin' in the Rain.* After a few notes from the movie's title song, the music escalated into an electronic-music rendition of "Singin' in the Rain" while Kelly began break-dancing. At the commercial's finale he appeared next to a parked Golf GTI.

Explaining why DDB used Kelly's likeness for the spot, Martin Loraine, the creative director at the agency, told the *New Zealand Herald,* "We looked for things which were icons. We thought about the Golf GTI when it came out. There are not many cars that invent a genre, which is what we thought was the most prominent thing about the GTI. It wasn't just a fast car or a nice car, it was an original, which is rare."

Starting in 1998 Arnold Worldwide advertised Volkswagen's New Beetle with its "Drivers Wanted" campaign. Television spots initially targeted nostalgic baby boomers with copy declaring "Less Flower. More Power" or "If you sold your soul in the '80s, here's your chance to buy it back." At first the New Beetle's popularity skyrocketed. More than 64,000 units were sold during its first year. By 2003, however, New Beetle sales began waning; critics referenced Volkswagen's problems to the quick boom-and-bust cycle that had haunted Chrysler's PT Cruiser after its 2000 release. In 2005 Volkswagen ended its contract with Arnold Worldwide and awarded

TOUGH LOVE

For the MINI Cooper "Counterfeit" campaign the advertising agency Crispin Porter + Bogusky created a spoof website titled www.CounterfeitMini.org. The site supposedly warned consumers about counterfeit MINI Coopers flooding the car market. In one section of the website, titled "TOUGH LOVE," a visitor could use his or her mouse to slap a counterfeit MINI Cooper owner who had supposedly bought an antique car, fashioned with MINI Cooper fog lamps and racing stripes, thinking it was a MINI Cooper.

its $400 million advertising account to Crispin Porter + Bogusky.

MARKETING STRATEGY

The "Counterfeit" campaign displayed MINI Cooper's signature characteristics, such as the car's colorful graphics and performance capabilities, in a way that "entertains and engages people," Alex Bogusky, Crispin Porter + Bogusky's principal, told *Adweek.* "You can't just push things into enough eyeballs anymore," he said. "It has to be so much fun that it's worth their time, that you've entertained them and taught them about the product at the same time."

On February 14, 2005, a 60-second commercial began appearing across cable channels such as Spike TV, Speed Channel, Sci-Fi Channel, and Outdoor Life Network. The spot posed as a public-service announcement from the fictional Counter Counterfeit Commission (CCC). The CCC was supposedly alerting the public about a recent outbreak of counterfeit MINI Coopers. The spot first explained the counterfeiting of luxury watches, sunglasses, and most recently, MINI Coopers. Footage showed high-end watch and sunglass knockoffs in Brazil's Rio de Janeiro flea markets, followed by a dilapidated car that was decaled with racing stripes. The spot then announced the availability of a 10-minute DVD that educated consumers about fake MINI Coopers and included testimonials from previously defrauded consumers. A man with his face obscured and voice altered admitted, "I bought a MINI for $1,200 bucks. 'Let's Motor,' right?" To which the voice-over answered, "Wrong!" The commercial continued with additional humorous footage of counterfeit MINI Coopers, followed by beautiful images of the real thing. The commercial ended with voice-over explaining, "To order Counterfeit MINIs, visit CounterfeitMINI.org or send a self-addressed-stamped-envelop to the Counter Counterfeit Commission."

The DVD, which sold for $19.95, provided more tongue-in-cheek information about counterfeit MINI Coopers. Besides the campaign's main website, www.CounterfeitMini.org, which provided detailed informational about counterfeit and authentic MINI Coopers, another website was created that supposedly auctioned counterfeit MINI Coopers. Conveniently, the auctions had all been closed. Bryan Buckley directed the campaign's filming in Rio de Janeiro. The footage was later edited to compose the 60-second television spot, the DVD, and the additional footage that was posted on the website. Collectively, it offered "an hour's entertainment, maybe, and that's a good trade for your time and your attention," Bogusky told the *Wall Street Journal.* To further validate the CCC's warnings, a pop-up message on www.MINIUSA.com directed consumers to call the CCC hotline if counterfeit MINI Coopers were spotted. Fictional brochures were also inserted in consumer magazines to warn about counterfeit MINI Coopers.

One of the campaign's challenges was its limited $25 million budget. To compete against Volkswagen, which spent an estimated $400 million on advertising in 2005, Crispin Porter + Bogusky devised a campaign outside of traditional formats. "Given that there is not a lot of difference among products in any given category, advertising is the differentiator," Chuck Porter, chairman of Crispin Porter + Bogusky, told *Television Week.* "We believe that making a brand a part of pop culture [is more effective]."

Some analysts criticized the campaign's deceptive quality, which could leave its target audience feeling betrayed. Also, for consumers to experience the full breadth of the campaign, they needed to visit the website, an extra step that complicated the campaign's message. Many advertising agencies, fearful of the strategy's overall risk, avoided such "call to action" campaigns. Tim Mellors, who had executed "call to action" campaigns as chief creative officer of WPP Group's Grey Worldwide North America, explained the benefit of this strategy to the *Wall Street Journal*: "You know perfectly well that most people won't bother, but when you get it right, it's another stage of involvement that's never been there in the past."

OUTCOME

The "Counterfeit" campaign yielded success soon after its launch. In March 2005 MINI Cooper recorded its highest monthly sales posting ever and surpassed the previous March's earnings by 44 percent. Fairing well at award shows, the campaign won a Gold Lion Award at the Cannes International Advertising Festival in 2005 and also received a Titanium Lion. The latter was given to the four campaigns considered most effective at using multiple mediums. "Counterfeit" was the only American campaign to win a Titanium Lion in 2005.

Crispin Porter + Bogusky also noticed a surge of chatter in automotive blogs and MINI Cooper chat rooms regarding the "Counterfeit" ads. Alex Bogusky, serving as a guest writer for *Advertising Age's Creativity,* stated, "I'm very happy to see the MINI 'Counterfeit' work getting recognized. It was a massive undertaking and a labor of joy for so many people at the agency, and it's the kind of work that gives us personally the greatest joy because the interaction with consumers, from the TV to the web, is so fun to watch. You actually get to see and read e-mails and blog entries from people who are being persuaded and entertained by MINI and the MINI brand. The relationship between brand and consumer is created so transparently and quickly, it's almost like creating advertising live on stage."

FURTHER READING

Beaton, Alistair. "Mini Cooper Model Stolen at Balmedie." *Aberdeen Press & Journal,* September 28, 2004, p. 3.

Bogusky, Alex. "Awards: Why We Care." *Advertising Age's Creativity,* August 1, 2005, p. 6.

Connelly, Walt, Hal Riney, and Jon Soto. "The Work." *Advertising Age's Creativity,* May 1, 2005, p. 24.

Convey, Eric. "Motor Mouth; Fun Mini Cooper S Has Small Flaws." *Boston Herald,* April 30, 2005, p. C16.

Curry, Sheree R. "Dump the:30 Spot and Embrace On-Demand." *Television Week,* July 25, 2005, p. 60.

Diaz, Ann-Christine. "Top Directors." *Advertising Age's Creativity,* June 1, 2005, p. 40.

Fera, Rae Ann. "Miami Agency Rules Online Space." *Boards,* August 1, 2005, p. 28.

Guyer, Lillie. "Mini's Spoof Ads Warn of Knockoffs." *Automotive News,* May 16, 2005, p. 38B.

Matier, Phillip, and Andrew Ross. "A Mini Cooper with Lights and Siren." *San Francisco Chronicle,* April 3, 2005, p. A21.

McAleer, Michael. "Mini Cooper S Works." *Irish Times* (Dublin), August 3, 2005, p.8.

Steinberg, Brian. "'Call to Action' Ads Give Clients Results They Can Measure." *Wall Street Journal,* March 22, 2005, p. B1.

Wentz, Laurel. "At Cannes, the Lions Say 'Grrr.'" *Advertising Age,* June 27, 2005, p. 1.

Zagor, Karen. "Road Test: 2005 MINI Cooper S: She Drives." *Globe and Mail* (Toronto), March 3, 2005, p. G15.

Kevin Teague

MINI ROBOTS CAMPAIGN

OVERVIEW

In 1967 a safety mandate forced the antiquated, cheaply made British Mini Cooper to discontinue sales in the United States. In 1994, when Bayerische Motoren Werke AG (BMW) attained control of the Mini Cooper brand, executives were perplexed about how to reintroduce their newly acquired microcar to the United States. Finally reappearing in the United States in 2002, followed by a prolific magazine, Web-based, and outdoor campaign, the MINI, as it had come to be spelled, was a screaming success. By 2004 MINI made up 11 percent of BMW's sales. Company executives were nervous, however, about the boom-and-bust pitfalls that haunted other trendy cars, like the New Beetle and PT Cruiser. It was for this reason that "MINI Robots," formulated as a "viral" campaign, a term referring to advertising that relies on word-of-mouth contagiousness, was launched in March 2004.

With an estimated budget of $15 million, "MINI Robots" was developed by Miami-based ad agency Crispin Porter + Bogusky. First a site was developed on the Internet to herald a clandestine project that assembled robots from MINI parts. The project's mastermind, a fictional Dr. Mayhew, was a retired scientist who posted daily video clips of his experiments. Shortly afterward a second site was published, with sightings of robots slinking through the moonlit streets of Oxford, England, and preventing traffic accidents. Later Crispin Porter + Bogusky inserted a novelette, "Men of Metal," into consumer magazines like *National Geographic, Rolling Stone, Men's Health,* and *Men's Journal.* The 40-page insert chronicled a journalist's quest to find Dr. Mayhew and the people rescued by his robots. To perpetuate the joke, Crispin Porter + Bogusky created websites for Dr. Mayhew, along with a home page for Casson, the fictitious publishing company of "Men of Metal," and a personal site for the novelette's author.

According to an interview with Jack Pitney, vice president of MINI USA, in the *Wall Street Journal,* customers appreciated the joke: "They like to come upon something in an interesting way and learn about it on their own terms." One week after the appearance of "Men of Metal," more than 46 million hits were registered on the "MINI Robots" main website. Success reached BMW's bottom line as well. During the first year of "MINI Robots," 36,000 MINIS were sold, surpassing the 34,000 units sold the previous year. By the end of 2004 MINI orders were outstripping supply, with a six-month waiting list for cars with some of the newer features.

HISTORICAL CONTEXT

Prompted by the Suez fuel crisis, Sir Alec Issigonis designed the Mini in 1959 to be Britain's first "classless" car. Meager but efficient, the tiny Mini was sold in the United States for only seven years, until collapsible steering wheels were mandated in 1967. In 1994 BMW acquired the Rover Group, which included the Mini brand. The German automakers initially were unsure about how to reawaken interest in the car, especially in the United States. Even after engineers had modernized the interior, upgraded the MINI with a 115-hp Chrysler engine, and increased the length by 20 inches, it was still the smallest car in the U.S. market. By 2001 consumer trends, including the burgeoning markets for SUVs and full-size trucks, suggested a daunting forecast for the MINI. "If we'd listened to the market research, we'd have never done the MINI," Pitney admitted to the *Cleveland Plain Dealer.*

Crispin Porter + Bogusky oversaw the U.S. marketing launch for the MINI. At the start of 2002 the budget was a meager $15 million, with Crispin Porter + Bogusky introducing cost-effective magazine and outdoor advertisements that *Brandweek* called a series of "one-offs," individual ads that were not part of an integrated campaign. *Playboy* allowed MINI to "pose" for its June 2002 centerfold spread, complete with a list of likes and dislikes. "The end to a perfect day: A hand-washing with warm, sudsy water and a nice wax," the ad read. In 2003 MINI punch-out kits, which allowed people to construct their own paper models, could be found in consumer magazines. Ford Expeditions were driven across the United States with MINIs strapped to their roofs. "We have to be creative in our marketing and look for clever ways to have $1 seem like $2," Pitney told *Autoweek.* "Everything we do has to reflect the unique, fun, cheeky nature of the MINI brand in a holistic, 360-degree MINI way."

From 2001 to 2003 brand recognition for the MINI rose more than 400 percent in the United States. Despite consumers' inclination toward larger cars, MINI sales rose from 20,000 units in 2002 to more than 34,000 in 2003. Kerri Martin, manager for marketing communications at MINI USA, was quoted in the *New York Times* as saying, "We're constantly going left when everyone is going right." It was in this vein of unorthodox thinking that the "MINI Robots" campaign was created.

TARGET MARKET

MINI USA and Crispin Porter + Bogusky anticipated that "MINI Robots" would resonate with the 20- to 30-year-old demographic of mechanically minded males who were put off by women's praise of the car as "cute." This was also a group, as Pitney told the *Wall Street Journal,* that does not like "being hit in the face with traditional advertising."

In an interview with *Shoot,* Andrew Keller, a Crispin Porter + Bogusky creative director, said, "[Given] the nature of the car, its target audience is what I call a creative mindset. They are people that go to the Web, and believe the car is a means of self-expression—it is that sort of vibe. However, we had to zero in on a target at the beginning, and it is twenty- to thirty-year-old males." He added, "But that is more tactical than anything right now because ultimately, the MINI should be something that everybody wants. The queen drove one and a plumber can drive one, and that is what we want to maintain."

Although a variety of men's magazines featured the novelette "Men of Metal," the references to the story were placed on the Internet. Thus, passing over a lower-income audience, "MINI Robots" was aimed at a target market with access to a computer and an Internet connection.

THE ITALIAN JOB

BMW's MINI made cameo appearances in movies like *Bourne Identity* and *Austin Powers, Goldmember,* but the little car's biggest role was in the 2003 remake of *The Italian Job.* While British Motor Corporation had refused to supply cars for the 1969 version, with Michael Caine, BMW donated more than 30 MINIs for Paramount's remake.

COMPETITION

J.D. Power and Associates stated in 2002 that MINI USA had not only reintroduced the brand in the United States but also created a new automotive sector, the premium small car. Other critics found categorizing the MINI more difficult and usually compared it to Volkswagen's New Beetle or to Toyota's Scion. The New Beetle was introduced in 1998 with the tagline "Drivers Wanted," which was similar to MINI's "Let's Motor." Volkswagen's ad agency, Arnold Communications, initially catered to nostalgic baby boomers, with copy declaring "Less flower. More Power" or "If you sold your soul in the '80s, here's your chance to buy it back." After its launch in 1998 demand for the New Beetle skyrocketed, and according to the *Financial Times,* by October 1998 Volkswagen had sold 64,000 units. By 2003, however, sales of the New Beetle had slowed

THE BEATLES DROVE MINIS

Despite selling a mere 10,000 units in the United States during the 1960s, Mini still managed to surface in the American psyche via celebrities. As *Out Motoring* stated, "It is always the 1960s for which it will be remembered... These 10 years saw the Mini go from a 'housewives shopping car' to a must have fashion accessory." James Garner, Twiggy, the Beatles, Peter Sellers, and even Steve McQueen drove Minis.

drastically, and between 2001 and 2002 Volkswagen reduced production by 18 percent. "Volkswagen's New Beetle and Chrysler's PT Cruiser... often prove to be 'fashion statements' with relatively quick boom-and-bust cycles," wrote Paul Eisenstein in the *Cleveland Plain Dealer.*

According to *Forbes* magazine, Toyota introduced the Scion in 2004 with substantial success. In its first year sales of the Scion matched those of the MINI. Compared to the MINI, however, Scion explicitly targeted a younger market, Generation Y, those born between the early 1980s and the late 1990s. In 2004 Toyota spent 70 percent of its Scion marketing budget on lifestyle events, including nightclubs and small-venue concerts. Scion even allowed consumers to accessorize the car over the Internet before stepping foot on a lot. Jim Farley, vice president of Scion, told *Ward's Dealer Business* that more than 50 percent of Scion customers had configured their vehicles online, adding an average of $1,200 in accessories.

MARKETING STRATEGY

According to an interview with Martin in the *New York Times,* the planning for the "MINI Robots" campaign began in late 2002 after Crispin Porter + Bogusky had requested a comic book or novel about robots. The campaign was developed over the following 18 months and launched in March 2004. "[The campaign] started as, 'Hey, let's build robots out of car parts,'" said Alex Bogusky, partner and executive creative director of the agency. It slowly morphed into a detailed campaign in the belief that, "if people are involved with it, they spend a lot of time with it, a good 45 minutes to an hour."

Beam, an outside company, assisted Crispin Porter + Bogusky with the "MINI Robots" main website, http://www.r50rd.co.uk. Zoic Studios supplied the video clips depicting Dr. Mayhew's daily experiments, including colossal MINI robots reaching down to grab SUVs before they plowed into test walls. Four additional websites were created by Crispin Porter + Bogusky. The first was a website for the fictional journalist Rowland Samuel. The second, for Samuel's fictitious publishing company, Casson, depicted mock upcoming releases about Bigfoot, Loch Ness, and alien crop circles. The last two were Geocities websites, on Yahoo, including a personal website for Dr. Mayhew and one posting the latest MINI robot sightings around Oxford.

After the websites were up, the 40-page insert "Men of Metal: Eyewitness Accounts of Humanoid Robots" appeared in such consumer magazines as *Motor Trend, National Geographic,* and *Rolling Stone.* The insert was written by the fictional Samuel, a freelance writer who bumped into an acquaintance at an Oxford party. The two began one-upping each other with urban legends, until Samuel's acquaintance claimed a friend had photographed a giant robot that saved a car from hydroplaning. Enticed by the story, Samuel probed others connected to the photograph in order to prove or disprove the story. Using testimonials and photos as evidence, "Men of Metal" duped a significant portion of its readers.

Ambiguity fueled the buzz over "MINI Robots." For the first two months of the campaign MINI logos and branding were omitted from the websites and the novelette. "We wanted people to experience it without us making a big announcement," Bogusky told the *New York Times.* The robots were not demystified until April, when Crispin Porter + Bogusky put up posters throughout New York City and Los Angeles featuring the MINI logo above the robot images. A "Robots" option appeared as well on the drop-down menu of the MINI USA website, allowing visitors to accessorize the robots with MINI-like features. Though "some people will be disappointed" after discovering the truth behind the "MINI Robots" campaign, Bogusky told the *New York Times,* "most people appreciate you doing something different."

OUTCOME

Public response to "MINI Robots" was almost immediate. Crispin Porter + Bogusky reported that a week after its introduction the "MINI Robots" main website had received more than 46 million hits. By October 2004 it had attracted more than 1 million visitors. MINI USA received E-mails from people who said that they enjoyed the campaign so much they were going to a dealer.

MINI seemed to be avoiding the boom-and-bust pitfalls that had haunted the New Beetle and the PT Cruiser. BMW projected selling only 25,000 MINIs in 2002–04, the first three years of its reintroduction in the

United States, but in the first year alone more than 20,000 units were sold. This increased to 34,000 in 2003 and 36,000 in 2004, by which time the MINI was making up 11 percent of BMW's total sales. In 2004 sales of the MINI were still outstripping the supply, with a six-month waiting list for cars with certain features. Bogusky boasted about the success of "MINI Robots" to the *New York Times:* "I've never gotten e-mails about a billboard or a television commercial saying, 'I'm going to buy a car because of this.' Here, we've gotten several."

Many industry critics, as well as Crispin Porter + Bogusky and MINI USA, believed that the "MINI Robots" campaign had created a new model in the advertising industry. For example, other viral marketing campaigns appeared in 2004. To market its liquid-crystal Aquos television, Sharp disseminated rumors that $3 million was stashed in hidden urns that could be located by using its website. For Lee Jeans, Fallow created a blog and answering-machine message supposedly left by a 90-foot model. "MINI Robots," along with Sega's "Beta-7" campaign, created a paradigm that treated consumers as willing participants, not passive observers. "We're going from the Golden Age of advertising to the Information Age of advertising," Bogusky told *Advertising Age's Creativity.* "And it's not going to be as easy for this generation to judge the brilliance of this new age."

FURTHER READING

Anderson, Mae. "Tall Tales: Advertising Steps into Interactive Fiction: Where the Buzz Is Real—Even When the Stories Aren't." *Adweek,* October 11, 2004, p. 28.

Eisenstein, Paul. "Will U.S. Drivers Pay Big to Think Small? Mini Cooper's Success Makes Automakers Rethink Strategy." *Cleveland Plain Dealer,* February 15, 2004, p. F1.

Elliot, Stuart. "Pursuing Marketing Buzz." *New York Times,* May 10, 2004, p. 8.

Granatstein, Lisa. "Crispin Porter + Bogusky: Spending between $10 Million and $25 Million: Best Use of Magazines." *Adweek,* June 23, 2003, p. SR6.

Greenberg, Karl. "A Year of Firsts in an Age of Belt Tightening." *Brandweek,* April 20, 2005.

Guyer, Lillie. "BMW Dares to Be Different with Mini Ads." *Automotive News,* August 4, 2003, p. 4M.

Halliday, Jean. "Scion Builds Buzz with Event Marketing." *Advertising Age,* November 8, 2004, p. 24H.

Hoag, Christina. "Coconut Grove, Fla., Advertising Agency Sweeps Top Awards." *Miami Herald,* June 30, 2003.

"The Others..." *Advertising Age's Creativity,* December 1, 2004, p. 30.

Steinberg, Brian. "'Call to Action' Ads Give Clients Results They Can Measure." *Wall Street Journal,* March 22, 2005, p. B1.

Suydam, Margot. "Let's Motor: CP+B Taps Integrated Approach to Spread the Mini Cooper Message." *Shoot,* December 5, 2003, p. 19.

Twomey, Brian. "Original and the Best." *Rear View Mirror,* August 13, 2004, pp. 38–39.

Voight, Joan. "Mini's Wild Ride: How CP+B Crafted Its Award-Winning Work for BMW's Quirky Car." *Adweek,* June 2, 2003, p. 24.

Kevin Teague

THE HIRE CAMPAIGN

OVERVIEW

In 2000 Bayerische Motoren Werke AG (BMW) posted total sales of $33 billion, a slight decrease from its 1999 earnings of $34 billion. Afraid of further backsliding, the Bavarian automaker decided to reshape its advertising to better target the Internet-savvy BMW customer. Before 2001 the company's advertisements had typically consisted of product-driven campaigns with immaculate BMWs clinging to mountain roads. BMW asked its longtime advertising partner, Fallon Worldwide, to create something different. In 2001 five action-packed short films emerged under the campaign title "The Hire," which became one of the most acclaimed campaigns in advertising history.

After working with BMW to develop the idea of a James Bond-type hero who drove various BMWs, Fallon enlisted David Fincher's film-production company, Anonymous Content. Fincher then successfully wrangled some of Hollywood's biggest guns—including directors Guy Ritchie and John Frankenheimer and actors Madonna, Forrest Whittaker, and Mickey Rourke—to create the five short films. Three more films were created in 2002 to promote BMW's new Z4 roadster. All eight starred Clive Owen (*Croupier, The Bourne Identity*) as the "hired" driver who found himself driving a BMW in every spot. "The Hire" was promoted much like a feature film would have been, with movie trailers, print ads, and Web ads.

The five initial films cost an estimated $15 million, and the three made in 2002 cost about $10 million. "The Hire" catapulted BMW's exposure into film festivals, awards shows, and even an exclusive BMW DirecTV channel. By 2002 BMW sales were up 17 percent, while some of its competitors, such as Volkswagen and General Motors, floundered. By June 2003 more than 45 million people had viewed the films, overshooting the original goal of reaching 2 million viewers. "The Hire" garnered numerous ad industry awards. The campaign's final spot, "Beat the Devil," aired November 21, 2002.

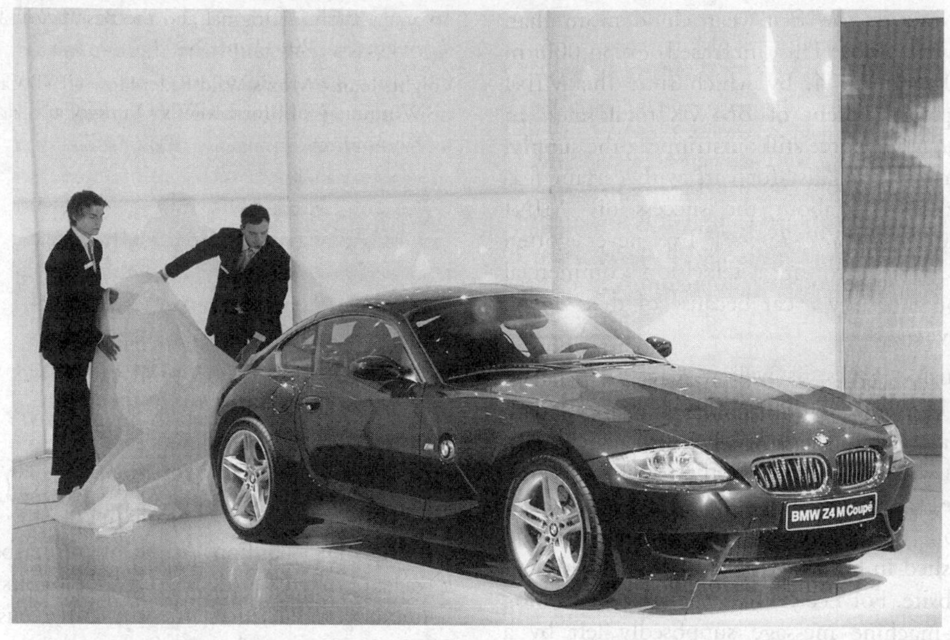

BMW's Z4M. © SANDRO CAMPARDO/EPA/CORBIS.

HISTORICAL CONTEXT

BMW, founded in Germany in 1913, awarded most of its advertising work to the Minneapolis-based agency Fallon in the mid-1990s. Three different BMW/Fallon campaigns preceding "The Hire" had mostly consisted of "hard-driving, product-focused efforts designed to show what it's like behind the wheel of a BMW," Jim McDowell, vice president of marketing at BMW North America, told *Advertising Age.* BMW and Fallon felt their campaigns' flavor had been so overused by competitors that the original uniqueness had washed out. Wanting to launch a more unprecedented campaign, BMW asked Fallon for something new, but Fallon's creatives felt confined within the restraints of traditional television spots. They wanted to show BMWs for longer periods of time and to truly push BMW's performance to the point of damaging the car, which was something unheard of for a car commercial. "In response to our plea," Bildsten said in an interview with *Shoot,* "[BMW] sent us this letter that was just amazing. They were telling us, 'Take off the gloves. Do whatever you want. We want you to really stretch.'"

After finishing a Timex campaign that included the use of video clips in Internet advertising, David Carter and Joe Sweet, two of Fallon's art directors, were eager to try different filming techniques. "One night I challenged [Carter and Sweet] to come up with something cinematic," Bildsten told *Brandweek.* "They came back the next morning with the whole idea almost completely worked out." When they took it to BMW, "it took us about 30 minutes to present and 10 seconds for them to give us a green light."

TARGET MARKET

"The Hire" largely arose from Fallon and BMW's growing concern that past campaigns had been missing the company's target audience: well-to-do, high-achieving males who usually researched purchases using the Internet and lacked the time to watch network television. Research showed that consumers inclined to purchase BMWs were also broadband-connected, tech-savvy males and that 85 percent of this population studied BMW's cars online before even stepping into a showroom. As far as whom the campaign would appeal to, McDowell explained to *Advertising Age,* "We would have guessed that our central tendency would have been 25-year-olds, but actually from our early measurements we got people older and more affluent than that." Knowing that the mature target audience was keener on the viewing experience than on the interactive experience, Fallon purposely avoided using gaming software on the campaign's website, http://www.bmwfilms.com.

To study the effectiveness of "The Hire," BMW and Fallon devised units of measurement called "BMW minutes," which calculated how much time viewers spent with the new Internet campaign compared to previous television campaigns. "We were astonished to discover that a major fraction of the total BMW minutes were

SUBPLOTS IN "THE HIRE"

Short subplots, which loosely linked the campaign's first five storylines, were filmed quickly, and with a digital video camera, by Ben Younger and Director of Photography William Rexer. The filming of one scene, which looked like a real-life occurrence to most onlookers, involved a "car thief" slamming a "hit man" onto a car hood in New York. "Some of the reactions I got from people who weren't real extras were so good that we had to hunt people down [to get permission to include them in the films]," Younger said in an interview with *Shoot* magazine. "I loved the reaction of one armored-car guy, so we paused the frame, took down the name on the side of the truck, and called the company to get a waiver from him."

Internet minutes," McDowell told *Advertising Age.* Males made up 68 percent of the viewers, 42 percent of whom came from households with incomes greater than $75,000. The second suite of "The Hire" films featured BMW's new Z4 roadster, which aimed at a demographic that could hopefully afford them. In late 2002 BMW began running its eight films on an exclusive BMW channel for DirecTV. The channel, which was available for a limited time, interspersed the films with behind-the-scenes footage and special "subplot" spots.

COMPETITION

Mercedes-Benz, the German luxury arm of DaimlerChrysler, was the top-selling luxury brand in the United States in 1999, a position it maintained until losing ground to BMW and to Toyota's Lexus in 2002. For the same year's first 10 months Mercedes units sold dropped by 1,500, losing out to BMW's incredible 17 percent sales growth that year. "Mercedes has been improving its quality but it hasn't been keeping pace with the rest of the U.S. industry," Brian Walters, director of quality research at J.D. Power and Associates, explained to *Bloomberg News.* In an attempt to reproduce BMW's campaign success, Mercedes's London-based ad agency, Campbell Doyle Dye, faked a movie trailer for a supposed upcoming film called *Lucky Star.* Never admitting to be just an advertisement, the movie "trailer" broke in U.K. movie theaters July 4, 2002. *Lucky Star* pretended to be the next release from producer Michael Mann (*The Aviator, Collateral*) and portrayed Benicio Del Toro as a man acting independently to clean up Chicago's commodities exchange. The spot periodically showed Del Toro masterfully speeding through Chicago in a $90,000 Mercedes 500 SL.

Toyota Motor Corp.'s Lexus luxury division rose up to be the luxury-car industry leader, selling more units than BMW or Mercedes in 2001. Besides the sales success, Lexus dominated as the most reliable in its industry; according to J.D. Power and Associates, Lexus cars had fewer than half of the problems, after four and five years, that the average cars and trucks had. In 2001 Lexus decreased its ad spending. By 2002 the carmaker's ad agency, California-based Team One Advertising, had focused its efforts on the remodeled ES300 sedan.

MARKETING STRATEGY

Initially, Fallon and BMW had decided to film one serialized 45-to-60-minute film featuring a suave hero who saved, kidnapped, and escorted people using different BMW models. Fallon approached production company Anonymous Content, headed by David Fincher (director of *Se7en* and *Fight Club*), to produce the film. Fincher recommended that the spots be broken into five different films in order to facilitate file downloading and allow more flexibility in attracting talent to work on the project.

Following Fincher's advice, Fallon developed scripts for five short films. In producing "The Hire," Fincher and Fallon went so far as to create a dossier, complete with FBI and CIA files, just to flesh out the films' hero. Fincher then solicited some of Hollywood's top directors. The final list included Ang Lee (*Crouching Tiger, Hidden Dragon*), John Frankenheimer (*The Manchurian Candidate*), Wong Kar-Wai (*Chungking Express*), Guy Ritchie (*Snatch*), and Alejandro González Iñárritu (*Amores Perros*). The scripts, ranging from dark to hilarious, were distributed according to each director's style. Anonymous Content chairman Steve Golin told *Shoot,* "The good news is that these weren't commercials. We had very few restrictions. The budgets were equivalent to [those of] high-end commercials."

Fallon flipped the advertising equation upside down by spending 90 percent of its budget on production and only 10 percent on media. The reduced media expenditure was initially seen as a huge risk. According to *Advertising Age's Creativity,* a BMW rep warned Fallon, "Either nobody will notice, or this will be a smashing success."

For each of the six-to-seven-minute films, subplots were also created in an attempt to weave the film storylines together. British actor Clive Owen, whose character became the common thread for the entire campaign, always played the skillful hired driver. Frankenheimer's "Ambush," the campaign's debut film, first became

> ### MADONNA PLAYING THE SPOILED DIVA
>
> The campaign's fourth film, "Star," featured a spoiled diva who received her comeuppance after whining and complaining about the slow speed of Clive Owen's driving. After smirking through a few minutes of her wrath, Owen slammed down the accelerator and ping-ponged the "star" in the backseat for a solid two minutes. Guy Ritchie, the director and cowriter of "Star," talked his wife, Madonna, into playing the part. "When he signed on, we didn't think she'd be along, we just desperately wanted him," Fallon's Bildsten told *Shoot,* adding that the actresses originally considered for the role "were a little more washed-up than her."

available for download on http://www.bmwfilms.com on April 26, 2001. It featured the hired driver saving a diamond smuggler from machine-gun toting assailants in a cargo van. Fallon released each of the following four spots every two weeks. Typical Hollywood methods, including broadcast spots, billboards, and free posters, were used to promote the films. Print ads ran in Hollywood trade magazines *Vanity Fair, Entertainment Weekly,* and *Rolling Stone.* The trailers for "The Hire," resembling regular movie trailers, aired on VH1, Bravo, and the Independent Film Channel. One of Fallon's biggest challenges was to pitch the films as entertainment but to still disclose BMW's involvement. "We wanted to avoid the 'microbrew syndrome,'" Bildsten explained to *Brandweek,* "like where you look down and see that [your beer] was actually made by Anheuser-Busch." "The Hire" was also uniquely filmed to fit computer screens. "No one had ever done an internet project of this magnitude, and we had a lot to learn," Fallon producer Robyn Boardman told *Advertising Age's Creativity.* "There are different things to keep in mind when shooting for the web. File size, for starters, and the fact that wide shots don't play well."

Due to overwhelming Web traffic, ad-industry praise, and BMW's bottom-line success in 2002, a "second season" consisting of three films began airing October 24, 2002. The second crop involved an equally renowned roster of names. Instead of Anonymous Content, all spots were produced by Ridley Scott (director of *Blade Runner* and *Gladiator*), who recruited directors Tony Scott (*Top Gun*), John Woo (*Face/Off*), and Joe Carnahan (*Narc*). The actors included Gary Oldman, James Brown, Don Cheadle, Ray Liotta, and of course, Clive Owen, returning to star in the final three films. The last of the films was released at the end of 2002. Even though BMW ended their 10-year relationship with Fallon in 2005, the eight films remained available on http://www.bmwfilms.com.

OUTCOME

"The Hire" raked in a plethora of advertising awards, including two Grand Clio Awards and a Grand Prix Cyber Lion at the International Advertising Festival in Cannes, France, along with Best of Show at the One Show Interactive competition. The campaign was praised not just by the ad industry; it earned kudos within the entertainment arena as well. "Hostage," from the second series of films, earned the award for Best Action Short during the Los Angeles International Short Film Festival in 2002. Entertainment magazines began reviewing the films. Even the *New York Times* gave the films a favorable review. Their entertainment value garnered media coverage not accessible to typical advertisement. "We'd hoped for a good response, but we never thought it would be as strong as it was," Bildsten told *Shoot* in 2001. "BMW recorded over eleven million film-views. And according to their research, it really worked. [The films] got people to not just pay attention, but to buy cars."

By June 2003 the films had been viewed more than 45 million times. BMW's sales rose 17.2 percent between 2001 and 2002, helping the automaker to outsell Mercedes and placing it second only to Lexus in the luxury-car market. From an ad industry perspective, the greatest pinnacle of "The Hire" may have been winning the first-ever Titanium Lion, the highest honor at the Cannes International Advertising Festival. The award recognized a campaign that caused "the industry to stop in its tracks and reconsider the way forward."

FURTHER READING

DeSalvo, Kathy. "BMW Weaves through the Web with Five Filmmakers." *Shoot,* May 11, 2001, p. 1.

Dill, Mallorre. "Movie Magic: Fallon's BMW Films Wins Top Honors at the One Show." *Adweek* (eastern ed.), May 13, 2002, p. 27.

Gaylin, Alison. "Drive On: BMW Breaks New Ground with Internet Series." *Shoot,* December 7, 2001, p. 30.

Hatfield, Stefano. "In BMW's Wake, Mercedes in U.K. Tries Its Own 'Movie.'" *Advertising Age,* July 22, 2002, p. 21.

Horn, Gabi. "Campaign of the Year: BMWfilms.com." *Advertising Age's Creativity,* December 1, 2001, p. 32.

Howe, Jeff. "BMWfilms.com." *Brandweek,* November 12, 2001, p. 5.

McCarthy, Michael. "BMW Cars to Star in Online Movie Sequel." *USA Today,* June 7, 2002, p. B3.

———. "BMW Drives into New Ad World: PC Mini-film." *USA Today,* June 6, 2001, p. B3.

McKissack, Fred. "Commercials Masquerade as TV Films." *Capital Times,* October 8, 2002, p. 1D.

Takaki, Millie. "Dirs. Scott, Woo, Carnahan Answer 'The Hire' Calling: RSA USA, Fallon Team on Three Web-Based Short Films for BMW." *Shoot,* August 16, 2002, p. 1.

Vagnoni, Anthony. "Behind the Wheel: BMW and Fallon's Web Films Widen Horizons for Entertaining Ways to Brand." *Advertising Age,* July 23, 2001, p. 12.

Wilcha, Kristin. "Short Route: BMW Tops One Show." *Shoot,* May 17, 2001, p. 1.

Kevin Teague

BC Dairy Foundation

3236 Beta Avenue
Burnaby, British Columbia V5G 4K4
Canada
Telephone: (604) 294-3775
Fax: (604) 294-8199
Web site: www.bcdairyfoundation.ca

DON'T TAKE YOUR BODY FOR GRANTED CAMPAIGN

OVERVIEW

The BC Dairy Foundation (BCDF) was established in 1974 to promote milk consumption in the Canadian province of British Columbia. Dividing its resources between in-school educational efforts and mainstream media campaigns, the organization, like most milk marketers in Canada, primarily targeted adults in its advertising. For much of the 1980s and 1990s, however, rates of milk consumption in British Columbia, as in other parts of North America and the world, declined substantially. In 2003, enlisting agency Palmer Jarvis DDB (later referred to as DDB Canada, Vancouver), BCDF changed its marketing strategy and targeted teens and young adults in a bold, risky campaign called "Don't Take Your Body for Granted."

Rather than preaching to young people about the nutritional virtues of milk, "Don't Take Your Body for Granted" instead took the idea of bodily neglect to an absurdly humorous extreme. In TV, film, print, and outdoor advertisements, bodiless humans—beings made of heads attached directly to feet—were shown in ordinary situations that, without a body, were extremely difficult. For instance, a TV/film spot showed an elderly bodiless woman attempting to walk her small dog but instead being dragged through the streets of her neighborhood, and print ads featured such scenarios as a terrified head being toyed with by a cat and a befuddled male head looking up at an impossibly high public-restroom urinal. A companion website allowed users to create their own scenarios using the bodiless humans from the commercials. Despite a having budget of only $3 million a year during its 2003–04 run, the campaign was able to break through to its target market by using bold humor and memorable imagery.

"Don't Take Your Body for Granted" attracted favorable media attention and won numerous advertising awards. Milk consumption rates, which had been declining for roughly 20 years in British Columbia, increased by 1 percent in 2003.

HISTORICAL CONTEXT

Though many consumers in the English-speaking world associated milk advertising with the "Got Milk?" campaign that in the 1990s began running in California and then throughout the United States, advertising on behalf of regional and national consortiums of North American dairy farmers was a well-established practice prior to that campaign. The concept of depicting celebrities wearing milk mustaches (associated with a well-known U.S. campaign of the 1990s), in fact, was first used in the 1970s in a Canadian campaign called "Wear a Moustache,"

A still from "Dog Walker," the television campaign launched by BC Dairy Foundation for their "Don't Take Your Body for Granted" campaign. PHOTO COURTESY OF DDB CANADA FOR BC DAIRY FOUNDATION. REPRODUCED BY PERMISSION.

crafted by the Toronto office of ad agency Ogilvy & Mather for the Ontario Milk Marketing Board. Likewise, the Milk Calendar, first produced in 1976 by Toronto agency Allard Johnson for the Dairy Farmers of Ontario (in partnership with the provincial milk boards of Alberta, British Columbia, Manitoba, and the Maritimes), featured milk-centric recipes and images of health and wellness and was distributed free to millions of daily-paper subscribers in Canada. The Milk Calendar became part of the fabric of Canadian culture, gaining the loyalty of multiple generations of Canadians and accounting for measurable increases in milk consumption upon its yearly release.

The BC Dairy Foundation (BCDF) was established in 1974 to serve as the public voice of British Columbia's dairy producers and processors. A nonprofit organization dedicated to increasing milk consumption in that Canadian province, BCDF pursued its goal in two primary ways: by partnering with the provincial school system to educate children about the nutritional benefits of drinking milk, and by marketing and promoting fluid milk and cream in the province.

For most of the 1970s, 1980s, and 1990s Canadian milk advertising in all provinces targeted adults, while milk producers used educational programs to reach children in the schools. During this time declines in milk consumption became a seemingly permanent fact of North American life. When in 2002 BCDF embarked on an agency search for a new media campaign, it decided to change advertising tactics. The organization selected one of Canada's top advertising agencies, Palmer Jarvis DDB of Vancouver (later called DDB Canada, Vancouver), to craft a new campaign that would appeal to young people.

TARGET MARKET

BCDF and Palmer Jarvis DDB selected 16- to 24-year-old British Columbia residents as their target for the "Don't Take Your Body for Granted" campaign. This group was notoriously fickle and difficult to reach, especially by advertising on behalf of milk, which, far from having any fashionable brand attributes, was not even a brand but a raw product fully lacking in properties that might be considered "cool." These teenagers and young adults, however, were particularly vital to the project of increasing milk consumption in the population at large, because the age of 16 or 17 marked the time in life when most people ceased consuming milk regularly.

Palmer Jarvis DDB enlisted its youth-marketing sibling shop, DDB Kid Think, to undertake substantial research on its target group, gleaning insights from interactions with high school and college students. Based on this research Palmer Jarvis DDB concluded that teens could be convinced to drink milk neither with a pitch suggesting that it was cool to do so nor with preachy messages about the health benefits of milk consumption. To substantially alter milk-consumption patterns among the target group, the agency felt, it had to do no less than make young people see milk in a new way. It thus began the search for a governing concept that was, according to *Marketing Magazine,* "unpredictable, slightly outrageous, and purposely non-adult."

SURVIVAL OF THE FITTEST

The BC Dairy Foundation followed up its "Don't Take Your Body for Granted" campaign with a similarly daring 2005 campaign tagged "It's Always Been Survival of the Fittest. Drink Milk." The campaign's TV spots were set in the Stone Age, which BCDF described in a press release as "a time when making nutritional food choices could have an immediate impact on survival." In the commercials cavemen were shown making poor beverage choices that resulted in their failure to survive. For instance, one spot showed a caveman who stumbled upon a soda can on a desert plain. While tilting the mostly empty can to try and get the remnants of the drink into his mouth, he was trampled by a dinosaur, who was shown trying to scrape the man from his foot at the end of the commercial.

COMPETITION

The other Canadian provinces each had individual organizations similar to BCDF. Rather than compete with one another, they each had the same goal of increasing milk consumption in their respective provinces. Several parallel milk advertising campaigns thus ran at once in Canada during this time, representing a variety of tactics and messages, while the most recognizable milk campaign of all time was airing in the United States.

One of the most lauded Canadian milk campaigns of the late 1990s and early 2000s was the work of the Quebec milk-producers group Fédération des producteurs de lait du Québec and its agency BBDO Montreal. Launched in 1998, the campaign targeted adults with the theme "Jamais sans mon lait" (never without my milk) and used French songs by classic recording artists such as Gilbert Bécaud, Charles Trenet, and Edith Piaf, together with sentimental, everyday scenes showing the defining presence of milk in the various stages of life. The immense popularity of the campaign led the milk federation to release *The White Album,* a CD compilation of the songs featured in the commercials. The album sold 250,000 copies. In 2001 an English-language segment of the campaign was unveiled for the benefit of the 800,000 Anglophones living in Quebec.

In the early 2000s the organizations representing dairy farmers in Alberta, Saskatchewan, and Manitoba pooled their resources and marketing skills for another noteworthy Canadian campaign, crafted by Vancouver's Cossette Communication-Marketing. These organizations targeted 9- to 17-year-olds, reasoning that children in this age group had more autonomy than in previous generations and therefore needed to be persuaded to make their own choice of milk over other beverage options. Like BCDF, these marketers understood that a pitch relying on the health benefits of milk would not be effective with young people. Using the tagline "Never Stop. Milk," individual TV spots employed images that dramatized such issues as first love, emotional loss, and the power of the imagination, all of which played on the idea of growth that never stopped. Milk was not featured explicitly in the commercials but rather was linked to physical and intellectual growth.

The best-known milk advertising campaign during this time—and of all time—was "Got Milk?" It was created by agency Goodby, Silverstein & Partners for the California Milk Processor Board. "Got Milk?" began as a California campaign in 1993, ran nationally in the United States from 1995 to 1998, and continued to run in its state of origin through the early 2000s. It took as its conceptual basis scenes in which the lack of milk resulted in humorously serious predicaments. Although "Got Milk?" was associated with the well-known print and outdoor campaign featuring celebrities with milk mustaches, which ran nationally in the late 1990s and through the 2000s, the two were actually separate campaigns. The defining "Got Milk?" spot was called "Aaron Burr," and it featured a bookish history buff who could not provide the answer to a radio trivia contest—listeners were asked to name the person who shot Alexander Hamilton (the answer was Aaron Burr)—because his mouth was full of peanut butter and he had no milk. The celebrity milk-mustache campaign, created for the nationwide Milk Processor Education Program by agency Bozell (and based on a 1970s Canadian campaign), began its run with the tagline "Where's your mustache?" When it discovered that consumers already believed that "Got Milk?" was the mustache campaign's tagline, the Milk Processor Education Program purchased the usage rights to "Got Milk?" from the California Milk Processor Board. "Got Milk?" became one of the best-known ad slogans in recent memory as well as a brand in its own right. The California Milk Processor Board created a briskly selling line of retail products—baby clothes, toys, ice-cream scoops, and aprons among them—with the tagline imprinted on them.

MARKETING STRATEGY

In "Don't Take Your Body for Granted," which was launched in January 2003, Palmer Jarvis DDB attempted to satisfy its mandate of changing the way teens looked at milk with an absurdly humorous visual conceit: the campaign theme was dramatized through images of human beings who literally had no bodies. They instead consisted of normal heads attached directly to feet, and each of the campaign's many TV, cinema, print, and outdoor executions illustrated the difficulty of life without a body.

For instance, one TV/cinema spot, "Dogwalker," showed the bodiless head of a grandmotherly woman being dragged behind the poodle she was attempting to walk. Another spot, "Bus," centered on a public-bus driver who, because he consisted only of head and feet, could not effectively reach either the pedals or the steering wheel of the vehicle; meanwhile, his bodiless passengers rolled about on the bus's floorboards. These commercials generated substantial tension and drama as the bodiless humans struggled unsuccessfully to regain control of their respective situations—situations that would have been ordinary but that had become positively harrowing in the absence of bodies. At the conclusion of each suspenseful action sequence, a white screen appeared with the message "Don't take your body for granted" imprinted upon it. This screen was then replaced with a second white screen reading "Drink Milk."

Print and outdoor ads used the same concept, with the tagline printed along the bottom of each image. One print/outdoor ad, "Urinal," showed a bodiless man looking up at a public-restroom urinal, which towered over him and presented an obviously insurmountable challenge. In "Cat" a cat toyed with a fearful head instead of a nearby ball of yarn, and "Escalator" showed the upturned, high-heeled feet and panicked head of a bodiless woman whose hair was caught in the teeth of an escalator.

An online component of the campaign, accessible at the website http://www.drinkmilk.ca, supported the media placements by offering an interactive experience with the campaign's bodiless humans. Users were asked to create their own 3-D images—employing their choice of backgrounds, characters, objects, speech bubbles, and motion lines—illustrating the difficulties presented by the lack of a body.

One of the initial difficulties Palmer Jarvis DDB faced was selling its conservative client on the outrageous idea it was suggesting. It therefore made a highly unusual proposition: if BCDF was not satisfied with the results of "Don't Take Your Body for Granted," the ad agency would create another campaign for free. BCDF took Palmer Jarvis DDB up on its offer, deciding to risk its reputation on the innovative campaign. The agency's director of brand management, Bill Baker, told *Strategy* magazine that, faced with negative feedback from constituents in the organization, one board member responded by saying, "Listen, I'm not sure I entirely get this campaign either.... But my teen-aged kids love them. They laugh hysterically every time they see them, and that's what we're trying to do here."

The arresting nature of the campaign's individual executions was particularly necessary given another of Palmer Jarvis DDB's key obstacles: a budget of only 3 million Canadian dollars, which did not allow it to place the commercials with the frequency that was usually necessary to reach its target market effectively, and which did not remotely approach comparable ad spending on behalf of branded beverages. Palmer Jarvis DDB creative director Alan Russell told *Boards,* "Apart from being a strategically smart campaign, the ads will draw tremendous attention because of their originality. The concept, the story lines, the visual craziness and the surprising payoff are all so unexpected for the milk category that I can't imagine not recalling these commercials, even after one viewing."

OUTCOME

Creativity said of the "Don't Take Your Body for Granted" campaign, "The fact is, our neighbors to the north at Palmer Jarvis DDB have out-mooed 'Got Milk?' with a disembodied piece of genius youth marketing." The campaign won numerous Canadian and international awards, including a Bronze Lion at the Cannes International Advertising Festival for the TV spot "Dogwalker" and a Bronze Clio for the 2004 print campaign. Market research found that, despite the limited TV and cinema placement of the campaign's spots—an unavoidable result of its minimal budget—80 percent of young people in British Columbia saw at least one of the commercials in 2003, compared to the 56 percent norm for campaigns with the same budget. Ninety-two percent of the young people who had seen individual spots agreed with descriptions of them as unique and different, and 83 percent deemed the commercials enjoyable. British Columbia's milk consumption climbed by 1 percent in 2003, at a time when the dairy industry hoped at best for modestly declining—rather than rapidly declining—sales. The consumption of flavored milk by teens and young adults climbed by 11.5 percent in 2003 as well. The campaign ran through 2004.

FURTHER READING

"B.C. Dairy Searches Alone." *Marketing Magazine,* May 20, 2002.

"Campaign: B.C. Dairy." *Creativity,* April 2003.

Christie, Brendan. "They're at It Again." *Boards Online,* February 6, 2003. Available from http://www.boardsmag.com/articles/online/20030206/moo.html

Dobson, Sarah. "Moo Juice Marketers." *Marketing Magazine,* May 26, 2003.

Gray, Gary. "Sour Milk." *Marketing Magazine,* March 1, 2004.

Katz, Hélène. "Milking Nostalgia." *Marketing Magazine,* April 5, 2004.

Lazarus, Eve. "The Cool Appeal of Milk." *Marketing Magazine,* December 8, 2003.

Lepage, Florence. "BC Dairy Foundation." *Marketing Magazine,* April 21, 2003.

Loughlin, Katherine. "Peer Pressure." *Marketing Magazine,* March 8, 2004.

Vinakmens, Kristen. "In the Hands of a Good Doctor." *Strategy Magazine,* November 3, 2003. Available from <http://www.strategymag.com/articles/magazine/20031103/relations.html>

Voight, Joan. "Dairy's Queen." *Adweek,* April 14, 2003.

Mark Lane

Binney & Smith

1100 Church Lane
Easton, Pennsylvania 18044
USA
Telephone: (610) 253-6271
Fax: (610) 250-5768
Web site: www.binney-smith.com

MAKE PLAY CAMPAIGN

OVERVIEW

Crayola was the most recognized brand name in children's art products, but as the twenty-first century dawned, the company that made Crayola—Binney & Smith of Easton, Pennsylvania (founded in 1885, a subsidiary of Hallmark since 1984)—grew more and more concerned that brand perception had boxed it into a corner. The public saw that Crayola had only crayons and markers, and for that reason 90 percent of its sales came during the late summer, when children were preparing to return to school. Furthermore, most new Crayola products were so overshadowed by the brand's two main items that sales in other areas were poor. Lastly, many viewed the line as old-fashioned, as even art supplies had moved into the electronic age.

To correct this perception Binney & Smith turned to its advertising agency of record, Leo Burnett of Chicago. In response to the challenge, the agency devised an award-winning television campaign on a budget of less than $1 million. The campaign, which aired on television for three weeks in spring of 2003, was titled "Make Play." Two ads, "Night" and "Fin," highlighted the new Crayola products while showing that children could enjoy Crayola year-round.

The campaign was effective enough to garner a 2004 Silver EFFIE Award. It also set the tone for future Crayola campaigns that emphasized the product line as being more diverse than simply crayons and markers.

HISTORICAL CONTEXT

Coincidentally or not, 2003 marked the centennial anniversary of the Crayola brand. For most of those 100 years the product held a secure place in the market—more than 120 billion crayons were sold worldwide—and therefore change came slowly to Crayola. Aside from expanding the number of colors (the 48-count box debuted in 1949, the 64-count box with sharpener in 1958) and occasionally renaming the colors (in 1962, for instance, "flesh" was renamed "peach"), the Crayola brand pretty much adhered to its tried-and-true formula. In 1978 markers became part of the product line, and for the next 25 years the company was perceived in light of those two products, despite the fact that in 1976 Binney & Smith had bought the highly successful product Silly Putty.

Crayola periodically reinforced itself in the public mind for most of that quarter of a century with marketing efforts that encouraged people to come up with names for new colors or rename old colors. Research and development was not, however, dormant at Crayola. Among the newer Crayola products was Window Writers, color markers that enabled children to write on windows and that were easily wiped off. In 2002 Window Writers were given the seal of excellence

© LWA-SHARIE KENNEDY/CORBIS

by the Quebec Consumers Association, which tested toys with 199 children aged 6 months to 12 years. In June 2002 Binney & Smith took another tack in its effort to push its products beyond the once- or twice-a-year buying spurts. The company opened what was referred to as a "branded destination site" in Hanover, Maryland, a suburb of Baltimore. Leslie Kaufman of the *New York Times* described Crayola Works as "a hybrid store and creative arts studio."

By 2003 Crayola's annual output was stupendous. According to Kathy Flanigan writing in the *Milwaukee Journal Sentinel,* it amounted to 1.5 million bottles of paint, 9 million Silly Putty eggs, 110 million sticks of chalk, 465 million markers, 600 million colored pencils, and a staggering 3 billion crayons. Still, there remained the problem of overcoming the perception that Crayola was a once-a-year buy. Sales of paints, modeling compound, and activity kits had decreased to such an extent that in November 2002 Binney & Smith announced it was dropping the third shift of its plant in Bethlehem, Pennsylvania. The company also moved some production to Mexico.

TARGET MARKET

Part of the challenge of the "Make Play" campaign was to shift Crayola's traditional target market from parents (primarily mothers) to children aged six to nine. It was parental buying habits that contributed greatly to the notion of Crayola products as simply back-to-school items. In other words, what Crayola had to do was appeal directly to those people using its products—kids—in order to break a century-old, ingrained shopping habit. In the "brief of effectiveness" that it submitted for the EFFIE Awards, the Leo Burnett agency explained that, in order to fuel sales growth throughout the year, Crayola needed to make kids themselves excited about the products. Further, it stated, "The brand also needed to go beyond the same old basic school-supply crayons and markers and focus on innovative products to drive category enthusiasm with kids." In other words Crayola was going to appeal to its new target market, six to nine year olds, by offering products that might not be seen as school supplies.

COMPETITION

Crayola's competitors within the children's-arts-and-crafts category included Alex, Rose Art, Faber Castell, Imaginarium (the in-house brand for Toys "R" Us), and Newell Rubbermaid, Inc. A century of name recognition, however, made Crayola dominant in the field. In 2001 Crayola controlled about 75 percent of the market, with Rose Art a distant second at 13 percent. With regard to market share the competition was almost negligible, though in more upscale toy stores, brands such as Alex, Rose Art, and even Faber Castell sometimes predominated. The relative newcomer to the field was Newell Rubbermaid, which had acquired pencil-maker Sanford in 1992. In 2001 Newell Rubbermaid announced that it

THE CRAYOLA NAME

The name "Crayola" was devised in 1903 by Alice Binney, the wife of Edwin Binney (who, together with his cousin C. Harold Smith, had invented the crayons). She combined *craie,* the French word for chalk, with "ola," short for oleaginous or oily. Literally, "Crayola" meant "oily chalk." A survey conducted in 1999 indicated that 99 percent of Americans recognized the Crayola name.

was reviving Sanford's Colorific brand and taking on Crayola's hegemony in the crayon-and-marker market, which was then valued at some $800 million. Newell's goal was to acquire a 10 percent market share by 2003.

Crayola faced stiffer competition for children's time from products outside the category of children's arts and crafts. First and perhaps foremost were television and its ancillary products, such as videos, DVDs, and video games. Competition was also provided by other children's toys specific to the age category of Crayola's target audience. Whether the competitors' toys (outside of the arts-and-crafts field) were electronic or not, they were still seen as year-round activities. Despite the fact that coloring was also a year-round activity, it was not seen as such with regard to consumer spending. Still, the Leo Burnett agency, in conjunction with Binney & Smith, believed that Crayola's newer items were enough of a basis upon which to build year-round demand, a demand that would center on the intrinsic value of the products.

MARKETING STRATEGY

Arts-and-crafts toys were essentially the opposite of electronic games and toys in that they stimulated a child's imagination rather than dulled it. The strategy of the "Make Play" ad campaign of 2003 was to reinforce this premise while focusing on new Crayola products, Twistables, a crayon created in response to the Glitz Stix put out under Sanford's Colorific brand; Click Em On Markers, which enabled a child to engage in two different activities, drawing and building; and Model Magic, a new type of modeling clay that dried overnight, allowing children more or less to create their own toys. These new products were to help achieve the campaign's goals of stimulating brand sales beyond the back-to-school period and expanding Crayola's already dominant market share of the children's-arts-and-crafts category.

Because the campaign's budget was limited to less than $600,000, television was the medium of choice. In fact, no other advertising medium was used to support the campaign. As reported in Leo Burnett's EFFIE Award brief for the campaign, "After evaluating a variety of media vehicles, TV ranked highest for the target's media consumption, affinity, mass reach, and ability to drive awareness of our product." The belief was that the television spots would ignite in the six- to nine-year-old target market what the agency dubbed "pester power"—children asking their parents to buy them something.

The television spots came out during the third week of April 2003, just prior to the Easter holiday. Traditionally this time of year was the third-heaviest period for children's advertisers (the top two were the back-to-school period and the weeks leading up to Christmas). The spots featured two commercials: "Night," which advertised Crayola Twistables, and "Fin," which showcased Click Em Ons. Lewis Lazare, an advertising critic for the *Chicago Sun-Times,* rated the former spot over the latter. He also stated, "the ads make clear that Crayola has moved beyond the simple crayon with the introduction of products aimed at today's sophisticated youngster, for whom simplicity isn't necessarily a virtue."

In discussing the Crayola spots Lazare wrote: "'Fin'... promotes Click Em Ons, a new marker that doubles as a set of sticks that click together to build things... The spot shows a boy using Click Em Ons to make [paper] shark fins that he places around his nearby pet dog. Then the boy snaps together the markers to build a protective cage for the pooch. The spot ably demonstrates how the product works." Lazare took exception, however, to the background music, arguing that it contributed to what he thought was a moody tone. As for the other spot, "Night," he said that it had "a lighter, more fanciful aura, as well as some lovely visuals." The commercial's first scene showed a boy playing with a glowing orb, pretending that it was a basketball. In the second scene the boy was at his desk looking through his window at his muse: a full moon. He was drawing with Twistables, a crayon designed so that the user did not have to peel paper to reveal more wax when the tip had worn down.

OUTCOME

In 2004 the "Make Play" campaign received a Silver EFFIE Award. EFFIEs were given in recognition of a campaign's effectiveness in the marketplace. The campaign, at least in the short term, accomplished both goals that had been set. Regarding stimulating sales beyond the back-to-school period, Model Magic experienced a 42.6 percent increase during the three-week advertising period. Subsequently sales tapered off, and for a number of weeks they remained at a plateau that was slightly higher than the pre-advertisement figures before settling to pre-advertisement levels in the summer of 2003.

The improvement in sales of Click Em On Markers was more dramatic. During the weeks of the "Make Play" campaign the markers experienced a 64 percent increase in sales compared to the six weeks prior to the campaign. Furthermore, in the week following the campaign's end, sales actually increased compared to the campaign's final week. In the second week after the campaign, sales were off only slightly from the campaign's final week. Both of these weeks represented substantial increases over the immediate pre-advertisement period. The campaign's second goal was to increase Crayola's share of the children's-arts-and-crafts market. To that end the campaign was also successful. Crayola gained 1.8 market share points over the same period in 2002.

Binney & Smith continued to find ways of maintaining Crayola products as items for year-round purchase, including expanding the product line. One lucrative strategy was to keep the Crayola brand name in people's minds through licensing. The Crayola brand had been licensed since the early 1990s, but in June 2003, soon after the "Make Play" campaign had run its course, Binney & Smith opted to maintain a booth at the Licensing Show (an annual trade event at which companies showcased their brands for prospective promotional partners) for the first time. As Amanda Burgess reported in the trade magazine *KidScreen,* Binney & Smith was attempting to expand its Crayola brand by creating a network of "A-list partners in toys, stationery/school supplies, apparel, accessories, bed, bath, home, publishing, and food."

In 2004 Binney & Smith ended its association with the Leo Burnett agency. That same year the company strengthened its grip on the arts-and-crafts category when the company started Big Yellow Box, a direct-sales venture that used independent representatives to market craft kits.

FURTHER READING

Baar, Aaron. "Binney & Smith Pulls Out of Burnett." *Adweek,* July 2, 2004.

Burgess, Amanda. "Crayola's Licensing Agenda Is Set to Get More Colorful." *KidScreen,* June 1, 2003.

Cornacchia, Cheryl. "Play Favourites: Lego and Crayola Markers among Top Toys Reviewed by Quebec Consumers Association." *Gazette* (Montreal), October 24, 2002.

"Crayola Is 100 Years Old. Orange You Tickled Pink?" *Washington Post,* October 7, 2003.

Flanigan, Kathy. "A Colorful Century from Crayola." *Milwaukee Journal Sentinel,* March 3, 2003.

Gallun, Alby. "Newell's New Colors; Ends Acquisition Binge to Focus on Boosting Existing Brands." *Crain's Chicago Business,* June 4, 2001.

Garland, Susan B. "So Glad You Could Come. Can I Sell You Anything?" *New York Times,* December 19, 2004.

Kaufman, Leslie. "PBS Is Expanding Its Brand from the Television Screen to the Shopping Mall." *New York Times,* June 27, 2002.

"KGOY but Can Brand Owners Keep Up?" *Brand Strategy,* November 2, 2001.

Lazare, Lewis. "2 Spots Tout New Crayola Products." *Chicago Sun-Times,* April 23, 2003.

"MediaBin Software to Help Market Toys." *Atlanta Journal-Constitution,* April 17, 2002.

Frank Caso

The Body Shop International PLC

Watersmead
Littlehampton
West Sussex, BN17 6LS
United Kingdom
Telephone: 44 1903 731500
Fax: 44 1903 726250
E-mail: info@bodyshop.co.uk
Web site: www.the-body-shop.com

RUBY CAMPAIGN

OVERVIEW

In 1976, when the cosmetics industry was making exaggerated claims about scientific advancements in skin care, Anita Roddick opened a store, The Body Shop, in a seaside town on the southern coast of England. Her product line, based on natural ingredients and age-old beauty secrets from Polynesia and the Amazon rainforest, was a vast departure from the patented laboratory-created, animal-tested products that promised to stop the aging process, eradicate dark circles under the eyes, and otherwise correct a woman's flaws. The products were plainly packaged, and they were not tested on animals and not promoted through extravagant advertising campaigns. In 1988 Roddick opened her first store in the United States, and by that time—through various social initiatives such as the "Stop the Burn" campaign to save the Brazilian rainforest (the source of many of the company's natural ingredients) and strong support of employee volunteerism—The Body Shop name had become synonymous with social activism and global preservation worldwide. The company had also become immensely profitable.

By the mid-1990s, however, The Body Shop faced growing competition, forcing it to begin its first major advertising initiative, the most prominent part of which was the "Ruby" campaign. The campaign was personified by Ruby, a doll with Rubenesque proportions who was perched on an antique couch and who looked quite pleased with herself and her plump frame. Randy Williamson, a spokesperson for The Body Shop, said, "Ruby is the fruit of our long-established practice of challenging the way the cosmetic industry talks to women. The Ruby campaign is designed to promote the idea that The Body Shop creates products designed to enhance features, moisturize, cleanse, and polish, not to correct 'flaws.' The Body Shop philosophy is that there is real beauty in everyone. We are not claiming that our products perform miracles."

The Ruby doll, a computer-generated image, appeared on posters, stickers, and T-shirts and in magazine ads. The campaign was launched in the United States in September 1997 following its successful introduction in several other countries.

HISTORICAL CONTEXT

The Body Shop was founded in 1976 in Brighton, England. From her original shop, which offered a line of 25 different lotions, creams, and oils, Roddick became the first successful marketer of body care products that combined natural ingredients with ecologically-benign manufacturing processes. Her company's refusal to test products on animals, along with an insistence on nonexploitative labor practices among suppliers around the world, appealed especially to upscale, mainly middle-class women, who were and have continued to be the company's primary market.

Part of the secret of The Body Shop's early success was that it had created a market niche for itself. The company was not directly competing against the traditional cosmetics companies, which marketed their products as fashion accessories designed to cover up flaws and make women look more like the fashion models who appeared in their lavish ads. Instead, The Body Shop offered a line of products that promised benefits other than appearance—healthier skin, for instance—rather than simply a better-looking complexion.

During the 1980s, when The Body Shop dominated the niche it had created, it avoided the kinds of traditional marketing used by the more fashion-driven cosmetics companies. This "antimarketing" strategy defied conventional wisdom in several important ways: the company had no advertising agency, it did not hire fashion photographers to photograph beautiful women wearing its products, and it did not advertise in the usual women's magazines. Instead, it relied on in-store promotions, including posters and educational materials that targeted its own customers, who then passed the word to their friends. This word-of-mouth approach, often regarded as the most effective form of marketing thanks to its built-in credibility factor, was augmented by a huge amount of favorable publicity generated largely by Roddick herself.

Roddick was outspoken in her views on environmentalism and social justice, and in the 1980s her beliefs ran against the prevailing political and social climate in a way that appealed to her target market. One of the company's best-known stands was its hard-line opposition to animal testing for cosmetics. It also instituted a Community Trade Programme, which attempted to find the company's natural ingredients from grassroots cooperatives and other community-based groups, thus helping to ensure that the profits went to people in need rather than to exploitative subcontractors. The Eastern European Relief Drive, designed to fund orphanages in Romania, and the Brazilian Healthcare Project, which provided care for 28 villages in the Amazon, were other company projects having little to do with cosmetics and everything to do with building a positive image for its socially conscious customers.

These initiatives generated an ongoing stream of favorable press attention, and The Body Shop, along with the American ice cream maker Ben and Jerry's, was hailed as a new breed of green, or environmentally conscious, business. As sales boomed, even the conservative financial markets approved of The Body Shop's impressive profit picture, and a public stock offering in 1984 was successful. An expansion campaign followed. In 1988 the company entered the U.S. market by opening a store in New York City, and by 1997 the company boasted 1,500 stores, including franchises, in 47 countries. Antimarketing seemed to be smart marketing, at least as far as The Body Shop was concerned.

TARGET MARKET

With its emphasis on natural ingredients and ethical processes, The Body Shop made it clear from the beginning that it was creating products for women who cared not only about their health and appearance but also about the environment. The company's success, in fact, was built on its ability to blend a product line with an environmentally conscious philosophy, which was particularly attractive to the generation of women who grew up in the 1960s and '70s. These women saw the Body Shop as an ethical alternative to the beauty-at-any-price stance of the more fashion-driven cosmetics companies. But it was also an emotional appeal, one that promised customers that in buying its products they were doing something good for the planet. In its early years The Body Shop's customers tended to be young middle-class women who could afford the extra expense that high-quality natural ingredients often entailed but who also bridled at the high prices attached to designer cosmetics. Over the years, as these early customers aged, many retained their "global" sensibilities, and The Body Shop continued to be a reliable source of products they could believe in.

Beauty in the traditional sense as portrayed by other cosmetics companies was never a concern either in The Body Shop's products or in its marketing. Thus, the "Ruby" campaign, which questioned the ideal of a thin body for every woman, was consistent with the company's long-standing principles. The campaign was also in line with another of the company's beliefs—truth in advertising—which had strong appeal to its target market. If The Body Shop was not going to make exaggerated claims for its products, it certainly was not going to pretend that every woman could, or should, try to look like the extremely thin models that filled women's magazines.

COMPETITION

By the mid-1990s The Body Shop's once invincible hold on its market began to loosen. Competitors, including The Limited's Bath & Body Works, Crabtree & Evelyn, and Aveda, had launched their own lines of natural cosmetics, often through their own chains of stores. The resulting glut precipitated a market shakeout in which smaller, undercapitalized companies began to be forced out of business, and even the larger companies faced flattening growth curves.

NOT FOR WOMEN ONLY

In the 1990s The Body Shop attempted to extended its market to include men. Although they were slow to accept "cosmetics," men, especially those who had grown up in the 1960s and 1970s, were open to shaving lotions and suntan oils. As a result, The Body Shop introduced lines of men's lotions and oils made with natural and ethically produced ingredients.

In June 1997, prior to the "Ruby" campaign, The Body Shop displayed in its stores a poster that depicted a man with a bottle protruding from his bathing suit. The poster was advertising The Body Shop's self-tanning lotion. The poster offended some people, and in North Carolina there were protests. Unwilling to be pressured by what it perceived to be a double standard in sexual stereotyping, the company refused to remove the poster from its stores.

The Body Shop found that, especially in the United States, its antimarketing style was having difficulty in the face of much more aggressive efforts by its competitors. American consumers, long accustomed to being actively campaigned for by advertisers, were less loyal to brands than the English and were more apt to be tempted by new products, new brands, and new packaging. Gift giving—for Mother's Day, Valentine's Day, and other holidays—was important in the United States, but The Body Shop's European management was late in realizing how great an impact this could have. By 1995 its profits from U.S. sales were falling, and as share prices responded to the disappointing profit figures, The Body Shop's relationship with the financial community also became strained. In 1996, its 20th anniversary, the company faced a crisis that seemed to demand a new marketing strategy.

MARKETING STRATEGY

In 1995 The Body Shop responded to its eroding market share by doubling its U.K. marketing budget while dramatically slowing the rate at which it was opening new stores in the United States. It also broke tradition by creating an in-house marketing department, something it had always resisted, and it named a marketing director and added marketing managers for individual product lines. In 1994 The Body Shop had hired the London office of the American advertising agency Chiat/Day (since renamed St. Lukes), though only in a "marketing consultancy" role, and by the following year the company was poised to regroup its marketing efforts.

At the same time The Body Shop was careful to back up its high, marketing profile with a series of initiatives aimed at convincing customers that the changes were more than just skin deep. These included a complete packaging redesign, a new hairstyling line, relaunches of the hair care and skin care lines, and several new fragrances. The company also announced a new direct home-shopping service and took its message directly to the American market with a 300-square-foot show truck that toured selected cities with product demonstrations. And for the first time the company began to entertain the possibility of direct advertising at the local level in the American market. Ads began to appear, though not in any orchestrated media campaign and mostly in smaller alternative publications such as *Mother Jones*.

With these initiatives starting to take effect throughout 1996, the company was planning its boldest marketing effort yet, the "Ruby" campaign. Part of a broader "Love Your Body" campaign, the "Ruby" campaign in the United States began with in-store posters and an ad in *Self* magazine. In keeping with The Body Shop's iconoclastic tradition, the company positioned itself squarely against an idea that had long dominated the fashion industry, the notion that there was an ideal beauty to which all women should aspire and that the ideal was decided by experts in Paris, New York, and London. The "Ruby" ad showed a redheaded, decidedly Rubenesque nude doll (hence the name Ruby) lounging luxuriously on a green velvet sofa. The headline had a blunt message: "There are 3 billion women who don't look like supermodels and only 8 who do."

The concept was created in-house by a team that included Roddick; her husband Gordon, who was the company's chairman; and Marina Galanti, the former international communications and media director for Benetton Group, the Italian clothing company known for its ads featuring social issues rather than clothes. In a U.S. interview with National Public Radio, Roddick described the setting of Ruby's creation: "The girls in [British fashion magazines] are exactly what the media wants . . . they have no bodies, they're too thin. They are passive. They are, you know, beaten up. So, we—three of us in my office—we came up with this broadsheet which was called 'Full Voice.' It was like a pamphlet on the body and self-esteem." While working on the pamphlet, they found a computer image of a doll they altered, blowing it up to an ever greater size until it became the Ruby of the campaign. The Body Shop placed the image in 400,000 newspaper inserts, and soon afterward the campaign took off.

It was notable that, like the Benetton campaigns, The Body Shop's new ad did not feature any products. It was satisfied to identify itself with a movement already well under way that held that a woman's sense of well-being, self-esteem, and beauty should arise from qualities such as health and happiness rather than from external ideals. A company statement at the time proclaimed, "As the personification of The Body Shop's commitment to self-esteem, Ruby is more than just an image; she's a state of mind—strong, independent and informed. She doesn't weigh her self-esteem against false standards. She loves her body and is true to herself."

Although this was an unusual message for a line of skin and hair care products, it came at a time when other companies were also making ads that questioned conventional images of beauty. In print ads for Freeman Cosmetics, for example, a woman was shown with her back to the camera. The caption asked, "How much do you need to see to know I'm beautiful?" An ad for Dove soap declared that its bar was "for the beauty that's already there." Even more blunt was a Canadian ad for Kellogg's Special K cereal. Featuring a very thin model, the ad asked, "If this is beauty, there's something wrong with the eye of the beholder." But among the advertising campaigns in this trend, the "Ruby" ad was among the most provocative because it not only questioned the ideal of an exceptionally thin body—which most women could not attain—but also promoted a nude "size 18" doll as an example of beauty.

Concurrent with the ad, The Body Shop produced Ruby stickers, postcards, and refrigerator magnets for sale in its stores and installed 40- by 60-foot banners of the doll in 289 selected stores in the United States. Though by far the most noted part of the company's new advertising initiative, "Ruby" was actually just one of a trilogy of issues-oriented campaigns that focused on body image, domestic violence, and aging. For the campaign on domestic violence, launched in October 1997, The Body Shop sold special whistles designed to call attention to what it had identified as another hot-button issue for women. The third issue, aging, with its natural tie-in to wrinkles and skin care, came closest to being a traditional product supporter.

These campaigns were supported by *Full Voice,* which, beginning as a broadsheet, was transformed into a company magazine. Produced in-house, the magazine was used to promote all of the company's ongoing environmental and social causes. Its reasoned explanations of emotionally resonant issues fit well within the company's overall strategy of appealing to the whole woman rather than just her body.

OUTCOME

The "Ruby" ad generated immediate attention both in the press and among the public. The *New York Times* and *Good Morning America* both ran stories, and the advertising press took note. Simon Green, creative partner at the advertising agency BDDH in London, wrote approvingly of the ad for the *Independent:* "Most women know that they are not supermodels, but there is no advertising out there that recognizes them for who they are without being condescending or patronising... I'm not even in the target audience, but even as a man it makes me have more empathy for The Body Shop." During the campaign the company reported a boost in sales in some of its markets, including a 12 percent sales increase in Australia and Switzerland.

Not everyone, though, was fond of the campaign. National Public Radio, which interviewed pedestrians passing by a Ruby poster in New York City, found mixed reactions. One person said, "I think it's too bitterly honest. It looks kind of degrading." Another pedestrian remarked, "It's representative, but they could have made her look more appealing... put a slip or something on her." Still another said, "It looks like a Barbie Doll that went wrong." But others in the interview were impressed. "It makes you feel better about yourself," a pedestrian said, reflecting one of the main goals of the campaign. The Body Shop, in fact, received thousands of calls and letters from women expressing gratitude for Ruby's realistic portrayal of beauty—gratitude, the company hoped, that would translate into increased sales for its products. But Sean Larkins, corporate public relations manager for The Body Shop, said, "We don't see profits as the be-all and end-all. We feel that business has a social responsibility to the self-esteem and well-being of its customers."

FURTHER READING

"The Body Shop Gets Real with Ruby." *Household & Personal Products Industry,* September 1997, p. 10.

Davis, Donald A. "Glut Indeed." *Drug & Cosmetic Industry,* November 1996, p. 22.

Elliott, Stuart. "The Body Shop's Campaign Offers Reality, Not Miracles." *New York Times,* August 26, 1997, p. C8.

Fallon, James. "Body Shop's American Agenda." *Women's Wear Daily,* May 12, 1995, p. S10.

Lee, Julian, and Patrick Barrett. "Body in Need of Reshaping." *Marketing,* April 4, 1996, p. 10.

Walker, Sophie. "Body Shop Barbie Ad Spawns New Campaign." *Financial Express,* September 4, 1997.

Patrick Hutchins

Borders Group, Inc.

100 Phoenix Drive
Ann Arbor, Michigan 48108
USA
Telephone: (734) 477-1100
Fax: (734) 477-1965
Web site: www.bordersgroupinc.com

THIS SEASON, IT'S THE ORIGINAL THOUGHT THAT COUNTS CAMPAIGN

OVERVIEW

Borders Group, Inc., the second-largest American book retailer after Barnes & Noble, Inc., adjusted to a trend of dwindling mall traffic by erecting more and more superstores, which tallied 435 by 2003. Hoping to dissuade consumers from shopping for books, CDs, and videos over the Internet, Borders strove to provide at each of its stores a customer-friendly setting equipped with cafés, furnished with comfortable seating, and set up so that customers could preview books and music before making a purchase. In April 2003 Borders ended its relationship with the Campbell-Ewald Company, the agency that had created Borders' "Find Out" campaign. Shifting away from price-oriented advertising and focusing instead on the meaningfulness of gift-giving, Borders released its "This Season, It's the Original Thought That Counts" campaign for the 2003 holiday season.

Borders awarded Crispin Porter + Bogusky's Venice, California, office its first account, estimated at $15 million, in September 2003. On November 30 Crispin Porter + Bogusky launched "This Season, It's the Original Thought That Counts" across print and outdoor advertising, with all advertising displaying the campaign's title as the tagline. The print ads, which appeared as inserts in newspapers nationwide during the weeks before Christmas, featured copy on one side that described the joys of receiving books as gifts. The insert's other side looked and felt like holiday wrapping paper. In addition to the book-themed newspaper inserts, DVD-themed wrapping paper was placed in *Rolling Stone Magazine* to suggest that movies made thoughtful gifts. With the same sentiment in mind, images of CD cases appeared in the *New Yorker*. All inserts could be removed and used to gift wrap a regular-size book, CD, or DVD.

The campaign garnered a plethora of ad-industry awards, including a Silver Pencil and a Best in Show recognition at 2004's ATHENA Awards competition, sponsored by the Newspaper Association of America. Borders saw a 3.78 percent sales growth in 2003, with 35 percent of its sales occurring during the quarter in which the campaign ran.

HISTORICAL CONTEXT

Prior to Crispin Porter + Bogusky's involvement, Borders had run a long campaign titled "Find Out," launched by Campbell-Ewald in the mid-1990s and lasting until April 2003. The campaign, which borrowed from earlier work done by ad agency Perich + Partners, focused on the experience of browsing in a bookstore. During the duration of "Find Out," Borders held promotional events such as book readings, author signings, lectures, and local-musician showcases. By April 2003 the campaign only appeared across print.

The company also cross-promoted with Children's Books & Toys, Inc., the parent company of FAO Schwarz. Borders recommended and delivered its books, music, and movies to Children's Books & Toys stores. In return the toy stores provided products for Borders and Waldenbooks, a mall-based bookstore chain owned by the Borders Group. But Borders, along with other bookselling superstores, tended to lack strong advertising outside the stores themselves. Mike Spinozzi, chief marketing officer for Borders, explained in *Adweek* that the company's marketing had in the past depended largely on "competitive square footage." He later referred to the approach as an "if you build it, they will come" model.

Hoping to build the emotional content of its brand, Borders hired the Zyman Group (consultants) in March of 2003. Spinozzi told *Adweek* that Borders assigned Zyman the task of defining the "functional and emotional benefits of the brand." A few months later Borders settled on Crispin Porter + Bogusky to handle its advertising, largely based on the quality of the agency's advertising for IKEA and on its vision about how the Borders brand should be developed. Tim Roper, creative director at Crispin Porter + Bogusky, commented to *Adweek* that if America's two book-superstores were on a college campus, "Barnes & Noble would be the law library, and Borders would be the smaller, funkier, cooler place." Roper, who also wrote copy for "This Season, It's the Original Thought That Counts," wanted to convey the idea that there was at least one item at Borders that was a perfect fit for everybody.

TARGET MARKET

The campaign targeted holiday shoppers within all age, income, and cultural parameters. Roper explained that its goal was "to intervene in the robotic buying patterns that usually result in catch-all gifts like sweaters, toasters or stainless-steel pen sets. We're talking to virtually anyone who aspires to give a gift that is truly meaningful and can be tailored to the individual recipients' personality and tastes." Borders hoped to connect gift-giving's meaningfulness to the Borders brand. To facilitate this connection, the "This Season, It's the Original Thought That Counts" campaign associated wrapping paper with the Borders logo. Massive retailers such as Wal-Mart and Costco could offer CDs, DVDs, and books at lower prices than Borders, which meant that Borders could not target consumers from a price orientation. "Borders has the opportunity to be a really cool brand," Roper told *Adweek*. "They know the need for differentiation and identity. Why buy the Tom Clancy book there rather than 15 other places?"

ECHO DEVELOPING DIGITAL TECHNOLOGY

In mid-2003 Borders became a member of Echo, a consortium working on the development of technology to regulate the licensing and retailing of digital music. Echo was founded in January 2003 by Best Buy Co., Hastings Entertainment, MTS, Incorporated (Tower Records), Trans World Entertainment Corporation, Virgin Entertainment Group, and Wherehouse Entertainment.

Borders offered consumers an informed staff and information centers that provided insight into books, CDs, and DVDs. "This is the beginning of our conversation with the consumer about the meaningfulness of content," Roper continued to explain to *Adweek*. He later pointed out that mass merchants did not offer much insight into products similar to those sold at Borders. He also remarked that the giant retailers sold music, movies, and books almost as an afterthought.

COMPETITION

Changing advertising agencies regularly, Barnes & Noble, the largest U.S. bookseller, contracted more than four different agencies to run ads between 1999 and 2005. Advertising that appeared during 2003, the same year as Borders' "This Season" campaign, was executed primarily in-house by Barnes & Noble. For 2002 the company spent a reported $6 million on advertising, undershooting what Borders spent the following year by $9 million. One print ad released in 2003 made the case that the company's superior size enabled it to provide a better selection. It showed a black-and-white illustration with two stacks of books, one stack grossly larger than the other, and text that boasted, "Bigger means more, OK?"

The primary strategy Barnes & Noble employed to bolster sales was similar to that of Borders: to merely build more superstores, some topping out at 60,000 square feet. Hoping to compete with Amazon.com, Barnes & Noble sold a large percentage of its website business, barnesandnoble.com, to Bertelsmann AG, which owned, among other things, the publisher Random House, Inc. By 2003 Barnes & Noble was trying to regain control of its website by buying Bertelsmann's shares.

WALDENBOOKS' NAMESAKE

Waldenbooks, owned by the Borders Group, was founded in 1933. The bookstore was named after Walden Pond, the Massachusetts pond that inspired Henry David Thoreau to write his renowned transcendentalist work *Walden*.

The dilemma for both Borders and Barnes & Noble was twofold. One, as a result of waning mall traffic, both companies' smaller bookstores—Waldenbooks belonged to Borders, and Doubleday was owned by Barnes & Noble—were losing money. Second, even though both companies recorded sales growth quarter after quarter, they continuously needed to provide reasons for people to enter their stores. Many consumers enjoyed the experience of buying books online from Amazon.com. To attract consumers inside their doors, Barnes & Noble used promotions similar to those employed by Borders, such as readings, book signings, and lectures. Its stores also featured comfortable seating and in-store cafés. In 2003 Barnes & Noble's sales grew more than 11 percent, surpassing the 3.78 percent growth Borders experienced that year.

MARKETING STRATEGY

To maximize the campaign's limited budget, Crispin Porter + Bogusky wanted to create print ads that consumers could interact with. On November 30 "This Season, It's the Original Thought That Counts" appeared in three different executions across print and outdoor mediums. Roper and David Steinke, the project's art director, were challenged to create spots that conveyed the meaningfulness of certain gifts, especially the kind sold at Borders. The campaign portrayed other kinds of presents, such as purely functional items, as involving less sentiment and as therefore less desirable. "Price and selection and convenience can only get you so far," Roper told *Adweek.* "You have to start with more of a brand perspective. If you think about the offerings in a place like [Borders], it's a far more personal statement or gift than a sweater or curling iron—if it's chosen right."

The first set of ads appeared in more than 40 newspapers nationwide, including the *Chicago Tribune* and the *Washington Post.* When discovered by the reader, the insert first appeared as folded wrapping paper embellished with reindeer. Once unfolded, the back of the wrapping paper displayed a life-size image of a book jacket. Copy appeared as review endorsements, such as, "Ever notice how when you gift wrap a book, everyone can always tell it's a book? They don't have to pick it up, shake it or put their ear to it. They look and they know." "Hmm, a book," appeared below in faded text. The insert was large enough to gift wrap most books.

The second execution, inserted in *Rolling Stone* magazine, was a snowflake-themed piece of wrapping paper with an actual-size photograph of a DVD case on the back. Consumers could place their DVDs directly onto the advertisement and gift wrap DVDs. Copy that mimicked the formatting seen on the back of most DVDs read, "A lot of other gifts, besides a DVD, can fit in this 5.5" × 7.5" rectangle. A small box of monogrammed handkerchiefs, for one. But after wrapping paper and ribbons have settled, nobody will curl up on the couch, belly stuffed with turkey sandwiches, to watch the climactic battle scene between a pair of designer socks." To the left of the photograph appeared the Borders logo and the campaign's tagline. Wrapping-paper inserts for gift wrapping a CD case were run in the *New Yorker.*

Outdoor ads appeared on mall kiosks and billboards, displaying copy such as, "If the pen is mightier than the sword, all original ideas can beat the you-know-what out of a toaster." Another image showed a woman catching snowflakes on her tongue, and each snowflake bore a title of a movie, book, or CD. The campaign ran through December of 2003.

OUTCOME

The "This Season" campaign made its mark in the advertising industry, collecting awards such as a silver at the One Show, a Bronze Lion award at the Cannes Advertising Festival, and a silver at the Clio Awards. The campaign's newspaper execution earned a Silver Pencil and won Best in Show at the 2004 ATHENA Awards competition. John E. Kimball, senior vice president and chief marketing officer for the Newspaper Association of America, remarked on ATHENA's website, "This year's Best in Show winner, in particular, demonstrates how a little 'outside-the-wrapper' thinking can have a tremendous impact."

For 2003 Borders posted a 3.78 percent growth in sales from the previous year, and 35 percent of the company's 2003 sales took place during the quarter that "This Season, It's the Original Thought That Counts" took place. The industry leader, Barnes & Noble, posted significantly higher growth: 11.62 percent. Borders struggled to define its brand in 2003 and to gain on Barnes & Noble; but as Candace Corlett, a partner at the marketing consultancy WSL Strategic Retail, told

Adweek, Crispin Porter + Bogusky's campaign was definitely "a step in the right direction."

FURTHER READING

Borst, Barbara. "Author! Author! Artist's Love of Books Led to Barnes & Noble Portraits." *Pittsburgh (PA) Post-Gazette,* November 25, 1997, p. D3.

Corrigan, Patricia. "Big Books, Little Prices." *St. Louis Post,* December 1, 2004, p. E1.

Elliot, Stuart. "Crispin Porter Moves Operations to Miami." *New York Times,* May 17, 2004, p. 10.

Fabrikant, Geraldine. "Top Honors Taken by Miami Agency." *New York Times,* September 23, 2004, p. 2.

Flass, Rebecca. "Borders to Consumers: 'It's the Thought That Counts': Toasters Get Snubbed in Crispin Porter + Bogusky's New Holiday Ads." *Adweek,* December 1, 2003, p. 9.

———. "Why Crispin Porter + Bogusky Decided to Bail on Building an L.A.-Area Agency." *Adweek,* May 24, 2004, p. 14.

Jensen, Trevor, and Rebecca Flass. "Crispin Porter + Bogusky Sees Borders as the 'Funkier, Cooler' Bookstore: L.A. Office Lands $15 Mil. Account as Client Refocuses on Image." *Adweek,* September 22, 2003, p. 10.

Mack, Ann M. "How Online Retailers Are Luring Holiday Shoppers." *Adweek,* December 6, 2004, p. 10.

Marcel, Joyce. "The Morrow Family and Manchester's Northshire Bookstore." *Vermont Business Magazine,* December 1, 2004, p. 15.

May, Jeff. "Booksellers Have a Read on What Customers Want: Big Stores." *Newark (NJ) Star-Ledger,* May 17, 2004, p. 24.

Milliot, Jim, and John Mutter. "Booksellers Anxious about Holiday '04 Prospects." *Publishers Weekly,* November 22, 2004, p. 5.

Saewitz, Mike. "Plaza Regaining Some of Past Glory." *Sarasota (FL) Herald-Tribune,* November 29, 2004, p. BS1.

Kevin Teague

Boston Beer Company, Inc.

75 Arlington St.
Boston, Massachusetts 02216
USA
Telephone: (617) 368-5000
Fax: (617) 368-5500
Web site: www.bostonbeer.com

IT'S WHAT'S INSIDE CAMPAIGN

OVERVIEW

In August 1998, after a two-month review, the Boston Beer Company, Inc. replaced its longtime ad agency, Carmichael Lynch, with Interpublic Group's McCann-Erickson. The New York-based agency's first work for the Samuel Adams Boston Lager brand retained the aspirational thrust of the final campaign from Carmichael Lynch but adopted a more straightforward approach that defined both the beer and its consumers. The resulting campaign, "It's What's Inside," was introduced later in the year and included both television and radio spots. Cofounder and CEO James Koch expressed confidence in the new tag line, which appeared to be borne out by the brand's performance in 1998.

HISTORICAL CONTEXT

Koch, who owned 27 percent of the Boston Beer Company, emerged from a long family line of brewers. His great-great-grandfather Louis once owned a brewery in St. Louis that operated in the shadow of Anheuser-Busch. His father, Charles Joseph, Jr., worked as a brewmaster at several breweries in Cincinnati. Koch himself gave up a promising career in business to pursue the family dream of owning and operating his own brewery. At the time, in the early 1980s, Americans' taste in mass-marketed beers had drifted toward light, pale brews like Budweiser. Koch proposed to buck the tide by marketing a more full-bodied lager made of choice ingredients, a connoisseur's beer brewed in the Old World tradition.

Koch founded the Boston Beer Company in 1984, raising $400,000 from friends and business associates and exhausting his personal savings of $100,000. For his recipe Koch retrieved his great-great-grandfather's old beer formula from his father's attic in Cincinnati. For the label of his flagship brand, Koch chose to honor Samuel Adams, the American Revolutionary hero who had once worked as a soaker and drier of barley (not a "brewer," as stated on the label).

The early days of the Boston Beer Company were difficult ones. Many Boston-area distributors doubted that consumers would pay $6 per six-pack for an American beer. And so Koch and his "sales staff" (consisting in its entirety of Koch's former secretary Rhonda Kallman), traveled from tavern to tavern hawking Samuel Adams in person. Koch also entered his beer in the Great American Beer Festival and won the consumer preference poll. He built his early advertising campaign around the award, saturating newspapers and radio waves with the tag line "The Best Beer in America." The ads stressed the idea that Samuel Adams beer was brewed in small batches by Yankee craftsmen. "I'd had no idea whether we'd find 100 customers or a million," Koch declared.

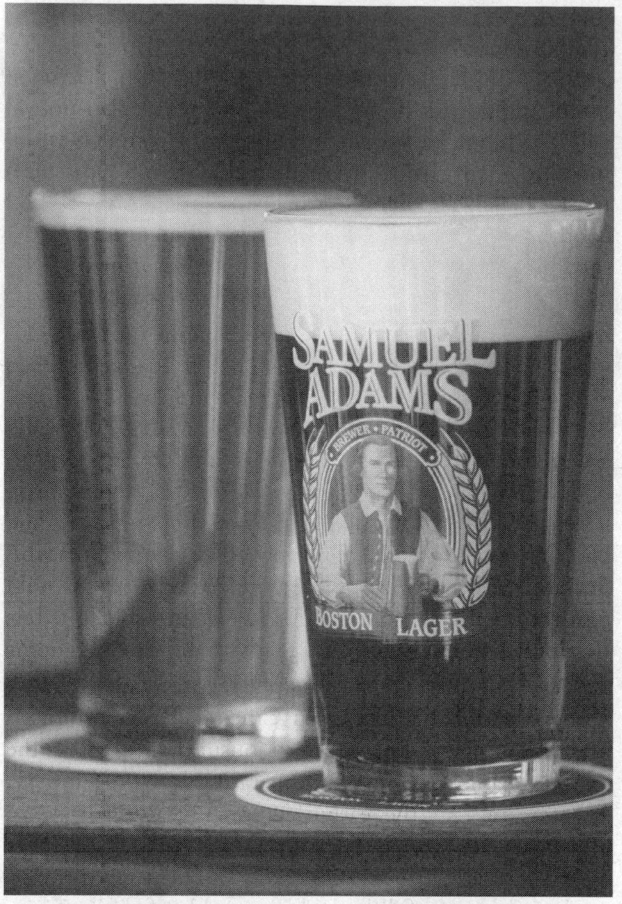

© DAVE BARTRUFF/CORBIS.

"I hoped to sell 5,000 barrels in five years, but we got to that goal in four months."

Once the company had posted those kinds of numbers, larger distributors began to show an interest. Samuel Adams beer became one of the first American specialty brews in decades to become a nationally distributed product. Annual sales of the Boston Beer Company grew at a 57 percent clip a year in the early 1990s. In 1996, 12 years after its launch, the company made $8.3 million in profits on sales of $214 million.

It was thus that the Boston Beer Company rose from obscurity to become one of America's leading craft brewers. The company eventually produced about 20 seasonal and year-round varieties of craft-brewed beers at its Boston and Cincinnati breweries, as well as through contracts with five others breweries across the United States. Each year nationwide it sold nearly 1.2 million barrels of lager (such as its flagship Samuel Adams Boston Lager), ales (in Oregon Original and Samuel Adams brands), and cider (Hard Core brand), and its brews were also distributed internationally.

In the mid-1990s, however, the market for craft brews began to slacken. Some analysts credited the slide to aggressive line and product extensions by companies like Boston Beer. Increased competition from the mass-market brewers, who marketed their own "craft brew" brands under names like Red Dog and Icehouse, also helped slow the growth of the segment. By this time even the best-known of the craft brews, Samuel Adams, had become a victim of diminishing investor expectations. Boston Beer's stock fell from a high of $32.50 in November 1995 to less than $10 in April 1998. The Samuel Adams advertising tag line, "All in due time," which attempted to equate the consumers and the beer, was criticized for being confusing. "We swung for the fences, and we missed," said one executive who worked on the campaign.

Koch initially laughed off some of the company's advertising miscues, saying, "If you brew a bad batch, you can drink your mistakes. In advertising, you suck it up in another way." In June 1998, however, after sales had continued to decline, Boston Beer initiated a two-month review of its advertising with the aim of replacing its longtime ad agency, Minneapolis-based Carmichael Lynch. New York's McCann-Erickson and Boston's Hill, Holliday, Connors, and Cosmopulos emerged as finalists in the competition, with McCann-Erickson named the winner of the estimated $12-$15 million account in August. The ad shop's first campaign for Samuel Adams lager, using the tag line "It's What's Inside," was unveiled in the autumn of 1998.

TARGET MARKET

The principal target market for Samuel Adams lager was young males. Beer industry research showed that 20 percent of American beer drinkers consumed about 80 percent of the beer produced domestically. Most of this 20 percent was composed of males aged 21 to 40. Craft beers like Samuel Adams were specifically targeted at a particular segment of this market, identified as "premium packaged lager trial lists." These consumers tried different brands but were not loyal to any particular one. Studies indicated that they made up about 12 percent of premium-packaged lager drinkers and accounted for 20 percent of volume. They were consumers who liked to keep up with the latest fashions in beer drinking and who believed that what they drank said a lot about them.

Boston Beer Company marketers also enjoyed success in the late 1990s at marketing their beer to women. In 1999 Samuel Adams became one of the first major beers to advertise during the television coverage of the NCAA women's basketball tournament. An ad aired during the telecasts of the final-four games represented a "major breakthrough" in beer advertising, according to

Bill Greer, director of media services at Mintz and Hoke advertising. And although Samuel Adams had a completely different profile than Budweiser or Miller, he said that the ad suggested that advertisers recognized that not only women watched women's basketball. "I think it's an evolutionary thing," Greer said. "And next year, it may be a revolution."

COMPETITION

In 1998 players in the tiny but influential craft beer market all drafted campaigns calling for new images, new promotions, and new market focuses. They did so in response to the overcrowding of the segment with an attendant sales slump. "The differentiation game has begun in earnest," declared Jerome Chicvara, marketing director for Full Sail Brewing Company.

According to the Institute for Beer Studies, as of 1998 there were about 1,250 small brewers in the United States, up 14 percent from 1996. Craft brewers, however, faced significant challenges in promoting their brands because they lacked the huge marketing budgets of the major brewers. Boston Beer Company, for example, spent a meager $6.1 million on advertising in 1996, according to Competitive Media Reporting.

The number two player in the craft brew segment, Pete's Brewing Company, embarked upon a major marketing makeover in 1998. Past ads had trumpeted Pete's brands as party beers without touting their quality. The brewer suffered an $8.9 million operating loss through the third quarter of 1997, however, prompting it to halt all consumer advertising and reevaluate its approach. In 1998 Pete's opted to escalate its use of public relations, introduce a golden ale, and eliminate weaker beers from its portfolio.

Full Sail Brewing Company opted for a different tack to set it apart from the competition. The West Coast specialty brewer used its 1998 ads to hammer home the message that Full Sail brews were full-bodied "big beers." The company spent an estimated $100,000 on print advertising for 1998, a fourfold increase over the previous year.

A third major Boston Beer competitor, Pyramid Ales, introduced its first concerted consumer ad effort in 1998, after years of focusing on trade publications. The brewer launched a $250,000 campaign in the San Francisco and other key West Coast markets. "We're reacting to the fact that the market is so overcrowded that [trade] marketing strategies are canceling each other out," said CEO George Hancock.

While Pyramid was expanding its advertising effort, the Maryland-based Frederick Brewing Company was pulling back and trying to use money more wisely after launching its first consumer campaign in 1997. During

THE EMPIRE STRIKES BACK

The ability of craft brewers like the Boston Beer Company to put a dent in the sales of the major mass-market brewers did not go unnoticed in the halls of Anheuser-Busch. Over the years the giant St. Louis-based brewer had tried to persuade wholesalers, who were often dependent on Budweiser sales, to stop selling specialty brews. The company also challenged Boston Beer's trademark for its Winter Lager just before the statute of limitations had expired.

But perhaps Anheuser-Busch's most concerted assault came in the summer of 1996, when America's number one brewer filed a complaint with the government arguing that Samuel Adams's labels were misleading. Boston Beer was a contract brewer, which meant that it hired bigger companies to help make its beer, but its labels noted only that the beer was "Brewed by Boston Beer Company, Boston, MA, and Under Special Agreement, Pittsburgh, PA." (The second city was the location of the contract brewer.)

Undaunted, Boston Beer's CEO, Jim Koch, defended his policy of not mentioning the contract brewer by name, insisting that to do so would give consumers the impression that Samuel Adams beer made, for example, at a Stroh's brewery was a Stroh's product. To which Francine Katz, an Anheuser-Busch vice president, countered, "How can you logically argue against a labeling standard that simply requires honesty?" Perhaps recognizing the logic of Katz's argument, Lucy Shaum, a spokesman for Boston Beer, conceded to an interviewer for *Beer and Beverage Monthly,* "Sure, we're jerking people's chains, but that's what advertising is all about, isn't it?"

While most consumers remained oblivious to the labeling flap, the controversy did, nevertheless, cost Koch's company. After an NBC news program broadcast a segment in October 1996 criticizing Boston Beer's labeling, the company's stock price fell 20 percent, the start of a protracted slide. Even so, Koch, who had about 95 percent of his net worth wrapped up in the stock, remained unbowed. "You don't create a whole new national market in the beer business by being frightened," he said. "Anheuser-Busch's campaign just makes us the underdog again."

1998 Frederick Brewing opted to focus its ad efforts on its brands' core markets in and around the District of Columbia. It earlier had run a far-flung campaign that reached into weaker markets such as Atlanta. "We're taking advertising to markets where we have the distribution to warrant it," said CEO Marjorie A. McGinnis.

MARKETING STRATEGY

The media budget for Samuel Adams's "It's What's Inside" campaign was split evenly between television and radio. Two 30-second ads were unveiled on national television, with three radio spots targeted to 23- to 35-year-old men. The ads fell into the category of so-called aspirational advertising, that is, ads depicting the consumers as they would like to be. In this case the ads were designed to appeal to young males' desire to live lives of danger, adventure, and intrigue. The product, Samuel Adams lager, was then associated with these qualities and, by extension, so was the consumer.

One of the best-known spots in the campaign, "Destiny," opened in black and white and was shot from the interior of a car traveling along a desolate country road. "As you get closer, your eyes get wider. Your heart beats faster," a male voice-over intoned over a musical backdrop. As the car rounded a curve, a big-city skyline came into view. "This is not gonna beat you. Oh, it's loud. And it's dirty. And it's big. But so are your plans. Hey John Boy. You ain't in Kansas anymore. From here on in, every day's gonna be a test." The spot then cut to a long "pour shot" of the amber beverage: "Those who pass deserve a great beer. Sam Adams. It's what's inside." The tag line, "It's what's inside," was created to refer to both the lager and the consumers who drank it, according to Koch. "The fundamental idea feels right to me. It's about the beer and the drinker and it evokes where we came from," he said. "In 1984, all we had was what was inside those bottles and we believed in our ourselves. These ads talk very much about that."

OUTCOME

Led in part by the "It's What's Inside" campaign, the Boston Beer Company enjoyed success in 1998. For the year barrels sold and net sales were 1,227,000 and $183.5 million, respectively, compared to 1,352,000 and $183.8 million in 1997. The company's gross profit margin for 1998 was 51.3 percent, up marginally from 51.0 percent in 1997. A confident Koch declared victory in his end-of-year statement to shareholders. "Despite the turmoil in the craft segment of the beer market and a modest erosion in volume, our leading market position and aggressive programs combined to produce very satisfactory operating results in 1998," he explained. "This performance continues to validate our strong business proposition."

FURTHER READING

Hwang, Suein. "McCann Gets Sammy." *Wall Street Journal,* August 4, 1998.

Warner, Judy. "Soul Searching for Samuel Adams." *Adweek,* November 2, 1998.

Robert Schnakenberg

Boston Market Corp.

14103 Denver W Pkwy.
Golden, Colorado 80401-4086
USA
Telephone: (303) 278-9500
Fax: (303) 216-5678
Web site: www.bostonmarket.com

EAT SOMETHING CAMPAIGN

OVERVIEW

NOTE: Since the initial appearance of this essay in the 1998 edition of *Major Marketing Campaigns Annual,* Boston Chicken Inc. changed its name to Boston Market Corp. The essay continues to refer to the company's former name, as that was the official name of the organization when the campaign was launched.

In the late 1990s Colorado-based Boston Chicken Inc. was one of the leaders in the burgeoning restaurant category of home meal replacement, or HMR. The term home meal replacement applied to restaurant-style food for taking home, including, of course, such traditional take-out options as pizza and burgers and fries. But many Americans began to draw the line at having that kind of meal too often. Consequently, a market emerged for more thoroughly prepared and nutritionally beneficent "comfort foods."

Boston Chicken, Inc. began franchising and operating retail food service stores under the brand name Boston Market. The restaurants, located in 38 states, offered home meal replacement in the form of comfort foods, which included rotisserie-roasted chicken, roast turkey, baked ham, and meat loaf, as well as fresh vegetables, salads, and other side dishes. By mid-1998 there were 1,149 Boston Market stores in 38 states and the District of Columbia, of which 936 were company owned. Boston Chicken also owned a majority interest in Einstein/Noah Bagel Corp., and its subsidiary company, Progressive Food Concepts, marketed a line of prepared foods via supermarkets.

Boston Market made its name in the home meal replacement category by offering dinner entrees. In January 1996, however, it expanded its line to attract the lunch crowd. It introduced a line of "Carver" sandwiches containing ham, turkey, or meat loaf. The next year saw the rollout of the Extreme Carver, a larger sandwich containing bacon and cheese in addition to meat. The marketing campaign for the Extreme Carver was accompanied by a coupon offer granting 20 or 25 percent off the new sandwiches. A series of television commercials was created by the Santa Monica, California, ad agency Suissa Miller. The new spots parodied commercials for other products, specifically the spare, artsy ads for Calvin Klein designer fragrances. Filmed in black and white, the spots starred the sardonic ESPN sports anchor Keith Olbermann (who appeared in color for comic effect). They were designed to capitalize on the sports maven's appeal among 18- to 29-year-old men, one of the key target markets for Extreme Carver sandwiches.

HISTORICAL CONTEXT

Boston Chicken was founded in 1988 by entrepreneur George Naddaff, one of the first men to see the potential of the burgeoning home food replacement industry. Brought up in Boston's South End by parents who emigrated from Lebanon, Naddaff was shining shoes at age 10 and went through the auto shop course at Brighton High School before learning that he was allergic to grease. He switched his career interests to sales, starting out peddling baby furniture to expectant parents in their homes and using leads provided by the manufacturer.

Naddaff began his franchising career in 1967, when he bought a regional franchise for Colonel Sanders' Kentucky Fried Chicken, opening 22 shops before selling the business in 1970. Having learned the fundamentals of business, he teamed with an early-childhood education specialist, Grace Mitchell, to start Living and Learning Centres Inc., a chain of child-care centers that grew to 48 locations in 10 years. They sold the chain in 1980 to Kinder-Care Learning Centers Inc. By that time Naddaff was involved with the start-up of VR Business Brokers Inc., which franchised local brokerages that listed small businesses for sale. Naddaff took the company public and sold 250 franchises, then sold the entire operation to a British group in 1987. The following year he used his venture capital connections to launch Boston Chicken, one of the first of the so-called home meal replacement franchises.

A spate of studies in the late 1990s confirmed that the home meal replacement trend that Naddaff foresaw was no fad. Consumers opted for a takeout dinner at home 61 percent more often than they did in the late 1980s, whereas they chose to eat dinner in a restaurant 4 percent less often, according to a 1995 NPD Group survey. "Time poverty" was the catalyst, and the underpinnings of the take-home trend seemed unlikely to change. In double-income families neither income earner had the time, energy, or desire to cook (or clean up after a meal). And while burger and pizza chains once satisfied Americans' need for carryout, fast-food ennui set in. Customers were seeking ever-changing variety and freshness for dinner.

Naddaff served as chairman and CEO of Boston Chicken from 1988 to 1992, when he sold the company to a group of executives from Blockbuster Entertainment. By 1996 the company had expanded to more than 1,000 stores across 38 states and was spending $90 million a year on advertising. Under a so-called "virtual advertising plan," the chain divided its creative work among three agencies, each commissioned to devise a campaign for individual Boston Market products. Suissa Miller was charged specifically with handling the ads for the Boston Carver sandwich line.

Suissa Miller's 1996 ad campaign "Don't Mess with Dinner" featured ordinary looking consumers searching for ways to feed their families home-cooked dinners with a minimum of fuss. In 1997, in order to target a more youthful crowd of sandwich enthusiasts, the company used wan models to spoof a popular series of Calvin Klein fragrance commercials. The campaign, called "Eat Something," proved successful in audience tests and with the targeted audience. "Don't Mess with Dinner" spots remained in use to promote the brand's line of Family Meals, but they increasingly took on the mocking tone of the "Eat Something" campaign. One such spot spoofed super hero television shows and movies. The commercial, called "Searchlight," features a harried mother trying to decide the best way to feed her family. She solves her problem only by flashing the giant image of a chicken into the night sky—much like Batman's "Bat Signal." Across town her husband picks up the signal and knows he must pick up Boston Market food for dinner.

TARGET MARKET

In general, Boston Market aimed to capture the business of time-pressed and cooking-shy consumers (many of whom had discretionary income to burn) who craved freshly prepared take-home meals that were a step up from traditional fast food. These consumers wanted the fruits of a chef's labor, but they wanted it without a wait. And they wanted to enjoy it in their own home.

With its line of Extreme Carver lunch sandwiches, introduced in 1997, Boston Market was specifically targeting young adult males, the most avid consumers of fast food. The accompanying ad campaign "Eat Something" was designed to appeal to this more cynical "Generation X" demographic through parody and the appearance of smart-aleck ESPN sports anchor Olbermann, who hosted the nightly *Sportscenter* sports highlight show.

COMPETITION

Boston Market in the late 1990s was one of the few restaurant chains catering to the home food replacement market. But that did not mean there was not vigorous competition to service harried consumers looking for home-cooked meals. Supermarkets were rushing in with expanded delis, packaged meals, rotisserie chicken, and sushi bars, blurring the lines separating fast-food emporiums, restaurants, and grocery stores. Feeding the trend further were specialty groceries and delis offering such items as tea-smoked duck, grilled portobello mushroom sandwiches on focaccia, and herb-roasted beef tenderloin with aioli.

Because many consumers wanted foods that they would cook themselves if they had the time, Boston

NEW MARKET MEANS NEW JARGON

Dinner patterns in America have changed rapidly. In the late 1990s people felt they had less and less time, and it seemed they did not want to spend lots of it making (or even planning for) dinner. As a result, many meals eaten at home were bought somewhere else, and food industry gurus have termed this practice "home meal replacement," or HMR. Not surprisingly, a whole litany of attendant marketing terms and acronyms began to spring up and have been flung across restaurant industry conference tables nationwide. They include: "Access Mode" (the way a consumer chooses to use a restaurant—dining in, delivery, takeout, and drive-through are access modes); "Center-of-the-Plate Protein" (the food portion that generally defines what is being eaten—mostly meat and poultry); "Daypart" (most consumers call this "lunch" if it occurs around noon, but the industry prefers calling it "afternoon daypart"); "QSR" (or quick-service restaurant, better known as a fast-food establishment); "HFFU" (pronounced hoofoo, the acronym stands for "heavy fast-food user," which tended to be young and male); and "Share of Stomach" (the ultimate goal of restaurant industry operators, this signified the portion of foods from restaurants and supermarkets that occupied a consumer's stomach).

Market's menu leaned heavily toward American comfort foods. But many industry observers expected the home meal replacement market to take a turn for the ethnic and adventurous in the first decade of the twenty-first century.

Newer home meal replacement players wanted to go beyond Boston Market-style carryout in hopes of stealing more grocery sales from supermarkets. Joining the category in Dallas was Eatzi's Market and Bakery, an 8,000-square-foot establishment that was a cross between a gourmet grocery store and take-home deli/restaurant. The Eatzi's experiment has attracted plenty of customers and attention.

MARKETING STRATEGY

Boston Market's "Eat Something" spots were part of a trend toward parody advertising that gained steam in the mid-1990s. Commercials such as Sprite's "Obey Your Thirst" drew their comic force from mocking the pomposity of other, more serious ads, usually for unrelated and noncompetitive products. These commercials attempted to place the mocking company or brand on the other side of the media "wall," commenting on the pretensions of advertising. They were primarily aimed at hip, young consumers who may have felt jaded or too media savvy to be fooled by commercials that erect a farcical image or pitch a product's miraculous effects. In the case of the "Eat Something" spots, the commercials poke fun at the pomposity of designer fragrance campaigns.

The first spot in this Boston Market campaign, "Eat Something," was filmed in black and white by director John Mastromonaco. The 30-second piece features stringy-haired, emaciated-looking young models affecting bored, vacant stares along a rocky shoreline. "Emptiness, emptiness," moans one such waif. "How can I fill this void of emptiness?" Emerging from out of nowhere, sports anchor Olbermann (who appears in full color) offers one possible answer: "Eat something!" What is the "burning from within" that the world-weary models feel? "It's called hunger," Olbermann quips. He then suggests that the models fatten up on the Extreme Carver sandwich, with its "ooey gooey" cheese sauce.

In another "Eat Something" commercial, entitled "Angst Band," a grunge rock band is shown rehearsing one of its downbeat songs. "I feel empty, nothing inside," the singer keens. Olbermann then enters, advising: "Hey Mozart, eat something!" Additional spots in this campaign spoof daytime soap operas and the relationship between professional athletes and their agents. All the spots rely on the element of surprise to turn consumer expectations upside down, while at the same time skewering the overly thin look that was prevalent among models.

The strategy was based on the premise that consumers tended to tune out straightforward advertising messages in an age of media overload. "Humorously portraying universally recognized cultural icons is an effective way to break through the intense media clutter in today's marketplace," said Bill McDonald, Boston Market's chief marketing officer. "Consumers relate to our having some fun with common images from popular culture." Having a laugh at other advertisers' expense was not, however, the only goal of the ads. Added McDonald: "Our new advertisements are humorous, but also deliver an important message to consumers that Boston Market stores offer quick, quality meal solutions for a variety of occasions." Trey Hall, Boston Market's vice president of marketing, stressed the importance of the ads in positioning Boston Market products as fun and enjoyable.

OUTCOME

Boston Market's "Eat Something" commercials proved fairly popular with consumers but were judged not to be very effective. A *USA Today* poll found that just over 25 percent of those polled liked the spots a lot. Only 14 percent deemed them "effective." The "Eat Something" commercials did prove to be highly effective at sticking in the minds of consumers, however; audience testing elicited recall in 95 percent of viewers who saw the spots. Popularity was slightly higher among Boston Market's targeted group of consumers, males between 18 and 29 years old; 31 percent of those in this age range polled by *USA Today* reported they liked the ads a lot, compared with 26 percent among 30- to 49-year-old consumers.

Among industry observers and insiders, the spots were given credit for their humor but were generally faulted on strategic grounds. Writing in *Advertising Age* magazine, columnist Bob Garfield conceded the ads were very funny. "Not since Marshall McLuhan popped out of the movie line in Annie Hall to deflate the academic blowhard has there been a more welcome intrusion into our suspension of disbelief," Garfield opined. He also found the casting of Olbermann inspired. Garfield, however, criticized the strategy behind the ads, calling "Eat Something" "a very good commercial for a very bad marketing idea." "Boston Market has neither the number nor the character of locations to compete with the sandwich slingers of the world," Garfield groused. "So why, for the sake of whatever marginal growth they might enjoy by attracting a few hungry teenagers, dilute the brand meaning, brand message, and media budget?"

Competitors in the fast-food sector were no more kind. Scott Lippitt, an account manager at fast-food giant Arby's, cast doubt on the idea of spoofing products outside the comfort food category. "What point is Boston Market trying to make," Lippitt complained to *Shoot* magazine, "other than saying, 'We're relevant to this younger target [market]?' The last time I looked, people weren't deciding to make a choice between spending money on eating at Boston Market or buying perfume."

FURTHER READING

Cuneo, Alice Z. "Boston Market Shifts Billings to Suissa Miller." *Advertising Age,* July 28, 1997.

Enrico, Dottie. "Boston Market Spoofs Klein, 'Eat Something' Is Popular, if Not Effective Advice." *USA Today,* June 30, 1997.

Garfield, Bob. "Boston Market Gets Laughs, Misses Point." *Advertising Age,* March, 1997.

Oberlag, Reginald. "It's Spot vs. Spot as Commercials Cannibalize Their Own for Impact." *Shoot,* May 30, 1997.

Reidy, Chris. "New Extreme Carver Ads Slice Up Calvin Klein Images." *The Boston Globe,* March 2, 1997.

Reuteman, Rob. "Use of Coupons Cut Boston Chicken's Dinner Sales; Boston Chicken's Beck Blames Self for Laying an Egg." *Rocky Mountain News,* June 8, 1997.

Robert Schnakenberg

Brigham's, Inc.

30 Mill Street
Arlington, Massachusetts 02476
USA
Telephone: (781) 648-9000
Fax: (781) 646-0507
Web site: www.brighams.com

REVERSE THE CURSE CAMPAIGN

OVERVIEW

At the beginning of the twenty-first century Brigham's, Inc., well known in New England for its ice cream and restaurants, looked to expand its product line to include the kinds of chunky ice cream flavors (with products such as candy bars mixed in) made popular by Ben & Jerry's. The first attempt was a flavor called "The Big Dig," but three years passed before the company was ready for a second launch. In 2003, as part of a 90th-anniversary promotion, Brigham's sponsored a contest to name a new flavor. The winning entry, revealed in April 2004, was "Reverse the Curse." The name was a reference to the supposed curse on the Boston Red Sox baseball team, which had not won the World Series since trading the legendary Babe Ruth to the New York Yankees.

The campaign to introduce the new flavor operated on a modest $250,000 budget and ran from April through late October 2004. It consisted of radio spots announced by a Red Sox player, print ads, a billboard, and in-store posters. The crux of the campaign, however, was a series of promotional events, which garnered a great deal of free media because the New England region that year was fascinated more than ever by the exploits of the Red Sox and anything associated with the club.

To the delight of Brigham's, the Red Sox won the World Series in 2004, and the curse was lifted. The ice cream was then renamed "Curse Reversed." As a result of good fortune and strong marketing work, which was recognized by the dairy industry, Reverse the Curse became Brigham's most successful product launch.

HISTORICAL CONTEXT

Brigham's was a well-entrenched New England brand at the start of the twenty-first century. The company was known both for its chain of restaurants, which had served Brigham's-brand ice cream for decades, and for its premium supermarket ice cream, which debuted in 1983. At its peak in the mid-1980s Brigham's operated more than 100 restaurants, but prepacked supermarket ice cream increasingly became its main source of revenue. In addition, the Elan brand of frozen yogurt was acquired to bring the company in line with the tastes of modern consumers. More importantly, Roger Theriault, appointed CEO of Brigham's in the mid-1990s, was able to complete the turnaround and transform the company from one that was merely holding its own into one that was actually profitable.

Brigham's best-selling flavor of ice cream—and one that was very much a New England tradition—was vanilla; it accounted for about one-third of all sales. While Brigham's Vanilla Ice Cream remained a favorite, the marketplace since the mid-1980s had seen an influx of ice creams that came in flavors with unusual ingredients mixed in, a trend that was first popularized by the Vermont-based company Ben & Jerry's. To stay current Brigham's introduced Big Dig, a vanilla ice cream with brownie pieces, caramel swirls, and chocolate chunks mixed in; the name played on the nickname of Boston's long-term Central Artery highway project. The flavor enjoyed a successful launch, but Brigham's did not follow up with any new flavors, instead turning its attention to ice cream bars and the expansion of its geographic reach.

In fall 2003 the company was approaching its 90th birthday, and it commemorated the occasion by holding a contest to concoct and name a new ice cream flavor. A large number of entries paid tribute to the Boston Red Sox, New England's highly popular Major League Baseball team. It was also no surprise that many of these names referred to the legendary "Curse of the Bambino" that supposedly afflicted the Red Sox; the team had not won a World Series championship since 1918, when, as a star pitcher and part-time slugger, Babe Ruth (George Herman Ruth, also referred to as "the Bambino") played a prominent role. Strapped for cash, the team sold the Babe to the New York Yankees in the winter of 1919. Ruth gave up pitching except for a rare mound appearance and proceeded to revolutionize the sport as a home-run hitter and its biggest star. While the Red Sox lapsed into mediocrity, the Yankees, which before adding Ruth had played second fiddle to the New York Giants, became the dominant team in baseball for the rest of the century. To explain their team's fall from grace, Red Sox fans created the myth that the Boston team was cursed because of the sale of Babe Ruth to the Yankees, and many nourished a comforting sense of fatalism even as they cheered on their team. More than one entry to the Brigham's contest offered the name "Reverse the Curse." The company selected the best of the accompanying recipes: Brigham's vanilla ice cream mixed with chocolate-covered peanuts (representing baseballs), caramel cups (representing bases), and swirls of Brigham's popular fudge sauce. The selection was made in secret, and only those with a need to know were told, while a marketing campaign to launch the new flavor was developed.

TARGET MARKET

Brigham's traditional target audience was mothers aged 24 to 54, because they were the people who did most of the grocery shopping and were likely to make the decision to purchase a Brigham's product. For the "Reverse the Curse" campaign the focus was broadened to include adults in general, although a baseball promotion was sure to attract the attention of children as well. Baseball in New England was followed by a wide range of people, from celebrities such as author Stephen King and actor Matt Damon to firemen and nurses. The ad agency aimed the campaign at a broad audience. The billboard that Brigham's rented near Fenway Park (the home ballpark of the Red Sox) off the Massachusetts Turnpike was seen by all demographics, and the radio spots were played on eight stations, each with a different format that appealed to every type of listener, from classical music to sports-talk radio. Brigham's was ultimately looking to reach anybody who liked ice cream, a market that cut across all demographics.

> ### NO, NO, HARRY!
>
> The Boston Red Sox owner who sold baseball star Babe Ruth to the New York Yankees in 1919, thereby earning the eternal enmity of Boston fans, was theatrical agent Harry Frazee, best known for backing the musical *No, No, Nanette* (1925). He supposedly sold off his star players to cover his theatrical losses.

COMPETITION

As a premium brand that cost more than most ice creams, Brigham's faced direct competition from Ben & Jerry's and Breyers, but after 90 years in business it was well entrenched in its market. Brigham's did not directly compete with another venerable New England brand, Hood, which concentrated on selling high volumes of less-expensive ice cream. Brigham's did, however, see Hood as an impediment to forging a link with the Red Sox. Hood had a long-standing relationship with the team, including some ownership ties. Hood was the only ice cream sold at Fenway Park, where the Red Sox played home games, and Brigham's was prevented from advertising on the park's huge message board. Brigham's was not even allowed to offer samples within the several-block pedestrian zone that surrounded the ballpark. Nevertheless, by introducing Reverse the Curse, conducting baseball-related promotions, leasing a highway billboard outside Fenway Park, and hiring one of the Red Sox players to serve as the spokesperson, Brigham's was able to outflank Hood to reach the Red Sox audience. While the Brigham's campaign could have been interpreted as a direct challenge to Hood, according to Brigham's vice president of marketing, Darryln Leikauskas, the "Reverse the Curse" campaign took little note of the competition. "It wasn't about them, it was about us," she said in a 2006 interview.

MARKETING STRATEGY

An initial goal of the "Reverse the Curse" campaign was to build up interest by keeping the new flavor a secret until the campaign was launched in April 2004 with the start of the baseball season. While manufacturing plans were made to produce "Reverse the Curse," Leikauskas told only a handful of people about the contest winner. Because packaging had to be ordered in January, Brigham's had to share the secret with a Maryland vendor, but no one that far way was interested in leaking the news. Brigham's sent samples (using generic packaging) to a variety of New England–affiliated sports and entertainment celebrities, asking for their comments in exchange for a cash donation to their favorite charity. They included actors Ben Affleck and Matt Damon, comedians Jay Leno and Denis Leary, football player Doug Flutie, and basketball player Dave Cowens. The campaign also included print ads in yearbooks produced by minor league teams in Lowell, Massachusetts, and Pawtucket, Rhode Island. Because of production deadlines, ads had to be supplied before the announcement of the new flavor. For the first editions, therefore, the ad depicted a group of the company's "all-star" flavors. A blank silhouette where Reverse the Curse was to be located offered the caption "Future Hall-of-Famer."

The campaign elements included radio spots, print ads, a billboard, in-store posters, and promotional events. Given the limited budget of $250,000, the campaign relied heavily on the promotional events, which garnered free attention from newspapers and television. The campaign kicked off in April 2004, shortly after the start of the new baseball season. Shipments of the product were timed to begin April 27, the anniversary of Babe Ruth Day, when, in 1947, Ruth was celebrated in every baseball park in the United States and Japan. To play further on the Babe Ruth curse, Brigham's conducted another event on May 13, making the case that ritualists often attempted to break curses on the unlucky 13th. A pair of psychic advisers who several months earlier had performed a ceremony at Fenway Park to undo the curse were enlisted to do the same at the Brigham's ice cream plant. A public rally was held the same day at a Brigham's Restaurant in Arlington, Massachusetts, at which a Babe Ruth impersonator appeared and offered attendees the first complimentary samples of Reverse the Curse. Next, Brigham's held a contest that was launched on a popular morning radio show: die-hard Red Sox fans were asked to send E-mails describing what they were willing to do to help the team break the curse. The winner was a young woman, a strict vegetarian, who offered for the sake of the team to eat 86 hot dogs, representing the number of years since Boston's last World Series triumph. She fulfilled her pledge on the afternoon of September 26, before a critical game against the Yankees at end of the season. (She was ultimately helped by family, friends, and other supporters in eating the hot dogs.) During the baseball postseason Brigham's also hosted an elementary-school rally in Dedham, Massachusetts, which included a surprise Reverse the Curse ice cream party, an event that received a good deal of local media attention.

For the advertising portion of the campaign Brigham's hired Boston-area Rattle Advertising. Elements included in-store signage and radio, print, and outdoor advertisements. The biggest commitment was to radio, which also included the largest expense of the campaign: hiring a Red Sox player to serve as a spokesperson. Because of the small budget Brigham's settled on one of the team's support players, first baseman Kevin Millar, who was nevertheless very popular with fans. He recorded a 60-second spot that was also edited into a 10-second version. It played during June, July, and August on eight area stations that offered a wide variety of formats; for instance, WMJX played soft rock, WBMX offered contemporary hits, and WCRB was a classical music station. The station that received the most ad dollars, however, was WEEI, a sports-talk radio station. In addition Millar made some promotional appearances.

Print ads were limited to the yearbooks of the two minor league teams that Brigham's had already been sponsoring. An ad also appeared on the back of a widely distributed summer guide of local events as well as within the pages of programs for the concert series at the Tweeter Center for the Performing Arts in Boston and other entertainment events. The headline of the ads read, "The Ice Cream of the Eternal Optimist." The lone billboard of the campaign was leased for the month of June. In stores Brigham's hung posters touting Reverse the Curse and featuring a nostalgic baseball scene.

OUTCOME

With the Red Sox trailing the New York Yankees three games to zero in the best-of-seven American League Championship Series of 2004, it appeared that Boston fans would have to suffer with their curse for yet another season. Then, in a dramatic reversal of fortune, the team rebounded to win four straight games and vanquish its hated rivals; it was the first time in baseball history that a team had recovered from such a deficit. The Red Sox then won the World Series, ending the so-called curse. From the start of the "Reverse the Curse" campaign, Brigham's had promised to change the name of the ice cream when the curse was lifted. It now hastily put together another contest to rename the flavor. In the meantime large stickers were applied to the in-store posters, proclaiming "Curse Reversed." It also became the eventual winner, saving the company some money on redoing the signage.

In large part because of the Red Sox's dream season, Reverse the Curse became the best product launch in Brigham's history. For the year it ranked number five in package sales for the company, representing 6 percent of all Brigham's sales, despite being available for less than the entire year. The Big Dig, in contrast, ranked number eight during its first full year, with 4.4 percent of sales. There was no doubt that the team's success fed into the success of the ice cream, but the marketing campaign behind the product was also an important element. The work was recognized by the International Dairy Foods Association, which presented Brigham's with a pair of awards: Best Overall Public Relations Campaign for the entire 90th-anniversary effort and Best Overall Mixed Media Campaign for "Reverse the Curse" in particular.

The campaign also brought with it benefits that were not easily detected. According to Leikauskas, "Reverse the Curse" changed Brigham's image from a stodgy brand to one that was more fun and innovative, helping to pave the way for future product launches.

FURTHER READING

Bulkeley, William M., and Mark Maremont. "Reversal of Fortune." *Wall Street Journal,* October 25, 2004, p. A1.

Jewell, Mark. "Red Sox Title Reverses Marketing of Curse." *Lawrence (KS) Journal-World,* October 30, 2004.

"Pitching to the Red Sox Nation." *BusinessWeek Online,* October 4, 2004. Available from <http://www.businessweek.com/smallbiz/content/oct2005/sb20051004_642313.htm>

"Play Ball." *Prepared Foods,* July 2004, p. 67.

Robinson, Alan. "'Curse' Reversed!" *Frozen Food Age,* September 2005, p. 10.

Silverstein, Clara. "Ice Cream, Ale and More Let Sox Fans Savor Success." *Boston Herald,* May 26, 2004, p. 44.

Ed Dinger

Budget Rent A Car System, Inc.

6 Sylvan Way
Parsippany, New Jersey 07054
USA
Telephone: (973) 496-3500
Fax: (973) 496-7999
Web site: www.budget.com

■■■

UP YOUR BUDGET CAMPAIGN

OVERVIEW

In 2005 Budget Rent A Car System, Inc., a key unit, with Avis, of the Cendant Car Rental Group, made its first foray into advertising on blogs (website digests typically maintained by one person or a small group of people). Blogs often focused on specific topics and thus attracted niche audiences, and they were known for their conversational tone and opinionated content. With a collective readership estimated at more than 30 million in 2005 and with extremely low advertising rates compared to TV, print, and traditional online placements, blogs represented an exciting, if relatively untested, opportunity for marketers. The Budget campaign, called "Up Your Budget," ran in October and November 2005 and represented one of the most notable marketing uses of this new medium to that date.

At the center of "Up Your Budget" was a series of treasure hunts in 16 American cities that took place during the campaign's four-week run. Information about the treasure hunts, each of which offered a cash prize of $10,000, was accessible only at the website www.upyourbudget.com, which took the form of a blog, and contest participants were enlisted in the further creation of the site's content. The event was advertised with flash-animation cartoons placed on 177 of the most popular blogs of the time; those placements cost approximately $20,000 to run, bringing the campaign's total budget to approximately $180,000. This amount was less than the cost of airing a single commercial on a top prime-time TV program. There was no off-line publicity of the event.

The campaign was well received within the realm of blogs (the so-called blogosphere), and www.upyourbudget.com drew more than 100,000 unique visitors over the four weeks that the contests ran. While the Budget campaign was believed to point the way toward the future of blog advertising, Cendant executives acknowledged the difficulty of judging whether a blog campaign was a marketing success or not, given the medium's newness and its dissimilarity to traditional marketing channels. Nevertheless, Budget planned to continue its blog-centered marketing efforts.

HISTORICAL CONTEXT

Founded in 1958 as a car-rental agency targeting value-conscious travelers, Budget Rent A Car expanded rapidly over the next several decades. In the 1980s and 1990s the company changed hands twice, and in 2002 it was acquired by Cendant Corporation, a global group of companies concentrated in the travel and real-estate industries. Cendant also owned the car-rental company Avis, a key component, with Budget, of the Cendant Car Rental Group.

In the 1990s and 2000s the advertising industry found its primary communication models threatened by a convergence of trends that were reshaping consumers' relationships to media outlets. Among the most noticeable of these trends was the increasing importance of the Internet to consumers' business, personal, and social lives. The Internet both upset traditional notions of marketing and offered an abundance of new advertising possibilities. One promising new outlet for online advertising was the blogosphere, the collective world of online blogs. A blog (the word was short for Weblog) was a website typically created by one person or a small group of people as a forum for personal expression or discussion on a particular topic (e.g., U.S. politics, contemporary literature, or celebrity gossip), with frequently updated postings whose content was often derived from and/or linked to other websites. Because bloggers, as those who maintained blogs were called, were subject to few if any institutional restraints, blogs were often characterized by their opinionated and irreverent approach to topics treated more cautiously by the mainstream media.

Blogs' growing influence on American culture was initially felt most keenly in the realm of politics. A 2002 post on the blog *Talking Points* led the mainstream media to scrutinize racially problematic comments made by Senate Majority Leader Trent Lott at a private party; the scrutiny eventually resulted in Lott's resignation from the leadership post. For the 2004 U.S. presidential election, moreover, organizers of both major American parties blanketed political blogs with campaign advertisements, underscoring the wider marketing potential of the emerging media outlet. The interrelated system of links characteristic of blogs—bloggers typically offered links to their own favorite blogs, so that the most popular blogs could have hundreds of so-called "inbound" links—meant that the medium especially lent itself to viral marketing, or marketing that used social networks to spread messages in a way that recalled the spread of viruses. By the end of 2004 it was clear that blogs, though they were not individually organs of the mainstream media, had certainly arrived in the consciousness of mainstream America: dictionary publisher Merriam-Webster declared "blog" its "Word of the Year" for 2004 (based on the number of times it was looked up in its online database), and a study conducted in November 2004 by the Pew Internet & American Life Project predicted that, by the new year, more than 30 million Americans would be readers of blogs.

TARGET MARKET

"Up Your Budget" attempted to lure a cross-section of the blog-reading populace to www.upyourbudget.com, itself a blog that served as the home base for the 16-city treasure hunt that was the campaign's focal point. Ads directing blog readers to www.upyourbudget.com ran on 177 blogs, including blogs focused on new technology, celebrity gossip, media affairs, and life in specific urban centers. Though individual blogs had their own niche audiences, blogs in general tended to attract young, technology-savvy consumers, and Budget saw a blog-focused advertising campaign as a way of linking itself with attributes that might differentiate it in an industry not typically defined by fierce brand loyalty. "We really wanted to try something new and different for our brand," the Cendant Car Rental Group's executive vice president of marketing, Scott Deaver, explained to *New Media Age* (an ad-industry magazine focusing on new media). "We had heard about the power of viral marketing and wanted to see if this was a way to cut through the clutter and do something totally new."

The potential to imbue a brand with coolness via a blog-focused advertising campaign, however, did not come without substantial risk. Bloggers and blog readers could be a tough audience for the uninitiated. Not only were the proprietors of blogs themselves relatively uninhibited, but also blogs by definition solicited comments from readers. "It's very easy to mess up because the space is very vocal," Steve Hall of the advertising blog *Adrants* told *New Media Age.* "If you don't blog, it's very likely you'll look stupid entering the space without an in-depth knowledge of it. Anyone interested in doing something in the space should work with a blogger." Budget thus enlisted blogger, author, and consultant B.L. Ochman for the campaign. Ochman was responsible for selecting the blogs on which the ads appeared and, along with the Impax Marketing Group of Philadelphia, helping to craft the campaign's overall strategy and content.

COMPETITION

With 30 percent of the market at the top 180 airports in the world, the Hertz Corporation was the leading car-rental company by a wide margin as of 2004. Hertz was more expensive than most other car-rental companies, but it was also perceived as having superior services; during the late twentieth century, accordingly, it was the most popular rental-car brand among corporate travelers. Hertz advertising campaigns in the early 2000s, however, included efforts to appeal to those who traveled on behalf of small businesses and who tended to be more budget-conscious than their corporate counterparts. After becoming a wholly owned subsidiary of Ford Motor Company in 2001, Hertz advertising often promoted Ford cars. An agreement extending this practice through 2010, under the terms of which Ford supplied half of Hertz's advertising budget, was projected to continue

HOW MUCH DO THEY CHARGE?

Rates for ad space on blogs varied at the time that "Up Your Budget" ran. In general the rates depended not just on the number of readers a blog attracted but also on the degree to which specific target markets were drawn to particular blogs. For instance, a celebrity-gossip blog might have a daily readership of 200,000 or more but charge weekly prices for ad space of only a few hundred dollars because of the muddied demographics of its broad readership. A more tightly focused and lucrative target group, however, was worth much more to advertisers even if the blog's readership was only 10,000. That said, the most popular of all blogs (as measured by the number of inbound links driving readers from other blogs to their sites) were generally also the most sought-after spaces for advertisers. The technology-focused *Boing Boing,* for instance, averaged 1.7 million readers monthly as of early 2006 and charged $8,000 a week for premium ad space.

even as Ford divested itself of its Hertz holdings in late 2005.

Beginning in 2002 car-rental companies moved increasingly large amounts of money into Internet advertising. This trend was especially evident among Budget's most direct competitors, those companies catering to value-conscious consumers, such as Thrifty car rental, part of the Dollar Thrifty Automotive Group. In 2002 Thrifty directed 25 percent of its total $9.8 million budget to the Internet and increased that percentage substantially in the following year. "The [I]nternet caters at this point to the value shopper and our brands are very well suited to that," Scott Anderson, Dollar Thrifty's senior executive vice president for global marketing and franchising, told *Advertising Age.* Thrifty's website experienced traffic increases that outpaced those of the other major brands in 2003.

MARKETING STRATEGY

The centerpiece of "Up Your Budget" was a series of treasure hunts held in 16 American cities—4 cities per week over the course of four weeks—between mid-October and mid-November 2005. The prize for individual winners in each city was $10,000, for a total prize package of $160,000. To win the prize contestants logged onto www.upyourbudget.com for daily clues and videos that helped them identify first the individual cities in question and then a location within each city where a yellow sticker had been placed. The first contestant in each city to find the sticker, call a toll-free number printed on it, and provide video or photographic proof of the discovery was the winner. There was also a treasure-hunters' blog linked to the site, where participants could submit their own hints or ideas about the official clues as well as report on their experiences.

In addition to the $160,000 in prizes, Budget spent approximately $20,000 on advertising placed solely on blogs. The advertisements, meant to drive traffic to www.upyourbudget.com, were simple flash-animated cartoons created by one of the world's best-known bloggers, Hugh Macleod, whose own blog was called *Gaping Void.* The images were of semihuman figures making humorous gestures and faces, and they were paired with copy such as "The Adventure Begins etc. etc." or "Hunt the Treasure... like it was a Wild Animal."

The exceedingly low price of advertising on blogs relative to TV, print, and mainstream online sites—Budget's total spending on the campaign was less than the cost of a 30-second spot on a highly rated prime-time TV show—made them attractive to marketers, but the medium's capacity for effective brand communication was still largely speculative. Among the campaign's more obvious goals of driving sales and building the Budget brand was that of measuring blogs' capacity to rival traditional marketing. "I wanted to promote 'Up Your Budget' only through bloggers, advertise only on blogs and let it accelerate virally from there," B.L. Ochman explained to *New Media Age.* "I wanted to prove that we could operate entirely without traditional media and still build brand awareness with a campaign that wasn't overly commercial." Budget did not even announce the campaign with an official press release. News of the campaign was first reported by blogs, including *Adrants, Boing Boing,* and *MarketingVox.*

One of the defining risks of viral marketing was the relinquishing of control over the brand's message, and this was a new experience for Budget's marketers. Scott Deaver told *New Media Age,* "To be asked to sit back and let the viral do its job was a complete leap of faith for us." Not only was it impossible to control the specific nature of the messages being spread virally, but because of the uncensored nature of blogs, the brand also risked being linked to controversial content.

OUTCOME

"Up Your Budget" was well received in the blogosphere, generating hundreds of blog posts and more than

100,000 unique visits (Web visits made by users from different Web addresses, excluding repeat visitors and thereby giving a more accurate sense of audience size) to www.upyourbudget.com over the four weeks of the campaign. The blog pages on which ads for the treasure hunt appeared were viewed 19.9 million times, resulting in approximately 60,000 click-throughs to www.upyourbudget.com; this meant that in the field of blog advertising the campaign was one of the most successful at driving online traffic to an advertised site. Thousands of people signed up to participate in the contest and to create content for the Budget treasure-hunter's blog, an unprecedented feat for a commercial blog to that date. Nevertheless, Deaver expressed ambivalence about the approach in an interview with the *New York Times.* "[T]he jury's still out . . . I'd be lying if I said I know what to measure to determine success . . . the real determination is, what do we learn? Are we smarter when we do it next time?" At the conclusion of "Up Your Budget," Budget announced that it would hold another such contest in 2006.

FURTHER READING

"Ad Blogging: Blogging in the US: Budget Car Rental." *New Media Age,* February 2, 2006.

Beirne, Mike. "Budget Rent A Car Takes Detour into Blogosphere." *Brandweek,* November 28, 2005.

"Budget Launches Blog-Based, Sixteen City Treasure Hunt." *Adrants,* October 24, 2005. Available from <http://www.adrants.com/2005/10/budget-launches-blogbased-sixteen-city.php>

"Budget Rent A Car Launches Blog-Focused Treasure Hunt Campaign." *MarketingVox,* October 24, 2005. Available from <http://www.marketingvox.com/archives/2005/10/24/budget_rent_a_car_launches_blogfocused_treasure_hunt_campaign/index.php>

Elliott, Stuart. "Placing Ads in Some Surprising Spaces." *New York Times,* November 25, 2005.

Halliday, Jean. "Car Renters Flock to Internet." *Advertising Age,* October 27, 2003.

Thompson, Clive. "The Haves and Have-Nots of the Blogging Boom." *New York Magazine,* February 20, 2006.

Mark Lane

Bureau of Engraving and Printing

14th and C Streets SW
Washington, D.C. 20228
USA
Telephone: (202) 874-3019
Web site: www.moneyfactory.gov

THE NEW COLOR OF MONEY CAMPAIGN

OVERVIEW

With the availability of digital technology such as scanners and high-quality color printers, the ability of counterfeiters to produce excellent facsimiles of U.S. currency forced the U.S. Treasury to introduce new note designs on a more regular basis. In addition, high-tech security measures had to be developed to counteract the advances made by counterfeiters. In 2003 a new $20 bill—featuring new colors and graphics as well as anticounterfeiting devices such as watermarks and embedded security strips—was ready to be introduced to the public. Public relations firm Burson-Marsteller was hired to take charge of a marketing campaign to unveil the new twenty and create a smooth transition when the notes entered the economy.

The $32 million campaign was a multipronged effort seeking to reach as many people in the United States as possible. In addition to using materials such as posters, brochures, and training videos aimed at alerting cashiers to the new security measures, "The New Color of Money" tried to reach a mass audience through entertainment channels, in particular television. The campaign included television spots, but it also relied on product placements, akin to the marketing of consumer goods. The new $20 bill was highlighted on television game shows as well as on prime-time dramas. It became the subject of conversations on morning news programming and of jokes by late-night comedians. The twenty also appeared on billboards, atop taxi cabs, in subway cars, and on Internet ads.

The "New Color of Money" campaign came to a close after the new $20 bill was formally unveiled in October 2002, accompanied by ceremonies staged across the country. The campaign achieved a great deal of recognition for the twenty with the general public. The transition was not without some bumps, however, nor did it lack critics who questioned the need to spend tax dollars on something people had no choice but to use.

HISTORICAL CONTEXT

The United States government had always taken steps to thwart forgery of its currency, in large measure to its experience in breaking away from the British; as part of its war effort Britain counterfeited the new Continental currency to make it worthless and wreck the economy of the fledgling republic. In about 1820, as an example of an early countermeasure, copper printing plates were replaced with steel ones because they produced uniform engravings and allowed for more complicated patterns on banknotes, thus complicating the task of counterfeiting. Nevertheless, counterfeiters continued to ply their trade, aided by the lack of a uniform currency. By the time of the Civil War some 1,600 state banks were issuing their own bills, resulting in about 7,000 varieties of notes,

© Joseph Sohm; Visions of America/Corbis

which made the task of determining real from fake all the more difficult. The Secret Service, today known for its role in protecting the president of the United States, was actually formed in 1865 to thwart counterfeiting. It was not until 30 years later that its agents began moonlighting as bodyguards for President Cleveland.

A common way to deter counterfeiting in the twentieth century was to change the design of the notes regularly. Most countries altered patterns every 15 to 20 years, although the United States tended to wait longer. By the 1990s, however, new technology made the job of the counterfeiter much easier, forcing the U.S. government to begin changing the design of its notes on a regular basis, roughly every seven years. In 1996 new $100 notes were introduced, followed by $50 notes in 1997, $20 notes in 1998, and $5 and $10 notes in 2000. The U.S. Department of the Treasury hired public-relations firm Burson-Marsteller in 1996 to spearhead a worldwide public education campaign to introduce the newly designed currency.

In 2002 Burson-Marsteller was hired again, this time to introduce the new colorized $20 bill, which would be followed by other denominations. The most noticeable changes to the new $20 bill were cosmetic. According to Tara Ross, a Texas attorney writing for the *American Enterprise,* "Peach and blue colors appear on the bill, but they are subtle. Andrew Jackson remains, but without the oval that used to surround his portrait. A blue eagle now appears to his right and a smaller eagle to his left. Several dozen little yellow [20s] appear across the back on the bill." In addition to the first use since 1905 of colors beyond green and black, the new $20 bill included several new anticounterfeiting features, including color-shifting ink, so that colors changed as the note was tilted; a watermark pressed into the paper and visible from both sides when held up to the light; and a security thread (a plastic strip) embedded in the paper, that in small print spelled out the denomination of the bill.

Unlike the previous rollout of new currency, however, this time Burson-Marsteller was joined by the Hollywood talent agency William Morris Agency, which would endeavor to secure "bit parts" for the new $20 bill on television shows and in movies. Omnicom Group's Davie-Brown Entertainment was also engaged to help in the marketing effort. It was all part of the $32 million

MONEY MATTERS

Although hard currency remained highly important in the United States, at the time that the campaign "The New Color of Money" appeared, cash was used to make purchases less frequently than in the past. According to the Nielson Report, 25 percent of purchases made in the United States in 1990 involved cash. By 2002 that number had dropped to 19 percent. The share was expected to be just 10 percent by 2020.

"The New Color of Money, Safer. Smarter. More Secure," marketing campaign to introduce to the world the new $20 bill, which was set to begin distribution through commercial banks on October 9, 2003.

TARGET MARKET

While in a sense the target audience for the "New Color of Money" campaign was every person in the world who was old enough to spend money, the focus of the campaign was on the United States. (A global public education effort would follow, highly important because 60 percent of U.S. currency was held overseas.) The campaign's purpose was to ensure a smooth transition to the new $20 bill, making sure that the general public expected the change and understood that both old and new currency would be accepted. Perhaps of even more importance was making people who handled cash as part of their jobs, especially cashiers, aware of the new security measures. Richard I. Mintz, chairman of the public-affairs division of Burson-Marsteller, told Betsy Streisand of the *New York Times* that the goal of the campaign was relatively simple: "We want to build awareness—then we can begin to change behavior." Streisand added, "The behavior that he wants to change includes stuffing the $20 bill, the most frequently counterfeited in the United States, into a pocket or cash register before checking its authenticity by, say, holding it up to a light or feeling for the security thread."

COMPETITION

The main competition for the new $20 bill was fake $20 bills. The elaborate security measures incorporated in the new note came in response to readily available digital technology—scanners, color printers, and software—that gave rise to casual forgers, such as college students color-copying a $20 bill to fool the pizza-delivery person, and provided powerful new tools for criminal forgers. It was estimated that less than 1 percent of counterfeit notes uncovered in the United States in 1995 were digitally produced. By the time the new $20 bill was introduced, that number had ballooned to almost 40 percent. On another level the new twenty faced competition in the media, because its message had to vie with countless others for the attention of the public. It was for this reason that the William Morris Agency was hired; by placing the new note in a variety of different situations on television, the chances of reaching a mass audience were greatly increased.

MARKETING STRATEGY

The "New Color of Money" campaign entailed the distribution of more than 37 million items of training materials, such as brochures, posters, training videos, and CD-ROMs, geared for cash-handling workers. There was also a website, www.moneyfactory.gov/newmoney, where people could learn more about the new anticounterfeit devices. A certain amount of coverage could also be expected from the news media. But in order to cast as wide a net as possible, the campaign also included television spots, promotional events, product placements, and joint marketing efforts. In addition, the new note even became fodder for late-night comedians. David Letterman commented that it looked like it had undergone a makeover from the guys on the hit show *Queer Eye for the Straight Guy.* It was not a surprising moment, given that representatives from the William Morris Agency had met weeks earlier with the writers for Letterman, *The Tonight Show with Jay Leno,* and other late-night programs to tell them about the new $20 bill. They did not care if the hosts poked fun at the bill, as long as they brought attention to it.

Other exposure through entertainment channels included appearances on the game shows *Wheel of Fortune, Pepsi Play for a Billion, Who Wants to Be a Millionaire,* and *Jeopardy.* Joint marketing deals were arranged with such partners as Wal-Mart and Pepperidge Farm. The latter put a picture of the new bill on its Goldfish cracker packages. The crackers themselves were colored to match the twenties, and the company also developed a contest around the new bill, offering a trip to Washington, D.C., as a prize. Like contemporary consumer products, the $20 bill was placed in movies and television shows, including *CSI: Miami, The West Wing,* and *Law & Order.* It was even electronically superimposed on the field during college football games on ESPN and during NFL games on *Monday Night Football* on ABC.

The campaign employed outdoor elements. A major billboard in New York City's Times Square was leased. Taxi toppers were procured in New York, Philadelphia,

Los Angeles, and San Francisco. Posters were put up in subways and bus shelters in such cities as Philadelphia, Washington, D.C., and San Francisco.

"The New Color of Money" also included a pair of television spots. In one a man withdrew money from an ATM and paused to inspect the new $20 bills that he received. While he displayed obvious pleasure in what he saw, an announcer commented, "You can see right away that things are different. We've added color and changed the portrait." The man then bought flowers from a vendor, who was equally impressed. After noting the security features and assuring the audience that both old and new twenties were legal tender, the announcer closed with the "safer, smarter, more secure" tagline. In the second spot, called "Sleight of Hand," a man in a music store received a new $20 bill in change after buying a CD. While the announcer listed the new features of the bill, accompanied by guitar riffs and record scratching, the man spun the bill on his finger and performed a number of other special-effects tricks, impressing the store clerk, who applauded at the end of the demonstration. A woman then stepped up to the counter and asked, "Can I get a new twenty?"

On the day the bill began distribution, the campaign organized a number of promotional events that received widespread news coverage. It was featured on NBC's *Today Show,* and cohost Katie Couric became the first New Yorker to purchase something—a cup of coffee at Dean & Deluca—with the new twenty. In Washington, D.C., the first of the new $20 bills was used by the head of the Bureau of Engraving and Printing to buy stamps from a vending machine. It was a calculated choice: in the 1990s the introduction of the new $20 bill was marred by problems with the same Post Office machines, which had not been properly prepared to accept the notes. More than 30 other similar events took place in cities across the country.

OUTCOME

The "New Color of Money" campaign succeeded in its core mission of garnering attention for the release of the new $20 bill. According to Burson-Marsteller, the campaign achieved an 82 percent awareness level for the twenty in the United States. The campaign also set the stage for the introduction of the new $50 note in 2004 and $10 note in 2005. But there were also problems. According to Ross of the *American Enterprise,* the campaign did not accomplish a smooth transition: "Several major grocery store chains received notice of the new [bills] mere weeks before they appeared on the market. As a result, self-checkout lanes across the country were not prepared to accept the new bills when they were introduced to the market."

Ross was one of a number of people critical of spending tax dollars on a marketing campaign for the new $20 note. She stated, "the Secret Service reported that $44.3 million in counterfeit notes were passed last year—not much compared to the cost of the marketing and all the upgrades to ATMs and other machines we now need. Rather than redesigning, marketing, and incorporating a new $20, $50, or $100 bill into our lives once every few years, it would be much cheaper and more effective to simply spend more time finding and prosecuting counterfeiters." *Brandweek* writer Philip Van Munching was even more caustic in his observations about the campaign, maintaining, "It isn't so much that our government thinks its constituents are stupid people; it's that the government is apparently comprised of stupid people, who naturally assume we're their intellectual equals—I don't question that the new $20 bills are different, but do we need to be sold on it?"

For its work on "The New Color of Money" Burson-Marsteller received advertising industry accolades. In 2004 it won top honors for Global Campaign of the Year at the PRWeek Awards, present by *PRWeek,* a trade publication serving the public-relations field. Moreover, the new $20 bill itself was named one of the "Best Products of 2003" by *BusinessWeek* and *Fortune* magazines.

FURTHER READING

Anderson, Gordon T. "It's Real Money Now." *CNN Money,* October 10, 2003.

Atkinson, Claire. "New Hollywood Star: The $20 Bill." *Advertising Age,* September 15, 2003, p. 3.

Buncombe, Andrew. "A Peach of a Job." *Independent* (London), September 30, 2003, p. 14.

"The Color of Money." *Wall Street Journal,* May 16, 2003, p. W17.

Goldstein, Steve. "U.S. Spending Money to Advertise Newly Designed $20 Bill." *Philadelphia Inquirer,* October 14, 2003.

Ross, Tara. "The New Color of Money . . ." *American Enterprise Online,* December 4, 2003. Available from <http://www.taemag.com/printVersion/print_article.asp?articleID=17804>

Streisand, Betsy. "Need Change for a $20 Bill? Call Hollywood." *New York Times,* September 28, 2003, p 3.

Van Munching, Philip. "Don't Show Us the Money." *Brandweek,* November 10, 2003, p. 22.

Walker, Rob. "The Money Pitch." *Slate,* October 27, 2003.

Ed Dinger

Burger King Corp.

5505 Blue Lagoon Drive
Miami, Florida 33126
USA
Telephone: (305) 378-3000
Fax: (305) 378-7262
Web site: www.burgerking.com

LUNCH BREAK CAMPAIGN

OVERVIEW

Because of what appeared to be a revolving door in its executive suite, as well as a steady drop in customer traffic, which was blamed on inconsistent food quality and poor customer service, Burger King was in search of a way to reestablish its brand identity and to rebuild sales. According to *Advertising Age,* in January 2004 Burger King had at the helm its nineteenth chief executive in its 50-year history, and at the same time the fast-food chain was struggling with a 22 percent decline in customer traffic that had begun in the late 1990s. Adding to the company's problems was a lack of consistency in its advertising. As *Advertising Age* noted, "Advertising has often been the scapegoat for sliding sales, with fours shops getting axed in the past four years."

Although Kevin Keller, a marketing professor at Dartmouth College, told *Advertising Age* that Burger King had "a brand problem, not an advertising problem," the company joined with the Miami-based advertising agency Crispin Porter + Bogusky to help implement a turnaround. The agency reintroduced "Have it your way," a popular tagline from the 1970s, and in February 2004 launched a marketing campaign, "Lunch Break," designed to appeal to its target audience, 18- to 34-year-olds who ate fast food and many of whom worked in offices. A series of television spots, which resembled an abbreviated sitcom, featured a cast of office workers ordering lunch from Burger King.

Burger King's return to the "Have it your way" tagline and the new "Lunch Break" campaign seemed to achieve the company's goals of reconnecting with its target audience and rebuilding sales. According to Burger King, for 10 consecutive months following the launch of the campaign, sales increased. Same-store sales in November 2004 were up 8.6 percent in franchised restaurants and up 14.2 percent in company-owned restaurants. The campaign was also recognized with awards at the 2004 Cannes Lions and the Clios.

HISTORICAL CONTEXT

Since opening its first restaurant in 1954, Burger King had grown to more than 11,200 restaurants in all 50 U.S. states and in 60 other countries, and it reported systemwide sales of $11.1 billion in the fiscal year ending June 30, 2003. The company aired its first television spot, "Home of the Whopper," in 1958, and its first major advertising campaign, "The Bigger the Burger the Better the Burger," was launched in 1968. Other campaigns followed, including the company's best-known and most successful, "Have It Your Way," which was introduced in 1974.

Despite the success of "Have It Your Way," the campaign was scrapped and replaced by what *USA*

© Roland Weihrauch/dpa/Corbis

Today described as "forgettable themes," including "Best Darn Burger" in 1978, "Burger King Town" in 1986, and "The Whopper Says" in 2001. Burger King seemed constantly to be changing its ad campaigns, but the new themes failed to resonate with consumers. As Burger King's customer traffic continued to slip, it appeared that the number-three fast-food chain, Wendy's, was ready to push Burger King from its second-place position and to settle in behind the number-one chain, McDonald's. In an effort to draw its customers back and to rebuild sales, Burger King took action in 2004 by reintroducing the "Have it your way" tagline in the "Lunch Break" campaign.

TARGET MARKET

Crispin Porter + Bogusky's Steve Sapka said that the "Lunch Break" campaign targeted "burger-craving Gen X and Gen Yers who demanded personalization and customization in every aspect of daily life. With much of that audience spending day after day at the office, BK knew that the relationships reflected in the 'Lunch Break' campaign would resonate well and get the brand message and product attributes out in an entertaining and relevant way."

Reintroducing the "Have it your way" tagline also appealed to another market, baby boomers who were looking for products and symbols reminiscent of their childhoods. In a discussion of the retro trend in culture and of its influence on the ways in which companies were marketing their products, Schuyler Brown, managing director of trends for Euro RSCG, told *USA Today,* "We're all nostalgic for the loss of our childhood. Kids are getting too old too fast. Adults are trying to hold on to their youth."

Although an Ad Track survey by *USA Today* reported that "consumers overall have mixed feelings about the return to 'Have it your way'... the ads score highest in likability and effectiveness with 18- to 24-year-olds." Russ Klein, the chief marketing officer of Burger King, told *USA Today* that it was all right that the survey results were skewed toward the young: "Our core group is 18 to 34 years old. We understand it's more important to be provocative than pleasant with this group."

COMPETITION

During an early ad campaign Burger King had referred to itself as "America's Burger King," but over the years it remained firmly entrenched in second place behind the fast-food giant McDonald's and just ahead of the number-three chain, Wendy's. As the *Evansville Courier & Press* noted, "McDonald's and Burger King have been going burger-to-burger for more than 30 years, with Wendy's and smaller companies also fighting for consumers' hearts and appetites... A price war between the two that stepped up in 2002 weakened profits and produced only mixed results, with Wendy's steering clear and picking up steady gains."

To try to bounce back from weakened profits, McDonald's, according to *USA Today,* had reinvented itself "as a place for the young and hip—not just for the Happy Meal set." In 2003 McDonald's introduced a new theme, "I'm Lovin' It," and planned its first global ad campaign to coincide with the new marketing approach. Jurgen Krauss, the CEO of Heye & Partner, the agency based in Munich, Germany, that had created the new theme, said that his "plan is to make McDonald's 'a lifestyle' not just a place to eat." *USA Today* reported that "McDonald's has reason to crow" about its marketing strategy, since the chain's same-store sales experienced the biggest increase in four years, with stock shares climbing close to a nine-month high.

While Wendy's sales grew during a Burger King-McDonald's price war in 2002, the death in that year of Dave Thomas, the company's founder and key spokesman, created new problems for the chain. Following Thomas's death, Wendy's struggled but failed to find an effective method to reach consumers, and according to *Advertising Age,* same-store sales for 2002 dropped in company-owned and franchised restaurants by 2.9 and 1.8 percent, respectively. In 2005, however, Wendy's changed its marketing strategy by "shedding its folksy

BURGER KING RETURNS TO POP CULTURE TO LAUNCH NEW BURGER

With the success in using popular television shows like *The Office* and *Seinfeld* as the theme for its "Lunch Break" marketing campaign, which featured a sitcom-style cast of 20-something office workers ordering lunch from the fast-food restaurant, Burger King turned in 2005 to another pop-culture venue—reality TV—to launch a new product and to support its marketing campaign. For this campaign Burger King partnered with business mogul Donald Trump for the season premiere of his reality TV show, *The Apprentice.*

According to the company, the challenge for the two teams on Trump's show, called "Street Smarts" and "Book Smarts," was to "name, build, market, and sell a new menu item at Burger King restaurants." At the end of the episode the Street Smarts team had won, with its product—the Angus Steak Burger—available to customers for a limited time at Burger Kings nationwide. Russ Klein, the company's chief marketing officer, said of the project, "At Burger King, our have it your way philosophy puts our customers in charge. It's all about empowerment and getting what you want, when you want it. That's why we couldn't wait to take this burger from the boardroom to the lunchroom."

image and one-size-fits-all message," reported AdAge.com. Wendy's new theme, "Do What Tastes Right," was designed to set the company apart from the competition, reflect the flexibility of its menu, and appeal to three consumer groups: baby boomers, who were Wendy's core customers; young adults; and Generation Zers, that is, the teens who were the customers of the future. Much as Burger King turned back the clock by reintroducing the "Have it your way" tagline, Wendy's returned to its "square hamburger roots." The company also increased its marketing budget, and while it did not introduce a global ad campaign, as McDonald's had, it did venture into Internet advertising. Speaking of the new marketing strategy, Ian Rowden, Wendy's executive vice president and chief marketing officer, told AdAge.com, "We can leverage what we have to different groups. One message at one time broadly targeted for one group doesn't play anymore for Wendy's."

MARKETING STRATEGY

Burger King stated that its advertising campaigns had contributed to the company's success, and to keep that success going Brad Blum, the company's CEO in 2004, said in a January 2004 press release, "We must have groundbreaking, next-level, results-oriented, and innovative advertising that strongly connects with our core consumers." Greg Brenneman, who replaced Blum as CEO in 2005, told *Newsweek* that the company's core consumers were identified when he reviewed a market study "that showed hard-core fast foodies made up only 18 percent of the population but accounted for 49 percent of business." Brenneman's priority became providing food options that appealed to the target audience of 18- to 34-year-old men "who like football and are 'gray collar' workers, because their jobs aren't a bright spot in their lives." Burger King's Klein told *USA Today* that the return to "Have it your way," the tagline that had worked well in the past, was long overdue: "When you have an ad campaign that sticky, it's foolish to go against it," he said. Andrew Keller, creative director at Crispin Porter + Bogusky, added, "At a time when self-expression and mass customization are critical elements of culture, the line makes total sense."

In the "Lunch Break" spots a cast of sitcom-style characters known as the "Lunch Break gang" ordered from Burger King, competing to see who could concoct the most unusual Whopper. The competition between the 20-something office staffers heated up with each new commercial. In one spot two coworkers clashed when one "copied" the other's Whopper order, and in another spot a worker claimed the title as "champion" when he ordered his Whopper with "no lettuce, extra ketchup, double bacon, double mayo, and two extra beef patties." Crispin Porter + Bogusky's "Lunch Break" campaign aimed to achieve three goals. It reached the primary target audience of 18- to 34-year-old office workers, it restored Burger King's cultural relevance by bringing back the "Have it your way" tagline, and it reestablished brand identity.

According to the agency's Sapka, "With little room for personalization in the fast food experience, BK had the opportunity to own customization in the category, which was the campaign's intent." Sapka said that it was because the "Lunch Break" gang's unique sandwich orders were so effective at promoting Burger King and at returning the "Have it your way" mantra to pop culture that they returned at the end of 2004 in ads tied to the *SpongeBob SquarePants* movie. In 2005 they were back promoting the Angus Steak Burger, the Tendercrisp, and the Big Fish. Brian Gies, Burger King's vice president of marketing impact, told *Chain Leader,* "As long as it [the "Lunch Break" campaign] stays fresh and relevant, we'll continue to keep it in the mix."

OUTCOME

The "Lunch Break" ads were believed to have had a strong influence on the resurgence of sales at Burger King. Gies told *Chain Leader* that the ads had been "an important contributor to the brand's momentum. The campaign has done great things for brand recall, message recall, and likeability."

WWD recognized two of the "Lunch Break" spots by including them on its list of the 10 most effective new TV commercials launched during the last week of February 2004, and *Adweek* included the campaign in its list of best spots. *Adweek* wrote that Burger King's campaign "managed to create characters who, despite their oddball antics (or maybe because of them), feel familiar and almost always funny... The casting and dialogue are superb, and the spots also seem to spark stomach rumbling, so CP+B must be doing something right." "Lunch Break" campaign spots also won the Silver Award at the 2004 Cannes Lions and Bronze Awards at the Clios.

Not every review of the campaign was positive, however. Lewis Lazare, writing for the *Chicago Sun-Times,* called the "Lunch Break" spots "a stylistic mish-mash if ever there were one." Lazare wrote that the "story line and underlying message are confusing... And, sadly, the message about getting burgers done your way at Burger King seems to be diminished by all the silent sturm und drang." According to *USA Today*'s weekly poll, Ad Track, only 14 percent of those familiar with the ads liked them "a lot" and thought that they were "very effective," while 30 percent were found to "dislike" the ads.

FURTHER READING

Begun, Bret. "A Really Big Idea—Burger King's CEO Has Turned Around Chain with a Radical Notion: Give People What They Want." *Newsweek,* May 23, 2005.

Chapman, Mary Boltz. "Cast of Characters: Burger King Hopes Fast-food Fans Will Relate to Its Lunch Break Campaign Evolution." *Chain Leader,* January 1, 2005.

Cummings, Betsy. "On the Crest of the Wave: Agencies Try to Strike While Pop-culture Fads and Trends Are Hot." *Adweek,* September 13, 2004.

Elliott, Stuart. "Burger King Takes a Product from TV to the Table." *New York Times,* January 21, 2005.

Horovitz, Bruce. "McDonald's Lovin' Turnaround." *USA Today,* June 30, 2003.

Howard, Theresa. "Burger King Appeals to Young Workers with 'Your Way' Ads." *USA Today,* April 10, 2004.

Johannes, Amy. "Burger King Cooks Up a Winner." *Promo,* May 1, 2005.

Lazare, Lewis. "Message Confusing in Burger King Ads." *Chicago Sun-Times,* March 3, 2004.

Macarthur, Kate. "Wendy's Overhauls Marketing Strategies." May 19, 2005. Available from <http://www.AdAge.com>.

———. "Wendy's Struggles to Serve Up Success: Hopes Hipper Image Helps in Post-Dave World." *Advertising Age,* February 21, 2005.

———. "What's Eating Burger King: 'Brand Problem Not Ad Problem,' Experts Say, as Chain Calls In Crispin." *Advertising Age,* January 26, 2004.

McCarthy, Michael. "Burger King Tries Old Slogan Again: 'Have It Your Way' Returns to Some Mixed Reviews in Kitschy New Ads." *USA Today,* May 23, 2005.

"McDonald's Widens Gap over Burger King in Fast-Food Wars." *Evansville Courier Press,* January 28, 2004.

Parpis, Eleftheria. "Best of the Rest in 2004." *Adweek,* April 2004.

"TV Advertising Recognition: The 10 Most Effective New TV Commercials Launched between Feb. 16 and Feb. 29." *WWD,* December 13, 2004.

Rayna Bailey

SUBSERVIENT CHICKEN CAMPAIGN

OVERVIEW

By 2004 Burger King's position as the second-largest hamburger company in the world was waning. With a worsening brand image and an unshakable image for poor food quality, the chain was forced to shut down hundreds of stores. Following a flurry of CEO and ad agency turnovers, Burger King awarded Miami-based ad agency Crispin Porter + Bogusky a $350 million advertising budget to reshape its image. "We weren't a brand that suffered from lack of awareness," Russ Klein, Burger King's chief marketing officer, told *Advertising Age,* "but we were a brand that suffered from a lack of emotional attachment." Crispin Porter + Bogusky resurrected Burger King's 1974 tagline "Have it your way" for "Subservient Chicken," one of its first campaigns for the firm. The campaign was launched on April 8, 2004, immediately following Burger King's introduction of the Tendercrisp Chicken Sandwich.

The campaign began with E-mail messages that directed recipients to SubservientChicken.com. A week later three 30-second spots were aired on network television, followed by a print ad that also directed people to the website. The website, which served as the core of the campaign, featured a person wearing a chicken costume who acted out whatever command was typed into the command bar. More than 400 commands had been filmed by Crispin Porter + Bogusky beforehand to correspond to possible commands. The website had the feel of a webcam, suggesting that the chicken was standing inside an apartment just waiting to act out the visitor's next prompt.

Considered a bold approach when it first appeared, the "Subservient Chicken" campaign collected a number of creative awards, including Best in Show at the One Show Interactive, the Grand Clio, and the Yahoo Big Idea Chair Award. Within the first 24 hours the website had received more than a million hits, with this number soaring to an impressive 385 million hits by April 2005. Visitors spent an average of six minutes interacting with the site. Not only did the "Subservient Chicken" campaign see Burger King's 21-month sales decline stop, but sales actually improved so much that in 2004 Burger King's growth surpassed its principal competitor, McDonald's Corporation.

HISTORICAL CONTEXT

Founded in 1954, Burger King had grown to include more than 11,000 fast-food restaurants, most privately owned franchises, by 2005. Early on, Burger King allowed franchisees to buy stores, which stimulated rapid expansion. Quality and consistency varied between stores, however, a flaw that had haunted Burger King for decades. From the beginning Burger King also used the "Have it your way" tagline to emphasize its restaurants' ability to prepare food to accommodate customers' tastes, a stab at the fixed menu of McDonald's. With the emergence in the late 1990s of restaurant chains touting healthier food, such as Starbucks Corporation and Jamba Juice Company, competition grew even fiercer among fast-food giants like Burger King, McDonald's, Wendy's, and Jack in the Box. To adjust to the emphasis on healthier eating, Burger King introduced low-carbohydrate options, including more salads. Brad Blum, CEO of Burger King in 2002, increased sales by adorning the menu with the Angus Steak Burger and Fire-Grilled Salads.

Burger King continued to fire agencies that created commercials with close-up shots of food, also known in the industry as "playing up the grill," a common technique used in McDonald's advertisements. Young & Rubicam, the agency that preceded Crispin Porter + Bogusky, had introduced Burger King's "Fire's Ready" campaign, but the agency was sacked after only 10 months. "There's a young guy product that basically all of the greatest advertising in the world is built around—that's beer. Here we have the exact same audience [as beer marketers]. Yet, in general, you have some of the worst advertising in the world," Alex Bogusky, a partner at Crispin Porter + Bogusky, told *Brandweek.* "Since they both have the same target there's no reason the fast food category has to be so lame. It's just gotten that way."

Until Wendy's released its own chicken sandwiches, Burger King's Original Chicken Sandwich had been the market leader in this food item. In response to Wendy's move, Burger King began using higher grade meat and other ingredients to create its new Tendercrisp Chicken Sandwich. A month after the sandwich was introduced, in March 2004, Crispin Porter + Bogusky launched the "Subservient Chicken" campaign. It was a time when Burger King was floundering. "It's not like you know you're getting the chance to work on a resurgent brand. You get a chance to work on a damaged brand. When we started on this, business was not too good [for Burger King]," Bogusky told *Brandweek.* "They were ready to take some risks."

TARGET MARKET

The "Subservient Chicken" campaign targeted 16- to 35-year-old males who were engaged with "online nontraditional" advertising. Crispin Porter + Bogusky hoped that the campaign would deviate from Burger King's traditional strategy, which was simply to mimic McDonald's advertising. Copying the strategy of the market leader, according to Crispin Porter + Bogusky, made Burger King seem to be just a smaller version, which was not something the public wanted. Crispin Porter + Bogusky attempted to make Burger King "popular" with its target market, believing that the popularity of the brand would then spread into other demographics. Jeff Hicks, Crispin Porter + Bogusky's president, told *Brandweek,* "We talk a lot about the 'cool uncle.' The voice of the brand is that cool uncle who may be closer to your age than your father's. He's the kind of guy who might say, 'Hey, take a year off from college and go travel.' He's got a little more of an adolescent voice than your parents but he's also got a little bit of experience. That's the voice we like for the brand."

Known for creating interactive, viral campaigns, that is, advertising spread by word of mouth, Crispin Porter + Bogusky began by steering away from traditional media. "What struck me was their holistic view," Klein told *Advertising Age's Creativity.* "They solve brand problems from the ground up. They don't necessarily gravitate to thirty-second TV commercials as a tonic for every marketing problem. They are not only a big believer but also a practitioner of word of mouth marketing—they understand what it takes to generate strong advocacy among the core customer." Neither Burger King nor Crispin Porter + Bogusky wanted a mass-market campaign, choosing instead to use a specific channel for reaching 16- to 35-year-old male Internet users. "If you

CHICKEN GARTER BELT

The bizarre chicken outfit, spoofing other more salacious websites, came complete with a garter belt. The costume was designed by Stan Winston, the same designer involved in movies like *Aliens, Terminator,* and *Jurassic Park.*

are going to be targeted," Klein continued, "you have to deliver something that is relevant to that target."

COMPETITION

McDonald's, the giant of fast-food firms, was founded in 1948 and by 1962 had served its billionth hamburger. "Billions served" became the company's tagline, and by 2002 McDonald's was spending more than $600 million per year on advertising. By 2002 the company operated more than 30,000 stores, almost triple the number of Burger King's. Each McDonald's restaurant obtained food from an authorized supplier, ensuring that a Big Mac tasted the same in Miami, Florida, for example, as it did in Anchorage, Alaska. McDonald's advertising campaigns traditionally included cross-promotions that involved toys and movies, with Walt Disney Studio Entertainment being one of its longest-running partners. The McDonald's Teenie Beanie Babies giveaway of 1997, for example, proved to be one of the company's biggest successes. By 2005, however, McDonald's was aggressively fighting to retain its breakfast market. Between 1995 and 2005, 36 percent of its breakfast customers had left for retailers like Starbucks, which served higher-priced Arabica coffees. Research showed that coffee, unlike breakfast sandwiches, brought consumers back to the same store every day, and so McDonald's responded by introducing a richer Robusta blend titled "Premium." An aggressive ad campaign followed, with one television spot showing a woman sipping McDonald's Premium coffee and enjoying a McGriddle sandwich while fantasizing, "I fired my boss" and "I married a rock star."

With more than 6,000 stores by 2002, Wendy's had gained the position of the third-largest fast-food chain in the world. Wendy's, which had a substantial menu that included alternatives to hamburgers, presented itself as a higher-quality alternative to McDonald's and Burger King. Dave Thomas, who had founded the company in 1969, often served as its spokesperson, and over the years he appeared in more than 800 commercials. The corporation's best-known ad campaign—"Where's the Beef?" with actress Clara Peller—appeared in 1984, and Wendy's market share immediately jumped 12 percent. When Thomas died in 2002 Wendy's turned to more conventional advertising, however. By 2005 the corporation was suffering losses from the rising price of beef, the emergence of healthier fast-food alternatives, and a hoax by a woman who claimed that she had found a severed finger in her Wendy's chili.

MARKETING STRATEGY

To add a healthier chicken sandwich to its menu Burger King introduced the high-quality Tendercrisp Chicken Sandwich on March 19, 2004. It was while planning another spot for Burger King that Jeff Benjamin, Crispin Porter + Bogusky's interactive creative director, came up with the idea of the "Subservient Chicken" campaign. He instructed his crew to film an actor wearing a chicken costume that had been designed by the Stan Winston Studio. The actor was instructed to perform more than 400 short actions. The filming took place inside the apartment of a friend of Benjamin's that was furnished with only a modest lamp and two couches. "Our approach has always been, 'Follow the work,'" Crispin Porter + Bogusky's Jeff Steinhour told *Fast Company.* "Meaning if ever you're in doubt about a decision, simply ask whether it's going to make the work better."

Benjamin activated the campaign website, SubservientChicken.com, on April 9, 2004. Once a visitor had entered the website, the text "Contacting the chicken" appeared on a black background and with the Burger King logo. Below, in a command bar, visitors were prompted, "Get chicken just the way you like it. Type in your command here." The chicken waited patiently, supposedly before a webcam, for the commands. Included in the chicken's repertoire were commands like "Dance," "Cluck," "Play baseball," and "Get into the Lotus position." If the chicken was asked to perform something inappropriate, impossible, or not on the list, it simply approached the camera and wagged its finger in admonishment. The overall effect was that the chicken seemed to be executing commands live.

As the project neared completion, on April 8, Benjamin E-mailed 20 people the website's URL. Without any serious promotion the website had registered more than one million hits by the end of the day. The following week three 30-second spots were aired on late-night network television. The spots featured scenes from the website, for example, the chicken acting out commands before young adults. In another spot a man commanded the chicken to try on different clothing. Only one print ad was released for the campaign. This

> ## BURGER KING VS. A GIANT
>
> To put the size of McDonald's into perspective, in 2002 it boasted over 30,000 stores, more than those of Wal-Mart, Carrefour SA, and Royal Ahold N.V. combined. McDonald's employed more people than Ford and General Motors. Because McDonald's owned the land beneath its restaurants, it also was the world's largest commercial holder of real estate.

ad, which featured a cutout of a chicken mask, appeared in an October issue of ESPN's magazine.

"I would describe what we're doing as making BK unique," Bogusky told *Brandweek.* "Sometimes that makes people uncomfortable. Viewers may look at the advertising and say, 'You can't talk that way' or 'That's kind of weird.' It's only weird because there's only been one voice [in the category] with any consistency and that's been McDonald's. So we're all conditioned to say, that's how fast food advertising should look, be and sound."

OUTCOME

Despite the low cost of the "Subservient Chicken" campaign, it garnered some of the advertising industry's foremost honors, including a Grand Clio, Best in Show at the One Show Interactive, and the Yahoo Big Idea Chair Award. After being online for only one month, the chicken had performed its millionth request. After one year the site had had approximately 14 million visitors and 396 million hits. Andy Bonaparte, a Burger King ad director, told *Adweek* that the campaign helped "sell a lot, a lot, a lot of chicken sandwiches." During the campaign Burger King's 21-month sales decline stopped and turned around. Burger King's sales growth was soon outperforming McDonald's. Sales of the Tendercrisp sandwich consistently increased at an average of 9 percent a week until it eventually sold more than the firm's other chicken offering, the Original Chicken Sandwich.

Matt Vescovo, one of the judges responsible for honoring the "Subservient Chicken" campaign with a gold during the Viral Awards show, was effusive in his praise of the campaign. He told *Adweek,* "To take that idea [that you can have chicken any way you like it] for something that really isn't that exciting—a chicken sandwich—and to so seamlessly put it into such an innovative use of technology, it just really hit so many sweet spots for me."

FURTHER READING

Anderson, Mae. "Out and About at the Clios: Ad Industry Luminaries from Around the Globe Mingled at the 43rd Annual Show." *Adweek,* June 13, 2005.

———. "Subservient Chicken Tunes In." *Adweek,* November 15, 2004, p. 26.

Creamer, Matthew. "Crispin Ups Ante: Widely Applauded Creative Shop Sheds Its 'Underdog' Label via BK Win; Shows Capability to Solve Problems on Mass Scale." *Advertising Age,* January 10, 2005, p. S1.

D'Innocenzo, Lisa. "Don't Be an Ass." *Strategy,* September 17, 2004, p. 8.

Howard, Theresa. "Burger King Promotes Tongue-in-Beak Chicken Fight: 15-Minute Main Event 'Ad' Airs Only on DirecTV." *USA Today,* November 5, 2004, p. B4.

Ives, Nat. "Crispin Porter Wins 12 Awards from One Club." *New York Times,* May 16, 2005, p. 11.

Lippert, Barbara. "A Royal Welcome: CP+B Is Dead-On with a Pair of Bizarre Burger King Spots." *Adweek,* September 27, 2004, p. 28.

Sanders, Holly. "Chicken Jerk & Alien Bees: 'Viral' Ads Create Buzz, but May Not Sell." *New York Post,* November 14, 2004, p. 34.

Story, Louise. "The Subservient Chicken and Other Award Winners." *New York Times,* June 13, 2005, p. 8.

Underwood, Ryan. "Like Just About Everything Crispin Porter + Bogusky Does, the Subservient Chicken Ad Campaign Is Risky and Extreme: It's Also Very, Very Smart." *Fast Company,* April 1, 2005, p. 70.

Wheaton, Ken. "Adages: Just Say No; The Subservient Chicken Does." *Advertising Age,* May 16, 2005, p. 56.

Wilker, Deborah. "Clio Spot-Light on Chicken 'n' Car." *Hollywood Reporter,* May 26, 2005.

Kevin Teague

WHEN YOU HAVE IT YOUR WAY, IT JUST TASTES BETTER CAMPAIGN

OVERVIEW

Despite its overall sales success, Burger King in 1998 embarked on what senior vice president of marketing James Watkins called an "aggressive evolution" of its brand. With industry leader McDonald'shaving taken steps to address a series of high-profile marketing missteps by rolling out a new cooking system designed to improve the taste of its products, Burger King responded with a marketing strategy that focused on the superior taste of its food. The chain's three-year-old "Get Your Burger's Worth" slogan was scrapped and replaced with a line that hit McDonald's in its self-acknowledged weak spot. "When You Have It Your Way, It Just Tastes Better," boasted the new Burger King television campaign from Ammirati Puris Lintas. "We will stake Burger King's future on taste," said Paul Clayton, president of the company's North American operations.

Since the founding of Burger King in 1954, the Miami-based chain had made food customization, encapsulated by the "Have It Your Way" tag line, a hallmark of its competitive strategy. Burger King restaurants offered traditional fast-food fare in addition to Whopper and BK Broiler sandwiches. The company had grown to become the number two fast-food hamburger chain, with franchisees operating more than 9,800 restaurants in all 50 U.S. states and in 55 countries and territories around the world. Now a subsidiary of London-based Diageo, PLC, one of the world's leading consumer products businesses whose international portfolio of food and drink brands included Guinness, Pillsbury, Green Giant, Häagen-Dazs, Old El Paso, Progresso, Smirnoff Vodka, Bailey's Original Irish Creme, and J&B Rare Scotch Whisky, Burger King enjoyed systemwide sales of $10.3 billion in fiscal year 1998.

HISTORICAL CONTEXT

Burger King was founded by James McLamore and David Edgerton, both of whom had had extensive experience in the restaurant business. They founded the new restaurant around the simple concept of providing the customer with reasonably priced quality food that was served quickly in attractive, clean surroundings. Powered by America's postwar fast-food boom, the company grew briskly over the ensuing decade. By 1967, when the company was acquired by the Minneapolis-based Pillsbury Company, 8,000 employees were working in 274 different Burger King locations nationwide.

Burger King's success was predicated on its leadership in such areas as product development, decor, service, and advertising. The Whopper sandwich, introduced in 1957, proved an immediate hit and paved the way for future menu innovations. In the late 1990s the Whopper retained its place as one of the best-known hamburger sandwiches in the world, with more than 1.4 billion being sold annually.

Restaurant decor was a second pillar of Burger King's success. Burger King was the first fast-food chain to introduce dining rooms, allowing customers a chance to eat inside. Drive-through service, designed to satisfy customers on the go, was introduced in 1975 and as of 1999 accounted for approximately 50 percent of Burger King's business. The company developed a tradition of taking great care in the design and construction of its restaurants.

Burger King's advertising campaigns also contributed to the company's success. The company's first television ad ran on Miami's only VHF station in 1958. The year after Burger King became a Pillsbury subsidiary, in 1968, the company's first major promotion, "The Bigger the Burger the Better the Burger," debuted. In 1974 the landmark "Have It Your Way" campaign was created. Other memorable Burger King advertising campaigns included "America Loves Burgers and We're America's Burger King," "Make It Special, Make It Burger King," "Battle of the Burgers," "Burger King Town," "We Do It Like You'd Do It," "Sometimes You've Gotta Break the Rules," and "Your Way, Right Away."

The road to the "When You Have It Your Way, It Just Tastes Better" campaign began in late 1993, when Clayton, Burger King's president, and James B. Adamson, its chief executive officer, initiated an agency review. As a result New York-based Ammirati Puris Lintas was tapped to revive the chain's "Have It Your Way" theme. In 1996 Burger King executed the new strategy with ads focused on foods and set to popular music from the 1970s and '80s. The musical spots helped consumers make an emotional connection with Burger King. Two years later "Have It Your Way" returned as an integral part of the burger giant's advertising.

TARGET MARKET

The fast-food sector was one of the most highly developed in the restaurant industry, with the fast-food hamburger category being perhaps the most competitive. There seemed to be McDonald's, Wendy's, and Burger King outlets on every corner, and consumers were using increasingly sophisticated criteria to decide where and how to spend their money. In this environment gains in market share became critical. One way in which Burger King had traditionally differentiated itself from its competitors and gained market share was by appealing to customers on the issue of customization. The basic idea, embodied in the "Have It Your Way" slogan, was that consumers had individual needs and were best served by products that could be easily customized for them.

There was statistical evidence to indicate that there was a large market for customized products. For example, two-thirds of consumers in a poll done by the consulting firm of Kurt Salmon Associates reported difficulty in finding clothes that fit well. About 36 percent of the respondents said that they were willing to pay 12 to 14 percent more for custom clothes and shoes. It was felt that the same principal applied to other areas, including fast food. This was supported by the fact that in 1998 Burger King enjoyed sales gains when it offered a customized option in side dishes with its value meal items.

IF YOU REBUILD IT, THEY WILL COME

Burger King's "When You Have It Your Way, It Just Tastes Better" may have represented a throwback to the company's past, but in other areas the fast-food giant was striding boldly into the future. At the same time that the chain was revamping its national advertising, it was looking to boost performance by paying more attention to restaurant operations, new-product development, and broader marketing.

In 1998 the chain announced that it was embarking on a three-year initiative to spruce up tired stores. Slated for retirement was the tan-and-brick color scheme used in Burger King restaurants, to be supplanted by cobalt blue. Exteriors were to be made brighter with the addition of yellow and red stripes, while the inside walls would be painted a mustard yellow. Even the time-honored Burger King-in-a-bun logo was to be refurbished with a new style of lettering.

Other new features included an interactive "virtual fun center" designed for use by children, who were among Burger King's most important customer; a space-age drive-through in which patrons could access electronic screens showing them what they had ordered and how much it would cost; and a computer-controlled broiler chamber that could heat more slowly, allowing for thicker patties such as a planned half-pound burger, tentatively called the Great American.

For many Burger King customers the changes were long overdue. Patrons had complained for years about hard-to-read menu boards, crowded eating areas, and tables bolted to the floor. What was their overall impression of the chain? "'Boring' would be the right word," cracked Jacqueline McCook, Burger King's head of strategic planning. "But they love the food." Consumers, McCook added, were sending Burger King a simple message: "If you make it a more pleasant environment, we'd come more often."

Paul Clayton, president of Burger King's North American operations, agreed with this assessment. "The best local-store marketing is a well-run restaurant," he told *Advertising Age.* "The better the restaurant delivers the brand, the better they will be. If we have a strong national marketing platform and execute it at the local level, it is a combination that can't be beat."

"Burger King has been customizing its sandwiches since the company was founded in 1954," said Rob Calderin, vice president of USA Marketing for Burger King, in announcing the program. "Now, we have taken this one step further. In addition to having great tasting food served just the way you like it, customers can have their choice of french fries or onion rings as part of their Value Meals."

COMPETITION

After world leader McDonald's Corp., Burger King was the number two hamburger fast-food chain. It had about 20 percent of the U.S. market, compared to 45 percent for McDonald's. In 1997, emboldened by a series of marketing missteps by McDonald's—including the ill-fated Arch Deluxe rollout and an abortive 55-cents pricing scheme—Burger King launched an all-out product war. In rapid succession it introduced a new burger, the Big King, and reformulated its french fries. Both were supported with major ad campaigns. According to figures from Competitive Media Reporting, McDonald's spent $578 million on advertising in 1997, 3.3 percent less than in 1996. At the same time Burger King boosted its ad spending 17.2 percent, to $423 million.

With consumer research consistently citing "better taste" as the basis for Burger King's appeal, McDonald's in 1998 took steps to improve the quality of its food. Costs to develop, install, and market a new high-tech cooking system were projected at $500 million, with franchise owners picking up at least $300 million of the tab. New toasters were designed to heat buns in just 10 seconds through a combination of radiant and convection heat, 14 seconds faster than the existing system. Holding cabinets with special moisture controls were installed to keep cooked beef and chicken patties hot for up to 20 minutes without drying. In addition, computer software was developed to more accurately project, often within seconds, what items would likely be ordered at specific times of the day.

To accompany the new approach, a new marketing slogan, "Made for You," was developed. It had echoes of Burger King's "Have It Your Way" slogan, something that did not go unnoticed at the headquarters of the number two chain. "We've offered 'Have It Your Way' since 1974," scoffed Burger King spokesperson Kim Miller. "What's the big deal?" Nevertheless, the renewed emphasis on food quality represented a sea change for McDonald's, which had long relied on heat lamps to keep precooked burgers warm.

MARKETING STRATEGY

Burger King had made customizing its sandwiches a hallmark of company philosophy since its founding in

1954 but only began fully promoting the "Have It Your Way" option in 1974. The tag line and its accompanying jingle became synonymous with Burger King in the minds of many consumers.

In 1998 Burger King revived the slogan with the rollout of what was called "the ultimate Have It Your Way meal" at its more than 7,600 restaurants in the United States. Beginning on October 19, Burger King customers could choose french fries or onion rings with any value meal at no extra charge. The side-order option was considered a logical extension of the "Have It Your Way" concept.

To emphasize the connection with the past, the burger giant assigned Matthew Berger, son of the original "Have It Your Way" jingle writer, Dennis Berger, to update the lyrics. "Value meals with rings or fries/Still cost the same with one great price," warbled singers in a new set of radio and television commercials. "You don't have to ask us twice to have it your way." To spearhead the new campaign, Burger King continued using popular ads that mixed food shots and classic rock and soul songs, while also adding more spots showing customers enjoying the chain's food.

As the campaign progressed, Burger King developed a series of new big-budget image- building television ads. In one a drill sergeant berated a group of recruits who must do everything the sergeant's way, except when it came to "having it their way" at Burger King. A second spot blended part of a 1973 ad with new footage to create a striking retro effect. A third ad took a more whimsical approach. Two men wearing 1970s leisure suits walked into a Burger King and ordered a Whopper without pickles. Three women emerged from behind the counter and began singing the "Have It Your Way" song. The ad then cut back to 1998, as the same two men, now balding and graying—but still clothed in polyester—ordered onion rings instead of fries and received the identical serenade.

An even more imaginative execution of the "When You Have It Your Way, It Just Tastes Better" theme was staged in time for the Fourth of July. On the holiday weekend Burger King for the first time aired brand image television spots directed exclusively to children that stressed the longevity and practical application of its customization process. "Burger King has been customizing burgers since being established in 1954 and we plan to pass that core equity message on to a new generation," said Calderin. "These advertisements send that message. As most parents would agree, kids can be fairly choosy eaters. The children's television spot in particular, lets them know they can have it their way at Burger King."

In addition to the television spot, on July 2 Burger King placed a full-page advertisement in *USA Today* saluting the Declaration of Independence and the Fourth of July. The ad playfully reminded readers that America's founding fathers were the first group to "have it their way." "Burger King and Independence Day have a lot in common," remarked Calderin. "We both adhere to the 'Have It Your Way' principle. This nation's founding fathers set the tone a long time ago by having it their way, and we've followed their lead."

OUTCOME

Burger King's new commercials reprising the "Have It Your Way" jingle may have scored points for nostalgia, but they did not prove popular with consumers. In a survey conducted by *USA Today,* only 17 percent of participants said that they liked the commercials "a lot." Of those surveyed, people with a household income of $25,000 to $35,000 a year responded most favorably to the ads. Thirty-three percent of African Americans said that they liked the commercials a lot, compared with 14 percent of whites. Perhaps more encouraging for Burger King was the response of young people, a key target for fast-food companies. Respondents between the ages of 25 and 29 were more enthusiastic than other age groups, with 26 percent of them reporting that they liked the commercials a lot. The commercials did receive higher scores for effectiveness, with 23 percent of respondents rating the commercials as "very effective."

Despite the lukewarm response in the survey, Burger King officials remained satisfied with the "When You Have It Your Way, It Just Tastes Better" theme. The company's ad director, Andy Bonaparte, reported that the commercials increased traffic in Burger King restaurants. "Response has been positive so far," he told *USA Today.* Many corporate image specialists agreed that the retro ads would prove to be a compelling platform for the chain. "'Have it your way' was the biggest idea Burger King ever had, and it's still very relevant today," claimed Allen Adamson of Landor Associates. "No one else has grabbed that positioning, so they're smart to bring that back."

FURTHER READING

Gibson, Richard. "Burger King Seeks New Sizzle." *Wall Street Journal,* April 14, 1999.

Horovitz, Bruce. "Re-inventing McDonald's." *USA Today,* February 20, 1998.

Wells, Melanie. "Not Their Way: Burger King Spots Lose with Consumers." *USA Today,* December 21, 1998.

Robert Schnakenberg

Business Leaders for Sensible Priorities

10 W. 18th St., 9th Fl.
New York, New York 10011
USA
Telephone: (212) 243-3416
Web site: www.sensiblepriorities.org

MOVE OUR MONEY CAMPAIGN

OVERVIEW

In 1997 Ben Cohen, cofounder of the superpremium ice cream company Ben & Jerry's Homemade Inc., was shocked to learn that Congress had decreased spending on social programs but had increased the Pentagon's defense budget. The following year Cohen founded Business Leaders for Sensible Priorities (BLSP), a nonprofit organization dedicated to transferring 15 percent of the $281 billion defense budget into educational funding. By 1999 he had mobilized more than 500 BLSP members, which included corporate executives, retired generals and admirals, and celebrities. Hoping to make education funding the key issue of the 2000 presidential elections and compel the next U.S. president to transfer money away from defense and into education, BLSP released its "Move Our Money" campaign.

The ad agency Hill, Holliday, Connors, Cosmopulos Inc. worked pro bono to create one television spot, one radio spot, and four print ads for the campaign. The radio and television spots featured Jack Shanahan, a retired vice admiral of the U.S. Navy, who explained that even though America had enough nuclear weapons to destroy the world several times over, the U.S. government was still building more. Shanahan explained that the government could allocate a small fraction of its defense budget to help improve America's education system without compromising the country's defense. Print ads created by Hill, Holliday's creative directors Dave Gardiner and Joe Berkeley featured provocative copy, such as "No wonder our bombs are smarter than our students." The campaign ran from December 1999 to January 2000 to target the New Hampshire and Iowa primary elections. It resurfaced in September 2000 to target the general electorate before the presidential election.

The campaign garnered a plethora of ad industry accolades, winning, for example, the Newspaper category at the 2001 International ANDY Awards. According to BLSP, polls tracking public opinion in Des Moines, Iowa, showed that support for shifting 15 percent of the defense budget to education jumped from 45 percent to 72 percent by the Iowa primary's completion. Unfortunately for BLSP, George W. Bush, who won the 2000 presidential election, supported an increase in military spending.

HISTORICAL CONTEXT

Even though Cohen still served on Ben & Jerry's board of directors in the late 1990s, he was no longer responsible for the business's daily operations. The extra time allowed the entrepreneur to channel his energy into social issues. After he learned of Congress's plans to balance the national budget by cutting back on social programs to

Ben Cohen, co-founder of Ben & Jerry's ice cream. © SHAUN HEASLEY/REUTERS/CORBIS.

increase the Pentagon's defense budget, Cohen rallied support for shifting the country's spending priorities. "Congress had added nine billion more onto the military budget than the Pentagon had even requested," Cohen said in *America's Graphic Design Magazine.* "And they were going to slip it by in the middle of the night, at the very end of the legislative session."

Cohen established BLSP to mobilize America's business leaders, celebrities, and retired military personnel to help shift 15 percent of the Pentagon's defense budget to education funding. In April 1999 BLSP launched a bus tour titled "U Slice the Pie," a campaign that used pie charts to illustrate the federal government's distribution of funds. Inflatable pie charts, cookies with pie charts in their frosting, and ballpoint pens with pie chart banners were dispensed at political rallies during the 20 months preceding the 2000 presidential election. BLSP was bipartisan and existed in a "pre-9/11 world," noted Berkeley.

Even the ex-Navy Republican presidential candidate John McCain, who ran for president in 2000, explained in the *Boston Globe,* "Look, we've been buying C-130s for 10 years" (referring to the C-130 Hercules, a military cargo plane). "We're going to have a C-130 in every schoolyard in America; there's no need for much of the equipment we are purchasing."

In 1999 Cohen asked Hill, Holliday to create a pro bono campaign for BLSP. "We talked about doing an emotional visual campaign illustrating school kids who were being cheated by shrinking school funding, but when Ben started giving us the facts about Pentagon spending versus education spending, we were astounded," explained Gardiner. "The Pentagon was still stockpiling arms and still spending at Cold War levels even though the Cold War had ended with the fall of the Berlin Wall. It made us think that if we could just find a way to present the facts provocatively, people would have the desired emotional reaction."

TARGET MARKET

According to Duane Peterson, the manager of BLSP, the December 1999 to January 2000 leg of "Move Our Money" targeted those living within the presidential primary election states of New Hampshire and Iowa. Republican and Democratic pollsters conducted a survey for BLSP, which determined that 45 percent of the Iowa electorate was willing to reduce defense spending by 15 percent. According to the *Bulletin of the Atomic Scientists,* when the same group was told that a 15 percent cut in defense spending would be used to improve education, health care, and other domestic causes, those supporting the defense cut jumped to 59 percent. The majority of those surveyed also agreed that U.S. allies should pay more for their own defense.

In 1999 Preston Daniels, mayor of Des Moines, told Reuters, "As a lifelong Iowan, I know that we do indeed support sensible priorities, given our state's populist spirit and unique role in the presidential election." He went on to state, "Iowans are patriotic, and I do believe we've got to stand behind our fighting troops."

Once "Move Our Money" rematerialized in September 2000 before the presidential election, its target extended to the entire electorate. Gardiner and Berkeley, the campaign's primary architects, designed the campaign to target people who thought about social issues but were misinformed about how the federal budget was distributed. Andrew Greenblatt, a spokesperson for BLSP, explained the general public's misconception in the *Pittsburgh Post-Gazette.* "The public agrees with us," Greenblatt said. "Give them a pie chart and ask them to cut it up the way they think reflects our actual spending, and they give a lot less to the military and a lot more to other pressing domestic needs, including education. When you show them the disparity between what we

PAUL NEWMAN

The actor Paul Newman was one of the celebrities to join Business Leaders for Sensible Priorities (BLSP), a nonprofit organization established in 1998 to decrease defense spending and increase educational funding. Explaining in *NEA Today* why he joined the organization, Newman stated, "For the cost of one F22 fighter plane—$188 million—we can build 20 new schools. For the $13 billion a year savings we'd gain by reducing nuclear weapons, we could enroll every eligible child in Head Start and cover every uninsured child in America."

and other nations spend on our military, and when you show them the disparity between what we spend on the military and what we spend on other needs, they can't believe it."

COMPETITION

The journalist Mark Weisbrot wrote in the *Las Vegas Review-Journal* that the Pentagon had historically posed two rationalizations for its exorbitant defense budget. First, defense spending bolstered overall employment and economic growth. Secondly, military research improved the innovation of other industries such as aerospace, computers, and electronics. John W. Douglass, president of the Aerospace Industries Association of America, disputed the "Move Our Money" campaign in the *New York Times.* "Just to try to say that Americans have two choices, education or Pentagon waste, is just an outrageous oversimplification and unfair statement," Douglass said.

Defense contractors such as the Boeing Company, the Northrop Grumman Corporation, and the Lockheed Martin Corporation never launched advertisement to discredit "Move Our Money." Peterson identified the campaign's main opposition as "latent support for authority, deference to the 'experts,' and the say-nothing approach of some candidates." Some critics blamed the politicians' blasé attitude on the source of their campaign funding. According to Iowa State University's *U-Wire,* defense contractors spent $32.3 million on political contributions between 1991 and 1997. The world's largest defense contractor, Lockheed Martin, posted more than $25 billion in sales for 2000, a year of relative global peace.

MARKETING STRATEGY

Along with Hill, Holliday's account executive Stever Aubrey, Berkeley and Gardiner developed the advertising strategy that "if we reduce Pentagon spending a little, we can improve education a lot," according to Gardiner. This concept was derived from information originally provided by Cohen. With a working precept for the campaign, Berkeley and Gardiner set out to create provocative black-and-white newspaper ads that would be ready before the January 2000 New Hampshire primary elections. One newspaper ad featured 1,000 tiny illustrations of nuclear bombs that were divided into 20 rows of 50. The ad's headline read, "The first row obliterates civilization. The rest destroy our schools." Another print ad featured a bar graph that displayed the Pentagon's $300 billion defense budget towering over the $33 billion education budget. The ad's headline read, "If only we could blow them away with our S.A.T. scores."

Berkeley, who wrote the campaign's copy, explained, "We wanted candidates to discuss real issues in the upcoming election instead of focusing on character assassination." The campaign's most awarded print ad, "Smarter Bombs," featured the copy "No wonder our bombs are smarter than our students" above the bar graph comparing the defense and education budgets. All print ads included the tagline "Move Our Money."

In late 1999 Cohen performed one of his BLSP demonstrations for the creatives at Hill, Holliday. Cohen dropped one ball bearing (BB) into a cup for every active U.S. nuclear warhead. Berkeley and Gardiner later cast Shanahan to use the same demonstration for a 60-second radio spot. Shanahan began the spot by stating, "I believe we can improve education in America without compromising our national security. To illustrate my point, I have some BBs here. Imagine each BB is a nuclear bomb." After one BB clinked into a metal cup, Shanahan continued, "[that] could destroy Hiroshima 15 times over." After five more clinks, Shanahan explained "[that] wipes out all of Russia. Now, after using those six bombs, this is how many the U.S. has left." The clinking of thousands of BBs followed. Shanahan concluded the spot saying, "By reducing our nuclear weapons, we could save billions of dollars. That money could be educating our kids. Let's get the politicians to talk about the real issues."

Gardiner conceived the campaign's only television spot from his childhood memory of the movie *Patton,* which starred the actor George C. Scott as General Patton. Berkeley explained, "When [Gardiner] was a kid, he went to see the movie *Patton.* He was late so the only seats available were in the front row (it was still the era of big movie screens). The movie opens with an extended monologue by General George S. Patton. He

> **DESTROYING THE WORLD'S CITIES × 10**
>
> In 1999 the United States spent 17 times more on defense than any potential adversary. It also maintained 12,000 nuclear warheads, enough to destroy every city in the world 10 times over. Its number of warheads was more than double the number of nuclear weapons maintained by China, Russia, Iran, Syria, North Korea, and Cuba combined. By maintaining a nuclear arsenal capable of destroying the world's cities only four times over, America could save $15 billion a year.

makes a speech to unseen troops. He stands on an enormous stage, dwarfed by a gigantic American flag behind him. It's the kind of image that sticks with you." Shanahan starred in the television spot, and much like Scott was in *Patton,* he was featured on a stage before a large screen. Shanahan then delivered a message that was similar to his radio spot's dialogue about the Pentagon's overstocking of nuclear warheads. Instead of using BBs to vivify America's stockpile of nuclear weapons, the screen behind Shanahan filled with hundreds of nuclear weapons. The commercial ended with the tagline "Move Our Money."

OUTCOME

The "Move Our Money" campaign created by Hill, Holliday collected a Gold and Bronze Pencil at the 2000 One Show Awards. One print ad earned a Bronze Lion at the 2001 Cannes Lions International Advertising Festival. It also garnered awards (two silver and one bronze) at the Clio Awards. At the 2001 International ANDY Awards, the print ad "Smarter Bombs" was the overall winner in the Newspaper category, one of the most prestigious awards in the advertising industry. Poles tracking public opinion in Des Moines, according to BLSP, showed that support for reallocating 15 percent of the defense budget to education jumped from 45 percent to 72 percent by the 2000 Iowa primary's completion.

Unfortunately for BLSP, President-Elect George W. Bush announced plans for increasing military funding before he acceded to office. The terrorist attacks on September 11, 2001, propelled Congress to further increase the Pentagon's budget. In 2002 the Defense Department chose Lockheed Martin as the lead contractor for the Joint Strike Fighter program. The contract was worth an estimated value of $200 billion.

FURTHER READING

Borosage, Robert L. "America Spends Billions Overseas—but Mainly in Military Aid, Not Development." *Nation,* May 8, 2000, p. 37.

Brown, Justin. "How Many Weapons Is Too Many? The Pentagon, Defending a $300 Billion Budget, Argues That America's Military Superiority Remains Vulnerable." *Christian Science Monitor,* November 4, 1999, p. 1.

Cocco, Marie. "Ice-Cream Man Asks Congress to Try New Flavor." *Newsday,* September 16, 1999, p. A51.

Isaacs, John. "Fortifying Fortress America." *Bulletin of the Atomic Scientists,* March 1, 1999, p. 24.

Killian, Larita J. "The Ice Cream Man Cometh: Ben Cohen of Ben and Jerry's Fame Tries to Take a Scoop Out of the Defense Budget." *Government Executive,* July 1, 2000, p. 122.

Merina, Antia. "Interview: Paul Newman—Working for New Priorities." *NEA Today,* February 1, 2000, p. 19.

Myers, Steven Lee. "'Pentagon Maverick' Sounds Alarm." *New York Times,* January 18, 1999, p. 15.

Nyhan, David. "Bush Aims His Blunderbuss at the Wrong Target." *Boston Globe,* December 5, 1999, p. D4.

Quinones, Eric. "Attacking Military Excess, from the Executive Office." *New York Times,* June 13, 1999, p. 4.

Rasberry, William. "Big Guns? We Need Stronger Brains." *Pittsburgh Post-Gazette,* October 19, 1999, p. A13.

Reidy, Chris. "Hill Holliday Winds Award." *Boston Globe,* May 13, 2000, p. C1.

Warner, Judy. "Hill, Holliday Breaks Ads for Bipartisan Cause." *Adweek,* December 13, 1999, p. 5.

Weltman, Eric. "Military Spending vs Everything Else." *Dollars & Sense,* January 1, 2000, p. 7.

Kevin Teague

Cadbury Adams USA LLC

389 Interpace Parkway
Parsippany, New Jersey 07054
USA
Telephone: (973) 909-2000
Fax: (973) 909-3051
Web site: www.cadburyadams.com

FOUR OUT OF FIVE DENTISTS CAMPAIGN

OVERVIEW

When pharmaceutical company Pfizer Inc. bought its competitor Warner-Lambert Company in 2000, it also acquired its Adams confectionary division and its gum brands Trident, Dentyne, and Chiclets. At the time, sugarless chewing-gum brands were taking the lead in retail gum sales as health-conscious consumers chose alternatives to sugary treats. In 2003 total sales of sugarless gum sales were $578.5 million, while sugared gum achieved $309.3 million in total sales. The top market position that year was held by Wm. Wrigley Jr. Company's brand Extra, with a 26 percent dollar share. Wrigley's Eclipse, with a 16 percent dollar share, held the number two spot. Number three was Pfizer's Trident, with sales of $82.6 million and a 14.8 percent dollar share.

To help Pfizer drive sales of Trident, ad agency J. Walter Thompson created a new marketing campaign for the brand that was based on Trident's 30-year-old claim that it was recommended by four out of five dentists to their patients who chewed gum. The campaign, which was limited to television, put a humorous spin on the answer to the question of why the fifth dentist did not recommend Trident. "Four Out of Five Dentists" spots began airing in January 2003. A month later Pfizer sold its Adams division, including the Trident brand, to London-based company Cadbury Schweppes. Cadbury Schweppes created an American subsidiary called Cadbury Adams and continued the "Four Out of Five Dentists" campaign through early 2005. Specific spending figures for the campaign were unavailable, but a report in *Adweek* noted that Cadbury spent approximately $5 to $10 million advertising the Trident brand in 2003.

The Trident television spot "Squirrel" earned accolades from the industry, including a mention on *Adweek*'s Best Spots list. Not all comments about the Trident commercials were positive, however. An article in *Advertising Age* questioned whether consumers under 35 years old—the brand's target audience—would get the reference to the old slogan. Some consumers also complained that the "Ride" spot, which showed the fifth dentist falling off a roller coaster, was in bad taste.

HISTORICAL CONTEXT

In 1899 a collaboration between Thomas Adams, Edward Beeman, and William White resulted in the founding of the American Chicle Group and the creation of chewing-gum brands such as Chiclets. In 1916 the company introduced the first gum touted as having oral-hygiene benefits: Dentyne. Following concerns expressed by consumers about the effects of sugar on their dental health, the company introduced Trident, a sugarless

ORIGINATOR OF TRIDENT'S "FOUR OUT OF FIVE DENTIST" CLAIM DIES

Longtime advertising executive Henry Kornhauser died on September 14, 2005. He was 73 years old. While working as an account executive for the Trident sugarless gum brand in the mid-1960s, Kornhauser provided the information that led to Trident's marketing claim that "Four Out of Five Dentists" recommended the product to their patients who chewed gum. Kornhauser began his career in the mail room of New York–based Katz Agency and eventually became an executive at ad agencies that included the well-known Cunningham & Walsh. During the 1970s he served as president of Dusenberry Ruriani & Kornhauser and then of Clyne Dusenberry and Kornhauser & Calene. Another famous slogan he helped create was Black Flag Roach Motel's "Roaches check in, but they don't check out."

gum, in 1964. Warner-Lambert Company, a pharmaceutical manufacturer, acquired the American Chicle Group in 1962; three decades later Warner-Lambert changed the name of its U.S. confectionary division from American Chicle Group to Adams.

In 2000, following a three-month takeover battle, pharmaceutical giant Pfizer bought the Warner-Lambert Company for $90 billion. Referring to the Adams segment as a "noncore" business, Pfizer sold it to Cadbury Schweppes in February 2003 for $4.2 billion. Just weeks prior to the sale, Pfizer launched Trident gum's "Four Out of Five Dentists" campaign. After the acquisition Cadbury Adams USA LLC was created as a U.S. subsidiary of London-based Cadbury Schweppes. Among the new subsidiary's products were the gum brands Chiclets, Dentyne, and Trident, the mint brands Clorets and Certs, and Halls cough drops. Cadbury Adams also handled the historical gum brands that carried the names of American Chicle Group's founders Thomas Adams and Edward Beeman: Adams Blackjack and Beeman's. Despite the change in company ownership, the "Four Out of Five Dentists" campaign for Trident gum was continued by Cadbury Adams through March 2005.

TARGET MARKET

Trident gum's "Four Out of Five Dentists" campaign targeted consumers in the 18- to 34-year-old demographic. According to the company, this group linked Trident gum with dental-health benefits (because it was sugarless it did not cause cavities) but often did not associate it with other health issues. The purpose of the new campaign was to stress the relevance of Trident sugarless gum in consumers' lives, not only as a means of preventing cavities but also to help with other health concerns. Based on information released by the Centers for Disease Control (CDC), 44 million Americans were considered obese in 2001, and 16.7 million were diagnosed with diabetes that year. Further, in 2003 the National Center for Health Statistics reported that the rate of obesity in kids aged 6 to 11 years old had quadrupled in the past 25 years. Research indicated that increased consumption of sugar by Americans of all ages was a contributing factor to the rising rate of obesity and related health complications such as diabetes.

COMPETITION

Since the introduction of its Juicy Fruit chewing gum in 1893, the Wm. Wrigley Jr. Company had held the top spot in sales of gum in the United States. But the company had been slow to jump into the sugarless-gum market. That changed in 1984, when Wrigley introduced its first sugarless brand, Extra, which by 1989 had become the country's best-selling sugar-free gum. It added Eclipse sugarless gum to its U.S. product line in 1999. Playing on the success of Extra and the growing popularity of sugarless gum, in 2001 Wrigley introduced another such product, Orbit, to American consumers. In 2003 the Extra brand held the number one spot with U.S. sales of $141 million. That year Eclipse was the number two sugarless gum, and Orbit followed in the number five spot with sales of $60.9 million. To help boost Orbit's sales and push it closer to the number three brand, Cadbury Adams' Trident, Wrigley launched an advertising campaign that poked fun at its competitor. The campaign, which began in February 2003, compared Orbit to "Brand T" gum, a product that resembled competitor Trident. Orbit advertisements also made fun of Trident's "Four out of five dentists recommend" claim. The Orbit ads featured an attractive spokeswoman with a British accent who showed what happened when a construction worker switched from "Brand T" to Orbit. After giving the man a kiss, the spokeswoman said, "Orbit cleans another dirty mouth. That's why four out of five construction workers prefer the good clean feeling of Orbit, no matter what."

Although the Hershey Company was best known for chocolate confections, such as its famous Hershey's Kisses, in 2000 the iconic chocolatier joined the gum market with the acquisition of Nabisco Holdings Corp.'s gum and mint business. The $135 million deal included Nabisco's Ice Breaker sugarless gum. In 2002 it appeared that Hershey itself would be sold, with potential buyers that included competitors Cadbury Schweppes and Wrigley. In late 2002 Hershey rejected a $12 billion bid made by Wrigley, and changes to the controlling Hershey Trust Board membership resulted in the company no longer being for sale. To enhance its gum brand and reach a wider segment of consumers, in 2002 Hershey expanded its Ice Breaker brand to include Unleashed, which targeted Generation Y youths, or kids 16 to 24 years old. Ice Breaker added a breath-freshening flavor, Spearmint, in 2003. The brand was ranked number six in 2003, behind Wrigley's Orbit.

MARKETING STRATEGY

In 2003 Adams, owned at the time by pharmaceutical company Pfizer, decided to break into the club of Super Bowl advertisers with a commercial for its Trident brand chewing gum. The company's ad agency, J. Walter Thompson, created a television spot that would stand out among the Super Bowl commercials that promoted everything from beer and soft drinks to tax preparers and athletic shoes. J. Walter Thompson created a spot that played on Trident's long-running tagline, "Four out of five dentists recommend." It used humor to answer the question that was raised by the tagline: Why did dentist number five not recommend the gum to his or her patients? The campaign was limited to television and included three spots.

The first of the three spots, which made its debut during Super Bowl XXXVII, was titled "Squirrel." It depicted a panel of five dentists sitting at a table, while a voice-over asked, "Four out of five dentists surveyed recommend Trident for patients who chew gum. But what about the fifth dentist?" The camera focused on the first four dentists as each one responded, "Yes." As the fifth dentist prepared to answer the question, a squirrel that had made its way into the room through an open window ran up the hapless dentist's pant leg. There was a loud crunching noise as the squirrel chomped onto one of the dentist's body parts, which was followed by the man screaming in pain, "No." The voice-over concluded: "One thing's for sure. Long-lasting Trident is good for teeth."

A second television spot was released in mid-January as a follow-up to the Super Bowl spot. Titled "Fly," it showed the panel of dentists again sitting at a table, but in front of each was a box with two buttons, one green and labeled "Yes," and one red and labeled "No." The voice-over asked the same question about the fifth dentist as in the "Squirrel" spot, but rather than verbally responding "Yes" to the question, each of the first four dentists pressed the green button, and the word "Yes" lit up. As the fifth dentist prepared to respond by pressing one of the buttons, a fly buzzed into the room and landed on his forehead. The dentist sitting beside him smacked the fly with a clipboard, knocking dentist number five unconscious; he fell forward, landing on the red button and lighting up the word "No." The voice-over again concluded with the statement "There are many theories, but one thing's for sure. Long-lasting Trident is good for teeth."

The final spot, "Ride," was created to support the launch of Trident's Cool Rush flavor variety, which was introduced in 2003. In this commercial the five dentists were shown riding a roller coaster at an amusement park. Following the same format used in the "Squirrel" and "Fly" commercials, before the unfortunate fifth dentist could respond to the question, the safety bar on his roller coaster car failed to swing all the way around, and he toppled out of the seat when the ride inverted.

OUTCOME

The humor of the spots, particularly "Squirrel," appealed to both consumers and the advertising industry. The spot earned recognition as one of *Adweek* magazine's 50 Best Spots of 2003. Finally providing an answer to the long-running question of why the fifth dentist did not recommend Trident to patients who chewed gum added to the interest. In his ratings of the Super Bowl commercials, *ESPN.com* columnist Eric Neel gave the "Squirrel" spot an Honorable Mention. On the other hand, while*Advertising Age* columnist Bob Garfield described the spot as "cute," he also voiced doubts about the effectiveness of the campaign's central joke: "Will anyone under 35 remember the old 'four-out-of-five dentists' claim?" Some consumers criticized the "Ride" spot, stating that it was in bad taste given the number of real amusement-park accidents related to roller coasters. The campaign's television spots ran through March 2005. In May of that year Trident launched a new campaign, "Little Mouth," which featured a set of animated false teeth caught in dangerous situations, such as falling into a cup of coffee and nearly drowning. In each spot the teeth were rescued by a pack of Trident sugarless gum, and the new tagline stated, "A mouth's best friend."

FURTHER READING

"Adams Acquisition Gives Cadbury Schweppes New Muscle." *MMR,* February 10, 2003.

Anderson, Mae. "JWT's Trident Smiles in Print, Not TV." *Adweek,* May 25, 2004.

Beirne, Mike. "Category Wars: Showdown in Sugar-Free Gum." *Adweek,* October 27, 2003.

"Best Spots of the Year: 2003." *Adweek,* February 9, 2004.

Fuhrman, Elizabeth. "Sugar-Free Sizzles: Gums Find Success with Sugar-Free and Line Extensions." *Candy Industry,* October 1, 2003.

Garfield, Bob. "Garfield's Super Bowl Review: Ads that Sell? Super." *Advertising Age,* January 27, 2003.

"Gum Offers More than Chewing." *MMR,* May 31, 2004.

"Hershey to Acquire Nabisco's Gum, Mints Business." *Professional Candy Buyer,* November 1, 2000.

"Ice Breakers Unleashed." *Confectioner,* December 12, 2002.

Kirk, Jim. "Wrigley Rolls Out Red Gumball to Boost Blue Extra." *Chicago Tribune,* March 28, 2003.

———. "Wrigley's Orbit Ads Launch Jabs at Gum Rival." *Chicago Tribune,* February 27, 2003.

Pennington, Gail. "Animals Rule the Super Ads." *St. Louis Post-Dispatch,* January 26, 2003.

"Trident's 'Four Out of Five Dentists' Claim to Fame to Air on Super Bowl XXXVII." *Business Wire,* January 22, 2003.

Rayna Bailey

Cadbury Schweppes Americas Beverages

5301 Legacy Drive
Plano, Texas 75024
USA
Telephone: (972) 673-7000
Fax: (972) 673-7980
Web site: www.cadburyschweppes.com
www.snapple.com

BOTTLES PERSONIFIED CAMPAIGN

OVERVIEW

In the 1990s Cadbury Schweppes Americas Beverages' subsidiary Snapple Beverage Corporation, long known for its quirky advertising, underwent a series of ownership changes that led to the brand losing its focus. In 2002 the company and its advertising agency, Deutsch New York, attempted to recapture the amateurish feel of the television commercials that had made Snapple a major success story of the early 1990s. Deutsch created the "Bottles Personified" television spots, in which Snapple bottles wearing wigs, clothes, and accessories were animated using the crudest of puppetry techniques.

The campaign, reported to be budgeted at $40 million, was introduced with six spots, including the well-regarded "House Party," in which a teenage Snapple-bottle daughter throwing a wild party was caught by her parents. Customers became involved by submitting their ideas for future commercials in the "What's Your Story" contest. The campaign was also supported by a mobile barbershop that gave out free haircuts in the styles worn by the Snapple-bottle stars. New TV spots, which featured Snapple employees introducing the animated bottles, followed in 2004.

The "Bottles Personified" campaign was popular enough to run for more than two years, but it never registered with the younger demographic to the extent that the marketers had hoped. Snapple underwent a marketing shakeup; different leadership was brought in, and Deutsch was replaced by a new ad agency in May 2004, at which point the "Bottles Personified" campaign came to an end.

HISTORICAL CONTEXT

Snapple, which essentially invented the alternative-beverage category, enjoyed explosive growth in the early 1990s, when it was the fastest-growing beverage company in the world. Much of its success was attributed to its quirky, almost amateurish advertising, which consumers found endearing. Beginning in 1991 Snapple commercials featured the spokesperson Wendy the Snapple Lady, a straight-talking native New Yorker. In 1994 Quaker Oats bought the brand for $1.7 billion, but it struggled under corporate ownership, and Snapple lost its edge. After three years Quaker Oats gave up on Snapple and unloaded it for just $300 million. The new owner, Triarc, reestablished the zaniness of the brand, bringing back the Snapple Lady in commercials. In three years Triarc was able to regain lost sales and cashed in by selling Snapple to Cadbury Schweppes for $1.45 billion.

Snapple's new corporate parent continued to fund the "Little Fruits" advertising campaign begun under Triarc. In these television spots Snapple bottles were dressed in fruit costumes. Their activities moved from innocent high jinks to more adult themes such as parent fruits trying to tell teen fruits about sex. According to Vivian Manning-Schaffel writing for Brandchannel.com, "Snapple's research showed that the earlier 'Little Fruits' ads appealed to kids and folks in their 40s, but those in the in-between ages were more interested in the newer, racier spots. Taking this into consideration, the brand came up with an idea to raise the cool quotient of Snapple to teenagers through 34-year-olds by vamping up the brand image." The result was the "Bottles Personified" campaign, developed by ad agency Deutsch New York.

BARTENDER, ANOTHER SNAPPLE

The Snapple brand was developed by Unadulterated Food Products, Inc., a company founded in Brooklyn in the early 1970s to sell pure fruit juices to area health-food stores. The company introduced a carbonated apple juice in 1978, calling it "Snapple," after buying the rights to the name for $500.

The product got off to a surprising start, with a number of distributors calling up to request the product. Only when tops started to pop off the bottles in the warehouse did the company realize that the juice had been fermenting and that it had been unintentionally selling hard cider.

TARGET MARKET

While Snapple wanted to appeal to all potential customers, especially its core 25- to 44-year-old market, the "Bottles Personified" campaign was especially geared toward "Generation Y," 18- to 24-year-olds who were not as familiar with Snapple's reputation as a pioneer of alternative beverages. It was also an important demographic because on a per-capita basis young people consumed more beverages than any other age group. Moreover, they could be persuaded to try a new product. Maura Mottolese, Snapple's vice president of marketing, told Kate MacArthur of *Advertising Age,* "Young beverage consumers tend to be flavor explorers, so they're not as loyal as older consumers." In order to make the "Bottles Personified" campaign more appealing to this demographic, many of the television spots played on the theme of teenage rebellion. Snapple also partnered with Viacom, a media company that enjoyed a strong presence with the target age group. Viacom's MTV unit produced the first wave of spots, which were subsequently shown on Viacom television channels, including the UPN network and the cable channels MTX, MTV2, BET, VH1, Nick at Nite, CMT, and TNN. According to Steve Jarmon, Snapple's vice president of corporate communications, the "Bottles Personified" campaign engaged "younger viewers without alienating our loyal customers. It seems to appeal to both older and younger Snapple drinkers."

COMPETITION

Snapple had to contend with a crowded beverage category, with scores of companies spending millions to advertise their products. In the carbonated category the likes of Coca-Cola and Pepsi regularly introduced new products, such as Vanilla Coke and Pepsi Twist. Not only did Coke and Pepsi have hefty advertising budgets to support their products, but they also enjoyed the benefits of a far-flung distribution network to make their products ubiquitous in the marketplace. They were also able to leverage these advantages in noncarbonated beverages. In the water category Pepsi's Aquafina and Coca-Cola's Dasani occupied two of the top three spots. They also offered direct competition to Snapple, in particular in the form of Coke's Nestea product and Pepsi's Lipton Brisk, the latter the category leader in the iced-tea segment. Snapple battled with AriZona Beverages for second place among teas and vied for sales with a multitude of private-label iced-tea brands. Snapple's fruit drinks also faced competition from juice makers such as Ocean Spray Cranberries, Inc., and Minute Maid (which was owned by Coca-Cola).

MARKETING STRATEGY

Explaining the genesis of the "Bottles Personified" campaign (also referred to as "Real Experiences" in the early days of the campaign, "Snapple was looking to go back to [the brand's original] quirky, homemade feeling," David Rosen, a Deutsch assistant creative director, told Sarah Woodward of *Shoot,* "We wanted to make advertising that looked as if two guys who worked at Snapple had to create the campaign, and did it by cutting wigs off Barbie dolls and gluing them on the bottles." The six spots in the initial wave of the campaign were shot in three days at Occidental Studios, Hollywood, and edited into 5-, 10-, 15-, and 20-second versions, which the marketers hoped would help the spots stand out in a television landscape dominated by 30-second spots. In addition, they hoped that, by giving viewers less, they would make viewers eager to see more of the animated bottles. While the brevity of the spots made editing somewhat difficult, the use of the Snapple bottles as actors allowed the directors to focus on the story. Codirector Jonathan Dayton explained to Woodward, "Every shot was a product shot. So we could just concentrate on the story and not worry about the gratuitous product placement." To enhance the amateur feel, the commercials were shot on digital video rather than film.

The first six spots were "Skateboard," "Boy Band," "Shower," "UFO," "Breakdance," and "House Party." Versions were also developed for print advertising. The spots began airing on April 15, 2002. Especially well received was "House Party." In this commercial Snapple bottles that were dressed like parents—Dad wore a necktie, Mom a string of beads—returned home to find that their house had been trashed by their daughter's friends. The pigtail-wearing daughter was caught kissing a Snapple bottle outfitted as a punk. Crude puppetry made her appear to be quaking with fear when she saw her parents. Instead of Snapple's usual tagline, "Made from the best stuff on earth," "House Party" and the other spots simply closed with the pop of a vacuum-sealed bottle being opened. Examples of other spots were "Shower," in which a bottle dressed as a female gym teacher caught boy bottles peeping into the girls' shower, and "Skateboard," which showed a Snapple-bottle skateboarder wiping out on a trick and ending up in the hospital.

Building on the successful launch of the "Bottles Personified" campaign, Snapple conducted the two-month, 13-city "Dye Hard Snapple Tour," which was developed to reach the 18- to 24-year-old target audience. A mobile barbershop offered free alternative hairstyles, similar to the Mohawks and mullets adorning the Snapple bottles in the television spots. Dye jobs inspired by Snapple flavors were also available. Free bottles of Snapple's newest flavors were handed out along with T-shirts and bandanas. The tour was not only well received by consumers but also garnered a good deal of media attention, appearing on some 30 television programs and accounting for more than two hours of coverage.

Another supporting element of the "Bottles Personified" campaign was the "What's Your Story?" contest, which allowed customers to submit their ideas for a new commercial. Of the more than 1,400 entries, the one chosen, by UCLA freshman C.J. Yu, depicted a smoky concert venue where a Snapple bottle dove off the stage for some crowd surfing, only to land on the floor with a thud. The contest was held again throughout 2002, resulting in more than 25,000 entries.

In April 2003, a year after the campaign broke, Snapple offered six more television spots, including the grand prize winner of the "What's Your Story" promotion, "Bouncing Car," which featured a hydraulic car that ejected the Snapple-bottle driver instead of impressing the Snapple girls on the sidewalk; "Pamplona," in which Snapple bottles ran with the legendary bulls—really guinea pigs with horns; and "Yard Sale," in which a Snapple bottle got in trouble with his mother when he tried to buy a stereo. The last spot also served as a springboard for a "Yard Sale" promotion, in which customers could exchange bottle caps for prizes at yard-sale-themed promotional events held in major cities. Other elements added to the "Bottles Personified" campaign included fortune-cookie messages, air banners flown over beaches and other summer spots, and advertisements on pizza boxes and deli bags.

The "Bottles Personified" campaign continued in 2004 with four 30-second television spots and two 15-second spots. In this execution, however, the dressed-up bottles were joined by employee costars who narrated the bottles' "epics." For example, one spot supported the introduction of a new flavor, Super Sour Lemonade, with a bottle dressed up like a superhero. A part of this final phase of the campaign was a 12-week summer sweepstakes called Snaffle. During this time trivia was printed on the Snapple caps, and each week four winning caps were announced; holders of all four caps won a weekly grand prize.

OUTCOME

While Snapple rolled out the final spots in the "Bottles Personified" campaign, the company's marketing team was being restructured by Cadbury. Overall the commercials were well received. In April 2002 the influential advertising magazine *Adweek* named "House Party" one of its "Best Spots." Often difficult to please, *Advertising Age* critic Bob Garfield called the spots "delightful" and "hilarious." Snapple also saw sales improve in 2002, but a year later, at a time when noncarbonated beverages enjoyed a boom, Snapple experienced a 4 percent drop in sales.

In 2004 Snapple's vice president of marketing, Maura Mottolese, admitted to Kate MacArthur of *Advertising Age* that the "Bottles Personified" campaign had done a good job connecting with its core 25- to 44-year-old consumers but that Snapple was still "trying to increase [its] relevance with 18- to 24-year-olds." Deutsch would run out of chances to address that problem, however. In May 2004 Cadbury replaced the agency, giving the Snapple account to Cliff Freeman and Partners. The newly appointed agency had previously worked with Randy Gier, the new chief marketing officer for Cadbury's American Beverages division, which included Snapple. A new campaign was soon developed that ditched the animated bottles for a reprise of Snapple's "real people" approach that had worked so well in the early 1990s, including the return of the popular spokesperson Wendy. Writing for *Adweek,* Kathleen Sampey and Kenneth Hein quoted one Snapple bottler who liked the new spots that were unveiled at a bottlers' meeting in October 2005. The writers added, "The bottler was appreciative of the changes, saying the personified bottles work from Deutsch was expected to be 'our Budweiser frogs. They weren't.'"

FURTHER READING

"Creative Best Spots: April." *Adweek,* May 13, 2002, p. 28.

Flass, Rebecca. "Metal and Glass." *Adweek* (eastern ed.), June 3, 2004, p. 14.

Garfield, Bob. "New Snapple Ads Hold Genius, and a Lesson for Kevin Costner." *Advertising Age,* May 6, 2002, p. 63.

Hein, Kenneth. "Snapple to Drinkers: We Dye Harder." *Brandweek,* December 9, 2002, p. 18.

———. "Surging Snapple Orders $12M Refill for Bottle Ads." *Brandweek,* February 2, 2004, p. 5.

MacArthur, Kate. "Snapple Appeals to Gen Y to Boost Sales." *Advertising Age,* May 10, 2004, p. 4.

Manning-Schaffel, Vivian. "Snapple—The Best Stuff." *Brandchannel.com,* January 20, 2003. Available from <http://www.brandchannel.com/print_page.asp?ar_id=107§ion=profile>

Sampey, Kathleen, and Kenneth Hein. "Cliff Freeman Brings Back Wendy the Snapple Lady." *Adweek,* October 25, 2004, p. 9.

Woodward, Sarah. "The Skateboarding Snapple Bottle, and Other Tales." *Shoot,* April 26, 2002, p. 16.

Ed Dinger

GO FOR ZERO CAMPAIGN

OVERVIEW

Royal Crown Company, which introduced Diet Rite in 1958, prided itself on being a pioneer of the soft-drink industry. Not only was Diet Rite the world's first diet carbonated soft drink (CSD), but it was also later the first CSD made with Splenda brand sweetener, a low-calorie sugar substitute extracted from sucrose. Diet Rite was purchased by Cadbury Schweppes Americas Beverages in 2000. Later that year a reformulated Diet Rite was released that had no carbohydrates, calories, caffeine, sugar, or sodium. The Coca-Cola Company's Diet Coke and PepsiCo, Inc.'s Diet Pepsi were Diet Rite's fiercest competitors, but neither offered a zero-calorie CSD made with Splenda, which was deemed a healthier sugar substitute than the commonly used sweetener aspartame. Hoping to increase its market share by 10 percent, Cadbury released its Diet Rite "Go For Zero" campaign.

The $8 million campaign was created by the advertising agency Brand Buzz and the public-relations firm Cohn & Wolfe. The first television commercial aired in August 2004. Other media included radio advertisements and a cross-promotion with the Zero Gravity Corporation (or ZERO-G), the world's first provider of flights that allowed the public to experience weightlessness. According to a Brand Buzz spokesperson the campaign was intended to brand Diet Rite on what the agency called a "zero messaging platform" by touting the drink's "zero carbs, zero calories, zero caffeine, zero sugar, and zero sodium" recipe. The campaign's first 30-second spot featured computer-generated zeros bubbling from each of Diet Rite's seven flavors.

Diet Rite's market share within diet CSDs increased by 46 percent during the campaign, and its entire CSD market share grew 59 percent. The campaign also garnered a Bronze EFFIE Award in the Beverages/Carbonated category in 2005. Nonalcoholic-beverage-industry critics praised the campaign for its ability to gain market share for the Diet Rite brand within an industry dominated by such titans as Coke and Pepsi, who spent $25 million to $50 million advertising their diet CSDs in 2004.

HISTORICAL CONTEXT

The soft-drink industry changed forever after Royal Crown Company introduced the world's first diet CSD, Diet Rite, in 1958. Royal Crown had originally created Diet Rite as a specialty drink, but after it excelled in a small test market, the company released Diet Rite nationwide under the tagline "Feel All Right." In 1962 it was the fourth-highest-selling cola in America. The sales of Royal Crown brands, such as RC Cola and Diet Rite, receded over the following decades until Cadbury Schweppes, the owner of CSD brands Seven Up and Dr Pepper, purchased Royal Crown in 2000. Although Diet Rite was the first calorie-free soft drink to use Splenda, Cadbury ran little Diet Rite advertising prior to "Go For Zero." Diet Rite television commercials had not aired since 1996. Critics such as Stephanie Thompson of *Advertising Age* referred to Diet Rite as an "out-of-vogue" soft drink.

Diet Rite's outlook improved in 2003 after the main website for the Atkins diet, a low-carbohydrate, high-protein weight-loss program, suggested Diet Rite over other diet CSDs. Not only did the Atkins website suggest drinking Diet Rite, but it also recommended using Diet Rite in its chicken marinade recipes. According to *Beverage Digest* editor John Sicher, the Atkins endorsement helped Diet Rite's sales jump 21 percent while the entire soft drink industry only grew 0.6 percent.

The Atkins website recommended food products that used the sugar substitute Splenda, which was deemed healthier than aspartame, a chemical that some scientists believed incited brain cancer. John Stanton, professor of food marketing at Saint Joseph's University in Philadelphia, told *Advertising Age* that the success of the Atkins diet had made previously unpopular brands such as Diet Rite popular again and had opened a window of opportunity for all other products containing Splenda. As people on the Atkins diet turned to Diet Rite in 2003, Cadbury began formulating a campaign that would expand its burgeoning base of health-conscious consumers.

TARGET MARKET

"Go For Zero" targeted what Brand Buzz dubbed "Label-Reading Wellness Women" between the ages of 35 and 49. Brand Buzz understood this target as a health- and diet-conscious population of females who balanced work, family, and other responsibilities. Aware that many women read the labels on their diet soft drinks, Brand Buzz designed the campaign to tout Diet Rite as the only Splenda CSD without calories. Coca-Cola produced a Splenda soft drink titled C2, and Pepsi produced the Splenda drink Pepsi Edge, but both combined Splenda with sugar, which resulted in an estimated 70 calories per 12-ounce can. Diet Rite's "zero messaging platform" hoped to attract all women pursuing a healthier diet, whether it was "zero-sugar" for Diabetes, "zero-sodium" for high blood pressure, or "zero-calories" for weight loss.

"We know that now more than ever people are looking for products that meet their needs for a health-conscious lifestyle," Tony Jacobs, vice president of marketing for Diet Rite at the company's Cadbury Schweppes Americas Beverage unit, was quoted in the *Wall Street Journal.* According to Jacobs, at the beginning of 2004 women made up 40 to 60 percent of Diet Rite's consumer base. Alongside the campaign's television spots, radio advertisements, and cross-promotion with ZERO-G, "Go For Zero" targeted "Label-Reading Wellness Women" by sponsoring Oprah Winfrey's *Live Your Best Life Tour,* a three-city event during which Winfrey hosted seminars about personal growth. Diet Rite also sponsored the American Diabetes Association and Speaking of Women's Health, an organization encouraging women to eat healthier and exercise more.

COMPETITION

C2, made by Coca-Cola, and Pepsi Edge were Diet Rite's largest competitors in mid-2004. Both combined Splenda with high-fructose corn syrup to create diet CSDs that tasted much like their non-diet counterparts, but with half the calories. In 2004 Coca-Cola launched a $50 million-plus marketing campaign to announce C2 with commercials featuring the Rolling Stones song "You Can't Always Get What You Want" and the Queen song "I Want to Break Free." Created by Berlin Cameron/Red Cell, an ad agency based in New York, the spots featured the tagline "Half the carbs. Half the cals. All the great taste." More than 12 million samples of C2 were distributed nationwide.

ASPARTAME

Many diet soft drinks, including Diet Coke and Diet Pepsi, contained a sugar-substitute called aspartame, a sweetener made from the combination of two building blocks of protein. Although the U.S. Food and Drug Administration (FDA) approved aspartame in 1981, public-interest groups such as the Community Nutrition Institute and the Center for Science in the Public Interest petitioned the FDA for another ruling. John Olney of Washington University in Saint Louis fanned the controversy when he released a medical study in 1996 that showed that brain cancer rates had jumped 10 percent in the United States since aspartame's approved by the FDA. In an earlier study laboratory rats that were fed aspartame also formed a significantly higher number of brain tumors. Advocates for aspartame claimed that the sugar-substitute had been proven safe in more than 200 laboratory tests and that aspartame was safe because it was composed of chemicals commonly found in meat, fish, cheese, eggs, and milk.

The $25 million Pepsi Edge campaign was also released in 2004, under the tagline "With full flavor and 50 percent less sugar and carbs, why not?" The campaign was created by advertising agency BBDO New York. Commercials featured normal men completing tasks while sportscasters Stuart Scott of ESPN's show *SportsCenter* and Rich Eisen of the NFL Network commented on them. Humorous print ads congratulated people on such prosaic accomplishments as wearing socks. The print's copy stated, "This moment deserves a Pepsi Edge."

Pepsi and Coca-Cola walked a fine line with their advertising messages. They could not advertise Pepsi Edge or C2 as aspartame-free CSDs without degrading their aspartame-laden brands, such as Diet Pepsi and Diet Coke. The similar taglines for Pepsi and Coca-Cola drew criticism from analysts. "These companies are selling the same product. What are they doing to differentiate themselves?" Tom Pirko, president of BevMark, a beverage-industry consulting firm, said to *Advertising Age.* "They're virtually indistinguishable."

MARKETING STRATEGY

The underlying message behind Diet Rite's $8 million "Go For Zero" campaign was that Diet Rite tasted just as good as CSDs made with high-fructose corn syrup, but that only Diet Rite contained "zero carbs, zero calories, zero caffeine, zero sugar, and zero sodium." Initially the campaign aired one television spot, which featured effervescent zeros rising from Diet Rite's seven flavors: cola, white grape, tangerine, red raspberry, golden peach, black cherry, and kiwi strawberry. The commercial's computer-animated zeros were created by Digital Domain, a special-effects company that had worked on such movies as *Apollo 13* and *Titanic.* Hoping to target "Label-Reading Wellness Women," Cadbury spent $2.7 million to air the commercial across cable networks such as TLC, Lifetime, HGTV, and the Food Network. These channels were selected based on their programming, which Brand Buzz believed resonated with the target's dietary and fitness interests. To reach a wider audience an additional $1.8 million was spent to release the commercial across network stations.

Cadbury expanded Diet Rite's "zero messaging platform" by partnering with ZERO-G, the world's first provider of zero-gravity flights for the public. In September 2004 Diet Rite and ZERO-G hosted "Go For Zero" promotions in Newark, Los Angeles, Dallas, Detroit, Atlanta, and Fort Lauderdale, where select consumers could experience weightlessness inside a modified Boeing 727-200. By descending at a speed that counteracted Earth's gravitational pull, the plane, called G-Force One, created a zero-gravity environment within its fuselage. ZERO-G typically charged $3,000 per flight, but consumers chosen for the promotion flew for free. ZERO-G's weightlessness technique was the same used by National Aeronautics and Space Administration (NASA) to prepare future astronauts for the weightlessness of space travel.

Cadbury hired the entertainment-marketing company EMCI to set up the ZERO-G promotion. "We believe this event will capture the imagination of America and break through all of the low carb clutter with a clear and powerful statement for Diet Rite," Jay Coleman, CEO of EMCI, told the *PR Newswire.* Spokespeople for Cadbury pushed the Diet Rite brand's "zero messaging platform" throughout the September event. Randy Gier, executive vice president and chief marketing officer of Cadbury Schweppes Americas Beverages, explained to the *PR Newswire,* "This new partnership with ZERO-G is a way for us to bring to the excitement of zero to life and to consumers around the country." Some critics frowned on ZERO-G's decision to endorse Diet Rite. Gary Ruskin, the head of Commercial Alert, a nonprofit watchdog group against intrusive advertisement, remarked in the *New York Times* about the partnership, "It's the creep of advertising into every nook and cranny of our lives and culture and even space."

OUTCOME

In 2005 "Go For Zero" earned Cadbury and Buzz Brand a Bronze EFFIE Award in the Carbonated Beverages category. During the campaign Diet Rite's market share catapulted 46 percent, far surpassing the original goal of a 10 percent increase. Amongst all CSDs, diet and non-diet, Diet Rite's market share increased 59 percent. Cadbury executives had also hoped "Go For Zero" would increase Diet Rite's baseline sales volume by 5 percent during the campaign's advertising period; it exceeded these expectations by increasing 11.4 percent even though the CSD industry was growing at a much slower rate.

Cadbury sales suggested that the success of "Go For Zero" did not just result from the endorsement from the Atkins diet. During the month of August, when the sole "Go For Zero" television spot aired, Diet Rite sold 10 percent more cases than the month before or the October afterward. Analysts attributed the success to Diet Rite's clear "zero messaging platform," while larger competitors such as C2 and Pepsi Edge fumbled with their advertising messages. Also, it became apparent that dieters wanted CSDs without any calories instead of CSDs with just half of the calories.

FURTHER READING

Berk, Christina Cheddar. "Cadbury Adds to Diet Rite Promotion." *Wall Street Journal,* July 14, 2004, p. B2C.

Elliott, Stuart. "Diet Rite's Promotion Shakes out Too Many Names for Promised Ad." *USA Today,* July 11, 1988, p. 2B.

Frank, John. "Diet Rite Reaches Out to Health Media." *PR Week US,* March 6, 2000, p. 9.

Fromm, Emily. "Soda-Pop Culture." *Adweek* (eastern ed.), February 21, 2000, p. 5.

Kirk, Jim. "Royal Crown Pops Top on New Diet Rite Recipe." *Chicago Sun-Times,* March 21, 1997, p. 49.

Kramer, Louise. "Healthy Cola? Diet Rite Tries Unusual Strategy." *Advertising Age,* October 25, 1999, p. 1.

MacArthur, Kate. "Pepsi's Edge, Coke's C2 Get Flat Reception; Brands Seen as 'Indistinguishable.'" *Advertising Age,* July 15, 2004, p. 3.

Schwartz, John. "Going to the Moon, Sponsored By M&M's." *New York Times,* October 10, 2004, p. 12.

Theodore, Sarah. "Diet Rite Goes Aspartame-Free." *Beverage Industry,* December 1, 1999, p. 19.

Thompson, Stephanie. "Low Carb Haute Cuisine." *Advertising Age,* July 12, 2004, p. 1.

Toops, Diane. "Old Favorite Diet Rite Reinvents Itself." *Food Processing,* March 1, 2003, p. 18.

Vaughn, Glenn. "The Incredible Rise and Fall of Diet Rite." *Georgia Trend,* June 1, 1995, p. 33.

Kevin Teague

California Department of Health Services, Tobacco Control Section

MS 7206
PO Box 997413
Sacramento, California 95899-7413
USA
Telephone: (916) 449-5000
Web site: www.dhs.ca.gov/tobacco

■■■

ANTITOBACCO CAMPAIGN

OVERVIEW

For decades tobacco manufacturers had glamorized smoking through widespread marketing campaigns and promotions, but as the negative health effects of such behavior grew increasingly clear toward the end of the twentieth century, health officials in the United States sought to educate the public about the ills of tobacco. California was the first to organize a statewide advertising and education effort, one that was funded by smokers themselves through a state-legislated cigarette tax. Between 1989, when the campaign first began, and 1997, California spent almost $116 million on antitobacco advertising. Although this was a significant amount, it paled in comparison to the ad budgets of leading tobacco makers, which spent several billion dollars a year on advertising.

In 1997 the California Department of Health Services (CDHS) stepped up its efforts in the antitobacco battle by launching an estimated $67 million, three-year advertising campaign designed to reduce and prevent smoking among youths and adults. The aggressive campaign, developed by Asher & Partners (Asher/Gould Advertising, Inc., until late 1997) of Los Angeles, consisted of television, radio, and print advertising, including billboard ads. Ads geared toward minorities and specific ethnic groups were also included in the campaign. These were created by specialty agencies Imada Wong Communications Group Inc., Valdes Zacky and Associates Inc., and Carol H. Williams Advertising.

The following year, in June 1998, the second phase of the three-year effort was launched. The approximately $22 million campaign again consisted of an extensive series of print, television, and radio ads that focused on bringing to light the manipulative marketing practices of the tobacco industry, the dangers of secondhand smoke, and the link between smoking and impotency. This last topic was the focus of one of the best-known television spots of the campaign, "Gala Event," which suggested to the male audience that smoking could adversely affect their sex lives. The campaign also focused on the increasing popularity of cigars and on the smoke-free bar and restaurant policy that was implemented in the state at the beginning of 1998. Kim Belsh, the director of California's DHS, explained the overall goal of the campaign in an interview with Daniel Zwerdling of National Public Radio, stating that "the whole focus of our media campaign is really to de-normalize tobacco use. And de-normalizing tobacco use means changing the perception of tobacco from something that is viewed as acceptable and even glamorous to a more realistic

The "Truth vs. Advertising" print ad from the "Antitobacco" campaign aimed at making cigarette smoking less glamorous.
CALIFORNIA DEPARTMENT OF HEALTH SERVICES. REPRODUCED BY PERMISSION.

perception of tobacco as dangerous, addictive, and socially unacceptable."

HISTORICAL CONTEXT

In 1988 California voters passed Proposition 99, an initiative that increased the tax on tobacco by 25 cents per pack of cigarettes, with the revenue to be used to fund antitobacco programs and healthcare services for underprivileged residents. In that year about 26.7 percent of Californians were smokers. The percentage declined rapidly as the tax-funded media effort began churning out aggressive advertising, and by 1995 only 16.7 percent of Californians smoked. The rate began to rise, however, when the administration of California governor Pete Wilson diverted $67 million in antitobacco funds in 1994 to pay for failing healthcare projects. In addition, television spots with an anti-industry tone, including one that featured tobacco industry executives testifying before the U.S. Congress that nicotine was not addictive, were discontinued because of pressure from the tobacco industry. Although antitobacco efforts continued, they were toned down both in character and in number, and in 1996, 18.6 percent of California adults smoked. The change in advertising, reported a research team from the University of California at San Francisco, led to an increase in tobacco sales between 1994 and 1998 of more than $1 billion, or an additional 840 million packs of cigarettes. Also alarming were statistics for young smokers. In 1992, according to the DHS, 8.7 percent of Californians aged 12 to 17 smoked. In 1995 the percentage was up to 11.9 percent. A survey conducted by the tobacco research center at the University of California at San Diego found that the percentage of youths aged 17 who were addicted to cigarettes had risen from 9.9 percent in 1993 to 12 percent three years later.

The increase in the number of California smokers, though considerably less than the national population of adult smokers, which hovered around 25 percent, was still cause for alarm among antitobacco activists, and many criticized the Wilson administration. Alan C. Henderson of the American Cancer Society of California said in the *Los Angeles Times,* "The Legislature and the governor need to wake up and smell the secondhand smoke. This is an embarrassment to the state that has been the leader in

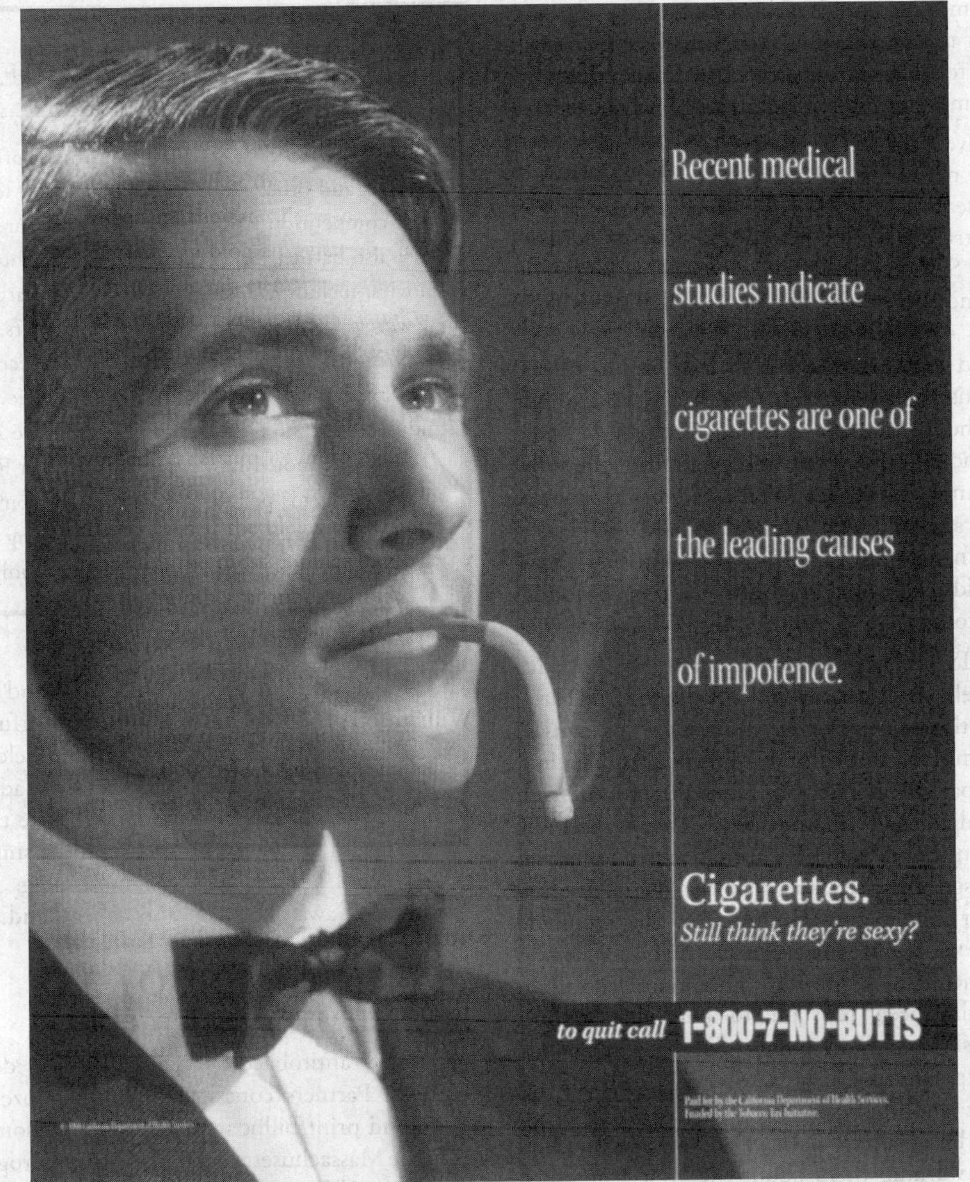
Recent medical
studies indicate
cigarettes are one of
the leading causes
of impotence.
Cigarettes.
Still think they're sexy?
to quit call 1-800-7-NO-BUTTS

A still from the "Gala Event" television ad aimed at desexualizing smoking. CALIFORNIA DEPARTMENT OF HEALTH SERVICES. REPRODUCED BY PERMISSION.

fighting tobacco." In response, the Wilson administration established a three-year contract with Asher & Partners to produce a major media campaign. In 1997, after some delays, the CDHS launched its first new advertising campaign since 1995 as a part of plans to reinvigorate the fight against tobacco. Sandra Smoley, secretary of California's Health and Welfare Agency, announced in a press release, "This advertising is some of the most aggressive, hard-hitting material that California's tobacco education media campaign has ever produced . . . These ads prove, once and for all, that this Administration is wholly committed to the anti-tobacco cause."

TARGET MARKET

The CDHS aimed its antitobacco advertising toward a number of audiences, but the agency primarily hoped to sway youths, including those who smoked and those who were susceptible to starting. More than 100,000 youths, a study at the University of California at San Diego discovered, took up smoking each year, and one-third of them would die from smoking-related diseases such as heart disease, cancer, or emphysema. Other studies indicated that it would take most of the addicted youths 16 to 20 years to quit smoking, and that almost 90 percent of smokers picked up the habit before reaching the age of

18. If youths made it past 18 without smoking, chances were high that they would not start. The studies made it glaringly clear to the CDHS that it was necessary to try to prevent teen smoking.

To effectively address youths, who often felt invincible and were not easily persuaded by advertising, it was important, researchers found, to inform them that the tobacco industry was trying to control them. One 1997 ad, "Voicebox Smoker," featured Debi Austin, a woman who began smoking at the age of 13. The spot, shot when she was 46, showed a hole in her throat where her larynx had been cut out because of her smoking habit. Still, Austin had not quit smoking; she smoked through the hole. She explained in the commercial, "When I found out how bad smoking was, I tried to stop. Believe me. I wish I could. But I can't." Belsh, discussed the strategy behind the ad in *USA Today,* saying, "You need to push emotional buttons . . . You need to give kids real evidence that they're being manipulated by the tobacco industry."

The CDHS targeted adult smokers with its media campaign as well, with ads focusing not only on the harm inflicted upon the smoker but also on the damage caused to loved ones and others through secondhand smoke. For the 1998 campaign the CDHS tackled two new issues. Because all California bars and taverns became smoke-free at the beginning of 1998, ads were deemed necessary to convince disgruntled smokers that this was a positive policy. Another issue the CDHS hoped to spotlight was the link between smoking and impotence. This time the focus was on men between 18 and 30, an age group that had traditionally been resistant to altering smoking habits. As Belsh, explained in the *Toronto Globe and Mail,* "Our experience has demonstrated that warning these guys that smoking will affect their health later in life has not been a very effective inducement to quit . . . Maybe warning them about the effects on their sex lives will be more powerful." The problem was not one to be taken lightly, for numerous studies, including the Massachusetts Male Aging Study, had indicated a significant link between smoking and impotence.

STARS AND SMOKES

Not only did the California Department of Health Services and other antitobacco forces have to contend with competition from tobacco manufacturers, but they also battled Hollywood. Many blockbuster movies, including *Reality Bites* and *My Best Friend's Wedding,* featured chain-smoking characters, portrayed by Winona Ryder and Julia Roberts, respectively. First lady Hillary Rodham Clinton criticized the movie industry for its focus on smoking, with the *Los Angeles Daily News* quoted her as commenting on Roberts's character: "This portrayal of a modern woman so reliant on cigarettes is particularly troubling given that more young women are taking up the deadly habit."

COMPETITION

The most powerful adversary of the CDHS was the tobacco industry, which consisted of the biggest advertisers in the United States. Philip Morris Companies Inc., the parent company of number one tobacco maker Philip Morris U.S.A., was the third leading U.S. advertiser in 1996 and also in 1997, despite a 5 percent reduction in ad spending. Philip Morris U.S.A., which produced such brands as the top-selling Marlboro, Benson & Hedges, Virginia Slims, and Merit, supplied about half of all the nation's cigarette shipments. Others included R.J. Reynolds Tobacco Company and Brown & Williamson Tobacco Corp. These powerful companies boasted immense advertising coffers and held the advantage of history. Tobacco companies had advertised and marketed their products for decades before the 1970 ban on radio and television cigarette advertising, making a strong and lasting impression among the public. Antitobacco awareness, on the other hand, was still in its infancy.

MARKETING STRATEGY

The 1998 antitobacco media campaign developed by Asher & Partners consisted of several dozen television, radio, and print/billboard ads, including some borrowed from the Massachusetts Tobacco Control Program's media campaign. Although the dangers of smoking were by then common knowledge in the United States, antitobacco messages were still a hard sell. As Bruce Dundore of Asher & Partners admitted in *Adweek,* "It is a very challenging account . . . It's tough to get people not to buy stuff, especially when it's a product equated with pleasure."

Ads that publicized the implementation of California's smoke-free policy for restaurants and bars began running in late 1997, and radio and television spots addressing the increased popularity of cigars began to air in the spring of 1998 while the full campaign continued to be developed. The cigar effort centered on the theme "Cigars, the big new trend in cancer," and the single television spot "How Many?" focused on the amount of nicotine in each cigar. A business suit-clad character named Chad relaxed with a cigar as the narrator questioned him about how many cigarettes he thought might equal the nicotine of one cigar. As he offered guesses, the corresponding number of cigarettes appeared in Chad's mouth. The narrator finally informed Chad that he would need to smoke more than 70 cigarettes to equal the nicotine in the cigar, and 70 cigarettes were seen stuffed into Chad's mouth. The spot ended with the narrator asking, "Need a light, Chad?"

In June 1998 the full CDHS campaign was launched. "Gala Event," the television spot that emphasized the link between smoking and impotence, was set at a festive affair. A handsome man in a tuxedo caught the eye of a beautiful woman across the bar, and the two exchanged long gazes as he suavely lit a cigarette. His cigarette suddenly went limp, and the woman was gone. The voice-over explained, "Now that medical researchers believe cigarettes are a leading cause of impotence, you're going to be looking at smoking a little differently." The spot then focused on three men smoking cigarettes. An attractive woman sauntered by, and the three men stared after her, only to find their cigarettes going limp. Embarrassed, the men covered their cigarettes or removed them from their mouths. The narrator then asked, "Cigarettes. Still think they're sexy?" "For decades, the tobacco industry has tried to link its deadly products with virility and sex appeal," explained Belsh, of the CDHS. "It's ironic that medical science shows smoking to be one of the leading causes of male impotence."

"Baby Smokers" focused on the problems of secondhand smoke and showed photos of young children and infants with lines such as "Nicholas Steele. Smoking since birth" and "Chris McDonald. Pack-a-week smoker" superimposed on the photos to emphasize how a parent's or guardian's habits could directly affect children. The tag line read, "Secondhand smoke is a first-rate killer." "Waitresses" featured various waitresses from restaurants and bars explaining the health hazards they experienced as a result of working in smoke-filled environments. They also voiced their support of the smoke-free restaurants and bars policy. "Ironic Quotes" showed a bedridden patient named Aaron. After quoting a tobacco industry executive, who claimed that people did not die from smoking, Aaron stated, "Let me clear things up for him. My doctor says I have less than one year to live." The tag line read, "The Tobacco Industry—They can bury the victims, but they can't bury the truth." A print ad, "Truth vs. Advertising," featured a circle of 20 cigarette print ads—ads that focused on the glamorous aspects of smoking and led consumers to believe that their lives would be enhanced by cigarettes—with the dates they ran. Printed alongside the ads were messages revealing what tobacco companies knew about cigarettes, for example, "The tobacco industry has known that nicotine is addictive since 1963. They denied any knowledge before Congress in 1994. Four years later they finally admitted it."

OUTCOME

The 1998 antitobacco campaign received considerable media attention, particularly "Gala Event," which brought to light a traditionally taboo subject. The number of smokers in California appeared to be on the decline as well, with the percentage of adult smokers dropping from 18.6 percent in 1996 to 18.2 percent in 1997. Smoking among youths also dropped, from 11.2 percent in 1996 to 10.9 percent in 1997. "I'm encouraged by the decline in smoking," announced Belsh, in a press release. "Smoking among youth in California has dropped for two years in a row, despite rising rates of youth smoking around the rest of the country. The adult smoking rate remains lower than any other state, with the exception of Utah." Also encouraging was the reduction in illegal sales of tobacco goods to minors in California, which dropped to 13.1 percent in 1998, an impressive 40 percent in one year.

Although the CDHS continued with its aggressive antitobacco media campaign in 1999, the word about the ills of smoking began to spread beyond a few select states such as California, Massachusetts, and Arizona. Out of the $206 billion settlement reached between tobacco companies and 39 states, which were suing to recoup the healthcare costs generated by tobacco-related illnesses, about $1.45 billion was tagged to pay for a five-year national antitobacco educational campaign. The newly formed National Tobacco Control Foundation was thus poised to launch the largest and most unified antitobacco advertising campaign ever developed, with an estimated $150 to $225 million marketing budget for 1999.

FURTHER READING

Morain, Dan. "New State TV Ads Link Smoking to Impotence in Men." *Los Angeles Times,* June 2, 1998, p. A3.

"New State Anti-Smoking Campaign Announced: California Department of Health Unveils $22 Million Advertising and Education Effort." *Sacramento Observer,* June 10, 1998, p. A9.

Parpis, Eleftheria. "Up in Smoke: Kicking Butt." *Adweek,* October 13, 1997, p. 33.

Takaki, Millie. "California Sends Anti-Smoke Signal to Stogie Smokers." *Shoot,* April 17, 1998, p. 7.

———. "California Ups the Anti-Smoking Ante, Unveils 11 Spots." *Shoot,* June 12, 1998, p. 7.

Mariko Fujinaka

TOBACCO CONTROL SECTION MEDIA CAMPAIGN

OVERVIEW

In 1988 California voters passed Proposition 99, a measure that imposed a tax hike on cigarettes and earmarked the revenues thereby generated for antismoking efforts, including statewide media campaigns. The Tobacco Control Section of the California Department of Health Services (CDHS) thus pioneered the high-profile, taxpayer-funded, big-budget antismoking advertising efforts that would ultimately become common across the United States. The California campaigns consistently attracted media attention and industry awards, but in 2000 CDHS decided on a change of course for its advertising. Hiring the Los Angeles–based agency Ground Zero, CDHS set itself the task of supplementing its ongoing educational, secondhand smoke, and cessation efforts with a more direct and confrontational assault on the integrity of tobacco companies and their personnel.

Budgeted at $125 million over five years, the Ground Zero work for CDHS first took the form of 2001 television spots as well as outdoor and print ads tagged, "Do you smell smoke?" The television spots featured a fictional tobacco executive named Ken Lane, who was shown disclosing despicable trade secrets in discussions with colleagues. In 2002 Ground Zero crafted a particularly powerful spot aimed at convincing current smokers to quit, and in 2004 the agency introduced its "Undo" theme, which used images of people blowing bubbles instead of smoking, among other arresting visual schemes, as a way of asking Californians to imagine a world without cigarettes.

California continued to post decreases in its adult smoking rates throughout the years that the Ground Zero–crafted antitobacco campaigns ran, building on the declines that had been initiated beginning with Proposition 99. Only Utah boasted fewer smokers per capita among its adult population.

HISTORICAL CONTEXT

Beginning in 1967, the Federal Communications Commission required television broadcasters to donate airtime to one antitobacco advertiser for every four tobacco commercials that appeared. The antitobacco spots produced in subsequent years by groups such as the American Cancer Society proved extremely effective, and cigarette consumption in America began dropping for the first time in the twentieth century. Tobacco companies thus supported a ban on the television advertising of their own products, since such a move would largely spell the end of donated airtime for antitobacco groups, and since these groups would find it difficult to buy their own time or otherwise place public service spots during peak viewing hours. After the eventual Congressional ban on the television advertising of tobacco products was enacted, and through most of the 1970s and 1980s, antismoking commercials were generally relegated to off-peak hours and were not considered effective. Tobacco companies, meanwhile, devoted their extensive resources to other media and to high-profile sponsorships. The smoking declines initiated in the late 1960s slowed.

The economics of antitobacco advertising began to change dramatically, however, when California voters passed Proposition 99, the California Tobacco Health Protection Act of 1988. The act introduced a new statewide cigarette tax of 25 cents per pack and allocated the resultant revenues to a group of complementary antismoking initiatives, including education programs in California schools, funding for tobacco-related research, and a media campaign. Among the media campaign's early efforts were spots that pointed out the moral bankruptcy of the tobacco industry; for instance, one commercial showed individual industry executives testifying in a congressional hearing that they did not believe tobacco was addictive. The best-known work in the first decade of California's media campaign was crafted by the Los Angeles advertising agency Asher/Gould (successively renamed Asher & Partners, Asher/Gal & Partners, and Italia/Gal). Among the agency's most lauded campaigns was a 1997 series of billboards featuring two cowboys on horseback in imagery that recalled the famous "Marlboro Man" ads. "I miss my lung, Bob," read the text in one such billboard. "Bob, I've got emphysema," read the text in another.

The California antismoking campaign was the first of its kind and scale in the world, and its success inspired Massachusetts, Florida, and Arizona, among other U.S. states, to embark on similar taxpayer-funded campaigns. CDHS's approach to antitobacco advertising, as well as its larger strategy for the denormalization of tobacco use, likewise served as a model for such organizations as the Centers for Disease Control and the World Health Organization. Between 1988 and 1999 adult smoking rates in California fell more than 32 percent, and California's declines in teen smoking well outpaced declines in other states.

TARGET MARKET

CDHS's 2000–05 antismoking media campaigns ran statewide in California, with the bulk of the messaging and budget devoted to a general market but with supplemental, language- and/or culture-specific commercials designed for Asians and Pacific Islanders, Latinos, African-Americans, and American Indians. CDHS placed great emphasis, through educational programs and other facets of its overall antismoking strategy, on a teenage audience, noting that 88 percent of smokers were introduced to cigarettes before age 18 and that the tobacco industry subtly continued to target teenagers despite legal rulings ordering it to cease doing so. The media campaign did not appeal strictly to teenagers, however. Part of the state's overall antismoking strategy was to denormalize tobacco use in the culture at large, which would presumably, in both the short and long term, make the activity less appealing to impressionable youngsters. It was especially necessary to spread an antitobacco message to a general audience, CDHS felt, given the tobacco companies' own concurrent efforts at normalizing their corporate images through court-ordered public-service advertising as well as voluntary image-crafting efforts. Many of the Ground Zero–crafted spots created between 2000 and 2005 focused on showing that tobacco companies, far from being normal businesses, were in fact morally reprehensible, villainous entities. The campaign also featured spots aimed at current smokers, which, in an effort to encourage them to quit, employed hard-hitting dramatizations of the dire health risks they were taking by engaging in the habit.

TARGETING CHILDREN

In a website companion to its media campaign, http://www.tobaccofreeca.com, the California Department of Health Services detailed ways in which tobacco companies continued to target minors despite the laws prohibiting them from doing so. CDHS pointed out, for instance, that images of the Marlboro Man, an icon specifically created to appeal to young people, was still, as of 2004, prominently featured in Philip Morris's advertising. The website cited a 2001 Stanford University study finding that almost half of California's convenience stores had tobacco advertising materials placed at a height of three feet or lower, at eye level with young children, and that in 23 percent of the state's convenience stores, cigarettes for sale were located less than six inches away from candy displays. In 2002, CDHS reported, R.J. Reynolds was caught advertising in youth-oriented publications. And in 2003 the Tobacco Enforcement Committee of the National Association of Attorneys General discovered that four different tobacco corporations had run ads in school editions of major U.S. newsweeklies.

COMPETITION

One of the first states to use the California model for battling the tobacco industry's influence was Massachusetts, whose Department of Health and Safety in 1994 increased taxes on cigarettes and invested the revenues in an ambitious marketing campaign crafted by the Boston advertising agency Houston Herstek Favat. Called "Truth," the campaign's television spots, like some of the early California commercials, sought to expose the tobacco companies' morally compromised business practices. Patrick Reynolds, a grandson of tobacco scion R.J. Reynolds, appeared in one spot providing information about the numerous harmful chemicals in cigarettes. "Why am I telling you this?" Reynolds asked. "I want my family to be on the right side for a change." Print ads attempted to generate public support for legislative measures aimed at reining in tobacco companies.

In 1998 the state of Florida likewise launched a marketing campaign funded by increased taxes on cigarettes. Created by Miami agency Crispin Porter + Bogusky and named "Truth" (like the Massachusetts campaign), the Florida campaign's highlights included spots pairing the congressional testimony of tobacco-industry executives with a sitcom laugh track, as well as spots showing teenagers who phoned tobacco corporations to ask pointed questions such as, "What is it about Lucky Strike cigarettes that's lucky? Is it that I might live?"

Following the 1998 master settlement agreement between four major tobacco companies and 46 U.S. states, which resolved lawsuits filed by state attorneys general, the tobacco companies were required to run their own antismoking advertising. Some critics, however, contended that these campaigns warned against smoking via methods that actually made smoking seem rebellious and therefore attractive to teens. Tobacco companies also took significant voluntary steps to recast their corporate images. Philip Morris Companies, for instance, changed its name to the comparatively nondescript Altria and markedly increased its food brand holdings.

Another noteworthy result of the 1998 tobacco settlement was the formation of a public advocacy group with national reach, the American Legacy Foundation (ALF), funded by $1.5 billion of the total $206 billion in settlement money. Beginning in 2000 ALF spent more than $150 million a year on nationwide, antismoking advertising cocreated by Boston's Arnold Worldwide (which had merged with Houston Herstek Favat) and Crispin Porter + Bogusky. The two agencies, leveraging their combined experience on the Massachusetts and Florida campaigns, had formed a team called the Alliance to bid for the ALF account. Unprecedented in scope and budget resources compared to previous antismoking projects, this campaign was, like its Massachusetts and Florida predecessors, also called "Truth," and it went to previously unexplored inflammatory lengths. One of the Alliance's first efforts involved filming activist teens piling body bags outside Philip Morris's corporate headquarters in New York. The resulting spots proved too controversial for the major television networks and were pulled off the air, along with another commercial shot at Philip Morris headquarters, after the tobacco companies involved in the 1999 settlement publicly complained.

MARKETING STRATEGY

CDHS's August 2000 hiring of Ground Zero for a five-year, $125 million advertising effort represented a change of direction for the state's antismoking campaigns. Like the nationwide "Truth" campaign then getting under way, the Ground Zero work focused more intensely than ever on overt vilification of tobacco companies. The campaign's television spots broke in early 2001 and ran during prime-time network programming like CBS's *Survivor* season finale and the NBC shows *ER* and *The West Wing.* Supporting outdoor, print, and online work reinforced the tagline "Do you smell smoke?" which, as Ground Zero's chairman Jim Smith told *Adweek,* referred to the premise that "the tobacco companies use smoke and mirrors, and we're suggesting maybe you smell smoke, and there's no smoke without fire."

The "Do You Smell Smoke?" television spots provided a documentary-like, fly-on-the-wall look inside the offices of a fictional tobacco company and centered on an amoral executive named Ken Lane, who explained ways in which the tobacco industry duped consumers. In "Lights," Lane was shown expounding on the fallacious perception that light cigarettes were better than regular cigarettes for one's health, explaining the manufacturing details that supposedly reduced tar and nicotine but in actuality did not, and marveling at the effectiveness of industry advertising that spread this misconception. A print ad running under the same tagline meanwhile pointed out the tobacco companies' alleged targeting of children despite the fact that the practice had been outlawed. Showing a young boy standing at a convenience store counter surrounded by numerous tobacco advertisements and transfixed by a large image of the Marlboro man at eye level, the ad's copy read, "Kid: 45 inches" and "Poster: 45 inches."

Ground Zero supplemented the anti-industry advertising with work that addressed the dangers of secondhand smoke and work that encouraged cessation. One 2002 television spot promoted the latter objective with particular force. Called "Echo," the spot featured a series of young, healthy-looking smokers who gave common excuses for why they could not quit smoking. Each statement in turn was juxtaposed with a statement from an overtly suffering, but not noticeably older, former smoker. A young man opened the commercial by noting with a smile that he could not "go more than a few hours without a cigarette," and his statement was followed by that of an emaciated man with tubes in his nose grimly saying, "I can't go more than a few feet without the oxygen tank." Similarly a healthy woman explained that she tried to quit smoking but gave up because she gained five pounds; her speech gave way to that of a female cancer patient saying, near tears, "I've lost twenty-five pounds." The spot closed with on-screen text that said, "Quitting is hard. Not quitting is harder."

No strategic changes were made to Ground Zero's CDHS work until 2004, when the theme "Undo" was applied to the campaign's television, print, outdoor, and online advertising as a means of asking consumers to visualize a world without smoking. One television spot used the tagline "Undo tobacco everywhere" and images of people in commonplace smoking locations and positions who instead of smoking were blowing bubbles. Another spot, tagged "Undo the exploitation," returned to the theme of tobacco-executive villainy by equating excellence in the business with a willingness to exploit the most vulnerable of all possible targets, young children. Another 2004 spot, "Growth," showed tobacco executives in a conference room who began uncontrollably birthing clones from their chests until suit-wearing clones covered the city streets outside the company offices. The image of irrepressible growth intentionally conflated tobacco-industry market gains and cancer, an idea underscored by on-screen text reading, "The more they grow, the more we die."

OUTCOME

The 2001 Ken Lane commercials so effectively impugned the integrity of tobacco-industry executives that the tobacco companies R.J. Reynolds and Lorillard filed a lawsuit alleging, as *Adweek* reported, that the spots "violated their constitutional rights and had a prejudicial effect on potential jurors in lawsuits related to smoking." The lawsuit was ultimately rejected. "Echo" was voted one of *Adweek* 's Best Spots of 2002. California's adult smoking rates remained lower than those in all other U.S. states except Utah: only 16.2 percent of the California population, as of 2003, were smokers, down from the 1988 rate of 22.8 percent. In 2004 the state's smoking rate reached a historic low of 15.4 percent, and state public health officer Dr. Richard J. Jackson announced, "Our messages about the dangers of tobacco use, secondhand smoke and the tobacco industry's misleading marketing practices are resonating with all Californians." Jackson further noted that California's smoking-related cancer rates were then declining three times faster than were rates among other Americans and declared that California would continue to spread its antitobacco message as long as tobacco products were sold.

FURTHER READING

Buyikian, Teresa. "Anti-Smoking Gets Personal." *Adweek* (western ed.), June 8, 1998.

Cooper, Ann. "Clearing the Smoke." *Print,* May/June 2001.

"Creative Best Spots 2002." *Adweek,* January 27, 2003.

Flass, Rebecca. "Ground Zero Takes Aim at Big-Tobacco Executives." *Adweek* (western ed.), April 30, 2001.

———. "Ground Zero Work Looks to 'Undo' Smoking in California." *Adweek,* February 9, 2004.

Lipin, David. "Ground Zero Nabs Anti-Smoking Biz." *Adweek,* August 28, 2000.

Parpis, Eleftheria. "Up in Smoke: Kicking Butt." *Adweek,* October 13, 1997.

Takaki, Millie. "Growth." *Shoot,* July 5, 2004.

"United States: Just Say No." *Economist,* December 9, 2000.

Woodward, Sarah. "CDHS Campaign Exposes Big Tobacco Hypocrisy." *Shoot,* December 8, 2000.

Mark Lane

California Milk Advisory Board

400 Oyster Point Blvd., Ste. 220
San Francisco, California 94080
USA
Telephone: (650) 871-6455
Fax: (650) 583-7328
E-mail: askus@realcaliforniacheese.com
Web site: www.RealCaliforniaCheese.com

HAPPY COWS CAMPAIGN

OVERVIEW

In an effort to promote the state's dairy products and to deal with its growing milk surplus, the California Milk Advisory Board (CMAB) established the "Real California Cheese" campaign in 1982. With the creation of the "Real California Cheese" label, the active marketing of the state's cheese began. During the first campaign, which used the tagline "California cheese is great cheese," California surpassed Wisconsin as the leading U.S. dairy state and jumped into the number two spot in the production of cheese. In 1995 "It's the Cheese" was introduced as the new tagline. The "Real California Cheese" campaign continued to be extremely popular and helped California to close in further on Wisconsin as the national leader in cheese production. The tagline "Great cheese comes from Happy Cows. Happy Cows come from California" was introduced in 2000 with the clear intent to take over the number one spot.

Supported by a $33 million marketing budget, the "Happy Cows" campaign was created by the advertising agency Deutsch LA. Television advertisements first appeared on local stations and then, beginning in December 2003, appeared on national cable channels, where the "Happy Cows" campaign would eventually have an audience of more than 500 million viewers. The spots aired during the 2004 and 2005 Super Bowls were especially important. Using humor and a sense of fun to convey their message, the television spots portrayed the lives of California cows as being carefree. In "Ding Dong," for instance, a couple of cows broke into fits of giggles as they played the "ring-doorbell-and-run" trick on their farmer. In addition to television spots there also were radio commercials, ads for buses and bus shelters, and outdoor billboards.

The "Happy Cows" campaign met with incredible success. It was overwhelmingly popular with the public, and it won various advertising awards, including being named by *Adweek* to its list of Creative Best Spots. The campaign was accompanied by increased sales of California cheese as well as of California dairy products generally. Partly as a result of the campaign's success, California was able to narrow the gap in cheese production between itself and Wisconsin. In 2004 the production of cheese in California neared 2 billion pounds, which was an increase of 163 million pounds, or 8.9 percent, over 2003. Although cheese production in Wisconsin in 2004 was almost 2.5 billion pounds, the CMAB continued its campaign to help California eventually take the lead.

HISTORICAL CONTEXT

The CMAB was established in 1969 in an effort by the California Department of Food and Agriculture to

California Milk Advisory Board's Happy Cows. © 2006 CALIFORNIA MILK ADVISORY BOARD. REPRODUCED BY PERMISSION.

promote the state's high-quality dairy products and to deal with the state's developing milk surplus. The state was producing 10.8 billion pounds of milk annually by 1975, and in the following years the amount increased dramatically. By 1982 it had become clear that California needed to face the problem of an ever-growing production of milk, which coincided with a declining rate of consumption. With the assistance of the Stanford Research Institute, the CMAB developed the idea that cheese might be a solution to the problem. Because 10 pounds of milk were generally needed to make 1 pound of cheese and because the nation's rate of cheese consumption was rising, this seemed to be a sensible solution. The "Real California Cheese" campaign was the result.

Although the "Real California Cheese" campaign began somewhat cautiously, starting with local markets and only slowly expanding nationwide, it quickly gained success. Within a decade of its introduction the campaign had helped make California the biggest dairy state in the United States, surpassing Wisconsin and bringing tremendous revenue to the state. Initially the tagline for the campaign was simply "California cheese is great cheese." Targeted mostly toward California women between the ages of 25 and 54, the "Real California Cheese" campaign represented an attempt to create an emotional connection to products made in the state. To achieve their goals, the advertisements were marked by intelligence and sincerity, along with a sense of humor.

In 1995 the "Real California Cheese" campaign introduced a new tagline, "It's the Cheese." This series of popular ads played on the humorous claim that the real reason people traveled to California was for its cheese. The advertisements used a representation of the "Real California Cheese" seal with the tagline, "It's the Cheese," next to it. Even the words in the ads were made of cheese. Running from 1995 to 2000, these ads appeared everywhere—on television; in outdoor advertising, including billboards, buses, and bus shelters; in retail stores; and on coupons and other printed materials. The success of the campaign helped to pave the way for the "Happy Cows" campaign, which was introduced in 2000. Like its predecessors, this campaign relied on a combination of humor and love for the state in its marketing of California cheese.

TARGET MARKET

With some 60 makers producing more than 250 varieties of cheese, the target market of the "Happy Cows" campaign was diverse. In a breakdown of California cheese production that was done in 2004, the major types were identified as follows: 45 percent mozzarella, 27 percent

ARE THEY REALLY HAPPY?

When People for the Ethical Treatment of Animals (PETA) sued the California Milk Advisory Board (CMAB) over its "Happy Cows" campaign, a superior court judge in 2003 sided with the defendant, but only on a technicality. PETA, arguing that the ads wrongfully idealized the lives of dairy cows as being pastoral and peaceful, had sued the CMAB for false advertising. The judge did not rule against PETA on the grounds that the cows were happy. Instead, he cited the fact that the government was exempt from the laws on false advertising that applied to private individuals.

cheddar, 15 percent Monterey Jack, 4 percent Hispanic-style, 3 percent Parmesan, 2 percent provolone, and 4 percent other. This wide variety, which included many higher-priced specialty cheeses, resulted from an extraordinarily diverse consumer base that ranged from ordinary families to individual connoisseurs.

Though the "Happy Cows" campaign, as well as previous campaigns, targeted any consumer of cheese, the primary focus was on women between the ages of 25 and 54. Women in this age range were thought to have slightly higher incomes than other women, and they were more likely to be mothers and, thus, often the grocery shoppers for a household. It was for this reason that television spots were aired more often during daytime programming than during the evening (60 percent versus 40 percent).

While the "Real California Cheese" campaign began by focusing on the local market, by the time of the "Happy Cows" campaign the marketing goals had been expanded, and the effort had become national. Thus, the "Happy Cows" campaign promoted California's cheese far beyond the state's borders.

COMPETITION

Although Wisconsin remained the number one producer of cheese in the United States, California appeared to be catching up. Wisconsin was working hard, however, to keep its number one spot. After California surpassed Wisconsin as the nation's top dairy producer in 1993, the Wisconsin dairy industry threw additional resources into its cheese industry, including $150 million for the expansion of production facilities. Under the guidance of the Wisconsin Milk Marketing Board, established in 1983, there were continuing efforts to maintain the state's leading position. Ventures such as the Chef Ambassadors Program, which published recipes calling for the use of various Wisconsin cheeses, were established for this purpose. Advertising campaigns such as "Where It Comes from Matters," which was launched in 2005, got right to the point, asking customers, "Why order your cheese from anyplace but Wisconsin?"

Cheese manufacturers located in other parts of the United States, such as the Tillamook County Creamery Association in Oregon and Agri-Mark, Inc., in New England, provided smaller-scale competition for California. Tillamook, a co-op owned by 150 Oregon dairy farmers, offered a range of dairy products, including milk, butter, ice cream, yogurt, sour cream, and dry whey. Still, Tillamook's focus was on cheese, in particular, cheddar, which accounted for 85 percent of the company's overall production. Agri-Mark, another privately owned co-op of farmers in Vermont, Massachusetts, and New York, had sold cheese since its startup in 1916. The co-op's cheese offerings included both the Cabot and the McCadam brands. Tillamook's sales in 2003 were $270 million, while Agri-Mark's were $600 million.

MARKETING STRATEGY

In 2000 "Great cheese comes from Happy Cows. Happy Cows come from California" was introduced as the campaign's new tagline. The tagline proclaimed that happy cows produced great cheese and that, because of the many things that made California great, California cows would, of course, be happy. The campaign, developed by the advertising agency Deutsch LA, began appearing in local television, radio, and print ads as well as in outdoor venues.

Several television spots were aired in rotation. Hailed as funny, clever, and cute, the commercials portrayed cows thinking and acting like humans. California loyalists, the cows affectionately revealed various aspects of life in the state, including the good weather, the beautiful scenery, and even earthquakes. "Cloud," for example, showed cows fleeing in panic from a tiny cloud in the sky, calling attention to California's sunny climate. "Race," which played on the carefree lifestyle of California, highlighted a race between cows, with a couple of bulls looking on. "Keep your eye on Doris; she's a rocket out of the gate," said one bull to the other. When the race began, Doris took the lead. "I'm winning!" she exclaimed; "I'm winning!" But when a fresh patch of dandelions, as well as the other runners, distracted her, the race was over. "We gotta move that finish line closer," said one of the bulls. The spot ended with the "Great cheese comes from Happy Cows. Happy Cows comes from California" tagline.

Although they started locally, the advertisements of the "Happy Cows" campaign appeared on national television beginning in December 2003, and they eventually reached the homes of more than 500 million viewers. As part of the national campaign, "Happy Cows" spots aired during both the 2004 and 2005 Super Bowls. There were further promotions in print and on the radio, and retail promotions included in-store coupons and a sampling program. There also were comprehensive public-relations and food-service promotions, as well as promotions through the "Real California Cheese" website, which covered the "Happy Cows" campaign in detail. The site even allowed visitors to view a selection of "Happy Cows" television commercials. The total annual budget for the campaign reached $33 million in 2004.

OUTCOME

The public loved the "Happy Cows" campaign. Consumers from around the United States submitted comments about the ads to the "Real California Cheese" website. One Idaho viewer said, "When your ads come on everything comes to a stop, people run in from different rooms just to watch because they are so wonderful . . . the sheep are adorable, they look just like ours! Too bad we didn't have you design an ad campaign for Idaho potatoes! Thank you again for giving us a few minutes of pure fun." The ads not only made the general public smile, but they also won numerous advertising awards, including being chosen by *Adweek* for its list of Creative Best Spots.

The "Happy Cows" campaign also seemed to spread the word about California cheese and to support the general "Real California Cheese" undertaking. By 1993 California had become the nation's largest supplier of milk and the largest dairy state overall. A decade later, after the debut of the "Happy Cows" campaign, milk production in California had increased by another 44 percent, to 36.4 billion pounds per year. Further, by 2004, through the efforts of the CMAB and the "Real California Cheese" program, California was selling 40 percent of its milk production—in the form of cheese, butter, and powdered milk—out of state. In addition, between 1983 and 2004 the production of cheese in California increased by an astonishing 609 percent, seven times the national growth rate. Over this period California had become the second-largest manufacturer and distributor of cheese in the United States.

Of course, the eventual goal of the CMAB was to replace longtime leader Wisconsin as the number one state in cheese production, and some strides toward this goal seemed to have been made. For example, in 2004 California was producing 25 percent of all mozzarella cheese in the United States. Being a top cheese producer and distributor had tremendous economic benefits for the state. In 2003 the U.S. cheese industry posted $40 billion in total sales. By 2002 the dairy industry in California was bringing in $35 billion year, approaching the income from the state's lucrative wine industry, which made $45 billion in that same year.

It appeared that California got into the right business at the right time, with a good product supported by an effective advertising campaign. The "Happy Cows" campaign and the remarkable success of "Real California Cheese" not only sparked the interest of cheese lovers across the United States but also gained the attention of academics. In 2005 Columbia University's Graduate School of Business published a case study of the CMAB's "Real California Cheese" campaign. The 34-page study, which was created as a teaching study at Columbia, was made available for use in business schools worldwide. As the case study's author, Michelle Greenwald, put it, "The growth of the California cheese industry over the past twenty-plus years is nothing short of a tremendous success story."

FURTHER READING

"Court Throws Out 'Happy Cows' Lawsuit." *San Diego Union-Tribune,* March 27, 2003.

Egelko, Bob. "Dairy Farms Can Keep Milking Their 'Happy Cows' Campaign." *San Francisco Chronicle,* January 12, 2005.

Emert, Carol. "California Looks to Expand Market." *San Francisco Chronicle,* January 30, 1999.

Fitzgerald, Tom. "Top of the Sixth." *San Francisco Chronicle,* January 8, 1998.

Fletcher, Janet. "Happy Cows Make a Better Cheese." *San Francisco Chronicle,* February 27, 2003.

Greenwald, Michelle. *It's the Cheese—Real California Cheese.* New York: Columbia University, School of Business, 2005.

"Happy Cows Make Better Lattes." *Houston Chronicle,* March 17, 2004.

Kirschenbaum, Carol. "What Does California's Bay Area Have that We Haven't Got? Glad You Asked." *St. Petersburg (FL) Times,* September 8, 1998.

Matier, Phillip, and Andrew Ross. "The Cheese Stands Alone." *San Francisco Chronicle,* May 19, 1996.

Parker, Penny. "Cheesy Campaign Comes to State: Move Over Wisconsin; California Claims to Be the Real 'Big Cheese.'" *Denver Post,* January 24, 1999.

"Real California Cheese: Tremendously Successful Long-Term Campaign." *Cheese Reporter,* April 8, 2005, p. 1.

Resler, Jerry. "California Takes a Cheesy Shot at Wisconsin: Tongue-in-Cheek Ads Play Off Friendly Dairy Competition." *Milwaukee Journal Sentinel,* November 12, 1995.

Roberts, Alison. "Value Added." *Sacramento Bee,* July 17, 2003.

Weise, Elizabeth. "PETA: 'Happy Cows' Ad Is a Lie." *USA Today,* December 11, 2002.

Candice Mancini

California Milk Processor Board

1801A Fourth Street
Berkeley, California 94710
USA
Telephone: (510) 883-1085
Fax: (510) 883-1085
E-mail: press@gotmilk.com
Web site: www.gotmilk.com

GOT MILK? CAMPAIGN

OVERVIEW

In the mid-1990s, with the emergence of new juices, fruit drinks, iced teas, coffee drinks, bottled waters, and soft drinks, Californians were drinking less milk every year. Milk consumption per capita in California had dropped 6 percent between 1987 and 1992. Before 1993 most of California's dairy advertising was funded either by the National Dairy Board (an organization of dairy farmers) or by the government-run California Milk Advisory Board. Together the two spent an estimated $13 million to promote the statewide consumption of dairy products. The budget was meager compared with those of other beverage companies. Dairy farmers could not compete with titans such as PepsiCo, Inc., and the Coca-Cola Company. The latter spent $100 million in 1992 to advertise just one of its brands, Coca-Cola Classic. Realizing that the dairy industry needed outside assistance, the California Department of Food and Agriculture formed the California Milk Processor Board (CMPB) in 1993. A few months later the CMPB released its "Got Milk?" campaign.

The ad agency Goodby, Silverstein and Partners (GS&P) created "Got Milk?" with the CMPB's $23 million annual budget. Previous campaigns had been aimed at people who did not consume milk, but the agency's research led it to target a different audience: people who were already milk drinkers. It concluded that "milk is usually consumed with something else, and that the only time people really think about milk is when they've run out of it." The print, television, radio, and billboard campaign debuted on October 29, 1993, with a television spot titled "Aaron Burr." The spot featured a history scholar who lost a radio trivia contest because his mouth was full of a peanut-butter sandwich and he was out of milk. "Got Milk?" continued for more than a decade and included television spots parodying steroid abuse in Major League Baseball and aliens that abducted cows for their milk.

Awards given to the first spot foretold the campaign's eminent success. "Aaron Burr" garnered three Gold Clios, the Grand Prix Clio for Commercial of the Year, one Gold EFFIE, and one Silver Lion at the 1994 Cannes International Advertising Festival. One year after the campaign began, milk sales in California had increased 7 percent.

HISTORICAL CONTEXT

According to the California Milk Advisory Board, from 1980 to 1993 annual milk consumption in California dropped from 30 to 24.1 gallons of milk per person. Before the formation of the CMPB the two leading entities that advertised dairy products in California were the National Dairy Board, an organization of dairy farmers that spent an estimated $2 million annually on television commercials, and the California Milk Advisory Board, which was formed in 1969 by the California Department of Food and Agriculture to promote dairy products. In 1992 the latter spent an estimated $11 million to advertise milk and other dairy products. One of its most memorable campaigns was "Milk. It Does A Body Good," created by the ad agency McCann-Erickson in the 1980s. Despite such efforts, milk was losing business to larger beverage makers, and eventually the state intervened. The California Department of Food and Agriculture established the California Milk Processor Board in February 1993. The fledgling CMPB was allocated $23 million for an advertising campaign.

Jeff Goodby, the cochairman of the ad agency Goodby, Silverstein & Partners, helped win CMPB's account by offering a compelling explanation for most consumers' need for milk. He suggested building a campaign around his theory that the only time consumers really wanted milk was when they had run out of it. Goodby then challenged his agency's creatives to develop stories of people who needed milk more than others. He suggested that, as a guideline, they use Steven Spielberg's 1971 thriller *Duel,* in which a malevolent truck driver hunted down a business commuter. "Imagine that truck was pursuing another semi, cutting it off and ramming it from behind," Goodby told his team, according to *Adweek.* "When the camera pulled back, you saw it was a cookie truck chasing a milk truck and the driver of the cookie truck had his mouth full of cookies and nothing to drink."

The guideline catalyzed a campaign titled "Got Milk?," in which actors were featured in humorous predicaments that resulted from their need to wash down food with milk. "We're going to jolt Californians out of their milk malaise," Jeff Manning, executive director of the CMPB, announced in the news service *Business Wire* days before the campaign was released. "Our focus is on action, not just attitude change. Increasing milk consumption at home is our only objective."

TARGET MARKET

GS&P market research used two key studies in different phases of this campaign: a 1993 MARC continuous telephone survey of a representative sample of the population in California, and a qualitative study of focus groups and one-on-one interviews led by GS&P. Other research included a national Nielsen household panel, from which California data were extracted. This study provided in-home scanner systems for participants to record their grocery buying from all kinds of food outlets. Additionally, Gallup conducted a tracking study based on daily telephone interviews designed to record milk consumption habits statewide. The Gallup study reported that three major reasons that people were drinking less milk were perceptions that milk was high in fat, that it was a children's drink, and that milk was boring compared with other drinks, especially sodas. The Gallup study also found that many Californians believed that they should drink more milk.

Previous campaigns had tried to stop the decline by portraying milk as cool, fun, and cutting-edge, much like advertising for sodas. As GS&P put it, campaigns for milk "had lively jingles, and healthy looking people with lustrous hair, perfect teeth and fine muscle definition [who] sang [about] it, jogged with it, and danced with it."

GS&P decided that previous advertising had been aimed at the wrong people. A CMPB study found that 70 percent of Californians used milk frequently. The agency concluded that most of the past advertisements had been targeted at the 30 percent of people who were not using any milk or who were using it less than the average person. GS&P decided to aim its campaign at the 70 percent who were ignored by the earlier campaigns, convincing them to use milk more frequently or to drink it in larger amounts. A representative of the ad agency explained, "persuading people who are *not doing something* to do it (whether again or for the first time) tends to be harder than persuading people who are *already doing it* to do it more often."

GS&P's research showed that 88 percent of milk was consumed at home. It was typically used as an accompaniment to food, and the food was frequently considered of more interest than the milk. Milk was rarely the center of attention, as previous ads had portrayed it. Backing up Jeff Goodby's original suggestion, the research concluded that "the only time people even think about milk at all is when they don't have any."

When focus-group participants (who had not had any milk for a week) got together, they reported that they usually did not think about milk at all but that "they had been painfully aware of it in its absence over the previous few days. And that absence had been all the more painful and frustrating in the context of certain foods," such as peanut-butter-and-jelly sandwiches, cereal, brownies, and chocolate-chip cookies. These foods were not the same without milk. One side effect of the research was that the participants experienced "powerful cravings" when they talked about the foods that went with milk. Some later said that on the way home from the focus groups they went shopping to buy some of the craved foods.

COMPETITION

In 1993 milk was competing against a beverage industry crowded with juices, fruit drinks, iced teas, bottled

IMITATION IS THE BEST FORM OF FLATTERY

Perhaps the best indicator of the campaign's effectiveness was Dairy Management, Inc.'s decision to take the California "Got Milk?" campaign nationwide in 1995, with an $80 million media spend. The organization, which promoted dairy products on behalf of America's dairy producers, paid the California Milk Processor Board (CMPB) to use the campaign, and the California group put the money back into media. SMI, Chicago, measured the national campaign and found that its success mirrored that of the CMPB.

waters, and soft drinks. One of milk's closest competitors was Snapple, a natural tea-based drink that was initially sold in health food stores. The brand was popular among consumers looking for healthier alternatives to soft drinks. Throughout the 1990s Snapple advertised its exotic flavors with its reoccurring spokeswoman the Snapple Lady, who was played by the company's own employee Wendy Kaufman. An illustration of Kaufman was featured on the bottle of Snapple Orange Tropic; it showed a reposed Snapple Lady wearing a floral dress against a tropical island backdrop. In many of the Snapple TV commercials the Snapple Lady simply answered the letters of real-life Snapple fans. The brand had a serious setback after being purchased by the cereal giant the Quaker Oats Company in December 1994. For two years Quaker Oats released high-budget commercials without the Snapple Lady, hoping to draw customers away from cola giants such as Coca-Cola and Pepsi. The strategy backfired, and advertising analysts lambasted Quaker Oats for misconstruing Snapple's brand identity. During Quaker Oats' two-year control of the brand Snapple sales declined 21 percent. Snapple was finally sold to Triarc Companies in 1997, and that year the Snapple Lady resurfaced as the brand's spokeswoman.

Throughout the 1990s the slogan "Got Milk?" grew more popular than slogans used by the competition. Pepsi advertised its flagship beverage, Pepsi, with a $500 million campaign titled "Generation Next," created by the ad agency BBDO New York in 1997. The world's largest soft-drink manufacturer, the Coca-Cola Company, spent $500 million on just its sporting-event advertisements in 1996. Despite the competition's deep pockets, "Got Milk?" proved more recognizable to consumers throughout the decade. According to the *U.S. Newswire,* 9 out of 10 Americans could identify the phrase in 2003.

MARKETING STRATEGY

There were three objectives to the "Got Milk?" campaign: to change the public's behavior regarding milk; to create the idea of "milk occasions" by associating the product with certain foods; and to curb the decline in sales by convincing people to buy milk more often and in larger quantities. Changing behavior, in addition to attitudes, was done with carefully placed media. A consumption strategy focused on coordinating the appropriate food with the time of day that a commercial was aired (for example, a cereal commercial in the morning or late at night), because most milk drinking occurred at home.

The campaign's first spots aired on October 29, 1993. "Aaron Burr," one of the 60-second debut spots, featured a man eating a peanut-butter sandwich and listening to a radio trivia contest. When the DJ asked, "Who shot Alexander Hamilton?" the man looked at the portrait on his wall that showed Burr and the bullet he had used to kill Hamilton. Because he was out of milk the history buff garbled, "Aaawwon Buuuhh," with a mouth full of peanut butter. The spot ended with the "Got Milk?" tagline. In 1997 the campaign included a series of black-and-white spots set in the fictional town of Drysville, where town officials had enforced a prohibition of milk. In 2002 the CMPB sparked media attention when the organization promised to donate heavily to the school board of the first Californian town that changed its name to "Got Milk?" None of the towns petitioned changed their names. The campaign then parodied Major League Baseball steroid abuse with a series of spots that featured athletes using milk as a performance-enhancement substance. After baseball authorities requested that the spots be stopped, "Got Milk?" advertised the high-calcium benefits of milk. In 2006 the campaign shifted into a humorous alien theme with spots featuring cows that had been abducted by aliens in search of milk.

GS&P intended to create a desire for the "complementary food item, then milk consumption would follow." The agency fashioned a kind of deprivation strategy, showing complementary food with no milk. Taking the milk away "provides the blow that links the action to a viewer's own refrigerator. The message is: go to the refrigerator, check the milk, make sure you have enough, if there isn't enough go and buy some, and maybe even have some right now." The ad agency heard focus-group anecdotes of eating complementary foods without milk to help them come up with creative ideas based on common, real-life experiences—"truths," as the creative team said, "that could then be dramatized to make them more impactful."

OUTCOME

According to the ad agency and the CMPB, the original objectives of the campaign were exceeded. Bruce Horowitz of the *Los Angeles Times* wrote in May 1994, "Since the ad campaign began . . . it has developed a near-cult following." In the first three months the effort reached a 60 percent aided recall level. MARC reported that "Got Milk?" had overtaken the "long-running 'Does a Body Good' campaign in top-of-mind awareness by mid-1994."

The campaign objective to change behavior and increase milk consumption was also met. Nielsen panels found that household penetration had increased from 70 percent in 1993 to 74 percent in 1995. The Nielsen household panel results showed that, except for the first two months of the campaign, milk consumption in California increased over the previous year, while it declined nationally—the reverse of the situation before the campaign began.

By 1994 the sales decline reported by California milk processors in 1993 had been halted. According to Nielsen scanner data, California milk sales increased 7 percent from 1993 to 1994, while national sales figures were unchanged. A GS&P report noted that sales grew by 13.5 million gallons, or $34 million. The 3.5 percent decrease in 1993 sales, together with the 1994 percentages, represented "a swing of 5.3 percent, or 40 million gallons, or $100 million dollars." The "Got Milk?" campaign made its mark in advertising by collecting nearly every industry award, including multiple Clio awards, several EFFIEs, a number of gold ADDY awards, a Silver Lion at the Cannes International Advertising Festival, and a David Ogilvy Research Award.

According to GS&P, a 1999 national survey revealed that awareness for the tagline "Got Milk?" was 12 times greater than the slogan for Pepsi, 6 times greater than the sports drink Gatorade's tagline "Life's a sport. Drink it up," and 4 times greater than Coke's slogan "Enjoy." Jeff Manning, executive director of the CMPB, explained in a 2003 issue of *Brandweek,* "A brand's strength and power comes from the immovable belief that it will live forever. Start acting on that belief and every decision, every idea, every waking moment begins to take focus and direction. The same holds true for a campaign or a tagline. 'Got Milk?' will live forever because we, the dairy industry, will it so. Not very scientific, but true nonetheless." In 2003 the CMPB reported that the campaign had a 97 percent awareness rate in California.

FURTHER READING

Adelson, Andrea. "Advertising." *New York Times,* June 14, 1994, p. D19.

"Beverages/Non-Carbonated: Calif. Fluid Milk Board." *Brandweek,* June 12, 1995, p. 12.

"Dairy Groups Reach 'Got Milk' Accord." *New York Times,* May 26, 1995, p. D4.

"Got Milk?" *Adweek* (eastern ed.), August 5, 1996, Special Planning Section, p. 6.

Horovitz, Bruce. "Meet the Milk Man." *Los Angeles Times,* May 27, 1994, p. E1.

Laue, Christine. "Got a Catchy Ad?" *Omaha (NE) World-Herald,* May 8, 2003, p. 1E.

Lazarus, George. "Half 'n' Half Milk Promotion May Not Flow." *Chicago Tribune,* February 10, 1998, sect. 3, p. 3.

"Milk Campaign Expanding Markets." *New York Times,* November 3, 1994, p. D23.

Voight, Joan. "Dairy's Queen." *Adweek,* April 14, 2003, p. 32.

———. "Goodby Changes Tack on 'Got Milk?'" *Adweek* (eastern ed.), September 1, 1997, p. 5.

Vranica, Suzanne, "Advertising: Milk Campaign Drops Calcium Pitch," *Wall Street Journal,* October 12, 2005, p. B4.

Wynter, Leon E.. "Business and Race: Group Finds Right Recipe for Milk Ads in Spanish." *Wall Street Journal,* March 6, 1996, p. B1.

Allison I. Porter
Kevin Teague

Calvin Klein Cosmetics Company

1325 Avenue of the Americas, 34th Fl.
New York, New York 10019
USA
Telephone: (212) 479-4300
Fax: (212) 479-4399
Web site: www.calvinklein.com

■■■

CK BE CAMPAIGN

OVERVIEW

Calvin Klein Cosmetics Company, a subsidiary of Coty, marketed fragrances under the name of Calvin Klein and cK. In August 1996 Paulanne Mancuso, CEO and president of Calvin Klein Cosmetics, announced the arrival of the latest cK unisex fragrance, cK be. The sequel to the company's extremely successful cK one, cK be was described as a "raceless, genderless, ageless, and shared statement." Each Calvin Klein ad campaign had its own characteristic image and its own particular target market. While the ads for cK one, Calvin Klein's first unisex fragrance, portrayed groups of young, multicultural, mostly androgynous urban men and women, the "cK be" campaign featured an intimate and raw close-up of the individuals within the cK one groups. According to Mancuso, "The 'cK be' campaign pulls you into these people's lives."

There were several similarities in the marketing of cK one and cK be, but the Calvin Klein marketers went further in launching cK be. The advertising of cK one involved images of sharing, groups, and similarities, whereas that of cK be was based on the idea of having the freedom to express oneself while living among a group and about the values and the lifestyles of the generation being portrayed. Whereas cK one was billed as "a fragrance for a man or a woman," cK be was described as "the new fragrance for people."

The ads, which were the creation of Calvin Klein's in-house advertising agency, CRK Advertising, were shot by the photographer Richard Avedon. He featured both well-known and unknown subjects in the commercials and black-and-white portraits. The portraits were paired with "be" statements such as "Be good. Be bad. Just be" and "Be shy. Be bold. Just be." Some magazines ran multipage ads in which the first page was all black with the statement "to be" printed in white. The next page or two contained only black-and-white portraits, while the last page, which also was black, had the words "or not be" printed in white. The last page was also accompanied by a portrait and a pull-apart scented tab.

Avedon took care to portray his models as real, imperfect people. He had the models look directly into the camera as if they were speaking revealingly and intimately about themselves. Most of the models were unusual looking, with many having tattoos and body piercings, and some appeared unkempt. In short, they did not fit the fashion industry's idea of all-American beauty, the type that usually graced slick magazine ads. Perhaps the most recognizable spokesperson for the "cK be" campaign was the model Kate Moss, who bared all of her blemishes and freckles while she also bared her soul. The photograph of Stacey McKenzie emphasized unforgettable lips, freckles, and hair. Other subjects included Theo Kogan, a member of the alternative band Lunachicks; Jason Olive, a popular African American model; and Vincent Gallo, a musician, actor, and writer and director.

The text of the ads was equally provocative. The guitarist Billy White announced, "I find whatever's in my mind is better kept up there. You know what I mean?" In one of the longer ads for cK be a young man told viewers, "You could get hurt. You could get sick. You could do all these things, and if you don't have intimate relationships that are strong, you're really alone. But alone is something I know how to do. Intimacy comes and goes. Alone is forever. Be single. Be plural. Just be." The androgynous female Felix N'Yeurt proclaimed, "I never have to wait in line for the bathroom."

HISTORICAL CONTEXT

Calvin Klein, president and chief executive of Calvin Klein, Inc., said that he first found a fragrance and then created an image to fit it—"It all starts with the scent." If a company wanted to develop and sell a new fragrance, it contacted several manufacturers. When the desired scent was formulated, a national campaign was introduced to create the image the company's marketing specialists believed would best sell the product. According to Rudy Detz, president of Creative Fragrances Manufacturing, "Without the images associated with brand recognition, the perfume that sells for $150 an ounce simply wouldn't." Detz added, "No one just goes shopping for perfume. They go as a response to the national ads and will ask specifically for a brand." A specific image had already been created with the campaign for cK one, and after the perfume had been on the market for a time, Calvin Klein Cosmetics was able to learn a great deal about the social values, attitudes, and consumer habits of Generation Xers. Marketers knew exactly what to do and where to go when it was time to launch cK be.

The cK be fragrance was developed by Givaudan-Roure, with Ann Gottliebas consultant. The fragrance was described by Klein as sensual, sexy, and personal. In the fragrance industry scents were defined by what were called top, middle, and bottom notes, which were wrapped in a "peace accord." cK be's top note included bergamot, juniper berry, mandarin, mint, and lavender; its middle note was a blend of light spices, magnolia, and peach; and its bottom note was sandalwood with opoponax and tonka bean. According to the company, "cK be contains an exclusive peace accord, made up of clean white musks, that travel throughout the fragrance, wrapping all three notes in sheer sensuality."

Many of Calvin Klein's ad campaigns were controversial. One of his most memorable featured the model Brooke Shields, who, while photographed in various poses wearing Calvin Klein jeans, stated that nothing came between her and her Calvin's. Some of the company's ads were even characterized as "kiddy porn" or as "heroin chic." In contrast, some Calvin Klein ad campaigns portrayed happier, wholesome types. Ads for the Calvin Klein fragrance Eternity portrayed a young family, and those for the men's fragrance Contradiction focused on a virile 26-year-old man with three children. The women's version of Contradiction used the clean-cut model Christie Turlington and the caption "She is always and never the same."

Those who criticized the cK image as one that promoted "skankiness" may not have realized that symbols of Generation Xers such as tattoos (other than the hearts and butterflies of the 1960s), body piercing (other than ears), and Dr. Martens had practically become mainstream. Advertisers knew how to seduce someone in their target market, and one did not have to be a practicing addict to look like one. It was all about image.

TARGET MARKET

People over age 40 tended to use classic fragrances or to use a fragrance they had been using for years, but people between 25 and 40 were more experimental and tended to buy a variety of fragrances. An even younger crowd, those between 18 and 25, tended to buy newer fragrances and spent most of their money on themselves. While cK one targeted this younger group, market research showed that the fragrance was purchased by people as young as 12 and as old as 50. The hip urban image was clearly attractive to a wide age group. Nonetheless, marketers narrowed the target group for cK be to those between 18 and 29 and tailored its ad campaign accordingly. According to Klein, "The whole idea of the cK fragrances stems from Generation X, or people who think that way, who have a young attitude."

Marketers knew that there were always groups of potential consumers outside a specific target market. Perhaps cK be would be attractive to those who were "earth-conscious," for example. The bottle was made of recyclable glass, aluminum, and plastic, and the exterior packaging was constructed of 100 percent recycled fibers. For those who were attracted to an androgynous image, the store displays were no-frill. In both the men's and women's cosmetic areas cK be was displayed on free-standing shelves, not behind a counter, making it highly accessible. Mimi Avins, fashion editor of the *Los Angeles Times,* suggested that the cK be image might be attractive to feminists and to former members of the counterculture, such as the hippies of the 1960s. Contrary to critics of cK images, Avins wrote, "Their subtext is the perfect antidote to the mendacity of the infuriatingly successful, The Rules: Time-Tested Secrets for Capturing the Heart of Mr. Right (Warner, 1996). If the lessons of that

ANTI-CALVIN KLEIN

Attacks on various aspects of Calvin Klein campaigns were not uncommon, with the charges often centering on the images used in the ads. There were even anti-Calvin Klein websites on the Internet. Nevertheless, his fragrances, fashion apparel, and home fashions remained among the most popular brands.

backward manual for mentally impaired Cosmo girls were distilled into cK be's haiku, it would read, 'Be fake. Be manipulative. Be gamey. Don't just be.' The Rules advises desperate women to hide behind a false image of perfection for as long as they can hold the pose. The cK be confessions champion honesty, an appropriate tack in this age of full disclosure... The generation that once didn't trust anyone over 30 is now skeptical of anyone who clings to an image that's too squeaky clean."

COMPETITION

In 1995 Americans spent $5 billion on fragrances. Approximately 60 percent of the market was in women's fragrances, with the remaining in men's, but it was women who purchased the majority of all scents. It was estimated that more than a hundred new fragrances were introduced every year, with advertisers spending millions of dollars on a new scent before it ever hit the retail market. There were classic scents such as Chanel No. 5, Joy by Jean Patou, Arpege by Lanvin, and Shalimar by Geurlain, all of which had been around for years and did not need aggressive advertising. Some fragrances could be purchased only at certain exclusive retail stores, while other could be found at department stores and at duty-free shops. Still others were sold in drugstores, supermarkets, and discount stores. The points of purchase often reflected exclusivity, trendiness, and price.

cK be had an introductory budget of $20 million, compared to cK one's $17-18 million, which may have given it the largest budget for any of the so-called prestige fragrances introduced in 1996. The introductory budget for Elizabeth Taylor's Passion, for example, was between $4 million and $6 million. Other prestige fragrances introduced at the same time included Ocean Dream by Giorgio Beverly Hills and Cosby Estee Lauder. Some consumers may have been confused by the fact that, at the time cK be was launched, Bebe also introduced its new fragrance, called 2be. Like Calvin Klein, other clothing designers such as Ralph Lauren, Perry Ellis, and Tommy Hilfiger were also introducing fragrances for both men and women, often to go along with a line of apparel. Also riding on the designer fragrance bandwagon were apparel stores such as Gap, American Eagle, Abercrombie & Fitch, and even Eddie Bauer, all of which had introduced fragrances with their own particular images. What was new about the cK fragrance line was that the same scent was marketed for both men and women.

MARKETING STRATEGY

Even before cK be was in stores, teaser ads appeared on billboards, on the sides of buses, and on bus shelters. Other outdoor advertising included images projected onto a surface comprised of a thin mist of water (hydro-illumination) and the world's largest air banner, which was flown over selected beaches during the 1996 Labor Day weekend.

During the launch period cK be scent strips were put in a variety of magazines popular with young women, including *Cosmopolitan, Vogue, YM,* and *W,* and in magazines read mostly by men, including *GQ* and *Playboy.* The scent strips were also put in magazines like *Vanity Fair,* which had a balance of male and female readership, and in magazines like *Spin, Vibe, Paper,* and *Ray Gun,* which had a large young male and female readership. In total, cK be was advertised in 48 publications. About a month or so before the fragrance was due to be stocked in stores, full-page ads depicting the brand concepts of individuality and freedom began to appear in magazines. There were also 30-second radio spots, and billboards and posters appeared in some 15 markets. In September 1996 the Avedon commercials debuted during the season premieres of several television shows popular with the target market, including *The X-Files, Friends, Melrose Place,* and *Suddenly Susan.*

Perhaps the most significant marketing strategy was an innovative promotional deal between Calvin Klein Cosmetics and Ticketmaster. Calvin Klein's Mancuso thought that "taking the scent to where these guys live" was an effective way to reach their target market. Ads for cK be were printed on the backs of tickets and in *Live,* the Ticketmaster magazine. Both the tickets and their envelopes were scented with cK be, with 9 million tickets being been sold during September and October 1996 alone. Another innovative departure from the traditional scent strips found in magazines was the distribution of 4 million wristbands with resealable fragrance strips. In addition, 3 million sample vials of cK be were attached to magnets and distributed at various events, concerts, and stores. To attain additional direct contact with the target market, Calvin Klein Cosmetics helped sponsor, along with Tower Records and *Rolling Stone* magazine, a 15-day nationwide tour featuring three of Capitol

Records' newest alternative bands—The Figgs, Smoking Popes, and Jimmy Eat World.

OUTCOME

cK be was the most successful of all fragrances launched in 1996, and it did well both in the U.S. and in global markets. It was expected to generate $30 million during the first season but actually generated $45 million. Further, cK be placed in the number 10 spot among all fragrance brands in 1996. In 1997, however, cK be ranked number 21 and by mid-1998 had dropped to number 51. In addition to having success in sales, the Calvin Klein marketers continued to impress the fragrance industry and consumers with their use of provocative advertising.

FURTHER READING

Albers Jackson, Barbara. "It's Time to Raise a Stink about That cK be Perfume Ad." *Tennessean,* October 24, 1996.

Avins, Mimi. "By Letting Be, Klein's Ads Break the Rules." *St. Louis Post-Dispatch,* January 2, 1997.

Born, Pete. "Calvin's New Contradiction." *Women's Wear Daily,* June 12, 1998, p. 29.

———. "cK be: Chart Buster's Sequel." *Women's Wear Daily,* May 24, 1996, p. 6.

———. "An Industry with Be's in Its Bonnet." *Women's Wear Daily,* August 30, 1996, p. 4.

Do Re Be *Women's Wear Daily,* August 23, 1996.

Elliott, Stuart. "Campaign for New cK Emphasizes Youthful Look." *Harrisburg Patriot,* August 20, 1996.

———. "$20 Million Plus Ad Campaign Kicks Off New Klein Scent." *Ottawa Citizen,* September 12, 1996.

Kroh, Joseph. "The Sweet Smell of Success: Millions of Advertising Dollars Are Behind All Those High-Priced Colognes and Perfumes." *Business First of Louisville,* September 2, 1996.

Christine Miner Minderovic

Campbell Soup Company

1 Campbell Place
Camden, New Jersey 08103-1799
USA
Telephone: (856) 342-4800
Fax: (856) 342-3878
Web site: www.campbellsoup.com
www.pepperidgefarm.com

GOLDFISH CRACKERS CAMPAIGN

OVERVIEW

Pepperidge Farm, Inc.'s Goldfish crackers, introduced in 1962, had by 2004 evolved into a megabrand available in more than 24 individual flavors and varieties, from the original cheddar to peanut-butter-filled sandwich crackers and crispy rounds. At the end of that year Goldfish sales in the United States were $168.5 million, making it the number two snack-cracker brand behind Nabisco's Ritz crackers. But despite its ranking the Goldfish brand was slipping; in 2004 sales of the crackers dipped 8.3 percent from the previous year.

To lift its iconic brand out of the doldrums, Pepperidge Farm, a division of the Campbell Soup Company, looked beyond its agency of record—Young & Rubicam Advertising in New York—for creative help. The company charged BrightHouseLive, a small Atlanta-based agency known for its unique approach to marketing and advertising, with developing a clever new marketing campaign for the Goldfish brand. BrightHouseLive created a television-focused campaign that featured an animated goldfish character named Finn. The campaign, which began in January 2005, also included in-store and online marketing and new packaging for the Goldfish crackers. A budget for the campaign was not announced, but according to TNS Media Intelligence/CMR, a unit of the United Kingdom–based market research firm Taylor Nelson Sofres, in 2003 Pepperidge Farm spent $16.3 million on advertising for its Goldfish brand, a figure that was almost unchanged from its spending in 2002.

The new campaign, as well as its spokescharacter, Finn, seemed to resonate with consumers and helped increase sales of Goldfish crackers by about 5 percent within several months of its launch. Media insiders also praised the campaign, using a variety of adjectives to describe Finn, from lovable and funny to spunky and irreverent. Additionally the Campbell Soup Company credited the campaign and its spokescharacter with boosting Pepperidge Farm's sales in 2005.

HISTORICAL CONTEXT

According to its website, Pepperidge Farm's humble beginnings in 1937 were in the kitchen of Margaret Rudkin, the mother of three children. To ease the allergies of one of her children, the industrious mom began baking bread for her family that contained none of the preservatives or artificial ingredients found in commercially baked bread. Her efforts in the kitchen soon evolved into a small business named for the family farm in Connecticut: Pepperidge Farm. The first product, whole-wheat bread, gained in popularity with consumers and in the 1940s, as the business grew, the line was

© ENVISION/CORBIS.

expanded to include oatmeal bread, dinner rolls, and stuffing mix. The peripatetic Rudkin also added to the product line by collecting recipes during her international travels, including European-style cookies that she discovered while traveling in Belgium in the 1950s. In 1961 the Campbell Soup Company acquired Pepperidge Farm. The following year Goldfish crackers were introduced after Rudkin discovered the snack cracker during a trip to Switzerland and returned with the recipe and permission to market it.

Ogilvy & Mather had served as the Pepperidge Farm ad agency for 40 years. In 1995 it resigned from the Pepperidge Farm and Goldfish crackers account, reportedly because of a business conflict, and agency Saatchi & Saatchi/New York took over the account. When a smiling face was added to the original goldfish in 1997, "Smiley" the Goldfish icon was born. Saatchi & Saatchi created the accompanying tagline, "The snack that smiles back." In 1998, following a consolidation by the brand's parent company, Campbell Soup, Young & Rubicam Advertising in New York won the Goldfish account. The agency introduced a new campaign for Goldfish crackers in 2003 that included the theme song "Jingle for Goldfish." The campaign, which targeted kids 8 to 12 years old, featured two scruffy, longhaired musicians playing acoustic guitars and singing the jingle. Television spots placed the singing duo in a variety of settings, including on a school bus and in a classroom. At the request of Pepperidge Farm, Atlanta-based BrightHouseLive joined the team in 2004. BrightHouseLive created an updated campaign for Goldfish crackers that featured a new animated spokescharacter, Finn the goldfish. The campaign was released in January 2005.

TARGET MARKET

Any parent, babysitter, or other person who had ever quieted a fussy toddler with a cup of Goldfish crackers could appreciate the value of the tasty fish-shaped treat. But with the new campaign featuring Finn, a personable animated goldfish, the goal was to help create an even closer bond between the popular Pepperidge Farm brand and the children who enjoyed Goldfish crackers. As an added benefit, the clever spots connected with the adults who purchased the product. The animated Finn also was designed to continue Goldfish crackers' appeal to tweens—kids 8 to 12 years old—and teens who had been given the fish-shaped crackers as toddlers but had perhaps stopped eating them in favor of other snacks. To further reach its target market, Pepperidge Farm introduced a Goldfish website, www.pfgoldfish.com, that enabled older kids to go online and play games featuring Finn. The site also offered a variety of activities that parents or caregivers could play with kids aged three to five years old, such as determining how many goldfish crackers tall the child was. In addition, new packaging (the milk-carton box was replaced with a bag similar to what was used for other products in the line) added to the appeal of the brand for consumers of all ages.

GOLDFISH CRACKERS REPLACED WITH COOKIES ON BOOK COVER

Pepperidge Farm's Goldfish crackers could be found almost everywhere, from the lunch boxes of elementary school kids to strategic placement in the movie *Christmas with the Kranks.* But when the fish-shaped cracker appeared on the cover of a new novel, the waters got choppy. The book, *Little Children* by Tom Perrotta, was about what happened in a suburban neighborhood when a convicted child molester moved in. To the dismay of Pepperidge Farm, featured on the cover of the novel were Goldfish crackers. The book's publisher, St. Martin's Press, had failed to get permission to use the crackers on the cover, so the book cover got a makeover: the Goldfish crackers swimming across the front of the book were replaced with chocolate-chip cookies.

COMPETITION

In the snack-cracker wars, flavor, as always, was paramount, but in the early 2000s part of the battle was about the shape of the cracker. Pepperidge Farm's fish-shaped crackers were near the top of the list, with 98 percent of Americans surveyed saying that they recognized and were familiar with Goldfish crackers. Nabisco, which claimed one of the top spots in the snack-cracker market with its Ritz brand, went one step too far in its competition with Pepperidge Farm when it introduced its own fish-shaped crackers in 1998. Nabisco's new crackers were planned as a tie-in to the Nickelodeon television network's program *CatDog.* The new crackers resulted in a lawsuit, pitting Nabisco against Pepperidge Farm. The latter alleged that Nabisco's new crackers infringed on its Goldfish brand trademark. In 2000 a federal court upheld Pepperidge Farm's claim and ordered Nabisco to discontinue production of its fish-shaped cracker. Later in 2000 Kraft Foods acquired the Nabisco brand for $18.9 billion. While Nabisco's Ritz cracker brand claimed the number one spot in the snack-cracker market at the end of 2004, with $232.6 million in annual U.S. sales, the company was still looking for a niche in the shaped-cracker market. Nabisco introduced dinosaur-shaped puffed crackers under its Ritz brand in 2005. The new Ritz Dinosaur crackers were created in direct response to Pepperidge Farm's Goldfish crackers and targeted the same young consumers and their parents.

In 2005 the Kellogg Company introduced its own character-shaped cracker under its Keebler Sunshine cracker brand, Cheez-It. Rather than a fish or prehistoric creature, however, Keebler Sunshine's new crackers were shaped like the cartoon character SpongeBob SquarePants and directly targeted the kids who munched on Ritz Dinosaur and Pepperidge Farm Goldfish crackers. Targeting an older audience, in 2004 Kellogg introduced Twisterz, another variation on its Cheez-It crackers. The new shape, a twisted cylinder rather than the traditional square, was launched in time for the end of college basketball season and included combination flavors designed to please college-age consumers: Cheddar & More Cheddar, Hot Wings & Cheesy Blue, and Cool Ranch & Cheddar. The new product launch was supported by a marketing campaign created by Leo Burnett/Chicago and continued the brand's tagline, "Get your own box." With $140.1 million in sales, the Cheez-It cracker brand ranked fourth in the snack-cracker market at the end of 2004.

MARKETING STRATEGY

Although New York–based Young & Rubicam Advertising remained the agency of record for Goldfish crackers and other Pepperidge Farm brands, in 2004, when Pepperidge Farm wanted to put a different spin on the advertising for the fish-shaped cracker and update the brand, it partnered with BrightHouseLive, an agency based in Atlanta, Georgia. BrightHouseLive had opened its doors in 2003 but had quickly earned a reputation for devising unusual advertising campaigns. The creative idea developed by the agency was a primarily television campaign that featured an animated goldfish named Finn. A specific budget for the campaign was unavailable, but according to a report in *Adweek,* in 2004 Pepperidge Farm spent approximately $14 million from January through September on advertising for the Goldfish cracker brand.

Prior to the creation of the campaign Pepperidge Farm devoted more than one year to conducting market research about Goldfish crackers. Included were interviews with mothers and children to determine what the brand meant to consumers. The company also worked with Character, a leading character-development agency within the film industry, to help establish the personality of the new spokescharacter, Finn.

For the campaign BrightHouseLive created a series of four 30-second and three 15-second television spots. The initial two 30-second spots, which were first aired in January 2005, highlighted Goldfish crackers' cheddar-flavored variety. Subsequent spots featured the brand's Flavor Blasted and Sandwich Snackers varieties. Each spot showed Finn interacting with other Goldfish crackers as he made plans to help protect them from being eaten by hungry humans reaching for a snack. Finn warned, "To avoid being eaten, you've got to avoid the bowl, avoid the baggies. Cool?" One spot had Finn's advice being ignored by the other Goldfish crackers. As the crackers laughed and jumped into a bowl on a kitchen counter, a person reached into the bowl and took a handful of the crackers. A voice-over stated: "Tasty Goldfish crackers, baked with real cheddar cheese. It's a wonder they're not extinct." Finn sighed and returned to the package to try again to warn the remaining Goldfish crackers about how to avoid becoming a snack for humans. The spot ended with Finn exclaiming, "So much for fish being brain food."

In addition to television spots, the campaign included in-store advertising and Internet promotions on a new website for the product that featured games and activities for kids to play alone or with their parents. As part of a brand update, the company designed new packaging for the crackers. In an interview reported in *Business Wire* prior to the release of the campaign, Pepperidge Farm's vice president of youth snacks, Steve White, said that, by bringing to life the familiar goldfish as the spokescharacter Finn, "we feel confident that kids of all ages are going to love the character as much as they love the snack."

OUTCOME

At the time of the new campaign's 2005 launch, Pepperidge Farm's Goldfish crackers were among the world's most popular snack crackers, with American consumers devouring more than 85 billion Goldfish crackers annually. Within six months of the start of the campaign Pepperidge Farm reported that sales of Goldfish crackers were up more than 5 percent. Parent company Campbell Soup also noted the success of the campaign in its third-quarter report for the period that ended May 2005. The report stated, "Sales of 'Pepperidge Farm Goldfish' snack crackers experienced good gains due to continued momentum of the base brand and the favorable impact of new advertising featuring the new animated character, 'Finn.'" Besides resonating with consumers and spurring sales, the campaign was well received by media insiders. Writing in the *Chicago Sun-Times,* Lewis Lazare described Finn as a lovable advertising icon that was "funny and irreverent" with "spunk and soul."

FURTHER READING

"Alien Invaders Attack with a Vengeance." *Snack Food & Wholesale Bakery,* June 1, 2005.

Baar, Aaron. "Jingle Backs Intro of Cheez-It Twisterz." *Adweek,* April 5, 2004.

Elliott, Stuart. "Campbell Soup Is Looking Beyond Its Big Agency for Ideas to Pump Up the Sales of Goldfish." *New York Times,* November 24, 2004, p. 5.

Janoff, Barry. "Pepperidge Farm Floats Fish Story." *Adweek,* January 18, 2005.

Jones, Malcolm. "Fiction: New Snack Attack." *Newsweek,* May 24, 2004.

Lazare, Lewis. "Hair-Brained Cartoon Ad a Disconnect." *Chicago Sun-Times,* January 11, 2005.

Lee, Richard. "Norwalk, Conn.-Based Pepperidge Farm Places Goldfish in 'Kranks' Movie." *Stamford (CT) Advocate,* December 18, 2004.

Lovel, Jim. "BHL Brings Goldfish Snack to Animated Life." *Adweek,* January 7, 2005.

Malovany, Dan. "Snack Attack: Many Cracker Manufacturers Are Adding New Products, Promotions and Marketing Programs that Not-Too-Subtly Resembles the Successful Strategies Used by Traditional Salted Snack Producers." *Snack Food & Wholesale Bakery,* December 1, 2004.

McMains, Andrew. "Pepperidge Farm Adds BrightHouse on Goldfish." *Adweek,* November 24, 2004.

"Pepperidge Farm Goldfish Character Brought to Life in New Advertising Campaign." *Business Wire,* January 10, 2005.

"Pepperidge Farm Hooks Animated Star." *Brandweek,* January 10, 2005.

Simon, Ellen. "Nabisco, Pepperidge Farm Battle over Cheese-Cracker Rights." *Knight Ridder/Tribune Business News,* January 19, 2000.

Rayna Bailey

MAKE IT CAMPBELL'S INSTEAD CAMPAIGN

OVERVIEW

Campbell Soup Company, long the dominant force in the American canned-soup market as well as a player in many other food and beverage categories, saw consistent sales losses in its all-important original Campbell's soup line throughout the 1990s and into the new millennium. These condensed soups still constituted the best-selling soup brand in the country and had one of the most recognizable labels in the world, the iconic red-and-white can, but condensed soup was being progressively upstaged by ready-to-eat brands (including Campbell's own Chunky soup) prized for their convenience. Having unsuccessfully tried numerous tactics in the attempt to revive its core business, Campbell's in 2003 hit on a combination of manufacturing, packaging, shelving, and communications tactics that positioned it to make an integrated bid, on behalf of all of its soup products, for consumers' attention. A major part of this effort was a decisive change in marketing tone, targeting, and strategy, embodied in the "Make It Campbell's Instead" campaign of 2003–4.

"Make It Campbell's Instead," crafted by Campbell's longtime ad agency BBDO New York, used an estimated $100 million budget and employed the conventions of reality television, which was extremely popular at the time, in a series of commercials designed to encourage the consideration of Campbell's full range of soups as replacements for a variety of meal types and snack foods. The spots were hosted by the pushy yet charming Gordon Elliott, the star of his own Food Network reality show, in which he stopped passersby and knocked on strangers' doors, asking them to try dishes that he himself cooked. The Campbell's commercials used this same premise—with Elliott intruding on ordinary families at mealtime, drivers of cars stopped at intersections, and the homes of celebrities—in order to suggest the consumption of a particular Campbell's soup variety.

"Make It Campbell's Instead" made a crucial contribution to the ongoing attempt to revitalize the Campbell Soup Company, an attempt that saw its first signs of success during the campaign's run. In 2004 the company's famed condensed-soup line saw its first sales gains since the 1980s, surprising analysts who had predicted the brand's continued decline.

HISTORICAL CONTEXT

Campbell's soup, long one of America's most recognizable packaged foods, fell precipitously out of favor with consumers in the 1990s and early 2000s. The demand for ever-more-convenient food products translated into the ascendance of ready-to-eat soups such as the Campbell Soup Company's own Chunky and Select brands and General Mills' Progresso. Such products took market share away from the Campbell's condensed varieties, which were sold in the famous red-and-white can—an ironic development considering the fact that a primary attribute of Campbell's condensed soups had always been the ease with which they could be prepared. Though Chunky and Select posted consistent sales gains, the core brand, condensed soup, accounted for approximately 70 percent of the company's soup operations and 35 percent of its profits, so Campbell remained committed to reviving it. In the 1990s and early 2000s the marketing strategy for Campbell's soup—with creative work chiefly crafted by ad agency BBDO New York—underwent drastic revision almost yearly, as did the roster of Campbell executives charged with reviving the brand. Industry observers characterized these changes as desperate attempts to update the product's image, and corporate analysts predicted that the declines in condensed-soup sales would continue indefinitely.

In 2002 Campbell launched a new product line, Soup at Hand, America's first "sippable" soup, which was packaged in a microwaveable container designed to fit in a person's hand for on-the-go consumption. This increase in portability, positioning soup to compete against snack and fast foods generally perceived as less wholesome and nutritious, translated into the company's most successful product launch since the introduction of the Chunky variety almost 30 years earlier. Meanwhile, the company's new president of U.S. soup, Jeremy Fingerman, encouraged innovation in Campbell's soup advertising. Long pitched to stay-at-home moms via wholesome TV imagery, the brand in late 2002 targeted college students with wry outdoor ads in select cities—Boston, Philadelphia, and Cincinnati—as a means of testing the core brand's ability to grow market share outside its traditional audience. In 2003 Campbell's attempt to assure consumers that soup was, as Fingerman put it in an interview with *Advertising Age,* "the superior simpler meal," gained further momentum. It included such measures as the reformulation of the condensed soups' recipes, the addition of pop-top lids to the condensed-soup cans, the introduction of new Soup at Hand flavors, the offering of Chunky and Select in microwaveable containers, and a renewed focus on supermarket shelving strategies.

TARGET MARKET

"Make It Campbell's Instead" was rooted in the company's attempt to convince consumers that soup was a better option for those seeking a simple and healthy meal. BBDO and Campbell used reality-based TV spots, some of which were scripted and some of which were not, to update the soup brands' images and make them seem relevant to "today's diverse consumer population," as president of Campbell North America, Larry McWilliams, said in a press release. The reality-based approach was, industry observers noted, a significant departure from Campbell's heritage as a traditional advertiser targeting stay-at-home moms with images of wholesome domesticity.

The commercials featured a single spokesperson, the Australian-born Gordon Elliott, star of the Food Network show *Door Knock Dinners.* Modeled on that program, in which the pushy but charismatic Elliott confronted people at home or on the street and asked them to eat a meal that he had prepared, the Campbell's spots showed Elliott urging strangers and celebrities to try Campbell's soup products in place of other snack or meal options. Individual commercials targeted different audiences, depending on the object of Elliott's attentions. While the spot that showed Elliott intruding on the home of TV personality and restaurateur B. Smith appealed to adult women, spots in which Elliott focused his antics on younger people were meant to appeal to

M'M! M'M! GOOD! TO GO

In early 2003, prior to the "Make It Campbell's Instead" campaign, Campbell unveiled a marketing, packaging, and promotions platform uniting its portable lines of soups. Recasting the well-known Campbell's slogan, "M'm! M'm! Good!"—which dated from the 1930s—the "M'm! M'm! Good! To Go" initiative consisted of the introduction of single-serve microwaveable soups as well as the inclusion of the Campbell's Soup at Hand "sippable" brand under the new "To Go" banner. Packaging and in-store materials directed attention to the convenience-enhancing innovations of the "M'm! M'm! Good! To Go" products, and a significant portion of Campbell's overall advertising budget was devoted to spreading awareness about the new and repackaged products. The "M'm! M'm! Good! To Go" soups represented one of the most promising avenues for Campbell's growth, and their inclusion in the umbrella "Make It Campbell's Instead" campaign increased the credibility of that broader effort's primary claim, which was that Campbell's products were a convenient and wholesome substitute for a wide range of meals and snacks.

kids. For instance, Elliott played basketball with the 16-year-old rapper Bow Wow in one commercial for Campbell's Chicken Noodle Soup. Other spots supported newly developed Soup at Hand varieties expressly developed for children, such as Pizza, Taco, and Mexican noodle flavors. The campaign marked Campbell's first sustained targeting of children.

COMPETITION

In addition to being an internally significant change in strategy, the fact that Campbell aimed its soup advertising at children was a noteworthy development in the intensifying competition with rival soup brand Progresso. Progresso's most successful recent advertising campaign, and its first to include national TV commercials, attempted to make the case that Campbell's was kids' fare but that Progresso—which was not condensed and claimed, for instance, such attributes as white meat and chunky vegetables in its chicken noodle variety—was worthy of adult palates. Launched in 1998, the Progresso campaign was called "Discover the Better Taste of Progresso," and it targeted women aged 25 to 54. One TV spot showed a male office worker eating Chicken & Stars soup from a bowl, which was positioned alongside a juvenile lunchbox and a can clearly meant to suggest Campbell's. A female coworker approached the man and said, "You know, Chicken & Stars used to be my favorite. Then I learned to ride a two-wheeler. Come on, you're an adult now. There's a better tasting soup." Print ads took the comparative concept even further, identifying Campbell's by name. Progresso sales climbed by 12 percent during the 1998–9 soup season—fall through spring—and research indicated that a large proportion of these sales increases could be attributed to the campaign. Progresso's gains were likewise in line with the industry-wide trend away from condensed soups. By 2003 Progresso's annual sales had climbed to $424 million, a marked improvement over its 1998 total of $258 million.

Progresso's most direct competitor was not Campbell's condensed lines, however, but Campbell's Chunky brand, which likewise employed messages of food quality and flourished at least partly at the expense of the original Campbell's brand. Chunky's most recent advertising retained the long-running tagline "The soup that eats like a meal" and featured professional football players being accosted by their mothers (usually played by actors), who used various humorous ruses to ensure that their sons were eating Chunky soup. Launched in 1997, the campaign ran for many years, corresponding with a period of enormous Chunky sales growth, despite the fact that industry critics typically disliked the spots' lack of subtlety and unsophisticated attempts at humor.

MARKETING STRATEGY

"Make It Campbell's Instead," which ran on television during the 2003–4 soup season—fall through spring—at an estimated cost of $100 million, represented a sizable risk for Campbell, because it departed from the company's previous advertising in more ways than one. The tonal dissimilarity of the irreverent, reality-based TV spots to the emotional, family-oriented advertising of Campbell's more successful past was perhaps the most obvious change in the eyes of consumers, but the unification of Campbell's full line of soups under one advertising platform was an important strategic shift as well. Larry McWilliams stated in a press release, "[W]e're single-minded in our focus to change how people think about soup. A unified platform will maximize the impact and efficiency of both our message and our media buying . . . Our aim is to shake consumers up with a very different creative effort that will get them thinking about soup in new ways." The campaign also featured far more individual spots than a typical Campbell's campaign, which allowed the ad agency to use a variety of different pitches tailored to specific targets and products. This comparatively drastic rethinking of the company's advertising strategy was supported by the changes in product formulation, packaging, and shelving that had recently been announced.

The TV spots were shot on location with small crews using handheld video cameras instead of film, a strategy aimed at generating a look of immediacy that was in keeping with the reality TV shows of the time. The first spot was called "Anthem," and it showed host Elliott confronting a succession of ordinary people in an office setting and on a street, asking them to try the Campbell's products newly available in microwaveable containers. Other unscripted commercials showed Elliott barging into real families' homes during meals and arguing that they should "Make it Campbell's instead" and putting Soup at Hand containers in the hands of drivers stopped at street intersections. Reflecting on the usefulness of these encounters for the purposes of advertising, Elliott told *Advertising Age,* "Nothing works better than letting real people tell you what they think."

These commercials alternated with others featuring celebrities who were paired with specific brands in ways that leveraged the appeal each had among particular groups of TV viewers. Elliott arrived at the home of trendsetting New York restaurateur B. Smith in one commercial, with the suggestion that she try Campbell's Select Italian Wedding soup, one of the company's most popular upmarket offerings, rather than cold sandwiches. In another commercial Elliott traveled to the Indiana home of the Dilley sextuplets, where he demonstrated for the benefit of the six siblings and their parents various ways of creating interesting new meals by adding common household mixings and toppings to Campbell's Tomato Soup. In the spot featuring rapper Bow Wow, Elliott and the 16-year-old star squared off for a game of one-on-one basketball, with the winner to receive a meal of Campbell's Chicken Noodle Soup. In a slight twist on the other commercials' concept, one spot showed Sandra Lee, who had her own Food Network show and was the author of the best-selling cookbook *Semi-Homemade Meals* (in which she offered recipes that used ready-made products such as Campbell's Cream of Mushroom Soup), instructing Elliott in the preparation of Campbell's Seafood Tomato Alfredo.

The commercials depended, for much of their effectiveness, on Elliott's personality and his ability to generate off-the-cuff humor and enthusiasm for the brand. Leavening his brazen intrusiveness with charm and poise, Elliott was able to disarm participants in the unscripted spots, and he showed considerable personal magnetism onscreen. His behavior in the commercials was meant to seem a daring update of the long-established advertising practice of employing spokespeople.

OUTCOME

The "Make It Campbell's Instead" concept remained in place through 2004, and the company put particular emphasis on extending the appeals to children, preteens, and teens that had first been tested in the Elliott-helmed commercials. Campbell also adapted the "Make It Campbell's Instead" theme to its new Carb Request soups, aimed at low-carbohydrate dieters, and to a series of Soup at Hand efforts aimed at women who tended to skip or skimp on lunch. Overall Campbell's change in approach—from marketing within the soup category to marketing its products as the answer to a wide variety of snack and mealtime occasions—was credited with spurring the company's long-awaited turnaround, and this change was substantially driven by the "Make It Campbell's Instead" campaign. In 2004, for the first time since the 1980s, Campbell's core condensed-soup brand not only stabilized its losses but also showed sales gains, topping the $1 billion mark in total sales. Campbell's company-wide sales growth began outpacing analysts' predictions, and the company was finally credited with arriving at a workable model for generating sustained success in an evolving soup marketplace.

FURTHER READING

Atkinson, Claire. "Campbell Pits FCB, Roster Shops." *Advertising Age,* December 30, 2002.

Cassidy, Hilary. "Campbell Soup Hot for Sports; Mr. Phelps Accepts New Mission." *Brandweek,* December 8, 2003.

Ellison, Sarah, and Suzanne Vranica. "Campbell Warms Campaign to Heal Soup Sales—Reversal of Slide Is Vital as Restructuring Proceeds." *Wall Street Journal,* December 26, 2002.

Garfield, Bob. "Four Campaigns Demonstrate the True Meaning of Creative." *Advertising Age,* December 8, 2003.

Reyes, Sonia. "Campbell Soup Bolsters Ad Team." *Adweek,* November 10, 2003.

Thompson, Stephanie. "Campbell Bets $100 Million on Edgy Ad Effort." *Advertising Age,* August 4, 2003.

———. "Campbell Flagship Suffers Sales Slide." *Advertising Age,* September 16, 2002.

———. "Campbell Soup Chief Energizes Marketing." *Advertising Age,* January 27, 2003.

———. "Mobile Meals Gaining." *Advertising Age,* June 23, 2003.

———. "Souping Up a Classic." *Advertising Age,* May 2, 2005.

Mark Lane

Canadian Film Centre

Windfields
2489 Bayview Avenue
Toronto, Ontario M2L 1A8
Canada
Telephone: (416) 445-1446
Fax: (416) 445-9481
E-mail: info@cdnfilmcentre.com
Web site: www.cdnfilmcentre.com

■■■

2004 TORONTO WORLDWIDE SHORT FILM FESTIVAL CAMPAIGN

OVERVIEW

The 2004 Toronto Worldwide Short Film Festival was the tenth in this series of prestigious events. The festival was sponsored by the Canadian Film Centre, a nonprofit organization based in Toronto that was dedicated to preparing future generations of filmmakers. Because the festival relied on government and corporate funding for its survival, growth from year to year was important. It was also important that the festival develop and maintain an identity separate from that of the noted Toronto International Film Festival, which was dedicated to feature-length films. Although they shared a home city, the two festivals were not connected.

The Canadian Film Centre worked with Taxi, a Toronto-based agency, to develop a campaign promoting the 2004 festival. Taxi did the work pro bono, continuing a relationship between the festival and the agency that dated to 2000. The campaign was built around a series of humorous television spots, broadcast on Canadian cable stations, that were designed to draw in a wide audience of moviegoers. Because the spots were done on behalf of a nonprofit center, they were considered public-service announcements, and the airtime, estimated to be worth about $3 million, was donated by the stations. One group of commercials featured a character named Ian Heidegger, a pretentious acting-teacher who demonstrated various techniques, which were invariably absurd, for performing in short films. One spot, titled "Special FX," featured Heidegger walking around with a cigarette stuck to his pants as a "special effect" for generating smoke. Taxi also created spots that underscored the fact that the festival was devoted to short films. At the same time, the spots cited aspects in common between short films and full-length features, such as special effects, to emphasize the similarity between the two mediums.

Like previous campaigns created by Taxi on the behalf of the festival, the 2004 spots were considered to be a success. Attendance continued to climb at a consistent pace—it had risen about 25 percent every year since Taxi began working with the festival—and submissions continued to come in from around the world. The campaign was also a hit with critics, and the "Special FX" spot won a 2005 Gold Clio Award. This was, however, the last campaign created by Taxi for the festival. In 2005, citing other commitments, the agency declined an offer to continue the relationship.

A scene from an Ian Heidegger commercial for the 2004 Toronto Worldwide Short Film Festival.
PHOTO COURTESY OF TAXI CANADA.

HISTORICAL CONTEXT

The Toronto Worldwide Short Film Festival was sponsored by the Canadian Film Centre, based in Toronto. The center was founded in 1988 by Norman Jewison, a Canadian native who had achieved success in Hollywood. It offered hands-on instruction to young Canadians who wanted to make a career in the film industry. The center typically took about 85 residents per year, all of whom received training from veterans of the film industry. The center's residents also collaborated on short film projects.

The center's 2004 festival was held from May 11 through May 16. It was the tenth year for the festival, and it featured entrants from around the world. As with past festivals, the entrants were grouped in two separate competitions, one for Canadian filmmakers and another for international participants. Although the festival was primarily designed to celebrate short films, it also served to promote the center.

The festival included films that were not entered in the competition itself. In 2004, for example, there was a screening of a short film titled *Destino*, a joint creation of the surrealist artist Salvador Dali and the animation pioneer Walt Disney. The project was begun in 1946, but it had been abandoned soon after. The film was finally finished by the Walt Disney Company in 2003, using storyboards and animation that remained from the original effort. Both Dali and Disney, of course, had died several decades before the film's completion. The festival also featured special programs, which in 2004 included a focus on Mexican films and a spotlight on music videos.

The festival was important for the city of Toronto in a number of ways. Tourism had suffered after Toronto experienced a mild outbreak of sudden acute respiratory syndrome (SARS) in 2003, and the 2004 festival served to help boost tourism in the city. In addition, along with the Toronto International Film Festival, the festival of short films continued to build upon Toronto's reputation as a major city for the art of film.

TARGET MARKET

The campaign for the Toronto Worldwide Short Film Festival was specifically targeted at moviegoers, especially those who were thought to be inclined to go to film festivals. At the same time the campaign was broad based, aimed at attracting as large an audience as possible. Maintaining a solid attendance at festival events was important, since the Canadian Film Centre operated strictly on a nonprofit basis. This meant that much of the funding for both the center and the festival came from government grants and corporate donations. One way to ensure that grants and donations continued was to keep the festival growing. In addition, because those who attended were charged admission, higher attendance helped fund the festival and the center. All money raised went back into the festival budget, meaning that higher attendance offered the opportunity to screen more films in future festivals.

COMPETITION

While there was no direct competition to the Toronto Worldwide Short Film Festival, since it was the only major event of its kind in the city, it was important that the festival try to prevent being eclipsed by the Toronto International Film Festival. Run by the Toronto

NORMAN JEWISON: A NORTHERN STAR

The Canadian Film Centre was founded in 1986 by the noted director and producer Norman Jewison in an effort to foster the film community of his native Canada. Born in 1926, Jewison received his education at the University of Toronto before embarking on a career in Hollywood. He was especially interested in exploring racism and racial issues, inspired in part by a journey across the Deep South of the United States during the Jim Crow era.

Jewison's best-known film, *In the Heat of the Night* (1967), dealt with America's racial politics head-on. The film starred Sidney Poitier and Rod Steiger as police officers who had to work together to find a murderer. Poitier played Virgil Tibbs, a Philadelphia police detective who, while on vacation in the South, was accused of murder by a local police chief, played by Rod Steiger. Eventually, despite mutual distrust, the two learned to cooperate in order to find the real killer. Other Jewison movies, such as *The Hurricane* (1999), which starred Denzel Washington, had similar themes. In this film, based on the life of Rubin Carter, an African-American boxer was wrongly accused of murder.

Other well-known Jewison films included the screen adaptations of *Fiddler on the Roof* (1971) and *Jesus Christ Superstar* (1973), as well as the 1968 hit *The Thomas Crown Affair*, which starred Steve McQueen. In recognition of his contributions to American film, Jewison received the Irving G. Thalberg Memorial Award at the 1998 Academy Awards ceremony.

International Film Festival Group, this latter event, which had begun in 1976, had over the years become one of the most prestigious film festivals in the world. In 1999, for example, the noted film critic Roger Ebert claimed that the Toronto International Film Festival was even more influential than the festival held in Cannes, France.

While the Toronto International Film Festival was held in the fall, after the festival of short films, it always threatened to overshadow the earlier event. For one thing full-length films had a greater hold on the public's imagination. Although a short film like *Destino,* the Dali-Disney collaboration, might hold interest for filmmakers, it could never achieve the audience enjoyed by many full-length feature films. For example, the Chinese film *Crouching Tiger, Hidden Dragon,* which had its North American premiere in Toronto in 2001, went on to gross more than $128 million in the United States and Canada. Thus, campaigns for the Toronto Worldwide Short Film Festival had to make the case for short films as an art form in their own right and help the festival define itself on its own terms.

MARKETING STRATEGY

Taxi, which had handled advertising for the Toronto Worldwide Short Film Festival since 2000, was a Canadian-based advertising agency with offices in Toronto, Calgary, and Montreal, as well as in New York City. The festival was a nonprofit event, and Taxi offered its work pro bono. Because the festival was a nonprofit event and received government support, the advertising counted as public-service announcements. Hence, local cable stations donated airtime, which was estimated to be worth $3 million.

The main concern of Taxi was to show that short films were not all that different from longer features. In addition, the agency felt that the spots needed to be light in tone so as to project a sense of fun. The 2004 campaign included three 30-second television spots that featured the character Ian Heidegger, an acting teacher. They were titled "Special FX," "Love Scene," and "Good Cop, Bad Cop."

"Special FX" began with a shot of a classroom in which "Short film workshop–Special F/X" was written on the blackboard. As smoke gathered around him, teacher Ian Heidegger walked around the room. He discussed various ways of producing smoke and the different characters he could play. A shot then let the viewer know that the smoke was coming from a cigarette the teacher had attached to the front of his pants. The lesson continued as the teacher asked his students who he could be, "a gorilla in the mist" perhaps. He ended the lesson by declaring, "You're all wrong. It's me, Ian Heidegger. I'm acting. Magic," as his students looked on in consternation. The spot than concluded with the Toronto Worldwide Short Film Festival logo, as Ian repeated his self-assessment: "Magic."

In "Love Scene" the Ian Heidegger character gave another lesson. Here "Short film actor's workshop–love scene" appeared on the blackboard. The spot began with the teacher, who this time was not named, standing at the front of the class with two students. After a moment he looked at them and gave the instruction, "Steve, John, make passionate love to each other." Confused by their teacher, the two students hugged awkwardly. He then interrupted them and told them to sit down. After reminding the class that they were learning about short films, he called another student, Ron, to the front of the class. The teacher then took off his shirt and told the class he would teach them how to make love in "three seconds." The spot closed with the instructor running full bore at his terrified pupil. Again, the spot concluded with the festival logo.

A third Heidegger spot was titled "Good Cop, Bad Cop." In this spot "Short film workshop–Good Cop/Bad Cop" appeared on the blackboard. Heidegger watched as three students enacted the Hollywood good cop/bad cop routine. In a scene reminiscent of a Hollywood action move, one "cop" was rude to the "suspect," while another was friendlier. The teacher eventually interrupted and told the students that the scene was "too long" for a short film. He then showed them "the Heidegger method" for the good cop/bad cop routine. The teacher sat down next to the suspect and said, "Confess, bitch. Nice hair." He nodded to the class, and the festival logo appeared.

The effect of the spots was to satirize pretentious Hollywood actors. The Ian Heidegger character was over-the-top in his mannerisms and voice, which served to make his special effect look even more ridiculous and his techniques seem all the more unhinged. Even his name, an echo of the noted twentieth-century philosopher Martin Heidegger, sounded pretentious. The tone of the spots was important to Taxi, which felt that humor would be more effective in getting people's attention.

Other commercials in the campaign centered on an imaginary short film titled *Livid.* These spots all made sport of how short the film was. A spot titled "Score," for example, featured a performance of the film's sound track, which was three notes long. Another spot, "Director," summed up the plot of the film in one sentence. Again, humor was the key to the success of the spots.

OUTCOME

The campaign for the 2004 Toronto Worldwide Short Film Festival was considered to be a success. Once again attendance rose, continuing a trend of roughly a 25 percent increase in every year between 2000 and 2004. The number of submissions also was up, with the festival in 2004 drawing more than double the number received in 2000.

The campaign, especially the Ian Heidegger spots, was also a hit creatively. "Special FX" was singled out for the 2005 Gold Clio Award in the television category. The 2004 campaign, however, was the last Taxi agreed to develop for the festival. In 2005, despite the Clio for their work on behalf of the 2004 festival, Taxi decided to stop offering pro bono work for the event. Because of an expanded client base, the agency felt that it could no longer give the attention the festival needed. Taxi continued, however, to do other projects for the Canadian Film Centre, including design work for its 2006 winter gala.

FURTHER READING

Ashenburg, Katherine. "What's Doing in Toronto." *New York Times,* August 22, 2004.

Dixon, Guy. "Short Films Have to Make Their Point Quickly." *Toronto Globe and Mail,* June 14, 2005.

Howell, Peter. Rare Disney Dalliance with Dali Opens Festival. *Toronto Star,* May 11, 2004.

Menon, Vinay. "Some Quick Takes on Canadian Shorts." *Toronto Star,* January 28, 2004.

Rea, Peter W., and David K. Irving. *Producing and Directing the Short Film and Video.* 2nd ed. Woburn, MA: Focal Press, 2001.

Sanati, Maryam. "Festival: Got 'Em by the Shorts." *Toronto Globe and Mail,* June 10, 2005.

Sheridan, Sherri. *Developing Digital Short Films.* Boston: New Riders, 2004.

Story, Louise. "The Subservient Chicken and Other Award Winners." *New York Times,* June 13, 2005.

Thurlow, Clifford. *Making Short Films: The Complete Guide from Script to Screen.* New York: Berg, 2005.

Worldwide Short Film Festival website. <http://www.worldwideshortfilmfest.com>

Guy Patrick Cunningham

Canon U.S.A., Inc.

1 Canon Plaza
Lake Success, New York 11042-1198
USA
Telephone: (516) 328-5000
Fax: (516) 328-5069
Web site: www.usa.canon.com

85 SECOND PHOTO LAB CAMPAIGN

OVERVIEW

In 2001 Canon U.S.A., Inc., a subsidiary of the Japanese printer, copier, and peripherals manufacturer Canon Inc., introduced a compact digital-photo printer, which offered speed and the convenience of being able to connect directly to a digital camera. The category was small but growing, prompting Canon in the fall of 2003 to launch the "85 Second Photo Lab" campaign, developed with New York's DCA Advertising. The goal was not only to support the launch of a new printer, the CP-300 Card Photo Printer, but also to bring energy to the category.

The $5 million "85 Second Photo Lab" campaign consisted of three television commercials, all of which demonstrated how a digital-camera user could quickly connect to a Canon Card Photo Printer and have a quality print in hand less than a minute and a half later. The television spots were supported by three print ads, which appeared in a variety of consumer magazines. They showed the Canon printer in typical picture-taking situations, such as at a child's soccer game, at a wedding, and at a vacation destination.

Ending in the early weeks of 2004, the campaign succeeded in boosting sales and brand awareness, and it set the stage for the launch of the next generation of Canon compact printers. It also won an EFFIE award, which singled out the campaign for creative achievement.

HISTORICAL CONTEXT

Canon's founders developed Japan's first 35-millimeter camera in 1934 and incorporated their business three years later. Canon gained a foothold in the U.S. market after World War II, when American servicemen returned home with the high-quality Japanese cameras they had bought at military base exchanges. The company branched into business machines in the 1960s, first with calculators and then with photocopiers, a market in which Canon became a serious challenger to Xerox. In addition to successfully diversifying its business, Canon proved to be a savvy marketer over the years. Although Nikon produced better quality cameras, Canon was able to surpass Nikon as Japan's top-selling camera brand in the early 1980s. In the United States, Canon also scored marketing triumphs with its EOS (electronic optical system) line of cameras in the late 1980s.

By the early 1990s only one-fifth of Canon's revenues came from camera sales, putting the company in a better position than Japanese rivals such as Minolta and Nikon, which suffered when camera sales dropped as a result of the market maturing. Canon was also less exposed than other camera companies as digital photography began to change the landscape at a rapid pace in the 1990s, and consumer electronics companies like Hewlett-Packard, Sony, and Nokia entered the field and used their marketing prowess to gain significant shares in the digital arena. Old-guard competitors such as Kodak, Polaroid, and Fuji miscalculated how rapidly digital technology would eclipse film, the sale of which had been highly profitable and difficult to give up.

But by the start of the 2000s there was no doubt that digital had arrived. It was also becoming clear that, just as control of the film market had been the key to the success of Kodak and Fuji, whoever was able to stake a claim to the output side of digital photography (that is, prints) would be better positioned for the long term, especially given that cameras were evolving into just another consumer electronics product, one from which it became increasingly difficult to squeeze out a profit. At first, buyers of digital cameras made far fewer prints than expected, but the industry believed that eventually consumers would grow tired of being limited to just seeing their digital pictures on their computers, which was where pictures ended up when transferred from cameras or received by E-mail. Photo labs made it increasingly easy to have prints developed from digital files, and a number of competitors developed self-service kiosks, which were widely distributed to drug stores and other retail outlets.

Canon, already in the printer business, offered ink-jet printers capable of printing photographs, but it also launched a Card Photo Printer called the CP-10, a small portable unit that a camera could connect to directly, producing high-quality four-by-six-inch photos, with or without borders. The printer used dye-sublimation technology, which applied wax in layers of color to produce sharper snapshots, making the photos more durable and resistant to liquids. The digital-still-photography market was small but growing. By the summer of 2003 Canon had a 15 percent share of the $204 million market, second only to Sony's 18 percent. In the fall of 2003 Canon decided to relaunch the second-generation Card Photo Printer, the CP-100, while introducing the new CP-300 with more marketing muscle via the "85 Second Photo Lab" campaign.

TARGET MARKET

The "85 Second Photo Lab" campaign cast a wide net, essentially aiming to appeal to all consumer digital-camera owners. But within that large group there were specific audiences to target. The younger demographic, 25- to 35-year-olds, was especially attracted to the innovative technology as well as to the convenience of Canon's Card Photo Printers, particularly the less-expensive CP-100. One element of the campaign was a nine-college campus tour, developed in conjunction with *Glamour* magazine, during which the easy-to-use compact printers were demonstrated.

Another product demonstration effort was arranged with Saks Fifth Avenue, taking place at 55 of the department stores across the country. This facet was in keeping with another target of the campaign: middle-class women. According to research conducted by Kodak, about three-quarters of all family pictures were taken by women. Moreover it was wives and mothers who mostly maintained the family photo albums, for which they needed prints. An easy-to-use and fast printer was a perfect addition to a digital camera, but having already spent a lot of money on a camera, memory card, and other accessories, many consumers were not willing to shell out further for a Card Photo Printer, especially when photo labs, self-service kiosks, and online services could provide prints. Consequently the "85 Second Photo Lab" campaign also had to target consumers with a certain level of disposable income. Hence much of the advertising was tied to the kind of interests these people pursued, such as travel, music and entertainment, and home decorating.

COMPETITION

Canon's Card Photo Printers faced competition on a number of fronts. Because part of their appeal was speed and instant gratification, the company had to contend with Polaroid's instant cameras. Polaroid, still wedded to film, had been devastated by digital technology, but it continued to enjoy a measure of success selling to the teen market its line of small I-Zone and JoyCam cameras and the small adhesive-backed "sticky film" they used.

CANON FODDER

Canon was established as Precision Optical Company in Japan in 1937. That same year the company dubbed the 35-millimeter camera it had developed the Kwanon, the name of the Buddhist goddess of mercy. In 1947 the name "Kwanon" was dropped in favor of the similar sounding, and more universal, "Canon," which meant "precision" in Latin. The company changed its name as well, and Precision Optical became Canon Camera Company Limited. In 1966 Canon U.S.A., Inc., was formed, and three years later the parent company, which had successfully branched into office products by this time, shortened its name to Canon Inc.

One-hour photo labs offering cheap, high-quality prints were also serious competitors with Canon, as were online services and the self-service kiosks produced by a number of companies, including Kodak, Polaroid, Olympus, IBM, Mitsubishi, Sony, and other, smaller players.

In addition Canon's new printers competed with home ink-jet printers, which were offered by a host of companies, such as Epson, Hewlett-Packard, and Canon itself. Direct competition came from other makers of specialty printers. Kodak offered an easy-to-use printer dock (employing continuous-tone thermal dye-transfer technology), and it spent large sums to pitch it to women as a portable party printer. Other companies also made small printers that used dye-sublimation technology, including the Olympus Camedia P-200, the Sony DPP-MP1, the Sony DPP-SV88, and the Panasonic PV-PD2100. In addition there were compact printers that relied on other technologies. Fujifilm's NX-500 used a thermo-autochrome process, while Hewlett-Packard's PhotoSmart 100 Compact was the only printer in the category to rely on ink-jets.

MARKETING STRATEGY

In October 2003 Canon and DCA launched the $5 million "85 Second Photo Lab" television and print campaign to promote the new CP-300 digital photo printer as well as to relaunch the less expensive CP-100 printer. Rather than position the products as just printers, the marketers chose to portray them as part of the entire picture-taking experience. The television spots and print ads both employed a square neon sign that read, "85 Sec Photo Lab." The origins of the sign grew out of a personal experience. DCA creative director Rob Rosen told *Adweek* 's Deanna Zammit, "We passed these one-hour-photo-lab signs and we thought, 'That's a good icon.'...Once we had that little mnemonic, we were able to lend it to print and TV."

The television commercials were aired on national cable channels and in local television markets that were also high-volume digital-camera markets. The three television spots were "Italian Woman," "Half Pipe," and "Sea Monster." In the first, a 30-second spot, a sultry Italian woman dressed in red walked down a street, attracting the attention of a number of men (and a bulldog), including a young American tourist sitting at a sidewalk café table. He snapped a digital picture using a Canon camera, which he quickly connected to a Card Photo Printer to produce an instant picture. In the background could be heard the sounds of a car crash. The snapshot, held up to blend in with the scene of the village square, was removed to reveal the steaming car wreck, no doubt caused by the Italian woman. The spot's voice-over commented, "Canon's Card Photo Printer. Great prints easily. Anywhere you take pictures. The 85 second photo lab. Digital revolutionized photography. We revolutionize digital." The spot also incorporated the "85 Sec Photo Lab" neon sign in the background.

The 15-second "Half Pipe" spot featured a young woman taking a picture of a man performing a bicycle stunt at an extreme-sports half-pipe competition. As she quickly developed a print using her Canon Card Photo Printer, the sound of a siren could be heard. Once again the print was held up against the background, and when it was removed, the extreme bike rider was shown being loaded into an ambulance. The voice-over offered a variation of the "Italian Woman" text. The last of the three spots, the 15-second "Sea Monster," showed a young man taking a picture of an unseen subject. He held up the photo, which showed a sea monster against a watery background, but when he removed the picture there was nothing visible but a ring of bubbles. The voice-over text was similar to that of "Half Pipe."

Neither of the two 15-second spots used the neon-sign image, but the campaign's three print ads did. They also used Canon's corporate tagline, "Canon Know How." One ad showed a Card Photo Printer turning out a picture at a wedding reception. Another placed the printer next to a soccer goal with a game in progress. The final print ad showed a Canon Card Photo Printer on a wicker table in a tropical paradise setting. The subject matter of the ads reflected the audiences the campaign targeted: families and consumers with enough income to afford traveling. The ads appeared in a variety of travel and lifestyle magazines.

OUTCOME

The "85 Second Photo Lab" campaign continued into the spring of 2004 and succeeded in garnering recognition for Canon's compact photo printers. The campaign was also successful on a creative level. In 2005 the campaign won the prestigious gold EFFIE award in the Computer Peripherals for Business/Personal Purposes category, presented by the New York American Marketing Association to honor creative achievement in the advertising industry. The award also recognized the campaign for "the results it generated in terms of measurably increased sales, market and mind share," according to the press release announcing the selection. The campaign also set the stage for Canon in April and May 2004 to introduce the next generation of the line: the CP-220 and CP-330. Among the enhancements was adding the ability to print on four-by-eight-inch paper, which allowed users to create and print their own greeting cards. The upgraded printers were also able to print sequences from movie clips as thumbnail images on a four-by-six-inch card.

FURTHER READING

Blachere, Kristina. "Stylish Dye-Sub Printer for On-the-Go Photos." *Computer Shopper,* February 2004, p. 64.

Bulik, Beth Snyder. "Sony, Kodak Lead U.S. Battle for Share in Digital Cameras." *Advertising Age,* May 31, 2004, p. 12.

"Canon's New Compact Photo Printers CP-200 and CP-330 Add Ease-of-Use, Flexibility and Style to Direct Photo Printing." *Business Wire,* March 31, 2004.

"Direct Photo Printer." *Poptronics,* July 2002, p. 6.

"Meet the IMA: Canon U.S.A., Inc." *Incentive,* May 2001, p. 54.

Morris, John. "Pint-Size Printers Deliver Big Results." *Computer Shopper,* May 2003, p. 38.

Portnoy, Sean, Stephen Bigelow, Kristina Blachere, Barbara Krasnoff, Chris Robertson, and Dong Van Ngo. "Photo Finish." *Computer Shopper,* April 2003, p. 114.

Sholik, Stan. "Specialty Printers Expand Photo Options." *Petersen's Photographic,* July 2002, p. 68.

Wasserman, Todd. "Kodak Focuses on Processing." *Brandweek,* May 24, 2004, p. 15.

Zammit, Deanna. "Canon on New Printer: You Can Take It with You." *Adweek,* October 20, 2003, p. 16.

Ed Dinger

CareerBuilder Inc.

8420 West Bryn Mawr Ave., Ste. 1000
Chicago, Illinois 60631
USA
Telephone: (773) 527-3600
Fax: (773) 399-6313
Web site: www.careerbuilder.com

TIME TO MOVE ON CAMPAIGN

OVERVIEW

By the 1990s newspapers were facing increasing competition from Internet job sites. In 1995, in order to compete with online sites for advertising revenue, the Tribune Company newspaper chains (whose publications included *Newsday,* the *Chicago Tribune,* the *Los Angeles Times,* and the *Baltimore Sun,* and Knight Ridder, publisher of the *Kansas City Star,* the *Miami Herald,* and the *Philadelphia Inquirer,* among others) partnered to create their own online job site, which ultimately evolved into CareerBuilder.com. Their aim was to level the playing field with the online competition, which included Monster.com and HotJobs.com, and to win back help-wanted advertisers. In 2002 the Gannett Company, with publications that included *Florida Today,* the *Arizona Republic,* and the *Fort Collins Coloradoan,* became an equal partner with the Tribune Company and Knight Ridder in the online venture.

Visitors to CareerBuilder.com's site increased 50 percent from December 2002 to December 2003, helped in part by the marketing campaign "Smarter Way to Find a Job," created by the company's Chicago-based ad agency, Cramer-Krasselt. CareerBuilder kicked off 2004 with a new campaign, titled "Time to Move On." Also created by Cramer-Krasselt, this $17 million campaign was aimed at employed but unhappy workers.

The "Time to Move On" campaign, which was launched on January 5, 2004, and ran until the end of the year, was a success both with job seekers and with the marketing industry. Not only did it increase traffic to the website to 16.2 million unique visits in the weeks following its launch, up from 7.5 million visits for the same period in January 2003, but it also received EFFIE and Tempo awards, with one television spot, "Bank Teller," being named an *Adweek* Best Spot.

HISTORICAL CONTEXT

As the popularity of online career sites grew in the early 1990s, newspapers were feeling the threat from their Internet competitors. Revenues from print help-wanted ads were slipping, as companies shifted their advertising dollars to Internet sites like Monster.com and HotJobs.com. In an effort to compete in the dot-com marketplace and to win back its ad dollars, two of the country's top newspaper chains—the Chicago-based Tribune Company and Knight Ridder, based in San Jose, California—joined forces to create their own employment website. The fledgling company, which began in 1995 as NetStart, Inc., was renamed CareerBuilder Inc. in 1998. By offering access to 130 newspapers and 400 job sites, CareerBuilder.com soon was going head-to-head with online job site

Monster.com and was pushing past HotJobs.com. In 2001 CareerBuilder.com reported more than 5.5 million unique monthly visits and 300,000 job listings. The Virginia-based Gannett Company joined the partnership in 2002, further increasing its reach online and giving CareerBuilder.com an edge over both Monster.com and HotJobs.com.

Cramer-Krasselt was hired in 2002 to help CareerBuilder with its marketing and advertising. In 2003 the company launched a national campaign designed to reach potential job seekers and to encourage them to visit its website, stating that this was "the smarter way to find a better job." The campaign was awarded a Gold EFFIE in 2004 for successfully changing the rules for how online job sites were advertised, including the decision to decline in joining Monster and HotJobs in buying advertising spots during the Super Bowl. In August 2004 CareerBuilder struck a blow at rival Monster when it won a five-year deal with Microsoft's MSN, valued at $150 million, a contract that had previously been held by Monster. Through the agreement, CareerBuilder was to provide the content for MSN's career channels. In addition, in a deal valued at $115 million over a four-year period, CareerBuilder replaced Monster in providing similar services to America Online (AOL). To maintain the momentum, the "Time to Move On" campaign was launched in 2004.

CAREERBUILDER JOINS RANKS OF SUPER BOWL ADVERTISERS

Based on the success of earlier marketing campaigns that had helped place CareerBuilder.com among the top three online job sites, the dot-com announced a national marketing blitz in 2005 to be launched during Super Bowl XXXIX. With its new campaign, CareerBuilder joined the ranks of online job sites Monster.com and HotJobs.com to run television spots during the annual football showdown. The campaign, with the tagline "A better job awaits," was the company's largest brand awareness effort since its inception in 1995. Besides the four Super Bowl spots, the campaign included additional television and radio spots and print and outdoor ads.

TARGET MARKET

At a time when online job sites typically targeted large companies in search of highly skilled technical workers, CareerBuilder looked at the statistics and the job market and realized that things were changing. Following the dot-com collapse, tech jobs had become scarce, and according to a report by the Associated Press, hourly workers—those in blue-collar and service professions—made up 60 percent of America's labor force. Adjusting to these changes, CareerBuilder added blue-collar and while-collar hourly workers to its target audience by introducing an effort in January 2003 to connect both unemployed skilled and unemployed hourly workers with employers.

Then, in December 2003, there appeared a report in *HR Magazine* indicating that a survey done by the Society for Human Resource Management and the *Wall Street Journal*'s CareerJournal.com had found that nearly two-thirds of all gainfully employed people were "extremely likely" to begin searching for new jobs within the coming year. Kirk Scott, Cramer-Krasselt's director of advertising for CareerBuilder, noted further that 85 percent of the people going online in search of jobs were already employed. "Given the way things in the economy have gone, there is an increased level of dissatisfaction of workers," Scott said. Although CareerBuilder's previous campaigns had targeted unemployed people looking for jobs, the company's 2004 campaign shifted its marketing focus toward employed people unhappy in their jobs, whether they were white-collar or blue-collar workers.

COMPETITION

The Internet division of Monster Worldwide, Inc. emerged in 1995 when the company acquired a recruitment firm that included an online job site designed to bring together job seekers and employers. The site, which became Monster.com, was a huge success. It primarily attracted high-tech job seekers, who could post their résumés online free of charge, and Fortune 1000 businesses willing to pay for access to the résumés and to post job positions that were open. Monster.com's revenues jumped from almost nothing in 1995 to $536 million in 2001, and by 2002 it had become the number one online job site, bumping HotJobs.com from the top spot. Monster.com began slipping, however, as competition from upstart CareerBuilder.com heated up. In 2003 the number of monthly visitors to Monster.com dropped 19 percent, to 15.3 million, from the previous year, and revenue dropped nearly 30 percent as well. As the job market changed and the site's former clients went the way of the burst dot-com bubble, they took their advertising money with them. In response, Monster.com followed the lead of CareerBuilder.com and began targeting health care, blue-collar, service, and other salaried workers. To emphasize the opportunities for skilled and hourly jobs on its website, Monster.com's marketing in 2003 included a television spot that showed an out-of-control, driverless semi racing down a road while an unemployed truck driver had a cup of coffee. Despite its efforts, however, Monster.com barely held its lead against the competition. In 2004 it reported 19.6 million visits, compared to CareerBuilder's 19.3 million. It then launched a new marketing campaign, "Today's the Day," designed to encourage job seekers not to delay looking for a new job and to do their search on Monster.com.

HotJobs.com, Ltd., founded in 1997, was ranked at the top of the online job sites by 2001. In 2002 the company was voted the "The Best General Purpose Job Board for Job Seekers," and it was ranked 14 on the *Bloomberg Personal Finance Magazine* 's Tech 100 list. It was already beginning to slip against the competition, however. The business was also on the sales block, with its closest competitor, Monster Worldwide, poised to buy it. Yahoo! landed the deal, however, and in February 2002 HotJobs.com became a wholly owned subsidiary of the Internet communications company. In an effort to turn around its declining site visits, the company launched a new campaign, titled "Rainbow Connection," in 2003. The campaign, which kicked off with television spots during the Super Bowl, targeted underemployed workers and featured people in various job situations singing "Rainbow Connection," the song made popular by Kermit the Frog in *The Muppet Movie.* Using the tagline "Dreams found faster," it also promoted the benefits of searching for a better job online at HotJobs.com. Within 24 hours of the first broadcast of the spot, the company reported that site visits had jumped 40 percent and that submissions of new résumés had increased 53 percent over the same period in the previous week. Although the campaign was considered to be a success, by 2004 the company was firmly entrenched as the number three online job site, behind CareerBuilder.com and Monster.com.

MARKETING STRATEGY

The challenge of the Chicago-based agency Cramer-Krasselt was to develop a marketing campaign that would achieve CareerBuilder's goal of reaching people who were unhappy in their jobs. The new campaign also aimed to increase brand awareness among job seekers and to convince them that CareerBuilder.com was not only sympathetic to their plight but also could connect them with more employers than competing online job recruitment sites. The new $17 million campaign, "Time to Move On," was launched nationwide in January 2004 with three television spots. It was supported with additional radio spots, as well as print and outdoor ads. Television spots appeared during early-morning news broadcasts, prime-time shows, and sports programs on network and cable channels. The print ads were published in newspapers owned by CareerBuilder's parent companies, the Tribune Company, Knight Ridder, and the Gannett Company.

The three kickoff TV spots featured dissatisfied employees fantasizing about how they could escape their wretched jobs. One spot showed a white-collar office worker being berated by perhaps the nastiest boss in the country. When the boss's tirade finally ended and he walked away, the suffering employee began eating lunch at his desk. Noticing a smear of ketchup on his lip, the employee pretended to be seriously injured, and an ambulance was called to take him to the hospital. At the first opportunity the unhappy employee jumped out of the ambulance and ran off. Another spot was set in a bank. An unhappily employed teller jumped onto the counter, pretending that the bank was being robbed. After telling everyone to get down, she leaped off the counter and quietly tiptoed out the door. The third spot portrayed a frustrated factory worker making his escape by crawling inside an oversized toy bear. In each spot the voice-over stated, "There comes a time in some careers when you just need to move on. Plan your great escape at the only job-search engine with over 350 leading newspapers and professional organizations." The tagline, "The smarter way to find a better job," was carried over from CareerBuilder.com's 2003 campaign.

Print ads pictured disgruntled employees in situations similar to those in the television spots. In one ad an employee neatly dressed in a trim skirt, sweater, and pumps was working in the stockroom of a men's clothing store. As she leaned over to sort through a cardboard box filled with folded dress shirts, a naked male mannequin behind her swung his foot and placed a swift kick on the unsuspecting woman's backside, as if to boot her out the door. The copy read, "Maybe it's time to move on." Another ad showed a harried-looking man sitting at his desk. The photograph was taken through a half-filled water cooler, giving the impression that the man could not keep his head above water. The copy asked, "Will you know when it's time to move on?"

OUTCOME

CareerBuilder.com's advertising struck a chord with frustrated employees everywhere who were contemplating job changes in the new year. Within one month of the launch of the campaign on January 5, 2004, the company had jumped to become the share leader in the online job search category, with a 117 percent increase in site visits. According to the company, more than 16 million individual visitors logged on to the site in January

2004, following the campaign's launch, compared to just 7.5 million visitors in January 2003.

In 2005 the "Time to Move On" campaign received a Gold EFFIE Award and two Tempo awards. The EFFIE honor recognized the campaign for successfully moving CareerBuilder.com from the number three online job site to number one by showing that the company understood job seekers and was sympathetic to their problems. The Tempo awards were presented by the Chicago Association of Direct Marketing to recognize leading marketing and creative programs, with "Time to Move On" winning in the broadcast category for both marketing (first place) and creativity (second place).

FURTHER READING

Bethany McLean. "A Scary Monster: Monster Worldwide Has a Cute Mascot, Memorable Super Bowl Ads, a Rising Stock Price—and a Host of Problems." *Fortune,* December 22, 2003.

"CareerBuilder.com to Tackle the Super Bowl in 2005." *PR Newswire,* June 15, 2004.

Hein, Kenneth. "CareerBuilder to Launch $17 Mil. Campaign." *Editor & Publisher,* December 15, 2003.

———. "Hunt for the Disgruntled." *Editor & Publisher,* December 15, 2003.

"HotJobs to Make a 'Rainbow Connection' with New Ad during Super Bowl: Consumers Offered Sneak Preview of New Spot on Yahoo! and HotJobs." *Business Wire,* January 24, 2003.

Jensen, Trevor. "CareerBuilder's New Tack: The Great Job Escape." *Adweek,* December 15, 2003.

"Monster and CareerBuilder Lead in Local Online Recruitment Revenue." *PR Newswire,* May 17, 2004.

"Monster.com Leads in 27 of 50 Top U.S. Job Markets, Newspapers Still Struggle to Understand Online Sales, according to Report by Classified Intelligence." *Business Wire,* April 22, 2004.

"New HotJobs Commercial Connects with Super Bowl Audience." *Business Wire,* February 5, 2003.

Oser, Kris. "CareerBuilder Looking to Do a Job on Monster: Site Gaining Visitors, Running Super Bowl Ad." *Crain's Chicago Business,* January 24, 2005.

Schramm, Jennifer. "Brace for Turnover." *HR Magazine,* December 1, 2003.

"Strategy: CareerBuilder.com Offers Online Options." *Adweek,* December 15, 2003.

Sylvester, David A. "Help Wanted Advertising Plummets Along with Jobs." *Knight Ridder/Tribune News Service,* April 1, 2003.

"U.S. Job Recovery Pushes 30 Percent Growth for Online Career Sites, according to Nielsen/NetRatings: Monster.com, CareerBuilder, and Yahoo! HotJobs Take Top Rankings." *PR Newswire,* July 16, 2004.

Rayna Bailey

Cargill, Inc.

15407 McGinty Road West
Wayzata, Minnesota 55391
USA
Telephone: (952) 742-7375
Fax: (952) 277-4455
Web site: www.cargill.com

■■■

COLLABORATE>CREATE> SUCCEED CAMPAIGN

OVERVIEW

Cargill, Inc. decided at the end of the 1990s to recast its image as a staid commodities company to an innovative provider of solutions for its food industry customers. The company developed a 10-year plan to change the way it operated and was perceived in the world. A new logo was created to announce that change was under way at Cargill, and a fresh branding message was conceived. In the fall of 2003 an integrated marketing campaign dubbed "Collaborate>Create>Succeed" was launched to articulate Cargill's new vision.

The campaign's main target was director-level officers in food industry companies, the goal being to show them through concrete examples how Cargill could partner with them to solve problems and in the end help them make more money. The TV spots and print ads laid out a real-world problem and then revealed the Cargill solution that proved profitable to the customer. For example, one ad centered on Cargill's efforts to help confectioners develop a better-tasting, low-sugar chocolate. Similar ads also presented these same stories on the Internet.

The long-term campaign, the budget of which was not publicly disclosed by Cargill, succeeded in improving the company's image with the target audience, which also indicated that it was now willing to pay more for Cargill products and services. The "Collaborate>Create> Succeed" theme also galvanized the Cargill rank and file as they began taking to heart the concept of partnership with customers. One of the print ads in the campaign won a prestigious honor, awarded first place for the Best Single Advertisement in the American Business Media's Creative Excellence in Business Advertising (CEBA) competition.

HISTORICAL CONTEXT

As the twentieth century came to a close, Cargill, the largest private corporation in the United States, with annual sales approaching $50 billion, found itself highly diversified yet typecast in the mind of its customers. The company was involved in virtually all aspects of the food-supply chain yet remained pigeonholed as a trading company and low-cost processor. Cargill's sheer size also worked against it, as customers had a difficult time associating such a behemoth with innovation, let alone possessing concern about the plight of the smaller companies it did business with. During the customer research phase of the "Collaborate>Create>Succeed" campaign, one respondent summed up an all-too-common opinion: "When Cargill says its believes in a win/win, they mean Cargill wins twice."

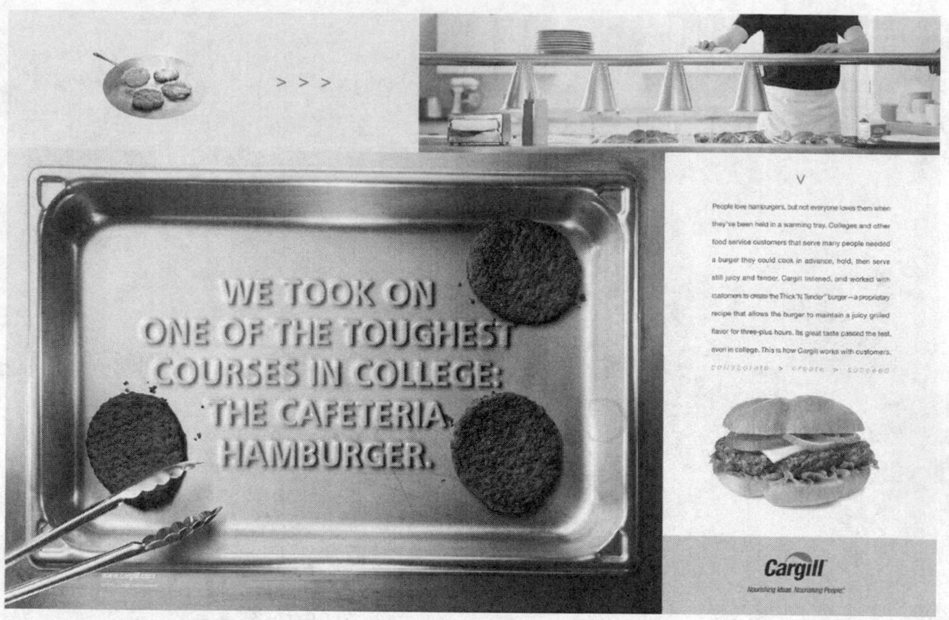

An ad from Cargill's "Collaborate>Create>Succeed." campaign.
PHOTO COURTESY OF MARTIN WILLIAMS, INC. REPRODUCED BY PERMISSION.

In 1999 Cargill initiated a 10-year plan called Strategic Intent, to reorganize the company for the new century and change its image. The stated goal was "By 2010, Cargill will be the recognized global leader in providing agriculture and food chain customer solutions that enable them to succeed in their businesses." The achievement of this goal required a reorganization of the way Cargill did business, a communications effort to change the mind-set of its workforce, and a major marketing campaign to change the perception of Cargill with its customers. More importantly it wanted to make the case that Cargill was more than just commodities and that despite its size it wanted to partner with customers to help them solve their problems to the benefit of both parties. Cargill was restructured into 90 business units, thus allowing employees to focus on the needs of their customers. The company then began to reposition the Cargill brand, in 2001 setting up the Cargill Brand Council, comprising senior executives from the business units as well as public affairs and marketing people, to coordinate the introduction of a new logo and develop a new message. In essence Cargill became a master brand applied to a wide variety of products and services. The new logo was unveiled in February 2002, and in the autumn of that year Cargill began conducting customer research to flesh out the brand strategy. In May 2003 the new brand-positioning strategy was formulated, and in September 2003 the "Collaborate>Create>Succeed" campaign was launched to articulate that message to current and potential customers on an international stage.

TARGET MARKET

While "Collaborate>Create>Succeed" tried to communicate to the world a new image of Cargill, it was primarily a business-to-business advertising campaign aimed at every level of the food industry, including processors, marketers, and retailers. But the ultimate target were primary decision makers, the C-suite, generally those executives with "chief" in their title (chief executive officer, chief financial officer, chief operating officer), who held the levers of power in the food-processing, food-service, and grocery retail industries. These were the people who established a company's strategy and determined how money was to be spent. While changing the perception of Cargill among the lower ranks was good public relations and might trickle up to influence the C-suite, the campaign sought to reach senior executives directly, change their perception of Cargill, and lead to new business opportunities. In this way the company would continue to move farther away from the commodities model, selling large quantities of raw substances at cheap prices, to become a provider of more profitable value-added services—becoming a partner rather than a mere supplier. The campaign also targeted Cargill's employees, making them more aware of the company's new mission and encouraging them to buy into the program and begin seeing customers as partners. In the

IOWA ROOTS

Minnesota-based Cargill, Inc., was established in 1865 by William Wallace Cargill when he bought his first grain business in Iowa. He was later joined by his younger brother Sam and in 1868 moved to Minnesota, where the company established its headquarters and began to take advantage of the post–Civil War western expansion of the railroad and agriculture.

end it was the rank and file that would have to make sure that the new campaign was a promise to fulfill and not mere puffery.

COMPETITION

With close to 100 business units, Cargill competed against a multitude of companies in a wide range of fields and virtually everyone in the food-processing, grocery, and restaurant industries. One of its chief rivals on the global stage was Archer Daniels Midland Company, one of the largest processors of oilseeds, corn, and wheat in the world, generating about half the amount of revenue of Cargill. A somewhat smaller competitor, Bunge Ltd., focused on soybean, grain trading, and fertilizer. In terms of the "Collaborate>Create>Succeed" campaign, however, Cargill's competition was not the chief concern. There were not competing messages in the marketplace to address. Rather, Cargill was in a sense competing against the prevailing image of itself. The message was not that Cargill was better than ADM or Bunge but that it had more to offer to customers than they realized, that Cargill was not a complacent giant but a vibrant and innovative company.

MARKETING STRATEGY

The task of the "Collaborate>Create>Succeed" campaign was challenging because of Cargill's sheer size. "Cargill is quite a complicated company," Ann Ness, the company's director of advertising and brand management, told Nicole Garrison, writing for the *Minneapolis/St. Paul Business Journal.* "What we've found is that there is so much more that we offer that our customers don't know about. They might know us as an egg company, but not know us as a meat company. They might know us as a meat company, but not know us as a chocolate company." The last marketing campaign Cargill offered, almost three years earlier, promoted the idea that Cargill played a major role in "the world's diverse appetite for food." While it boosted the company's image, the advertising failed to tell the world what Cargill actually had to sell. "Collaborate>Create>Succeed," on the other hand, sought to provide concrete examples of what Cargill did. More importantly these examples were crafted into stories that followed the same pattern: if a customer had a need that could not be met in the general marketplace, then Cargill intervened to use its expertise to address that customer problem. Thus a major task for the marketing team was the selection of the case studies that would make the most compelling stories to illustrate the campaign's message. The case studies were categorized within three general challenges facing customers: how to grow new products; how to simplify a complex supply chain; and how to improve the health and nutrition of a product.

"Collaborate>Create>Succeed" was an integrated campaign with elements that included radio spots, online media, and a campaign microsite, but the anchors were 8 television spots, 12 print ads, 8 banner ads, and a website. An example of a success story told on television was the spot called "Better Beef," which juxtaposed images of cattle-driving cowboys and people pushing shopping carts on the range in search of a better cut of beef. The spot's voice-over explained how Cargill worked with supermarket chains to "round up" a line of high-quality hand-cut beef, followed by the tagline "This is how Cargill works with customers." Another spot, "Sugar-Free Chocolate," began with the problem facing people who loved chocolate but had to cut back on sugar. The solution was Cargill using its knowledge of sweeteners and sugar replacers to team up with candy makers to produce a new generation of better-tasting sugar-free chocolate.

Five of the six television spots had a corresponding print ad that made the same point but added some detail. In the "Better Beef" print execution, the cowboys were seen sitting on the railing of a supermarket parking lot "cart corral." The text made the point that Cargill focused on the "entire ranch to retail process." The "Sugar-Free Chocolate" print ad used a child for its image rather than a young woman, but the text made the same point about how Cargill used its expertise to help develop new better-tasting sugar-free chocolate. The print ads also relied on the tag "This is how Cargill works with customers." Other ads showed how Cargill helped Italian cheese makers increase the production of Parmesan cheese by providing a specialized feed for the cows supplying the milk; how Cargill established a culinary school for sales reps so they could better serve the needs of chefs and restaurant managers; how Cargill helped baking companies to develop a new "heart-healthy" bread; and how Cargill worked with food-service customers to create the Thick'n Tender hamburger, a proprietary recipe for a burger that could remain in a warming tray for extended periods of time without losing its taste. Because a major goal of the "Collaborate>Create>Succeed" campaign was to educate the audience about the breadth of what Cargill had to offer, the print ads that touted success in one area of the food industry were run in a trade publication covering a different aspect. For people who wanted further information, the campaign's website offered details on the case studies that were the germ of the TV spots and print ads.

The media strategy of the campaign had to take into account the nature of the C-suite target audience. Hard working and pressed for time, they watched little television, aside from business programming. Hence the television spots were shown mostly on national cable news channels, including CNN, Fox News, and CNBC. Airtime was also purchased on certain sporting events, like golf and the Olympics. The target audience read a great deal, so the campaign's print ads ran in a range of publications, from trade publications to general business publications, such as *Forbes* and the *Wall Street Journal.* Ads also appeared on a number of websites, including WSJ Online, MarketWatch.com, and SmartBrief (a repository of daily food industry news). The online elements proved highly influential, as many executives increasingly turned to the Internet for up-to-the-moment information not available through other channels.

OUTCOME

The "Collaborate>Create>Succeed" campaign met its intended goals. An Annual Awareness and Attitude Study conducted by Cargill in 2005 demonstrated that as a result of the campaign, decision makers in the food industry were now more likely to see Cargill as a partner able to offer innovative solutions. Moreover they were willing to pay more for Cargill products and services. "Collaborate>Create>Succeed" generated a great deal of interest in Cargill, reflected by the more than 50,000 visits to the microsite during the first four months after the campaign broke. The balance sheet also showed improvement, as Cargill experienced double-digit sales and profit growth in each of the two years immediately after the campaign began in 2003.

"Collaborate>Create>Succeed" was also recognized by the advertising industry. In the autumn of 2005 one of the campaign's print ads, the "TNT Burger," won first place for Best Single Advertisement in the American Business Media's Creative Excellence in Business Advertising (CEBA) competition. But perhaps most important of all was the effect the campaign was having on the Cargill corporate culture. The "Collaborate>Create>Succeed" slogan was incorporated in almost all internal and external communications and became something of a rallying cry among employees—as the message and the behavior began to reinforce one another and play a major role in Cargill, making the goal of its 10-year plan a reality.

FURTHER READING

Baar, Aaron. "Cargill Nourishes Brand Image." *Adweek* (midwest ed.), January 8, 2001.

———. "Martin/Williams Takes Charge of Cargill's Image." *Adweek* (midwest ed.), July 27, 1998, p. 3.

"Cargill, Inc." In *International Directory of Company Histories,* vol. 13. Farmington Hills, MI: St. James Press, 1996.

Coakley, Debbie. "Nourishing Ideas." *Agri Marketing,* November–December 2003, p. 26.

Garrison, Nicole. *Minneapolis/St. Paul Business Journal,* October 6, 2003.

Reinan, John. "Cargill Grows a Better Web Site." *Star Tribune* (Minneapolis), October 25, 2004, p. 7D.

Salvage, Bryan. "Creating a Deli $ensation." *Meat & Deli Retailer,* May 2004, p. 16.

Ed Dinger

Carl's Jr.

6307 Carpinteria Ave., Ste. A
Carpinteria, California 93013
USA
Telephone: (805) 745-7500
Fax: (714) 780-6315
Web site: www.carlsjr.com

■■■

SIX DOLLAR BURGER CAMPAIGN

OVERVIEW

As Carl's Jr., one of the country's leading fast-food burger chains, prepared to celebrate its 60th anniversary in 2001, the brand was feeling the pains of an aging icon. Despite its reputation for serving quality burgers and for introducing innovative options not usually found at early fast-food establishments, such as self-serve beverage counters, the company was losing customers to a new niche: fast-casual restaurants. These restaurants had higher prices and better-quality food than found at fast-food places. Carl's Jr. was hurt further by the deep discounts on products that competing fast-food chains, such as Burger King and McDonald's, were offering customers. A Carl's Jr. press release stated that the company's practice of offering a small but quality selection of menu items and limiting discounts had contributed to a continuing weakness in same-store sales.

To remedy the situation, Carl's Jr. took a closer look at the fast-casual niche and saw it as an opportunity to expand its business. The business-lunch crowd was typically in a hurry but hungry for a quality meal. To entice these customers, Carl's Jr. began offering a new product, the Six Dollar Burger. The burger gave customers the best of both worlds: a restaurant-style burger that was as convenient as fast food. To support the burger's introduction, a campaign was created by Los Angeles–based Mendelsohn/Zein Advertising, at an estimated cost of $50 million. It kicked off with a series of television spots that not only praised the Six Dollar Burger but also spoofed casual-dining businesses such as T.G.I. Friday's. One TV commercial showed hapless customers who were forced to join the birthday celebration of a diner at a nearby table, and another showed an overenthusiastic waiter pushing dessert on diners before the main course was served. Radio spots also promoted the product.

Consumers ultimately bought the concept. The company reported that, following the launch of the "Six Dollar Burger" campaign, same-store sales took a positive turn and reversed the downward slide Carl's Jr. had experienced for the previous three periods. In addition the campaign won a bronze EFFIE award and was presented a Silver Skillet award by *Restaurant Business* magazine.

HISTORICAL CONTEXT

In 1941 Carl Karcher went into business for himself by setting up a hot-dog cart in Los Angeles. By 1946 his business had grown into a drive-in restaurant with hamburgers as one of the featured menu items. As Carl's Jr. continued to expand, it earned a reputation for serving delicious charbroiled hamburgers. In 1997 CKE Restaurants, owner of Carl's Jr., purchased a floundering

© KIM KULISH/CORBIS.

Midwestern burger chain, Hardee's. Rather than proceeding with CKE's initial plans to convert Hardee's to Carl's Jr. shops, the two sister chains maintained separate but similar identities and menus, which confused consumers. In addition, as the core customers of Carl's Jr.—baby boomers—aged, their tastes changed. Although these baby boomers had grown up with fast food, they also possessed significant disposable income and were looking for higher quality food like the kind served in casual-dining restaurants. Carl's Jr. went into a slump as customers fled to its high-end competitors and as sister chain Hardee's carried it along on its own downward spiral.

To win back its former customers and lure new customers, Carl's Jr. began carving out a new niche for itself as a fast-food chain serving restaurant-quality food. After experimenting with a variety of larger burgers and testing four prototypes with consumers, Carl's Jr. introduced the Six Dollar Burger in 2001. With its launch Carl's Jr. joined the ranks of other fast-food chains (such as Noodles & Co., Chipotle Mexican Grill, and Boston Market) competing with casual-dining restaurants by promoting their businesses as "fast-casual" dining establishments.

TARGET MARKET

According to the Oklahoma City *Journal Record,* Carl's Jr. launched its Six Dollar Burger because it "[viewed] the fast casual niche market—the hybrid between quick service and casual dining—as offering a strong business opportunity, especially with the average lunch hour being just 36 minutes these days." While Carl's Jr. targeted its core customers who had left the chain in search of a quality dining experience, the new burger and marketing campaign also appealed to time-strapped office workers, especially women, by offering a casual-dining restaurant meal without the hassles and costs associated with eating in a midscale restaurant.

Carl's Jr. also did not alienate the consumer group most likely to eat fast food: young men aged 18 to 35. At $3.95 the Six Dollar Burger fit the budgets of most men in that demographic. Weighing in at almost one-half pound of beef, and with toppings that included two thick slices of cheese, the burger could also satisfy the appetites of most hungry young men. To make sure this group of consumers got the message that Carl's Jr. was the place to go for burgers, the "Six Dollar Burger" campaign eventually evolved to include commercials featuring attractive young women in provocative situations.

SIZZLE IS COMING FROM MORE THAN THE BURGERS IN NEW CARL'S JR. SPOTS

In 2001 Carl's Jr. introduced its successful Six Dollar Burger and an accompanying campaign. The burger, which cost $3.95 but was designed to replicate more pricey casual-dining fare, was a hit with consumers. To keep the momentum growing, the chain in November 2003 expanded its offerings to feature a full line of premium burgers. In an effort to reach its target audience of men 18 to 35 years old, Carl's Jr. simultaneously launched a new campaign of provocative TV spots starring Playboy founder Hugh Hefner and a bevy of Playboy bunnies.

The sizzling commercials may have been hot to the target audience, but they offended other consumer segments, including Thomas Aquinas College president Thomas Dillon. After the ads aired Dillon asked Andrew Puzder, president and chief executive officer of Carl's Jr. parent company CKE Restaurants, to resign his position on the college's board of governors. Prior to Puzder's resignation from the board, CKE issued a statement regarding the Hefner ad campaign, stating, "As a pop icon, Hefner appeals to our target audience and credibly communicates our message of variety."

COMPETITION

For Carl's Jr. the key competitors were number one burger chain McDonald's Corporation and number two

CARL'S JR. JUMPS ON LOW-CARB BANDWAGON

With the influence of diet-conscious consumers helping to determine the menu offerings at many dining establishments, Carl's Jr. adjusted its product line in response to one of the latest diet crazes: low-carbohydrate meals. An estimated 32 million Americans at the time were on a low-carb diet. Starting in December 2003 burger lovers could get their favorite Six Dollar Burger with all the trimmings except one: the bun. To reduce the carbohydrate count of the half-pound burger from 61 grams to a skimpy 6 grams, Carl's Jr. wrapped the burger in iceberg lettuce, reduced the amount of ketchup, and switched from sweet to dill pickles.

chain Burger King Corporation. Both were also struggling icons trying to reach the time-strapped business-lunch crowd, and both launched new campaigns in the early 2000s. McDonald's and Burger King also took a cue from Carl's Jr. by giving consumers what they wanted: big, juicy burgers like those found in casual-dining restaurants but served up fast and at a good price.

Using a group of 20-something office workers known as the "Lunch Break Gang" as spokespersons, Burger King in 2004 began a campaign promoting its Whopper hamburger and reintroduced its well-known slogan "Have It Your Way." To further appeal to the casual-dining crowd, the chain began offering an upgraded burger made with Angus beef, which it called the Western Angus Steak Burger. The campaign was a success for the chain, which reported monthly sales increases in the 10 consecutive months following its launch.

In 2003 McDonald's launched a campaign with the slogan "I'm Lovin' It." The chain's advertising agency stated in an interview with *Money* magazine that the plan was "to make McDonald's a 'lifestyle,' not just a place to eat." The new campaign became the first that McDonald's had launched internationally. After the "I'm Lovin' It" campaign appeared, McDonald's was named "Marketer of the Year" by *Advertising Age* for the brand's "marketing achievements around the world."

MARKETING STRATEGY

Introducing the Six Dollar Burger when many other fast-food chains were discounting their burgers was something of a risky strategy for Carl's Jr. The company explained, however, that the "Six Dollar Burger" campaign was designed to create a marketing concept that would set the chain apart from the competition. It also hoped that, by positioning the product as the first restaurant-quality burger offered by a fast-food chain, it could win back its market share from high-end and midscale casual-dining restaurants.

The campaign's television and radio commercials, created by ad agency Mendelsohn/Zein, were designed to reach burger lovers who craved restaurant-quality burgers but wanted them without the annoyances or high prices of sit-down restaurants. Television spots that kicked off the campaign portrayed the traditional restaurant-dining experience as less than desirable. One commercial featured diners who were forced to listen to a neighboring customer being sung to on his birthday, while another showed a pushy waiter encouraging customers to order dessert before their main course was served. At the end of each spot a voice-over asked, "Wouldn't it be nice if you could just get one of those great $6 restaurant burgers . . . without the restaurant?" The radio ads employed a man-on-the-street format, with people sampling the Six Dollar Burger and then commenting on the product in their own words.

OUTCOME

Following the launch of the "Six Dollar Burger" campaign, the *Orange County Register* reported that sales at Carl's Jr. restaurants made a turnaround and that for 14 straight months CKE reported positive sales at Carl's Jr. restaurants open more than one year. Restaurant analyst Bob Sandelman noted that the campaign successfully reinforced the company's message that Carl's Jr. was at the high end of fast food. Noting the success of the Six Dollar Burger, sister chain Hardee's introduced a similar product, called the Thickburger, within months. Hardee's customers received the new burger with the same enthusiasm that Carl's Jr. customers had, which helped boost the chain's falling sales. Based on the popularity of the Six Dollar Burger and the success of the campaign, Carl's Jr. introduced in 2003 a complete line of Six Dollar Burgers with five flavor varieties and an expanded marketing campaign that featured sexy commercials designed to appeal to men 18 to 35 years of age.

In 2002 the "Six Dollar Burger" campaign won a bronze EFFIE award for achieving the company's goal of developing a unique marketing concept and setting the chain apart from the competition. In addition Carl's Jr. won a Silver Skillet award, which was presented by *Restaurant Business* magazine in recognition of "exceptional innovation in new food or beverage items and uniqueness in product and marketing strategy."

Although the campaign was a success for Carl's Jr., there was one negative outcome: Dallas-based casual-dining restaurant chain T.G.I. Friday's filed a lawsuit against Carl's Jr. parent company CKE, alleging false advertising. The suit, which was settled in U.S. District Court in Los Angeles, according to *Nation's Restaurant News,* was related to one of the Carl's Jr. ads, which included the claim that its $3.95 Six Dollar Burger was "like the burger I just paid about $6.25 for at Friday's." Both companies declined to comment on the settlement or to divulge its terms.

FURTHER READING

"Burger Lovers: Carl's Jr. Has More of What You Want." *PR Newswire,* November 3, 2003.

"Carl's Jr. Celebrates 60th Anniversary." *PR Newswire,* July 12, 2001.

"CKE: Hardee's Sales Soar in '$6' Promotion." *Nation's Restaurant News,* February 11, 2002.

"Friday's, CKE Settle Suit over '$6 Burger' Ad Claim." *Nation's Restaurant News,* June 10, 2002.

Lansner, Jonathan. "You Hope Alan Greenspan's Been Hitting Some Drive-Through Windows." *Santa Ana (CA) Orange County Register,* March 19, 2002.

"Marketing Magic." *Restaurants & Institutions,* August 1, 2001.

"McDonald's Named 'Marketer of the Year.'" *PR Newswire,* December 13, 2004.

Montgomery, Tiffany. "Bigger Burgers with Better Beef Boost Business at Carl's Jr., Hardee's Eateries." *Santa Ana (CA) Orange County Register,* August 19, 2004.

"New and Noteworthy." *Los Angeles Daily News,* July 4, 2001.

Parpis, Eleftheria. "Best Spots of 2004." *Adweek,* June 6, 2005.

Peters, James. "CKE Slips despite Gains from '$6' Burger." *Nation's Restaurant News,* September 16, 2002.

"The Six Dollar Burger Sheds Its Buns and 55 Grams of Carbohydrates in Time for New Year's Resolutions." *PR Newswire,* December 15, 2003.

Spector, Amy. "On the Fast Track: QSR Chains Race to Adopt Casual Approach." *Nation's Restaurant News,* July 16, 2001.

"Targeting the Casual Niche." *Oklahoma City Journal Record,* August 22, 2001.

Zuber, Amy. "The Best of Both Worlds." *Nation's Restaurant News,* October 1, 2001.

Rayna Bailey

Carnival Corporation

3655 NW 87th Avenue
Miami, Florida 33178-2428
USA
Telephone: (305) 599-2600
Fax: (305) 599-2600
Web site: www.carnivalcorp.com

FUN SHIPS CAMPAIGN

OVERVIEW

Beginning in the mid-1980s Carnival Cruise Lines emerged as a leader in the global market, and within a decade the Miami-based carrier had become the world's leading cruise operator. With a total of more than 30 ships and a broad base of holdings, Carnival Cruise Lines had become Carnival Corporation in 1994. By that time it had long since established a winning ad campaign, with television spots featuring entertainment personality Kathie Lee Gifford. Beginning in early 1997, however, the company took a new approach, using animated figures—most notably dancing fish—in place of human performers, with Gifford retained for the voice-over.

The agency of record, HMS Partners, typically employed a budget of $20 million to present two spots per year for the campaign, which was loosely titled "Fun Ships" and ran through 2000. The individual commercials, featuring their respective "stars"—the computer-generated images—cavorting to a calypso beat while Gifford's voice-over touted Carnival, were part of a continued branding effort in which Carnival sought to present itself as the "Fun Ships" line. "We own fun," senior vice president of marketing Vicki Freed told Jeffery D. Zbar in the *Fort Lauderdale Sun-Sentinel.* "We've been investing in fun for 20 years now. All the research tells us that our brand is known for fun."

As a result of this campaign and other moves by Carnival—such as the purchase of rival lines, the construction of new ships, and innovative marketing methods—bookings on Carnival ships continued to grow in 1998, 1999, and 2000, as they had grown for many years preceding. With expanded fleet capacity and more ships slated to be finished in the early years of the new century, however, Carnival and other cruise lines were especially vulnerable to the downturn in the larger travel and tourism industry following the terrorist attacks on September 11, 2001.

HISTORICAL CONTEXT

In 1972 Ted Arison, a former executive with Norwegian Caribbean Lines, joined forces with Meshulam Riklis of American International Travel Service (AITS) to form Carnival Cruise Lines. The latter, an AITS subsidiary, launched its first ship, the *Mardi Gras,* shortly thereafter. Like some farcical version of the *Titanic,* the *Mardi Gras* ran aground on its maiden voyage. With this inauspicious start, the nascent line was soon heavily in debt, and in 1974 Arison bought out Riklis for almost nothing.

By 1975, however, Arison had turned a profit by careful positioning with regard to Carnival's target market. He added a second ship in 1976 and a third the following year. In the midst of a market depressed by high inflation during the late 1970s and early 1980s, Carnival prospered under the leadership of Arison and his son Micky, who became CEO in 1979. By 1987, when it went public, Carnival was the leading cruise operator in the world.

In the late 1980s Carnival diversified, adding short cruises to, and a gambling casino in, the Bahamas. There were also land tours, a hotel chain, and—following the 1989 purchase of Holland America Line—luxury cruises. By the mid-1990s the newly renamed Carnival Corporation had established a heavy presence in Europe that culminated with the early 1998 purchase of the upscale Cunard line of Great Britain for half a billion dollars.

TARGET MARKET

From the mid-1970s Ted Arison had shown an ability to recognize the target demographic of Carnival Cruise Lines, and more than 20 years later his son seemed to have inherited the trait. Furthermore, Micky Arison, with his family-controlled 45 percent of the company, continually worked to refine Carnival's focus on its target market.

The elder Arison recognized early that the cruise line's customer base was built around youngish middle-class adults, and he designed the shipboard entertainment—including discos, live music, and gambling—accordingly. Hence the focus on fun, evident in Freed's statement that the line had been "investing in fun" for two decades. The first two spots in the new campaign, released in 1997, featuring dancing fish and swaying palms respectively and included a voice-over by Gifford, saying, "I guess some vacations are just more fun than others." Gifford, whose contract with the cruise line continued until mid-1999, presented a somewhat longer, but still fun-oriented, tagline in the 1998 spots: "Looks like one vacation is just more fun. We guarantee it. Carnival. The most popular cruise line in the world."

Awareness of the target market motivated more than the company's attempts to associate fun with its image, however. Journalist Kitty Pilgrim, interviewing Micky Arison for Cable News Network Financial News (CNNfn) in 1998, noted the high numbers of Americans who would have reached "the prime cruising age" within a few years. According to one analyst, Pilgrim commented, by 2005 there would be 81 million Americans between the ages of 40 and 59. Arison, when asked if he expected an increase in ticket sales to coincide with this trend, not surprisingly said that business had long been good and was only going to get better; nonetheless, he conceded, "There is no question that the aging of the baby-boom generation is falling into really our prime target market for cruising."

To accommodate the aging baby-boom market, along with growing health concerns among the population, in November 1998 Carnival launched its first-ever smoke-free cruise ship, the *Paradise.* The latter would sail a seven-day route between Miami and the eastern or western reaches of the Caribbean. Arison explained to Pilgrim that surveys had shown a decline in the numbers of smokers among Carnival customers. At present, he said, no more than 22 percent of the company's passengers smoked, so it made sense to dedicate at least one ship to a completely smoke-free environment.

Carnival also used price as a means of drawing in the large numbers of Americans who had never taken a cruise before in their lives—92 percent of the U.S. public, according to a study referred to in *Advertising Age* in early 1997. The Cruise Line International Association reported that in 1996 fewer than 5 million Americans took cruises, leaving a market of more than 270 million untouched.

In addition, given trends in the market, the company could be expected to attract female travelers. According

TITANIC RESULTS?

Did the 1998 hit *Titanic*—a huge box-office success as well as the winner of several Academy Awards, including Best Picture—hurt ticket sales for cruise ships? One would assume that it would have: after all, the central event of the film was the sinking of an ocean liner. But that would be an incorrect assumption, according to Carnival Corporation CEO Micky Arison. "I think exposure to the industry is clearly positive," Arison told Kitty Pilgrim of Cable News Network Financial News (CNNfn), on the program *In the Game* in November 1998. "And while we weren't expecting a boost from *Titanic* . . . the reality is that it did show some of the glamour of cruising's past, and the first half of the movie . . . was pretty positive."

The first half of the film took place before the sinking of the majestic *Titanic* on the night of April 14, 1912. One scene in particular that seemed to have captured viewers' imaginations, Arison told Pilgrim, was the one in which star Leonardo Di Caprio climbed onto the bow, placing himself at the very front of the ship. Arison stated, "We do have people trying to get out on the bows to feel fresh air because of the movie . . . Captains are constantly complaining that they've got to take people down from the bows of the ship."

to a study conducted by About Women, a business research firm, in late 1996, women were more likely to take cruises than men, more likely to plan their vacations carefully, and more likely to spend a greater amount of money. One of the chief concerns of women travelers—both in the leisure as well as business segments—was security. They wanted to know they would be safe in their rooms, whether in a hotel or on board a ship. Uniglobe Travel senior vice president Michele Desreux gave Carnival high marks for its treatment of female customers: "There are progressive suppliers," she told the *Worcester Sunday Telegram,* "such as Hyatt Hotels and Resorts and Carnival Cruise Lines, that take special care with women travelers."

COMPETITION

At the same time that Carnival brought out its first round of "dancing fish" spots in early 1997, archrival Royal Caribbean Cruises also broke new advertisements. With six television spots created by ad agency McKinney & Silver of Raleigh, North Carolina, the Royal Caribbean campaign centered on the tagline "Like no vacation on earth." Royal Caribbean's commercials, like Carnival's, departed from existing industry standards, which tended to call for shipboard scenes; the competitor's spots used "fly-by" scenes of a ship cruising on the water.

As Zbar reported in *Advertising Age,* "Other competitors ha[d] already charted new courses" in their adverting as well. In September 1996 Celebrity Cruise Line introduced a new campaign using animated figures created by Korey, Kay & Partners of New York City. Norwegian Cruise Lines had, in 1995, presented a series of spots built around the tagline "It's different out here"—advertising that used "attractive models and provocative themes," in Zbar's words, to make a departure from typical cruise-ship advertising.

Pointing out the common denominators underlying these advertisements, Zbar reported that "executives noted the merits of selling the emotional experience of cruising, as opposed to the rational approach"—i.e., selling the sizzle rather than the steak. He quoted Adam Goldstein, vice president of marketing for Royal Caribbean: "We wanted to strike out in a new direction that gets people who historically might have been put off by yet more classic cruise imagery, to say that the kind of vacation we offer is connected with some of the most fundamental vacation and personal needs."

MARKETING STRATEGY

For 12 years, starting in the mid-1980s, Carnival advertising had centered on celebrities, usually depicted on board a Carnival ship. Julie Weingarden in *Adweek* described the typical Carnival ad lineup as "second-tier celebrities like Richard Simmons and Willard Scott rubbing elbows with perky ship hostess/spokesperson Kathie Lee Gifford."

Then in January 1997 came the first in a new line of television spots, which Zbar described in *Advertising Age*: "Realistic, computer-animated tropical fish and swaying palms replace longtime spokeswoman Kathie Lee Gifford—retained as voice-over talent—as the central characters. As the fish dance to an original mambo tune, a Carnival ship is seen plying the water's surface. And as palms sway to a calypso beat, a ship sails into view. 'I guess some vacations are just more fun than others,' says Ms. Gifford's voice-over."

The new television campaign had emerged from a 1996 print campaign using the theme of fun, and whereas Carnival had spent $30 million on total advertising in the preceding year, in 1997 it intended to devote $20 million to the new campaign alone. The company certainly was not having to spend money on celebrity talent: the "stars," as Weingarden called the main attractions in the commercials, were computer-generated. Behind the new spots was the work of Digital Domain, a computer production facility in Venice, California, that had also provided visuals for the film *Titanic.*

In 1998 the company proceeded with what Zbar called "a continued shift from shipboard shots and toward branding its 'Fun Ships' concept." Again there were two spots that replaced their predecessors on national television in October, and again the theme of fun was built around the antics of images created with the help of a computer. In "Starfish," a school of those multilegged sea creatures danced to a calypso beat, and the same musical backing appeared in "Beach Chairs & Umbrellas"—a spot that showed yet more cavorting on the part of nonhuman actors. Both spots included Gifford's voice-over: "Looks like one vacation is just more fun. We guarantee it. Carnival. The most popular cruise line in the world." The campaign continued with little alteration through 2000.

OUTCOME

Results for Carnival in the late 1990s seemed to indicate that the company's leadership was justified in straying from cruise-ship advertising tradition. In 1999 Wall Street analyst Brian Egger of Donaldson, Lufkin and Jenrette, a specialist in the cruise and gaming industries, described Carnival as "extremely well positioned." According to Suzanne Koudsi of *Leisure Travel News,* Egger called Carnival his "favorite company" and noted, "Carnival is best known for going after a customer that's never taken a cruise."

The fall of 2000 saw Carnival depart even further from the celebrity-focused platform that had defined its advertising prior to 1997. The new campaign adopted the conventions of so-called "reality TV" as a means of updating Carnival's image and addressing negative stereotypes about the cruising experience. Amateur actors were sent on Carnival cruises and then interviewed after the fact; the hope was that the actors would appear to be disinterested, third-party endorsers. The first-time cruisers told stories of negative expectations overcome, and in the process they described highlights of their individual Carnival vacations. The previous tagline, "The most popular cruise line in the world," remained in place.

The booming cruise industry of the late 1990s had led Carnival, along with its competitors, to increase the size of its fleet dramatically. The consequences of such overbuilding were already cause for concern by 2000, but the September 11, 2001, terrorist attacks turned the situation into a full-blown problem. The declines in travel and tourism following the attacks forced Carnival and its competitors to resort to deeply discounted fares in the scramble to fill what had become an overabundance of berths. Although the subsequent years were difficult ones for all cruise lines, the long-term outlook for the cruise industry remained strong, and Carnival was well positioned for future growth in the event of a rebound, thanks in no small part to its marketing-generated identity as the "fun" cruise line.

FURTHER READING

"Carnival Reports Revenue Hike in 1st Quarter." *Travel Weekly,* April 3, 1995, p. 39.

Determan, Wendy. "Carnival's New Line of Luxury." *Leisure Travel News,* April 12, 1999, p. 17.

Goetzl, David. "Cruising to Nowhere." *Advertising Age* (midwest ed.), November 12, 2001.

Koudsi, Suzanne. "Analysts Optimistic for Cruise Industry." *Leisure Travel News,* January 25, 1999, p. 21.

———. "The Cruise Buzz." *Leisure Travel News,* December 14, 1998, p. 598.

———. "Selling Cruises Made Easy?" *Leisure Travel News,* March 8, 1999, p. 4.

"Record Carnival Result." *Lloyd's List,* December 23, 1994, p. 2.

Scott, Diana. "Travel Is Up for Women of All Ages, but Survey Reveals a Troubling Note" *Worcester (MA) Telegram & Gazette,* January 26, 1997, p. F1.

Weingarden, Julie. "Carnival Cruise Turns to 'Toons to Show It's Still the 'Fun Ship,'" *Adweek* (southwest ed.), January 13, 1997, p. 5.

Zbar, Jeffery D.. "Carnival, Royal Caribbean Ads Depart from Tradition: Dancing Fish Bump Beaming Kathie Lee from Starring Role in Cruise-Ship Ads." *Advertising Age,* January 6, 1997, p. 6.

———. "Fun Ads for the 'Fun Ships': Carnival Sets Sail into World of Computer Animation." *Fort Lauderdale (FL) Sun-Sentinel,* October 3, 1998, p. 15C.

———. "Miami-Based Carnival Cruise Lines to Debut New 'Reality-Based' Television Ads." *Fort Lauderdale (FL) Sun-Sentinel,* November 8, 2000.

Judson Knight
Mark Lane

Cellco Partnership

180 Washington Valley Road
Bedminster, New Jersey 07921
USA
Telephone: (800) 214-3555
Fax: (908) 306-6927
Web site: www.verizonwireless.com

CAN YOU HEAR ME NOW? CAMPAIGN

OVERVIEW

Cellco Partnership, which operated under the name Verizon Wireless, was the largest mobile-phone service provider in America during 2002. Rated best by consumers in customer satisfaction, Verizon was spending an estimated $1 billion every 90 days to improve service quality and to expand its coverage "footprint" (the term given to a mobile-phone reception area). Although its smaller competitors, such as Sprint PCS Group and Cingular Wireless LLC, began price wars using lower-priced calling plans, their footprints and sustained-call rates were lacking. Subscribers using Cingular were four times more likely to drop (lose service during) a call than Verizon's customers. Avoiding the price wars completely and rebranding itself as a premium service provider, Verizon launched its "Can You Hear Me Now?" campaign on January 14, 2002.

"Can You Hear Me Now?" was created by Bozell, a New York-based ad agency that operated as part of the Interpublic Group of Companies. The television spots starred actor Paul Marcarelli as a Verizon field tester who dropped in on locations ranging from the outlandish to the mundane. In each spot he asked, "Can you hear me now?" into a mobile phone. After hearing an affirmation, Testman, as Marcarelli's character was dubbed, replied, "Good!" By 2003 Verizon was spending $300 to $400 million annually on the "Can You Hear Me Now?" campaign, with an additional $700 to $800 million on direct mail and in-store promotions. Only 10 percent of the campaign's budget went into print advertising.

Although the "Can You Hear Me Now?" campaign did not receive many advertising awards, it did help establish higher-ground branding for Verizon during intense industry competition. The number of Verizon subscribers increased from 32.5 million at the campaign's launch to 37.5 million in 2003. By the start of 2004 the number of subscribers was 43.8 million, which indicated that quality was indeed a strong selling point for cell-phone consumers. Verizon remained the number one wireless provider in America until February 2004, when Cingular purchased AT&T Wireless Services for $41 billion.

HISTORICAL CONTEXT

Cellco Partnership, doing business under the name Verizon Wireless, formed in 2000 when Bell Atlantic merged with Vodafone, the world's largest mobile-phone service provider. Together the partnership had 32 million subscribers, making Verizon an overnight industry leader. Starting in August of 2000 Verizon Wireless began the largest renaming campaign in history. Print ads featured Verizon employees promising customers that they would receive the same dependable and reliable service they had

© BRAD SWONETZ/ZEFA/CORBIS.

experienced with Bell Atlantic and Vodafone. The campaign was created by four separate advertising agencies working together: the Lord Group, Burrell Communications, Temerlin McClain, and La Agencia de Orci & Asociados.

After conducting an analysis of its own quality and that of its competition, Verizon realized that its network provided the most dependable coverage in the industry. It quickly positioned itself as the reliable alternative and continued pouring capitol into improving its already reliable network. In 2003 the Federal Communications Commission (FCC) mandated "number portability," allowing subscribers to keep their phone numbers when they changed wireless providers. Soon afterward many new subscribers turned to Verizon.

"We're not the low-cost provider. We're not the most aggressive with promotional deals and headset giveaways," Marvin Davis, vice president of advertising for Verizon Wireless, told *USA Today.* "Our brand message is important, because the market recognizes it's a higher-quality service. People are willing to pay more to get more." $4 million was spent improving Verizon's network in 2004, and $5 million was spent in 2005. According to Consumers Union (a publisher of consumer reports), Verizon was receiving the least amount of customer complaints in the industry. Cingular, the market leader since 2004, garnered the most, with 289 complaints per million subscribers.

CONTAGIOUS QUESTIONS

With its "Can You Hear Me Now?" campaign, Verizon joined other advertising campaigns that had reached iconic status by asking questions not always meant to be answered. Wendy's International, Inc., achieved similar contagiousness with its "Where's the Beef?" campaign in the 1980s. Anheuser-Busch had everyone asking "Whassup?" after the 2000 Super Bowl. In 1997 the McDonald's Corporation also made ad history with its question, "Did somebody say McDonald's?"

TARGET MARKET

The campaign targeted 25- to 54-year-olds who treasured their phone's ability to place calls anytime and anyplace. To reach this target, every "Can You Hear Me Now?" spot featured 34-year-old actor Paul Marcarelli as a technician who was always validating Verizon's superior network. At the beginning of the campaign neither Verizon nor Bozell would identify the actor playing Testman. Verizon even denied the press interviews with Marcarelli. The reticence was an attempt to make the spokesman seem as if he lived only inside commercials and to encourage the target audience's perception of Testman as a one-dimensional character.

By 2003 half of all Americans owned cell phones. Price wars continued among most wireless providers besides Verizon, which held its stance on service quality. Verizon averaged $49 per month on calling plans, targeting users with higher incomes. *USA Today* surveyed the audience reaction to the "Can You Hear Me Now?" ads in its regular Ad Track feature. Results showed that 20 percent of viewers liked the ads "a lot." Although this was lower than Ad Track's average of 21 percent, the campaign scored higher than any other wireless ad for the two years prior.

COMPETITION

Cingular was formed in 2000 with the union of SBC Communications and BellSouth. Early ad efforts for Cingular focused on "Jack," the company's X-shaped, orange mascot, who never spoke yet stood for "self-expression." Using the tagline "Cingular fits you best," its campaign promoted services such as Family Talk and Rollover minutes. "We're seeing very strong results, and I think 'Cingular fits you best' is a big contributor," Daryl Evans, Cingular's vice president of advertising

CAMPAIGNING A CULTURAL ICON

Testman, the character constantly asking "Can you hear me now?" into his Verizon phone, appeared in more than 100 spots. Some featured him on the sets of TV shows *Jeopardy* and *Fear Factor.* References to the character and his tagline became widespread. *Saturday Night Live* used the slogan to lampoon President Bush, showing him asking Israeli prime minister Ariel Sharon, "Can you hear me now?" *The Tonight Show* got on board by depicting Alexander Graham Bell repeating the question into one of his earliest telephones. Verizon pushed the Testman craze so far as to stage a Testman look-alike contest in Wisconsin.

and marketing communications, told *USA Today.* "Cingular recognizes that people use wireless in all kinds of different ways."

By 2002 Cingular was spending $428 million on advertising. Two years later Cingular acquired AT&T, giving Cingular enough subscribers to emerge as the industry leader. AT&T's infrastructure allowed Cingular to increase its coverage "footprint" instantly. The new leader began targeting Verizon's market in October 2004 with its "Raising the Bar" campaign, which referred to the "bars" on a cell phone's signal-strength meter. Nevertheless, when the broadcast-monitoring group TNS Media Intelligence/CMR conducted customer-loyalty testing in early 2005, asking random cell-phone users to compare their service with that of an ideal wireless provider, Verizon customers proved to be the most loyal, followed by Sprint PCS and T-Mobile. Cingular ranked fourth, with four times as many service complaints as Verizon.

Sprint spent $481 million on advertising in 2002, with a campaign that starred a spokesman referred to as "Sprint guy." In television spots "Sprint guy," played by a tall, blue-eyed actor clad in a black trench coat, explained different Sprint services to people. One commercial featured him demonstrating Sprint's camera phone to a family on a beach. Another spot, hinging on deadpan humor, showed him consoling a support group of disgruntled wireless customers. "Sprint guy" appeared in more than 100 television spots, mostly promoting features such as no-roaming fees, Sprint's all-digital network, and high-speed wireless Internet service.

MARKETING STRATEGY

Before the "Can You Hear Me Now?" campaign began, Verizon discovered that consumers struggled to differentiate between wireless brands. The campaign's greatest challenge was to establish higher ground in an industry undergoing fierce price wars. Unable to lower subscriber fees, Verizon focused the campaign on Verizon's premium coverage. According to a statement released by Bozell, the campaign was intended "to position Verizon Wireless as a superior wireless company that relentlessly strives to be the most reliable national wireless provider in the country."

The campaign's first spot was launched on January 14, 2002. Over the course of the campaign more than 100 similarly themed "Can You Hear Me Now?" television spots were made. All featured the same spectacled man, dressed as a Verizon test engineer, traveling the country to validate Verizon's infrastructure. Testman, as his character was called, appeared in wheat fields, on snowy mountains, on the set of the TV show *Jeopardy,* and in airports. In most spots Testman quickly asked, "Can you hear me now?" After supposedly hearing an affirmation through his phone, he replied "Good!" Later spots varied. A 2004 commercial showed Testman standing nervously in an office-building lobby. A woman finally exited the women's restroom and handed Testman a mobile phone. "Works fine," she said. A voice-over then stated, "When you're testing the largest, most reliable network in the nation, you can't let anything stop you." The spot ended with Testman making one last call, asking, "Can you hear me now?"

"Can You Hear Me Now?" print ads (many, but not all of which featured Testman) appeared in magazines such as *Entertainment Weekly, People, Sports Illustrated,* and *Rolling Stone.* During the first year television spots were created by Bozell, but after Bozell merged with another Interpublic-affiliated agency, Lowe, in early 2003, the campaign was produced by Lowe & Partners Worldwide. It eventually moved into the hands of McCann-Erickson (also a division of Interpublic). One of Bozell's early challenges was casting the Testman character. "We were looking for someone memorable. Something that would cut through the advertising clutter," Melanie Vandervalk, vice president of marketing and sales for Verizon Wireless, told the *Washington Post.* Verizon settled on Paul Marcarelli, a 34-year-old actor from New York. At the campaign's onset, Verizon restricted the press' access to Marcarelli. Verizon would not answer questions about his identity or allow interviews. "He needs to stay one-dimensional and [Verizon] needs to control him. It turns from advertising to PR," Kristie Nordhielm, assistant professor of marketing at Northwestern University's Kellogg School of

Management, explained to *Advertising Age.* "To expose him is a tradeoff between getting additional exposure for free and losing control of his image, but it's not because they don't want him to be an icon."

Some experts felt the campaign's tagline had been repeated ad nauseam. "'Can you hear me now?' [has become] annoying because of the repetition, but I think it drives home the point, and it works for that reason," Robin Hafitz, cochair of Mad Dogs & Englishmen, an advertising firm in New York, told the *Washington Post.* Verizon further catapulted Testman to the status of a cultural icon by sponsoring look-alike contests in Wisconsin. "I think the key to the Verizon [Wireless] guy is his understatement," Nordhielm continued in *Advertising Age.* "These things go in cycles and right now we seem to be in 'less is more' time with the Dell guy [Steven] being 'more is more.' To identify a cultural icon is like rolling the dice. It's the right place, right time, right icon."

OUTCOME

"Can You Hear Me Now?" was connected with some of Verizon's earliest and greatest successes, including reducing customer turnover to 1.8 percent, a 2.5 percent drop from 2000. "You can see that the commercials have really resonated with consumers," said Sue Marek, a former industry analyst who covered the wireless sector for *Wireless Week,* told the *Baltimore Sun.* "It's really paid off for them in a big way." While competitors had to drop prices to maintain market share, Verizon was able to maintain its average monthly service revenue per user at $49. During the first year of "Can You Hear Me Now?" Verizon sales grew 10 percent. Overall, Verizon achieved the campaign's two main goals: increasing the subscriber base and establishing itself as a premium service provider.

At the start of the campaign Verizon had 32.5 million subscribers; in 2003 it had 37.5 million, and at the beginning of 2004 Verizon subscribers numbered 43.8 million. The increases indicated that cell-phone consumers were just as concerned about quality as they were about price. Linda Barrabee of market research firm the Yankee Group said to *USA Today,* "If you only feed customers lower prices, that's all they are going to think of you as. If you give them something compelling, they'll consider staying with you."

FURTHER READING

Dill, Mallorre. "Keep On Testing." *Adweek* (eastern ed.), June 3, 2002, p. 20.

Elliott, Stuart. "In a Surprise Move, Verizon Wireless Stays with Interpublic." *New York Times,* April 28, 2004, p. 6.

Howard, Theresa. "'Can You Hear Me Now?' a Hit; Simple 'Testman' Ads Help Verizon Wireless Stay Strong." *USA Today,* February 23, 2004, p. B8.

———. "Wireless Ads to Tap into Services." *USA Today,* July 29, 2003, p. B3.

Jette, Julie. "HIGHWAYMAN; On-Road Testing Key to Cellular Success; Verizon Tracking of Dropped Calls a Marketing Tool." *Quincy (MA) Patriot Ledger,* March 10, 2005, p. 24.

McMains, Andrew, and Ann M. Mack. "Verizon to Hear New Ideas from 3 IPG Shops." *Broadcasting & Cable,* May 24, 2004, p. 26.

Noguchi, Yuki. "Wireless Gets the Priciest Plugs; Carriers' Megabuck Ads Flood Airwaves." *Washington Post,* October 31, 2003, p. E1.

Sabatini, Patricia. "Hear This: Testman Is No Nerd." *Pittsburgh (PA) Post-Gazette,* May 12, 2003, p. 1C.

Sampey, Kathleen. "Quick Turnaround for Verizon Spot." *Adweek,* May 3, 2004, p. 7.

Sanders, Lisa. "Breaking: Verizon Gets Testy: Bozell Campaign for Wireless Leader Features 'Testman.'" *Advertising Age,* January 14, 2002, p. 2.

Steinberg, Brian. "Advert Mailbox." *Wall Street Journal,* December 17, 2003, p. B4A.

York, Emily Bryson. "Verizon Keeps 'Testman' on Short Leash." *Advertising Age,* August 25, 2003, p. 7.

Kevin Teague

The Charles Schwab Corporation

101 Montgomery Street
San Francisco, California 94104
USA
Telephone: (415) 627-7000
Fax: (415) 636-5970
Web site: www.schwab.com

SMARTER INVESTOR CAMPAIGN

OVERVIEW

Known as a discount broker in a world of traditional full-service investment firms, the Charles Schwab Corporation diversified during the 1980s and 1990s. In keeping with an industry-wide trend toward offering customers one-stop financial services, it expanded into banking, annuities, bond trading, and mutual funds. With the rise of the Internet, Schwab's core brokerage business evolved to allow trading on its website, making it America's leading online broker by the late 1990s. While a host of upstart, low-fee online trading services challenged Schwab from below, the company also needed to position itself against a wide range of consolidated financial-services companies. In response to these pressures, and amid an unprecedented bull market on Wall Street, Schwab rapidly increased its marketing profile at the end of the millennium, an effort that culminated with the well-received "Smarter Investor" campaign, which began in 1999 and ran through 2000.

Created by the New York office of Omnicom Group's BBDO agency for an estimated first-year price tag of $50 million, "Smarter Investor" began as a series of four television commercials featuring sports celebrities. According to the agency, the use of celebrities was meant to make Schwab seem accessible and good-natured, in touch with ordinary Americans' interests, and the athletes' humorously surprising grasp of the intricacies of investing terminology suggested that anyone, no matter what their previous level of financial expertise had been, could become a smarter investor with Schwab's help. Supporting print ads used the campaign's tagline, "Creating a world of smarter investors." Subsequent TV spots featured entertainment celebrities, and then the campaign evolved to shift the focus away from celebrities and onto Schwab's retirement-planning products and services.

The campaign attracted favorable industry attention and awards, but a sputtering stock market led Schwab to rethink the do-it-yourself ethos embodied by the "Smarter Investor" campaign. The terrorist attacks of September 11, 2001, dramatically heightened the investing public's already palpable anxiety, and Schwab further changed its advertising message, in the subsequent months and years, to suit a more anxious investing public.

HISTORICAL CONTEXT

Stanford graduate Charles Schwab founded his eponymous company (then Charles Schwab & Co.) as a full-service brokerage firm in 1971. When the Securities and Exchange Commission banned fixed brokers' commissions in 1975, Schwab's competitors responded by increasing commissions. Schwab instead lowered commissions and

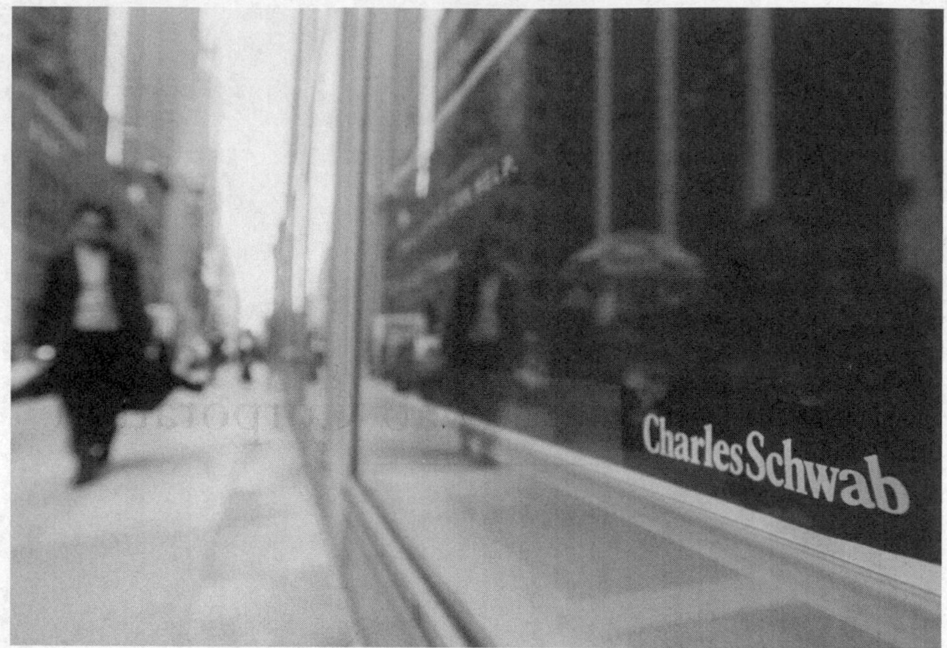

© JAMES LEYNSE/CORBIS.

positioned itself as a no-frills alternative to traditional full-service brokers. Between 1977 and 1983 Schwab revenues grew by a factor of 30. Throughout the 1980s and 1990s Schwab diversified into banking, retirement, personal investment advising, mutual funds, and other products similar to those offered by its full-service rivals. But those rivals also diversified during this time, as did most other key players in the financial-services industry. Schwab had, however, built an unparalleled system of local branches over the course of its first three decades, along with a corresponding reputation for accessibility and value that distinguished it from its pricier rivals.

In addition to competing against this wide range of financial-services giants, Schwab had to contend with new down-market rivals as well. The number of online investing services went from none in 1995 to 82 in 1998, and though Schwab was early to establish itself in the online brokerage wars, upstart companies continued to undercut one another (and Schwab) in pricing, with online transaction fees falling below $10, a significant difference from Schwab's fee of $29.95.

By 1998 more than 50 percent of Schwab's brokerage customers were trading online, and Schwab had almost 30 percent of the online trading market. To maintain its position atop the online investing industry, and to remain competitive with higher-priced rivals, Schwab embarked on its first concerted effort at brand-building (it had focused most of its previous advertising on specific products). When it hired BBDO in 1998, Schwab dramatically increased its advertising budget, setting out to unify its products and services under an umbrella concept and to define its image for the investing public. Initial BBDO spots included documentary-style branding work featuring ordinary Schwab customers praising the company.

TARGET MARKET

Though it continued to stress Schwab's accessibility and usefulness to a wide range of investors, the 1999 "Smarter Investor" campaign took Schwab beyond BBDO's initial ordinary-investor approach and into glitzier territory. As a broad corporate-image campaign, "Smarter Investor" did not focus on specific Schwab products or segments of investors but instead sought to communicate the firm's position amid the wide range of available financial-services companies.

According to BBDO's creative director, Jimmy Siegel, the agency wanted to play up Schwab's reputation for offering "a very down-to-earth, honest way to invest," and the use of celebrities underscored the firm's desire to seem affable and in tune with the interests of ordinary people. Each spot revolved around the humorous use of investing jargon by people who were well known for reasons other than their stock-market savvy, which sent the message that anyone, with Schwab's help, could become knowledgeable about investing. Poised between

FUNNY BUSINESS

Schwab's "Smarter Investor" campaign was a departure from much financial-services advertising in its reliance on humor, but "Smarter Investor" was not Schwab's first foray into the business of trying to be funny. In 1998, advertising shop BBDO's first year helming Schwab's corporate-image efforts, the agency came up with a series of spots employing the tagline "Ready to Move Up?" The ads featured such professionals as a plastic surgeon and an airline pilot who, because they had to spend so much time thinking about their finances, botched their primary, high-stakes jobs. Schwab pulled the campaign following complaints by organizations such as the American Medical Association, and BBDO went with a more palatable brand of humor in the ensuing "Smarter Investor" spots.

the world of conventional full-service brokers and that of discount, limited-service online brokers, Schwab wanted investors to see it as unique in that it did not charge exorbitant fees but still provided its customers with solid advice and market knowledge. The idea that Schwab was in the business of creating knowledgeable investors was, in the words of BBDO senior creative director Charlie Miesmer, "a compliment to investors and Schwab alike."

COMPETITION

E*TRADE Financial Corporation, second to Schwab in online-brokerage market share, spent more than a quarter of its 1998 revenues on the rollout of its new website. Targeting investors who used the web to research financial matters but who did not yet use it for trading, the E*TRADE push included direct-mail promotions offering $50 signing bonuses to select new customers. The company also ran text-heavy print ads detailing the site's features. TV spots were aired on cable television, and a significant portion of the advertising budget was devoted to online media.

Merrill Lynch & Co., the nation's largest brokerage firm at the time, was hardly immune to the challenges of the evolving financial-services marketplace. With its "Human Achievement" campaign it had positioned itself as a desirable, people-focused firm that was preferable to the electronic realm of online brokerages. Observers were surprised, therefore, when Merrill did an about-face in June of 2000, announcing that it would begin offering low-cost online trading. Merrill phased out the "Human Achievement" message and began the process of refining a marketing approach that could reconcile the company's full-service brokerage heritage with its new discount online offerings.

FMR Corp., also known as Fidelity Investments, was the world's leading mutual fund company in addition to offering a range of financial services, such as brokerage, life insurance, trust services, and securities clearing. Fidelity had in the preceding years been using a significant proportion of its marketing resources to spread the word about its capabilities beyond mutual funds, focusing on its brokerage business in particular. In 2000 the company launched the "See Yourself Succeeding" campaign, which showed Fidelity advisers teaching customers about new products or helping them find solutions to investment problems.

MARKETING STRATEGY

The factors that set Schwab apart from other companies—its heritage of no-nonsense investing capabilities and customer service provided via its comprehensive branch system—formed the basis of BBDO's vision for the "Smarter Investor" campaign. Additionally, the campaign's reliance on humor was a departure from traditional financial-services advertising, a contrast, in the words of BBDO co-CEO and chief creative officer Tedd Sann, to the "heavy and amorphous" marketing of competitors. Celebrities had the obvious advantage of attracting attention to the ads, and further, as *Adweek* columnist Barbara Lippert noted, the presentation of the celebrities as "knowing users of complicated information" was a refreshing departure from typical endorsement ads.

The first four spots in the campaign began running in late August 1999. They were featured during CBS's coverage of the U.S. Open tennis tournament as well as during tennis, golf, and football programming on both network and cable stations throughout that year. The professional athletes featured in the ads were tennis players Anna Kournikova and Mary Joe Fernandez, football players Shannon Sharpe and Jason Sehorn, skier Picabo Street, and basketball player Dikembe Mutombo. In each case an athlete showed an unexpectedly sophisticated grasp of financial matters while engaged in his or her acknowledged field of expertise. For example, in one spot Fernandez remarked about the Russian Kournikova (known for her attractive appearance as well as for her tennis playing), "I'm not really friends with Anna Kournikova. First of all, there's that whole language thing." The scene then shifted to Kournikova telling an umpire, "A P/E ratio is price divided by earnings," before she turned to a group of tennis students and asked, "Can anyone say asset allocation?"

In another spot, called "Trash Talk," New York Giants cornerback Jason Sehorn bemoaned the verbal abuse he had received from Denver Broncos tight end Shannon Sharpe. Sharpe was shown, at the line of scrimmage, bad-mouthing Sehorn with putdowns such as "Your mama pays full commission!" and "I bet you pay transaction fees on your mutual funds!" The ads used the voice-over line "When we created a smarter kind of investment firm, we created a smarter kind of investor," and the primary campaign tagline was "Creating a world of smarter investors." Print ads featuring the tagline alone ran in such publications as the *Wall Street Journal, Forbes,* and *Fortune.*

The second series of television spots featured non-sports celebrities and employed the same concept and tagline. In one ad, first aired during the 2000 Super Bowl, Beatles drummer Ringo Starr was shown rhyming various financial catchphrases with the word "elation." Another spot depicted two lovers on a seaside balcony, with a female voice-over supplying their dialogue. The man asked, "What's wrong?" and the woman replied, "My portfolio is totally unbalanced. My mutual funds are underperforming." The voice behind the dialogue was revealed to be that of romance writer Jackie Collins, supposedly reading from her new novel.

Schwab similarly featured celebrities in a humorous way to pitch its retirement-planning capabilities during and after the main campaign's run. In "Retirement Home" a group of sports superstars who had only recently passed their prime were gathered at a retirement home, variously napping, knitting, and playing bingo or shuffleboard. A voice-over stated, "These days, it's never too early to think about retirement." Another spot featured baseball slugger Barry Bonds, who was then on the verge of breaking Hank Aaron's career home-run record, being subliminally encouraged by Aaron, via a stadium loudspeaker, to think about retiring.

OUTCOME

Schwab's "Tennis Player" ad, featuring Fernandez and Kournikova, was named an *Adweek* Best Spot of 1999. The "Jackie Collins" spot also garnered *Adweek* Best Spot honors in April 2000. "Retirement Home" won a Silver Lion at the 2000 International Advertising Festival in Cannes, France. Barbara Lippert called the campaign "truly deft, delightful work, mostly because it's smartly written and well-executed."

But as the stock market declined, Schwab began to phase in new messages and marketing approaches, beginning with spots featuring the company's founder, Charles Schwab, comforting anxious investors in a town-hall setting. During the September 11 terrorist attacks Schwab lost its World Trade Center headquarters, but all of its employees survived. The company was the first financial-services firm to launch a new campaign after the attacks, running spots that compared Schwab advisers to the most trustworthy people in investors' lives. Because the stock market had plunged and consumer trading had fallen dramatically, Schwab had to cut its advertising budget, and it dropped BBDO without a review in 2002. Instead it appointed GSD&M, the Austin, Texas shop that had been in charge of advertising for Schwab online, as its primary creative agency. Between 2000 and 2003 Schwab laid off more than a third of its workforce and struggled to return to the levels of profitability it had enjoyed in years prior.

FURTHER READING

Barney, Lee. "Schwab and MassMutual Initiate Ad Campaigns to Remake Their Images." *Mutual Fund Market News,* September 13, 1999.

Buckman, Rebecca. "On-Line Brokerage Firms Advertise Big as Volume of Stock Trading Skyrockets." *Wall Street Journal,* September 11, 1998.

Buckman, Rebecca, and Kathryn Kranhold. "Schwab Serves Up Sports-Themed Ads." *Wall Street Journal,* August 30, 1999.

Cardona, Mercedes. "Financial Firms Press On with Advertising Plans." *Advertising Age,* October 1, 2001.

Gasparino, Charles. "Merrill Hopes New Ads Can Integrate Its Image as Full-Service Firm, Leading Online Broker." *Wall Street Journal,* January 3, 2000.

Gianatasio, David. "A Solid Investment." *Adweek,* December 11, 2000.

Hein, Kenneth. "Charles in Charge." *Brandweek,* March 19, 2001.

Linnett, Richard. "Personality Plus." *Adweek,* August 30, 1999.

Lippert, Barbara. "Star Power." *Adweek,* December 6, 1999.

Parpis, Eleftheria. "Best Campaigns of 1999." *Adweek* (western ed.), January 24, 2000.

Petrecca, Laura, and James B. Arndorfer. "Schwab Enlists BBDO for $50 Mil in Brand Ad Work." *Advertising Age,* June 26, 1998.

Warner, Bernhard. "Taking Stock of the Web." *Adweek* (western ed.), September 21, 1998.

Woodward, Sarah. "BBDO New York Puts Its Money Where the Mouth Is." *Shoot,* September 17, 1999.

Mark Lane

Chevron Corporation

6001 Bollinger Canyon Road
San Ramon, California 94583
USA
Telephone: (925) 842-1000
Fax: (925) 842-1000
Web site: www.chevron.com

A WORLD OF ENERGY CAMPAIGN

OVERVIEW

NOTE: Since the initial appearance of this essay in the 1999 edition of *Major Marketing Campaigns Annual,* Texaco Inc. and Chevron Corporation merged. The essay continues to refer to the company's name as Texaco, as that was the official name of the organization when the campaign was launched.

In 1997 Texaco was the fifth-largest marketer of crude oil, natural gas, and other related products. On the list of rival companies that were outperforming Texaco were the Exxon Corporation, the Royal Dutch/Shell Group, BP p.l.c., and Mobil Corporation. To boost its market share Texaco needed to increase sales, but the brand's image had been tarnished during the early 1990s. Texaco had been accused of polluting rainforests, overpricing its products, and institutionalizing racism in the workplace. Texaco executives calculated that improving their brand's image would help sales; it was with this goal in mind that Texaco introduced its "A World of Energy" campaign.

"A World of Energy" was the most expensive campaign in Texaco's 95-year history. The New York office of the BBDO Worldwide ad agency released the print and television campaign with $30 million, which was half of Texaco's annual marketing budget. Commercials debuted on Labor Day weekend in 1997. The actor Paul Newman provided the voice-over: "See Texaco run and develop, invent, visualize, hypothesize, explore, discover, and relentlessly search. Seek . . . and find the energy the world needs to run. Run world, run." As Newman said, "See the world run," the spot showed a baby gazing at a revolving toy complete with moving cars, planes, and trains. The scene shifted to quick shots of a helicopter taking flight, a nun operating a lawn mower, a line of Texaco's tanker trucks carrying fuel, and Texaco workers searching for oil under the sea and in rugged mountains. Honoring the Screen Actors Guild strike in 2000, Newman did not provide a voice-over for the campaign's last spots, which aired during the 2000 Summer Olympics. The campaign ended a few months later.

Texaco reported an annual revenue drop from $45.5 billion in 1996 down to $35.7 billion in 1999. According to ad critics, however, the campaign did help Texaco's image. Texaco improved its relationships with companies that were operated by minorities, and the government-appointed committee monitoring Texaco stated that the company had improved its ethics by diversifying its workforce.

HISTORICAL CONTEXT

Initially known as Texas Company, Texaco was founded in 1902 by Joseph "Buckskin" Cullinan and Arnold

Schlaet, who struck oil near Beaumont, Texas, in 1903. Texaco's first geophysical laboratory was established in 1919 to create durable seismic recorders for use in the fields where underground reservoirs of oil and natural gas were found. By the 1930s the firm was established throughout most of the United States, in addition to having ventures in numerous other countries, and it had begun marketing oil from the Middle East. In the 1950s and 1960s Texaco sold more gasoline than any other U.S. oil company, but its profits declined during the 1970s as the price of oil from the Middle East began to rise. American consumers responded by purchasing less gasoline, and Texaco closed many of its filling stations. After losing $10.3 billion in a lawsuit involving a merger dispute in 1985, Texaco filed for bankruptcy, from which it emerged in 1988. At the time, it was the largest firm in U.S. history to declare bankruptcy, and the legal judgment against it was the largest that had ever been awarded in a U.S. court, according to *Time* magazine. By 1998 Texaco ranked third among the nation's oil companies and was operating about two dozen refineries and 23,000 gas stations.

One of Texaco's most successful early marketing efforts was its sponsorship from 1948 to 1956 of the *Texaco Star Theater,* a television program with entertainer Milton Berle as the master of ceremonies. The show featured singing "men from Texaco... who work from Maine to Mexico." Another popular marketing campaign, "You Can Trust Your Car to the Man Who Wears the Star," was launched in 1962 and continued for more than two decades. It featured a memorable theme song and emphasized the bright red star-shaped logo that appeared on Texaco service stations throughout the country. In 1974 singer and comedian Bob Hope became "the man who wears the star," personifying the Texaco brand in a long series of commercials. In 1988 the "Star of the American Road" campaign was launched to depict Texaco as a modern business with an all-American heritage. Television commercials in the campaign featured a stirring jingle that said, "Wherever you are, trust the Texaco star. Up ahead it's there, shining bright." One spot showed a family driving through a storm, running low on gasoline, and finding a Texaco station thanks to the star shining in the gloom.

The "Star of the American Road" campaign was discontinued in 1995 when corporate advertisements to build the Texaco brand were introduced. The new "Add More Life to Your Car, Take It to the Star" campaign used humor, rock music, and special effects to create a more modern image for Texaco. In 1997 Texaco launched "A World of Energy," its largest corporate advertising and public-relations effort to date. Over the years the company had been accused of damaging the environment, conducting business in a racially biased manner, overpricing its products, and other unpopular practices. The new advertisements were intended to redefine the company's image, portraying Texaco as a widely diversified firm that provided energy that improved the lives of people around the world.

WORLDWIDE OPERATIONS

Texaco and its affiliates found, produced, and distributed oil and natural gas through a vast network of operations in more than 150 countries. The company conducted deepwater exploration primarily in the Gulf of Mexico, Latin America, and West Africa. Its major production facilities were located in the United States, the United Kingdom, the North Sea, the Middle East, and the Pacific Rim.

TARGET MARKET

Because gasoline, motor oil, and related products were not commodities that consumers saw or touched when they purchased them, the difference between various brands was not readily apparent. Therefore, packaging and brand image were paramount for an oil company trying to persuade people to buy its products instead of a competitor's. Texaco had been working to establish a strong global brand identity since the 1980s, when it had begun cultivating a new image with the Texaco star as a focal point. In 1996 the company decided to launch a bold campaign that would distinguish the Texaco brand from its competitors and emphasize the firm's worldwide operations and diverse, dedicated personnel. Most of Texaco's previous advertising had been geared toward selling gasoline and other products, but "A World of Energy" aimed to alter the general public's perception of Texaco as a corporation. The campaign specifically targeted opinion leaders, Texaco's shareholders, other companies that might someday form joint ventures with Texaco, and governments of foreign countries such as Indonesia and Angola where Texaco operated. It was thought that Texaco's stock price would rise and the company's reputation would improve as the brand image became stronger. The advertisements were also intended to boost morale among Texaco employees following a period in the early 1990s when the company had laid off large numbers of mid-level managers.

COMPETITION

The $850 billion petroleum industry included about 20 major oil producers and refiners with operations in the

United States, about 40 global companies, and hundreds of smaller firms. According to CNNfn Online, Exxon led the overall U.S. petroleum industry at the end of 1998, Mobil was second, and the recently formed BP Amoco was third. Shell was the largest oil company in the world, followed by Exxon, BP Amoco, and Mobil. In 1998 Exxon had worldwide sales of $100.7 billion, Shell had $93.7 billion, BP Amoco had $68.3 billion, Mobil had $46.3 billion, Texaco had $31.7 billion, and Chevron Corporation had $26.2 billion.

The industry changed rapidly during the 1990s as rival companies entered into cooperative marketing arrangements or merged their businesses. Royal Dutch/Shell Group (a joint venture between Royal Dutch Petroleum and "Shell" Transport and Trading) operated 47,000 service stations around the world and owned or had interests in 1,700 companies, including its subsidiary Shell Oil Company. In 1998 Texaco formed joint ventures with Shell Oil and Saudi Refining, Inc., to combine certain refining, marketing, transportation, and lubricants operations in the United States. The two new companies, known as Equilon Enterprises LLC and Motiva Enterprises LLC, were estimated to be the nation's largest retailers of gasoline, controlling about 15 percent of the U.S. market. The joint ventures marketed products under both the Shell and Texaco brand names.

Texaco had formed other alliances with its competitors over the years. Its Caltex company—a joint refining and marketing venture with Chevron—had operated in Asia and other regions around the Pacific Rim since 1936. As other rivals consolidated their operations, Chevron and Texaco considered merging, but in June 1999 Texaco declined the proposal. In 1998 the U.S. leader, Exxon, acquired Mobil for $80.1 billion to form a huge conglomerate named Exxon Mobil Corporation. The merger gave the new company about 13 percent of U.S. gasoline sales. Another oil giant, BP Amoco, was formed near the end of 1998 when British Petroleum acquired Amoco Corporation for $48.2 million. BP Amoco had 10.5 percent of U.S. gasoline sales in 1998.

For many years Shell Oil had been known for its corporate advertising, including the "Come to Shell for Answers" and the subsequent "Answer Man" campaigns, which involved the insertion of informational booklets in magazines such as *U.S. News & World Report* and *National Geographic.* Exxon had applied most of its advertising budget in 1989 and 1990 toward revamping its tarnished reputation after its *Valdez* tanker ran aground and spilled millions of gallons of crude oil along the pristine shoreline of Alaska. Like Texaco, other oil companies sometimes ran ad campaigns to point out the petroleum industry's good deeds. In 1999 a magazine advertisement for Phillips Petroleum Company featured a large, beautiful photograph of migratory waterfowl in silhouette against a gold and purple sunset. The headline read, "Thanks to Phillips, weary travelers will always have a place to stop and refuel." The text said that the company had donated land to the Cactus Playa Lake Project in Texas, providing habitat for hundreds of thousands of birds that needed a place to rest during seasonal flights across the central United States. "It's yet another example of what it means to be The Performance Company," the ad concluded.

SPONSORSHIPS

In conjunction with "A World of Energy" advertising, Texaco improved its brand image by sponsoring the U.S. Olympic Team through the year 2004, the XIX Winter Olympic Games in Salt Lake City, the US Open Tennis Championship tournament, auto racing, and the Metropolitan Opera.

MARKETING STRATEGY

Texaco's corporate advertising campaign, "A World of Energy," was created by the New York office of the BBDO Worldwide advertising agency to strengthen the familiar Texaco brand and to set a unifying tone for the company's communications. The campaign emphasized that Texaco's diverse operations improved the lives of people all over the world by providing energy and other benefits. In a press release Peter I. Bijur, chairman and chief executive officer of Texaco, said, "Texaco plays an integral role in the global energy market, and our objective with this long-term campaign is to focus on the commitment of Texaco employees and their dedication to pursuing energy sources and delivering energy products to people around the globe. Our campaign embodies this idea, and illustrates the value we bring to the quality of life for people whose lives we touch through the exploration, production, refining, distribution and marketing of energy products, and as caretakers of our valuable resources."

Ted Sann of BBDO added, "This new campaign builds on, and burnishes, Texaco's strong brand heritage for a new era. We traveled the globe to capture the vision and dedication of Texaco workers and the innovative technologies they are using to keep the world running. We want to convey that the lives we enjoy are fueled, in great part, with Texaco energy, represented by both the people of the company and its products."

"A World of Energy" received $30 million of Texaco's annual advertising budget of more than $60 million. Television commercials in the campaign were launched on Labor Day weekend 1997 during Sunday morning programs and coverage of the US Open tennis tournament, National Football League games, and golf competitions. The commercials also ran during shows such as *National Geographic Explorer* on TBS, *Fangs* on the Discovery Channel, and *Extreme Machines* on the Learning Channel. A spot called "Anthem" showed a world in fast motion—British commuters hurrying to catch trains, a Michigan child stepping out of a school bus, airplanes flying above the port of Rio de Janeiro—juxtaposed with shots of Texaco's geologists, oil rig crews, and other workers of various races providing energy to keep the world's machines operating. "We're always going, to keep you coming. To keep your whole world running," said the lyrics to the commercial's powerful theme song, "Do You See the Star?" Another spot showed Texaco workers on an oil platform, in high-tech operations centers, in a laboratory, under the ocean, and on mountaintops. A narrator (Newman) said, "They go to the strangest places, work in the tightest quarters, and gladly keep the oddest hours. Who are they? Forever probing and prodding, digging and exploring. Who are these people? They are Texaco. And they do what they do to find the energy the world needs to keep on running."

In addition to television commercials the campaign included magazine advertisements and full-page ads in newspapers throughout the United States. An advertisement in *Smithsonian* magazine featured a large photograph of three barefoot children happily eating watermelon in the golden glow of sunbeams. The headline read, "One day while finding energy, we found a way to get water to watermelons." The text explained that, while drilling for oil, Texaco often found underground water reserves. The company channeled some of that water to farms in the arid Central Valley of California, where not only watermelons but apples, oranges, and many other crops were irrigated to feed people throughout the United States. The text concluded, "It's one more way our relentless pursuit of energy keeps the world running. Looks like that water made quite a splash." The red Texaco logo and the slogan "A World of Energy" were centered prominently at the bottom of the ad.

The campaign concluded after the 2000 Olympics, during which Texaco released three commercials that tied the Texaco brand to athletics. Because of a strike enforced by the Screen Actors Guild, Paul Newman did not provide a voice-over for the final spots, and ad critics believed that his absence hindered the campaign's effectiveness. One spot featured children improving their athleticism via trial and error. "Life on the playing field is not much different than life in the oil field," explained a voice-over. "Sometimes, when you wonder how you'll ever find the energy to go on, you just dig down a little deeper. And there it is." Another Texaco spot venerated the company's employees. The voice-over explained that many Texaco employees found time to volunteer as youth coaches, because "finding energy is their full-time job." Ironically, on October 16, 2000, Texaco and Chevron merged to create the world's fourth-largest oil company, and as a result 4,000 employees lost their jobs. The merged companies changed their name to Chevron Corporation in May 2005.

OUTCOME

The campaign's tagline, "A world of energy," became a general corporate signature and was used in other advertising campaigns during 1999, unifying the company's marketing efforts. To demonstrate Texaco's sensitivity to racial issues and its appreciation for its diverse customers and employees, two campaigns that targeted African-American and Hispanic consumers were developed by minority-owned ad agencies. The tagline was translated into Spanish as "*Un mundo de energia*" for use in markets such as Texas, California, Arizona, and Colorado and for publication in magazines such as *Latina* and *Hispanic Business.* In May 1999 Texaco launched a television campaign to publicize Havoline motor oil with the slogan "Add more life to your car." The commercials revolved around youth and aging. One spot starred Dick Clark, a celebrity who had been famous for decades but never seemed to age. In June 1999 the joint venture between Shell Oil and Texaco released a $40 million advertising effort consisting of separate campaigns for two types of consumers: the drivers who patronized Shell's full-service stations and the drivers who patronized Texaco for its "car friendly" gasoline. The Shell campaign featured the tagline "Count on Shell to keep you going." The Texaco campaign's tagline was "Get that 5th tank feeling," which referred to a claim by Texaco that its gasoline improved an engine's performance by the fifth tank. While a worldwide economic slowdown and an oversupply of oil and gasoline caused prices to plummet and created a significant slump in the industry, U.S. demand for gasoline actually increased by 2.4 percent in 1998. (The United States was home to 5 percent of the world's population but used 30 percent of all energy produced.) Texaco reported revenues of $45.5 billion in 1996, $46.7 billion in 1997, $31.7 billion in 1998, and $35.7 in 1999. From an ad-industry perspective the campaign received little praise. According to some critics the campaign did, however, improve Texaco's brand image, which had been marred during the early 1990s.

FURTHER READING

Beatty, Sally Goll. "Happy Faces Abound in Texaco's First Corporate Advertising Drive." *Wall Street Journal* (Marketing & Media-Advertising), August 29, 1997.

Castro, Janice. "Texaco's Star Has Fallen: Facing a $10 Billion Penalty, the Oil Company Chooses Bankruptcy." *Time,* April 20, 1987, p. 50.

Dill, Mallorre. "Olympic Energy." *Adweek* (eastern ed.), August 7, 2000, p. 44.

Elliott, Stuart. "Olympic TV Commercials Win Few Gold Medals." *New York Times,* October 3, 2000, p. 1.

Fest, Glen. "KJS Marketing Accents Texaco's Hispanic Message." *Adweek* (southeast ed.), October 27, 1997.

Garfield, Bob. "Texaco Gushes about Being 'Energy Giant,'" *Advertising Age,* September 8, 1997.

Green, Jeff. "All Pumped Up." *Brandweek,* May 24, 1999, p. 1.

Hill, Dee J. "Texaco Pumps Up Its Emotions." *Adweek* (southwest ed.), June 19, 2000, p. 6.

Lawrence, Jennifer. "Bankrupt Texaco to Polish Its Star." *Advertising Age,* April 20, 1987, p. 3.

Mack, Toni. "Can Texaco Catch Up?" *Forbes,* March 25, 1996, p. 60.

Solomon, Jolie. "Luke Lends His Cool Hand to Texaco." *Newsweek,* October 6, 1997, p. 52.

"Texaco Partners with Communications Group." *National Petroleum News,* January 1, 1999.

Susan Risland
Kevin Teague

Church & Dwight Company, Inc.

469 N. Harrison Street
Princeton, New Jersey 08543-5297
USA
Telephone: (609) 683-5900
Fax: (609) 683-5900
Web site: www.trojancondoms.com

TROJAN MAN CAMPAIGN

OVERVIEW

Until 2001 Carter Products Division, a division of Carter-Wallace, Inc., owned the world's largest condom brand, Trojan. Although the condom industry had enjoyed an increase in profits in the late 1980s and early 1990s, by the mid-1990s growth had stagnated. Carter Products hoped to regain customers and to attract new consumers for its Trojan brand with a humorous marketing approach. Public discussion of condoms had been discouraged because the subjects of sex and contraception were considered taboo, but Carter Products believed a lighthearted advertising touch would break through these barriers and make condoms accessible and acceptable. Hoping to make using condoms "cool" and eventually increase sales, Carter Products released its "Trojan Man" campaign.

Created by Carter Products' longtime ad agency, Bates USA, Inc., the "Trojan Man" campaign started with radio commercials in 1996 and expanded into the television arena in 1998. The campaign was financed with Carter Products' estimated $7 million annual advertising budget. In the commercials a superhero-like spokesperson known as Trojan Man showed up during intimate moments between couples or friends to offer Trojan condoms. The spots ended with the tagline "Trojan. America's #1 Condom. Trusted for over 80 years." The "Trojan Man" campaign began as a brand-enhancing endeavor, but in 1997 Carter Products geared it toward the introduction of new condom products. After Carter Products sold its Trojan brand to Church & Dwight Co. (the maker of Arm & Hammer baking soda) in 2001, similarly themed print, radio, Internet, and television advertisements featuring the horse-riding Trojan Man appeared until 2005. Hoping to appease networks that would in turn grant Trojan more airtime, Church & Dwight stopped using "Trojan Man" in favor of a more reverent campaign titled "Make a Difference."

Trojan condoms accounted for 74 percent of the condom market by 2004, far surpassing the 50 percent market share it held in 1998. Ad critics praised "Trojan Man" for reshaping attitudes that once held condom commercials to be catalysts for promiscuity. Instead, critics argued, the American public began to consider condoms as an alternative to unprotected sex.

HISTORICAL CONTEXT

Condoms had existed since at least the sixteenth century, but even into the 1990s they were not thought to be a suitable topic for open conversation or for television commercials. In fact the National Comstock Law of 1873 made the sale of condoms for contraceptive purposes illegal and disallowed the distribution of information regarding birth control. Laws also stated that condoms could only be marketed as products designed to protect people from sexually transmitted diseases (STDs). Advertising condoms as birth control devices was forbidden up to the 1970s, and this created some complications for condom manufacturers who wished to advertise their products.

Even as laws became less stringent, the public was deemed unready for televised condom advertisements. In 1975 a local television station in San Jose, California, ran the first commercial advertising condoms, a spot that promoted Trojan brand condoms. The station received numerous disapproving calls, and as a result it conducted a public poll during the evening news broadcast. Although the majority of the viewers found the commercial acceptable, the station chose to cease airing the spots for fear of public backlash.

The role of the condom in American society shifted with the rise of AIDS (acquired immunodeficiency syndrome) and HIV (human immunodeficiency virus) in the 1980s. A National Public Radio report noted that in 1987 the surgeon general endorsed the promotion of condoms when he declared on network television: "The threat of AIDS is so great that it overwhelms other considerations, and advertising, I think . . . is necessary in reference to condoms, and would have a positive public health benefit." Despite the surgeon general's statements, however, public service announcements televised on national networks in 1988 focused not on condoms but on increasing AIDS awareness. The networks still refused to air brand-specific condom commercials, but condom companies such as Carter Products did benefit from the publicity provided by AIDS-awareness campaigns. The *Encyclopedia of Consumer Brands* referred to findings by the *Wall Street Journal* that indicated 40 to 50 percent yearly growth in condom sales following the publication of the surgeon general's 1986 report declaring the usefulness of latex condoms in protecting people against HIV infection. The sales growth dropped considerably in the early 1990s, however, as American citizens grew weary of AIDS prevention messages.

Television networks continued to provide obstacles in the 1990s. When professional basketball player Magic Johnson publicly announced that he was HIV positive, Fox Broadcasting Company was the only national television network to reverse its policy against airing condom commercials. Carter Products took advantage of this policy change and created a spot focused on STD prevention, conforming to Fox's stipulation that the ads could not discuss contraception, only disease prevention. Other national television networks still considered advertising condoms too controversial. *Entertainment Weekly* in 1991 spoke with ABC's director of media relations, Janice Gretemeyer, who indicated, "We don't believe it's appropriate to take ads on controversial issues." NBC's manager of corporate communications, Richard Cutting, stated, "some segments of the public feel that advertising condoms would encourage promiscuity."

Carter Products and other condom manufacturers received a boost from the federal government when the Centers for Disease Control and Prevention (CDC) attempted to counter the decline in condom sales with a marketing campaign in 1994 that promoted latex condoms as suitable protection against the AIDS virus. The initial 1988 CDC television ad campaign had not endorsed condom use because of pressure from political groups and television networks. The director for the CDC's national AIDS information and education program, Fred Kroger, in 1991 told *Entertainment Weekly*: "Many stations still won't accept them [public service announcements] if the focus is on condoms. It's one thing to talk about prevention, it's another to promote it." The CDC had thus created ads that described scientific facts regarding the disease, educating the public regarding the basics of AIDS. According to William DeYoung, a Harvard University health communications specialist who had worked with the CDC, the campaign's message had not gone far enough. He told National Public Radio that "once people are aware of the problem, they need to start thinking about how to deal with the problem, how to prevent the problem, and that's where the effort falls down." The 1994 campaign, on the other hand, openly discussed condoms and their effectiveness in providing protection against STDs, specifically HIV infection. The national networks had reservations, but most agreed to air the commercials during adult viewing hours.

The 1994 CDC advertising campaign may have set the stage for the loosening of network guidelines. More local television stations began allowing commercial condom advertisements, and in 1996 spots by Carter Products' competitor Ansell Consumer Products, the manufacturer of LifeStyles condoms, appeared on several network affiliate stations; the spots were limited to adult viewing hours or aired only after midnight. The rise of cable television stations such as MTV and Comedy Central provided a new arena for condom commercials as well. The major networks, however, still refused to show paid condom advertisements, and this in combination with network affiliate restrictions guaranteed the scarcity of televised condom spots.

TARGET MARKET

Trojan brand condoms' target market first consisted of young males, including teenagers. Carter Products discovered that this target group generally shunned condom use because condoms were considered unacceptable and not "cool." In a National Public Radio report Thomas Coates, a professor of medicine at the University of California in San Francisco, elaborated on reasons why some individuals did not use condoms: "We know that people don't use condoms because they are afraid of loss of sensation, we know that people don't use condoms because they're afraid their partners might object, they might think that they're loose or immoral or fast-living or in the fast lane. We know that women are reluctant to bring up condom use for fear that the man will reject her." Carter Products wished to address the concerns of its target group and change the negative perception of condoms.

By 1998 the campaign's target had expanded to include women. More female-centered styles of Trojan condoms had been made available since the campaign's launch in 1996. Richard Kline, vice president of marketing for Carter-Wallace, explained to *Adweek* (eastern edition) that women were beginning to purchase condoms. One spot that aired in 2001 featured two women chatting in a café. "I didn't sleep a wink," one boasted. Appearing off-camera, Trojan Man interrupted, "I guess everyone is enjoying new Extended Pleasure condoms from Trojan."

Carter Products was initially propelled by statistics concerning its core consumer market. The National Campaign to Prevent Teen Pregnancy reported in 1996: "One out of every three girls has had sexual intercourse by the age of 15, and one out of two by the age of 18"; in addition, "Three out of every four boys have had sexual intercourse by the age of 18." The American Social Health Association discovered in 1996 that "over 12 million people become infected with STDs . . . each year, with two-thirds occurring in people under the age of 25." Not only did Carter Products wish to reach consumers to increase sales, but the company also felt the need to educate them about STDs and pregnancy.

Carter Products chose to incorporate humor in the "Trojan Man" marketing campaign to maximize Trojan brand condoms' appeal and to influence its target market. The company's research had shown that humor appealed to teenagers and young adults and was ranked as the best approach for advertising. The "Trojan Man" campaign thus used humor to downplay the delicate nature of the subject matter, to attract the audience's attention, and to send a message about the importance of using condoms, particularly Trojan brand condoms. Carter Products hoped its target consumers would react positively to the campaign and that their perceptions regarding condoms would change—it wanted condom use to be considered not only responsible but also "cool."

WHERE ARE THE CONDOMS?

Condom sales were restricted to drugstores for many years. It was not until the 1990s that condoms began to appear for sale in supermarkets, vending machines, and discount stores. Condoms were also given away on high school and college campuses in conjunction with AIDS and STD awareness campaigns.

COMPETITION

In 1998 Carter Products manufactured deodorants, home pregnancy tests, hair-removal products, and tooth polish in addition to 23 varieties of condoms. According to the company, its Trojan brand condoms accounted for more than 50 percent of all retail sales of condoms in the United States and thus dominated the category. Carter Products' main U.S. competitors included Durex Consumer Products, a subsidiary of London International Group Plc (LIG) and manufacturer of Ramses, Sheik, Touch, Fourex, Avanti, Gold Circle Coin, and Saxon brand condoms; and Ansell, maker of LifeStyles brand condoms.

Carter Products ranked highest in U.S. sales and was second to LIG in the global condom market. The *Market Share Reporter* published data from *Drug Topics Today* that reported Trojan and Trojan-Enz condoms were the top contraceptive brands according to 1996 sales. The combined market share was 41.8 percent. LifeStyles condoms followed Carter Products with 10.5 percent, and Sheik had 5.2 percent. Also in *Market Share Reporter* a ranking of the best-selling condom brands in supermarkets taken from *Supermarket Business* indicated that Trojan and Trojan-Enz brands were the most popular. In 1996 Trojan brand condoms topped supermarket sales at 30.7 percent, followed by Trojan-Enz with 22.5 percent. LifeStyles came in a distant third with 14.1 percent, and Sheik Super possessed 4.6 percent of the market share.

MARKETING STRATEGY

Carter Products' concerns when planning the "Trojan Man" campaign involved the stagnation in U.S. condom sales and consumers' lack of interest in using condoms. Education about the importance of using a condom appeared not to interest the public; the *Dallas Morning News* cited industry reports declaring the decline of condom sales among those aged 25 and younger. The director of the Gay and Lesbian Latino AIDS Education Initiative, David Acosta, stated that educational programs had proved ineffective and explained: "The whole idea that knowledge equals practice is bogus... People may know all the right things. They know about seat belts. They know about cigarettes." Though Trojan brand condoms' core consumer group understood the repercussions of not using condoms, it was not enough to instigate habitual condom use. Unease discussing the subject and the belief that condoms decreased sexual pleasure added to the abandonment of condoms. Carter Products sought to address all of these issues with the humorous "Trojan Man" campaign and hoped to sway the male target group while also appealing to those new to the category and the female market as well. Capturing the loyalty of customers to ensure long-term consumption was also an objective.

To accomplish its goals Carter Products and its advertising agency of more than 50 years, Bates USA, decided to launch a national radio campaign to enhance Trojan condoms' brand identity. The first batch of radio spots, therefore, focused not on a particular style of condom but on the Trojan brand. The five 60-second spots produced throughout 1996 all ended with the tagline "Be a Trojan Man. Help reduce the risk with Trojan. America's #1 condom. Trusted for over 80 years." The spots also stated, "more people trust Trojan condoms than all other brands combined," and "Trojan latex condoms help provide the protection you need and the sensitivity you demand."

In 1997 Carter Products shifted gears and produced two radio spots promoting a new product, Trojan Ultra Pleasure condoms. The 1996 campaign had established Trojan condoms' brand identity and introduced listeners to the comical Trojan Man character who appeared out of nowhere with his horse to provide Trojan brand condoms and straightforward advice. Laurel Dobalo, director of condom marketing for Carter Products, told *Chain Drug Review,* "The messages are serious, but conveyed in a way to appeal to young people." The new spots ended with a slightly different tagline: "New Trojan Ultra Pleasure. Trojan, America's #1 condom. Trusted for over 80 years." One spot, called "My Pleasure," took place in an apartment and featured a couple getting ready for an evening out. They became distracted by romantic possibilities but were interrupted suddenly by Trojan Man, who was introduced by singers in the background singing, "Trojan Man." The man asked, "Trojan Man, what brings you here?"; Trojan Man responded, "The stairs." Trojan Man provided the couple with Ultra Pleasure condoms and then departed. In the second spot, called "Sailor," Trojan Man interrupted a couple on a boat. The man recognized Trojan Man and asked, "Trojan Man. How'd you get here?"; Trojan Man answered, "Australian crawl. It's my fastest stroke." He continued, "I couldn't wait to tell you about new Trojan Ultra Pleasure latex condoms," and then explained the features of the condoms, not forgetting the important message about protection. Trojan Man and his horse then splashed into the water and swam away.

In addition to the radio campaign Carter Products launched an interactive website that provided free condoms, trivia games, product information, educational data regarding safe sex, and more. The company licensed the Trojan brand and began selling clothing and accessories that featured the Trojan name. Carter Products was also active in college and spring-break events and other promotional activities.

In August 1998 Carter Products released its first Trojan television commercials. One spot featured a couple enjoying a romantic dinner. When the man suggested that his date "share some chocolate mousse," she replied, "I'd share anything with you." The couple was abruptly interrupted by Trojan Man, who handed them a Trojan Shared Sensation condom and quipped, "It looks like you're pretty close to dessert." The second spot featured Trojan Man interrupting an intimate couple rowing a boat across a moonlit lake. The commercials marked a shift in the campaign because they targeted both men and women. "More and more women are also buying condoms to help provide protection in their intimate relationships," Kline of Carter-Wallace said to *Adweek* (eastern edition) in 1998.

Church & Dwight purchased the Trojan brand in 2001 and used the ad agency Bates Worldwide to continue the "Trojan Man" campaign. In July 2005 the company replaced the campaign with "Make a Difference," a more somber campaign created by the ad agency Kaplan Thaler Group to warn consumers about the consequences of unprotected sex. Church & Dwight hoped the different tone would convince large networks such as Fox, CBS, and NBC to air Trojan commercials earlier than 9:00 p.m.

OUTCOME

The "Trojan Man" campaign met with positive results, according to Carter Products. Since 1996 Trojan brand's dollar market share rose more than six points to capture more than 60 percent of the U.S. condom market as measured by A.C. Nielsen. Carter Products referred to results of June 1998 Teen and Adult Omnibus studies that reported an improvement in Trojan brand's performance since 1996. Trojan brand awareness increased from 38 percent to 49 percent among adults and from 53 percent to 74 percent among teens. Gains in advertising awareness were even more impressive. Among adults who were aware of any category advertising, 45 percent recalled a Trojan ad in 1996 compared to 69 percent in 1998. In contrast only 9 percent of adults and 10 percent of teens recalled the advertising of the next most cited competitor.

"It can make a serious subject approachable," Kitty Ravenhall, senior vice president and management representative at Bates, told *Adweek* (western edition) in 2001. "[The Trojan Man] is a voice of authority and purveyor of a serious message, but he does it in a way that people can relate to." The campaign changed advertising trends across the condom industry. After "Trojan Man" debuted, condom makers' advertisements emphasized not only safety but also pleasure. In 1998, for instance, Durex released "Set Yourself Free," its first-ever campaign that did not caution consumers at all about unprotected sex.

During the campaign's last full year Trojan was not just leading the pack; it was setting a high-water mark for the industry. Trojan held an incredible 74 percent of the total condom market in 2004, surpassing the 50 percent market share it posted in 1998. Sales for Church & Dwight grew 8 percent in all channels in 2004, and Trojan sales generated $166.3 million in all outlets excluding Wal-Mart.

FURTHER READING

"Condom Ads Sneak on TV." *Editor and Publisher,* November 16, 1996, p. 38.

Hank, Kim. "Carter-Wallace." *Adweek* (eastern ed.), August 17, 1998, p. 25.

McCormick, Rachel. "Message of 'Hip-Hop' Condoms Questioned." *Milwaukee Journal Sentinel,* July 27, 2004, p. 1E.

Meyers, Kate. "TV's Last Taboo. The Big Three TV Networks Still Say No to Running Condom Ads." *Entertainment Weekly,* November 22, 1991, p. 16.

Neff, Jack. "Trojan Takes Health Tack, Eyes Break into Prime Time." *Advertising Age,* February 14, 2005, p. 8.

O'Konowitz, Tom. "Condom Ads Primed for Prime Time." *Arlington Heights (IL) Daily Herald,* June 2, 2005, p. 1.

Parpis, Eleftheria. "Risky Business." *Adweek* (western ed.), August 13, 2001, p. 18.

Wells, Melanie. "Sex May Sell, but as for Condoms, Networks Aren't Buying." *USA Today,* November 30, 1998, p. 09B.

Mariko Fujinaka
Kevin Teague

Church's Chicken

980 Hammond Dr. NE, Ste. 1100
Atlanta, Georgia 30328
USA
Telephone: (770) 350-3800
Fax: (770) 512-3920
Web site: www.churchs.com

FULL FLAVOR, FULL POCKETS, FULL LIFE/FULL FLAVOR, FULL POCKETS CAMPAIGN

OVERVIEW

Church's Chicken, owned by AFC Enterprises, had a reputation for serving traditional Southern-fried chicken as well as other Southern favorites, such as fried okra and biscuits with honey. But the chain was falling behind its competitors and had just a 6 percent market share in 2001. To reestablish brand identity and reconnect with consumers, the chain launched three marketing campaigns in as many years. Beginning in 2000 the company launched "Maybe It's Your Cooking," which was followed in 2001 by the reintroduction of one of its classic themes from the 1980s, "Big Pieces, Little Prices." When those campaigns failed to get the results the company wanted, it launched, in 2002, the "Full Flavor, Full Pockets, Full Life" slogan and marketing campaign. Shortly after its launch the campaign was renamed "Full Flavor, Full Pockets."

Developed by the company and its Atlanta-based agency BaylessCronin, the campaign was described by AFC Enterprises as "the most powerful brand launch in its history." The $15 million campaign included television spots, radio, print, and billboard ads, and an interactive website tie-in. It also launched the company's new theme, "Full Flavor, Full Pockets, Full Life," and introduced the chain's cartoon mascots, named Full Flavor and Full Pockets. Church's chief marketing officer, Ann Stone, said of the characters, "Since they don't resemble anyone, they can be anyone, and our guests in market research validated that."

While the campaign was created to capture the brand's true essence and to resonate with consumers, it fell flat. Prior to the campaign's launch Church's sales were climbing; following its 2002 introduction sales began to fall, and customers failed to connect with the cartoon mascots. In 2003 the company shifted most of its creative work from BaylessCronin to Gecko Motion, an agency based in Johannesburg, South Africa, and the campaign was revamped. "Full Flavor, Full Pockets" was replaced in 2004 with a new campaign, "We Got the Crunch," aimed at the chain's multicultural, multiethnic, urban customers.

HISTORICAL CONTEXT

From its beginnings in 1952 as a single restaurant serving only Southern-fried chicken and located across from the Alamo in San Antonio, Texas, Church's Chicken grew to the nation's number two chicken franchise business by the late 1980s. In 1989 Church's Chicken merged with the number three chain, Popeyes Chicken & Biscuits. Despite the merger the two operations remained separate, each offering its own distinct brand of fried chicken and menu offerings—Church's with a Southern style and Popeyes serving up Cajun. Three years later the two chains were acquired by AFC Enterprises, and change was soon in the air. Top on the agenda for parent AFC was reimaging the brands and upgrading the restaurants of both chains. In addition AFC began an expansion effort with Church's. By 2002 the chain had grown from 1,078 stores to 1,517, with locations in eight countries besides the United States.

To emphasize its quality food and reasonable prices, Church's in 2001 revived its successful ad campaign "Big Pieces, Little Prices," which had first been used in the mid-1980s. Created by Atlanta-based agency BaylessCronin, the tagline clearly identified the brand and struck a chord with many consumers, who remembered it from the first time it was used. Church's Chicken prepared to celebrate its 50th anniversary in 2002 with improved customer service, a redesigned kitchen concept, and plans to increase its product offerings. It also scrapped its reintroduced "Big Pieces, Little Prices" campaign and replaced it with "Full Flavor, Full Pockets, Full Life."

TARGET MARKET

According to the *Food Institute Report,* Church's Chicken identified two-thirds of its customers as African-American and Latino. The chain also had a high concentration of restaurants in older urban communities. But with sales lagging, the chain designed its "Full Flavor, Full Pockets, Full Life" campaign and the cartoon characters featured in the ads to reach a broader audience. The company described the target audience for the ads as consumers who lived full lives, had families, and were on a budget.

Full Flavor and Full Pockets, the campaign's cartoon mascots, had beige dots for heads and were voiceless and faceless. A spokesman for the company said that, based on market research, creating characters without faces made it possible for them to be anyone. "Customers will say, 'That could be me,' and identify with the product," he told the *Atlanta Business Chronicle.*

COMPETITION

The weak economy in 2001 and the terrorist attacks on September 11 had a negative impact on the bottom lines of many fast-food restaurants, including Church's Chicken and its top two competitors, KFC Corporation and Chick-fil-A, Inc. To help boost sales number one KFC and number two Chick-fil-A upgraded their restaurants, introduced new menu items, and launched new marketing campaigns at the end of the year.

AFC SELLS CHURCH'S CHICKEN CHAIN FOR $390 MILLION

In 1992 AFC Enterprises acquired the Church's Chicken fast-food chain and Popeyes Chicken & Biscuits (Church's and Popeyes had merged in 1989). After devoting 12 years to "reimaging," "upgrading," and "modernizing" the chains, according to the *Nation's Restaurant News,* AFC in 2004 sold the struggling Church's chain to Cajun Holding Company, an affiliate of Crescent Capital Investments, for $390 million. Quoted in the *Atlanta Journal-Constitution,* Frank Belatti, AFC's chief executive officer, said the sale of Church's had completed "a process that began early last year to reshape our portfolio and focus on Popeyes as our growth vehicle for the future."

The *Atlanta Journal-Constitution* described Belatti's comments when discussing the sale of the Church's chain as resembling those of a parent proud of a child finally stepping out on her own. But a statement included on the Church's website read as if the child had for some time been ready to take wing and fly: "After 12 years under the AFC umbrella, Church's Chicken declared December 26, 2004 their Independence Day." Under its new leadership Church's stated that it planned to go head-to-head with the competition by adding spicier offerings to its menu selections and that by 2010 it would expand to 2,500 restaurants worldwide, up from some 1,500.

True to its word, Church's in 2005—just months after its sale by AFC—introduced spicy chicken in the largest product launch in the company's history. Church's chief operating officer, Harsha V. Agadi, who replaced company president Hala Moddelmog after the chain's sale, told*Business Wire,* "We are going beak-to-beak with our competitors with this new product and we are going to make a huge impact on the market." Among the competitors was former sister chain Popeyes Chicken & Biscuits, known for its spicy Cajun-style chicken offerings. Agadi said, "Now we can compete head-on with Popeyes, as well as with KFC and Chick-fil-A, and I would strongly advise Popeyes to fasten its seat belt."

In 2001 KFC launched its "Hot and Fresh" program, which required stores to prepare menu items in smaller batches to assure customers were served the freshest food possible. KFC celebrated its 50th anniversary in 2002 by upgrading the interior design of its stores with sophisticated lighting, bistro-style tables, and lower booths not typically found in fast-food restaurants. The *Nation's Restaurant News* reported that the company also pursued "an aggressive strategy of multibranding its concepts" with other chains, such as teaming with A&W Restaurants in more than 80 restaurants. An ad campaign featuring Jason Alexander, best known for his role as George Costanza in the television series *Seinfeld,* was launched in 2002 as well.

Chick-fil-A's marketing campaign featuring a herd of clever cows that encouraged consumers to eat more chicken continued to be a hit in 2001, six years after its introduction, but the company also introduced a line of wrap sandwiches that were popular with fast foodies. According to the *Nation's Restaurant News,* the wraps were the first new product launched by the company since the mid-1990s. To further expand its reach in underserved markets such as Denver and Phoenix, the company announced plans to increase the number of restaurants in those cities from a total of 19 to 75 by 2007.

MARKETING STRATEGY

With the launch of Church's "Full Flavor, Full Pockets, Full Life" campaign, the company's strategy was to expand its focus on offering good value to include spokescharacters that would be associated with the brand and establish a bond with customers. The campaign, which launched with TV spots featuring the cartoon mascots Full Flavor and Full Pockets, was the company's first nationwide television campaign. The company said that the new campaign was one of the most aggressive rebranding efforts in its history. Along with six TV spots the campaign included radio, print, and billboard ads.

The initial television spots portrayed the two mascots (bright yellow, chubby, faceless cartoon characters with beige dots for heads) in stressful situations seeking relief with Church's Chicken. One ad featured Full Flavor paying bills and deciding that eating a piece of Church's chicken topped with jalapeño juice would make the chore more pleasant. Another ad showed Full Pockets riding a motorcycle up to a Church's drive-through window to place an order and discovering the order was too large for him to carry. In each ad the characters wielded a magic marker that helped solve their problems. The bill-paying mascot used the marker to draw a cool drink to go with his spicy chicken; the motorcycle-riding mascot used his marker to draw a sidecar to carry his order. A company spokesman explained that the ads were meant to show busy consumers that Church's could help relieve the stress in their lives. Making the characters headless was intended to send the message that Full Flavor and Full Pockets were everyone. Their names also reinforced the brand's qualities: good food for reasonable prices.

To further connect with consumers and increase awareness of its new campaign, Church's launched an interactive website that featured the cartoon characters Full Pockets and Full Flavor. The site provided nutrition information for the products and a restaurant locator with details about in-store promotions. Consumers visiting the site also had access to the campaign's print ads and television and radio spots.

OUTCOME

Despite high expectations for the "Full Flavor, Full Pockets, Full Life" campaign, following its launch the company reported that sales at stores open for at least one year dropped 5 percent in the first quarter. In addition the *New York Times* wrote that, prior to the introduction of the new theme, Church's sales had been increasing on a year-over-year basis, but after the campaign began, sales began dropping at stores that had been open for at least a year. Reluctant to call the campaign a failure, company president Hala Moddelmog said, "We thought the animation [used in the advertising] would stand out among the clutter better than it did at the end of the day."

Amid complaints from franchisees concerning falling sales and customer confusion about the campaign's message, Church's Chicken, within a year of launching the "Full Flavor, Full Pockets, Full Life" campaign, was rethinking its strategy. "I'm evaluating this campaign head to toe," Moddelmog told the *New York Times.* To begin addressing the problems associated with the campaign, the company revamped the ads to include real people interacting with the cartoon characters. The chubby mascots also seemed to send the message that eating Church's chicken was fattening, so the characters were slimmed down for the new ads.

In addition to revamping the campaign, the chain also switched most of its creative work from its agency BaylessCronin, which had created the campaign, to Gecko Motion. "I'm not quick to jump to change an agency when things aren't moving well, or change a campaign, but in this case I think it's called for," Frank Belatti, chief executive officer of parent company AFC, told the *New York Times.*

FURTHER READING

Cavanaugh, Bonnie Brewer. "Something to Cluck About: Church's, Popeyes Celebrate Milestones." *Nation's Restaurant News,* May 20, 2002.

Cebrzynski, Gregg. "Church's Breaks Its 'Most Powerful' Brand Promotion—Church's Chicken Launches Marketing Campaign." *Nation's Restaurant News,* July 22, 2002.

"Chicken Hawked." *Restaurants & Institutions,* August 8, 2002.

"Church's Chicken Brings Brand to Full Life with Most Powerful Brand Launch in Company History." *QSR Online,* July 9, 2002.

"Church's Chicken 'Full Life' Ads, Available on Redesigned Web Site." *Nation's Restaurant News,* January 6, 2003.

"Church's Chicken Gets Spicy; Spicy Chicken Launch Is the Largest in Company History." *Business Wire,* July 19, 2005.

"Church's Chicken Turns to Advertising to Take on Bigger Chains." *Food Institute Report,* July 15, 2002.

Frumkin, Paul. "Chicken Chains Hatch New Products, Marketing Campaigns to Boost Sales." *Nation's Restaurant News,* June 24, 2002.

Hayes, Jack. "Church's Adds Spice to Menu, Growth Plan Following Crescent's Acquisitions." *Nation's Restaurant News,* February 14, 2005.

MacArthur, Kate. "Yet Another AFC Exec Flies Coop: Church's Chicken CMO Resigns." *Advertising Age,* July 14, 2003.

Mehegan, Sean. "Church's Chicken Tried a New Approach and Disappointed Franchise Owners." *New York Times,* July 1, 2003.

Saporta, Maria. "When AFC Gives Church's Its Wings, Exec on Her Own." *Atlanta Journal-Constitution,* November 4, 2004.

Stafford, Leon. "Atlanta-Based Fast-Food Firm Completes Sale of Church's Chicken." *Atlanta Journal-Constitution,* December 30, 2004.

Woods, Walter. "Church's Turns 50 by Revamping Stores, Menu." *Atlanta Business Chronicle,* July 12, 2002.

Rayna Bailey

Cisco Systems, Inc.

170 W. Tasman Drive
San Jose, California 95134-1706
USA
Telephone: (408) 526-4000
Fax: (408) 526-4100
Web site: www.cisco.com

THE SELF-DEFENDING NETWORK CAMPAIGN

OVERVIEW

Cisco Systems, Inc., the world's largest producer of Internet switches and routers, released advertising prior to 2004 that simply encouraged people to use the Internet more. As Internet use increased, more Cisco hardware was needed to expand Internet networks. Between 2002 and 2004 Cisco acquired six Internet-security companies, including Protego Networks, Inc., for a combined price of $339 million. At first Cisco was incorporating Internet-security technologies into its own products only to boost consumers' confidence in the Internet's ability to stop destructive hackers, viruses, Trojans, and worms. Because Cisco's Internet security proved, however, to be more effective than actual Internet-security providers, Cisco decided to offer Internet security as a separate service from its switches and routers. To persuade information technology (IT) departments and their corporate officers to start purchasing Cisco's Internet security systems, Cisco launched its "The Self-Defending Network" campaign.

The advertising agency Ogilvy & Mather released the $20 million campaign across television, radio, print, direct mail, and the Internet in early 2004. Instead of showing Cisco's security systems protecting other technology, commercials featured Cisco security systems protecting people. In the spot "Sarah's Escapade," for example, an executive told his daughter, "I'll be right back, honey," just before leaving her unsupervised in his office. The bored girl began clicking on her father's computer mouse until a message popped up on his monitor stating, "Worm Detected." The young girl panicked. "Worm Isolated," was the computer's next message, followed by "Worm Destroyed." The girl threw up her arms in celebration. The spot ended with the voice-over, "Defending the network from human nature. This is the power of the network. Now."

Not only did the campaign garner a Gold EFFIE Award in the computer software category in 2005, but the industry-analysis firm Millward Brown showed a 950 percent increase in the business audience's willingness to use Cisco for IT security. Cisco's share in the security-provider market jumped seven points, and Cisco Systems totaled $175 million in sales for 2004.

HISTORICAL CONTEXT

Besides being one of the Nasdaq's fastest-growing stocks during the late 1990s, Cisco was also the world's leading producer of switches and routers that directed traffic across the Internet. In 1998 Cisco released advertising that encouraged Internet usage, which in turn increased the demand for Cisco's hardware. Two years later Cisco's ad agency, Hill, Holliday, Connors, Cosmopulos, Inc., introduced a $43.8 million campaign with the tagline "Empowering the Internet generation." The campaign's television spots, including one titled "Factory," featured Cisco's hardware increasing businesses' Internet usage, which indirectly boosted the businesses' profits.

After the technology sector plummeted in late 2000, Cisco did not release a campaign for almost three years. In June 2002 Cisco awarded its advertising account to DarkGrey, the technology unit of Grey Global Group. For its first few months doing business with Cisco, DarkGrey developed a campaign with the tagline "Advancing the human network." None of the DarkGrey advertisements were actually released, however. When Marilyn Mersereau became Cisco's new vice president for corporate marketing in late 2002, she turned Cisco's advertising account over to Ogilvy & Mather, an agency she had worked with as vice president of global advertising at International Business Machines Corporation (IBM).

In 2003 Ogilvy & Mather released the largest campaign in Cisco's history, the $10–$150 million "This is the power of the Network. Now" campaign. With the goal of positioning Cisco as a leader in networking technologies for businesses and individual consumers, the campaign focused on associating Cisco's brand with ingenuity. In a television spot titled "Olive," the CEO of an olive distributor was humorously shown reducing his company's costs by optioning for an Internet-based phone system. Another commercial featured a mischievous young girl using one of Cisco's home products, a Linksys router, to antagonize her older brother's new girlfriend.

From 2002 to 2004 Cisco purchased a total of six small Internet security businesses. In 2003 alone, security breaches had wreaked more than $17 billion in damage for U.S. businesses. After integrating a plethora of smaller security systems into its core products, Cisco believed it offered a holistic security solution unlike Cisco's competitors. To brand Cisco as a leader in Internet safeguarding, Cisco released its "The Self-Defending Network" campaign in February 2004.

COMPUTER WORMS, TROJANS, AND VIRUSES

The term "computer virus" was first used in 1983 to describe computer software that had mutated inside a computer and had become destructive. By the late 1990s the term was used to describe unwanted software that was usually installed unknowingly by the computer's owner or operator.

Worms were a subclassification of the computer virus. They copied themselves without assistance or permission from their hosts and often spread via E-mail. Once it finished installation, a worm E-mailed itself to other unsuspecting recipients on the host's contact list. Trojans, also a subclassification of the computer virus, hid inside seemingly benign files, such as images or text documents, that consumers typically saved for extended periods of time. Although viruses, worms, and Trojans infected computer systems differently, their shared intent was to destroy or steal information. Hardware, such as the Internet routers and switches produced by Cisco Systems, were also susceptible to Viruses, worms, and Trojans.

TARGET MARKET

To become the world's largest supplier of Internet routers and switches, Cisco spent years forging relationships with data-networking experts who purchased hardware needed for Internet expansion. When Cisco began advertising itself as an Internet security provider in 2004, it focused on a new target: those in charge of purchasing firewalls (the systems protecting networks from hackers), spam filters (filters restricting unwanted E-mail), and virus scans (scans that removed unwanted software, such as viruses, Trojans, or worms, that was designed to damage or steal information.)

Cisco separated its new target into two groups: "technology decision-makers" and "business decision-makers." The first group consisted of IT specialists involved in every step of a business' security purchasing. The second group, "business decision-makers," consisted of c-level (e.g., chief information officer, chief technology officer) executives concerned about the effects of corporate security on overall profit. Cisco hoped the campaign would appeal to executives complying with regulations that were implemented after the terrorist attacks of September 11, 2001, such as the Anti-Money Laundering Act, which enforced tighter restrictions on electronic money transfers. Another post-9/11 regulation made CEOs personally liable for providing accurate information in their financial reports, a ruling partially responsible for an increase in executive jail sentences. Executives became increasingly protective of their businesses' internal networks where financial data was stored. Chief information officers were even required to report on the potential damage a network breach could render on their business.

Cisco felt that prior to the release of "The Self-Defending Network," "technology decision-makers" and "business decision-makers" considered Cisco products a satisfactory starting point for security, but not a comprehensive solution. The campaign aimed to adjust both groups' perception of Cisco's brand as a fully integrated security platform.

COMPETITION

Even though the security provider Barracuda Networks, Inc., was founded in 2002, by 2005 it dominated as the world's leading provider of security systems for enterprise-level business. Its clients included IBM, the National Aeronautics and Space Administration (NASA), the US. Department of the Treasury, and Barnes & Noble. Dean Drako, the president, CEO, and cofounder of Barracuda Networks, attributed his company's success to the fact that it designed all the security systems in-house and did not rely on outside software applications. "We did that because we didn't want to have to have any per-user fees," Drako told *Computer Reseller News.* "That was important because we want to make it easy to buy. So instead of 45-page-long price lists, like some of our competitors have, our price list has five items on it—for the five models of Barracuda."

Barracuda Networks also attributed its success to a channel distribution strategy, in which Barracuda relied on outside distributors to handle its marketing, sales, and distribution. The company signed a number of resell agreements with distributors such as SYNNEX Information Technologies, which outfitted companies with computer networks and security systems. "We didn't want to have our own professional services organization. We are a product company. And we believe the channel is absolutely the best mechanism for delivering security, where customers are looking for people who know more than they do," Drako continued in *Computer Reseller News.*

One of Barracuda Networks' few marketing efforts involved creating podcasts, or digital audio files, that educated businesses about the dangers of spam, worms, Trojans, and viruses. By going to the website www.PodTech.net, consumers could download the free files and listen to them on MP3 players or computer music programs. Drako was the featured speaker for the podcasts.

MARKETING STRATEGY

Cisco was the leading producer of Internet switches and routers, and Ogilvy & Mather hoped that titling its campaign "The Self-Defending Network" would suggest Cisco's additional leadership in the field of network security. Instead of focusing on the technical procedures of stopping spam, hackers, viruses, and worms, the campaign conveyed the human stories affected by such attacks. All television spots portrayed consumers who were, unbeknownst to them, victims of a security breach but protected by Cisco's security systems.

On February 30, 2004, the first two commercials aired across Sunday morning programming, including *Meet the Press, This Week, Face the Nation,* and *CBS Market Watch.* In the television spot titled "Inside Job," an assistant told a chief financial officer (CFO) that their company's network had just been infiltrated. "How could that happen?" the CFO asked, just as his visiting daughter stepped from his office to brag about a new game she had downloaded onto his computer. The CFO's expression suggested that he had identified the unknowing culprit. The *Sydney Morning Herald* quoted Cisco's global marketing chief, James Richardson, as saying, "If you're going after the business market, then you have to be pragmatic and deliver a value proposition. It's hard to introduce humor into that equation. But you can do that with issues close to the consumer, such as security and mobility."

To reach a broader audience, television spots also aired across prime-time shows such as *The West Wing, CSI, Law and Order,* and *60 Minutes.* The television spot titled "Sarah's Escapade" aired February 30 as well. It featured a girl who accidentally downloaded a worm onto her father's work computer. Luckily for her, Cisco's virus scan detected, isolated, and removed the worm before it caused any damage. The spot ended with a voice-over that said, "Defending the network from human nature. This is the power of the network. Now." The commercial "Silent Hero," which aired March 30, featured a dinner table of executives complaining about their networks crashing. A woman remarked to the only quiet man at the table, "Jeff, you're awfully quiet." He replied, "Our network didn't go down," referring to the stability offered by Cisco's product. Two final commercials, "Espresso Time" and "New Glass," began airing on July 30.

The print ads "Woman on Pillow" and "Little Girl" appeared in newspapers such as the *Wall Street Journal* and the *Washington Post*; they also appeared in business magazines such as *Fortune, Forbes,* and the *Economist.* Billboards announcing "The Self-Defending Network" were posted throughout the technology-laden communities of Silicon Valley and San Francisco. For the first time in advertising history, an advertisement was employed that temporarily filled a member's computer screen after he or she logged into his or her online *Wall Street Journal* account. The ad announced Cisco's "The Self-Defending Network." Internet banner advertisements also ran across the tops of the *Economist* and *BusinessWeek* websites. E-mails about Cisco's security systems were sent to more than 46,000 individuals responsible for a business' IT-related decisions.

OUTCOME

Ogilvy & Mather and Cisco considered "The Self-Defending Network" a solid success. Not only did it snag a Gold EFFIE Award in 2005, the campaign also had a positive halo effect on Cisco's entire brand. According to Ameritest/Cy Research, a consumer test group, a survey conducted during March 2004 found that Cisco scored higher than average on brand leadership measures such as: "Is technically innovative," "Is a technology leader," and "Offers products that help your organization stay competitive." Across the Internet the campaign's growth could be measured by a 96 percent increase in traffic to www.Cisco.com's security pages. Cisco's share in the security-provider market jumped seven points in 2004. By the campaign's end analysis firm Millward Brown showed a 950 percent increase in the willingness of the business audience to use Cisco for IT security.

The Yankee Group, a market research firm, stated in 2004, "Cisco was the only IT networking firm to rank as one of the most trusted security providers, alongside other security specialists like Symantec and Verisign." VeriSign and Symantec Corp. were well known for providing secure telecommunications services, digital commerce, and consumer virus protection. "This survey result is really a testament to the power of Cisco's remarkable brand recognition," Phebe Waterfield, Yankee Group Security Solutions and Services analyst, was quoted in *Business Wire*.

FURTHER READING

Baker, David R. "New Ad Campaign for Cisco." *San Francisco Chronicle*, February 18, 2003, p. B1.

Bannon, Lisa. "EToys Readies $20 Million Blitz to Hit Homes for the Holidays." *Wall Street Journal*, September 27, 1999, p. B10.

Barns, Emma. "Cisco Appoints MBA to Develop Business Campaign in Europe." *Campaign*, August 6, 2004, p. 7.

Fahey, Alison. "21st Annual Agency Report Cards." *Adweek*, April 12, 2004, p. 25.

Garner, Rochelle. "Barracuda Networks." *Computer Reseller News*, August 22, 2005, p. 35.

Gordon, Andrew. "Cisco to Search for a Corp Agency of Record in the US." *PR Week*, June 6, 2003, p. 6.

Hwang, Suein L. "3Com to Kick Off Ad Campaign Tying Products to Internet Boom." *Wall Street Journal*, October 25, 1999, p. B14.

Kaplan, David, Justin M. Norton, and Kathleen Sampey. "Cisco, DarkGrey to Part Ways." *Adweek* (western ed.), September 16, 2002, p. 2.

Lee, Julian. "Cisco Injects Humor to Appeal to Consumers." *Sydney Morning Herald*, March 25, 2004, p. 30.

Madden, Normandy. "Northwest Uses Unusual Ad Platform." *Advertising Age*, August 1, 2005, p. 10.

Maddox, Kate. "Integration Spurs OgilvyOne Growth." *B to B*, October 10, 2005, p. 29.

———. "Ogilvy's Award-Winning Creative in 'Demand.'" *B to B*, March 8, 2004, p. 26.

O'Connell, Vanessa. "Cisco Says the Time Is Right to Roll Out a New Campaign." *Wall Street Journal*, February 18, 2003, p. B4.

Kevin Teague

Citibank

399 Park Avenue
New York, New York 10022
USA
Telephone: (212) 559-1000
Web site: www.citibank.com

IDENTITY THEFT SOLUTIONS CAMPAIGN

OVERVIEW

Note: Also see essay for Citigroup Inc.

In fall of 2003 Citibank, a subsidiary of Citigroup Inc., the world's largest financial services conglomerate, set out to bolster its consumer divisions' "Live Richly" umbrella campaign with a set of television, print, and outdoor advertisements that introduced its new Identity Theft Solutions service for credit-card holders. The service was a timely response to Americans' growing fears about the crime of identity theft and was intended to distinguish Citibank from its consumer-banking competitors and to thereby build on the people-friendly image cultivated in previous "Live Richly" spots.

The idea of identity theft was inherently terrifying, but Citibank and its main U.S. ad agency, Fallon Worldwide of Minneapolis, wanted to communicate the potential severity of the danger posed to consumers without resorting to scare tactics. The resulting series of four television ads, which cost an estimated $750,000 to produce, featured ordinary, sympathetic characters who channeled, via lip-synching, the voices of the sinister but humorously intriguing criminals who had victimized them. This technique directly dramatized the idea of someone assuming another person's identity, and the wild disparity between the characters' appearance and his or her dialogue was both comical and disturbing. Print and outdoor ads similarly employed pictures of innocent-looking people juxtaposed with copy indicating the out-of-character crimes or debts for which that person was supposedly responsible.

"Identity Theft Solutions" was named *Adweek* 's Best Campaign of 2003, and an individual campaign spot won a 2004 Emmy for Outstanding Commercial. Citibank's consumer divisions, and particularly its credit-card operations, sustained the parent company through extremely difficult financial times. The campaign ran through 2004.

HISTORICAL CONTEXT

Citibank hired Fallon Worldwide's Minneapolis shop to take over the brand's U.S. advertising in 2000, a move widely seen as an attempt to humanize its faceless corporate image. Fallon, a rising star known for its quirkiness, promised to produce ads that were "unbanklike," while still managing to live up to the challenge that, according to *Adweek,* Citibank had set: to "unite the varied and various elements of its consumer division—including banking and credit cards." The company wanted to distance itself from the financial-services advertising of the 1990s, which concentrated on wealth for its own sake, and Fallon helped the company do so by creating an umbrella concept titled "Live Richly," which focused on presenting financial well-being as a means to living fully rather than as the object of life.

© *Alan Schein Photography/Corbis Reproduced by permission.*

Though the message "There's more to life than money" struck some observers as disingenuous coming from a bank, the campaign's theme proved well suited to an historical moment characterized by the dot-com crash, the terrorist attacks of September 11, 2001, and several high-profile corporate scandals. In this climate of widespread anxiety about the American economy and personal security, Citibank pinpointed a further danger to consumers—identity theft—and introduced a service to protect them from it.

As businesses relied more and more on computer technology, identity theft—the criminal use of an unwitting individual's private information to open false credit-card accounts, secure home and car loans, or commit other criminal acts—increasingly became an issue for Americans. Identity-theft complaints rose 73 percent between 2001 and 2002, and they continued to multiply in the years following. Further, the fear of terrorists using forged identities to commit crimes raised public awareness of the problem. Victims of the crime typically found themselves answerable for large sums of money owed, and criminal acts committed, in their names, and the process of rehabilitating their lives and credit histories was a daunting, months-long affair. Citibank accordingly inaugurated its Identity Theft Solutions service, a free benefit that provided customers with access to specialists who would, in cases of identity theft, help victims contact credit bureaus and police, help them monitor their credit reports, and otherwise be available for support and consultation until their individual cases were closed.

TARGET MARKET

"Identity Theft Solutions" dovetailed with the larger "Live Richly" campaign, which targeted, in Citibank's words, "balance seekers" whose household incomes were between $60,000 and $100,000 a year. Fallon's Anne Bologna told *Newsweek* that Citibank defined balance seekers as "people who have always believed that money is not the end, but the means to an end," and company executives estimated that 90 million Americans fit this description. The initial phases of the "Live Richly" campaign had appealed to this audience by de-emphasizing the importance of money with messages such as "He who dies with the most toys is still dead" and "People make money. Not the other way around."

With "Identity Theft Solutions" Citibank wanted to communicate the urgency of the danger that gave rise to their new service while maintaining the lighthearted tone of the "Live Richly" campaign. It was important, in the company's view, to let potential customers know that identity theft could happen to them without simply frightening them. By making consumers aware of the danger and showing that Citibank alone had an answer to it, the campaign "was designed to be relevant, differentiating and a motivating factor for consumers to switch banks," as a company executive told *Bank Systems & Technology Online*.

Fallon's creative team satisfied its assignment using a simple, surprising, darkly funny vehicle: a drastic disconnect between a speaker's voice and his or her appearance. In television spots, for instance, a beer-drinking,

BEHIND THE SCENES

In addition to ordinary auditions for its "Identity Theft Solutions" spots, Fallon's creative team allowed itself some less traditional casting flourishes. For instance, a nosy neighbor kept pestering agency personnel on location during the New Jersey shoot for "Flaps," a commercial in which an elderly woman speaks in a gruff male voice about her fraudulent purchase of a pickup complete with "them mud flaps with the naked ladies on 'em." The filming crew responded by seamlessly incorporating the neighbor into the ad as the woman's husband. Unconventional casting had its hazards, however. When the team used a photograph of Fallon colleague Emily Frazee for print ads, some people in Frazee's hometown of Kahoka, Missouri, missed the point of the copy that stated that there were three warrants out for her arrest. About a dozen people became worried and called her parents, Frazee told *Adweek.* "Everybody thought I was in trouble."

middle-aged man sits in his easy chair while speaking, in the voice of a Valley girl, about a shopping binge during which he bought a $1,500 leather bustier that "lifts and separates." Showing a vividly real character inhabited by another fully developed character's voice served to illustrate with chilling but entertaining directness the phenomenon of identity theft. Print and outdoor ads used the same principle of juxtaposition, pitting a character's photographic portrait against drastically out-of-character copy.

COMPETITION

According to *U.S. Banker,* between 2000 and 2003 retail bank advertising expenditures grew at unprecedented rates, primarily as a response to consolidation at the corporate level. Consolidation made for bigger advertising budgets, but as was the case with Citibank, many large financial institutions wanted to avoid being seen as inhuman monoliths. Several banking companies—including American Express and Capital One—ran memorable campaigns contemporaneously with the "Identity Theft Solutions" spots.

American Express had a long-standing reputation for innovation in advertising, and it continued to push the envelope with an online campaign featuring Jerry Seinfeld and an animated Superman in "webisodes" that were several minutes long. In them Seinfeld and Superman acted much like Jerry and his friends had in the sitcom *Seinfeld,* and an American Express card was always woven into the plot. The interactive American Express website included behind-the-scenes footage and photos of Seinfeld and Superman, and in 2004 the webisodes were picked up by the TV stations NBC and TBS.

Morgan Stanley, meanwhile, used offbeat humor in a campaign that dramatized just how committed the firm's financial advisers were to its clients. In one spot, a woman was shown cheering enthusiastically at a children's soccer game. When asked which child was hers, she explained that she was the financial adviser of one of the children's parents.

Capital One continued to run its popular "What's in Your Wallet?" spots, which promoted its "No-Hassle Card" and raised brand awareness to 97 percent, according to *Advertising Age.* Bank One launched its "Individual Answers" campaign, which showcased the personalized features its customers could access and ended with montages of individual faces and the assertion that no two people were alike.

MARKETING STRATEGY

Fallon's Steve Driggs told *Adweek* that the concept for the "Identity Theft Solutions" was inspired by stories of real-life victims of identity theft. Voice-overs for the original four TV spots were recorded prior to shooting, and the actors lip-synched the dialogue. The precisely calibrated lip-synching vividly illustrated the idea of one person inhabiting another's identity. The visible characters in each spot were easy for viewers to sympathize with, and the villainous voices, as Barbara Lippert wrote in *Adweek,* "stay away from stereotypical criminal situations and the usual thug voices we're used to seeing and hearing in police dramas and anti-drug commercials." In "Geek," for instance, a hip young African-American woman channeled a nasal, laughing male voice: "Firewall? Like that could stop me! Once I got her account number, I couldn't spend it fast enough: 64-inch plasma-screen monitor, 10 4.2-megahertz wireless routers, and 20,000 bucks to complete my robot. My girl robot. This is gonna be the best prom ever!" An announcer then said, as the Citi logo appeared onscreen, "Help getting your life back—that's using your card wisely," a message that underscored the human touch that Citibank had been cultivating for years. The tagline "Live Richly" was included under the logo, linking the new spots to the previously established umbrella campaign.

Adweek reported that, in developing the print advertising, Fallon used an Episcopal church's directory to find faces that embodied the innocent look of someone whose identity had been stolen. Unable to secure the rights to use the actual directory photos, the creative team shot its own photos of one churchgoer, Jack Wiborg. The resulting image was of an affable, bespectacled, portly man with a double chin. Underneath the picture was copy that absurdly read, "I had $23,000 worth of liposuction." A Fallon colleague, Emily Frazee, was used as the model for the "innocent cheerleader" type Citibank had wanted for another print ad. The accompanying copy stated, "There are three warrants for my arrest. One of them involves smuggling."

In addition to being entertaining, the ads immediately "positioned Citi as an ally for cardholders in crisis," according to *American Banker.* The bank was not simply boasting about its size and status; it was offering a valuable service that distinguished it from other banks. The ads addressed a growing consumer fear and, in showing that Citibank cared about what was important to its customers, supported the "Live Richly" message.

A second series of three TV ads followed the initial set, introducing new characters and extending the lip-synching concept without substantial alteration. Other television ads used a different concept but a similar brand of humor in playing up the degree to which people had become afraid of giving out personal information. In one spot, a young couple in bed debated the merits of disclosing their names to one another, just before a nine-year-old boy leapt onto the mattress saying, "Hi Mommy. Hi Daddy."

OUTCOME

Citigroup's consumer operations sustained the conglomerate during the time that the "Identity Theft Solutions" campaign aired, a time when the company's capital-markets divisions were facing notably inhospitable conditions. Added to a sluggish investment-banking climate were Citigroup's difficulties stemming from its role in the Worldcom scandal and from its publicized regulatory violations in Japan. Citigroup's consumer divisions grew vigorously, however, led by Citibank's credit-card operations, which were the primary beneficiaries of the "Identity Theft Solutions" message.

Adweek named "Identity Theft Solutions" its campaign of the year for 2003, citing "those wickedly funny juxtapositions, Fallon's seamless production and its simple but entertaining way of conveying a difficult message." *American Banker* also called the Fallon campaign one of the industry's best for that year. *U.S. Banker* noted the influence that the Citibank spots had on industry insiders: "Ad execs, brand consultants, and bankers all give Citi and its agency, Fallon Worldwide, kudos for the piercing spots." The print campaign was a finalist in the Magazine Publishers of America's Kelly Awards in 2004, and the individual spot "Outfit," featuring the man speaking in a Valley-girl voice, won the 2004 Emmy Award for Outstanding Commercial. *Boards* magazine named Fallon its Agency of the Year for 2004, drawing particular attention to its "Identity Theft" campaign.

FURTHER READING

Anderson, Mae. "The Fine Print." *Adweek,* June 7, 2004.

Cardona, Mercedes M. "Capital One." *Advertising Age,* November 17, 2003.

Cardona, Mercedes M., and Hillary Chura. "Citibank Choice of Fallon Signals Edgier Approach." *Advertising Age,* August 7, 2000.

De Paula, Matthew. "In '04, Bank Ads Scored Big. Message Delivered." *U.S. Banker,* January 2005.

"Duly Noted." *Creativity,* October 2004.

Garfield, Bob. "Four Campaigns Demonstrate the True Meaning of Creative." *Advertising Age,* December 8, 2003.

"Lessons in Rich Living from the King of Wealth." *Financial Services Marketing,* February 4, 2002.

Lippert, Barbara. "Look Who's Talking." *Adweek,* November 24, 2003.

McGeer, Bonnie. "Memorable: Citi, Bank One, Citizens of R.I. Ads." *American Banker,* March 10, 2004.

Noonan, David. "Wall Street's New Pitch." *Newsweek,* March 12, 2001.

Parpis, Eleftheria. "Campaign of the Year: Citibank." *Adweek,* February 9, 2004.

Pytlik, Mark. "Fallic Worship." *Boards,* January 1, 2005.

Schneider, Ivan. "Citibank ID Theft Campaign May Lead to Back-Office Efficiencies." *Bank Systems & Technology Online,* July 13, 2004. Available from <http://www.banktech.com/showArticle.jhtml?articleID=23900534>

Vines, Emily. "Citibank Shines Bright Spot on Identity Theft." *Shoot,* December 12, 2003.

Mark Lane

Citigroup Inc.

399 Park Avenue
New York, New York 10043
USA
Telephone: (212) 559-1000
Fax: (212) 793-3946
Web site: www.citigroup.com

LIVE RICHLY CAMPAIGN

OVERVIEW

Note: Also see essay for Citibank.

Citibank, a subsidiary of Citigroup Inc., the largest financial-services company in the world, offered consumer and corporate banking services through some 1,400 offices in more than 40 countries. In the early twenty-first century, amid a strong U.S. economy, Citibank initiated research for an advertising campaign to promote its personalized services, attract financially savvy consumers seeking options for investing their new wealth, and strengthen brand recognition. With the help of newly hired advertising agency Fallon Worldwide of Minneapolis, Citibank launched the "Live Richly" advertising campaign in 2001.

The rebranding campaign, with an estimated budget of $100 million, was built around the tagline "Live Richly." The television, print, and billboard campaign featured slogans such as "People with fat wallets are not necessarily more jolly," "Holding shares shouldn't be your only form of affection," and "He who dies with the most toys is still dead," emphasizing the importance of living life to the fullest while downplaying the focus on money. In addition to promoting the Citibank brand, the campaign sought to highlight Citibank's credit-card division as well as its retail bank operations.

Several of the "Live Richly" television commercials were named "Best Spots" by *Adweek* magazine. The campaign ran through 2004 and inspired such related campaigns as "Identify Theft Solutions," which promoted Citibank's security solutions for credit-card customers. "Live Richly" succeeded in raising interest in Citibank and its offerings: following the unveiling of ads for Citibank's new financial service Citipro, the number of information requests for Citipro at retail branches increased 47 percent.

HISTORICAL CONTEXT

Founded in 1812 as the City Bank of New York, this urban merchant's bank continued to expand and diversify its services over the next century. The bank changed its name to Citibank, N.A. (National Association), in 1976, following its parent holding company's change to Citicorp. In 1998 Citicorp and the Travelers Group completed a $76 billion merger to form Citigroup, Inc. Citicorp was at the time the second-largest commercial bank, and Travelers Group was a leading international insurance/investment-banking firm. The Citicorp-Travelers merger thus represented a new era of horizontal expansion.

Citigroup then began an acquisition spree that included acquiring in 2002 Golden State Bancorp (the parent company of First Nationwide Mortgage and California Federal Bank), a move that added 352 branches and approximately 1.5 million new customers to Citigroup. By then the company was well on its way to having 3,000 bank branches and consumer-finance offices in the United States and Canada, plus an additional 1,500 locations worldwide.

The terrorist strikes of September 11, 2001, initiated changes in American opinions regarding finances. While Americans were left reordering their priorities to allow more time at home with family, Citibank was creating a "new standard" in consumer retail banking. "In a down economy people want to hear that money isn't important," said Al Ries, chairman of Ries & Ries, a marketing consultancy in Atlanta, Georgia. Though the market research for the "Live Richly" campaign had been completed prior to 9/11, Citibank, with its simple and reassuring ads, benefited from consumers' fears of corporate layoffs and the stock-market instabilities of a down economy.

"Live Richly" was Citibank's first major advertising campaign since "The Citi Never Sleeps," which ran in the 1980s and early 1990s. "The Citi Never Sleeps" was developed by ad agency Foote, Cone & Belding's Chicago division and promoted individual banking products. In 1996 agency J. Walter Thompson followed "The Citi Never Sleeps" with an international campaign designed to promote Citibank's international services, such as traveler's checks and a global ATM network. The campaign sported the tagline "Your Bank, Your Money, Your World."

In 1997 Citibank shocked the advertising world by hiring yet another new ad agency, Young & Rubicam, and giving the agency responsibility for all its advertising and direct-marketing needs, in total worth an estimated $500 to $700 million. Prior to 1997 Citibank had divided its marketing assignments among several major agencies, which were blindsided by Citibank's decision. In 2000 Citibank again shopped for a new agency. From seven contenders, Fallon Worldwide was selected.

NOT EVERYONE WAS LIVING RICHLY

Not everyone found Citibank's "Live Richly" advertising campaign to be charming and warmhearted. Some rejected as a ruse Citibank's message that there was more to life than money. In 2003 the Rainforest Action Network, an environmental organization, launched a contest calling for fake advertisements that highlighted Citibank's allegedly corrupt business practices and environmental and social destruction. Patterned after the "Live Richly" print ads, the submissions were posted on a website. Examples of fake ads included "Funny how nobody ever calls it forest destruction" and "Forest Destruction and Global Warming? We're banking on it!"

TARGET MARKET

In order for Citibank to reach its goal of becoming a global brand with one billion customers by 2010, it needed to appeal to a broad population. The campaign aimed to attract middle-income consumers, some 90 million Americans, and intended to accomplish this by convincing them that Citibank understood their values. Specifically, Fallon targeted what it defined as "balance seekers." Balance seekers were not driven by money but used it to fund parts of their lives that made them happy. According to Anne Bologna, director of planning at Fallon, the agency conducted more than 20 focus groups to better understand consumers' relationships with their money. Bologna explained, "We found more than 90 million adults in this country are looking for balance in their lives. They're not striving to become millionaires, and money isn't their end goal. They view money as a tool to help them attain balance and live their priorities."

In addition to luring middle-income balance seekers, Citibank targeted young urban consumers, including the segment of the population labeled Generation X (people born between 1965 and 1980). Members of Generation X had a reputation for avoiding all things stodgy. Known for seeking alternative approaches to life, Generation X consumers after 9/11 seemed to assiduously avoid the corporate norm, opted for flex time, and often worked from home. Citibank hoped to connect with these consumers through humor and "un-banklike" advertising. In a 2001 press release Fallon Minneapolis president and executive creative director David Lubars commented, "Citibank's new creative is a significant departure from advertising traditionally seen in this category. We've used humor and emotion in the ads to help Citibank connect with people on a more human level than is typically seen from a financial brand. The work establishes Citibank as a consumer ally and friend, not an institution."

COMPETITION

Citigroup reportedly reaped $47 million in net profits a day in 2004 and ruled the financial-services industry. Competitors, among them JPMorgan Chase, Bank of America, Merrill Lynch, and Morgan Stanley, worked to chip away at Citibank's market share. Though Bank of America fell behind Citigroup in the United States in terms of assets, it was the third-largest U.S. bank and boasted the country's most extensive branch network. In fall of 2000 Bank of America launched a one-year, $100 million advertising campaign. It included television, radio, and print advertising and was introduced during the 2000 Olympic Games. Designed to strengthen the Bank of America brand and send the message that Bank of America could help customers grow financially, the campaign focused on two themes, "Grow" and "Why Not?" Bank of America marketing executive Barbara Desoer stated in a 2000 press release, ". . . our goal is to build and sustain awareness of what Bank of America stands for—a customer-driven company that provides innovative financial solutions through a variety of channels."

In 2001 Chase Manhattan and JP Morgan & Company merged to form JPMorgan Chase. By 2002 it was the nation's second-largest financial services firm, and in 2004 it had sales of more than $56 billion. Also in 2004 JPMorgan Chase acquired Bank One, the sixth-largest bank in the United States. JPMorgan Chase's advertising consisted primarily of smaller, more targeted campaigns. In 2002, for instance, the firm unveiled a marketing campaign aimed at Hispanic consumers, and the following year its online investing arm, BrownCo, initiated a $10 to $12 million campaign to attract active traders.

MARKETING STRATEGY

Citibank committed itself to the "Live Richly" campaign in 2001 by bolstering its advertising budget, increasing it to some $100 million; in comparison, according to *Competitive Media Reporting,* Citibank's U.S. advertising budget for the first nine months of 2000 was only $14.6 million.

In creating the "Live Richly" campaign, Fallon Worldwide avoided typical bank stuffiness, and, according to Maggie Shea of Fallon, it also did not want to talk about consumers and their money in a "sappy way." Instead Fallon worked to create an "emotional connection that felt fresh, modern, sophisticated and reassuring," Shea explained to *Adweek.* Rather than focusing on milestone events such as buying a home, having children, or graduating college, this bank campaign focused on "the everyday role of money."

The six-week newspaper component, budgeted at just under $2 million, consisted of a series of simple and quirky ads. They appeared in 19 daily newspapers across the United States, including the *New York Times,* the *Chicago Tribune,* the *Miami Herald,* and *El Nuevo Herald,* the Spanish-language edition of the *Miami Herald.* Initial ads were placed in unexpected sections of newspapers, such as the movie section and the comics. Larger, more detailed ads then appeared in main sections of newspapers for five weeks. Though newspaper advertising was thought to be old-fashioned by some in the advertising industry, it proved to be a key element in the "Live Richly" campaign. Fallon believed that newspapers had a dedicated readership and appealed to a wide variety of consumers. The agency estimated that 30 million consumers were exposed to the campaign through newspaper ads alone.

The print ads sought to appeal to readers on a human level. Lisa Seward, Fallon's media director, noted in *Adweek,* "The banking category across the board is guilty, I think, of speaking to consumers as account numbers and not as people. So [with this campaign], we're trying very hard to acknowledge customers as human, with human motivations." One ad that ran in the comics section declared, "Sometimes wealth is having time to read these." Other ads stated, "Sometimes wealth is buying the $6 popcorn and not obsessing over the fact that you just paid $6 for popcorn," and "If you gave up your morning coffee for a year, you could make an extra mortgage payment. But man, you'd be grumpy." Seward explained that the ads were not intended as attention grabbers. "They did pop off the page, but [they] were small and charming, in a quiet voice."

The television component focused on three areas: boosting the Citibank brand, pushing Citibank's credit-card division, and promoting local branch business. Acclaimed documentary filmmaker Errol Morris directed the brand-building commercials, which starred non-actors. One spot featured snippets of everyday life along with appropriate phrases—a child was swung around in the air by the father, accompanied by the text "Count your blessings"; a teenager made silly faces, and the text on screen read, "Investments mature. You don't have to"; an older gentleman joyously played the trombone to the text, "Dirty, rotten, filthy, stinking happy." All spots ended with the tagline "Live Richly."

Brief Citibank messages were shown on billboards, phone kiosks, bus shelters, subway stations, and construction bridges across six different cities in the United States. The slogans included messages such as "Healthy credit is good, but keep an eye on your cholesterol, too," "Hugs are on a 52-week high," and "The word 'splurge' loses meaning if it becomes a regular daily event." In 2003, in order to fund $2 million in church restorations, the prominent Grace Church at Broadway and 10th Street in New York posted above its portico a huge billboard with the Citibank logo and its "Live Richly" slogan; the ad's text read, "If happiness is just around the corner, turn often."

OUTCOME

Fallon's Citibank advertising continued in this humorous and nonthreatening vein for the following five years. In this time the "Live Richly" umbrella campaign spawned other, more targeted campaigns, including "Identity Theft Solutions" and "Thank You." The former promoted Citibank's anti-identity theft services for its credit-card clientele, while the "Thank You" campaign introduced Citibank's Consumer Rewards Program, which was also for its credit-card customers.

The "Live Richly" campaign's "Tire Swing" commercial was named one of *Adweek* magazine's "Best Spots" of 2004. Analyst Paul Jamieson of Gomez Advisors believed that Citibank's "Live Richly" ads sent an attractive message to consumers, and he commented in *Financial Services Marketing,* "What they're really speaking to is what consumers desire these days, which has less to do with saving money and more to do with saving time. They're saying: 'Concentrate on the things that make life rewarding; we'll take care of the complicated stuff.' It's a great message." The advertising industry agreed, and "Live Richly" won a Gold EFFIE Award in 2002.

FURTHER READING

Beckett, Paul. "Citibank Unveils Advertising Campaign." *Wall Street Journal,* January 15, 2001.

Carvell, Tim. "Citi of Fear." *Moneybox,* July 31, 2002.

Case, Tony. "Fallon." *Adweek,* June 18, 2001.

Elliott, Stuart. "Citibank Consolidates, Stunning Madison Ave." *New York Times,* August 8, 1997.

Gordon, Joanne. "Do You Really Need That?" *Forbes,* March 19, 2001.

Hogue, Ilyse. "The Cost of Living Richly: Citigroup's Global Finance and Threats to the Environment." *Multinational Monitor* 23, no. 4 (April 2002).

Kapler, Bob. "Living Richly at Citibank Means There's More to Life than Money." *Financial Services Marketing,* March 20, 2001.

Lamport, Joseph. "Wake Up and Smell the Subterfuge." *Salon.com,* February 4, 2002.

"Off the Mark." *Delaney Report,* February 12, 2001.

Wasserman, Todd. "Banking on Upturn, but '01 Woes Add Up." *Brandweek.com,* April 11, 2005.

Bridget McGinniss Kerr

Clairol, Inc.

1 Blachley Road
Stamford, Connecticut 06922
USA
Telephone: (203) 357-5000
Fax: (203) 357-5000
Web site: www.clairol.com

■■■

TOTALLY ORGANIC CAMPAIGN

OVERVIEW

Clairol, Inc.'s Herbal Essence was a top-ranked shampoo in the 1970s. Although it retained a following in California, by the 1990s it had dropped in popularity elsewhere. In 1994 Clairol introduced a new Herbal Essences brand that offered a variety of shampoos and conditioners made from organic materials. Other Herbal Essences hair-care products followed. Instead of imitating the marketing strategy of other shampoo brands, Clairol, a subsidiary of Bristol-Myers Squibb Company, wanted to advertise the sensual experience of washing hair, not how its shampoo made hair shiny or silky. Hoping to increase sales and make the Herbal Essences brand stand out against the noise of competing advertisers, Clairol introduced a campaign titled "Totally Organic."

The print, television, and radio campaign, created by the ad agency Wells Rich Greene BDDP in New York, was released in 1994. *Adweek* estimated its budget to be between $15 million and $20 million. The natural makeup of the new shampoos was a strong selling point, but it was advertisements using sexual humor that helped Herbal Essences gain recognition over other environmentally sound competitors. Commercials featured women who simulated sexual ecstasy while shampooing their hair, usually in a public setting such as a crowded supermarket. The campaign shifted its strategy in 2000, when pop singer Britney Spears recorded a song for Herbal Essences titled "I've Got the Urge to Herbal" and posed for print ads. Her contribution lowered the campaign's female target age range from 18 to 49 down to 16 to 49. Despite the brand's ownership changing hands and the campaign being transferred to a second ad agency, "Totally Organic" continued until 2004.

While using sex in advertising was a controversial, or in some views anachronistic, approach, incorporating humor made the Herbal Essences ads contemporary and effective. The "Totally Organic" campaign was considered a solid success by Clairol executives, and it inspired a relaunch of another Clairol standard, Nice 'n Easy hair color. "Totally Organic" helped the brand triple its market share between 1994 and 1999—making Herbal Essences the second-largest shampoo brand in America.

HISTORICAL CONTEXT

In 1994 Clairol, a division of Bristol-Myers Squibb, introduced Herbal Essences, a collection of four shampoos and four conditioners sold in 12-ounce bottles for $3.29. Marketing began in 1995 with approximately $20 million in print and television advertising. Styling products—gels, mousses, and spritzes—and body-wash products were added to the line in 1996, and in 1997 Herbal Essences products were introduced to the United Kingdom and other markets.

The new product traded on the name recognition of a previous Clairol product, Herbal Essence, which was ranked the number three shampoo in the early 1970s, with an 8 percent market share. That share had fallen to 0.1 percent by the 1990s, however. Herbal Essence was not a natural product, while the new Herbal Essences products were made almost exclusively of herbs, botanicals, and other plant ingredients derived from renewable resources. The formulas were biodegradable and not tested on animals, and the packaging material was made out of recyclable plastic.

Clairol said that the old Herbal Essence would be continued because it retained favor with Hispanic consumers. To avoid confusion between the two products, however, it would be merchandised separately from the new Herbal Essences line.

CONNECTIONS

Clairol advertised its reformulated Nice 'n Easy hair coloring during the final episode of the sitcom *Seinfeld,* on May 14, 1998. The spots starred comedian Kristen Johnston of the sitcom *3rd Rock from the Sun. Seinfeld* star Julia Louis-Dreyfus had been a former spokeswoman for Nice 'n Easy.

TARGET MARKET

An association with nature was part of the original Herbal Essence shampoo's appeal, but the product's green credentials were more image than fact. "Consumer research has shown us that people remember Herbal Essence as a natural product, even though it really wasn't," said Jeanne Matson, Clairol's marketing director for hair care. The new Herbal Essences products, said to be 99 percent natural, were created and marketed with environmentally informed consumers in mind. "With companies like the Body Shop and Aveda introducing natural hair products in the specialty arena, it seemed like the perfect time to revive Herbal Essence and make it truly natural and environmentally sound," Matson said.

A trend toward upgrading shampoos for the mass market had resulted in a new niche. This new market was for hair-care products that offered salon-quality treatment—such as alpha hydroxy acid—or natural ingredients—such as those used in specialty shampoos from companies like the Body Shop or Aveda—at less than salon or specialty prices. At $3.29 for 12 ounces, a bottle of Herbal Essences shampoo was more expensive than the old Herbal Essence, which continued to be merchandised at $2.99 for a 14.5-ounce bottle, but it was still inexpensive.

The new Herbal Essences was first aimed at "women aged 18 to 49 who are interested in natural products and do not mind paying premium prices in order be environmentally sound," said Jane Owen, senior product manager. This demographic group apparently included fans of television shows like *Seinfeld,* programs noted not for their environmental stance but for pushing the envelope in questions of taste. A controversial but effective marketing strategy used by Clairol for its new Herbal Essences products sidestepped the environmental question altogether and instead focused on the sensual act of shampooing by playing the word "organic" off "orgasmic." After adding print and radio spots featuring 18-year-old singer Britney Spears in 2000, the campaign's target expanded to include women between the ages of 16 to 49.

COMPETITION

Clairol was the number one hair-products company in the United States. Procter & Gamble, however, dominated the shampoo market in 1997, with its leading product, Pantene. Nonetheless, Clairol's Herbal Essences was "making plenty of noise," as characterized by market reports. The company's shampoo sales rose 89.3 percent, to $52.8 million, for the year ending August 25, 1996, and conditioner sales were up 94 percent, to $31.8 million. The Body Shop and Aveda were the two competitors most commonly cited by the creators of Herbal Essences. These companies sold environmentally sound products at above-average but not exorbitant prices, and the Body Shop especially appealed to the global consciousness of consumers.

MARKETING STRATEGY

Competition, even within specific categories, was becoming increasingly intense in television advertising in the 1990s. Stock products had been done to death and without much originality, according to Judith Werme, group creative director at ad agency DDB Needham Chicago. "A blitzed-out population has become increasingly blasé," said Mark Crispin Miller, professor of media studies at New York University. "So there's an accelerating desperation to make an impression, to stand out."

Print copy for Clairol's Herbal Essences shampoos and conditioners stated that they contained a combination of natural organic herbs, botanicals, and spring-water, giving users "a totally organic experience." Television commercials, however, turned this straightforward environmental description into a whole different story. A TV spot developed by Wells Rich Greene

EMPLOYEE COMMUTER PROGRAM

Clairol, Inc., based in Stamford, Connecticut, spruced up its Employee Commuter Program to reflect the images used to market environmentally friendly products such as Herbal Essences. The Clairol shuttle bus, which transported employees to and from the Stamford train station, was decorated with depictions of fresh herbs and flowers so as to resemble the design of the new shampoo bottles. The Clairol Employee Commuter Program provided the train-station shuttle, low-cost vanpooling, and emergency rides home for commuters who needed them. In 1995 Clairol won the Governor's Circle Transportation Award, presented annually to recognize individual and corporate contributions to alternative transportation that helped to improve Connecticut's air quality and reduce congestion on its highways.

BDDP, New York, showed a woman "really, really enjoying her shampoo," wrote Tom Soter for *Shoot* magazine. "In the piece, a woman shampooing her hair in the shower murmurs, 'Feels so good,' then progresses to 'yes, yes, yes,' until the spot ends with an orgasmic cry. The punchline is lifted straight out of the famous deli orgasm scene in When Harry Met Sally." A woman watching the commercial on television at home then said, "I want to get the shampoo she's using." Another version showed a woman who, to the puzzlement of the passengers overhearing her, moaned with pleasure as she shampooed with Clairol Herbal Essences in the restroom of an airplane.

The $15 million to $20 million campaign was an example of "shock advertising," which Bob Garfield, critic for *Advertising Age,* described as "calculatingly taking license to offend and inflame." But Linda Kaplan Thaler, who developed the Herbal Essences advertisements for Wells Rich Greene BDDP—and who soon after took the entire Clairol account to her new company, Kaplan Thaler Group—described the Herbal Essences "Totally Organic" campaign as based on "the theory of disruption." "If the convention in the shampoo category is to show the benefit of making hair shiny and healthy, we would go against that. Instead of finding some molecule of evidence that our product made hair slightly shinier, we thought we'd get more bang for the buck by doing something that everyone else isn't doing, but is equally as inviting. We said, 'Why not concentrate on the actual experience of washing hair rather than the end benefit? When you're cleaning yourself, it's a cathartic experience—you're naked, it's deeply sensual."

The commercials were developed within a climate of permissiveness in television in 1994, manifested in shows such as *Seinfeld, Friends,* and *NYPD Blue* as well as on MTV. "There is such an onslaught of wild, weird and wacky stuff on MTV," explained DDB Needham's Werme, "that in advertising, there's almost nothing you can't do." But programs such as *Seinfeld* and *Friends,* while pushing the boundaries for acceptable topics and language, also operated in a climate of sensitivity to women's rights and, perhaps, with ennui toward a sex-saturated medium. "It's not acceptable to have T&A in beer advertising anymore," commented Jeff Funicular, creative director at ad agency Leo Burnett, Toronto. "It's not acceptable to have women draped over the hood of a car." If sex was going to sell or even be noticed, it had to be self-deprecating and witty. "We decided a comedic experience would work best," said Kaplan Thaler about the Herbal Essences advertisements.

Other television spots that featured racy material with a high quotient of humor included those for Fruit of the Loom underwear, Westin Hotels, Coca-Cola, Mercedes-Benz, and the Bermuda Department of Tourism. "Television permissibility was clearly enjoying a renaissance," wrote Soter in *Shoot,* but humor was a key ingredient for success.

In late 1997 another disruption spot was created for Clairol by Kaplan Thaler to launch a new hair-care line called Daily Defense. The spot showed a fleet of stylists at a commercial shoot grooming the opulent blond tresses of a model. The scene was interrupted with images of a no-nonsense brunette explaining the benefits of Daily Defense, said to provide protection from damaging environmental effects, including pollution, solar radiation, and chlorine from swimming pools. "We're poking fun at what goes on behind the scenes at many [shampoo] commercials," said Kaplan Thaler. Research showed that many women were tired of seeing "unrealistic" females in ads, she added. A simple scientific look was planned for the product's packaging. "This is about a product that is high-tech," said Bill Decker, president of Clairol's retail division. "It is not a natural or sensory story."

In 1999 the ad agency Kaplan Thaler Group, New York, was awarded the Herbal Essences account. The all-female agency, helmed by the campaign's creator, Linda Kaplan Thaler, released new television spots and print ads with the expanded $30 million Herbal Essences ad budget. One courtroom-themed spot featured the sex therapist Dr. Ruth promoting the new Herbal Essences body wash while a female lawyer delved into a sensuous hair-washing daydream. Handsome men in the courtroom began singing, "She's got the urge to Herbal." Pop star Britney Spears recorded her own 60-second version of "She's Got the Urge to Herbal" for a 2000 radio spot. Her song was also used for a preconcert video presentation during Spears's 50-city summer concert tour, which was sponsored by Clairol. In addition Spears posed for Herbal Essences print ads, which appeared in youth-oriented magazines such as *Teen People, Seventeen,* and *YM.* Spears lowered the campaign's target age to girls as young as 16.

The Procter & Gamble Company purchased Clairol from Bristol-Myers Squibb in 2001 and renamed the company P&G-Clairol, Inc. In March 2001 members of the boy band 98 Degrees appeared in provocative print ads and television spots for Herbal Essences. In addition Herbal Essences sponsored the band's 2001 spring concert tour. In 2003 the campaign featured *Sex and the City* star Kim Cattrall, who provided spots with voice-overs. The blonde bombshell was shown moaning in a shower while shampooing her hair in one commercial—drawing a backlash from the watchdog group the American Family Association. In 2004 Herbal Essences put its 10-year-old "Totally Organic" campaign on hiatus in America, according to *Advertising Age,* in favor of a campaign that was less sexually charged.

OUTCOME

A *USA Today* Ad Track survey of 41 commercials in 1997 showed that only 8 percent of those questioned responded that they liked the Herbal Essences ads "a lot." A mere 14 percent rated the ads "very effective." Nonetheless, Clairol was pleased with the campaign. "This has been Clairol's most successful product launch in the history of the company," said Bill Susetka, senior vice president and general manager of Clairol U.S. "It has greatly exceeded our initial expectations."

In 1997 Clairol reported a 36 percent increase in sales, which was attributed to its Herbal Essences line. That year the line had a sales increase of 168 percent, to $351 million. Herbal Essences products were introduced or expanded in more than 40 countries. Clairol became a market leader in Peru and Puerto Rico in 1997, and in Asia Clairol's Herbal Essences product line "put it on the map," according to Steve Sadove, president of worldwide Beauty Care & Nutritional at Bristol-Myers Squibb (then the parent company of Clairol). "It's the most successful thing we've done at Clairol," Sadove added. "We believe Herbal Essences has the potential to be a mega brand spanning many different product categories."

During the first five years of "Totally Organic" Herbal Essences tripled its market share and eventually became the second-largest shampoo brand, behind Pantene. In 2003 its consumer-awareness scores were higher than that of any other shampoo, according to the newspaper the *Hamilton Spectator.* By 2004 some ad analysts had begun criticizing the campaign for its lack of fresh material. Such accusations were later validated by Herbal Essences' bottom line. In the campaign's final full year in the United States, the brand lost 1.9 market-share points in shampoo and 1.1 market-share points for conditioner.

FURTHER READING

Berkowitz, Harry. "Sex Sells in Latest TV Commercials: Even Cautious Mercedes Has Racy Run in New Ads." *Newsday,* May 10, 1996.

Elliott, Stuart. "A Vivid-Livid Divide: Madison Ave.'s New Explicitness Is Open to Debate." *New York Times,* June 19, 1998.

Enrico, Dottie. "'Seinfeld' Finale Advertisers Put On Game Faces." *USA Today,* April 29, 1998.

"How the Ad Track Ads of 1997 Stack Up." *USA Today,* December 29, 1997.

Kagan, Cara. "Styling Products Take Shape for Clairol's Herbal Essence." *Women's Wear Daily,* February 9, 1996, p. 6.

Kim, Hank. "Kaplan Thaler Unveils TV Spot." *Adweek* (eastern ed.), December 8, 1997.

———. "2 Assignments For Kaplan Thaler." *Adweek* (eastern ed.), January 19, 1998.

Neff, Jack. "P&G Retains Clairol Planners." *Advertising Age,* March 18, 2002, p. 3.

Robb, Jay. "Ads You Can't Wash Out of Your Hair." *Hamilton (ON) Spectator,* December 9, 2003, p. G15.

Soter, Tom. "Sex-Smitten." *Shoot,* September 27, 1996.

Tode, Chantal, "Clairol's Daily Defense Strategy." *Women's Wear Daily,* July 18, 1997.

Megan McNamer
Kevin Teague

CNS, Inc.

7615 Smetana Lane
Eden Prairie, Minnesota 55344
USA
Telephone: (952) 229-1500
Fax: (952) 229-1700
Web site: www.cns.com

■■■

BACK IN THE SACK CAMPAIGN

OVERVIEW

During the early 1990s Breathe Right nasal strips, manufactured and marketed by CNS, Inc., enjoyed a meteoric rise in sales. This success was largely attributed to the influence of certain prominent athletes, who wore the strip to enhance performance. It also succeeded to an extent as a cure for problem snorers but had difficulty breaking into the more crowded cold and allergy field. While the product gained brand recognition, it became typecast as a specialized product for star athletes. Sales peaked in the mid-1990s, as did the price of CNS stock, and the company launched several marketing efforts aimed at reaching a family audience. In particular, women were targeted because they bought most of the cold remedies in the house, and since a greater number of men than women had snoring problems, women were the ones most affected by snoring and more motivated to seek a product to curb the problem. In an attempt to appeal to married problem snorers, generally 50 years and older, CNS in 2004 introduced its "Back in the Sack" campaign, developed by ad agency Olson & Company. The strategy was to convince couples that Breathe Right nasal strips could ease the snoring that hurt so many relationships.

With a budget of less than $1 million, "Back in the Sack" was in essence a direct-response campaign. The goal was to convince consumers to request a six-night sample pack of nasal strips either by calling a toll-free telephone number or by registering at a dedicated website. CNS felt confident that if people tried the product they would become customers. The TV spots ran late at night or early in the morning, the times when the problem of snoring was most on the minds of consumers. Morning radio personalities who tried the strips to alleviate their own snoring and offered their own testimonials played a major role in the campaign, as did a print ad that ran in a Sunday newspaper coupon insert. The website also provided educational information and the chance to send a humorous Snore-O-Gram E-mail message to loved ones, urging them to give Breathe Right a chance to address their snoring problem.

Despite its limited budget the "Back in the Sack" campaign far exceeded its goals. The response rate to the sampling effort was five times the target, while sales increased at more than twice the anticipated rate. The campaign also won a prestigious EFFIE award in 2005 and continued to drive sampling and sales for CNS.

HISTORICAL CONTEXT

After receiving Food and Drug Administration approval in late 1993, the Breathe Right adhesive nasal strip, used to keep nasal passages open, found a ready market not with chronic snorers but with athletes. The company that

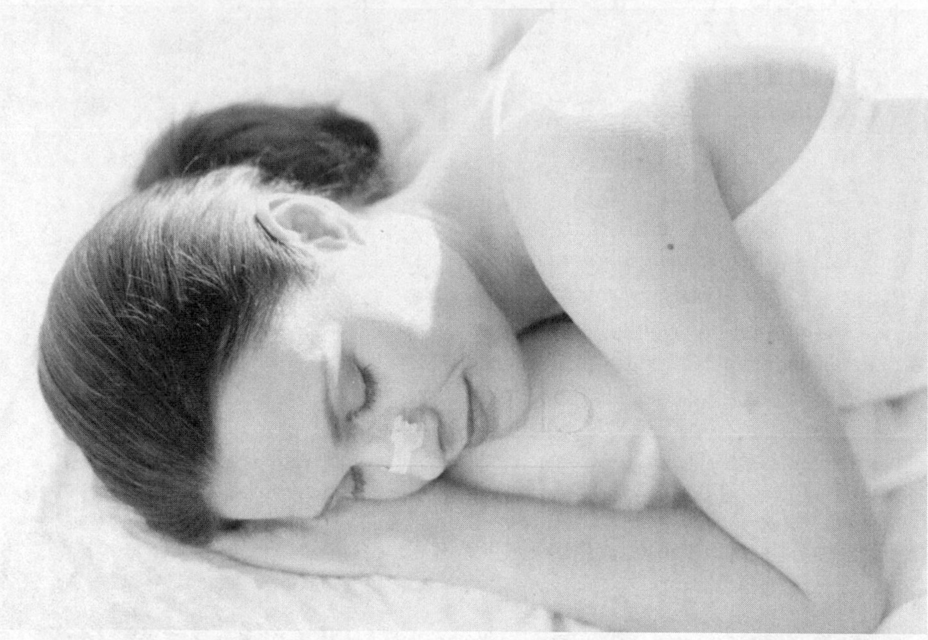

© MICHAEL KELLER/CORBIS. REPRODUCED BY PERMISSION.

produced the product, CNS, Inc., mailed samples to National Football League trainers, people who were more likely than most to understand the biology behind the strips. The Philadelphia Eagles were the first to give the product a try, applying it to the nose of running back Herschel Walker, who at the time was suffering from a cold, before he rushed for 269 yards and scored a pair of touchdowns. Star San Francisco 49ers' wide receiver Jerry Rice then wore the strip for a Monday Night Football game, generating national attention for the Breathe Right brand and jump-starting its marketing campaign. A wide assortment of athletes used the product, many of them providing unpaid endorsements.

Sales exploded for Breathe Right, peaking around $65 million in 1996 before beginning to slip. "The problem," according to Monte Hanson, writing for *Finance and Commerce Daily Newspaper,* "was that the strips marketed as a product worn by professional athletes to enhance performance and by men who had snoring problems had limited consumer appeal." A new president, former Pillsbury executive Marti Morfitt, was hired in March 1998 as the price of CNS stock began to plummet. He began an effort to break out Breathe Right beyond its athletic typecasting and position it as a product for the entire family, able to help people suffering from nasal congestion caused by colds or allergies. A product containing Vicks mentholated vapors as well as decorated nasal strips for kids were introduced. The 1999 "Breathe Right. All Night" campaign promoted the product as a way to relieve nighttime nasal congestion. One of the TV spots showed a woman using the strip to ease nasal congestion. The subsequent "On the Nose" campaign also attempted to target women, a market that CNS believed was untapped because it viewed Breathe Right as a product for athletes or men with snoring problems. Women were important because they were often the ones who bought the product for spouses with snoring problems and were generally the family member responsible for buying cold remedies. A major goal of the "On the Nose" campaign was to urge women to see Breathe Right as a product for themselves.

The "On the Nose" campaign, launched in January 2000, succeeded in raising consumer awareness and increased sales and even won a prestigious EFFIE award for CNS and its advertising agency, Campbell Mithun, but it did little to convince women to overcome their reluctance to wear an adhesive strip over their noses. Nevertheless CNS learned over the years that if it could persuade people to try the product, there was a good chance they would buy it. According to a 2003 study, people who tried the strip were seven times more likely to purchase it. The goal of the "Back in the Sack" campaign, developed by Olson & Company and launched in the summer of 2004 in a number of test markets, was to get as many nasal strips on the noses of potential customers as possible.

TARGET MARKET

The "Back in the Sack" campaign targeted married snorers, which already accounted for the bulk of Breathe

DESPERATION: THE MOTHER OF SOME INVENTIONS

The Breathe Right nasal strip was invented by Bruce Johnson, a man who suffered from allergies as well as a deviated septum. In his attempts to keep his nasal passages open, he resorted to such desperate measures as putting straws up his nose and even using paper clips to keep his nostrils open. His inspiration for Breathe Rights came one day when he drove past an archway at the University of Minnesota and he realized that he could pull open his nasal passages from the outside rather than from within. This insight led to his creation of an adhesive strip that could be applied over the nose.

Right sales, but because the budget was less than $1 million, the company could not effectively reach a wider family market. It was also a vast market, given that studies indicated more than half of U.S. households had a problem snorer. Typically, problem snorers were men who were not affected by their snoring and, thus, lacked the motivation to try Breathe Right strips. Their wives, however, were highly motivated, eager to find a product to alleviate their husbands' snoring, to get some sleep, and, in many cases, to save their relationships. Moreover problem snoring grew worse with age, providing older women with more motivation than younger women to take action. The campaign, as a result, targeted adults 50 years and older.

COMPETITION

As a product to relieve congestion, Breathe Right faced competition from well-established brands—the likes of Vicks, Claritin, and Benadryl—that had spent hundreds of millions of dollars to establish themselves in the marketplace. But they could not claim to eliminate or even alleviate snoring. It was this opening that CNS wanted to exploit, and once consumers had gained relief from snoring there was a good chance they would try Breathe Right for congestion. Competition in the snoring aid category was varied but limited. There were some 300 patented devices intended to solve problem snoring, as well as such homemade nostrums as sewing a sock with a tennis ball inside it to the pajama back to force the snorer to sleep on his side (because snoring grew worse from sleeping on the back). On the market consumers could find slumber sleep masks, contour pillows, an assortment of sprays and pills, as well as "Chin-Up" strips, which kept the mouth closed and forced a user to breathe through his nose. There were also competing nasal strips, the best known being Clear Passage, produced by giant pharmaceutical Schering-Plough. Additionally drugstore chains offered private-label nasal strips, but Breathe Right was the dominant brand in the category.

MARKETING STRATEGY

Since the introduction of Breathe Right a decade earlier, CNS had received hundreds of letters from satisfied customers offering their testimonials. A large portion of them said that Breathe Right not only alleviated a snoring problem but perhaps saved a relationship. Taking this cue, the marketers decided to focus on the emotional benefit of using Breathe Right to curb snoring: rekindling relationships and—in the language of the campaign—getting couples "back in the sack."

The campaign was a multifaceted, integrated effort to attract, and in some cases reattract, problem snorers. Media elements of the campaign included television, radio, newspaper, direct mail, public relations, and interactive/online. In order to make the message resonate, especially important given the limited budget, the direct-response television spots were aired at times when the problem of snoring was most on the minds of people affected by it: overnight and early in the morning. One spot showed a tattered half of a picture of a man on a bed pillow in the shadows of the night, his snoring heard in the background. The other half of the picture, that of his wife, was shown on the other pillow, with the sound of a ticking click representing her sleeplessness. After the voice-over made the case for Breathe Right strips, able to alleviate snoring in six nights, the halves of the picture were seen reunited. The direct response of the ad came at the close with a toll-free number people could call to receive a free six-night sample pack of the product. The pack itself served an educational purpose: consumers learned that the body needed to retrain itself in order to breathe differently and to stop snoring. Moreover the consumers were developing a nightly habit of applying the strip, a habit that would carry over once they experienced results and began to purchase the product.

Radio also proved effective in convincing people to request a product sample. Popular radio station morning "drive" personalities who themselves suffered from snoring were located. They were then given Breathe Right strips to use and, once they had success with the product, were enthusiastic in their praise of Breathe Right the next morning. The last major element in the campaign was the Sunday newspaper coupon inserts, which a large number of the target audience scoured for bargains before doing their grocery shopping. CNS ran a four-color front page ad on the SmartSource coupon inserts. All told, the campaign spent less than $500,000 on media.

NOT QUITE BRAIN SURGERY

When CNS, Inc., maker of Breathe Right strips, was founded in 1982 by a pair of neurologists, they had no intention of becoming involved in over-the-counter pharmacy items. The company's purpose was to develop brain-wave monitors for surgery. Because insurance companies were reluctant to cover the use of such technology, CNS switched its attention to making sleep-disorder diagnostic equipment. When the inventor of the Breathe Right nasal strip, Bruce Johnson, showed his prototype to CNS chairman Dr. Dan Cohen, he was not laughed out of the office, as had been the case in his previous company pitches. Instead, Cohen recognized the potential of the product and signed an exclusive deal to sell the strips.

The campaign's website, GetBackInTheSack.com, also played a major role. Not only could consumers sign up online for the sample pack, but the site also provided interactive educational material that showed how the strips worked. Many of the testimonials CNS had received from couples were posted online, lending credibility to the campaign's theme of Breathe Right saving relationships. The website also included whimsical Snore-O-Grams, E-mail messages that could be sent to loved ones to encourage them to do something about their snoring.

OUTCOME

One of the objectives of the "Back in the Sack" campaign was to double the response rate of prior sampling efforts, from 0.9 to 1.8 percent. A further goal was to increase sales by more than 8 percent over the same time period of the previous year. On both counts the campaign more than exceeded the target. The response rate to the sample offer was 9.12 percent, a 1,103 percent increase over the historic average and far beyond the 1.8 percent goal. This success then had an impact on sales, which grew 17 percent, a rate increase that more than doubled the campaign's goal. What started out as a trial effort was rolled out nationwide in 2005, and investors soon took note of the campaign's success. They bid up the price of CNS stock, which topped the $25 mark for the first time since the heady days of 1996. Then the stock would dip below the $5 mark within two years. This time, however, CNS had record revenues in fiscal 2005 to support the stock's price.

The "Back in the Sack" campaign was also recognized by the advertising industry. In 2005 it won the Gold in the Health Aids/Over-the-Counter Products category of the EFFIE Awards, presented annually by the New York American Marketing Association to honor outstanding advertising campaigns.

FURTHER READING

Anthony, Neal St. "CNS Investors Breathing Easier Again." *Star Tribune,* July 26, 2005, p. 1D.

Black, Sam. "CNS Targeting New Market with Product." *CityBusiness* (Minneapolis, MN), December 29, 2000, p. 2.

"CNS Launches Breathe Right National Advertising Campaign." *Drug Store News,* March 15, 1999, p. CP42.

"Creating a Brand—Out of Thin Air." *Drug Stores News,* December 14, 1998.

Groeneveld, Benno. "Take a Breath." *CityBusiness* (Minneapolis, MN), July 7, 2000, p. S10.

Hanson, Monte. "Shareholders of Nasal Strips Maker Call for Change." *Finance and Commerce* (Minnesota), August 9, 2001.

Ed Dinger

The Coca-Cola Company

1 Coca-Cola Plaza
Atlanta, Georgia 30313-2499
USA
Telephone: (404) 676-2121
Fax: (404) 676-6792
Web site: www.cocacola.com

■■■

KEEP PLAYING CAMPAIGN

OVERVIEW

Although the Coca-Cola Company was well known for its carbonated-soft-drink brands, by the late 1980s a different type of beverage was attracting consumers and capturing a rapidly increasing market share: isotonic beverages, or sports drinks. In 1992 Coca-Cola jumped into the sports-drink arena with the introduction of PowerAde. Despite its marketing and promotion efforts, the brand struggled to gain a foothold with consumers. Five years after its launch in 1997, PowerAde had only managed to reach a 15.1 percent market share, far behind powerhouse brand Gatorade, which had a 73 percent share. In 1999 PowerAde eked out just $77 million in sales, while Gatorade claimed $631 million. Adding to Coca-Cola's woes was that, under pressure from its investors, in 2000 the company withdrew its $16 billion bid to acquire Gatorade and its parent Quaker Oats Company, only to see its competitor PepsiCo land the deal for $13.4 billion.

To boost Coca-Cola's struggling PowerAde brand, in 2000 ad agency McCann-Erickson New York created a new marketing campaign that used humorous television spots to send the message that athletes drank PowerAde before, during, and after the game or competition. The campaign featured athletes at all levels, from high school kids to pros, going through pregame rituals and superstitions as they prepared for competition. Each spot included the voice-over "Whatever you do to get up for the game, stay up," and the tagline "Keep playing." A specific budget for the campaign was unavailable, but a report in *Adweek* noted that Coca-Cola's media spending for PowerAde through November 2000 was $31.2 million.

The television spots were well received by consumers and the advertising industry. One spot, "Bus Ride," featuring high school basketball players on the team bus getting mentally pumped up for their looming game, earned an *Adweek* magazine Best Spot honor. But the campaign failed to increase PowerAde sales as planned. In 2001 Coca-Cola hired Wieden+Kennedy, a Portland, Oregon–based agency, to create a new campaign for PowerAde. The campaign had the tagline "Very real power," and it featured the Atlanta Falcons football team's quarterback Michael Vick in a series of television spots.

HISTORICAL CONTEXT

Since its introduction in 1886 of a sparkling beverage sold at drugstore soda fountains, Coca-Cola was best known as a producer of carbonated soft drinks. Its brands included the flagship and eponymously named Coca-Cola (Coke) as well as a list of products added to the company's lines over the years, such as Sprite and Tab, added in the 1960s, and Mr. Pibb, added in the 1970s.

In 1967 isotonic drinks—sports beverages that were designed specifically for athletes to replace body fluids and some nutrients lost while exercising—appeared on the market with the introduction of Gatorade. The product quickly grew in popularity with elite athletes and eventually gained acceptance among health-conscious consumers who turned to Gatorade as the beverage of choice to recharge after exercising or playing sports. By 1989 some 40 different sports drinks were on the market, including PepsiCo's Mountain Dew Sport. Sales of sports drinks increased 17 percent from 1988 to 1989, with Gatorade earning the lion's share of the sales. Sports-drink sales hit the $500 million mark in 1990 and were growing quickly. At that time Coca-Cola introduced its own sports drink, a powder that the consumer mixed with water. The product, Max, failed to advance past test markets, but in 1992 Coca-Cola began selling PowerAde with greater success. The company supported the new product's launch with an ad campaign that included displays, posters, and television spots. In a *Time* magazine article Coca-Cola touted PowerAde as "a drink made for athletes and anyone who works up a sweat."

Winning market share from sports-drink giant Gatorade proved difficult for Coca-Cola's PowerAde. Sales of isotonic drinks hit $801 million in 1999, up 12.8 percent from $712 million in 1998, but PowerAde had captured just $77 million in sales in 1999, versus Gatorade's $631 million. By 2000 Coca-Cola was reevaluating its struggling PowerAde brand and was considering acquisition of Gatorade and the brand's parent, Quaker Oats Company. When it became known that Coca-Cola was considering a $16 billion stock offer that would involve exchanging 1.9 Coke shares for each share of Quaker Oats, investors fled Coca-Cola, sending its stock into a downward spiral. Coca-Cola executives abandoned the plan to buy Quaker Oats. Competitor PepsiCo acquired the company and its Gatorade brand in 2000 for $13.4 billion. With Gatorade under the banner of Coca-Cola's top competitor, PepsiCo, the company redirected its energies toward revamping and promoting PowerAde.

TARGET MARKET

Isotonic sports drinks first targeted serious athletes. But as the beverages became more familiar, athletes of all ages and at all skill levels were increasingly choosing them over carbonated beverages or drinks such as iced tea or plain water to recharge after a workout or competition. According to Coca-Cola, from the time of its introduction PowerAde's target audience had always been young men in the 18- to 30-year-old demographic. A Coca-Cola spokesman said that the company's consistent youth-focused target market was maintained with the "Keep Playing" marketing campaign. He added, however, that in addition to targeting PowerAde's traditional audience, the campaign also began shifting some of the focus to younger consumers and introduced a multiethnic approach to promoting the product.

POWERADE FEATURED DURING ESPN/ABC PROGRAMMING

Coca-Cola and ESPN/ABC entered a marketing partnership in 2000 that would give PowerAde, Coke's sports-drink brand, an increased presence on ESPN, a cable network owned by ABC. As part of the deal, "PowerAde Break" segments would be included during ESPN's popular show *SportsCenter,* and PowerAde was also featured during select ABC network sports programming. In addition to traditional television advertising, the deal provided an opportunity for Coke and ESPN/ABC to partner on nontraditional marketing efforts such as promoting their brands in high schools and movie theaters.

COMPETITION

PepsiCo joined the sports-drink market in 1994 with its new beverage All Sport. Although the brand, like other sports drinks, targeted athletes of all ages and ability levels, in 1998 the All Sport brand was expanded to include Body Quencher. The new product specifically targeted kids 6 to 15 years old and was offered in kid-friendly flavors such as Fruit Punch, Cherry Slam, and Raspberry Burst. But the All Sport brand failed to attract consumers, and in 1999 its sales slipped 22.4 percent to $31.1 million, or just 3.7 percent of the sports-drink market. By 2000 PepsiCo was reevaluating its role in the sports-drink arena, and the company was considering purchasing Quaker Oats Company and its Gatorade sports-drink brand. Quaker Oats rejected the initial offering of $14 billion that PepsiCo made in November 2000, but one month later Quaker Oats accepted PepsiCo's $13.4 billion offer that included assuming $750 million in debt. PepsiCo's addition of Gatorade to its product mix led the Federal Trade Commission to question whether it violated antitrust regulations, so in 2001 the company sold its All Sport sports-drink brands to Monarch Beverage Company, an Atlanta, Georgia–based company with a drink lineup that included Dad's

Root Beer and Moxie, a cola-style carbonated beverage popular in America's New England states.

Gatorade, the original sports beverage, was the market leader in 1999, holding a 79 percent share of the sports-drink market with $631 million in sales. The beverage was developed in 1965 by the University of Florida to help its football players finish an entire game under the hot, humid conditions typical in Florida. The new drink was named Gatorade as a tribute to the school's mascot, the Gators, and in 1967 an agreement was reached with Stokely-Van Camp, Inc., to produce Gatorade. At the time Stokely-Van Camp produced canned vegetables and was best known for its canned pork and beans. During the 1967 Orange Bowl the sports drink burst onto the national scene with the Gators' victory over Georgia Tech; Georgia Tech's coach attributed the win in part to the Florida team's use of Gatorade during the game. Quaker Oats Company purchased Stokely-Van Camp, which included Gatorade, in 1983. Gatorade got another national boost in 1987 when Super Bowl fans watching the game saw New York Giants players pour a full cooler of Gatorade over their coach's head in celebration. In 1991 Gatorade signed on basketball legend Michael Jordan as spokesman and launched its "Be Like Mike" campaign. In a twist as tart as Gatorade's lemon-lime flavor, in the late 1980s Quaker Oats granted PepsiCo licensed manufacturing rights to Gatorade in select countries. About nine years later, in 1998, Quaker Oats sued PepsiCo for using Gatorade's secrets to develop its own sports drink, All Sport. Quaker Oats won the lawsuit but ultimately lost the battle when PepsiCo finalized its purchase of Quaker Oats and the Gatorade brand in 2000.

MARKETING STRATEGY

To promote Coca-Cola's sports drink PowerAde in 2000, the agency McCann-Erickson New York created a campaign that put a humorous spin on the efforts that athletes of all levels, from high school students to professionals, took to get psyched up to play the game. The campaign, which was limited to a series of television spots, focused on the unique superstitions of each athlete and how they worked through them before each game. No specific budget was available for the campaign, themed "Keep Playing," but according to information published in *Adweek,* Coca-Cola's marketing budget for PowerAde through November 2000 was $31.2 million.

In April a television spot titled "Bus Ride" aired. It showed a high school basketball team in a school bus on its way to play in a game. A screen graphic read: "Monroe H.S. basketball team 44 minutes before tipoff." The kids rhythmically beat on the backs of the bus seats with their fists, and a voice-over stated: "Whatever you do to get up for the game, stay up." The spot closed with the tagline "Keep Playing."

Subsequent television spots that aired through 2000 featured national and international athletes from a variety of sports. The spots included "Sheldon," "Wrestler," and "Garlic." The "Sheldon" spot depicted Buffalo Bills football player Sheldon Jackson sitting in the team locker room. Dressed only in his underwear and his football shoulder pads, Sheldon was shown painting his fingernails purple, a pregame routine that he had begun while playing college ball to help him focus on the upcoming competition. In "Wrestler" South African amateur wrestler Steven Van Eden was depicted standing in front of a mirror beating on himself before a match. Part of his ritual included tossing a threatening sneer at the mirror. The spot "Garlic" showed Flavio Davino, one of Argentina's top professional soccer players, rubbing garlic all over his body and inside his shin guards. This was a pregame ritual that Davino believed would ward off evil spirits. Another spot featured U.S. Olympic track star Maurice Green writing his goal race time on a piece of paper and putting it inside his running shoe. A spot that did not air on American television featured a Korean basketball team, not pounding on the backs of bus seats like the U.S. high school basketball team but chanting in front of an alter. Like the initial television spot, "Bus Ride," each commercial included the screen graphic "Whatever you do to get up for the game, stay up." Background music was by the 1960s garage-rock band the Monks.

OUTCOME

Adweek advertising critic Barbara Lippert described as "amusing" the PowerAde television spots showing athletes preparing to play by working through their various pregame superstitions. In 2000 the television spot "Bus Ride," which showed a bus full of high school basketball players on the way to a game, was named a Creative Best Spot by *Adweek.* At the end of 2000, however, despite the advertising effort by McCann-Erickson, PowerAde was still a struggling brand. In 2001 Coca-Cola introduced a new marketing campaign with the tagline "Very real power," created by Portland, Oregon–based agency Wieden+Kennedy. Serving as celebrity spokesman in the television spots was the Atlanta Falcons football team's quarterback Michael Vick.

FURTHER READING

"The Allure of Gatorade." *CNN/Money,* November 21, 2000.

"Creative: Best Spots of April." *Adweek,* May 22, 2000.

DeMasters, Karen. "Be Aggressive!" *Supermarket News,* February 21, 2000.

"Good Sports: Coke, Pepsi, Monarch and Quaker Sports Drinks Purchases." *Prepared Foods,* June 1, 2001.

Leith, Scott. "New Powerade Game Plan Afoot; Michael Vick Ads Part of Promotion." *Atlanta Journal-Constitution,* August 14, 2001.

Lippert, Barbara. "Powerade: Power Plays." *Adweek,* July 31, 2000.

"Marketing: Sports Drinks: Gotta Get That Gator." *BusinessWeek,* November 27, 2000.

Nellen, Christopher. "Enhancing Athletic Performance with Sports Drinks." *Health Products Business,* August 1, 2000.

"Pepsico-Quaker Oats Deal Changes Competitive Landscape for Coca-Cola." *Knight Ridder/Tribune Business News,* December 4, 2000.

Petrecca, Laura. "Coke Boosts ESPN/ABC Presence in $20 Mil Deal." *Advertising Age,* March 27, 2000.

Theodore, Sarah. "Sports Drinks Leave Room for Many Players." *Beverage Industry,* June 1, 2000.

Unger, Henry, and Scott Leith. "Coke Might Be Looking to Join Gatorade Dance." *Atlanta Journal-Constitution,* November 4, 2000.

Rayna Bailey

OBEY YOUR THIRST CAMPAIGN (1998)

OVERVIEW

First marketed in 1961 by the Coca-Cola Company, the lemon-lime soft drink Sprite was in the late 1990s one of the fastest growing carbonated soft drinks in the United States and around the world. As of mid-1998 Sprite was the number-three soft drink in the world and the number-five soft drink brand in the United States. From 1994 to 1998 the brand experienced global double-digit growth. This period of dramatic expansion coincided with the launch of the brand's ad campaign "Obey Your Thirst."

Introduced in 1994, the "Obey Your Thirst" campaign—created by Lowe & Partners/SMS of New York—established Sprite's distinct brand personality through humorous, tongue-in-cheek spots that reinforced the "trust your instincts" concept. The campaign aimed to speak directly to the drink's target market, teenagers, rather than talking down to them.

From its inception "Obey Your Thirst" relied on the power of a 1990s trend toward "anti-advertising." The commercials in this campaign parodied those for other products that used hype and image-building to appeal to consumers. "Consumers are jaded by advertising," declared Lee Garfinkel, cochairman and chief creative officer at Lowe & Partners/SMS. "In order to reach certain people, advertising that doesn't take advertising too seriously is appreciated by the consumer."

The "certain people" that Garfinkel had in mind were mostly teenagers, particularly inner city teenagers. To go along with its ads, Sprite marketers designed an aggressive marketing campaign to appeal to this demographic. Co-promotions with the National Basketball Association (NBA), including appearances by some of its emerging stars in Sprite commercials, helped erect an image for Sprite as the brand of hip, sometimes cynical young people everywhere.

HISTORICAL CONTEXT

Sprite started out in a niche category—lemon-lime soft drinks—but by the mid-1990s had clearly broken away and transcended into a mainstream brand. In 1994 Sprite passed the one-billion unit case mark worldwide—a significant milestone in terms of the size of the brand. An aggressive marketing strategy aimed at urban youth has been credited with Sprite's explosive growth. Since 1994 Sprite has been the official soft drink of the NBA, a growing worldwide sports property that has been particularly popular with youth. Adding to Sprite's appeal, its packaging was distinctive and attention getting; graphics introduced in 1994 added a crisp blue color to Sprite's traditional green.

In 1994 Sprite retired its upbeat ad campaign "I Like the Sprite in You" for an edgier approach designed to appeal to Generation X. The new tag line, in its full iteration, read: "Image is nothing. Thirst is everything. Obey your thirst." Among the first commercials in the campaign, targeted at teens and young adults, was one featuring basketball star Grant Hill in a parody of pretentious fashion commercials. Oddball humor, the use of basketball endorsers, and the appeal to youth culture were to remain staples of the "Obey Your Thirst" campaign.

By 1996 Coca-Cola USA was spending $55.7 million to advertise Sprite in the United States alone. The brand's innovative spots helped Sprite move $1.2 billion cases worldwide that year, and the beverage zoomed to the number-four position among U.S. soft drinks. Still, the parent company looked to increase its ad budget for 1997. "The more the brand grows, the more we spend," declared Sergio Zyman, Coca-Cola's chief marketing officer, in the pages of the *Atlanta Journal-Constitution.* In a bid to spur even further growth, Coca-Cola ordered a tune-up of the Sprite advertising strategy. In April 1997 the company unveiled five new Sprite commercials under the "Obey Your Thirst" rubric. The new spots, created in partnership with Lowe & Partners/SMS, were said to mark a creative new direction for the brand.

MARKETING TO "GEN X" HAS ITS DOWNSIDE

Sprite has reaped much success from its "Obey Your Thirst" commercials playing to the cynical attitudes of 1990s youth. The ads gained their satirical punch from the debunking of other ads that relied on hype and image building. This approach was said to appeal to jaded Generation X consumers raised in an age of media manipulation. But playing to the apathy of the public has not always been successful. In fact, as Coca-Cola USA discovered when it tried to market the first Generation X soft drink, it can backfire spectacularly.

The concoction was called OK Soda and was the brainchild of Coca-Cola USA marketing chief Sergio Zyman (who would later develop the New Age beverage Fruitopia). Introduced in selected cities in mid-1994, OK Soda brandished matte-gray cans featuring downbeat drawings by underground comic book artists. The emblazoned slogans were equally doleful. "What's the point of OK soda?" read one representative caption. "Well what's the point of anything?"

Advertising for the seemingly depressing drink was created by the prominent Portland ad house of Wieden & Kennedy. A 1-800-I-FEEL-OK hotline was offered, where callers could record comments, listen to the cynical (and agency-crafted) ramblings of others, and take a Generation X "personality test." OK Soda's advertising message failed to overcome its reputed deficiencies of taste. The nine-city campaign failed, and the product was quietly withdrawn from circulation.

TARGET MARKET

By sharpening the focus and defining Sprite's personality—energetic, edgy, and straightforward—Sprite's marketers made the brand more relevant to its target audience. The goal of Sprite advertising in the 1990s seemed simple—to convey that Sprite was a thirst-quenching drink with an attitude that connected with teenagers. This approach proved to be very appealing to young people who did not want to be "marketed to" in the traditional sense. Sprite's commercials humorously poke fun at hard-sell tactics while focusing on one basic premise: Sprite may not make consumers more popular, more beautiful, or even NBA superstars, but it will quench their thirst.

Sprite's marketers designed this message to be pertinent around the world. The brand's "edge" and unpretentious attitude were crafted to speak to youth in all different cultures. According to official company press materials, "Teens around the world share the desire to be able to express themselves and make their own choices. Sprite aims to encourage and represent this attitude."

COMPETITION

Once considered a "niche" product, Sprite in the 1990s was no longer viewed as competing in the lemon-lime category but rather as competing against other mainstream soft drinks. In fact, Sprite sales surpassed those of its principal lemon-lime competitor, 7-Up, in 1993. But there still was one niche market that Sprite advertisers continued to try to capture: young people. With "Obey Your Thirst," Coca-Cola USA aimed Sprite ads at specific age groups. At the same time, rival soda maker PepsiCo Inc. was turning away from this practice. It believed that trying to execute a niche strategy in the soft drink industry carried too many risks because companies invariably fail to reach any customers outside the target audience.

In 1996 the Sprite brand concluded one of its most spectacular years of market performance. Sales surged an impressive 17.6 percent, displacing venerable Diet Pepsi along with Mountain Dew and Dr. Pepper to become America's fourth-ranked soft drink. 7-Up, in eighth place, dropped 0.2 percent in volume. "Sprite has been highly successful . . . much of it at the expense of 7-Up," observed Paine Webber analyst Emanuel Goldman in the *Atlanta Journal-Constitution.* Sprite's strong performance, together with the robust sales of Coke and Diet Coke, gave Coca-Cola USA three of the four top soft drink brands for the first time since 1985.

In response to the challenge from Sprite, Dr. Pepper/Seven Up Inc. in 1997 announced plans to reformulate 7-Up, making it less sweet and giving it a crisper taste. Industry analysts expected the reformulation to make 7-Up taste more like Sprite. The company also planned to introduce new graphics for 7-Up packages as well as a new advertising campaign.

MARKETING STRATEGY

In addition to relating a straightforward message that Sprite was a light, crisp, and refreshing beverage, Sprite marketers wanted to convey that Sprite was not pretentious. Since the introduction of the "Obey Your Thirst" campaign in 1994, the Sprite brand spoke to legitimacy and integrity, encouraging consumers to trust their instincts and, in a sense, saying to teenagers, "Exercise your own judgment." The earliest "Obey Your Thirst" commercials parodied the pomposity and pretense of commercials for other products. Specifically in Sprite's crosshairs were spots for Canon cameras featuring tennis star Andre Agassi, in which the tennis star declares, "Image is everything." A series of humorous Sprite spots inverted this concept and those of similar commercials.

Coca-Cola USA's 1997 advertising strategy for Sprite retained the "Obey Your Thirst" tag line and the irreverent, icon-bashing tone of previous spots for the brand. The newer spots continued to poke fun at other company's ads. But they also took on an edgier tone, as Coca-Cola USA sought to meet its goal of capturing 50 percent of domestic market share by the turn of the century.

There were five new spots in all, all created by Lowe & Partners/SMS. Perhaps the most daring—and the most critically well-received—was a commercial that parodied Coca-Cola's own commercials from the 1980s by providing information on Jooky, a mythical newfangled soft drink. A group of youthful party goers are shown living it up with their Jookies on the beach when the camera pans back to show two slack-jawed gawkers watching the "commercial" on television. When they pop the tops on their own Jookies, however, no party breaks out. "Oh, man," says one. "Mine's busted." The voice-over then instructs: "Trust your taste buds, not commercials."

The other spots in the campaign were similar in tone. One poked fun at product demonstrations. Another took aim at the venerable Budweiser frogs, showing a bear eating out of a tin can while a frog snacked on a slimy worm. In another, perennial "Obey Your Thirst" pitchman Grant Hill fends off offers from an agent to do television shows, books, and record albums. The spot was seen as an oblique parody of Pepsi commercials featuring basketball star Shaquille O'Neal. A third commercial told visitors to Hollywood to bring along their own Sprite because "a place this concerned with image just doesn't have any." This was a clear spoof of the popular Visa credit card commercials that urge viewers to "bring along your gold card" to various hot spots.

Accompanying the new ads was a packaging overhaul. The Sprite "dimple bottle" was designed to differentiate the brand from other beverage choices, particularly in the important single-serve segment. The proprietary plastic packaging, featuring vertical rows of "bubbles" indented on the bottle wall, was reminiscent of Sprite's familiar green glass bottles and was designed to reflect the brand's "cool, refreshing" personality. Sprite launched the new packaging in grocery and convenience stores with a flier announcing, "We're smiling so wide our dimples are showing."

Building a brand relevant to consumers sometimes involved more than traditional advertising tactics. Sprite endeavored to reflect its distinct, straightforward personality through a complete marketing mix in a way that was relevant to teenagers. Accordingly, a series of cross-promotions with youth-oriented enterprises was launched. Three popular NBA players—Kobe Bryant of the Los Angeles Lakers, Juwan Howard of the Washington Wizards, and number-one draft pick Tim Duncan of the San Antonio Spurs—all agreed to give away their team jerseys and basketball shoes to 150 winners of the Sprite "Own 'Em" contest. In addition, six grand prize winners got to drive away in a sport utility vehicle that had actually been driven by the players. Consumers could win instantly by looking under the cap of 20-ounce and one-liter bottles of Sprite or by checking the inside packs of Sprite 12-pack and 24-pack can wraps to reveal prizes. Launched in November 1997 to coincide with the start of the NBA season, the promotion ran through the end of March 1998.

Keeping with its basketball theme, Sprite marketers also launched the Sprite Playground at NBA Jam Session, an interactive attraction offering a wide variety of basketball activities for fans to test their skills, play out-of-the-ordinary games, and win prizes. The activities area, which traveled to various state fairs around the United States during the summer of 1997—was surrounded by NBA photos and life-size player images. The strong connection between Sprite and professional basketball was explained by Pina Sciarra, Sprite brand manager for Coca-Cola USA, in a company press release: "Sprite is the only soft drink that embodies the lifestyle and attitude of NBA players."

Other national "Obey Your Thirst" promotions also sought to appeal to urban youth. An under-the-cap promotion teamed Sprite with apparel manufacturers Fishpaw Industries and Shabazz Brothers Urbanwear, both of whose clothing lines appealed to inner-city youths as well as markets outside the urban boundaries. In this promotion consumers had a one in six chance of winning free products, or they could win apparel from Fishpaw and Shabazz by simply twisting off the cap and reading the message imprinted under the top of 16-ounce, 20-ounce, and one-liter bottles of Sprite. The Sprite "Under the Cap 'Obey Your Thirst' Promotion" began March 1, 1997, and ran through September 30, 1997.

In a promotion aimed more specifically at the African-American community, Coca-Cola USA signed on as a major advertiser and exclusive soft drink sponsor of the annual *Soul Train Music Awards* show on March 7, 1997, in Los Angeles's Shrine Auditorium. *Soul Train* was a popular, nationally syndicated television dance and music show founded by Don Cornelius. A "Sprite Nite" celebrity party was held on the eve of the *Soul Train*

Music Awards show and was televised live on Black Entertainment Television (BET). In addition to performances by rhythm-and-blues and hip-hop artists, the Sprite Image Breaker of the Year Award was presented. Coca-Cola USA aired commercials for Sprite and Coca-Cola Classic during the awards program.

OUTCOME

Measured in sales impact, "Obey Your Thirst" was a successful campaign. The "Obey Your Thirst" message helped Sprite secure 5.8 percent of the national soft drink market in 1996, up from 5.1 percent the previous year. In 1997 Sprite's global volume jumped by 13 percent while domestic volume increased 10 percent. Beverage industry analysts were impressed with Sprite's ability to create sustained growth in a competitive sector. "Coke's marketing of Sprite has been laser-like in its focus and very successful," John Sicher, the editor of *Beverage Digest*, told a writer for *Newsday*.

Some advertising critics, however, found the strategy behind the ads too cynical. "If image is nothing and taste is everything," asked Bob Garfield in *Advertising Age* magazine, "why is not one of the ads about taste? Why are none of the ads about anything intrinsic to Sprite? Why does the famous athlete send up use Grant Hill, a famous athlete?" The answer, according to Garfield, was because "as far as this advertising is concerned, image is not nothing. Image is everything."

FURTHER READING

Edwards, Jim. "Notes from Underground (Anti-Advertising Becoming Mainstream)." *Adweek,* August 18, 1997, p. 23.

Garfield, Bob. "Sprite Raps 'Image' While Embracing It." *Advertising Age,* April 21, 1997, p. 63.

Roush, Chris. "Sprite Ads Poke Fun at the Icons." *Atlanta Journal-Constitution,* April 15, 1997, p. B2.

———. "Sprite Moves Up in Rankings." *Atlanta Journal-Constitution,* February 5, 1997, p. C1.

Robert Schnakenberg

OBEY YOUR THIRST CAMPAIGN (2004)

OVERVIEW

In late 2003 the Coca-Cola Company's lemon-lime soft-drink brand, Sprite, reigned as America's fifth-best-selling soft drink and the highest-grossing lemon-lime soda in America. Even though Sprite appeared to be the clear leader over all lemon-lime soft drink brands, its market share was rapidly slipping to Sierra Mist, a lemon-lime soft drink sold by the Pepsi-Cola Company. Reusing its long-running tagline that was conceived by the ad agency Lowe & Partners in 1994, Sprite released a new variation of the "Obey Your Thirst" campaign to keep its product relevant to its 16- to 24-year-old target demographic.

The WPP Group's advertising agency Ogilvy & Mather released three television spots in February 2004 that introduced Sprite's new mascot, Miles Thirst, a 10-inch-tall puppet. Hoping to attract the youth of the hip-hop and basketball cultures, Miles Thirst's wardrobe consisted of flashy hip-hop garb. The wisecracking puppet proclaimed his love for Sprite in two television spots. In a third commercial, titled "LeBron," LeBron James, the National Basketball Association (NBA) all-star, gave Miles Thirst a tour of his decadent home. The puppet appeared unimpressed until James led him into his kitchen, which was equipped with a Sprite vending machine. The campaign's 2004 budget was estimated at $45 million. Besides the television spots, media included online advertisement, a Miles Thirst website, and the passing out of free posters, magnets, stickers, and T-shirts featuring Miles Thirst. The campaign and tagline ended in 2005 after Sprite dropped Ogilvy & Mather for the Miami-based advertising agency Crispin Porter + Bogusky.

Overall success for the 2004 campaign was mild. Besides collecting a Bronze One Show Award in the category of Promotional and Point of Purchase Posters in 2004, the campaign was also appreciated by a majority of its target market. "Obey Your Thirst" commercials were "liked a lot" by 18 to 24 year olds, according to the weekly consumer poll Ad Track, conducted by *USA Today.* Unfortunately for Sprite, sales fell 3 percent in 2004, and its overall 5.7 percent share of the soft-drink industry was dwindling.

HISTORICAL CONTEXT

After Lowe & Partners created the "Obey Your Thirst" campaign in 1994, Sprite enjoyed strong market growth into the late 1990s. It was the fastest-growing Coca-Cola brand in 1997 and sold 6 percent more cases over the previous year. By 2001, however, sales had begun to wane, and Coca-Cola executives feared that Sprite and other Coca-Cola brands were falling out of style with the younger crowd. Hoping a different ad agency would reenergize its lemon-lime brand, Coca-Cola awarded its Sprite advertising account to Ogilvy & Mather in 2001. To bolster Sprite's image Coca-Cola also paid NBA superstar Kobe Bryant to endorse the lemon-lime soft drink. Bryant was featured in commercials that used the tagline "Obey your thirst," along with an additional tagline, "What's your thirst?" Tom Pirko, president of the beverage-industry consulting firm Bevmark, told

Advertising Age, "Coke has been attacked as being dowdy and ultra-conservative, so they want to stay relevant." Sprite stopped airing commercials featuring Bryant in 2003 after a 19-year-old Colorado woman accused him of rape.

The 2003 television spot "Rikkia" was the first Sprite advertisement released by Ogilvy & Mather. It featured the race-car star Rikkia Miller speeding around the racetrack to music by the rock group the Donnas. Miller also provided a voice-over for "Rikkia" in which she explained her love for racing. Just before drinking a Sprite at the spot's conclusion, Miller looked into the camera and asked, "What's my thirst?"

Sprite's sales jumped 12 percent in the second quarter of 2003 after the brand released its new flavor Sprite Remix, a lemon-lime soda with a twist of tropical fruit "Sprite is a great brand, but it has been in decline for several years. It badly needs a shot in the arm," John Sicher, editor and publisher of *Beverage Digest,* an industry publication, told the *Dow Jones News Service.* "Remix will help, but additional aggressive steps are also necessary." That same year Sprite negotiated a $2 million-per-year endorsement contract with basketball all-star LeBron James. Hoping to regain relevance within its target market, Sprite in February 2004 released a version of "Obey Your Thirst" that featured James along with Sprite's new mascot, a puppet named Miles Thirst.

LEBRON JAMES

Born on December 30, 1984, LeBron James was the youngest NBA basketball player to receive the Rookie of the Year award (2003–2004). The six-foot-eight-inch forward, who began endorsing the lemon-lime soft drink Sprite in 2003, was one of only three rookies in NBA history to average 20 points a game.

TARGET MARKET

"Obey Your Thirst" targeted 16 to 24 year olds. According to KPMG Consumer Markets Insider, a company that analyzed different industry trends, teenagers did not respond to advertisements in the same way as adults. Teenagers typically listened to "brand ambassadors," young celebrities or fellow teenagers that established credibility amongst their peers. To endorse the soft drink, Sprite hired NBA star LeBron James, who was only 20 years old during the 2004 leg of "Obey Your Thirst." The new Sprite mascot, Miles Thirst, a 10-inch puppet dressed in hip-hop clothing such as oversized watches, baggy pants, and gold chains, was also featured in Sprite advertisements in 2004 and 2005. "Thirst was the perfect choice for Sprite," John Carroll, group director for Sprite, told the *PR Newswire.* "Not only does Thirst represent everything Sprite stands for, he recognizes and represents the aspects of youth culture that are inherent to Sprite drinkers. Plus, you couldn't ask for a better last name."

Although Miles Thirst was an African-American puppet, the campaign did not solely target an African-American demographic. "Hip-hop is a $1 billion-a-year industry that could not survive on just black people," Shawn Prez, president of the urban-marketing group Power Moves, remarked in *USA Today* about Miles Thirst and his hip-hop appeal. "When you're making this kind of money, [hip-hop] has crossed gender, race and age groups. The white audience for hip-hop is much larger than the black audience at this point." In 2004 white, suburban teenage males spent more money on hip-hop products than any other group, according to *USA Today.*

COMPETITION

Ranking third in soft-drink sales (behind Coca-Cola and PepsiCo, Inc.), Dr Pepper/Seven Up, Inc., struggled to bolster its own flagship lemon-lime brand, Seven Up, in 2004. Young & Rubicam Advertising had handled Seven Up's $25 to $45 million yearly advertising budget since 1995. Initial campaign taglines touted Seven Up as the "uncola," referencing the drink's lack of cola, an ingredient found in Pepsi and Coca-Cola soft drinks. Next, the "Are You an Un?" campaign was launched, but it was quickly discontinued in 1999 after its appeal to 12 to 24 year olds proved ineffective. The sales of Seven Up's 192-ounce cases dropped from 174 million sold in 2002 to 126 million sold in 2003. In 2004 Seven Up advertisements featured the tagline "Make 7Up Yours." The avoidance of using "un" or "cola" was an attempt by Young & Rubicam to make Seven Up appeal to younger consumers unfamiliar with the cola reference.

According to Gary A. Hemphill, senior vice president of the Beverage Marketing Corporation, which offered research and consulting services to the soft-drink industry, the drop in Seven Up sales resulted from the growing success of Sierra Mist, a lemon-lime soft drink sold by Pepsi under the tagline "shockingly refreshing." After the brand was introduced in early 2001, its sales climbed 89.3 percent between 2002 and 2003. The successful new competitor prompted Seven Up and Sprite to rethink their marketing strategies. Sprite created commercials with Miles Thirst. Hoping to regain its slipping market share, Seven Up approached several different advertising agencies outside of Young & Rubicam.

SOFT-DRINK EMPIRE

The Coca-Cola Company was the world's largest producer of soft drinks in 2004. With nearly 400 brands in more than 200 countries, the soft-drink mogul owned the lemon-lime brand Sprite, the citrus drink Squirt, Dasani water, the sport drink Powerade, and even the entire suite of Fanta brands.

MARKETING STRATEGY

In 2003 Sprite signed a $12 million dollar, six-year deal with the NBA Rookie of the Year LeBron James. Ogilvy & Mather also created a mascot for Sprite, Miles Thirst, a wisecracking puppet whose mouth remained closed while speaking. Reno Wilson, an actor who had frequently appeared on the hit television program *The Cosby Show,* provided Miles Thirst's voice. The puppet portion of "Obey Your Thirst" kicked off on February 14, 2004, when three commercial spots, "LeBron," "Two Sprites," and "What's Better Than Sprite?" aired during the NBA All-Star game. In all the spots Miles Thirst was shown in several different wardrobes reflecting hip-hop fashions. Ogilvy & Mather hoped the combination of James's endorsement and a humorous Sprite-loving puppet would compel 16 to 24 year olds to drink Sprite.

In the 30-second spot titled "LeBron," James gave Miles Thirst a tour of his luxurious home. The spot mimicked the MTV program *Cribs,* in which celebrities allowed MTV camera crews to tour their houses. During "LeBron," Miles Thirst appeared disinterested in James's furnishings, which included a king-size waterbed and a plasma television. The puppet became suddenly excited about the tour when he noticed a giant Sprite vending machine in James's kitchen. In the spot "Two Sprites," Miles Thirst explained to curious onlookers why he preferred to have two extra-large Sprites in the cup holders of his movie theater seat. "Never be too far away from the big, thirst-quenching taste of Sprite," the puppet explained The commercial's humor hinged on the beautiful women flanking Thirst at the spot's conclusion. The spot "What's Better than Sprite?" featured Thirst challenging his friends to name one thing better than Sprite. Suddenly two beautiful women passed, prompting Thirst to rephrase the challenge: "Alright! Name two!" Miles Thirst ended each spot by demanding, "Show me my motto." The screen then displayed the tagline "Obey your thirst."

Adweek magazine's Barbara Lippert wrote of the campaign, "The set-up—a sexualized vinyl doll spouting street lingo—could easily devolve into an obvious, annoying, pandering and even racist attempt to get-down-in-the-hood-with-the-bros. Instead, it's quick, funny and real enough." Other critics were not as pleased. The Rainbow/Push Coalition, a discrimination watchdog group founded by the Reverend Jesse Jackson, accused the puppet of propagating negative African-American stereotypes. "We've had some conversations with Coke about Miles. We let them know that we think the character is ill-advised," Janice Mathis, a Rainbow/Push vice president, told *Brandweek.*

The website www.milesthirst.com was created for the campaign. Miles Thirst also appeared on MTV as a guest, and 1,500 Miles Thirst dolls were mailed to "key trend influencers around the country," according to *USA Today.* In May 2004 Ogilvy & Mather released further commercials with Miles Thirst explaining Sprite's "Thirst Out" promotion, in which consumers could win video rentals, digital music downloads, and mobile-phone ring tones.

OUTCOME

Lisa Speakman, senior brand manager for Sprite at Coca-Cola, told *Brandweek* that the 2004 segment of "Obey Your Thirst" was the highest rated in recent Sprite history. "Our internal brand-health scores are increasing on the Sprite brand. This indicates the marketing is having its desired effect over time," she said in April 2004. The campaign also garnered a Bronze One Show Award for Promotional and Point of Purchase Posters in 2004. Despite higher ratings and an advertising-industry award, however, the campaign failed to halt Sprite's drop in sales. The soft-drink's sales dipped 3 percent in 2004, according to *Beverage Digest,* a publication covering the nonalcoholic-beverages industry.

Sprite was not the only lemon-lime soft drink to lose sales in 2004. Seven Up was knocked from the list of top-10 soda brands, a change that many analysts attributed to the rising popularity of Pepsi's Sierra Mist, a lemon-lime drink released in 2001. Sierra Mist sales grew 89.3 percent in 2003 compared with 2002. Sprite's 2005 sales slump prompted Coca-Cola to end Ogilvy & Mather's advertising for its Sprite brand and to discontinue its "Obey your thirst" tagline.

FURTHER READING

Delaney, Kathy. "The Work." *Advertising Age's Creativity,* September 1, 2002, p. 30.

Elliott, Stuart. "A Division of Cadbury Schweppes Solicits Ideas from Smaller Agencies on Ways to Market 7Up." *New York Times,* April 27, 2004, p. 12.

Erickson, Chris. "On the Bubble—Wizards of Fizz Aim New Sodas." *New York Post,* July 27, 2005, p. 44.

Garfield, Bob. "Sprite's Latest Won't Help It Escape Confines of Dorkville." *Advertising Age,* August 5, 2002, p. 41.

Hastings, Michael. "Coca-Cola Test-Marketing a Soda-Energy Drink." *Winston-Salem (NC) Journal,* August 24, 2005, p. 2.

Howard, Theresa. "Coke Creates Hip-Hop Figure to Inject Sprite with Attitude." *USA Today,* April 26, 2004, p. B.12.

Laborde, Errol. "The Cure." *New Orleans Magazine,* August 1, 2005, p. 8.

Lazare, Lewis. "Sprite to Put 'Thirst' out Front." *Chicago Sun-Times,* February 13, 2004, p. 75.

Leith, Scott. "Shine Is off Sprite's Star." *Atlanta Journal-Constitution,* November 29, 2001, p. G1.

Lippert, Barbara. "Sprite's Small Wonder." *Adweek,* February 23, 2004, p. 30.

Martin, Philip. "Spirits: A Pint of Pimm's Cup Is British Refreshment." *Little Rock, Arkansas Democrat Gazette,* October 7, 2005, p. 77.

McKay, Betsy, and Suzanne Vranica. "Coca-Cola Is in Talks to Consolidate Ad Accounts." *Wall Street Journal,* October 1, 2002, p. B12.

Sampey, Kathleen. "Fight for Sprite Will Include Newcomers." *Adweek,* July 21, 2003, p. 6.

Thomaselli, Rich. "Feat over Pepsi: James' Coke Deal Sets New Endorser Standard." *Advertising Age,* August 25, 2003, p. 3.

Kevin Teague

REAL CAMPAIGN

OVERVIEW

Despite being the top soft-drink company in the world, the Coca-Cola Company showed signs of struggle in the 1990s, when consumers worldwide started demonstrating a strong preference for healthier beverages. Coca-Cola's subsequent marketing efforts, including the 2003 "Real" campaign, reflected this change.

The multimillion-dollar "Real" campaign, which used a combination of music and celebrity presence to promote Coke Classic, was reminiscent of Coca-Cola ads from the 1960s to the '90s. The "Real" campaign's message itself, that Coke is the "Real" thing, was a reminder of the company's long heritage. The campaign's numerous television and radio spots, as well as print ads, were targeted toward a teen and young-adult market, just as Coke advertising had long been. It was with these consumers in mind that the company signed on such actors as Penelope Cruz and Courtney Cox Arquette, as well as musicians Common and Mya, to promote the product.

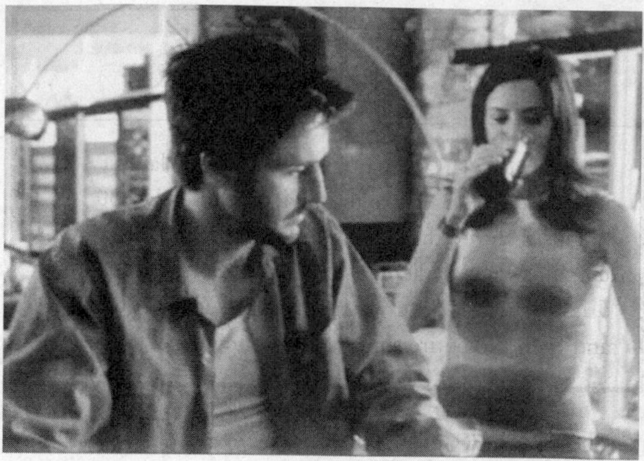

Courtney Cox Arquette and David Arquette in a still from Coca Cola's "Real" campaign. IMAGE COURTESY OF THE ADVERTISING ARCHIVE LTD. REPRODUCED BY PERMISSION.

The campaign was attention grabbing, catching the eyes and ears of its target audience. Most consumers who were polled claimed to like the ads "a lot." The press seemed equally entertained by the campaign, raving about its advertising success, especially compared with the past three botched advertising attempts that Coke had recently endured. In fact, many ad critics thought the "Real" campaign marked the first Coke advertising success in a decade. The success, however, was not a financial one. Despite the campaign's popularity, sales of Coke products, especially Coke Classic, continued to dwindle. Coke Classic in 2003 experienced a disheartening 3 percent decrease in sales. "Real" ran until 2005, when it was replaced by "Make It Real," an extension of the previous campaign.

HISTORICAL CONTEXT

In May 1886 Jacobs' Pharmacy in Atlanta sold the first serving of Coca-Cola. Invented by John Pemberton (a Civil War veteran and pharmacist), the soft drink contained syrup, sugar, and carbonation, along with the caffeine-rich kola nut and the drug cocaine. The name Coca-Cola was invented by Pemberton's bookkeeper, Frank Robinson, who also wrote the distinct script that has been sprawled on all Coca-Cola products to date. The beverage was not an instant success. In its first year at Jacobs' Pharmacy, approximately nine servings were sold each day. Pemberton ended up with a $20 loss overall. But success, though not immediate, was right around the corner.

By the late 1890s Coca-Cola had become one of America's most popular fountain drinks. And soon thereafter it was being sold all across the United States and Canada. Advertising played a key role in Coca-Cola's early success, and for some time to come advertising would continue to contribute to its success. Its 1930s Santa advertising helped to create the modern image of Saint Nick, as well as an increased personal connection between consumers and Coke. In 1971 (while war persisted in Vietnam) a similar result was found with a television commercial showing young people gathered on a hilltop in Italy, singing, "I'd like to buy the world a Coke." More than two decades later the "Always Coca-Cola" campaign, which introduced the very popular Coke-drinking polar bears, also ended with positive results. But advertising success would not come so easily in the future.

"Always Coca-Cola" continued through 2000, when it was replaced by "Coca-Cola. Enjoy." Neither campaign met with success. In 2001 Coca-Cola launched "Life Tastes Good," but the campaign was pulled in the wake of the terrorist attacks of September 11, 2001. Largely because of consumers' increasing preference for healthier beverages, sales of Coca-Cola were steadily declining. But perhaps consumers simply missed the polar bears and the entertaining campaign that featured them. With the thought that consumers might be won over by another successful advertising campaign, Coca-Cola threw millions into its 2003 "Real" advertising campaign.

TARGET MARKET

Since the 1990s Coke Classic had experienced a decrease in market share and volume in the beverage industry, especially among its younger consumers. Largely as a result of a nationwide focus on obesity and other health issues, which resulted in healthier eating habits (especially among the young), tastes for beverages changed. According to *Beverage Digest,* during each year between 1996 and 2000, Coke Classic's sales either fell flat or reflected a decline. In 2000 there was a 0.1 percent increase. Younger people simply drank less cola than had earlier generations, preferring instead such beverages as bottled water, juices, and flavored sodas.

Coke's 2003 "Real" campaign targeted the younger generation the company felt it was losing. While many longtime consumers had remained loyal to Coke, most of these represented an aging population. Young adults, in contrast, had the potential to be targeted for years to come. Because of this Coke's "Real" campaign had a celebrity-heavy focus. Such big names as Cruz and Cox Arquette starred in new Coke commercials. The campaign premiered its first advertisement (the television commercial "Real Compared to What") during the 2003 American Music Awards, an event that typically drew a young audience.

NINETEENTH-CENTURY BIG-BUDGET ADVERTISING

In 1892, six years after Coca-Cola was first sold (for five cents a glass, in Atlanta's Jacobs' Pharmacy), the company had an advertising budget of $11,401 (accounting for inflation this would represent $234,006.49 in 2005). A budget of this size was highly unusual for the time. The advertising agenda included hiring salesmen to travel across the country to sell Coca-Cola to various businesses. To convince business owners to order the soda, the company often offered free merchandise (for instance, prescription scales and decorative clocks) that displayed the Coca-Cola logo. Another strategy involved the distribution of coupons, which allowed proprietors to try Coca-Cola for free. Lastly Coca-Cola began placing its name everywhere: on newspapers, outdoor posters, wall and barn signs, streetcar cards, and many other places. The combination of these efforts proved quite successful, and before long Coca-Cola had become a household name.

COMPETITION

The Coca-Cola Company's three main competitors were PepsiCo, Cadbury Schweppes, and Nestlé. Presenting the most challenging competition for Coca-Cola was PepsiCo, which had also long ago branched out beyond cola. Coke had extended its reach far into the "other beverages" market with Fanta, Sprite, Barq's, Minute Maid, and Dasani water, among others, to a tune of some 400 drink brands in all, including coffees, juices, sports drinks, waters, and teas. PepsiCo had similarly expanded its "other beverages" market, having acquired, for example, Tropicana orange juice and Aquafina water (the top seller of bottled water in the United States). But PepsiCo also had gone beyond beverages by adding a number of nonbeverage food products, including Frito-Lay (the world's number one distributor of corn chips and potato chips) and Rold Gold Pretzels.

Although Cadbury Schweppes and Nestlé might have seemed the less-obvious competitors of Coke products, they each succeeded in taking market share from the world's leading soft-drink company. Largely associated with its chocolates, British-owned Cadbury, after merging with Schweppes in 1969, became a top competitor in the beverage business. With a long list of beverages offered (including 7 UP, A&W Root Beer, Canada

Dry, Dr Pepper, and Hawaiian Punch), Cadbury Schweppes managed to place itself third among the world's top soft-drink providers. Nestlé, the top-selling food company in the world, became the world leader in coffee sales and one of the world's largest makers of bottled water.

Although Coca-Cola was the world's leading soft-drink distributor (with a 44 percent market share in 2003, a clear lead over second-place PepsiCo, at 31.8 percent), some of its competitors brought in significantly larger overall sales. In 2004, for instance, Nestlé's total sales exceeded $76 billion and PepsiCo's was in the neighborhood of $29 billion, while Coca-Cola's was less than $22 billion. (Cadbury Schweppes trailed the pack at approximately $13 billion.)

MARKETING STRATEGY

Coca-Cola wanted to remind consumers of its past, its authenticity, its "realness" in its 2003 "Real" campaign. Created by ad agency Berlin Cameron/Red Cell in New York, the new slogan played off Coca-Cola slogans of the past: "It's the real thing" and "Can't beat the real thing." (Initially the job of coming up with a new campaign was assigned to both Berlin and McCann-Erikson Worldwide Advertising in New York. With its "Real" idea Berlin took over the new campaign.)

Coca-Cola believed the "Real" campaign could return the company to a level of success that at least equaled what it had experienced during its "Always Coca-Cola" campaign years of 1996–98. (During that period the Coca-Cola Company had enjoyed an average 5 percent increase in volume change per year.) To achieve this goal Coke and Berlin relied heavily on a musical and celebrity presence. The campaign debuted with a 90-second "Real Compared to What" television commercial during the 2003 American Music Awards. In the commercial R&B singer Mya and hip-hop artist Common performed a remake of the 1960s jazz hit "Compared to What." The commercial's debut followed the duo's presentation of the Coca-Cola New Music Award to the top unsigned artist or band.

In another television commercial, "Penelope," Cruz walked into a restaurant, guzzled a Coke Classic, burped, and giggled. "The Arquettes" was filmed on a set that copied the real home of Cox Arquette and husband David Arquette. A motive of the commercials was to reveal celebrities during "real" moments in which they enjoyed a "real" soft drink. In all more than a dozen television spots were filmed for the campaign. They featured a variety of celebrities, including late-night talk-show host Craig Kilborn, cyclist Lance Armstrong, and members of Coke's NASCAR racing team.

The campaign also included a major tie-in with the 2003 NCAA basketball tournament and a summer promotion that awarded families trips to theme parks. And in addition to its television presence, "Real" advertising was found in print, online, and on the radio waves. As to the latter Coke went all out, introducing "Coke FM," in which 60-second spots featured well-known musicians. In all mediums the advertising efforts represented an attempt by Coca-Cola to return to the values of past campaigns. Coke wished to reveal its "real" values. As one consulting firm adviser pointed out, the "Real" campaign was something that easily could have been done in any decade since the 1960s. The question was, would consumers go for it?

OUTCOME

Consumers were positive in their ratings of the "Real" advertisements. For instance, shortly after the campaign debuted a Harris study revealed that 25 percent of respondents claimed to "like the ads a lot," while only 8 percent claimed to "dislike the ads." Of those who liked the ads "a lot," the largest presence was among 25- to 29-year-olds, followed by 18- to 24-year-olds. Thus Coke's target market had indeed been reached. Financially, though, the campaign did not measure so successfully. Coca-Cola finished 2003 with a small decline in volume, down 0.2 percent from 2002. The results for Coke Classic were far less desirable: a 3 percent decrease from 2002.

Regardless of the popularity of the "Real" campaign, which generated a multitude of positive press, there was not much hope to promote Coke Classic in a marketplace that was squeezing out sugary colas. Contrary to the campaign's message, consumers, who had been seeking healthier, lighter drinks, might actually have preferred the "unreal" thing. This could later be demonstrated by the notable success of Diet Coke with Lime (2004) and the introduction of other varieties of Diet Coke by 2005, including calorie-free Coca-Cola Zero (designed to taste more like Coke Classic than like Diet Coke).

Even as the "Real" campaign did not send consumers in droves to purchase Coke Classic, Coca-Cola hoped the campaign's popularity would have lasting effects, prompting consumers to purchase the Coca-Cola brand product that better suited their tastes. To launch the new, healthier version of the classic, the 2005 Coca-Cola Zero campaign ("Everybody Chill") took an approach similar to that of the "Real" campaign by reviving the 1971 "I'd Like to Buy the World a Coke" television spot. Thus "Everybody Chill" repeated the trend of looking to the past in the quest to find future customers.

FURTHER READING

Aitken, Lucy. "Analysis—Coca-Cola Review Speculation Grows after Changes at the Top." *Campaign,* July 30, 2004.

Bhatnagar, Parija. "Coke, Pepsi Losing the Fizz." *CNN Money,* March 8, 2005.

"The Coca-Cola Company Announces Launch of Coca-Cola C2: The Great Taste of Coca-Cola with Half the Sugar, Carbohydrates and Calories." *Financial News,* April 19, 2004.

"Coca-Cola to Launch New No-Calorie Drink." *Financial News,* March 21, 2005.

Day, Sherri, and Stuart Elliot. "The Media Business: Advertising—Coca-Cola Goes Back to Its" Real" Past in an Effort to Find Some New Fizz for Its Classic Brand." *New York Times,* January 10, 2003, p. C4.

Dobhal, Shailesh, Abir Pal, Amanpreet Singh, et al. "The Real Thing." *Business Today,* May 23, 2004.

Hays, Constance L. *The Real Thing: Truth and Power at the Coca-Cola Company.* New York: Random House, 2004.

Howard, Theresa. "Things Go Better for New Ad Campaign." *USA Today,* March 16, 2003.

"Iconic Ads: A Case of History Repeating." *Marketing Week,* June 23, 2005.

Leith, Scott. "Coca-Cola Zero Latest in Entry in Diet Derby." *Atlanta Journal-Constitution,* March 22, 2005.

Liu, Betty. "Palumbo Faces Fight to Put Fizz Back into Coca-Cola: The World's Most Valuable Brand Has Become One of the Hardest to Sell." *Financial Times* (London), July 7, 2003.

Pendergrast, Mark. *For God, Country and Coca-Cola: The Definitive History of the Great American Soft Drink and the Company That Makes It,* 2nd ed., revised and expanded. New York: Basic Books, 2000.

"Race Tightens in Carbonated Soft Drinks." *Business and Industry MMR,* June 28, 2004.

Watters, Pat. *Coca-Cola: An Illustrated History.* New York: Doubleday, 1978.

Candice Mancini

YOU ARE WHAT YOU DRINK CAMPAIGN

OVERVIEW

The marketing of diet products has been fraught with unique challenges because of their focus on physical appearance. Issues such as cultural ideals of beauty, physical health, gender roles, sexuality, and personal identity all hover implicitly or explicitly around the diet products phenomenon. Such concerns constituted only one minefield for the Coca-Cola Company in its advertising of Diet Coke. Another was the word "diet" itself, associated with self-denial. By the mid-1990s few foods or drinks other than diet sodas still carried the label. New products that had no negative "diet" connotations, such as iced teas and flavored waters, began to take market share. Yet Diet Coke's brand equity was entrenched and powerful. Diet Coke, along with regular Coke, was a flagship product for Coca-Cola. Thus, Coca-Cola needed to maintain and strengthen a positive association based on Diet Coke's already significant market share, as well as to maintain and increase that share.

In 1995 Coca-Cola dropped Diet Coke's longtime tag line "Just for the taste of it" and shifted focus from taste to the less direct, lifestyle-oriented benefits of drinking Diet Coke. The company tapped its agency, Lowe & Partners/SMS of New York, for an ad campaign estimated to cost $40 million and that comprised three television spots demonstrating the positive effects of drinking Diet Coke. Using the tag line "You are what you drink," the campaign opened in May 1997 and aired across the United States as well as in the United Kingdom, Canada, South Africa, and Australia. But the campaign's message and humor were misunderstood, negative feedback was received, and Lowe and Coca-Cola quickly retrenched with new spots. These problems occurred, in large part, because of the difficulty of navigating through the treacherous sea of issues attached to the marketing of products tagged "diet."

HISTORICAL CONTEXT

Diet colas had been on the market over 10 years when Coca-Cola introduced Diet Coke in 1982. In the 1960s and 1970s the R. C. Cola Company pioneered the diet cola product category. PepsiCo introduced Diet Pepsi in the 1970s as well. Diet Coke's launch was one of the most successful ever; it rapidly took the lead in market share for diet colas. Better taste was part of that success, as Diet Coke was the first diet cola to use the artificial sweetener NutraSweet. Hence, its first tag line "Just for the taste of it" promoted this benefit. The tag line was to be used on and off for a decade. By April 1988 Diet Coke held 10.1 percent of the $40 billion soft drink market based on supermarket sales, while Diet Pepsi held 6.9 percent.

The diet soft drink category hit its stride in the 1980s, expanding to 30 percent of the soft drink market. During that decade, diet colas drove the growth of the soft drink market, with consumption growing four to five times faster than for sugared sodas. This coincided with changes occurring among the baby boomers: they were aging, and they began exercising with a vengeance and watching calories. But they did not want to give up flavor. "Having it all," it seemed, included undiminishing beauty and fitness as well as enjoyment of food and drink. The tag "Just for the taste of it" fit this mind-set. The implication that the products' taste was good enough to be appreciated for its own sake neutralized the negative association of the word "diet."

The swift growth of the diet drink category stopped abruptly in the 1990s. Sales stayed relatively flat, while the growth of sugared sodas went up. In 1990 diet colas accounted for 21.3 percent of cola sales; this fell to 18.7 percent by 1996. According to *USA Today,* "both Coca-Cola and Pepsi saw their diet cola shares dip in retail stores two-tenths of a percentage point during the first half of 1997."

Several analysts identified key factors in the sluggish 1990s diet drink sales. John Sicher of *Beverage Digest,* speaking to *USA Today,* mentioned "the strong performances by bottled waters and the fact that many dieters now focus more on fat than calories." In the same article, Michael Bellas of *Beverage Marketing* noted that "health-conscious consumers also have some misgivings about artificial sweeteners and caffeine." Manny Goldman, a Paine Webber analyst speaking on National Public Radio's *Morning Edition* in May 1997, commented that in the 1990s "people were becoming a little more self-indulgent, and they were concerned with satisfying their own basal desires, like things that taste good. They were willing to take on some calories to do that." The baby boomers were actually mellowing out. The fight against the effects of time and gravity was ultimately unwinnable, so they chose to adapt. In the meantime, a new market, Generation X, was emerging, and their very different mind-set had to be addressed if Diet Coke was to maintain or improve market share.

As these forces played out, Senior Vice President of Marketing Sergio Zyman guided the company's marketing style. Often described as brilliant, mercurial, and temperamental, he was dubbed by Cynthia Mitchell of *The Atlanta Journal and Constitution* "one of the architects of contemporary advertising." Zyman became known as the person who launched Diet Coke, a huge and immediate success. This was followed in 1993 by the launch of New Coke, a huge and immediate failure. Acting as fall guy, Zyman left the company.

Zyman's approach to the marketing process was innovative and iconoclastic. For example, he increased Coke's agency network to over two dozen shops. Moreover, he rapidly changed the marketing of Diet Coke, a strategy complicated by the fact that the market for diet soft drinks was itself rapidly changing. "It is unpredictability that has confused diet Coke's message to consumers," concluded Benzera and Parpis of *BrandWeek.*

A summary of the major advertising campaigns of the 1990s illustrates this unpredictability and the resulting fragmentation of brand image. In January 1990 a series of 30-second Diet Coke ads featured celebrities saying goodbye to sugared Pepsi Cola in favor of Diet Coke. The campaign's theme was "The move is on." This was a clear effort to grab soft drink market share: Diet Coke was third overall with 8.9 percent, and Pepsi Cola was second with 18.3 percent. In January 1993 Diet Coke dropped the tag line "Just for the taste of it" and presented two new slogans: "One awesome calorie" and "Taste it all," splitting the message into two different directions. A famous—or infamous—1994 spot created by Lowe & Partners reversed stereotypical gender roles by having office women ogle a shirtless construction worker drinking a Diet Coke on his break.

In 1995 Zyman returned to Coca-Cola and resumed his marketing of Diet Coke. He was "charged with shaking up the company's marketing efforts," noted Mitchell. It is questionable whether the company needed shaking up as much as it needed focus. One relatively conceptual 1995 spot that received critical approval featured a swimming elephant; it was created by the Minneapolis agency Fallon McElligot. Although visually engaging, the spot failed to mesh thematically with other Diet Coke commercials. Another spot produced the same year took a decidedly nonesoteric approach, featuring supermodel Stephanie Seymour dismissing a male admirer at a lunch counter. Diet Coke did grow in 1995 by 3.6 percent, compared with less than 2 percent for other diet soft drinks, but the growth was less than that of Coca-Cola's other soft drinks. And given that the 1995 Diet Coke sales were flat in grocery stores, convenience stores, and gas stations, the miscellany of commercials was not working. Diet Coke's share of the soft drink market dropped three-tenths of a percent from 1991 to 1995.

In 1996 Coke spent $72 million on commercials for Diet Coke. A 1996 campaign from Lowe featured variations on the "Just for the taste of it" jingle, such as "Just for the fun of it." Diet Coke sponsored the Grammy Awards in 1996 and based an early 1997 promotion, "Diet Coke Untapped," on that sponsorship. Then in January 1997 Diet Coke started an $18 million-plus campaign featuring music stars and prizes.

The varied nature of the market required several types of ads. Yet the campaign needed an overarching plan allowing its impact to build over time. This would have required a disciplined strategic partnership between Coca-Cola and the primary agency, Lowe, with consistent direction provided by Coca-Cola as a foundation for the agency's sustained creative activity.

TARGET MARKET

Part of the difficulty of marketing Diet Coke resided in the diversity of its market, each segment of which had it own hot spots and red flags. Because by 1997 the taste

DIET COKE TAG LINES

"Just for the taste of it": 1982–1992, 1995–1997.

"One awesome calorie": 1993.

"Taste it all": 1992.

"This is refreshment": 1994.

"You are what you drink": 1997.

issue was no longer news, Coca-Cola needed to focus on the concerns of Diet Coke drinkers and potential drinkers. The company teamed with Lowe early that year to create three new television spots with the tag line "You are what you drink." The spots were based on the premise that the product helped people to look and feel their best.

Specifically, the effort was targeted at what Coca-Cola identified as three "attitudinal groups," distilled from the diverse Diet Coke market. The "fit and confidents" were the younger and hipper group, 20-something men and women who did not need to diet but feared gaining weight. The "reluctant dieters" were men and women in their 30s who wanted to look good without sacrificing taste. The "aggressive dieters" were women 35 and over who worked hard to stay fit. Coca-Cola intended this effort not only to spur greater usage of Diet Coke among current Diet Coke drinkers but also to bring back some lapsed users and pull in some drinkers of regular Coke as well.

COMPETITION

Although many diet sodas have tried to corner the market over the years, Diet Coke and Diet Pepsi have been locked in a head-to-head battle from the start, with Diet Coke gaining and holding the greater market share but Diet Pepsi always too close for comfort, particularly in terms of brand recognition and popularity among retail consumers. Together, Coca-Cola and Pepsi brands controlled 75 percent of the soft drink business by 1997, with their diet colas alone earning more than $10 billion in sales.

An incident occurring in the 1980s exemplifies the intensity of the Diet Coke-Diet Pepsi competition. Diet Coke at that point held 10.1 percent of the soft drink market and Diet Pepsi 6.9 percent. Pepsi produced a TV ad in which boxer Mike Tyson told reporters that Diet Pepsi "beat the taste of Diet Coke" in consumer taste tests. Tyson had just beaten Leon Spinks in a major match, which Pepsi had exclusively sponsored. Coke challenged the methodology behind the claim, demanded that Pepsi produce its research, and asked the networks to withdraw the ads (which they did not). Pepsi submitted documentation to the networks and challenged Coke's own testing methods. Another component of the $4.4 million campaign was a full-page ad in the *New York Times* showing Tyson holding a can of Diet Pepsi. The ad copy read, "After a couple of pops in the mouth, it was over. Diet Pepsi had won the title. In head-to-head taste tests, Diet Pepsi decisively beat the taste of Diet Coke."

The market share percentages of the two competitors shifted in the mid-1990s even more in Diet Coke's favor. In 1995 Diet Coke was third among all soft drinks in market share, with 8.8 percent, the same as the previous year. Diet Pepsi was fifth, the same place as in 1994, but lost 0.1 percent. By the last quarter of 1996 Diet Pepsi had fallen to seventh place, in spite of a 1.6 percent gain in sales volume. In its previous number four spot was Coca-Cola's soda Sprite. Just $243,000 was spent on advertising Diet Pepsi in 1996, but in early 1997 PepsiCo completely repositioned its strategy with a new $19 million campaign.

MARKETING STRATEGY

In the first half of 1997, Diet Coke kept its number three position in the soft drink lineup, diet sodas overall continued to lose market share, and Diet Pepsi launched its new campaign featuring the slogan "This is diet?" During that time Coca-Cola had performed extensive research and positioning studies that led to the articulation of a new strategy: "Diet Coke helps you look and feel your best." This was based in large part on the fact that, after all was said and done, there was nothing new, such as a better sweetener, on which to construct a more exciting message. Promoting taste alone was no longer an option. Moreover, Diet Pepsi had just launched its taste-oriented "This is diet?" ads. Lowe & Partners/SMS worked with Coca-Cola to produce three TV ads for the campaign, "Aunt Rosalina," "Blizzard," and "Queen." The campaign followed swiftly on the heels of an image revamp for the brand, executed by SBG Partners, San Francisco, which consisted of a silvery new package and new graphics for the drink. It was designed to align the brand with various consumer lifestyles and represented the first genuine strategy for the brand since 1994. Coke executives believed that "the repositioning would re-energize the static diet category," according to *MediaWeek.* The campaign broke on May 19, timed for the start of the summer season, and ran on network and cable.

The "Blizzard" spot showed two men commenting on women walking by who were bundled up against the cold. The women who drank Diet Cokes through their scarves were the ones the men favored. The "Queen" commercial showed a mirror telling a queen that she no longer was fair; rather, a girl drinking Diet Coke was.

"Aunt Rosalina," the most controversial spot in the series, was set in an Italian village. After watching a parade of beautiful, fit women who stroll by proudly holding cans of Diet Coke, a lovely little girl asks her old aunt, "If I drink Diet Coke, will I be beautiful too?" Aunt Rosalina replies, "I never had a Diet Coke, and look at me." The camera moves to reveal her to be an ugly hag. The ad was rotated with "Blizzard" and "Queen" and received far less weight—166 spots out of 844. Approximately 60 percent of the commercials were shown during primetime, 20 percent during the day, and 10 percent during late night.

The tag line for these commercials, "You are what you drink," was meant to be tongue-in-cheek and lighthearted while conveying the message that drinking Diet Coke could help the consumer look and feel good. In "Aunt Rosalina" this message was reinforced by the attractive women who were drinking Diet Coke. Intentionally they were caricatures rather than characters; the viewer was not expected to think she magically would look that way by drinking Diet Coke. In that sense the ad spoofed in a subtle way the goal of ideal physical beauty. Sergio Zyman, quoted in *USA Today,* explained that "this latest wave of advertising is less about well-recognized intrinsic attributes of the brand, such as taste and one-calorie refreshment. It is more about how someone feels and the self-confidence they project when they hold a Diet Coke." Zyman told *The Wall Street Journal Europe* that for Coke to continue to rely on the theme of "taste and one-calorie is kind of beating a dead horse" and that the aim now was to "broaden the definition of Diet Coke. I would like to see people walking around with Diet Coke." Or, as *AdWeek* 's Debrah Goldman put it, the real message of the campaign was "to establish Diet Coke as a fashion accessory,. . . la Evian."

OUTCOME

Consumer and critical reaction to the commercials was fast and harsh, and the airing of "Aunt Rosalina" ended on July 20, 1997, three months after it began. Coca-Cola received letters from customers criticizing its "sexist" approach. A nationwide poll reported in *USA Today* of 271 adults who had seen the Diet Coke commercials showed that 10 percent of all respondents liked the ads a lot, but this fell to only 3 percent for 18-to-24 year olds. Fully 21 percent of respondents disliked the spots. But a significant percentage, 16 percent, said the commercials were very effective, and almost two-thirds considered them somewhat effective, indicating conflict over the message. Responses of critics revealed that the intended playfulness of the commercials missed the mark. The milder commentary critiqued the spots for presumptuousness and lack of subtlety. Goldman of *AdWeek* wrote, "These spots are a classic case of a campaign with its briefs showing. Sure, Coca-Cola wants you to be what you drink, just as other advertisers hope you are what you wear or drive.... But an advertisement's job is to elicit that reaction, not to assume it, or, worse, to pretend that it already exists."

On National Public Radio's *Morning Edition,* Joshua Levs questioned Coca-Cola's Bob Bertini, who presented the rationale behind the commercials. Then Levs zeroed in: " 'You are what you drink'—who wants to be carbonated water, caramel color, aspartame, and potassium benzoate?" That he could even consider such a literal reading of the line—the very week the spot first aired—signaled serious problems with the commercial for Coke. Bob Garfield of *Advertising Age* opened his review of "Aunt Rosalina" with "This just in: Men are pigs." He interpreted the commercial as affirming that the value of women lies in their slenderness and attractiveness to men. He did not see or accept that the spot's humor actually poked fun at this attitude. The "troubling new spots," he wrote, "remind women how important Diet Coke is in their relentless pursuit of svelteness, men's attraction and self-esteem.... In the end, for all their tongue-in-cheek exaggeration, these spots don't lampoon the cult of beauty. They validate it."

The "feel your best" component of the message seemed to have evaporated. The media budget was reduced as a result of this negative response, and creative development was undertaken to rectify the situation. Lowe produced two commercials, "Big Wrestlers," which featured Sumo wrestlers who sincerely compliment each other's appearance despite their tremendous size, and "It's Him," centered on an invisible man who is admired by attractive women in a bar, presumably because of his confidence and demeanor. These new spots, however, were attempts to breathe life into positions consumers had already rejected; "look and feel your best" had died. They received little weight in the last quarter of 1997 and were shelved in early 1998.

Shortly after "Aunt Rosalina" flopped, Wieden & Kennedy of Portland, Oregon, was assigned six 30-second Diet Coke commercials in a last-ditch attempt to get some traction. This spurred media speculation that Wieden would become the new agency for the brand. The spots were not well received. After that Coca-Cola recognized the need to step back and undertake "extensive research... to determine a strategy and long-term direction for the brand." Two earlier spots produced by Lowe were aired then and continued to be aired through the summer of 1998.

In March 1998 Sergio Zyman resigned from Coca-Cola. The man who replaced Zyman, Charles S. Frenette, was Zyman's opposite in terms of personality and operations background. Frenette continued to work with Lowe & Partners. He indicated that he planned to take a longer-term strategic approach to the Coke-Lowe partnership, so critical for the marketing of Diet Coke during times of cultural and demographic upheaval.

FURTHER READING

Benezra, Karen. "Coke Ad Push to Give Diet Direction." *BrandWeek,* May 12, 1997, Part 4, p. 1.

Benezra, Karen and Eleftheria Parpis. "Chasing Sergio." *BrandWeek,* March 30, 1998, p. 30.

"Coke Tries to KO Diet Pepsi Ads Featuring Mike Tyson." *Los Angeles Times,* July 6, 1988, p. 1.

"Cola Wars Lite: Joshua Levs of Member Station WABE in Atlanta Reports Coca-Cola and Pepsi Are Launching New Offensive in the Ongoing Cola Wars." *Morning Edition,* National Public Radio, May 20, 1997.

Enrico, Dottie. "Diet Coke Ads Unpopular but Effective." *USA Today,* September 29, 1997, p. 12B.

Garfield, Bob. "Diet Coke's Approach Quickly Wears Thin." *Advertising Age,* May 19, 1997, p. 85.

Goldman, Debrah. "It's the Bottle, Stupid." *AdWeek,* May 26, 1997, p. 38.

Mitchell, Cynthia. "Coke's New Attitude Ads with Women Ogling a Hunk Weren't Always Coca-Cola, but New Products and Revamped Marketing Signal Big Changes on North Avenue." *Atlanta Journal and Constitution,* April 10, 1994, p. H1.

Cynthia Tokumitsu

Columbia Sportswear Company

14375 NW Science Park Drive
Portland, Oregon 97229-5418
USA
Telephone: (800) 547-8066
Fax: (503) 985-5960
Web site: www.columbia.com

■■■

MOTHER BOYLE CAMPAIGN

OVERVIEW

By 2005 the Portland, Oregon–based Columbia Sportswear Company was the largest seller of skiwear in the United States and an industry leader worldwide. Founded in 1938 by German immigrants Paul and Marie Lamfrom and their daughter Gert, the company grew into a billion-dollar-a-year enterprise by 2003. Much of Columbia's growth was attributed to the 1984 launch of its signature "Mother Boyle" advertising campaign, which placed Gert Boyle, who became the company's CEO in 1970, front and center as the company's spokesperson. The grandmother with the fake "Born to Nag" tattoo proved an instant success as the personification of Columbia Sportswear's no-nonsense durability.

Beginning in 1984 the print ads and television spots created by Columbia's advertising agency, Portland-based Borders Perrin Norrander, cemented the company's reputation for manufacturing coats, hats, and other cold-weather apparel that could stand up to the harshest weather conditions. The implication of the humorous advertising, especially the television spots in which Gert inflicted torture on her real-life son, Tim, the company's president and CEO since 1995, was that Columbia's products, particularly the heavy-duty parkas, were as tough as the "one tough mother" who ran the company. A typical television spot from 2000 featured Gert driving a Zamboni across an ice rink. When she passed over a drinking straw poking through the ice, viewers saw Tim embedded in the ice, using the straw to breathe. Presumably his Columbia parka made the frigid temperature bearable. As Columbia's primary marketing campaign, "Mother Boyle" received the lion's share of the company's advertising budget over the years, which in 2004 alone amounted to $15 million.

The success of the campaign was evident through its longevity. For more than 20 years Gert Boyle played the company's stone-faced matriarch, exposing her son to heinous conditions in the television spots and scolding readers in print ads. When the campaign began in 1984, Columbia Sportswear's annual sales were $13 million; by 1997 that number had reached $358 million. Most importantly the campaign gave the company a recognizable public face. Gert Boyle proved irresistible to reporters, who flocked to profile her, thereby giving the company free publicity in magazines such as *Time* and *Forbes,* a writer from which dubbed her "a Leona Helmsley with humor." In 2005 Boyle capitalized on her popularity by publishing her autobiography, *One Tough Mother: Success in Life, Business, and Apple Pies.*

HISTORICAL CONTEXT

Columbia's marketing strategy relied heavily on Boyle's rags-to-riches life story and her supersized personality.

The tale of a homemaker with three children who was thrust into the business world after her husband suddenly died was as American as apple pie. Having the moxie to stand up to the bankers and lawyers who wanted her to sell the company for pennies and persevering long enough to turn it into a major brand made her a hero in the business world. "Early to bed, early to rise, work like hell and advertise" was her oft-stated motto.

Columbia Sportswear hit its stride in the early 1980s when it introduced the Bugaboo ski jacket, a two-in-one system comprising a detachable liner and an outer shell, both of which could be worn separately. Apart from the product, the timing was right. People were beginning to spend more time outdoors and were also adopting a more casual approach to outerwear than in previous years. The fitness craze made outdoor sports, skiing in particular, more popular than ever before. The Bugaboo jacket became the company's signature product, selling millions of units over the next two decades.

Gert Boyle assumed the helm of the company in 1970 following the unexpected death of her husband, Neal Boyle, who had taken over from Gert's father several years earlier. Lawyers urged her to sell the struggling company, but she refused. For the paltry sum they were willing to pay her, she figured it made more sense for her to run the company into the ground herself.

Growth was slow. For several years Columbia Sportswear subsisted by selling its designs to other companies, such as Eddie Bauer and L.L. Bean. Then, as Tim Boyle explained to *CNN/Money,* the breakthrough came when he realized "that brands are really all you have to sell, and products are just extensions of the brand." With that thought in mind Columbia Sportswear set out to redefine their image.

By 1983 executives from Columbia, along with representatives from Borders Perrin Norrander, decided the company needed to distinguish itself from the competition. "Back in 1983," Gert told a writer for *Inc. Magazine,* "our advertising was about how our products weren't just manufactured, they were engineered. The trouble was, everybody else in our industry was advertising the same way. So our advertising agency asked us, 'What's different about Columbia Sportswear?'" The answer was Gert Boyle. Not everyone, however, was convinced that the self-described "little old lady" could win the brand loyalty of hard-core sportsmen and athletes. They gave it a shot anyhow. The first ad read, "Before it passes Mother Nature, it has to pass Mother Boyle." A campaign was born.

ADVERTISING STRATEGY: BAWDY HUMOR

In 2002 Borders Perrin Norrander, Columbia Sportswear's longtime advertising agency, launched a print ad for the company's Jr. Fire Ridge Parka, a winter coat for children. The ad's copy offered the first of two major guffaws: "You can freeze your sperm. You can freeze your embryos. But last we checked it was still illegal to freeze your children." Mother Boyle piped in at the bottom: "Early signs of hypothermia include poor coordination and confusion. Two things best saved for puberty."

TARGET MARKET

The campaign targeted sports aficionados. Columbia's print ads ran predominantly in sports-themed magazines, such as *Outdoors, Hiking, Backpacker,* and *Sports Illustrated,* and many of its television spots ran on niche cable channels, including ESPN, MTV, and Comedy Central. Though Columbia Sportswear products were readily available at high-end sports retailers, such as REI and Cabela's, they were often also available at many department stores and even in the company's own flagship stores in Portland, Oregon; London, England; and Paris, France. Indeed the "Mother Boyle" campaign proved to have international appeal. Gert Boyle told a reporter for *CNN/Money* that the campaign was well received in Australia. "They have the same sense of humor as we do. You know, they all have mothers."

Apart from targeting those interested in sports, the "Mother Boyle" campaign appealed to people who lived and worked in cold climates and relied on quality outerwear to get them through long, frigid winters. By emphasizing durability over style, the advertising zeroed in on those who valued a reasonably priced product that served its purpose season after season. With casual dress becoming the standard in almost every sector of the population, Columbia's advertising capitalized on the middle-class consumer who was driven more by comfort and price than style.

COMPETITION

In terms of sportswear, Columbia's closest competitors were Timberland and North Face, although it also competed with the apparel divisions of Reebok and Nike. Timberland's print and television advertising, including its catchphrase "Make It Better," focused on the durability of the company's products and featured the same rugged outdoor terrain that could be found in Columbia's advertising. The message was similar to Columbia's "Mother Boyle" ads, minus the humor and

ONE TOUGH MOTHER: THE BOOK

In 2005 Gert Boyle published her autobiography, *One Tough Mother: Success in Life, Business, and Apple Pies.* The book's cover showed Boyle brandishing the "Born to Nag" tattoo featured in early ads for Columbia's "Mother Boyle" campaign.

the indelible image of a no-holds-barred woman running the show.

North Face, a high-performance outerwear manufacturer, offered expensive items that attempted to keep pace with fashion trends, a strategy eschewed by Columbia. Part of Gert Boyle's appeal was her dedication to practicality over style, as evidenced by the fact that the design of Columbia's Bugaboo jacket never changed in more than 17 years of production. North Face, by comparison, focused its advertising around the stars of "extreme" sports, such as Alpine mountain climbing, and marketed its product as a "prestige" brand, as opposed to Columbia's dedication to its practicality, durability, and functionality. This made North Face more vulnerable to the finicky marketplace, as the company found out in the 1990s when its sales plummeted.

"Everybody else's ads in the outdoor-clothing business are the same," Gert Boyle told *Inc. Magazine.* "There's always a young, firm body. Sometimes, with a little luck, there are two firm bodies intertwined with each other . . . But if you put your finger over the name of the people who are advertising, you couldn't tell whose ad it is. Well, ours are different."

MARKETING STRATEGY

Gert Boyle credited the originality of the "Mother Boyle" campaign for Columbia's success. "You can look at nine-tenths of the manufacturers of outerwear, skiwear, anything like that—they're all the same ads. All these gorgeous people who couldn't possibly do on skis what they're supposed to be doing. Then you've got the little old lady. That's what sets us apart. Not because we make better clothing, but because the advertising gets your attention," she told David Whitford of *Fortune Small Business.*

As Paul Swangard of the Warsaw Sports Marketing Center told Bryan Brumley of the Associated Press, corporate success "starts with leadership. And it starts with the company defining its brand through its ownership. Gert has been synonymous with the identity that one equates with Columbia." As the public face of Columbia, Boyle was an anomaly. "If you see any ad of an outdoor company, you see beautiful young people. What makes Columbia different—there is this little old lady," she told a reporter for the *Financial Times.* Yet her high profile was more than just vanity. Jack Peterson, of Borders Perrin Norrander, told a writer for *Adweek* that she also "embodies everything the brand is about—uncompromising quality, toughness."

In addition to toughness, the "Mother Boyle" ads occasionally employed ribald language that was unusual for the normally staid field of outerwear. "There's nothing motherly about mother nature," read the headline of a 2002 ad for Columbia's Boundary Peak Parka. "Except maybe her big mountainous breasts." Below that, Gert Boyle piped up, "I've got hot flashes to keep me warm. You'll need something that zips." For an industry typically consumed with testosterone-influenced machismo, this female-centric viewpoint was bold and funny. Peterson told *Adweek* that despite the controversial nature of the ads' text, research revealed 97 percent approval ratings for the campaign. The controversy also helped differentiate Columbia from marketing behemoths such as Nike. "It's always been a Columbia trademark to be a sharper nail rather than a heavier hammer," Peterson said.

The company's television spots for 2005 featured two new "Mother Boyle" ads. In one Gert Boyle operated a cement mixer, which excreted an assortment of odd objects down its trough. The last object was Tim Boyle, wearing a pristine Columbia parka. In the "Dart" spot Tim addressed a group of business associates in a conference room during a meeting. Mother Boyle took aim from the hallway and blew a dart into his neck. The next shot revealed Tim abandoned in a vast snowy wilderness as his mother departed in a helicopter.

Beyond Gert Boyle's charisma, the "Mother Boyle" television spots worked because of the dynamic between her and her son. Not many corporate CEOs would agree to be the punch line of a joke, but Tim Boyle was philosophical about it. "It's very effective, so I guess I have to suck it up," he told a reporter for *CNN/Money.*

OUTCOME

Over the years the "Mother Boyle" campaign not only increased Columbia Sportswear's sales but it also earned respect in the advertising business. Three of the ads were shortlisted for Clio Awards: 1998's print ad "Three Reasons to Own a Good Pair of Boots," 1998's "When You Are as Old as the Hills," and 2001's television spot "Sled Dogs."

Anchored by the "Mother Boyle" campaign, the company showed earnings in 2000 that had increased

70 percent over the previous year, with revenues surpassing $600 million. By 2005 sales had reached $1 billion. As Gert Boyle entered her 80s (in 2004), she left the company's daily business to her son but continued to star in television spots and retained her position as chairman of the board, with no plans to retire. As she wrote in *Fortune Small Business,* "They asked Tim once, 'What's going to happen to the ad when your mother dies?' He said, 'We'll have her stuffed.'"

FURTHER READING

Barron, Kelly. "Tough Mama." *Forbes,* December 25, 2000, p. 232.

Boyle, Gert, and Tim Boyle. "Our Company, Ourselves." *Inc. Magazine,* April 1998.

Boyle, Gert, and Kerry Tymchuk. *One Tough Mother: Success in Life, Business, and Apple Pies.* Portland, Oregon: Westwinds Press, 2005.

Boyle, Gert, and David Whitford. "How We Got Started." *Fortune Small Business,* September 8, 2003.

Boyle, Tim. "Executive Life: The Boss." *New York Times,* January 18, 2004.

Brumley, Bryan. "She's Mother of All Sportswear Firms." *Deseret Morning News,* April 7, 2005.

"Columbia Sportswear Ads Lay It on the Line: Tough Clothes Made by a Tough Lady." *CNN/Money,* October 9, 1998. Available from <http://money.cnn.com/1998/10/09/busunu/columbia_pkg>

Flass, Rebecca. "Columbia Sportswear Pushes Some More Buttons: Gert Boyle Again a Fixture of Irreverent $10 Mil. BPN Campaign." *Adweek,* September 23, 2002, p. 5.

Gert, Tim. "Return in Ads for Columbia Sportswear." *Brandweek,* September 19, 2005, p. 3.

Holmes, Stanley. "Gert Gets the Last Laugh." *BusinessWeek,* June 10, 2002, p. 100.

———. "Talking with One Tough Mother." *BusinessWeek,* April 7, 2005.

Jung, Helen. "Profits Tumble at Columbia Sportswear." *Oregonian,* July 29, 2005.

"Mother Boyle's Star Touch Keeps Columbia Shining." *South China Morning Post,* June 9, 2002.

Kathy Wilson Peacock

ConAgra Foods' Feeding Children Better Foundation

1 ConAgra Drive
Omaha, Nebraska 68102-5001
USA
Telephone: (800) 771-2303
E-mail: FeedingChildrenBetter@conagrafoods.com
Web site: www.feedingchildrenbetter.org

CHILD HUNGER CAMPAIGN

OVERVIEW

ConAgra Foods, the $14 billion packaged-food giant, created its Feeding Children Better program in 1999 in response to the growing problem of childhood hunger in the United States. In conjunction with the Advertising Council and America's Second Harvest, ConAgra's Feeding Children Better program launched a multitiered public service campaign to increase awareness and understanding of childhood hunger, which, at the time, affected approximately 14 million American children.

The "Child Hunger" public service campaign, which started in 2001, used television, print, radio, Web banners, and pamphlets, reaching 57.5 million people in its first year alone. Created by advertising agencies Bartle Bogle Hegarty of New York and Euro RSCG Tatham Partners of Chicago, both of whom volunteered their services free of charge, the ads conveyed to the public the realities of being poor and hungry. The first part of the campaign, conceived by Bartle Bogle Hegarty, used the tagline "The sooner you believe it, the sooner we can end it" and involved heartbreaking television spots drawn from real-life stories. In "Shared Food," for example, a girl prepared a meager meal for the younger children in her family but neglected to feed herself. Euro RSCG, which took over the account in 2002 and changed the tagline to "Hunger. A choice no one should have to make," created equally poignant TV commercials. "Rent or Food," "Heat or Food," and "Medicine or Food" were all created in an attempt to disclose the terrible choices many poor families had long had to make.

In the end the "Child Hunger" campaign was considered successful. More than $45 million of media was donated to promote the campaign, accomplishing ConAgra's goal of gaining free media exposure for the problem and thus making the other tasks more easily attained. There were 285,250 hits on Feeding Children Better's website (the URL was displayed in all advertising materials), there was an increased awareness that childhood hunger existed in America, and in response to the campaign the U.S. Department of Agriculture donated 9 million lunches to schools in the summer of 2001.

HISTORICAL CONTEXT

The Feeding Children Better program was established in 1999 by ConAgra Foods, a leading packaged-food company offering such brands as ACT II, Healthy Choice, Kid Choice, Peter Pan, and Parkay. Feeding Children

Better—which became the largest corporate-backed program to fight child hunger—was divided into three major components: Kids Cafe, Rapid Food Distribution System, and Public Awareness Campaign. In a combined effort the three divisions were able to donate food, to assist in its distribution to the hungry, and to raise awareness both of the organization and of child hunger in the United States.

To help run Feeding Children Better, ConAgra partnered with the national nonprofit group America's Second Harvest, the largest charitable domestic hunger-relief organization in the United States. America's Second Harvest had evolved into a network of more than 200 food banks, which, in total, dispensed food and grocery products to approximately 50,000 charitable hunger-relief agencies. The organization administered Feeding Children Better's Kids Cafes and Rapid Food Distribution System. To operate the Feeding Children Better program, ConAgra also teamed up with the Center on Hunger and Poverty, a research center based at Brandeis University that had long been dedicated to serving the needs of low-income Americans.

Feeding Children Better's "Child Hunger" campaign developed as a result of a hunger-awareness initiative conducted in 2001 by ConAgra Foods, the Advertising Council, and America's Second Harvest. In ConAgra's words (from the Feeding Children Better website), "By educating the public about child hunger, ConAgra Foods' Feeding Children Better program seeks to be a catalyst and encourage others to get involved in the fight against child hunger. The ultimate goal is to insure that American children have the capacity to grow, to learn in school and to reach their full potential."

TARGET MARKET

At the campaign's start 14 million American children had been classified by America's Second Harvest as "food insecure," meaning that they were hungry or at risk of hunger. In a country of great prosperity, this ever-growing problem went largely undetected. "Child Hunger" advertising directly targeted hungry children and their families, letting them know who to contact if they needed food assistance. ConAgra desired to bring attention to this group during the summer months, when the national free-lunch program would reach far fewer children than during the school year. Only about 2.2 million kids would be fed during the summer, compared with 14 million during the school year. For this reason the campaign was released during the summer.

Those who could directly benefit from food distribution were not the only ones targeted by the "Child Hunger" campaign. Raising awareness in all Americans was the goal. Thus the campaign directed viewers to the Feeding Children Better website, where they could become better educated about hunger and, in particular, about child hunger. Providing such information as "Every fourth person standing in a soup kitchen line is a child," "13 million kids live in households that do not have an adequate supply of food," and "One in five children in the U.S. is hungry or at the risk of hunger every year," ConAgra Foods and Feeding Children Better hoped to spread compassion for the poor and to find donors for the program.

"STOP THE WASTE!"

Results from a 2004 study revealed that nearly half of all the food in the United States went to waste. The University of Arizona study, led by anthropologist Timothy Jones, looked at food loss over a 10-year period and concluded that of all food ready for harvest, 40 to 50 percent never got eaten. Jones stated that if measures were made to diminish waste, each year tens of billions of dollars would be saved—money that, he suggested, could be used to fight hunger via contributions to such programs as America's Second Harvest.

COMPETITION

There had been a great many other hunger-prevention programs developed in the United States. The Food Research and Action Center (FRAC) was one such program. A national organization, FRAC was founded in 1970 as a public interest law firm and grew to be a key player in the fight to decrease hunger in America. Like Feeding Children Better, FRAC focused on child hunger. In particular the organization engaged in ongoing research to document national hunger and its effect on low-income families with children.

Share Our Strength (SOS), with the motto "It takes more than food to fight hunger," was another leading antihunger advocate. The program, founded in 1984 and based in Washington, D.C., had raised more than $180 million in the fight against hunger and poverty, both in the United States and worldwide. SOS's approach centered on teaching cooking and nutrition classes to low-income families. It also managed a number of corporate-backed campaigns, such as "Charge against Hunger," which operated from 1993 to 1996 and was sponsored by American Express. By donating three cents from every fourth-quarter transaction, the credit-card company raised $21 million for SOS.

Meanwhile ConAgra Foods (a top producer of food in the United States), which provided funding for Feeding Children Better and which in 2004 had sales exceeding $14 billion, faced steep competition in its sale of packaged foods. ConAgra's main competitors were Kraft Foods (with 2004 sales exceeding $32 billion) and Nestlé (with 2004 sales totaling more than $76 billion). Neither megacorporation had backed a major nonprofit in the specific way that ConAgra had with Feeding Children Better, although they had historically given to many charitable organizations, often in connection with nutrition. Kraft, for instance, created a "Kraft Cares" global philanthropy program, which focused on two main areas: hunger and healthy lifestyles. Still these efforts tended to be shorter term and promotion oriented, instead of long-term, nationwide commitments like the one ConAgra had made to Feeding Children Better. Further ConAgra was the only company to run a public service campaign specifically to fight childhood hunger in the United States.

MARKETING STRATEGY

The "Child Hunger" campaign aired in 2001 as a series of public service announcements, with advertisements created by volunteer ad agency Bartle Bogle Hegarty, based in New York City. The announcements' main objective was to raise awareness about hunger, especially child hunger, in the United States and to increase empathy toward parents of hungry children. With the "Child Hunger" campaign ConAgra, the Ad Council, and America's Second Harvest wanted to change the general perception of child hunger as being a result of a lazy parent not doing his or her job. The advertising was intended to reveal the difficult choices these parents had long had to make, such as deciding whether to spend money on rent or food. Further they aimed to expose the damaging physical and mental effects of hunger on children. Another objective was to provide opportunities for citizens to take action against childhood hunger. These would prove difficult tasks, because, in addition to the negative opinions the public had formed about hungry children and their parents, there was an inaccurate national perception that hunger barely existed in the United States.

Using the tagline "The sooner you believe it, the sooner we can end it," the tragic television spots, directed by Joe Pytka of Bartle Bogle Hegarty, were drawn from real-life stories. In "Ketchup Soup" a mother scavenged ketchup packets from take-out restaurants in order to make ketchup-and-water soup for her young family. In "Chicken Pox" a young girl talked her brother into attending school when he had chicken pox just so he could receive his free lunch. Finally "Shared Food" portrayed a girl preparing a meager meal for her younger siblings. At the end of the spot the camera backed up to reveal that the older girl did not eat anything, leaving her portion for the others.

In 2002 Bartle Bogle Hegarty's contract ended, and Euro RSCG Tatham Partners continued the campaign, which took on a different tagline, "Hunger. A choice no one should have to make." The agenda, however, remained the same: to spread the word about childhood hunger in the United States, with a focus on the terrible choices poor families continually have had to face. Additional TV spots were released. In one, titled "Rent or Food," a mother, with her children listening nearby, tried to explain to her landlord that she could not pay the rent because she needed the money to feed her children. Other spots, including "Heat or Food" and "Medicine or Food," depicted the same message.

In addition to television, the campaign appeared in various forms, including radio, print ads, Web banners, and pamphlets. Among the print ads was one about "Julie," who was cold and suffered from what the ad called "Chicken Skin." Every ad directed the audience to a toll-free number, 1-800-FEED-KIDS, as well as to a website, http://www.feedingchildrenbetter.org. All were made possible through donated media that exceeded $45 million in value. The campaign continued through 2003.

OUTCOME

The efforts of Bartle Bogle Hegarty and Euro RSCG Tatham Partners were met with accolades from the advertising industry. Among the campaign's many awards were an International Andy award and a silver EFFIE award, the latter of which judged campaigns on the basis of their results. More importantly the ad agencies and organizations behind the campaign considered it to have achieved its goals.

The campaign's first objective—gaining free media exposure—was exceedingly met. While in 2001 the average Ad Council campaign received $28.6 million in donated media, "Child Hunger" received $45.3 million. Second, the ads also successfully inspired action: from June through December of 2001, the campaign's 800 number received 2,677 calls, while its website received 285,250 hits. By the campaign's end the number of website hits had reached 507,400. Ninety percent of telephone calls had been inspired by the television and radio spots. Third, awareness of childhood hunger in America increased dramatically. In a public-opinion study run by the Ad Council, 50 percent of participants in 2001 said that they believed childhood hunger existed in the United States. In 2002 the number jumped to 87 percent. When participants were asked if they thought that the problem existed in their own community, only 10 percent in 2001 said yes. In 2002 the number increased to 39 percent. The campaign also achieved its goal of generating a collective concern and discussion so that the problem would no longer be hidden. As a direct result of the campaign, in the summer of 2001 the U.S. Department of Agriculture donated to schools 9 million lunches for children in need. On a wider scale the advertising reached more than 57.5 million people, who either read, watched or heard about the issue through means of the "Child Hunger" campaign.

FURTHER READING

Broder, David S. "No Recess for Hunger." *Washington Post,* June 4, 2003, p. A27.

Brunt, Cliff. "Companies, Workers Give Food, Clothes, Toys." *Omaha (NE) World-Herald,* December 25, 2002, p. 1B.

"ConAgra Foods' Feeding Children Better Foundation." *PND News,* February 25, 2003.

"ConAgra Foods, Minor League Clubs Team Up to Feed Kids." *Progressive Grocer,* June 16, 2005.

Cone, Carol L., Mark A. Feldman, and Alison T. DaSilva. "Align Your Brand with a Social Cause." *Harvard Business Review,* July 14, 2003.

Grace, Erin, Jeffrey Robb, et al. "ConAgra Donating Trucks to Food Banks." *Omaha (NE) World-Herald,* May 7, 2002, p. 2B.

Hauser, Andrea. "Web Site Fights Summer Hunger." *Omaha (NE) World-Herald,* June 13, 2001, p. 21.

Lazare, Lewis. "New Ad Campaign Targets Hunger." *Chicago Sun-Times,* August 8, 2002, p. 51.

Maki, Amos. "Bakers Have Recipe to Fight Child Hunger." *Atlanta Journal-Constitution,* July 10, 2003, p. 1JH.

Palmer, Jane. "Two Kids Cafes Open for Omaha Children." *Omaha (NE) World-Herald,* July 21, 2001, p. 61.

Riskind, Jonathan. "Hunger Grows in This Land of Prosperity." *Columbus (OH) Dispatch,* March 3, 2002, p. 3F.

Sarasohn, David. "Fighting the Battle on the Food Front." *(Portland, OR) Oregonian,* October 26, 2001, p. C11.

Candice Mancini

Conseco, Inc.

11825 N Pennsylvania St.
Carmel, Indiana 46032
USA
Telephone: (317) 817-6100
Fax: (317) 817-2847
Web site: www.conseco.com

PROTECT/CREATE WEALTH CAMPAIGN

OVERVIEW

Although Conseco, Inc., an insurance and financial services company, had become large and successful through acquisitions, it had little name recognition even among agents working for its various units. In order to establish the Conseco name as a brand, the company hired the advertising agency Fallon McElligott, Inc. to develop a print campaign to run in trade publications, followed by a $15 million television campaign, "Protect/Create Wealth," targeted toward consumers with household incomes between $25,000 and $75,000 per year. The consumer campaign, Conseco's first-ever on television, began running in February 1998 on ESPN and during the CBS broadcast of the NCAA basketball tournament, after which it moved to cable television. In a departure from the warm, sentimental advertising of insurance companies in the past, the campaign used edgy humor to make the point that life did not always go as expected and that a person needed to be financially prepared for bad or good times, either by having insurance or a financial plan. The company followed up with a $5 million print campaign in April 1998. The "Protect/Create Wealth" campaign ended in December 1998.

HISTORICAL CONTEXT

Conseco was founded in 1979 as Security National of Indiana Corp. by Stephen C. Hilbert, a former encyclopedia salesman from Terre Haute. In 1982 the company made the first of many acquisitions that would be the key to its growth, and in 1983 the company changed its name to Conseco, Inc. According to the company's annual report filed with the U.S. Securities and Exchange Commission on March 31, 1999, from 1982 through 1998 Conseco acquired 19 insurance groups. By January 1998 the company was a $36 billion entity that sold life and health insurance and annuities under 25 names, including Colonial Penn Life and Casualty, American Travellers Life, Bankers Life & Casualty, and Capitol American.

Despite the fact that Conseco had grown into one of the country's largest life and health insurance companies, few knew the company name. According to company spokesperson Jim Rosensteele, "Our research showed that even agents currently doing business with a Conseco company have very low awareness of the Conseco name. For many years, we've been thought of as a collection of companies." The company thus decided to develop the Conseco name as a brand. At the same time Conseco decided to diversify beyond insurance into the realm of financial services, and in 1997 the company began to market its own over-the-counter mutual funds. The following year, Conseco spent $6.5 billion to acquire

Green Tree Financial Corp., which added home loans, credit cards, and home equity loans to its offerings.

Another reason to seek name recognition was Conseco's need to begin growing from within by increasing the sales of the companies it had purchased. One market observer claimed that 1998 would be a "make-or-break year" for Conseco, noting, "So far, they've built [success] on the bodies of a number of companies without a lot of brand recognition. They're probably not going to have any significant acquisitions this year, so they've got to digest the acquisitions they've already made and show some internal growth."

Conseco was aware of the need to increase sales and in 1996 began to work on a new marketing plan. By January 1998 the company had a new logo, which featured a series of steps rising from the Conseco name, illustrating the company's focus on performance. Conseco hired advertising agency Fallon McElligott to create a print campaign targeted toward the nation's 190,000 independent insurance agents. The campaign emphasized Conseco's financial success. One advertisement read, "Q: What do you call an insurance company that has an unyielding grasp on the bottom line? A: Your friend." It went on to say, "We are unapologetically profitable... PERFORMANCE IS WHAT MATTERS." Conseco set aside $10 million for the agent campaign, which ran in the *Wall Street Journal, Sports Illustrated, Newsweek,* and *Forbes,* as well as in trade publications. The company then spent $15 million for a consumer campaign, its first-ever on television.

TARGET MARKET

Conseco's consumer-oriented campaign sought to establish the company's name as a brand for a diversity of services, including insurance and investments. In February 1999 *American Banker* described Conseco's target segment as American households that earned $30,000 to $70,000 per year, rather than the very rich, saying that it was a "long-neglected segment of U.S. consumers." Company founder Hilbert said that his goal was to make Conseco the "Wal-Mart of financial services."

The first spot ran on February 26, 1998, on ESPN and then ran on CBS during the NCAA basketball tournament in March 1998. "If you look at the crowd that watches college basketball, they are college-educated people. It's an excellent target audience to reach," said Sandy Deem, a spokesperson with First Union, a company that ran advertising during the 1999 tournament. College basketball viewers were reported to have higher salaries and more education than other sports fans. Conseco spokesperson Rosensteele said, "There's nothing like the NCAA tournament to really build exposure with the audience we're targeting. We really want to build brand awareness with both agents and consumers." Rosensteele also acknowledged that Conseco had a special connection with college basketball, which "is very big here in Indiana."

FALLON MCELLIGOTT: FROM MINNEAPOLIS TO THE BIG APPLE

Minneapolis advertising agency Fallon McElligott opened a branch in New York in April 1995, and by September 1997 it had $120 million in billings. One major reason for its success, according to an article in *Shoot,* was the agency's chairman, Andy Berlin, who had helped launch the San Francisco-based Goodby, Berlin & Silverstein in 1983.

In addition to Conseco, Fallon McElligott boasted a client list at the time that included Coca-Cola, Tidy Cat, the NBA, Conde Nast publications, the *Washington Post,* Metropolitan Health Care, the National Symphony Orchestra, the Kennedy Center for the Performing Arts, Bankers Trust Worldwide, and Bancomer, the largest bank in Mexico.

Berlin said that one thing setting the agency apart from others was that the creative people worked "unusually closely" with account planners while campaigns were being developed. According to Berlin, the agency was also structured with as few layers as possible and featured a very young and prolific group of creative talent.

Berlin believed that finding an "original voice" was the most important thing he contributed to Goodby, and he continued to hold that philosophy at Fallon McElligott. "The world doesn't need another Young & Rubicam or another Ogilvy & Mather," he said. "It needs fresh voices."

COMPETITION

According to an article in *National Underwriter Life & Health* on January 12, 1998, the insurance and financial services industries had just gone through a "watershed year—the year in which it became apparent that the life insurance industry was no longer able to stand apart from the fundamental restructuring occurring within the financial services industry." One major development was the "unprecedented level of merger and acquisition

MUTUAL FUNDS PARTNER WITH SPORTS FOR MARKETING ADVANTAGE

At one time the business and sports worlds had little to do with each other, at least from a marketing standpoint. During the 1990s, however, both mutual funds and sports became increasingly popular among men and women of all ages with money to invest. A marketing match was thus created.

According to a July 18, 1999, article in the *Arizona Republic,* in 1998 financial firms spent an estimated $850 million on global sports advertising. Among other things mutual fund companies became high-profile sponsors of professional sports teams and athletic events. Stadiums and sports arenas were being named after financial companies, despite occasional fan protests. Conseco Field House, home of the Indianapolis Pacers, was just one example, along with Safeco Field in Seattle and the Philadelphia 76ers' new venue, First Union Center.

"Financial-services firms have been increasingly turning to professional sports to raise brand-name recognition," according to Cerulli Associates, a Boston consulting firm. "Sports sponsorships offer a unique benefit over traditional advertising: consumers often form an emotional attachment to sports teams."

activity in the financial services industry." Significant mergers and acquisitions took place in the life and property/casualty markets, as well as in the managed care and brokerage segments. In the life insurance market companies were driven to consolidate by the desire to expand their scale, volume, products, distribution, and expertise. In addition to Conseco, other companies using acquisitions to stay competitive included Aegon N.V., American General Corp., ING Groep N.V., Jefferson-Pilot Corp., and Lincoln National Corp.

"From a fragmented industry composed of thousands of competitors we are being driven toward a concentrated financial services market with a few national-level players in each segment," *National Underwriter Life & Health* reported. "Insurance companies that once specialized in a single line or market now face hulking competitors like Travelers-Salomon Brothers, G.E. Capital, Zurich-Kemper, and Morgan Stanley-Dean Witter, along with the likes of American General, Aegon USA, and ING." Only three months later, in April 1998, Citicorp and Travelers Group Inc. announced that they were merging to form Citigroup Inc., "the world's first supermarket for banking, insurance and financial services," according to Reuters news service. The merger created a megacompany with $698 billion in assets.

MARKETING STRATEGY

Conseco's $15 million television campaign aimed at consumers was part of a long-term strategy to establish the company as a brand name in order to engender greater customer loyalty and to enhance sales. This would allow the company to grow without relying as heavily on acquisitions as it had in the past. As reported in February 1998 in *Adweek,* the television campaign was launched with five commercials—three 30-second spots and two 15-second spots—that used storytelling to make the point that Conseco could provide a variety of financial services.

The 30-second spots explored negative themes, but with an upbeat twist at the end. Fallon McElligott used edgy humor in the commercials in order to set Conseco apart from other companies, which had traditionally used sentimentality or warmer humor. In one 30-second spot, "Grim Reaper," a couple was relaxing at home when, unbeknownst to them, the Grim Reaper came to their front door. Before he could knock, a female Reaper appeared and lured him away by lifting her skirt to flash a bit of leg bone. The two ran off together, and the couple remained blissfully unaware of the close call. The voice-over said, "You never know when your number is going to be up. That's why you need protection against the unexpected." In another 30-second spot, "Italian Woman," a woman was told that her man had been seen with another woman in a jewelry store. As she stomped to the store with a rolling pin in hand and a crowd in tow, the voice-over said, "Sometimes you need health insurance. Sometimes you need life insurance." When she discovered that the "other woman" was actually a store clerk and that the man was buying her a ring, she dropped the rolling pin and the voice-over said, "And sometimes you need investments for the future." The third 30-second spot, "Boxer," explored similar bad news/good news themes, showing a young boxer being beaten up in the ring but telling the viewer that he had won a $2 million purse in the process. One of the 15-second spots simply showed a squirrel jumping from branch to branch in a tree, only to fall out of sight on his final leap. The narrator said, "You know the saying, 'Look before you leap?' Well, it's especially true when you make financial decisions. So, maybe you should be talking to Conseco." The tag line for the campaign was "Create wealth. Protect wealth. For life."

The campaign was designed to encourage consumers to use Conseco for a variety of financial services and to emphasize that things did not always go according to plan. "Life can go either way, and we want to show that Conseco is there," said account supervisor Mary Ann Harris. The company was also interested in standing out from the crowd, particularly since it was a relatively late arrival in consumer marketing. The company and the advertising agency believed that the edgy approach was a welcome change from the messages of the past, that people were tired of "warm and fuzzy advertising" and were "ready to hear a different message." Bill Schwab, a cocreator of the campaign with Fallon McElligott, remembered one member of a focus group member who said, "If I see one more insurance-company ad where some child is tugging at her mother's skirt, I'll throw up."

It was reported that Conseco planned to run 51 commercials on CBS during the NCAA tournament alone. In addition, the advertising appeared on such cable networks as ESPN, CNN, A&E, and the History Channel. Within weeks after the television advertising began, the *Indianapolis Star* reported that the Conseco name was gradually being used by the company's subsidiaries and added to products, part of the move to publicize Conseco as a brand name. In April a $5 million print campaign followed in financial and news magazines.

OUTCOME

According to Victor Kimble, the Conseco account supervisor at Fallon McElligott, the campaign succeeded in getting the Conseco message out in a nontraditional way. Kimble believed that it put Conseco "on the awareness map" and "gave them the buzz they needed" to get started. Conseco used Fallon McElligott for its next wave of national advertising, created for television and print and launched almost exactly one year after the 1998 campaign. Kimble said that the strategy was refined for the 1999 campaign, which featured commercials in which a bride and groom were forced to cater their own wedding and a man in a wet suit went snorkeling for coins in a fountain to fund his retirement. The latter spot won a Silver Lion at the Cannes Film Festival in the product category of "investment, insurance and property development."

Observers judged Conseco's marketing efforts to the lower-income segment to be well-timed. According to James Bell, a senior partner with New York corporate brand specialist Lippencott & Margulies, there has been "a hiatus" in effective advertising to this market, with most marketing aimed toward "slicked-back guys with wire-rimmed glasses getting on airplanes in first class."

Stewart Stockdale, Conseco's executive vice president of marketing and strategic planning, said in July 1999 that he was "very pleased" with the recognition Conseco advertising was getting. "We are even more pleased that our campaign to build a nationwide consumer brand focusing on financial services for middle America—households with $25,000 to $75,000 in annual income—is working. Awareness of Conseco has doubled in the past year. Even more importantly, we've seen healthy increases in overall preference for our brand, in consumer receptivity to purchase our products, and in the number of positive traits consumers associate with our brand. Brand-building is a long-term effort, but we're off to a great start."

FURTHER READING

Ambrose, Eileen. "Conseco, Finish Line Make Tourney Advertising Campaigns Designed to Create National Brand-Awareness." *Indianapolis Star,* March 17, 1998, p. B6.

Baar, Aaron. "Fallon Launches National TV Effort for Conseco." *Adweek* (Midwest Edition), February 23, 1998, p. 3.

"Breaking: Conseco: Dollars and Sense." *Advertising Age,* March 9, 1998, p. 51.

"Conseco to Launch New Tagline." *Fund Marketing Alert,* November 30, 1998, p. 5.

"Conseco TV Commercial Receives Top Award at Cannes Festival," *Business Wire,* July 13, 1999.

Koenig, Bill. "Conseco Reports Sharp Rise in Earnings." *Indianapolis Star,* February 26, 1998, p. D1.

McMains, Andrew. "A Simple Plan." *Adweek* (Eastern Edition), February 22, 1999, p. 28.

Palmer, Joel. "Silliness Sells Securities." *Business Record,* March 29, 1999, p. 14.

Pletz, John. "Conseco Planning $25 Million Ad Blitz." *Indianapolis Business Journal,* January 19, 1998, p. A3.

"Road to Final Four Gets New Billboards; NCAA Hoop Commercials Shift From Macho to Money." *Hartford Courant,* March 26, 1999, p. D1.

Scism, Leslie. "Conseco Takes a Light Approach to Sell Serious Insurance Products." *Wall Street Journal* (Eastern Edition), March 3, 1998, p. B8.

Timmons, Heather. "Conseco Bids to Make a Bundle Selling to People at the Low End." *American Banker,* February 24, 1999, p. 4.

Debbi Mack

Cunard Line Limited

24303 Town Center Dr., Ste. 200
Valencia, California 91355
USA
Telephone: (800) 728-6273
Fax: (661) 284-4748
Web site: www.cunard.com

CAN YOU WAIT? CAMPAIGN

OVERVIEW

The Cunard Line Limited boasted one of the cruise industry's most storied pasts, having carried the Royal Mail across the Atlantic for England before building one of the grandest and most respected fleets of passenger ships during the early twentieth century. The rise of passenger aircraft, however, all but eliminated the demand for transatlantic ocean travel, and by the turn of the millennium Cunard had a fleet of two ships, only one of which continued to travel the once-prominent route between North America and Great Britain. The world's largest cruise-ship company, Carnival Corporation, purchased Cunard in 1998; later that year Cunard announced its plan to construct what would be the largest and most luxurious passenger ship of its time, the *Queen Mary 2.* The ship was slated to make regular transatlantic voyages, which would be evocative of the golden age of ocean travel, as well as select Caribbean, South American, and New England cruises. To build awareness about the new ship preparatory to its January 2004 maiden voyage, Cunard enlisted the New York office of ad agency TBWA\Chiat\Day to helm a marketing campaign for 2003.

The campaign, budgeted at an estimated $8 million, began in spring 2003, with the intent of helping Cunard achieve full booking of *Queen Mary 2* 's maiden voyage and 60 percent booking on the rest of the ship's 2004 trips. Because construction of the ship was still underway, TBWA\Chiat\Day could not showcase the product itself, so the campaign instead conveyed the idea that a *Queen Mary 2* voyage was an event worthy of intense anticipation. Print ads used images of overdressed women in everyday situations, such as a stylish mother serving her children breakfast while wearing a ball gown, together with the "Can You Wait?" tagline. To enhance the ship's upscale allure, the brand names of luxury products and services to be featured on the *Queen Mary 2* itself were included in the ads' copy.

The *Queen Mary 2* sold out its berths by July 2003, approximately four months after the campaign began, and the occupancy goals for the ship's entire 2004 schedule of voyages were exceeded shortly thereafter. The campaign won a Gold EFFIE Award in 2004.

HISTORICAL CONTEXT

The Cunard Line was established in 1839 as a transatlantic carrier of the Royal Mail from Britain to Canada and the United States, and by the early twentieth century it had expanded to become one of the world's premier shipping lines. Cunard lost 22 ships during World War I, including the *Lusitania,* whose sinking by German U-boats while crossing from New York to

Liverpool contributed to America's entrance into the conflict. Transatlantic shipping's golden age came in the 1920s and 1930s, and Cunard remained a major player in the industry, employing the well-known marketing tagline "Getting There Is Half the Fun" during those years. In 1934 Cunard's *Queen Mary* became the first vessel ever launched by a member of the British royal family, Her Majesty Queen Mary (wife of the then-reigning king, George V), and the *Queen Elizabeth* was unveiled in 1938, named for Queen Elizabeth, wife of King George VI, who had assumed the throne. Winston Churchill credited his country's enlistment of these ships during World War II with shortening the conflict by at least a year. By the 1950s Cunard carried one-third of all passengers crossing the Atlantic, but at the end of that decade commercial passenger jets began making the transatlantic journey. Thus began the steady erosion of transatlantic boat travel until, by the late twentieth century, the practice seemed part of history. Though Cunard's *Queen Elizabeth 2,* which was introduced in 1969, continued to make transatlantic voyages, the company went through several changes of ownership and struggled to reinvent itself for a new age. Cunard was purchased in 1998 by cruise-ship giant Carnival, which hoped to leverage the brand's rich legacy and reputation for luxury in a bid to return the venerable line to profitability.

Among the centerpieces of Carnival's attempt to revive Cunard was the building of the largest and most luxurious passenger ship in existence, the *Queen Mary 2,* to take over the *Queen Elizabeth 2*'s transatlantic route in addition to making Caribbean voyages. Slated to make its maiden voyage in late 2003, the *Queen Mary 2* was intended to appeal to nostalgia for the golden age of transatlantic ship travel while also updating the experience to suit the expectations of modern luxury vacationers. Not only was the *Queen Mary 2* being prepared, at great expense, to travel a route that was nearly obsolete, but its construction also coincided with a sharp downturn in luxury travel as a result of a slowing U.S. economy and fears regarding terrorism. Complicating Cunard's new agenda even further was the fact of serious overcapacity within the cruise industry. After years of consistent fleet enlargement (plans largely put into place before the economic downturn), in the early 2000s cruise lines found themselves forced to cut fares dramatically to attract passengers. This was not, however, an option for the *Queen Mary 2,* which was billed as the jewel not just of Cunard's fleet but of the entire cruise industry.

TARGET MARKET

Because the *Queen Mary 2* represented an occupancy increase of 60 percent for the Cunard fleet (which consisted of two other ships at the time), it was imperative that with the new campaign TBWA\Chiat\Day expand Cunard's target market not just for the initial months after the ship's christening but also in the long run. The agency sought out these new customers among wealthy, status-conscious Americans who already owned and had experienced many of the things they wanted in life. Such people, the agency deduced, had traveled widely and frequently traveled outside the United States. Their travels were characterized by a need to take ever more exotic or impressive vacations, at least partly because of the bragging rights this gave them among others in their social class. Though jaded in many ways, this target group still sought out proximity to famous and prestigious people, brands, and experiences.

Thanks to its upscale legacy, the Cunard brand had the potential to satisfy the traveling desires of this market, and Cunard augmented its brand strength by partnering with other upscale names, including Veuve Clicquot (the makers of a renowned champagne), Canyon Ranch (a luxury spa company), and Todd English (a Boston-based celebrity chef). This gathering of upscale brands, mentioned in the ads' copy, was meant to work together with the idea of anticipation communicated by the ads' imagery and tagline to make a *Queen Mary 2* cruise alluring to the status-conscious target.

Cunard mixed traditional and modern in its choice of brand partners as well as in its onboard amenities—for instance, the *Queen Mary 2* had a grand staircase and furnishings evocative of the stately ships of an earlier age, and each cabin was outfitted with a high-speed Internet connection. This blend of classic and cutting-edge was a further reflection of the target market's desires and expectations. While Cunard specifically appealed to consumers' desire to step back in time to a supposedly more elegant and ceremonious age, these consumers did not want to sacrifice the comfort and convenience available to them in the present.

HOW BIG? HOW MUCH?

Upon entering service in January 2004, the Cunard Line's *Queen Mary 2* was the largest cruise ship ever built. It was almost as long as four football fields laid end to end, and its above-water height (accommodating 17 passenger decks) was the approximate equivalent of a 23-story building. Unsurprisingly, the *Queen Mary 2,* whose construction costs reached $800 million, was also the most expensive ship ever built.

COMPETITION

Cunard's corporate parent, Carnival Corporation of Miami, owned many of the top cruise lines in American and European markets during this time, including Princess Cruises, the Holland America Line, and the world's most popular and profitable cruise brand, Carnival Cruise Lines. Of these brands, Carnival Cruise Lines, which marketed comparatively affordable cruises to a mainstream audience, had by far the highest marketing profile. For decades prior to the turn of the millennium, Carnival had cultivated a positioning as "The Fun Ships," and in 1985 it used this brand image in the first-ever cruise-industry spots to appear on network television. The commercials featured celebrity spokesperson Kathie Lee Gifford (then Kathie Lee Johnson) singing about the Carnival experience. After moving away from this strategy in the late 1990s, Carnival experimented with reality-based advertising in the 2000s before returning to an emphasis on its "Fun Ship" identity.

The world's second-largest cruise company, Miami-based Royal Caribbean Cruises Ltd., was responsible for perhaps the most noteworthy cruise-industry advertising campaign of the early 2000s. The company offered trips to the Caribbean as well as to Alaska, Europe, and elsewhere. Having indulged significantly in the fleet expansion characteristic of the cruise industry in the late 1990s, and with further expansion planned for the 2000s, Royal Caribbean's namesake line, Royal Caribbean International, addressed the inevitable need to expand its target market by crafting a new and more vibrant brand image in a long-running campaign tagged "Get Out There." In an attempt to change the popular notion that cruise vacations were for the elderly, the campaign's TV spots employed fast-paced cutting between images of adventurous off-ship activities together with the high-energy Iggy Pop rock song "Lust for Life." This repositioning was considered a success, and the average age of Royal Caribbean customers dropped substantially. The problem of industry overcapacity, however, remained.

MARKETING STRATEGY

"Can You Wait?" was budgeted at approximately $8 million. The *Queen Mary 2* 's maiden voyage was firmly scheduled for January 2004 (the preliminary completion date of late 2003 having been revised during the ship's construction); the marketing campaign accordingly debuted in spring 2003. Its central goals were to generate sufficient awareness to sell out the maiden voyage and to sell 60 percent of the berths for the *Queen Mary 2*'s entire 2004 schedule. In addition to the difficulties stemming from industry overcapacity and the waning taste for transatlantic ocean travel, TBWA\Chiat\Day faced the challenge of marketing a product that did not yet exist. Though the *Queen Mary 2* promised to set an industry standard for grandeur and elegance, it was under construction during the campaign's run and so could not be used to supply visual examples of that grandeur and elegance.

TBWA\Chiat\Day thus settled on anticipation as the campaign's controlling theme. Building on the idea that vacationers enjoyed anticipating their travels as much as the travels themselves, the agency employed imagery and copy meant to stimulate desire for the experience of crossing the Atlantic on the *Queen Mary 2* while allowing prospective travelers to imagine the exact nature of the experience for themselves. The resulting print ads ran in trade magazines as well as national consumer magazines owned by Condé Nast, including *Gourmet, Vanity Fair, W, Bon Appétit, Architectural Digest,* the *New Yorker,* and *Condé Nast Traveler.* The consumer ads each featured an image of a woman dramatically overdressed for her commonplace surroundings. One ad, for instance, showed a woman serving breakfast to her children while wearing a full-length ball gown. Another showed a husband and wife in bed, the husband shirtless under the bedcovers and the wife sleeping beside him in a ball gown and high heels. Copy included the "Can You Wait?" tagline, the brand names of Cunard's luxury-product partners, and the Cunard and *Queen Mary 2* logos. Together—and especially as buzz began to build about the *Queen Mary 2* —these elements suggested the idea that a voyage on the new ship was an event worthy of anticipation of the highest degree.

As part of the marketing agreement that resulted in the exclusive placement of *Queen Mary 2* ads in Condé Nast magazines, TBWA\Chiat\Day and the publisher designed promotional events geared to the readership of each title. The campaign also included direct-mail and online components in keeping with the overall theme.

OUTCOME

By July 2003 Cunard had sold all 2,620 berths for the *Queen Mary 2* 's January 2004 maiden voyage. This represented the earliest sellout for any voyage in Cunard's long and storied history, as well as an industry-wide record for the number of berths sold before a ship's construction had been completed. Bookings for all of 2004 substantially exceeded Cunard's precampaign goals. Surveys involving readers of *Architectural Digest,* one of the publications in which the "Can You Wait?" ads ran, revealed that 69 percent of those surveyed recalled the *Queen Mary 2* ads; according to the survey results the ads also ranked first among ads in the magazine for attracting and holding readers' attention. Cunard's own research supported these findings across the group of publications in which the ads ran. More than 50 percent of passengers booked for 2004 *Queen Mary 2* vacations had not previously sailed on a Cunard ship. "Can You Wait?" was awarded a Gold EFFIE Award in 2004 in the Travel/Tourism/Destination category. The EFFIE Awards, one of the most prestigious events in the advertising industry, were hosted annually by the New York American Marketing Association.

FURTHER READING

Birmingham, Stephen. "Unflappable New York, Wide-Eyed at Last." *New York Times,* May 2, 2004.

Davidson, Carla. "Long Live the Queens." *American Heritage,* September 2005.

Elliott, Stuart. "Cunard Selects TBWA\Chiat\Day." *New York Times,* July 27, 2001.

Goetzl, David. "Cunard Sets Sight on a Bygone Era." *Advertising Age,* December 11, 2000.

Griswold, Alicia. "Carnival Calls Review for Cunard." *Adweek,* May 7, 2001.

Schama, Simon. "Sail Away." *New Yorker,* May 31, 2004.

Scull, Theode W. "Queen Mary 2." *Cruise Travel,* May/June 2004.

Wakin, Daniel J. "Restoring the Queens' Glamour." *New York Times,* August 19, 2001.

White, Randy Wayne. "Fine Liner." *Outside,* October 2004.

Young, Susan J. "Crowning a Queen." *Travel Agent Magazine,* March 24, 2003.

Mark Lane

CVS Corporation

One CVS Drive
Woonsocket, Rhode Island 02895
USA
Telephone: (401) 765-1500
Fax: (401) 766-2917
Web site: www.cvs.com

LIFE TO THE FULLEST CAMPAIGN

OVERVIEW

In 2002 CVS Corporation's drugstore chain, CVS/pharmacy, was approaching its 40th anniversary, and as a result of steady growth it was nipping at the heels of the nation's number one drugstore chain, Walgreens. Although much of CVS's growth had been the result of acquisitions and was limited to specific regions of the United States, including New England and the Northeast, the drugstore chain was planning a push for national expansion. To reach consumers in markets where CVS was a new face as well as to enhance its brand image in areas where consumers were familiar with the chain, CVS turned to its advertising agency, Boston-based Hill, Holliday, Connors, Cosmopulos (often called Hill Holliday).

The campaign Hill Holliday created, "Life to the Fullest," was CVS's first national campaign. It was designed to enhance the company's brand image as well as shift its marketing focus from products to consumer lifestyles. A budget was unavailable, but CVS typically spent about $35 million a year on advertising. Included in the campaign were television spots that aired on cable and network channels that had a large female audience. Print ads also appeared in *People* magazine, which had a high female readership. Both print ads and TV spots featured people in environments such as a living room, a restaurant, and a public restroom, but with store-aisle markers hanging over their heads that listed each person's recent purchases and the benefits of buying the items at a CVS store.

While the campaign failed to garner any industry awards, it did capture the attention of consumers. Following its launch CVS reported an 8.7 percent increase in sales over the previous year and a 73 percent jump in net income for the same time period. Hill Holliday's efforts on behalf of the drugstore chain were recognized by the magazine *Advertising Age,* which named the company one of its Advertising Agencies of the Year for 2002. Praise for the campaign also came from *Adweek.* The magazine described one television spot as a refreshing change from the routine "ho-hum" advertising in the retail-beauty-products segment.

HISTORICAL CONTEXT

When Ralph Hoagland and brothers Stanley and Sidney Goldstein opened the first CVS store in 1963 in Lowell, Massachusetts, the business offered busy consumers a one-stop shop for a variety of over-the-counter health-care products and beauty aids. Four years later the company added prescription drugs to its product mix when it opened pharmacies in its stores. By 1970 the chain had 100 stores serving customers throughout the northeastern United States. Without abandoning the vision of its founders, which was focused on meeting the needs of customers, the company began expanding. At the end of 1989 the chain reported 789 stores and sales of $1.95 billion. In the 1990s acquisitions and consolidations of small regional chains—including in 1990 the Peoples Drug Stores with 500 stores, in 1997 the Revco chain with 2,552 stores, and in 1998 Arbor Drugs with 207 stores—boosted CVS to the United States' number two drugstore chain in outlets and sales, behind Walgreens. In 1996 the chain changed its name to CVS Corporation. CVS was originally the acronym of the stores' name, Consumer Value Stores, but as the business evolved, company executives said that the CVS stood for Customer, Value, and Service.

As CVS grew, it used a variety of marketing strategies to reach consumers in the markets where the chain was expanding. In 2000, working with the tagline "Care that touches everyone, one at a time," CVS promoted the idea that its business was based on customer service. A CVS in-house team created print advertising, from sales signs displayed in stores to newspaper ads and weekly circulars. Television and radio spots were created by the chain's advertising agency, New York–based Bates USA, which had signed on with CVS in 1997. CVS initiated its ExtraCare customer-loyalty-card program in 2001, supporting its introduction with a marketing campaign created by Boston-based agency Hill, Holliday, Connors, Cosmopulos. The ExtraCare launch was successful, and as CVS planned a national expansion into new markets, it dropped Bates USA and shifted its advertising work to Hill Holliday. The chain's first national brand-image campaign, themed "Life to the Fullest," was released in 2002.

REDESIGNED CVS STORES TO ENHANCE WOMEN'S SHOPPING EXPERIENCE

Hoping to appeal to women, its core audience, CVS Corporation began a makeover of its drugstore chain in 2004. Among the planned changes were cheerful turquoise and magenta walls and short shelves that enabled a woman of average height (five feet four) to see all over the store in a quick glance. An open path at the entrance of each store was designed to allow busy moms to avoid having to traverse a cluttered maze of aisles. To further pamper busy women, remodeled stores would have a beauty counter staffed by trained cosmetics and skin-care consultants. The chain's newest marketing strategy was expected to help add to the more than three million customers who shopped at CVS stores each day.

TARGET MARKET

CVS conducted market research to help identify the target market for the chain's new advertising campaign. The research included reviewing data from 45 million members of the chain's ExtraCare loyalty-card program, for which advertising and marketing had been created by Boston advertising agency Hill Holliday in 2001. The ExtraCare program offered customers rebates on purchases while enabling CVS to track buying trends. The data identified three customer profiles: young moms in their 30s, working mothers in their 40s with older children living at home, and retired women in their 60s and older. Data also revealed income levels of the average shopper, how much they typically spent each time they visited a CVS store, and what nonprescription products they usually purchased. Based on the information, the "Life to the Fullest" campaign was designed to appeal to women in a variety of age groups and incomes, but it specifically targeted the chain's core customer, working mothers of all ages. The campaign was also intended to create an emotional link to the women it targeted and sought to reinforce the idea that CVS understood women and their shopping needs. Reporting for *Drug Store News,* Rob Eder noted that, although the ads emphasized the quickness and efficiency of shopping at CVS, they also strove to avoid making the shopping experience seem dull.

COMPETITION

Walgreens, founded in 1901, was the United States' number one drugstore chain based on sales. Although CVS, with $24.2 billion in annual sales in 2003, was closing in on Walgreens, the older chain clung to its top spot. At the end of 2003 Walgreens operated 4,291 drugstores and reported annual sales of $32.5 billion. To encourage customers to shop the stores' front end (an industry term for the part of the store that was not the pharmacy) for a wide variety of nonprescription items and to send the message that the chain was more than a place to pick up prescription medications, in 2002 Walgreens released a marketing campaign themed "Perfect." Created by Omnicom Group's Chicago-based division, Downtown Partners, the television spots sent the message that Walgreens offered shoppers convenience, good service, and large product selection. The spots were set in the mythical village of Perfect and showed a dreamy image of everyone doing things they were supposed to do and everything working out right.

At the end of the spots a voice-over noted, "Of course, we don't live in Perfect, so we have Walgreens, where we can get what's needed for the real world." Not wanting to abandon its pharmacies, which accounted for about 64 percent of the chain's annual sales, Walgreens in 2002 introduced a second campaign that focused on the pharmacy aspect. The campaign was referred to as "Rx Safety Net" and was designed to differentiate Walgreens pharmacies from the competition and show the benefits of choosing Walgreens for prescription-drug services.

The number three drugstore chain, Rite Aid Corporation, owned 3,400 stores in 2003 and had annual sales of $16 billion. Despite falling in behind CVS and Walgreens, Rite Aid reported that its front-end business was one of the strongest in the chain-drugstore industry. One of Rite Aid's goals was to further build its pharmacy business by encouraging front-end shoppers to become pharmacy customers. John Learish, the chain's senior vice president of marketing, told *Chain Drug Review,* "The brand starts with the pharmacy. It's the heart and soul of what we do." With that in mind, rather than devising marketing campaigns to drive pharmacy customers to shop the front ends of their stores, as CVS and Walgreens did, in 2003 Rite Aid took a different approach. The chain released a campaign themed "With Us It's Personal," which focused on its pharmacy services and the relationship customers had with in-store pharmacists and sales associates. In addition, the campaign intentionally lacked a catchy tagline because, Learish noted, "The customer is pretty savvy. A slogan alone won't do it." He added that the effort was more than an advertising campaign: "It's a new approach to the way we do business."

MARKETING STRATEGY

Before planning its new marketing campaign, CVS and its ad agency, Hill Holliday, invested time in market and consumer research to determine everything from who they should target to what products the consumer was shopping for during stops in CVS stores. Working with the data gathered, Hill Holliday created the "Life to the Fullest" campaign. It began in October 2002 with a series of six television spots and a dozen print ads. No budget was available, but a report in *Adweek* noted that the drugstore chain spent approximately $35 million annually on advertising.

Television spots aired in the morning during network news programs, including *Good Morning America* and *Today.* During prime time the spots were shown on cable networks with a large female audience, such as Lifetime, the Food Network, and Home and Garden Television, as well as during programs that attracted a younger female audience, including *Survivor, The West Wing,* and *Gilmore Girls.* Spots relied on visual techniques to show viewers how products available in CVS stores could enhance their lives and how shopping at the chain could save them time. Each spot placed a typical shopper in her normal environment, but with a CVS store-aisle marker over her head. On the aisle marker's left side was a list of the shopper's CVS purchases, and on its right side was a list of the benefits the person derived from shopping at the chain. In one spot a woman flirted with a handsome 20-something guy at a nightclub. The left side of the aisle marker above her head read, "Calcium, Iron Supply, Haircolor," while the right side stated, with each phrase on a separate line, "Still / Grooving / At 50." When the woman turned away from the man and toward the camera, it was evident she was no longer a 20-something. Another spot showed a woman ready to relax in a peaceful swimming pool. The left side of the aisle marker over her head stated, "SunBlock, Lip Balm, and Skin Care," while the right side read, "And Hubby / Has the / Kids." A spot targeting older women had a couple of senior ladies showing off a confident and playful attitude while primping in a public restroom with cosmetics purchased at a CVS store.

Print ads, which ran in *People* magazine, followed a format similar to the television spots. One ad featured a woman sitting on her living-room sofa while she gave herself a manicure and pedicure. The aisle marker over her head read, "Cotton balls, nail polish, chocolate, extra bucks can be extra indulgent." Another print ad showed a couple sitting in the candlelit booth of a romantic restaurant. The woman was holding a present, and the aisle marker above her head stated, "Greeting cards. Gift wrap. Chocolate. He's finally getting it."

OUTCOME

Following the 2002 launch of the "Life to the Fullest" campaign, CVS reported a chainwide upswing in sales. According to a report in *Chain Drug Review,* in 2001 CVS had failed to meet its business goals, reaching just $413.2 million in net income. But in 2002 the company's net income increased 73.4 percent to $716.6 million. Further indication that the campaign was helping drive consumers into CVS/pharmacy stores was a jump in 2002 sales to $22.2 billion, an 8.7 percent increase over 2001 sales. In 2003 *Advertising Age* magazine named Hill Holliday one its Agencies of the Year, in part for its creative efforts on CVS's "Life to the Fullest" campaign. A report in *Adweek* praised the television spot that showed elderly women primping together in a public restroom with cosmetics purchased at a CVS drugstore for injecting life into what was typically a "ho-hum retail segment."

FURTHER READING

"Ads Tout Belief in Customer Service (CVS Corp. Advertising Strategy)." *Chain Drug Review,* December 11, 2000.

Aoki, Naomi. "CVS to Undergo Makeover; Drugstore Chain Redesigns Stores with Women in Mind." *Boston Globe,* May 2, 2004.

"CVS Makes Things Easy for Customers." *Chain Drug Review,* July 21, 2003.

"CVS Names Hill, Holliday as Lead Ad Agency." *Business Wire,* June 19, 2002.

Eder, Rob. "CVS Breaks New Lifestyle-Oriented Ads." *Drug Store News,* October 21, 2002.

Gatlin, Greg. "CVS Aims Ads at Busy Women." *The Boston Herald,* October 10, 2002.

Gianatasio, David. "CVS to Live 'Life to the Fullest'." *Adweek,* October 19, 2002.

"Hill, Holliday, CVS National Campaign: 'Life to the Fullest'." *Adweek,* October 14, 2002.

Kirk, Jim. "Chicago Tribune Marketing Column." *Chicago Tribune,* January 10, 2002.

"New Campaigns: Cleaning Up on Aisle Seven, Eight, Nine…" *Brandweek,* October 21, 2002.

"Rite Aid Aims to Break Out from the Pack (Building a New Rite Aid)." *Chain Drug Review,* October 27, 2003.

"Time-Starved People Need Good, Quick Service." *Chain Drug Review,* July 21, 2003.

"TV Spots Highlight Convenience." *Chain Drug Review,* April 29, 2002.

Rayna Bailey

Cyan Worlds Inc.

14617 Newport Hwy.
Mead, Washington 99021-9378
USA
Telephone: (509) 468-0807
Fax: (509) 467-2209
Web site: www.riven.com

RIVEN CAMPAIGN

OVERVIEW

NOTE: Since the initial appearance of this essay in the 1999 edition of *Major Marketing Campaigns Annual,* the Riven product was acquired by Cyan Worlds Inc. The essay continues to refer to The Learning Company, as they owned Riven when the campaign was launched.

An advertising campaign that used spectacular screen shots from Riven: The Sequel to Myst helped make the product the leading computer game in the United States within two months of its release. Riven and its phenomenally successful predecessor, Myst, were the two most popular PC games in 1997, and they remained among the highest-ranked computer games throughout 1998. Like Myst, Riven was a nonviolent adventure game that involved the exploration of fabulous islands and the solving of puzzles to the accompaniment of an eerily beautiful sound track. Advertisements for Riven emphasized that it was a continuation of the mysterious story introduced in the first game. One television commercial began with a close-up of a book embellished with curious symbols that swept the audience into a world full of abandoned structures, towering cliffs, meandering pathways, and intriguing machines, all new but similar to the sights gamers had found on the islands of Myst. The campaign also included radio commercials, print ads, and a network of hyperlinks on the Internet. In addition, promotions for Riven had begun building anticipation a year before the game was released in October 1997. The campaign for Riven, which ran during 1997 and 1998, was developed by Saatchi & Saatchi Advertising. The game was designed by Cyan, Inc., was published by Brøderbund Software, Inc., and was marketed by Brøderbund's Red Orb Entertainment division.

HISTORICAL CONTEXT

Cyan was a software development company founded in 1988 in Spokane, Washington, by brothers Rand and Robyn Miller and a friend, Chris Brandkamp. Richard Vander Wendelater joined Cyan to help develop Riven. The firm's early successes included three games for children: Spelunx and the Caves of Mr. Seudo, Manhole, and Cosmic Osmo. The publisher of Myst and Riven, Brøderbund, was founded in 1980 by brothers Doug and Gary Carlston to market their computer games Galactic Empire and Galactic Trader. The firm soon became widely known for its imaginative games and for its interactive software for homes, schools, and small businesses. The company's most successful products included Family Tree Maker, Print Shop, Living Books, 3D Home Series, and an educational game named Carmen Sandiego. Brøderbund's Red Orb Entertainment division, formed in 1997, developed high-quality computer games, and it published and marketed entertainment software made by Cyan and other companies. Red Orb's most successful games included Warlords, The Journeyman Project, and Prince of Persia.

When Myst was launched in October 1993, it was among the first CD-ROM games with three-dimensional graphics. This technological breakthrough allowed consumers to enjoy realistic adventures on their personal computers. In addition to its groundbreaking animation, Myst featured a hauntingly beautiful sound track and an intriguing concept. The player was transported to five mystical islands complete with deserted buildings, a spaceship, a sailing ship, a lighthouse, and a tree with an elevator in it. By piecing together clues and using logic to operate generators and other equipment, the player solved a mystery involving the family that had built the structures. Although players felt a sense of suspense while exploring the islands, the game involved no violence. Myst was regarded as one of the most "immersive" games of its day, making players feel as if they had actually entered an alternate reality. At the time a computer game was considered successful if it sold a total of 100,000 copies, but Myst sold half a million copies in its first year. Also impressive was its continued success over time. It was the third most popular software of any kind in 1995, its sales surpassed only by Quicken and the program to upgrade Microsoft Windows. By the spring of 1998 consumers had purchased more than 4 million copies of Myst, making it the best selling CD-ROM entertainment title to date. By the fifth anniversary of its release approximately two copies of Myst had been sold for every minute the game was on the market. People who had enjoyed Myst waited with great excitement for the release of Riven: The Sequel to Myst in the fall of 1997.

RELATED PROMOTIONS

Other promotions ran in conjunction with the advertising campaign for Riven. Sound tracks to computer games were sometimes sold to generate publicity and additional revenues from consumers who did not own computers but who wanted to experience part of what the games had to offer. By February 1998, when Virgin Records and Cyan, Inc., released the sound track to Riven: The Sequel to Myst, consumers had already purchased 70,000 copies of the Myst sound track by mail order. The music of Myst was released for sale through retail outlets in April 1998. Only 300 units of the Riven sound track sold during the first week, but Cyan expected sales to increase over time, since games tended to remain popular for years. To commemorate the fifth anniversary of the release of Myst in October 1998, Red Orb Entertainment began marketing Ages of Myst, a software package that included Myst, Riven, a video that discussed the making of Riven, a dedication from the brothers who had created the titles, and a journal in which players could take notes to help them solve puzzles in the games. Ages of Myst was promoted with its own seven-figure advertising campaign.

TARGET MARKET

Traditionally marketed toward young males, many computer games were promoted with advertisements that emphasized violence, but the campaign for Riven emphasized the mystery and beauty of a surreal world. Although male consumers 18 to 45 years old were a primary market for Riven, Myst had also been unusually successful with a mainstream audience of women (who accounted for about a third of its sales), children, and older people. The campaign for Riven targeted the millions of people who had already purchased the first game, and it was designed to entice consumers who had heard about Myst but never played it. In fact, Riven was expected to attract a large number of people who seldom played computer games. It was designed for consumers with various skill levels and various reasons for playing. Some enjoyed exploring a realistic fantasy world as if they were experiencing an adventure vacation. Others were more interested in solving logical problems. Riven required little manual dexterity, only the ability to point and click with a computer mouse, and its lack of violence made it an appealing choice for families. Because of its complex puzzles, however, it was intended primarily for adults who liked to think.

COMPETITION

In 1997 North American retail sales of computer games reached $5.1 billion. During the first half of 1998 the computer gaming industry grew by about 30 percent. Sony Corporation's PlayStation and other console video games designed to be played on television sets had dominated the emerging industry for years, but as more consumers purchased personal computers with CD-ROM drives and other technological innovations, computer games became increasingly popular. By the late 1990s thousands of titles were available, including chess, flight simulators, games that mimicked football and other sports, adventures that used characters and settings from motion pictures, and games designed for small children. Some of the most popular titles involved graphic violence, while others revolved around such intellectual challenges as the building of cities and the solving of puzzles. In 1998 Scrabble, Monopoly Game, and Frogger—all marketed by Hasbro Interactive—were among the top 20 computer games. The leading title in 1998 was StarCraft, marketed by Havas Interactive, Inc., which also marketed the popular Diablo and Titanic: Adventure out of Time.

Riven and Myst were generally considered to be part of the strategy, action, and adventure segments of the industry, which included games that simulated wars and big-game hunting. Two of the most widely known titles in the segment were Doom and Quake (both made by id Software, Inc.), which required players to navigate mazes while gunning down enemies. Quake II ranked 16th out of the top 20 PC games in 1998. Another long-running favorite, Tomb Raider, was in 12th place in 1997 but dropped out of the top 20 in 1998. The game, marketed by Eidos Interactive, starred a scantily clad heroine with a flair for gunfights and gymnastics. Some action games featured battling knights, dragons, and other fantasy characters who fought with primitive weapons. "Heft your broadsword and mete out punishment in a purely medieval manner!" proclaimed the text in an advertisement for King's Quest, marketed by Sierra On-Line, Inc. In science fiction games the player was often pitted against futuristic weapons and gigantic robots in a fight to dominate entire worlds. "The wreckage just doesn't stop!" read the headline in a magazine advertisement for Total Annihilation, marketed by Cavedog Entertainment, a division of Humongous Entertainment, Inc. Two products related to the *Star Wars* series of motion pictures—Jedi Knight: Dark Forces II and X-Wing vs. TIE Fighter—were among the top 20 PC games of 1997. Both were marketed by LucasArts Entertainment Company, which also made the popular adventure game Grim Fandango.

Other adventure games more closely resembled Myst and Riven. Timelapse, marketed by Hammerhead Entertainment, a division of Barracuda, Inc., involved a search for a missing archaeologist and the discovery that ancient civilizations in Egypt and the Americas had been in contact with beings from another planet. An advertisement in *Family PC* magazine showed beautiful, colorful scenes from the game, including an artist's rendition of a technologically advanced Atlantis, a Mayan pyramid, and a boat docked beside an Egyptian temple. A game named Temujin, developed by SouthPeak Interactive, was launched in mid-October 1997, allowing its promoters to take advantage of the publicity surrounding the release of Riven two weeks later. Like Riven, Temujin was a nonviolent adventure with high-quality graphic art, a series of puzzles to solve, and no action figures. SouthPeak's $650,000 advertising campaign in print media and on the Internet, launched in March 1997, called attention to the similarities and differences between Temujin and Riven.

MARKETING STRATEGY

After four years of product development and one year of publicity to build anticipation, the advertising campaign for Riven broke late in the summer of 1997. The game itself was released on Halloween amid great excitement from consumers, who looked forward to purchasing the sequel to Myst. Although extensive advertising for a CD-ROM game was unusual, the promotional campaign from Saatchi & Saatchi included public relations support, network and cable television commercials, radio spots, and ads in *Rolling Stone* and other magazines for young adults. Brøderbund budgeted $10 million for the marketing effort, half for traditional advertising media and half for Internet promotions. On the World Wide Web a network of hyperlinks led consumers to numerous so-called immersive sites, where they could sample demonstration versions of the game. To generate suspense, these sites were launched in succession over a period of time. Other sites provided fans with background information about the worlds and characters in Riven, and they listed related merchandise such as daggers and costumes that consumers could purchase. The marketing plan included agreements with on-line gaming sites and search engines, including Excite, Webcrawler, and Yahoo!, to lead consumers to Riven promotions. In addition, Red Orb Entertainment formed a retail marketing partnership with Toshiba Corporation to make shoppers aware of Riven and to provide opportunities for the public to try a demonstration of the game. Early in 1998 consumers who purchased Riven also received a demonstration version of a new Brøderbund game named Journeyman Project 3: Legacy of Time. The retail promotions helped Riven compete for valuable display space in the 19,000 stores in which it was sold.

Television commercials used scenes from Riven to give consumers a quick, intriguing tour of an alternative reality full of water, cliffs, peculiar buildings, and sophisticated machinery. In one spot a narrator said, "The grounds have been prepared, the paths raked. Everyone and everything is in place. All is in its final state of readiness. You may enter whenever you choose. Leaving, however, is another matter." The commercial opened by showing a book on a golden circle. To the sound of eerie music, the turning of pages, and water dripping in a vast cavern, the book opened to show a black rectangle in which a watery world suddenly materialized. The audience was swept inside, flying past the rocky shore of an island and along a walkway to a strange round structure. The scene shifted to a view from inside a dark cave, looking through a rickety gate. The camera moved outside and climbed a pathway meandering up a hill. A new scene showed a whalelike animal waving its fins in the air and then shifted to a narrow opening in another dark cave, looking out on sunbeams illuminating a ship's wooden deck and rigging. The camera seemed to drop as an elevator descended quickly, revealing glimpses of towering rock formations, blue sky, and mysterious shadows. The elevator stopped at a pathway leading to another curious structure. The scene switched back to the book, which slammed shut with a loud bang while mysterious music played. Fire and darkness gave way to a picture of the game's box and the words "Riven. The Sequel to Myst" on a black background with mist drifting across it.

OUTCOME

In 1997 Riven was the most popular game for both PC and Macintosh users, and Myst was the second most popular PC game. PC Data reported that, in the seven years the company had tracked software sales, Riven was the first entertainment title to reach number one in the category in just over two months. Consumers purchased more than 95,000 copies of Riven on its first day in stores, generating $4.4 million in sales. More than 474,000 copies of Riven were sold within the first month after its release in October 1997. By March 1998 sales of Riven had skyrocketed to approximately 1.5 million copies. By the end of 1998 Riven had dropped to 11th place on the computer game charts, and Myst had slipped to 3rd. At that time the average retail price for Myst had been discounted to $18 (down from $47 in 1996), while Riven's average price was $39. Riven was widely acclaimed and won a 1998 craft award for outstanding achievement in art and graphics from the Academy of Interactive Arts and Sciences. Cyan planned to recap the story line of the two games in novels and was considering a feature film.

Robyn Miller retained his position as co-owner of Cyan but also in 1998 founded Land of Point, a firm that developed computer-animated feature films with the same type of geographic and cultural detail as those found in Myst and Riven. In 1997 Cyan had an estimated $20 million in sales, up 33.3 percent over 1996. In 1998 Brøderbund's Red Orb Entertainment division introduced a new action game, Warbreeds, a combination of fantasy and science fiction that used real-time strategy and characters with complex backgrounds. Aimed primarily at adults, Warbreeds involved the building of structures and the harnessing of power, but unlike Riven, it included violent battles and interaction with alien creatures.

The success of Riven, supported by the continued demand for Myst, was the primary reason Brøderbund had revenues of $81.3 million during the first eight months the game was on the market, compared to $21.8 million for the same period in the previous year. Nevertheless, the company reported a net loss of $2.7 million for the financial quarter that ended on May 31, 1998. The cost of royalties for Riven and Myst contributed to the loss. In addition, the company had increased its sales and marketing budget by about 38 percent, including a 77 percent increase in its advertising budget. In September another software firm, the Learning Company, acquired Brøderbund with a stock swap valued at $420 million. The Learning Company moved Riven to its Mindscape Entertainment division, which marketed an assortment of action games. By the end of the year the Learning Company had become a division of Mattel, Inc., one of the largest firms in the toy industry.

FURTHER READING

Armstrong, Larry, and Steve Hamm. "CD-ROMs: The Giants Rule." *Business Week,* October 6, 1997, p. 156.

Browder, Seanna. "More Magic from the Makers of Myst?" *Business Week,* October 5, 1997, p. 160.

Gatland, Laura. "Big Game Hunting: 'Temujin' Fights 'Riven' for a Piece of the CD-ROM Game Market." *Marketing News,* January 5, 1998, p. 1.

Guttman, Monika. "Two Mavericks Become Moguls: The Miller Brothers Are Working Hard to Create a Sequel to 'Myst,' Their Bestselling CD-ROM Game." *U.S. News & World Report,* January 15, 1996, p. 48.

Kelly, Sean. "Rand Miller: Riven Driven." *Computer Life,* April 1997, p. 46.

Langberg, Mike. "'Riven' Succeeds Computer Game Sensation 'Myst,'" Knight-Ridder/Tribune Business News, November 4, 1997.

McCabe, Kathy. "Video Game Wars: Hasbro Interactive Fights for Share in Crowded Market." *Boston Globe,* June 2, 1999, p. D1.

Scally, Robert. "PC, Video Game Software Sales Hit Record High in 1997." *Discount Store News,* March 9, 1998, p. 65.

Shatz-Akin, Jim. "Not to Be Myst." *Computer Life,* January 1998, p. 121.

Thomas, Susan Gregory. "Good, Clean Adult Fun: Not Every Exciting PC Game Has to Involve Mayhem." *U.S. News & World Report,* November 24, 1997, p. 119.

Warner, Bernhard. "ROM Realm." *Brandweek,* February 17, 1997, p. 1.

White, Ron. "Adventure." *PC/Computing,* December 1997, p. 320.

Susan Risland

DaimlerChrysler Corp.

1000 Chrysler Dr.
Auburn Hills, Michigan 48326-2766
USA
Telephone: (248) 576-5741
Web site: www.daimlerchrysler.com

EMPLOYEE PRICING PLAN PLUS CAMPAIGN

OVERVIEW

The Chrysler Group, based in Auburn Hills, Michigan, was the American subsidiary of DaimlerChrysler, responsible for the sales, marketing, and manufacturing of vehicles from the Dodge, Chrysler, and Jeep brands. In 2005 one of Chrysler's key competitors, the General Motors Corporation (GM), had planned a major sales initiative that combined price reductions with rebates and promised to make the price of GM vehicles extremely competitive. In an attempt to head off this move the Chrysler Group developed its own program, Employee Pricing Plan Plus, slated for June 2005. The initiative combined regular rebates (cash-back programs for consumers purchasing vehicles) with 4 to 5 percent discounts on the factory price. This led to price reductions of thousands of dollars for certain vehicles.

To spread the word about this new program the Chrysler Group asked its primary advertising agency, BBDO Detroit, to develop a campaign that would alert a wide audience to the steep discounts on Chrysler vehicles. BBDO decided to reach into the automaker's past and bring back Lee Iacocca to serve as the company's spokesperson. Iacocca, who from 1978 to 1992 served as president and then as chairman of Chrysler Group's predecessor, the Chrysler Corporation, had starred in a number of successful television spots on behalf of the automaker during the 1980s. The new spots, however, featured Iacocca in situations unfamiliar to those who remembered him from earlier campaigns. Instead of seriously addressing the camera, Iacocca informed consumers about the Employee Pricing Plan Plus through onscreen discussions with entertainers, his granddaughter (played by an actress), and a television set. One particularly memorable spot featured Iacocca playing golf with gangster-rap pioneer Snoop Dogg. The campaign also used print ads, which did not feature Iacocca.

The campaign was a success. July 2005 sales increased 32 percent over the same month in 2004, convincing Chrysler to extend the Employee Pricing Plan Plus until the end of the model year. Sales for the entire year were up about 5 percent.

HISTORICAL CONTEXT

The Chrysler Group was a subsidiary of the Germany-based automaker DaimlerChrysler. Headquartered in Auburn Hills, Michigan, the Chrysler Group was responsible for selling vehicles in the Dodge, Chrysler, and Jeep brands. It was created following the 1998 merger between the Chrysler Corporation and Daimler-Benz. Daimler-Benz itself was formed in 1926 through the merger of two German automakers. While Chrysler had been struggling when it joined forces with Daimler-Benz, by 2004 the company was reporting solid sales growth. That year the Chrysler Group sold more than 2.2 million units of its Chrysler, Jeep, and Dodge vehicles, a 4 percent increase from the previous year. The best-selling Chrysler Group vehicle in 2004 was the Dodge Ram pickup, 426,000 of which were moved that year.

The Chrysler Corporation was founded in 1925 by Walter P. Chrysler. Along with the Ford Motor Company and the General Motors Corporation, Chrysler was known as one of the "Big Three" U.S. automobile manufacturers that dominated the international automotive industry through much of the twentieth century. By the 1970s, however, Chrysler was in serious trouble, and it reached near bankruptcy in 1980. The company was saved from bankruptcy in part by a 1980 bailout from the federal government that was engineered by Chrysler's new top executive, Lee Iacocca.

Iacocca became president of Chrysler in 1978 and chairman of the company one year later. In addition to securing federal support, he made substantial changes to how the company operated. He streamlined its management structure by removing many of the company's executives, and he cut costs by negotiating with the powerful United Auto Workers union to institute a reduction in wages and benefits.

By 1983 the company was making enough of a profit to repay all of the money the U.S. government had loaned it in 1980. The company introduced the first minivan in 1984, creating a new market that Chrysler continued to dominate through the beginning of the twenty-first century. Iacocca also became Chrysler's most visible spokesperson, appearing in a long string of television commercials in the 1980s. Most of those spots ended with the executive's famous catchphrase: "If you can find a better car, buy it." He retired from the company in 1992.

In 1995, however, the former savior of the company alienated many at Chrysler when he joined investor Kirk Kerkorian's unsuccessful attempt to take over the company. As a result, relations between Iacocca and the Chrysler Corporation, which later became part of DaimlerChrysler, were strained for much of the next 10 years. The market pressures that Kerkorian's takeover bid exposed later helped push Chrysler to merge with Daimler-Benz.

LEE IACOCCA

During a career that lasted nearly five decades, Lee Iacocca built a reputation as one of the most successful executives in the automotive industry. Most of that time was spent at the Ford Motor Company, where he began his career in 1947. While at Ford, Iacocca helped develop the brand's signature Ford Mustang muscle car. He became president of the company in 1970 but was forced to leave that position in 1978 after a dispute with Henry Ford II, the son of the company's founder. Soon afterward Iacocca joined the Chrysler Corporation as that company's president. He became chairman the following year.

Chrysler's subsequent turnaround from near bankruptcy made Iacocca a major celebrity. His autobiography, *Iacocca* (published in 1984), topped the best-seller lists, and he became Chrysler's public face, starring in a series of commercials that ran throughout the 1980s. Iacocca's public reputation was so good that many people urged him to run for president of the United States in 1988. He declined. Instead Iacocca continued at Chrysler until his retirement in 1992. He angered many at Chrysler in 1995 by participating in billionaire investor Kirk Kerkorian's unsuccessful bid to take control of the company; the situation led to years of acrimony between Iacocca and an organization that many credited him with saving. Chrysler and its onetime hero executive finally patched things up in 2005, when Iacocca became the company's spokesman once again.

TARGET MARKET

On July 9, 2005, Chrysler introduced its Employee Pricing Plan Plus program. It was a very competitive mix of reduced prices and consumer rebates (through which customers could earn cash back from vehicles purchased) meant to compete with parallel sales that rival automakers—particularly General Motors—were offering that summer. The program was aimed at all consumers who were often more price-conscious than other buyers and especially at those younger than 49 years of age.

COMPETITION

In 2005 the General Motors Corporation (GM) was offering a major price-incentive plan through its dealers, reducing the prices of most GM vehicles. At the time GM was the world's largest automaker as well as the top-selling automobile manufacturer in the United States. Using the tagline "You pay what we pay," GM cut prices aggressively in an attempt to convince consumers that they would get a good deal on a GM car purchased in July 2005. This put the pressure on GM's rivals to match these low prices or get left behind.

To counter GM, the Chrysler Group developed an offer that it dubbed the Employee Pricing Plan Plus. The program covered most Chrysler Group vehicles, including the Chrysler PT Cruiser and the Dodge Ram pickup. Planned for July 2005, the program featured discounts of 4 to 5 percent off the dealer invoice. Any existing rebates would also continue to be honored. The effect was steep reductions in sales prices. For example, the price of the Dodge Durango SUV was cut by up to $9,000 with a rebate.

MARKETING STRATEGY

The Chrysler Group decided to tout its Employee Pricing Plan Plus with a $75 million television campaign to run in July and August 2005. It enlisted advertising agency BBDO Detroit to develop the campaign. BBDO determined that the best way to introduce Chrysler's new pricing program was to turn to someone from the company's past. After a 20-year hiatus from television commercials, Lee Iacocca returned as the pitchman for Chrysler Group vehicles. Although he retired from the company in 1992, Iacocca was still closely identified with the automotive giant. He also maintained a high profile in his own right through his work with the Iacocca Foundation, a charitable organization that raised money for diabetes research. Iacocca had created the foundation in 1984, after the death of his wife. In 2005 he donated his entire paycheck from making the commercials to the foundation. In addition, the Chrysler Group agreed to become a partner of the Iacocca Foundation, pledging to help raise more than $6 million.

The campaign began with three 30-second television spots: "Desk," "Channel Surfing," and "Granddaughter." The first spot, "Desk," featured Iacocca discussing the new pricing plan with Jason Alexander, an actor widely known for his role as George on the hit sitcom *Seinfeld.* It aired beginning July 9. In the spot "Channel Surfing," Iacocca was shown watching a commercial for Chrysler's 2005 vehicle line. After the commercial for the vehicles ended, Iacocca pointed out that it had failed to mention the company's new Employee Pricing Plan Plus, which he than explained. The spot used Iacocca's outgoing, irreverent personality to connect with audiences.

The third spot, "Granddaughter," used a setup similar to that of "Desk," in which Iacocca was engaged in a conversation with someone about the new "Employee Pricing Plan Plus." This time it was a young girl, said to be his granddaughter (the girl was actually played by an actress). In August the final commercial, "Golfing Buddies," premiered. It depicted Iacocca golfing with famed rapper Snoop Dogg, who was one of the major innovators of the rough-edged "gangster rap" of the early 1990s. The spot's entertainment value came from the incongruousness of the sight of the hip-hop star golfing at a country club with the aging business icon. Adding to the humor was Iacocca's use of hip-hop slang during the spot. All of the commercials featured Iacocca's 1980s tagline, "If you can find a better car, buy it."

Even 13 years after his retirement, Lee Iacocca was a well-known figure who carried high name recognition with consumers. He also had the advantage of being known for his work in the automotive industry; indeed he was arguably the most acclaimed auto executive of his generation. This gave him an ability to connect with car buyers that few could match. Also, he was a proven success as a pitchman, having starred in a number of successful campaigns in the 1980s. The pairings with entertainers Snoop Dogg and Jason Alexander especially caught TV viewers' attention. Even those unswayed by Iacocca's reputation could still find humor in the scenario of the aging executive hanging out with irreverent pop-culture figures.

The Employee Pricing Plan Plus campaign also included a major three-page print spread in *USA Today.* Referring to the company's competitors, it featured the tagline "First, we beat them at the show. Now, we're taking it to the showroom." Similar print advertisements later ran in local publications throughout the United States. Iacocca was not depicted in the print ads.

OUTCOME

The television spots for Chrysler's Employee Pricing Plan Plus were immediately successful. Although only 15 percent of respondents to *USA Today*'s Ad Track survey rated the spots favorably, the commercials produced strong bottom-line results. Sales in July 2005 improved 32 percent over July 2004: the Chrysler Group sold more than 240,000 units that month, a company record for monthly sales. Competitor GM's pricing program, however, generated even bigger sales gains; it moved 41 percent more units in July 2005 than in the previous year. Although the Employee Pricing Plan Plus program was originally slated for July 2005, because of its effectiveness it was extended through the rest of the summer. For the year Chrysler Group saw U.S. sales jump 5 percent, with more than 2.3 million units sold.

The spots worked best with the young driver they were meant to target. In the Ad Track survey 18 percent of consumers aged 25 to 49 stated that they liked the spots a lot, the best of any age group. Between 66 and 74 percent of these respondents recognized Iacocca (it varied depending on the particular commercial). Older viewers, however, were more aware of who Iacocca was. Between 82 percent and 91 percent of respondents aged 50 and over recognized the famed businessman when they saw the commercials.

FURTHER READING

Clanton, Brett. "Iacocca Back as Chrysler Voice." *Detroit News,* July 7, 2005.

Hakim, Danny. "As the Going Gets Tough, Chrysler Calls on Its Old Pitchman." *New York Times,* July 7, 2005.

———. "Hip-Hop Argot Meets Corporate Cant, All to Sell Chryslers." *New York Times,* August 5, 2005.

Howard, Theresa. "Iacocca Return: Win-Win Deal." *USA Today,* October 2, 2005.

Iacocca, Lee. *Iacocca: An Autobiography.* With William Novak. New York: Bantam Books, 1984.

———. *Talking Straight.* With Sonny Kleinfield. New York: Bantam Books, 1988.

Maynard, Micheline. "Openers: Suits; Generizzle, Fo' Shizzle." *New York Times,* November 13, 2005.

Peters, Jeremy W. "'Employee Discounts' Push July Auto Sales to a Record." *New York Times,* August 3, 2005.

Vlasic, Bill, and Bradley A. Stertz. *Taken for a Ride: How Daimler-Benz Drove Off with Chrysler.* New York: W. Morrow, 2000.

Yates, Brock. *The Critical Path: Inventing an Automobile and Reinventing a Corporation.* Boston: Little, Brown, 1996.

Guy Patrick Cunningham

ENGINEERED TO BE GREAT CARS CAMPAIGN

OVERVIEW

Automobile advertising has historically constituted not only one of the most visible but also, in sheer dollar volume, one of the largest aspects of the marketing industry. Thus in the 1990s Chrysler, which in 1998 merged with German automaker Daimler-Benz to create DaimlerChrysler AG, had an advertising budget of $1 billion. This certainly dwarfed the budgets of most companies, but even the amount it dedicated to its Chrysler line in 1998—as opposed to other lines such as Plymouth or Jeep—was impressive at an estimated $200 million. Michigan agency Bozell, Southfield handled the entire account, which included television, radio, and print advertising, with an emphasis on television. The company's overall theme was "Great cars. Great trucks." As for the Chrysler brand itself, it replaced its 1997 campaign, "What's in Your World?," with the tag line "Engineered to be great cars."

Chrysler's 1998 advertising promoted models such as the Concorde and the LHS, the latter introduced in 1994. But the biggest news was the 300M, a semiluxury model whose design suggested earlier styles. And well it might, for the *M* in its name signified a return to the popular 300 "letter series" of the 1950s and 1960s. During that time Chrysler had produced a new model each year, identified by successive letters of the alphabet. The launch of the 300M also marked the return of a distinctive winged logo that Chrysler had not used for more than 60 years.

Advertising for the 300M and other lines emphasized luxury in an attempt to overcome negative images associated with the company's recent past. In the 1970s Chrysler had nearly gone bankrupt, and even under the leadership of the charismatic Lee Iacocca in the 1980s, it had been unable to shake the perception of its product as drab and utilitarian. Perhaps it was ironic then that Chrysler's 1998 advertising also stressed the theme of heritage. But in this case "heritage" suggested something much larger than the company's actual history; rather, the theme carried with it images of a luxurious past—and a prosperous future.

HISTORICAL CONTEXT

In 1920 the Maxwell Motor Car Company hired former General Motors (GM) vice president Walter Chrysler to turn around its failing enterprise. Chrysler became president of the revitalized company in 1923 and in the following year introduced the Chrysler model with a distinctive winged symbol as its trademark. A year later, in 1925, the company was renamed Chrysler, and in 1928 it purchased Dodge, a company that produced the Plymouth and DeSoto lines.

After a strong start, however, by mid century Chrysler began to slip. At a time when rivals GM and Ford, responding to postwar prosperity, regularly introduced new models, innovation at Chrysler came to a standstill. The company even dropped the winged symbol in the mid-1930s, adding to the impression of Chryslers as unexciting cars. Then, in the mid-1950s, the automaker showed that it still retained Walter Chrysler's ability—Chrysler himself had retired in 1935—to revive his company's fortunes.

"In 1955," wrote Jennifer Lach in *American Demographics* in 1998, "Chrysler needed a new icon. It had no [Chevrolet] Corvette, no [Ford] Thunderbird for young crew-cuts in blue jeans to drool over. That was the year the company found its muscle car: the C-300." Promoted as "America's most powerful car," the C-300 proved enormously popular, and during the next decade Chrysler introduced a new model every year, each with a letter attached to the end of the name. With the 300Lin 1965, however, the so-called letter series ended.

Chrysler itself fell on hard times in the 1960s and 1970s. First it introduced smaller models before the public was ready for them, and then it returned to larger vehicles just in time for the oil crisis of the 1970s. The company persisted in producing gas-guzzlers throughout the decade, and soon Chrysler was in so much trouble that it applied for and received $1.5 billion worth of loan guarantees from the federal government.

Iacocca, former Ford president, became head of Chrysler in 1978, launching yet another turnaround. During the 1980s the company paid off its government loans, beat its competitors by introducing the first minivan, and introduced a series of sturdy if unexciting vehicles called "K cars." Iacocca left the company in 1992, and in 1998 it was acquired by Daimler-Benz, a vast European auto manufacturer whose best-known product was the upscale Mercedes-Benz.

TARGET MARKET

With the Chrysler 300M sedan, launched in 1998, the company made a push for mature, prosperous buyers with a penchant for luxury. The target for the 300M model, according to Jean Halliday in *Advertising Age,* was people 35 years of age and older, with buyers expected to be about 40 percent female. For its LHS sedan, another luxury model first introduced in 1994, the company expected buyers to be 45 years old and older, with about 30 percent female. Its appeal was to what Lach in *American Demographics* called the "near-luxury" segment.

Hence the emphasis on heritage, certainly not a theme a company would apply in marketing to very young consumers, along with a program of marketing in a number of venues, many of them decidedly upscale. The first print ads for the 1998 line appeared in October 1997 in *Coastal Living, Food and Wine, Vogue, GQ, Martha Stewart's Living,* and a number of other publications, including the more broadly based *Business Week* and *Sports Illustrated.*

Television advertising ran the gamut, though again the thrust was toward more seasoned viewers. Hence the company placed spots on ABC's *Nightline* and NBC's *Tonight Show,* as well as on ABC and CBS telecasts of college football. Other television advertising in the 1998 campaign also placed an emphasis on mature viewers. Thus in January the company ran its "Wings" spot on the telecast of the Bob Hope Chrysler Classic golf tournament, the Golden Globes film awards, and the popular show *ER.* Meanwhile, Chrysler eyed the demographics of the future. Chrysler executive Steven Bruyn told Lach that the company already had its eye on the 2003 market, when it predicted that what were called "personal luxury cars"—that is, two-seater sports cars—would be all the rage. "Once the kids are gone" to college, an industry analyst suggested, "[baby] boomers are going to trade in their SUVs [sport utility vehicles] and indulge in a two-seater."

COMPETITION

On the one hand, Chrysler faced its traditional foes in the U.S. auto industry: Ford, whose Lincoln Continental line competed with Chrysler's luxury models, and GM, with its Buick Park Avenue and other models. On the other hand, there were the many upscale imports such as the Lexus and the BMW. But the theme that appeared again and again, as the advertising and automotive industries examined the "new" Chrysler—both the car and the company—was that of the company's own conflicts over image.

Indeed, image problems perhaps posed the greatest competition to Chrysler. "To some," wrote Robyn

GETTING INSIDE CONSUMERS' BRAINS

"At first glance," wrote Jeffrey Ball in the *Wall Street Journal,* "DaimlerChrysler AG's new PT Cruiser looks like a massive gamble. Set to go on sale starting at about $16,000 early next year [2000], it's part 1920s gangster car, part 1950s hot rod, and part London taxicab." Yet as Ball went on to relate, its creation was the product of a thorough and innovative new program in marketing research that would soon find imitators if it proved successful. Chrysler, which dubbed its new offering "a sure-fire 'segment buster,'" certainly believed so.

French-born medical anthropologist G. Clotaire Rapaille, who had first gained notoriety for his experiments with teaching language to children with severe autism, oversaw the studies. Using theories related to a "mental imprint," Rapaille set out to help Chrysler discover consumers' "reptilian hot button"—an instinctive, preverbal part of the brain that would show what they really wanted. The result was what Ball described as "a series of freewheeling, three-hour focus-group sessions in the U.S. and Europe."

Having shown participants a prototype of the vehicle, Rapaille presented them with questions such as "I'm from another planet and I don't even know what you do with that [vehicle]. What is the purpose of this thing?" In what Ball described as the "most bizarre—but also the most productive" part of the sessions, Rapaille "dimmed the lights, began playing tapes of soothing music, and told the group to relax their bodies." He then gave them pen and paper and asked them to write stories about the vehicle prototype. The stories revealed, in Rapaille's words, the view that "it's a jungle out there... People want to kill me, rape me. Give me a big thing like a tank."

Meredith in the *Houston Chronicle* in January 1998, "the Chrysler name conjures the image not of a car but rather of a company that taxpayers bailed out of near-bankruptcy almost two decades ago." Tanya Gazdik and Teresa Buyikian noted in *Adweek* at the same time that "Chrysler is hoping to change customers' perception of its brand with a new spot breaking on Jan. 11." Chrysler/Plymouth/Jeep division general manager Marty Levine admitted that "consumers still see the 'K cars' of the 1980s when they think of the brand."

With its new campaign, David Kiley wrote in *Brandweek,* Chrysler hoped to "boost sales of Chrysler brand, which has underperformed expectations, and close the gap between what the company feels is the reality of Chrysler brand cars and the lingering perception of dullness left over from the brand's dowdy days in the 1970s and '80s." It faced what Meredith in the *Houston Chronicle* called "an identify crisis, the root of which is the name the brand shares with its corporate parent."

MARKETING STRATEGY

With its 1998 campaign, which first appeared in September 1997, Chrysler and Bozell sought to firmly imprint the company's brand image in consumers' minds with an emphasis on heritage and luxury. Its overall corporate theme remained the same: "Great cars. Great trucks." But in place of Bozell's earlier tag line, "What's in your world?," the new campaign was built around the phrase "Engineered to be great cars." Advertising included television, radio, and print, but as was often the case with automobile advertising, TV led the way.

Television advertising prominently featured the "new" Chrysler winged logo—actually the old one, resurrected after a hiatus of more than 60 years. Jay Kuhnie, Chrysler-Plymouth communications manager, announced in a press release to accompany the launch that "Chrysler's winged badge symbolizes the [company's] proud heritage of design and engineering while serving as a hallmark for the brand." Three of the four TV spots were entitled "Badge," "Decisions," and "Sunbeam," and the initial launch also included six print ads. Both print and TV showed champagne-colored vehicles, which the company had selected because of their elegant appearance, and a print ad for Chrysler Town & Country announced that the car was "what a penthouse looks like on the ground floor." In total Chrysler ran 17 electronic spots and 23 print ads for all lines, including Plymouth, Jeep, and Eagle.

The second salvo of advertising appeared on network television in January, during the National Football League play-offs leading up to the Super Bowl. According to Gazdik and Buyikian in *Adweek,* "The spot, set to ethereal music, features a montage of winged objects, such as butterflies and airplanes, intertwined with champagne-colored Chryslers." This was the "Wings" spot, in which a voice-over announced, "For ideas to take flight they must have wings." Soon afterward the company ran a number of TV spots and print ads for the Chrysler Concorde, advertising that a January 15 press release stated would "develop the concept of 'ideas in flight.'"

To promote the 300M in May, the company brought out perhaps the most distinctive of its television ads, one it had actually begun creating more than four decades before. "Chrysler uncovered an old industrial film," wrote Halliday in *Advertising Age,* "with Bob Roger, chief engineer on those cars [the letter series], and many of his comments from snippets of the film appear in three new 30-second spots for the entry-luxury 300M." The new spots added a tag line to go with "Engineered to be great cars," announcing, "The technology has changed. But the soul lives on."

OUTCOME

"Bringing a car to market is a $1 billion to $4 billion investment," Bruyn told Lach in *American Demographics.* "As a result, you like to be right." By the end of the year it appeared that Chrysler had been. According to information compiled by the Automotive News Data Center, in one month—August 1998—Chrysler sold nearly 4,500 of the new 300Ms. This was more than one-third of the car's total sales since it had appeared earlier in the year. Within the so-called near-luxury market, the 300M already had a 10.8 percent share, a figure exceeded only by the Volvo 70 series and the Lexus ES 300.

Chrysler appeared to be on the upswing, and increased sales spread to other models. Meanwhile, it prepared to launch its PT Cruiser, an unusual-looking entrant in the sport utility category that Jeffrey Ball of the *Wall Street Journal* described as "part 1920s gangster car, part 1950s hot rod, and part London taxicab." The vehicle was the product of an innovative strategy in marketing research pioneered by French medical anthropologist G. Clotaire Rapaille. Rapaille's studies with language and his attempts to teach autistic children in Switzerland during the 1960s led him to the ideas that he believed would help researchers discover consumers' hidden and most instinctive desires. Whatever the results of the PT Cruiser, it was sure to live up to the promise of a Chrysler engineer, who told Ball, "We didn't make a generic vehicle."

The PT Cruiser's unusual design was a hallmark of Chrysler's strategy: melding the best of the past with the most prominent elements of the future. Wrote Lach, "The egg-crate grille [of the 300M] harks back to earlier styles in the letter series, and simple analog dials dot the dashboard." Inside, however, the car suggested quite a different era, with plush leather seats, a climate-control system, and a nine-speaker stereo system. Given the company's interest in marketing to the future—which included changing demographics, with more and more baby boomers becoming empty nesters—Lach asked, "Is a 300 convertible on Chrysler's drawing board? Only time will tell."

FURTHER READING

Ball, Jeffrey. "But Does It Make You Feel?" *Wall Street Journal,* May 3, 1999, p. B1.

"Chrysler Brand to Launch All-New 1998 Chrysler Concorde Ad Campaign." *PR Newswire,* January 15, 1998.

"Chrysler Launches Campaign for Sedan." *Adweek* (Eastern Edition), May 4, 1998, p. 60.

"Chrysler/Plymouth/Jeep/Eagle Division Launches New 1998 Advertising." *PR Newswire,* September 15, 1997.

Gazdik, Tanya. "Bozell Gives Chrysler New Look: Bozell Worldwide to Handle Spot TV and Print Ads for the Automaker." *Adweek* (Midwest Edition), September 15, 1997, p. 2.

Gazdik, Tanya, and Teresa Buyikian. "3 Automakers Unveil New Campaigns for 1998." *Adweek* (Eastern Edition), January 5, 1998, p. 10.

Halliday, Jean. "Chrysler Moves into 'Great' '98 Model Advertising: New Ads Begin This Week as Part of Nearly $1 Bill in Ad Spending." *Advertising Age,* September 15, 1997, p. 4.

———. "New Chrysler Sedan Looks to Past for Ad Inspiration: Snippets from Old Film Used in New Campaign." *Advertising Age,* May 4, 1998, p. 8.

Kiley, David. "Chrysler Set to Break Flurry of Ads for Corporate, Chrysler, Plymouth; Launches a New Ad Campaign for Its Chrysler & Plymouth Brands." *Brandweek,* September 15, 1997, p. 7.

Lach, Jennifer. "Boomers on the Drawing Board." *American Demographics,* November 1, 1998, p. 48.

Meredith, Robyn. "Chrysler Rescue Effort Takes Wing in Big Way." *Houston Chronicle,* January 18, 1998, p. 9.

Washington, Frank S. "Chrysler Ads Stress Engineering, Power." *Automotive News,* September 15, 1997, p. 36.

Judson Knight

JEEP CAMPAIGN

OVERVIEW

NOTE: Since the initial appearance of this essay in the 1998 edition of *Major Marketing Campaigns Annual,* The Chrysler Corp. merged with German automaker Daimler-Benz to create DaimlerChrysler. The essay continues to refer to the company's former name, as that was the official name of the organization when the campaign was launched.

In the 1990s Chrysler Corporation ran a prolonged branding campaign for its four-wheel-drive Jeeps. Although Jeep was one of the oldest and best-known sport utility brands in the United States, it had encountered intense competition as the popularity of four-wheel-drive automobiles (dubbed "sport utility vehicles," or SUVs) exploded among American consumers. In order to bolster the Jeep brand, Chrysler directed the advertising agency Bozell Worldwide, Inc. to create a television advertising campaign for Jeep's product line: the Jeep Wrangler, Jeep Cherokee, and Jeep Grand Cherokee. Three of the ads, "Snow Covered," "El Toro," and "Quicksand," were designed not only to elevate sales but also to distinguish Jeep from the 40-odd other models of SUVs that were flooding the market and vying for consumers' new car dollars.

To reach its upscale target market, Jeep chose to run its ads primarily during highly rated, prime-time network television shows and special events. "Snow Covered," "El Toro," and "Quicksand" each used a combination of humor and fantasy to catch viewers' attention, and each was an element of what Bozell's managing partner and creative director Bill Morden termed "the consistent, constant visual of building the brand." "Snow Covered," a 60-second spot that first aired during the 1994 Winter Olympics, had, according to *USA Today,* "one of the longest runs of any TV ad produced by a car company." The commercial featured a Jeep burrowing under a deep blanket of snow as an arresting way of conveying the power and tenacity of the vehicle. Interestingly, the ad did not picture an actual Jeep model. The 30-second "Quicksand," which debuted in September 1995, showed a Jeep Grand Cherokee trapped in a tropical landscape by a massive water buffalo that refuses to move out of the way. After the car sinks down into a mire of quicksand, the buffalo ambles away. The Jeep then drives itself up out of the muck and goes on its way. "El Toro," another 30-second spot, first aired in September 1996. It depicts the romantic attraction of two animals for a bright red Jeep Grand Cherokee. The car is first pursued by a bull and drives into a river to escape. As the car emerges, dirty, muddy, and dripping, it is chased by a smitten pig.

Although Jeep could not draw a direct correlation between the television commercials and its sales figures, it pronounced itself pleased with the results of the campaign. Jeep sales rose during the period the ads were being broadcast, and polls demonstrated their popularity with consumers. In addition, the ads won a number of advertising awards, generating further publicity for Jeep and its vehicles.

HISTORICAL CONTEXT

The Jeep brand originated during World War II when the U.S. Army required a rugged vehicle that could master off-road terrain and the brutal conditions of battle. Partly because of Jeep's popularity among American GIs, the American Motor Corporation continued to produce the sturdy car after the war. Seemingly half-car and half-truck, the vehicle with its four-wheel-drive capacity had a reputation for being able to go anywhere. Jeep never lost the macho image it garnered during the war. It was a car for the outdoors, for the rugged individual, for the free spirit. In the 1980s, however, a growing market for "passenger-friendly" four-wheel-drive vehicles developed. Drivers wanted the robust look and image of a four-wheel drive outside but the comfort and smoothness of a sedan inside. Jeep responded by shifting its product line, discontinuing some models, and introducing new ones to conform to this trend.

Jeep Cherokee first came on the market in 1984 and quickly attained great popularity. Jeep Wrangler, a smaller and more economically-priced model, appeared in 1986. The following year Chrysler Corporation acquired the American Motor Corporation and incorporated Jeep into its new Jeep/Eagle division. In 1993 Chrysler launched the Jeep Grand Cherokee, a luxurious and premium-priced four-wheel-drive vehicle, with a slew of amenities. By the mid-1990s these three models made up the whole of Jeep's product line. The Wrangler, which in 1997 cost about $13,000, appealed to a younger market. The Cherokee, on the other hand, suited a slightly older consumer who might need more space for a growing family. Finally, the Grand Cherokee, with optional leather seats, was the four-wheel-drive vehicle for the affluent consumer who appreciated the luxury of the model but also sought the cachet of the Jeep brand.

Jeep's product line was evolving in tune with the American car market. By 1997 pickup trucks, SUVs, and minivans—all three were termed "light trucks"—accounted for one out of every two vehicles sold in the United States. Indeed, the sale of sport utility vehicles increased 74 percent in 1997 alone. According to the London *Independent,* analysts expected SUV sales to rise an additional 35 percent by 2006. Even more noteworthy was the fact that the fastest growing sector of this market was for the so-called luxury SUVs, which included the Jeep Grand Cherokee. The company's website explained the allure: "This vehicle is proof you can have a true off-road vehicle without giving up . . . luxuries and amenities."

TARGET MARKET

The higher-end sport utility vehicles appealed to a far different group of consumers than the early Jeep models: the average Jeep Grand Cherokee buyer was 44-years old. *Advertising Age* declared that the success of the car was "largely due to the acceptance of upscale SUVs by buyers in their forties." The vast majority of sport utility vehicle drivers no longer even took their cars off-road. Rather, the appeal of the SUVs was due more to the perception that they were safer than smaller, more fuel-efficient cars. Not only were SUVs a great deal larger and heavier (they weighed about 5,000 pounds) than the average car, they also afforded the driver a clearer view of the road because they were so tall. As *The Fort Worth Star-Telegram* asserted, "Sport utility vehicles appeal to an aging population desperately seeking security at a time of corporate downsizing, family breakups, and crime." Moreover, by providing more cargo and passenger space, SUVs were ideal for families.

But more than anything else, an SUV-like Jeep provided a crucial intangible factor—image. A spokesperson for Mercedes-Benz told the London *Independent* that SUVs were "an expression of individuality, lifestyle, and an active enjoyment of life." Both men and women enjoyed the sense of power and hearty individualism that Jeep seemed to convey.

Jeep's advertising sought to reinforce that image. "Snow Covered," which did not portray an actual Jeep model, was solely a brand-building campaign. "Quicksand" and "El Toro" specifically touted the Grand Cherokee, but Bozell's Morden emphasized that "every ad we do is a deposit in that brand equity bank." According to *USA Today,* the three spots used fantasy and humor "to appeal to the company's yuppie target."

The commercials reached out to their target not only through humor but also through their narrative structure. Unlike the "standard" car commercial, the Jeep spots were not catalogs of features. Instead, they told a story that was intended to captivate the audience and communicate to them the values and nature of the brand. Each of the three spots played on key themes: Jeep's ability to bring the driver into nature; to afford the driver the "reach" to go anywhere and do anything in a Jeep; and to give the driver the mastery and capability the brand promised. "Quicksand" and "El Toro" were specifically designed to remind the viewer that the Grand Cherokee was not just another luxury car. According to Morden, the commercials told their target audience that "underneath all the leather, it's still a Jeep."

COMPETITION

Jeep was not the only brand of sport utility vehicle trying to attract the wealthy yuppie with the soul of an adventurer. In fact, the SUV segment of the auto industry had become one of the most crowded. The number of SUV models surged from 21 in 1987 to nearly 50 ten years later. All told, by 1997 SUV sales accounted for 15 percent of total new car sales. "When we created

THE AMERICAN APPEAL

Jeep's rugged and outdoorsy image appealed to consumers outside of the American market, too. In England, where Jeep's most direct competition was Range Rover, ads for the Grand Cherokee played up the quintessential "Americanness" of the Jeep brand. Commercials featured shots of Western landscapes filled with sunsets, open spaces, and tough dirt roads. English consumers responded strongly to these images and to the Jeep mystique.

'Snow Covered' in 1994 we pretty much stood alone," said Bill Morden. "But now there are 60 or 70 commercials a week trying to do the same thing as us." Jeep's competition encroached on both the high and low ends of the SUV sector. Toyota's Land Cruiser and 4Runner, Chevrolet's Suburban, Land Rover, Range Rover, Mercedes-Benz's M-Class, Lexus's RX300, and Lincoln-Mercury's Mountaineer presented fierce competition for the more upscale new car buyer Jeep sought to attract to its Grand Cherokee. On the other end of the spectrum, Toyota's RAV4, Geo's Tracker, Suzuki's Samurai, and Mitsubishi's Montero threatened to encroach on the less affluent, younger crowd who had previously coveted the Jeep brand and purchased the more affordable Wrangler or Cherokee. By 1996 the Ford Explorer had risen to become the best-selling sport utility vehicle with an 18.8 percent market share. The Grand Cherokee was second, with 13 percent. Cherokee and Wrangler were fourth and ninth, respectively, with 6.9 percent and 3.8 percent.

Jeep's competitors also initiated their own big-budget campaigns. Lexus launched a campaign for its 1999 RX300 that used the tag line, "It's not just another sport utility. It's like no other vehicle on earth." Lexus, like Jeep's Grand Cherokee, targeted consumers in their early 40s. Both Ford and Mercury's marketing efforts for the Explorer and the Mountaineer stressed the versatility and practicality of the vehicles. Ford spent an estimated $44.3 million advertising the Explorer and Expedition in 1996, while Toyota devoted $37.7 million to the 4Runner. In an effort to prevail in this fiercely competitive market, however, Jeep outspent its competitors by a substantial margin. In 1996 Chrysler spent $76.3 million marketing the Grand Cherokee, as well as an additional $42.5 million on the Cherokee and $21.6 million on the Wrangler.

MARKETING STRATEGY

As the self-proclaimed leader in the SUV sector, Jeep shied away from overtly acknowledging its numerous competitors in the ads. "We seldom, if ever, compare ourselves specifically to other brands," Morden said. Instead, Bozell created commercials that attempted to connect consumers with the benefits of the brand on a more emotional level. "It's all personality," Gary Topolewski, executive creative director and managing partner at Bozell, told *Adweek.* "Cars are an emotional purchase. Bottom line, you want to feel good about the car you're driving." Few Jeep spots featured the aptly named "laundry list of features." Instead, Jeep used the narrative style ads in order to distinguish itself from other SUV campaigns.

Jeep chose to bring its message to a more "upscale, forward-thinking audience," said Morden. In order to do so, the company pinpointed select prime-time television shows to carry the ads. "Snow Covered" aired on such programs as the 1994 Winter Olympics and the 1997 Aloha Bowl. "Quicksand" was seen on shows such as ABC's *20/20* and NBC's *National Geographic,* as well as during Fox Network's broadcasts of the National Hockey League's conference semifinals and finals and NBC's airings of the National Basketball Association's play-off games. "El Toro" ran during popular shows like *Mad About You, Murder One,* and *Star Trek Voyager,* as well as on NBC's broadcasts of National Football League games.

OUTCOME

"Snow Covered," "Quicksand," and "El Toro" won the admiration of the advertising industry. In 1994 "Snow Covered" won the coveted Grand Prix Award at the Cannes Festival. Analysts lauded both Jeep and Bozell for the witty and innovative ads. Certainly the polished ads helped to bolster Jeep's image as the preeminent SUV on the market. As *USA Today* commented, "Innovative ads get noticed."

Although Bozell was quick to assert that drawing a direct correlation between sales figures and specific ads was difficult at best, Morden did assert that "these spots continued to fit Jeep products into the brand. People saw them as being very positive to the brand's identity." Jeep sales soared 13 percent the year Jeep took home the Grand Prix for the spot. In addition, *USA Today* 's *Ad Track* consumers survey revealed that it ranked as one of the ten best-liked ads of 1997; thereby proving its popularity.

FURTHER READING

Bradsher, Keith. "Power Trip. Yes, They're Safe. Yes, They Can Carry a Lot. But Sport-Utility Vehicles Also Offer the Allure of Control." *The Fort Worth Star-Telegram,* March 25, 1997.

Enrico, Dottie. "Jeep Plows Winning Turf. Long Running Ads on Track With Critics and Viewers." *USA Today,* April 7, 1997.

Enrico, Dottie. "Top Honors Help Ad Agencies Hype Themselves." *USA Today,* June 28, 1996.

Green, Gavin. "Motoring: More Leap onto the Off-Road Gravy Train." *London Independent,* October 18, 1997.

Horton, Cleveland. "Requires Artful Ad Buys and Attention to Segment Lifestyle." *Advertising Age,* April 1, 1996.

Parpis, Eleftheria. "New Directions." *Adweek,* January 27, 1997.

Rebecca Stanfel

THERE'S ONLY ONE CAMPAIGN

OVERVIEW

Jeep was a division of the Chrysler Group, a Detroit-based subsidiary of the DaimlerChrysler Corporation that was responsible for the manufacturing, sale, and marketing of the Chrysler, Jeep, and Dodge brands in the United States. The Grand Cherokee, which was introduced in 1992, was a major vehicle for Jeep. It had helped initiate the market for smooth-handling, road-friendly, midsize sport-utility vehicles (SUVs) in the 1990s and was still a leader in that category. Competition from other midsize vehicles, such as the Ford Explorer, combined with customer migration to both bigger and smaller SUVs meant that by 2000 the Grand Cherokee had to fight to hold onto its market share.

Jeep enlisted ad agency Foote Cone & Belding (FCB) to run a new campaign for model year 2001 that was intended to help Jeep stand out in a crowded field. The effort, titled "There's Only One," centered around "Shake," a humorous spot that featured a muddy Grand Cherokee shaking itself clean in the manner of a dog. First airing in the fall of 2000, it attempted to show consumers that, even though the Grand Cherokee was a luxury midsize SUV, it was still rugged and hard-nosed, just like Jeeps had always been. The campaign's tagline, "Jeep—There's Only One," subtly built on Jeep's name recognition and status as an originator of the off-road and SUV categories. The brand's greatest asset was its name; ever since the vehicle's wide use by the U.S. military during World War II, Jeep had been one of the most recognizable brands in the world. The company wanted to capitalize on this as much as it could.

The "Shake" spot was a big hit with critics and took home a Bronze Clio in 2001 in the television/film commercial category. It also helped the Grand Cherokee to be recognized—according to surveys conducted by automobile-industry data collectors R.L. Polk & Co.—as the midsize SUV with the highest degree of customer loyalty in 2001.

DaimlerChrysler's Jeep. © AARON HOROWITZ/CORBIS.

HISTORICAL CONTEXT

The Jeep name originally referred to a military vehicle widely in use by the U.S. Army during World War II. Combining elements of a car, a truck, and an armored vehicle, its durability and ability to travel made it essential to the war effort. The Jeep was developed by the Willys-Overland company of Toledo, Ohio, though other manufacturers also built Jeeps during the war. After the conflict was over, Willys began to market the brand to civilians. The High Mobility Multipurpose Wheeled Vehicle (also called the Humvee, or Hummer), a larger, more heavily armored vehicle, later came to replace the Jeep for most military uses.

Jeep had a number of owners, including American Motors, before being scooped up by Chrysler in the late 1980s. Chrysler was one of Detroit's most profitable companies in the 1980s, but by the end of the following decade its fortunes had begun to fade. In 1998 the automaker merged with German car manufacturer Daimler-Benz (most famous for its Mercedes brand automobiles), creating the DaimlerChrysler Corporation/DaimlerChrysler AG. Jeep became a part of the Chrysler Group, a subsidiary of DaimlerChrysler that also handled the manufacture, sales, and marketing of the Chrysler and Dodge brands.

The Jeep Grand Cherokee was first introduced at the 1992 North American International Auto Show. It replaced the Grand Wagoneer as Jeep's midsize SUV. The vehicle was larger than the original Cherokee, which, along with the Wrangler, served as Jeep's touchtone vehicle. It helped create a new market for midsize, rugged SUVs. Despite its off-road capabilities, the vehicle proved popular with suburban and urban drivers, and it was one of the leading SUVs throughout the 1990s. It offered a roomier, more luxurious feel than many other midsize SUVs in the early 1990s.

In 1998 Jeep introduced the second generation of the Grand Cherokee, radically redesigning the car in the face of competition from the Ford Explorer and Chevrolet TrailBlazer. The new Grand Cherokee featured the Quadra-Drive system, which helped the driver maintain control of the vehicle even if only one wheel had traction. This improved the Grand Cherokee's off-road performance and made it safer in the snow. It also featured a powerful V-8 engine and a driver-side airbag. This second-generation model proved so successful that Jeep did not significantly alter the Grand Cherokee again until model year 2005.

Unfortunately, the SUV market was starting to get crowded. Smaller imports, such as the Honda Odyssey, had begun to make tentative inroads into the U.S. market. Also alarming from the Grand Cherokee's point of view was the rise of larger luxury SUVs, such as the Cadillac Escalade. With younger, lower-income SUV drivers buying smaller imports and wealthier buyers moving on to bigger vehicles, midsize SUVs felt a crunch. By 2001 these larger and smaller SUVs had seen their market shares rise 37 percent and 42 percent, respectively. Meanwhile the midsize category remained flat. This presented a challenge. Jeep had to distinguish itself and the Grand Cherokee from an ever-growing field of rivals within the SUV market.

TARGET MARKET

The Grand Cherokee was a midsize SUV. These vehicles had proven particularly successful at connecting with image-conscious families who wanted a large vehicle to transport their children but did not want to buy a "stuffy" minivan. Also, the Grand Cherokee's size and Quadra-Drive system gave it a reputation among drivers as a safe car, one that would offer good handling in the snow and protect the driver in the event of a crash. The safety aspect appealed to suburban moms and dads. In addition, the Grand Cherokee was an imposing vehicle, and it had considerable off-road capabilities. This made it popular among males in their 20s and 30s who were looking for a rugged, fun car.

THE JEEP EXHIBIT

In 2000 Jeep released its "There's Only One" campaign. The campaign's tagline underscored the Jeep's iconic status as an off-road vehicle; the Jeep was developed by the Willys-Overland Motors for use in World War II. But DaimlerChrysler wanted to recognize the iconic brand's history in a more direct way. In honor of Jeep's 60th anniversary, in 2001 the Walter P. Chrysler Museum, in Auburn Hills, Michigan, created an exhibit titled "The Mighty Jeep: A Legend Turns 60." It featured the original Jeep along with 26 other vehicles and prototypes. The Walter P. Chrysler Museum, which opened in 1999, was created by DaimlerChrysler to spotlight the history of its American vehicles. This served in part to offset the fact that Chrysler—one of the "Big Three" U.S. automakers—in 1998 came under the control of a European parent, DaimlerChrysler AG.

COMPETITION

Despite efforts by Toyota, Honda, and Nissan, the primary competition for the Grand Cherokee came from fellow American midsize SUVs, such as the Chevrolet TrailBlazer, Ford Explorer, and Dodge Durango. In fact, these four vehicles together commanded a whopping 72.9 percent of the midsize-SUV market share in the United States.

Though Chrysler Group stablemate the Dodge Durango also competed with the Grand Cherokee, GM's Chevrolet TrailBlazer and especially the highly successful Ford Explorer were considered to be the major competitors for Jeep. The Explorer, available in two- and four-door models, was the leading vehicle in the segment in terms of sales. In fact, the Explorer had been the top-selling vehicle in the segment every year since its introduction in 1991, and by 1998 Ford was selling more than 430,000 units of the vehicle in the United States alone. The Explorer especially appealed to families because of its smooth ride and attractive appearance. That helped the Explorer stand out in a crowded segment. Jeep wanted its new campaign to accomplish something similar for the Grand Cherokee.

MARKETING STRATEGY

Jeep sought a clever campaign that would emphasize the Grand Cherokee's reputation as a rugged vehicle that could be taken off-road, while also distinguishing the vehicle and the brand from the flood of SUVs on the market. To implement its new plan, Jeep turned to Foote Cone & Belding (FCB), a Southfield, Michigan–based subsidiary of True North Communications. FCB had a long history working with the brand, and Jeep was confident in the agency's abilities. The campaign would include billboards and print ads focusing on the vehicle's rugged appearance. The key to the campaign, however, was a new television spot called "Shake."

FCB hired Gerard de Thame Films, a production company based in London, to put the spot together. It was directed by Gerard de Thame, who had previously directed music videos for the famed British musician Sting. The commercial, which first aired in fall of 2000, began with a mud-coated Cherokee pulling into a suburban driveway. After a couple got out of the Cherokee and walked toward the house, the vehicle shook itself off in a quick back-and-forth motion reminiscent of a dog. Now mud was everywhere, including all over the couple who owned the car. A voice-over then said, "Even though the Jeep Grand Cherokee is more refined and civilized than ever, it still hasn't lost its animal instincts." The spot closed with the campaign's tagline, "Jeep—There's Only One." The humor of the spot allowed the company to spotlight Jeep's rugged reputation in a subtle way. By revealing a clean-cut suburban couple to be the drivers of the muddy Grand Cherokee, the spot implied that even Grand Cherokee drivers who lived in the suburbs had "messy" wild sides.

The campaign's tagline, "There's Only One," also called to mind the Jeep's storied past. The vehicle's ubiquity in the military during the massive mobilization for World War II injected it straight into popular culture. By 1942 the vehicle merited a mention in the film *Holiday Inn,* starring Fred Astaire. The Jeep, with its distinctive vertical front grille, quickly became an icon and would become synonymous with rugged, off-road vehicles. Even by 2000, with SUVs a major force in the U.S. auto market, many people still referred to every vehicle in the class as a "jeep." The "There's Only One" tagline was a subtle reminder that these "jeeps" were not the same thing as a real Jeep. It also underscored Jeep's position as the longtime leader in the SUV category.

OUTCOME

The campaign was a solid success, and the "Shake" commercial was awarded a Bronze Clio in the television/film category. A Clio was one of advertising's most prestigious awards. The Clio Awards originated in the late 1950s as a way to honor the best in advertising. Subsequent television spots continued to underscore what people loved about the Grand Cherokee. In October 2001 the Polk Automotive Loyalty Awards were announced, and the Grand Cherokee was ranked the number-one SUV for customer loyalty. The awards were given annually by the Michigan-based R.L. Polk & Co., a firm that collected and analyzed information about the automotive industry.

Despite Jeep's satisfaction with Foote Cone & Belding's work, the Chrysler Group dropped the agency in late 2000, in the interest of consolidating all of the company's advertising and marketing efforts with one firm. It awarded its account to Omnicom, an agency that had been working with other Chrysler brands. Later that year Foote Cone & Belding became a part of the New York–based Interpublic Group.

FURTHER READING

Bradsher, Keith. "Auto Sales Keep to Torrid Pace Even as Loan Costs Rise." *New York Times,* May 3, 2000.

Cobb, James G. "Carmakers Go Online and Off Road at Detroit Auto Show." *New York Times,* January 16, 2000.

Hakim, Danny. "A Buyer's Market for Autos Is a Tough Development for Chrysler." *New York Times,* October 11, 2001.

Healy, James R. "Chrysler Again Runs Low on Financial Fuel." *USA Today,* January 30, 2001.

Kurylko, Diana. "DaimlerChrysler Vehicles Reflect a New Game Plan." *Automotive News,* August 21, 2001.

Reuwee, Brian M. "Big 3 SUVs Dominate Market, J.D. Power Study Says." *AutoWeek,* November 30, 2001.

Statham, Steve. *Jeep Color History.* Osceola, WI: Motorbooks International, 1999.

Wald, Matthew L. "Preliminary Review Is Begun for Jeep Grand Cherokees." *New York Times,* July 5, 2001.

Wilson, Kevin. "Exhibit Traces Jeep Origins and Heritage." *AutoWeek,* December 3, 2001.

Guy Patrick Cunningham

Darden Restaurants, Inc.

5900 Lake Ellenor Drive
Orlando, Florida 32809
USA
Telephone: (407) 245-4000
Fax: (407) 245-4000
Web site: www.redlobster.com

LIFE ON LAND IS DRY CAMPAIGN

OVERVIEW

Darden Restaurants, the largest casual-dining restaurant group in the world, operated three distinct restaurant concepts: the Olive Garden, Bahama Breeze, and Red Lobster. With about 700 locations, Red Lobster was the nation's leading full-service seafood restaurant chain, offering fresh seafood at moderate prices. Red Lobster had a disappointing year in 1997, with same-store sales falling 3.9 percent on average unit sales of $2.6 million. Hoping to increase sales and revitalize the Red Lobster brand, Darden Restaurants released its "Life on Land Is Dry" campaign.

Created by the ad agency Euro RSCG Tatham, the $80 million radio and television campaign began in October 1997 and portrayed the seafood restaurant as an escape from life's dry daily routine. To reinforce the slogan, Euro RSCG Tatham created spots that contrasted images of dry, barren landscapes with images of couples and families frolicking at the seashore. The new campaign—which began with television spots during programs like the Major League Baseball playoffs and prime-time programs *Friends* and *3rd Rock from the Sun*—carried the theme "Life on Land Is Dry." The commercials, together with ancillary marketing changes like new menus and the addition of an elevated bar to some restaurants, were designed to create a more energetic personality for the Red Lobster chain. The campaign ended in mid-2000.

"Life on Land Is Dry" marked a strategy shift for Red Lobster. The campaign promoted Red Lobster as a fun-loving restaurant instead of promoting the chain's prices, selection, or food quality. The strategy proved to be effective. During the campaign's second year Red Lobster reported double-digit gains in same-store sales for the first time in nearly a decade.

HISTORICAL CONTEXT

Red Lobster was a pioneer in television advertising among casual-dining chains, putting commercials on the public airwaves long before similar chains such as Chili's, Bennigan's, and T.G.I. Friday's joined the fray. For many years Red Lobster advertisements employed the tagline "Red Lobster for the Seafood Lover in You," developed by its longtime partner Grey Advertising, one of the world's largest ad agencies with billings of more than $5 billion. Grey Advertising's other accounts included Cover Girl makeup, Pantene shampoo, and Kool-Aid fruit drink.

Over time, however, casual-dining competition grew keener, with a host of clever ads vying for the attention of consumers. As Red Lobster's sales began to decline in the mid-1990s, Grey Advertising tried to come up with a new approach that would differentiate the seafood chain from its rivals. In 1997 the agency created a campaign for Red Lobster that provided more emphasis on fresh seafood. The slogan was "Prepared so fresh you can taste it." This campaign reflected Red Lobster's desire to expand its audience not only to those looking for lobster and shrimp but also to people who enjoyed fresh fish. It did not, however, resonate with consumers. "That wasn't the personality we were looking for," Red Lobster spokesman Andrew Dun said. "In today's restaurant world, having a fresh product isn't enough to be differentiated."

In the first quarter of 1997 Red Lobster sales of $475.3 million were about 1 percent below the same period a year earlier. Same-store sales, a measure that excluded new and closed outlets, were down 3.6 percent. The chain worked feverishly to combat the sales slump by introducing a new menu, lowering prices, and sinking more money into employee training to ensure that servers and managers understood the new menu.

None of this seemed to work, however, and in the summer of 1997 Darden Restaurants announced it would review its Red Lobster advertising and consider switching agencies. Prominent ad agencies were asked to submit proposals as part of the review process. *Adweek*, an industry trade publication, reported that campaigns Darden rejected early on included one by Saatchi & Saatchi that said, "Life is a beach. And we've got the food." The company also passed on a J. Walter Thompson proposal with the theme "Inside every Red Lobster there is a great little seafood place." After extensive review, incumbent Grey Advertising, New York–based Deutsch, and Euro RSCG Tatham, a Chicago ad agency with a strong consumer-products resume, emerged as finalists for the $90 million account. A test of the three agencies' ad strategies determined the winner.

In September Darden selected Euro RSCG Tatham to develop the new Red Lobster campaign. At the time Euro RSCG Tatham was the world's eighth-largest advertising agency, with billings of $7 billion. It had no significant restaurant accounts, although it was working with consumer-product and food companies promoting brands such as Sara Lee, Head & Shoulders, and Old Spice. Euro RSCG Tatham began work immediately on the estimated $80 million campaign. Its contract for the Red Lobster account was structured with an incentive. The more Red Lobster improved, the greater the revenue for the ad agency. Grey Advertising continued to handle Darden's Olive Garden business.

Tatham officials soon began dropping hints in the trade press about the direction of the new Red Lobster campaign. The agency said that it would continue advertising Red Lobster on television but that it would also look at more targeted advertising, such as direct mail and the Internet. New advertisements would include an emphasis on atmosphere as well as on food. "Red Lobster has more to sell than food on the plate," a Tatham official declared. "They have a place, an attitude, a feeling . . . all of which we will portray in the advertising." Tatham's new ads, featuring the tagline "Life on Land Is Dry," debuted on October 6, 1997.

TARGET MARKET

Red Lobster was a leading player in the market category known as casual dining, whose appeal was primarily to aging baby boomers. This was the group that came of age simultaneously with fast food. As they aged, analysts said, these customers would want full-service, sit-down dining. Although more receptive to ethnic influences on the menus, they still wanted familiar food at moderate prices. "The major challenge [in appealing to this market] would be the economy," said Ron Paul, president of the restaurant-industry consulting firm Technomic. "Casual dining is doing very, very well now because consumers are willing to spend the dollars it takes." But when the economy took a downturn, he noted, consumers traded down to fast food.

COMPETITION

The 1990s were a golden age for casual dining establishments. The restaurants' themes, or concepts, varied, but their menus did not stray far from mainstream tastes. Some companies stuck with one specialty, such as Uno Restaurant Corp. and its famous deep-dish pizza of Chicago. Many chains, however, developed several concepts. Darden Restaurants, for example, was able to establish the two dominant chains in casual dining—the Red Lobster seafood concept and the Olive Garden, which had an Italian theme.

With its focus on seafood, Red Lobster was in the enviable position of having no serious national competitors. Its closest rival, Landry's Seafood Restaurants, operated about 120 seafood restaurants in 26 states. The nation's number two operator of casual-dining seafood restaurants, Landry's operated four chains: Landry's Seafood Houses, the Crab House, Joe's Crab Shack, and Willie G's Oyster Bar. By contrast, steak chains such as Outback Steakhouse and Lone Star Steakhouse & Saloon were in a crowded field and struggled to trumpet points of differentiation.

MARKETING STRATEGY

"We're taking a brand that already has a lot of positive attributes and making it more casual, more energetic," said Wyman Roberts, executive vice president of marketing for Red Lobster, upon announcing the chain's new ad campaign. "Like all brands, we need to evolve into something appropriate for these times."

RESTAURANT MAKEOVERS—NEXT OPRAH!

What could be done when a restaurant's image had become stale, its identity out of step with the times? The same thing an individual would do in order to spruce up his or her personal appearance: get a makeover. "Re-imaging" was what restaurant industry analysts called it, and it worked wonders for a number of older chains, including Red Lobster. Some of the other operations that successfully reinvented themselves were:

- KFC. The old gray Colonel just ain't what he used to be. In June 1997 bearded Southern patriarch Harland Sanders (long since deceased in real life) saw his image reconfigured into an edgy "supergraphic" designed to attract younger customers. The restaurant formerly known as Kentucky Fried Chicken also added a host of nonfried items to its menu, including Rotisserie Gold roasted chicken, Chunky Chicken Pot Pie, and the Bacon Ranch Chicken Twister, KFC's take on the popular "wrap" sandwich.
- The Melting Pot. Fondue just did not have the same appeal it had in the 1970s. As a result, this Tampa, Florida–based chain of 43 fondue restaurants found itself in a prolonged sales slump. Market research indicated that the Melting Pot was perceived as a romantic, special-occasion restaurant that the average customer visited only once or twice a year. To combat this perception the chain unveiled a new logo, remodeled its interiors and exteriors, and launched a new ad campaign positioning itself as "an out-of-the-ordinary dining experience" suitable for any night of the week, not just special occasions.

In Red Lobster's judgment the times called for repositioning the restaurant as a welcome break from the otherwise dry world. The first two 30-second television spots, entitled "Escape" and "Pack Your Bags" and featuring the tagline "Life on Land Is Dry," began airing in October 1997 during prime-time programs such as *Monday Night Football, Friends, 3rd Rock from the Sun, Home Improvement,* and the Major League Baseball playoffs. The new commercials set footage of Americans of all ages enjoying fun on the beach to upbeat original music. The beach images, shot on both U.S. coasts, in Cape Cod and Los Angeles, were designed to associate the fun and excitement of water experiences with the freshness of Red Lobster fish and seafood. "By tapping into people's memories of great beach vacations and sunny days spent relaxing in backyard pools, we capture their passion for life by the water including their hunger for fresh fish and seafood," said Gary Epstein, managing partner of Tatham.

Subsequent spots in the campaign used contrast to make the same point. Scenes of people doing everyday, mundane tasks on land, using shots of the Los Angeles freeway and the deserts of Lancaster, California, were juxtaposed against the "escape" implied in Red Lobster seafood. "Research showed that our customers long for experiences that take them away from the grind of their everyday routines," Roberts observed. "With this understanding of our customers' needs, we hope to get them excited about seafood and the entire experience of dining at Red Lobster restaurants. In fact, this ad campaign is the first chapter in the larger story of efforts to restructure and rejuvenate Red Lobster."

The "Life on Land" campaign also included a number of beach-themed commercials featuring musical accompaniment from big names such as Rod Stewart and LeAnn Rimes. One spot launching a promotion for snow crab legs featured three older women cavorting across the sand while Rod Stewart's song "Hot Legs" played in the background. The promotion offered one pound of crab legs for $9.99. Another spot employed country-and-western prodigy Rimes's baleful rendition of "Blue" to promote a $14.99 Maine lobster dinner. "It's the story of the end of the season and a woman reflecting on the great summer and the experiences she's had at the seashore. Red Lobster is trying to do a good job of just tapping into that," said Roberts.

To complement its brand-building efforts on network TV, Red Lobster also released a $12 million radio campaign focusing on promotional messages. Radio stations in 60 markets across the country aired 60-second spots supporting the "Life on Land Is Dry" theme. The initiative, which doubled Red Lobster's annual radio spending without eating into TV buys, followed successful local tests that involved sponsorships of local disc jockeys.

In 1999 the campaign aired another beach-based commercial, titled "Wingtips," which featured a woman walking barefoot across a pristine beach. The spot's voice-over encouraged consumers to "Breathe. Smile. Eat. Make a mess. Make a memory." The spot deviated from the campaign's other commercials by ending with the tagline "Escape to Red Lobster." The "Life on Land Is Dry" campaign ended in mid-2000.

In addition to the multimedia advertising push, Red Lobster also made a number of cosmetic changes designed to improve the restaurant experience for both its patrons and employees. Dress-code changes for staff allowed servers to wear shorts and colorful shirts with fish motifs instead of the traditional black pants, white shirts, and ties. The company also eliminated its long-standing ban on beards for male workers. The changes were designed to improve morale in this notoriously high-turnover industry.

Significant additions were also made to the Red Lobster menu. More boldly flavored entrees like Louisiana Lacy's Catfish and Hickory Planked Salmon were added, together with a new seafood pasta line backed by TV commercials. "In the past, I think we were guilty of creating a menu that leaned toward the middle of the road," said Tim Rosendahl, the seafood chain's vice president of food and beverage. "Now our seafood gumbo, for example, is much more authentic. It's got a real kick."

Finally, Red Lobster announced a renewed effort to increase awareness of the restaurant's alcoholic beverage offerings. Elevated bars, akin to the ones seen in Bennigan's and T.G.I. Friday's outlets, were installed in select Red Lobster restaurants, while a teal-colored corrugated roof was designed to provide a tavern-on-the-beach feel. With this push the chain hoped to tap a potential new profit engine, since its alcohol sales were only about half the industry average. In the past, Roberts explained, "We did not really push or even acknowledge in our restaurants that it's OK to have a drink."

OUTCOME

Red Lobster's sales slump appeared to have bottomed out by the end of 1997. Sales of $417.8 million, with 49 fewer restaurants, were more than 4 percent below the prior year. Sales on a comparable store basis were down 0.2 percent. On the plus side, profit margins were substantially improved over 1996 because of lower cost of goods sold and reduced selling expenses. More importantly, the company was satisfied with the new course being charted by Euro RSCG Tatham. "Red Lobster has made great progress compared to one year ago and is in the midst of a refocusing on guest satisfaction similar to that successfully undertaken by [t]he Olive Garden," said Joe R. Lee, Darden Restaurants chairman and CEO. "While we celebrate the improvements, we realize we must maintain our focus on great food and great service in order to provide an outstanding dining experience every time."

The company continued to make progress through 1998. After nearly a decade of stagnating or declining fortunes, the chain saw double-digit gains in same-store sales in the third quarter of that year. The 11.6 percent increase marked the biggest such gain in eight years. Analysts credited much of the sales success to the revamped ad campaign. "It's a much classier campaign," observed Stacy Jamar, a restaurant analyst for Salomon Smith Barney. "It's a more appealing image than before." "They [Euro RSCG Tatham] have really done a good job with established brands," added Lehman Brothers analyst Mitchell Speiser. "It has taken a while to turn Red Lobster around because there was a negative perception that it was an old chain and not too relevant. They have done a great job of changing the perception and pruning the portfolio."

FURTHER READING

Howard, Theresa. "Red Lobster Goes Overboard for Diners." *USA Today,* May 7, 2001, p. B4.

Jensen, Trevor. "Red Lobster Keys on Food, Fun." *Adweek* (midwest ed.), November 6, 2000, p. 7.

Kramer, Louise. "Red Lobster Ads, Make-Over Seen Turning the Tide." *Advertising Age,* October 12, 1998.

"A Lobster Campaign." *Oklahoma City Journal Record,* October 15, 1997.

Mehegan, Sean. "Red Lobster Fights a Drop in Customers with a Campaign Inviting Diners to 'Share the Love.'" *New York Times,* July 7, 2003, p. 8.

Strother, Susan. "Red Lobster Goes Fishing in Ad Market." *Orlando Sentinel,* May 2, 1997.

Robert Schnakenberg
Kevin Teague

Davidson Development Inc.

101 E. Town Place, Ste. 200
Saint Augustine, Florida 32092
USA
Telephone: (904) 940-5050
Fax: (904) 940-5057
Web site: www.wgv.com

REPOSITIONING CAMPAIGN

OVERVIEW

Davidson Development Inc. was the primary engine behind the project that came to be known as World Golf Village, an upscale development located between Jacksonville and Saint Augustine, Florida, combining residential, commercial, and recreational zones. The Village's centerpieces were the World Golf Hall of Fame and a course designed by legendary PGA (Professional Golfers' Association) champions Arnold Palmer and Jack Nicklaus, called King & Bear in honor of the two players' respective nicknames. Initial attempts at marketing the area to home buyers took golf purists as their target market, but after several years of lackluster sales in its Estates of World Golf Village subdivision, Davidson turned to Atlanta–based agency Cole Henderson Drake (CHD) for a marketing campaign that would remake the development's image.

The Estates of World Golf Village "Repositioning Campaign" made use of a $700,000 annual budget during its 2003–04 run. CHD sought to change consumer perception of World Golf Village by drawing attention to the opportunities for gracious living present in the development rather than focusing solely on the golfing amenities, and it calibrated its message not for male golfers but for baby-boomer women, who were believed to play a larger role than their husbands in making home-buying decisions. The campaign primarily consisted of a series of two-page print spreads, with black-and-white photos and copy emphasizing the elegance and inspirational nature of the Estates lifestyle.

The campaign coincided with a 170 percent sales growth of Estates properties, and Davidson's revenues far outpaced precampaign goals. A tracking study indicated, furthermore, that CHD had successfully recast World Golf Village's image. In 2005 the "Repositioning Campaign" won a Silver EFFIE Award in the Real Estate category.

HISTORICAL CONTEXT

The PGA Tour's World Golf Hall of Fame in Pinehurst, North Carolina, was opened in 1974, but in the 1980s the PGA began searching for a site on which to build a similar facility that would honor golfers not eligible for the World Golf Hall of Fame. In the early 1990s a location between Jacksonville and Saint Augustine, Florida, was donated to the cause, and a number of worldwide golf clubs and associations pledged their support. The PGA eventually decided to close its Pinehurst facility and combine operations with the Florida facility under the name World Golf Hall of Fame. Construction began in 1996, and the Hall opened in 1998, boasting the support of 26 golf organizations from around the world.

Jack Nicklaus (L) and Arnold Palmer, April 6, 2001.
© REUTERS/CORBIS.

World Golf Village was the name given to the multifaceted development surrounding the Hall of Fame. Conceived as a golfers' resort destination as well as an upscale residential area, the development featured two golf courses, the more notable of which was called King & Bear, named after its designers, the golf greats Arnold Palmer and Jack Nicklaus. The development mixed retail, commercial, residential, and resort amenities, but for a variety of reasons initial sales of the mostly high-end real estate did not meet expectations. The location itself (in a previously little-developed area) was faulted by some in the local real-estate industry, and a related lack of vehicle traffic made it difficult to create buzz in the community. Prospective buyers and members of adjacent communities did not have a clear understanding of the development's aims outside of serving as a site for the World Golf Hall of Fame, and the lack of inhabitants made potential homeowners question the vibrancy of the community into which they were being asked to buy. In many cases these criticisms were shared or propagated by important local opinion makers, including real-estate agents and the press. The lack of enthusiasm surrounding the project led to stalled plans for further development of the site as well as reductions in investment on behalf of the project's backers. If the development was to satisfy investors' initially grand visions, it needed an image makeover.

Previous marketing on behalf of World Golf Village had focused on the Hall of Fame and the golf courses in an attempt to appeal to a logical target market—golf-obsessed men—but this strategy had not so far resulted in a sufficiently attractive image to drive developers' and investors' sales goals. Davidson thus enlisted Atlanta agency Cole Henderson Drake (CHD) to create a print campaign for the Estates of World Golf Village, a community within the larger development featuring homes priced at $500,000 and higher. The agency needed to respond to the perceived shortcomings of the World Golf Village image while offering fresh strategic insights.

TARGET MARKET

CHD took the lackluster sales results so far posted by the Estates subdivision as evidence that previous advertising efforts had been wrongly conceived. Though the exclusive targeting of male golf enthusiasts was clearly a commonsense approach to the image-building project of a development featuring world-class golf courses and a shrine to the sport's greatest players, CHD observed that women tended to have the most influence in selecting a community and home. CHD particularly focused on women of the baby-boom generation with upscale habits and tastes—many of whom still had kids at home—rather than the retirees or empty-nesters who might also have been likely to have the financial resources to buy into the Estates neighborhood. These women, CHD believed, valued the emotional attributes of a potential home. The apparent lack of vibrancy in the World Golf Village community was thus a formidable barrier to these key home buyers, as was the idea that the development was strictly for golfers. Though the target group of women appreciated the amenities typically found in upscale golf communities, the golf attractions themselves were only tangential factors in their decision making. They primarily wanted assurance that the community they were choosing was healthy, balanced, and had a promising future.

CHD further decided to market the Estates beyond the local area, targeting affluent residents of the northeastern United States in addition to regional and local women. Prospects from outside the immediate area would not be affected by local perceptions and would be more accustomed to the premium prices of the homes in the Estates neighborhood. The Estates' affiliation with an entity as prestigious as the World Golf Hall of Fame,

INSIDE THE HALL OF FAME

The World Golf Hall of Fame, the centerpiece of the larger World Golf Village development, was the definitive storehouse of the sport's legacy and the officially sanctioned tribute to its heroes. The 72,000-square-foot structure housed exhibits tracing the story of golf's invention and development in Scotland all the way through the new millennium, and the 104 inductees admitted to the Hall's membership as of 2005 were honored with permanent exhibits throughout the building. A rotating series of exhibits focused on individual members, whose exploits and personalities were chronicled at greater length, and each member's story was further told in the Member Locker Room. The Member Locker Room devoted one locker apiece to each inductee, and each locker was filled with personal items that helped make golf lovers' heroes come more vividly to life. Another of the Hall's signature spaces was the Trophy Tower, which provided visitors with up-close views of some of the game's most fabled championship trophies.

as well as the fact that home sites were adjacent to a world-class golf course, made this a reasonable if ambitious expansion of the target.

COMPETITION

The years 2000–05, though they were marked by a struggling American economy in general, saw one of the country's most substantial real-estate booms in history. Real-estate companies of various sorts, flush with profits thanks to the boom, turned increasingly to the image-building power of advertising, which generally represented an attempt not just to spur sales but also to hedge against the ever-present threat of a market downturn.

Among real-estate agencies, several nationwide firms were actively engaged in brand-building efforts. Re/Max was the U.S. market leader, and it increased ad spending by 10 percent in 2002 before turning to Los Angeles agency davidandgoliath for a $30 million national campaign, which was released in 2004. Century 21 boosted ad spending by more than 60 percent in 2002, up to an annual ad budget of roughly $25 million. It ran a 2003 campaign tagged "Real estate for your world." Meanwhile, Coldwell Banker in 2003 launched a $14 million national campaign touting the realtor's "Concierge" program, which provided logistical aid to new home owners.

Some notable innovations in advertising were made by new-home developers during this time as well. Ryland Homes, a home builder with offices across the nation, worked with the media-sales firm WorldLink and a TV distributor to create an original syndicated TV program called *America's Moving To...* The show, which named Ryland as a sponsor and featured content specially designed to resonate with the company's target consumers, ran in local markets with a Ryland presence and highlighted housing choices in cities around the country. A group of developers of new-home subdivisions in the San Francisco Bay area turned to a similar concept in 2003, banding together to underwrite the show *Bay Area New Home Living Featuring Sunset Magazine.* The half-hour show featured two- to three-minute segments sponsored by and showcasing the developments of individual home builders. These segments were interspersed with decorating, architectural, and lifestyle content sponsored by *Sunset Magazine.*

MARKETING STRATEGY

The "Repositioning Campaign" ran during 2003 and 2004. It focused on print executions but also included outdoor ads, direct mail, public relations, and promotional tie-ins. Its yearly budget was a relatively minimal $700,000, and hence a premium was placed on effective selection of magazines rather than on blanket coverage. The ads were placed primarily in lifestyle magazines with editorial content that included travel, finance, and style. This was a departure from previous World Golf Village advertising, which had run mostly in local and regional newspapers. Not only did lifestyle magazines allow Davidson and the Estates to appeal to upscale consumers outside the region, but they also served as a more appropriate context for the new ads' elegantly understated visuals and two-page-spread formatting.

The core message that CHD sought to communicate with the series of print ads was that the people who lived at World Golf Village were as special as the golf opportunities that were available. In keeping with the target-market shift, the agency wanted to alter the image of World Golf Village from that of a golf purists' community to that of a fashionable, inspiring, exclusive, and yet approachable place to live. CHD took it for granted that consumers would understand the golf-centric elements of the development, and many ads used little golf imagery, focusing instead on the elegant lifestyle and prestige of the Estates in fashionable black-and-white photographs. Frequently these photographs were supported by nods to the prestige of the World Golf Hall of Fame and the King & Bear golf course, with logos appearing along with copy that detailed important information about the development. When an ad did focus explicitly on golf, that focus underscored the lifestyle pitch. For instance, one ad showed a man from behind, surveying a dramatic golf-course backdrop, and the accompanying copy stated, "Some refer to it as one of the top courses in the world. A lucky few refer to it as their backyard." Overall, the campaign was meant to create a much-needed persona for the development rather than emphasize the quality of the homes and golf amenities.

Along with the series of print ads, CHD used event-focused marketing of the Estates. Regular open houses spearheaded by the agency allowed local prospects to see the world-class development in their midst and resulted in a much-needed increase in traffic to the site. Out-of-town vacation packages, offered through direct mail, were also paired with tours of properties. Materials given to prospects after such tours and used by realtors carried messaging and images consistent with the print ads' theme. The World Golf Village was also the exclusive real-estate sponsor of the Bloomberg financial service's website.

OUTCOME

During the two years of the campaign's run, the Estates of World Golf Village saw its sales grow 170 percent, with sales revenues far outpacing Davidson's goals. Traffic to the development substantially increased, according to CHD, and the ratio of prospects to sales drastically improved. Before CHD released the "Repositioning Campaign," the ratio of prospects to purchasers of homes in the Estates neighborhood was greater than 1:100. By 2004 this ratio had narrowed to 1:10, well ahead of industry norms, which were approximately 1:20. CHD also pointed to strong evidence from a tracking study indicating that perceptions of World Golf Village were changing. Davidson vice president of marketing Alayna Kimball said in a press release, "We are very pleased with the campaign and its consistent message for the Estates. The ads were effective and instrumental in helping us exceed our sales goals." The campaign won a Silver EFFIE Award in the Real Estate category in 2005, a testament to its effectiveness in the marketplace.

FURTHER READING

Patton, Charlie. "Golf Village 'Awesome' but Often Idle." *Jacksonville Florida Times-Union,* February 6, 2002.

———. "World Golf Village Courts More Visitors." *Jacksonville Florida Times-Union,* March 20, 2002.

Smits, Gary. "Marketing a Shift in Strategy with a Massive Remodeling and Media Blitz, the World Golf Hall of Fame Is Being Given a New Image." *Jacksonville Florida Times-Union,* July 17, 2004.

Mark Lane

Dell Inc.

1 Dell Way
Round Rock, Texas 78682-2222
USA
Telephone: (512) 338-4400
Fax: (512) 283-6161
Web site: www.dell.com

■■■

DUDE, YOU'RE GETTING A DELL CAMPAIGN

OVERVIEW

In 2002 Dell Inc. experienced its first-ever yearly decline in net revenue. In 2001 sales hit $31.9 billion, but the next year they fell to $31.2 billion. The drop in sales coincided with an overall decline in computer sales worldwide, and the mail-in computer giant was far from doomed. Still, it was at this time that Dell shifted its advertising approach, introducing its "Dude, You're Getting a Dell" campaign in 2001. The advertisements starred Steven, a "surfer dude" teen, and were intended to attract high school and college students and their parents.

The Chicago office of ad agency DDB created the campaign, which consisted of approximately 20 television commercials that placed Steven in various scenarios in which he could promote the computer, using the ubiquitous tagline "Dude, you're getting a Dell." Such instances occurred during a high school graduation speech, in a college classroom, and during a computer-store sales pitch. Throughout the campaign Steven persistently promoted Dells in a way that appealed to teens and both charmed and annoyed adults. The "dude" became incredibly popular with TV viewers, prompting Dell, from 2000 through 2002, to spend a large portion of its $200 million annual advertising budget on the campaign.

Steven became an instant pop-culture icon. But sales, which had begun to decline in 2001, did not rebound in 2002, and some people at Dell wondered if the popular character was overshadowing the product. Dell and DDB therefore began preparations to move away from the "Dude" campaign by phasing Steven out in late 2002, replacing him with a group of fictional interns. "Dude" fans were outraged, but sales did not suffer. In fact Dell shipments increased by 25 percent in the quarter following the introduction of the intern ads. Sales continued to grow, and Dell more than rebounded from the losses it had experienced in 2002. By the end of 2003 annual revenue had grown past $40 billion, and it increased to nearly $50 billion the following year. Regardless of the effectiveness of the "Dude, You're Getting a Dell" campaign, however, the "dude" was regarded as one of the most memorable figures in the history of advertising.

HISTORICAL CONTEXT

Michael Dell began working with computers at age 15, when he took apart a brand-new Apple computer to see if he could rebuild it. He could. In the 1980s Dell began rebuilding and selling computers from his University of Texas at Austin dorm room, naming his company PCs

A still from Dell's "Dude. You're Getting A Dell" television campaign featuring Steven, the Dell "dude." DDB/NEEDHAM, CHICAGO. REPRODUCED BY PERMISSION.

Limited. In 1985 the company developed its own computer, the Turbo PC, which was advertised for direct sale in national computer magazines. Consumers were attracted by the low prices, so much so that the company grossed $6 million in its first year of business. In 1987 PCs Limited changed its name to Dell Computer Corporation, and in 1992 *Fortune* magazine listed Dell as one of the world's 500 largest companies. Sales climbed dramatically, giving even the century-old IBM something to worry about. Within a decade Dell had become the largest seller of personal computers in the United States. It lost that spot to Hewlett-Packard in 2002 but regained it within a year. In subsequent years the two continued to battle for the number one spot.

Dell's concentration remained on direct sales even as it moved away from relying solely on its mail-order catalog to reach customers. During the shift Dell used larger and larger advertising campaigns to promote its products and its direct sales approach. Its $70 million "Be Direct" worldwide campaign of 1998 emphasized the advantages of Dell's direct-to-customer business philosophy. But the customer-service team that was then operating Dell's direct sales was often criticized by consumers. Complaints about unknowledgeable and rude sales representatives were made public. There were also accusations about cheap and undependable parts. In response Dell launched "Dell4me," a $30 million ad campaign that was accompanied by the theme "Your thoughts exactly." This campaign shifted the focus from Dell's technical specifications to the company's ability to help consumers get the most out of that technology. Although "Dell4me" represented an attempt to appeal more directly to individual consumers, it was not altogether personable in its approach. To improve Dell's image, a more upbeat advertising campaign was deemed necessary. Thus "Dude, You're Getting a Dell" was introduced in 2001.

TARGET MARKET

Prior to the "Dude" commercials, Dell had been known as a company that primarily targeted business accounts, a fact reflected in its advertising campaigns. The Steven character was intended to broaden the company's appeal to individual consumers. In particular Dell wished to target first-time computer buyers (and their parents). The company reasoned that these customers might be especially intimidated by the task of purchasing a computer that was not available in stores. Steven helped to make Dells seem far less daunting, thus bridging the gap between the computer company and customers.

According to *Newsweek,* in 1990 about 15 percent of U.S. households owned a computer. Within a decade the

DUDE, YOU'RE UNDER ARREST

Benjamin Curtis, the actor who played Steven in the "Dude, You're Getting a Dell" commercials, was arrested on February 9, 2003, for buying a bag of marijuana. He was apprehended after a police officer witnessed him buying the drugs on a street in Manhattan. After spending a night in jail, Curtis was released, and the charges were later dismissed.

number jumped to 50 percent. Further a large percentage of homes with computers were occupied by teenagers. In 2001, when "Dude, You're Getting a Dell" was launched, an incredible 78 percent of American teens had computers and Internet access in their homes. Because many of these computers were purchased by parents, Dell's campaign had to simultaneously target teens and parents. Steven, played by actor Benjamin Curtis, who was 21 in 2001, was himself a representative of the lucrative young-adult demographic. In the "Dude, You're Getting a Dell" television commercials, Steven spoke most directly to parents who were purchasing computers for their high school and college-age kids. The character became a phenomenon among consumers in the 13-to-24 age bracket.

COMPETITION

Dell Inc. was not the only computer company experiencing rapid growth at the end of the twentieth century. Hewlett-Packard (HP), in particular, offered fierce competition for Dell. Since 1999 the two companies had been vying for the spot of number one seller of PCs in the United States and subsequently in the world. The rivalry was amplified by the two companies' battle for Compaq (in 1999 Dell took over Compaq; in 2002 Hewlett-Packard acquired the company). In 2002 Hewlett-Packard launched its "Everything Is Possible" campaign, which, inspired by HP customers' success stories, focused on the company's positive relationship with its customers. HP followed it with the "You + HP" campaign in 2003. "You + HP" won accolades, including being named Campaign of the Year by *Adweek.* With a wide range of products, including PCs, printers, and servers, as well as high sales (in 2004 sales approached $80 billion) and a soaring net income (in 2004 it was $3.5 billion, representing a one-year net income growth of 37.7 percent), the company gave Dell stiff competition.

Another computer giant, IBM, had long competed with Dell in the field of computer products. In 2004 its sales exceeded $96 billion, with a net income nearing $8.5 billion. The latter reflected an 11.2 percent growth since 2003. But while Dell was finding success with its "Dude" advertising, IBM was met with disdain for its 2001 "Peace, Love and Linux" campaign, which promoted the Linux operating system. For the campaign IBM hired ad agencies to spray-paint stenciled side-by-side images of a peace symbol, a heart, and a penguin (the Linux mascot) on sidewalks in Chicago and San Francisco. Local officials and business owners demanded that the images, which they considered vandalism, be removed.

Following the lead of its rival Dell, Gateway in 2004 closed down all of its computer stores but continued selling its merchandise by phone and through its website. Prior to the shift Gateway had been experiencing major financial difficulties. Its chain of stores was far from profitable, and from 2001 to 2003 the California-based company had lost money during most quarters. From 2002 to 2003 Gateway's revenue plunged from $4.2 billion to $3.4 billion. Even its long-standing and popular spotted-cow advertisements could not help. Closing the stores had some immediate positive results: by 2004 sales had improved nearly $2.5 billion.

In the field of network computing—including corporate networks and websites as well as workstation computers—Sun Microsystems offered challenging competition for Dell. Its sales and net income, though nowhere near Dell's, were admirable. In 2004 its sales exceeded $11 billion, and it had a net income nearing $400 million.

MARKETING STRATEGY

Dell had used the character of Steven prior to the "Dude" campaign. Two agencies, DDB New York and Lowe Lintas, created the character in earlier concepts. In the first Steven ad, which aired during the 2000 holiday season, actor Curtis played a teenage boy asking his parents for a Dell computer for Christmas. When DDB's Chicago office took over the campaign in 2001, it decided to play up the Steven character and gave him the "Dude" tagline.

The goal of the new campaign was to move away from the technology-focused ads that mostly appealed to businesses and the particularly computer-savvy individual. With Steven, Dell could better identify itself with consumers across the board in a personable and familiar way. The company spent a significant amount of money to promote Steven and his "Dude, You're Getting a Dell" slogan. For each year between 2000 and 2002, Dell spent approximately $200 million on advertising. A large chunk of this was used for the "Dude" TV commercials, which began airing in the spring of 2001.

In two years Curtis made approximately 20 commercials with Dell. The spots ran during both daytime and prime-time TV shows and appeared on all major networks.

The "Dude" commercials did not vary much from one to another. In each ad Steven, an annoying but somewhat lovable young guy, was seen relentlessly and enthusiastically pushing Dell computers at every opportunity. In one series of three commercials Steven, playing Santa's helper in an elf suit, told kids they wanted a Dell for Christmas. In another spot Steven was with a date in his father's car (trying to pass the car off as his own) when he advised a computer-seeking neighbor, Mr. Foster, to buy a Dell. Steven was also seen giving a speech at a high school graduation, throwing his sales pitch at the end; at a computer store, announcing his Dell pitch on the loudspeaker; and writing his tagline on a blackboard in a college classroom. During the two years that the "Dude" commercials ran, Steven's task seemed to be to connect with teens and annoy adults (such as a high school principal, a store manager, and a college professor). The spots, although not changing in theme, progressed with Steven's fictional life: he was depicted first in his messy bedroom in his parents' home and subsequently graduating from high school, working part-time jobs, and attending college.

OUTCOME

"I would choose a Dell over a Gateway because Steven is cuter than Gateway's cow," claimed one teen, referring to Gateway's long use of the cow in its advertisements. Steven became a cult figure in advertising akin to Clara Peller, star of Wendy's famous "Where's the Beef?" campaign of the 1980s. Steven fan sites popped up on the Internet, Steven fan mail was sent to Dell, and Curtis was recognized everywhere he went. The campaign's effectiveness in selling Dell products, however, was less clear.

From the third to the fourth quarter of 2000—after the holiday-season introduction of Steven—Dell sales rose 38 percent. But while some credited the "Dude" character for this, others linked the sales to the fact that Dell had lowered its prices. In 2001, when the first 10 or so "Dude" commercials were aired, net revenue actually declined slightly. Dell did not fare much better in 2002; even at $35.5 billion, revenue was down from 2001. By this time Dell was preparing to shift away from ads featuring the Steven character. In the fall of 2002, with plans to fade Steven out, the company introduced a new campaign involving a fictional group of young interns. One of the first three intern commercials ended with an appearance by Steven repeating his familiar tagline. In the other two the phrase "Dude, You're Getting a Dell" was spoken by a voice-over announcer who was not Steven.

Steven fans felt betrayed by Dell. Replacing the character, however, turned out to be perfect timing for the company. Soon after the change Curtis was arrested for possession of marijuana, a situation that would have presented Dell with a PR nightmare. The shift may have also resulted in significant monetary benefits. Dell shipments increased by 25 percent in the quarter following the launch of the intern commercials; the same period after the start of the "Dude" campaign had produced an increase of just 16 percent. The intern commercials were nowhere near as popular as the "Dude" spots. But as Dell's CEO and founder, Michael Dell, put it, "We're not running the Steven TV show." Still, regardless of whether the Steven character took attention away from the computers themselves and whether the "Dude" campaign was in fact responsible for an immediate skyrocket of sales, the campaign did significantly raise awareness of the brand.

FURTHER READING

"Dell Says Ads Helped Boost Bottom Line." *Houston Chronicle,* January 19, 2002, p. 2.

"Dell's Disappointing News Shakes US Further." *Scotsman,* November 11, 2000, p. 6.

Elliot, Stuart. "Agency to Quit the Dell Account." *New York Times,* April 6, 1999.

———. "Dell to Focus More on Consumers." *New York Times,* September 23, 1999.

Harrison, Crayton. "Dude from Dell Gives Sales a Lift." *Seattle Times,* December 26, 2001.

Howard, Theresa. "Dude! You've Been Replaced." *USA Today,* March 9, 2003.

Kessler, Michelle. "Dude, Dell's Service Has Slipped, but Company's Working on It." *USA Today,* April 29, 2002.

Lazare, Lewis. "Dell Campaign Starts Oct. 1." *Chicago Sun-Times,* September 21, 2001, p. 70.

Musgrove, Mike. "Gateway's Changes Yield Little Reward." *Washington Post,* January 11, 2003, p. E01.

O'Harrow, Robert. "Dell Sales Projection Sends Market Down; Vote Concern a Factor; Nasdaq at Low for Year." *Washington Post,* November 11, 2000, p. E01.

Ross, Barbara, Alice McQuillan, and Greg Gittrich. "Total Bummer for Dell Dude." *Daily News,* February 11, 2003, p. 5.

Scheiber, Dave. "Dude, You're Getting a Career." *St. Petersburg Times,* January 28, 2002.

Vranica, Suzanne, "Viewers Go Wild for Dell's Surfer Dude." *Ottawa Citizen,* January 11, 2002, p. F1.

"You're Gettin' New Ads, Dude! Dell Plans for Life without Steven." *Ottawa Citizen,* October 17, 2002, p. F8.

Candice Mancini

Delta Air Lines, Inc.

1030 Delta Boulevard
Atlanta, Georgia 30320-6001
USA
Telephone: (404) 715-2600
Fax: (404) 715-5042
Web site: www.delta.com

■■■

LET YOURSELF FLY CAMPAIGN

OVERVIEW

Although Delta Air Lines, Inc., was the number three air-passenger carrier in the early 1990s, by 1996 it was feeling the pressures of low-cost carriers such as Southwest Airlines. Budget-conscious air travelers were embracing cheap tickets and willingly giving up first-class seating, onboard meals, and other frills offered by older carriers such as Delta, United Airlines, and American Airlines. When Southwest expanded service into the lucrative Florida leisure-traveler market in 1996, Delta realized that its customers were abandoning it for that airline. To compete with Southwest, in 1996 Delta unveiled a low-cost carrier called Delta Express. Although Delta Express was initially a success, discount fare wars and consumers' brand confusion, among other problems, caused the carrier to falter. In 2002 Delta announced plans to close Delta Express and introduce a new low-cost carrier, Song Airlines, in its place.

To assure that Song's launch was a success and to send the message that low cost did not have to mean low quality, Delta planned a major branding campaign with a budget estimated at $10 to $12 million. Working with its advertising agency, Kirshenbaum Bond + Partners, as well as the agency's units Media Kitchen (media strategy) and Lime (public relations), Delta developed a unique marketing strategy that included print ads, television spots, and outdoor efforts. Also part of the creative team were Andy Spade, who had served as creative director of various ad agencies, and Spade's wife, fashion designer Kate Spade, who was responsible for creating new uniforms for Song's customer-service staff and flight attendants.

Song's branding strategy was a resounding success. The company reported that, within five months of the "Let Yourself Fly" campaign's launch, brand awareness had jumped from zero to as much as 44 percent in key target markets. In early 2005 the original campaign was replaced with a new one, "Fly Your Own Song," created by Shepardson Stern & Kaminsky, New York. Later that year Song, along with its parent, Delta Air Lines, filed for bankruptcy. Delta reported that Song Airlines would be discontinued in 2006.

HISTORICAL CONTEXT

After starting as a crop-duster service in 1924, Delta Air Lines' first passenger-carrying flight took off in 1929. The fledgling airline served customers traveling between Dallas, Texas, and Shreveport, Louisiana. Within one year Atlanta was among the destinations, along with Monroe, Louisiana, and Jackson, Mississippi. Through a series of mergers with other airlines—Northwest in 1972, Western in 1987, and Pan Am in 1991—Delta grew and expanded its routes to become a global carrier.

© LARRY DOWNING/REUTERS/CORBIS.

By the mid-1990s Delta was the number three air-passenger carrier, ranking behind number one American Airlines and number two United Airlines.

By the mid-1990s customers were abandoning the carrier for discounters such as Southwest Airlines, especially in the popular Florida leisure-travel market. To try and win back passengers, in 1996 Delta launched its own no-frills, low-cost airline, Delta Express. It was initially successful, but as other low-cost airlines—including JetBlue Airways—started up, Delta Express's business began slipping. In 2002 Delta announced plans to disband Delta Express and launch a new low-cost airline, Song. The new airline was planned to compete directly against other low-cost airlines that continued to win Delta's customers. Song's first target markets were those dominated by JetBlue's service: Orlando and Fort Lauderdale, Florida, and cities in the Northeast, including Boston and New York.

TARGET MARKET

According to the Travel Industry Association of America, in 2003 the core customers of most airlines were business travelers, although they accounted for just 28 percent of all air travel. The rest of air travel was leisure (59 percent) and combined business/leisure travel (13 percent). As Delta Air Lines prepared for the launch of its low-cost subsidiary, Song, the company had its eyes on a nontraditional target market: women. Tim Mapes, the new air carrier's managing director of marketing, told *Adweek* that, while most airlines targeted male business travelers, Song was the only airline "targeting female leisure and business travelers." The women that Song was trying to reach were described as sophisticated people with discerning taste who loved bargains and hated typical airline food. More specifically, Song's target market was any frequent traveler in the airline's primary markets, New York and Boston. Also targeted were those leisure travelers in Florida who had used Song's key competitor, JetBlue Airways.

COMPETITION

JetBlue Airways Corporation, based at John F. Kennedy International Airport in New York, was launched in February 2000 and set the standard for a new breed of low-cost air-passenger carriers. The airline offered only coach service, but it included first-class amenities such as additional legroom and wider leather seats, free snacks during flights, and video entertainment, including DirecTV, in every seat. More importantly, JetBlue's focus was on customer service. It offered the convenience of e-ticketing, toys in airport terminals to occupy children waiting for flights, and blue-corn tortilla chips onboard. The strategy seemed to work; the airline reported boarding its 500,000th passenger within eight months of its first flight. To promote its services and build brand identity, in September 2000 JetBlue released its first marketing campaign. Created by the Boston office of Arnold Communications, the $1 million campaign's initial advertisements were billboards that emphasized the frustration that air travelers felt as a result of

SONG AND NYC MEATPACKING DISTRICT ALLIANCE ANNOUNCED

In a unique effort to separate itself from the crowd of low-cost air carriers, Song Airlines, a subsidiary of Delta Air Lines, Inc., formed an alliance in late 2003 with the fashionable New York City neighborhood the Meatpacking District. According to the alliance, the Meatpacking District Initiative, an organization composed of businesses located in the neighborhood, would receive financial support from Song to increase awareness of the area's retail shops and restaurants. Song would benefit from the alliance by increasing its opportunities to reach the upscale customers who lived in the Meatpacking District or frequented the shops and restaurants there. Although Song officials planned no traditional signage or advertising in the neighborhood, the airline's logo appeared on a map of the area that was widely distributed to travel agents and New York City hotels.

high prices and poor service. Television spots followed in October. By 2003 JetBlue was serving customers, especially those traveling for leisure, in 20 cities in Florida, in the Northeast, and on the West Coast. Also in 2003 JetBlue introduced flights between Long Beach, California, and Atlanta, home of Delta Air Lines. The flights between Atlanta and Long Beach seemed to be a direct response to Delta's plans to introduce its low-cost carrier, Song, with flights between New York and Florida, JetBlue's primary market.

United Airlines took on JetBlue and Delta's Song in November 2003 with the introduction of its own low-cost carrier, Ted. It made its first flight in February 2004. Described as an airline-within-an-airline, Ted—its name was derived from the last three letters of "United"—was based in Chicago and operated within the United brand. It offered passengers opportunities not typically provided by discount carriers, such as the ability to earn United's Mileage Plus miles and to upgrade from economy to economy plus (with more legroom at each seat). Ted also targeted leisure travelers, who accounted for 59 percent of all air travel, rather that the smaller business-traveler market. Once Ted was established, United planned to drop United service from its Denver hub to cities likely to be visited by leisure travelers—such as Las Vegas; New Orleans; Phoenix, Arizona; and Orlando, Florida—leaving those destinations to be covered by Ted. Passengers on Ted were served snacks (pretzels and biscotti) on morning flights and could buy more substantial snacks or light meals on longer flights. To support the launch of its new airline, United worked with agencies Fallon Worldwide, Minneapolis; Frankel, Chicago; and Pentagram, New York, to create a branding program, which *Adweek* said was "lighthearted" and "comfortable." But Ted's purpose was twofold. It took the place of United's original discount carrier, Shuttle by United, which operated for seven years until it was disbanded in 2001; and it was hoped the new low-cost carrier would attract customers, build business, and help the struggling United emerge from bankruptcy, for which it filed in 2002.

MARKETING STRATEGY

To guarantee that its spin-off airline, Song, would stand out from the crowd of discount airlines, Delta embarked on a major branding campaign for the new carrier that was intended to convince consumers it was offering more than just low-cost tickets. The effort involved every aspect of the new airline, from the uniforms of the customer-service agents and flight attendants to the food and entertainment provided on board. Marketing for the new airline supported the message that Song was unique and would provide customers an experience equal to air travel in the 1960s, when flying was an adventure in glamour and sophistication rather than simply a way to arrive at destination B from point A. In addition to the work of Delta's advertising agency, New York–based Kirshenbaum Bond + Partners, work on the project was provided by Andy Spade, former creative director at ad agency TBWA\Chiat\Day and husband of fashion designer Kate Spade, who developed Song's new uniforms. Kirshenbaum Bond + Partners divisions Media Kitchen and Lime worked on Song's media and public relations/promotions accounts.

Kirshenbaum Bond + Partners and Andy Spade partnered on Song's marketing campaign, with the agency handling outdoor advertising and Spade creating print ads. Television spots were also a part of the campaign. Print ads, which ran in publications such as *InStyle, Travel & Leisure, Food & Wine,* and the *New York Times Magazine,* were two- or three-page spreads, each depicting a Song customer who matched the specific publication's readers. The *InStyle* spread portrayed a 20-something woman dressed in jeans and a striped shirt, her red hair flying out behind her as she held onto a tree. The copy read: "Kate isn't afraid of flying, she's afraid of conformity." A spread that appeared in the *New York Times Magazine* featured an older woman with coiffed white hair. She was posed in front of rosebushes with her hands on her hips, and the copy read:

"Magdalena could fly in first, but she'd rather save $600 and not meet another CEO." The ads visually alluded to flying; for instance, the redhead's hair was flying behind her, and the older woman's arms on her hips hinted at the shape of wings. Ads also included the slogan, "Founded by optimists, built by believers," the tagline "Let Yourself Fly," and a list of Song's variety of product offerings.

Television spots for the campaign followed a format similar to the print ads, using imagery that evoked flight. The spots also used the theme and tagline of the campaign, "Let Yourself Fly." During an interview on PBS television's *Frontline,* Spade described the spots as "kind of a morph between a music video and a commercial." One commercial featured a small group of people laughing and running across a meadow while flying a kite in a crystal-blue sky. Text on the screen stated, "Now boarding happy people," followed by a list of Song's benefits (such as organic food and low fares) and the tagline "Song. Let yourself fly."

In addition to print ads and television spots, Song's marketing strategy included outdoor work by Kirshenbaum Bond + Partners' media-strategy division, Media Kitchen. One of the projects entailed hiring skywriters to fly over beaches on the East Coast, such as those on the Jersey shore, Martha's Vineyard, and Florida, writing in the sky the message "Wish you were here. Fly Song.com." The outdoor effort also featured signage that read, "Fifth Avenue style at Lower East Side prices," and that was placed in fashionable locations in New York City, such as the corner of Broadway and Houston Street. The agency's public-relations unit, Lime, opened a Song retail store in New York's SoHo neighborhood. The shop gave consumers an opportunity to try out Song's leather seats, sample its food, view the onboard entertainment options, and book a flight.

OUTCOME

With its initial "Let Yourself Fly" campaign, which created a brand identity for Song that established it as a stylish and fun way to travel and set it apart from other low-cost air carriers, Song emerged as one of the fastest-growing travel brands. In an interview with *Adweek,* Tim Mapes, the airline's managing director of marketing, noted that, five months after its launch, Song had established a brand awareness of 44 percent among consumers in target markets such as New York and Boston.

After a three-year run, in May 2005 Song replaced its "Let Yourself Fly" campaign with a new campaign titled "Fly Your Own Song." The effort was created by New York agency Shepardson Stern & Kaminsky and featured a series of print ads supported by outdoor and online advertising. The ads focused on Song's options that allowed passengers to personalize their travel experience. The campaign was released in select markets, including New York, Boston, and Los Angeles, before being expanded to other areas served by the airline.

Despite the success of its multimillion-dollar branding effort and of the follow-up campaign, in September 2005 Song Airlines filed for bankruptcy protection along with its parent Delta Air Lines. At the time Delta reported that Song would continue operation until 2006 and then would be absorbed back into its parent, Delta Air Lines. Gerald Grinstein, Delta's chief executive officer, told the *Los Angeles Times* that many of the best aspects of Song, such as additional legroom for passengers and high-tech entertainment options, would be incorporated into Delta as the airline continued to evolve as a more passenger-oriented carrier.

FURTHER READING

Baar, Aaron, and Deanna Zammit. "Roster Shake-Up at Delta." *Adweek,* May 28, 2003.

Beirne, Mike. "Are These the Little Airlines that Could?" *Brandweek,* March 29, 2004.

———. "Variety's the Spice Aboard Song." *Adweek,* April 25, 2005.

Bernstein, James. "Ted, Meet Song/Major Carriers Try to Make a Mark with Discount Airlines." *Cincinnati Post,* March 24, 2005.

Grantham, Russell. "Delta Tunes Up for New Song Low-Cost Airline to Take Off in Spring." *Atlanta Journal-Constitution,* January 29, 2003.

Howe, Peter J. "A Swan Song for an Airline Brand." *Boston Globe,* October 29, 2005.

Kesmodel, David. "United's Little Ted Gets Off to Flying Start Low-Fare Airline Fills 82 percent of Seats, Beats Expectations." *Denver (CO) Rocky Mountain News,* March 12, 2004.

Lippert, Barbara. "Song: Not So Catchy." *Adweek,* December 8, 2003.

Muskal, Michael. "Delta to Eliminate Discount Carrier Song." *Los Angeles Times,* October 28, 2005.

Rawls, Linda. "Kate Spade to Help Delta's Discount Airline Song Go for Stylish Look." *Palm Beach (FL) Post,* August 18, 2003.

Schmuckler, Eric. "The Media Kitchen." *Adweek,* June 21, 2004.

Thomaselli, Rich. "Song Sponsors NYC 'Hood." *Advertising Age,* November 24, 2003.

Tsui, Bonnie. "JetBlue Soars in First Months." *Advertising Age,* September 11, 2000.

"United Airlines Says Ted Is Good to Go." *Brandweek,* November 28, 2003.

Rayna Bailey

ON TOP OF THE WORLD CAMPAIGN

OVERVIEW

"Millions of reasons to fly today; only one that matters to you" was the central message of the "On Top of the World" campaign for Delta Air Lines, Inc. The campaign acknowledged that customers had individual reasons for flying, and it assured them that the airline would strive to meet their needs. To the accompaniment of ethereal music, some of the television commercials focused on individual passengers dreaming that they were being pampered by airline employees and then awakening to discover that the reality of a Delta flight was almost as pleasant as the dream. One woman was gently fanned by attendants as she slept on a bed of feathers. In another spot a man danced while an orchestra played just for him. Later spots showed people writing down their reasons for flying on Delta, attaching the pieces of paper to balloons, and watching them float into the air. Delta employees gathered the papers and placed them on airplane seats to indicate that they had assumed responsibility for ensuring that each customer's needs were met. The fantasy advertisements were intended to change the company's image and to portray the comfortable conditions in Delta's new transatlantic business-class seats. The "On Top of the World" campaign, which was created by Saatchi & Saatchi Advertising, began in May 1997 and was scheduled to run through the fall of 1999 in various media.

HISTORICAL CONTEXT

Delta Air Lines was founded in 1924 as Huff Daland Dusters, the first business to offer aerial crop dusting. C.E. Woolman, B.R. Coad, and George Post were instrumental in the formation of the enterprise. A division of Huff Daland Manufacturing, a New York firm that made airplanes, the dusting company began operations in Macon, Georgia, and then moved to Monroe, Louisiana. In 1928 the enterprise was sold to a group of Louisiana businessmen, and its name was changed to Delta Air Service in honor of the Mississippi delta region where it operated. During the 1940s the company moved its headquarters to Atlanta, and its name was changed to Delta Air Lines, Inc. The company offered crop-dusting services in the United States until 1966. Meanwhile, the firm began transporting passengers and mail among cities throughout the South. Mergers with Chicago and Southern Air Lines (C&S) in 1953, Northeast Airlines in 1972, and Western Air Lines in 1987 expanded Delta's operations nationwide. By 1998 the airline was making more than 5,000 daily flights to 318 destinations in 41 countries.

Over the years Delta's advertising slogans included "Trunkline to sunshine," introduced in 1945; "Delta is ready when you are," used from 1968 to 1984; "We love to fly and it shows," introduced in 1987; and "You'll love the way we fly," introduced in 1994. The airline often emphasized passenger comfort and personal service in its marketing efforts. "We take the time and effort to make you feel comfortable and relaxed on each Delta flight. Because we care," said an advertisement in *Sunset* magazine in 1986. In 1996 the $20 million "Delta Marathon" campaign during the Olympic Games showed the worldwide travels of British actor Nigel Havers, who had appeared in the film "Chariots of Fire." The commercials were intended to enhance Delta's status as an international carrier by appealing to the general public but also to frequent business travelers, who were becoming increasingly important to airlines.

Before 1978, when the U.S. airline industry was deregulated, advertising campaigns for Delta and other carriers were typically designed to promote a brand image. During the chaotic competition of the 1980s and 1990s the emphasis shifted to affordable prices as airlines launched fare wars and incentives such as frequent-flier programs to build customer loyalty. The industry lost enormous amounts of money, and many new carriers went out of business. After surviving economic difficulties during the early 1990s, Delta embarked on a dramatic cost-cutting program called Leadership 7.5, which streamlined its operations and increased passenger traffic but lowered employee morale and customer service. By 1997 the company was moving away from Leadership 7.5 and adopting a bold new marketing strategy that would change the airline's image and strengthen the Delta brand.

TARGET MARKET

The "On Top of the World" campaign was aimed primarily at business travelers flying on expense accounts. Because corporate travelers tended to fly frequently, they valued comfort and service during their trips. Since their fares were being charged to a business, these passengers tended to be less concerned about price. Nevertheless, they often traveled in the moderately priced business-class section because their employers were not willing to pay for the more costly first class. Some customers paid for less expensive seats and then used their frequent-flier credits to move into first class, reducing the airline's profits from the first-class section. During 1997 Delta's business-class market increased four times as fast as its first-class market, and the airline adjusted to the changing times by introducing a new transatlantic business class. (International operations, particularly transatlantic flights, accounted for about 20 percent of the company's revenues.) In 1998 Delta reconfigured its first-class and business-class sections into one group of luxury seats known as BusinessElite, which offered passengers greater legroom and space to recline. One newspaper advertisement in the "On Top of the World" campaign called attention to the more spacious seating arrangement by stating, "Delta presents the last news today's hardened business executives would expect to hear from a company. 'We're upsizing.'" The campaign also emphasized the sincere, courteous service for which Delta had always been noted.

COMPETITION

In 1998 Delta transported 105 million passengers, more than any other airline in the world. According to *Aviation Week & Space Technology,* United Airlines, Inc., was in first place in the United States, with American Airlines second, Delta third, Continental Airlines, Inc., fourth, Northwest Airlines Corporation, fifth, and US Airways Group, Inc., sixth. During 1998 Delta considered a marketing and code-sharing alliance with United Airlines, since the two carriers served more than 200 destinations but competed in only 34 of them. The virtual merger, which would have given the two firms nearly 39 percent of all U.S. traffic, was opposed by government officials on antitrust grounds, and it was abandoned when Delta's pilots withdrew their support. In the same year Northwest and Continental began planning a similar alliance, which would control about 16 percent of U.S. traffic, but the partnership was delayed as the two companies awaited antitrust clearance from the U.S. Department of Justice. Meanwhile, American and US Airways considered a cooperative arrangement, which would control 25 percent of the market, but they ultimately converted the proposal into little more than a reciprocal frequent-flier plan. Because the three alliances would have created three gigantic airline blocs controlling 82 percent of the market, they were opposed by government regulators, consumer groups, and smaller airlines.

Like Delta, other airlines were using new advertising slogans in 1998. United, a subsidiary of UAL Corp., had abandoned its familiar "Come fly our friendly skies" tag line and in 1997 launched a candid campaign called "Rising," which admitted that air travel was not always pleasant. The campaign promised that United would rise to the challenge and improve its performance. One magazine advertisement said, "We figure by the time you reach the gate agent, you've had enough red tape." The text explained that the company had given its gate agents the power to resolve problems for customers without consulting a supervisor or asking the customer to wait. In one television commercial the narrator promised, "Air travel needs to be easier, more professional, especially for people who do it most. Now it will be, because, compared to the rest of the industry, United Airlines is headed in a different direction."

LIVING BILLBOARD

While competing for the Delta Air Lines, Inc., account, Saatchi & Saatchi Advertising submitted an idea for a "living billboard" that would feature a 44-foot-long section of a Delta jet and actual people playing the roles of passengers and flight attendants. The billboard would showcase the appetizing food, individual movie screens, and comfortable conditions on the airline's new business-class flights to Europe. Saatchi & Saatchi expected Delta to commend the creative effort and then request a less unusual approach. Instead, Delta executives were so enthusiastic about the idea that they asked the agency to have the display completed within two months. The billboard was erected near the Port Authority Bus Terminal in Manhattan, where it was seen by an estimated 1.5 million people each day. *Adweek* estimated that Delta received more than $2 million worth of publicity, thanks in part to testimonials from the billboard's passengers and widespread coverage by print and broadcast media. The promotion, which lasted six days and cost $250,000, won a 1998 *Mediaweek* Plan of the Year Award.

Continental Airlines, a subsidiary of Continental Air Holdings, also had a new marketing slogan, "Work hard. Fly right." Like Delta, Continental advertised a business-class fare (known as BusinessFirst) that offered first-class perks to attract international fliers. The 1990s were a time of flux for Continental, which operated at a loss early in the decade and filed for bankruptcy protection, from which it emerged in 1993. By 1997 Continental was generating $7.2 billion in annual revenues and was growing faster than any other major U.S. carrier, but because one of its primary investors was attempting to withdraw from the company, Continental was viewed as a possible takeover target. Delta considered merging with Continental during 1997, and in January 1998 Continental received takeover proposals from both Delta and Northwest, but no agreement was reached during the year.

Northwest lost $224 million during the third quarter of 1998 because of a pilot strike that lasted from June to September. The company had revenues of $10.2 billion in 1997, and in 1998 it reported a profit of $71 million during the first quarter and $49 million during the second quarter. Northwest's marketing efforts in 1998 included a notable advertising campaign for the company's E-Ticket service, which allowed customers to purchase tickets electronically via the Internet. Northwest was also known for its popular "What in the World" advertisements in *USA Today,* which was based on interesting facts, for example, the number of glasses of milk a cow produced in its lifetime tied to the line "Milk your vacation for all it's worth."

Another top competitor, American Airlines, emphasized the familiarity of its brand during 1998. In its advertisements international travelers felt as if they were almost home when they saw the company's red, white, and blue emblem. American, a subsidiary of AMR Corporation, had led the U.S. airline industry in 1992, with a market share of 20.3 percent, compared to 19.3 percent for United and 16.8 percent for Delta. By the late 1990s American held the second largest market share in the United States but was generating more revenue than any other carrier in the world.

MARKETING STRATEGY

By 1997 Delta was ready to move away from the straightforward themes and simple melodies of its earlier advertisements and to try a daring new strategy to change its image. It hired a new agency, Saatchi & Saatchi Advertising, to design a consistent, multimedia ad campaign that would build the Delta brand. The campaign revolved around the message that Delta was a global carrier that treated customers as individuals and made them feel as if they were "on top of the world." Gayle Bock, vice president for consumer marketing at Delta, explained, "We all know the rational reasons for choosing an airline: schedule, convenience, frequent flier miles, and cost. However, to connect an airline brand with its customers, it is essential that we also understand their emotional needs. In this regard, Delta already has a long history of commitment to personal customer service. No courtesy is too small to extend to any customer, anywhere in the world. The new branding campaign demonstrates that Delta professionals recognize customers individually. It is who we are, and it is our competitive advantage."

The surreal quality of the "On Top of the World" campaign was underscored by its chantlike theme music, a New Age song called "Adiemus." The first five television commercials in the U.S. campaign, launched in the spring of 1997, looked a great deal alike and had the same overall tone. They showed passengers dreaming that airline chefs, flight attendants, and other personnel were catering to them as if there were no other travelers on the plane. When the passengers awoke, they discovered that Delta's transatlantic business class was almost as pleasant as their dreams. A second series of television commercials began airing in the fall of 1997 and ran through 1998.

POP MUSIC

"Adiemus," the unusual theme song in the "On Top of the World" campaign, had been used in European advertising for Delta Air Lines since 1994. The music was so successful that the London Philharmonic Orchestra recorded a longer version, which climbed the popular music charts to reach number 13 across Europe and number 8 in Italy. Consumers purchased more than 100,000 copies of a compact disc that featured the song.

Like the first spots in the campaign, they featured the song "Adiemus" and voice-over narration by actress Christine Lahti, star of the television series *Chicago Hope.* In the spots that aired during 1998 Lahti said, "There are millions of reasons to fly today. Only one that matters to you. At Delta Air Lines, it is our pleasure to get you to the place you want to be." The fantasy television commercials depicted a wide range of passengers who wrote their reasons for flying on Delta Air Lines (using words such as "success," "fun," "home," "the deal," and "the thrill") on pieces of paper, attached them to balloons, and watched as the messages floated into the sky. Delta employees collected the pieces of paper and assumed responsibility for meeting the customer needs written on them.

The "On Top of the World" campaign was a global promotion initially launched in the United States and Europe. It included print and billboard advertisements, radio spots, and network television commercials aired during programs such as *ER, Good Morning America, 20/20,* and sportscasts. The campaign received a large percentage of Delta's estimated $100 million annual advertising budget. According to Competitive Media Reporting, Delta spent $30.8 million on all advertising during the first half of 1997, compared to $31.9 million for United Airlines and $28.6 million for American Airlines. In the previous year Delta had spent $70.2 million for advertising, United $71.2 million, and American $61.3 million.

OUTCOME

The "On Top of the World" campaign was acclaimed for its style and creativity. One of the television commercials in the European campaign, "Synchronized Flying," which starred dolphins swimming together as if in a water ballet, won a Golden Kompass Award in 1995, and the public frequently called to learn when it would air so that they could tape it. "Adiemus" won a gold Clio in 1998 for original music.

Delta's research indicated that most consumers understood the central message of the promotion, but some people were mystified by the surreal advertisements. A new multimedia campaign promoting the airline's intercontinental BusinessElite service was launched in April 1999 with the tag line "Delta BusinessElite, outclassing business class."

In January 1999 *Air Transport World* named Delta the global airline of the year. In May 1999 *Aviation Week & Space Technology* named Delta the industry's best-managed major airline, citing the company's organizational strength and ability to compete in the global marketplace.

FURTHER READING

Beirne, Mike. "Delta Sets First Class Perks at Biz Price." *Brandweek,* December 14, 1998, p. 8.

Caranicas, Peter. "Something Special on the Air." *Shoot,* June 6, 1997, p. 4.

Martin, Ellen Rooney, and Michael McCarthy. "New Delta and United Ads Take Flight, Target Business Travelers." *Adweek* (Eastern Edition), May 5, 1997, p. 5.

Mundy, Alicia. "Paulette Stout." *Adweek* (Eastern Edition), December 7, 1998, p. 44.

Nelms, Douglas W. "Image Is (Nearly) Everything." *Air Transport World,* May 1995, p. 71.

"Pulling Delta Out of Its Dive." *Fortune,* December 7, 1998, p. 157.

Roush, Chris. "Ad Agency Resigns from Delta Air Lines Account." Knight-Ridder/Tribune Business News, March 7, 1997.

———. "Delta Air Lines Brings Out New Ads." Knight-Ridder/Tribune Business News, September 25, 1997.

———. "Saatchi & Saatchi to Give Delta Air Lines a New Look, Slogan." Knight-Ridder/Tribune Business News, March 14, 1997.

Walker, Karen. "US Alliances Face Scrutiny." *Airline Business,* July 1998, p. 10.

Woolsey, James P. "On Top of the World." *Air Transport World,* July 1997, p. 30.

Susan Risland

THE PASSENGER'S AIRLINE CAMPAIGN

OVERVIEW

Delta Air Lines was the number three air-passenger carrier in 1999, behind number one American Airlines and number two United Airlines. Delta's goal was to move up in the rankings to number one, at least in the eyes of its customers. But as consumer dissatisfaction with the airline industry overall continued to increase, Delta's main challenge was to convince people that air travel did not have to be a negative experience.

To reverse the negative perception consumers had of air travel, and to win over customers, Delta in 1999 replaced its longtime ad agency BBDO with the Leo Burnett Company. Leo Burnett created a branding and advertising campaign for Delta that began in March 2000. Titled "The Passenger's Airline," the campaign was unique in that it had no specific tagline, theme song, or celebrity spokesperson. Rather, the television spots, radio spots, and print ads focused on passengers, their needs, and how Delta was working to meet those needs.

The campaign reached its target audience, and in 2001 it received a Silver EFFIE Award for achieving its goal of mending the damaged relationship between Delta and its customers, particularly frequent business fliers. Following the September 11, 2001, terrorist attacks in the United States that included the hijacking and crashing of four commercial airliners, consumers fled from air travel. Because Delta's "The Passenger's Airline" campaign had resonated so well with the airline's customers, the Leo Burnett Company's team revamped it for the circumstances. With the title "Person to Person," the modified campaign remained passenger-focused and was designed to show how Delta could help bring people together.

HISTORICAL CONTEXT

In 1924 Huff Daland Dusters was founded as the world's first aerial crop-dusting company. The company quickly evolved to offer passenger service under the name Delta Air Service. Delta's first passenger flights began in 1929, carrying passengers from Dallas, Texas, to Shreveport, Louisiana, and from Monroe, Louisiana, to Jackson, Mississippi. In 1930 service was expanded to include Atlanta, Georgia, followed in 1934 with a name change to Delta Air Lines. In 1946 Delta's millionth passenger climbed on board. Delta Air Lines merged with Northwest Airlines in 1972, becoming a key carrier in the New York/Boston market. Delta continued to grow, merging with Western Airlines in 1987 and purchasing Pan Am's transatlantic routes in 1991 to become a global carrier. *Air Transport World* magazine named Delta the global airline of 1998.

To promote its flights between Chicago and Miami, Delta in 1945 hired the Montclair, New Jersey–based advertising agency Burke Dowling Adams (BDA) to create a marketing campaign. The $150,000 campaign had the tagline "Trunkline to Sunshine." BDA merged with another agency, BBDO of Atlanta, in 1964. In 1968 BBDO launched the campaign "Delta Is Ready When You Are," which was used by Delta for 16 years.

The "We Love to Fly and It Shows" campaign followed in 1987. In 1994 BBDO repositioned Delta's marketing to focus on the airline's customer service and introduced the slogan "You'll love the way we fly." But in 1997, after 51 years of serving as Delta's creative agency, BBDO resigned the airline's account when Delta opened the door to other ad agencies. According to a report in the *Atlanta Journal-Constitution,* Delta's decision to pursue other agencies was based on the failure of BBDO's 1996 campaign, "Delta Marathon," which was designed to promote the Atlanta Olympics. At the time BBDO stated that it preferred not to compete with the three other agencies vying for Delta's account: Ogilvy & Mather, Ammirati Puris, and Saatchi & Saatchi. BBDO stated further that during the review process it came to believe that Delta had already removed the agency from consideration.

When the dust settled, Saatchi & Saatchi, an agency based in New York, was selected to handle Delta's $100 million advertising account. In September 1997 "You'll love the way we fly" was pulled, and Saatchi's new campaign for Delta, "On Top of the World," was launched. The agency's relationship with Delta did not have the staying power that BBDO's did, however. In 1999, amidst management upheaval at the airlines and complaints that the theme "On Top of the World" was obtuse and unsuccessful, Delta again looked for a new agency to handle its account. Besides Saatchi & Saatchi, in the running were the Leo Burnett Company, TBWA Worldwide, and Grey Advertising. Leo Burnett won the $100 million account and in March 2000 launched Delta's global campaign, "The Passenger's Airline."

AIRLINE ALLIANCE ADS PROMOTE CUSTOMER SERVICE

In 2000 SkyTeam, an alliance between Delta Air Lines and its partners Air France, AeroMexico, and Korean Air, introduced a new marketing campaign designed to promote the customer service and benefits the separate airlines offered consumers. Themed "Putting You Back in the Picture," the campaign included television spots and print ads. Delta and its partners formed the alliance in late 1999 to develop code-share agreements, which enabled the partners to sell seats on each other's planes. According to Delta, one year after forming a code-share agreement with Air France in 1998, it had generated some $400 million in extra sales. To benefit consumers the SkyTeam Alliance connected more than 6,000 flights daily and carried approximately 174 million passengers to 98 countries each year. Other such alliances and their partners included Star Alliance, led by United Airlines and Lufthansa, and Oneworld Alliance, led by American Airlines and British Airways.

TARGET MARKET

In 1999 Delta conducted a study of its customers, and the results revealed that, although the airline typically reported high ratings for customer satisfaction, it was experiencing the effects of a negative perception of the airline industry. Many business travelers had become distrustful of airlines and their broken promises of better service, shorter check-in and boarding lines, on-time departures and arrivals, and no lost luggage. Delta considered such travelers to be one of its key market demographics. According to a report submitted for consideration by the EFFIE Awards, the airline's primary target audience was "Road Warriors," that is, 25- to 54-year-old men who flew on more than six trips annually. Steve Crawford, executive vice president of client services at Leo Burnett, told *Adweek* that the "Passenger's Airline" campaign was designed to address a split between the airline and its customers. "There's a relationship between the business traveler and the airlines that's really important," Crawford said. Recognizing the importance of that relationship, Lisa Bennett, executive creative director at Leo Burnett, added that the two-phase campaign would focus on the passenger's experience of flying Delta Air Lines and on addressing customer concerns.

COMPETITION

As the skies became more crowded and passenger numbers inched up, reaching more than 700 million travelers boarding 9 million flights in 2000, complaints about airline service were also on the rise. A report by the National Institute for Aviation Research at Wichita State University found that, despite promises by airlines to improve their services in 2000, overall they had not. The U.S. Transportation Department reported that from 1999 to 2000 the number of complaints had risen 20 percent, to nearly 3 complaints for every 100,000 passengers. The number one airline, American Airlines, a subsidiary of AMR Corp., and low-fare upstart Southwest Airlines Company, were among the companies reviewing methods to attract passengers and to respond to complaints of everything from long lines in the terminals to cramped quarters on the planes.

American Airlines focused on making passengers more comfortable once they were on board. In 2000

American expanded the free space inside its planes by removing two rows of coach seats in each of its 700 jets. The project cost an estimated $70 million. To support the effort American launched what it described as an amusing advertising campaign themed "More Room throughout Coach." Developed by ad agency TLP-Dallas, it was specifically aimed at business travelers, those who fly most. The campaign was twofold: it promoted the additional legroom on the planes, and it responded to the question of what had happened to all the seats that had been removed. The "Great American Seat Take-Off" portion of the campaign gave people a chance to win two of the removed seats and two round-trip coach tickets to any American Airlines destination. Ads for the promotion ran in major daily newspapers across the United States. "More Roomobile," part two of the campaign, was a traveling trailer set up like the inside of a remodeled American jet. It toured to 27 cities and gave people along the route the opportunity to play games and win prizes such as American Airlines golf tees, baggage tags, and T-shirts.

Southwest Airlines targeted business travelers, typically men between 25- and 54-years-old. In 2000 the airline signed a four-year sponsorship deal with the National Hockey League that was designed to reach hockey fans who also fell into Southwest's target demographic. The agreement included a deal with ABC television that included broadcast commercials, sponsorship during hockey-game intermissions, and showing Southwest's logo on goal replays. Also in 2000 Southwest worked with its Austin, Texas–based agency GSD&M to launch a marketing campaign to promote its website. The campaign's tagline, "A symbol of e-freedom," was a variation on Southwest's familiar "A symbol of freedom" slogan. TV spots portrayed people in unpleasant daily situations adjacent to images of them enjoying pleasant vacations. The message was: "When the going gets tough, get going to southwest.com to book a quick getaway."

MARKETING STRATEGY

The Leo Burnett Company, which had created the successful "Fly the Friendly Skies" theme for United Airlines, was hired by Delta Air Lines in 1999 to develop a new global branding and advertising campaign for the air carrier. A report in the *Cincinnati Post* stated that, prior to developing the campaign, Leo Burnett's team interviewed thousands of the airline's passengers and employees. The interviews considered every aspect of a traveler's experience with the airline, from making phone reservations to gate announcements in the terminals and employee uniforms. Based on the information it gathered, Leo Burnett created Delta's "The Passenger's Airline" campaign.

The $100 million worldwide campaign did not sing Delta's praises with catchy taglines or songs, and there was not a celebrity spokesperson in sight. Rather, the campaign focused on strengthening Delta's business relationship with its passengers by promoting what Delta had to offer from the perspective of passengers. Included was a redesigned delta.com website, more casual uniforms for employees, and advertising with television and radio spots and print ads. Lisa Bennett, executive creative director for Leo Burnett, told *Adweek,* "We didn't want this campaign to come across as corporate in nature. Rather than Delta saying, 'This is who we are,' we wanted to sign off with the passenger point of view."

Kick-off television spots aired on CBS during the 2000 NCAA basketball tournament. The commercials featured a variety of air travelers, from backpackers looking for a bargain to a businessman dressed in a suit. In each spot a text bubble appeared over the passenger's head with thoughts such as "Wants a window seat" and "Nap" followed by a voice-over asking, "How do you want to fly?" Other spots entailed airport vignettes that focused on passengers' needs. One portrayed a passenger stopping in an airport terminal ice-cream shop and lingering over a cone. The message was that the passenger had time to enjoy the ice cream because he had used Delta's E-ticketing and avoided long lines at the airline's terminal counter. It concluded with the statement, "Check in at the curb and go straight to the plane." Some spots closed with shots of personalized luggage tags on which passengers wrote their desires. In one spot a group of passengers were shown waiting at a baggage carousel, and the tag read, "Fly . . . understood." Print ads, which appeared in major magazines, were similar to the TV spots. In one promoting Delta's BusinessElite international service, the baggage tag read "Fly . . . like an '80s bond trader."

OUTCOME

Despite the lack of a catchy tagline or theme song to resonate with consumers, "The Passenger's Airline" campaign achieved it goals. The campaign was presented a Silver EFFIE Award in 2001 for its success in reconnecting the airline with business travelers, for joining the company's complete roster of product offerings under one umbrella, and for increasing brand regard at a time when consumers had a deep distrust of airlines. But by the end of the year Delta was embroiled in disputes with its employee unions. In November 2000 the airline was forced to cancel 375 flights because of a pilot shortage, affecting thousands of its customers. Under threats of delayed or canceled flights, Delta was struggling to maintain the consumer confidence the campaign had helped build.

The terrorist attacks on September 11, 2001—in which four commercial airliners were hijacked and crashed into the twin towers of the World Trade Center in New York, the Pentagon, and a field in Pennsylvania—further eroded consumer confidence in air travel and in airlines as a whole. Delta was forced to take another look at its successful marketing campaign. Rather than abandon the campaign, however, the Leo Burnett agency modified it for the circumstances. Maintaining the same focus on customers that "The Passenger's Airline" had used, the revamped campaign introduced a new series of advertisements, themed "Person to Person," designed to reinforce the importance of people being together in person.

FURTHER READING

Barr, Aaron. "Delta Gets in Passengers' Heads." *Adweek,* March 13, 2000.

"Delta Air Lines Debuts 'Person-to-Person' Advertising." *PR Newswire,* November 6, 2001.

Fonti, Nancy. "Delta Ads to Focus on Longing to Connect with Friends, Family." *Atlanta Journal-Constitution,* November 6, 2001.

Frook, John Evan. "Southwest Hooks NHL Sponsorship; Four-Year Agreement Designed to Put Male Business Travelers on More Flights." *B to B,* September 11, 2000.

Goetzl, David. "Delta's New $100 Mil Push Signals Shift in Branding." *Advertising Age,* March 13, 2000.

Grantham, Russell. "Delta, Global 'Sky Team' Partners Launching Ad Campaign Today." *Atlanta Journal-Constitution,* June 23, 2000.

Herschel, Gordon Lewis. "Advertising's Confusion Factor—Delta Air Lines Advertising." *Direct,* November 15, 1999.

Knapp, Kevin. "Airlines Vie for Online Runway." *Advertising Age,* March 20, 2000.

Reed, Dan. "American Airlines to Give Coach-Class More Legroom." *Knight Ridder/Tribune Business News,* February 6, 2000.

Stammen, Ken. "Delta Parades Its Deluxe New Jet Comforts: PC Ports, Seats Made for Sleep." *Cincinnati Post,* March 28, 2000.

———. "Delta Unveils Ad Drive, Turns Focus to Passengers." *Cincinnati Post,* March 8, 2000.

Thurston, Scott. "CEO of Delta Air Lines Makes Progress toward Repairing Image of Company." *Atlanta Journal-Constitution,* April 20, 2000.

———. "Delta Airlines' New Advertising Campaign Highlights Simple Pleasures." *Atlanta Journal-Constitution,* March 7, 2000.

"TLP, Inc. Partners with American Airlines to Promote 'More Room throughout Coach' Campaign." *Business Wire,* August 16, 2000.

Rayna Bailey

DHL Holdings (USA), Inc.

1200 S. Pine Island Rd., Ste. 600
Plantation, Florida 33324
USA
Telephone: (954) 888-7000
Fax: (954) 888-7310
Web site: www.dhl-usa.com

COMPETITION. BAD FOR THEM. GREAT FOR YOU. CAMPAIGN

OVERVIEW

In June 2004 Plantation, Florida–based DHL Holdings (USA), Inc., a subsidiary of DHL, which was headquartered in Belgium and was itself a subsidiary of the privately owned German postal service Deutsche Post World Net, ended a more-than-20-year absence from the U.S. television advertising market with a three-spot campaign that announced increased competition in the U.S. express and ground parcel market. The company, which had gone through a number of changes in the years just prior to the campaign, hired Ogilvy & Mather of New York to produce the campaign.

The campaign sported the tagline "Competition. Bad for them. Great for you." It consisted of television spots as well as print and online advertising and outdoor signage. In addition to the campaign proper, Ogilvy PR Worldwide conducted a public-relations campaign to assist in reintroducing the brand. The cost of the campaign was approximately $150 million.

The "Competition" campaign not only reintroduced DHL to United States customers but also introduced new colors for the company and made consumers aware of a fourth option (after UPS, FedEx, and the United States Postal Service) in the U.S. express shipping market. The campaign ended in February 2005, but DHL's two subsequent U.S. advertising campaigns followed up on what "Competition" had achieved and further cemented the company's presence in the U.S. market. *B to B* named it the best integrated campaign of 2004.

HISTORICAL CONTEXT

Founded in 1969 by Adrian Dalsey, Larry Hillblom, and Robert Lynn (whose surname initials gave the company its name), DHL was originally an express-courier service that carried documents such as bills of lading between San Francisco and Honolulu. During the next two decades DHL focused on international express delivery. In the 1970s DHL first initiated service to Pacific Rim countries (except China) and followed this up with service to Europe, Latin America, the Middle East, and Africa. In the 1980s the company began air-express service to Eastern Europe and the People's Republic of China. A television ad campaign of the early 1980s was memorable for its visuals of flying company vans. During this period DHL was content to relinquish the U.S. express market to rivals United Parcel Service (UPS) and Federal Express (now FedEx). That attitude changed in the early years of the twenty-first century.

The new approach toward the U.S. express-shipping market came with a new owner. In 2002 the German company Deutsche Post World Net completed its

© THIERRY ROGE/REUTERS/CORBIS.

acquisition of DHL (the process had begun in 1998). The following year DHL, in an effort to expand its ground-delivery capabilities, made a $1.1 billion offer to buy the ground-delivery service of Seattle-based Airborne Express. Airborne, initially an air-delivery company, had only recently begun its ground-package service in 2001. The deal was held up for five months while the U.S. Department of Transportation examined it closely. The department's two concerns were reduced competition and—because of the climate of heightened security following the terrorist attacks of September 11, 2001—foreign ownership. Ultimately the acquisition went through: the Airborne ground service was merged with DHL Americas, while Airborne's air operations became part of a new independent company called ABX Air, which was owned by Airborne stockholders. In this way the issues of foreign ownership and reduced competition were bypassed.

TARGET MARKET

The target market for the "Competition" campaign was the combined group of owners of small- and medium-sized U.S. businesses. Theresa Howard wrote in *USA Today,* "Historically both DHL and Airborne courted larger companies, overlooking the smaller businesses that generate 75 percent of new jobs and 52 percent of the gross domestic product, according to *Inc.* magazine." It was by tapping into this overlooked market that DHL in 2004 hoped to expand upon its meager share of the U.S. ground-express market while not overlooking its core customer base of larger companies.

In addition the humor of the spots was designed to grab the attention of customers under age 40, whether or not they were business owners. In this way DHL laid the groundwork for its future customer base. Finally, as at least one media critic, Barbara Lippert of *Adweek,* recognized, the spots were also intended to boost morale among DHL employees and solidify the company's effort to expand its share of the express- and ground-delivery market.

COMPETITION

While the United States Postal Service (USPS) competed with DHL, there was never any doubt about who the company was really focused on overtaking. UPS and FedEx held such larger percentages of the U.S. express- and ground-delivery market that DHL Americas CEO John Fellows referred to them as duopolists. In an article in *South Florida CEO,* Rochelle Broder-Singer quoted Fellows, who saw some advantage for the smaller DHL Americas. "Within the U.S., our competitors are very inflexible [because of their size] and often arrogant. We'll ensure that our brand is flexible." Flexible or not, UPS had effectively rebranded itself with its "What Can Brown Do for You?" campaign, which cost some $45 million. The campaign broke in February 2002, during the Winter Olympics. For its part FedEx responded in October 2003 with its $90 million, award-winning "Relax, it's FedEx" campaign.

That FedEx and UPS saw DHL as a potential threat was obvious from the roadblocks that they threw up

DEUTSCHE POST WORLD NET

While technically tracing its roots back to 1490 and the founding of the modern postal system in what later became Germany, Deutsche Post World Net itself came about in 1995, after the unification of Germany and following the second postal reform. Originally the company was called Deutsche Post AG, with the government as a majority stockholder. The company went public in 2000 and became the largest IPO (initial public offering) of the year in Germany, raising 6.6 billion euros. By the time of its 2002 acquisition of DHL, which became a wholly owned subsidiary, the company was known as Deutsche Post World Net. Its headquarters were in Bonn, Germany. In addition to the express delivery and logistics (i.e., managing a customer's specific transportation and warehousing needs) services provided by DHL, the company retained its original mail service and also offered financial services through its Deutsche Postbank division.

when the company sought to take over Airborne Express. Still, compared to them DHL was a very small player in the U.S. market. According to SJ Consulting, a Pennsylvania-based transportation-industry consulting firm, in 2004 UPS held 51 percent of the U.S. parcel market, FedEx had a 27 percent share, and the USPS captured 13 percent of the market. DHL trailed with 7 to 8 percent.

MARKETING STRATEGY

The strategy for the advertising campaign was twofold: to reintroduce the brand to customers and to position DHL as a serious alternative to UPS and FedEx in the United States. DHL executives felt that increasing the company's share of the U.S. market was crucial to the company's global positioning. In her *USA Today* article, Howard quoted Richard Metzler, then executive vice president of marketing for DHL Americas, who said, "There can't be a strong DHL globally without a strong DHL in the U.S."

The campaign was DHL's first U.S. advertising in two decades, and it used simple humor to get the point across, never leaving any doubt that the company was taking on the giants in the U.S. express market. In one television spot UPS and FedEx trucks waited on opposite sides of a railroad crossing while a long line of flatcars passed, each carrying DHL trucks. Another spot showed a FedEx truck and a DHL truck racing through a city trying to arrive first at the same destination. The race ended in a two-way tie for second place: a DHL driver was walking out of the building just as they arrived. The spots featured the tagline "Competition. Bad for them. Great for you." The passing-train spot particularly reinforced the new DHL colors, red and yellow. Previously DHL trucks had been painted white. The spots aired early in the morning, on prime-time broadcast and cable programs, and during late-night talk shows.

Metzler, who had worked in FedEx's marketing department prior to coming to DHL, also discussed the spots in a *B to B* article by Mary Ellen Podmolik. "We had to nail it on creative, and we did," he said. Podmolik noted that because of the lengthy gap between DHL's ad campaigns, "Metzler considered it critical to refer to FedEx and UPS by name so as to define [DHL's] own abilities in the express delivery market to U.S. customers."

In addition to the television commercials, print ads were run in leading business publications, ads were placed online, and billboards were installed in strategic locations around the United States. One of DHL's most prominent, and telling, billboard ads was located at the Memphis, Tennessee, airport, across from the FedEx hub. (FedEx was headquartered in Memphis.) As further proof that the "Competition" campaign was the first salvo in DHL's plan to become a major shipper in the U.S. market, the company announced in September 2004 that it had leased space in Memphis for a new sorting center, the third of a planned seven new hubs. The *Commercial Appeal,* a Memphis daily, quoted two DHL officials on the subject. Steve White, at the time the head of DHL's hub and gateway operations, explained, "Memphis will allow us to expand our overnight delivery to parts of Arkansas, Tennessee, Mississippi, and Kentucky." Dan McDonald, then head of DHL network planning, had a more competitive take on the expansion into Memphis: "Memphis is geographically in the center of the country. FedEx found it works for them, and that we're in FedEx's backyard is just icing on the cake."

Ogilvy PR Worldwide complemented the ad campaign with a public-relations campaign that aimed, according to a June 2004 press release published in *Business Wire,* "to reintroduce the global express and logistics leader to core constituents and opinion leaders." In that same press release Metzler said, "Using a full 360-degree arsenal of marketing channels, we are showcasing the DHL brand's value message to current and potential customers across all points of contact."

DHL enhanced its ad campaign by signing a deal that made it the "Official Express Deliver and Logistics Provider" of the U.S. Olympic team for the 2004

Olympic Games, which were held in Athens. As such DHL also signed an exclusive U.S. broadcast agreement with NBC, the network that aired the Athens Olympics. The agreement locked out UPS and FedEx from national television advertising during the Olympics broadcast. This was not DHL's first sponsorships of a high-profile sporting event; in 2002 the company was one of the official sponsors of the British soccer team during the World Cup tournament.

OUTCOME

There was no doubt that the reintroduction of the DHL brand was successful, though, as expected, gaining a larger share of the market was less so. Nevertheless, in the *USA Today* weekly poll Ad Track, 23 percent of those familiar with the spots liked them "a lot." This was a slight increase over the Ad Track average of 21 percent. Among those polled in the 30-to-39 age group, 33 percent liked the spots "a lot," while 27 percent considered them "very effective." The Ad Track average for the latter was also 21 percent. Furthermore, as Howard noted in her November 2004 *USA Today* article, "tests of DHL's unaided consumer brand awareness show a 40-point climb." Because of the Airborne Express acquisition and the $1.2 billion expansion project, DHL's U.S. operations lost money in 2004 and 2005, though parent Deutsche Post World Net boasted that the company would reach the break-even point by 2006.

Being more or less the groundbreaker in the United States for the new DHL, the "Competition" campaign was bound to influence the company's subsequent campaigns. In early 2005 DHL launched a baseball-themed campaign as part of a sponsorship deal with Major League Baseball. DHL became the official delivery service for the league, the National Baseball Hall of Fame, the website MLB.com, and individual teams. One of the baseball spots featured Johnny Damon, who at the time was a star outfielder for the 2004 World Series champion team the Boston Red Sox. By associating the company with one of the touchstones of American culture, the baseball connection demonstrated DHL's commitment to increasing its share of the U.S. market. In September 2005 DHL introduced a new integrated campaign that emphasized customer service. "Last year we wanted people to understand that we were here and that we were a choice in . . . shipping," said Karen Jones, DHL vice president of brand, advertising, and promotions, in an *Adweek* article by Kenneth Hein. "Then the task was coming up with a unique and different message to tell the world why they should choose DHL."

FURTHER READING

Aufterbeck, Sigrid. "Airborne Express Shareholders Approve Sale to DHL." *Seattle Times,* August 15, 2003.

Broder-Singer, Rochelle. "Fighting the Duopoly." *South Florida CEO,* May, 2004.

Creamer, Matthew. "DHL Bets on Flexibility as It Moves on FedEx, UPS in U.S." *Advertising Age,* September 6, 2004.

"DHL Brings Competition and Choice to U.S. Delivery Business with New Campaign." *Business Wire,* June 14, 2004.

"DHL. Campaign Close-Up." *Sales & Marketing Management,* August 2004.

"DHL Joins U.S. Olympic Team." *Brandweek,* July 7, 2004.

"DHL Launches $150 Mil. Campaign." *Adweek,* June 21, 2004.

Gillie, John. "Seattle-Based Airborne Inc. in Talks to Sell Ground Delivery Unit." *Tacoma (WA) News Tribune,* March 25, 2003.

Hannon, David. "Small Package Market Changes Could Benefit Buyers." *Purchasing Magazine Online,* March 17, 2005. Available from <http://www.purchasing.com/article/CA510904.html?text=hannon>

Hein, Kenneth. "'Service Is Back' in New DHL Spots." *Adweek,* September 12, 2005.

Howard, Theresa. "DHL Dispatches Its Message to USA." *USA Today,* November 11, 2004.

Maddox, Kate. "Karen Jones, VP-Advertising, Brand and Promotions, DHL Express USA." *B to B,* July 11, 2005.

Roberts, Jane. "FedEx Rival to Open Sorting Hub in Memphis, Tenn., 'Backyard.'" *Memphis (TN) Commercial Appeal,* September 17, 2004.

Frank Caso

Diageo plc

8 Henrietta Place
London, WIG OMD
United Kingdom
Telephone: 44 20 79275200
Fax: 44 20 79274600
Web site: www.diageo.co.uk

KEEP WALKING CAMPAIGN

OVERVIEW

Diageo plc's Johnnie Walker was one of the world's top scotch brands in the late 1990s and early 2000s, but blended scotch as a category was in long-term decline. Among distilled spirits, meanwhile, vodka was booming, largely as a result of effective youth-oriented marketing. Trying to shed a perception that scotch drinkers were stodgy, suit-wearing business types, Johnnie Walker in 1999 unveiled a global branding campaign called "Keep Walking" that continued to associate scotch drinking with success while widening the definition of success to appeal to young drinkers. The U.S. version of this campaign, which began in 2001, celebrated the maverick entrepreneurial ideas of the 1990s, but its message fell prey to changing perceptions of exactly such entrepreneurs following the dot-com crash and successive corporate scandals. In 2003 Johnnie Walker's U.S. agency, Bartle Bogle Hegarty (BBH) of New York, set out to update "Keep Walking" to accommodate yet another definition of success.

The new installment of "Keep Walking," which had a budget of approximately $15 million, focused on life as a journey and offered Johnnie Walker as a product that helped people navigate the uncertainties of that journey. The Striding Man logo, an image of an aristocratically dressed man in midstride, had been used in the campaign's prior incarnations to represent the idea of personal progress; now the logo was used to suggest the determination required to weather the many obstacles and strange turns one encountered in life. The campaign's print ads paired the Striding Man and the "Keep Walking" tagline with stories of individual career paths that had taken unpredictable turns, while outdoor executions featured the Striding Man as their central character, who was shown having emerged from difficulties represented by simple visual symbols, such as walls, rainclouds, and stock-market graphs.

BBH exceeded its goals of drawing attention to the Johnnie Walker brand and to the Striding Man as a brand icon. The update of "Keep Walking" won a Silver EFFIE Award in 2005. The concept behind the outdoor component of the campaign was extended in a subsequent series of print and outdoor ads launched in late 2004.

HISTORICAL CONTEXT

Blended scotch whiskey fell drastically out of favor among American consumers during the 1980s and 1990s, losing more than 20 percent of its sales volume as young people in particular turned to clear liquors. While vodka brands such as Absolut and, later, Grey Goose built up-to-date, premium product images that appealed to people in their twenties and thirties—high-volume consumers essential to the long-term health of any alcohol brand—scotch advertising on the whole did not keep pace with the times.

Predictable appeals, such as using stereotypical Scottish imagery or connecting traditional ideas of business success with scotch drinking, were ineffective in communicating with young people.

Diageo's Johnnie Walker attempted to remedy this image problem by turning, in 1999, to a global branding platform called "Keep Walking," crafted by Bartle Bogle Hegarty of London. Featuring the Striding Man logo—an image of a walking man decked out in a top hat, boots, and cane, which made its first appearance on the Johnnie Walker bottle in 1909—"Keep Walking" was meant to suggest the idea of personal progress; the perpetually walking figure signified the determination necessary to realize one's dreams and goals. In print ads as well as TV spots such figures as Abraham Lincoln and the actor Harvey Keitel, as well as artists and philosophers, were employed to stress the long-established connection between success and scotch-drinking, but the campaign effectively broadened the definition of success to encapsulate worlds beyond the country clubs and private libraries of macho businessmen.

A U.S.-specific campaign running under the "Keep Walking" umbrella was launched in early 2001, at the height of enthusiasm regarding the so-called "new economy." Print ads assuring consumers that "A simple idea can change the world" depicted napkins on which the big entrepreneurial ideas of the 1990s—like selling coffee for $4.95 or opening an online bookstore—were shown in embryonic form, sketched on cocktail napkins, matchbooks, and other scraps of paper. A corresponding online promotion offered entrepreneurs a shot at $500,000 in grant money to realize their own business dreams. In the wake of the dot-com crash, the terrorist attacks of September 11, 2001, and a wave of corporate scandals, however, the limitations of this inspirational, shoot-for-the-moon message became clear. Diageo enlisted its U.S. agency, the New York office of Bartle Bogle Hegarty, to further recast the "Keep Walking" idea in 2003.

TARGET MARKET

Urban men aged 25 to 34 were Johnnie Walker's primary target, but the 2003 update of the "Keep Walking" concept marked a key shift in the brand's approach to this group. Previous installments of the campaign had been aimed at stimulating demand among the target group regardless of whether they already drank Johnnie Walker or, for that matter, scotch in general. The new version of "Keep Walking," by contrast, was aimed at scotch drinkers who were already familiar with the brand. BBH New York sought to take advantage of the fact that most people chose their alcohol brands based on social factors; the agency felt that if those who occasionally drank Johnnie Walker could be encouraged to drink it regularly, then they would serve, ultimately, as brand representatives among their friends and acquaintances. By strategically narrowing the target market in this way, moreover, BBH was able to make better use of a limited advertising budget.

BBH believed that in a scandal-ridden, recession-era business world, it did not make sense to emphasize material riches exclusively. The agency found poll numbers suggesting that a large majority of young men would, if given the choice, prefer two extra weeks of vacation to a 10 percent raise in pay. The new installment of "Keep Walking," then, emphasized life as a journey and offered models of success that were much more down-to-earth than those presented in the prerecession campaign of 2001. Gone were references to simple, world-altering ideas; in their place there appeared profiles of accomplished men, complete with references to the setbacks, humiliations, and unpredictable turns that characterized their paths to success. The Striding Man logo was transformed into a symbol of endurance rather than of simple inspiration.

COMPETITION

"Keep Walking" supported Johnnie Walker's two blended scotches, its Red Label and Black Label products. Johnnie Walker Red was the more affordable and more popular of the two and was America's second-leading scotch brand, behind Dewar's. Johnnie Walker Black, the fourth-best-selling scotch in the United States at the time of the campaign's launch, was a rival to premium brand Chivas Regal, then the country's number five scotch.

Dewar's, like Johnnie Walker, was at this time attempting to update its image and appeal to a younger audience. In 2000 the brand changed its approach to print marketing, entering into advertising partnerships with a few strategically selected publications, rather than continuing to run ads in as many as 20 magazines at a time. One prominent Dewar's partnership, with *Men's Journal,* resulted in a 2003 project called "Conquer the Highlands," an adventure story of two young men on an "extreme" tour of Scotland, which ran as a print insert described as an "advertorial," meaning it was intentionally similar to the magazine's content. This blurring of the boundaries between editorial and advertising content tested magazine-publishing conventions of the time. The theme was also adapted into a cable-television program, a one-hour adventure show that likewise mixed the two young men's adventures with product placement.

Rather than continuing to compete with vodka and other clear spirits for the youth market, Chivas Regal in 2003 instead began repositioning itself to appeal to an older male market. In a global ad campaign called "The Chivas Life," the brand made no apologies for its luxury roots, celebrating bold life choices such as going ice fishing in Alaska, "crossing the room like you own it," and

THE LABELS

Johnnie Walker brands included not just its consistent top sellers, Johnnie Walker Red Label and Johnnie Walker Black Label, but also Blue Label and Gold Label versions. All of Johnnie Walker's products were blended scotches, as opposed to single malts, with the difference in label color (and purchase price) indicating a difference, primarily, in the age, rarity, and quality of each individual whiskey in the Johnnie Walker blend. Red Label was considered a smooth scotch suitable for everyday drinking, whereas Black Label, consisting of more than 40 whiskeys, each of which was at least 12 years old, was intended for more luxurious times and settings. Blue Label was comprised of rarer whiskeys still and was intended to hearken back to the blending style of the company's namesake. The component whiskeys in Gold Label were each at least 18 years old. Johnnie Walker suggested that Gold Label be served frozen, in a chilled glass, with a snack of bitter chocolate.

embarking on a sailing trip, the destination of which was decided by throwing a dart.

Vodka, meanwhile, was the distilled-spirits industry's fastest-growing market segment and one in which consumers' purchasing choices, according to many observers, were almost exclusively tied to marketing and brand image. In the 1980s and 1990s Absolut vodka had risen from obscurity to become one of the hippest brands in the world and, ultimately, the number three distilled spirits brand in America, thanks to a long-running advertising campaign that turned the product's bottle into an iconic, fashionable emblem. In the first few years of the new millennium, however, Absolut's yearly sales growth could not keep pace with the vodka market at large, which was growing rapidly because of new designer brands such as Grey Goose. Using a taste-test platform whose findings were called into question from the start, together with aggressive marketing to bar owners, the Grey Goose brand grew faster, between 2000 and 2004, than any alcohol product in recent memory, becoming the vodka of choice for urban consumers of pricey specialty cocktails.

MARKETING STRATEGY

The new "Keep Walking" campaign had an estimated budget of $15 million and involved distinct print and outdoor components meant to accomplish different tasks. The "Journeys" print series, which featured profiles of men who had achieved success in unconventional ways, was meant to connect with consumers by making them evaluate their own conceptions of personal progress and by showing them that Johnnie Walker understood their lives. The outdoor portion of the campaign, called "Icons," was less personal and more overt in its branding, showing the Striding Man continuing to move forward despite difficulties, which were represented by simple but suggestive graphics against a black background.

The "Journeys" ads included "Bar," which showed a young man standing behind the bar of his own cutting-edge drinking establishment. A horizontal yellow timeline cut across the image, with copy reading, chronologically across the page, "First Business Loan," "Second Mortgage," "Third Migraine," and "Fourth Location." Similarly, "Cave" summarized an unconventional career path, showing a rear view of a man who was standing at the mouth of a cave that opened on to the ocean. The copy keyed to the various stages of the timeline graphic read, "Discover Caving," "Discover Perfect Cave," "Discover Others Will Pay to Be Guided There," and "Discover Perfect Job." "Producer" depicted a preoccupied man sitting in front of an enormous audio-mastering console. The story of his career path, as told via the accompanying timeline, was, "Terrible Guitarist," "Incompetent Drummer," "Laughable Lead Singer," and "Double-Platinum Producer." In each ad the Striding Man logo appeared above the "Keep Walking" tag at the far right end of the time line, suggesting the pictured individual's determination.

The "Icons" ads sent similar messages, but through symbolic images rather than via individual profiles. For instance, the Striding Man was shown emerging from the precipitous valley of a stock market graph and climbing a slope indicating an upswing, a clear reference to the recent economic woes that had affected many among the Johnnie Walker target market. "Wall" depicted the Striding Man on the other side of a wall he had just walked through, and "Cloud" showed him continuing to walk after having weathered a rainstorm.

In addition to point-of-service promotions, which linked imagery from the national campaign to retail displays of the product, the campaign included a less traditional element called a "Mentorship" program. The program involved sending E-mail invitations that directed Johnnie Walker drinkers to a website where they could register for social gatherings staged by the brand. These gatherings put the "mentors" in a position to spread their brand enthusiasm to Johnnie Walker neophytes.

OUTCOME

BBH exceeded many of its goals for attracting attention to the Johnnie Walker brand. The agency met its goal of increasing awareness of the Striding Man as brand logo. Whereas only 22 percent of consumers were aware of the logo's connection to Johnnie Walker before the campaign ran, 50 percent made the connection after the ads had been running for three months. While BBH had not staked the value of its campaign, which was more concerned with building brand equity and identity, on its capacity to generate immediate sales increases, a comparison of sales figures from the same three-month period the previous year showed a dollar-sales increase of 3.7 percent and a volume-sales increase of 3 percent. The campaign was awarded a Silver EFFIE Award in 2005.

The concept behind the "Icons" outdoor ads was extended in a print and outdoor campaign that was launched in late 2004, in which the Striding Man was shown, as before, against a black background, having successfully endured an obstacle represented by symbolic graphics. More than 50 such ads were generated, and each was tailored to its medium, the timing of its appearance, or (in the case of outdoor placements) its physical location. The "Keep Walking" tagline and the Striding Man logo remained Johnnie Walker's controlling umbrella concepts in subsequent advertising both globally and in the United States.

FURTHER READING

Beck, Ernest. "Johnnie Walker Scotch Tries a New Tack." *Wall Street Journal,* November 16, 1999.

Branch, Shelly. "Johnnie Walker Targets a Younger Market." *Wall Street Journal,* February 7, 2001.

Elliott, Stuart. "Chivas Regal and Johnnie Walker Start Preaching to the Choir in Campaigns Aimed at Scotch Lovers." *New York Times,* October 3, 2003.

"International Brand Development." *Marketing,* June 12, 2001.

Mason, Tania. "Johnnie Walker Plans 'Keep Walking' Shows." *Marketing,* July 5, 2001.

McCoy-Pinderhughes, Paula. "Anything's Possible." *Black Enterprise,* June 2001.

McMains, Andres. "Johnnie Walker Celebrates Ideas." *Adweek,* January 22, 2001.

"Stride Right." *Creativity,* December 2004.

Mark Lane

NOT EVERYTHING IN BLACK AND WHITE MAKES SENSE CAMPAIGN

OVERVIEW

NOTE: Since the initial appearance of this essay in the 1998 edition of *Major Marketing Campaigns Annual,* Guinness was acquired by Diageo. The essay continues to refer to Guinness, as that was the name of the organization when the campaign was launched.

In 1996 Guinness initiated a new advertising campaign for its famous stout beer. With a history dating back to 18th-century Ireland, the brand had a venerable image. Not only was the black-colored beer the best-selling stout in the United Kingdom and Ireland but it was also exported to 150 different countries. Abroad, Guinness was able to capitalize on its association with all things Irish to drive sales. But at home in the British Isles, Guinness found that newer Irish stout beers such as Bass and Murphy's were threatening to encroach on Guinness's domination of the declining stout category. Most importantly, Guinness had not captured the younger generation of 18 to 34 year olds. For the most part these younger drinkers considered the dark brew to be more their parents' beer of choice than their own.

The "Not Everything in Black and White Makes Sense" campaign was conceived to reposition the Guinness brand to appeal to younger drinkers. The surrealistic-style commercials created by advertising agency Ogilvy & Mather attempted to make people reconsider Guinness. The campaign set out to do so in two ways. Not only were the commercials creative, humorous, and eye-catching but they also presented implausible situations that encouraged viewers to form their own opinions—about the spots and about Guinness itself. The intent was to enable viewers to drop their preconceptions about Guinness, including common notions that the beer was too bitter, fattening, or not chic enough. "We decided we had to more or less revamp the brand and everything it stood for—re-invent it as it had re-invented itself many times already, and reconnect it to the new Ireland," Guinness marketing director Tim Kelly told the *Sunday Business Post.*

The launch spots of the campaign—"Bicycle" and "Old Man"—were both directed by Tony Kaye and encouraged viewers to take a new look at Guinness. "Bicycle," which was filmed in a style reminiscent of 1940s movies, depicts a world without men. Against a backdrop of the song "I'm Gonna Wash That Man Right Out of My Hair," the commercial portrays women in jobs traditionally held by blue-collar men. After these women drink beer, arm wrestle, and shoot pool, the commercial moves to a scene of a starkly empty maternity ward. Gloria Steinem's famous quote, "A woman needs a man like a fish needs a bicycle," flashes on the screen. What follows is the image of a fish riding a bicycle and the campaign's tag line, "Not everything in black and white makes sense." "Old Man" similarly set out to shock the viewer with its surprising ending. The commercial sets out with the sad scene of an old man dressing alone in his apartment. Singer Pete Townshend's quote appears on screen: "I hope I die before I grow old." It turns out, though, that the old man is donning his formal wear to marry a heavily pregnant buxom blonde.

While Guinness's sales rose over the life of the campaign, the company was not entirely pleased with Ogilvy & Mather's efforts. Two spots in particular sparked firestorms of controversy, which were not the sort of notoriety Guinness was hoping to achieve with its advertising. One, involving sadomasochistic practices, was decried as a reference to the death by hanging of a conservative member of Parliament that was rumored to have had sexual undertones. The other, which never actually ran, featured two gay men enjoying a tranquil breakfast. Tabloid newspapers, which got wind of the proposed commercial, chastised Guinness for condoning homosexual behavior. When the company responded by denying that it ever intended to do so and that it never would in the future, the gay community was outraged. Ultimately, Guinness fired Ogilvy & Mather and shifted its advertising business to Abbott Mead Vickers. That agency's first campaign for the stout giant featured more traditional advertising focusing on the quality of the beer.

© JOEY NIGH/CORBIS.

HISTORICAL CONTEXT

Guinness beer was founded under near-mythic circumstances in 1759, when Arthur Guinness took over an abandoned brewery at St. James Gate in Dublin, Ireland, and began producing a dark beer called porter. In later years the company named one of its strongest brews Guinness Extra Stout Porter. The porter appellation was in time dropped, and thus the stout category of beer was born. Guinness's distinctive black color derived from the fact that some of the barley used in the production was roasted, rather like coffee beans. The darkness of the beer contrasted with the "blonde" foam that resulted from the beer being poured or "pulled" from the tap.

The company also had a venerable history of advertising. Beginning in the 1930s the SH Benson ad agency coined the slogan "Guinness is good for you." At the same time the "My Goodness, My Guinness" poster ads, which featured a balding zookeeper whose Guinness was perpetually stolen by larcenous animals, received critical and popular acclaim. Even as early as the 1930s, however, the company used advertising to reposition the brand. *The Guardian* newspaper has explained that, for example, the "Guinness for Strength" campaign of that decade, which portrayed an archetypal workman in the midst of his labor, was designed to give the beer "a more masculine, macho image." Nearly 40 years later the company sought to again reposition itself. In order to appeal to women and to soften the brand's primary association with working-class men, Guinness designed glossy, stylish ads that appeared in British fashion magazines.

In the 1980s Guinness again shifted its image through its advertising campaign. The seven commercials of the "Guinnless" campaign targeted 24- to 34-year-old men by depicting humorous scenarios of Guinness drinkers who were deprived of their coveted brew. In the late 1980s Guinness signed on with ad agency Ogilvy & Mather and released the "Man with the Guinness" campaign, which once more deliberately tried to reposition the brand—this time "as a drink for strong, confident individuals," according to *The Guardian.*

Yet by the mid-1990s the cultural world of which Guinness was a part had again shifted. Not only had other Irish stout beers entered the market with their own distinctive advertising campaigns, but stout beers as a whole were losing British drinkers. Guinness became convinced that viewers had become too comfortable with the overwhelmingly popular seven-year "Man with the Guinness" campaign. To reinvigorate its marketing, the company went back to the drawing board with Ogilvy & Mather and nearly two years later released the first two "Black and White" commercials.

TARGET MARKET

The target of Guinness's new campaign revealed once more a strategic repositioning of the brand. As of 1996 the stout sector of the beer market was in decline. Although 79 percent of British drinkers over the age of 55 drank stout, only 35 percent of young adults consumed it. Thus, while Guinness held more than 80 percent of the draught stout market, the company's growth could not be fueled by gaining more within the segment. Instead Guinness had to focus on winning over younger drinkers to its distinctive stout beer. As a result, the brewing titan targeted its new campaign to 18- to 34-year old males. "Guinness need[ed] . . . consumers to rethink their choice of beers," reported *Advertising Age International.* The goal, in short, was to appeal to the target market to "rethink stubbornness when making up one's mind."

In order to reach out to its target, the campaign sought to reflect the values of young adults in the 1990s. In an era dominated by postmodern philosophy that posited the ultimate relativity of all things including truth, the campaign resonated perfectly with the abundant insecurity and introspection of the times. "Research shows people today are more inwardly focused," said the *Independent-London.* "The current message is: think again about life, your inner self, Guinness. All is not how it appears at first glance." Each of the commercials opened with a statement that appeared to be categorical, but as the commercial progressed the assertion became more tenuous and open to debate.

Moreover, the look of the campaign was crafted to reach out to its target audience. It was stylish enough to appeal to a segment of the population that was raised with television and advertising. And it did not resort to the exclusivity that was the hallmark of other beer advertising. "Bicycle" was decidedly non-sexist and attempted to challenge the viewer with issues of gender. Ogilvy & Mather even produced a commercial that featured two gay men together at the breakfast table engaging in a decidedly normal kiss. The spot was leaked to tabloid newspapers before its release, however, and in the ensuing ruckus Guinness chose not to release the commercial.

COMPETITION

While other stout beer producers were not challenging social mores in quite the same way, Guinness did begin to feel pressure from stout brands that challenged Guinness's hegemony. Irish brands, including Murphy's Irish Stout, Caffrey's, Beamish, and Bass Ale, were expanding their market share at Guinness's expense. Many of these brands laid claim to an Irish heritage through their advertising. These Gaelic ties were significant because, as the largest minority group in Britain, the Irish wielded considerable spending power. More importantly, however, was the fact that both in Britain and abroad (especially in the United States), the love of Irish culture had exploded in the 1990s to the point that all things of Ireland were trendy. Murphy's sought to capitalize on this dynamic with the "Vincent Murphy" campaign. In one spot the quintessentially Irish Vincent Murphy sips his beer while he observes a ranting old man at the pub. As the man complains, Murphy quips, "Unlike the Murphy's, he's very bitter." This underhanded dig at Guinness's supposed bitter taste also subtly conveyed Murphy's "genuine" Irish heritage. Caffrey's ads, on the other hand, focused on the "New Ireland." "There's warmth and lyricism mixed with cosmopolitan and contemporary appeal," a spokesperson for the company told the *Independent-London.* Beamish trumpeted its status as the "only brand that brews only in Ireland."

According to *The Guardian,* the "Black and White" campaign served to reassert "Guinness's superiority in a marketplace that had suddenly become saturated with Irish stouts." On the one hand, the explicit premise of the campaign—that not everything was as it appeared or claimed to be—addressed Guinness's rival's claims of cultural integrity as well as the competitors' snipes at Guinness itself. The campaign also sought to reflect Guinness's clout in the market. Controlling nearly 80 percent of the stout sector and 4.4 percent of total beer consumption in Great Britain, Guinness was, without question, the dominant beer in its category. The creativity and quality of the "Black and White" commercials sought to highlight the status of the beer itself.

A FROTHING GOOD IDEA

One of the distinctive features of Guinness was the light head atop the dark body when a pint was poured from the tap. Guinness wanted to be able to offer that signature look in its line of canned beer as well. To do so, the company invested five years and better than $7.5 million in an effort to come up with an in-can system that could replicate the pint pour. After investigating such methods as pouring the beer through nylon stockings and sandpaper-lined cans, Guinness's engineers came up with the widget. This device, a plastic chamber with a small hole placed at the bottom of the can, generated enough pressure when the can was opened to create the desired head.

MARKETING STRATEGY

As the definitive leader in its category, Guinness could not count on converting drinkers of rival stout brands as a means of continuing to expanding the brand. Instead, it had to win the loyalty of those who did not drink stout beer or had never tasted the black ale. In short, the campaign had to convince consumers to reevaluate their choice of beers. According to the *Sunday Business Post,* the goal of the "Black and White" campaign "was three-fold: to bring non-draught Guinness drinkers into the brand, to make Guinness a regular choice for occasional drinkers, and to dissuade regular drinkers from switching to competitive stouts."

Part of this agenda involved "updating" the brand's image among younger British consumers. The campaign set out to accomplish this goal through daring commercials that clearly reached beyond Guinness's solid, middle-age base. One of the more infamous spots of the "Black and White" campaign portrayed a sadomasochistic man hanging by chains from the ceiling (in a leather straightjacket) beneath a picture of British Prime Minister John Major. Other commercials in the campaign displayed similar moxie. A series of print ads featuring a satanic priest and an overweight nudist appealed to a more youthful audience. The company not only used mainstream publications to display the campaign's ads but also selected smaller magazines that directly reached the campaign's target. The sadomasochistic ad, for instance, ran solely in *FHM,* a publication with a circulation of only about 500,000 readers, most of whom, however, were young men drawn to the magazine's glossy coverage of "fashion, football, and women," according to the *London Sunday Telegraph.*

Guinness strove to reposition itself outside the realm of television and print also. The company sponsored the Cheltenham festival in Britain as well as the Fleadh Irish Music Festival in New York. By aligning the brand with international rock stars such as Sinead O'Connor, Van Morrison, and Shane MacGowan, Guinness sought to increase its allure with a younger and more cosmopolitan segment of the British population.

OUTCOME

The Guinness "Black and White" campaign was deemed a success from the outset. According to the company's marketing department, the brand achieved its highest-ever share of the beer market—5.2 percent—after the campaign broke. The November 1997 *Adwatch* survey revealed a 56 percent recall among consumers across socioeconomic and gender lines. The survey also emphasized that the commercials performed especially well among the target audience. The campaign garnered industry accolades as well. Bob Garfield acknowledged the spots in *Advertising Age International.*

In March 1998, however, Guinness indicated in a bold fashion that it was not entirely pleased with the high-profile "Black and White" campaign when it left Ogilvy & Mather and placed its advertising account with Abbott Mead Vickers instead. Officially the company stated to the *Times of London* that "part of the Guinness ethos has always been to move on before we have to" and that "Ogilvy & Mather's work cannot be delivered any further." Yet the rift between Guinness and Ogilvy & Mather ran deeper. The spot featuring the two gay men (which never ran) unleashed a storm of protest from conservative viewers and shareholders. After Guinness furiously backpedaled in response, claiming that "at no time, did we set out to make a so-called 'gay' ad, nor will we be screening one," the gay community became outraged. Later the spot picturing the hanging sadomasochistic man drew another round of criticism, especially from Tory politicians who insisted the ad was a reference to the death by hanging of Tory Member of Parliament Stephen Milligan.

Furthermore, Guinness hinted that the "Black and White" campaign was "elitist" and inaccessible to younger consumers. Analysts speculated that the commercials had not touted the brand's essential "Irishness" enough or that they had cultivated too serious an image for the beer. Guinness followed "Black and White" with Abbot Mead Vickers's "Good Things Come to Those Who Wait." These new commercials were decidedly non-surreal and lacked the "artistic" feel of the grainy "Black and White" spots. One spot portrays an elderly swimmer attempting to cross the village bay before his pint of Guinness, poured by his bartender brother, has settled. The old-fashioned style of the commercial contrasted with "Black and White's" postmodern style.

FURTHER READING

"The Big Pint Is Not Going Down Too Well, But That's the Point, Says Guinness." *Sunday Business Post,* April 13, 1997.

"Campaign of the Week: Guinness." *Marketing,* November 6, 1997.

Carter, Meg. "The Miracle of St. Patrick." *Independent-London,* March 17, 1997.

Davies, Jim. "Marketing: Potting the Black. A New Ad Campaign on the Way This Friday." *The Guardian,* May 11, 1998.

"A Fish on a Bike? Must Be a Guinness Ad." *Sunday Business Post,* March 10, 1996.

Garfield, Bob. "Shades of Grey Emerge in Rethinking Guinness." *Advertising Age International,* February 17, 1997.

Hatfield, Stefano. "Les Boys Removed from the Black Stuff." *Times of London,* November 14, 1997.

Rivlin, Richard, and James Hardy. "Tories Rage over 'Perverted' Guinness Advert." *London Sunday Telegraph,* January 5, 1997.

Rebecca Stanfel

Dial-A-Mattress

31-10 48th Ave.
Long Island City, New York 11101
USA
Telephone: (718) 472-1200
Fax: (718) 482-6561
Web site: www.mattress.com

ALWAYS OUT THERE CAMPAIGN

OVERVIEW

By repositioning Dial-A-Mattress, a seemingly fly-by-night operation with B-grade commercials, as a company on the cutting edge of so-called anti-advertising, the "Always Out There" campaign demonstrated the importance of taking chances. Dial-A-Mattress first took a chance by hiring Dweck & Campbell in New York, a young agency with a penchant for guerilla marketing, such as spray painting brand names on Manhattan sidewalks, to handle most aspects of the makeover. Dweck, in turn, took a chance by selecting 30-year-old John O'Hagan to direct the three introductory commercials in the campaign. Hagen, a 1996 graduate of New York University Film School, had directed an award-winning documentary for his thesis but no television spots. Dweck, which had very strong creative people but no staff producer, according to 31-one-year-old producer Larry Shanet, took a further chance by hiring Shanet to produce the spots, his first freelance assignment after working for four years at Siquis Ltd. in Baltimore.

This willingness to take risks culminated in a series of three 30-second television spots described as "very odd" and even "demented," terms that translated into compliments in the contemporary advertising lexicon. Dweck mirrored the atmosphere of the commercials with oddball marketing tactics, such as advertising on carry-out pizza boxes and Chinese take-home cartons. The campaign also initiated a number of changes that transformed the face that Dial-A-Mattress presented to the public, including a script for its customer service representatives to use when fielding orders over the telephone, new uniforms for its delivery people, and a redesigned company logo that was painted on the sideboards of its truck fleet.

The commercials introduced these changes by following the misadventures of two imperturbable deliverymen as they deposited mattresses in the households of customers who revealed themselves to be very strange. "Arctic Ground Squirrel" featured a man in a squirrel costume who intended to hibernate all winter in his basement; "Wrestlers" featured a husband-and-wife team re-creating the antics of pro wrestlers; and "Wannabe" featured a uniform freak who dressed up in a Dial-A-Mattress uniform. The spots generated humor by focusing on the contrast between the eccentricity of the customers and the unflappability of the deliverymen, who seemed to have seen it all.

HISTORICAL CONTEXT

Dweck & Campbell president Michael Dweck described his client Dial-A-Mattress succinctly: "It's the FedEx of mattress companies." More precisely, Dial-A-Mattress amounted to a marriage of a phone-order catalog company and an overnight delivery service. Customers phoned in an order to Dial-A-Mattress, and then one of the company's delivery trucks, which were on the road 24 hours a day, arrived at the customer's home with a choice of three mattresses to compare. The ultimate resting place of the product—the customer's own bedroom—thus served, quite appropriately, as the showroom.

In 1999 an article in *Advertising Age* pointed out that "prior to [the 'Always Out There'] campaign, Dial-A-Mattress was known in the New York area for painfully bad TV spots." In fact, the constraints of advertising budgets across the bedding category created a genre of advertising so uniformly awful that it generated a sub-genre of ads that parodied the stereotypical bedding commercials. So Dial-A-Mattress was well positioned to use parody in its advertising, provided it could find an agency attuned to the subtleties of irony but willing to work on a low-budget, regional account.

Dweck & Campbell fit the bill perfectly—the start-up shop's first account in 1992 revitalized New Jersey-based Giant Carpet with a series of 30-second commercials, aired on *Saturday Night Live,* that cost about $1,000 each to produce. Mining the same vein of presidential mockery as *SNL* cast member Dana Carvey's impersonation of George Bush, the commercials recast the cut-rate carpet retailer from cheesy to hip. By 1997 the agency, founded by Dweck and vice president/creative director Lori Campbell, collected billings estimated at $20 million from clients such as Pepsi, Time Warner, and Seagram's. Servicing these staid names earned Dweck inflated clout and budgets, but the shop maintained its cutting-edge reputation by continuing to take risks.

After seeing the story boards for the Dial-A-Mattress campaign, about 150 directors sent in reels from respected companies such as bicoastal Harmony Pictures and the bicoastal/international firm Propaganda. From these Dweck chose O'Hagan on the endorsement of Bryan Buckley, a partner at Hungry Man production company, which was in the process of signing the young director. Buckley backed the rookie by agreeing to codirect the spots; while Buckley showed up on the sets daily, he allowed the young director to take the reins of the production. Even without Buckley's recommendation, O'Hagan's work spoke for itself, as his student film *Wonderland,* which documented the eccentric inhabitants of Levittown, New York, had won the 1997 Cable Ace Award as well as a nomination for O'Hagan as the best director at the DGA Awards.

O'Hagan, a Brown University graduate who was born in Dublin, Ireland, but grew up in a Maryland suburb of Washington, D.C., listed photographers Diane Arbus, Robert Frank, and Bill Owens as well as fiction-writer Flannery O'Connor as his prime artistic influences. "They all have a way of capturing the absurd and the poetic in the everyday," O'Hagan said in an article by Scott Jones in a 1998 issue of *Shoot.* Dweck sought a director who could similarly capture the absurd and the poetic in the everyday, hence the choice to chance a newcomer. O'Hagan captured the absurdity of the everyday by allowing his actors enough room to spontaneously create genuine moments where they were guided less by the script or the director's instructions than by their own intuition of the natural flow of the situation. "I don't tell [the actors] how they have to say it or that they have to hit all the words on the line," O'Hagan commented in Jones's article. "They can put their spin on it, direct it, keeping it as real and spontaneous as possible." The key was to get his actors "to a place where they try things, where they aren't just saying things they think you want them to say," O'Hagan continued.

TARGET MARKET

Consumers in the regional area targeted by Dial-A-Mattress were familiar with the name of the company, but they were not aware of its unique selling process. "With Dial-A-Mattress, we did studies and found out that people who didn't buy from them knew the company well—through 10 years of advertising—but didn't know where the mattresses came from," said Dweck in a 1998 *Shoot* article by Richard Linnett. "They didn't see any outlets, no salesmen," he continued. Part of Dweck's challenge consisted of educating the consumers about the process, so the commercials portrayed it, focusing on the deliverymen who visited customers' homes with the products. The spots also featured exaggerated versions of the target audience. By depicting customers who were unusual, Dial-A-Mattress identified its customers as individualistic. By exaggerating the quirkiness of the portrayals, the spots set consumers' minds at ease by assuring them that the deliverymen would not consider them weird, as they had probably seen even stranger behavior.

COMPETITION

The "Always Out There" campaign was a direct reaction to a decline in sales at Dial-A-Mattress as a result of increased competition from Sleepy's, another regional bedding retailer that followed the traditional strategy of wooing customers into showrooms. Dial-A-Mattress also competed against department stores, which maintained showroom displays that captured the attention of customers who were not even shopping specifically for bedding. Dial-A-Mattress distinguished itself, however, as the only retailer that delivered the bed to its future setting as a part of the selling process, allowing for a purchasing experience tailored to the individual.

ONE MAD SQUIRREL

Director John O'Hagan of Hungry Man production company harnessed some of the energy generated by conditions on the set of the "Arctic Ground Squirrel" shoot for Dweck & Campbell client Dial-A-Mattress. The actor portraying the squirrel got hotter and hotter in his costume, so he vented some of his frustration in his performance. As well, some of O'Hagan's directives proved frustrating, according to an article in *Shoot.* "And there was the point when [the squirrel was] down in the basement, in his hibernating room with the mattress men," O'Hagan recalled. "I wanted him to look up at the ceiling, like he's yelling at his wife, but every time he tilted back to look up, the squirrel head would fall off."

MARKETING STRATEGY

Dweck & Campbell took on the responsibility for a complete overhaul of Dial-A-Mattress with the understanding that greater visibility with a revamped image would require changes in the company itself. Market research revealed that consumers were wary of a retailer with no showroom and no tangible structure upon which to pin an image. "We had to build trust," recounted Dweck in Linnett's article. "So we said, let's redesign the trust. What [Dial-A-Mattress operators] say when customers call, how they say it, how [customers are] treated after the purchase—we'll control that whole cycle. And then there's radio ads, there's outdoor; we're creating wardrobe, too, [and] we designed their uniforms."

The "Wannabe" spot highlighted the new uniforms, as the commercial centered around a customer with a uniform fetish. In an odd twist, the customer greeted the deliverymen dressed exactly as they were, and the wanna-be joined them in unloading the mattress. While displaying the screwball humor of the other ads in the campaign, this spot also paved the way for the shift to new uniforms. "Of course, we don't want people to think this is a weird transition, an overnight transformation, like if the post office suddenly showed up with bright orange trucks," Dweck observed. "You'd say, 'What's up? What'd you do with my mail?' We want to make the transition nice and smooth, but fast, too." Dweck & Campbell used existing ad space as well to support the transition. Dial-A-Mattress maintained a fleet of "50 trucks that are always out there," Campbell pointed out. "So we are using them as billboards and a way of introducing their new logo—'Always Out There.' "

The new logo highlighted not only the pervasiveness of Dial-A-Mattress delivery trucks and the availability of its telephone operators but also the "out there" quirkiness of the new campaign and the company's attitude more generally. The two other spots accentuated this message. "Wrestlers" featured a suburban couple garbed in outlandish wrestling outfits. "Honey, it's here," the husband announced as the deliverymen appeared with the mattress. The wife proceeded to pin her husband on the mat and then kick him in the groin. "What's wrong?" she inquired lovingly, before continuing to thrash him. The two deliverymen shrugged off the couple's actions as commonplace, everyday behavior.

"Arctic Ground Squirrel" exaggerated the absurdity of the situation. In this spot, a man greeted the deliverymen in a squirrel costume, acting out his identification with the rodent who wanted to hibernate, although he had not yet been able to do so because he was too busy cleaning the gutters and roof. The costumed man escorted the deliverymen to his den in the basement and informed them that "Anybody with half a brain knows an Arctic ground squirrel is down by now." The spot hinted at the reason behind his desire to burrow into the ground when his wife upstairs began loudly berating him through basement ceiling. The man tried to enlist the sympathy of the deliverymen, but all they offered was a clipboard to sign for his delivery. The impassive demeanor of the deliverymen provided both the humor and the sales pitch: these guys did not deliver therapy or interpretation or even reaction—all they delivered were mattresses.

OUTCOME

Dweck & Campbell believed in the maxim that word-of-mouth advertising worked best of all. So they targeted their advertising at triggering discussion from its audience. It pleased O'Hagan to overhear random strangers quoting his spots, confirming that the commercial had made a memorable impression on them. "Right after ['Arctic Ground Squirrel'] came out, I overheard some guys on the subway telling each other to 'Shut your piehole!' " O'Hagan recalled in Jones's article in *Shoot.* "It felt good to do something that people were responding to," he continued. O'Hagan designed his films to elicit responses from his audience by leaving them open to interpretation, by not spelling out the meaning of his message: "If you're just shoving things down people's throats, there's nothing for them to talk about . . . I like to give the audience more credit than that. People do pick up on the subtleties. They enjoy them." The "Always Out There" campaign generated much talk value in these terms.

Shoot magazine's Linnett called the "Arctic Ground Squirrel" spot "magnificently absurd." He expressed reservations about the "Wrestlers" spot after viewing a rough cut at MacKenzie Cutler, a postproduction boutique in the revitalized Flatiron district of Manhattan, where Dave Coza edited the films. "Although it's a funny concept, the piece at this stage begs less fight and more personality," stated Linnett. The addition of the wife's fleeting concern for her husband injected personality into the spot. "That one plaintive moment captures her character and gives the entire spot a sense of texture and personality," Linnett pronounced.

Advertising Age, in its May 31, 1999, ad review, called the "Arctic Ground Squirrel" spot a success. "The unexpected nature of the spot and others in the campaign, along with the genuinely funny executions, helped drive Dial sales up significantly." "Arctic Ground Squirrel" won a coveted Gold Lion in the retail category at the 1998 Cannes International Advertising Festival. A year later the spot picked up a Gold Clio in the Home Furnishings/Appliances category and a bronze medal in the Consumer Television under $50,000 Budget category at the twenty-third annual One Show Awards held in New York City's Lincoln Center. In August 1998, however, Dweck & Campbell resigned the $5 million account, even though the agency was producing award-winning work on the campaign. Dweck explained in an article in *Advertising Age* that "philosophical differences over direction" forced him to resign the account. Although the "Always Out There" campaign was short-lived, it gained attention from the critical community of the advertising field as well as the attention of everyday consumers.

FURTHER READING

"Jack in the Box's Dick Sittig Deserving of a Bigger Canvas: Retail." *Advertising Age,* May 31, 1999.

Jones, Scott. "John O'Hagan: Rookie Walks Away with a Big Gold trophy." *Shoot,* October 16, 1998.

Krol, Carol. "Dweck Resigns 1-800-Mattress: Differences over Direction Cited as Agency Drops $5 Mil Account." *Advertising Age,* August 31, 1998.

Linnett, Richard. "X Marks the Spot: On the Town with an Indie Producer and Alternative Agency Types." *Shoot,* February 13, 1998.

William D. Baue

The Dial Corporation

15501 N. Dial Boulevard
Scottsdale, Arizona 85260
USA
Telephone: (480) 754-3425
Fax: (480) 754-1098
Web site: www.dialcorp.com

YOU'RE NOT AS CLEAN AS YOU THINK CAMPAIGN

OVERVIEW

In 2001 Dial, the Dial Corporation's mainstay brand in the soap market for more than 50 years, was the only brand with an all-antibacterial line of products. The challenge in promoting it was that focus-group research showed that many consumers did not think they needed their soap to be antibacterial. In its maiden voyage as Dial's ad agency, Austin, Texas–based GSD&M came up with a high-impact national TV campaign called "You're Not as Clean as You Think." With the goal of increasing sales by reinvigorating the public's interest in the brand's soaps and body washes, the campaign was released in January 2002.

GSD&M created two television commercials to kick off the campaign, which had a budget of somewhere between $18 and $25 million. The effort not only used the tagline "You're not as clean as you think," but also resurrected the slogan "Aren't you glad you use Dial?" One spot began with a close-up, from a toilet bowl's point of view, of a thirsty dog lapping up a drink of toilet water. The dog's owner then arrived home to have her face licked enthusiastically by the pooch. This spot, as well as a second one that took place in a gym locker room and featured an inadvertently shared towel, employed gross-out humor. They were, however, constructed carefully to keep the message up front and offense to a minimum.

The campaign hit its mark. Sales of Dial-brand products increased 5 percent in the first half of 2003, placing the company more solidly in the number two position behind Dove's Unilever. *USA Today*'s Ad Track polls in 2003 showed good numbers for the Dial commercials, particularly with regard to women, an audience Dial had hoped to woo. Dial retained the "You're Not as Clean as You Think" theme in 2004, using it in a cross-promotion with the movie *Shrek 2,* a partnership that the company described as successful.

HISTORICAL CONTEXT

The Dial Corporation's signature brand was established in the mid-1940s, when meatpacker Armour & Company developed an unlikely new product, deodorant soap. It named the new soap "Dial" to underscore claims that the product supplied 24-hour protection from odors caused by bacteria. The soap was introduced in 1948 with a full-page advertisement in the *Chicago Tribune* that featured a unique attention-getting element: it was printed with scented ink. Dial soap was an instant hit, and by the 1950s it had become the best-selling deodorant soap in the United States. In 1953 the company's famous advertising slogan, "Aren't you glad you use Dial? Don't you wish everybody did?" was born.

The Dial brand was expanded beyond soap to include other deodorant products and shaving creams. In 1970 the brand was passed from one unusual corporate parent to another when Canadian bus company Greyhound bought Armour and moved the company to a new headquarters in Phoenix, Arizona, under the moniker Armour-Dial. In 1987 the bus line was sold off. Two years later Liquid Dial soap, the first antibacterial soap of its kind, was introduced. The product was so well received that it spawned many imitators. In 1991 the company took the name of its best-known brand and became the Dial Corporation.

The Dial Corporation struggled in the 1990s, as competition increased and sales flattened. In the late 1990s it employed a campaign themed "Doesn't That Feel Better." The TV spots were created by agency DDB Worldwide, a subsidiary of the advertising conglomerate the Omnicom Group. Set to Judy Garland's rendition of "Somewhere Over the Rainbow," the spot was composed of black-and-white images of a child washing with the bar soap. The voice-over said, "You can get there and feel clean, healthy, restored," and then followed with the tagline "Doesn't that feel better?" The campaign garnered little attention and failed to make any sales breakthroughs. When Herb Baum, formerly of Hasbro and Quaker State, took the reigns as CEO of Dial in fall 2000, his task was to streamline the operation in preparation for a change of ownership that was planned to take place in 2004, when Dial would become a subsidiary of the German consumer-products company Henkel KGaA. Austin, Texas–based agency GSD&M Advertising, which, like DDB, was part of the Omnicom Group, won the $18 to $25 million Dial Corp. account in June 2001. The maverick agency developed a campaign that made consumers and industry observers take notice and that in the process even managed to reinvigorate the old slogan "Aren't you glad you use Dial?"

TARGET MARKET

Young mothers and other young bacteria-conscious consumers were the focus of the new "You're Not as Clean as You Think" campaign. "We have a 40-plus group that has been very loyal," explained Steve Tooker, general manager of Dial's personal care division, in a 2003 *USA Today* article. "They grew up with 'Aren't you glad you use Dial?' What we were missing along the way was picking up the younger group and the younger mom." GSD&M's memorable TV spots had to walk a fine line between funny and too gross. Male audiences would appreciate the bathroom humor, but the commercials also needed to avoid offending young female household buyers, in whom Dial wanted to instill concern regarding unseen dirt and bacteria.

Focus groups revealed that the widely recognized gold bar of Dial soap was often thought of as a masculine product. The company felt that the TV spots' shock factor communicated the idea that their soap was essential for cleaning as well as protection and would resonate with mothers in particular. Although Dial asserted that it was not trying to make the brand more youthful, in 2004 it chose a kids' movie, *Shrek 2,* the sequel to the hugely successful animated feature about an ogre named Shrek, for the brand's first movie promotion. TV spots featured the characters from the film demonstrating the theme "You're Not as Clean as You Think." These spots may have been aimed at moms and tots alike, but the packaging, which included a limited-edition ogre-shaped dispenser, was clearly meant to appeal to children's purchasing influence on their parents.

AGENCY THRIVES IN AUSTIN

In 1971 the fact that Chicago and New York had been centers of the advertising industry almost since there was an ad industry did not phase the six University of Texas graduates who started GSD&M Advertising as a way to stay and work in their beloved Austin. The agency's revenues grew in a little more than 30 years to $1.5 billion. GSD&M won some of the country's most sought-after clients, including the king of the discount retailers, Wal-Mart. The company eventually included a Chicago office. GSD&M became part of media giant the Omnicom Group in 1998.

COMPETITION

According to global research firm Mintel, from 2000 to 2003 more than 250 antibacterial products were available for sale in the North American market. Dial may have invented the antibacterial segment, but by 2002 it was running second in the $950 million bar-soap category as a whole. At 16 percent it was well behind the 25 percent share boasted by Unilever's Dove soap. Those figures, compiled by market-information firm Information Resources, Inc., omitted Wal-Mart, a significant Dial retailer, but there was still cause for concern. Research company TNS CMR reported that Dove was outspending Dial as well. In the first nine months of 2001 Dove's media spending was $29 million, compared to $11.5 million for Dial.

A number of other soap manufacturers served as challengers to Dial's variety of personal-cleansing products. Colgate-Palmolive's Irish Spring bar and Softsoap liquid were top sellers in the late 1990s and the first few years of the new millennium. With longstanding loyalty among consumers, conglomerate Procter & Gamble's Ivory and Safeguard brands were formidable competitors as well. By 2001 the glut of competitors had forced the midsize Dial Corp. to set itself apart by getting creative in a normally unexciting advertising category.

MARKETING STRATEGY

In 2001 Dial was unique in that it was the only brand with an all-antibacterial line, but research showed that many consumers did not think that they needed their soap to be antibacterial. Rich Tlapek, a vice president and group creative director at GSD&M, described the dilemma in a 2002 issue of *Advertising Age.* "In focus groups, people would all say they thought they were clean or clean enough. That left us in a difficult situation of how do we increase the relevance [of the antibacterial position] if people think they're already clean?" GSD&M won the Dial account in 2001 with a plan to use high-impact TV spots that would remind consumers just how germ-ridden they might be on any given day. The budget for "You're Not as Clean as You Think" was reported to be between $18 million and $25 million, with almost half of it spent on testing the campaign in order to ensure efficacy once it was released in January 2002.

Two 30-second TV commercials ran on prime-time network and cable channels, primarily during sitcoms but also during some morning shows. The first spot opened with a close-up of a thirsty dog enjoying a drink from a toilet. Upon hearing the arrival of his owner, the dog ran downstairs to greet her with an enthusiastic face licking. The second spot took place in a gym locker room. A sweaty man wiped not only his armpits but also his privates with a towel and then replaced it where he had found it. A second man, who had just come from the sauna, took the same towel to dry his face. Both spots were capped off with a voice-over saying, "You're not as clean as you think," which was then followed by Dial's old slogan, "Aren't you glad you use Dial?"

Dial and GSD&M were aware that they ran the risk of turning people off. "We definitely don't want to be in the fear-mongering business," said Bill Puentes, director of marketing at Dial, to *Advertising Age.* "That's why we took a humorous approach." The goals of the campaign were to grab consumers' attention, communicate why people needed Dial products, and reinforce the brand's national presence. The spots were designed to hook viewers with likable yet cutting-edge content while also maximizing brand recognition by drawing upon Dial's advertising heritage.

Other spots followed in 2003, expanding on the same theme. In one a man in a pool heard the boy swimming next to him tell his mother that he no longer needed to use the restroom. Another spot showed a bus that had been transporting nudists to a retreat; after it dropped them off, it changed its sign and took on riders for a garden tour—without a cleaning in between. Bolstered by the success of the campaign, Dial undertook its first movie cross-promotion, forging an affiliation with the 2004 animated film *Shrek 2.* TV spots featured the lovable but not-too-tidy cartoon ogre Shrek extracting wax from his ear; the substance was later mistaken by his friend, Donkey, for hair gel. The tagline remained essentially the same: "You're not as clean as you think you are." During the movie's highly successful run Dial sold Shrek-themed products, including bottles of Liquid Dial featuring pumps shaped like Shrek and Donkey and ogre-apple scented body wash.

OUTCOME

The Dial Corporation and GSD&M had a winner with "You're Not as Clean as You Think." Brand sales grew 5 percent in the first half of 2003, and the company gained ground on market-share leader Unilever. The campaign received positive press from both ad-industry publications and the mainstream media, and consumer brand awareness increased. *USA Today* 's Ad Track poll reported good numbers for the commercials in 2003. The newspaper surveyed those familiar with the campaign, and 25 percent of these respondents said that they liked the spots "a lot," which was above the Ad Track average of 21 percent. Perhaps more important was the fact that 26 percent of women, a key target of the campaign, liked the commercials "a lot." In an August 2004 issue of *USA Today,* Tom Ennis, Dial's director of marketing, said that the *Shrek 2* cross-promotion was good for the movie studio as well as Dial, stating that the promotion had "overachieved its sales estimates."

FURTHER READING

Bittar, Christine. "Cranking Up the Dial." *Brandweek,* March 24, 2003, p. 24.

———. "Dial Continues to Shower Attention on 'Dirty' and Germ-Ridden Locales." *Brandweek,* March 31, 2003, p. 8.

Howard, Theresa. "Dial's Glad Viewers Like Its New Ads." *USA Today,* September 19, 2003. Available from <http://www.usatoday.com/money/advertising/adtrack/2003-09-15-dial_x.htm>

———. "Shrek and Donkey's Waxy—Uh, Wacky—Ad Dials Up Winner." *USA Today,* August 2, 2004. Available from <http://www.usatoday.com/money/advertising/adtrack/2004-08-01-track-dial_x.htm>

Kleinman, Marty. "A New Generation of Hand Soaps." *Global Cosmetic Industry,* April 2002, p. 28.

MacArthur, Kate. "Dialing for Dollars Is a Dirty Business." *Advertising Age,* January 14, 2002, p. 3.

McCarthy, Michael. "P&G Hopes to Clean Up with Liquid Soap Sequel." *Adweek,* February 10, 1992, p. 5.

Parker-Pope, Tara. "Dial Soap Campaign Aims to Calm Fears of a Germ-Ridden World." *Wall Street Journal,* January 20, 1998, p. 1.

Parpis, Eleftheria. "Some Like It Hot." *Adweek,* October 7, 2002, p. 18

Robertson, Anne. "Brand New." *Business Journal of Phoenix,* May 31, 2002, p. 1.

Van Arnum, Patricia. "Did Dial Take Henkel to the Cleaners?" *Chemical Market Reporter,* January 26, 2004, p. FR3.

Weintraub, Arlene. "Wish Everyone Used Dial? Dial Does; The Soapmaker's Profits Are Going Down the Drain." *BusinessWeek,* September 25, 2000, p. 132.

Simone Samano

Diamond Foods, Inc.

1050 South Diamond Street
Stockton, California 95205-7087
USA
Telephone: (209) 467-6000
Fax: (209) 461-7309
Web site: www.diamondnuts.com

EMERALD NUTS MARKETING CAMPAIGN

OVERVIEW

In 2004 Diamond Foods, Inc., a company known for producing culinary nuts, created a high-quality selection of snack nuts called Emerald Nuts, which came in packaging that fit automobile cup-holders. The canister lids measured out 1.5-ounce servings. To create national brand recognition and to move away from its image as making nuts that were only for cooking, Diamond released its "Emerald Nuts Marketing Campaign" in early 2004.

The "Emerald Nuts Marketing Campaign," created by Goodby, Silverstein & Partners, appeared in print, Internet, and television formats. The agency created 15 television commercials that all played on the initials "E.N." The first two spots, "Encouraging Norwegians" and "Exercising Newscasters," aired in Northern California markets during the 2004 Super Bowl. "Encouraging Norwegians" showed a portly Norwegian man standing next to a bull's-eye target while someone off camera fired arrows at it. The man gave encouragement, such as "Good shot," while snacking on Emerald Nuts. The spot ended with a voice-over stating, "Encouraging Norwegians love Emerald Nuts." Diamond spent an estimated $9.9 million on advertising during the first 10 months of 2004.

The campaign's bottom-line success was measured in July 2004, when Diamond reported an annual net revenue of $350 million, which was $50 million above the previous year. In a daring move Diamond gambled almost the entirety of its advertising budget to air a 30-second spot (which diverged from the "E.N." theme) during the 2005 Super Bowl. "We can buy one spot, and we can make one ad for that one spot," Sandra McBride, Emerald's vice president of marketing, told the *Boston Globe.* The gamble paid off when Diamond sales grew 56.3 percent during the three months following the game. The "Emerald Nuts Marketing Campaign" also garnered a gold EFFIE in 2005.

HISTORICAL CONTEXT

Diamond, an established brand in California since 1912, was owned by more than 1,800 growers at the start of 2004. This farmers' cooperative, doing business as Diamond, led the world in culinary walnut production and in-shell walnuts. Diamond paid nut growers 3.5 cents a pound over the industry average, which was 1.8 cents a pound. In January 2004 the cooperative took a stab at the burgeoning snack-nut market by creating Emerald Nuts, a brand that offered nuts in exotic flavors, curvy containers, and larger sizes, with fewer peanuts in the assorted packages. The snack-nut sector only had one major player, Planters Nuts, one of the many brands owned by Kraft Foods. Besides taking advantage of a

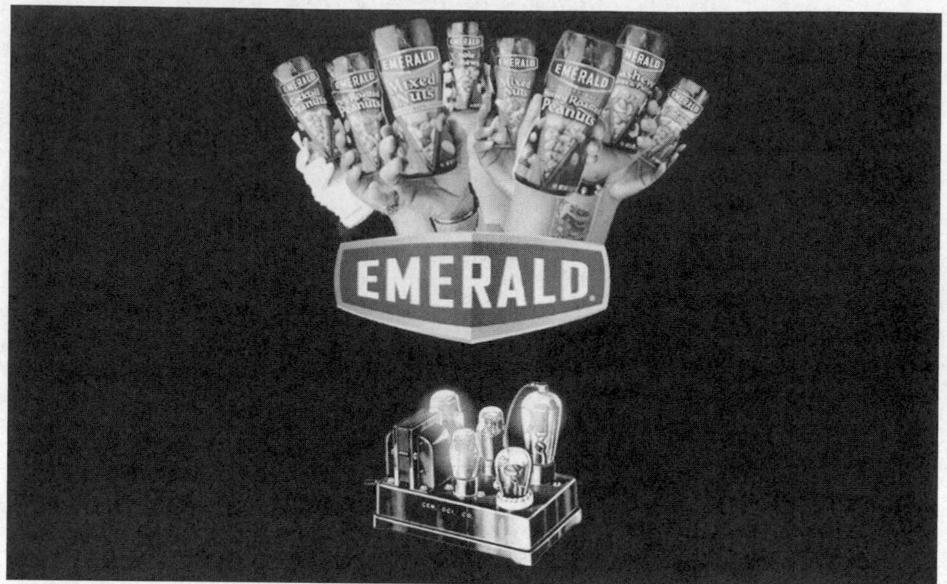

Photo courtesy of Diamond Foods, Inc. Reproduced by permission.

sector with only one main competitor, Emerald Nuts were intended to capitalize on the popularity of the Atkins diet, a high-protein and low-carbohydrate weight-loss plan that encouraged nut consumption. Further, the nut sector reported 12.7 percent growth in 2004. Analysts attributed this sharp rise to a heightened demand for high-protein foods and to the U.S. Food and Drug Administration's announcement that nuts reduced heart disease.

"What we're doing with Emerald Nuts is building a new consumer franchise over in the snack-nut aisle," McBride told the Stockton *Record* Previously Diamond products had been located solely in supermarkets' baking aisles. One of the greatest challenges for the "Emerald Nuts Marketing Campaign" was successfully introducing the public to an unheard-of brand. "It does cost somewhere between 20 and 30 million dollars to build a brand name," Suzanne Walchli, an assistant professor of marketing at University of the Pacific, explained to the *Record.* "It's rather difficult to break even on a brand in the first year."

The advertising climate during the period between the 2004 and the 2005 Super Bowls welcomed the innocent silliness of Emerald Nuts' branding. When Janet Jackson's wardrobe "malfunctioned" during the 2004 Super Bowl halftime show and exposed her breast, more than 500,000 complaints poured into the Federal Communications Commission (FCC). In response the FCC instituted massive censorship restrictions across most media channels. Therefore the climate for 2005's Super Bowl, the one that Diamond poured a majority of its Emerald Nuts advertising budget into, was increasingly sensitive. "Everybody was paying more attention this year," McBride told the *Record.* "That attention was good for Emerald."

TARGET MARKET

The "Emerald Nuts Marketing Campaign" targeted 25- to 45-year-old males and females. Surveys showed that faster-paced Americans were drifting away from traditional sit-down meals. "In a survey last month, we found that more than 62 percent of adults polled admit to replacing a meal with a snack at least once per week," Michael J. Mendes, Diamond's president, said in an interview with *Business Wire.* "We want to convey the message to general consumers, and professional or armchair Olympic athletes, that not all nuts are created equal. Emerald sets a higher standard in snacking, providing a quality alternative to less healthy snacking options."

Sports enthusiasts were continuously targeted during the 2004 leg of the campaign. After the 2004 Super Bowl, 15-second television spots were shown during the Athens Summer Olympics and then during the World Series. The 30-second spot that aired during the 2005 Super Bowl was viewed by 89.2 million people and ranked as one of the campaign's greatest expenditures. "Even at a rate of $2.4 million for 30 seconds of air time, advertisers said, the Super Bowl is among the cheapest advertising available when you factor in the cost per eyeball," according to Naomi Aoki, a writer for the *Boston Globe.* A survey conducted by Penn, Schoen &

THE ANGRY LEPRECHAUN

In an attempt to increase the staying power of its 2005 Super Bowl commercial, Diamond continued the 30-second spot's storyline by creating a side website, http://www.angryleprechaun.com, that featured a leprechaun character who was angry about being cut from the final commercial. The spot, which Diamond spent a majority of its 2005 advertising budget on, featured a father who avoided sharing his Emerald Nuts with his young daughter by telling her that if she ate Emerald Nuts, unicorns would disappear forever. Magically, a unicorn, Santa Claus, and the Easter Bunny sequentially appeared in the living room to challenge the father's lie. A leprechaun character was filmed for the spot as well but was cut in the commercial's final edit. The agitated leprechaun, Finnegan O'Reilly, had purportedly created the website to urge visitors to E-mail Emerald Nuts and demand the leprechaun spot be added and an extended commercial be aired.

Berland Associates, a strategic communications firm, determined that the majority of Super Bowl viewers would rather miss the actual game than the Super Bowl's commercials.

COMPETITION

Nabisco Holdings Corp. owned Planters Nuts until Kraft purchased Nabisco in 2000. Up until 2004 Planters was the only nationally branded snack nut and dominated supermarket's snack-nut aisles. "Planters is like the Big Brother of salty snacks. We had to come up with creative that stood out, was fun and that just sticks with you beyond 15 seconds," Jeff Goodby, the Goodby, Silverstein & Partners cochairman who helped formulate the Emerald Nuts campaign, explained to *Brandweek.*

In 2003 ad agency Foote Cone & Belding created commercials for Planters that depicted the brand's mascot, Mr. Peanut, dancing to disco music in one spot and break-dancing in another. Using computer-generated imagery, other Mr. Peanut commercials showed Mr. Peanut's life as a young legume. Baby Mr. Peanut was shown receiving his first monocle, despite being an infant, followed by his first hat and cane. The spot was an attempt to "contemporize" the brand and spin the mythology behind Mr. Peanut. Commercials released closer to Christmas showed Mr. Peanut with Santa Claus and a reindeer.

Up until 2004 Planters had packaged its nuts inside cans and bags. A few months after Emerald Nuts introduced its sleekly packaged nuts, however, Planters released its own range of multiflavored peanuts called Nutcases, which came sealed in reusable, brightly colored pots. Flavors included sour cream and jalapeño. Rob Woodall, marketing director at Trigon Foods, the primary manufacturer of Planters products, told *Brand Republic,* "The opportunity was to create a lighter-eating nut-snack, which would appeal to a younger audience."

MARKETING STRATEGY

Two 15-second television spots, "Encouraging Norwegians" and "Exercising Newscasters," kicked off the "Emerald Nuts Marketing Campaign" during the 2004 Super Bowl. The first containers of Emerald Nuts had been released only a few weeks prior, and only in Northern California supermarkets. Because of the brand's limited availability, the Super Bowl spots only aired in Northern California. After Diamond increased the range of Emerald Nuts' distribution, nationwide spots began airing during the Athens Summer Olympics. A total of 15 spots, each 15 seconds in length, were created, all with nonsensical titles, such as "Entangled Nine-Year-Olds" and "Extreme Nurses." The spots depicted their amusingly named groups just long enough for the viewer to understand the title. One spot, "Envious Nomads," showed two dusty, travel-worn nomads standing with a camel on a sidewalk. The out-of-place male nomad snacked on Emerald Nuts while admiring a typical suburban house and yard. The voice-over ending the spot explained that "Envious Nomads love Emerald Nuts."

To compensate for the campaign's limited budget, Goodby, Silverstein & Partners purposely created short television spots. They were then placed as "bookends" on commercial breaks, with one spot airing at the beginning and one at the end of the break. "As a result, we get tickled by the first spot and afterward, given a minute or two to ponder it, we're hit with a second spot straight away to cement the brand name in our minds," ad critic Seth Stevenson explained on National Public Radio.

The television spots primarily focused on brand awareness, and Diamond was criticized for not explaining why consumers should pick their nuts over Planters'. Diamond executives, however, boasted positive results after the campaign's 2004 beginning. "We saw an active response at shelf level and we just had a flood of consumer e-mail that showed a very, very strong response to the campaign and the product," McBride told the *Record.*

The campaign's boldest move occurred in early 2005, when Diamond placed a majority of its budget into one 30-second nationwide television commercial to be aired during the Super Bowl. The spot deviated from the previous "E.N." format, showing a father snacking on Emerald Nuts next to his daughter. When the daughter asked, "Daddy, can I have some Emerald Nuts?" her father replied, "Honey, if you eat an Emerald Nut, unicorns will disappear forever." A talking unicorn, Santa Claus, and even the Easter Bunny sequentially appeared to admonish the father for lying. The spot ended with the text, "They're kind of hard to share."

According to a Diamond spokesperson, the Super Bowl spot was discounted from $2.4 million to $2 million because of its fourth-quarter game placement. Diamond scored, however, when the fourth quarter became the second-most-watched segment of the game as the losing team rallied during the final minutes. Most of the campaign's television spots, along with deleted scenes, were posted on the brand's website, http://www.emeraldnuts.com.

OUTCOME

The primary objective of the "Emerald Nuts Marketing Campaign" was to establish brand awareness of Emerald Nuts at a national level. Diamond quickly met with success at the local level. Just a few months after the campaign launched, an early campaign survey showed that 77 percent of Northern Californians recognized the Emerald Nuts brand. By July sales for Diamond were $50 million above the previous financial year's sales.

The company took a big risk by sinking a majority of its 2005 advertising budget into one 30-second Super Bowl commercial. Grant Pace, creative director at ad agency Conover Tuttle Pace, which created Budweiser's "Bud Bowl" Super Bowl campaign, approved of the strategy, saying to the *Boston Globe,* "People aren't going to think hard about it . . . What you want is for people to see you in the store and think, 'I saw these guys on Super Bowl. It must be pretty decent stuff.'" Diamond was pleased with the results of its Super Bowl advertising. The Monday after the game, the Emerald Nuts website reported 24,308 unique visitors, significantly more than the 1,182 average-per-day reported during the previous October. Sales after the Super Bowl increased 56.3 percent between February and April.

FURTHER READING

Aoki, Naomi. "Taking a Shot at the Big Time." *Boston Globe,* February 4, 2005, p. D1.

De Marco, Donna. "Ad-stravaganza: Companies Being 'Super' Careful during This Year's Game." *Washington Times,* February 3, 2005, p. C8.

Elliot, Stuart. "Ad Reaction Claims Super Bowl Casualty." *New York Times,* February 3, 2005, p. 1.

———. "Ameriquest Mortgage Spots Emerge as Surprise Winners in Super Bowl Competition." *New York Times,* February 9, 2005, p. 7.

Fahey, Alison. "21st Annual Agency Report Cards." *Adweek,* April 12, 2004, p. 25.

Fonte, Diwata. "Walnut Growers Will Go Public." *Fresno (CA) Bee,* July 2, 2005, p. C1.

Lippert, Barbara. "A Star Is Born: Planters' Mini-Mr. Peanut Is a Sweet Antidote to the Snow- and Santa-Filled Clichés of the Season." *Adweek,* December 15, 2003, p. 30.

Niedt, Bob. "Convenience on Display." *Syracuse (NY) Post Standard/Herald-Journal,* March 9, 2005, p. 51.

Palazzo, Suzanne. "Nuts for On-the-Go Snackers." *Grocery Headquarters,* May 1, 2005, p. 72.

Parpis, Eleftheria. "January (Creative Best Spots)." *Adweek,* February 16, 2004, p. 18.

Stafford, Leon. "Last to First: CIBA Moves Super Bowl Ad—Lens Maker Opts for Costlier Spot in Game." *Atlanta Journal-Constitution,* February 4, 2005, p. F1.

Turcsik, Richard. "Ones for the Heart." *Progressive Grocer,* April 15, 2004, p. 56.

Kevin Teague

The Diamond Trading Company

17 Charterhouse St.
London, EC1N 6RA
United Kingdom
Telephone: 44 20 74044444
Fax: 44 20 74303022
Web site: www.dtc.com

RAISE YOUR RIGHT HAND CAMPAIGN

OVERVIEW

The Diamond Trading Company (DTC), the London-based marketing subsidiary of the international diamond company De Beers SA, had earned a reputation for its success at creating buzz for diamond jewelry and reaching untapped consumer niches to help expand the sale of diamonds. With its promotion of eternity rings, diamond tennis bracelets, and three-stone anniversary jewelry, DTC's advertising resonated in particular with American consumers. According to the trade organization Jewelers of America, in 2000 retail sales of diamonds in the United States reached record levels, accounting for more that half of the $57.5 billion in retail diamond sales worldwide. Always watching for ways to introduce classic diamond jewelry to new market niches, in 2003 DTC introduced the right-hand ring.

With the support of its longtime advertising agency, New York–based J. Walter Thompson, the right-hand ring was introduced with a multimillion-dollar campaign that sent the message that diamond rings were no longer just for engagements and weddings. Themed "Raise Your Right Hand," the campaign featured print ads in fashion magazines and targeted baby-boomer women with annual household incomes of $100,000 or more. Ads included photos of fashion models dressed in evening clothes showing off the rings; the copy declared, "Your left hand says 'we.' Your right hand says 'me.'" Women were encouraged to change their way of thinking about diamond rings. Not only could women wear them to express their individual style, but they could buy the rings for themselves rather than waiting to get a diamond as a token of a man's love.

The campaign was a success. It was awarded a Gold EFFIE Award in 2005 for, among other things, achieving 39 percent awareness of the right-hand ring in the year following the introduction of the campaign. In addition, the campaign helped boost diamond-ring sales in the nonbridal categories by 15 percent in the year after its launch. In 2005 the ads were revamped to depict "women next door" wearing the rings, and the Diamond Trading Company's U.S. marketing arm, Diamond Promotion Service, partnered with the Internet retailer Jewelry.com to promote October as "Right-Hand-Ring Month."

HISTORICAL CONTEXT

Since its beginnings in 1888 as a South African diamond-mining operation developed by the Oppenheimer family, De Beers SA had grown to a conglomerate as multifaceted as the gems it mined. To establish a market and build social status for the diamonds it was mining, in the 1930s De Beers turned to Hollywood, draping stars and starlets in diamond jewelry for photo opportunities. Also at that time De Beers created the Diamond Trading Company to serve as its London-based sales and marketing arm. By the 1940s the company was emphasizing the link between diamonds and romance. Its advertisements encouraged men to shower their significant others with diamonds set in rings, necklaces, and other jewelry as a symbol of their undying love. In 1947 De Beers's ad agency introduced "A diamond is forever," a slogan that lasted for almost 60 years.

To promote the diamond engagement ring in Brazil, Germany, and Japan, in 1967 De Beers hired New York–based advertising agency J. Walter Thompson to develop an ad campaign. The campaign, which portrayed the diamond ring as a symbol of love, was only moderately successful in Brazil and Germany, but it was a hit in Japan. By 1981 more than 60 percent of the brides in Japan were receiving a diamond ring as a symbol of engagement. The professional relationship between De Beers and the J. Walter Thompson advertising agency was a success, too. The Diamond Trading Company's U.S. marketing arm, Diamond Promotion Service, was a division of J. Walter Thompson, and its public-relations side, the Diamond Information Center, maintained an office in J. Walter Thompson's New York offices.

De Beers created new outlets for its diamonds and joined the list of diamond retailers in late 2000 when it joined forces with luxury-goods company LVMH Moët Hennessy Louis Vuitton to create a new retail jewelry brand. *Women's Wear Daily* reported that the two companies planned to invest $400 million over a five-year period in the venture, with the first store, named De Beers, to open in London. At that time the De Beers name became the sole property of LVMH; all subsequent generic diamond advertising by De Beers would feature the company's new "Forever" trademark, and marketing would fall under the banner of the Diamond Trading Company.

TARGET MARKET

Since stepping in as the sales and marketing arm of De Beers SA in 2000, the Diamond Trading Company (DTC) had shown a flair for building interest in and driving sales of fine diamond jewelry. In early 2001 the DTC told upscale women that a diamond tennis bracelet, a classic design in which a single line of diamonds encircled the wrist, was the perfect piece of jewelry to complete any fashionable outfit, and women listened. Following the terrorist attacks on September 11 of that year, fashion jewelry such as diamond tennis bracelets fell from favor, but the DTC reintroduced the three-stone diamond anniversary ring in a two-part campaign. The first part targeted men, encouraging them to buy the rings as symbols of the past, present, and future of a relationship. The second, aimed at women, promoted three-stone diamond earrings and necklaces as a way for a woman to celebrate life with her significant other.

The challenge of bringing back to the fashion forefront the outdated cocktail rings buried at the bottom of women's jewelry boxes led to creation of the so-called "right-hand ring." But the right-hand ring also provided an opportunity to reach a previously untargeted niche of nearly 77 million people: 45- to 65-year-old professional women, both married and single, with household incomes of $100,000 and up. "This woman knows herself, she's proud. . . . She reflects her confident style through a luxury purchase," Lynn Diamond told *Israel Diamonds* magazine. Diamond, the managing director of Diamond Promotion Services, the United States division of the DTC, said that the right-hand ring created a category for, and gave meaning to, diamond rings not classified as engagement, bridal, or anniversary jewelry and encouraged women to buy the rings for themselves as a way to express their personal style.

COMPETITION

Although De Beers supplied more than half of the market's rough diamonds, two other companies vied with De Beers for market share: BHP Billiton, with headquarters in Melbourne, Australia (BHP Billiton Limited), and London (BHP Billiton Plc); and Aber Diamond Corp. of Toronto, Ontario. Both companies produced diamonds in the rough, and both also pursued relationships with high-end retailers to create branding, marketing, and consumer sales outlets for their gems.

Aber directly supplied diamonds to high-end jewelry retailer Tiffany & Company Then in a twist, in 1999 Tiffany purchased almost 15 percent of Aber at a cost of $71 million in order to assure a steady supply of quality diamonds for its jewelry. According to *Jewelers Circular Keystone,* while it was not uncommon for miners like Aber and De Beer to turn retailer, Tiffany's acquisition of a percentage of Aber was the first time a jewelry retailer had turned miner. In what was considered more the norm, in 2004 Aber acquired 51 percent of jeweler Harry Winston for $85 million. With its purchase of a share of Harry Winston, one of the leading retail jewelers to the rich and famous since 1932, Aber developed a broader presence in the diamond industry, eliminated the middleman for its diamond sales, and gained a foothold in the profitable U.S. market.

BHP Billiton, the largest diversified natural-resources business in the world, reported that diamonds were both its smallest business unit and its fastest-growing one. Following the 2001 merger of Australia-based BHP Limited and London-based Billiton Plc, the company seemed to be on a mission to increase its diamond assets and involvement in the diamond industry. The heart of the company's diamond business was the Ekati mine in Canada, which accounted for approximately 6 percent of

NEW DTC CAMPAIGN HOPES TO CHANGE WEDDING ANNIVERSARIES

The Diamond Trading Company (DTC) was always on the lookout for new ways to market diamonds. In 2001 the DTC convinced many women that a casual outfit was not complete without a diamond tennis bracelet, then it later assured women that they could have a diamond ring without an engagement and that it could be worn on their right hand as well as their left. In 2005 the DTC took on wedding anniversaries. According to the company's research, 65 percent of women interviewed reported that they would like to receive diamond jewelry from their husband as an anniversary gift; however, only 6 percent actually got diamonds. To help get the message across to men that diamonds could be a wife's best friend, the DTC launched a marketing campaign designed to encourage men to commemorate their wedding anniversary with a gift of diamonds. The campaign hoped to replace the phrase "happy anniversary" with the tagline "I forever do," a combination of "I do" and "Diamonds are forever." Its goal also was to increase diamond sales. Based on DTC estimates, if just 10 percent of married women received a piece of diamond jewelry on their anniversary, the market would jump $3.2 billion.

the world's rough diamond production in 2000. To brand polished diamonds from Ekati, in 2000 the company created Aurius Diamonds, a marketing division based in Australia. By 2001, following the introduction of Aurius, sales had doubled monthly in Australia, producing $393 million in sales. In 2003 BHP Billiton announced plans to offer the Aurius brand in retail stores in the United States, Canada, and Singapore in addition to Australia.

MARKETING STRATEGY

Following the success of its three-stone-jewelry campaign, which promoted rings, earrings, and necklaces as symbols of love and enduring relationships, in 2003 the Diamond Trading Company launched a new campaign to sell not just diamond rings, but an idea. Working with its ad agency, J. Walter Thompson, DTC introduced the right-hand ring and through clever marketing launched a fashion trend. Additionally, the campaign reached a previously unmarketed-to demographic: independent, financially well-off, older women. Unlike previous campaigns that portrayed the diamond ring as a symbol of love, the "Raise Your Right Hand" campaign promoted the diamond ring as a badge of individual style. Claudia Rose, director of marketing strategy at J. Walter Thompson, said that the right-hand ring campaign was different because it linked diamond rings to fashion rather than romance. "This gives women another message," Rose said. "Diamonds also can represent a woman's unique style and be expressive as something like their favorite leather goods."

For the multimillion-dollar campaign, J. Walter Thompson developed a series of print ads that ran in fashion magazines, including *Elle, Vogue,* and *In Style.* Ads also appeared in publications likely to be read by the target demographic—upper-middle-class women 45 to 65 years old—such as *Condé Nast Traveler* and *Town and Country.* In developing the ads J. Walter Thompson used fashion models younger than the women being targeted. Explaining the strategy, Diamond Promotion Service, De Beers's U.S. marketing arm and a division of the J. Walter Thompson agency, said that regardless of their own ages, women identified more readily with younger women in print ads. The ads had edgy, evening-wear-clad fashion models showing off right-hand rings Each ad also featured a significant message to distinguish the right-hand ring from the engagement and wedding ring worn on the left hand. Among the statements were: "Your left hand says 'we.' Your right hand says 'me,'" "Your left hand likes to be held. Your right likes to be held high," "Your left hand is your heart. Your right hand is your voice," and "Your left hand lives for love. Your right hand lives for the moment." Each ad included the tagline "Women of the world, raise your right hand." By the end of the year the print campaign was expanded to include television spots.

Jewelry designers were encouraged to develop rings that matched De Beers's prototype right-hand rings, which were trendy and fashion-conscious To avoid being confused with traditional diamond engagement and wedding rings or with the popular three-stone anniversary rings, right-hand rings had one diamond of 20 points or larger and as many additional smaller diamonds as desired as long as it was not limited to three. A report in *Israel Diamonds* noted that more than 300 designs were submitted by manufacturers hoping to be a part of the campaign. From the original submittals, 10 ring designs were selected. An additional 6 ring designs were commissioned by Diamond Promotion Services, resulting in the 16 rings that were featured in the ads.

OUTCOME

The "Raise Your Right Hand" campaign was a marketing success for the Diamond Trading Company. Prior to the campaign's launch, diamond-ring sales were at the low end of the diamond-jewelry market, representing 28 percent of diamond jewelry, or $3.3 billion in sales, in 2003. Following the introduction of "Raise Your Right Hand," in 2004 nonbridal ring sales increased 15 percent. The campaign also created a cultural phenomenon by convincing single women that they could have a diamond ring without an engagement or in addition to a bridal set. And while the campaign originally targeted women with household incomes of $100,000 or more, right-hand rings soon were available at stores from Costco and Wal-Mart to Tiffany & Company and ranged in price from a couple hundred dollars to several thousand. Besides appearing on the right hands of stars such as Cameron Diaz, Charlize Theron, Halle Berry, and the female cast members of *Sex and the City,* women in all income brackets were soon sporting the rings. Clothing designers such as Betsey Johnson and Zac Posen, recognizing a growing trend, paired right-hand rings with their 2004 spring ready-to-wear styles.

In 2005 the campaign garnered a Gold EFFIE Award from the New York American Marketing Association for "exceeding its objectives of bringing ring growth into line with total diamond jewelry growth." The campaign was also recognized for pushing single women into the diamond-jewelry-buying market and achieving 39 percent product awareness among consumers in the year following its launch. Also in 2005 the DTC revamped the campaign, introducing new ads that were similar to the original but with a softer and less fashion-forward tone, replacing hard-edged fashion models with women dressed in cardigans. The right-hand ring category was broadened as well to include almost any ring that allowed women to express their individual identities. To further encourage women to raise their suitably adorned right hands, Diamond Promotion Services, the DTC's U.S. marketing arm, partnered with Jewelry.com, the premiere Internet jewelry site, and named October "Right-Hand Ring Month."

FURTHER READING

Bates, Rob. "Can These Three Words 'I Forever Do' Change the Anniversary?" *Jewelers Circular Keystone,* March 1, 2005.

———. "DPS Claims Campaign's 'a Success': Get Ready for a 'Broader' Right-Hand Ring Campaign." *Jewelers Circular Keystone,* June 1, 2005.

———. "Tiffany's New Setting: How the Famed Jeweler Became the World's First Retailer-Turned-Miner." *Jewelers Circular Keystone,* September 1, 2003.

Benson, Steven. "A Giant Moves In." *Israel Diamonds,* October 1, 2001.

"BHP Takes Shine to De Beers' Game." *Australasian Business Intelligence,* September 5, 2001.

"De Beers Touts Right-Hand Rings." *Jewelers Circular Keystone,* April 1, 2003.

Johnson, Marylin. "Style: On the Other Hand Diamonds (and Other Gems) are an Independent Girl's New Best Friend in Chic Right-Hand Rings." *Atlanta Journal-Constitution,* November 23, 2003.

Kletter, Melanie. "Rings Reflects Women's Rights." *Women's Wear Daily,* October 20, 2003.

"Looking Downstream." *Israel Diamonds,* June 1, 2001.

"Mining Company to Buy Winston." *Women's Wear Daily,* December 1, 2003.

Overholt, Alison. "The Right-Hand Ring Craze." *Cosmopolitan,* October 1, 2004.

Payne, Melanie. "Diamond Sellers Launch Marketing Campaign for 'Right-Hand Rings' for Women." *Sacramento Bee,* December 2, 2003.

"Right-Hand Rings. The Next Big Thing." *Israel Diamonds,* August 1, 2003.

"Women of the World Raise Your Right Hand." *Business Wire,* June 3, 2005.

Yee, Blythe. "Diamond Merchants Dub 'Right-Hand Ring' Next Big Thing." *Chicago Sun-Times,* August 15, 2003.

Rayna Bailey

DirecTV Group, Inc.

2230 East Imperial Hwy.
El Segundo, California 90245
USA
Telephone: (310) 535-5225
Web site: www.directv.com

CELEBRITIES READ FAN MAIL TO DIRECTV (BECOME A DIRECTV FAN NOW) CAMPAIGN

OVERVIEW

In June 2003 the DirecTV Group, Inc., provider of satellite television, launched a new marketing campaign featuring commercials with A-list Hollywood actors giving dramatic readings of actual fan letters received by the client. The use of celebrities was intended to help elevate DirecTV above its competition: cable television providers and direct-broadcast satellite rival Dish Network, both of which had begun imitating DirecTV's successful commercials featuring Dan the installer.

Developed by ad agency Deutsch/LA, the new $100 million-plus campaign consisted primarily of TV spots, which included such actors as Joan Cusack, Danny DeVito, Robert Duvall, Laurence Fishburne, and Andy Garcia. Comedian Dennis Miller anchored radio spots, and a print ad was introduced featuring a picture of actor Dennis Hopper. The TV spots were shot against a bare background with nothing more than a stool. What made them powerful was the enthusiasm of the customers' letters and the ability of veteran actors to read the letters with equal conviction. The atmosphere was kept lighthearted, resulting in impromptu remarks that found their way into the commercials. In one, for example, DeVito, following his rant called "Lies," asked the crew in a joking manner, "Did I capture the guy's anger?"

"Celebrities Read Fan Mail to DirecTV (Become a DirecTV Fan Now)" lasted little more than a year, ending in July 2004. While it proved a boon to DirecTV, which enjoyed four straight quarters of increased subscribers, the same could not be said of Deutsch. Despite its good work and excellent relationship with DirecTV's marketing people, the agency lost the account even before the campaign closed.

HISTORICAL CONTEXT

Deutsch/LA established its relationship with DirecTV in 2000 when it won a creative project for Sunday Ticket, the exclusive National Football League package of Sunday games. Deutsch won the entire creative account later in the year when DirecTV put up its business for review. With just under 9 million subscribers, DirecTV was the dominant player in its category but, after a solid run of several years, it had become engaged in a fight for survival, threatened on one side by rival satellite providers and on the other by digital cable. In the fall of 2000 DirecTV ran the first television commercials developed by Deutsch. Centered around Dan the DirecTV installer, these commercials became the focal point of DirecTV's marketing campaign for the next year and a half. While successful, the installer campaign led some viewers to mistake DirecTV for a hardware company. The installer concept grew even less attractive when Dish Network and cable companies began using installers in their own ads.

With the installer becoming everybody's spokesperson of the moment, DirecTV felt that the waters had been muddied and its brand diminished in the process. The company believed it was imperative that DirecTV launch a new marketing campaign that would not only reinforce its position as an entertainment company but also reassert its leadership position and restore some luster to the brand.

TARGET MARKET

In the campaign that would succeed Dan the installer, DirecTV targeted existing customers, hoping to keep them on board. The company also wanted to appeal to potential new subscribers, especially ones with higher levels of disposable income, people who were not only attracted to premium brands but also likely to purchase DirecTV's higher-end programming combinations, pay-per-view events, and high-margin sports packages. To achieve that end DirecTV asked Deutsch/LA to create a campaign that leveraged the influence of celebrities.

COMPETITION

DirecTV faced entrenched competition from cable television systems (whether mom-and-pop operations or larger systems) around the country, but none could match the number of channels and digital picture and sound quality that DirecTV had to offer. Early on DirecTV faced satellite competition from PrimeStar, but after DirecTV swallowed PrimeStar's 2.2 million subscribers in 1999, that left only Echostar's Dish Network. Because the satellite dish and receivers were manufactured by Echostar, Dish Network was able to offer lower programming costs as well as lower equipment prices, making it a formidable foe.

By 2000 DirecTV and Dish Network battled each other but also received stiffer competition from cable operators, who began rolling out their own digital packages that not only rivaled the quantity of channels found on direct broadcast satellite systems but also offered movies on demand, high-speed Internet access, and Internet phone service as well. And on the horizon was another satellite provider, VOOM (owned by a subsidiary of Cablevision Systems Corporation), slated for a 2004 launch. VOOM eventually positioned itself as a high-definition television service, but it never caught on and ceased operations in April 2005. Nevertheless, in the early 2000s VOOM, backed by Cablevision's deep pockets, was not a venture DirecTV could afford to take lightly.

ON THE CUTTING-ROOM FLOOR

It should not have come as a surprise that, when DirecTV hired A-list Hollywood actors to give dramatic readings of actual customer letters, some quality material would be left out. According to Deutsch/LA associate creative director Michael Bryce, Robert Duvall's best performance was not used in the DirecTV campaign. Given a letter written by a Southern minister, Duvall put on a white suit and then, adopting the evangelical preacher persona he used so convincingly in the film *The Apostle,* sang the praises of DirecTV and issued a fire-and-brimstone denunciation of cable. Although everyone involved considered it a brilliant performance, the film *The Passion of the Christ* was controversial at the time, and DirecTV thought better of airing a commercial that might generate negative publicity.

MARKETING STRATEGY

Since taking over the DirecTV account, the Deutsch/LA creative team had become aware of the client's unusual fan mail—mostly handwritten, usually quirky, generally humorous, and incessantly enthusiastic about DirecTV's service, especially when compared to cable, which the writers skewered with a passion. In fact, DirecTV executives adorned their walls with their favorite letters. After DirecTV requested a campaign that featured celebrities, the Deutsch team began sampling the letters, which the agency had already used in a small way on the DirecTV website in promoting Sunday Ticket. Although the team was attempting only to get a feel for DirecTV subscribers, it soon became apparent that the fan letters were a treasure trove of material. "It was stuff you couldn't make up," Mark Musto, a Deutsch creative director, told *Shoot.* "We kept saying to ourselves, 'If there is a way we can get this passion and emotion into our TV commercials, we'd be in a great place.' So then we started kicking around the notion of getting big Hollywood actors to present these letters."

The creative team selected a pool of letters, all of which possessed "that special something that set the letter apart—whether it was a quirkiness or a passion or something that was real human that you could hang your hat on," Musto recalled. Then the team began the laborious task of tracking down the letter writers and securing permissions. People who agreed to allow their letters to

NO WAY!

All the actors hired to dramatize DirecTV fan mail were initially dubious about the unabashed enthusiasm of the letters. In fact they suspected that the letters had actually been written by the agency.

be read were given a $500 thank-you. In several cases, however, a favorite letter had to be discarded when the writer balked. While the agency secured the permissions, a director, Baker Smith of Harvest Productions, was hired.

The team had no interest in simply impressing consumers with how big a name it could buy to endorse DirecTV. Rather, the goal was to match the material to a specific actor, to deal with emotions that everyone could connect with while hopefully establishing a relationship between the audience and the celebrity. Securing the kind of A-list Hollywood talent DirecTV and Deutsch had in mind presented a challenge, however. While actors at this level might lend their voices to commercials or accept a paycheck for pitching a product in Japan, they avoided showing themselves in U.S. television commercials in the belief that overexposure might tarnish their star power. A wish list of actors was developed, and feelers were made through their agents—but only with money on the table. The first group of actors to sign on were DeVito, Fishburne, and Garcia. Another element in the campaign, a kicker, was that the actors were also DirecTV customers, although, in truth, DirecTV was ready to make them customers if necessary.

Initially the commercials were to be shot on an ornate set in the Culver Studios in Culver City, California. As the day of production neared, however, the soundstage was stripped down, finally consisting of nothing more than a glossy black floor, a blue background, a stool, and a simple spotlight. The creative team began to worry that by taking such a minimalist approach the commercials might fail to engage the audience. But as soon as the actors stepped into the spotlight and began performing the letters—quickly demonstrating to everyone assembled why they became stars in the first place—it became apparent that in terms of production value less was definitely more. The sparse set actually accentuated the power of the actor and the passion of the letter writer.

Each actor was given three letters for filming, one of which was in keeping with a familiar persona and others that might even go against type. Smith intentionally kept the atmosphere loose to make the crew into a ready audience to help draw out a performance. As a result the actors were willing to take chances and try out a number of deliveries. Smith told *Boards Magazine* about his experience directing Fishburne: "I didn't know Laurence from a hole in the ground, but I'd give him simple suggestions like, 'Try reading the letter as if you're a 17-year-old surfer dude,' and this 40-year-old black guy turned into a 17-year-old white surfer. I watched the transformation. Then we read like Shakespeare and Orson Welles, got way fucking serious, and again the body language changed." In the end Fishburne used a Shakespearean delivery for a letter that read, "Dear DirecTV, This morning I turned on the telly and all I can say is jumpin' ja hos se fat! Yee haw!"

For his spot DeVito performed a letter the team called "Lies," in which he delivered a passionate screed: "Dear DirecTV, Cable says reception quality is poor with satellite TV. Lies! My reception is way better with DirecTV than it ever was with cable!" Garcia's spot, "Even Greater Than Greatest," was intense but a shade quieter than the others: "Dear DirecTV, There's not a word to describe how great DirecTV is. It's not great. It's not greater than great. It's even greater than greatest." The convivial atmosphere on the set also elicited some off-the-cuff remarks from the actors as they slipped out of character, such as DeVito quipping, "Did I capture the guy's anger?"; Fishburne wondering, "How was that? Was that too over the top?"; and Garcia remarking to the letter writer, "I think I'm going to have you write my next review." These comments then served as taglines to close the commercials.

The first three 30-second commercials began airing in June 2003, presented in letterbox format with the name of the actor and writer appearing in subtitles. "Celebrities Read Fan Mail to DirecTV" also included radio and print elements. The radio spot used Miller, who read a letter from a customer expressing her joy about calling her former cable company to say, "Please disconnect my cable." The print ad showed 21 faces of DirecTV customers and fans, one of which was Hopper. Joining the campaign in September 2003, actor John Goodman cut a television commercial to promote Sunday Ticket. He read a letter from a satisfied Indianapolis Colts fan.

In March 2004 DirecTV and Deutsch launched a second phase of the campaign, which ran until July 2004. It featured television commercials by Cusack and Duvall. Cusack offered a screwball interpretation of a letter written by a fan in love with the word "great." Duvall, adopting the tone of a proper Southern gentleman, pondered the qualities of a DirecTV customer service representative that he longed to see in his wife.

OUTCOME

"Celebrities Read Fan Mail to DirecTV" was considered a success by DirecTV, which signed up new customers at a healthy pace during the course of the campaign. But even before the second leg kicked off, DirecTV elected to sever its relationship with Deutsch/LA. The company hired a new executive vice president of marketing, Neal Tiles, who decided to consolidate the DirecTV account with agencies owned by Omnicom Group, including BBDO Worldwide, which took over the Deutsch business. BBDO had recently hired executive creative director Eric Silver, who had previously worked with Tiles. Deutsch managing partner Eric Hirshberg told *Adweek,* "I look back on our four years with DirecTV as a satisfying client-agency relationship . . . It was a good run."

FURTHER READING

Champagne, Christine. "Baker Smith Opens DirecTV Mailbag for Deutsch LA." *Shoot,* July 4, 2003, p. 7.

Davis, Wendy. "DirecTV Breaks $20 Mil Effort from Deutsch." *Advertising Age,* January 22, 2001, p. C2.

Deutsch, Claudia H. "DirecTV Makes an Unexpected Move." *New York Times,* February 27, 2004, p. C2.

Flass, Rebecca. "$100M Dish for DirecTV." *Brandweek,* June 16, 2003, p. 20.

———. "To Keep Its Edge, DirecTV Picks Celebs over Installer." *Adweek,* June 16, 2001, p. 9.

Howard, Theresa. "DirecTV Enlists A-Team of Stars to Sing Its Praises." *USA Today,* October 5, 2003.

Sampey, Kathleen. "Ties Bind BBDO to DirecTV Business." *Adweek,* March 1, 2004, p. 7.

Solman, Gregory. "Deutsch Releases Final Spots for DirecTV." *Adweek* (western ed.), March 1, 2004.

Wakelin, Simon. "A Mighty Wind." *Boards Magazine,* December 1, 2003, p. 45.

Ed Dinger

Discovery Communications, Inc.

One Discovery Place
Silver Spring, Maryland 20910
USA
Telephone: (240) 662-2000
Fax: (240) 662-1868
Web site: www.discovery.com

■■■

TWO GUYS CAMPAIGN

OVERVIEW

In September 1995 Discovery Communications, Inc., made the move to the World Wide Web when it invested $10 million to launch Discovery Channel Online (Discovery.com). The new website featured news, nonfiction articles, options such as online shopping, and information about Discovery Channel's programming. At the time of its launch, Greg Moyer, president and chief operating officer of Discovery Networks, said the company was "extremely bullish" about the fast-growing online medium. Within five years of its launch, 4 million users each month were logging on to Discovery.com. In February 2000 the company made the decision to take advantage of the dot-com surge and combine its Internet and other media assets into a new business unit at an investment of $500 million spread over a five-year period.

To promote its new and improved website, Discovery.com (a subsidiary of Discovery Communications) and its agency, Publicis & Hal Riney, San Francisco, launched a national marketing campaign themed "Two Guys" with the tagline "Discover something new every day." The campaign, part of Discovery.com's $70 million consumer advertising budget for the year, included print ads, Web elements, and television spots that ran on the Discovery Channel and sister networks Animal Planet and the Travel Channel. The advertising featured two middle-aged men poorly disguised as a variety of characters, from mosquitoes to meteors, discussing things they had learned on the Discovery.com website just before meeting an untimely and unusual demise. In a TV spot one of the mosquito men gets swatted by his victim, and in another the meteor guys both burst into flames.

The campaign was a hit with consumers. Following its June 2000 launch the number of users visiting the Discovery.com website increased one percentage point (based on the number of people using the Internet at any particular moment). Although the ads resonated with consumers, in August, at the end of its preplanned summer run and without comment from Discovery.com, the campaign was canceled.

HISTORICAL CONTEXT

Discovery Communications launched the cable network Discovery Channel in June 1985 with 156,000 subscribers. As it grew Discovery Communications continued to add networks and subscribers, and in 2000 the company listed Animal Planet, the Travel Channel, BBC America, and the Learning Channel among its cable network holdings. In addition the company had begun to expand internationally into countries that included Latin America and Asia. Total subscribers for its combined networks had reached 269 million households by 2000.

As part of its expansion, Discovery Communications in 1995 invested $10 million in a new venture and launched its website, Discovery.com. In 2000 the company expanded the Discovery.com website and developed it as a new wholly owned subsidiary with a planned financial investment of $500 million spread over a five-year period. While the investment in the project seemed huge, Gary Alden, principal analyst of Arlen Communications, told *Broadcasting & Cable,* "Five hundred million is not that much money in Internet terms. It's a traditional media company in the era of Time Warner–AOL doing what it has to do to launch new kinds of businesses."

The reinvented website combined the resources of all of Discovery Communications' networks into one location on the Internet. It also offered users E-mail and messaging features and included plans to add options such as "Discovery Be-There Adventures" using advanced video technology. The company described Discovery.com as a "super-vertical" website that offered users information about travel, lifestyle, health, animals, kids, and other topics. Discovery Communications chairman and chief executive officer John Hendricks said of the new venture, "We're layering on a very successful online service," and he explained various possible options to help finance the project, including an IPO or existing shareholders' investments.

To promote Discovery.com and to encourage people browsing the Internet to visit the site, Discovery Communications planned to increase the site's on-air advertising by 200 percent. Shortly after the upgraded website's introduction, Discovery Communications launched its "Two Guys" marketing campaign.

TARGET MARKET

Discovery Communications had built a following of 180 million total subscribers familiar with its offerings of "nonfiction entertainment" from nature documentaries to informational programming airing on its various networks. The mission of the "Two Guys" campaign was to attract Discovery's traditional viewers to its upgraded and relaunched website and to encourage younger audiences connected to the Internet to visit the site when searching for information on a broad range of topics from travel destinations to health-care questions. Using over-the-top humor and what *PR Newswire* described as a "hip, pop-savvy attitude," the campaign was designed to reach consumers across all age demographics and show them they could find information relevant to their day-to-day lives on Discovery.com in each of seven categories: health, discoveries, lifestyle, travel, school, animals, and kids. According to *Adweek Western Advertising News,* Discovery.com executives explained, "The campaign is built on the traditional Discovery brand, but tries to play to a younger consumer with an offbeat sense of humor."

REDESIGNED DISCOVERY WEBSITE SUFFERS DOT-COM WOES

Discovery Communications' Internet business unit, Discovery.com, took a hit in late 2000 after the bubble burst in the dot-com industry. By November of that year, citing lower-than-expected e-commerce and advertising revenues, Discovery.com executives announced a sweeping reorganization of the company. As part of the changes, Discovery.com laid off 45 percent of its full-time staff, eliminated some 150 contract jobs, and refocused its plans for the online division. Its website was redesigned in 2001 to shift the focus from original content to promoting Discovery Communications' 200 retail outlets, including the Nature Company stores, and 11 cable networks, including Animal Planet, the Travel Channel, and the Learning Channel. The strategy, however, failed. Emily Meehan, a senior analyst with the Yankee Group, told *Multichannel News,* "When you think about the myriad of travel, learning, and health destination sites already out on the Web, Discovery's notoriety in these categories becomes diluted in the Web world."

COMPETITION

In 2000 the National Geographic Society was an icon more than 100 years old. Besides publishing its namesake magazine, through its wholly owned subsidiary National Geographic Ventures, the society had established a presence on television with its cable network, National Geographic Channel US, listing 25 million households as subscribers, and on the Internet with its website, nationalgeographic.com. As Discovery.com was making changes to its website, National Geographic announced efforts to expand its presence on the Internet as well, but rather than revamping its existing site the company formed alliances with two existing companies having websites: Novica.com and iExplore.com.

Novica.com was an online marketplace that specialized in selling handcrafted works from artisans in developing countries. According to a report in *Business Wire,* the terms of the alliance gave National Geographic a 19 percent share in the dot-com, with rights to increase that to almost 30 percent. Rick Allen, president and chief executive officer of National Geographic Ventures, told *Business Wire,* "For more than a century National Geographic has enabled hundreds of millions of people to travel to the far corners of the globe—at least from their armchairs. Novica makes it easy for individuals to experience another culture through its art."

For those who preferred to leave their armchairs at home, National Geographic in 2000 also acquired a 30 percent share in iExplore.com, an online resource for adventure travel. National Geographic added iExplore.com's database of some 5,000 trips to 152 countries to its website, and iExplore.com added National Geographic Expeditions to it site.

A&E Television Networks, with 80 million total subscriber households in 2000, also announced plans to increase its Internet offerings. In addition to having websites (including AandE.com, historychannel.com, and biography.com) tied to its various cable channels, one proposed site (wildlifestories.com) was developed to compete directly with Discovery Communications' website, Discovery.com, according to Todd Tarpley, vice president of A&E's interactive unit, as reported in *Multichannel News.* Additionally the company launched an updated version of its most popular site, historychannel.com, which attracted more than one-third of the combined 1.1 million people using the company's six sites.

MARKETING STRATEGY

Cable subscribers who regularly tuned in to the Discovery Channel were familiar with the network's unique documentaries that included up-close-and-personal views of wildlife, from the common to the rare, as well as other nonfiction programming on a variety of topics. Discovery Communications' challenge was attracting those television viewers to its upgraded and relaunched website, Discovery.com. To encourage its viewing audience to join the 4 million people visiting its site each month, Discovery.com and its agency, Publicis & Hal Riney, San Francisco, launched the "Two Guys" campaign with the tagline "Discover something new every day."

The national campaign, part of Discovery.com's overall $70 million advertising budget, kicked off in June and included print ads in magazines and newspapers, television spots running on Discovery Communications' various cable networks, and Web elements. Tim Maleeny, senior vice president and account director with Publicis & Hal Riney, San Francisco, described the campaign as raw, bold, and edgy. "We thought it was time to use humor to present the Discovery brand from a different perspective," he told *Adweek Western Advertising News.*

Television spots featured shots of bugs, animals, and other things found in nature that Discovery Channel viewers expected but with a twist: the parts were played by two guys in bad disguises. One ad showed the guys, dressed as mosquitoes, land on someone's arm. The mosquito men discuss Discovery.com's many positive qualities while sucking up the victim's blood through straws. In true mosquito fashion, one of the insects is squashed by a well-placed smack from the victim. Another spot had the two guys dressed as meteors sharing information they found on Discovery.com. Just as one meteor guy comments that he learned meteors burn up in the earth's atmosphere, the camera zooms in to show the two guys burst into flames.

OUTCOME

The "Two Guys" campaign was a success if measured by consumer response. According to *Broadcasting & Cable,* Discovery.com's user traffic, which was estimated at 4 million online visits per month prior to the campaign, increased by a full percentage point based on the percentage of all people using the Internet at any point in time. Despite the campaign's popularity with consumers and the increased site visits generated by the television spots and print ads, Discovery.com, without comment, canceled the entire campaign at the end of its preplanned summer-only run.

FURTHER READING

"Adventure in Partnership." *TravelAge West,* September 4, 2000.

"A Wrap for Fish." *Broadcasting & Cable,* August 28, 2000.

"The Big Push: Fact and Friction from Discovery.com." *Advertising Age,* June 12, 2000, p. 76.

Cole, Richard. "Discovery Puts Previews on Web Site." *Cable World,* December 18, 2000.

DeMarco, Donna. "National Ad Campaign Is Invitation to Discovery on Line." *Washington Times,* June 12, 2000.

"Discovery.com Launches New Advertising Campaign, Inviting Consumers to 'Discover Something New Every Day.'" *PR Newswire,* June 6, 2000.

Donohue, Steve. "A&E Bulks Up Web Sites." *Multichannel News,* March 6, 2000.

Granger, Rod. "Discovery Commits $10M for Online Venture." *Multichannel News,* July 3, 1995.

Moss, Linda. "Different Bites of the Same Apple." *Multichannel News,* October 16, 2000, p. 20A.

"National Geographic and Novica.com Announce Strategic Alliance: 112-Year-Old Organization Sees Synergy with Young Web Site." *Business Wire,* December 12, 2000.

Norton, Justin M. "Discovery.com Debuts 'Two Guys.'" *Adweek Western Advertising News,* June 19, 2000, p. 7.

Stump, Matt. "Discovery.com Takes Hit, Slashes Staff." *Multichannel News,* November 20, 2000.

Tedesco, Richard. "Discovery Sets Big Net Play." *Broadcasting & Cable,* February 7, 2000.

Rayna Bailey

Doctor's Associates Inc.

325 Bic Drive
Milford, Connecticut 06460
USA
Telephone: (203) 877-4281
Fax: (203) 876-6674
Web site: www.subway.com

JARED FOGLE CAMPAIGN

OVERVIEW

In the late 1990s, despite being the leader in the submarine sandwich fast-food niche with an estimated 27 percent market share, Subway sandwich shops' sales were flat and showed no signs of improving. That changed, however, when one of the chain's loyal customers, an overweight Indiana University senior named Jared Fogle, took the chain's promise of serving healthy, low-fat sandwiches to heart and went on a diet of Subway sandwiches. The "Subway Diet" was a success—Fogle lost 245 pounds eating the chain's sandwiches twice a day—and Subway had a new spokesman to attract diet-conscious consumers to its restaurants.

On the advice of its advertising agency, Hal Riney & Partners, Subway hired Fogle to pitch its low-fat menu options. Using Fogle's weight-loss success story as its theme, Subway launched a $75 million advertising campaign in 2000. The first television commercial featuring him was a 30-second spot that opened by showing the pre-diet, 425-pound Fogle, followed by the trimmed-down Fogle ordering a Subway sandwich and eating it while seated on a park bench. An announcer stated, "We're not saying this diet is right for you. You should talk to your doctor first. But it's food for thought."

The campaign resonated with people looking for healthy, high-quality, low-fat alternatives to the typical fast-food choices of greasy burgers and fries. The company was careful to avoid responsibility for promoting a diet plan, however. A Subway spokeswoman told the *Cincinnati Post,* "We're pleased that our low-fat sandwiches could fit into [Jared's] meal plan, but it's not a diet that we endorse by any means." Commenting on the success of the "Jared" campaign, Subway said that, following Fogle's 2000 appearance in a television advertising spot for the chain, his weight-loss success story had captured the attention and imagination of millions consumers and television viewers. Fogle subsequently starred in eight additional commercials for Subway and was the featured speaker at hundreds of public appearances.

HISTORICAL CONTEXT

In 1964 people craving a submarine sandwich either made it at home or went to a local sandwich shop or Italian restaurant. That changed in 1965, when recent high school graduate Fred DeLuca, worried about finding money to pay his college tuition, talked with his family's friend, Peter Buck. Rather than offering to pay DeLuca's tuition, Buck had a different suggestion: he would loan the money for Fred to open a sub sandwich shop. Ten years later there were 16 Subway shops in business and one goal on DeLuca's mind: expansion. By 2004 the chain had grown to more than 21,000 stores in 75 countries. Commenting on the growth during an interview with *Advertising Age,* Subway's director of development, Don Fertman, said, "Goal-setting has always been important. Besides being No. 1 in every market we serve worldwide, our main goal was to look at what the possibilities can [lead to]."

Beginning as early as 1989 Subway was using its menu of sandwiches made with fresh-baked bread, fresh ingredients, and low-fat meats such as turkey-based cold cuts, to promote itself as the restaurant choice for people wanting to eat healthy. In 1992 Subway added veggie and cheese and roast chicken breast sandwiches to its menu selection, further strengthening its image as the low-fat fast-food chain. Subway promoted itself through various marketing campaigns as the healthy alternative to greasy fast food. It launched its first national television campaign, "Subway—It's My Way," in 1990, and the theme "The Way a Sandwich Should Be" was introduced in 1996. The chain's 1998 "Eat Smarter" marketing included television spots portraying overweight people in various situations, such as a clearly heavy man floating in the water behind a motorboat waiting to be towed on his skis. When his friend revved the boat's engine the boat would not move. The camera panned to a partially eaten burger and fries while a voice-over said, "Eat less fat." It was not until the 2000 campaign featuring Jared Fogle, however, that the chain's low-fat options finally captured the attention of consumers. April Y. Pennington wrote in *Advertising Age,* "You can lose weight eating Subway sandwiches! everyone cried, and the rest was history."

REAL MEN WANT RED MEAT, AND SUBWAY RESPONDS WITH STEAKBURGERS

Typical Subway customers were women and men working in white-collar jobs who headed to the chain's restaurants during lunch breaks to enjoy its healthy selection of low-fat sandwiches. Research revealed, however, that 12- to 34-year-old males, many working in blue-collar jobs, were not concerned about fat or calorie content and wanted juicy burgers and other red-meat options not available at Subway. In response to that unfilled niche, Subway introduced the Steakburger, a sandwich made with a chopped-beef patty. At nine grams of fat but with a selection of cheeses, fresh vegetables, and condiments as toppers, the burger fit within Subway's commitment to provide consumers healthy options, but it fell just outside the chain's goal of offering menu items with less than 350 calories and 6 grams of fat.

The company introduced the Steakburger with television ads featuring a 30-something construction worker demanding, "Gimme a Subway Steakburger." Although originally planned as a short-term product offering, the success of the "Hot News for Burger Lovers" campaign had franchise owners asking that it be added to the permanent menu.

TARGET MARKET

As the new millennium approached, obesity in the United States was a growing problem. According to research conducted in 2000 by the American Obesity Association, 30 percent of children aged 6 to 11 years old were overweight, and 15 percent were considered obese. The numbers for adolescents aged 12 to 19 were similar. Further, 127 million American adults were considered overweight, and 60 million were obese. One factor blamed for these statistics was high-fat, high-calorie fast food. From the mid-1980s Subway began reaching out to consumers of all ages by promoting itself as an alternative to hamburgers and fries. With Fogle as the poster boy for thin people everywhere trapped in overweight bodies, the new Subway ads focused on attracting consumers wanting to lose weight and make healthier eating choices while still having a fast meal.

COMPETITION

To help build a brand identity and lure customers away from the top two chains, Subway and Blimpie, the number three sub sandwich chain, Quiznos, launched a marketing campaign that featured the company's cofounder, Jimmy Lambatos. "Chef Jimmy" used quirkiness and a grandfather-next-door approach to establish an image of quality for Quiznos. In the television ads he smiled and waved, stressing the importance of fresh, high-quality ingredients when making a good sandwich. "Chef Jimmy" was so passionate about making a perfect sandwich that he forgot to put on his pants. During an interview with Kelly Pate of the *Denver Post,* Quiznos's chief executive officer, Rick Schaden, said that the company was counting on the personality of "Chef Jimmy" to drive sales and help push the restaurant into the fast-casual niche, defined as restaurants with higher-quality food than typical fast-food places. "Our next step is to take everything we do and make sure it's in line with that," Schaden explained.

Despite its distinction of being the oldest sub sandwich chain—it was founded in 1964—Blimpie International had been pushed by Quiznos from its number two spot by 2004. As the company prepared to celebrate its 40th birthday, it was struggling to reinvigorate its brand. Blimpie chief marketing officer Mark Mears said to *PR Newswire* that the company's new plan was consumer focused and encouraged restaurant franchisees to treat customers "The Blimpie Way." Mears explained that the new slogan "permeates all levels of the Blimpie system and will serve as the foundation for revitalizing a brand that until recently stood still and resisted change while our competitors adapted to meet the needs of today's consumers." He added, "We also plan to 'take off the gloves' in a new, aggressive marketing campaign."

MARKETING STRATEGY

Promo's Peter Breen noted that, while Subway was a 15,000-restaurant chain worldwide with an estimated $3.2 billion in sales, it lacked the advertising budget to compete with chains like McDonald's and Taco Bell. But he noted that Subway was "fairly confident they can compete with the big boys when it comes to offering healthier food and better service." A limited budget was not enough to prevent Subway from moving ahead with the "Jared" campaign. Breen wrote that the chain's marketing team was taking its healthy-alternative theme in a different direction with the introduction of an upgraded menu, a more appealing service plan, and a $75 million advertising campaign. As part of the campaign Subway dropped its four-year-old tagline, "The way a sandwich should be," and replaced it with the slogan "Eat fresh." The campaign included television spots featuring weight-loss champion Jared Fogle as well as Billy Blanks, the creator of Tae Bo, a workout program that combined elements of karate, aerobics, boxing, and dance.

While Blanks's message reached consumers who were already exercising and living a healthy lifestyle, Jared Fogle and his weight-loss success story resonated with consumers fighting the battle of the bulge. Fogle was a student at Indiana University in 1998 when he saw Subway's commercials promoting the chain's "Seven under Six" low-fat sandwiches. Believing the promise of eating healthier food suggested in the Subway ads, Fogle, who weighed more than 400 pounds, put himself on a diet in which he ate nothing every day but a cup of coffee for breakfast, a Subway six-inch turkey sub for lunch, and a foot-long veggie sub for dinner. He also had a bag of chips and diet soda with each sandwich. One year later, helped by his diet of Subway low-fat sandwiches and a daily exercise regimen, Fogle had dropped almost half his body weight and had become Subway's unexpected champion.

When Fogle's weight-loss story made its way into an article in the *Indiana Daily Student* newspaper, word quickly spread and appeared in the national news. From there the story was picked up by Subway officials, who asked him to star in a commercial. The initial television spot portrayed the 425-pound Fogle and then switched to a shot of him, 245 pounds leaner, ordering a Subway sandwich and eating it while sitting on a park bench. Blanks became the chain's first celebrity spokesman when his spot aired. It featured Blanks leading a Tae Bo class in a series of kicking and punching moves and telling students to head to Subway after the class for a healthy lunch. The spot included an offer giving away coupons for Blanks's workout videos with Subway sandwich purchases. William Schettini, Subway's chief marketing officer, told Breen, "Blanks and Fogle gave Subway a one-two kick, so to speak, with Blanks appealing to the already health-conscious and Fogle inspiring those who want to be health-conscious."

Chris Carroll, director of marketing for the Subway Franchisee Advertising Fund Trust, said in an interview with *Promo* that Subway's marketing ultimately had to show how the chain's products benefited the customer. He explained, "What we've decided to do, at least over the next 12 to 18 months, is to have our promotional message be about our products. Every piece of creative will have a promotional theme to it, but in our case, we've got these new sauces, we've got these new breads, and that becomes the promotional message, the incentive to try us out."

OUTCOME

The health-focused campaign was so successful that the company delayed the launch of a new $75 million branding campaign in 2000 in order to continue running the Jared Fogle and Billy Blanks spots. Subway, which had believed the low-fat theme had lost its appeal, reportedly was surprised by the success of the campaign. Carroll told *Advertising Age,* "We've been doing low-fat for 3 1/2 years and did well, but driving the business 15 percent to 20 percent is unbelievable." And although Subway had grown steadily since its opening in the early 1960s, the chain experienced a rapid boom following the introduction of Jared Fogle as spokesman, growing to 17,700 U.S. locations, versus 13,000 for McDonald's by 2004. Also in 2004 Subway launched a new campaign themed "F.R.E.S.H. Steps," which took aim at childhood obesity. Designed to encourage kids to strive toward a healthier lifestyle, the campaign included 11 commercials featuring Fogle and three non-actor children talking about how their lives had been changed by eating healthy food. Based on the success Fogle had connecting with consumers, both adults and children, the chain signed him on for additional advertising that was planned to continue into 2005.

FURTHER READING

Berry, Kate. "Big Mac Attack: McDonald's Prepares to Challenge Subway's Dominance." *Los Angeles Business Journal,* November 29, 2004.

"Blimpie International." *Franchising World,* October 1, 2004.

Breen, Peter. "Companies; A Cut Above." *Promo,* August 1, 2000.

Buss, Dale. "Catching the Diet Craze." *Chief Executive,* December 1, 2003.

Garfield, Bob. "Subway Ads Are Lean on Laughs and Overstuffed with Laziness." *Advertising Age,* September 29, 2003.

Kaelble, Steve. "Ask Jared: Great Gig: TV Viewers Can't Get Enough of Hoosier Subway Spokesman." *Indiana Business Magazine,* November 1, 2003.

Kung, Howard. "Jared and Jim: Subway's Conflicting Posterboys." *Charlottesville (VA) Cavalier Daily,* September 4, 2001.

MacArthur, Kate. "Subway Heats Up in Fighting Off Underdog Quizno's." *Advertising Age,* June 14, 2004.

———. "Subway Sales So Strong Marketer Delays New Ads; Tae Bo's Blanks, Man Who Has Lost 245 Pounds Sparks a Surprise." *Advertising Age,* June 19, 2000.

———. "Subway's Tasteful Theme Shifts Low-Fat Positioning." *Advertising Age,* April 3, 2000.

Pate, Kelly. "Owners Hope to Distinguish Quizno's Sub Shops with Fast-Casual Approach." *Denver Post,* February 2, 2003.

Pennington, April Y. "Neck and Neck: Being Number 1 in the Franchise Race Has Its Advantages, but There Will Always Be Others Nipping at Your Heels." *Entrepreneur,* January 1, 2004.

Thompson, Stephanie. "Subway Burger Targets Working-class Men; Sandwich Fits Chain's Ongoing Health Profile." *Advertising Age,* March 6, 2000.

Wessel, Harry. "Sub Shops Battle for Business." *Orlando (FL) Sentinel,* April 25, 2005.

Rayna Bailey

Dr. Martens Airwair USA LLC

10 NW 10th Ave.
Portland, Oregon 97209
USA
Telephone: (800) 460-3885
Web site: www.drmartens.com

■■■

BELIEFS CAMPAIGN

OVERVIEW

In May 1997 Airwair Ltd. assigned the creative portion of its Dr. Martens advertising account to the Dallas-based agency Pyro. Dr. Martens was a brand of work boots and shoes known for their industrial outer appearance. The boots already had an antiestablishment and youth-culture image; Pyro was asked to create a branding campaign that would continue to define that image. Pyro responded with a series of four print ads—none of which contained a product shot—that appeared in consumer magazines and as in-store posters. The expression of the Dr. Martens brand through unconventional images and messages maintained consistency with the company's reputation for nontraditional marketing strategies. Television advertising developed by the British agency Harrison Carloss followed up on the print campaign, which continued into 1998. This U.S. campaign also extended into an international campaign.

Concurrent with this campaign, Dr. Martens extended its brand name by producing and distributing alternative music compilations that complemented its brash image. Then, in 1998, it launched the Dr. Martens record label to continue this marketing strategy by promoting shoe sales through CD giveaways. The move tied into the brand's historical connection to alternative musical trends, from the days of the British invasion in the 1960s to the eruption of punk in the 1970s to the breaking of new wave in the 1980s to the grunge movement of the 1990s. Dr. Martens sought to use its brand recognition as a means of leveraging publicity for up-and-coming bands while at the same time benefiting itself by adding a further compulsion to the consumer's purchase decision. Dr. Martens also tied into the World Cup soccer tournament in 1998 with a series of boots featuring national flags countries competing in the event.

HISTORICAL CONTEXT

Dr. Klaus Maertens, a German M.D., teamed up with Dr. Herbert Funk, an engineer, to design shoes to relieve the sore feet of Munich women in the wake of World War II. The shoes also provided relief to Maertens himself after he suffered a skiing accident. The secret to the design was the process of heat-sealing the sole so as to create a pocket of air that cushioned footfalls. In 1959 Maertens transferred production to Britain, licensing the brand to the Benjamin Griggs and Septimus Jones Company (later known as R. Griggs Group), manufacturers of industrial footwear since 1901. The anglicization of the name to Dr. Martens occurred in this transition, simplifying the spelling for the purpose of exporting the shoes to new markets. The Griggs company produced its first Dr. Martens boot on the first of April, 1960, naming the model 1460 after this date.

Guitarist Pete Townshend initiated Dr. Martens' connection to rock and roll. He wore 1460s on stage because the boots proved solid enough for stomping on smashed guitars when his band, the Who, took to destroying its equipment during distortion-filled encores. The gesture of youthful rebellion became embodied in the shoes, which were too bulky to be fashionable but turned into a fashion statement anyway. Subsequent generations of rebels wore them as an expression of their angst. This earned DMs, as the boots were dubbed, an underground following in the skinhead, punk, and new-wave movements. The Dr. Martens World Wide Web site asserted that "classic punk bands such as The Clash, the Stranglers, the Damned and Buzzcocks [wore] the boots almost religiously."

In 1995 Dr. Martens tied into this connection with the alternative music scene by releasing a compilation CD entitled *Unlaced* (playing off the popularity of MTV's live acoustic series *Unplugged*) featuring the music of Blur, New Order, and Suede. Music & Media Partnership, a company specializing in connecting branded businesses with record companies, orchestrated this strategy. The CD was a success, reaching the top 20 on the charts with sales of more than 100,000. Dr. Martens followed up with more compilations, shifting from over-the-counter sales to purchase-incentive gifts. One such compilation, released through Warner Brothers, moved 450,000 CDs (and shoes) in a month. "There's no way we would have shifted nearly half a million pairs of shoes in the space of a few weeks but for the promotion of that shoe," said Dr. Martens music strategist Karl Nielsen in York Membry's *Music Week* article.

Subsequent compilations did not move quite so well. *Shoe Pie,* by the label 4AD and featuring Lush, Throwing Muses, and the Breeders, sold only 200,000 copies in the United States and 80,000 in the United Kingdom. Nielsen stressed that moving product was not necessarily the primary objective of the promotions—Dr. Martens was "not just in it to buy market share quickly. The Dr. Martens philosophy is to be supportive of youth culture, especially through music, but not overtly commercial," said Nielsen in Membry's article. Dr. Martens supported the music of youth culture in multiple ways. It sponsored stages at the Phoenix and Reading festivals in 1996. In 1998 it sponsored the Glastonbury Festival and sponsored a stage during the Lollapalooza U.S. tour. Dr. Martens also supported individual bands, sponsoring Soul Coughing on its 1998 U.K. tour and sponsoring a live recording of Logical Progression III during Christmas 1997.

TARGET MARKET

"Music is a great way for a brand such as Dr. Martens to reach its target market," said Rick Blaskey of Music & Media Partnership, who helped seal the deal with Dr. Martens. That target market consisted primarily of youths aged 13 through 25. This connection to youth culture both honored the roots of the brand's success while also generating future success by hooking in devotees early on. Arkady Ostrovsky profiled Dr. Martens's "dream customer" in his 1998 *Pittsburgh Post-Gazette* article, introducing her simply as Ann, a 26-year-old native of San Francisco working in New Zealand. "I have been wearing DMs since I was 13. First at school, then at university. My boyfriend was a punk and he had red hair and 20-eyelet boots." Her current boyfriend, by contrast, was a derivatives trader, and she bought him a jumper from DM's limited clothing line. Dr. Martens thus became the item that nonconformists could carry with them to symbolize their latent rebellious spirit as their lives conformed more to the norm.

Ostrovsky commenced his article by quoting a joking Stephen Griggs, chairman of the R. Griggs Group, his family's company, which had been manufacturing Dr. Martens since 1960. "We had Madonna and the Pope wearing DMs, but my mom does not get on too well with them. She thinks they are too clumpy." Though Dr. Martens did not have plans of targeting older mothers of corporate executives, the brand did aspire to expand its target market. However, demographic growth would prove more challenging than geographic growth, so Griggs thought more in terms of expanding distribution, not expanding marketing. "I am very uncomfortable about the U.S. being 60 percent of our sales. Obviously, I do not want our American sales to drop, but I want to increase the share of other markets to counter the U.S.," Griggs stated in Ostrovsky's article. Specifically Griggs envisioned China and Latin America as the brand's biggest potential growth markets.

COMPETITION

Dr. Martens advertising did not position the product as a work boot, but rather as a fashion statement identifying the wearer with youth culture. The brand therefore competed against other brands that identified themselves with youth culture, especially those growing out of the rebellious skateboard movement, such as Vans, Air Walk, and Caterpillar. Dr. Martens held an advantage, though, as most of these brands produced sneakers, whereas no other boot held sway over youth fashion as did Dr. Martens. In this sense Dr. Martens had successfully carved its own niche in the youth market without any threatening competition. Dr. Martens's main challenge, then, became growing its own market without commercializing its image, which would appear to its antiestablishment target market as selling out. "We have to convince people that DM shoes are still the same; it is

THE DR. MARTENS-HARLEY-DAVIDSON CONNECTION

Dr. Martens marketing maintained several affinities with Harley-Davidson marketing. Both brands appealed to consumers at opposite ends of the spectrum, but both brands hyped the fact that their loyalists existed outside the mainstream. While this tactic risked segmenting the target market into a small niche, both companies remained true to their devotees, trusting that the genuine nature of their fans' rebelliousness would gain respect from the mainstream. Both companies supported their nonconformist brand image through brand extensions, or brand stretching. Harley-Davidson developed a comprehensive merchandising and licensing program that proliferated the Harley logo as well as the Harley attitude pervasively.

Dr. Martens achieved a similar proliferation of its brand image through alternative music, eventually launching its own record label. While some critics questioned the move as a mere marketing ploy, Dr. Martens's marketing strategist Simon Mills said the strategy was more of a commitment to the youth culture and alternative music culture that supported DM for so long. "We have a genuine desire to support new British bands and that is why we're [launching the Dr. Martens record label]," Mills said in a 1997 article in *The Independent.* "It's not just a marketing ploy. Our brand is big enough for us not to have to spend on conventional advertising, so we are able to support other avenues and not seek too much recognition for doing it."

just now we are making more of them," said Griggs in Ostrovsky's article.

MARKETING STRATEGY

Pyro's product-free campaign, which marked the return of Dr. Martens advertising after a year-long hiatus, commenced with a series of four print ads that ran in consumer magazines such as *Rolling Stone* and *Details,* as well as those with a more alternative edge, such as *Bikini, Raygun,* and *Spin.* Thematically, the ads advanced the notion of individualism, inherently suggesting that wearing Dr. Martens expressed individualism. One headline read, "The mainstream is polluted," while another ran: "You start out and end up just like everyone else. What happens in between is up to you." The ink from one headline—which read: "The world is full of generic, mass-produced, homogenized products. Don't become one" —bled into the shape of a bar code, punctuating the message of the text. In Steve Krajewski's 1997 *Adweek* article Pyro creative director Todd Tilford explained the rationale behind the product-free message ads. "What the client liked about our work is that we try to blur the line between advertising and 'brand art.'"

Following up on its success with CD compilations, Dr. Martens created its own eponymous record label, launching the project by releasing a compilation entitled *Generation To Generation,* which tied together different periods of the music listened to by Dr. Martens wearers. Alternative bands of the '90s such as Box Office Poison and Lynus covered '60s anthems "Louie Louie" and "My Generation," respectively, as a means of tying together the first wave of DM music to the current crop of DM music. The collection also included tracks from '80s bands such as the Lambrettas and the Untouchables. The long-term goal for the label was to "push young British talent to an audience who wouldn't otherwise hear them" by running promotional giveaways throughout all the areas covered by Dr. Martens distribution, according to Dr. Martens marketing strategist Simon Mills.

The painted-boots tie-in with World Cup soccer in 1998 was an idea that originated with the Norwegian distributor of the brand to celebrate his home team's qualification for the tournament. The distributor ordered 40,000 pairs of boots with the Norwegian flag in hopes of catching the wave of his country's nationalistic fervor. Similarly Dr. Martens sought to capture the patriotism of soccer fans with the Stars and Stripes, the Union Jack, and St. Andrews flags.

Dr. Martens also ventured into broadcast ads in 1998 with the campaign created by Harrison Carloss of Newcastle-under-Lyme. It ran concurrently with the Pyro campaign. In the United Kingdom the ads ran exclusively in cinemas, while France and the United States added television to the media mix. Print ads also ran in fringe magazine titles such as *Loaded, FHM, Maxim, ID, The Face, Arena, Dazed & Confused, Frank, Sugar,* and *Bliss.*

OUTCOME

Between 1980 and 1998 Dr. Martens sales increased tenfold, reaching $395.2 million in 1998, as the brand sold 12 million pairs of boots and shoes globally. In 1997, when Pyro began creating advertising for DM, the brand racked up pre-tax profits of $54.56 million, a significant increase over the figure of $35.2 million in pre-tax profits for 1996. At the conclusion of 1998

Airwair began making preparations for the 40th anniversary of Dr. Martens by shopping for an ad agency that could handle a global account. In April 1999 Airwair awarded the $10 million account to the British agency TBWA GGT Simons Palmer, London, thus consolidating the brand's advertising at one agency to create a cohesive global campaign, targeting the core markets of Britain, France, Italy, Germany, the Benelux countries, and the United States. TBWA creative director Trevor Beattie reacted to the announcement with enthusiasm, calling Dr. Martens "a great name, a cult brand and a fabulous creative challenge. People are fighting to work on the account."

FURTHER READING

"Dr. Martens Flags New Boots for World Cup." *Marketing Week,* February 12, 1998.

Krajewski, Steve. "Unseen 'Doc Martens' Reappear in U.S. Ads." *Adweek,* October 6, 1997.

Membry, York. "Dr. Martens Kicks In." *Music Week,* March 7, 1998.

Ostrovsky, Arkady. "Dr. Martens Steps Up Its Growth." *Pittsburgh Post-Gazette,* August 21, 1998.

"These Boots Are Made For Your CD Player." *The Independent,* March 2, 1997.

William D. Baue

Dr Pepper/Seven Up, Inc.

5301 Legacy Drive
Plano, Texas 75024
USA
Telephone: (972) 673-7000
Fax: (972) 673-7000
Web site: www.dpsu.com

THIS IS THE TASTE CAMPAIGN

OVERVIEW

After an upturn in its fortunes in the highly competitive soft-drink industry, in 1997 Dr Pepper/Seven Up Inc., a subsidiary of Cadbury Schweppes, reigned as the leading noncola soft-drink business in North America. Its spicy beverage Dr Pepper was the third-best-selling noncola soft drink in America and was outsold only by PepsiCo's Mountain Dew and the Coca-Cola Company's Sprite. Analysts within the soft-drink industry attributed Dr Pepper's success partly to its unrivaled position as the leading spicy soft drink. In contrast, Dr Pepper's sister brand 7 UP was competing against other successful lemon-lime soft drinks, such as Sprite. Dr Pepper had been advertising with the cumbersome tagline "Now Is the Time. This Is the Place. Dr Pepper, This Is the Taste." In an effort to continue its sales growth and streamline its previous tagline, Dr Pepper/Seven Up released a campaign called "This Is the Taste."

The ad agency Young & Rubicam created "This Is the Taste" with Dr Pepper's estimated $55 million advertising budget. The campaign, which consisted of print ads and television spots, debuted on January 1, 1998, with four commercials that emphasized the unique flavor of Dr Pepper. Young & Rubicam conceived commercials that attempted to "deliver [this] hard-hitting claim in a humorous way," John Swan, an agency partner, explained to *Adweek.* One of the spots depicted John Madden, a former National Football League (NFL) coach, searching a deserted stadium trying to find the elusive meaning of the game. His journey ended in success at a Dr Pepper vending machine. The campaign continued into 1999 with soccer-themed commercials featuring American and Mexican athletes. All spots closed with the "This Is the Taste" slogan. The campaign ended January 1, 2000.

"This Is the Taste" was proclaimed a success by both Dr Pepper and industry experts. In 1999 Dr Pepper's sales grew at a faster rate than that of the overall soft-drink industry. The campaign's final year marked the 15th consecutive year of sales growth for Dr Pepper.

HISTORICAL CONTEXT

Founded in 1885, Dr Pepper was the oldest of the major soft-drink brands in the United States. But despite its distinctive taste, the beverage had never achieved the mass acceptance of Coca-Cola or Pepsi. For most of its history Dr Pepper's advertising had tried to make a virtue of this outsider image. After billing itself as the "most original soft drink ever" for much of the 1970s, the company switched to the funky and popular "Be a Pepper" campaign in 1977. Following the conclusion of its "Hold Out for Out-Of-the-Ordinary" campaign in 1987, Dr Pepper was the fifth-best-selling soft drink in the country. "We're pretty comfortable with the idea that consumers know we're different," a company spokesperson told *USA Today.*

Dr Pepper's uniqueness was again to be a significant asset during the 1990s. Beginning in 1990 Americans' love affair with colas began to wane. According to the *Wall Street Journal,* the combined share of colas in the United States dropped from 72 percent in 1990 to 64 percent in 1996. In place of colas, consumers swilled ever greater amounts of so-called noncolas—primarily Dr Pepper, Mountain Dew, and Sprite. By 1995 Dr Pepper was the fourth most popular soft drink in the country, and its year-end sales were up 6.9 percent, far surpassing the remainder of the industry, which grew by only 3 percent. Despite this remarkable growth spurt, however, its two noncola counterparts, Sprite and Mountain Dew, outpaced Dr Pepper. After a year of record-breaking sales, Sprite displaced Dr Pepper as the leading noncola beverage in 1996, when its sales volume jumped 12 percent from 1995. Mountain Dew also performed well. In response, Dr Pepper created "Now Is the Time. This Is the Place. Dr Pepper, This Is the Taste," to add momentum to the Dr Pepper brand. Nevertheless, while 1997 proved to be another growth year for Dr Pepper, Sprite and Mountain Dew continued to sell better. Prior to its inauguration of the 1998 "This Is the Taste" commercials, Dr Pepper possessed 5.8 percent of the domestic soft-drink market, while Mountain Dew and Sprite respectively controlled 6.3 percent and 6.2 shares. "We will only be content when Dr Pepper is growing at a faster rate than any other major soft drink," promised Jack Kilduff, the company's president, when he announced the marketing agenda for 1998.

TARGET MARKET

To reach its ambitious goals, Dr Pepper needed to capture an essential demographic group. John Clarke, Dr Pepper's chief advertising officer, told *Adweek* that the new spots targeted 12- to 34-year-olds. Especially important was the narrower market of teenagers within this broad group. Part of their significance lay in their sheer numbers. As the progeny of the massive baby-boomer generation, these members of the so-called Generation Y (or "echo-boomers") accounted for 28 percent of the American population. Moreover, these consumers, who were between the ages of 10 and 18, were rapacious soft-drink guzzlers. For example, in 1993 alone teens spent $3 billion of their own money on soda, reported the newsweekly *Time.* Marketing a product to these echo-boomers was a difficult proposition, however. They were, *Time* explained, "inoculated against pitches from having grown up with television jingles at breakfast." Members of Generation Y not only commanded a greater spending power than any prior generation but also recognized that "their main area of [authority was] as a consumer," said *Time.*

According to the *Daily News Record,* the most effective way to address this audience was to "under promise;" that is, to avoid the typical strategy of touting an inanimate product as the path to happiness or popularity. Generation Y-ers were far too media savvy to succumb to this questionable logic. Consequently, "This Is the Taste" avoided scenes of gorgeous young adults drinking Dr Pepper and suddenly enjoying newfound prowess or popularity. Instead the commercials focused on Dr Pepper's taste and, as *Brandweek* noted, on "consumers' undying devotion to the product." Moreover, "This Is the Taste" retained the spirit of Dr Pepper's long-standing quirky image advertising. This decision was grounded in the tendency of teens to rebel against the conventional and accepted. Dr Pepper's spots did show people going to extreme lengths for a swig of the beverage, but these folks were presented as unique and unconventional, quite unlike the portraits of everyday, hardworking Americans who were the mainstay of many Coca-Cola campaigns.

Of course, while it assiduously courted Generation Y, Dr Pepper did not want to alienate consumers over the age of 20. Unlike Pepsi's campaigns, which had long sought to position that soft drink primarily as a youth brand, "This Is the Taste" strove to achieve a cross-generational appeal. No scenes of screaming teens or smart-talking kids were used. Instead "This Is the Taste" relied on a tongue-in-cheek humor, catchy story lines, and an ensemble of characters that catered to adults as well as teens. For instance, John Madden's presence provided the campaign with a means to connect with older consumers, as did a commercial released in December 1998 featuring the notoriously intense Bill Cowher, coach of the Pittsburgh Steelers NFL team. Because they did not resort to doling out the heavy-handed cynicism and obvious antiadvertising stance that was supposed to be popular among teenagers and their Generation X counterparts, "This Is the Taste" commercials had to be "more creative than ever to effectively convey our message," Dr Pepper's Clarke told *Adweek.*

COMPETITION

Sprite and Mountain Dew, Dr Pepper's foremost competitors, also strove to appeal to a youth market. Unlike Dr Pepper, though, both these brands more directly and unabashedly targeted Generation Y consumers. Sprite's 1998 marketing effort stemmed from its parent company's 1993 decision to end "I Like the Sprite in You," a peppy campaign that mainly attempted to differentiate Sprite from its fellow lemon-lime beverage 7 UP. In its place Sprite and its ad agency, Lowe & Partners/SMS,

GOING GLOBAL

In addition to being Dr Pepper's most expensive campaign, "This Is the Taste" led to the company's first-ever television commercial for international markets. Shot in Buenos Aires, Argentina, this spot portrayed an assortment of rural and urban images in an attempt to establish a global look for the brand. Dr Pepper's John Clarke declared the spot "a real masterpiece" and explained that its goal was to prompt international consumers to try the beverage. "With a name like Dr Pepper and a truly unique taste, some people might be reluctant to try it, but when they do, they love it," he added.

developed "Image Is Nothing. Taste Is Everything. Obey Your Thirst," a campaign that set its sights directly on Dr Pepper and Mountain Dew. As Lee Garfinkle, the chairman of Lowe & Partners, told *Adweek* on November 6, 1995, "the challenge was... to make Sprite relate to today's kids and bring it into the '90s." The way that "Obey Your Thirst" accomplished this aim was to ridicule the styles and fluffy messages of traditional soft-drink commercials and instead cultivate a pronounced antiadvertising stance. The commercials used cutting-edge hip-hop music and scenes of teens skateboarding, skiing, and playing basketball. Although "Obey Your Thirst" incorporated celebrities, such as National Basketball Association (NBA) star Grant Hill, the spots derided the entire notion of using a celebrity endorser. One component commercial depicted Grant Hill stylishly dunking the ball on the court and then pausing to take a sip of Sprite. As a young boy watched him and followed his example, the voice-over declared, "If you want to make the NBA, practice. If you want a refreshing drink, obey your thirst. Sprite." A company spokesperson explained the campaign's strategy to *Advertising Age* in 1998: "The approach is that we're not talking down to our audience. We know teens are smart enough. We know they know we're selling them a product." The brand's sales increased immediately after the campaign's launch. After becoming the fastest-growing soft drink in 1996, *Advertising Age* proclaimed that Sprite had "transcended the lemon-lime category to become a mainstream soft drink." Its successes continued in 1997 as it garnered a 6.2 percent share of the soft-drink market.

Mountain Dew reaped similar rewards from its strategy of targeting teenage boys. Created by BBDO Worldwide, its fast-paced commercials resembled music videos more than advertisements. Extreme athletes—representing sports that were tremendously popular with the echo-boomers, such as skateboarding and snowboarding—were a staple of Mountain Dew's advertising. In one 1999 spot skateboarders raced along the tops of New York skyscrapers. In another spot scenes of extreme athletes crashing and falling off their skateboards, surfboards, and snowboards were set to the old folk tune "Dem Bones." Mountain Dew aired a Super Bowl commercial in 1999 and was a prominent sponsor of the X-Games, an extreme sport extravaganza broadcast by ESPN. Like Sprite, Mountain Dew often adopted a more jaded outlook in its advertisements. Mountain Dew's 1997 performance was even more outstanding than Sprite's. It gained the distinction of being the fourth most popular soft drink that year and triumphed in "clever brand differentiation," noted *Advertising Age.*

MARKETING STRATEGY

Dr Pepper had described its goal for "This Is the Taste" as that of "position[ing the brand] more as a leading soft drink rather than simply as the leading noncola soft drink," Dr Pepper's Clarke explained to the *Dallas Morning News.* The company viewed the campaign as its vehicle into the mainstream cola market. Although Dr Pepper was far less interested in claiming converts from Pepsi and Coke's flagship colas, it did feel that by not billing itself exclusively as a fringe drink, it could cannibalize Sprite and Mountain Dew's share of the market. Therefore, "This Is the Taste" was "more aggressive and more of a call to action," said Clarke to the *News.* "We believe we're as much of an icon to consumers as Coke or Pepsi."

Dr Pepper realized that establishing its brand in the mainstream of the soft-drink market would require a concentrated marketing push. Both in 1997 and 1998 Dr Pepper budgeted more to promote itself than it did in any prior advertising campaigns. The outlay in 1998, in fact, was 50 percent higher than in 1997. "This increased marketing investment will ensure greater consumer exposure to Dr Pepper in 1998 than ever before," predicted Dr Pepper/Seven Up's president. The company built upon the solid foundation laid in 1997 with "This Is the Taste" ads—which had appeared during high-profile events such as the NFL conference championships games. In 1998 Dr Pepper branched out and ran its commercials during new programming as well. Along with big-ticket sporting events, "This Is the Taste" spots ran during the Golden Globe Awards and Rosie O'Donnell's talk show. In addition to its television spots, Dr Pepper used print ads. These did not share the images from the commercials but instead touted their own message. The company also sponsored a car in the NASCAR circuit in a bid to raise its visibility. "We've pulled together all the elements needed to propel Dr Pepper into the number one noncola soft drink position in the U.S.," raved the company's president at a bottler's convention.

The campaign continued into 1999 with a January release of three 30-second TV commercials. Titled "Anthem," "Latin," and "Halftime," they featured Americans and Mexicans playing soccer. The decision to tie Dr Pepper in with soccer melded with the agency's decision in 1999 to advertise Dr Pepper's international appeal. Although it was not the most popular sport in America, soccer was internationally referred to as "The World's Favorite Pastime."

The campaign officially ended on January 1, 2000, when Young & Rubicam released the subsequent campaign, "Dr Pepper Makes the World Taste Better." Clarke explained in the *PR Newswire* news service that the 2000 campaign made sense as the next step for Dr Pepper's advertising. "Now, we're going to provide the answer to the logical question, 'Why is Dr Pepper the taste,'" Clarke said. "Because no matter where you are, and no matter what you're doing—a Dr Pepper will make life taste better. In fact, as our new tagline declares, 'Dr Pepper Makes the World Taste Better.'"

OUTCOME

The noncola category of the soft-drink industry had another banner year in 1998. Dr Pepper sales rose 5.8 percent during the year. Nevertheless, Dr Pepper could not match the gains its rivals made. Mountain Dew catapulted past Diet Coke to become the third-best-selling soft drink, with its sales growing a stunning 9.9 percent in 1998. Sprite held onto its position as the number five beverage in the category, while Dr Pepper remained lodged in sixth place. In significant ways the company was hindered by its bottling and distribution systems. Because Dr Pepper/Seven Up owned no private bottling plants, it was dependent on independent operations or those controlled by Coca-Cola or Pepsi to perform this crucial step of moving the beverage from production to market. Moreover, its giant competitors had better distribution systems and more clout with retail and fast-food chains. Indeed, Dr Pepper/Seven Up was "in a tooth-and-nail struggle with larger rivals Coke and Pepsi for every inch of space it now occupies in supermarkets, convenience stores, soda fountains, and vending machines," *Brandweek* asserted.

Despite these liabilities, Dr Pepper's future looked bright. The noncola sector showed no signs of slowing, and the brand had a loyal following of consumers. In 1999 Cadbury Schweppes sold its non-U.S. DrÊPepper business and several other brands to the Coca-Cola Company. Cadbury Schweppes also decided to merge its bottling plant, the Dr Pepper Bottling Company, with the Carlyle Group's bottling plant American Bottling to form the consolidated Dr Pepper/Seven Up Bottling Group.

Dr Pepper executives attributed the brand's increased sales growth to the "This Is the Taste" campaign along with the improved bottling. Dr Pepper sold 5 percent more cases than in the previous year—marking its 15th consecutive year of sales growth. The brand's achievement was praised as "a phenomenon" by John Sicher, the publisher and editor of the industry newsletter *Beverage Digest.* Because of Dr Pepper's lack of competitors, Sicher referred to the drink as "an unstoppable freight train." Dr Pepper was the third-fastest-growing U.S. soft-drink brand in 1999, surpassed only by Mountain Dew and Sprite. Unfortunately for Dr Pepper/Seven Up, the company's second-largest brand, 7 UP, recorded a 3 percent sales decline the same year.

FURTHER READING

Benezra, Karen. "Dr Pepper/7-Up Beat Marketing Drums, But Is Pepsi Alliance in Offing?" *Brandweek,* September 22, 1997.

Cooper, Ann. "The Genie Inside the Bottle." *Adweek,* November 6, 1995.

Cox, James. "Sinatra Sings for a Winner." *USA Today,* June 1, 1987.

Deogun, Nikhil. "Coca-Cola May Purchase Orangina." *Wall Street Journal,* December 22, 1997.

Garfield, Bob. "Bob Garfield's Ad Review." *Advertising Age,* April 21, 1997.

Gladfelter, Elizabeth. "A Consultant Says that Gen X, Gen Y, and Boomers Have Starkly Different Characteristics, and Marketers Should Proceed with Caution." *Daily News Record,* November 9, 1998.

Gleason, Mark. "Sprite Leads the Pack in Soft Drink Growth." *Advertising Age,* February 12, 1996.

Greenwald, John. "Will Teens Buy It?" *Time,* May 30, 1994.

Howard, Andrew, and Theresa McMains. "Humor Softens Y&R's Dr Pepper Sell." *Adweek,* October 5, 1998.

Howard, Theresa, "7Up's New Jingle." *Brandweek,* August 23, 1999, p. 1.

Zimmerman, Martin. "Dr Pepper Changes Taste in Advertising." *Dallas Morning News,* October 26, 1996.

Rebecca Stanfel
Kevin Teague

Dreyer's Grand Ice Cream Holdings, Inc.

5929 College Avenue
Oakland, California 94618
USA
Telephone: (510) 652-8187
Fax: (510) 450-4592
Web site: www.dreyersinc.com

UNBELIEVABLE CAMPAIGN

OVERVIEW

To herald the launch of not just a new product line but also an entirely new manufacturing process, Dreyer's Grand Ice Cream Holdings, Inc., initiated in May 2004 what was to become the largest and most aggressive marketing campaign in the company's history. Founded in 1928 as a partnership between William Dreyer and Joseph Edy, Dreyer's (which was known as Edy's east of the Rockies in the United States to avoid confusion with rival Breyers) rose to become the largest ice-cream maker in the United States by 2005. After five years of research and development Dreyer's had come up with a proprietary new way to blend its ice cream that resulted in a richer-tasting but lower-fat version of its traditional product. The San Francisco–based agency Goodby, Silverstein & Partners created an ad campaign that was intended to attract consumers to this new product by building on the established brand name Dreyer's Grand Light yet giving ice-cream buyers a new reason to reach for a product that many felt was inferior to the "real" thing.

The comprehensive campaign, named "Unbelievable," featured four prime-time television spots, backed by print, billboard, and radio advertising. Dreyer's spent $20 million on the campaign. The theme of the TV spots was imitative of classic spy-thriller films, with various people expressing absolute incredulity that the new ice cream could possibly be lower in fat and calories than the original and accusing a fictitious Dreyer's executive of fraud and deceit.

The campaign was both a critical and financial success, winning a Gold EFFIE Award for the ad agency and boosting 2004 sales of Dreyer's Grand Light by 68 percent and overall sales of the company's products by 49 percent over the previous year. "Unbelievable" ran from May through November 2004.

HISTORICAL CONTEXT

Ice cream had reached a household penetration level of 90 percent by 2004. This meant that almost everyone in America bought ice cream; those who were apt to buy it already had it in their freezers, and those who did not would be difficult to persuade to put it there. As a result, the ice-cream manufacturing industry relied heavily on slight tweaks of established products (such as new shapes, sizes, or flavors) to boost sales. As was often case with mature products, there had been little innovation in the industry for decades. Whether on a stick, on a cone, dipped in chocolate, cut into bite-sized pieces, spread between two cookies, or blended with nuts and caramel, the product remained what it had always been: a frozen concoction made from sugar and cream. In 2004 the per capita consumption of ice cream in the United States was 44 pints per year, the highest in the world. Trying to convince consumers to buy even more of the product was also dicey, because few people thought that ice cream was a healthy food choice to begin with.

The ice-cream industry was not immune to trends, and because of their product's market saturation the manufacturers were quick to capitalize on shifts in consumer attitudes in the hope of increasing sales. In the mid-1980s, when low-fat diets reached a national fever pitch, the ice-cream industry was stymied. People were being told to eat a low-fat diet. Ice cream, as the very name implied, relied on milk fat to produce its rich, creamy taste. Sales of ice cream dropped as Americans turned to lower-fat alternatives. After a few years of both product and market research, in 1987 Dreyer's introduced its Grand Light line of lower-fat ice creams. Sales were initially strong but quickly stagnated as customers found the taste not rich or smooth enough, according to the company's internal research. It seemed that people would rather cut calories and fat in other parts of their diet and eat traditionally fattening ice cream if they ate it at all.

Diets fads came and went, and by the late 1990s the new trend of low-carbohydrate diets was leading the pack. While elimination of fats from consumers' plates was no longer the dietary thrust, reducing refined sugars and calories was, and again ice-cream sales took a hit. Most manufacturers of ice cream jumped the trend by using artificial sweeteners to reduce the sugar and calories in their products or by using fat substitutes to make their ice creams healthier. Unfortunately, "low fat," "low carbohydrate," and "healthy" were synonyms for "tastes bad" in many consumers' minds. For this reason Dreyer's took the innovative step of formulating not new ingredients but a new processing method to produce a version of their traditional ice cream that was lower in fat and calories but much closer in taste to the original.

The end result of a five-year and $100 million investment (in research and development, marketing, and infrastructure improvements) was a proprietary new "slow-churned" process of making ice cream. By employing a significantly lower temperature and higher pressure than traditional methods, the new churning method broke up and flattened the fat molecules in the cream, thereby increasing the number of molecules and their collective surface area while distributing them more evenly throughout the product, resulting in a richer and creamier texture. The manufacturing process took three times longer than with regular ice cream, hence the term "slow churned." One serving of traditional ice cream had 11 grams of fat and 175 calories, while the new product had only 3.5 grams of fat and 100 calories. Dreyer's had great hopes that this new product line, absent artificial or substitute ingredients, would revitalize the static "good-for-you" segment of the ice-cream market and find a welcome reception from health-conscious consumers or those who just wanted to reduce the guilt in an age-old guilty pleasure.

TARGET MARKET

With more than 60 percent of Americans classified as overweight, and with organic, natural, and lower-calorie foods seeing brisk sales going into 2004, Dreyer's aimed to sell its new product across a wide spectrum of consumers, but it intended specifically to target women—traditionally the grocery shoppers in most families—in the hopes that once inside the household the new ice cream would catch on with all members of the family. Research suggested that women were more likely to reach for a healthy alternative to regular ice cream, while men and children were more resistant to anything other than the real thing. In addition, the aim of the campaign was to attract lapsed buyers of "light" ice cream who had abandoned the category on the basis of poor taste as well as people who avoided eating ice cream in general because of its unhealthy nutritional profile.

COMPETITION

Dreyer's was acquired by Nestlé in 2003, making the combined company the world leader in ice-cream production and sales, followed by Unilever PLC, maker of the Breyers and Ben & Jerry's brands. In 2004, however, the Breyers brand had total annual U.S. sales of $529.1 million, whereas the Dreyer's brand's U.S. sales topped out at $422.2 million. Dreyer's had for years distributed the Ben & Jerry's brand of ice creams through its own distribution channels. Moving a competitor's product into the marketplace might seem counterproductive, but Dreyer's CEO Gary Rogers explained in an interview with CNN that, with an enormous fleet of its own freezer trucks, Dreyer's had the only direct-to-store distribution network in the United States. Because the Dreyer's distribution business accounted for more than half of its annual profits, it made fiscal sense to extract additional profit from a competitor even if that company's products ultimately sat next to the Dreyer's products on supermarket shelves.

While Dreyer's was the first to market with its new lower-fat ice creams, Unilever was close behind, introducing a "double-churned" version of its Breyers line in 2005. It used a similar process to create a more flavorful and creamy-textured ice cream with less fat and fewer calories. In a widespread TV and print campaign Breyers used the tagline "At Breyers, we believe good things get better... when they're doubled!" and paired it with soothing images from nature of "doubles," such as a double rainbow and a two-pronged waterfall. The advertisements then explained the "double-churned" process.

> ## WHAT'S IN A NAME?
>
> In 2004, when Dreyer's introduced a new slow-churned version of its original low-fat ice cream, Dreyer's Grand Light (introduced in 1987), it hyped the new technology used to produce the ice cream but kept the same name for the product, not wanting to confuse consumers and hoping to rebuild the stagnant light-ice-cream category on the back of its established brand name. Despite a $20 million media campaign to promote the new product, however, Dreyer's came to learn that the name itself, Grand Light, was an impediment to sales because a certain segment of the population was resistant to anything describing itself as healthy or "light." Halfway through the campaign Dreyer's retooled its packaging to de-emphasize the "light" aspect of the ice cream and to promote its slow-churned manufacturing process more forcefully. Advertising the new ice cream by its process instead of its low-fat and low-calorie content helped boost sales further. From that point on, the packaging featured a larger version of the words "Slow Churned" and a deemphasized "Light" name, so that it effectively read "Dreyer's Slow Churned."

MARKETING STRATEGY

What Dreyer's determined from its exhaustive research was that most people had an aversion to low-fat or healthy products, believing them to taste significantly worse than foods full of fat and calories. Rather than promote its slow-churned ice cream as a healthy alternative to regular ice cream, Dreyer's, in conjunction with ad agency Goodby, Silverstein & Partners, chose to tackle the problem of skepticism head-on: the crux of the campaign was to tout the incredulous fact that the new ice cream tasted almost as good as the real thing. In fact, in preliminary national blind taste tests, 8 out of 10 people thought that they were eating a full-fat premium ice cream rather than a "light" version. Bolstered by this research, Dreyer's embarked on a $20 million national media campaign, the largest in company history. It featured TV spots, print ads, billboards, radio spots, and commercials that aired in movie theaters prior to feature films.

The company was ambitious in its goal for the campaign, which was to increase stagnant sales of its light ice creams in 2004 by at least 50 percent over the previous year. Considering that the product was not rolled out until May, this amounted to a target increase of 50 percent for only seven months of the year (a period that would, however, include the ice-cream "selling season," which corresponded to the hottest months of the year, May through September). Dreyer's also hoped to create a "halo effect" in the sales of its traditional ice-cream lines as well. Even though no advertising was planned for its regular Grand Ice Cream line in 2004, Dreyer's was counting on its increased media presence to draw customers to all of its products, not just the advertised Dreyer's Grand Light line.

Four TV spots provided the backbone of the campaign. Goodby, Silverstein & Partners' approach was to build on and play off of the skepticism most consumers had about any sort of reduced-calorie dessert product. Rather than try to educate people about the technological innovations of the new product, the ad agency set out to forestall the viewer's incredulity by acknowledging it and taking it a step further. Using a classic-film-noir approach, each of the four spots featured a fictitious Dreyer's executive named Jim who was approached in sinister or underhanded ways by other employees who were so skeptical about the low-fat content of the new slow-churned ice cream that they accused him of passing off real ice cream as the new "light" product. In one spot Jim got into his car in the company parking lot after hours only to have a fellow employee lean forward out of the shadowed back seat and claim, "I know what you're up to." In another commercial Jim was approached by a woman at a company picnic who told him, "It's just not right, what you're doing." In a third Jim was accosted by a security guard who threatened to expose his secret unless Jim provided five gallons of ice cream per week to keep him quiet. The spots were utterly serious in tone, shot in high-contrast filmic style. The deadpan tone belied the silly message, but the point was driven home that this ice cream must be good enough to fool people, even people who worked for Dreyer's. These three spots were edited into one additional commercial that ran like a movie trailer, with fast edits and a voice-over saying, "A man stands alone, accused of a terrible crime." This commercial was played on television and in movie theaters in the advertising time before a feature film.

The print campaign took a similar approach, highlighting the "unbelievable" claim that the new light ice cream was, in fact, a reduced-fat product. One billboard featured a photo of a half-gallon container of the ice cream with the tagline "Introducing New Dreyer's Grand Light." The ad was then made to look as though it had been defaced by graffiti, with the words "no way this is" inserted between the words "Grand" and "Light," resulting in an ad that effectively read: "Introducing New Dreyer's Grand 'no way this is' Light." The radio spots resembled public service announcements, with a deadpan male voice stating, "This message is a public service announcement from Dreyer's Corporation," and then explaining that consumers may have been confused as to whether they had purchased a "light" or regular ice cream because the taste was so similar.

OUTCOME

Dreyer's more than met its goals with the campaign. Sales of the Grand Light ice creams rose 83 percent during the campaign's run and 68 percent for the year. Sales of all Dreyer's products increased $429 million, or 49 percent for the year. Clearly the "halo effect" approach had worked as hoped. Even the competition could not deny Dreyer's successful innovation and reinvigoration of the light-ice-cream category. John Cutter, CEO of Friendly Ice Cream Corporation, stated in a 2004 earnings conference call, "One thing that Dreyer's has done very effectively is they've come out with some very good 'better-for-you' products. They have a slow churned ice cream that is very good."

Goodby, Silverstein & Partners won a Gold EFFIE Award (Packaged Food, Diet/Health/Light category) for the campaign; the EFFIEs, held annually by the New York American Marketing Association, was one of the most prestigious award programs in the advertising industry. The campaign also generated a significant amount of press. In addition to numerous write-ups in food-industry magazines, *Newsweek* ran a piece on the new manufacturing process, CEO Rogers was interviewed on CNN, and the product was taste-tested by the anchors of *The Today Show* during a food segment.

Dreyer's was ultimately able to jump-start sales in a category that had seen flat sales for the previous three years, and it inspired just about every other major competitor to follow suit. More than 100 "low-carb" ice creams were introduced in 2004, versus only 19 in 2003 and zero in 2000. By positioning itself soundly in the marketplace with its sweeping ad campaign, Dreyer's achieved its goals and put itself ahead of an industry-wide trend.

FURTHER READING

Clancy, Maureen. "Matters of Taste." *San Diego Union-Tribune,* July 27, 2005, p. E1.

Funderburg, Anne Cooper. *Chocolate, Strawberry, and Vanilla: A History of American Ice Cream.* Bowling Green, OH: Bowling Green State University Popular Press, 1995.

Horovitz, Bruce. "Makers Put Fattening Ice Cream on a Diet; Tasty Fat, Sugar, Carbs Get Pinched to Curb Melting Retail Sales." *USA Today,* June 21, 2004, p. A1.

Phillips, David. "Looking for a Churn Around: Sales Have Softened in the Past Year, But Ice Cream Makers Have Rolled Out A Slew of Better (for You) Products Designed to Resurrect the Category." *Dairy Foods,* March 1, 2004, p. 44.

———. "Surf's Up for Lighter Ice Cream: The Food Industry Is Moving toward the Center with Products that Offer True Nutritional Balance." *Dairy Foods,* March 1, 2005, p. 22.

Reyes, Sonia. "New Products Dreyer's Has the Scoop to Please Ice Cream Skeptics; Keeping the Taste while Losing the Fat Is Key to New $20M Effort." *Brandweek,* May 10, 2004, p. 3.

Riell, Howard. "Indulging In Health; Health Concerns Continue to Drive a Lot of New Product Development in Ice Cream and Frozen Novelties, but Indulgence Remains the Rule of the Day." *Frozen Food Age,* May 1, 2004, p. 33.

Setoodeh, Ramin. "Corporate Last Licks; Can Dreyer's, the Largest U.S. Ice Cream Maker, Figure Out How to Market Its Newfangled Low-Fat Product?" *Newsweek,* May 9, 2005, p. 36.

Wellman, David. "Cool Treats, Hot Formulations: New Manufacturing Process and Formulations Play a Key Role in the Latest Round of Entries." *Frozen Food Age,* February 1, 2004, p. 28.

Wherry, Rob. "Who They Kidding? Ice Cream Wars." *Forbes Global,* April 14, 2005, p. 17A.

Jonathan Kolstad

drugstore.com, inc.

411 108th Ave. NE, Ste. 1400
Bellevue, Washington 98004
USA
Telephone: (425) 372-3200
Fax: (425) 372-3800
Web site: www.drugstore.com

A VERY HEALTHY WAY TO SHOP CAMPAIGN

OVERVIEW

When drugstore.com launched its website in 1999, the competitors in the online-drugstore segment were primarily a site introduced that year by CVS, a traditional "brick-and-mortar" drugstore, as well as several "pure-play" Internet retailers (those with online stores only), including PlanetRx.com and Rx.com. By 2000 PlanetRx.com and Rx.com had closed their sites, drugstore giant Walgreens had introduced an online presence, and drugstore.com was growing, with reported revenues of $34.8 million its first year and nearly 724,000 unique visitors to its site in one month (February 2000). To drive business during its first year, drugstore.com spent $28.5 million on advertising created by ad agency McCann-Erickson. Despite its marketing efforts and growing consumer interest in the site, however, drugstore.com lost $115.8 million in 1999. Pushed by its partners—General Nutrition Center (GNC) and Rite Aid drugstores—drugstore.com dropped McCann-Erickson and signed on Fallon McElligott as its new agency in August 1999 (the agency shortened its name to Fallon in 2000).

To help establish drugstore.com as a force on the Internet as well as a solid alternative to traditional drugstores, to further increase brand identity, and to drive shoppers to drugstore.com's website, Fallon created a new marketing campaign for the e-tailer that began in March 2000. The $30 million campaign targeted drugstore.com's core customers, women aged 25 to 54. It included television and radio spots, print ads, and online advertising, all with the theme "A Very Healthy Way to Shop."

The campaign won a 2001 Bronze EFFIE Award and achieved its goals, increasing overall brand awareness by 48 percent and pushing the number of weekly visits to the site up 18 percent. Sales also increased, jumping to $110 million in 2000. But drugstore.com continued to operate in the red, losing more than $193 million in 2000. As part of its budget-cutting measures, drugstore.com canceled its campaign and eliminated all off-line media spending.

HISTORICAL CONTEXT

Drugstore.com hung out its virtual shingle in 1999 with the goal of providing consumers with first-rate pharmacy services and a wide selection of health, wellness, and beauty products not often available at traditional brick-and-mortar drugstores because of space limitations. Coupled with the variety of products was convenience; busy consumers could shop for what the company described as "drugstore stuff" from the comfort of their own home or office simply by logging onto the Internet.

Partnerships with companies such as General Nutrition Center (GNC) and the Rite Aid drugstore chain helped drugstore.com expand its market reach. Within 13 months of drugstore.com's introduction the company announced that its one-millionth customer had shopped at the site. *Chain Drug Review* reported that, according to Peter Neupert, drugstore.com's CEO, by May 2000 more than two million Internet users were visiting drugstore.com's site each week.

Helping drive consumers to the new website was an advertising campaign created by the agency McCann-Erickson, Seattle. San Francisco–based Left Field Advertising, which had been responsible for all of drugstore.com's advertising prior to McCann-Erickson taking over off-line efforts, continued to handle drugstore.com's online advertising. Shortly after drugstore.com began its partnership with GNC and Rite Aid, McCann-Erickson lost the drugstore.com account based on complaints by the two chains that the advertising strategy touted online shopping at the expense of brick-and-mortar stores. Also, at the end of 1999 Left Field dropped the drugstore.com account. Drugstore.com moved quickly to find a new agency. After a four-week review the company named Minneapolis-based Fallon McElligott its new agency, with McCann-Erickson to be assigned work on a by-project basis.

Drugstore.com stipulated that Fallon McElligott (which became simply Fallon in 2000) needed to create the new branding campaign quickly, but the agency's president and creative director, David Lubars, said that Fallon was up to the speedy challenge the job posed. During an interview with *Adweek,* Lubars said, "All of these [dot-com] companies want to go fast. It's good for us as an agency to move quickly." And move quickly Fallon did. The agency was hired by drugstore.com in August 1999, and its first work for the online business—television spots with the tagline "Let the drugstore come to you"—broke that November. In March 2000 Fallon released a new campaign for the e-tailer themed "A Very Healthy Way to Shop."

THE CHARITABLE WING OF DRUGSTORE.COM

Founded in 1999, drugstore.com used 200,000 shares of its initial public offering (IPO) to create a nonprofit charitable organization, the drugstore.com Foundation. According to drugstore.com, the foundation "funds programs that facilitate emotional and economic self-sufficiency and improve the health, dignity and well-being of people in need." Its focus is on communities where drugstore.com has physical facilities.

The drugstore.com Foundation has donated money to numerous organizations, including Washington Women in Need, the AIDS Coalition of New Jersey, the American Red Cross, and National Meals on Wheels. Donations are selected by drugstore.com employees. For example, in 2001 an employee committee at drugstore.com's southern New Jersey distribution center donated $25,000 to three nonprofit organizations in the state: the Visually Impaired Co-Partners of Gloucester County, the Emmanuel Cancer Foundation, and the AIDS Coalition of Southern New Jersey.

TARGET MARKET

Drugstore.com's director of communications, Erik Moris, succinctly stated the company's target market during an interview with *Advertising Age.* "We're building this company around women," he said. Moris noted that even the use of a bathtub as the focal point of the marketing campaign specifically targeted women, because men took showers and not baths. Women 25 to 54 years old were drugstore.com's core audience. Additional studies identified head-of-household women, known as the family's gatekeeper, as a key target because they were the consumers who made decisions about what products to buy and where to shop for them. The campaign was designed as a way to show busy, working women how drugstore.com could help simplify their lives and give them more time for the things they enjoyed, including spending time with family and friends and simple pleasures such as bubble baths. The campaign also drove home the point that by shopping for their various non-grocery purchases, from prescriptions to cosmetics, on the drugstore.com website, they could reduce the number of weekly trips they made to a bricks-and-mortar drugstore.

COMPETITION

Since 1901, when pharmacist Charles R. Walgreen, Sr., opened his drugstore in Chicago, his business goal was always to provide customers what they needed at a good price. By 1910 Walgreen had two stores and a growing customer base. The business continued to expand and had reached 525 stores by 1929. Recognizing the value of advertising to reach customers, Walgreens (as the chain became known) relied on newspapers to carry its ads, but in 1931 the company launched the largest marketing campaign in its history. The effort cost $75,000 and included both print and broadcast advertising. In 2001

Walgreens was the number one drugstore chain in the United States, with $21.1 billion in sales. The company had 3,300 stores and projected opening a total of 425 new stores annually. The company was slow to become an e-tailer, however, falling behind the competition on the Internet. That changed when Walgreens went online in 2000. The launch of the new website, walgreens.com, was supported by a national marketing campaign designed to introduce consumers to Walgreens' new service and build online brand awareness. The campaign was created by Euro RSCG Tatham, Chicago, and included four television spots.

CVS opened its first store in Lowell, Massachusetts, in 1963, offering customers a selection of beauty items and over-the-counter health products. Pharmacies were added to the stores in 1963. By 1970 the chain had grown to 100 stores serving customers in the Northeast. The drugstore chain continued its expansion, and beginning in 1990 growth was driven by acquisitions. In 1990 CVS acquired the 500-store People Drug, which served the Mid-Atlantic states; in 1997 the Revco chain was purchased, adding an additional 2,552 stores in the Midwest and Southeast; and in 1998 Arbor Drugs, with 207 stores in Michigan, was acquired. In 1999 CVS paved the Internet highway for other brick-and-mortar drugstores when the chain became the first fully integrated online pharmacy in the United States. To help promote the new service, CVS signed a multimillion-dollar sponsorship agreement with Microsoft Corp.'s MSN.com. As part of the deal CVS agreed to advertise through the online company's network and to sponsor the MSN Health Channel, MSN WomenCentral's Health, and MSN Hotmail's Pharmacy Quicklink. In return, the Health & Wellness Channel of MSN's e-commerce site, eShop, offered links to CVS.com's various sections. Other marketing for CVS included newspaper circulars and television and radio spots with the tagline "Care that touches everyone, one at a time." The New York office of ad agency Bates USA was responsible for the company's television and radio spots, while print ads were created in-house by a CVS team.

MARKETING STRATEGY

Fallon's "A Very Healthy Way to Shop" campaign for drugstore.com quickly followed the agency's first effort for the health and beauty e-tailer, "Let the Drugstore Come to You," which was a series of television spots that broke during the 1999 holiday season. "A Very Healthy Way to Shop" was an expansion on drugstore.com's effort to establish brand identity, to position the online-only business as a preferred alternative to brick-and-mortar drugstores, and to drive consumers to shop at the site. The campaign began in March 2000 with television and radio spots, special sales promotions, and online advertising. The budget was estimated to be $30 million.

Precampaign research by Fallon identified key markets based on consumers' income, education level, and access to the Internet. Eight metropolitan areas where the campaign would be released were targeted: Boston, New York, Chicago, Denver, Seattle, San Francisco, Austin (Texas), and Washington, D.C. Research also noted that many women with an extra hour in their day would spend it taking a bath, which led to a continuation of Fallon's earlier work for drugstore.com that featured a woman soaking in a bathtub.

Television spots for the new campaign had the busy career woman back in her tub, where she made decisions, helped family and friends, and ordered health and beauty items from drugstore.com while she soaked in a bubble bath. In the first spot the woman was shown running a business meeting from her bathtub and helping one of her staff members by ordering necessary items from drugstore.com via her laptop computer, which was securely resting on a tray across the middle of the tub. A follow-up spot showed the woman chatting with her upset preteen daughter and again turning to her laptop to order products that would make her daughter feel better. The third spot in the series featured the woman hosting a cocktail party from the foamy comfort of her bathtub. The spots aired for the first time during the broadcast of the Academy Awards. Additional network programming during which spots aired included ratings giants *Friends, ER, The West Wing,* and *The Late Show with David Letterman.*

Radio spots followed a similar format and aired in the target cities on news/talk stations and on stations that played music ranging from adult contemporary to oldies, jazz, and classic country. Integrated online and off-line efforts included an alliance with Discovery Health Media, a multimedia company consisting of a health-information website (http://health.discovery.com) and the Discovery Health Channel, a new cable channel run by Discovery Communications. The agreement entailed placing drugstore.com advertisements on the Discovery Health website and running television spots not only on the Discovery Health Channel but also on other Discovery cable networks, such as the Learning Channel and the Travel Channel.

OUTCOME

Although drugstore.com's marketing campaign was funded with a limited budget, the effort successfully achieved the goals of increasing brand awareness, reaching its target consumers, and driving business to drugstore.com's website. According to Fallon, in the markets where radio and television spots aired, brand awareness was 52 percent higher than in markets where drugstore.com had not been promoted. Further, brand awareness overall increased to 48 percent in less than one year. Visits to drugstore.com's website increased significantly following the start of the campaign. Just over one year after opening its online business and within one month of the campaign's introduction, drugstore.com reported that it had reached its one-millionth unique paying customer. A review of online health and beauty retailers by *Drug Store News* noted that visits to drugstore.com's site increased 24 percent through June 2001 compared to the same period the previous year. In 2001 the "A Very Healthy Way to Shop" campaign won a Bronze EFFIE Award in the General Retail/Etail category. Despite the campaign's success and rapidly increasing sales, the company was losing money. In response to the mounting deficit, all off-line media spending was eliminated in July 2000, four months after the campaign began, cutting the total media expenditure to less than $20 million.

FURTHER READING

"Ads Tout Belief in Customer Service (CVS Corp. Advertising Strategy)." *Chain Drug Review,* December 11, 2000.

Baar, Aaron. "Drugstore.com a Balm for Women in Fallon Ads." *Adweek,* March 20, 2000.

———. "Online Pharmacy Picks Fallon." *Adweek,* August 23, 1999.

"CVS.com Complements Brick-and-Mortar Units (CVS Corp. Web Site)." *Chain Drug News,* December 11, 2000.

"Drugstore.com Achieves One Million Online Shoppers; Passes 'Paying-Customer' Milestone Faster than Key Online Players." *Business Wire,* April 4, 2000.

"Drugstore.com Donates $25,000 to Charities." *Drug Store News,* August 6, 2001.

"Drugstore.com Gives Consumers Options." *Chain Drug Review,* May 1, 2000.

"Drugstore.com Launches Consumer Advertising Campaign Featuring 'Life in the Tub'." *Business Wire,* March 20, 2000.

Goetzl, David. "Drugstore.com Hunts Supermoms." *Advertising Age,* March 20, 2000.

Kelly, Jane Irene. "Left Field Drops Amazon, Drugstore.com." *Adweek,* August 30, 1999.

Kirk, Jim. "Chicago Tribune Marketing Column." *Chicago Tribune,* February 9, 2001.

Parks, Liz. "Chains Utilize Web Sites as an Aid, Rather than Business Model." *Drug Store News,* July 23, 2001.

———. "Soft Economy Has Yet to Deter Online Shoppers Completely." *Drug Store News,* September 24, 2001.

"Walgreens Launches First Marketing Campaign for Walgreens.com." *Advertising Age,* February 8, 2001.

Rayna Bailey

Dyson Ltd.

Tetbury Hill
Malmesbury, Wiltshire SN16 0RP
United Kingdom
Telephone: 44 870 5275104
Web site: www.dyson.com

DOESN'T LOSE SUCTION CAMPAIGN

OVERVIEW

After experiencing years of success in Europe, the high-priced, British-made Dyson vacuum began appearing in the United States in 2002 during a time of recession and a waning U.S. vacuum industry. Nevertheless James Dyson—the vacuum's creator and Dyson Ltd.'s president and spokesman—stood resolute that his filterless, bagless vacuum would succeed stateside. Awarded Dyson's advertising budget in 2002, the ad agency Fallon Worldwide launched the "Doesn't Lose Suction" campaign to tote Dyson's superior technology in an industry that, according to Dyson, needed improvement.

With a $14.4 million budget, Fallon released "Doesn't Lose Suction" across television and print during the second week of October 2003. James Dyson appeared in some 30-second television spots while only providing the voice-overs for others. In the first spot James Dyson soberly explained the shortcomings of traditional vacuums, specifically, the clogging of their filters and bags. He then admitted to spending 14 years developing a vacuum that used centrifuge technology to spin the dirt out of air at 100,000 times the force of gravity. Dyson vacuums were easy to empty, never clogged, and boasted more suction power than traditional vacuums. The spot ended with a black-background shot of the new Dyson vacuum.

Soon after the campaign's release Dyson vaulted past its competitors and went from a zero percent market share to being America's top-selling vacuum in 2005. The success of Dyson vacuums, which retailed between $399 and $550, actually increased the entire vacuum industry's price tags, which had previously averaged $95 to $125. "Our goal is to completely change the way vacuums are marketed in the U.S.," Doug Kellam, president of Dyson, Chicago (the company's U.S. headquarters), told *Advertising Age.* Dyson's marketing involved blatantly stating its technical advantages over the competition and then unflinchingly attaching an exorbitant price tag. Besides increasing Dyson's sales the campaign also snagged a silver EFFIE advertising award in 2005.

HISTORICAL CONTEXT

In 1970, while studying at the Royal College of Art, the inventor and designer James Dyson released his first creation, the Sea Truck. His subsequent inventions included a wheelbarrow and a boat ramp that used inflatable balls instead of wheels. He started working on a bagless vacuum cleaner in 1978. Before Dyson decided to market the revolutionary vacuum himself, he approached the Hoover Company in the 1980s with his bagless, filterless vacuum idea. "Hoover wouldn't give it the time of day. They said: 'Bags are best. Bags will always be best.' Then they copied it," the inventor said in *The Story of Dyson,* a booklet included with every Dyson vacuum.

James Dyson spent 14 years perfecting his vacuum. It used centrifugal force to keep dirt spinning along the inner cylinder's insides while the suction chamber remained unobstructed. The effect was similar to that of a tornado. The first Dyson model, the Dyson Cyclone, was released in the United Kingdom in 1993. The company put almost all profit back into development over the next 12 years, expanding Dyson's team from 3 scientists to 350. In an interview with *Advertising Age,* Dyson's global marketing director, Clare Mullin, reiterated the company's commitment to development, saying, "We're an engineering-led company, not a marketing-led company." Most of Dyson's European success was attributed to word of mouth.

Many analysts believed Dyson vacuums would flop in America. When the product arrived in 2002, the United States was in a recession, and analysts doubted that consumers would be able to justify spending $429.99 on a vacuum. James Dyson disagreed. Speaking to the *Times* of London, he explained, "Vacuum cleaners are quite recession-proof because people retrench back into the home. If you look back historically, the sales don't drop at the time of recession." As evidence he mentioned Dyson's strong sales during the United Kingdom's recession in 1993.

According to the *Times* of London, the company decided to use Fallon as its ad agency because, in the words of James Dyson, "We liked the style, they are educational." Believing that Americans would be drawn to Dyson's technology, Fallon crafted Dyson spots to be instructive. Dyson further explained, "Our ads are never funny, they are almost boring. I think vacuuming is serious and I don't think it's something to joke about." By mid-2005 Dyson and Fallon, citing strategic differences, had discontinued their relationship.

TARGET MARKET

"Doesn't Lose Suction" targeted 30- to 40-year-olds along with a subgroup of allergy sufferers and pet owners. With the latter in mind, Dyson promoted its vacuums at dog and cat shows. One of the product's technological advantages over bag or filter vacuums was its ability to collect fine dust and ash without the particles affecting vacuum suction. "Suction to consumers is very important, and Dyson as a marketer claimed something that resonated with consumers," Bill McLaughlin, executive editor at *HomeWorld Business Magazine,* told *Advertising Age.*

Dyson had reportedly spent very little on advertising in Europe, where raves about the vacuum's advantages were spread by word of mouth. But the company took a different approach to America because, as the *Times* of London stated, "the US is too big a place to rely on conversations over the garden fence." At the end of 2003 Dyson aired television spots across major American network and cable channels. "It's mad for us not to have been here. If we are just half as successful as we have been in Britain, we'll be selling 3.5 million vacuum cleaners," James Dyson told the *Times* of London.

DYSON'S WASHING MACHINE

James Dyson set out to improve another household appliance: the washing machine. "A lot of the things I used every day irritated me," James Dyson told the *Providence Journal.* "I wanted to have a go with them." In 1996 James Dyson asked his research team to investigate all factors that might enhance the performance of washing machines. Researchers experimented with detergents, water temperatures, and washing motions. After four months a remarkable fact was uncovered: clothes that were washed by hand for 15 minutes were cleaner than clothes washed inside a washing machine for 67 minutes. The discovery prompted Dyson engineers to design a two-chambered washing machine, later dubbed the CR01, that simulated hand washing.

Before Americans could even buy the vacuum, skeptics claimed that Dyson's price tag would deter consumers. "Dyson is a leading brand in Europe at those high prices, but the American consumer's mentality is price, price, price," Gerry Beatty, a senior editor at *Home Furnishings News,* told *Advertising Age.* Dyson vacuums arrived first in American specialty stores and then in Target stores. As the brand's popularity blossomed, its vacuums were sold by Best Buy, Home Depot, and Linens 'N Things. Reflecting upon Dyson's success, Norman Axelrod, chairman and CEO of Linens 'N Things, explained to *Advertising Age,* "[The Dyson vacuum] becomes our best seller simply because there is something new and something exciting about it, so there is not a resistance to price points."

COMPETITION

When Dyson vacuums first appeared in America in 2002, the Hoover brand, owned by the Maytag Corporation, was leading the American vacuum industry with a 25 percent market share. After an incredible two-year spurt, Dyson knocked Hoover down to a 16 percent market share and claimed 21 percent. Hoover tried scrambling back by releasing vacuums outfitted with the Fusion Cyclonic Filtration System, a technology modeled after Dyson's vacuums. By 2005 Hoover was spending

$47 million on advertising with its new, Dyson-like tagline, "No Loss of Suction." Hoover also released a vacuum model, called WindTunnel, that boasted 56 percent more suction than Dyson. The claim appeared in Hoover's television spots, which were created by Element 79 Partners.

The Louisiana-based Oreck Corporation, manufacturer of upright and canister vacuums, took Dyson to court in 2005 after claiming Dyson's "Doesn't Lose Suction" tagline was "literally false." Dyson countersued with a similar accusation about Oreck's tagline "Maintains Suction Power." Oreck's main advertising push used infomercials and direct mailers, but the company occasionally aired television spots starring David Oreck, the company's founder and spokesperson, on cable and broadcast TV. One 30-second spot in 2005 showed him outfitted as a magician, asking, "Want to make your pet hair magically disappear?" The spot then cut to David Oreck promising that an Oreck vacuum could "clean every rug in your home," while his toupee fluttered from vacuum suction. The spot ended with an owl clinging to the end of his Oreck XL broom. *Advertising Age* reported that David Oreck venomously attributed Dyson's success to the "superior advertising of an inferior machine."

MARKETING STRATEGY

"Doesn't Lose Suction" spots first aired in October 2003 on network and cable channels such as A&E, Lifetime, HGTV, and TLC. To reach the company's 30- to 40-year-old target market, print ads appeared in conscientious magazines such as *Metropolitan Home, Parenting,* and *O: The Oprah Magazine.* Print ads, like the television spots, dwelled on product innovation. One ad read, "While everyone else was fiddling with headlights or stiffer bristles, someone went and reinvented the whole machine."

Initial television spots for the campaign featured either James Dyson or his voice-over convincingly explaining his vacuum's advantages. The campaign's second spot started with the camera panning across sad-looking vacuums from the competition. James Dyson's steady British voice began, "Ever since the vacuum cleaner was invented, it's had a basic design flaw. Bags, filters: they all clog with dust and then lose suction. The technology simply doesn't work." The camera then stopped on Dyson standing, literally, behind his product. He continued, "So I spent 14 years developing one that does. The Dyson Cyclones create 100,000 times the force of gravity to spin the dirt out of the air. So nothing gets clogged—ever."

The "Doesn't Lose Suction" campaign employed promotions outside traditional vacuum-industry mediums. Dyson's DC11 canister vacuum appeared in a window display at the upscale department store Barney's New York. As part of Fallon's strategy to target pet owners, Dyson vacuums were given away in competitors' goody bags at the Westminster Dog Show. Similar to what Dyson's brand had experienced in Europe, people in the United States were talking about their Dyson vacuums. Mullin told *Advertising Age* that all economic groups were "buying it literally because of the performance of the vacuum cleaner." The clear shell and different shape of the Dyson vacuum warranted its exhibit at the Metropolitan Museum of Art in New York, the San Francisco Museum of Modern Art, the Science Museum in London, and the Pompidou Centre in Paris.

In developing the campaign Fallon was challenged to deviate outside traditional vacuum advertising, which included direct mailers and huckster-style television spots. "We knew from the beginning what we didn't want," Michael Hart, copywriter and group creative director at Fallon, told *Brandweek.* "No dancing moms vacuuming. No long-haired cats shedding in the background. No bowling balls being sucked up. Just the vacuum, the man who invented it and why it's better."

Dyson increased measured media spending from $755,200 in 2002 to $14.4 million by 2003. In 2004 Dyson continued increasing its advertising budget, bringing the sum to $16.1 million in the first seven months. During the "Doesn't Lose Suction" campaign Dyson released new models, such as the DC15, a machine that employed an inflatable ball for a more agile wheelbase. James Dyson continued providing the voice-overs for the DC15 spots. "James does a very good job of being himself on camera," Mike Gibbs, group creative director at Fallon, told *Advertising Age.*

OUTCOME

Defying industry analysts, excelling from zero U.S. market share to U.S. market leader in three years, and revolutionizing one of the world's most popular appliances, Dyson underwent an incredible amount of growth during its "Doesn't Lose Suction" campaign. "They have a radically different thing going... It's a great new brand," David Lubars, president and executive creative director at Fallon, told *Adweek.* The campaign also earned a silver EFFIE award in the Household Furnishings and Appliances category in 2005.

Many critics praised the campaign for its frank, confident delivery, which portrayed James Dyson as a man so moved by his own invention that he himself believed Americans would be compelled to buy it after hearing his explanation. The approach, according to Dyson, not only worked but also prodded the entire vacuum industry to improve hardware and advertising. David Oreck, the founder of Dyson's fierce competitor Oreck, agreed with this assessment, telling *Advertising Age* that Dyson's strategy of focusing on its vacuums' technology instead of on price points had helped America's vacuum industry to undergo a "constructive" change.

FURTHER READING

Arditi, Lynn. "Filling a Vacuum—Inventor Brings Good Design Home." *Providence (RI) Journal,* May 6, 2005, p. F1.

Baar, Aaron. "Fallon to Bow Dyson." *Adweek,* July 22, 2002, p. 6.

Cuneo, Alice. "Dyson Takes On Vacuum Giants: $15M Push for High-Priced Cleaner." *Advertising Age,* October 13, 2003, p. 6.

———. "No. 2 in Market Share: Dyson Hoovers Up Vacuum Business." *Advertising Age,* December 4, 2004, p. 1.

Elliot, Stuart. "And Now, the Awards for the Best and Worst Commercials during the Oscar Broadcast." *New York Times,* March 2, 2005, p. 5.

Frazier, Mya. "You Suck: Dyson, Hoover and Oreck Trade Accusations in Court, on TV as Brit Upstart Leaves Rivals in Dust." *Advertising Age,* July 25, 2005, p. 1.

Garfield, Bob. "Dyson Ad Succeeds by Saying Precisely How Product Sucks." *Advertising Age,* December 6, 2004, p. 37.

———. "10 Ads I Loved." *Advertising Age,* December 20, 2004, p. 14.

Gemperlein, Joyce. "Vacuums, Sweeping Us Away: Eager Consumers Get Sucked Up in the Marketing Frenzy." *Washington Post,* August 7, 2005, p. 5.

Homan, Becky. "A Minute of Your Time: Trends, Tidbits." *Akron (OH) Beacon Journal,* July 9, 2005, p. 15.

Palmer, Camilla. "MCBD Resigns Dyson after Creative Clashes." *Campaign,* November 15, 2002, p. 5.

Rayner, Abigail. "Dyson Prepares to Clean Up as He Enters American Vacuum." *Times* (London), October 4, 2002, p. 29.

Reinan, John. "Fallon Agency Snags Several Effie Awards." *(Minneapolis, MN) Star-Tribune,* June 8, 2005, p. 2D.

Kevin Teague

Eastman Kodak Company

343 State Street
Rochester, New York 14650-0002
USA
Telephone: (800) 698-3324
Telephone: (585) 724-4000
Fax: (585) 724-1089
Web site: www.kodak.com

ADVANTIX CAMPAIGN

OVERVIEW

Eastman Kodak Company ran one of the largest advertising campaigns in its history to publicize the Advanced Photo System (APS), a new type of camera, film, and related products developed jointly by Kodak and a number of competitors. Kodak's APS cameras were designed primarily to make photography easier for the snapshooter, the consumer who took pictures to remember birthdays and other such occasions.

Because the public was still confused about APS after an initial marketing campaign in 1996, the company hired ad agency Ogilvy & Mather of New York to design new advertising for 1997 to explain the advantages of APS products. These commercials ran until they were replaced by the next phase of APS promotions, which began in the summer of 1998. Kodak spent far more than its competitors to promote APS, which helped consumers equate APS with Advantix, the Kodak brand of APS products.

The 1997 "Advantix" television campaign ran in two stages. The first was a spot that asked, "Can your camera do this?" and then explained three of an Advantix camera's innovative features; drop-in film loading, choice of three picture sizes, and an index print. The second stage consisted of three humorous scenarios, one for each special feature of the Advantix system, which showed photographers experiencing problems they could have avoided if they had used APS. One spot, for example, showed an elderly woman who had fulfilled her lifelong dream of having her picture taken in front of the Eiffel Tower. When she had the pictures developed, she was horrified to see that the photographer had cropped off most of her head so that the tower would fit into the picture. The ad concluded, "She should've had a Kodak Advantix camera with three picture sizes for better pictures."

The campaign also included print advertisements that illustrated the three distinctive features of APS products. Each ad displayed color photographs against a Kodak yellow background and was accompanied by a brief explanation of one of the features and of Kodak's general corporate signature, "Take Pictures. Further."

HISTORICAL CONTEXT

In helping to develop the Advanced Photo System to make photography easier for the average consumer, Kodak was staying true to its roots. The company had been founded in 1888 on the slogan "You push the button, we do the rest." Kodak had a history of introducing new products, including photographic equipment and supplies, projectors, and copiers. In 1997 Kodak was a multinational corporation with nearly 100,000 employees, one of the 25 largest companies in the United States.

The "Tall Tales" commercials ran in the same year as the first ads to promote the new Advantix camera. The initial campaign, launched in February 1996, was designed by J. Walter Thompson, which had been Kodak's primary ad agency for more than 60 years. The commercials opened with the customary Kodak moment, as when a bearded hippie admired a spectacular mountain vista and commented, "Some people see mountains. I see personalities." After the point had been made that every photographer captured pictures from a unique point of view, the voice-over said, "Now Kodak introduces a new technology that will let you take those pictures further than you've ever imagined." The commercial concluded by summarizing the three innovative features of APS cameras and film.

In 1997, when J. Walter Thompson was replaced by Ogilvy & Mather, the "Advantix" campaign began. Kodak had invested a great deal of money in researching and developing APS, and it allocated $100 million to promote Advantix products worldwide.

TARGET MARKET

Kodak believed that its core customers would take more pictures of a broader range of subjects if they were provided with cameras, film, and other merchandise that would make photography easier. The company wanted to attract new customers but was primarily interested in appealing to those who were already familiar with its products. A large percentage of Kodak's customers were mothers who took pictures during birthday parties, holiday celebrations, vacations, and other family occasions. Kodak's previous advertising had focused on this type of situation, but as its customers became more adept at photography, the company's commercials featured a wider variety of possibilities.

Although many customers had learned how to use the more complex 35-mm equipment that had been their best option before the advent of the Advanced Photo System, they were not particularly interested in creating professional-looking photographs. Instead, they wanted convenient equipment that was easy to use and would produce pictures of good quality. It was thought that they would appreciate the compact size of the Advantix cameras, the "foolproof" drop-in loading that would help them avoid frustrating mechanical problems, and the choice of three picture sizes for each shot. In addition, they would welcome the index print, which, like a proof sheet, showed miniature replicas of each shot on the roll of film. The index print would allow users to see what they were getting when they ordered reprints without having to deal with negatives. The marketing campaign pointed out each of these advantages in a simple way that could be grasped by watching a 30-second television commercial or by reading a few sentences in a print ad.

SPILLOVER EFFECTS

Although the "Advantix" campaign focused on just one of Kodak's products, it helped increase overall sales. One reason for the company's success was its family orientation and reputation for trustworthiness. Its advertising traditionally revolved around the "Kodak moment," an emotional portrait of a consumer capturing a heartwarming experience on film. This had helped Kodak cultivate a wholesome image, but research showed that the company was not particularly appealing to younger consumers. In 1996 Ogilvy & Mather tried a new angle with its humorous "Tall Tales" commercials that portrayed unconventional uses for various Kodak products. For instance, one ad featured a consumer using Kodak's Image Magic digital enhancement station to disguise the dents in a Gremlin automobile. The campaign was well received, particularly among young adults.

COMPETITION

Each of the five companies—Kodak, Canon U.S.A., Minolta, Nikon, and Fuji Photo Film U.S.A.—that cooperated in developing the Advanced Photo System had its own brand of APS products, and they were designed to meet the needs of somewhat different target markets. In general, all provided the three basic APS features, and Fuji also introduced a line of APS film. Kodak's Advantix camera tended to be slightly less expensive than some of the other APS brands and was generally easier for snapshooters to use. Consumers did not have the option of changing lenses with the Advantix camera, but it did have a built-in zoom lens.

In contrast, one of Canon's four APS cameras, the EOS IX, was designed to accept more than 50 lenses and hundreds of accessories. The company also introduced the credit card-size ELPH, the world's smallest shutter camera with a 2x zoom lens. The ELPH had several sophisticated features, including an active autofocusing mode that used an infrared emitter and sensor and a passive mode that could discern variations in contrast. Another model, the Canon ELPH 490Z, featured a 4x zoom lens. In television commercials a woman with an elfin air about her inquired, "Have you seen the ELPH?" as a series of ultracompact cameras floated past. The ads ended with the tag line "It's so advanced . . . it's simple." Another Canon slogan said, "ELPH: the big name in the Advanced Photo System."

During 1997 Fuji offered rebates of up to $15 to develop and print a roll of its Fujicolor SmartFilm when customers purchased certain Fujifilm Endeavor APS cameras. To publicize the rebates, the company ran a full-page ad in *USA Today* and other ads in 15 key markets. The campaign was launched in September 1997 to coincide with holidays such as Thanksgiving and Christmas. In addition to promotional efforts for its APS films, Fuji expanded its network of photographic laboratories in Europe and the United States and offered digital imaging services. Fuji's net sales increased 12 percent in 1997.

Minolta and Nikon also advertised their cameras and accessories, but Kodak spent far more to publicize APS than did all the other companies combined. In addition to its "Advantix" campaigns, Kodak participated in co-op ads with the other companies to educate the public about APS.

Kodak's $100 million budget to advertise Advantix products amounted to about 85 percent of the total all five companies spent to publicize APS products in 1997. Fuji initially allocated about $13 million, twice its previous ad budget, to promote its SmartFilm brand. Minolta allocated $10 million, about 150 percent of its previous ad budget, to promote its Vectis brand of APS products. Kodak's total spending on advertising in 1994, just before APS was introduced, was $65.4 million. In 1997 the company budgeted about $60 million for advertising Advantix in the United States alone.

MARKETING STRATEGY

At the end of the 1996 campaign introducing the Advanced Photo System equipment and film, consumers still seem confused. As a result, Ogilvy & Mather introduced the "Can Your Camera Do This?" spot. The 1997 round of ads was intended primarily to promote the Advantix brand and only secondarily APS. The challenge was to communicate the basics of a new, complex technology in print ads and television commercials.

In April 1997 Kodak began airing television ads that asked, "Can your camera do this?" They stressed the three features of Advantix cameras—drop-in film loading, the choice of three picture sizes, and an index print. This first phase of the campaign was designed to explain the functional benefits of APS.

The next series of television ads were humorous, depicting common problems that photographers could eliminate by using Advantix products. The print ads gave more details. For example, one television spot showed a couple who were having a reprint made so that they could enter the photo in a cute-baby contest but who chose the wrong negative and inadvertently submitted a picture of a chubby grown-up. The commercial ended with the line "They should've had the Kodak Advantix system with an index print so you can see what you're ordering." The corresponding print ad showed an example of an index print and included explanatory text: "Choosing your favorite smile is a lot easier when you can actually see the smile. When Kodak Advantix film is processed, your pictures come back with the negatives in their original film cassette and with an index print that gives you a miniature version of every shot. Ordering reprints is easy, and you can get them in any of the three sizes. So no more squinting at negatives, trying to tell a grimace from a grin."

The broadcast ads were aired on network, cable, and syndicated television programs, particularly during the Academy Awards and the coverage of the Winter Olympics in Nagano, Japan. In addition to the United States, they ran in the United Kingdom and in other countries. In non-U.S. markets the "Can your camera do this?" spots were shown more often than the humorous ads. The print ads ran primarily in consumer magazines in the United States. Some appeared in publications that focused on new parents and travel so as to reach readers who were likely to be taking more than the average number of photographs. The ads also appeared in general-interest magazines and in various other publications.

The ads highlighting the three features of the Advantix camera ran into the summer of 1998, when the next stage of the promotion began. Kodak's promotion of Advantix products and APS had been designed to encompass several years, allowing the company to expand gradually on the basic message.

OUTCOME

Kodak and Ogilvy & Mather analyzed the public's reaction to the campaign and found that it scored high on every positive indicator. When asked to tell what they recalled about the advertisements, people were able to repeat the words almost exactly. One of the spots was included on *Adweek* 's list of the best ads of 1997. During 1997 Kodak saw strong growth for its other merchandise as well, in part because of the promotion of such products as Max film and Goldfilm.

FURTHER READING

Cardona, Mercedes M. "Kodak Media-Buying Biz Follows Creative to O&M." *Advertising Age,* June 23, 1997.

Enrico, Dottie. "Kodak Campaign Clicks, Develops Tech-Savvy Image." *USA Today,* September 16, 1996.

Garfield, Bob. "Kodak's Split Image Lights Up Advantix." *Advertising Age,* February 1, 1996.

"Kodak Ends an Era, Calls It Quits with JWT." *Advertising Age,* June 17, 1997.

Wilke, Michael. "Kodak, JWT Snap Closer with Advantix Push." *Advertising Age,* February 5, 1996.

———. "Kodak Tries Humorous Tack in $60 Mil Advantix Effort: Ads Strive to Create Human Attachment to New Tech." *Advertising Age,* June 9, 1997.

Susan Risland

THE BEST PART OF PHOTOGRAPHY IS THE PRINTS CAMPAIGN

OVERVIEW

One of the most successful brands in the history of the United States, Eastman Kodak Company, whose founder had invented popular photography in the 1880s, was slipping as it entered the twenty-first century. Although it was a pioneer in the development of digital photography, Kodak had continued to focus on its highly profitable film products, conceding much of the digital-photography market to a host of competitors. Realizing it was falling behind, the company in 2003 decided to concentrate on its digital lines. To promote Kodak's easy-to-use printing systems—which were available through either self-service kiosks or camera docks that connected to a personal computer—Kodak and its advertising agency, Ogilvy & Mather Worldwide, launched a campaign in 2004 titled "The Best Part of Photography Is the Prints."

The campaign's print and television advertisements played off the question "Where are my pictures?"—touching upon the frustrations many digital-camera users encountered when trying to get hard copies of the photos they had taken. The commercials targeted women, who, according to market research, took the vast majority of family pictures and maintained the family photo albums.

The "Best Part of Photography Is the Prints" campaign won a 2005 EFFIE award and helped Kodak to increase the sales of its digital lines. But as the sale of traditional film products eroded further, the company continued to struggle financially. In the hopes of reestablishing its prominent position in the shifting photography marketplace, the company in 2005 replaced the campaign with a new marketing effort promoting Kodak's cutting-edge digital cameras.

HISTORICAL CONTEXT

Kodak had essentially invented the amateur photography industry in the 1880s, when bank clerk George Eastman founded the Eastman Dry Plate and Film Company and introduced the first Kodak brand camera. From the start the company proved to be a savvy marketer, as evidenced by its initial slogan, "You press the button—we do the rest." While Kodak made money from the sale of cameras and especially from its film, over the decades the company wisely associated itself with the picture-taking process and lifestyle rather than with the merchandise—which included many innovative items, such as the $1 Brownie camera in 1900 (with film costing 15 cents a roll), the world's first true color negative film in 1942, and the Instamatic camera in 1963. Kodak embraced television advertising early on, establishing fruitful relationships with television stars such as Ozzie and Harriet Nelson, variety show host Ed Sullivan, and sitcom actor Dick Van Dyke. The company later employed campaigns urging consumers to put "open me first" cards on Christmas presents containing Kodak cameras so that pictures could be taken when the rest of the presents were opened. Kodak's marketing triumphs peaked in the early 1990s, when it tapped into the vernacular phrase "Kodak moment" to promote its cameras and film. But with the rise of digital photography people began to seriously question whether Kodak's moment had come and gone.

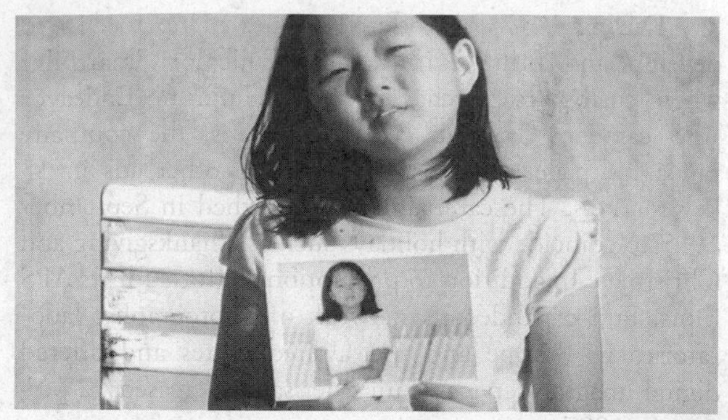

A still from "The Best Part of Photography Is the Prints" campaign. EASTMAN KODAK. REPRODUCED BY PERMISSION.

Ironically, although Kodak was a pioneer in digital camera technology, garnering a number of key patents, the general public was mostly unaware of these accomplishments. The company, failing to anticipate how quickly digital technology would surpass traditional cameras and film, allowed a number of companies, some with no association with cameras at all, to stake significant claims in the growing new market.

In the mid-1990s Kodak dropped its longtime advertising agency, J. Walter Thompson Company, in favor of Ogilvy & Mather and attempted a corporate makeover to appeal to younger consumers. But Kodak still gave short shrift to digital photography by continuing to emphasize traditional photography and film, especially in China and in developing countries in Eastern Europe. Revenues began to erode, declining four years in a row by 2003, and the price of Kodak stock followed suit. The company found itself at a crossroads: it could either remain in the high-profit-margin film business or fully commit to digital technology, where margins were lower and, like those of all high-tech electronics, dropping. To complicate matters, Kodak lacked the reputation in digital it had enjoyed for so many years in traditional photography.

In September 2003 the company announced it was casting its lot with digital technology. Money that had gone to promoting the film business in developed markets would instead be directed toward selling such technologies as ink-jet printers and high-end digital printing. A large number of digital-camera users were not making prints of their photographs, but Kodak believed that eventually they would see the value of having hard copies. Sensing an opportunity, the company decided to emphasize its kiosk printers and home-printing camera docks, which became the focal point of the campaign, titled "The Best Part of Photography Is the Prints." In a larger sense, however, Kodak wanted to position itself as a player in the entire digital process, from capturing the image to outputting it.

DON'T MESS WITH THE CLOTHES

The founder of the Eastman Kodak Company, George Eastman, was a frugal bank bookkeeper whose only extravagance was photographic equipment, which at the time included heavy glass plates and chemicals. According to lore, during a vacation he made the mistake of packing the chemicals along with his clothes, which were ruined by a leak. Disgruntled by the wet-plate process that had cost him part of his wardrobe, he examined the new dry-plate process—which had emerged only a few years earlier—and soon perfected a longer-lasting version. Eastman next eliminated the glass altogether, coating paper with gelatin and photographic emulsion and rolling it on a spool. He then invented a simple camera to use the film. He called it the Kodak, a word without meaning but one that quickly became associated with popular photography.

TARGET MARKET

While in general Kodak's "Best Part of Photography Is the Prints" campaign was aimed at all digital-camera users, the company had a more specific target in mind: wives and mothers. Kodak research had revealed that 70 to 80 percent of family pictures were taken by women. Moreover women were generally the keepers of family memories and maintained the photo albums. It was with women in mind that the company had earlier introduced its EasyShare system, which included a camera, software, and an easy-to-use dock for transferring pictures to a computer. Later it offered an EasyShare printer dock, which allowed photos to be printed straight from a camera, without using a computer. The company said that women generally placed the printer dock in the kitchen and often took it with them as a party printer. But as Carl E. Gustin, Jr., Kodak's chief marketing officer, explained to Claudia H. Deutsch of the *New York Times,* the company also realized that the target customer would want a printing option that did not involve owning a home ink-jet printer. He stated, "So if digital photography and printing is going to be a truly mass phenomenon, then self-service retail has to be a big part of it." Thus promoting Kodak's kiosks at retail stores was also a priority for the company and the new marketing campaign.

According to Beth Snyder Bulik, writing for *Advertising Age,* the target audience was "women, ranging from teens to grandmothers." Because consumers in the younger demographic tended to E-mail pictures to one another and to view Kodak as a stodgy brand, the company had decided not to pursue this group aggressively. Nevertheless Kodak also hoped to begin connecting with young people by promoting its cutting-edge technology. For example, Kodak possessed high-definition OLED (organic light-emitting diode) display technology, which allowed for thinner cameras and mobile phones with picture-taking capabilities. The company was optimistic that when tech-savvy members of the younger generation began to realize the implications of this and other Kodak innovations, they would begin to change their view of the brand.

COMPETITION

Kodak faced competition in the digital arena on a number of fronts. Its digital cameras competed against established camera companies, such as Canon, Fuji, Minolta, and Olympus, but also against newcomers, such as Hewlett-Packard, LG Electronics, Nokia, Samsung, and Sony. All of the latter group had arrived in the photography market via their successes in digital technology and had the deep pockets to support aggressive marketing campaigns. On the home-printing front Kodak's main competitor was market leader Hewlett-Packard (although Kodak led in the sale of the ink-jet paper on which digital photos were printed).

Digital pictures that were saved on memory cards and CDs could also be dropped off like film rolls at a local photo shop or drugstore counter for processing, but increasingly consumers were turning to do-it-yourself digital-photo kiosks where pictures could be selected, edited, and printed on the spot. It was in this category that Kodak was able to leverage its brand to establish itself as a major player in the digital-photography industry. It forged alliances with drugstore chains, such as CVS in the United States and Boots in the United Kingdom, and with superstores, such as Wal-Mart and Target. Nevertheless kiosks remained a competitive sector, the direct competition coming from the likes of Polaroid, Olympus, PMI/KIS, IBM, Mitsubishi, Sony, and a host of smaller companies.

MARKETING STRATEGY

Kodak continued to follow its century-long strategy of playing up the lifestyle of taking pictures rather than the cameras or film themselves. The difference was that digital products were made the priority, and Kodak allocated the necessary resources to promote them. According to TNS Media Intelligence, out of the $109 million Kodak spent in 2004 on measured media (that is, TV, radio, and print), $71 million was devoted to digital cameras, home-printing solutions, and self-service kiosks. The thrust of the "Best Part of Photography Is the Prints" campaign, composed of both television and print elements, was on ease of use, in particular in printing digital photos. This was a market, unlike digital cameras, where Kodak could truly use the strength of its brand to its advantage. In a three-month companion campaign developed by HSR Business to Business, Cincinnati, the Kodak Professional unit promoted its line of digital-photo printers through print ads aimed at professional photographers.

Nicola Bell, worldwide executive group director at Ogilvy & Mather, told Claudia H. Deutsch of the *New York Times,* "Our research shows that even people who love their digital cameras are still frustrated about how to get prints." The strategy of the new television spots was relatively straightforward. "We have to position the kiosks as friendly little machines that guarantee good, long-lived pictures," Bell explained.

Writing for *Advertising Age,* Beth Snyder Bulik maintained that the strategy of the new campaign could be encapsulated in the question asked in each ad: "Where are my pictures?" She interviewed Pierre Schaeffer, Kodak's vice president and director of business strategy and marketing services, who said that many people could relate to the catchphrase, adding, "There has been a brainwashing in digital cameras that suggests you need to be a computer expert. We try to break that image... ' You press a button, we do the rest. We're the experts in photography, you don't have to be.' "

The "Best Part of Photography Is the Prints" campaign broke in late May 2004. In the new TV spots Kodak customers talked about how they loved digital photography but lamented the fact that they never actually got their photos printed. One commercial featured the EasyShare digital camera and printer dock. Another promoted the picture maker kiosk. In the *International Herald Tribune,* Deutsch described the commercials as featuring "a panoply of people—young and old, male and female, black and white and Asian—professing love for their digital cameras. Then it pans to one young man crying plaintively, 'Where are my pictures?' The answer, of course, is readily at hand—if he would only go to his local self-service kiosk and make them." Other TV spots focused on consumers using the EasyShare printer dock at home.

The campaign's print ads also divided their focus between the self-service kiosks and the easy-to-use home printer dock. Other aspects of the campaign included monthly educational E-mail newsletters, a holiday mailing, and booths at NASCAR races.

OUTCOME

Kodak's Schaeffer told *Advertising Age* that the different elements of the company's "Best Part of Photography Is the Prints" campaign "all paid off big-time." Kodak gained U.S. market share on Sony, improving from 15.3 to 18.3 percent in the first half of 2004. On the kiosk side of the business, Kodak was enjoying tremendous growth, due in large measure to advertising and to the distribution of Kodak kiosks throughout the marketplace. Not to be discounted, however, was the quality of the product, which ranked at or near the top of the three different categories defined by the Digital Imaging Marketing Association: stand-alone units, kiosks linked to remote printing equipment, and combination kiosks that could either print locally or send files to a remote digital-photo minilab for development. Also of great importance was that an increasing number of people were turning to kiosks for their prints. According to market research about 39 percent of digital-camera users tried kiosks in 2004 compared with 28 percent in 2003. The campaign also garnered recognition for Ogilvy & Mather, which won a bronze in the Consumer Electronics category at the 2005 EFFIE Awards, given out annually by the New York American Marketing Association in recognition of the year's most effective advertising campaigns.

Kodak made strides in positioning itself in the digital marketplace in 2004, and its digital sales were growing at a strong clip, but the traditional film business was slipping even faster than expected, putting additional pressure on Kodak's marketers to promote the digital lines to make up for shrinking film sales. In the first quarter of

2005 Kodak generated sales of $2.83 billion, down from the $2.92 billion it had reported for the same period a year earlier. In the second quarter the company suffered a net loss of $143 million. Ogilvy & Mather's next major market effort, launched in 2005, pursued the theme "Keep it forever. Keep it Kodak," another attempt to retain Kodak's connection to the past while portraying the company as an innovator. In addition Kodak was undergoing a large makeover that ranged from revamping product design and styling to updating operating systems.

FURTHER READING

Bulik, Beth Snyder. "Kodak EasyShare." *Advertising Age,* November 2004, p. S2.

———. "Kodak Scores with Digital Cameras but Film-Biz Losses Cloud Big Pictures." *Advertising Age,* April 25, 2005, p. 4.

———. "Sony, Kodak Lead U.S. Battle for Share in Digital Cameras." *Advertising Age,* May 31, 2004, p. 12.

Denn, Rebekah. "Digital Photo Kiosks Are Dandy, but Not All Are Created Equal." *Seattle Post-Intelligence,* November 30, 2004.

Deutsch, Claudia H. "Get the Pictures?" *International Herald Tribune,* July 21, 2004, p. 16.

———. "The Post-film Photo Industry Promotes Kiosks for Turning Digital Images into Print." *New York Times,* July 20, 2004, p. C9.

Howard, Theresa. "Kodak Ads Build Up Its Digital Image." *USA Today,* August 18, 2005.

Jardine, Alexandra. "Is This a Kodak Moment?" *Marketing,* October 13, 2004, p. 28.

Wasserman, Todd. "Kodak Focuses on Processing." *Brandweek,* May 24, 2004, p. 15.

Ed Dinger

TAKE PICTURES. FURTHER. CAMPAIGN

OVERVIEW

In the mid-1990s the Eastman Kodak Company was not just the leading manufacturer of photographic film, paper, and chemicals; it was listed as one of the top companies in America. In both 1996 and 1997 the stock-market researcher EquiTrend selected Kodak as the number one brand for quality in the United States. At that time digital photography had not yet reached critical mass, and Kodak wanted to promote its new Kodak Advantix Photo System. Advantix was pitched as an "error-free, drop-in film" that allowed consumers to download film images onto a computer. At the same time camera makers such as Canon Inc. and Sony Corporation were developing digital cameras. Hoping to brand Kodak for a younger market and promote Advantix, Kodak released its "Take Pictures. Further" campaign.

The television, radio, outdoor, and print campaign was funded by Kodak's $100 million marketing budget and debuted in April 1996. Created by the ad agency Ogilvy & Mather of New York, the campaign was separated into different executions. "Anthem" consisted of five 60- and 30-second spots with the actor Luke Perry repeatedly answering the question "What can a picture be?" The second execution, titled "Tall Tales," featured two 60-second commercials that each told a story through images. Campaign spots that were not connected to "Anthem" or "Tall Tales" aired later. The headline in an advertisement in *People* magazine asked, "Isn't it time you had a new box to keep your pictures in?" A second magazine ad featured a photograph of workers mining vivid yellow sulfur on a steaming volcano. The text explained that Kodak Ektachrome Elite II amateur slide film could capture vibrant, pure colors under varying light conditions. The campaign officially ended in March 2001.

"Take Pictures. Further" began just as digital photography was entering the mainstream culture. Advantix was not as popular as Kodak had expected. From 1999 to 2001 the company's sales dropped from $14.1 billion to $13.2 billion. Because the campaign branded Kodak with film technologies instead of emerging digital technologies, the advertising community blamed it for outdating the Kodak brand while digital photography blossomed.

HISTORICAL CONTEXT

Kodak traced its roots to Eastman Dry Plate Company, founded in 1880 by George Eastman and Henry Strong. Dry plates represented a significant improvement over the chemically treated wet plates of glass that photographers had previously used to expose one picture at a time in their cameras, a procedure that required considerable expertise. In 1884 the company patented the first roll film, a long strip of paper coated with emulsion that was sensitive to light. In 1888 Eastman began marketing the Kodak, a portable box camera that cost $25 and was loaded with enough film for 100 pictures. The invention of this type of camera and film was important in the growth of the motion-picture industry, and it opened the field of photography to amateurs.

Emphasizing that its new cameras were simple enough for the average consumer to use, Eastman Company advertised with the slogan "You push the button, we do the rest." At the turn of the century the firm increased its mass-market appeal by introducing a small Kodak camera called the Brownie at the inexpensive price of $1. By that time the enterprise was known as Eastman Kodak Company. Among its many noteworthy innovations were the introduction of color film in 1935 and the launch of the Kodak Instamatic camera in 1963. Ease of use remained a primary theme in the company's marketing efforts. "Kodak Instamatic Cameras load instantly! Automatically shoot and take sharp, clear pictures time after time!" said an advertisement in *Good Housekeeping.* "No threading. No fumbling. No rewinding."

With a market share that averaged 60 to 70 percent, Kodak led the industry for decades. By 1997 it was one of the 25 largest companies in the United States. Its products included photography equipment and supplies, film, projectors, and copiers. Units such as Sterling Drug had been acquired over the years but were divested in the early 1990s as part of a general overhaul that focused the company on imaging products. During the late 1990s the firm kept up with changing technology by rapidly expanding and improving its digital equipment and services. These innovations allowed consumers to store their photographs on compact or floppy disks, view them and alter them on computer screens, and transmit them over the Internet. Kodak offered numerous state-of-the-art products and services, and it formed marketing alliances with companies such as America Online and Intel Corporation to encourage customers to use their photographs in new ways.

Over the years Kodak had cultivated a family-oriented image with advertising that revolved around the "Kodak moment," a portrait of a consumer capturing a heartwarming experience on film. Many people were not aware, however, that Kodak offered more than film and cameras. In addition, research showed that consumers thought the company was old-fashioned. In 1996 Kodak released the "Take Pictures. Further" campaign to change its image and to publicize its many products along with the possibilities they offered to consumers.

TARGET MARKET

Kodak had cultivated a loyal following among consumers at least 35 years old, but it was not particularly appealing to most younger people. The new corporate-image campaign was intended to retain Kodak's traditional customers while reaching teenagers and young adults, with a particular emphasis on consumers who were interested in mastering the most recent technologies. The first advertisements to use the "Take Pictures. Further" theme were aimed at the parents (ages 25 to 55) of school-age children, at young adults who used computers and had a college education (ages 18 to 34), and at business managers and department heads (ages 35 to 64). These ads promoted products such as Image Magic service, which allowed consumers to crop and enlarge their photographs using Advantix, and the Fun Saver, a camera designed to be used only one time. Later advertisements also showcased innovative products. "Introducing the easiest way to get your pictures into your PC. The new Kodak Advantix film drive," said a magazine ad that ran in 1998.

Some advertisements targeted the company's core clientele of snap shooters 25 to 54 years old, primarily women, who took pictures to remember events such as birthday parties and family vacations. Kodak had become the industry leader by making it easy for people to take good photographs, and as the company introduced digital cameras and other innovations, its advertising assured consumers that photography would still be easy and more fun than ever. One advertisement in *Travel & Leisure* promoted Kodak Max film with the headline "I don't care about f-stops. I don't care about shutter speeds. I just want to take a picture." The ad showed three badly exposed photographs labeled "Before Kodak Max" and three correctly exposed photographs labeled "After Kodak Max."

By showing new ways for people to enjoy their photographs, Kodak encouraged its customers to do more with their pictures than toss them in a drawer or file them away in a photo album. Of the 70 to 80 billion photographs that Americans snapped each year, only 2 percent were reprinted or enlarged. The "Take Pictures. Further" campaign urged consumers to use new technology such as E-mail to share photographs with their families and friends, to incorporate more photographs into documents created on their computers, and to improve photographs by altering their appearance. In addition to promoting Kodak's digital products and services, the campaign was intended to revive interest in traditional film and cameras by explaining the many ways that average people could work with visual images.

KODAK.COM

Kodak's home page on the Internet (http://www.kodak.com) was redesigned in 1998 with easier navigation and expanded content. It included a new section called "Further," which targeted consumers who were adept at using the latest technology. It was one of the few marketing efforts by Kodak in 1998 that connected Kodak's brand to digital photography. The website section explained how consumers could use digital photography, animation, and other innovations. Kodak.com also contained articles for general audiences. The site had been launched in 1995, received more than 66 million page views in 1997, and consisted of more than 25,000 pages by 1998.

COMPETITION

One of Kodak's primary rivals was a company with headquarters in Japan, Fuji Photo Film U.S.A. Both Kodak and Fuji made film and photographic papers for professionals and amateurs, both firms had acquired large film processing companies nationwide to increase their share of the photo-finishing market, and both had begun manufacturing products such as digital cameras to compete in the emerging field of digital technology. Fuji had earned a reputation for low prices and high quality. In the spring of 1997 it suddenly slashed the price of its film, saying that one of its largest distributors had switched to Kodak and left Fuji with 2.5 million rolls of excess film to sell. During that summer Kodak's film sometimes cost as much as 30 percent more than Fuji's. According to *Brandweek,* Kodak's share of the $3 billion U.S. film market slipped from 85 percent in 1988 to about 70 percent by the summer of 1997 and 65 percent by June 1998. Fuji had about 15 percent of the film market in 1998, up from 10 percent in 1996, and it also controlled about 15 percent of the photo-finishing market. Lacking the brand loyalty that Kodak had cultivated over the years, Fuji attempted to strengthen its corporate brand image in 1998 with an advertising campaign that used bright colors, surreal scenes, and the slogan "You can see the future from here."

Kodak also competed with companies that made cameras and related products. In 1998 Canon U.S.A. promoted its Advanced Photo System camera, the ELPH, with the tagline "So advanced . . . it's simple." The company's "Wildlife as Canon Sees It" series of magazine ads featured large, beautiful photographs of wildlife above text that characterized each animal and mentioned Canon's efforts to protect endangered species. Each ad included a small photograph and description of a Canon product. Another camera maker, Pentax Corporation, asked, "Aren't your pictures worth a Pentax?" The campaign showed customers explaining that they had been able to take spectacular photographs thanks to certain features on their Pentax cameras. Minolta Corporation continued its "Only from the Mind of Minolta" campaign, while Olympus America Inc. used the slogan "Focus on Life."

MARKETING STRATEGY

Kodak had been using 200 advertising agencies worldwide but reduced that number to 4 during a general restructuring of its marketing program in 1994 and 1995. The company then increased its advertising expenditures for film, cameras, and its first image campaign. Kodak's U.S. advertising budget was $65.4 million in 1994, $82 million in 1995, and about $100 million from 1996 through 1998. Each of the four agencies (Ogilvy & Mather, J. Walter Thompson, Uniworld, and Saatchi & Saatchi) promoted a specific group of products, with the separate advertising campaigns all using the new slogan "Take Pictures. Further." Ogilvy & Mather was responsible for the overall corporate-image effort. Kodak's trademark yellow served as the dominant color in the advertisements, helping to unify the brand message. In print ads the tagline was positioned beside or below the red and yellow Kodak logo, often near the address of the company's home page on the Internet, which was also designed around the "Take Pictures. Further" theme.

The tagline first appeared in advertisements designed by J. Walter Thompson to publicize Kodak's new Advantix camera and accessories, which were launched in April 1996. Ogilvy & Mather handled the Advantix campaign in 1997 and 1998, still using the "Take Pictures. Further" slogan. Ads for Advantix products explained that the camera could take pictures in three sizes, that it featured drop-in film loading, and that the consumer received an index print when the film was developed. In 1997 Kodak spent about $60 million to advertise the Advantix brand in the United States. Ogilvy & Mather also created the "Tall Tales" execution, which had a budget of $20 to $40 million and ran during 1996 and 1997. These humorous scenarios, which aired on television and at movie theaters, showed people using products and services such as Kodak Gold and Max films and Kodak premium processing. One spot showed a young man accidentally photographing a flying saucer, then being pursued by government agents and rescued by space aliens. In another spot a consumer used Kodak's Image Magic digital enhancement station to hide the dents in a photograph of a Gremlin automobile.

Many executions in the "Take Pictures. Further" campaign emphasized Kodak's digital products. A two-page ad in *Reader's Digest* in 1998 featured a photograph of three boys playing soccer. The headline read, "Your son was a blur as he raced down the field. But every detail will be crystal clear when you print out your pictures." The opposite page showed a digital camera with text explaining that the product allowed consumers to preview pictures, delete whatever they disliked, store the

OUTDOOR ADVERTISING

The "Take Pictures. Further" theme was used in the Kodak Image Expo at the 1996 Olympic Games and on kiosks and signs at Turner Field, the ballpark of the Atlanta Braves professional baseball team.

digital images on a picture card, use a computer to E-mail them to family and friends, and print them on high-quality paper. An ad in *People* magazine in 1998 also showed boys playing soccer next to the headline "This kick went clear across the country." A coupon was included, inviting consumers to try Kodak PhotoNet (an online service for E-mailing photographs, ordering reprints, and purchasing gifts via the Internet) or Kodak Picture disk (a floppy disk that allowed consumers to view photographs on their computer monitors and incorporate pictures into documents).

Kodak continued to use the slogan in new advertising campaigns during the late 1990s to promote three digital-imaging products that allowed amateurs to enlarge or crop their photographs, remove the red that flash photography sometimes caused in a subject's eyes, add messages to the image, and place decorative borders around their pictures. Noting an increase in the number of teenage consumers, Kodak began slanting more of its U.S. advertising toward teenage girls. One spot, titled "Tattoo," featured a girl who wanted a tattoo. Adhering to her mother's advice to "shoot your friends' tattoos, and we'll look at the options," she used an Advantix camera to photograph four different tattoos she liked. After having a nightmare in which the phrase "Viva Macarena" was tattooed across her forehead, the teen decided against getting a tattoo.

Unifying its global advertisements, the company launched its first worldwide image campaign in 1999. The effort built on the earlier campaign's "Tall Tales" commercials and featured more fantastic stories told through photographs taken with Kodak products.

OUTCOME

During the six-year span of "Take Pictures. Further," Kodak's uncontested dominance over the photography industry began to wane. The enterprise lost business not to other film companies but to the skyrocketing popularity of digital photography. According to Kodak executives and advertising analysts, the problem with "Take Pictures. Further" was that it failed to promote Kodak's own advancements in digital technology. In 1996 Kodak was one of the first companies to introduce a range of pocket-size digital cameras. Instead of marketing the digital cameras, however, Kodak promoted Advantix, which did not offer as many features as digital photography and cost more for consumers to develop. Belinda Parmar, an Ogilvy & Mather representative who worked on the campaign, told *Marketing* that Kodak's greatest problem was that "[i]t may have promising digital technology, but it has failed to communicate this effectively and convince consumers that Kodak is a digital brand."

Sales for Kodak steadily declined during the campaign's final three years. Kodak released several digital cameras throughout this period, but technology critics believed that digital Kodak cameras lacked the functionality and form of cameras made by Sony and Canon. In 2001 Kodak also made a late entry into online photo development with its launch of www.Ofoto.com, a website onto which consumers could upload their digital images and later receive the printed images in the mail. Kodak was offering digital products, but its campaign pushed the more expensive and less popular film products. "Kodak is well placed to become a success in home printing, particularly as the sector moves from high-end to mass market," Parmar continued in *Marketing*. "But first," she said, "it must focus its marketing communication on why, rather than how, people print out digital."

FURTHER READING

Crain, Rance. "Capturing the Kodak Moment Fast Becoming a Sad Memory." *Advertising Age,* November 24, 1997, p. 25.

Desmond, Edward W. "What's Ailing Kodak?." *Fortune,* October 27, 1997, p. 185.

Freeman, Laurie. "Shooting for Share." *Supermarket Business,* February 1999, p. 47.

Gelsi, Steve. "Putting the Big Picture Back in Focus: Kodak, Revamping Staff and Budget, Takes an Edgy Tack to Get Back on the Growth Track." *Brandweek,* November 25, 1996, p. 18.

Jardine, Alexandra. "Kodak: Is This a Kodak Moment?" *Marketing,* October 13, 2004, p. 28.

Kim, Hank. "Ogilvy Helming Global Kodak Effort." *Adweek* (eastern ed.), November 23, 1998, p. 5.

"Momentous Shifts." *Brandweek,* June 1, 1998, p. 26.

Panczyk, Tania D. "HSR Set to Push Kodak to Pros." *Adweek,* November 25, 2002.

Street, Rita. "Making Pretty Pictures Hip." *Shoot,* October 18, 1996, p. 25.

Susan Risland
Kevin Teague

TALL TALES CAMPAIGN

OVERVIEW

In the early 1990s Kodak, the venerable photo products company, found itself in increasing difficulties. Despite a long history of pioneering products and dominating the market, the company was up against strong competition, and it also faced rapidly changing new technology. In trying to keep up, Kodak had ventured unsuccessfully outside its core market of imaging, which for Kodak included photography, digital imaging, color management systems, and image and document storage systems.

In this digital age most consumers were unaware that Kodak had digital products; rather, Kodak was seen as the "yellow box" company. By 1993 Kodak posted a $1.5 million loss. The company still dominated in film sales, but it was perceived as old-fashioned and out of touch with younger consumers.

The company took several steps to revitalize its image. It created the tag line "Take Pictures. Further" for all of its advertising in order to show consumers the many possibilities available to them in taking and developing their photos. Kodak also turned to the New York advertising agency Ogilvy & Mather to create the "Tall Tales" corporate brand campaign for television, the first such effort for Kodak. The campaign had a twofold objective: to establish the Kodak brand as one offering a multitude of possibilities for pictures and to make the company more relevant to potential new customers in the generation X age group.

"Tall Tales" was made up of two series of spots, each minimovies of 60 seconds, which ran during 1996 and 1997 on television and at movie theaters. The 1996 series was highly successful, winning a Gold Effie and a number of other awards. In 1997 Kodak followed with a second set of "Tall Tales."

HISTORICAL CONTEXT

Kodak was founded in 1881 by George Eastman and became a household name and market leader with the introduction of the Brownie camera in 1900, color film in 1935 and, above all, the Kodak Instamatic camera in 1963. Eastman believed in reaching ordinary people, and his mission was to make photography, then a cumbersome procedure, something anybody could do and enjoy. "You push the button, we do the rest" was the Kodak slogan, and it was a tremendous success. It made Kodak far and away the market leader for a century, maintaining a 60-70 percent market share.

When CEO George Fisher took over the reins at Kodak at the end of 1993, his goal was to refocus Kodak on what it does best. He was in a sense returning to the vision of George Eastman but placing his efforts firmly in the context of digital technology—meaning the use of computers and other digital media to create, manipulate, send, and store images. Fisher began selling off the new ventures that had led the company off its path—which had included Sterling Drug, L&F Products (makers of Lysol and related products), and the Clinical Diagnostics division—and refocused the company on imaging.

Kodak's marketing dilemma was that it had failed to position itself as a digital imaging innovator. Surveys showed that few consumers were even aware that Kodak had digital products. Indeed, as the magazine *Sales and Marketing Management* reported in early 1997, only very technology-savvy consumers were aware of the range of possibilities for enhancing photographs. During the 1990s, of the 60 million photos that were taken annually around the world, fewer than 2 percent were enlarged, manipulated, hung for display, or used commercially. Most went into a photo album or shoe box.

To resolve this dilemma Fisher created the new position of Chief Marketing Officer and in 1995 appointed Carl Gustin to fill it. Gustin left a position with the computer giant Apple to join Kodak and had also worked for a number of prestigious marketing agencies. Thus, he embodied exactly the talents Fisher sought to position Kodak for the digital age. The marketing department led by Gustin sat atop the business units and created centralized corporate branding and strategic planning. The new system was a dramatic change for Kodak. Whereas formerly each business division had carried out single-product advertising, Kodak changed to system advertising, which was planned through the corporate marketing division.

"Our goal is to go beyond 'You push the button' and take customers toward a future where they 'Take pictures. Further'," Fisher told *Sales and Marketing Management.* "But we'll do this in a way that makes it just as easy to take pictures further as it was to push the button. We want our imaging technology to be easy to use. Consumers want more and better pictures, not technology for its own sake."

TARGET MARKET

The "Tall Tales" campaign was directed at three separate and distinct groups. It focused first on parents of school-age children. More specifically, this group, generally 25 to 55 years old, was college-educated, used a PC at home, often subscribed to an on-line service, and took pictures. The group was also thought to influence the technology decisions of mainstream Kodak consumers who were less comfortable with technology.

A second major focus group was the "wired generation," adults 18 to 34 years old who were college-educated and PC and Internet users. It was thought that this group influenced other young consumers, as well as technology providers. Finally, the campaign focused on business managers and department heads, aged 35 to 64, who might have been part of the decision-making process for technology purchases in medium and large businesses. This group was likely to influence the technology considerations of fellow business executives, managers, and employees. All three groups were considered influential in the "Information Age."

KODAK OUT OF THE PICTURE IN JAPAN

In 1995 Kodak filed a petition with the United States government (under section 301 of the Trade Act of 1974) asking the government to investigate and remedy what it saw as anti-competitive trade practices in the Japanese market for consumer photographic film and paper. Japan was the second-largest market for consumer photographic products in the world, but Kodak's share of the film market there was less than 10 percent. The company had a much higher market share in other industrialized nations, including other Asian countries. The company said that its market research had shown that Japanese consumers were aware of the Kodak brand but cited "lack of availability" as their primary reason for not trying Kodak products.

Kodak's position in the conflict was strengthened in mid-1996, when an investigation by the U.S. trade representative confirmed the existence of trade barriers to imports of photographic film and paper in Japan. In February 1997 the U.S. government filed suit against Japan with the World Trade Organization (WTO) in Geneva, charging the government of Japan with preventing foreign importers from gaining a meaningful share of the Japanese market for consumer photographic products. The WTO ruled against Kodak later that year, but in early 1998 the U.S. government announced that it would hold the government of Japan to market access commitments it had made during the course of the dispute.

COMPETITION

For much of its history Kodak had been without serious competition. However, the company met with new threats to its market position, during the 1970s and 1980s. Companies like Fuji and Konica successfully entered the film business and companies like Microsoft, Apple, Sony, and Hewlett Packard became leaders in the arena of new technologies. Because Kodak initially failed to position itself as a player in the digital age, it posed little threat to key digital competitors. Few consumers saw Kodak as a forward-thinking and innovative company; many did not even know of Kodak's digital products and services. But Kodak retained strong brand recognition. In 1996, for example, branding expert Interbrand Schechter Inc. called it the world's fourth strongest brand, surpassed only by McDonald's, Coca-Cola, and Disney.

Kodak saw Fuji as a particularly strong competitor in the film business. The two companies engaged in a protracted dispute over Kodak's share in the Japanese film market during the 1990s, with Kodak asserting that it had been denied a fair chance to reach out to Japanese consumers. Although Kodak lost the battle legally, it had the backing of the U.S. government and was able to wring some concessions from the Japanese government.

MARKETING STRATEGY

Prior to the "Tall Tales" campaign, Kodak had used single-product advertising, parceling out its $300 million advertising budget among some 200 agencies worldwide. By 1996 Gustin had consolidated these 200 agencies to four: Ogilvy & Mather, J. Walter Thompson, Uniworld, and Saatchi & Saatchi, assigning each to focus on specific products worldwide. In a further consolidation, Ogilvy & Mather became the sole agency for the "Tall Tales" executions, which combined product and image advertising in Kodak's first-ever corporate brand campaign.

The campaign had very specific goals. It sought to position Kodak as a digital technology innovator among those most influential in the Information Age; to develop Kodak brand awareness among the young wired generation, a good number of whom did not own cameras; and to increase awareness that Kodak had digital imaging products for both home and business uses.

The point of the campaign, which cost between $20 million and $40 million, was to convince the target groups that Kodak could best help them unleash the power of pictures. Kodak's products were perceived by consumers as being both reliable and of high quality, and evoked images of family values. On the other hand, consumers also saw Kodak as an old-fashioned and stodgy company that mostly made little yellow boxes of film to capture "Kodak moments." The campaign sought to draw on the long-held positive values to reposition Kodak as an innovative company more focused on the future than on treasured moments of the past. At the same time, Kodak was concerned that it not alienate its core group of older consumers. In other words, the campaign needed to promise the digital future without abandoning a long and worthy heritage.

During the first phase of the "Tall Tales" campaign, buses at the 1996 Olympic Games in Atlanta carried Kodak advertising, and a CD-ROM containing video clips and company materials was distributed to selected members of the press. The campaign included Internet marketing as well. The Kodak website was redesigned around the "Take Pictures. Further" theme for both 1996 and 1997.

The 1997 series consisted of three "60-second movies" that linked life events with Kodak products. Among the products and services the campaign showcased were the Funsaver single-use camera, Kodak premium processing, Kodak Gold film with color sharp technology, Gold Max film, and Image Magic cropping and enlarging features.

In the first television spot, "Tattoo," a teenager desires a tattoo. Rather than prohibiting it outright, her mother proposes a compromise: she can photograph her friends' tattoos, and they will study the results together. The girl uses a Kodak camera to take snapshots of her friends' tattoos: Mickey's bulldog, Rachel's rose, Daphne's lizard, and Uncle Leo's faded and indecipherable "something." That night she awakens screaming from a nightmare in which "Viva Macarena" is tattooed onto her forehead. To her mother's visible relief, she announces the next day that she has decided to forego the entire project. In another spot, called "Saturday," a bouncy teenager takes pictures of scenes from an ordinary suburban day. Her bright and colorful pictures of feet, socks, a dog, and a bowl of cereal are fun and offbeat, and unexpectedly a museum curator offers the young photographer $100,000 to exhibit them. She accepts eagerly and basks in the spotlight of instant fame. Finally, in "Stacy" a young man sweeps his girlfriend off her feet with a digitally enhanced Kodak photo, paving the way for the couple's dreams of marriage and a long life together.

Specific network, cable, and syndicated programs made up the television media plan. The airings were planned to reach viewers of lighter television shows and those with an interest in technology and innovation. "Tattoo" had its prime-time debut on the *Drew Carey Show* on March 12, 1997; "Saturday" made its first appearance also on March 12 on the Fox Network; and "Stacy" premiered on *The Simpsons* on March 9. "Saturday" was also shown during the Academy Awards on March 24. The broadcast schedule ran May through July 1996 and during March 1997.

OUTCOME

Kodak executives viewed the "Tall Tales" campaign of 1996 and 1997 a success, declaring that the campaign had effectively redefined Kodak as a serious player in the Information Age. A 16-country tracking study showed a 3 percent gain in brand equity (or confidence in the brand), which the company attributed to "re-energizing, rather than abandoning a focus on memories," as CEO Fisher expressed it in a letter to the magazine *Advertising Age.* The campaign's commercials of 1996, which won a Gold Effie, registered an "enjoyability" score higher than 97 percent of all spots ever tested by Millward Brown International (MBI). In the category "uniqueness," "Tall Tales" received the best MBI score ever. Post campaign ad surveys by MBI Ad Trackers found that target consumers had changed their brand perceptions and that Kodak was seen as a more forward-thinking technological innovator after the campaign.

The wired generation also found more relevance in the Kodak brand. MBI found that the perception of the Kodak brand as "contemporary," "cool," and, above all, relevant rose by 25 percent in this group. Looking at the target audience as a whole, MBI found increased awareness that Kodak offered a variety of products for home and business users and that Kodak was more than just the "yellow box" company.

The campaign also had an immediate short-term effect on film sales for the second quarter of 1997. Still, despite the positive outlook, many financial experts felt it was too soon to judge the success of the "Tall Tales" campaign and questioned whether customers had truly accepted the company as a digital leader. "Kodak is in the midst of a long-term transition," Tom Graves of Standard & Poors told *Sales & Marketing Management.* "But if Kodak offers innovative, affordable products, it can be accepted as a leader in digital technologies."

FURTHER READING

Conlon, Ginger. "Getting into Focus: Carl Gustin is Leading Kodak's Effort to Reinvent Itself for the Future." *Sales & Marketing Management* January 1, 1997.

Gelsi, Steve. "Kodak Eyes Edgier Ads via Creative Consortium." *Brandweek* October 28, 1996.

Nelson, Emily, and Sally Goll Beatty. "Eastman Kodak Takes Thompson out of Picture, Focuses on Ogilvy." *The Wall Street Journal* June 17, 1997.

Wilke, Michael. "Kodak Studies 'Low' Interest by Kids: Working toward Global Ad Effort, Using Saatchi's Kid Connection." *Advertising Age,* April 14, 1997.

Susan M. Steiner

eBay Inc.

2145 Hamilton Avenue
San Jose, California 95125
USA
Telephone: (408) 376-7400
Fax: (408) 369-4855
Web site: www.ebay.com

ABBREVIATED CAMPAIGN

OVERVIEW

In 1995 eBay Inc. was founded in San Jose, California. It was an online site, located at www.ebay.com, that enabled users to buy and sell items from other users. Rather than sell items itself, eBay made money by charging fees on completed transactions and by charging for advertisements on its website. In 2003 more than 900 million items were posted for sale on eBay. These items included automobiles. Because of their relatively high prices, automobile sales generated larger fees than many other kinds of sales. In the arena of used-car sales, however, the company faced competition from online search engines such as Google and Yahoo! as well as from traditional newspaper advertisements.

EBay charged the ad agency Goodby, Silverstein & Partners, based in nearby San Francisco, with developing a radio spot that would inform consumers of the benefits of using eBay to sell automobiles. The result was a humorous 60-second spot called "Abbreviated." The spot featured a narrator using an "abbreviated" language culled from newspaper classified ads. Rather than just telling listeners that classified ads did not provide enough space to adequately describe an automobile, the narrator demonstrated this through his own speech. Then he touted the benefits of selling cars on eBay.

The spot was a hit with critics. In 2005 it won a Silver Lion at the International Advertising Festival, a 2005 Bronze Clio Award, and the top prize at the annual Radio Mercury Awards. These awards, however, came after eBay's decision in March 2005 to part ways with Goodby, Silverstein & Partners. The company elected to work with BBDO on future campaigns. EBay felt that the larger New York–based agency was better equipped to handle integrated campaigns that combined online, televised, and radio elements. Both agencies were part of the larger communications company the Omnicom Group.

HISTORICAL CONTEXT

The San Jose–based eBay was created to capitalize on the increasing expansion of the Internet into everyday life in the United States and around the world. The company provided sellers and consumers a platform where they could find each other and conduct transactions. Sellers offered a wide range of goods via the eBay website, www.ebay.com, including sneakers, automobiles, furniture, clothing, and collectibles. The site was best known for the online auctions that it enabled. Sellers posted an item on www.ebay.com, and buyers could view the item and bid on it. The highest bidder purchased the item.

As the Internet became more popular, eBay was able to expand quickly, and the company set up companion sites around the world. Soon eBay began describing itself as "The World's Online Marketplace." The company's profits came via fees it collected on each transaction as well as from advertising it sold on its assorted websites. The approach was largely successful, and in 2003 alone more than 900 million items were listed on eBay. By 2004 eBay was offering the PayPal service, which enabled buyers to pay sellers through their credit cards or via secure account transfers. There were several subsections to the eBay site, including one for automobile sales, labeled "eBay Motors." Consumers could search cars by make and model or by price. Because higher-priced items generated higher fees, the company made more money from automobile sales than it did from many other items sold via www.ebay.com.

At the outset eBay relied on word of mouth to promote its business. As the company became more successful, it branched out into print and radio advertising. In 2002 eBay conducted its first television campaign, "Do It eBay," which was developed by Goodby, Silverstein & Partners. The San Francisco–based agency had been responsible for all of the company's radio advertising through 2004 as well. Goodby, Silverstein & Partners was best known for its award-winning "Got Milk" campaign on behalf of the California Milk Processor Board. The agency was founded in 1983 by Jeff Goodby and Rich Silverstein, who had previously worked together at the Ogilvy & Mather agency.

ONLINE AUCTIONS

The most common type of transaction on eBay's website was an auction. To list an item for auction, a seller was required to register with eBay. Then he or she chose whether or not to offer a "Buy It Now" option for the item. This was a feature that allowed a buyer to purchase the item outright, bypassing the auction. After setting a "Buy It Now" price, the seller posted a minimum bid for the item. Then the seller determined how long the auction should last and set a minimum bid increment. A minimum bid increment was the minimum amount over the current bid a buyer was allowed to offer. For example, if someone bid $5 for an item, and the minimum bid was $1, then the minimum for the next bid was $6.

Buyers bid by entering into the site the maximum amount they were willing to pay. Their bid appeared as the minimum allowed at that time, and then it moved up as more people bid. For example, in the above scenario, if the buyer chose to bid $10 instead of just $6, his or her bid first appeared as $6 and then rose as new bids were made. If someone else saw the item and bid $7, the first buyer's bid moved up to $8. Bidders were allowed to increase their maximum bids. The person with the highest bid when the auction ended won the item.

TARGET MARKET

EBay usually aimed for a very large target market. The company wanted to be the destination of choice for anyone shopping online. The website had always been especially popular with collectors, who used the site to track down rare and hard-to-find items, such as out-of-print records or idiosyncratic household goods.

The site listed many types of items for sale, however, and it was also a major attraction for bargain shoppers and consumers who were comfortable doing their shopping online. The company also allowed people to sell automobiles on the site. These were expensive items, which meant that the company collected higher fees on such transactions. The kind of shopper that bought an automobile on eBay was a typical used-car shopper: younger and on a budget. The company saw automobile sales as a prime candidate for growth.

COMPETITION

The most serious competitor for eBay, especially for big-ticket items such as automobiles, was the search engine Google. Like eBay, Google did not sell anything itself. Instead, consumers used Google's website to search for items online. For example, a used-car dealer or an individual would post on a website the vehicles they had for sale, and buyers would find the site via Google. Other search engines, such as Yahoo!, offered similar services. In fact, Yahoo! even allowed sellers to post ads that would appear in the Yahoo! Autos section of the search engine's website, www.yahoo.com. Although neither of these companies provided online auction services, they competed with eBay by providing an alternative way for consumers to buy automobiles online.

The company was even more concerned, however, about its off-line competitors. While certain products, such as music files, collectibles, or books, seemed to attract online buyers easily, most consumers were accustomed to buying automobiles through off-line means, such as classified advertisements in newspapers. To grow its automobile-selling business eBay needed to lure more of these people into buying (and selling) automobiles on ebay.com.

MARKETING STRATEGY

Goodby, Silverstein & Partners was the agency of record on the 2004 radio campaign, which consisted of a

60-second spot titled "Abbreviated." It was part of the $250 million in U.S. advertising that eBay purchased in 2004. Later that year eBay augmented its radio efforts with a television campaign, also engineered by Goodby, Silverstein & Partners. This campaign, which carried the tagline "The Power of All of Us," ran in the fall and winter shopping season. It did not focus on automobiles.

The "Abbreviated" radio spot was fairly straightforward. It featured a man speaking directly to the audience, without any music or sound effects. In the ad the speaker communicated in short, abbreviated words, like those used in a typical classified ad in a local newspaper. He explained to consumers—especially potential sellers—that the abbreviated language used in newspaper classifieds was too unclear to give potential buyers an idea of what the car was actually like. In contrast, eBay allowed sellers a chance to post more detailed text and pictures, so buyers knew just what they were getting.

"Abbreviated" was distinctive both for its message and for its quirky vocabulary, which entailed shortening words by leaving out most of the vowels and many of the consonants. By referring to a car as "cr," for example, the spot captured the listener's attention. It began with the announcer saying, "If YR FMLR with the CLSIFDS section of the NWSPPR, you PRBLY understand this MSSG quite well." This strange-sounding language was scattered throughout the spot, driving home its central thesis—that classified ads offered too little space for sellers to describe a vehicle properly—by demonstrating it. At one point the speaker described a car using the abbreviated language of newspaper ads, and the results sounded like gibberish.

The commercial also touted eBay's Vehicle Protection Program, which guarded consumers against being stuck paying for a car that was not in as good a condition as the advertisement had claimed. Finally it reminded listeners that eBay offered a nationwide customer base, as opposed to the local reach of most newspapers. Even when describing eBay's own services, the narrator still slipped into abbreviated words occasionally, using them sporadically enough that his meaning was not lost but often enough to keep the spot's humor going.

"Abbreviated" referred specifically to "eBay Motors" instead of just "eBay"—even though "eBay Motors" was only a category on www.ebay.com, as opposed to an actual separate entity. This distinction was made for consumers who were used to thinking about eBay as a place to buy smaller items, such as household goods or clothing. It also reinforced the idea that eBay was not only a place where automobiles were available for sale but also a natural place to go shopping for these kinds of items. This subtle gesture allowed the spot to concentrate on the benefits of selling cars on eBay without having to clear any hurdle the listener might have about shopping for an automobile that way. The commercial was recorded at the GSP Post studio in San Francisco. It was produced for Goodby, Silverstein & Partners by Brian Coate and was written by Tyler McKellar. GSP Post served as the production company.

OUTCOME

The spot was a success, although it also marked the end of eBay's account with Goodby, Silverstein & Partners. In March 2005 eBay ended its relationship with the agency, replacing it with the New York–based BBDO. The company believed that BBDO, a larger agency, was better equipped to provide integrated marketing campaigns that would combine Internet, television, print, and radio elements.

Regardless, "Abbreviated" was particularly successful with critics. It received a Silver Lion in the Radio category at the 2005 International Advertising Festival in Cannes, France. Called the "Olympics of Advertising," the Cannes festival was among the most prestigious in the world, with campaigns and agencies from all over the globe under consideration. "Abbreviated" also won a Bronze Clio that year; the Clios were one of the largest international advertising award programs. In addition Goodby, Silverstein & Partners won the $100,000 first prize at the 2005 Radio Mercury Awards for the "Abbreviated" spot. Based in New York, the Radio Mercury Awards were begun in 1992 to offer an exclusive recognition for excellence in radio advertising. All of these awards were announced after eBay had terminated its relationship with Goodby, Silverstein & Partners.

The effort contributed to a solid year for eBay. The company finished 2004 with consolidated net revenues of $3.27 billion, a 51 percent improvement from 2003. The company also reported a record 1.4 billion listings during 2004, up more than 45 percent from the previous year. More than $34 billion of transactions took place in 2004 via eBay's online auctions and listings. Therefore, the "Abbreviated" commercial appeared to succeed in helping traffic at www.ebay.com continue to grow.

FURTHER READING

Anderson, Mae. "Goodby Gets Radio-Mercury Grand Prize." *San Francisco Chronicle,* June 8, 2005.

———. "'Grr,' 'Real Men' Tally at Cannes." *San Francisco Chronicle,* June 25, 2005.

Cohen, Adam. *The Perfect Store: Inside eBay.* Boston: Little, Brown and Company, 2002.

———. "PayPal and Other Post-Bubble Signs of Life on the Internet." *New York Times,* February 6, 2002.

Guernsey, Lisa. "EBay at a Crossroads: Can 'Buy Now' Share Space with 'Bid Now'?" *New York Times,* December 7, 2004.

Howard, Theresa. "EBay Spends Bigger on Advertising." *USA Today,* January 2, 2005.

Lacy, Sarah. "Easier Shopping Around—Online." *BusinessWeek,* December 8, 2004.

Mullaney, Timothy J., and Robert D. Hof. "E-Tailing Finally Hits Its Stride." *BusinessWeek,* December 20, 2004.

Raine, George. "EBay Dumps S.F. Ad Agency." *San Francisco Chronicle,* March 31, 2005.

Stross, Randall E. *EBay: The First Inside Account of Venture Capitalists at Work.* New York: Crown Business, 2000.

Guy Patrick Cunningham

EBAY 2004 TELEVISION CAMPAIGN

OVERVIEW

The San Jose, California, company eBay, Inc., was an online-based auction and selling community that in 2004 serviced 115 million shoppers, who purchased items ranging from clocks to shoes to automobiles. The company did not sell anything itself, instead making money from advertising and by charging sellers listing fees for using the company's website, ebay.com, to sell items. In 2004 eBay restructured its listing fees, charging higher fees for more expensive items, in an effort to encourage sellers to offer lower opening prices for auctions. This carried the risk that some sellers would be less inclined to use eBay, because they might want to avoid the fees. Although eBay was the most popular online-auction site, it faced pressure from other Internet companies, such as Amazon and Google, whose own services diverted consumers away from eBay.

In order to maintain strong visibility in the face of this pressure, eBay earmarked $250 million for marketing in 2004. From its inception eBay had only run one major television campaign, relying on word of mouth, Internet ads, and print campaigns to attract consumers. In 2004, however, the company commissioned Goodby, Silverstein & Partners, an agency based in San Francisco, to run a new television campaign. There were four spots in all, rolled out that October and November. The most popular spot was known as "Toy Boat." It featured a boy losing his toy boat at sea, only to find it again as an adult after a fisherman found it and posted it for sale on eBay. The commercial featured a voice-over by Hollywood actress Rosanna Arquette. Other spots appealed to the sense of community offered by eBay. The campaign was meant to differentiate eBay from impersonal sellers such as Amazon or search engines like Yahoo and Google.

The spots were a hit with critics. The Directors Guild of America singled out Noam Murro, director of "Toy Boat," for Outstanding Directorial Achievement in Commercials. The commercials helped eBay's fourth-quarter revenues jump 24 percent compared to the same period in 2003. The campaign also marked the end of eBay's relationship with Goodby, Silverstein & Partners. In 2005 eBay offered its business to BBDO, a larger advertising agency based in New York City.

HISTORICAL CONTEXT

The Internet-centered company eBay, Inc., was founded in September 1995 and was based in San Jose, California, near the state's famous "Silicon Valley," so called because it was home to a number of technology-related businesses. By 2004 eBay employed about 9,000 people and operated around the world. It was intended to provide a global trading platform where consumers could trade or auction different items. EBay allowed vendors and consumers to buy and sell a wide range of items, ranging from clothing to electronics to celebrity collectables to cars. To describe its business it adopted the slogan "The World's Online Marketplace." Throughout the 1990s the company expanded, adding local eBay sites to service countries that included Australia, China, India, and France.

EBay offered buyers the choice between either bidding in an online auction or buying an item outright for a predetermined price. All sales took place via the company's website, which in the United States was located at www.ebay.com. The company made a profit not by selling items itself but by taking a percentage of the sales price of the items sold on the site. EBay collected listing, feature, and final-value fees from all of the registered sellers that used the site. Advertising on the site itself provided another source of income. The company also expanded its business by offering PayPal, an online payment system that could be used on other websites. In 2004 eBay purchased a 25 percent stake in the online community Craigslist, which offered online "classified ads" for people to buy and sell items. It had thus been emerging as a potential competitor for eBay.

In eBay's early years the company primarily relied on word of mouth to attract buyers and sellers to ebay.com. Even in the early 2000s the company stuck to more conservative print campaigns. The company's first major television campaign was released in 2002; it was created by Goodby, Silverstein & Partners, a San Francisco–based agency that was especially known for its work with technology companies. The campaign later won a 2004 Gold EFFIE Award in the retail category. The spots helped eBay's online community expand to 115 million shoppers.

© LANCE IVERSEN/SAN FRANCISCO CHRONICLE/CORBIS.

TARGET MARKET

EBay's target market was anyone interested in buying or selling things online. Because younger people were often more comfortable with technology such as the Internet, consumers under 40 were especially important to eBay. Collectors, who used the site to track down hard-to-find items such as out-of-print books and CDs, were also considered to be valuable users of the site.

After eBay raised its listing fees in January 2004, there was concern that some sellers might be more inclined to avoid listing on the site. The company had raised prices by about 9 percent across the board, but increases were as high as 45 percent on more expensive items. EBay hoped that this would convince some sellers to use a lower starting price for auctioned items, which would attract more bargain-conscious consumers, who then might be tempted to bid on more and more items. To prevent competitors from cutting into its core business, eBay decided that it needed to run another television-based marketing campaign. The company wanted to make sure that consumers still thought of eBay as the best place to buy things online.

COMPETITION

By 2004 eBay was the dominant online-auction site in the world. Because of the nature of the Internet, however, the company did not only compete with other auction-oriented sites. EBay made its money through the sales conducted on its site and via advertising on that same site. Both required the company to keep attracting a large numbers of visitors to the site. While eBay did not sell anything directly, it needed brisk sales to generate fees. Therefore, one of its biggest competitors was the online retailer Amazon. Amazon sold a variety of products, ranging from books to electronics. It conducted high-profile radio and television campaigns. Its direct sales often competed with the sellers that used eBay, so the auction site had to be sure to keep its own profile on par with Amazon.

Perhaps the most dynamic force on the Internet in 2004 was the search engine Google. Google and other search engines, including Yahoo, did not sell anything directly, but users could find individual sellers via such search engines. Users went to Google's website and searched for a particular product or seller; then they could connect with these sellers directly. Google did not have any connection with such sellers, instead making money from advertising sold on the google.com website itself. Google even added a special search called "Froogle," with which users could filter a search to show only online sellers. This cut into eBay's business, because if buyers could find sellers directly through Google, they would have no reason to shop at eBay. It also meant that sellers could sell items on their own websites and avoid paying eBay any fees.

MARKETING STRATEGY

In 2004 eBay earmarked about $250 million for U.S. advertising. Once again, Goodby, Silverstein & Partners

DESPERATELY SEEKING EBAY

When eBay released a major television campaign for only the second time in the company's history, it knew that the spots needed to connect quickly with customers in order to distinguish the online-auction site from Internet sellers such as Amazon and search engines such as Google. To do that the company enlisted a familiar voice to star in the spots: Rosanna Arquette.

Arquette was a part of an acting family that included sister Patricia (star of the film *True Romance* and the television show *Medium*) and brother David (of the *Scream* trilogy). Their father, Lewis, was an actor as well, having appeared in numerous television and film projects in the 1970s and 1980s.

One of Rosanna Arquette's first high-profile roles came in 1985, when she starred in *Desperately Seeking Susan.* In the film Arquette's bored suburban housewife switched places with a New York bohemian (played by pop singer Madonna). She later acted in critically lauded films such as *New York Stories* (1989) and *Pulp Fiction* (1994) along with box office hits *Hope Floats* (1998) and *The Whole Nine Yards* (2000). Arquette also appeared as a guest star on many of the biggest television hits of the day, including *The Practice, Malcolm in the Middle,* and *Grey's Anatomy.* As a result, she was familiar to a vast range of people. This breadth of recognition made her ideal for work with eBay, which attracted a variety of users.

ran the campaign. The San Francisco–based agency had made its reputation designing innovative campaigns for online-based businesses such as E*Trade. It had handled eBay's only other television campaign in 2002.

The new campaign centered on four television spots, two that launched in October and two more that followed a month later. The spots were intended to promote the idea of eBay as a community, differentiating it from the impersonal retailer Amazon or the sprawling Web that the search engine Google harnessed for its users. By underscoring the communal aspect of eBay, the company hoped to lure consumers into spending more time—and therefore making more purchases—at ebay.com. The campaign used the slogan "The Power of All of Us." One spot featured shots of people doing good deeds for each other, including opening doors for people and delivering food to shut-ins. On-screen text explained to the audience that eBay's online community "proved" that people were "good." The spot was an appeal to the sense of community that had inspired some eBay users to set up collectors' clubs built around particular products sold on eBay.com.

The most popular spot, "Toy Boat," was designed to underscore the perceived benefits of online auctions in general and eBay in particular. It began with a shot of a young boy playing with his new toy boat. The boat then was swept out to sea by the receding tide and apparently lost forever. Years later, however, it turned up in a fishnet. The fisherman who found it decided to make some money selling the toy on eBay. The now-adult boy discovered it there, posted in an online auction. The spot closed with the tagline "What if nothing was ever forgotten? What if nothing was ever lost?" Voice-over for the spot was provided by the actress Rosanna Arquette, known for her work in such films as *Pulp Fiction* and *Desperately Seeking Susan.*

Another commercial featured a man dusting off his clock collection. Soon his home was filled with other collectors offering him new clocks. He chose his favorite and added it to his current group of clocks. This spot appealed directly to collectors, people especially drawn to the site in hopes of finding a rare or unusual item. These kinds of items—a strange clock, for example—were not easy to find on sites like Amazon that focused on new, practical items, or via Google, which offered searches that showed popular (not quirky) products at the top of its listings.

OUTCOME

Critics and audiences enjoyed the new spots. One, "Toy Boat," garnered special recognition at the Directors Guild of America Awards for 2004. The spot's director, Noam Murro of the production company Biscuit Filmworks, was honored for Outstanding Directorial Achievement in Commercials for "Toy Boat" and two other spots. EBay's television commercials also helped boost the company's sales in the last quarter of 2004, which coincided with the campaign's run. U.S. revenues at the company were up 10 percent from the previous quarter and had increased a solid 24 percent compared to the previous year's fourth quarter.

While the increase was below the 38 percent growth the company had seen in the same quarter between 2002 and 2003, it was still a healthy pace. EBay nevertheless discontinued its relationship with Goodby, Silverstein & Partners soon after the campaign finished, moving to New York City–based BBDO for future campaigns. The agency was larger and operated a more diverse portfolio than Goodby, Silverstein & Partners.

FURTHER READING

Cohen, Adam. "PayPal and Other Post-Bubble Signs of Life on the Internet." *New York Times,* February 6, 2002.

———. *The Perfect Store: Inside eBay.* Boston: Little, Brown and Company, 2002.

Guernsey, Lisa. "EBay at a Crossroads: Can 'Buy Now' Share Space with 'Bid Now'?" *New York Times,* December 7, 2004.

Howard, Theresa. "Ads Pump Up eBay Community with Good Feelings." *USA Today,* October 17, 2004.

———. "EBay Spends Bigger on Advertising." *USA Today,* January 2, 2005.

Lacy, Sarah. "Easier Shopping Around—Online." *BusinessWeek,* December 08, 2004.

Mullaney, Timothy J., and Robert D. Hof. "E-Tailing Finally Hits Its Stride." *BusinessWeek,* December 20, 2004.

Richtel, Matt. "EBay Buys 25% Stake in Craigslist, an Online Bulletin Board." *New York Times,* August 14, 2004.

Stross, Randall E. *EBay: The First Inside Account of Venture Capitalists at Work.* New York: Crown Business, 2000.

Tedeschi, Bob. "E-Commerce Report; The Three Big Internet Portals Begin to Distinguish among Themselves as Shopping Malls." *New York Times,* April 8, 2002.

Guy Patrick Cunningham

Electronic Data Systems

5400 Legacy Drive
Plano, Texas 75024
USA
Telephone: (800) 566-9337
Web site: www.eds.com

■■■

CAT HERDERS CAMPAIGN

OVERVIEW

Although Electronic Data Systems (EDS), the Plano, Texas–based company founded by H. Ross Perot in 1962, was the acknowledged inventor of the information technology (IT) services industry, by the end of the twentieth century EDS, despite continued growth, had fallen behind its competitors—especially regarding its public image. To correct that, EDS chose Fallon McElligott (later Fallon Worldwide), an independent Minneapolis ad agency, as its lead agency in May 1999. Fallon, in conjunction with new corporate management at EDS, saw its mission as changing the EDS image not only with respect to the company's present and future customers but also for EDS employees, whose morale was low. The ad campaign set out to do this by creating brand awareness where either none had existed or the awareness had petrified over the years.

"Cat Herders" (the name applies to the initial television spot and the campaign), which played off the industry expression "it's like herding cats," served both these purposes. It gave EDS employees an image that was serious, despite the humor of the commercial, and it highlighted EDS's problem-solving capabilities for its customers. The initial campaign used television, print, the Internet, and the COMDEX trade show at a cost of approximately $8 million. The campaign was presented as a trilogy. The first television spot, "Cat Herders," was a huge success, while the second and third spots, "Airplane" and "Running with the Squirrels," were eye-catching follow-ups but lacked the impact of the initial spot.

The "Cat Herders" spot ran through 2001 and won numerous awards, including an Emmy Award nomination. EDS also enjoyed an improvement in employee morale and corporate image, along with new contracts and acquisitions. In 2000 EDS reported fourth-quarter earnings of $5.2 billion, a 5 percent increase from the previous year and a new quarterly high for the company.

HISTORICAL CONTEXT

Throughout the 1960s, 1970s, and 1980s, EDS experienced phenomenal growth and was the recognized leader in the IT services industry, enjoying government, military, and commercial contracts. In 1984 EDS became a division of General Motors (GM), and three years later, when EDS celebrated its 25th anniversary, it reported global revenues of $4.4 billion. In 1996 EDS severed its relationship with GM and once again became an independent company. The 1990s, which saw the rise of the dot-com businesses, was a decade in which EDS slipped behind newer competitors in the race for customers. Although EDS expanded globally throughout the decade, its image was that of a lumbering dinosaur whose primary ties were to the military. In an October 2000 article, Associated Press writer David Koenig quoted then EDS president and chief operating officer Jeffrey M. Heller on the company's decline. "By '96," Heller said, "technology had changed and skills had changed. We didn't change fast enough." Koenig noted that 1996 was also the year that IBM overtook EDS as leader in the IT services industry, though the computer giant had only been in the industry a few years.

Events leading to the EDS ad campaign trilogy occurred quickly in 1999. In January Richard Brown was named chairman and CEO. Fallon was chosen as lead agency, and Don Uzzi, named marketer of the year in 1995, came on board. Almost from the beginning Uzzi injected a bold style into staid EDS when he invited broadcast and print reporters to EDS's Plano headquarters to witness the company's handling of the Y2K transition. It was a successful PR move that was topped only by the ad campaign.

H. ROSS PEROT: THE MAN WHO WOULD BE PRESIDENT

Born in Texarkana, Texas, in 1930, H. Ross Perot first came to the attention of the general public when he funded an operation to rescue two of his employees at EDS from an Iranian prison in 1979. Perot, a graduate of the U.S. Naval Academy, had started EDS in 1962, virtually inventing the IT services industry while building his company into a multi-billion-dollar international corporation. He sold EDS to General Motors in 1984, thereby gaining a seat on GM's board. Two years later he quit the GM board and sold his remaining shares in EDS to the parent company. (EDS became an independent company in 1996.) In 1988 Perot started Perot Systems, also a computer company.

Perot is best known for his two quixotic presidential candidacies in the 1990s. In 1992 he garnered 19 percent of the presidential vote, the highest percentage for an independent or third-party candidate since Theodore Roosevelt in 1912. His percentage helped defeat incumbent George Bush Sr. and elect Bill Clinton president. Perot opposed the North American Free Trade Agreement (a pet Clinton project) and was the prime mover in the formation of the Reform Party in 1995. His second run for president was as that party's candidate in 1996. Perot was excluded from the televised debates and went on to receive just 8 percent of the vote.

TARGET MARKET

With the ad campaign itself, EDS relied again on the press to help get its message across. Fallon, in its Brief of Effectiveness (submitted to the EFFIE Awards committee), stated, "We were after the editorial staff at key business and IT vehicles such as the *Wall Street Journal, New York Times,* ZDNet, etc. For them, EDS represented the Old Economy in a changed world. Reporters typically ignored or dismissed EDS as a company with little news value."

Other groups targeted by the ad campaign were technology decision makers and EDS employees and possible recruits. The first group consisted of company IT directors, marketing directors of e-commerce divisions, and top-level corporate executives: CEOs, COOs, and CIOs. The second group, employees and recruits, was targeted to reinvigorate corporate culture at EDS.

COMPETITION

No company, even one that essentially invented an industry as EDS did, could remain without competitors for long. While EDS, especially during the Perot years, had successfully fended off challengers in the IT industry and grown into a multi-billion-dollar business, others sought to carve their own niches in the fast-growing IT services industry. Most notable among EDS's competitors was top computer hardware manufacturer IBM and its computer services division, IBM Global Services. Despite being the industry leader, IBM, too, suffered from a somewhat stodgy image. The firm tried to soften and humanize its reputation with a $100 million branding campaign in 1995. Entitled "Subtitles," the campaign emphasized IBM's global reach and power by featuring people in different countries using IBM products. In the television spots the actors spoke in their native tongues, and subtitles appeared on the screen. A strong element of humor put a positive spin on IBM's international dominance.

EDS's market share was also cut into by such startup companies as Scient Corp., founded in 1997 in San Francisco; then New York–based Razorfish (now known as Avenue A/Razorfish and headquartered in Seattle), which was founded in 1995; and Viant Corp. of Boston, originally Silicon Valley Internet Partners. Though each of these companies experienced its own troubles when the dot-com bubble burst, at the time they were viewed as hipper and more nimble—able to solve technology problems that were arising in the new information age that had come to fruition in the 1990s.

MARKETING STRATEGY

The first spot, "Cat Herders," set the tone for the trilogy. It provided a humorously visual description of the well-known phrase "it's like herding cats." In Silicon Valley parlance this phrase had come to mean working on extremely hard technology problems. The spot showed range-hardened cowboys on the trail, but instead of cattle they herded cats across a river. The visual united the new (Silicon Valley lingo) with the established (an image of a cowboy—rather fitting for a company located in Texas). It also gave EDS's employees a new identity and feeling of self-worth. As "cat herders" they were the tech people who could get anything done. Brand identification for viewers was provided by a final voice-over, which intoned, "EDS, managing the complexities of e-business."

The "Cat Herders" commercial made its debut in the most glamorous, and perhaps most expensive, of all television advertising venues, the Super Bowl. It aired on January 30, 2000, during Super Bowl XXXIV. EDS and Fallon chose to show the commercial during major televised sporting events, noting that the target group of technology decision makers was more likely to be viewing such programs. Subsequently the "Cat Herders" spot appeared during the U.S. Open golf tournament, in June; the National Basketball Association finals, also in June; the U.S. Open tennis tournament, in late August to early September; the Presidents Cup golf tournament, in October; and Monday Night Football. Fifty percent of the "Cat Herders" portion of the campaign went to television. The television spots were reinforced by print ads in such publications as the *Wall Street Journal, Fortune, Forbes,* and *Wired.* Ads also appeared in the online magazine *Salon.*

The second spot in the campaign was "Airplane," and it made its debut later in 2000. EDS and Fallon stuck to the winning strategy of breaking the commercial during a prime televised sporting event; "Airplane" appeared during the Thanksgiving holiday National Football League network broadcasts. The spot also appeared during broadcasts of Monday Night Football. "Airplane" depicted a group of mechanics assembling an airplane while in flight. Like its predecessor, "Airplane" was a visual manifestation of a well-known business expression, in this case "building an airplane on the fly." Explaining the spot's connection and symbolism, David Lubars, then president and executive director at Fallon, as quoted over the PR Newswire, said, "This is the second commercial in the series. The first, 'Cat Herders,' talked about the importance of aligning a company's scattered technologies and moving them in the right direction. The message of 'Airplane' is a natural follow-up in that it answers the question, 'Now I know what to do, how do I do it without messing up my company in the process?'"

"Running with the Squirrels" was the final spot in the trilogy, and it debuted on January 28, 2001, during the broadcast of Super Bowl XXXV. The ad parodied the famous running of the bulls in Pamplona, Spain. This was a bit of a departure from the first two spots in the series in that it did not depict a popular industry maxim. The humor aspect aside, squirrels were chosen because of their speed and agility. The commercial, at least the actors' part of it, was shot in Pedrazza, Spain, not far from Madrid; the squirrels (some real but most computer generated) were filmed on a California soundstage. Following Super Bowl XXXV, "Running with the Squirrels" ran in rotation with the previous two spots in the series.

OUTCOME

"Cat Herders" was an unqualified success for EDS. The campaign won numerous advertising awards, including a First Boards Award in 2000, a Cannes Silver Lion in 2000, a bronze Clio in 2001, *Advertising Age*'s Best Visual Effects Award in 2001, and a silver EFFIE Award in 2001. EDS also estimated that its initial investment of about $8 million brought in an additional $12 million in "incremental PR"—233 outlets mentioned EDS in their pre- and post-Super Bowl coverage (according to the EFFIE Awards Brief of Effectiveness submitted by Fallon). The ad was even referred to by President Bill Clinton.

Speaking a year after the fact, Uzzi, EDS's senior vice president for global advertising, as quoted by Stefani Eads in *BusinessWeek Online,* said, "The Super Bowl [ad] played out in spades for our business. The first week after the Super Bowl, we had 10 million hits to EDS.com, which is five times our normal rate. And brand awareness increased 40 percent year-on-year in 2000, something we attribute greatly to the commercial's success." Uzzi's summation was echoed by Fallon boss Lubars in an article in the *Minneapolis Star Tribune,* written by Ann Merrill. Speaking a few days prior to Super Bowl XXXV, Lubars observed, "Last year the Super Bowl ad got an incredible internal buzz at EDS." Merrill also noted that there was "an influx of resumes" at the company following the "Cat Herders" airing.

The effectiveness of the latter two spots in the series was less clear cut. Critics were generally silent on "Airplane," but "Running with the Squirrels" provoked a mixed reaction. Some media critics, such as Ellen Neubourne, questioned the commercial's effectiveness in putting across its message. Writing in *BusinessWeek Online,* she gave "Running with the Squirrels" a thumbs-down, commenting that "the sure sign that the ad is in trouble comes at the end when text has to pop onto the screen and explain to the viewer that the squirrels are meant to represent small and nimble competition. If we got all the way to the final five seconds without getting it, the ad didn't work."

Other media critics, analysts, and advertising professionals felt "Running with the Squirrels" was as funny as "Cat Herders" but too much like the previous spot to be effective. Nevertheless EDS continued to prosper throughout 2001; the company reported fourth-quarter revenues of $5.9 billion and net income of $405 million. The "Cat Herders" campaign ran through 2001 and was replaced by a series of 50 thirty-second television spots that ran over the course of 17 days during the 2002 Winter Olympics.

FURTHER READING

Eads, Stefani. "Can Thousands of Squirrels Lift EDS? It Made a Splash at Super Bowl XXXV with Another Creative Ad—but That Doesn't Mean It Will See a Payoff." *BusinessWeek Online,* January 30, 2001. Available from <http://www.businessweek.com/bwdaily/dnflash/jan2001/nf20010130_999.htm?campaign_id=search>

"EDS Builds Airplane in Midflight in New TV Spot." *Computer Publishing & Advertising Report,* December 4, 2000.

"EDS: Cat Herders." *EFFIE Awards Brief of Effectiveness,* 2001.

"EDS Debuts Second in Series of Epic TV Ads at COMDEX; New Ad Shows How Company Can Help Transform Business 'On the Fly'; Company Continues Campaign That Started with Award-Winning 'Herding Cats' Spot." *PR Newswire,* November 15, 2000.

"EDS Selects Fallon McElligott as Ad Agency of Record; Fallon McElligott/Duffy Design to Reinvigorate EDS' Marketplace Image." *PR Newswire,* May 26, 1999.

"EDS Signals New Marketing Posture at Super Bowl XXXIV; Company Uses Epic Humor, High-Visibility Venue to Spotlight Its E-Business Leadership; Reaffirm Corporate Commitment and Culture." *PR Newswire,* January 17, 2000.

Gaither, Chris. "Electronic Data's Earnings Are Better Than Expected." *New York Times,* February 8, 2001.

Hays, Constance L. "Herding Cats, Lassoing Viewers." *New York Times,* February 13, 2000.

Koenig, David. "EDS Strikes Boldest Stroke Yet in Makeover Campaign." Associated Press, October 20, 2000.

LeSueur, Steve. "Boss Brown Says EDS Has Shed Dinosaur Ways." *Washington Technology,* March 30, 2000. Available from <http://washingtontechnology.com>

Merrill, Ann. "Local Entries in the Super Bowl of Advertising; After Months of Planning, Filming and Editing, Ads Created by Twin Cities Agencies Are Prepared to Compete for the Hearts of About 120 Million Viewers." *Minneapolis Star Tribune,* January 25, 2001.

Neuborne, Ellen. "Scoring Supe XXXV's Commercials." *BusinessWeek Online,* January 29, 2001. Available from <http://www.businessweek.com/bwdaily/dnflash/jan2001/nf20010129_211.htm>

Frank Caso

Eli Lilly and Company

Lilly Corporate Ctr.
Indianapolis, Indiana 46285
USA
Telephone: (317) 276-2000
Fax: (317) 277-6579
Web site: www.lilly.com

PROZAC PRINT CAMPAIGN

OVERVIEW

Since its introduction in 1987, Prozac's sales had boomed, generating significant revenue for its manufacturer Eli Lilly and Company. But the success of this new type of antidepressant—a selective serotonin re-uptake inhibitor (SSRI)—soon spawned intense competition in the $4 billion per year antidepressant market. By mid-1996 Prozac's sales growth was slowing, and drugs such as Zoloft and Paxil were eating into its market share. In response, Lilly initiated a new advertising campaign for Prozac in 1997. The campaign was a radical shift in Lilly's marketing strategies for the little green pill. Instead of focusing solely on convincing doctors of the benefits of Prozac for their patients, Lilly reached out directly to consumers for the first time. The Prozac print campaign, which appeared in over 20 general-interest magazines, targeted both adults who suffered from depression and those who shared their lives. The ads used visual metaphors to describe the experience of depression and subsequent recovery through effective treatment and were designed most specifically to reach those who were depressed but had not sought any form of medical assistance.

Lilly selected the Chicago-based advertising firm of Leo Burnett USA to help spread the message to consumers that "Prozac Can Help." The original ad was a three-page magazine spread that featured sharply contrasting images portraying the darkness experienced by a person suffering from depression and the light that a patient felt when the illness abated. The first page consisted of a gray cloud on a black background accompanied by the line "Depression Hurts." The opposite page was a vibrant blue with a highly stylized drawing of a yellow sun captioned with the campaign's signature line: "Prozac Can Help." Beneath both pictures were six paragraphs of text that described some of the symptoms of depression. The final paragraph encouraged readers to seek medical care if their symptoms matched those described in the ad and closed by stating that "Prozac has been prescribed for more than 17 million Americans. Chances are someone you know is feeling sunny again because of it. Prozac. Welcome back." The third page contained the disclosure information and product warnings mandated by the Food and Drug Administration (FDA).

In the months following the publication of the initial ad, Lilly released two companion ads. Each featured the same text, and all were thematically similar. One of the new ads substituted a broken vase and a vase holding flowers for the gray cloud and the yellow sun of the original ad. The other, which ran only in November and December 1997, displayed a limp Christmas tree on one page and a sturdy, upright tree on the opposite page.

Although the actual execution of the campaign was the work of Leo Burnett, the creative inspiration for the images came from focus groups conducted with depressed patients. Not only did Lilly and Burnett use these groups to evaluate the effectiveness of the proposed campaigns, but the companies actually used ideas generated by the patients themselves. After having patients draw the "experience of depression and recovery," Burnett used this raw material to design the final campaign.

Although the Prozac print campaign received some criticism for its efforts to influence potential consumers directly, many others praised the campaign for removing some of the stigma attached to depression and mental illness in general. Lilly pronounced itself pleased with the results and doubled its advertising budget for 1998 in order to expand the campaign.

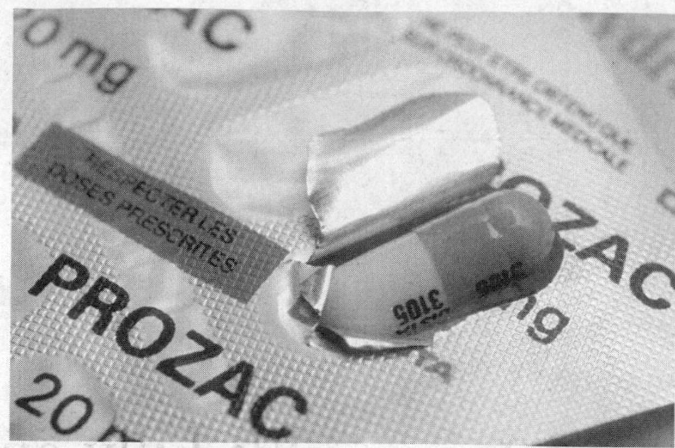

© ANNEBICQUE BERNARD/CORBIS SYGMA.

HISTORICAL CONTEXT

Eli Lilly introduced Prozac in 1987. The antidepressant immediately revolutionized the treatment of depression. As the first SSRI, Prozac acted to increase the available levels of the brain chemical serotonin. Not only did the medication have fewer side effects than older classes of antidepressants such as tricyclics, but it also worked remarkably well. By 1996 Prozac had been prescribed to more than 17 million Americans and had achieved $2.36 billion in sales worldwide. It was used to treat bulimia and obsessive-compulsive disorder, as well as depression. Since Prozac accounted for 29 percent of Lilly's sales by the fourth quarter of 1997, the drug was quite important to Lilly's continued success.

By the mid-1990s, however, the astronomical growth of Prozac sales had begun to taper off. According to the *Chicago Sun-Times,* "sales were no longer growing at previous levels." Lilly's drug met increasing competition from more recently introduced SSRIs, which eroded Prozac's dominance of the antidepressant market. Analysts were also predicting that the burgeoning antidepressant market—which by 1996 was expanding by almost 33 percent annually—would become saturated by the turn of the century. Furthermore, Lilly's exclusive patent on Prozac was to expire in 2003, at which time generic makers could enter the field, a development that would greatly reduce the drug's profitability.

In light of these changes, Lilly recognized the necessity of revamping its advertising strategy. Traditionally the company had marketed Prozac in two ways, both of which centered on physicians. The company maintained a vast sales force that traveled "door-to-door" to doctors' offices. The sales representatives met with both primary care physicians and psychiatrists to explain the benefits of prescribing the medication to their patients and handed out free samples. Lilly also advertised in professional medical journals in hopes of swaying more doctors to prescribe Prozac for depressed patients. Increasingly, though, Lilly—like others in the pharmaceutical industry—realized the incredible potential in targeting patients directly.

TARGET MARKET

The campaign was intended to reach depressed adults and the people closest to them. By 1997 17.5 million Americans suffered from depression, according to *Med Ad News.* Depression, however, was a seriously underdiagnosed and undertreated illness. Eli Lilly claimed that two out of every three depressed individuals did not receive treatment. By targeting those who were reluctant to seek professional help for their symptoms, the campaign attempted to appeal to a substantial number of people. Victoria Murphy, a spokesperson for Eli Lilly, explained her company's strategy to the *Fort Worth Star-Telegram*: "The goal is very simple: to encourage people suffering from depression to get into treatment."

By expanding its advertising focus to include depressed people who had not yet tried its medication, Lilly hoped to see its Prozac sales rise. Mike Grossman, Director of Public Relations for Leo Burnett, saw his project as one of "assisting people in their depressed stupor to raise their hand for help . . . [T]hey might not recognize their condition or know that help is out there." In order to do so, however, the campaign had to overcome the stigma that surrounded depression and other mental illnesses. The wording of the ads' text was carefully selected to describe the symptoms of depression in a nonthreatening way: "So you may have trouble sleeping. Feel unusually sad or irritable. Find it hard to concentrate. Lose your appetite. Lack energy. Or have trouble feeling pleasure . . . ." The ads also sought to dispel some of the prevalent misconceptions and fears about depression.

PEPPERMINT PROZAC

Shortly after the introduction of the direct-to-consumer print campaign, Lilly also brought out a liquid Prozac. The company claimed that this peppermint flavored product was targeted at elderly patients who could not swallow the pill version. Critics such as author/columnist Arianna Huffington, however, claimed that the company was trying to reach a far younger audience by using "child-like" graphics in its ads.

"[I]t isn't just feeling down. It's a real illness with real causes.... Some people think you can just will yourself out of a depression. That's not true." Grossman summed up Burnett's goal for the ads' text: "We wanted it to be dignified."

Because the visual elements of the advertisements were inspired by patients' illustrations of their own feelings about depression and recovery, the campaign clearly intended to connect with depressed readers (or their family members and friends) on an emotional level. The simple yet powerful symbols of darkness and light were developed to be inclusive. "We wanted patients and depressed people to be able to respond to the ads," said Grossman.

COMPETITION

Eli Lilly's strategy of appealing directly to consumers indicated that the company had "decided to fend off competition from other drug companies by going over doctors' heads and targeting patients," the Chicago *Sun-Times* reported. By expanding its potential market, Eli Lilly was attempting to reinvigorate flagging sales. When it was first released, Prozac was the only medication of its kind. Both doctors and patients appreciated the drug's ability to combat depression effectively, in many cases without causing disruptive or dangerous side effects. Over time, though, Prozac's solitary reign ended. Other pharmaceutical companies began to create and market their own SSRIs. Smith Kline Beecham's Paxil and Pfizer's Zoloft competed head-to-head against Prozac in the "modern antidepressant" category. Other SSRIs joined the increasingly crowded field. Effexor, manufactured by American Home Products Corp., and Bristol-Myers Squibb Company's Serzone began to encroach on Prozac's territory. In addition, the older tricyclic family of antidepressants continued to be readily prescribed by doctors. Even nonprescription remedies for depression gained adherents. Hypericum, a derivative of the St. John's wort plant, was touted as the "natural Prozac."

By July 1997 Prozac commanded less than 50 percent of the $4 billion market for "modern antidepressants" that it had previously dominated. Zoloft, introduced in 1992, was gaining in popularity and had captured nearly one-third of this market. In 1997 Zoloft's global sales grew to $1.51 billion, while third-ranked Paxil topped $1.45 billion. Prozac's sales for that year totaled $2.56 billion. Recognizing these developments, the *Wall Street Journal Europe* declared in 1996 that "the king of antidepressants is under attack." Claiming that its medication had fewer side effects than Prozac, Pfizer marketed Zoloft aggressively. Indeed, Pfizer's sales force outmaneuvered Lilly's, visiting almost 70,000 more doctors' offices in 1996 than the Lilly team. In the process, Pfizer's sales representatives passed out many Zoloft samples to these physicians, who in turn dispensed them to depressed patients. Pfizer also placed advertisements in medical journals that implicitly reminded doctors of Prozac's drawbacks, especially the fact that it was reputed to provoke anxiety in some patients. "Consider Safety. Consider Effectiveness. Consider Zoloft...," the ads suggested. The fact that Pfizer priced Zoloft 20 percent below Prozac also contributed to that drug's rapid rise by attracting cost-cutting Health Maintenance Organizations.

While its market dominance was being eroded, Lilly, like a number of other drug companies, took notice of a new development in medical advertising. Rogaine (an anti-hair loss product) and Nicoderm (a smoking cessation aid) had realized tremendous gains in profitability thanks to direct-to-consumer television campaigns run in 1994. These campaigns sparked a broader trend toward direct-to-consumer marketing of an array of pharmaceutical products. Peter Labadie of William-Labadie Advertising told the *Chicago Tribune* that this shift "started with hair replacement products. Marketers felt that advertising was moving the products." Thus, in addition to increasing its sales force and promoting Prozac more strongly to primary care physicians, Lilly embarked on its own direct-to-consumer print campaign in an effort to outflank its competitors. This was the first such effort that Lilly had made on behalf of Prozac. At the time, it was also the largest direct-to-consumer campaign for a "modern antidepressant." American Home Products Corp. had run a regional campaign for Effexor that featured tributes to the powers of the medication ("I got my marriage back," declared one), but Lilly's Prozac campaign appeared nationwide.

MARKETING STRATEGY

After Eli Lilly chose Leo Burnett to create its direct-to-consumer campaign, the ad agency devised a number of possible ads. The one that was best received by patients in

Lilly focus groups was, not surprisingly, the series partially inspired by the experiences of patients. The dual metaphorical images of dark and light accurately expressed to them what depression and a return to health felt like. Lilly also sought input from doctors and mental health advocacy groups before releasing the original ad to the public.

In order to reach a large and varied group of people, Lilly chose to run the campaign in general-interest magazines with wide circulations. The ad first appeared in 20 such publications, including *Family Circle, Good Housekeeping, Sports Illustrated, Cosmopolitan, Men's Health, Newsweek, Time, Parade Magazine,* and *Entertainment Weekly.* In keeping with data indicating that the incidence of depression among women was twice as high as that among men, the magazine list was "skewed toward women," according to Grossman. As *Med Ad News* pointed out, women accounted for 60 percent of doctor visits and were twice as likely as men to request a specific brand of medication.

Lilly selected a print medium in part because of limitations that the FDA had placed on direct-to-consumer television ads. Regulations in force at the time prohibited pharmaceutical companies from drawing an explicit connection between a medical condition and a medication. Print ads, which were not circumscribed by such restrictions, were therefore a better way for Lilly to convey its message to consumers. Moreover, consumers had more time to reflect on a print ad then on a 30-second television spot, which was ideal for Lilly's purposes. Indeed, according to the *Indianapolis Star,* the ad encouraged the reader to muse actively over symptoms. As Gary Mitchell, a professor at the Indiana University Medical Center, told the *Indianapolis Star,* "You're on Paxil and you see the Prozac ad, and ask yourself, 'Why am I not on that drug?' "

OUTCOME

Although it is difficult to correlate sales increases to the campaign, Lilly expressed pleasure with the results. In fact, the company announced to *Health News Daily* that it was doubling its 1998 advertising budget in order to obtain "a full year effect" from the campaign. Industry analyst Myron Holubiak took a clearer stance on the effect of advertising in *The Commercial Appeal:* "That drug companies are creating a demand through consumer advertising can be proven, and physicians will prescribe drugs their patients ask for." Prozac's sales rose 9 percent in 1997 to reach $2.56 billion; 1997 fourth quarter earnings were up 15 percent.

Not everyone, however, approved of Lilly's direct-to-consumer efforts. The American Medical Association condemned all advertising that targeted patients. Erik Parens' column in the *Washington Post* was indicative of the outcry directed at the Prozac campaign. "Of course, doctors can—and should—say no to anyone who doesn't need a particular medication. But let's not fool ourselves: If doctors are under pressure from their patients to prescribe a particular medication, they must become strong gatekeepers to prevent misuse."

Despite the negative response from some columnists and consumer advocacy groups, a great many doctors and mental health alliances praised the campaign's efforts to educate a large number of individuals who suffered, undiagnosed and untreated, from an often debilitating illness.

FURTHER READING

Campbell, Laura. "Demand via Direct Ads Hikes Firms' Health." *The Commercial Appeal,* February 22, 1998.

Kirk, Jim. "FDA May Relieve T.V. Advertisers." *Chicago Tribune,* July 8, 1997.

Langreth, Robert. "Prozac Finds Itself Losing Market Share to Newer Rivals." *Wall Street Journal* (Europe), May 10, 1996.

"Lilly's Prozac Promotional Efforts Will Double in 1998." *Health Daily News,* January 30, 1998.

"Lilly Sheds Light on Depression." *Med Ad News,* August 1, 1997.

"No End in Sight." *Med Ad News,* October 1, 1997.

O'Malley, Chris. "Lilly Takes Prozac to the People." *Indianapolis Star,* July 1, 1998.

Parens, Erik. "The Problem of Mixing Drugs with Ads." *Washington Post,* October 26, 1997.

"Prozac Ads Hope to Lure Patients." *Chicago Sun-Times,* July 6, 1997.

Taylor, Holly. "Prozac Ads Cloud Issue of Therapy's Role, Experts Say." *Fort Worth Star-Telegram,* July 19, 1997.

Rebecca Stanfel

Energizer Holdings, Inc.

533 Maryville University Drive
St. Louis, Missouri 63141
USA
Telephone: (314) 985-2000
Fax: (314) 985-2000
Web site: www.energizer.com

■■■

BUNNY CHASERS CAMPAIGN

OVERVIEW

The pink Energizer Bunny first marched across American television screens in 1989 to advertise the Eveready Battery Company's Energizer batteries. Eight years later Eveready Battery (which eventually became Energizer Holdings, Inc.) was America's second-largest battery manufacturer, behind Duracell, Inc. After the Energizer Bunny's debut proved highly successful, Eveready continued to spin off similar campaigns throughout the early 1990s. One television spot began as a hemorrhoid-cream commercial but was soon interrupted by the marching Energizer Bunny. The voice-over message never varied, with the announcer proclaiming, "Energizer batteries. They keep going and going and going..." In 1997 Eveready and its longtime ad agency, TBWA\Chiat\Day, struggled to develop fresh Energizer Bunny campaigns. That year, in an attempt to revitalize the bunny's image and replace Duracell as the industry leader, Eveready introduced its "Bunny Chasers" television campaign, which borrowed the storyline from the previous summer's blockbuster tornado thriller *Twister.*

"Bunny Chasers" started in summer 1997, when *Twister* was released on video. TBWA\Chiat\Day created the campaign's seven TV spots with Eveready's $50 million advertising budget. The campaign featured teams of young, obsessed scientists who chased the Energizer Bunny much like meteorologists chased tornadoes in the movie. The spots were filmed to resemble documentaries: handheld cameras were used, and the dialogue was ad-libbed. At various bunny "sightings" the actors stepped outside of their "Bunny Chaser" van for staged interviews with director Phil Morrison. The campaign ended in late 1997, but campaigns featuring the Energizer Bunny continued for several more years.

Ad Track, *USA Today*'s consumer poll about ad campaigns, revealed that audiences enjoyed "Bunny Chasers" but felt that the commercials were ineffective. Although ad analysts offered slight praise to the campaign for presenting the Energizer Bunny in a new format, ad publications such as *Advertising Age's Creativity* criticized TBWA\Chiat\Day for not retiring the Energizer Bunny earlier. The overall sales growth for the company in 1997 was less than the sales growth for the overall battery industry.

HISTORICAL CONTEXT

The battery market in the United States had traditionally been a fairly quiet category in terms of advertising. But the proliferation of household appliances, toys, pocket calculators, handheld computers, audio players, and other electronic devices that required batteries had steadily boosted sales into the $2 billion range. By the mid-1980s the field was highly competitive, with the major players being Duracell and Eveready, although Rayovac held on to approximately 10 percent of the market. It was at this point that Eveready and its Energizer brand of alkaline batteries launched the campaign that would create a lasting impact on the battery business and on American popular culture as well.

Created by the Los Angeles-based ad agency Chiat/Day (before its mid-1990s merger with TBWA and at the peak of its decadelong creative preeminence in the advertising industry), the campaign tapped into a widespread public weariness with clichéd advertising forms. Adopting as its mascot the most innocent-seeming of icons, a decidedly low-tech pink toy bunny, the campaign used wicked irony to infiltrate a wide range of insufferable commercials on the way to gaining the awareness of its target market. The spots worked by creating faux advertising that was just close enough to the real thing to provide a genuine sense of surprise—and in many cases, relief—when the actors droning on about hemorrhoid cream or some other numbingly familiar product were interrupted and thrown into confusion by the mute but energetic rabbit. Energizer's "going and going" tagline quickly became part of the national vocabulary. Having hit a winner with the campaign, Eveready and its agency stuck with it, creating successive versions of the bunny's adventures that worked ever harder to avoid becoming parodies of themselves. Advertisers typically did not use the same advertising theme for eight years, but Eveready believed that the Energizer Bunny was still viable.

REMAKING WAKITA

In 1997 the Eveready Battery Company introduced an advertising campaign for its Energizer battery that parodied the pervious summer's blockbuster movie *Twister,* which starred Helen Hunt and Bill Paxton. During the making of the tornado-themed action movie, the downtown section of Wakita, Oklahoma, was demolished for a scene in which a tornado wreaked havoc on the Great Plains. The Warner Bros. studio then paid for Wakita's downtown to be rebuilt and donated a new fire truck to the town.

TARGET MARKET

Because nearly everyone used portable devices requiring power—be they flashlights, radios, or handheld computers—the market for alkaline batteries was all but universal. Thus, category advertising attempted to be broad in its scope and appeal. Use among multiperson households was strong, given the prevalence of battery-powered toys and small appliances such as clocks and radios. That Duracell's Copper Top advertising often featured an animated family of battery-using toys illustrated the point. Even so, the market was directed toward men in general, who tended to be the predominant users of gadgets, and toward young men in particular, who were especially drawn to portable music systems, computer devices, camcorders, and other "high-drain" devices. In addition, the market was subject to a strong seasonal spike around the Christmas holidays, when the national spasm of gift spending created a strong demand for batteries to power millions of toys and other items. An estimated 40 percent of battery sales were connected to end-of-the-year gift giving, and this important market segment clearly centered on the parents who tossed a pack or two of batteries into the shopping cart along with the latest power-gobbling supertoy. Eveready's "Bunny Chasers" campaign, however, took as its primary target young men, the so-called Generation Xers who had grown up with television, knew its advertising inside and out, and had become immune to its tired tropes. The one thing this ultrahip cohort would respond to was irony, and "Bunny Chasers" had that in spades.

COMPETITION

The big three in the battery industry were Duracell, owned by Gillette; Eveready, a Ralston-Purina company; and Rayovac, which had been acquired by the Thomas H. Lee Company, a Boston investment house. The three were vying for a market valued by Information Services at $2 billion a year. Of that, an estimated 60 percent was made up of the disposable alkaline batteries commonly used in toys and household appliances. The remainder included nonalkaline and rechargeable batteries. Although, as tested by *Consumer Reports,* there was little actual difference in performance among the various brands of alkaline batteries, both of the leaders maintained that their own tests demonstrated real, even dramatic advantages in longevity.

When it came to marketing, the competition between Duracell and Eveready for the number one position was especially fierce, with Duracell's Copper Top traditionally edging out Eveready's Energizer. According to estimates from Merrill Lynch, Duracell recorded $800 million in sales in 1996, while Eveready followed closely with $701 million. Meanwhile, number three Rayovac reported a distant $211 million. Beginning in 1992 Rayovac had put most of its efforts into rechargeable batteries, but in 1997 the company threatened to stir the competitive soup when it signed superendorser Michael Jordan to help promote its newly redesigned Maximum alkaline batteries.

In terms of advertising budgets, Competitive Media Reporting pegged Eveready's 1996 Energizer budget at $65.6 million, while Duracell, running a campaign that featured computer-animated, battery-powered toy characters, spent $60.7 million. With its new Michael Jordan campaign, Rayovac was expected to spend $25 million in 1997. The competition between Duracell and Eveready was waged both on and off the advertising field. Duracell's longtime claim that "No other battery lasts longer" was openly challenged after Eveready introduced its new High Drain battery, designed for devices like camcorders and minidisc players that required more power. Energizer demanded that the television networks stop running Duracell's advertising unless the company changed the commercials.

MARKETING STRATEGY

Like any company hoping to extend a successful advertising campaign, Eveready, along with agency TBWA\Chiat\Day, faced the challenge of topping its previous efforts. In its eight-year run Energizer had become so well known in pop culture that any new incarnation would be watched very closely, both by a public that had established its own emotional bond to the bunny and by the advertising industry, some of whose members had long tired of the award-winning concept. Yet Eveready was strongly committed to its spokesrabbit. Observed Mark Larsen, the company's newly hired category manager of communications for Energizer, "We really wanted to dial it up and connect back with the consumer even stronger." To make that connection, Larsen and the TBWA\Chiat\Day creative team linked the Energizer Bunny with the 1996 movie *Twister* to create a campaign with Eveready's $50 million annual advertising budget.

One of the previous summer's special-effects extravaganzas, *Twister* chronicled a group of tornado-chasing scientists who, because of their obsession with the violent storms, kept going and going no matter the hardship or danger. As it happened, the obsessed scientists also fit right into the product's target profile. They were young males who used battery-operated gadgets. The agency knew, however, that their target consumers were media-wise and would respond best to irony and humor, and so the campaign was created as a deadpan parody of what had been a rather straightforward adventure movie. The obsession of the bunny chasers matched the endurance of the battery-driven bunny. The spots, shot in a documentary style—even to the point of having the actors ad-lib their lines—were classic image advertising, as the campaign had always been. No product was shown, only an attitude and the single benefit of longevity.

Commercial director Phil Morrison was hired to direct the "Bunny Chasers" campaign in part because he was known for his humorous style. In creating a documentary look and feel for the spots, he loaded his actors—chosen for their nonglamorous looks and ability to improvise—into an equipment-laden van and then drove through the countryside. At various "sightings," the whole crew would pile out, and Morrison would "interview" them. This technique yielded the very first installment of the seven-spot campaign, a teaser called "Woodchuck" in which the team located its quarry only to discover that it was not the bunny at all but a woodchuck. The woodchuck line was the spontaneous invention of one of the actors who had decided on his own that the first sighting should be a false alarm.

OUTCOME

USA Today's Ad Track poll indicated that, as one more installment of the overall Energizer Bunny campaign, "Bunny Chasers" was popular among audiences but nevertheless lacked effectiveness. *Adweek* named the commercial "Woodchuck" a Best Spot in 1997. Other critics attacked TBWA\Chiat\Day for overusing the Energizer Bunny and for not inventing something entirely new for Eveready. In the December 1, 1998, issue of *Advertising Age's Creativity,* the agency's creative director, Clay Williams, explained his reluctance to replace the Energizer Bunny: "It's hard to turn your back and move away from a campaign that has as much equity as this one."

In addition to disappointing the advertising critics, "Bunny Chasers" did little to help Eveready outperform its competition. Although Eveready's profits were up 3.3 percent in the second quarter of 1997, they lagged behind rival Duracell's 7.3 percent growth during the same period. Moreover, Eveready trailed the overall industry, which recorded a 4.2 percent gain during the quarter. Retailers, too, saw little direct impact from the advertising. Said Michael Polzin of Walgreens, the nation's largest drugstore chain, "We can't really recognize how the brand advertising affects that particular brand's sales. It does heighten awareness, however, among consumers that they need batteries, and so it helps our battery sales overall."

Nevertheless, the company was pleased with its 1997 skirmish in the battery wars, however substantial or insubstantial its impact on sales turned out to be. Said Eveready's Larsen, "The bunny is and always will be" a part of American culture. Although "Bunny Chasers" ended in 1997, the use of the bunny continued the next year for an Energizer campaign with a pit-stop theme. Actors playing mechanics in the commercials inserted new Energizer batteries into turbocharged, high-speed bunnies. Despite the fact that Eveready's sales fell even further behind Duracell in the late 1990s, in the months leading up to the November 2000 election Eveready revived its earlier strategy of using fake commercials, releasing spots in which the Energizer Bunny humorously interrupted TV promotions for the fictitious politician Bob Fremgen.

FURTHER READING

"Ask the Bunny." *Advertising Age,* June 3, 1991, p. 22.

Berger, Warren. "Agency of the Year." *Advertising Age's Creativity,* December 1, 1998, p. 28.

Clark, Michael. "Morrison, TBWA Chiat/Day Proclaim Bunny Season." *Shoot,* November 15, 1996.

Cuneo, Alice Z. "The Marketing 100: Energizer: Mark Larsen." *Advertising Age,* June 30, 1997.

Enrico, Dottie. "Humor Remains Top Tool for Ad Campaigns." *USA Today,* September 30, 1996, p. 3B.

———. "Viewers Want Bunny Back; Energizer Battery Ads Skip a Beat with Current Twist." *USA Today,* February 24, 1997, p. 9B.

Goldrich, Robert. "Former C/D Creative Enters into First Spot Shop Affiliation." *Shoot,* June 13, 1997.

"How the Bunny Charged Eveready." *Advertising Age,* April 8, 1991, p. 20.

Martin, David M., Elaine Rowland, and David Bourgeois. "Taste Test—TBWA Chiat/Day Inc.'s 1997 Advertising Campaigns." *Shoot,* December 12, 1997, p. 50.

McCarthy, Michael. "TBWA Re-energizes Advertising 'Icon.'" *Adweek* (eastern ed.), November 13, 1995, p. 57.

Mehegan, Sean. "The Bunny—Energizer Challenges Duracell at the Networks." *Brandweek,* September 1, 1997.

"Real Money." *Mediaweek,* June 30, 1997.

Siwolop, Sana. "Now a Pure Play among Top Battery Makers." *New York Times,* November 23, 1997.

Wentz, Laurel. "Judges Boot Copycat 'Bunny,'" *Advertising Age,* June 25, 1990, p. 56.

Patrick Hutchins
Kevin Teague

ESPN, Inc.

ESPN Plaza
935 Middle Street
Bristol, Connecticut 06010
USA
Telephone: (860) 766-2000
Fax: (860) 766-2213
Web site: www.espn.go.com

THE RICK CAMPAIGN

OVERVIEW

ESPN began in the late 1970s as the first 24-hour cable channel devoted exclusively to sports news and the airing of such minor sports as Australian Rules football and tractor pulls. By the 1990s, however, it was a powerhouse ready to extend its brand in every direction, including internationally. On the domestic side, a radio network was launched in 1992; a second cable channel, ESPN2, made its debut in 1993; and a website was introduced in 1995. Then in the fall of 1996 ESPN launched its third cable channel, ESPNews, a 24-hour sports-news service. ESPN hired ad agency Ground Zero to develop a new television and print campaign to promote the channel. The result was an effort titled "The Rick."

The Rick was a fictional obsessive sports fan who rarely left a bedroom bedecked with all manner of memorabilia. Based on a composite of real-life fans, The Rick embodied the dedication of ESPNews to the minutiae of the sports world. In the television spots the character often showed off his collection of sports memorabilia, including sports figurines, which he insisted were vital artifacts and not mere dolls.

Although it was difficult to say how much of a role "The Rick" played, ESPNews outlived its main competition, CNN-SI, which failed to achieve high enough ratings and was taken off the air. The Rick himself, while not especially well received by critics, was popular with ESPN's core audience. The character was brought back to promote the ESPN website as well as the ESPY Awards, a sports-award show organized by and aired on ESPN.

HISTORICAL CONTEXT

A new era in televised sports began on September 7, 1979, when ESPN, the Entertainment and Sports Programming Network, went on the air. Backed by $10 million in start-up money from Getty Oil, the network was the brainchild of William F. Rasmussen, a broadcaster whose original idea was to televise school sports in Connecticut. ESPN's employees initially numbered about 75, and the network was available in some 1.4 million American homes.

The first program telecast, and to this day the centerpiece of ESPN programming, was *SportsCenter,* the network's daily wrap-up of sports news. Its success enabled ESPN to begin broadcasting around the clock on September 1, 1980. With few live events to cover, the network relied on a hodgepodge of monster-truck shows, tractor pulls, Australian Rules football, and business programming to keep viewers entertained. Although advertiser interest remained tepid, on May 31, 1981, ESPN reached the 10-million subscriber plateau, an important milestone for a start-up network.

The next three years were a period of exponential growth for ESPN. By August 1983 the network had 28.5 million subscribers and had surpassed Turner Broadcasting's WTBS to become the largest cable network in America. The next year ESPN acquired its first major sports programming, college football. "That was the first property we had that the networks wanted," said Steve Bornstein, the chief executive officer of ESPN. Also in 1984, ABC Video Enterprises bought ESPN from Texaco, which had taken over Getty Oil. ESPN concluded the year with its first profitable quarter and became available in all 50 U.S. states.

In 1985 Capital Cities Inc. bought ABC and acquired ESPN for $237.5 million. In July of that year the ticker known as *Sports Update,* which offered scores and news flashes on the half hour, made its debut as *28/58.* Continuing to pursue football, the big game of sports programming, ESPN in 1987 inked a first-of-its-kind cable deal with the National Football League (NFL), allowing it to televise 13 games per season. Later that year ESPN became the first cable network to reach 50 percent of American homes with television, some 43.7 million households. ESPN International was launched in 1988, and within 10 years it was sending American sports worldwide, with broadcasts in 14 languages. Major league baseball joined the ESPN roster in 1989.

In 1991, in its 12th year, ESPN went to an all-sports format, dropping the morning program *Nation's Business Today* in favor of rebroadcasts of *SportsCenter.* On January 1, 1992, the ESPN Radio Network was introduced, offering 16 hours a week of sports news, commentary, and information. Reflecting a trend toward round-the-clock coverage of sports news, the ESPN Phone Update was introduced in 1993. The 900-number service offered scores, news, and information 24 hours a day.

In October 1993 ESPN expanded its family of television networks domestically for the first time when ESPN2, or "the Deuce" as it was known, became available to some 10 million households. The new network offered programming similar to that of ESPN but with a more youthful orientation and a commitment to covering alternative, or "extreme," sports.

In 1995 "ESPNet SportsZone" (later "ESPN SportsZone") was launched on the World Wide Web. This sports resource quickly emerged as one of the most-visited content sites on the Internet, setting a record for usage by registering a high point of 21.6 million hits in one day a year after it was introduced. Also in 1995 ESPN India went on the air, becoming ESPN's 16th network outside the United States. Commentary was provided in English and Hindi. By this time ESPN programming could be heard in 14 languages worldwide. In the United States ESPN could now boast of reaching 70 percent of homes with television, the first U.S. cable network to achieve this level of penetration. Total subscribers had reached 67.1 million.

Impressed by the network's development and the potential for further growth, the Walt Disney Company in 1996 bought ESPN, thus forging a partnership between Disney-owned ABC and the cable network. In the autumn of 1996 ESPNews—the 24-hour all-sports news network—was launched. Five charter advertisers quickly signed on: Coors Brewing Co., General Motors Corp., Levi Strauss & Co., McDonald's Corp., and Procter & Gamble Co. Several of the companies already advertised heavily on ESPN and ESPN2. ESPNews hired 11 new anchors for the network, adopting a format of consecutive 30-minute programs throughout the day. It replayed ESPN's showpiece *SportsCenter* program each night and featured ESPN commentators such as Peter Gammons on baseball and Chris Mortenson on the NFL. ESPN2 was used to help expose ESPNews to a wider audience by carrying the service between periods in its hockey coverage and at halftime during college basketball games.

At the end of the 1990s the ESPN family of networks, publications (including *ESPN the Magazine,* a biweekly publication that first appeared in March 1998), and services seemed poised for continued growth. Estimates of the value of ESPN and ESPN2 ranged as high as $5 billion, or about one-quarter of the $19 billion Disney had paid for the entire ABC-Capital Cities empire. By 1999 ESPN, the "mother network," was reaching 73 million, or almost 75 percent, of all homes with television in the United States as well as more than 90 million worldwide. This impressive level of market penetration allowed ESPN to aggressively cross-promote its other networks, including the infant ESPNews.

TARGET MARKET

"The Rick" targeted one of advertising's most coveted demographic groups: young men. These viewers were increasingly tuning out mainstream network television fare in favor of specialized programming geared to their interests, such as that found on ESPN and ESPNews. "Male viewers are continuing to be difficult to target in prime time," observed Larry Goodman, president of news sales for Turner Broadcasting. "For concentrated male viewership, in general, you have to look at cable."

Fortunately for sports news networks such as ESPNews, this male demographic group had few places to turn to in the market. "There's such a shortage of male viewers in broadcast network prime time that any

NOT THE FIRST TIME

"The Rick" was not ESPN's first foray into the realm of offbeat, humorous promotional advertising. In fact, in the eyes of many the network was a master at blending reality and whimsy.

In 1993, for example, ESPN signed a deal with ad agency Wieden+Kennedy, based in Portland, Oregon, to produce a series of promos for its nightly sports news broadcast. Entitled "This Is SportsCenter," the humorous spots featuring big-name athletes achieved a sizable cult following. Some of the more memorable spots in the campaign included one in which *SportsCenter* anchor Charley Steiner punched out the Syracuse Orangemen mascot, another in which anchors Keith Olbermann and Dan Patrick performed surgery on the knee of Indianapolis Colts quarterback Jim Harbaugh, and a third in which the rotund Steiner took over the role of a pool attendant on TV's *Melrose Place* when actor Andrew Shue was brought in to replace him on *SportsCenter*.

As the cornerstone of ESPN's 24-hour sports programming, *SportsCenter* was one of the network's core equities. ESPN's aim in developing the humorous campaign was to solidify the powerful ESPN brand image as not just a TV network but also as a huge sports fan itself. The *SportsCenter* anchors were allowed to convey their distinct personalities, and the spots gave sports fans an exaggerated documentary look at the show's inner workings. Based on the response the spots received at industry awards shows and in the trade press, they also provided viewers with many reasons to smile.

branded network specializing in the 25–54 demo is always going to be valuable," said Goodman.

COMPETITION

Although it was the first 24-hour all-sports news network, ESPNews was soon joined by a formidable competitor, CNN-SI, a joint venture of CNN, the Cable News Network, and *Sports Illustrated* magazine. A third major player in cable sports programming, Fox Sports Net, emerged in the late 1990s as a challenger to ESPNews sister network ESPN.

The networks shared many characteristics, but for the purpose of capturing the interest of viewers, they tended to emphasize their differences. Jim Walton, CNN senior vice president in charge of CNN-SI, saw the "hard news" cachet implicit in the CNN brand as the principal point of differentiation. In an interview soon after CNN-SI's launch, he was quick to point out that the satellite system PrimeStar had placed the network in two different areas of its service: news and sports. Nevertheless, Walton was not sure that the point was getting across to consumers. As he said in comparing his product with ESPNews, "I see us as different, but I don't know if consumers perceive us differently."

All three of the networks exerted considerable promotional muscle in their efforts to win the allegiance of sports-obsessed consumers. CNN-SI relied on *Sports Illustrated* as a built-in weekly promotional vehicle. ESPN and Fox aggressively advertised their services and programming with on-air and off-network promos. By the end of the 1990s all three of the networks remained viable, despite the suspicion in some quarters that the sports segment had become saturated. While no ratings data were available for CNN-SI and ESPNews, the networks reportedly boasted cable subscribers of 1 million and 1.5 million, respectively, minuscule numbers by cable standards but worth fighting over in the eyes of programmers and marketing officials.

MARKETING STRATEGY

ESPNews conceived of its fictional spokescharacter in the "Rick" advertisements as "the most knowledgeable sports fan in the history of the universe." He was an obsessive collector of everything related to sports, from a mouth guard belonging to hockey star Eric Lindros to a jar of pickle juice that Hall of Fame pitcher Nolan Ryan had used to prevent blisters on his fingers. As an exaggerated representation of the hard-core sports aficionado, the character was designed to reflect the target audience of ESPNews.

Television spots for the "Rick" campaign were directed by Christopher Guest of bicoastal Moxie Pictures. A veteran comic actor and director, Guest was best known for his work on NBC's *Saturday Night Live* in the mid-1980s. He also cowrote and costarred in the 1983 cult comedy hit *This Is Spinal Tap.* The creative team at ad agency Ground Zero consisted of creative directors Court Crandall and Kirk Souder, art director Guy Shelmerdine, copywriter Steve O'Brien, and agency producer Patricia Phelan. To play the part of The Rick, Crandall recruited a college friend, Boston-born Mike O'Malley, a rising actor with a number of credits on his resume, including a stint as a host of the Nickelodeon game show *Guts*.

The campaign was the brainchild of copywriter O'Brien. Relying on memories of his youth growing up in New England, he based the character depicted in the "Rick" commercials on his brother Pat and a group of sports-obsessed friends who, like ESPNews, prided themselves on always knowing the latest scores and all manner of minutiae. As a model for the character's cluttered bedroom, O'Brien envisioned his brother's old bedroom, its shelves crammed full of sports memorabilia. "We blew it out to the next level," O'Brien said, commenting on the real-life basis for the obsessive character. "We imagined a kid who is really, really into sports and kept growing in that knowledge and adding to his room until he had this awesome collection of sports-related items."

A sports fan in his own right, O'Brien also drew on himself for inspiration. At one point he brought some of his sports figurines into the Ground Zero offices and conducted fanciful "interviews" with them, as if he were a television broadcaster. In one of the "Rick" spots the spokescharacter did the same thing.

The other spots in the "Rick" campaign followed a similar pattern. In one the character proudly displayed a basketball net obtained for $15 from the grounds crew at North Carolina State University. In another he again trotted out his collection of sports figurines, this time to defend them as vital artifacts, "not toys, not dolls." In a third spot he played with a set of racing cars, defending his sports hobbies while dismissing other pastimes, such as reading Franz Kafka, whose story *The Metamorphosis* he erroneously described as concerning a man who turned into a cocker spaniel.

In 1998 The Rick was enlisted to promote ESPN.com, replacing a character called Net Boy who was not popular enough to retain after a website of the same name lodged a legal challenge. But The Rick's popularity also played a role. According to ESPN ad director Alex Kaminsky, quoted in *Brandweek,* "our audience related so well to 'The Rick,' that we really thought it was time to put him back into prime time." The new spots included The Rick demonstrating the versatility of "Rickwear," an Astroturf jacket that could double as a practice putting green. In another execution The Rick tried to convince ESPN to partner on a joint venture, "the official website of The Rick." In 2004 ESPN brought back The Rick once again, this time to promote the ESPN sports-awards program the ESPYs. Wearing his usual Boston sports garb, The Rick offered to trade used nasal strips worn by NFL players for tickets to the ESPYs.

OUTCOME

"The Rick" was recognized with a number of advertising-industry awards, a sign that it had accomplished the goal of breaking through the clutter of sports commercials. For the spot "Slot Cars—Scenarios," Ground Zero in 1998 won the 32nd annual Belding Award for the top low-budget commercial from the Advertising Club of Los Angeles. In 1999 Ground Zero was awarded the Belding Bowl for an ESPNews package made up of two TV spots, "Colors" and "Big Heads—Little Bodies," and a print ad entitled "The Rick, Rosin."

Not all reviewers reacted favorably to the campaign, however. Some did not find the spots to be funny and even thought that they were a bit unsavory. Writing in the *Los Angeles Times,* ad critic Denise Gellene observed, "In these spots, aimed at sports fans and cable programmers alike, The Rick comes off as a genuine sports-aholic. But his obsession lacks the zany quality of sports fanatics depicted in ads for other ESPN services. It seems The Rick needs to get a life—or at least a shower."

Despite the critics, The Rick was popular with ESPN's target audience, and the campaign played its part in successfully launching ESPNews. CNN-SI, in the meantime, failed to catch on and was ultimately dropped. When ESPN tapped The Rick to promote the ESPYs, ESPN received some of the best ratings it had experienced in several years for the program. "The Rick" campaign also helped to advance the acting career of O'Malley. He starred in the disastrous sitcom *The Mike O'Malley Show,* which was cancelled after two episodes in 1999, but found sitcom success as the star of the CBS sitcom *Yes, Dear,* which debuted in 2000. O'Malley also landed roles in such films as *Pushing Tin* and *28 Days.*

FURTHER READING

Elliott, Stuart. "ESPN Campaign Uses a 'Hostile' Web Site to Send Viewers Its Way." *New York Times,* February 27, 2001, p. C6.

Gellene, Denise. "ESPN Fumbles on 'The Rick,'" *Los Angeles Times,* March 5, 1998.

Jensen, Jeff. "Cable TV: Battle Gets Nasty for Eyes and Ears of Sports Junkies." *Advertising Age,* April 14, 1997.

Lefton, Terry. "ISL Latest to Shop College Grid Playoff with $2.4 Billion Plan." *Brandweek,* December 14, 1998, p. 16.

Seaman, Debbie. "What's the Big Idea?" *Advertising Age,* April 1, 1998.

Steinberh, Brian, and Suzanne Vranica. "ESPN Brings Off the 'Rick' Trick." *Wall Street Journal,* July 20, 2004, p. B8.

Takaki, Millie. "Ground Zero Tops Belding TV Competition." *Shoot,* May 7, 1999.

Robert Schnakenberg
Ed Dinger

THIS IS SPORTSCENTER CAMPAIGN

OVERVIEW

ESPN was launched in 1979 in Bristol, Connecticut, as the first cable television channel devoted exclusively to sports, although it had limited access to sports programming. One way to fill airtime was to run a daily sports-highlight show. Called *SportsCenter,* this program could offer much greater depth than the traditional five minutes reserved on the local news. It proved highly popular with viewers. In 1993 ESPN hired ad agency Wieden+Kennedy to promote the SportsCenter brand. What resulted was the "This Is SportsCenter" campaign, which would become one of the most popular and longest-running campaigns on television.

The campaign's television spots were humorous, topical vignettes that featured ESPN anchors, top athletes, mascots, and other celebrities. One of the most popular spots of the entire campaign parodied the fears of Y2K (also known as the millennium bug, which, it was believed, would cause many computers to crash when their clocks attempted to change the year from 1999 to 2000) by showing an ESPN Y2K test gone bizarrely awry. Chaos ensued in the darkened studios: sirens blared, and star athletes were out of control. The spot closed with crazed anchor Charlie Steiner holding a lantern, a tie wrapped around his head, and his face painted. "Follow me," he screamed, "Follow me to freedom!" The phrase became so associated with Steiner that in 2002, when he was invited to lead the crowd in the singing of "Take Me Out to the Ballgame" at Wrigley Field, he closed by exclaiming, "Follow me to freedom."

The "This Is SportsCenter" campaign was popular with ESPN's audience as well as critics, as reflected by its longevity. The campaign also won numerous awards, including the 1997 Best of Show (TV category) at the American Advertising Federation's ADDY Awards, the 1996 Ad Age Best of Show, and the 1997 Broadcast Best of Show at the American Advertising Awards. In 1999 *TV Guide* listed the campaign among the 50 greatest commercials of all time, and in 2002 the Cable & Telecommunications Association for Marketing inducted the "This Is SportsCenter" campaign into its Hall of Fame.

HISTORICAL CONTEXT

In 1979 Bill Rasmussen founded the first cable channel devoted entirely to the coverage of sports events and news. ESPN, or the Entertainment and Sports Programming Network, was headquartered on a remote tract of land in Bristol, Connecticut. Before ESPN and *SportsCenter,* which debuted with the network, sports news was "confined to the five minute ghetto on the eleven o'clock news," John Walsh, ESPN senior vice president, told the *Boston Globe.* ESPN expanded quickly, fueled in part by the evolution of sporting events into a pop-culture phenomenon. Athletes like Michael Jordan were no longer merely viewed as competitors; they were powerful celebrities in their own right. By 1998 ESPN reached 73 million homes, and, according to the *Boston Globe,* it was "hailed as cable's most financially successful experiment."

No longer just a single sports-broadcasting channel, ESPN had become a sports empire. The network grew to include numerous ventures that capitalized on the reputation and success of the original cable channel: ESPN2, a second sports cable channel that targeted a younger audience; ESPN International; ESPNews, a channel devoted exclusively to 24-hour sports news; ESPN SportsZone, a sports information and news site on the World Wide Web; and *ESPN Magazine,* a sports magazine intended to challenge *Sports Illustrated.* In addition, the network planned to expand further to include a chain of restaurants, ESPN Grill, and merchandise stores. By 1997 ESPN was worth an estimated $8 billion.

As ESPN's good fortunes grew, so did those of *SportsCenter,* which had become the network's most popular and best-known show. "It represents the network in its entirety," Tom Clendenin, ESPN's director of advertising, said of the program. "It represents ESPN as a franchise." *SportsCenter*'s anchors, including Chris Berman, Dan Patrick, and Keith Olbermann (who later left to host a news show at MSNBC), became celebrities virtually as popular as the athletes they covered. While ESPN and *SportsCenter* became more polished and creative, ESPN's promotions, according to *Advertising Age's Creativity,* "reflected that of a pretty conservative, straightforward cable programmer."

This would change in 1993, however, when ESPN hired Wieden+Kennedy, the same advertising agency that had turned the Nike logo into a universally recognized symbol. Together, Wieden+Kennedy and ESPN shifted the network's marketing strategy. They "wanted people to fall in love with ESPN the brand, and not just the programs," said Wieden+Kennedy's Larry Frey. Judy Fearing, ESPN's senior vice president of marketing, elaborated in *Advertising Age's Creativity*: "Wieden [was] . . . very involved in developing a personality for ESPN so that you don't just look at us and think highlights, you see an identity and an attitude." Before the "This Is SportsCenter" ads Wieden+Kennedy produced several well-received campaigns, including "Kooky College Tunes," in which lounge singer Robert Goulet serenaded NCAA basketball teams. The "This Is SportsCenter" campaign, however, represented the culmination of

Wieden+Kennedy's efforts to craft a memorable image for both *SportsCenter* and ESPN.

TARGET MARKET

The campaign's message, delivered with a deadpan humor that was reminiscent of the style of the *SportsCenter* anchors, was that ESPN was the hub of all sporting events. The amusing vignettes starring athletes, *SportsCenter* anchors, celebrities, coaches, and referees made clear the premise that ESPN was the world of sports. In this way the campaign reached out to any viewer with a passing interest in news of the day's sports. But men between the ages of 18 and 34 were consistently both ESPN's and *SportsCenter*'s core audience, and it was this group the network particularly wanted to target with the advertisements.

A combination of topicality and humor was the preferred method for reaching out to the core group. In its satirical style the campaign alluded to many of the same issues that sports fans followed on *SportsCenter.* Commercials were based on events such as the gutting of the Florida Marlins after their championship season of 1997, the penny-pinching practices of team owners, and boxer Mike Tyson's carnivorous tendencies. For instance, one spot featured the "trade" of the *SportsCenter* anchor Charley Steiner to *Melrose Place* in exchange for one of the good-looking actors from the soap-opera drama. Another spot, "Marlins Trade," featured batboys cut by the champion baseball team and hired as camera operators for *SportsCenter.* A spot called "KidsCenter" spoofed the match in which Mike Tyson bit off a chunk of Evander Holyfield's ear.

The campaign also spoofed athletes' personas, exaggerating their personality traits by placing them in incongruous situations. In one popular spot Grant Hill, a basketball player for the Detroit Pistons and a noted nice guy, played the piano, in uniform, in the lobby of the ESPN building in much the same manner as a pianist in a hotel bar. The slickness of the commercials, coupled with their implicit message that the viewer was in on a terrific inside joke, was intended to appeal directly to ESPN's target audience.

COMPETITION

The campaign's claim that ESPN was the dominant voice in sports reflected a certain reality. *SportsCenter* was far and away the most watched sports show on television, and ESPN landed several lucrative contracts to broadcast NFL and major-league baseball games. But ESPN faced emerging competition in the sports cable industry, often from channels that deliberately imitated the snappy tone and informal feel of *SportsCenter.* CNN-SI, launched after the merger of Time Warner (the owner of *Sports Illustrated*) and CNN, posed a threat because of its huge talent pool of CNN journalists and *Sports Illustrated* print reporters. But CNN-SI reached only 10 million homes and ultimately fell by the wayside. Fox Sports Network also looked hungrily at ESPN's revenues and popularity, but it lacked ESPN's strong sense of identity. *SportsCenter* faced more potent competition from local cable sports channels like Comcast in Philadelphia and Washington, D.C., which hosted *SportsNite,* a 30-minute program devoted exclusively to hometown teams. But when it came to covering sports on a national basis, *SportsCenter* simply had no peer.

"When you think about it, [everybody does] what they're doing—highlights, scores, and the controversial athlete soundbite of the day," declared an analyst to the *Boston Globe.* "They've distinguished themselves largely because of their attitude." The intangible attitude that distinguished *SportsCenter* from its cable-channel competitors was precisely what the "This Is SportsCenter" campaign strove to convey. But the commercials also tried not to diminish ESPN's reputation as the single most authoritative source of sports information.

In the view of ESPN its competition was not limited solely to other sports cable channels. It considered any program on any television network that went against *SportsCenter* as a competitor. Even programs such as *The Tonight Show* and *Late Night with David Letterman* were challengers. ESPN's Clendenin encapsulated his network's philosophy when he said, "SportsCenter is more than a sports show. It's an entertainment show."

FUNNY BUT TRUE

SportsCenter anchors stressed that, despite the zaniness of the "This Is SportsCenter" campaign, the show remained the preeminent voice in sports broadcasting. Dan Patrick told the *San Diego Union-Tribune,* "Amid the foolishness, SportsCenter has compromised nothing."

MARKETING STRATEGY

In 1995 Alan Broce, who was then ESPN's director of advertising, met with Wieden+Kennedy and elaborated the network's goals for the *SportsCenter* campaign. Hank Perlman, an avid *SportsCenter* fan and a copywriter for the agency, provided much of the early inspiration for the campaign. At a brainstorming session he hit upon a unique idea. "We were blown away by the silliness of this little industrial-park town which sports fans think is the place where it all happens," Perlman told

Entertainment Weekly. "So we decided, why not make Bristol the center of the sports universe?" Perlman went on to write most of the first 80 spots in the campaign. By 1997 the campaign had yielded more than 120 spots, yet they never appeared to lose their freshness or to become fragmented. According to *Advertising Age,* the strength of the campaign was that each spot stood for the spirit of the whole. The relatively low budget (the first 70 spots cost in total less than a million dollars to produce) provided Wieden+Kennedy with the flexibility to continually mine current events for creative advertising ideas.

Two of the most popular spots released in 1997, "KidsCenter" and "Broadcast News," received a great deal of attention. In "KidsCenter" Evander Holyfield, the heavyweight boxing champion, was overseeing a daycare center for the children of ESPN employees. Linda Cohn, one of the SportsCenter anchors, described the unique "skills" these children learned. Holyfield watched over the children as they boxed and admonished them "not to bite," a sardonic reference to the match in which Mike Tyson bit off a portion of Holyfield's ear. Holyfield continued his instruction as he warned the children, "Don't go out without your gloves on." Dutifully, the children left with boxing gloves. In "Broadcast News," a spoof of the movie of the same name, a relay race of athletes frantically rushed to get a tape on the air. The spot ended with Drew Bledsoe, the star quarterback for the New England Patriots football team, trampling the University of South Carolina basketball team's mascot.

Although the "This Is SportsCenter" campaign was primarily designed for television, the network released a series of print ads that appeared in sports magazines and in general-interest publications such as *Rolling Stone, Spin,* and *Entertainment Weekly. Advertising Age* reported that Wieden+Kennedy overcame the difficulties in "translating the humor from a TV campaign to a print campaign." The agency used still images to convey the campaign's fictional documentary style. For example, the television spot featuring Hill playing the piano in his basketball uniform was transformed in print to a single photo. The copy provided additional humor by noting that he was able to play only a couple of times a week during the basketball season.

Most of Wieden+Kennedy's efforts in the *SportsCenter* campaign were devoted to television. The commercials were aired on both ESPN and network television programs, primarily during prime-time sporting events such as NBA and NFL games. According to *Advertising Age's Creativity,* the overall strategy behind the network spots was "not only to increase use of regular viewers but to attract the occasional stray fan as well." In addition to snaring new viewers and convincing others to watch the network more often, the campaign was run on network television to increase the brand's visibility. "The goal was to make SportsCenter a talked-about brand," ESPN's Fearing told *Entertainment Weekly.*

The "This Is SportsCenter" campaign remained fresh and popular as the new century dawned. The television spots continued to maintain their humorous sensibility, and top athletes were eager to participate for the twice-yearly commercial shoots, willingly accepting their $1,000 fee, paid to the charity of their choice. The most significant change was the way the spots were unveiled to the public. In 2000 the latest batch of spots was first released as content on the ESPN website, www.ESPN.com. With only a limited amount of promotion, the initial spot posted on the first day was downloaded about 64,000 times. These four spots featured hockey player Ken Daneyko, basketball player Jerry Stackhouse, and comedian Carrot Top, who supposedly joined the *SportsCenter* staff in a bid to keep up with *Monday Night Football*'s hiring of comedian Dennis Miller.

In July 2002 *SportsCenter* aired its 25,000th installment, and to help commemorate the occasion Wieden+Kennedy produced new television spots in the "This Is SportsCenter" campaign. They featured Hilltopper, the Western Kentucky University fuzzy pink mascot, logging in past tapes of the show in the subbasement of the ESPN headquarters, as well as Los Angeles Clippers basketball player Elton Brand.

Instead of the usual array of star athletes, in 2004 the campaign focused on the winner of the national spelling-bee championship, covered by ESPN earlier in the year. The young champ, David Tidmarsh, was challenged by ESPN's Scott Van Pelt to spell "Pujols," the last name of the Saint Louis Cardinals' star player. There appeared to be no letup to the campaign. In fact, in 2006 ESPN found yet more ways to deliver the television spots to its viewers. They were available on demand at ESPN.com, delivered on DVDs, and in 2006 became downloadable as videos for use on MP3 players.

OUTCOME

The "This Is SportsCenter" campaign generated nearly constant attention from the media. Tom Shales, TV critic for the *Washington Post,* included the spots in his list of "the 35 things to be thankful for in television." He wrote that "the promos make you want to watch the show even if you hate sports and hate promos." *Entertainment Weekly* raved that the spots "have delivered some of the freshest entertainment on the tube." The campaign collected numerous industry awards, including Best of Show (TV) at the 1997 American Advertising Federation's ADDY Awards, the 1996 Ad Age Best of Show, and the 1997 Broadcast Best of Show at the

American Advertising Awards. In 1999 *TV Guide* ranked the campaign number 22 on its list of the 50 greatest commercials of all time. The Cable & Telecommunications Association for Marketing inducted the campaign into its Hall of Fame in 2002. Trade magazines such as *Shoot, Adweek,* and *Advertising Age* regularly ran articles lauding the innovation of the campaign. ESPN considered the buzz to be a sign of success. "Anytime you develop an advertising campaign that is talked about, you know that you've hit a home run," Fearing told the *Sacramento Bee.*

The *SportsCenter* campaign also succeeded in galvanizing public attention and moving the show into the realm of entertainment in the public consciousness. Photos of *SportsCenter* anchors Patrick and Olbermann were splashed across the same page in *TV Guide* as those of *Entertainment Tonight* cohost-turned-pop-singer John Tesh. The spots so captivated people's imagination that strangers on the street shouted out lines from specific *SportsCenter* promos when they caught sight of Patrick and Berman. Fearing again summed up ESPN's delight to *Entertainment Weekly* when she said, "Now SportsCenter is part of pop culture."

ESPN monitored the response through a telephone survey of hundreds of viewers. The results indicated that the campaign had indeed broken through. Ratings figures rose as more viewers tuned into the show, but even more importantly, viewers increasingly recognized the ESPN brand. "The consequence has been continuous ratings growth, unprecedented brand recall...and a positive buzz among sports elite," an ESPN executive told *Advertising Age.* Indeed, athletes as popular as Tiger Woods and Dennis Rodman called ESPN to request a spot in the commercials. But perhaps the best indication of the success of the "This Is SportsCenter" campaign was the spate of copycat spots inspired by the campaign. Companies such as the Weather Channel featured spots with the same documentary style and offbeat humor of the *SportsCenter* campaign. Fearing told *USA Today* in 2000 that she hoped the campaign ran forever, noting, "As long as there's athletes and pop culture to tap into, we'll keep doing it." Several years later the campaign was running strong with no end in sight.

FURTHER READING

Cuneo, Alice. "MPA Kelly Awards: The 1996 Finalists." *Advertising Age,* May 13, 1996.

Friedman, Wayne. "ESPN Treats Promos as Programming." *Advertising Age,* November 13, 2000, p. 8.

Garfield, Bob. "Best Awards: ESPN Scores Best of Show." *Advertising Age,* May 27, 1996.

Gough, Paul J. "ABC Sports, ESPN Tackle iTunes." *Hollywood Reporter,* January 4, 2006, p. 4.

Hogan, Monica. "ESPN Celebrates Milestone 'SportsCenter,'" *Multichannel News,* July 15, 2002, p. 98.

Jurkowitz, Mark. "They Know the Score with a Mixture of Fast Talk, Wacky Cultural Allusions, and Professional Expertise." *Boston Globe,* February 1, 1998.

McCarthy, Michael. "ESPN's 'SportsCenter' Ad Campaign Going Strong." *USA Today,* April 17, 2000.

Miller, Stuart. "SportsCenter: 25 Years of Excellence." *Broadcasting & Cable,* November 8, 2004, p. S48.

Nelson, John. "ESPN Scores with Ad Campaign." *Sacramento Bee,* April 23, 1996.

Quindt, Fritz. "Primo 'SportsCenter' Promos Make Fans Watch, Talent Known." *San Diego Union-Tribune,* April 26, 1996.

Shapiro, Leonard. "ESPN Ads Generating Talk." *Fort Worth Star-Telegram,* May 24, 1996.

Snierson, Dan. "Center of Attention with Assists from Athletes and Celebs." *Entertainment Weekly,* October 24, 1997.

Vagnoni, Anthony. "Head Games: ESPN Has Taken the Sometimes Lowbrow Image of the Sports Fan and Turned That into Ultra Cool." *Advertising Age's Creativity,* September 1, 1996.

Rebecca Stanfel
Ed Dinger

WITHOUT SPORTS CAMPAIGN

OVERVIEW

Beginning with its 1979 cable-television launch, ESPN, Inc. (then officially known as Entertainment and Sports Programming Network), strove to build a brand that was synonymous with sports. After progressively acquiring broadcasting rights to college basketball and football and then, one after another, to each of the major professional sports leagues, ESPN became the dominant sports network on television as well as a cable-industry model for success. Indeed, the proliferation of specifically targeted cable channels in the 1990s and 2000s owed a great deal to ESPN's example of successfully targeting sports-obsessed men. At the same time, the wide selection of channels that became available to most consumers made it ever more imperative that networks offer a clear brand image. In late 2002 ESPN unveiled its first overall branding campaign, "Without Sports."

Created by the New York office of ad agency Wieden+Kennedy (W+K), the "Without Sports" television spots ran during ESPN's own programming. The campaign attempted to reinforce the network's brand image as the sports-fan's lifeblood while simultaneously transcending the core audience of 18- to 34-year-old men to make the point that nearly everyone was, at bottom, a sports fan. Offering honest and at times humorous depictions of the intense ways in which sports and everyday life were inextricably linked, each commercial asked viewers to consider a particular element of human life that would be lost if sports did not exist. In the campaign's first season, for instance, a spot called "Coach" showed a wide cross-section of sports fans who, in the throes of complete emotional involvement with televised games, continually offered advice to the players. The commercial ended with the onscreen type, "Without sports, there'd be no one to coach." A spot in the campaign's second season showed a father and son playing basketball and postulated, "Without sports, how would we close the gap?"

"Without Sports" won a Gold Lion at the 2003 International Advertising Festival in Cannes, France, and ESPN research indicated that the campaign helped increase ratings as well as brand recognition in its first several years on the air. ESPN remained the premier cable network in the eyes of cable operators, viewers, and marketers during the campaign's multiyear run.

HISTORICAL CONTEXT

Started by entrepreneur Bill Rasmussen with funding from Getty Oil, ESPN made its television debut on September 7, 1979, at a time when fewer than 14 percent of American households had cable and the big-three broadcast networks could count on 90 percent of the country's television audience. Cable as a medium did not yet have a clear identity, and existing cable networks, such as HBO and WTBS, offered programming aimed at general audiences. More than just the first all-sports network, ESPN was the first network to target a specific segment of the American viewing public: namely, sports fans, the overwhelming majority of whom were men.

In its early years ESPN filled its programming schedule with a range of non-mainstream sports broadcasts, ranging from college baseball to tractor pulls to Australian Rules Football, and was further defined, in the public imagination, by the groundbreaking sports-news and highlights show *SportsCenter,* which ran nightly for one hour. The network was also instrumental in the popularization of college basketball; throughout the early 1980s ESPN attracted its largest audiences during its annual coverage of the NCAA men's basketball tournament and initiated the tournament-time phenomenon that came to be known as "March Madness." ESPN increased its profile further by acquiring broadcasting rights to college football games in 1984, but the network's watershed moment came with its first NFL football programming deal, in 1987; its subsequent *Sunday Night Football* broadcasts routinely topped the cable ratings. After cementing additional deals with Major League Baseball, the National Hockey League, and eventually the National Basketball Association, ESPN could legitimately claim to be "the ultimate destination for sports fans and the advertisers chasing them," as *Mediaweek*'s Keith Dunnavant put it.

ESPN's success proved, in the words of the network's first president, Chet Simmons, "that you could survive and prosper with a relatively small audience as long as you succeeded in targeting the right audience," and a wide range of niche networks followed in ESPN's wake, transforming television for both viewers and marketers. ESPN itself spawned six additional television networks as well as a successful magazine, the premier website of its kind, and numerous related ventures both in the United States and abroad. In the increasingly competitive cable-TV marketplace, the necessity for network branding became more apparent. Seeking to reinforce and extend its image as the premier source for sports on TV, ESPN enlisted ad agency Wieden+Kennedy's New York office to prepare the network's first-ever overall branding campaign in late 2002.

TARGET MARKET

ESPN had built its brand on the simple idea of appealing to men via 24-hour sports coverage. Among all men, 18- to 34-year-olds formed ESPN's core audience, a segment of the population that was both intensely coveted by marketers and notoriously difficult to reach. The network had further found, according to company executive Artie Bulgrin, that "if you target a demo like men 18 to 34, you aren't likely to alienate teens and you aren't likely to [alienate] the older viewers." This strategy had made ESPN the most effective network in reaching men, according to Jason Kanefsky of the media-consulting firm Media Planning Group. He explained, "ESPN delivers the double whammy of being able to attract a broad range of men with franchises like the NBA and NFL while also reaching the younger demos with hockey or the X Games."

The "Without Sports" commercials, which ran during the network's own programming, were designed to show this base of sports fans that ESPN was, according to Wieden+Kennedy art director Kim Schoen, "the world's biggest sports fan." At the same time, Schoen told *Creativity,* ESPN wanted to transcend the values of its traditional target audience "to make the point that sports are part of everybody's life in some way or another. Even if you don't think you're a sports fan, you probably are." The spots therefore focused on moments demonstrating essential connections between sports and ordinary life and asked viewers to consider various ways in which their lives would be less rich without sports.

WHO WOULD CHEER FOR THE NIMRODS?

Among the commercials in the second year of the ESPN "Without Sports" campaign were three 30-second spots featuring the real-life Watersmeet High School Nimrods' basketball squad from Michigan's Upper Peninsula. In addition to Nimrods players, the commercials included community members, such as the 1940 graduate who sang the school fight song and George Peterson, who, in addition to coaching the Nimrods, served as the school's athletic director and principal and as the school district's superintendent. All of the "Without Sports" commercials asked viewers to consider the consequences of a world without sports, and the Nimrods spots, intended to show the ways that sports could unify communities, phrased the question in the following way: "Without sports, who would cheer for the Nimrods?" Peterson told *Advertising Age* that, in the months following the spots' release, the school was deluged with mail and website hits and sold $40,000 worth of Watersmeet Nimrods athletic wear.

COMPETITION

During this time cable and satellite subscribers routinely had access to literally hundreds of television channels; therefore, it became increasingly necessary for networks to define their brands for consumers. Several prominent network-branding campaigns ran at the same time as "Without Sports."

The Turner Broadcasting System's TBS Superstation, historically associated with rebroadcasts of movies and live broadcasts of Atlanta Braves baseball games, had recently shifted its focus to syndicated reruns of comedy series, including *Sex and the City, Seinfeld,* and *Everybody Loves Raymond.* The network thus tapped the ad agency Publicis USA of New York to craft a 2004 campaign repositioning it as a comedy-focused outlet. Publicis used an absurdist setup suggesting that TBS was an authority on comedy; the spots showed ordinary people contacting TBS representatives at a call center to ask whether situations they had witnessed were funny or not. The TBS representatives walked the callers through a set of questions in order to derive an estimate of the situation's comic value. The spots ran with the tagline "TBS. Very funny."

The USA Network was likewise attempting, during this time, to craft a new image. The network enlisted 72andSunny, an agency based in Los Angeles, to dramatize USA's distinctiveness, and the agency came up with a series of promotions, including a 2004 spot using characters from two of the network's programs. Called "Dueling Disorders," the commercial featured Tony Shalhoub, the actor who played the obsessive-compulsive, eponymous hero of *Monk,* and Anthony Michael Hall, who played a psychic on the show *The Dead Zone.* In the commercial the two heroes encountered one another and were mutually repelled by their respective oddities.

The Fox Entertainment Group's Fox Sports Networks meanwhile hired San Francisco–based agency TBWA\Chiat\Day in 2001 to advertise the network's coverage of Major League Baseball and National Hockey League games and to craft the network's brand image. Fox Sports, which supplied content to roughly 20 regional networks, also developed spots focusing on its regional sports coverage.

MARKETING STRATEGY

Wieden+Kennedy's New York office, ESPN's primary agency since the mid-1990s, won the network's branding account with a spring 2002 pitch centering on a made-up game called Shelfball, which resembled baseball and involved a ball, a bookshelf, and an ornate compendium of rules. Supposedly invented by bored W+K staffers as early as 1999, Shelfball and the inexplicable intensity its players brought to the game served as one of the key concepts underlying the "Without Sports" idea. W+K's Kevin Proudfoot, a copywriter and creative director on the campaign, said that "Without Sports" was meant to capture "instances where sports and our lives intersect." Six spots revolving around the playing of office Shelfball aired in the initial months after the campaign's December 2002 launch, highlighting the contrast between the sport's foolishness and the players' complete seriousness in the heat of competition. The spots were comical, but they also conveyed the campaign's central idea of the almost mystical power that sports exerted on human life. The tagline for each of the Shelfball spots was "Without sports, a shelf would just be a shelf."

Other initial "Without Sports" spots were less reliant on humor and more sincere in addressing, as *Advertising Age*'s Bob Garfield phrased it, "the mystery of sports." The campaign's first-year flagship commercial, "Coach," showed, Garfield said, "fans from all walks of life, of all ethnicities and both major sexes, gripped in the pleasure-pain of a close game in progress, beseeching players to do the right thing." The action was punctuated by the tagline "Without sports, there'd be no one to coach." Another spot, reminiscent of a music video, featured hip-hop star Nelly rapping about sneakers while dressed, like his backup singers, in professional sports apparel. The commercial closed with the tagline "Without sports, there'd be nothing to wear."

In 2004 the campaign continued to depict true-to-life scenes illustrating the powerful ways in which sports and life were intertwined. "Makeshift" showed children energetically playing a variety of pickup sports games using improvised playing areas and equipment, like a laundry basket for a hoop and a pizza box for home plate. A series of three spots featured the Watersmeet High School Nimrods, an actual basketball team from Michigan's Upper Peninsula, in an attempt to show, as Proudfoot said, "how sports plays a role in bringing communities together." Another 2004 spot, "Foul Me," focused on how sports helped bring family members together, featuring a dad and his son playing basketball and using the tagline "Without sports, how would we close the gap?" For the 2005 NCAA basketball tournament ESPN focused on the idea of "Cinderella stories," those instances when long-shot teams overcame the odds to win emotional tournament victories. Using ESPN parent company Disney's classic cartoon *Cinderella,* W+K altered footage to show a sneaker-wearing Cinderella riding in a basketball-shaped carriage, in conjunction with the tagline "Without sports, Cinderella wouldn't wear sneakers."

OUTCOME

"Without Sports" generated favorable attention within the advertising industry and the press from its inception, and it won a Gold Lion at the 2003 Cannes International Advertising Festival. As of February 2004 ESPN could claim a ratings increase of 14 percent over the previous year and an increase of 41 percent over 2002, the year that closed with the airing of the first spots of the campaign. According to a January 2004 brand-relevance survey conducted by the network, 33 percent more people, as compared with results from the previous year, attested that they identified with the ESPN brand. As Lee Ann Daly, senior vice president of marketing at ESPN, told *Advertising Age,* "I don't think there's any question the campaign had something to do with it." As of 2005, according to Beta Research (a marketing-research firm), cable operators, viewers, and advertisers all ranked ESPN as the number one network in a variety of categories relative to perceived value, satisfaction, brand image, and marketing potential.

FURTHER READING

Anderson, Mae, and Celeste Ward. "Creative Briefs." *Adweek,* March 7, 2005.

Berelowitz, Marian. "They Shoot, They Score." *Adweek,* March 10, 2003.

"Campaign: ESPN." *Creativity,* January 2004.

"Campaign: ESPN." *Creativity,* March 2003.

Cisterna, Fred. "Acne." *Shoot,* March 28, 2003.

———. "Channel Surfing." *Shoot,* June 11, 2004.

Dunnavant, Keith. "Changing the Game." *Mediaweek,* July 26, 2004.

"ESPN 'Makeshift.'" *Creativity,* April 2005.

Garfield, Bob. "ESPN Plays on Spiritual Sway of Sports in Wieden Campaign." *Advertising Age,* February 3, 2003.

Thomaselli, Rich. "ESPN Vaults Tiny H.S. from Obscurity to Fame." *Advertising Age,* March 15, 2004.

Whitney, Daisy. "Where the Boys Are." *Television Week,* September 6, 2004.

Mark Lane

E*TRADE Financial Corp.

135 East 57th Street
New York, New York 10022
USA
Telephone: (646) 521-4300
Fax: (888) 276-9771
Web site: www.etrade.com

MONKEY TRILOGY CAMPAIGN

OVERVIEW

In early 2000 the high stock prices of America's technology industry were reaching their zenith. E*TRADE Financial Corp., along with other brokerage firms, such as Charles Schwab & Co., Inc., and TD Ameritrade Holding Corp., allowed stock traders to monitor and trade stock online. The flippant buy-sell behavior of day traders—along with the overvaluation of technology companies—was greatly responsible for the stock market's drastic collapse in mid-2000. Although E*TRADE was considered a dot-com, meaning it was a business that existed primarily online, its financial services included ATM retail banking, institutional brokerages, and asset management. E*TRADE released its "Monkey Trilogy" campaign to suggest that it was not just another half-baked dot-com but a formidable brokerage that could compete with established firms such as Charles Schwab and Merrill Lynch & Co., Inc.

The campaign consisted of three commercials created by the ad agency Goodby, Silverstein & Partners. The first spot, "Monkey," aired during the 2000 Super Bowl. At that time the technology sector was still flourishing. Of the game's 36 spots, 17 were purchased by dot-coms. "Monkey" featured two disheveled men clapping while a chimpanzee danced to the Mexican folk song "La Cucaracha" in a garage. The spot concluded with the copy "Well, we just wasted two million bucks. What are you doing with your money?" At the 2001 Super Bowl, after the technology industry had imploded, E*TRADE aired "Monkey II." The spot featured the same chimpanzee walking through a ghost town consisting of failed dot-com companies. The final Super Bowl commercial, in 2002, featured an E*TRADE executive firing the chimpanzee for creating an over-the-top E*TRADE commercial complete with dancing showgirls and big-band music.

Many advertising critics considered the "Monkey Trilogy" an insightful commentary on the rise and fall of America's technology industry. The first commercial garnered a Gold Lion at the Cannes International Advertising Festival. In 2000 *Shoot* magazine ranked "Monkey" above all other Super Bowl spots with its "Top Spot of the Week" rating. Audiences polled by *Adweek* also rated "Monkey" as the most memorable commercial out of all the 17 dot-com spots.

HISTORICAL CONTEXT

Trade Plus first surfaced in 1982 as an electronic brokerage firm for companies such as Charles Schwab. Ten years later Trade Plus created E*TRADE, an online service available only to stockbrokers. When www.etrade.com launched in 1996, E*TRADE's services also became available to the general public. Soon afterward the firm hired Christos Cotsakos as CEO, and the new executive took the firm public. The technology boom in the late 1990s fueled the popularity of purchasing and selling stocks online, which boosted E*TRADE's sales; in addition, the company's own stock price flourished.

In 1999 Goodby, Silverstein & Partners pitched its services to E*TRADE's Cotsakos, who quickly undermined the ad agency's concepts. Goodby, Silverstein & Partners' cochairman Rich Silverstein explained the experience in *Campaign,* an advertising-industry magazine. "The first meeting with him was like boot camp," he said. "It was really, really awful. Someone in our team—and I won't say who—came out saying they would never work for the man. He was challenging us to go to war with him, to see what we were made of. You don't usually get attacked in the first interview—usually it's a love fest. But he would ask you a question and you'd answer and he'd say, 'Wrong! Next!' " Despite an unfavorable start, however, E*TRADE awarded its ad account to the agency. Goodby, Silverstein & Partners soon released the "It's Time for E*TRADE" campaign, which collected a Gold EFFIE from the American Marketing Association in 2000.

Rich Silverstein explained the demands that Cotsakos placed on the agency leading up to the 2000 Super Bowl. "Christos always wanted to [advertising during] the Super Bowl," Silverstein continued in *Campaign.* "And he beat us up for six months. 'What's the Super Bowl commercial? What's the Super Bowl commercial?' It was unbelievable. Yeah, it was more pressure than anyone needs."

The agency believed that other dot-com ads were funny but that few connected their humor back to the brand. As a result, even though audiences enjoyed the commercials, they could not recall what was actually being advertised. The observation prompted Goodby, Silverstein & Partners to comment on its competitor's wasted advertising money and then contrast the wastage with E*TRADE's prudence.

GARAGE DOOR

Christos Cotsakos, the CEO of the online brokerage firm E*TRADE, had an atypical approach to leadership, according to *Campaign,* an advertising magazine. Inside an office building that served as E*TRADE's Menlo Park headquarters (the company moved to New York city in 2004), Cotsakos installed a regular garage door along an office hallway. The out-of-place furnishing was to remind E*TRADE employees that "behind some garage door somewhere, someone else could be working on ideas better than theirs."

TARGET MARKET

The original "Monkey" spot targeted the free-spending consumers who were still enjoying the technology boom at the beginning of 2000. One year later America's economic landscape had changed. Internet-based companies that could afford a $2 million Super Bowl spot in 2000, such as Pets.com, were no longer in existence. The economic slump of 2001 and 2002 changed the "Monkey" campaign's target. The second and third "Monkey Trilogy" commercials targeted America's growing jobless population that had once worked for dot-coms. It also targeted the suddenly sheepish investors that were recoiling from the damaged stock market. "E*TRADE always wants to be timely and on top of things," Dave Gray, Goodby, Silverstein & Partners group creative director and art director, explained to *Shoot.* "So, basically, [Monkey II] was just an observation of the condition of the market now&a lot of [dot-coms] are now out of business. The fact that there were only three [dot-com] companies advertising on the [2001] Super Bowl made it perfect timing."

With an estimated 135 million viewers during the 2000 Super Bowl and 131 million during the 2001 Super Bowl, the campaign reached one of America's largest audiences. Talking to *Shoot* magazine, Paul Cappelli, the president of the advertising service the Ad Store, New York, lightheartedly described the Super Bowl audience as "a bunch of morons sitting around a TV, watching a football game and drinking beer." Cappelli also explained that this target expected Super Bowl commercials to be funny. When the commercials were not, audiences sometimes felt confused.

The three "Monkey Trilogy" spots parodied other dot-com commercials. According to advertising analysts, using parody was a cost-effective method of reaching large audiences. Parody poked fun at something the target market already understood; it avoided the risk of creating an entirely new joke. "Advertising is one of our most popular forms of entertainment. So making jokes about ads can be a fun, 'in' thing to do," the marketing and advertising consultant Michael Markowitz explained to *USA Today.*

COMPETITION

On December 31, 1999, Merrill Lynch, one of the world's largest financial-services companies, released a $150 million campaign to herald its new online services under the tagline "Be Bullish." Although Merrill Lynch dwarfed competitors such as Charles Schwab, Ameritrade, and E*TRADE, the Merrill Lynch brokerage division had been criticized for its late delivery of an online trading service. Television spots for "Be Bullish" aired on cable channels such as CNN and USA. The campaign's premier television spot, which resembled a large-budget action movie, featured commandos rappelling from helicopters that were hovering above Manhattan. The helicopter squadron subsequently airlifted the 7,000-pound bull statue that was commonly associated with the New York Stock Exchange and Merrill Lynch's logo. "We're bringing the bull back," James Gorman, chief marketing officer at Merrill Lynch, said to *USA Today,* referring both to the company's logo and to an aggressive attitude within the stock market.

Charles Schwab reigned as America's largest online brokerage firm in 2000. Charles Schwab's "Smarter Investors" surfaced during the 2000 Super Bowl with three spots created by the ad agency BBDO New York. Until the Super Bowl "Smarter Investors" had only featured high-profile athletes such as tennis star Anna Kournikova and football player Shannon Sharpe. Hoping to stand out from the athletic climate of the Super Bowl, one Charles Schwab Super Bowl spot titled "Ringo" featured former Beatles drummer Ringo Starr explaining the stock market to younger musicians. "Using a non-sports personality, such as Ringo Starr, helps demonstrate the depth and breadth of this campaign," Ted Sann, cochief executive officer and chief creative officer of BBDO, said in a press release published in the PR Newswire news service.

MARKETING STRATEGY

The first "Monkey Trilogy" commercial cost an estimated $2 million. The 30-second spot "Monkey" began in front of a suburban-looking garage. Inside it one older man sitting on an ice chest was beside another man in a lawn chair. Next to them was an overturned bucket supporting a boom box. A chimpanzee dressed in an E*TRADE T-shirt pressed play on the boom box, which played the Mexican song "La Cucaracha." The ape began dancing; and the two men struggled to clap in time with the song. At the spot's conclusion copy read, "Well, we just wasted two million bucks. What are you doing with your money?"

The spot was originally conceived by Goodby, Silverstein & Partner's creative director Dave Gray and associate creative director Gerry Graf. Bryan Buckley of the production company Bicoastal/International Hungry Man directed the spot. Buckley explained his first impression of the commercial to *Shoot* "Gerry and Dave called me and said, 'OK, there's two guys clapping, and a monkey standing on a street corner, and it just goes on for thirty seconds,' and I'm thinking, 'This spot sounds terrible,'" Buckley mused. After he heard the spot's punch line, however, Buckley said, "I just laughed out loud because you just never expected that."

CHIMPS VS. HUMANS

Dave Gray, the group creative director and art director for the ad agency Goodby, Silverstein & Partners, helped film a commercial for the online brokerage firm E*TRADE. The spot, titled "Monkey," poked fun at dot-coms wasting money on poorly conceived Super Bowl commercials. "Monkey" featured two old men trying to clap while a chimpanzee danced to the song "La Cucaracha." Gray explained to *Shoot* magazine how working with the chimpanzee proved easier than working with humans. "You'd tell the monkey to run up the driveway, jump over the boom box, turn it on, jump up on the garbage can and start tapping its foot, and he'd nail it every single time," Gray said. "You tell the guy on the right to stop smiling and he'd start clapping."

Buckley explained that two of the spot's main challenges were choosing the right actors and selecting a filming location. Instead of using a street corner Buckley chose an unassuming garage for the location. One of the men cast in the spot was not even an actor, but the father of an actor with whom Buckley had worked previously.

Buckley then directed the 2001 E*TRADE commercial titled "Monkey II," which also used the chimpanzee from "Monkey." Instead of parodying wasted dot-com advertising, "Monkey II" commented on the bankruptcy that had plagued dot-coms since mid-2000. Only three dot-com companies, E*TRADE, Hotjobs.com, and Monster.com, aired commercials in the 2001 Super Bowl; a drastic difference from the 17 companies featured in 2000's game. "Monkey II" began with the chimpanzee riding his horse through a ghost town of fictional startup companies such as Pimentoloaf.com and TieClasp.com. The vanity plates of an abandoned Porsche Boxster read "DOT COMER." After a wrecking ball smashed through the "LeSocks.com" building, the sock-puppet dog that had starred in the previous year's Pets.com commercial landed at the chimpanzee's feet. "Monkey II" was not entirely humorous. For the conclusion, tears began running down the chimpanzee's cheek, and the copy "Invest wisely" appeared with E*TRADE's logo.

The final spot, "Monkey Musical," aired during the 2002 Super Bowl. Although the spot continued

E*TRADE's previous wasted-money theme, it received less acclaim from the advertising industry. The spot began with a chimpanzee bedecked in a shiny green suit before an ensemble of Las Vegas showgirls. After a 30-second musical act the white copy "Tomorrow morning" appeared on a black background. The chimpanzee was shown sitting in the office of E*TRADE's CEO, Christos Cotsakos. The disapproving executive held a newspaper with the headline "Monkey Flops" and berated the chimpanzee for advertising with a musical. He fired the chimp but set him up with a new job manning space flights for NASA.

OUTCOME

The first two "Monkey Trilogy" spots collected some of advertising's most coveted awards. In 2000 "Monkey" won a Gold Lion at the Cannes International Advertising Festival (in the investment, insurance, and property-development category). The same spot collected an ANDY Award in the financial products and services category of the International ANDY Awards, given out annually by the Advertising Club of New York. In the banking and financial category of the Clio Awards, it won a silver in 2001. "Monkey II" also collected an ANDY Award in the television category in 2002. It was short-listed in the investment, insurance, and property-development category at Cannes.

From 2000 until 2002 Goodby, Silverstein & Partners created other E*TRADE advertisements that coincided with "Monkey Trilogy." The combined effort safeguarded E*TRADE against the very thing "Monkey" accused other dot-coms of doing: wasting money. E*TRADE weathered the stock-market recession between 2000 and 2002 better than Merrill Lynch or Charles Schwab. Both posted a sales loss of 37 percent between 2000 and 2002. Even though it was grossly outsized by both Schwab ($4.4 billion in 2002 sales) and Merrill Lynch ($28.3 billion in 2002 sales), E*TRADE only decreased 13 percent during the same three-year-period. Sales for E*TRADE were $1.9 billion in 2002, a 13 percent decrease from the $2.2 billion posted in 2000.

FURTHER READING

Cuneo, Alice Z., and Richard Linnett. "Graf Lands at BBDO Again, Digs Straight into Doritos," *Advertising Age,* September 25, 2000, p. 4.

DeSalvo, Kathy. "DGA Nominees Reflect on Best Spot Director Honor." *Shoot,* February 9, 2001, p. 1.

———. "Evolution: Monkey See, Monkey Cry." *Shoot,* February 2, 2001, p. 16.

Dill, Mallorre. "Post-Game Wrap Up." *Adweek,* February 7, 2000, p. 20.

Elliott, Stuart. "Ad Bowl 2001 Will Be a Rout." *New York Times,* January 26, 2001, p. 1.

———. "Big Plays, Surprise Heroes, Shocking Defeats and Other Super Bowl XXXIV Marketing Memories." *New York Times,* February 1, 2000, p. 10.

———. "The Super Bowl XXXV Commercials, from Pleasant Surprises to Whose Idea Was This." *New York Times,* January 30, 2001, p. 8.

Garcia, Sandra. "Buckley Plays Monkey in the Middle for E*Trade." *Shoot,* February 4, 2000, p. 14.

Gaylin, Alison Sloane. "Bryan Buckley." *Shoot,* March 24, 2000, p. 24.

Hall, Amanda. "The Man Who Made a Monkey out of Advertising." *Campaign,* September 15, 2000, p. 40.

Kelly, Michael. "Prep Grad's Monkey Ad." *Omaha World-Herald,* February 1, 2001, p. 11.

Mark, Michael. "Boring Bowl." *Shoot,* February 9, 2001, p. 4.

Marshall, Caroline. "The Cream of Cannes." *Campaign,* July 7, 2000, p. 26.

McCarthy, Michael. "Marketers Turn Out Spoofs to Connect Quickly with Viewers." *USA Today,* April 23, 2001, p. B03.

Takaki, Millie. "Getting into the KQED 'Swing' of Things." *Shoot,* March 2, 2001, p. 11.

Vranica, Suzanne. "Advertising." *Wall Street Journal,* December 22, 2000, p. B3.

Wells, Melanie. "On the Cover." *Forbes,* January 24, 2000, p. 70.

Wilkinson-Ryan, Tess. "The Work." *Advertising Age's Creativity,* March 1, 2001, p. 15.

Kevin Teague

WHY WOULDN'T YOU? CAMPAIGN

OVERVIEW

A pioneer of online stock trading, E*Trade Financial Corp., spending heavily on advertising that used irreverent humor, established itself in the minds of consumers during the 1990s. As long as the stock market and economy were booming, this marketing approach proved quite successful. That all came to an end in the early 2000s as the economy stalled, the dot-com bubble burst, and the stock market collapsed. People who dabbled in the market with their online accounts grew cautious. Faced with a severe erosion in business, E*Trade retrenched, bringing in new leadership that slashed the advertising budget and diversified the company's product offerings. When the stock market rebounded in 2003, E*Trade initiated a change in marketing strategy, hiring Minneapolis-based Martin/Williams Advertising to handle the advertising account. The agency developed the "Why Wouldn't You" campaign, which began in February 2004.

The new campaign featured a pair of television spots that repositioned the E*Trade brand while specifically promoting the company's mutual fund and mortgage products. Print elements, direct marketing, and in-store promotional pieces also played a part in the effort, which was slated to spend $90 million over the course of the year.

Only weeks after the "Why Wouldn't You" campaign began, however, E*Trade changed marketing heads. Although Martin/Williams soon lost the account, the campaign it created succeeded in helping E*Trade to add some 372,000 new accounts, significantly grow its mutual fund and mortgage business, and increase its overall assets by 35 percent over the previous year.

HISTORICAL CONTEXT

E*Trade essentially invented online trading in 1991. As the economy soared in the second half of the 1990s and Internet ventures became the darlings of Wall Street, it enjoyed phenomenal growth. E*Trade spent heavily on advertising, about $140 million a year at one point. Like another newcomer in the brokerage business, Ameritrade, E*Trade used irreverent humor to establish its brand and appeal to a younger demographic, suggesting that stock trading was like playing a game while mocking traditional stock brokers, portrayed as stodgy and being interested only in customers who had already made their fortunes. The culmination of these free-spending days for E*Trade was a 2000 Super Bowl television spot that featured a chimpanzee and the text "Well, we just wasted 2 million bucks. What are you going to do with your money?"

Soon the dot-com bubble burst, and E*Trade was hurt like all the other Internet companies. And because the economy collapsed as well and the stock market tanked, people no longer saw stock trading as a game. Even consumers who harbored no desire to play day trader were hurt, as their 401(k) accounts and mutual funds suffered major losses. E*Trade lost almost half its customer base and in response slashed its ad budgets. Moreover, there was little money to be made in stock transactions themselves, prompting old-line firms to get out of the business. In early 2003, following a corporate shakeup, a new CEO was installed and E*Trade looked to revamp its business model. To mitigate the risk of becoming a niche player in the volatile online stock trading niche, E*Trade looked to diversify—an effort that was actually under way—moving into such areas as institutional trading, market making (acting as middleman in stock transactions), mutual funds, banking, lending, mortgages, and stock plan administration services. Along with adopting a more conservative, product-centered strategy, E*Trade also decided to reconsider its advertising.

E*Trade's advertising account, now estimated to be worth $35 to $45 million a year, was put up for review with five agencies participating. Incumbent Goodby, Silverstein & Partners, responsible for the Super Bowl chimp spot, opted not to participate. In October 2003 Martin/Williams emerged the winner. The new agency was charged with the task of repositioning the E*Trade brand as a safe haven for serious money. At the same time, E*Trade wanted to take advantage of an upswing in the stock market and promote its trading division. While humor would remain a key element in the E*Trade approach, the company looked to avoid the pure zaniness of past advertisements.

TARGET MARKET

Martin/Williams's first task was to determine the target customer for what would become the "Why Wouldn't You" campaign. The agency zeroed in on self-directed investors, the kind of people who mistrusted the traditional financial companies, perceiving them to be controlling and unapproachable. Although Morgan Stanley, Goldman Sachs, Merrill Lynch, and the like were now preaching "partnership," the consumers that E*Trade targeted were somewhat skeptical of this pitch, especially in light of recent Wall Street scandals in which some of these very same firms had knowingly sold marginal stocks to smaller clients while saving the prime issues for themselves and favored customers. Starting with the self-directed investor, Martin/Williams narrowed this target audience into what it saw as three focused subsegments, which research indicated was responsible for more than 60 percent of all brokerage accounts, online banking, and mutual fund investing. At least on the brokerage side, E*Trade and its online rivals were also "targeting a warier and more tech savvy customer than the newcomers who helped set the heady tone for the online broker industry in the 1990s," according to Kate Fitzgerald writing in *American Demographics,* eschewing "the soccer-mom day trader making a killing in her kitchen during the late 1990s" in favor of "the most active and experienced traders who generate the most profits."

COMPETITION

E*Trade's most direct competitor was Ameritrade Holding Corp., which had pursued a similar irreverent, free-spending marketing approach during the 1990s. Ameritrade continued to promote its brokerage services through humorous television spots. Shortly after Martin/Williams won the E*Trade account, Ameritrade launched its "Good Idea. Bad Idea" campaign to tout its flat pricing approach and other benefits. In one spot a man getting in a New York taxi said, "One flat rate, right? L.A. please." "Flat rate pricing," explained a voice-over. "Bad idea for taxis. Good idea for online trading." Another competitor

"WE BELIEVE WE HAVE A GOD-GIVEN RIGHT TO MARKET SHARE"

For seven years, from the mid-1990s to the early 2000s, E*Trade was headed by CEO and chairman Christos M. Cotsakos, a former Vietnam infantryman, who brought with him a foxhole mentality: you have to trust the person next to you. He became known for his team-building exercises and initiation rites, such as having newcomers stand on a chair to reveal something about themselves before a group of coworkers. He once had his managers attend cooking school and then work together to create a gourmet dinner. Cotsakos was also extremely aggressive, telling *BusinessWeek,* in a 2000 profile, "At E*Trade, we're an attacker, we're predatory. We believe we have a God-given right to market share." But with the popping of the Internet bubble—and after it was revealed that his salary was $80 million in 2001, a year in which his company lost more than $240 million—Cotsakos went from being regarded as a visionary to becoming a poster child for dot-com excess, after it was revealed that his salary was $80 million in 2001, a year in which his company lost more than $240 million.

in this sector was Fidelity Investments, which at the time was promoting its "active trade services." Taking a more emotional approach, this campaign featured a TV spot in which a man appeared to be a high-powered investor or fund manager executing offers from his well-apportioned office only to have it revealed, once the door was opened, that he was at home. Other online trading rivals included Charles Schwab & Company and TD Waterhouse Investor Services, Inc.

In its new businesses, E*Trade faced competition from numerous angles, as a wide swath of companies were positioning themselves as one-stop shopping centers of financial services. It was not just firms like Merrill Lynch, Goldman Sachs, and Citigroup subsidiary Salomon Smith Barney that E*Trade had to contend with in this arena. There were also a multitude of insurance companies, banks, and even mutual fund companies, such as giants Fidelity Group and the Vanguard Group, which also provided stiff competition.

MARKETING STRATEGY

In keeping with its changing business model, E*Trade looked to evolve its marketing message and brand positioning. Because the targeted self-directed consumer exhibited an antipathy for old-guard financial firms, which the consumer saw as primarily interested in feathering their own nests, E*Trade wanted to portray itself as a sort of consumer advocate, one that was looking out for the little guys and offering them trustworthy ways to build wealth.

In addition to promoting its online trading service to take advantage of the rebounding stock market, the new E*Trade campaign also looked to target new services, like mutual funds and mortgages. Many customers, viewing their E*Trade accounts as "play" money, dabbled in the stock market without much worry. They generally put their "safe" money, however, in mutual funds. One of the tasks of the marketers was to assure these customers that E*Trade, despite its history of wacky television commercials, was a reliable harbor for their money. It was an opportune time to enter the field, given that the mutual fund industry faced allegations that it engaged in illegal trading and overcharging customers. In keeping with the consumer advocacy approach, E*Trade made the marketers' job easier by a change in fund structuring, in particular the 12b-1 fees that many mutual funds charged customers to cover the cost of promoting the funds. E*Trade became the first in the industry to rebate half of those and other service fees to its mutual fund customers. In the mortgage area E*Trade also gave the marketers something to work with by streamlining the way a mortgage was arranged and by launching the Mortgage on the Move program, allowing customers to move to a different market but keep their low mortgage rate. Again the company depicted itself as a consumer advocate.

As important as it was to position the brand, to maintain that E*Trade was looking out for the little guy, E*Trade still had to find a way to close the deal, to make potential customers take action. The strategy of the new ads was to get people to question their behavior and to present them with a tangible benefit, urging them to take advantage of it. In essence the benefit was a no-brainer, and E*Trade asked people, "So why on earth wouldn't you?" The phrase "Why on earth wouldn't you?" became the theme and encapsulation of the new campaign.

As the "Why Wouldn't You" campaign broke in February 2004, E*Trade announced that it planned to double its advertising budget in 2004 to $90 million. The first two television spots pursued the new theme and reintroduced the brand while specifically promoting some of E*Trade's new products. The first spot, titled "Purse," pitched the company's mutual funds by playing up its fee rebate program. In it a man was seen running with a purse through a crowded city street. The commercial then cut to a woman who appeared to be chasing him, presumably because he had stolen her purse. She got on a bus, and in an unexpected twist, the commercial showed the man catching up to her to return the purse. In a further surprise the woman opened the purse to find that it contained more money than when she had lost it. A voice-over by actor Kevin Bacon then asked, "If you could own the same mutual funds and get cash back every year, why on earth wouldn't you?"

A second spot, titled "New Neighbors," promoted E*Trade's Mortgage on the Move program. In it a suburban couple watched their new neighbors move in. Out of the car and moving van emerged a host of horrors, including crying babies, armed skinhead adolescents, screaming adults, barking dogs, dirt bikes, alligators, and killer bees. In this spot Bacon intoned, "When it's time to move, E-Trade's new mortgage on the move goes with you. If you could move and keep your low mortgage rate, why on earth wouldn't you?"

The new E*Trade television commercials aired on a variety of national cable channels. They also aired on network television during the NCAA basketball tournament in March. In addition to these spots (which were the primary focus of the "Why Wouldn't You" campaign), other elements included a companion print campaign that ran in national newspapers and magazines, some direct marketing, in-store promotional pieces for E*Trade's walk-in branches, and an Internet component that included Web banners.

OUTCOME

E*Trade's chief marketing officer resigned two months after the "Why Wouldn't You" campaign broke and was replaced in June 2004 by Nicholas Utton, who soon put the account up for review once again. Martin/Williams was part of Omnicom Group, and Utton was portrayed in the press as an "Interpublic Group loyalist." While head of marketing at JP Morgan Chase and MasterCard International, he had forged a successful relationship with Interpublic shops McCann Erickson, Foote Cone & Belding, and the Martin Agency. It was not surprising, therefore, when E*Trade and Martin/Williams severed their relationship in July 2004. By all accounts it was an amicable parting. Martin/Williams spokesman Steve Rudolph explained to the press, "It's a business of relationships," while in a released statement, president Steve Collins noted, "With a change in marketing leadership often comes changes in agencies and we wish E*Trade the best as they move forward."

Although Martin/Williams did not have the chance to roll out additional phases, the "Why Wouldn't You" campaign succeeded in improving E*Trade's overall business as well as benefiting the firm's mutual fund and mortgage products. According to the agency E*Trade added nearly 372,000 new accounts in the six months after the campaign began. E*Trade also experienced a 35 percent increase in overall assets compared to the previous year. Moreover these assets were spread across a wider range of products. The campaign's mutual fund component, according to Martin/Williams, succeeded in attracting a higher-value customer, resulting in a 22 percent increase in E*Trade's mutual fund business. Likewise E*Trade's mortgage operation enjoyed a 33 percent increase in direct mortgage originations, although the company also benefited from a refinance boom caused by low interest rates. The campaign garnered no advertising awards, but it accomplished the goals laid out by the client. It was only a change in management at E*Trade that was responsible for Martin/Williams losing the account.

FURTHER READING

Baar, Aaron. "E*Trade Boosts Marketing Budget." *Adweek,* February 19, 2004.

———. "E*Trade, M/W Go Separate Ways." *Adweek,* July 27, 2004.

———. "Martin/Williams Is Selected for E*Trade." *Adweek,* September 24, 2003.

———. "Trading Co.'s Adspend Takes Off with Market." *Adweek,* February 23, 2004, p. 12.

Fabrikant, Geraldine. "E*Trade Parts with Martin/Williams." *New York Times,* July 29, 2004, p. C3.

Fitzgerald, Kate. "The New Cautious Optimists." *American Demographics,* April 1, 2004.

Janoff, Barry. "Beware of the Ghoul Next Door." *Brandweek,* March 15, 2004, p. 34.

Kaplan, David. "No Joke: How Money Talks Now." *Broadcasting & Cable,* April 26, 2004, p. 24.

Steinberg, Jacques, and Matthew Preusch. "E*Trade Chooses Martin/Williams." *New York Times,* September 26, 2003, p. C4.

"Tricks of E*Trade." *BusinessWeek,* February 7, 2000, p. EB18.

Ed Dinger

Euromarket Design, Inc.

1250 Techny Rd.
Northbrook, Illinois 60062
USA
Telephone: (847) 272-2888
Fax: (847) 272-5366
Web site: www.crateandbarrel.com

CRATE & BARREL 1998 PRINT ADS CAMPAIGN

OVERVIEW

In October 1998 Euromarket Design, Inc. launched an advertising campaign for Crate & Barrel, its chain of housewares and furniture stores. With an estimated budget of $3.5 million, Chicago-based ad agency McConnaughy Stein Schmidt Brown (MSSB) created a visually striking print campaign that appeared in national publications and regional magazines. While most of Crate & Barrel's previous advertising had focused on selling individual products, the new campaign attempted to burnish Crate & Barrel's overall brand image and distinguish the company from its various rivals. Although the market for housewares was growing—as consumers' real wages rose, new home construction surged, and aging baby boomers spent more on redecorating—Crate & Barrel faced increased competition from other housewares retailers, ranging from other upscale stores such as Williams-Sonoma Inc.'s Pottery Barn to the mass merchandiser Target, owned by the Dayton Hudson Corp.

Crate & Barrel did not abandon specific products completely in its effort to promote its new image. Instead, the 1998 print ads paired shots of individual offerings with scenes of nature or buildings. The copy for the ads was somewhat lengthy and relied on a subdued wittiness to convey the campaign's message—that Crate & Barrel offered timeless products that imbued one's life with simplicity. For instance, one of the five ads queried, "What does one of our tables have in common with an afternoon in the country? Or one of our chairs with a lakeside sunset?" The copy continued, "Well, all warmly embrace the concept of simplicity: Clearly a plus in an age when three-fourths of the world's surface is covered with water, but four-fifths is wired for cable." An elegant, classic table was portrayed next to a scene of a wooden bridge expanding out over the ocean to the horizon line. The company's logo was discreetly placed in the corner of the piece. Other ads depicted a Crate & Barrel chair (along with a deserted shoreline), a goblet (with a snow-covered pastoral scene), plates (with a country chapel), and stockings stuffed with presents (with another snowy landscape). While some of the print executions were clearly holiday oriented, they nevertheless attempted to impart the campaign's overall theme, that Crate & Barrel was "not just a local housewares shop," as Heidi Musachio, an account supervisor at MSSB, told *Adweek.*

Like most other retailers, Crate & Barrel's peak business was during the holiday season. Accordingly, the campaign ran through December 1998 and then ended. Although the company's sales figures rose during the duration of the campaign and the ads received plaudits from the advertising community, Crate & Barrel shifted its advertising account to the recently formed Chicago ad shop Tucker Tapia and returned to more product-focused spots.

HISTORICAL CONTEXT

Crate & Barrel's humble origins gave no indication of its future status as a housewares and furniture "powerhouse," as the *Chicago Tribune* described the company. Founded in 1962 by Gordon and Carole Segal, the first Crate & Barrel store was housed in an abandoned elevator factory in Chicago and stocked with specialty housewares items. Because they could not afford expensive merchandise fixtures, the Segals displayed their wares on packing crates and barrels, thereby hitting upon the catchy name for their venture. "I knew plenty of young people like us with good taste and no money," Gordon Segal told *HFN: The Weekly Newspaper for the Home Furnishing Network.* "Who was catering to them?" As the company expanded and opened new stores, Crate & Barrel won the allegiance of the baby boomer generation—who increasingly earned more money to complement their "good taste"—with its distinctive and well-made products.

In the early 1990s Crate & Barrel broadened its offerings to include furniture. In fact, by 1995 furniture accounted for one-third of the company's sales. After its 1994 revenues topped $272 million, Crate & Barrel opened a Manhattan store in 1995 with a splashy campaign. By 1996 Crate & Barrel had grown to 62 retail outlets in 15 U.S. markets and did a brisk catalog business as well. Segal teamed up with German mail-order giant Otto Versand in 1998 to help fuel expansion of the privately held company. At the time the 1998 Crate & Barrel print campaign debuted, Segal boasted to the *Chicago Tribune* that "we've never had business better."

TARGET MARKET

Crate & Barrel's success was due in part to the financial well-being of its core customers, those consumers aged 35 to 60. According to *Gifts and Decorative Accessories,* the bullish U.S. economy had created "new pockets of affluence," in which "5 percent of the population [was] made up of households with incomes of more than $100,000." Leading the pack were baby boomers, who had sown their wild oats in the 1960s and 1970s and had settled down into middle age and family life by the 1990s. As a result, as the *Chicago Tribune* noted, these consumers chose "to spend their cash on decorating, remodeling, and expanding their homes." In 1997 "boomer-led families making more than $70,000 a year spent almost $100 billion on home-related products," the *Los Angeles Times* reported. Crate & Barrel's furniture sold especially well among baby boomers, who were more apt than their younger counterparts to devote thousands of dollars to new furniture. The company recognized that it would need to attract these mature consumers with its 1998 print campaign.

To reach this audience, Crate & Barrel incorporated themes that resonated with the group. After the rampant consumerism that had characterized much of the 1980s, the affluent classes of the 1990s largely eschewed this worldview and at least paid lip service to the notion of simplicity—of living with less and thereby living more fully. Moreover, as baby boomers aged, they grew nostalgic for the past. Crate & Barrel incorporated both of these sentiments into its 1998 print campaign. One of the ads, which depicted an oversized chair with classic lines and minimal detailing as well as an empty wooden bench facing the seemingly infinite span of the sea, proclaimed that "things were simpler 'then.' Or so we often hear. But if things were simpler 'then' does that mean they have to be more complicated now? Not by a long shot. At Crate & Barrel we've got a veritable store full of classic designs that prove 'then' doesn't own simple. It merely has a time share." The message was clear. Not only were Crate & Barrel's products themselves attractively and stylishly straightforward, but they could also seamlessly connect consumers to a less complicated past. As Segal told *HFN,* "We're selling concepts and lifestyles, not items."

Baby boomers were not the only consumer group interested in housewares, however. "American consumers' passion for the home spans to the young," noted *Gifts & Decorative Accessories.* First-time home buyers and newlyweds were crucial customer groups for Crate & Barrel as well. In an effort to draw in the soon-to-be-married (and those who wished to lavish gifts upon them), the company had become one of the first non-department stores to offer a gift registry. By 1997, 17 percent of its sales were derived from this tremendously popular service. One of the 1998 print pieces spoke directly to this group. The spot, which featured Crate & Barrel dishes and a photo of a humble-looking church, declared that "the average person spends 26 years finding the right partner. 13 months finding the right church. 8 months finding the right caterer. And 6 months finding the right honeymoon spot. Which just may explain why the average person ends up with the wrong plates." According to Jim Schmidt, MSSB's creative director for the campaign, the ad's use of tongue-in-cheek humor and visually arresting images was intended to appeal to younger consumers, an important demographic group for the retailer. While older consumers, who were at the apex of their careers and thus their earning capacities, had more disposable income, younger consumers—who were often embarking on their first housewares purchases—were crucial to Crate & Barrel's long-term success. Brand allegiances were formed early in life and lasted for a long time, and the company that could garner a following among the young would have a significant competitive advantage.

ON-LINE VENTURES

In addition to its fall print campaign, Crate & Barrel ventured into other new territories in 1998. In June the company teamed up with Fry Multimedia to launch its first website. Just as the print ads attempted to convey the "feel" of the Crate & Barrel experience, so too did the on-line effort. According to *DM News,* Fry Multimedia incorporated photographs "to create a light and airy ambiance, a look consistent with Crate & Barrel's other sales channels."

COMPETITION

Crate & Barrel faced considerable competition. According to the *Arizona Republic,* "The retailing landscape [was] packed with companies trying to cash in on the home craze." On the one hand, Crate & Barrel was challenged by other upscale housewares stores, especially Pottery Barn and Restoration Hardware Inc. On the other hand, mass-merchant retailers had begun to offer inexpensive imitations of the items found in more expensive stores. Target proved a particularly potent adversary for Crate & Barrel in this segment. Moreover, as a furniture seller, Crate & Barrel competed against more traditional furniture retailers. "Everybody is your competition nowadays," Segal told the *Wall Street Journal.* "The whole marketplace is more dynamic and aggressive."

In the realm of specialty stores, Pottery Barn primarily appealed to a younger, hipper customer. With its slightly less expensive products and dim store interiors, Pottery Barn attracted consumers with what *Forbes* termed its "relaxed contemporary" merchandise. The Swedish company Ikea AB, a chain of rapidly expanding furniture and housewares stores, drew an even younger core audience, often including college students and others furnishing their first apartments. At the other end of the demographic spectrum was Restoration Hardware, which, according to *Business Week,* "cannily play[ed] off childhood memories of nesting baby boomers." Founded in 1979 by Stephen Gordon after he had been unable to find authentic-looking fixtures for a remodeling project, the chain evolved into far more than the average neighborhood hardware store. Pricey furniture shared the floor with mirrors, lamps, and a number of knickknacks such as old-style toys. Each store had a hardware section, but Restoration Hardware's focus was predominantly on its housewares and furniture. Gordon's brainchild was also engaged in rapid expansion. At the close of 1998, 65 stores were in operation, often in close proximity to Crate & Barrel's venues. "Their customer is our customer," Bette Kahn, a Crate & Barrel representative, told *Business Week.*

Although Kmart Corp. had made headway into a more upscale market with its line of Martha Stewart Everyday housewares, Target was the clear leader among the giant retailers in drawing more affluent customers, those who might otherwise frequent Crate & Barrel. According to *Fortune,* Target's average customer was a college-educated woman with an income above $50,000. The more than 850 Target stores had seen a 26 percent increase in sales between 1997 and 1998, and the company's stock had risen a stunning 527 percent since 1995. Target's success stemmed from its persistence in "always looking to have the latest things," a retail analyst told *Fortune.* As *HFN* explained, "Instead of trying to copy a department store, Target's MO has been to emulate a Pottery Barn or a Crate & Barrel, and to translate those colors and trends to the masses." Designer Michael Graves offered a line of futuristic housewares exclusively at Target, which expanded the home section of its superstores to highlight such offerings. The chain also began to carry elite brands, such as the cookware line Calphalon, which once would have been considered too upmarket for Target. As part of its ongoing branding efforts, Target inaugurated the "Grab Your Own Style" campaign in 1998, which stressed the company's more sophisticated image. The campaign kicked off with a 16-page insert in *Bon Appetit,* a food and cooking magazine that catered to older and more affluent readers. With its focus on the coordinated home decorating ideas available at Target, "Grab Your Own Style," like Crate & Barrel's 1998 print campaign, touted notions of simplicity and fashion more than individual products.

MARKETING STRATEGY

Crate & Barrel strove to forge a distinct brand image for itself with its 1998 print effort. "The goal of the campaign was to reaffirm in people's minds that when you buy something from Crate & Barrel it is classic and timeless," MSSB's Schmidt explained. While Pottery Barn imbued its stores with a more funky aura and Restoration Hardware banked on a warm nostalgia, Crate & Barrel's 1998 print ads stressed elegant simplicity. Of course, to impress this message upon consumers, the ads had to be noticed. Schmidt emphasized that the executions were intended to stand out from the page in order to capture the reader's attention. Half black-and-white and half color, the spots were indeed striking. For instance, one piece depicted a single goblet, which was photographed to reveal every simple detail, every line, and every reflection of light from its surface. This artful presentation made it seem much more than a glass; it became an image, representing the essence of the Crate & Barrel brand.

By posing the goblet next to the scene of a snowy landscape, Crate & Barrel further refined the aura of simplicity. The ad copy humorously reinforced this notion by undercutting any sense of pretentiousness that might be conveyed by the photo: "It's the time of year when we raise a glass to our family and to our friends. To our pasts and to our futures. It's the time of the year when we raise a glass to our dreams and to our hopes. In short, it's the time of the year when there's a lot of pressure on a glass." Segal explained the principle underlying Crate & Barrel's advertising (as well as its store presentation) to *HSN:* "To be a good retailer, you've got to have that theatrical ego-centricity. You're setting an atmosphere and the architecture." Crate & Barrel ran the pieces in publications that were read by the upscale, home-oriented audience it sought. These included *Martha Stewart's Living* and *Metropolitan Home,* as well as the Sunday magazines of the *New York Times* and the *Chicago Tribune.*

The timing of the 1998 print campaign was also carefully calculated. Unlike some other industries, housewares retailers did a substantial portion of their business during the holidays, when consumers purchased new items either for their own entertaining or to give as presents. The campaign therefore debuted in October and ran through this peak period. In addition to the goblet piece, Crate & Barrel employed the holiday theme in an ad that portrayed three stockings stuffed with wrapped packages. Above another snowy scene, the copy expressed every parent's Christmas reality: "5:05am: Can we go downstairs now? 5:10am: Can we go downstairs now? ... 5:34am: Can we go downstairs now?" The spots featuring the company's tables and chairs stayed away from holiday motifs, however, since furniture sales tended to be less seasonally sensitive.

OUTCOME

By all accounts Crate & Barrel's 1998 print campaign achieved impressive results. According to MSSB's Schmidt, the company's sales during the holiday shopping season rose between 5 and 10 percent. The ads were also praised by advertising critics. In addition to being recognized at several Chicago awards shows, the campaign was ranked among the year's best by Communications Arts. Nonetheless, because of the business cycle in the housewares industry, Crate & Barrel ended the campaign at the close of the holiday season.

In April 1999 Crate & Barrel switched ad agencies, settling on Tucker Tapia. Its new campaign, launched that month, returned to the more product-focused style of earlier Crate & Barrel ads. The theme of this effort was the Crate & Barrel "cocktail," in which large pieces of furniture were paired with small housewares. In one, for example, a sofa was shown on end balanced on a martini glass. The company also anticipated returning to television advertising in the fall of 1999 after a two-year hiatus.

FURTHER READING

Berner, Robert. "Crate & Barrel Sells a Majority Stake to German Mail-Order Firm Versand." *Wall Street Journal,* February 13, 1998.

Branch, Shelly. "How Target Got Hip." *Fortune,* May 24, 1999.

Chandler, Susan. "Furnishing a Sea Change: A Raft of New Retailers Are Redrawing the Furniture Landscape, and Many Traditional Stores Are Suffering." *Chicago Tribune,* February 28, 1999.

"Crate & Barrel in Holiday Mood." *Adweek,* October 26, 1998.

Creno, Glen. "Chain Expands to Valley Scottsdale." *Arizona Republic,* September 3, 1998.

Goldman, Abigail. "A Fine Time for Sellers and Consumers of Housewares: Boomers and Others Are Eating Up the Fancy yet Affordable Items." *Los Angeles Times,* February 25, 1999.

Marsh, Ann. "Retailing: What a Niche Home." *Forbes,* January 26, 1998.

McAllister, Liane. "Licensing Comes Home." *Gifts & Decorative Accessories,* May 1, 1998.

Neuborne, Ellen. "Welcome to Yuppie Hardware." *Business Week,* December 21, 1998.

Tisch, Carol. "Crate & Barrel Plans Home Store Rollout." *HFN: The Weekly Newspaper for the Home Furnishing Network,* June 15, 1998.

Vincenti, Lisa. "Aggressive Target Launches a Marketing 'Glitzkrieg,'" *HFN: The Weekly Newspaper for the Home Furnishing Network,* May 18, 1998.

Wray, Christina. "Impact's Call to Action (Ideas of Crate & Barrel Chief Executive, Gordon Segal)." *HFN: The Weekly Newspaper for the Home Furnishing Network,* February 19, 1996.

Rebecca Stanfel

FedEx Corp.

942 S. Shady Grove Rd.
Memphis, Tennessee 38120
USA
Telephone: (901) 818-7500
Web site: www.fedex.com

BE ABSOLUTELY SURE CAMPAIGN

OVERVIEW

Founded in the 1970s, Federal Express (FedEx) quickly carved out a niche in the express package business, helped in large part by its aggressive advertising. In the early years FedEx relied on a fast-talking spokesman who anchored the "Absolutely, Positively Overnight" campaign that ran from 1978 to 1983. By the 1990s it was facing increasing competition from rival express firms offering cheaper service. Despite being far younger than United Parcel Service (UPS) and the United States Postal Service, by this time FedEx was able to portray itself in its advertising as a well-established, reliable shipper.

The "Be Absolutely Sure" campaign, which broke in January 1998, offered humorous examples of what could occur if someone relied on a cut-rate shipper rather than FedEx. In one spot a 30-something swimming-pool cleaner finally received his acceptance letter to Harvard University, news that, if received 20 years earlier, might have made a profound difference in his life. In another spot toy soldiers in a mock commercial were reduced to wearing dresses because their uniforms did not arrive on time.

The "Be Absolutely Sure" campaign ended at the close of 2000. During its three-year run it produced a number of memorable commercials. The spot "Apology," which was little more than a television test pattern and an abject apology for not having sent the tape of the real commercial by FedEx, was recognized as one of the best commercials of 1999. The toy-solider spot, "Action Figures," was nominated for an Emmy Award in 2000.

HISTORICAL CONTEXT

When Fred Smith returned from the Vietnam War in the 1960s, he entered Yale University in New Haven, Connecticut. The undergraduate Smith wrote a term paper in which he presented the idea that, with the fast-emerging service economy of the United States in the latter half of the twentieth century, what America needed was a good, reliable package delivery service. His professor gave him a C. This grade, however, did not deter Smith from raising investment capital, and by 1971 he had almost $140 million in operating funds. Bank loans accounted for $90 million of this amount, and Smith had raised another $40 million from investors. The remaining $8 million was loaned by family members. Obviously, Smith had a lot riding on this deal, and with his capital in place he proceeded to launch the largest venture-capital-funded start-up corporation in history: Federal Express. Smith reportedly chose the name because "Federal" suggested the U.S. government, a connotation that was still largely positive despite the unpopular war in Vietnam. And "Express" was chosen because it recalled the legendary Pony Express of the 1860s.

During the 1970s Federal Express—or FedEx, as it came to be called—grew rapidly alongside competitor United Parcel Service (UPS). Both profited from the fact that airlines were getting out of the parcel service and from the bankruptcy of rival REA Express. FedEx also benefited from a 1974 strike by UPS union workers, not to mention a strong record of advertising. Years later, in 1997, writers at *Entertainment Weekly* voted FedEx's 1981 "Fast-Paced World" spot the second greatest commercial of all time, behind Energizer's "Escape of the Bunny." In the spot, created by Ally & Gargano, actor John Moschitta managed to say 450 words in one minute, or seven words per second, as a way of illustrating FedEx's speed.

In the mid-1980s FedEx hit on a loser when it introduced the idea of ZapMail, which promised document delivery in two hours. It might have been a success if fax machines had not begun making their appearance, thereby eliminating the need for the service. The company ended up losing $300 million on ZapMail in 1986. It recovered handsomely in the 1990s, however, greatly expanding its international service and again profiting from a UPS strike in 1997. In the following year it created the FDX Corporation as a holding company for Federal Express and its other companies.

TARGET MARKET

Federal Express attained its position by appealing to businesses both big and small. The 1990s saw two opposing trends: the continued growth of large corporations through acquisitions and mergers and the concomitant growth of small business. As corporations became bigger and more impersonal, it seemed that more and more people were leaving salaried employment and setting up new businesses in their homes. At the same time, corporations outsourced more of their work and also allowed many employees to work from their homes. FedEx, like its competitors, benefited both from large corporate business and the growth of small business, which meant that more businesspeople were sending more packages.

The growth of telecommunications and a global economy helped spur an increase in international business, and here, too, FedEx was poised to reap a bountiful harvest. During the 1980s it expanded its international service greatly by acquiring companies in Italy, Japan, and other countries, and in 1995 it became the first U.S. express carrier to establish direct service to the People's Republic of China—perhaps the world's fastest-growing economic powerhouse. The mid-1990s also saw the creation of Latin American and Caribbean divisions, and in 1997 FedEx established a service hub in Miami to lead the way for greater Latin American expansion. It also set up its first hub in Europe, at Charles de Gaulle Airport in Paris.

FedEx illustrated the breadth of its customer base with 1997 ads that showed a wide array of people, separated by gender, race, ethnicity, and nationality, but united in their use of FedEx as a preferred service. According to Dottie Enrico in *USA Today,* a consumer poll conducted in 1997 found that FedEx's advertising was most popular with people in the 30 to 49 age group. The poll also showed that the advertising had proven particularly well received by African-American consumers, with 45 percent of black respondents judging the FedEx ads "very effective."

Later executions of the "Be Absolutely Sure" campaign had more specific targets. The 1999 television spots were aimed at companies doing business with Internet companies. A year later the campaign touted FedEx's new direct routes to China, targeting companies that were shipping to and from China.

COMPETITION

In the express-delivery market segment, FedEx's two largest competitors were UPS and DHL Worldwide, but by the mid-1990s it faced a new and formidable competitor: the United States Postal Service (USPS). The latter was a hybrid: formed as a part of the U.S. government, it became an independent entity in 1970, but it still maintained a monopoly over door-to-door mail delivery in the United States. Its dimensions dwarfed those of any competitor: as the USPS had often noted, it delivered more mail in a week than the combined forces of FedEx and UPS did in a year.

Yet as an independent entity, the USPS sought to go after the competition in its advertising to promote its Priority Mail service. There ensued a lengthy battle between FedEx and the Postal Service over ads that compared USPS's and FedEx's prices and asserted that it was cheaper to send packages through Priority Mail. FedEx took the Postal Service to court, and in April 1997 a Memphis federal judge, in the first ruling in the case, overturned an appeal by the USPS to throw the suit out of court. The USPS had claimed that, due to the Lanham Act, which protected certain federal agencies from lawsuits, it could not be sued, but the judge ruled that "by placing its no-holds-barred advertisements on national television, USPS embarked on an excursion into the commercial world unique to a federal entity."

Then there was UPS, which was nearly shut down between August 4 and 18, 1997, because of a strike by 185,000 of its employees, members of the Teamsters union. "When the Teamsters walked out on Atlanta-based United Parcel Service," wrote Tim Triplett in *Marketing News,* "they delivered an unexpected windfall

FROGS, PUMPS, AND BARS: JUST ANOTHER SUPER BOWL

The Super Bowl was not only one of American sports' biggest events, it was also one of advertising's business events of the year, as companies vied for airtime before audiences estimated at over 100 million. Among the most notable commercials aired during the 1998 Super Bowl was a Federal Express spot that caught the attention of Bob Garfield, who described it in *Advertising Age:* "Somebody sent the ad to the network by a competing overnight service, so all we see is color bars. Absolutely, positively a breakthrough idea."

Among the biggest headline-grabbers at the Super Bowl were the Budweiser frogs, the ultrapopular amphibians employed by Anheuser-Busch to promote its star brand. Garfield called the Budweiser spot, in which Louie the Lizard attempted to electrocute the frogs, "a bit uncomfortably morbid but a lot funnier than the parallel soap opera playing out in Washington"—a reference to the sex scandal involving President Bill Clinton and White House intern Monica Lewinsky.

Another spot lauded by Garfield was a commercial for Mail Boxes Etc., which had turned over its commercial to a customer—a minuscule corporation that manufactured a pocket pump for inflating basketballs. "This low-production-budget commercial within a commercial not only taps vicarious excitement for the lucky entrepreneurs," Garfield wrote, "it underscores MBE's dedication to small business."

Garfield, who reviewed a plethora of Super Bowl commercials, was not so enthusiastic about a spot for Qualcomm phones in which "a man wakes up in a foreign hotel room, spooked and disoriented." The man walked to the balcony to find a crowd cheering; thinking the applause was directed at him (rather than the actual object, a dictator on the next balcony), the man raised his Qualcomm digital phone in a show of triumph. "And the point of this stunning, enigmatic, surrealistic spot?" Garfield asked. "Good question."

to the U.S. Postal Service and Memphis-based Federal Express Corp., among other parcel shipping competitors. But whether UPS's rivals can hang onto that newfound business remains to be seen." UPS, the world's leading package delivery service, estimated that it permanently lost 5 percent of its business due to the strike, but it sought to recover its position with an advertising campaign in which it apologized for the strike. Meanwhile, FedEx reported that it delivered an extra 9.5 million packages during the period of the strike.

MARKETING STRATEGY

FedEx began the "Be Absolutely Sure" campaign by airing a TV spot called "Apology" during the Super Bowl in January 1998. It proved to be one of its most notable commercials of the year. The Super Bowl, with more than 100 million viewers, was always a prominent arena in which companies advertised their wares, and many opted for a glitzy approach to build on the hype. Not so with FedEx and BBDO: their spot consisted simply of a test pattern made up of colored bars. A voice-over explained that FedEx's advertising agency—a fictionalized entity—had mistakenly sent its commercial via a competing package service. Of course it had not arrived, the voice-over explained, and therefore viewers would not see its planned spot, which was to have featured dancing kangaroos and country music superstar Garth Brooks.

This tongue-in-cheek approach won the company high praise, particularly from within the advertising industry. Bob Garfield of *Advertising Age,* often a stern critic of Super Bowl commercials, called it "Absolutely, positively a breakthrough idea." FedEx followed this spot up with an even more attention-getting spot, whose first airing it also tied to a football event, ABC-TV's *Monday Night Football* on September 14. The spot, "Opportunity Knocks," featured Mort, a figure described in a FedEx press release as "a swimming pool cleaner in his late 30s." Mort "receives a letter—20 years too late—from a generic delivery company." In fact the van that delivered Mort's delayed letter bore the name "Lucky Shamrock Expediting." "Had Mort received the letter on time," the press release went on, "his destiny could have been totally different: 'You've been accepted to Harvard University,'" the letter announced. "'And awarded a scholarship. Please respond by August 1978.'" The spot then reminded viewers to 'Be absolutely sure,' and ship with FedEx.

Another commercial in the first round of executions showed what could happen if a shipper other than FedEx was entrusted with the delivery of the Stanley Cup hockey trophy. Rabid fans who had gathered at Detroit's Joe Louis Arena to celebrate their champion Red Wings watched the team be presented not with the Stanley Cup but with a bag of donkey feed, while thousands of miles away the Cup was displayed to a group of Bolivian peasants in a marketplace.

The "Be Absolutely Sure" campaign continued in 1999, targeting businesses selling over the Internet. In one notable spot a website design team, composed of nerds and a raving madman smashing a computer, made its pitch to three befuddled executives. The message of the spot was simple: pick whoever you want to design your Web page, but stick to FedEx when it comes to shipping your packages.

During the 1999 NCAA Bowl Championship Series in January, FedEx aired more "Be Absolutely Sure" spots. This set of commercials took a less humorous approach. The 30- and 60-second spots were collectively entitled "Takeoffs" and showed FedEx planes taking off for various cities, along with songs that suggested their destinations: "April in Paris"; "Chicago"; "18 Miles from Memphis"; "Oklahoma"; and "Sweet Home Alabama."

In 2000 FedEx aired the most popular television commercial of the campaign. The spot, which highlighted the shipper's direct route to China, was unveiled on New Year's Eve 1999 during the Liberty Bowl college football game. Called "Action Figures," it was a parody of a low-budget toy commercial. The G.I. Joe–like dolls, Combat Rangers, were put through their paces: parachuted out of helicopters, plunged into mud. But the soldiers wore women's clothing and accessories, including pink handbags and blow-dryers. Watching the commercial was a trio of businessmen, one of whom asked why the Combat Rangers were wearing dresses. "That's because the commander uniforms didn't arrive from China on time," he was told as the underlings then blamed one another for not using FedEx as their shipper.

The "Be Absolutely Sure" campaign played itself out by the close of 2000. Before it ended, famed television crocodile hunter Steve Irwin made an appearance. In his spot he was bitten by a poisonous snake and reassured the audience that he had some antivenom that had been shipped via Federal Express, only to learn that someone had chosen a different carrier and the serum had not arrived. Irwin collapsed, the screen went blank, and the "Be Absolutely Sure" slogan and FedEx Logo appeared. In January 2001 FedEx retired "Be Absolutely Sure" in favor of a new approach that featured the slogan "This is a job for FedEx."

OUTCOME

As FedEx noted in its press release, the "Opportunity Knocks" spot was in line with memorable Federal Express ads throughout the years. Among those campaigns was "Absolutely, Positively Overnight," which included the famous fast-talker spot; the campaign, which ran from 1978 to 1983, had won advertising's EFFIE Award. Then there was "It's Not Just a Package, It's Your Business" from 1987 to 1988; "Our Most Important Package Is Yours," which aired from 1991 to 1994; and the short-lived "Absolutely, Positively Anytime" (1995).

Despite his sad story, Mort the pool cleaner—along with "Apology" and the entire "Be Absolutely Sure" campaign—won praise from the advertising industry. *Adweek* listed "Opportunity Knocks" among its "Best Spots" in the October 1998 issue. *Advertising Age* included "Apology" in its list of best spots in 1998, calling it an example of "zigging while everyone else zagged"—that is, pursuing a strategy that set the company apart. Though some in the industry had suggested that the spot might seem like an advertising inside joke, *Advertising Age* held that it "stood out amongst all the other overhyped TV ads . . . and cut through the clutter like the sound of one hand clapping." The most acclaimed spot of the entire campaign was "Action Figures," which, along with four other commercials, was nominated for an Emmy Award in 2000.

FURTHER READING

"Best Spots." *Adweek* (eastern ed.), October 12, 1998.

Campbell, Laurel, et al. "Here's Lookin' at Priciest Ads at Super Bowl: They Better Be Incredible." *Memphis (TN) Commercial Appeal,* January 31, 1999, p. C-1.

"Cut to the Chase." *B to B,* November 20, 2000, p. 34.

Enrico, Dottie. "FedEx Advertising Campaign Delivers Effective Message." *USA Today,* August 25, 1997, p. B-4.

"FedEx Wins Ruling in USPS Lawsuit." *Traffic World,* April 14, 1997, p. 31.

Garcia, Sandra. "Not Using Fed Ex Can Be a Drag for 'Action Figures,'" *Shoot,* January 7, 2000, p. 14.

Garfield, Bob. "Bud Lizards Electrify Super Bowl Ads." *Advertising Age,* January 26, 1998, p. 1.

———. "Super Bowl Advertisers Set the World Back 30 Years with Naked Appeals to Guys." *Advertising Age,* February 1, 1999, p. 1.

"Heart Defects, Bones, and Other Cases of Zigging When Others Zag: Miscellaneous." *Advertising Age,* May 31, 1999, p. S-10.

Hill, Dan. "The Post Office's Priority." *Brandweek,* February 23, 1998, p. 18.

Linnett, Richard. "Some Like It Hotter." *Adweek,* January 3, 2000, p. 18.

Mull, Angela. "FedEx Ad Wins Local Agency Nods." *Phoenix (AZ) Business Journal,* January 30, 1998, p. 3.

"New FedEx Ad Reminds Viewers to 'Be Absolutely Sure' about Shipping; Campaign to Break Tonight During Monday Night Football." *Business Wire,* September 14, 1998.

Salomon, Alan. "FedEx Delivers New Ads via College Bowl Blitz: Delivery Service Stresses Global Reach in Latest Commercials." *Advertising Age,* January 4, 1999, p. 8.

Triplett, Tim. "Teamsters Deliver Windfall to UPS Competitors, but Can They Retain It?" *Marketing News,* November 24, 1997, pp. 2-3.

Judson Knight
Ed Dinger

OUR OFFICE IS YOUR OFFICE CAMPAIGN

OVERVIEW

On February 12, 2004, the Memphis, Tennessee–based express shipping giant FedEx Corp. (founded in 1973 as Federal Express) expanded in a new direction when it purchased the Dallas, Texas–based Kinko's photocopy center chain, which was founded in 1970 in Santa Barbara, California. The purchase was not a complete surprise to industry analysts—FedEx had already been using many Kinko's copy centers as drop-off points for customers, and the purchase consolidated these services, among other things. After rebranding the company as FedEx Kinko's Office and Print Services and the outlets themselves as FedEx Kinko's Office and Print Centers, FedEx began to implement an ad campaign designed to attract small business owners as well as a more mobile customer, one who would find FedEx Kinko's services convenient as an "office on the road." The ad campaign was tagged "Our Office Is Your Office."

The campaign was created by BBDO New York, FedEx's lead agency and creators of the award-winning 2003 campaign "Relax, It's FedEx." Using the offbeat humor that had become a hallmark of FedEx advertising, the $25 million rebranding campaign broke with four 30-second television spots. Other spots were added later. In addition to television the campaign used radio, the Internet, print, and direct mail. The campaign had the important task of reintroducing a known entity to the public with ads titled "First," "Luggage," "Welcome Aboard," "Cloud Nine," and "Plastic."

"Our Office Is Your Office" intended to cement FedEx Kinko's new identity into customers' psyches. Several of the spots earned accolades from the advertising industry. Sales at FedEx Kinko's failed to soar as much as management had hoped, but for fiscal year 2005 the company still managed to report revenues of $2.1 billion, an increase over the previous year.

HISTORICAL CONTEXT

At a glance the combination of FedEx and Kinko's would seem an unlikely merger. The former was an established shipping company that practically reinvented the package delivery industry by concentrating on express delivery via jets. Kinko's, on the other hand, was one of the leaders in the print and photocopy field. At the time of the buyout, Kinko's was operating approximately 1,200 stores worldwide, serving 215 countries. The company estimated its annual revenue for calendar year 2003, which was just prior to the buyout, at nearly $2 billion. However, the relationship between FedEx and the privately owned Kinko's, which stretched back to the 1980s, had been growing more intertwined over the years. In 1988 FedEx became Kinko's exclusive shipper, and by the end of 2003 FedEx was conducting full-service retail business in 134 Kinko's stores.

Kinko's profitability aside, a further incentive for the buyout was a shift in corporate thinking at FedEx. Since its inception the company had been the leader in express delivery services, pioneering domestic and international air shipment. The financial downturn of the first years of the twenty-first century, however, was a major factor in the flattening out (and in some fiscal quarters a slight decline) in the company's express shipment sector. During this same time FedEx Ground experienced seven consecutive quarters of double-digit growth. Clearly customers were choosing a lower price over the convenience of fast delivery. With the corporate shift toward focusing more effort on its ground delivery service and the already solid relationship between FedEx and Kinko's, plus the high profitability of mobile customers who used the FedEx drop-off points in Kinko's stores, the decision to expand into the print and copy industry seemed an almost foregone conclusion in the information age.

The announcement of the buyout came in December 2003. At that time, as reported in *Brandweek,* FedEx chairman, president, and CEO Frederick Smith declared, "The FedEx and Kinko's combination will substantially increase our retail presence worldwide and will enable both companies to take advantage of growth opportunities in the fast-moving digital economy. Our two companies share a similar background, culture and customer focus, and that common ground is extremely important as we prepare for future growth and success." In February 2004 FedEx paid approximately $2.4 billion in cash to acquire the global operations of Kinko's.

TARGET MARKET

Aimed at small business owners and casual and regular customers in need of the office and shipping services the new FedEx Kinko's could provide, the "Our Office Is Your Office" campaign relied on offbeat humor—practically a FedEx trademark. The spots made several points, primarily that the busy mobile customer and small business owner, who might not be able to afford or have the

RETAIL MERCHANT

By the end of 2005 FedEx Kinko's was certainly venturing far from the roots of its progenitor companies. That year the company established an online office supply and furniture outlet. In doing so FedEx Kinko's expanded its competition from its traditional rival, the UPS Store, to include Staples, Office Depot, and OfficeMax. In a *New York Times* article by Bob Tedeschi, Kenneth A. May, FedEx Kinko's chief operating officer, noted some concern but pointed out, "They're competitors who have also been marketing at the sweet spot of our space." In other words, the aforementioned superstores offered copying, printing, and shipping services. Kinko's, on the other hand, had been selling office supplies for 15 years. While the giant office supply companies seemed unfazed by the FedEx Kinko's move into their territory, the midsize and smaller supply houses were clearly upset, especially those that had been using FedEx as their shipper. Meanwhile analysts saw the move as a response to consolidation in that sector of the retail industry.

inclination for permanent office space, let alone myriad office equipment, could find satisfaction at FedEx Kinko's. The ad campaign targeted casual, more mobile customers because they, and to a lesser degree small business owners, were more likely to pay higher shipping rates in addition to making use of the full range of printing, copying, shipping, and electronic services—the latter dealing with electronic transfer and delivery of scanned and documents and PDF files.

FedEx Kinko's also intended to lure customers away from the UPS Store, the leading provider of shipping, postal, and business services in the world. The UPS Store not only offered identical services as FedEx Kinko's, but it also provided mailbox rentals. To attract these UPS Store customers, "Our Office Is Your Office" focused on FedEx Kinko's lower shipping rates.

COMPETITION

From the outset the main competition for FedEx Kinko's was the UPS Store. Shipping rival United Parcel Service (UPS) had actually led the way in diversification with its 2001 purchase (for $191 million) of Mail Boxes Etc., which was rebranded the UPS Store in 2003. In 2004 UPS opened 525 additional outlets, which raised the total number of UPS Stores to 3,771. This was approximately three times the number of FedEx Kinko's outlets.

Regarding their retail pack-and-ship outlets, UPS had a strategy that differed from that of FedEx in three important ways. First, the UPS Stores were franchised as opposed to being a subsidiary company. The second difference was location. FedEx Kinko's were concentrated in urban areas, while UPS Stores were located in suburban and rural areas, though by early 2005 UPS Stores were expanding into urban neighborhoods as well as college campuses, military bases, and convention centers. Third, while both were after the growing retail shipping market, FedEx Kinko's offered more print and copy services than the UPS Store.

Dave Hirschman, writing in the *Atlanta Journal-Constitution* soon after the "Our Office Is Your Office" ad campaign broke, noted that while FedEx Kinko's lagged behind the UPS Store in terms of physical numbers, its urban stores took in "far more revenue on average than suburban UPS Stores." Nevertheless, and despite its expansion elsewhere, UPS Stores remained wedded to the suburbs. On this subject Mark Davis, a senior analyst at FTN Midwest in Cleveland, as quoted by Sandra O'Loughlin in *Brandweek,* observed, "UPS is very focused on the next battleground, which they believe is out in the suburbs and rural areas. That's where they feel the next opportunity exists for them to enhance their relationships with customers and provide an additional point of contact for them in their competition with both FedEx and DHL, but also the U.S. Postal Service."

In time as FedEx Kinko's services evolved, the "Our Office Is Your Office" ad campaign would seem to foreshadow a whole new dimension. By 2005 FedEx Kinko's was in competition not only with the UPS Store (as an extension of UPS itself) and DHL but with office suppliers Staples and Office Depot as well.

MARKETING STRATEGY

The "Our Office Is Your Office" campaign was the first for FedEx Kinko's. The campaign debuted during the first week of July 2004 with nine television spots along with radio, print, direct-mail, and Web elements. The campaign's goal was to immediately position FedEx Kinko's as a less expensive, more convenient alternative to the UPS Store. The "Welcome Aboard" spot did this by specifically mentioning savings of up to 35 percent. As quoted in *Business Wire* at the time of the launch, Gary Kusin, president of FedEx Kinko's, declared, "These ads reflect the value that FedEx Kinko's offers to our customers. In addition to the industry's broadest range of services—copying and printing, computer rental, Wi-Fi Internet access, videoconferencing, and

FedEx shipping—we plan to launch a complete pack-and-ship capability before the peak holiday season." And FedEx executive vice president T. Michael Glenn (quoted in the same article) noted, "FedEx Kinko's powerfully redefines the future of the business services marketplace by offering customers a fully functional office on the road." Many business journalists picked up on and advanced that theme.

From the outset the campaign strategy was to take on the UPS Store directly. When FedEx purchased Kinko's it went full steam into waters it had previously only been testing. While the number of domestic UPS Stores was far greater than the number of FedEx Kinko's, the latter relied on location—urban versus suburban—and its wider range of services to attract new customers.

The spots "First" and "Welcome Aboard" both touted FedEx Kinko's over its main rival, the UPS Store. "First" used sight and sound gags to show the availability of FedEx Kinko's as opposed to the UPS Store and empathized with customer frustrations over not finding a UPS Store open. The spot depicted a man pointing out different company artifacts (the first dollar, which was framed, and the first letter from a satisfied customer) to a woman. The third artifact was a chair embedded in a wall, which signified the first tantrum. The man in the commercial, as quoted by Barry Janoff in *Brandweek,* went on to explain, "because we had to ship a package and the UPS Store was closed."

In "Welcome Aboard" a boss and an employee argued over whether the employee had been fired or quit. The spot ended with the worker being rehired after mentioning that by using FedEx Kinko's instead of the UPS Store he had saved up to 35 percent. Thus the humor had a very competitive edge to it.

In another spot, "Luggage," the convenience of utilizing FedEx Kinko's services was highlighted. Two would-be entrepreneurs struggled as they tried to unload office equipment from an airline carousel. One finally suggested that perhaps they ought to have gone to FedEx Kinko's.

OUTCOME

In comparing FedEx Kinko's with the UPS Store, Jack Aaronson, CEO of the Aaronson Group, an award-winning strategy and design firm, noted in his online column "Customer Relations" in September 2004 (two and a half months after the "Our Office Is Your Office" campaign broke) that the FedEx Kinko's "rebranding was a lot more successful in terms of user perception. Users know both brands [FedEx and Kinko's] and the core competencies of each . . . No questions remain in consumers' minds as to what these newly rebranded stores can do . . . FedEx Kinko's commercials and online ads tell you everything you can expect from the stores. They reaffirm the consumer really does get the best of both worlds."

Despite Aaronson's high marks for the rebranding effort and the "Our Office Is Your Office" ad campaign, the public was slower to make use of the wide range of services at FedEx Kinko's Office and Print Centers than had been hoped by company executives. Nevertheless in the first quarter of fiscal 2006, FedEx Kinko's reported revenues of $517 million. This was a 6 percent increase over the first quarter of the previous fiscal year. Operating income, however, had declined 16 percent over the first quarter of fiscal 2005. The increase in revenue was attributed to the traditional FedEx services that were available at the Office and Print Centers: FedEx Ground and FedEx Express delivery. There was a decline in revenue in the copy product line.

Despite the decline in revenue for "traditional" office services at FedEx Kinko's Office and Print Centers, corporate officials felt that the "Our Office Is Your Office" ad campaign had successfully implanted the notion of integrated services in customers' minds. The ad industry seemed to agree, as "Cloud Nine" was designated as one of *Adweek* magazine's Best Spots of 2004, and "Plastic" won an international bronze Andy award in 2005.

By the end of the first quarter of fiscal 2006, FedEx Kinko's claimed more than 1,450 employees with service in more than 11 countries. One year after the launch of the campaign, FedEx Kinko's was making plans to triple its number of domestic stores. In August 2005 the parent company took the office notion one step further when it began selling office supplies and furniture online.

FURTHER READING

Aaronson, Jack. "The Rebrand Challenge: UPS/MBE vs. FedEx/Kinko's." September 30, 2004. Available from <http://www.clickz.com/experts/crm/crm_strat/article.php/3414121>

"FedEx Changing Kinko's Brand Name to FedEx Kinko's." *New York Times,* April 27, 2004, p. 4.

"FedEx Delivers $2.4 B to Acquire Kinko's." *Brandweek,* January 5, 2004.

"FedEx Expands Operations with Kinko's Buy." *Brandweek,* December 30, 2003. Available from <http://www.brandweek.com>

"FedEx Hits the Road to Tout Kinko's." *Brandweek,* July 6, 2004. Available from <http://www.brandweek.com>

"FedEx Launches New Ad Campaign: Positions FedEx Kinko's as Your 'Office on the Road.'" *Business Wire,* July 6, 2004.

"FedEx Taps BBDO for Kinko's Advertising Campaign." *Memphis Business Journal,* July 6, 2004. Available from <http://www.bizjournals.com/memphis/stories/2004/07/05/daily1.html>

Hirschman, Dave. "FedEx, UPS Tactics Diverge: Retail Shippers a Top Priority." *Atlanta Journal-Constitution,* July 13, 2004.

Janoff, Barry. "If Your Ex Comes Knocking, Start Rocking." *Brandweek,* July 12, 2004.

O'Loughlin, Sandra. "Strategy: UPS Eyes Retail Growth in Urban, College Locations." *Brandweek,* March 7, 2005.

Tedeschi, Bob. "New Level of Competition: When a Supplier Gets into Its Customers' Business." *New York Times,* September 26, 2005.

Frank Caso

RELAX, IT'S FEDEX CAMPAIGN

OVERVIEW

Witty and engaging ads, a hallmark of the Memphis-based FedEx Corp. for more than two decades, had helped propel the success of the shipping and transportation company. In September 2003, however, in response to an economic downturn and highly competitive television advertising from rival United Parcel Service (UPS), FedEx sought to redefine itself to the public. That year the company launched "Relax, It's FedEx," its most ambitious ad campaign. Unlike past advertising, the "Relax, It's FedEx" campaign placed more emphasis on ground delivery and international shipping. It also emphasized the appeal of FedEx's integrated services in helping businesses solve their shipping problems.

Created by ad agency BBDO New York, the campaign initially kicked off with a series of eight spots created for television, but it eventually included print, radio, and Internet components. Television, as expected, consumed between 65 and 70 percent of the campaign's $90 million budget. Each of the humorous spots contained the campaign's tagline, "Relax, It's FedEx," reinforcing the point that harried workers need not worry about shipping dilemmas. The eight spots in the initial phase of the campaign were titled "Call Center," "Career Maker," "Chinese Office," "Crate," "Drama," "MBA," "Problems," and "Remind Me." In "Drama," for example, two workers melodramatically repeated that they were "doomed," believing that they would not be able to get a shipment to Houston by the next day. Each repetition of the word "doomed" became more melodramatic than the previous one. But the final voice-over announced, "You can try, but we've taken all the drama out of shipping overnight."

The campaign was successful enough for FedEx to continue running it through 2005. It also won a number of awards. In 2004 the spot "Drama" garnered a Gold Addy Award, while "Chinese Office," with the entire commercial spoken in Cantonese without English subtitles until the company name was mentioned at the end, won a Silver Addy Award. The campaign also won an Andy Head Award and an LIAA (London International Advertising Awards) Trophy in 2004. FedEx enjoyed an increase in sales, reporting revenues of $24.7 billion for fiscal 2004, up from $22.5 billion the previous year.

HISTORICAL CONTEXT

Since FedEx's founding in 1973 as Federal Express, the company had concentrated on air shipping—on its first day of operation it shipped 186 packages—as the key to successful express delivery. Over the next three decades the company remained the leader in that sector of the delivery industry, and by May 2003 FedEx was making 2.7 million air shipments per day. Yet the number marked a decline of four-tenths of a percent over FedEx's previous fiscal quarter. In fact FedEx's air shipment numbers declined in 9 of the 10 fiscal quarters between 2001 and May 2003. Meanwhile, the company's ground delivery service enjoyed double-digit growth for seven consecutive quarters.

FedEx Ground came into being in 1998 after the company purchased Roadway Package Service. Within five years its popularity with customers, based on its lower costs, was on the verge of altering the company's original approach. The move by customers away from express delivery was attributed to the stalled economy, in which cost had taken preference over an item's "absolutely positively" —an earlier FedEx tagline—arriving quickly, though FedEx took great pains in the ads to assure that it would. This reality was acknowledged by Laurie A. Tucker, a FedEx senior vice president, in a *Wall Street Journal* article by Suzanne Vranica and Rick Brooks that appeared the day the "Relax, It's FedEx" campaign kicked off. "The [domestic] express industry took a big hit," she admitted. Tipping off *Wall Street Journal* readers as to the content of the upcoming ad campaign, Tucker observed that the industry's immediate future was in ground shipping and international express shipping.

TARGET MARKET

The wry tone of the new ad campaign was a return to the style of earlier FedEx campaigns. Since "Relax, It's FedEx" was the company's first campaign to focus on ground and international express delivery, however, the target market was therefore expanded from the core audience the company had previously sought to reach. Whereas "Chinese Office," for example, emphasized the reliability of FedEx's international delivery, "Call Center" took a different approach by humorously emphasizing the company's prompt home delivery

© ALAN SCHEIN PHOTOGRAPHY/CORBIS

service. The latter commercial showed a man whose shower had been interrupted by a FedEx delivery calling the service department of a company he had done business with to complain that he had not expected his package so soon. While these ads highlighted the shift in FedEx thinking, the spots also appealed to the company's important target market of middle management and small-business owners. The ads also highlighted FedEx's Internet service. Spots such as "Drama," "MBA," and "Remind Me" were aimed at midlevel shippers or poked fun at the boss.

COMPETITION

A sluggish economy was not the only factor contributing to the shift in FedEx's thinking. The company's major rival and the leading ground shipper, UPS, launched its own successful ad campaign with the tagline "What Can Brown Do for You?" In the *Wall Street Journal* article by Vranica and Brooks, Alan Brew of Addison Branding & Communications in San Francisco declared, "Brown has put some pressure on FedEx." The writers mentioned Brew's observation that the UPS campaign employed an important branding strategy—personalization—which, inadvertently or not, had been emphasized by Brew himself in his use of the term "Brown" for UPS. Furthermore, UPS had been outspending FedEx in advertising. In 2002 UPS spent $163.8 million on advertising, while FedEx spent only $84.6 million. FedEx enjoyed a modest improvement in its share of the ground delivery market in 2003, though more than half of all ground deliveries in the United States were made by UPS. In 2004 UPS had revenue totaling $36.6 billion.

The United States Postal Service (USPS) ranked second in ground deliveries, but its 2004 revenue totaled $69 billion. As Douglas P. Shuit pointed out in *Workforce Management,* however, the revenue for those services that placed the USPS in competition with the privately owned companies—priority and overnight mail and package delivery—totaled approximately $7.4 billion per year. Also in 2003 another rival, the German-owned DHL International, sought to make inroads in the express delivery market. The purchase of Airborne Express was part of its $1.2 billion investment plan in the U.S. market.

MARKETING STRATEGY

The "Relax, It's FedEx" campaign debuted with two 30-second spots on October 4, 2003, during a telecast of the first game of the National Football League season. The game, between the Washington Redskins and the New York Jets, was played on the Redskins' home field, FedEx Field, thus reinforcing the company's brand name. FedEx had also purchased naming rights to the arena that was home to the Memphis Grizzlies of the National Basketball Association, and the company was a sponsor of the Orange Bowl and of Professional Golfers Association events. In an article published in *Traffic*

SNAPPY TAGLINES, FUNNY ADS

In 2003 "Relax, It's FedEx" became the latest in a series of memorable advertising taglines used by the company, some of which, because of their humor, survived in an expanded cultural context. In 1975 FedEx, then known as Federal Express, debuted its first television commercial with the tagline "America, you've got a new airline." This was followed in 1977 with the simple "Hellooo Federal." It was in 1979, however, that Federal Express commercials really began to leave their mark on the public consciousness, beginning with the tagline "When it absolutely positively has to be there overnight." That tagline was parodied on *Saturday Night Live* in a skit about a company called Einstein Express: "When it absolutely positively has to be there the day before yesterday." Federal Express embraced the humor and further defied industry standards with its "Fast-Talking Man" ads of the 1980s, which used the line, "Peter, may I call you Pete?" In this instance the memorable line did not even mention the company name. Nevertheless, the humor served as subliminal reinforcement.

World soon after the first ads appeared, Angela Greiling Keane quoted Brian Philips, FedEx's vice president of U.S. marketing, as saying, "We rely heavily on sports to reach the decision makers in our industry. We can track a return on investment for each and every sponsorship property we engage with." But FedEx was not about to put all of its advertising eggs in one basket, and the company's television spots showed up more and more on cable specialty programs. In addition, the "Relax, It's FedEx" ads encompassed the full range of the media.

As the campaign progressed through 2004, FedEx made further efforts to secure a larger portion of the ground delivery market. The preparation for this had been made in December 2003 when the company purchased Kinko's, the Dallas-based photocopying chain, for more than $2 billion. Kinko's was the largest such chain in the world, with more than 1,200 stores, located primarily in the United States. FedEx, which already had drop-off centers in Kinko's stores, planned to expand the chain into Europe and Asia, thus facilitating electronic transfer and the delivery of scanned documents and PDF (Portable Document Format) files.

In December 2004 the company announced that it would extend the "Relax, It's FedEx" campaign into 2005 with six new 30-second television spots, which previewed that month. BBDO New York once again produced the spots. Highlighting FedEx's integrated services—express delivery, international delivery, ground delivery, FedEx.com, and FedEx Kinko's—the ads turned on the same winning formula of wry humor. The six spots in the second series were titled "Bus," "Job Counselor," "Shower," "Sweeps," "Tom," and "Wrong." "Job Counselor," in which a pirate was interviewed for a job in a company's shipping department, highlighted FedEx.com. China was again the focus of one spot—"Tom"—promoting FedEx's international delivery service. In the spot the world's seemingly most inept worker was still able to ship to China by using FedEx. "Wrong," a commercial for FedEx ground delivery, featured a befuddled worker whose coworkers were constantly pointing out his linguistic and other confusions: the leaning tower of pizza, French benefits, and actor James Dean and singer and sausage pitchman Jimmy Dean.

In keeping with its policy of advertising heavily on sports broadcasts, thus directing the spots primarily to males between the ages of 25 and 55, the second series of ads debuted throughout the Bowl Championship Series of college football during the first weekend of 2005. Another ad was shown during the Super Bowl in February of that year.

OUTCOME

The ads not only won awards in the advertising industry and recognition from the public, but they were accompanied by an upturn in FedEx business. As the United States emerged from the recession of the early years of the twenty-first century, FedEx market shares also improved. In fiscal 2004 FedEx Ground had revenues of $3.9 billion. Its share of the ground delivery market in 2004 ranged from 27 percent, according to Pittsburgh analysts SJ Consulting, to 31 percent, according to J.P. Morgan. Both figures showed that FedEx was making significant inroads into what was formerly seen as unassailable UPS territory.

In May 2005 the Atlanta consulting firm the Colography Group confirmed a trend that the "Relax, It's FedEx" campaign not only capitalized on but also nurtured. The Colography Group estimated that the year would see FedEx Ground and FedEx Freight handle 50.1 percent, or more than half, of the company's shipments. Without commenting directly on the shipping percentages for these two segments, FedEx officials gave tacit approval to this figure. As quoted by Jane Roberts in the *Memphis Commercial Appeal*, the president of the Colography Group, Ted Scherck, noted, "This is a watershed because you have the carrier that defined the concept of air express now providing more shipments on the ground than in the air. . .The mode of transportation is increasingly irrelevant to shippers."

In 2004 the U.S. Department of Transportation awarded FedEx 12 additional flights to China, including the sole direct flight from the United States to the Pearl River Delta area, which was one of China's major economic and manufacturing centers. In 2005 FedEx signed an agreement to use the Guangzhou Baiyun International Airport as its Asian transfer hub beginning in 2008.

In the first quarter of fiscal year 2006, which ended on August 31, 2005, FedEx reported that "total combined average daily package volume at FedEx Express and FedEx Ground grew 5 percent year over year for the quarter, due to continued growth in international express, U.S. domestic express and ground shipments." The company further reported that its overall revenues were up 10 percent, to $7.71 billion as opposed to $6.98 billion the previous year. Net income rose 3 percent, from $330 million to $339 million. These increases were reflected in the various segments of FedEx services. FedEx Express revenue was up 11 percent over the previous year, to $5.12 billion, and FedEx Ground revenue increased 14 percent, to $1.22 billion. The daily package volume had increased 6 percent in comparison with the previous fiscal year. Revenue in the FedEx Freight segment increased 11 percent, to $882 million, while FedEx Kinko's saw a 6 percent increase, to $517 million. This last increase was largely attributed to the growth of FedEx Ground and Express services in conjunction with the conversion of FedEx World Service centers to FedEx Kinko's Ship Centers.

FURTHER READING

"FedEx Companies Star in New Advertising Campaign." *Business Wire,* September 4, 2003.

"FedEx Continues to Relax in 2005." December 30, 2004. Available from <http://www.brandweek.com>

"FedEx Scores with NFL Breakout." September 5, 2003. Available from <http://www.brandweek.com>

"FedEx, UPS to Set Up Transfer Hubs in China." *Comtex News Network,* July 21, 2005.

Janoff, Barry. "BBDO Freshens FedEx 'Relax' Campaign." *Adweek,* December 30, 2004.

Keane, Angela Greiling. "Relax, It's a FedEx Ad." *Traffic World,* September 15, 2003.

Link, Jonathan. "Relax, Nothing Has Changed." *Boards,* October 1, 2003.

Maddox, Kate. "BBDO New York's 'Imagination' Sparks a Big Year." *Business to Business,* March 8, 2004.

Roberts, Jane. "FedEx Likely to Ship More Packages by Ground in 2005." *Memphis Commercial Appeal,* May 22, 2005.

Shuit, Douglas P. "Packing in Customers." *Workforce Management,* May 1, 2005.

Vranica, Suzanne, and Rick Brooks. "FedEx Recasts Itself on the Ground." *Wall Street Journal,* September 4, 2003.

Weber, Henry R. "UPS, FedEx Rivalry a Study in Contrasts." May 20, 2005. Available from <http://www.boston.com/business/articles/2004/05/20/ups_fedex_rivalry_a_study_in_contrasts>

"AAF Awards: Addy; The Creative Spirit of Advertising." October 23, 2005. Available from <http://www.aaf.org/awards/addys_silver_2005.html>

Frank Caso

THE WAY THE WORLD WORKS CAMPAIGN

OVERVIEW

Federal Express Corporation (FedEx), founded in the 1970s, built its success on an innovative business model, offering the business world the first overnight shipping service. But savvy marketing also played a key role in the rise of the company. Just one year after becoming operational, FedEx released its first advertising campaign. Increased sales resulted, as did more advertising. In 1978 FedEx introduced the award-winning "Absolutely, Positively Overnight" campaign, which featured a fast-talking spokesman. It ran until 1983. Other memorable FedEx campaigns that followed were "It's Not Just a Package, It's Your Business," which ran in 1987 and 1988; "Our Most Important Package is Yours," which ran from 1991 to 1994; and "Absolutely, Positively Anything," a 1995 campaign. Reliability and speed were at the heart of the message in these campaigns. Then, in 1996, FedEx released a campaign called "The Way the World Works" that emphasized the company's position as a leader in global shipping.

"The Way the World Works" was designed to communicate the idea that FedEx could help customers, particularly small businesses, cultivate contacts all over the globe. The company's longtime advertising agency, BBDO Worldwide of New York, designed the advertisements, which showed customers in various countries using FedEx delivery and warehousing-inventory services to market their goods.

FedEx considered "The Way the World Works" to be one of its most successful marketing efforts. According to the company, it increased awareness levels of FedEx to new highs. Nevertheless, by autumn 1998 the company was ready for a change, and it returned to a more humorous approach with the "Be Absolutely Sure" campaign that followed.

HISTORICAL CONTEXT

When it began operations with 14 small aircraft in 1973, Federal Express was the first company of its kind to offer overnight shipping. At the time it delivered to 25 cities from New York to Florida. The next year the company launched its first advertising campaign with a budget of $150,000 and the tagline "Federal Express—a whole new airline for packages only." After the first commercial was broadcast, the company's shipping volume shot up from 3,000 to 10,000 packages a night. By the end of 1997 the company had a fleet of more than 600 aircraft and some 40,000 other vehicles, and it was handling 3 million packages worldwide every day.

Because it was the first company to offer express delivery services, Federal Express created its own market. Demand grew quickly, and Federal Express became the first company in the United States to achieve revenues of $1 billion within 10 years. Revenues mushroomed to nearly $35 billion by 1996, and, according to the company's 1997 annual report, they were expected to reach more than $250 billion worldwide before the year 2020.

Over the years Federal Express became known for its humorous advertising campaigns, including pitchmen who spoke at a frenetic speed and an employer who pretended to be his secretary when he telephoned to check on a package. With "The Way the World Works" the company took a more serious approach, stressing brand image and the ability to help businesses compete in the global economy. The latest campaign also meshed with the general FedEx tagline, "The World On Time," which had been introduced along with the company's updated logo in 1994. It was not only the tone but also the message of the company's advertising that changed. In the early 1990s the message was that consumers could rely on Federal Express to deliver packages quickly. The ads emphasized the company's technological features, such as software for tracking shipments. The principal message of "The Way the World Works," however, was that FedEx could deliver worldwide.

TARGET MARKET

According to Steve Pacheco, manager of advertising for FedEx, "The Way the World Works" campaign was targeted primarily at three groups of consumers: professional managers who were 25 to 54 years old and who earned at least $35,000 annually, small shippers and owners of small businesses who were 25 to 54 years old and who earned at least $50,000, and people who made decisions and influenced opinions in corporations, a largely male group 35 to 64 years old and with household incomes of at least $60,000. Although in the past, small businesses had not had much opportunity to buy and sell merchandise in other countries, this was becoming important to compete globally. "Federal Express is an enabler that allows them to do business all over the world," Pacheco explained.

NAME CHANGE

In conjunction with the launch of its "The World On Time" campaign in 1994, Federal Express also changed its logo and brand name to FedEx, the name by which the company and its services had informally come to be known. The logo, which used an arrow to symbolize speed and efficiency, was done in the trademark purple and orange, and the company's planes and ground vehicles were repainted to match.

FedEx could not only ship goods quickly, but it could also track the precise location of a package, and it offered a money-back guarantee if the item did not arrive on time. A business could predict when merchandise would arrive or exactly when it needed to be shipped. This allowed businesses to lower their operating costs by maintaining smaller inventories. Because a large percentage of inventory was in transit at any given time, FedEx planes and trucks, in effect, became mobile warehouses for the company's customers. The concept of shipping and receiving merchandise "just in time" became increasingly popular. The taglines "The World On Time" and "The Way the World Works" thus helped FedEx convey the message that it understood modern business practices and could be an important element in a company's operating strategy.

Pacheco said that FedEx hoped that the ads would surprise people who were not familiar with everything the company had to offer. At the same time the campaign was intended to broaden the company's appeal to its established customers and to encourage them to make better use of its services.

COMPETITION

FedEx was the largest express transportation company in the world. Thanks to its vast network of aircraft and trucks, it could deliver to more than 200 countries within 48 hours. It had the only routes in and out of China and exclusive rights to many other routes in Asia, where 7 of the 10 fastest-growing economies were located.

By 1997, although FedEx still dominated express delivery with a market share of about 43 percent, it had lost ground to competitors. According to the Colography Group, United Parcel Service (UPS) had 27 percent of the market, Airborne Express 15 percent, and the U.S. Postal Service 5 percent, with all other services combined claiming 8 percent. Worldwide, the total revenues from express shipments for FedEx were 50 percent more than those of its nearest competitor.

In terms of all shipping, however, UPS had grown to be twice the size of FedEx. In 1995 UPS shipped 3 billion packages every day and had revenues of $21 billion. By contrast, in 1997 FedEx shipped about 3 million items daily, and it reported revenues of $10.2 billion in 1996 and $11.5 billion in 1997. To better compete with UPS, FedEx merged with Caliber System and thereby acquired the RPS trucking company, which was the second-largest ground carrier after UPS.

FedEx also benefited from a 15-day strike of UPS workers in August 1997. UPS saw its share of the package delivery market drop from about 80 percent before the strike to an estimated 70 percent after. FedEx employees put in overtime to cope with the flood of extra packages during the strike, and the company reported that its earnings more than doubled for the quarter because of the additional volume. FedEx estimated that it retained 15 percent of the extra volume after the UPS strike had ended. During the strike FedEx ran a print ad thanking its employees for helping the company handle the additional workload, and it rewarded its workforce with a $20 million bonus. Among other things, the ad told the public that customer service was important to FedEx personnel.

The U.S. Postal Service competed with both FedEx and UPS by advertising its Priority Mail service, priced beginning at $3, which was notably cheaper than its competitors' charges of $6 to $12 for two-day delivery. FedEx sued the Postal Service for false advertising, because Priority Mail did not guarantee two-day delivery. Instead, it offered "two- or three-day" delivery and in 1996 delivered only 81 percent of its packages within two days. An advertising industry watchdog council said that the ads were acceptable, however, for the public understood the difference between what the Postal Service and its competitors were offering. The ads and the lawsuit continued, and the Postal Service maintained that, by promoting Priority Mail at an inexpensive price, it had pressured FedEx to lower its charges by a third.

MARKETING STRATEGY

"The Way the World Works" campaign was created at the request of Frederick Smith, founder and CEO of Federal Express, who had asked the senior management of the company to organize a campaign that would focus on the global economy. BBDO produced the commercials.

SPECIAL ADS FOR NEW SERVICES

Over the years Federal Express had also done special advertising to promote new services and technology. The "AsiaOne" campaign, for example, promoted the company's delivery services in Asia, the "Early A.M." a new service within the United States, and "FedEx Ship" its enhanced computer capabilities. Such innovations kept FedEx a leader in its business, and they also put pressure on competitors.

BBDO, known for the use of emotion and human interest in its advertising, tapped into the idea that FedEx empowered individuals to realize their dreams. The dream might involve designing avant-garde furniture and selling it to someone on the other side of the world or shipping a dress from Italy to Japan so that a wedding would come off perfectly. FedEx wanted people who saw the commercials to perceive them as heartfelt messages. What was implied was that the company cared as much about every package as it cared about the wedding dress.

FedEx's Pacheco said that the campaign's five key objectives were to "magnify the scope of Federal Express, show the global and international capabilities, add value to the FedEx brand, communicate all of our high-tech innovations, and position Federal Express as a leader." Previous ads had touched on some of these points, but "The Way the World Works" took a new direction by calling attention to global delivery services. The word "world" in the tagline was significant, because it emphasized FedEx's ability to deliver worldwide. In addition, it referred to the fact that the people who worked for FedEx were of all races and lived in many countries. "Early on, we identified the need to be as culturally diverse as we could. You'll see people from all around the world in the campaign," said Pacheco. Just as important was the word "works," which conveyed the idea that FedEx helped its customers get their work done by helping them solve their delivery problems.

The campaign featured six TV spots—five 30-second commercials and one 60-second commercial—that were introduced in late 1996. The spots ran mainly on highly rated television programs, including prime-time shows and sports and news broadcasts. In one spot a dressmaker in Italy shipped bridal gowns to customers in Japan. Another scenario showed pop-up books published in Wales being sent to classrooms in England and Thailand. The warm, distinctive voice of actress Linda Hunt asked, "How did such ordinary people come by such extraordinary powers? Believe it or not, all it took was the wave of a wand." In a humorous spot called "Doug," an employee had entrusted an important package to a delivery company other than FedEx. When the package failed to arrive on time, Doug's manager locked him in a closet and berated him while the rest of the staff looked on. Each commercial ended with a picture of a revolving globe and the tagline "The Way the World Works."

The spots were translated into various languages for the 20 markets in which BBDO handled FedEx advertising. Although they were broadcast in various countries, the commercials were created primarily for the United States. In fact, the campaign was the first that FedEx had not customized to individual countries.

OUTCOME

It was generally felt that FedEx's "The Way the World Works" campaign achieved its goals. For one thing the commercials improved the company's image with the public. "The campaign spiked our awareness level up almost to all-time high levels," Pacheco said. In a survey reported in *USA Today,* 28 percent of consumers said that the spots were very effective, while 15 percent said that they "liked the ads a lot." A mere 4 percent said that they disliked the campaign. The spots were most popular with people 30 to 49 years old. Pacheco claimed that the commercials were actually more popular than the *USA Today* survey indicated. He noted that FedEx and BBDO had conducted their own awareness studies and had found that the campaign was one of the most effective the company had ever undertaken. For example, multiple telephone surveys conducted to judge the public's perception of the FedEx brand over a period of time showed a strong, positive response to the commercials.

Perhaps one of the most important indicators of the campaign's success was the number of people who contacted FedEx directly after seeing the spots on television. One woman in New York City liked the wedding dress in the commercial so much that FedEx put her in touch with the dressmaker and gave her permission to use a copy of the gown for her own wedding. Another person used classical music from the campaign as a tribute at the funeral of a loved one. A third person obtained some 20 red chairs like those used in one of the spots. Pacheco noted, "I think FedEx, because of its closeness with its customers, probably gets more customer reaction like this."

"The Way the World Works" came to a close in 1998, when FedEx elected to shift gears, as the company now faced competition from a number of upstart overnight shippers, such as DHL. The company returned to a more humorous approach with the "Be Absolutely Sure" campaign, which offered comical examples of what could occur when someone relied on a cut-rate shipper rather than FedEx.

FURTHER READING

Enrico, Dottie. "FedEx Ad Campaign Delivers Effective Message." *USA Today,* August 25, 1997.

"FedEx Will Quit Joking Around Overseas Marketing: The Company Decides Humorous Ads Don't Work Globally." *Los Angeles Times,* January 21, 1997.

Fisher, Anne. "The World's Most Admired Companies." *Fortune,* October 27, 1997.

Garcia, Shelly. "Federal Express' New World View: Delivery Company Breaks Global Ad Campaign Created by BBDO." *Adweek* (eastern ed.), September 16, 1996.

Grant, Linda. "Why FedEx Is Flying High." *Fortune,* November 10, 1997.

"How the Ad Track Ads of 1997 Stack Up." *USA Today,* December 29, 1997.

Janah, Monua, and Clinton Wilder. "FedEx? Try . . . LogistEx." *Information Week,* October 27, 1997.

Levering, Robert, and Milton Moskowitz. "The 100 Best Companies to Work For in America." *Fortune,* January 12, 1998.

"Reshaping the Postal Service to Fit a Changing World." *Postal Record,* June 1997.

Rosato, Donna. "FedEx Delivers Strong Earnings on UPS Strike." *USA Today,* September 16, 1997.

Susan Risland
Ed Dinger

Fila USA

1 Fila Way
Sparks, Maryland 21152-3000
USA
Telephone: (410) 773-3000
Fax: (410) 773-3000
Web site: www.fila.com

GRANT HILL 4 CAMPAIGN

OVERVIEW

Between 1994 and 1996 Fila USA climbed from seventh place in the athletic-footwear category to an impressive third place. Although the company made shoes and attire for a variety of sports, basketball-shoe sales proved Fila's biggest success. An endorsement deal with Detroit Pistons' player Grant Hill played a clear role in this achievement. After introducing Hill's signature shoe in 1995, Fila's basketball shoe sales shot up 52 percent in one year, putting it right behind the industry leader Nike. Image problems, however, continued to nag Fila. In the United States athletic-shoe sales were driven by both technology and style. Fila was struggling to transform its image from that of fashionable shoes to functional shoes. By 1997 Fila had still not found a solid niche among young consumers, the lifeblood for athletic-shoe sales. During the first half of the year retail orders were weaker than expected and sales were stalled, forcing Fila to do heavy discounting. Even Hill's endorsement seemed less meaningful to teens than it had been a few years earlier. A young player in a New Jersey basketball league was asked by *Bloomberg News* about Fila shoes. He summed up the problem: "Look around—nobody's wearing them."

Despite the waning effectiveness of Hill's endorsement, Fila renewed his contract in 1997 and created a new advertising campaign to promote the Grant Hill 4 basketball shoe. It was reported that Hill's new seven-year endorsement agreement with Fila was valued at $80 million. The campaign began in early November to tie in with the start of the National Basketball Association's new season. Four initial television spots focused on Hill's personality rather than the shoe's new high-performance technology and featured the tagline "Change the game." Subsequent print ads followed the same theme as the television spots.

The campaign failed to achieve its goal of driving sales. Based on 1997 sales, in 1998 Fila had dropped to number four in the U.S. market, behind competitors adidas, Nike, and Reebok. Further, in the first quarter of 1998 Fila's U.S. sales plummeted 52 percent. Leo Burnett USA was hired as the agency of record for Fila in July 1998 and was charged with creating a new campaign to support the launch of the Grant Hill 5 shoe.

HISTORICAL CONTEXT

Fila was founded in Italy in 1926 as a knitwear company and introduced its first line of athletic sportswear in 1973. During the 1980s and early 1990s Fila's U.S. footwear was produced by another company under a licensing agreement. In 1991 Fila made the strategic decision to regain direct control of its footwear line and bought back the license to make its own shoes. Over the years Fila had positioned itself as a source for fashionable athletic footwear and apparel. The fashion niche had helped distinguish Fila from its more technically oriented competitors, but it marred Fila's image as a maker of functional shoes.

In 1993 Fila began remedying its lackluster sports image by signing a number of marquee athletes to endorse the shoes. In the basketball market the roster included players Jerry Stackhouse, Jamal Mashburn, and Hersey Hawkins. Bringing Detroit Pistons basketball player Grant Hill into the fold in 1994 helped the company climb from seventh place in the athletic-footwear category to third. Fila senior vice president of advertising and communications Howe Burch credited Hill's alliance with taking the company to a new level. He told the *Washington Post* that Hill "bridged the two markets for us, urban and suburban." Hill's endorsement meant a lot to footwear buyers for sporting-good stores as well as to the kids who bought the shoes. A buyer for City Sports in North Reading, Massachusetts, told *Footwear News* that he considered Hill's selling power second only to Chicago Bulls' basketball great Michael Jordan.

The endorsement strategy worked well initially. In the athletic-shoe category Fila moved into the number three slot, behind Nike and Reebok. For basketball shoes the company's sales were second only to Nike. The original Grant Hill basketball shoes, introduced in 1995, were unique and sold out quickly. But young consumers proved fickle about their athletic shoes. Many were unimpressed with the design of the second and third version of the Grant Hill shoes. Pairs were sitting on retailer's shelves and being discounted. "Sell-through" (the percentage of inventory sold by retailers per week) on the Grant Hill model introduced in October 1996 was just 10 to 15 percent. By contrast, the first version had sold through at as high as 70 percent. In 1997 *Bloomberg News* asked players on the New Jersey basketball league what they thought of Fila. One 17-year-old said, "They look ugly, with those big Fila words."

Part of the problem was that basketball shoes as a category were in a slump. Fila also acknowledged that releasing the shoes prior to the start of the basketball season might have been a mistake. Alan Sisson, owner of Slam Dunk, New York, told *Footwear News* in September 1997, "Fila was one of my best vendors a year ago. They've definitely slipped, but I feel they'll come back."

Others were more critical of Fila for continuing to play up the style of its shoes rather than emphasizing technological innovation. Young consumers who had grown up in the age of technology expected to hear about a shoe's technical features. Company president Bob Liewald justified Fila's positioning in *Sporting Goods Business,* saying, "Our mission is to create a unique blend of creativity and function. We're not ashamed of who we are. The name works against us and for us."

TOP 10 ENDORSERS OF 1997

NBA players held the top two spots on the list of most coveted sports spokesmen of 1997. The ranking took into account money earned from endorsements and a subjective evaluation of demand that Brian Murphy of the *Sports Marketing Letter* called the "heat index."

Athlete and annual endorsement income in millions: (1) Michael Jordan: $40.0, (2) Grant Hill: $26.9, (3) Tiger Woods: $25.0, (4) Shaquille O'Neal: $23.0, (5) Arnold Palmer: $19.2, (6) Andre Agassi: $17.0, (7) Jack Nicklaus: $16.0, (8) Joe Montana: $12.0, (9) Ken Griffey, Jr.: $6.0, (10) Deion Sanders: $6.0.

TARGET MARKET

Several years after Fila began producing its own athletic shoes, the company held a pivotal focus group with 12- to 18-year-olds that altered the direction of the company's marketing efforts. The youths said that they could not relate to Fila at all. Fila shoes seemed more like fashion statements than something to wear for playing sports. According to *American Demographics,* most athletic shoes were actually worn in nonathletic situations where style was more important than performance. For most wearers, what mattered was looking cool in school. Nonetheless, even the least athletic kids were looking to inner-city basketball courts for cues to what shoes to wear, and they did not see Filas there.

Capturing young buyers' interest was crucial for Fila and other athletic-sportswear companies. According to the Athletic Footwear Association, most athletic-footwear firms actively targeted consumers in the 12- to 24-year-old range. Not only did this group make up 28 percent of the total sales market, but they also tended to spend more per pair and stick with a brand as they grew older.

COMPETITION

Few retail categories had as formidable a leader as athletic footwear did in the mid-1900s. In 1996 Nike dominated the market with 44 percent of U.S. athletic-footwear sales. Reebok held 16 percent of the market, Fila 7 percent, adidas 5 percent, and New Balance 3 percent.

By 1998 Nike was running its "I Can" campaign, a successor to the wildly successful "Just Do It" campaign. Nike's new ads, however, had not resonated with the youth market as its previous ads had. Consumers were apparently growing tired of Nike's win-or-else attitude and its glorification of athletes. In addition, by becoming the industry leader, the shoes had lost some of their trendiness. Evan Cameron, a partner and head of planning at Berlin, Cameron & Partners, which handled part of the Reebok account, said that teens in his focus groups referred to the Nike symbol as a "swooshstika."

During the 1990s Reebok followed in Nike's footsteps, making heavy use of athlete endorsements to impart the message that it too was a performance brand. Although the strategy had paid off by earning the company the number two sales spot, Reebok was also facing poor sales in the late 1990s. In fact, athletic-shoe sales had cooled for the entire industry. Companies were realizing that imitating Nike would no longer earn them easy sales. "Nike created a vocabulary ten years ago, and everybody's been using that same kind of imagery and vocabulary ever since," Bill Heater of Heater Advertising, the lead agency for Reebok, told *Advertising Age.* "The same athletes, the same photographers. There's a suffocating sameness in the category."

The athletic-footwear companies that showed any substantial growth in 1997 were those with offbeat approaches to marketing. Adidas's advertising, for instance, relied less on athlete endorsements and more on regular Joes. One series of TV commercials for adidas that was successful in courting new customers actually portrayed a group of fat Yankee fans. The "brown shoe" phenomenon was another factor in declining sales of athletic shoes. Kids were taking off their basketball shoes and putting on hiking boots and lug-soled shoes made by smaller labels, such as Wolverine's, Hush Puppies, and Caterpillar. To complicate the matter, they were also flocking to designer-label sneakers from such companies as DKNY and Tommy Hilfiger.

MARKETING STRATEGY

In September 1997 Fila renewed its contract with basketball star Grant Hill, signing him to an $80 million, seven-year endorsement deal. Analysts had speculated earlier that losing the endorsement would have been a crippling blow to Fila. There were other indications, however, that buyers did not necessarily want any more sports celebrity endorsements. In years past, a celebrity endorsement was a surefire way to sell athletic shoes, but many insiders believed that the trend had outlived its usefulness. Executive director Gregg Hartley of the Sporting Goods Manufacturers Association told the *Boston Globe,* "There are only about four athletes in the whole world who can actually sell product." According to Hartley, the athletes that were worth their fees included basketball star Michael Jordan and golfers Tiger Woods and Greg Norman. Other athletes did not necessarily earn "a bang for their marketing buck," noted editor Sean Brenner of *Team Marketing Report,* an industry newsletter.

Fila was banking on Hill's cachet to lend credibility to its footwear line. They had good reason to think it would; more than $100 million had already been generated from Hill's signature shoes. But with the NBA season about to get under way, Fila still faced a considerable roadblock. "They don't have the shoes that kids want to buy," Peter Russ, an analyst with Shelby, Cullom Davis & Co., bluntly told *Bloomberg News* in mid-1997. Kids wanted shoes that blended the latest street looks with the hottest technology. Fila's reputation as a company that sacrificed performance for fashion continued to hurt sales. The new Grant Hill 4 basketball shoe had the potential to overcome that image problem. It was built on the company's proprietary 2A technology, which consisted of a matrix of high-performance, thermoplastic cylinders that provided cushioning and stability.

Arnell Brand Consulting Group, New York, created the advertising campaign for the Grant Hill 4 shoe. The campaign's debut tied into the beginning of the NBA season in November. For most marquee basketball shoes, footwear companies could count on a window of four to six weeks in which to sell their brands. "After a week," says Mark Westerman, director of advertising at Fila, "you know if the campaign is working." The four 30-second television commercials for the Grant Hill 4 shoe played up Hill's personality and image, which Westerman described as "a champion, a winner, a good guy." The spots, which employed the tagline "Change the game," communicated what it took to win, using a more low-key, introspective style than past campaigns. For instance, "Anthem" interspersed images of Hill playing basketball with close-ups of him as he listened to the national anthem before a game. "4 on the Floor" used rap lyrics to draw attention to the Fila shoe. In both "Tunnel" and "Shower," viewers saw Hill quietly getting himself psyched up for a game. Print ads that complemented the television spots appeared in *Slam, Source,* and *Sports Illustrated,* and a mural of Hill on a wall in downtown Detroit carried the theme as well.

OUTCOME

The campaign did not spark the sales that Fila needed. In 1998 Fila announced that its overall sales were worse than expected in the United States. "We had an exceptionally high level of close-out sales which killed the market," Fila spokesman Andrea Nacmias told *Footwear*

News. $480 million in 1997 U.S. sales gave the brand a share of about 6 percent, which meant that it trailed adidas as well as Nike and Reebok. Fila's 1998 first-quarter U.S. footwear sales figures were also grim, dropping 52 percent to $78.8 million. "[Fila] essentially [has] no shelf space left. It can only go up from here, I suspect," said Flavio Cereda, an analyst with the London office of ABN Amro. "They've got to do something about their presence in the U.S." Fila did not need an industry analyst to state the obvious. By that time it had already hired companies to study branding and logistics and brought on board a new advertising agency to release the Grant Hill 5 shoe.

Fila was not alone in posting poor sales for basketball shoes. The Athletic Footwear Association reported that basketball shoes accounted for only 20.2 percent of total athletic-shoe sales in 1997, compared to 28 percent in 1998. Other styles, such as running shoes, were on the rise, perhaps in a backlash response to bulky basketball shoes. Even with rising sales in certain categories, however, the entire athletic-footwear industry—including Nike—suffered that year. Consumers seemed to be moving away from big brands and toward smaller, more individualistic labels. Many companies were reevaluating their marketing strategies, particularly their use of endorsements by athletes. Jim Andrews, editor of *IEG Endorsement Insider,* a newsletter that tracked endorsements, said he thought that shoe companies had "oversaturated the market. So many players had signature footwear, it was no longer unique." Although Grant Hill's endorsement had undeniably helped put Fila on the map, even Howe Burch acknowledged that "kids just aren't as inspired by athletes because a) there are too many of them and b) because of their behavior. It's contributed to the overall cynicism and distrust of sports personalities." Reebok was a visible example of a company that chose not to renew its contract with its star athlete, basketball player Shaquille O'Neal.

Sporting Goods Business reported that Fila was shifting its focus more toward performance sports. "We put the needs of the street ahead of the performance needs of the athletes," said John Eberle, vice president of communications at Fila. "We'll return to making innovative products." Sources indicated to *Advertising Age* that the next brand push, released in 1999 by newly hired ad agency Leo Burnett, would position Fila around performance and technology and might also leverage the company's Italian heritage. The first ads promoted the newest Grant Hill shoe, the Grant Hill 5, and they were followed by additional work to promote the Fila brand. And while Fila was committed to its contract with Hill through 2004, ankle injuries had the basketball star sidelined for much of the 2000–01 season. Frank Fudo, a partner at the sports-marketing firm 16W Marketing, told ESPN that Hill excelled on the basketball court, "but him not playing doesn't help Fila too much."

In 2000 Fila began its first consolidated global campaign with BDDP/TBWA of Paris and Merkley Newman Harty of New York serving as the creatives. The new tagline that enhanced the various ad images, "Sport Life Fila," was designed to send the message that there was more to life than sports. Television spots featured Hill, Chicago Cubs star Sammy Sosa, and U.S. women's soccer team captain Carla Overbeck. The new campaign portrayed the athletes actively participating in their specific sports but also showed their human side outside of the sports arena.

FURTHER READING

"Fila Close-Outs Wreck Quarter." *Footwear News,* July 20, 1998.

"Fila Grant Hill 5 Advertising Campaign Links to Proprietary Website." *PR Newswire,* November 12, 1998.

"Fila Tries to Put Spring Back in Its Step." *Chicago Tribune,* August 17, 1997.

Fisher, Eric. "Fila Hopes Restructuring Can Put a Bounce Back in Step." *Washington (DC) Times,* November 23, 1998.

Gorant, Jim. "Slam-Dunking Hoop Shoes." *Popular Mechanics,* December 1, 1997.

"International News." *Advertising Age,* April 10, 2000.

Jensen, Jeff. "Fila Names Burnett to $20 Mil Account: New Shoe Intro First Task for Former Reebok Agency." *Advertising Age,* July 6, 1998.

"Retailers See Green in Fila's New $80M Grant Hill Deal." *Footwear News,* September 29, 1997.

Tedeschi, Mark. "Fila Plans '98 Retreat." *Sporting Goods Business,* February 25, 1998.

Walpert, Bryan. "Fila Gains Foothold in Athletic Shoe Market." *Washington Post,* April 7, 1997.

Kim Kazemi
Rayna Bailey

Ford Motor Company

1 American Road
Dearborn, Michigan 48126
USA
Telephone: (800) 392-3673
Web site: www.ford.com

■■■

DRIVING AMERICAN INNOVATION CAMPAIGN

OVERVIEW

Ford Motor Company, based in Dearborn, Michigan, entered 2005 in a difficult position. The automaker had sold only 3.15 million vehicles in the previous year, a million units less than what it had sold annually at the beginning of the decade. The company had been hemorrhaging market share as well, dropping to 18.6 percent in 2004 after spending much of the 1990s with more than 25 percent. Competition was especially fierce from Toyota Motor Sales, U.S.A., whose Japanese parent company, Toyota Motor Corporation, in 2004 displaced the Ford Motor Company as the world's second-largest automobile company in terms of sales for the first time (Ford's traditional rival, General Motors, remained number one).

To improve its overall image Ford mounted a brandwide advertising initiative called "Driving American Innovation" in 2005. The company wanted to bolster its reputation for innovation and address criticism from environmentally conscious consumers that the company's vehicles were not fuel efficient. To accomplish this Ford relied on two agencies owned by the communications-services conglomerate WPP Group—Penn Schoen & Berland and Ogilvy & Mather Detroit—to develop an advertising campaign. The effort included television, print, and Internet elements. Television spots and print ads featured the company's CEO, William "Bill" Ford, Jr. The TV commercials combined archival footage of previous Ford Motor Company successes, such as the famous Model T, with images of contemporary Ford vehicles. In the spots Bill Ford discussed how the company was building on its history of innovation and touted new products such as Ford's fuel-efficient hybrid vehicles. The campaign began in October 2005 and ran through the end of the year.

Because the campaign was designed to bolster the entire Ford brand's image, its success was difficult to gauge. According to marketing-information firm J.D. Power and Associates, in 2005 Ford drivers remained loyal to the brand at higher rates than was typical in the industry. Nevertheless, the company continued to lose market share.

HISTORICAL CONTEXT

Based in Dearborn, Michigan, Ford Motor Company was the third-largest automaker in the world in 2005 in terms of units sold. The company was founded in Michigan in 1903 by Henry Ford. In 1908 the company introduced the Model T. The car quickly became one of the most successful vehicles in U.S. automotive history, selling more than 15 million units from its inception through its cancellation in 1927. The Model T helped

William (Bill) Clay Ford, Jr., Chairman of the Board and Chief Executive Officer of Ford Motor Company. © JAMES LEYNSE/CORBIS.

make Ford the world's largest automaker at that time. In fact, in 1918 nearly half of all cars owned in the United States were Model Ts. While Ford was eventually overtaken by General Motors as the world's largest automobile manufacturer, the company continued to prosper throughout the twentieth century.

By 2005 Ford was employing more than 320,000 people worldwide and selling vehicles under the Ford, Lincoln, Mercury, Land Rover, Mazda, Volvo, Jaguar, and Aston Martin nameplates. The company also faced substantial challenges. In January 2004 the Toyota Motor Corporation, based in Japan, passed Ford to become the second-largest automaker in the world. Toyota was able to overtake Ford in part because the latter's sales fell sharply in the first few years of the twenty-first century.

In 2004 Ford sold 3.15 million units worldwide, more than a million fewer units than it had sold in 2000. The company had maintained a market share of 25 percent through the mid-1990s, but by 2004 that was down to 18.6 percent. More worrisome was the fact that Ford had failed to turn a profit in 2004. As a result there were a number of shakeups at Ford in 2005, as the company introduced a slate of new top executives in September in the hopes of turning around its sales decline. In October 2005, just before the "Driving American Innovation" campaign began, the company reported a quarterly loss of $284 million.

Because Ford sold a number of large vehicles, such as the Explorer sport-utility vehicle (SUV), that got few miles to the gallon, Ford's sales were especially sensitive to high gas prices. In 2005 gas prices rose to as high as $3 per gallon in the United States, in part as a result of market pressures caused by war in the oil-rich nation of Iraq. One way to reduce demand for gasoline was to offer hybrid vehicles. A hybrid vehicle combined two energy sources for propulsion: an internal combustion engine and an electric motor. The electric components reduced the need for gasoline, allowing the car to go further on less gas. In 2005 Ford produced about 24,000 hybrid vehicles. At the time the only Ford hybrid available was the Ford Escape Hybrid SUV, introduced earlier that year.

TARGET MARKET

Ford was interested in promoting the entire brand, not just one or two vehicle lines. This was an unusual move in the industry; most automotive campaigns tended to spotlight a particular vehicle or group of vehicles. Hence the new campaign would have to be accessible to a notably wide audience (essentially, any potential car buyer). The purpose of the campaign was to improve Ford's overall corporate image. The automaker wanted to project an image as an innovative company that was at the cutting edge in designing safer, more environmentally friendly vehicles. In addition, any Ford campaign would have to

FORD'S STAR EXECUTIVE

William Clay "Bill" Ford, Jr., was born in Detroit, Michigan, in 1957. He was the great-grandson of Henry Ford, the founder of Ford Motor Company. His father, William Clay Ford, Sr., also worked at Ford as chairman of the company's finance committee. After graduating from Princeton University in 1979, Bill Ford joined Ford Motor Company, working as a product-planning analyst. In 1987 he became managing director of Ford Switzerland, a Ford affiliate based in Europe, before being elevated to the company's board of directors the following year. He became chairman of that board on January 1, 1999, and was named CEO on October 21, 2001.

A professed environmentalist, Bill Ford promised to make the Ford Motor Company a "greener" automaker, speaking out about global warming and air pollution. Upon becoming CEO he directed the company to publish its first report outlining the environmental impact of its vehicles and operations. In addition, he pledged in 2001 to improve fuel efficiency by 25 percent by 2005. He withdrew that goal in 2003, however, saying that market conditions made it untenable. This attracted heavy criticism from environmental groups such as the Sierra Club, which accused him of going back on his word.

In addition to his work at the Ford Motor Company, Bill Ford was a trustee at Princeton. He also served as the vice chairman of the Detroit Lions, a National Football League franchise. His father, William, was the company's president and owner, having purchased the club in 1964.

emphasize performance, because according to internal data, 52 percent of Ford drivers were also racing fans.

Ford was also interested in reaching out to environmentally conscious consumers. Although Bill Ford made environmental innovation a focus of his tenure as CEO, the company drew the ire of many environmental groups. Various organizations, including the Sierra Club, the Bluewater Network, and the Rainforest Action Network, staged protests against the automaker.

COMPETITION

The two automakers that Ford traditionally competed against were General Motors and the Chrysler Group, the U.S. affiliate of Daimler Chrysler. Commonly referred to as the "Big Three," these three major American automakers had dominated the industry for most of the twentieth century. General Motors was the largest automaker in the world, and its Chevrolet brand was the best-selling brand in the United States. Chevrolet's success stretched back for decades: 1 out of every 10 cars in the United States was a Chevrolet in 1964. By 2004 Chevrolet's TrailBlazer sport-utility vehicle was making inroads against the Ford Explorer, the most popular vehicle in the segment. The TrailBlazer moved 283, 384 units in 2004, versus 339, 333 units sold by the Ford Explorer.

By the late twentieth century, however, the U.S. automotive market had changed. Toyota Motor Sales had made substantial gains in the U.S. market. In 2004 it sold 2,060,049 units in the United States alone. Sales were buoyed by vehicles such as the Toyota Camry, a midsize sedan that was the best-selling car in the United States in seven out of eight years between 1997 and 2004 (1997–2000 and 2002–04). Toyota's sales gains were helped by the automaker's reputation for innovation, safety, and quality.

MARKETING STRATEGY

Ford decided to bolster its reputation with a brandwide campaign. Two different agencies, Penn Schoen & Berland and Ogilvy & Mather of Detroit, worked in concert to create this major initiative. Both were part of the WPP Group, a media and communications services holding company. The theme of the campaign was "Driving American Innovation," a title that was intended to reflect both Ford's history of innovation and its stated commitment to developing new technologies, particularly in regard to safety and fuel efficiency. The campaign celebrated the company's enduring "spirit" of innovation. Its centerpieces were two television commercials, the 60-second "Innovation" and the 30-second "Compass." Eventually another 30-second spot, "Rebirth," also appeared, following a similar format.

All three spots combined archival footage from the automaker's history with scenes of the company's CEO, Bill Ford, discussing the Ford brand and its history. Ford, a descendent of the automaker's founder, had been with the company since 1979 and had taken over as CEO in 2001. He had previously starred in a 2002 television campaign. In the commercial titled "Innovation" Ford discussed how important innovation had always been to the Ford Motor Company, calling it "the compass that guides this company moving forward." The spot further illustrated the company's innovation by highlighting famed early Ford vehicles, such as the Model T. The Ford GT, which the company billed as a "supercar," was also shown. The vehicle, which had first appeared in 2003, was an expensive (costing in excess on $150,000) sports car that featured a racing-style design.

Ford, a self-described environmentalist, also discussed the company's efforts to increase the production of hybrid vehicles, which would help reduce the release of greenhouse gasses into the environment by using less gasoline to power their engines. "Innovation" helped underscore this by featuring the Ford Escape Hybrid, a sport-utility vehicle (SUV) with a hybrid engine. The spots were broadcast during hit television programs with wide audiences. These included Oprah Winfrey's syndicated talk show, ABC's prime-time adventure drama *Lost,* the ABC nighttime soap opera *Desperate Housewives,* CBS's immensely popular police drama *CSI,* and televised games of the National Football League.

The campaign also included print and radio components. Some print ads featured blueprint-style images of new Ford vehicles and touted the company's current innovations. One two-page spread that appeared in major dailies, including the *Wall Street Journal,* consisted of a photograph of Bill Ford along with text from a speech on innovation that was attributed to him.

OUTCOME

In September 2005 the Ford Motor Company announced plans to boost the production of hybrid vehicles to about 250,000 units per year by 2010. The Ford Escape Hybrid garnered the North American Truck of the Year award at the 2005 North American International Auto Show. That year Ford was especially successful with its midsize sedan the Fusion; that vehicle managed to sell more than 23,000 units during the period from its October 2005 introduction to the end of the year. This did not, however, mollify the company's detractors in the environmental movement. In November the Rainforest Action Network staged demonstrations at 12 different Ford dealerships in the Dearborn area in protest of the poor gas mileage of vehicles such as the popular Ford Explorer SUV.

The campaign also appeared to bolster Ford's customer loyalty. According to J.D. Power and Associates, a marketing-information firm, a 51 percent majority of all Ford customers who traded in vehicles in 2005 did so to get another Ford. This was about two percentage points higher than the industry average. The company's market share continued to slip, however, hitting 17.4 percent for the year.

FURTHER READING

Adubato, Steve. "Message, Messenger Must Quickly Click." *Newark (NJ) Star-Ledger,* February 12, 2006.

Banham, Russ. *The Ford Century: Ford Motor Company and the Innovations that Shaped the World.* New York: Artisan, 2002.

Carty, Sharon Silke. "Bill Ford Carries On Family Name with Grace." *USA Today,* February 27, 2005.

Elliott, Dorinda. "Can This Man Save the American Auto Industry?" *Time,* January 30, 2006.

Greenberg, Karl. "Ford Chairman Is Ready for His Close-Up." *Adweek,* October 20, 2005.

Krebs, Michelle. "In Detroit, the Dogs Have Their Day." *New York Times,* January 9, 2005.

Maynard, Micheline. "A Comeback for the Car Species." *New York Times,* January 5, 2006.

O'Donnell, Jayne. "Ford Touts Volvo Safety Link in Ads but Not Trials." *USA Today,* January 16, 2006.

Taylor, Alex, III. "Bill Ford: Market Share Bleed Stops Now." *Fortune,* January 8, 2006.

Wilson, Kevin. "The Way For'd: Dearborn Sets Sail on a New Tack." *AutoWeek,* January 23, 2006.

Guy Patrick Cunningham

LIFE IN DRIVE CAMPAIGN

OVERVIEW

In October 2005, Ford Motor Company introduced the new Ford Fusion. Inspired by the company's futuristic Ford 427 concept car, the Fusion was a four-door sedan aimed at young, upwardly mobile drivers. It replaced the discontinued Taurus model. The Fusion was launched into a competitive segment that featured established vehicles such as the Nissan Altima, the Honda Accord, and the best-selling car in the U.S. market, the Toyota Camry. Ford hoped that the Fusion's unique visual design, which included a distinctive three-bar front grille, would help the vehicle stand out.

The J. Walter Thompson agency, also based in Detroit, was responsible for developing a launch campaign for the Fusion. The resulting "Life in Drive" campaign kicked off in October 2005 and featured a mix of traditional and new-media advertising. Its centerpiece was a series of television commercials. There were several 15-second spots, along with two 30-second spots. The spots often ran back-to-back, with a 15-second commercial leading into one of the two longer spots. The 15-second spots all featured a contrast between "life"—illustrated by images of people performing dull, frustrating tasks, such as trying to open a CD case—and "Life in Drive," where the viewer saw the Fusion on a drive through a hip cityscape depicted via quick cuts. The campaign also featured an innovative online component, which included a "Photo Fusion" feature on the Ford website. Consumers could post pictures of themselves along with brief descriptions of what the photos contained. Posters were then given an opportunity to view other consumers' pictures based on shared keywords in their descriptions. This interactive program was meant to attract young consumers who were comfortable with seeking information online.

The campaign met with solid success. Ford sold more than 23,000 units between the Fusion's October 2005 debut and the end of the calendar year, with sales climbing every month. The vehicle sold so well that dealers reported having trouble keeping the new Fusion in stock, forcing Ford to increase production of the vehicle.

HISTORICAL CONTEXT

The Ford Motor Company was founded by Henry Ford on June 16, 1903. Based in Detroit, Michigan, the company was responsible for one of the most important innovations in automobile manufacturing, the assembly line. This 1913 innovation helped make Ford the second-largest automaker in the world (after General Motors) for much of the twentieth century. By the beginning of the twenty-first century the Ford Motor Company was selling vehicles under eight different brands: Ford, Lincoln, Mercury, Land Rover, Mazda, Volvo, Jaguar, and Aston Martin.

Ford decided to create a new four-door family sedan to replace the Taurus, an older model that consumers no longer found exciting. After considering other names, the company called the new vehicle the Ford Fusion. The design of the vehicle was inspired in part by the Ford 427, a concept vehicle that had been met with general acclaim at a number of auto shows. The Fusion featured a spacious interior, a stiff chassis for better handling, and a distinctive exterior design. The car was meant to look sleek and speedy, in contrast to other, more staid midsize sedans, such as the Taurus. Most notable was the vehicle's three-bar front grille and its unique triangular taillights.

Ford also created a racing version of the Fusion, which competed in National Association for Stock Car Auto Racing (NASCAR) events. In fact, Ford's racing division provided some input on the car's design. Internal data showed that Ford's market share was 6 percent higher among NASCAR fans than it was nationally. The Fusion would debut at the Ford Championship weekend at the Homestead-Miami Speedway, which featured the final race of the 2005 NASCAR Busch series. The event was planned for November 17 and 18, 2005.

In October 2005 Ford introduced the Fusion for model year 2006, with a base price of $17,795. Ford was already in the midst of a strong year, with sales up 12 percent from 2004 through September. It hoped to be able to establish the Fusion as a vehicle that could sell up to 160,000 units annually.

TARGET MARKET

The Fusion was designed to appeal to consumers between the ages of 25 and 35. These consumers were identified by the company as being strongly interested in music and technology. Ford wanted to connect with middle-income consumers who were both established in their careers and upwardly mobile. While some of these buyers gravitated toward sportier cars, such as the Ford Mustang, or toward large SUVs, internal data at the automaker led Ford to believe that drivers in this age group were becoming more interested in midsize sedans. In effect, the Fusion would serve as the next step for the young drivers who had previously driven smaller cars such as the Ford Focus. As a family sedan the Fusion was especially geared toward young families, people with younger children, or those considering starting a family soon.

COMPETITION

The Fusion competed most directly with other midsize vehicles. These included imports such as the Honda Accord, the Nissan Altima, and the Volkswagen Jetta and domestic models such as GM's Chevrolet Malibu. The giant of the midsize field, however, was the Toyota Camry. First introduced in 1980, the Camry had been the biggest-selling car in the United States in seven out of the eight years between 1997 and 2004. In 2004 it sold an impressive 426,990 units. It usually sold for between $19,000 and $25,000. The Camry was not a flashy car; its popularity rested primarily on its reputation for quality. It was a safe, durable vehicle and held its resale value well.

Ford hoped that by pricing the Fusion between $17,995 and $21,000, it would distinguish itself from its competitors. Prices for the other major midsize cars on the market began around $18,400 and could climb as high as $25,000 for so-called luxury versions of the vehicles. Ford believed that its aggressive pricing might help offset the fact that many established brands had built-in customer bases.

MARKETING STRATEGY

Ford designated the Detroit-based ad agency J. Walter Thompson with developing a launch strategy for the new Fusion. The resulting campaign, released in October 2005, was named "Life in Drive," and it mixed

FUSION FLASH CONCERTS

A key part of the Ford Motor Company's introduction of the Ford Fusion in 2005 was its sponsorship of a series of free concerts in the months leading up to the vehicle's launch. The series was a joint effort between Ford and Sony Pictures Digital, a division of the Sony Corporation of America. After registering on a special Ford Fusion website, consumers were notified about the concerts via text message. These concerts were inspired by "flash mobs," outdoor gatherings created on the spur of the moment by using the text-messaging features of cell phones and other mobile communication devices. Often organizers of flash mobs would alert a small number of people about a gathering, and then word would spread organically as those people contacted others.

The first Fusion Flash Concert was held in July 2005 in New York City. It featured the alternative hip-hop act the Roots. Later concerts presented a mix of rock acts, including Collective Soul, the Wallflowers, Yellowcard, Pete Yorn, and Staind, as well as hip-hop performers Jermaine Dupri, Fat Joe, and Frankie J. Each band appeared at their own individual concerts. Registered consumers were notified about each performance at the last minute, meaning that the entire event would come together in a "flash." Each concert took place in a different urban area, including Dallas, Philadelphia, Los Angeles, and Chicago. The most successful of the Flash concerts was the hard-rock band Staind's August 9 appearance in Boston, which drew an audience of 12,000 people.

traditional television and print advertising with online efforts and live events. Print ads appeared in *USA Today* and in local newspapers. The campaign was preceded by a series of Fusion Flash Concerts, featuring bands such as alternative hip-hop stars the Roots, popular rapper Fat Joe, and rock bands Staind and Collective Soul. The Staind event was a particular success, drawing 12,000 people to a free concert in Boston. Organizers had only expected a showing of about 500.

The "Life in Drive" campaign began in earnest with a series of 15-second teaser spots directed by Grammy-winning director Joseph Kahn, who had previously directed music videos for rock band U2 and rapper Eminem, among others. One commercial, "Trash Day," began with a half-dressed man taking out the garbage. He was too late and missed the garbage truck, and a voice-over declared, "This is life." Suddenly, rock music blared, and a series of quick cuts showed a Fusion driving around a city. The voice-over returned to say, "This is life in drive." Another 15-second spot, "Doggie," showed a young woman cleaning up after her dog, leading to the same voice-over and quick cuts. The spot titled "CD" featured the same setup, only this time it began with someone having difficulty opening a CD case. Each commercial closed with the text tagline "Life in D," which then gave way to the Ford Fusion logo. The "D" resembled the "D" (for "drive") that appeared on the Fusion's gearshift.

Kahn also directed two 30-second spots for the campaign. These premiered on October 31, 2005. The most important, "Particle," drew attention through its prominent use of the Apple iPod as a prop. A portable music player known for its distinctive white color and sleek design, the iPod was first introduced in 2001 and quickly became the most popular digital-music player on the market. It was particularly popular among drivers in the Fusion's target demographic. Some critics felt that by trying to associate itself with a trendy new product, Ford risked allowing the Fusion to look stale and uncool by comparison. One critic noted that the Fusion did not even have an adapter that would allow the iPod to play in the vehicle.

"Particle" began with a man on a subway listening to the device. As he listened, particles that looked like bubbles began to rise out of the iPod. These bubbles then drifted up from the subway car and onto a dance floor, where they circled a young woman. The bubbles continued to circulate, moving past rollerbladers and a flat-screen television. Finally they reached a traffic intersection, where they "fused" together to become a Ford Fusion vehicle. The other 30-second spot, "Ignition," featured a similar theme. This time the Fusion itself generated the energy, which in turn revitalized a worn-out urban neighborhood. Both commercials ended with a voice-over declaring, "a car shouldn't just use energy, it should create it," before concluding that the Fusion represented "more innovation from Ford." Often Ford packaged one of the 15-second spots back-to-back with one of the longer commercials, creating a 45-second advertising block.

The campaign quickly branched out into new media. In November Ford began an effort at three major Web portals: Yahoo!, AOL, and MSN. The Fusion was represented via prominent ads and banners on all three sites. Ford also used an innovative "Photo Fusion" feature on its own website. The feature allowed customers to post personal pictures on the site. When they did so, consumers were also asked to describe their photos. Based on those descriptions, the Photo Fusion feature would then show other consumers' pictures to the poster, based on similar keywords in both descriptions. This interactive system was meant to appeal to young consumers who were more interested in actively navigating the Web than in watching TV commercials. The company also posted selected "Life in Drive" television spots on the company's website.

OUTCOME

The Fusion met with solid success. After its October 2005 introduction the vehicle saw sales increase every month. By November Ford had already sold 15,481 units (a number that included precampaign sales). In December the Fusion sold 7,568 units, its best monthly figures for 2005. According to internal studies, customers rated the Fusion's unique design as the number one reason for purchasing the vehicle. The car managed this without the heavy incentives, such as cash rebates, that many automakers used to help sell new vehicles. The vehicle proved so popular that Ford dealers had a difficult time keeping it in stock. As 2006 began, Ford ramped up production to meet the ever-growing demand. In an effort to expand its appeal, the company also announced that it would develop a hybrid version of the Fusion for model year 2008.

FURTHER READING

Banham, Russ. *The Ford Century: Ford Motor Company and the Innovations that Shaped the World.* New York: Artisan, 2002.

Bowens, Greg. "Ford Looks beyond Traditional Audience at It Tilts New Fusion Campaign toward Hip Youth." *Automotive News,* December 1, 2005.

Chura, Hillary. "Throwing All Cultures into the Marketing Pot." *New York Times,* February 21, 2006.

Cobb, James G. "Diamonds Out of the Distress of 2005." *New York Times,* January 1, 2006.

Krebs, Michelle. "In Detroit, the Dogs Have Their Day." *New York Times,* January 9, 2005.

Maynard, Micheline. "A Comeback for the Car Species." *New York Times,* January 5, 2006.

Rashbaum, Alyssa. "Fat Joe, Roots, Jermaine Dupri Coming Soon to a Parking Lot Near You." *Vibe.com,* July 11, 2005. Available from <http://www.vibe.com/news/news_headlines/2005/07/fatjoe_flashconcerts/>

Stevenson, Seth. "Apple Jacking: Car Ads that Look Like iPod Ads." *Slate,* January 30, 2006. Available from <http://www.slate.com/id/2135009/?nav=navoa>

Wilson, Amy. "Ford Dealers Can't Get Enough Fusions." *Automotive News,* December 16, 2005.

Wilson, Kevin. "The Way For'd: Dearborn Sets Sail on a New Tack." *AutoWeek,* January 23, 2006.

Guy Patrick Cunningham

STORYTELLING CAMPAIGN

OVERVIEW

For 15 years Ford Motor Company, the number two automaker among Detroit's big three, had advertised its vehicles with the slogan "Have you driven a Ford lately?" In 1998 the company launched a new campaign with the tag line "Ford Cars: Built to Last." The campaign, developed by advertising agency J. Walter Thompson, used a storytelling approach and ran in print and broadcast media as well as on the Internet. It was based on the notion that people enjoyed hearing other people's stories.

The "Storytelling" campaign centered around everyday people who owned Ford vehicles, and the ads used humor and emotion to reach consumers. As its spokesperson Ford chose John Corbett, best known as the philosophical disc jockey on the television series *Northern Exposure,* a man with a pleasant, relatively low-key demeanor that fit well with the campaign. His role in the commercials closely resembled his work from the hit show, in which he had been something of a narrator. Corbett and country superstar Alan Jackson, another Ford spokesman, appeared together in an ad for National Ford Truck Season beginning in October 1998, and they were also featured on the company's website.

The company launched the campaign during the Winter Olympics in February 1998 with six television spots. The campaign included ads for the Mustang, Taurus, Escort ZX2, and pickup truck models. Six months later, Ford decided to expand the campaign to all of its 1999 vehicles.

HISTORICAL CONTEXT

The Ford Motor Company, founded in 1903, has experienced its share of highs and lows. Its founder, Henry Ford, was described by Ed Crews in an August 11, 1998, article in the *Richmond (Virginia) Times-Dispatch* as "a mythic figure in American business history. He comes down to us as a contradictory mix of inspired tinkerer, backyard mechanic, captain of industry, eccentric and

Actor John Corbett. © LYNN GOLDSMITH/CORBIS.

capitalist oppressor. Sometimes it is impossible to see where the myth ends and the man begins."

In 1908 Ford introduced the popular Model T. Also known as the "Tin Lizzie," it was said to be the "universal car," built to be rugged, reliable, and easy to operate. When Ford incorporated the assembly line into his company's production process, he revolutionized not only the auto industry but also all industries. Increased efficiencies allowed Ford to keep prices down and expand into overseas markets. By 1915 Ford had produced its millionth car. In 1916 Ford made half of all the American cars built and accounted for 40 percent of the world's auto production.

But success may have blinded Henry Ford to the need for change. By the 1920s competing automakers were producing models with more style, comfort, and power than the Tin Lizzie. Ford dragged his feet on producing a new model, and the company continued to make the Model T into the late 1920s. Only when it became absolutely clear that the car would not sell at any price did Ford throw in the towel. He shut down production for six months in order to retool the plants for a new model. The successor Model A enjoyed good sales, but by 1932 General Motors (GM) had taken the number one spot from Ford, and GM held it for decades.

Over the years Ford introduced many successful models, including the Thunderbird, Escort, Taurus, and, perhaps most notably, Mustang. It also produced the Edsel, a spectacular flop, and from time to time the company suffered financial setbacks. Ford became known for its pickup trucks and sport utility vehicles, including the F-Series truck and the Explorer. Despite its successes, however, for the most part Ford remained an also-ran to number one General Motors. In addition, Ford and other U.S. automakers eventually had to contend with inroads made by foreign auto manufacturers, primarily the Japanese.

TARGET MARKET

The "Storytelling" campaign was developed with both male and female consumers in mind. For instance, "Hands," a commercial for the F-Series truck, showed close-ups of the hands of a hardworking but sensitive mechanic named Joe. Shots of Joe's hands working with a blowtorch and gripping the wheel of his Ford truck were interspersed with shots of him holding a small child. Jan Klug, Ford Division's marketing communications manager, said, "The 'Hands' story is the highest rated F-Series spot we have tested among men and women. It really touched a chord with consumers, who could relate to a guy and his truck balancing work and family."

Ford took care to ensure that the campaign would appeal to women even if it did not target them exclusively. Three of the six television spots used to launch the campaign featured women. One spot informed viewers of Ford's support for Race for the Cure, a national breast cancer charity. In addition, because "Built Ford Tough," the popular tag line used for trucks, tested poorly with women, Ford dropped the idea of also using it for its car ads. Instead, the tag line "Built to Last" tag was created for Ford cars.

Seven months after the campaign launch, *Adweek* reported that Ford intended to increase its spending on ads that targeted Hispanic and African American consumers and, for the first time, to make some of the advertising targeting African Americans part of the general market pool. Uniworld, New York, was hired to handle the African-American marketing, while Zubi Advertising of Miami handled the Hispanic advertising.

COMPETITION

Ford, General Motors, and Chrysler (which in November 1998 merged with Daimler-Benz AG to become DaimlerChrysler AG) made up Detroit's big three automakers. For years GM had enjoyed the number one spot in U.S. auto manufacturing, followed by number two Ford and number three Chrysler. In November 1997, however, *Ward's Auto World* reported that all three were losing market share in passenger cars to light trucks and sport utility vehicles. At the same time there was increasing pressure on the Detroit automakers to keep prices down. GM offered various financial incentives, including cut-rate financing programs and cash rebates on 1998 cars and light trucks. Ford and Chrysler offered similar incentives as well. The *Wall Street Journal* reported in November 1997 that, despite healthy sales and a robust economy, U.S.-based automakers were also

JOHN CORBETT: FROM STEELWORKER TO SPOKESPERSON

John Corbett, an ex-steelworker from West Virginia who went into acting after being injured on his job, was probably best known for his role as small town disc jockey Chris Stevens in *Northern Exposure.* Corbett also served a shorter stint on the Fox sci-fi series *The Visitor,* in which he played a passenger on an alien spaceship that crash-landed in Utah.

The Ford campaign was not Corbett's first experience as an auto spokesperson. During his time on *Northern Exposure,* Corbett also provided the voice-over for Isuzu Trooper commercials. A spokesman for the Isuzu advertising agency said that Corbett was chosen because "we wanted someone who was observant, who had a compassionate voice that would present a situation and then make it relevant." Perhaps Ford observed those same qualities in Corbett when it signed him on as its storyteller.

facing increased price pressures from Japanese imports as a result of the weak yen and reduced production costs.

During 1998 General Motors reportedly lost market share, and in August 1998 the *Wall Street Journal* noted that "GM's total sales and market share fell below those of No. 2 automaker Ford Motor Company for the first time since a national strike against GM in 1970." Ford's market share for April 1999 was reported to have dropped by 0.9 percent from that of the previous three months, however.

MARKETING STRATEGY

The launch of a new advertising campaign in February 1998 was a major event for the company. According to Art Spinella, the automotive director for CNW Marketing Research, "Ford tends to hand on to its ad campaigns for a long time." The new campaign featured a new tag line. The slogan that Ford had used for 15 years—"Have you driven a Ford lately?"—was replaced with "Ford Cars: Built to Last." The tag line "Built Ford Tough" continued to be used in truck advertising.

The television ads told stories of everyday people with humor and emotion in order to strike a chord with consumers. In choosing a spokesperson, Ford looked for someone who was not such a megastar that he or she would overshadow the product. Corbett, known from *Northern Exposure,* tested well. In fact, his role in the commercials closely resembled his role in the television series, in which he served as something of a narrator.

In a written statement issued several months after the campaign had started, Ford described its approach as "down-to-earth" and "a real change in Ford's approach to advertising." According to Ford's Klug, "When we launched the campaign in 1998, we discovered that everyone has a favorite story about a car or truck. This campaign is all about communicating on an emotional level—not just price and features." According to Ford, the spots dealt with "the human spectrum of experience, from the humorous to very emotional themes." Klug noted that the campaign "is all about building mind-changing communication, and to do that we need to make an emotional connection with our customers. One of the benefits of the campaign is the ability to tell stories that capture the personality of individual vehicles, but in a consistent, unified way that conveys the values that stand behind the Ford name."

Examples included an ad in which two friends—Charlie and Ray—made a wager over the capabilities of the F-Series truck. Charlie bet that Ray's truck would not be able to tow an 8,000-ton ship, and, of course, he lost. Another example was an Escort ad in which two women in a ZX2 tried to elude a strange van that was chasing them. When the van passed them, they realized that it was Publishers Clearing House trying to give them a prize.

Ford reportedly earmarked $80 million for the campaign, double the amount spent the year before. Six 30-second television spots were introduced during the coverage of the Winter Olympics, with the models advertised including the Mustang, Taurus, Escort ZX2, and F-Series pickup truck. One of the ads focused on Ford history, and another emphasized Ford's commitment toward Race for the Cure.

OUTCOME

After six months of running the ads, Ford decided to expand the campaign to all of its vehicles—cars and trucks—with the release of the 1999 models. Corbett was enlisted to appear in 13 new commercials, which included the "Hands" spot and another called "Charlie's Parents," in which two overprotective parents took comfort in knowing that a Taurus was helping keep their son Charlie from harm. Another humorous spot showed two women talking about their boyfriends' Mustangs, only to realize that they might be talking about the same man. In addition to the 13 new spots, several old ones were carried over from the 1998 campaign.

Ford also decided to change its 1999 marketing strategy to focus on its primary brands—Ford, Lincoln,

FORD TRUCK ADS COME ON STRONG

For its 1999 advertising efforts Ford decided to do more than just tell nice stories about its trucks. In fact, in a departure from precedent the company decided to come on stronger. In addition to referring to competitors by name, Ford's truck advertising took on a somewhat confrontation tone. Paul Morel, Ford Division's truck group brand manager, called the ads "very hard-hitting and confident for a very tough and competitive market." In one ad a factory foreman announced to the plant that a Ford F-Series truck in the parking lot had its lights on, and he watched in dismay as all of the workers cleared out to check on their trucks. One print ad showed a Ford F-Series truck driving through the rain with the text "You're not going to find a better truck anywhere. Not even if you look under a rock." The reference was reportedly to advertising for the General Motors C/K Series truck in which Bob Seger sang "Like a Rock."

"Ford hasn't been doing in-your-face advertising with their competitors before. So I think the strategy they're taking with their truck represents forward thinking," said Tanya Gazdik, the Detroit bureau chief for *Adweek*.

Mercury, Jaguar, and Mazda—rather than individual models. Jim Schroer, Ford's executive director of marketing strategy and brand management, believed that past marketing efforts had tended to promote specific nameplates, such as Taurus and Explorer, too heavily and did not connect with or reinforce the primary brand. "The change is to make sure each nameplate strengthens the primary brand it is under," he said.

Spinella of CNW Marketing Research predicted, "This new campaign looks like it has some legs under it and Ford should be able to use it for another 10 to 15 years." Ford's Klug thought that the storytelling approach was effective. "Storytelling is part of the human DNA," she said. "People can really relate to it. You can tell stories that revolve around the personalities of our products."

FURTHER READING

Berkowitz, Harry. "TV Advertisers Go for the Gold." *Newsday,* February 5, 1998, p. A53.

"Ford Ads to Bolster Truck Lead." *Calgary Sun,* October 2, 1998, p. A18.

"Ford Division Launches New Internet Website." *PR Newswire,* October 13, 1998.

"Ford Expands 'Storytelling' Advertising Campaign for 1999 Model Year." Ford Division Public Affairs, September 28, 1998.

"Ford Readies '99 Effort." *Adweek* (Midwest Edition), September 28, 1998, p. 8.

Gazdik, Tanya. "Ford Tries New Tagline, Approach." *Adweek* (Southeast Edition), February 9, 1998, p. 41.

Halliday, Jean. "Ford Division Expands Storytelling Ads For '99." *Automotive News,* August 24, 1998, p. 49.

———. "Ford Switches Directions to Push Primary Brands." *Advertising Age,* November 16, 1998, p. 6.

Ramirez, Charles E. "Ford Gets New Ad Theme." *Detroit News,* February 5, 1998, p. B1.

Teegardin, Carol. "Ford Ad Campaign Takes On Competition." *Detroit Free Press,* October 3, 1998.

Winter, Drew. "Feisty Ford." *Ward's Auto World,* May 1996, p. 63.

Debbi Mack

Fortune Brands, Inc.

300 Tower Parkway
Lincolnshire, Illinois 60069-3640
USA
Telephone: (847) 484-4400
Fax: (847) 478-0073
Web site: www.fortunebrands.com

SIGN BOY CAMPAIGN

OVERVIEW

FootJoy, owned by Fortune Brands, Inc., sold more golf shoes during the 1990s than any other company by keeping their innovative shoes on the feet of the world's best golfers. Two events in 1996, however, caused the company, which also made socks and gloves, to restrategize its advertising. Not only did Nike, Inc., announce it would begin designing golf shoes, but it agreed to pay champion golfer Tiger Woods $8 million a year to endorse them. Fearful that Nike would dominate the burgeoning younger market of golfers, FootJoy released its quirky "Sign Boy" campaign to attract young players.

In 1998 FootJoy awarded its estimated $5 to $7 million advertising budget to ad agency Arnold Worldwide Partners. Print ads and television spots appeared in January 1999 starring comedian Matt Griesser, who played the campaign's character titled "Sign Boy," a moniker for the standard-bearer or person carrying the cumbersome scoreboard from hole to hole during golf tournaments. In the first eight commercials Sign Boy pestered golfers, sometimes mid-swing, with his overzealous blathering and obsession over FootJoy shoes. With a background in improvisational comedy, Griesser ad-libbed every commercial, which appeared on channels such as ESPN, NBC, and ABC. In one spot Sign Boy dove into a water hazard while wearing nothing but FootJoy shoes. The golfers Phil Mickelson and David Toms looked on in horror. Another spot showed Sign Boy slinking into a locker room just to sniff the FootJoy shoes of professional golfers. Another featured him nabbing Ernie Els's toothbrush. With the exception of a yearlong hiatus in 2002, the "Sign Boy" campaign expanded to include Internet ads as well as on-site promotions where Griesser would actually heckle players during golf tournaments.

The campaign collected a Silver EFFIE Award in 2001 and helped increase FootJoy sales 10 percent in the market of people under age 30. Andy Jones, marketing vice president at FootJoy, told the *Palm Beach Post,* "Ultimately the judge of any advertising campaign is market-share growth. During the campaign we've experienced significant market-share growth in both golf shoes and golf gloves."

HISTORICAL CONTEXT

Fortune Brands, the corporation that owned alcohol brands such as Jim Beam and Knob Creek, purchased FootJoy in 1986. Running non-humorous advertising that usually featured golfers, FootJoy dominated the golf-shoe industry during the 1990s. It was only after Nike announced its upcoming golf shoe that FootJoy rethought its entire marketing strategy. Not only had Nike dominated the outside-athletic-shoe industry, but the titan was showing a growing interest in golf, first with its introduction of Nike golf apparel. Then it offered world-champion golfer Tiger Woods an $8 million endorsement in 1996. Woods, who was playing Masters Tournaments by the age of 19, appealed to the under-30-year-old age group. Soon afterward FootJoy senior product manager Tim Murphy told *Adweek* (eastern edition) that FootJoy had experienced an erosion in its market share among younger customers since Nike engaged Woods.

In 1998 FootJoy asked Arnold Worldwide to rebrand the company's shoes for a younger audience. Arnold Worldwide's senior vice president, Jamie Graham, worked on the project with Ron Harper, the agency's senior art director. Graham explained to *Shoot,* "We were in the right place at the right time, because Nike was coming along, doing some very cool stuff with Tiger Woods. FootJoy was worried about being perceived as old-fashioned, so they gave us more [freedom] than they might otherwise have done."

The Sign Boy character was first conceived by Harper, who recalled a friend raving about serving as a standard-bearer at a tournament. Harper and Graham began strategizing FootJoy's first humorous television commercial. For the casting call they titled their scripts after player nicknames such as "Philly Mick" for Phil Mickelson and "DL3" for Davis Love III. After screening 100 candidates Harper and Graham chose actor-comedian Matt Griesser, who not only picked up on the nickname references but also began lampooning different golfers during the cast selection. "He nailed David Duval's swing in the audition room. We couldn't get rid of him, in fact," Graham said to the *Palm Beach Post.*

TARGET MARKET

The "Sign Boy" campaign targeted golfers and golf enthusiasts under 30 years old. It also hoped to retain FootJoy's core golf customers while maintaining the brand's rank as the golf-shoe industry leader. To reach this younger demographic, the campaign used humor, a quality not typically found in golf commercials before 1999. "A lot of golf commercials in the past were just Lee Trevino telling people to use Top-Flite," Griesser told the *Florida Times-Union.* "FootJoy was trying to reach a younger audience and one way to do it is with humor." In a spot with British Open champion David Duval, Sign Boy began testing wind speed for the golfer and then rambled on about what club he should use. The spot ended with Sign Boy heaping praise upon Duval's choice of FootJoy shoes. Sign Boy also made appearances at tournaments. During Rhode Island Country Club's CVS Classic, Griesser told driving-distance record holder John Daly that he needed to lengthen his already lengthy backswing if he was serious about driving the golf ball.

SECOND CITY

Before his role as the blundering sign carrier in a FootJoy shoe campaign titled "Sign Boy," Matt Griesser performed improvisational comedy for the Los Angeles troupe of Second City. Second City was a Chicago-based entertainment program famous for launching the careers of, among others, comedians John Candy, Eugene Levy, and Martin Short.

Aware that its target market would grow tired of seeing the same three or four commercials played over and over, Arnold Worldwide filmed eight commercials total. Graham explained to *Shoot,* "People who watch golf watch it religiously, so the same people who watch golf this weekend will see all the golf advertising over and over again. They appreciate the fact that we give them more, rather than less, commercials. Sign Boy himself has a cult following on the tours. He makes appearances and goes to charity golf events."

COMPETITION

In 1998 Etonic Athletic Worldwide, one of America's leading makers of golf shoes, ran television and prints advertising that claimed their new plastic-cleated shoes caused less damage to fairway turf than FootJoy shoes. The print, created by ad agency Greenberg Seronick O'Leary & Partners of Boston, ran in *Golf Digest, Golfweek,* and *Golf Magazine.* FootJoy immediately sued Etonic, stating that FootJoy had been making spikeless, fairway-friendly shoes since 1959. FootJoy demanded Etonic stop the campaign and pay damages.

In August 1996, while donning a black Nike hat with the company's "swoosh" emblem, Tiger Woods won his third U.S. Amateur Championship. After the tournament he announced that he would begin endorsing Nike, which analysts estimated would earn Woods $8 million per year. At the Greater Milwaukee Open that took place the following weekend, Woods dressed in more Nike apparel, which included Nike golf shoes. Bob Wood, president of Nike Golf, said to *Brandweek,* "Our philosophy at Nike Golf, as well as at Nike, is to start with the best players, make product that works for them, and establish ourselves that way." Not only would Tiger Woods continue endorsing Nike shoes, but Nike also rolled out its own line of golf balls in 1999 and had introduced clubs by 2002. After Woods first announced the relationship with Nike, one retailer, Susan French, told the *Portland Oregonian* that she immediately sold

TIGER WOODS

In 1996 world-champion golfer Tiger Woods was featured in a Nike Golf television spot that exposed racist policies still lingering on a small group of American golf courses. In the spot, which aired during a Monday night NFL football game, Tiger stated, "There are still golf courses in the United States that I cannot play because of the color of my skin. I'm told I'm not ready for you. Are you ready for me?" The spot was followed by Nike Golf's tagline, "It's time to change."

out of her 3,000 Nike hats and ordered an additional 750 to keep up with demand. "They want the hat, they want a shirt, they want any sort of memento," she said. Nike continued using Woods's endorsements, each of which featured the tagline "It's time to change."

MARKETING STRATEGY

The "Sign Boy" television spots first appeared on January 8, 1999, during the Mercedes Championship on ESPN, and later rotated across network channels NBC, CBS, and ABC and on the cable channel USA Network. Initial commercials ended with the FootJoy taglines "The No. 1 shoe in golf" or "The No. 1 glove in golf." The first eight spots were also filmed unscripted. Professional golfers featured in the spots, such as Davis Love III, Justin Leonard, Phil Mickelson, David Duval, and Jesper Parnevik, were asked to react with Sign Boy as they would any tournament volunteer. Sign Boy, played by Griesser, pestered, distracted, and admired the golfers with overzealousness as they attempted to golf. "We use him in a specific relationship with all the pros, mashing on them and telling them what superb footwear they have," Graham explained to *Shoot.* "His particular obsession is that he knows every single style and brand of shoe inside out. We engage him in good-natured banter with the pro golfers."

The "Sign Boy" campaign took a hiatus in 2002 when FootJoy released its poorly received "Golf Gods" campaign, which featured animated golfers receiving superpowers from their FootJoy shoes. Graham told the *Palm Beach Post,* "[FootJoy] got hundreds of e-mails, hundreds and thousands of e-mails saying, 'Hey, where's Sign Boy? What have you people done? And by the way, we hate these Golf Gods.'" Andy Jones, FootJoy's vice president for marketing, said to *Shoot,* "I think the best thing we can say about it is that it was a mistake.... We pushed the envelope with Sign Boy and we were trying to push the envelope again." By 2003 the "Sign Boy" campaign had resumed with five new spots, including one that featured Incredible Technologies, Inc.'s video-golf game Golden Tee. By 2005 the campaign included Internet banner ads, and its budget had escalated from an estimated $5 million to $7 million.

As the campaign progressed Griesser increased his public appearances at tournaments. In 2005 Sign Boy stumbled into the audience at the CVS Charity Classic golf tournament. Craig Stadler, a well-built professional golfer with thick facial hair, sat beside his son and other golfers waiting for the father-son tournament to begin. According to the *Providence Journal,* the crowd exploded with laughter as Sign Boy pointed back and forth between both Stadlers and said, "Walrus. Little Walrus. Walrus. Little Walrus." Next he teased Jay and Bill Haas by repeating, "Big Haas. Little Haas. Big Haas. Little Haas."

Each year the campaign released more commercials than most industry competitors. "We shoot them at breakneck speed," Graham stated to *Shoot.* "I think the thing with humor is, the more you have—as long as it's funny—the better. You don't want to tell the same joke over and over again. So even though some of these spots don't air nearly as much as a purist would say they should, it satisfies us because it never gets boring."

OUTCOME

The "Sign Boy" campaign earned a Silver EFFIE Award in 2001, increased FootJoy sales 10 percent with the under-30 market, and stoked FootJoy's lead over the rest of the industry. The campaign also injected golf advertising with humor, something it had lacked before the campaign's 1999 release. In 2001 Griesser said to the *Portland Oregonian,* "Now you can see more humor in golf ads all the time. I like to think that the ads I've been in also have served to reveal more of the golfers' personalities." The campaign reaped praise from cable station the Golf Channel and from sports publications such as *Golf Magazine, Sports Illustrated, Golf Plus, Golfweek,* and *Golf World.*

During the campaign's first five months FootJoy sales increased 16 percent over the previous year-to-date figures. The campaign's lighthearted humor, according to some analysts, simultaneously appealed to older and younger consumers. Graham told *Brandweek,* "Only FootJoy can talk about tour dominance, which they do via these ads in a way that appeals to young players without putting off the older guy." Griesser's personality as Sign Boy far exceeded the creatives' expectations for the character, which originally called for "a doofy-looking guy who walks around in very long shorts." Arnold Worldwide originally gave the campaign a life expectancy of three years, and was pleased to be proven wrong when it exceeded five years.

FURTHER READING

Champagne, Christine. "J.J. Sedelmaier Goes Golfing with Gods." *Shoot,* January 25, 2002, p. 14.

Diaz, Ann-Christine. "Special Report: Top Production Companies." *Advertising Age's Creativity,* September, 1, 2005, p. 44.

Dolbow, Sandra. "FootJoy's 'Sign Boy' Goes inside Ropes." *Brandweek,* June 19, 2000, p. 17.

Duckworth, Ed. "Golf: The CVS Charity Classic." *Providence (RI) Journal,* July 11, 2000, p. D5.

Long, Rani. "Golf Shoes Fore Sale." *Shoot,* December 10, 1999, p. 54.

Griesser, Matt. "Sign Boy: After a One-Year Hiatus, the Bungling FootJoy Pitchman Played by Matt Griesser Is Back On the Air." *Sports Illustrated,* February 10, 2003.

Manning, Jeff. "Woods Lays Claim to New Kind of Green." *Portland Oregonian,* August 29, 1996, p. A1.

McCabe, Jim. "Score One for Yuks: 'Sign Boy' Character Is Back for Another Round." *Boston Globe,* January 19, 2003, p. C17.

———. "'Sign Boy' Character Holds Fans' Attention." *Boston Globe,* March 23, 2000, p. F2.

O'Brien, George, "Spalding Goes for the Rebound." *Business West,* October 1, 2000, p. 6.

Robinson, Bob. "Notebook: 'Sign Boy' Lends Hand to Stunt by Mickelson." *Portland Oregonian,* August 8, 2001, p. E4.

Smits, Garry. "Sign (Boy) of the Times Dives into Job." *Florida Times-Union,* June 8, 2003, p. C6.

Tays, Alan. "Fits Him Like a Glove." *Palm Beach (FL) Post,* April 27, 2005, p. 10C.

Thornton, Carolyn. "CVS Charity Classic: 'Sign Boy,' Jacobsen Leave Them Laughing." *Providence (RI) Journal,* June 28, 2005, p. D4.

Kevin Teague

Foster's Group Limited

77 Southbank Blvd.
Southbank, Victoria 3006
Australia
Telephone: 61 3 96332000
Fax: 61 3 96332000
Web site: www.fostersgroup.com

■■■

HOW TO SPEAK AUSTRALIAN CAMPAIGN

OVERVIEW

In 1990 Foster's Lager, owned by Foster's Group Limited (previously Foster's Brewing Group) and distributed and marketed by Miller Brewing Company in the United States, began pursuing a U.S. strategy of associating itself with "Australianness." After a detour away from this marketing strategy, Miller and its Foster's agency, Angotti, Thomas, Hedge of New York, in 1994 released "How to Speak Australian," which became one of the longest-running and most popular beer advertising campaigns of its time.

"How to Speak Australian" began with spot placements in regional markets and an estimated budget of $3 million. In 1997 Miller made it a national campaign and increased the budget to approximately $10 million. From 1994 to 2001 the campaign's central idea remained consistent. TV spots introduced a word or term, such as "Room Service," and then showed what that term meant in Australia; in this case, it meant a live chicken and a meat cleaver delivered to a hotel guest's room. Following such arresting redefinitions of commonplace terms was an image of the Foster's can, labeled "Beer." The commercials closed with the tagline "Fosters. Australian for Beer." Print, outdoor, and radio executions followed this basic model, which seemed virtually inexhaustible. Four to six new TV spots were crafted each year, and the consistency of the platform also meant that old spots could be recycled as long as they remained fresh.

"How to Speak Australian" won a Silver EFFIE Award in 1994 and a Gold EFFIE in 1995, and the Foster's brand grew rapidly in the United States through 1998. The campaign remained popular, and the brand continued to grow, but by 2000 Foster's sales had begun to be eclipsed by other beers in the imported-beer market. Some analysts believed that Miller had missed an opportunity to turn Foster's into an import stalwart along the lines of category-leading Corona Extra. After the dissolution of Angotti, Thomas, Hedge in 2001 Miller assigned the Foster's advertising account to Chicago's J. Walter Thompson agency. J. Walter Thompson made an unsuccessful attempt to reinterpret what was by then a classic advertising campaign, and in the following years Miller continued searching for the right agency to update the Foster's identity.

HISTORICAL CONTEXT

In the 1980s the Foster's Brewing Group (which later bought heavily into wine brands and dropped "Brewing" from its name) set out to make its undistinguished namesake brew stand out from the pack of Australian beers by raising its profile internationally. As the brand attained

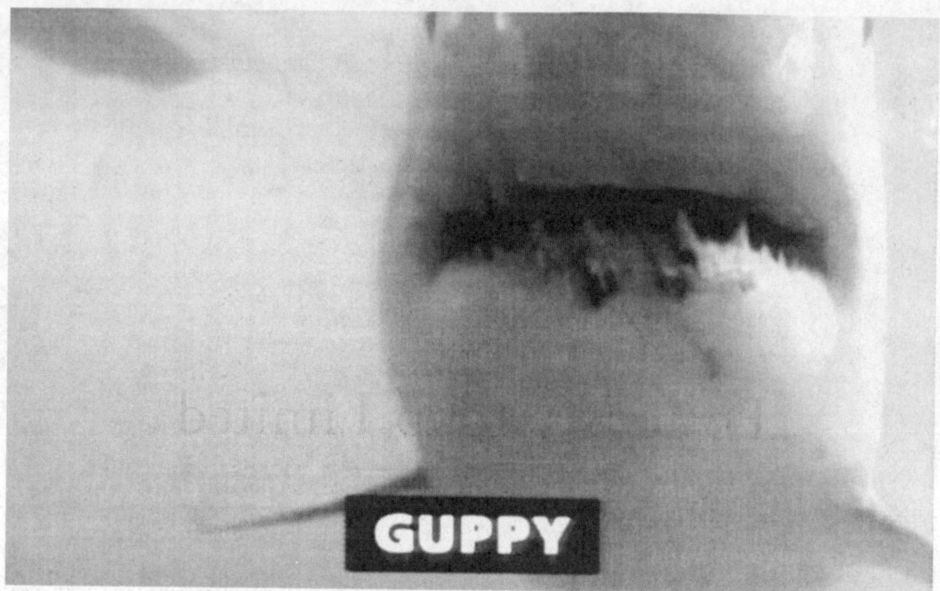

A still from the "Guppy" television ad for Foster's "How to Speak Australian" campaign.
MILLER BREWING COMPANY. REPRODUCED BY PERMISSION.

status outside of Australia, Australians themselves began drinking it in larger numbers. By the mid-1980s Foster's was at the top of the Australian beer heap, and its international image was strengthened by a series of commercials in the United Kingdom featuring the actor Paul Hogan, then a TV personality trafficking in the supposedly quintessential Australianness that he would go on to parlay into international fame in the movie *Crocodile Dundee* (1986). Foreign sales became a prime source of Foster's revenue, and in the early 1990s the company set out to brand itself in the United States by playing up its Australian roots. An unproductive detour away from this strategy was scuttled in 1994, when Foster's U.S. agency, Angotti, Thomas, Hedge, settled on the "How to Speak Australian" platform that, together with the tagline "Australian for Beer," would define the brand's marketing for years to come.

During the 1990s and into the first half of the following decade, Foster's was distributed and marketed in the United States according to a succession of complex corporate arrangements in which its Australian parent company partnered with the Canadian beer maker Molson and the United States' Miller Brewing. Although the specific terms of these agreements shifted over the course of the "How to Speak Australian" campaign, Miller was, practically speaking, responsible for Foster's marketing in the United States. The arrangement allowed Foster's to take advantage of Miller's extensive distribution network, but at the same time Foster's parent company did not have control over the brand's marketing. This became cause for concern when, because of the terms of the three-way partnership, Foster's advertising budget was calibrated not just according to its own performance but according to the performance of Molson, whose fortunes were then in decline in the United States. Thus, despite Foster's sales growth, Miller capped spending on "How To Speak Australian" at approximately $10 million annually through 2000.

TARGET MARKET

As Foster's beer became established in numerous countries, advertising for the brand was no longer aimed chiefly at Australians but at a broader audience of people who may not have known much about the Australian way of life. In the United States in 1997 the "How to Speak Australian" campaign was directed primarily at male consumers of legal drinking age, 21 to 34 years old, who favored imported beer. That group of consumers had been the main target for the brand's U.S. advertisements for some time. "This audience is very advertising-savvy. They want commercials to not only give them a reason to drink Foster's, but they also want to be entertained. We feel these ads succeed on both levels. Our Foster's ads try to entertain, show the product attributes, and provide a humorous look into the Australian lifestyle," said Marino. "Our research shows that Foster's is viewed as a very unassuming, approachable brand that appeals to both blue-collar and white-collar audiences."

A still from Foster's "How to Speak Australian" campaign. MILLER BREWING COMPANY. REPRODUCED BY PERMISSION.

COMPETITION

When, in 1997, the "How to Speak Australian" campaign moved from spot and regional placements to become a national campaign, the leading imported beer brands in the United States were Heineken and Corona Extra. In 1997 Heineken ran an advertising campaign to establish the company's symbol—a red star on a green background—as a widely recognized icon. One print ad featured a red star floating on the Chicago River, which had been turned green for Saint Patrick's Day. Another showed a star-shaped display of red Christmas lights against green electrical cord. The campaign had been launched in 1996 with a teaser that consisted of a solitary, unidentified red star on buildings and outdoor billboards. The campaign's broadcast advertisements showed the Heineken star on objects such as sunglasses and cocktail napkins. Actual conversations among people drinking beer in social situations were recorded and then performed by actors for the commercials. In one spot a man expressed his amazement that his date did not know who wrote *Moby Dick,* and the woman snapped at him in return. In another spot a man boasted about his state-of-the-art computer system. His companion commented, "That's psychotic. What are you gonna do with all that?" The man answered, "I don't know. Go online. Meet girls." Another spot showed people discussing the significance of a white radiator on display at an exhibit of modern art. The commercials were intended to convey the message that Heineken was "authentic" while faddish microbrews were not. Heineken spent more than $30 million on print and broadcast advertising in 1997, an increase of 55 percent over its budget for 1996.

Another competitor, the top-selling import brand Corona Extra, had experienced slow sales during the late 1980s but had seen a 35.7 percent sales surge in 1996. The Mexican beer was marketed in the United States by two companies, Barton Beers and Gambrinus Co., that operated separate regional promotions. The brand's U.S. advertising, which revolved around fun and sun at the beach, was widely viewed as instrumental in the brand's rise to the top of the U.S. import market. Corona's unwavering commitment to this marketing strategy through the end of the century and beyond was rivaled, among beer advertisers, only by the consistency of Foster's positioning.

The leading American beers during this time were Budweiser, Bud Light, Miller Lite, and Coors Light. These brands, led by the Bud sibling brands, leveraged marketing budgets 5 to 15 times larger than that of Foster's.

MARKETING STRATEGY

Foster's U.S. marketers and the agency Angotti, Thomas, Hedge initially grappled with the problem of creating brand awareness in an environment dominated by big-budget domestic-beer campaigns. The campaign ran during 1994, 1995, and 1996 in markets including San Francisco, Los Angeles, San Diego, Phoenix, Denver, Atlanta, and New York. A warm reception and sales gains

HOW TO SPEAK "FOOTY"

The "How to Speak Australian" campaign was supplemented by various other marketing endeavors, including sponsorship of weekly parties for fans of the Australian Football League. Posters and a booklet were printed to help fans learn "How to Speak 'Footy,'" the slang term for this wild sport resembling a cross between rugby and cricket in which the players wore no protective padding. The posters featured a photograph of players crashing into each other above the words "Australian for Football," then a picture of Foster's in a glass, a can, and a bottle over the tagline "Australian for Beer."

led Miller, in 1997, to take the effort national, raising the initial budget from an estimated $3 million to the $10 million figure that was to remain constant, with slight variations, through 2001. During this time the campaign remained extremely faithful to the original concept developed by Angotti, Thomas, Hedge. "What we're trying to do is position Foster's for both a domestic audience and an imported audience," Angotti account director Michael Stoner told *Brandweek*. "It has an easygoing, laid back personality. We tried to get that through in the ads." The TV, print, outdoor, and radio executions used Australia's reputation as a refreshingly untamed land inhabited by tough, no-nonsense, offbeat men and women as a corollary to the values Angotti hoped to attach to the Foster's brand identity.

The 15-second television commercials opened with an announcer saying in a thick Australian accent, "How to Speak Australian." The announcer pronounced a word or phrase, and then the commercial illustrated a humorous definition. For example, the spot that defined "room service" showed a live chicken and a meat cleaver being delivered to a guest's motel room. Another early spot showed the Australian definition of "No": a woman casually tossing a man out of a bar. The spots each ended with an image of a can of Foster's and the caption "Beer," followed by a close-up of the brand's logo and the tagline "Foster's. Australian for Beer." Similarly, a billboard used a picture of a dagger labeled "Australian for dental floss" and a picture of a Foster's can labeled "Australian for beer." The tagline made it sound as if Australians were so fond of Foster's that they equated it with the word "beer" and would drink no other brand. Although this was not strictly true—Foster's was, during the 1990s, Australia's second-biggest beer brand—all of the various executions during the campaign's life worked together to convey that single brand message.

As the campaign became well known across America, Angotti's challenge became to keep the commercials fresh through consistently surprising and humorous interpretations of the central conceit. "Witness Protection Program" featured a man dressed in a kangaroo suit living with a gang of kangaroos in the desert. In "Wake-Up Call" an innkeeper tossed an alarm clock through an open motel window, striking a rugged male guest, who grinned as he awoke and sat upright. "Marriage Counselor" depicted a woman winning an arm-wrestling match with a man in a bar, after which a referee said, "That settles it, mate. Her mum moves in." Another spot showed a great white shark with the caption "Guppy." Each year Angotti typically produced four to six new executions, and because of the campaign's consistency, commercials from previous years could be reused seamlessly alongside new spots. The campaign became so successful that the parent company of Foster's adapted it for use in Canada, Argentina, Brazil, Chile, the Caribbean, and numerous European countries.

OUTCOME

The "How to Speak Australian" campaign won a Silver EFFIE Award for advertising effectiveness and creativity in 1994 and a Gold EFFIE in 1995. Consumers tended to be more familiar with the Foster's brand than any other brand except Budweiser, and Foster's commercials were the most popular among brands in the category, according to the Australian American Chamber of Commerce in Los Angeles. Jim Mullahy, senior brand manager for Foster's lager, said, "We have a lot of fun with Foster's advertising, and viewers clearly enjoy that humor. Research indicates that 'How to Speak Australian' is one of the most widely recognized and memorable ad campaigns for beer. The strong brand-building advertising was integral to Foster's tremendous sales growth, which has been in the double digits for the last five years. In 1997 alone the brand increased more than 25 percent."

Foster's sales again handily outpaced those of the fast-growing import segment as a whole in 1998, ending the year up 20.6 percent, but 1999 saw the brand's growth slow markedly, to 9.2 percent. By 2000 Foster's was growing more slowly than the imported-beer category as a whole, and beer-industry analysts routinely spoke of the brew as a missed opportunity for Miller. Because of the Miller-Molson-Foster's agreement, Miller had never raised spending on Foster's to the levels that the immense popularity of "How to Speak Australian" seemed to warrant. By the time this restrictive corporate arrangement was reconfigured in late 2000, analysts

PACKAGING COUNTS

When Foster's beer was first marketed in the United States, it was presented in 25-ounce "Oil Cans" instead of the standard 12-ounce bottles and cans. The unusually large packaging made Foster's stand out on the shelf and was the perfect complement for the "How to Speak Australian" campaign, which had a rugged, masculine, exaggerated quality. Later Foster's was also offered in 12-ounce bottles and in kegs.

wondered whether Foster's might not have missed its chance for sustained success. Although spending was raised to more than $15 million in 2001 and was projected to rise in future years as high as $25 million, Foster's was not able to capitalize on these increases. By 2003 the brand was in decline in the United States, with sales losses of 7 percent.

In 2000 Angotti, Thomas, Hedge was dissolved. Miller awarded the Foster's account to J. Walter Thompson of Chicago, and the new agency crafted a 2001 reinterpretation of the "How to Speak Australian" that applied the original campaign concept to urban-dwelling Australians. J. Walter Thompson had lost the account by 2002, however, and its successor, Wieden+Kennedy, held the Foster's account for 10 months without selling Miller on any of its "How to Speak Australian" executions. In June 2004 Miller gave the account to another of its roster agencies, Ogilvy & Mather, which was charged with the job of applying the "Australian for Beer" tagline to escapist imagery of the sort that had propelled Foster's competitor Corona to its spot at the top of the imported-beer market in the United States.

FURTHER READING

"Beverages/Alcohol: Foster's." *Brandweek,* June 12, 1995.

Chakravarty, Subrata N. "Soap Opera Down Under." *Forbes,* February 15, 1993.

Cooper, Ann. "Foster's Beer." *Brandweek,* May 9, 1994.

"Foster's Brewing Olympics Tie to Aid in Image at Home." *Wall Street Journal* (eastern ed.), March 24, 1999.

Khermouch, Gerry. "Aussie Rules." *Brandweek,* October 16, 2000.

———. "Molson, Foster Seen Clamoring for More Marketing Control in U.S." *Brandweek,* August 21, 2000.

———. "Translating Australian." *Brandweek,* May 10, 1999.

Levere, Jane L. "Foster's Beer Is Putting a New Twist on Its Longtime 'How to Speak Australian' Campaign." *New York Times,* March 6, 2001.

McDowell, Bill. "Miller Devotes More Focus to Import Beer Portfolio: Foster's Ads Air on Network TV, while Molson Turns to Hockey." *Advertising Age,* February 24, 1997.

Panczyk, Tania D. "JWT Bows First Foster's Work." *Adweek* (midwest ed.), March 5, 2001.

Susan Risland
Mark Lane

Fox Entertainment Group, Inc.

1211 Avenue of the Americas, Ste. 302
New York, New York 10036
USA
Telephone: (212) 852-7111
Fax: (212) 852-7145
Web site: www.foxsports.com

■■■

NHL ON FOX CAMPAIGN

OVERVIEW

The Fox Entertainment Group was a division of Rupert Murdoch's News Corporation, a global media and entertainment empire. News Corporation published newspapers (including the *Times of London*), magazines (including *The Weekly Standard*), and books (HarperCollins). The company owned an 81 percent stake in the Fox Entertainment Group, one of the largest entertainment conglomerates in the world. Fox Entertainment Group produced, developed, and distributed TV and motion picture programming (including *Ally McBeal, The X-Files,* and *Titanic*) through its Fox Filmed Entertainment and Twentieth Century Fox units. It also owned America's Fox Television Network as well as 22 TV stations across the United States. In addition, Fox Entertainment had interests in cable TV channels and major league sports teams.

Fox Entertainment's Fox Sports division gained instant credibility in 1993 when it acquired the rights to broadcast National Football League (NFL) games. While the exorbitant rights fees the league commanded made the property a "loss leader" for the network, the cachet of professional football—especially among Fox's core youthful male demographic—made the acquisition worthwhile. Using ultramodern graphics, "in your face" promos, and a highly energetic pregame show, Fox took over an already successful product and enhanced it. Two years later Fox took a bigger gamble when it paid $155 million for broadcast rights to National Hockey League (NHL) games for the next five years. In doing so the network had acquired an underperforming TV property that traditionally drew lower ratings than bowling. It hoped to repeat its NFL success on the ice.

For the first three years of Fox coverage, ads for the NHL were handled by various agencies on a project basis. Then in late 1997 Fox Sports named the New York-based advertising agency of Cliff Freeman & Partners to handle advertising for its broadcast coverage of NHL games. The agency immediately initiated a campaign designed to win hockey a wider audience through the use of offbeat humorous promos.

The Fox NHL promo campaign, directed by Christopher Guest through bicoastal Moxie Pictures, was composed of five ads based on the premise that many sports would be better if they were played like hockey. In one typical spot a female bowler was knocked to the floor by a competitor trying to prevent her from making a game-winning strike. Other spots depicted hockey's violence and aggression applied to the sports of billiards, golf, and squash. The spots proved enormously popular with viewers and critics alike, earning Cliff Freeman & Partners a host of advertising industry awards. Fox continued to struggle to broaden the viewership for professional hockey, however, and in 1998 when the network's contract ran out, ABC acquired the NHL broadcast rights for the 1999–2000 season and beyond.

HISTORICAL CONTEXT

Fox Sports acquired the right to telecast professional hockey at a time of great promise, when the NHL's ratings on other networks were rising. Ratings for ESPN's Sunday night NHL games were up 67 percent in 1993–94, while the Canadian Broadcasting Corporation's telecasts were up 59 percent. Fox officials believed they could increase the average rating for hockey telecasts to a 2, which would represent a 12 percent increase over the 1.6 rating earned by ABC in a limited number of games in 1993-94.

The NHL was also optimistic about the partnership. "This is our first over-the-air contract in 20 years," said Bernadette Mansur, NHL vice president for corporate communications. "There's no doubt that ESPN has done a tremendous job in producing and promoting the NHL, but Fox gives us a national network contract. It takes us to another level."

A labor dispute between the league's owners and players unfortunately delayed the start of the 1994–95 NHL season. When the lockout finally ended in January 1995, Fox Sports aired its first slate of promotional ads for its broadcasts of NHL games. The spots featured the offbeat humor that would become a hallmark of Fox hockey ads over the next few years. In one ad New York Islanders winger Benoit Hogue was shown shooting raisin bagels at a goal. In another Florida goalie John Vanbiesbrouck parodied 1950s child icon Jerry Mathers for a spot called "Leave It to Beezer."

The ads aired frequently, paving the way for Fox's initial broadcast on April 2, 1995. That Sunday's slate of six regional games boasted a panoply of new technical innovations designed to enhance the viewing experience. These "bells and whistles" included animated graphics, a theme song, five to eight cameras (with a robotic camera at the main game site), Dolby surround sound, super slow motion, and the "Fox Box," a score/clock graphic that Fox had previously introduced during its NFL broadcasts. The broadcast was preceded by a 15-minute pregame show hosted by former basketball player James Brown, with commentary from former NHL player Dave Maloney. The anchors returned during intermissions for analysis that featured a few unconventional touches, including an in-studio roller rink, which analysts used to demonstrate skills and techniques.

After a shaky first season ratings-wise, the NHL on Fox, as it was dubbed, began to show signs of success over the ensuing seasons. During the 1996–97 NHL season, for example, national television demographic results posted increases in key areas. There was a 36 percent increase in NHL on Fox viewership among women aged 18 to 24, with an 86 percent increase during the Stanley Cup Finals. At the same time there was a 5 percent increase in NHL on Fox viewership among men aged 18 to 34, with a 32 percent increase during the Stanley Cup Finals. There was a 3 percent increase in viewership among male teens 12 to 17, with a 22 percent increase during the Stanley Cup Finals. The demographic improvements, however, may have had more to do with a renewed interest in hockey generally rather than a reflection of Fox's broadcasts or promotional strategy. During the same season, by contrast, NHL on ESPN viewership rose 22 percent among women 18 to 24, with a 106 percent increase during the Stanley Cup Finals. There was a 14 percent increase in NHL on ESPN viewership among men 18 to 34, with a 52 percent increase during the Stanley Cup Finals.

Ratings did not continue to improve over the next season, however, and in the fall of 1997 Cliff Freeman & Partners of New York was awarded the Fox NHL account after a presentation to Neal Tiles, senior vice president for marketing at Fox Sports in Los Angeles. Spike DDB, owned by filmmaker Spike Lee and the DDB Needham Worldwide unit of Omnicom Group, continued to handle advertising for NHL games on Fox Sports Net, a cable television joint venture of News Corporation, Tele-Communications Inc., and Liberty Media, a unit of Tele-Communications.

TARGET MARKET

Having inherited rights to broadcast hockey at a point of record viewer interest in the sport, Fox marketing officials believed the only way to "grow" the audience for its broadcasts was to appeal to casual fans of the sport. "If we put on a production for purists, hockey is going to fail," declared Ed Goren, an executive in the Fox Sports division. "A lot of people have done it well, but the bottom line is that hockey hasn't been able to attract a national audience. The most important mission we have is broadening the audience. If we do the greatest show in the world and all we get is a 1.6 [rating], we've failed."

To capture a youthful audience, Fox from the beginning relied on humor, high-tech effects, and the lure of larger-than-life personalities to sell hockey to fans who rarely watched the sport on TV. "Right now, hockey is like soccer," said Goren. "Millions of kids play it, but they don't watch it, because there are no heroes. We have to give them heroes. We have to sell these players as athletes and as personalities."

COMPETITION

Despite a major marketing push in recent years, the NHL, as far as the major professional team sports went,

THE CURIOUS CASE OF THE GLOWING PUCK

No feature symbolized Fox's ill-fated attempt to broaden the audience for televised hockey more than its infamous "glowing puck." Officially known as FoxTrax, the glowing puck was designed to remedy a frequent viewer complaint about hockey on television: that the tiny, fast-moving puck was impossible to follow on the flat screen of a TV set.

FoxTrax relied on sophisticated computer technology to track the puck and then laid graphics on top of it, creating the effect of a glowing blue disk with a comet tail that changed colors depending on how fast the puck was moving. Almost immediately critics attacked the idea, claiming among other things that it could not possibly work. Fox officials were quick to refute that charge. "We tested that by shooting pucks out of cannons at a wall, and none ever failed," said Stan Honey, executive vice president of technology for News Corporation, Fox's parent company.

Others complained that the glowing puck cheapened the game by introducing an element of technological gimmickry into the telecasts. The decision to use it, however, was fully in keeping with Fox Sports' stated intention to bring hockey to the masses. "The point is, some people needed FoxTrax to learn the game," NHL on Fox game analyst John "J.D." Davidson explained. "Others, who are hard-core fans, didn't like it. It's a shame we couldn't find a way to have a remote control that you could either have it or not have it through your clicker. That would have been ideal."

Fox's inability to generate significant viewer interest in its hockey eventually prompted it to abandon FoxTrax. The glowing puck was retired, presumably to a museum of technology. No viewer complaints were recorded at its demise.

remained a decided fourth among viewers, behind the NFL, Major League Baseball, and the NBA. Hockey remained a low-rated sport that nevertheless had solid advertiser appeal for companies seeking a young, male demographic target. Hockey's major competitor in the fall/winter sports market was the NBA, which had arguably surpassed baseball as the second most popular sport after the NFL in the United States. Its ability to reach 18- to 34-year-old males made it an attractive property for those wishing to sell autos, soft drinks, and athletic shoes. Like hockey, though, the league had some problems—lower scoring games, the threat of labor strife, growing pains for the new breed of players, and the aging of its longtime current star system. As of 1999, however, the NBA appeared unthreatened by the NHL as a television property.

MARKETING STRATEGY

From the day it won the rights to broadcast NHL hockey games, Fox Sports pursued an aggressive promotional strategy designed to whip up interest among viewers who had previously not tuned in to hockey telecasts. From the ads to the broadcasts themselves, this strategy was marked by innovation, risk taking, and a "rewriting the rules" approach. "We're telling our people there is no right or wrong," said Goren.

There was, of course, an inherent danger in this strategy. If Fox reached too far to pull in new fans, it could alienate hard-core fans who preferred a more traditional approach. The network was willing to take that risk, however, betting that hard-core hockey fans would realize that the TV audience for the sport must expand if it were to grow in the next century.

To promote its 1997–98 slate of telecasts, Fox Sports turned to Cliff Freeman & Partners. Cliff Freeman landed the assignment from Fox Sports personally after making a presentation to Tiles, the senior vice president of marketing for the sports division of Fox. "I'm a big fan of Cliff Freeman's work," said Tiles. "We need a highly creative message to break through the clutter, because we are the clutter."

Freeman's first ads broke in fall 1997, while the main campaign kicked off in January during Fox's broadcast of the annual NHL All-Star Game. The new campaign consisted of four spots, all conceived by copywriter Eric Silver. In the first, "Bowling," a woman bowler was shown about to make a crucial shot to win a match. From behind her back her opponent suddenly charged into her and knocked her to the floor, causing her to drop the bowling ball. "Bowling would be better," a caption declared, "if it were hockey." The other three ads played off the same juxtaposition. In "Billiards" a pool player needing to make one final shot was assaulted from the side by his opponent, who went on to sink the ball himself. "Golf" playfully sent up the solemnity of TV golf broadcasts, as a golfer's rolling putt was shown being swatted away from the hole by another player, hockey goalie style. "Very smoothly done," commented the unseen announcers dryly. And in "Squash" two elderly competitors were shown ferociously checking each other into the court's walls as they traded shots. The spot concluded with one man savagely pressing the other's face into a clear glass pane. Once again, a caption proclaimed that the sport would be better "if it were hockey."

All four spots were designed to capture viewer interest with what looked like a real sporting event, then concluded with a humorous twist in which the violent ethos of hockey was introduced. This style was in keeping with research that showed that young viewers—jaded by a lifetime of watching conventional TV commercials—responded most favorably to offbeat ads marked by humor and surprising and violent twists.

OUTCOME

Cliff Freeman & Partners won numerous awards for its "NHL on Fox" campaign. An entry comprised of "Billiards," "Bowling," and "Golf" earned the agency the Grand Clio in television at the 1998 Clio Awards Gala, held at Lincoln Center. Freeman's work for Fox collected four Golds in various TV categories. The Fox ads were also awarded a Gold Lion as a media campaign at the 45th annual International Advertising Festival in Cannes, France, in July 1998.

Despite all the accolades, the quirky spots did little to boost the ratings for Fox's NHL telecasts. The network's NHL ratings plummeted to a 1.4, the lowest in four years. Fox admitted to losing a fortune on its $155 million rights fees. As a consequence, in August 1998 Fox lost its NHL rights to Disney (ABC, ESPN, and ESPN2) for a staggering five-year, $600 million bid. "In our own way, I guess we elevated the awareness of the game to a point where the folks at Disney decided it was worth a lot of money," commented Fox Sports' Goren.

The outcome of the "NHL on Fox" was more favorable for at least one player in the campaign. The ad shop of Cliff Freeman & Partners was kept on by Fox to create a series of offbeat commercials for the network's game of the week baseball broadcasts. The slapstick spots retained the same wacky perspective and odd, cartoonlike characters of the agency's NHL campaign.

FURTHER READING

Berkowitz, Harry. "NYC Agency Gets Top Clio Award: Cliff Freeman Wins for Hockey Spots." *Newsday,* May 15, 1998.

DelNagro, Mike. *NHL Has Serious TV Marketing Problem,* Gannett News Service, February 26, 1999.

Robert Schnakenberg

French Connection Group PLC

30 Old Burlington St.
London, W1S 3NL
United Kingdom
Telephone: 44 20 73997000
Fax: 44 20 73997001
Web site: www.frenchconnection.com

SCENT TO BED CAMPAIGN

OVERVIEW

In 1997 the French Connection Group PLC embarked on a rebranding of its flagship French Connection line of clothing, which was sold in both department stores and stand-alone company stores throughout the world. The company's agency, TBWA\London, used an internal company moniker, FCUK (French Connection United Kingdom), as the conceptual basis for a newly brash brand image. Featured on product labels, storefronts, and in advertising that overtly encouraged the subliminal rearrangement of the acronym, the letters FCUK proved an immensely successful marketing device. The brand name was exported to North America in 1998, and subsequent advertising campaigns used the near-obscenity to incite predictable and, for French Connection, lucrative controversies. A 2003 print and promotional campaign on behalf of a line of FCUK fragrances, however, was bolder than previous FCUK campaigns, and it met with more mixed results.

The 2003 campaign, called "Scent to Bed," leveraged a projected $10 million budget to introduce American teens and young adults to the fragrances FCUK Him and FCUK Her. The obvious implications of the tagline and product name were bolstered by an image, in print ads, of an attractive, nearly nude couple in an intimate bedroom situation. The ads ran in men's and women's fashion magazines as well as in teen magazines. Planned promotional tie-ins included in-store handouts labeled "License to FCUK," which touted a "Scent to Bed" website.

French Connection was not, however, able to mobilize the campaign's full budget or promotional capacities. Widespread protests by religious and concerned-citizens' groups led the country's largest department-store company—Federated, the owner of Macy's, Bloomingdale's, and Goldsmith's—to remove all FCUK products from its inventories, and the "Scent to Bed" ads were pulled from the teen magazines in which they had been placed. Though French Connection reported strong sales of the FCUK fragrances, the marketing campaign was put on hold. The company's next American advertising campaign did not use the FCUK acronym at all.

HISTORICAL CONTEXT

Stephen Marks worked in the British fashion industry in the 1960s before starting his own company in 1972. Named after Marks's favorite movie, French Connection established itself as a British wholesaler of midpriced, upscale, casual clothing aimed at a fashion-conscious target market consisting primarily of teens and young adults. The French Connection brand expanded to continental European, Asian, and North American markets. Marks took the company public in 1984.

In the 1990s French Connection shifted its emphasis from wholesale to retail operations; the company undertook a corresponding broadening of its product offerings and renovation of its stores' appearance. The retail fashion market was highly competitive and fragmented, however, and French Connection needed a clearer market positioning. In 1997 founder Marks enlisted TBWA\London's Trevor Beattie, a creative director who had achieved fame in the advertising industry for creating an overtly provocative (and very successful) campaign for Wonderbra, to helm a rebranding of French Connection. Beattie decided that the company needed to promote an image of irreverent hipness in keeping with its core target market, but he had not settled on any unifying icon for the rebranding project when, while at French Connection headquarters, he noticed the letters "FCUK" in a company fax header. The letters stood for "French Connection United Kingdom" and were used in communications with the company's Hong Kong office (FCHK), but Beattie immediately saw the brand-building potential of the near-obscenity. French Connection was rebranded as FCUK, a move that generated extensive controversy while fueling unprecedented company growth. Outdoor advertisements in London, tagged "FCUK fashion," were outlawed by Britain's Advertising Standards Authority after widespread outrage; the company responded with ads whose tagline, "FCUK advertising," did little to quell citizens' complaints.

In 1998 the FCUK logo began appearing in the United States, on T-shirts and on the company's U.S. storefronts. Print ads explicitly encouraged the logo's subliminal associations, using transposed language such as "night all long" and "I you want." An outdoor campaign that ran on top of New York City taxicabs paired the brand name with the tag "Think your clothes off"; it was pulled after only a few days. Another New York print and taxi-top campaign followed, using copy that stated, "Brave but not free / FCUK censorship."

TROUBLE HERE, TROUBLE THERE

French Connection had a larger market presence in the United Kingdom than in the United States, and in the 2000s it leveraged the FCUK brand for a variety of U.K. ventures, including a line of alcohol (which was eventually recalled in reaction to complaints that it targeted minors). In 2004 the company launched an Internet-based radio station under the FCUK brand. Advertisements on behalf of FCUK radio were characteristically bold, reading, "FCUK FM from PNUK to RCOK and back. Nonstop FNUK. FCUK FM." Britain's Advertising Standards Authority ruled that the ad was offensive and required that all FCUK ads for the following two years be submitted for preapproval. Soon after this ruling, which came on the heels of FCUK's marketing troubles during the U.S. "Scent to Bed" campaign, French Connection temporarily dropped the FCUK logo from its advertising.

TARGET MARKET

The primary target for the FCUK Her and FCUK Him fragrance lines was 18- to 25-year-olds, but FCUK also placed "Scent to Bed" advertisements in publications primarily read by much younger teenage girls. Given the ubiquity of sexual imagery in the media at the time, sexual appeals to young people had to be extremely explicit or daring to stand out. FCUK's ability to make a splash in a hypersexual environment was primarily a function of its products' brand name, which, in combination with the clear sexual implications of the ad imagery and the "Scent to Bed" tagline, amounted to one of the bluntest sexual appeals in recent mainstream U.S. advertising.

Given FCUK's history of courting controversy as a means of spurring sales, industry observers took it for granted that the company welcomed the inevitable public uproar surrounding the fragrances' launch. As religious and concerned-citizens' groups began to mount predictable protests, Michael Wood, vice president of the media consultancy Teenage Research Unlimited, told *USA Today,* "The more people say, 'How dare them,' the more interest they get from the teen market." Other analysts pointed out a potential pitfall of this approach: teens were dependent on their parents for the money required to make most of their purchases.

COMPETITION

The American fashion-industry standard for sexually explicit marketing had arguably been established by Abercrombie & Fitch (A & F) in the late 1990s and early 2000s. Indeed, one of the most prominent groups protesting the "Scent to Bed" campaign, Concerned Women for America, described the FCUK campaign as "Abercrombie & Fitch on Viagra." Despite the suggestion that A & F's marketing was tame by comparison, the popular retailer of clothing for college-age young adults had become one of the most roundly protested advertisers of the time, regularly provoking the ire of concerned citizens across the political spectrum. Most of this outrage centered on the company's signature "magalog" (a hybrid of magazine and mail-order catalog), the "A & F Quarterly," which integrated racy editorial content with art-quality photos of nearly nude young men and women. An early issue of the magalog ran a widely condemned feature called "Drinking 101," which encouraged college students to "drink creatively" and provided recipes for such cocktails as the "Brain Hemorrhage." Another notorious issue, from the 1999 holiday season, featured a cover image that included a male model's pubic hair as well as an image of Santa and Mrs. Claus engaging in sadomasochistic sex acts. A 2003 Christmas issue touting "group sex and more" generated a last round of outrage but proved the last installment of the publication; it was retired amid ongoing controversy and, perhaps more to the point, flagging in-store sales.

American Apparel, an upstart wholesaler of high-quality T-shirts and other basic knitwear, was responsible for another prominent advertising campaigns that flirted with pornography. The American Apparel print and outdoor campaign, introduced to coincide with the opening of the brand's first retail outlets in late 2003, was largely masterminded and executed by the company's founder, Dov Charney. It featured overtly sexual, casual snapshots of employees and other nonprofessional models. Balancing this pronounced appeal to sexual appetites with a sweatshop-free corporate model, American Apparel successfully targeted young, fashion-conscious urban progressives. Regularly outpacing the garment industry in yearly sales, American Apparel grew rapidly, expanding its stable of retail stores from two to more than 50 during the first two years of the campaign's run.

MARKETING STRATEGY

FCUK Him and FCUK Her were the company's first global fragrance products, and they became available worldwide in French Connection stores and department stores starting with a September 2003 launch in the United States. The "Scent to Bed" print and promotional campaign, developed by TBWA\London (FCUK's agency of record since the 1997 rebranding), was a U.S.-specific element of the global push that was timed to coincide with the fragrances' introduction. The projected campaign budget at the start of the campaign was $10 million.

Print ads ran in magazines that included *Cosmopolitan, Marie Claire, Maxim,* and *FHM* as well as in the magazines *Seventeen* and *Teen People,* whose readerships consisted primarily of girls in their early and middle teenage years. The "Scent to Bed" tagline was superimposed over an attractive young couple in an intimate bedroom situation. This combination of imagery and text, supported by the subliminal reading of the accompanying brand name, sent an unmistakable sexual message to young people. Many assumed, judging from FCUK's history of parlaying controversy into sales gains, that the company was hoping for some amount of buzz-generating backlash. The company itself remained coy about its strategies. "Whether it shocks you or amuses you," Andrea Hyde, president of French Connection Holdings, told *USA Today,* "FCUK certainly makes the consumer think."

Promotional elements of the campaign included invitations to a FCUK fragrance launch party that were shaped like "do not disturb" signs for hotel doorknobs and that read, "FCUK in progress." At the time of the campaign's September release, plans were in place for a holiday promotion involving "License to FCUK" cards to be distributed by stores that carried the fragrance. The cards were to include a code to be used at a "Scent to Bed" website, allowing consumers access to a list of effective pickup lines and the chance to win a free six-person Club Med vacation.

OUTCOME

A "Scent to Bed" backlash gained steam immediately upon the FCUK fragrances' American introduction. "It's very disgusting and highly offensive," Roberta Combs, president of the Christian Coalition of America, told *USA Today.* "It's a sad day when people have to do this type of advertising, especially toward our youth." The American Family Association initiated a large-scale E-mail and phone drive to file complaints with participating department-store chains, and French Connection began experiencing trouble with the department stores that carried the FCUK brand. In the first two weeks after the fragrances were introduced, they ranked no lower than eighth among top-selling fragrances at Sephora stores and no lower than fourth at Bloomingdale's. The controversy soon began to affect stores, however. The department store Kaufmann's ceased using in-store "Scent to Bed" displays, while the largest department-store corporation in America, Federated Department Stores—which owned Macy's, Bloomingdale's, and Goldsmith's, among others—pulled not just the FCUK fragrances but all FCUK-labeled products from its stores within a month after the campaign's launch. In October 2003 the magazines *Seventeen* and *Teen People* both announced that they would no longer run FCUK ads, and French Connection discontinued the campaign.

The fragrances remained available in French Connection stand-alone stores and sold well. According to Zirh International, the company that manufactured the fragrances for French Connection, the launch exceeded sales expectations as well as production capacities. Unused portions of the campaign budget were redirected to in-store initiatives and to other international markets. In November the company submitted to a relabeling of its products as "French Connection United Kingdom" in an attempt to get them back on Federated Department Stores shelves. The advertising campaign on behalf of the fragrances remained on hold indefinitely.

According to *Advertising Age,* chairman and CEO Marks remained convinced that the campaign was right for its target market. French Connection's North American sales continued to grow, reaching $84 million for 2003, more than double the company's sales figures for 1997. After a separate 2004 controversy in Great Britain resulted in an order by the Advertising Standards Authority that all FCUK outdoor advertising be preinspected, French Connection temporarily discontinued the use of its notorious acronym. A 2004 U.S. campaign featuring TV, print, and outdoor components used models posing as bikers in the American desert. The campaign's copy included, "Something beginning with F," and "Don't make us say it." "We think it's revolutionary," Marks told *Women's Wear Daily.* "Who else would advertise without using their name?"

FURTHER READING

Conti, Samantha. "FCUK's Disappearing Logo." *Women's Wear Daily,* September 13, 2004.

Estell, Libby. "Well, 'FCUK' You, Too." *Incentive,* November 2003.

Hall, Emma. "Stephen Marks: French Connection Group." *Advertising Age,* January 26, 2004.

Howard, Theresa. "Teen Fragrance's Titillating PR Push Could Create a Stink." *USA Today,* September 10, 2003.

Jardine, Alexandra. "FCUK Ads Raise Ire of U.K. Watchdog." *Advertising Age,* July 19, 2004.

Jardine, Alexandra, and Laurel Wentz. "French Connection Gives FCUK a Rest." *Advertising Age,* August 23, 2004.

Lindsay, Greg. "An FCUKing Brilliant Idea; French Connection Was Struggling in America—Until Its Bad-Boy Adman Found Salvation in Four Not-So-Naughty Letters." *Business 2.0,* August 2004.

Lippert, Barbara. "All FCUKed Up." *Adweek* (eastern ed.), October 11, 1999.

Neff, Jack. "FCUK Abandons Abbreviation to Get Perfume Back in Stores." *Advertising Age,* November 24, 2003.

Neff, Jack, and Jon Fine. "Magazines, Retailers Ban Racy FCUK Scent." *Advertising Age,* October 13, 2003.

O'Loughlin, Sandra. "French Connection UK Turns Radio on Its Ear." *Brandweek,* March 15, 2004.

Mark Lane

Frito-Lay Inc.

7701 Legacy Dr.
Plano, Texas 75024
USA
Telephone: (972) 334-7000
Fax: (972) 334-2019
Web site: www.fritolay.com

THE LOUDEST TASTE ON EARTH CAMPAIGN

OVERVIEW

Frito-Lay Inc., the world's largest maker of snack foods, launched an advertising campaign in 1997 to focus on a narrow market for its Doritos brand of flavored tortilla chips, to introduce new Doritos products, and to increase the international sales of tortilla chips. Doritos were the top-selling tortilla chips in the United States, but previous advertising had targeted a broad audience, and public awareness of the brand had begun to decline. With "The Loudest Taste on Earth" campaign, the company targeted consumers who were 16 to 21 years old and who appreciated the freedom to make noise. The campaign emphasized that Doritos were flavorful, that they made a loud crunch when they were eaten, and that it was acceptable for young people to be exuberant and uninhibited.

One television commercial showed a middle-aged man going berserk because three young men were eating Doritos to the accompaniment of deafening rock and roll. The older man cried out in frustration as he rushed past the young men to unplug their stereo, but the music continued. He then cut down a power pole, causing a citywide blackout. The music stopped abruptly, and he looked relieved. The young men glanced mischievously at each other while one of them crumpled an empty Doritos bag. He then ripped open a new bag, the music started again, and the older man bellowed in exasperation. The voice-over said, "Doritos tortilla chips. The loudest taste on earth."

The campaign, which was launched in April 1977 and ran into 1998, was developed by BBDO Worldwide, New York, an agency that had been doing business with Frito-Lay's parent company, PepsiCo, for decades. In 1997 the ad budget for Doritos was increased significantly, to $40 million. "The Loudest Taste on Earth" campaign ran in the United States, where Doritos were already popular, and then in several other countries. PepsiCo's net sales increased during 1997, with the Doritos brand showing particularly strong growth.

HISTORICAL CONTEXT

The Frito Company began operations in San Antonio, Texas, in 1932 and merged with H. W. Lay & Company to form Frito-Lay in 1961. Four years later, Frito-Lay merged with the Pepsi-Cola Company to form PepsiCo, and during the 1990s the snack food division became known as the Frito-Lay Company. In 1997 Frito-Lay expanded its product lines in Europe, Australia, and South America by purchasing salty snack brands in countries there, and in the United States it acquired the Cracker Jack brand of candy-coated popcorn and peanuts.

Frito-Lay made nine of the 10 top-selling brands of snack chips in the United States, including Lay's and

Ruffles potato chips, Cheetos cheese puffs, Rold Gold pretzels, and Tostitos and Doritos tortilla chips. The company's first product had been Fritos corn chips, which were promoted for years by a character called the Frito Kid and later with the tag line "Munch a Bunch! of Fritos Brand Corn Chips." Humor had worked well in marketing for various Frito-Lay brands. A 1996 ad campaign for Baked Lay's potato crisps featured a popular puppet character named Miss Piggy and three fashion models devouring the low-fat snack without worrying about gaining weight. The ads produced a rush to buy the product, and Baked Lay's went on to become the most successful new product in Frito-Lay's history, generating more than $250 million in sales in its first year. Another campaign that began in 1994 and ran for several years featured comedian Chris Elliott as a good-natured man who could liven up any occasion by producing a bag of Tostitos tortilla chips. The tag line was "You Got Tostitos, You Got a Party." In one spot Elliott displayed Tostitos in an attempt to impress women, but the women took the Tostitos and rejected him.

Frito-Lay's "better-for-you" low-fat products generated $1 billion annually, but controversy arose in 1996 when some consumers reported gastrointestinal problems after eating foods that contained olestra, a fat replacer also known by the brand name Olean. A one-ounce serving of Doritos MAX Tortilla Chips with Olean had one gram of fat and 90 calories, compared to seven grams of fat and 140 calories in a serving of original Doritos. "The idea of no-fat snacks is hugely appealing to millions of people," said Dennis Heard, Frito-Lay's senior vice president of technology and operations. "Our testing of olestra is to determine whether this new ingredient can be made to work and deliver that important benefit to our customers. As with any new product, ultimately the consumer must decide." He added that "Frito-Lay would never make any product that intentionally could cause people to become sick."

In 1995 and 1996 Frito-Lay's low-fat products accounted for 47 percent of the company's growth, and they figured prominently in its marketing plans. A campaign for Reduced Fat Doritos debuted on the telecast of the Summer Olympics in 1996 and extended into 1997. The commercials showed physicians examining a man who had tried the new tortilla chips and was so startled by their good flavor that an expression of surprise had frozen on his face. In addition to the advertising campaign, Frito-Lay launched a nationwide promotion in which 5 million consumers in 4,500 supermarkets were given "mystery samples," black bags that contained Reduced Fat Doritos. The words "So . . . what is it? The answer is in the bag!" were printed next to a bright yellow and red question mark on the front of the package. On the back were the words "It's not what you think it is." Inside was a coupon and a printed message identifying the tortilla chips as Reduced Fat Doritos.

A HIT IN ISRAEL

In August 1997 Frito-Lay launched "The Loudest Taste on Earth" campaign in Israel. Television commercials were supplemented by advertisements on 600 billboards, promotions in Israel's largest supermarket chains, and sponsorship of music festivals attended by the target market of young people. The Doritos brand was enthusiastically welcomed in Israel, where in Tel Aviv a $5.7 million production plant had been built by Elite Foods, the company that manufactured Doritos. "Before we even started advertising, the product was flying off the shelves," said Gidi Landsberger, the Elite Foods marketing director.

TARGET MARKET

In 1997 Frito-Lay decided to reposition Doritos as the snack of choice for a specific group of consumers. A 1996 campaign called "Get a Life" had targeted a broad market, primarily consumers 12 to 34 years old, with the message that Doritos was "everybody's snack." One spot, for example, featured a masseur who was energized by snacking on Doritos. In contrast, "The Loudest Taste on Earth" campaign was intended to appeal to a narrower market of consumers, people 16 to 21 years old. These consumers, known as Generation Xers, tended to enjoy alternative music and had grown up watching rock videos on MTV.

Tortilla chips were particularly popular in the United States, where per capita consumption of the crunchy corn snack was nearly five pounds a year. In an average month one bag of Doritos was sold for each household in the country. Many consumers snacked on tortilla chips instead of cooking, a practice that Frito-Lay hoped to encourage by positioning its chips and dips as convenience meals. For consumers who were concerned about gaining weight, Frito-Lay promoted its low-calorie lines during the same months "The Loudest Taste on Earth" campaign was being broadcast.

COMPETITION

With more than $1 billion in annual sales, Doritos was the top-selling brand in the flavored tortilla chip category and was popular throughout North and South America. Doritos accounted for 10 percent of Frito-Lay's annual

THE CINEMA IN FRANCE

To publicize the brand in France, Frito-Lay gave away 800,000 bags of Doritos at the cinema during 1996. A $5 million television advertising campaign ran concurrently with the promotion. In addition, Frito-Lay worked with its parent company, PepsiCo, to sponsor a movie festival called the Doritos Pepsi Show.

sales of about $10 billion worldwide. The company sold its products in 40 countries, was the leader in five of the 10 largest snack food markets, and had 54 percent of the salty snack market in the United States. Its closest competitors, Procter & Gamble and Borden, had 4 percent each. Pringles potato crisps, made by Proctor & Gamble, were the only top 10 snack chips in the United States not made by Frito-Lay. A third competitor, Anheuser-Busch, had given up the snack food business in 1996, selling its processing plants to Frito-Lay and its Eagle brand to Procter & Gamble.

Thus, Procter & Gamble constituted Frito-Lay's principal competition in the United States. During 1997 Procter & Gamble continued a $40 million television advertising campaign for Pringles that had been running since 1995. The commercials originally had featured young people drumming on the cans in which Pringles were packaged, but eventually the campaign included people of all ages. The tag line, "Once You Pop, You Can't Stop," called attention to the brand's unusual packaging, complete with lids that could be popped open and snapped shut again. Procter & Gamble said that the commercials helped increase brand awareness and improved sales of Pringles, which was the third most popular brand of potato snack in the country. According to the Snack Food Association, the brand gained 1.5 percentage points of market share in supermarkets during 1997, up from 10.2 percent in 1996. Procter & Gamble had introduced a tortilla chip line of Pringles in 1996 and was preparing to launch Fat Free Pringles, made with Olean, in 1998. Pringles containing Olean had been tested in a few markets in 1996, and within a year the brand's sales in those markets had risen by 25 percent.

MARKETING STRATEGY

Frito-Lay planned to make Doritos a priority in 1997 by introducing new lines and airing blockbuster commercials in the United States and in other countries. In January the company asked ad agency BBDO Worldwide, New York, and affiliated agency DDB Needham Worldwide to present ideas for a new Doritos campaign. DDB Needham had been handling the company's Cheetos, Rold Gold, and Fritos accounts. BBDO had been doing business with Pepsi-Cola for more than 30 years and was handling Frito-Lay's Tostitos, Ruffles, and Lay's accounts, among others. BBDO was awarded the Doritos account and developed "The Loudest Taste on Earth" campaign, with the Lay's account given to DDB Needham soon afterward. At the end of the year, however, PepsiCo reviewed the way its national television commercials, worth about $170 million annually, were being planned and purchased. Several ad agencies were considered, but in the end all of the Frito-Lay accounts were consolidated with BBDO.

"The Loudest Taste on Earth" campaign stressed that Doritos were flavorful tortilla chips that made a loud crunch when they were eaten. Because making a noise while eating was frowned upon in many social situations, the joy of being "allowed to be loud" was intended to appeal to young people, who liked to challenge the rules of etiquette. With their driving rock and roll sound tracks, the commercials also brought to mind the many times such young people had heard their parents tell them to lower the volume of their music. Above all, the campaign conveyed an attitude of unrestrained exhilaration. The people in the ads were having a good time with their friends as they snacked on Doritos.

"The Loudest Taste on Earth" campaign was launched in April. The first of 20 spots, "Boy," opened with an angelic looking woman with short, platinum blond hair. In a clear, sweet voice she sang, "There once was a boy who wanted everything to be loud." The camera showed a long-haired teenager tearing open a bag of Doritos, with the words "LOUD LOUD LOUD" flashed across the screen as the music changed into pounding rock and roll. "You're allowed to be loud," the song continued, as a series of wildly colorful music video images followed. The boy began to fly, a plastic cow fell down, a walking Doritos bag paraded along a runway like a fashion model, people rode Doritos bags through city streets, and an enormous Doritos tortilla chip tumbled down an avenue. "The hundred decibel, in-your-face taste of Doritos," said the voice-over, and the singer concluded, "The loudest taste on earth." The woman in the ad was Crushing Underground's Mary Wood, a performer and jingle producer who had helped write the music for "Boy." She also performed in another spot in the campaign, introducing a line called Spicy Nacho Doritos. In addition to spots that looked like music videos, the campaign featured three television commercials that focused on the Doritos logo.

One of Frito-Lay's goals was to make sure that its advertising budget went toward campaigns consumers would remember and discuss. "It's got to be a great idea first—that's where the dollars will flow," said Roger Berdusco, Frito-Lay's vice president of marketing. To place its messages before the largest number of consumers, the company tended to run commercials during major media events, such as the Super Bowl or the Academy Awards, but some of "The Loudest Taste on Earth" spots aired during programs with young audiences, such as science fiction programs on cable.

OUTCOME

With the relaunch of Doritos and the introduction of less fattening lines of several brands, including Baked Lay's and Reduced Fat Doritos, Frito-Lay's sales had been increasing for several years. The Doritos brand showed particularly strong growth in 1997, the year "The Loudest Taste on Earth" campaign was launched. According to Hoover's Company Capsules, Frito-Lay experienced growth of 7.2 percent in 1997. Sales totaled $10.4 billion, up from $9.7 billion in 1996.

"The Loudest Taste on Earth" campaign continued to run into 1998, even as Frito-Lay prepared to keep the brand's momentum going with the launch of two more lines, Doritos 3D's Tortilla Chips and Doritos WOW! Nacho Cheesier Tortilla Chips, made with Olean. In addition, "The Loudest Taste on Earth" campaign was scheduled to be broadcast in several other countries as Frito-Lay attempted to position the brand as the most popular snack for young adults around the world.

FURTHER READING

"AMA Cites Frito-Lay." *Advertising Age,* April 26, 1996.

Chakravarty, Subrata N., and John R. Hayes. "The Pure-Play Syndrome." *Forbes,* October 20, 1997.

"DDB Wins $50M Pan-Euro Frito-Lay Account." *Advertising Age,* May 28, 1997.

"Doritos Ads Go Global." *Advertising Age,* March 29, 1996.

"Doritos Woos French." *Advertising Age,* June 4, 1996.

Enrico, Dottie. "Chipper Pitchman: Comedian Chris Elliott Touts Low-Fat Tostitos." *USA Today,* April 8, 1996.

———. "Consumers Pig Out on Baked Lay's Campaign." *USA Today,* October 7, 1996.

Merrill, Christina. "New Directions for Doritos: BBDO Breaks Campaign That Saved the Business in Pitch Versus DDB Needham." *Adweek* (Eastern Edition), April 28, 1997.

"P&G to Roll Out Fat-Free Pringles." *Advertising Age,* October 15, 1997.

"PepsiCo Puts Its Weight Behind Doritos' Israeli Launch." *Advertising Age,* August 20, 1997.

Petrecca, Laura, Judann Pollack, and Mark Gleason, "Frito-Lay's Doritos Sets Agency Shootout: DDB Needham, BBDO Vie for $40 Mil Business." *Advertising Age,* January 27, 1997.

Soter, Tom. "Ear Candy: Shoot's Fall Top Three Spot Tracks Are Cheesy, Ultra Hip, and an Old Favorite with a Twist." *Shoot,* October 31, 1997.

Willman, John. "Salty Snack Attack on Europe." *Financial Times,* February 2, 1998.

Susan Risland

Fuji Photo Film U.S.A., Inc.

200 Summit Lake Drive
Valhalla, New York 10595
USA
Telephone: (914) 789-8100
Fax: (914) 789-8295
Web site: www.fujifilm.com

■■■

MEET THE GREENS CAMPAIGN

OVERVIEW

With the rise of digital photography in the 1990s, Fuji Photo Film U.S.A. found itself in danger of being marginalized as nothing more than a film company despite offering a wide range of digital products and services. In 2000 New York advertising agency Publicis was hired to help reposition Fuji as an image and communications brand. To help achieve this end, Fuji in November 2002 launched a new campaign, "Meet the Greens," that featured a modern family that used the full range of Fuji products, both digital and traditional. In addition to high-tech Dad and low-tech (and very pregnant) Mom, the family included teenage daughter Kellie and six-year-old Stewart.

The $20 to $25 million multimedia campaign featured three television spots, as well as print ads, newspaper inserts, outdoor advertising, and an online sweepstakes. An example of the humorous approach the campaign took was the television spot "Miracle," which showed Mrs. Green using her Fuji QuickSnap disposable camera to capture what she and the children considered to be the miracle of all miracles: Dad vacuuming.

Fuji hoped to exploit the Green family concept for an extended period of time, but after a second sweepstakes, in which participants were asked to submit names for the Greens' new twins, the campaign petered out in 2003. The television spots were generally well received, but the concept did not prove to work well in print ads.

HISTORICAL CONTEXT

When Publicis took over the Fuji account in 2000 it faced the difficult challenge of expanding the brand beyond an immediate association with film. According to Claudia Deutsch writing in the *New York Times* in 2001, that association "galls them. FujiFilm sells developing equipment, photo processing services, printers, coated papers and cameras... the many lucrative things that can help film companies survive the encroachments that digital photography is making into the film market." Indeed the emergence of digital technology in the 1990s had turned the photography industry upside down. Traditionally the lion's share of profits had come from the sale of film. While consumers might buy a camera every few years, they had to regularly purchase film, a highly profitable business for traditional photo companies like Kodak and Fuji. Digital technology brought in a host of new competition from the electronics arena, and as was the case with all consumer electronics, the price of cameras dipped to the point that it was difficult to make money from selling them. And with an increasing number of consumers embracing digital technology, the need for film diminished, forcing an old-line photography company like Fuji to adjust to the new business reality. Having "film" in its name was no longer an advantage, and years of brand development that equated "Fuji" with "film" in the mind of consumers now created a drag on the company's efforts to advance into the future.

"We have simply got to reposition Fuji as a communications company," Fuji's vice president for advertising Joan C. Rutherford told Deutsch. Jennifer Garr, chief marketing officer for Publicis, added, "Pictures aren't just about archiving, but about communicating... We want the Fuji brand to be top of mind when consumers think about using images." According to Deutsch repositioning the Fuji brand was more than a hope: it was a "survival strategy." From a sales point of view, however, the goal had not changed much. The money in photography had always been on the "output stream." As Deutsch explained, "He who dominates the output side—that is, sells the most prints, developing chemicals and such—will rule the market."

To begin the process of repositioning the brand, Fuji launched a $20 million campaign in the fall of 2001 that also highlighted the company's digital cameras, scanners, printers, and new digital developing equipment. The campaign's three television commercials showed how Fuji products could be used to solve real problems, however exaggerated they might be. In the spot titled "Poodle" a young man in an elevator was enamored with a beautiful lady who clearly adored her pet poodle. He used a Fuji digital camera to take a picture of a pet store poodle and then uploaded the image to the Fuji website. Next he returned to the elevator wearing a sweatshirt with a poodle printed on the front, catching the attention of the young lady. The tagline for all the spots was "Do you speak Fuji?"

"The overall theme running throughout the new campaign is that 'if you speak Fuji your communication will be enhanced,'" Rutherford explained in a press release. "The new campaign extends pictures beyond memories and takes the mystery out of digital imaging. It brings to life the concept of better communication through pictures. What is particularly important is that each ad demonstrates the fun and easy practical benefits of digital imaging and relates those benefits to everyday life."

A year later Fuji and Publicis took the concept further by embodying Fuji's consumers in a single family: the Greens. The name was an allusion to Fuji's longtime association to the color green in its distinctive packaging.

TARGET MARKET

Because the "Meet the Greens" campaign was part of a larger brand repositioning effort, it was aimed at a wide target audience that included consumer, professional, business, and retail customers. Previous ad campaigns had targeted early adapters of new technologies, but digital photography had moved beyond this stage, prompting Fuji and the competition to appeal to general consumers. On a more specific level the new Fuji ads hoped to reach women, in particular mothers 24 to 41 years of age. According to research conducted by Kodak, 70 to 80 percent of family pictures were taken by women. They were the ones who maintained family photo albums, so they had to be educated about the ways to get prints from their digital cameras, whether it was from home printers, sending the digital files to a lab for development, or using Fuji self-serve kiosks at a drugstore. The use of a family in the new campaign, featuring domestic situations that would have appeal to women, was intended to reach this key demographic. Only to a small extent did the marketers attempt to target men and children, although both were represented in the Green family concept. The younger demographic, for instance, was not of prime concern because they tended to share pictures with one another via E-mail and were less likely to make prints.

COMPETITION

For many years Fuji's chief competitor had been Eastman Kodak. The two companies vied for film customers. Fuji had done particularly well with lower-priced film and disposable cameras, which it introduced into the market in the mid-1980s. But because Fuji's product offerings now extended beyond film and disposable cameras to include a wide range of digital cameras and output solutions, it faced a host of new competitors. In the digital camera field Fuji had to contend with old-guard brands like Kodak, Minolta, Olympus, and, to a lesser degree, upscale Nokia. But of equal threat were the newcomers to photography through digital technology, such as Hewlett-Packard, Samsung, Sony, and LG, all of which had successful product lines outside of photography and possessed the financial wherewithal to fund aggressive

CRAZY ABOUT THE MOVIES

Fuji Photo Film Company was founded in Japan in 1934 to take over a factory that intended to produce black-and-white motion picture film for local consumption. The facility, located in a small village in the shadow of Mount Fuji, was chosen because of its clean water and air and close proximity to Tokyo, located about 50 kilometers west of the city.

TALE OF THE TAPE

The first commercial blank videotape was offered in 1956 by the 3M Corporation at a price of $307 per reel. Fuji Photo Film Company was the first non-U.S. company to produce videotape.

marketing campaigns. It was their combined marketing heft that was a key factor in the speed in which digital photography overtook film, catching both Fuji and Kodak by surprise. In the home printer market Fuji competed against category leader Hewlett-Packard as well as an increasingly aggressive Kodak, which was heavily promoting its EasyShare system and home printing dock. Kodak was also a chief rival in the all-important self-service digital photo kiosk business. Such units were cropping up at drugstore chains and other retail establishments, allowing customers to select, edit, and print digital pictures on the spot, and were becoming an increasingly important offset to the loss of film sales. Kodak was especially effective in leveraging its brand to become a major force in this category, but Fuji also faced competition in kiosks from major players like Polaroid, Olympus, PMI/KIS, IBM, Mitsubishi, and Sony, as well as from a number of smaller companies.

MARKETING STRATEGY

The Green family—reminiscent of an irreverent suburban television sitcom family, a la *The Simpsons* or *Malcolm in the Middle*—was crafted to include every type of picture taker. According to a Fuji press release when the campaign was launched in November 2002, "Mr. Green is an advanced amateur photographer who loves to shoot with Fujifilm's range of digital cameras. Mrs. Green likes to use Fujifilm 35 mm and QuickSnap one-time-use cameras. Kellie, their teenaged daughter, is a fan of Fujifilm's Nexia Q1, a trendy-looking APS film camera. And Stewart, the always-scheming six-year-old, is happy to take pictures with whatever camera he can get his hands on." The "Do you speak Fuji?" tagline of the previous campaign was dropped in favor of "Get the picture," a slogan Fuji had actually used several years earlier and which the company believed offered more universal appeal. "Get the picture" was also catchy because of its ambiguous meaning. As an imperative, "Get the picture" urged the audience to take pictures as well as to make prints. As a question, "Get the picture" asked the audience if it understood—in essence asking if it was in the know and hip enough to embrace the Fuji message. The multifaceted campaign, estimated to have a budget of $20 to $25 million, included television spots, print ads, newspaper inserts, outdoor advertising, and an online sweepstakes.

The linchpin of the "Meet the Greens" campaign was the three TV spots, which broke on national television during an episode of NBC's *Crossing Jordan.* The spots also appeared during other primetime network shows, such as *Alias, NYPD Blue, The Practice, ER, Law & Order,* and *The West Wing.* Cable television stations that aired the commercials included Discover, Nick at Nite, TLC, VH1, USA, and TBS. The spots also ran during syndicated reruns of such popular shows as *Seinfeld* and *Just Shoot Me.*

The three commercials were structured as humorous, offbeat vignettes, each one highlighting a specific Fuji product or service while showing the Green family involved in everyday picture-taking situations. In the spot called "Date," Mr. Green and Stewart decided to have fun with Kellie's nervous young date, Chad. In answer to Mr. Green's implied question, "So, Kellie tells me you're on the football team," bratty Stewart quipped, "He's the mascot." Chad then had the misfortune of accepting an offering of messy candy. When Kellie finally made her appearance, he had candy stuck to his braces and smeared around his mouth. "Let's get a picture," Mr. Green announced, after which he picked up his Fujifilm FinePix F401 camera to get a candid shot of a smiling Chad and mortified Kellie. The focus of the second spot, "Miracle," was a Fujifilm QuickSnap Flash disposable camera. The commercial opened with Mrs. Green and the children frantically in search of something. Finally she found a QuickSnap camera buried beneath the cushions of the couch. She and the children then rushed upstairs to capture a picture of a "miracle," which turned out to be Mr. Green vacuuming. In the last of the three spots, "Charade," Fuji's self-serve digital photo kiosk was the centerpiece product. In the ad Mr. Green was shown using an in-store kiosk (the Aladdin Digital Photo Center) to develop pictures of his wife and kids. At home he laid out the pictures on the couch and started playing charades by himself. When the family walked in on him, Stewart offered a guess at the subject of the charade: "Night of the Living Dead?"

The "Meet the Greens" campaign also featured a pair of print ads. In one Mr. Green was shown taking a close-up picture of blades of grass, accompanied by the cheeky caption "Mr. Green Gets Hooked on grass," a marijuana allusion geared toward a baby boomer audience. The ad ran in such publications as *Popular Photography* and *Wired.* A second print ad featured Kellie taking a picture of her brother listening to the swollen belly of a very pregnant Mrs. Green. The headline read, "Stewart listens for a change." The ad appeared in mainstream publications like *People.* Another print element was an insert in 100 million newspapers that featured the Greens and included coupons for Fuji film and one-time cameras. The "Meet the Greens" campaign also included outdoor advertising that pictured the Greens' mailbox filled with a complete array of Fujifilm products. The text read, "What Cool Families Use." The mailbox concept was then carried over into the online sweepstakes that was launched later in November and promoted on the Fujifilm website as well as on Yahoo.com, Nickjr.com, ABCnews.com, Babycenter.com, and a number of other sites.

OUTCOME

The "Meet the Greens" advertising ran through the rest of 2002 and were supposed to be followed with a new series of commercials in the spring of 2003 and a third series in the fall of 2003. In April 2003 Fuji launched another sweepstakes by way of an ad in *Good Housekeeping,* inviting participants to offer names for the twins Mrs. Green was set to have. The twins were also expected to be featured in new television spots. The spots never materialized, however, as the Green family concept failed to resonate with the audience as well as the marketers had hoped. While the television spots were engaging—"Date" was highlighted as one of the best recent spots in a December 2002 issue of *Adweek* —the concept did not translate well to the print medium. Nevertheless Fuji had made strides in its effort to recast its brand as more than just film.

FURTHER READING

Deutsch, Claudia. "Fuji and Kodak Are Trying to Expand Their Images and Their Horizons beyond Just Traditional Film." *New York Times,* September 5, 2001, p. C2.

———. "A Fuji Campaign Features the Everyday Moments of the Greens—Captured on Film, of Course." *New York Times,* December 2, 2002, p. C10.

"Fuji Stays in Step with Changes in the Market." *Chain Drug Review,* June 21, 2004, p. 192.

Havlik, Dan. "Move Over 'Simpsons' and Make Way for 'The Greens.'" Imaginginfo.com, December 1, 2002.

Hoffman, Mala. "In Process Fujifilm USA Takes Off in Westchester." *Westchester County Business Journal,* September 30, 2002, p. T1.

Mack, Ann M. "The Greens' Scene." *Adweek,* November 11, 2002, p. 4.

———. "Photo Finish." *Adweek,* September 10, 2001, p. 30.

"Publicis Catches Fuji Photo Film." *Adweek* (eastern ed.), April 17, 2000, p. 88.

Wasserman, Todd. "Fuji Expecting Green Family Additions." *Brandweek,* April 14, 2003, p. 8.

———. "Meet the Greens." *Brandweek,* November 11, 2002, p. 1.

Ed Dinger

Game Show Network

2150 Colorado Ave., Ste. 100
Santa Monica, California 90404
USA
Telephone: (310) 255-6800
Fax: (310) 255-6810
Web site: www.gsn.com

YOU KNOW YOU KNOW CAMPAIGN

OVERVIEW

The Game Show Network (GSN), the only 24-hour cable channel in the United States dedicated to game shows and interactive game playing, was founded in 1995. By 2000 its ratings were at an all-time high, and the network said it was attracting a growing number of viewers. Its goal, however, was to expand the number of cable outlets offering GSN and to increase its viewer base from 25 million subscribers to 50 million within three years.

To accomplish this goal, GSN launched its first-ever consumer-marketing and brand-awareness campaign in March 2000. Signed on to create the campaign, which was estimated to cost between $5 million and $10 million, was TBWA\Chiat\Day, an ad agency based in San Francisco. Themed "You Know You Know," the campaign featured three television spots showing ordinary people in different locations, each shouting the same word. At the end of the spots it was revealed that the people were watching a game show on television and yelling the answer to a question.

Within seven months of the campaign's launch its success was evident. According to Nielsen Media Research, the Game Show Network had added five million new subscribers. The campaign also garnered a long list of awards, including two Clio Awards, a Cannes Lion Award, and recognition as one of *Adweek*'s top 20 spots of the year. The company said, "The remarkable growth of the network continues to exceed our expectations... we have significantly impacted our sales efforts in the past six months."

HISTORICAL CONTEXT

Game shows were popular programming in the early days of television, but they dropped off the viewing radar in the 1950s when it was revealed that cheating was rampant on such hit shows as *The $64,000 Question.* By the mid-1960s and 1970s forgiving viewers were again tuning in to game shows, including *The Gong Show, The Price Is Right,* and *The $10,000 Pyramid.* Seeing a unique niche, in December 1994 the Game Show Network hit the airwaves. The new network, jointly owned by Sony Pictures Entertainment and Liberty Media Corporation, offered cable subscribers 24 hours of nonstop programming from its library of classic game shows. In addition to *The Price is Right,* GSN's library included *Match Game, Password, Family Feud,* and *To Tell the Truth.* For insomniac gamers, the network offered Black & White Overnight, a block of programming that featured game shows from the 1950s and 1960s, such as *I've Got a Secret, Beat the Clock,* and *What's My Line?*

But despite a full programming line up and a base of 25 million subscribers, by 2000 the network was struggling to survive. To attract a broader audience GSN added new programming that allowed viewers to participate in the on-air games; they could win money or other prizes by playing along while watching the program and calling a special telephone number. Noting that game shows were interactive by nature—viewers often shouted answers at their televisions before the on-screen contestants responded—the network also moved playing opportunities to the Internet. Gamers could go online and play a game while it was on television. Other additions were new game shows original to the network, including *3's a Crowd,* and special-event programming such as Y2PLAY, which ran on New Year's Eve 1999 and featured the final episodes of popular game shows of the past. The "You Know You Know" campaign, the network's first marketing effort, was launched in 2000 in an attempt to expand GSN's reach and to increase consumer awareness of the network.

INTERACTIVE SITE LETS GAMERS PLAY ON TV AND WEB

Game Show Network fans were able to be active participants in their favorite games without leaving the comfort of their living rooms. The network's updated interactive website, gameshownetwork.com, included features that enabled players to watch a game on television while playing along on the Internet. As part of the website's launch the network gave players a chance win more than $10,000 in prize money playing "What's in the Box," a trivia-type game. Also available on the site was related merchandise for sale, such as *Hollywood Square* T-shirts. For viewers who listed game show-hosts among their heroes, the site gave them a chance to chat online with such legends as Wink Martindale, who hosted 19 game shows during his career, including *Tic-Tac-Dough.*

TARGET MARKET

When it was introduced, the Game Show Network struggled under the perception that game shows only attracted older, less-upscale audiences. It also had to change perceptions that successful shows such as *Jeopardy* were known as "quiz shows" but that programs called "game shows" were losers. GSN founder and president Michael Fleming said that the challenge was getting out the message that game shows had a broad appeal for all audience demographics, from preteens to older viewers. Early in 2000 GSN executives reported that its viewer base of 25 million subscribers was expected to double by 2003. That prediction of increased viewers was based in part on the success of game-show programming on non-cable networks, such as ABC's *Who Wants to be a Millionaire,* which pushed cable operators to take a closer look at the Game Show Network.

While the "You Know You Know" campaign's primary target was households with cable providers offering GSN, it was presented in a way that encouraged game-show fans not receiving the network to request that their cable ompanies add the channel. The campaign also was designed to tickle the secret superiority complex of many average game-show viewers—those viewers who sat on their sofas in front of their televisions and shouted out the correct answers before the game's on-air contestants.

COMPETITION

In the 1990s viewership of the big-four television networks—ABC, CBS, NBC, and FOX—was steadily declining, and cable channels were gaining viewers. In addition, the Game Show Network was in the unusual position of trying to woo viewers away from competing cable networks at a time when viewers were asking for fewer game shows and more educational fare. A 1997 *Wall Street Journal* poll indicated that 79 percent of respondents wanted television programming to include more documentaries and shows related to history and the arts, while 60 percent wanted to see fewer game shows.

As the Game Show Network moved ahead with plans to boost its program lineup with a new game show set in the Mall of America in Minneapolis, Minnesota, and with interactive gaming options on its website, cable channels Bravo and Discovery were applying similar strategies to attract viewers. Bravo, the artsy cable channel that sent programming into 79 million U.S. homes, turned to England when it decided to add a new show to its offerings. The new series, *Cold Feet,* was added to the 2001 program mix along with the long-running hit shows *Queer Eye for the Straight Guy* and *Inside the Actors Studio.* The new program was supported by a marketing campaign that included television, radio, and print advertising as well as Internet marketing. Also in 2001 the network gave a fresh look to its year-old tagline, "Not your everyday . . . everyday on Bravo Network," which had helped increase viewership by about 30 percent after its introduction. The network's revamped on-air look was designed to capture the attention of its target audience, viewers between 25 and 54 years old with discriminating tastes. Besides on-air ads that featured images of average people doing everyday things such as answering the phone, the campaign included print ads and website tie-ins.

In 2000 the Discovery Channel, a cable network with a subscriber base of 78 million homes and best known for its spectacular documentaries, turned its advertising focus to its Internet division, Discovery.com. The new "Two Guys" campaign, described as humorous and edgy, had the tagline "Discover something new every day." Although the commercials remained loyal to the Discovery brand, complete with close-ups of insects and flaming meteors, they had a twist designed to appeal to younger viewers. In one spot, mosquitoes landed on a man's arm, but a closer look revealed the insects to be two men dressed as bugs. As the bug-men began sucking their victim's blood through straws, one bug was smashed, in true mosquito style, by the victim. Another spot featured two men dressed as meteors. When one man commented that meteors burned up in the Earth's atmosphere, there was a flash and the camera showed both men bursting into flames. The Discovery.com campaign included TV spots on the Discovery Channel as well as print and online ads. Despite its popularity with viewers—the ads increased the number of Internet users logging onto Discovery.com by one percentage point—the campaign had been canceled by the end of the year, with the network offering no explanation for the decision.

ABC and NBC were also trying to win back defecting viewers and to keep viewers who continued to tune in. Both networks had launched major marketing campaigns in late 1997. ABC's "TV Is Good" campaign included ads in newspapers and magazines as well as television spots. NBC's campaign, "Must See TV," took a similar approach. In addition, ABC offered direct competition to the Game Show Network with its game shows *Wheel of Fortune* and *Jeopardy,* two of the highest-rated first-run syndicated shows on television.

MARKETING STRATEGY

The GSN's "You Know You Know" campaign was the network's first foray into consumer marketing since its inception in 1995. The brand-awareness campaign kicked off in March 2000 with three television spots in limited markets that included Boston and Philadelphia. Also a part of the campaign were outdoor ads and other promotional events. The campaign was multipurposed: it was designed to encourage cable operators not offering the network to subscribers to add GSN to their channels, and it was aimed at getting the cable and satellite subscribers who were already receiving the channel to tune in and watch.

"You Know You Know" television spots, which ran on cable channels such as Comedy Central, Lifetime, and Nickelodeon (during its "Nick at Nite" programming), featured ordinary people in unusual situations, each repeating the same word. At the end of each commercial it was revealed the people were shouting the answer to a game-show question on television. In one spot a woman getting a massage shouted, "Sputnik," while another woman checking coats for customers shouted the same word, and a man in an office did also. The camera shifted to show a woman on television asking, "Sky Lab?" A buzzer sounded, the woman on television lost, and it became clear that the correct answer was "Sputnik." The tagline "You Know You Know" followed. In the "Botulism" spot the incorrect answer was "salmonella," and the wrong word in the "Marsupial" spot was "rodent."

The television portion of the campaign was supplemented by a live contest that featured a GSN van towing a huge box to different locations with the question, "What's in the Box?" Clues about what was in the box were announced each day. Contestants were able to register their guesses with either local sponsors of the game or by calling a posted phone number.

In an effort to further promote its brand, in August the campaign was expanded to include seven additional markets: Sacramento, Los Angeles, Saint Louis, Kansas City, Indianapolis, Charlotte, and Raleigh-Durham. The network explained that the decision was made to expand the campaign because it resonated well with cable providers and consumers. "These spots do an incredible job capturing the fun, unpredictable, and involving nature of game shows.... By expanding the reach of the campaign, we can continue to increase GSN awareness and encourage consumers to tune in to GSN," a company spokesman said.

OUTCOME

The "You Know You Know" campaign was named one of the 20 best advertising spots of 2000 by *Adweek.* Additional accolades for the campaign quickly followed. The "Botulism" television spot won a Silver Lion at the International Advertising Festival in Cannes, France, and the "Marsupial" spot was included on the Cannes Lion Shortlist. The Game Show Network also earned two Promax Judge's Choice awards, given for overall outstanding work by Promax & BDA, an international association of promotion, marketing, and design professionals in electronic media. Promax presented the entire campaign with a Gold Award in its Branding and Imaging category, and the "Sputnik" spot was recognized separately. Silver and Bronze Clio Awards and a nomination for a Mark Award (an honor given out by the Cable & Telecommunications Association for Marketing) in recognition of excellence in cable-television marketing, were added to the campaign's honors.

Dena Kaplan, the network's senior vice president of marketing, said that the success of the campaign exceeded the company's expectations. *Business Wire* quoted Kaplan as stating, "It is exciting to see the 'You Know You Know' television campaign play well with consumers as well as the advertising community. Our brand campaign has been successful in expanding the awareness and distribution of the network."

FURTHER READING

Adalian, Josef. "All-Game Network Plans Next Steps." *Variety,* January 1, 2000.

"Bravo, Game Show Plan Series Pushes." *Multichannel News,* November 13, 2000.

"Game Show Network Debuts Its First Consumer Marketing Campaign." *Business Wire,* April 3, 2000.

"Game Show Network Hits 30 Million Subscribers." *Business Wire,* November 28, 2000.

"Game Show Network Receives Cannes 2001 Lion Award and Prestigious Promax Judge's Choice Recognition for 'You Know You Know' Marketing Campaign." *Business Wire,* July 11, 2001.

"Game Show Network Relaunches gameshownetwork.com, the One-Stop Game Show Site on the Internet." *Business Wire,* February 18, 2000.

"Game Show Network You Know You Know Clio." *Business Wire,* June 7, 2001.

"Game Show Network's First Consumer Marketing Campaign Expands Its Reach." *Business Wire,* August 3, 2000.

"Game Show Network's First Consumer Marketing Campaign Honored as One of Year's Best." *Business Wire,* March 6, 2001.

Hogan, Monica. "Bravo Updates On-Air Look." *Multichannel News,* February 5, 2001.

Lipschultz, David. "Sony Spies a Jackpot." *Internet World,* April 1, 2000.

Norton, Justin M. "Discovery.com Debuts 'Two Guys." *Adweek,* June 19, 2000, p. 7.

Voight, Joan. "TBWA Touts Game Show Network," *Adweek* (western ed.), April 10, 2000, p. 9.

"The Work." *Advertising Age's Creativity,* May 1, 2000, p. 12.

Rayna Bailey

Gap Inc.

2 Folsom Street
San Francisco, California 94105
USA
Telephone: (800) 333-7899
Fax: (415) 427-2553
Web site: www.gap.com

FOR EVERY GENERATION CAMPAIGN

OVERVIEW

In 1999 Gap Inc., with a reputation for offering consumers affordable casual clothing basics such as khakis, jeans, and T-shirts, shifted its marketing focus to teen shoppers. To attract teens to its stores, Gap began offering trendy merchandise such as glitter-decorated denim jackets and body-hugging shirts. The strategy backfired when Gap's core customers, baby boomers who had relied on the chain's basic, casual styles, took their clothing dollars elsewhere. Gap's sales went into a downward spiral, and in April 2002 the company reported a 24 percent drop in sales at stores that had been open for a year or more.

In 2002, in an effort to win back its core customers and reverse its declining sales, Gap again changed its focus. Working with the New York–based advertising agency Laird + Partners, the chain launched a global marketing campaign titled "For Every Generation," which was aimed at a broader audience. Although executives declined to release the campaign's budget, a spokesman for Laird + Partners stated that it was one of the largest projects Gap had undertaken in several years. The campaign included television spots, print and billboard ads, and direct mailings. Commercials featured a roster of some 50 celebrities dressed in their own Gap clothes.

By the end of 2002 it had become clear that Gap's marketing strategy had accomplished its goal. Prior to the campaign's launch, the chain had reported 29 consecutive months of declining sales. Following its launch in October 2002, Gap's sales were on the rise, up 1 percent compared with a 17 percent drop in the same month the previous year. In addition *USA Today*'s weekly poll Ad Track concluded that consumers, especially adults between the ages of 25 and 64, found the ads highly appealing.

HISTORICAL CONTEXT

In 1969 Doris and Don Fisher opened the first Gap store in San Francisco. According to the company Don Fisher's motivation for opening the store was "to make it easier to find a pair of jeans." In an effort to update the look of its merchandise, Gap in the late 1990s turned away from its founder's original idea and began selling trendy fashions geared toward teens instead of the basics preferred by baby boomers. As a result it lost many of its core customers, sending the company into a financial free fall. In 1999, prior to the shift in product, the company had reported \$1.13 billion in earnings. After the switch in 2001 Gap reported a loss of \$7.8 million. In early 2002 Gap reported its worst financial performance in its 30-year history.

Gap's product switch was partly a result of a shift, in the late 1990s, in fashion trends away from basic casual clothes to a flashier look favored by young women. In 2002 the *Washington Times* described Gap's product change as a fashion faux pas. The paper stated, "Gap's problems started well before this season as the company moved away from the look that made it famous and added trendy clothes like denim jackets with glitter and tight-fitting fashions to its product mix." Customers walking into their favorite Gap store in search of a pair of basic khakis fled when they instead saw orange and turquoise cropped jeans embellished with silver studs. The chain also found itself losing business to its sister chain, Old Navy (also owned by Gap Inc.), which sold products similar to Gap's but at lower prices. Further confounding Gap Inc. was what many analysts saw as the company's lack of focus when it came to establishing an identity for the Gap brand that would help distinguish it from Old Navy.

When the brand launched its new campaign in 2002, it returned to its roots and original philosophy of enabling people of all ages to buy Gap products and adapt them to fit their personal styles. The company admitted that chasing fickle teens with trendy clothes was a no-win plan. Kyle Andrew, vice president of marketing for Gap, said in a *Women's Wear Daily* interview, "Let Gap be Gap. Let's not try to be trendy." For the new campaign, in addition to returning to its offerings of basic jeans, khakis, and tees, the company also revived and slightly modified a slogan it had used in the past but had failed to take full advantage of: "For every generation, there's a Gap."

TARGET MARKET

Although Gap's "For Every Generation" campaign alienated trend-obsessed teens, it shifted the company's focus back to a broader range of customers. The consumers Gap's new campaign targeted ranged from infants to senior citizens. It also was designed to win back its former core customers, baby boomers who had always relied on the chain's quality, affordable basic clothing styles.

Explaining the new strategy, company president and CEO Millard Drexler told *Business Wire,* "Gap speaks a common language that everyone understands, and this campaign reflects the connection that people of all ages have with Gap. Whether you are six, sixteen or sixty, nothing is more universal than a pair of Gap jeans. That's the kind of classic style, product and message we stand for."

COMPETITION

As Gap struggled to reverse more than 22 months of negative same-store sales, one of its top competitors, Abercrombie & Fitch, was embroiled in its own problems related to marketing and product offerings that many considered offensive. Also among Gap's top competitors was American Eagle Outfitters, which was on the opposite end of the marketing spectrum from Abercrombie, with climbing sales and a reputation for offering wholesome advertising and merchandise.

Abercrombie & Fitch was founded in 1892 as a purveyor of quality camping, hunting, and fishing clothing and equipment, and by 1917 it was the world's largest sporting-goods store. Among the store's customers were Teddy Roosevelt, who purchased gear at the store before setting off on an African safari, and Ernest Hemingway. In 1988 the chain was bought by the Limited (which also owned Victoria's Secret) and shifted from selling sporting clothes and equipment to outfitting suburban kids.

The Limited phased out its ownership in 1998, and Abercrombie became an independent public company. The chain's marketing and merchandise, produced in-house, turned toward the explicit and sexual. In 2002 the company was listed by *PR Newswire* as producing one of the 10 worst public relations blunders of the year. The publication reported that Abercrombie had offended the public with its thong underwear for prepubescent girls

GAP, OLD NAVY, AND BANANA REPUBLIC

With Gap promoting the idea that it was for everybody, *Women's Wear Daily* wondered who Gap Inc. expected to shop at its other chains, Old Navy and Banana Republic. Gap's vice president of marketing, Kyle Andrew, explained that many customers would shop at all three chains but that efforts were being made to separate the brands. "Old Navy is more family and value shopping. Gap can move up to be a more stylish place, and Banana Republic can move up to be an even more stylish place." Gap was also especially known for its jeans, a feature the company emphasized in its fall 2002 line. By 2002 Old Navy was being pressured by—and losing customers to—discount stores that carried similar merchandise but that also offered the convenience of one-stop shopping. Because of its higher customer profile and merchandise offerings that were trendier or more stylish, the other store in the trio, Banana Republic, was having fewer problems keeping its customers.

and its T-shirts that portrayed stereotyped images of Asian-Americans. Despite pulling the controversial merchandise from its product line, the company remained known for the "sex sells" theme in its marketing. The company's 2002 catalog, titled "XXX," included sexually suggestive photographs on more than half of its 280 pages. Despite consumer complaints about its merchandise, Abercrombie reported a 21 percent sales increase in October 2002 compared with the same period the previous year. It noted, however, that same-store sales had dropped 5 percent from January through November 2002.

American Eagle Outfitters, founded in 1977, was originally known for selling men's outdoor gear. In 1992 it underwent a rebranding and became known for its classic American, mainstream style, which successfully appealed to its target market: mature teens and young adults. By 1997 the chain had begun making additional improvements to its selection of merchandise, and it introduced marketing—which included ads in such magazines as *Mademoiselle, Seventeen,* and *Spin*—intended to broaden the brand's customer base by promoting its affordable, casual, and basic clothing. American Eagle reported that first-quarter sales overall in 2002 were up 14.9 percent over the same period in the previous year; however, same-store sales for the first quarter of 2002 were down about 2 percent.

MARKETING STRATEGY

As Gap's "For Every Generation" campaign was prepared for its launch, a company spokesman said that the new marketing strategy had been created to broaden its appeal to consumers and to attract people of all ages back to the chain. In addition the campaign was the first one the company had used for all Gap divisions, including adult, kids, and baby.

The campaign starred some 50 celebrities of all ages from a variety of fields (such as movies, music, art, and fashion) in TV spots and print ads. The latter included a 48-page portfolio in *Vanity Fair* magazine. Personalities featured in the print campaign ranged from country music icon Willie Nelson and up-and-coming singer Taryn Manning to comedian Whoopi Goldberg. Among the film stars dressing in their favorite Gap fashions for the ads were Sissy Spacek, Lauren Hutton, Salma Hayek, and Christian Slater. Trey Laird, president and executive creative director of Laird + Partners, explained to *Business Wire,* "We selected a broad range of personalities who each have a highly defined individual style. We worked with each person to create their own look in Gap jeans—keeping it personal, authentic and real."

Each ad featured a celebrity wearing a pair of Gap jeans combined with other Gap items as well as their own clothes and accessories. Nelson appeared in a TV spot wearing his Gap jeans and performing a guitar version of the Hank Williams classic "Move It On Over." Another TV spot starred models Shalom Harlow and Alek Wek showing off the comfort and style of their Gap jeans while dancing to the 1960s hit song "Bend Me, Shape Me." In one print ad Kelly Klein, socialite, photographer, and ex-wife of fashion designer Calvin Klein, paired her Gap jeans with one of her favorite lacy tops.

OUTCOME

With more than two years of negative same-store sales results at the end of 2002, following the launch of its "For Every Generation" campaign, the company reported that, while its earnings remained down, they still came in above expectations. Although in October its same-store sales had been up only 1 percent, this was a turnaround from a 17 percent drop during that month the previous year. A report in *USA Today* stated that, based on the data, "It looks like Gap's more familiar basic merchandise and new ad campaign are working." Gap executives also said that the campaign appeared to be moving the company back in the right direction.

According to information gathered by Ad Track, *USA Today* 's weekly consumer poll, about 21 percent of those surveyed liked the ads "a lot." The commercials also scored higher with two key groups—women and adults ages 25 to 64—indicating that Gap was reconnecting with its former core customers. An article in *Women's Wear Daily* noted that Gap's "increased advertising, and increasingly amusing advertising, [had] helped expand sales in recent months" for the retailer. It further noted that, while the chain's rebirth was not complete, it was clearly occurring.

FURTHER READING

"Abercrombie & Fitch, Martha Stewart, Jerry Falwell, N.Y. Yankees on List of 10 Worst 2002 PR Gaffes: Eighth Annual PR Blunders List Unveiled." *PR Newswire,* December 5, 2002.

"American Eagle Outfitters Wins Abercrombie & Fitch Lawsuit in U.S. Court of Appeals: For the Third Time in Four Years AE Prevails in Court against A & F." *PR Newswire,* February 18, 2002.

Atkinson, William. "Specialty Apparel Retail Survivors." *Shopping Center World,* May 1, 2002.

De Marco, Donna. "Gap Goes Back to Basics to Stop Sales Slouch: Retailer Returns to Less Flashy Clothes." *Washington Times,* May 10, 2002.

Forson, Lindsye. "Abercrombie & Fitch Too Sexy for Young Kids." *Battalion,* June 5, 2002.

"Gap Launches 'For Every Generation.'" *Business Wire,* August 8, 2002.

Howard, Theresa. "Gap Swings Back into Action." *USA Today,* November 18, 2002.

Lockwood, Lisa. "Gap's New Ad Plan: Market to Boomers, Not to Fickle Teens." *Women's Wear Daily,* August 6, 2002.

———. "Gap's New Ads Target Former Customers: Troubled Specialty Store Chain Will Kick Off New Television Campaign on Aug. 15." *Daily News Record,* August 12, 2002.

———. "Laird Adds Gap Stores Account to His Fledgling Ad Agency." *Women's Wear Daily,* March 14, 2002.

Weitzman, Jennifer. "Gap's Transition." *Women's Wear Daily,* December 10, 2002.

———. "Second Straight Profit for Gap." *Women's Wear Daily,* August 16, 2002.

Young, Kristin. "Chains Aim at Core." *Women's Wear Daily,* August 21, 2002.

Rayna Bailey

HOW DO YOU WEAR IT? CAMPAIGN

OVERVIEW

As Gap, Inc., approached its 35th birthday in early 2004, the 1,500-store chain was experiencing an upswing in profits and sales, reporting steady increases since 2002. First-quarter profits in 2004 were up 55 percent, and sales were up 9.4 percent compared with the same period the previous year. To celebrate its birthday and maintain the profit and sales momentum, Gap charged its advertising agency, Laird + Partners, New York, with creating a new global marketing campaign to be released in summer 2004.

For the "How Do You Wear It?" campaign Laird + Partners turned to what had worked well for the chain in the past: celebrity-centered television spots and print ads. Signed on as the celebrity spokeswoman was *Sex and the City* star and fashion idol Sarah Jessica Parker. Although no specific budget for the campaign was available, *Adweek* reported that Gap's advertising budget the previous year was $140 million. Further, Gap reportedly paid Parker $38 million for her three-season, six-month contract. Besides Parker, other celebrities featured in the campaign's different television spots and print ads included singer Lenny Kravitz, actress Jada Pinkett Smith, and New England Patriots football star Tom Brady.

Despite the success of previous celebrity-centered campaigns, Gap's new effort failed to drive sales or resonate with consumers. Within months of the campaign's start Gap reported its worst overall sales performance in two years. The spokeswoman of the campaign, Parker, also took a hit as consumers posted their criticisms on the Internet. When Parker's contract expired in spring 2005, Gap replaced her with a new spokeswoman: 17-year-old British singing star Joss Stone.

HISTORICAL CONTEXT

The Gap chain of retail clothing stores got its start in 1969, when the first store was opened in San Francisco by Doris and Don Fisher. Motivated by the desire to provide customers with an easy option for finding jeans, when the store opened, it sold only one product: Levi's jeans for men and women. By 1970 Gap had grown to six stores, and in 1974 the rapidly expanding chain introduced its own private-label jeans as well as accessories. Over time Gap expanded its brand to include other basic casual styles, such as khakis and tees for men, women, and children. It stopped selling Levi's in 1991. In late 1999 the chain was beginning to show its age, and as its marketing focus and product mix shifted from its core customers—baby boomers—to teens, sales fell into a steady 22-month decline. In April 2002 the chain reported a 24 percent drop in sales at stores open at least one year. Furthermore, in May of that year the company reported that overall sales for the month fell to $962 million compared with sales of $1.2 billion for the same month one year earlier.

In an effort to reverse the downward spiral, in 2002 Gap replaced its agency, Modernista! of Boston, with New York–based advertising agency Laird + Partners. The agency worked with the chain's in-house marketing team on a new advertising campaign that would target a broader audience than the teens on whom Gap had been focusing. The partnership resulted in the "For Every Generation" campaign. Featuring a list of celebrities ranging from country-music icon Willie Nelson to comedian Whoopie Goldberg and actress Christina Ricci, the campaign moved Gap back to its roots of offering basic casual clothing for consumers of all ages and showed how Gap fashions were adaptable to each person's individual style. Following the campaign's introduction, the chain reported a sales increase of 1 percent in October 2002. While small, the sales improvement was significant considering the 17 percent drop reported for October 2001.

In 2004, as the chain prepared to celebrate its 35th anniversary, Gap also planned to release a new global marketing campaign. Based on the success of its celebrity-centered campaigns, which included the first such effort, "Individuals of Style," which ran from 1988 through 1993, and the 2002 "For Every Generation" campaign, Gap and its agency stuck with what had worked in the past. Laird + Partners' new campaign, "How Do You Wear It?" featured celebrity and fashion icon Sarah Jessica Parker as well as other celebrities who would connect with consumers and send the message that

Gap offered clothes that enabled people to express their individual style.

TARGET MARKET

Through the use of celebrities of all ages and genders in its marketing campaigns, Gap attempted to reach a broad range of consumers: men and women, teens to baby boomers. Earlier campaigns featured celebrities such as counterculture writer Jack Kerouac, country-music elder statesman Willie Nelson, and 20-something actress Christina Ricci wearing Gap clothes. The campaigns were designed to send the message that everyone, regardless of age or sex, could find a Gap style perfectly suited or adaptable to his or her personal taste.

When, in 2004, the chain released its "How Do You Wear It?" campaign with 39-year-old actress Sarah Jessica Parker as its spokeswoman, it was clear that women were the target market. Parker's TV show *Sex and the City* was highly popular with women. In addition, the actress was the ideal person to convey the idea of individuality, because she was closely linked with her character's eclectic, cutting-edge style, a combination of vintage and couture clothes and pricey Manolo Blahnik shoes. According to a Gap press release, Parker's spots were intended to connect with "women of all ages and to help them understand the versatility of our products and our spirit of individual style." Not forgetting its male target, for some spots Gap's campaign partnered Parker with singer Lenny Kravitz, also wearing Gap clothes, while additional print ads featured top athletes and actors who resonated with male consumers.

COMPETITION

American Eagle Outfitters, Inc. (AE), which had 828 shopping-mall-based stores scattered throughout the United States and Canada in 2004, got its start in 1977 selling outdoor gear. By 1992 the retailer's product line had been expanded to include a wide selection of casual attire, from polo shirts and khaki pants to shorts, sweaters, and skirts. For the brand's target market—men and women 15 to 25 years old—the high quality and reasonable prices of AE's merchandise were particularly appealing. By 2004 the chain was ranked 9th among the country's top 10 specialty retailers. The company reported a 19.9 percent sales jump to $350 million in the three months ended May 2004 compared to the same period the previous year.

Keeping its marketing eye on its target audience of high school and college students, in 2004 AE began a new marketing campaign, "AE Jeans Will Rock You." The campaign kicked off in September at 22 college football stadiums across the country. Each time the 1977 hit rock song *We Will Rock You* by Queen was played during football games, AE product giveaways were announced. To reach the high-school crowd, campaign television spots featuring the Queen song aired on MTV as teens prepared to go back to school. In addition to its new marketing campaign, in 2004 AE also began a redesign of its stores, replacing its original beach-house-themed decor with a trendy city-lofts theme featuring concrete floors, high ceilings with skylights, and plasma televisions running AE ad spots.

Abercrombie & Fitch (A & F) was also founded as a provider of outdoor gear. But unlike AE, which was a relative newcomer in the market, A & F opened its doors in 1892 and had counted author Ernest Hemingway and U.S. president Theodore Roosevelt among its clients. In 1988 the chain was bought by the Limited, which operated the women's clothing chains the Limited and Victoria's Secret. After the acquisition A & F's product focus shifted from outdoor gear to contemporary casual clothes for upper-class suburban teens and 20-somethings. Ten years after its purchase of A & F the Limited phased out its ownership of the chain. As an independent public company, A & F took a new approach to its marketing strategy.

GAP HOPES TO LURE SHOPPERS WITH NEW STORE DESIGNS

The year 2005 was marked by store makeovers for San Francisco–based clothing chain Gap, Inc. In April the chain reopened seven of its stores in Colorado following extensive remodeling. The new store designs were planned with older consumers with deeper pockets in mind, rather than the teens it had been targeting previously. The overhaul was also the first store-upgrading effort undertaken by the chain in at least 10 years. Hoping to win back its core customers—baby boomers—who had fled the Gap when its merchandise and advertising began targeting a younger crowd, the redesigned stores offered a variety of perks. Included was free bottled water in the dressing rooms and a lounge area with magazines, newspapers, and books for shoppers to read while taking a break. The redesigned Colorado stores were prototypes for all Gap stores, with a nationwide store renovation on the schedule. Later in 2005 the Gap introduced a new store design in Omaha, Nebraska, that included four of the chain's brands—Gap, GapKids, BabyGap, and GapBody—under one roof.

In 2002 the chain's in-house marketing team developed a campaign that included a 280-page sales catalog titled "XXX." The title clearly portrayed the catalog's contents, which featured sexually suggestive photographs on more than half its pages. The catalog targeted high school and college students, but it raised the ire of parents and consumer watchdogs. It also pushed sales at the chain up 18 percent. By 2004, however, A & F was experiencing a sales decline, reporting an 11 percent drop in same-store sales in the quarter that ended January 2004. For the same quarter, overall sales chainwide inched up slightly (4.8 percent) to $560.4 million. Acknowledging that the chain's marketing had occasionally crossed the line, A & F's chief executive officer, Michael Jeffries, told *Women's Wear Daily* of plans for changes to the strategy. A & F introduced a new national advertising campaign in 2004 that included ads in magazines and outdoors as well as a 60-page catalog. The promised changes to its marketing strategy were evident. While the catalog featured photos of bare-chested young men and young women in bathing suits or skimpy outfits, it lacked the nude models in suggestive poses found in previous publications. The summer 2004 catalog was also plastic-wrapped and had a tag noting that it was not for sale to anyone under 18 years old.

MARKETING STRATEGY

Since the 1980s Gap had relied on celebrities to promote its brand in several advertising campaigns. Celebrities were featured in its "Individuals of Style" campaign, which ran for six years beginning in 1988, and in its "For Every Generation" campaign, which was created for Gap in 2002 by Laird + Partners. Based on the success of its previous celebrity-centered campaigns, when Laird + Partners designed its "How Do You Wear It?" campaign for Gap, stars were front and center in the television spots and print ads. Signed to a three-season, six-month, $38 million contract as the campaign's spokeswoman was actress Sarah Jessica Parker, known for her role as fashionista Carrie Bradshaw on the hit television show *Sex and the City*.

A 90-second television spot featuring Parker and musician Lenny Kravitz first aired during the *MTV Video Music Awards* in August 2004. In the spot Parker danced while Kravitz performed a mix of his songs *Lady* and *Are You Gonna Go My Way*. As Kravitz sang and played the electric guitar, Parker added to her outfit, showing the variety of ways that Gap jeans could be worn. Eventually six different versions of Parker appeared to be dancing with Kravitz. Parker was shown in Gap jeans customized with everything from velvet ribbons to millions of dollars worth of antique jewelry. During the spot Kravitz's Gap clothes also were customized with a variety of items, including studs, grommets, and gold-braided ribbon. The campaign also included a series of 30-second spots and 15-second teaser spots, which aired on all major networks and cable channels in the United States and Canada.

Print ads began running in September in national magazines, including *Vogue, Vanity Fair, Harper's Bazaar,* and *Essence*. In addition to Parker, the print ads featured other stars from television, music, fashion, and sports, such as actresses Jada Pinkett Smith and Jessica Alba. Ads also broke in men's magazines such as *GQ* and *Details*; these versions featured Kravitz as well as New England Patriot football star Tom Brady and actors Michael Vartan and Josh Duhamel.

Other marketing elements of the campaign were outdoor, direct mail, in-store, and online efforts. The online aspect included a special website, www.howdoyou.com, that allowed customers to post photos of themselves showing how they personalized their Gap clothes. Customers who logged onto the site could also vote for their favorites of the posted pictures, view the campaign's TV spots, and get fall fashion tips.

OUTCOME

Although the strategy of relying on celebrities to promote its brand worked for Gap in the late 1980s through the early 1990s, the idea seemed to fall flat in the first decade of the new century. The chain's "Individuals of Style" campaign, which ran from 1988 through 1993 and featured a variety of celebrities, boosted sales and earnings an average of 43 percent from 1990 to 1993. The sales growth for 1993 alone was a reported 30 percent. In 2002 the chain released a campaign, "For Every Generation," that also featured a long list of stars and contributed to a slight turnaround in declining sales. The celebrity spokespersons also helped establish Gap's reputation as a cool brand. But whether it was a sign of changing consumer tastes or the increasing retail options available to shoppers, Gap's subsequent celebrity-centered campaigns, including a single television spot featuring singers Madonna and Missy Elliot, failed to resonate with customers. Wendy Liebmann, president of the New York–based marketing consulting firm WSL Strategic Retail, told *Advertising Age* that the Gap had lost its meaning and edge. She said, "It's the name everyone knows but aren't real sure what it stands for anymore . . . there are other choices that mean more to consumers anyway today."

The 2004 "How Do You Wear It?" campaign also failed to accomplish its goal of driving sales, and despite her image as a fashion icon, its celebrity spokesperson, Sarah Jessica Parker, failed to enhance Gap's former cool image. The *Advertising Age* report stated that, following the campaign's introduction, the chain reported its worst sales performance since 2002. Additionally, comments that consumers posted about the advertisements on the New York–based blog *Gothamist* (www.gothamist.com) were generally less than kind about both the Gap clothing featured in the spots and about its celebrity spokeswoman. One writer described the print ad in which Parker had cut her Gap jeans off at the knees and embellished them with black velvet bows as "weird." Another described Parker's appearance in the same ad as looking like "Little Bo Peep on acid." Another asked the question, "Could those pants be any less flattering?"

In March 2005, just weeks after announcing a new series of advertisements featuring Parker, the star's three-season contract with Gap expired, and the chain reported that it was replacing her with a new celebrity spokeswoman: up-and-coming 17-year-old British singing sensation Joss Stone.

FURTHER READING

Alexander, Deborah. "Gap Opens 4 Stores under a Single Roof." *Omaha (NE) World-Herald,* November 9, 2005.

"American Eagle Outfitters Reinforces 'AE Jeans Will Rock You Campaign' with Innovative Advertising Initiative." *Business Wire,* September 29, 2004.

Arellano, Kristi. "Gap Upgrades Design of Colorado Stores to Cater to Older, Upscale Customer." *Denver Post,* April 22, 2005.

Frazier, Mya. "Star-Struck Gap Follows Celebs off a Sales Cliff; News Analysis: Decline Due to Many Factors, but Ad Campaign Isn't Helping." *Advertising Age,* November 28, 2005.

"Gap Taps Sarah Jessica Parker for Ads." *Adweek,* May 28, 2004.

Greenberg, Julee. "American Eagle's City Escape (American Eagle Outfitters Revamps Store Design)." *Women's Wear Daily,* June 17, 2004.

"In Brief: Adidas Olympic Sponsorship. . .Trimming Down. . .No Gaps." *Women's Wear Daily,* January 25, 2005.

"Parker Parked? Gap Gets Stone(d)." *Cincinnati (OH) Post,* March 16, 2005.

Roberts, Roxanne. "40, but Sporting a $38 Million Figure." *Washington Post,* March 23, 2005.

"Sarah Jessica Parker and Lenny Kravitz Show Us How They Wear It in New Gap TV Campaign." *PR Newswire,* August 27, 2004.

"Sarah Jessica Parker Enjoys Being a Girl in Gap's New Spring TV Spot." *PR Newswire,* March 1, 2005.

Weitzman, Jennifer. "A&F to Revamp Approach." *Women's Wear Daily,* February 18, 2004.

Williams, Mark. "Abercrombie's Cover-Up/Retailer's New Photo Essay: More Clothes, Less Skin." *Cincinnati (OH) Post,* June 16, 2004.

Young, Kristin. "Sarah Jessica Parker Inks Deal with Gap." *Women's Wear Daily,* May 27, 2004.

Rayna Bailey

KHAKIS CAMPAIGN

OVERVIEW

On April 23, 1998, Gap Inc. launched a global advertising campaign for its chain of nearly 1,600 casual-clothing stores. This campaign, created by Gap's in-house agency, Gap Direct, focused on the company's khaki pants. The U.S. khakis market was growing at a rapid rate. Younger consumers fueled the expanding market as they increasingly eschewed blue jeans, the traditional badge of youth culture, because their baby-boomer parents often wore denim. Furthermore, "business casual" clothes, including khakis, were gaining acceptance as appropriate professional attire. In an effort to claim a greater portion of the khakis market, as well as to burnish the Gap brand, Gap dedicated an estimated $20 to $30 million to its 1998 "Khakis" campaign.

The initial three commercials sought to "reinvent khakis," according to a Gap news release. Each spot was set to a distinct type of music and featured active young adults sporting different styles of Gap khakis. In "Khakis Rock," skateboarders and in-line skaters executed moves to the music of the alternative rock band Crystal Method, while "Khakis Groove" portrayed energetic hip-hop dancers and funk music from Bill Mason. The most popular and acclaimed ad of the trilogy was "Khakis Swing," in which stylish khaki-wearers expertly swing danced to Louis Prima's "Jump, Jive an' Wail." The spots, which ran during such high-profile programs as *Ally McBeal* and *ER,* used Gap's trademark white background and showcased Gap's newest varieties of khakis—flat front, low rise, slim fit, and cargo. Print and outdoor ads also appeared in major markets and in national magazines such as *Spin* and *Details.* "It's about what you bring together to khakis, and what you want that look to say about you," a Gap representative stated in the May 25, 1998, *Daily News Record* in an effort to explain the underlying premise of the campaign. Once known as comfortable "old man's" clothes and then as the preppy pants of the 1980s, khakis were presented as the ultimate in cool in this campaign.

The campaign was an immediate success. Consumers were effusive about the commercials, and Gap's sales soared after the release of the ads. A *USA Today* AdTrack survey revealed that younger consumers—a key target for the campaign—responded particularly favorably to Gap's new message. By March 1999 the company had created a new trio of "Khakis" ads: "Khakis A-Go-Go," with a 1960s-inspired soundtrack; "Khaki Soul," set to soul music; and "Khaki Country," which featured line dancers and the music of country star Dwight Yokum.

HISTORICAL CONTEXT

The Gap was founded in 1969 when Doris and Don Fisher opened a San Francisco store that primarily offered Levi's blue jeans. Although the couple had originally planned to name their business PAD, they settled instead on the Gap, in honor of the generation gap that defined the young baby boomer generation. The company rapidly expanded in the 1970s, debuting private-line labels, of which "Gap" eventually became the only brand offered in the stores. The company developed a loyal following of teenagers and young adults, who responded to the catchy "Fall Into the Gap" advertising campaign that ran from 1974 to 1979. In 1981 the Gap acquired the chain of Banana Republic stores, and in 1986 it launched its children's-clothing venture, GapKids.

A seminal moment in Gap history occurred in 1983 when Fischer brought aboard Mickey Drexler as his deputy. Not only did Drexler hire new designers and renovate stores, but he also honed and simplified the Gap's brand image. Gap's advertising reflected its new, carefully cultivated cachet. In 1988 the company began its "Individuals of Style" campaign, a series of striking black-and-white print ads that portrayed famous individuals in simple articles of Gap clothes. Actress Kim Basinger appeared in a crisp white Gap shirt and pearls, while Dizzy Gillespie donned a black turtleneck. As the May 15, 1998, edition of *Women's Wear Daily* explained, Gap "flouted the convention of showing fashion models in pretty poses, [instead] featuring poets and musicians." Gap continued this theme—described by *Fortune* as "extraordinary people in ordinary clothes"—in its 1993 to 1995 "Who wore khakis?" campaign. These print ads incorporated photos of past celebrities, such as Pablo Picasso, Marilyn Monroe, and Ernest Hemingway, clad in khakis.

Gap's design and marketing formula of studied simplicity proved imitable, however. "Apparel companies from J.C. Penney to Armani had started selling 'basics,'" said *Fortune*. With new competitors, such as Abercrombie & Fitch, gaining the loyalty of teenagers and 20-somethings, Gap's sales dwindled. By 1995 store sales were flat. As part of a broader effort to bolster both its sales and its image, Gap launched its first television campaign in 12 years in 1997 with ads for its Easy-Fit jeans. The campaign starred a variety of performers, including L.L. Cool J., Lena Horne, and David Arquette, and revived the "Fall Into the Gap" tag line. For its efforts Gap was named 1997 "Marketer of the Year" by *Advertising Age*.

TARGET MARKET

One of the primary target audiences of the "Khakis" campaign was teenagers. These members of the so-called Generation Y (or "echo boom") provided obvious opportunities to the company that could capture their allegiance. In 1999 there were 31 million consumers between the ages of 12 and 19, comprising 28 percent of the American population. This group spent an estimated $149 billion of its own money in 1998, according to *Long Island (N.Y.) Newsday*, and also heavily influenced many family purchasing decisions. In an effort to appeal to Generation Y, Gap sought to create "Khakis" commercials that expressed the values and activities of this segment. "Khakis Rock," for instance, featured in-line skating and skateboarding, sports that the November 9, 1998, *Daily News Record* labeled as "Gen Y pastimes." The khaki pants modeled in the spot were of the baggy style popular among teens. The music choice in "Khakis Rock"—the pulsing alternative sound of Crystal Method—was in tune with teens' tastes. The ad, which was produced to look more like a music video than a traditional commercial, was designed to appeal to a group raised on MTV. Although a Gap spokesperson cautioned the *Newark (N.J.) Star-Ledger* that the "Khakis" campaign was meant to curry favor with "all ages," she did emphasize that "we think the campaign is very young and high energy."

The "Khakis" campaign also attempted to court the notoriously cynical Generation X, those consumers born between 1964 and 1979. "X-ers are decidedly anti-marketing [and] anti-hype," an analyst told the *Daily News Record*. This demographic group, which came of age during economic recession and the onset of the AIDS epidemic, tended to be pessimistic and reluctant to respond to standard hard-sell advertising messages. "Khakis" ads were accordingly stylish in their execution but deliberately understated in their pitch. "With us, it's about entertaining as much as it is about fashion," a Gap spokesperson explained to the *Chicago Tribune*. The "retro" craze that captivated Generation Xers was also apparent in the "Khakis" campaign. Twenty-somethings in the 1990s embraced cocktails, cigars, and lounge music with a fervency that had eluded their parents, and "Khakis Swing" featured young people swing dancing with aplomb. Moreover, all the actors appearing in the "Khakis" ads were young adults, a calculated choice that conformed to Generation X's "prefer[ence for] images that portray people like themselves," according to the *Daily News Record*.

While the "Khakis" campaign tended to skew toward younger consumers, Gap took care not to alienate baby boomers. The "business-casual" boom of the 1990s meant that more employees—of all ages and positions—took to wearing khakis to work more often. Indeed, in September 1997, Gap handed out free khakis on the floor of the New York Stock Exchange and convinced the exchange to relax its strict suits-only dress code for one day. The "Khakis Swing" ad exploited boomers' "nostalgia for the old days," an industry analyst told the *Daily News Record*. In fact, the *Daily News Record* concluded that the "Khakis Swing" commercial "reach[ed] all three generations."

A SWINGING INFLUENCE

Although Gap's "Khakis Swing" commercial was influenced by the resurgence of "retro" culture among young consumers, the ad itself did much to boost further interest in swing dancing. "I think that ad did more for swing dance than it actually did for those pants," a swing commentator told the *Quincy (Mass.) Patriot Ledger.*

COMPETITION

Gap was not the only company seeking to capture younger consumers. Levi Strauss & Company launched its $50 million "One Leg At A Time" advertising campaign for its Dockers division in March, 1998. Founded in 1986, Dockers dominated the khaki sector, controlling 26 percent of the market in 1998. While Dockers had experienced considerable success with its "Nice Pants" campaign (which ran from 1995 through 1998), Dockers, like Gap, expected growth to come from Generation Xers and echo boomers, according to *Advertising Age.* This new campaign, conceived by Foote, Cone & Belding was intended to draw in younger consumers. "One Leg At A Time" had different components, including television commercials (which appeared during programming such as the NCAA basketball championships and prime-time shows), print, and outdoor spots. Dockers also utilized more unconventional marketing strategies. The brand sponsored independent film festivals, showed movie clips from these festivals on the walls of buildings in trendy neighborhoods, and sent free khakis to cutting-edge figures such as Harmon Lee and Omar Sosa. "We don't want to be the big corporation, banging you over the head with our message," a Dockers spokesperson told the *Daily News Record.* "We'll try to set ourselves apart by making ourselves a part of life on the street level." In July 1998, however, Dockers ended "One Leg At A Time," citing increased advertising pressure from Gap. In its place Dockers tried a new strategy when it "dropp[ed] the ordinary guy image it has had since its launch, [and] switch[ed] to a sexier approach," according to *Advertising Age* on January 18, 1999. Two new commercials—both of which featured attractive young men who receive considerable attention from women because of their pants—aired mostly during sports and male-oriented programming.

Gap faced other challengers as well. Like Dockers, the Haggar Clothing Company sold its khaki pants at retail stores. In June 1998 the company debuted print ads that portrayed model Billy Brown clad only in Haggar khakis. "The ad," said the *Washington Post,* "communicated the sentiment that khakis, specifically those from Haggar, are cool." Recognizing that women purchased nearly half of all men's clothing for their partners, Haggar's new campaign targeted females. Thus the ads appeared in publications popular among women, such as *Glamour* and *Marie Claire.* Tommy Hilfiger, a trendy casual-wear designer, represented an additional threat to Gap. *Advertising Age* called Hilfiger a "marketing titan" and the "sportswear choice" for fashion-minded 20- and 30-somethings. After launching a women's sportswear line in 1996 to augment its successful men's line, Hilfiger and Miramax films teamed up to tout the 1998 movie, *The Faculty.* Stars from the film appeared in print and television ads (wearing Hilfiger creations, of course) that ran on MTV, VH1, and Comedy Central and in magazines such as *Teen People, Spin, Details,* and *Rolling Stone.* Gap also faced competition from hip retail chains such as Abercrombie & Fitch, which targeted consumers below the age of 30. The bulk of Abercrombie & Fitch's sales were derived from its glossy catalogue, but the company also operated a chain of 159 stores across the United States.

MARKETING STRATEGY

A year before the launch of Gap's "Khakis" ads, the company's designers and marketers had determined that "1998 would be the year of the khaki," said *Fortune.* In addition to conceiving the campaign Gap developed new styles of the classic tan pants in hopes of capitalizing on booming khakis sales. (Total khaki sales were 12 percent higher in 1997 than 1996, and 1996 sales had been 22 percent higher than 1995.) While Gap certainly hoped to sell large quantities of khakis, the massive effort it devoted to the campaign undergirded its overarching goal: to strengthen and contemporize the Gap brand. Khakis offered the Gap a means to draw a broad cross-section of American consumers into the company's stores. As the *Daily News Record* asserted, "[i]t's rare for one item to stretch its legs from the golf clubhouse to urban streets to the corporate boardroom." Khakis did just this, however, proving to be popular school attire for teens, "casual day" garb for employees, and clubbing clothes for Generation Xers. The "Khakis" campaign attempted to reach all of these distinct demographic groups.

Since Gap sought to reach across demographic divides, the company used different media to carry its "Khakis" message. Television commercials were the foundation of the campaign. For the most part Gap selected programs that garnered a younger audience of Generation X and Generation Y viewers, including *ER,*

Ally McBeal, The Practice, and *The X-Files.* When the company "re-debuted" these ads in August 1998 it added to its roster *Felicity,* a hit show among teens, and *Party of 5,* a drama that had a cult-like following among teens and 20-somethings. Gap also ran "Khakis" commercials during more high-profile programming. In May 1998 the company spent an estimated $1.7 million to advertise on the final episode of the tremendously popular sitcom *Seinfeld.* The 1999 installment of "Khakis" ads first appeared during the Academy Awards telecast, which was a "major hit with women and young people and dr[ew] a more affluent audience than the Super Bowl," according to the *San Jose Mercury News.* Print "Khakis" ads were published in more youth-oriented magazines, such as *Spin, Details, Vibe, Vanity Fair, Vogue, ESPN, Teen People,* and *Entertainment Weekly.* Bus and billboard ads were also used in key markets.

Since the campaign had the dual purpose of enhancing the image of the overall Gap brand, the company was careful to ensure that the "Khakis" ads projected the Gap's desired image. The look and feel of the spots, with their stark, white backgrounds and minimalist feel, shared the design principle of Gap stores. Moreover, despite their music-video undercurrent, the commercials remained focused on Gap's khakis and the Gap logo that silently appeared at the end of each spot.

OUTCOME

The "Khakis" ad were lauded by viewers and critics. A *USA Today* AdTrack survey revealed that the spots were "very effective and very popular with consumers of all ages." The survey indicated that the "Khakis" spots scored "especially well among young consumers." Teen marketing studies showed that "Khakis" ads were the second most popular of any advertisement among teenagers and that consumers under 20 ranked Gap fifth among brands they liked most.

Advertising critics and apparel industry analysts were equally enthusiastic. The *New York Times* named "Khakis Swing" one of the year's best ads, and the *Chicago Daily Tribune* declared that the "Khaki" ads "created the biggest cultural stir of any TV spot" since a popular 1997 ad. An analyst for the *Wall Street Journal* reported that the "Khakis" commercials had bolstered Gap's brand: "They have a brand, not just retail stores. People are buying the brand, not just something to cover their nakedness."

Gap stores experienced a stunning 24 percent gain in same-store sales during May 1998 alone, which *USA Today* credited to the "Khakis" advertising. Year-end figures for 1998 revealed that Gap had increased its sales nearly 40 percent during the year. The *San Francisco Chronicle* praised Gap's "high-energy advertising" for "fueling" this rapid growth.

FURTHER READING

Berkowitz, Harry. "Marketers' Dilemma: What Gets Teens To Buy?" *Long Island (N.Y.) Newsday,* January 24, 1999. Detailed discussion of the teenage market that "Gap Khakis" attempted to reach.

Berner, Robert. "Gap Launches TV-Ad Campaign to Boost Sales At Its Retail Stores." *Wall Street Journal,* April 28, 1997.

Carter, Kelly. "In the Swing." *Quincy (Mass.) Patriot Ledger,* October 12, 1998.

Cox, Ted. "The Gap's 'Khakis Rock' Ad a Jivin' Blend of Past and Present." *Arlington Heights (Ill.) Daily Herald,* June 15, 1998.

Cuneo, Alice. "Dockers Aims to Equal Jeans Sales: Levi Strauss Sets $50 Million Campaign Seeking Younger Buyers for Brand." *Advertising Age,* March 9, 1998. Descsribes Dockers advertising campaign.

Cuneo, Alice."Dockers Takes A Sexier Approach in New Ad Push." *Advertising Age,* January 18, 1999.

Dodd, Annmarie. "Dockers Bringing Khaki Message to Urban Areas." *Daily News Record,* June 3, 1998.

Dodd, Annmarie. "In Today's Bottoms Business, Comfort is Spelled K-H-A-K-I-S." *Daily News Record,* May 25, 1998.

Emert, Carol. "Gap Sizzles." *San Francisco Chronicle,* April 26,1999.

Enrico, Dottie. "Viewers Find Gap Ads Toe-Tapping Good." *USA Today,* June 8,1998.

Givhan, Robin. "Rhapsody in Beige." *Washington Post,* June 7, 1998.

Gladfelter, Elizabeth. "A Consultant Says that Gen X, Gen Y and Boomers Have Starkly Different Charactersitics, and Marketers Should Proceed with Caution." *Daily News Record,* November 9, 1998. Compares and contrasts the different demographic segments "Gap Khakis" ads targeted.

Grant, Lorrie. "Retailers Report Strong Sales Gains in May." *USA Today,* June 5, 1998. Describes rising sales in the wake of the "Gap Khakis" campaign.

Grogan, Leigh. "Gap Fills in Void of Television Advertising with Some Real Toe-Tappers." *Sacramento Bee,* May 20, 1998.

Haber, Holly (with Sharon Edelson). "Retail Ads: Upping the Ante." *Women's Wear Daily,* May 15, 1998.

McCollum, Charlie. "Khakis Taking Jeans' Place as Wardrobe Staples." *Newark (N.J.) Star-Ledger,* June 8, 1998.

———. "Oscar Ceremony Becomes Advertising Event." *San Jose Mercury News,* March 22, 1999.

Munk, Nina (with Michelle McGowan). "Gap Gets It: Mickey Drexler is Turning His Apparel Chain into a Global Brand." *Fortune,* August 3, 1998. Outlines Gap's history and marketing strategies.

Patterson, Philana. "Gap Shares Hit 52-Week High After 'Blow-Out' May Sales Report." *Wall Street Journal,* June 5, 1998.

Smith, Sid. "Nice Pants." *Chicago Tribune,* June 4, 1999.

Rebecca Stanfel

THIS IS EASY CAMPAIGN

OVERVIEW

Gap, Inc. was established in 1969 with the purpose of selling one product: Levi's jeans. In 1991 Gap cut its ties with the Levi's brand and limited its merchandise offerings to Gap's private-label brand of jeans, khakis, and colorful one-pocket T-shirts, which had been introduced beginning in 1974. Despite the company's profit and sales growth through 1991, sales went into a slump in 1993 and 1994, increasing just 1 percent each year. The chain reported no sales growth in 1995. As the downward slide continued, Gap began looking for ways to expedite a turnaround. Part of the strategy included opening more than 200 new stores in 1996, and in 1997 its in-house marketing team created a new brand-building campaign titled "This Is Easy."

Gap's $15 million "This Is Easy" television campaign was introduced in April 1997 to promote the company's line of Easy Fit Jeans. Although a few Gap commercials appeared on television during the early 1990s, the "This Is Easy" campaign marked the company's first significant journey into television advertising since the mid-1980s, when the Gap opted to put its marketing efforts into print advertising. The spots were intended to renew enthusiasm and boost sales at Gap stores, which in 1996 showed the poorest sales performance of the three Gap Inc. divisions—Gap, Old Navy Clothing, and Banana Republic. Gap was also responding to the highly competitive market for denim jeans by reasserting its strong brand image.

The renewed foray into television and increased spending on advertising helped Gap achieved its goal of growing sales and boosting its brand image. Following the campaign's launch in 1997, sales increased 23 percent from the previous year. *BusinessWeek* listed Gap 17th on its 1998 list of best-performing companies, and the chain announced plans to open 300 new stores that year. Also in 1998, Gap began a new global marketing campaign that was a modified version of its "This Is Easy" campaign.

HISTORICAL CONTEXT

The Gap skated along relatively smoothly after its inception in 1969 until the mid-1990s, when management realized that other retail companies were imitating its store design and products, essentially relegating the Gap to being just another retailer. The stacks of jeans, khaki pants, and multicolored one-pocket T-shirts that could be purchased at every Gap turned up in other stores, often at lower prices. Sales figures reflected this turn of events. *BusinessWeek* reported that, although profits at stores that had been open for more than a year had grown an average of 12 percent from 1986 to 1991, earnings skidded in the mid-1990s. Sales grew a mere 1 percent in both 1993 and 1994, and there was no growth in 1995. Donald Fisher, Gap founder and chairman, confessed to *BusinessWeek,* "We were looking at ourselves as a store rather than a brand. When you do that, you draw thick, heavy lines around your freedom."

Marketing strategies were shifted, and the company's upper management made efforts to solidify Gap's brand image. Millard "Mickey" Drexler, Gap's president and CEO, studied companies with strong brand presence, such as Coca-Cola, McDonald's, and Nike, and concluded that Gap should follow in their footsteps. According to *BusinessWeek,* Drexler discovered that "the first thing that hits you is that you can buy [such highly branded products] in a lot more places than you can buy Gap." The company, therefore, opened 203 new stores in 1996 alone. Drexler also introduced new products, such as nail polish and perfume, and he decided to invest more time and money in advertising. Drexler told *Advertising Age* that, in addition to building the brand, "We also realized we had to expand what advertising and marketing mean to this company." The Gap, reported *BusinessWeek,* increased its advertising budget and spent an estimated $90 million in 1996, compared to $64 million in 1995, and comparable store sales (sales at stores open for more than a year) jumped from being flat in 1995 to a 5 percent increase in 1996.

TARGET MARKET

The Gap's appeal had spanned generations, and thus its target market was also wide-ranging. When the company opened its first store in 1969 and sold Levi's jeans, it appealed largely to the youth market, consumers between the ages of 15 and 25. The Gap attempted to expand its core consumer group in the 1970s by adding additional clothing items and active wear, but for the most part its popularity through the 1980s remained with teenagers and the youth market. In the 1990s, however, Gap began to open more stores and offer new products to expand its consumer base.

The Gap customer, regardless of age, appreciated comfortable, simple clothes and went to the Gap for its ease of shopping and inventory of classic styles. In a conversation with *MSNBC Business Video,* Warren Hashagen, Gap's senior vice president and chief financial officer, explained the diversity of its consumers: "[The Gap] is certainly a company that likes to think of itself as relevant to the youth of America as well as people of all ages." Through its merchandise the company "give[s] a consistent message to the customer how easy it is to take clothes from our store and mix with their own wardrobe for their own style." June Beckstead, Gap's vice president of product design for the women's division, asserted that

Gap clothes appealed to the full spectrum of consumers. She told the *Wall Street Journal,* "We dress America. . . . You walk down the street, and you see people wearing our clothes. They're young and old, they're hip and they're not."

For the "This Is Easy" campaign the Gap chose to hone in on the target market that consisted of younger men, including teenage boys. The men's line had not performed as well as the other divisions, and Gap wanted to lure back male customers. Alice Ruth, an analyst at Montgomery Securities, told the *Wall Street Journal* that the men's clothing line had suffered because it had gotten a bit too trendy and because the Gap had deviated from its reputation as a store that offered wardrobe basics such as jeans, khaki pants, and solid-colored T-shirts. The Gap hoped to reassert its position in men's clothing by focusing again on the basics. In the *Wall Street Journal* McCadden explained the "This Is Easy" campaign's message to men: "Gap offers you all the pieces. No matter who you are there is something at the Gap for you."

COMPETITION

Because the Gap was a major retail clothing chain as well as a manufacturer of private-label clothes, it faced competition in virtually every corner. When asked during *Biz Buzz,* a business-oriented show on the cable network CNN, about the companies that provided competition, McCadden responded, "In the case of Gap, probably just about everyone. I mean we're [a] very large, very broad brand . . . I think how we view the brand and how we manage the personality and the message of the brand really isn't in relation to competitors." Hashagen, in an interview with *MSNBC Business Video,* agreed with McCadden and stated that the Gap provided a level of quality and service that set the company apart from its competitors. Hashagen noted, "there's always a tremendous amount of competition in retail. We think of our business as being a great value . . . The quality of the product, how long it will last, how well it works with your other wardrobe items or our store, the service level you get, how easy the store is to shop and all of that is meant to give a good value overall."

Regardless of whether Gap stores possessed a competitive edge over other retail and private-label companies in terms of value and brand identity, the lack of sales growth in the early 1990s indicated that the company needed to adopt new strategies to boost profits. Competition from stores that imitated Gap's core products and display styles prompted the company to strengthen its brand identity and provide a constant flow of new products. In fact, approximately every six weeks Gap stores introduced and rotated styles. Robyn Waters, the trend director for Dayton Hudson's Target Stores, told the *Wall Street Journal,* "If there is anything we emulate it's [Gap's] great core product and the constant flow of newness and fresh product all the time."

According to figures from the market-research specialists NPD Group, published in the *San Francisco Examiner,* the jeans industry exploded in the 1990s, hitting $8.7 billion in sales in 1996 alone. This reflected a 10 percent increase over sales in 1995. Beverly Butler, a spokesperson for Gap, said, "It's a really crowded market and getting more so." Designer labels such as Tommy Hilfiger and Nautica entered the jeans market, and private-label jeans by Sears and J.C. Penney grew in popularity. *BusinessWeek* published data compiled by NPD Group that indicated a considerable increase in the market shares of private-label jeans, from 16 percent in 1990 to 25 percent in 1997. The Gap, as the largest manufacturer of private-label jeans, held some of this valuable market, but as flat earnings demonstrated, it needed more.

A NEW COMPETITOR

When the Gap first opened its doors in San Francisco, its competitive edge came from the bell-bottom Levi's it offered for sale. When in 1991 the Gap stopped selling Levi's jeans to focus exclusively on its own label, it bid farewell to an ally and said hello to a new competitor.

MARKETING STRATEGY

The Gap's brand-building "This Is Easy" campaign debuted on prime-time television on April 27, 1997. In the initial two-week period the first six spots were aired nationally more than 600 times on the major networks and also on cable channels, including MTV, ESPN, and Comedy Central. As McCadden explained to the *Los Angeles Times,* "That whole campaign of easy-fit jeans really springs off a 28-year history at Gap of personal style . . . What we're doing right now is simply taking what's been a core equity and carrying it to new mediums." The resurrection of the "Fall into the Gap" theme and jingle served both a nostalgic and marketing purpose. McCadden elaborated, "It subtly says to someone, 'This brand has a great history. You've trusted this brand for a long time.' " Jeans were selected as the Gap product that best represented the brand image.

The decision to return to national television advertising in full force after a hiatus of nearly a dozen years was necessary to achieve the ubiquity of a well-known brand. As Drexler related to *Advertising Age,* "TV was critical for us... You can't consider yourself a serious marketer without, in fact, having a major presence in TV long-term." Hank Wilson, a consumer-goods analyst for Hambrect & Quist, voiced his agreement in the *Los Angeles Times* when he stated, "The Gap is of a size and scale where traditional television advertising can yield the kinds of awareness improvement that they would probably like to see."

The "This Is Easy" television spots featured jeans-clad celebrities singing, playing musical instruments, dancing, or performing other artistic specialties they considered to be easy. The Gap's choices of celebrities were designed to attract as wide a range of viewers and consumers as possible. Younger stars drew in the youth market, while older celebrities were chosen to appeal to a more mature crowd. Each spot was filmed against a stark white backdrop to evoke the Gap's simple and easy style and ended with the Gap logo and the tagline "Easy Fit Jeans."

The first spot starred rapper and actor LL Cool J. Outfitted in Gap jeans and T-shirt, LL Cool J offered his take on what he considered to be "easy." McCadden explained the concept of including celebrities in the television spots in his conversation on CNN's *Biz Buzz* when he said, "The whole idea of that campaign is about personal style, and what we do is we invite the stars to come, and the first 20 seconds is about them. It's what's easy for them. They wear our easy fit jeans. LL arrived on the set and had actually written that entire rap himself about the Gap." The pervading theme of what is easy also conveyed the message that Gap provided ease in shopping, especially for males. McCadden told the *Los Angeles Times,* "The message is that we've figured it out for you. We're going to make this as easy as it can be."

LL Cool J's rap started with "I know you like your outfits stylish. Any other line but the Gap is childish. Everybody working there's a personal stylist. You're fallin' once you hear the Gap callin'," and it included "'G' is for gritty, 'A' is for always, 'P' is for power and the people." To conclude the 30-second spot, LL Cool J stated, "How easy is this? Fall into the Gap," and he then threw a kiss to viewers. Although the spots promoted Gap's Easy Fit Jeans, the company and product being pushed were not revealed until the end of the ads, when the tagline and Gap logo appeared.

"This Is Easy" included four additional television spot during the initial campaign launch. Two spots featured actors Lukas Haas and David Arquette, with Haas playing the keyboard while Arquette accompanied on the trumpet. Arquette ended by stating, "This is definitely easy," and the "Fall into the Gap" theme was heard. Rounding out the ads were two spots with actor Eric Mabius, who beat on conga drums and concluded, "This is really easy."

At the beginning of July 1997 the company initiated a radio campaign and introduced several new television spots. The two radio spots featured LL Cool J and the musicians Junior and Tanya Rae Brown and ran in major markets that included Los Angeles, San Francisco, Chicago, New York, and Boston. One of the new television spots showed ballet star Nikolaj Hubbe dancing in jeans and sneakers, with jazz piano music in the background. Hubbe announced, "This is super easy," and he finished by performing pirouettes to the "Fall into the Gap" theme. The Hubbe spot debuted in United Artists Cinemas, where it ran for a month before moving to television. The other new spots featured actors Peter Berg and William H. Macy and country music stars Junior and Tanya Rae Brown. Macy, who appeared in the motion picture *Fargo,* played a harmonica, and Berg, star of the television show *Chicago Hope,* strummed an electric guitar. Junior Brown performed on his "guit-steel," a guitar and slide steel combination he created, while his wife played a guitar. Brown surmised, "This is totally easy," and the spot closed with the signature theme.

The Gap continued its tradition of using the print medium and invested heavily in outdoor advertising. The company also used its stores as an advertising venue, putting approximately 170,000 posters in its windows. Billboards displayed the Gap ads, and enormous outdoor signs known as spectaculars, which were large enough to cover the entire side of an office building, appeared in major cities. McCadden, in his discussion on *Biz Buzz,* explained, "The whole idea behind them is to really present Gap jeans in a different format... [W]e like the idea of the walls because they just present it to the consumer in sort of a new... light. And they're also—you know, they're larger than life."

In 1998 the campaign was revised and a new series of commercials was released to promote another of Gap's jeans styles: Original Fit Jeans. The new campaign included television spots and prints ads that followed a format similar to that of the "This Is Easy" effort. No specific budget for the campaign was released, but a company spokeswoman told *Women's Wear Daily* that it was Gap's "biggest campaign to date." The four 30-second television spots, which were released in July, featured music stars from various genres, from blues and jazz to hip-hop and rap. Appearing in the spots were blues guitarist Kenny Wayne

Shepherd, singer and rapper Missy Elliott, legendary trumpeter Herb Alpert, and hip-hop group Run-DMC. In a press release Gap described the campaign as a "tribute to originality." Each spot included the chain's familiar white background and the theme "Fall into the Gap." The print ads showed models dressed in Gap's Original Fit Jeans. Ads ran in consumer magazines such as *Vanity Fair, Vogue,* and *Rolling Stone* beginning in August. The campaign also included billboards displayed in 24 cities worldwide that featured models wearing Gap Original Fit Jeans.

OUTCOME

The return to television and the increase in spending paid off for Gap. According to *BusinessWeek,* Gap's 1997 sales increased 23 percent from 1996, and the company ranked 17th on *BusinessWeek*'s 1998 list of best performers. Industry executives applauded the Gap's marketing efforts and brand-building campaign, and it became the company to emulate. Alan Millstein, a retail analyst and publisher of *Fashion Network Report,* told *Advertising Age,* "They made their name into a brand... They are one of the few retailers that has that luxury." Sergio Zyman, senior vice president and chief marketing officer at Coca-Cola, agreed: "The Gap accelerated to the point that the brand is on fire... There is no competitor who has a kind of brand essence that can pose a threat."

The Gap showed no signs of slowing down. The company announced plans to open 300 new Gap stores in 1998, and by May 1998 the company operated more than 1,000 Gap stores, up 15 percent from the previous year. Hashagen told *MSNBC Business Video,* "I think if you have a good store, a destination people want to shop at, you can have quite a few of them." The Gap appeared poised to become ubiquitous. According to *Stores,* Fisher believed that there was plenty of room for more Gap stores: "When you look at the total number of dollars spent on our kind of apparel, we're a small market share player. I think Wal-Mart does $30 billion and they continue to grow, so I have every reason to believe that we will continue to grow as well."

While the 1997 and 1998 marketing campaigns and store-expansion efforts seemed to pay off with increased sales and praise from industry insiders, trouble was looming on the horizon for Gap, and it was coming from its sister chain Old Navy. In 1999 Gap was reporting that sales were flat or down compared to the previous year, versus Old Navy, which had increases of 20 percent. Old Navy, with its bargain-basement prices on products that were similar to those that Gap was selling, was winning away Gap's customers. Gap's clever advertisements with music stars that crossed generations were beginning to have a negative effect as well. Analysts complained that Gap lacked focus. Bob Buchanan, an analyst with A.G. Edwards, told *BusinessWeek,* "I've got a problem when I see Gap trying to appeal to people age 12 to 60." In late 1999 Gap announced plans for a new marketing campaign to kick off the 2000 spring season. It shifted its focus from jeans and basic khakis and tees to its fashion-forward sportswear in bright colors. Also in a change from its 1997 and 1998 efforts, the new campaign had no tagline.

FURTHER READING

Becker, Ingrid. "Gap Tries to Refashion Image for a Better Fit." *Los Angeles Times,* October 2, 1997, p. D5.

Berner, Robert. "Gap Launches Television-Ad Campaign to Boost Sales at Its Gap-Store Division." *Wall Street Journal,* April 28, 1997, p. B8.

———. "How Gap's Own Design Shop Keeps Its Imitators Hustling." *Wall Street Journal,* March 13, 1997.

Byrnes, Nanette, Amy Barrett, Steve Hamm, Andy Reinhardt, and Gary McWilliams. "The Business Week Fifty." *BusinessWeek,* March 30, 1998, pp. 76–85.

Callebs, Sean. "Vice President in Charge of Marketing for the Gap Discusses Marketing." *Biz Buzz (CNNfn),* August 7, 1997.

Cuneo, Alice Z.. "Gap Returns to TV in $15 Mil Campaign." *Advertising Age,* April 28, 1997, pp. 1f.

———. "Gap TV Spots Take Jeans beyond the Blues; Maverick Musicians Tune in to Original Fit Jeans." *PR Newswire,* July 17, 1998.

———."Marketer of the Year: The Gap." *Advertising Age,* December 15, 1997.

Himelstein, Linda. "The World according to Gap." *BusinessWeek,* January 27, 1997.

Lee, Louise. "People: Trend Spotters: Why Gap Isn't Galloping Anymore." *BusinessWeek,* November 8, 1999, 1997.

Lockwood, Lisa. "Gap Ads Will Sing Blues to Sell Jeans in Major Campaign." *Daily News Record,* July 20, 1998.

Neuborne, Ellen, and Stephanie Anderson Forest. "Look Who's Picking Levi's Pocket." *BusinessWeek,* September 8, 1997, p. 68.

Reda, Susan. "Donald G. Fisher, Chairman of The Gap Inc." *Stores,* 1997.

Sundius, Ann. "One on One Interview with Warren Hashagen, Chief Financial Officer and Senior Vice President, Gap Inc. (GPS)." *MSNBC Business Video,* September 26, 1997.

Tanaka, Wendy. "Denim Derby." *San Francisco Examiner,* May 20, 1997, p. C1.

Mariko Fujinaka
Rayna Bailey

Gateway, Inc.

7565 Irvine Center Drive
Irvine, California 92618
USA
Telephone: (949) 471-7000
Fax: (949) 471-7041
Web site: www.gateway.com

PEOPLE RULE CAMPAIGN

OVERVIEW

In August 2000, in the midst of a collapse of the global personal-computer market, direct marketer Gateway, Inc., launched the "People Rule" branding campaign. Developed by New York advertising agency McCann-Erickson Worldwide, the campaign was built on the premise that average consumers were not getting the most out of their computers and would welcome more support from a PC maker.

"People Rule" extended beyond television, radio, and prints advertising. It also included free help at Gateway Country stores in the form of weekly "Ask-a-Tech" sessions and clinics that taught the rudiments of computers and the Internet. The advertising portion of the campaign also included the company's first use of a celebrity spokesperson: actor Michael J. Fox.

The $150 million campaign petered out in 2001, as Gateway underwent changes in the top ranks of its management and as McCann-Erickson was dismissed as the company's ad agency. The campaign was disjointed from the start; all along McCann-Erickson was second-guessed by Gateway's founder, who, in the middle of the campaign, brought in a documentary filmmaker to create a pair of television spots that clashed with the style of the ads the agency had developed. "People Rule" did little to prevent Gateway from losing a major slice of the market, and economic conditions were such that, in all likelihood, it had been a doomed effort from the start, no matter how effective individual parts of the campaign may have been.

HISTORICAL CONTEXT

In only a handful of years, Gateway, Inc., founded in 1985, grew from a $10,000 startup in Sioux City, Iowa, into one of the leading direct retailers of personal computers in the world, with annual sales approaching $10 billion. From the time it began advertising, Gateway took a folksy approach and played off its rural roots, featuring pictures of cows and even shipping its products in white boxes adorned with black spots resembling the markings of a Holstein cow. The company developed an in-house marketing team in the early 1990s but in 1997 hired an advertising agency, D'Arcy Masius Benton & Bowles. Gateway's young founder, Ted Waitt, brought in an AT&T veteran, Jeffrey Weitzen, to run the company in January 1998, and one of Weitzen's first moves was to change ad agencies. He hired McCann-Erickson Worldwide, with whom he had worked closely while at AT&T.

Business was booming for Gateway when McCann-Erickson took over the account, but the relationship with the client soon began to sour. In 1999 McCann-Erickson won Microsoft's huge advertising account, after which Gateway officials became increasingly dissatisfied with McCann's level of service. More importantly, in 2000 the global PC industry was hit by the worst slump in its brief history. Because Gateway relied greatly on the consumer and small-business markets, the hardest-hit sectors, it began to see a serious erosion in sales. Although revenues reached a record $9.2 billion in 2000, Gateway's sales tailed off severely during the course of the year. Weitzen was under great pressure from Waitt to stop the bleeding, as was McCann-Erickson, Weitzen's hand-picked ad agency, which Waitt also criticized, considering its approach "more corny than folksy," as reported by Aaron Baar and Kathleen Sampey of *Adweek*. It was under these difficult circumstances that McCann-Erickson launched its "People Rule" campaign in August 2000.

TARGET MARKET

Earlier in 2000 Gateway had employed the "Gateway@work" campaign, which targeted medium-size businesses to boost sales in that market. The "People Rule" campaign focused on the other key sector, consumer sales. The company commissioned research that revealed that there was "a disconnect between people and technology," as Brad Heimdichner, one of Gateway's "technology ambassadors," told Lyn Berry of the *Denver Business Journal*. According to Berry, a random sampling of 750 Americans showed that "69 percent of people who own personal computers believe they are not maximizing the potential of their personal computers. Only 32 percent said they even know the full potential of their computer." The survey also revealed that 44 percent did not believe they had enough training on how to use their computers and did not have enough available technical support. Furthermore, just 15 percent believed that their computers delivered everything their manufacturers had promised. It was these dissatisfied, less technologically knowledgeable consumers that the "People Rule" campaign hoped to reach. As Heimdichner explained, "It's Gateway's promise to always put people before technology, and that's why we're focusing more than ever on helping people understand their technology."

COMPETITION

As the "People Rule" campaign broke in 2000, Gateway faced competition in the commercial market—in which Gateway ranked fifth at the time—from another direct marketer, Dell, as well as from IBM, Hewlett-Packard, and Compaq Computer Corp. About 70 percent of Dell's sales came from large corporations and government organizations, but it had begun to commit greater resources to competing in the home-PC market, Gateway's strength.

HAVING A COW

The association of Gateway, Inc., with cows—they appeared in its advertisements and were evoked by the black Holstein spots on its white shipping boxes—was a reflection of the company's roots. Founder Ted Waitt learned the computer business while working for nine months at a computer store in Des Moines, Iowa. Confident that he knew enough to start his own business selling computers, he borrowed $10,000 from his grandmother in 1985 and set up a mail-order operation in a farmhouse at his father's sagging cattle brokerage in Sioux City, Iowa. After the business outgrew the farmhouse, Waitt moved it to Sioux City's Livestock Exchange building. Gateway started advertising in computer magazines in 1988. Given the company's connection to livestock, it was not surprising that the first full-page ad featured a picture of his father's cattle herd. Thus, a motif was born.

Gateway ranked third in the global consumer-PC area with a 13.9 percent market share, trailing top-ranked Compaq and the number two company, Hewlett-Packard. But it was Dell that emerged as Gateway's greatest threat in this market. Dell had perfected a build-to-order model that kept down costs by not keeping hardware stockpiled, and with its size came buying power that allowed it to offer PCs at low prices that Gateway and the others were unable to match. Moreover, a seemingly unlimited marketing budget allowed Dell to promote its affordable PCs around the clock on television and through other media. Ironically, it was a similar strategy of building affordable computers that had made Gateway an overnight success in the late 1980s, when Waitt found a way to assemble off-the-shelf components to make a computer that offered customers a better value than the competition. Gateway might have been able to undercut some of its other rivals in price, but it could not come close to matching Dell, which, at the time the "People Rule" campaign began, was starting a price war that crippled the competition. Dell quickly assumed the top spot in global PC sales, while Hewlett-Packard and Compaq joined forces through a merger and Gateway struggled to hang onto market share.

MARKETING STRATEGY

Gateway's "People Rule" campaign was part advertising campaign, part educational program. The company leveraged its chain of 290 Gateway Country stores to offer a range of programs, a number of them free, to demystify technology for both consumers and businesses and to help them get the most out of their computers. Full-time computer experts, called "technology ambassadors," were hired for the stores, which hosted weekly "Ask-a-Tech" sessions at which consumers could get free advice and have their computer problems analyzed. The ambassadors also held free mobile clinics and conducted outreach programs with local community groups. Free weekly clinics at the stores taught PC users—whether or not they were Gateway customers—a wide range of subjects, including PC and Internet basics, online investing, and the elements of digital photography and digital music. Gateway also increased the number of classroom and online training sessions it offered. The company's Web presence was beefed up with the introduction of a "supportal," a website intended to augment the technical support Gateway made available to its customers over the phone.

The $150 million "People Rule" campaign included television, print, and radio elements. Because it was in essence part of a long-term positioning of the Gateway brand, the advertising portion of "People Rule" focused on the brand more than on specific products. In the words of a press release announcing the launch of the campaign, the goal was to expand "the definition of 'Gateway Country' from the name of its revolutionary retail concept to a more human way to approach technology."

The first of four television spots McCann-Erickson developed showed a typical living room with a PC sitting unused, ignored by family members; two girls played while a father opened bills. A voice-over described the many uses of a computer but stated that none of them mattered if a person was not shown how to use it. Viewers were then urged to call or visit a Gateway Country store for help in unlocking the power of their PCs. In another of the early television spots a boy traded in his computer for a new one and then tried to trade in his little sister for a scanner. An ad called "Apartment," which debuted later in 2000, was especially well received. It featured a young woman entering her date's apartment and being surprised to see a series of framed pictures in which he posed with an odd assortment of celebrities: boxer Evander Holyfield, rock singer David Lee Roth, actress Marilyn Monroe, and Lassie, the canine star of TV and film. A voice-over posed the rhetorical question, "Wish you could add a little something to your photographs?" Viewers were then told that Gateway would help teach them all about digital photography. The television spots appeared on network television and national cable channels as well as on local television on a spot-market basis (as time slots opened up at attractive prices at the last minute).

To accompany the initial TV spot, a two-page print ad on the same subject appeared in a number of national and local newspapers. Further print ads were employed throughout the campaign. One of them incited the ire of Maryland's state comptroller, however. A Gateway ad that ran in the *Baltimore Sun* on September 12, 2000, read, "Buy one now and we'll pay the sales tax." But "sales tax" was crossed out, ostensibly by a Gateway lawyer who in a handwritten note commented, "Can't say this! Must say 'we'll offer a discount equal to the sales tax rate.'" It was intended to poke fun at the legal maneuvers in advertising but did not amuse the comptroller, who charged the ad was misleading and violated Maryland's tax code prohibiting "tax sales." He instructed his compliance division to force Gateway to drop the ad or change it.

The run-in with the state of Maryland was just one of a number of distractions McCann-Erickson faced as it launched the "People Rule" campaign. In late October Gateway, at the insistence of Waitt, circumvented the agency and began running a pair of commercials produced by documentary filmmaker Henry Corra, whose low-key, no-frills work included *George,* a film about his autistic son. Corra and Waitt had become friends in the mid-1990s, and the filmmaker had done some work for Gateway shortly before McCann-Erickson took over the account. Corra's two new commercials were at odds with McCann-Erickson's work. According to Stuart Elliott of the *New York Times,* Corra's spots, "which are fast-paced and mix footage of actual shoppers shot in black-and-white as well as color, contrast markedly with McCann's, which are shot conventionally and feature actors." McCann-Erickson was initially diplomatic about the situation, stating, through spokesman Stewart Alter, "The 'people rule' brand platform is a big one and it can accommodate a documentary approach." But Elliott reported that a few months later, after McCann-Erickson and Gateway had parted ways, agency heads called Corra a "behind-the scenes thorn in our sides" and accused him of trying to "undermine the agency in many ways." For his part, Corra commented, "I don't think McCann understood what I did."

The relationship between McCann-Erickson and Gateway was clearly falling apart in the final weeks of 2000. At the same time, with the severe drop-off in sales during the fourth quarter of the year, Weitzen's tenure as Gateway's head was coming to an end. *Adweek* reported in December 2000 that Gateway was talking with East Coast ad agencies. When Waitt dismissed Weitzen and reassumed the CEO post in January 2001, McCann-Erickson's prospects of keeping the Gateway account dimmed further. The agency made one last stab at saving the "People Rule" campaign. Actor Michael J. Fox was hired as Gateway's first celebrity spokesman. In recent months he had been diagnosed with Parkinson's disease and had established a foundation dedicated to find a cure for it. As part of the Fox advertising Gateway became the technology partner for the foundation. The premise of the new humorous television spots featuring Fox was that he was just like the target audience, overcoming technology challenges. Two weeks after the Fox portion of the campaign debuted, the McCann-Erickson ads were scrapped as Gateway dropped the agency.

OUTCOME

Early in 2001 Gateway was on the verge of hiring Minneapolis-based agency Fallon to replace McCann-Erickson, but Fallon too ran afoul of Waitt after it proposed a complete rebranding of Gateway. The company decided to handle its advertising in-house once again, trying its best to make use of Fox's celebrity. But he proved ill suited to the task. As Frank Priscaro noted in *MC Technology Marketing Intelligences,* "One of the most important rules of using a spokesperson is to pick someone who tied in with the product in some way. Pretending that Mr. Fox is going through the rigors of buying a new computer himself doesn't wash . . . Barring an obvious tie-in, a spokesperson should be famous, but not too famous, so he doesn't steal the show. It's nice that Mr. Fox would do these commercials, but he's a lot bigger than Gateway is, and so he overshadows the campaign."

Aside from the problems that cropped up during the "People Rule" campaign, the effort appeared to have been ill fated from the start. No one questioned that consumers wanted help in getting the most out of their computers, but when it came time to buy a new PC, they generally opted to get the most features for the lowest price—a lesson Gateway itself had taught the market. At the time, Gateway simply could not match Dell in terms of price, and no amount of in-store tech sessions, art-house commercials, or celebrity endorsements could stem the tide of eroding sales.

FURTHER READING

Baar, Aaron, and Kathleen Sampey. "Creative, Connections Help Fallon Gain Gateway." *Adweek,* February 12, 2001, p. 2.

Berry, Lyn. "Most Computer Users Fail to Maximize PC Potential." *Denver Business Journal,* September 1, 2000, p. 10A.

Elkin, Tobi. "Troubled Gateway Turns to New Shop as Earnings Fall." *Advertising Age,* February 12, 2001, p. 4.

Elliott, Stuart. "A Computer Company Again Asks a Filmmaker for a Fresh Creative Slant." *New York Times,* October 30, 2000, p. C18.

Hachman, Mark. "'People Rule' Shows Who's Minding Shop at Gateway." *TechWeb,* September 2, 2000.

Kady, Martin, II, Chris Silva, Mike Sunnicks, Suzanne White, and Owen T. Davis. "Gateway's Taxing Predicament." *Washington Business Journal,* September 15, 2000, p. 2.

Linnett, Richard. "Regarding Henry." *Advertising Age,* March 26, 2001, p. 1.

Linnett, Richard, and Tobi Elkin. "Gateway Ads Set to Return to House Unit." *Advertising Age,* February 26, 2001, p. 1.

Mallorre, Dill. "Power to the People." *Adweek* (eastern ed.), September 4, 2000, p. 32.

Piven, Joshua. "Is Shakeout Looming for PC OEMs?" *Computing Technology Review,* February 2001, p. 6.

Priscaro, Frank. "Peer Review: Tear Sheet." *MC Technology Marketing Intelligences,* April 2001, p. 48.

Rodrigues, Tanya. "Adweek Names Gateway, Jack in the Box Ads among 50 Top Spots." *San Diego Business Journal,* February 12, 2001, p. 22.

Sampey, Kathleen, and David Gianatasio. "Gateway Meets Quietly with a Handful of Agencies." *Adweek,* December 18, 2000, p. 3.

Stamler, Bernard. "Gateway Splits with McCann-Erickson." *New York Times,* February 8, 2001, p. C6.

Ed Dinger

GEICO

One GEICO Plaza
Washington, DC 20076
USA
Telephone: (301) 986-3000
Web site: www.geico.com

■■■

GECKO CAMPAIGN

OVERVIEW

Relatively obscure until the 1990s, GEICO, a direct marketer of auto insurance, began to make its mark when it expanded beyond direct-mail solicitation and spent money on other media, especially television. Unlike rival insurers, GEICO took a lighthearted, humorous approach to its television spots, which produced steady growth for the company. Nevertheless, many consumers were still not certain about the pronunciation of the company's name, often referring to it as "gecko" when calling for a rate quote. In the summer of 1999 GEICO aired a 15-second television spot that featured a cartoon gecko, a tropical lizard, conducting a press conference to tell people that it was not he but GEICO that could save them money on their car insurance and to please stop calling him.

The gecko spot was just a single quirky commercial and was not intended as the start of a long-term campaign. But in reaction to an actors' strike, GEICO instructed its advertising agency, the Martin Agency of Richmond, Virginia, to develop more gecko spots. The character became popular, and GEICO added more human features to him and created a new series of commercials featuring the gecko. In 2002, in a spot titled "The Meadow," he ran through a field hand in hand with an adoring female customer. In "Big News," a spot that aired in 2005, he urged fellow lizards to spread the news that GEICO could save people money. In the meantime GEICO released two other campaigns that ran alongside the "Gecko" campaign, which had become a general brand-building effort for the company but still received a hefty share of the more than $200 million that GEICO spent on advertising each year.

Although it never garnered any major advertising awards, the "Gecko" campaign proved popular with consumers and played a major role in GEICO's emergence as one of the leading auto insurers in the United States. In 2005, during New York's Advertising Week, an annual industry event hosted by the American Association of Advertising Agencies, the gecko was named one of advertising's top icons.

HISTORICAL CONTEXT

For 60 years, starting in the 1930s, GEICO was a relatively unknown automobile insurer that targeted federal government employees and noncommissioned military officers with its direct-mail pitches. By concentrating on customers with sterling driving records, it was able to offer low rates and carve out a profitable niche in the marketplace. In the 1990s GEICO, by then the seventh-largest auto insurer in the United States, looked to expand its client base. In 1994 it hired the Martin Agency to handle its advertising and add television, radio, and print to the marketing mix. The public company soon came into the orbit of Berkshire Hathaway, Inc., controlled by legendary stock-market investor Warren Buffett, who had owned GEICO stock since 1951. He took GEICO private in 1996 and made it a Hathaway subsidiary.

Commercials for car insurance were traditionally straightforward, serious appeals. To make GEICO stand out and to humanize car insurance, Martin decided to rely on humor. It also developed a brand promise in a slogan that would be reinforced campaign after campaign: "Fifteen minutes could save you 15 percent or more on car insurance." Inherent in the promise was another key element in the marketing strategy: a call to action. Because GEICO insurance was not sold to brokers, customers had to be moved to mail in a response, call a toll-free phone number, or, with the advent of the Internet, visit the company's website. To assure that GEICO was to customers more than a computer screen or a voice on the telephone, the agency also had to put a face on GEICO itself.

The new advertising emphasis quickly produced solid results for GEICO. The company had been writing approximately 26,000 premiums a year, but that number improved to 39,570 in 1995 and to 69,600 in 1996. When Buffett took control, GEICO was told to accelerate the pace of its growth strategy even more. Hence, ad spending increased from $10 million in 1995 to $270 million in 2000. With a great deal of money at its disposal and significant creative latitude, the Martin Agency produced a variety of humorous ads. In 1999 the creative team at Martin considered the common mispronunciation of GEICO as "gecko," the small tropical lizard. This brainstorming session led to a single 15-second television spot, which gave birth to an advertising icon and initiated a long-term campaign for GEICO.

TARGET MARKET

GEICO and other automobile insurers tried to reach one of the broadest markets possible: virtually everyone who drove a car. "Who is GEICO selling to?" asked Seth Stevenson, writing for the online magazine *Slate.* "Pretty much everyone—man or woman, gay or straight, black or white, hip or hick. If you drive a car, they want your business." Because older drivers tended to stick with their longtime insurers, GEICO hoped to appeal to a younger audience, roughly 25 to 40 years of age. GEICO vice president of marketing Edward Ward told *USA Today* 's Michael McCarthy in 2005, "We have a lot of information that [says] those are the people who shop. We want to fish where the fish are biting."

COMPETITION

GEICO had to contend with well-entrenched competition. King of the hill since the 1940s was State Farm, which controlled nearly a fifth of the market. It had spent considerable sums to establish its own brand promise, one that did not rely on price: "Like a good neighbor, State Farm is there." Second to State Farm was Allstate, with a share of more than 10 percent. It also had a well-known slogan: "You're in good hands with Allstate." Less entrenched was the Progressive Corporation, which quickly stepped up its ad spending to fend off GEICO. Progressive also focused on price, making its mark through the use of the Internet and the promise to present its best quote alongside those of its chief competitors.

The heavy marketing activity of Progressive and GEICO forced Allstate to begin competing on the basis of price. While State Farm continued to remain above the fray in terms of pricing—stressing instead service and reliability—it felt enough pressure from the competition to increase its own advertising budget significantly. Furthermore, because of several factors, there were now greater profits to be made from car insurance, prompting insurers to scramble for more customers. One reason for the increased profits was that during the 1990s there were major improvements in the way cars were built, which resulted not only in fewer repairs but also fewer accidents. Also of importance was the graying of America: as baby boomers grew older, they began driving slower, again leading to fewer accidents, fewer claims, and greater profits for insurers. The fastest-growing segment of the auto insurance business was the direct model, as pursued by GEICO. In addition to State Farm, Allstate, Progressive, and other companies selling policies through agents—such as Travelers, Hartford, Nationwide, and AIG (American International Group)—GEICO had to deal with a new breed of direct marketers leveraging the power of the Internet. Another challenge was the fact that old-guard firms were beginning to use the Internet to add direct-sales capabilities to their offerings.

MARKETING STRATEGY

In July 1999 GEICO ran a television spot that featured a computer-generated cartoon gecko holding a press

WELL SPOKEN

Despite being a reptile, GEICO's gecko spokesperson was known for his distinguished British accent. Over the years a number of actors supplied his voice. The first was Kelsey Grammer, star of the hit TV situation comedy *Frasier.*

conference at which he declared, "I am a gecko, not GEICO. Please stop calling me." GEICO's Ward told Jim Lovel of *Adweek,* "It was a throwaway 15-second spot...It was an odd spot that didn't fit, but we thought it was funny." According to Lovel, "The gecko could have disappeared after the spot, if professional actors had not gone on strike that year. Because of the absence of talent, GEICO asked Martin to produce more spots with the gecko. The company was inundated with calls and letters from people who wanted to see more of the lizard."

The Martin Agency developed a number of television spots in 2000 in which the gecko, with his refined British accent, made the same point repeatedly: he could not save viewers money on their car insurance—only GEICO could. At the beginning of 2001 the agency proposed a change of tack to GEICO. Martin's Steve Bassett, a senior vice president and group creative director, told *Shoot* magazine's Sloane Gaylin that the agency's creatives had thought it would be an interesting twist if the gecko gave up on telling people not to call him and decided instead to finally start working for the company. Out of this idea flowed several new gecko spots. In the one called "Audition" the gecko tried to land the GEICO spokesperson position and encountered an out-of-work veteran of television commercials, the Taco Bell Chihuahua. Other spots in the series, " 'Hands,' " "Tail," "Employees of the Month," and "Food," showed the gecko working at the GEICO office. In "Action Figures," a parody of the movie *Toy Story,* a gecko doll broke up a fight between two action figures in a sleeping child's bedroom while telling them about the GEICO's affordability.

In order to make the gecko more suitable to these new scenarios, the animators reworked him to include more human attributes. In the press conference commercial the gecko had crawled on the microphone on all fours, but in later spots he moved on two feet and carried himself more like a person. Thus, in the 2002 spot "Meadow" he was able to hold hands, run down a beach, and spin around in a field with a woman.

Although the gecko commercials proved popular, Martin developed two other television campaigns that ran in parallel: "Good News," which consisted of comical spots in which someone told an unsuspecting person that they had just received good news, only to reveal that the news was that they had saved money on their car insurance; and a series of "mini campaigns" featuring a mix of humorous commercials. The three campaigns each carved out their own territory in GEICO's overall marketing strategy. The "Good News" spots focused mostly on the cash-savings message, while the gecko spots became more of a brand-building vehicle, keeping the GEICO name front and center in the minds of consumers.

GEICO added another twist to the gecko-as-spokesperson spots in the fall of 2005. In the commercial "Big News," the gecko, after two years of spots in which the only words he spoke were "well, hello," delivered a pep talk to a group of other lizards in the woods, sending them forth to spread the big news that, by visiting geico.com, people could save hundreds of dollars on car insurance. Other spots featured the gecko encouraging other lizards to pitch GEICO. To exploit the gecko character even further, GEICO introduced an amateur filmmaking competition, giving people a chance to submit their "15-second conceptual movie trailers" involving the gecko character. The goal was to appeal to the 18- to 34-year-old demographic as well as to a create a viral campaign, one that would take on a life of its own and perhaps drum up some new ideas for using the gecko in future commercials.

OUTCOME

In the year after GEICO introduced the gecko character, the company generated sales of $5.6 billion. By the end of 2003 revenues had grown to $7.8 billion. It was impossible to say how much of that success could be attributed to the "Gecko" campaign, and with the launch of two parallel campaigns in 2003 and 2004, it became even more difficult to determine. There was no doubt, however, that the gecko had achieved the status of pop-culture figure. During New York's Advertising Week in September 2005, the gecko tied with Juan Valdez, the face of Colombian coffee since 1960, as America's favorite ad icon. The honor was determined by consumer votes. GEICO and the Martin Agency were still having fun with the character, as evidenced by the accolades they showered upon the gecko after it gained iconic status. In a press release Martin's Basset commented, "He's cute, he's green, he works hard, he's got a great attitude, and he could save people a lot of money on their car insurance."

FURTHER READING

Elliott, Stuart. "GEICO Lightens Up a Successful Campaign while Trying to Keep What Made It Work." *New York Times,* August 8, 2003, p. C2.

Frazier, Mya. "Progressive, GEICO Prod Auto Rivals into Price War." *Advertising Age,* February 28, 2005, p 4.

Gaylin, Sloane. "Leaping Lizards." *Shoot,* August 2, 2002, p. 18.

Janoff, Barry. "It's Easy Being Green." *Brandweek,* December 5, 2005, p. 28.

Lovel, Jim. "Gecko Gets More GEICO Airtime." *Adweek* (southeast ed.), November 17, 2005.

———. "Loving the Lizard." *Adweek,* October 24, 2005, p. 32.

McCarthy, Michael. "Buffett Wants to Know: Do GEICO Ads Get Job Done." *USA Today,* January 24, 2005.

Nudd, Tim. "Koenigsberg and the Gecko." *Adweek* (southwest ed.), July 2, 2001, p. 26.

Rayner, Bob. "After Some Lean Years, Richmond, Va., Ad Agency Wins Back Big Accounts." *Richmond (VA) Times-Dispatch,* March 29, 2004.

———. "Born Here, GEICO Gecko Goes for Ad-Industry Glory." *Richmond (VA) Times-Dispatch,* September 17, 2005.

Edward Dinger

GOOD NEWS CAMPAIGN

OVERVIEW

By the mid-1990s direct auto insurer GEICO had already enjoyed strong growth through the use of mass-market advertising, expanding beyond direct mail to include humorous television commercials. At the start of the new century GEICO scored a hit with its commercials that featured a cartoon gecko. In the spring of 2003 GEICO released a second, complementary effort, the "Good News" campaign.

"Good News," developed by the Martin Agency of Richmond, Virginia, was essentially a television campaign, although some of the material was recycled for radio spots. The commercials played off the familiar pattern of "good news, bad news" jokes. In each spot someone was told by another that there was "good news," then learned that the good news had nothing to do with their predicament. Rather, the bearer of glad tidings had just saved a "bunch of money" on his car insurance by switching to GEICO. In one of the early spots, for example, a prisoner thought that his sentence had been commuted, only to learn that his lawyer's good news concerned car insurance.

The "Good News" campaign was effective in carrying GEICO's money-saving sales pitch, while the gecko advertisements served more to build the brand image, and a third campaign focused on a younger demographic. The company did not disclose how much of its more than $200 million ad budget was devoted to "Good News." But it was clear that it worked: after the campaign began, GEICO's brand recognition improved among consumers, and sales soared. Moreover, the "Good News" reversal-of-expectation ploy began to be adopted by consumers for comedic purposes, and they invariably mentioned GEICO by name. The value of such free advertising was incalculable.

HISTORICAL CONTEXT

A direct marketer of auto insurance that for nearly 60 years was dependent on direct-mail advertisements, GEICO began to spend an increasing amount of money on television spots in the 1990s. When legendary investor Warren Buffett acquired control of the company in 1996 through his holding company Berkshire Hathaway, Inc., GEICO allotted even more money to its advertising budget in order to meet the kind of growth that was expected. To get noticed GEICO and its ad agency, the Richmond, Virginia–based Martin Agency, looked to exploit humor in an industry that had traditionally adopted a serious tone in its advertising. Lacking the support network of State Farm, Allstate, and other agent-based insurers, GEICO made its humorous pitch on the basis of price and found a strong brand promise in the slogan "Fifteen minutes could save you 15 percent or more on car insurance." Furthermore, because GEICO lacked the personal contact of an insurance salesman, it used humor to make the company seem less impersonal to potential customers, who needed to feel comfortable and confident, not to mention motivated, to place a telephone call—or later, log onto the Internet—to purchase a policy.

With an increasing amount of ad dollars at its disposal, the Martin Agency developed a wide variety of advertisements for GEICO. One, a television spot featuring a gecko (customers often mispronounced the GEICO name as "gecko"), struck a chord in 1999 and became the anchor for the company's marketing and the inspiration for a long-term advertising campaign. In 2003 GEICO and Martin developed the "Good News" television campaign, which ran alongside the gecko spots, sometimes back-to-back in 15-second clips. The gecko spots began to focus on reinforcing the GEICO brand, while the "Good News" spots reminded consumers of the insurer's low-price promise.

TARGET MARKET

In general GEICO's advertising targeted every person who owned a car and was required by law to carry insurance. But because older drivers tended to be loyal to their insurance companies, GEICO focused a great deal of its attention on a younger demographic, essentially 25 to 40 years of age, in hopes of peeling away customers from rival insurers. Younger drivers were especially attractive potential customers because they had not built up a relationship with an insurer and by nature were more willing to look around for a better rate. Having less money than most older drivers, they were also more price-sensitive and especially open to GEICO's lower cost. For this group the absence of a personal relationship with an insurance agent was not deemed as significant a

GOOD NEWS FOR "GOOD NEWS"

Few advertising slogans actually became part of pop culture. GEICO's marketers knew that their "Good News" campaign had reached such status when, on a late night television show, popular actor Jim Carrey told host Conan O'Brien, "Good news! I just saved a bunch of money on my car insurance by switching to GEICO." More importantly, the audience erupted in laughter, well aware of the reference.

factor as the price of the policy. With their often irreverent and playful tone, the "Good News" commercials were especially effective in reaching younger consumers.

COMPETITION

When GEICO began its advertising push in the early 1990s, it was seventh in a crowded field of companies offering car insurance. As it moved up the ranks, its main competition was winnowed down to market leader State Farm, which had less than 20 percent of the business; Allstate, with about half that amount; and the Progressive Corporation, a distant third. The big two spent hefty sums on advertising to remind the public of their individual brand promises: State Farm with "Like a good neighbor, State Farm is there," and Allstate with "You're in good hands with Allstate." They were well entrenched with a strong core of loyal customers, and as conservative companies, it was not surprising that these insurers produced conservative advertising that focused mostly on their honesty and concern for their customers. Making a sales pitch on the basis of price was not part of the strategy and was almost beneath their image. Moreover, by emphasizing price State Farm and Allstate risked turning car insurance into nothing more than a commodity, the buying and selling of which was based on the lowest price possible.

Progressive, with more to lose to GEICO, quickly followed suit and increased its ad budgets. Thus, Progressive and GEICO forced their larger competitors to spend more advertising dollars as well. Allstate even began to compete in terms of price. But there was another reason why these insurance companies began to spend more on advertising: there were more profits to be made. Cars were better built and less prone to accidents. Moreover, the large baby-boomer population was growing older, driving slower, and experiencing fewer accidents. With fewer claims to pay out, insurers made more money, even if they lowered rates to lure business away from their rivals.

Because direct marketers such as GEICO did not have the expense of an agent network to support and could offer the lowest rates, the direct model became the fastest-growing segment of the auto insurance industry. GEICO had to continue to spend heavily on advertising to fend off a new breed of Internet direct marketers of car insurance. Traditional agent-based companies such as Nationwide, Hartford, Travelers, and AIG (American International Group) also began pursuing the direct model through their websites.

MARKETING STRATEGY

The "Good News" campaign broke on March 1, 2003, and adhered to GEICO's successful three-part strategy. First, it used humor to make the television spots stand out; second, it reinforced the company's brand promise, "Fifteen minutes could save you 15 percent or more on car insurance"; and finally, it made a strong appeal for action, urging the audience to initiate contact with GEICO, especially via the Web.

The campaign began with a series of three television spots. In "Lawyer" a man waited in prison while his lawyer took a call and then pronounced, "Good news." The prisoner hoped that he had gained his freedom but learned that, in fact, the good news was that his attorney had just saved "a bunch of money" on car insurance by switching to GEICO. This reversal of expectation was the pattern followed by all subsequent commercials in the campaign. In another of the initial spots, "Pitcher," a baseball manager visited a pitcher on the mound with good news. The pitcher thought that he would be allowed to stay in the game but instead was told that his manager just saved money on GEICO; the pitcher was still on his way to the showers. The last of the three spots, "News," featured a news anchor covering a volcano eruption. He told viewers not to worry because, despite the obvious disaster unfolding, there was good news: he had just saved money on his car insurance.

The first wave of "Good News" commercials were effective but drew criticism as being somewhat nasty. Bob Garfield, critic for *Advertising Age,* called them "strikingly cruel." The reason they were effective, according to executives at GEICO and the Martin Agency, as cited by Stuart Elliott of the *New York Times,* was "the added twist that the person being told the good news is on the outside looking in, almost chumplike, and is not invited to share in the good fortune." Moreover, Elliott wrote, "The approach defies the hoary rules of so-called slice-of-life advertising, which require that the person serving as the sponsor's proxy welcomes everyone else to change their lives wonderfully, too, by buying the product."

Although GEICO and the Martin Agency maintained that they received few complaints about the "Good News" commercials, the second round of five spots, which began airing in August 2003, were softer in tone. They also veered further away from the slice-of-life approach, as four of them focused on tricking viewers by parodying typical television fare. Brian Steinberg of the *Wall Street Journal* called them "situational commercials, ones designed to play off the shows consumers are watching." One of the new spots spoofed a soap opera: a man told his lover the good news about his car insurance only to watch her storm out as he pleaded, "I saved. I thought that meant something to you." Other programming that became grist for the mill included home-improvement shows, televised congressional hearings, and infomercials (such as a parody of a hair-loss-treatment product spot). To make the spots even more effective GEICO took care to shoot them on video rather than film and to air them during the type of programming that they tried to imitate—for instance, running the soap opera spot during soap operas and the prisoner spot with courtroom dramas.

GEICO and Martin also developed what they called "Mini- Campaigns," a collection of humorous spots that began airing in 2004 along with "Good News" and the long-standing gecko spots. GEICO was now running three campaigns simultaneously, saturating the airways with 15-second spots that espoused the GEICO brand promise. In addition, each of the campaigns emphasized a different part of the marketing strategy. The gecko spots became more of a brand-polishing effort, while the "mini campaigns" mostly targeted younger viewers with their off-the-wall humor. For its part, "Good News" focused on GEICO's savings pitch.

The "Good News" spots were rotated constantly, with new ones occasionally added to the mix. In the spring of 2005, for example, GEICO unveiled a pair of new spots. "Speed Racer" was a parody of the classic cartoon series of that name. In it the hero, Speed, received a call from Trixie warning him that the bridge was out and that he was headed for disaster. "But I have good news," she declared, then delivered the standard punch line to the bewilderment of Speed. The second spot featured personal trainer Tony Little, familiar to television viewers for his infomercial pitches. Once again, the viewer was tricked into thinking that the commercial was actual programming.

OUTCOME

It was impossible to determine how much credit the "Good News" campaign deserved for GEICO's success, since it was initially paired with the gecko ads and then became one of three simultaneous TV campaigns. But there was no doubt that GEICO was pleased with the "Good News" effort. In August 2003 Edward Ward, GEICO's vice president of marketing, told Elliott of the *New York Times* that, since the campaign had begun, the company was "ecstatic with the volume of phone calls and Web activity and sales." He also told Elliott that results were "running at record levels."

The spots clearly resonated with consumers, who, much to the delight of the marketers, began to use the campaign as a source of humor in their own telling of jokes. "When a campaign slogan makes it into the common vernacular of popular culture, you know you've got yourself a hit," wrote Rae Ann Fera for *Boards* in 2003. "Two famous instances of the tag being used—without duress or influence—are when an airline pilot and an on-air weatherman relayed bad news to their audience while following up with the good news that they [had] switched to GEICO." Fera also reported that, after the spots began airing, GEICO's unaided brand recall was the highest in company history.

FURTHER READING

Elliott, Stuart. "GEICO Lightens Up a Successful Campaign while Trying to Keep What Made It Work." *New York Times,* August 8, 2003, p. C2.

Fera, Rae Ann. "The Good News Is GEICO's Back." *Boards,* August 27, 2003.

Frazier, Mya. "Progressive, GEICO Prod Auto Rivals into Price War." *Advertising Age,* February 28, 2005, p. 4.

Janoff, Barry. "License to Drive Us Crazy." *Brandweek,* April 25, 2005, p. 42.

Lovel, Jim. "Loving the Lizard." *Adweek,* October 24, 2005, p. 32.

"The Martin Agency Erupts for GEICO." *Shoot,* April 11, 2003, p. 12.

McCarthy, Michael. "Buffett Wants to Know: Do GEICO Ads Get Job Done." *USA Today,* January 24, 2005.

Rayner, Bob. "After Some Lean Years, Richmond, Va., Ad Agency Wins Back Big Accounts." *Richmond (VA) Times-Dispatch,* March 29, 2004.

Steinberg, Brian. "Newest TV Spinoffs: 'Situ-mercials.'" *Wall Street Journal,* March 2, 2004, p. B11.

Ed Dinger

MINI-CAMPAIGNS

OVERVIEW

Starting in the mid-1990s GEICO, a direct marketer of automobile insurance, began spending an increasing amount of money on advertising, particularly television spots. The company's ad agency, the Martin Agency of Richmond, Virginia, produced a wide variety of commercials. Unlike traditional car insurance advertising that took a serious tone and focused on accidents, GEICO spots were lighthearted and humorous. In 1999 GEICO introduced a gecko cartoon character that became a company mascot and the subject of its own advertising campaign. In 2003 GEICO released its popular "Good News" campaign, a "good news, bad news" comedic formula that spoofed television programming, from soap operas to congressional hearings. Both of these campaigns were joined by a simultaneous effort, "Mini-Campaigns," which was unveiled in 2004.

"Mini-Campaigns" played on older GEICO formulas, such as explaining that in the time it took to do a particular thing, a person could purchase car insurance from GEICO. The campaign also introduced a group of sophisticated cavemen offended by GEICO's claim that its website was so easy to use, even a caveman could do it. They became the subject of a series of spots. The wide-open campaign also allowed the creative team to pursue television-programming parodies that fell outside the "Good News" formula. The reality-TV spoof "Tiny House" proved to be particularly popular.

"Mini-Campaigns" became one strand in a three-part, $200 million-plus advertising strategy for GEICO. Commercials from all three campaigns inundated the airways, keeping the GEICO message front and center with consumers and helping to drive increasing sales.

HISTORICAL CONTEXT

GEICO was a relatively obscure auto insurance company until the 1990s. For nearly 60 years it had operated as a niche player, using direct-mail pitches to attract customers with excellent driving records. In this way GEICO was able to offer cheaper rates than its competitors. The company almost failed in the 1970s as it adjusted to changes in the marketplace, but it found a savior in renowned stock-market investor Warren Buffett, who had held stock in the company since the 1950s. By the 1990s GEICO was the seventh-largest auto insurer in the United States and was eager to grow even larger and attract a wider customer base. In 1994 it hired the Martin Agency to serve as its ad agency and began for the first time to spend money on mass-advertising efforts, which quickly resulted in strong growth. When Buffett acquired GEICO for his investment vehicle, Berkshire Hathaway, Inc., two years later, the company was told to grow even faster, and the advertising budget swelled.

GEICO honed its pitch into a brand promise that would anchor all of its subsequent campaigns: "Fifteen minutes could save you 15 percent or more on car insurance." The Martin Agency also proved adept at crafting humorous television commercials, a significant departure for the staid car insurance industry, which had traditionally adopted a serious tone. Not only did the humor help GEICO to stand out from the crowd, but it also put a human face on a company that did not rely on agents. Instead, people's interaction with the company was a voice on the telephone or an impersonal computer screen.

In the summer of 1999 GEICO aired its first commercial employing a cartoon gecko, playing off of the common mispronunciation of the GEICO name. A series of spots featuring the gecko followed and became a staple of U.S. television commercials. In 2003 GEICO launched a second successful campaign, called "Good News." Commercials in this series featured someone, often in dire straits, being told by another that there was good news. Their expectations were dashed, however, when it was revealed that the good news was that the other person had saved a lot of money on their car insurance by switching to GEICO. The insurer ran both the "Gecko" and "Good News" campaigns simultaneously, with the former keeping the GEICO brand in the forefront and the latter focusing on the company's money-saving message. GEICO's ad budget swelled beyond $200 million a year, and with a mandate to achieve outstanding growth, the marketers released yet another campaign in 2004. Called "Mini-Campaigns," the new effort was a collection of humorous television spots that provided the creative team with a outlet for ideas that did not fit into the "Gecko" or "Good News" models but continued to build on GEICO's humor and brand image.

TARGET MARKET

Because every person who drove a car in the United States was required by law to carry car insurance, GEICO targeted a vast audience, young and old, male and female, and all ethnic groups. GEICO tended to focus on a younger demographic, however, because a major part of its marketing strategy was convincing people to take action, to call GEICO or visit the company website and change insurance carriers. Older drivers tended to stick with their insurance agents, making it natural that GEICO should focus most of its appeal on younger drivers, essentially those 25 to 40 years of age. It was this demographic that the company believed was most likely to shop around for a better rate and ultimately do business with GEICO. The television spots that made up the "Mini-Campaigns" appealed to an even younger demographic: drivers between the ages of 18 and 34.

COMPETITION

By the time of the "Mini-Campaigns," GEICO had grown to become the fourth-largest auto insurer in the United States. At the head of the list since the 1940s was State Farm, controlling about 18.5 percent of the market.

GEICO'S HERITAGE

GEICO stood for Government Employees Insurance Company, a name that led to the common misperception that it was a government agency. In fact, it was founded in Texas in the 1930s by Leo and Lillian Goodwin, who decided to sell car insurance only to people with sterling driving records. In this way they would be able to offer lower premiums, attract new business, and carve out a niche in the auto insurance field. Their initial market consisted of federal government employees and the top three grades of noncommissioned military officers. It was not until the early 1990s that GEICO began to expand aggressively beyond that pool of customers.

It had spent hundreds of millions of dollars on marketing over the decades and had one of the best-known slogans in all of advertising: "Like a good neighbor, State Farm is there." Next in line, with just over 10 percent of the market, was Allstate, another well-entrenched competitor with its own timeworn slogan: "You're in good hands with Allstate." Coming in third and fourth were the Progressive Corporation and GEICO, with 7.1 percent and 5.5 percent market shares respectively. State Farm and Allstate did not wish to compete with GEICO on price, a move that the top-two companies feared would relegate car insurance to mere commodity status—a generic item people bought because it was the cheapest. The big two were not just selling insurance; they were selling their reputations. Progressive, not as well entrenched, was quick to follow suit with GEICO, increasing its ad budgets and emphasizing price.

Eventually Allstate made some price appeals, and even State Farm beefed up its ad spending. But a major reason they were willing to join GEICO and Progressive in the car insurance ad wars was that there were more profits than ever to be made in the business. In the 1990s cars became better built, resulting in fewer repairs, fewer accidents, and consequently fewer insurance claims. In addition, the population was growing older on average, and typically the older people became, the slower they drove, again leading to fewer accidents. Thus, GEICO had to contend with companies larger in market share as well as a pack of smaller insurers also eager to attract more customers and reap the benefits of higher profits in the industry. Rounding out the top 10 in direct premiums written in 2004 were Farmers Insurance Group (4.9 percent), Nationwide Group (4.5 percent), United Services Automobile Association Group (3.5 percent), American International Group (3 percent), Liberty Mutual Group (2.8 percent), and American Family Insurance Group (2.2 percent).

MARKETING STRATEGY

Having enjoyed success with "Gecko" and "Good News," both of which became populist campaigns embraced by consumers, GEICO and the Martin Agency launched "Mini-Campaigns" in September 2004. The freewheeling, humorous effort contained variety in hopes of touching a chord with consumers and perhaps giving birth to another popular ad concept.

The initial wave of the campaign comprised nine spots. Three featured cavemen and were intended to drive traffic to GEICO's website as well as to appeal to younger drivers. In the first of the series, "Insult," a TV announcer made the claim that the GEICO website was so easy to use that "even a caveman can do it." A caveman who was part of the TV crew, however, took offense at this supposedly politically incorrect remark, shouted, "Not cool!" and stormed off the set. The second spot, "TV," showed a pair of urbane caveman in their finely apportioned living room watching the first spot and grumbling, "What's that supposed to mean?" In the third spot, "Apology," the announcer tried to make peace by inviting the two cavemen to a trendy eatery. "We had no idea you guys were still around," he pleaded, only to be dismissed with a suggestion that in the future he should do a little research first.

Three of the "Mini-Campaigns" commercials offered new humorous variations on an old GEICO commercial formula that used the phrase "In the time it takes . . ." For example, a husband was asked by his wife, who was modeling a new dress, "Does this make me look fat?" Only half listening, he replied, "You betcha." The voice-over then commented, "In the time it takes you to pull out the sofa bed, you could save 15 percent or more."

The final three spots were parodies of infomercials and reality TV shows, territory the "Good News" campaign had been adept at exploiting. One spot spoofed an Old Navy commercial, making the point that the clothes would not save a person money on car insurance, while another was a takeoff of a Super Glue infomercial. The most widely acclaimed spot of all nine was a reality-TV parody called "Tiny House." Taking its cue from the hit film *Being John Malkovitch,* which featured an absurdly low-ceilinged office space that was located between elevator floors, "Tiny House" appeared to be a promo for an upcoming reality show in which a newly married couple would have to spend a year in a miniature house.

"The marriage was built to last," intoned the announcer, "but the house was too small." Snippets were shown of the marriage unraveling because of the confined space. The announcer then said, "The drama will be real, but it won't save you any money on your car insurance." The spot fooled viewers and critics alike, many of whom praised the execution. "Why do I love this Tiny House thing so much?" wrote Barbara Lippert of *Adweek.* "First of all, its meticulous production expertly mimics every squalid detail of the reality-promo genre (the cutting and pacing, the typeface, the music). And there's a clever, deeper insight here: 'living concept' shows like Big Brother are awful precisely because they make the viewer feel claustrophobic."

GEICO added a pair of new executions to "Mini-Campaigns" in April 2005. Both of the 30-second spots focused on the ease of buying a GEICO policy online by contrasting it with the difficulty of everyday situations. In one spot the wheels from a set of rolling luggage came off. In another children in a spelling bee were presented with an extremely difficult word to tackle.

OUTCOME

"Mini-Campaigns" became a useful outlet for a variety of ideas for GEICO television commercials. While it was impossible to determine how much money the campaign added to GEICO's balance sheet, there was no doubting the role the entire advertising strategy played in the company's strong growth. Just to keep pace, GEICO would have to continue to advertise aggressively, and "Mini-Campaigns" served a valuable function, acting as a depository for spots outside the "Gecko" and "Good News" formulas as well as providing a breeding ground for potentially popular new formulas. According to Seth Stevenson, writing for the online magazine *Slate,* GEICO pursued a "scattershot approach" because it had to appeal to such a broad group of people. "Some ads are straightforward and tame (aimed at older drivers), while some are absurd (the kids seem to like this). All for a single product. Still, it's not just the range, but the volume of ads that's so astonishing. It seems like there's a GEICO spot every time you turn on the TV." Given the heated competition in the auto insurance field, that situation was not likely to change for some time to come, and the "Mini-Campaigns" concept was well suited to providing GEICO with new iterations of time-tested themes.

FURTHER READING

Elliott, Stuart. "GEICO Lightens Up a Successful Campaign while Trying to Keep What Made It Work." *New York Times,* August 8, 2003, p. C2.

Frazier, Mya. "Progressive, GEICO Prod Auto Rivals into Price War." *Advertising Age,* February 28, 2005, p. 4.

Janoff, Barry. "Car Insurance Salesmen Come Out of the Cave." *Brandweek,* September 27, 2004, p. 38.

Lippert, Barbara. "Keeping It Real." *Adweek,* September 20, 2004, p. 36.

Lovel, Jim. "GEICO TV Campaign Evolves at Martin." *Adweek,* April 25, 2005.

———. "Martin Withholds GEICO's Gecko." *Adweek,* September 13, 2004.

McCarthy, Michael. "Buffett Wants to Know: Do GEICO Ads Get Job Done." *USA Today,* January 24, 2005.

Rayner, Bob. "After Some Lean Years, Richmond, Va., Ad Agency Wins Back Big Accounts." *Richmond (VA) Times-Dispatch,* March 29, 2004.

Steinberg, Brian. "Newest TV Spinoffs: 'Siti-mercials.'" *Wall Street Journal,* March 2, 2004, p. B11.

Stevenson, Seth. "The Best Ad on Television." *Slate,* July 25, 2005. Available from <http://www.slate.com/id/2123285/>

Ed Dinger

General Electric Co.

3135 Easton Turnpike
Fairfield, Connecticut 06828-0001
USA
Telephone: (203) 373-2211
Fax: (203) 373-3131
Web site: www.ge.com

IMAGINATION AT WORK CAMPAIGN

OVERVIEW

Since 1979 General Electric Co. (GE) had relied on one of the most successful branding slogans in history: "We bring good things to life." But along the way the company had become almost exclusively associated with its lighting and appliance products, which by the end of the twentieth century represented only a small percentage of the company's business. With the installation of a new chief executive, Jeffrey R. Immelt, who replaced the legendary Jack Welch, the company decided to rethink its branding in order to better position GE as an innovative and forward-looking company. The result was a new slogan, "Imagination at work," which became the focus of a campaign aimed at consumers, business partners, and investors as well as GE employees.

The $100 million "Imagination at Work" campaign, developed by BBDO Worldwide Inc., began in January 2003. In addition to TV spots, it included print ads and Web elements. The advertisements simultaneously repositioned the brand and directly promoted one of GE's many businesses. In one commercial, for example, Lassie, the heroic canine star of vintage TV and films, warded off a cougar with an array of karate moves as a way to talk about GE's security technology. In time the campaign also spread to Europe and Asia.

Despite taking some criticism for dropping "We bring good things to life," GE expressed satisfaction with the campaign and continued to build on it. Market research detected a change in consumers' perceptions of GE: more people were viewing GE as a high-tech company rather than as a relic from the smokestack era. Moreover the new slogan became something of a rallying cry within the company, spurring on employees to make innovative contributions.

HISTORICAL CONTEXT

Throughout its history General Electric Co. enjoyed the benefits of a consistent marketing message. From the 1930s to the 1950s the company relied on the slogan "Live better electrically," which was followed by two decades of variations on the word "progress," such as "Progress is our most important product." In 1979 GE unveiled "We bring good things to life," a cornerstone to one of the most successful corporate branding campaigns in history, backed by about $1 billion in advertising. The company also had consistent leadership in the form of John F. "Jack" Welch, who became chairman and CEO in 1981. The charismatic leader sought to build up GE's status in all of the technology, service, and manufacturing areas that the company participated in. By the time Welch announced that he would retiring in 2001, GE, fast growing and profitable, had a market capitalization of $505 billion, making it second only to Microsoft.

Welch's tenure at the top, however, ended on a sour note when GE failed in its bid to acquire a major rival, Honeywell International.

Welch was succeeded by Immelt, who set out to put his own imprint on GE by, among other things, revamping the company's marketing. According to Diane Scarponi, writing in the *Seattle Times,* "Immelt said shortly after he was appointed in September 2001 that he wanted to rethink the company's image." Beth Comstock, head of communications at GE, told Scarponi, "Immelt has really been pushing a technology focus, a reinvigoration of technology at GE around the world. We wanted our communications to match that." The company conducted research that suggested that most consumers connected the "We bring goods things to life" slogan with GE's lighting and appliance business. Since the introduction of the slogan a generation earlier, however, the company had grown in so many directions that lighting and appliances had come to account for only 6 to 7 percent of revenues. Management decided that GE needed a new articulation, one that was part mission, part vision, and part strategy. After 18 months of research, brainstorming, and testing, the company and BBDO Worldwide coined a new slogan, "Imagination at work," and began to plan a marketing campaign to support it.

TARGET MARKET

One goal of the "Imagination at Work" campaign was to reach a broader range of consumers. Instead of concentrating on Sunday-morning television programming, the new GE spots would try to appeal to prime-time audiences by advertising on such shows as the hit sitcom *Friends.* In defining its target market the company took care to include Hispanic consumers, who accounted for nearly 13 percent of the U.S. population, a figure that was expected to reach 17 percent by 2020.

Because the contemporary GE was essentially a business-to-business company, the campaign also sought to communicate with other companies, who were GE's business partners. In addition it needed to reach GE's investors. The launch of the new campaign came at a time when the company had seen significant erosion in its stock price. A public company, GE wanted to assure investors that, because of its continuing ability to develop innovative products, it was a corporation with a large amount of untapped potential. GE employees were also a target audience; the campaign provided a directive to them to create the new products that would meet the needs of consumers and create the growth that investors expected. Moreover, because GE was a global company, the new campaign had to reach a worldwide audience of consumers, businesses, and investors.

IMAGINATION WORKING OVERTIME

General Electric Co. grew out of Thomas Edison's 1879 invention of the first commercially feasible lightbulb. Over the course of his lifetime, the former newsboy and telegraph operator received more than 1,300 patents associated with such inventions as the stock ticker, the phonograph, the movie camera, and the alkaline battery. He generally slept 4 hours a night and was known to work 40 to 50 hours at a stretch.

COMPETITION

As a multifaceted global company involved in 11 different businesses, GE faced competition on a multitude of fronts. Direct global competition came from a variety of companies, since GE was involved in such diverse areas as aircraft engines, television, amusement parks, commercial lending, environmental control products, plastics, medical technology, and robotics. As a result GE competed against a panoply of multinational corporate giants, including Citigroup, General Motors Corporation, Honeywell International, J.P. Morgan Chase & Co., the News Corporation Limited, Rolls-Royce, Time Warner Inc., Toshiba Corporation, the Walt Disney Company, and Whirlpool Corporation. Hence the "Imagination at Work" campaign had to promote GE in a broad enough way to position the brand in a myriad of markets, taking on countless competitors.

Because a bulk of its advertising was on television, GE, and its message, also had to contend with indirect competition in the form of a host of other voices vying for viewers' attention. Further, given that the campaign was based on the idea that GE was imaginative and innovative, the pressure was on the marketers to demonstrate that quality in the advertising itself.

MARKETING STRATEGY

Judy Hu, GE's general manager of advertising and brand, explained the company's rebranding strategy to Kate Maddox and Beth Snyder Bulik of *B to B:* "We wanted to highlight some of our 'wow' products and services—things that were unexpected and that people didn't know GE was involved in . . . The overall objective was aligning our market position with our future and creating a truly integrated campaign." Furthermore she said, "It had to be global, touch our external and internal constituencies and use as many different types of media as possible." Because they had the best stories to tell in terms of

NEEDS A LITTLE WORK

Before coming up with the much-admired slogan "We bring good things to life" in 1979, General Electric's ad agency offered the client a slightly less refined version: "We make the things that make life good."

innovation, three divisions—GE Aircraft Engines, GE Plastics, and GE Medical Systems—became the focal point of the initial advertising efforts.

The $100 million "Imagination at Work" campaign broke on January 19, 2003, with television, print, and Internet advertising. A week earlier GE had introduced the program to its employees by giving out promotional items such as mouse pads because, as Hu told *B to B,* "We wanted everyone to understand why we were doing it and what it meant." GE also held an online trivia question about the company. The winner was given a trip to the Golden Globe Awards, during the telecast of which the new commercials would first air—a further reflection of GE's desire to appeal to a prime-time audience. The first set of TV spots tried to establish the new slogan and reposition the brand while at the same time drawing attention to a specific GE business. In one commercial the company promoted its aviation products by wondering what would have happened 100 years ago if the Wright brothers had strapped a GE jet engine to their box-kite airplane, which, at the close of the commercial, morphed into a contemporary jet. Another spot compared GE's medical technology with a genius clerk able to locate medical records quickly in an immense storage room.

The "Imagination at Work" campaign also included print and Internet elements and even an upgrade of the GE logo, traditionally rendered in black and white but now available in 14 different bright colors and pastels. According to Maddox and Bulik of *B to B,* the print ads used "the 'wow' factor to highlight GE's various businesses. The ads featured dramatic photos of products such as a wind turbine, Evolution locomotive and GE image-guided surgery, while providing additional information on the nuts and bolts of the products." The ads ran in such mainstream publications as the *New York Times,* the *Wall Street Journal, BusinessWeek,* and *Forbes* as well as in trade magazines, including *Automotive Design and Production, Building Operation Management, Plastics Technology,* and *Power Engineering.* To promote GE online and to help reeducate consumers, the company launched the "Pen" subcampaign, developed by Omnicom's OMD unit. "Pen" introduced an interactive Web space in which users could put their own imaginations to work by making drawings that could be E-mailed to others, who could then add their own touches.

GE built on the successful launch of the "Imagination at Work" campaign by adding new TV spots and expanding other elements. In one commercial promoting GE Commercial Finance, Christopher Columbus charmed the queen of Spain into providing him with three small ships. According to the voice-over, "Without proper financing, even the best ideas in the world can fall flat." Perhaps the most memorable of the subsequent television spots was "Lassie," a black-and-white commercial that played off of the old television series featuring Lassie, a collie, and her owner, Timmy, to promote GE's security technology. In it Lassie protected Timmy from the threat of a ferocious cougar by rising up on her hind legs and, with the help of computer-generated imagery, unleashing a set of martial-arts moves. The graphics and voice-overs of three of the later television commercials were translated into Spanish and then ran for 10 weeks on Spanish television channels in seven markets, including Dallas, Houston, and Miami.

The "Pen" subcampaign also warranted a second generation; an enhanced website was launched in September 2004. Called "Imagination Cubed," it allowed up to three people to collaborate on illustrations at the same time while communicating through a chat interface. The "Imagination at Work" campaign expanded beyond the United States as GE began advertising in Asia and Europe, where the campaign included outdoor advertising. In May 2005 GE introduced an initiative called "Ecomagination" to promote its environmentally friendly products. This initiative, the largest marketing effort in the "Imagination at Work" campaign, broke with eight-page inserts in four major newspapers and later included TV spots, more print ads, and another online element.

OUTCOME

Dropping the slogan "We bring good things to life" in favor of "Imagination at work" was met with criticism from both inside and outside GE. Some suggested that, rather than making such a radical departure, the company would have been better served to build on the previous slogan, which had been so successful. It was also suggested that, as a slogan, "Imagination at work" was far from imaginative: Black & Decker used "Ideas at work," Sony had "Innovation at work," and three companies, including Ford, were mining the phrase "Ingenuity at work." But Robert Lauterborn, a former GE marketing executive turned college professor, approved of the change, telling Sean Callahan of *B to B,* "It's a return to GE's roots as one of the great innovative and manufacturing companies on earth."

Regardless of what others thought, GE's management appeared pleased with the change. About a year after the campaign began, market research indicated that half the respondents perceived GE as "dynamic," 40 percent saw it as a company able to deliver high-tech solutions, and 35 percent considered it "innovative." Comstock told Marv Balousek, writing for the *Wisconsin State Journal,* that "Imagination at Work" was more than just a tagline, explaining, "It's really become a rallying cry. It's allowed us a platform to reinvigorate marketing."

FURTHER READING

Callahan, Sean. "GE Campaign Brings 'Good Things' to an End." *B to B,* February 10, 2003, p. 3.

———. "GE Continues to Develop 'Imagination.'" *B to B,* October 25, 2004, p. 22.

———. "New GE CMO Taps 'Imagination.'" *B to B,* August 11, 2003, p. 3.

Creamer, Matthew. "GE Sets Aside Big Bucks to Show Off Some Green." *Advertising Age,* May 9, 2005, p. 7.

Elliott, Stuart. "GE to Spend $100 Million Promoting Itself as Innovative." *New York Times,* January 16, 2003, p. C1.

Maddox, Kate, and Beth Snyder Bulik. "Integrated Marketing Success Stories." *B to B,* June 7, 2004, p. 20.

Scarponi, Diane. "GE Bringing New Ad Slogan to Life." *Seattle Times,* January 17, 2003, p. C2.

Soter, Tom. "On the Job: Finding the Right Match for a Spot's Soundtrack." *Shoot,* March 12, 2004, p. 13.

Ed Dinger

General Mills, Inc.

One General Mills Boulevard
Minneapolis, Minnesota 55426
USA
Telephone: (763) 764-7600
Fax: (783) 764-7384
Web site: www.generalmills.com

STORIES CAMPAIGN

OVERVIEW

In 2003 General Mills, Inc.'s brand Cheerios was the top-selling cold-cereal brand in the United States, claiming $334 million in sales of the $8 billion cereal market. But General Mills believed that the aging brand, which had been introduced in 1941 as Cheerioats, was losing its edge. The company began looking for ways to move the brand out of the kitchen cupboard and to make the cereal part of American families on a more emotional level.

To help achieve that goal, the Cheerios packaging was changed, replacing the bowl of Cheerios on the box's front with a heart. And General Mills' agency, Saatchi & Saatchi New York, which had worked with the company for almost 80 years, was charged with creating a new advertising campaign that focused less on the nutritional message that the brand's oat ingredients were healthy and more on the emotional benefits of the cereal. Saatchi & Saatchi's co-chief operating officer Mike Burns said in an interview with *Fast Company,* "It became very much about motherhood and nurturance—that Cheerios is an expression of love and doing the best for your family." The "Stories" campaign, which presented a series of television spots sharing the true experiences of consumers that involved Cheerios, began in 2003.

According to Saatchi & Saatchi, the campaign succeeded in reaching mothers as well as consumers of all ages, which helped to drive sales. The campaign also inspired consumers to log on to the "Stories" website to post their own heartwarming family experiences involving Cheerios and to read those of others. In addition, the ongoing campaign was recognized by the advertising industry, beginning in 2003 with one spot, "Breakfast in Bed," being named a Best Spot by *Adweek.* In 2005 the "Heartbeat" spot won a Gold EFFIE Award, and the "Adoption" spot garnered four ADDY Awards, including the National Gold.

HISTORICAL CONTEXT

General Mills introduced Cheerioats in 1941 with a marketing strategy that included a cute little-girl spokescharacter named Cheery O'Leary and the tagline "Cheer up with Cheerioats." The brand also signed on in 1941 as sponsor of the radio Western *The Lone Ranger,* and it maintained the relationship during the program's run through 1949. The popularity of the masked man and his show pushed sales of Cheerios to nearly 1.8 million cases of the cereal in the first year of sponsorship. When the program moved to television in 1949, Cheerios stayed on as its sponsor until the 1960s. During the years that it sponsored *The Lone Ranger* the brand experienced numerous changes.

In 1945 the cereal's name was changed to Cheerios, and sweet little Cheery disappeared into the cereal-character history books. The tagline was changed to

"Cheerios: the first ready-to-eat cereal." In the 1960s General Mills began promoting the health benefits of its Cheerios brand with marketing taglines such as "Go with the goodness of Cheerios" (introduced in 1964), which was followed by "Nutrition: that's the Cheerios tradition" (1971). Almost from the beginning, Cheerios' marketing targeted children, and in 1974 it got a boost with moms as the preferred first finger-food for their toddlers when pediatricians began recommending it to parents. In 1994 the tagline "The one and only" was introduced, and when the "Stories" campaign began in 2003, the long-running tagline continued to be used.

TARGET MARKET

According to Saatchi & Saatchi, the "Stories" campaign targeted and was designed to resonate with anyone who had a tender spot in their heart, regardless of their age. But beyond that, the campaign targeted moms by portraying real situations that busy women could relate to. In an E-mail correspondence Saatchi & Saatchi representative Blair Meisels wrote, "We know the world isn't perfect and neither is her family, but it's the special moments when they come together that make it all worthwhile." The campaign also targeted all generations of consumers looking for diet support for a healthier life by promoting the product's cholesterol-lowering benefits as well as its value as a nutritious first finger-food for toddlers.

COMPETITION

The Kellogg Company was the number one breakfast-cereal maker in the United States in 2004, with a 33.5 percent share compared to General Mills' 31.5 percent share. With its Frosted Flakes brand falling in at number two behind General Mills' Cheerios, a long-standing favorite with parents of toddlers, Kellogg determined to meet the competition head-on by introducing its own toddler-friendly cereal. The new brand, Tiger Power, was tagged "food to grow" and targeted the mothers of toddlers and preschool-age children. Supporting the new cereal's launch was a $20 million television, print, and Internet marketing campaign created by Leo Burnett Chicago. It used Tony the Tiger, Kellogg's iconic spokescharacter for the Frosted Flakes brand. Even though the new cereal resembled Cheerios (it had three O-shapes connected to form a triangle) and had a strong supporting campaign and a well-known spokescharacter touting it as "Gr-r-reat to grow," Tiger Power lacked power and failed to grow. The new cereal hit the shelves in January 2005, and by May sales had reached only $3.4 million, a small number compared to Cheerios' reported $550 million in sales in 2004. Kellogg announced plans to increase the advertising budget for the new brand, but according to a report in *Advertising Age,* some were questioning whether the cereal would still be on store shelves by the end of the year.

Kraft Foods, Inc., the number one food company in the United States, was best known for its expansive line of cheeses, crackers, and cookies. Also in the Kraft Foods arsenal was the Post Cereals line with more than 23 varieties. One was Grape-Nuts, which was introduced to consumers in 1897 and was one of the first ready-to-eat cereals, and another was kid-targeted Alpha-Bits (introduced in 1957), cereal shaped like the letters in the alphabet and loaded with sugar. Despite its broad selection of cereals, Post ranked a distant third behind Kellogg and General Mills, claiming just a 16 percent market share at the beginning of 2000. To help drive sales, in 2000 Post began a promotional effort that included offering items from the Universal Studios *Land Before Time* movies, a dinosaur-themed series that had been a hit with kids aged two to seven. The effort was supported by print advertising that targeted mothers of children in that age group, but it seemed futile, as Post reported a 1.9 percent drop in sales in 2001 from the previous year. In a 2003 promotion Post put mini-bobblehead statues of Major League Baseball players in boxes of its different cereal brands, including Alpha-Bits. Again the effort did not noticeably increase sales. Post took a different approach to reach moms and their kids in 2005; it reformulated its Alpha-Bits cereal, making it sugar free and whole grain. To promote the improved cereal as a healthy finger food for toddlers, Post partnered with the

CHEERIOS PROJECT PROMOTES CHILDREN'S LITERACY

To promote children's literacy, General Mills' Cheerios brand kicked off its "Spoonfuls of Stories" project in 2002. During the holiday season that year the company packaged one of five different children's book titles in five million boxes of Cheerios. The first free books, in what was planned as an annual holiday giveaway, included *Rosie's Walk; Alexander and the Terrible, Horrible, No Good, Very Bad Day; Sylvester and the Magic Pebble; Cloudy with a Chance of Meatballs;* and *Salt in His Shoes: Michael Jordan in Pursuit of a Dream.* Supporting the project was a new website, www.spoonfulsofstories.com, that had a variety of age-appropriate activities and stories that parents and their children could share. The books were published by Simon & Schuster.

Reach Out and Read program to introduce letter recognition and reading to young children. The children's literacy effort included distributing new books to children ages six months to five years old through pediatricians' offices. In addition, learning activities using the alphabet cereal in what the company described as "eat-ertainment" could be found on the website www.alpha-bits.com.

MARKETING STRATEGY

Cheerios was the top-selling cold cereal in the United States in 2003, but General Mills wanted to give the brand a creative edge that promoted the cereal's health benefits while also connecting with consumers on a meaningful and emotional level. Saatchi & Saatchi, which had been General Mills' agency for nearly 80 years, was charged with creating a new marketing campaign for Cheerios that would achieve the desired edge for the brand, connect with consumers, and drive sales. Working with the idea that customers' real-life experiences with Cheerios would resonate with consumers, the agency developed the "Stories" campaign. It was released in 2003. No specific budget for the campaign was announced, but according to a report in *Advertising Age,* in 2003 General Mills spent $40 million advertising the Cheerios brand overall.

The campaign, limited to television, told the true stories of various customers' life experiences in which Cheerios had played a role. The 10 unique spots included the titles "Breakfast in Bed," which aired in 2003, and "Heartbeats" and "Adoption," both of which aired in 2005. "Breakfast in Bed" depicted a young boy in the wee hours of the morning carrying bowls, spoons, and a bottle of milk into the semidark bedroom where his parents were sleeping. He used a box of Cheerios as a tray, and he advised his sleepy parents, "You've got to take some cholesterol off of you." In the "Heartbeat" spot, a small boy was shown cuddling with his father on a sofa. The boy said, "I hear something. Thump, thump, thump." The father said that the sound was his heart talking to the boy. The little boy then asked, "Does it ever say anything else?" A voice-over stated the health benefits of eating Cheerios. This was followed by the boy saying, "I hear gorp, gorp," to which the man responded, "That's my stomach." The boy asked, "Your stomach talks too?" The spot ended with the Cheerios tagline, "The one and only." In "Adoption" a young couple was shown riding in the back seat of a car in an unknown but clearly foreign city. They were picking up two small children who they were adopting. Both children were reluctant to leave the orphanage or foster home where they had been living, but the couple had an opportunity to begin bonding with the children when they offered them Cheerios as a treat.

Supporting the campaign was a new website, www.cheerios.com/stories, that enabled consumers to share their own "Cheerios Moments" and read those of others. The stories shared on the website touched upon Cheerios lovers from all generations. Many of the posted stories were from parents whose children were adults but continued to eat Cheerios. In one story, "Cheerios Bandit," the mother of a toddler wrote that her daughter began walking at 10 months old and quickly learned how to help herself to the box of Cheerios, earning her the nickname that titled the story. Another person said that her daughter, who had eaten Cheerios since she was a toddler and was then 23 years old, still considered Cheerios her favorite "comfort" food. The writer of "88 Years of Dedication" told of the person's 88-year-old mother, who ate a bowl of Cheerios for breakfast every day and occasionally a bowl of the cereal before bed if she was hungry. It noted that the elderly mother was in good health, volunteered, and cut her own grass using a riding mower. People who visited the website could also view the "Adoption" television spot.

OUTCOME

The "Stories" campaign was well received by consumers and was recognized with numerous advertising-industry awards. Consumers motivated by the television spots took time to log on to the "Stories" website to share their own "Cheerios Moments" stories, read the stories of others, and comment on the commercials. One customer who posted her comments on the site wrote that the spot featuring a young boy serving his parents breakfast in bed was "the most wonderful, delightful, and adorable ad I've ever seen."

The commercial "Breakfast in Bed" was named an *Adweek* Best Spot in 2003. The campaign's spot "Heartbeat," telling the story of a young boy hearing his father's heart beating, garnered a 2005 Gold EFFIE Award. The award's summary credited the campaign with boosting Cheerios' sales and getting to the heart of what was important to consumers. In addition, the "Adoption" commercial, which related the story of a couple on their journey to pick up the two small children they had adopted, won four 2005 ADDY Awards in the cinema and television categories, including the National Gold award. The American Advertising Federation presented the awards each year in recognition of creative excellence in advertising.

FURTHER READING

"Best Spots." *Adweek,* February 17, 2003.

Lee, Thomas. "Tony vs. Cheerios; Kellogg Co. Is Taking On General Mills' Cheerios Brand with a New Cereal Aimed at Toddlers and Touted by Venerable Pitchman Tony the Tiger." *Minneapolis (MN) Star Tribune,* January 8, 2005.

"Multimedia Available: More than Nutrition Packed in This Cereal: Free Children's Books inside Millions of Cheerios Boxes." *Business Wire,* November 17, 2003.

Reinan, John. "Keeping the 'O' Rolling." *Minneapolis (MN) Star Tribune,* July 20, 2003.

Scourtes, Mary D. "Brief Bites. Cheering On Cheerios." *Tampa (FL) Tribune,* December 4, 2002, p. 1.

Sicherman, Al. "Tidbits. Alpha-Bits: How Sweet It Isn't." *Minneapolis (MN) Star Tribune,* August 11, 2005.

"Sound Source Interactive Teams with Kraft Foods Unit in National Promotion for 'The Land Before Time.'" *Business Wire,* May 10, 2000.

"Spots: Cheerios." *Advertising Age,* April 28, 2003.

Thompson, Stephanie. "Cheerios Crushes Tony as Kellogg Launch Flops." *Advertising Age,* June 13, 2005.

———. "Kellogg Pounces on Toddlers; Tiger Power to Wrest Tot Monopoly Away from General Mills' $500M Cheerios Brand." *Advertising Age,* December 6, 2004.

Tischler, Linda. "How Do I Love Thee? Let Me Plot the Graph." *Fast Company,* July 1, 2004, p. 64.

Rayna Bailey

General Motors Corporation

300 Renaissance Center
PO Box 300
Detroit, Michigan 48265-3000
USA
Telephone: (313) 556-5000
Web site: www.gm.com

AN AMERICAN REVOLUTION CAMPAIGN

OVERVIEW

Chevrolet was a division of the General Motors Corporation (GM), the largest car manufacturer in the United States. Long facing pressure from Japanese automakers such as Toyota, the company decided to revamp its vehicle lineup in 2004 by launching 10 new and redesigned models under a single campaign, "An American Revolution." This marked Chevrolet's first division-wide marketing push in more than a decade.

The campaign was headed by Michigan-based ad agency Campbell-Ewald. Beginning with a television commercial on December 31, 2003, during *Dick Clark's Primetime New Year's Rockin' Eve,* "An American Revolution" featured dozens of TV spots, each featuring a vehicle in the company's fleet. Key spots promoted the sports-car model Corvette C6 and the SSR truck. Chevrolet reached out to many demographics, using "An American Revolution" as a flexible umbrella that encompassed many targeted mini-initiatives. This included a male-focused print campaign for the Silverado truck and a hip-hop themed radio and television campaign for the Impala and HHR. The campaign relied on exposure during key events, including New Year's Eve, the Super Bowl, the Vibe Awards, and the 2004 Summer Olympics.

The campaign was mostly successful. Many models, such as the Corvette and the Impala, had strong sales numbers. Consumers responded favorably to the new commercials, which all fared well in *USA Today*'s Ad Track surveys, with 26 percent of respondents giving the campaign the highest score possible (against an industry average of 16 percent). At 98 percent, dealer participation was impressive. The company also generated significantly more traffic at its website and maintained its high public profile. Nevertheless, some individual lines, especially the SSR, did not sell well.

HISTORICAL CONTEXT

Chevrolet was founded in 1911 by Louis Chevrolet, a Swiss-born race-car driver, and William Durant, a former executive at General Motors. By producing cars such as the 1912 Classic Six, a five-passenger sedan, the company soon became successful enough for Durant to buy a majority of GM's voting stock. Soon thereafter Chevrolet merged with GM and became a separate division of the older company. GM dominated vehicle sales in the United States throughout the twentieth century, with Chevrolet as its premier line. By 1963, in fact, 1 out of very 10 vehicles sold in the United States was a Chevrolet.

The brand featured a number of well-known vehicles over the years, including the 1957 Bel Air, which would later be known as the "'57 Chevy," and the most

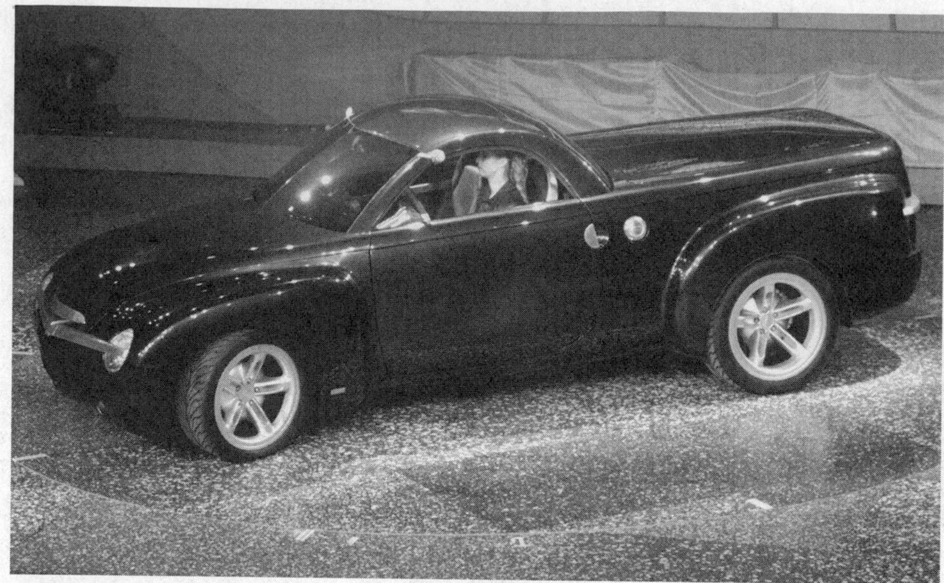

Chevrolet's Super Sports Roadster (SSR) concept pickup truck. © REUTERS/CORBIS.

recognizable American sports car, the Corvette. The Corvette was introduced in the early 1950s and became the most famous vehicle in the entire Chevrolet line. Production on the car continued through the twenty-first century, making it Chevrolet's most established vehicle.

In the face of strong competition from such competitors as the Toyota Motor Corp., Chevy decided to update much of its fleet in a 20-month period beginning in January 2004. Ten of the vehicles would be launched in that period: the cars models Malibu Maxx, Aveo, Cobalt, Corvette C6, Uplander, and Impala; the trucks SSR and Colorado; and the sports utility vehicles (SUVs) Equinox and HHR.

As Chevrolet's signature car, the Corvette was to be the centerpiece of the campaign. The SSR was also important to the launch. Based on Chevy's midsize SUV, the Trailblazer, the SSR was a stylized, convertible truck that Chevrolet hoped would prove popular enough to boost the sales of its other trucks.

TARGET MARKET

The target market for the campaign varied from vehicle to vehicle. The SSR and Colorado trucks were aimed at men, especially those in their 20s and 30s. At a price of more than $40,000 per vehicle, the SSR would have to find a lucrative audience of young professionals to be successful.

Chevrolet also used the "American Revolution" campaign to reach out to minority consumers, particularly African-Americans. The Impala and HHR were especially important to that outreach. The company also made a push for Latin-American consumers. The Accent Marketing agency of Miami was hired to run the parallel Spanish-language "Subte" (Join Us) campaign. The campaign featured television spots that aired on Spanish-language stations such as Telemundo and Univision as well as radio spots and print ads.

COMPETITION

Chevrolet's traditional competition came from GM's primary American competitors, the Ford Motor Company and the Chrysler Group (the American division of DaimlerChrysler, responsible for the Chrysler, Jeep, and Dodge brands). The company was also under pressure from the Japanese automaker Toyota Motor Corp., whose subsidiary, Toyota Motor Sales, U.S.A., was making heavy inroads in the U.S. market. In 2003 Toyota passed Ford to become the second-largest automaker in the world, right after Chevrolet's parent, GM. The Japanese automaker moved 6.78 million units worldwide in 2003 alone, versus 8.6 million units sold worldwide that year by GM.

Chevrolet was especially concerned about the SSR's sales prospects. It would be entering the already crowded light-truck field. Nevertheless, Chevy hoped to move at least 13,000 units of the SSR. This was a relatively conservative number that reflected the strength of the light-truck market in the United States. Both the SSR and the Trailblazer faced stiff competition from the Ford Explorer, which remained the top-selling vehicle in its

A BLOCKBUSTER ADMAN

Chevrolet kicked off its major "An American Revolution" campaign on December 31, 2003, during the TV program *Dick Clark's Primetime New Year's Rockin' Eve,* with a commercial titled "Car Carrier." The spot had to be a blockbuster, because it would introduce six brand-new and newly designed vehicles as well an initiate an umbrella campaign that would last 20 months. To ensure success Chevy turned to a blockbuster director: Michael Bay.

Bay had been one of Hollywood's most successful action-movie directors since his 1995 debut film, *Bad Boys,* which helped make Will Smith a major movie star. He also directed one of the biggest hits of 1996, *The Rock,* starring Sean Connery and Nicolas Cage. His most successful picture, however, was the Bruce Willis vehicle *Armageddon,* which was the highest-grossing film globally in 1998. Though often derided by critics as vapid, Bay's films were almost always major box-office hits.

Bay had long been a successful director of commercials. His first spot, for the American Red Cross, won a prestigious Clio Award. Spots directed by Bay also won several Gold Lions at the Cannes International Advertising Festival, an event dubbed the "Olympics of advertising" for its competitiveness and respect within the industry. Bay did work for a number of the world's most recognized brands, including Budweiser, Nike, Levi's, and Coca-Cola.

class in 2003. The Corvette, Chevrolet's biggest name, would be challenged by other sports cars, including the Porsche 911, the Audi 350Z, and the BMW Z4.

MARKETING STRATEGY

Chevrolet was faced with the daunting task of introducing new models for 10 separate vehicle lines, or half of its fleet. To meet this challenge the company unified all of its advertising under one overarching campaign, "An American Revolution." This tagline reflected the dynamic new products Chevy was introducing. The campaign was created by the Michigan-based agency Campbell-Ewald and cost a reported $800 million to implement.

Chevrolet had many goals for the campaign. Most importantly, it wanted to establish strong sales for all of its new vehicles, especially key models such as the Corvette C6. Dealer participation in the company's most recent campaign, "We'll Be There," had been only about 20 percent. Chevy wanted this number to improve significantly. It also wanted to maintain a high level of customer awareness for the company in general.

The campaign was the first company-wide initiative since the "Heartbeat of America" campaign in the 1980s. It kicked off on New Year's Eve 2003–2004, during the television special *Dick Clark's Primetime New Year's Rockin' Eve.* Chevrolet was the primary sponsor of the event, the most-watched New Year's celebration on American TV. It also bought a major billboard in Times Square to capitalize on the New Year's Eve publicity.

The first spot of the campaign—and the focus of Chevy's New Year's advertising—was the "Car Carrier" spot. Helmed by major Hollywood director Michael Bay, whose films included the blockbusters *Armageddon* and *The Rock,* it featured six new Chevrolets that were being introduced in 2004. The spot starred the premier vehicle in Corvette's fleet: the Corvette. Each new vehicle made an appearance as it was loaded onto a car carrier. The SSR received prominent placement, dramatically backing into the frame at the end of the spot.

The New Year's launch underscored one of Chevrolet's key goals for the campaign: to advertise at major events. This approach continued with the debut of two major spots at the Super Bowl just a few weeks later. The SSR was the star of one of these spots, titled "Soap." It featured children getting their mouths washed out with soap after their response to seeing the SSR for the first time. The commercial met with controversy for its implied profanity and only ran for a few months. It made an impression on viewers, however, and was regarded as one of the best spots on the broadcast, which was acknowledged to be the biggest night in TV advertising.

The Summer Olympics gave Chevrolet a chance to premiere a TV commercial featuring its Silverado truck. The spot depicted a Silverado acting as a tow truck for a car carrier. It recalled the New Year's spot that kicked off the entire campaign while also underscoring the sturdy, reliable power of Chevrolet's signature truck. Later, another key move of the campaign focused on the Silverado as well. In order to unite all of its advertising under one banner, Chevrolet discontinued its popular "Like a Rock" campaign, which had run for more than a decade. Featuring the eponymous song by Bob Seger, the "Like a Rock" spots had helped the Silverado become one of the most popular trucks in the United States. In anticipation of a 2006 redesign, however, Chevrolet decided that a new approach was needed to keep the brand fresh.

To reach the male consumers that composed the major target market for Chevy trucks, Chevrolet used both television spots and print ads. The key spot of the campaign featured the catchphrase "Men love trucks. Why? Because trucks don't ask why." The print campaign was built around a 10-page insert called "Men, Woman, and the Truck: A Relationship Handbook." These inserts were placed in publications with large male readerships, such as *Popular Mechanics* and *Men's Health*. The ads were meant to underscore the Silverado's appeal to men in a humorous way, by tweaking traditional "macho" notions about men and women. In addition, retired National Football League (NFL) star Howie Long was signed on as a spokesman for entire Chevy truck line.

For the HHR and Impala lines, Chevrolet devised commercials around the rap group Slum Village in an effort to reach younger fans of hip-hop music. Several television and radio spots were produced, including two 60-second radio spots for the Impala. The television commercials, with stylized visuals and quick-cut edits, were meant to look like music videos. They featured the song "EZ Up," a single by Slum Village. The group itself was chosen because of its Detroit roots, and the spots prominently featured Detroit scenes. These commercials were intended to show the hipness of the Chevrolet brand. They also targeted urban consumers and ran during popular hip-hop themed events, including the Vibe Awards. Created by *Vibe* magazine, one of the most successful urban-music-themed publications, the awards spotlighted the best hip-hop performers in the United States.

OUTCOME

The campaign was successful on most fronts. Chevrolet accomplished its goal of increasing dealer participation. Ninety-eight percent of United States Chevy dealers participated in the campaign. Traffic at the company's website increased significantly, with individual vehicles, such as the Aveo, seeing 280 percent more visitors than they were before 2004. The campaign's television commercials drew praise from critics, who found them bold and interesting. More importantly, consumers responded to the spots. According to a Millward Brown study conducted in late 2004, the "American Revolution" campaign was the seventh-most-recognized campaign at that time.

The spots as a group drew a positive response in *USA Today*'s Ad Track survey as well, with 26 percent of respondents holding a highly favorable view of the campaign, versus an industry average of only 16 percent. Sales were solid. The Corvette C6, which featured prominently in the campaign's kickoff, sold out for the year. The Impala also performed impressively, moving 290,259 units to become the top-selling domestic four-door passenger vehicle in 2004; and the Trailblazer, with 283,384 units sold, made stiff inroads against the class-leading Ford Explorer's 339,333 units. Some lines disappointed, however. The SSR had surprisingly weak sales, moving less than 9,000 units. Chevrolet later discontinued the line.

FURTHER READING

Carter, Bill, and Stuart Elliott. "New Creative Director for Chevrolet Account." *New York Times,* May 19, 2004.

Geist, Laura Clark. "Silverado Joins Chevy Revolution." *AutoWeek,* November 18, 2005.

Greenberg, Karl. "Chevy Silverado Sheds 'Like a Rock.'" *Adweek,* October 07, 2005.

Howard, Theresa. "'Revolution' in Ad Campaign." *USA Today,* October 17, 2004.

Krebs, Michelle. "In Detroit, Home Teams Swing for the Fences." *New York Times,* January 4, 2004.

———. "In Detroit, the Dogs Have Their Day." *New York Times,* January 9, 2005.

Piligan, Ellen. "Chevrolet Greets the New Year with an Ambitious Campaign to Introduce 10 Vehicles in 20 Months." *New York Times,* December 19, 2003.

Robinson, Eugene. "GM's Collapsing Ladder." *Washington Post,* November 25, 2005.

Sanneh, Kelefa. "Mixing Rednecks and Blue States." *New York Times,* November 8, 2004.

Smith, Stephanie. "Publishers Ponder Auto Ads." *Adweek,* December 05, 2005.

Guy PatrickCunningham

BREAK THROUGH CAMPAIGN

OVERVIEW

Cadillac, a division of Detroit-based auto giant General Motors Corporation (GM), had long been GM's luxury division, offering higher-priced, roomier vehicles. The brand had been in trouble for several years, however, and saw sales tumble almost 10 percent between 2000 and 2001. One of the primary culprits was Cadillac's aging customer base. By the early 2000s the average age of Cadillac buyers was 65 years old. Younger drivers tended to prefer European and Japanese luxury automobiles such as BMW, Mercedes, and Lexus. To help reach younger consumers, Cadillac developed the CTS, a sedan that was priced as an "entry" luxury car, along the lines of the BMW 3 Series.

Cadillac earmarked nearly a quarter of a billion dollars for a new campaign, which was implemented by advertising agency D'Arcy Masius Benton & Bowles.

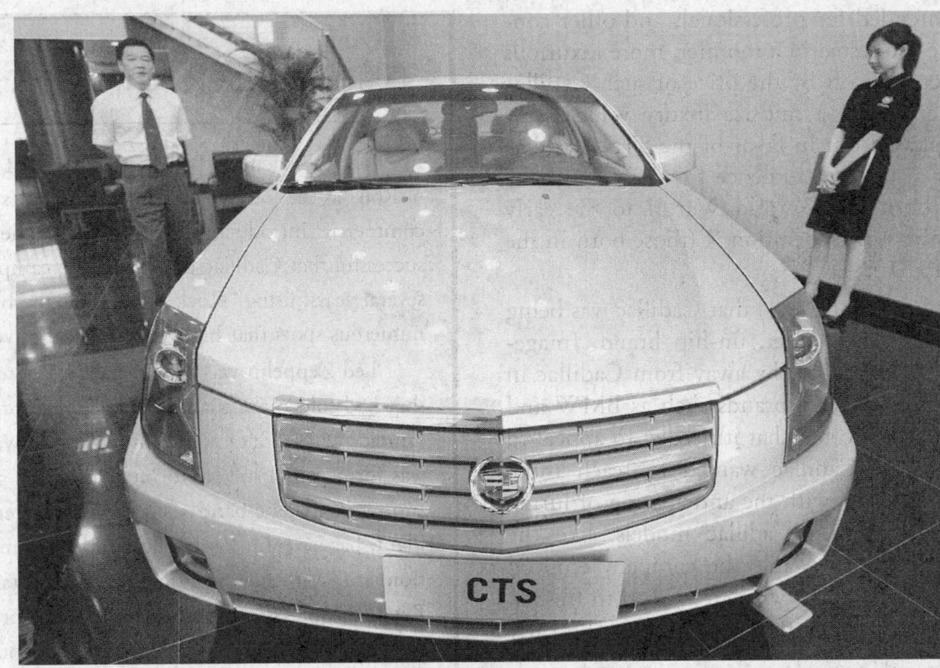

A Cadillac CTS © CARLO CORTES IV/REUTERS/CORBIS.

Titled "Break Through," the campaign revolved around a television spot that premiered at the 2002 Super Bowl. The commercial first invoked the brand's post–World War II heyday by showing a young professional driving a 1959 Cadillac. The commercial really kicked into gear with the arrival of the new CTS, which passed the 1959 vehicle on the open road while Led Zeppelin's "Rock n' Roll" played in the background. Led Zeppelin was one of the most successful rock bands of the 1960s and 1970s, and Cadillac believed that the band's iconic status and hard-rock sound offered the right combination of nostalgia and edge.

Representing a major achievement for the campaign, the average CTS buyer was 55 years old. Cadillac expanded the "Break Through" campaign for several years, making it a division-wide affair. It became a key component in the company's efforts to revitalize itself.

HISTORICAL CONTEXT

Cadillac rose from the remains of the Henry Ford Company. After Ford left the company, his former partners decided to continue in the automobile business. In 1902 they formed the Cadillac Automobile Company. The organization took its name from Antoine de la Mothe Cadillac, the founder of the company's home city of Detroit. In 1909 Cadillac was purchased by General Motors. As the twentieth century progressed, GM grew to become the largest automaker in the world.

Cadillac developed into GM's luxury brand. The vehicle never sold well outside the United States, but within the country Cadillac became synonymous with quality and luxury. By the early 2000s, however, the brand was under pressure from European and Japanese luxury brands such as Lexus and BMW. Between 2000 and 2001 the company's sales dropped about 9 percent, bringing to 40 percent the sales slide that had been going on since the mid-1980s.

As Cadillac's customer base aged, the brand began to get a reputation as an "older" company aligned with establishmentarian attitudes. In fact, by 2001 the average Cadillac buyer was 65 years old. This presented a problem for GM because the division's future depended on attracting baby boomers—people who were in their 40s and 50s in 2001. The company also had trouble getting women to purchase its vehicles. In an effort to reach out to younger drivers, for model year 2003 Cadillac replaced its sagging Catera model with the CTS, which was designed to be sleeker and flashier than the Catera. The CTS operated on a 5-speed transmission, reminiscent of that used in BMWs, and it used a 220-horsepower V-6 engine, which provided a smooth ride. It also offered OnStar, a computerized guidance system.

TARGET MARKET

The new CTS was positioned as an entry-level luxury car for drivers who tended to be well established in their careers. It was intended for professionals and other consumers who were interested in a roomier, more luxurious ride but who were put off by the price of such Cadillac mainstays as the Seville, a midsize luxury vehicle that would soon be phased out in favor of the STS. Cadillac hoped to attract a younger audience for the CTS: baby boomers (those born from World War II to the early 1960s) and members of Generation X (those born in the late 1960s and 1970s).

The company was concerned that Cadillac was being seen by consumers as an older, un-hip brand. Image-conscious boomers tended to shy away from Cadillac in favor of flashy foreign luxury brands such as BMW and Lexus. The company also felt that it needed to appeal to more women drivers. Cadillac wanted to reach those consumers with the CTS, with the anticipation of luring them to buy higher-priced Cadillac models, like the Seville/STS, in the future. While the company enjoyed its reputation as a classic luxury car, it wanted to freshen up that image to help meet the challenges of the early 2000s.

COMPETITION

As an affordable, entry-level luxury car, the CTS competed with similarly priced vehicles from other luxury automobile brands. Chief among these was the Lexus ES 300, manufactured by the Toyota Motor Corporation's Lexus division. The ES 300 was the latest in the popular ES sedan line, first introduced in 1989. Lexus introduced the ES 300 in model year 2003, at the same time that Cadillac brought out its new CTS. Because the ES 300 launch was a major priority for Lexus, the CTS faced intense competition from the beginning.

Acura would also be launching a new design of its luxury vehicle the TL, though with less fanfare than Lexus. Other imports that competed directly with the CTS included the Mercedes-Benz C-Class, the Audi A4, the BMW 3 Series, and the Infiniti G35, made by a subsidiary of Nissan. The Ford Motor Company's Lincoln luxury division was long considered a chief competitor for GM's Cadillac division. Lincoln, however, did not have a strong entry-level vehicle available at the time. Its flagship model, the Town Car, did draw from some of the CTS's market share, but it was more expensive and competed more directly with the Cadillac Seville.

MARKETING STRATEGY

Cadillac wanted its new campaign to accomplish many different things. Most importantly, it needed to introduce the CTS successfully. Its other goals were to reverse the previous year's substantial decline in sales and to burnish the company's image in relation to import luxury brands. Cadillac enlisted ad agency D'Arcy Masius Benton & Bowles, based in Troy, Michigan, to run its new campaign, which would cost more than $240 million. The agency had worked with Cadillac before and understood the company's concerns.

To drum up advance publicity, Cadillac offered the CTS for use in *The Matrix Reloaded,* the 2003 sequel to the popular science fiction movie *The Matrix.* At the core of the campaign was a series of several television spots, all of which featured the Led Zeppelin song "Rock n' Roll." Led Zeppelin, who recorded nine studio albums between 1968 and 1980, was one of the first hard-rock bands and also one of the most enduringly popular. While the band still appealed to younger fans, its original loyal fan base was now comfortably middle-aged.

It was believed that Led Zeppelin's music possessed a combination of nostalgia and edge that would appeal to baby boomers. The band's untitled fourth record,

THE CADILLAC OF ROCK BANDS

In 2002 Cadillac used Led Zeppelin's 1971 song "Rock n' Roll" as the soundtrack to the company's Super Bowl commercial introducing the new CTS. The spot was so successful that Cadillac continued the campaign for several years, using "Rock n' Roll" as the backdrop for numerous spots that highlighted its other vehicles.

Led Zeppelin was a British-based hard-rock band that had sold more than 100 million records in the United States alone by the time the spot was filmed. It was formed in 1968 by former Yardbirds guitarist Jimmy Page. The band also featured singer Robert Plant, bassist John Paul Jones, and drummer John Bonham. With such songs as "Whole Lotta Love," Led Zeppelin quickly established itself as the premier hard-rock band of its era. Its untitled fourth album, released in 1971, was its most successful outing. The album featured "Rock n' Roll" as well as the band's best-known song, "Stairway to Heaven," which for decades was one of American radio's most-requested songs.

The band continued to record and tour throughout the 1970s, releasing multiplatinum albums such as *Houses of the Holy* (1973) and *Physical Graffiti* (1975), until the tragic death of John Bonham on September 5, 1980. While the band reformed for 1985's Live Aid benefit concert, and Page and Plant recorded together again in the 1990s, the band never toured or recorded again.

featuring the classic-rock staple "Stairway to Heaven" as well as the hard-charging "Rock n' Roll," was one of the best-selling records of the 1970s and was seen by some baby boomers as a touchtone of their youth. Because Led Zeppelin had an outlaw reputation in its heyday, attracting various stories and urban myths about its members' over-the-top parties and decadent lifestyle, the band never acquired a stuffy reputation, even with the passage of time. Also, the band's classic status—it was in the Rock n' Roll Hall of Fame and was generally regarded as the exemplar of the hard-rock genre—helped to underscore Cadillac's reputation as the classic luxury car.

The campaign kicked off during the 2002 Super Bowl on Fox television, at a cost of more than $10 million. The event, which served as the championship game for the National Football League, was typically the most watched television event of the year, and the advertisements that ran during it garnered not only a large audience but also a significant amount of media attention. The Cadillac spot began by showing a young professional driving a vintage 1959 Cadillac. He was stuck in a traffic jam but then managed to turn off down a side street, which led to an open highway. At this point the Led Zeppelin music began, and a CTS appeared in the rearview mirror. A unseen announcer then declared: "A legend—reborn." Soon the CTS passed the older car and rocketed down the open road, as the music played louder and louder. The spot closed with the tagline "Break Through."

Other brands, including Coors Light beer and Sheraton Hotels, also used popular 1960s and 1970s songs in their advertisements during this time. As baby boomers aged, they continued to buy products that celebrated 1960s and 1970s recording artists, such as the *Beatles Anthology* CDs. Led Zeppelin itself had released several popular box sets in the 1990s, and in 2003 it put out a successful collection of live performances recorded in 1972.

On January 27, 2004, Cadillac paid to become the official vehicle of Super Bowl XXXVIII, which was broadcast on CBS. Cadillac featured a new 60-second spot called "Turbulence" that expanded upon the "Break Through" campaign. It featured a voice-over by the actor Gary Sinise, who had played a major role in the Oscar-winning 1994 film *Forrest Gump.* The commercial retained "Rock n' Roll" on the soundtrack and highlighted four key Cadillac models: the Escalade and SRX sports utility vehicles (SUVs), the XLR, and the CTS. The spot showed the four cars driving in the desert. The CTS, Escalade, and SRX all met at an intersection, creating a swirl of "turbulence" that eventually subsided to reveal an XLR with its top down, driven by a young woman. Cadillac ran three other spots during the broadcast, featuring the Escalade, SRX, and XLR individually. All three ended with the "Break Through" tagline.

The musical focus of the spot dovetailed with Cadillac's decision to offer XM radio in its DeVille, Seville, CTS, and Escalade models. XM was a popular satellite-radio service that provided a diverse array of music, sports, and entertainment channels. The subscription service required a special radio, which Cadillac began to offer for the CTS and other lines.

OUTCOME

The CTS did not fare well competing head-on with BMW or Mercedes, but its competitive pricing—it came in at under $35,000—meant that Cadillac could reorient its campaign to take on the Honda Accord and Toyota Camry. Otherwise, the campaign met with success. Automobile journalists awarded the CTS the North American Car of the Year at the Detroit-based North American International Auto Show in 2002.

Cadillac was pleased with the "Break Through" campaign results. Eventually the company's website even carried the "Break Through" tagline. As late as 2005, 85 percent of respondents to an internal survey still saw the campaign as fresh and different. Most importantly, within nine months of the "Break Through" campaign's inception, the average age of CTS buyers was down to 55, a marked improvement over the Cadillac division's average of 65. Nearly 40 percent of those consumers were women. Internal data showed that approximately half of CTS buyers would not have previously considered purchasing a Cadillac.

FURTHER READING

Cantwell, Julie. "The Big Idea Is Even More Important Now." *Automotive News,* January 14, 2002.

———. "Cadillac Launches 'Break Through' Ad Campaign to Reverse Sales Slide, Change Image." *Automotive News,* January 28, 2002.

Elliott, Stuart. "Despite Millions of Viewers, the Super Bowl Is Not Quite So for Madison Avenue." *New York Times,* February 1, 2002.

Guilford, David. "A Cadillac Century: At 100, Cadillac Shows Signs of Life." *Automotive News,* August 22, 2002.

Hendry, Maurice, et al. *Cadillac, Standard of the World: The Complete Seventy-Year History.* New York: Dutton, 1973.

Howard, Theresa. "Hard-Rocking Ads Aim for All Ages." *USA Today,* July 27, 2003.

Salmieri, Stephen. *Cadillac.* New York: Rizzoli, 1985.

Walker, Rob. "Ad Report Card: Cadillac's Rock of Ages." *Slate,* April 15, 2002. Available from <http://www.slate.com/id/2064338/>

Yorke, Ritchie. *Led Zeppelin: The Definitive Biography.* Lancaster, PA: Underwood-Miller, 1993.

Guy Patrick Cunningham

THE CADDY THAT ZIGS CAMPAIGN

OVERVIEW

Although ownership of a Cadillac was for decades widely considered a part of the "American Dream," Cadillac Motor, a division of General Motors, saw its share of the luxury-car market begin to decline in the 1990s. The company also saw the rise of a new subcategory in the luxury-car field, the entry-level luxury car (or "entry-lux"), exemplified by new models such as the Lexus and new, lower-priced Mercedes models. Cadillac responded to these trends by taking a risk in 1997 with a new entry-lux model, the Catera. The sporty, comparatively affordable Catera was unlike anything Cadillac had ever sold before. It was also the first Cadillac made entirely overseas (in Germany).

To launch this groundbreaking new model, Cadillac implemented a marketing campaign unlike any it had done before, calling the Catera "The Caddy that Zigs." The campaign—which included a variety of television and print advertisements—used humor and clever copy to communicate to car buyers that the Catera was a whole new kind of Cadillac. The campaign even used a quirky red cartoon duck as a prominent symbol, another move that broke with the more staid marketing usually associated with Cadillac.

The campaign received harsh criticism from media and auto-industry critics. Surveys also showed the public had a mixed reaction to the campaign (especially the duck). But Cadillac executives were pleased with the sales figures for Catera's first year, and they reported that the campaign overall had made a positive impression on the public's traditional perceptions of the car maker.

HISTORICAL CONTEXT

Since its early days Cadillac was a company that specialized in luxury cars. Eventually car buyers identified the Cadillac name as synonymous with American luxury cars ("Cadillac" even appears in some dictionaries with the definition "luxurious"). Marketing campaigns emphasized the car maker's tradition and quality and were aimed at an older, wealthy, male demographic.

But the emergence of luxury cars from foreign manufacturers made a dent in Cadillac's market share. Competitors like Mercedes-Benz, BMW, and Lexus gradually eroded Cadillac's long-time dominance of the luxury field: from 1990 to 1996 Cadillac's share of the luxury-car market plunged dramatically from 22.2 percent to 14.8 percent.

One of the reasons for the drop was that other car makers were building the popular entry-lux vehicles. Traditional luxury vehicles controlled 52 percent of the overall luxury market in 1991 but only 34 percent four years later. During the same time period, the market for entry-lux cars grew from 25 to 39 percent.

TARGET MARKET

The typical buyer of a Cadillac automobile was male, in his late 50s or 60s, affluent, and usually but not always college-educated. David Nottoli, Cadillac's Catera brand manager for 1997, said the Catera campaign sought a different market. "We were looking at the 45–50 age bracket," he said. In addition to this narrow market, Cadillac wanted to expand on its traditional customer base by pursuing more female customers. The car maker was hoping 50 percent of Catera customers would be women. In addition, Cadillac hoped to draw an audience that was almost 100 percent college-educated. Nottoli added that non-General Motors customers were also targeted by the Catera campaign.

According to the Catera Brand Book for Cadillac dealers, "The target buyer for this car is young enough to be the son (or, just as likely, daughter) of people currently driving DeVilles [a larger, older Cadillac model]. Their definition of luxury bears no resemblance to their parents' generation. For them . . . BMWs, Volvos, and Infinitis say more than Cadillacs and Lincolns. When it comes to luxury, Cadillac is status quo. And these buyers don't want status quo."

COMPETITION

By 1997 Cadillac was increasingly concerned about its decreasing market share as well as the growing popularity of entry-lux autos. The buyers in this new market tended to be younger, more performance-conscious, and more open to automobiles built overseas such as Mercedes-Benz and Lexus. Cadillac executives' attention was especially drawn to the cases of two competitors' vehicles launched in the 1990s: The Lexus ES 300, which sold 39,367 units in its first year (1992); and the Mercedes-Benz C class, which sold 23,793 units in its launch year (1994).

Cadillac's Nottoli noted that these cars were introduced with essentially the same marketing strategies traditionally used for upscale automobiles. Television and print ads were geared for an affluent audience, with dignified shots of cars rolling along country roads or displayed in luxurious settings. Cadillac knew it had to pursue a different style of marketing campaign for its Catera, as it wanted to make a major impact in the competitive entry-lux market.

MARKETING STRATEGY

To launch its ambitious Catera campaign Cadillac worked closely with its national advertising agency, the Bloomfield, Michigan, office of the international firm

SUPER BOWL SPOT NOT SUPER FOR CADILLAC

It was the 1997 Super Bowl, the most prestigious advertising platform available to companies seeking a prime audience. Cadillac bought a 45-second spot during the second quarter of the game. They then readied an ad starring supermodel Cindy Crawford and the red cartoon duck used as a spokes-symbol for the Catera. The car maker hoped Crawford and a witty script would give Catera the younger buzz they were looking for.

The spot aired and won a few raves. But then the criticism started. As the *London Daily Telegraph* described it, "There in the driving seat was supermodel Cindy Crawford, kitted-out in black leather micro skirt and thigh-high leather boots, looking like she was on her way to an Emma Peel fan-club meeting. What's more, Ms. Crawford is discussing the car's finer qualities with a cartoon duck, informing the feathery fellow that 'This is the Caddy that zigs'—presumably followed by a particularly impressive zag." Women's groups were outraged at the choice of clothing for Crawford, especially the leather miniskirt and go-go boots. They did not find the clever copy amusing, either.

Facing a firestorm of criticism, Cadillac pulled the spot from rotation. When combined with the widespread criticism of the poor maligned duck, the 1997 Catera campaign confronted more than its share of slings and arrows.

D'Arcy Masius Benton & Bowles (DMB&B). The car maker spent an estimated $40 million on the campaign. According to Nottoli, Cadillac knew most car buyers saw the company as the manufacturer of serious, luxury automobiles. To challenge this perception, Cadillac wanted to emphasize a lighter side in the Catera campaign. "We tried to focus on fun," he said.

They started with the campaign's slogan, "The Caddy that Zigs." Although auto enthusiasts and Cadillac owners had long called the cars by the "Caddy" abbreviation, the company had never used the shortened term in any advertisement before the Catera. This simple break with tradition was an important one for Cadillac, as the company wanted to emphasize that the Catera was different from any car the maker had produced before.

When Cadillac and DMB&B faced the issue of which symbol or spokesperson to use for the campaign, they turned to the family crest of the founder of Cadillac (the crest is on each automobile made by the company). That crest featured six ducks—actually mythical birds called merlettes that are similar to ducks. In the crest all six ducks face left. Cadillac officials decided to play off the crest—a symbol rooted in years of family and company tradition—for its Catera "spokesperson." Cadillac and DMB&B creative teams decided to turn one of the ducks in the crest to the right. The idea was that the duck "zigged" away from Cadillac tradition, just like the Catera. Thus the slogan "The Caddy that Zigs" was born.

The use of a cartoon duck—red, no less—was meant to emphasize fun and irreverence, Nottoli said. Cadillac knew the use of a cartoon animal to promote a luxury car was not without its risks, but the company also knew it had to take chances to reach its younger target market. "The goal of the duck was to show how luxury and fun could come together," Nottoli said. "It was representative of a whole attitude."

The 1997 Catera campaign got off the ground in January with a spot in a prime advertising location: the Super Bowl. The Catera spot, featuring the red duck and model Cindy Crawford, generated quite a bit of attention—not all positive—for the car maker. Several more television spots followed, all emphasizing the duck and a younger, irreverent attitude. One full-page magazine advertisement played on this attitude with a paean to "duck logic": "Ducks think differently than you and me. They would never forget a birthday. They have never sponsored a negative political ad. They avoid talk shows like the plague. They dance in the rain and take great pains not to walk around the puddles." Ads later in the year noted the performance features of the car. One 30-second television spot was set on a curving, mountain road. The Catera drove along with two competing entry-lux cars following. The voiceover announced, "You follow the leader. You follow the pack. Then you get a Catera. Suddenly, you don't follow anything." The background music was upbeat techno-pop, and the spot closed with the "Caddy that Zigs" slogan and the duck.

In a unique promotional move, Cadillac displayed Cateras at an Atlanta mall for five weeks in January and February 1997. Cadillac-trained specialists were on hand to answer questions about the cars, and special kiosks were set up for curious shoppers. The idea was to expose the Catera to the public in an environment not traditionally associated with automobiles, with the goal of interesting consumers who might not normally consider buying a Cadillac in test driving a Catera. Figures showed about 70,000 people visited the mall display.

Other innovative direct marketing techniques were employed. One Cadillac dealer took Cateras to golf and tennis tournaments, events populated by affluent, younger car buyers. The same dealer also used Cateras to taxi people to and from National Symphony Orchestra performances. In another unique move, a six-page foldout ad, which ran in fashion magazines, tied the Catera's styling to the work of trendy fashion designers.

OUTCOME

There were strong, divergent views on how successful the 1997 Catera campaign was. For Nottoli, the campaign was a winner for bottom-line reasons: the Catera sold well in its launch year. "In the end you judge the outcome based on results," Nottoli said. Those results included the sale of 25,411 Cateras in the vehicle's first year, surpassing Cadillac's sales goal of 25,000. But Nottoli remarked that sales figures were not the only measure of success for the Catera campaign. He noted that the age of the typical Catera buyer—a factor that had been a crucial part of the marketing strategy—was lower than that of other Cadillac buyers. While Cadillac and industry experts differed on what the median Catera-buyer age was (while Cadillac claimed the median age was 52 years old, 13 years younger than the median age for traditional Cadillac buyers, auto industry observers claimed the age was closer to 58), Nottoli said the undeniable fact was that the car was bought by younger consumers.

The gender makeup of Catera buyers was also promising, Nottoli said. About 51 percent of Catera buyers were male, which was right on target for Cadillac's goal of having an equal number of female and male buyers. This gender equity was much different from the typical Cadillac customer base, and Nottoli said the Catera marketing campaign played a big part in drawing female customers.

In addition, Nottoli said the Catera was successful as a "conquest vehicle," an auto industry term for a car that brings in buyers who had previously not purchased a vehicle from that brand. In the case of the Catera, the campaign helped draw non-General Motors buyers into the Cadillac showrooms, another of the campaign's key goals.

While Nottoli considered the 1997 Catera campaign a success, he acknowledged problems, most notably the red duck. While Cadillac originally adopted the duck as a spokes-symbol to emphasize fun and irreverence, the cartoon character soon began receiving too much attention. "We couldn't get people off the duck," Nottoli said. "People took it too far. They had a love-hate relationship with the duck."

Criticism of the Catera campaign was consistent and strong. From the beginning of the campaign, viewers were critical of the use of the duck. They also questioned whether the target market would accept a Cadillac. *USA Today*'s fourth annual survey of advertising agency creative directors reported it as one of the worst campaigns of 1997, writing, "More than a third of the panelists name Catera as their first choice for 1997's worst ad. Cadillac wants to attract younger viewers to its $30,000 car, but ad executives say it was a mistake to link a luxury brand in a commercial with a wise-cracking cartoon duck." In addition, *USA Today*'s Ad Track survey reported that only 9 percent of consumers surveyed liked the Catera duck (below the 22 percent average) and only 11 percent found the ad campaign very effective (compared to a 25 percent average).

Cadillac dealers were also critical of the campaign, complaining that the Catera campaign focused too much on fun and not enough on the car's features. "We don't need a quack as our spokesman," Jacques J. Moore, president of a Cadillac dealership, told the *Washington Post*. "The Catera is a heck of a good car, an excellent car. We need an advertising campaign that sticks to the merits of the car, that emphasizes the quality of the Cadillac name."

Nottoli responded by saying that Cadillac was aware of the campaign's weaknesses. He added that his one regret was the campaign was a little too "silly" and not sophisticated enough. But, he added, "We took a risk. I'm glad we did."

Nottoli said focus groups conducted by Cadillac showed solid awareness of the Catera, but that awareness did not necessarily bring buyers to the point where they bought the car. He added that many focus group participants did not consider the Catera a Cadillac; they considered it to be a different car altogether. Cadillac owners also did not consider the Catera a "real" Cadillac, but rather a "little Cadillac," he said.

Nottoli said this was part of the "Cadillac baggage" the Catera marketing campaign fought to overcome. Cadillac's traditional image as a maker of big luxury cars for older people played a big part in the acceptance of the "Caddy that Zigs" message. "We didn't start with a clean slate," Nottoli said. "The Cadillac baggage hurt us."

In 1998 Catera advertising downplayed the duck and emphasized the car's performance features. The duck only appeared at the end of ads as an icon. Catera sales for 1998 were up considerably over sales in 1997, and the age of Catera buyers continued to decrease, Nottoli said, demonstrating the effectiveness of the "Caddy that Zigs" campaign.

FURTHER READING

Brown, Warren. "The Caddy They Ducked; Sporty Catera Hasn't Steered Younger Buyers to GM's Flagship Division." *Washington Post*, September 11, 1997.

"Cadillac Goes after Customers by Taking Catera to the Mall." *Automotive News*, June 26, 1997.

Crain, Rance. "If It Walks Like a Duck... Then Caddy Rises to Defense of its 'Entry Lux'." *Advertising Age,* September 29, 1997, p. 28.

Enrico, Dottie, and Melanie Wells. "Campaign 1997: Some Ads Win Kudos, Others in Death Throes." *Salt Lake Tribune,* December 21, 1997.

Halliday, Jean. "Caddy's Catera Will Be a Tough Sell." *Advertising Age,* August 19, 1996, p. 12.

"How the Ad Track Ads of 1997 Stack Up." *USA Today,* December 29, 1997.

Jackson, Kathy. "Catera Report Card: Missing Boomers on First Attempt." *Automotive News,* September 1, 1997, p. 3.

Pepper, Jon. "Cadillac Catera Ad Team Flying against Tradition." *Detroit News,* Jan. 26, 1997.

Simison, Robert L., and Rebecca Blumenstein. "Cadillac, Lincoln Struggle to Get Back in Luxury-Car Race." *Wall Street Journal,* July 3, 1997.

Washington, Frank S. "Caddy Hopes Catera Lures Younger Buyers." *Automotive News,* October 28, 1996, p. 6.

Washington, Frank S. "Cadillac: Pluck the Duck, Dealers Urge." *Automotive News,* February 10, 1997.

Washington, Frank S. "Catera Finds Red Duck Is a Lame Icon." *San Diego Union-Tribune,* December 6, 1997.

Alden ScottCrow

EV1 INTRODUCTION CAMPAIGN

OVERVIEW

In December 1996 General Motors Corporation (GM) became the first major automaker in almost 80 years to market an electric car, dubbed the EV1. The car's debut came just months after the California Air Resources Board had reluctantly decided to postpone a mandate requiring that 2 percent of cars sold in the state by 1998 be powered by electricity. Regulators agreed to change the mandate to 10 percent by 2003, but only if automakers began voluntarily introducing electric cars. With the EV1, GM effectively shifted the discussion about electric cars from the fringe to the mainstream.

By most accounts, the car was a technological marvel. Its sporty aerodynamic design, which included an all-aluminum frame, magnesium seats, and low-resistance tires, earned GM engineers 23 patents. But while the introduction of the EV1 was undeniably a watershed event, there were obstacles to the car's success. It could travel just 80 to 90 miles before needing to be recharged, which took about three hours. The price was high, with lease payments coming to about $480 a month after various federal, state, and local tax incentives. And since there were only a handful of public charging sites, drivers would need to lease a charging unit for their garages or workplaces for another $50 a month.

Thanks to a steady stream of media coverage, there was pent-up curiosity about the EV1 when it became available on December 5, 1996. The $10 million advertising campaign developed by Hal Riney & Partners of San Francisco added to the mystique of the EV1. The campaign did not delve into the intricacies of the car's technology but instead was aimed at building awareness and excitement about the fact that an electric car was available and that GM was behind it. While the target market for the EV1 was expected to be affluent people with an interest in technology and the environment, the early stage of the campaign was aimed at reaching a broader, more general audience. Teaser billboards and newspaper ads inaugurated the campaign, which was kicked off in full force on December 5, 1996, with the broadcast of a $1.5 million television commercial that featured an endearingly lifelike brigade of home appliances.

HISTORICAL CONTEXT

During the 1990s California earned the dubious distinction of having the dirtiest air in the nation. Car and truck exhaust could be blamed for at least half of the state's air pollution, which spurred regulators to create a mandate for electric-powered vehicles. Similar clean-air mandates were in the works in other states, such as New York and Massachusetts that were also alarmed by worsening air quality. The laws that were passed varied, but in general they required automakers to begin offering vehicles that met the ultra-low-emissions-vehicle (ULEV) standard or the zero-emissions-vehicle (ZEV) standard.

The mandates were controversial. The principal question was whether states should mandate production of the cars and hope that consumers and ample public charging stations followed or if consumer demand should determine how many electric cars automakers built. GM's research suggested that consumers were receptive to electric cars, even if it meant sacrificing some of the conveniences they enjoyed with gas-powered automobiles. The lack of a public infrastructure was worrisome but not insurmountable to GM. In southern California, for example, utility companies had already begun installing charging sites in locations such as shopping centers, restaurants, hospitals, theaters, and public parking structures. By being the first to bring a car to market, GM would be able to stake a claim to technological leadership going into the next century.

Many in the industry believed that the EV1 and other electric cars could legitimize a new approach to transportation that would dramatically lessen air pollution. John Dunlap III, the chairman of the California Air Resources Board, was enthusiastic about the EV1: "This

General Motors' EV1. © KIM KULISH/CORBIS SYGMA.

has the potential of being a revolutionary step." Others, however, worried that if the EV1 failed it could set back development of alternative-fuel vehicles for years to come.

TARGET MARKET

Not surprisingly, GM selected California as a launch state for the EV1. Arizona, the other launch state, also made sense, for its warm climate allowed for optimal performance of the car's battery. A key marketing decision was made that, while the car would carry the GM badge, it would be leased through the Saturn Corporation subsidiary. The two-seater EV1 seemed to be a good fit with Saturn's young, environmentally conscious buyers. Moreover, by offering the EV1 at Saturn dealerships, where 73 percent of sales were to people whose second choice was not a GM vehicle, GM saw an opportunity to reach import-loyal customers.

Oddly enough, marketing the EV1 was as much about determining who should not drive it as who should. GM was quick to point out that the EV1 was not right for everyone. Joseph Kennedy, the Saturn vice president for marketing, told *Popular Science,* "Because the EV1 is a two-seat vehicle and does not have the long-distance range [of] 200 miles or 300 miles, it will play a role in the owner's portfolio of vehicles." He explained that the EV1 was not a primary household vehicle that could fulfill all driving needs but one appropriate for "shorter, quicker uses around town."

The groundwork for introducing the EV1 was laid in 1994, when GM's PrEview Drive Program gave people in 12 cities the chance to drive a prototype model for two weeks. "We saw that it wasn't going to be an ordinary buyer," Necole Merritt, manager of corporate communications for Saturn, observed. "It was someone attuned to innovation, the kind of person who bought the first cell phone or first computer." The PrEview Drive Program and other research suggested that potential drivers would be affluent college graduates, usually white, middle-aged men who were leaders in their fields. They were expected to be 35 to 54 years old, with an annual family income of more than $125,000 and a high interest in technology and the environment. Frank Pereira, GM's EV1 brand manager, noted that the car "really speaks to those who have a desire to be in the forefront of directing the evolution of technology."

Once the vehicle was in the Saturn retail facilities, sales consultants narrowed the target market even further. Each facility had a consultant trained in EV1 technology who screened customers to be sure that an electric vehicle was appropriate for their needs. Next, would-be customers made an appointment with an electric vehicle marketing specialist who spent up to 12 hours making certain that their driving habits and expectations were a good fit with the EV1. "It's important they convey to customers what this car can and cannot do," explained Donald Young, Saturn's representative for the EV1 program. "We don't want to sell it to someone who drives 60

FROM PLANES TO CARS

General Motors' commitment to the development of an electric car can be traced to a 1977 airplane flight. The plane, called the *Gossamer Condor,* was the first human-powered plane to fly a difficult three-mile course. Designed by engineer Paul MacCready, it had transparent wings spanning 96 feet, virtually no fuselage, and a minuscule cockpit in which the pilot sat and pedaled. The success of the delicate craft led to the creation in 1979 of the *Gossamer Albatross,* a human-powered plane that was able to cross the English Channel. Two years later MacCready built a solar-powered aircraft that accomplished the same feat.

Engineers at GM financed the next MacCready project, which was an aerodynamic, solar-powered vehicle called *Sunraycer.* When the vehicle won a 2,000-mile race in Australia in 1987 against fierce international competition, GM decided to hire MacCready's research firm to build a prototype electric vehicle. This car, called the Impact, debuted at an auto show in Los Angeles in 1990 to tremendous public response. Its innovative design and technology established the direction for what was to become the EV1.

miles to work each way." The specialists also coordinated a home and garage inspection to determine how to install the EV1's charging unit.

COMPETITION

In 1996 a reporter for the *Los Angeles Times* wrote that, "while other major auto makers have held their electric vehicle cards close to the vest, GM has been center stage." Every major automaker, however, was under the same clean-air mandate, and they all kept watchful eyes on the public's reaction to the EV1. What they observed was a market, albeit a small one, emerging.

Other automakers followed on GM's heels. Toyota produced an electric version of its RAV4sport utility vehicle, but for government or company fleet leasing only. In 1997 Ford produced an electric vehicle for fleet use. Ford, however, seemed to be taking a different approach from GM, with its efforts directed at creating alternative-fuel vehicles that would meet ULEV standards. *Consumers' Research Magazine* reported that Ford offered the best range of "street-worthy" alternative-fuel vehicles, including the electric Ranger pickup truck, a Taurus sedan that ran on methanol and ethanol, and several other sedans that ran on compressed natural gas.

In May 1997 Honda presented the most formidable challenge to GM's electric car yet when it introduced its EV Plus, which boasted a longer-life nickel-metal hybrid battery and a greater driving range. Advertising for the EV1, however, did not address any of the emerging competitors. For the time being there was plenty of room for all electric carmakers on the playing field.

MARKETING STRATEGY

To build public awareness of the EV1's introduction, GM hired Hal Riney & Partners, the same marketing and communications partner that had created Saturn's award-winning advertising. Teaser billboards in Los Angeles and San Diego were the first element of the campaign to be unveiled. The billboards displayed a lightning bolt and the words "You can't hear it coming, but it is." The day the cars went on sale, new billboard ads went up with a photograph of the EV1 and the words "The electric car is here."

The campaign's centerpiece was a 90-second television commercial that showed animated household appliances greeting the battery-powered EV1. Its eye-catching special effects were created by Industrial Light and Magic, a studio started by *Star Wars* creator George Lucas. The commercial began with a thunderstorm that knocked the electricity out in a home. When the power came back on, the appliances sprang to life. They unplugged themselves and waddled out the door to watch as the EV1 approached on the street. "It's intended as a celebration of the arrival of the electric vehicle," explained Saturn's Kennedy. Both 30- and 60-second versions of the commercial also aired for 12 weeks in late 1996 and early 1997.

Newspaper ads during the introductory campaign tried to show consumers what a dramatic departure the EV1 was from gasoline-powered cars. For instance, a two-page ad in the *Los Angeles Times* depicted reeds blowing in the wind as the car drove by. It read, "There is no noise. No pistons. No valves or exhaust. Just the whir of an AC motor. And the wind. And your thoughts, of course. As you drive the electric car." Because the automobile was available only in limited markets, the heaviest concentration of newspaper advertising was regional. Newspapers ads appeared in the California edition of the *Wall Street Journal* and in the *Los Angeles Times, Arizona Republic,* and *Phoenix Gazette.*

Magazine advertising during the introductory period was placed to reach leaders in technology and innovation. The media plan included such periodicals as *Business Week, Inc., Scientific American, Wired,* and *American Benefactor.* Magazine ads had the same thoughtful, laid-back

NOTHING NEW

Electric-powered vehicles were anything but a new invention. In fact, in the early 1900s battery-powered cars were all the rage, accounting for about 30 percent of the market. They were quiet and easier to start than gas-powered cars, which had to be cranked. After improvements, however, gasoline-powered cars quickly eclipsed electrics, for they were faster and could go farther. By the 1920s electric cars were a thing of the past.

approach as the newspaper ads. One ad, for instance, showed the blur of the car on a stretch of highway and read, "You will never again use the words 'fill'er up.' Or 'check the oil.' Never utter the need for a tune-up. Or a smog check. Nope. You will simply say, 'Unplug the car and let's go.' When you drive the electric car."

Following the 12-week introductory campaign, the marketing efforts for the EV1 shifted into a lower gear. The remainder of the advertising budget went primarily into direct-mail pieces and a handful of ads in magazines favored by technology buffs.

Time magazine's Margot Hornblower criticized the marketing approach used for the EV1. Describing a billboard that showed a single headlight in the darkness and the words "Electrohydraulic power steering, digital clock, EV1," Hornblower wrote, "The low-key print campaign has been so esoteric as to be nearly incomprehensible." This subtle approach also was frustrating to members of the EV1 Owners Club, who felt that the car's features should be spelled out more clearly in order to lure potential drivers. In fact, Marvin Rush, cofounder of the club, purchased airtime on KFI in Los Angeles with his own money and ran unauthorized spots for four weeks in early 1998. Rush told the *Los Angeles Times* that EV1 owners "consider ourselves evangelists. We're trying to get GM to change its advertising." In the end GM's lawyers reviewed the radio ads for misstatements, found none, and opted to let the renegade campaign run its course. "They're actually pretty good," EV1 brand manager Frank Periera confessed to the *Los Angeles Times.*

OUTCOME

The EV1 advertising campaign received critical kudos. Bob Garfield, a reviewer for *Advertising Age,* wrote that the television commercial used "eye-popping digital effects to communicate the revolutionary significance, the drama and the exciting implications of this introduction." He added, "The march of the electronivores! It's a wonderful concept, wonderfully realized. Even the unplugged among us will not be able not to stare at the futuristic vehicle Californians and Arizonans can buy right now." A print ad for the EV1 took home the prized $100,000 cash Kelly Award for best magazine advertising as well as nonmonetary Kelly Awards for meeting the campaign's objective and for design and graphics.

While the EV1 got rave reviews for its advertising, the car itself had no shortage of critics. Automotive analyst Christopher Cedergen told CBS News, "Overall, the electric car concept is premature. The technology really isn't there yet." Richard de Neufville, professor of transportation at the Massachusetts Institute of Technology, was quoted in *Time* magazine as saying, "They gave a party, and nobody came." GM declined to make sales projections when the EV1 rolled out, but industry sources speculated that fewer than 2,000 would be leased in the first year. That figure proved to be optimistic, for only 300 EV1s were actually leased. Some speculated that the advertising had missed the mark by failing to link the EV1 with Saturn dealerships. Joe Ricciardi, who led GM's EV1 effort in Arizona, acknowledged in the *Arizona Republic* that "there are a lot of people who don't know it [the electric car] is out there and don't know where to find it."

To some the EV1 was most remarkable in its role as a stepping-stone to other clean-air transportation solutions. Phil Hodgetts, president of the Electric Vehicles Association of Southern California, said in the *Los Angeles Times,* "The biggest advantage of the EV1 has been to excite public interest in cars that will be nonpolluting, in pure electric vehicles running on batteries. I think it's the start of something big." GM executives contended all along that the goal of the EV1 was to build a market for alternative-fuel vehicles and that sales volume was less important than giving early drivers a good experience. Despite tepid leasing numbers in 1997, GM's commitment to the EV1 remained firm going into 1998. The car was introduced in the metropolitan areas of San Francisco and Sacramento, the advertising budget was increased from $10 million to $15 million, and GM stepped up efforts to create an infrastructure by committing $750,000 for the development of public charging sites in the car's markets.

While the basic approach remained the same, advertising leading into 1998 introduced a welcome touch of humor to the sometimes awestruck tone of the 1997 campaign. A few print ads even cleverly capitalized on the public's dubiousness. An ad that ran in newspapers in northern California, for example, showed an overhead view of the EV1 and stated, "All the skepticism in the world can't stop it. The electric car is here."

FURTHER READING

"Charge over Electric Cars." *Newsday,* February 13, 1997, p. A75.

Cogan, Ron. "The Electric Experience." *Popular Science,* November 1, 1996, p. 81.

Gardner, Greg. "GM Flips EV1 'On' Switch." *Ward's Auto World,* March 1, 1996, p. 89.

Garfield, Bob. "EV1 Provides Saturn with Charge of Pride." *Advertising Age,* November 1996.

Gellene, Denise. "Electric Car Owner Spots GM Some Ads." *Los Angeles Times,* May 22, 1998, p. D1.

Golfen, Bob. "GM Trying to Spark Interest in EV1: Allowing Car's Sale Could Be Next Step." *Arizona Republic,* March 29, 1997.

Hornblower, Margot. "Is This Clean Machine for Real? Electric Cars Hum down the Road but Face Obstacles of High Cost, Limited Range, and Unlimited Politics." *Time,* December 15, 1997, p. 62.

Maynard, Michelle. "Only A List Can Buy New E Car." *USA Today,* August 28, 1996, p. 1.

Nauss, Donald W. "GM's EV1 Gears Up amid Charge of the Ad Brigade." *Los Angeles Times,* November 26, 1996, p. D3.

———. "GM Rolls Dice with Roll-Out of Electric Car." *Los Angeles Times,* December 5, 1996, Home Edition, p. A1.

Peters, Eric. "Alternative Fuel Vehicles." *Consumers' Research Magazine,* October 1, 1997, p. 35.

"Reality Check on Electric Cars." *Los Angeles Times,* September 1, 1996, p. B4.

Kim Kazemi

HUMMER CAMPAIGN

OVERVIEW

When General Motors Corporation (GM) acquired the commercial marketing rights to the Hummer truck, the civilian version of the U.S. Army's Humvee, it faced the challenge of promoting a vehicle that was never intended to be sold in high numbers. Part of the solution was to design smaller, less-expensive versions, the H2 and H3, but much of the success would have to depend on the marketing. Rather than turning to a roster of ad agencies it usually worked with, GM hired a young Boston creative boutique, Modernista!, in 2000.

The initial goal of the $35 million campaign, begun in August 2001, was to establish Hummer as a luxury brand. Thus, images of mud-splattered Hummers that played up the vehicle's off-road capabilities were scrapped in favor of shots that made it seem jewel-like. Once the brand was repositioned, the marketers' goal was to pitch the lower-priced H2 and H3 to a wider market, hopefully to more women.

Factors such as rising gas prices and the perception that the Hummer was oversized for most consumers proved to be major hurdles for the marketers. However, by the end of 2003 the campaign had succeeded in redefining the Hummer brand, and with the introduction of the H3 in 2005, the marketers took on a new challenge: selling the Hummer to a mass market.

HISTORICAL CONTEXT

The Humvee was designed for the U.S. Army in 1979 by AM General Corp., based in South Bend, Indiana. The 3.5-ton vehicle became a star of the 1991 Persian Gulf War, spurring consumer demand for a civilian version, which was introduced in 1992 as the Hummer. It catered to an exclusive market, as demonstrated by the fact that Arnold Schwarzenegger was one of the first buyers. The vehicle never received much advertising support; AM General spent less than $1 million on marketing the Hummer in 1999, when it sold about 700 of the trucks. Nevertheless, AM General did enough business to attract the attention of General Motors, and in the end bought the Hummer brand in late 1999.

GM signed a seven-year contract with AM General to produce the next generation, GM-designed version, the Hummer H2 sport-utility vehicle (SUV). The agency Modernista! was hired to promote the brand. Prior marketing efforts had played up the military connection and the Hummer's off-road capabilities, billing the vehicle as "the world's most serious 4x4." Modernista! won the account because it was the only agency that attempted to fashion a wider appeal by going beyond the tough-guy, army-truck image.

The principals involved in the campaign did not lack experience in selling cars. Modernista!'s cofounder, Lance Jensen, had worked with Hummer's advertising director, Liz Vanzura, when she was at Volkswagen of America and he was with the Boston-based ad agency Arnold Communications. Both played key roles in developing Volkswagen's award-winning "Drivers Wanted" campaign. Vanzura commented that, while the Volkswagen ads were aimed at "cool, young people," her new mission was to sell Hummers to "cool, rich people."

TARGET MARKET

Even before hiring Modernista!, GM had done a great deal of market research. According to Ted Evanoff, writing for the *Indianapolis Star,* "In 1999 researchers stumbled across the notion that an unlikely cross-section of America—surgeons, dot-com millionaires, rock stars, high school students, corporate execs—prized their individuality. And they regarded the rugged Hummer as a symbol of individuality, especially compared with the typical sport-utility common in suburbia." Modernista! was given 2,200 pages of market data to distill into an advertising message. The agency was also handed a brand that skewed very much toward males, averaging 50 years

© NAJLAH FEANNY/CORBIS.

in age and with an annual household income of more than $200,000. The target buyer for the less-expensive H2, while still male, was 42 years old on average and had a household income above $125,000. Vanzura told Chris Reidy of the *Boston Globe* that the coveted audience included "rugged individualists, adventurous entrepreneurs, and adrenaline junkies." In other interviews she described the target market as "successful achievers" and "style leaders." She also told Evanoff that Hummer had to vie with other purchases the well-to-do might consider, such as yachts or vacation houses, stating, "We're really not competing in an automotive category."

COMPETITION

The yacht, vacation house, and other status symbols notwithstanding, Hummer competed in the luxury-SUV category against other SUVs, including the Lincoln Navigator, Land Rover's Range Rover, and the Lexus LX 470. But Hummer's chief opponent was DaimlerChrysler's Jeep Wrangler. Boasting similar military roots but extending back to World War II, Jeep had defined the SUV category and at its height in 1993 controlled nearly 30 percent of the traditional SUV market. Over the following several years, however, the brand failed had to introduce new models, and its less-expensive ones faced increasingly stiff competition, resulting in a severe erosion of sales. As long as Hummer was not a direct competitor, DaimlerChrysler took little notice of it, but as soon as GM acquired the right to mass-market the Hummer, DaimlerChrysler recognized the threat at the high end of the SUV category and became determined to hold on to Jeep's reputation as the premier heavy-duty, off-road brand.

The two vehicles had slightly different target markets, however. Jeep appealed to consumers who loved the outdoors and might attend one of the dozens of Jeep Jamboree off-road events held throughout the year. Typical Hummer customers, on the other hand, wanted the off-road capabilities the vehicle had to offer but were more interested in the image it created. They were as likely to drive their Hummers to an upscale mall as up a mountain.

MARKETING STRATEGY

In preparation for marketing the lower-priced H2, Modernista! instituted a bridge campaign, paid for by AM General, to sell the H1 while repositioning the brand. As Will Uronis, an associate creative director at Modernista!, explained to the *Boston Herald*'s Greg Gatlin, "Hollywood had defined what Hummers stood for—war, explosions and arrogance... We just took a look at another facet of the truck." Jensen added, "We went out and talked to guys that drove them... they don't all hunt and kill things." Nevertheless, Hollywood movies had done a good job of making consumers aware of the Hummer. Market research conducted in 1999 indicated that as many as one in five buyers of full-size SUVs considered purchasing the Hummer. The bridge campaign was intended to play to the "rugged individualists" who, research revealed, were

FAMILY FEUD

Hummer and its chief rival, Jeep, shared a common heritage. American Motors bought the Jeep business from Kaiser Jeep in 1970, forming the basis of a military unit that was spun off as a subsidiary, AM General Corp. In 1979 AM General designed the Humvee for the U.S. Army as a military transport vehicle and incorporated Jeep's seven-slot grille. When Chrysler acquired the Jeep business in 1987, the two vehicles parted ways. AM General introduced the civilian version of the Humvee, the Hummer, in 1992. Although Chrysler did not initially object to sharing the Jeep's distinctive grille, that changed in 1999, when GM acquired the rights to market Hummer and became a direct threat to the Jeep franchise. In February 2001 DaimlerChrysler sued General Motors, alleging that the Hummer's front grille too closely resembled that of the Jeep. DaimlerChrysler lost, and the cousins continued to share a family resemblance.

attracted to the Hummer and to set the stage for the launch of the H2 by creating an emotional attachment to the brand that transcended the hard-edged image fostered by Hollywood. According to Evanoff, writing in the *Indianapolis Star,* the promotion of the H1 was intended to create a "halo" over the brand, providing "the foundation for a brand image that will carry the smaller H2."

The first national ads for the GM-owned Hummer began appearing on August 13, 2001. It was an all-print campaign that featured photographs of the vehicle in lush locales in Chile. Not only did the pictures suggest where the H1, with its off-road prowess, could take the viewer, but they also made the big truck look small. It was the first time Hummer was not portrayed covered in mud or linked to the military. Reinforcing the visual message of the ad was the text, which included the headline "How did my soul get way out here?" and the concluding text "Sometimes you find yourself in the middle of nowhere. And sometimes in the middle of nowhere you find yourself. The legendary H1." Hummer's longtime tagline, "World's most serious 4x4," was replaced by "Like nothing else." The four ads ran through the rest of 2001, appearing in such publications as the *Wall Street Journal, Barron's, Esquire, Spin, Wired,* and *Red Herring.* Hummer's 50 dealers were also encouraged to use the ads created by Modernista! to bring continuity to the brand's makeover, with some of their media costs being reimbursed by a cooperative advertising program.

The H2, based on GM's Chevrolet Tahoe full-size SUV, was introduced in July 2002. A second model featuring a small pickup bed and a cargo door was supposed to be offered at the same time, but the launch was pushed back, partly because the vehicle needed more work but also as a way to extend the marketing buzz the brand was creating. The new H2, with a base price of $48,000, was about half the price of the H1 and, despite being called the "baby Hummer," essentially the same size. But it featured a smaller, less noisy gas engine rather than a cumbersome diesel one, and it had comforts and customizable options the H1 lacked but that were expected in a luxury SUV.

The introduction of the H2 was supported by another print campaign developed by Modernista! While the "Like nothing else" tagline of the previous ads was retained, the look of the new ads was markedly different, relying on dramatic close-ups set against bold, sky-blue backgrounds.

Like the first ads, the new ones ran in a wide range of magazines, with the text tailored to the publication. For example, in the *Robb Report,* which covered all things luxurious, the text read, "Excessive. In a Rome at the height of its power sort of way." The *Vanity Fair* text read, "Threaten the men in your office in a whole new way," part of an effort to increase the number of women buying the vehicles. Another ad proclaimed, "Perfect for rugby moms." About 10 percent of H1 owners were women, and one goal of the H2 campaign was to increase that number to 25 percent. Outdoor ads were also produced, running in 14 major markets, including New York, Los Angeles, Chicago, and Detroit. Print and outdoor ads were made available for the use of dealers.

The first Hummer television ads aired in mid-August 2002. The initial three 30-second spots, intended to romanticize the truck, were shot in Iceland and in Vancouver, British Columbia, and featured both natural and urban locations. They showed friends in a Hummer speeding over the tundra of Iceland or a professional woman weaving through traffic in a city. Set to rock music, the only words in the spots were text statements such as "Maybe if you can, you will." A second phase of the television campaign played on people's perception of the Hummer as a gas-guzzling road hog. In one spot a young boy constructed a small wooden version of the Hummer to enter in a soapbox derby, while The Who's "Happy Jack" played in the background and the little girl next door looked on. At the start of the big race the other boys scoffed at little Jack and his less-than-streamlined racer, but he prevailed by abandoning the asphalt course, breaking the rules to go cross-country and win the race and the girl. Through the humor of the spot Jack was portrayed not as a blatant cheater but as a heroic iconoclast, offering subliminal reassurance to potential Hummer customers who might feel guilty about buying a vehicle that got about 13 miles to a gallon of gas on the highway. A second Hummer spot, also displaying a tough side, hearkened back to the Asteroids video game of the 1980s, with a spaceship blasting boulders only to confront an indestructible Hummer, which chased the ship off the screen.

OUTCOME

GM and Modernista! succeeded in introducing Hummer to a wider market, but after a strong showing in 2003, sales began to tail off, partly because of high gas prices. To regain lost ground, in 2004 GM introduced the H2 SUT (sport-utility truck). This was followed by the unveiling in 2005 of the H3, a midsize Hummer priced from $29,500 to $32,000. Almost 17 inches shorter, 1,700 pounds lighter, and more fuel-efficient at 20 miles per gallon, it was a vehicle GM hoped women and younger drivers would find more appealing.

In pitching the vehicle to a mass market, Hummer and Modernista! faced a new task. Putting a positive spin on the challenge, Jensen told Jeremy W. Peters of the *New York Times,* "The brand has a lot of different personality levels . . . You can do the serious capability stuff, the real rough-and-tumble rock climbing stuff, the peaceful back-to-nature stuff." Industry analyst Mary Ann Keller disagreed, telling the *New York Times* that it was impossible to sell Hummer to the masses: "How in the world can you possibly fathom that something that looks like a military vehicle is practical for the average driver?"

FURTHER READING

Cantwell, Julie. "General Motors Is Trying to Wipe the Mud Off Hummer." *Automotive News,* August 6, 2001.

Evanoff, Ted. "GM Blazes a New Trail with Its Marketing Strategy for Upscale Hummer." *Indianapolis Star,* August 12, 2001.

Garfield, Bob. "Garfield's AdReview." *Advertising Age,* July 7, 2003, p. 25.

Greenberg, Karl. "Liz Vanzura: GM's Ad Director Is on a Roll." *Brandweek,* April 7, 2003.

Hakim, Danny. "Spots for the Hummer and the Hybrid Prius, Opposites on the Road." *New York Times,* September 11, 2003, p. C5.

Halliday, Jean. "Of Hummers and Zen." *Advertising Age,* August 6, 2001, p. 29.

Irwin, Tanya. "GM's Hummer Choice Reflects Desire for Daring." *Adweek,* October 16, 2000, p. 6.

———. "Modernista! Launches $20 Mil. Hummer Campaign." *Adweek,* July 8, 2002, p. 5.

———. "Modernista! Repositions Hummer." *Brandweek,* August 6, 2001, p. 5.

Peters, Jeremy W. "How to Market Hummers to the Masses." *New York Times,* June 28, 2005, p. C3.

Reidy, Chris. "Boston Ad Agency Hopes Hummer Ads Juice General Motors Profits." *Boston Globe,* August 16, 2001.

Wells, Melanie. "Muscle Car." *Forbes,* July 22, 2002.

Ed Dinger

LOOKING FOR MR. GOODWRENCH CAMPAIGN

OVERVIEW

In the early 2000s General Motors Corporation (GM) found itself the victim of its own success. Improved quality in its vehicles had resulted in less warranty work for the service centers of GM dealerships, which very much depended on the revenues. All of GM's 7,400 dealers were brought under the Goodwrench program (a national chain of GM dealer repair shops), and the ad agency chemistri (later called Leo Burnett Detroit) was given the task of building up the brand to attract more nonwarranty work to the service centers. The marketers decided to revive the Mr. Goodwrench character, not seen in GM ads for almost a generation but still alive as a cultural icon. The result was the "Looking for Mr. Goodwrench" campaign.

Rather than portray Mr. Goodwrench as an actual person, as was done from 1975 to 1985, chemistri revisited the concept by creating an oblivious reporter character, played by comedian Stephen Colbert, known for a similar role on Comedy Central's program *The Daily Show.* He set off on a never-ending quest to find the one and only Mr. Goodwrench, never quite able to comprehend that every one of GM's 80,000 technicians was, in essence, Mr. Goodwrench. In addition to 30-second TV spots, the campaign consisted of radio spots and print ads, supplemented by an updated website.

In the first year GM spent $50 million on the "Looking for Mr. Goodwrench" campaign, which began in March 2003 and succeeded in elevating the Goodwrench brand in the minds of consumers. Colbert's rising stardom also helped the campaign, and he was retained for a second set of TV spots, launched in October 2004, and for a third in 2005.

HISTORICAL CONTEXT

To promote its network of dealership service centers, in 1975 GM's Service and Parts Operations (SPO) introduced Mr. Goodwrench, the everyman of General

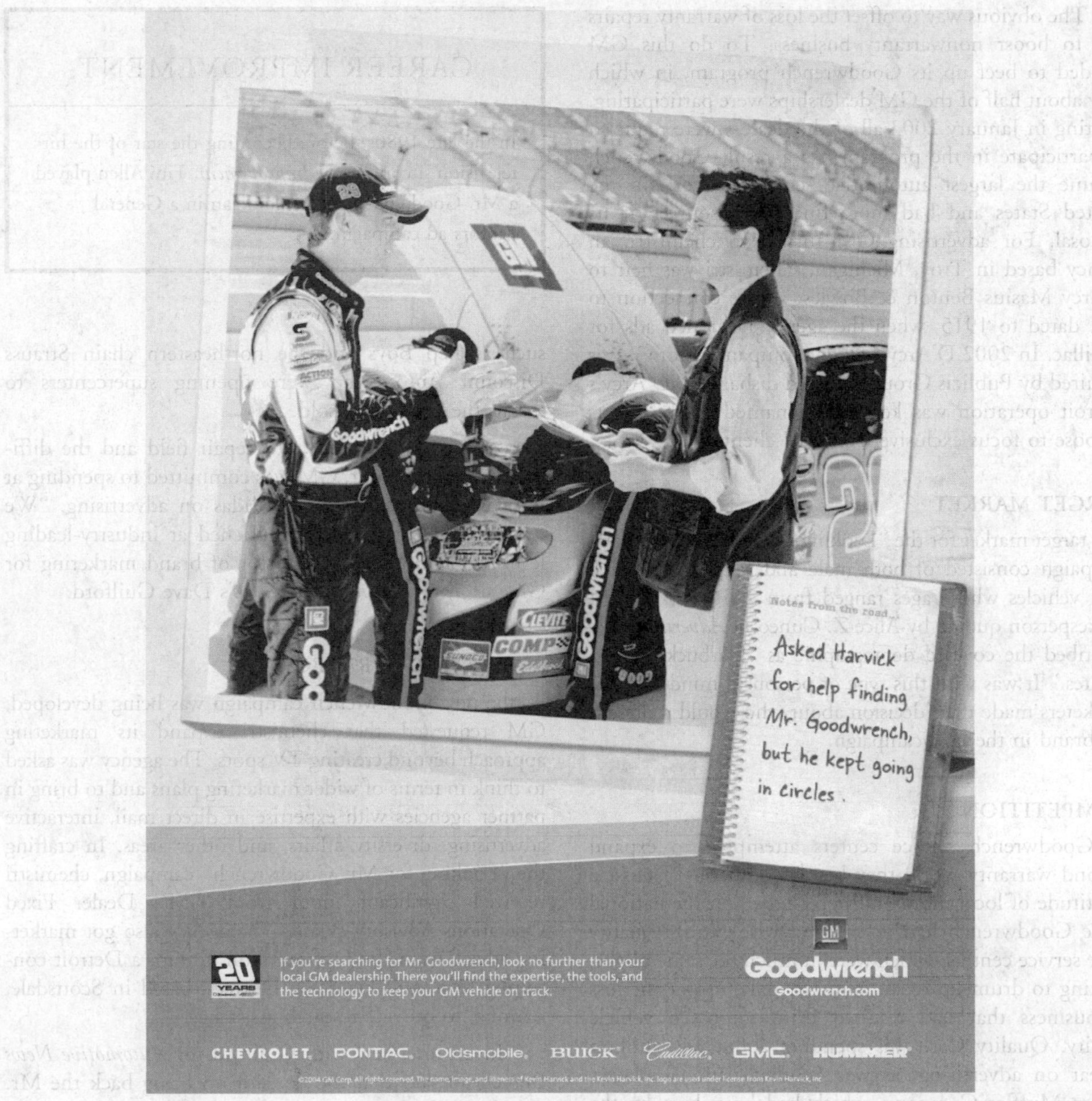

Steven Colbert looking for Mr. Goodwrench. **PHOTO COURTESY OF LEO BURNETT DETROIT. REPRODUCED BY PERMISSION.**

Motors technicians, along with the slogan "Keep that great GM feeling with genuine GM parts." The character remained the focal point of GM SPO ads for a decade. In the ensuing years, however, GM SPO received fewer advertising dollars and produced no memorable campaigns. In the meantime the quality of General Motors cars improved, resulting in a significant erosion in income for the shops, which concentrated on performing warranty work. In 2002, for example, GM cars had 130 problems per 100 vehicles, an 11 percent improvement over the prior year, placing the company third in quality behind Toyota and Honda. Because their cars had fewer problems, GM consumers also became lax about taking them in for scheduled maintenance and repairs, adding further to the loss of business at GM repair shops. It was estimated that dealers performed 15 to 20 percent less warranty work in 2002 than in 2001. GM dealers became concerned that the loss of warranty work would reduce the amount of money they could invest in mechanics' training and service facilities and that this would produce a downward spiral of diminished service quality, poor reputation, and further erosion of sales.

The obvious way to offset the loss of warranty repairs was to boost nonwarranty business. To do this GM decided to beef up its Goodwrench program, in which only about half of the GM dealerships were participating. Starting in January 2003 all of the dealers were required to participate in the program. As a result Goodwrench became the largest automotive service network in the United States and had more financial resources at its disposal. For advertising GM turned to chemistri, an agency based in Troy, Michigan. Chemistri was heir to D'Arcy Masius Benton & Bowles, whose connection to GM dated to 1915, when the agency fashioned ads for Cadillac. In 2002 D'Arcy's parent company, Bcom3, was acquired by Publicis Groupe SA and disbanded. D'Arcy's Detroit operation was kept and renamed chemistri, its purpose to focus exclusively on GM clients.

TARGET MARKET

The target market for the "Looking for Mr. Goodwrench" campaign consisted of both male and female owners of GM vehicles whose ages ranged from 24 to 54. A GM spokesperson quoted by Alice Z. Cuneo in *Advertising Age* described the coveted demographic as "Starbucks suburbanites." It was with this type of person in mind that the marketers made their decision about who would represent the brand in the new campaign.

COMPETITION

As Goodwrench service centers attempted to expand beyond warranty work, they began competing against a multitude of local mom-and-pop shops. On the national scene Goodwrench had to contend with Ford's Quality Care service centers, which were in much the same plight, looking to drum up repair work to make up for the loss of business that had resulted from improved vehicle quality. Quality Care was spending about $40 million a year on advertising, as was another national player, Midas Muffler Company, which had been hurt by the introduction of longer-lasting mufflers in the 1990s. Midas was attempting to reposition itself as a general car maintenance center instead of just a muffler shop, and it had the benefit of a well-recognized brand to aid in the effort.

Goodwrench also faced regional competition from smaller muffler shops, such as Meineke Discount Mufflers, which had changed the name of its 900 shops in Canada and the United States to Meineke Car Care Center. Although it lacked the budgets of other companies, Meineke had the advantage of a celebrity pitchman, boxer George Foreman. Another muffler chain stepping into the fray was the 600-unit Monro Muffler and Brake. Moreover, the repair field was crowded with competitors of a different type: auto parts retailers—such as Pep Boys and the northeastern chain Strauss Discount Auto—who were opening supercenters to install the parts they sold.

> ### CAREER IMPROVEMENT
>
> In the late 1980s, before becoming the star of the hit television sitcom *Home Improvement,* Tim Allen played a Mr. Goodwrench-like technician in a General Motors ad campaign.

Given the crowded auto repair field and the difficulty of standing out, GM was committed to spending at least as much as Ford and Midas on advertising. "We want to get this program launched at industry-leading levels," Jon Brancheau, director of brand marketing for GM SPO, told *Automotive News*'s Dave Guilford.

MARKETING STRATEGY

As the new Goodwrench campaign was being developed, GM requested that chemistri expand its marketing approach beyond creating TV spots. The agency was asked to think in terms of wider marketing plans and to bring in partner agencies with expertise in direct mail, interactive advertising, diversity affairs, and other areas. In crafting the "Looking for Mr. Goodwrench" campaign, chemistri received significant input from GM's Dealer Fixed Operations Advisory Board. The agency also got marketing advice from the Optimization Group, a Detroit consulting firm, and hired Six Degrees, based in Scottsdale, Arizona, to provide research assistance.

In an interview with Guilford for *Automotive News* Brancheau said that the decision to bring back the Mr. Goodwrench character, even though he would be nothing more than a phantom, was a "no-brainer." Research showed that, despite an 18-year absence, Mr. Goodwrench remained firmly entrenched in the mind of consumers. The marketers elected to use humor, but because it was important to portray the technicians as skilled professionals, they had to walk a fine line. The challenge, therefore, was to find a way to relay serious information—such as the fact that dealer technicians used the latest in diagnostic tools and had received more then one million hours of combined training in the previous year—and still be funny. Humor also helped to address another potential pitfall: focusing too much on the need for service, which might carry the implication that GM products were not trustworthy. Moreover, humor helped spice up what was a less-than-exciting subject for consumers. Marketing

A COMEDY VET

Born in South Carolina, Stephen Colbert, star of the "Looking for Mr. Goodwrench" campaign, studied acting at Northwestern University. He got his start with the Second City comedy troupe in Chicago, then moved to New York with fellow cast members to create the sketch comedy show *Exit 57* for Comedy Central. After two seasons Colbert joined *The Daily Show* in 1997. He was also a creator and star of the acclaimed program *Strangers With Candy,* which aired on Comedy Central from 1999 to 2000.

director Beth Grotz told Theresa Howard of *USA Today,* "Your typical automotive service ad is a technician or service manager pleading with you to come in. We thought we'd take a little different approach to see if we could get more interest in the category."

To serve as the focal point of the new Goodwrench campaign, GM elected to hire a comedian and settled on Stephen Colbert, a reporter on Comedy Central's *The Daily Show,* a satire of an evening news program. Colbert's deadpan delivery and well-honed dimwit persona made him an ideal choice to play the role of a reporter searching to find the one and only Mr. Goodwrench. While many people may not have recognized Colbert at the time, he was well known by the target market.

The "Looking for Mr. Goodwrench" campaign was multifaceted. In addition to TV spots, it included radio, print, and Internet elements. Print ads appeared in such magazines as *People, Newsweek, Time, Sports Illustrated, Better Homes and Gardens,* and *Ebony.* All ads mentioned the Goodwrench website, where consumers could find additional information and locate their nearest service center.

The focus of the campaign was four 30-second television spots, which aired during both network and cable programs. In addition, chemistri created five spots that dealers could air on their own, and GM established 30 local marketing groups to fund local advertising. The national ads first appeared in March 2003, in time to be shown during telecasts of the NCAA Men's Basketball Championship. They were also shown during other sporting events, including NASCAR races, a major venue for promoting anything automotive. Moreover, GM Goodwrench sponsored a race car, which would be featured in one of the TV spots.

All four of the first wave of ads in the "Looking for Mr. Goodwrench" campaign featured Colbert's clueless reporter attempting to uncover the identity of the man called Goodwrench. The spot called "Service Bay" showed Colbert in a safari vest that would become the character's trademark. He interviewed three GM service technicians, asking, "Mr. Goodwrench—who is this one and only GM expert?" They all claimed to be Mr. Goodwrench, confusing Colbert, who resorted to a bullhorn to ask the real Mr. Goodwrench to please step forward. The spot closed with the line "Find Mr. Goodwrench at over 7,000 GM dealerships nationwide." A second spot, "Mitre Saw," was broken into two parts. First, when told that Mr. Goodwrench had more than one million hours of training, the disbelieving reporter quipped, "Doesn't leave much time for Mrs. Goodwrench now, does it?" Colbert then asked a technician what kind of tool Mr. Goodwrench would be if he were a tool. When the bemused technician answered, "Wrench," Colbert was quick to reply, "No, the correct answer is mitre saw."

The final two spots in the initial "Looking for Mr. Goodwrench" campaign took Colbert out of the service center. In "NASCAR Garage" he visited with the driver of the GM Goodwrench-sponsored race car, Kevin Harvick. Colbert was again skeptical when Harvick confirmed that Mr. Goodwrench knew GM cars better than he did and could be found both at the track and at GM dealerships. The spot closed with Harvick expelling Colbert from his race car, where Colbert was pretending to be a driver. In the last spot, "On the Street," Colbert approached people to question them about Mr. Goodwrench, capping off the interviews by outlandishly asking whether he did root canals as well as service work on GM vehicles.

There was no doubt that Colbert's work on the TV and radio spots was the cornerstone of the success of the "Looking for Mr. Goodwrench" campaign. When the ratings of *The Daily Show* improved dramatically during the U.S. presidential campaign of 2004, Colbert's visibility grew. The show's "Indecision 2004" coverage was especially popular with a younger demographic, part of which admitted to getting most, if not all, of their real news from the fake news show. GM's Goodwrench service centers enjoyed Colbert's reflected popularity. GM even became a sponsor of *The Daily Show*'s website. Market research indicated that, after the launch of the campaign, GM experienced significant gains in unaided brand awareness, ad awareness, and brand consideration.

In October 2004, in an attempt to build on the momentum created over the previous year, GM began airing two new spots in the "Looking for Mr. Goodwrench" campaign. Colbert was again featured, this time joined by a sidekick, comedian Brian Posehn. Together they traveled in a tiny three-wheeled truck with "Looking for Mr. Goodwrench" emblazoned on the side. In the spot titled "Stakeout" they tried using high-tech equipment in a dealership parking lot to find Mr. Goodwrench. In the second spot, "APB," Colbert asked a mounted police officer to put out an all points bulletin (APB) for Mr. Goodwrench, noting that Mr. Goodwrench claimed to spend more than a million hours a year training. "Do you know what that means?" he asked. "Expertise?" suggested the officer. "Two words," replied Colbert, then offered three: "Labor law infraction."

Three new "Looking for Mr. Goodwrench" ads appeared in the summer of 2005. While the little truck made an appearance when Colbert challenged Harvick to a race, Posehn did not. Instead, Colbert was solo once again, questioning technicians and customers alike in his ongoing search for Mr. Goodwrench, a concept that continued to provide the copywriters with enough humorous situations to exploit Colbert's talent and promote the Goodwrench brand.

OUTCOME

GM was extremely pleased with the "Looking for Mr. Goodwrench" ads. As Grotz told the online resource the Auto Channel, "GM has broken away from the pack... Most vehicle service ads feature a technician holding a part in his or her hand, but we moved away from the typical spot and connected with consumers through unique settings in addition to the dealership environment, and through humor." The campaign was recognized by the advertising industry, winning a Bronze EFFIE Award (Automotive Aftermarket Products and Services category) in 2005. Meanwhile, Colbert's high profile, both in films and on Comedy Central, added luster to the ongoing campaign.

FURTHER READING

Baker, Ross K. "Logo-Types." *American Demographics* 11, no. 3 (March 1989): p. 68.

Bonamici, Kate. "The Daily Show Shill." *Fortune,* November 29, 2004, p. 64.

"Chemistri Continues Search for Mr. Goodwrench." *Adweek,* October 5, 2004.

Cuneo, Alice Z. "Marketers, Politicians Clamor for 'Daily' Fix." *Advertising Age,* September 27, 2004, p. 12.

Guilford, Dave. "GM Boosts Goodwrench Advertising." *Automotive News,* March 17, 2003, p. 8.

Halliday, Jean. "GM's New Goodwrench Ads Seek Trust in Dealer Service." *Advertising Age,* June 7, 1999, p. 20.

———. "Goodwrench Rolls First Ads in 2 Years." *Advertising Age,* August 18, 1997, p. 25.

Howard, Theresa. "GM Revives Mr. Goodwrench Ads, Throwing in Comedic Twist." *USA Today,* December 5, 2004.

Irwin, Tanya. "New GM Spots Look for Mr. Goodwrench." *Brandweek,* March 17, 2003, p. 12.

Jackson, Kathy. "D'Arcy Takes a New Name." *Automotive News,* March 17, 2003, p. 22.

Miller, Duane. "Driving Service Business during Car Care Month." *Automotive News,* April 11, 2005, p. 2.

"Mr. Goodwrench Cranks up Fresh Pitch for GM Service." *Brandweek,* March 17, 2003, p. 7.

Ed Dinger

START SOMETHING CAMPAIGN

OVERVIEW

Once the crown jewel of the General Motors Corp. (GM), the Oldsmobile division had fallen on hard times. As a result, GM went so far as to contemplate terminating the venerable Oldsmobile nameplate, but it opted to reinvent the division instead. Beginning in 1994 Oldsmobile introduced new cars designed to appeal to younger consumers and help win back sales from competitors. Moreover, GM designated Oldsmobile as its import-fighting wing. To this end Oldsmobile created the Alero, a compact car designed to take on such best-sellers as Honda Motor Co.'s Accord and Toyota Motor Corp.'s Camry. With a planned launch date of September 1, 1998, Oldsmobile turned to its longtime ad agency, the Leo Burnett Company, to create a campaign that would generate excitement about the Alero.

For this $80 million kickoff campaign, Oldsmobile adopted the tagline "Start Something." The commercials were unlike anything Oldsmobile had ever done before. In both the 15-second teaser commercials (which debuted August 3, 1998) and the 30-second commercials (which began on September 1), quick-cutting images were set to a pulsing electronic sound track, scenes of screaming teenagers were interspersed with shots of the Alero, and red ovals spelled out such commands as "Start to Scream" and "Stop Commuting. Start Driving." Every spot closed with the "Start Something" moniker. Leo Burnett also created print pieces and savvy Internet ads.

The Alero and its supporting marketing campaign were deemed a success by General Motors executives as well as industry insiders. The campaign also managed to reach its target audience of younger consumers. GM predicted that 1999 sales of the Alero would reach or surpass 100,000 vehicles. Based on its success, the campaign was continued in 1999 and expanded to include the entire Oldsmobile line of vehicles. Early in 2000 the tagline "Start Something" was modified depending on which vehicle was being promoted in the specific spot. The initial success of the Alero was brief, however, and by the end of 2000 Oldsmobile sales were again on the decline. In December 2000 GM announced that it was ceasing production of Oldsmobiles.

HISTORICAL CONTEXT

Oldsmobile had once been perceived as a "status" car, a high-powered American car for the stylish executive with a family, said an article in the July 15, 1991, *Adweek*. Between 1983 and 1986 the division sold more than one million cars per year. In 1987, however, Oldsmobile's fortunes waned. GM's policy of "badge engineering" resulted in Oldsmobile's vehicles becoming indistinguishable from other GM lines, diluting the brand's cachet. In addition, the company was slow to introduce new products that kept up with consumers' tastes. Although Oldsmobile's 1988 campaign, "This Is Not Your Father's Oldsmobile! This Is a New Generation of Olds," was lauded by ad critics and popular with consumers, it did little to bolster the brand's sinking sales. By 1996 Oldsmobile's share of the U.S. car market had reached an all-time low of 2.2 percent (down from its 1995 share of 2.6 percent). Its 1996 sales were 14.5 percent lower than in 1995. According to *Fortune* magazine, Oldsmobile's loyal customers were aging and had either "died or defected to Buick."

The division took stock of its situation in the mid-1990s and committed itself to revamping its entire product line. In 1994 Oldsmobile debuted the Aurora, which served as "the centerpiece of [the company's] strategy to boost sagging sales by attracting buyers younger than its traditional sixty-something crowd," noted *USA Today*. The redesigned Bravada sport-utility vehicle (model year 1996), the Silhouette and Cutlass (1997), and the Intrigue (1997) followed. So adamant was Oldsmobile to reach younger drivers that in 1997 it teamed up with *The X-Files,* a show that had a cultlike following among Generation Xers, for a major promotion. Nevertheless, Oldsmobile had no entry-level car that could draw consumers into the Oldsmobile line, so as the entire Oldsmobile line struggled to shed its geriatric image, Alero was pegged as the division's entry-level vehicle.

TARGET MARKET

Priced between $17,500 and $22,000, the Alero was designated as the entry-level vehicle of the Oldsmobile line. The division intended it to be a high-volume car and set a prelaunch goal for Alero of eventually accounting for 40 percent of Oldsmobile's sales. "Start Something" was grounded in the premise that the bulk of the consumers who would ultimately drive these sales would be those between the ages of 30 and 50. Within this broad demographic group, Oldsmobile focused on "well-educated singles or young families with children," according to the *San Diego Union-Tribune*. The division's lingering reputation for "fogey-mobiles" made this a challenging audience to win over. Nevertheless, it was an important segment for Oldsmobile to capture. The grail for all car companies was to have consumers "grow" within a line of cars—to start with low-end vehicles and progress to ever-more expensive cars as they became older and wealthier. Market research had shown that brand allegiances were often formed early and tended to be long lasting. If Oldsmobile were to survive, it had to introduce consumers to its line.

To indicate that the Alero represented a new direction for Oldsmobile, Leo Burnett crafted a campaign that was meant to stand out from the array of other car commercials and seize viewers' attention for itself. "At first glance, it doesn't look like car advertising—it's not supposed to," the division explained in an August 26, 1998, press release. To add to the aura of uniqueness, Oldsmobile opted not to use actors in the commercials. "These are real people with real lives and passions. They closely reflect the attitude and character of the Alero," said Mike Sands, Oldsmobile's director of advertising. Moreover, the commercials had a high-energy, youthful feeling. Images of children, teens at a concert, a martial artist, and a man jumping off a mountain into the snow were the core of the spots. The sound track was modern and pulsing, and the quick-cutting cinematography resembled a music video more than a standard car commercial. "We want people who are willing to try something new," Sands told *Automotive News.* But Oldsmobile was careful not to position itself too far outside the mainstream. The company wanted women to account for 50 percent of its sales, and conventional wisdom held that this demographic responded well to family-oriented messages. As a result, the division included upbeat domestic scenes in many of its ads. "The spots are trying to communicate a certain way of thinking and living," a Leo Burnett spokesperson told *Adweek*. "[The campaign] speaks to a consumer set that is very new to Oldsmobile."

Oldsmobile pitched the Alero not only to younger drivers but also to minority groups, most notably Hispanics and African-Americans. The U.S. Census predicted that Hispanics would account for 42 percent of America's population growth between 1998 and 2008, while only 2.3 percent of Oldsmobile's 1997 sales had come from Hispanics. African-Americans were also underrepresented among Oldsmobile consumers. "There is a huge potential for the Alero to gain Hispanic and African-American customers who had never before considered buying an Oldsmobile," Oldsmobile's brand manager Bob Clark explained to *Automotive News* in September 1998. In its bid to pitch Alero to Hispanic and African-American consumers, Oldsmobile created

REAR VIEW?

One interesting aspect of the "Start Something" teaser spots for the Alero was that each commercial ended with a shot of the Alero backing up, seemingly out of the commercial. The image was probably meant to help differentiate "Start Something" ads from the visual cacophony of other car advertising.

separate ads that targeted these distinct communities. For instance, Alero's Hispanic-oriented advertising used the tagline "Vivelo," which meant "To Live," because "Start Something" translated poorly.

COMPETITION

As GM's "import-fighting" line, Oldsmobile wanted the Alero to compete against comparable compact sedans by the established import players—the Honda Accord, the Toyota Camry, the Nissan Altima, and the Mazda 626. Alero's task was a difficult one because it involved "mak[ing] conquest sales in a shrinking market segment," according to *Automotive News.* Sales in the lower mid-range segment that Alero sought to enter had seen shrinking sales, as increasing numbers of consumers bought sport-utility vehicles and other light trucks instead of cars. It was a highly competitive market, and Alero's rivals conducted savvy campaigns designed to keep their share of the market. Claiming converts would be a challenge.

Foremost among the Alero's rivals was the Toyota Camry, which was the best-selling car in the United States in both 1997 and 1998. Since fall 1997 Toyota's ad agency, Saatchi & Saatchi, had advertised the Camry as part of the company's overall branding campaign: "Everyday People." The Camry figured prominently in these print and television spots that showed the versatility and practicality of Toyota. Toyota's overall share of the U.S. market grew from 8.1 percent in 1997 to 8.7 percent in 1998.

The Honda Accord was the second-best-selling car in the United States in 1997 and 1998. For model year 1998 Honda had launched a completely redesigned Accord. Spots by Rubin Postaer & Associates used the tagline "An Accord Like No Other" to tout the Accord's roomier interior, performance, and quiet engine. This $100 million campaign "was almost paying homage to the Accord over the past 22 years," a Honda spokesperson told *Advertising Age.* In October 1998 Honda switched strategies with two new national Accord commercials (also by Rubin Postaer) that did not use "An Accord Like No Other." Instead the spots presented the Accord not just "as a car you need," but more as "a car you want," a Honda representative explained in the October 5, 1998, issue of *Advertising Age.* In one a frazzled woman left an airport, and, by using her remote-control key, was able to freeze all action around her until she reached her Accord. The tagline proclaimed, "It's not just a car. It's a state of mind." Honda's overall share of the U.S. car market rose from 6.2 percent in 1997 to 6.5 percent in 1998.

Oldsmobile also viewed the Mazda 626 and the Nissan Altima as direct competitors of the Alero. Since spring 1998 Mazda, which controlled a 1.5 percent share of the U.S. car market, had used the slogan "Get In. Be Moved." in advertising for all its offerings. As part of this campaign, Mazda's ad agency, W.B. Doner & Co., created a commercial for the 626 that sought to build a more energetic and sophisticated image for the car. Set to David Bowie's song "Rebel Rebel," the commercial portrayed an attractive woman driving across town in her 626. She stopped at a sign announcing a PTA meeting and walked inside carrying a cake. "Do not go gentle into that good PTA meeting," the voice-over intoned, in a spoof on Dylan Thomas's famous poem, "Do Not Go Gentle into That Good Night." Mazda ran a similar commercial for the 626 in May 1999. Nissan, whose share of the U.S. car market was an impressive 4.0 percent, pulled the plug on its "Enjoy the Ride" branding campaign in 1998 and initiated more product-specific spots that failed to have their desired effect. The company consequently inaugurated a new branding campaign in 1999 with the tagline "Driven."

MARKETING STRATEGY

"Start Something" was designed to generate excitement for the launch of the Oldsmobile Alero. Just as the component advertisements strove to convey the car's fun-to-drive and distinct image, Oldsmobile's marketing efforts attempted to make the Alero's introduction highly visible to the car's target audience. "We really need to establish this vehicle with a big splash," Oldsmobile's Sand was quoted in the August 17, 1998, *Adweek.* The teaser commercials were an essential component of this plan. Even before the Alero had arrived at dealers, these 15-second spots "offer[ed] more of a sneak preview than a full disclosure of what l[ay] ahead," Oldsmobile explained in a press release. By the time the full 30-second spots aired on September 1, Oldsmobile had piqued viewers' curiosity. Print ads ran in major monthly magazines and newsweeklies after September 1.

Oldsmobile employed atypical media strategies to ensure that the Alero received a considerable amount of attention. The Internet figured prominently in the "Start

Something" campaign. According to *Brandweek,* the Internet was the "centerpiece of its media blitz." In addition to scores of banner ads displayed on popular websites, Oldsmobile even offered test drives at home for consumers who signed up online. Incorporating the Internet into its marketing venues was a logical choice for Oldsmobile. "We think the Internet is used by very youthful, very technologically savvy consumers who are similar to the consumer profile that we want to attract with the Alero," Sands told *Automotive News.* To raise the Alero's profile further, Oldsmobile announced its "Start Something Tuesdays on ABC Sweepstakes" in August 1998. This promotional tie-in with ABC's Tuesday evening prime-time lineup encouraged viewers to enter a sweepstakes in which 200 Aleros would be awarded.

Because Oldsmobile included Hispanic and African-American consumers in its target audience, the division used slightly different methods to reach these groups. For instance, Alero advertisements bearing the "Vivelo" tagline appeared in national Hispanic magazines and on Spanish-speaking networks. Oldsmobile concentrated its Hispanic-oriented efforts on large cities such as Los Angeles and Miami, as well as in regions with substantial Hispanic populations, such as Texas and the Southwest. GM declared October 13, 1998, to be "GM Hispanic Awareness Day." At the company's Miami symposium that day, a GM executive said, "I think the Alero speaks volumes about our commitment to, and expansion into, the Hispanic community."

In 1999 GM expanded the "Start Something" campaign to encompass all of its Oldsmobile vehicles in what company executives described in *Advertising Age* as a "divisional branding campaign," or "divisional effort." Karen Francis, Oldsmobile's general marketing manager, told *Advertising Age* that in 1999 Alero's marketing tagline, "Start Something," was being moved to all Oldsmobile vehicle models and that the expanded campaign would kick off with television spots during the 1999 Super Bowl. A new campaign to support the introduction of the Oldsmobile Aurora sedan began in April 2000; it featured the "Start Something" theme, but with a subtle twist. Francis explained to *Advertising Age* that each vehicle in the Oldsmobile line would have a different word after "Start." For the Aurora the tagline was "Start Obsessing," and the Alero's modified tagline was "Start Connecting." The strategy took a different spin in late 2000 when GM announced that the redesigned Bravada sport-utility vehicle would be the last vehicle released under the Oldsmobile brand. Leo Burnett created just one 30-second TV spot supporting Bravada's launch; it was scheduled to appear on syndicated cable for three weeks followed by a run during the "March Madness" basketball coverage. The spot featured a Bravada racing down a road with a herd of wild horses running alongside it. A voice-over stated, "A new beast on the road."

OUTCOME

Both GM officials and industry analysts heralded the Alero's launch as a success. Although GM's overall 1998 performance was sluggish, the *Wall Street Journal* called the Oldsmobile division GM's "one bright spot" and stressed the importance of the Alero to Oldsmobile's positive results. Sands informed the January 11, 1999, *Adweek* that the Alero campaign was the first Oldsmobile effort that had "truly resonated" with this younger target audience. "It was like a light bulb went off in [consumer's heads] that Oldsmobile had changed," he exclaimed. An Oldsmobile dealer further emphasized the division's turnaround to *Automotive News* on February 15, 1999: "We're attracting non-Oldsmobile owners into the showrooms to buy Oldsmobiles." The company predicted 1999 sales of the Alero to exceed 100,000.

The Alero's debut was made all the more impressive by the challenges it overcame. In June 1998 a labor dispute led to strikes at major GM production facilities, which delayed the Alero's initial release. Some dealers and analysts therefore predicted a tepid reception for the car. "We've got a lot of advertising support and market interest generated and now people come in the door and there's nothing to show them," one dealer complained to the *Capital Times.* But these fears proved to be overblown.

Following a brief rise on the crest of the "Start Something" campaign, in December 2000 Oldsmobile sales took a disappointing nosedive. GM executives soon announced that the entire Oldsmobile line would be phased out. The launch of the redesigned Bravada sport-utility vehicle in 2001 would be the brand's swan song. According to an *Advertising Age* report, Oldsmobile's plans for a 2001 first-quarter divisional branding campaign were canceled. "Obviously, we're not into brand building, we're into brand selling," a GM spokesman said. Further, amidst complaints from Oldsmobile dealers that the advertising failed to clarify fully the brand's new positioning, the unit's general manager Karen Francis and advertising director Mike Sands both resigned, and Oldsmobile conducted an agency review. Included in the review were incumbent Leo Burnett; McCann-Erickson Worldwide, which was the agency for the Buick line; and E. Morris Communications, the agency handling Oldsmobile's African-American advertising. Following the review Leo Burnett retained the account and created the final advertising for Oldsmobile. In 2004 the last new Oldsmobile rolled off the assembly line.

FURTHER READING

Akre, Brian. "GM Strike Has Dealers Fretting over Inventory." *Capital Times,* June 19, 1998.

Halliday, Jean. "Curtain Call for Oldsmobile; GM's 103-Year-Old Unit Going Out with Bravada—and a $10 Mil Push." *Advertising Age,* March 19, 2001.

———. "Honda Ads Stick Simplicity." *Advertising Age,* October 5, 1998.

———. "How to Sell a Dying Brand; GM Agencies Confront Uphill Challenge of Marketing to Consumers Who Worry about Servicing Their Olds." *Advertising Age,* December 18, 2000.

———. "The Marketing 100: Honda Accord." *Advertising Age,* June 29, 1998.

———. "New Olds Effort Evolves Tagline; Automaker Starts 'Obsessing' for Aurora and 'Connecting' for Alero." *Advertising Age,* February 28, 2000.

———. "Olds Suffers Sales Slide, Dealers' Dissatisfaction; New Ad Director to be Named at Troubled GM Unit." *Advertising Age,* October 16, 2000.

———. "Olds to Buck GM Trend, Plans Division Brand Ads: Effort Likely in 1st Quarter 2000, Says Francis." *Advertising Age,* June 21, 1999.

Jaffe, Andrew. "Is Olds Making an Intelligent Choice?." *Adweek,* July 15, 1991.

Maynard, Mark. "The New Olds Alero." *San Diego Union-Tribune,* April 5, 1998.

"Oldsmobile." *Adweek,* August 10, 1998.

Taylor, Alex, III. "GM: Time to Get in Gear." *Fortune,* August 28, 1997.

Warner, Fara. "GM's Sales Fall by 5% in the US." *Wall Street Journal,* December 4, 1998.

Washington, Frank. "Olds' Goal: 400,000 '99 Sales." *Automotive News,* February 15, 1999.

———. "Olds Plans an Aggressive Ethnic Pitch." *Automotive News,* September 14, 1998.

Rebecca Stanfel
Rayna Bailey

Gill Foundation

2215 Market Street
Denver, Colorado 80205
USA
Telephone: (303) 292-1594
Web site: www.gillfoundation.org

TURNOUT CAMPAIGN

OVERVIEW

In 2004 the issue of same-sex marriage catapulted into the media spotlight when San Francisco's newly elected mayor, Gavin Newsom, allowed city officials to issue marriage licenses to same-sex couples. Colorado became a focal point for the issue after two of its politicians, U.S. Representative Marilyn Musgrave and U.S. Senator Wayne Allard, proposed an amendment that banned same-sex marriage. Also based in Colorado, the Christian group Focus on the Family Action began campaigning to preserve what it considered "traditional" marriage. In response Denver-based Gill Foundation, America's largest contributor to lesbian, gay, bisexual, and transgender (LGBT) organizations, launched the "TurnOut" campaign to drum up voter support for same-sex marriages and sexual-orientation antidiscrimination laws.

Between 1994 and 2004 the Gill Foundation invested nearly $54 million in LGBT-related issues, and in 2003 it contracted advertising agency DDB Seattle to create the "TurnOut" campaign for the months preceding the 2004 presidential elections. Television and print advertising appeared in July and targeted cities that had no laws to protect Americans from losing their jobs because of their sexual orientation. Six television spots played like minidocumentaries, showing real people coming out in their workplaces. These employees described what it was like to keep their personal lives secret at work and explained how they planned to disclose their sexual orientation to coworkers and management. The spots ended by directing viewers to http://www.TurnOut.org, a website that revealed the results of each person's effort and explained other key LGBT issues.

Although Musgrave was reelected in 2004 and Allard was reappointed to serve as a deputy majority whip in 2005, a survey showed that, by the end of the "TurnOut" campaign, its audience felt more receptive to same-sex marriage issues. From an ad industry standpoint "TurnOut" was highly successful; it won five awards at the 51st Annual Cannes Lions International Advertising Festival as well as a Clio Award.

HISTORICAL CONTEXT

In 1992 Colorado voters passed an amendment to their state constitution that negated the power of laws protecting Americans from sexual-orientation discrimination. Four years later the U.S. Supreme Court struck down the amendment. The issue, remaining relatively undisturbed for years, exploded in 2004 when San Francisco's mayor allowed the city to issue marriage licenses to same-sex couples.

In 2004 Colorado Republicans Musgrave and Allard proposed an amendment to the U.S. Constitution that banned same-sex marriage. If passed the amendment would affect survivor benefits for children and spouses in same-sex families. At the time, same-sex families were also denied more than a thousand federal benefits that opposite-sex families qualified for. At the state level only three states granted same-sex marriages the same rights and responsibilities bestowed upon so-called traditional marriages.

The Gill Foundation, which had been founded by software tycoon Tim Gill in the 1990s, reacted by rallying voters to support same-sex marriages and antidiscrimination laws. As part of the "TurnOut" campaign, voter-mobilization tool kits were sent to some 250 organizations around the country, encouraging voters to elect candidates such as Colorado's Stan Matsunaka, who did not support the proposed amendment. Ted Trimpa, a Colorado attorney and gay-rights lobbyist, told the *Rocky Mountain News* that it was time to politically "go after people who go after us." Many in LGBT communities feared that if the wrong candidates were elected, they could hinder the rising momentum of the gay-rights movement. "We can't afford to lose," Trimpa continued in the *Rocky Mountain News.* Gill Foundation organizers were telling volunteers to encourage similar-minded voters to "vote like your civil rights depend on it."

Television spots for the "TurnOut" campaign focused on antidiscrimination issues, specifically in the workplace. At the time, only 14 states protected citizens from being fired because of their sexual orientation. Surveys conducted before the campaign indicated that mainstream voters felt sympathetic about the problem of workplace discrimination.

TARGET MARKET

According to Eric Gutierrez, a creative director at DDB, "TurnOut" targeted voters who "might be open to a discussion about rights in the workplace." Polls conducted by the Gill Foundation showed that, out of a wide range of LGBT issues, equal rights in the workplace was considered highly important; more than 80 percent of straight people felt that everyone should have such rights. These findings prompted DDB to center the campaign's most prominent aspect, the television spots, on this issue. Rodger McFarlane, executive director of the Gill Foundation, told *Business Wire,* "Numerous studies, including our own, reveal that a majority of 'straight' people are appalled when they know that non-discrimination protections don't exist for many lesbian, gay, bisexual and transgender citizens." The campaign was also aimed at the 56 percent of Colorado voters who did not support gay issues.

The "TurnOut" television spots showed six real people dissatisfied about hiding their sexual orientation from coworkers. Filmed as minidocumentaries, the spots featured the employees coming out at work. Lisa Herrera, for example, ended five years of silence about her personal life by placing a picture of her girlfriend on her desk. Steve Calhoun, a prototype tester at Detroit's Ford Motor Company, said his coworkers were not supportive when he came out. Each person also lived in a state that permitted employers to fire people for being gay, lesbian, bisexual, or transgender.

Gill Foundation volunteers told the *Rocky Mountain News* that the biggest challenge for "TurnOut" was getting straight, like-minded voters, specifically those under the age of 35, to vote. Even though volunteers felt that they could make a bigger impact by talking to voters one-on-one, "TurnOut" allowed the Gill Foundation to make gay-rights issues visible inside voters' homes.

THE GILL FOUNDATION'S FOUNDER

Tim Gill, founder of the Gill Foundation, was one of only two openly gay individuals to make the Forbes 400 list in 1997. After borrowing $2,000 from his parents in 1981, Gill founded Quark, Inc., a company that grew to create high-end software for page-layout design. In the mid-1990s Gill established the Gill Foundation and subsequently provided millions of dollars for lesbian, gay, bisexual, and transgender groups and HIV/AIDS charities, including the Colorado AIDS Project.

COMPETITION

Focus on the Family Action (FOTFA), a political lobbying organization spearheaded by James Dobson to ban same-sex marriage and abortion, targeted the Evangelical Protestants that made up 23 percent of the U.S. electorate in 2004. Frustrated by previous Supreme Court decisions, Dobson began endorsing political candidates he thought would galvanize his religion-charged agenda. He appeared on TV talk shows such as ABC's *This Week* and on Fox News to express his distaste for same-sex marriage, claiming that it exacerbated what he referred to as a "culture war." Despite Dobson's influence, President George W. Bush refused to screen Supreme Court appointees according to their position on same-sex marriage. Bush also condoned civil unions if the state law allowed it.

Leading up to the election, FOTFA organized mass voting drives intended to register at least 1 million voters. Latinos were targeted with paid radio programming that aired across Spanish radio. FOTFA sponsored groups

RESTRICTED SURVIVOR BENEFITS

One of the most prominent cases involving the rights of same-sex couples involved Peggy Neff. After her partner of 18 years, Sheila Hein, was killed inside the Pentagon during the terrorist attacks of September 11, 2001, Neff petitioned for survivor benefits under the Virginia Victims of Crime Act. The state denied her the award, declaring that only a "surviving spouse, parent, grandparent, sibling, adult child, or legal dependent of a deceased victim" was eligible. Neff eventually sought compensation at the federal level. In 2003 she was granted $557,390 from the federal funding set aside for the victims' relatives.

called "family policy councils," which operated in 35 locations throughout the United States. One such group based in Ohio even sponsored the initiative that eventually banned same-sex marriages in that state.

Dobson's personal efforts included barnstorming the battleground states in the months before the election. He urged Christians to "vote their values" at a rally titled "Mayday for Marriage" that FOTFA organized in Washington, D.C. More than 13 thousand Hispanic churches were sent mailers that outlined how the congregation should vote. Also the group donated some $60,000 to support an Oregon measure banning same-sex marriages. Many analysts credited FOTFA for Bush's reelection, the placement of congressmen opposed to same-sex marriage, and the ousting of Democratic Senate Minority Leader Tom Daschle, who had previously blocked a vote on an amendment prohibiting gay marriage.

MARKETING STRATEGY

When the Gill Foundation awarded DDB its advertising work, it presented the ad agency with research. One study showed that more than 80 percent of Americans believed that discrimination on the basis of sexual orientation should not be tolerated in the workplace. Making this statistic its starting point, DDB, in collaboration with director Doug Pray of the production company Oil Factory, filmed minidocumentaries to expose work-related discrimination. According to Gutierrez, "TurnOut" had been originally slated for early 2004, but after San Francisco's mayor stirred up media attention by issuing marriage certificates to same-sex couples in February, DDB and the Gill Foundation delayed the launch. The foundation feared that the political climate had become too volatile for "TurnOut," the intent of which was to encourage a more cerebral discussion of LGBT issues.

With the November election approaching and the media fervor about LGBT issues showing no sign of abating, the Gill Foundation finally aired the first "TurnOut" television spots on July 5, 2004. The minidocumentaries appeared on TV in states that allowed employees no legal recourse if they were discriminated against because of their sexual orientation. Modeling the campaign after past civil-rights cases, DDB wanted to portray real people coming out in the face of opposition. Finding volunteers to do it was difficult but necessary, according to Pray, who filmed the spots. Gutierrez told *Advertising Age's Creativity,* "In our concepting phase, we realized there's probably no moment in the Civil Rights era that better illuminated white folks than the Rosa Parks bus incident. Her small act of courage served as a great national commercial for civil rights."

Detroit native Herrera came out by setting a picture of her girlfriend on her work desk. Calhoun, another subject for "TurnOut," sent a note that explained to his bosses that he was gay and about to be in a commercial. The six television spots then directed viewers to http://www.TurnOut.org to read about the outcomes of the employees' actions. All six employees received a range of responses. Kimya Ayodele was fired after she came out. According to the *Denver Post,* her tires were also slashed, and coworkers verbally abused her after she dated someone from work. Herrera had a different experience. "More people would come up and talk to me," she told the *Denver Post.* "Everyone is more helpful. It's more like a team now. I don't feel like the outside person."

Once people visited http://www.TurnOut.org, they were exposed to a wider range of issues regarding LGBT rights. One bullet read, "Did you know... Forty-six states have failed to enact laws that address crimes motivated by prejudice against gender identity?" Other campaign efforts involved sending voter-mobilization tool kits to more than 250 organizations with a collective audience of 4 million voters. Three different print ads appeared, featuring copy such as, "For gays and lesbians, America is 14 states that recognize our right to live free from job discrimination, and 36 states that don't." The campaign's website went offline after the election.

OUTCOME

Making its mark in the ad industry, the campaign in 2004 snagged a Clio Award in the Integrated Campaign category. At the 51st Annual Cannes Lions International Advertising Festival, the "TurnOut" television spots won 5 of the 89 available awards. According to postcampaign surveys, unaided awareness for "TurnOut" increased more than 50 percent with exposed populations—meaning that most people who saw the spots remembered them. Data also showed that individuals exposed to the campaign were more receptive to discussing LGBT rights, one of the campaign's main objectives. Nadine Smith, executive director for the advocacy group Equality Florida, told *Business Wire,* "Encouraging greater civic involvement around LGBT issues is critical for any positive, lasting change to occur."

Election results in 2004 were more daunting. Many candidates who supported LGBT rights were replaced by conservatives who did not. Nonetheless DDB and the Gill Foundation felt that the campaign was a success in that it educated its audience and encouraged wider public participation in LGBT issues, two achievements that were necessary for the expansion of civil rights.

FURTHER READING

Beller, Gerald. "GOP Tapped Growing Christian Fervor." *Charleston (WV) Gazette,* November 22, 2004, p. P5A.

Champagne, Christine. "DDB Seattle Creates Uplifting HIV/AIDS Awareness Ad." *Shoot,* February 6, 2004, p. 12.

Dwyer, Kelly Pate. "Going inside the Decision to Come Out: Four Featured in Ads about Gays in the Workplace Share Their Experiences." *Denver Post,* August 13, 2004, p. C1.

Gorski, Eric. "Dobson Shifts Power to Focus on the Politics." *Denver Post,* November 14, 2004, p. A1.

Gutierrez, Eric. "On the Issue of Selling Issues." *Advertising Age's Creativity,* April 1, 2004, p. 6.

Herel, Suzanne. "Newsom's First Veto Upheld by Board." *San Francisco Chronicle,* March 31, 2004, p. B4.

Ives, Nat. "To Get Their Messages Across, More and More Nonprofit Organizations Are Going Commercial." *New York Times,* February 20, 2004, p. 4.

Kirkpatrick, David. "Rally against Gay Marriage Draws Thousands to Capital." *New York Times,* October 16, 2004, p. 12.

Knight, Heather. "Wong to Resign as Director of Port of S.F." *San Francisco Chronicle,* April 1, 2004, p. B4.

Mack, Ann M., and Eleftheria Parpis. "Jurors Take 'Fun' Route to Grand Prix." *Adweek,* June 28, 2004, p. 6.

Miller, Robert. "Junior League Ball Is 'Hot' Stuff." *Dallas Morning News,* January 27, 1994, p. 3D.

Olvera, Javier Erik. "Girding the Gay Vote: Collaborative Effort Under Way to Elect Friendly Candidates." *Rocky Mountain News,* July 5, 2004, p. 12A.

Weinkopf, Chris. "Different Renegades, Different Media Portraits." *American Enterprise,* April 1, 2004, p. 51.

Kevin Teague

GlaxoSmithKline plc

980 Great West Rd.
Brentford, Middlesex TW8 9GS
United Kingdom
Telephone: 44 20 80475000
Fax: 44 20 80477807
Web site: www.gsk.com

POWER TO QUIT CAMPAIGN

OVERVIEW

NOTE: Since the initial appearance of this essay in the 1998 edition of *Major Marketing Campaigns Annual,* SmithKline Beecham merged with Glaxo to form GlaxoSmithKline plc. The essay continues to refer to the company's former name, as that was the official name of the organization when the campaign was launched.

NicoDerm CQ, a sticky patch that adhered to the skin and delivered a steady flow of nicotine to help ease the physical withdrawal symptoms associated with quitting smoking, was introduced by its manufacturer, the pharmaceutical company SmithKline Beecham, as a prescription drug in 1991. The product was a success, climbing to the top of the prescription smoking-cessation market and winning a prestigious R&D 100 Award for 1992. By the mid-1990s, however, NicoDerm's sales had flattened, and SmithKline decided that the product's future lay in the over-the-counter drug market. The company received approval from the Food and Drug Administration (FDA) in mid-1996 to sell NicoDerm as an over-the-counter medication rather than by prescription only. Hoping to attract the broad base of American smokers who had either been unsuccessful in prior attempts to quit smoking or who were contemplating quitting for the first time, SmithKline hired the advertising agency Jordan, McGrath, Case, Taylor, New York to design its initial advertising blitz. The pharmaceutical company dedicated $35 million to advertise NicoDerm and in August 1996 launched a multimedia campaign featuring a barrage of print, radio, and television spots.

The campaign pitted NicoDerm most directly against its main competitor—Johnson & Johnson subsidiary McNeil Consumer Products Company's Nicotrol, another transdermal nicotine replacement product. Both products vied for the vast market of smokers of either gender between the ages of 25 and 64. The two companies vigorously sought to win over consumers. SmithKline's NicoDerm campaign consisted of two kinds of advertisements, one that focused on NicoDerm's effectiveness and the other that favorably compared its product to Nicotrol. For example, the commercial "Morning Break" relates the fate of two office workers who both recently quit smoking. One used NicoDerm while the other tried to give up the habit "cold turkey." The man who used the patch remains calm and collected, but his co-worker suffers from constant cravings, nervousness, and an inability to concentrate. Another spot, "Pharmacy," shows NicoDerm spokesperson, Carolyn McCormick, explaining the differences between NicoDerm and Nicotrol. Because NicoDerm supplied three different dosages of nicotine patches and Nicotrol only one, she emphasizes that NicoDerm is the better product because it allows smokers to taper. Testimonial ads—which featured personal accounts of how NicoDerm had eased the difficulties in quitting smoking—were often used as well. All of the ads bore the same tag line, "The power to quit, the power to comfort, the power to quit successfully," and were careful not to understate the difficulty of quitting. Instead, they emphasized that with NicoDerm it was possible to do so.

The campaign was a resounding success. Marketing surveys discovered that consumers considered the ads highly effective. Backed by its ubiquitous commercials, NicoDerm quickly assumed a dominant position in the over-the-counter smoking-cessation aid market. By 1998 the product's power had nearly forced Nicotrol to abandon the field. McNeil severely curtailed Nicotrol's advertising budget and chose to refocus its promotional efforts on a new antismoking nasal spray available only with a prescription. SmithKline, on the other hand, intended to continue its broad-based advertising campaign in order to protect NicoDerm's position in the field against encroachment by other antismoking products.

HISTORICAL CONTEXT

In 1991 SmithKline Beecham released its prescription-only nicotine patch, which was designed to be attached—rather like an adhesive bandage—to the skin of a person attempting to quit smoking. NicoDerm delivered a steady flow of nicotine, the highly addictive substance in tobacco, transdermally so that the ex-smoker did not experience the uncomfortable symptoms of nicotine withdrawal. The product came in three dosages: 21, 14, and 7 milligram patches. Heavy smokers began using the 21 milligram patch and, through the full ten weeks of the "three step" NicoDerm program, progressively decreased their dosage of nicotine until they were not only smoke-free but also patch-free. Those who smoked less could begin the regime with the 14 milligram or 7 milligram patch. Although early sales for this prescription program were strong, demand for the patch tapered off by the mid-1990s, and its revenues plateaued. NicoDerm was, however, the clear leader in this sector of the prescription drug market.

In a major policy shift the FDA decided to approve nicotine replacement products for over-the-counter use in 1996. NicoDerm was the second patch to become available after this development, following McNeil Consumer Products' Nicotrol. SmithKline's own Nicorette, a nicotine-laced chewing gum that served the same end as the transdermal patches, also hit the over-the-counter market before NicoDerm. Although its chief competitor, Nicotrol, became available to consumers first, NicoDerm had the advantage of having controlled nearly 40 percent of the prescription market.

Analysts expected nicotine replacement therapies to sell well over the counter. "Once you eliminate the need to visit a doctor, sales will increase dramatically," George Quesnelle, a SmithKline Beecham marketing executive, told the September 13, 1996, edition of *USA Today.* "The ability to walk into the local pharmacy and buy these products will make a world of difference." Still, experts concurred that advertising would play a substantial role in determining which of the nicotine patch brands would win over smokers.

TARGET MARKET

NicoDerm's big-budget campaign had a wide audience to reach. Of the 48 million American smokers, nearly 16 million tried to give up smoking each year. According to *Brandweek,* NicoDerm's ads especially targeted those smokers aged 25 to 64. Not all who tried NicoDerm were first-time quitters. The Centers for Disease Control declared that only 2 million of the 16 million people who attempted to kick the habit each year actually succeeded. Moreover, nearly a quarter of those who did had made up to five attempts at quitting. "The consumer has to have made a very important decision about his own health and welfare before he ever considers this kind of product," a marketing analyst told *USA Today.*

Appealing to this target market could be a delicate task at times. Instead of creating slick ads that downplayed the enormity of the challenge facing the soon to be ex-smoker, Jordan, McGrath focused on relating to the concerns of its desired audience. Joe Martin, a senior brand equity manager for NicoDerm CQ, told the March 31, 1997, edition of *USA Today* that the ads wanted to reassure consumers that "it is difficult to quit smoking." The commercials and print ads never trivialized the symptoms such as anxiety, restlessness, and withdrawal that might have been experienced by NicoDerm's potential users during past attempts at quitting smoking.

The campaign also strove to appeal to its target market by not being pejorative. Smokers had come to inhabit a world that increasingly condemned their habit. Not only were most smokers fully aware of the negative health risks associated with the vice, they were also constantly reminded of these by their doctors, spouses, co-workers, newspaper articles, and the antismoking commercials funded by some states. Jordan, McGrath realized that harping on this theme would not boost NicoDerm's sales. "We aren't here to preach the horrors of smoking; we're here to advertise a product that is available to smokers once they've convinced themselves it's time to quit," Ilon Specht of Jordan, McGrath told *USA Today.*

Although the ads did not seek to impress the viewer like some of the more flashy campaigns for athletic shoes or cars, they did try to capture a certain earnestness in an attempt to win the trust of their audience. "A key

OFF TO THE RACES

In possibly its most creative effort to reach its smoking audience, NicoDerm sponsored a car at the 1997 Marlboro 500 auto race at the California Speedway. This marked the first time a smoking-cessation product had sought to enter the heavily cigarette-sponsored auto world. Danny Vitolo, the driver of the NicoDerm car, thought that the connection was logical. "[Quitting smoking] takes a commitment," he told the September 25, 1997, edition of *Florida Today.* "It's very similar to racing. In racing, you must be very committed and determined." As part of the promotion SmithKline also promised to donate $500 to the American Cancer Society for each member of Championship Auto Racing Teams who quit smoking.

motivating factor is for consumers to feel comfortable purchasing a product without a doctor's prescription or advice," said Don Stuart of the marketing-consulting firm Cannondale Associates. The ads did need to motivate viewers, though. Since so many people had unsuccessfully attempted to stop smoking in the past, the NicoDerm spots explicitly stated that their product, and theirs alone, could help end an ongoing struggle to become tobacco-free. Jordan, McGrath's testimonial ads were designed to serve this purpose. The message conveyed in these was: "If I could do it, so can you."

COMPETITION

The smoking-cessation aid market exploded after NicoDerm and Nicotrol began being sold over the counter in 1996. Total revenues for the industry in 1997 reached nearly $650 million, more than double the previous year's volume. Analysts believed this expansion would continue. "I still see growth in the [smoking-cessation aid] category," Barbara Kuhn, a buyer for a major drug-store chain, told the October 6, 1997, edition of *Drug Store News.* "I don't think it's peaked yet, with more companies going to non-smoking policies and more public places being restricted." On the strength of its 40 percent share of the prescription drug market at the time of its shift to over-the-counter status, coupled with a $50 million advertising blitz, NicoDerm surged to a commanding lead in the field. Its 1996 sales were more than $134 million, as compared to $52 million for its most direct competitor, Nicotrol.

Nicotrol, however, had no intention of remaining in second place and decided that advertising was its key to success. McNeil Consumer Products unleashed a full-scale advertising barrage on behalf of its brand, spending more than $53 million between March 1996 and March 1997 alone. Nicotrol was promoted via print, radio, and television spots, coupon offers, and brochures sent directly to doctors. The company bought air-time for commercials on such highly rated network television shows as *ER.* Some of these ads featured celebrities such as actress Patricia Kalember, who had appeared in the television shows *Sisters* and *thirtysomething.* Others were "reality-based" spots that tracked the progress of three Ann Arbor, Michigan, residents as they used Nicotrol to help themselves quit smoking. These testimonial commercials in particular proved to be quite popular with consumers. "We discovered that the best way to reach smokers who are ready to quit is to have other smokers talk to them," McNeil Consumer Products spokesman Ron Schmid told *The Detroit News.*

Although Nicotrol was the only other transdermal patch available over the counter, NicoDerm faced competition from prescription smoking-cessation aids as well. In June 1997 pharmaceutical titan Glaxo Wellcome introduced an oral tablet designed to curb smokers' cravings for nicotine. It supported this new product, called Zyban, with a strong direct-to-consumer marketing campaign. Novaritis's Habitrol, which did not make the shift from prescription to over-the-counter status with NicoDerm and Nicotrol, remained a market player as well. Although its sales were relatively small compared to NicoDerm, the National Advertising Division of the Council of Better Business Bureaus (NAD) noted that the prescription/over-the-counter distinction "does not remove competition between [NicoDerm and Habitrol] or reduce Habitrol to bit player status." Johnson & Johnson was also developing an antismoking nasal spray. The increased competition had an impact on NicoDerm's share of the market. By the second quarter of 1998 NicoDerm's sales had dropped 18 percent, although sales of Nicorette, SmithKline Beecham's nicotine gum, continued to rise. SmithKline's NicoDerm, though, still enjoyed a substantial lead over its rivals.

The battle between the manufacturers of these smoking-cessation aids was heated. McNeil Consumer Products and Novaritis both filed complaints with the NAD, which served as a watchdog agency monitoring the accuracy of consumer advertising; the companies alleged that SmithKline Beecham had made misrepresentations in its advertising for NicoDerm. SmithKline filed two complaints against Nicotrol as well. The NAD sustained both of the complaints against NicoDerm and admonished SmithKline to alter some of its ads. It rejected one of the complaints against McNeil Consumer Products but sustained the other, mandating changes in ad copy. SmithKline and McNeil also went to court over one of these disputes, eventually reaching a confidential settlement on the matter.

MARKETING STRATEGY

Because its target market—adult smokers between the ages of 25 and 64—was so broad, NicoDerm employed a range of strategies to appeal to its potential customers. It ran ads directed at narrow segments of the market, such as smoking couples who were thinking about having children. One commercial featured a young couple using NicoDerm to stop smoking before trying to get pregnant in order to have a healthier baby. SmithKline also secured an exclusive sponsorship deal with the American Cancer Society (ACS) in August 1996. In return for payments of at least $1 million per year in sales royalties over the three years of the arrangement, the ACS permitted NicoDerm packages to be emblazoned with the society's logo as well as with a reference to the partnership between NicoDerm and the ACS for promoting the cessation of smoking.

The company also sought to increase NicoDerm's sales through its association with special television programming. NicoDerm was a primary sponsor of New Year's-themed programming on the TBS, Nickelodeon, and Family Channel cable networks that ran on and around New Year's Eve 1997. For example, NicoDerm's sponsorship earned it very visible signs on stage during "Comedy Cure II," a movie marathon on the TBS channel hosted by comedian Rodney Dangerfield. Whenever Dangerfield or other comedians performed, NicoDerm's logo was prominently displayed. In addition, the product received further billing during the course of interviews with passers-by about their new year's resolutions. As NicoDerm's media manager Nancy Louvre explained to the December 16, 1996, edition of *Adweek*, "It made sense for us to partner with programming that would showcase our product. This is our most critical time of the year, and we're very heavy in both TV and print ads with a New Year's resolution theme."

Creating effective advertising was a challenge, however. A writer in *USA Today* remarked on September 13, 1996: "Glitzy ad campaigns, attractive coupon offers, scare tactics, and other tried-and-true marketing tactics that help sell other over-the-counter medications may not work with heavy smokers." SmithKline decided that emphasis on a simple, straight-forward message was the best way to promote the product. "Smokers know the problem with smoking," said George Quesnelle, a vice-president of medical marketing and sales for SmithKline Beecham's consumer-health unit, in the May 22, 1996, edition of *The Wall Street Journal Europe*. "You might say they've been beaten over the head by it. What they need to know is that [quitting] is possible."

Building on this message, Jordan, McGrath devised two classes of ads to increase NicoDerm's sales. The first, termed "equity ads," strove to strengthen the cachet of the NicoDerm brand, stressing that NicoDerm was a product capable of helping even the most addicted smoker break the habit. The second type of ad, dubbed "competitive ads," focused on distinguishing NicoDerm most directly from Nicotrol but also from its other competitors. It was these ads, with their specific claims about NicoDerm in contrast to other smoking-cessation products, that gave rise to the complaints that Nicotrol and Novaritis filed with the NAD. While NicoDerm was forced to alter particular statements in two of its ads in response, it continued to employ "competitive ads" as a way of defending and increasing its share of the market.

NicoDerm employed a saturation strategy for these ads across television, radio, and print media. On television NicoDerm sought to reach all segments of its target market. It advertised on soap operas and other daytime shows, early morning programming such as the *Today* show, late night chat shows, and even syndicated and cable television broadcasts. Although SmithKline did make the occasional ad-purchase on prime-time shows, the company felt that the cost of such slots generally outweighed the benefits they brought in return.

NicoDerm ads also ran frequently on an assortment of radio broadcasts. SmithKline liked radio spots because they were comparatively inexpensive, allowing the company to bombard listeners with information about NicoDerm. Additionally, SmithKline advertised heavily in large-circulation magazines, such as *Life, Better Homes and Gardens, Sports Illustrated, Readers Digest,* and *U.S. News & World Report.* The company's goal for this multimedia approach was to reach the maximum possible number of consumers.

OUTCOME

NicoDerm's advertising campaign was a tremendous success. Despite the handicap of coming onto the over-the-counter market a month after its closest competitor, NicoDerm was backed by SmithKline's marketing muscle and quickly established itself as the leading brand in the field. It continually refused to relinquish this position, even as other smoking-cessation aids came on the market or strove to challenge its supremacy. By mid-1998, in fact, Nicotrol had effectively ceded the patch field to NicoDerm. A health-care marketing consultant told the June 8, 1998, edition of *Advertising Age:* "There comes a time when you're spending more than you're selling, and you cut your losses." McNeil slashed its advertising budget for Nicotrol and shifted its focus to promoting a new antismoking inhaler available only by prescription. But NicoDerm's drop in sales volume through the early part of 1998, coupled with the $15 million McNeil planned to spend advertising its new product, as well as Glaxo's heavy spending on Zyban—$20 million in the fourth quarter of 1997 alone—indicated that NicoDerm would need to continue to fight to maintain its primacy in the field.

Although the ads promoting NicoDerm were not particularly innovative or cutting edge, surveys demonstrated their value. *USA Today* 's "Ad Track" poll on advertising success reported that only 14 percent of consumers gave NicoDerm's ads high popularity marks. But more then 20 percent of the people exposed to NicoDerm commercials said the ads were effective, an impressive response level for the industry. Buoyed by feedback such as this, SmithKline planned to continue its multimedia campaign in order to support and expand NicoDerm's share of the smoking-cessation aid market.

FURTHER READING

Enrico, Dottie. "NicoDerm CQ Smokes Competition in Sales." *USA Today,* March 31, 1997.

———. "Targeting Quitters: Cashing in on Kicking a Habit." *USA Today,* September 13, 1996.

Hwang, Suein L. "U.S. TV Ads by Drug Firms Promote Quitting Smoking." *Wall Street Journal Europe,* May 22, 1996.

"Indy-Car Driver to Deliver Anti-Smoking Message." *Florida Today,* September 25, 1997.

Kulpa, Jennifer. "Family Planners Could be Untapped Market for Smoking Cessation Products." *Drug Store News,* October 6, 1997.

Matzer, Maria. "NicoDerm Puts Stamp across New Year's TV to Net Resolvers." *Brandweek,* December 16, 1996.

"SmithKline NicoDerm CQ 'Only' Three-Step System Claims to be Modified." *The Tan Sheet,* January 19, 1998.

Wilke, Michael. "McNeil Counters Nicotrol's Sales Slide with RX Extension." *Advertising Age,* June 8, 1998.

Rebecca Stanfel

SOCIAL ANXIETY DISORDER CAMPAIGN

OVERVIEW

In 1999 Paxil, manufactured by SmithKline Beecham (now GlaxoSmithKline plc), was third among the pharmaceutical industry's best-selling SSRIs, a class of drugs then used primarily to treat depression and anxiety-related maladies. The drugmaker's strategy for gaining ground on rivals Prozac and Zoloft included extending Paxil's market by winning approval by the U.S. Food and Drug Administration (FDA) to treat other forms of mental illness. When, in May of that year, the FDA made Paxil its only approved treatment for social anxiety disorder, the drug finally found itself in a position, after seven years on the market, to outsell its rivals. Social anxiety disorder was a little-known condition at the time, but estimates by SmithKline Beecham put the number of potential Paxil customers in the United States at close to 10 million. Enlisting the public relations firm Cohn & Wolfe as well as Paxil's advertising agency of record, McCann Erickson Consumer Health, SmithKline Beecham mounted a combined physician, PR, and direct-to-consumer branded campaign that was meant to inform Americans about social anxiety disorder and to let them know that Paxil alone had been approved to treat it.

Immediately after learning of the FDA ruling, SmithKline Beecham increased its spending on physician-targeted ads to get the word out about the new Paxil designation. Meanwhile, the drugmaker funded a public-service campaign meant to spread awareness of social anxiety disorder. Then, in September 1999, a $30 million push of the Paxil brand began its run on television and in magazines with national circulations. SmithKline Beecham focused its message about social anxiety disorder on professionals between the ages of 18 and 34, with an emphasis on men, who were believed more likely to seek help for the condition because of career concerns.

The PR campaign resulted in more than a billion media references to social anxiety disorder, up from roughly 50 in previous years, almost all of which mentioned that Paxil was the only approved treatment for the condition. Seven months after its launch, the campaign had made the Paxil brand name one of the most recognized prescription drugs in the United States, and the drug was responsible for a sizeable increase in the anxiety medication category. Paxil gained on its SSRI rivals and experienced sustained sales growth, a trend that continued as the drug won further treatment designations, and the company adapted its marketing accordingly in the following years.

HISTORICAL CONTEXT

In 1987 Eli Lilly and Company won U.S. approval to sell Prozac, the first among a class of drugs called selective serotonin reuptake inhibitors (SSRIs) that treated clinical depression by elevating levels of serotonin—a chemical believed crucial to regulating mood—in the brain. Prozac's effectiveness and lack of side effects compared to existing medications for depression revolutionized not only the way mental illness was treated by psychiatrists but also the way it was perceived by the public. By 1992, when Pfizer and SmithKline Beecham introduced their own SSRIs, Zoloft and Paxil, respectively, depression had lost much of its stigma in the United States. In the following years SSRIs became one of the best-selling prescription drug categories.

For its first several years on the market, Paxil remained in third place among SSRIs, and SmithKline Beecham set its sights on new markets for the drug. In the mid-1990s Paxil won FDA approval for the treatment of anxiety-related conditions like panic disorder and obsessive-compulsive disorder. Though these markets led to substantial growth for the brand, it was the FDA's approval of Paxil in 1999 as a treatment for a little-known condition called social anxiety disorder that gave the drug its first significant advantage over competitors. Social anxiety disorder, or debilitating shyness, was a condition that, according to SmithKline Beecham, affected as many as 10 million Americans, and Paxil was the only FDA-approved treatment.

SmithKline Beecham was aided in its attempt to reach this untapped market by an easing of FDA regulations in 1997 that governed the advertising of prescription drugs. The policy shift almost immediately changed the nature of the advertising of prescription drugs, as pharmaceutical companies, which traditionally had focused on physicians and other medical professionals in their marketing efforts, began to rely on advertising their products directly to consumers, much as was done with other consumer goods. Though restrictions remained regarding the disclosure of side effects and though the FDA retained a role in approving advertisements, direct-to-consumer pharmaceutical marketing quickly became ubiquitous in the United States, increasingly putting patients rather than their doctors in the position of deciding which drugs might best satisfy their needs.

TARGET MARKET

The social anxiety disorder campaign targeted professionals aged 18–34 who, despite appearing normal, experienced overwhelming fear in social or work-related situations. SmithKline Beecham estimated that the total number of people suffering from the condition in the United States numbered 10 million, and the company believed that only 5 percent of these people were being treated. The company thus set out to define social anxiety disorder for an enormous untapped market, to let people know that they were not alone in their suffering, and to urge people to seek out Paxil, the only available FDA-approved treatment. As the Paxil product director, Barry Brand, told *Advertising Age,* "Every marketer's dream is to find an unidentified or unknown market and develop it. That's what we were able to do with social anxiety disorder."

The National Institute of Mental Health, however, placed the number of sufferers from social anxiety disorder at around 5 million. This discrepancy pointed to a controversy surrounding the subjectivity of diagnosis and, by extension, SmithKline Beecham's marketing of Paxil. While SmithKline Beecham argued that it was catering to an overwhelming need and helping relieve previously untreated suffering, critics believed that the drugmaker was artificially creating a market for Paxil by encouraging the merely shy to diagnose themselves with the more debilitating form of social phobia.

It was estimated that twice as many women suffered from social anxiety disorder as men, but in a departure from conventional wisdom men appeared more likely to seek treatment for the condition. In most medical matters men were less likely to seek treatment, but as McCann Erickson's Nan Dillon told *Advertising Age,* "This tends to be the exception because social anxiety disorder can actually damage a man's career."

COMPETITION

When the Paxil social anxiety campaign was launched, Prozac was the SSRI market leader and Eli Lilly's biggest earner, with annual sales approaching $3 billion. In the summer of 1999 a Prozac campaign narrowly preceded Paxil's social anxiety disorder ads to become the first-ever TV marketing of a psychiatric drug. The centerpiece of the Prozac campaign was a 30-minute infomercial that aired on local and cable networks late at night and on weekends, when people with untreated depression were believed likely to be watching. The infomercial featured a mostly female cast of Prozac users giving testimonials, as well as imagery of presumably depressed people and informational segments with doctors talking about depression and its treatment. Mental health experts were divided on the question of whether it was appropriate to pitch Prozac under the cover of public-service programming. The company supported the infomercial with 30-second TV spots offering a toll-free number to call for more information.

Paxil's other major competitor in the SSRI market, Pfizer's Zoloft, whose 1999 sales were estimated at $2 billion, had not yet used direct-to-consumer advertising. In early 2000, however, Pfizer initiated an account review with the intention of moving the duties for Zoloft advertising away from health care specialists Lyons Lavey Nickel Swift to a general-market agency. Deutsch Inc. won the review and began preparing a Zoloft direct-to-consumer message. Having already won approval for treatment of post-traumatic stress disorder, Zoloft was well positioned to benefit from the dramatic increase in SSRI prescriptions following the terrorist attacks in the United States on September 11, 2001.

PUBLIC SERVICE?

In the years before and after the social anxiety disorder campaign, blurring the line between public service and marketing became a staple of the prescription drug business, and the practice went well beyond the framework of traditional advertising. As the *Wall Street Journal* reported in 2001, with the rise of prescription drug branding, it became increasingly common for drug companies to pay celebrities to mention their products on television, as though for altruistic or personal reasons. Singer Donny Osmond, for instance, credited Paxil with curing his social anxiety disorder. Former Olympic gymnast Bart Conner touted Celebrex's salutary effects on his osteoarthritis, while his near contemporaries Bruce Jenner and Dorothy Hamill were hired to talk about their use of Vioxx to treat their own painful joints.

The stories of celebrity triumphs over illness often were picked up by news outlets that were not aware they were covering paid endorsements for drugs. As with other drug marketing that offered itself as a public service, many health care professionals frowned on the dishonesty of the practice, while others defended celebrity plugs as a useful technique for spreading a message of relief to millions of suffering people.

In late 1999 Bristol-Myers Squibb Company launched a direct-to-consumer campaign supporting BuSpar. One of only two drugs approved to treat generalized anxiety disorder at the time, BuSpar was also used to treat depression. Unlike its competitors among psychiatric drugs, BuSpar was not associated with such side effects as drowsiness and loss of libido. The BuSpar campaign targeted women via magazines like *Good Housekeeping* and *People* and, using an image of a cartoon female with symptoms of anxiety, on broadcast and cable TV.

MARKETING STRATEGY

Soon after the FDA decision in May 1999 allowing Paxil to be marketed as a treatment for social anxiety disorder, SmithKline Beecham increased its spending on physician-targeted ads by $1 million, according to *Medical Marketing and Media.* The company changed the copy in medical journals from "Paxil means peace... in depression, panic disorder, and OCD" to "Show them they can... the first and only approved treatment for social anxiety disorder."

Meanwhile, SmithKline Beecham funded an informational and public relations campaign to spread awareness about social anxiety disorder. Sponsored by a trio of advocacy organizations—the American Psychiatry Association, the Anxiety Disorders Association of America, and Freedom From Fear—the campaign was orchestrated by the New York PR firm Cohn & Wolfe and was designed, according to *PR News,* "to educate reporters, consumers, and, in some cases, physicians, in an effort to encourage diagnosis and treatment." Featuring posters placed at bus stops across the country and the tagline "Imagine being allergic to people," the PR campaign did not explicitly mention Paxil or SmithKline Beecham. Likewise, Cohn & Wolfe technically represented the nonprofit organizations and the doctors involved, even though SmithKline Beecham paid for the campaign. Virtually all of the sizeable media coverage Cohn & Wolfe generated mentioned not just the Paxil name but also the fact that it was the only FDA-approved treatment for the condition.

In September 1999 SmithKline Beecham launched its first Paxil direct-to-consumer ads, a TV and print campaign crafted by McCann Erickson Consumer Health and with an estimated cost of $30 million. Like the public relations efforts, the branded advertising was intended to define the condition for potential Paxil users and to give afflicted Americans comfort by sending the message that they were not alone. This portion of the campaign also sought more directly to raise awareness of the Paxil name.

In an attempt to reach its core target of 18- to 34-year-old professionals, SmithKline Beecham bought airtime on prime-time shows like *Ally McBeal* and ran the print ads in magazines that included *Rolling Stone* and *Sports Illustrated.* Both the television spots and the print ads used the tagline "Your life is waiting," and they directed consumers to ask themselves whether they experienced anxiety that made them avoid social interaction, that resembled a panic attack, or that was detrimental to their social or professional life. The 60-second TV spot informed viewers that more than 10 million Americans suffered from social anxiety disorder and that sufferers were a mix of male and female professionals engaged in productive office and social activities. In keeping with the belief that men were more likely to seek treatment for social anxiety disorder, the print ads primarily targeted male professionals, with the primary image being a distraught man in business clothes.

OUTCOME

PR News reported that, as a result of the campaign to advertise social anxiety disorder, media references to the condition climbed to more than 1 billion articles, up from 50 in 1997 and 1998, with 96 percent conveying the information that Paxil was the only FDA-approved treatment then available. After the campaign had been running for seven months, according to *Medical Marketing and Media,* Paxil scored third among advertised prescription drugs in unaided recall, behind Viagra and Claritin. Paxil's market share among anxiety drugs from December 1998 to May 1999, the months immediately preceding the campaign, was 9.3 percent of 6.7 million prescriptions. From June to October 1999, as the campaign ran, Paxil's market share not only grew to 11.5 percent but was responsible for half of the increase in the entire market, which grew to 7.2 million prescriptions.

In 2000 British rival Glaxo Wellcome merged with SmithKline Beecham. In its 2000 annual report the new entity, GlaxoSmithKline, claimed that Paxil "became number one in the U.S. selective serotonin reuptake inhibitor market for new retail prescriptions in 2000." In 2001 GlaxoSmithKline won FDA approval to market Paxil for both generalized anxiety disorder and post-traumatic stress disorder. Paxil continued to outpace its rivals in sales growth. The terrorist attacks in the United States on September 11, 2001, resulted in a dramatic increase in prescriptions for all antidepressants and anxiety drugs. During this time Paxil's advertising positioned it as an answer to the uncontrollable feelings of fear and helplessness that many people felt in the aftermath of the attacks.

FURTHER READING

Andelman, David. "Misleading or Not, Ads Boost Drug Makers' Earnings but Raise Cost to Consumer." *New York Daily News,* February 12, 2001.

"Drug Makers Pay Sick Celebrities to Gain News Play." *Wall Street Journal,* January 3, 2001.

"Experts Saddened by Medication Infomercial." *Marketing News,* June 7, 1999.

Goetzl, David. "Anxiety Level on the Rise with High-Profile DTC Ads." *Advertising Age,* December 20, 1999.

———. "Paxil." *Advertising Age,* June 26, 2000.

———. "Paxil Anxious to Get Message Out." *Advertising Age,* September 27, 1999.

Hawkins, Beth. "Paxil Is Forever." *City Pages,* October 16, 2002.

Koerner, Brendan. "Coming to You Direct." *U.S. News & World Report,* June 21, 1999.

Liebman, Milton. "Head-to-Head Marketing... May the Best-Promoted Drug Win." *Medical Marketing and Media,* November 2000.

McMain, Andrew. "Pfizer Places Zoloft's $50 Mil. Biz in Review." *Adweek,* January 31, 2000.

Parpis, Eleftheria. "Fear Factor." *Adweek,* November 12, 2001.

"Patient Testimonials Reintroduce an Old Drug in a New Market." *PR News,* May 15, 2000.

Vedantam, Shankar. "Drug Ads Hyping Anxiety Make Some Uneasy." *Washington Post,* July 16, 2001.

Mark Lane

Global Gillette

Prudential Tower Bldg.
Boston, Massachusetts 02199
USA
Telephone: (617) 421-7000
Fax: (617) 421-7123
Web site: www.gillette.com

ANYTHING ELSE WOULD BE UNCIVILIZED CAMPAIGN

OVERVIEW

NOTE: Since the initial appearance of this essay in the 1998 edition of *Major Marketing Campaigns Annual,* Gillette was acquired by Procter & Gamble. Global Gillette now operates as a subsidiary company. The essay continues to refer to the company's former name, as that was the official name of the organization when the campaign was launched.

The Gillette Company enjoyed a position of dominance in men's toiletries, a broad category that included not only deodorants and antiperspirants but also such items as pre- and aftershave products. Deodorants and antiperspirants, however, remained the largest product categories in toiletries, with Gillette's Right Guard brand among the leaders. Gillette had attained its leadership in the market through a combination of new product development, technological innovation, and an expanding global presence.

By the mid-1990s marketers of deodorants and antiperspirants were no longer emphasizing protection against odor but rather various aesthetic factors. New developments included products that were clear and that left no residue on clothing as well as protectants that were formulated to glide on easily. This new approach in product development and marketing came at a time when sales of antiperspirants and deodorants had begun to stagnate, a sign that the market was saturated.

With the advent of clear gels and sticks, however, the market began growing again. Not unexpectedly, industry leader Gillette was in the forefront of the growth. Seeking continuity in its marketing, it rolled out its clear stick and clear gel products under the banner of its long-running "Anything Else Would Be Uncivilized" campaign, using famous athletes in unlikely situations to promote the new items. Although response to the campaign was mixed, Gillette was able to maintain and even improve upon its market share.

HISTORICAL CONTEXT

For almost a century Gillette had been the worldwide leader in products for male grooming, a category originally comprising blades, razors, and other shaving accoutrements. But toiletries for men came to form only a portion of the company's vast global sales. Gillette also achieved a dominant market position in writing implements, correction products, and toothbrushes and oral care appliances. Relying on its traditional strengths of research and development, advertising, and geographic expansion, the company managed to continue to sustain its growth.

Founded in Boston in 1901 by King C. Gillette, the company introduced the world's first safety razor two

Advertisement for Gillette Right Guard Clear Stick deodorant. GILLETTE COMPANY. REPRODUCED BY PERMISSION.

years later. A patent for the device followed in 1904. In 1905 Gillette expanded outside the United States, establishing a sales office in London and a manufacturing operation in Paris. The famous Gillette Blue Blade was introduced in 1932 and an innovative dispenser that eliminated the need to unwrap razor blades after World War II.

Gillette diversified its operations after the war. In 1955 it acquired the Paper Mate Pen Company, an expansion into the area of stationery that it has maintained since. Hoping to secure its grip on the toiletries market, Gillette introduced Right Guard aerosol deodorant in 1960. Brisk sales of the deodorant, along with innovations in shaving products, pushed annual Gillette sales past the $1 billion mark for the first time in 1973. In the 1980s Gillette continued to expand by acquiring Liquid Paper Corp., a maker of correction products, and Oral-B Laboratories, a toothbrush manufacturer. But the company had to fend off numerous hostile takeover bids, and it embarked on a dramatic restructuring program in order to increase profitability. In 1990 the company introduced the Sensor shaving system in 16 countries.

Since that time Gillette has continued to seek competitive advantage in its three businesses: personal grooming products, stationery products, and small electrical appliances. By 1997 sales exceeded $10 billion. With a workforce of 44,000 in 63 facilities worldwide, the company distributed its products in more than 200 countries and territories around the globe.

By sharing resources among its units to optimize performance, Gillette hoped to nurture sustained sales and profit growth. Its plan was to maintain its market dominance by shrewdly investing in the technologies that were vital to success in each of its core businesses. This strategy informed the 1993 launch of Gillette Series Clear Gel antiperspirant. This product was followed in 1996 by the introduction of clear stick products under the Gillette and Right Guard brand names. The company's stated mission, however, remained unchanged—"to offer consumers products of the highest level of performance for value."

TARGET MARKET

"Anything Else Would Be Uncivilized" was first introduced as the tag line in Right Guard ads in 1986. The New York advertising agency NW Ayer & Partners had created the commercials to appeal to sports-loving male

Basketball player Scottie Pippen in a scene from Gillette Company's "Uncivilized" television commercials. **GILLETTE COMPANY. REPRODUCED BY PERMISSION.**

consumers. Early spots featured such sports celebrities as the basketball player Charles Barkley, football's Brian Bosworth, baseball player Kirk Gibson, boxer Marvin Hagler, and wrestler Terry "Hulk" Hogan, along with action film star Chuck Norris. The common trait of these celebrity spokesmen was an aggressive nature and tough-guy demeanor.

With the launch of Right Guard Clear Stick Antiperspirant and Deodorant in 1996, Gillette again turned to NW Ayer to create an appeal to the active male. The agency developed a new print and television ad campaign featuring Scottie Pippen of the National Basketball Association (NBA) champion Chicago Bulls. By placing a highly recognizable sports star in an unfamiliar visual context—in this case on a croquet lawn—the ad team hoped to provide a juxtaposition that would grab the attention of the male sports fans who bought Right Guard.

ATHLETES AS PITCHMEN

The practice of using professional athletes as endorsers is always fraught with peril. Agencies have to be lucky enough to snare an athlete at the top of his or her game and then pray that declining performance or personal controversies do not torpedo a promising campaign. When Converse Sneakers terminated its contract with basketball player Latrell Sprewell for his off-court behavior (trying to strangle his coach), it found itself the object of a lawsuit. The fact that Converse ultimately won its case did not altogether calm nerves at ad agencies across the country.

COMPETITION

By the mid-1990s Gillette had reasons to be concerned about its toiletries business. According to data from Information Resources, sales of deodorants and antiperspirants in food, drug, and mass-merchandising stores fell 1.1 percent in 1996 to $1.4 billion. Among the top five leading brands, only Procter & Gamble's Secret and Colgate-Palmolive's Mennen registered sales gains. The dollar sales of Secret rose 3 percent, while Mennen's sales increased 13.1 percent. According to Mennen's own figures, its Speed Stick grew two to three times faster than its other brands.

The tremendous rise in Speed Stick sales could be explained by three key factors: the introduction of Speed Stick gel in March 1996, improvements to the traditional stick formula that kept cannibalization of existing products to a minimum, and an aggressive marketing program that motivated consumers. Because of the success of Speed Stick, Gillette moved quickly to replicate the formula.

MARKETING STRATEGY

In the category of clear antiperspirants, Gillette chose to focus its efforts on promoting its existing line instead of launching a new one. Accordingly, in 1996, when Peter Clay was named vice president for business management of Gillette toiletries, he was given a simple mission—to take the technology already in use on Gillette Series Clear Gel and put it into an antiperspirant stick form. Gillette poured $30 million into research and development on the clear stick.

The first fruit of Clay's mandate was Gillette Series Clear Stick, introduced in the summer of 1996. This was followed later in the year by Right Guard Clear Stick. Together the two products were the first truly clear antiperspirant sticks on the market that did not leave white residue on the body or clothes. "It's an antiperspirant formula that's a challenge because it's hard to get the efficaciousness of a stick without white residue," Clay explained to *Advertising Age.* To emphasize the difference, Clay decided to make the packaging clear, and, to drive home the distinction even further, he had stickers bearing the legend "No White Residue" placed on every package. Under the aegis of Clay and his staff, NW Ayer created the product's $25 million ad campaign.

For its national ad campaign Gillette commissioned the agency to create a series of television commercials using the slogan "Anything Else Would Be Uncivilized." The tag line had been a staple of Right Guard spots since 1986. Industry veteran Stan Schofield was selected to direct the ads, and Scottie Pippen of the NBA champion Chicago Bulls was chosen to appear in the spots as celebrity spokesman. The sports connection was obvious, since many previous Right Guard spots had used superstar athletes. But Gillette had other reasons for choosing Pippen. "We decided to utilize Scottie because he is a driving force on the most powerful team in the NBA and truly embodies the spirit of Right Guard," Carole Johnson, Gillette's vice president for personal care products, told *PR Newswire.*

To provide humor that would help make the ad memorable, NW Ayer's creative team attired Pippen demurely in an Edwardian cable knit sweater vest and placed him on a croquet lawn. His mouthing of the campaign's tag line thus became the blithe comment of a sophisticate who has finally found a deodorant that will not jeopardize the aesthetics of his leisure ensemble. For Gillette's Johnson, the use of a basketball player was winningly apropos. "On the court, he's a tough competitor and a highly respected player," she told *PR Newswire.* "Portraying him in an unexpectedly gentle and reserved manner provides a contrast that is both attention-getting and humorous." The first ads of the new campaign began airing in January 1997. The commercials appeared in prime time on broadcast networks and cable television outlets in 15- and 30-second versions. The accompanying print campaign ran in sports and general-interest publications.

In January 1997 the 10-year relationship between Right Guard and NW Ayer & Partners came to an end. Gillette shifted its account, whose value was estimated at $10 million, to New York-based Saatchi & Saatchi Advertising. The new agency now faced the challenge of putting a fresh twist on the "Anything Else Would Be Uncivilized" campaign. In January 1998, Saatchi & Saatchi debuted its first television commercials. The 15- and 30-second spots were shown during NBC's national telecast of the FedEx Orange Bowl college football game. Retaining the "Anything Else Would Be Uncivilized" tag line, the new spots again placed a prominent athlete in an unlikely situation, this time Dallas Cowboys running back Emmitt Smith as the master of a team of show dogs.

"When one is competing for the eye of the judges," Smith remarked in the 30-second spot, as he held a pack of bulldogs at bay, "one must keep a firm leash on odor and perspiration." The dogs then performed tricks at Smith's command. The spot ended with Smith accepting a trophy for best of show as he uttered the tag line. The commercials were followed by print ads in sports and general-interest periodicals. Some critics questioned the choice of Smith, a veteran on the downside of his career, as the new spokesman. But Gillette was quick to offer a defense of its new standard bearer. "Emmitt's championship attitude and tenacious style of play mirror the Right Guard image and make him a great candidate for the campaign," said Clay. "He is a driving force on the field and a highly respected player by both teammates and fans; depicting him as reserved and genteel is a contradiction that is entertaining and humorous."

OUTCOME

Despite favorable reaction in the media, the Right Guard "Anything Else Would Be Uncivilized" ads failed to impress consumers. *USA Today*'s Ad Track measured the popularity and effectiveness of the Pippen commercials in the spring of 1997. A scant 11 percent of respondents who had seen the spots at least three times reported that they liked them a great deal. The Right Guard commercials thus ranked among the least popular campaigns measured by Ad Track in its first two years of polling.

There also were mixed results among demographic groups. Older consumers tended to like the ads, with 19 percent responding very favorably. The spots were clearly targeted at the young, however. But only 14 percent of those polled between the ages of 18 and 24 gave high popularity marks to the ads. Even more vexing for Right Guard's marketers was the lukewarm response of male consumers, the campaign's core market. Only 9 percent of men liked the ads a lot, compared with 14 percent of women.

When Ad Track sought to measure consumer recall, the Right Guard ads elicited more positive responses. More than 60 percent of those surveyed reported that they had seen an "Anything Else Would Be Uncivilized" ad on more than one occasion. Industry observers credited the campaign's high recall numbers to its effective use of humor.

It remained to be seen whether the Saatchi & Saatchi ads featuring Smith would do anything to improve the poll numbers. The initial critical response to the ads was less than encouraging. At best, Gillette was faulted for bad timing in choosing Smith to do the ads. For the first time in seven seasons the Dallas Cowboys had failed to make the National Football League play-offs, and Smith himself was widely seen as being headed for retirement. "Smith is a likable athlete," said Denise Gellene in the *Los Angeles Times,* "but for now, at least, he isn't a winner."

Although the deodorant category as a whole was flat in 1997, Gillette, along with other top brands, posted sizable gains. According to Information Resources, sales of Gillette's Right Guard grew 4.9 percent during the year.

FURTHER READING

Alm, Richard. "Advertising Spot No Sweat for Emmitt." *Dallas Morning News,* January 1, 1998, p. 1D.

Enrico, Dottie. "Searching for Deodorant Ads That Stick." *USA Today,* April 28, 1998, p. 5B.

Gellene, Denise. "Timing Is Off for Right Guard Spokesman." *Los Angeles Times,* January 15, 1998, p. D4.

"Gillette Moves Right Guard to Saatchi." *Adweek,* October 7, 1996, p. 6.

Lefton, Terry. "Pippen Gets Civilized with Gillette." *Brandweek,* December 2, 1996.

"Marketing in Brief: Right Guard." *Rose Sheet,* January 5, 1998.

"Scottie Pippen Shoots Croquet for Right Guard." *PR Newswire,* January 28, 1997.

Robert Schnakenberg

Go Daddy Software, Inc.

14455 N. Hayden Rd., Ste. 219
Scottsdale, Arizona 85260
USA
Telephone: (480) 505-8800
Fax: (480) 505-8844
Web site: www.godaddy.com

■■■

GODADDY.COM SUPER BOWL COMMERCIAL CAMPAIGN

OVERVIEW

By 2004 Go Daddy Software had become a leader in the Internet domain-name registration industry, buying available domain names and then selling them to individuals and businesses for a yearly fee. In 2004 the company embarked on its first national marketing effort, contracting New York agency the Ad Store to help make Go Daddy and the GoDaddy.com website known to mainstream America via a TV spot for Super Bowl XXXIX. That Super Bowl, played on February 6, 2005, was the first since the infamous "wardrobe malfunction" that had resulted in pop singer Janet Jackson's breast being exposed on the air during the previous year's halftime show. Among the results of the public outcry following the incident was increased pressure on Super Bowl advertisers to avoid risqué images and themes. Go Daddy chose to fly in the face of this pressure by running a sexually suggestive commercial that lampooned the prevailing climate of censorship.

With a 30-second Super Bowl spot costing $2.4 million, Go Daddy's decision to advertise twice during the game represented a considerable risk for such an unknown company. Additional production expenses approached $1 million. The spot featured a buxom woman undergoing Congressional questioning in order to gain approval to appear in a commercial for GoDaddy.com. As the woman pointed to the GoDaddy.com logo on the front of her tight tank top, one of the shirt's straps broke, a wardrobe malfunction that was met with camera flashes and shocked exclamations as the woman continued to explain what GoDaddy.com was. The commercial aired as planned during the first quarter of the Super Bowl, but then, apparently because of the protests of a National Football League executive, Fox neglected to run the spot during the second on-air slot that Go Daddy had purchased.

The spot was rated one of the Super Bowl's most memorable, but it was the controversy surrounding the network's refusal to air it a second time that proved to be Go Daddy's true marketing coup. The numerous media stories about Fox's censorship of a commercial about censorship gave Go Daddy nearly $12 million in free publicity. The company continued to run TV spots featuring the tank-top-clad woman, including a spot during Super Bowl XL that made reference to the previous year's commercial.

HISTORICAL CONTEXT

Bob Parsons sold his first successful company, Parsons Technology, in 1994, and in 1997 he used the proceeds to start a new company, Jomax Technologies. Unsatisfied with the Jomax name, Parsons and his staff came up with the more arresting moniker Go Daddy. As Parsons told *Wall Street Transcripts,* the name worked "because the domain name GoDaddy.com was available, but we also noticed that when people hear that name, two things happen. First, they smile. Second, they remember it." After an unsuccessful attempt to establish the company as a source for website-building software, Parsons reinvented Go Daddy as a registrar of Internet domain names, buying unused website names and then reselling them to individuals and businesses in need of an online presence. Go Daddy also offered auxiliary services and products enabling customers to launch their sites after the domain-name purchase, including (as in the company's early days) software for building sites. Domain-name registration, however, was a burgeoning industry as America became increasingly wired and more and more businesses found it essential to establish a Web presence. By 2004 Go Daddy had sold nearly seven million domain names and was the world's leading registrar of domain names. Up to that point the company had done little marketing, relying primarily on word-of-mouth buzz and low prices; Go Daddy offered domain names for $8.95, compared with fees of $35 at the industry's high end.

In late 2004 Go Daddy enlisted New York agency the Ad Store for its first sustained offline advertising campaign. The company announced that the campaign would make its TV debut during the 2005 Super Bowl, a move that drew widespread criticism, partly because of the recent history of Super Bowl advertising undertaken by dot-com companies. Dot-com advertising on the Super Bowl had been prevalent in the late 1990s and in the first few years of the new century but had been nearly absent from the game since the bursting of the Internet bubble, leading many industry observers to connect such Super Bowl airtime purchases with the fiscal irresponsibility characteristic of failed dot-coms. Parsons argued that his company was different. As he told *Brandweek,* "Back in '99 . . . dot-coms raised money on ideas that weren't viable. But we are the leader in our industry and actually do make money."

The 2005 Super Bowl presented a uniquely restrictive environment for advertisers. During the previous year's Super Bowl halftime show a much-publicized "wardrobe malfunction" had occurred that resulted in the on-air exposure of pop singer Janet Jackson's breast. The uproar surrounding this incident led some critics to address what they saw as the related indecency of much of that year's Super Bowl advertising. 2004 Super Bowl commercials singled out for censure had included a Budweiser spot featuring flatulent Clydesdale horses and numerous commercials promoting erectile-dysfunction drugs. Both the National Football League and the Federal Communications Commission were exerting pressure on Fox, the broadcaster carrying the 2005 game, to ensure that newly rigorous standards of decency were upheld during Super Bowl XXXIX.

TARGET MARKET

Parsons told *Brandweek* that Go Daddy targeted "everyone who wants a [W]eb presence." Go Daddy's domain-name prices were among the industry's least expensive, and it offered a range of website-management services that comparably priced competitors did not; therefore, Parsons and his colleagues believed that the company would continue to grow rapidly as long as it could make a wider public aware of its brand. The Super Bowl, of course, offered one of the last giant television audiences in an age of fragmenting viewership, and it was annually the most watched television program in America by a wide margin. Super Bowl XXXIX was expected to reach 130 million U.S. viewers, though the actual number of viewers watching the game at any given time was estimated at closer to 90 million.

If Go Daddy could make a splash with an audience of this size, it could count on a much greater degree of brand awareness among the American population at large. Though that year's restrictions on the content of Super Bowl commercials limited the degree to which advertisers could use provocative imagery and messages, Go Daddy and the Ad Store nevertheless charted an intentionally controversial course as a means of standing out from the field of high-profile advertisers. The Go Daddy commercial thus featured an attractive female model in sexually suggestive attire and in a context that directly parodied the political hysteria surrounding the previous year's halftime incident.

COMPETITION

Among Go Daddy's top competitors was Network Solutions, which was introduced as a technology-consulting company in 1979, making it a veritable ancient in the online world. Network Solutions was awarded a grant from the National Science Foundation in 1993 to create a single domain-name registration service for the Internet, which effectively gave the company a monopoly in the industry of domain-name registration until 1999, when the field was opened to competition. The Internet-security and telecommunications company VeriSign acquired Network Solutions at the height of the dot-com bubble in 2000, for $15 billion (the largest Internet merger in history at that point). The company's 2003 sale to Pivotal Equity was a measure of the changes in the dot-com world in the interim: the purchase price this time was $100 million.

Register.com was another of Go Daddy's rival domain-name registrars. The company was founded as

LAYERS OF MEANING

The Go Daddy commercial that ran during Super Bowl XXXIX made obvious reference to Janet Jackson's "wardrobe malfunction" in the previous year's Super Bowl halftime show, but the spot included other veiled references as well. The "Broadcast Censorship Hearings" providing the commercial with its backdrop were supposedly being held in Salem, Massachusetts, suggesting that the then-current restrictions on Super Bowl advertisers were not unlike the famous seventeenth-century witch trials for which that town was famous. More obscure, and perhaps less meaningful, inside references came in the form of the characters' names. The central character in the spot, Nikki Cappelli, was named after the 17-year-old daughter of Paul Cappelli, the creative director and copywriter of the commercial. One of the Congressional committee members shown questioning the Nikki Cappelli character was named Bob Parsons, after Go Daddy's founder and CEO, and another committee member was named Tom Rossano, after a member of the team from Hungry Man, the production company that worked on the spot.

a domain-name registrar in 1994, and it was one of the five original companies selected for entry into the newly opened market in 1999. Like Network Solutions, Register.com had Internet-bubble baggage. The company made its initial public offering on March 3, 2000, a week before the Nasdaq peaked, at a price of $24 per share; by the end of that first trading day, Register.com was priced at $57.25 per share. Register.com shares climbed to $116 before the dot-com bubble definitively burst. By 2005 the company's shares were hovering between $5 and $6 and were considered by many analysts to be a good value for the money.

MARKETING STRATEGY

The official price for 30 seconds of Super Bowl XXXIX airtime was $2.4 million, and Go Daddy bought two such blocks of time, intending to run the same commercial twice, once in the first quarter of the game and once just before the two-minute warning at the game's end. (Media-industry insiders contended, however, that publicized Super Bowl advertising rates were akin to sticker prices on automobiles and that advertisers ultimately did not pay the full amount.) Go Daddy's expenses were not limited to the media-buying cost; the company invested close to $1 million in production of its Super Bowl commercial, an amount of money equivalent to the yearly marketing budget of comparably sized companies. Part of this expense was a result of unforeseen problems with Fox in the weeks leading up to the game. As Tim Arnold, managing partner at the Ad Store, recounted after the fact in *Adweek,* Fox approved storyboards of the Go Daddy commercial on December 3, 2004 (just over two months prior to the Super Bowl, which was played on February 6, 2005), only to withdraw that approval on December 22, after the commercial was already in preproduction. After Fox placed new restrictions on the commercial—including a demand that the words "wardrobe malfunction" be removed from the script—the Ad Store shot "16 and a half" versions of the spot to account for all possible objections the network might yet make. The network continued to reject proposed versions of the commercial until the week before the game, at which point Go Daddy finally received grudging permission to use the airtime for which it had already paid in excess of $4 million.

The commercial reproduced the look of the C-SPAN network (known for its live coverage of Congressional matters), with a banner at the bottom of the screen informing viewers that they were witnessing "Broadcast Censorship Hearings" in Salem, Massachusetts. A woman named Nikki Cappelli (played by Candice Michelle), wearing a tight-fitting tank top and jeans in an otherwise formally dressed crowd, explained to the Congressional committee that she wanted to be in a commercial. When asked what she was advertising, she stood and pointed to the chest of her tank top, on which the GoDaddy.com name was printed, and as she began to inform the panelists about the company's identity, a strap on her top snapped, threatening to reveal her breasts and triggering a flurry of camera flashes and gasps from onlookers. Asked what she would do in the commercial, Cappelli stood and performed a dance with her arms in the air, again triggering shocked gasps and camera flashes. A Congressional panelist then said, "Surely by now you must realize that you're upsetting the committee." Cappelli earnestly replied, "I'm sorry, I didn't mean to upset the committee," as an elderly committee member was shown putting an oxygen mask to his face. A black screen featuring the message "See more coverage at GoDaddy.com" then appeared—a reference to an uncensored and more sexually suggestive version of the "hearings" that was available for viewing on the website—and the commercial closed with the voice of a female committee member saying, "May I suggest a turtleneck?"

The commercial never made its second appearance on the Super Bowl. After airing it in its assigned first-quarter spot, Fox decided not to run it in the fourth quarter, reportedly because of complaints made by a high-level National Football League executive.

OUTCOME

During the Super Bowl traffic to GoDaddy.com spiked by 378 percent, and a survey conducted one and then two days after the Super Bowl found that the Go Daddy commercial was the most memorable of all spots that ran during the game. It was the story of Fox's decision not to air the commercial a second time, however, that proved most useful to the company. The censorship of a commercial that itself poked fun at overzealous censorship proved irresistible to the media, especially in the context of the ongoing commentary about standards of broadcast decency. As word of this incident spread, Go Daddy became by far the most talked-about Super Bowl advertiser. The buzz surrounding the brand in the game's aftermath—measured as "share of voice," the percentage of times that Go Daddy was mentioned in stories about the Super Bowl that ran on national, cable, and the top 50 local TV networks—was calculated at 51.4 percent between February 7 and 11, 2005. Go Daddy received nearly $12 million in free publicity, and many of the TV stories about the incident replayed portions of the commercial. Bob Parsons said in a press release, "Go Daddy accomplished exactly what it set out to achieve with its first-ever Super Bowl ad—increased brand awareness. Today, millions of people now know about GoDaddy.com, which in turn has generated significant new business." The magazine *Business 2.0* declared the Go Daddy Super Bowl effort the "Smartest Ad Campaign" of 2005.

Though Go Daddy allowed its contract with the Ad Store to expire soon after the 2005 Super Bowl, moving its creative duties in-house, the company's subsequent advertising conformed closely to the model established by the Super Bowl commercial. The actress who played Nikki Cappelli, Candice Michelle, continued to appear in Go Daddy spots that drew overt attention to her sexual appeal, and she became known as the "Go Daddy Girl." In 2006 she appeared in a Go Daddy spot that ran during the NFL Playoffs, and Go Daddy again struggled to get a spot approved for the Super Bowl. The Super Bowl XL commercial, which rehashed material from the previous year's spot, again ran in an extended form on the company website, as did alternate versions of other Go Daddy commercials. Website visitors could read a detailed history of Go Daddy's attempt to gain approval for its 2006 Super Bowl entry and could also view numerous spots that had been denied, suggesting that the company's battles against censorship had become increasingly self-conscious and premeditated. Go Daddy continued to grow rapidly.

FURTHER READING

Anderson, Diane. "GoDaddy.com Strives to Make Name for Itself." *Brandweek,* December 13, 2004.

Anderson, Mae. "GoDaddy.com Tops ACNielson Recall Index." *Adweek,* February 28, 2005.

Arnold, Tim. "Who's Your Daddy?" *Adweek,* February 21, 2005.

"CEO Interview: Bob Parsons—GoDaddy.com." *Wall Street Transcript,* October 26, 2004.

Crawford, Krysten, and Matthew Maier. "And the Winners Are . . . Our Picks for the Brainiest Businesses and Businesspeople of the Year." *Business 2.0,* January/February 2006.

Doty, Cate. "A Win-Win for Advertisers." *New York Times,* February 14, 2005.

Elliott, Stuart. "GoDaddy.com Is Ending Contract with Ad Store." *New York Times,* March 29, 2005.

———. "A Super Bowl Spot Meant to Be Provocative Apparently Succeeds after Only One Broadcast." *New York Times,* February 8, 2005.

Fass, Allison. "Super Pricey." *Forbes,* February 14, 2005.

Garfield, Bob. "Fear Wins in Super Bowl Rout." *Advertising Age,* February 7, 2005.

Hein, Kenneth. "Study Says Some Should Take Pass on Super Bowl." *Brandweek,* January 24, 2005.

Lippert, Barbara. "The Disabled List." *Adweek,* February 7, 2005.

Van Munching, Philip. "ABC, Tell Daddy Where to Go." *Brandweek,* January 23, 2006.

Zammit, Deanna. "The Ad Store." *Adweek,* January 31, 2005.

———. "GoDaddy Severs Ties to Ad Store." *Adweek,* March 28, 2005.

Mark Lane

The Goodyear Tire & Rubber Company

1144 East Market Street
Akron, Ohio 44316-0001
USA
Telephone: (330) 796-2121
Fax: (330) 796-2222
Web site: www.goodyear.com

ON THE WINGS OF GOODYEAR CAMPAIGN

OVERVIEW

Upon regaining its title as the world's largest tire manufacturer in 1999, the Goodyear Tire & Rubber Company broke sales records and was busy collecting the tattered market shares of its competitors. Its competitor Bridgestone/Firestone Retail & Commercial Operations suffered notably in 2000, when tires made by the company malfunctioned, causing some 200 deaths. In an attempt to gain even more ground over the competition and create a campaign outside of its traditional format, Goodyear decided to embark upon a new campaign.

Goodyear awarded its $60 million advertising contract to San Francisco–based Goodby, Silverstein & Partners. The resulting television and print campaign, called "On the Wings of Goodyear," began over Labor Day weekend in 2001. The agency tailored "On the Wings of Goodyear" for viewers who were previously unresponsive to product-centered tire commercials. "It really wasn't about the tires. It was more about the role that tires, and specifically Goodyear tires, play in people's lives," Cathryn Fischer, Goodyear's vice president and chief global marketing officer, told the *PR Newswire.* Three different 30-second spots, all centering on the experience of travel, aired across network and cable programming. The commercials continued into 2003 and focused on universal travel themes; for instance, one spot depicted families from different cultures on road trips, all with children asking, "Are we there yet?" from the backseat. Aiming at a wider target than past campaigns, six print variations of "On the Wings of Goodyear" appeared in consumer magazines.

By 2003 Michelin North America and Bridgestone had rallied back, knocking Goodyear to the number three position. Analysts attributed Goodyear's market slip to its restructuring attempts, which involved consolidating factories and performing cost-cutting measures. Even though "On the Wings of Goodyear" did not draw many accolades from the ad industry, it forced all tire makers to rethink using a technical pitch to sell their products to Americans. In 2004 Goodyear ended its relationship with Goodby, Silverstein & Partners and reassigned responsibilities to Arnold Worldwide, but the company continued to use the tagline "On the Wings of Goodyear."

HISTORICAL CONTEXT

Goodyear was founded in 1898 and led the world's tire market by 1916. Throughout the twentieth century it oscillated in and out of the number one spot in the tire industry. By 1990, however, Goodyear had been suffering so drastically that it lost money for the first time since the Great Depression. With the help of CEO Stanley Gault, Goodyear by 1999 had rallied back and regained its position as market leader. Gault moved the company's tire sales outside Goodyear's retail stores by forging partnerships with Wal-Mart, Kmart, and Sears. Goodyear also benefited from the misfortune of its competitor Firestone when Firestone Wilderness AT tires malfunctioned on Ford Explorers. Ford replaced them with Goodyear-made tires.

In 2001 Goodyear ended its 15-year relationship with ad agency J. Walter Thompson, which had orchestrated Goodyear's straight-shooting "Serious Freedom" campaign. The campaign included spots that explained to consumers the inner workings of tires. Advertising commentators criticized "Serious Freedom," along with campaigns launched by Michelin and Bridgestone, for not differentiating the brands from one another. Except for a handful of tire enthusiasts, most consumers described tire commercials "simply as a lot of tires," Fischer told the *PR Newswire.* In an attempt to reach a wider audience, Goodyear hired Goodby, Silverstein & Partners to craft its advertising. Saul Ludwig, an industry analyst, said to the Cleveland *Plain Dealer,* "Goodyear is getting in with their new ad program, while Firestone is on the sidelines, and Michelin is in the process of changing their advertising. Goodyear hasn't had a brand problem. Goodyear is acting out of strength, not out of weakness."

TARGET MARKET

Goodyear's new campaign targeted a much broader market than its previous "Serious Freedom" campaign, which had appealed to male, sports-orientated tire consumers. In contrast "On the Wings of Goodyear" focused on safety-minded consumers with an affinity for travel. Awareness about tire-safety issues, however, did not automatically translate into brand awareness. "Surprisingly, even with all the Firestone stuff, it's not on people's minds," Harold Sogard, general manager of Goodby, explained in an interview with the *Plain Dealer.* "If you go ask your neighbors what kind they are driving on, they don't have a clue." Research conducted before the campaign showed that most consumers never purchased tires with a brand in mind. The company concluded that explaining tire safety with a heartfelt narrative would make a more vivid impression.

To make sure the ads connected with consumers, Goodyear first screened the campaign for 20,000 of its employees. A.J. Faught, vice president of Goodyear affiliate Northwest Tire & Service in Flint, Michigan, told *Tire Business,* "So many tire ads look so technical, which doesn't appeal to anyone other than the enthusiast. This campaign goes straight to the point about safety. Safety is a big issue right now with consumers, who don't want to have to worry about their tires." Goodyear employees felt that the new campaign was more "touchy-feely" and that it would indeed strike a chord with a larger demographic.

"WHAT'S THE THIRD PEDAL FOR?"

During production for the television spot "Family Vacations," casting called for speakers of one of the African click languages. The spot featured a family road-tripping across Africa in a Land Rover. Two boys in the backseat, using their own tribal dialect, incessantly asked their parents when they would reach their destination. Director Bryan Buckley found an actor in Los Angeles to play the father, but at the last minute it was discovered that he could not drive the Land Rover. As Buckley told *Shoot,* "We asked everyone we cast three things: Can you drive, do you have a license and can you drive a standard transmission? Well, of course, this guy says 'yes' to all three, but when he steps into the vintage Land Rover we have on the set, he asks, 'What's the third pedal for?' and it becomes obvious that he has no idea how to drive a stick... So for safety reasons, I tell him he can't do the commercial, and I'm wondering just where I'm going to be able to find a replacement... Fortunately, the 'mother' stepped forward, and, as it turns out, in addition to speaking the click dialect perfectly, she could drive a stick like nobody's business."

COMPETITION

Bridgestone/Firestone had worked its way up to be the world's largest tire manufacturer by 2003. This was despite the fact that Firestone tires had notoriously shredded on Ford Explorers in 2000, leading to the deaths of more than 200 people. Further investigation into the tragedy's causes shifted blame onto Ford. One source quoted a Ford Motors spokesperson as admitting, "Something about the car caused it to roll over and crash, no matter what tires it was riding on." In 2000 Bridgestone/Firestone reported a $2.8 billon loss over the previous year. By 2002 Bridgestone had rebounded with a sales growth of 16.5 percent, reaching almost $19 billion and surpassing Goodyear's $13.8 billion. Until 2001 Bridgestone had primarily advertised with sponsorships at motor-sports events. After 2000 the company began moving advertising into wider markets, shifted efforts from Firestone to Bridgestone, and premiered two TV spots at the start of the 2002 Olympic Games. For the first six months of 2001 Bridgestone spent $12 million on advertising, a significant increase from the $400,000 the same period the year before. Despite the accidents Bridgestone continued marketing Firestone tires. Grey Worldwide, the advertising firm handling the Bridgestone account, told *Advertising Age* in 2002, "We are not going to abandon a more than 100-year-old brand. Firestone has a rich heritage and it's the tire you can rely on."

While Goodyear's "On the Wings of Goodyear" campaign ran, its competitor Michelin drifted between being the second- and third-largest tire manufacturer in the world. Focusing most of its efforts in North America, the South Carolina corporation had $7 billion in sales during 2002 and grew 14 percent. In 2002 Michelin launched a television, print, and outdoor campaign that featured Michelin's longtime mascot, Bibendum, the plump character made of white tires. The campaign's first TV spot, "Guardian Angels," was created by Palmer Jarvis DDB and capitalized on the consumer's need for safety. The 30-second commercial featured Bibendum making snow angels, followed by the tagline "Your guardian angel this winter." Another Michelin spot, "Shuttle," featured Bibendum entering a NASA space shuttle, which also used Michelin tires, just before its launch. The campaign focused primarily on consumer satisfaction and safety issues, as opposed to tire performance.

MARKETING STRATEGY

Before releasing the "On the Wings of Goodyear" campaign, Goodyear had 20,000 of its employees preview the first television spots in August of 2001. Each 30-second commercial centered on a specific theme: carpooling, family vacations, and the morning commute. All three aired for the public during Labor Day weekend, and six print ads began appearing in consumer magazines such as *Time, People,* and *Newsweek.* Goodby, Silverstein & Partners wanted to venture outside Goodyear's previous target market, sports-centric males. The television spots ran during a wide range of prime-time television programs, including *60 Minutes, The Drew Carey Show, Everybody Loves Raymond,* and *48 Hours.*

Firestone's disaster had made the public acutely sensitive to tire safety, a concept Goodby drove home with "On the Wings of Goodyear." The campaign attempted to imply that Goodyear's tires would keep drivers and passengers safer, which in turn would increase consumer desire for Goodyear tires. One 30-second spot, "Carpooling," which dwelled exclusively on the theme of safety, featured a young girl being carpooled. The spot's voice-over warned, "She's not your daughter, but if you give her a ride home, she might as well be." Another spot, "Morning Commute," carried a lighter tone and featured a car full of office workers. The driver was constantly swerving to avoid random furniture and housewares left in the road.

One of the campaign's most memorable spots, first airing on September 1, 2001, featured four families from different ethnic backgrounds on road trips. The spot, directed by Bryan Buckley of the production company Hungry Man, played on the universality of bored children enduring family road trips. The commercial began with an American family traveling in a midsize sedan. A little girl in the back seat asked, "Are we there yet?" to which the father grunted, "No." The next shot featured a second family road-tripping through snow-capped mountains, and a similar "Are we there yet?" exchange took place, but in subtitled Russian. A third road trip, in the middle of a rainstorm, unfolded, but this time the family spoke Chinese. The last shot featured an African family all speaking a tribal click dialect and speeding across the desert in a Land Rover. Two young boys in back asked if they had arrived at their destination yet. The mother finally snapped, "If you ask me that again, I have to stop this car!"

Later television spots, gravitating around similar themes of safety and introducing Goodyear's Run-Flat technology, broke in 2003. One television spot, "Screw," showed a screw tumbling from a skyscraper and onto the street. After a car ran over it, a voice-over explained, "Sharp steel is no match for smart rubber. Tires with Run-Flat technology." Print ads ran during 2003 as well. Harry Cocciolo, creative director for Goodby, Silverstein & Partners during 2003, told *Adweek,* "We tried to find ways to remind people that tires can really make a difference. The Run-Flat technology is being used by Humvees in the military. These are really great proof points that haven't been taken advantage of."

Adweek selected the Goodyear commercial "Bouncing Balls" as one of the best spots of April 2003. The surreal spot featured a driver heading down a street that suddenly filled with bouncing balls. Seconds later children began chasing the balls. The driver slammed on his brakes, and a voice-over remarked, "The unexpected can be planned for. Tires with proven stopping power."

OUTCOME

By 2003 Goodyear had again slipped to number three among tire makers. But despite the fact that "On the Wings of Goodyear" coincided with a decline in Goodyear's sales (from $14.1 billion to $13.8 billion in one year), the campaign was important for reshaping the advertising paradigm that tire makers had used for years. As John Polhemus, president of Goodyear's North American operations, told *Tire Business,* "It's a dramatic departure from the type of product-and-technology-focused advertising that Goodyear has used in the past, and quite frankly, a departure for the tire industry itself." In 2002 Michelin and Bridgestone began tailoring advertising efforts around safety and brand awareness instead of product design.

The majority of industry analysts blamed Goodyear's 2002 backslide on the company's restructuring efforts rather than on Goodby's campaign work. The closing of factories and laying off of thousands of workers resulted in an $85 million decrease in annual operating costs. In 2003 Goodyear also sold most of its stock in Sumitomo Rubber Industries, which had sustained the company for decades. To exacerbate Goodyear's problems even further, it became entangled in an age-discrimination lawsuit.

"On the Wings of Goodyear" did score minor ad-industry points when *Adweek* chose the "Bouncing Balls" commercial as one of the best spots of April 2003. By 2004 Goodyear had signed its creative efforts over to Arnold Worldwide, but it continued using the tagline "On the Wings of Goodyear."

FURTHER READING

Chappell, Lindsay. "Bridgestone Gets a Big Boost: Ad Dollars Surge as Focus Shifts from Firestone." *Advertising Age,* November 26, 2001, p. 31.

Diedrick, Brian. "Director Buckley Goes On the Road, Family Style." *Shoot,* September 21, 2001, p. 12.

Ethridge, Mary. "Goodyear Begins Ad Campaign for Assurance Line of Tires." *Akron (OH) Beacon Journal,* April 27, 2004.

Frazier, Mya. "Goodyear Ads Go Road Least Traveled." *Cleveland (OH) Plain Dealer,* September 4, 2001, p. C2.

Halliday, Jean. "Fighting Tire Slump: Leading Brands Up Ad Budgets as Sales Deflate." *Advertising Age,* February 25, 2002, p. 4.

Irwin, Tanya, and David Gianatasio. "Dunlop Consolidation Advances: Final Shootout Comes Down to Goodby, BBH and Arnold." *Adweek* (eastern ed.), February 18, 2002, p. 3.

Jeffers, Michelle. "Goodyear Tires Take on Hazards: Rubber Balls, Screws Are the Enemy in New Goodby Spots." *Adweek,* April 21, 2003, p. 7.

Norton, Justin. "Goodby Crafts Interactive Racing Site for Goodyear." *Adweek* (western ed.), September 23, 2002, p. 4.

Ransom, Kevin. "It's Lights, Camera, Action for Goodyear Tire Effort." *Adweek,* April 26, 2004, p. 15.

Sanders, Lisa, and Alice Cuneo. "Goodyear Changes Ad Agency." *Rubber & Plastics News,* June 14, 2004, p. 26.

Stumpf, Todd. "Yep, 2001 a Real Head(line) Banger." *Tire Business,* December 17, 2001, p. 11.

Zielasko, Dave. "Goodyear's Taking Flight: New Marketing Promo 'Wings' It." *Tire Business,* September 10, 2001, p. 1.

Kevin Teague

William Grant & Sons Ltd.

Glenfiddich Distillery
Keith
Grampian, AB5 4DH
United Kingdom
Telephone: 44 1340 820000

■■■

SINGLE MALT CAMPAIGN

OVERVIEW

Having established what constituted a high advertising budget for its Glenfiddich brand of scotch, nearly $1.7 million, William Grant & Sons Ltd. at the end of 1998 moved its account from New York-based McCann-Erickson Worldwide to a much smaller firm, Gyro Worldwide in Philadelphia. The change marked the end of McCann's three-year "The Friday Scotch" campaign.

Scotch whisky was not usually a product whose advertising attracted enormous attention in the United States, simply because it was not marketed on television or radio. Nor had Glenfiddich or its family-owned Scottish distillery attained enormous exposure in the American market—despite the fact that it was the world's leading brand of single-malt scotch. For that matter Glenfiddich's 1998 advertising itself did not make headlines: the real story was the gathering resurgence of scotch in general and of single-malt scotch in particular—a trend on which Glenfiddich and its competitors sought to capitalize. "About five years ago," wrote Jerry Shriver in *USA Today* in 1998, "a wave of well-heeled consumers began rebelling against the prevailing low-fat/abstemious lifestyle." Shriver went on to note, "distinctive and pricey single-malt scotches began elbowing aside generic blend whiskies. Then, cigar smokers helped revive cognac, port, and bourbon sales."

Despite the renewed interest in scotch among the youthful set, single-malt scotch whisky still suffered from an association with old age, according to Lisa Buckingham in the *Guardian:* "Think of whisky and the picture which most readily springs to mind is that of a greying cardigan wearer, nestled contentedly in a high-backed armchair. It is an impression most distillers would give their right arm to eradicate." Age and the changing of the guard between generations were themes that had animated the advertising of Glenfiddich for many years.

HISTORICAL CONTEXT

Scotch whisky received its name for a simple reason: it came only from Scotland, which in the 1990s had some 100 distilleries. Most of these were of long standing, though few had remained in the hands of their founders' descendants from the beginning. Thus William Grant & Sons, established in the 1850s and led some 140 years later by the great-great-grandchildren of the founders, was an exception.

The term "single-malt scotch" had little meaning until the latter part of the nineteenth century. Up until that time all scotch was made from malted barley and was distilled unblended; then a distiller by the name of Usher began blending high-grade scotch with less expensive varieties of whisky, using water to further extend the mixture. The resulting whisky was not only cheaper than single-malt but also weaker, which actually proved to be an advantage since it made it more appealing to a wider range of drinkers.

Another benefit to the distiller was the fact that blends were easier to control. Each batch of single malt tended to have its own level of quality, which was consistent throughout the whole batch but did not extend to future batches. The many variables in a blend actually made it more predictable, since a distiller could use varying mixtures to correct for anomalies such as bitterness.

Thanks to these factors, single-malt had all but disappeared by the end of World War II. Scotch itself continued to be popular, but by the late 1960s liquor consumption began to decline and was increasingly confined to older and older drinkers. The young, who became ever more health-conscious in the 1980s, saw liquor as something their parents drank.

Yet in the early to mid-1990s there came a popular backlash against those values of the 1980s. This was accompanied by the stigmatization of "political correctness" and an embracing of fashions from the 1950s and early '60s, albeit reinterpreted for the '90s. The change in the zeitgeist extended to diet: thus red meat, vilified for many years, was in again. So were martinis, cigars instead of cigarettes, and single-malt scotch.

A BIT OF SCOTLAND IN INDIA

At first glance it might seem—to an American at least—that there was little connection between Scotland and India. But of course there was a strong historic link between the two places, thanks to the British Empire, which introduced British phenomena such as cricket and scotch whisky to the Indian subcontinent. Thus when William Grant & Sons vice chairman Grant Gordon wanted to establish a stronger Indian presence for the Glenfiddich brand in 1998, it made perfect sense to sponsor the Triangular Cricket Tournament.

Cricket remained India's most popular sport, with whisky one of its most popular alcoholic beverages. Gordon told *Business Line*'s Indian edition, *The Hindu,* that his company, which invested $1 million in the tournament, held an 8 percent share of the blended whisky market in India. Gordon invited Indian tourists in Scotland to visit the Glenfiddich distillery, which had welcomed more than two million visitors since it first opened its doors to the public in 1976.

TARGET MARKET

Driving the new trends toward single-malt scotch and other fashions was the same youthful market that made crooner Tony Bennett one of the most popular performers on MTV. In 1998 James B. Arndorfer of *Advertising Age* speculated that William Grant would introduce "shooter-type drinks aimed at young adults," and though a William Grant executive declined to comment on this supposition, vice chairman Grant Gordon—great-grandson of one of the company's founders—told a reporter for the Indian edition of *Business Line* that "Our target-group all over the world is the 25-30 age." Gordon went on to add something that seemed to contradict his first statement: "Whisky is for mature drinkers." What he meant, of course, was that it was not for people who had merely reached legal drinking age, a clientele more inclined toward beer. The youngest drinkers, after all, would not typically be able to afford the prices associated with higher grades of scotch. According to Peter Simoncelli, food and beverage director at the Four Seasons hotel in Chicago, "the trend is to order the 18- or 25-year-old selections at prices up to $23 a pour."

Such prices fit with the upscale "menus" of cigar bars. "Cigar rooms in restaurants provide a clublike setting," said Curt Burns of Chicago's Hudson Club, quoted in the *Orlando Sentinel,* "and since it takes time to smoke a great cigar, it's tempting to sip a special spirit too. The need to spend $10 to $18 for a snifter hasn't scared anyone off." Burns was referring to brandy or cognac, but similar rules applied to single-malt scotches. Yet price, combined with the long-standing image associated with scotch, meant that brands such as Glenfiddich had to overcome resistance among the young. According to Mike Dennis in *SuperMarketing,* a British survey in 1997 revealed that 62 percent of regular whisky drinkers were 50 years old or older.

COMPETITION

The British study also showed that 61 percent of vodka drinkers, by contrast, were in the 18-to-34 age group. Vodka, the star component in the martini, thus represented one of Glenfiddich's primary competitors. Then there were the 100-plus makers of scotch whisky.

Dominating the scotch industry, in terms of quality appraisal if not sales, were six distilleries that earned a five-star rating from British connoisseur Michael Jackson, arguably the world's leading authority on scotch. These six distilleries were the Macallan, Auchentoshan, the Glenlivet, Highland Park, Lagavulin, and Springbank. As for the top scotch in terms of U.S. sales, that position was held by Dewar's; but Glenfiddich still held the lead in Great Britain, with a 22 percent market share, and in the world, where it enjoyed a 27 percent share.

According to an October 1998 report in the *Herald,* three brands had managed to overcome vicissitudes in the market, such as a decline in overall growth of whisky sales in Europe and North America. These three brands were Glenfiddich, Laphroaig, and Glenmorangie, each of which had reached a "respectable" 13 percent increase in sales during the year. Of Glenfiddich, a commentator in *Off Licence News* ("off licence" is the British term for a liquor store) wrote, "It is sold in 190 nations. Considering [that] the United Nations has just 185 members, that's pretty impressive brand penetration." Hence William Grant marketing manager Patrick Tully spoke proudly of Glenfiddich as the "category captain."

Certainly maintenance of a distinct identity proved crucial in a heavily segmented industry. William Rice in the *Orlando Sentinel* quoted Ronny Millar of United Distillers as saying, "One thing is clear: if you try to duplicate a whisky at another distillery, it won't work." But in the sudden rush to single-malt brands that characterized the market during the late 1990s, numerous scotch makers either attempted to get on the bandwagon or to shore up existing offerings. Dewar's announced plans in 1998 to introduce a "high malt content" 12-year-old scotch, and Bowmo represented a "cask strength" malt. The latter had a higher alcohol content than most single malts, up to 120 proof; Glenfiddich also marketed its own cask strength variety.

MARKETING STRATEGY

In 1996 Glenfiddich and McCann-Erickson ran 90-second spots on British television in a campaign that cost 1.5 million pounds, or about $2.5 million. The spots focused on a father and son, whose dialogue emphasized the concept of scotch as a tradition passed down through generations. At the end of the commercial, the two shook hands, and the father handed his son a small bottle of Glenfiddich.

This advertising represented a shift from past Glenfiddich marketing, which was built around images of Scottish heritage and time-honored techniques of distilling. In the United States at about the same time, McCann-Erickson launched "The Friday Scotch," a series of print ads centering around the idea of scotch as an element of good times and celebration. During this period William Grant dramatically increased its advertising, establishing an annual budget as high as $10 million for all its brands. In 1997 it devoted $3 million to Glenfiddich and Frangelico alone, and by 1998 it was spending 1 million pounds, or about $1.68 million, on Glenfiddich.

"We have outstanding brands," Mark Teasdale, senior vice president for marketing, told *Advertising Age* in April 1998, "and we're going to aggressively get back to building their upscale status." At the same time William Grant moved away from its exclusive relationship with McCann, first by signing Grace & Rothschild of New York to handle all brands except for Glenfiddich. Teasdale suggested that the company would be reviewing its "Friday Scotch" campaign but declined to discuss future plans; meanwhile, as Arndorfer reported in *Advertising Age,* Glenfiddich sales in the stateside market had leveled off at 95,000 cases in 1996, the last year for which sales information was available.

By December 1998 Glenfiddich was running a new campaign in Britain. Posters displayed at bus stops and shopping centers asked "How much do you love your next-door neighbour?" and "How much do you love your father-in-law?" According to a report in *Off Licence News,* First Drinks Brands, distributor of Glenfiddich in Great Britain, had conducted research which showed that "consumers hold their beloved bottle of single malt in such high esteem that they are likely to hide it away when expecting a high influx of visitors, and offer their guest less prized drams instead."

OUTCOME

William Grant spent one million pounds on the British poster campaign and by the end of 1998 was prepared for a new assault on the U.S. market—with a new advertising agency. Thus on one of the last business days of the year, December 22, the *New York Times* reported that the company was prepared to drop its "Friday Scotch" campaign. According to Teasdale, the latter had run "for about three years and delivered some solid numbers," but apparently it was time for a change.

That change came with the December selection of Gyro Worldwide as the U.S. agency for Glenfiddich. McCann would still handle other advertising throughout the world, but the choice of Gyro represented a clear desire to appeal to a more youthful, MTV-influenced market. The Philadelphia agency, as the *New York Times* reported, was "known for provocative campaigns aimed at consumers in the 20's and 30's for such products as clothing, alcoholic beverages, and cigarettes." Gyro's techniques had not always won praise from critics of advertising: its print ads for clothing retailer Zipper Head, for instance, showed convicted mass murderer Charles Manson along with the headline, "Everyone has the occasional urge to go wild and do something completely outrageous."

In 1999 a new William Grant marketing director, Heather Graham, signaled the company's interest in a new agency to handle its British advertising, primarily on television. During the spring of that year, it launched an agency review with the help of pitch consultant Agency Assessments, and by July BMP DDB had won the British account for William Grant. Universal McCann would continue to oversee media buying in the British market.

If anything was clear about William Grant in general, or its Glenfiddich single-malt advertising in particular, it was the fact that changes were afoot. As *Off Licence News* reported in November 1998, "there are clearly busy times ahead for Glenfiddich and William Grant. Whether the brand succeeds in maintaining the momentum in the malt market or not over the next few years, no one will be able to turn around and accuse it of not trying."

FURTHER READING

Arndorfer, James B. "Wm. Grant Hikes Budget for Upscale Liquor Brands: Spirits Marketer Enlists Grace, Eyes Product Introductions." *Advertising Age,* April 13, 1998, p. 12.

Buckingham, Lisa. "Single Malt Can Survive Drowning in Cola; It's the Pipe and Slippers That Are Damaging One of Scotland's Key Export Industries." *Guardian* (London), April 10, 1999, p. 28.

"By the Single File: Whisky Industry Needs Strategy Re-Think." *Herald* (United Kingdom), October 8, 1998, p. 27.

Cozens, Claire. "Agencies Vie for William Grant Whisky Business." *Campaign,* April 2, 1999, p. 1.

Dennis, Mike. "Spirited." *SuperMarketing,* November 20, 1998, p. 22.

"Like Your Scotch Neat? On the Rocks? Pretension, Be Gone. A New Campaign Portrays It as Way Cool." *New York Times,* December 22, 1998, p. C1.

"New Glenfiddich Posters." *Off Licence News,* December 4, 1998.

Olmsted, Larry. "Scotch Drinking: What's New in Old Whisky?" *Investors Business Daily,* February 20, 1998, p. A1.

Purdom, Nick. "Consumer PR—Scots Persuaded Back to Whisky." *PR Week,* June 4, 1999, p. 8.

Rice, William. "Scotch Drinkers Becoming Single-Minded in Their Pursuit: Lovers of Fine Whisky Are Willing to Pay Plenty for the Distinctive Taste of Aged Spirits." *Orlando Sentinel,* January 15, 1998, p. H7.

Shriver, Jerry. "Demystifying Spirits." *USA Today,* December 11, 1998, p. 7D.

"We Intend to Stay in the News and Tap the Huge Whisky Market." *Business Line* (The Hindu), May 7, 1998.

Judson Knight

H&R Block, Inc.

4400 Main Street
Kansas City, Missouri 64111
USA
Telephone: (816) 753-6900
Web site: www.hrblock.com

WORRIED ABOUT BILL CAMPAIGN

OVERVIEW

In 2000 the largest tax-preparation company in the Unites States, H&R Block, Inc., was venturing beyond the niche industry in which it had excelled for 45 years. After a series of acquisitions and changes in upper management, the firm known for preparing tax returns began touting its new mortgage and brokerage services, financial-planning services, and line of personal-finance software. The company's executives also wanted to brand H&R Block as a financial service available to all Americans, not just high-profile businesses. Assimilating all of the company's changes into one advertising message, H&R Block released its "Worried about Bill" campaign.

Created by the advertising agency Young & Rubicam, "Worried about Bill" broke nationally on January 12, 2000. H&R tripled its advertising budget to finance the $100 million campaign, which employed television, radio, print, and outdoor advertisements. Most of the campaign's 21 television spots featured the fictional character Bill, who, as the April 15 tax deadline approached, grew increasingly anxious while preparing his taxes. The commercials depicted the frazzled Bill becoming so obsessed with the task that he ignored his wife's attempts at seduction, allowed his daughter to stay out all night, and eventually looked to his daughter's boyfriend for financial advice. The campaign's storyline culminated with Bill, delirious from reading his 1099 tax form, incinerating his financial records in the backyard barbecue.

The campaign collected the Best of Show and two Gold awards for the broadcast category at the 32nd annual American Advertising (ADDY) Awards. It also garnered two Gold awards in the television competition at the One Show's 2001 ceremony. Besides its ad-industry success, the campaign helped H&R Block boost its 2000 sales 38 percent over the previous year's sales. David Byers, the company's chief marketing officer, explained to *USA Today,* "We're very happy with the creativity. The feedback we've gotten from consumers has been that it's been enormously successful for us." Much to Young & Rubicam's astonishment, H&R Block opened its advertising account up for review only a few months after "Worried About Bill" began.

HISTORICAL CONTEXT

Henry and Richard Bloch, brothers from Kansas City, Missouri, first offered their tax-preparation services in 1946 under the name United Business Company. The business quickly grew after the Bloch brothers franchised it. Wanting to change the name United Business Company but afraid that consumers would pronounce their last name as "blotch," Henry and Richard renamed the business H&R Block in 1955. Later in the 1970s

Henry appeared in television spots for the company and assured his audience that their taxes were safe with H&R Block.

In 1996 Young & Rubicam won the firm's advertising account. Some of the agency's early work for H&R Block included a 20-second radio spot titled "Proctor," which stressed the importance of privacy by humorously featuring a street-corner proctology exam. The magazine *Advertising Age* deemed "Proctor" the best radio commercial of 1998. That year H&R Block spent an estimated $30 million on advertising. In 1999 the firm spent $28 million on advertising during the first nine months.

Believing that his company could offer more services to its preexisting customers, newly elected H&R Block president Mark Ernst wanted to brand the business as more than just a tax preparer. In 1993 the company had purchased the personal-finance-software company MECA Software; to expand its mortgaging services H&R Block purchased Fleet Financial Group's Option One Mortgage; and in 1999 the company expanded its brokerage services by acquiring discount brokers Olde Financial Discount. By late 1999 the firm wanted Young & Rubicam to unify its services under the H&R Block brand. The *Delaney Report* quoted H&R Block chief marketing officer David Byers as saying in 1999, "We're going through a major transformation—moving from being a one product company to a financial services powerhouse. H&R Block is a brand that is ubiquitous. We want to capitalize on that as well as on the high degree of trust the consumer has in the brand."

TARGET MARKET

"Worried about Bill" targeted its preexisting small and medium-sized business customers that trusted H&R Block for their tax preparation but that still relied on brokerages such as the Charles Schwab Corp., Morgan Stanley, and Merrill Lynch & Company for financial planning, mortgaging, and investing. In addition to businesses, the campaign also targeted individuals with similar financial needs. Differing from H&R Block's advertising during the late 1990s, which suggested that H&R Block was the best firm for preparing taxes, "Worried about Bill" communicated to audiences that the firm offered a wider range of financial services. According to Greg Farrell of *USA Today,* the campaign attempted the transform "H&R Block from tax preparer to full financial services company for Middle America."

By early 2000 the surge of young entrepreneurs within the burgeoning technology sector had expanded America's newly wealthy crowd. According to market researcher Spectrem Group, the number of U.S. households with more than $1 million in assets had doubled from 3.45 million in 1994 to 7.1 million in 2000. Spectrem Group also reported that 44 percent of this population felt overwhelmed by the amount of time needed to manage their assets. Sixty percent of the same population believed that there was too much information regarding financial planning. "Worried about Bill" suggested that using H&R Block's services would make organizing their finances easier.

FALSE CLAIMS

During an advertising campaign launched in January 2000, the financial-services provider H&R Block created a Refund Rewards program that placed its clients' tax returns on ATM cards. As part of the promotion the ATM cards were eligible for discounts on brands such as Sears, General Motors, RadioShack, and US Airways. One ad for Refund Rewards appeared in the *Virginian Pilot,* a Virginia newspaper, and read, "Spend more quality time with your refund. Why wait six weeks for your tax refund when H&R Block can give you your refund amount in as little as two days?" Liberty Tax Service, one of H&R Block's tax-preparing competitors, filed a lawsuit against H&R Block stating that the advertising made false claims. Refund Rewards ATM cards were not actually carrying the balance of tax refunds but rather small loans that were to be paid off after the real tax returns arrived. A three-judge federal court of appeals banned the Refund Rewards advertisement and forced H&R Block to pay Liberty $325,000 in legal costs.

COMPETITION

The ad agency Emmerling Post released a series of print ads for the asset-management branch of financial holding company the Phoenix Companies in 2000. One print ad featured the text "Money. It's not what it used to be," above a picture of a queen dressed in ostentatious clothing beside another woman wearing black leather and a tiara. Other print ads stated, "Some people still inherit wealth, the rest of us have no choice but to earn it." Specifically targeting an audience composed of the newly wealthy, a third print ad featured a casually dressed young man standing beside a dapper-looking gentleman with the copy, "New money is different than old money. For one thing, it's younger." Instead of repeating the trends of other asset-management firms that placed print ads in financial magazines, Phoenix Companies placed the ads in "lifestyle books read by the well-to-do," according to *Advertising Age.*

On December 31, 1999, Merrill Lynch, which provided financial services for private, institutional, and government clients, launched a $150 million campaign to herald its new online services under the tagline "Be Bullish." Television spots for the campaign aired on cable channels such as CNN and USA. The campaign's premier television spot consisted of a large-budget commercial that began with a squadron of helicopters descending upon Manhattan. As the commercial progressed, commandos rappelled from the helicopters and later airlifted the 7,000-pound bull statue that was commonly associated with the New York Stock Exchange. Merrill Lynch's logo also featured the image of a bull. "We're bringing the bull back," said James Gorman, chief marketing officer at Merrill Lynch, referring to both the company's logo and an aggressive attitude within the stock market. "The icon is much loved, but modernized. The bull is entering the digital age."

MARKETING STRATEGY

The "Worried about Bill" campaign's first spot, "Block Air," did not feature the campaign's lead character, Bill. Young & Rubicam hoped the 30-second television spot would herald H&R Block's newer services without distracting from its tax-preparation reputation. "Block Air" parodied airline commercials by featuring a pilot, purportedly flying for H&R Block's new airline, giving his mechanics and then his crew a thumbs-up. The spot's voice-over asked, "How much has H&R Block changed?" It then answered, "Not this much."

Twenty television spots followed "Block Air" and ranged from 15 to 60 seconds long. Throughout the bulk of the campaign, the character Bill grew increasingly frazzled as the April 15 tax deadline approached. The campaign excluded all images of accountants, tax-preparation software, or handshaking, the kinds of themes that, according to *Adweek* critic Barbara Lippert, were typically used in financial-services advertisements. Instead the commercials featured the average disorganized consumer. Bill was shown so consumed with preparing his own taxes that when his teenage daughter asked for money in the spot "Dad, Can I Have Some Money—Tax Day 6," he offered her his entire wallet. When she told him she would be out all night, Bill replied, "Have a good time." His preoccupation caused him to ignore his wife's attempt at seduction in a spot titled "W-2—Tax Day 5."

"The humor is intended to build on the brand's reputation of accessibility," explained Byers to *Adweek.* "We're a brand that mainstream America feels comfortable doing business with." In the television spot "Please Be Quiet—Tax Day 20," Bill's daughter and wife were featured silently reading in their living room with only the sound of a clock ticking. Bill burst into the room and screamed, "Dad needs quiet!" The campaign's 60-second television spot, which shared the campaign's title, "Worried about Bill," began with Bill appearing chipper and very sane. As Bill read through his tax forms, he grew paranoid and even began confiding in the family cat. After tax preparation completely wore down his sanity, the wild-eyed Bill piled his financial statements into the backyard barbecue. The spot ended with Bill's wife calling for professional help and the appearance of the tagline "Get help."

"Taxes can be such a downer, and we don't want H&R Block to be," Young & Rubicam's group creative director John Matejczyk told *Adweek.* Although the $100 million campaign was not the first humorous advertising that Young & Rubicam had developed for H&R Block, it was by far the most expensive the agency had created for the firm.

OUTCOME

The campaign was awarded Best of Show and received two Gold awards for the broadcast category at the 32nd annual ADDY Awards, conducted by the American Advertising Federation. It also garnered two Gold awards in the television competition at One Show's 2001 ceremony. Barbara Lippert, critic for *Adweek* magazine, praised the campaign, saying, "It conveys that the brand is not only alive, but responsive and even hip to the 21st century. That's no small feat." In 2000 H&R Block posted $2.2 billion in sales, a significant increase over the previous year's sales figure of $1.5 billion.

The ad agency seemed convinced of its client's delight with the campaign. "Young & Rubicam helped H&R Block achieve four consecutive record-breaking years for its business," Howard Breen, the agency's president and CEO, stated to *Knight Ridder/Tribune Business News* in April 2000. "They've been happy with our efforts... In fact, the current work we've done for them has effectively repositioned the company in a stylish, contemporary and relevant way, and has been well-received by both consumers and the media."

Unfortunately for Young & Rubicam, two of the campaign's creators, John Matejczyk and David Skinner, resigned in March 2000. Even though more than 50 people were involved with the campaign, the two resignations prompted H&R Block to reopen its advertising account for review. Although it was invited to, Young & Rubicam did not compete for the account. The ad agency Campbell Mithun took over the firm's advertising on June 19, 2000.

FURTHER READING

Baar, Aaron. "H&R Block Focuses on Taxes." *Adweek* (midwest ed.), January 15, 2001, p. 4.

Cardona, Mercedes M. "H&R Block's $100 Mil Review Jolts Y&R: Marketer Pleased with Creative but Cites Key Departures for Move." *Advertising Age,* April 3, 2000, p. 67.

———. "Investors Opening Arms to Nouveau Riche Clients." *Advertising Age,* August 14, 2000, p. S2.

———. "Marketing 1000." *Advertising Age,* October 8, 2001, p. S20.

Champagne, Christine. "Back in Action." *Shoot,* April 7, 2000, p. 40.

Cisterna, Fred. "Craig Gillespie." *Shoot,* October 12, 2001, p. 22.

Dill, Mallorre. "Chip off the Old Block." *Adweek* (eastern ed.), July 10, 2000, p. 26.

Elliott, Stuart. "Chicago Agencies Win Addy Awards." *New York Times,* June 9, 2000, p. 6.

Farrell, Greg. "Ad Agency's Reward for Good Reviews: Hit the road, Jack." *USA Today,* April 17, 2000, p. 8B.

———. "Merrill Lynch Upgrades Bull from Bronze Age to Digital Era." *USA Today,* December 27, 1999, p. 8B.

Goddu, Jenn. "H&R Block Goes Beyond Taxes." *Adweek* (midwest ed.), January 17, 2000, p. 4.

———. "H&R Block in Play." *Adweek* (midwest ed.), April 3, 2000, p. 8.

Lippert, Barbara. "Taxing Times." *Adweek* (eastern ed.), March 6, 2000, p. 28.

O'Reilly, Terry. "Our Radio Doesn't Suck." *Marketing Magazine,* July 12, 1999, p. 9.

Wilcha, Kristin. "Cliff Freeman and Partners Tops One Show Awards." *Shoot,* May 11, 2001, p. 7.

Kevin Teague

Hallmark Cards, Inc.

2501 McGee St.
Kansas City, Missouri 64108
USA
Telephone: (816) 274-5111
Fax: (816) 274-5061
Web site: www.hallmark.com

SNEAK A PEEK CAMPAIGN

OVERVIEW

With its "Sneak a Peek" advertising campaign, Hallmark Cards, Inc., hoped to convince consumers to insist on buying only Hallmark greeting cards and to check the brand insignia on the backs of cards they received. "This campaign hinges on the concept that there is only one thing consumers need to know: it's Hallmark, cards that say what they think and feel, the brand they trust," said Brad Van Auken, the company's director of brand management and marketing. The television spots for the campaign featured a young married couple either exchanging greeting cards between them or picking out cards to give to others. The woman attempts to teach her husband the best techniques to discreetly check whether or not the cards he receives are from Hallmark. The campaign played on the company's long-running slogan, "When you care enough to send the very best."

Hallmark, the dominant greeting card company in the United States, had a wholesome image and was known for its emphasis on excellence. The company had a long history of successful marketing endeavors, including the award-winning "Hallmark Hall of Fame" series of television programs. Hallmark and its two major competitors, Gibson Greetings, Inc. and American Greetings Corporation, branched out in 1997 by marketing their merchandise via the Internet and offering related products, such as cards that consumers could print at home on their computers. The "Sneak a Peek" commercials won an Effie Award and were popular among consumers, especially with women, who were the primary target market. The campaign was launched in 1996 and ran through 1997. As in previous years, Hallmark's sales accounted for nearly half of the $7 billion in revenues generated by the greeting card industry in 1997.

HISTORICAL CONTEXT

The Hallmark company was established in 1910, when a penniless teenager named Joyce C. Hall arrived in Kansas City, Missouri, and began marketing his two shoeboxes full of picture postcards through a mail-order business. The business grew rapidly and was soon producing greeting cards, ornamental gift wrap, party decorations, and jigsaw puzzles. In 1984 the company acquired Binney & Smith, which manufactured Crayola products, Magic Markers, and Liquitex art supplies. By 1997 Hallmark Cards was a global firm employing more than 20,000 people, including hundreds of artists, designers, writers, editors, and photographers. In addition to the Hallmark brand, the company made Ambassador Cards, Shoebox Greetings, and several other lines. Hallmark products were sold at a chain of stores owned by the company but also at drug stores and other retail outlets. Since

AP IMAGES.

consumers wanted the convenience of finding Hallmark products wherever they shopped, the company launched a new line of cards, Expressions from Hallmark, in 1996. Unlike some other Hallmark brands, the Expressions line was available in supermarkets and other mass-merchandise stores. By encouraging consumers to check the insignia on the back of cards, the "Sneak a Peek" campaign helped call attention to the fact that Expressions was a Hallmark line.

Some of the company's advertisements were tailored to promote specific products, such as Ambassador Cards. Others, like the "Sneak a Peek" campaign, were intended to generate awareness of Hallmark products in general. In 1951 the company had begun a long-term sponsorship of the popular and critically acclaimed "Hallmark Hall of Fame," a series of television programs for family viewing. In 1997 alone Hallmark sponsored 87 films and miniseries for television, including *Gulliver's Travels* and Larry McMurtry's *Streets of Laredo.* In 1996 the company spent $23 million to publicize the Hallmark Hall of Fame and $102 million on advertising designed to draw consumers into Hallmark Gold Crown stores, which carried greeting cards and specialty items. The print and broadcast ads promised, "You'll Feel Better Inside."

A Hallmark survey in the spring of 1997 showed a 93 percent approval rating for the programs and an 86 percent approval rating for the company's advertising. The "Hallmark Hall of Fame" broadcasts won numerous Emmy Awards, and the Hallmark commercials that accompanied the programs were recognized for their tastefulness and creativity. Joyce Hall's motto, "Good taste is good business," had helped the company establish a wholesome image. The company's slogan since 1944, "When You Care Enough to Send the Very Best," was a reference to Hall's memoirs *When You Care Enough.* For many years the slogan was incorporated into the company's advertising. Consumers age 50 and over tended to be particularly fond of Hallmark's sentimental, family-oriented advertising. In 1997 the company's Internet site included a Nice-O-Meter, an interactive survey that allowed visitors to measure how nice they were.

TARGET MARKET

In 1997 the market for greeting cards, stationery, and other correspondence products was increasing steadily. Hallmark's research showed that 29 percent of consumers were writing more than they had previously, 46 percent of grandmothers said they received correspondence from their grandchildren, and 58 percent of mothers said their children wrote them thank you notes. A poll in *Adweek* said nearly a third of the people in the United States planned to correspond more frequently than they had in the past. Consumers liked to give cards that expressed the feelings that they did not have the courage to say aloud. "If the message in a card rings true, people identify with it and see themselves in it," said Ellen McKeever, manager of the Shoebox Greetings division of Hallmark. "If a character on a card reminds people of someone they

INNOVATIVE MARKETING

Hallmark Cards was the first greeting card company to advertise nationally. That initial ad, in the *Ladies Home Journal* in 1928, was ridiculed as "Hall's Folly" because it was thought that consumers took no notice of brand names when they purchased greeting cards. But the venture was a success. Hallmark later generated publicity by sponsoring a radio program in which poems and other writings from greeting cards were read.

know, or if they just like the character or find it funny, they will choose that card." The perception was that the exchange of cards made people feel good and enhanced their relationships. The "Sneak a Peek" campaign played up these feelings by emphasizing that sending a Hallmark greeting was the ultimate demonstration of caring.

The company had conducted extensive research to determine what its customers, who were 90 percent women, wanted in greeting cards. "From all the information we've collected directly from greeting card purchasers, three things are abundantly clear," said Mark J. Schwab, the company's vice president of strategy and marketing. "First, consumers want to find great products that are a good value... Second, the time-pressed consumer longs for a convenience-based greeting card offering from Hallmark, a company she knows and trusts.... Third, we have to make it crystal clear to the consumer that the card shop is simply the best place to shop for our category of products, an exciting, vibrant site from which to reinforce Hallmark brand equity." The "Sneak a Peek" campaign encouraged consumers to have such faith in the Hallmark brand that they would not bother looking at anything else.

COMPETITION

Hallmark was the dominant greeting card company in the United States, with a market share that averaged about 42 percent, according to *USA Today* 's *Ad Track.* American Greetings Corporation came in second with 35 percent, and Gibson Greetings, Inc., was third. In 1996 American Greetings had entered a small but expanding market—interactive entertainment for girls—by developing books and video games that featured several of the company's popular characters, including Strawberry Shortcake, the Holly Hobbie Blue Girl, and the Popples. In 1997 the company worked with Avery Dennison Corp. to produce a line of greeting cards for inkjet printers. Television commercials and ads in women's magazines were planned to target women 25 to 54 years old who had children less than 18 years old. American Greetings was involved in various other marketing endeavors during 1997, including advertising on the Internet site of Hearst HomeArts, which featured several magazines published by the Hearst Corporation.

The World Wide Web offered vast opportunities for selling greeting cards, candy, and related merchandise, a market estimated to be more than $219 million in 1998. In December 1997 American Greetings tapped into the world of electronic commerce by promoting its cards, flowers, chocolates, and gifts via America Online at a site that had previously been known as AOL's Card-o-Matic store. American Greetings invested $3 million initially, committed to the arrangement for three years, and agreed to pay millions more in the future. The venture, which had been announced in October, was launched at about the same time that Hallmark began an on-line marketing partnership with the company operating Yahoo!, an Internet search engine. Although some of Hallmark's on-line cards were free, American Greetings charged for all its cards.

American Greetings was also one of 65 businesses that began marketing merchandise through CompuServe's Electronic Mall on the World Wide Web in March. In addition, the company collaborated with SmarTalk TeleServices in an on-line promotion before Mother's Day, from April 22 through May 11. Customers who purchased American Greetings merchandise were awarded free telephone time, and customers could follow a link to SmarTalk's site on the Internet. American Greetings products were also featured at the redesigned Internet site of a third company that offered telephone services, MCI Communications Corp.

Meanwhile, Gibson Greetings invested $6 million for an equity in Greet Street, an Internet site where the company could market its cards. Gibson also made an agreement with Firefly, a software company, to market cards through Firefly products. By the end of the year Gibson was preparing to launch its first television advertising campaign to promote its popular bean bag toys. The company had lost $28.6 million in 1994 but had made a profit of $900,000 in the first half of 1995. In that year Gibson wanted to sell either its greeting card business or its Cleo, Inc., gift wrap division. Although American Greetings expressed interest in merging with the greeting card division, Gibson would not agree to the arrangement because of possible antitrust complications.

MARKETING STRATEGY

One of Hallmark's strongest selling points was the popularity and widespread recognition of the brand. In a

HALLOWEEN PROMOTIONS

Research by Hallmark Cards revealed that Halloween was the eighth most popular occasion for exchanging greeting cards in 1995. The company estimated that nearly 30 million Halloween cards were distributed that year. The holiday was second only to Christmas in regard to marketing efforts. In 1990 Halloween ranked third on the list of most popular occasions for adults to attend parties, behind New Year's Eve and the Super Bowl.

1995 survey by UPS Equitrend, consumers preferred the Hallmark brand more than 18 times as often as its closest competitor. When asked to name a brand of greeting cards, 91 percent of consumers mentioned Hallmark, and 84 percent mentioned Hallmark first. The company had built its brand equity by insisting on excellence, continually pushing its creative staff to be innovative, developing new ways to help Hallmark outlets and other retailers market the company's merchandise, and conducting research to determine consumer response to the company and its products. "The marketplace is changing, and consumers' needs are always evolving, but excellence remains at the top of our priority list," said Hallmark's Van Auken. "Through our products, our advertising, our retail environments, and even our World Wide Web site, Hallmark creates experiences to strengthen the tremendous equity of the Hallmark brand. So the real good news is, we're on the right track, and consumers see it."

In 1996 Hallmark had begun to employ a new, multifaceted marketing strategy that included launching the "Sneak a Peek" advertising campaign to promote general awareness of the brand. Of the $175 million Hallmark spent each year for marketing, it budgeted $50 million for the "Sneak a Peek" campaign in 1996 and $44 million in 1997. The campaign, developed by the Leo Burnett USA advertising agency in Chicago, was intended to motivate consumers to act on their preference for the Hallmark brand when they purchased greeting cards and other personal expression products. The campaign centered on a consumer's impulse to look at the back of a greeting card to see whether it was a Hallmark. "Sneaking a peek" was portrayed as a commonplace indulgence that required enviable adroitness. The broadcast commercials featured a young couple who verified that they "cared enough to send the very best" by glancing furtively at the backs of cards they received from each other. Celebrities appeared in some of the television commercials during 1997; one spot showed three women checking for the Hallmark insignia on the backs of Valentine's Day cards they had received from singer Ray Charles. Another spot showed a baby in a bassinet looking at the "Hallmark" on a card. The commercials aired during popular prime-time television programs such as *Friends, Frasier, Mad about You,* and *Home Improvement.* The campaign also included advertisements in print media. These ads, which made the back covers of magazines such as *Good Housekeeping* and *National Geographic* look like the backs of Hallmark cards, ran in 115 publications in 1996 and 125 publications in 1997. Most of them featured a single line of text that was tailored for each magazine. Other ads on the backs of more than 100 magazines consisted of the Hallmark name only.

OUTCOME

The "Sneak a Peek" campaign received an Effie Award in 1996 for effectiveness and creativity in advertising. Hallmark's research from the spring of 1997 indicated that 86 percent of consumers felt positive about the company's advertising. In October 1997 Hallmark's brand equity was ranked fourth among 282 national brands in a study by Total Research Corporation. The study analyzed how well consumers recognized each brand and their perception of the quality associated with it. In another survey *USA Today's Ad Track* reported that 31 percent of respondents liked the "Sneak a Peek" campaign, compared with a survey average of 22 percent. The campaign was particularly popular with its primary target market; 36 percent of women liked the ads. In contrast, 21 percent of men liked them. Only 4 percent of the respondents said they disliked the ads, compared with a survey average of 12 percent. Consumers age 65 or older liked the campaign best; 37 percent gave it the highest scores for popularity. The Hallmark ads were among only a few in the survey to receive high marks for both popularity and effectiveness.

The company maintained its dominance in the $7 billion greeting card industry with sales of $3.4 billion in 1997, $3.6 billion in 1996, and $3.4 billion in 1995. The market remained strong and was expected to expand because the average age of the population was increasing, and older people tended to send more greeting cards. Additional sales were expected as card companies customized more of their products for target markets.

FURTHER READING

"America Online Formally Announces Plans for American Greetings Business." *Advertising Age,* October 10, 1997.

"American Greetings Launches Mother's Day Promo." *Advertising Age,* April 23, 1997.

Cuneo, Alice Z. "Avery Taking on Epson with Help from Saatchi; Market Could Boom to $500 Mil. in Two Years; Hallmark May Be Next." *Advertising Age,* June 23, 1997.

Enrico, Dottie. "Viewers Open Up to Greeting-Card Ads." *USA Today Ad Track,* May 27, 1997.

Fitzgerald, Kate. "Hallmark Going for the Gold." *Advertising Age,* April 29, 1996.

"Gibson Greetings Bows on the Web." *Advertising Age,* December 9, 1997.

"Hallmark Ads Support Low-Price Card Lines." *Advertising Age,* February 9, 1998.

"Hallmark Dons on Web." *Advertising Age,* November 19, 1996.

"Hallmark Promotes Equity of Its Brand." *Chain Drug Review,* June 23, 1997.

"Hot Spot: Valentine's Day Ads: Burnett Buddies Up for Valentine's." *Advertising Age,* February 10, 1997.

"How the Ad Track Ads of 1997 Stack Up." *USA Today,* December 29, 1997.

"If It's News Today, It's in a Birthday Card Tomorrow." *PRNewswire,* July 28, 1997.

"Resurgence in Letter, Card Sending at Home, in Office." *PRNewswire,* January 23, 1997.

"Today's Ad: Hallmark." *USA Today Ad Track,* May 27, 1997.

Troy, Mike. "Demographic Merchandising Zeros in on Niche Card Givers." *Discount Store News,* April 1, 1997.

Susan Risland

Hardee's Food Systems, Inc.

505 N. Seventh St., Ste. 2000
St. Louis, Missouri 63101
USA
Telephone: (314) 259-6200
Fax: (314) 621-1778
Web site: www.hardees.com

■■■

REVOLUTION CAMPAIGN

OVERVIEW

In 1997, when it was acquired by CKE Restaurants, Hardee's Food Systems was a struggling chain in the Midwest and Southeast with a growing reputation for poor service and substandard food. By 2002 the chain had launched 10 different marketing campaigns in nine years, each designed to turn the chain's business around. The campaigns met with little success. To try and carve out a niche somewhere between inexpensive fast-food chains and pricier "quick-casual" restaurants, as well as to win back customers, Hardee's executives initiated the Hardee's "Revolution" in select test markets. The rebranding effort included a scaled-down menu featuring the chain's new premium Thickburgers, renovated restaurants, and a new emphasis on customer service.

In 2003 the "Revolution" program was expanded to the rest of the chain with a supporting marketing campaign created by Mendelsohn/Zein Advertising, an agency based in Los Angeles. Andrew Puzder, president and chief executive officer of Hardee's, told *Nation's Restaurant News* that the chain planned to devote all of its marketing energy in 2003 to the "Thickburger Revolution." According to *Nation's Restaurant News* the campaign had an estimated budget of $50 to $60 million. The commercials, which ran on television and radio, were honest and apologetic about the company's slip into substandard food and service. Puzder was featured in some spots, where he admitted that the food the chain used to serve was bad. In other spots former customers stated why they no longer ate at Hardee's.

Although it seemed that Hardee's was taking a risk by introducing higher-priced premium burgers at a time when competitors were slashing prices, the strategy paid off. In 2004, following the launch of "Revolution," the chain's fourth-quarter same-store sales increased 9.2 percent over 2003. In addition the "Revolution" campaign was awarded an EFFIE in 2005.

HISTORICAL CONTEXT

Hardee's started out in 1960 in Greenville, North Carolina, as a simple walk-up counter business owned by Wilbur Hardee. It eventually grew into a small-town hero to hungry diners throughout the South and Midwest. The chain built a reputation for good quality, nontraditional fast-food fare such as roast beef sandwiches and "made from scratch" biscuits. For a brief time, before Hardee's became known as the place to avoid if you were hungry for hamburgers, the chain bumped Wendy's International from its number three spot. But by 1990 its downward spiral had begun. The chain's food quality was unpredictable, and menu changes left customers confused, while poor service sent them running for the door.

In 1997 CKE Restaurants, which already owned the burger chain Carl's Jr., acquired Hardee's with a plan to transition the entire chain to Carl's Jr. restaurants. Hardee's franchisees and executives bitterly rejected the plan. Hardee's and Carl's Jr. maintained their separate identities, but the former became known as Star Hardee's and sported the Carl's Jr. happy-star logo on its signs. The menu at Hardee's also underwent changes to more closely match the offerings served by its sister chain, and stores were haphazardly remodeled to make their decor resemble that of Carl's Jr. The changes did little to boost business for Hardee's, and the brand slipped to number six among fast-food burger restaurants. In 2003 Puzder, who had become president of Hardee's in 2000, determined it was time to reestablish the brand's identity and to rebuild the neglected chain's business and reputation. The Hardee's "Revolution" was launched.

TARGET MARKET

Sister chain Carl's Jr. had focused its energies on being the place for young men to go for big, juicy burgers, but the goal for Hardee's was to appeal to adults by offering a broader range of menu items that included fast, tasty breakfasts and restaurant-style burgers for lunch or dinner. "The Hardee's brand is broader—it has more breakfast business, it's more adult," Brad Haley, the company's executive vice president for marketing, told *Restaurants & Institutions.*

The two brands not only appealed to different consumer groups but also were distinguished from each other by regional differences, which made it difficult to create a single marketing theme for both brands. Hardee's was centered in the Midwest and Southeast, whereas Carl's Jr. served the West. Haley said, "In the Southeast, Hardee's is a very strong breakfast brand. In other regions it's more a lunch/dinner [concept]. So when you're looking at the brand, it's not one-size-fits-all."

COMPETITION

While Hardee's was taking a risk by offering customers the kind of thick burgers served at casual-dining restaurants and selling them at a higher price (about $4 for a burger), the chain's key competitors, McDonald's (the number one burger chain) and Burger King (the number two chain), were promoting discount prices to attract customers. The tactic was dubbed the "99-cent menu war" by Jim Kirk of the *Chicago Tribune.* He wrote, "With No. 2 burger chain Burger King preparing a major national marketing assault around 99-cent menu items, executives at McDonald's are making their own value strategy a priority with franchisees."

McDonald's launched a national marketing campaign focused on its "Dollar Value Menu" in October 2002. Burger King launched its campaign just a month ahead of that of McDonald's. The *Atlanta Journal-Constitution* reported that, faced with complaints that fast-food restaurants were causing American obesity, the two chains had earlier "tinkered with their menus to add healthier choices and more sophisticated flavors. Now they're turning to price to win back customers." Individual items on the 99-cent value menu at McDonald's included two sandwiches, fries, salad, and beverages; Burger King's 99-cent offerings included hamburgers, tacos, and chili.

For both chains the strategy behind the 99-cent value menu was to attract price-conscious consumers who were limiting their visits to restaurants because of the weak economy. Harry Balzer, vice president of the market research firm NPD Group, told the *Atlanta Journal-Constitution,* "The average cost of preparing a meal at home is $1.96, making it tempting to turn the cooking over to someone else for just a few pennies more." The 99-cent value menu strategy produced mixed results and

HARDEE'S SPOT FEATURING PARIS HILTON TOO HOT FOR SOME TO HANDLE

When Hardee's added the Spicy BBQ Thickburger to its popular line of Angus Thickburgers in 2005, it turned to hotel heiress and reality-TV star Paris Hilton to promote it. The resulting spot, which featured a bathing-suit-clad Hilton washing a Bentley automobile while eating a BBQ Thickburger, was first used by Carl's Jr. That chain pulled the controversial spot in early June, but Hardee's launched it later in the month, changing the product name and logo. The commercial came on the heels of another Hardee's spot, which starred a young woman described by the *St. Louis Post-Dispatch* as "seductively riding a mechanical bull." Brad Haley, executive vice president of marketing for Hardee's, explained that sexy women were used in the commercials to appeal to the young men that constituted the chain's target market. The Hilton spot may have resonated with the target audience, but some media watchdogs and consumer groups, such as the Los Angeles–based Parents Television Council, denounced it as "soft-core porn." Despite such complaints, the commercials produced results. Hardee's reported that its revenues had climbed 11 percent in 2004 and that for the first time since 1999 it was profitable.

weakened profits for the dueling chains. As Burger King's global marketing officer Chris Clouser noted during an interview with *Time* magazine, the problem with promotions offering deep discounts was that "you train customers to come only when there's a blue-light special."

MARKETING STRATEGY

"Revolution" was created to set the Hardee's chain apart from other fast-food restaurants and to establish it as a premier-burger specialist, according to Jack Hayes, writing for *Nation's Restaurant News.* The company was also trying to lure customers by carving out a niche somewhere between typical fast-food chains and higher-priced quick-casual dining establishments. To accomplish that, Hardee's introduced a selection of Angus-beef burgers and eliminated about 40 percent of its lunch and dinner items. The breakfast menu, popular with customers, was left intact.

In addition to a menu overhaul, the campaign included a series of television commercials that boldly tackled the chain's reputation for bad food and poor customer service. One spot, which opened with a scene shot in black-and-white, featured a young man stating that, while Hardee's "used to be cool," he no longer went there because when he wanted a burger, he wanted a big, juicy one. The spot then switched to a color shot of a Thickburger and the tagline "It's how the last place you'd go for a burger will become the first place." Other commercials featured company president Puzder humbly agreeing with customer complaints that the food quality at Hardee's had deteriorated and that service was substandard. The spots had been developed based on consumer research that included reviewing comment forms customers had filled out and left in suggestion boxes at Hardee's restaurants.

The "Revolution" campaign also signified the chain's shift away from the low-cost—and often low-quality—approach to fast-food menu items that had dominated the quick-service food arena almost since its beginnings. Puzder said that the chain's new campaign was intended to set Hardee's apart from the competition and to build its brand identity as the premium-burger specialist among fast-food restaurants. In an interview with *QSR Magazine,* he explained, "We not only made the burgers bigger and began using higher quality Angus beef, we also improved the quality of virtually every ingredient on the burgers . . . At a time when most of our competitors have turned to discounting tactics, Hardee's is banking on America's ongoing love affair with truly great burgers."

OUTCOME

After declining steadily for more than 10 years, Hardee's experienced a swing in the other direction following the January launch of "Revolution." The chain reported a 9.2 percent increase in same-store sales in the fourth quarter of 2003 compared to the same period the previous year. Sales growth continued, and Hardee's reported same-store sales increases for eight consecutive months through March 2004 at stores open for one year or more. Haley told *QSR Magazine,* "This was a pure quality strategy and it's very reassuring to see that fast food consumers appreciate what we have done." The success of the campaign was enhanced when CKE, reversing its original strategy, applied the Hardee's approach to sister chain Carl's Jr. and introduced to the latter's menu not only Thickburgers but also some of the Hardee's breakfast items. Further recognition of the campaign's success came in 2005, when it was awarded an EFFIE for meeting its goals of increasing sales, regaining consumer confidence in the brand, winning back the company's core customers (men aged 16 to 34), and earning credibility as the best place to go for a great burger.

FURTHER READING

Cantrell, Kate. "Hardee's Ad Featuring Paris Hilton Will Not Run in the Southeast." *Fayetteville (NC) Observer,* July 12, 2005.

Eisenberg, Daniel. "Can McDonald's Shape Up? The Fast-Food King Thinks Better Service, Nicer Décor and Bigger Bargains Will Get Business Cooking Again." *Time,* September 30, 2002.

Feldstein, Mary Jo. "Hardee's Goes to Paris for New Burger Campaign." *St. Louis Post-Dispatch,* May 14, 2005.

"Flame Out? CKE Is Trying Again to Rejuvenate Hardee's." *Restaurants & Institutions,* April 1, 2002.

Gilligan, Gregory J. "Changes at Hardee's Restaurants Pay Off." *Richmond (VA) Times-Dispatch,* May 2, 2004.

"Hardee's Breaks Rank from Competition with New Premium Burger Menu." *QSR Magazine,* January 21, 2003.

Hayes, Jack. "Hardee's Thins Menu with Thickburger Focus." *Nation's Restaurant News,* February 3, 2003.

Kirk, Jim. "Burger King, McDonald's Expected to Grapple at 99-cent Level." *Chicago Tribune,* May 7, 2002.

Lee, Elizabeth. "Burger Giants Put Bargains on the Menu." *Atlanta Journal-Constitution,* October 4, 2002.

MacArthur, Kate. "Hardee's Tries Big-Burger Line: Thickburgers Anchor Pared-Down Menu." *Advertising Age,* January 27, 2003.

"Parental Group Says Hilton Ads Too Hot." *AP Online,* May 25, 2005.

Smith, Samantha Thompson. "Hardee's New Marketing Campaign Deprecates Former 'Skinny' Burgers." *Raleigh (NC) News & Observer,* July 12, 2003.

Stewart, Al. "Big Burgers Boosting CKE Bottom Line as Strategy Pays Off." *Los Angeles Business Journal,* July 5, 2004.

Tritto, Christopher. "'Hardee's Revolution' Spreads to West Coast, Carl's Jr." *St. Louis Business Journal,* April 16, 2004.

Rayna Bailey

Harley-Davidson Motor Company

3700 W. Juneau Ave.
Milwaukee, Wisconsin 53208
USA
Telephone: (414) 343-4680
Fax: (414) 343-8230
Web site: www.harley-davidson.com

■■■

THE BOOK OF HARLEY-DAVIDSON CAMPAIGN

OVERVIEW

As a symbol of brawny industrial power, no-nonsense technological prowess, and pure American individualism, it would be difficult to surpass the Harley-Davidson motorcycle. Even as flagship Americans products, from automobiles to television sets, were overtaken, outdesigned, and outmarketed by competitors from Asia and Europe, the Harley stood defiantly apart, refusing to give an inch, much like its famous champions, the Hell's Angels-style bikers of modern legend. At least that was the image most people held after nearly two decades of ambitious product development by the company, helped along by generally inspired advertising from its agency. And as demand for the high-priced motorcycles exceeded supply, the company launched a line of "genuine" Harley-Davidson accessories and clothing, including cigarettes and cologne. These marketing successes, however, came at a cost. Potential Harley buyers, unable to ride away on the bike they wanted and unwilling to wait the average two years until it became available, were turning to Japanese brands. Japanese companies had begun marketing a line of Harley clones, heavy cruising bikes designed to capture the low-slung style of the classic Harley, sometimes with more power and features. At the same time, Harley's very success in selling to a wider market was causing some of its core riders to question the company's commitment to its values. Company research found that "a small but vocal group of core riders are saying that Harley is 'selling out.'"

To counter this trend, a new advertising campaign was launched in 1997. The campaign, dubbed "The Book of Harley-Davidson," was designed to remind core consumers that the company that "wrote the book" on Harley was not about to stray from its principles. In this way the campaign hoped to reinforce positive brand perception among new buyers, while reversing any negative perceptions core riders might have. The company had ambitious sales objectives as well, for it hoped for a 10 percent increase over 1996 figures. Sticking mostly to print advertising, the campaign presented a series of spread ads in national men's magazines as well as in books for enthusiasts. Each ad was a "chapter" that sold the romance of both the motorcycle and the American road. For example, chapter 5, which sold touring bikes, was titled "Waking Up in Strange Places," while chapter 8 was called "Is That Thing Street Legal?" an appropriate headline for an ad touting racing bikes. By all measures, the campaign succeeded in meeting its objectives. By 1998 unit sales had increased, positive perceptions by new buyers had improved, and negative perceptions by core riders had been cut in half.

HISTORICAL CONTEXT

Founded in 1903, the Harley-Davidson Motor Company was among the original companies building and selling

A 1997 model Harley-Davidson motorcycle. AP IMAGES.

motorcycles to racers and other thrill seekers. Among a crowded field of starters, it had the distinction of being the only motorcycle company to survive the next 80 years, and thus it came by its legendary status honestly. During the late 1970s, however, the company was troubled by a reputation for poor quality, lagging innovation, and serious competition from abroad, most notably from Japanese manufacturers. During an unfortunate period of ownership by AMF Corporation, the company even produced Harley-Davidson golf carts. Finally, after a group of investors bought the company back, it began a remarkable turnaround. In 1979 the company hired the Minneapolis ad agency Carmichael Lynch Spong to help reverse some of the negative perceptions that were plaguing it. Jud Smith, group creative director of the agency team that worked on the account at the time, said in an *Adweek* article, "The image was that it [the motorcycle] was owned by dirtballs and decidedly uncool." Although Harleys were seen as distinctively designed, honest machines, many of the competitors were offering more user-friendly motorcycles, especially for less-experienced riders. Easier to maintain, some of the other bikes were even faster than the legendary Harley. Still, Harley-Davidson had developed a near fanatical following of riders whose deep emotional attachment to their bikes had already crept into American culture. Harley "Hogs" were perceived as simple but tough and as embodying the rebellious facet of the national character.

By 1984 Harley-Davidson had turned an important corner under its new management, introducing a new line of bikes while significantly improving quality. The advertising began to communicate the changes, and at the same time it drew upon the passion the motorcycle inspired in its core riders with themes like "Things are different on a Harley" and "Harley through and through." The advertising even broke with its rule of always making the bike the hero of the ad by employing high-profile—and highly passionate—Harley riders like Malcolm Forbes, Jay Leno, and Mickey Rourke, who agreed to do the ads for a dollar if it would help their favorite motorcycle company. By the 1990s an improved product and savvy marketing had turned Harley-Davidson from the motorcycle of "dirtballs" to the choice of free-spirited American individualists. Along with them came a legion of consumers who wanted to own part of a legend and could afford to pay as much for a bike as most people paid for a car. Despite the long waiting period, sales edged ever upward.

TARGET MARKET

Harley-Davidson's core rider had always defined its primary target market. That rider was most likely to be a male (91 percent), although his mate, if he had one, tended to be as enthusiastic about the bike as he was. He rode the motorcycle and lived the lifestyle. Yet, unlike consumers of many other high-ticket products, Harley owners spanned a broad socioeconomic spectrum. Visitors to the massive Harley-Davidson meets that took place in Sturgis, South Dakota, and in Daytona Beach, Florida, encountered riders from every strata of American life. But all of them embraced, if only for a weekend, the Harley credo of freedom, self-reliance, and individualism. The advertising invariably addressed itself to those riders

MEET THE NEW BOSS

As advertising campaigns went, Harley-Davidson's award-winning print campaign was fairly inexpensive to produce. Carmichael Lynch Spong's Rowley noted that in some cases the agency stretched its photography budget by using existing images. This was possible because, unlike new cars, Harleys were not restyled each year. For instance, one photograph from the campaign showed a glistening, black Fat Boy Harley-Davidson parked under a clothesline as the sun set behind it. Just a year earlier, the same bike had been a glistening, yellow Fat Boy, but, thanks to the magic of digital imaging technology, the expensive image could be reused.

who lived the credo, who in fact already owned a Harley. Jack Supple, for many years the executive creative director on the account at Carmichael Lynch Spong, described bluntly the tight focus Harley-Davidson's advertising maintained on the core rider: "We don't pander to the broader public."

Yet there was a secondary target market the advertising also reached, the segment of the broader market that was interested in Harley-Davidson motorcycles because of their reputation. In many ways this segment was every bit as important as the primary group, for it was from this group that increased sales came. Existing Harley owners might buy a new bike from time to time, but they would never fuel 10 percent or higher annual growth. This market also tended to be predominantly men who had grown up with the Harley legend in some form or other but who did not own one. It was a tribute to the company, the advertising, and the motorcycle itself that these men did not need to be convinced of the superiority of the product, as they might if they were shopping among Japanese bikes. They merely needed to be exposed to the legend frequently enough.

COMPETITION

Any company that owned 50 percent of its category, as Harley-Davidson did of cruiser motorcycles, might easily be thought of as not having serious competition. Yet because demand was exceeding supply and creating a remarkable two-year waiting period for buying a Harley, the door was open to a handful of competitors, each looking to increase its share of the market at Harley-Davidson's expense. Foremost among these were the four big Japanese motorcycle manufacturers—Honda, Yamaha, Kawasaki, and Suzuki—each of which had begun building its own heavy cruiser motorcycle in the previous three years. These Harley clones were characterized by big engines and an authentic look. Each could be mistaken by a non-Harley novice for the real thing. Unlike the real thing, however, these motorcycles were ready to be driven away from the showroom.

More troubling in some ways were a pair of companies preparing to offer an alternative American bike right in Harley's own neighborhood. In Minneapolis, Excelsior Henderson, a classic American motorcycle company that had failed, was threatening to come to life again and produce its own, truly authentic line of bikes. At the same time Polaris, a large manufacturer of snowmobiles, had plans—and the resources—to market a moderately priced cruiser in the $8,000 to $10,000 range. Against this background Harley-Davidson was not content to rest on its laurels, even if it could still sell many more bikes than it actually produced.

MARKETING STRATEGY

Harley's strategy for the campaign flowed quite naturally out of the company's unique history and place in the market. The shape of the campaign, however, was determined primarily by the need to reassure the core ridership that the company had not "sold out," in the words of Craig Rowley, account supervisor at Carmichael Lynch Spong. The campaign's theme, "The Book of Harley-Davidson," was devised by a team led by creative directors Kerry Casey and Jim Nelson. They relied primarily on print media because of its ability to reach the target market most cost-efficiently. Although two television spots were shot for the campaign, they were designed to be used by dealers and not broadcast nationally. The print ads consisted of spreads, each purporting to be a chapter from "The Book of Harley-Davidson," although only three actual chapters were represented in the campaign. These chapters were supplemented by a series of similar spreads selling parts and accessories, although not in chapter form. Headlines in the series said, for instance, "She's a full-figured gal," referring to a fully decked-out Electra-Glidecruiser, and "Drop the wrench. Stand back and look. Laugh evilly," over a gorgeous shot of a Heritage Softail Classic. The ads ran in media catering to motorcycle enthusiasts, including *Harley Woman,* and also in national general-interest men's magazines such as *Men's Journal, Rolling Stone,* and *Sports Illustrated,* a sure indication of the company's focus on the large secondary market of non-Harley-owning men.

It should be noted that the campaign was supplemented by Harley-Davidson's exceptionally thorough dealer support programs, which included a catalog that was virtually a collector's item among Harley enthusiasts. Rowley reported that many dealers would not give a catalog to a prospective customer until he bought a bike, the catalog then serving as a surrogate until his motorcycle was delivered two years later. The company also earmarked a significant portion of its marketing budget in support of its owners groups, known as HOGs, or Harley Owners Groups, a practice that Harley-Davidson had pioneered long before Saturn automobiles, for instance, began announcing picnics for owners and related support programs.

OUTCOME

Judging the Harley-Davidson campaign by the most common measure—sales figures—would be somewhat misleading, given that the company could have sold every motorcycle it built with or without advertising. Indeed, Harley-Davidson exceeded its goal of selling 10 percent more bikes in 1997, reaching 13 percent, for a total of 96,216 units. But this was due to, if nothing else, a 13 percent increase in production. Had the factory turned out 50 percent more Harleys, the company could have reported a 50 percent sales increase. Yet, based on its own extensive polling of its customers and on the market, management considered the campaign a success. Based on its data, the "perception of Harley-Davidson as 'a strong and appealing brand' increased by sixteen percent during the campaign," according to an agency press release. At the same time the number of core riders who described the company as "selling out"—admittedly small to begin with—fell by more than half. Positive publicity continued to generate itself as the media rushed to align itself with the Harley phenomenon, always a sure sign that a brand was hot. In the area of creativity, one of the dealer television spots won a Gold Lion at the Cannes International Advertising Festival, one of advertising's most coveted honors.

FURTHER READING

Cooper, Ann. "Believers in the Power of Print." *Adweek* (Eastern Edition), April 12, 1993, p. 34.

Damashek, Harris, and Junu Bryan Kim. "Echo Award Winners Diverse but Represent Fields Top Work." *Advertising Age,* October 28, 1996, p. S4.

Flint, Jerry. "No Sweat." *Forbes,* April 10, 1995, p. 22.

"Harley-Davidson Returns to TV." *Adweek* (Eastern Edition), August 19, 1996, p. 36.

"Newswire Roundup." *Adweek* (Eastern Edition), August 10, 1998, p. 49.

"1996 Echo Awards: Spotting the Trendsetters." *Direct Marketing,* November 1996, p. 10.

"Partnerships in Engineering Excellence." *Forbes,* November 9, 1992, p. 218.

Smith, Geoffrey N. "Live to Ride." *Financial World,* September 26, 1995, p. 6.

Watanabe, Laurie. "How the Midwest Was Won." *Dealernews,* July 1998, p. 22.

Patrick Hutchins

Heineken USA Inc.

360 Hamilton Ave., Ste. 1103
White Plains, New York 10601
USA
Telephone: (914) 681-4100
Fax: (914) 681-1900
Web site: www.heineken.com

IT'S ALL ABOUT THE BEER CAMPAIGN

OVERVIEW

In the 1990s Heineken beer (imported from Dutch parent company Heineken NV and sold in America by Heineken USA Inc.) had an outdated image. An icon of 1980s luxury and excess, Heineken had not adapted to changing trends in the United States. Heineken USA understood that its future growth hinged on making the brand more approachable in the U.S. market and on connecting with the beer industry's all-important audience of 21 to 35 year olds. The company also wanted to maintain its reputation for superior beer. Enlisting agency Lowe & Partners (later called Lowe Lintas & Partners), Heineken in 1999 launched an advertising campaign that balanced these prerogatives while reinventing the brand's image.

"It's All About the Beer"—the central component of Heineken USA's estimated measured-media spend of $34 million for 1999—focused on so-called "beer moments," situations in ordinary life that became dramatic or otherwise noteworthy because of the presence of Heineken. With irreverent humor and down-to-earth backdrops, the new television spots took Heineken off its pedestal and communicated an updated, youth-conscious sensibility. At the same time, as the campaign's tagline and theme suggested, the commercials' focus was solidly on the quality of the beer itself.

The campaign helped fuel consistent increases in Heineken sales and was credited with positioning the beer for healthy long-term growth. These successes were likewise reflected in increased ad spending, as the brand's measured-media budget grew to an estimated $50 million by 2001. Despite changing agencies twice in two years, Heineken stuck with the "It's All about the Beer" concept and tagline and continued to target a youthful audience in the following years.

HISTORICAL CONTEXT

The first barrels of Heineken reached the United States in the 1880s, and by 1972 the brand had become America's top imported beer. Heineken's fortunes in America improved even further in the 1980s, as it, like other luxury items, was a prime beneficiary of the conspicuous consumption for which that decade was known, a cultural trend that was especially pronounced in Heineken's biggest market, New York City. Heineken likewise adapted, in the 1980s, to the emerging light-beer phenomenon, introducing Amstel Light and imbuing it with an upscale image similar to that of its older sibling. Marketing on Heineken's behalf had long been geared toward making the brand a status symbol and identifying it as the beer of choice for urban sophisticates.

Heineken's pedestal positioning did not serve it as well in the 1990s, however. Sales slumped, and the company

© THE COVER STORY/CORBIS.

struggled to craft an up-to-date image for the beer that would make it relevant to a new generation of younger drinkers. "We had an aging franchise," Heineken's senior vice president of marketing, Steve Davis, told *Beverage Industry.* "We didn't conjure up in consumers' minds much energy and excitement, and we were becoming kind of 'your father's Oldsmobile.' We got high marks from everybody saying we were a great beer; what they weren't saying is that we were a great beer for them." The company recognized that, if it were to increase its U.S. market share, it needed to mute its elitist image and win over young domestic-beer drinkers. After an unsuccessful marketing campaign designed to make the red star on Heineken's label an icon comparable to Nike's "swoosh" symbol, Heineken initiated an agency search, dismissing Wells Rich Greene and hiring Lowe & Partners of New York (which later merged with Ammirati Puris Lintas to become Lowe Lintas & Partners), whose chief creative officer, Lee Garfinkel, had previously helmed an effort that successfully recast Mercedes, in much the way Heineken hoped to reinvent itself, as a more approachable brand.

TARGET MARKET

Heineken's effort to expand the U.S. market for its beer depended on appealing to younger drinkers. As *Beverage Industry* noted, "a 25-year-old averages 65 gallons of beer per year, while a 55-year-old sips 15 gallons." Among 21 to 35 year olds Heineken particularly focused on urban-dwelling trendsetters, ordinary but sophisticated beer drinkers. Davis told *Brandweek* that Heineken's ideal consumers were younger people "who tend to be opinion leaders. They are visible, self-confident, and risk-takers." The brewer also needed to counteract these drinkers' perception that Heineken was a beer strictly for special occasions in bars and restaurants but not for everyday, off-premise consumption. To thus broaden its appeal, the brand had to strike a delicate balance between its hard-won image as a superior product and its desire to appear more ordinary.

"It's All About the Beer" accordingly used irreverent humor while showing the product, in television spots, being consumed in settings far less rarefied than those traditionally associated with the brand. The campaign focused on universal "beer moments," occasions when the presence of Heineken significantly affected otherwise ordinary behavior. This approach enabled the brand to show its lighter, more populist side, while also managing to keep the focus on the high quality of its beer.

COMPETITION

In its push to broaden its market in America, Heineken necessarily took aim at beer-industry heavyweights such as Anheuser-Busch and its flagship brew, Budweiser. Anheuser-Busch, in addition to possessing an almost 50 percent market share of the country's beer market, had an advertising budget far larger than those of its nearest competitors. Despite declining sales of Budweiser, the brewer continued to support the "King of Beers" with blockbuster ad campaigns in the late 1990s and early 2000s. Budweiser commercials featuring talking frogs that croaked "Budweiser" in combination with one another gave way to a competing cast of lizards and an evolving swamp-creatures storyline, and then Budweiser made an even bigger splash with "Whassup?!" a campaign featuring a group of friends who greeted one another using the idiosyncratic, slang question that gave the campaign its name. A true measure of Heineken's success, in the eyes of industry commentators, was the fact that, during this time, Anheuser-Busch used a "Whassup?!" spot to poke fun at stereotypical Heineken drinkers, thereby acknowledging its much smaller competitor as a threat. In the commercial, preppy types greeted each other with a hyper-articulate rendering of "How are you doing?" while drinking beer from green bottles clearly meant to suggest Heineken.

AUSTIN POWERS AND HIS HEINEKEN

During the first year of the "It's All about the Beer" campaign, Heineken and ad agency Lowe Lintas also linked the beer to the movie *Austin Powers: The Spy Who Shagged Me,* which starred comic Mike Myers as a lusty, mod-style British detective. Though this marketing effort was separate from "It's All about the Beer," it was coordinated with the overall goal of broadening Heineken's reach among young people. The beer maker bought product-placement rights in the movie and ran a television spot in which Powers was shown receiving a massage from an attractive woman. "Why did you stop?" Powers asked the masseuse when she paused in her work. "I was just admiring your Heine," she answered, speaking of his beer, not his body. The eight-week promotional effort was considered an integral part of the successful push—anchored by "It's All about the Beer"—to appeal to younger drinkers.

Corona Extra doubled its share of the American import market between 1995 and 2000, going from a 13.5 percent market share to 27.3 percent and overtaking Heineken as the country's best-selling import. The brand's marketing strategy, which attempted to make the Mexican beer synonymous with seaside relaxation and escape from the everyday, was widely credited with providing fuel for such rapid growth. Taglines such as "Miles Away from Ordinary" and "Go Someplace Better" ran in concert with beach scenery, as Corona extended its tried-and-true advertising formula into the early years of the millennium.

MARKETING STRATEGY

"It's All About the Beer" premiered two weeks before the 1999 Super Bowl, during telecasts of the National Football League (NFL) conference championship games. This choice of venue was a strategic move by Heineken to counteract Anheuser-Busch's dominance in Super Bowl advertising by achieving comparable visibility for a fraction of the cost, while effectively taking center stage as the only advertiser offering Super Bowl–quality spots during those earlier games. Further, for the big game itself Heineken skirted Anheuser-Busch's Super Bowl exclusivity agreement with the Fox network, which prohibited other brewers from buying national airtime during the big game, by buying time on selected local affiliates. Heineken spots ran during the Super Bowl in markets that included New York, Los Angeles, Chicago, and Atlanta, cities accounting for 70 to 80 percent of the brand's American sales.

In its bid to appeal to a younger and more down-to-earth audience, Heineken took calculated risks of various types in the campaign's individual spots. Commercials that broke in 1999 and ran through 2000 included "Mood Swing," in which a fan in a basketball arena was shown doing something that had been unthinkable in an earlier era's Heineken advertising: drinking the brew from a plastic cup. The dramatic crux of the spot came when the fan's enthusiasm for his team caused him to spill his Heineken. Another spot, "The Weasel," showed a man bringing a Budweiser-like beer to a house party and then filching another guest's Heineken from the refrigerator. "Premature Pour" showed a man and woman pouring Heineken while eyeing one another seductively; excited, the man poured too much beer too quickly, and spilled it. "The Male Bonding Incident," meanwhile, parodied heterosexual men's hang-ups about homosexuality. The spot showed two sports-watching men accidentally holding hands while passing a Heineken bottle, before both recoiled in horror. While the sexuality and humor of these spots was in keeping with the tone of much beer advertising of the period, Heineken was almost alone among industry competitors in linking such human situations explicitly to its product. Each of the "beer moments" dramatized in the campaign, regardless of the human behavior exhibited, hinged on the presence not just of beer but of Heineken.

Later executions of the "It's All About the Beer" theme included a group of spots keyed to Heineken's introduction of a keg-shaped can. In "The Envy," which ran through 2002, two men stood next to one another at public urinals. Both set their beers on top of the receptacles, but one of the men could not stop looking at the other's keg-shaped Heineken can. The Heineken drinker, rattled by the attention, left the restroom abruptly. In "The Poachers," two friends in the checkout aisle of a supermarket stealthily moved the grocery divider on the conveyor belt so that another customer's case of Heineken would be included among their own purchases.

OUTCOME

Heineken's U.S. sales grew consistently with the introduction of "It's All About the Beer." The brand's estimated sales were at 35 million cases in the mid-1990s; by 1999 that figure had grown to 47 million cases, and in 2000 Heineken saw another 10 percent increase, with sales of 54 million cases. The sales increases were seen as directly tied to Heineken's new brand image, and the brew's measured-media spend of an estimated

$34 million in 1999 grew to $50 million by 2001. Additionally, Lowe Lintas was tapped, in 2000, to adapt the concept of the campaign for Heineken markets worldwide. Hillary Chura noted in *Advertising Age,* "Heineken's game plan—to broaden the brand's appeal—allowed the lager to break records, shatter stereotypes and register consecutive years of healthy growth." Gerry Khermouch of *Brandweek* said of the campaign, paraphrasing Heineken's Steve Davis, "It clicked on all three requirements for a winning campaign: it broke through, was entertaining and offered a provocative, relevant message . . . By contrast, even the best work on Bud and Miller often clicks on just the first two criteria."

In 2002 Heineken moved its advertising account from Lowe Lintas to D'Arcy Masius Benton & Bowles, because Lee Garfinkel, the most instrumental figure from the outset of the campaign, had himself taken a job at D'Arcy in January of 2001. Heineken waited for Garfinkel's non-compete clause to expire before moving its account to his new agency. D'Arcy continued the "It's All about the Beer" campaign in work that paired the established beer-centered theme with holiday subject matter. Heineken changed agencies again in 2003, enlisting Publicis New York, but stayed on message, extending "It's All About the Beer" in well-received TV spots as well as outdoor ads and radio spots in the following years.

FURTHER READING

Beirne, Mike. "Heineken Seeing More Green on TV, In-Store." *Brandweek,* November 10, 2003.

———. "Heineken's New Summer Creative Is a Case of Déjà vu All Over Again." *Brandweek,* July 1–July 8, 2002.

Chura, Hillary. "Heineken Sips Success." *Advertising Age,* October 22, 2001.

Elliott, Stuart. "Favoring Creativity, Heineken Will Take Its U.S. Campaign to a World Audience." *New York Times,* May 25, 2000.

Halleron, Chris. "Heineken USA." *Beverage World,* May 15, 2001.

Khermouch, Gerry. "It's All about the Beer Ads." *Brandweek,* October 16, 2000.

Lippert, Barbara. "Last Laugh: Lowe Crafts a Final Round of Sly, Subtle Work for Heineken." *Adweek,* April 22, 2002.

Mack, Ann M., and Kathleen Sampey. "At Publicis, It Ain't Easy Being Green." *Adweek,* June 2, 2003.

McCarthy, Michael. "Risky 'Premature Pour' Ad Sells Beer with Sex, Humor." *USA Today,* July 24, 2000.

Sampey, Kathleen. "Reason to Be Jolly." *Brandweek,* October 28, 2002.

Theodore, Sarah. "Rising Star." *Beverage Industry,* July 2002.

Weinbach, Jonathan B. "Heineken Orchestrates Super Bowl Play." *Wall Street Journal,* January 22, 1999.

Mark Lane

The Hershey Company

100 Crystal A Drive
Hershey, Pennsylvania 17033-0810
USA
Telephone: (717) 534-6799
Fax: (717) 534-6760
Web site: www.hersheys.com

THE CRISP YOU CAN'T RESIST! CAMPAIGN

OVERVIEW

Hershey supported the launch of ReeseSticks wafer bars with a campaign that emphasized the product's connection to its predecessor, the popular Reese's Peanut Butter Cup. ReeseSticks had a different texture and taste because they contained crisp wafers in addition to the creamy peanut butter and milk chocolate found in peanut butter cups. A television commercial featured a round peanut butter cup in the form of a buzzsaw, cutting a wafer in half and covering it with chocolate and peanut butter. An advertisement in *Reader's Digest* in May 1998 simply showed two Reese's Peanut Butter Cups above the word "original" and two ReeseSticks above the words "new extra crispy." One of the ReeseSticks was broken apart to reveal that it contained layers of peanut butter between wafers, all coated in milk chocolate. The tag line "The Crisp You Can't Resist!" was centered below a picture of the new product in the trademark orange Reese's wrapper.

ReeseSticks were the latest in a series of innovative line extensions that had helped make Reese's the company's most successful brand. Reese's was one of the first widely popular candies that combined chocolate and peanut butter. Competing with Hershey, the industry leader, other confectioners introduced their own crispy chocolate-and-peanut butter candies. Advertising for ReeseSticks was so effective, however, that demand exceeded supply shortly after the product was launched nationally in the spring of 1998. "The Crisp You Can't Resist!" campaign of television commercials and print advertisements was created by the New York office of Ogilvy & Mather. It was introduced in print and broadcast media early in 1998 and continued into 1999.

HISTORICAL CONTEXT

Hershey traced its roots to Lancaster Caramel Company, founded in 1886 by Milton S. Hershey. A subsidiary, Hershey Chocolate Company, opened in 1894. Milton Hershey retained the chocolate business when he sold the caramel operation for $1 million in 1900. He used the money to open what would become the largest chocolate factory in the world. He also founded a utopian community named Hershey, Pennsylvania, for the company's workers, and he established an orphanage and ensured that it would continue to receive a large percentage of the firm's profits after his death. By the 1990s the company was called Hershey Foods. It manufactured ice cream toppings, chocolate syrup, chocolate chips and other baking products, milk products, and various brands of pasta. The company led the U.S. candy industry with brands such as Hershey's milk chocolate bars, Hershey's Kisses, Hershey's Nuggets, Kit Kat chocolate bars, Cookies 'n' Creme white chocolate bars with cookie bits, York Peppermint Patties, and Twizzlers licorice. In 1996

Hershey also acquired Leaf North America, which made Jolly Rancher, Milk Duds, Whoppers, and PayDay candies. In 1998 Reese's was the largest and most popular of Hershey's brands and was valued at $350 million, according to *Advertising Age.*

Reese's Peanut Butter Cups were launched in 1928 by Harry Burnett Reese, the founder of H.B. Reese Candy Company. Hershey acquired the firm for $23.5 million in 1963 and began marketing Reese's Peanut Butter Cups nationally. The product consisted of specially processed peanut butter in a disk-shaped, milk chocolate shell with fluted edges. It was packaged in bright orange wrappers that contained two peanut butter cups. The first line extension, Reese's Crunchy Peanut Butter Cups, was launched in 1976. Other line extensions introduced over the years included small candies called Reese's Pieces, peanut butter Easter eggs and Christmas trees, peanut butter baking bits, peanut butter in a jar, peanut butter ice cream, and peanut butter puffs cereal. According to *Brandweek,* Hershey's total advertising budget for all its Reese's products was $33 million in 1997, up from $22.6 million in 1996.

From 1969 to 1988 Reese's Peanut Butter Cups were promoted with the tag line, "Two great tastes that taste great together." In 1988, after market research showed that consumers had developed individual, ritualistic ways of eating Reese's Peanut Butter Cups, the company launched a humorous campaign called "There's No Wrong Way to Eat a Reese's" that was still running in 1999. The new ads highlighted the candy's unique qualities and the many eccentric ways it could be eaten. One magazine advertisement that ran in 1998 showed two miniature peanut butter cups above two captions that both said, "'I eat them just like my brother.'" A second line of text explained, "(Don and Dan, identical twins.)"

In 1995 Hershey supported its recently introduced Reese's Nutrageous candy bar—a crunchy combination of chocolate and peanuts—with a $9.5 million advertising campaign. In 1997 the company spent an estimated $10 million to launch another line extension, Reese's Crunchy Cookie Cups, which contained peanut butter, milk chocolate, and a chocolate cookie. The promotion included the distribution of 50 million coupons and 8 million free samples of the product. Later in the year Hershey began selling ReeseSticks wafer bars in limited markets. The "The Crisp You Can't Resist!" campaign was launched early in 1998 to support the national introduction of ReeseSticks.

TARGET MARKET

Targeting a broad audience of people who enjoyed the taste of creamy peanut butter and rich milk chocolate together, "The Crisp You Can't Resist" appealed to consumers who enjoyed Reese's Peanut Butter Cups but who wanted to try a line extension with a new texture and slightly different taste. Hershey intended the new product to move beyond the candy market and compete with cookies and cakes in the snack market. Lisa Kronmuller, new products manager of Hershey's marketing department, said in a news release: "Consumers love the taste of peanut butter and chocolate together. ReeseSticks provide a unique combination of sweet and salty tastes with an extra crispy texture—a perfect snack item for chocolate candy, cookie, and snack cake lovers." The ads emphasized the similarities and differences between ReeseSticks and Reese's Peanut Butter Cups. The campaign's lighthearted tone entertained the audience and conveyed the message that candy was a fun, enjoyable treat. The ads also showed that ReeseSticks were more complex than some other candies, since they contained three ingredients assembled in layers.

> **DESCRIPTIVE NAMES**
>
> Hershey considered calling one of its candy bars "Acclaim" but rejected the idea after consumers in focus groups guessed that the product being described was most likely a four-door sedan. The candy was eventually dubbed Reese's Nutrageous, a name that immediately evoked an image of peanuts and caramel.

COMPETITION

Hershey led the U.S. candy industry in 1997 with sales of $4.3 billion. Its closest rival was Mars, Inc., which owned brands such as M&M's Chocolate Candies, Snickers, Twix, 3 Musketeers, and Milky Way. In third place was Nestlé SA, a company based in Switzerland, with brands that included Baby Ruth, Butterfinger, and Crunchbars. The chocolate-covered cookie and wafer category was valued at $155 million that year. Information Resources, Inc., reported that Reese's Crunchy Cookie Cups had sales of $20 million and controlled 12.9 percent of the category. Reese's Crunchy Cookie Cups Halloween Candy generated an additional $7 million in sales. Hershey's Kit Kat brand had sales of $61 million, and Twix had sales of $49.9 million. For the year ended November 8, 1998, all Reese's products had sales of $108.9 million; Kit Kat had $60.5 million, and Hershey's Mr. Goodbar had $9.5 million, according to *Brandweek.* From mid-August 1997 through mid-August 1998 Twix had sales of

$70.5 million in grocery stores, drug stores, and mass merchandise outlets.

Advertising Age reported that Mars spent $67.3 million to advertise its products in 1998. Of that amount, $58.9 million went for television commercials and $7.2 million went for print ads. A large percentage of Mars' marketing budget was used to promote M&M's, a popular product that came in two styles—chocolate and chocolate-covered peanuts—with multicolored candy coatings. An M&M's Crispyline extension was launched late in 1998 with a $40 million advertising campaign.

During the first half of 1998 Mars spent $11.9 million to promote another popular brand, Twix chocolate-covered wafer, with the tag line "Two for me, none for you." The print ads and television commercials revolved around the idea that although Twix was sold in packages of two, the product tasted so good that people were not willing to share it. One commercial showed a man who had just been awarded two expensive vehicles in the brand's "Double or Nothing" instant-win game. As he wondered what he would do with identical Jeep Wranglers, his companion mused, "Maybe give one to your best friend." Television commercials in the campaign aired during programs for young people, including *Buffy the Vampire Slayer* and *Party of Five.*

Hershey's other primary rival, Nestlé promoted its Butterfinger brand with an advertising campaign that starred cartoon characters from the popular television program *The Simpsons.* Ads for another crunchy candy, Baby Ruth, used the tag line "This baby gets you going!" to position the brand as a source of energy for active people. In 1997 Nestlé spent about $5 million on advertising to support the launch of White Crunch, a bar of white chocolate with crisped rice and peanut pieces. Nestlé also introduced four varieties of a new brand, Treasures, which consisted of milk chocolate shells filled with peanut butter, Butterfinger Bits, the crisped rice used in Crunch bars, or caramel. An advertisement in *People* magazine featured the headline, "This would read even better if you were curled up with some Nestlé Treasures." The tag line "From you to you" suggested that Treasures were a good choice for consumers who wanted to indulge themselves.

Another rival, Russell Stover Candies, launched Russell Stover Peanut Butter & Jelly Cups. Sold two to a package or individually wrapped in large bags, the product consisted of round chocolate shells with a peanut butter filling and either grape jelly or raspberry jam. One advertisement featured the tag line "Gushing with Flavor" in type that looked as if it had been written with purple and red jelly. The text said, "For the first time ever, Russell Stover combines the world's most popular flavors: peanut butter, jelly, and milk chocolate." The ad included a coupon that could be redeemed for 50 cents toward the purchase of the product and another coupon that consumers could redeem for a free sample.

MARKETING STRATEGY

Hershey originally picked ReeseSticks as the most promising contender among a field of four new products made with wafers and peanut butter. The company spent three years conducting focus groups, distributing free samples in locations such as shopping malls, and surveying several hundred consumers as it adjusted the recipe to achieve the most popular balance of chocolate, peanut butter, and wafers. Hundreds of names, including "Reeskies," were considered before the product was christened. The New York office of Ogilvy & Mather created advertisements that emphasized the new line extension's taste, texture, and connection to the familiar Reese's Peanut Butter Cups. In a 15-second television commercial called "Sawmill," the blade of a buzzsaw—shaped like a round Reese's Peanut Butter Cup on its side—sliced a crisp wafer in half. The chocolate and peanut butter of the blade melted in the process and coated the divided wafer to form two ReeseSticks. The commercial included the tag line "The Crisp You Can't Resist!" The *Los Angeles Times* said that during the week of April 13-19, commercials for ReeseSticks aired 16 times on daytime network television, placing the message in 70 million homes.

In addition to television commercials, the national launch of ReeseSticks in February 1998 was supported by advertisements in magazines such as *People,* and *Sports Illustrated.* More than 10 million samples of the product were given away at retail outlets, and 40 million coupons were either attached to the product's packaging or inserted in *Parade* magazine in April. Standard packages of ReeseSticks sold for about 50 cents, but to encourage consumers to sample the new candy, trial-size ReeseSticks were priced at 25 cents for a short time after the product's launch. Beginning in April some of the product's packaging featured a tie-in to the motion picture *Godzilla,* which was scheduled for release on Memorial Day. When the National Football League season started, Hershey included ReeseSticks in its second annual $1 Million Kick promotion, which offered consumers an opportunity to kick a field goal during the Super Bowl.

"The Crisp You Can't Resist" ad ran in conjunction with the popular "There's No Wrong Way to Eat a Reese's" campaign, which promoted Reese's Peanut Butter Cups and the Reese's brand in general. Hershey sometimes alternated the two campaigns in consecutive issues of magazines such as *Reader's Digest. Advertising Age* reported that Hershey spent $86.2 million to advertise its candies in 1998, up from $84.5 million in 1997, with $60.6 million going toward television commercials and $23.3 million going toward print ads. Hershey budgeted an estimated $15 million for "The Crisp You Can't Resist!" in 1998.

OUTCOME

Soon after the launch of ReeseSticks in February, the candy was so popular that Hershey could not manufacture enough to keep up with demand. The company briefly scaled back its advertising until a larger supply of the product became available. Hershey's earnings per share rose from 33 cents to 39 cents by June 1998, and the increase was attributed primarily to sales of ReeseSticks. The company continued to dominate the U.S. chocolate industry with a market share of 45 percent in the spring of 1999.

FURTHER READING

Beirne, Mike. "Crispy Cruncher." *Brandweek,* September 14, 1998, p. 1.

———. "Twix." *Mediaweek,* September 28, 1998, p. 52.

"Candy & Snacks." *Discount Store News,* October 20, 1997, p. 32.

Liebeck, Laura. "Candy Show Set to Launch." *Discount Store News,* January 26, 1998, p. 25.

"Mars Extends M&M's Crisp-Ward." *Brandweek,* June 29, 1998.

Mehegan, Sean. "Hershey Bets $15M to Grow Reese's Again." *Brandweek,* December 1, 1997, p. 1.

Thompson Stephanie. "Candy." *Mediaweek,* May 18, 1998, p. 30.

Warner, Mary. "Sweet Success: Reese's Sticks [sic] Debut Today." *Harrisburg Patriot,* February 9, 1998.

Susan Risland

THERE'S NO WRONG WAY TO EAT A REESE'S CAMPAIGN

OVERVIEW

The Hershey Company acquired the H.B. Reese Candy Company in 1963, and with the acquisition came a popular peanut-butter-filled, chocolate-coated candy, Reese's peanut butter cups. The Reese's brand expanded over time to include Crunchy Peanut Butter Cups, Reese's Nutrageous candy bar, and Reese's Pieces, which in 1982 were made famous as the preferred treat of a lovable alien in the movie *E.T. the Extraterrestrial.* For almost 20 years, from 1969 to 1988, Hershey promoted its Reese's peanut butter cups with the familiar tagline "Two Great Tastes that Taste Great Together" and with humorous television spots. That changed after research revealed that people had developed various methods of eating Reese's peanut butter cups.

After reviewing the research, the company's ad agency, Ogilvy & Mather of New York, created a series of humorous TV spots and print ads that emphasized the unique character of peanut butter cups and the people who ate them. Themed "There's No Wrong Way to Eat a Reese's," the campaign began in 1988, with new advertisements introduced each year through the 1990s. Some played up the shape or composition of the candy, while others hinged entirely on the traits of the person eating the peanut butter cup. One print ad depicted four Reese's peanut butter cups with bites taken out of them to make them look like the four phases of the moon. The caption said, "I eat them in phases. (Richard Chandler, Astronomer)."

The positive reactions to the new campaign showed that, while its long-running predecessor was a success, consumers had been ready for a change. As the "There's No Wrong Way to Eat a Reese's" campaign continued what would become a nearly 15-year run, studies conducted by the agency revealed that consumers enjoyed the ads, related to them, and connected them with the Reese's brand. In the late 1990s an agency executive commented that, even after 10 years, the campaign "really worked."

HISTORICAL CONTEXT

Reese's peanut butter cups were invented in the 1920s by Harry Burnett Reese, who had worked at the dairy of Milton S. Hershey, the founder of Hershey Foods Corporation. Inspired by Hershey's success, Reese quit his dairy job and founded the H.B. Reese Candy Company. Reese's peanut butter cups, the company's most popular product, were shells of Hershey's milk chocolate filled with specially processed peanut butter. In 1963 the company was sold to Hershey for $23.5 million. The Reese's brand grew steadily and was expanded to include Reese's Crunchy Peanut Butter Cups, Reese's Pieces, Reese's Nutrageous candy bars, peanut butter Easter eggs and Christmas trees, peanut butter in a jar, baking bits, and peanut-butter-puffs cereal. Reese's became the top seller among the Hershey brands, which included Hershey's Kisses, Kit Kat chocolate bars, York Peppermint Patties, and Twizzlers licorice. In 1996 Hershey also acquired Leaf North America, which made Jolly Rancher, Milk Duds, Whoppers, and PayDay candies. In addition, Hershey sold chocolate syrup, ice-cream toppings, baking products, pasta, peanut butter, milk products, and other foods.

From 1969 to 1988 the tagline in two advertising campaigns for Reese's peanut butter cups was "Two Great Tastes that Taste Great Together." Commercials in the first campaign, "Collisions," featured two people, one carrying chocolate and the other carrying peanut butter, who accidentally collided and jammed their snacks together. They were always delighted with the taste of the new combination. Some of the unlikely collisions happened as people rounded corners, climbed out of manholes, and watched video games. The lively, fun tone of the commercials was intended to reflect the enjoyment consumers would experience as they tasted a Reese's. After the campaign had run for a decade, the company began developing more contemporary advertising that would appeal to consumers 12 to 34 years old. The "Collisions" advertisements had emphasized that chocolate and peanut butter were individual ingredients. In contrast, the "Near Misses" campaign stressed the fact that Reese's taste was a result of the combination of the two. This campaign, which ran from 1986 to 1988, used less slapstick and more sophistication in its humor. In 1988 the "There's No Wrong Way to Eat a Reese's" campaign was developed to emphasize the candy's unique qualities and the many ways it could be eaten.

TARGET MARKET

Because advertisements for candy had to appeal to consumers of all ages, they tended to be amusing and offbeat. A catchy jingle that children would sing at school was part of many successful campaigns. According to some experts, adult consumers were most apt to buy candy that was advertised humorously regardless of the price or taste of the product. The "There's No Wrong Way to Eat a Reese's" campaign used humor to emphasize the fact that peanut butter cups were different and more complex than some other types of candy and that they could be eaten in various ways. In fact, the company had discovered that many consumers had formed a strong emotional attachment to Reese's peanut butter cups and often ate them ritualistically. The act of consuming a rich, flavorful candy with a variety of textures could be a highly satisfying experience. The advertising campaign emphasized this individuality and self-indulgence in a lighthearted way.

In 1995 the United States ranked eighth in the world for total annual chocolate consumption. Americans ate a total of 3.1 billion pounds of chocolate in 1996. The average American ate 11.7 pounds of chocolate that year, up from 9.7 pounds in 1983. The average per capita consumption of all candy was 24.3 pounds, up from 17.9 in 1983. Candy sales climbed during the Halloween, Christmas, Easter, and Valentine's Day seasons.

COMPETITION

In the 1990s the U.S. retail chocolate industry was worth $13 billion annually, according to the Chocolate Manufacturers Association, and most of the top-selling chocolate candies were made by either Hershey or Mars, Inc., a private company owned by one of the nation's wealthiest families. Hoover's Company Capsules placed the value of the Mars company at $13 billion. The *Arizona Republic* reported that Mars had more than $1 billion in annual sales in 1997. The company's products included M&M's, Snickers, Three Musketeers, Milky Way, Skittles, and Starburst candies; Twix snacks; Uncle Ben's rice; and several brands of pet food. Hershey led the overall candy market in the United States, and Mars was second. According to *Candy Industry Magazine,* Reese's peanut butter cups were the fourth most popular chocolate candy bar in 1997, with 9 percent of the market. M&M's Chocolate Candies were the leading chocolate candy worldwide and had 16 percent of the market in the United States. Hershey's chocolate bars had 10 percent; Snickers bars had 8 percent; Butterfinger bars and York Peppermint Patties each had 4 percent; Crunch bars, Three Musketeers bars, and Russell Stover chocolate bars each had 3 percent; and Reese's Nutrageous bars had 2 percent. Hershey's Kisses and Kit Kat bars, made by Hershey, were also popular.

The top-selling Mars brand and Reese's main competitor, M&M's, had a series of enormously successful campaigns. In the past the brand had been marketed with the tagline "M&M's Melt in Your Mouth, Not in Your Hands." In a 1996 promotion consumers had voted to replace tan M&M's with blue. Advertising in 1997 featured animated M&M characters named Red, Yellow, and Blue to represent the three main colors of M&M's. Mars also designed its Internet site to look like a tour of a movie studio where each animated character had a trailer full of photographs and other fanciful possessions. In 1997 Mars responded to consumer suggestions and added a female Green character, and the ads featuring her played on the old myth that green M&M's were an aphrodisiac. The campaign featuring these characters included celebrities such as Dennis Miller, B.B. King, and Tia Carerre playfully interacting with the M&M's. The celebrities helped draw the attention of adult audiences, but the animated characters took center stage in

PUBLICITY COUP

The Reese's brand experienced a rush of popularity in 1982, when the main character in the blockbuster movie *E.T.* used a trail of Reese's Pieces to find his way through a forest.

the commercials. In a 1996 survey by *USA Today* 's Ad Track the commercials ranked second out of more than 60 campaigns in the poll, with 45 percent of respondents saying they "liked the ads a lot." In a 1997 survey by the American Marketing Association, fifth-grade students in Dallas listed spots for M&M's among their favorite commercials. Competitive Media Reporting calculated that Mars spent about $20 million on television commercials for M&M's during the first half of 1996.

The other top-selling Mars candy, Snickers, also had a popular campaign attached to it. Snickers had long been advertised as the perfect snack to satisfy hunger, but since 1995 the message had taken on a more lighthearted slant. A strategy revolving around the tagline "Hungry? Why Wait?" was developed to target males 18 to 22 years old, and more commercials were aired during sports programs on television. In one spot an elderly man had just finished painting a giant-size logo of the Chiefs football team between a pair of goalposts when a player commented, "Hey, that's great. But who are the Chefs?" The painter stared at the misspelling, muttered "Great googily moogily!" and took comfort in a Snickers bar as he resigned himself to the fact that the entire logo would have to be repainted. A voice-over said, "Not going anywhere for a while? Grab a Snickers." In another spot a coach informed a football team, "Listen up. This year we gotta be a little more 'politically correct' with the team prayer." A priest began the prayer, but the coach interrupted him to let a Rabbi take over, then a Native American shaman, a mystic from India, an Eastern Orthodox priest, and a long line of other religious leaders. "Not going anywhere for a while?" asked the announcer. "Grab a Snickers." The "Team Prayer" spot was among the 10 most popular ads of 1997, according to a survey by *USA Today* 's Ad Track. Nearly a third of respondents said they "liked the ad a lot," and 26 percent said it was effective. About 40 percent of consumers with household incomes of at least $50,000 said they liked the campaign. *Advertising Age* reported that Snickers generated sales of $277 million from March 1997 to March 1998, an increase of 2.3 percent from the previous year. Competitive Media Reporting estimated that the 1996 advertising budget for Snickers was $42.2 million.

MARKETING STRATEGY

Previous marketing had first stressed the two main ingredients of Reese's—chocolate and peanut butter—as individual elements. Next, the combination of the two was emphasized. In 1987, however, the company's research revealed that consumers could not replicate Reese's by combining chocolate and peanut butter at home. The product's unique taste was identified as a key selling point. In addition, the research showed that many consumers had peculiar ways of eating Reese's peanut butter cups. The "There's No Wrong Way to Eat a Reese's" campaign featured the humor that consumers expected of the brand, and they were strongly focused on the product.

> ### PUBLIC RELATIONS
>
> The Hershey Company promoted one of its top-selling chocolate candies with the Hershey's Kissmobile, a specialty vehicle more than 25 feet long and 11 feet tall, which looked like a row of three enormous Hershey Kisses. The vehicle traveled thousands of miles every year, stopping at children's hospitals, parades, festivals, and retail outlets. The promotion increased awareness of the brand and helped raise donations for the Children's Miracle Network, a nonprofit organization that supported children's hospitals.

The first six commercials in the campaign began airing in 1988, and additional spots were released in waves. Five of them ran in 1997. The campaign initially consisted of television commercials and included print ads after 1994. One print advertisement showed a Reese's peanut butter cup with four holes that made it look like a button. The caption read, "I make my own special alterations. (William Hamilton, Tailor)." In another print ad the candy had been nibbled into the shape of the United States. The caption said, "I start in Seattle and work my way around. (Miss Moore, Geography Teacher.)" A third showed a vampire leaving two fang marks where he had sucked the peanut-butter center out through the chocolate shell. The campaign featured a lively cast of additional characters, including a barber, a dragon, a secret agent, a private detective, a golfer, an Internal Revenue Service agent, a postal worker, and a mentalist.

Television spots included one that began with an announcer saying, "How domino champ Charlie Armstrong eats a Reese's Peanut Butter Cup." A drum roll accompanied a close-up of a little boy peering around a row of carefully balanced candy packages. To the sound of falling dominoes, the boy tipped over the first package, and the camera followed the rapidly falling Reese's across the table until the last package flipped one piece of candy into the boy's hand. The boy said, "Yeah." Clapping and cheers were heard in the background. As the camera zoomed in on two peanut butter cups and their wrapper, the announcer concluded, "There's no wrong way to eat a Reese's." Another began with an announcer saying,

"How librarian Harriet Causbie eats a Reese's peanut butter cup." The words also appeared on the screen in gold letters against an orange and chocolate-brown background, the trademark colors of Reese's candies. The scene then shifted to a library, where a serious woman in a gray suit sat at her desk. A sign over her head said, "Quiet please." She held a piece of candy and shook her finger at the camera as she whispered, "I eat them as quietly as I can." At that moment the sign fell with a crash, but she continued eating her candy. The commercial ended with a view of two peanut butter cups and their wrapper against an orange and brown background. A voice-over stated, "There's no wrong way—Shhh—to eat a Reese's."

In March 1997 Hershey began promoting a new product in the Reese's line, Reese's Crunchy Cookie Cups, with an estimated $10 million advertising campaign that appeared in print media and on television. Reese's Crunchy Cookie Cups consisted of peanut butter, milk chocolate, and a chocolate cookie, which gave the product an interesting texture. In April the company distributed 50 million coupons and 8 million free samples of the new product. Later in the year the cookie cups were included in the "There's No Wrong Way to Eat a Reese's" campaign. Another line extension, the Reese's Nutrageous candy bar, had been introduced in 1994. It received $9.5 million for advertising in 1995 and $5.4 million for the first six months of 1996. In comparison, the company spent $16.2 million to advertise regular and crunchy Reese's peanut butter cups in 1995 and $9.2 million for the first six months of 1996.

OUTCOME

The effectiveness of the "There's No Wrong Way to Eat a Reese's" campaign was demonstrated in tracking and copy tests conducted by ad agency Ogilvy & Mather. "It's run for almost ten years, and it's a campaign that really worked. Consumers identify with it," said Amy Robertson, an account executive with the agency. The tests showed that people remembered the advertisements, related to them, and associated them with the Reese's brand.

With a growth rate of 5.4 percent, the retail-confectionery category was one of the most rapidly expanding food markets in the United States in 1997. Hershey had record net sales of about $4.3 billion, up from about $4 billion in 1996, and the company said that its candy business in North America was the chief contributor to the increase in earnings. At the end of 1997 Hershey was preparing a new television and print advertising campaign, coupons, and a sampling promotion to introduce another line extension, ReeseSticks wafer bars, in February 1998.

After a successful 15-year run, in 2002 the "There's No Wrong Way to Eat a Reese's" campaign was replaced. A new campaign created by Ogilvy & Mather had the theme and tagline "Get Lost in a Reese's." It targeted young men ages 18–24 who typically enjoyed candy on the run, but it also appealed to consumers in other age groups. In addition to the new campaign, to help the brand stay relevant to consumers the company updated its product packaging and introduced another line extension: FastBreak candy bars. "Get Lost in a Reese's" supported the launch of FastBreak.

FURTHER READING

Associated Press. "Green Means Go for M&M's." *Tampa Tribune,* January 24, 1997.

DeKok, David. "Chocolate Wars." *Harrisburg (PA) Patriot & Evening News,* October 13, 1995.

"Divine Ms. Green Lives Up to Name in M&Mland." *Arizona Republic,* February 18, 1997.

Enrico, Dottie. "Consumers Sweet on M&M Ads." *USA Today,* July 28, 1996.

Enrico, Dottie, and Lydia Gibson. "Snickers' 'Why Wait?' Ads Hit Sweet Spot." *USA Today,* April 21, 1997.

"Food Ads Are Top with Kids." *Adweek,* April 24, 1997.

Garfield, Bob. "Snickers Ads Grab the Elusive 'Big Idea.' " *Advertising Age,* September 2, 1996.

Grant, Tracy, and Judith Evans. "Honey, Pass the Green M&M's." *Washington Post,* January 27, 1997.

Gustin, Carl, Jr. "Ogilvy Clients Talk about the Agency and Its Work: Partnerships and Brand-Building Are Stressed." *Advertising Age,* September 21, 1998.

"Hershey Sets Reese's Crunchy Launch." *Adweek, Eastern Edition,* October 28, 1996.

"How the Ad Track Ads of 1997 Stack Up" *USA Today,* December 29, 1997.

"Late News. (Advertising/Marketing News Briefs)." *Advertising Age,* June 17, 2002.

Mehegan, Sean. "Hershey Keeps Reese's Growing with $10M Intro of Cookie Cups." *Brandweek,* October 28, 1996.

"The Power and the Passion: Reese's Is Just One of Hershey's Power Brands. Here's the Punch behind It." *Confectioner,* October 1, 2002.

Susan Risland
Rayna Bailey

Hewlett-Packard Company

3000 Hanover St.
Palo Alto, California 94304
USA
Telephone: (650) 857-1501
Fax: (650) 857-5518
Web site: www.hp.com

BUILT BY ENGINEERS, USED BY ORDINARY PEOPLE CAMPAIGN

OVERVIEW

In early 1996 the Hewlett-Packard Company began to rethink its role in the electronics products industry. Undisputedly the market leader for printers and other electronic products, Hewlett-Packard (HP) nevertheless saw the competition at its heels. Even more important, as technology became more "personalized" and accessible to the average person, the company was not sure it could rely solely on its history as a purveyor of electronic goods to businesses and institutions.

Hewlett-Packard turned to the San Francisco advertising firm Goodby Silverstein & Partners to create an ad campaign that would give it a more human face and present it as a company responsive to the needs of its customers. Goodby Silverstein designed "Built by Engineers, Used by Ordinary People," a campaign focusing on the new Mopier business printer and the 690 series of DeskJet printers for the home. The campaign, which ran from late 1996 until about the middle of 1997, was designed to appeal to both HP's core customers—businesses—and to recreational or home users of electronics. The consumer ads showed people in situations that could easily be made simpler by the use of Hewlett-Packard products, while the business ads showed the imagination and flexibility of HP's engineering capacity.

HISTORICAL CONTEXT

Like many pioneering companies of the 20th century, Hewlett-Packard was born in a garage. It was founded by engineers David Packard and Bill Hewlett in 1938. At the time the mission was to develop and market a resistance-capacity audio oscillator that could be used to test sound equipment. Hewlett and Packard's $538 in founding capital carried them through until the Walt Disney studios ordered eight of their devices. Then in 1941 the United States entered the Second World War, and an immediate overwhelming need for HP's instruments was created. After the war ended, the company lost its mainstay government orders and decided to seek clients in the private sector. Hewlett-Packard introduced its measuring devices into the flourishing post-war electronics industry. In 1972 the company pioneered personal computing with the world's first handheld scientific calculator, and it then went on to introduce the first desktop mainframe (in 1982) and the LaserJet printer (the first and most prominent of a line of printers for business and home), as well as copiers and scanners.

TARGET MARKET

Although Hewlett-Packard held its position as the world's leading supplier of hard-copy products

HP GETS ANOTHER MAKEOVER

At the end of 1997 Hewlett-Packard launched a second advertising campaign, this one with the tag line "Expanding Possibilities." "Expanding Possibilities" grew out of reflections at the company that it was still perceived by consumers simply as the company that makes computer printers. HP had failed to establish a strong corporate identity in the way it wanted to be perceived: as an interesting, even sexy, maker of products that are relevant to the ways ordinary people live.

"Expanding Possibilities" differed greatly from "Built by Engineers, Used by Ordinary People" in that it did not focus on specific products. Rather, in recognition of the increasing role technology plays in everyday life, it asked viewers to think about the company as more than just the maker of business-related gadgets.

One way it did this was to make changes, albeit not drastic ones, in the company's use of color. Until then the boxes used to house the company's computers and printers had been a simple white, suggesting scientific prowess and accuracy but also sterility and lack of emotion. The company began using strong, vivid colors on its boxes, consumer manuals, and store displays.

Television ads (also developed by Goodby Silverstein & Partners) that began running in November showed new ways for people to use the company's products to make and transmit images. In one spot new parents use a Hewlett-Packard camera and computer to send out birth announcements over the Internet. In another, former Negro League baseball player Buck O'Neil uses HP printers, scanners, and computers to make and sell Negro League baseball cards online.

(LaserJet and DeskJet printers, DesignJet large-format printers and plotters, ScanJet scanners, OfficeJet printer-fax-copiers, CopyJet color printer-copiers, and HP FAX facsimile machines), the company became concerned in 1996 that it projected an image too cold and technological for the home-electronics user to relate to. Since HP had a growing customer base of individual consumers, it decided to focus on making its technology seem more accessible.

The resulting television and print advertising in the "Built by Engineers, Used by Ordinary People" campaign targeted two audiences: families with children and business professionals, particularly corporate executives, management information system (MIS) experts, and end users. Creative elements were designed to appeal to low-end users while at the same time showing off the products' high-tech features to viewers well versed in information technology.

COMPETITION

Although Hewlett-Packard remained the market leader for printers, its largest competitors—Canon, Xerox, and Lexmark—were making strenuous efforts to narrow the gap. Also, as high technology moved into people's living rooms, the company saw that other makers of computers and electronic goods—such as Microsoft and Apple, among others—had been able to position themselves as interesting and cutting edge while Hewlett-Packard was viewed by consumers as reliable but stodgy.

Canon, the giant Japanese maker of business machines, cameras, and other optical products, presented a formidable challenge to Hewlett-Packard with its line of laser and BubbleJet printers. Marketing its products under the tag line "You *can* with a Canon," the company experienced strong growth in its printers during 1997. Canon targeted businesses with such products as the Digital GP215, a multifunctional digital device for networked workgroups that printed, faxed, copied, and scanned. The company also introduced the MultiPASS L90, another multifunctional system, and a new color laser printer, the CLBP 360PS. The BubbleJet continued to defend its market share with a very small and light personal model, the BJC-50, weighing only 900 grams.

Xerox Corporation, which introduced the first (manually operated) commercial xerographic product in 1949 and the first automatic office copier in 1959, made its first laser printer in 1977 and by 1991 was developing an extensive printer line. To highlight the company's evolution from copy machines to a wide range of business products, Xerox in 1994 adopted the tag line "The Document Company, Xerox" as its new corporate signature. As a document company, Xerox in 1997 introduced an array of specialized printer products for business, including a color printer for signs, banners, and billboards; a printer designed specifically for engineering needs; and the Xerox Productivity Centre System, which allowed users to scan, store, manage, electronically collate, distribute, print, and copy wide-format documents such as those used by architects, mapmakers, and graphic artists.

Lexmark brought up the rear in this august assemblage, but it was able to chip away at the other companies' lead during 1997. Lexmark, based in Lexington,

Kentucky, was smaller than its competitors and had a narrower product range. It concentrated on laser, ink jet, and dot matrix printers and associated supplies that were comparable but lower-priced than Hewlett-Packard models. In November 1997 Lexmark won the first Annual Peripherals Excellence Award for network laser printers, beating out Hewlett-Packard and Apple.

MARKETING STRATEGY

The Hewlett-Packard advertising account had been held since 1988 by Saatchi & Saatchi in San Francisco, but the company decided against asking them to carry out the new campaign. According to the *San Jose Business Journal,* this was partially because of a 1995 print campaign that cost more than $30 million but failed to leave any lasting impression on consumers. Arlene King, peripherals-advertising manager at Hewlett-Packard, had another explanation for the move. "We wanted to get more visible advertising than we did in the past. We had been with Saatchi for eight years and we were becoming too alike." In May 1996 HP chose Goodby Silverstein & Partners in San Francisco to head the $40 million printer advertising account (Saatchi did, however, retain the PC portion of the Hewlett-Packard account). Goodby Silverstein & Partners had previously been known for creative and popular campaigns such as the "Got Milk?" ads for the California Milk Processor Board.

In consumer research, Goodby Silverstein found that most people associated Hewlett-Packard with technical strength and reliability. Therefore, the new campaign needed to link Hewlett-Packard's heritage as an engineering company and its reputation for building reliable products with the usefulness of HP products in "ordinary" situations. In short, the challenge was to humanize the face of technical prowess by giving complicated engineering a human face.

The $10.5 million Goodby Silverstein campaign for Hewlett-Packard, "Built by Engineers, Used by Ordinary People," solved the dilemma by poking gentle fun at its own engineers while illustrating the excellence of HP products, particularly the 693 DeskJet printer, for use in the home, and the LaserJet 5si Mopier (multiple originals copier), a network printer for large-scale commercial use.

The year-long campaign was two-pronged, targeting both individual consumers and corporate entities. It featured television spots that ran from late November 1996 through late February 1997 on CNN and national networks. Those were supplemented by print ads in publications like *Newsweek,* the *Wall Street Journal, Business Week, Fortune, PC Magazine, PC Week,* and *PC Computing* that ran beyond the close of the television segment. In addition, the San Francisco-based interactive ad agency Red Sky developed an interactive ad that could be viewed on the Internet though the end of February 1997.

The Goodby Silverstein television spots showed both the ordinary and the extraordinary uses to which Hewlett-Packard printers can be put. In "Mower," the first of the "corporate side ads," a nerdy-looking announcer sporting a bow tie lists what a Mopier can do (print, staple, collate) and then jokes that the only thing it cannot do is mow the lawn. That serves as enough of a challenge to HP engineers, who immediately begin reconfiguring the printer. In the next scene the Mopier is turned on its side charging around an overgrown field, having been transformed by the company's engineers into a lawnmower.

In a second spot, "Translation," the interviewer asks an HP engineer to explain exactly how a Mopier works. The engineer answers in highly technical jargon, which is translated for the layperson in a running voice-over. In both of these spots the engineers were actual Hewlett-Packard employees.

In the consumer-oriented spots, the usefulness of HP products in personal situations was demonstrated. In the "Baby-sitter" spot, an elderly man babysitting his infant granddaughter panics when she wakes up and begins to cry for her mother. Suddenly he has a brilliant idea: he grabs a picture of the mother and turns on his DeskJet printer. When the mother returns, she sees the grandfather—with a color print of the mother pasted on his face—holding the peacefully sleeping baby.

In a similar ad ("Room"), a teenager whose mother checks up on him through the key hole on his bedroom door fools her into thinking he has finally cleaned his extremely messy room by making a color printout of a picture of the room in a pristine state and positioning it just beyond the key hole.

The interactive ad developed by Red Sky was an extension of the television and print campaign into the electronic medium. It carried on the playfulness of the television spots but was also very different, using as it did the interactive capabilities of online advertising. As Joel Hladecek, Red Sky's chief creative director, told the *San Francisco Business Times,* "There are two rules of advertising in this medium. The audience has the ability to choose what it's interested in, and people will avoid advertising if they can."

Red Sky responded by burying the advertising message within entertainment. Their 1997 Pong advertising banner for Hewlett-Packard, promoting the LaserJet Mopier, played off the print and television tag line. Viewers used Shockwave technology to play games of Pong with an engineer named Jerry. They were initially drawn to the ad by the familiar sound of a ping-pong game. They then discovered that the ad was more than just a banner: it was an interactive game in which they could use their mouse to actually play along. The ad ran through February 1997 at various sites.

OUTCOME

The "Built by Engineers, Used by Ordinary People" campaign was pronounced an unqualified success by the company. Post-campaign quantitative research showed that the campaign had been very effective in reaching the desired targets. Those assessments were confirmed by the number of awards the campaign won during 1996 and 1997.

At the ICON Awards, sponsored by *Marketing Computers* and *Business Week* to honor excellence in high technology marketing and advertising, "Built by Engineers" won 1996 Best of Show ICONs for "Baby-sitter," "Room," and "Mower"; platinum in the best advertising campaign, broadcast category; and gold in the best advertising/television campaign category.

At the international Clio Awards, which recognize excellence and creativity in consumer advertising, "Baby-sitter," "Room," and "Mower" won best national campaign certificates, and "Baby-sitter" was also a certificate winner. In addition, *Adweek,* which publishes an annual list of the 10 best spots of the year, declared "Baby-sitter" to be one of the best spots of 1996. The spots won other awards as well, both in local advertising industry shows, such as the San Francisco Show, and in New York-based shows, such as The One Show.

In Europe the campaign also won a Directors and Art Directors Silver Pencil Award in London for "Baby-sitter." Finally, "Baby-sitter" won a Silver Lion at the Cannes Advertising Festival.

The Red Sky interactive ad also garnered acclaim, in this case from critics of Internet advertising. *Microscope,* a weekly online Web ad review magazine, rated the banner ad "a perfect 10" and called it "the most attention-getting ad on the Web." *PC World* followed suit, awarding it the number one position in *PC World* 's Top 10 Advertiser Achievement Awards. The ad went on to win a Platinum Award in the 1997 *Marketing Computers/Business Week* ICON Award for the multimedia category.

FURTHER READING

Beatty, Sally Goll. "H-P to Get Marketing Makeover." *Wall Street Journal,* November 11, 1997.

Bennis, Warren, and Patricia Ward Biedermann. *Organizing Genius: The Secrets of Creative Collaboration,* Addison-Wesley Publishing Co, Inc., 1998.

Charry, Tamar. "H-P Gently Mocks Its Own Nerds in Ads." *Denver Post,* January 6, 1997.

Ginsberg, Steven. "HP Hopes New Agency, Campaign Can Attract Reams of New Customers." *San Jose Business Journal,* December 16, 1997.

Hemmila, Donna. "Red Sky Warning: Interactive Ad Firm Creates Strange Digital Worlds." *San Francisco Business Times,* April 24, 1998.

"Hewlett-Packard: HP Plays Ping-pong with Mopier Ad." *M2 Presswire,* February 13, 1997.

"HP Breaks First Work From Goodby With New Effort Promoting Printers." *Computer Publishing & Advertising Report,* November 25, 1996.

"New Television Ad Campaign Unveiled for HP Printers." *Business Wire,* November 8, 1996.

Scrupski, Stephen. "The Curse of Normality." *Electronic Design,* March 17, 1997.

Voight, Joan. "Ads Soften Hewlett-Packard Image: Goody Silverstein Promotes Printers for 'Normal People'." *Adweek Eastern Edition,* November 18, 1996.

Susan M. Steiner

EXPANDING POSSIBILITIES CAMPAIGN

OVERVIEW

Although it was widely known and respected in the business world for its solid engineering and reliable products, Hewlett-Packard, a huge company with 121,900 employees and revenues of $42.9 billion in 1997, found itself relatively unknown to the general public. Beginning in the late 1990s, Hewlett-Packard sought to expand its presence in the consumer market. To do so, the company initiated a $75 million consumer brand strategy that included an advertising campaign called "Expanding Possibilities." It was the first time in Hewlett-Packard's 60-year history that it had tried to shed its reputation as an engineering and business firm for a more consumer-oriented image. In 1997 the consumer business accounted for only a quarter of Hewlett-Packard's revenue, but the company saw this segment as being the place where growth would come most rapidly. As the general public became more focused on technology, Hewlett-Packard wanted to have a more prominent place in the consumer's mind.

The "Expanding Possibilities" campaign first appeared in the United States on November 11, 1997, in the form of three television spots that featured color printing applications people could employ in everyday situations. The ads ran through January 1998. They were aired in prime time on CBS, ABC, NBC, CNN, A&E,

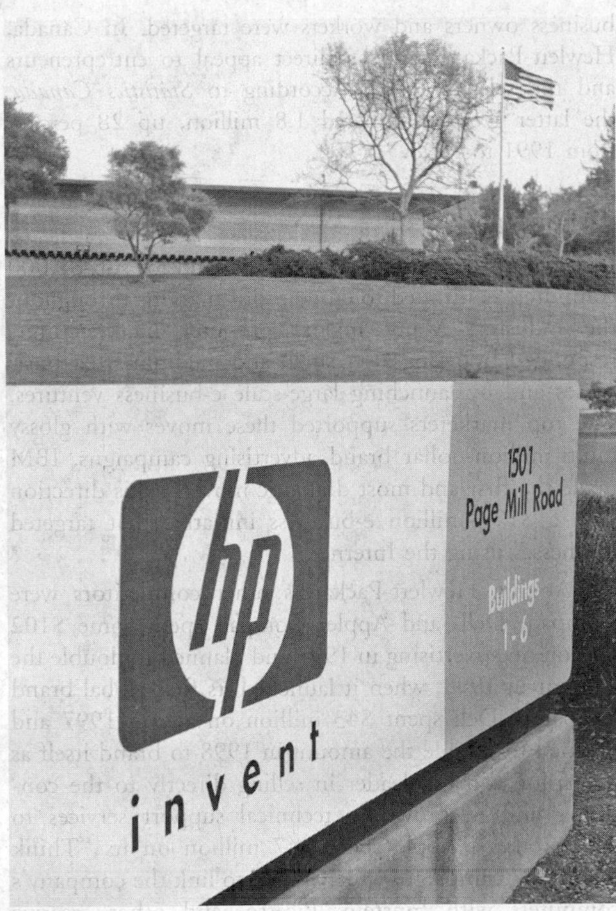

Hewlett-Packard Company headquarters in Palo Alto, California. AP IMAGES.

and the Discovery Channel. In Canada the spots ran on the Hockey Night, Bravo!, Showcase, Discover, and Life Network channels. Goodby, Silverstein & Partners of San Francisco created the spots. The original "Expanding Possibilities" campaign was budgeted at $15 million for the United States and at $40 million globally.

The "Mason" spot showed a couple capturing their newborn baby's wrinkled image on a Hewlett-Packard digital camera. The father downloaded the image onto a Hewlett-Packard computer, created a birth announcement, and E-mailed it to relatives. "Herta" featured a grandmother who took family photographs off the wall, scanned them into her Hewlett-Packard PC, and made a family history book for her children and grandchildren. "Buck" centered on a former Negro Leagues baseball player, Buck O'Neil, and a young friend who created their own baseball cards with O'Neil's Hewlett-Packard scanner, PC, and printer and then sold them on the Internet.

In March 1998 Hewlett-Packard added a $12 million brand campaign with two more television spots and a print element, all created by Saatchi & Saatchi of San Francisco. The two 30-second spots ran during sports and news programs in the company's top 10 regional markets in the United States. The schedule later included national exposure on CNN, ESPN, the Discovery Channel, and the Learning Channel. This round of the campaign, unlike the original ads, was aimed toward businesses. In one spot, for example, an airline maintenance worker discovered that it would take five months to produce a revised manual telling workers not to remove the plug in a plane's oil pan. As an alternative, he quickly updated the manual via the Internet. The print ads appeared in the *Wall Street Journal* for a month. A third group of "Expanding Possibilities" ads that were released in October 1998 used print media, on-line services, and radio to reach corporate customers, small businesses, home users, and students.

HISTORICAL CONTEXT

Two Stanford University engineers, William Hewlett and David Packard, founded the company with $538 in a Palo Alto garage in 1939. Their first major customer, Walt Disney, bought oscillators to help make his film *Fantasia.* In the 1970s and 1980s Hewlett-Packard became known as an entrepreneurial high-tech company, and it has been credited with establishing Silicon Valley. For years it made the lists of America's best-managed companies. By the late 1980s, however, the company seemed entrapped in a bureaucratic jungle, with burdensome decision making by consensus and other organizational problems. In 1990 Hewlett-Packard was reorganized, and cost-cutting measures included voluntary severance and early-retirement programs. The company's single sales force was divided by product lines, and administrative and manufacturing areas were consolidated.

During its history Hewlett-Packard had always been much better known in the business community than among general consumers. It was the world's second largest computer supplier and a leading provider of electronic products and systems for computing, measurement, and communications. But it did not use advertising to appeal directly to consumers. Lewis Platt, then the chairman, president, and CEO of Hewlett-Packard, said that 18 months of focus group testing showed that the public felt the company to be trustworthy and reliable but did not view it as innovative. Hewlett-Packard's reputation stemmed from its engineering-dominated culture, and while people judged its products to be of high quality, they perceived the company as being technical and impersonal.

In addition, the company's decentralized structure contributed to its fragmented marketing efforts and prevented it from taking full advantage of consumer interactions. For example, the owners of Hewlett-Packard's 75 million ink-jet printers bought from two to five new cartridges a year, but the company did not have a plan to take advantage of these customer contacts.

Hewlett-Packard's vision of the future included a blending of consumer electronics, including PCs and communications and entertainment products, with new product categories emerging. The company's goal was to prepare to become the largest consumer electronics supplier by the early 2000s. This would mean becoming much better known among consumers. As the technology battleground moved into the home, however, Hewlett-Packard had to prepare to compete with electronics and entertainment companies such as Sony and General Electric that already had a much higher profile with consumers and that were viewed in more positive terms.

TARGET MARKET

The primary target of the initial "Expanding Possibilities" ads was families with children, but the company also wanted to become better known among small businesses, microbusinesses, and the owners of home businesses. Both business owners and workers were targeted. In Canada, Hewlett-Packard made a direct appeal to entrepreneurs and the self-employed. According to *Statistics Canada,* the latter group numbered 1.8 million, up 28 percent from 1991 to 1998.

HEWLETT-PACKARD EARNS HIGH RANKINGS

Hewlett-Packard's reputation could be gleaned from the following rankings:

- first worldwide in sales of ink-jet printers, photo-quality printers, and laser printers
- first worldwide in sales of acute-care patient-monitoring systems
- first in reliability for notebooks, desktop PCs, and PC servers (*IDC* and *Dataquest*)
- first in on-site support staff responsiveness, technical knowledge of phone staff, and remote automated diagnostics (*Computerworld*)
- second most-admired computers/office equipment company (*Fortune,* March 1, 1999)
- third most-admired company in Asia (*Asian Business,* May 1, 1998)
- tenth best company to work for in the United States (*Fortune,* January 11, 1999)

COMPETITION

In 1997 and 1998 the consumer demand for sub-$1,000 computers continued to erode profit margins throughout the industry. Many major computer manufacturers responded by going after small and medium-sized businesses and by launching large-scale e-business ventures. The top marketers supported these moves with glossy multi-million-dollar brand advertising campaigns. IBM made the first and most dramatic move in this direction with a $130 million e-business initiative that targeted businesses using the Internet.

Among Hewlett-Packard's other competitors were Compaq, Dell, and Apple. Compaq spent some $102 million on advertising in 1997 and planned to double the amount in 1998, when it launched its first global brand campaign. Dell spent $43 million on ads in 1997 and planned to double the amount in 1998 to brand itself as the originator and leader in selling directly to the consumer and in providing technical support services to its customers. Apple spent $47 million on its "Think Different" campaign, which aimed to link the company's computers with Einstein, Picasso, and other creative people.

MARKETING STRATEGY

To demonstrate the excitement of its new campaign, Hewlett-Packard hosted a gala announcement event in San Francisco on November 11, 1997. At the kickoff event Hewlett-Packard chairman Platt described the company's image as "a lab coat that was empty." The company had excelled at engineering prowess but never at savvy self-promotion. The new campaign aimed to add to the company's strengths a new spirit of excitement, creativity, and innovation. Along with the new advertising, Hewlett-Packard introduced new product packaging, in-store merchandising, and vending machines for its ink-jet printer supplies.

The introduction of the "Expanding Possibilities" campaign meant dropping Goodby, Silverstein & Partners' award-winning campaign that used the tag line "Built by engineers. Used by normal people." One reason for the switch was to dispel the notion that the company was dominated by engineers. "The consumer brand strategy and advertising campaign aim to make the HP brand more relevant to consumers by revealing the company's dynamic side and dispelling the idea that HP is only a printer company," said the firm's Antonio

Perez. "People used to say HP was a great stealth marketer," said Jill Kramer, the company's marketing communications manager, in *Adweek*. "There's been growing recognition with HP that our brand is truly an asset and that is something we should be investing in. We are becoming more visible and more aggressive."

Part of the reason for a move toward consumers was the rapid pace of change. With technology and products evolving so quickly, consumers were easily confused and often felt behind the times. Executives at Hewlett-Packard felt that a finely honed brand identity might attract consumers looking for a guide through the digital and technology jungle. In addition, the company recognized that the market for traditional business products was expanding to include in-home and consumer use. Lower-cost, higher-quality printers, scanners, and all-in-one machines made the products attractive outside the typical corporate or business setting. The campaign also called attention to Hewlett-Packard's Internet products, something it had been producing for years but had never promoted to the public.

Hewlett-Packard sometimes referred to the new campaign as "the real life campaign" because the strategy was to shine the spotlight on people not usually associated with technology. Grandparents and children were highlighted, and they shared their stories in their own words. The intent was not just to show what people could do with Hewlett-Packard products but also to demonstrate what the products could help people achieve. Hewlett-Packard products were presented as engines for consumers' creative thinking.

Although Hewlett-Packard wanted to change its image with the "Expanding Possibilities" campaign, there were certain elements in its marketing effort and image that were retained. The company logo and the display of the Hewlett-Packard name with the logo remained the same. The company also maintained continuity with its advertising agencies. Goodby, Silverstein & Partners continued handling the ads for Hewlett-Packard printers and scanners and for the company's other computer equipment. Saatchi & Saatchi Advertising continued the advertising for the company's Pavilion line of personal computers, and Winkler Advertising continued to create the company's ads for laser printer supplies.

OUTCOME

Independent research showed that the ads were successful in changing the perceptions of consumers. According to Goodby, Silverstein & Partners, studies showed that the ads had helped Hewlett-Packard come to be perceived as a company that "empowers people to 'make exciting things happen.' " People's awareness that Hewlett-Packard made more than just printers also increased.

In March 1998 the *Business Journal* of San Jose reported that Hewlett-Packard led the market as the top seller of workstations running off Microsoft Windows. It sold nearly 155,000 Windows-based workstations, or 42 percent of the market, in 1997. The journal attributed part of Hewlett-Packard's success to the "Expanding Possibilities" campaign.

The original three "Expanding Possibilities" spots won two Icon Awards, and "Buck" won a silver Clio.

FURTHER READING

Elkin, Tobi. "Upfront: The Clients—Brands: Computer." *Adweek,* May 18, 1998.

"HP's New Brand Advertising Campaign Demonstrates How Consumers Can 'Expand Possibilities,' " Business Wire, November 12, 1997.

Johnson, Bradley. "Seeing Opening, HP Rushes New Global Ad Effort." *Adweek,* March 2, 1998.

"The Pack." *Brandweek,* September 28, 1998.

Chris John Amorosino

YOU + HP CAMPAIGN

OVERVIEW

Long known as a reliable but predictable maker of computer printers, Hewlett-Packard Company (HP) was, in 2003, engaged in a recasting of its moribund image, a project initiated by HP's chief executive officer, Carly Fiorina, after a divisive 2002 merger with computer company Compaq. That year HP unveiled its most ambitious consumer advertising campaign ever. The new campaign, called "You + HP," featured HP's digital cameras and imaging products, a segment of the Fortune 100 company's operations that was seen as a major growth opportunity.

"You + HP" supplemented an ongoing enterprise campaign that had introduced the "+" graphic as a means of showcasing HP's partnerships with other companies and institutions and that further positioned the old-line company as a forward-looking, glamorous company in tune with twenty-first-century lifestyles. Developed by HP's main U.S. advertising agency, Goodby, Silverstein & Partners of San Francisco, the campaign broke in October 2003 with the risky use of 20-page print inserts, first in *USA Today* and later in trendsetting magazines, and went on to feature some of the most talked-about television spots of the time. Directed by François Vogel, the television spots dramatized the digital-photography revolution with visuals integrating still frames and live

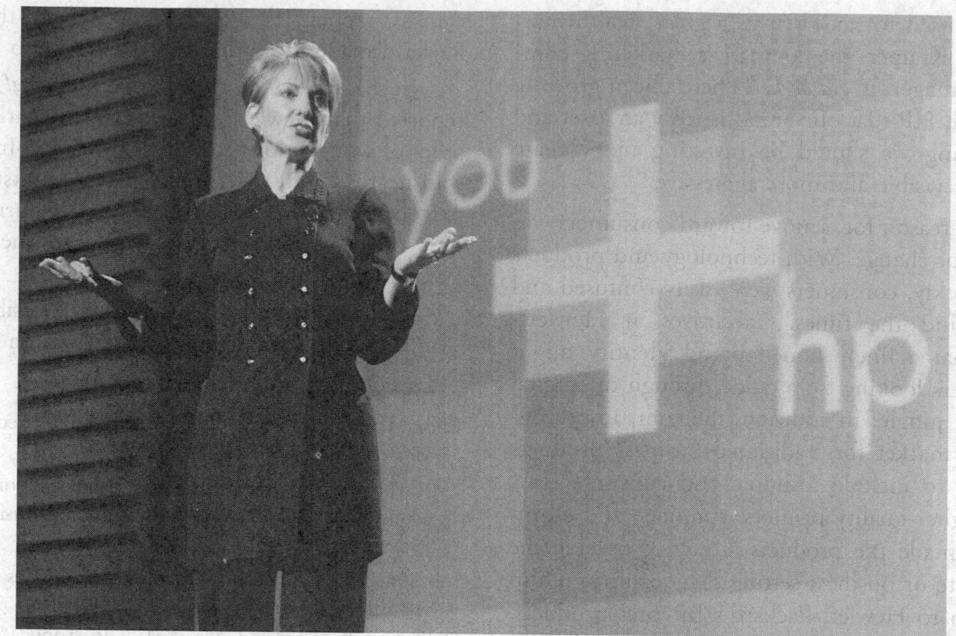

Carly Fiorina, January 8, 2004. © STEVE MARCUS/LAS VEGAS SUN/REUTERS/CORBIS.

action, while catchy pop music by the Cure (in the campaign's first year) and the Kinks (in the second year) played as the spots' sound track.

The print and television portions of "You + HP" were well received by industry commentators as well as the general public, and the campaign was credited with effectively updating HP's image for a new generation of consumers. The campaign continued to evolve, and the company's broader marketing efforts kept the "+ HP" idea as their starting point. HP's change in direction, however, was not welcomed by all; the company's board of directors ousted Fiorina in 2005.

HISTORICAL CONTEXT

HP had a storied history of innovation and was a Fortune 100 company when Carly Fiorina took over as chief executive officer in 1999. Though the company was well known for its quality products and particularly for its printers, "it had become clear," according to *Advertising Age,* "that HP had to do something to change its consumer image." HP's takeover of its rival Compaq in 2002—at a time when PC sales (the heart of Compaq's business) were abysmal—raised further questions about the company's direction in the precarious postbubble marketplace. Fiorina and Allison Johnson, HP's senior vice president for global brand and communications, asked agency Goodby, Silverstein & Partners to answer these questions by showcasing the merger itself and then by focusing on other high-profile but previously unpublicized HP partnerships in a large-scale rebranding push that broke in the fall of 2002.

Ads touting the merger used an "HP + Compaq" graphic to show the strength of the partnership, and the "+" sign was then used as a unifying visual symbol in the larger branding campaign, which extolled HP's contributions to an impressive array of corporate and institutional partners. The campaign was launched with "Anthem," a television spot that, as *Creativity* magazine noted, "linked HP technology to bigger and cooler things—Dreamworks' imagemaking, FedEx's efficiency, BMW's Formula 1 need for speed." Other memorable ads were "Restore," which brought figures from a Dutch master painting to life in order to illustrate the role HP played in restoring art for London's National Gallery, and "The Next Shift," which featured iconic toys—Slinky, Elmo, Spiderman, and others—commuting to work in Manhattan as a way of illustrating HP's involvement in keeping Toys "R" Us stores stocked and ready for business. *Creativity* selected Goodby's HP branding work as its campaign of the year for 2003, arguing that the spots had worked together to "render formerly square HP a magnetic new personality."

Meanwhile the rapid rise in popularity of digital cameras presented one of the few bright spots in the dismal technology sectors of the struggling American economy. As the 2003 holiday season approached, digital cameras were poised to overtake traditional cameras in yearly sales for the first time. Though HP was not known for its cameras, its wide portfolio of products meant that

TOO COOL?

Though no one argued that Carly Fiorina had been a bold, decisive leader during her tenure at HP, her February 2005 dismissal generated plenty of speculation about the overall value of her contributions to the company. Many pointed to the Compaq acquisition—narrowly approved over the open hostility of Walter Hewlett, son of the company's founder—as an outright blunder, moving HP as it did into a heavy investment in PCs at the expense of its lucrative printer business. Some observers even wondered whether Fiorina's drastic makeover of the HP image, celebrated though it had been in advertising circles, could be classified a success. As analyst Rob Enderle told the *San Francisco Chronicle,* "When she took over, HP was kind of stuck in the mud. Now, it's clearly a much more vibrant company, but it's harder to tell what it is. It used to have a clear identity—like your grandpa five years after retirement, really nice but not going anyplace. Now, it has a faster-moving capability, but it would have been nice to keep the warm, fuzzy part."

it was positioned to offer consumers an integrated system for home digital photography.

TARGET MARKET

"You + HP" specifically targeted consumers, which distinguished the campaign from other HP enterprise and business-to-business efforts. Digital-imaging products were becoming integral to the personal lives of ordinary Americans, so these products in particular offered HP the opportunity to position itself as "the ultimate lifestyle technology company," in the words of *Advertising Age.*

Because most of those who were buying digital cameras were first-time purchasers, it was imperative that HP emphasize the simplicity of the new technology. At the same time, simplicity could not be the campaign's main message, because HP did not want to appear to be pointing out consumers' ignorance. Goodby and HP therefore pitched the company's digital-imaging products as vehicles for promoting individuals' creativity and fulfillment. Scott Berg, director of worldwide media for HP, told *Adweek,* "Our position was to say the digital camera could become a natural extension of, or appendage to, your being, that you are free from the tyranny of the photo lab." By linking the HP brand image with the inspirational notion of personal fulfillment, Fiorina aimed at making the tech giant a true pop-culture brand along the lines of Coca-Cola or Nike. The "You + HP" campaign, then, was meant to cut across demographic lines, and it dwarfed all previous HP attempts to target consumers.

To make the pitch specific to HP, the campaign pointed to the company's full range of products, suggesting that the seamless transition from picture taking to picture printing was possible because HP could satisfy every step of the process. Consumers could take pictures with an HP camera, store and manipulate them on an HP personal computer, and print them using an HP printer, ink cartridge, and paper.

COMPETITION

Given its sprawling portfolio HP competed with a wide range of companies, but its "You + HP" campaign, while leveraging and further establishing its overall brand identity, directly pitted the company against other digital-camera manufacturers. At the time of the campaign it was number six among digital-camera vendors in the United States, well behind segment leaders Eastman Kodak Company and Sony Corporation.

Kodak's success, according to *Advertising Age,* was chiefly attributable to its "century-long simple stance that Kodak equals pictures." Though hampered somewhat by losses in the rapidly diminishing film-photography side of its business, Kodak could claim, like HP, to offer simple solutions to the entire picture-making process, especially as PCs became unnecessary for printing. Kodak had the industry-leading photo printer as well as the industry-leading online printing and storage site (called the Kodak EasyShare Gallery), and it had kiosks at major retail stores, such as Wal-Mart and CVS, that allowed consumers yet another outlet for printing pictures. Kodak's digital-imaging ads therefore focused on ease of use while reinforcing the company's history of photographic excellence.

Sony likewise made appeals to consumers based on its legacy, but that legacy was one of "quality technology and cutting-edge design," according to *Advertising Age,* rather than one of film photography. This image merged neatly with the company's digital-imaging marketing efforts, which drew attention to the convenient size and sleekness of Sony cameras. In 2005 Sony reinforced its image by unveiling the tagline "WorryFree Digital Products," orchestrating a marketing push with partner retailers to head off the concerns of first-time digital-camera buyers and assure them that its products were simple and easy to use.

MARKETING STRATEGY

"You + HP" was launched with a 20-page print insert in the October 2, 2003, edition of *USA Today.* The idea of spending $10 million on such an insert, designed to run in about a dozen publications, went against the grain of traditional print advertising for photography brands, which tended to focus on maximum coverage and frequency. Because the campaign was "more lifestyle-oriented than anything else," as Berg told *Adweek,* the company "had to find a way to stand out in unique environments" rather than take a blanket approach to print placement. Goodby's creative team decided that the magazines in which the insert would appear after its launch should be ones whose editorial focus celebrated the power of photography; the team thus chose such titles as *Vogue,* the *New Yorker, People, Entertainment Weekly, InStyle, ESPN: The Magazine, GQ, Travel + Leisure,* and *Condé Nast Traveler.* The inserts put the consumer at the center of HP's message, featuring the word "You" in a prominent position on nearly every page, employing vibrant photo collages and statements such as "You are a point-and-shoot revolutionary with an itchy shutter finger" and "You are the Van Gogh of pic files." The ads featured the full range of HP digital-imaging products, pointing out the brand's coverage of the entire picture-making process but forgoing the usual listings of technical specifications.

The campaign's initial television spots, directed by Vogel and shot in Barcelona, further underscored the revolutionary nature of digital-photography technology. In both "You" and "Statue," people in social settings and on city streets were frozen in still frames suggesting photographs, while the scenes' action moved on briskly and a continuous stream of individual moments were framed before dissolving back into motion. The fluidity of the movement from human interaction to still frame, along with the profusion of photographic possibilities suggested, communicated the limitless options available to the digital-camera owner while dramatizing the integration of artistic expression and ordinary life. The arresting visual effects worked with the Cure's moody 1989 hit song "Pictures of You" to create, as *Adweek* put it, "an emotional paean to digital photography."

In 2004 Goodby's creative team planned a second series of television spots to be paired with the upbeat Kinks song "Picture Book." This time the challenge was to go beyond illustrating picture-taking possibilities and find a visual method for dramatizing the ease of printing photos. In a test spot filmed as his bid to direct the new series, Vogel shot himself at his desk putting empty white frames around his head while coolly singing along to the Kinks song playing in the background. Vogel then tweaked the footage until it appeared that he was effortlessly creating a series of casual self-portraits from thin air. Not only did this test ad get him the job, but it was reshot with little alteration as the 30-second spot "François." In the spot "Picture Book" the principle of picking photographs out of thin air was applied to crowds of people. At the start of the commercial, two rows of people held frames to their faces, after which the frames became pictures, and then the people traded these self-portraits with one another. In "Relay" the photographic frame was passed like a baton between groups and individuals. Photos transformed into dynamic real-life scenes and vice versa as the frame made its way through a hypnotic flux of distinctive people and moments.

OUTCOME

"You + HP" was widely acknowledged as a key contributor to the ongoing transformation of the company's image from, as *Advertising Age* put it, "well-regarded though stodgy into a brand akin to sexier rivals such as Sony Corp." For the print insert that launched the campaign, which "cut through in a medium that HP's rivals have dominated for decades," Goodby was awarded *Adweek*'s Media Plan of the Year for Best Use of Magazines. Goodby's market research indicated that the inserts raised consumers' likelihood to buy HP digital-imaging products by 8 percent. The 2004 television spots generated, according to Goodby and HP, more consumer feedback than either had ever gotten from an ad, and *Adweek* named "You + HP" its Campaign of the Year for 2004. *TV Guide* 's praise went beyond the realm of advertising, claiming that the spot "Picture Book" was the best 60 seconds of television then on the air.

In 2004 HP extended the "You + HP" concept to digital music, partnering with Apple to sell HP-branded iPods and offering iTunes software on its PCs. The iPod, an MP3 player that allowed consumers to mix and match music to suit their personalities, offered HP a further vehicle for connecting the personal-expression ethos to its brand image. A business-to-business campaign called "Change + HP" was likewise launched in 2004, using the company's new cutting-edge image to appeal to information-technology decision makers in the rapidly evolving tech marketplace. "You + HP," along with the umbrella "+ HP" idea and HP's image, continued to evolve through 2005. Whether HP's change in direction was a welcome one remained an open question, however, at least to the company's board of directors. Fiorina was ousted as chief executive officer in February 2005.

FURTHER READING

Anderson, Mae. "Campaign of the Year: Hewlett-Packard." *Adweek,* February 7, 2005.

Bulik, Beth Snyder. "Hewlett-Packard." *Advertising Age,* December 13, 2004.

———. "Kodak Scores with Digital Cameras but Film-Biz Losses Cloud Big Picture." *Advertising Age,* April 25, 2005.

———. "Sony, Kodak Lead U.S. Battle for Share in Digital Cameras." *Advertising Age,* May 31, 2004.

"Campaign of the Year: HP." *Creativity,* December 2003.

Champagne, Christine. "Agency Producer: Josh Reynolds." *Adweek,* January 24, 2005.

Dolliver, Mark. "Creative: Portfolio." *Adweek,* October 20, 2003.

"Goodby, Silverstein & Partners." *Advertising Age,* January 12, 2004.

Granatstein, Lisal. "Goodby, Silverstein & Partners." *Adweek,* June 21, 2004.

"HP 'Francois.'" *Creativity,* April 2005.

Khermouch, Gerry. "Can HP Make Consumers' Hearts Race?" *Business Week Online,* October 2, 2003.

Maddox, Kate. "HP Demonstrates Power of Partnerships." *B to B,* October 25, 2004.

Parpis, Eleftheria. "Creative All-Stars." *Adweek,* January 19, 2004.

Said, Carolyn. "Fiorina: 'Wicked Smart' but Ultimately Unsuccessful." *San Francisco Chronicle,* February 10, 2005.

Wasserman, Todd. "HP Puts More Focus on Digital Cameras." *Brandweek,* September 1, 2003.

Woodward, Sarah. "Francois Vogel." *Shoot,* March 26, 2004.

Mark Lane

Hilton Hotels Corporation

9336 Civic Center Dr.
Beverly Hills, California 90210
USA
Telephone: (310) 278-4321
Fax: (310) 205-7678
Web site: www.hiltonworldwide.com

IT HAPPENS AT THE HILTON CAMPAIGN

OVERVIEW

Ownership of the Hilton Hotel brand had been split apart in 1964. As a result, the hotel chain was controlled by two distinct groups—Hilton Hotel Corporation (HHC), which held the rights to the brand in the United States, and Hilton International Company (HIC, a division of the Ladbroke Group PLC), which owned the brand abroad. Since their breakup, HHC and HIC had maintained separate marketing and public relations efforts. In 1997, however, facing intense competition in both domestic and international markets, the two companies formed the Hilton Alliance, which was committed to creating a single global image for the hotel chain. After changing the Hilton logo, the companies selected advertising agency Bozell Worldwide to produce a branding campaign that would differentiate Hilton from its competitors. The company wanted a unique message to position itself advantageously among the other massive global hotel chains competing for the patronage of business and leisure consumers. The result was the "It Happens at the Hilton" campaign, which debuted on October 5, 1998, and used photographs of celebrities and everyday travelers to "convey the strength of the Hilton name and its association with quality, achievement, innovation, and timeless style," said Robert Dirks, the senior vice president of marketing for HHC.

Hilton allocated a budget of approximately $10 million for the first three months of the campaign, which was comprised mainly of print ads. "It Happens at the Hilton" sought to epitomize the Hilton experience for its audience. Unlike traditional advertising for major hotel chains, which typically focused on the nuts and bolts of the visiting experience—mainly rooms or services—Hilton's campaign used striking photos of past and present celebrities at various Hilton hotels. One spot featured ex-Beatle John Lennon and his wife Yoko Ono during their "Bed-in for Peace" at the Amsterdam Hilton. Political figures Winston Churchill and Nelson Mandela, as well as celebrities Larry King and Naomi Campbell, also appeared in ads bearing the "It Happens at the Hilton" tag line. To ensure that consumers were not alienated by a celebrity-laden campaign, however, Hilton also ran a substantial number of ads that portrayed average Hilton guests, ranging from CEOs and other business people to families on vacation. One print piece, for instance, depicted a family at a Hilton pool. "Relaxation now available in a convenient family size," the copy chirped. The company's goal was straightforward. "We want to show that so many things happen at the Hilton, from weddings to romance, and that Hilton is part of the community," Dirks told *Advertising Age International.* Hilton declared itself pleased with the campaign's result.

HISTORICAL CONTEXT

The Hilton chain had come a long way from its beginning in 1925 when Conrad Hilton built the first hotel to carry his name in Dallas, Texas. By 1998 more than 400 Hilton hotels—ranging from resorts and casinos to airport business hotels—were operating in 50 countries. The company's 1964 decision to spin off its global properties into a separate entity, however, impeded Hilton from developing a consistent worldwide image. After Hilton's international wing was acquired by Trans World Airlines, HHC and HIC agreed not to develop their franchises in the other's zones. Nevertheless, the erstwhile siblings bickered over trademarks.

In the early 1990s HHC had struggled to forge an identity. Pernicious price wars among upper-class hotels led HHC, and its ad agency McCann-Erickson, to craft ads focused more on price and perks than on the chain's own attributes. The result was a frequently chaotic marketing strategy that relied heavily on special promotions, often to the detriment of HHC's bottom line. In an effort to rectify this situation, HHC severed its relationship with McCann in 1992 and hired Daley & Associates to develop a new ad campaign. The resulting "Take Me to the Hilton" effort helped the company overcome some of its difficulties, but HHC was still hampered by its inability to expand in overseas markets. The burgeoning travel market, both domestically and internationally, had generated a wave of consolidations in the industry, as hotel chains teamed up in order to offer broader options to consumers. As an industry insider explained in the January 16, 1995, issue of *Brandweek,* "just to be a domestic brand does not insure long-term visibility." HIC faced similar limitations by virtue of its exclusion from the sizeable U.S. market. Recognizing the importance of presenting a more unified front to its rivals, HHC and HIC linked their advertising, sales, loyalty programs, and development strategies, and then sought to leverage this new alliance into enhanced business opportunities.

TARGET MARKET

According to *Advertising Age International,* "It Happens at the Hilton" strove to appeal to people between the ages of 35 and 50 who were "active achievers among business and leisure groups." It would certainly be a challenge to attract an audience this broad within the confines of a single campaign. To do so, HHC opted to use a diverse array of photographs in the "It Happens at the Hilton" ads in the hope that this multifaceted approach would connect with consumers on various levels. For example, HHC chose to use images of celebrities from different generations at Hilton hotels both to grab people's attention with the famous faces and to reinforce the notion that Hilton had a long and storied history. The use of political icons such as Nelson Mandela and Winston Churchill was intended to lend the campaign a particular *gravitas,* which was calculated to appeal to the elite business travelers Hilton wanted to reach.

At the same time, the images of iconoclast John Lennon and supermodel Naomi Campbell ensured that the campaign would appear neither stuffy nor dated. In fact, the incorporation of celebrities such as these into the branding campaign let Hilton speak to a more status-conscious and upscale group of travelers. "The implied message to Hilton customers is, 'If it happens for these people at Hilton, it can happen for me too,'" Dirks explained. In a period when affluent business and recreational travelers had a slew of hotel options, "It Happens at the Hilton" provided the hotel chain a certain cachet that played well to its more status-oriented guests.

But Hilton was careful not to pursue this more upscale and business-oriented identity at the expense of other travelers. "We wanted consumers to know the hotel is accessible, not just for the rich and famous," Ken Sakoda, a Bozell vice president, said in the October 5, 1998, issue of *Advertising Age.* The company therefore presented a variety of scenes of everyday people enjoying the Hilton's amenities in order to balance the celebrity shots. Bozell also injected humor into these projects, and stressed the pleasure and convenience Hilton could bring to any vacation. In an ad for Hilton's line of resorts, a couple is shown sprawled in lounge chairs on the beach. "Tailored vacations call for a fitting," the tag line declared. By presenting real-life scenarios—such as weddings or stressed-out families in dire need of respite—Hilton made it possible for a whole other sector of consumers to relate to the scenes.

AN INCLUSIVE CAMPAIGN

"It Happens at the Hilton" was praised by South Africa's Commission for Racial Equality for its presentation of prominent black figures, such as Nelson Mandela and Naomi Campbell. Mandela was pictured at a Hilton in London during an African National Congress meeting, while Campbell was captured at the National Italian American Foundation Banquet at a Washington, D.C. Hilton. "It is always good to see black people portrayed in a positive light," a CRE spokesperson told *The Voice.* "However, all this does is emphasize how easy it is to produce a good advertisement and how biased other campaigns can be."

COMPETITION

Hilton's quest to forge a unified brand image occurred while many of its rival upscale hotel chains were striving to do the same. According to the *Wall Street Journal,* hotel occupancy rates in 1998 had reached a four year low because of overbuilding. At the same time, the industry was in the midst of a significant consolidation. Chains such as Marriott and Renaissance merged with each other to help bolster their presence on a national and global scale. The result of these agglomerations was a degree of industry-wide uniformity, as local or regional properties with their distinct characteristics, selling points, or histories, were folded into often generic multinational conglomerates. "If you ever stay in a three- or four-star hotel, they are increasingly offering more or less the same product and levels of comfort," Greg Delaney, one of the creative forces behind "It Happens at the Hilton," told *Marketing Week.* While hotels had once used such features as excellent service or a four-star dining room to differentiate themselves, by the mid-1990s, "these [were] standard in each sector," noted *Marketing Week.* "The only way that hoteliers [could now] stand out [was] through brand building."

One of Hilton's most formidable rivals was the Hyatt Hotels Corporation, which embarked on an updated global branding campaign in 1999. Created by agency Cramer Krasselt, these print ads targeted individual business and leisure travelers, meeting planners, travel agents, and corporate travel planners. While the campaign built upon Hyatt's slogan from a pre-existing campaign, "Feel the Hyatt Touch," it avoided the conventional formula of using service and traveler bonus programs as its focal point. Like Hilton, Hyatt acknowledged that "in the minds of our target audience, the difference between major hotel chains is becoming less and less apparent," a Hyatt spokesperson told *Advertising Age* on October 19, 1998.

Another large hotelier, Holiday Inn Worldwide, had launched its first branding campaign in 1997 to support its Crowne Plaza chain of high-end hotels. This campaign, "Get to Know Us, We'll Get to Know You," used famous "business personalities . . . to give the somewhat stony corporation a relatable face," explained the January 27, 1997, *Brandweek.* With agency Scaros & Casselman, Crowne selected celebrities who reflected the interests of its targeted guests to appear in its ads. For instance, Crowne used Armour Golf CEO Michael Magerman in a television spot that humorously showed hotel staffers so accustomed to Magerman's indoor golfing that they gracefully avoid golf balls flying across lobby floors as a matter of course. "A lot of upscale hotel users' principal hobby is golf," Crowne's marketing vice president told *Brandweek.* "Michael Magerman is an up-and-coming CEO, and, at 34, a prototypical Crowne Plaza user." Other spots depicted various comparable business leaders.

Some of Hilton's other competitors began to institute similar marketing programs as well. Marriott International, which had acquired Renaissance in 1997, consolidated its massive ad account in 1998 in order to better broadcast its message. Promus Hotels Corporation's Doubletree and Wyndham Hotels and Resorts, on the other hand, continued to stress the traditional attributes of pleasant rooms and attentive service, according to the June 28, 1999, issue of *Advertising Age.*

MARKETING STRATEGY

Hilton's challenge was to distinguish its brand from the numerous competing upscale hotel chains. It's first objective was, therefore, to make "It Happens at the Hilton" stand out from other hotel advertising. "There is a lot of hotel advertising out there, but if you take the logo off, they are almost interchangeable," a Bozell executive told *Advertising Age* on October 5, 1998. Using celebrities to represent the brand was essential to this agenda. But this approach was not without its danger. While "celebrity-driven ad campaigns [were] immediate attention-getters" that could break "through the clutter," of other advertising, the *Chicago Tribune* noted, Hilton's effort ran the risk of having consumers confuse its brand with those of other companies the celebrities had endorsed in the past. Alternately, consumers might assume that Hilton was too exclusive, if the likes of Naomi Campbell lodged there. "We had been concerned that the creative concept featuring personalities might not be relevant to everyday guests," Dirks said to *Advertising Age International.* To alleviate this risk, Hilton and Bozell conducted extensive pre-launch testing in key Hilton markets, such as Los Angeles, New York, and London, to ensure that "It Happens at the Hilton" was accessible to its target audience.

Having cleared this hurdle, Hilton's next task was to bring the message of the campaign—that guests should expect a memorable experience when staying at the Hilton—to its chosen audience of elite business and leisure travelers. Print was the predominant medium used because of its ability to hone in on select niches. For instance, since frequent business travelers were a key market, Hilton erected poster versions of the spots at international airports and ran them in in-flight magazines such as *American Way* and *Delta Sky.* To address business people even when they were not on the road, Hilton also advertised in publications including the *Financial Times, Business Week, Time, Newsweek, U.S. News & World Report,* as well as major market newspapers, such as the *Wall Street Journal, USA Today,* and the *New York Times.*

Moreover, Hilton utilized travel magazines so that it could connect with consumers planning leisure travel. Hilton placed ads in *Travel & Leisure* and *Conde Nast Traveler* as well as in family-focused magazines such as *Family Fun* and *Travel & Leisure Family.* Finally, Hilton pitched "It Happens at the Hilton" to meeting planners at large corporations by printing the pieces in meeting planner magazines. There was also a small portion of the campaign devoted to television. For the most part, Hilton would trade rooms for airtime on programs such as *Entertainment Weekly* and broadcasts of the Oscars and Grammys. These short 15-second spots employed the "It Happens at the Hilton" tag line.

The campaign was global in its scope, running on four continents. The first two print pieces broke not only in the United States and Canada, but also in Australia, the United Kingdom, Germany, and various Asian nations. Publications in each country were used, such as the *Frankfurter Allgemeine Zeitung* in Germany. The international focus was imperative if Hilton was to reach the growing market of American business people who traveled frequently, as well as international business travelers around the world. According to a company press release, Hilton wanted the campaign to be seen by more than three-quarters of international business travelers.

OUTCOME

Hilton was delighted with the results of "It Happens at the Hilton." Consumer surveys indicated that the campaign had performed well above expectations in reaching its target audience. Moreover, research revealed that Hilton had successfully negotiated the risks of incorporating famous personalities, according to Hilton's vice president of marketing. Despite the company's concerns, the campaign had remained rooted to the product it touted. Consumers understood that the celebrity photos were used to underscore the unique qualities of the hotel—that things "happened there"—and did not feel put off by them. Hilton continued the campaign into 1999.

The company was so impressed with the effectiveness of "It Happens at the Hilton" that it extended the campaign for internal use. Just as "It Happens at the Hilton" signaled to consumers a new identity for the venerable old hotel, the company inaugurated "Hilton Pride Makes It Happen" to bring this same message to its staff. These posters strove to remind employees that the "new" Hilton was their creation and responsibility and that they should take pride in the hotels where they worked.

FURTHER READING

Cuneo, Alice. "Hilton Touts Some Famous Hotel Goers." *Advertising Age,* October 5, 1998.

Fannin, Rebecca. "Hilton Features Celebrities, Reaches for Everyday Guests." *Advertising Age International,* January 11, 1999.

Goetz, Thomas. "Hotel Occupancy Rates Hit Four Year Low." *Wall Street Journal,* May 14, 1998.

Killgren, Lucy. "Hotel Chains Wake Up to the Power of Branding." *Marketing Week,* January 11, 1999.

Lazarus, George. "Star Power Gets the Lead in New Hilton Campaign." *Chicago Tribune,* September 28, 1998.

Salomon, Alan. "Hilton Hotels: Alison Kal." *Advertising Age,* June 28, 1999.

———. "Hyatt Slates $6 Million for '99 Branding Campaign." *Advertising Age,* October 19, 1998.

Underwood, Elaine. "Hilton versus Hilton." *Brandweek,* January 16, 1995.

———. "$7 Million Crowne Push Taps CEO Power." *Brandweek,* January 27, 1997.

Rebecca Stanfel

Hollywood Entertainment Corporation

9275 SW Peyton Ln.
Wilsonville, Oregon 97070
USA
Telephone: (503) 570-1600
Fax: (503) 570-1680
E-mail: info@hollywoodvideo.com
Web site: www.hollywoodvideo.com

■■■

WELCOME TO HOLLYWOOD CAMPAIGN

OVERVIEW

Hollywood Entertainment Corporation hurtled into 1998 at a screaming expansion pace for its chain of Hollywood Video retail stores—the company planned to open more than 353 new stores in 1998 to bring the total number up to 1,260 by year's end. The decade-old chain of superstores had quickly become the second largest video-rental chain in the nation, and chairman, founder, and CEO Mark J. Wattles believed that Hollywood Video had ample opportunity for growth. "[In 1993] we were a 15 store chain and embarked on a very aggressive store opening schedule." Wattles announced in a prepared statement. "Last week [April 13, 1998] we opened our 1,000th video superstore and we plan on opening our 2,000th within the next three years. With over 20,000 employees, and a very strong management team, we are not only focused on growth, but the continued improvement of our operations, as well."

To position Hollywood Video as the superlative entertainment store, Hollywood Entertainment launched its first major branding campaign in May 1998. Developed by New York-based Cliff Freeman and Partners, an agency known for its creative, cutting-edge work, the "Welcome to Hollywood" campaign consisted of nine television spots and eight radio ads. The radio ads followed the theme "Sixty Second Theater" and provided humorous synopses of popular movie plots. The television ads were set in Hollywood Video stores and featured store employees in amusing behind-the-scenes situations. Wattles discussed the purpose of the campaign—estimated to have cost anywhere from $11 million to $20 million—at the company shareholders' meeting in May 1998. "We want to be a brand so powerful that when you think of movies you think of Hollywood [Video]," he said. President and COO Jeff Yapp agreed. "We want our customers to think of Hollywood Video as their inside connection to Hollywood and the world of entertainment," Yapp said in a prepared statement. "As our mission statement says, 'We are Hollywood. We are entertainment.'"

HISTORICAL CONTEXT

Hollywood Video first opened its doors in 1988 with one store in Portland, Oregon, run by owner Wattles and his wife. From the outset Hollywood Video stores were large, brightly lit with an abundance of neon, and had 50 to 70 television monitors blasting the latest video offers. Employees dressed in red bow ties and cummerbunds. Every detail was designed to mimic the excitement and bright lights of Hollywood. And like Hollywood and the movie industry, Hollywood Video moved quickly and aggressively—only five years after its formation and with a total of 16 stores, the company went public.

With the acquisition of Texas video-rental chain Video Central in 1994, the number of Hollywood Video stores rose to 100, and by 1995 the company was the third largest video-rental chain in the United States. By 1996 Hollywood had assumed the number-two position, and the company reported net income in 1996 of $20.63 million, a surge of 75 percent over net income in 1995, which was $11.79 million. The company had more than 500 stores in 29 states by October of 1996. Wattles told the *Portland Oregonian,* "In the third quarter [of 1996], we averaged better than a new store opening every 36 hours... and in the fourth quarter we plan on averaging over a new store every 24 hours." In 1997 the company opened 356 new stores, and net income continued to rise—in the second quarter of 1997, Hollywood enjoyed an 83 percent increase in profits.

THE PRICE OF FAME

Though Don LaFontaine's voice was familiar to many moviegoers, his face was not, and this may have motivated his acceptance to sit in the small cabinet for multiple takes. Cliff Freeman's executive creative director, Arthur Bijur, told *SHOOT* that voice talents "probably live for the moment that their voice is attached to their face." Tate & Partners' Baker Smith, who directed the commercial, agreed, noting that LaFontaine must have been eager to participate in that ad because "we didn't find out until we were shooting that he is slightly claustrophobic and asthmatic, and here we are shutting him up in a dark little cabinet, and when we opened it up to check on him he would be in there taking hits off his medicine inhaler."

TARGET MARKET

More than 80 percent of households in the United States owned VCRs in the late 1990s, and these households were filled with potential Hollywood Video customers. As a result Hollywood's target audience was quite broad. The company's advertising agency indicated that Hollywood's target market consisted of those aged 18 to 45 as well as suburban families with children. Wattles discussed the company's consumer target in an interview in the *Wall Street Transcript* in 1994 and said, "... when the advertising agencies ask what your demographic profile is, I say, 'Alive.'" Nearly everyone, Wattles elaborated, enjoyed watching movies. "One thing that's nice about our business is our demographic profile. It's so simple. Obviously there are demographic profiles of people who watch more movies than others but the curve is very slight. We're not just a teenage business, or a midlife business, or an X-generation business." To appeal to this wide audience, Hollywood Video stores focused on the one thing all the customers shared—the love of movies. "Our store design, our marketing, and our advertising reflect the name and image of Hollywood," he explained. "We try to create an exciting environment that is movie and/or movie star oriented."

Though Hollywood Video's audience was sizeable, many viewers were growing increasingly distracted by new entertainment technologies and options, such as pay-per-view television programming, digital video disks (DVD), the Internet, and expanded offerings from cable television and direct broadcast satellite. Industry analysts labeled the video-rental market mature, with little growth left. According to a study for the Video Software Rental Association, total revenue from the rental market declined 4.2 percent in 1997. Tom Wolzien, an analyst with Sanford C. Bernstein, pointed to a 1996 poll of 1,000 households with satellite television programming that discovered a 70 percent drop in video rentals. Still, many believed an audience for video rentals remained. Roffman Miller Associates' Marvin Roffman told the *Los Angeles Daily News:* "There were a lot of people on Wall Street that were giving the death knell to the industry... [b]ut it's probably not going to die for a long time. Home video is still a very viable business." Hollywood Video believed this as well, and to continue to attract customers the company implemented many customer-oriented policies, such as lower rental prices, guaranteed availability of popular rentals, and five-day rentals on every video in the store. According to the *Portland Oregonian,* Wattles was not intimidated by new technologies or forecasts of doom; Hollywood Video would, Wattles stated, change with the times and with clientele tastes. "As long as interest in movies continues,... there will be opportunities," Wattles vowed.

COMPETITION

Generating three times as much revenue as the theatre arena, the home video market was extremely lucrative and, as a result, highly competitive. Number-one ranked Blockbuster Inc. (previously Blockbuster Entertainment Corp.), which was three times the size of Hollywood Video, had dominated the field for a decade and at the end of 1997 boasted 4,000 stores in the United States and 6,000 globally. Purchased by entertainment giant Viacom Inc. in 1994, Blockbuster enjoyed a commanding market share of 25 percent at the beginning of 1998. Hollywood, though expanding rapidly, had just fewer than 1,000 stores by Christmas 1997 and a market share of about 5 percent, according to the *Portland Oregonian.* Blockbuster was not invincible, however, and the company struggled in 1996 and 1997 as a result of financial and marketing blunders. Hollywood Video, meanwhile, enjoyed rapid expansion and healthy profits.

Though media reports made much of the competition between Blockbuster and Hollywood, Wattles maintained that he did not view Blockbuster as a rival or an enemy. "[W]hile Blockbuster is certainly the Goliath, I would not describe us as the David at all. We are not out to slay Goliath," Wattles said in the *Wall Street Transcript* in 1994. He referred to Blockbuster as "our friendly competitor" and insisted there was room in the market for both superstore chains. Still, the two appeared to be rivals—Hollywood claimed to have the largest number of titles, offered guaranteed availability of popular releases, and had aggressive pricing and rental strategies. Blockbuster, with a new CEO and renewed focus on video rentals, responded in late 1997 by lowering its prices, extending rental periods, providing incentives for returning rentals early, and offering more new releases. Blockbuster also launched a new advertising campaign in early 1998 with the theme, "Get your movie . . . and go home happy."

Blockbuster and Hollywood Video were the clear leaders in the video-rental market, but both companies had to contend with independent retailers as well as national and regional chains such as third-ranked Video Update Inc. and Suncoast Motion Picture Company. The independents, on the other hand, complained that they could not compete with video giants, which were capable of instituting revenue-sharing deals with movie studios that allowed them to purchase videos at much lower costs and thus offer larger numbers of popular titles—the Independent Video Retailers Group stated that independent stores located within three miles of a Blockbuster store suffered from an 11 percent decline in revenues during the first half of 1998.

MARKETING STRATEGY

By the time Hollywood Video launched its "Welcome to Hollywood" campaign in mid-1998 the company had a strong first quarter under its belt—it had opened 88 new stores and reported revenue of $170 million, a 54 percent jump from the first quarter of 1997. The company also launched a new store design that emulated the allure of Hollywood to a greater degree—the bright lights and monitors were accompanied by Hollywood memorabilia and photos of movie stars. The campaign's ads appeared in major U.S. markets and spotlighted Hollywood Video's new releases, promotions, guarantee policies, and, as Wattles said in the *Portland Oregonian,* "that we love movies. . . . We are Hollywood." Arthur Bijur, Cliff Freeman's executive creative director, explained in *SHOOT* that the campaign was designed to show consumers that Hollywood Video "really gets Hollywood and everything about it, . . . to show that it's more a place which is really all about movies." To accomplish this, Bijur said, the spots focused on things that were uniquely and utterly Hollywood.

"Action" was set in the action/adventure section of a Hollywood Video store. An older cowboy dressed in black attempted to teach two male employees how to throw a fake punch as customers looked on in curiosity. The employee practicing to hit ran into some trouble with the maneuver. The cowboy explained, "That was a good start, but we don't actually want to hit the person." The puncher tried again but was unsuccessful. On the third punch the second employee slumped to the ground as the cowboy exclaimed, "That was so close!" Another television spot, "Don," lampooned movie trailers and featured Don LaFontaine, who actually provided voice-overs for many trailers. In the ad a couple approached the counter with a video and asked the employee to tell them a bit about the movie. The employee knocked on a cabinet underneath the counter and LaFontaine, dressed in a suit, emerged. The employee handed him the tape, and LaFontaine read in his instantly recognizable voice: "From Flesh to Steel. From Blood to Blade. From Man to Mutant. Evil has a new enemy. Justice has a new weapon. And the world . . . has a new hero." LaFontaine then handed the tape back to the employee and crawled back into the cabinet. Cliff Freeman art director Matt Vescovo explained in *SHOOT* that "the whole idea is that Hollywood Video is totally Hollywood, and one of the things we associate with Hollywood is this guy's voice. So what better guy is there to describe a movie to customers than this guy who's an authority and knows everything about every movie and everybody has heard his voice a million times?" Other spots included "Birds," which parodied Alfred Hitchcock's movie of the same name, "Musical," which featured two male employees dancing and singing about the store's five-day rental policy, and "Credits," which spoofed the final credits of a movie.

The "Welcome to Hollywood" campaign also included several radio spots. All followed the "Sixty Second Theater" theme and provided a humorous glimpse into the plots of such popular movies as *Tomorrow Never Dies, As Good As It Gets, Scream 2,* and *Good Will Hunting.* In the ads the announcer began, "Hollywood Video presents Sixty Second Theater, where we try, unsuccessfully, to pack all the action and drama of a two-hour Hollywood production into 60 seconds." A comical take-off of the plot ensued, complete with actors impersonating the celebrity voices. The *Good Will Hunting* spot ended with the announcer stating,

"If this doesn't satisfy your urge to see *Good Will Hunting,* and we can't say we blame you, then rent it today at Hollywood Video, where *Good Will Hunting* is guaranteed to be in stock, or next time it's free."

OUTCOME

The "Welcome to Hollywood" campaign was well received and resulted in numerous honors. Not only did the campaign garner several awards at the 40th annual Clio Awards Festival but the radio portion of the campaign received a gold award at the One Show, and several of the spots were recognized at the national Addy Awards. "Action" was named on *Adweek's* "Best Spots of the Year—1998" list, and the campaign took honors at the 46th International Advertising Festival in Cannes, France. Cliff Freeman was selected as the Agency of the Year by both the Clio Awards and *SHOOT.*

Hollywood Entertainment managed to open about one store per day in 1998, and by mid-1999 there were more than 1,300 Hollywood Video stores in 43 states; Hollywood Video's market share was about 10 percent. For the quarter ended September 30, 1998, Hollywood reported revenue of $184.1 million, a 48 percent increase from the same period in 1997. Same-store sales enjoyed an increase of 7 percent. For the first quarter of 1999 the company reported revenue of $260 million, up 53 percent from the same period in 1998. Same-store sales jumped by 18 percent, and net income climbed 92 percent. In October 1998 Hollywood purchased Reel.com, Inc., a leading Web-based video retailer, thus expanding its distribution channels. As the company's Web site indicated: "The past success of Hollywood Video is apparent and the future is bright. If the Hollywood Video story were a movie, the final frame of this action packed adventure would not read 'The End,' but rather 'To Be Continued . . .'"

FURTHER READING

Garcia, Sandra. "Tales from the Script." *Advertising Age's Creativity,* September 1, 1998, p. 30.

Hill, Jim. "Hollywood Continues its Rapid Expansion." *Portland Oregonian,* May 29, 1997, p. B1.

———. "Hollywood Kicks Off Big Ad Push." *Portland Oregonian,* May 28, 1998, p. C1.

Oberlag, Reginald. "Smith Pokes Fun at Movie Trailers for Hollywood Video." *SHOOT,* August 14, 1998, p. 14.

Mariko Fujinaka

Home Box Office, Inc.

1100 Avenue of the Americas
New York, New York 10036
USA
Telephone: (212) 512-1000
Fax: (212) 512-1000
Web site: www.hbo.com

IT'S NOT T.V. IT'S HBO CAMPAIGN

OVERVIEW

Founded in 1972, Home Box Office (HBO) was the oldest and largest premium pay television channel in the United States. Unlike network television and most other cable channels, which raised revenue by selling advertising spots during programming, HBO relied exclusively on subscribers' monthly fees to generate income. As consumers' entertainment choices multiplied dramatically over the years, HBO strove to construct a distinctive niche for itself and to stand out amid competitors, which included other television channels, movies, home video rentals, and the Internet.

In 1996 HBO launched an innovative $60 million television advertising campaign in an effort to draw attention to itself and to strengthen its brand recognition. The spots, conceived by ad agency BBDO New York, sought to reflect the spirit and the programming of HBO. Instead of previewing upcoming events or providing a traditional "tune-in" message, the "It's Not T.V. It's HBO" campaign attempted to present the viewer with a sample of HBO's programming. The five spots making up the campaign deliberately strove to be humorous, creative, and original.

According to the company, based on surveys prior to and following the launch of the campaign, "It's Not T.V. It's HBO" achieved its goal of increasing the network's brand image and awareness among consumers. Further, the campaign earned praise from the media and advertising industries. "Chimps," the first commercial of the campaign, was awarded the first ever commercial Emmy. In 1997 the "Chimps" spot received a Gold Clio Award in the Television/Cinema category. As the campaign continued, its focus shifted, and the slogan evolved into the network's mantra, setting HBO apart not only from other pay television channels but also from all TV networks. The Cable & Telecommunications Association for Marketing (CTAM) named the campaign its Hall of Fame winner in 2003.

HISTORICAL CONTEXT

In its early days HBO primarily showed Hollywood movies and high-profile sporting events such as boxing. In the mid-1980s, however, HBO began to emphasize original productions, which included critically acclaimed made-for-HBO movies such as *And the Band Played On* and *From the Earth to the Moon,* comedy shows such as *The Larry Sanders Show,* and dramatic series such as *Oz.* The shift toward original programming was fueled in part by the arrival of the VCR, which enabled viewers to rent at their convenience the same Hollywood movies broadcast by HBO. By the mid-1990s the network also offered original documentary films, animation specials, children's and family programming, extensive sporting events and shows, and coverage of contemporary music concerts. At the time of the "It's Not T.V. It's HBO" campaign, 30 percent of HBO's programming was original. By 1997 HBO reached roughly 23 million subscribers, approximately one-fourth of the viewing public. That same year it also won 19 Emmy Awards for its original films and shows, the most ever garnered by a cable television channel.

HBO's programming was recognized for being innovative and daring. The *New York Times* lauded the channel's "willingness to take a chance on unconventional programming and to allow writers and directors to operate with minimal interference." HBO produced movies dealing with such issues as abortion, AIDS, and racism. As a pay television channel independent of advertisers' pressures and demands, HBO had the flexibility for controversial and bold programming. "We're not selling ads," Jeffrey Bewkes, the company's CEO, told *BusinessWeek*. "We're not selling our audience to advertisers. We're selling our programming service to you." HBO's mandate, and the key to its survival and profitability, was to continue to expand its subscriber base.

Like the cable industry as a whole, HBO was subject to "churning," the phenomenon of tremendous fluctuations among subscribers. Each month a huge number of viewers disconnected their HBO service for a variety of reasons. Some signed up for a specific event, such as a high-profile tennis tournament, and then disconnected the next month. Others subscribed to HBO only during the winter months, when they knew they would spend more time indoors, and canceled the service in the spring and summer. Some lost their jobs or suffered other financial hardships, and some disconnected when they moved. Despite the constant drain of viewers, however, an even greater percentage signed up either as first-time or repeat subscribers.

There were other factors that made it challenging for HBO to attract and retain subscribers. Potential customers had a wide array of entertainment choices. Network and cable television, premium cable channels like HBO, Showtime, and the Disney Channel, and video rentals, movie theaters, and even chat rooms on the Internet—all vied for the consumer's entertainment time and dollars. It was in this competitive situation that HBO developed the "It's Not T.V. It's HBO" campaign. The goal was not only to distinguish HBO from its competitors but also to reflect the originality of much of HBO's programming. The commercials, with their quirky humor, compelling plots, and high-tech execution, were intended to encapsulate the strengths of HBO and keep the channel prominent in the consumer's mind.

GOODALL'S ROLE

Jane Goodall agreed to the "Chimps" commercial only when HBO and BBDO New York pledged to film wild chimpanzees, not captured, "entertainment," animals. Despite the fact that she only charged her normal speaking fee, Goodall was criticized for entering the commercial realm. She stated, however, that her goal was to help the plight of chimpanzees through the exposure of the commercial.

TARGET MARKET

With its huge base of subscribers, HBO had a diverse viewing audience. For that reason the "It's Not T.V. It's HBO" campaign did not target a narrow demographic group. HBO hoped to reach all segments of the American consumer market from ages 18 to 49. The image ads conceived by BBDO were considered an ideal means to reach this broad-based target. Because the spots did not focus on one aspect of HBO's programming but instead tried to hone the overall image of the channel, the campaign could appeal to all viewers. "The campaign tries to convey that we are a total entertainment package—that there is something for everyone," said Chris Donlay, HBO's manager of corporate affairs.

"We were not looking for a market share or Nielsen ratings," said Nancy Parmet, HBO's vice president of marketing, who oversaw the "It's Not T.V. It's HBO" campaign. "We were looking to break through the clutter." *USA Today* acknowledged the competitive and multifaceted state of the entertainment industry when it declared that to thrive "HBO must remain top-of-mind with consumers."

COMPETITION

In striving to establish a strong brand identity for HBO, the campaign had to differentiate the channel from its competitors. HBO's most direct competitors were other pay television channels. Although it was by far the most watched pay television station, HBO faced stiff competition from other cable channels. Networks such as Showtime and TNT followed HBO's lead in offering more original programming. "There was a time when HBO's programming was the only thing worth watching on cable, but that's not the case anymore," a television industry analyst told the *New York Times*.

HBO's long-term success involved more than simply staying afloat in the premium channel television industry. The channel was also competing against different types of entertainment sources. HBO felt that it could not compare itself only to other TV channels. It had to get people's attention. In an era in which the average person could choose to watch a sitcom on network television, tune in to CNN on a basic cable package, rent a movie from a local video store, drive to a nearby theater to see the latest Hollywood film, or pay for HBO's movies and shows, the image ads were intended to equate HBO with entertainment. According to Parmet, "The ads needed to be cutting edge. We wanted to make the kinds of ads that people would talk about the next day at work."

MARKETING STRATEGY

HBO gave BBDO New York the project of creating a memorable campaign. After HBO briefed the ad agency on its specific needs and concerns, BBDO took over the creative aspects of the campaign. In a brainstorming session, Michael Patti, the vice chairman and executive creative director of BBDO, and Don Schneider, the agency's senior creative director, hit upon a striking concept. The two envisioned a commercial in which a parrot would recite famous movie lines because it saw into a neighboring apartment, where a television was tuned to HBO. The idea quickly evolved into the award-winning spot featuring lip-synching chimpanzees steeped in movie lingo.

The 1996 spot, titled "Chimps," featured renowned primatologist Jane Goodall and a group of wild chimpanzees in the Gombe preserve in Africa. Frame-by-frame animation made it appear as though the chimps were actually speaking famous lines from classic Hollywood movies. The premise of the spot was the powerful impact HBO exerted on its viewers. The commercial opened with a proud chimp uttering lines spoken by Marlon Brando in *The Godfather*: "He never could have outfoxed Santino. But I didn't know until this day that it was Barzini all along." Another chimp replied with lines from *Forrest Gump*: "Mama says that stupid is as stupid does." As a third chimp tossed a stick to the ground, he repeated a line from *Network*: "I'm mad as hell and I'm not going to take it anymore." A father chimp spoke Darth Vader's well-known line from *Star Wars*—"The force is with you, young Skywalker"—as he patted a small chimp on the head. After a group of chimps chanted, "Toga! Toga! Toga! Toga!..." from *Animal House*, the camera panned to a bewildered Goodall writing in her journal. Her voice-over said, "September 19: Their inexplicable behavior continues." A chimp then bellowed, "Yo, Adrian, I did it," a line from *Rocky*. The camera cut back to Goodall's cabin, where her television was tuned to HBO, and she continued, "Got to go now. *Braveheart* is on." A black screen followed with a graphic and the campaign's tagline, "It's Not T.V. It's HBO."

Producing the spot proved to be quite a challenge, however. The chimpanzees were filmed at their feeding sites in the Gombe preserve. Frame-by-frame animation was then used to create the illusion that the animals were reciting movie lines. Sherri Margulies, a film editor who worked on the spot, told *Shoot* that, while other commercials had used similar effects, "the elaborate attention to detail... on this spot [was] completely unique." All told, the special effects took approximately 20 to 30 hours per chimp, requiring the ad agency to work around the clock for a month.

In 1997 HBO followed "Chimps" with four new television spots, each intended to elevate the HBO brand. Using tongue-in-cheek humor, the spots attempted to convey the uniqueness of HBO's programming. In "Haircuts" the men of an idealized American small town sported bizarre, patterned haircuts. It turned out that Carl, the town barber, had become engrossed in HBO's programming as he cut his customers' hair, the result being freakish haircuts. In another spot, "Roach Motel," an enthusiastic pest exterminator was unable to rid a home of its roaches by using sprays or bombs. He succeeded only by luring the cockroaches into a roach "motel" with a neon sign that advertised "Free HBO." The campaign's ironic wit continued in a spot featuring a sadistic repairman who tormented an entire town by plugging in and unplugging their cable in the midst of a captivating HBO program. A final commercial, "Glee Club," related the tale of a disgruntled neighbor who gave the local barbershop quartet free HBO in the hope of distracting them from practicing at all hours.

In order to reach the maximum number of potential viewers, HBO aired the commercials during its own programming, on other cable channels, and, most notably, on network television. All five spots ran during prime-time network shows, including top-rated programs such as the 1997 World Series, *Seinfeld, Chicago Hope,* and *ER*. The network commercials were intended to reach both current HBO subscribers and those who had either never subscribed or had allowed their subscription to lapse. HBO hoped that the commercials would remind current subscribers of the quality and value of the channel's programming, while at the same time reaching millions of other viewers who had not signed up for HBO. "We wanted to inform nonsubscribers of what they are missing," said Parmet.

In 1998 the network continued the campaign with two new spots, including one that debuted during a *Monday Night Football* game. HBO also reported that the spots would be shown on as many as 20 other cable networks. Like the original spots, the new commercials relied on humor and high production values to assure that they would stand out. One spot, "Guardian Angel," showed a person hit by a falling piano when his guardian angel was distracted by a television in a store window. The mishap was explained by the campaign's tagline, "It's not T.V. It's HBO." The second spot starred actor

George C. Scott serving as the general of an army of germs fighting for control of a television remote. The campaign's focus shifted in 1999 from the original brand strategy. Although its emphasis remained on the central theme, "It's Not T.V. It's HBO," the advertising spots became focused on marketing specific HBO programming.

OUTCOME

HBO pronounced the "It's Not T.V. It's HBO" campaign an unequivocal success. In the company's estimation, the campaign achieved its primary goal of elevating the brand's image in the market. Extensive precampaign and postcampaign surveys indicated that the commercials had made viewers more aware of the HBO brand. According to the December 8, 1997, edition of *USA Today,* HBO's membership increased from 21.1 million in 1996 to 22.7 million in 1997. But HBO stressed that it was difficult to correlate the number of subscribers with its high-profile ad campaign because of the variety of factors that influenced fluctuations in membership. For 25 years HBO had seen the number of its subscribers increase each year.

The media and the advertising industry responded positively to the spots. On December 9, 1996, *USA Today* heralded the campaign as one of the "rare knockouts" in advertising. Trade publications such as *Adweek* and *Shoot* extolled the technical wizardry of the commercials. "Certainly there is something to be gained for an entertainment provider merely by being entertaining," declared the November 4, 1996, *Advertising Age.* In September 1997 "Chimps" received the first ever Emmy Award for a commercial. It beat out other well-liked campaigns, such as those by Nike and Levi's, to be named the best commercial of the year. Also in 1997 the "Chimps" spot received a Gold Clio Award. The Clios were international advertising awards presented annually in recognition of creative excellence and innovation in advertising.

Viewers also responded well to the campaign. *USA Today* 's Ad Track, a poll measuring the popularity and effectiveness of national campaigns, revealed that consumers consistently liked the HBO spots, often ranking them among the 10 best commercials. According to the newspaper, "the spots were especially effective with consumers aged 18–24." Larry Gerbrandt, a senior analyst at Paul Kagan, told *USA Today* on December 8, 1997, that "the ads worked well for HBO. The name HBO is practically synonymous with pay TV."

Yet the campaign's positive impact on HBO's subscriber figures was less clear. Although 33 percent of respondents in the December 29, 1997, Ad Track survey declared that they liked the HBO campaign "a lot," only 20 percent thought that the campaign was "very effective." In a similar vein, *Advertising Age* criticized the campaign for not providing enough information about HBO's actual programming.

"Chimps" in particular generated a great deal of controversy. Many journalists were outraged that the basic premise of the spot was false. Goodall did not watch HBO; in fact, the pay channel was not available in the remote region of Africa where she lived. The spot drew more criticism when it was learned that the voice attributed to Goodall was not hers. HBO, however, felt the media were taking the commercial far too seriously, and the company itself was pleased with the results of its efforts.

In 1998 the campaign was expanded to include print, radio, and direct mail. As the campaign morphed from a branding strategy for the network into its operating mantra in 1999, the marketing also shifted to specific programming. According to network executives, the strategy evolved based on the success of two of its shows—*The Sopranos* and *Sex and the City*—as well as of original movies that the network was producing and sporting events that it aired. The new marketing effort resulted in HBO being named Cable Marketer of the Year in 2000 by *Advertising Age.* The original "It's Not T.V. It's HBO" campaign was named to the Cable & Telecommunications Association for Marketing (CTAM) Hall of Fame in 2003, which, according to the organization, honored the "finest and most influential campaigns in the history of cable."

FURTHER READING

Applebaum, Simon. "Hall of Fame. (The 2003 CTAM Hall of Fame Winner Goes to HBO for Its 'It's Not TV. It's HBO' Campaign)." *Multichannel News,* July 21, 2003.

Berger, Warren. "At 25, Excellence and Big Budgets for a Late Bloomer." *New York Times,* November 9, 1997.

Bernstein, Paula. "Branding Bolsters Expectations. (HBO at 30)." *Variety,* November 4, 2002.

Eberle, Ed. "Sherri Margulies: Editor Explains Assembling HBO's 'Chimps.'" *Shoot,* September 19, 1997.

Enrico, Dottie. "HBO Ads Tickle Primal Funny Bone." *USA Today,* January 13, 1997.

Friedman, Wane. "HBO Finds Humor in Roaches." *USA Today,* December 8, 1997.

———. "HBO; Original Programming Choices Drive Viral Marketing Strategies that Include Word-of-Mouth, Touring Caravans, Parties in Major Markets, and Massive Direct Marketing Campaigns for HBO." *Advertising Age,* November 27, 2000.

Garfield, Bob. "Chimps Are Champs at Ad Entertainment." *Advertising Age,* November 4, 1996.

Hogan, Monica. "HBO Makes Heavy Cable Buy for New Spots." *Multichannel News,* October 26, 1998.

Stevens, Elizabeth Lesly. "Call It Home Buzz Office." *BusinessWeek,* December 8, 1997, pp. 77–78.

Wells, Melanie. "The Good, The Bad, The Ugly of 1996." *USA Today,* December 9, 1996.

Rebecca Stanfel
Rayna Bailey

Honda Motor Company

2-1-1 Minami-Aoyama
Minato-ku
Tokyo, 107-8556
Japan
Telephone: 81 3 34231111
Fax: 81 3 54121515
Web site: www.world.honda.com

■■■

THE POWER OF DREAMS CAMPAIGN

OVERVIEW

In 2002 Honda Motor Company was the number-three Japanese automobile manufacturer in the world, behind Toyota and Nissan. While Honda's automobile sales in Japan and the United States were considered strong, sales in the United Kingdom and mainland Europe were thought to be weak, even though automobile production in the United Kingdom had been ongoing for a decade. Further, Honda vehicle sales had been declining in these regions since 1998. In response to these problems Honda hired ad agency Wieden+Kennedy's London office to create an advertising campaign that would directly address the issues.

"The Power of Dreams," released in 2002, was an omnipresent campaign in the United Kingdom and beyond, using television, direct mail, radio, posters, press, interactive television, cinema, magazines, motor shows, press launches, dealerships, postcards, beermats (coasters), and even traffic cones. It built upon Honda's company slogan, "Yume No Chikara," which was first endorsed in the 1940s by the company's founder, Soichiro Honda. Translated into English, it meant to "see" one's dreams. Wieden+Kennedy used this phrase as the basis of its question to consumers: "Do you believe in the power of dreams?" The global campaign, which centered on this tagline, included print and television components starring ASIMO, a humanoid robot developed by Honda. While the ASIMO ads gained widespread recognition, the 2003 television commercial called "Cog" was clearly a pinnacle of the campaign. In a single take with no special effects, more than 85 individual parts of the new Accord interacted in a complicated chain reaction. The spot won 37 advertising awards.

Honda considered "The Power of Dreams" an advertising success. Worldwide sales of Honda vehicles rose dramatically from 2002 through 2005, from 2.6 million units per year to 3.2 million units per year. In the United Kingdom sales improved by 28 percent. In Europe sales in 2002 increased from 170,000 to 196,000, which rose to 217,000 in 2003. The campaign also won IPA Advertising Effectiveness awards, British Television Advertising awards, and even a 2003 Gold Lion at the Cannes International Advertising Festival.

HISTORICAL CONTEXT

In April 1964 Honda spent $300,000 to sponsor the Academy Awards, becoming the first foreign corporate sponsor in the event's history. With the tagline "You Meet the Nicest People on a Honda," the Honda advertising campaign was a success, becoming one of the best-remembered advertising campaigns in the company's history. Nevertheless, although the campaign promoted

Honda's motorcycles well, it did little to sell Honda vehicles. The reality was that Honda was better known for its motorcycles than it was for its cars. This long remained the case in most of the countries where Hondas were sold. In Japan, where big-splash promotional efforts for Honda's cars were common, the problem was not so severe. The 1981 campaign to promote Honda's model the City, for one, was omnipresent in Japan, incorporating large-scale TV, radio, and print advertising. There was even a variety of City novelty goods for sale and a specialty magazine called *City Press.*

Meanwhile, in the United Kingdom, Honda automobile production had yet to begin. Honda cars had been available there as imports, but not enough units were ordered to establish a presence. Further, the prices of imported cars could not compete with that of vehicles manufactured within the country. Thus, at the time, any sales push in the area focused on Honda motorbikes. In 1992, when Honda automobile production began in the United Kingdom, the shift toward promoting Honda automobiles there began, albeit slowly. But the potential market for the new manufacturing plant was huge: located in Swindon, England, it was responsible for producing vehicles well beyond the United Kingdom, including mainland Europe, the Middle East, and Africa. As such, Honda felt the need to begin a major campaign within the United Kingdom. Eventually it happened.

"The Power of Dreams" replaced the 1999 global tagline "Do You Have a Honda?" This earlier campaign employed print, radio, and television, and portrayed the dreams of Honda's founder, Soichiro Honda, who envisioned providing the world with all the possible means of travel. Soichiro Honda himself had repaired and created bicycles and motorcycles as well as both road cars and racing vehicles. The "Do You Have a Honda?" ads thus incorporated images of all of these means of transportation as well as more creative means, including a hot-air balloon and a cable car. Although the "Do You Have a Honda?" ads spread worldwide, the United Kingdom was barely affected by the campaign. From 1998 to 1999 Honda automobile sales in Europe dropped from 240,000 to 235,000. The decline continued through 2002. In the United Kingdom, Honda auto sales began to drop in 2000.

In 2002 "Do You Have a Honda?" was replaced with the campaign "The Power of Dreams." Although the tagline was part of a larger global focus, the campaign, under the leadership of ad agency Wieden+Kennedy in London, centered on promotional efforts within the United Kingdom.

WERE THOSE BALLOONS REALLY COMING OUT OF THEIR EARS?

Honda wanted real balloons to inflate from actors' ears in its 2005 "Dreams/Yume No Chikara" television commercial. To achieve this effect, devices were placed inside the ears; each had a small tube that was pulled behind the ear and taped to the actor's back. As the actors were playing their roles, the devices popped out, and the balloons (representing ideas considered by the actors) filled with air.

TARGET MARKET

"The Power of Dreams" targeted a large and diverse audience. While Honda wished to attract younger buyers, they were not the company's only focus. With a wide range of car models, from the lower-priced Civic to the higher-end Accord, Honda could potentially appeal to drivers within all age groups and socioeconomic statuses. All potential new buyers, whatever their age, represented Honda's target market. Thus, of the many different media that "The Power of Dreams" employed, television advertising, with its ability to reach a wide audience, was expected to be the most effective. Further, by portraying Hondas as hip and fun, the commercials appealed to a broad range of potential buyers.

Honda's new campaign mainly focused on raising public awareness of its cars—especially in Europe and the United Kingdom, where Honda was largely associated with motorcycles—and, in particular, getting new customers to visit Honda showrooms. There was also an emphasis on pleasing return customers. The company wished to improve communications with Honda owners and thus make them feel good about their choice of Honda; this in turn would convince them to buy a Honda the next time around.

COMPETITION

Worldwide, Honda was largely associated with its motorbikes. Toyota Motor Corp., on the other hand, was synonymous with Japanese automobiles. Japan's number one carmaker, Toyota brought in huge revenue from around the globe. While Honda was spending millions promoting its campaign "The Power of Dreams," Toyota was enjoying incredible revenue increases: from $129 billion in 2003, to $154 billion in 2004, to $173 billion in 2005. The sales were generally connected to Toyota's solid reputation for quality and value. To enhance this reputation, Toyota advertisements around the globe had been consistently reminding customers of the economical excellence of Toyota cars. At the same time another message had been spread: Toyota's concern for the environment (and for the price customers were paying for gasoline). In 2003 Toyota began a global campaign for its hybrid automobile, the Prius, which had been released in Japan in 1997. Toyota claimed that in 2003 Prius grabbed 90 percent of the worldwide hybrid-car market. Among its top competitors in the category was Honda, which had created two hybrid automobiles of its own: the Insight (developed in 2001) and the Civic Hybrid (developed in 2003).

In 2002 Japan's second-largest automaker, Nissan Motor Company ran a global marketing campaign of its own, titled "Shift." With the tagline "Shift can change a person, a life, the world, or it can simply change the way you move through it," it was Nissan's first-ever global campaign. Its launch coincided with the reintroduction of the popular Nissan Z, a sports car that had been sold from 1969 through 1996. When the Z was revived as the 350Z for model year 2003, those who had not preordered the vehicle had a difficult time getting one. To further confirm the car's success, the 350Z was named one of *Car and Driver*'s "Ten Best" for 2003. Nissan's revenue climbed dramatically between 2002 and 2004. From 2002 to 2003 revenue increased from $47 billion to $57 billion. By 2003 the number had jumped to $70 billion.

While Honda's 2003 fiscal revenue of $66 billion reflected an 8.6 percent increase from the year prior, its revenue from auto sales was not quite enough to take over Nissan's number two spot in Japanese auto sales. Honda's 2003 automobile revenue was $54 billion, just below that of Nissan. But sales continued to rise during its "The Power of Dreams" campaign, bringing in $78 billion in revenue in fiscal 2004 and $81 billion in fiscal 2005.

MARKETING STRATEGY

In 2002 Honda wished to increase worldwide familiarity with its automobiles, especially within the European market. The use of ad agency Wieden+Kennedy in London confirmed a strong focus on the United Kingdom in particular. Before the launch of "The Power of Dreams," Honda thought that its name was too often connected to its motorcycles only, especially in Europe and the United Kingdom. Honda wanted to be equally known for its automobiles. Thus, Honda and Wieden+Kennedy attempted to convey that it was in fact a distinctively innovative car company. As a first step in doing so, Wieden+Kennedy developed "The Book of Dreams." Colorful and eclectic, it was part scrapbook, part information packet. It was fun, and it helped to illustrate Honda's identity, which the agency dubbed "Honda-ness." The book was used as a springboard for many of the campaign's subsequent ads. Next Honda formed "The Dream Factory," a committee with the task of maintaining a consistent philosophy while placing the campaign everywhere, including on television, in the mail, on posters, in the press, cinema, and magazines, and at motor shows.

In its print ads Honda depicted simple, everyday objects: a perfume bottle with the Honda name; a banana; a pencil; a stamp. Other ads displayed parts of the Honda vehicle, such as a stick shift, tires, and a muffler. There was a traffic cone draped in leopard fur and a brightly painted birdhouse. More complicated advertisements also were used: in one, a Honda CR-V was shown driving on a road lined with trees growing traffic lights on their branches, and in another the car drove past traffic-cone mountains. The television spots were equally diverse and interesting. Children played on a colorful jungle-gym model of a Honda in "Play." Honda Jazz vehicles were seen driving through cartoon worlds in "Pecking Order," "Seats," and "Bus Lane."

In the much-acclaimed TV spot "Cog," more than 85 individual parts of the new Accord interacted in a highly complicated chain reaction, ending with a voice-over that asked, "Isn't it nice when things just work?" The television spot was expensive to produce. The final 10 seconds used the voice of Garrison Keillor, voice of Public Radio's program *Prairie Home Companion.* In addition, the spot, which reportedly used no special effects, required the film crew to shoot it 606 times to get it right. At two minutes in length, air time for the complete commercial was extremely costly. The spot, first run during the Brazilian Grand Prix in April 2003, was met with awe.

The eclectic advertisements, still toting the tagline "The Power of Dreams," continued in 2005. "Dreams/ Yume No Chikara," broadcast that year, showed Tokyo business leaders discussing different ideas. The ideas came out of their ears as real balloons, inflating, deflating, popping, or flying away. One balloon formed perfectly, representing a dream becoming reality. The campaign's radio commercials included "Doodle," "Big Grin," and "Oblonger."

"The Power of Dreams" also featured ASIMO, Honda's ever-evolving humanoid robot. Honda presented its first humanoid robot in 1986, under the name EO. By 2000 it had evolved into ASIMO, whose legs and arms moved like a human's. This was an incredible feat in the field of robotics. ASIMO first appeared in a TV spot in an earlier campaign in 2002. That year, when "The Power of Dreams" took over as the new tagline, the robot became even more omnipresent, both in Honda ads and in other contexts. ASIMO hosted many Honda promotional events; the robot rang the opening bell at the New York Stock Exchange's 25th anniversary in 2002 and shook hands with the Belgian prime minister in 2005. Such public appearances contributed to the widespread recognition and success of the ASIMO global branding ads in "The Power of Dreams" campaign. In 2005 Honda released "Run," a global corporate TV spot featuring ASIMO. The commercial gained international renown for its clever portrayal of a "race" in an airport between the robot and an elderly Japanese businessman. The global campaign also released two variations of posters titled "ASIMO and a Boy," set in the same airport, substituting the businessman with a young boy. In the U.K. version of the campaign, however, ASIMO played a more minor role.

OUTCOME

"The Power of Dreams" was widely recognized within the industry, receiving IPA Advertising Effectiveness awards; AD&D awards for Radio Advertising; British Television Advertising awards; and Advertising Creative Circle awards. The television spot "Sense," portraying a collection of daily situations in which power sources "sensed" when they needed to turn on or shut down (to promote Honda's Integrated Motor Assist Engine), gained 13 awards and recognitions. "Cog" brought in 37, including the highly prestigious Gold Lion (Cars category) at the International Advertising Festival in Cannes, France, in 2003. In addition to advertising awards, "Cog" (also known as the "Rube Goldberg ad," after the legendary American cartoonist and sculptor) brought Honda the status of creating an advertising phenomenon. Like Wendy's "Where's the Beef?" campaign of the 1980s, "Cog" was regarded as advertising legend, becoming one of the most talked-about television commercials in advertising history.

The "Power of Dreams" also met with monetary success. From the start of the campaign through 2005, Honda's unit auto sales worldwide increased from 2.6 million units to 3.2 million units per year. In the United Kingdom sales improved by 28 percent. Later in the campaign, from 2004 through 2005, unit sales of Hondas in Asia increased by 50 percent. Other positive results were more subtle: Honda recognition increased, including acknowledgement of its advertising as being "cool." Media coverage was intensive, and free media value was generated (for instance, CNN ran two features on the campaign, and the Discovery Channel ran a documentary on it). Showroom visits rose, and even sales of used Hondas increased. Internally, there were also benefits. In the United Kingdom, Honda was included in the *Sunday Times* newspaper's "Best Companies to Work for" list for the first time ever in 2003; it was number 18. By 2004 the company had moved up to number 16. Staff turnover was low, and 89 percent of workers said that they were proud to work for Honda. The goal of reaching 100,000 annual unit sales in the United Kingdom by 2005 was reached.

FURTHER READING

"Advertising Imitates Art." *Sunday Telegraph* (London), April 20, 2003.

Bold, Ben. "Honda Takes 'Power of Dreams' into Mail." *Marketing,* January 5, 2005.

Cookson, Clive. "Robots Show What's Afoot in Cornell Lab." *Financial Times* (London), February 18, 2005.

Elliott, Stuart. "Wieden Is Top Winner in Awards for TV Work." *New York Times,* June 18, 2004.

"Kim Papworth and Tony Davidson, Creative Directors, Wieden & Kennedy." *Financial Times* (London), November 9, 2004.

Le, Thuy-Doan. "Can-Do-Robot, at Your Service." *Sacramento Bee,* April 1, 2005.

Manning, Jeff. "Mechanical Marvel." *Portland Oregonian,* April 29, 2003.

"Market Review—Beemers Hit the Buffers." *Motor Industry Magazine,* July 2004.

Mills, Dominic. "Ad of the Week." *Daily Telegraph* (London), April 9, 2002.

Parshotam, Arthur. "Direct Choice: Honda Welcome Pack." *Marketing,* February 16, 2005.

"Pick of the Week: Honda." *Campaign,* April 29, 2005.

"Private View." *Campaign,* March 4, 2005.

"Process: Honda—Yume No Chikara." *Creative Review,* June 2, 2005.

"Robots Welcome the Expo Visitors." *Journal of Japanese Trade & Industry,* March 1, 2005.

"Wieden and Kennedy Create Honda Ad." *Marketing Week,* April 14, 2005.

Candice L. Mancini

Honda UK

470 London Rd.
Slough, Berkshire SL3 8QY
United Kingdom
Telephone: 44 845 2008000
Web site: www.honda.uk

■■■

GRRR CAMPAIGN

OVERVIEW

One of the world's best-known carmakers, the Honda Motor Company, Ltd., had popularized economy and midsize cars for decades. In 2003 the company struck out in a new direction when it began selling in the United Kingdom a version of its popular Accord powered by a newly designed diesel engine. The advertising campaign to promote the diesel engine (the Accord also came in a standard gasoline-engine model) was even bolder than the product itself. Titled "Grrr," it was a masterpiece of counterintuitive thinking and presentation.

The campaign was designed by Wieden+Kennedy London and consisted of a television and cinema spot backed by radio, print, and Internet advertisements. It broke on September 24, 2004, in cinemas in the United Kingdom. The spot featured a retro 1960s neopsychedelic look, complete with flying diesel engines, a rainbow, animated bunnies, and a folk song sung by radio humorist Garrison Keillor. The song also backed the radio commercial. The point of the spot was to show that a new, modified diesel engine had been designed by Honda, one that was cleaner and less noisy.

The "Grrr" campaign and the television spot in particular won numerous awards in the United Kingdom, the United States, and elsewhere. The television spot won the Epica D'Or at the Epica Awards (which recognized creativity in European advertising); four gold British Television Advertising Awards, including TV Commercial of the Year (2004); the Grand Prize at the ANDY Awards in New York; two gold and eight silver D&AD (Design and Art Direction) awards, including the first D&AD gold for music; Best in Show at the One Show Awards; a Titanium Lion (for the radio spot) and the Grand Prix at the International Advertising Festival in Cannes, France; and a Gold Clio and the Grand Clio.

HISTORICAL CONTEXT

While the Japanese automobile maker Honda enjoyed modest success in the United Kingdom, innovation was always the watchword. In the early twenty-first century that theme intersected with British and European drivers' growing preference for diesel-powered over regular gasoline-engine autos. For Honda and its chief designer, Kenichi Nagahiro, the diesel engine was a new adventure. Although Honda had been producing hybrid cars (which used an internal combustion engine with an electric motor) since 2001, the company had yet to produce a diesel engine, and Nagahiro professed to despise them. (Honda had sold diesel-powered Civics, but the engine was produced by Isuzu.) The diesel market, however, was growing fast in Europe and the United Kingdom in the early years of the twenty-first century, and Honda, a company noted for the high quality of its engines, had no choice but to follow the trend or lose customers.

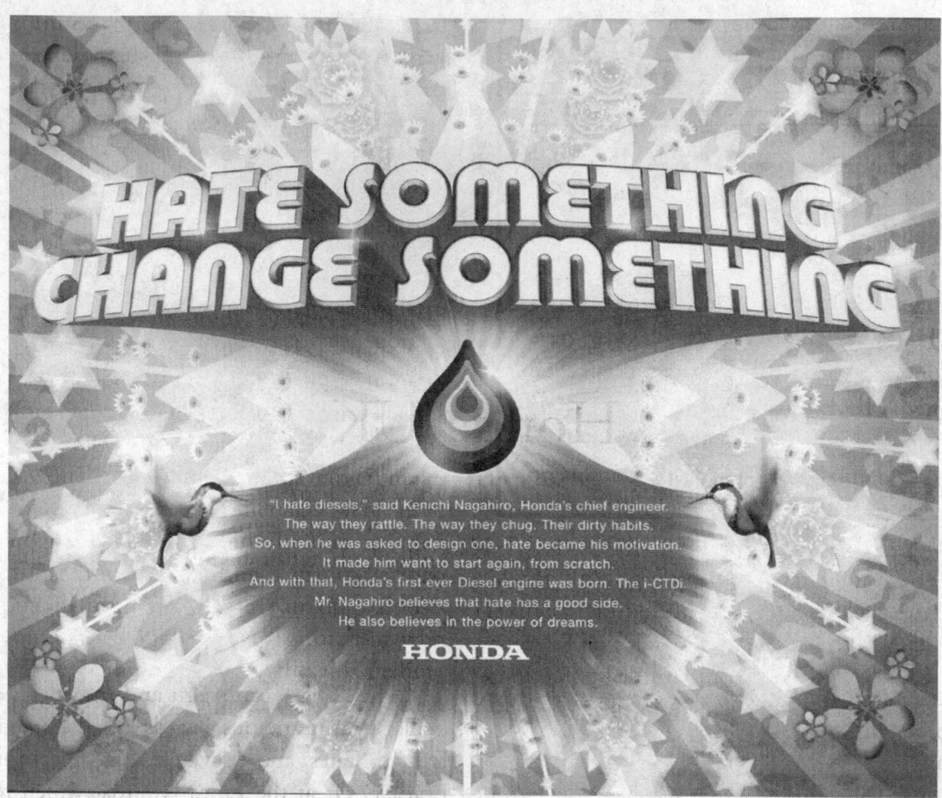

A still from Honda's "Grrr" campaign. IMAGE COURTESY OF THE ADVERTISING ARCHIVE LTD. REPRODUCED BY PERMISSION.

Nagahiro's dislike of the diesel engine was in fact one of the motivating forces behind his desire to make a quieter, cleaner one. The model he and his team came up with, the 2.2i CTDi, was placed in the Accord in 2003 (and later in the CR-V and the FR-V, Honda's compact multipurpose vehicle) for distribution throughout the United Kingdom, Ireland, and the more diesel-conscious European market. In a January 2004 article for the London newspaper the *Sun,* Ken Gibson wrote that in 2003 diesel-powered automobile sales in the United Kingdom "increased to 710,000—29 percent of the market—with diesel converts driving everything from superminis to executive cars."

The Accord itself had been reintroduced to consumers in the United Kingdom and Europe with Honda's previous advertising campaign, "Cog." This Rube Goldbergesque television spot, which followed a chain reaction of Accord parts, beginning with ball bearings and including tires that roll uphill, was itself critically acclaimed.

TARGET MARKET

The "Grrr" campaign focused on the increasing number of diesel auto drivers in the United Kingdom as well as on those willing to make the switch to a diesel-powered auto. In continental Europe the percentage of diesel drivers was even higher, with some pockets reaching as high as 70 percent. The television—and to a lesser extent radio—spots were also aimed at aging baby boomers, who presumably had families and for whom the TV spots' look and sound would have a humorously nostalgic feel. They were also geared toward a younger generation with families and disposable income, but who would view the spots as retro. The Accord, into which the 2.2i CTDi diesel engine was originally placed, was considered a family car, as was the popular CR-V sport-utility vehicle, the second Honda to be powered by the 2.2i CTDi.

COMPETITION

In addition to competing in the United Kingdom and throughout Europe with other Japanese carmakers, Honda was considered on a par with the low-end BMW models and the high-end Volkswagens. But as more than one car critic noted, the diesel engine took Honda to a higher level. In the *Sun,* Gibson wrote, "The Honda Accord is everything good about diesel power—the only surprise is that it took Honda so long to develop

THE DIESEL ENGINE

The diesel engine got its name from its inventor, Rudolf Diesel (1858–1913), who received a patent for the engine in 1893. The prototypes for his engine ran on coal dust, and he even produced a demonstration model in the 1890s that was fueled by peanut oil. By 1897 Diesel had built an engine that ran at a theoretical 75 percent efficiency.

The main difference between a diesel engine and a gasoline engine was that a spark was not required in a diesel (hence, no spark plugs). In the early diesel models air compression within the engine's cylinders caused the fuel combustion. The early diesels were large and were used only in heavy machinery, ships, and trains. In the 1920s an injection-pump design was implemented in the diesel engine. This advance was responsible for smaller engines, making them viable for automobiles. The first auto manufacturer to employ a diesel engine was Mercedes Benz in the 1930s. By the end of the twentieth century more and more drivers were recognizing the efficiency of the diesel, which in turn led to more innovations on the engine.

the model . . . [T]he 2.2 litre [engine] in the Accord shows they have been fine tuning an exceptional engine that sets new levels of excellence. In fact the Honda power unit is so good only top-of-the-range executive diesels from Mercedes, BMW and Audi can compete with it." Edward Stephens of the *Birmingham Evening Mail* declared the new vehicle "a diesel that performs just like a petrol engine in terms of acceleration, quietness and responsiveness . . . [T]his diesel is certainly one of the best—if not the best—in its class."

Nevertheless, Honda started out well behind other carmakers in the race to attract diesel car buyers in the United Kingdom and Europe. Audi had introduced its Avant in 1998 with support from a campaign that included a print ad that depicted a crushed pink rabbit with a drum on a road (a reference to battery manufacturer Energizer's well-known "Energizer Bunny" commercials). The ad read: "Audi TDi. Keeps on going. No other diesel looks like it or lasts like it." Volkswagen introduced its diesel Passat soon afterward, while BMW had preceded both.

MARKETING STRATEGY

A number of factors contributed to the style and message of the "Grrr" campaign and of the television spot in particular. These included chief engineer Nagahiro's disdain for diesel engines, the whimsy of the "Cog" campaign, and competitor Audi's 2003 campaign that featured animation in its television spot (though the spot advertised a gasoline-powered auto). The difference with "Grrr" was that Wieden+Kennedy took what some media critics described as a counterintuitive route.

The "Grrr" spot, with its 1960s retro look and feel, invoked that decade's idealism, but with a twist. The message, as filtered through Nagahiro's experience, was that hate could be a catalyst for change. In a June 2005 article in *Adweek* Mae Anderson quoted Sean Thompson, a senior copywriter for Wieden+Kennedy, who admitted, "When we were asked to do an ad for launching the new diesel engine, we got really interested in this hate thing, how hate can push you forward. In tandem with that, we started thinking about a song, because a song is happy—so what if we wrote a song of hate?" In fact, throughout the animated spot the word "hate" was spelled out numerous times as visual reinforcement while smoky, dark diesel engines flew through the air and assorted feel-good animals such as bunnies, birds, and fish gamboled about. Backing this was a song sung by radio personality Garrison Keillor, who crooned: "Can hate be good? / Can hate be great? / Can hate be good? / Can hate be great? / . . . Hate something / Change something / Make something better . . ." By the end of the spot the old, dirty diesel had been transformed into a thing of beauty: a quiet, clean, efficient diesel engine, the 2.2i CTDi. Meanwhile Honda had expounded a new concept, "positive hate."

The version of the spot that launched the "Grrr" campaign on September 24, 2004, in cinemas throughout the United Kingdom was 90 seconds in length. The television version was edited into 90- and 60-second lengths and was supported by radio, print, and Internet advertising. The idea of "Grrr" was to build on the success of the "Cog" campaign. This had been Honda's manufacturing strategy as well. While "Cog" reintroduced the Accord to the public, "Grrr" went a step further by introducing a diesel-powered Accord model as well as the diesel CR-V sport-utility vehicle. The ingenious part was that the spots were not about the cars at all. The focus was completely on the new diesel engine that Honda offered; the automobiles were therefore passively advertised. Because prospective buyers were already aware of the qualities of the Accord and CR-V, what they needed to be reassured about was the fact that Honda's proprietary diesel was an improvement over competitors' engines (and the Isuzu diesel used in the Civic). By concentrating on what was really new, a Honda-built diesel engine, the "Grrr" spots provided that reassurance in a positive yet quirky manner.

OUTCOME

The "Grrr" campaign was an excellent follow-up to "Cog." If anything, it surpassed its acclaimed predecessor in the number of advertising awards it garnered. As a tandem, the two campaigns boosted sales of the Accord and, by extension, Honda autos in general. Total sales of the Accord went from 34,879 in 2003 to 51,235 in 2004, an increase of 46.9 percent. Total Honda sales throughout Europe in those two years increased from 217,473 to 255,721, a jump of 17.6 percent.

More remarkable was what the "Grrr" campaign accomplished on its own. The rise in sales of diesel-powered Accords was astonishing. In 2003, the year the diesel-powered Accord was introduced, 518 were sold. In 2004, the year the "Grrr" campaign came out, 21,776 were sold. That figure represented 42.5 percent of all Accord sales. It was almost twice as much as the 2004 sales figure for the diesel-powered Civic (which had an Isuzu engine), which totaled 12,025. On the strength of its success with the diesel engine, Honda went ahead with its plans to produce diesel-powered CR-Vs and FR-Vs in 2005. Honda also announced that in 2004 its manufacturing plant in Swindon had set a production record of 193,456 cars, a 4.75 percent increase from 2003.

With all of that in place Honda predicted a good year for 2005 for its United Kingdom and European market. While the overall market was down in 2005, Honda experienced a 7.8 percent growth in sales that year. This was second only to BMW, which tallied a 9.3 percent increase in 2005. In calendar year 2005 Honda's sales in Europe totaled 285,924, an 11.8 percent increase from 2004. (This was a 31.4 percent increase compared to Honda's 2003 European sales numbers.)

More important, along with the Accord, the CR-V and FR-V, both with diesel engines, played crucial roles in Honda's continued upswing in Europe and particularly the United Kingdom, where Honda was the ninth-largest auto company in terms of sales. A brief, unsigned article that appeared in the *Daily Post* of Liverpool in July 2005 reported, "Honda has hit 50,000 sales in the UK within the first half of the year—equalling the firm's full year sales figure in 1996. The result has been made possible by a dramatic boost in Accord diesel sales, continuing demand for the CR-V . . . and the successful introduction of the FR-V."

By the end of 2005 Honda held 4 percent of the U.K. market, a half percentage point behind BMW. Since its introduction in 1995 the Honda CR-V had been the best-selling gasoline-powered SUV in the United Kingdom, so offering a diesel option was a logical step. Commenting on that move in the *Daily Telegraph* of London, Andrew English wrote, "[It] would be difficult to find a safer, better engineered and more socially and environmentally responsible example than the Honda CR-V . . . Start up and the diesel gives little indications of its origins, unless you have the window open, whereupon the industrial growl leaks in. In fact there are few occasions when you are aware that this is a diesel other than the occasional turbo whistle and momentary injector rattle. In that respect it's a match for the best German and French units." With a follow-up advertising campaign to "Grrr" in the works, and with new innovations to is diesel-powered autos, Honda remained optimistic for 2006.

FURTHER READING

Anderson, Mae. "The Conception of 'Grrr' and How It Came to Warm So Many Hearts." *Adweek,* June 20, 2005.

Comyn, Paddy. "New Accord Takes a Power Trip; Honda May Be a Little Late to the Diesel Engine Party, but Their Latest Executive Car Demands Serious Attention." *Sunday Tribune* (Dublin), February 22, 2004.

English, Andrew. "Making the Best of a Flawed Idea. First Drive: The New Diesel Engine Is Beautiful and Honda's CR-V Is among the Best of Its Kind." *Daily Telegraph* (London), January 15, 2005.

Gibson, Ken. "Honda Finds Peace with New Diesel." *Sun* (London), January 2, 2004.

"Honda Going Diesel in Europe." *Nikkei Weekly* (Tokyo), May 24, 2004.

"Honda Joins the Chorus of Support for 4x4s." *Sentinel* (Stoke-on-Trent, England), January 1, 2004.

Letts, Quentin. "And That's What Sells the Car." *Sunday Telegraph* (London), April 13, 2004.

McAleer, Michael. "Ending the Fuel Discord." *Irish Times,* March 10, 2004.

———. "Honda Diesel a Three-Times Winner." *Irish Times,* January 21, 2004.

"Motoring: Honda Record." *Daily Post* (Liverpool), July 13, 2005.

Mutel, Glen. "BBH Promotes Audi A4 Engine with Fish Theme." *Campaign,* February 14, 2003.

Stephens, Edward. "Motoring: Diesel Is First among Equals." *Birmingham Evening Mail* (Birmingham, England), September 8, 2004.

Frank Caso

Iconix Brand Group, Inc.

215 W. 40th Street
New York, New York 10018
USA
Telephone: (212) 730-0030
Fax: (212) 730-0030
Web site: www.candiesinc.com

■■■

JENNY MCCARTHY FOR CANDIE'S CAMPAIGN

OVERVIEW

In 1978 Candie's shoes, especially a model called the Slide (a high-heeled slip-on), became a "must have" fashion accessory for America's teenage population. The shoe's popularity, as well as the company's fortunes (which peaked at approximately $190 million in sales in 1984), waned as fashion fads changed in the late 1980s. In the mid-1990s Candie's Inc. was still designing and manufacturing women's and girl's casual and fashion footwear, but its brand was considered passé by its core market of teenage girls. Hoping to revive its brand and trigger a sales upsurge similar to the one in 1978, Candie's released its "Jenny McCarthy for Candie's" campaign.

The $4 million campaign was conceived by Candie's CEO Neil Cole and Candie's in-house advertising agency, InMarketing, Inc. "Jenny McCarthy for Candie's" surfaced in February 1997 as a print campaign with risqué images of the former Playboy Playmate of the Year and NBC sitcom star Jenny McCarthy. The ads featured McCarthy in a variety of poses (most of them in the bathroom) wearing Candie's shoes. One of the most contentious images featured an almost-nude McCarthy sitting on a toilet wearing nothing but her panties and a pair of Candie's shoes. Despite the ads being rejected by almost every consumer magazine except for *Spin,* the controversy surrounding them brought Candie's back into the limelight. McCarthy returned in 1998 for two Candie's TV spots titled "Just Screw It," which parodied a Nike shoe commercial. In 2001 McCarthy was featured in a Candie's campaign that consisted of a set of print ads and one television spot that doubled as public service announcements discouraging teenage pregnancy. The actress reappeared in 2004 to advertise Candie's shoes with print ads that paired McCarthy with *American Idol* singing-contest winner Kelly Clarkson.

Although the majority of the campaign was deemed by many to be in poor taste, it catapulted Candie's into the headlines over and over again. In 1998 *Fortune* listed Candie's, which was later renamed Iconix Brand Group, Inc., as one of the top 25 fastest-growing companies in the United States.

HISTORICAL CONTEXT

The history of the Cole family shoe business and the Candie's brand was full of ups and downs. When Neil Cole and his brother Kenneth were boys, they spent much of their time in and around their father's dilapidated shoe factory in Brooklyn, New York. The company, called El Greco, was moderately successful until 1978, when father Charles and son Kenneth took a trip to Italy. There they stumbled upon a shoe unlike any

Jenny McCarthy with her advertisement for Candies.
© MITCHELL GERBER/CORBIS.

El Greco had ever made. The backless, toeless slip-on had a chunky wooden wedge sole and a 2 1/2-inch, pencil-thin high heel. The Coles bought 600 pairs on sight and began importing them to the states. When actress Olivia Newton-John wore a similar style in the 1978 hit movie *Grease,* the shoe's popularity took off. Within five years the Cole's small family business had sold more than 14 million pairs of Candie's Slides and increased its sales 60 times over.

Young women aged 14 to 30 who aspired to be part of the fashion in-crowd were constantly bedecked in their skintight Jordache or Sasson jeans, tiny tube tops, and Candie's Slides. Advertising for the shoes took a straightforward "sex sells" attitude, as print ads and television commercials depicted scantily clad coeds running around college dormitories (wearing their Candie's, of course).

In 1982 son Kenneth left to start his own shoe company. The Kenneth Cole brand became one of the best-known designer shoe labels in America. He developed a unique advertising style by integrating issues of the day (usually political) in his ads. Through the years Kenneth Cole ads featured messages related to AIDS, the homeless, the rain forest, cloning, right-wing politics, and even presidential intern Monica Lewinsky. By 1997 Cole had built his business to more than $148 million in sales. In 1985 it was Neil's turn to go out on his own. He went into the jeans business, registering the name "No Excuses." Continuing the family tradition of controversial advertising, Cole used "notorious" models in his print ads and television commercials, including Donna Rice, the former mistress of presidential candidate Gary Hart.

By that time the shoe business was beginning to slide. Candie's were out of fashion and piling up in bins at discount stores. Charles Cole retired, and the business was sold in 1986. But Neil decided he wanted it back, so along with a group of individual investors, he purchased the company in 1991.

At first Cole brought out new designs of Timberland-style hiking boots, practical sneakers, and comfortable sandals with thick heels. Advertising was simple, earthy, and home-oriented, featuring lace curtains and bowls of fruit. *Forbes* magazine quoted Cole as saying, "We've traded the flash and trash of the Eighties for a more Nineties look. I'm no longer interested in fads that are here today, gone tomorrow."

But the "Nineties look" was not selling. So Cole, tuning in to the "retro" trend in fashion (the return of styles from the 1970s and 1980s) and besieged with requests for Candie's Slides from fashion editors and buyers, decided to bring the line back. To attract Candie's original customers who remembered the shoe from their own teen years, Cole introduced an upscale version of the shoe by forming alliances with four of the country's top women designers. In 1996 Cole announced that Anna Sui, Betsey Johnson, Nicole Miller, and Vivienne Tam would each be designing a line of Candie's Slides. In 1997, with the introduction of the Jenny McCarthy campaign, Candie's once again became a household word.

TARGET MARKET

In many an American household the Candie's name became one more crack in the typical rift between teenagers and their parents. Although some products may have had crossover appeal, attracting numerous age groups, Candie's Slides were clearly and purposely marketed to 12- to 24-year-old females. When the shoes first came out in the late 1970s, many parents forbade their daughters to wear them, disapproving of the "image" they created. Naturally, young girls only became more determined to wear them. Many of those women, grown up and with teenagers of their own, voiced their disapproval of Candie's in the 1990s—not so much of the

MCCARTHY WAS NOT ALONE ON THE POT

Candie's toilet-based advertisements featuring Jenny McCarthy may have generated the most controversy in 1997, but they were not the only ones that appeared that year. In a much tamer ad for Vanish toilet bowl cleaner, a woman named Pat Mayo (a real person) from Hometown, Illinois (a real place), stood next to her porcelain treasure and told viewers, "I have the cleanest and nicest-smelling bathroom in the neighborhood. If anybody doesn't believe me, ring my doorbell and you can smell my toilet!" And, lest little children feel left out, Mattell introduced a toddler-sized doll called Potty Training Kelly. Commercials for the toy showed a child playing with the doll, pulling down its pants, sitting it on the toilet, and listening to it "tinkle."

shoes but of the Jenny McCarthy advertising campaign. Once again, those protests only served to spur on Candie's sales.

In 1997 Jill Kilcoyne of Teen-age Research Unlimited in Northbrook, Illinois, estimated that U.S. teenagers spent $84 billion of their own money and $38 billion of their parents' money. Candie's was targeting this strong spending market, and alienating parents was a way of creating a bond with its young customers. Jenny McCarthy was Candie's way of cementing that bond. Focus groups showed that teens loved her flamboyant personality and off-center sense of humor. When asked about the Candie's bathroom ads, David Conn, Candie's director of marketing, told Anne Moncreiff Arrarte of the *Houston Chronicle,* "Our audience finds the visuals cute and funny. Granted, there's a fine line between what is gross and what is cute, but we care about how our customers react—not adults." One of the main reasons McCarthy was chosen to model Candie's was that teens identified with her and parents did not. In fact, Candie's CEO Neil Cole told Marcia Pledger of the *Cleveland Plain Dealer* that the company did not want teens to know that their mothers had worn the Slides 15 years earlier. Said Cole, "We think this girl wants to think she's discovering fashion and that she's a part of a fashion trend."

COMPETITION

The retro fashion trend that was so beneficial to Candie's did not spill over to all shoe companies. Two of Candie's largest competitors, Nike and Nine West, were plagued by negative publicity and disappointing earnings. Nike's success in signing golf champion Tiger Woods just before he won the Masters tournament at the age of 20 was a marketing coup for the company. Nike faced tough national criticism, however, when reports surfaced about human-rights violations and unfair labor practices in its Asian plants. Nine West reported lower-than-expected earnings for 1997, partly as a result of the fact that the Securities and Exchange Commission was investigating its accounting practices.

Athletic endorsements for shoe companies were as popular as ever. Converse signed controversial basketball star Dennis Rodman to a multiyear endorsement deal, and Fila USA inked a seven-year, $80 million contract with Grant Hill. Yet among all the celebrity endorsements, Candie's McCarthy campaign was a standout. In December 1997 *Footwear News* stated, "Candie's will be remembered in 1997 for one of the most indelible ad images, featuring unforgettable MTV diva Jenny McCarthy in a spunky, tongue-in-cheek print campaign."

MARKETING STRATEGY

In the mid-1990s Candie's conducted an extensive search for someone to represent the Slide to its target market. That search revealed that MTV's Jenny McCarthy rated most popular with those 12 to 24 years old. McCarthy, who originally studied to be a nurse, had become Playboy's Playmate of the Year in 1994. Within the next few years her career skyrocketed. She became a guest veejay on MTV then got the job as host of that channel's irreverent version of *The Dating Game,* called *Singled Out.* Soon she had her own skit-oriented show on MTV. She later starred in her own sitcom on NBC, although it lasted less than one season. During this time Candie's chose her to be the spokeswoman for its $4 million print campaign, and on February 10, 1997, she made her first personal appearance at New York's famed Macy's department store. Hundreds of teenage fans waited in line for hours to catch a glimpse of her and to get her autograph.

Candies and its then in-house advertising agency, InMarketing, Inc., showed McCarthy three advertising concepts, and she chose the "bathroom" theme. In an E!Online interview with McCarthy she was asked if she sought out controversy. She replied, "I really don't. I didn't want to be, like, the Madonna shock wave of the entertainment industry. I thought of [the ads] as something that made fun of myself."

Celebrity and fashion photographer Davis Factor, a member of the legendary Max Factor family, shot the print ads. They depicted McCarthy in a series of bathroom scenes: as a sultry nightclub performer singing into the shower head wearing a red sequined dress, as a glamorous femme fatale painting her finger nails while dressed in a sophisticated full slip, and as a sexy maid at work scrubbing the toilet in a bubblegum-pink nightie.

The most controversial ad was shot in two versions. In both McCarthy was sitting on the toilet with her panties down around her ankles. In one she was wearing an orange T-shirt and a pair of orange Candie's. In the second she was wearing nothing but the shoes. The company claimed that there was no message to this edgy advertising. Its marketing director David Conn told the *Northern New Jersey Record* that Candie's was simply attempting to sell shoes. "We're a $100 million company trying to compete with the like of Hilfiger and Guess," said Conn. "We can't outspend them, so we have to create a stir." CEO Neil Cole told *Footwear News* in February 1998, "Our advertising philosophy is to create brand awareness. We don't think people buy product either way based on whether they like the ad. With our advertising, the key is to drive them to be intrigued by the brand."

With a spike in sales following its 1997 print ads, the next year Candie's tripled its ad spending to an estimated $13.5 million. In August 1997 most television stations, including New York's WCBS and WNBC, rejected a Candie's commercial featuring McCarthy that was designed to sell Candie's Durango ankle boots. In the spot the actress was talking on the phone while a plumber worked under her sink. "I'm getting my crack fixed," she told her friend. "It's so big, it's smiling at me." McCarthy then climbed down and joined the plumber, exposing her own backside in the process.

On February 1, 1998, McCarthy was featured in two TV spots with the tagline "Just Screw It," in which she demonstrated her lack of athletic prowess as she wore the new line of Candie's fashion sneakers. Fearing litigation for the commercials' adulterated use of Nike's "Just Do It" tagline, MTV and other networks refused to air the spots. Three years later McCarthy and the pop group Destiny's Child made public appearances to promote the Candie's Foundation, a new organization created by Neil Cole to discourage teenage pregnancy in America. In one spot for the organization McCarthy warned a teenage couple not to have unprotected sex and then handed the girl a wailing newborn to heighten the reality of pregnancy. Print ads also featured McCarthy wearing a new Candie's clothing line and included text that advised against teenage pregnancy. In 2004 McCarthy surfaced again to promote Candie's shoes in ads that hinted at her controversial 1997 images. Sitting on a toilet, McCarthy wore little besides Candie's shoes. This time she appeared alongside singer Kelly Clarkson, winner of the contest *American Idol,* who wore nothing but Candie's shoes while soaking in a bathtub. The ads ran in the April and May issues of magazines popular with the teen-girl target, including *YM, Teen People, Elle Girl, Teen Vogue, Hollywood Life,* and *Jane.*

OUTCOME

Despite the controversy, or more likely because of it, Candie's campaign became one of the most successful marketing events of 1997. In December of that year *Footwear News* reported that since the campaign began, brand recognition for Candie's had increased by 90 percent. Sales for the first quarter of 1997 jumped to $16.9 million from $6.8 million in the previous quarter. During the same time period the company's earnings went up to $823,338, or 6 cents a share, compared with a loss of $423,338, or 5 cents a share, during the same period in 1996.

The campaign, like most of Candie's history, had its ups and downs. It was originally scheduled to appear in national magazines including *Allure, Cosmopolitan, Elle, Glamour, InStyle, Mademoiselle, Marie Claire, Seventeen, Vogue,* and *YM.* Several of the magazines, including *Seventeen, InStyle, Cosmopolitan,* and *Vogue,* refused to run some of the ads. The only magazine that ran the ad of McCarthy without her T-shirt was *Spin,* and the ad only ran once.

Candie's also aborted an attempt to have McCarthy sell a sneaker the company called "microsoft." The shoe was part of a line of computer-themed footwear with names such as Dot Com, Mega Byte, Web Site, and Crash. The company, however, did not get permission from Microsoft to use its name, and, after being "asked" by Bill Gates's legal department to stop using the name, Candie's pulled the ads.

To top it off, *Time Magazine* chose the Candie's campaign as the worst advertisement of 1997, saying, "Candie's bathroom humor, even when good, is still, well, bathroom humor. Putting the scatological Jenny McCarthy on a toilet, panties wrapped around her calves, to sell Candie's shoes couldn't raise this print campaign above the level of potty chic."

Nonetheless Jenny McCarthy—along with later Candie's spokeswomen that included Kelly Clarkson, the actress Hillary Duff, the pop singer Ciara, and the country-rock trio the Dixie Chicks—helped Candie's reclaim the status it had in the late 1970s and early 1980s. When asked by *Footwear News* in February 1998 why the company was focusing so much on advertising and promotions, Neil Cole replied, "We think of ourselves as a marketing company that happens to be in footwear."

For 1998 the brand posted shoe sales of $93 million, considerably less than the company's 1984 high-water mark of $190 million. During the years of the campaign Candie's continued to meet with success. Between 2003 and 2004 the company's stock more than doubled. In July 2005 Candie's changed its name to Iconix Brand Group, Inc.; Candie's had already sold licenses for most of its brands, including Candie's, the Bongo footwear line, and the recently acquired clothing line Badgley Mischka. Neil Cole wanted the enterprise's name changed as it expanded beyond just being a footwear designer and into a brand-management company.

FURTHER READING

Arrarte, Anne Moncreiff. "Ads Use Shock Value to Reach Rebellious Demographic." *Houston Chronicle,* June 29, 1997.

"The Best and Worst of '97." *Time Magazine,* December 19, 1997.

Fox, Danielle, "Skin Trade; As Footwear Companies Continue to Sex Up Their Marketing Images, Many Are Left Wondering." *Footwear News,* February 26, 2001, p. 50.

Ivry, Bob. "Shock of the Rude: Selling to Gen-X." *Bergen County (NJ) Record,* October 3, 1997.

Krol, Carol, and Laura Petrecca, "Footwear Marketer Candie's Seeks Shop for Brand Project," *Advertising Age,* September 21, 1998, p. 3.

Kroll, Luisa. "Like My Shoes." *Forbes,* April 7, 1997.

Lenetz, Dana, "Candie's Celeb Ads Tell Teens to Be Survivors." *Footwear News,* May, 7, 2001, p. 6.

Pledger, Marcia. "Girl Power Makes Waves with Retailers." *Cleveland Plain Dealer,* April 1, 1998.

Quick, Rebecca, "Candie's Restates Results, as SEC Probes Accounting." *Wall Street Journal,* September, 23, 1999, p. B19.

"Sweet Success." *Footwear News,* February 9, 1998.

"Year on the Edge." *Footwear News,* December 29, 1997.

Sharyn Kolberg
Kevin Teague

IKEA International A/S

Box 640
Helsingborg, SE 25 106
Sweden
Telephone: 46 42 267100
Fax: 46 42 132805
Web site: www.IKEA.com

UNBÖRING CAMPAIGN

OVERVIEW

In 2002 IKEA was the world's largest home-furnishing retail chain and had just released plans to open 60 to 70 new stores across Asia, Europe, and North America. Although most people in U.S. metropolitan areas were already familiar with the Swedish home retailer, many Americans living in smaller cities and suburban areas were not. To increase its brand recognition in the United States, IKEA launched its "Unböring" campaign, the title of which was fashioned with a fake umlaut as a tongue-in-cheek reference to the company's Swedish heritage.

After 11 years with Deutsch Inc. as its ad agency and a brief contract with Carmichael Lynch, in 2002 IKEA signed over its advertising budget, estimated at $45 million, to Crispin Porter + Bogusky, an agency based in Miami. For the new campaign the agency focused on a phenomenon that it called "furniture guilt" or "old furniture gravity," which it described as Americans' compulsion to keep outdated furniture. "Lamp," the first television spot, featured an old red lamp that had been replaced by a new IKEA lamp. The lamp's curbside doom was accompanied by poignant piano music. In the spot's final few seconds a man with a Swedish accent appeared and scoffed at the audience's sympathies. "Many of you feel bad for this lamp. That's because you [are] crazy. It has no feelings. And the new one is much better." "Unböring" continued into 2005; all ads featured the word "Unböring" at the end. Print, Internet, and billboard ads were employed along with a heavy catalog launch at North American IKEA stores.

"Unböring" earned several awards and occurred during a critical point in IKEA's U.S. market expansion. The first television spot, "Lamp," received the campaign's greatest accolades, snagging the Grand Prix at the Cannes International Advertising Festival along with the Grand Clio. IKEA sales in the United States, which was IKEA's second-largest market, increased by 8 percent between 2002 and 2003. "There was a lot of discussion about the whole IKEA campaign," Clio juror Bob Scarpelli told *Adweek*. "We agreed that it plays with your emotions and perception the way few commercials do. You feel uneasy when you see it. That's great. It makes you think."

HISTORICAL CONTEXT

With its first store appearing in Sweden in 1958, IKEA climbed to the position of world's top furniture retailer by designing hip, Bauhaus-inspired furnishings and shipping them unassembled to reduce labor costs. The first U.S. IKEA opened in Philadelphia in 1985, and in the early nineties, Los Angeles became the site of the first West Coast IKEA. In 1989 IKEA awarded Deutsch, an agency based in New York, the company's advertising

© JERRY MCCREA/STAR LEDGER/CORBIS.

budget. Linda Sawyer, managing partner and CEO for Deutsch, told *Advertising Age,* "Ikea was pivotal to us. Its growth paralleled our own. It was the reason we invested in direct marketing, the reason we moved into interactive." The agency created commercials for IKEA that some considered controversial, including a 1994 spot featuring a gay couple picking out a dining-room table from IKEA. The agency's contract lasted 11 years, at which point IKEA briefly signed with the Minneapolis-based shop Carmichael Lynch.

With plans to expand its retail presence in North America, in 2002 IKEA switched agencies again, choosing Crispin Porter + Bogusky after seeing the agency's work. "They identified in the pitch a real strategic opportunity that we now see translated into the creative, and that was to challenge the home furnishing that is out there," Christian Mathieu, external marketing manager for IKEA, told *Advertising Age.* Mathieu said that the company had been especially impressed by the agency's ads for MINI Cooper cars and its "Florida Truth" anti-tobacco campaign, saying, "We're an advocate of trying to break conventions, and you see that in those campaigns."

In developing an advertising strategy to support IKEA's expansion, Crispin Porter + Bogusky suggested that American sales would be stimulated by a campaign that shattered America's persistence to accumulate outdated furniture. Speaking to the *New York Times,* Irma Zandl, president of the Zandl Group, a market research and consulting company, offered an analysis of the reasoning behind the campaign: "IKEA's cheap prices are a plus, as are its contemporary designs. But it has a spotty reputation for quality. The campaign may be seeking to 'put a positive spin' on that disadvantage, suggesting that you will want to replace something anyway, so that it doesn't matter that it doesn't last very long."

TARGET MARKET

Alex Bogusky, creative director at Crispin Porter + Bogusky, told *USA Today* that the original "Unböring" spots, "Lamp" and "Moo Cow," were aimed at Americans who "spend wildly on 'fashion' purchases, such as clothes and shoes. They still cling to a 'till death do us part attitude' with their furniture." According to Crispin Porter + Bogusky, these consumers had a guilt-induced, Puritan attachment to Colonial remakes. Before the campaign Crispin Porter + Bogusky's planning group conducted research showing that, in one American lifetime, people had the same average number of dining room tables as they did spouses: 1.6. Even affluent consumers who decorated every year or two held tightly to old furniture. Crispin Porter + Bogusky ran the first segment of the campaign hoping to break Americans of this inclination and to get them to view furniture as fashion items. "People here just don't approach furniture as a fashion category at all," Bogusky told *Shoot.* "But in the Bahamas, people tend to redo their homes every year, with this year's colors and styles. It's another culture." Furniture-industry analyst Jerry Epperson told the *Washington Post* that the average sofa was kept for eight years by Americans. Bedroom furniture stuck around for 16 to 20 years. Recliners were replaced every six years; not because they fell out of fashion but because their parts and padding were worn out.

COMPETITION

By 2005 Bed Bath and Beyond (BBB) was considered the largest domestic retailer in the United States, with 660 stores and $5.1 billion in sales. In 2000 BBB had begun relying exclusively on circulars, catalogs, and word of mouth to advertise. All BBB stores were divided into two main departments: domestics (which included kitchen fixtures, bathroom accessories, and bedroom items) and home furnishings. BBB rarely held sales, focusing instead on what it called "everyday low prices." One expense BBB budgeted into passive advertising was the creation of its website. Designed by R/GA, an agency specializing in interactive advertising, http://www.bedbathandbeyond.com was called "Best E-Commerce Site" by *Advertising Age* in 2000.

In 2002 and 2003 Linens 'n Things (LNT) ranked 21st out of all U.S. home retailers. The company almost doubled its sales between 2001 and 2003. By 2005 it was considered the second-largest U.S. retailer of home

THE OLD RED LAMP

Crispin Porter + Bogusky and Spike Jonze considered a variety of lamps before settling on the red, lonely desk light that was left curbside in the television spot "Lamp." Explaining why Crispin Porter + Bogusky settled on that particular lamp, Ari Merkin, the spot's writer, told *Shoot,* "This one stood out as the most pathetic. It was the kind of thing you'd have in your dorm room. I actually think I did have a lamp like this in my dorm room at school." After the shoot someone not from Crispin Porter + Bogusky took the prop home. When the agency asked for it back, the lamp's new owner mimicked the "Lamp" commercial by sending Crispin Porter + Bogusky a note that stated, "See, you've fallen for it. See, you've grown attached to it, and you are crazy."

textiles, housewares, and decorating accessories. Realizing that home fixtures were more lucrative than linen, LNT had begun marketing "things" more aggressively by 2003. Advertising created by the Richards Group targeted women aged 25 to 54 with a "recipe" message. One television spot depicted people cooking together in a kitchen during a casual dinner party, with a voice-over listing visible items as if they were recipe ingredients. TNS Media Intelligence/CMR, a business information service, stated in *Adweek* that LNT spent almost $4 million on newspaper, radio, magazine, and outdoor advertising in 2002. The majority of its $60 million ad budget was spent on circulars and direct mail.

MARKETING STRATEGY

During the last weeks of September 2002 Crispin Porter + Bogusky unleashed IKEA's "Unböring" campaign, which cost an estimated $45 million, across television, the Internet, print, and outdoor advertising, all ads containing the pronouncement: "Unböring." Outdoor billboards featured enormous IKEA price tags with actual furnishings, such as bookcases and sofas, attached to the signs. "Unböring" posters were pasted on walls in New York City and Chicago, and "Lamp" and "Moo Cow" television commercials aired during the World Series and during popular network shows such as *Frasier* and *Friends.* Magazine ads appeared in *Spin, Cosmopolitan, Vogue, Entertainment Weekly, Essence,* and *Vibe.*

The campaign's first television spot, "Lamp," garnered the most awards. It was directed by Oscar nominee Spike Jonze, who also directed *Being John Malkovich.* Bogusky explained to *Shoot* why Jonze chose the script: "He loved the idea of trying to make you feel for this inanimate object. He loved that challenge." The spot featured a red desk lamp that a woman removed from her apartment and set on the sidewalk. A moody piano score accentuated the lamp's doom as heavy rain began to fall. A newer, more contemporary lamp appeared in the window overhead, which the old lamp seemed to be hopelessly gazing at. The commercial ended with Jonas Forlander, a Swede, scolding the audience for caring about an old lamp's fate.

Filmed back-to-back with "Lamp," the next television spot, "Moo Cow," depicted a couple passionately embraced on a table. The woman, perturbed by the gaze of a cow-shaped ceramic creamer, smacked it onto the floor. Forlander appeared once again to state, "You feel sad for the little creamer. This is because you are crazy. Tacky items can easily be replaced with better IKEA."

Wes Anderson, director of *Rushmore,* helmed IKEA's next two commercials, "Kitchen" and "Living Room." The spots, which first aired in November of 2002, drifted from the original "old furniture gravity" concept of the first two and focused exclusively on IKEA's brand. The spots portrayed a family and a couple arguing inside an IKEA showroom. In the spot "Living Room," a family appeared to be arguing inside their living room, which was furnished with IKEA products. By the spot's conclusion it had become apparent they were actually inside an IKEA showroom. Bogusky explained the two spots in *Shoot.* "The way you are allowed to use their showroom is extremely interactive. They don't mind if you take naps on a piece of furniture. We wanted to play on that and take some broader ground from a brand point of view that we're a life-at-home company, not just a furnishings company."

The next television spots, which were designed by Crispin Porter + Bogusky and StyleWar, a collective of Swedish designers and directors, refocused on IKEA's affordability by explaining how easily people could fit new IKEA furnishings into their household budgets. The commercials showed living rooms and kitchens being magically remodeled. "Maybe you have $120. Maybe you have $650. Maybe you have $2,300," a female voice explained in the spot titled "Thugs." Each time a price was quoted, different IKEA products appeared in the room. The "Unböring" campaign continued into 2005, bolstering IKEA for the opening of its 50 new U.S. stores between 2005 and 2012.

OUTCOME

"Unböring" ran during a time in IKEA's history when its U.S. sales were rising (they increased 8 percent between

SPIKE JONZE

Spike Jonze, the director of "Lamp," also directed the films *Being John Malkovich* and *Adaptation* and starred in *Three Kings.* Although Jonze was nominated for a best-director Oscar for *Being John Malkovich* in 1999, the family of his ex-wife, Sophia Coppola, clearly collected more rewards from the Academy of Motion Picture Arts and Sciences. In 2004 Sophia Coppola won the Oscar for best original screenplay. Her father, the director Francis Ford Coppola, grandfather, the composer Carmine Coppola, and cousin, the actor Nicolas Cage, had all won Oscars.

2002 and 2003). It helped push global sales to $15.4 billion by 2004. In 2003 most ad industry pundits had predicted that Wieden & Kennedy's Honda commercial "cog" would win the Grand Prix at the International Advertising Festival in Cannes, France, but "Lamp" snatched the award. Crispin Porter + Bogusky creative director Paul Keister, surprised about winning the Grand Prix, told *Shoot,* "It's a very simple, strong idea, and the strategy came through without any sort of compromises. It wasn't bogged down with information. It was just pure branding for IKEA." "Lamp" also won the 2003 Grand Clio for television.

FURTHER READING

Anderson, Mae. "'Crazy' at the Clios: TV Back in Spotlight with CP+B's 'Lamp' Coup." *Adweek,* May 26, 2003, p. 26.

Beer, Rebecca. "Close-Up: Live Issue—Crispin Porter & Bogusky. The US Ad Agency That Trounced 'Cog' at Cannes." *Campaign,* July 4,2003, p. 16.

Dunlap, Bill. "Flying Right: Crispin Porter + Bogusky Has an Award-Winning Year, Topped with Continuing Creativity." *Shoot,* December 5, 2003, p. 15.

Elliot, Stuart. "IKEA Challenges the Attachment to Old Stuff, in Favor of Brighter, New Stuff." *New York Times,* September 16, 2002, p. 6.

Garcia, Sandra. "Home Makeover: Crispin Porter + Bogusky Highlights Style and Affordability for IKEA." *Shoot,* December 5, 2003. p. 17.

Griswold, Alicia. "Off-road Trip: Crispin Porter + Bogusky Explores New Terrain with Mini, IKEA and Molson." *Adweek,* January 20, 2003, p. 26.

Hales, Linda. "Jeepers, Keepers!; IKEA Ads Deride Attachment to Old Furniture." *Washington Post,* September 21, 2002, p. C2.

Lazare, Lewis. "IKEA Makes Argument; Angry Couples at Center of New Spots for Retailer." *Chicago Sun-Times,* November 14, 2002, p. 63.

Lippert, Barbara. "Broken Homes: Unboring, Yes, but Also Cheerless. Bring Back the Swede!" *Adweek* (eastern ed.), November 25, 2002, p. 22.

McCarthy, Michael. "IKEA Pulls an Upset to Win Top Ad at Cannes Lions." *USA Today,* June 23, 2002, p. B2.

Soter, Tom. "New Frontiers: Crispin Porter + Bogusky Production Department Is on Top of New Trends." *Shoot,* December 5, 2003, p. 16.

Van Dusen, Christine. "Who's Afraid of IKEA?" *Atlanta Journal-Constitution,* June 26, 2005, p. C1.

Wilcha, Kristin. "IKEA's 'Lamp' Shines at Cannes Advertising Festival." *Shoot,* June 27, 2003, p. 1.

Kevin Teague

InBev USA

101 Merritt 7
Norwalk, Connecticut 06856-5075
USA
Telephone: (203) 750-6600
Fax: (203) 750-6699
Web site: www.inbev.com

■■■

GRAB A ROCK CAMPAIGN

OVERVIEW

NOTE: Also see essay for Labatt USA.

After years of outperforming other beers in its category, the Latrobe Brewing Company's Rolling Rock, then owned by Labatt USA (a division of Belgium's Interbrew that became known as InBev USA following the parent company's 2004 merger with AmBev), set out in 2002 to reverse the previous year's sales decline. Rolling Rock's recipe for success had included a positioning based on the brand's perceived authenticity and quirkiness as well as a push to capture the loyalty of entry-age drinkers. Building on the success of a rock-music festival called the Rolling Rock Town Fair in the brewery's hometown of Latrobe, Pennsylvania, but moving away from its previous emphasis on radio advertising, Labatt USA charged agency McCann-Erickson of New York to craft a national TV campaign. The result was "Grab a Rock."

"Grab a Rock," a four-commercial campaign that was part of the $25 million spent annually to promote Rolling Rock in North America, focused on peculiarities of male behavior and bonding codes and targeted men aged 21 to 34. Within this target, however, Labatt USA further honed its message by aiming two spots at the younger subset of the larger group and two spots at the older subset. The campaign began in January 2002 and was supported by a promotional partnership with ESPN. In addition to sports-programming placements, airtime was purchased on a variety of other cable networks during male-oriented shows.

The campaign was credited with helping to arrest the previous year's sales slide and with contributing to a 2 percent gain in Rolling Rock sales for 2002. The success of the first four spots led Labatt USA to commission four more for 2003. The 2004 merger between parent company Interbrew (which owned such best-selling European brands as Stella Artois, Bass, and Beck's) and Brazil's AmBev (maker of the world's third-most-popular beer, Latin America's Skol) made Rolling Rock's new ultimate parent the largest beer producer in the world.

HISTORICAL CONTEXT

The Rolling Rock brand was introduced in 1939 by Latrobe Brewing, an entity created by five brothers from the Tito family of Pittsburgh when, speculating that President Roosevelt would repeal Prohibition a year before he actually did, they purchased what had been the Loyalhanna Brewing Co. in Latrobe, Pennsylvania. Rolling Rock, with its distinctive green bottle featuring painted-on horse imagery and the mysterious number 33, saw consistent sales gains in the 1960s and sold 720,000 barrels in 1974 before beginning a decade-long decline. Throughout this time, however, the Tito family maintained and renovated their brewery, and the company survived even as many local breweries nationwide went out of business. In 1985 a Japanese beverage manufacturer called Sundor bought Latrobe Brewing and then sold the company at a profit to Labatt USA in 1987.

Labatt USA continued to invest heavily in production and bottling capability, but it also added a key ingredient to the Rolling Rock sales strategy: marketing, a tactic the Tito family had believed unnecessary. In the 1990s the brand relied mostly on radio advertising and continued to build a consumer following, especially in the Northeast, the Great Lakes region, and California. Rolling Rock outperformed most players in the so-called superpremium beer category, which included imports and microbrews along with other beers priced higher than the mainstream beer brands, and targeted newly legal drinkers with the first Rolling Rock Town Fair, a rock-music festival near Latrobe, in August 2000. After experiencing record sales that year Rolling Rock saw its position weaken in 2001, with declines of 8 percent in volume. Although the brand supplemented its Town Fair positioning with targeted TV spots featuring aspiring alternative-rock bands, Labatt USA continued to allot the bulk of its Rolling Rock ad spending to radio. As it took the Town Fair concept to 15 other cities in 2001 and embarked on a new round of production-enhancing upgrades at the Latrobe brewery, Rolling Rock faced increasing competition from both imports and microbrews in the U.S. market. Labatt USA began, with agency McCann-Erickson of New York, planning Rolling Rock's first large-scale national TV effort.

WHAT DOES IT MEAN?

The 33 on the Rolling Rock beer bottle had long been seen as a brand asset, helping to inspire loyalty among drinkers. Since the beer's 1939 debut, consumers had obsessively guessed at the 33's meaning and provenance, but Latrobe Brewing and its subsequent corporate owners guarded the secret closely, wisely assuming, according to observers, that the mystery was worth much more to marketers than any explanation could be. Among theories regarding the meaning of the 33 were that it was the racing number for the horse pictured on the bottle, that it referred to the 33 paces separating the brew house from the brewmaster's office, and that it referred to the year 1933, which marked the repeal of Prohibition. Another long-held theory held that the 33 was a typo, a word count of the print generated for the original Rolling Rock label, which erroneously made it onto the proofs for the bottle label and stayed put because the brewery's original owners did not want to waste the bottles that had been made before the error was caught.

TARGET MARKET

"Grab a Rock," whose four TV spots had in common an emphasis on humorous, peculiarly male codes of behavior, primarily targeted 21- to 34-year-old men, who were far and away the beer industry's most voracious consumers. Within this market, however, the campaign made separate appeals: two of the spots targeted the 21- to 24-year-old subset of the overall target, while the other two were geared toward the older men of the group. Rolling Rock's shift in its advertising emphasis from radio to television made sense, as Rolling Rock director of marketing David Van Wees told *Brandweek,* because "Our target spends more time watching TV—20 hours a week—than they do listening to radio, reading or going online combined."

The spots aimed at the younger segment featured correspondingly young actors in humorous situations involving bar behavior and pizza eating, while the other two commercials focused on marriage and backyard barbecues, issues more pertinent to those in their late twenties and early thirties. All of the spots featured cameos of the number 33, the mystery number on the Rolling Rock bottle. The tendency of Rolling Rock aficionados to speculate about the meaning of the number was perceived to be a factor in the brand's allure.

COMPETITION

Though Rolling Rock's ultimate parent, Interbrew (later known as InBev) of Belgium—which bought Labatt in 1995—rivaled Anheuser-Busch at the top of beer markets around the world, it did so not through the global marketing of individual brands or images but by tailoring the image of individual beers to individual markets. Thus, while Rolling Rock was Interbrew's top U.S. product, and although Interbrew was an international powerhouse, Rolling Rock was not—and was never intended to be—a top product outside of North America. In the United States Rolling Rock necessarily competed with domestic full-calorie beers such as Budweiser and also with superpremium beers, those priced higher than the mainstream brands.

Anheuser-Busch, in addition to having an almost 50 percent market share of the country's beer market, had an advertising budget far larger than its nearest competitors. Despite declining sales of Budweiser, the brewer continued to support the "King of Beers" with blockbuster ad campaigns in the late 1990s and early 2000s. Among the most noteworthy campaigns on behalf of Budweiser were the series of commercials featuring frogs whose croaks sounded out the brand's name and a long-running follow-up effort in which the scope of the swamp motif was widened to include talking lizards. Budweiser made what may have been its biggest advertising splash ever, though, with the "Whassup?!" campaign, which focused on four friends' trademark, slang greeting and became a pop-culture phenomenon in 2000.

Heineken, one of Rolling Rock's top competitors in the superpremium category, unveiled its long-running "It's All About the Beer" campaign in 1999. Focusing on universal "beer moments," situations in ordinary life that hinged on the presence of Heineken, the campaign was designed to broaden the brand's U.S. market, especially among young people, by counteracting consumers' elitist associations regarding the classic Dutch brew. At the same time, the tagline and content of the commercials strove to communicate the superiority of the actual product.

Corona Extra, meanwhile, had recently eclipsed Heineken as the United States' top imported beer. The brand's rapid growth in the 1990s was chiefly attributable, in the eyes of many industry watchers, to its marketing strategy. In a succession of campaigns that each built on the same idea—equating Corona with a beach vacation—the brand's marketers established a clear and appealing product image that was distinct from that of all competitors. Between 1995 and 2000 Corona Extra's share of the American import market went from 13.5 percent to 27.3 percent.

MARKETING STRATEGY

Labatt USA declined to release budget figures for "Grab a Rock," Rolling Rock's biggest advertising campaign ever, but senior brand manager Daniel R. Hilbert indicated that the campaign represented a tripling of spending on advertising in support of the brand and yet still accounted for only a fraction of the $25 million spent annually to promote the beer in North America. The campaign built on the youth-oriented marketing push fueled by the Rolling Rock Town Fair concerts and also relied on the perception of authenticity and mystery that supposedly surrounded the brand. New packaging, unveiled almost simultaneously with "Grab a Rock," retained Rolling Rock's traditional horse and steeplechase imagery but highlighted the mystery number 33, which had always appeared on the brand's bottles but the meaning of which had never been disclosed. Likewise, a $14.5 million upgrade of Latrobe Brewing's bottling capacity indicated that Rolling Rock was poised to grow by up to half a million barrels in sales per year.

"Grab a Rock" broke during a January 2002 telecast of a National Football League (NFL) game on ESPN, and the spots continued to appear during that network's *SportsCenter* sports news show as well as on live coverage of athletic events such as college basketball tournaments and the National Hockey League (NHL) playoffs. "Grab a Rock" spots also appeared on the major networks Fox and CBS and during NFL pregame coverage. Airtime was purchased on cable channels such as TBS, VH1, and the Discovery Channel. Rolling Rock additionally sponsored 33 hours of comedy on the cable channel Comedy Central, a deal that included numerous placements of the "Grab a Rock" commercials.

In one of the campaign's spots aimed at 21- to 24-year-olds, two young men were seen sending hand signals to one another across a crowded nightclub, as one was invited to play pool with an attractive woman and the other was buying Rolling Rocks for the group. A deadpan voice-over provided a humorous translation of the signals. In the other spot aimed at the target market's younger end, the voice-over explained the principle of the "reverse blow," a coping strategy for the young man who had just bitten into an extremely hot piece of pizza. The real solution to the young man's dilemma was, of course, to drink a Rolling Rock.

The commercials that were meant to appeal to the target's older subgroup dealt with more domestic issues but still emphasized male codes of interaction and the ways in which Rolling Rock figured into the lives of men. In "Barbecue," for instance, several critical onlookers ridiculed a host's burger-grilling technique, calling him a "rookie" when he ran out of steak sauce. By pouring Rolling Rock over the sizzling meat, however, he regained his credibility as grill master. Similarly, in "Wedding Rock," set at a wedding reception, the groom took a break from the ceremonial festivities to share a Rolling Rock with his friends. "Did she give you a hall pass, or what?" one friend asked. Another poked fun at him with the question, "What's it like to wear jewelry?" The groom coolly responded, "This old thing?" and opened the beer with his new wedding ring, as the voice-over proclaimed, "And thus the groom maintains his status among the pack."

In April 2002 Rolling Rock supported its airing of the "Grab a Rock" spots on ESPN by entering into a promotional partnership with the network. A *SportsCenter* basketball-highlights segment titled "Shooting the Rock," which showcased great shooting plays, was introduced. Additionally, "Grab a Rock" commercials were preceded, on *SportsCenter,* by a Rolling Rock billboard highlighting a consumer scavenger hunt called "Hunt for 33," in which viewers were encouraged to locate the hidden 33s in the TV spots and report their findings on ESPN.com, where they had the chance to win 33 tickets to sporting events of their choice. The promotion lasted for six weeks.

OUTCOME

After "Grab a Rock" was launched in January 2002, brand manager Hilbert told *Knight Ridder/Tribune Business News,* "Sales for February absolutely crushed our plan [for the month] and were well ahead of last year.... Our orders so far for March look to be 8 percent above plan. So we're on a roll, and things are going well." As these trends continued through the year, Labatt USA commissioned four new "Grab a Rock" spots in November 2002. Like the first batch, these commercials, which aired in 2003, focused on male behavior, and especially male-female relations, while prominently showcasing Rolling Rock and its trademark green bottle. A heavy emphasis on sports programming continued, and another promotional partnership with ESPN's *SportsCenter* ran during the spring of 2003. Sales figures for 2002 showed an overall gain in volume of 2 percent, confirming that the declines of 2001 had been reversed.

The Rolling Rock Town Fair was extended, along with "Grab a Rock," into 2003. In 2004 Interbrew merged with Brazil's AmBev, and the resultant company was called InBev. The merger made InBev the world's leading beer producer, surpassing Anheuser-Busch. Latrobe Brewing's official U.S. owner became known as InBev USA. In 2004 Rolling Rock tried to sidestep new commercial-excising TV technologies (such as TiVo) with an emphasis on product placement in TV shows, including CBS's *Ed* and NBC's *The West Wing.*

FURTHER READING

Barbieri, Kelly. "On a 'Roll': Sponsorship a Hit for Beer Company." *Amusement Business,* September 17, 2001.

Beirne, Mike. "Labatt Alternative Ads Target Rolling Rockers." *Brandweek,* April 30, 2001.

———. "Marketers of the Next Generation: David van Wees." *Brandweek,* April 7, 2003.

———. "Rolling Rock Orders Up More TV Ads after Campaign Spurs Sales Spike." *Brandweek,* November 11, 2002.

———. "Rolling Rock Trades Radio for Television." *Brandweek,* October 29, 2001.

Cassidy, Hilary. "ESPN to Rock Viewers With '33' Roll." *Brandweek,* March 25, 2002.

Khermouch, Gerry. "Follow-Up: Rock Rolls." *Brandweek,* August 21, 2000.

McKay, Jim. "Expanded Production, New Ad Campaign Raise Profile, Reach of Rolling Rock Beer." *Knight Ridder/Tribune Business News,* March 2, 2002.

"Rolling Rock Beer Plans New TV Ad Campaign." *Pittsburgh Business Times,* October 31, 2001.

Tomlinson, Richard. "The New King of Beers." *Fortune,* October 18, 2004.

Mark Lane

ING Groep N.V.

ING House
Amstelveenseweg 500
Amsterdam, 1081 KL
Netherlands
Telephone: 31 20 5415411
Fax: 31 20 5415412
Web site: www.ing.com

■■■

ING LAUNCH CAMPAIGN

OVERVIEW

In 2000 ING Groep N.V. (spelled ING Group in the United States) was a financial powerhouse in Europe, offering a diverse range of insurance, banking, and asset-management services through offices in 60 countries, but the company had not made its way into the U.S. financial arena. That changed in late 2000, when ING finalized the acquisition of three American insurance companies: ReliaStar, Aetna Financial Services, and Aetna International. With the acquisitions complete ING was positioned to pursue a position in the U.S. financial marketplace.

To boost its identity and attract customers in the United States, ING partnered with New York advertising agency Jordan McGrath Case & Partners (JMCP) to create an integrated branding and marketing campaign. The campaign, estimated at $20 to $30 million, began in May 2001 and took a humorous approach to introducing the ING name to consumers. It included television spots and print ads that featured the ING name and company logo—a stylized orange lion—on the back of a park bench. The name appeared to be the suffix of a verb, the first part of which was obscured by someone sitting on the bench. The tagline was "It's not an ending, it's a beginning." In 2002 the campaign evolved to include Internet ads on specific financial websites.

Although the campaign increased awareness of the ING name among American consumers, the financial climate in the United States at the time prevented the company's business from increasing. Further, in June 2001, just one month after the campaign began, ING ended its relationship with JMCP; it awarded the account to DDB Worldwide in August. That October JMCP's parent, Havas Advertising, combined the agency with another of its companies, Arnold Worldwide, to create Arnold McGrath New York. ING reported that the follow-up Internet advertising effort resonated with consumers, with 35 percent who viewed the ads saying that they would use ING's services.

HISTORICAL CONTEXT

ING Group, based in Amsterdam, the Netherlands, was established following the 1991 merger of two financial institutions in the Netherlands: the insurance company Nationale-Nederlanden and the bank NMB Postbank Group, both of which had roots stretching back to the nineteenth century. The combined companies, known as Internationale Nederlanden Group, formed the first bancassurer (a bank with a subsidiary insurance company) in the Netherlands. Also in 1991 its name was shortened to its initials: ING. The company soon emerged as an international financial force through acquisitions of related companies, including Brussels Lambert Bank of Belgium and BHF-Bank of Frankfurt, Germany.

In 2000 ING acquired three U.S. insurance companies: Minneapolis-based ReliaStar Financial Corp. for $5 billion in September and Aetna Financial Services and Aetna International, both divisions of Aetna, Inc., of Hartford, Connecticut, for $7.7 billion in December. With the American companies added to its business holdings, by 2001 ING Group boasted more than 100,000 employees in 65 countries, including 11,000 employees in the United States. Following integration of its U.S. acquisitions into its group, ING's stated goals included spending up to $50 million to build brand identity with its existing U.S. customers as well as to attract new American customers. As part of the effort ING announced plans to begin a national marketing campaign in early 2001. The company hired Jordan McGrath Case & Partners of New York to develop a campaign that would both present the company's name and its correct pronunciation—"eye-en-gee"—and let consumers know that it was now a player in the American financial industry.

ING FOUNDATION SUPPORTS UNSUNG HEROES: TEACHERS

Through its philanthropic foundation ING U.S. Financial Services, a division of ING's U.S. operations, the company supported educators in all 50 states with the Unsung Heroes Awards. The awards recognized 100 outstanding teachers each year, with at least one teacher (and his or her school) from each state selected to win a $2,000 monetary prize. The 100 teachers were selected by Scholarship America, a nonprofit education-support and student-aid organization. From the 100 finalists, 3 were chosen by ING's Educators Advisory Board, composed of six top educators from across the United States, to receive an additional financial award—$25,000 for first place, $10,000 for second place, and $5,000 for third place—for an exceptional educational project.

TARGET MARKET

Although people in all income demographics needed a variety of financial services, when ING launched its business in the United States it had its corporate eye on what industry officials described as the "sweet spot." This consisted of consumers in the middle-income markets and "evolving-affluent" markets (the latter category referred to people who were in the process of advancing beyond the middle-class market into the upper-income market). Specifically, ING's campaign was designed to resonate with men and women aged 35 to 54 with annual household incomes of $75,000 or more. This group of consumers was believed to be the most likely to need the financial products and services offered by ING both for the protection of their wealth and for access to methods that would help their accumulated money grow.

COMPETITION

Citigroup Inc. entered the financial marketplace with the founding of City Bank of New York, which was opened in 1812 with the goal of serving a group of New York's business owners. In 1864 the bank's name was changed to National City Bank of New York. By 1894 it had grown to become the largest bank in the United States, and three years later it was the first to establish a foreign department and begin foreign exchange trading. In 1914 the bank opened a branch in Buenos Aries, Argentina, becoming the first U.S. national bank with a foreign office. The stock market crashed in 1929, the same year that National City Bank became the world's largest commercial bank. The bank holding company First National City Corporation became the parent of the bank in 1968. The parent corporation's name was changed to Citicorp in 1974, and two years later National City Bank became Citibank. In 1998 the company's Citicorp and Travelers Group divisions were merged to create Citigroup Inc. To help reach consumers with the message that Citigroup could be their partner in managing all aspects of their finances, it launched an advertising campaign in 2001 with the theme and tagline "Live Richly." Advertising was created by Fallon Worldwide and appeared on television, in print, and in outdoor executions. The campaign ran through 2003 in New York City, Chicago, San Francisco, Los Angeles, Miami, and Washington, D.C.

AXA Financial was a U.S. division of the Paris-based company AXA. The latter was formed in the early 1980s when Mutuelles Unies, a group of insurance companies, acquired the Drouot Group, France's leading private insurance company. By 1982 Mutuelles Unies-Drouot was France's largest non-state-owned insurance company and was expanding internationally with services that included life insurance, financial management, and real-estate investment. In 1985 the company was becoming better known as the "Bebear Group" for its chairman and chief executive officer, Claude Bebear. To reverse the growing trend of using the incorrect name, company officials began searching for a new one. After compiling a list of suggested names, three settled at the top: Argos, AXA, and Elan. The top choices were presented to company employees, who voted for their favorite. "Elan" was the preferred name, but executives in the company's Canada offices complained that the name meant "moose" in French, and according to Canadian myth the moose was considered to be unintelligent. "Argos" was eliminated when it was learned that another company had already claimed the name. By default, in 1985 "AXA" became the new company name of Mutuelles Unies-Drouot. To increase brand awareness and inform U.S. consumers of the variety of financial services that AXA Financial offered, in 2002 the company announced a new advertising campaign created by the Martin Agency of Richmond, Virginia. Its television spots had the tagline "Your Future. Your Way," and included the music and words from the song *My Way* by Frank Sinatra.

MARKETING STRATEGY

Although ING was a well-known integrated financial services company throughout Europe, when it decided to enter the U.S. market, it was faced with building brand identity and name recognition. The challenge for the company's agency, Havas Advertising's Jordan McGrath Case & Partners of New York (JMCP), was to create a marketing campaign that would launch the company in the United States while clearly sending the message that ING was a name and not a suffix. JMCP signed on with ING in November 2000 and developed a campaign that took a humorous, tongue-in-cheek approach to the ING brand. Included in the effort were television spots and print ads. In an interview with *Adweek,* Rochelle Klein, chief creative officer for JMCP, explained that the campaign was designed to introduce ING to American consumers as "a new player in the financial industry and [to] get [its] name across."

Television spots for the branding and marketing effort, which had an estimated budget of $20–$30 million, began airing in May 2001. The kick-off spot opened with a man and his dog walking in a park. When the man got near a park bench where some people were sitting, he noticed the large letters "ING" on the back of the bench. Curious about the word that appeared to be partially hidden, the man asked a woman, "You have any idea what that says?" She answered, "ING." Not satisfied with her answer, he asked, "Do you know what's before it?" When the woman did not answer, the man looked at the bench and shouted, "What's that say?" The tagline for the spot was "It's not an ending, it's a beginning." Other spots featured various characters clearly pronouncing the company's name as three letters: "I-N-G." The spots also stressed that ING was an integrated financial services company. Spots aired during network and cable programs, including the popular *Friends* and *The West Wing.*

Like the television spots, print ads featured the ING name and stylized lion logo on a partially obstructed billboard. The full billboard was eventually revealed, showing the person reading the sign that he or she was seeing the company's entire name and not the end of a word. Also as in the TV spots, the tagline was "It's not an ending, it's a beginning." Print ads appeared in the *Wall Street Journal* and *USA Today* as well as in other national business and consumer magazines and trade publications read by financial-services professionals.

In the following year, 2002, the campaign was expanded to include advertising on the Internet. The ads appeared on financial news sites such as Fool.com, Forbes.com, and Smartmoney.com. In one ad every *ing* that appeared in the news text turned orange to match ING's corporate color. Another Internet ad was an extension of the television spots and print ads and featured the man and his dog looking up at an ING billboard. When the man asked, "What is ING?" another man responded, "It's a financial services company." His reply, however, was drowned out by a passing herd of sheep. Still another Internet ad displayed a number with the headline "People in the U.S. who don't know what ING does." Each time someone viewed the ad, the number decreased by one. The New York office of Tribal DDB (the interactive and online division of the agency DDB Worldwide) created the Internet advertising.

OUTCOME

Although the campaign succeeded in familiarizing American consumers with the ING name and helped create brand identity, the company reported in a press release that "the reality of today's depressed and volatile U.S. equity markets has kicked the industry and put an unwelcome dent in our nine-month performance." Following the start of the campaign ING reported that its 2002 pretax results for its U.S. financial-services division were $462.6 million, down from $717.7 million for the same period in 2001. The 2002 Internet effort that followed the television and print launch, however, did help drive business and further increased the company's name and brand recognition among consumers. According to an ING survey, 35 percent of consumers who saw the online ads stated that they planned to use ING's services.

Shortly after the start of its branding campaign in June 2001, ING ended its relationship with the agency Jordan McGrath Case & Partners (JMCP). The account was awarded to Omnicom's DDB Worldwide New York in August 2001. Further, in October 2001 JMCP's parent company, Havas Advertising, folded JMCP into another of its agencies, Arnold Worldwide, to create Arnold McGrath New York. That agency was ultimately folded into Arnold Worldwide.

FURTHER READING

"Breaking: ING Americas; ING Lets the Dogs Out." *Advertising Age,* May 21, 2001.

"A Brush with Greatness, Financial Services—Citigroup Ads." *Brandweek,* April 30, 2001.

Bryan, Scott. "European Financial Firm Land-ING in America." *Brandweek,* May 21, 2001.

———. "ING Breaks U.S. Ads." *Adweek,* May 21, 2001.

"A European Scope: ING Group." *Global Finance,* July 1, 2001.

Green, Heather, and Pallavi Gogoi. "Online Ads Take Off—Again." *BusinessWeek Online,* May 5, 2003. Available from <http://www.businessweek.com/magazine/content/03_18/b3831079_mz063.htm>

"Hotline (The ING Group Goes into Review)." *Adweek,* June 18, 2001.

Howard, Theresa. "Discover Goes for Funny Bone." *USA Today,* March 12, 2001.

"ING Americas Announces Integrated Management and Organizational Structure." *Business Wire,* December 14, 2000.

"ING Group Banks $50 M on Boosting Identity in the U.S." *Brandweek,* November 6, 2000.

"ING Launches First Major U.S. Ad Campaign; Campaign Marks the Next Phase in ING's U.S. Strategy—Building Name Awareness." *PR Newswire,* May 21, 2001.

Mack, Ann M. "ING Uses Web to Build Awareness." *Adweek,* October 22, 2002.

Stephens, Erica. "ING Ad Campaign Focuses on Products and Name." *Atlanta Business Chronicle,* May 25, 2001.

"The Washington Times Advertising and Media Column." *Washington (D.C.) Times,* September 30, 2002.

Rayna Bailey

Intel Corporation

2200 Mission College Blvd.
PO Box 58119
Santa Clara, California 95052-8119
USA
Telephone: (408) 765-8080
Fax: (408) 765-9904
Web site: www.intel.com

BUNNY PEOPLE CAMPAIGN

OVERVIEW

During the 1980s the popularity and performance of personal computers (PCs) experienced phenomenal growth. Chip maker Intel Corporation, based in Santa Clara, California, produced a major share of the microprocessors powering those PCs, leading the way in both consumer recognition and sales and claiming a 90 percent market segment share by the late 1990s. By 1990 Intel had begun to focus its marketing on shaping the corporate brand with newly hired agency EURO RSCG DSW Partners, Salt Lake City. The agency set out to create a brand image for Intel's chips as "The computer inside," a concept that, in a 1991 campaign, hit the bull's-eye. "Intel inside" became more than a campaign tag line; it was an industry icon.

Throughout the 1990s the PC industry faced an ever-increasing demand from consumers for faster, high-performance microprocessors for their personal computers. In 1997 Intel responded by introducing its most enhanced technology in 10 years, MMX and the Pentium II processor. Acknowledging the increasing trend to use PCs for entertainment as well work, Ann Lewnes, Intel's director of worldwide advertising, stated, "[The company's objective] is to create awareness and excitement among consumers. We wanted to position the product as fun, particularly for multimedia applications."

Intel was the only tech company to purchase ads for the 1997 Super Bowl's coveted commercial slots. During Intel's 30 seconds, "Bunny People" did the disco. These Bunny People were modeled after chip technicians who work in the hyperclean manufacturing rooms of fabrication plants. Their spacesuit like "cleansuits," or "bunny suits," are worn to prevent even the tiniest of particles from contaminating the processors. In the spot a group of Bunny People danced about in brightly colored lam, bunny suits. Said Lewnes, "These commercials are humorous, high-tech fantasies that show how fun computing can be with MMX technology." Another spot in the campaign featured *Seinfeld* star Jason Alexander as a hapless character hoping to impress potential blind dates via Intel's video phone. These spots, together with related print ads, radio spots, and promotions, spurred both consumer approval and rival spoofing and was the most comprehensive campaign ever undertaken by Intel.

HISTORICAL CONTEXT

By the 1980s computers had begun to move from a largely scientific and industrial market into the personal user market. Intel's 1989 ad campaign with Shafer & Shafer, an Irvine, California, tech agency, prompted consumers to upgrade their systems with the latest technologies. Intel had just released its 386 chip, an upgrade of

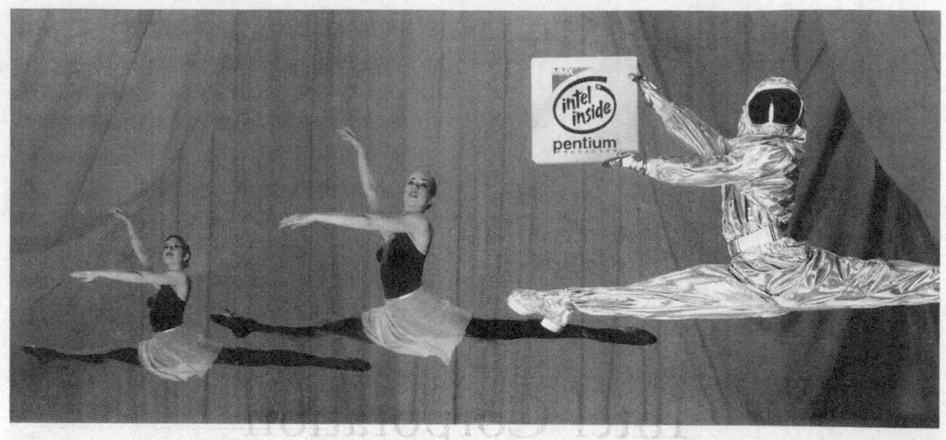

Bunny Man ballet, from Intel's "Bunny People" campaign. © 2006 INTEL CORPORATION. REPRODUCED BY PERMISSION.

its 286 chip. When computer makers and buyers did not rush to upgrade, a striking "Red X" campaign was designed. Print ads and billboards featured graffiti-esque red spray paint x-ing out "286" and scrawling in "386SX" in an effort to move consumers along the upgrade food chain. In 1990 Intel signed on EURO RSCG DSW Partners. That year's campaign, "The Computer Inside," focused on building the corporate brand. In 1991 the company launched "Intel Inside." The success of the "Intel Inside" campaign was due in part to brilliant co-op marketing—that is, paying PC makers to feature the logo in ads. Through a combined marketing effort between Intel and computer makers, the "Intel Inside" logo on PCs became a seal of approval in the minds of consumers.

Between the years 1989 and 1996 Intel's revenues soared from $3.1 billion to $20.8 billion, net income rose from $391 million to $5.2 billion, and market segment share grew from under 60 percent to 80 percent. The "Intel Inside" campaign had solidified Intel's image of superior performance, outweighing the fact that the company's microprocessors cost considerably more than those available from its competitors. Intel became a cash cow, with sales increasing a whopping 30 to 50 percent every year between 1994 and 1997.

As Intel's enviable success was turning heads and profits, their competitors were carving a different niche. Prior to 1997 the average PC price was $2,000. In that year Compaq Computer Corporation set an industry precedent by offering a high-powered PC at a bargain-basement price of $999, powered by rival Cyrix Corporation's MediaGX chip. The sub-$1,000 PC market proved irrepressible. Within a year nearly all major PC makers were offering the new price point, resulting in a segment sales increase from 7 percent of the U.S. retail market in 1996 to approximately 25 percent in 1997. Intel's president and CEO Dr. Andrew S. Grove explained the company's response to this competition to *Business Week:* "For us to walk away from a market whose size is going to be measured in tens of millions of units per year, maybe bigger, is inconceivable.... It is very important for us to participate at both ends of the wire." The company planned to make up for meager profits on the low end with increased volume and on the high-end with sales directed at server and workstation markets.

TARGET MARKET

The success of Intel's brand identification could largely be summed up in two words: "Intel Inside." The tag line had proven enormously successful in whispering "performance inside" into the ears of PCs buyers. Consumers wanted an assurance that their PC could go the distance double-time as they cruised the Internet, developed intricate audio and animation programs, and played power-hungry computer games.

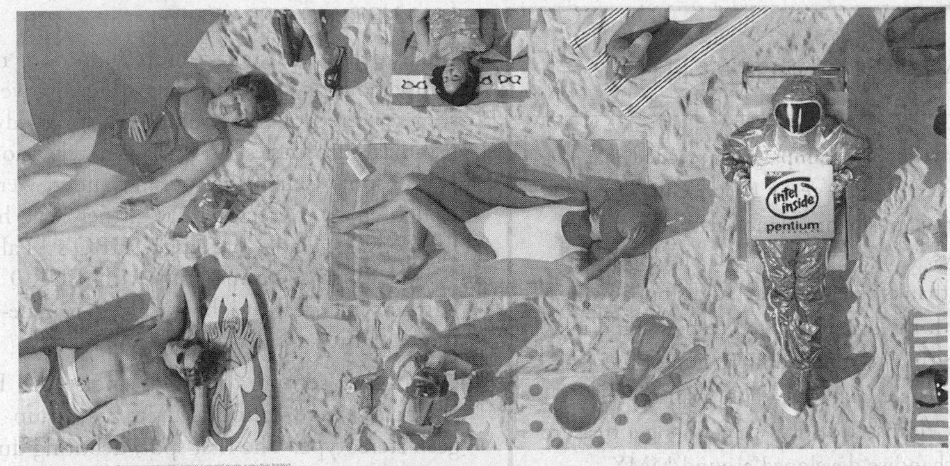

Bunny Man at the beach, from Intel's "Bunny People" campaign. © 2006 INTEL CORPORATION. REPRODUCED BY PERMISSION OF INTEL CORPORATION.

The age market for such a product was widespread—PC users from their late teens to late 40s. To reach such a diffuse target, the "Blind Date" and "Bunny People" spots were aired on such programs as *ER, Seinfeld,* and *Veronica's Closet,* with cable TV spots purchased on The History Channel, CNN, and A&E. The women's market was targeted with print ads placed in *Self, Vanity Fair, Gourmet,* and, for the first time, *Martha Stewart Living.*

The "Bunny People" spots proved the most popular aspect of the campaign. The mood set by Wild Cherry's boogie-down tune, "Play That Funky Music," hit home with those at both ends of the Baby Boomer generation. Boomers who had come of age during the 1970s identified with the disco reference from firsthand experience. The theme spoke to younger Boomers as well because the campaign was launched during a late 1990s nostalgia for anything from the 1970s. The hints of '70s nostalgia in the disco-themed ads proved a winner with the youngest target market segment as well. Intel's campaign had successfully caught the ears of all ages within its intended market.

COMPETITION

By the 1997 release of MMX technology, Intel had a decided claim on the title of world's top selling chip maker. Primary competition came from Cyrix Corporation's MediaGX processor and Advanced Micro Devices's (AMDs) K6chip. Intel had already earned a distinguished reputation for performance, if not low-end pricing. Rivals Cyrix and AMD set out to develop a reputation for high quality at a more competitive price than Intel's. Cyrix's 1997 marketing goals were strikingly similar to Intel's, with one exception. "People want to be entertained in their living room—they don't want just a productivity tool. Through our innovative processor and system technology, we've made possible an easy-to-use home infotainment system with PC capability that people can actually afford," stated Cyrix's vice president of corporate marketing, Steve Tobak, on the company's website. Intel's rivals had an edge in competing in the sub-$1,000 PC market, because their processors continued to be available at prices well below the Pentium's. Consumers had been offered a sub-$1,000 PC that could perform, and they scooped them up. Market segment share for the price point jumped from 10 percent in 1996 to upwards of 20 percent the following year. "It's the first time in many years that there has been a viable alternative [to Intel] at the low end," IBM senior vice president Samuel J. Palmisano told *Business Week.* His company tapped AMD's K6 chip for their low-end line of PCs. Intel's monopoly on high performance chips that could run desirable software had been challenged, and at a considerably lower cost to PC makers.

AMD's fall 1997 campaign, developed by Hill, Holliday Advertising, sent out just this message. One spot featured a secret agent held captive by an evil mastermind whose plot to rule the world is foiled when the processor in his expensive PC cannot deliver. Thanks to the AMD processor in his PC, the secret agent handily

PLAYING IS THE THING

Intel's "Bunny People" campaign succeeded in transforming supposedly geeky MMX chip technicians into fun-loving, dance-at-the-drop-of-a-keystroke guys. The ads were popular in consumer surveys, and thanks to Intel merchandising, anyone enamored with the brightly suited techies could take home an eight-inch beanbag doll version of their very own. Bunny People character dolls, available in an assortment of cleansuit colors, were among a treasure trove of merchandise developed around MMX technology. Consumers could pick up a Bunny People doll at their favorite computer outlet or log on to Uniquely Intel, the company's Internet merchandise catalog (http://www.intel.com), to scoop up Bunny People embellished beach towels, bags, tumblers, watches, and apparel.

escapes. On AMD's website, Tom Stites, vice president of communications, said, "These television spots target personal computer consumers. Our intent is to show that buying PCs based on the AMD K6 processor is a smart choice. The message is that no matter how much or how little consumers are prepared to spend for a similarly configured system, they will get better performance with the AMD K6. Our message of performance and value is compelling, but our primary competitor outspends us on advertising by almost twenty to one. In order to be heard above the noise, commercials from AMD must break through with humor and excitement."

Apple Computer, Inc., could not have agreed more. In 1997 Apple joined forces with TBWA Chiat/Day for the first time in over a decade. This team was responsible for having produced Apple's legendary "1984" campaign, voted the best ad of all time by advertising professionals. In early 1998 the team followed their cerebral 1997 "Think Different" campaign with the "Toasted Bunny" spot, a direct spoof on Intel's disco dancing "Bunny People." Apple had already made fun of Intel's vaunted processor speed in a spot of a garden snail crawling along with a Pentium II chip on its back. Their "Toasted Bunny" spot featured a guy in a shimmering blue cleansuit, accompanied by the 1970s classic "Disco Inferno." As the foil-clad techie dances to the beat, his feet burst into flames, and he has to be doused by a fireman. Apple's website deepened the tease with, "Ah, there's nothing sweeter than the smell of toasted chips in the morning."

MARKETING STRATEGY

Intel's decision to take a more humorous marketing tack came about as chip suppliers were discovering that consumers were not responding well to ads dwelling on the technical intricacies of PCs. On television two "Blind Date" spots, starring Jason Alexander, were the first ads to lighten up. Director Jim Gartner, who had brought to life Pepsi's "Dad's Blessing," HBO's "Falling TV" and Visa's "Burro," teamed up with EURO RSCG DSW Partners in creating the spots, a tongue-in-cheek portrayal of Intel's video phone capabilities.

In the second round of spots, the Bunny People characters were introduced in a send-up of the boring geek stereotype. The first spot, debuting during the 1997 Super Bowl, contrasted a traditional fabrication-plant setting with a more free-spirited MMX technology department. Within this more fun-loving environment, the Bunny People danced the workday away, suggesting the PC user could experience new heights of fun with the aid of MMX technology. The Bunny People showed up on television spots throughout the year, and during the fall an international flavor was added by having the Bunny People travel the globe in a "TechMobile," created by Batmobile designers Trans FX of Los Angeles. In the "Road Trip" spot the Bunny People became so excited about Pentium II technology, they were inspired to build the TechMobile to help them spread the word around the world. In a second spot the TechMobile delivered the beloved Bunny People to Hong Kong, where they were hailed by crowds in awe of the marvels of Pentium II.

The television and print campaigns were complemented by radio commercials and an interactive sweepstakes. On the websites of MTV, Interzine, Gamespot, MPlayer, Hotwired, and Hollywood Online, users were supplied with clues for the official sweepstakes found on Intel's website.

Intel continued its proven track record of co-op marketing in 1997. The home PC buyer's awareness of the Intel microprocessor increased from 20 percent at 1992's campaign launch date to 80 percent in 1996, according to Dennis Carter, vice president of sales and marketing for the company. Even more impressive was the 90 percent recognition in the business market. Carter told *Advertising Age* magazine that 70 percent of home PC buyers and 85 percent of business buyers preferred Intel and were willing to pay the higher price the "Intel Inside" logo commanded.

Since the inception of "Intel Inside," consumers had shown a strong allegiance to the company's co-op efforts. According to a September 15, 1997, issue of *Advertising Age,* Intel had an estimated advertising budget of $900 million in 1997, $750 million of which went into co-op ads. As of 1997, approximately 1,500 PC makers were participating with Intel in co-op marketing, wherein they received a 6 percent rebate on chip purchases by tacking the Pentium logo on their PCs and ads. PC makers would come up with one-third of the cost of print ads and one-half that of broadcast costs. For the first half of the year, nearly 80 percent of the $202.9 million spent on U.S. PC advertising in computer and business publications featured the "Intel Inside" logo according to Sheila Craven, president of Adscope, an ad tracking company. Intel's contributions toward shared advertising proved irresistible, with every major Intel-based PC maker participating by 1996.

OUTCOME

Intel's "Bunny People" campaign proved a strong success, thanks to the uplifting image provided by Wild Cherry's "Play That Funky Music." A *USA Today* Ad Track survey found the spot among the top 10 favorite ads among baby boomer consumers, making it the most popular tech campaign ever measured by the poll. It ranked in the top 20 of 90 campaigns measured by Ad Track in a two-year period. The breakdown showed that 30 percent of those answering the survey claimed they liked the MMX ads a lot, with 38 percent of those between 18 and 24 giving the ads a thumbs up. A mere 8 percent of those polled felt the television spots were ineffective. Consumers said they felt the disco-dancing Bunny People imparted a fun, consistent image for the brand. Ricky Banaag, Intel Microelectronics country manager for the Philippines, told *Newsbytes News*, "Our research shows that the Bunny People characters have been a positive influence on Intel's brand personality. Bunny People characters have helped make the Intel brand more friendly and accessible."

Industry insiders were not necessarily so positive. Apple executive Allen Olivio called the "Bunny People" ads frivolous in *Entertainment Weekly*. "It's what happens to advertisers when they don't have anything to say." Marketing consultant Gary Stibel showed concern that Intel's funky ads might threaten the reputation for high quality secured with its earlier "Intel Inside" identification, and he suggested to *USA Today* that Intel should stick to a consistent image. A president of an undisclosed ad agency for a major computer client, commenting on Intel's focus on co-op marketing, told *Advertising Age*, "Most people that buy computers don't even know that that chip is in there. They care about the performance of the computer. It really doesn't matter what the chip is." But John Dahlin of EURO RSCG DSW Partners responded, "Ultimately the success of your work is the success of your client. What we do is produce advertising that works great for the problems that our client has. If it doesn't win a lot of awards . . . as long as a billion people buy Pentium, I can handle that." Intel could well handle its year-end report for 1997: revenue totaled $25.1 billion, with net income at $6.9 billion. It was the eighth consecutive year of earnings and revenue record setting for the world's largest chip maker.

FURTHER READING

Abrams, Judith. "Hearing Footsteps in Sub-$1,000 Market." *Multimedia Monitor,* November 1, 1997.

Armstrong, David. "Computers; Loose Connections." *The Press,* December 23, 1997.

Enrico, Dottie. "Consumers Bought into Real-World Ads in '97." *USA Today,* December 29, 1997.

———. "Consumers Flip for Hip Chip Ads but Is Intel's Image Being Squandered?" *USA Today,* May 12, 1997.

———. "For Advertisers, Age Starts to Matter." *USA Today,* September 22, 1997.

Goldfisher, Alastair. "Apple Torches Bunny in Latest TV Campaign." *The Business Journal, San Jose,* March 23, 1998.

"Intel Bunny People to Invade Aussie Living Rooms." *Newsbytes News Network,* February 26, 1997.

"Intel Launches $100+ Million Worldwide Ad Campaign." *Computer Publishing & Advertising Report,* September 29, 1997.

"Intel Unveils Global Pentium II Processor Ad Campaign." *M2 PressWire,* September 16, 1997.

Jacobs, A. J., and Shawna Malcom. "Spoof in Advertising: Imitation Is the Sincerest Form of Parody." *Entertainment Weekly,* April 10, 1998.

Johnson, Bradley. "Challenge for Intel: Boosting Tech Market." *Advertising Age,* September 15, 1997.

Reinhardt, Andy, Ira Sager, and Peter Burrows, "Cover Story: Intel." *Business Week,* December 22, 1997.

Seaman, Debbie. "What's the Big Idea?" *Advertising Age's Creativity,* May 1, 1998.

Stahlman, Mark. "MMX Is Great, But Do We Need It?" *Computer Reseller News,* February 10, 1997.

"US $10 Million Intel Media Blitz for Asia Pacific." *Newsbytes News Network,* November 17, 1997.

Barbra Brady

TIME FOR A PENTIUM II PROCESSOR? CAMPAIGN

OVERVIEW

Intel Corporation, the world's largest manufacturer of computer chips, had used a consistent marketing strategy to make its brand universally recognizable. Since 1991 Intel had advertised its line of chips directly to consumers with the tag line "Intel Inside." By 1998, 80 percent of all active computers were powered by Intel's Pentium chip, and its share of the global chip market was also an impressive 80 percent. According to the *National Post,* Intel so "thoroughly dominate[d] the microprocessor industry that [its] slogan [had] become a defining reality of personal computing." Intel had thrived in part because its advertising had convinced consumers and business users to upgrade repeatedly to its latest products. As *Advertising Age* explained, Intel's marketing premise was to bill itself as providing "the fastest, latest, and greatest chips." In May 1997 Intel introduced the Pentium II, a microprocessor that was more powerful than its predecessors and also contained innovative MMX technology, which allowed for improved multimedia functions.

After initially pitching the Pentium II to the business side of the market, Intel decided that 1998 was the year in which to explain to a mass consumer audience why they should also buy personal computers containing the Pentium II. In September of that year, Intel launched its "Time For A Pentium II Processor?" campaign, which consisted of a trio of television commercials created by Messner Vetere Berger McNamee Schmetterer/Euro RSCG—the first work this agency had produced for Intel. The purpose of the three spots was "to dramatize the question of what would happen if the deficiencies of Pentium II's competitors (and progenitors) insinuated themselves" into the real world, noted *Advertising Age* on September 28, 1998. Although Intel's lead in the microprocessor market was substantial, its competitors had begun to make inroads by offering budget chips. Consumers were becoming increasingly unwilling to pay premium prices for Intel's cutting-edge technology when they could purchase computers powered by cheaper chips, that—although slower—were still capable of executing a variety of tasks.

The three "Time" spots humorously and hyperbolically illustrated the difficulties a failure to use a Pentium II processor could create. One ad depicted a sky diver whose parachute unfurls at a glacial speed. As he plummets towards the ground, a message box pops up on screen: "Processing parachute, please wait." Another commercial portrayed a soccer match in which the goalie had not fully downloaded. As the opposing team advances with the ball, only his legs have materialized and a similar "please wait" message is displayed. The final commercial featured a baseball game where the pitcher's fastball never arrives at home plate. "Whoaaa," the broadcaster exclaims as the ball hangs in the air, "the pitch hasn't processed yet. Aw, this slow processing thing is a tough break for this young kid." Another "window" appears—"Processing fastball"—to explain the delay. Each commercial closed with a voice-over querying, "Time for a Pentium II Processor?" accompanied by the "Intel Inside" logo. Intel was quite pleased with the spots. Not only did they boost sales of the Pentium II itself but they were lauded by consumers and advertising industry insiders alike.

HISTORICAL CONTEXT

Intel's greatest marketing innovation was to target a mass audience with its microprocessors. Beginning in 1989 with its famous "Red X" campaign on behalf of its 386 chip, Intel recognized the rewards afforded by hawking its wares directly to a broad range of consumers rather than simply aiming for technophiles. This approach was significantly at odds with what was then conventional wisdom concerning technology advertising. According to the September 15, 1997, issue of *Advertising Age,* ad critics derided Intel's consumer-based efforts because "most people that buy computers don't even know that the chip is in there…They care about the performance of the computer [not] what chip the chip is." Microprocessor manufacturers typically touted their products to original equipment manufacturers (OEMS), who assembled personal computers and then sold machines to the public. Intel, by contrast, believed that it could create demand for its products through savvy ads, and that by doing so it could get personal computer users to pay attention to microprocessor brands and even ask specifically for computers containing Intel.

"Intel Inside," which was conceived by Dahlin Smith White and debuted in 1991, consistently delivered the message that Intel's chips were superior. The first "Intel Inside" ads were designed to promote Intel's 486 chip (the successor to the 386), and the company continued to use the campaign as it rolled out new generations of ever more speedy and advanced chips including the Pentium and then the Pentium Pro chips. Early "Intel Inside" commercials took viewers on a high-tech voyage through the innards of a computer that ended at the processor, the "brain" of the machine. Later ads were more sophisticated, such as the company's "Bunny People" spots, which first aired during the 1997 Super Bowl, and depicted disco-dancing technicians adding fun to Pentium chips. (These "Bunny People" commercials were also the first to feature the Pentium II chip.) In addition to the television, print, and radio campaigns that ran under the umbrella of "Intel Inside," the company also sponsored an advertising co-op, in which it paid a portion of an OEM's marketing costs if the manufacturer would announce that its machines had "Intel Inside," generally accomplished by way of a sticker affixed to each computer made. By 1997 every major computer maker participated in the co-op, including Compaq, IBM, Packard-Bell, and Hewlett-Packard. Contrary to the glum forecasts of tech insiders, Intel's consumer-targeted campaigns were an unequivocal success. The company's revenue had grown from $3.1 billion in 1989 to $20.8 billion in 1996, and "its Pentium brand has become synonymous with the rise of the PC," declared *Marketing*.

The Pentium II was not only faster, but it also performed multimedia functions better than its predecessors. In May 1997 Intel launched a campaign for the Pentium II that sought to reach business PC users. This $20 million print and Internet campaign used the slogan "The Next Chapter in PC Technology," and appeared in newspapers such as the *New York Times, Wall Street Journal,* and *USA Today*.

TARGET MARKET

After completing the campaign aimed exclusively at business PC users, Intel focused on a mass consumer audience with "Time." While the market for technical products had once been dominated by a computing elite, one-third of all American households owned a PC by 1994, according to the *Wall Street Journal* on September 20, 1994. Reaching such a vast and diverse audience was a challenge. As *Advertising Age* explained on October 7, 1996, Intel's overarching goal was to craft advertisements that were "relevant to consumer and business targets" alike, across demographic and geographic divides.

The primary way "Time" attempted to appeal to a broad audience was to avoid technical terms and jargon that would alienate some consumers (albeit while catering to a more computer-savvy segment). This was a key shift from the "Bunny People" approach, which had reached a more technology-oriented audience with its focus on the chip-making process. Instead, the "Time" spots "cleverly connect[ed] the cold concept of computer processing power to real-life situations," according to the *Orange County Register*. Without resorting to a discussion of megabits or graphic interface, Intel perfectly illustrated the campaign's underlying premise that computer speed was a necessity. In this way, the campaign reflected the computing reality of the mass of people who used their machines mainly as tools to word process, surf the Internet, and download information from favorite Web sites. The spots tapped into the "frustration [such a consumer] feels if [her] PC isn't working as fast as it might," a Messner executive told *Marketing*. The campaign hoped to play off the frustration everyone felt at some point, as they sat by idly while their computers slowly downloaded a file. The "message bar" incorporated in the commercial ("Processing parachute") was nearly identical to those that cropped up on all machines during a download.

"Time" simultaneously strove not to alienate those whose computer skills transcended this basic tool level.

INTEL HITS A HOMER

Shortly after the debut of "Time for a Pentium II Processor?" Intel broke a more general branding spot featuring an unlikely hero—Homer Simpson of the hit comedy show *The Simpsons*. The animated commercial depicts the famously stupid Simpson getting a Pentium chip implanted in his brain. He becomes a brilliant professor, who formulates a sort of unified pastry theory. The spot, which appeared after November 8, 1998, closed with a shot of the back of Homer's head—on which was stamped the famous "Intel Inside" logo. An Intel marketing executive explained in a press release that "Homer Simpson is the perfect vehicle to communicate that having an Intel processor makes your computer smarter... If an Intel chip can turn Homer Simpson into a scholar, imagine what it can do for your PC."

As the *Dow Jones News Service* noted, Intel had to "reach the 'in' crowd while amusing the rest of the audience." The ironic humor of the spots helped fulfill this goal by ensuring that regardless of a viewer's level of technical know-how, the spots would be engaging and witty.

COMPETITION

Despite Intel's overwhelming past success in its consumer advertising, "Time" was launched at a crucial point for the company. In what the *National Post* termed "a rare, but costly stumble," Intel had "failed to foresee that many users would prefer low-cost PCs that handle[d] typical computing tasks with alacrity" instead of "costlier machines based on Intel's fastest and most lucrative processors." By the summer of 1997, the *San Jose Business Journal* reported the results of a survey conducted by ZD Market Intelligence, which indicated that a stunning 34 percent of U.S. businesses would consider buying PCs with a chip other than a Pentium, and 25 percent claimed they were "highly interested" in purchasing a non-Intel PC.

Advanced Micro Devices Inc. (AMD) was one of Intel's competitors that was winning over OEMs and customers alike with its inexpensive chips. According to the *National Post,* AMD controlled 50 percent of the chip market for PCs costing less than $1,000 by 1998, and it was supplying chips for the consumer computer lines at OEMS, such as Compaq, IBM, and Packard-Bell, that had previously been Intel's exclusive domain.

Part of AMD's strategy was to make consumers aware of its offerings. In 1996 the company launched a television campaign with the tag line "amd@work." Created by Hill, Holliday, Connors, Cosmopulos, the spots detailed how AMD chips "make the technology that people use today more affordable, more powerful, easier to use," an AMD spokesperson told *Advertising Age* on October 7, 1996. In May 1997 AMD announced that it would price its chips 25 percent below the cost of a comparable Intel microprocessor. In 1998 AMD aired humorous spots that demonstrated the 3-D capabilities of its chips.

Cyrix, a unit of National Semiconductor Corp., also gained a foothold in the low-end computer chip market. In November 1998 Cyrix inaugurated its first branding campaign. As its focal point, Cyrix stressed its cheaper prices and positioned itself as an egalitarian product. The print and television campaign "intended to let consumers know that Cyrix is enabling the PC manufacturers to deliver high-performance computers ... for well under $1,000," Cyrix's director of advertising told the November 2, 1998, *Brandweek*. The ads, which were designed by Goldberg Moser O'Neilland targeted first-time PC buyers, used bold drawing done in the Russian constructivist style to augment the campaign's tag line "The Liberation of Information." One print piece, "Liberty and Access for All," made its proletarian pitch: "Gen X-ers, empty nesters, boomers, cocooners, closet capitalists, web surfers, gainers, educators, unite."

In addition to this pressure at the less expensive end of the market, Intel also encountered more aggressive marketing from one of its high-end competitors, Apple Computer. After breaking out of its long slump, Apple debuted three competitive ads in March 1998. Crafted by TBWA Chiat/Day, these spots directly attacked the Pentium II. In one, a man wearing a suit identical to those of Intel's "Bunny People" has to be hosed down. As he looks at the camera with smoke pouring from his helmet, the voice-over (performed by actor Richard Dreyfus) declared, "Apple Computer would like to apologize for toasting the Pentium II processor in public." Apple claimed its G3 chip, which was a joint project between Apple, IBM, and Motorola, was twice as fast as the Pentium II. "Apple has to make some very strong product statements here," a company executive told the *Wall Street Journal* on March 26, 1998.

MARKETING STRATEGY

Intel selected television as the means to convey the message of "Time." Since the company sought to reach a mass audience, it selected an array of programs, ranging from *The X-Files* to major sporting events to late night chat shows, on which to air its spots. To heighten the impact, the campaign debuted during the season premieres of heavily watched shows such as NBC's Thursday night titans *Seinfeld* and *ER*. The company also used web banner ads to spread its message. These efforts featured a slow moving download screen similar to the television executions.

Intel's goals for the campaign were two-fold. Since the company wanted to drive sales for the Pentium II, the product's name featured prominently in the tag line in each commercial. On the other hand, because Intel was increasingly under siege from competitors who sold bargain chips, Intel needed the campaign to reinforce its overall branding message. Therefore, while the commercials used the speed of the Pentium II's as a specific product selling point, the implicit message was "to educate our consumer audience about what role the processor plays in their PC and the value of it," Joanne O'Brien, Intel's manager of consumer advertising, told *Brandweek* on October 26, 1998.

Ever since Intel had first ventured into consumer advertising, it was faced with a challenge. Because its chips grew exponentially more advanced every few months, Intel was continually in the midst of introducing a new microprocessor. Its advertising had somehow to cultivate consumers' desire for the latest and fastest chip. As the September 15, 1997, *Advertising Age* explained, "Intel's future depends as much on marketing as it does on technology ... it must continue to create demand for its ever-faster chips." "Time" strove to incite this demand. By presenting the problems of the technical world in the "real" world of the commercials' soccer game and skydiving, Intel sought to make the speed of one's processor less a concept of computing and more about computing's growing power over life. The divide between reality and virtual reality was blurred in the spots. The campaign's chief goal was to encourage viewers to feel a sense of concern over matters technical, and then to find a solution in the message of the ads. "Time" worked to make consumers "feel comfortable with a ... product that was impersonal," according to *USA Today*.

OUTCOME

Intel expressed satisfaction with "Time." The humorous vignettes combined with Intel's persistent use of the "Intel Inside" tag line, helped fuel sales of the Pentium II. In addition, the campaign was credited with reinforcing the Intel brand before an even more massive launch campaign—the one for the Pentium III microprocessor early in 1999.

"Time for a Pentium II Processor?" was also quite well-received by its target audience. Consumer surveys revealed that the "Time" ads were the best-liked advertising Intel had ever released. Moreover, advertising critics were enthusiastic. While many of Intel's previous efforts had been soundly panned within the ad industry, "Time" spots received plaudits from advertising critics. *Advertising Age* 's Bob Garfield praised the campaign on September 28, 1998, for focusing on the product and successfully distinguishing its from its competitors. "Anyone who has ever tried to multitask or download video understands" the spot's moniker, he noted.

FURTHER READING

Beatty, Sally Goll. "Apple's Ads Scorch Intel Bunnies." *Wall Street Journal,* March 26, 1998.

Garfield, Bob. "Intel Downloads Chip Woes into Real World." *Advertising Age,* September 28, 1998.

Goldfisher, Alastair. "Intel Plants New Brain in Homer: Chipmaker Latest to Air Consumer-Oriented Commercials." *San Jose Business Journal,* November 9, 1998.

Goldman, Kevin. "Computer Companies Try TV Ads' Mass Appeal." *Wall Street Journal,* September 20, 1994.

"If Only Homer Simpson Had a Brain! It Happens, in New Intel Campaign." *Brandweek,* October 26, 1998.

Johnson, Bradley. "Advanced Micro Devices Spreads Word on Its Chips." *Advertising Age,* October 7, 1997.

———. "Challenge for Intel: Boosting Tech Market." *Advertising Age,* September 15, 1997.

———. "Computer World's Task: Sell 1 Brand to 2 Targets." *Advertising Age,* October 7, 1996.

McLuhan, Robert. "Speed Is the Issue for Intel." *Marketing,* December 3, 1998.

Nguyen, Peter. "Short Cuts." *Orange County Register,* October 11, 1998.

Piller, Charles. "Intel's Dominance under Siege." *National Post,* February 26, 1999.

Wells, Melanie. "Toon Town Takes Over Baby Boom." *USA Today,* November 4, 1998.

Rebecca Stanfel

Intercontinental Hotels Group PLC

3 Ravinia Drive, Suite 100
Atlanta, Georgia 30346
USA
Telephone: (770) 604-2000
Fax: (770) 604-5403
Web site: www.ihgplc.com

HOLIDAY INN BRAND REJUVENATION CAMPAIGN

OVERVIEW

In 1996 Holiday Inn, then owned by the British brewing conglomerate Bass PLC but subsequently acquired by Intercontinental Hotels Group PLC (IHG), embarked on a $1 billion renovation program that forced franchises to improve their facilities or lose their association with the brand. Holiday Inn wanted not only to publicize the physical improvements it was making but also to revitalize consumers' ideas about the chain. After dominating the roadside hotel market for decades, the chain had been struggling since the 1980s to distinguish itself from a host of new competitors. Parent company Bass brought in ad agency Fallon McElligott (later Fallon Worldwide) of Minneapolis to modernize the Holiday Inn image and rebuild the brand's reputation for quality and consistency.

Fallon launched its brand-rejuvenation efforts with a splash during the 1997 Super Bowl, using the tagline "On the way" to tell consumers about the physical makeover in process at many Holiday Inns. The television campaign "Mark" followed, running to wide acclaim from 1999 to 2002 and significantly raising the brand's profile. After "Mark," Holiday Inn left television for two years, focusing on print, airport displays, and outdoor ads in its "What Matters Most" campaign. A 2004 television campaign on the children's network Nickelodeon followed, and in 2005 Fallon adapted the concept behind the "What Matters Most" campaign for placement on a variety of cable television networks.

The success of the brand-rejuvenation strategy was most evident during the "Mark" campaign, but Holiday Inn's evolution was complicated by the economic downturn following the terrorist attacks in the United States on September 11, 2001, as well as by the growing consumer preference for budget accommodations. Holiday Inn remained the heart of IHG, and the parent company continued to look for ways of leveraging the brand's heritage while appealing to changing consumer tastes.

HISTORICAL CONTEXT

The first Holiday Inn was opened near Memphis, Tennessee, in 1952. Entrepreneur Kemmons Wilson conceived his chain of hotels as an antidote to the uneven selection of accommodations then available along America's highways. As the brand expanded, its consistency from location to location set it apart from competing mom-and-pop establishments, as did innovations like free ice cubes, swimming pools, in-room televisions, air-conditioning, and kids-stay-for-free room rates. A computerized reservations system revolutionized trip planning and triggered a large-scale franchising push. Holiday Inn's famed "Great Sign," as it was called, loomed over highways across the nation and came to symbolize dependable, unpretentious comfort for weary travelers. By 1972 a new Holiday Inn opened its doors for business every three days.

But the 1970s oil embargo reduced the number of vacationers on the nation's roads, and in some ways the wild success of Holiday Inn's first two decades became a hindrance to the brand's continued development. The large number of franchises the chain sold during its boom years threatened to undermine the very consistency that had set Holiday Inn apart in the beginning, and competing chains, having adopted Wilson's innovations exactly, began using them in varying combinations to attract specific subsets of the everyman traveler who had always been Holiday Inn's target customer. Holiday Inn itself eventually spawned subbrands—such as Hampton Inn, Crowne Plaza, and Holiday Inn Express, Select, and SunSpree—to compete in the fractured travel market, and though Holiday Inn's parent company performed well, by the 1980s the original brand had lost not only its authority but also its identity. The Great Sign was retired in favor of a supposedly more modern, back-lit plastic model, and consumers could no longer say with confidence what to expect from a stay at any given Holiday Inn.

BAD IDEAS

Though the innovations of Holiday Inn founder Kemmons Wilson in roadside lodging amenities transformed the American hotel industry and landed him on the cover of *Time* magazine in 1972, his entrepreneurial instincts were not infallible. According to *USA Today,* Wilson demanded that all Holiday Inn rooms come with flyswatters before realizing that "it probably wasn't sending the right kind of message." Likewise, the notion of equipping every franchise with a trampoline was banished to the scrap heap of hotel history when "a youngster bounced too high and crashed (unhurt) through Wilson's office window."

TARGET MARKET

During preliminary market studies Fallon found that Holiday Inn had an incredibly strong base of consumer loyalty and that this loyalty cut across cultural barriers. Individuals who participated in Fallon's study, according to the *Atlanta Journal-Constitution,* recalled fond childhood memories of Holiday Inn vacations and spoke of Holiday Inns "as places where 'good people' stay." The overwhelming sentiment was that consumers of all backgrounds wanted Holiday Inn once again to become a brand they could trust. This information dovetailed with Holiday Inn's age-old definition of its core target as the everyman traveler. "It is a heartland, middle-market brand," Fallon's chairman, Pat Fallon, told the *Minneapolis Star Tribune.* Accordingly, the resulting campaign emphasized middle-American values and the sensible, standard features that had constituted the brand's reliability in earlier years.

At the same time Fallon's creative team believed that consumers, and young people in particular, needed an initial shock in order to be encouraged to take another look at what they believed to be an outdated brand. The campaign thus made an intentionally risky television premiere with a 1997 Super Bowl spot in which an extremely attractive female at a high school reunion turned the heads of her male classmates before they discovered that she was their former classmate Bob Johnson, now a transsexual. This dramatic metaphor for Holiday Inn's renovation project was followed, in the campaign's first year, with spots that used a more mainstream brand of humor to communicate the brand's return to consistency.

As the campaign developed, Holiday Inn and Fallon increasingly tailored the brand-rejuvenation message to the 25- to 54-year-old businesspeople among their everyman audience, those who by 1999 accounted for 70 percent of the chain's guests. This focus on business travelers was especially apparent in the "Mark" television campaign, which used the ongoing story of a 37-year-old slacker who lived at home with his parents. In repeatedly making it clear that he could not expect the amenities at home to compare to those of a Holiday Inn, Mark's parents pointed out to business and other travelers the specific advantages of staying at the chain's hotels.

COMPETITION

The scope of the rejuvenation campaign and Fallon's unconventional approach to the brand placed Holiday Inn among the most striking of hotel advertisers on the national stage at the time, but competitors across the market spectrum likewise had noteworthy campaigns. Accor Economy Lodging's Motel 6 had met with sustained success in its radio spots featuring the voice of National Public Radio personality Tom Bodett and his well-known tagline "We'll leave the light on for you," supporting the chain's own billion-dollar renovation of its properties. These spots eventually moved to television. Holiday Inn's sibling brand in the budget sector, Holiday Inn Express, boasted an acclaimed ongoing campaign called "Stay Smart," also the handiwork of Fallon, that showed hotel guests making absurdly intelligent statements about matters on which they had been ignorant before getting a good night's rest at a Holiday Inn Express. Cendant's Days Inn chain used its "There You Go" campaign to position itself as a brand whose extensive global presence took the guesswork and inconvenience out of travel.

Other chains tried to appeal to children, who, it was believed, could strongly influence their parents' lodging decisions. Embassy Suites, a leader in the family leisure sector, used characters from Nickelodeon's long-running *Rugrats* series in television commercials that were filmed, like the popular cartoon, from the point of view of children. Comfort Inn and Comfort Suites used a promotional tie-in with Pokemon, the cartoon character trading-card phenomenon that became a movie in 2000, which they publicized via national radio and print outlets.

MARKETING STRATEGY

From the time Fallon pitched the Holiday Inn account, it was apparent to all that reviving the brand would be an extremely difficult, long-term project. The belief that Holiday Inn was a mediocre chain whose time had come and gone was as widespread as consumers' affection for the brand. Likewise, the massive renovation project behind the claim that Holiday Inn was changing did not yet apply to all franchises. At the time the campaign opened, only about one-third of the chain's hotels had been renovated. "This puts us in a conundrum," Fallon's president and creative director, Bill Westbrook, told the *Atlanta Journal-Constitution*. "We need to have another way [aside from detailing the renovation project] to tell consumers about Holiday Inn but not to get them to expect too much."

The first phase of the campaign was launched with the Super Bowl ad in which, according to Holiday Inn's John Sweetwood, transsexual Bob Johnson served as a "wake up call to consumers across America." The commercial indeed attracted attention, but much of it was negative, and the ad was pulled from circulation rather than being used, as planned, in combination with the other spots in the ongoing campaign. The television spots that followed up the campaign's launch reminded consumers of the Holiday Inn they had once trusted and used the tagline "On the way" to indicate that the chain was in the process of reviving its prior standards of excellence. Print and outdoor ads supported this message of ongoing improvement.

Once the idea of renovations and a return to excellence had been publicized, the popular "Mark" campaign, which ran on television from 1999 to 2002, pointed out specific perks available to business and leisure travelers. A jobless 37-year-old living at home with his parents and grandmother, Mark's demands for amenities like free rent ("kids should stay for free"), better breakfast, and business services led his mother to ask, "What do you think this is, a Holiday Inn?" In its second year Mark's parents continued to ask that brand-defining question, and the tagline "More is better" was added to promote features like high-speed Internet connections and large work spaces. In his third year on the air Mark took the logical step of moving into a Holiday Inn, where he was shown eating leftovers off a room-service tray in the hallway and interrupting a "Symposium for Global e-Thinking" to ask if anyone could direct him to the pool.

The emphasis of the brand-rejuvenation strategy then shifted to print and outdoor advertisements as the "What Matters Most" campaign again emphasized Holiday Inn's all-American roots, down-to-earth personality, and basic features. The ads brought back the iconic Great Sign, pictured against a sunrise or sunset in a way meant to duplicate the feeling of arriving at a Holiday Inn. Witty copy like "Close to downtown. Near the airport. As far from trendy as you can get" reinforced the convenience and no-nonsense image that Fallon and Holiday Inn had long been trying to reestablish. Another popular spot referred to the widespread practice of filching hotel towels: "About the towels, we forgive you." In late 2003 the "What Matters Most" ads focused on the quality of Holiday Inn breakfasts to distinguish the chain from budget competitors who provided little or no breakfast choices. These ads ran in publications such as the business-friendly *Wall Street Journal* and *USA Today* and were placed in dioramas in the Hartsfield-Atlanta International Airport.

In 2004, for the first time since the "Mark" campaign had ended in 2002, Holiday Inn commercials returned to television, beginning a two-year partnership with the children's cable network Nickelodeon. The initial Nickelodeon spots featured a cartoon family with enormous noses who found freedom from their insecurities at a Holiday Inn. As part of the Nickelodeon deal, Holiday Inn became the official hotel sponsor of *The SpongeBob SquarePants Movie* and its DVD release. In 2005 the brand-rejuvenation effort moved beyond Nickelodeon to a wide variety of cable networks with "Signs," a television campaign derived from the "What Matters Most" print ads.

OUTCOME

During the "Mark" portion of the brand-rejuvenation effort, Holiday Inn's advertising strategy met with its clearest signs of success. According to Holiday Inn's

Greg Price, unaided awareness of the brand grew by roughly 50 percent in the "Mark" campaign's first two years. But the U.S. lodging industry as a whole suffered during the economic downturn that followed the terrorist attacks in 2001 and the bursting of the stock market bubble, with the midscale-with-food-and-beverage sector—Holiday Inn's sector—losing out in particular as more and more travelers opted for budget hotels.

Holiday Inn remained the heart of IHG's portfolio, with 1,484 hotels worldwide. In 2004 IHG unveiled a new prototype Holiday Inn in Gwinnet County, Georgia, that showcased artwork celebrating the brand's past, employed a modernized Great Sign, and had streamlined kitchen operations with an eye toward greater profitability.

FURTHER READING

Alexander, Keith L. "Hotel Ad May Get Early Checkout." *USA Today,* January 28, 1997.

Baar, Aaron. "Holiday Inn Offers More Mark." *Adweek,* March 13, 2000.

———. "Renovations Done, Holiday Inn Touts Amenities." *Adweek,* March 8, 1999.

Bly, Laura. "Come Inn off the Highway." *USA Today,* May 24, 2002.

Gleason, Mark. "Fallon's Challenge: Make Holiday Inn More 'In.'" *Advertising Age,* September 2, 1996.

"Hello Again, Great Sign." *Lodging Hospitality,* July 15, 2003.

Lazare, Lewis. "Holiday Inn Brings Back Successful Mark Campaign." *Chicago Sun-Times,* July 2, 2001.

Lippert, Barbara. "Marking the Spots." *Adweek,* April 5, 1999.

Merrill, Ann. "Ad Agency Fallon McElligott Captures Holiday Inn Account: Minneapolis Company Will Get Foot in Door of Travel Market as It Creates Campaign to Shed Hotel Firm's Outdated Image." *Minneapolis Star Tribune,* August 20, 1996.

Petrecca, Laura. "Holiday Inn Makes Its Mark to Tout Amenities: Ads' Yutzy Guy Wants More than Comforts of Home." *Advertising Age,* March 8, 1999.

Rauscher, Susannah Vesey. "The Holiday Inns of the Future: Polishing a Dated Image the First Task." *Atlanta Journal-Constitution,* October 17, 1996.

Rich, Motoko. "Holiday Inn's TV 'Slacker' Is Leaving Nest." *Wall Street Journal,* March 22, 2001.

Sheehan, Patricia. "Ship Shape." *Lodging Hospitality,* May 15, 2005.

Siebert, T.W. "Gotta Stay at Them All!" *Adweek,* June 12, 2000.

Steinberg, Brian. "Ads Target Stay-at-Home Travelers—Hotel-Industry Marketers Seek to Imprint Brands as Domestic Trips Gain." *Wall Street Journal,* June 6, 2003.

Mark Lane

STAY SMART CAMPAIGN

OVERVIEW

In 1998, after being in business for seven years, Holiday Inn Express, the limited-service offshoot of the famed but ailing Holiday Inn brand, had no clear identity apart from its namesake and was in danger of being left behind in a burgeoning segment of the hotel industry. Its parent at the time, Bass PLC (the Holiday Inn brands later became part of the Intercontinental Hotels Group PLC), enlisted Fallon McElligott (later renamed Fallon Worldwide) of Minneapolis to establish a personality for the young brand. The result was the "Stay Smart" campaign.

Aimed at male business travelers aged 25 to 54 and supported by a mere $3.5 million estimated annual ad budget in its early stages, the "Stay Smart" campaign made use of the premise that such travelers felt emotional validation at the idea that, in choosing a limited-service rather than a full-service hotel, they had acted sensibly. Exaggerating this idea of intelligent hotel choice for comic effect, the early TV spots in the campaign showed ordinary people opining about subjects in the manner of true experts, even though they had no training or education in these subjects. In lieu of knowledge, these individuals offered the following explanation for their mastery of complicated disciplines: "I did stay at a Holiday Inn Express last night." Though the content of the commercials went through various alterations over the campaign's multiyear run, the premise as well as the line "I did stay at a Holiday Inn Express last night" remained unchanged.

The campaign's punch line was picked up and used to humorous effect by journalists, editorial writers, and talk show hosts, among others, and the "Stay Smart" concept was given credit for effectively putting Holiday Inn Express on the industry map. The chain became the fastest-growing hotel in its category and outpaced its own sales goals during the campaign's run. "Stay Smart" saw its budget grow over the course of its run, and it was awarded a 2004 EFFIE that acknowledged its long-running effectiveness.

HISTORICAL CONTEXT

The Holiday Inn brand was launched in the 1950s by Memphis entrepreneur Kemmons Wilson, who, as a result of his own struggles to find reliable overnight lodging while traveling across the country, saw the need for a standardized set of hotels. The first links in the Holiday Inn chain grew up around Memphis, and their overwhelming success led Wilson to expand nationwide. Thanks to reasonable rates and amenities, like free ice, swimming pools, in-room televisions, and air-conditioning, Holiday Inn prospered, setting the standard for the roadside lodging industry in the 1960s and 1970s. In the 1980s, however, the chain began to suffer from its size and success. The number of franchisees operating under the Holiday Inn banner had grown unmanageably in the chain's boom years, and the disparity in quality between individual franchises undermined the brand's promise of reliability. In addition, as competitors copied the Holiday Inn model, Holiday Inn itself was no longer a unique lodging option. The unpretentious, reliable hotelier for the masses had become a shabby, lesser version of its old self in consumers' minds.

The Holiday Inn Express subbrand was launched in 1991 by then parent Bass PLC as a means of capitalizing on another developing trend in the lodging industry. Travelers increasingly were choosing less expensive accommodations, foregoing the full-service model established by Holiday Inn for limited-service hotels offering, in lieu of a restaurant, a free breakfast requiring minimal kitchen facilities and preparation. The established leaders in this segment included Hampton Inn and Courtyard by Marriott. After its first several years in business, Holiday Inn Express could claim no clear brand identity separate from its older sibling. The introduction of other Holiday Inn subbrands like Crowne Plaza, Sunspree, and Select in the 1990s further muddied consumers' perceptions of the brand family's individual members.

A DISSENTING VIEW

Thanks to their outrageous brand of humor, the "Stay Smart" ads on behalf of Holiday Inn Express immediately registered with consumers, but some critics, including prominent industry analyst Bob Garfield, an *Advertising Age* columnist, derided the premise of ordinary people developing extraordinary knowledge after a night's stay at the hotel chain. The idea that someone became "smart" about a matter like orthopedic medicine, as happened in one spot, after staying at a Holiday Inn Express had no logical connection, Garfield argued, to the intelligence required to choose a sensible hotel. There was no mention of the amenities that made Holiday Inn Express a smart choice and no explanation of how the subbrand differed from the regular Holiday Inn brand.

TARGET MARKET

Ultimately Bass and Fallon wanted the "Stay Smart" message to resonate with all travelers, but budgetary constraints made such a broadly aimed pitch untenable, especially at the outset of the campaign. Thus, they narrowed the target market, tuning the campaign's message so that it would resonate with the group of consumers most essential to the health of Holiday Inn Express and others in its market category, namely, men aged 25 to 54 who traveled frequently on business. The business travelers most likely to patronize Holiday Inn Express were those whose expenses were not fully reimbursed by their employers. These travelers were, therefore, expected to be economy minded and inclined to choose hotels for pragmatic reasons.

Fallon research indicated, moreover, that such travelers felt emotionally validated for choosing limited-service hotels like Holiday Inn Express. The idea that they had chosen no-nonsense comfort rather than unnecessary niceties presumably made these businessmen feel intelligent and sensible. The agency therefore arrived at its "Stay Smart" message, which acknowledged and encouraged this feeling of validation. The appeal to feelings was intended to establish a deeper connection with business travelers than would a more traditional hotel campaign touting amenities. Fallon also placed a premium on delivering the "Stay Smart" message in a way that distinguished Holiday Inn Express, in business travelers' minds, from the more established brands in its category. The campaign thus utilized absurdist scenarios and relied heavily on humor, departures from most hotel advertising of the time.

COMPETITION

Hotels had traditionally used print and television advertising to reinforce ideas about the cleanliness and comfort of their rooms and the quality of their customer service. As the differences between major hotel chains became insubstantial, many in the lodging industry turned to awards programs to distinguish themselves and to inspire brand loyalty. The awards tactic also became a casualty of standardization, however, as numerous hotel chains came to offer similar programs and airline partnerships. In this climate, hoteliers like Marriott, Starwood—whose holdings included Westin and Sheraton—and Hilton—the owner not only of its eponymous chain but, thanks to a recent merger, of Doubletree, Embassy Suites, and Hampton Inn—added features and elite levels to their awards programs. Among these companies, Starwood attempted to break out of this pattern by renovating its hotel rooms with an eye toward giving them a signature, marketable look. Another option for differentiating hotel brands was, of course, advertising.

Bass and Fallon were among the first hotel advertisers to use risky advertising as a way of breaking out of this impasse of sameness, and their branding work for

Holiday Inn was, along with the "Stay Smart" campaign, among the hotel industry's most notable marketing at the time. As part of the project to rejuvenate the ailing brand, and in concert with a large-scale push to renovate aging Holiday Inn properties across the country, Bass and Fallon courted controversy with a 1998 Super Bowl ad that used a transsexual as a symbol of the changes then occurring within the organization. This ad was followed up by TV spots assuring viewers "We're on the way" and showing housekeepers entering Holiday Inn rooms with chainsaws when the guests left for the day. After the change in brand identity and the message of the renovation project were established, Holiday Inn unveiled its lauded "Mark" campaign, in which an aging slacker named Mark who lived at home with his parents kept demanding amenities and services from his family. The family's response—"What does this look like, a Holiday Inn?"—was met with hilarity by Mark's elderly grandmother and was meant to reinforce the notion that Holiday Inn was, indeed, the standard for comfortable lodging in America.

Another hotel brand that had managed to create a distinct personality at least partly through marketing was Motel 6. In 1987 the discount chain began to use the voice of down-home radio personality Tom Bodett and the signature phrase "We'll leave the light on for you" in a radio campaign. The campaign, which was effective in establishing the brand's earthy, no-frills image, ran for more than a decade, eventually moving to television with a message of large-scale property renovations in the 1990s and continuing through the turn of the century.

MARKETING STRATEGY

The "Stay Smart" campaign, with an original budget estimated at $3.5 million, was launched in May 1998 on cable TV networks, with particular emphasis on sports programming. The initial group of three 30-second spots took the idea of guests' intelligence to a logical extreme, showing ordinary individuals who, after staying at a Holiday Inn Express, found themselves capable of giving extremely nuanced professional advice despite the fact that they had no qualifications for doing so. In one commercial, for example, a motorist stopped on the side of the road to tend to an injured cyclist. After declaring that the man was suffering from a dislocated patella, the Good Samaritan informed him that he was going to reset the bones. When the cyclist asked, "You are an orthopedic surgeon?" the Good Samaritan replied, "No, but I did stay at Holiday Inn Express last night." Copy reading "It won't make your smarter, but you'll feel smarter" ran on-screen.

The TV campaign's first significant update came in 2000, with two 30-second spots that maintained the central premise of the 1998 spots while scaling back the extremity of the humor. Rather than showing people who had become absurdly knowledgeable, the new spots showed people making intelligent decisions in humorous real-life situations. One spot, set in the waiting room of a dentist's office, featured a patient who, while waiting for his name to be called, overheard his dentist having a heated phone exchange involving a trip to the police station. Someone, it became clear as the patient listened, had suffered a life-threatening injury at the dentist's hands, and the dentist was supremely unconcerned with the person's well-being. At the end of the conversation the camera cut away from the insensitive dentist and back to the waiting room, revealing that the patient had fled. A caption reading "Stayed at a Holiday Inn Express last night" appeared on-screen.

In the spring of 2001 the concept was given a new twist in a TV spot featuring, or so it seemed, the rock band KISS. The musicians, in trademark face paint, were shown leaving the stage after a riotous encore, only to be revealed, once they had removed their makeup, as impostors. "You guys aren't KISS," a band manager asserted, and one of the members said, "No, but we did stay at a Holiday Inn Express last night." A simultaneous promotion took the "Stay Smart" theme in another direction, as Fallon put the operating idea behind the campaign—that those who stayed at a Holiday Inn Express should be commended for their intelligence—to the test. A promotion called "Express Your Smarts" asked ordinary people to write their own scripts for a "Stay Smart" commercial. Entry forms were available in Holiday Inn Express lobbies, online, and at branches of Gold's Gym, and contestants were required to use the campaign's now well-established punch line. The winning spot aired on the Discovery Channel.

By 2003, thanks to the success of the campaign's first five years, the budget had nearly doubled, and for the first time new creative work was used to bolster specific hotel amenities. In that year the "Stay Smart" theme was applied to spots introducing the chain's spruced-up breakfast bar, which featured special coffee roasts and a cinnamon roll developed especially for the hotel. In 2004 the campaign was adapted to publicize an upgrade of all bathrooms in the franchise, including the installation of high-powered "Stay Smart" showerheads manufactured exclusively for the hotel by Kohler. New Fallon-scripted TV spots showed guests arriving at inspired business ideas while showering, with accompanying text reading "If you do your best thinking in the shower, imagine how smart you'll be under our new showerhead." The enduring tagline "No, but I did stay at a Holiday Inn Express last night" remained in place.

OUTCOME

The "Stay Smart" message entered quickly into the American pop-culture lexicon. Ordinary people, as well as journalists and commentators, recycled the "No, but I did stay at a Holiday Inn Express last night" tagline. Mentions on *The Late Show with David Letterman* and National Public Radio were measures of the idea's pervasiveness, as was presidential candidate Al Gore's adoption of the tagline for his own humorous purposes during a speech in the run-up to the 2000 election. Holiday Inn Express became the fastest-growing hotel chain in its market segment and surpassed its own goal of generating $1 billion in sales a year ahead of schedule, in 1999 rather than 2000. Brand awareness of Holiday Inn Express grew 40 percent during the campaign's first three years, and in 2004 "Stay Smart" won a Gold EFFIE in the Sustained Success category, an honor based on the complete life of the campaign and its salutary effects on sales and brand image.

FURTHER READING

Baar, Aaron. "Advertising? Do-It-Yourself." *Adweek,* April 23, 2001.

———. "Fallon Airs Debut Spots for Holiday Inn Express." *Adweek,* May 4, 1998.

———. "New Holiday Inn Express Spots Closer to Reality." *Adweek,* April 17, 2000.

Beirne, Mike. "Breaking Out of the Hotel Rut." *Brandweek,* June 5, 2000.

———. "Holiday Inn Express Does Breakfast." *Brandweek,* November 11, 2002.

———. "Holiday Inn Express Launches Ad Contest." *Adweek,* May 28, 2001.

Garfield, Bob. "No Room for Logic at Holiday Inn Express." *Advertising Age,* May 11, 1998.

"Holiday Inn Express Ads Support New Bathrooms." *Hotels,* November 2004.

Rich, Motoko. "Holiday Inn's TV 'Slacker' Is Leaving Nest." *Wall Street Journal,* March 22, 2001.

Salomon, Alan. "Holiday Faces Future Aiming for Stability." *Hotel & Motel Management.* April 7, 1997.

Mark Lane

International Business Machines Corp.

New Orchard Road
Armonk, New York 10504
USA
Telephone: (914) 499-1900
Web site: www.ibm.com

CAN YOU SEE IT? CAMPAIGN

OVERVIEW

In 2002 the world's largest provider of computer products and services, International Business Machines Corp. (IBM), was relishing the comeback it had begun to experience eight years earlier. The computer titan had consolidated its scattered advertising accounts into a single account with one agency. By 2003 IBM was emerging not only as a leader in the production of computers but also as a consultant for e-business, a term referring to the integration of technologies such as E-mail servers, internal networks, call centers, and online inventory technology. To attract c-level (e.g., chief executive officer or chief technology officer) executives to its products and e-business consulting service, IBM released a campaign titled "Can You See It?"

The company's ad agency, Ogilvy & Mather Worldwide, created the campaign using IBM's $600 million annual advertising budget. Print and television spots first appeared on April 21, 2003. Print ads featured businesses that were flourishing with IBM's e-business consulting. One ad displayed a bank's exterior and read, "A bank discovers a source of new customers. Existing customers. Can you see it?" Ads appeared in the *Wall Street Journal, Computerworld,* and *Information Week.* With a less serious approach than the print ads, the campaign's television spots featured c-level executives explaining their business-related nightmares to therapists. In the 30-second spot "Museum," for instance, an executive explained his recurring nightmare about being on exhibit at a natural history museum. In his dream the executive was trapped inside a glass case while a museum guide explained to visitors that "Executiva Obsoletus" had become extinct after not adapting to contemporary business demands. The campaign continued until the end of 2003.

In 2004 "Can You See It?" won Best of Show at the ICON Awards, an event that recognized achievements in advertising. During the first nine months of 2003 IBM also posted a $1.5 billion income gain over the same period of 2002. The ad critic Barbara Lippert praised the television spots in *Adweek,* stating, "There's no overt sexual interpretation, as with Freud, but the commercials do make the solving of abstruse business problems like outsourcing and e-business on demand a little sexier, smarter and more fun."

HISTORICAL CONTEXT

In early 1994 IBM's stronghold on the computer industry was giving way to younger companies such as Compaq Computer Corp. and Dell Computer. Advertising for the 83-year-old IBM was delegated to 42 different advertising agencies. Lisa Baird, vice president of worldwide advertising for IBM, explained to *B to B* that using so many ad agencies had created problems for the company. "We had different logo presentations, the pieces of the IBM story were being told everywhere and were different country to country and business unit to business unit, and we weren't using our competitive advantage end to end to help customers be more successful." Hoping to consolidate its image and improve sales, IBM awarded its entire $500 million advertising account to the agency Ogilvy & Mather in 1994.

In 1997 the ad agency marketed IBM using the tagline "e-business," a term coined by IBM and which referred to the integration of technologies such as E-mail servers, internal network services, call centers, and online inventory technology. IBM's focus expanded at the beginning of 2002, when its new CEO, Sam Palmisano, changed the company's tagline to "e-business on demand" to emphasize its dedication to the ever-changing demands of customers.

The tagline "e-business on demand" was first used in IBM's "Gizmo" campaign, released in October 2002. Humorous television spots for the campaign featured executives from the fictitious electronics company Bagotronics evaluating inventions such as an elixir that granted omniscience and a "business time machine." Executives in the spots considered using the latter to go back in time and amend underbudgeted jobs and dead-end consulting projects. The spots ended with copy explaining that IBM's e-business consulting and e-business products provided reality-based solutions to such problems. Whereas "Gizmo" targeted both c-level executives and information technology (IT) employees, the "Can You See It?" campaign was aimed primarily at c-level executives.

TARGET MARKET

The campaign's target market consisted of c-level (e.g., chief executive officer, chief technology officer) executives who typically affected purchasing decisions for corporations. Ogilvy & Mather aired the commercials on news channels such as CNN and MSNBC to target an audience that treated television more as a resource than as a source of entertainment. Print ads appeared in similar-minded publications such as the *Wall Street Journal, Computerworld,* and *Information Week.*

Research conducted by Ogilvy & Mather before the campaign revealed that high-level executives worried about large-scale problems. To connect with this target, television spots featured c-level executives explaining corporate-level problems to their therapists. One executive loathed her business's lack of focus. Another expressed doubt about his company's ability to adjust quickly to future changes. Chris Wall, a senior partner at Ogilvy & Mather, explained to *B to B* that even levelheaded executives agonized over their business's future. "The whole notion of anxiety really resonated. It was simply an exaggeration of something that is quite real," Wall said. "Executives watching these spots should come away thinking, this company gets it, it understands me and my problem."

The "Can You See It?" message did not necessarily tout IBM's technology. Instead it suggested that IBM understood business and sold services to help c-level executives. Creatives at Ogilvy & Mather did not want the target to order IBM products after viewing the spots, but instead wanted the spots to prompt executives into a discussion about using IBM as a technology consultant. Using humor, each spot featured a therapist attributing his or her client's nightmares to business problems. Copy then explained that IBM offered a viable solution to similar problems. Barbara Lippert wrote in *Adweek,* "Not only does this IBM campaign manage to talk e-business with all the 'c-level' executives it needs to reach, it also manages to make fun of corporately correct speech and procedures, no doubt learned at '90s-style touchy-feely, walking-on-coals, being-blindfolded-to-learn-to-trust bonding retreats."

COMPETITION

The computer company Sun Microsystems posted sales in 2002 that were only 15 percent of IBM's sales. Servers, the large computers that businesses used for their networks, were Sun's flagship product. Sun also introduced in 1995 a software language called Java, which could be used to create applications for the Internet, video games, mobile phones, and computers.

In 2003 the ad agency J. Walter Thompson released the first Sun advertising campaign that targeted consumers instead of only businesses. The campaign advertised Sun's Java software, which was increasingly being used for mobile-phone video games. Sun's website featured pop star Christina Aguilera holding a mobile phone that played Java-based games. The campaign was intended to strengthen Java's image and subsequently boost the sales of Java products. "What we would like to create is demand for all things Java," Ingrid Van Den Hoogen, a Sun senior director of marketing, said about the campaign in the *Wall Street Journal.*

In June 2003 Sun released a multimillion-dollar campaign to discredit IBM. Similar to the concept of a personal computer using Microsoft's Windows operating system, all of Sun's servers used an operating system called Unix. IBM instead used the Linux operating system for its servers along with software titled AIX, which was IBM's proprietary version of Unix. Referring to IBM's blue icon, Sun's print ads read, "Attention AIX users: Sun is here to help . . . Unfortunately, our friends in Blue have a problem with licensing contracts that could

TABULATING SUCCESS

The salesman Thomas Watson saved the struggling punch-card processing company Computing-Tabulating-Recording (C-T-R) Company from bankruptcy when he joined C-T-R in 1914. Watson aggressively marketed his new company, which soon landed contracts with the U.S. government during World War I. In 1924 C-T-R changed its name to International Business Machines (IBM) and soon dominated the global market of tabulators, time clocks, and electric typewriters.

make things very expensive for anyone running AIX." The ad's mention of "licensing contracts" referred to a lawsuit filed by the computer retailer the SCO Group, Inc. The SCO Group claimed that IBM's Linux software had stolen code from Unix. The print ads appeared in the *Wall Street Journal* and the *San Jose Mercury News.*

MARKETING STRATEGY

The "Can You See It?" television spots appeared less than six months after IBM's "Gizmo" campaign began and borrowed some of its predecessor's qualities. First airing on April 21, 2003, "Can You See It?" spots even featured actors that had played Bagotronics executives in the "Gizmo" commercials. Just as in "Gizmo," the executives depicted in "Can You See It?" needed help with their businesses. The television spots aired on CNN and MSNBC, which were channels commonly watched by c-level executives.

In the 60-second spot "Balloon" a business executive described a recurring nightmare to a therapist. While resting on a leather couch, he said that in this dream he and his colleague were "falling to our doom" inside the basket of a hot air balloon. The two executives threw everything they could out of the basket, but the balloon continued to plummet. The therapist explained that the nightmare was rooted in the executive's "fixed cost fixation" and recommend he "let go." At first the executive assumed the therapist was suggesting he fire his colleague, which was later revealed to be the executive's brother-in-law Phil. The therapist assured him that that was not necessary. Framed by IBM's trademark blue borders, the commercials copy then stated, "It's an on demand world. Jettison fixed costs. Not Phil." The spot ended with the tagline "e-business on demand" followed by the IBM logo.

Further spots showed therapists connecting the nightmares of c-level executives back to their c-level business problems. Text at the finale of each spot explained that IBM offered e-business consulting or e-business products to solve such problems. Lippert wrote in *Adweek,* "The work shows that you don't have to be even slightly neurotic, given the reality of business these days, to feel awash in anxiety and worry or that you might just be sunk."

The campaign's print ads, which appeared in business publications, featured images of businesses that were prospering from IBM's advanced e-business products and consulting service. In the print ad "Retailer" an image showed a store selling men's business clothing. The ad's headline read, "A retailer does less selling. Yet gets more sold. Can you see it?" Copy below the headline explained that the store's IBM inventory system had helped a clothing retailer monitor its inventory. Another print ad explained how a Tokyo scooter seller with limited showroom space sold twice the amount of scooters it featured by using IBM. Other ads continued to ask, "Can you see it?"—referring to the audience's ability to "see" how IBM was helping businesses meet the demands of customers. The campaign continued until the end of 2003.

OUTCOME

"Can You See It?" won a gold award and Best of Show at the 2004 ICON Awards, an event that recognized achievements in advertising. IBM's income during the first nine months of 2003 skyrocketed 30 percent compared to the same period in 2002. Advertising critics, citing how difficult it was to blend humor with business-to-business (b-to-b) advertising, praised the IBM campaign. Ellis Booker, the editor of the business magazine *B to B,* was referring to "Can You See It?" when he wrote, "We give special kudos to humor when it's done well in b-to-b advertising. Because the best of these ads, even as they wink at us, show they know what they're talking about, that there's something important beneath the levity—something we ought to know, think about or do." Booker further explained that campaigns that failed in their attempts to be funny eventually offended the business crowd they were trying to amuse.

"Can You See It?" helped IBM continue its string of success following the consolidation of its advertising account in 1994. Even as the technology sector began crumbling in 2000, IBM remained relatively stable, drawing on its steady capital and decades of experience. "Can You See It?" reinforced IBM's legacy as a business that was determined to help its customers succeed. Lippert praised the campaign in *Adweek,* stating, "So in these tricky times, forget about buying from some ex-dot-com operator who can't get himself arrested—go to the old guys who will do it comprehensively (but expensively) and correctly, so you can stay nimble and responsive. You might get a better night's sleep in the bargain, and even manage to make it [to] your meeting."

FURTHER READING

Allossery, Patrick. "Big Blue Playing to Win: IBM Canada Targets Mid-sized Companies in New, More-spirited E-business Campaign." *National Post* (Don Mills, Ontario), May 13, 2002, p. FP8.

Bernstein, Roberta. "2003 Ad Agency of the Year." *MC Technology Marketing Intelligence,* May 1, 2004, p. 24.

Booker, Ellis. "Finding the Funny in B-to-B Ads." *B to B,* July 11, 2005, p. 10.

Cuneo, Alice Z. "IBM Puts Push behind Linux; Sees It as Tool to Fight Microsoft." *Advertising Age,* September 8, 2003, p. 89.

D'Innocenzo, Lisa. "Beating Brand Fatigue." *Strategy,* November 17, 2003, p. 1.

Kaplan, David. "Into the Blue." *Adweek* (eastern ed.), July 8, 2002, p. 12.

Kohnstamm, Abby. "Special Report: Power Players." *Advertising Age,* October 4, 2004, p. P14.

Lippert, Barbara. "IBM's Nightmares on Wall Street." *Adweek,* May 5, 2003, p. 26.

Maddox, Kate. "Creative." *B to B,* June 13, 2005, p. 37.

———. "IBM, Ogilvy Celebrate 10 Years." *B to B,* June 7, 2004, p. 1.

———. "IBM's Strategy Keeps It In and On Demand." *B to B,* October 25, 2004, p. 24.

McArthur, Keith. "IBM Launches New Campaign." *Globe and Mail* (Toronto), May 24, 2004, p. B12.

Silverman, Gary. "IBM Deletes Its 'e' on Demand." *Financial Times* (London), May 20, 2004, p. 20.

Kevin Teague

E-BUSINESS CAMPAIGN

OVERVIEW

Long associated with mainframe computers, International Business Machines Corporation (IBM) struggled in the late 1980s because it was unable to deal with a world dominated by personal computers and other changes in the marketplace. The fortunes of the giant corporation spiraled downward and touched bottom in 1993. A management shakeout led to a major change of direction as IBM rebranded itself as a solutions company. The company introduced its "Solutions for a Small Planet" marketing campaign in 1995. The tagline from this campaign was then used on the "E-Business" campaign that was released in April 1997.

The "E-Business" campaign, created by ad agency Ogilvy & Mather, targeted small businesses and corporations alike. A multifaceted effort, it featured television spots, prints ads, and Internet elements, all of which emphasized how IBM could help companies take advantage of the business possibilities of the Internet. Each of the early spots, filmed in black and white, presented a typical business problem that IBM, with the power of Internet technology, was able to solve. One spot showed young Web designers who were able to create a flaming logo but were unable to create a website capable of integrating suppliers and customers.

Due in large measure to its marketing efforts, IBM successfully recast itself as a solutions company. The "E-Business" campaign then broke off into a number of directions, focusing, for example, on wireless products and infrastructure. Nevertheless, as IBM entered the new century, the term "e-business" remained at the center of its marketing. The "E-Business" campaign and some of its commercials were also recognized with several advertising-industry awards.

HISTORICAL CONTEXT

The advent of the Internet opened a myriad of opportunities for IBM. The company aggressively promoted the concept of electronic commerce under the trademarked name e-business. E-business combined IBM's strength in networks, information storage, and data management with the global reach of the Internet to create a worldwide marketplace. According to research firm Forrester Research, the trade of goods and services via the Internet was projected to increase from $7.8 billion in 1997 to $105 billion by the year 2000. Although Forrester conceded that this amount accounted for only a small portion of the U.S. gross national product, many clamored to stake claims to it, including IBM. As Jerry Michalski, managing editor of a newsletter focused on computers and communication, told *Fortune,* "Over time, a portion of practically every transaction will touch the Internet." IBM's CEO, Louis V. Gerstner, Jr., agreed. He explained to *U.S. News & World Report,* "For 11 years I ran one of the world's most electronic businesses, the American Express Card.... It's a great example of an e-business, a network business—millions and tens of millions of people doing business in hundreds of countries, and it's all done electronically."

IBM's previous advertising campaign, "Solutions for a Small Planet," which began in 1995, was designed to enhance the IBM brand and to assert the company's global yet human image. The television spots showcased various IBM products and services but focused primarily on the IBM brand. "E-Business" leveraged the strength of the brand that "Solutions" had worked to promote and narrowed the focus to IBM's Internet technologies and e-business products and services. "E-Business" was essentially an extension of the "Solutions" campaign, and thus all of the commercials shared the same tagline.

TARGET MARKET

The "E-Business" campaign targeted businesspersons, particularly those in high-tech industries and those involved in making decisions and directing corporate strategies. As *Fortune* stated, "The advertising is effectively aimed at Everybusinessman, from the FORTUNE 500 to the startup, from the risk-averse 50-something middle manager to the frustrated Gen Xer. But in particular, it is also skewed toward small and medium-sized businesses, which may have thought IBM was out of their league and which also, some believe, provide the greatest e-business growth opportunity for IBM in the near term as big business slowly warms up to the idea." So while the audience appeared broad, its members shared one critical trait: all were involved in businesses that depended heavily on computers and that could benefit from jumping on the Internet bandwagon.

IBM hoped to emphasize the relevance of e-business and to assert its dominance in the field, and one way to accomplish this was to target smaller-sized businesses with which IBM had no prior history. When Irving Wladawsky-Berger, general manager of the company's Internet division, discussed IBM's customer base in an interview with *MSNBC Business Video,* he indicated that existing customers showed the earliest interest in e-business. He also explained the importance of attracting smaller businesses and the potential power they could wield in an environment such as the Web, where all were created equal. Wladawsky-Berger also explained why IBM generally targeted businesses and businesspeople rather than individual consumers, stating that "for the most part, we know how to work with businesses—large business, mid-sized businesses, more and more small businesses.... That's our forte, and the kinds of things we offer are very attractive to them." IBM's strategy was to help the businesses, and they in turn would reach the consumers.

To entice the target audience, IBM incorporated humor into the "E-Business" campaign, which featured office employees felled by common computer problems such as a malfunctioning printer and telephone glitches during a conference call. It was hoped that office workers and managers, because they had experienced similar frustrations, would be drawn in by the spots. Viewers in the target group would then realize that IBM could help them solve their daily technological trials. An executive at advertising agency Foote Cone & Belding commented on a print portion of IBM's "E-Business" campaign in *Fortune,* saying, "it has taken a subject that was terribly esoteric, about which everyone is uncomfortable, and explained it. This is not the arrogant, awesome IBM; this is a very helpful and supportive IBM."

E-COMMERCE VS. E-BUSINESS

In the mid-1990s IBM coined the term "e-business," which referred to the infrastructure of E-mail servers, network servers, and even call centers used by a business. The term was commonly confused with the existing term "e-commerce," which referred to business conducted over the Internet.

COMPETITION

The *Wall Street Journal* noted that, despite losing market share and suffering immense losses in the early 1990s, IBM's PC business seemed to be recovering in the second half of the decade. Information on market shares from Dataquest indicated that IBM's take of the U.S. computer market in 1996 was 8.7 percent, which placed the company third behind Compaq, with 13.3 percent, and Packard Bell-NEC, with 11.6 percent. IBM also fared well in the services market. According to the *Star Tribune,* the company's services division became the second-largest producer of revenue in the first quarter of 1996, posting sales of $3.2 billion and passing the software business for the first time. Although IBM faced competition from EDS, Computer Sciences, and Andersen Consulting, CEO Gerstner felt confident that the company could be a formidable force in the services sector. He told the *Star Tribune* that, as the largest manufacturer of computers, software, and disk drives, "We can build a very successful model for growth around services."

IBM was not impregnable, however, and the company faced considerable competition in many fields. IBM struggled to earn market share in the global arena, and International Data reported that, although the worldwide information technology market grew 13 percent in 1996, IBM's once dominant 21 percent share in 1987 had dropped to 12 percent in 1996, down even from 15 percent in 1993. An executive at the North American unit of British Airways told the *Wall Street Journal,* "Ten years ago, IBM would have been the obvious lead choice.... There are a lot more situations [today] where IBM has to make much greater efforts to win the work." These situations included the relatively new playing field

IBM DROPS THE BALL AT THE OLYMPIC GAMES

As IBM regained footing in the precarious high-tech industry, the company also indulged in high-profile events to announce its comeback. IBM may have jumped the gun, however, when it stepped up as the exclusive provider of computing services for the 1996 Olympic Summer Games in Atlanta. An official sponsor, IBM handled everything from the tabulation of results and scoring to the management of schedules, and the company greatly publicized its involvement. While the world watched, however, IBM stumbled, for the system responsible for transmitting results to the news media was slow and inaccurate, and news organizations resorted to copying down scores from telecasts or to sending assistants to sports arenas to collect results by hand. A wiser, much more low-key IBM arrived at the 1998 Winter Games in Nagano, Japan, determined to win a quiet victory the second time around.

of e-business, where competitors such as Microsoft, Netscape Communications, and Yahoo! would certainly line up for a piece of the action. Microsoft's Eric Koivisto told *Fortune,* "A lot of companies share the desire to be the one people think of when they want to conduct commerce using the Web."

MARKETING STRATEGY

The purpose of the "E-Business" campaign was to convince customers that IBM was the company that could offer the best solutions for their e-business and Internet problems. The first phase of the campaign began in April 1997 with four television spots, a print effort, and Internet ads. The second phase, which started in October with a budget of $200 million, was touted as a new promotion. Many of the television commercials focused on a business problem occurring in an office environment and then introduced IBM as the company that could help. Stylistically unique, the spots were filmed in black and white, with a blue border surrounding each frame. Steve Hayden of the ad agency Ogilvy & Mather explained the message of the "E-Business" spots to *Adweek* when he said, "There have been a lot of communications saying you can get on the Internet overnight and suddenly everything is rosy." He noted that the Internet "does change everything about the way you do business, but it's not quite that simple." The spots emphasized that, while technological problems arose constantly, IBM was there to help.

The first batch of television spots included "Whizzy," "Whizzy Website," "Conference Call," and "Virus." The last showed problems that could arise from computer viruses. A group of office employees tried to solve a printing problem only to discover that a coworker had downloaded a virus off the Web. The spot promoted IBM's virus scanning products. "Whizzy Website" showed two men reviewing various websites on the Internet and animatedly discussing features they could put on their own site. One commented, "Wait until the guys in marketing see this!" The other said, "We could get a flaming, dancing logo," and the two men both shouted, "We can do anything!" Their spirits were tempered, however, when one asked the other, "Can you order any of this stuff?" and the other responded, "No." The spot then cut to a frame with the words "IBM Internet Solutions," with the voice-over saying, "IBM helps business websites do business." The spot ended with the familiar tagline from the "Solutions" campaign. IBM's Michael Reene explained the strategy behind the spot at an industry forum: "E-business isn't about twirling logos and fire-breathing web sites. It's about being more competitive . . . and profitable. It's about expanding global market opportunities."

Other spots included "Restaurant," "On Hold," "Websters," "Christmas," "Web Jam," "Hype," and "Knowledge." "Restaurant" featured a group of businessmen discussing the online purchase of golf clubs. One asked, "Are you crazy?" and another said, "Your life may be ruined." The spot promoted IBM's encryption technology. Both "Hype" and "Web Jam," which were part of the October promotion, included a frame with IBM's "e-business solutions" logo, with the *e* graphically encased in a circle. "Hype" featured two men sitting in a conference room, one reading documents while the other typed on a laptop. The reader said, "It says here the Internet is the future of business." He paused, then continued, "We have to be on the Internet." The other asked, "Why?" The reader replied, "Doesn't say." With catchy piano music in the background, the text explained, "IBM helps thousands of companies do real business on the Web." "Web Jam," which continued with the previous theme, featured two male office employees dealing with a website problem. When one said, "Check out the flame now," the other showed alarm. He later said, "We should have upgraded this server," to which the other replied, "Can't. It's not scalable." The spot culminated in a frame that explained, "IBM Scalable Web Servers mean never having to say you're sorry." Although the spots were lighthearted and humorous, the problems featured could seriously damage a business's operations.

Wladawsky-Berger summed up IBM's intent when he told *MSNBC Business Video,* "We want people, first of all, to agree that something dramatic is happening and that this is something they need to get on with, and if they say—what do I do next? We want them to think—well, call IBM." Carla Hendra, Ogilvy & Mather's president, explained to *Mediaweek* in 1999 how the different elements of the campaign worked together: "We used television for brand awareness and to drive traffic to the Web. Business print was used for more in-depth messaging to opinion leaders. Web advertising was meant to show the medium is the message."

In an expansion of the "E-Business" campaign, launched in October 1999, IBM focused on what it called "e-culture," highlighting customer testimonials and the depiction of real-life solutions IBM offered its customers. A few months later, in a related effort, IBM released a campaign called "E-Business People" that focused on IBM employees who provided the solutions. The "Solutions for a Small Planet" slogan continued to be used in 2000 when IBM turned its attention to the emerging wireless market. These e-business spots, for example, showed a young woman in Italy using a cell phone to arrange a credit-card purchase from a vending machine. By this time a major portion of IBM advertising was devoted to e-business. In a 2000 article *Brandweek* quoted an unnamed IBM representative as saying, "People ask us 'What comes after e-business?' More e-business."

OUTCOME

The "E-Business" campaign did not end so much as it branched off into a number of directions, as "e-business" in effect became the IBM brand. In 1998 IBM began to promote what it called e-business tools. This effort was followed by "E-culture," "E-Business People," and the wireless spots. In 2002 IBM was still flying high despite the collapse of the dot-com sector. It introduced a new campaign, "E-Business Is the Game. Play to Win," which focused on the need to maintain a robust computer infrastructure. A subsequent campaign, "E-Business On Demand," showed how companies could leverage that infrastructure to better serve their customers in a fast-paced world.

The "E-Business" campaign met with varied reactions among viewers. *USA Today* 's Ad Track, a poll that measured an advertising campaign's popularity and effectiveness, found that a mere 11 percent of those surveyed actually liked the spots a lot. Forty-three percent were neutral, and 7 percent of viewers did not like the advertisements. In terms of effectiveness, the campaign earned higher ratings, with 24 percent of men polled finding the ads highly effective. In contrast, only 11 percent of women surveyed considered the spots highly effective. IBM representatives noted that Ad Track generally polled a diverse group, and because the campaign was aimed at a specific target group, this could explain the low scores. IBM declared the campaign a success, and others agreed. *Adweek* voted "E-Business" the best campaign of the year in 1997, and the spots "Virus" and "Whizzy Website" both won awards at the 1997 Cannes International Advertising Festival. In 2004 the "E-Business On Demand" effort won an EFFIE Award; hosted by the New York American Marketing Association, the EFFIEs were one of the most prestigious awards programs in the advertising industry.

FURTHER READING

Ditlea, Steve. "Big Blue Is Back." *Mediaweek,* January 4, 1999, p. 28.

Enrico, Dottie. "IBM Ads Compute Low Popularity Score." *USA Today,* January 19, 1998, p. B6.

Garfield, Bob. "IBM Finds Solution to Become Relevant." *Advertising Age,* April 7, 1997, p. 53.

Kaplan, David. "Into the Blue: How Ogilvy & Mather Gave IBM a Dash of Color—and a Pile of New Business." *Adweek* (eastern ed.), July 8, 2002, p. 12.

Marchetti, Michele. "IBM's Marketing Visionary." *Sales & Marketing Management,* September 2000, p. 52.

Morris, Betsy. "IBM Really Wants Your E-Business." *Fortune,* November 10, 1997, p. 36f.

Parpis, Eleftheria. "Best Spots 1997." *Adweek,* February 2, 1998, p. 21.

Wasserman, Todd. "IBM Mines Wireless Gold in New TV Ads." *Brandweek,* September 11 2000, p. 6.

Mariko Fujinaka
Ed Dinger

GIZMO CAMPAIGN

OVERVIEW

After consolidating its advertising account in 1994 from 42 advertising agencies to just one (Ogilvy & Mather), International Business Machines Corp. (IBM) resurrected its image from an outpaced computer company to that of an innovative leader within the computer industry. Besides streamlining its advertising account, IBM also benefited from the dot-com collapse that started in 2000. While younger companies without IBM's experience and capital perished, IBM expanded its scope by providing more infrastructure hardware, increased software development, and e-business consulting. The term "e-business," coined by IBM in the mid-1990s, referred to the infrastructure of technologies—such as internal networks, E-mail, call centers, and the Internet—used by a business. To tout the ability of IBM's e-business products to meet the ever-changing demands of customers, IBM released its "Gizmo" campaign.

Drawing on the company's estimated $500 million advertising budget, the New York office of Ogilvy & Mather created "Gizmo." The campaign first appeared on October 29, 2002, with a series of teaser television commercials, online ads, and print ads. The campaign included the launch of bagotronics.com, a website belonging to a fictional company called Bagotronics. The majority of the "Gizmo" spots featured the Bagotronics executives troubleshooting their e-business problems with fantastical products such as an elixir that granted omniscience, a time machine that would help amend past mistakes, and a "Universal Business Adapter" that connected any electronic device to any other electronic device. At the end of each spot, copy explained that the featured product did not exist but that IBM's e-business products could provide a realistic solution to a similar problem. The "Gizmo" campaign included nine television spots along with print and online ads. All the commercials featured the tagline "e-business on demand."

During the campaign's first three months, ad awareness for IBM increased 20 percent compared with the three months before the campaign. Among other ad-industry awards, "Gizmo" won a 2004 Silver EFFIE Award in the Corporate Reputation/Image/Identity category. IBM reported an income of $4.9 billion during the first nine months of 2003, a major improvement from the $3.4 billion reported for the same period in 2002.

HISTORICAL CONTEXT

In 1994 sales were waning for the 83-year-old IBM. Its advertising account was spread across 42 different advertising agencies, and its future as a technology leader was diminishing. "The IBM brand, though once heroic and famous and incredibly valuable, declined in relevance," Brian Fetherstonhaugh, the chief operating officer managing IBM's account at Ogilvy & Mather, explained to *Adweek*. "IBM was rated the 283rd most valuable brand in the world. In addition to a new-business model and positioning, the brand needed to attract people or it faced going out of business."

After awarding its estimated $500 million advertising account in 1994 to just one agency, Ogilvy & Mather, IBM began an extraordinary comeback. The newly appointed ad agency advertised IBM with what it called a "360 degree" approach. Explaining this approach in *MC Technology Marketing Intelligence,* Carla Hendra, president of Ogilvy & Mather's OgilvyOne North America division, said, "A lot of other agencies create an ad and then extend it out into other channels. We bring together the integrated team at the outset, and look for a kind of media-agnostic solution."

> ### NATIONAL GEOGRAPHIC IMAGE COLLECTION
>
> In November 2002 the National Geographic Society, the company that for more than a century was responsible for publishing *National Geographic,* a magazine that focused on culture, adventure, and nature, began selling 10,000 of its archived images on www.ngsimages.com. The website was made possible by IBM's e-business software and hardware infrastructure technology.

In 1997 IBM released its "E-business" campaign. The term referred to a business's infrastructure, or the integration of different technologies, such as customer call centers, internal computer networks, Internet servers, security services, and E-mail servers. The campaign suggested that businesses could integrate their technologies using IBM infrastructure products. One of the campaign's commercials featured a Web designer trying to please a client with a spinning logo. The unamused client had originally asked the designer not to make a new logo but rather to put his entire supply chain online, one of the services provided by IBM.

In March 2002 Sam Palmisano replaced Lou Gerstner as CEO of IBM. One of Palmisano's first decisions as CEO was to expand IBM's "e-business" tagline to "e-business on demand." The addition of the phrase "on demand" was intended to emphasize the fact that IBM's flexible products and services could fill the fluctuating demands of customers.

TARGET MARKET

Graham Calderwood, senior partner at Ogilvy & Mather's Toronto office, explained to *Strategy* that a campaign did not become successful by chance. "It happens through a disciplined approach, and the first part of that is to understand what's going on in the customer's head. You have to make that connection between the advertiser and the target customer." Ogilvy & Mather used focus groups, individual interviews, and workshops to understand the "Gizmo" campaign's target market, which consisted of two groups. First, the campaign targeted the information technology (IT) employees that typically oversaw the purchasing of products used for E-mail, networking, security, and phone systems. The campaign also targeted c-level (i.e., chief information officer, chief technology officer) executives that made purchasing decisions for a company.

Although the campaign appeared across traditional television channels, Ogilvy & Mather hoped to target the IT demographic with video spots on ESPN.com, CNN.com, and other websites popular with IT employees. This group tended to use Internet news sources rather than watch television news programs. The campaign targeted c-level executives by releasing print ads in business magazines.

"Gizmo" also avoided technical details about IBM products. Instead it reached its target market with humor and a strong human element. The majority of the campaign's commercials featured executives of the fictional company Bagotronics listening to an IT employee explain an absurd gizmo that would hopefully solve business problems. Although the ads focused on Bagotronics, Ogilvy & Mather's initial audience testing showed that the audience had a clear idea of which brand was being advertised.

COMPETITION

Carly Fiorina, the CEO of the computer and printer company Hewlett-Packard (HP), spearheaded the largest acquisition in tech-sector history in 2002 after she convinced HP's shareholders to approve the $19 billion acquisition of the computer maker Compaq Computer. To quell the shareholders' doubts, Fiorina argued that the acquisition of Compaq would strengthen HP enough to take infrastructure business away from IBM. Undermining the IBM tagline "e-business on demand," HP titled its $400 million campaign "Demand More." The campaign, released in early 2003, used the tagline "Everything is possible."

"Everybody is doing this," Paul Phillips, manager of competitive strategy for the computer company Sun Microsystems, said to *Reuters News*. "[HP is] trying to move [itself] closer to the IBM model but without the depth and experience IBM has." To promote its own management software, Sun created a similar campaign titled "N1."

Before HP acquired Compaq, consumer polls showed that the HP brand was still associated only with printers. With "Demand More" HP hoped to expand its reputation into the realm of personal-computer systems, imaging and printing systems, enterprise infrastructures, and services. During the campaign HP released more than 150 new products that could be used to improve business infrastructures. HP updated its infrastructure software OpenView with a self-fixing technology. It also reshaped its ProLiant blade servers so that more server hardware could be stacked on shelves. The new design freed up computer storage space for businesses and reduced the energy needed to keep the servers cool.

NICE FACADE. BAD INFRASTRUCTURE.

IBM released a television commercial in 2001 that touted the company's superior infrastructure technology. One spot featured the Leaning Tower of Pisa and copy that read, "Nice facade. Bad infrastructure." As two people attempted to photograph the structure in the commercial, the tower collapsed. The spot ended with the copy "Infrastructure: Sooner or later, it matters." IBM stopped airing the commercial immediately after the terrorist attacks of September 11, 2001, in which the two World Trade Center towers in New York were destroyed.

MARKETING STRATEGY

The "Gizmo" campaign first surfaced on October 29, 2002, with a series of teaser commercials and print ads that hinted at the existence of Bagotronics, a fictional company created for the campaign. IBM was not identified as the advertising source until later. The campaign would extend into 2003 and include nine television spots, several online ads, and print ads with the "Gizmo" theme. Ogilvy & Mather even created a Bagotronics website.

The campaign's commercials spoofed business problems such as underbudgeted projects, network problems, and missed deadlines. In each spot the Bagotronics executives invited an IT representative to pitch the latest gizmo in the company's boardroom. The spot "Time Machine," for instance, began with the Bagotronics CEO studying a glass contraption filled with twirling parts. When he asked his IT representative what the gizmo was, the IT rep replied, "It's a business time machine." He then proceeded to explain that Bagotronics could use the machine to amend past business mistakes. The executives appeared delighted with the contraption. When a female executive asked about the company's "dead-end consulting project," the IT employee smugly insisted that the time machine would make sure the project "never happened." After a few more questions and answers, the IT employee warned that the time machine was just a prototype and therefore dangerous. Pointing to an executive on his right, the CEO said, "Phil, you go first." The spot then flashed through several screens displaying the copy "THERE IS NO BUSINESS TIME MACHINE" and "YOU SHOULD CALL IBM FIRST." The spot ended with the campaign tagline, "e-business on demand," and a final image of the IBM logo.

In promoting IBM's e-business solutions Ogilvy & Mather faced the challenge of making infrastructure technology appear interesting to the campaign's target market. "How do you get people engaged in something they may not be interested in to begin with?" Chris Wall, Ogilvy & Mather senior partner, asked in *B to B.* The agency resorted to humorous situations with which c-level executives and IT personnel could readily identify. "There was a time when [business-to-business advertising] was thought of as very serious and austere," Wall continued. "Now, business has become like sports, where people follow businesses and stocks like they follow sports scores. That is a pretty big shift. You find us talking about business in a more entertaining way."

Further television spots showed the same Bagotronics executives considering the use of magic server pixie dust, magic business binoculars, and a magic elixir that could offer powers of omniscience. Print ads displayed similar gizmos. The print's copy explained that, unlike magic elixirs and pixie dust, IBM offered a reality-based solution to e-business problems.

OUTCOME

Advertising critics deemed "Gizmo" a quantifiable success. Four days after the campaign was released, the Bagotronics.com website recorded 17,131 unique visitors. IBM's connection to Bagotronics was explained in the "read our ad" section of the website, which was viewed more than 41,000 times. According to *B to B,* ad awareness for IBM was 20 percent greater during the campaign's first three months than during the three months before the campaign. As "Gizmo" continued into 2003, IBM's business skyrocketed. The company's reported income was 30 percent greater during the first nine months of 2003 than during the first nine months of 2002. The New York American Marketing Association awarded "Gizmo" a prestigious Silver EFFIE in the Corporate Reputation/Image/Identity category in 2004.

Chris Wall stated that one of the achievements of the "Gizmo" campaign was illustrating IBM's ability to deliver on the promises made by less-experienced companies during the 1990s. "We had the go-go years of the dot-com era, then we kind of had a hangover after the crash, and now we have an in-between stage," Wall explained to *B to B.* "[The possibilities] talked about in the late '90s [are] starting to happen, but the companies that are doing it are companies you know and trust, not 20-year-old kids."

FURTHER READING

Allossery, Patrick. "Big Blue Playing to Win: IBM Canada Targets Mid-sized Companies in New, More-spirited E-business Campaign." *National Post* (Don Mills, Ontario), May 13, 2002, p. FP8.

Bernstein, Roberta. "2003 Ad Agency of the Year." *MC Technology Marketing Intelligence,* May 1, 2004, p. 24.

Booker, Ellis. "Finding the Funny in B-to-B Ads." *B to B,* July 11, 2005, p. 10.

Cuneo, Alice Z. "IBM Puts Push behind Linux; Sees It as Tool to Fight Microsoft." *Advertising Age,* September 8, 2003, p. 89.

D'Innocenzo, Lisa. "Beating Brand Fatigue." *Strategy,* November 17, 2003, p. 1.

Kaplan, David. "Into the Blue." *Adweek* (eastern ed.), July 8, 2002, p. 12.

Kohnstamm, Abby. "Special Report: Power Players." *Advertising Age,* October 4, 2004, p. P14.

Lippert, Barbara. "IBM's Nightmares on Wall Street." *Adweek,* May 5, 2003, p. 26.

Maddox, Kate. "Creative." *B to B,* June 13, 2005, p. 37.

———. "IBM, Ogilvy Celebrate 10 Years." *B to B,* June 7, 2004, p. 1.

———. "IBM's Strategy Keeps It In and On Demand." *B to B,* October 25, 2004, p. 24.

McArthur, Keith. "IBM Launches New Campaign." *Globe and Mail* (Toronto), May 24, 2004, p. B12.

Silverman, Gary. "IBM Deletes Its 'e' on Demand." *Financial Times* (London), May 20, 2004, p. 20.

Kevin Teague

LINUX CAMPAIGN

OVERVIEW

The world's largest computer company, International Business Machines Corporation (IBM), was one of the first large computer companies to sell its mainframe servers with an operating system called Linux. Linux was developed in 1991 by a software developer searching for a free alternative to the costly operating system called Unix. Unlike Unix and operating systems such as Microsoft Corporation's Windows, Linux was free, or "open-source," and available without patent or copyright protections. To cut down on software costs, IBM shipped 15 percent of its servers with the free Linux operating system in 2002. To increase consumer faith in Linux and wean more of IBM's customers off of Unix and

Microsoft operating systems, IBM released its "Linux" campaign.

Ogilvy & Mather Worldwide drew upon IBM's $600 million annual advertising budget to create the campaign. The first "Linux" spot, a 90-second commercial titled "Prodigy," began airing on September 5, 2003. It featured an alert 10-year-old boy who sat inside a stark, brightly lit room. The boy, whom Ogilvy & Mather used to represent a computer operating with Linux, listened attentively to lessons given by individuals such as the academician Henry Louis Gates, the director Penny Marshall, a plumber, an airline pilot, and the boxing champion Muhammad Ali. Similar television spots ensued, including a 30-second, $2.3 million Super Bowl commercial in 2004. The campaign included print ads, postcards, E-mail, and Web banners. Using the word "open" to emphasize Linux's open-source use, the campaign used the tagline "LINUX. THE FUTURE IS OPEN. IBM."

"Linux" earned a Bronze EFFIE Award in 2005 within the Computer Software category. For the first half of 2004 IBM posted $45.4 billion in global revenues, which surpassed IBM's revenues during the same period a year before by nearly 9 percent. Ad critics praised the campaign for blending elegance with simplicity. The ad critic Barbara Lippert wrote in *Adweek* that the serious tone of the campaign's 2004 Super Bowl spot set IBM apart from the clutter of humorous spots vying for attention.

HISTORICAL CONTEXT

Created by the Finnish student Linus Torvalds in 1991, Linux became a popular nonproprietary operating system that could be used in lieu of more expensive products such as Microsoft's Windows and Sun Microsystems' Unix. Not usually installed in personal computers, Linux was instead used in servers, which were the large computers powering networks. IBM wanted to sell more servers with Linux in order to reduce its reliance on expensive operating systems. "IBM has seen that Linux opens doors . . . it takes expenses away from IBM, it makes life simpler because the software helps unify IBM's diverse products," Dan Kusnetzky, vice president of systems software research at the technology market research firm International Data Corp., said to Reuters News. "IBM sees that by making the Linux market bigger, IBM's slice of that market will be bigger," he explained.

According to Reuters News, IBM was responsible for a 2001 guerrilla marketing campaign called "Peace, Love, and Linux," in which Linux's penguin logo was spray painted, along with a heart and a peace symbol, on the sidewalks of San Francisco, New York, and Chicago. In 2002 IBM stated that 6,000 of its business customers were using Linux and that 15 percent of IBM servers were shipped with the free operating system. IBM was not the only computer company taking advantage of Linux. International Data Corp. reported that, during the first quarter of 2003, Hewlett-Packard shipped 29.4 percent of its servers with Linux, and Dell shipped 22.1 percent.

"Linux" was IBM's first large advertising campaign to focus on Linux. Executives at IBM wanted to use IBM's brand equity to persuade information technology (IT) employees and c-level (e.g., chief executive officer, chief technology officer) executives to rely on Linux. Speaking with Reuters News in 2003, Lisa Baird, head of global advertising at IBM, stated that awareness of Linux had reached "a tipping point" and that the campaign was meant to encourage interest in the operating system. "We are only one of many companies committed to it," she said. "We are certainly doing everything to increase the momentum of that interest."

DIGITAL FOOTBALL

In 2003 the National Football League (NFL) designated IBM as its official technology partner. In return for the NFL's endorsement, IBM began converting 80 years of football film footage into a digital format that could be accessed instantaneously by the public. The NFL hoped that its new digital archive would cut costs and make the league more efficient.

TARGET MARKET

"Linux" television spots reached a mass audience by airing across popular sports programming, including the 2004 Super Bowl. With the campaign IBM hoped to foster trust among consumers in general, but it was more specifically aimed at technology decision makers. Marketing analysts explained that, even though IT employees and c-level executives watched less television than the general population, they still watched broadcasts of high-profile sporting events such as the Super Bowl. To resonate with the broader audience that may not have understood the intricacies of Linux, the campaign used little technical information. Instead the commercials employed a highly emotional content backed by A-list celebrities and IBM branding.

Speaking to *Computerworld,* Christopher Williams, a strategist at the marketing firm Idea Engineering, described the three groups most affected by the 2004

"Linux" Super Bowl spot: "In reaching the mainstream, [IBM is] reaching the IT decision-makers, the company's stakeholders, and the IBM shareholders." The latter two, stakeholders and shareholders, may not have understood the difference between Unix and Linux, but the campaign suggested that IBM was making the right decision by choosing Linux. The spot used endorsements by celebrities such as boxer Muhammad Ali to establish Linux "as a good business decision for you and your bosses," said Williams.

Some IBM stakeholders feared that, by using an operating system without an entity responsible for its production, no one could be held accountable for failure. "Users still have concerns about the viability of Linux vendors over time," Dan Kusnetzky of International Data Corp. said to the *San Jose Mercury News.* "They have concerns about staff expertise for administering Linux, and they worry there is no one throat to choke because it's developed by a community of developers."

COMPETITION

In January 2004 Microsoft, the world's largest software company, launched a global advertising campaign that claimed that its Windows Server 2003 was 10 times cheaper to use than Linux. The campaign, titled "Get the Facts," was based on findings unearthed by independent market-research firms such as Giga Research and Meta Group. In addition to print ads, the campaign included an updated section on Microsoft's website; titled "Get the Facts on Windows and Linux," it allowed visitors to download the comparison results between the two operating systems. One magazine ad began with the headline "Weighing the cost of Linux vs. Windows? Let's review the facts." Even though Linux was free, explained the ad, the installation, development, and service of Linux would make it a more expensive alternative to Windows Server 2003.

"As Linux became more mainstream, as Linux became more commercial, as IT professionals wanted to make more pragmatic decisions on it, they needed a set of data to help them sort through their decisions," Martin Taylor, Microsoft's general manager of platform strategies and its lead media contact for Linux issues, said to the *Seattle Post-Intelligencer.* Taylor explained that the campaign was merely an effort to collect and organize outside information that discredited Linux.

Some advertising critics lambasted the campaign for using research that claimed to be "independent" even though it was financed by Microsoft. In August 2004 the Advertising Standards Authority (ASA), a U.K. advertising watchdog, concluded that the "Get the Facts" campaign was flawed. According to the ASA, Meta Group used more expensive hardware to operate Linux for the price comparison between Windows Server 2003 and Linux. The unnecessary expense tipped the results in Microsoft's favor.

MUHAMMAD ALI

Although he was a highly public figure during the 1960s and 1970s, the retired heavyweight boxer Muhammad Ali began a slow retreat from public appearances after being diagnosed with pugilistic Parkinson's syndrome in 1984. Much to the advertising world's surprise, the boxer appeared in three commercials during the 2004 Super Bowl: IBM's "Linux" commercial, Global Gillette's "Gillette" commercial, and a "Choose to Vote" public service announcement. Ali's wife, Lonnie, explained to *Women's Wear Daily* that her husband was using the advertisements to reassure the public that he was alive and active. The boxer was opening a museum that promoted the legacy of Muhammad Ali the following year.

MARKETING STRATEGY

During the first week of September 2003 IBM released "Linux" print ads, postcards, E-mails, and Web banners with the tagline "LINUX. THE FUTURE IS OPEN. IBM." The campaign was IBM's first bold statement of support for Linux. On September 7 the campaign's first TV commercial, a 90-second spot titled "Prodigy," broke during the opening games of the National Football League. The spot also appeared on CBS during the men's finals of the US Open tennis tournament.

"Prodigy" featured a 10-year-old boy sitting inside an all-white room that *New York Times* ad critic Nat Ives described as reminiscent of the movie *2001: A Space Odyssey.* The commercial began with a male voice and a female voice discussing the boy, who was sitting quietly on a white plastic chair. The male voice-over stated, "I think you should see this." The female replied, "It's just a kid." For the remainder of the spot, the boy sat silently as professionals from various disciplines explained subjects such as problem solving, plumbing, Latin, guitar, astronomy, and history. The boy's focused expression suggested that he comprehended the information as quickly as it was disseminated. After the boxer Muhammad Ali told the boy, "Speak your mind, don't back down," the two off-camera voices from the spot's beginning finished their conversation. "Does he have a name?" the woman asked. "His name is Linux," the man answered. The spot ended with the tagline "LINUX. THE FUTURE IS OPEN. IBM." Ogilvy & Mather used the word "open" to remark on Linux's open-source software, which allowed the public to use it for little or no fee.

Further spots with the same 10-year-old boy continued into 2004. The 30-second spot titled "Muhammad Ali," which cost an estimated $2.25 million, aired during the 2004 Super Bowl. It featured the boy watching television footage of the world heavyweight champion Muhammad Ali winning a boxing match. After the match Ali shouted, "I shook up the world!" The television set disappeared. Then the more recent 62-year-old Ali appeared to encourage the boy to "Shake things up. Shake up the world." Ali, famous for his unorthodox boxing style and his spectacular results, was considered to be an ideal endorsement for Linux. John Lucy, a spokesman for IBM, told the *Herald-Sun,* "Linux is the underdog, as Ali was. Both developed a global cult following by taking on the big boys and proving they were ultimately the most powerful and popular contenders."

Super Bowl ad critics praised the dignified nature of the "Muhammad Ali" commercial. While so many other brands used humor during the game, "Muhammad Ali" stood apart with its inspirational message. "The way you differentiate yourself is to have a different tone, a different creative feel in the midst of the guffaws," Deirdre Bigley, vice president of advertising at IBM, explained to Reuters News. "I think we are going to grab attention by being more elegant."

OUTCOME

The "Linux" campaign did not score well in some audience polls. One survey, conducted in Canton, Ohio, which was the location of the Pro Football Hall of Fame, rated "Muhammad Ali" as the fifth-worst commercial aired during the 2004 Super Bowl. The campaign garnered more praise from ad critics, many of whom admired the campaign's creative strategy and classy execution. Praising the Super Bowl spot "Muhammad Ali," *Adweek* advertising critic Barbara Lippert explained on *CBS News: The Early Show,* "I liked the Linux one.... I thought it looked great. It was startling. It changed the tone."

The commercial "Prodigy" earned the campaign a Bronze EFFIE in 2005 in the ceremony's Computer Software category. Aside from ad-industry success, the campaign was also credited with boosting IBM's profit. During the first half of 2004 IBM posted $45.4 billion in global revenues, which surpassed IBM's revenues during the same period a year before by nearly 9 percent.

The campaign's failure to impress the broader Super Bowl audience was attributed by some critics to the general confusion about Linux. Audience polls, including *USA Today*'s Ad Track survey, showed a general dislike of the campaign. Some advertising critics believed that, if given enough time, audiences would embrace the "Linux" campaign. For instance, Paul Cappelli, president of the ad agency the Ad Store, wrote in *Shoot,* "I'm aware [that the Muhammad Ali spot] didn't score all that well with *USA Today,* but the exposure on the game will help that ad. As it airs some more, I think you'll see it climb in its effectiveness."

FURTHER READING

Allossery, Patrick. "Big Blue Playing to Win: IBM Canada Targets Mid-sized Companies in New, More-spirited E-business Campaign." *National Post* (Don Mills, Ontario), May 13, 2002, p. FP8.

Bernstein, Roberta. "2003 Ad Agency of the Year." *MC Technology Marketing Intelligence,* May 1, 2004, p. 24.

Booker, Ellis. "Finding the Funny in B-To-B Ads." *B to B,* July 11, 2005, p. 10.

Cuneo, Alice Z. "IBM Puts Push behind Linux; Sees It as Tool to Fight Microsoft." *Advertising Age,* September 8, 2003, p. 89.

D'Innocenzo, Lisa. "Beating Brand Fatigue." *Strategy,* November 17, 2003, p. 1.

Kaplan, David. "Into the Blue." *Adweek* (eastern ed.), July 8, 2002, p. 12.

Kohnstamm, Abby. "Special Report: Power Players." *Advertising Age,* October 4, 2004, p. P14.

Lippert, Barbara. "IBM's Nightmares on Wall Street." *Adweek,* May 5, 2003, p. 26.

Maddox, Kate. "Creative." *B to B,* June 13, 2005, p. 37.

———. "IBM, Ogilvy Celebrate 10 Years." *B to B,* June 7, 2004, p. 1.

———. "IBM's Strategy Keeps It In and On Demand." *B to B,* October 25, 2004, p. 24.

McArthur, Keith. "IBM Launches New Campaign." *Globe and Mail* (Toronto), May 24, 2004, p. B12.

Silverman, Gary. "IBM Deletes Its 'E' On Demand." *Financial Times,* May 20, 2004, p. 20.

Kevin Teague

SOLUTIONS FOR A SMALL PLANET CAMPAIGN

OVERVIEW

International Business Machines (IBM) Corporation was undeniably a powerful and influential presence during the early days of the computer boom. In the 1970s and early 1980s IBM dominated the computer market. The company was largely responsible for the success of the personal computer industry, and major corporations and the federal government relied on its mainframe systems. IBM's profits reached $6.6 billion in 1984, and the company's stock reached an all-time high in August 1987. Increased competition led to a drop in profitability, however, and by the 1990s Big Blue, as the company was known, had lost its omnipresence.

A revitalization effort began in 1993 with the hiring of a new CEO. The advent of the Internet also boosted IBM's prospects. The company hoped to become a major contender in electronic commerce by combining its long-standing strength in network computing and research with the global capabilities of the Internet. To accomplish these goals, IBM needed to present a more user-friendly image while leveraging its powerful brand name. IBM's "Solutions for a Small Planet," which debuted in early 1995 with a budget of $100 million, was a brand-building campaign designed to reveal the company's global reach. To emphasize the company's universal relevance, the print and television ads depicted people throughout the world using various IBM products in their everyday lives.

The "Solutions for a Small Planet" campaign continued through 1998 and included more than 25 television spots. The campaign, initially launched in the United States, soon made its way to Canada, Latin America, Europe, the Middle East, Africa, Asia, and elsewhere. At the commencement of the worldwide campaign, IBM's Scott Brooks told *USA Today,* "This campaign will be seen by millions of people in over four continents.... It was designed to reflect IBM's universal appeal all over the world."

HISTORICAL CONTEXT

IBM had a number of problems when Louis V. Gerstner, Jr., became CEO in April 1993. The company had lost $16 billion between 1991 and 1993, and its stock plunged to a low of $40 in 1993. (The high, which was reached in 1987, had been $175.) In seven years the company, long known for its no-layoff policy, had undergone five major restructurings and cut its workforce by half. Plans to split IBM into smaller divisions were in the works, which distracted the company and blurred its focus. IBM's two mainstays, mainframe computer systems and personal computers, lost market share in the early 1990s as well. Mainframes seemed destined for obsolescence, and small, aggressive upstarts entered the personal computer market and gobbled up profits. These young companies sped past the large and unwieldy IBM in terms of product development and introduced new systems to the public while IBM fumbled. In 1992 computer consultant Ulric Weil told *Time* magazine, "IBM is no longer the monolithic monster that strikes fear in the hearts of competitors.... It has proved to be quite mortal after all." No one seemed to possess much confidence that IBM could recover, not even Gerstner. He had not been thrilled with the offer to head the flailing IBM, and he told *Fortune,* "It just looked like it was going into a death spiral. I wasn't convinced it was solvable."

When Gerstner took the reins, he slashed jobs, decided against dividing the company, and chose not to give up on mainframes. He also shifted the focus to support services and systems and acquired software companies in order to compete with Microsoft. In an unprecedented move, in 1994 Gerstner severed ties with IBM's 40 advertising agencies and consolidated all advertising, an estimated $400 to $500 million in global spending, at one agency—Ogilvy & Mather. A worldwide agency, Ogilvy & Mather had branch offices in 59 countries at the time. Gerstner hoped to present a unified brand image in its global advertising, and it was thought that a single agency would be best equipped to deal with such a task.

Ogilvy & Mather's first major effort as IBM's sole advertising agency was the "Solutions for a Small Planet" campaign, which began on New Year's Day in 1995. IBM needed the brand-enhancing campaign to be successful if it were to regain its reputation as a technological leader. Marketing consultant Al Ries told *USA Today* that the campaign was "the make-it or break-it campaign" and that "if this flops, IBM's reputation with consumers will suffer." Forrester Research's Bill Bluestein agreed and said that IBM "has been surpassed by Microsoft, even Intel, as a technological powerhouse, and this kind of an ad effort could help change people's minds about IBM."

TARGET MARKET

According to a *USA Today* interview with an IBM marketing executive in 1995, the "Solutions for a Small Planet" campaign initially targeted "affluent, well-educated, mostly male consumers." This group represented those most likely to have had prior experience with and knowledge of IBM and its products. IBM purchased commercial ad time on sports- and news-related shows to reach these consumers, and *USA Today* 's Ad Track, a poll designed to measure a campaign's popularity and effectiveness, found that the strategy had worked. When Ad Track surveyed 1,255 adults, it discovered that more than one-third had not seen any of IBM's spots. Those who had seen the commercials, however, were predominantly members of IBM's target audience. While approximately one-third of the women polled had seen the ads, more than one-half of the men had viewed them. In terms of popularity, the high-income viewer earning more than $50,000 a year liked the spots more than those who made less than $7,500 a year.

While IBM may have hoped to capture the attention of the high-income consumer at the beginning of the "Solutions for a Small Planet" campaign, it then adopted a more egalitarian approach by placing the spots on national network television during prime time. And because the reach of computers was growing at an exponential rate throughout the 1990s, so was IBM's target market. Although the spots featured foreign languages and countries, they showed common people discussing technological issues in an everyday manner, sending the message that technology affected everyone. For instance, one of the spots showed a group of Czechoslovakian nuns discussing the Internet and IBM's OS/2 Warp. One nun said, "I'm dying to surf the 'net," and another was beeped on her pager. Another spot was set in Marrakech, Morocco, with one man confessing in Arabic, "Hey, I'm no wirehead," something that many in the United States could understand. The idea was to show empathy for those who felt that technology was passing by them and to suggest that IBM could be the company to provide the solution.

DOES ANYONE GET IT?

One of the spots in the "Solutions for a Small Planet" campaign featured the fictitious rock band Spinal Tap. The commercial was shown during the 1996 Summer Olympic Games and was intended to be funny. Unfortunately for IBM, many viewers were unfamiliar with the 1984 faux documentary *This Is Spinal Tap,* in which the band originated and which parodied heavy metal rock and band tours. In the IBM spot the musicians' dialogue was subtitled, which kept with the "Solutions for a Small Planet" strategy, for the loud music drowned out the voices. The band members discussed the launch of a comeback tour and surmised that, if IBM could help manage the Olympics, the company could certainly handle the logistics of its tour. The spot was supposed to surprise and engage viewers and dispel IBM's uptight image, but viewers were at most surprised.

COMPETITION

There was a time when IBM ruled the computer industry and had no direct competition. A 1992 *Star Tribune* article stated, "So tight was IBM's market grip that it was practically impossible for any computer company to do business without being tied in some way to the Big Blue colossus." IBM's glory days passed in the late 1980s and early 1990s, however, as the high-tech industry blossomed and new competitors arose. IBM chose to stand by its cash cow—mainframes—but, unfortunately for IBM, sales declined as more users opted for personal computers. IBM was slow to enter the personal computer market, and competitors such as Apple, Compaq, and Packard Bell had a healthy head start. *Time* noted that IBM's PC business ailed in 1992, with revenues and market share dropping.

After Gerstner joined IBM, profits began to pick up, and IBM's future did not appear as grim. According to Dataquest, IBM ranked third in the U.S. computer market in 1996, with a market share of 8.7 percent. Compaq led the group with 13.3 percent of the market, followed by Packard Bell-NEC with 11.6 percent. After IBM came Dell, with 6.9 percent, and then Apple, with 6.7 percent. According to Dataquest, IBM also placed third in the home PC market for 1996, with 8.1 percent. Packard Bell ranked first, with a 27.3 percent share, and Compaq came in second, with 12.2 percent. Gateway, Apple, and Acer, respectively, followed IBM.

IBM also provided Microsoft with competition in software. After IBM acquired Lotus Development in 1995, *U.S. News & World Report* indicated that the two company's software businesses were comparable in size, with IBM's growing successfully. IBM's personal computers were preloaded with Lotus software, which significantly increased the chances that those using the 624,000 IBM PCs sold in 1996 would use Lotus rather than Microsoft.

Although IBM had gotten back in the game, the company still faced fierce competition. The *Wall Street Journal* noted that revenue in 1997 had increased 40 percent from 1987 and that nearly two-thirds of the company's revenue was attributed to personal computers and services. (In 1992 only about 40 percent of IBM's revenue had come from PCs.) Although these statistics seemed impressive, profits had gone up only 3.2 percent during the decade. According to the *Wall Street Journal,* "That means IBM labored mightily to add more than $20 billion in yearly revenue—all to produce less than a penny of profit on each extra dollar." While IBM's revenue went up 5.6 percent in 1996, Hewlett-Packard's increased 19 percent and Intel's rose 29 percent. In other words, "IBM added $4 billion in new revenue last year [1996], but Hewlett-Packard, half IBM's size, added $6.9 billion; and Intel, one-third as big as IBM, tacked on $4.6 billion."

MARKETING STRATEGY

The aim of the "Solutions for a Small Planet" campaign was to demonstrate IBM's global reach while giving the company a friendly, unintimidating image. The spots were filmed in the languages of the countries depicted and carried subtitles. While the ads were shown worldwide, none was televised in the country of its native language. Using foreign languages was intended to draw in viewers and hold their interest. Ogilvy & Mather's Matt Ross told *Newsday* that using a foreign tongue "draws people in and causes them to become a lot more involved in the spots.... It's hard not to pay closer attention when a foreign language comes on." The spots showed common people discussing IBM, computers, and technology to illustrate the company's universal reach. Greek fishermen, Argentine tango dancers, Italian farmers, and Irish shepherds were among those featured.

IBM increased advertising spending significantly to ensure that the campaign would reach as many viewers as possible, with *Business Marketing* reporting that its broadcast spending increased by 866 percent in 1995. The campaign continued through 1997 and into 1998 and included several Olympic-themed spots to inform viewers of IBM's Olympic sponsorship. IBM also invested in other advertising campaigns and, as the "Solutions for a Small Planet" campaign aged, gradually placed less emphasis on its spots. Many of IBM's ads, whether or not they were part of the campaign, shared the tag line "IBM. Solutions for a Small Planet."

Several ads appeared on U.S. network television during 1997. Some were humorous and all depicted interesting scenarios. The "Fashion Models" spot featured two Scandinavian models walking down a runway during a fashion show. They conversed in Swedish about IBM's "data mining" services, with English subtitles to guide U.S. viewers. One of the models asked the other how her line of knee socks was selling, and the second responded that business had improved since she contacted IBM. She explained, "See, IBM's got a fab way of looking at data and coming up with zillions of ideas you'd just never think of. It's called 'data mining.'" The first model then replied, "Data mining? Sounds like the edge I need for my chain of Tire and Auto Centers." The spot introduced an IBM service and solution in an alluring and unexpected manner.

Another ad, "Japanese Surgeons," took place in an operating room and featured two Japanese surgeons, one male and one female. As they prepared to perform surgery, they discussed in Japanese their personal computers. The patient, still conscious, laid on the operating table listening. The female surgeon asked the male how his children were enjoying their new computer. The male surgeon responded, "It's not up and running yet. You know me. All thumbs." The patient's eyes widened at this remark. The female surgeon then said that her family loved their IBM Aptiva: "It's got CD-ROM... lots of software... It's ready to go right out of the box." The male then asked if the computer was difficult to set up, to which the female surgeon replied, "It's not brain surgery." The spot ended with a shot of the patient's alarmed and surprised face and the tag line. The intent of the spot was to introduce IBM's line of Aptiva home computers in an engaging and humorous manner.

IBM's campaign attempted to cover a large number of IBM products and services in many foreign countries. A Hungarian organ grinder showed interest in an IBM ThinkPad laptop computer, and Tibetan monks discussed the advantages of Lotus Notes. Singers in South Africa discovered children's software, actresses in a Chinese opera house discussed the benefits of IBM's technical support for PC owners, and a water taxi driver in Bangkok told a businessman passenger about IBM's consulting services. Every spot showed how IBM affected individuals in varying professions and of varying ages spanning the globe and how IBM offered solutions for all of them.

OUTCOME

The "Solutions for a Small Planet" campaign lasted through 1998, although IBM supported various other advertising endeavors during the duration of the campaign. The other campaigns complemented the "Solutions for a Small Planet" ads, placing heavier emphasis on specific products and services rather than promoting only the IBM brand. "Nuns" and "French Guys," both early spots, won Clio Awards for 1995, and "Ships," developed by Ogilvy & Mather's Paris branch and televised during the 1998 Winter Olympic Games, won an award at the 1997 Cannes International Advertising Festival.

IBM had progressed considerably since its near death days of the early 1990s. According to *U.S. News & World Report,* IBM's record-setting 1997 revenues of $78.5 billion provided a clear indication that the company had been resurrected. Because of economic downturns in foreign markets, however, IBM saw profits fall in early 1998. Nonetheless, the declining revenues had been expected, and others in the computer industry were affected as well. IBM became a contender in an industry in which the company had been written off, but as IBM's chief financial officer, G. Richard Thoman, told the *Wall Street Journal,* "We've done a lot, but we still have a lot to do."

FURTHER READING

Enrico, Dottie. "IBM Launches 'Small Planet' Ads to Boost Image." *USA Today,* December 30, 1994.

———. "IBM's Subtle 'Solutions' Target Affluent Men." *USA Today,* May 22, 1995.

Garfield, Bob. "Spinal Tap Drops Torch in IBM Effort." *Advertising Age,* May 27, 1996.

"International Flavor: Advertisers Sprinkle in a Little Foreign Language." *Newsday,* January 29, 1995, p. E5.

Mariko Fujinaka

Isuzu Motors America, Inc.

13340 183rd Street
Cerritos, California 90702-6007
USA
Telephone: (800) 255-6727
Web site: www.isuzu.com

THE CALL CAMPAIGN

OVERVIEW

In an effort to diversify its vehicle lineup, Isuzu Motors America, Inc., designed a new sports utility vehicle (SUV), the Axiom, for model year 2001. At that point Isuzu sold only trucks and SUVs that offered a rugged, truck-like ride. This made the company vulnerable to fluctuations in the truck market in ways that other, more diverse automakers were not. Essentially, every Isuzu line featured vehicles designed to be driven off-road. The company designed the Axiom to offer a smoother ride, in the hopes of luring young suburban drivers. This presented a challenge for the company since the SUV field was a crowded one and Isuzu suffered from poor brand visibility.

Isuzu's low profile was a result in part of its failure to run a major television marketing campaign since 1999. In an attempt to raise its profile, in 2001 the company budgeted $15 million for advertising. It decided to return to TV and contracted San Francisco–based ad agency Goodby, Silverstein & Partners to produce a spot that brought back Isuzu's famed "pitchman" Joe Isuzu. Played by the actor David Leisure, Joe Isuzu had achieved widespread notoriety from 1986 to 1990, when he starred in a series of Isuzu commercials. The humor in the spots came from the over-the-top exaggerations Joe used to "sell" Isuzu vehicles, including claiming one Isuzu had a greater seating capacity than the Houston Astrodome. The new Joe Isuzu spot, "The Call," depicted a now-overweight Joe getting back into shape following a call from Isuzu asking him to come back to work.

Unfortunately the spot, which ran from spring through fall of 2001, did not jump-start Axiom sales. The vehicle missed a modest goal of 12,000 units sold, and Isuzu failed to attract the new consumers that it wanted. The spot met with a mixed reaction and did not enter the national consciousness on the same scale as the original Joe Isuzu spots. Some observers felt that the Axiom's poor sales may have been partially due to the company's decision to offer stronger customer incentives to other SUVs in the Isuzu fleet, the Rodeo and the Trooper. The spot did, however, boost Isuzu's overall brand recognition.

HISTORICAL CONTEXT

Isuzu Motors America, Inc., was the American subsidiary of the Tokyo-based company Isuzu Motors Ltd. Created in 1981, Isuzu Motors America was responsible for the marketing and distribution of Isuzu vehicles in the United States. In 1971 Isuzu Motors Ltd. began a close relationship with U.S. auto giant General Motors (GM). By 2001 GM had taken a 49 percent capital interest in the Japanese manufacturer. The two companies cooperated in the production of new technologies; for example, beginning in 1997 Isuzu took over most of GM's diesel development. A year later Isuzu assumed most of the responsibility for engineering GM's commercial-vehicle fleet.

The automaker specialized in making trucks. In fact, at the turn of the twenty-first century Isuzu did not sell a single car in North America. This lack of diversity led the company to be vulnerable to downturns in the truck-buying market. As Japan's economy went through a sustained rough patch in the 1990s, Isuzu took major sales hits in its home market. In the late 1980s Japanese drivers bought 190,000 trucks per year, but by 2002 that number had dropped to some 70,000 units. This led to a financial crunch at Isuzu. More pressing for Isuzu Motors America was the struggles at its one North American factory in the late 1990s and early 2000s. Subaru-Isuzu Automotive, Inc., was a joint venture of Isuzu and Fuji Heavy Industries, Ltd., which was responsible for the manufacturing of vehicles for Isuzu and for Fuji's Subaru subsidiary. Combined production at the plant topped out at about 216,000 units per year in 1998, before falling to a mere 186,317 units in 2001. Isuzu was looking to sell its share of the plant to Fuji, though the automaker did not want to abandon the lucrative U.S. market altogether. After the sale to Fuji was completed in 2002, Isuzu would have to rely on partners such as GM to supply more manufacturing aid in the United States. As part of the deal to take full control of the plant, Fuji agreed also to provide up to 30,000 units of the Rodeo and Axiom per year for sale in the North American market.

Isuzu decided that it needed to diversify its lineup. At the time the automaker was known primarily as a producer of durable, high-performance off-road vehicles. Though the company did not want to stray too far from its roots as a truck manufacturer, it felt that a sports utility vehicle (SUV) with some car-like features might give the brand more flexibility. The vehicle would be built on a platform similar to that of the Isuzu Rodeo. It would feature a lower ride height than most SUVs. The auto was primarily designed for street driving. This contrasted with the Rodeo, which was a rugged, off-road vehicle. While still rugged, the Axiom would offer a smoother ride than most trucks. Isuzu hoped that this would open up its brand to drivers who might not ever be inclined to drive off-road.

Isuzu's troubles were compounded by its lack of a strong presence on U.S. television. The company had not run a major TV campaign since 1999, which hurt its visibility among consumers. In the past the automaker had had notable success with the Joe Isuzu character. Joe Isuzu, played by the actor David Leisure, starred in a series of commercials for various Isuzu vehicles from 1986 to 1990. The character, who billed himself as a "company spokesman," was created by the ad agency Della Femina, Travisano, and Partners.

Joe was famous for his outrageous exaggerations (and outright lies) on behalf of Isuzu's vehicles. One spot for the Isuzu Trooper featured Joe promising that if he was lying, lightning would strike his mother. After Joe proceeded to tell the audience that the Trooper was big enough to carry an entire symphony orchestra, that was just what happened. Text often appeared on the screen, chiding Joe for his dishonesty (sometimes a caption would bluntly declare: "He's lying.") His most visible moment was in several well-received spots that aired during Super Bowl XXI in 1987, the most-watched sporting event of the year. The character Joe Isuzu quickly entered the nation's consciousness as an emblem of dishonesty, leading President Ronald Reagan to compare Sandinista leader Daniel Ortega, whose Communist regime in Nicaragua was a Cold War adversary of the United States, to the TV pitchman.

TARGET MARKET

Isuzu hoped that by concentrating on drivability, it could lure middle-class SUV buyers. The Axiom's price, which ranged from $26,595 to the low $30,000s, would make the car accessible to the SUV-buying public. Isuzu wanted new drivers, people who might not be inclined to purchase its more rugged Rodeo or Trooper lines. Like many SUVs, the Axiom appealed to drivers in their 20s and 30s. Because the Axiom was largely unknown to this target group, Isuzu set a modest goal of selling 12,000 units for model year 2001.

It was believed that the cynical humor of Joe Isuzu would resonate particularly well with the younger buyers that the Axiom needed to attract. The Isuzu Axiom suffered most from a distinct lack of visibility with its target market, which was exacerbated by the company's absence from television advertising for several years. Because it was anticipated that Joe Isuzu's return would also attract free publicity in the media, the character offered a low-cost way to garner additional attention for the brand.

COMPETITION

Isuzu's main concern was positioning the Axiom against other rugged midsize SUVs. The company felt that the Toyota 4Runner and Ford Explorer were comparable vehicles. Toyota, as a Japan-based automaker with a high reputation for quality, was an especially important competitor. Isuzu also considered the Lexus RX 300 and the Volvo V70 Cross Country to be important models to watch. Though both were slightly more expensive than the Axiom, these luxury brands offered similar driving experiences, and many consumers saw them as comparable vehicles.

DAVID LEISURE: THE MAN BEHIND THE LIAR

Through both his original run in the late 1980s and his brief return in 2001, the character of Joe Isuzu in the Isuzu television commercials was played by David Leisure. The actor first made an impression on audiences with a small but memorable turn as an unnamed Hare Krishna in the 1980 hit comedy *Airplane!,* directed by Jim Abrahams and the Zucker brothers, David and Jerry. The peak of Leisure's visibility came in 1986, however, when he first played Joe Isuzu. From 1986 to 1990 the serial liar Joe was the company's pitchman. The Joe Isuzu commercials featured Joe making obviously inflated claims about various Isuzu products, once claiming that a new Isuzu had "more seats than the Astrodome." The character was so popular that in 1988 Burger King "borrowed" him for a joint promotion with Isuzu.

Leisure was able to use his newfound visibility to land a major role on NBC's sitcom *Empty Nest.* The show, which ran from 1988 to 1995, focused on recently widowed Dr. Harry Weston, played by Richard Mulligan. Leisure costarred as Charlie Dietz, Weston's womanizing neighbor. Leisure was a key source of comic relief on the show. After *Empty Nest* left the air, Leisure continued to work steadily on TV, making guest appearances on such shows as *Touched by an Angel, Diagnosis Murder, General Hospital,* and *Sabrina, the Teenage Witch.*

Other Asian automakers were making major gains in the early 2000s. Their combined market share in 2001 rose to approximately 19 percent, up from about 17 percent the year before. Isuzu had concerns about being overshadowed by these fellow Japanese imports, especially since several featured successful SUVs in their 2001 fleet. By running high-profile marketing campaigns, these competitors had attained much more visibility than Isuzu in recent years. Isuzu felt that it needed to reestablish its presence on TV and then quickly boost the Axiom's visibility.

MARKETING STRATEGY

Isuzu enlisted the agency Goodby, Silverstein & Partners to run the company's fist television-driven campaign of the decade. In order to connect quickly with its target audience, Isuzu centered its marketing drive on the best-known figure in the company's marketing history: Joe Isuzu. Goodby would be resurrecting a character created by another agency, Della Femina, Travisano, and Partners, which no longer did business with Isuzu. The key spot featured Joe Isuzu's return to the company following a 15-year "retirement." Isuzu also used other means to get the word out about its street-friendly new Axiom. One of the most prominent of these was a product placement in *Spy Kids,* a hit family film produced by the Walt Disney Company's Miramax subsidiary. In an unorthodox move Isuzu also cooperated on a remote-controlled toy Axiom that would be sold at RadioShack.

Goodby, Silverstein & Partners was a major advertising agency based in San Francisco. It had created a number of major campaigns, included "Got Milk?" for California Milk Processors. The agency was founded in 1983, and by 2001 it had become a part of the advertising and marketing conglomerate the Omnicom Group.

The return of Joe Isuzu relied on a single 30-second spot titled "The Call." It featured an overweight Joe Isuzu at home, railing against Isuzu's mediocre post-Joe commercials. Suddenly a call came through from Isuzu, calling Joe to work for the company again. To the strains of "The Eye of the Tiger," a hit 1983 song by Survivor that was featured prominently in the film *Rocky III,* Joe began to work out. Partly because of the sound track, the spot recalled the training montages of the popular "Rocky" film series, though it was not a direct homage. Over the course of 20 seconds the audience saw Joe slim down to his original weight, and the spot closed with him grinning before the camera, ready to resume pitching Isuzu vehicles.

The company decided to bring the character back as a shortcut, instead of launching the Axiom with a brand-new campaign that might need some time to register with consumers. Because of the original spots' popularity, Joe Isuzu was a cultural artifact. He would be instantly recognized by viewers, who would then be more likely to remember the new Axiom. The spot ran for a relatively limited time, beginning in the spring of 2001 and closing in October. It was also made available on the Internet through Isuzu's website.

OUTCOME

The response to the campaign was mixed. The advertisements helped Isuzu's brand recognition climb up to 25 percent across all models. The spot fared poorly in *USA Today*'s Ad Track survey, with 21 percent of respondents rating the spot negatively, compared to a survey average of 13 percent. The spots were particularly unpopular with older consumers; 36 percent of respondents over the age of 50 gave the commercial an unfavorable rating.

The negative reactions of mature viewers did not bother the company, however, because "The Call" was intended for younger consumers, and they had a higher opinion of the spot. On the bright side, 48 percent of consumers told Ad Track that they considered the spot effective.

Sales for the Axiom, however, were deeply disappointing. By August 2001 only about 2,700 units had been sold, and the company was not able to make up the difference by the end of the year. This was blamed on a number of factors. Many observers said that Isuzu did a poor job of targeting sales incentives at Axiom buyers. In fact, by concentrating its incentives for the year on its other SUVs, the Rodeo and the Trooper, Isuzu might have undercut the Axiom's sales. Also, the units' base price of $26,595 might have been too high for a newcomer to the crowded SUV field. The Axiom did not put up the kind of numbers Isuzu wanted and did not help the company reverse its poor fortunes. It was eventually discontinued in 2004. Isuzu also parted ways with Goodby, Silverstein & Partners in 2002.

FURTHER READING

Belson, Ken. "G.M. Moves to Increase Control of Some Isuzu Units." *New York Times,* August 15, 2002.

Graham, Laurie. *On the Line at Subaru-Isuzu: The Japanese Model and the American Worker.* Ithaca, NY: ILR Press, 1995.

Halliday, Jean. "'Slow, Painful Death': Troubled Isuzu Cuts Production, Spending." *Advertising Age,* September 23, 2002.

Kohn, Joe. "Lost in SUV Crowd, Axiom Sales Disappoint Isuzu." *AutoWeek,* October 3, 2001.

Krebs, Michael. "Joe Isuzu Is Back, and He Has a New Sport Utility to Sell." *New York Times,* July 1, 2001.

May, Jeff. "Carmaker Jump-Starts Joe Isuzu Ad." *Newark (NJ) Star-Ledger,* March 9, 2001.

McCarthy, Michael. "Marketers Bring Back Vintage Ad Icons." *USA Today,* August 7, 2001.

Tanikawa, Miki. "Isuzu Motors Moves to Cut Losses." *New York Times,* May 30, 2001.

Yamaguchi, Yuzo. "Isuzu Will Sell Stake in U.S. Plant; Sagging Sales of Sport-Utilities Blamed." *AutoWeek,* October 29, 2002.

Yamaguchi, Yuzo, and Lindsay Chappell. "Flagging Sales Forcing Isuzu to Reconsider Its Venture in U.S." *AutoWeek,* October 18, 2002.

Guy Patrick Cunningham

J.C. Penney Company, Inc.

6501 Legacy Drive
Plano, Texas 75024
USA
Telephone: (972) 431-1000
Web site: www.jcpenney.net

■■■

IT'S ALL INSIDE CAMPAIGN

OVERVIEW

The J.C. Penney Company, Inc., had been a fixture in the retail world for nearly 100 years when sales started to drop in the late 1990s. The Plano, Texas, company realized that Americans had lost interest in J.C. Penney and developed a five-year strategy to bring it back from the brink of financial failure. In 2000 Chicago-based advertising giant DDB was engaged to replace Dallas-based Temerlin McClain, which had been J.C. Penney's agency since 1991. DDB had launched the "It's All Inside" campaign by the fall of 2000, setting the stage to rebrand the company inside and out.

The $200 million advertising effort reached all levels of media, from television to print, and also included using in-store signage and updating the look of the company's catalog, stores, and online shopping site. "Fresh and contemporary" was how Bob Scarpelli, DDB's chief creative officer, described the new J.C. Penney look in a September 2000 article of *Adweek* (southwest edition). Television spots debuted that same month and were carefully crafted to prompt core female consumers—who had either deserted the chain or ignored it altogether—to rethink their perceptions of the merchandise as well as of themselves. One commercial that typified this mission depicted an attractive everywoman whose clothing and personal style changed to reflect her moods as she went about her day. The song "Never the Same Girl Twice," by the band Supreme Beings of Leisure, underscored the sentiment of a J.C. Penney that had something for everyone.

J.C. Penney's debt had decreased by 50 percent at the end of 2004, keeping one of the nation's oldest retailers alive and kicking. The new logo, a red square with a crisply written "JCPenney," was the cornerstone of a new image for Penney's, and although ad slogans evolved, the tagline "It's all inside" remained integral to the logo (it was placed directly adjacent to the red square) throughout the five-year restructuring period. Under the new leadership of retail veteran Allen Questrom, J.C. Penney consolidated its product buying, redesigned stores, and began repositioning itself in the national mindset. Sales growth over the next five years met or exceeded the company's goal of 2 percent each year.

HISTORICAL CONTEXT

James Cash Penney opened his first store in Kemmerer, Wyoming, in 1902. He named it the Golden Rule to signify that he had set out to make value and fair dealing the hallmark of his retail business. At the time, many merchants operated under the motto "caveat emptor," meaning let the buyer beware. Penney's service-oriented philosophy was a welcome change for customers, and his business flourished. The company's first of many private brands, Big Mac, hit the shelves in 1922 (by which time the name Golden Rule had been replaced with "J.C. Penney

JC Penney store located in the Garden State Plaza Mall, Paramus, New Jersey. © NAJLAH FEANNY/CORBIS.

Company"). Private brands became a mainstay of Penney's merchandise success. The J.C. Penney catalog debuted in 1963, and the company continued to grow. It struggled through the 1980s and even more so in the 1990s, but that did not stop it from opening a new 1.9 million square-foot headquarters in Plano, Texas, in 1992.

From its inception J.C. Penney had relied on word of mouth and traditional advertising for its local stores. In 1948 the company made its first foray into movie tie-in promotion when stores gave away patterns based on the popular Oscar-winning song "Buttons and Bows" from the Bob Hope film *The Paleface.* The year 1953 saw an even more unusual tie-in. J.C. Penney dressed more than 50 mannequins exposed to an atomic-bomb test at Yucca Flat, Nevada. The clothes were then displayed at stores across the country to prove that J.C. Penney clothes offered the best protection in an atomic blast. The first time that the company participated in national advertising was in 1956, when it ran a series of ads in the hugely popular *Life* magazine. In 1969 it hired its first advertising agency, LaRoche, McCaffrey, and McCall. Through the end of the century J.C. Penney continued to use notably conservative advertising to promote its brands and services. By 1991 sales of $16.2 billion reflected a drop in revenue for the company.

The 1990s were not kind to the national retailer. Its bonds were reduced to junk status, and the store's merchandise proved unappealing to the buying public. "We found [that] a lot of our problems were self-inflicted," said Michael Boylson, Penney's chief marketing officer, in an April 2004 issue of *Advertising Age.* The company's advertising during this period was created by Dallas agency Temerlin McClain. Consumers were moved neither by the company's slogan, "The look. Look who. J.C. Penney," nor by TV commercials that tried too hard to be hip. In early 2000 J.C. Penney severed ties with Temerlin McClain in favor of a more cohesive marketing program from global mega-agency DDB of Chicago. Retail-turnaround expert Allen Questrom, credited with the recent rebound of Federated Department Stores, Inc., came on board as chairman and CEO of J.C. Penney in September 2000. His mission—to centralize buying, redesign product, and get the message out to the consumer—affected the nearly 1,100 department stores that the company operated. By its 100-year anniversary in 2002 J.C. Penney's recovery was underway, thanks to the combination of advertising and product overhaul that typified the "It's All Inside" campaign.

TARGET MARKET

Through a century of doing business J.C. Penney remained focused on serving the needs of the consumer's whole family. In the June 2002 issue of *Retail Merchandiser* Questrom reaffirmed this description of the company's core market as "mainstream American families," a group earning somewhere between $30,000 and $80,000 a year and seeking value. Still, as a new millennium began, it became clear that the J.C. Penney consumer was overwhelmingly female; women accounted for 80 percent of sales, and they were buying for not only themselves but also for their families.

Prior to the "It's All Inside" campaign the Penney's marketing team worked to identify its target and settled on two categories of customer. The "Starting Outs" were young people between 18 and 35 who were beginning careers and families. "Modern Spenders" were consumers 35 to 54 with two incomes and more discretionary dollars at their disposal. Within these two groups women were still believed to be the primary buyers, and Penney's recognized that their attitudes were changing. Traditionally large department stores such as J.C. Penney

J.C. PENNEY LOOKS TO HISPANICS FOR SALES BOOST

By the time that J.C. Penney approached the end of its five-year recovery plan, American working families—historically the bedrock of Penney's sales—had found the retailer again. In 2004 J.C. Penney turned a significant portion of its marketing attention to a new and growing segment of the population: Hispanics. A price-conscious and family-centered demographic, Hispanics were a natural focus for Penney's. That year the company dedicated $15 million in advertising dollars to wooing Hispanic consumers, a group that encompassed a wide variety of nationalities. Omnicom's Dieste Harmel & Partners in Dallas was hired to coordinate merchandise, store signage, promotions, and TV spots that would make the cultural connections necessary to win over what had become the country's largest minority group.

had been in a position to set the trends for consumers who had scant retail choices. The explosion of retail variety in the late twentieth century gave women more freedom to reject J.C. Penney lines whose style had not kept up with the times. The "It's All Inside" tag was meant to draw women's attention to the fact that Penney's merchandise was catching up to the needs of a variety-oriented customer. Not only did Penney's change its logo, but also it revamped buying practices and reconfigured its distribution at the same time in order to allow quicker response to market demand.

COMPETITION

J.C. Penney's historical rival was Sears. Founded in 1886, Sears predated J.C. Penney in the catalog market by several decades and also had a formidable private-brand business. In the 1980s J.C. Penney faced even stiffer competition from young upstarts that took its philosophy of value-for-less and ran with it. Target came on the scene in 1962 as the discount-merchandising face of department-store giant the Dayton Company. Target's slick marketing and appealing, trendy merchandise outhipped everyone in the field, and by year 2000 the company had 1,300 stores in 47 states and was doing billions of dollars in business. Kohl's was a much more blatant copy of the J.C. Penney model but managed to do better at providing an enjoyable value-shopping experience. The conservative-looking Kohl's stores were easy to navigate, and the company's fashion lines were quality approximations of the latest styles. By 1999 Kohl's had recorded its fourth consecutive year of growth exceeding 30 percent, while J.C. Penney struggled to stay afloat.

Customers were losing interest in Penney's formerly strong brands, such as St. John's Bay and Arizona Jean Company. Sales were suffering in the wake of Target's success in commissioning designers to create exclusive Target lines, such as Liz Lange maternity and Michael Graves housewares. J.C. Penney had tried a similar strategy in the 1980s with lines from Mary McFadden and Halston, but these particular designer labels, along with a less-attractive shopping space, did not hit the right note with consumers. Also stealing some of J.C. Penney's pie was the Wal-Mart chain of superstores. A frequent destination for low-cost home items but not necessarily apparel, Wal-Mart began offering more up-to-date fashion in the 1990s. That company's founder, Sam Walton, had been a Penney's employee in 1940 and had used many of the J.C. Penney principles in the founding of his own business.

MARKETING STRATEGY

A five-year recovery plan that began in 2000 was implemented with the goal of making J.C. Penney the "driveway decision" for consumers, meaning that it would be their first destination on shopping excursions for apparel and housewares. The company's new agency, DDB of Chicago, was allotted $200 million for TV spots and radio, print, direct mail, and in-store efforts. DDB came up with a winning slogan, "It's All Inside." The tagline was intended to communicate that there was a fresh change in the brands and decor at J.C. Penney stores while also addressing the consumers' state of mind. J.C. Penney and DDB wanted customers to reevaluate how they felt about the store and themselves.

Three television spots specifically geared toward that huge buying group of women debuted during the Emmy Awards telecast in September 2000, with additional runs on popular sitcoms and the hit prime-time game show *Who Wants to Be a Millionaire.* One spot depicted a couple excitedly preparing for the arrival of an adopted daughter. Another commercial took a playful tone, showing a woman using a pile of shoes to play fetch with her dog. Finally, in the spot that best embodied Penney's new appreciation for its female customer, a woman was depicted whose outfits transformed throughout the day to match her change in mood. The music behind each spot was provided by stylish electronic-pop band Supreme Beings of Leisure. The commercials conveyed a feeling of being up-to-date without looking overly trendy. In a September 2000 *Brandweek* article, DDB's Scarpelli said that the agency's goal for J.C. Penney was "to make people think about [the company] in a new way." He continued, "Our whole strategic insight was self-expression."

In that same 2000 issue of *Brandweek,* Stephen Farley, then chief marketing officer for J.C. Penney, reflected on his expectations of the new agency: "In the past, we had to manage five or six different resources. Now, we're asking DDB to manage those resources for us in a full integration effort." Making the J.C. Penney brand more prominent as well as more universally appealing was key to DDB's mission. To this end the Penney's online shopping site was revamped at this time. The new logo, a bright red box surrounding "JCPenney" with the directly adjacent tagline "it's all inside," anchored the corner of every Web page. The color scheme of red, white, and gray may have taken a page from Target's red bull's-eye logo, but J.C. Penney managed successfully to present its own clean, contemporary Web destination reflecting the company's revitalized personality. DDB left no stone unturned, enlisting its sister agencies for specific tasks: Optimum for media planning, Omnicom's OMD for media buying, Rapp Collins for direct-marketing duties, and Spike DDB for ethnic and urban marketing. The new, more sophisticated look of J.C. Penney was consistent through all the company's public appearances, creating an approachable, inviting image, whether a potential customer was leafing through the mail-order catalog or looking at a newspaper insert.

OUTCOME

In its five-year turnaround plan the J.C. Penney Company had set the goal of achieving a 2 percent increase per year from 2000 to 2005. *Retail Merchandiser* reported that J.C. Penney had surpassed that goal, with a sales increase of 3.3 percent in 2001, a year that saw the company's store and catalog sales reach a desirable $18 billion. The sluggish economy throughout the period actually highlighted Penney's strengths. With household incomes remaining low, consumers were willing to give the revamped J.C. Penney another shot at their dollars. Although the "It's All Inside" campaign was not a favorite with ad-industry reviewers, it did resonate with the most important audience: consumers. By 2004 the company's daunting debt was cut in half, and the first quarter was a strong start, promising to keep J.C. Penney growing steadily into the fifth year of its comeback plan.

FURTHER READING

Baar, Aaron, and J. Dee Hill. "DDB Gets Fresh for Penney." *Adweek,* September 11, 2000, p. 5.

Cardona, Mercedes. "'One-Trick Pony' No More: Penney's Markets Way to Turnaround." *Advertising Age,* April 26, 2004.

Curry, Mary Elizabeth. *Creating an American Institution: The Merchandising Genius of J.C. Penney.* New York: Taylor & Francis, 1993.

Dolbow, Sandra, Aaron Baar, and J. Dee Hill. "Penney's 'Inside' Pitch, via DDB, Seeks Relevance with Core Target." *Brandweek,* September 11, 2000, p. 6.

Halkias, Maria. "Top Advertising, Marketing Executive Resigns from J.C. Penney." *Dallas Morning News,* November 21, 2000.

Hill, J. Dee, and Aaron Baar. "Penney Takes an 'Inside' Track." *Adweek* (southwest ed.), September 11, 2000, p. 4.

Lazare, Lewis. "JCPenney Ads Lack Broad Creative Theme." *Chicago Sun-Times,* February 25, 2004, p. 84.

"Special Report: Power Players." *Advertising Age,* October 4, 2004, p. 12.

Stankevich, Debby Garbato. "Penney Turns on a Dime." *Retail Merchandiser,* June 1, 2002, p. 55.

Thau, Barbara. "Penney Seeks Happy Medium between Online, Catalog Sales." *HFN,* December 18, 2000, p. 6.

Wells, Devona. "Former J.C. Penney CEO to Speak at Bakersfield, Calif., Business Conference." *Bakersfield Californian,* October 13, 2000.

Williamson, Richard. "JC Penney Dresses Up for Oscars." *Adweek,* February 17, 2005.

Simone Samano

Jack in the Box, Inc.

9330 Balboa Avenue
San Diego, California 92313-1516
USA
Telephone: (858) 571-2121
Fax: (858) 571-2121
Web site: www.jackinthebox.com

JACK'S BACK CAMPAIGN

OVERVIEW

In the late 1990s Jack, the clown spokesman for Jack in the Box restaurants, was at the center of a comeback for the fast-food chain. Jack in the Box had used a clown as its mascot until 1980. In that year a commercial showed the clown being blown up as a means of signifying the chain's move into fare with an adult appeal. The chain was hard hit in 1993 when an outbreak of *E. coli* bacteria in its Seattle restaurants led to the hospitalization of hundreds of customers and the deaths of four who had eaten tainted burgers sold by the restaurants. For the company the challenge in the mid-1990s became to rebuild its brand and win back customers.

In 1994, with a campaign orchestrated by the Venice, California, office of TBWA\Chiat\Day, Jack made his return. Thereafter, Jack in the Box advertising was built around the theme "Jack's Back." Production for the campaign was almost entirely TV-based. Spending figures were not disclosed. Most prominent among the Jack TV spots in 1998 was the award-winning "The Visit." It was a parody of the TV show *Cops* and showed Jack beating on a door, demanding to see a Brad Haley. Jack then confronted Haley, a smart-aleck kid who had bad-mouthed the chain's food. When Haley tried to flee, Jack chased him down and forced him to eat a burger, which Haley admitted was "tasty." "You're not just saying that because I'm kneeling on your spine?" Jack asked. The humor of the commercial was further compounded by the fact that Jack in the Box's vice president of marketing communications, one of the people most responsible for the "Jack's Back" campaign, was named Brad Haley.

The campaign's success was undeniable. The "Visit" spot won numerous awards, including a Gold Lion at the International Advertising Festival in Cannes. After Dick Sittig, creator of the Jack campaign, resigned from TBWA\Chiat\Day, Jack in the Box moved its account to Sittig's new agency, which had the unlikely name of Kowloon Wholesale Seafood Company. Sittig's agency continued to create new television spots using the "Jack's Back" theme. The ongoing campaign won a Bronze EFFIE in 2003 and a Silver EFFIE in 2005.

HISTORICAL CONTEXT

In 1941 Robert Peterson founded Topsy's Drive-In in San Diego, California. He later renamed it Oscar's, and by 1950, when he changed the name to Jack in the Box, the company had four restaurants. It was among the first drive-in restaurants in America, and the appeal of Jack in the Box was heightened by its mascot, a clown whose head appeared on the restaurant's distinctive logo and signage.

The company became Foodmaker, Inc., during the 1960s, but the restaurants remained under the Jack in the Box name, and by 1968, when Peterson sold Foodmaker to Ralston Purina, it had some 300 restaurants. In 1969

Jack in the Box became the nation's first fast-food restaurant to serve breakfast, and within a decade it had more than 1,000 locations around the United States. In 1979, however, it decided to scale back its operations, selling 232 facilities in the East and Midwest and focusing its business on the West Coast and in the southwestern United States.

Ownership of Foodmaker fell into the hands of management after a leveraged buyout in 1987, and the company began to franchise many of its formerly company-owned stores. Foodmaker hit on hard times in 1993, an event painfully remembered five years later by CEO Robert Nugent, then chief operating officer. "Sunday morning, January 17, 1993," he told Jennifer Waters of *Restaurants & Institutions,* "I got a call from our head marketing guy. He said, 'We have a problem in Seattle. It's food poisoning.'"

The cause was the *E. coli* bacteria, which had tainted ground beef, causing hundreds of people to be hospitalized and killing four others—including a nine-year-old boy. Nugent, the father of two daughters, remembered this as "one of the most devastating things I've ever experienced." But Foodmaker responded in an exemplary fashion. It halted all hamburger sales in its more than 1,100 U.S. restaurants and removed the meat from all its facilities. Facing huge lawsuits, company executives met regularly in prayer groups, and Foodmaker developed a food inspection program later cited by the Food & Drug Administration (FDA) as a model to the industry. Foodmaker weathered the storm, including the lawsuits and huge losses, and by the late 1990s had reemerged stronger than ever.

TARGET MARKET

In a bid to draw in more adults, Foodmaker in 1980 had gotten rid of its Jack logo, the trademark clown; in fact, a television spot actually showed Jack being blown up. The end of the logo was meant to symbolize a shift in direction, with a greater appeal to adults rather than children. This was accompanied by a change in the menu. By 1994, however, Foodmaker had decided it was time to bring Jack back, so in the first of a new wave of commercials, Jack announced his return—"thanks to the miracle of plastic surgery."

"If that sounds like serious business," wrote Linda Mae Carlstone of *Franchise Times* in February 1997, "be aware that the new Jack is seven feet tall—part clown, part man—with a giant spherical head, a permanent painted smile, and a pointed yellow hat. Let's also point out [that] he blows up the boardroom in the lead ad." Brad Haley, vice president of marketing communications for Jack in the Box, told Carlstone that "Jack was carefully planned." As Carlstone noted, "Company research showed the biggest fast-food hamburger consumer is the 18-to-34-year-old male, so the humor is targeted to this group that is," in Haley's words, "jaded about advertising in general, mistrustful, and typically [without] a character to relate to." Carlstone went on to note that "Jack is liked by older adults and kids. His likeness appears in kids' meals and toy promotions." Said Haley, "I'd like to say the broad appeal was part of our thinking, but it was a pleasant surprise."

Garcia of the *Los Angeles Times* specifically linked the appeal of Jack to Generation X: "The secret behind Jack lies in his disarming personality," she wrote. "Gen-Xers distasteful of advertising view him as a parody of hyped celebrity pitchmen—and like him because of it." She also noted that he was "a hit with males in their late teens up to their 30s—voracious consumers of cheeseburgers, shakes, and fries."

WEBISODES

In *Nation's Restaurant News* Gregg Cebrzynski described the following vignette, which might have seemed at first sight like something from a Jack in the Box TV commercial: "Jack is driving along the freeway, the top down on the car. Suddenly, thunder is heard. Lightning flashes in the sky. Jack never loses the grin on his face. He reaches next to him on the seat and grabs a Jumbo Jack sandwich. Rain starts to pour down. It's pouring so hard that Noah's Ark can be seen in the distance. But it's not raining in Jack's car. It's illuminated by its own little sunshine because Jack is having so gosh darn much fun eating a Jumbo Jack that even a storm can't darken his day."

In fact, this was not a television commercial, but a potential part of a new phenomenon called "webisodes," a term coined by Johann Liedgren of Seattle's Honkworm. The latter, along with Rocket Pictures, also of Seattle, had teamed up to produce animated commercials on the Internet, spots that would feature longer, more involved stories than would be possible on television. In the future, Cebrzynski suggested, visitors to the Jack in the Box website might be able to access such webisodes. According to Cebrzynski, Liedgren and his partner, Dan Pepper of Rocket Pictures, "have not signed up any restaurants as clients yet, but they believe Jack in the Box, Taco Bell, and McDonald's, because of their strong brand images, would be perfect candidates."

COMPETITION

Another powerful California-based fast-food chain, Carl's Jr., made its own appeal to the young in 1998 with what Robert Wisely, president of parent company CKE Restaurants, called "the big messy, drippy advertising campaign." Dennis Pollock of the *Fresno Bee* described one of the chain's most controversial spots: "The burger drips and the couple strips down inside a coin-operated laundry. In a television commercial that has brought howls of protest in the [San Fernando] Valley and elsewhere, her melting ice cream bar prompts her to disrobe while he strips down to his paper bag from Carl's Jr."

Although Jordin Mendelsohn, managing partner of the agency that created the spot, told Pollock, "I can sell a lot of hamburgers," many viewers found such advertising a turnoff. In another spot a young man "slobbers," in Pollock's words, over a double-bacon cheeseburger from Carl's Jr. before a blonde in a Porsche caused him to toss the burger on the ground and jump in with her. A voice-over announced, "If you ever find anything hotter and juicier than a Carl's Jr. Double Western, go for it." Wisely dismissed detractors as people "from the Central Valley, which seems to have more Midwestern values. The [complaint] calls have come from grandparents and mothers with young children who see it as an affront to their lifestyle."

By 1999 Carl's Jr. had acquired North Carolina–based Hardee's, which had been the nation's fourth-largest burger chain after McDonald's, Burger King, and Wendy's. This put the California chain into a southern market where West Coast advertising styles were not likely to be as popular; meanwhile, Foodmaker made its own push into the southeast with Jack in the Box. As for Jack, many observers saw him as one of the most effective weapons in Foodmaker's arsenal, which would give the company an edge over even McDonald's Ronald McDonald or Wendy's popular Dave Thomas. Foodmaker poked fun at one competitor's symbol in a spot where Jack appeared at the gate of a mansion and said, "Let me speak to the Colonel, founder-to-founder." The spot promoted the company's new chicken sandwich, competition for Kentucky Fried Chicken.

MARKETING STRATEGY

From the time of the 1994 reintroduction of Jack, Foodmaker worked with TBWA\Chiat\Day. In 1996, however, the new Jack's creator, Sittig, left TBWA\Chiat\Day to form his own agency in Santa Barbara. Foodmaker moved the account in March 1997 to follow Sittig, and @radicaL.media handled production for television commercials.

Television spots for Jack in the Box during 1998 were seemingly endless, and indeed the campaign consisted of perhaps two dozen different commercials. These developed the story line of Jack's existence, along with his personality as a witty, sardonic iconoclast. Central to this advertising was the idea that Jack was the true CEO of Jack in the Box, a concept he reinforced with phrases such as "Since I regained control of the company"—a reference to his return from suspended animation four years earlier.

In January 1999 Eric Celeste of the *Fort Worth Star-Telegram* reviewed some of his favorite Jack commercials. In a spot called "Spicy Crispy Chicks," for instance, Foodmaker seemed to lampoon efforts by competitor Carl's Jr. to use sex as a means of selling hamburgers. An underling showed Jack an intended commercial showing the scantily clad "Spicy Crispy Chicks Dancers" cavorting to music. Disgusted, Jack told the lackey, "You are so fired." Thus Foodmaker managed to simultaneously use sex and make fun of the concept. Celeste described another spot, titled "Focus Group": "Jack and his corporate suits are conducting a focus group composed of meat-lovers, asking them what they think of the company's new Ultimate Cheeseburger, which contains only meat and cheese. The men complain about the use of a bun. 'Lose that bun,' says one, 'and you got somethin'.' Jack storms in and screams that their suggestion is ridiculous because 'your hands would be covered with MEAT and CHEESE!'" At the end, however, he sighed and said of the "no-bun theory," "All right, we'll look into that."

Based on the campaign's continued success, new spots were created that targeted a broader audience and featured Jack poking fun at the chain's fast-food competitors. In 2000, working with a measured-media budget of $61.6 million, Jack in the Box released television commercials that included several aimed at the Hispanic market. One Spanish-language spot featured Jack talking to a tarot-card reader at a carnival; another spot, released in time for the holidays, spoofed 1970s dating-game shows. One spot that aired in 2002 was aimed at the burger chain's competitor, the Subway sandwich chain, and its famous weight-loss spokesman Jared. The spot, titled "Jared," showed Jack walking onto a train platform to introduce the restaurant's Ultimate Cheeseburger to people. Jack approached a 20-something man named Jared and asked him where he was from. Jared, reluctant to talk to a man with a giant Ping-Pong ball for a head, responded, "The subway."

In 2003 the campaign was modified to expand its target market beyond burger-hungry 18- to 34-year-old men to include women and older adults. Described as a "brand reinvention" by the *San Diego Business Journal,* the effort included spots featuring Jack in situations that promoted the chain's upgraded food and the restaurants' move from fast food into the trendier "fast-casual dining" category. A spot released in 2004 and titled "No French" showed Jack being interviewed by a French newscaster, who asked why Jack was calling French fries "natural-cut fries." Jack cracked under the pressure of the newscaster's "You have a problem with the French" attitude and responded with an undiplomatic "Eh."

The introduction of Jack car-antenna attachments led to the creation of sidekicks for Jack, little Ping-Pong heads who began developing a story line of their own in some commercials. During the summer, with Congressional campaigns afoot, Jack ran a political campaign in which he demonized his opponent as "a milkshake-hating extremist." Denise Gellene of the *Los Angeles Times* called this spot "a sendup of political advertising" that managed, in just 30 seconds, to make fun of "every cliché of political advertising." But perhaps the biggest news of Jack's ersatz political campaign was the fact that he had a wife—a normal-looking woman, without the Ping-Pong head.

OUTCOME

"The Visit," the spot in which Jack confronted Haley, won a Belding Award from the Advertising Club of Los Angeles in April 1998, as well as a Gold Lion at the 45th International Advertising Festival in June. In October "The Visit" won still more awards at the Excellence in Advertising for Television and Excellence in Advertising for Radio Awards. In December Gellene chose Jack's political campaign as one of her top three ads of the year.

While Jack gathered awards and kudos, his company prepared for a push into the southeastern United States. According to Louise Kramer, writing in *Advertising Age* in February 1999, "The move east will be backed by TV commercials from Jack in the Box agency Kowloon Wholesale Seafood Co.... They will introduce the concept to consumers, and use the same theme as the long-running campaign featuring the Jack character."

In May 1999 Warren Berger of *Advertising Age* celebrated Jack, along with "Got Milk" and a few others, as examples of campaigns whose impact had not faded. According to Berger, "Haley says research has shown that consumers can't wait to see what Jack's going to do next. And unlike more human founders of other burger chains, Sittig believes this character can go on indefinitely as spokesperson—because 'this is one company founder who doesn't age.'"

As the campaign's run continued, the awards also continued to pile up. In 2002 the "Jared" commercial was named one of *Adweek* magazine's Best Spots. The campaign earned a Bronze EFFIE Award for Sustained Success in 2003, and in 2004 *Adweek* again honored one of the campaign's spots, "No French," as one of the publication's Best Spots. Another EFFIE for Sustained Success, this time a Silver, was awarded in 2005.

FURTHER READING

Bell, Diane. "Jack's Wife Is Normal: No Fat Head." *San Diego Union-Tribune,* July 28, 1998, p. B-1.

Berger, Warren. "Jack in the Box: Explosive Staying Power." *Advertising Age's Creativity,* May 1, 1999, p. 30.

Carlstone, Linda Mae. "Clown Returns Home to Help Jack Up Sales." *Franchise Times,* February 1, 1997, p. 20.

Cebrzynski, Gregg. "Marketing & Media." *Nation's Restaurant News,* July 13, 1998, p. 18.

Celeste, Eric. "We Do Know (and Love) Jack: Edgy Jack in the Box Commercials Funnier than Most TV Fare." *Fort Worth (TX) Star-Telegram,* January 12, 1999, p. 1.

Garcia, Shelly Nina. "Clowning Glory: Never Mind His Looks, Icon's Personality Gives Fast-Food Chain the Last Laugh." *Los Angeles Times,* October 9, 1997, p. D-4.

Gellene, Denise. "Campaign Spoof Wins for Pitch with Appeal." *Los Angeles Times,* July 30, 1998, p. D-6.

"Jack Pez to Do Battle against Taco Bell Chihuahua: It's Dog vs. Pez in World of Fast Food." *Santa Ana (CA) Orange County Register* March 24, 1999.

Kramer, Louise. "Jack to Burst Out of Its West Coast Box: Fast-Food Chain Eyes 500 Sites in Southeast." *Advertising Age,* February 1, 1999, p. 3.

Lansner, Jonathan. "Can You Top This? In the Fast-Food War for Your Belly and Your Buck, Tackiness Is King." *Santa Ana (CA) Orange County Register,* July 8, 1998, p. C-1.

Lewis, Connie. "A Test in Taste: Jack in the Box Offers New Fare, but Quality May Still Be Job No. 1." *San Diego Business Journal,* October 13, 2003.

MacArthur, Kate. "Jack's Fighting at Fifty; Jack in the Box Struggles with Image and Rivals." *Advertising Age,* February 19, 2001.

Pollock, Dennis. "Sex, Burgers and Outrage: Carl's Jr.'s 'Big Messy, Drippy Advertising Campaign' Proves Profitable, but Complaints Are Piling Up." *Fresno Bee,* October 2, 1998, p. C-1.

Waters, Jennifer. "Back in the Black." *Restaurants & Institutions,* July 1, 1998.

Judson Knight
Rayna Bailey

Jenny Craig, Inc.

5770 Fleet Street
Carlsbad, California 92008
USA
Telephone: (760) 696-4000
Fax: (760) 696-4009
Web site: www.jennycraig.com

■■■

KIRSTIE ALLEY CAMPAIGN

OVERVIEW

With 64 percent of American adults considered overweight or obese in 2004, weight loss was big business in the United States. An estimated 44 percent of women and 29 percent of men were trying to lose weight in 2004, and they were spending about $44 billion on diet programs. That amount was expected to increase steadily to nearly $48 billion by 2006. As the number of overweight people looking for a magic bullet for weight loss grew, so did fad programs promising to make the task of dieting easier. Diet crazes such as the Atkins low-carbohydrate diet plan began winning consumers away from traditional programs, such as Jenny Craig, that took a conservative approach to dieting. By 2004 the number of people signing on with Jenny Craig weight-management centers was stagnating.

To win back customers, in 2004 Jenny Craig made two changes: it added to its roster a new diet program that offered clients more flexibility than its original plans, and it signed on J. Walter Thompson New York as its advertising agency, replacing its former agency, Johnson/Ukropina of Irvine, California. The first task for J. Walter Thompson was to create an advertising campaign supporting Jenny Craig's new diet program, Jenny YourStyle. Although the campaign began in September 2004, it was replaced just months later, in January 2005, with a new set of advertisements that featured actress/comedian Kirstie Alley as its celebrity spokeswoman. No budget for the new campaign was available, but according to a report in the *New York Times,* the preceding campaign, "Jenny YourStyle," cost $30 million.

The "Kirstie Alley" campaign was an immediate hit with consumers. American dieters drawn to Alley's humorous approach to her own weight problem and dieting efforts rushed in droves to Jenny Craig Centres to sign up. Following an appearance by Alley on *The Oprah Winfrey Show,* calls to Jenny Craig centers increased 81 percent. Based on its success a series of new television spots were added to the "Kirstie Alley" campaign and began airing in December 2005.

HISTORICAL CONTEXT

Before Jenny Craig became an international weight-management company, she was a 50-year-old woman with a supportive husband, Sid Craig, and a dream. She wanted to help people improve their lives through balanced nutrition, physical activity, and lifestyle. In 1982 Jenny Craig opened her first eponymous weight-loss center in Melbourne, Australia. The Craigs established additional centers in New Zealand, and in 1985 the company expanded into the United States with 12 centers in Los Angeles. By 2004 there were more than 650 company-owned and franchised Jenny Craig Weight Loss

Actress Kirstie Alley. © JIM RUYMEN/REUTERS/CORBIS.

Centres in Australia, New Zealand, Canada, Guam, Puerto Rico, and the United States. The company steadily increased memberships at Jenny Craig Weight Loss Centres by using marketing methods that relied on customer testimonials similar to those promoting other weight-loss programs. Included were commercials featuring ordinary consumers sharing their personal weight-loss success stories.

As the number of overweight and obese people increased, so too did the number of weight-loss companies and programs vying for their share of the diet industry, which had climbed to an estimated $44.6 billion in 2004. Low-carbohydrate fad diets such as Atkins and South Beach, which promised weight loss by only eating foods low in carbs, began winning away dieters from traditional programs like Jenny Craig. In 2004 Jenny Craig responded to the new diet plans with the introduction of Jenny YourStyle, a more flexible plan that allowed participants to continue many of their dietary habits while still losing weight. Wanting a fresh approach to its advertising to support its new weight-loss program, Jenny Craig also began looking for an advertising agency to replace Johnson/Ukropina of Irvine, California.

Agencies competing for the business included Interpublic Group of Companies, based in New York; Newport Beach, California–based independent agency Heil-Brice; and Bartle Bogle Hegarty, which withdrew from the competition prior to the final round. J. Walter Thompson New York (JWT) eventually won the account. To prepare for the competition and become familiar with the client, executives at JWT went on a Jenny Craig diet, and in addition to winning the account, they lost a total of 50 pounds. JWT's first creative effort for Jenny Craig was a $30 million campaign that was released in September 2004 and helped introduce the new Jenny YourStyle program. It also was designed to reintroduce Jenny Craig as the diet center of choice for consumers looking for sustainable weight loss. In December 2004 JWT prepared to begin a campaign featuring celebrity spokeswoman Kirstie Alley, who signed on to promote Jenny Craig after going on the Jenny YourStyle weight-loss program. The first television spot starring Alley aired in January 2005.

TARGET MARKET

According to *U.S. News & World Report,* 64 percent of Americans were overweight or obese in 2004. Further, at that time 44 percent of women and 29 percent of men said that they were trying to lose weight. In 2005 nearly an equal number of men and women said that they were actively trying to lose weight: 30 percent and 31 percent, respectively. Reaching the men and women already on a diet program as well as those considering starting a program was the goal of J. Walter Thompson's 2005 "Kirstie Alley" campaign. Jenny Craig's chief operating officer, Jim Evans, noted in *PR Newswire* that the new campaign featuring Alley "was designed to resonate with anyone looking to lose unwanted weight with a safe, scientifically proven, lifestyle-focused method."

COMPETITION

Weight Watchers International, based in Woodbury, New York, was established in 1963. In 1997 Weight Watchers signed on as spokeswoman British royal and ex-wife of Prince Andrew, Sarah Ferguson, the Duchess of York. The stunning, red-haired "Fergie" was the ideal spokeswoman for Weight Watchers: she was a celebrity, an emotional eater struggling with weight loss, divorced, and a busy, working single mom. The *Tampa Tribune* described her as "both glamorous and ordinary." She also connected with American women, who followed her lead and embraced the Weight Watchers diet program, flocking to its weekly weigh-ins and meetings held in communities nationwide. In 2001 the privately held Weight Watchers went public, and by the following year it reported that sales had increased 127 percent to $620 million. Sales jumped to $944 million two years later. But by 2004, despite having some 1.5 million members, Weight Watchers was slipping. Many dieters, frustrated with the hassles of the program's system for counting

WHAT'S FOR DINNER? OR BREAKFAST? OR LUNCH? GOURMET DIET FOOD

More and more people, regardless of their weight, were discovering the convenience of having gourmet diet meals delivered right to their doors, ready to heat and eat. Jenny Direct, the home-delivery division of weight-loss management company Jenny Craig, Inc., reported that in 2004 its service had grown to more than 8,000 clients in the United States. The nutritious meals were growing in popularity with dieters and nondieters alike who had neither the time nor the inclination to prepare three home-cooked meals plus snacks each day. Participation in the Jenny Direct program cost on average $15 per day, and it included delivery by Federal Express or United Parcel Service. Meals arrived frozen with instructions about what should be eaten at each meal, removing all the guesswork and ensuring that hungry gourmands or dieters had perfectly balanced meals three times a day with little effort on their part beyond turning on a microwave oven.

calories, were abandoning Weight Watchers. Others were wooed away by the newest fad diets, such as Atkins and South Beach, which espoused losing weight while eating what you wanted as long as it was low in carbohydrates. To reverse the trend, during the summer of 2004 Weight Watchers ran a series of television spots created by its agency, the Seiden Group of New York. The commercials featured women who told not only of their weight-loss successes with the program but also of the side benefits, such as developing more self-esteem and achieving more quality time with their families. Weight Watchers also responded to the low-carb diet craze and introduced a selection of low-carbohydrate, ready-to-eat meals and a new program, the TurnAround plan, that focused less on counting calories and more on food choices. In November 2004 Weight Watchers replaced the Seiden Group with ad agency Young & Rubicam of New York, but then it partnered with Foote Cone & Belding, Chicago, to launch a new advertising campaign with the tagline "Watch yourself change" in January 2005.

In 1996 the Internet took dieting to a new level with the introduction of the website eDiets.com. It was described by its founders as the "premier one-stop online diet and healthy-living destination." Included on the site were personalized information, products, professional advice, and other services for consumers who wanted not only wanted to lose weight but also to improve their lives through fitness and nutrition. Relying solely on online advertising, eDiets.com had attracted more than 1.5 million members worldwide by 2003. Its target market was women aged 25 to 54 years old with an average weight-loss goal of at least 50 pounds. The site offered more than 20 different diet plans, including Atkins and the Mayo Clinic Diet, and won the praises of *Forbes,* which named it "Best of the Web" in the diet and nutrition category. Hoping to reach a broader range of consumers, in early 2004 eDiets.com released a series of four television spots created by the Ad Store, an agency based in New York. The $1.5 million effort paid off, nearly doubling the number of visitors to the site. Later that year eDiets.com announced plans to double its budget for television advertising to $3 million.

MARKETING STRATEGY

J. Walter Thompson's creative effort for Jenny Craig featuring actress/comedian Kirstie Alley was twofold: it expanded on an earlier, albeit brief, campaign developed to promote Jenny Craig's new weight-management program titled YourStyle, and it built on Alley's self-deprecating sense of humor. The new campaign followed Alley's efforts to lose more than 50 pounds by adhering to the Jenny YourStyle weight-loss program, which was also the basis of her new Showtime television show, *Fat Actress.* Campaign spots were loosely based on the theme "Have you called Jenny yet?"

Television spots for the new campaign were released during the first week of January 2005, a critical time for companies in the diet business, because it was when many people were enthusiastic about their New Year's resolutions to lose weight. In the initial spot Alley was shown on a set with little decor beyond a chair and an oversized pink telephone. Alley picked up the phone handset and called Jenny Craig's founder. She then told an unseen person at the other end of the line that the call was "in regards to me being fat." Alley then looked directly at the camera, as if speaking to every overweight person watching the commercial, and said, "Hey, you're chubby too! Let's lose weight together! They have really yummy food.... They have chicken fettuccini!" At the end of the spot Alley's call was finally put through, presumably to Jenny Craig herself, and Alley said, "Jenny! Hey, listen girl, I'm fat!" Unlike the first-person testimonials usually used in diet-program ads, Alley's spot appeared believable.

Subsequent spots followed Alley on her weight-loss adventure and featured her sharing her personal experiences with dieting and the Jenny Craig program. Spots also maintained the sense of humor used in the initial spot while focusing on Alley's increased energy and emphasizing the variety of foods available through the plan. People who missed the spots when they aired could log onto the company's website, www.jennycraig.com, and read Alley's blog entries, which were updated each week. Television spots could also be watched on the website.

OUTCOME

When Jenny Craig launched a new advertising campaign featuring Kirstie Alley as its spokeswoman, consumers quickly embraced the star as she pursued weight loss through Jenny Craig. More importantly, record numbers of overweight Americans enrolled in the program. According to a *PR Newswire* report, the company claimed that the campaign resonated with consumers because the commercials were humorous, honest, and lacked the "outlandish 'magic bullet' claims" typically seen in ads for other weight loss plans. *Adweek* critic Barbara Lippert also praised the campaign for its honesty, commending it for avoiding political correctness and for not being afraid to use the "f" word—fat—in weight-loss television spots. Five months after the campaign began, Alley appeared on *The Oprah Winfrey Show* to announce that she had lost more than 33 pounds, reaching the halfway mark of her weight-loss goal. Alley's statements during the show resulted in an 81 percent increase in callers to Jenny Craig inquiring about the weight-loss program. In a press release commenting on the campaign, Jenny Craig's chief operating officer, Jim Evans, said, "Our business has been very strong since Kirstie Alley joined our program." The campaign was so successful that it was extended. J. Walter Thompson created a new series of television spots featuring Alley that began airing at the end of 2005, and it continued the tagline "Have you called Jenny yet?"

FURTHER READING

"EDiets.com Ranks as No. 1 Health, Fitness & Nutrition Site, According to Nielsen/NetRatings." *PR Newswire,* January 14, 2004.

"'Fat Actress' Kirstie Alley Chooses Jenny Craig to Lose Weight; Actress to Star in New Advertising Campaign." *PR Newswire,* December 20, 2004.

Ives, Nat. "Eat Carbs, Lose Weight. Jenny Craig's New Campaign Touts Flexibility." *New York Times,* September 10, 2004, p. 5.

"Jenny Craig Phones Jump after Kirstie Alley's Appearance on 'The Oprah Winfrey Show.'" *PR Newswire,* May 24, 2005.

"Jenny Craig Unveils New Twists in Its Next Round of Kirstie Alley Commercials." *PR Newswire,* December 16, 2005.

Lawlor, Vera. "Not for Dieters Only: Gourmet Breakfast, Lunch, and Dinner—Delivered." *Bergen County (NJ) Record,* August 4, 2004.

Lippert, Barbara. "Barbara Lippert's Critique: The Weighting Game." *Adweek,* January 10, 2005.

Oser, Kris. "EDiets Launches Digital Magazine for 13 Million." *Advertising Age,* January 24, 2005.

"Rethinking Weight." *U.S. News & World Report,* February 9, 2004.

Sanders, Lisa. "J. Walter Thompson Diets Its Way to Review Victory." *Advertising Age,* June 10, 2004.

Thompson, Stephanie. "After the Carb Craze: Diet Marketers Bet on Balanced Options." *Advertising Age,* January 3, 2005.

Thompson, Susan H. "Britain's Fergie Brings Her Message of Inspiration and Weight Loss." *Tampa (FL) Tribune,* February 1, 2004.

"Weight Watchers Woodbury, N.Y." *Adweek,* November 1, 2004.

"Y&R Wins $45 Mil. Weight Watchers' Account." *Adweek,* November 16, 2004.

Zammit, Deanna. "Ediets.com Beefs Up TV Budget." *Adweek,* June 16, 2004.

Rayna Bailey

JetBlue Airways Corporation

118-29 Queens Boulevard
Forest Hills, New York 11375
USA
Telephone: (718) 286-7900
Fax: (718) 709-3621
Web site: www.jetblue.com

JETBLUE LAUNCH CAMPAIGN

OVERVIEW

JetBlue Airways was the brainchild of David Neeleman, an aviation expert. It was Neeleman's third foray into start-up discount airlines; he launched the Salt Lake City, Utah–based Morris Air in the late 1980s and helped to develop WestJet, a Canadian low-fare carrier, in the mid 1990s. The key priorities for the new airline, according to an *Advertising Age* report, was providing the "best coach for the best price" and remembering that quality service would result in return business and drive positive word of mouth from customers. The company's stated philosophy was "people are travelers, and not cargo."

Prior to its launch in February 2000, JetBlue was generating buzz without any advertising efforts. Magazine feature articles profiled the start-up airline in December 1999 and January 2000. As the airline prepared for its first flight, however, its advertising agency, Merkley Newman Harty, New York, created a print-only campaign themed "Unbelievable" to reinforce the new airline's amenities and low fares. As JetBlue evolved, its marketing strategy shifted as well. Although the "Unbelievable" campaign was reaching consumers, in July 2000 the company, without review, hired Arnold Communications Boston as its agency and axed Merkley Newman Harty. Despite Arnold's successful efforts, including creating the airline's first television campaign, JetBlue dumped the agency and began looking for a replacement in 2001. JetBlue hired independent New York agency the Ad Store to replace Arnold, but the company also turned to BBDO and Ground Zero New York to create additional campaigns that year.

While JetBlue's early marketing strategy and relationships with its various agencies may have seemed tempestuous, the approach also seemed to work. Not only did each agency's campaign efforts reach consumers and help build the discount carrier's brand identity, but the campaigns built business. Within eight months of its first flight, JetBlue reported that it was profitable and that its 500,000th passenger had climbed aboard. Further, by September 2001 the company reported that its income had increased more than 20 percent from the same period the previous year. *Advertising Age* named JetBlue its 2001 Marketer of the Year.

HISTORICAL CONTEXT

When he laid the groundwork for JetBlue, founder David Neeleman already had a solid background in start-up airline experience. Neeleman's first commercial airline, Salt Lake City, Utah–based discount carrier Morris Air, was sold to Southwest Airlines in 1993 for $130 million in stock. In 1996 Neeleman helped found Canada's discount airline WestJet, modeled after Southwest Airlines. Based on his airline experience, in

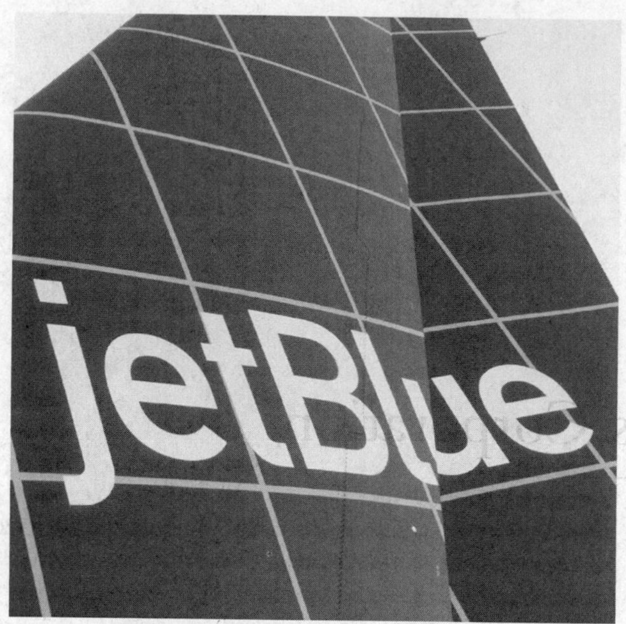

© JAMES LEYNSE/CORBIS.

1999 Neeleman put together a management team and $130 million in capital funding with plans to launch a new discount carrier that the company's website stated "would bring humanity back to air travel."

Based at New York's John F. Kennedy International (JFK) Airport, JetBlue offered its first flight in February 2000, with amenities not typical of a discount airline, including new planes, leather seats with extra legroom, and free in-flight satellite television at each seat. The company also took a unique approach to its marketing. It reported that it had allotted an ad budget of $12.8 million to support its launch. This was a pittance compared to other airlines' ad spending; for instance, competitor Southwest Airlines reported a $107.6 million advertising budget in 2000. JetBlue worked instead with the theory that it was more important to get everything about the product right first and then consider advertising. Helping JetBlue reach consumers and build brand identity without extensive spending on advertising was free publicity, such as articles profiling the start-up airline that appeared in issues of *Condé Nast Traveler* and *New York* magazine before the first flight ever took off. When JetBlue put its marketing budget to work, it partnered with Merkley Newman Harty New York for its first campaign. Within months of the campaign's start in 2000, Merkley Newman Harty was replaced by Arnold Communications Boston. Arnold created JetBlue's first television spots, which hit the air in October 2000. Arnold introduced a new campaign for JetBlue in June 2001, but the airline was already looking for a new agency. During 2001 three separate agencies created campaigns for JetBlue: the Ad Store, BBDO, and Ground Zero New York.

TARGET MARKET

Following research and serious number crunching, JetBlue's executives determined that the new airline's target market was the eight million people who lived within a five-mile radius of New York's JFK Airport, JetBlue's home base, as well as anyone living in Manhattan. According to a report by Jonah Bloom in *Advertising Age,* the numbers were accurate. He wrote, "Manhattanites have flocked to the airline in the thousands." As JetBlue expanded its service area, the target market also was expanded to include college students, young professionals, and middle-aged travelers looking for a bargain. The reach also extended beyond bargain hunters to target more affluent consumers, or what JetBlue's executives described in *Advertising Age* as "travel snobs." Noting JetBlue's reluctance to restrict its target market to younger, hipper consumers, the company's CEO, David Neeleman, said that age was irrelevant: "We are an every person airline."

COMPETITION

When JetBlue's founders planned the new low-cost airline, their model was the granddaddy of discount air carriers, Southwest Airlines. Southwest began operating in Texas in 1971 with the notion of getting passengers to their destinations on time, offering the lowest possible price, and assuring that the customers enjoyed the trip. Not only did that idea attract customers, but it also set the standard for other low-cost carriers. Southwest's first flights served the Texas cities of Dallas, Houston, and San Antonio. At the end of 1999 Southwest was ranked the number-four air-passenger carrier, and it included on its list of destinations 58 cities in 29 states. Southwest kicked off 2000 with a new marketing campaign designed to encourage travelers to visit its website, www.southwest.com, for everything from researching destination information to booking flight tickets, rental cars, and hotel rooms. The new campaign's tagline, "A symbol of e-freedom," put a spin on Southwest's ongoing tagline, "A symbol of freedom." Television spots used humor to portray people in a variety of unpleasant situations juxtaposed with the same people enjoying a fun vacation. The voice-over said, "When the going gets tough, get going to southwest.com to book a quick getaway."

To compete with discount carriers such as Southwest and start-ups such as JetBlue, in 2000 Fort Worth, Texas–based American Airlines added some perks to its aircraft in hopes of enticing new customers and keeping its existing ones. Citing customer complaints about comfort aboard its planes, in February 2000 American

JETBLUE PASSENGERS GET FREE IN-FLIGHT TV

When passengers boarded a JetBlue plane, they could do something not available on any other airline: settle back in their seats, put on a pair of headphones, and watch programs on 24 television stations. The satellite programming was offered to each individual passenger through seat-back screens. Despite being a low-cost carrier that looked for ways to save money and cut expenses, JetBlue's LiveTV was a free service for passengers. But the free TV was originally planned as a pay-to-use service with a $5 price tag. The plan to charge for the service was dismissed by JetBlue executives, however, when they determined that the goodwill gained from offering the perk for free was worth more than the estimated $810 additional revenue per flight that would be generated by charging for the service.

announced plans to remove two rows of seats from each of its more than 700 jets, thereby giving coach-class passengers more legroom. The effort kicked off in August and was supported by a marketing campaign tagged, "Make More Room throughout Coach." Global marketing agency TLP, Inc., of Dallas created the campaign, which included the "Great American Seat Take Off" contest to respond to the question: Where did all the seats go? The goal of the contest was to find owners for the seats American removed from its planes. To promote the campaign, print ads ran in major daily newspapers, including the *New York Times,* the *Chicago Tribune,* the *Boston Globe,* the *San Francisco Chronicle,* and the *Los Angeles Times.* The following year American took another step to make the insides of its narrow-body planes more passenger-friendly, increasing the size of the overhead storage bins to allow more room for carry-on luggage.

MARKETING STRATEGY

When JetBlue took to the skies in February 2000, it was introduced to consumers in the first two cities it included on its flight route—Buffalo, New York, and Fort Lauderdale, Florida—with a marketing campaign created by the fledgling airline's agency, Merkley Newman Harty. Themed "Unbelievable," the initial campaign, which began in January 2000, also was designed to help establish the brand. It was limited to print and featured full-page ads in local newspapers that touted the new airline's "unbelievable" low fares and amenities not typically provided by a discount air-passenger carrier. Text in one ad read: "$79 to Fort Lauderdale? What, as a stowaway?" At the time of the "Unbelievable" campaign's launch, future campaigns were planned that would apply the same theme to outdoor efforts and television spots.

In May 2000 JetBlue hired Arnold Communications Boston to replace Merkley Newman Harty. Arnold created a multimedia campaign for JetBlue that included newspaper, outdoor, and broadcast advertising. The cost of the new marketing effort was estimated at $10 million, and new ads were slated to begin running in the summer of 2000. These ads, which like the "Unbelievable" campaign ran only in cities served by JetBlue, lacked a specific tagline and were designed to drive customer traffic rather than establish a brand image for the airline. One new billboard that appeared in New York City at the Queens Midtown Tunnel stated: "$79 to Florida. Quite a bargain considering it's $3.50 to Queens." Print ads focused on humor to inform consumers of the airline's perks as well as its efforts to keep costs in check, such as not offering passengers hot meals. In one print ad a caricature of a chicken was shown with the text: "Nature never intended it to fly. Really low fares. Free live TV. No rubber chickens." Television spots aired during the World Series, which was played that year between New York's two teams. Arnold Communications created a new campaign for JetBlue that launched in June 2001. With the tagline "Somebody Up There Likes You," it focused on customers and employees of the airline. The new campaign's advertisements appeared in print, broadcast, and outdoor formats and ran in the cities served by JetBlue.

Shortly after the "Somebody Up There Likes You" campaign began, JetBlue replaced Arnold with independent New York creative shop the Ad Store. A new campaign by the Ad Store that concentrated on the New York market began running on television after the September 11, 2001, terrorist attacks in which commercial airliners were crashed into the World Trade Center towers in Manhattan. The Ad Store's work included spots that emphasized travel, customer service, and the airline's humanity. One spot portrayed what it would be like if a subway train were a JetBlue plane. In a crowded subway car, crew members put pillows under passengers' heads and blankets over their bodies, poured coffee in a cup that a beggar was holding out to collect change, and more—all executed to the classic pop song by Jackie DeShannon, "Put a Little Love in Your Heart."

BBDO also created a television campaign for JetBlue following the September 11 terrorists attacks. Titled

"New York Miracle," the campaign positioned the airline as the first passenger carrier to use humor in its advertising to encourage people to return to air travel after the attacks. The commercials poked fun at New York institutions, celebrities, and cultural stereotypes. In one spot the camera panned across a lavish, upper-class New York holiday party, settling on a woman pouring her friend a glass of wine. A voice-over with a British accent stated, "New Yorkers are known for their exceptional taste. So what is New York's favorite wine?" The joke of the spot was a pun: the first socialite responded in a nasal whine, "I want to go to Florida!" and her friend added, "Me too!" A second television spot showed a New York man sitting on an armless leather chair in a room sans decor other than a blinking Christmas tree and a bouncing robotic puppy. The voice-over said, "We've got a warm spot for you." The man responded with a smile.

When JetBlue expanded its California services in September 2001, the airline turned to Ground Zero New York to create a marketing campaign. The agency described its effort in *Adweek* as a "guerilla-marketing campaign." It promoted JetBlue's service between New York's JFK Airport and Long Beach Airport in California. Included were JetBlue-branded Volkswagen Beetles, T-shirts, maps, and bumper stickers with the slogan "Goodbye LAX" (a reference to the Los Angeles area's major airport) that blanketed Southern California. Signs stating, "Goodbye airfare shock. Goodbye parking agony. Goodbye getting lost," appeared on airport shuttle buses at both the JFK and Long Beach airports.

OUTCOME

JetBlue's strategy of keeping its advertising small and targeting it to specific markets rather than embarking on a major branding effort seemed to pay off for the passenger carrier, but not necessarily for its agencies. Although Merkley Newman Harty's "Unbelievable" campaign initially was limited to full-page ads that ran in major newspapers in Florida and New York, it succeeded in attracting customers and creating buzz about the carrier. According to a report in *World Airline News,* the company stated that the launch of the campaign and the airline's new website resulted in more than half of consumer inquiries becoming flight bookings. JetBlue's director of communications, Gareth Edmondson-Jones, further noted, "As it is, each inquiry is being converted into two bookings." Within six months of its first flight, JetBlue had boarded half a million passengers and had its first month of profitability.

Despite the campaign's success, without review JetBlue replaced Merkley Newman Harty with Arnold Communications barely six months after the "Unbelievable" campaign began. Arnold's work for the airline also succeeded in conveying the message that, while JetBlue was low cost, it was also high class. Again, within one year JetBlue ended its contract with the agency. Stepping in were the Ad Store, BBDO, and Ground Zero New York. The efforts of all three agencies succeeded in increasing awareness of the airline, but BBDO's television spots raised complaints from some industry insiders. *Adweek* critic Barbara Lippert commented that the stereotyping used in the spot featuring the socialites, who she described as "Jewish American Princesses," was offensive. She added that, while the spot depicting the well-to-do man in his loft was "simple and kind of cute," it also made no sense.

Noting that JetBlue was thriving and growing on the buzz created by customers' word-of-mouth praise as much as from JetBlue's mixed advertising efforts, *Advertising Age* named the airline its 2001 Marketer of the Year.

FURTHER READING

Gianatasio, David. "Arnold Retools JetBlue Message." *Adweek,* June 11, 2001.

———. "Arnold Soars with JetBlue Air." *Adweek,* June 4, 2000.

Goetze, David. "JetBlue Asks Sponsors to Pick Up TV Tab." *Advertising Age,* July 21, 2000.

Higginbotham, Keith. "JetBlue Kicks Up Promotion Level for Two New Flights from Long Beach, Calif." *Long Beach (CA) Press-Telegram,* August 16, 2001.

"JetBlue Airways Awards Integrated Marketing Campaign to Arnold Communications." *Business Wire,* May 31, 2000.

"JetBlue Airways Open for Business." *Business Wire,* January 11, 2000.

"JetBlue Opens Reservation Center, Launches Ad Campaign." *World Airline News,* January 14, 2000.

"JetBlue Seeks 'Smaller' Partners." *Adweek,* August 14, 2001.

Knapp, Kevin. "Airlines Vie for Online Runway; Southwest Rolls New Campaign; United Woos Specific Segments." *Advertising Age,* March 20, 2000.

Lippert, Barbara. "Barbara Lippert's Critique." *Adweek,* December 3, 2001.

Mack, Ann M. "Ground Zero's Hour." *Adweek,* September 3, 2001.

Reed, Dan. "American Airlines to Give Coach-Class Customers More Legroom." *Knight Ridder/Tribune Business News,* February 6, 2000.

"Southwest Airlines Unveils Destinations and Fares from Palm Beach International Airport." *PR Newswire,* October 19, 2000.

"TLP, Inc. Partners with American Airlines to Promote 'More Room throughout Coach' Campaign." *Business Wire,* August 16, 2000.

Tsui, Bonnie. "JetBlue Soars in First Months." *Advertising Age,* September 11, 2000.

Rayna Bailey

John Hancock Financial Services Inc.

John Hancock Place
Boston, Massachusetts 02117
USA
Telephone: (617) 572-6000
Fax: (617) 572-9799
Web site: www.johnhancock.com

INSURANCE FOR THE UNEXPECTED. INVESTMENTS FOR THE OPPORTUNITIES. CAMPAIGN (1996)

OVERVIEW

NOTE: Since the initial appearance of this essay in the 1998 edition of *Major Marketing Campaigns Annual,* John Hancock Mutual Life Insurance Company changed its name to John Hancock Financial Services Inc. The essay continues to refer to the company's former name, as that was the official name of the organization when the campaign was launched.

With assets of $62 billion, John Hancock Mutual Life Insurance Company ranks among the nation's 15 largest life insurance companies. But the 136-year-old company also sells a growing number of investment management products and services for which it generally has not been recognized. In 1996 John Hancock was better known as an insurance company at a time when consumers were showing less interest in insurance and more interest in investments.

With its "Insurance for the Unexpected. Investments for the Opportunities" campaign, launched in 1996, the company sought to raise consumer awareness of its investment management expertise and to reinforce its position as a leading life insurance provider. Hancock also wanted to emphasize the need for financial self-reliance and to show consumers that it recognized their changing needs and desires.

For this high budget television campaign, the long-standing Hancock agency Hill Holliday Connors Cosmopulos created five spots (in both 60- and 30-second versions). Contrasting tender family moments with tough financial decisions, the spots addressed financial planning for various life situations, such as saving for college tuition and retirement and adjusting financially to single parenthood. Actress Sigourney Weaver supplied the voice-over, while the music was provided by Mark Knopfler, songwriter for the rock group Dire Straits. Tony Kaye of Tony Kaye & Partners, West Hollywood and London, directed the spots.

Shot in black and white, the campaign featured the same personal style that had distinguished Hancock's critically acclaimed "Real Life, Real Answers" campaign in the late 1980s and early 1990s. The company launched the ads in April of 1996 with a media buy concentrated around the 1996 Summer Olympics (Hancock is a Worldwide Olympic Sponsor). The spots ("Triple Squeeze," "Shepherds," "Subway," "Alone," and "Freedom") took six months to create. Expense was not the first consideration; getting the appropriate feeling and message was.

"Triple Squeeze" opened with a few shots of well-dressed children and grandparents in a field, followed by a title card that read, "Your parents, your children, yourself." Video of a girl walking between an older man and woman gave way to another title card that completed the first. It read, "Who do you love the least?" The black and white video continued showing small children and elderly grandparents as Weaver's voice-over said, "You owe it to your parents . . . for they brought you into this world. You owe it to your children . . . for you did the same for them. But the day may arrive when both debts come to you. When you may have no choice but to borrow from your own retirement . . . to educate a child or care for a parent. And into whose eyes can you look and say you just can't help, for in both you will surely see your own?" All the spots ended with the tag line "Insurance for the Unexpected. Investments for the Opportunities," followed by the Hancock logo and website address.

The 60-second version of "Subway" started with shots of a flower and a man's profile superimposed on an electrical tower. The first title card read, "Will you want to work when you're 65?" Next the viewer saw a lone man standing in the middle of an empty downtown city street, then walking into a subway station as the voice-over began, "You will wake up one day and there will be no subways." A second title card, responding to the first, read, "Will you have to?" As the viewer watched a man alone at an airport, a plane taking off, and other stark business shots, the voice-over continued, "There will be no time sheets or corporate ladders to climb. You will find in that moment, life will change from a thing to be conquered to a time to be savored." Video for the second half of the ad, when retirement is discussed, showed a man in a business suit with bare feet and his pants rolled up as he wades in the water on a beach. The voice-over continued, "If retirement is a bridge to be crossed when we get there, then we must accept whatever lies in store for us. If it is one we must build, then let us begin."

Another spot opened with senior citizens wading in the ocean's surf as the voice-over explained that as an insurance company it is Hancock's business to predict how long people will live. The commercial continued by explaining that as a leading investment firm it is also Hancock's business to help people save enough money should they happen to live longer and prove the company's predictions wrong. Each spot used Knopfler's haunting music to heighten the emotional impact.

HISTORICAL CONTEXT

This campaign followed the long-running "Real Life, Real Solutions" campaign that debuted in 1985 and focused on John Hancock as an insurance provider. By 1996 management wanted to position the company as a provider not only of insurance but also of investment services.

Although Hancock's life insurance sales continued to grow throughout the 1990s, industry-wide sales were flat, having decreased by 3 percent in both 1994 and 1995, according to the market research trade group LIMRA International. Tillinghast-Towers Perrin reported that from 1970 to 1996 the life insurance industry's share of people's personal assets dropped from 20 percent to 14 percent. Many insurers dealt with this decline by offering fewer new insurance products and more wealth accumulation or investment-type products.

By 1997 annuities, mutual funds, and specialty products were providing more and more of the leading companies' revenue. According to LIMRA International, annuities and pensions increased to 66 percent of the industry's business, making accumulation products the dominant force in the life insurance industry.

Hancock's strategy was to offer a wide range of protection and investment products through many different distribution channels. Although the company was well recognized for life insurance products, Hill Holliday research revealed that the brand had lower recognition with its investment products (variable annuities and mutual funds). The company lacked credibility and awareness as an expert in the high interest investment arena.

TARGET MARKET

The traditional Hancock market was middle income households with annual salaries of $35,000 and up. "Real Life, Real Answers" had aimed at this broad audience. The new campaign moved upscale, aiming for 16 million "Investment Enthusiasts,"—adults, ages 35-64, with annual household incomes of $75,000 or more and with assets or interest in both insurance and investments. Hancock's research suggested that these consumers faced a triple financial concern: saving for their children's education, caring for aging parents, and saving for their own retirements.

But unlike many other insurers, Hancock also sought to serve the needs of more modest, nontraditional households. For example, in 1997 the company used ads similar to but less costly than those in the "Insurance for the Unexpected. Investments for the Opportunities" campaign to target a narrow market segment—single parents. Hancock hired a small strategic planning firm to sift through its customer database, interview a range of potential customers, and use that research to fine tune both its products and its advertising. To these consumers, Hancock advertised lower-cost term life insurance that they could purchase over the telephone or the Internet.

Q & A WITH THE ART DIRECTOR

Jamie Mambro, Art Director for Hill Holliday, on John Hancock's "Insurance for the Unexpected. Investments for the Opportunities" campaign:

Q: Is insurance a difficult product to create ads for?

A: No, because it's dealing with a lot of fears and anxieties that everyone shares. It's pretty close to home.

Q: Did you need to be aware of the competition so you could distinguish John Hancock in this campaign?

A: Not really. John Hancock has been distinguished in this category for quite a while. They, in a way, have defined the category, at least emotionally.

Q: How did you start the campaign?

A: It started about a year before we worked on the creative. Our research showed what people's issues were. Two writers and myself took that research and began to talk among ourselves about the issues each one of us faced in terms of older parents who might need care . . . children who need college . . . retirement. The ideas came out of our own life experiences.

Q: Is there a core idea behind the campaign?

A: It centers around the issue of self-reliance. You have to rely on yourself to provide for your financial needs.

Q: Why two writers?

A: I went to both of them—both are excellent writers (Mike Sheehan and Ernie Schenck)—and asked them to write because we had six spots to do. I wanted the scripts to stay fresh. Sometimes when you have one writer on six scripts some scripts tend to be stronger than others.

Q: What happened to the sixth spot?

A: It never ran. The client didn't like the visual imagery or the music we chose. The great thing about the client, David D'Alessandro, is he really believes in powerful work. He wants to do things that he believes are going to make a mark for his company. He's really, for a lot of us, the best creative director we've ever had. He has great taste. Even though he might want to kill something we listen to him because he's the one who's been responsible for creating the work.

Q: Was there any additional pressure following up such a successful campaign as "Real Life, Real Solutions"?

A: Yes, in the beginning there was, but we let it work for us. No one's going to deny that "Real Life, Real Answers" is one of the greatest campaigns this agency's ever produced. But following that up was a challenge and something we looked forward to. It was a good kind of pressure.

COMPETITION

The life insurance industry's largest company, Prudential, ran its "Be Your Own Rock" campaign during the same time period as the Hancock campaign. Some observers found the two similar. Both were shot in black and white, addressed major life questions, featured voice-overs, and urged people to actively confront their own financial realities. In one Prudential spot a man snowshoed through a mountain meadow as the voice-over said, "Somehow, at some deep level, we're responsible for what happens to us . . . I mean, you're the best investment you've got. You're the best investment you'll ever have." To streamline production, Prudential began producing commercials with its own internal advertising agency. Early in 1998 the company's crews produced 35 spots in a five month period.

Many other insurers—such as CIGNA, ReliaStar, and SunAmerica—began increasing their television advertising budgets in 1996 and 1997. The life insurance industry spent $255 million on network television spots in 1996—a 78 percent increase over 1995, according to Television Bureau of Advertising numbers. In 1998 Hancock planned to spend $15-20 million. While other insurance companies like Prudential, Metropolitan Life, and Northwestern were clearly Hancock's main competition, the company also considered the large mutual funds, brokerage houses, and banks to be competitors. They, too, were increasing ad spending. Janus, Fidelity Investments, American Century, and T. Rowe Price all began or greatly expanded their television advertising in 1997. Although John Hancock was outspent five to ten times by some insurance, investment, and brokerage competitors, the company believed its brand recognition was at parity with its higher spending competitors.

One advantage John Hancock had was a close, 14-year relationship with Hill Holliday. The agency constantly monitored the financial services industry and had built up a comprehensive and proprietary research database.

MARKETING STRATEGY

Traditionally, life insurance advertising has emphasized the insurer's financial strength. Much like banks, insurance companies have tried to convey the sense of security and safety they offer to customers.

As it had with the "Real Life, Real Solutions" campaign, Hancock broke from the traditional and emphasized the need for financial self-reliance. "Much insurance advertising is still stuck in the world of Ozzie and Harriet," Fred Bertino, creative director at Hill Holliday, told *Shoot* magazine. "This is a campaign that's not afraid to tell you what's going on." The ads presented Hancock's empathy for its customers facing tough financial problems and then offered solutions and motivation for people to take action. Hancock believed consumers felt increasing anxiety about their ability to meet all their own and their family's financial responsibilities and that they needed and wanted to become more astute, self-sufficient, and focused on their financial future.

As with the previous campaign, Hancock sought to turn the camera around with these spots. The company strove to portray the consumer's perspective and to do so in a way that no other financial services company had done. Each spot attempted to reinforce what consumers deeply felt about their financial future and empower them to act.

OUTCOME

Hill Holliday measured consumer viewpoints before the April 1996 launch and compared them with a sampling taken after the Olympics in August. Results showed increases in several investment attributes. There was a 38 percent increase in the number of consumers who saw Hancock as an investment industry leader; a 75 percent increase in people who thought Hancock was a smart, sophisticated company; and a 67 percent increase in consumers who thought the company offered flexible products that change with customers' needs.

Financially, Hancock did well in 1997. Net gain from operations hit a record $506 million. Assets under management increased 11 percent, to $116 billion. Life insurance sales increased while the industry as a whole continued to drop. Company sales of annuities and mutual funds, its two core investment products, rose 117 percent and 175 percent of goal, respectively.

Creatively the campaign was a huge success as well, garnering critical praise and numerous industry awards. The campaign earned the TV Grand Clio at the 38th annual Clio Awards on May 14th, 1997, as well as Silver and Bronze Lions at the 1997 Cannes International Film Festival. It also won a pair of Clios in the insurance ad and copywriting categories. The campaign captured Best of Show in the Northeast region's top creative award show, the Hatch Awards. The New England Broadcasting Association presented the campaign with its Gold Award and another Best of Show.

FURTHER READING

Dunlap, Bill. "When All the Stars Align: The Creative Minds Behind Award-Winning Spots Tell How They Came Together." *Shoot* June 20, 1997.

Goch, Lynna. "Don't Touch that Dial." *Best's Review,* Property-Casualty Insurance Edition, January 1998, p. 63.

McGavin, Patrick Z. "Vital and Innovative." *Shoot* March 21, 1997.

Reidy, Chris. "Pinpointing a Market." *Boston Globe* June 12, 1998, p. C4.

Savan, Leslie. "The Pause that Refrightens: Reality... What An Ad Concept." *Village Voice* June 11, 1996.

Chris John Amorosino

INSURANCE FOR THE UNEXPECTED. INVESTMENTS FOR THE OPPORTUNITIES. CAMPAIGN (2000)

OVERVIEW

In 1996 John Hancock Financial Services, Inc. (then called John Hancock Mutual Life Insurance Company), began updating its acclaimed "Real Life, Real Answers" campaign, which had been running since 1985 and which used real-life situations to point out the wide range of insurance and financial-services products the company offered. John Hancock adopted the tagline "Insurance for the Unexpected. Investments for the Opportunities" and extended the emphasis on the dramas ordinary people faced. In 2000 the company leveraged its sponsorship of the Olympic Games in Sydney and of Major League Baseball's World Series to launch a series of four television commercials running under the four-year-old tagline.

Created by long-time John Hancock agency Hill, Holliday, Connors, Cosmopolous of Boston, the 2000 TV campaign built on the realism of the company's previous advertising by featuring families in moments of crisis or joy and continued to position John Hancock as a company equipped to respond to the financial needs of all such human situations. The campaign's most noteworthy spot featured a lesbian couple arriving in the United States with their newly adopted Asian baby.

The lesbian-themed spot, one of the first mainstream advertisements ever to showcase a same-sex relationship, generated the bulk of the media attention given to the campaign. Applauded by gay and lesbian advocacy groups and criticized by some conservatives, the commercial was altered after its first airing to make the nature of the relationship more ambiguous. John Hancock's research indicated an increase in brand awareness as a result of the campaign, which was estimated to cost $12 million, and the "Insurance for the Unexpected. Investments for the Opportunities" tagline was retained in subsequent advertising.

HISTORICAL CONTEXT

In the 1980s, like many of its competitors, John Hancock expanded beyond its primary business of life insurance to enter a broad range of financial-services business sectors. Intent on bolstering its core insurance business while simultaneously informing consumers of its wider portfolio of products and services, and likewise hoping to counteract the negative image most Americans had of insurance companies and agents, the company launched the "Real Life, Real Answers" campaign in 1985. Using print ads and TV spots, the campaign focused on people rather than on the company itself, employing story lines that revolved around the everyday financial difficulties and decisions faced by real people. The ads thereby positioned John Hancock as a sympathetic supplier of financial services that answered a variety of ordinary but critical needs. The "Real Life, Real Answers" campaign immediately generated critical acclaim for its realism and emotional force, and it translated into increased brand awareness and sales. The campaign won the Grand Prix at the Cannes International Advertising Awards Festival in its first year, ran for 10 years, and in 1998 was named one of the top 20 campaigns of the preceding 20 years by *Adweek*.

In 1996 John Hancock and Hill, Holliday undertook the task of replacing the by-then legendary campaign. The new campaign had simultaneously had to distinguish itself from "Real Life, Real Answers" and to deliver comparable doses of humanity and emotional charge. Using the updated tagline "Insurance for the Unexpected. Investments for the Opportunities," the new campaign similarly focused on ordinary people faced with difficult financial decisions. Though the execution of the new campaign differed in substantial ways from that of "Real Life," relying more on voice-overs than the docudrama scenarios that had characterized the long-running campaign, "Insurance for the Unexpected" worked to maintain the same brand image and market positioning John Hancock had been cultivating for the previous decade.

As part of its long-term branding strategy, John Hancock was a sponsor of high-profile sporting events, and it was a perennial sponsor of the Olympic Games. Like the "Real Life" campaign, "Insurance for the Unexpected" relied especially heavily on placement during Olympic television coverage. In 2000 John Hancock renewed its contract with the Olympics and entered into a five-year sponsorship with Major League Baseball, which made it the exclusive financial-services partner of the league.

TARGET MARKET

The 2000 television campaign was designed to appeal to members of households earning more than $75,000 in annual income, but the spots were otherwise not meant to split consumers along traditional demographic lines. As Steve Burgay, who was then John Hancock's vice president of advertising and corporate communications, put it, "Our advertising has always tried to honestly and respectfully depict what's going on in the world. We don't target a segment. We speak to a need, an emotion, a financial uncertainty or opportunity." Above all, the campaign sought to communicate a human touch. *Adweek* columnist Barbara Lippert remarked on the same quality, which in her view distinguished the John Hancock ads from other, more specifically targeted campaigns of the time: "What's impressive about the campaign is that it mirrors the rhythms and dissonances of life. More than appealing to segments, it's human—and that's what connects."

By featuring ordinary people in situations with which a diverse range of middle-class Americans could identify, John Hancock sought to convince consumers that it understood their everyday issues and situations and had a suite of products to meet their needs. Like "Real Life" and previous incarnations of "Insurance for the Unexpected," the campaign put the focus on consumers. The individual scenes on which each commercial turned returned to the mode of the "Real Life" commercials, with a storytelling style reminiscent of short nonfiction films. There was no mention of the company or interruption in the drama, and at the close of each spot the John Hancock logo and tagline appeared silently on the screen. Such a gentle promotional style worked to send John Hancock's brand message of understanding and concern rather than to showcase particular products.

COMPETITION

John Hancock's top competitors, Prudential Financial, Inc., and MetLife, Inc., were similarly trying to maintain their core business of life insurance while building consumer recognition of their increasingly diverse range of financial-services products. Prudential and MetLife were

UNDER FIRE

John Hancock aroused predictable protests from conservative groups in the wake of its "Immigration" spot, which featured lesbian partners bringing an adopted Asian child back to the United States, but the company also found itself under fire from international adoption advocates. The commercial did not specify the adopted child's ethnicity, but some advocates believed that the child was Chinese. Since China prohibited the adoption of its country's children by gay parents, the Joint Council on International Children's Services worried that the ad might provoke China to ban all adoption by unmarried parents.

consistently among the most-recognized names among insurers, thanks to long-running ad campaigns that had become part of the fabric of American culture, but both were transitioning into new marketing phases during this time.

Prudential, thanks to its long-running "Get a Piece of the Rock" campaign, was a top-of-mind brand among consumers, but most Americans thought of the Rock, as the company was sometimes called, strictly as a provider of life insurance. In the middle and late 1990s Prudential struggled to capitalize on the equity of its Rock identity and spread awareness of its expanded financial-services capabilities. A well-regarded campaign created by the Minneapolis-based agency Fallon McElligott in 1996 aimed to update the company's image and support all of its business units by using the slogan "Be Your Own Rock." After Fallon and Prudential parted ways, the company moved its advertising in-house, before initiating separate account reviews for specific divisions like Prudential HealthCare and Prudential Investments. In the late 1990s and early 2000s a variety of specific campaigns ran on behalf of individual Prudential products and services, but the parent company did not embark on any noteworthy branding work.

MetLife likewise had enormous brand recognition thanks to its association with Charles Schulz's *Peanuts* characters and its long-time use of Snoopy as the company's "spokesbeagle." The slogan "Get Met, It Pays" was well known among consumers and intimately associated with the *Peanuts* characters, but as with Prudential and John Hancock, the company's established image was that of an insurer, despite its expansion in previous years. In 1999 MetLife shifted away from the Snoopy-based imagery and began featuring real people in its advertisements, though Snoopy continued to appear at the end of television commercials, dancing above the MetLife logo. The "Get Met, It Pays" tagline was replaced in a 2001 rebranding campaign with the slogan "Have you met life today?" The new campaign, intended to raise awareness of the company's financial-advising capabilities, was described by MetLife as a "celebration of life, beginnings and the financial freedom that leads to life significance."

MARKETING STRATEGY

After a preview during the women's qualifying events for gymnastics, the 2000 "Insurance for the Unexpected" campaign took advantage of John Hancock's renewal of its Olympic sponsorship agreement to make a network launch during the Sydney games, which were held in September 2000. The spots ran throughout the games before going on to appear again during that year's World Series, as part of the company's new five-year sponsorship agreement with Major League Baseball.

Each of the four commercials captured, as a John Hancock spokesman told *Annuity Market News,* "a moment of crisis, wonder or glory." The commercials made it clear, moreover, that such moments potentially created the need for financial products. By focusing on the stories being told rather than on the company, John Hancock intended to forge an emotional connection with consumers while informing them, through the range of situations featured in the ads, that it had products to meet the needs of a variety of situations ordinary people might encounter. John Hancock wanted to distinguish itself from companies claiming that their financial products would substantially alter customers' lives. Instead, the "Insurance for the Unexpected" campaign painted a picture of a company whose products were designed to support individuals' lives no matter what shape those lives took.

Three of the spots set out to accomplish this task by using relatively mainstream imagery and characters and by focusing on moments of difficulty. "Tour" took as its subject a middle-aged man who was preparing to put his father in a nursing home and who became highly emotional when an employee took him on a tour of the facilities. "California" focused on a divorced couple in the midst of a whispered argument about the ex-husband's role in their son's life. The father insisted that he was doing enough just before announcing that he and his new companion were thinking of moving to California. "Saturday Night," meanwhile, introduced viewers to a single mother who had to rush home after a date with her boyfriend to avoid making the babysitter stay late. As a solution to such inconveniences, the boyfriend proposed that they get married, but the woman declared that she and her daughter could take care of themselves.

One of the four spots, however, represented a bold departure from themes traditionally broached in mainstream advertising, and it accordingly attracted far more attention than the other three, easily breaking through the clutter created by the many corporate heavyweights who were also advertising during the Olympics. Titled "Immigration," the spot showed two women in an airport marveling over their new Asian baby, with whom they had obviously just arrived in the United States. On the way to customs one of the women remarked that the other would be a "great mom," and the other replied, "So will you." The clear implication that the women were lesbian domestic partners, and the treatment of this fact as completely normal, made the commercial unique in mainstream marketing history. As Lippert said, "I can't remember any other national spot in ad history so effortlessly featuring homosexuals, except for the Ikea ad years back showing two gay men proving their commitment by buying a dining-room table." Predictably, the ad met with a substantial number of complaints, and after its first showing it was edited to make the nature of the women's relationship more open to interpretation. Most prominently, the "great mom" exchange was excised from the revised version. Explaining the change, John Hancock issued a statement saying, "People focused a great deal of their attention on what was going on between the adults. It was important to us to focus them, instead, on the real message of the spot, which is however a child comes into a family, that child is entitled to financial protection, and John Hancock can help."

OUTCOME

Most of the media attention paid to the 2000 "Insurance for the Unexpected" campaign centered on the "Immigration" spot. Gay and lesbian advocacy groups were virtually unanimous in applauding the breakthrough treatment of homosexuality in the original version of the ad, but the revised version drew mixed reviews. Mike Wilke of the Gay Financial Network called the spot "one of the most honest, nonsensational looks at a same-sex couple in mainstream advertising ever to come along" but criticized John Hancock for "backpedaling away from it." Scott Seomin of the Gay and Lesbian Alliance against Defamation applauded John Hancock and defended the revised version, saying that "it's a great ad even without the dialogue."

John Hancock's research both before and after the Olympics indicated an increase in brand recognition as a result of the 2000 "Insurance for the Unexpected" campaign. The company extended both the concept and the tagline of the campaign, modifying it to suit the marketplace but continuing to stress the same message. In 2004 John Hancock continued to emphasize real people and the company's potential role in their lives but focused a new campaign on children, returning the spotlight to its core life insurance business with the tagline "It's Not Your Life You Insure."

FURTHER READING

"Be Your Own Rock." *Adweek,* July 21, 1997.

Dill, Mallorre. "Creative Briefs." *Adweek* (Midwest ed.), September 18, 2000.

Gianatasio, David. "Hancock Ads Take Some Chances." *Adweek* (New England ed.), August 14, 2000.

Goch, Lynna. "Don't Touch That Dial." *Best's Review,* January 1998.

———. "Hancock Returns to Olympics, Signs Major League Baseball." *Best's Review,* April 2000.

"Hancock's Ad Draws Fire." *BestWire,* September 19, 2000.

Lippert, Barbara. "A Time for Us." *Adweek,* September 11, 2000.

McNatt, Robert. "Did Hancock Go a Mom Too Far." *Business Week,* September 25, 2000.

"MetLife Reinvents Its Identity with Launch of Ad Campaign." *Best's Review,* June 2001.

Pizzani, Lori. "Hancock Skips Gloss in New Ads." *Annuity Market News,* November 2000.

Reidy, Chris. "Hancock Re-edits Ad for Olympics: Company Tones Down Commercial Featuring Gay Couple with Baby." *Boston Globe,* September 13, 2000.

Riedman, Patricia. "Reel Life, Reel Answers." *Advertising Age's Creativity,* September 1996.

Warner, Judy. "Mike Sheehan." *Adweek* (western ed.), February 10, 1997.

Mark Lane

Kellogg Company

1 Kellogg Square
Battle Creek, Michigan 49016-3599
USA
Telephone: (616) 961-2000
Fax: (616) 961-2871
Web site: www.kelloggcompany.com

GOTTA HAVE MY POPS CAMPAIGN

OVERVIEW

The Kellogg Company's humorous "Gotta Have My Pops" campaign, which had been airing on television since 1988, continued to increase brand awareness of Kellogg's Corn Pops ready-to-eat cereal throughout 1997. Like many cereal ads, the campaign was aimed primarily at children. The advertisements depicted friendly scheming among people who wanted to make sure they got their Corn Pops, particularly if the cereal was in short supply. In one spot a teenage boy searched for a box of Corn Pops while his grandmother sat nearby at the kitchen table with a bowl of cereal. Realizing that she was about to eat the last of the Corn Pops, the boy tried to think of a plan to take them away from her. She guarded the bowl and laughed to herself, knowing what he was thinking, but when he gave her a mournful, pleading look, she handed them over to him.

Although Kellogg led the cold-cereal industry in the United States and worldwide, it had been losing market share gradually since 1988. Consumers were switching to generic brands, in part because of the rising price of name-brand cereals. In fact, the four dominant cereal companies had raised their prices so often that the U.S. Congress had considered launching an investigation of the industry. After a competitor slashed its prices in 1996, Kellogg followed suit and suffered a loss of revenues as a result, but the company's profits began to rise again in 1997. Kellogg said the "Gotta Have My Pops" campaign had helped the brand gain market share and had increased sales of Corn Pops.

HISTORICAL CONTEXT

Kellogg had been in business since 1906. It made more ready-to-eat cereal than any other company in the world and sold its products in about 160 countries. Cereal constituted 80 percent of its sales, but Kellogg also made other grain-based foods, including Eggo frozen waffles, Pop-Tarts toaster pastries, Lender's bagels, Kellogg's Nutri-Grain cereal bars, and a cereal-based snack called Rice Krispies Treats. In 1997 the company made 12 of the top 15 brands of cold cereal. But its share of the $8 billion U.S. market had dropped to 33.2 percent from a peak of 40.5 percent in 1988, and its net income had fallen by about 20 percent since 1992, to $546 million. Although competition in the industry was intense, with more than 200 brands of cereal on the market, the top four manufacturers had raised their prices steadily for years. Kellogg had increased its prices as often as twice a year, until some of its brands cost about $5 a box. In response, consumers began buying less expensive generic cereals available at supermarkets and large stores such as Wal-Mart. In addition, growth had almost leveled off in the cereal market as consumers turned to muffins, bagels, and other breakfast foods they could eat on the way to work or school. Although Americans were buying 2.7 billion packages of cereal each year, Kellogg's sales had increased by only 3 percent annually from 1992 to 1996.

Like some of its competitors, the company ran expensive coupon promotions to encourage consumers to buy its brands, even as the price of the cereal continued to rise. But analysts said the strategy was not cost-efficient. One professor of agricultural economics at Purdue University said manufacturers who used coupon promotions spent an amount equivalent to 20 percent of their sales for coupon distribution, reimbursement to retailers and clearing-houses, and executive salaries. In November 1996 Kellogg Chief Executive Officer Arnold Langbo said that the company would do whatever it took to regain its market share. Since 1995 he had closed some of the company's manufacturing plants and laid off 1,000 workers to reduce costs. He had also bought back $2.4 billion worth of the company's stock to keep the price from falling. In response to price cuts by competitors, Kellogg had reduced the price of two-thirds of its products by an average of 19 percent in 1996. To increase sales further, the company launched two new line extensions, Honey Crunch Corn Flakes in 1996 and Cocoa Frosted Flakes in May 1997.

Kellogg's Corn Flakes and Kellogg's Frosted Flakes were the most popular brands of ready-to-eat cereal in the world in 1997. Frosted Flakes had been advertised for years with a cartoon character named Tony the Tiger, who enthusiastically proclaimed that Frosted Flakes were "grrrrrreat." Well-known characters associated with other Kellogg brands included Toucan Sam, Corny the rooster, Dig 'Em the frog, and a trio of elves called Snap, Crackle, and Pop. Kellogg's best selling cereal brands included Frosted Flakes, Corn Flakes, Rice Krispies, Raisin Bran, Special K, and Corn Pops.

TARGET MARKET

Young people had been the only target for Kellogg's Corn Pops advertising until 1993, and they were the primary target of the "Gotta Have My Pops" campaign in 1997. But like Kellogg's Frosted Flakes campaign, the Corn Pops campaign sought to appeal to adults as well as children. The "Gotta Have My Pops" campaign portrayed Corn Pops as a food that was so fun to eat and so flavorful that people would plot to take the cereal away from each other. Cold cereal was a favorite breakfast for children, since all but the youngest of them could prepare it without help from an adult. It provided a quick meal before the early morning rush to school, and some children and adults ate it as a snack at other times of the day. Not all cereals were popular with children, however. The "Gotta Have My Pops" campaign featured young people of various ages having a good time as they ate Corn Pops instead of reluctantly eating some other brand at the insistence of an adult.

INTERNET ADVERTISING

Kellogg's "Gotta Have My Pops" campaign was featured on Sony Corporation of America's "The Station," an interactive, entertainment website (http://www.station.sony.com). Kellogg was one of eight major advertisers that signed on when the network was launched in March 1997. The site featured shopping, games, music, chat rooms, children's programs, and online versions of the popular game show *Wheel of Fortune* and the television soap opera *Days of Our Lives.*

COMPETITION

More than 85 percent of the ready-to-eat cereal sold in the United States was made by four companies: Kellogg, General Mills, Inc., Post Cereals, and the Quaker Oats Company.

General Mills, in second place behind Kellogg, had sales of $5.6 billion in 1997. The company made the nation's most popular cold cereal, Cheerios, in addition to Wheaties, Chex, Total, Lucky Charms, Cocoa Puffs, and other brands. General Mills also made Betty Crocker and Bisquick desserts and baking mixes, Hamburger Helper dinner mixes, Gold Medal flour, Fruit Roll-Ups and Bugles snacks, Yoplait yogurt, and Pop Secret microwave popcorn. In 1997 the company continued its long history of promoting the health benefits of Wheaties, "The Breakfast of Champions," by featuring sports stars on the cereal boxes. General Mills had sponsored the first televised sports broadcast in 1938, and through the years its products had been promoted by such television and radio personalities as the Lone Ranger, George Burns and Gracie Allen, and cartoon characters Rocky and Bullwinkle. In 1997 another well-known cartoon character, the Trix Rabbit, continued its 20-year quest for a taste of Trix cereal, only to be foiled as usual. The commercials ended with one of the most famous lines in advertising: "Silly rabbit. Trix are for kids." General Mills had reduced prices on more than 90 percent of its brands four times since 1993, including a cut that averaged 11 percent in 1994, but the company adjusted for inflation by raising prices an average of 2.6 percent in July 1997.

In third place was Post (a division of Kraft Foods, which was owned by Philip Morris Companies, Inc.), the manufacturer of brands such as Shredded Wheat and Grape Nuts. Although the company had spent large amounts of money to promote its products, its market share had fallen from 16.8 percent in 1995 to 15.6 percent in 1996. The president of Kraft said that if Post had done nothing to halt the slide, its share would have dropped to 13 percent. In 1996 Post and its sister company Nabisco rocked the industry by cutting prices about 20 percent, an average of $1 a box. Post's market share promptly increased by 4 percent while Kellogg's share dropped. Post had conducted a survey and found that 59 percent of consumers were angry about the steadily rising price of cold cereal. Some of the major brands cost as much as $4 or $5 a box, while the price of similar generic brands was about $1 less. Much of the additional money was being used to finance a marketing war among the nation's top cereal companies. For a package of cereal priced at about $3.50, $1 was spent on advertising and promotions, 40 cents on ingredients, 31 cents on packaging, the manufacturer made a profit of 45 cents, the grocery store made 68 cents, and the remainder went for operating expenses. In 1995 Congress had considered an investigation to determine whether cereal makers were guilty of overpricing their products. Also in that year the U.S. Bureau of Labor Statistics had reported that between 1983 and 1995 retail cereal prices had climbed 93 percent, an increase that was much greater than the increase in the cost of manufacturing cereal. After Post reduced its prices, other major manufacturers were pressured to follow suit and consequently experienced lower profits. Post also cut promotional costs by issuing a single coupon that could be used to purchase any of its brands, instead of running one coupon for each brand.

The fourth-place cereal maker, Quaker Oats, responded to the pricing problem by offering nine of its brands in bags instead of boxes, which reduced the cost by 35 to 40 percent. At $2 a bag, the cereals experienced 73 percent growth during 1997. Quaker's sales of bagged cereal for the year were $160 million, but its profit margin on those cereals was 3 percent, compared to 20 percent for branded cereals in boxes. Although its profit from bagged cereals was only $5 million, Quaker gained 2 percent of cereal market share in 1997. The company also appealed to consumers by manufacturing cereals, such as Frosted Flakers, that were similar to competitors' brands but less expensive. Quaker's top selling brands included Quaker Oats, Cap'n Crunch, and Life Cereal. During 1997 the company revived an ad campaign that had aired more than 20 years earlier. The original ads had featured "Mikey," a picky eater who amazed his brothers by enthusiastically eating Life Cereal. The brothers had exclaimed, "He likes it! Hey, Mikey!" In the new promotion more than 35,000 children entered the "Be the Next 'Mikey' Contest," which ran from January through June 1997. The winner, four-year-old Marli Brianna Hughes, was judged the most photogenic embodiment of the Mikey personality: energetic, independent, and confident. Sales of Quaker's boxed cereals increased 11 percent in 1997, but the company's total sales decreased by 4 percent to $5.02 billion, primarily because Quaker sold its Snapple beverage business in May.

MARKETING STRATEGY

Because most cereals were made from similar basic ingredients—mostly grains and sugars—manufacturers relied to a large extent on advertising, colorful artwork on the boxes, games on the back, sometimes a prize inside, and endorsements from celebrities to persuade consumers to choose their brands. Some companies called attention to the health benefits of eating certain types of cereal. Commercials aimed at children tended to emphasize the taste of the product and to portray cereal as food that was fun to eat. The "Gotta Have My Pops" campaign had been developed in 1988 by the Leo Burnett ad agency as a new creative idea to generate interest and excitement for the Corn Pops brand. It had been airing for nearly 10 years, and new spots had been added as the campaign progressed. Of the four commercials that ran in 1997—"Roofdeck," "Tickets," "Guests," and "Grandma" —two were new, and two had run in 1996. The ads aired on television in the United States and Canada but did not appear in print media.

In the spot called "Guests," a teenage boy was babysitting his younger sister and her friends, who were in the living room eating the last box of Corn Pops. The boy schemed to get some of the Corn Pops and finally went outside and rang the doorbell. Then he opened the door and shouted, "Look! It's Barney!" Thinking that they were about to meet one of their favorite animated characters—a purple dinosaur named Barney—the girls screamed in delight and rushed outside, and the boy hurried to snatch up the box of Corn Pops.

OUTCOME

Kellogg felt that the "Gotta Have My Pops" campaign had succeeded in helping to build the Corn Pops brand, and the campaign was continued into 1998. The company reported that sales of Kellogg's Corn Pops had increased since the campaign began, and the brand had gained market share. Overall, however, Kellogg brands of cold cereal continued to lose market share in the United States, dropping from 33.8 percent in 1996 to 33.2 percent in 1997, according to *Fortune* magazine. Net sales for all Kellogg products were $6.83 billion in 1997, an increase of 2 percent since 1996. In 1997 Kellogg sold 3.9 percent more cereal in the United

States than it had in 1996, when it had weathered the price cuts by Post. But Kellogg was still the number one cereal maker in the nation and in the world. At the end of 1997 the company was promoting its cereals as healthy food with a new television and print campaign called "Cereal. Eat It for Life."

FURTHER READING

Baumohl, Bernard; Jane Van Tassel; William A. McWhirter; and Adam Zagorin. "Cereal Showdown." *Time,* April 29, 1996.

Carvell, Tim. "Grape-Nuts Monday. Cereal Wars: A Tale of Bran, Oats, and Air." *Fortune,* May 13, 1996.

Enrico, Dottie. "Frost Flakes Ads Receive Soggy Reviews." *USA Today Ad Track,* September 9, 1996.

"FDA Finalizes First Food-Specific Health Claim for Oatmeal." *PR Newswire,* January 21, 1997.

Grant, Linda. "Where Did the Snap, Crackle & Pop Go?" *Fortune,* August 4, 1997, p. 223.

"Life Cereal Searches for the Next 'Mikey'." *PR Newswire,* January 7, 1997.

Norton, Rob, and Kerry Hubert. "Are There Too Many Breakfast Cereals?." *Fortune,* March 3, 1997.

"Quaker Oatmeal Celebrates 120 Years on America's Breakfast Table." *PR Newswire,* September 17, 1997.

Schay, Alex. "Two Scoops of Competition." *Motley Fool,* July 31, 1998.

"Schumer, Gejdenson Remarks Don't 'Bag' Everything; Quaker Bagged Cereals Offer Taste, Quality at 40 Percent Less than Boxed Every Day." *PR Newswire,* July 24, 1997.

Van Tassel, Jane. "Cereal Siege: Kellogg's Answers Post's Cuts, But It's Not a Price War." *Time,* June 24, 1996.

Susan Risland

SPECIAL K KICK-START DIET PLAN CAMPAIGN

OVERVIEW

The Kellogg Company had been a dominant force in the ready-to-eat cereal market for a little more than a century, but in 2001 the company's cereal division failed to register a significant profit increase for the company. In order to grow sales quickly for one of its flagship brands, Special K, Kellogg reintroduced a diet plan in 2002 that it had floated successfully a few years before. The Special K Kick-Start Diet instructed participants to replace breakfast and lunch with a bowl of Special K and skim milk, promising a loss of up to six pounds in two weeks. The "Kick-Start" campaign, sometimes called the "Un Testimonials" campaign, offered body-conscious consumers an alternative to complex and unsatisfying weight-loss options.

Ad agency Leo Burnett USA enlisted the help of its media agency, Starcom, to replant the Special K flag. With a budget of approximately $9 million for TV, print, outdoor, and online advertising, the Special K Kick-Start Diet first reached the public at holiday time in late 2002 and early 2003. This period was determined to be the perfect opportunity to reach adults resigned to address their weight concerns in the new year. A set of television commercials dubbed "Un Testimonials" showed everyday men and women discussing all the weight-loss tactics that had failed them in the past, such as "the downsize diet," in which one ate a personal pizza instead of a whole one, or the unappealing "corn juice" diet. Contrasted with these fad diets, the Special K plan was presented as a sensibly delicious weight-loss solution. Starcom was responsible for hundreds of wallboards (indoor billboards) that were placed in locations where women in particular would be thinking about their appearance or health. For instance, in a hair salon the ad would read, "The right hair cut can make you look slimmer. This actually helps make you slimmer."

The ads resonated with consumers. Special K was rewarded with a 22 percent increase in sales by the end of 2002, an important step in resurrecting brand interest. There was also significant improvement for Kellogg's cereal division, which recorded a 7 percent rise in retail sales in 2003. In 2004 Leo Burnett USA won a coveted Gold EFFIE (Packaged Food category), an industry award measuring effectiveness in advertising, for the campaign. The two-week diet was also successfully used to promote Kellogg's new cereal Smart Start.

HISTORICAL CONTEXT

Cereal products got their start in 1894, when W.K. Kellogg stumbled upon the recipe that inspired Corn Flakes in the kitchen of the Battle Creek Sanitarium in Battle Creek, Michigan, where he was employed by his brother, Dr. John Harvey Kellogg, as an accountant, business manager, and jack-of-all trades. An early proponent of "health food," Kellogg later marketed his product, and the Kellogg Company as well as the entire cereal industry was born. In the century that followed, the Kellogg Company, headquartered where it began, in Battle Creek, grew to become a world leader in the production of convenience foods, manufacturing in 17 countries and marketing its brands in 180 countries. The company reported sales nearing $10 billion at the end of 2004.

Throughout the twentieth century Kellogg often touted the nutritional value of its cereals. Special K was introduced in 1955 as a high-protein, quick breakfast alternative. Advertising for many brands was also closely tied to iconic characters, such as Tony the Tiger for Frosted Flakes; Snap! Crackle! and Pop! for Rice

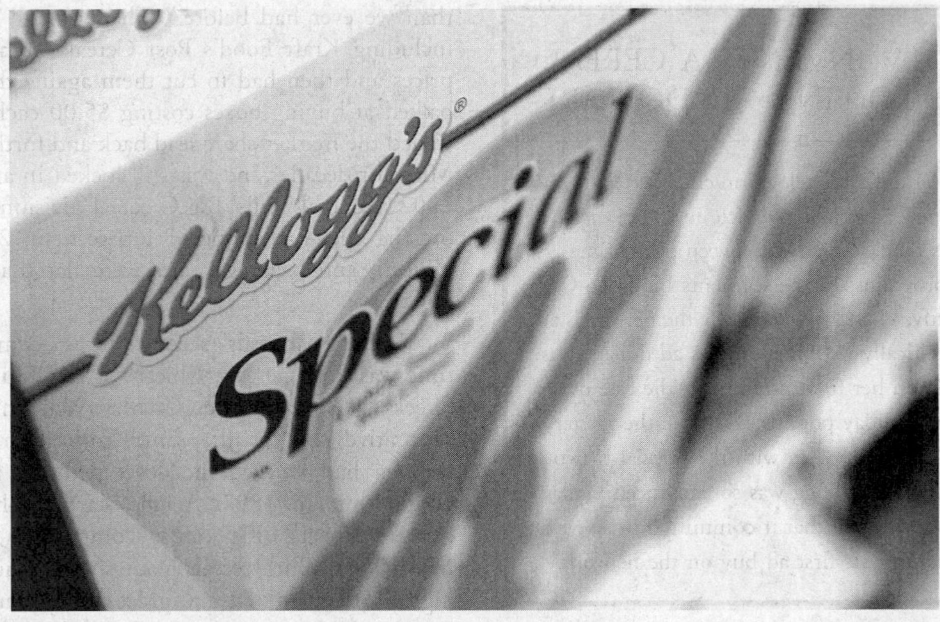

© RAMIN TALAIE/CORBIS.

Krispies; and the Corn Flake's rooster. Special K's brand images were more body-conscious in nature. One of the brand's most enduring TV images was a lingering shot of the body of a model-thin woman in a white one-piece bathing suit who bent to a position that then allowed her to morph into the Special K logo, a letter *K.* The vast Kellogg empire used more than one advertising agency to get the message across for all its various brands, chiefly employing Leo Burnett and J. Walter Thompson.

In the late 1990s Kellogg found new ways to emphasize the health aspects of its brands, including Special K. Jon Cashen, vice president and creative director of Leo Burnett, stated in a 1997 *New York Times* article that the agency's mission was to "weave a tapestry of the goodness of cereal and the goodness of life." It zeroed in on specific health concerns for women. One print ad showed a mother playing with her child; the caption read, "A bowl of cereal may help reduce the risks of osteoporosis," emphasizing that five Kellogg cereals, including Special K, provided recommended daily amounts of calcium. Later in 1999 Kellogg took an even bolder step by positioning its cereal as diet food for the first time. The Special K Two-Week Challenge Diet was developed by Kellogg and backed by Purdue University professor of foods and nutrition Richard Mattes. The plan, which was described on the backs of cereal boxes as well as in print ads and television spots, was simply to replace breakfast and lunch with a bowl of Special K and skim milk in order to lose up to 6 pounds in two weeks. One early TV commercial for the diet proved to be a misstep. It featured a doll named Diet Debbie who followed crash diets and exercised after each meal. This was followed by an image of Special K cereal and the tagline "Let's just eat sensibly all year." Despite the exhortation to eat sensibly, many consumers believed that the use of a Barbie-like doll could be misconstrued as endorsement of dieting to young girls. The company next successfully revisited a "Reshape Your Attitude" campaign directed at women and stressing positive body image, self-worth, and sensible eating. One extremely successful TV spot during this time showed men of all sizes in a bar worrying about their weight. The ending showed an average-looking guy in his late 40s saying, "I have my mother's thighs. I just have to accept that." The tagline that followed stated, "Men don't obsess over these things. Why do we?"

TARGET MARKET

The "Special K Kick-Start Diet" campaign began in late 2002. Kellogg needed to give adults a compelling reason to choose Special K and then keep them coming back for more. Mike Greene, vice president of customer marketing at Kellogg, described the company mindset in a November 2002 article in *Progressive Grocer.* "From 2001 to 2002 there has been an increase from 21 percent to 35 percent of adults that are dieting," said Greene. He explained that consumers looked for a diet that easily fit into their lifestyles. "We heard back from consumers that

COURT TV INVENTS A CEREAL SLEUTH TO FIND AD DOLLARS

In January 2004 the cable television channel Court TV introduced a new advertising vehicle in the form of short vignettes that were aired between prime-time investigative programs. In the segments Linda Lo-Cal, a female detective character created by the network's ad sales team specifically to win Kellogg's ad dollars, was featured taking on her first assignment: the case of unwanted extra holiday pounds. To solve the mystery, advertiser Kellogg stepped in with the Special K two-week diet challenge. Kellogg was so convinced Linda Lo-Cal could do the job that it committed to a seven-figure deal, marking its first ad buy on the network.

using cereal for weight loss had the highest level of satisfaction out of any other form of dieting. It's easy, simple to do, and it tastes good." Women, making up the majority of weight-conscious adults, were particularly on the minds of the marketers at Kellogg.

Starcom's part of the ad push consisted of positioning wallboards and brochures; the agency was even more specific about its target market, describing it as consisting of women who were "concerned with looking and feeling good." Starcom even took into consideration the intended female consumer's state of mind at certain locations, such as the doctor's office or dressing rooms. "We know a lot about our target and its habits around resolution time," said Amy Hume, associate media director of Starcom in a June 2003 issue of *Mediaweek*. She continued, "People get energized around the holidays—they get a new hairstyle to start the year fresh, they schedule a physical, new health club memberships peak. And it's a huge time for wedding dresses—you order in January for a June wedding." The media team honed in on the places where women tended to think about their weight, thus ensuring that their target consumer viewed the Special K ads when they were probably most receptive to the weight-loss message.

COMPETITION

In the 1990s consumers increasingly left cereal behind for other breakfast alternatives, such as bagels and breakfast bars. In 1997 Kellogg's Jon Wilson, executive vice president for consumer and customer engagement, acknowledged this to the *New York Times,* saying, "We are cognizant that we have more competition for breakfast than we ever had before." That year all cereal makers, including Kraft Food's Post Cereals brands, had raised prices and then had to cut them again when consumers balked at buying boxes costing $5.00 each. Kellogg had traded the market-share lead back and forth with General Mills for decades and was still locked in a tight battle in 2002. General Mills' Big G cereal division was floundering (its sales had dipped 3.1 percent in 2001, to $2.17 billion), and Kellogg's sales were flat that year at $2.2 billion.

Kellogg's cereals' second-biggest competitor at the time was Post Cereals, which was also founded in Battle Creek, Michigan. After Charles William Post spent a restorative stay at the same sanitarium where W.K. Kellogg had worked, he developed the flagship cereal Grape-Nuts in 1897. At the start of the twenty-first century Special K's direct competition was General Mills' Total. Both cereals made similar claims of offering high protein, low fat and great taste. General Mills was not timid when it came to ad spending. In January and February of 2002 it spent $39 million, compared to Kellogg's $32 million in ad spending for that same period, according to TNS/CMR, a provider of advertising and marketing information.

MARKETING STRATEGY

To reinvigorate interest in and consumer devotion to Special K, the Kellogg Company enlisted the help of mega-agency Leo Burnett USA as well as its media buying partner, Starcom. It was decided that the end of 2002 and the beginning of 2003, a span of months referred to by Amy Hume of Starcom as "resolution time," would be ideal to launch a new incarnation of their two-week diet challenge, the Special K Kick-Start Diet. It was aimed at adults susceptible to fad dieting who felt that most weight-loss options were difficult stick with. A set of television spots called "Un Testimonials" aired showing several examples of the perennial "man or woman on the street" recalling various outrageous diets that they had tried—and failed—to follow. The doomed diets included the "one-meal-a-day," "olive oil," and "all-garlic" diets. Later that year another round of similar spots highlighted the presummer months, when the target audience increased once again as people took stock of their physiques in anticipation of bathing suit season.

Andy Jung, senior director of advertising and media services for Kellogg, stated to *Mediaweek* that the company spent $8 million to $12 million per year in support of the Special K diet challenge. A standout component of the Kick-Start Diet campaign was designed by media agency, Starcom, and executed for under $1 million. Hundreds of wallboards with brochures, which described the diet and included a progress-tracking grid, were placed in more than a dozen markets. Locations were chosen carefully. In addition to health clubs, the boards went up in dressing rooms, bridal shops, and beauty salons. Ad copy was tailored to the location. In doctor's offices the ads read, "The doctor will see (less of) you now!" and in a bridal salon they stated, "Your bridesmaids' dresses don't have to look bad for you to look good." Jung told *Mediaweek* that the strategy broke new ground, stating, "It took brand advertising more into immediacy marketing."

The most creative tactic may have been the diet itself. The Kick-Start Diet ensured that each individual following the plan would need to purchase three boxes of cereal over a two-week period. If the consumer did experience weight loss, presumably he or she would go on after the two weeks to include Special K in his or her eating routine, either as a continuation of the diet or because he or she had had a positive experience with the cereal. Kellogg also introduced a website to support its newly created community; at the site Kick-Start dieters could network, keep a progress journal, or find nutrition and exercise information.

OUTCOME

Consumer reaction to the Special K Kick-Start Diet plan translated into positive numbers for the company, which only the year before had seen no sales growth and previous to that had been trailing General Mills. In the markets where Kellogg had concentrated the campaign, Special K in 2002 gained 22 percent in dollar volume over the year before. Smart Start, a newly introduced Kellogg brand, which was also promoting its own two-week challenge, experienced a significant increase as well. By 2003 retail cereal sales as a whole had increased by 7 percent for Kellogg, contributing to the nearly $9 billion the company ultimately took in that year. The "Un Testimonials" spots and Kick-Start campaign were also recognized with a Gold EFFIE Award in 2004 for Leo Burnett and Starcom. These prestigious industry awards were given annually by the New York American Media Association to honor effective ad campaigns. Kellogg's success with weight-conscious Americans did not go unnoticed by the competition. In late 2005 Post Cereals began a weight-loss campaign of its own that was remarkably similar to the Special K plan: replace two meals a day with Post "Healthy Classics" cereals and lose 10 pounds.

FURTHER READING

"Breakfast Smarts." *Advertising Age's Creativity,* April 1, 2003, p. 25.

Carmichael, Mary. "Third Helping for Kick-Start." *Grocer,* May 31, 2003 p. 46.

Emerson, Bo. "Crunch Time: For Many, Cereal Is the 24/7 Food of Choice." *Atlanta Journal-Constitution,* March 7, 2002, p. 1C.

Hellmich, Nanci. "Riding the Subway to Fitness." *USA Today,* February 5, 2002, p. 1D.

Kane, Courtney. "Kellogg Promotes Its Family of Cereals, Even the Sugary Ones, as Components of a Healthy Diet." *New York Times,* September 3, 1997, p. D7.

Lafayette, Jon. "Court TV to Feature Ad Vignettes." *Television Week,* November 17, 2003, p. 3.

"PMA Reggie Awards: Bronze Winners." *Brandweek,* March 22, 2004, p. R13.

Schmuckler, Eric. "Starcom." *Mediaweek,* June 23, 2003, p. SR10

Sege, Irene. "Kellogg's Eats Its Ad." *Boston Globe,* January 20, 1999, p. C1.

Thompson, Stephanie. "Kellogg's Kick-Start." *Advertising Age,* January 2, 2002, p. 2.

———. "Kellogg's Retakes Lead." *Advertising Age,* May 13, 2002, p. 2.

Turcsik, Richard. "The Battle Plan from Battle Creek." *Progressive Grocer,* November 15, 2002, p. 48.

Simone Samano

KFC Corp.

1441 Gardiner Lane
Louisville, Kentucky 40213
USA
Telephone: (502) 874-1000
Fax: (502) 874-8291
Web site: www.kfc.com

CHICKEN CAPITAL USA CAMPAIGN

OVERVIEW

Despite 50 years of selling "finger lickin' good" fried chicken, Kentucky Fried Chicken in the early 1990s Corp. decided to change with the times. Besides changing its menu offerings to include healthier choices, such as roasted chicken and salads, the company further distanced the brand from its greasy past by dropping its full name and adopting the moniker "KFC." An editorial in *Advertising Age* stated, "It made sense then to diversify the menu . . . But the chain's jettisoning of a venerable name—and distancing from the word fried—was ill-conceived and damaging. It made a clear brand fuzzy." Even worse for the company, the strategy failed. KFC's business went into a downward spiral. After trying several tactics to win back customers—including a series of advertising efforts promoting its fried chicken as health food, which landed the chain in trouble with the Federal Trade Commission—in 2003 KFC returned to its Southern-fried roots and launched a new marketing campaign called "Chicken Capital USA."

The campaign, created by KFC's agency Foote Cone & Belding, kicked off with a television spot that promoted a "Fried with Pride" tagline and featured country-music star Trace Adkins singing while average people declared their love for chicken. The company also dropped its initials and returned to using its full name. Additional marketing had the chain joining forces with NASCAR heavyweight Dale Earnhardt, Jr., to sponsor the Chance 2 Motorsports racing team.

Writing for the *Nation's Restaurant News,* Gregg Cebrzynski said of the campaign, "[It] adheres to the fundamental approach of staying true to the brand and the product, giving consumers a reason to try the product and entertaining viewers along the way . . . This campaign is just what KFC needed: presenting fried chicken as fun to eat—the fat calories be damned." In addition, the Ad Age/IAG Quarterly Ad Performance Report (based on research conducted by the firm Intermedia Advertising Group) listed one of the "Chicken Capital USA" campaign's spots as "the most-recalled new TV ad of the second quarter of 2004."

HISTORICAL CONTEXT

In 1992 Kentucky Fried Chicken abandoned its full name if favor of its initials, shifted its product focus from what it did best—fried chicken—to roasted chicken, and dropped the well-known tagline that helped build the brand, "Finger Lickin' Good," for less memorable slogans such as "America Loves What the Colonel Cooks" and "Kitchen Fresh Chicken." The changes brought trouble to the 50-year-old company that had come to represent old-fashioned comfort food to many consumers.

An editorial in *Advertising Age* stated that, while it made sense to add healthier options to its menu offerings, "particularly for a chain that sells lots of family meals and needs to offer something for family members who don't want traditional fried chicken," it did not make sense for the company to drop its name. "It implied there was something unmentionable about KFC's former middle name." The editorial said that in making the changes "KFC violated basic rules that ailing marketers often forget when a business and market is in flux. Marketers need to be what they are, be authentic, be real. If you sell a product, make it the best you can, be proud of it, and don't waffle."

It took 14 years, but Kentucky Fried Chicken finally recognized that its success was in its roots. A company spokeswoman told *Advertising Age,* "People have asked why we changed the name back in the '90s and that was because we offered more non-fried products. Consumers tell us they love Kentucky Fried Chicken and many of our customers never stopped calling us Kentucky Fried Chicken." The chain reverted back to its full name and offered its fried food with pride but kept its healthier products on the menu as well. It launched the "Chicken Capital USA" campaign to let people know that it was moving back to its Southern roots.

BLENDING CONTEMPORARY COOL WITH OLD-FASHIONED HERITAGE

In 2005 Kentucky Fried Chicken opened a store in Louisville, Kentucky, featuring a new logo and an updated, more youthful, and slimmer image of the original Colonel Sanders caricature that had been used to promote the product since its beginnings. The restaurant's interior featured low tables, ottomans, and a digital jukebox. Added to the contemporary decor was a new menu that harkened back to the chain's Southern roots and featured its core menu item—fried chicken—along with other Southern-style comfort foods, such as popcorn shrimp, collard greens, and sweet-potato pie.

In an interview with the *Nation's Restaurant News,* Tre Musco, chief creative officer of KFC's brand-imaging agency, said that the chain's "current image is a little dated and doesn't have a feel and contemporary image that relates to younger consumers who are looking for a healthier lifestyle. So what we want to do is bring a lot of respect to the heritage of the brand in a more contemporary way. The 'old-school cool' approach takes KFC's brand heritage and reinterprets it in a fresh, hip way."

The *Nation's Restaurant News* reported that the new Louisville restaurant followed the remodeling of a store in Washington, D.C. Company spokeswoman Bonnie Warschauer told the publication that sales rose 20 percent at the Washington restaurant following its remodeling and reopening. She explained that KFC planned to update 50 test stores in the chain's other locations.

TARGET MARKET

Kentucky Fried Chicken's main target had always been busy families hungry for affordable, quick, and complete meals. Fried chicken was the chain's mainstay and the reason its customers flocked to the restaurant. KFC spent years promoting its various fried foods and "finger lickin' good" crispy chicken. But customers' tastes had changed, and to appeal to those who had become worried about the health detriments associated with eating fried food, KFC introduced rotisserie chicken. The effort was a dismal failure when the roasters did not work properly, and diet- and health-conscious consumers continued to avoid the restaurant. Then in 2004 the chain's "Chicken Capital USA" campaign was introduced along with new menu items such as baked chicken. The old favorite, fried chicken, was still on the menu. The campaign was meant to broaden KFC's reach to include 20-something women and men, middle-class adult Americans, and even diet-conscious consumers. Company president and chief concept officer Gregg Dedrick told Cebrzynski of the *Nation's Restaurant News* that the new product offerings were a way to "offer lunch and dinner options for everyone in the family."

COMPETITION

While Kentucky Fried Chicken struggled to return to its fried roots and recapture customers, the number two fried chicken chain, Chick-fil-A, Inc., with more than 1,100 outlets nationwide and $1.5 billion in sales in 2003, embraced its heritage and attracted customers to its stores with a marketing strategy that included carnival-like parties and the offer of free food at new stores. To promote the opening of a new Chick-fil-A restaurant in Texas in 2004, the company celebrated with music and prizes, and the first 100 adults in the door received coupons good for a year's worth of free combo meals. A report in the *Dallas Morning News* stated that fans of the chain's fried chicken had gathered outside the store up to 24 hours in advance of its opening, "with the devotion of followers seeking front-row concert tickets." According to the report, "It's at least the 45th such event nationwide since the program was launched." Jerry Collins, a Dallas-based marketing and advertising consultant, estimated that the cost of the Texas event, including the 100 free meals, was about $50,000. He told the *Dallas Morning News* that, while the expense was high for a single restaurant, "For brand image and brand identity, that's cheap."

Chick-fil-A also promoted its brand through a campaign themed "Eat Mor Chikin" that featured cows encouraging consumers to avoid eating beef. The long-running campaign—the title of which was misspelled because cows had purportedly written it—starred the bovines on merchandise such as calendars, stuffed toys, and clothing as well as in radio and television spots and on billboards. Following the introduction of the campaign Chick-fil-A's brand awareness increased 44 percent in the chain's top 27 markets, and system-wide sales tripled. Like KFC, the chain also used a race-car driver in its marketing, partnering with stock-car legend Kyle Petty to sponsor the "Kyle Petty Charity Ride across America."

Number three in the fried-chicken market, Popeyes Chicken & Biscuits (held by AFC Enterprises, Inc.), followed the path of Kentucky Fried Chicken and moved away from its fried history and into the health-food arena by offering what the *Gazette* of Colorado Springs described as "chicken in slimmed-down versions." Popeyes also ignored the labels other chains used to avoid the fried stigma, such as "tender strips" or "crispy nuggets," opting instead for humor and honesty, calling its lighter offering "Naked Chicken." Along with the unbreaded chicken, Popeyes offered dieting customers seasoned green beans instead of fries.

Unlike its competitors, Popeyes did not use race-car drivers to promote its product offerings. Its marketing, themed "Stand Up for Flavor," used humor, featuring comedian Bruce Bruce in a series of spots designed to maintain the chain's sales momentum. And although Bruce was "a heavy guy," whose appearance may have reminded consumers that fried chicken and mashed potatoes were not diet food, the company's chief marketing officer, Rob Calderin, told the *Atlanta Journal-Constitution* that the comedian's main job "would be to appeal to the chain's core audience, especially African-Americans, who have been loyal customers. He was the right person at the right time for our brand. The notion of humor and the irreverence of Bruce Bruce is what our food is all about."

MARKETING STRATEGY

Speaking of Kentucky Fried Chicken's campaign to revert to its roots, revive its brand, and win back customers, David Aaker, a professor of marketing at the University of California, Berkeley, said in an interview with *Advertising Age,* "Every time a brand gets into trouble, one way to get out of it is to go back to your heritage and figure out what you used to be." Another marketing professor, John Swan of St. John's University in New York, added, "KFC has an authenticity that's less about fried chicken than it is about family gatherings after church or for a hearty lunch.... They finally understood the essence of the brand." To help with KFC's rebranding, or the re-embracing of its heritage, Foote, Cone & Belding created the "Chicken Country USA" campaign.

"Chicken Country USA" featured a variety of spots with country-music star Trace Adkins singing catchy jingles while average Americans—from truckers and football players to kids and sexy young women—enjoyed a chicken meal. One spot had a child eating chicken while dressed in a T-shirt that proclaimed "I'm in the Colonel's Army." Another spot, aimed at women, featured a "diva" going through a KFC drive-through to pick up some roasted chicken. Building further on the success of the "Chicken Capital USA" campaign, the chain partnered with race-car driver Dale Earnhardt, Jr., to sponsor six races in the NASCAR Busch Series in 2004. As part of the promotion the company issued limited-edition KFC commemorative buckets signed by Earnhardt with his quote, "My Favorite Chicken," beneath his picture.

According to a report in the *Nation's Restaurant News,* the new campaign clearly presented both the brand and the product message. Additionally, it successfully used contemporary images to present an aging brand that was a distinct switch from the dull campaigns the chain had used in the past. David Novak, chairman and chief executive officer of KFC's parent company, Yum Brands, took a cautionary approach to KFC's "everything old is new again" strategy, however. He said to *Nation's Restaurant News,* "A brand's heritage can either take you forward or it can hold you back. What we don't want to do is live in the past at KFC."

OUTCOME

Kentucky Fried Chicken's marketing strategy paid off, as indicated by the fact that TV spots for "Chicken Capital USA" occupied 4 of the top 10 spots on *Advertising Age* magazine's list of most-recalled commercials. In addition, the magazine named one KFC commercial as the most-recalled new television spot of the second quarter in 2004. An editorial in *Advertising Age* stated, "Kentucky Fried Chicken takes a risk in putting attention back on 'fried' even as critics blame fatty fast food for Americans' obesity. That's a risk worth taking. Kentucky Fried Chicken is an iconic brand that can thrive if it makes a product as good as its name."

Improvements in the company's sales also were attributed to the campaign's success. Five months after "Chicken Capital USA" kicked off, Yum Brands, KFC's parent company, reported that the chain had "posted a 2 percent increase in U.S. same-store sales for the quarter, ending a prolonged slump," and linked this success with the "Chicken Capital USA" campaign.

FURTHER READING

Cebrzynski, Gregg. "KFC, Facing Slump, Serves Up 'Roasted' Items." *Nation's Restaurant News,* May 24, 2004.

———. "Latest TV Spots for KFC Send Strong Message about the Brand." *Nation's Restaurant News,* July 5, 2004.

"Editorial: No Shame in KFC's Real Name." *Advertising Age,* May 2, 2005.

Frumkin, Paul. "Beak to the Future: Chicken Chains Take Flight." *Nation's Restaurant News,* June 27, 2005.

Horovitz, Bruce. "KFC to Boast about Roasted Chicken." *USA Today,* April 27, 2004.

"KFC Most-Recalled Ad of Quarter." *Advertising Age,* August 2, 2004.

"Late News; Red Cell's Daley Said to Be in Talks about Role at FCB." *Advertising Age,* May 3, 2004.

Lewis, Herschell Gordon. "Fried Chicken from the Chicken Hearted." *Direct,* July 1, 2004.

MacArthur, Kate, "KFC Spells It Out: Chain Takes Pride in Being Fried." *Advertising Age,* April 25, 2005.

Powell, Jennifer Heldt. "Kentucky Fried Roots Return." *Boston Herald,* April 21, 2005.

Schreiner, Bruce. "Yum Brands Reports 13 Percent Earnings." *AP Online,* October 5, 2004. Available from <http://www.highbeam.com/library>

Spielberg, Susan. "KFC Eyes Return to 'Kentucky Fried' Roots." *Nation's Restaurant News,* May 2, 2005.

Rayna Bailey

Kimberly-Clark Corporation

351 Phelps Drive
Irving, Texas 75038
USA
Telephone: (972) 281-1200
Fax: (972) 281-1490
Web site: www.kimberly-clark.com

KLEENEX ANTI-VIRAL CAMPAIGN

OVERVIEW

The Kimberly-Clark Corporation, in business since the 1870s, had long been servicing the sick with its medical supply brands and consumer paper brands. By the first years of the twenty-first century health and infectious illness had become a hot global topic. In 2004 a flu vaccine shortage was predicted for the United States. It was at this time that one of the Irving, Texas, company's top brands, Kleenex, was serendipitously poised to introduce a new entrant into the facial-tissue market. Kleenex Anti-Viral tissues hit store shelves in August 2004 in anticipation of the upcoming cold and flu season. The supporting campaign, released in October, was focused on getting the word out to consumers that the product could help stop the spread of seasonal illnesses.

To introduce Kleenex Anti-Viral to American families, the $30 million campaign used television, cinema, print, radio, and online advertisements as well as education programs, coupon inserts, and public relations. Ad agency J. Walter Thompson New York, part of communications conglomerate WPP Group, was responsible for the campaign. The most widely visible element, a humorous TV and cinema commercial called "Guru," came nearly a year after the product's introduction. In it a robed, spiritual-looking man walked through a scenic landscape. Gentle music played as he was shown saving small creatures from certain death. Back at home he sneezed and grabbed the Kleenex Anti-Viral tissue in front of him, only to be mortified when he saw that the tissue box stated that the product "kills 99.9 percent of cold and flu viruses."

Demand for the product exceeded Kimberly-Clark's expectations. In its first months as a retail offering, Kleenex Anti-Viral captured 4 percent of the $1.5 billon tissue market. Research showed that a third of the consumers who bought the product were new to the facial-tissue category. Major media outlets covered the product as a news story prior to its introduction. By the end of 2005 the product's market share was up another point to 5 percent.

HISTORICAL CONTEXT

Kimberly-Clark Corporation was founded in 1872 as a paper mill in Neenah, Wisconsin, but it soon branched out into product innovation. The company boasted a stable of brands, which by the year 2000 included national household names such as Scott, Huggies, and Kleenex. In the early years one of the company's most important innovations was a creped cellulose wadding called Cellucotton. A substitute for cotton bandages, it was used to treat wounded soldiers in World War I and soon afterward led to the development of Kotex feminine pads and Kleenex facial tissue. Kleenex, originally

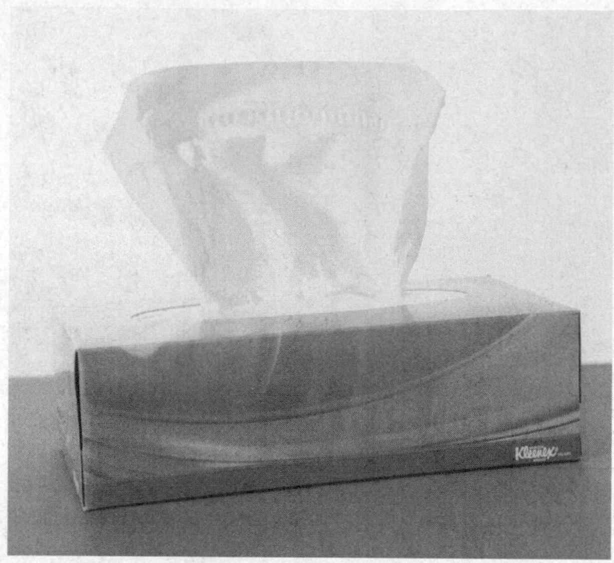

© SGO/IMAGE POINT FR/CORBIS.

introduced in 1924 as a disposable towel for removing cold cream, became a cornerstone of the Kimberly-Clark paper and personal-product empire. Consumers quickly found another use for Kleenex, and in 1930 marketing was changed to show the products as disposable handkerchiefs. Sales skyrocketed. In 1932 print ads showed a homemaker uncomfortably holding by her fingertips a used cloth handkerchief that she was about to launder. The copy read, "World's Worst Job Ended."

The Kleenex name became synonymous with facial tissue, and the company dominated the new market that it had created. Through the years advertising included cartoon ads, the first of which appeared in 1941, when a contest called "True Confessions" was introduced. It challenged the public to come up with a new, creative use for Kleenex tissue; the winners' entries would appear in the comics section of their local papers. In the 1950s the popular cartoon character Little Lulu appeared in the product's first television commercials, giving her "timely tips" for tissue use and singing the jingle "Soft, Strong, Pops Up, Too." The strength of the tissue was the selling point in the 1960s, when Harry James, a well-known bandleader, was shown blowing on his horn with an intact Kleenex tissue secured around the bell. In the 1980s the product was promoted with an award-winning campaign called "Kleenex Says Bless You." Kleenex ColdCare tissues, the company's first significant tissue innovation, was introduced in September 1996 with a campaign created by ad agency Foote Cone & Belding of Chicago. These ultrasoft tissues with aloe and a menthol scent combated competitor Puffs' introduction in the late 1980s of tissues containing aloe lotion.

The 1995 merger of Kimberly-Clark with Scott Paper, a top producer of paper towels and toilet paper, cemented the company's place as the world's leading maker of paper products and put it on the global Fortune 100 list. Unfortunately for agency Foote Cone & Belding, the marriage with Scott also precipitated a change in advertising strategy. The ad agency J. Walter Thompson, or JWT, had already done creative work for the Scott brand when it won the $100 million tissue account for Kleenex and sister brands Scottex and Andrex in North America and Europe in 1999. Kleenex moved on to a new slogan, "Thank Goodness for Kleenex," and was working on making an emotional connection to consumers with a promotion called "Kleenex Moments" to be tied into the upcoming 2004 Olympics. Kimberly-Clark's medical-supply business was also increasing during this time. At the start of the new millennium, consciousness about germs was on the rise, and there was a corresponding increase in the number of hand-sanitizing products and antibacterial soaps. In response to this growing health-focused trend, in 2004 Kimberly-Clark was set to introduce the next big Kleenex extension product.

TARGET MARKET

Kleenex began as a cold-cream-removal product that was originally aimed exclusively at women. Once the product changed its focus, families became its primary target. Kleenex Anti-Viral was no exception. Because Kimberly-Clark's research revealed that families with children were more likely than those without kids to develop colds throughout a season, the new product was designed with family needs in mind. In the press release announcing the launch of Kleenex Anti-Viral, Robert P. van der Merwe, group president of Kimberly-Clark's North Atlantic Family Care division, said, "Through research, we learned that it's increasingly important to consumers to protect their families against common cold and flu viruses." As the major purchasers of household and personal-care items, women, or more specifically mothers, were secondarily targeted by the Anti-Viral campaign. The company saw women as the primary caregivers, often the ones responsible for doctor visits and health maintenance. The Kleenex website thus provided "Mom's Stay-Well Tips" and "Mom's Remedies" as well as recipes, symptom lists, and scenes of caring family interaction.

COMPETITION

Global consumer-products giant Procter & Gamble bought Charmin Paper Company in 1958 and then renamed its tissues Puffs in 1960. Since then Puffs had been a determined second in the race for facial-tissue market share. Even though the word "Kleenex" had long been synonymous with tissue, the supersoft Puffs

UNMENTIONABLE PRODUCTS

Kimberly-Clark and Scott Paper, which eventually became one company in the 1990s, built their fortunes on products that everyone wanted and needed but that were not considered suitable for advertising. During World War I Kimberly-Clark discovered that army nurses were using the company's Cellucotton bandage products for feminine-hygiene purposes. As a result Kimberly-Clark developed Kotex feminine pads, but in the 1920s it faced opposition from many newspapers and magazines, which would not allow advertising for the product. Likewise, stores would not permit point-of-purchase advertising displays and even kept the product off shelves, stocking it behind the counter. Kimberly-Clark persisted and eventually broke those marketing barriers, creating another world-famous brand.

developed a strong and loyal following. By 1996 it had a nearly 33 percent share of the market, compared to Kleenex's formidable 48 percent. Still, Procter & Gamble beat Kleenex to punch in 1987 with its line extension Puffs Plus with Lotion. With this new line Procter & Gamble began to dip into traditional Kimberly-Clark territory: product innovation.

When Kleenex added another specialized tissue, Kleenex Anti-Viral, to its roster in 2004, Puffs did not have an answer in the form of a competing product. Its parent company, Procter & Gamble, did, however, start what it called an "education campaign," according to an article published in the December 6, 2004, issue of the *Toledo Blade.* The article stated that Procter & Gamble had hired a public relations firm to spread the word that Kleenex Anti-Viral would probably not prevent colds and flu.

MARKETING STRATEGY

By the closing decades of the twentieth century, line extensions of core brands had become an increasingly important tool for companies such as Kimberly-Clark, whose Kleenex-brand tissues had dominated the market for 80 years. Kimberly-Clark was encouraged in its development of Kleenex Anti-Viral partly because of the growing popularity of germ-fighting soaps and other personal products. In August 2004 the company launched its Anti-Viral tissues, the first product of its kind. That October a $30 million campaign began; timed to coincide with the start of cold and flu season, it consisted of print ads, cable and network television spots, cinema and radio advertising, special events, consumer sampling, coupons, and educational programs. The initial emphasis was on the product and the science behind it. Packaging was an important element. An image of an undulating yellow banner wrapped every new box of Kleenex Anti-Viral, announcing "Kills 99.9 percent of cold & flu viruses." The tissue itself was designed to look effective, with blue dots making a subtle pattern on each sheet. Graphics on the Kleenex website magnified the blue-dotted middle layer, explaining that it was a unique moisture-activated system designed to trap and kill viruses.

Promotion and education was important for the Kleenex brand. Prior to the release of the campaign in October, Kimberly-Clark was successful in publicizing the attributes of the new Kleenex product through means other than advertising. In July 2004 media outlets such as *USA Today* and CNN's *American Morning* ran stories about the upcoming product. The cable news show featured its medical correspondent, physician Sanjay Gupta, demonstrating the actual Kleenex Anti-Viral tissues and packaging. Gupta stated that the tissues' ability to kill viruses would probably help to slow the spread of illness to others.

Television spots did not follow until October 2005, when the next cold and flu season began. JWT New York created a clever TV spot that aired on U.S. television and in cinemas and in the United Kingdom as well. Creative director Ty Montague oversaw the agency's production of the spot, called "Guru." In it a robed monk walked through a serene landscape rescuing tiny creatures, including a goldfish and a spider, from dire circumstances. Mystical-sounding music played as he arrived at his spartan domicile. He looked as if he were about to sneeze and then reached for a tissue as a voice-over stated, "Kleenex Anti-Viral tissues trap and kill 99.9 percent of cold and flu viruses in the tissue..." The guru sneezed into it and expressed relief until he read the virus-killing claim on the box. The narrator continued, "That's right, kills." The guru looked stunned and then gazed up to the sky as the voice-over concluded, "Thank goodness for forgiveness. Thank goodness for Kleenex."

OUTCOME

When Kimberly-Clark bought Scott Paper for $9.4 billion in 1995, the company's market share in some products made great increases, but the merger put a strain on Kimberly-Clark as it tried to integrate the two operations. By 2004 it had gone through a reorganization and needed a winning new product. Hopes were high for Kleenex Anti-Viral, and early statistics indicated that the new product had contributed to improved overall sales for Kimberly-Clark. The company reported that its consumer-tissue revenues, which accounted for 36 percent of the company's total revenues, were a healthy $5.8 billion worldwide in 2005. In the August 6, 2005, issue of *Grocer,* Matt Muniz, Kleenex Anti-Viral brand manager, described a promising breakthrough: "In the U.S. we found that after six months 35 percent of Kleenex Anti-Viral tissues buyers were new to the facial tissue category." In its first months Kleenex Anti-Viral captured 4 percent of the $1.5 billon tissue market. As 2005 came to a close, the new product had increased its market share to 5 percent and had posted more than $50 million in sales, not counting those at the nation's largest retailer, Wal-Mart, or other discount outlets.

FURTHER READING

"Ad Notes. . . ." *Wall Street Journal,* February 24, 1999, p. 1.

Bach, Pete. "Tissue, Paper Towel Making a Growing Business in Valley." *Appleton (WI) Post-Crescent,* February 5, 2006.

"Branding the Sneeze." *Retail Merchandiser,* August 2005, p. 28.

Kirsche, Michelle L. "Consumables: Reporter's Notebook." *Drug Store News,* August 23, 2004, p. 47.

Lewis, Diane E. "Flu-Wary Massachusetts Firms Attack Germs." *Boston Globe,* November 8, 2004.

Lindeman, Teresa F. "Retailers Scramble to Fill Gap Left by Flu Shot Shortage." *Knight Ridder/Tribune Business News,* October 12, 2004, p. 1.

Mehegan, Sean. "Tissue of Buys." *Brandweek,* September 2, 1996, p. 1.

Neff, Jack. "Flu Fear Equals Marketer Bonanza." *Advertising Age,* October 25, 2004, p. 8.

Raju, Narisetti. "Plotting to Get Tissues into Living Rooms." *Wall Street Journal,* May 3, 1996, p. 6.

Rosenwald, Michael S. "Fear of Flu Sparks Home-Remedy Sales." *Washington Post,* December 22, 2004. p. E01.

Wasserman, Todd. "A Fertile Environment for New Germ Killer PS." *Brandweek,* January 30, 2006, p. 5.

———. "Forget Tissues, Kleenex Is Branding 'Moments': Olympic Tie-In Will Include Plugs from Athletes' Moms." *Brandweek,* December 19, 2005, p. 9.

Simone Samano

Kmart Corp.

3100 West Big Beaver Road
Troy, Michigan 48084
USA
Telephone: (248) 463-1000
Web site: www.kmartcorp.com

KMART JOE BOXER LAUNCH CAMPAIGN

OVERVIEW

Joe Boxer built its reputation in the underwear field by being offbeat. It was the first to offer glow-in-the-dark boxers and was known to stage outrageous stunts, such as sending 100 pairs of underwear to President Bill Clinton in 1993 to mark his first 100 days in office. The accompanying note read, "If you're going to change the country, you've got to change your underwear." But Joe Boxer was sold in department stores, where it had to fight for shelf space, and saw sales drop off as consumers began opting to shop at specialty stores. In 2001 the company was sold and the new owner soon struck an exclusive deal with Kmart. Although Kmart was the second largest retailer in the United States, it could not hope to compete on price with the top retailer, Wal-Mart, and had attempted to carve out a place in the market by creating celebrity brands, such as the Martha Stewart line of products. Joe Boxer was the first major department store brand to make the switch to Kmart, and its launch took on even greater importance for Kmart, which in the meantime had to file for Chapter 11 bankruptcy protection and contend with the uncertainty of the future of Martha Stewart, who was involved in an insider stock trading scandal that ultimately led to her imprisonment. Thus the Joe Boxer launch not only sought to introduce Joe Boxer's expanded line of apparel and other lifestyle products but also hoped to infuse some energy into Kmart, sorely in need of a spark.

The Joe Boxer kickoff was part of a larger back-to-school effort in the summer of 2002. Developed by ad agency TBWA\Chiat\Day, it consisted of the usual oddball promotional stunts, such as shooting people wearing Joe Boxer clothes out of a cannon, as well as a special pullout section in Kmart's weekly advertising circular, mailed to 10 million people. The core of the campaign, however, was the television spots, and one in particular, "Vaughn," grabbed the spotlight. In it a muscular young African-American man happily danced his Boxer Boogie, wearing nothing more than a pair of white boxers and a toothy smile. The pure joy of his routine won over viewers, and the dancer, Vaughn Lowery, not only received his 15 minutes of fame, making television appearances and becoming the object of press interviews, but also provided Joe Boxer and Kmart with some much appreciated attention and momentum.

The Joe Boxer launch only lasted through August 2002 and the end of the back-to-school sales push, but it resulted in an immediate surge for Joe Boxer products. The emergence of Lowery as the Boxer Guy also set the stage for a pair of equally popular holiday ads and an elaborate dance-number TV spot that was part of the 2003 back-to-school campaign, which also marked the one-year anniversary of the Joe Boxer launch. The brand, in spite of its solid start, began to lose its place with Kmart, which emerged from bankruptcy and was swallowed up by Sears. The company subsequently began deemphasizing Joe Boxer, seen as little more than a men's underwear and women's intimates brand.

HISTORICAL CONTEXT

In 2001 a struggling retailer, Kmart, and a struggling underwear maker, Joe Boxer, joined forces in an effort to reverse their fortunes. The latter, established in 1985 to make novelty ties, had made its mark with its irreverent, wacky approach to boxer shorts, including the Imperial Hoser, a red tartan boxer with a detachable raccoon tail; boxers with a $100 bill silk-screened on them; and the industry's first glow-in-the-dark underwear. The company branched into loungewear and sleepwear for men and women and enjoyed strong growth during the 1990s, supported by unusual, attention-grabbing marketing efforts, such as the first-ever in-flight underwear fashion show. The brand took steps toward becoming a lifestyle brand, introducing a licensed Timex watch, for example, but Joe Boxer focused on department stores—including Saks Inc., Marshall Field's, Dillard's, May Department Stores, and Federated Department Stores—where it never received the shelf space the company wanted. More importantly, target customers began turning to specialty stores, a move that had an adverse impact on Joe Boxer's sales. In 2001 Joe Boxer was acquired by apparel holding company Windsong Allegiance Group, LLC. A short time later the company signed a long-term, exclusive agreement with Kmart. It was a down-market move for a major department store brand, but it gave Joe Boxer an opportunity to launch new lines of home and apparel products, as well as a chance to reintroduce the brand in a major marketing campaign with the resources of America's second largest retailer behind it.

For years Kmart had done well creating a series of exclusive brands—including Disney, Sesame Street, Kathy Ireland, Jaclyn Smith, and Martha Stewart—to drive sales. With Stewart in legal trouble because of insider stock trading charges, Kmart was eager to lure its first major department store brand in Joe Boxer, which also appealed to a younger customer. The retailer planned to promote the Joe Boxer–exclusive with a back-to-school campaign, but before that could take place Kmart was forced to file for Chapter 11 bankruptcy protection. Nevertheless the company pressed ahead with its plans for Joe Boxer, the launch of which took on even greater importance as Kmart more than ever needed something to change the topic away from finances and Martha Stewart and bring some energy to the business.

TARGET MARKET

The target customer for Kmart was a married woman, 35 to 45 years old, with children. The retailer's top brand, Martha Stewart, was also skewed toward older women. What made the addition of Joe Boxer so appealing to Kmart was that it targeted a younger demographic, the 14- to 34-year-old age range, and appealed to both women and men. As an exclusive Kmart brand, the Joe Boxer product lines were greatly expanded beyond underwear and sleepwear, practically infiltrating every department in the store. The brand was applied to all manner of apparel, from infant clothing to jackets and jeans, as well as shoes, jewelry, clocks, and picture frames. Given that the Joe Boxer launch was tied in with a back-to-school push, the target audience of the campaign was expanded to include the wider family market.

FOOTLOOSE AND IVY LEAGUE

Vaughn Lowery, the Boxer Guy who gained sudden popularity dancing in his boxer shorts in a 15-second ad for the Joe Boxer launch with Kmart, was born in Detroit in modest circumstances. Although his family lived in a federally subsidized housing community, he grew up with a strong desire to go to college. He graduated from Cornell University with a degree in labor relations. He also wanted to pursue acting, and with that in mind he moved to Los Angeles two years before landing his first Joe Boxer commercial.

COMPETITION

As a department store underwear and sleepwear brand, Joe Boxer competed against the likes of Calvin Klein, Ralph Lauren, and Donna Karan—all of which possessed greater clout in terms of brand recognition and financial resources. The move to Kmart put Joe Boxer in competition with down-market underwear brands, like Fruit of the Loom and Jockey International, and with other mass merchants, like Wal-Mart and Target. But the expansion into other product categories turned Joe Boxer into a lifestyle brand. Because of its iconoclastic, somewhat irreverent approach, Joe Boxer had carved out a unique niche and lacked any direct competitor, other than companies with competing lifestyle visions, such as Calvin Klein, Ralph Lauren, and other designers.

MARKETING STRATEGY

In July 2002 the campaign to introduce the Joe Boxer brand to Kmart was kicked off in typical Joe Boxer fashion. Two men dressed in Joe Boxer clothes and underwear were shot from a cannon in the parking lot of a Detroit Kmart store. "We definitely needed to get out there with the message of what you'd expect from Joe Boxer is still there, and now it's at Kmart," Kmart marketing executive Steven Feuling told Sherri Day of the *New York Times.* A few days later a round of four television commercials, developed by TBWA\Chiat\Day, were unveiled. Kmart also used its weekly advertising circular, sent to more than 10 million households, to promote the brand. An eight-page pullout featured Joe Boxer merchandise. Also in keeping with the brand's fun promotional events, Joe Boxer held a fashion show later in July on the escalator of the Astor Place Kmart store located in New York's Greenwich Village. Joe Boxer's founder, Nick Graham, riding on the back of a convertible, headed a parade that included the New York Police Department pipe and drum band. Graham then hosted the fashion show that featured teens modeling back-to-school apparel and presided over a mock wedding of Joe Boxer and a woman representing Kmart. "Do you, Joe, take this woman as your wife, even though she has 1,800 stores and gets around a lot?" he asked.

The centerpiece of the campaign, however, was the four 15-second TV spots, which focused on Joe Boxer's core underwear and clothing items. With the younger demographic in mind, the spots relied on an upbeat, bossa nova music track and featured young models wearing Joe Boxer underwear and clothing. In the spot titled "Guy's Trend," for example, young men 14 to 24 years of age were targeted. In it one male model wore a hooded sweatshirt with Joe Boxer on the chest, and as he pulled it over his head he commented that he loved to wear his boxers on his head. Another model wearing a Joe Boxer jacket claimed to put on his boxers "one arm at a time." A companion spot called "Girl's Trend" featured young women wearing skirts and studded blue jeans. One of the models commented that "a girl can never have too many studs."

Another of the first wave of spots, titled "Vaughn," was created spontaneously and proved so popular that it changed the entire direction of the Joe Boxer launch at Kmart. In the commercial a smiling, muscular African-American model dressed only in white cotton boxers danced to the campaign's bossa nova music in what would become known as the Boxer Boogie, something of an homage to rope-skipping fighters. The text "Why is this guy so happy?" flashed across the screen. The spot quickly developed a fan following, as did the model, 28-year-old Vaughn Lowery.

Lowery, an aspiring actor who moved to Los Angeles and turned to modeling, attended an audition for the Joe Boxer spots. He twice read from the script, asked to deliver the line "They're tight and they're white." The director had urged the actors to have fun and just be themselves, so on his third shot Lowery deviated from the script. "They played the music and I went crazy, dancing like my little cousins and I do in the living room," he told Sarah Freeman of the Associated Press. "Then I stripped down to my Joe Boxers and kept on dancing... At first it was like, 'Oh, my God, what did I just do?' But then all the Joe Boxer people, Kmart people, production people, they were all standing, whistling and clapping." TBWA creative director Patrick O'Neill called it an inspired performance, telling Freeman, "He didn't just audition to get the job; he created a combination of things we didn't foresee. It was what we call a happy accident." In short order Lowery was brought into the studio and did 25 takes of his dance; a commercial was fashioned out of his moment of spontaneity.

The "Vaughn" spot caught the attention of *The Tonight Show,* which played it with the head of band-leader Kevin Eubanks (who looked a lot like Lowery) superimposed over the dancer's face. Lowery gained a fan club and began making television appearances, including *The Tonight Show,* and granted press interviews. The spot was so popular that Kmart set up a separate website to accommodate fans who wanted to download the clip.

OUTCOME

According to Lorene Yue, writing for the *Detroit Free Press,* Kmart, because of "Vaughn," hadn't "seen this much attention paid to its commercials since Rosie O'Donnell and Penny Marshall strolled the aisles from 1997 to 1999." The spot was a key element in a brief campaign that created a very positive buzz about Kmart and Joe Boxer, "helping Kmart sell roughly $20 million in Joe Boxer apparel a week after the line was introduced," wrote Yue. For Kmart, dealing with Chapter 11 bankruptcy reorganization, the success with the Joe Boxer launch was a major boost to the balance sheet as well as company morale.

Lowery took advantage of his sudden fame to land a costarring role on the NBC sitcom *Scrubs* and appear in other advertising campaigns, and he figured prominently in subsequent Kmart efforts to promote Joe Boxer. He appeared in a pair of holiday spots in late 2002, dancing in one while wearing just a silver-wrapped box and in the other performing an "antler dance" with several women. These ads proved popular as well, leading to Lowery appearing in an ad that was part of the 2003 back-to-school marketing campaign. It offered a more elaborate, Broadway-like dance number in which Lowery made his entrance on a swing and joined in a group boogie.

The back-to-school campaign and the final Vaughn spot were held up when Kmart and TBWA\Chiat\Day became involved in a dispute over fees: $2.4 million to the agency and another $1.1 million to vendors used by the agency. Kmart eventually made the payments but parted ways with the agency that had been instrumental in the successful launch of Joe Boxer with Kmart. But the retailer, which emerged from bankruptcy in May 2003, had more pressing issues to address than building on the momentum of Joe Boxer. Kmart then merged with Sears, after which the Joe Boxer brand was cut back, and the focus returned to men's underwear and women's intimates.

FURTHER READING

Anderson, Mae. "Ad Libs: A Little Spontaneity on Set Can Go a Long Way." *Adweek,* October 13, 2003, p. 28.

Baar, Aaron, and Rebecca Flass. "A Popular Pitchman's Next Step: Videogame Fame." *Adweek,* February 24, 2003, p. 10.

Day, Sherri. "Kmart Will Shoot Two Men in Joe Boxer Shorts from a Cannon in a Brand-Promotion Effort." *New York Times,* July 25, 2002, p. 14.

Elliott, Stuart. "After a Bitter Parting, Kmart Picks Finalists to Succeed 2 Agencies." *New York Times,* August 19, 2004, p. C3.

Freeman, Sarah. "Boxer Boogie Brings Fame." *Associated Press,* December 18, 2002.

Garcia, Sandra. "Song and Dance: Joe Boxer and Kmart Get in the Groove." *Shoot,* May 9, 2003, p. 21.

Irwin, Tanya. "Kmart Diversifies Holiday Spots." *Adweek,* November 25, 2002, p. 4.

Nudd, Tim. "The Odd Couple: Graham Puts the Blue in Blue-Light Special." *Adweek* (eastern ed.), August 5, 2002, p. 22.

Robinson, Gaile. "Under It All, the Joe Boxer Dancer Is a Zany Guy." *Fort Worth Star-Telegram,* December 27, 2002.

Walker, Rob. "Boxer Rebellion." *Slate,* September 9, 2002.

Young, Vicki M. "Rolling with the Punches." *WWD,* July 21, 2005, p. 1.

Yue, Lorene. "Joe Boxer Commercial Brings Kmart Big Bucks." *Detroit Free Press,* September 4, 2002.

Ed Dinger

MARTHA STEWART EVERYDAY CAMPAIGN

OVERVIEW

In 1997 Kmart Corporation wooed Martha Stewart back. She had taken the position of Kmart lifestyles consultant and Home Division spokesperson in 1987 but had, according to Stewart, been alienated through "unimaginative" retailing and "no quality control." As Stewart ascended to the status of lifestyle maven for American culture at large in the early 1990s, she worked her way out of her contract with Kmart, which was descending to the verge of bankruptcy. In 1995, however, Floyd Hall took over the helm of Kmart and orchestrated a turnaround. Even before he began to transform the existing Kmart format into the more shopper-friendly Big Kmart and Super Kmart formats, Hall sought to reestablish the chain's relationship with Stewart. Hall recognized that Stewart's reputation for a commitment to quality and economy suited Kmart's rebuilding plans perfectly.

Working together, Kmart and Stewart developed a video that featured each category in Stewart's Everyday brand and explained how to coordinate the various products in the line. The effort was an in-store, point-of purchase video. Additionally, Kmart released a $60 million marketing campaign to support the new brand that included television spots, print ads, and direct mailings to consumers. The remarriage succeeded, for Stewart, by establishing her own corporation, Martha Stewart Living Omnimedia, LLC, had leveraged enough power to oversee quality control. Although Stewart, a renowned perfectionist, could prove hard to please, the arrangement benefited Kmart, because it retained not a cardboard character as spokesperson but rather a well-oiled machine in the form of the 30-person staff at Stewart's company that paid attention to details. In return, Stewart benefited from the increased exposure Kmart gave her name and concept through the Martha Stewart Everyday line. Kmart and Stewart thus established a symbiotic relationship.

Brand extensions and new commercials were added in 1999 and 2000, but trouble was looming. In 2000 Kmart dropped its agency, Campbell Mithun Esty, Minneapolis, and replaced it with TBWA\Chiat\Day New York. Despite reviving its BlueLight Special in 2001 and releasing a new marketing campaign supporting it as well as a new round of commercials promoting the Martha Stewart Everyday brand, Kmart filed for bankruptcy in 2002. Stewart encountered her own legal problems in 2002 when she became embroiled in an insider-trading scandal.

HISTORICAL CONTEXT

According to Marcia Heroux Pounds in a 1998 article in the *Ft. Lauderdale Sun-Sentinel,* in 1987 Boca Raton-based marketing consultant Barbara Loren-Snyder was searching for "the Ralph Lauren for the masses of the ['90s]," someone to pair with Kmart to boost profits in its housewares department. Stewart's 1982 book *Entertaining* caught Loren-Snyder's eye on a bookstore shelf, and a visit to Stewart's Westport, Connecticut, home, with its painted floors, confirmed Loren-Snyder's hunch that she had identified a candidate with flair and style. Loren-Snyder's advice outweighed that of the other three consultants assigned to the project, and Kmart gave Stewart the nod, negotiating what amounted to a licensing agreement with her. Stewart appeared in television commercials for Kmart, and Kmart featured Stewart's

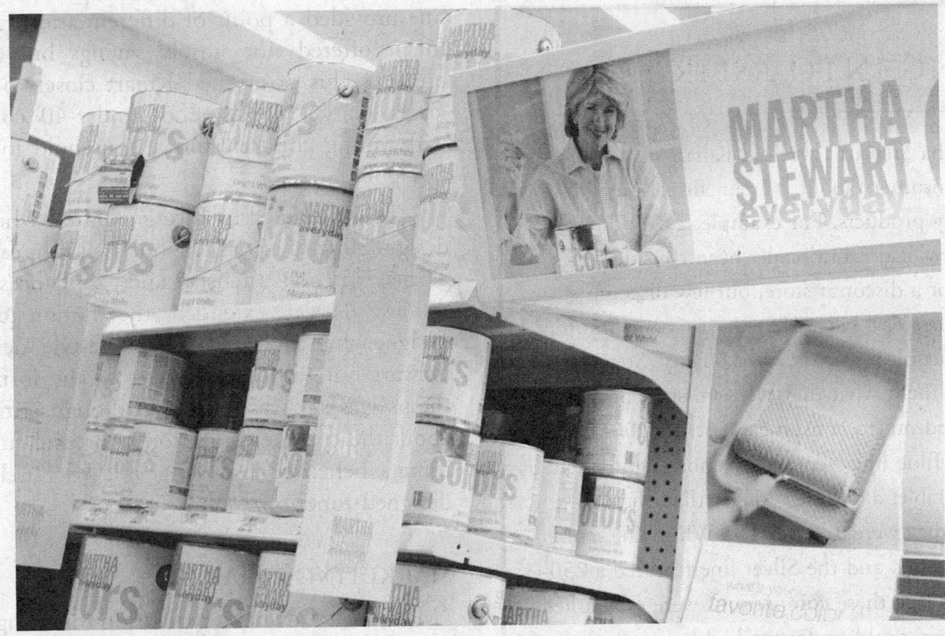

Martha Stewart and Kmart joined forces in 1997 to form a lucrative partnership.
© NAJLAH FEANNY/CORBIS.

name on some of its products. The agreement, however, did not prevent Stewart from backing out when she experienced difficulty dealing with Kmart, which was on a downslide at the time.

Under chief executive officer Joseph Antonini, Kmart started to founder in the early 1990s. The discount retailer posted a staggering loss of $974 million in 1993. It rebounded in 1994 with a slight profit but sank back into red ink in 1995, losing $571 million. Much of the blame for the slide fell on Antonini, who resigned in March 1995 at the urging of shareholders and the board of directors. The board replaced Antonini with Hall, the former chief executive of rival discount retailer Target who had since headed Grand Union supermarkets and cofounded his own business in museum reproductions. Hall strategized a turnaround by restructuring the existing Kmarts instead of expanding; in fact, he closed some 200 locations that were lagging in sales. The Big Kmart format featured wider aisles and brighter lighting. In addition, it expanded the grocery section by 35 percent, hoping to lure one-stop shoppers with low-margin groceries in addition to high-margin apparel. These and other strategies succeeded, and Kmart posted profits of $249 million in 1997.

At the same time that Kmart was rebounding, Stewart was eclipsing her previous success. She continued to publish books as well as *Martha Stewart Living* magazine, which reached a circulation of 2 million. She had a syndicated newspaper column, a daily radio feature, and a television program. She also mastered interactive media, maintaining a World Wide Web site that hosted 300,000 visits a week. Just as Kmart approached her to reestablish their relationship, Stewart was consolidating these diverse enterprises under one umbrella, her company Martha Stewart Living Omnimedia, which she bought from Time Inc. in 1997. Thus, what distinguished the second union between Kmart and Stewart was that both sides were now operating from a position of strength.

TARGET MARKET

Kmart's target market consisted of women aged 25 to 49 who came from households with incomes of $20,000 to $60,000. Kmart had traditionally offered low prices for low-quality merchandise, but Hall changed this formula. Stewart represented the key to the transformation, with the success of the Martha Stewart Everyday line, symbolizing the overall repositioning of Kmart. Stewart's name was synonymous with quality, but she also promoted common sense, which included economizing. In fact, Stewart helped usher in the trend toward sensible shopping. In the 1980s shoppers had displayed their ability to overspend. The recession of the early 1990s reversed this dynamic. It became "chic to save," according to Kurt Barnard, president of *Barnard's Retail Trend Report,* as reported by Marty Hair in the *Newark Star-Ledger.*

Stewart did not act only to lower the bar, however. She also raised the bar in terms of Kmart's clientele.

TAPPING INTO ASPIRATIONS

Part of Martha Stewart's work at Kmart involved educating consumers about the benefits of buying higher-quality products. For example, a 180-thread-count bedsheet had traditionally been considered a good value for a discount store, but few discount-store shoppers understood what 180-count meant. In order to convince people to buy a better quality, Stewart had to explain to them what they were missing. Stewart simply pointed out to consumers that the 200-count sheets in her Blue line were woven more tightly, felt more comfortable, and lasted longer than the 180-count sheets they were used to. The White line sported a 230-count sheet, and the Silver line featured a 250-count sheet. Once these comparisons were established, Kmart shoppers could understand why they might consider paying a little more (though still a reasonable price) for a slightly better product. Hence the success of the White line, the next step up in the Martha Stewart Everyday product range, and of the Silver line, the top tier. Stewart and Kmart were simply tapping into shoppers' aspirations.

Shoppers who would not otherwise have frequented the discount chain were lured in specifically by her line. Even though *Martha Stewart Living* magazine categorically avoided advertising the Martha Stewart Everyday line, cross-fertilization nevertheless occurred on the strength of Stewart's reputation. Kmart and Stewart anticipated and facilitated this dynamic of higher-income women shopping at a discount store by offering three tiers of products: Blue, White, and Silver lines. The uninitiated could work their way up from the bottom tier, the Blue line, but those accustomed to high quality could find what they wanted from the start in the top tier, the Silver line.

COMPETITION

In reputation Kmart positioned itself between Wal-Mart and Target, and it fell between them in market share as well. Wal-Mart appealed to hard-core discount shoppers, while Target appealed to younger and higher-income shoppers. According to a 1998 article by George White in the *Los Angeles Times,* Wal-Mart had 22 percent of the discount retail market, while Kmart controlled 9 percent and Target 5 percent. The Martha Stewart Everyday line provided a point of differentiation from Wal-Mart, for it offered not simply savings but also value and quality. This positioned Kmart closer to Target, whose target market consisted of under-40 college graduates with young children and a household income of about $47,000.

Target reacted by hiring architect Michael Graves to design a line of affordable but stylish housewares, such as clocks, kitchen utensils and appliances, and picture frames. Target extended the notion of branding a designer by choosing not a lifestyle designer such as Stewart but rather a designer of the forms and objects themselves such as Graves. Although critics complained about the commercialization of architecture, Target customers benefited by being able to purchase pleasantly designed functional items.

MARKETING STRATEGY

"Martha Stewart has a reputation for doing things right," said Kmart shopper Janet Day in George White's *Los Angeles Times* article. "I'm sure she wouldn't allow anyone to use her name on a product unless she was happy with it." Although it might have been easy to exploit such a reputation, Stewart worked hard to gain integrity and to sustain it. Thus, she oversaw quality control of the Martha Stewart Everyday line. "We don't advise. We don't approve. We do it," said Sharon Patrick, president and chief operating officer of Martha Stewart Living Omnimedia. Steve Ryman, Kmart divisional vice president and brand director of Martha Stewart Everyday, agreed. "They have total control. But," he added, "they listen well." As explained by Patrick, Stewart and Kmart shared a vision: "We want to engineer quality into mass market products."

The central considerations behind the Martha Stewart Everyday line were function and coordination. Individually, each product in the line was designed to fulfill a specific function properly. More important, however, Stewart designed her products to correspond in color and style across categories. This design symmetry removed the burden of matching from Kmart consumers, many of whom were not prepared to undertake the task. The designer, in this case Stewart, thus had the most important role in creating the brand. Martha Stewart Everyday epitomized the "designer brand," as Stewart herself was both the designer and the brand, exemplifying the 1990s trend toward the branding of designers, as with Graves. The strength behind the brand was the equity Stewart had accumulated by investing in her own identity, which at this point had a tangible salability.

Kmart and Stewart produced an in-store, point-of-purchase video that showed all of the categories in the Martha Stewart Everyday line—bedding, towels, paints, and so forth—and explained how to coordinate items. The video also explained the progression from the different tiers of products, from the Blue to the White to the Silver line. Kmart further supported the Martha Stewart Everyday line by devoting a 4,500-square-foot area in each store exclusively to the products. In early 1998 these products accounted for 55 percent of Kmart's "soft home" business, and by the end of the year they accounted for 70 percent of Kmart's sales of domestic products. Kmart and Stewart agreed, however, that the line should not represent Kmart's entire offerings in domestic products, for some products were not appropriate to the Stewart concept. On the other hand, Kmart announced its intentions to expand the Martha Stewart Everyday line into other appropriate categories.

Kmart supported the Martha Stewart Everyday brand with its most extensive marketing campaign ever. The discount retailer spent $60 million on television and print advertising, direct mailings, and special events to promote the line. In March 1998 Kmart relaunched a national television spot that showed Stewart hanging sheets across the Grand Canyon, and it produced a new spot for the summer. It supported the new spring line of products with print advertising, direct mail, Sunday newspaper inserts, and magazine ads.

As promised, in 1999 Kmart and Stewart launched an extension of her Everyday brand with the introduction of Martha Stewart Everyday Garden, which included outdoor and patio furniture. In 2000 Everyday Kitchen, another brand extension featuring more than 650 cooking and entertaining items, such as dinnerware, bakeware, and cutlery, hit Kmart's shelves. The Everyday Keeping collection of home-storage items followed in 2001 and included such products as closet organizers, hangers, ironing boards, and airtight glass and plastic containers. Also introduced in 2001 was the Everyday Decorating line, with lamps, mirrors, picture frames, and other home-decor products. Each new line extension was supported by television spots, print ads, and direct mailings. Stewart, shown putting her products to good use, figured prominently in all of the commercials. One spot supporting the Everyday Kitchen product launch featured Stewart setting her table for dinner guests with a selection of items from her Kitchen collection.

OUTCOME

Measuring strictly by the book, Kmart's Martha Stewart Everyday campaign succeeded beyond expectations. In 1998, its second year, the brand had $800 million in sales, up from $450 million in the first year. The success stemmed from each category of the line performing in top form. The Martha Stewart Everyday brand of towels was outsold only by Cannon, which had been in the business for more than 100 years. Success also stemmed from the coordination of the lines under the larger umbrella. The White line, the intermediate tier, outperformed all expectations, and the Silver line also did better than projected. Only the Blue line merely met sales expectations.

Kmart and Stewart won a slew of awards for their coordinated marketing efforts. The Big Kmart layout, with 4,500 square feet devoted to the Martha Stewart Everyday line, won the 1997 *Discount Store News* Supply Performance Award by Retail Category, (SPARC/3M Award) for its unique and effective design. Kmart was named the 1998 LIMA Retailer of the Year specifically for the Martha Stewart Everyday line in domestics and nonfurnishings. The American Marketing Association awarded both Kmart and Martha Stewart Living Omnimedia its silver and bronze Edison Best New Product Awards for the Martha Stewart Everyday line in its introductory year. In addition, the association awarded Stewart herself the Edison Achievement Award, bestowed upon executives who distinguished themselves through exemplary business careers.

The success of the Martha Stewart Everyday line became the benchmark for Kmart's potential under the restructuring orchestrated by Hall. One key feature of the success was its sustainability as the Martha Stewart Everyday line was extended into other categories. In spring 1999 Kmart introduced the Martha Stewart Everyday Garden collection, which included 10 patio furniture sets as well as gardening supplies such as bamboo rakes, organic fertilizers, gloves, hoses, and flowerpots. In the future the retailer planned to extend the horticultural line with the addition of live plants, bulbs, and seeds. Kmart also announced plans to launch the Martha Stewart Everyday Baby layette collection and later to add kitchen products, the area in which Stewart, on the strength of her cookbooks, had initially earned her reputation. According to a 1999 article by Mike Duff in *Discount Store News,* Andy Giancamilli, president of U.S. Kmart Stores, said, "Once we've extended her into kitchen, that's it. Then we build." Martha Stewart Everyday brand director Ryman agreed with his colleague. "I think it's best to say we're just at the beginning and have a lot of product development, marketing and advertising to accomplish," he was quoted as saying in Duff's article. "You haven't seen anything but the tip of the iceberg. We have just started to see the effects of Martha Stewart at Kmart," Ryman concluded.

Although the Martha Stewart Everyday line was a success, Kmart was struggling in the marketplace and in search of more edgy advertising to try and win customers from its competitor Target. In 2000 Kmart moved its

$100 million advertising account to TBWA\Chiat\Day New York. The new agency did not tamper with the Stewart campaign, but in 2001 it released a marketing campaign that reintroduced Kmart's BlueLight Special and the familiar announcement "Attention Kmart Shoppers..."

Despite the sales increases attributed to the Martha Stewart Everyday line, a new ad agency, and a new campaign, Kmart continued to face declining overall sales, climbing financial losses, and a particularly poor 2001 holiday shopping season. In January 2002 the chain filed for Chapter 11 bankruptcy. Adding to the retailer's woes, Martha Stewart was embroiled in her own legal problems after becoming tied to the ImClone Systems insider-trading scandal. A new series of commercials that Kmart released in October 2002, featuring Stewart promoting her line of bed and bath linens for the holidays, came under fire from the media and consumers. For subsequent holiday television spots promoting the Martha Stewart Everyday brands, Kmart dropped Stewart, using only her voice with an image of Santa Claus.

FURTHER READING

Baker, Chris. "Kmart Has No Comment on New Television Advertisements featuring Martha Stewart." *Washington (DC) Times,* October 11, 2002.

Connor, Tracy. "Kmart Drops Martha Stewart Visage from New Holiday-Houseware Ad Campaign." *New York Daily News,* November 15, 2002.

Cuneo, Alice. "Banking on Blue; Kmart Reinvents the Blue Light Special." *Crain's Detroit Business,* April 9, 2001.

Duff, Mike. "The Martha Miracle Takes Root in L&G and Blossoms in Baby." *Discount Store News,* March 22, 1999.

Gatlin, Greg. "Retail Giant Kmart Is Bankrupt." *Boston Herald,* January 23, 2002.

Hair, Marty. "Martha Pays Attention to Detail... and Kmart Shoppers." *Newark (NJ) Star-Ledger,* April 7, 1999.

Heroux Pounds, Marcia. "Martha Stewart and Kmart: A Match Made in Boca." *Fort Lauderdale (FL) Sun-Sentinel,* March 13, 1998.

Liebeck, Laura. "The Mileage of Martha Stewart Keeps Extending Every Day." *Discount Store News,* March 9, 1998.

Meyer, Nancy. "Kmart Launches Martha Stewart Garden Furniture." *HFN: The Weekly Newspaper for the Home Furnishing Network,* January 25, 1999.

White, George. "K-Ching! Kmart Trying to Boost Image, Products." *Los Angeles Times,* February 20, 1998.

William D. Baue
Rayna Bailey

ROSIE O'DONNELL AND PENNY MARSHALL CAMPAIGN

OVERVIEW

In 1994 Kmart Corporation came close to bankruptcy. In October of that year the company—then the second-largest retailer in the United States—posted its seventh consecutive quarterly decline in profits, closed 100 of its 2,350 stores, cut the ranks of management by 10 percent, and laid off 5,350 hourly employees. In March 1995 Kmart's board of directors forced the company's president and CEO to resign. And in April of that year Kmart ended its 25-year association with the advertising firm of Ross Roy Communications when it announced that it had chosen Minneapolis-based Campbell Mithun Esty (CME) to handle its $175 million account.

In November 1995 CME introduced a new Kmart holiday advertising campaign starring television and movie celebrities Rosie O'Donnell and Penny Marshall. The campaign included 10 commercials directed by comedian David Steinberg. They depicted the two women as Kmart shopping buddies, with shopping-savvy O'Donnell pointing out featured merchandise and great values to novice shopper Marshall. The goal of the spots was not only to increase sales but also to build awareness of Kmart as a fun place to shop. According to a CME executive, the message was that "Kmart is changing. The merchandise is better, it's more fun to shop there, and I can still get great deals."

The campaign was a success, despite polls that showed consumers had lost faith in celebrity endorsements. According to *USA Today*'s Ad Track, 31 percent of women who had viewed the commercials described them as "very effective." Television spots featuring O'Donnell and Marshall also helped drive sales, and as the campaign continued, so too did its success. In December 1997 the campaign moved into its second year with new commercials, and Kmart reported that sales had increased 2.9 percent over the same period the previous year, with overall earnings in 1997 up 43 percent. Based on the campaign's success, new spots were released in 1998 and 1999. At the end of 1999, however, O'Donnell's relationship with Kmart ended as a result of complaints from consumers about her advocacy of gun control. In 2000 Kmart also moved its account to ad agency TBWA\Chiat\Day New York as it planned to shift to edgier advertising.

HISTORICAL CONTEXT

From modest beginnings in 1899 as the S.S. Kresge Co. Store in downtown Detroit, rapid expansion took Kresge to 85 stores and annual sales of $10 million by 1912. In

1929 a Kresge store became part of the first suburban shopping center, Country Club Plaza in Kansas City, Missouri. The Kresge company launched its first newspaper advertising in 1930 and in the 1950s added radio advertising. It was during this time that the discount store came into being. Kresge opened its first discount store in Garden City, Michigan, in 1962 under the name Kmart. By 1998 Kmart had some 2,100 stores in the United States, Puerto Rico, Guam, the U.S. Virgin Islands, Canada, and Mexico and employed more than 300,000 people.

The growth of the company was not all uphill. From the late 1970s through the early 1990s the company instituted an aggressive program of expansion and acquisition. It acquired all or parts of such companies as Waldenbooks, Sports Giant, Sports Authority, and OfficeMax. By the mid-1990s Kmart seemed to have lost focus, and the company began to reevaluate its holdings. According to CME spokeswoman Ginny Vonckx, "Despite a presence in thousands of towns across America and elsewhere, its identity with consumers had declined.... Consumers questioned if it was still a great store that delivered great merchandise at a great value."

In the early 1990s Kmart instituted a five-year store renovation project. Commercials promised consumers that stores would be brighter and better stocked. As Jennifer Negley reported in *Discount Store News,* however, "... consumers overall were not convinced to switch their allegiance to 'the new Kmart,' particularly when there were freshly built, cleaner, better-stocked Wal-Marts and Targets just down the road."

When new management took over the company in late 1994, there was a move to shore up the chain's sagging image. Before it hired CME as its ad agency, Kmart's slogan had been "Low prices and extras you won't find anywhere else." Consumer research showed that the advertising led customers to expect to find great deals, a pleasant shopping atmosphere, and a good selection of merchandise. Shoppers had difficulty, however, matching the advertising with the reality of a visit to a Kmart store. Thus, by late 1995 Kmart was experiencing severe image problems and was rapidly losing credibility with its customers and shareholders. David Tree, chief creative officer of CME, told *Adweek*'s Jean Halliday and Ellen Rooney Martin that Kmart's previous advertising had been "self-important and over-reaching. It missed the target."

As a way of improving communications with customers, CME introduced O'Donnell and Marshall as ambassadors for Kmart. O'Donnell had been a stand-up comic before beginning a movie career in 1992, when she was selected by director Marshall to costar in *A League of Their Own.* Other film credits included *Sleepless in Seattle, The Flintstones, Exit to Eden,* and *Harriet the Spy.* She made her Broadway debut in 1994 as Rizzo in Tommy Tune's revival of *Grease* and in 1996 began her own variety and talk show. Marshall was perhaps best remembered for her role in the situation comedy *Laverne and Shirley,* which ran for more than seven seasons on ABC. She moved to the forefront of Hollywood directors with the film *Big,* the first movie directed by a woman to take in more than $100 million at the box office. Since then she had directed numerous other movies, including the Academy Award–nominated *Awakenings.*

The pair was chosen because it was believed that Kmart shoppers could identify with them because they were down-to-earth and had the ability to relate to the average consumer. In a 1995 interview in *Advertising Age,* R. Fulton Macdonald, president of International Business Development, applauded Kmart's choice. He told reporter Leah Haran, "Rosie is very credible, and the biggest thing Kmart needs is credibility. That is going in the right direction—getting credible women to vouch for Kmart without making false pretenses. She is no-nonsense and tells it like it is."

TARGET MARKET

During the years Kmart was undergoing its program of expansion and acquisition, it also tried to change its identity. The company made efforts to broaden its traditional blue-collar appeal and to include a more upscale market by, for example, instituting exclusive items such as a designer clothing line by former *Charlie's Angels* actress Jaclyn Smith. When the O'Donnell-Marshall campaign was created, however, the idea was to appeal to the company's original target market. This market consisted of women between the ages of 25 and 49 who had children and household incomes of $20,000 to $50,000. Research showed that 87 percent of America's children came from such households and that these women were heavy discount shoppers. The idea was to relate directly to these women in a humorous way.

COMPETITION

The problems that Kmart was experiencing in attracting consumers were caused in part by what retail consultants Management Horizons called the "overstoring of America." Stores such as Wal-Mart, Sears, Target, and J.C. Penney created intense competition for customers, and they did so partly through substantial increases in advertising. In the early 1990s, for example, Wal-Mart increased its ad spending by 14 percent and Target its spending by 47 percent. During the same two years Kmart's spending on advertising dropped almost 32 percent.

By 1998 Wal-Mart was the world's number one retailer, bigger than Sears, Kmart, and J.C. Penney combined. Its commercials focused on the store's low prices

ROSIE O'DONNELL'S ROSIE O'DOLL

The success of Rosie O'Donnell's talk show took many people by surprise, including toy makers. During the holiday shopping season of 1996, O'Donnell talked about one of her new favorites, a toy called Tickle Me Elmo by Tyco. This generated a national buying frenzy for the doll, as well as Tyco's immense gratitude. To say thanks, the company made a doll in O'Donnell's likeness and presented it to her. Rosie O'Doll was a 16-inch soft-bodied toy that, when squeezed, uttered O'Donnell-inspired phrases like "What a cutie patootie!" and "Dreams come true with Rosie." O'Donnell was so taken with the doll that she suggested to Tyco that they mass-produce it and work with selected retailers to donate a portion of the proceeds to the For All Kids Foundation.

Naturally, one of the retailers chosen was Kmart. Bill Dunlap, chairman of Campbell Mithun Esty, told Stuart Elliott of the *New York Times,* "Rosie puts fun into shopping, and she's very interested in kids, which is a big part of the Kmart mix." The doll also made a cameo appearance in the 1997 commercial "Toy Mania," perched on a shelf above O'Donnell and Penny Marshall as they answered questions on the toy hotline.

as well as the friendliness of its staff, with many of the commercials featuring actual employees talking about the great values that could be found at a Wal-Mart store. Sears, another of Kmart's principal competitors, faced its own image problems. Its solution was a long-running campaign created by Young & Rubicam that featured the slogans "The Many Sides of Sears" and "The Softer Sides of Sears." If Kmart were to stay afloat, it needed to make the experience of shopping in its stores more desirable for the target customer and address the negative perceptions of its stores.

MARKETING STRATEGY

Kmart took a four-pronged approach to restoring its image and its profits. First, it built on the popularity and credibility of the two spokeswomen, O'Donnell and Marshall, to instill confidence in consumers. The company then strengthened its exclusive celebrity brands, including Jaclyn Smith's sportswear, Kathy Ireland's swimwear and lingerie, Martha Stewart Everyday housewares, and *Sesame Street* children's merchandise. The third step was to refurbish stores to create a more pleasant shopping experience. And, fourth, in 1998 the company began to reposition the chain as Big Kmart, relying on big-name celebrities like Bob Hope, featured in one of the first Big Kmart commercials, to bring added credibility to the turnaround.

All of Kmart's efforts were successful in bringing the company back to life, but it was the O'Donnell-Marshall commercials that most people came to associate with the Kmart name. From the beginning consumers enjoyed the two women's sharp-tongued yet good-natured banter. One of the first commercials in the series had Marshall looking for toys while she and O'Donnell hurried through a Kmart store. "They got Hot Skate Barbie?" asked Marshall. "Right here," said O'Donnell. "They got Hot Wheels Criss Cross Crash?" asked Marshall. "Right here," said O'Donnell. "What about Dr. Dreadful?" asked Marshall. To which O'Donnell replied, "Oh, we broke up months ago."

But even Kmart could not have foreseen the success of the *Rosie O'Donnell Show.* When the comedian went on the air with her own talk show in 1996, it was an immediate hit. She and her guests referred to Kmart frequently, and O'Donnell even began to refer to herself as "the Kmart lady." Marshall was sometimes a guest on the program, and she and O'Donnell recited Kmart escapades. When O'Donnell hosted *Saturday Night Live,* none other than Marshall made a special guest appearance. In the show's opening segment Marshall complimented O'Donnell on her outfit, asking her where she had bought it. "Kmart," replied O'Donnell. "Who knew?" Marshall answered, repeating a refrain from a Kmart commercial.

O'Donnell and Marshall celebrated their first anniversary with Kmart in November 1996 with another series of 10 holiday commercials. The first two were "Toy Mania," which showed the two women in a Kmart playing with Legos, which was featured in a store-wide promotion, and "Trim-A-Home," in which O'Donnell used soap opera terms to discuss the happenings in her illuminated ceramic Christmas village. Their anniversary series also marked the pair's first 60-second spot (previous spots had been 30 seconds long), a parody of the "Twelve Days of Christmas."

In 1997 the two celebrities were featured in Kmart's holiday commercials for the third straight year. Larry Davis, Kmart's vice president of marketing, told *Adweek* 's Aaron Baar, "Customers tell us that, as they're in the midst of their own holiday preparations, they look forward to seeing how Rosie and Penny fare." Two of the 1997 spots were once again directed by comedian Steinberg. One spot, "Holiday Magic," showed how

O'Donnell moved from the present to the Renaissance and back again with a click of her fingers. Marshall attempted to re-create the feat but to no avail. She then found herself sporting reindeer antlers and lamenting that she would like to go shopping but would not fit in the car. O'Donnell told her not to worry because "you'll pull it." "Santa's Workshop" found the pair at the North Pole, where they observed busy elves readying a wide variety of holiday merchandise for Kmart stores. At the conclusion of the tour, O'Donnell asked Marshall, "So what we have learned?" "We need elves," Marshall replied.

The campaigns were fully integrated with Kmart promotions. Items fitting the campaign strategy were also prominently featured in Sunday newspaper circulars, and store signs promoted such themes as "Toy Mania." When a major in-store promotion was scheduled, O'Donnell and Marshall were used to generate awareness and highlight the promotion. One Thanksgiving commercial, for example, featured the pair waiting at dawn for a Kmart store to open so they could get a free fanny pack with $70 in coupons. The spot was coordinated with a promotion offering the free gift and coupons to the first 500 customers at each Kmart store.

The campaign continued in 1998 with the introduction of a new series of holiday-season television spots featuring the popular duo. The spots debuted in November during the NBC *Sunday Night Movie* and ran through mid-December. Playing up O'Donnell's well-known passion for Broadway, two of the spots promoted the "big show" at Kmart, according to a report in *PR Newswire.* One spot, titled "That's Entertainment," had O'Donnell and Marshall doing a song-and-dance routine riddled with pratfalls and featuring a guest appearance by Godzilla. Another spot, "Be a Santa," featured the two performing with singing elves.

As the 1999 holiday shopping season unfolded, Kmart and other traditional retailers were confronted with competition from the Internet as more and more shoppers preferred to do their gift buying online. In an *Advertising Age* report analysts predicted a "bleak Christmas for the inert traditional retailers." Kmart released a new round of commercials and television specials featuring its top spokeswomen, O'Donnell and Marshall. In a break from the humorous spots featuring O'Donnell and Marshall, the chain also introduced a new campaign that targeted women and starred the country-music mother-daughter singing team Naomi and Wynonna Judd.

OUTCOME

Although a 1996 *USA Today* Ad Track poll showed that consumers were losing faith in celebrity endorsers, the Kmart commercials proved to be an exception to the rule. CME's Tree told *USA Today* reporter Melanie Wells that consumers were responding more favorably to Kmart since the campaign had begun airing. "We're not looking for celebrities to be shills for the company," said Tree. "They're there as actresses. They're an exaggeration of the Kmart customer. They are 'ordinary people' who tell it like it is."

The strategy seemed to work. According to *USA Today*'s Ad Track, more than one-third of the women polled liked the spots, compared with less than one-fifth of men. The spots were said to be "very effective" by 31 percent of the women, as opposed to 19 percent of the men. According to Dottie Enrico, "... the campaign performed well with all adult consumers. An impressive 29 percent of those who'd seen the ads three times or more [said] they liked them a lot. The ads were especially popular with consumers over 25." The ad agency was pleased with the campaign's results; CME's Vonckx stated, "our own research, and research done by third parties, has told us repeatedly how much our consumers like these ads. And they like them because they can relate to these two friends as shoppers, and they're rewarded for watching them with a story that's entertaining too."

Writing about the campaign in *Discount Store News,* reporter Negley stated, "The casting of two women with strong blue collar appeal and working class bonafides not only speaks straight to Kmart's core customer, it's proved something of a public relations master-stroke." That masterstroke seemed to have been successful in getting Kmart on the road back to the position it once held. In 1998 Kmart was the country's third-largest retailer, and its stock was trading at more than three times the value it had before the O'Donnell-Marshall spots began running. Kmart's holiday sales in December 1997 rose a small but significant 2.9 percent over the same period in 1996, with Wal-Mart's sales rising 7.2 percent and Target's 6.4 percent, while J.C. Penney's was falling by 2.3 percent. Overall earnings at Kmart in 1997 were $330 million, a 43 percent increase over the previous year.

In 1999 O'Donnell and Kmart announced that the company's popular spokeswoman was ending her five-year association with the company when her contract expired in December. A *Knight Ridder/Tribune Business News* report attributed the decision to O'Donnell's pro-gun-control views and subsequent complaints from angry consumers. According to *Knight Ridder/Tribune Business News,* after O'Donnell publicly criticized actor Tom Selleck for appearing in a commercial for the National Rifle Association, "Kmart received hundreds of angry phone calls from National Rifle Association supporters." It was uncertain whether or not Marshall would continue to appear in commercials for Kmart without her sidekick. Kmart announced in 2000 that it was moving its $100 million account to TBWA\Chiat\Day New York.

FURTHER READING

Baar, Aaron. "Rosie and Penny Check In." *Adweek,* November 11, 1997.

"Broadway, Family Entertainment and Goodwill Take Center Stage in Kmart Holiday Promotions." *PR Newswire,* November 12, 1998.

Cuneo, Alice Z.. "Holiday Shopping Showdown; Turning Point: Traditional Retailers Could Find Their Usual Tactics Outdated by Cyber-Selling." *Advertising Age,* November 15, 1999.

———. "Kmart Targets Target as It Taps TBWA for Ads; Retailer Seeks Creative Boost, Awards Account to Chiat/Day." *Advertising Age,* October 2, 2000.

"Detroit Free Press Michigan Memo Column." *Detroit Free Press,* September 23, 1999.

Elliott, Stuart. "A Soft-Bodied Toy and Cause-Related Marketing." *New York Times,* November 26, 1997.

Enrico, Dottie. "Women Like Kmart's Rosie and Penny Ads." *USA Today,* October 14, 1996.

Goldman, Kevin. "Kmart Gives Campbell Mithun Blue Light." *Wall Street Journal,* April 18, 1995.

Halliday, Jean, and Ellen Rooney Martin. "Kmart Greets Holidays." *Adweek,* November 13, 1995.

Haran, Leah. "Kmart Gets Real as It Maps Road to Survival." *Advertising Age,* October 16, 1995.

Herzog, Boaz. "Gun-Control Stance Leads Rosie O'Donnell to Leave Kmart Ads." *Knight Ridder/ Tribune Business News,* November 23, 1999.

Liebeck, Laura. "Over the Hump, but Not the Mountain." *Discount Store News,* June 23, 1997.

Negley, Jennifer. "Attention Kmart Shoppers." *Discount Store News,* December 12, 1996.

Wells, Melanie. "All's Not Well in Celebrity Pitchdom." *USA Today,* November 4, 1996.

Sharyn Kolberg
Rayna Bailey

Kraft Foods, Inc.

3 Lakes Dr.
Northfield, Illinois 60093-2753
USA
Telephone: (847) 646-2000
Web site: www.kraftfoods.com

IT'S HOW TO UNPLUG CAMPAIGN

OVERVIEW

The "It's How to Unplug" advertising campaign, handled by the New York office of Young & Rubicam, encouraged women to pause during busy days and relax with a cup of General Foods International Coffees, made by Kraft Foods, Inc. "Inhale the subtle cinnamon aroma. Sip slowly until you unplug," suggested a magazine advertisement announcing that Cafe Vienna—one of the brand's many varieties—had been reformulated with a richer, creamier taste. Since their launch in the early 1970s, General Foods International Coffees had been marketed with an emphasis on the idea that drinking them was almost like taking a vacation, because they resembled beverages a traveler might enjoy while touring Europe and other faraway places. Although competing lines of flavored coffees continued to multiply while demand for instant coffees in general decreased throughout the 1990s, General Foods International Coffees remained one of the most popular brands in the United States. The "It's How to Unplug" campaign ran in print and broadcast media during 1997 and 1998.

HISTORICAL CONTEXT

General Foods International Coffees were introduced in 1973 by General Foods Corporation. Founded in 1895 by Charles William (C.W.) Post in Battle Creek, Michigan, the firm was originally called Postum Cereal Company Ltd., but in 1922 its name was changed to General Foods. In 1985 the company was purchased by Philip Morris Companies Inc. Three years later Philip Morris also acquired Kraft, Inc., a major manufacturer of cheese and other food products since 1903. The two firms were soon combined to form the nation's largest food company, Kraft General Foods, which was reorganized in 1995 as Kraft Foods, Inc.

The numerous brands made by General Foods included Grape Nuts and Post Toasties cereals, Jell-O gelatin, Log Cabin syrup, Calumet baking powder, Birdseye frozen foods, Oscar Mayer meat products, and a cereal beverage named Postum. For many years the company's Maxwell House coffee was advertised with the famous slogan "Good to the last drop." According to legend, the statement was originally made by President Theodore Roosevelt in 1907 when he tasted the blend in the Maxwell House Hotel in Nashville. In 1988 General Foods introduced Private Collection, a line extension of Maxwell House that featured eight varieties of gourmet coffee beans that consumers could grind at supermarket displays to suit their preferences. Private Collection was intended primarily for professional consumers more than 30 years of age with annual incomes of at least $35,000. In 1992 Maxwell House Cappuccino was introduced as a premium coffee aimed at women more than 35 years of age. General Foods also manufactured ground and instant Sanka, which had been introduced in 1927 as the nation's first decaffeinated coffee and which was most popular with older consumers. During 1998 Kraft promoted Sanka with the tag line "Everything you love about coffee." In addition to Maxwell House and Sanka, Kraft marketed ground and instant Yuban, a coffee made with Colombian beans and billed as "the richest coffee in the world."

General Foods International Coffees were powdered instant beverages complete with nondairy creamer, designed to be stirred into hot water or milk. All 18 varieties in the line were presweetened, but some contained no sugar, no fat, and no caffeine. Chocolate, cinnamon, nonalcoholic liqueurs, and other specialty ingredients were added to make blends such as Orange Cappuccino, Cafe Francais, Cafe Vienna, Irish Mocha Mint, Suisse Mocha, and Kahlua Cafe. Kraft also made a related line of powdered General Foods International English Teasin flavors that included English Breakfast Creme, Viennese Creme, and Island Orange Creme. They were promoted as "tea you scoop instead of steep."

Early advertising for General Foods International Coffees featured spokeswoman Carol Lawrence discussing her European travels and noting that she enjoyed coffee that reminded her of Vienna and other places. "Now I can have the flavor of a European coffeehouse in my own house," read the headline in a magazine advertisement in 1975. Another ad showed Lawrence seated among ferns that bordered an Italian-style lily pond. "I love Italy. I love coffee. I suppose that's why I love everything about Orange Cappuccino," read the headline. Later ads suggested combining the instant coffee with ice cream to make a cool summer drink. Some of the advertisement featured the tag line "It's our flavor that makes us special," while others used the long-running slogan "Celebrate the moments of your life." A campaign during the mid-1990s showed cups of coffee against uncluttered landscapes. "New Irish Cream Cafe. Escape to your own Emerald Isle," read one headline. Steam from the coffee cup formed the ghostly image of a castle against a background of velvety green pasture. Another ad showed the sun setting above the ocean while steam in the shape of a palm tree wafted from a coffee cup. "Escape to your own little island," read the headline.

MUSICAL KIOSKS

In 1994 General Foods International Coffees were advertised on interactive kiosks in music stores. Consumers could watch videos and read music reviews while listening to tracks from more than 40,000 albums. Between selections they saw 10-second advertisements aimed at specific ethnic or age groups or at people interested in certain types of music. To use the kiosks, consumers were required to reveal demographic information such as income, age, address, and favorite genre of music. By the end of November 1994 profiles of 820,000 people who used kiosks nationwide had been compiled into a customer database.

TARGET MARKET

Many advertisements for General Foods International Coffees revolved around visiting a friend, spending time with a husband and children, and other emotional moments. General Foods had identified the needs of its target market by conducting focus groups, often led by psychologists who asked women questions such as how they felt before and after drinking coffee, what sort of people they thought would drink General Foods International Coffees, and how the brand might be incorporated into a person's dreams. The research revealed that most women who purchased the product were amiable, warm, and employed but not obsessed with their careers. Early advertisements for the brand were slanted toward college-age women who had visited foreign countries or who planned to travel some day. The ads were also aimed at nurturing homemakers who drank flavored coffees as a special treat. Over the years the ads showed more interaction among family members, friends, and people who worked together. The "It's How to Unplug" campaign targeted the brand's traditional customers (women 25 to 54 years old) with an emphasis on the idea that General Foods International Coffees could be a pleasant, relaxing self-indulgence amid the pressures of everyday life.

During the 1990s demand for the plain ground coffee typically sold in supermarkets declined. Some Americans drank less coffee because they were concerned that caffeine might harm their health. In addition, many consumers experimented with trendy gourmet blends, while others switched to soft drinks. Positioned as a premium brand that offered a wide assortment of flavors, General Foods International Coffees were often seen as a substitute for a sweet snack. Further, because the coffees came in powder form, the consumer could control the strength of the drink.

COMPETITION

In 1990, at a time when total sales of instant coffee had declined by 9.4 percent in 12 months, sales of General Foods International Coffees increased by 11 percent to

$115.9 million. *Advertising Age* reported that by 1995, with 4.7 percent of the U.S. market, General Foods International Coffees was the fourth most popular coffee of any kind, behind Folgers with 27.4 percent, Maxwell House with 19.2 percent, and private-label brands with 7.6 percent. Hills Bros. and Maxwell House Master Blend each had 4.1 percent, and Taster's Choice had 4.0 percent.

Leading the trend toward specialty coffees, Starbucks Corporation expanded its market rapidly during 1998 by offering premium blends at 3,500 supermarkets in selected regions of the United States. Until 1997 the company had sold coffee primarily through its coffee shops, an idea inspired by the espresso bars of Italy. Founded at Pike's Place Market in Seattle in 1971, the Starbucks chain grew slowly to five cafés by 1982 and then mushroomed to 1,000 by 1996. During 1998 Starbucks opened its first coffee shops in Europe and launched a 250-page Internet site where customers could order coffee on-line. The site included a Coffee Taste Matcher to help consumers decide which of the company's numerous products they would like to sample.

In 1997, according to *Advertising Age,* Procter & Gamble Company spent $65.9 million to advertise its Folgers brand. In April 1998, after Procter & Gamble reduced the price of its instant and ground Folgers coffees by 10 cents, Kraft cut the price of selected Maxwell House coffees by about twice as much. Procter & Gamble had introduced Folgers Custom Blend in 1991 and followed with Folgers French Roast Regular Coffee and Custom Roast Folgers. The company also competed with Starbucks by purchasing the gourmet Millstone brand of specialty coffees in 1995. Within three years Millstone was available at 7,000 supermarkets.

Hills Bros. and Taster's Choice were both made by Nestlé SA, a company based in Switzerland. Its Nescafé brand, one of the first instant coffees launched in the United States and the most popular brand of coffee in the world, had U.S. sales of $14 million in 1998. Nestlé introduced Hills Bros. French Roast in 1992 and in 1994 launched Taster's Choice Flavored Coffee, an instant coffee that was available in Irish crème French vanilla, and hazelnut flavors. Taster's Choice had been advertised for years with the "Romantic Neighbors" campaign, a series of episodes that chronicled the budding romance between two sophisticated neighbors. In 1998 Nestlé launched a new ad campaign to announce that Taster's Choice had been reformulated. The campaign's first television commercial showed various people drinking coffee, and then, through special effects, the pictures were combined to form the image of a coffee cup and a jar of Taster's Choice.

DECORATIVE TINS

General Foods International Coffees were sold in rectangular or oblong tins with ring-pull opening tabs and resealable plastic lids. To help establish a brand identity and to increase sales, the limited-edition tins were sometimes decorated with special designs that encouraged consumers to collect and save them. When a new series of designs was placed on the market, many people purchased an entire set. Floral motifs, reproductions of quilts, European cityscapes, and landscapes were a few of the themes used over the years, with each promotion usually running for about six months. For one series contemporary artists were commissioned to create work that looked as if it had been done by four great European artists: Vincent van Gogh, Pieter Brueghel, Jean-Honor, Fragonard, and Jean-Baptiste-Camille Corot. Kraft sometimes packaged other products, such as Maxwell House Cappuccino, in designer tins as well.

Nestlé also made Coffee-Mate creamers in flavors such as Irish crème and amaretto. Although only 12 percent of American households tended to purchase flavored coffee creamers, the category was growing at a rate of more than 20 percent each year and had sales of nearly $400 million in 1998. Another company, Suiza Foods, made International Delight creamers in hazelnut, French vanilla, and Irish crème flavors. Aimed primarily at women, the product line included single-serve creamers that consumers often added to ordinary coffee at work or in other settings away from home.

MARKETING STRATEGY

The Young & Rubicam advertising agency developed the "It's How to Unplug" campaign to improve brand awareness and to encourage women to drink General Foods International Coffees more frequently. The ads conveyed the message that rich, creamy coffee was a satisfying indulgence to lift the spirits, alleviate stress, and help people enjoy the simple pleasures of life. The campaign ran in print and broadcast media during 1997 and 1998. According to Competitive Media Reporting, Kraft spent $41.2 million to advertise General Foods International Coffees in 1997 and planned to increase its budget by at least $4 million in 1998. *Advertising Age* reported that the brand's advertising budget had been $33.6 million in 1992 and $37.2 million in 1995.

In the fall of 1998 Kraft budgeted an estimated $7 million for television commercials, print advertisements, and freestanding inserts to support the relaunch of Viennese Chocolate Cafe. An advertisement in *People* magazine in November showed an Austrian style of building with a window framed by lace curtains. Bright red flowers below the window emphasized the red in an awning above, which looked exactly like a tin of Viennese Chocolate Cafe. In an elegant typestyle the headline read, "Take the time to stop and smell the chocolate." The ad featured only two additional lines of text: "It's the perfectly chocolate way to unplug. General Foods International Coffees." Viennese Chocolate Cafe had been introduced in 1992 and was relaunched in 1998 after the company's research indicated that chocolate ranked high among consumers' favorite flavors of coffee, second only to vanilla. In 1998 Kraft also launched Cappuccino Coolers, sweetened blends of General Foods International Coffees in hazelnut and French vanilla flavors intended to be mixed with milk and ice and served cold.

OUTCOME

For the fiscal year that ended May 24, 1998, General Foods International Coffees had 19 percent of the market for instant coffee, with sales of $165.7 million, according to *Brandweek.* That year the instant coffee segment of the beverage industry was valued at $855.3 million. Demand for instant coffees sold in supermarkets continued to decline during 1999, however, as consumers purchased Starbucks and other alternative brands. To attract younger consumers, Nestlé relaunched Taster's Choice Instant Coffees in 1999 and introduced a line extension of its Nescafé brand named Frothe, a foamy beverage available in six flavors. Frothe was intended to compete directly with General Foods International Coffees, particularly Cappuccino Coolers. Meanwhile, Procter & Gamble launched the Folgers Whole Bean line of six premium blends, including hazelnut, French vanilla, and French roast flavors.

In March 1999 Kraft ran a sweepstakes to celebrate the 25th anniversary of the launch of General Foods International Coffees. Prizes included two $2,500 cash awards and a trip for two to Paris. A new tag line for General Foods International Coffees, "It stirs the soul," was introduced in February. Like previous advertising for the brand, the new campaign emphasized the satisfying, contemplative state of mind that consumers experienced while relaxing with a cup of their favorite coffee. Television commercials featured actor Armand Assante narrating while women sipped coffee beside a fireplace and on the shore of a lake. One magazine advertisement featured a photograph of flowers, a garden path, an empty chair, and the sun setting over a grassy field. "It's that moment when you discover there's a resort outside your back door," read the headline.

FURTHER READING

"Brand Scorecard." *Advertising Age,* October 5, 1992, p. 16.

"Coffee and Tea Cup Runneth Under." *Marketing & Media Decisions,* October 1983, p. 179.

Freeman, Laurie. "Specialty Coffees' Thirst Grows Unquenchable." *Advertising Age,* September 30, 1996, p. S14.

Kanner, Bernice. "The Secret Life of the Female Customer." *Working Woman,* December 1990, p. 68.

Masterson, Peg. "Top 100 Succumbs to Specialty Coffees' Aroma." *Advertising Age,* September 29, 1993, p. 30.

McMath, Robert. "Multiplicity of Ways to Drink and Serve Coffee." *Brandweek,* October 12, 1992, p. 25.

Postlewaite, Kimbra. "Powder Potential." *Beverage Industry,* July 1998, p. 10.

Susan Risland

IT'S NOT DELIVERY, IT'S DIGIORNO CAMPAIGN

OVERVIEW

Owned since 1988 by the Philip Morris Companies, Inc., Kraft is the largest U.S.-based packaged food company in the world. It traces its history to three separate and successful entrepreneurs of the late-19th and early-20th centuries: J. L. Kraft, who began a wholesale cheese business in Chicago in 1903; Oscar Mayer, who in 1906 was one of the first meat packers to receive a Federal Meat Inspection stamp of approval; and C. W. Post, who put Grape-Nuts cereal on the market in 1897. Kraft owns and markets more than 70 major brands, many of which were the first of their kind and have become deeply entrenched in 20th-century American popular culture, most notably Velveeta cheese, Jell-O gelatin, Kool-Aid, Kraft cheeses, Oscar Mayer meats, Maxwell House coffees, Post ready-to-eat cereals, Stove Top stuffing mixes, and Miracle Whip salad dressing. In 1989 Kraft introduced a newcomer to that august family of products: DiGiorno brand refrigerated pastas and sauces. Kraft's long history of food industry firsts continued when the company expanded the DiGiorno brand line in 1995 by introducing DiGiorno Rising Crust Pizza, the first frozen pizza with a fresh-frozen, not precooked, crust.

Using an advertising campaign designed by Foote Cone & Belding, Chicago, that included in-store product sampling as well as television and print advertising, DiGiorno Rising Crust Pizza met with immediate positive response. The campaign, with a reported $11 million budget, kicked off on television in select markets in 1996 and 1997. Print advertising continued the campaign in 1998. The campaign was updated and enhanced in subsequent years to support extensions to the rising crust pizza line.

DiGiorno was a breakout success in its category; in its first year, even before it was in national distribution, it had sales of $125 million, and it ended 1997 with a sales volume of $200 million. In fact, DiGiorno became one of the fastest product successes ever at Kraft, rivaling Oscar Mayer Lunchables for its speed in breaking the $100 million sales mark while at the same time garnering a repeat purchase rate of 50 percent. The campaign's tagline, "It's not delivery, it's DiGiorno," successfully drove home the message with consumers that the DiGiorno was as good as the pizza delivered from their favorite take-out pizzeria.

HISTORICAL CONTEXT

In the summer of 1997 Kraft downsized its corporate structure, merging several divisions and creating a joint coffee and cereals division, a beverages and desserts division, and a "New Meals" division, into which category DiGiorno Rising Crust Pizza was placed. The reorganization fell together with changes in the executive ranks—Bob Eckert was named president and CEO following the departure of Robert Morrison in October 1997—and with an agency realignment. Kraft ended its relationship with the New York-based Grey Advertising, Inc. Its remaining agencies include Foote Cone & Belding and Leo Burnett, both of Chicago, and New York's Ogilvy & Mather, Y&R Advertising, and J. Walter Thompson. Foote Cone & Belding was chosen to create the advertising for DiGiorno Rising Crust Pizza and later for Tombstone Rising Crust Pizza, an in-house competitor.

The company architect of the DiGiorno Rising Crust Pizza phenomenon was Arthur Reingold, senior brand manager for DiGiorno Rising Crust from early 1994 to 1996. From formulation of the original idea to machinery to marketing, Reingold led a team that in effect let loose a frozen pizza revolution in 1996. When Reingold was assigned to the Kraft Pizza division in Glenview, Illinois, in 1994, he and his team began seriously discussing an idea that had been floating around for some time. The idea was the creation of a premium frozen pizza, a supermarket pie that could rival, and possibly beat, the offerings of a good pizzeria. This level of quality was considered an unattainable goal, but as Reingold discussed it with Frank Cole, who had been part of the General Foods (GF) organization in the 1980s—when GF had patented baking processes for other products to make them rise and bake up fresh in the oven—the idea took more concrete form. Cole retrieved the research, and Reingold and his team went to work on it. The result was the "rising crust" in DiGiorno Rising Crust Pizza. Unlike conventional frozen pizzas, DiGiorno's crust was not precooked. It baked in the oven as it was prepared, rising and creating a fresh-baked bread aroma.

In addition to quality, convenience was a prime consideration in the development of DiGiorno Rising Crust. The pizza was designed to go into the oven without preheating so that consumers could do other things while the meal was baking.

FIRST CHEESE

The cheese covering DiGiorno Rising Crust Pizza is not just any cheese—it is one of a long line of "firsts" Kraft has developed over the decades. Kraft cheese was the first to appear in many different forms and packages, some of which dramatically changed the way cheese was marketed and used by customers. Kraft processed cheese, developed in 1915 and patented in 1916 after many years of experimentation, was among the first and most successful of its kind. The new cheese had an extended shelf life and uniform flavor and was sold in convenient packaging. Kraft was also the first to sell processed cheese in individually wrapped slices (and later shredded or as strings); before that, cheese had been sliced by the retailer, so consumers could not know for sure which brand they were buying. It also had a short shelf life, quickly drying out or becoming moldy. Another first for Kraft was the development of nonfat cheese.

TARGET MARKET

The "It's Not Delivery, It's DiGiorno" campaign targeted an audience of adults aged 25 to 54. The tighter focus was on adults 44 and younger with incomes of $40,000 and above who were medium to heavy users of carry-out pizza parlors such as Pizza Hut.

COMPETITION

Supermarket frozen pizza was a hot sales category in 1997, growing by double digits in that year at least in part due to the extraordinary success of DiGiorno Rising

Crust. That success notwithstanding, DiGiorno Rising Crust Pizza still faced stiff competition on two fronts: among purveyors of fresh pizza and in supermarket freezers. DiGiorno Rising Crust had been created to go up against fresh take-out pizza, such as that sold by Pizza Hut, Papa John's, and others, and those remained its primary competitors. In the supermarket pizza category, a major new competitor to DiGiorno Rising Crust was Freschetta frozen pizza.

Although DiGiorno's place at the top of the list of rising crust frozen pizzas remained secure throughout 1997, Freschetta's $56 million in sales during its first year landed it the number 10 spot on the 1997 "Top 10 New Product Pacesetters" list drawn up annually by Information Resources, Inc., of Chicago. The makers of Freschetta, Schwan's Sales Enterprises of Minnesota, were newcomers to the rising-crust pizza market but long-time competitors of Kraft. Schwan's, which primarily marketed the Tony's and Red Baron brand pizzas, introduced Freschetta into four markets in October 1996 and had moved the product into about half of the country by May 1997. The Freschetta advertising campaign from Bozell Advertising, Minneapolis, included television spots, magazine ads, outdoor posters and billboards, coupons, and in-store sampling, Brand Manager Tom Bierbaum told *Advertising Age.* The name Freschetta, Bierbaum said, was created to suggest flavor "like the old country" and "to marry its authentic taste with freshness." Schwan's total budget for all pizza advertising was $7 million in 1996.

The overwhelming success of DiGiorno Rising Crust also spawned competition from within the company itself. Kraft competed with itself by marketing a similar entry into the frozen pizza market under the Tombstone brand name, which Kraft had acquired in 1986. During the research and development stage of DiGiorno Rising Crust, Kraft had at one point considered marketing the final product under the Tombstone name but instead decided on DiGiorno to help position it as a high-quality Italian meal. Retailing at a slightly lower price and planned specifically to go up against Freschetta, Tombstone Rising Crust likewise used ads from Foote Cone & Belding. The advertising plan included television spots, free-standing inserts, and sampling, with consumer promotions handled by Davidson Marketing. Television spots showed the Tombstone character in a variety of precarious situations, including sinking in quicksand and ready for hanging at the gallows. When asked what he wanted on his tombstone, he answered, "A crust that rises."

In April 1997 Tombstone was sold in about 80 percent of the country. Kraft also owns a third entry in the supermarket pizza category, Jack's, which is sold mainly in the Midwest and the South and did not seriously threaten DiGiorno's lead.

According to Information Resources, Kraft, including Jack's brand, held the largest share of the frozen pizza market in 1997, with 35 percent, while Schwan's, the makers of Freschetta, had a market share of 23.7 percent.

MARKETING STRATEGY

Reingold and his team took the finished product to focus groups, who were highly enthusiastic—in fact, their reaction, as Reingold recalled, was "wow." Bearing the pizza in one hand and stacks of glowing consumer group reports in the other, Reingold approached top management for funding for development of the rather complicated machinery that would be needed for mass production of the rising crust pizza. The product was introduced to a test market in about 6 percent of the country in 1995. In a departure from normal test market procedure, Reingold began tracking sales on a weekly basis and setting weekly goals. The product was an instant hit; by October of that year, distribution had doubled. In fact, demand was so much higher than expected that Reingold and other Kraft officials were initially unsure how much to produce. "How high was high?" Reingold wondered. "We didn't want to commit to markets we couldn't service."

The advertising agency Foote Cone & Belding had been brought into the project at the focus group stage. FCB developed television and print/outdoor advertising with the tag line "It's Not Delivery, It's DiGiorno," which featured consumers trying the product—at a party, for example—and finding it so good that they assumed it was pizzeria pizza. Because the test market had shown that sampling would be crucial to DiGiorno's success (*Advertising Age* reported that about 25 percent of the total budget went to sampling rather than advertising), the direct sales force sent into stores for in-store sampling received extra training. The company also developed the DiGiorno Travelin' Pizzeria, an 18-foot truck that could distribute samples at events and in parking lots.

The rollout continued, and by 1996 DiGiorno was available in about 80 percent of the United States. The Travelin' Pizzeria reached 63 different markets, and in July 1997 the "DiGiorno Hot Air Balloon Tour" was added to the list of marketing strategies. The enormous balloon was adorned with a huge "pizza" ("a larger than life crust that literally rises," as the company described it). It made stops across the country, offering balloon rides to members of the media as well as to consumers.

Kraft supported the DiGiorno introduction with an $11 million budget, a little more than the $9 million it allocated to its in-house rival Tombstone. Television advertising took place in selected markets around the country during 1996 and the first three quarters of 1997. In the last quarter of 1997, television spots were shown on national networks. Print advertising, which carried into 1998, was focused on general interest and entertainment publications, and included *Entertainment Weekly, Style, People, TV Guide, Rolling Stone,* and *ESPN Magazine.* Men were specifically targeted with ads in *Esquire* and *GQ,* and gourmet cooks with ads in *Bon Appetit.*

The campaign was expanded in 1999 to support the introduction of several new flavor varieties of the popular pizza brand. According to a report in *Frozen Food Age,* soft drinks are the top beverage consumed with pizza, and tapping into the information Kraft launched a joint venture with its DiGiorno brand and Coca Cola that included in-store displays and other merchandising.

In 2000, a new series of television spots were added to the campaign to support the launch of DiGiorno's Half & Half Rising Crust pizzas. One spot was based on a scene from the Alfred Hitchcock thriller, *Psycho,* and included the familiar tagline, "It's not delivery, it's DiGiorno."

A new spin was put on the "It's Not Delivery, It's DiGiorno" campaign in 2001 when Kraft launched a new promotion, "Be a DiGiorno Delivery Guy," with the prize for one winner, who would not deliver pizza, was $100,000 cash and a new Chrysler PT Cruiser. A television spot supporting the promotion showed a "slacker" visiting an unemployment office responding to a job offer on a DiGiorno pizza box. The woman working behind the counter said that DiGiorno is not delivery pizza. Print ads appeared in *People* magazine and an insert was included in newspapers. The promotion and campaign was repeated in 2002.

The tagline got a twist in a 2003 television spot that featured ESPN and ABC announcers for the National College Athletic Association, Bill Rafferty and Dick Vitale. During the spot the usually verbose Vitale was quiet as he enjoyed a slice of DiGiorno pizza. Rafferty thanked the pizza delivery guy for finding the secret to keeping Vitale quiet, but Vitale had the last word when he reminded Rafferty, "It's not deliver. It's DiGiorno, baby."

OUTCOME

The marketing campaign for DiGiorno Rising Crust Pizza was by all measures a resounding success. The level of sales and the results of the sales analysis were both very satisfying to the company. While Reingold and the others admitted to some spillover from buyers of the Kraft Tombstone and Jack's frozen pizzas, the greater part of sales came from increased frozen pizza usage.*Food and Beverage Marketing* reported that roughly half of DiGiorno volume was new to the category and that both category spending and household penetration had grown at a much higher rate in DiGiorno markets than in non-DiGiorno markets. Moreover, qualitative research indicated that many consumers were replacing some of their spending at pizza parlors with DiGiorno. Repeat purchase levels exceeded 50 percent, the second highest repeat levels in the history of Kraft foods.

Food and Beverage Marketing also described surveys that noted that a strong brand relationship had been established with consumers. The impact of the product, and the impact of the ongoing marketing campaign, was such that DiGiorno was able to establish brand equity in its first year in the nation's supermarket freezers. DiGiorno also received accolades from *Consumer Reports,* which declared in its January 1997 issue that DiGiorno Rising Crust "tastes almost as good as pizza-chain pizza and costs less."

The 2001 and 2002 "Be the DiGiorno Delivery Guy" promotions were a notable success. Andrea Brown, the brand's director of consumer promotion told *Promo* magazine, that the contest was run two years because "it resonated so well with consumers, retailers, and the sales force that it was a must to repeat." In 2002, *Promo* named DiGiorno Rising Crust pizzas as one of the year's Best Promoted Brands, due to the success of the ongoing "It's Not Delivery, It's DiGiorno" campaign. The "It's Not Delivery, It's DiGiorno" campaign was updated and enhanced each year as new products in Kraft's rising crust pizza line were added. In 2003, the campaign was recognized by *Frozen Food Age* for Excellence in Marketing. Some 10 years after the campaign's 1996 launch, it and the iconic tagline were still reminding consumers, "It's not delivery, it's DiGiorno."

FURTHER READING

"A Meal That's Easy as Pie." *Consumer Reports* January, 1997, p. 19.

"DiGiorno Raises Dough—Fast!." *Frozen Food Age,* August 1, 1997.

"Freschetta Pizza Makes IRI's Top 10 for 1997." *Frozen Food Age,* June 1, 1998.

Harrison, Dan. "DiGiorno Widens First Place Position in Pizza." *Frozen Food Age,* July 1, 1999.

Harrison, Dan. "Rising Crust Pizza Rolls On." *Frozen Food Age,* January 1, 1999.

"He Delivers! (DiGiorno Rising Crust Brand Manager Arthur Reingold)." *Food & Beverage Marketing,* April 1, 1997.

Kirk, Jim. "Chicago Tribune Marketing Column (Vitale Pitches Pizza)." *Chicago Tribune,* March 6, 2003.

Petrecca, Laura, and Judann Pollack. "Kraft Dumps Grey in Advertising Shift." *Crain's Chicago Business,* March 9, 1998.

Pollack, Judann. "Kraft's DiGiorno Sparks Rising Crust Pizza Rivals." *Advertising Age,* April 28, 1997.

Thompson, Stephanie. "DiGiorno Keeps Delivery Theme for New Promo; In a Twist on Tagline, Brand Pledges Big Payoff for Not Delivering Pizzas." *Advertising Age,* April 2, 2001.

———. "Tombstone Rings Dip Into Snacktime; Kraft's New Doughnut-Shaped Pizza to Arrive with Mom-Focused Ads." *Advertising Age,* March 20, 2000.

Susan M. Steiner
Rayna Bailey

Labatt USA

101 Merrit 7
Norwalk, Connecticut 06856
USA
Telephone: (203) 750-6600
Web site: www.labattblue.com

■■■

ROLLING ROCK ADS CAMPAIGN

OVERVIEW

NOTE: Also see essay for InBev USA.

In February 1998 Labatt USA, a division of Labatt, Inc., of Canada, increased its ad spending by 40 percent as part of a five-year plan to become the largest import/specialty beer marketer in the United States. A good portion of the increase was spent on an aggressive marketing push for Rolling Rock, a product of the Latrobe Brewing Company. Although Rolling Rock was the company's premier domestic brand, it was beset by stagnant sales. Labatt USA charged the New York-based ad agency Ammirati Puris Lintas with the task of creating a new campaign for Rolling Rock. Television spots made their debut later in 1998 and continued into 1999. The ads, which emphasized Rolling Rock's core equities of distinctiveness and quality, were supplied by bicoastal X-Ray Productions. The campaign also had a print component, created by the Bartle Bogle Hegarty agency.

HISTORICAL CONTEXT

Rolling Rock had been brewed in Latrobe, a town located in the Appalachian Mountains of Pennsylvania, about 25 miles east of Pittsburgh, since 1939. In its early days Rolling Rock was a core-market beer that was sold largely in seven-ounce bottles, called "ponies" or "pork chops" by the locals. Early radio ads for the brand proclaimed, "From the rolling hills of the Laurel Highlands: Rolling Rock."

Like most of the other medium-sized regional firms that survived the growth of national breweries in the postwar era, Latrobe plowed profits back into its physical plant and thus kept up with advances in brewing machinery and techniques. From around 3,000 barrels in 1939, Rolling Rock's output peaked at 715,000 barrels. But by 1987 sales had shrunk to 450,000 barrels a year. In order to allow sales to grow, the founding Tito family found itself forced to sell the brewery to a major player.

In 1987 Labatt USA acquired Rolling Rock, ushering in six years of rapid growth for the brand. Sales in Boston, New York, and other markets benefited from shrewd positioning by Labatt. The new owner took a brand that was a regional mainstream beer and reintroduced it to other markets as a specialty beer. On-premise sales were driven by a specially painted bottle. By 1993, however, the brand was once again stagnating. Sales stalled at about 1 million barrels in that year, just as "craft beers" from microbreweries started catching on. The craze for craft brews kept sales of Rolling Rock at about this level until 1997 when, after years of double-digit growth, the expansion of the craft brew segment slowed.

With microbrews clearly falling out of favor, Labatt USA concluded that it could boost sales of Rolling Rock by 5 percent with a plan that involved $12 million in media support, including the brand's first network television exposure. In early 1998 Labatt announced plans to spend more than $20 million in media advertising for the coming year. Its priorities included the first national network TV buy for Rolling Rock; new creative and increased spending for its Mexican beers Dos Equis, Tecate, and Sol; expanded TV support for the Canadian import Labatt Blue; and a campaign for the newly acquired Dutch brew Carlsberg.

TARGET MARKET

Males in their 20s were the principal target market for beer. About 75 percent of all beer in the United States was consumed by men. Since the late 1970s, however, the number of beer drinkers had been declining. The trade publication *Beer Marketer's Insights* reported a correlation between a decline in males aged 18 to 24 with a decline in beer sales in areas such as California, New England, and the mid-Atlantic states. Not only were there fewer young people, but fewer young people were drinking, and those who continued to drink were drinking less. A 1998 study conducted by the *Journal of Studies on Alcohol* found that the number of men who identified themselves as frequent drinkers of alcohol had declined and that the number of infrequent drinkers and abstainers had increased.

Some brewing companies responded to the shrinking target market by tailoring their advertising to create a strong relationship between their beers and their customers. "We've been dealing with a flat to declining market for close to a decade," said Susan Henderson, a spokeswoman for the Miller Brewing Company. "To have compelling branded messages that gain loyalty for responsible uses for our products is job number one." Other brewers chose not to target young drinkers specifically. "We're not constantly trying to figure out what the best way to talk to a 21-year-old is," commented Tom Cardella, a vice president of Labatt USA. As a higher-priced specialty brand, Rolling Rock had a marketing strategy that was not geared toward replenishing the supply of young beer drinkers. Instead, marketing efforts in the late 1990s focused on Rolling Rock's heritage as a small Pennsylvania brewer.

The aim was not to target all young beer drinkers but to appeal to a discrete portion of the market. "We have identified a group in the market called premium packaged lager triallists," explained Rolling Rock marketing manager Susan Keyes. "These people try different brands but are not loyal to any particular one. They are 12 percent of [premium-packaged lager] drinkers and account for 20 percent of volume." Rolling Rock's marketing research showed that young premium-packaged lager drinkers liked to keep up with the latest fashions in beer drinking. According to Keyes, "They believe what they drink says a lot about them. They have a 'live for the weekend' attitude." Wooing these consumers emerged as a priority for Rolling Rock in the late 1990s.

COMPETITION

Beer advertising took an unconventional turn in 1997 as competitors such as Miller Lite, Miller Genuine Draft, Heineken, and Bass Aleeach launched edgy campaigns designed to break the mold of the traditional approach. By the next year, however, puzzled responses from consumers and wholesalers prompted almost all of the brewers to abandon entertainment-oriented ads and to shift back to product and user themes.

Miller provided the most prominent example of this retrenchment. In 1997 the struggling number two brewer unveiled a series of quirky commercials for its two most popular brands, Lite and Genuine Draft. The ads in the Lite campaign featured a character dubbed Dick, a fictional advertising executive. One of the first commercials showed a man emerging from a field without pants, his genitals covered by a Miller logo. The Genuine Draft ads, shot in black and white, employed quick-cut editing and relied on music instead of a spoken narrative or dialogue, creating an effect that was akin to a music video.

Miller's sales initially improved, and company executives crowed that the ads deserved some of the credit. Several Miller wholesalers complained about the ads, however, and in 1998 sales resumed their decline. Some members of the advertising industry trade press criticized the ads for alienating Miller's older drinkers. "That's the danger of so-called 'edgy' humor," said former Heineken USA executive Philip Van Munching. "You get 'em with one ad and turn 'em off with the next. It's a stupid way to advertise your product."

Coors, the number three U.S. brewer, enjoyed more success with its unconventional approach. Its 1998 campaign featuring the tag line "Hey Beer Man" was targeted to young men. Coors also increased its ad support for Zima, a citrus-flavored malt beverage positioned as a hip alternative to beer.

MARKETING STRATEGY

According to Labatt USA's official positioning statement, Rolling Rock was "unique and distinctive from all other beers. Rolling Rock consumers tend to be people that are looking for things outside the mainstream. They want something different. Rolling Rock is a lager, so it's more like mainstream beers, but it has a little more body, a little more bite than the traditional lagers. Then there's the quirkiness of the brand, the 33 [printed on the bottle], the horsehead, the small town origin.

THE MYSTERY OF "33"

An element of Rolling Rock's appeal involved the unexplained "33" on the back of each silk-screened green bottle. What did it mean? Where did it come from? Why was it there? The number had provided hours of conversation in bars over the years, not to mention E-mails, Internet discussions, and late-night college bull sessions. The brand did its own promotions on the question, offering contests for the best explanations.

The most common answer was that the number referred to 1933, the year of the repeal of Prohibition in the United States. Other popular explanations were that 33 was the number of words in the original Rolling Rock advertising slogan, the number of letters in the ingredients of the beer (hops, malt, water, rice, corn, brewer's yeast), and the number of the race horse on the bottle (the horse's number was not shown).

Even the brewery's owners, Labatt USA, professed to be mystified about the origin of the number. "The 33 is the first thing people ask me about," said Darin Wolf, Labatt USA's director of marketing for the brand. Quirky ad campaigns were spun around the number, one noting the synchronicity of the number and Super Bowl XXXIII and another coinciding with the introduction of the 33-cent stamp.

What was the real truth about the mysterious 33? The straight story was this. The Latrobe Brewing Company was originally a satellite of the Pittsburgh Brewing Company, best known as the brewers of Iron City Beer. After the repeal of Prohibition, Pittsburgh sold off its smaller brewing facilities, and the Latrobe brewery was bought by five brothers from the town—Frank, Joseph, Robert, Ralph, and Anthony Tito. The Titos sold beer for five years but wanted to launch a new brand that would get sales going on an upward trend. They came up with a name, Rolling Rock, but were looking for a slogan that covered all of the salient facts without taking up too much space.

According to James Tito, a member of the family, whoever came up with the slogan proudly scrawled "33" at the bottom of it to show how concise it was. The brewery sent the slogan off on the original sheet of paper, forgetting to tell the printer that the "33" was not part of the advertising. Thousands of fairly expensive silk-screened bottles later, the brewery realized that it had a problem. After considering the price of destroying the bottles and of silk-screening new ones, the brewery decided to let them go out without explanation. It was a surprisingly smart move.

Everything we do tries to position the brand as different from other beers."

For many years Labatt USA did not do much to plant this image of Rolling Rock in the public mind. Stagnant sales, however, finally prompted the company to launch a full-scale restaging of the brand, aimed at changing its image from a laid-back discovery for 30-somethings to a leading-edge streetwise brew for 20- to 25-year-olds. The restaging dropped references to mountain springs to offset consumers' misperceptions that Rolling Rock was watery. It also cleared the way for a national rollout for a line extension, Rock Light, after two decades of being limited mainly to the core Pennsylvania and Ohio markets.

The 1998 Rolling Rock marketing initiative represented the biggest-ever TV buy for the brand. During the spring and fall of 1998, Labatt USA ran a mix of seven 30-second spots and four 15-second spots during sports telecasts and prime-time and late-night network and cable TV programming. The humorous ads from Ammirati Puris Lintas revolved around Rolling Rock's distinctive green, painted bottle.

On August 24 the print campaign for Rolling Rock, devised by Bartle Bogle Hegarty, was unveiled. The print ads challenged consumers to take actions depending on five rolls of dice. They included winking at a newsagent, growing a moustache, and asking a stranger the time in a Danish accent. The print ads, which carried the tag line "On a roll with a rock," ran in entertainment listings magazines, including *Time Out,* and were supported by a corresponding poster campaign. Labatt USA also ran a separate summer promotion in which consumers could get posters of artists' renditions of the Rolling Rock bottle.

Rolling Rock was a specialty product that relied on package design for its main means of brand recognition, and so its bottle played an important role in the repositioning of the brand. Rolling Rock officials considered its green glass, long neck, and mysterious "33" as core equities. "Everything revolves around the longneck bottle," according to Brad Hittle, group director of marketing at Labatt USA. "Consistency is the name of the game when you're a niche player." The taller container with the painted label provided "genuine character" to the brand, Hittle said. As for the green, blue, and white presentation, he added, "They're not sexy colors. But that's what the consumers like."

There was only one problem. Until 1998 the painted long-necked bottles of Rolling Rock were available only on-premise, that is, in bars and restaurants. Some years earlier, as a cost-cutting measure, the brand had gone to paper labels for off-premise sales. But according to Rolling Rock marketing executive Joe Gruss, the change had caused a problem. "We were known for the silk-screened bottles. People would drink it in those bottles on-premise. When they got to the store to buy beer to take home and saw paper labels, it was kind of a let-down. It was the same beer, it was just a perception change."

In 1998 Labatt decided to return to selling Rolling Rock exclusively in long-necked, painted bottles. Doing so required the brewer to raise prices almost 50 cents per six-pack, thus repositioning the brew between domestic premium and specialty beers. But the decision to go to the painted bottles exclusively had an unexpected result that made the higher costs a moot point. "When we made the decision to eliminate the paper labels, we did quite a bit of quantitative research on the change, and the perception of the new packaging," said marketing executive Darin Wolf. "Not only were consumers willing to pay more for the silk-screened bottles, they actually expected to pay more."

OUTCOME

Rolling Rock's 1998 ad campaign, stressing its Pennsylvania heritage and distinctive green bottle, was one of the big winners at the 14th Annual "Best of New York" Addy Awards honoring the best creative advertising of the year. The campaign won three Addies in the alcoholic beverages category for the spots titled "Thirsty," "History," and "Evolution."

The campaign also proved popular with Rolling Rock wholesalers, who seemed pleased that advertising support was finally being provided for the brand, even if they did not fully comprehend the strategy. "They seem to be working," one wholesaler said of the Rolling Rock ads. Then he added, in a comment typical of wholesalers on any brand of beer advertising in the 1990s, "Besides, I don't know what we're looking for in beer ads any more."

FURTHER READING

Khermouch, Gary. "Labatt to Juice Dos Equis, Rock in '98." *Brandweek,* December 15, 1997.

"Rocking and Rolling." *Grocer,* May 29, 1999.

Robert Schnakenberg

Las Vegas Convention & Visitors Authority

3150 Paradise Road
Las Vegas, Nevada 89109
USA
Telephone: (702) 892-0711
Web site: www.lvcva.com

VEGAS STORIES CAMPAIGN

OVERVIEW

Between 2000 and 2002 the number of visitors to Las Vegas dipped from 35.8 million to 35 million. Analysts blamed the slump on the terrorist attacks of September 11, 2001, and the sprawl of Native-American-owned casinos across America, along with a sudden increase in jurisdictions allowing gambling. The Las Vegas Convention & Visitors Authority (LVCVA), whose primary duty was to market Southern Nevada as a premier destination for leisure and business travel, drew its funding from Nevada's room tax. In hopes of branding Las Vegas as a leisure destination for people craving indulgence and an escape from their humdrum lives, LVCVA released its "Vegas Stories" campaign in January 2003. It differed from past LVCVA campaigns that advertised Las Vegas's exquisite hotels, golf courses, and entertainment.

The $58 million campaign was originally scheduled for 20 months and featured the tagline "What happens here, stays here." After achieving considerable success it continued into 2005. Conceived by the ad agency R&R Partners, the campaign appeared across print, Internet, outdoor, and television mediums. Suggesting that people did not always want to disclose what they did in Las Vegas, the spots were based on true stories. Several commercials merely featured people, usually in their twenties or thirties, who were suspiciously vague about what they actually did during recent Las Vegas vacations. When asked about their trip, the travelers grew quickly uncomfortable and fabricated hardly cohesive stories. Some spots featured people completely reluctant to talk about their Las Vegas trip.

Shrouded in controversy almost from its conception, "Vegas Stories" commercials were banned from airing during the 2003 Super Bowl. Las Vegas businesses also voiced their difficulty in hiring out-of-state employees after the campaign's tagline boasted of Las Vegas's immoral side. Despite the discord, the campaign prompted *Brandweek* magazine to bestow R&R Partners with its Grand Marketer of the Year award. The campaign also helped reverse Las Vegas's visitor decline. In 2004 the city hosted 37.4 million visitors, which was 2.4 million more than in 2002.

HISTORICAL CONTEXT

The LVCVA advertising account had been handled by Las Vegas–based R&R Partners since 1981. Not only had R&R Partners helped Las Vegas become one of America's fastest-growing cities by the late 1990s, but it had also helped brand Las Vegas as a popular destination for art, musicals, and world-class cuisine. Erika Brandvik, PR manager at LVCVA, told *PR Week US,* "The fact is 15 years ago there were only two states where you could gamble, and now you can engage in some form of gambling in 48 of the 50 states. So just being a gaming destination isn't going to do it for people anymore."

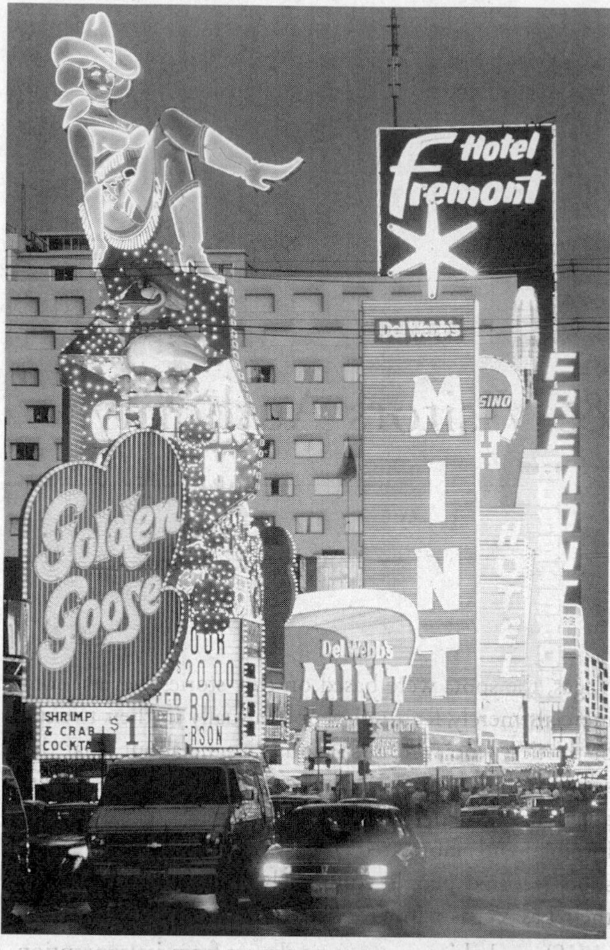

© DAVE BARTRUFF/CORBIS.

In March 1999 R&R Partners released a campaign titled "Las Vegas—It's anything and everything," which appeared during the same year that luxury hotels such as the Venetian, Mandalay Bay, Bellagio, and Paris opened along the Las Vegas strip. Soon afterward an R&R Partners survey revealed that most visitors were attracted to Las Vegas's unrestricted atmosphere. To hype the city's liberated environment the agency released a campaign called "Freedom Party." It involved the construction of the website www.vegasfreedom.com and ads announcing a fictitious presidential candidate who, incidentally, belonged to an equally fictitious "Freedom Party."

To stoke Las Vegas's convention business, the "We Work as Hard as We Play" campaign appeared just before the terrorist attacks of September 11, 2001. R&R Partners valued the campaign but wanted to also target leisure travelers by branding Las Vegas as a "commitment-free, pressure-free, judgment-free" destination. After fumbling with such taglines as "Las Vegas: You know how it goes," "Vegas: Keep it between us," and "Las Vegas: Get in on the secret," Jason Hoff and Jeff Candido, copywriters at R&R Partners, chose "What happens here, stays here," the previous motto of men misbehaving in remote locations.

TARGET MARKET

During the campaign's first year, "Vegas Stories" targeted 21- to 35-year-olds with a penchant for adult entertainment. The first television spots, aired in January 2003, suggested that Las Vegas was a place where businesswomen led double lives, coeds engaged in one-night stands, and groups of friends got so drunk at night that members of the party would be missing the next morning. As the campaign continued and its popularity increased, its target market was expanded. By 2005 the campaign's commercials became more ambiguous to broaden their appeal. Candido told the *Washington Post,* "They're successful because people can imagine more than what we show. A grandmother who sees these spots can imagine that [the debauchery] is spending too much time at the buffet. The 23-year-old bachelor party guys can have their own ideas about what went on." To widen their target R&R Partners also created spots that featured elderly couples, African-American and Latino women, middle-aged couples, and a sexually ambiguous character.

LVCVA and R&R Partners later began targeting different archetypes that they created for the campaign. One such archetype, titled "The Admiral's Club," was profiled as a heavy traveler and recreational gambler, usually 35 years of age or older, with a household income of more than $50,000 and who read magazines such as *Golf Digest, Sports Illustrated,* and *Playboy.* "The Cultured Pearl" was described as a high-power businesswoman whose household income exceeded $100,000. "Fashionistas" were flashy, domestic travelers who enjoyed recreational gambling, were sometimes college-educated, and watched TV shows like *Will & Grace, American Idol,* and *The Bachelorette* at night. The "Jack & Diane" archetype was described as a married-with-children suburbanite who took short vacations and enjoyed heavy recreational gambling. Lastly, "Mr. Saturday Night," was depicted as a unmarried man who earned more than $50,000 annually, preferred high-energy activities, was a modest gambler, and watched television shows like *Fear Factor, Survivor, The Apprentice,* and *The Contender.*

COMPETITION

As with Las Vegas, room tax also provided a marketing budget for the gambling-friendly city of Reno, located 450 miles north of Las Vegas. In 2003 Reno-Sparks

$1 DEAL

The Las Vegas Convention & Visitors Authority (LVCVA) formed a committee in 2005 to investigate its president and CEO, Rossi Ralenkotter. Without consulting his board members Ralenkotter had sold rights to LVCVA's popular slogan, "What happens here, stays here," back to the advertising agency that created it, R&R Partners, for the price of $1. After further investigation Ralenkotter's name was cleared. Analysts, however, criticized him for selling the slogan, which could have generated millions of dollars in licensing agreements. Before the sale R&R Partners convinced Ralenkotter that they were more prepared to protect the slogan from copycats and opportunists.

Convention & Visitors Authority (RSCVA) released a campaign titled "America's Adventure Place," referring to Reno, which was still reeling from the popularity of Native-American casinos and from public unease over possible terrorist attacks. Las Vegas was generating seven times Reno's gambling revenue; many of Reno's casinos were in desperate need of renovation. "We found Reno didn't have a great perception in our (tourist) market," Deanna Ashby, the RSCVA executive marketing director, told the *Reno Gazette-Journal.* She described Reno's previous image as "a place where you can get your teeth knocked out in a barroom brawl."

In 2004 the $1.5 million Truckee River Whitewater Park was built in the heart of downtown Reno. With 8,000 tons of concrete the city converted a 2,600-foot stretch of the Truckee River into class II and class III rapids for kayakers. Print and television spots for "America's Adventure Place" aired in California's Bay Area and Sacramento markets. Commercials portrayed Reno as a popular destination for nightlife, hiking, mountain biking, and white-water kayaking. Print ads with the tagline "360 Degrees of Adventure" showed panoramic collages of similar activities. Despite most of Reno's visitors being age 55 or older, the campaign focused on a younger demographic of outdoor enthusiasts. By 2004 Reno had finally stopped the diminution of its tourist industry, but the city still had not regained the 5.1 million visitor count it saw in 2000.

MARKETING STRATEGY

"Vegas Stories" was a major departure from previous LVCVA campaigns, in that it did not flaunt the famous Las Vegas strip, show the insides of casinos, or display forms of adult entertainment. Instead it strove to brand Las Vegas as a retreat for adults searching for guilt-free fun. For instance, in the 30-second spot "Parents," two parents confronted their teenage son, who had hosted a house party while they were away at Las Vegas. When asked what he had done all weekend, the son replied, "Nothing." When he asked his parents the same question, they sheepishly replied, "Nothing." In contrast to past LVCVA campaigns, the "Parents" spot was not even set in Las Vegas. "We're developing a brand rather than a product," Rob Dondero, an executive vice president of R&R Partners, told *Adweek.*

The campaign's first spots, which began airing in January 2003, were slightly more risqué and were eventually banned from appearing during the 2003 Super Bowl. Several Las Vegas businesses also claimed that the spots marred the city's reputation as a respectable place to work. Directed by Bryan Buckley, the commercials showed, for instance, a businesswoman impulsively marrying a handsome, non-English-speaking man and then hurriedly insisting, "I have to get back to my convention." In another spot a young woman justified her one-night stand to her girlfriends by insisting, "He's a juggler and he had very nice hands." In a commercial featuring a group of middle-aged men recovering from a night of overindulgence, one man asked, "We've got one guy missing in action. All we have are his dentures. What are we gonna say?" All spots ended with the tagline "What happens here, stays here."

After its 2003 backlash, the campaign released six new TV commercials on February 11, 2004, that were less explicit. In the spot "Unclaimed Luggage," a couple approached the front desk of a hotel in search of their luggage. When asked a few simple questions, for instance, about what room they stayed in or when they checked in, the couple confessed to never actually entering their room. Instead they had spent a sleepless night enjoying Las Vegas. "What we've tried to show is the precursor, and the aftermath, to a personal story, and let viewers fill in the details," Candid told the *Washington Post.* Another spot, titled "Silent Car," featured a limousine transporting what seemed to be an exhausted bachelorette party. At first the women appeared sullen, until one bridesmaid snickered, which sparked contagious laughter throughout the car. LVCVA spent an initial $58 million to run print ads and television spots. The latter aired across such networks as Comedy Central, E!, ESPN, ESPN2, Fine Living, Food Network, Fox News, and MSNBC until August 2004.

The campaigned continued into 2005 with five more television spots, all of them less provocative than their original counterparts. One 2005 commercial featured a boxer whose manager was relieved that he could not remember the night before. Another spot, portraying the ambiguity that Las Vegas offered its visitors, featured a woman who assumed the names of television characters. R&R Partners' chief executive, Billy Vassiliadis, told the *Washington Post,* "People always ask if the spots are about sex. If that's what you want to read into it, that's fine."

OUTCOME

In 2004 "Vegas Stories" overtook campaigns released by McDonald's Corp. and Apple Computer to win *Brandweek* magazine's Grand Marketer of the Year award. As the campaign continued and Las Vegas restored its dwindling tourist industry, even some of the campaign's toughest critics, such as Nevada's Governor Kenny Guinn, warmed up to its controversial tagline. After traveling domestically, the governor, who was addressing the 20th annual Governor's Conference on Tourism, was quoted by *Associated Press Newswires* as saying, "I can tell you that slogan is synonymous with Las Vegas, and they don't take it as a negative. Some of us did. I believe I did to begin with. But I've changed my mind because you need something that is attached to Las Vegas and the state of Nevada."

Not only had the visitor decline to Las Vegas stopped by 2004, but the city also boasted 2.4 million more visitors that year than in 2002. Furthermore, a *USA Today* Ad Track survey deemed "Vegas Stories" spots the most effective commercials on television and the sixth most likable.

FURTHER READING

Farhi, Paul. "Las Vegas Ads' Winning Streak." *Washington Post,* December 2, 2004, p. C01.

Friedman, Wayne. "Vegas Touchback." *Television Week,* February 14, 2005, p. 2.

German, Jeff. "Dollar Deal Is Costing LVCVA Big Bucks." *Las Vegas Sun,* September 11, 2005, p. 03.

Kanigher, Steve. "Misrepresenting Vegas Is a Sign of the Times." *Las Vegas Sun,* June 6, 2004, p. 04.

———. "Recommendations Made for LVCVA to Keep Ownership of Protected Slogans." *Las Vegas Sun,* September 7, 2005, p. 01.

Koch, Ed. "Controversy Absent on Famous Vegas Sign." *Las Vegas Sun,* July 27, 2005, p. 02.

McKee, David. "Difficult to Assign Dollar Value to Las Vegas Slogan." *Las Vegas Business Press,* July 25, 2005, p. 2.

———. "$27K at Center of Slogan Brouhaha." *Las Vegas Business Press,* August 15, 2005, p. 2.

Mihailovich, Steven. "'Las Vegas Stories' Wins Industry Award." *Las Vegas Business Press,* October 18, 2004, p. 2.

Smith, John L. "Ex-councilman Doesn't Like Las Vegans Losing Their Shirts in $1 Deal." *Las Vegas Review-Journal,* July 15, 2005, p. 1B.

Smith, Rod. "Tourism: Ad Effects, Terrorism Fears Fade." *Las Vegas Review-Journal,* April 24, 2004, p. 1D.

Wargo, Brian. "R&R Partners Hired to Launch Tourism Campaign." *Las Vegas Sun,* August 30, 2005, p. 03.

Wheaton, Ken. "Adages; Agency Brings out the Softer Side of Sin City." *Advertising Age,* September 19, 2005, p. 52.

Kevin Teague

La-Z-Boy Inc.

1284 N. Telegraph Road
Monroe, Michigan 48162
USA
Telephone: (734) 241-4074
Fax: (734) 457-2005
Web site: www.lazboy.com

■■■

THE NEW LOOK OF COMFORT CAMPAIGN

OVERVIEW

La-Z-Boy Inc. built its furniture brand on a single product, the ubiquitous recliner-rocker closely associated with TV-watching men in their middle and late years. Though the company began expanding into other furniture products in the 1980s, it had not by the late 1990s effectively enlarged its consumer base beyond its aging male loyalists. Still number one in the recliner category, La-Z-Boy wanted to make itself relevant to a new generation of Americans, especially women, who played the dominant role in the overwhelming majority of furniture transactions. The company progressively placed more emphasis on modern, fashionable furniture lines, and in 2000 it charged its longtime agency, Doner of Detroit, with the project of changing consumers' perceptions of the La-Z-Boy brand.

The resulting campaign, "The New Look of Comfort," paired La-Z-Boy's reputation for comfort with a style-focused pitch meant to resonate with young women. Drawing on an estimated $5 to $10 million budget, the campaign's print portion appeared in home-oriented magazines in the fall of 2000, and the campaign moved to television in the summer of 2001. Each print and TV execution focused on an individual La-Z-Boy product in a striking visual arrangement meant to draw attention to its elegant design features, while witty copy and voice-overs supplemented the fashionable sensibility on display.

"The New Look of Comfort" spurred sales of each of the individual products advertised in print and on TV and was extended as La-Z-Boy continued to build its fashion credentials. A 2002 charity event in which the company asked prominent designers to contribute recliner prototypes for auction eventually led to a sustained collaboration with Todd Oldham, a former New York fashion designer. The Todd Oldham collection debuted in 2003 and built further buzz around La-Z-Boy's evolution; advertising on behalf of the prominent new line retained the tagline "The New Look of Comfort."

HISTORICAL CONTEXT

La-Z-Boy began life in the garage of Edward Knabusch's father in Monroe, Michigan, when Knabusch and his cousin Edwin Shoemaker quit their jobs to start their own furniture company in 1927. In 1929 the pair introduced their first upholstered recliner, thus establishing the template responsible for the company's enormous success in subsequent decades. Recliner design took a step forward in the 1950s, when La-Z-Boy added built-in footrests, and the 1960s saw sales boom with the birth of the rocker-recliner, which became the industry standard. La-Z-Boy dominated the recliner category throughout the latter half of the twentieth century, becoming virtually synonymous with easy-chair comfort.

La-Z-Boy moved beyond the manufacture of recliners in the 1980s, but it remained almost exclusively associated with its signature product. Thus, in the 1990s the company pursued sales growth by outfitting recliners with numerous and varied gadgets, including telephones, modems, drink coolers, heaters, and massage equipment. These efforts did not substantially enlarge the company's market, and although La-Z-Boy remained the category leader, selling upward of 1 million recliners annually in the United States, its steady but unexciting consumer base of aging men offered no measurable avenues for growth.

In the 1990s the company began seeking growth via its other product lines, and this project necessitated the building of a new base of consumers. Though popular among baby boomers, La-Z-Boy out of necessity had to position itself to appeal to a new wave of Americans, and these young people were unlikely to adopt the style choices of their parents and grandparents. La-Z-Boy research indicated, moreover, that 85 percent of furniture purchases were initiated by women. The company accordingly moved into more modern furniture styles and pinpointed young women as the key demographic necessary for future sales growth. The La-Z-Boy brand remained so closely associated with unstylish recliners, however, that these typically fashion-conscious consumers did not take the new products seriously. The brand's well-developed reputation for comfort gave it a sizable advantage in the broader furniture market, but it had to overcome a corresponding reputation as a brand suited to suburban dads and granddads if it was to become an attractive option for young women.

TARGET MARKET

In previous years Doner had successfully helped La-Z-Boy maintain its image as a leader in furniture comfort with campaigns targeting married, college-educated consumers in their mid-20s to mid-50s, with household incomes of $50,000 or more. These men and women were expected to base their furniture-buying decisions more on comfort than on style. "The New Look of Comfort," by contrast, explicitly targeted fashion-conscious women between the ages of 25 and 44, both single and married, with incomes reaching into the upper ranges of the middle class. The campaign's intent was to encourage these consumers to rethink their notions of La-Z-Boy by linking the brand's heritage of comfort with a new, dramatically more stylish image. To attract the attention of a target group that did not necessarily take the brand seriously, La-Z-Boy needed to appear much bolder and more adventurous than it had in the past.

COUNTERPOINT

Known almost exclusively as the maker of comfortable recliners for couch potatoes, La-Z-Boy made serious efforts to update its image beginning in 2000 with its campaign "The New Look of Comfort." Some analysts, however, remained skeptical about the company's prospects for generating sales among fashionable young women, La-Z-Boy's key target for future growth. Analyst Laura Champine of the financial-services firm Morgan Keegan, for instance, acknowledged that La-Z-Boy's contemporary offerings, including the collection created by prominent fashion designer Todd Oldham, represented a valid attempt to reach beyond its core market of aging men, but she downplayed the suggestion that the brand had substantially changed consumer perception as of 2005. "It has taken them decades to establish their brand image," she told *Brandweek,* suggesting that a comparable period of time might be necessary to see La-Z-Boy through as dramatic a brand transformation as the one the company was then undertaking.

At the same time La-Z-Boy had to be careful not to alienate its more traditional consumer base, as conventional recliners continued to account for half of the brand's sales. The company simultaneously ran separate advertising efforts to speak to its traditional customers, but it was also mindful of the need to ensure that the fashion-oriented pitch of the new campaign could not be construed as a suggestion that the recliners upon which it had built its reputation were unsophisticated or outdated.

COMPETITION

The Ethan Allen brand, known for offering a full selection of home furnishings in a variety of styles, was during this time also attempting to appeal to young consumers. In 2000 the furniture maker and its retail network enlisted Grey Advertising of New York for a campaign in support of its new Horizons line, designed with 25- to 35-year-old consumers in mind. The campaign featured romantic storylines and surreal, dramatic imagery, such as an Ethan Allen bed placed in the middle of a dry desert lake bed. In 2002 the company intensified its efforts to reach young consumers, cutting prices on Horizons as well as on a more expensive line targeted at those who were beginning to upgrade their furniture after the first few years of home ownership. In an attempt to attract young families to its retail outlets, Ethan Allen likewise expanded its offerings of children's furniture and stepped up advertising on these new lines' behalf.

With its combination of sleek, modern design and low price, the Swedish furniture maker IKEA had become the brand of choice for young, urban men and women who wanted to balance style with economic considerations. Successful advertising crafted by New York–based agency Deutsch had positioned IKEA as the brand consumers turned to for the major purchases necessary during key transitional events, such as marriage or the purchase of a home. Deutsch later adapted this idea to allow for more company growth by extending the concept to smaller events in people's lives, effectively spurring consumers to visit IKEA stores more often. Later Deutsch work showed how mundane environments (including a bowling alley and a subway car) took on drama and life with the addition of IKEA furniture. IKEA and Deutsch ended their 11-year relationship in 2000, when the company solicited advertising ideas from other agencies. The company briefly gave its account to Minneapolis agency Carmichael Lynch before tapping agency Crispin Porter + Bogusky to take over its advertising in 2002. The agency began targeting a consumer subculture ranging from thrift-shop savants to the arbiters of underground fashion trends, urging them to see furniture as fashion items subject to changing trends rather than as settled fixtures in the home to be replaced only once or twice a lifetime.

Another manufacturer of recliners, Mitchell Gold, was, like La-Z-Boy, also attempting during this time to overcome that furniture category's fashion-related shortcomings. A 2001 Mitchell Gold print campaign targeting women suggested that the company made "recliners that don't look like recliners" and employed copy modeled after common women's-magazine exhortations, such as "Bring something a little daring into your relationship."

MARKETING STRATEGY

By 2000 La-Z-Boy boasted a full line of modern chairs, sofas, coffee tables, and other furniture that met the style demands of a younger, upscale, female target market, but these consumers either were not sufficiently aware of this fact or did not take La-Z-Boy's fashion credentials seriously because of the company's heritage. Doner's objective was to change these consumers' perceptions of La-Z-Boy and, accordingly, to spur sales of its new, fashionable lines. La-Z-Boy chose seven specific pieces of furniture and related fabrics to showcase. If the campaign could boost sales of these select items, then the company could more confidently proceed with the further cultivation of its new target market, thereby positioning itself for sustained sales growth. La-Z-Boy wanted to accomplish this goal without abandoning its image of comfort, a brand attribute that the company had been assiduously building for more than 70 years. The tagline for the new campaign, "The New Look of Comfort," was meant to update consumers' notions of what comfortable furniture could look like. Ideally Doner and La-Z-Boy wanted their female target to be pleasantly taken aback by the notion that the stylish new furniture lines carried the La-Z-Boy brand name.

La-Z-Boy spent an estimated $50 million on advertising annually; "The New Look of Comfort" initially accounted for $5 to $10 million of this total. Doner made the individual pieces of furniture the heroes of the campaign's introductory print ads, which ran, beginning in late November 2000, in publications that included *InStyle, Martha Stewart Living, Elle Decor,* and *Metropolitan Home.* Witty copy accompanied photo arrangements that, rather than showing La-Z-Boy furniture in standard domestic settings, used modern compositional elements to enhance the style-intensive message. For instance, a red recliner called the Carlyle, featuring sleek wooden arms and other retro-modern stylings, was shown surrounded by other red chairs with text reading, "Everybody needs a role model." A plum-colored sofa was showcased by itself in an ad advising, "We recommend a wallet-sized photo for those times when you absolutely have to leave the house." Another ad paired the same sofa's image with the copy "We thought it was about time furniture had a jazz section."

In June 2001 the campaign was extended to television with 15-second spots that were conceptually in keeping with the print ads. They ran on a range of cable channels, including Lifetime, Nick at Night, A&E, Discovery, USA, and Animal Planet. Doner also placed the commercials prominently on *The View,* an ABC morning talk show with a strong female viewership. As with the print ads, each spot focused explicitly on the furniture itself while using voice-overs (spoken by actress Courtney Thorne-Smith) similar to the print ads' copy. One spot opened with a shot of the Venus de Milo before showing a La-Z-Boy product called the Ava chair. Thorne-Smith intoned, "We thought our chair looks pretty good without arms, too." In another commercial the camera tracked paw prints through a forest, which led to the Catalina sofa; as it was shown, the voice-over declared, "Your other furniture will fear for its life."

OUTCOME

Before "The New Look of Comfort" began, none of the seven furniture and fabric combinations featured in the campaign were among La-Z-Boy's top-10-selling fabric-and-frame combinations. As of 2002, however, all seven advertised product combinations made the list. La-Z-Boy accordingly ventured further into the world of stylish furniture, partnering with seven fashion designers, including Tommy Hilfiger, Nicole Miller, MoMo Falana, and Todd Oldham, to create signature La-Z-Boy recliners. Two prototypes of each designer's chair were produced and auctioned to benefit a New York shelter for homeless victims of AIDS. In concert with the event La-Z-Boy ran a five-page spread in *InStyle* magazine using the tagline "The New Look of Comfort." La-Z-Boy particularly liked Oldham's approach to recliner design, and in 2003 the company announced a high-profile partnership with the former maker of popular shoes and jeans for the MTV generation. The resulting Todd Oldham by La-Z-Boy collection of urban-styled furniture generated substantial buzz upon its fall 2003 release. Supporting advertising on behalf of the Oldham collection retained the "New Look of Comfort" theme and tagline.

FURTHER READING

Appelbaum, Michael. "Comfy to Cool: A Brand Swivel." *Brandweek,* May 2, 2005.

Bloom, Jonah. "La-Z-Boy: Kurt Darrow." *Advertising Age* (midwest ed.), November 17, 2003.

Cuneo, Alice Z. "Lounging Shoppers Show Off Comfort in Ads for La-Z-Boy." *Advertising Age,* August 9, 1999.

Fitzgerald, Kate. "La-Z-Boy Maxim." *Advertising Age,* June 26, 1998.

Gunin, Joan. "La-Z-Boy's New Print Ads Key on Style, Humor." *Furniture/Today,* November 6, 2000.

Irwin, Tanya. "Designs on a La-Z-Boy." *Adweek* (midwest ed.), February 11, 2002.

———. "La-Z-Boy Targets Younger Buyers." *Adweek* (midwest ed.), November 20, 2000.

———. "La-Z-Boy Targets Young Women." *Adweek* (midwest ed.), July 16, 2001.

Palmeri, Christopher. "La-Z-Boy: Up from Naugahyde; Its Stylish Line, by Designer Todd Oldham, May Just Banish the Stodgy Image." *BusinessWeek,* April 12, 2004.

Perry, David. "La-Z-Boy Ads Let Product Be the Hero." *Furniture/Today,* August 13, 2001.

Mark Lane

LeapFrog Enterprises, Inc.

6401 Hollis St., Ste. 150
Emeryville, California 94608-1071
USA
Telephone: (510) 420-5000
Fax: (510) 420-5001
Web site: www.LeapFrog.com

■■■

LEARN SOMETHING NEW EVERY DAY! CAMPAIGN

OVERVIEW

Frustrated by the lack of educational toys, in 1995 Mike Wood, a California attorney, rewired a talking greeting card to help his son differentiate between phonetic sounds. Soon afterward Wood founded LeapFrog Enterprises, Inc., to fill what he considered a void in the $34 billion toy industry, which was dominated by the companies Mattel and Hasbro. While competitors focused on movie-licensed toys or one-hit products such as Beanie Babies, LeapFrog concentrated on high-quality educational toys. By 2001 LeapFrog had developed more than 100 products and recorded $222 million in sales. To codify its brand as the leading educational toymaker, LeapFrog released its "Learn Something New Every Day!" campaign.

In 2002 LeapFrog provided an advertising budget of $20 million to Ackerman McQueen, Inc., an agency that had handled LeapFrog's marketing since 1995. Released in 2002, "Learn Something New Every Day!" distinctly targeted mothers, along with gift-giving neighbors and grandparents. The strategy differed from those of other toy manufacturers, which targeted children. The campaign's television spots featured children learning different disciplines, including Spanish, reading, and phonics. All spots ended with the tagline "Learn Something New Every Day" below a green LeapFrog logo. In addition to television spots, the campaign's media included print, direct mail, point of purchase, and online advertisements as well as public relations.

Judges for the EFFIE Awards were so impressed with LeapFrog's sales jump and expanded brand awareness that they awarded the campaign the coveted Grand EFFIE Award in 2004. Between 2001 and 2002 LeapFrog sales skyrocketed 37 percent, brand awareness increased 21 percent, and the toymaker's electronic learning book, the LeapPad, held rank as the top-selling toy of 2002. "This is David and Goliath," Gene Dunkin, president of the New York American Marketing Association's Board of Directors, announced at the EFFIE Awards. "While the big agencies won lots of EFFIEs and are to be heartily congratulated, the big winner is a mid-size agency and a nine-year old startup that took the educational toy market by storm. Its success can be attributed in part to a smart advertising campaign that produced great results."

HISTORICAL CONTEXT

Ackerman McQueen had handled LeapFrog's advertising since 1995, after one of Mike Wood's friends recommended the agency to him. "I thought we would just do a couple of spec ads, and that would be it," Ackerman McQueen's president, David Lipson, told *Adweek*. "But the more we learned about LeapFrog, the more certain we became that it would be a big success."

Advertising critics attributed LeapFrog's rapid growth to its unprecedented strategy. Not only did LeapFrog design its applications' circuitry instead of outsourcing it, but every toy was also designed to improve what LeapFrog considered an "educational problem." The company kept more than 100 educators on staff. To oversee new toy development LeapFrog established an educational advisory board that was headed by Robert Calthey, the dean of the Stanford Graduate School of Education. To promote its educational edge over the rest of the industry, LeapFrog released a print campaign in 1997 that targeted parents with children under four years old. At the time LeapFrog's competitors were solely targeting children. LeapFrog's 1997 ads appeared in childcare and family magazines such as *Parent* and *Family Circle*. The campaign suggested that educating toddlers at an early age would help them learn when they were older. One ad featured an image of a young girl with the tagline "How she does on her SAT depends on how well she does on her ABCs."

Leading up to "Learn Something New Every Day!" was the economic downturn affecting the public school system. State budgets were being cut, and one in three students was reading below his or her grade level. LeapFrog conducted an in-home ethnographic survey to further understand its customer, who it dubbed the "LeapFrog Mom." The LeapFrog Mom believed that stimulating a child's mind at an early age would benefit him or her later on in life. She also spent five times more on toys than other mothers did, provided that the toys were educational. Also, the LeapFrog Mom was the primary mentor, protector, and educator for her preschool children. After uncovering this target's educational priorities, LeapFrog released "Learn Something New Every Day!"

TARGET MARKET

The campaign targeted the 25- to 49-year-old female subgroup titled "LeapFrog Moms" with children between the ages of 2 and 12. To unearth the LeapFrog Mom sensibilities, a precampaign survey was conducted by Flake-Wilkerson Market Insights, a marketing-research consultancy. The survey revealed that LeapFrog Moms believed that the earlier children's minds were stimulated, the better they performed later in life. The target mom was described as "adventurous," "confident," and "discerning." While non-LeapFrog mothers purchased movie-licensed Harry Potter, SpongeBob, and Spider Man toys that offered little educational merit and averaged $7 a toy, LeapFrog Moms were willing to spend an average of $40 on a toy if it was purported to aid child development. Two-thirds of LeapFrog Moms also passed educational toys on to other children, while non-LeapFrog moms treated toys as disposable objects.

The campaign's secondary target consisted of gift-giving aunts, uncles, and grandparents who appreciated lasting presents that made a positive difference in a child's life. This subgroup composed 30 percent of the campaign's target. The campaign treated LeapFrog Moms, not their children, as the ultimate decision makers, and aired commercials across adult television channels such as *Lifetime, Oxygen,* and *The Food Network,* and during programs that tended to have female audiences, such as *Oprah* and *The View*. Other toymakers, such as Mattel and Hasbro, targeted children by airing commercials during Nickelodeon's children's shows and Saturday morning cartoons. Such toy companies then relied on what LeapFrog referred to as the "nag factor," or children persistently asking their mothers for toys they had seen advertised on television.

LEAPSCANDAL

LeapFrog, a maker of educational toys, was the subject of scandal in 2004. The toymaker sold $1 million worth of products to Prince George's County Public Schools in Maryland. The sale included the brand's flagship product, LeapPad, an electronic platform that taught children disciplines such as reading, math, and geography. Controversy erupted when the public school board learned that its chief, Andre Hornsby, was living with a LeapFrog saleswoman at the time of the sale.

COMPETITION

According to Securities and Exchange Commission documents, LeapFrog commanded an estimated 75 percent share of the preschool toy segment in 2002. LeapFrog's largest competitor, Mattel, was the world's largest overall toymaker in 2002, with brands such as Hot Wheels, Barbie, and Fisher-Price. The latter was Mattel's preschool toy brand, which released the PowerTouch Learning System in 2003. Similar to the LeapPad, the PowerTouch was a laptop-sized platform that used software to teach preschoolers different subjects. One slight difference between the two products was that the LeapPad required a stylus; but PowerTouch could be operated with a child's finger. LeapFrog claimed that the stylus enabled children to interact with smaller letters, a quality conducive to developing early reading skills.

Fisher-Price advertised the PowerTouch with its "Play. Laugh. Grow." campaign in 2003. In addition to noting the similarities of the two brands' products, critics drew parallels between Fisher-Price and LeapFrog's marketing strategies. "Play. Laugh. Grow." solely targeted mothers. Fisher-Price's research revealed that for the first time in history, Generation-X mothers were outspending baby-boomer mothers on toy purchases. Baby-boomer mothers tended to treat learning and playing as two separate activities, but the new majority of Generation-X mothers combined the two activities. The $25 million "Play. Laugh. Grow." campaign featured television spots with children having fun while learning on a PowerTouch. The campaign helped Fisher-Price sales to increase 7 percent in 2004. The campaign's ad agency, Young & Rubicam Brands, also earned a Silver EFFIE Award in 2005 for the work. By 2005 "Play. Laugh. Grow." was radically repositioned to target Latina mothers, one of the fastest-growing demographics in America.

MARKETING STRATEGY

Treating the LeapFrog Mom as the ultimate decision-maker when it came to toys, "Learn Something New Every Day!" television spots only appeared on adult programming. Ackerman McQueen also realized that first-time mothers had not yet established a brand allegiance, so 12-page brochures advertising LeapBaby, a LeapFrog product aimed at newborns, were mailed to daycares, preschools, and hospitals. The brochure explained how LeapFrog products developed early cognitive skills. Print ads for LeapBaby appeared in magazines such as *American Baby* and *Child.*

Most of the $20 million campaign's commercials featured children learning to read with LeapPad, an electronic platform that taught different subjects depending on what software was inserted. In one spot, titled "Gifts," a preschool-aged girl kept receiving new LeapPad software in the mail from her grandfather. A voice-over for the commercial stated, "Learning to read has never been more fun." As the commercial progressed, the girl's reading level improved with every new package. For the spot's finale she telephoned her grandfather to say, "Hi Grandpa, I got a surprise for you." She then read him complete sentences from one of her latest LeapPad programs. The spot ended with the LeapFrog logo above the tagline "Learn Something New Every Day." Other spots featured subjects besides reading. "New Neighbor" showed a young boy learning phrases in Spanish so that he could introduce himself to his new Latino neighbors.

LeapFrog noticed that its competitors advertised toys either by featuring children enjoying the toy within an unrealistically fun situation or by using "over-the-top" commercials to generate hype about a product. "Learn Something New Every Day!" strove for relevant and honest advertising content. Ackerman McQueen cast "real-looking" actors to play moms, dads, and children. When young boys and girls were shown learning in television spots, they sometimes did so with difficulty. The commercials intent was to connect with moms working to teach their own children.

In addition to employing traditional media outlets, for "Learn Something New Every Day!" LeapFrog hosted promotional events with teachers to galvanize the brand's "educational position." To advertise one of its latest toys, LeapFrog presented teachers at several New York City public schools with donations and LeapFrog products. By 2004 more than 15,000 American classrooms were equipped with some type of LeapFrog toy. During the campaign LeapFrog's research also revealed that LeapFrog Moms were unsure about what learning toy was suitable for their child's age group. The brand's selection had jumped from one product to an overwhelming 134 in just nine years. To distinguish its toys better, LeapFrog deployed a classification system at retailers such as Target, Wal-Mart, and Toys "R" Us that was called "LeapLevels: The right stage for the right age." LeapLevels separated products into different age groups. The groupings were then explained with signage, floor graphics, shelf blades, and retailer circulars.

OUTCOME

Not only did the campaign win the Grand EFFIE, considered to be one of the advertising industry's most coveted awards, in 2004, but it also helped solidify LeapFrog as an industry giant. During the campaign's first year LeapFrog sales increased 37 percent, brand awareness rose 32 percent, and retailers allotted 68 percent more footage for LeapFrog products. The two top-selling toys in America were made by LeapFrog, and much of the toy industry started mimicking its advertising strategy.

By 2003 LeapFrog was the third-largest toymaker in the world. Fisher-Price eventually released a product similar to the LeapPad, resulting in LeapFrog filing a lawsuit over patent violation. In 2004, however, LeapFrog's success waned after a combined slowdown in the toy industry and rising operational costs plagued the company. That year LeapFrog posted an $8 million loss, a stark contrast to the previous year's $72 million profit.

FURTHER READING

Bainbridge, Jane. "Sector Insight: Traditional Toys and Games—Playing to Win." *Marketing,* November 17, 2004, p. 34.

Best, Paul. "Cool Tech." *The Age* (Melbourne), August 26, 2003, p. 9.

Buckleitner, Warren. "Smaller. Smarter. Plugs into Your TV." *New York Times,* August 11, 2005, p. 10.

Bullard, Dave. "Nib Wins Draw." *Herald-Sun* (Melbourne), July 13, 2005, p. C08.

Devine, Nancy. "Unlocking the World of Imagination." *Toronto Star,* November 27, 2003, p. G08.

Elliott, Stuart, and Raymond Hernandez. "Groups Recognize Agencies' Creativity." *New York Times,* June 14, 2004, p. 10.

Fest, Glen. "LeapFrog." *Adweek* (southwest ed.), November 17, 1997, p. 40.

Kim, Queena Sook. "Advertising: Fisher-Price Courts Gen-X Mothers." *Wall Street Journal,* September 19, 2003, p. B3.

Lomartire, Paul. "Toronto Firm's Toys Are Hot." *Milwaukee Journal Sentinel,* December 28, 2003, p. 10B.

Vavra, Bob. "Fun with the Basics: The Best-Selling Toys Don't Come with a Lot of Bells and Whistles." *Progressive Grocer,* October 15, 2002, p. 53.

Williamson, Richard. "The Ride's Far from Over at Ackerman McQueen." *Adweek,* August 2, 2004, p. 12.

Kevin Teague

Levi Strauss & Co.

1155 Battery St.
San Francisco, California 94111
USA
Telephone: (415) 501-6000
Fax: (415) 501-7112
Web site: www.levistrauss.com

IT'S WIDE OPEN CAMPAIGN

OVERVIEW

Clothing manufacturer Levi Strauss & Company entered the wide-leg jeans market in the summer of 1996. To celebrate the launch of its Wide Leg line, the company initiated a campaign aimed at a target market of boys age 9 to 14. The "Make Room" campaign featured television spots with male youths, looking rebellious and tough, tromping through urban settings.

In November 1996 Levi's followed up the "Make Room" campaign with the $40 million "It's Wide Open" campaign. The latter was designed to expand the target market from young boys to males up to 34 years of age. The "Elevator Fantasy" spot starred two strangers—a young man and woman wearing Levi's Wide Leg jeans—sharing an elevator ride. As the elevator descended, fantasies of romantic possibilities ensued, with visions of the couple getting married and having a child. The daydreams stopped, however, when the elevator reached its destination, and the pair emerged and parted without having spoken a word. Another spot in the "It's Wide Open" campaign was "Doctors," which spoofed television programs such as *ER* by showing surgeons and a patient singing and having fun in an emergency room.

Levi's goal in the "It's Wide Open" campaign was to engender popularity among trend-setting, jeans-wearing youth and to increase its market share in the highly competitive denim category. Both television spots were enthusiastically received by the public and the media, but they did little to boost Levi's denim sales.

HISTORICAL CONTEXT

One of the most widely known brand of jeans, Levi's was a major player in the market from its inception in 1850 to the early 1990s. Levi's became extremely popular in the 1950s among youth influenced by movie stars such as James Dean and Marlon Brando, who appeared in films wearing the company's jeans. The 1980s marked a decline in the jeans market, and Levi's profits fell as a result. Levi's then ventured into the casual clothing category and introduced its Dockers line in 1986, hoping to recapture sales especially with the baby boomer generation that had stoked Levi's popularity in the 1950s.

The denim market was revitalized in the 1990s as consumers opted for comfortable, casual clothing. The company enjoyed record sales of $7.1 billion in 1996 (with $4.3 billion attributed to U.S. sales), including $3 billion from Levi's products, but the company felt the need to increase its share of the jeans market by attracting new customers while also satisfying loyal Levi's consumers. *Business Week* reported that Levi's dominance in the jeans market had slipped from 30.9 percent in 1990 to 18.7 percent in 1997. The desire to reverse this decline and keep up with fashion trends was the impetus for the Wide Leg line and its accompanying marketing campaign.

The wide-leg style was popular with teenagers, particularly urban youths concerned with fashion and image. Other jeans manufacturers, however, had already introduced wide-leg and baggy jeans and established their presence in the market; Levi's had to scramble to catch up. As Alan Millstein, a New York retail consultant and editor of *Fashion Network Report,* stated in *Business Week,* "Levi Strauss was zagging when the world was zigging... The company totally missed the significance of the inner city and the huge impact it has on trends. It tells me they're sleepy in their marketing." Levi's had been preoccupied with the Dockers line and the launch of Slates, its men's dress clothing line, and may have neglected its denim division. Robert Haas, Levi's chairman and CEO, admitted in *Business Week,* "When you try to take on too many things, you are not as attentive to the warning signs."

Levi's first attempt to win back market share with its Wide Leg line of jeans was manifested in the "Make Room" campaign, aimed at younger boys. The campaign, launched in August 1996 in time to influence back-to-school purchases, included television ads of rebellious-looking boys traversing urban locales and making businessmen in suits nervous. The spots ran on prime-time network television shows popular with this age group such as *The Simpsons* and on cable channels such as MTV.

NOT ALL WERE AMUSED

Although many people found the "It's Wide Open" campaign humorous and enjoyable, some viewers were not amused at the "Doctors" ad. Critics found the ad to be in poor taste, arguing that it made light of serious medical situations. Jill Lynch, a Levi's spokesperson, defended the ad in *USA Today:* "The doctor spot is clearly a spoof of TV emergency room shows... It is not intended in any way to represent real-life situations."

TARGET MARKET

Levi's traditional target market included males between the ages of 15 and 25, but the "It's Wide Open" campaign was designed to attract men up to 34 years of age. Levi's initial Wide Leg jeans campaign, "Make Room," targeted the youth market in an attempt to gain popularity and loyalty. Because the wide-leg style evolved from the skateboarding craze generated by this age group, it seemed appropriate to gain its approval before progressing to older consumers. Fashions adopted by youths often influenced older customers as well, and Levi's hoped to benefit from this trend. In addition, the teen group was a lucrative market. Gus Floris, an associate publisher of the trade magazine *Sportswear International,* told the *San Francisco Examiner,* "... the biggest group buying jeans are teenagers. They own like eight pairs on average." Unfortunately for Levi's, its market share with the consumer group of 15- to 19-year-olds had dropped from 33 percent in 1993 to 26 percent in 1997. Gordon Harton, vice president for the Lee brand of jeans, a Levi's competitor, told *Business Week,* "It's very important that you attract this age group...By the time they're 24, they've adopted brands that they will use for the rest of their lives."

After responding to the youth market, Levi's quickly sought to broaden the market for Wide Leg jeans by targeting males up to age 34. "Wide leg is a huge trend for us," Steve Goldstein, vice president of marketing and research for Levi's USA, reported to *Advertising Age.* He added that males "are willing to and anxious to have more than one [cut of jeans] in their closet," indicating that Levi's felt there was a market for the trendy style with an older crowd.

COMPETITION

Although Levi Strauss & Company was the largest brand-name clothing manufacturer in the world in the 1990s, it was second to VF Corporation in the manufacture of jeans. According to the 1998 *Market Share Reporter,* VF, the maker of Lee and Wrangler jeans, held 30.1 percent of the U.S. market, compared to Levi's 16 percent. Stores such as the Gap and designer labels, including Guess, Tommy Hilfiger, Calvin Klein's CK, Nautica, Diesel, and Ralph Lauren's Polo, also posed competition for Levi's. As Millstein explained in the *San Francisco Chronicle,* "Tommy Hilfiger is king of the hill with inner-city youth...Levi's is terrified that their back-to-school business will be affected by the entry of Tommy into the jeans market."

Private-label jeans also honed in on Levi's market share. According to the *San Francisco Examiner,* J.C. Penney grossed $1 billion in 1996 with its Arizona line, and Sears, Roebuck's Canyon River Blues line enjoyed sales of $200 million in 1996 and the first half of 1997. Wal-Mart and Kmart also entered the jeans market with Route 66 and Faded Glory, respectively. Levi's jeans also were sold at these stores and thus were forced to share shelf space with the lower-priced labels.

Millstein told the *San Francisco Examiner,* "The party is over for Levi and Lee... They owned and dominated their collective brands in department stores and mass merchandisers through the '70s and '80s. Now nouveau competition is eroding their share of the market dramatically." As reported in the *San Francisco Chronicle,* Kurt Barnard, a New Jersey retail analyst, agreed, "The jeans business has become a cutthroat, highly competitive, overcrowded field that is extremely price oriented." Millstein summed things up in the *San Francisco Examiner* when he said, "There's only a finite amount of space in stores."

MARKETING STRATEGY

Levi's strategy for marketing its Wide Leg line of jeans was twofold: first, draw in the youth market, and then rely on the older male market to follow. After targeting teenagers with the "Make Room" campaign, Levi's introduced the "It's Wide Open" campaign to attract older customers without alienating the younger ones. According to *Advertising Age,* there was some concern that the "Make Room" ads with tough-looking young boys may have been interpreted as promoting intimidation. The "It's Wide Open" spots, on the other hand, were brazen yet humorous and played on the concept of wide-open possibilities. Geoffrey Thompson, creative director at Levi's advertising agency, Foote, Cone & Belding (FCB), indicated in the *San Francisco Examiner* that the spots were designed to appeal to the late teen and early 20s crowd "who are starting out on their own and appreciate irreverence." FCB account supervisor Ken Epstein told *USA Today,* "We were launching a new product, so we wanted to cut through the clutter and get consumers' attention." To accomplish this, FCB focused on originality and attitude rather than directly pushing the product.

The first television spot of the campaign, "Elevator Fantasy," aired in late 1996 on prime-time network television, and it was followed by "Doctors," which ran through early 1997. "Elevator Fantasy," which featured the young strangers, was set to a tune by the Partridge Family, a band easily recognized by those who grew up in the 1970s. The spot was thus progressive because it promoted a new line of Levi's jeans, yet nostalgic because the Partridge Family harkened back to the days when many members of the target market were children.

"Doctors" parodied popular television medical dramas. It presented a critically injured patient, clad in Wide Leg jeans, being rushed into an operating room. The staff hurriedly prepared to operate, with the beeping of medical machines heard in the background. The patient then pushed his oxygen mask aside and began to sing the techno-pop song "Tainted Love," a hit in the 1980s, in synchronization with the beeping. The surgical team appeared surprised, but then the head surgeon removed his surgical mask and joined in, followed by the rest of the team. They started dancing about the operating room, playing with the medical equipment and inflating surgical scrubs with oxygen tubes. The beeping suddenly stopped, replaced by a steady tone, and the patient became unconscious. A staff member yelled, "He's crashing!" and the surgical team worked to revive him. They succeeded, and the beeping resumed, allowing the patient and operating room personnel to finish the song. The spot ended with the Levi's Wide Leg logo and the tag line "Levi's Wide Leg Jeans. It's Wide Open."

According to the *Washington Post,* the "Doctors" spot was "intended to radiate originality and possibilities." Like the "Elevator Fantasy" ad, "Doctors" was modern and forward thinking because of the product it promoted and because it spoofed contemporary hit television shows. At the same time it evoked memories for the target market through the song "Tainted Love." Still, the spot was risky because it did not specifically focus on the product. Chuck McBride, the group creative director of FCB, admitted to the *Washington Post,* "The client was a little worried about its relevancy at first, ... but the kids got it right away."

OUTCOME

Both spots in the "It's Wide Open" campaign were successful in generating enthusiasm. According to Ad Track, a *USA Today* poll designed to measure the popularity and effectiveness of ads, of more than 85 campaigns reviewed since May 1995 "It's Wide Open" was among the top 20 in popularity. The spots were especially popular with those between the ages of 18 and 29, with 44 percent responding positively. In contrast, only 24 percent of those polled between the ages of 30 and 49 stated that they enjoyed the ads.

Both television commercials received nominations for Emmy Awards as the best commercial in 1997. "Doctors" and "Elevator Fantasy" were selected out of a pool of 237 entries that was narrowed down to 5 finalists. In addition, both spots took gold medals at the San Francisco Ad Club's annual creative competition in 1997, and "Doctors" received a Silver Lion at the 44th annual Cannes International Advertising Festival. The campaign earned a place on many lists of the best of 1996, including those of the *New York Times, Adweek,* and *Time.* FCB, Levi's advertising agency since 1930, was named the U.S. Agency of the Year for 1996 by *Advertising Age,* due in large part to its work for Levi's. Levi's Goldstein told *Advertising Age,* "They're hitting home runs... The Wide Leg campaign is the most celebrated work that's been done for us in many years."

Although the Levi's Wide Leg campaign received critical acclaim as well as recognition by the general public, it did little to boost Levi's market share in jeans. Ad Track reported that, though the spots ranked high in popularity, in terms of effectiveness they scored below the average of 26 percent. Only 21 percent of respondents considered the Wide Leg spots effective. Levi's profits reflected the poll's results, with 1997 worldwide sales of $6.9 billion, 4 percent below the record sales year of 1996.

FURTHER READING

Angwin, Julia. "Levi's Hopes Wide-Leg Jeans Will Grab Urban Youth Market." *San Francisco Chronicle,* July 26, 1996, p. B1.

Cuneo, Alice Z. "Advertising Age's Agency of the Year." *Advertising Age,* April 21, 1997.

Cuneo, Alice Z., and Pat Sloan. "Levi's Dresses Up to Battle the Competition." *Advertising Age,* July 29, 1996.

Emert, Carol. "Levi's Battles to Stop Slide in Market Share." *San Francisco Chronicle,* June 25, 1997, p. B1.

Enrico, Dottie. "Levi's Ads Wear Well with Target Audience of Young Consumers." *USA Today,* March 17, 1997, p. 6B.

Feuerstein, Adam, and Clifford Carlsen. "Levi Tries to Get Young People into Its Pants." *San Francisco Business Times,* April 14, 1997.

Garfield, Bob. "Jeans' Allure Hangs on Elevator Fantasy." *Advertising Age,* November 25, 1996.

Himelstein, Linda. "Levi's Is Hiking Up Its Pants." *Business Week,* December 1, 1997, p. 70.

Irvine, Martha. "Levi's Searching for a New Image." *Columbian,* November 6, 1997, p. D2.

"Levi's Refashions Its Wide Leg Ads." *Advertising Age,* August 5, 1996.

Span, Paula. "It Ads Up to an Emmy." *Washington Post,* September 6, 1997, p. D5.

Tanaka, Wendy. "Denim Derby." *San Francisco Examiner,* May 20, 1997, p. C1.

Mariko Fujinaka

LEVI'S TYPE 1 JEANS CAMPAIGN

OVERVIEW

Levi Strauss & Co., whose founder invented blue jeans, became the jeans brand of choice for America's youth around the mid-twentieth century, but during the 1990s this began to change. After peaking in 1996 the company's sales fell steadily each year through the early years of the new millennium. In response to the changing tides of fashion, Levi Strauss in 2003 began implementing a new, segmented strategy that focused on the launch of two prominent new lines of jeans. Levi Strauss Signature jeans were a mass-market line to be sold in discount stores such as Wal-Mart, and Levi's Type 1 jeans were meant to appeal to trendsetting youth via Levi Strauss's ordinary channels of distribution. While the Signature line was seen as essential to its long-term health, the company did not want the mass-market line to upstage the main brand. Virtually all of the company's U.S. marketing in 2003, therefore, was devoted to Type 1, in the interest of updating the Levi's image for younger men and women, many of whom were increasingly turning to designer labels. The "Levi's Type 1 Jeans" campaign started on January 2, 2003.

The campaign kicked off with a "Gold Rush" consumer promotion, an interactive online treasure hunt for a pair of jewel-encrusted jeans. The promotion culminated in the airing of the campaign's initial television spot, "Stampede," during the 2003 Super Bowl broadcast. That commercial, in combination with a series of similar spots, had been meant to run through August 2003 but was deemed unworthy of Levi's by critics, including company CEO Philip Marineau, and the campaign was retooled.

Two further spots began airing in the summer of 2003 before the campaign was discontinued in the United States. The domestic launch of the Type 1 line proved disappointing. Levi Strauss continued to struggle with the perception that it was an out-of-date brand.

HISTORICAL CONTEXT

Bavarian immigrant Levi Strauss made canvas pants for prospectors during the California gold rush in the mid-nineteenth century before deciding on the more durable fabric that became known as denim, which Strauss further enhanced with indigo dye and copper rivets. For the company's first hundred years, Levi's jeans were the standard work pant for a wide variety of American laborers, but in the 1950s they became fashionable casual wear among young people. The successful addition of pants line Dockers, together with expansion into Europe and Asia, aided Levi Strauss's growth in the late twentieth century, and the company's global sales peaked at $7.1 billion in 1996. Between 1996 and 2001, however, sales of Levi's among young Americans plummeted. According to the Zandl Group, a youth-marketing consulting firm, only 8 percent of young people in 2001 named Levi's as their favorite brand of jeans, compared with 31 percent in 1996. In 1999 and 2000 the company closed 35 U.S. manufacturing facilities and transferred most such operations overseas.

Long known for classic styles such as the 501 jean, Levi's began introducing new lines to appeal to changing tastes. Its agency at the time, TBWA/Chiat/Day, experimented with a variety of tactics and taglines during these years, including "Opt for the Original" and "Make Them Your Own," as well as a digitized visual gag called "Crazy Legs," which attracted attention but did little to drive sales. CEO Marineau, hired away from PepsiCo in 1999, began shopping for a new agency for the Levi's account in 2001. The New York office of Bartle Bogle Hegarty (BBH), the London-based agency that handled Levi Strauss's more successful European and Asian advertising, won the account.

BBH's first U.S. campaign, a 2002 effort on behalf of Levi's Low-Rise jeans, used the tagline "Dangerously Low" and was intended, according to a company press release, to build on the company's "iconic brand heritage and convey that signature modern, sexy, old school rock 'n roll look of Levi's." Panned by some critics as failing to connect to the brand's longstanding virtues, the campaign did little to arrest the slide in Levi's sales and image.

TARGET MARKET

In 2003 the company hoped to slow its sales decline by appealing to different market segments with the creation of two distinct brand lines. Levi Strauss Signature jeans, designed for a mass market in stores such as Wal-Mart, had a lower price than premium Levi's and were not branded with the trademark Levi's two-horse back patch or red tags. Though Signature, by giving Levi's an entrance into the growth market of discount stores, was seen as an essential part of the company's long-term U.S. sales outlook, the line was not supported by any out-of-store advertising nor mentioned in the Type 1 advertising.

The Type 1 line, conceived as a new flag bearer for the Levi's name, was designed to appeal to a fashion-conscious youth market of both genders. Type 1 jeans featured enhanced versions of the two-horse back patch, trademark rivets, and other characteristic Levi's detailing (in addition to the newly fashionable low waistband introduced in the preceding years). The jeans' new look and high-profile Super Bowl premiere were Levi Strauss's attempt, as the *Wall Street Journal* put it, "to convince people its brand is still cool."

Levi's and BBH envisioned this coolness as deriving from the company's authenticity and roots as well as from a modern sensibility. CEO Marineau told analysts, according to *Advertising Age,* that the purpose of the Type 1 ads "was to let consumers know Levi's was an 'innovation' icon, and 'no longer your mom and dad's jeans.'" The company website further described the new line as "perfect for people who make noise and speak—or sing—their minds to change the culture we live in." As the product launch progressed, Levi's research suggested that the jeans, though generally not selling as well among the youth market as the company had hoped, had found popularity among young male Hispanics and African-Americans.

> **ACROSS THE POND**
>
> Though Levi's was a struggling brand worldwide, it experienced measured success with Bartle Bogle Hegarty (BBH) advertising campaigns in England and Asia. In contrast to the American Type 1 campaign, the European launch of Type 1 jeans on February 13, 2003, had little to do with the brand's heritage and was well received by critics. The spot, created by BBH's London shop and using the tagline "A Bold New Breed," featured a gang of mouse-human hybrids who, while wearing Type 1 jeans, kidnapped a cat and successfully held it for ransom.

COMPETITION

Levi Strauss's largest U.S. competitor during this time was Greensboro, North Carolina–based VF Corporation, owners of a range of apparel brands that included Lee and Wrangler jeans. During this time Lee, sold in mid-market department and specialty stores, launched its One True Fit jeans, targeted at 18- to 34-year-old women and supported by a TV, print, point-of-purchase, and online advertising campaign. Lee also continued to develop its Series 66206 oversized pants and shorts line, which featured wide legs and multiple pockets, and it revived Pipes, a boys' line emulating fashions popular among skateboarders. Wrangler, meanwhile, focused on men with a 2003 advertising campaign behind its Five Star Premium Denim line. TV commercials ran during sports programming, and print ads ran in a variety of sports and outdoors magazines as well as women's publications (because women often bought clothes for men). The Five Star Collection, like the Wrangler brand generally, was sold through discount chains including Wal-Mart, Kmart, and Target.

Gap Inc.'s Gap retail chain was, like Levi's, adjusting to strategic difficulties during this time. After alienating its core customers (adult buyers of basic casual khakis, jeans, T-shirts, and polo shirts) with collections aimed at young women, Gap brought in a new CEO, Paul Pressler, who presided over the retail chain's return to an emphasis on its staple products. A 2002 holiday print campaign featuring portraits of actors such as Will Ferrell and Ray Liotta was followed by a similar 2003 holiday campaign behind its Fair Isle line for women, which showcased celebrities including Claudia Schiffer, Jamie Lee Curtis and her daughter Annie Guest, and Katie Holmes. A TV campaign supporting a new line of corduroy jeans broke in the summer of 2003, featuring singers Madonna and Missy Elliott.

MARKETING STRATEGY

To launch its Type 1 jeans, Levi's announced its "Gold Rush" promotion, an online treasure hunt whose centerpiece was, in the words of a company press release, "the boldest and most valuable pair of jeans in the world." The Type 1 design features, intended to play up the brand's iconic rivets, stitching, back patch, and other detailing, were themselves accentuated, in the prize pair of jeans, with diamonds, rubies, and gold. Valued at $85,000, the jeans were part of a $150,000 package (the remainder of which came in the form of gold and cash packed into the jeans) meant to commemorate the company's 150-year anniversary. To compete for the prize package, consumers logged on to the Levi's website during the four-week period leading up to the 2003 Super Bowl. Each week one question was posted, and a correct answer gave participants access to clues about the location of the bejeweled jeans; additionally participants could play games on the site to gain access to further clues. The promotion culminated in a final clue revealed during the introductory Super Bowl spot.

The Super Bowl spot, "Stampede," combined Old West imagery with an urban backdrop in an attempt, as a company press release phrased it, "to symbolize the fusion of Levi's rich heritage with the brand's modern design sensibility." In the 60-second spot a herd of buffalo was seen stampeding through an unnamed cityscape. When the stampeding herd approached a young, stylish couple wearing Type 1 jeans, all the animals magically came to a stop before galloping around them. The ad closed with the text "Levi's Type 1 Jeans. Bold since 1853," and then the date shuffled forward before stopping at 2003.

Despite the anticipatory buzz Levi's and BBH built up around the Super Bowl spot's premiere, sales of Type 1 jeans were disappointing, and CEO Marineau publicly blamed the spot in a meeting with analysts, saying, "It wasn't a Levi's ad. It didn't have a sense of humor about itself. It was certainly a poor Super Bowl ad." BBH was ordered to rethink the campaign's two remaining television spots, and "Stampede" finished its run in March, six months earlier than had been planned.

The other TV spots appeared in the summer of 2003, in time for the back-to-school season. "Car," again relying on Western motifs, involved a contemporary cowboy outfitted in Type 1 jeans and jacket, but the sense of humor Marineau found lacking in "Stampede" now found its way into the campaign. The cowboy chased down and lassoed a wild, bucking car. As *Adweek* columnist Barbara Lippert stated, "'Car' makes serious American references but also manages to be funny and wry." A second spot, "Horse," fit this same profile, showing a woman on horseback facing down a sleek, modern train.

OUTCOME

"Car" won a Bronze Lion at the International Advertising Festival in Cannes, France, and a Silver Clio in 2004, but sales of Type 1 jeans did not live up to company projections, nor did the Type 1 campaign significantly affect Levi Strauss's flagging overall brand. The company continued to cut costs via reorganization and facility closures, shuttering all of its North American manufacturing plants in addition to many factories overseas, which were replaced by independent contractors.

In 2004 Levi's and BBH launched a U.S. print campaign, its largest ever, that signaled a departure from the strategic underpinnings of the Type 1 work. Photographed by Richard Avedon and placed in such magazines as *Rolling Stone, Us Weekly, Glamour, Entertainment Weekly,* and *Allure,* the campaign introduced portraits of real Levi's wearers organized around the theme "A Style for Every Story." The ads supported various Levi's product lines rather than focusing on any single style, and no allusion was made to the jeans maker's Western heritage.

FURTHER READING

Beatty, Sally. "Levi's Strives to Keep a Hip Image—Some Retailer Discontent Gives It Reason to Promote 'Type One' Jeans at Game." *Wall Street Journal,* January 23, 2003.

"CEO Can't Duck When Ads Flop." *Advertising Age,* April 7, 2003.

Cuneo, Alice. "Levi's CEO Blames Slow Launch on Spots." *Advertising Age,* March 31, 2003.

Cuneo, Alice, and Richard Linnett. "Bartle Bogle Tapped to Cure Levi's Blues." *Advertising Age,* January 14, 2002.

Dill, Mallorre. "A Walk on the Wild Side." *Adweek,* July 1, 2002.

Dolbow, Sandra. "Starring Role for Wrangler's Five Star Jeans." *Brandweek,* July 29, 2002.

Garfield, Bob. "Lowered Expectations: Levi's Continues Tradition of Bad Ads." *Advertising Age,* July 29, 2002.

Grimm, Matthew. "False Consciousness." *Brandweek,* January 20, 2003.

"Levi's." *Advertising Age,* January 27, 2003.

Lippert, Barbara. "American Beauty." *Adweek,* July 14, 2003.

McMain, Andrew. "Levi's Has Stories to Tell of People and Their Jeans." *Brandweek,* March 29, 2004.

O'Laughlin, Sandra. "Celebs Fill Holiday Campaign from Gap." *Brandweek,* November 10, 2003.

———. "Lee Jeans Launching One True Fit in Move to Extend Market Share." *Brandweek,* January 13, 2003.

"Type 1 Gets Makeover." *Advertising Age,* June 30, 2003.

Mark Lane

THEY GO ON CAMPAIGN

OVERVIEW

Even though Levi Strauss & Company had been the cornerstone of the denim industry for over a century, declining sales plagued the company during the latter half of the 1990s. Jeans designed by competing brands such as Guess, Tommy Hilfiger, and Calvin Klein had encroached upon Levi's market share. Foote Cone & Belding, which had been Levi's ad agency since 1930, was set back after its executive creative director, Mike Koelker, resigned in 1994. Koelker had served as an adviser to Levi's chief executive, Bob Haas, and had also conceived the brand's most successful campaigns throughout the 1980s and early 1990s. Hoping to stop declining sales and revitalize its image, Levi's released its largest-ever advertising campaign, titled "They Go On."

The $90 million campaign began in 1997 and focused solely on the brand's image rather than specific products. Foote Cone & Belding created six television commercials, most 60 seconds in duration, interwoven in a dreamlike fashion. According to Levi's, the spots "are unusual in that they have no discernible beginning or end, and in many cases even rely on viewers to fill in the blanks." On September 22 the existing spots were merged with new ones to create a loosely connected drama that was released on the website NBC.com. The online segment also let viewers interact with the actors by posting messages on the website. The campaign ended in 1998.

Although increased competition in the jeans market had affected Levi's market share, the company contended that the "They Go On" campaign was intended as a celebration of the Levi's brand rather than a reaction to declining sales. The strategy proved ineffective. Even though some advertising critics initially praised the campaign, Levi's executives and ad critics later considered the campaign to be a total disaster. In 1998 Levi's reported its worst sales decline since World War II. It soon ended its 68-year relationship with Foote Cone & Belding and reassigned its account to TBWA\Chiat\Day.

HISTORICAL CONTEXT

Levi's, founded in 1850, had dominated the jeans industry for more than a century, surviving the ups and downs of the U.S. economy. When the denim market enjoyed revitalization in the 1990s, however, Levi's was slow to follow. Although Levi's was touted as the world's biggest apparel manufacturer and reported record sales of $7.1 billion in 1996, its market share in the jeans area had slipped. The *Los Angeles Times* reported figures from Tactical Retail Solutions, a firm specializing in tracking retail sales, that indicated a drop in Levi's share of the men's jeans market from 48.2 percent in 1990 to 26.2 percent in 1997. Previous efforts to restore its position had included the "It's Wide Open" campaign for Levi's Wide Leg jeans in 1996 and the ongoing "501 Reasons" campaign. Both campaigns garnered critical acclaim but failed to restore Levi's status as the jeans-market leader. Profits, in fact, rose only 1 percent during the first quarter of 1997, and in February Levi's announced that it would cut 1,000 jobs by year's end.

Spurred by declining jeans sales, the company turned to Foote Cone & Belding, its advertising agency since 1930, to help enhance Levi's image, and the decision was made to concentrate on the strength of the brand and to scrap individual product campaigns. Brad Williams, a marketing manager at Levi's USA, downplayed the significance of the new campaign strategy and explained to the *San Francisco Business Times,* "This is more of a campaign-driven shift than an overall strategy of the brand . . . Moving away from product advertising is a better way to characterize it than supplanting it." According to *Advertising Age,* Levi's ran a brand advertising campaign in March 1995, the first time it had done so in more than a dozen years. The campaign included two spots with the tagline "They're not Levi's jeans until we say they are," and it featured "Works Progress Administration era-style animation." The campaign was not well received, however, and the spots were short-lived.

TARGET MARKET

Levi's traditional market included males between the ages of 15 and 25, and "They Go On" was designed to include this consumer group as well as older demographics. Trying to please the 15–25 age group while not alienating older customers proved a difficult task. Tom Fanoe, president of Levi's USA, told the *San Francisco Chronicle,* "Our target consumer is 15 to 25 years old, so every few years we're dealing with a whole new set of consumers who may or may not [have the same taste] as their older brothers or sisters." Fanoe elaborated on this problem to the *Los Angeles Times,* admitting, "For many years, the Levi brand was the

CELEBRITY CAMEOS

Several of the spots in the Levi's "They Go On" campaign featured appearances by celebrities. Author Quentin Crisp appeared as a patron in a nightclub, and musician Lenny Kravitz was the rock star stuck at a gas station's pay phone. The bag boy in "Bag Boy Fantasy" was played by Brian Vaughan, the actor who had portrayed the young Brad Pitt character in the film *Seven Years in Tibet,* and the riled agent of the rock star was played by Bodhi Elfman, son of Danny Elfman, musician and member of the rock band Oingo Boingo.

uniform of younger people... and we were also able to nurture a relationship with people 25 years of age and older. In the last few years, that's been more problematic for us." CSC Consulting analyst Marie Drum Beninati agreed: "Boomers got older and started looking for more comfort than they can get from Levis. And while kids still wear jeans, it's a different kind of jeans—wide jeans, jeans hanging down over their derriere, jeans made from other materials."

Concurrent with Levi's loss of market share was a growing decline in popularity with the youth market that accounted for a large percentage of jeans purchases. In order to ensure future buyers, it was crucial to gain the allegiance of customers from a young age. Unfortunately for Levi's, its market share with the consumer group of 15- to 19-year-olds dropped from 33 percent in 1993 to 26 percent in 1997. Levi's learned that this statistic was not a fluke when a yearlong research project indicated that the "echo boomers," children of baby boomers, considered Levi's passé. Steve Goldstein, vice president of marketing and research for Levi's USA, told *BusinessWeek,* "Kids say they love the Levi's brand. But if you ask them whether it's 'with it,' they'll say no." Sixteen-year-old Irma Cruz stated in the *Columbian,* "Levi's are too straight, too plain... None of my friends wear them." Levi's needed to present a fashionable and modern campaign that would win over these consumers.

COMPETITION

As more players entered the lucrative denim market in the 1990s, Levi's faced growing competition. According to the 1998 *Market Share Reporter,* VF Corporation, the maker of Lee and Wrangler jeans, held 30.1 percent of the U.S. market, compared to Levi's at 16 percent. Designer labels also infiltrated the market, with Guess, Tommy Hilfiger, Calvin Klein's CK, Nautica, Diesel, and Ralph Lauren's Polo among the high-end labels fighting for market share. Gap, along with its Old Navy clothing line, also posed a threat. Private-label jeans, such as J.C. Penney's Arizona line and Sears, Roebuck's Canyon River Blues series, also entered the market and gobbled up valuable jeans dollars. According to the *Tactical Retail Monitor,* as reported in the *Los Angeles Times,* private-label jeans experienced a rise in market share from 3.2 percent in 1990 to 19.1 percent in 1997.

Alan Millstein, a New York retail consultant and editor of *Fashion Network Report,* told *Advertising Age,* "Levi's is in a pincers from the private-label and specialty brands in department stores and the designer brands." According to the *Los Angeles Times,* Tony Cherbak, a Deloitte & Touche retail-industry analyst, agreed with Millstein and stated, "For a long time, they were the only game in town... They were able to demand prices and dictate display. But as other brands ate into their market, retailers could turn elsewhere or make their own private label brands."

MARKETING STRATEGY

To boost its popularity with the younger market and to lure customers, Levi's chose to launch the $90 million image-building campaign based on the strength of its brand. Levi's Fanoe was quoted in the *San Francisco Chronicle* as saying, "The ads will be built around what the Levi's brand stands for: originality, independence and Levi's as an American icon." The biggest and most expensive campaign instigated by Levi's, "They Go On" included six television spots, five of which lasted 60 seconds and one 90 seconds. It debuted in August 1997 on prime-time network television and during telecasts of National Football League games on Fox as well as on MTV. The spots were also shown in movie theaters across the nation. The print and outdoor portions of the campaign began in October with print ads in magazines such as *Rolling Stone* and *Sports Illustrated.* Levi's home page on the World Wide Web provided additional ad information, and the campaign included bilingual spots in Spanish and English for viewers in the Los Angeles and Houston areas. Levi's expected 94 percent of its target consumers to see the campaign an average of 15 times each.

The six television spots shared a loosely interwoven narrative. Common elements linked the spots, but the elements were often random, and viewers had to pay close attention to notice the connections. As Amy Rosenthal, the senior marketing specialist at Levi's USA, explained to the *Dallas Morning News,* "We call it dream logic... There's no beginning, middle or end, just a series of little vignettes. Nothing much happens, but they are connected in interesting ways by interesting things." The strategy was similar to those adopted by competitors Lee and Guess, both of which produced television spots that were like minifilms that told stories, albeit nebulous ones, designed to push an image rather than a product. It was believed that this soft-sell approach would appeal to teenagers who had become jaded about pushy advertising. In the *Dallas Morning News* James Twitchell, author of *Adcult USA,* commented on the Levi's campaign by remarking, "It's the ultimate super-soft sell, so soft there's no sell at all... Advertising has become so omnipresent, the only way to cut through it is with something that doesn't look like an advertisement."

Levi's hoped that the target consumer would be engaged by the spots and encouraged to view all of them. Unlike other episodic campaigns that televised one spot at a time, Levi's chose to show the commercials in groups of two or three in an attempt to draw in the viewer and to signify that the spots were indeed related. Andy Berkenfield, Foote Cone & Belding account manager and vice president, told the *Dallas Morning News,* "You do worry with this sort of episodic storytelling that it will be confusing, so you try to make it pretty obvious, especially early on."

The first spot, the 90-second "Impala Man," featured a man wearing a cowboy hat who drove a Chevrolet Impala filled with stuffed animals to a diner. In the diner he talked to D.J. Marcus, a New York–bound disc jockey, and gave away a stuffed dinosaur. The following spot, "Car Chase," starred a Kojak-obsessed cab driver employed by a plainclothes policeman to chase a thief making a getaway on a moped. The cab driver engaged in a high-speed chase, with the nervous officer in the backseat. In the third spot, "Ice Cream Man," the disc jockey from the first spot returned as a disc jockey in a trendy nightclub, an ice cream man would not hand over ice cream to young children unless they correctly answered difficult trivia questions, and a rock musician spoke on a pay phone at a gas station. "Bag Boy Fantasy" showed the agent of the rock star on a cellular phone in a grocery store while the bag boy daydreamed of being a rock star. "Test Drive," the fifth installment, included a girl who took a car on a test drive, with the dealer in the backseat making sales claims. She stopped to pick up her boyfriend and then drove to a coffee shop. The final spot, "Car Wash," featured a goggles-clad man who drove an AMC Gremlin through a car wash with the windows rolled down, thus washing the inside and outside of the car. As he exited the car wash, the Impala from the first spot drove by.

A team of 40 engineers from NBC Digital Productions merged the six original spots with new commercials to create a drama series that debuted on September 22, 1997. The drama appeared exclusively on NBC.com, which used "They Go On" to promote the network's new Snap! website browser created by the technology publisher CNET. Returning characters such as D.J. Marcus and the Impala man were featured along with the new characters Chloe and Zack. At certain arranged times the actors interacted with website visitors via a message board.

It was revealed in the April 26, 1999, issue of *Adweek* (eastern edition) that both the online "They Go On" drama series and earlier spots were the result of a new advertising agenda set in place by Gordon Shanks, the president of operations in the Americas for Levi's. In early 1997 Shanks had requested that Foote Cone & Belding make the campaign "reinforce Levi's brand values across all consumers in all categories." In response, the agency's creative director Chuck McBride created a 30-second spot that spoofed the current baggy-pants trend while simultaneously touting Levi's own baggy Wide Leg jeans. The zany commercial featured a young man being operated on by dancing surgeons. Although representatives from Foote Cone & Belding believed the commercial would resonate well with younger consumers, Shanks rejected it. As a result, much of the agency's talent left, and the remaining creatives released the more elusive "The Go On" spots in August.

OUTCOME

When the campaign first aired, Levi's reported positive feedback regarding the "They Go On" campaign from young consumers, and it won critical praise for its originality. The *Los Angeles Times* rated the campaign a three out of four for effectiveness, and the *Orange County Register* scored it an A- for its concept. Bob Garfield, columnist and reviewer for *Advertising Age,* gave "They Go On" three out of four stars.

Unfortunately for Levi's the praise was short-lived. The company posted a 4 percent sales decline in 1997. That same year Levi's announced that it would close 11 U.S. factories and lay off nearly one-third of its workforce. Clothing-industry consultant Harry Bernard of Colton Bernard, Inc., told the *Columbian,* "I think ['They Go On' is] probably the most unfocused ad campaign that they've ever had... I think they've lost track of who and what they are." Other advertising analysts accused Levi's of specifically losing touch with its teenage customers. John Flanagan of the youth-marketing consultancy Thermostat explained to *Adweek* (eastern edition) that Levi's "wasn't monitoring the streets, they fell asleep."

In 1998 Levi's posted its worst sales loss since World War II. Furthermore, according to a study conducted by the retail-industry analysts Tactical Retail Monitor, Levi's market share of U.S. jeans plummeted from 31 percent in 1990 to 16.9 percent in 1998. Levi's executives partially blamed Foote Cone & Belding for their company's downturn. Agency representatives blamed Levi's Gordon Shanks for trying to target such a wide demographic. In early 1998 Levi's ended its 68-year relationship with Foote Cone & Belding, but it continued using the "They Go On" tagline until mid-1998.

FURTHER READING

Cuneo, Alice Z. "Insight into Brand Wins Levi's for TBWA Chiat/Day." *Advertising Age,* February 2, 1998, p. 3.

———. "Levi's Branding Blitz in Works." *Advertising Age,* March 31, 1997.

———. "Levi's Fights Back with Image Ads." *Advertising Age,* July 28, 1997.

Emert, Carol. "Levi's Battles to Stop Slide in Market Share." *San Francisco Chronicle,* June 25, 1997, p. B1.

Feuerstein, Adam, and Clifford Carlsen. "Levi Tries to Get Young People into Its Pants." *San Francisco Business Times,* April 14, 1997.

Garfield, Bob. "Levi's Heroes Vapid, but They Wear Well." *Advertising Age,* August 11, 1997, p. 29.

Gellene, Denise. "Levi Strauss Shoots for the Hip." *Los Angeles Times,* September 4, 1997, p. D4. Reviews the "They Go On" campaign.

Himelstein, Linda. "Levi's Is Hiking Up Its Pants." *Business Week,* December 1, 1997, p. 70.

Irvine, Martha. "Levi's Searching for a New Image." *Columbian,* November 6, 1997, p. D2.

Johnson, Greg. "Levi Strauss Is Trying to Give Its Product and Image a Better Fit." *Los Angeles Times,* November 6, 1997, p. D1.

Kelly, Jane Irene, and Michael McCarthy. "TBWA C/D to Levi." *Adweek* (eastern ed.), February 2, 1998, p. 5.

"Levi's Launches 'Funky' Ad Blitz." *San Francisco Examiner,* July 29, 1997, p. B1.

Maurstad, Tom. "Levi's Commercials Sell Soft and Cool." *Dallas Morning News,* October 19, 1997, p.1C.

Oberlag, Reginald. "NBC Continues TV/Internet Convergence with Snap! Alliance." *Shoot,* August 14, 1998, p. 22.

Outhier, Craig. "From Edgy to Ridiculous, TV Pitches Continue to Push the Envelope and Test Our Patience." *Orange County Register,* October 26, 1997, p. F10.

Voight, Joan. "An American Icon Fades Away." *Adweek* (eastern ed.), April 26, 1999.

Mariko Fujinaka
Kevin Teague

Lincoln National Corp.

1500 Market Street, Suite 3900
Philadelphia, Pennsylvania 19102-2112
USA
Telephone: (215) 448-1400
Fax: (215) 448-3962
Web site: www.lfg.com

HELLO FUTURE CAMPAIGN

OVERVIEW

In the late 1990s Philadelphia-based Lincoln National Corp., which marketed itself as Lincoln Financial Group, launched a successful branding campaign that targeted affluent consumers. But in the early 2000s it became clear that as baby boomers entered their retirement years and challenged preconceived notions about what retirement meant, Lincoln Financial Group would have to reposition its brand and message to remain relevant in the marketplace. The result was the "Hello Future" campaign that began in April 2005. It was aimed at both affluent baby boomers and the financial planners and other intermediaries that sold the Lincoln Financial Group products.

The "Hello Future" campaign, created by ad agency Martin/Williams of Minneapolis, Minnesota, presented an optimistic image of retirement as an opportunity to pursue dreams, whether they satisfied a lifelong interest or involved giving back to the community. One of the television spots, for example, featured an African-American woman who as a child was told by a guidance counselor to become a file clerk so she could meet eligible lawyers to marry. Instead she became a lawyer, then a judge, and finally, in retirement, a guidance counselor. Coming full circle, she advised a young girl to think higher than file clerk and to consider becoming a lawyer. In addition to television spots, the "Hello Future" campaign included radio, print, online, and alternative media elements. Although the budget was not made public, Lincoln Financial Group had reportedly spent $20 million in advertising the previous year.

The initial phase of the "Hello Future" campaign came to a close at the end of 2005. The dramatic increase in call-center volume and website traffic indicated that the message resonated with consumers. Moreover, the intermediaries were pleased and embraced the campaign.

HISTORICAL CONTEXT

Although it was nearly 100 years old by the late 1990s, Lincoln Financial Group was a little-known provider of financial services, operating under a variety of brand names, such as Lincoln Life, the Delaware Group, and Vantage Global Advisers. Working with ad agency Martin/Williams, the firm launched a branding campaign to bring all the subsidiaries under the Lincoln name and developed a logo that featured a silhouette of Abraham Lincoln. Moreover, the association of the great president with integrity, trustworthiness, and honesty was in keeping with the image Lincoln Financial Group wished to project as it began to target affluent consumers. Relying on the tagline "Clear solutions in a complex world," the campaign proved highly successful. According to research firm Wirthlin Worldwide,

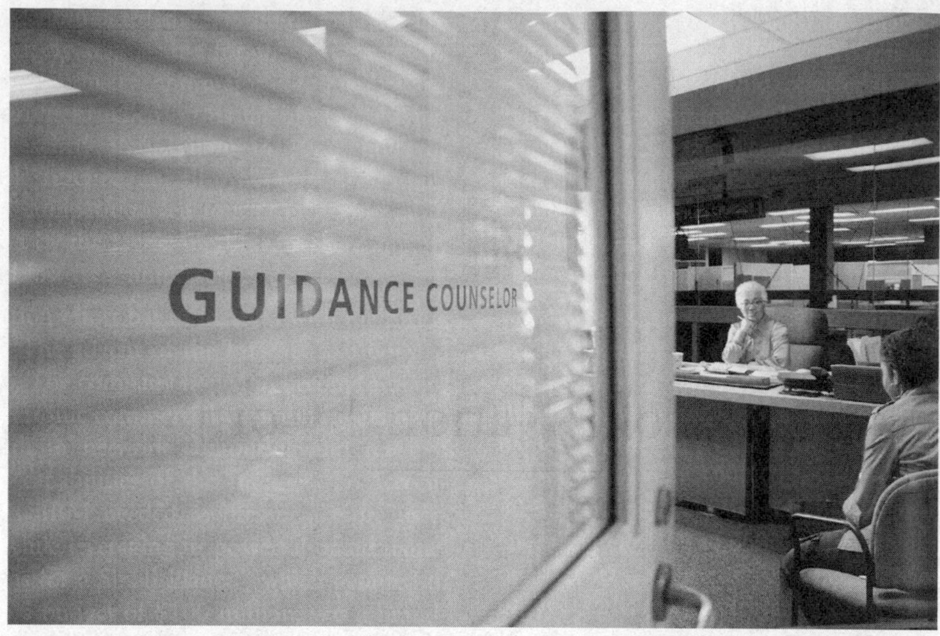

A still from "Guidance Counselor," a television ad featured in Lincoln National's "Hello Future" campaign. PHOTO COURTESY OF MARTIN WILLIAMS, INC. REPRODUCED BY PERMISSION.

between 1998 and 2000 aided brand awareness among consumers with assets between $250,000 and $500,000 increased from 22 percent to 36 percent. In addition, between 1999 and 2000 aided branded awareness among consumers worth more than $500,000 improved from 31 percent to 38 percent.

Lincoln Financial Group underwent another significant change in the early 2000s. It introduced a new channel of distribution, moving from a network of financial advisors to a wholesale force that sold products to financial intermediaries (such as brokers and financial advisors). But it soon became apparent that many potential intermediaries were not familiar enough with what Lincoln Financial Group had to offer. A series of print ads was then introduced to make the pitch that Lincoln Financial Group products would make the brokers and financial advisors heroes to their clients.

While Lincoln Financial Group had made great strides with both affluent consumers and intermediaries, it was operating in a changing marketplace. Aside from increased competition in the number and type of companies offering financial products, Lincoln Financial Group and Martin/Williams recognized that a major sea change was about to take place. Just as the baby-boom generation, throughout its iconoclastic development, had differed markedly from its elders, forever defying the conventional wisdom of marketers, it was now in the process of redefining retirement. Baby boomers, especially affluent ones, planned to not only live longer but also to pursue a far more active retirement than their parents had, whether that meant launching a second career, giving their time to the community, or pursuing travel and other interests. And with that shift in paradigm, the financial needs of an older demographic would change as well. Lincoln Financial Group, as a result, had no choice but to adapt, but it also recognized a chance to seize an opportunity, to distinguish itself from the crowded field of companies offering financial products and to stake out a position in a changing marketplace.

Lincoln began to reposition and increase recognition of its brand in 2004 when it acquired the naming rights to the new football-only stadium in Philadelphia. Lincoln Financial Field became the home of the National Football League's Philadelphia Eagles, one of the most successful and popular NFL franchises. The company also gained exposure through sports by sponsoring the prime-time made-for-television golf tournament Lincoln Financial Battle at the Bridges, showcasing the world's most popular golfer, Tiger Woods. In 2005 it also sponsored the Lincoln Financial NBC Sports Report that appeared during the televised coverage of such high-profile events as the Wimbledon and French Open tennis tournaments, Notre Dame college football games, and PGA golf tournaments. In April 2005 Lincoln Financial Group launched the "Hello Future" campaign, retiring

"Clear Solutions in a Complex World" after six years to take the next step in repositioning the brand.

TARGET MARKET

"Hello Future" targeted two audiences: consumers and intermediaries. As had been the case since the late 1990s, Lincoln Financial Group focused on affluent consumers, roughly 45 to 64 years of age with an annual income of at least $100,000 or income-producing assets of $250,000 and higher. The campaign tried to appeal to both men and women equally. Nor was age a prime consideration: research indicated that a person's mindset about retirement was more important. About 10 years before people planned to retire—whether that be 55, 65, or older—they began to think seriously about making sure their finances were in order and thus became open to the "Hello Future" message. Thus, the campaign had to be nimble enough to appeal to people in their 40s as well as their 60s.

The other target of the "Hello Future" campaign were the intermediaries, who would actually have to sell the Lincoln Financial Group products to consumers. Intermediaries were divided into four channels: wirehouse brokers like Merrill Lynch and Morgan Stanley; independent financial planners; banks; and insurance decision-makers.

COMPETITION

Lincoln Financial Group had to contend with strong competition on a number of fronts. It faced direct competition from dozens of firms, but the most prominent were the Hartford Financial Services Group, Pacific Life and Annuity Company, Genworth Financial, Prudential Financial, and Massachusetts Mutual Life Insurance Company. All of them had the financial resources to market their products effectively, making it more difficult for Lincoln Financial Group to cut through the clutter to have its message heard. Offering less direct competition was another crowded field, which included such firms as Fidelity National Financial and T Rowe Price Group and such Internet-oriented companies as E*Trade Financial Corp. Lincoln Financial Group was also in a sense competing against—and appealing to—the self-directed investor, who might be using the services of a discount broker or trading online through E*Trade or Ameritrade Holding Corp., both of which had spent many millions of dollars in humorous, sometime outrageous advertisements to gain name recognition. In the process they changed the nature of financial-services advertising, which was traditionally staid and played off the idea "we're the experts, we know what's best for you." Now old-line firms like Morgan Stanley were introducing humor into their advertisements and talking about earning trust, a key concept given the number of recent Wall Street scandals in which financial firms clearly did not have the best interests of their customers at heart.

A PICTURE WORTH MORE THAN A THOUSAND PENNIES

Lincoln National Corp. did not establish its corporate headquarters in Philadelphia, Pennsylvania, until 1998. Its roots actually stretched back to the early years of the century and to Fort Wayne, Indiana, where a man named Wilbur Wynant established a nonprofit fraternal insurance company in 1902. Two years later, however, he skipped town, leaving his local associates either to fold the company or make a stab at reviving the business. It was reorganized in 1905 as Lincoln National Life Insurance Company, with the Lincoln name invoked to suggest trustworthiness, an asset all too often lacking in the insurance industry at the time. The company wrote to Abraham Lincoln's only surviving son, Robert, requesting a picture of his father for use on the company's letterhead. Within days the younger Lincoln sent a photo with the reply: "I find no objection whatever to the use of a portrait of my father upon the letterhead of such a life insurance company named after him as you describe; and I take pleasure in enclosing you, for that purpose, what I regard as a very good photograph of him."

MARKETING STRATEGY

The underlying strategy of "Hello Future" was to show baby boomers that Lincoln Financial Group understood the changing nature of retirement and to project a positive image of retirement as a time of optimism and opportunity. In short, retirement was a beginning, not an ending. The resulting integrated campaign, which broke in April 2005 with a two-page full-color ad in the *Wall Street Journal,* included a wide range of elements, including television and radio spots, print ads, online marketing, and a variety of alternative media plays.

The five television spots of the campaign carried a crossover message. While they primarily targeted the customer, they were also intended to polish the image of Lincoln Financial Group to make it appeal to the intermediaries. Each of the spots provided examples of people embracing retirement. In the "Guidance Counselor" spot an African-American girl in the 1960s was advised by a school guidance counselor to become a file clerk: "It's a great way to meet eligible lawyers." Instead, she was shown going to college, becoming an attorney, then retiring as a judge to become a guidance counselor herself. The spot closed with her conferring with a student: "File clerk? Have you ever considered being a lawyer?" The voice-over then summed up the message: "The one thing you've always wanted to do? It's still out there, just waiting for you to say, 'Hello future.'" Another spot showed a classic-car garage owner telling a customer that he had decided to sell his business in order to pursue a dream before he was too old. The new owner was then shown. Ironically, he had bought the business to follow his own retirement dream. The voice-over stated, "Maybe you'll finish your life's work early. Or maybe you'll hear a second calling and say, 'Hello future.'" The other spots featured a retired man teaching physically challenged children to ski, a family returning to Russia to discover their roots, and a doctor volunteering in a distant country. The 30-second spots ran on national cable and network programming, including during the Lincoln Financial NBC Sports Report.

The radio spots and print ads of the "Hello Future" campaign mirrored one another in a number of ways. They primarily targeted intermediaries, although the message reached consumers as well. The 30-second radio commercials played on the Wall Street Radio network and in large part relied on similar text to what was found in the print ads. "Maybe you'll finish your life's work early. Maybe your next retirement party won't be your last. Maybe you prefer days filled with challenge and purpose. Maybe today you'll wake up and say... 'Hello future.'" The print ads appeared in the *Wall Street Journal* and in business and finance periodicals such as *Fortune* and *Money*.

Online elements of "Hello Future" included content sponsorship on the *Wall Street Journal Online* and on the *Smart Money* website. In terms of alternative media, the campaign participated in a co-branding insert that appeared in *Smart Money,* sponsored the Times Square ticker in New York City, and also provided plastic bags for the delivery of the *Wall Street Journal* in 10 top markets.

OUTCOME

According to an October 2005 interview with Stacy Hintermeister, vice president and group account director for Martin/Williams, there was no data available at the time to indicate what kind of impact the "Hello Future" campaign had on brand awareness. But other signs were positive, such as the doubling of call-center volume and website traffic. Anecdotally, the campaign was well received in the marketplace, and financial planners and other intermediaries expressed their approval and embraced the effort. Lincoln Financial Group was also pleased with the campaign, which helped in its efforts to strengthen strategic partnerships. Distribution in key segments increased, contributing to earnings growth in 2005. The campaign ran until the end of 2005, at which point it was reviewed and evolved for 2006.

FURTHER READING

Baar, Aaron. "Lincoln Focuses on Its Name." *Adweek,* July 22, 2002, p. 2.

———. "New Target for Lincoln Financial." *Adweek* (Midwest ed.), March 19, 2001, p. 5.

Frazier, Lynne McKenna. "Fort Wayne, Ind.–Based Lincoln Nation Raises Brand Profile." *Fort Wayne (IN) News-Sentinel,* October 6, 1998.

"Lincoln National Corporation." *International Directory of Company Histories,* Vol. 25. St James Press, 1999.

"M/W, Lincoln Financial in Storytelling Mode." *Adweek* (midwest ed.), April 28, 2005.

Rosenthal, Marshall M. "High-Yielding Assets." *American Demographics,* March 2001, p. S20.

Snyder, Beth. "Lincoln Financial Aims Ad Effort at Superrich in U.S." *Advertising Age,* March 15, 1999, p. 26.

Ed Dinger

Little Caesar Enterprises, Inc.

2211 Woodward Ave.
Detroit, Michigan 48201
USA
Telephone: (313) 983-6000
Fax: (313) 983-6390
Web site: www.littlecaesars.com

■■■

CLONING CAMPAIGN

OVERVIEW

Though few consumers would connect complicated mathematical equations and the latest scientific advances in biology with Little Caesar Enterprises, Inc., both figured into an early 1997 advertising campaign for Little Caesars Pizza, as the company is commonly known. Dreamed up by Cliff Freeman & Partners, who had been providing Little Caesars' wacky ads since 1986, the "Cloning" campaign was delivered to television audiences in March 1997.

Known for wildly improbable and quirky commercials, Cliff Freeman & Partners rolled out the "Cloning" campaign on the heels of one of the century's biggest biological bombshells—the cloning of Dolly the sheep. The campaign consisted of three television spots (the original 30-second spot, followed by 20- and 15-second versions), as well as print advertising for Little Caesars' latest bargain, the Unlimited Pizza. This product incarnation was available for only $6.99 and consisted of any size pizza, in round or square crust, with any combination of 12 toppings, which meant, mathematically speaking, hundreds of millions of available choices. The first Unlimited Pizza was only $6.99, and customers could order a second for $6.99 and receive a free order of Crazy Bread as well.

The Cloning commercial, launched March 31, 1997, portrayed a group of white-coated scientists (a writer for the Orange County Register likened them to something from an Ed Wood movie) watching a colleague in a glass-encased room with a sheep. As another scientist pressed a clearly marked red "cloning" button, a second sheep, identical to the first, appeared. The scientists, mad with glee, were interrupted by the arrival of two pizzas from Little Caesars. They were all so excited about the Unlimited Pizza deal that no one noticed that the pizzas were placed on top of the red button. As the red button then produced dozens of sheep, the slaphappy and blissfully ignorant scientists expounded on the excellent value of Little Caesars. The last shot showed the glass room overflowing with cloned sheep and the trapped scientist fruitlessly holding up a handwritten "help" sign.

HISTORICAL CONTEXT

Little Caesars was the brainchild of Michael and Marian Ilitch, who joined in the post-World War II pizza boom. Brought to the United States by Italian immigrants decades earlier, pizza took the country by storm after hundreds of thousands of enlisted men came home after eating it in Europe. The Ilitches' first restaurant debuted in 1959, where pizza became their most-requested menu item, and the first "Little Caesars" opened in 1962.

In 1998 Little Caesars boasted more than 4,800 outlets in the United States, Canada, the Dominican Republic, Guam, Honduras, Korea, Puerto Rico, and the

Czech and Slovak Republics. The Little Caesars chain was the third-largest pizza producer in the country, selling as many as four million pies (with the same recipe perfected in 1959) per week. At the time of the "Cloning" campaign, Little Caesars was struggling to maintain its market share and to juice sales after flat numbers for three years running. Though the Little Caesars brand was well known, consumers had an increasing number of choices for their pizza dollars—including fast food giants like McDonald's, which was test-marketing small pizzas.

The tag line "Pizza! Pizza!" was initiated by Little Caesars back in the early 1970s, when it began selling two pizzas for the price of one. Other pizza makers followed suit, at least for awhile, but most could not cover the costs; Pizza Hut and Domino's offered a second pizza for a nominal cost, such as four or five dollars. Little Caesars truly hit the big time in the 1980s and signed up with Cliff Freeman & Partners in 1986. Armed with about 5 percent of its annual revenues (which were $400 million in 1986), Little Caesars took a serious leap into television advertising, and its choice of Cliff Freeman & Partners was a favorable one. Known in the industry for such humorous classics as Almond Joy's "Sometimes You Feel Like a Nut" and Wendy's "Where's the Beef?" the creative team at Cliff Freeman soon put their spin on Little Caesars' products and turned out a series of goofy commercials that became the hallmark of Little Caesars' pizza.

Pizza carryout and delivery consumption heated up considerably in the late 1980s and early 1990s, and the Big Three—Pizza Hut, Domino's, and Little Caesars—used a myriad of approaches to differentiate themselves from one another in the consumer's mind. Although all touted value, Little Caesars was far and away the value leader. Pizza Hut's mainstay was its sit-down, red-roofed restaurants, and Domino's was better known for its delivery service. Pizza Hut and Little Caesars had also stepped up delivery (although Little Caesars originally delivered pizzas in the 1960s, it went to carryout only in the 1970s), but neither could top Domino's in this market segment. Little Caesars had some dine-in outlets, including "pizza stations" inside Kmart stores, but Pizza Hut ruled the sit-down segment with over 8,600 restaurants.

To bring greater awareness to its calling card—value—Little Caesars had to reinvent itself and its brand. As in the past, it turned to the creative minds at Cliff Freeman & Partners. Unfortunately for those at Cliff Freeman, the success of earlier campaigns like the "Conga Line," "Big! Big!" and "Safety Video" raised high expectations.

TARGET MARKET

Little Caesars' marketing has remained the same for each of its advertising campaigns—always targeting families and adults aged 18 to 49. Although the Unlimited Pizza's most recent predecessors (Pizza by the Foot and the Giant Caesar) appealed more heavily to crowds because of the sheer volume of pizza, the Unlimited Pizza appealed not only to this crowd but also to smaller groups or families who were more concerned with what was on their pizza than with gorging themselves. All of Little Caesars' pizzas were geared toward the budget-conscious; they were usually priced several dollars less than Pizza Hut or Domino's pizzas and provided enough food for at least one dinner and possibly leftovers as well. As a further bonus, if two Unlimited Pizzas were ordered at $6.99 each, Little Caesars threw in a complimentary order of Crazy Bread.

In addition to the age and income range of its customers, Little Caesars consistently targeted customers with a strong sense of the absurd, those who would laugh at highly improbable but humorous situations populated with bizarre characters. Cliff Freeman & Partners' commercials were always a bit left field, but they were well liked and remembered in consumer polls. The success of the quirky ads led consumers and Madison Avenue to expect more not only from Cliff Freeman & Partners but from Little Caesars as well.

COMPETITION

The fast food pizza segment had been ruled for decades by the Big Three until in the 1990s brought the emergence of the Louisville, Kentucky-based Papa John's International. Within a few short years, Papa John's

PIZZA AND GLADIATORS

Picture Nero noshing on a flat, breadlike substance covered with red sauce and varied ingredients as he hollers to bring in the lions. Yes, pizza has been around since the Roman Empire, at least according to Greg Hardesty of the *Orange County Register.* Early pies were probably topped with garlic, leeks, and herbs. Mozzarella cheese was not added until the seventh century, and by the 1880s pizza had become a staple for Italian royalty and peasants alike, with scores of immigrants bringing the dish to the United States. Soldiers ate pizza on the run during World War II, and the dish enjoyed a surge of popularity when they came back home, which in turn spawned Pizza Hut, Little Caesars, Domino's, and thousands of neighborhood pizzerias.

had risen from nowhere to become the seventh-ranked pizza chain in 1994, then the fourth in 1996 with phenomenal growth in units, robust same-store sales, and burgeoning overall sales. The Big Three, however, took turns suffering setbacks and debacles: Pizza Hut's Big Foot and Triple Decker pizzas were "boom-splats," a term the chain coined itself. Domino's dove into reckless spending, and its famous 30-minute guarantee was blamed for car accidents and spurred lawsuits. Little Caesars' national rollout of delivery services met with little enthusiasm, and its sales were falling.

Minor setbacks loomed large for the Big Three as Papa John's grew rapidly, but Little Caesars was the most vulnerable of the bunch. Not only had the company lost a 10-year veteran to rival Domino's, but both Domino's and Pizza Hut were taking direct aim at Little Caesars' customers. Both chains introduced huge, cheaply priced pizzas, and Domino's went so far as to create Twisty Bread, remarkably similar to Little Caesars' Crazy Bread, and to debut amusing television commercials with a cartoon character. For its part, Papa John's was not fiddling much with different products or over-the-top promotions—the company stressed a quality pizza that tasted good. Plenty of consumers agreed, often citing Papa John's as the best tasting pizza in surveys. The franchise was named "Best Pizza Chain in America" in 1998 by Restaurants & Institutions and also topped its food quality, service, and convenience categories. Papa John's expanded in all directions, opening a new outlet virtually every day, with hopes for 2,000 by the year 2000.

For Little Caesars, new product rollouts generally took two months from conception to the completed ad campaign. With heavy pressure to boost sales, Little Caesars rolled out two huge pizza products (the Giant Caesar and Pizza by the Foot) in quick succession in 1996, a time when its market share was eroding and same-store sales were weakening. The Unlimited Pizza's debut in early 1997 was still a statement in value but also heralded another approach: to concentrate on better pizza rather than simply more pizza.

MARKETING STRATEGY

Although the Cloning commercial was timely and as absurd as Cliff Freeman & Partners' usual television ads for Little Caesars, the company's print ads added another dimension to the campaign. Previous ad campaigns had consisted of a television commercial (usually in 30-, 20-, and 15-second versions), print ads, and radio spots, but the Unlimited Pizza rollout had no such accompanying radio spots, just print ads in newspapers and local direct mailers. Little Caesars' print ads were usually retreads of television commercials, yet in Unlimited Pizza's case, the print ads took another tack entirely. There was no reference to cloning sheep; a lesson in mathematics was given instead. By playing with numbers, signifying the nearly "unlimited" possibilities for its latest pizza rollout, Little Caesars was once again betting on its buzz word—value—but also on variety.

Value and variety were a complementary pair, successfully parlayed by Little Caesars with its Pizza by the Foot. In this three-square-foot behemoth, customers could enjoy a different topping on each one-foot section. The Unlimited Pizza, however, took variety to the extreme, offering any size (small, medium, or large) or shape (round or square) pizza, with any combination of 12 toppings. And herein was the mathematical lesson: if customers ordered two different Unlimited Pizzas, how many variations could be concocted? The folks at Little Caesars turned to finance professors at nearby Wayne State University, who determined that there were 302,002,176 possible combinations, more than enough to last a lifetime. In fact, according to Wayne State's professor Rob Wolf, you could "eat a different pizza every meal of every day for more than 275,000 years!"

The hype of the Unlimited Pizza's print ads appealed to younger pizza fans who delighted in experimenting, to those who loved pies with multiple toppings, and, with the very inexpensive price of $6.99, even to those who wanted only cheese and sausage. Little Caesars' only difficulty in enticing the younger generation was that most of its outlets did not have delivery, and younger, teenage consumers could not drive. Such consumers had to rely on a busy mom or dad or call another pizza maker.

In contrast to the Giant Caesar or Pizza by the Foot, the Unlimited Pizza did not require specially made pans and delivery boxes or as much oven space. At the outset, the new pizza product did not require extra spending because Little Caesars already had everything necessary to make the Unlimited Pizza—unless customers ordered so many more toppings than usual that there were shortages, which was unlikely.

OUTCOME

Although the Cloning commercial was not as popular with consumers and Madison Avenue as previous ad campaigns, the product did well enough to still be available at Little Caesars more than a year later. The television campaign, although oddly funny, did not produce the guffaws necessary to pull the company from its doldrums, which may have been the impetus for the next two moves made by Little Caesars. One was to return to the bigger-is-better theme by bumping up the size of its small, medium, and large pies by 4 inches each, from 10, 12, and 14 inches to 14, 16, and 18 inches. The other step, which was much more profound, was to put its $40 million advertising account up for review in early 1998, effectively ending its 12-year relationship with Cliff Freeman & Partners.

Despite the "Cloning" campaign's awards (a Silver Clio and two Communication Arts citations), rumors had circulated that the management at Little Caesars and Cliff Freeman were no longer seeing eye-to-eye on marketing strategy. With stagnant revenues of $1.8 billion for 1995, 1996, and 1997 and a host of other difficulties, Little Caesars needed a blockbuster ad campaign and felt a change of scenery might provide the boost. Yet regardless of what the future would bring, Little Caesars still had run more award-winning ad campaigns than any other pizza chain and could rest on its laurels for a while—if the words "Pizza! Pizza!" were uttered in quick succession, everyone immediately thought of Little Caesars.

So what was more important to pizza buyers: size, crust, or toppings? Cost or convenience? Little Caesars had geared its pizzas to just about every preference at some point, with Big! Big!, Giant Caesar, and Pizza by the Foot tackling size, with stuffed or seasoned crusts for dough lovers, and with the Unlimited Pizza for topping combinations. The chain always kept its price low and bet on the convenience factor by placing outlets in Kmart stores and Holiday Inn hotels, by rolling out credit card use in Utah, and by establishing plenty of neighborhood Little Caesars throughout North America and abroad. With lackluster sales in the late 1990s, the company needed some fine-tuning and perhaps a new product or variation so different it snapped consumers to attention. Little Caesars clearly hoped its new ad agency, Bozell Worldwide, would be the key to its rejuvenation.

FURTHER READING

Benezra, Karen. "Pizza Parting: Revamping Caesars Splits with Agency." *Brandweek,* February 23, 1998.

Child, Charles. "Domino's Preparing to Step up Pizza War." *Crain's Detroit Business,* May 31, 1993.

Enrico, Dottie. "Little Caesars Pleases, but Misses Topping Previous Ads." *USA Today,* July 21, 1997.

Frank, Robert. "Marketing and Media: Building a Better Pie—Pizza Hut Is Topping Rivals with Cheese...." *Wall Street Journal,* January 18, 1996.

Halliday, Jean. "Variety Is the Spice of Life in Domino's Pizza-War Plan." *Crain's Detroit Business,* August 2, 1993.

Hardesty, Greg. "More Dough: With Fast Food Consumption Up, New Pizza Players Battle Entrenched Chains for a Slice of the Profits." *Orange County Register,* June 22, 1998.

Howard, Theresa. "Pizza's 'Big Three' Hold the Gimmicks, Serve Simplicity." *Nation's Restaurant News,* January 13, 1997.

Lutton, Christine. "Sizing up the Pies: When It Comes to Monster Pizzas, Big Does Not Mean Better, Our Tasters Say." *Virginian-Pilot/Ledger-Star* (Norfolk), August 5, 1993.

Merritt, Jennifer. "Fast Food: Chains Have Long History of Gimmicks." *Knight-Ridder News Service,* January 7, 1998.

Outhier, Craig. "Time after Time: Commercial Appeal." *Orange County Register,* June 22, 1997.

Prewitt, Milford. "Pizza Chains Ditch Discounts in Back-to-Basics Bake-Off." *Nation's Restaurant News,* August 1, 1994.

Rose, Peter. "Pizzeria Owners Find Their Niche in Crowded Boise Market." *Idaho Business Review,* April 9, 1994.

Rubenstein, Ed. "Size Matters in New Campaigns Set to Attack the Competition." *Nation's Restaurant News,* September 22, 1997.

Taryn Benbow-Pfalzgraf

GRAND CANYON CAMPAIGN

OVERVIEW

Little Caesars, an international pizza chain of more than 4,800 units, is well known in the advertising industry for its quirky "Pizza! Pizza!" television commercials. Created with Cliff Freeman & Partners, the ads feature bizarre humor and absurd comic images while avoiding hard-sell directives.

A mainstay of Little Caesars pizza has always been value; the company provided customers with two pizzas for the price of one or bigger pizzas for less money than its primary competitors Pizza Hut, Domino's, and Papa John's. With the introduction of the "Giant Caesar" pizza in the fall of 1996, Little Caesars again demonstrated to consumers that it would always provide more pizza for the money, and to prove it the Giant Caesar pizza was more than 65 percent bigger than standard 14-inch large pizzas and sold for the very attractive price of $9.99 or $10.99 depending on the geographic area. The 8-slice, 18-inch pizza was also filled with larger-than-life ingredients, including three-inch pepperoni and giant-sized ham toppings.

The Giant Caesar pizza campaign revolved around the old adage that size does indeed matter, with the Little Caesars pizza dwarfing items generally considered huge or outsized, such as the Grand Canyon (from which the campaign took its name) and mainland China. The campaign even played on the most common "size" joke about male genitalia. The national television spot featured several straight-faced hayseeds eating the pizza in the first two (Grand Canyon and China) vignettes and an elderly couple in bed on their honeymoon in the third vignette. The ad had the tag line "The new Giant Caesar makes everything else look small." The 30-second commercial, launched on August 12, 1996, was run during popular prime-time television programming and during sporting events, and was accompanied by radio and print advertising.

HISTORICAL CONTEXT

The Little Caesars franchise—owned by parent company Little Caesar Enterprises, Inc.—has been in business for 40 years. Founded by husband-and-wife business partners Michael and Marian Ilitch in Garden City, Michigan, the original restaurant served a variety of food items from spaghetti to french fries to fried chicken as well as pizza. But pizza was the most popular product, and the Ilitches sold nearly 300 in their first week as restauranteurs. With their low-priced, flavorful pizzas selling about as fast as they could make them, the Ilitches soon realized they had a winner. The first Little Caesars franchise store, serving mostly pizza, was opened in the Detroit area in 1962.

The recipe the Ilitches used in the 1950s is the same one used today, though the pizza has varied by size, crust type, and toppings. Little Caesars has always used natural ingredients, eschewing synthetics such as manufactured cheese products and artificial flavorings. In the years since Little Caesars was established, many competitors have emerged, including small independent pizzerias as well as chains like Pizza Hut, Shakey's, Domino's, and latecomer Papa John's, which took the industry by storm in the early 1990s.

Though like Pizza Hut the company began as a sit-down establishment and later added delivery services, Little Caesars went to carry-out only in 1971, the same year the two-for-one program was initiated. The now-famous "Pizza! Pizza! Two Great Pizzas! One Low Price!" slogan became a permanent part of Little Caesars' marketing campaigns in 1975. Two years later, the company added drive-through windows, and in two more years it installed a conveyor oven to increase its capacity. Although technological advances continued to change certain elements in the pizza-selling and delivery business, value and taste had remained Little Caesars' claim to fame—until a series of catchy and undoubtedly original television ads came along.

By the time Little Caesars hired Saatchi & Saatchi's Cliff Freeman & Partners in 1986, there were 1,000 company franchises across the nation, and the company was ready to devote some serious dollars (about 5 percent of its revenues, which had reached nearly $400 million) to becoming a serious competitor. Cliff Freeman & Partners was at the zenith of its popularity as well, having produced several award-winning advertising campaigns, including the popular "Where's the Beef?" television ads featuring Clara Peller for Wendy's. Freeman's first efforts for Little Caesars marked the company's television advertising debut, with seven 30-second spots filled with silly characters, unusual situations, and quirky humor that became Little Caesars' advertising trademark.

Given that the pizza carry-out and delivery industry had heated up considerably in the late 1980s and early 1990s, Little Caesars began experimenting with its service operations. The company went back to delivery services, again putting it head-to-head with Domino's. Though the national introduction of delivery services wasn't nearly as successful as hoped, the company left it up to the individual franchisees whether to continue the service or not. Yet a bigger hit came through a remarkable deal with Kmart in 1992, placing self-serve Little Caesars "Pizza Stations" in over 400 Kmart stores. The success of these units led to hundreds more, and though these locations were later renamed KCafe and began serving other food brands, Little Caesars pizza was still the mainstay of the menu, and the association with the discounter provided an excellent promotional venue.

The introduction of the Giant Caesar was technically nothing new, as larger-sized pizzas—some up to 24 inches—had been offered by Pizza Hut, Domino's, and Little Caesars as well as by independents. Size, however, had been scaled down across the board when two-for-one deals became the norm in the 1980s. Additionally, bigger pizzas were not always cost-effective as they required larger pans and more ingredients, took up greater oven space, and required special packaging.

TARGET MARKET

Little Caesars' advertising has generally targeted families and adults from 18 to 49 years of age. The Giant Caesar and its corresponding Grand Canyon spots were aimed especially at families with several mouths to feed, as the Giant would satisfy the needs of the average-sized family (four to six members). The product was also a potential success with college students with their traditionally large appetites and tight budgets.

In addition to the age range of its customers, Little Caesars always targeted those with a slightly offbeat sense of humor, those who would find its commercials—with zany situations and often absurd-looking characters uttering equally absurd lines—worth a good guffaw. Both audiences and the advertising industry came to expect much from the company, which was both a blessing and a burden as it became necessary for Cliff Freeman & Partners to continually top itself.

COMPETITION

Little Caesars' competition grew exponentially as geographic areas were saturated with a wide range of fast food restaurants, including a variety of pizza producers. Though the company's sales outpaced industry growth

SIZE VS. SHAPE

The pizza wars between Pizza Hut, Domino's, and Little Caesars are legendary and have sparked fierce competition within the industry. Competitors, both large and small, have tried to steal customers by experimenting with their pizzas' size (up to 36 inches for Little Caesars' Pizza by the Foot), shape (round, square, rectangular, and football shaped, the latter courtesy of Little Caesars), height (for example, the Triple-decker by Pizza Hut, which was a disaster), crust (cracker thin, cheese stuffed, pan, hand tossed, spice brushed, and double dough), toppings (from three-inch pieces of pepperoni from Little Caesars to rose petals, egg, peanut butter, squash, rattlesnake, ostrich, buffalo, gator, tuna, chocolate chips, and jelly beans in some pizza joints), and cheese (whole-milk, skim-milk, and artificial mozzarella, as well as cheddar, goat cheese, feta, and others types of cheese).

by 24 percent in the early part of the 1990s, the middle and later years of the decade were not as rosy; Pizza Hut and Domino's hit their strides and were better at steering customers away from Little Caesars. Convenience often seemed to play a greater role than taste or price in the fast food war. Little Caesars hoped customers would return not only because its products were cheap and convenient, but also because they were better tasting than those of its two primary rivals. Additionally, the company hoped its unusual, funny ads would help consumers remember the Little Caesars brand.

Pizza Hut was clearly a formidable competitor primarily because of its size (over 7,200 restaurants) and available capital. A former subsidiary of PepsiCo, Pizza Hut had spun off in 1997 but still had considerable clout, especially after introducing delivery service. Domino's, on the other hand, with about 5,400 outlets nationwide, was immensely popular with the college crowd. Yet Domino's wanted to capture the family market, too, focusing on busy working Moms too harried to fix a sit-down meal every day.

Little Caesars' earlier initiative to provide two pizzas for the price of one made competitors sit up and take notice and forced both Pizza Hut and Domino's to offer their own interpretation of this deal. While they did not offer two-for-one deals, each did offer a second pizza for a cut-rate price. Then came Papa John's, which made the fight for market share even more fierce, and though the fast food industry as a whole was growing, it was overcrowded.

MARKETING STRATEGY

Little Caesars had dubbed itself the "value king of the pizza industry," and the Giant Caesar was meant to demonstrate the indisputable truth of this statement. According to Sue Sherbow, Little Caesars' vice president of Corporate Communications, many people believed "bigger is better, so we developed our Giant Caesar to satisfy people's appetites and purchasing trends." In marketing the Giant Caesar, the pizza was not only significantly bigger but somewhat different than Little Caesars' other pizzas. It was considered more "New York"-styled, with a more pronounced or rolled-over crust, and it looked more "homemade" than mass produced. The pizza had to capitalize on its most important asset—value—during a slowdown in the $25 billion pizza market. To achieve this goal, Cliff Freeman & Partners came up with the Grand Canyon campaign, illustrating just what was "big" and what was not.

Another hallmark of Little Caesars' marketing was to promote fun; the company did not take itself too seriously and wanted its products and advertising to reflect people enjoying themselves. Some of its previous ad campaigns by Cliff Freeman & Partners clearly promoted this creed, like the well-known Conga Line (featuring dancing poodles and humans) or the Delivery training sequence (would-be delivery drivers being put through a rigorous program). These commercials had been immensely popular and not only earned awards and citations but plenty of brand recognition. Although Pizza Hut had tried a mega-pizza called "Big Foot" and Domino's had created the "Dominator" (both were short-lived), and with Papa John's International putting even more pressure on the three major pizza chains, Little Caesars really needed a winner—in terms of product and sales, as well as effective advertising. As Anthony Vagnoni, an *Advertising Age* editor, commented to *USA Today* in a July 1997 article regarding Little Caesars, "Anything less than a belly laugh isn't good enough." Vagnoni also stated that Little Caesars' advertising was consistently well done and was "still far superior to ads . . . for other pizza products."

Yet lower sales and an $8 million shortfall when a quarter of its franchisees were late on their national ad fund payments in 1997 (according to *Competitive Media Reporting*) caused Little Caesars not only to cut back significantly on marketing dollars but to be cautious with the dollars that were spent. In addition to its advertising support, Little Caesars was busy trying a myriad of new promotional ventures, including opening pizza kiosks in Holiday Inn's busiest hotels near Walt Disney World in

Orlando, Florida; test-marketing the use of American Express cards in some of its Utah outlets; and offering slices at 39 cents each to celebrate its 39th anniversary.

OUTCOME

While the "Grand Canyon" campaign was clearly a success with consumers and the advertising industry, most viewers felt it was not as good as previous Little Caesars campaigns. The ads did propel sales, and the television and radio spots won 10 major awards, including both national and regional Addys, an Andy citation for best national campaign, and two Clios (a silver in the retail foods category and a bronze in the national campaign segment), all in 1997. Yet the industry's slump had weakened Little Caesars, resulting in rather flat sales for 1995, 1996, and 1997. Total or systemwide sales had hit $2 billion in 1994 and fallen to about $1.8 billion for the next three years.

Despite its many successes with Cliff Freeman & Partners, including the Grand Canyon spot, Little Caesars put the estimated $40 million account up for review in early 1998. The move prompted Freeman to resign and left several other agencies—including Bozell Worldwide; Grey, New York (who had previously pitched for Domino's); and the Minnesota-based Fallon McElligott—vying for the work. Though Cliff Freeman himself said it was time to move on—since he and Little Caesars' management no longer saw eye-to-eye on marketing strategy—he was quoted in a *Brandweek* article in February 1998 as saying, "They put us on the map and vice versa."

While it was not known what the next generation of Little Caesars promotions might be, consumers had come to expect a certain type of ad from this company. Given that Little Caesars had been voted the "Best Pizza Value in America" by *Restaurants & Institutions* magazine for 11 consecutive years, it seemed unlikely that their ads or their pizza would change much in the near future, despite any temporary difficulties. As for the Giant Caesar, although it was discontinued, Little Caesars increased the size of all its pizzas in response to positive reactions to the Giant Caesar.

FURTHER READING

"American Express Card Now Welcome at Utah Little Caesars Locations." *PR Newswire,* March 13, 1998.

Frank, Robert. "Marketing & Media: Building a Better Pie—Pizza Hut Is Topping Rivals with Cheese...." *Wall Street Journal,* January 18, 1996.

Howard, Theresa. "Kmart Corp.: Attention Shoppers—Retail Giant Hails 'Caesars' as a Big Guy." *Nation's Restaurant News,* January 1998.

———. "Pizza's 'Big Three' Hold the Gimmicks, Serve Simplicity." *Nation's Restaurant News,* January 13, 1997.

"Little Caesars Celebrates 39 Years in Business with 39-Cent Slices of Pizza." *Bison Franchise News,* May 6, 1998.

"Little Caesars Named Best Pizza Value in America by Consumer Survey." *Bison Franchise News,* March 26, 1998.

"Pepperoni the Size of Ferris Wheels." *Advertising Age's Creativity,* September 1, 1996.

Pittinger, Heather. "Popular and Profitable." *Hotel & Motel Management,* May 6, 1996.

"Pizza! Pizza!." *Adweek,* August 19, 1996.

"Pizzeria Rolls Out Extra-Large Pie." *Tampa Tribune,* August 14, 1996.

Rubenstein, Ed. "Size Matters in New Campaigns Set to Attack the Competition." *Nation's Restaurant News,* September 22, 1997.

Taryn Benbow-Pfalzgraf

SAFETY VIDEO CAMPAIGN

OVERVIEW

Consumers know Little Caesar Enterprises, Inc. for its absurd, funny commercials created by Cliff Freeman & Partners, including the very popular and award-winning "Safety Video" campaign. Rolled out near the end of 1996 to introduce its new Pizza by the Foot, the Little Caesars campaign not only elicited laughs from audiences but once again proved humor in advertising translated into dollars and sense.

With more than 4,800 Little Caesars outlets throughout the United States and Canada, the Dominican Republic, Guam, Honduras, Korea, Puerto Rico, and the Czech and Slovak Republics, the company was selling more than four million pizzas per week by 1998. Say "Pizza! Pizza!" and everyone thinks Little Caesars, just as consumers and the advertising industry alike had come to expect the ribald humor and bizarre antics in the company's commercials from the mid-1980s into the late 1990s.

Cliff Freeman & Partners' "Safety Video" campaign, like its predecessors, was not heavy-handed salesmanship, but goofy situational comedy. This time, the comedy resulted from the selling and buying of Little Caesars' new Pizza by the Foot, a three-foot-long rectangular pizza sold in a specially designed box along with a complimentary order of eight Italian bread sticks. The campaign's television spot, focusing on "safety" instructions for handling this unusual product, began with a video shown to customers by a Little Caesars employee and manager. The video was simple and straight forward, explaining the possible hazards of mishandling this potentially "dangerous" pizza and how to "observe a safe turning radius."

Ludicrously loopy, the customer in the commercial ignored the video, and mayhem resulted: the television monitor crashed to the floor, glass was shattered in the pizza outlet's doors, a customer approaching the door was decked, a passing bicyclist was whacked by the box, and so on. The Little Caesars manager intoned, "I don't think he was paying attention."

HISTORICAL CONTEXT

Little Caesars' rollout of Pizza by the Foot was its latest example of giving consumers more for their hard-earned bucks. As an originator of selling two pizzas for the price of one back in the 1970s, Little Caesars introduced Pizza by the Foot close on the heels of another bigger-is-better product, the Giant Caesar. The Giant Caesar had been introduced in August 1996, a mere month and a half before Pizza by the Foot debuted. Both products were meant to assure customers that Little Caesars was always willing to give them more pizza for every dollar and that the company would keep finding new ways to do so. Launching two outsized products in succession was part of a marketing drive to keep "value" synonymous with the company's name and products. Pizza by the Foot further emphasized value by giving customers a free order of Little Caesars' latest garnish, the new Italian Bread (fresh-baked bread sticks lightly brushed with olive oil and sprinkled with an Italian blend of spices).

Little Caesars was no novice in the fast food industry, having been around for four decades. Founders Michael and Marian Ilitch had begun their trade in Garden City, Michigan, with a full-service restaurant serving such staples as fried chicken, pasta dishes, and pizza. After selling almost 300 pizzas in their first week, the Ilitches decided to open another restaurant that concentrated on low-priced pizza; the first Little Caesars franchise store opened in the suburbs of Detroit in 1962.

Throughout the rest of the 1960s and the beginning of the 1970s, Little Caesars grew throughout the Midwest. The "Pizza! Pizza! Two Great Pizzas! One Low Price!" marketing concept was initiated in 1971, the same year the company stopped delivery in favor of carryout only. Over the next decade, Little Caesars added drive-through windows, installed conveyor ovens, and broadened its menu. When it hired Cliff Freeman & Partners in 1986, Little Caesars had 1,000 outlets across the nation and was prepared to spend about 5 percent of its annual revenues (or $20 million that year) on advertising. Cliff Freeman & Partners was well respected in the ad business, having produced a number of successful and award-winning campaigns like Wendy's "Where's the Beef?" and Almond Joy's "Sometimes You Feel Like a Nut." The partnership turned the increasingly well-known pizza chain into a media giant with a series of quirky 30-second commercials, featuring odd vignettes with even odder characters.

Because the pizza carryout and delivery industry had heated up considerably in the late 1980s and early 1990s (because of the falling price of high-quality cheese), Little Caesars resumed delivery services, but was not pleased with the results. The company therefore returned to its mainstay—value—by rolling out the Giant Caesar and Pizza by the Foot in quick succession. The only downside to producing Pizza by the Foot was its special packaging; yet the unique, handled rectangular box seemed to provide almost as much fun as the pizza inside. The "Safety Video" commercial was launched during prime-time family-oriented television programming and sports events on October 28, 1996. Lasting 30 seconds (subsequent versions also ran at both 20 and 15 seconds), the television commercial was accompanied by print advertising and three separate radio spots.

TARGET MARKET

Throughout its history, Little Caesars aimed its marketing at families and adults from 18 to 49 years of age. Both Pizza by the Foot and the Giant Caesar were created for college students, parties, and averaged-sized families. Pizza by the Foot was especially accommodating, because each one-foot section could have a different topping—thereby pleasing everyone. Lastly, the meal came with free Italian bread and was sold for the low price of $10.99. Pizza by the Foot, Little Caesars made clear, was the perfect crowd-pleaser for anyone on a budget.

In addition to appealing to customers in a particular age group and income range, Little Caesars consistently targeted folks with a screwball sense of humor, those who would get a good belly laugh from Cliff Freeman & Partners' ads. Consumers and the advertising industry not only consistently rated Little Caesars ads as effective and funny but also came to expect those involved to top themselves with ever more outrageous, bizarre campaigns.

COMPETITION

When Little Caesars developed a new product and gave Cliff Freeman & Partners the necessary information, a finished ad campaign was usually ready within two months. In the mid- and late 1990s, this was especially crucial due to fierce competition. Little Caesars had knocked Domino's off its second-tier spot in the early 1990s, when the latter suffered losses of $68 million in 1991 and $55 million in 1992. In 1994 and 1995, however, Domino's came back with a vengeance (in part because of the defection of a 10-year Little Caesars

PIZZA PIZZA SQUARED

Little Caesars has long been known by its advertising, and its "Pizza! Pizza!" tag line, coined in the 1970s, became recognized around the world. Not only did the "Pizza! Pizza!" motto become synonymous with the Little Caesars franchise, but it also stood for the "double" value in receiving two pies for the price of one. Unfortunately for Little Caesars, one of its major competitors Canada is a chain called Pizza Pizza—a higher-ranked rival that received a boost every time Little Caesars advertised using its "Pizza! Pizza!" slogan.

executive who joined Domino's) just as Little Caesars started experiencing its own problems. Then came Papa John's International, challenging not only Little Caesars but Domino's and Pizza Hut as well. In 1996, when Little Caesars' market share declined from 14.5 to 13.4 percent and sales fell by nearly 8.1 percent, Papa John's had excellent same-store sales (up 10 percent) and a phenomenal unit growth of 32.1 percent for the year (all figures according to *Nation's Restaurant News*).

On top of stiff competition came an industry slowdown, which seemed to hurt Little Caesars more than Pizza Hut, Domino's, or Papa John's. In this flooded marketplace, where convenience and availability often counted for more than taste and price, Little Caesars, with its 4,800 franchises, needed more than ever to imprint its brand on the consumer's mind. To compete with Pizza Hut's 7,200-plus restaurants, as well as 5,400 from Domino's and another 1,500 or so from Papa John's, Little Caesars had to differentiate itself from the pack. The company chose to entice them with silly and irreverent advertising, and hoped to keep them with variety and exceptional value.

MARKETING STRATEGY

Larger pizzas for less money was certainly nothing new, especially because Little Caesars had used that strategy with the Giant Caesar a few months earlier. Pizza by the Foot had to make its mark in a different way. Back in 1993, Pizza Hut had introduced Big Foot pizza, which was two square feet of pizza cut into 21 slices, and it did not make much more than an immediate and short-lived splash. For its part, Domino's debuted the Dominator, which was 30 inches long, and a new garnish called Twisty Bread, almost a carbon copy of Little Caesar's Crazy Bread. At the time, Little Caesars was offering its Big! Big! pizza, which was two feet long and plugged by George Burns in television spots.

Three years later, at the end of 1996, Little Caesars was not only topping the competition, but also itself, with Pizza by the Foot. It was bigger than Domino's largest pizza by half a square foot and Pizza Hut's by a whole square foot and came with a different topping on each one-foot section. With free Italian bread sticks the deal was touted as a great value. But the real kicker was the unique carrying case; by placing the emphasis on the specially designed box and secondarily on the pizza, consumers were drawn to try it at least once—and this was the focus of a new $10 million ad campaign by Cliff Freeman & Partners.

The "Safety Video" television commercial came in three versions, with the original at 30 seconds and the other two at 20 and 15 seconds each. To accompany the television spot, Cliff Freeman & Partners produced three equally creative radio spots and print advertising in newspapers and direct mailers. The three radio spots, called "Family Dinner," "Megaphone," and "Timmy," were as off-the-wall as the "Safety Video" commercial, with the first running in both 60- and 30-second versions and the other two running at 30 seconds each. "Family Dinner" featured a family attempting to converse while eating Pizza by the Foot; their conversations were stymied by the vast distance they had to put between them to accommodate the gigantic pizza. The "Megaphone" radio spot took the same premise one step further by having the family use a megaphone to speak to each other. The "Timmy" spot featured a father and son (Timmy) dining on Pizza by the Foot, with the son tossing a slice of pepperoni from his end of the pizza all the way to his dad, who was duly impressed by his throwing skills.

The nuts and bolts of the Pizza by the Foot campaign were simple—touting the enormous size and value of this new product through effective, original, and quirky advertising. Cliff Freeman & Partners' use of the Pizza by the Foot box was a stroke of genius. Even though the old directives of value and "more pizza for your money" were in the commercial, concentrating on the box opened a new world of "safety" gags. Given most people's intolerance for instructional media (from putting together a bicycle to cooking in the microwave) and the ridiculous lengths to which some companies and manufacturers go to instruct customers on safety, portraying a customer who pays little or no attention to the Safety Video was a universal jab at consumers and companies alike, making the resulting havoc all the more credible and hilarious.

Because Little Caesars considered itself the "value king of the pizza industry," bringing out a parade of bigger-is-better pizzas like the Big! Big!, the Giant Caesar, and Pizza by the Foot was supposed to propel the company's brand more decisively in the $25-billion pizza market. As company spokesperson Sue Sherbow commented in a January 1997 article in *Nation's Restaurant News,* "Little Caesars has always tried to emphasize value; that's our niche—and we will continue to look at innovation, value and fun." The last word of this statement, "fun," was a hallmark of Little Caesars ads—if the ads were fun and funny, consumers were entertained and apt to remember them longer.

OUTCOME

Pizza by the Foot fared well after its October 1996 debut. The item remained an optional menu item into 1998, and the Italian Breads pawned a sibling called Italian Cheese Bread. In its never-ending quest to provide more for less, Little Caesars went on to develop the Unlimited Pizza, offering any sized pizza and any topping for the low price of $6.99, and later bumping up the size of all its pizzas by four inches each.

Cliff Freeman & Partners' "Safety Video" television campaign was popular with both consumers and the advertising industry. The campaign won a slew of awards—in this sense reminiscent of previous Little Caesars winners like the "Conga Line" and "Cheeser! Cheeser!" campaigns—and was better received than the Giant Caesar's "Grand Canyon" commercials. "Safety Video" was voted Best TV Single by *Adweek,* garnered eight Addys (overall, national, and regional), two Andys, won Ad Age's Best of TV award, claimed two Clios (a silver in the retail foods category and a bronze in the national campaign segment), and was given the Silver Pencil from the One Show awards, all in 1997. The "Family Dinner" and "Megaphone" radio spots also won several awards, including Clio certificates, a Mercury award, and the Communication Arts' Radio Single award. Yet despite kudos from the advertising industry, Little Caesars was in a slump, with stagnant sales of about $1.8 billion for 1995, 1996, and 1997, after hitting over $2 billion in 1994 for systemwide sales.

Fraught with tepid sales, a shortfall in its national advertising fund, the layoff of 1 percent of its corporate workforce, and an oversaturated market, Little Caesars put its estimated $40 million advertising account up for review in January 1998. Cliff Freeman & Partners' response was to resign the account, stating that their objectives no longer matched those of Little Caesars. The Detroit office of Bozell Worldwide eventually won the account, and the advertising industry waited to see what direction Bozell and Little Caesars would take to shore up market share and renew the latter's brand in the minds of consumers.

FURTHER READING

Child, Charles. "Domino's Preparing to Step Up Pizza War." *Crain's Detroit Business,* May 31, 1993.

Frank, Robert. "Marketing and Media: Building a Better Pie—Pizza Hut Is Topping Rivals with Cheese. . . ." *Wall Street Journal,* January 18, 1996.

Halliday, Jean. "Variety Is the Spice of Life in Domino's Pizza-War Plan." *Crain's Detroit Business,* August 2, 1993.

Howard, Theresa. "Pizza's 'Big Three' Hold the Gimmicks, Serve Simplicity." *Nation's Restaurant News,* January 13, 1997.

Lutton, Christine. "Sizing Up the Pies When It Comes to Monster Pizzas, Big Does Not Mean Better, Our Tasters Say." *Virginian-Pilot/Ledger-Star* (Norfolk), August 5, 1993.

Polong, Travis E. "Firms Spar for Bigger Slice of Pizza Market." *San Antonio Business Journal,* July 30, 1993.

Prewitt, Milford. "Pizza Chains Ditch Discounts in Back-to-Basics Bake-Off." *Nation's Restaurant News,* August 1, 1994.

Rubenstein, Ed. "Size Matters in New Campaigns Set to Attack the Competition." *Nation's Restaurant News,* September 22, 1997.

Walkup, Carolyn. "Little Caesar Cuts 27 Management Posts at Headquarters." *Nation's Restaurant News,* July 14, 1997.

Weigel, George. "Big's the Word in the Industry." *Sunday Patriot-News* (Harrisburg), August 1, 1993.

Taryn Benbow-Pfalzgraf

TALKING PIZZAS CAMPAIGN

OVERVIEW

By the late 1990s the pizza market had become saturated, and Little Caesar Enterprises, Inc., a value-oriented player that had grown dramatically during the 1980s, saw its sales and market share flatten. The company decided to change its marketing strategy and early in 1998 hired Bozell Worldwide Inc., giving the agency the task of developing a new advertising campaign that would emphasize product quality in addition to value.

The Bozell "Talking Pizzas" campaign ran on television in the fall of 1998 and in direct-mail solicitations. In the two 30-second television spots two pizzas had a humorous conversation. The campaign was similar to previous efforts in that it offered a value-oriented promotion; major differences were that the ads used a gentler humor and emphasized product quality through the dialogue and close-up shots of the pizzas. The direct-mail advertising offered a money-back guarantee. The campaign was a marked change from the zany approach of the past and got a subdued reaction from critics and consumers.

HISTORICAL CONTEXT

Husband-and-wife team Mike and Marian Ilitch started their first restaurant in Garden City, Michigan in 1959. The restaurant served a variety of foods, including spaghetti and fried chicken, but pizza was clearly the most popular item. The Ilitches sold almost 300 pizzas during the first week of business. They eventually decided to make low-cost pizza the main item on their menu and opened the first Little Caesars franchise operation in Detroit in 1962. The small family pizza chain grew dramatically. Although it started out as primarily a sit-down restaurant, delivery services were later added. In 1971 Little Caesars changed to a carry-out only business and began offering two-for-one pizza deals. In the same year the slogan "Pizza! Pizza! Two Great Pizzas! One Low Price!" was introduced.

By the 1980s Little Caesars' business was booming, and in 1986 the company hired Cliff Freeman & Partners, known for its use of goofy humor in advertising, as its agency. The pairing resulted in award-winning ads and was widely regarded to have worked to the benefit of both parties. For more than a decade Little Caesars' advertising was known for its offbeat humor based on wacky sight gags and an animated toga-clad Roman who proclaimed "Pizza! Pizza!" and other double tag lines such as "Pan! Pan!" and "Big! Big!" at the end of each commercial. The advertising almost always revolved around the theme of getting more for the money at Little Caesars. "Value is our niche and emphasis and it's very valid for us," said Little Caesars spokesperson Sue Sherbow in January 1998. "It's how we expect to be doing business for years to come."

According to *Crain's Detroit Business,* by the late 1990s Little Caesars' sales had "stagnated" and its market share flattened. Evelyne Slomon, editor of *Pizza Today,* reported that the company was "feeling the financial pinch" from its unprofitable two-for-one specials. "I don't expect the company to go out of business, but their sales are going down, and they need to re-group," she said. The company cut its advertising spending by 22.8 percent in 1996 and overhauled its management. The *Detroit Free Press* reported in October 1998 that the company had downsized its staff twice in less than 14 months.

The company also had a history of bumpy relationships with its franchisees. In 1993 one group of franchisees sued the company in federal court, claiming that it had violated antitrust laws by overcharging them for supplies and not allowing them to deal with other suppliers. Franchisees reportedly worried about the company's financial situation and criticized its marketing approach as lacking in foresight, consistency, and effectiveness.

To make matters worse, Little Caesars was getting substantially less than rave reviews on quality. *Brandweek* reported in January 1998 that, regardless of value, "customers have to feel good about the pizza they get. And when it comes to taste, Little Caesars often loses. In its last pizza survey, Consumer Reports called Little Caesars offerings 'low in flavor, and the cheese can be so chewy it's almost rubbery.'" Bob Garfield, reviewer for *Advertising Age,* wrote in September 1998, "There's an old joke about a kvetching guest at a Catskills resort. Not only is the food terrible, he complains, but the portions are too small. It's supposed to be ridiculous, but with such a consumer in mind the Little Caesars marketing strategy was born." Garfield went on to compare the pizza to "wet flannel, minus the flavor." Nonetheless, Little Caesars received 11 consecutive awards for "best pizza value" based on consumer surveys by *Restaurants & Institutions* magazine.

When the company decided to rethink its marketing strategy, it began a quiet review of its advertising. This prompted Freeman to resign the account in February 1998, and Bozell was hired two months later. With the new advertising agency came a new emphasis on product quality that the company hoped would give it an edge in an increasingly competitive pizza market.

TARGET MARKET

Little Caesars had historically targeted families and adults in the 18-to-49-year age bracket. The value message was geared toward those who were conscious of budgets, including families with children and college students. The new campaign represented a shift in focus from value alone to one in which quality was also emphasized, although not to the exclusion of value. The campaign ran nationwide and featured two television spots that were shown during prime-time network and cable shows and during some college football games.

COMPETITION

Little Caesars ranked number three among the top four pizza chains. Pizza Hut, Inc., was number one, and Domino's Pizza, Inc., ranked second, with Papa John's International, Inc., in fourth place. Other, smaller players in the crowded pizza market included Sbarro, Italian Eatery, Round Table Pizza, ShowBiz Pizza Time, Inc.'s Chuck E. Cheese's, and Godfather's Pizza.

The pizza segment in general was stagnant in the late 1990s. *Brandweek* reported that pizza chain sales went up only a half of 1 percent in 1996, compared to the rise in total fast-food sales of 5.6 percent in the same period.

LITTLE CAESARS GOES FOR NEW LOOK

According to *Nation's Restaurant News,* in addition to promoting pizza quality, Little Caesars decided in 1998 to renovate its stores. At the annual convention of franchisees in early May, the company debuted a new prototype unit with higher ceilings, brighter colors and lighting, new countertops, and an expanded self-service drink station. "It incorporates our value and quality into the look of our stores, and it is a very family-friendly image that attracts customers," said Sue Sherbow, spokesperson for Little Caesars. She did not elaborate on the costs of the renovations but said that franchisees were not required to adopt the new design.

Bob Angona was one of the franchisees who liked the prototype. When Angona lost the lease on one of his two units, he relocated the store and used the new decor. While he would not discuss the cost, he said that sales were up 15 to 28 percent over the same period in the previous year. He attributed the increase to both the new design and the new location.

Other franchisees were concerned that the prototype had not been thoroughly tested and that the company might not stick with it. According to *Nation's Restaurant News,* the company had previously introduced unit models that did not pan out. Some franchisees said that the company should focus more on product quality than on a new store design.

During this time other segments fared significantly better than pizza, with burger sales rising 4 percent, chicken sales 10.5 percent, and sales of sandwich chains 4.8 percent. *Nation's Restaurant News* reported in September 1998, however, that Papa John's and Domino's had increased their market shares while Little Caesars' sales had lagged during the previous few years. The top three chains were particularly threatened by Papa John's, which, despite its relatively small size, had gained ground on its rivals through rapid nationwide expansion and growth in sales.

Large pizza chains, which historically had tried to boost sales with new product promotions, started to emphasize product quality, improve operations, and renovate units to revive business. They continued, however, to rely to some degree on promotions, with Pizza Hut adding new types of pizza to its menu, Domino's coming out with two new flavored crusts, and Little Caesars launching its "Big! Big!" campaign. Unlike its rivals, the up-and-coming Papa John's focused more on quality than on menu expansion. Chris Sternberg, Papa John's vice president of communications, said, "We continue to focus on our better-ingredients strategy. There are temptations to do line extensions and new-product rollouts, but we really believe that staying focused on doing one product better than anyone else helps us to continue to grow."

MARKETING STRATEGY

In the Bozell campaign, which first aired on September 2, 1998, the action in the two 30-second television spots—"Mutual Admiration" and "Home Movie"—revolved around two talking pizzas. As before, the television commercials were humorous, but there was more emphasis on the quality of the pizza. They put the spotlight on the product rather than on sight gags. Each commercial ended with the traditional "Pizza! Pizza!" tag line. Observers noted that the humor was more subdued than in the zany approach of Freeman. Gary Topolewski, Bozell's executive vice president and chief creative officer, said that the primary goal of the television commercials was "putting in the personality that is exclusively Little Caesars . . . It's not belly laughs; it's whimsical and a wink of the eye. And it's palatable, as opposed to talking starkly about the ingredients." Topolewski went on to observe, "Humor is a tough nut to crack to really make sure it works. You don't want the humor to overshadow the quality message."

In "Mutual Admiration" the two pizzas traded profuse compliments in exaggerated New York accents about the quality of each other's toppings. The first pizza said, "Look at you! You are lookin' good!" The second pizza replied, "Me? No my friend. It is YOU that is looking good . . . look at all those toppings!" The first pizza came back with "My toppings! Forget about it!" The conversation continued in this vein, with interjections such as "You're killin' me" and "Oh, stop it" thrown in. Pizza was featured in almost every shot in the commercial, and the conversation was filmed with quick side-to-side camera movements.

"Home Movie" showed two pizzas reminiscing about their "childhood" while they watched a "home movie," which, in this case, was a training film for Little Caesars employees on how to make pizzas. One pizza said, "Oh, look at that little ball of dough. Is that you?" The other responded, "You've got a very good eye. That is me." Growing wistful as they saw themselves in their "youth," they mused about how they had "grown up so fast." When one pizza asked if the other was crying, the second replied, "No, it's the onion."

VF ROLLS OUT PIZZAS FOR EMPLOYEES

When VF Corporation, makers of such apparel brands as Lee and Wrangler, found that there was a communications gap between the home office and company employees, it put some dough into solving the problem—pizza dough, that is.

Workforce reported in December 1998 that, according to research done the previous year, employees lacked knowledge of the VF brands, the role of the parent company, and the extent of its operations. In response VF decided to have 15,000 Little Caesars pizzas delivered on the same day to 40,000 employees at 185 plants and offices around the United States.

For trivia buffs: making the pizzas required some five tons of tomatoes, six tons of flour, and enough cheese to fill 34 bathtubs. It took the equivalent of 2,000 hours, or 83 days, to cook the pizzas. If the pepperoni from the pizzas were laid end to end, it would have traversed the length of 125 football fields. The pizzas placed together on the ground would have covered half an acre.

While *Workforce* did not report how much the national pizza party cost, the magazine described it as "a drop in the bucket when you consider VF's 1997 sales totaled $5.2 billion."

In a company press release Topolewski said, "Pairing light-hearted, entertaining copy, with virtually 30-seconds of product, the ads clearly make the pizza the focal point and reinforces the quality product. Additionally, using the talking pizzas throughout all communications will create a synergistic message to consumers that Little Caesars is committed to maintaining its value and quality position in the marketplace."

Although the emphasis was on quality, the new commercials continued to offer value in a promotion of two 12-inch pizzas with up to three toppings for $10.99. Direct-mail advertising supported the television campaign by offering a money-back guarantee with the new slogan "If it's not right, we'll take the bite!" The direct-mail advertising focused on the pizza's ingredients and the fact that the company still used its "authentic 1959 recipe." The money-back guarantee was not part of the television spots according to company spokesperson Sherbow because it was feared that it would obscure the message on product quality.

OUTCOME

According to company vice chairman Denise Ilitch, Little Caesars' sales rose during September and October of 1998. In November, however, *USA Today* described consumer response to the "Talking Pizzas" campaign as "tepid." According to an Ad Track poll, only 12 percent said that they liked the campaign "a lot," compared with an Ad Track average of 21 percent. Fifteen percent of men liked the ads, compared with 9 percent of women, and no one liked it as much as the previous year's campaign. According to the poll, 24 percent of consumers liked the Freeman commercials featuring sight gags about product size. More people thought that the Freeman ads were likeable rather than effective, however. The Bozell commercials, on the other hand, produced the opposite reaction, with 13 percent of consumers stating that they thought the ads were effective.

Reaction from advertising industry critics to the new campaign was not overwhelmingly favorable. Denise Gellene wrote in the *Los Angeles Times* that making the pizzas so prominent in the advertising "might be a mistake. The pizzas . . . look fairly ordinary, raising questions about what makes Little Caesars special." Garfield of *Advertising Age* disagreed with the company's description of the dialogue in "Mutual Admiration" as "clever banter," comparing it instead to "cheesy imitations of Frank and Louie, right up to the New Yawk accent." Garfield was kinder to "Home Movie," calling the dialogue "more charming and witty . . . but still not exactly laugh-out-loud delightful." While he acknowledged that the ads did "make the pizzas look tempting," Garfield cautioned that "now that Little Caesars has opened the quality issue, it had better be prepared to deal with the consequences if the reality in the box doesn't match the pictures on the tube."

FURTHER READING

Benezra, Karen. "Caesars' Fall." *Brandweek,* January 26, 1998, pp. 21-25.

———. "Pizza Parting." *Brandweek,* February 23, 1998, p. 1.

Cebrzynski, Gregg. "Pizza, Pizza: Little Caesar Ad Campaign Focuses on Product." *Nation's Restaurant News,* September 14, 1998.

Garfield, Bob. "Caesars' Pizza Patter Doesn't Really Cut It." *Advertising Age,* September 7, 1998.

Gazdik, Tanya. "Pizza Work to Fatten Bozell Staff." *Adweek* (Midwest Edition), April 6, 1998, p. 6.

Gellene, Denise. "Advertising & Marketing Ad Reviews." *Los Angeles Times* (Home Edition), September 17, 1998, p. D6.

Kosdrosky, Terry. "Let's Talk Pizza: Quality Is New Caesar Pitch; Franchisees Wary." *Crain's Detroit Business,* September 21, 1998, p. 1.

"Little Caesars Ads Aim for Pizza Lust." *USA Today,* November 16, 1998.

Parpis, Eleftheria. "Defend This?" *Adweek* (Eastern Edition), February 23, 1998, p. 3.

Petrecca, Laura, and Louise Kramer. "Little Caesars Calls Review; Freeman Out." *Advertising Age,* February 23, 1998, p. 1.

Teegardin, Carol. "Little Caesar's Tries to Reverse Sliding Pizza Sales." *Detroit Free Press,* October 16, 1998.

Zuber, Amy. "Pizza Hut-vs.-Papa John's Battle Signals Intensifying War among Segment Leaders." *Nation's Restaurant News,* June 22, 1998, p. 114.

Debbi Mack

Logitech International S.A.

Moulin du Choc
Vaud
CH-1122 Romanel-sur-Morges
Switzerland
Web site: www.logitech.com

WHAT WILL YOU DO WITH ALL THAT FREEDOM? CAMPAIGN

OVERVIEW

For many years Logitech International S.A. was well known among personal computer manufacturers, which bundled the company's computer mice with their machines, but to the general public Logitech was little known. Increasingly Logitech sought to build up its own brand identity as it tried to sell more upscale mice and keyboards under its own name rather than the brand of original equipment manufacturers (OEMs). Cordless mice and keyboards were ideal categories to pursue, and Logitech became the clear-cut industry leader. In the early 2000s Logitech needed to protect its franchise, threatened in particular by Microsoft. It also wanted to promote cordless products with a wider market. Hence in the autumn of 2003 it launched the "What Will You Do With All That Freedom?" marketing campaign.

The new campaign, created with ad agency Collaborate of San Francisco, featured the first television commercials in Logitech's history. The three 30-second spots in the $10 million campaign portrayed humorous situations in which people struggled with wired mice and keyboards and then discovered the freedom that came with cordless peripherals. The campaign also featured print ads that relied on images from the television commercials. In addition the "What Will You Do With All That Freedom?" campaign included in-store promotions and online elements.

Logitech succeeded in increasing awareness of its cordless products, preparing the ground for the introduction of less expensive products in this category in 2004. Sales grew at a rapid pace, and cordless products became a major sales driver for Logitech. The "What Will You Do With All That Freedom?" campaign, which ran into 2004, also won a prestigious Effie award in 2005.

HISTORICAL CONTEXT

Logitech was founded in 1981 by Stanford University classmates Pierluigi Zappacosta, born in Italy, and Daniel Borel, born in Switzerland, with the mission to design an electronic typesetting system. They soon learned about a Swiss watch-parts manufacturer that had developed a new computer mouse, which at the time was little more than a curiosity since communicating with a computer was commonly accomplished with a keyboard alone. Although the mouse was originally invented in 1964 for use in a graphical interface with computers, there was no market for such a device until the rise of the personal computer industry and Apple Computer introduced a user-friendly graphical interface. Zappacosta and Borel licensed the U.S. rights to the Swiss mouse and began selling mice to Apple for sale with their computers. The introduction of Microsoft's Windows operating system then opened up the market for Logitech to sell mice for IBM-compatible computers as well.

By the mid-1990s 17 of the top 20 computer companies were bundling Logitech mice with their systems, but few consumers were aware of the brand. Sales reached a plateau, earnings sagged, and Logitech was in danger of becoming a one-trick company. The company changed its fortunes in 1997 with the hiring of a new chief executive officer, Geurrino De Luca, who had served as the head of Apple's worldwide marketing. Logitech had always possessed top-notch engineering skills; it now had the marketing savvy to build the brand. De Luca recognized not only that PCs were becoming consumer-oriented appliances but that Logitech had to establish brand awareness with a mass audience. He pushed the company into the development of cordless input devices. "New generations of keyboards and remote controls will replace the mouse in the living room," he told David Einstein of the *San Francisco Chronicle*. "DVD and interactive digital TV will be integrated into the home computer, and this will create the need to have remote control functionality in the keyboard or in other types of control devices." Einstein added, "With that in mind, Logitech is putting a lot of effort into cordless mice, which can be used to control a PC from across the living room."

Logitech enjoyed a resurgence in the late 1990s, but as the new century dawned it faced the challenge of larger competitors, in particular Microsoft, looking to chip away at Logitech's core franchise of mice and keyboards. In 2002 the company conducted a search for a new advertising agency to launch a marketing push to ward off these challenges. It hired a small San Francisco shop called Collaborate, which had experience in promoting consumer products as well as computers.

TARGET MARKET

Logitech's target market had shifted over the years. Originally the company sold most of its mice to OEMs, which bundled the product with their PCs. In the 1980s a limited number of general consumers were willing to buy PCs, which still carried a high price tag, so sales came mostly from business customers. As prices came down, computers became easier to use, and the rise of the Internet provided further incentive to buy a PC for the home, the industry focus shifted to more of a mass market for both computer makers and providers of peripherals. Logitech sold most of its products to OEMs, but it also sold replacement and upscale items through retailers. These items were pitched toward consumers with more disposable income, people willing to pay more for sleek-looking, high-tech mice or keyboards. The "What Will You Do With All That Freedom?" campaign promoted Logitech's latest high-tech products, cordless mice and keyboards. Although the company hoped these would become mainstream items in time, the campaign targeted consumers more likely to buy the products at the time of the campaign: adults aged 25 to 54 with incomes of at least $75,000.

REMOTE POSSIBILITIES

Logitech's cordless mice and keyboards relied on radio-frequency technology. Unlike the competing infrared technology, which required a clear line of sight and had a range of about 30 feet, radio waves could penetrate walls and had a range of 150 feet. To prevent interference from typical cordless household telephones, which operated at a frequency of 900 megahertz, Logitech's cordless mice and keyboards operated at another part of the radio frequency spectrum, at 27 megahertz.

COMPETITION

In the 2000s people began to hold on to their computers longer, opting to buy peripherals to make them more versatile and useful. As a result competition for this business increased, expanding beyond the computer industry to include consumer electronics companies like Creative Technology and Philips Electronics. By building brand awareness Logitech was able to move beyond computer mice, keyboards, and joysticks (a product added for game players) to add speakers, headsets, microphones, and computer cameras. But Logitech's core products remained mice and keyboards, and it became the undisputed leader in wireless mice and keyboards. A major factor in hiring Collaborate was to protect this franchise and ward off giant Microsoft, which had decided to make a push on the computer component category by redesigning its products and becoming more aggressive in its marketing. Logitech was also threatened by smaller competition including Acer Inc. and Fujitsu Ltd., which were making strong bids to take away market share in the cordless category.

MARKETING STRATEGY

Because wireless products offered a higher profit and were the future of the category, Logitech, after a strategic review with Collaborate, chose to promote them as a way to drive sales in the "What Will You Do With All That Freedom?" campaign, which was budgeted at $10 million. The goal

TALE OF THE TAIL

The prototype of the computer mouse was made by Douglas C. Engelbart in 1964. In 1970 he received a patent on his "X-Y Position Indicator for a Display System" device, which was little more than a wooden shell with two metal wheels inside. Because a wire came out one end and looked like a tail, Engelbart nicknamed it a mouse.

was to convince the target audience to upgrade its traditional wired mouse and keyboard. The marketers decided to use humor to portray people in real-life (albeit exaggerated) situations in which mouse and keyboard cords got in the way and then to present the Logitech solution. Because the products were cord free, the idea of freedom became the core of the campaign, leading to the theme "What Will You Do With All That freedom?"

For the first time in its history, Logitech produced television commercials to anchor a campaign. "Until now, we've focused on channel promotion and advertising in vertical print and online media," commented Robin Selden, the company's vice president of marketing, in a press release announcing the launch of the new marketing effort. "What we've found, however, is that television is the ideal medium for this campaign, because sight, sound, motion and emotion help convey the benefits of our cordless products—and because it's time to reach out to a broader audience."

The "What Will You Do With All That Freedom?" campaign featured three 30-second television spots, which were unveiled on ABC's *Monday Night Football* on September 8, 2003. The one called "Multi-Tasker" showed a woman in an office trying to take a phone order while working on more than one computer workstation using wired mice and keyboards. Unfortunately a cat tried to play with a computer mouse, forcing the woman to try to move the cat while balancing the keyboard on her lap. She dropped the telephone, presumably losing a sale. On-screen text read, "Make multi-tasking less taxing." A voice-over common to all three spots declared, "The Logitech cordless keyboard and mouse. No cords to tie you up, slow you down or hold you back." The spot then showed the woman's work area refitted with wireless products, freeing her to wheel across the office floor—and accidentally run over the cat.

A second spot, "Lounge Chair," showed a man struggling to move a leather lounge chair into place. On-screen appeared the text "Comfort is a very relative thing." The humorous conclusion of the commercial, accompanied by the voice-over, was the sight of the man working his computer from across the room, where he had a wireless keyboard on his lap and a wireless mouse on the padded arm.

The last of the three spots, "Coffee Cup," showed a man working on his home computer but having trouble with his mouse, the cord of which had been knotted up and shortened. Because he could not pull the mouse into position, he spilled his paperwork, unintentionally highlighted text on his screen, and ultimately knocked over his cup of coffee. The complementary text read, "Don't tangle with your mouse." The kicker to the spot was the man putting his feet on his desk to happily work with a wireless keyboard on his lap—only to spill his coffee anyway.

The print element of the "What Will You Do With All That Freedom?" campaign drew on images from the television spots. For example, the man from "Coffee Cup" was shown in the print ad surrounded by a vast number of coffee mugs, along with the copy "Go ahead, live dangerously." Featured in another print ad was the man from "Lounge Chair." Looking quite comfortable in his T-shirt and pajamas, he used a wireless mouse and keyboard to operate his computer from his recliner. The print ads appeared in mainstream publications, such as *Time, Newsweek, Sports Illustrated,* and *BusinessWeek,* as well as in major newspapers.

The "What Will You Do With All That Freedom?" campaign also included direct mail, in-store promotions, and Internet elements. It ran into 2004. In a complementary effort for the holiday season, Logitech launched a print campaign in 22 European countries and also took steps to beef up and integrate its marketing in the Asia-Pacific region.

OUTCOME

The "What Will You Do With All That Freedom?" campaign succeeded in building awareness of Logitech's cordless products and set the stage for the introduction of new products in the category. In March 2004 Logitech began selling a new line of less expensive cordless mice and keyboards, tailored for the wider market targeted by the campaign. The one-time province of "early adopters," wireless devices were becoming a more mainstream peripheral and an important driver for Logitech's future growth. According to market research only 8 percent of the more than 250 million home PCs installed globally in 2003 used cordless mice and keyboards, providing Logitech with a large future sales opportunity. In fiscal 2005, for instance, Logitech reported that the sale of cordless mice had jumped by 69 percent over the previous year. The "What Will You Do With All That Freedom?" campaign was also successful creatively. It won the silver in the Computer Peripherals for Business/Personal Purposes category, presented by the New York American Marketing Association to honor creative achievement in the advertising industry.

FURTHER READING

"Collaborate Goes Free with Logitech." *Shoot,* November 28, 2003, p. 18.

Einstein, David. "Building a Better Mouse." *San Francisco Chronicle,* August 12, 1997, p. C1.

Flass, Rebecca. "Logitech Opts for TV's Motion and Emotion." *Adweek,* September 5, 2003.

Hall, William. "Logitech Proves No Mouse among Men." *Financial Times,* January 6, 2003, p. 15.

"Logitech Launches a New Television Ad as Part of Its $10 Million Campaign." *Advertising Age,* September 8, 2003, p. 93.

Murphy, Kate. "Cutting All the Cords: New Gadgets Let Your Computer Shed Its Wires." *BusinessWeek,* February 12, 2001, p. 100E1.

Norton, Justin M. "Logitech Review Narrowed to 4." *Adweek* (western ed.), October 7, 2002, p. 6.

———. "Logitech Taps Collaborate to Tout PC Components." *Adweek,* November 4, 2002, p. 4.

"Of Mice and Men." *Economist,* July 7, 1990, p. 69.

Rothman, Matt. "Logitech Inc.: Humanizing the Computer." *California Business,* February 1991, p. 9.

Saito-Chung, David. "PC Device Firm Grows Faster Than PC Makers." *Investor's Business Daily,* July 19, 2002, p. B08.

Ed Dinger

Lycos, Inc.

100 5th Ave.
Waltham, Massachusetts 02451
USA
Telephone: (781) 370-2700
Fax: (781) 370-3415
Web site: www.lycos.com

■■■

GO GET IT CAMPAIGN

OVERVIEW

Lycos, Inc. was founded in June 1995 and quickly grew into a vast Internet hub with services that included a search engine, comprehensive directories, personal home pages, E-mail, communities, and shopping functions. To help spur its growth, the company hired New York agency Bozell Worldwide to create an advertising campaign. The "Go Get It" campaign, which had the goal of attracting both new and experienced Internet users to visit Lycos.com, made its debut in November 1998 and continued into 1999. The $25 million campaign included television and print advertising.

In "Quick and Easy," the only 30-second spot in the campaign, a man showed a drawing to a black retriever and shouted, "Lycos, go get it!" The dog zoomed off and quickly returned with a frogman's flippers. The man showed Lycos another drawing, and this time he returned pulling a yellow sports car with his teeth. The voice-over said, "Unleash the new Lycos, and the Internet is at your command. So no matter what you're looking to retrieve, Lycos will hunt it down quicker and easier." In the final scene Lycos was shown a picture of fashion model Claudia Schiffer. The dog streaked off again, and viewers heard the voice of a woman saying, "Hi, I'm Claudia," as the Lycos logo appeared with its search button labeled "Go Get It."

The campaign included a 15-second version of "Quick and Easy" and two additional 15-second spots. In "Dinosaur" Lycos sped off in a black streak and returned with the skeleton of a dinosaur. A computer showed the Lycos search engine screen with the word "dinosaur" in the window. After the word changed to "investments," the spot ended with the company logo and search command key. The viewer heard the sound of coins and a voice saying, "Jackpot!" The other spot, "Earthquake," showed Lycos coming back apparently without anything until the scene shook, a rumble was heard, and a switch to the search engine screen revealed that the word being searched for was "earthquake." Next the word changed to "hockey," and the spot concluded with sounds of a stadium crowd and the voice-over saying, "Nice shot!"

A full-page print ad showed a stylized version of the dog, with one paw help up in an attentive, here-to-serve-you pose. Below appeared the headline "Now the fastest retriever in cyberspace." The ad copy read, "No matter what you're searching for on the Internet, from biographies to body piercing, you'll find it faster and easier when you unleash the new Lycos. All you have to do is log on to the Internet and say, 'Lycos, Go get it!'" The ad ended with the company logo, website address, and yellow search command key with the words "Go Get It!" in blue.

HISTORICAL CONTEXT

Jan Robert Horsfall, vice president of marketing for Lycos, said that the name came from a Latin word for a

Lycos's Labrador Retriever from the "Go Get It" campaign. BOZELL. REPRODUCED BY PERMISSION.

particular type of spider. Unlike most spiders, this one did not use a web to trap prey but instead left its web to hunt. The spider's unique approach and its aggressiveness fit the Lycos style.

In 1995 Lycos became one of the first companies to provide in-depth search services on the World Wide Web. Lycos became a publicly traded company on Nasdaq just 10 months after it was founded, making it the youngest company ever to go public. To grow, the company decided to expand by offering full services, with the aim of becoming one of the major destinations on the Web.

In early 1998 only 20 percent of Web users visited Lycos, but by the end of 1998 it was one of the most popular hubs on the Internet. A major reason for the growth was that Lycos bought up a stable of Internet properties. By 1999 it had built a network of linked sites that included Tripod, WhoWhere, Angelfire, MailCity,

RISE AND FALL

A Lycos news release in June 1999 showed that the audience for the portal had grown dramatically during the period from May 1998 to May 1999. Lycos had grown in audience reach from 39.4 to 48.4, an increase of almost 23 percent. Even though it remained the largest portal, the audience reach for Yahoo! had decreased 4.5 percent, from 53 to 50.6. Excite had an even more dramatic drop, of 16 percent, in audience reach, from 33.1 to 27.8.

HotBot, HotWired, Wired News, Webmonkey, Suck.com, and MyTime.com. Lycos had evolved from a search engine into an Internet hub that people could use not just to find something but also to chat, shop, send and receive E-mail, get news, and more.

TARGET MARKET

"Go Get It" aimed to attract both people who were new to the Internet and those who used other search engines. It also sought people who had not used the Internet but were considering doing so. Lycos kept an eye on category leader Yahoo! and, as it gained audience size and market share, was quick to compare itself to the larger company.

COMPETITION

In April 1996 Yahoo! launched its "Do You Yahoo!?" campaign in the New York, San Francisco, and Los Angeles markets. The $5 million television, radio and print campaign first aired on TV programs such as *Saturday Night Live, Star Trek, Seinfeld, The X-Files,* and *Late Night with David Letterman.* "Do You Yahoo!?" sought to convey both the benefits of getting on the Web and the irreverence and fun of the Yahoo! service. A 1997 spot, for example, poked fun at a young man's attempts to cover his baldness with a few remaining, lonely strands of hair. After conducting an Internet search, he was shown confidently bouncing down a busy street and turning heads with a bushy, three-foot-high Afro. Through 1998 Yahoo! remained the category leader, with the most recognized name and highly valued property on the Internet.

In July 1998 the NBC-owned portal Snap! began a campaign with the tag line "Don't suffer from information overload. Snap! out of it." One Snap! ad centered on a hearing-impaired boy who signed good-bye to his mother as he boarded the school bus. A classmate who witnessed the incident went on-line to look up sign language, and the next day he introduced himself using the signs he had learned on the Web.

Another competitor, Excite, which boasted strong search features, was the Web page for buyers of Dell computers. In October 1996 Excite introduced a $10 million campaign from Foote, Cone & Belding that featured the Jimi Hendrix song "Are You Experienced?" In December 1998 Excite premiered a new network and cable television campaign. Six 30-second ads showed people botching common activities in embarrassing, humorous ways. One spot told viewers that the woman pictured could send photographs to friends around the world using Excite. She then walked through a screen door she had just closed. In another spot a man was all thumbs as he installed an air conditioner, only to watch it plummet from his window. The spots ended with the suggestion that, if these people can use Excite, "you can too."

By 1998 the competition for Lycos had broadened beyond other search engines and portals to include major on-line services such as America Online (AOL) and Microsoft. The latter was spending $61 million on television ads built around the theme "Where do you want to go today?" Trying to outduel Microsoft, AOL spent $66 million on television advertising. AOL, with billions in Internet user fees, 15 million subscribers, and the longest track record as a content aggregator, had distinct advantages.

MARKETING STRATEGY

Lycos positioned itself as a network. Its mantra was that users could go to Lycos and find anything they wanted. The company differed from Yahoo! in that it did not put all of its properties under the same brand identity. Instead, Lycos built a system of distinct yet interrelated Internet services. According to an article in the *Boston Globe,* Lycos chief executive Bob Davis credited this cross-linking of sites for much of the company's rapid growth. Bo Peabody, a Lycos vice president and founder of the Internet community site Tripod, said, "We decided the best way to catch Yahoo! was to pursue a network of branded sites, rather than one megasite." The theory was to get people to use Lycos for its search capabilities and then to keep them there for the free Web pages. "This is the whole point about multiple brands. We don't care if we lose the user if they come to someplace we own," said Peabody.

Every Lycos site had links to the others woven into its fabric. From anywhere in the network a person could search the Lycos index. At the bottom of every Lycos search page viewers had the choice to run the same search on HotBot, another Lycos property that appealed to more experienced surfers. Viewers could not miss the many offers to sign up for free E-mail, do on-line shopping, look up phone numbers, or explore another Lycos service.

The company cast its net even wider and broke a written rule that portals only hosted, and did not develop, stores. In December 1998 it launched the Lycos store. This megastore offered a broad selection of consumer items from more than 200 brand name retailers, making Lycos the first major portal site selling directly to consumers.

The wide range of services helped make the "Go Get It" refrain ring true. In the "Go Get It" ads the black Labrador retriever named Lycos found anything the user was looking for and did so at speeds that made the search fun and easy. An earlier campaign had starred a Sherpa mountain guide, but Lycos decided that Sherpas were associated with dangerous situations. Danger might have been appropriate in the early days of the Web, when many users were concerned about getting lost and confused, but by 1998 people no longer viewed the Internet as a forbidding place. Lycos had considered using a bloodhound in the campaign, but focus groups showed that speed and friendliness were not considered traits of a bloodhound.

It was finally decided that a Labrador retriever gave the essential image—friendly, lively, fast, and great at going and getting what the master wanted. "I was worried initially about the dog," said Horsfall in *USA Today.* "You can bore people by using metaphors that are too basic. But from the first day the ad started airing, feedback has been overwhelmingly positive. It has given our brand real personality."

Speed, completeness, and fun rang through each spot. The dog found things fast. The items retrieved varied widely, from swimming flippers to investments to hockey to earthquakes. And the humor was evident. After retrieving the swimming gear, for example, the dog paused to shake the water out of his coat. At another point the dog appeared confused until the man realized that the drawing he was showing Lycos was upside down.

The basic theme of the campaign was to show people that there was more on the Web than they realized. Lycos tied the ads and its site together by using its search command key (yellow with the words "Go Get It" in blue) as the campaign tag line and as a signature element in all of the spots.

OUTCOME

In November 1998 Business Wire called Lycos's jump in audience reach (percentage of Internet users who touched down on the site) "unparalleled." A week after the campaign launch, Lycos experienced a 41 percent increase in traffic on its home page. Two months into the campaign Davis said that about 50,000 people were signing up for various Lycos Internet services every day, compared with a few hundred a day in early 1998. Lycos attributed much of the increase to the advertising campaign. *USA Today,* for example, reported that the first commercial was popular with consumers, with 22 percent of people who had seen it several times saying that they liked it "a lot."

On May 18, 1999, Lycos reported that revenues for the preceding quarter had been $35.1 million. This was a 132 percent increase over the comparable period from the previous fiscal year and a 15 percent increase over the quarter ending January 31, 1999.

FURTHER READING

Bray, Hiawatha. "Eyes Are the Prize: For Now a Transformed Lycos Looks to Boost Its Profile Not Profits, As It Seeks to Become a Destination for Net Users." *Boston Globe,* January 17, 1999, p. H1.

"Lycos Network Audience Reach Soars to 44.5%." Business Wire, November 18, 1998.

"The Lycos Network Launches First-of-a-Kind Program to Distribute Its Traffic-Building Services." Business Wire, December 13, 1998.

Reidy, Chris. "Lycos Unleashes $25 Million Ad Campaign." *Boston Globe,* November 2, 1998, p. B8.

Sparta, Christine. "Lovable Lab Takes Lycos Places." *USA Today,* May 3, 1999, p. B11.

Chris John Amorosino

Mail Boxes Etc., Inc.

6060 Cornerstone Ct., W
San Diego, California 92121-3795
USA
Telephone: (619) 455-8800
Fax: (619) 546-7488
Web site: www.mbe.com

■■■

SEE YOUR SMALL BUSINESS ON THE SUPER BOWL CAMPAIGN

OVERVIEW

Mail Boxes Etc., Inc. (MBE), a network of franchise centers that provided products and services for small businesses, generated widespread excitement among its primary customers by offering them a chance to win a free television commercial in the "See Your Small Business on the Super Bowl" campaign. Entrepreneurs were asked to write a brief essay describing their businesses and explaining what they would like to tell the public in a national television commercial. From thousands of entries Mail Boxes Etc. selected semifinalists, announced a smaller group of finalists several weeks later, and then named the winner a few weeks before the Super Bowl. Mail Boxes Etc. paid more than $1 million for a 30-second commercial during the Super Bowl and gave the spot to the winner of the contest. The campaign allowed the company to demonstrate its dedication to the small businesses that made up the bulk of its clientele. Through news releases, promotions at Mail Boxes Etc. outlets, and word of mouth, the "See Your Small Business on the Super Bowl" campaign generated publicity for months before and after the single airing of the winner's commercial. The campaign was handled by Kenneth C. Smith Advertising. It was launched in 1997 and was still running in 1999.

HISTORICAL CONTEXT

"Making Business Easier. Worldwide," was the corporate slogan for Mail Boxes Etc., a company that provided one-stop business, communication, and postal services in convenient locations such as shopping centers and commercial complexes. The typical Mail Boxes Etc. center was an independently owned and operated franchise where customers could make black-and-white or color photocopies, send and receive fax transmissions, transfer money, purchase office supplies, have documents notarized, have passport photographs taken, use computer workstations, rent mailboxes, have items packaged and shipped, and receive packages delivered by companies such as United Parcel Service of America, Inc. (UPS). The firm had begun in 1980 when Anthony DeSio opened a small business where customers could rent mailboxes and buy postage stamps. The company soon began offering voice mail and other services for customers with home offices and small businesses, and within one year it sold its first franchise. Mail Boxes Etc. had 1,000 franchises in operation by 1990, double that number by 1993, and more than 3,700 by 1998, making it the largest operation of its type in the world. In November 1997 Mail Boxes Etc. became a subsidiary of U.S. Office Products Company, a firm that provided business services, office supplies, office furniture, and break-room products such as coffee to corporations, schools, and other organizations.

Early advertising for Mail Boxes Etc. included only sporadic use of television, but by 1996 the company was spending about $12 million annually for national television commercials. The tag line for most of its ads that year was, "It's not what we do, it's how we do it." A holiday campaign launched in November 1996 carried the tag line, "If you can dream it up, we can pack it up and get it there." Those television commercials emphasized that Mail Boxes Etc. could handle packages of any size or shape. Earlier in the year, during the Super Bowl, Mail Boxes Etc. had run a $1.2 million television commercial that featured the Oscar Mayer "Wienermobile," a 27-foot-long vehicle shaped like a frankfurter. The Wienermobile's driver was depicted as the "ultimate road warrior," a customer who depended on Mail Boxes Etc. to provide services that a business owner needed while making frequent trips. During the Super Bowl in January 1997 the company ran a pleasant television commercial that showed a seaplane charter service making photocopies, sending fax transmissions, and shipping salmon at a Mail Boxes Etc. franchise in an isolated Alaskan community. For the next Super Bowl the company emphasized its commitment to small business by giving its television commercial to one of its customers in the "See Your Small Business on the Super Bowl" campaign.

THE AMERICAN DREAM

In November 1998 Mitch and Tracey Spence of Windsor, Wisconsin, won $50,000 when they mailed a package at a Mail Boxes Etc. (MBE) franchise and were given a scratch-off game card. They used the cash as down payment on a home. The owner of the Mail Boxes Etc. location commented: "It is such a thrill to be a part of this. I opened this MBE center about seven years ago, and it is really remarkable to be able to give something like this back to one of my customers. It's not every day that you help someone realize the American dream of owning a home." Among 7.5 million cards that Mail Boxes Etc. distributed during the promotion, the Spences' was the only one that awarded the bearer $50,000 in cash. Other customers won prizes such as free photocopies, a laptop computer, and a Hawaiian vacation.

TARGET MARKET

The "See Your Small Business on the Super Bowl" contest was open to U.S. companies with no more than 20 workers, self-employed entrepreneurs, and independent contractors who worked at home or in small offices. In a news release the company's president and chief executive officer, James Amos, said, "Mail Boxes Etc. is committed to serving the small-business market, and we wanted to demonstrate our dedication by featuring a small business during our commercial." In another news release Amos said: "Entrepreneurs…work long and hard to realize their dreams of owning a business. Small-business people are succeeding in every town in America. Their ambition and commitment deserve to be showcased on the Super Bowl, alongside commercials from some of the biggest companies in the world."

During the 1990s the number of small firms and home-based businesses in the United States increased rapidly. These consumers appreciated the convenience of a one-stop center where they could purchase office supplies, mail letters and packages, and use photocopy machines and other equipment that they did not have in their own offices. Many patrons used Mail Boxes Etc. to conduct business while they were away from home. In addition to its franchise outlets the company operated MBE Business Express centers in four major hotel chains for the convenience of business travelers. These unstaffed self-service centers—activated by the swipe of a credit card—featured photocopy machines, fax machines, computer workstations, Internet connections, and E-mail capabilities. Customers could also call a nearby Mail Boxes Etc. outlet from the business center to arrange for binding, packing, shipping, and other projects. In September 1998 Mail Boxes Etc. introduced MBE Online, an Internet site designed to help small-business owners with sales and marketing, business opportunities, human resources and management, professional and personal development, and strategies for investing money and retiring from a career. The package of services was intended to help entrepreneurs compete in the global marketplace.

COMPETITION

Mail Boxes Etc. dominated the business-services category. It competed with mail and parcel center franchise networks such as Pak Mail, Parcel Plus, PostNet, and Postal Annex+in addition to copy-service stores and office-supply stores. Companies that delivered letters and packages competed with Mail Boxes Etc. but sometimes also formed cooperative agreements with it. One of the nation's largest postal operations was the United States Postal Service, an independent government agency that reported sales of $60 billion in 1998. Mail and packages that customers brought to Mail Boxes Etc. outlets were transferred to the Postal Service or another carrier for delivery. Mail Boxes Etc. served as a drop-off point for UPS, one of the leading carriers. In 1998 UPS reported sales of $25 billion. Mail Boxes Etc. offered express shipping services through an agreement with another large transportation company, Federal Express Corporation (FedEx). For the fiscal year ended May 31, 1998, FedEx had revenues of $13.3 billion.

A primary rival for Mail Boxes Etc. was Kinko's, Inc., a network of business service centers with estimated sales totaling $1 billion in 1998. Kinko's had started by providing self-service photocopy machines to the public but had expanded into package mailing, binding and finishing, custom printing, computer rentals, and other business services. A large percentage of its customers operated small or home-based businesses. Kinko's installed high-speed Internet connections at its outlets and in 1997 formed a partnership with Microsoft Corporation's Hotmail to begin offering E-mail and communications services via the World Wide Web. Access to the Internet was included in the $12-an-hour fee that the company charged to use its computer workstations. The new service was publicized via online advertising, direct mailings to 300,000 customers, screen savers on computers at Kinko's centers, and promotional materials in Kinko's stores. The firm's general advertising slogan, "The new way to office," was introduced during the Super Bowl in 1996 and ran through 1998. The $20 million campaign was intended to emphasize the company's technological capabilities and to depict Kinko's as the best one-stop business center for consumers in the age of "virtual" offices.

Another major competitor, TRM Corporation, operated more than 33,000 TRM Copy Centers in outlets such as drug stores, hardware stores, convenience stores, gift shops, and stationery shops. Each TRM center featured a self-service photocopy machine, a machine stand, and promotional signs. TRM had sales of $57 million in 1998. In addition to photocopy centers Mail Boxes Etc. competed with office-supply stores, which often featured self-service photocopiers and other business equipment. One of the largest was Staples, Inc., which sold everything from pens and paper to telephones, computers, and software. Its humorous and popular "Yeah, We've Got That" advertising campaign, aimed at small-business owners and the general public, began airing on national television and occasionally on the radio in 1997 and continued into 1998. It was the second largest office supply store in North America that year, behind Office Depot, Inc., and ahead of OfficeMax, Inc.

MARKETING STRATEGY

In the "See Your Small Business on the Super Bowl" campaign, owners of small businesses throughout the United States were invited to describe in no more than 100 words how their operations showed the entrepreneurial spirit, why they should appear in a Mail Boxes Etc. commercial, and what they would say about their businesses to Super Bowl viewers. Entry forms were available at Mail Boxes Etc. franchises and at the company's Internet site. For the 1997-98 contest each of three finalists received $1,000, while the winner received a 30-second commercial and an additional $10,000. For the 1998-99 contest the second and third place winners received $2,000 each, while the first place winner received $5,000 and a free commercial. In 1998 Mail Boxes Etc. budgeted $16 million for advertising, according to *Adweek.* The company also used news releases and media coverage to generate excitement among entrepreneurs as the sweepstakes progressed. "On Super Bowl Sunday, during the big game, after a grand half-time show, in front of a huge audience, and among commercials for some of the largest corporations in the world, a monumental event will occur for one very small business," said one news release.

From several thousand contestants who entered the sweepstakes during September and October of 1997, 10 semifinalists were filmed in mini-commercials as part of the screening process, and three finalists were selected in early January 1998. The first made unique dog carriers; the second made customized bicycles; and the third made pocket-size air pumps that could be used to inflate basketballs, the liners of football helmets, and other sporting equipment in locations such as playing fields, parks, and beaches. The winner, Pocket Pumps, was announced on January 21, 1998, at the Super Bowl media party hosted by Mail Boxes Etc. at Sea World California. Robert Lange and Charles Davey, the owners of Pocket Pumps, appeared in the $1.3 million television commercial within a commercial during the Super Bowl on January 25, displaying their hand-held, squeeze-action air pump. In addition to demonstrating how the pump could inflate sports balls, the ad used trick photography to show the pump inflating and deflating Davey's head. The spot was produced on a low budget but was seen by an estimated 140 million viewers at a particularly exciting moment in the third quarter of the game. "It may be the biggest advertising touchdown any small business has ever scored," a news release noted. "Pocket Pump may also claim the unofficial title of 'Smallest Business to Advertise on the Super Bowl.'"

During the spring of 1998 other press releases tracked the progress of Pocket Pumps after the airing of the commercial, and the continued media exposure maintained public interest in the sweepstakes. Mail Boxes Etc. followed with the "See Your Small Business on the Super Bowl Search II" from August 1 through October 15. Twenty semifinalists were selected in November, 10 finalists were announced in December, and Jeremy's MicroBatch Ice Creams was named the winner on January 11, 1999. The home-based enterprise was owned by Jeremy Kraus, a 22-year-old entrepreneur who had used a mailbox at Mail Boxes Etc. as his business address when he sold ice cream during his years as a student at the University of Pennsylvania. Kraus wrote on his sweepstakes entry form: "Using MBE on the Penn campus made it possible for me to juggle school and my business. I am now my own boss, and heading a rapidly growing and delicious company." The $1.6 million commercial for Jeremy's MicroBatch Ice Creams aired during the second quarter of the Super Bowl on January 31. In conjunction with the second contest Mail Boxes Etc. also ran a national sweepstakes that awarded a trip for two to attend the Super Bowl game at Pro Player Stadium in Miami. The contest was not limited to owners of small businesses. The winner, announced in January 1999, was selected by random drawing from more than 18,000 entries. The prize included round-trip airfare, four days' and five nights' lodging, and tickets to the Super Bowl.

OUTCOME

Advertising Age called the "See Your Small Business on the Super Bowl" campaign the best idea among all the commercials that ran during the Super Bowl in both 1998 and 1999. The first winner in the contest, Pocket Pump, had received about 10 telephone orders a day for its product before the commercial aired. After the Super Bowl the company's orders skyrocketed to more than 6,000 calls a day. Pocket Pump's revenues for the first quarter of 1998 were 150 percent higher than its total revenues for the previous year. When Pocket Pump donated $5,000 of its newfound wealth to a San Diego burn center in April 1998, Mail Boxes Etc. matched the donation, a gesture that generated news coverage in several publications. In 1997 Mail Boxes Etc. ranked eighth in *Success* magazine's "Top 200 Franchises." For several years *Entrepreneur* magazine listed Mail Boxes Etc. among the top 10 franchises of all kinds, and in 1997, 1998, and 1999 the magazine named Mail Boxes Etc. as the number-one postal and business service franchise.

FURTHER READING

Associated Press. "Advertisers Go Long in Super Bowl Spots." *Chicago Sun-Times* (Financial Section), December 9, 1997.

Garfield, Bob. "High Voltage: A Shocking Development for the Budweiser Frogs: Bud Lizards Electrify Super Bowl Ads." *Advertising Age,* January 26, 1998.

———. "Super Bust: How Bad Were Bowl Ads? Best Starred Losing Candidate, Pigeons, Mosquito." *Advertising Age,* January 27, 1997.

Gantenbein, Barry. "Contest Can Give Small Business 30 Seconds of Fame." *Milwaukee Journal Sentinel* (Business Section), October 13, 1997.

Goldfisher, Alastair. "Super Bowl Commercial up for Grabs." *The Business Journal-San Jose,* September 14, 1998.

Johnson, Christina S. "Local Entrepreneurs Pumped over Ad During Super Bowl." *San Diego Daily Transcript,* January 27, 1998.

"Mail Boxes Etc. Announces Second National Search for a Small Business to Feature on Super Bowl Commercial." *Business Wire,* August 3, 1998.

"Pocket Pump Named Winner in Mail Boxes Etc.'s 'See Your Small Business on the Super Bowl' Search: Small-Business Owners Featured in Mail Boxes Etc.'s Super Bowl Commercial." *Business Wire,* January 22, 1998.

"Super Bowl Ad Meter Results." *USA Today,* January 31, 1999.

"Ten Entrepreneurs Named Semi-Finalists in Mail Boxes Etc.'s 'See Your Small Business on the Super Bowl' Search." *Business Wire,* December 1, 1997.

Susan Risland

Malden Mills Industries, Inc.

46 Stafford Street
Lawrence, Massachusetts 01841
USA
Telephone: (978) 685-6341
Fax: (978) 975-2595
Web site: www.polartec.com

FORWARD FABRIC CAMPAIGN

OVERVIEW

From its inception in 1906, Malden Mills Industries, Inc., was a leading American textile company. The firm's Polartec brand all-season synthetic fabrics, which helped pave the way for high-tech textiles, found their way into clothing made by companies like Patagonia, Columbia, and North Face. Although a fire in late 1995 destroyed the company's headquarters and all of its machinery and corporate records, a rebuilding effort had the firm back on its feet by 1997. Company reports indicated that sales reached nearly $370 million in 1997, just slightly less than the $400 million in sales prior to the fire. But a $150 million debt, caused in part by the rebuilding effort, forced Malden Mills into bankruptcy in 2001. Two years later the company emerged from bankruptcy.

With the bankruptcy in its past, Malden Mills took a new approach to promoting its flagship product, Polartec fabrics. In 2005 the company's advertising agency, Nail Communications, based in Providence, Rhode Island, replaced a previous campaign that had no tagline but that focused on outdoor sports. The new international marketing campaign focused on the Polartec brand. The campaign, estimated to cost more than $10 million, included print and outdoor advertising, television spots, and campaign-specific websites. Its theme, "Forward Fabric," was the first new tagline for the brand in more than five years.

The campaign was well received by the industry. Within weeks of the campaign's launch, *Adweek* published several articles praising the effort for its effectiveness and for being different from traditional advertising used by brands trying to connect with outdoor sports enthusiasts. In addition, the campaign reportedly received positive feedback from customers, such as Patagonia, that used Polartec fabrics in their garments.

HISTORICAL CONTEXT

Malden Mills, the textile company that became known for its Polartec all-season synthetic fabrics, had been founded in 1906 by Henry Feuerstein. In December 1995 a fire devastated the company. In addition to the 90-year-old building that housed the firm, all of the machinery used in its operations, along with the computer disks storing every textile design that had been created since the company's inception, also were lost. By June 1997, however, the company had rebuilt its facilities, and most of its 3,000 employees were back at work. But rebuilding the business was a greater challenge. Prior to the fire, the company had reported sales of about $400 million; in 1997 sales dropped to between $365 million and $370 million, according to a report in the *Daily News Record.* To establish an updated and a more fashionable image among consumers, Malden Mills shifted its advertising in 1997 away from special-interest publications to more mainstream and lifestyle magazines, such as *Men's Health* and *Sports Illustrated.* In addition, companies like Liz Claiborne and Polo agreed to include Polarfleece, an offshoot of Malden Mills' Polartec fabric, in their fall garment offerings.

Despite its efforts Malden Mills remained mired in a debt of more than $150 million, and in November 2001 the company filed for Chapter 11 bankruptcy. Aaron Feuerstein, the company's chief operating officer and grandson of its founder, had spearheaded Malden Mills through the rebuilding following the fire, but he lost control of the firm after filing for bankruptcy. In 2004 Feuerstein resigned and was replaced by Michael Spillane. Despite fears that he was planning to close the business or move the operations offshore, the new chief operating officer forged ahead with the business. To make sure that the company's focus on high-tech fabrics was in the forefront of customers' minds, Spillane allocated more than $10 million in 2005 for a new advertising campaign to promote the Polartec brand. The campaign, which used the tagline "Forward Fabric," was the first major advertising effort for the brand since 2000.

U.S. MILITARY PROTECTED WITH POLARTEC PRODUCTS

In 2000 Malden Mills entered into a $17 million, three-year contract with the U.S. military to provide Polartec fabrics for clothing made for members of the U.S. Marines. In the 2005 defense spending bill, the U.S. Congress approved $21 million to fund additional Polartec garments for American troops. The 2005 program was to include providing Polartec textiles for the Army Extended Cold Weather Clothing System, the Marine Corps Mountain Cold Weather Clothing and Equipment Program, and the Navy Air Warfare Center's Multi-Climate Protection System. Polartec textiles are also used to make garments for the U.S. Air Force and for Special Operations Forces.

TARGET MARKET

Alec Beckett, creative partner with Nail Communications, which handled the advertising for Polartec, said during an interview that marketing textiles to consumers was like marketing the chips used in a computer or the muffler on a new car. A connection must be made in the consumer's mind between the garment being bought and the fabric it was made with, just as, for example, a connection must be made between a computer and the chips inside. He compared Polartec to the Intel chips used in Dell computers. "The idea of this campaign is to have consumers know Polartec is in it [the garment] so they want it, like when they buy a Dell computer because it has Intel inside," he explained. Customers might not fully understand the technology behind the fabric or the computer chip, but they understood that it was of good quality, which made them want to buy products that contained it.

Nate Simmons of Backbone Media, Malden Mills' public relations and marketing firm based in Carbondale, Colorado, further noted that the "Forward Fabric" campaign targeted active, outdoor enthusiasts of all ages. The advertising was designed to make athletes of any age and at any skill level aware of the ways in which the Polartec fabric in their garments could help make their activities more comfortable or could enhance their performance. He said that because of the campaign's launch in late fall, it particularly targeted skiers getting ready for the ski season.

Besides educating consumers about Polartec fabrics, the campaign also targeted clothing manufacturers by highlighting the brand's technological innovations. Beckett said, "Polartec just makes the fabric, this advertising is aimed at the people who make the garments."

COMPETITION

W.L. Gore & Associates, Inc., best known for Gore-Tex, a waterproof and windproof fabric used in garments preferred by white-water rafters and snow skiers, began to market its textiles directly to consumers as well as to manufactures in 1976. In 1989 Gore enhanced its marketing program when it gave financial backing to the participation of the American explorer Will Steger in the International Trans-Antarctica Expedition. This eight-month, 4,000-mile ski and dogsled journey across Antarctica served as the heart of the company's new promotional strategy. When the company signed a marketing deal with the Weather Channel in 2000, it shifted the promotion of Gore-Tex and of products made from the fabric back to average consumers. The agreement included having meteorologists and other members of the Weather Channel crew wear Gore-Tex shoes and outerwear during on-air broadcasts. Then, in 2002 the company launched a print and television campaign under the theme "Comfort Is Where You Find It." This new advertising campaign featured people participating in a variety of activities while wearing garments made from Gore-Tex fabrics. Garments made of Gore-Tex, long a wardrobe staple of outdoorsy types, underwent a fashion makeover in 2004 when brands such as Polo RLX and

London Fog began using the fabric in some of their outerwear and casual clothing.

Burlington Industries, Inc., another company known for its waterproof and oil-repellant fabrics, was on the lookout for new technologies to improve its textiles when, in 1998, it invested in a startup specialty chemical firm, NanoTex LLC. This company's scientists had developed several fabric treatments, including Nano-Care, which made fabric stain repellant, and Nano-Dry, which helped fabric wick moisture away from the skin. Burlington then licensed the NanoTex products for use by other textile mills and marketed what it called its "nanotechnology" directly to apparel brands and retailers. The company also undertook a consumer campaign, with ads in such magazines as *Good Housekeeping.* Despite efforts to expand its business, Burlington struggled financially, however. Burlington Worldwide was formed in 2001, but in December of that year the company, once the world's largest manufacturer of textiles, filed for bankruptcy protection. In 2003 WL Ross & Company acquired Burlington and Cone Mills, another bankrupt textile manufacturer. Ross then combined the two companies in 2004 to create the International Textile Group, with Burlington operating as a subsidiary.

MARKETING STRATEGY

Nail Communications, which served as the advertising agency for Polartec beginning in 2001, created the "Forward Fabric" campaign to increase consumer awareness of high-tech fabrics and to end confusion about what they were. The campaign also shifted the brand's traditional marketing strategy to clothing retailers like North Face and Columbia and away from promoting itself as a product element. The new global campaign included print ads, television spots, and an Internet component. Ads appeared on billboards and in airports in selected markets as well, and the advertising was translated into four languages for use in European markets.

Print ads appeared in such U.S. magazines as *Outside, Shape, Freeskier,* and *Men's Journal* and in numerous European publications, including *Panorama* and *Terra.* The ads used humor as they combined images of Polartec scientists working in their labs with images of people participating in a variety of activities while dressed in apparel made from Polartec. One ad, for example, showed a scientist on the right side of the page reaching up to write an equation on a dry-ink board with a marker, while on the left side a young man wearing Polartec athletic pants and shirt was rock climbing. The text read, "We're not all that different. You live for adrenaline. We live for moisture vapor transmission rates. Okay, we're pretty different. But we share a common goal, namely, to make your dreams possible. And while ours aren't as dramatic, we get to use big words. So there." Another ad portrayed a scientist on one side of the page writing in a notebook while on the other side a ski jumper was airborne. The text read, "You dream of fresh tracks, blue sky, and big air. Us? We get pumped about dimensional stability. Thermal transmittance. Hydrostatic resistance. Before you mention how dorky that sounds, remember—your dreams would be pretty cold and damp without ours."

Television spots used a similar format, with a split screen portraying the research and development and the production processes of Polartec on one side of the screen and athletes in a variety of outdoor pursuits wearing garments made of Polartec fabric on the other. The TV spots aired on the Resort Sports Network in ski resort towns such as Vail, Colorado, and Sun Valley, Idaho. Billboard ads were placed in Times Square in New York City, in areas that attracted heavy skier traffic, such as Salt Lake City, Denver, and Boston, and in European cities, including Grenoble, France, and Innsbruck, Austria. Other ads were located in selected airports, including Denver International and Reno/Tahoe International in Nevada.

The Internet component of the "Forward Fabric" campaign was designed to appeal to a younger audience of consumers. Nail Communications created two unconventional websites for the campaign. ShaveMyYeti.com was a game in which users used a virtual razor to shave a hairy, scowling yeti. When the creature was completely shaved and left standing hairless in his boxer shorts, the user could dress it in warm, comfy Polartec garments. The smiling yeti then happily set off on a series of adventures, from kite flying by San Francisco's Golden Gate Bridge to ice skating in Manhattan's Central Park. The second website, SheepAreEvil.com, showed a sheep's head skull and crossbones against a black background. The text read as if it had been written by a bizarre conspiracy theorist who believed that sheep were plotting to take over the world. The introduction included the warning "We are the marionettes and they [the sheep] are the ones holding the strings." The site also included links such as "Nostradamus Prediction," "Crop Circles," and "Sheep and the Hindenburg."

OUTCOME

Although the biggest buying seasons for products made of Polartec were the fall and winter, shortly after the launch of the "Forward Fabric" campaign in September 2005 industry watchdogs were already praising the effort. An article in *Adweek* noted that the portrayal of outdoor enthusiasts participating in their favorite activities placed side by side with the Malden

Mills scientists in their offices designing the Polartec fabric used in the clothing worn by the athletes was a particularly successful strategy. Another *Adweek* article stated that the campaign took a "radically different approach—and to good effect." Simmons, of Backbone Media, noted that early in the campaign's run it also received positive feedback from manufacturers and retailers, such as Patagonia and REI, who used Polartec fabrics in their garments.

FURTHER READING

Bushnell, Davis. "Malden Mills Presses Product: Set to Launch Ads for Polartec." *Boston Globe,* June 9, 2005.

Carofano, Jennifer. "The Great Outdoors: Timberland Hits the Playground, Hi-Tec Sports Introduces a New Collection and Gore-Tex Take to the Tube." *Footwear News,* August 12, 2002.

Chirls, Stuart B. "Gore Is Hot on Marketing for the Cold." *Daily News Record,* March 27, 1989.

Dolliver, Mark. "Polartec High-Performance Fabrics." *Adweek,* September 19, 2005.

Fitzgerald, Michael. "Burlington's Future: Virtually Here." *Textile World,* March 1, 2003.

"Gore-Tex Dials into Weather Channel." *Footwear News,* August 28, 2000.

Greene, Joshua. "Textile Firms Try to Reel in Consumers." *WWD,* September 17, 2002.

Hye, Jeanette. "Malden Mills Rises from Ashes on Wings of Change: Fire Served as Catalyst for Creation of Greater Synergies." *Daily News Record,* April 4, 1997.

Malone, Scott. "New Textile Behemoth: Ross Forms $900M International Textile Group, Poised to Take on China." *WWD,* March 18, 2004.

———. "Spillane: Malden's Next Chapter." *WWD,* April 18, 2005.

Mitchell, Kim. "Versatile Fleece." *Wearable Business,* August 1, 2002.

"Nail Helps Polartec Move Fabric Forward." *Create Magazine,* August 15, 2005.

"Nail Helps Polartec Tell Left from Right." *Adweek,* August 17, 2005.

"U.S. Congress Awards Malden Mills Major Military Contracts for 2005: Polartec Fabrics and Electronic Textile R&D Funded in 2005 DOD Bill." *PR Newswire,* August 6, 2004.

Wilson, Claire. "The Gore-Tex Fashion Makeover: How W.L. Gore Slowly Took Its Brand Beyond—Way Beyond—Technical Activewear." *Daily News Record,* January 19, 2004.

Rayna Bailey

Marriott International

1 Marriott Dr.
Washington, DC 20058
USA
Telephone: (301) 380-3000
Web site: www.marriott.com

NEVER UNDERESTIMATE THE IMPORTANCE OF A GOOD NIGHT'S REST CAMPAIGN

OVERVIEW

NOTE: Since the initial appearance of this essay in the 1999 edition of *Major Marketing Campaigns Annual,* Marriott Hotels Corporation changed its name to Marriott International. The essay continues to refer to the company's former name, as that was the official name of the organization when the campaign was launched.

Marriott Hotels Corporation debuted a major television advertising campaign for its Courtyard by Marriott chain of hotels in May 1997. The five spots that made up the campaign showed hapless people making terrible blunders at work-related functions. Created by Lowe & Partners/SMS, the commercials were filmed in a grainy style reminiscent of home videos or live news broadcasts. Courtyard's forays into high-profile television commercials were part of its efforts to maintain its position in the extremely competitive mid-priced hotel market. Because other major chains such as the Hilton Hotels Corporation and Holiday Inn had entered the segment, travelers were faced with a dizzying array of hotel options from which to choose. With the "Never Underestimate the Importance of a Good Night's Rest" spots, Marriott sought to establish a memorable identity for the Courtyard brand, as well as to carve out a specific market niche for the hotel chain.

The humorous commercials all depicted the perils of working when not at one's best. In the award-winning "Missed Cue," a person scheduled to speak at a business conference was shown losing his bearings at the function. After this speaker was introduced, he burst into applause along with everyone else, until the man sitting next to him reminded him that he was the one who was supposed to talk. Startled and flustered, he leapt up to the podium and belatedly began his presentation. Another commercial captured an on-the-scene reporter, oblivious to the fact that he was on the air, holding his microphone and staring vacantly at a camera. In a similar vein a third spot portrayed a man struggling to find his way through a thick, red stage curtain to speak in front of a large (and waiting) crowd. Every spot closed with the campaign's tag line, "Never Underestimate the Importance of a Good Night's Rest." The implication was clear: unlike its competitors, Marriott's Courtyard hotels could ensure business travelers the rest that would allow them to function at an optimal level.

Courtyard by Marriott's campaign continued to run throughout 1998. In addition to receiving several major advertising awards, "Never Underestimate the Importance of a Good Night's Rest" was praised by industry critics and consumers alike for delivering its branding message in a lighthearted, yet powerful, way.

HISTORICAL CONTEXT

Although the Marriott family built their first hotel in 1957, the Courtyard by Marriott chain was not founded until 1983. The Courtyard franchise represented the company's initial entry into the mid-priced segment of the lodgings market. Marriott's previous offerings had been multistoried upper-end hotels, often located downtown in urban districts. But the company recognized that many of the successful hotels run by other firms in the lower-priced category were aging and that a new market entrant with more modern facilities could have success in the field. Confident that it could triumph in this venture, Marriott conducted extensive market research for two years before breaking ground with Courtyard. After determining the attributes that consumers sought in a hotel in this price range, Marriott set out to ensure that Courtyard would provide these things. The hotels were designed to look like country inns, complete with interior courtyards featuring walking paths. Although smaller than the more spacious accommodations at Marriott's flagship hotels, Courtyard's rooms were comfortable and well-equipped.

Courtyard was an element of Marriott's aggressive overall plan for segmentation. In 1988 the company had launched Fairfield Inn, a budget chain, and followed this debut with the creation of several other chains, each targeting a specific market. For example, Towne Place Suites, Residence Inns, and Spring Hill Suites each catered to various types of long-term business travelers. According to the *Wall Street Journal* on October 13, 1998, Marriott "brand[ed] hotels as if they were packaged goods," as it "blanketed the country with a range of brands."

The Courtyard chain proved to be an unequivocal success for Marriott. After a spate of building in 1996, the company operated more than 300 Courtyard hotels not only in the United States and Canada but also in Australia, Austria, England, China, France, and Germany. Like most other hoteliers, Marriott advertised Courtyard primarily through print and radio. For instance, in April 1997 Marriott used the opening of its 300th location to break its print and radio campaign called "Courtyard Hits 300." As part of this campaign, Marriott tracked the best hitters in Major League Baseball and gave prizes away to the winners of weekly radio trivia contests. But facing increased competition, Marriott decided to step up its advertising efforts on television with "Never Underestimate the Importance of a Good Night's Rest."

TARGET MARKET

The focus of Courtyard had always been on business travelers. In its bid to capture this market, the hotels eschewed the spacious lobbies and elegant restaurants of Marriott's flagship buildings. Instead, Courtyards provided fax machines, dual phone lines, comfortable in-room work environments, a semi-residential ambiance, and a reasonable price tag. As the *Wall Street Journal* noted on February 2, 1996, Courtyard's emphasis had always been "work first; play second." "Never Underestimate the Importance of a Good Night's Rest" targeted Courtyard's key clientele, which the *Journal* described as "road warriors," those frequent business travelers seeking affordable yet pleasant accommodations. This audience was a logical one, as the "mid-level business hotel ha[d] been one of the hottest segments of the hotel market," according to the January 11, 1996, *Wall Street Journal.*

"Never Underestimate the Importance of a Good Night's Rest" directly and cleverly portrayed the worldview of this group. Every scene in the campaign was work related, focusing on public "on-the-job blunders," as *USA Today* noted. Rather than dwelling on the details of why a Courtyard Inn would leave the weary traveler rested and refreshed, the campaign subtly addressed the latent fears of business people everywhere. Unlike most other hotel advertising, which usually described the service and spacious rooms available, "Never Underestimate the Importance of a Good Night's Rest" spoke to the reality of life on the road for a business traveler. A business hotel, the ads acknowledged to its viewers, could be gauged by one factor: did it allow the traveler to work well, to work efficiently, and to work without regret. No mention of extraneous details was made. It did not really matter if a bellman brought up luggage or if the restaurant served caviar. What was essential, the ads suggested, was the degree to which a hotel enhanced—rather than detracted from—a business traveler's business.

NEVER UNDERESTIMATE THE IMPORTANCE OF A PLEASED EMPLOYER

M.D. Asherton-Pickett, editor of an eponymous travel newsletter, explained the appeal of Courtyards and other hotels in its class to businesses. "It's the kind of hotel a boss has to love," Asherton-Pickett told the *Wall Street Journal* on February 2, 1996. "They can probably demand more work."

COMPETITION

The mid-priced, business-oriented hotel category to which Courtyard belonged was one of the more competitive in the industry, and Marriott faced many threats to its continued success. After taking note of Courtyard's achievements, several of Marriott's larger competitors also developed similar chains. As the *Wall Street Journal* noted on January 11, 1996, "a number of company's have sought to replicate the success of Courtyard." Furthermore, established entrants in the sector were spurred at least in part by Courtyard's success to renovate their existing buildings. One of Courtyard's fiercest rivals was Holiday Inn, which had been the mid-priced mainstay before Marriott's arrival. In 1997 Holiday Inn launched a $30 million ad campaign created by Fallon McElligott to announce its massive hotel renovation projects. An ill-fated Super Bowl ad, which portrayed a middle-aged person returning to a high school reunion after having a sex change, spearheaded the campaign. Subsequent spots were less sensational and stayed more closely on message. The campaign's tag line was direct and to the point: "We are out to make every Holiday Inn like the best Holiday Inn." A company spokesperson explained the impetus behind the campaign to the January 20, 1997, *Brandweek:* "We are the biggest, [and] at the same time, it's easy for people to take us for granted."

Having hammered home the fact that the chain had been "made over," Holiday Inn broke its first campaign for its Holiday Inn Express, a chain of hotels that directly competed with Courtyard. Also created by Fallon McElligott, this $10 million campaign was launched in 1998 and used humor to convey the advantages of the hotels. The component ads presented vignettes in which ordinary people felt empowered to take charge in dangerous situations. These people's confidence was rooted not in actual skill, however, but in the fact that they had spent the preceding night at a Holiday Inn Express. In one spot a man approached a cyclist who crashed. "Just stay still," he told the cyclist authoritatively. After a brief examination he concluded, "You've dislocated your patella. I'm going to have to set it. Hang on." "OK. But you are an orthopedic surgeon?" the cyclist asked. "No, but I did stay in a Holiday Inn Express last night," the would-be doctor replied. Another execution portrayed a female hiker being menaced by a large bear at a National Park receiving cockamamy advice from a besuited man who strode through the on-looking crowd. The ads all closed with the tag line "It won't make you smarter. But you'll feel smarter." This tongue-in-cheek sentiment gracefully conveyed the salubrious effects that Holiday Inn believed its hotels offered. "Our primary goal was to give guests a reason to stay with us rather than our competitors," a company spokesperson told *Advertising Age.*

Wingate Inn, a property of HFS, also entered the fray and introduced an awareness-boosting radio campaign in 1997. Like Courtyard, Wingate Inn "hope[d] to lure business travelers with amenities like data ports, fax machines, and portable phones," explained *Brandweek* on September 15, 1997. The radio spots featured Anne Winn and Garrett Brown, the duo who had pitched Molson Golden until 1988, and incorporated the tag line "Built for Business." The Promus Hotel Corp. also dedicated a considerable marketing budget to its mid-range business hotel chain, Hampton Inn. In February 1998 Hampton released a DDB Needham cable television campaign that jokingly portrayed the "Insomniacs Club" and promised, "We make it easy to take it easy."

MARKETING STRATEGY

Like its competitors, Marriott sought to distinguish Courtyard from the slew of other mid-priced hotels. According to the April 17, 1996, *Wall Street Journal,* the proliferation of brands and sub-brands in the category left many consumers "bewildered." As an industry analyst told the *Journal,* "[p]eople are coming across these brands, and they don't have a clue what they are." Forging a powerful brand identity in the face of this chaos was a particular challenge for hoteliers as compared to other purveyors of consumer products. "Because consumers don't stay in hotels every day, it takes a long time for brand differentiations to sink in," noted the *Journal.* To overcome these obstacles Marriott opted to use television as the vehicle to carry the message of "Never Underestimate the Importance of a Good Night's Rest," since television spots usually received far more notice than their print counterparts. To reinforce this strategy Marriott often ran the commercials during high-profile events, such as telecasts of National Football League games, to generate even more buzz and excitement about the campaign.

In keeping with its goal to make Courtyard stand out from its competitors, Marriott also strove to make the "Never Underestimate the Importance of a Good Night's Rest" spots distinctive and engaging. The style in which the commercials were filmed did much to accomplish this strategy. Unlike the bulk of television ads, which often relied on slick images and special effects, Courtyard's campaign was deliberately understated. One of the directors "took the low-grade video style of CNN footage and copied it bald-faced, as if the ads were actually chronicling people's out of step behavior," explained *Shoot.* Not only did the handheld camera footage provide the commercials with a unique visual feel, but—coupled with the potentially disastrous events unfolding in them—gave the spots an irresistible allure (viewers being unable to look away from the impending catastrophes). The humor of the campaign was also an essential element of its appeal. Its wittiness enabled

Marriott to reach a diverse group of viewers across demographic lines. As the December 21, 1998, edition of *USA Today* put it in lauding the campaign, "[a]nyone who has suffered sleep deprivation can appreciate [the 'Never Underestimate the Importance of a Good Night's Rest'] campaign."

Marriott embarked on other promotional efforts to complement the "Never Underestimate the Importance of a Good Night's Rest" campaign. To reward loyal customers and attract new ones across its diverse array of lodging options, Marriott unveiled its Marriott Rewards program in 1997. Marriott Rewards replaced the company's long-standing Honored Guest Awards program and differentiated it in a significant way. The Honored Guest program had let consumers accumulate bonus points for stays at individual Marriott brands. The new rewards program allowed consumers to amass points across the company's diverse holdings, thereby encouraging consumers to use Marriott brands regardless of their reason for traveling. At the same time Marriott co-branded credit cards with Visa U.S.A. and First Chicago Bank in order to put its name before consumers in a wider variety of situations. These cards also allowed consumers to accrue bonus points at the company's hotels.

OUTCOME

"Never Underestimate the Importance of a Good Night's Rest" was well-received by advertising industry critics. Both *USA Today* and *Advertising Age* ranked the Courtyard campaign among the best of 1998. In addition to winning an ANDY award, a component commercial ("Missed Cue") garnered a Gold Lion at the prestigious International Advertising Festival in Cannes, France.

Correlating the campaign's popularity to the company's performance in its category was difficult (mainly because Marriott's hotel holdings stretched across several price categories and continents), but the company expressed satisfaction with the effort. Marriott's profits for the financial quarter immediately following the ads' debut were up 16 percent. By July 1998 Marriott's revenues per available room had increased 6 percent. Courtyard remained the second-most profitable hotel in the mid-price category behind Holiday Inn.

FURTHER READING

Bigness, Jon, and Jonathon Dahl. "Soon, Hotels Only a Boss Could Love." *Wall Street Journal,* February 2, 1996.

Binkley, Christina. "Hotels: Marriott Outfits an Old Chain for New Markets." *Wall Street Journal,* October 13, 1998.

"HFS Break First Ads for Wingate." *Brandweek,* January 15, 1997.

Orwall, Bruce. "Hilton to Create Hotels Targeting Budget Travelers." *Wall Street Journal,* January 11, 1996.

———. "Multiplying Hotels Brands Puzzle Travelers." *Wall Street Journal,* April 17, 1996.

Petrecca, Laura. "Holiday Inn Express Intros 1st TV Campaign, Via Fallon." *Advertising Age,* May 4, 1998.

Sanders, Lauren. "Special Report: Directors/Fall Edition." *Shoot,* October 16, 1998.

Wells, Melanie. "Ad Experts' Best and Worst of 1998." *USA Today,* December 21, 1998.

Rebecca Stanfel

Mars, Inc.

6885 Elm Street
McLean, Virginia 22101
USA
Telephone: (703) 821-4900
Fax: (703) 448-9678
Web site: www.mars.com

THE ENERGY YOU CRAVE CAMPAIGN

OVERVIEW

In October 2003 renowned candy company Mars, Inc.'s newly created food division, Masterfoods USA, began a teaser campaign to let consumers know that a new energy bar was coming their way. Snickers Marathon bars, which came in two flavors, Multi-Grain Crunch and Chewy Chocolate Peanut, hit store shelves in January 2004. The new product was designed to appeal to the loyal candy-bar customer who already used the Snickers bar to satisfy hunger but wanted a healthier, protein-based energy bar more suited to their daily workout needs. The bars were aimed at taking some of the estimated $1 billion market away from industry leaders PowerBar and Balance Bar as well as an abundance of other nutrition-bar makers.

Advertising agency BBDO New York was responsible for generating high consumer awareness of the product in a short time. In fall 2003 print ads were placed in health and fitness magazines to pave the way for a comprehensive media campaign called "The Energy You Crave," which would coincide with the Marathon bars' retail appearance in January 2004. The budget for the campaign was estimated at $10 to $20 million. Television spots took up some 75 percent of ad dollars, with the rest split between print, outdoor, and online advertising as well as public relations, point-of-purchase displays, and promotional functions. The television spot that kicked off the campaign showed athletes at their limit, engaging in activities such as running and weight lifting. "Agony, anguish," said a female voice. A male voice took over, saying, "Despair. Pain. Words that should never define the taste of your energy bar." The spot was capped off by the campaign's tagline, "The Energy You Crave."

Mars, pleased with the performance of the campaign and product sales in the first months of 2004, introduced two more Snickers Marathon varieties at the end of that year. As 2004 came to an end, Snickers Marathon was among the top five fastest-selling energy bars in all stores. BBDO won a Silver EFFIE (a prestigious advertising-effectiveness award) for the campaign in 2005.

HISTORICAL CONTEXT

Since its introduction in 1930 the Snickers candy bar had been a key building block in the Mars, Inc., confection empire begun by Frank Mars in the early twentieth century. Along with the M&M's candies brand, Snickers bars became a staple of American snacking life, making the McLean, Virginia–based Mars the second-largest candy maker in the United States by the year 2000. Unlike its colorful little round cousins, however, Snickers developed a following not only for its reputation as a sweet treat but also as a hunger tamer. This meal-like quality was emphasized by Mars advertising, which consistently referred to the protein-supplying peanuts in the bar. Ads shored up the concept with the longtime slogan "Snickers really satisfies" and later with "Hungry? Why wait."

Energy bars started appearing in the 1970s but did not hit their stride until two decades later. Formerly a small niche product found in health-oriented outlets, energy or nutrition bars made up one of the fastest-growing food-product segments in 2003, with sales estimated at more than $1 billion. The bars' expansion into the mainstream market had not gone unnoticed by Mars, which had consolidated its food brands in 2002 under one division, Masterfoods USA, located in Hackettstown, New Jersey. The Mars mission had always included strengthening core brands. Drawing upon the long history of Snickers to create its own version of a protein bar, the company was looking for a way to break into a market not traditionally associated with a candy brand. According to Masterfoods spokesman Jeffrey Moran, Mars had been working on a Snickers-based energy bar for years before introducing the Snickers Marathon line in January 2004. He explained to *Drug Store News,* "We saw people using the Snickers candy bar for protein because of the peanuts. We wanted to take the taste of Snickers and grow it into a new and different category instead of trying to make candy healthy." The bars featured a protein-heavy blend (trademarked QUADRATEIN) of soy, peanut, casein, and whey, which was combined with carbohydrates and other nutrients.

ANGLING FOR SNICKERS MARATHON FANS

In February 2004 FLW Outdoors, the world's leading competitive-fishing organization, announced that Snickers Marathon bars would sponsor its upcoming fishing tournament season. The Mars brands Snickers and M&M's had been sponsors of the annual competitions since 2001. Confident of a loyal consumer mentality among the nation's more than 52 million anglers and their families, Mars had already used the venues for two other Snickers brand-extension launches, Snickers Crunch in 2001 and Snickers Almond Bar in 2003.

TARGET MARKET

The first Snickers Marathon bars, made available early in 2004, were aimed primarily at men in the 18-to-45 age range who were committed to physical fitness, working out during the week and possibly engaging in some amateur competition on the weekends. The ideal customer might be a fan of Snickers candy who was looking for a healthy alternative that would taste better than standard chalky nutrition bars. Mars was also looking to woo new customers, male and female, to the nutrition-bar market: people who had once thought that energy bars were only for professional athletes but were starting to consider them a mainstream snack-food choice.

The two original flavors, Multi-Grain Crunch and Chewy Chocolate Peanut, were aimed at men first but essentially at any active adult. In fall 2004 two subsequent bar recipes followed that had a different consumer target. The Snickers Marathon Protein Performance Bar was designed to attract the more focused athlete, while the Snickers Marathon Low Carb Lifestyle Energy Bar was offered with women in mind.

COMPETITION

Traditional leaders in the energy-bar category were PowerBar, owned by venerable Mars competitor Nestlé, and Balance Bar, owned by megacorporation Kraft Foods. PowerBar was reporting more than $100 million in annual sales when Nestlé, then the world's largest food and beverage company, acquired the Berkeley, California, company in 2000. Nestlé CEO Peter Brabeck was keen to use the brand as a major component in his plan to remake Nestlé into the world's leading health and wellness company. In the wake of a glut of new competition PowerBar held its own but did not experience the growth that Nestlé had expected. Still, PowerBar's reputation of being an originator in the category made it a major competitor against Mars' own product. Another challenge for Mars was Balance Bar. Balance Bars, designed on the popular nutritional philosophy of 40 percent carbohydrates, 30 percent protein, and 30 percent fat (40/30/30), came on the scene in 1992 and enjoyed success into the next decade.

At the same time that Mars introduced its Snickers Marathon bars, another longtime rival, the candy company Hershey, unveiled its own entrant into the nutrition-bar segment. Hershey's SmartZone bar was based on the elements of the hugely popular, protein-centered Zone Diet that was created by biochemist Barry Sears and introduced to the public in 1995. Hershey, like Mars, was hoping that its association with candy would be an asset, creating customer expectations that it would taste good. The SmartZone bars promised a healthier controlled release of sugar (low glycemic index), which would also keep eaters satisfied longer. The idea of satiety was treading directly on Snickers' long-held territory, and low glycemic index was also a foundation for the new Snickers Marathon bars. The list of competition was formidable and diverse. When introduced later in 2004 the Marathon Low Carb Lifestyle Energy Bar would face off against Atkins Diet Advantage bars, which reported sales of $63.8 million in 2003, and Cliff Luna bars for women, which took in $42.4 million that same year.

MARKETING STRATEGY

Advertising agency BBDO New York was charged with the task of convincing discerning, health-conscious consumers that Snickers Marathon was a nutritiously credible energy bar with the great taste of a candy bar. The campaign the agency created, "The Energy You Crave," began in fall 2003 with teaser print ads in health and fitness magazines. The ads emphasized the nutritional aspects of the coming Marathon bars while laying the groundwork for the mass-media assault that would follow in January 2004. A budget of $10 to $20 million was allotted to cover television, print, outdoor, and online advertisements. The bulk of the advertising money, about 75 percent, was spent on the TV aspect of the campaign, with a 30-second spot debuting on January 3 during the NFL Wild Card game. In the commercial athletes were shown running extreme distances, climbing dangerously high, surfing, and pumping iron with weights that had "torture" written on them. A female voice-over intoned, "Agony, anguish." A male voice-over continued, "Despair. Pain. Words that should never define the taste of your energy bar." The tagline that followed stated, "The Energy You Crave."

At about the same time that the first TV spot ran, print ads began appearing in general-interest magazines as well as in health and fitness publications. Billboard ads were placed in the top 10 energy-bar markets, regions that made up approximately 10 percent of the country's population. The campaign included an emphasis on public relations, point-of-purchase displays, and online banners placed on health-oriented websites. The multi-pronged media approach was necessary to achieve the much-needed name recognition that was so vital to a new product entering a well-established market segment. Ads and promotions relied on the Snickers name for that purpose. Speaking with the *Atlanta Journal-Constitution,* Scott Krugman, vice president of public relations for the National Retail Federation, the world's largest retail trade association, described this as a distinct advantage over other new category entrants. "They're bringing something to the market that a lot of other products don't have—a recognizable name that will get people to pick it up in the first place." The Snickers name could also have been a liability, however, if the advertisements had not sufficiently communicated that Snickers Marathon was a true energy bar and not just a candy-bar pretender.

The first goal of the advertising strategy was to create product awareness, but the second part, to get consumers to buy them once and then again, was even more vital. The universal criticism of products in this food category had always been the taste and flavor experience. Consumers often settled for the lesser of two taste evils when choosing a nutritional bar, thinking that if it served one's nutritional requirements, it probably could not taste good as well. Mars felt that it could win repeat business on the taste factor. Jeffery Moran explained the company's thinking in a 2004 issue of *Convenience Store News.* "We've seen continued focus on everyday energy, and Snickers has always had an underlying focus on endurance and sustainability." Moran continued, "The taste of Snickers has always been our point of differentiation, and we can bring our history and background of how to make things taste good into the energy bar category." The tagline carried on all advertising, "The Energy You Crave," perfectly conveyed that the bars were so tasty and energy-packed that consumers would actually look forward to eating them.

OUTCOME

In its first year Snickers Marathon lived up to the Mars company's consumer-awareness goals and sales expectations. According to Ipsos-ASI, an advertising-research firm, the Snickers Marathon TV spots scored a Copy Effectiveness Index of 232, well above the category norm of 70 to 130, which meant that viewers understood the message of the advertising copy "The Energy You Crave." Surveys by Ipsos-ASI also revealed promising results, reporting a 50 percent "intent to purchase" level, which was more than double the typical 22 percent. Near the end of 2004, approximately 11 months after it was introduced to consumers, Snickers Marathon was among the top five fastest-selling energy bars in every outlet. Even more encouraging for Mars, Snickers Marathon was number one in the convenience store category when compared to its two major competitors, PowerBar and Balance Gold 5, a popular Balance Bar product.

BBDO New York also picked up accolades within the advertising industry, winning a Silver EFFIE Award (Snacks/Desserts/Confections category) in 2005 for its "The Energy You Crave" campaign. That year the agency also won three Gold EFFIEs for other campaigns, prompting BBDO New York's president and CEO, John Osborn, to proclaim in a company press release, "This is like hitting a Grand Slam." Mars' Masterfoods USA division responded to the success of the first two

Snickers Marathon flavors by introducing more bar variations. By the end of 2005 there were eight Snickers Marathon bars to choose from that were in three nutrition categories: energy, protein, and low carbohydrate.

FURTHER READING

"The A-List." *Progressive Grocer,* September 1, 2004, p. 35.

Anderson, Mae. "Flipping for Snickers." *Adweek,* August 9, 2004, p. 20.

Beirne, Mike. "Confectioners Unwrap Low-Carb Strategies." *Brandweek,* June 14, 2004, p. 14.

Brenner, Joel Glenn. *The Chocolate Emperors: Inside the Secret World of Hershey and Mars.* New York: Random House, 1999.

Brown, Sandy. "Hotlines." *Adweek,* January 5, 2004, p. 4.

Cole, Leslie. "Bars as Big Business." *Portland Oregonian,* January 27, 2004, p. FD01.

Eckstein, Sandra. "Snickers Serves Up Energy Bar." *Atlanta Journal-Constitution,* May 13, 2004, p. 7NW.

Embrey, Alison. "The Energy Train." *Convenience Store News,* July 12, 2004

Kirsche, Michelle. "Better-for-You Bars from Candy Makers Bring Flavor, Variety to Nutrition Aisle." *Drug Store News,* October 11, 2004, p. 39.

Squires, Sally. "Belly Up to the Bars." *Washington Post,* July 27, 2004, p. F01.

Thompson, Stephanie. "Nestle Makes Nutrition Its No. 1 Priority in U.S." *Advertising Age,* March 21, 2005, p. 3.

———. "Snickers Marathon: Masterfoods Launches Energy Bar." *Advertising Age,* June 23, 2003, p. 8.

Simone Samano

INNER BEAST CAMPAIGN

OVERVIEW

Whiskas, a cat-food brand in Mars, Inc.'s Masterfoods USA division, was the world's leading cat food. Its sales performance and brand identity was inconsistent from nation to nation, however, and in the United States at the turn of the millennium it was a middle-of-the pack brand in an increasingly competitive category. Having failed to energize the Whiskas brand through a variety of marketing techniques and packaging changes, Mars switched advertising agencies in 2002, hiring the Los Angeles office of TBWA\Chiat\Day. TBWA's first campaign for Whiskas, "Inner Beast," represented a departure from conventional cat-food advertising.

Budgeted at $20 million and employing the tagline "What Cats Want," the "Inner Beast" campaign sought to show cat owners that Whiskas understood and catered to the instinctual nature of their pets. Rather than conform to the industry model of depicting cats as cute, lovable, semi-humans who were utterly dependent on their owners' benevolence, TBWA\Chiat\Day dramatized the atavistic ferocity of even the smallest house cats by showing them hunting large prey on the Serengeti. The agency achieved this image by splicing new footage of house cats into stock footage directly reminiscent of nature documentaries. Suspenseful music highlighted the absurd juxtaposition of 10-pound house cats chasing water buffalo, zebras, and impalas that weighed several hundred pounds, and a voice-over proclaimed, "Your cat has an inner beast. Feed it."

In market-research tests the campaign scored well in terms of memorability and entertainment value, and it was considered a successful category-defying new approach to cat-food advertising. Mars handed over an increasing amount of its global advertising duties to TBWA\Chiat\Day, and Whiskas continued to position itself not just as a supplier of cat food but as a brand that understood the true nature of cats.

HISTORICAL CONTEXT

In the 1990s and early 2000s Whiskas was the world's best-selling cat food, but its performance varied dramatically from market to market. While it was the leading cat food in the United Kingdom and Europe, it was only the sixth-best-selling in the United States and was in danger of becoming a stagnant brand there. Whiskas and its agency D'Arcy Masius Benton & Bowles, which was also the lead agency for other brands in Mars, Inc.'s Masterfoods portfolio, had tried a variety of approaches to jump-start sales growth and to make Whiskas stand out from competitors at the brand level. In general, however, they had failed at this task.

One of the most noteworthy among these divergent campaigns was a 1999 series of commercials designed not simply for cat owners but for cats themselves. Based on a concept first tested in Great Britain, where Whiskas was the leader in its category, the commercials opened with a 15-second intro asking cat owners to put their cats in a position to watch the sequence that would follow. What followed was a flurry of darting movements and geometrical patterns, with chirping birds, a scurrying mouse, and a mobile of reflective metal fish, among other images, running in tandem with a soundtrack that included noises undetectable by human ears. Though cat = were intrigued by the spots, according to animal behaviorists at the Mars-associated Waltham Center for Pet Nutrition in Leicestershire, England, their owners in America remained unmotivated to try the Whiskas brand in greater numbers.

In 2002 Mars relieved D'Arcy Masius Benton & Bowles of advertising duties on the various brands it serviced and renewed the search for marketing ideas that would help Whiskas rise above its middle-of-the-pack status in the United States. Mars hired TBWA\Chiat\Day's Los Angeles office to reinvigorate the Whiskas brand.

TARGET MARKET

The "Inner Beast" campaign targeted cat owners. Using the tagline "What Cats Want," the commercials defied industry trends emphasizing the cute and human-like attributes of cats—the unnatural attributes of cats, as TBWA\Chiat\Day saw it—focusing instead on convincing cat owners that Whiskas alone among cat-food brands understood the true nature of their pets. Cat owners, the ad agency felt, did not see their cats as stand-ins for children; rather, they prized the uniquely feline qualities of their pets, even when these qualities resulted in difficult or disturbing behavior. Cats' instinctual nature not only accounted for their most prized qualities, but it also directly dictated the foods they chose, allowing TBWA\Chiat\Day to tie the Whiskas brand logically to its concept. The "Inner Beast" spots attempted to communicate that Whiskas shared cat owners' appreciation for their pets, while raising the brand's profile through humorous, provocative imagery.

TBWA\Chiat\Day thus crafted spots that showed meowing house cats chasing water buffalo, zebra, and impalas on the Serengeti. One of the TBWA creative directors on the account, copywriter Gary Pascoe, told the *New York Times,* "Any cat owner will tell you, cats are unaware of their size and can't help the lion side of them from coming out. To 10-pound Fluffy at home, the couch is a gazelle and the carpet is the Serengeti."

COMPETITION

The leading cat foods in the United States at the time of the "Inner Beast" launch were Cat Chow, Iams, Friskies, Meow Mix, and 9 Lives. Industry-wide sales declines, together with a wave of corporate consolidation, beginning with Procter & Gamble's 1999 purchase of the premium brand Iams, had recently ratcheted up the levels of competition among these brands and made the Whiskas effort to craft a distinctive image all the more pressing. In 2001 Ralston Purina, the manufacturer of Cat Chow, Meow Mix, and Purina O.N.E. in addition to leading dog-food brands and other pet products, was purchased by Nestlé, the corporate owner of the Friskies brand. As part of the merger, federal regulators concerned about antitrust issues compelled Nestlé to sell the Meow Mix line, making Meow Mix one of the few independent cat-food companies. H.J. Heinz Company in 2002 sold the 9 Lives brand to Del Monte Foods.

Prior to the "Inner Beast" launch, Procter & Gamble was the only one of the major industry players to have recently increased its cat-food advertising budget. With the 1999 acquisition of Iams, the company immediately and drastically increased advertising spending on behalf of all Iams products for dogs and cats. As a result of its marketing and the moving of Iams beyond specialty pet-food stores and into supermarkets and mass merchandisers, Iams sales grew by roughly $200 million dollars during the brand's first year under the Procter & Gamble banner.

The newly independent Meow Mix Company went one better than the 1999 Whiskas commercial crafted for cats: in 2003 the company launched *Meow TV,* an actual show featuring segments designed for the enjoyment of cats. Budgeted at a miniscule $400,000, the series of two shows ran on the Oxygen cable network and created significant buzz around the brand. Sales, however, remained flat.

Nestlé, meanwhile, significantly scaled back total expenditures on its brands Cat Chow, Friskies, and Purina O.N.E. after the 2001 merger that placed them all under the same corporate umbrella. It allotted

BEHIND THE SCENES

John Payne and Gary Pascoe, the TBWA\Chiat\Day creative directors on the Whiskas account, had worked as an art director–copywriter duo for nearly a decade prior to the "Inner Beast" campaign. The two got to know one another in 1994 while taking cigarette breaks at their then-employer, advertising agency the Richards Group of Dallas. They were first assigned to work together on a table-card promotion for TGI Friday's jalapeño poppers and went on to work as a team on beer advertising as well as accounts for Motel 6 and Continental Airlines. They moved together to TBWA\Chiat\Day's Los Angeles office in 1997, where they won assignments for Taco Bell, Sony PlayStation, Infiniti, Levi's, and Nissan. Both credited their ability to come up with the "Inner Beast" concept—showing house cats hunting on the Serengeti—to the fact that they were cat owners. As *Creativity* reported, Payne had a black short-haired cat named P.T., and Pascoe had an "obese, mentally challenged calico named Barkley."

$29.9 million to the trio, down from pre-merger totals amounting to $39.9 million. In 2004 Nestlé's Purina lines were to be integrated into an unprecedented branded-entertainment effort on NBC. Created by ad agency Fallon Worldwide in concert with prominent network TV producers and writers, the show was to be a satire of the 2004 U.S. presidential election featuring the Cat and Dog parties, with Purina brands heavily integrated into the program. Despite significant excitement over the fact that the show would represent a new format for advertisers, the venture was scuttled because of Purina's financial difficulties.

MARKETING STRATEGY

"Inner Beast" represented not just a conceptual shift in Whiskas' advertising but also a return to its pre-2001 levels of ad spending. After spending only $14 million on Whiskas in 2002, Mars allotted TBWA\Chiat\Day an estimated $20 million a year for Whiskas. The campaign, which was launched in June of 2003, consisted of three TV spots—"Buffalo," "Zebra," and "Impala"—as well as print ads that conformed to the "Inner Beast" theme.

TBWA\Chiat\Day creative directors John Payne and Gary Pascoe, who helmed the "Inner Beast" effort as art director and copywriter, respectively, attributed their understanding of cat behavior in part to the fact that both of them were longtime cat owners. "Cats haven't sold out like dogs have," Pascoe told *Shoot.* "You can't get cats to lay down or roll over or do any of that silly stuff. They're true to their instinctual nature." When they spent time studying a large body of clips, however, Pascoe and Payne found that this understanding of cats was at odds with the bulk of the cat-food industry's advertising. Noticing the prevalence of unnatural behaviors—singing and dancing, for instance—fallaciously imposed on cats by industry advertisers, the team settled on a working concept of showing cats as they really were. This led them to the idea of dramatizing cats' instinctual aggressiveness in an over-the-top, humorous fashion, by depicting small domestic cats in predator-prey chase scenes reminiscent of nature documentaries.

Director Noam Murro of Biscuit Filmworks, Los Angeles, settled on the strategy for filming the "Inner Beast" spots. Because shooting on location in Africa was not a reasonable option, Murro used stock footage from nature documentaries and edited out the lions in pursuit of their quarry. Trained house cats were then filmed on California ranch land chosen for the similarity of its flora and fauna to that found in the stock footage. Shooting challenges included matching the cats' angles of pursuit in real time to that of the filmed lions, and the primary task confronting editors and effects technicians was the splicing of the individual cats into the chase scenes in a seamless fashion.

"Buffalo," "Zebra," and "Impala" each followed the same template, their primary differences being that of the species of quarry pursued by the house cat in each spot. The commercials opened with footage of groups of animals going about their daily routine, while suspenseful music reminiscent of soundtracks habitually employed in nature documentaries provided an obvious cue to viewers that a predator was lurking somewhere nearby. The suspense built as the hunted animals began betraying signs of fear, so that the revelation that the predator was a small, meowing house cat achieved maximum comic effect. The absurd chase scene then played out after the fashion of the genre, with the music building toward a crescendo as the tiny cat hid behind rocks, bounded across open plains, and closed in on animals that weighed several hundred pounds. A voice-over underscored the campaign's message: "Your cat has an inner beast. Feed it." Whiskas products then appeared onscreen, arranged on top of a rock, and the voice-over added, "Whiskas: made to satisfy a cat's natural instincts." Each spot ended with a purple screen on which the Whiskas logo and the tagline "What Cats Want" appeared.

Accompanying the "Inner Beast" TV spots were print ads that ran in newspapers with coupon inserts. These featured the "What Cats Want" tagline along with a predatory-looking cat lying in the grass as though waiting for its prey.

OUTCOME

According to testing undertaken by the prominent market-research firm Millward Brown, the "Inner Beast" campaign rated far higher in terms of memorability than other cat-food commercials; 63 percent of viewers enjoyed the spots (versus an advertising norm of 37 percent), and 81 percent felt that the work was superior to other cat-food advertising. Market research also revealed that the key message transmitted by the campaign was the one that TBWA\Chiat\Day had hoped to communicate: that Whiskas was the food that suited cats' instinctive preferences.

Mars was so enamored of TBWA\Chiat\Day's "Inner Beast" work for Whiskas that, over the next two years, it awarded the agency's worldwide network more than 40 percent of its international Masterfoods advertising business, including assignments in 70 different countries. Whereas Whiskas had been a minor account for the storied advertising agency, Mars's Masterfoods subsidiaries eventually became one of its most significant clients. The "Inner Beast" campaign was considered groundbreaking for its industry, and the theme of depicting cats' true natures remained in place in subsequent Whiskas marketing initiatives.

FURTHER READING

Champagne, Christine. "Dir. Murro Hunts Big Game for Whiskas." *Shoot,* July 18, 2003.

Diaz, Ann-Christine. "Gary Pascoe and John Payne, TBWA\Chiat\Day\LA." *Creativity,* February 2004.

Elliott, Stuart. "A New Pitch for Cat Food Is Based on Celebrating Fluffy's Inner Beast." *New York Times,* July 8, 2003.

Fera, Rae Ann. "Whiskas Feeds the Inner Beast." *Boards Online,* July 10, 2003. Available from <http://www.boardsmag.com/articles/online/20030710/whiskas.html>

O'Leary, Noreen. "U.S. Agency of the Year: TBWA\Chiat\Day." *Adweek,* January 10, 2005.

Pappas, Ben. "Transparent Eyeball." *Forbes,* June 14, 1999.

Parpis, Eleftheria. "The Tao of Clow: How a Surfer from West Los Angeles Became the Art Director of His Generation and the Soul of Chiat/Day." *Adweek,* November 17, 2003.

Thompson, Stephanie. "Category Spending Still Stagnant." *Advertising Age,* June 23, 2003.

———. "Mars Dumps D'Arcy, Citing Office Closure." *Advertising Age,* May 13, 2002.

"Whiskas: 'Buffalo.'" *Adweek,* July 14, 2003.

Mark Lane

M&M'S NEW MILLENNIUM CAMPAIGNS

OVERVIEW

In the years 2000 through 2005 M&M's candies remained a brand giant for Mars, Inc., manufacturer of other popular candies, including Skittles, Twix, Starburst, and Snickers. Several ad campaigns for M&M's were released during this period, including the "Global Color Vote" in 2002 and "Help Us Find Our Colors" in 2004. It was during this period that Mars embraced an integrated media philosophy that ensured that a product's television advertising, print ads, Internet elements, and point-of-purchase displays were coordinated seamlessly with packaging, public relations, and other media. Mars executive Peter Littlewood orchestrated the company's many media agencies that were responsible for different aspects of each campaign.

Often promotional in nature, the new integrated campaigns were usually linked to high-profile national events. Promotions also centered on the chocolate candies' famous colors and featured the characters known as the M&M's Spokescandies. The "Global Color Vote" asked consumers worldwide to vote on a new color in 2002. The campaign worked hard to portray this as a news event and succeeded when victorious purple was announced on news outlets such as CNN. Television advertising buys were concentrated on programs with notably huge audiences. For instance, the "Find Our Colors" tie-in campaign showed partying Spokescandies on the *Dick Clark's New Year's Rockin' Eve* telecast. When the clock struck midnight, the candies' colors vanished. For subsequent months in 2004, black-and-white M&M's were sold in special packaging until their colors were reclaimed on commercials that aired the night of the Academy Awards telecast in March.

The fiercely independent, privately held company generally kept profit details to itself, but *Investors Business Daily* reported in 2002 that M&M's was responsible for a healthy $2 billion-plus in company revenue, up from $1.5 billion the previous year. The "Global Color Vote" achieved results in the first three months of 2002, with growth reaching double digits for M&M's, while the category as a whole only grew by 3 percent. Most of the M&M's campaigns ran a cycle of about six months before moving onto the next promotion.

HISTORICAL CONTEXT

Mars, Inc., began as a privately owned family business captained by Frank Mars in the early decades of the twentieth century. M&M's milk chocolate candies got their start in Europe, however. Frank's son Forrest Mars was discouraged by his father's conservative business view, so the two parted ways in the 1930s. Forrest went to stake his claim in Europe. There he noticed a unique candy product: lentil-sized pellets of chocolate with a hard sugar coating that kept them from melting. Company legend had it that he saw soldiers with the candy during the Spanish Civil War. He brought the idea back to the states and, working independently of his father's company, introduced the first M&M's candies in 1940. Forrest was an innovator and a shrewd student of business. In what might be described as his first promotional tie-in coup, he managed to get M&M's included in U.S. soldiers' rations in World War II. Upon his father's death Forrest Mars took over Mars, Inc., and merged it with his own candy company.

The brown, yellow, orange, red, green, and violet (a color that was later replaced with tan) candy shells prevented the candies from melting and were a hit with consumers. Hence the memorable longtime slogan "The Milk Chocolate Melts in Your Mouth—Not in Your Hand" was born in the 1950s. Peanut M&M's soon followed as the company's first brand extension. The slogan was used for decades and only began to be phased out when a new long-term device emerged in the

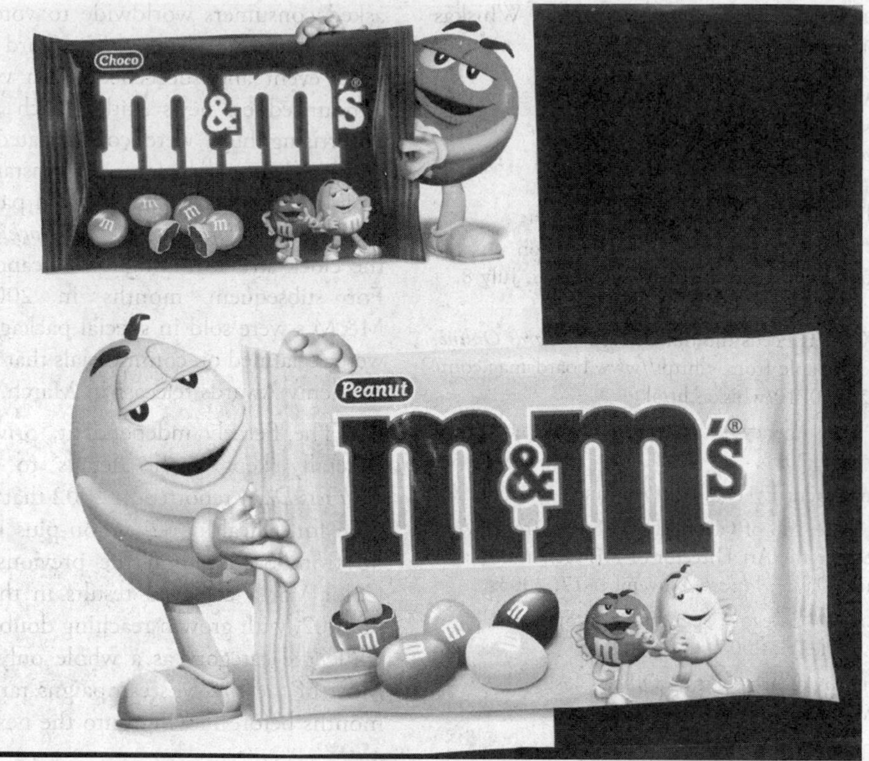

M&M Mars's Spokescandies. IMAGE COURTESY OF THE ADVERTISING ARCHIVE LTD. REPRODUCED BY PERMISSION.

form of "Spokescandies," cartoon M&M's candies with faces, arms, and legs. These brand characters were first used in advertisements in 1954 and finally appeared on packages in 1972. The original Red and Yellow characters were one-dimensional images. Later the characters became animated in three dimensions using Claymation techniques. Commercials using the Spokescandies were humorous or cute, intended to appeal to children in particular. There was a significant shift through the 1980s and into the next two decades, when the characters—rather than taste or eating experience—became the focus of the candies' advertising. Television spots in the 1990s paired the Spokescandies with such celebrities as actress Halle Berry and comedian Dennis Miller.

The M&M's brand was a pioneer in the world of advertising with its unique approach to promotions, tie-ins, and cohesive advertising strategies. In 1982 M&M's candies were first provided for astronauts on United States Space Shuttle trips. To highlight M&M's introduction to the international market in the 1980s, the candies became the "Official Snack Food" of the 1984 Olympics. It was in this period that color became another ongoing theme of M&M's advertising and promotion. Holiday-themed candies were introduced: red and green were packaged together at Christmastime, and pastels were sold for Easter. The 1995 color-vote promotion caught the attention at least 10 million Americans, who chose blue to enter the mix. As the year 2000 approached, the M&M's ad team was already thinking ahead. In 1998 it declared M&M's "the official candy of the new millennium." Capitalizing on the Roman numeral *M,* which meant 1,000, and a preoccupation with the coming millennium, it tied the product in with an enormous worldwide event without having to spend a cent on rights. "M&M's—blatantly exploiting the new millennium," was how one sarcastic, self-deprecating TV spot ended.

TARGET MARKET

M&M's advertisements and promotions were designed to appeal to a wide variety of consumers. Historically the brand's multifaceted campaigns had always considered every age group. The Spokescandies fit the bill perfectly and were honed with every new campaign to attract a broad range of consumers. Their appearance was designed to be cute for little kids, while their attitude was often wisecracking for teen appeal. M&M's aimed television spots in particular at an older audience. Spots that featured the Spokescandies in adult environments or situations were featured in 2001. For instance, satires of

PET FOOD PROFITS

Forrest Mars invented the canned-pet-food business back when he was in Britain in the 1930s. He convinced pet owners that it would be healthier for their animals than the usual table scraps. A new industry was born, resulting in the Kal Kan, Pedigree, and Whiskas brands that eventually made up 50 percent of sales for Mars, Inc.

an upscale hotel visit or the traditional big box of valentine chocolates that a husband gave a wife were rife with mature subtext. Voting promotions and games on the company website were carefully crafted to appeal to all ages.

COMPETITION

The leaders in chocolate convenience foods had for years been Hershey, Mars, and Nestlé, in that order. In 2001 Hershey's share of the U.S. confectionary market was 30.3 percent, nearly twice that of Mars (16.9 percent) and well above Nestlé (6.3 percent), according to Information Resources, a Chicago research company whose figures did not include sales at Wal-Mart. Hershey, wishing to create even more distance between itself and Mars, adopted Mars's business model of putting the bulk of ad dollars behind its top-three brands. In the October 29, 2001, issue of *Advertising Age,* Credit Suisse First Boston analyst Dave Nelson observed that Hershey's new president and CEO was "in line with how (Mars) sees the world." He continued, "By marketing big brands, you don't have to spend as much to connect with the consumer, so return on investment is naturally higher." Hershey may have been emulating its nearest competitor's ad strategies, but the advertising philosophies of the number one and number two candy makers remained unique. Hershey concentrated on branding, while Mars continually sought to create an emotional connection with the consumer.

Henri Nestlé invented milk chocolate in 1875, but it was Milton Hershey who made the sweet snack food a household name. Nestlé's lack of diversification of its chocolate offerings had kept it comfortably behind Mars for decades. In 2002, however, Mars had reason to be concerned when reports surfaced that Hershey was for sale. Nestlé was considered to be the prime candidate to snap up the iconic Pennsylvania company. But the sale did not materialize, and Hershey regrouped. Over the next two years the market-share ratios remained roughly the same for chocolate's big three. In 2005 Hershey introduced a new product called Kissables that was remarkably similar to M&M's candies.

MARKETING STRATEGY

Mars spent $195 million on U.S. confection brand advertising in 2000, much of that concentrated on its three top brands, which generated 67 percent of sales. It was at this time that Mars made a shift in how it drove and oversaw media functions, giving its marketing division a more "in-house agency" feel. Executive Peter Littlewood was the man credited with successfully coordinating the vast and various print, TV, public relations, Internet, and other media saturations that accompanied each new M&M's push. In a September 2002 issue of *Advertising Age,* Bob Gamgort, president of the North American division of Mars, described Littlewood as perfect for the job because of his "terrific experience in brand marketing and his strong interest in broadening outside traditional arenas." M&M's advertising methods for the new millennium were even more creatively geared toward the elements that had brought the brand success in the previous century: high-visibility promotions using the Spokescandies and the color theme in fully integrated cross-media campaigns.

In 2000 M&M's Spokescandies, introduced 50 years before and evolving ever since, were on their way to becoming iconic characters. Each one had a personality and had been growing along with consumers. The two originals were Red, a loveable and slightly pompous milk chocolate, and Yellow, an endearingly absentminded Peanut M&M. Later came supercool Blue and anxiety-ridden Crispy. The only female character, vivacious Green, was created with a wink at rumors suggesting that the green candies were aphrodisiacs. A fall 2001 campaign entitled "What Is It about the Green Ones?" featured a spot in which Green, a glamorous movie star, had her candy shell off when a producer entered her trailer. In another commercial she was a pinup girl on a poster in a teen boy's room. Her picture was stamped on the green candies during the campaign as well.

Color changes were a key tactic for generating interest. Color votes made consumers feel that they had a personal stake in the product. Blue became a permanent M&M's color by popular U.S. vote. The company had wanted M&M's to be part of the fabric of American life throughout the twentieth century, and with the turn of a new century M&M's was looking beyond U.S. borders. The year 2002 gave rise to the "Global Color Vote" campaign, a six-month effort. M&M's asked citizens of more than 200 countries to pick a new candy color; the choices were pink, purple, and aqua. Purple's victory, revealed on June 19, 2002, was covered on major news outlets such as CNN and on popular TV shows, including *The Tonight Show with Jay Leno.* Mars even conducted a poll that demonstrated that 40 percent of those polled were aware of purple's win.

Mars continued to find innovative color-themed promotions to renew interest or inspire continued loyalty in the M&M's brand. On a popular New Year's Eve show in 2003 the Spokescandies cavorted with host Dick Clark until the clock struck midnight, and then their colors dramatically disappeared. For the next two months all M&M's packages contained black-and-white candies only. A supporting sweepstakes was held proclaiming, "Help us find our colors." Each winner received cash or a Volkswagen Beetle in a color matching that of the candy they had found in the black-and-white packages. The colors returned to coincide with the Academy Awards ceremony in March 2004. Commercials featuring more vibrantly colored M&M's spokescharacters at a big Hollywood party introduced the slogan "Chocolate is better in color," which ran through May. This exemplified the kind of all-fronts campaign for which M&M's had become known. A buildup of advertisements and promotions that culminated in a focused event ensured high visibility throughout the first half of 2004.

Wherever an event of national significance occurred, Mars seemed to make sure that M&M's was linked to it. A noteworthy 2002 Super Bowl spot was called "Hotel." A man checked into a fancy hotel that promised a complimentary chocolate on the pillow. The next scene showed the man terrified to discover that he was sharing his bed with the Red M&M's spokescharacter. This spot not only stood out for its situational humor but also was even more effective because the audience had come to know Red's persona. "We continue to develop their personalities," said Scott Hudler, brand communications manager for Mars, in a February 2002 issue of *Brand Marketing.* He further explained, "We don't want them spouting the same lines over and over again." That year 30-second Super Bowl advertising slots were selling for a reported $1.9 million, but Mars purchased last-minute for a cut rate that was worth the high visibility. BBDO New York was responsible for the "Hotel" spot, but the company's integrated marketing campaigns also used the agency Grey Worldwide, New York. Other promotional support work for the brand had come from an unusually large variety of media firms, including but not limited to TJ Paul, Marketing Drive Worldwide, Mediaedge:cia, and Starcom MediaVest Group.

OUTCOME

Mars, Inc., continued to be committed to its private status, and at the close of 2005 it described itself as an $18 billion business. For the company's most celebrated brand, M&M's, the first five years of the new millennium were marked by global success. One of the largest M&M's promotions during that period, the "Global Color Vote" of 2002, produced a U.S. sales increase of 21 percent for the colored candies that year, an admirable feat when compared to category growth of only 3 percent overall. Profit details for the privately held company were rarely disclosed, but *Investors Business Daily* reported in 2002 that M&M's accounted for more than $2 billion in company revenue, up from $1.5 billion the previous year. In 2005 Mars continued to expand the brand by introducing Dark Chocolate M&M's and Mega M&M's with adults in mind.

FURTHER READING

Angrisani, Carol. "Character Traits." *Brand Marketing,* February 2002, p. 6.

Baker, Olivia, Maria Puente, and Jerry Shriver. "M&M Embraces Rumors about Those Green Ones." *USA Today,* p. 1D.

Beirne, Mike. "Calling All Candy Makers." *Brandweek,* February 4, 2002, p. 23.

———. "Tie-Ins: Masterfoods Sweetens '04 with M&M's, Shrek 2 Pushes." *Brandweek,* December 1, 2003

Deutsch, Claudia. "M&M's the Top Star on an Ad Walk of Fame." *New York Times,* September 20, 2004, p. C11.

Elliott, Stuart. "Despite Millions of Viewers, the Super Bowl Is Not Quite So for Madison Avenue." *New York Times,* February 1, 2002, p. C2.

———. "From Monkeys to M&M's, Madison Ave. Mostly Opts to Entertain the Super Bowl's TV Fans." *New York Times,* February 5, 2002, p. C6.

Hisey, Pete. "A Taste Explosion." *Retail Merchandiser,* February 2002, p. 58.

Linnett, Richard, and Jack Neff. "Media Consolidation: Masterfoods Starts Scrap for $300M Account; Review to End by December." *Advertising Age,* November 3, 2003, p. 1.

Richman, Michael. "Mars Found the Sweet Spot Innovate to Succeed: Candy Maker Crafted M&Ms, Snickers into Snack Staples." *Investor's Business Daily,* July 12, 2002, p. 3.

Thompson, Stephanie. "Peter Littlewood; VP-Marketing Services, Masterfoods USA." *Advertising Age,* September 30, 2002, p. S6.

Simone Samano

SNICKERS CRUNCHER CAMPAIGN

OVERVIEW

Mars, Inc., which entered the candy business in 1922, has long been one the top sellers of candy bars in the world. Also notable was that Mars, founded by Forrest Mars, Sr., has remained a privately owned family business, and the company has historically been run in an atmosphere of mystery. Mars has kept its formulas and business practices behind a wall of secrecy, and it has also ventured into new products with extreme caution. Yet the Snickers Bar, introduced in 1930, had long been the top-selling candy bar in the United States, and by 2001 an extension of the product seemed warranted. Mars initiated the expansion of the line that year by introducing the Snickers Cruncher, supporting it with a $40 million television and print campaign.

Mars hired ad agency BBDO New York to introduce the new addition to the Snickers family. In print and television advertising BBDO used the tagline, "Hungry? Crunch this," to portray the candy bar as a positive way to alleviate stress. Such television ads as "Car Alarm," in which a woman shoved a sofa out her apartment window to stop an annoying car alarm below, recommended the Snickers Cruncher as an alternative way to experience a satisfying "crunch."

Within a mere six months after its launch, the Snickers Cruncher became a top-10 candy bar in the chocolate confection category. While the popularity of the original Snickers Bar largely accounted for this success, the humorous campaign also played a role. In 2001 one of *USA Today*'s Ad Track surveys indicated that, within the 18- to 24-year-old age bracket (largely representing the target market of the campaign), 61 percent liked the ads "a lot." The launch of the Snickers Cruncher was so successful that it inspired the usually cautious Mars to introduce another new product in the Snickers line, the Snickers Almond Bar, the following year.

HISTORICAL CONTEXT

In her book *The Emperors of Chocolate: Inside the Secret World of Hershey and Mars,* Joël Glenn Brenner wrote, "Mars spends an estimated $400 million a year to advertise its products across America, but since its founding, the company itself has operated inside a fortress of silence." In 1989 Brenner was only the third member of the press known to interview anyone inside Mars since its founding in 1922. Established by Forrest Mars, Sr., the son of a struggling candy maker named Frank Mars, the family-owned business was one of the most secretive companies ever to exist.

The company found incredible success, making the Mars family one of America's wealthiest. Its first candy success was M&M's, introduced in 1940. Mars subsequently increased its offerings, although it did so with an air of caution. The addition of the Snickers Bar was one change that seemed to pay off spectacularly. An early model of the nougat-and-peanut candy bar was introduced in 1923, but without a chocolate coating. In 1930 Mars launched a milk-chocolate-coated version, which was an immediate success. The Snickers Bar continued to gain widespread recognition, especially from 1948 to 1952, when it sponsored *The Howdy Doody Show.*

The Snickers product line eventually expanded. In 1968 a small, fun-size version of the candy bar became available; two years later, the Snickers Munch bar, a candy bar modeled after peanut brittle, was launched. From 1989 to 1990 two more Snickers products hit stores: the Snickers Ice Cream bar and Snickers Miniatures (which were even smaller than the fun size). The Snickers Ice Cream Cone came around in 1996. Still, these products were developed not as new versions of Snickers but as separate products carrying the same theme. In 2001 the Snickers Cruncher, which got its crunchy texture from crisped rice, became the first product offered as a direct extension of the original Snickers bar.

Like many past Snickers products, the Crunchers were marketed with a theme of universal humor that both kids and adults could understand. The debut Cruncher ads, which showed consumers how they could "crunch" out their frustrations, used a similar approach to the then-current Snickers campaign, "Hungry? Grab a Snickers." One such Snickers ad portrayed a hungry football team that was too pumped up to find its way onto the field. This kind of wit was used in Snickers Cruncher advertisements.

TARGET MARKET

Snickers had become America's best-selling candy bar, not only among kids, but among adults, too. Therefore its advertising had to take an approach that would appeal across generations. To achieve this Mars promoted Snickers with a specific kind of humor that involved elements of silliness and wit, which made it appealing to both children and adults. In "Car Alarm," for instance, a woman threw her couch out of her apartment window onto a car below to stop an annoying car alarm. While children might laugh over the sheer ridiculousness of the situation, an adult could better relate to the satisfaction one might achieve from doing such a thing. Mars had established that the core target audience for Snickers was 12- to 24-year-olds, but at the same it kept its older snackers in mind. Such taglines as "Hungry? Grab a Snickers," or "Hungry? Why Wait," coincided with moments that both kids and adults would find funny. It was with a similar approach that Mars targeted the Snickers Cruncher Bar.

COMPETITION

The dramatic rivalry between Mars and the Hershey Company appeared to have been created in fiction. Between them, insults were traded and rumors were

EVERY LAST "M"

Mars Inc. aimed for perfection in the manufacturing of its products. Total cleanliness and meticulousness were essential at the company. According to Joël Brenner's book *The Emperors of Chocolate: Inside the Secret World of Hershey and Mars,* it was said that the bacteria level on a Mars factory floor was less than the average level in a household sink. Such perfection was a goal in all aspects of Mars's manufacturing. Every *m* on an M&M and each squiggle on top of a chocolate bar were scrupulously tracked. The slightest imperfection on a piece of chocolate caused it to be tossed into the trash, leading to the discarding of millions of M&M's candies on any given day.

spread. They battled for the spot of America's top candy maker, the world's top candy maker, and even the U.S. military's top candy maker. Mars had placed itself inside a fortress, guarded and mysterious. As a private company, it was able to sustain this image more easily than most. Hershey, too, maintained an element of mystery, especially when guarding its chocolate secrets. But as a public company, much more information was made available.

This public information did not appear to have hurt the Hershey Company, which had become the top candy seller in North America. With sales near $4.5 billion (with more than half of this from chocolate alone) and a net income of nearly $600 million, the company had been a phenomenon ever since it sold its first nickel bar in 1900. Over the decades Hershey expanded dramatically, ultimately producing many of the world's favorite indulgences, including Reese's Peanut Butter Cups, Twizzlers licorice, Mounds/Almond Joy bars, York peppermint patties, and Hershey's Kisses chocolates. The company also ventured into the grocery-goods business by selling such products as baking chocolate and peanut butter.

While Mars promoted its new Snickers Cruncher, Hershey was marketing several new products of its own. In 2001, for example, Hershey launched the Big Kat chocolate wafer bar (a larger version of its Kit Kat), which immediately competed with the Snickers Cruncher. But even more significant was Hershey's continual extension of its Reese's line, which represented the biggest competition for Snickers. The Reese's products had been expanding since the peanut butter cup was first introduced in the 1920s. New editions of the product included Reese's Fast Break as well as alternate versions of the peanut butter cup.

Meanwhile, the food giant Nestlé, which offered such chocolate treats as Nestlé Crunch and Smarties, had become the world leader in chocolate sales. In 2004 its sales of candy and cookies reached $7.1 billion. With overall sales exceeding $76 billion, Nestlé had become not only the world's top seller of chocolate but also the number one distributor of food. Among Mars's other competitors was London-based food giant Cadbury Schweppes, which took its own share of the chocolate market. The company, largely known in the United States for its Cadbury Creme Egg, also sold chocolate bars as well as soft drinks, juice products, and gum. In 2004 its total sales neared $13 billion.

MARKETING STRATEGY

Snickers added incredible wealth, in the form of over $250 million a year, to the already lucrative Mars, Inc. The Snickers Bar was first introduced in 1930, when it was sold for a nickel. Soon thereafter, it became an American favorite. In an attempt to reap further benefits from its popularity, in 2000 Mars launched an effort that would add several new products under the Snickers name.

In a $40 million television and print campaign, Mars and its ad agency, BBDO New York, launched Snickers Cruncher, which the Snickers website described as a "crispy, crunchy chocolate bar packed with roasted peanuts, caramel and milk chocolate that's not just crunchy. It's beyond crunchy." Filled with crisped rice, the candy bar seemed to have mimicked Hershey's Whatchamacallit, which was introduced in 1978. But although a goal of the campaign was to steal market share from rival Hershey's, competing with the Whatchamacallit was not the primary focus. In creating a new Snickers line of goodies, Mars intended to do with Snickers what Hershey had done to expand its Reese's line.

BBDO developed a series of creative and witty ads and commercials to promote the Snickers Cruncher. The television spots, including "SUV," "Telemarketer," "Car Alarm," and "Popular Phrases," provided humorous examples of people smashing or shattering things in order to alleviate frustration. In "Car Alarm" a woman, irritated by the sound of a car alarm, shoved a sofa out her apartment window, crushing the offending car. Another spot showed people buying annoying talking dolls from a street vendor, only so that they could stomp them to pieces. After each scene, a voice-over stated the tagline, "Hungry? Crunch this," which suggested that eating the Snickers Cruncher was a more positive way to act on one's urge to "crunch" something.

Mars also considered it important for the campaign to be consistent with advertising for the original Snickers Bar. As Bob Gamgort, the company's general manager for chocolate, explained to *USA Today*'s Theresa Howard, "The feel and humor of the Cruncher ads feels like Snickers.... This is a way to keep them within the Snickers franchise when they are looking for a crunchy texture. That is why the spots have a very simple message." The spots represented the new candy bar as the Snickers that consumers were already familiar with, but with a satisfying crunch.

OUTCOME

Snickers Cruncher met with immediate success. Within six months of its launch it became a top-10 candy bar in the chocolate confection category, according to the Chocolate Manufacturers Association of the United States. While the Snickers name helped to boost the new candy bar to the top, the multimillion-dollar ad campaign also played a role. The television spots, which used the clever humor of regular Snickers campaigns, were hugely successful with viewers. Six months after the campaign's debut, *USA Today* reported that 34 percent of respondents to its Ad Track survey liked the ads "a lot." This was significantly higher than the Ad Track survey average of 22 percent. Among those aged 18 to 24, the ads were incredibly popular, with 61 percent giving them positive ratings. Because the target market was 12- to-24-year-olds, this latter number marked a triumph of the campaign.

The "Snickers Cruncher" campaign's success contributed to the continuation of the new Snickers line. In 2002 Mars introduced the Snickers Almond Bar. This marked a time of expensive marketing efforts by Snickers. Simultaneously, the Snickers brand became a sponsor of the immensely popular *Survivor* reality-television show as well as an official sponsor of the NFL. In 2004 the Snickers line was expanded in a way that catered to healthier eaters, with the introduction of Snickers Marathon, an energy bar that boasted of 16 vitamins and surplus of protein. According to Mars, Snickers Marathon was "the first energy bar in history with a taste worthy of the Snickers brand name." The continued expansion of the line sparked new advertisements, which followed the old Snickers theme of smart humor.

FURTHER READING

Beirne, Mike. "Snickers Gives Birth to Cruncher." *Brandweek,* June 5, 2000.

"Beloved Bars Will Bounce Right Back." *Australian* (Sydney), July 4, 2005, p. 14.

Brenner, Joël G. *The Emperors of Chocolate: Inside the Secret World of Hershey and Mars.* New York: Bantam Dell Publishing Group, 2000.

Buckley, Neil, Jeremy Grant, and Juliana Ratner. "Candy's Dandy but Strategy Remains the Key." *Financial Times,* August 2, 2002, p. 24.

Elliott, Stuart. "Mars Unit Looks to Merge Marketing." *New York Times,* November 3, 2003, p. 13.

Fairclough, Gordon. "Mars Inc. Faces Unclear Future Due to Death." *Wall Street Journal,* July 6, 1999, p. 22.

Falcon, Mike. "Super Bowl Ads Neglect Nutrition." *USA Today,* January 29, 2001.

Guy, Sandra. "Chicago Hosts a Taste of Candymakers' Latest." *Chicago Sun-Times,* June 6, 2000, p. 54.

Hoffman, Ken. "Candy Bar Ice Cream Best of Both Whirls." *Houston Chronicle,* June 23, 2000, p. 7.

Howard, Theresa. "Candy Bar Breaks Crispy New Ground." *USA Today,* June 4, 2001.

Laucius, Joanne, and Zev Singer. "Mars Bars: The Tyrant's Chocolate of Choice: Sweet Treats Found in Tiny Hideout." *Ottawa (Ontario) Citizen,* December 16, 2003, p. A3.

"Mars Inc." *Washington Post,* April 25, 2005, p. T60.

Pandya, Nick. "Rise: Cool Companies: No 84 Mars Inc." *Guardian* (Manchester), July 27, 2002, p. 5.

"2 Candy Makers Raising Wholesale Prices." *New York Times,* December 12, 2002, p. 14.

Candice L. Mancini

Maryland State Lottery Agency

Montgomery Park Business Center
1800 Washington Blvd., Ste. 330
Baltimore, Maryland 21230
USA
Telephone: (410) 230-8800
Fax: (410) 230-8800
Web site: www.mdlottery.com

CASH IN HAND CAMPAIGN

OVERVIEW

As the Maryland Lottery, run by the Maryland State Lottery Agency, entered its 25th year in 1998, it found itself struggling. After the lottery first began in 1973, sales and popularity grew rapidly. By the mid-1990s, however, players had begun to lose interest, and they seemed inclined to hold out for enormous jackpots rather than play regularly. Despite new games and promotional efforts, the Maryland Lottery suffered from a 7 percent decline in ticket sales between 1996 and 1997. To turn around the ailing lottery, which had become the state government's third-largest source of revenue, a new director was brought on board, new games were introduced, and a new advertising agency, Eisner & Associates, Inc., was hired in 1997. In addition, Maryland's governor, Parris N. Glendening, proposed adding $2 million to the lottery's advertising budget for 1998, raising it to $13.7 million.

The lottery's new director, Buddy Roogow, explained to the *Baltimore Sun* that the lottery agency would adopt a new strategy for attracting customers and would stress the amusement aspect of playing the lottery over the possibility of becoming rich. Roogow stated, "We're fighting for the entertainment dollar." Eisner & Associates created the "Cash in Hand" campaign, which introduced a new game launched in early 1998. It was one of several promotions for various Maryland Lottery products. In keeping with Roogow's mission, the two television spots developed for the campaign were entertaining and humorous. They featured animated characters attempting to explain the basic concept of the Cash in Hand game—that the top prize of $500,000 was awarded in one lump sum, "all at once," rather than in annual allotments. The amusing spots aired on major network affiliates and cable channels during prime-time viewing hours.

The "Cash in Hand" campaign played a major role in reviving the fortunes of the Maryland Lottery, which, despite increased competition from Powerball and other multistate jackpots, was able to increase revenues in 1998. The campaign also received recognition from the advertising industry.

HISTORICAL CONTEXT

Citizens took to heart the Maryland Lottery's marketing slogan of the 1970s, "You've Gotta Play to Win!," making the lottery an instant success. When a daily game was introduced in 1976 to accompany the weekly drawing, lottery sales increased almost fivefold during the following two years. Annual sales of the daily game, Pick 3, reached a high point in 1985 at nearly $475 million. Proceeds from lottery sales went into the state's general fund and helped support such government services and programs as education, human resources, and public health. And as the third-largest revenue source for the state, after income and sales taxes, the state grew accustomed to and dependent upon the income.

The days of lottery fever, however, inevitably began to dwindle. In the mid-1990s the Maryland Lottery faced growing competition from ever-increasing casinos and other forms of gambling and gaming as well as from lotteries that cropped up in neighboring states and regions. As reported by Maryland's Department of Fiscal Services, lottery sales through April 20, 1997, were off by $56.5 million compared to the previous fiscal year. To boost sales, lottery director Roogow implemented an aggressive new strategy to renew enthusiasm and inject energy into the lottery. Roogow not only altered the prize rules of some games to enable more players to win smaller prizes, but he also developed cooperative business partnerships with private companies to transform losing lottery tickets into coupons and introduced several new games, including Cash in Hand. The agency also joined forces with several other states in 1996 to offer the Big Game, a jackpot game.

The Maryland Lottery, Roogow believed, also needed a change in image to generate interest, and the most effective means of accomplishing this was through advertising. To that end the lottery broke with its agency since 1982, Trahan, Burden & Charles Inc., and granted Baltimore-based Eisner & Associates a three-year contract. Roogow planned to do away with traditional lottery ads that showed mansions and fur coats and other luxuries. "We want to portray excitement," Roogow told the *Baltimore Sun,* "... and move away from the dreams and fantasies of other campaigns... Those images of mansions promote unrealism to people." With an increase in the advertising budget of 16 percent in 1998, Roogow hoped to promote the many products offered by the Maryland Lottery, rather than focusing on jackpot games, and to create an atmosphere of fun.

TARGET MARKET

The Maryland Lottery hoped to attract new players as well as those who had abandoned lottery games because of disinterest or for gaming alternatives, such as casino gambling. The agency also intended to lure players living in nearby communities, such as the Washington, D.C., area. Roogow told the *Washington Post,* "One of the important thrusts of new advertising money is to try to improve our presence in the Maryland suburbs of Washington... We believe that we can and should be able to do better there." In addition to more advertising,

> ### IT COULD BE YOU... BUT IT PROBABLY WON'T
>
> Buddy Roogow, director of the Maryland State Lottery Agency, was vocal and blunt about the remote chances of winning large jackpots and had a slogan of his own—"It could be you... but it probably won't." "It's not fair to give the implication that it's easy to win $1 million," Roogow told the *Wall Street Journal.* "There's a one in seven million chance to win the jackpot in the Lotto game. That's why we emphasize the fun of playing. A government body has to be socially responsible." To encourage people to play more frequently, Roogow shifted the Maryland Lottery's efforts toward instant-win games and scratch-off tickets, offering more players more chances to win.

Roogow believed that offering more "winning experiences," albeit smaller prizes, would also attract additional players, as studies had demonstrated that one of the reasons people stopped playing lottery games was because they did not win.

Although Roogow claimed that the Maryland Lottery did not direct its marketing toward a particular demographic group, reports indicated that those who played heavily and regularly tended to come from lower-income brackets. An annual survey conducted for the Maryland Lottery by Market Facts, Inc., found that in 1997, of heavy players (those spending at least $10 per week), nearly half did not hold a high school diploma, about half earned less than $20,000 a year, and more than 60 percent were of African-American descent. The study also noted that the state's players were "more likely to be male, less educated and more downscale" than nonplayers. Although the actual market for lottery products could be quantified, Roogow insisted in the *Washington Post,* "We do not try to appeal to a specific group of people."

COMPETITION

Lotteries were illegal from 1894 to 1964, but by the late 1990s more than 35 U.S. states offered state-run lotteries. Between 1970 and 1996, according to the *Atlantic Economic Journal,* lottery sales rose from $49.2 million to $34 billion, producing net revenues of $34 billion in 1996. With the possibility of such profits, it was no surprise that the Maryland Lottery found itself facing strong competition from neighboring states and communities, particularly Washington, D.C., and Virginia. The District of Columbia's lottery, which began in 1982, presented a threat to Maryland particularly between 1992 and 1995, when sales grew 57 percent, but beginning in 1996 its sales began to drop. Still, in 1996, according to *La Fleur's 1996 World Lottery Almanac,* the District of Columbia was the third-ranked state lottery in terms of per capita sales, while the Maryland Lottery was ranked eighth. And though the Virginia lottery, which started in 1988, made it only to number 19 on the list, it advertised aggressively and had a well-known marketing character known as Lady Luck.

Not only did the Maryland Lottery face competition from other lotteries, but it also struggled against those opposed to gaming. Economist Peter Reuter of the University of Maryland said to the *Journal Record,* "This is a large, terribly regressive tax on a service sold by a state monopoly." The prolottery contingent maintained that the lottery benefited the community by providing funds for education and other civic services and that playing the lottery was voluntary, but its arguments often fell flat. The University of Maryland's Julian Simon told the *Fort Worth Star-Telegram,* "The states do not simply offer their product to the public. They promote hard. Lottery advertisements are beguilingly seductive, and misleading to boot." And consumer activist Ralph Nader commented in the *Washington Post,* "The whole thing is unseemly, for the state to encourage gambling."

MARKETING STRATEGY

The "Cash in Hand" campaign, launched in early 1998, consisted of two television spots as well as some radio and point-of-sale promotions. The television commercials ran during such popular prime-time programs as *ER* and *NYPD Blue.* Eisner creative director Bill Mitchell discussed the concept behind the Claymation commercials in *Adweek* and said, "The key concept for this product is that if you match seven numbers between one and thirty-one, you win all the cash, all at one time." The agency's research had demonstrated that most people wanted to receive their prize money all at once rather than in increments. "We were looking for a simple, endearing and demonstrative way to communicate this message," Mitchell explained. Mitchell stated that he and writer Brian Kelley had come up with the idea behind the campaign while eating in a restaurant. "Surrounding us were all these great containers full of ketchup, sugar, oatmeal and syrup that could be used to demonstrate a lot pouring out—all at one time," Mitchell explained.

One of the spots, entitled "Diner," featured two male Claymation characters seated at a counter with large plates filled with breakfast foods. The brunet male put his newspaper down and said, "Imagine getting half-a-million dollars all at once." The blond male then asked, "All at once? What do you mean?" The brunet replied, "You know, all at once," and then, to demonstrate, he emptied an entire container of sugar into the blond's coffee cup. "Oh, I see. So this isn't all at once," the blond replied, putting some ketchup on the brunette's eggs, "but this is all at once." He then squeezed the ketchup bottle so that the entire contents squirted up into the air and landed on the brunet's head. The interplay continued, with the brunet placing a whole bowl of oatmeal in the blond's lower lip. The blond then picked up a meringue pie, ready to demonstrate "all at once" in the brunet's face. As the Cash in Hand logo appeared on the screen, the voice-over said, "Play Cash in Hand from the Maryland Lottery. It pays you half-a-million dollars all at once. Just like that." The spot then cut back to the Claymation characters, the blond still holding the pie. A third character walking by the counter overheard the two males and asked, "All at once? What do you mean?" To which the eyes of the two mischievous males grew wide.

The second spot, "Missed It," was also set at the diner counter and also starred two male Claymation characters. A heavyset character told his neighbor, "If my numbers win, I get half-a-million all at once." The thinner male, seated before a large salad, asked, "All at once?" The first male then attempted to demonstrate the concept by placing an entire baked potato in his mouth. The thin character was momentarily distracted, however, and looked away while the feat was being accomplished. When he turned back, he prompted the heavyset male, "Go ahead." The male then swallowed his steak all at once, but the thin man was once again looking away. At the end of the spot the heavyset male had a stack of empty plates in front of him, but his neighbor still had not seen him consume anything "all at once."

Aside from the creative success of the "Cash in Hand" campaign, Eisner made a fundamental change to the Maryland Lottery brand. Instead of focusing on the promise of riches, as embodied by the tagline from previous campaigns, "It Could Be You," the Maryland Lottery now emphasized the fun of playing lottery games, reflected by the new tagline: "Let Yourself Play." Not only was it a more honest approach, since the odds of winning remained low, but it also gave consumers "permission" to play lottery games even when they knew it was in many respects a poor investment.

OUTCOME

Thanks in part to clever and entertaining marketing, the Maryland Lottery enjoyed a stellar 1998. While other states were placing increased efforts on multistate jackpots such as Powerball, rather than investing in their own lotteries, the Maryland agency chose to advance its state lottery products. Although state lotteries that were not part of Powerball experienced about a 5 percent decrease in revenue in 1998, Maryland's lottery sales rose 3 percent, to $1.07 billion. And for the fiscal year ending June 30, 1998, Maryland gained profits of more than $400 million, a record and an increase of 2 percent over the previous year. Gross ticket sales grew 2.8 percent, reaching nearly $1.1 billion. The Maryland Lottery reported that more than $367.6 million was deposited into the state's general fund and that more than $566.1 million, 53 percent of gross sales, went toward prize monies. Cash in Hand players, for example, received a total of $5.8 million in prizes.

The "Cash in Hand" campaign succeeded in launching the Cash in Hand game, which proved popular enough to be offered until September 2002. The campaign was also recognized with a number of awards, including a Clio for "Diner" and recognition from the New York Festival's 41st Annual Television Advertising Awards. Moreover, Eisner continued to create winning campaigns, as well as products, for the Maryland Lottery. A television spot created for the "Pumpkin Chunkin" campaign was honored with the Best of Show award at the 27th Annual Best in Baltimore ADDY Awards in 2001. Every year that Eisner held the account, the Maryland Lottery increased sales and exceeded goals. The ad agency also succeeded in repositioning the lottery brand. Marketing surveys showed steady increases in important measures, in particular when respondents were asked if they agreed with the statement "the games are fun even if you don't win." After five years the Maryland Lottery account was put into review in 2002 as mandated by law, but no one was surprised when Eisner retained the business. "I believe they've done an outstanding job in the five years they've had the contract," Buddy Roogow, director of the Maryland State Lottery Agency, told the *Baltimore Sun.* "I'm very excited about the direction we've been going and where we're going in the future."

FURTHER READING

Arney, June. "Doner and Eisner Share Best-of-Show at Addys." *Baltimore Sun,* March 13, 2001.

———. "Eisner Wins Md. Lottery Deal." *Baltimore Sun,* April 18, 2002.

Babington, Charles. "Md. Trying to Attract More Lottery Players." *Washington Post,* September 24, 1997, p. B1.

Chinoy, Ira, and Charles Babington. "Lotteries Lure Players with Slick Marketing." *Washington Post,* May 4, 1998, p. A1.

———. "Low-Income Players Feed Lottery Cash Cow." *Washington Post,* May 3, 1998, p. A1.

Conklin, J.C. "Winning Lotto Motto: 'Could Be You... Probably Won't,'" *Wall Street Journal,* May 24, 1999, p. B1.

Fitzgerald, Nora. "All in One Lump Sum." *Adweek,* May 25, 1998, p. 4.

———. "Eisner's Creativity, Prize Are Right as It Captures Maryland Lottery." *Adweek,* May 5, 1997, p. 3.

Kappalman, Samantha. "Ad Firm Won Lottery Betting on Consumers." *Baltimore Sun,* October 3, 1997, p. C1.

Kline, Alan. "Lottery Seeks Firm that's Just the Ticket." *Washington Times,* January 13, 1997, p. D8.

Reed, Keith T. "Lottery Ad Campaign in Review." *Baltimore Business Journal,* January 21, 2002.

Mariko Fujinaka
Ed Dinger

MasterCard International

2000 Purchase Street
Purchase, New York 10577
USA
Telephone: (914) 249-2000
Fax: (914) 249-2000
Web site: www.mastercard.com.

■■■

PRICELESS CAMPAIGN

OVERVIEW

In 1997 MasterCard International, the largest subsidiary of the credit card company MasterCard Incorporated, was reeling from years of unfocused campaign strategies. The industry leader, Visa International, posted sales of $1.65 billion in 1996, nearly double MasterCard's posted sales. In a saturated credit card market where companies jostled to find a place in consumers' wallets, it was essential for MasterCard to forge a powerful brand image that would bring new customers to MasterCard and convince current cardholders to use their MasterCards more often. "The bottom line is that we want people to like us, and we want MasterCard to be the first card they pull out," Lawrence Flanagan, the company's vice president of advertising, told *American Banker*. Hoping to develop an emotional bond with consumers and improve the MasterCard brand image, the company released its "Priceless" campaign.

With an estimated cost of $85 million to $100 million, the television, print, Internet, and billboard campaign was created by the ad agency McCann-Erickson New York. The campaign broke in October 1997 with TV spots that presented a number of scenarios in which intangible rewards were obtained by virtue of the purchase of various items. For instance, "Father/Son" depicted a father taking his son to a baseball game. The prices of various items were listed: "two tickets ($28); two hot dogs, two popcorns, and two sodas ($18); one autographed baseball ($45)." The final item, "Real conversation with 11-year-old son," was tallied as "Priceless." The versatility of both the tagline and the concept enabled McCann-Erickson to target nearly any market with advertising that was either humorous or sentimental.

By 2004 the campaign had appeared in 96 countries and had been translated into 46 languages. In addition to winning more than 100 awards, including advertising awards, by 2006 "Priceless" was credited with boosting MasterCard's market share in the intensely competitive credit card sector. *Adweek* referred to "Priceless" as "one of the industry's most admired campaigns."

HISTORICAL CONTEXT

While MasterCard's chief competitor, Visa USA, had used the "It's Everywhere You Want to Be" campaign since 1985, MasterCard had struggled to devise a lasting brand image. MasterCard's "Master the Moment" campaign, which ended in 1993, attempted to position the card as a more upscale product. Component ads portrayed celebrities and other glamorous folk spending with carefree abandon. With its next campaign, however, MasterCard swung to another extreme. This effort, titled "It's More than a Credit Card: It's Smart Money," stressed the practicality of MasterCard. Rife with scenes of "everyday" people using MasterCard at ordinary places

A still from Mastercard's "Priceless" campaign. IMAGE COURTESY OF THE ADVERTISING ARCHIVE LTD. REPRODUCED BY PERMISSION.

like the supermarket, "Smart Money" was MasterCard's attempt to carve out a unique niche for itself that distinguished it from the more aspirational messages of Visa and American Express Company (AmEx).

Although MasterCard had sought to glorify middle-class values, the result was less than desirable. Its image seemed mired in stolid and unexciting connotations. While Visa had successfully represented itself as the universally accepted "globe-trotting card," "MasterCard was the everyday hardware-store card," a McCann-Erickson executive told *Adweek.* With its share of the domestic charge card market slipping to about 26 percent in 1996 (compared to Visa's 52 percent), MasterCard fired Ammirati Puris Lintas—its most recent ad agency—in March 1997 and turned to McCann-Erickson to revolutionize the way consumers perceived MasterCard.

TARGET MARKET

"Priceless" was a particularly strong campaign because it allowed MasterCard to address distinct audiences with individual commercials tailored to suit each market niche. With its broad goal of targeting consumers aged 18 to 54, MasterCard was faced with a seemingly formidable task of spanning generational and demographic divides. McCann's innovation was to maintain the overarching unity of "Priceless" at the same time that it pursued radically different groups. One important market for MasterCard was the massive baby-boom generation. The benefits of connecting with this audience were obvious. Not only were boomers vast in number, but they also wielded considerable spending power as they reached the pinnacles of their careers (and earning power). This niche of wealthy 40- and 50-somethings was the most sought-after segment in the credit card industry, according to *Advertising Age.* Catering to this population was challenging, though, and involved "subtly celebrat[ing] experience [while] squeamishly avoid[ing] terms like middle-aged," explained the *Washington Post.*

One way "Priceless" targeted boomers was to incorporate the realities of the generation into the campaign. Many of the advertisements featured attractive people in their 40s and 50s celebrating the rites of passage of midlife. "India" portrayed an American couple escaping to India for their 25th wedding anniversary, while "Ireland" narrated a woman's return visit to her homeland with her adult daughter. Even more important, though, was the fact that component "Priceless" ads presented the values and mind-sets of this crucial demographic group. As an industry analyst told the *Post,* for boomers, "[l]ife is supposed to be a series of new adventures." Accordingly, "India," which first ran in January 1998, showed the anniversary couple boldly exploring India as a means of marking their time together, not simply cozying up in a restaurant close to home. MasterCard rejected Paris as the couple's destination because "that was deemed insufficiently exotic for adventure-minded boomers," noted the *Post.* A print ad with the "Priceless" moment described as "learning Mozart at 48" (on a $7,000 baby grand piano, no less) subtly flattered boomers: not only were they spirited enough to embark on new challenges, but also, they were not too old to be able to do so.

Other demographic groups were important to MasterCard as well. While boomers controlled a substantial portion of the market, consumers in their 20s were in the process of forming lifelong brand allegiances. As *USA Today* noted, younger consumers "tend to stick with the first card they use." "Zipper," which debuted at the same time as "India," specifically targeted "people in their early twenties," a MasterCard spokesperson told *American Banker.* The commercial employed a wry humor in its portrayal of a young man clumsily trying to strike up a conversation with an attractive woman in a coffeehouse. Many "Priceless" ads opted for more universal appeals altogether. In September 1998 MasterCard used the backdrop of the race between baseball sluggers Mark McGwire and Sammy Sosa to break Roger Maris's long-standing home-run record. After cataloging the costs of the home-run extravaganza to scenes of the two players smacking long drives, the spot concluded "Sixty-two: Priceless."

COMPETITION

MasterCard's quest to bolster its brand and to incorporate its various products under one unified campaign was shared by its primary rivals, Visa and American Express. In the cutthroat credit card market, with consumers being constantly bombarded by new card offers, building a brand was the best way to remind consumers to use a specific card. Visa had mastered this strategy. Since 1985

A LITTLE TOO FLATTERING

In 1999 MasterCard International sued Home Box Office (HBO) over a "Priceless" parody the cable channel aired to promote its original series *Arliss.* The show featured a slimy and corrupt sports agent as its title character. The offending commercial portrayed Arliss engaging in various shady transactions and concluded with the tagline: "There are some men money can't buy. Arliss isn't one of them."

the company's "It's Everywhere You Want to Be" ads unstintingly trumpeted that Visa was the most universally accepted card in the world. Although this campaign directly attacked AmEx, it had also succeeded in marginalizing MasterCard. "Everywhere" had implied "that if Visa targets AmEx, then Visa makes MasterCard irrelevant," an industry analyst told *Card News.* "Everywhere" ads in 1998 pursued niche markets such as Generation X consumers, Internet shoppers, and affluent baby boomers.

In addition to "Everywhere," Visa launched its "Works Like a Check" campaign in 1997 to boost usage of its debit card, the CheckCard. These commercials, created by ad agency BBDO (which also handled the "Everywhere" account), featured easily recognizable celebrities, such as Bob Dole and Shirley MacLaine, who were thwarted in their efforts to write a check because they did not have identification handy. "Our long-term strategy is to move from being the world's best credit card to the world's best way to pay," a Visa spokesperson told *Advertising Age.* Visa also had several high-profile sponsorships, which further highlighted its name and brand messages. Especially effective were its affiliations with the National Football League, the Olympic Games, and horse racing's Triple Crown races—the Kentucky Derby, the Belmont Stakes, and the Preakness. But in a testament to the brutally competitive nature of the industry, Visa's share of the market declined slightly in 1997 despite all these efforts.

In 1996 AmEx began a massive branding campaign conceived by ad agency Ogilvy & Mather that sought to bring new customers to the American Express flock. Like "Priceless," AmEx's "Do More" strove to use the overarching campaign to promote all of AmEx's services and cards. Although it had long prided itself on its elite consumer core, AmEx had experienced a dramatic loss of market share in the early 1990s. To reverse this trend the company used "Do More" as a vehicle to attract younger consumers as well as a more diverse base of cardholders. Print ads and television spots in 1998 featured multiracial golf sensation Tiger Woods, comedian Jerry Seinfeld, snowboard pioneer Jake Burton, and basketball legend Earvin "Magic" Johnson. "The message is that American Express has a broad range of financial services for various life stages and lifestyles," said *American Banker.* After years of slippage AmEx's share of the market rose to 17 percent in 1997 from 16.4 percent the year before. In 1998, however, AmEx once more lost ground to Visa and MasterCard.

MARKETING STRATEGY

The hallmark of the "Priceless" campaign was its consistency. Every MasterCard commercial, regardless of the specific product touted or the intended target audience, bore the same tagline and the same format of "shopping list" and "priceless" moment. The reason was clear. In the ultracompetitive market staying "on message" was essential to convincing consumers to pull out MasterCard from their card-stuffed wallets. As one analyst told *Direct,* the key to credit card marketing was "to do something habit forming to build use of the card." MasterCard wanted its products inextricably linked to the "Priceless" theme in consumers' minds. To this end the company crafted "Priceless" ads for an array of offerings. For example, a commercial that debuted in June 1998 touted MasterCard's debit card: after showing a hardware store checkout line moving with glacial speed as a supervisor was called to approve a routine check purchase, the "Priceless" moment was described as "Never having to wait for Al"—the hapless manager—"again." MasterCard's Platinum card was the focus of both the "Ireland" and "India" spots. Even the company's corporate sponsorships were included. As the official sponsor of Major League Baseball MasterCard seamlessly incorporated its baseball-themed spots into "Priceless." In addition to the Sosa/McGwire commercial, MasterCard released a touching vignette about taking children to their first ball game in time for the 1998 World Series. MasterCard's sponsorship of World Cup soccer was the focus of yet another "Priceless" ad that used the patriotic image of the American flag as its "priceless" episode.

To keep its marketing message foremost in consumers' minds the company selected high-profile media venues to carry "Priceless" commercials. "Zipper" and "India" debuted during the 1998 Super Bowl because that game "is the showcase event . . . to reach the largest audience in one shot," a MasterCard executive told *American Banker.* Acquiring this massive viewership was crucial if MasterCard was to succeed in its quest "to become the Coca-Cola of currency," he added. Other "Priceless" commercials were aired during subsequent Super Bowls. On the broadcast of the 2004 game the cartoon character Homer Simpson appeared in a spot, using his

MasterCard to purchase items at a convenience store. The next year a 30-second spot depicted more than 10 advertising icons, such as Count Chocula and the Pillsbury Doughboy, gathering around a dinner table. The spot ended with the voice-over "Getting everyone together for dinner? Priceless." The 2006 Super Bowl featured the actor Richard Dean Anderson, who in the 1980s had starred in the popular TV adventure series *MacGyver,* escaping from a bomb-rigged building by using everyday items that he purchased with his Debit MasterCard.

MasterCard opted to debut its first-ever Internet-oriented ad on another prominent television program—the final episode of the popular show *Seinfeld.* This commercial, which hyped MasterCard's alliance with Excite, was MasterCard's attempt to introduce television viewers to the ease of online shopping. The commercial was a perfect illustration of MasterCard's plan to expand its markets through the "Priceless" campaign. The spot depicted a busy mother who purchased her children's clothes on Excite's shopping channel with her MasterCard. The time she has saved provided her with a "Priceless" moment of being able to relax. E-commerce afforded credit card companies tantalizing opportunities. Unlike typical retail transactions, Internet purchases were almost entirely made with credit cards. Even though only a small fraction of consumers had ever tried buying products online, many analysts foresaw an explosion of online retail business. Debit cards were becoming more common as well and—like Internet commerce—offered MasterCard the chance to win new customers without cannibalizing its base, as debit cards mainly competed against cash and checks as payment options.

The campaign branched out with side storylines carrying the "Priceless" theme. In 2004 the "Dog Trilogy" featured three spots telling the story of a lost puppy who was helped back home by various do-gooders. One of the commercials earned *Adweek*'s Best Spot recognition. The same year MasterCard released its first Ramadan-themed campaign that targeted consumers in the Middle East. One spot featured a traveling Arab businessman who used his MasterCard to spend time with his family.

OUTCOME

The campaign was an undisputed success. After only three months MasterCard noted a rise in consumer awareness about the brand. The company told *American Banker* that its "share of wallet" increased 0.4 percentage points in the first six months of "Priceless." The magazine attributed this to "MasterCard steadying its course." The company reported that its share of the domestic credit card market reached 26.9 percent in 1998, up from 26.4 percent in 1997. From 1997 until 2002 MasterCard's sales increased from $1.08 billion to $1.89 billion. "They've hit a grand slam with this one," an industry analyst told *American Banker.* If imitation was the sincerest form of flattery, the campaign's ability to boost consumers' awareness was also evidenced by the number of spoofs of the campaign that cropped up on programs such as *Saturday Night Live,* the *Late Show with David Letterman,* and *The Simpsons.* Joyce King Thomas, deputy creative director at McCann-Erickson, estimated in 2004 that the campaign had been parodied about 50 times. "It just says that it's part of popular culture when it's used on programming," she said in *Adweek.*

By the start of 2006 the "Priceless" campaign had aired in 105 countries and had been translated into 48 languages. The campaign collected more than 100 awards, including both a 2001 and 2006 Gold EFFIE Award in the Sustained Success category, which recognized campaigns with three or more years of sustained growth. It also won a Bronze Lion at the Cannes Lions International Advertising Festival, *Adweek* magazine's Spot of the Year award, and an Advertising Women of New York "Good" Award. In 2002 there were 590 million MasterCards in circulation. Nonetheless, an effective brand campaign from Visa had helped MasterCard's fiercest competitor remain number one as "Priceless" entered its fifth year. In 2002 Visa posted sales of 4.8 billion, more than double the $1.89 billion recorded by MasterCard.

FURTHER READING

Anderson, Mae. "National Lampoon." *Adweek,* August 9, 2004, p. 18.

Arndorfer, James. "Credit Card Industry Attempts to Build Usage in Tight Market." *Advertising Age,* October 5, 1998.

Bloom, Jennifer Kingston. "Card Brands to Clash in Super Bowl of Advertising." *American Banker,* January 23, 1998.

Boorstein, Jonathon. "Credit Card Crisis." *Direct,* December 1, 1998.

Chester, Rodney. "It's Been Parodied." *Courier-Mail* (Brisbane, Australia), July 1, 2004, p. 3.

Coulton, Antoinette. "MasterCard Ads Push for a New Consistency." *American Banker,* October 28, 1997.

Farey-Jones, Daniel. "MasterCard Takes to the Air and Online for Brits Campaign." *Brand Republic,* January 17, 2005, p. 1.

"Issuers' Advertising Strategies Target Consumer Values." *Card News,* May 25, 1998.

Kim, Hank. "Inside Priceless: MasterCard Moments." *Adweek,* April 12, 1999.

"MasterCard 'Dog Trilogy.'" *Advertising Age's Creativity,* April 1, 2005, p. 22.

Meece, Mickey. "Career Tracks: AmEx Goes Well Beyond Cards with New TV Spots Series." *American Banker,* June 18, 1996.

Span, Paula,"A New Wrinkle for Madison Avenue." *Washington Post,* March 24, 1998.

Rebecca Stanfel
Kevin Teague

Mattel, Inc.

333 Continental Boulevard
El Segundo, California 90245-5012
USA
Telephone: (310) 252-2000
Fax: (310) 252-2180
Web site: www.mattel.com

■■■

PLAY. LAUGH. GROW. CAMPAIGN

OVERVIEW

With the popularity of video games infringing upon the children's-toy industry, the largest toy manufacturers reported that the maximum age of children playing with toys dropped from 12 years old in 1981 to 8 years old by 2001. Even for children under 8, traditional toys were losing ground to electronic learning toys, a category that increased by 60 percent in four years. The rise was attributed to the developing population of Generation X mothers, who valued toys that combined playing with learning. Mattel, Inc., led the toy industry with brands such as Hot Wheels, Barbie, and Fisher-Price, but LeapFrog Enterprises, Inc., was one of the industry's fastest-growing competitors with its smash hit, the LeapPad, an electronic book that attempted to make learning fun. To rebrand itself as a toy maker that also fused playing with learning, Fisher-Price released its "Play. Laugh. Grow." campaign.

Created by ad agency Young & Rubicam Brands, "Play. Laugh. Grow." was estimated to cost $25 million, making it the most expensive campaign in Fisher-Price's history. It started in September 2003 and used print ads and television spots. Ten commercials appeared across network and cable channels to tout the brand's latest products, which included the PowerTouch, an electronic book-holder that taught preschoolers reading as well as subjects such as science, geography, and mathematics. One television spot showed preschoolers giggling and learning to read with PowerTouch. By 2004 the campaign had refocused on the burgeoning demographic of Latina mothers, and commercials began airing in Spanish across television and radio.

Even though the toy industry had been waning for years and Mattel posted a sales decrease in 2004, "Play. Laugh. Grow." helped Fisher-Price's sales increase 7 percent, making it one of Mattel's most successful brands. The campaign also won a Silver EFFIE Award in 2005. John Taylor, a toy analyst at Arcadia Investment, an institutional research group in Portland Oregon, explained in the *Wall Street Journal,* "This is Mattel's first salvo in a market LeapFrog dominates and is likely to dominate for a long time. But Fisher-Price isn't going away, and the final outcome of this battle won't be determined for some time."

HISTORICAL CONTEXT

When Mattel purchased Fisher-Price, a toy manufacturer for preschoolers, in the early 1990s, Mattel already owned such brands as Barbie and Match Box. The acquisition soon paid off for the industry leader. Top-selling Fisher-Price items, such as the brand's trademark lines Activity Table, Little People, Rescue Heroes, and See 'N Say, helped Fisher-Price increase sales by 26 percent in 2001. Fisher-Price formed strategic alliances with companies such as Procter & Gamble, which solicited new products to mothers in prenatal education classes. That same year ad agency Young & Rubicam formulated a campaign titled "Oh, the Possibilities!" which utilized print, including a direct mailer for expectant mothers entitled "The First Year." Fisher-Price began reducing its dependency on colossal retailers like Wal-Mart and Target by selling merchandise online and through direct-mail catalogues. By 2002, even though Fisher-Price was still increasing its sales, LeapFrog had gained significant market share by developing electronic learning toys, such as the LeapPad. From the mid-1990s to 2002 more than nine million LeapPads were sold, an achievement connected to the growing population of Generation X mothers, who preferred toys that combined playing with learning. A generation earlier baby-boomer mothers had treated learning and playing as two separate activities.

In 2003 toy brands were also rethinking their entire marketing strategies. Big sales on one-hit items such as Beanie Babies and Razor Scooters had become less frequent. "We're all transitioning from a phenomena-based, hit-driven business to a brand growth business as our center ground," Brian Goldner, president of the U.S. toys unit of toy company Hasbro, told *Brandweek.* "We're rediscovering the power of brands. The basics still ring true."

Young & Rubicam wanted to create a campaign that proved Fisher-Price was just as viable as LeapPad when it came to designing educational toys. "We want to remind today's mom that Fisher-Price is relevant and it's still important to their child," Chuck Scothon, senior vice president of marketing at Fisher-Price, told the *Wall Street Journal.*

SCIENCE OF PLAY

Fisher-Price, the maker of toys for preschool-aged children, was one of the few toy makers in the United States with laboratories to study what toys children liked. "The company has long realized and championed the importance of play in a child's development," the brand's United Kingdom marketing manager, Ruth Clement, told *New Media Age,* a magazine that covered the business of interactive media. "In the laboratories, children are observed by our researchers so we can get a better idea of the stages a child goes through and what toys can aid them in that."

TARGET MARKET

"Play. Laugh. Grow." initially targeted mothers who were part of Generation X, a classification of Americans and Canadians born between 1965 and 1976. By 2003 mothers in this age range were purchasing 65 percent more toys than baby-boomer (born in the 1940s through early 1960s) mothers. When it came to toy selection Generation X mothers preferred electronic learning toys that combined the process of learning with playing. Baby-boomer mothers tended to separate their learning toy purchases from play toys. Fathers from Generation X were also more involved with toy purchasing than baby-boomer fathers. To specifically target Generation X mothers, however, Fisher-Price created commercials that showed preschool children having fun while learning with Fisher-Price products.

In 2004 the campaign refocused on another target market. Influenced by research conducted by the U.S. Census Bureau, which stated one out of every five U.S.-born child was Hispanic, "Play. Laugh. Grow." began targeting the Latino communities of Los Angeles, Houston, and Chicago. It was predicted that by 2010 the number of Hispanic children under nine years old would increase by 22 percent, while the same age of non-Hispanic children would decrease by 1 percent. Fisher-Price contracted Market Vision, an Hispanic advertising agency, to create Spanish television and radio spots for the campaign. Bonnie Garcia, president of Market Vision, told the *PR Newswire,* "The Latina mom is young. Her child is at the center of her universe and she's very much involved in her family and in her community. As a brand of toys and juvenile products, Fisher-Price is uniquely positioned to offer her everything she needs to give her family the best possible start in life."

COMPETITION

Founded in 1995, LeapFrog developed electronic learning toys that used interactive games to teach children subjects such as phonics, reading, math, writing, music, geography, and spelling. Generation X mothers, looking for toys that made learning fun, quickly became fans of the brand's LeapPad, an electronic toy into which a book was placed; it taught preschoolers different subjects depending on what cartridge was inserted. LeapPad's popularity catapulted the brand's earnings. Net sales rose from $160.1 million in 2000 to $313.7 million in 2001. LeapFrog's success prompted Fisher-Price to strategize its own advertisement for the electronic-learning toys category. "People get the impression that Fisher-Price will

POPULAR BRANDS

Wunderman, a unit of advertising agency Young & Rubicam Brands, conducted a survey in 2002 to discover what brands were most popular with women. Fisher-Price was selected as one of the most popular, along with Starbucks, Tylenol, Google, and Discover. Among the least popular were Hertz, adidas, RadioShack, Avis, and PlayStation.

buy their way into the category," Mike Wood, LeapFrog's founder and chief executive, told the *Wall Street Journal.* "But we've got nine million parents telling other parents about how their children learned to read on the LeapPad."

As LeapFrog's popularity grew, so did its product line. The company continued developing products for newborn children all the way up to children 16 years of age. In 2003 the ad agency Ackerman McQueen, Inc. released a wildly successful campaign titled "Learn Something New Every Day!" The campaign earned a Grand EFFIE Award in 2004 and cost LeapFrog more than $20 million. While other brands ran ads on Nickelodeon networks and during Saturday-morning cartoon shows, commercials for "Learn Something New Every Day!" targeted 25- to 49-year-old-mothers by appearing during such shows as *Oprah* and *The View* and on the Oxygen Network. Television spots showed parents, grandparents, and neighbors eager to give LeapFrog products as gifts to children.

MARKETING STRATEGY

In September 2003 the $25 million "Play. Laugh. Grow." campaign appeared in print and on television. The TV spots aired across network and cable stations. It was the largest campaign in Fisher-Price's history and positioned the brand to attract 20- to 30-year-old mothers. Ten initial television spots were created by Young & Rubicam, each depicting preschoolers playing and learning with Fisher-Price products. One commercial featured children playing with Fisher-Price's Little People, plastic figurines that taught children about farming, transportation, and even historical subjects such as the Middle Ages.

Another 30-second spot featured Fisher-Price's new PowerTouch toy, a product similar to the LeapPad. When a PowerTouch book with embedded software, such as *Dora's Alphabet Adventure Game,* was placed into the PowerTouch cradle, the cradle would talk children through the book's storyline. Children could then interact with the book by pressing down on certain words, objects, or colors. The spot promoting the PowerTouch began with the copy: "Learning to read is easier..." with an off-screen woman also reading the words. Next, a preschool-aged girl exclaimed to a preschool-aged boy, "Look, my finger is magic!" She then placed her finger upon the word "cat," and PowerTouch pronounced the word through its small speaker. After the girl effortlessly taught the boy how to use PowerTouch, the spot ended with the Fisher-Price logo above the word "Learning." The words "Play. Laugh. Grow." appeared on the lower half of the white screen.

After the U.S. Census Bureau released information showing the Hispanic population to be the fastest-growing ethnic group in America, Fisher-Price altered its marketing strategy. On October 15, 2004, television and radio spots created by Market Vision and Young & Rubicam began appearing across Spanish channels. The Hispanic portion of the campaign was initially launched in Los Angeles, Chicago, and Houston. Outdoor ads appeared with the following tagline in Spanish: "Play with Them. Laugh with Them. Grow with Them."

At the beginning of the campaign Fisher-Price attempted to convince Generation X mothers that Fisher-Price could integrate playing and learning. Once the campaign shifted toward Latina mothers, Fisher-Price also had to overcome two common beliefs held by their new target market. One was that Fisher-Price was too expensive; the other was that Fisher-Price toys were for elementary school–aged children. "Our recommendation to Fisher-Price was to focus on these three top markets and make a deep connection with Hispanic families. Through traditional and non-traditional marketing vehicles, we can reach the Latina mom in her home, her neighborhood and even in her pediatrician's office," Bonnie Garcia stated in the *PR Newswire.* To increase brand loyalty with Latina mothers, Fisher-Price released heartfelt ads that emphasized the mother-child bond.

By 2005 "Play. Laugh. Grow." had been extended to Hispanic festivals across the United States, where children could sample Fisher-Price toys inside two 60-by-60-feet "play pens." Actors dressed as life-sized Fisher-Price toys interacted with children at the festivals as well. The 2005 portion of the campaign coincided with the brand's 75th-anniversary celebration.

OUTCOME

Even while Mattel's other brands reported losses in 2004—Barbie, for instance, was down 13 percent—Fisher-Price reported a 7 percent increase in sales. Much of the toy industry was suffering from a phenomenon that analysts called "age-compression," in which children stopped playing with toys at a younger age.

Brandweek reported that in 1981 the average age at which kids stopped playing with toys was 12 but that by 2003 the age had dropped to 8. Despite the change, the new age ceiling of 8 was still above Fisher-Price's preschool age. Mattel brands such as Pictionary, Tyco Electric Racing, and Barbie were more affected by age-compression, which explained why Fisher-Price performed better. Matt Bousquette, president of Mattel's boys division, told *Brandweek* that to overcome age-compression, "You've got to reinvent 80 percent of your base volume on an annual basis. You've got to continue to reinvent and keep the brand fresh every year."

In 2005 the campaign garnered a Silver EFFIE Award (Children's Products category) from the New York American Marketing Association. Overall the campaign helped Fisher-Price transition its brand from baby-boomer mothers to the developing Generation X market, and eventually, the even faster growing market of Latina mothers. "Play. Laugh. Grow." also branded Fisher-Price as a toy maker that melded playing with learning.

FURTHER READING

Bain, Helen. "Brand Gestures." *Dominion* (Wellington, New Zealand), April 26, 2001, p. 17.

Bellantonio, Jennifer. "Big Y&R Gets Bigger with Mattel Boys' Account Win." *Irvine (CA) Orange County Business Journal,* August 26, 2002, p. 45.

———. "Crossover Eyeing Second, Third Generation Hispanics." *Orange County Business Journal,* June 17, 2002, p. 12.

Coleman-Lochner, Lauren. "Despite Discounters, Game Isn't Over for Toymakers." *New York Times,* December 30, 2003, p. 13.

———. "Hunting for Value inside the Toy Box." *New York Times,* December 28, 2003, p. 7.

Finnigan, David. "A Knock-Down Drag-Out Fight." *Brandweek,* February 12, 2001, p. 21.

Flass, Rebecca. "Y&R Wins Big in Mattel's 3-Way Toy Review." *Adweek* (Southwest ed.), August 19, 2002, p. 5.

Goetzl, David, "Media Edge Media Agency of Year." *Advertising Age,* February 28, 2000, p. S2.

Hays, Constance. "Toy Retailers Find Prices at Wal-Mart Tough to Beat," *New York Times,* December 23, 2003, p. 1.

Kim, Queena Sook. "Advertising: Fisher-Price Courts Gen-X Mothers." *Wall Street Journal,* September 19, 2003, p. B3.

Lomartire, Paul. "Toronto Firm's Toys Are Hot." *Milwaukee (WI) Journal Sentinel,* December 28, 2003, p. 10B.

Pearlman, Jonathan, and Gerard Ryle. "Revealed: Deadly Bath Cradles in Thousands of Homes." *Sydney Morning Herald,* May 24, 2004, p. 1.

Sampey, Kathleen. "FCB Taps Y&R Exec: Corrigan to Steer J.P. Morgan Chase Account." *Adweek* (eastern ed.), May 27, 2002, p. 4.

Seckler, Valerie. "Study Reveals Women's Top 10 Favorite Brands." *Women's Wear Daily,* November 11, 2002, p.15.

Kevin Teague

McDonald's Corporation

McDonald's Plaza
Oak Brook, Illinois 60523
USA
Telephone: (630) 623-3000
Fax: (630) 623-5004
Web site: www.mcdonalds.com

■■■

CAMPAIGN 55 CAMPAIGN

OVERVIEW

In 1996, McDonald's, the world's biggest fast food restaurant chain, found itself in a proverbial pickle. A tight labor market, additional costs resulting from minimum wage increases, and price pressures on raw materials sent the burger giant's operational costs spiraling upward, which in turn helped to depress profits. All this came at a time when McDonald's major rivals, Wendy's International and Burger King Corporation, were using innovative marketing strategies to eat into the Golden Arches' share of the pie.

McDonald's first attempt to arrest these trends was the May 1996 introduction of the Arch Deluxe, a "premium" sandwich targeted at adult consumers. The strategy seemed valid at a time when inflationary forces were ascendant in the economy. In order to sustain profits, McDonald's needed to develop a product consumers would be willing to spend more money on. The only problem was that the Arch Deluxe proved to be unpopular with consumers. Furthermore, the ad campaign designed to promote the new entree featured grimacing children clearly turned off by the new "grown-up" burger. McDonald's had consequently alienated one of its core markets—little kids—in pursuit of invigorated sales to adult customers. As Arch Deluxes piled up on warming racks waiting for consumers who were not buying them, the burger giant scrambled to rethink its approach.

The result was an ambitious price-cutting promotion that seemed to fly in the face of the economic winds that had spawned the Arch Deluxe. The new campaign was heralded by months of anxious anticipation. In a statement to the press at the end of 1996, McDonald's announced that it was "on the threshold of an unprecedented value offering that will be good news for our customers, our franchisees, and our business . . . and bad news for the competition."

Consumers across the country got a taste of the new direction almost immediately. As of April 11, 1997, price promotions began to figure more prominently in McDonald's national advertising. Before then, these efforts were usually focused on the local or regional level. After two weeks of "national price point advertising," the new national campaign began on April 25, 1997. Dubbed "Campaign 55" for the year McDonald's was founded, the promotion lowered the price on a rotating slate of sandwiches with the purchase of french fries and a soft drink. A similar deal was launched on a rotating basis through the chain's breakfast menus. The value pricing plan was accompanied by a new advertising campaign, "My McDonald's," created by the Leo Burnett Agency, McDonald's longtime ad partner. As the overall architect of the campaign, Burnett received the bulk of the ad work, although McDonald's other roster shops, DDB Needham Worldwide and Burrell Communications, also received some assignments.

The stakes were enormous. McDonald's was luring its customers into restaurants with a 55-cent promise and risking their anger when they were hit with a $1.79 actual price tag after the mandatory purchase of fries and a drink. If consumers refused to accept the deal, they could view McDonald's as having reneged on a promise. More importantly, the chain's pursuit of sales volume came at the expense of franchisee profitability—a strategy that threatened to erode the sometimes tenuous bonds of trust between the parent company and its retail partners. "Campaign 55" would prove to be a marketing debacle for McDonald's and its partners at Leo Burnett. When the dust settled, the landscape of two of America's signature industries—fast food and advertising—had been dramatically changed.

HISTORICAL CONTEXT

In 1982 McDonald's, citing the need for a bigger agency, jettisoned Needham in favor of its crosstown Chicago rival, Leo Burnett. One of Burnett's first campaigns introduced consumers to the children of "Camp Nippersink," solidifying the burger giant's hold on the kids' market. By 1988, however, the Golden Arches began a long-term effort to win the hearts and minds of the adult dinner crowd. One of the first campaigns in this initiative, "Mac Tonight," parodied a familiar Brecht-Weillsong—to little apparent effect. The Arch Deluxe failure was thus only the last in a series of unsuccessful attempts to secure the adult market. That misstep, compounded by eight straight quarters of declining sales, prompted McDonald's executives to rethink its marketing approach. The end result was "Campaign 55."

In a December 1996 memo, McDonald's Chairman Jack Greenberg outlined the burger maker's overall market strategy. He wrote of the company's intention to "reenergize and focus . . . U.S. marketing efforts and develop a national value proposition." It was a significant departure for a company that had always offered its price promotions on the local and regional level. In late February 1997, several senior Burnett executives met at McDonald's Oak Brook, Illinois, headquarters to map out an advertising strategy for "Campaign 55." At the same time, McDonald's franchisees were being briefed on the new pricing strategy via closed-circuit television. Shortly thereafter, franchisees were given a chance to approve the national discount plan. At least 75 percent of the burger maker's 2,700 owner-operators needed to give a thumbs-up in order for the plan to go forward. They did so, but not without trepidation. Many owner-operators viewed the pricing plan as a drastic, even desperate move and an overreaction to the sales slump. Some expressed skepticism about whether the "home office" had done the research to make certain this was what consumers wanted. Many of these reservations would prove to be prescient in the weeks and months to come.

On April 4, 1997, McDonald's restaurants across the United States began offering 55-cent Egg McMuffin breakfast sandwiches with the purchase of hash browns and a drink. Three weeks later, on April 25, the promotion was expanded to Big Macs as well. Quarter Pounders were next up in the rotation, with their price reduction commencing in mid-June. McDonald's dedicated $66 million worth of national advertising to the value-pricing plan, much to the dismay of some regional shops, which had benefited enormously when McDonald's diverted $150 million from national to regional advertising in 1996.

TARGET MARKET

As a national campaign with an enormous advertising budget, "Campaign 55" was theoretically aimed at all fast food consumers across the United States. But in a fast food market dominated by large chains, the real target was those consumers who had strayed to other burger purveyors on the issue of value pricing. In the late 1990s, fast food was one of the most developed sectors in the restaurant industry, with the fast food hamburger category being perhaps the most competitive; there seemed to be McDonald's, Wendy's, and Burger King outlets on most every corner. And consumers were using increasingly sophisticated criteria to decide where and how to spend their money. In this environment the goal for these companies was market share gain.

McDonald's aim with "Campaign 55" was to convince customers to visit its restaurants instead of its competitors. Very often a promotion like a price-cutting program can play a big part in convincing the customer. Wendy's, with its 99-cent Super Value Menu, and Burger King, with its 99-cent Whopper and $2.99 Whopper Meal Combo, had stolen away some of McDonald's pricing edge, and had scored notable market share gains. McDonald's hoped that customers who had been wooed away by the promise of value would respond favorably to "Campaign 55."

COMPETITION

For quite some time, McDonald's had understood the root of its troubles: smaller chains were using seemingly tastier, more diverse menus and shrewd marketing to eat into their market share. Burger King in particular relied on product-focused ads to score sales increases of 2.6 percent per store for the year ending September 30, 1996.

While McDonald's overall sales remained strong, the company felt it had to do something to stem the market

LATE-NIGHT PUBLICITY

An old adage says that there is no such thing as bad publicity. But some say that an even older adage dictates: stay out of the monologues of late-night talk-show hosts. The latter could be a sure sign that one has turned into a national joke. And yet that is just what happened to venerable national icon McDonald's in the wake of its much maligned "Campaign 55" promotion. *Late Show* gabber David Letterman was the emcee for a round of good-natured knife twisting that took the form of a Top Ten List citing "Other Failed McDonald's Promotions." Among the "promotions" on Letterman's list were: "Happy Meals include small containers of nitrous oxide"; "Get 500 Quarter Pounders for the price of 499"; and "Buy any sandwich and have clown makeup permanently tattooed on your face." "The 55-cent McCoronary" topped the list.

share erosion. It responded initially by opening more restaurants. The thinking was that even if store volume did not increase, sales would go up because of the increased number of stores. In addition McDonald's could collect more rent and franchise fees. But franchisees soon called for a halt in expansion. They found their own profits plummeting as new outlets opened up close by, cannibalizing their sales. A program to introduce new sandwich items, such as the Arch Deluxe, also failed. McDonald's seemingly was left with no alternative but to slash prices.

As word leaked out about the nature of the promotion, industry observers began to fear a burger price war. The prospect of falling profit margins helped to depress stock prices for McDonald's and its major competitors, Wendy's International and Grand Metropolitan, the parent company of Burger King Corporation. Both companies rushed to announce that they had no plans to match McDonald's price cuts. "We've attached ourselves to a strategy that states it's not a great value if it's not a great tasting burger," said Andy Bonaparte, Burger King's director of advertising.

While the Golden Arches was using its partnership with the Walt Disney Corporation to tie into that company's 1997 summer movie releases, Burger King returned fire with adult-targeted tie-ins to the blockbuster film *Jurassic Park: The Lost World* starting on Memorial Day weekend. Ads for that onslaught were created by Ammirati Puris Lintas of New York. In a special promotion aimed at children, BK Kids Meals were offered with giveaway toys from director Steven Spielberg's *The Land Before Time* video series.

MARKETING STRATEGY

McDonald's marketing officials expected the value price promotion to spur consumer traffic and nudge patrons into paying full price for the chain's higher-margin french fries and soft drinks. Accordingly, the chain advised its franchisees to increase on-hand packaging and food supplies by 10 to 15 percent in anticipation of a corresponding hike in sales.

While the focus of the campaign was national, the media plan called for a window of local spot promotions in April 1997. McDonald's envisioned "Campaign 55" as an integral part of a summer marketing blitz tied to the June release of the Walt Disney Company's animated feature *Hercules* and the comedy-adventure film *George of the Jungle* in July. "Campaign 55 is not a short-term promotion," declared McDonald's spokeswoman Anna Rozenich. "It's designed to increase restaurant profit and cash flow over a long period of time." Indeed, the burger giant planned its marketing calendar around "Campaign 55" well into 1998, the idea being that every month or so a different sandwich would be featured at the discounted price. Initially, the price reduction was to be accompanied by a promise to offer the customer free food if an order was not served within 55 seconds. After complaints from owner-operators about the feasibility of this and all aspects of the marketing plan, however, this feature was abandoned.

Coincident with the April 4 price reduction promotion was the debut of the "My McDonald's" national television campaign created by Leo Burnett. The commercials showed McDonald's owner-operators and restaurant workers expressing the company's core values. Its only seeming relation to the price promotion was the emphasis on the year 1955—the year McDonald's was founded and when the "core values" presumably were formulated. "This is not in the least a price promotion," remarked McDonald's senior vice president of marketing Brad Ball.

The new strategy carried with it a number of inherent risks. First, it seemed to run counter to the economic trends of the day. With operational costs rising, a drastic cut in prices put McDonald's two strikes down in the effort to spur profit margin increases. This was difficult, especially for franchisees, who had already seen their margins erode due to the company's aggressive expansion program. Another risk McDonald's had taken was embarking on a dual campaign. In doing so, they faced one of marketing's toughest challenges: boosting sales while building a brand identity at the same time. There seemed to be little doubt that McDonald's needed to do both. Superior brand advertising by Burger King and Wendy's was having the effect of luring away once-loyal McDonald's customers; the accompanying drop in sales meant McDonald's had to sell more food. But the quest for a quick sales spike is not always consistent with the long-term goal of building a brand identity.

OUTCOME

Reaction to "Campaign 55" was sharply negative from its inception. Many observers were taken aback by the degree of discounts offered. Others saw the abrupt shift in strategy as a sign that McDonald's was confused about its marketing direction. "For the past year, McDonald's has bounced around in terms of its marketing strategy," said Stacy Jamar, a restaurant analyst with Smith Barney, "from last year taking the high road with deluxe sandwiches to this year's pseudo price discount." "I don't think it's a viable long-term solution to the problem they have in the U.S., which is a product problem," declared Damon Brundage of NatWest Securities. Indeed, many analysts saw "Campaign 55" as little more than a quick-fix—a pricing gimmick designed to stop the decline in sales while the company scrambled to devise and implement a real solution to its long-term problems.

For a while, the burger giant ignored these brickbats. The program had achieved some success at the breakfast level, because it spurred sales of combo meals, raising the average customer's bill. And in mid-May, McDonald's announced that unit sales of its Big Mac sandwich had more than doubled since the price reduction. The company enjoyed its strongest comparable April store sales in years. But part of that boost could be attributed to a popular "Teeny Beanie Baby" toy giveaway promotion that same month.

While official figures showed a spike in sales, there was anecdotal evidence to suggest that restaurants were not, in fact, selling more Big Macs than when the promotion began. And any increase in traffic was offset by customer confusion about where the deal actually was. "It's a price promotion that doesn't tell you the price," scoffed Ron Paul, an industry analyst and president of Technomics. His concerns were echoed by McDonald's owner-operators. "I think it's because the offer is confusing," said Dick Adams, the chairman of an independent association of about 100 McDonald's franchisees. "Customers come in expecting to buy a 55-cent Big Mac and they have to buy a conventional meal package." Many customers complained that they did not realize they had to buy fries and a drink to get the 55-cent price deal on their sandwich. Some customers quickly learned to supplement their entree with just a small drink and small fries. Under this arrangement franchisees found they actually lost money.

The ad campaign also proved to be ill-fated. There was considerable confusion over how the pricing plan tied in to the brand-building "My McDonald's" ad theme. As many analysts had predicted, the objectives of the dual ad campaign were not always complementary. While "My McDonald's" tried to build up an image for the brand, "Campaign 55" seemed to drag that image down by concentrating on dollars and cents details.

Finally, in mid-June, following an avalanche of bad press and a near revolt among franchisees, McDonald's discontinued the lunch and dinner components of "Campaign 55." The burger giant moved rapidly to devise a local price initiative to replace the national discount program. That move came as McDonald's prepared to implement a decentralization plan that divided the United States into regions in order to allow regional executives more power to make marketing decisions. And in August 1997, the other shoe finally dropped on "Campaign 55." Following a lengthy review process, McDonald's dropped Leo Burnett as its lead national ad agency and awarded the bulk of the estimated $350 million account to DDB Needham. This closed the book on what analysts considered one of the biggest misfires in marketing history.

FURTHER READING

Benezra, Karen. "McDonald's Looks for Rebound after Campaign 55 Flop." *Adweek,* June 9, 1997.

Edwards, Cliff. "McDonald's Franchisees Are Formidable Adversaries." *Star Tribune,* June 5, 1997.

"McDonald's Corp. Says Unit Sales of Big Macs Are Soaring Since It Cut Price of Sandwich." *Star Tribune,* May 12, 1997.

Whalen, Jeanne. "Beleaguered McDonald's Looks to Local Price Effort." *Advertising Age,* June 9, 1997.

———. "McDonald's 55 Cent Price Ads to Snare Most of Budget." *Advertising Age,* April 7, 1997.

Robert Schnakenberg

DID SOMEBODY SAY MCDONALD'S? CAMPAIGN

OVERVIEW

The world's largest fast-food chain by a sizable margin, McDonald's had experienced many years of unbridled growth, but it had faltered in the mid-1990s. Many blamed errors of judgment in marketing, including the introduction of an unpopular burger called the Arch

Deluxe in 1997 as well as a confusing discount offer on the chain's signature Big Mac hamburger in 1998. McDonald's, it seemed, had lost sight of the strengths that had made it the industry leader, most notably a keen sense of image that had been burned into customers' minds in the 1970s with classic advertising campaigns such as "You Deserve a Break Today."

As part of its efforts to rejuvenate its image, the company in late 1997 introduced the "Did Somebody Say McDonalds?" campaign with television spots aired throughout the United States. This marked the return of DDB Needham, the advertising agency that had worked with McDonald's from 1971 to 1981 during some of the company's best advertising years. DDB creative director Bob Merlotti created the tagline for the campaign, which ran throughout 1998 and into 1999. Specific spending on "Did Somebody Say McDonald's?" was not disclosed, but McDonald's reportedly spent $604 million on advertising from June 1996 to June 1997. This represented a 12 percent increase over the previous 12-month period.

With "Did Somebody Say McDonald's?" the company sought to return to the ground it had lost—both in the market and in the hearts of its once-loyal customers. But despite the optimistic outlook for the campaign, it failed to drive business and increase sales. In 1999 the company built on the campaign when, at a cost of $100 million, it introduced a local brand-building effort featuring singer Donna Summer. The following year a new campaign, "We Love to See You Smile," was released, replacing the "Did Somebody Say McDonald's?" campaign.

HISTORICAL CONTEXT

In 1948 brothers Dick and Mac McDonald opened the first McDonald's restaurant in San Bernardino, California. Several years later Chicago entrepreneur Ray Kroc happened to stop at the restaurant while on a business trip to Chicago and was instantly taken with the idea. Kroc inked a franchise agreement with the McDonald brothers in 1954 and the following year opened a McDonald's of his own in Des Plaines, Illinois. Fascinated by the idea of mass-producing and selling hamburgers, Kroc improved handsomely on the McDonald brothers' marketing ideas and by 1957 owned a string of McDonald's in the Midwest and California. Four years later he paid the McDonald brothers $2.7 million for their share.

Already by 1962 the chain had sold one billion burgers, and it charted its sales progress with a sign proudly displayed beneath the distinctive "Golden Arches" logo that set its facilities apart from all other fast-food chains. Of course, McDonald's had much more that set it apart: from the beginning Kroc had been taken with the simplicity of the McDonald brothers' stores, most notably the fact that these lacked the clutter typical of most roadside hamburger stands. As he began franchising units—which he did at a rate of more than 500 a year during the 1970s—Kroc issued stringent guidelines regarding virtually every aspect of restaurant operations.

McDonald's signature clown, Ronald McDonald, made his first appearance in 1963, and future years would find him with an array of friends, such as Mayor McCheese. Also in 1963 McDonald's offered its first menu extension, the Filet-O-Fish. Ronald and the expanded menu—which later included breakfast, chicken items, and salads—would become such fixtures of McDonald's that it was hard to imagine a time when they did not exist. Similarly, by the 1990s it was difficult to picture a McDonald's without a drive-through window, but these only made their appearance in 1975.

With the death of Kroc in 1984, McDonald's entered a new era. It expanded rapidly overseas as its U.S. operations began to run up against the inevitable: McDonald's had been so successful in the United States that it seemed likely, or at least possible, that the market would become saturated. Indeed, McDonald's executives would boast that the average customer had to drive no more than four miles to get to the nearest McDonald's. With more than 12,460 restaurants in America by the 1990s, there was one McDonald's for approximately every 290 square miles of U.S. territory; given the fact that the American landmass included vast uninhabited areas in Alaska and the West, this was an impressive figure indeed.

TARGET MARKET

Still, McDonald's sought to work its way into new U.S. markets. Thus in 1993 it began placing restaurants inside the ultra-popular Wal-Mart stores, following a trend toward fast-food restaurants in large retail facilities. By the mid-1990s, however, it seemed that McDonald's had lost sight of its market, as two costly marketing failures seemed to suggest. In 1996 there was the Arch Deluxe, promoted as a burger for adults—as opposed to most McDonald's fare, which, like Ronald McDonald himself, was targeted to children.

The problem with the Arch Deluxe was its relatively high price tag of $2.29, making it the most expensive single item on the McDonald's menu. Marketing for the Arch Deluxe, including billboards featuring children complaining about the "grown-up" burger, did little to spur sales. McDonald's followed this in 1997 with "Campaign 55," a discount promotion offering the signature Big Mac burger for a mere 55 cents. Instead of drawing in more customers, according to Harry Berkowitz of *Newsday,* this promotion merely "confused and annoyed" them.

ALGUIEN DIGO MCDONALD'S?

In March 1998 McDonald's unveiled six new Spanish-language spots designed to appeal to Hispanic customers. All featured the company's tagline, "Did somebody say McDonald's?," only in these commercials, created by del Rivero Messianu of Coral Gables, Florida, it was "Alguien digo McDonald's?" Three of the spots were tied to a recent Monopoly game promotion, and others promoted Happy Meals, French fries, and breakfast items. In "Point of View," which, according to Katy Eckmann and Scott Hume of *Adweek,* was the company's first image ad for Happy Meals, a man harangued his wife with a tale of a tough day on the job. All the while his young son listened thoughtfully, and then he offered his father a McDonald's Happy Meal.

"Some marketing experts," Berkowitz wrote in September 1997, "say McDonald's is wrong to focus on whether its burgers are better than the competitions, rather than on its warm, all-American family image." Said industry analyst John Grace, "They lost sight of what the brand stood for. They need to recapture the essence of the McDonald's brand, which is not in the products but in the consumer's mind." Louise Kramer of *Advertising Age* wrote in May 1999 that many consumers and others rooting for McDonald's in the burger wars wished for a return to the values expressed in the brand's classic "You Deserve a Break Today" campaign created by 1971 by Needham, Harper & Steers, an earlier incarnation of DDB Needham.

As McDonald's faltered during the 1990s, however, it was easy to put too much focus on what the company lacked and not enough emphasis on what it possessed. This was the position of *Newsweek International,* which in November 1997 listed a number of assets. Among these was "Happy hunting abroad." In contrast to the threatened saturation of the U.S. market, "each day, less than 1 percent of the people on the planet eat McDonald's. That's a lot of mouths yet to feed." There was also "A bodacious brand name. Last year McDonald's trumped Coke as the best known worldwide." And then there was perhaps the most important asset of all: "A lock on the hearts and tummies of American kids—and exclusive rights to Disney promotions through 2006. By then, the population of school-age kids could hit record highs—with record allowances."

COMPETITION

McDonald's was unquestionably the leader of the U.S. burger-chain market and of the fast-food market as a whole. In 1996 it had sales of $16.4 billion, dwarfing the $7.3 billion of Burger King. In fact, McDonald's sales exceeded the combined receipts of Burger King, third-place Pizza Hut, and fourth-place Taco Bell. Fifth in the fast-food market, and third among burger chains, was Wendy's, with $4.4 billion in sales. Next came KFC, followed by seventh-place Hardee's, a burger chain with $3.1 billion in sales in 1996. Below Hardee's were three non-burger chains: Subway, Domino's, and Arby's. In the burger market McDonald's in 1996 held a whopping 42 percent share, compared to Burger King's 19 percent and Wendy's 11 percent. Hardee's held a little more than 7.5 percent, and California-based Jack in the Box an additional 3 percent. All other burger chains rounded out the segment, with a 17 percent share.

Yet by the time it released "Did Somebody Say McDonald's?," the company faced extraordinarily stiff competition from Burger King. Berkowitz wrote, "Customers are gobbling up so many Big Kings—the chain's new, beefed-up version of its archrival's Big Mac—that [New York franchise owner Joe Della Monica] had to take down store signs promoting it at a sale price of 99 cents to avoid running out." This was welcome news to Della Monica, who said that four years earlier, in 1993, "We were in survival mode." At that time Burger King, owned by Britain's Grand Metropolitan PLC, was suffering under an advertising campaign "featur[ing] MTV grunge star Dan Cortese and the loud slogan 'I Love This Place,'" Berkowitz noted. In 1997, by contrast, it ran appealing commercials built around classic songs such as the Troggs' 1960s hit "Wild Thing."

Meanwhile, McDonald's floundered. In an effort to counter the Big King, it test-marketed the Mega Mac, an imitation of Burger King's Whopper that went nowhere. But the Whopper was flame-broiled, while the Big Mac was fried—another negative in the eyes of many consumers eager to minimize fast-food fat. Worse, McDonald's could not compete adequately with either Burger King or Wendy's in the area of special orders. The setup in McDonald's stores was simply too rigid to make special requests anything but a time-intensive exception to the rule; Burger King, by contrast, had proudly announced its ability to handle special orders with the "Have It Your Way" advertising campaign of the 1970s, which had imprinted on the consciousness of millions of customers. McDonald's in 1998 and 1999 experimented with new systems to aid in preparing special orders and to allow it to serve fresher product, as Burger King and Wendy's did, rather than allowing burgers to age under a warming lamp until someone bought them.

MARKETING STRATEGY

The "Did Somebody Say McDonald's?" spots first aired in October 1997. One showed a young man and young woman on a date in a movie theater; when the man turned to the woman and asked if she wanted to go to McDonald's after the movie, an actor on the movie screen asked, "Did somebody say McDonald's?" This caused a general stampede out of the theater, as moviegoers abandoned the feature in favor of the nearest Big Mac. Another spot showed an office worker who innocently announced to his colleagues that he was stopping by a McDonald's and would pick up a burger for anyone who needed one; before he could get out the door, he was besieged with requests.

Of the spots, which would continue airing throughout 1998, an industry analyst told Heather Pauly of the *Chicago Sun-Times,* "McDonald's has been playing by the other guy's rules by getting overly involved in price rather than reminding people of the emotional part of the product. I think this campaign does that." Likewise Courtney Kane, reporting for the *New York Times,* noted that "The goal of the campaign . . . is to bring back warm, fuzzy feelings about the purveyor of Quarter Pounders and Chicken McNuggets."

Meanwhile, McDonald's management and staff at its research kitchens worked on a reconfiguration of the production process so as to provide customers with fresh—and custom-made—burgers. They also experimented with a product called the Big Xtra, or MBX, as it was called at corporate headquarters. If successful, the Big Xtra would simultaneously replace the failed Arch Deluxe and take on Burger King's Whopper. McDonald's CEO Michael Quinlan also expressed an interest in revamping one of the company's most recognizable symbols, Ronald McDonald. "I think we can punch him up a little," Quinlan told Ralph Raffio in *Restaurant Business.* Raffio noted that the head of McDonald's marketing had indicated that Ronald might be due for a "tweaking." In the future, he suggested, McDonald's famous clown might even age a bit.

OUTCOME

In March 1999 McDonald's announced that it would invest a staggering $100 million in new local brand-building advertisements featuring singer Donna Summer. The latter would sing a version of her 1983 hit "She Works Hard for the Money," only instead of "She works hard for the money / so you better treat her right," the McDonald's jingle would say, "You get more for the money / 'cause McDonald's treats you right." It was the first time Summer—best known as the sexy queen of 1970s disco—had ever rerecorded a song for a commercial. In fact, she recorded it several times, in eight different styles, including swing, big-band, and country versions.

Arnold Communications, which handled local advertising for McDonald's, created the Summer commercials, but the idea of using the song was the brainchild of Maryland franchisee Cathy Bell. When she suggested it before a cooperative of local McDonald's franchisees, response was enthusiastic. Summer proved agreeable to the idea, and Bell told June Arney of the *Baltimore Sun,* "When I was told [Donna Summer] had agreed to a contract, I said, 'Wow, is this really happening?' Even if you didn't grow up when that song was around, you can relate to it. It's hip. It brings a jazzy overtone to the lyrics." At the end of the commercial Summer whispered, "Did somebody say McDonald's?"

From the introduction of the tagline in 1997, responses to the campaign had been mixed. Yet "Did Somebody Say McDonald's?" harkened back to the classic McDonald's image campaigns of the 1970s as few campaigns since then had managed to do. The company hoped that, given time—and some restructuring both in corporate operations and kitchen management—the tagline would capture popular sensibilities. But in 2000, as McDonald's dismal sales trend continued—a report in *Crain's Chicago Business* noted that sales averages were up 1.5 percent as a result of increased prices but that actual transaction counts were down about 6 percent—the "Did Somebody Say McDonald's?" campaign was discontinued. Replacing it was "We Love to See You Smile.," a $500 million effort created by DDB Needham.

FURTHER READING

Arney, June. "New McDonald's Ad Owes Idea to Howard Woman; TV-Radio Campaign Starts Today Here and in 9 Other Areas." *Baltimore Sun,* February 26, 1999, p. 1-C.

Berkowitz, Harry. "Battle of Burgers: McDonald's, Burger King Battle for Fast-Food Throne." *Newsday,* September 21, 1997, p. F-10.

"DDB Needham Worldwide: Did Somebody Say DDB Needham?." *Advertising Age,* March 30, 1998, p. S-16.

"Did Somebody Say McDoomed?." *Newsweek International,* November 17, 1997, p. 31.

"Donna Summer Stars in $100 Mil McD's Push." *Advertising Age,* March 8, 1999, p. 48.

Eckmann, Katy, and Scott Hume. "McDonald's Making Changes." *Adweek* (midwest ed.), March 23, 1998, p. 8.

Galloro, Vince. "McDonald's Debuts New Commercials (Did Somebody Say New Commercials?)." *Arlington Heights (IL) Daily Herald,* July 1, 2000.

Jensen, Trevor. "Scoring Touch." *Adweek* (eastern ed.), November 2, 1998, p. 28.

Kane, Courtney. "McDonald's Starts a Big Campaign to Revive Its Brand Image." *New York Times,* October 2, 1997, p. 5.

Kramer, Louise. "DDB's McPlan: Did Somebody Say Evolution? McDonald's Lead Shop Considers Ad Tweaks, Meeting Attendees Say." *Advertising Age,* May 10, 1999, p. 1.

MacArthur, Kate. "McD's Poised to Launch New Attack Strategy; Recruits Military-Style Consultancy to Battle Slump." *Crain's Chicago Business,* September 4, 2000.

———. "McD's Serves Up $500 Mil Smile with a New Logo; Slice-of-Life Commercial Kicks Off Long-Awaited Campaign This Week." *Advertising Age,* June 26, 2000.

Oestricher, Dwight. "Buffett Selloff Seen Making Buying Opportunity in McDonald's Stock." Dow Jones News Service, March 16, 1998.

Pauly, Heather. "Big Mac's New Ad Attack." *Chicago Sun-Times,* October 2, 1997.

Raffio, Ralph. "Did Somebody Say... McDonald's Was Hurting?." *Restaurant Business,* February 15, 1998, pp. 28–38.

Judson Knight
Rayna Bailey

I'M LOVIN' IT CAMPAIGN

OVERVIEW

By 2003, after nearly 50 years as the king of fast food, McDonald's Corporation was suffering an identity crisis. As *Time* magazine reported, "The challenges facing McDonald's come supersized. Its home market is all but saturated, its sterling reputation for fast, friendly service and cleanliness is tarnished, and customers are putting a growing premium on freshness and taste, neither of which McDonald's is renowned for." In addition, the company's revenues were shrinking, and it had lowered its earnings expectations for 2002. To reconnect with customers, the company planned remodeling projects in more than half of its U.S. stores, it revamped its menu offerings to include healthier choices, and, to rebuild brand identity, it launched a worldwide marketing campaign, "I'm Lovin' It," featuring singer Justin Timberlake.

Timberlake, however, was suffering his own identity crisis—he had been booed and pelted with water bottles by concertgoers during a performance in Canada—and some McDonald's executives were initially reluctant to sign a spokesman who was unpopular with the type of consumers the company was trying to reach. Nonetheless, Timberlake received a contract worth almost $6 million, and the "I'm Lovin' It" campaign was launched in 2003. Developing the campaign was a combined effort by McDonald's, ad agency DDB Chicago, and the German-based agency Heye & Partner, a division of DDB Worldwide. The campaign featured five television commercials with appearances by Timberlake that focused on the adult market. There were other spots created to "maintain the emotional connection the McDonald's brand has with families and kids," according to a report in the *New York Beacon.* In addition to the television spots, the campaign included window posters, signs on outdoor poles, ceiling danglers, and special kiosks. *Advertising Age* estimated the total budget to be $100 million.

The worldwide campaign, the first-ever global marketing effort for McDonald's, was introduced in Germany rather than the United States. As David McHugh reported in the *Bergen County (NJ) Record,* "Germany was chosen as launch venue because the slogan was dreamed up by a German ad agency, Heye & Partner." The new slogan replaced the company's previous tagline, "We Love to See You Smile," which had been introduced in 2000. Following its launch in Germany, the campaign kicked off in 100 other countries, including the United States. In 2004 the new marketing strategy paid off when *Advertising Age* named McDonald's the Marketer of the Year for the "brand's marketing achievements around the world."

HISTORICAL CONTEXT

As McDonald's celebrated it 50th anniversary in 2005, the company also could celebrate maintaining its lead in the fast-food burger race. According to *PR Newswire,* the company had grown from one restaurant in Des Plaines, Illinois, to more than 30,000 restaurants, most independently owned and operated, that served almost 47 million people in more than 100 countries every day. In a

A still from McDonalds' "I'm Lovin' It" television campaign. IMAGE COURTESY OF THE ADVERTISING ARCHIVE LTD. REPRODUCED BY PERMISSION.

2002 *Time* magazine article Daniel Eisenberg wrote, "McDonald's opens a new store somewhere around the globe every eight hours." Sales had climbed from $366.12 on opening day at the first restaurant to more than $19 billion in 2004.

In response to competition from other fast-food chains, such as number-two Burger King, and a crowded restaurant market that offered consumers upscale "fast-casual" dining options, McDonald's went on a mission to win customers and revitalize its business. Eisenberg reported that the company planned to bulldoze as many as 1,000 of its aging restaurants and give face-lifts to about 6,000 others. "Remodeling more than half its 13,099 U.S. restaurants, which could cost the company as much as $800 million over the next two years, is only part of CEO Jack Greenberg's latest plan to get bloated old Ronald McDonald back in shape," Eisenberg said.

Greenberg's plans included rolling out a "dollar value menu" for price-conscious customers, adding healthier choices to the menu, and developing new restaurant formats. The last included sit-down diners that would offer home-style menu items like meatloaf and chicken-fried steaks or three-in-one stores that would serve traditional burgers and fries along with Boston Market chicken and Donatos pizzas, both of which, as Eisenberg noted, were owned by McDonald's. In addition, Greenberg proposed launching a $20 million national ad campaign to promote its dollar menu items.

Dave Carpenter, business writer for *AP Worldstream,* reported that when James Cantalupo took over as McDonald's CEO in 2003 he introduced additional changes, including renewed efforts to "eliminate shoddy service, improve speed and add new menu items, including an entrée-sized salad and the McGriddle breakfast sandwich." Among other changes was the launch of the company's "I'm Lovin' It" campaign, designed to work in all languages and to dispel the chain's image as a fading icon by portraying it as "forever young."

TARGET MARKET

According to Carpenter, the "I'm Lovin' It" campaign was designed to attract "younger and hipper consumers…It's aimed at helping the restaurant chain connect better with customers—especially young adults, moms and kids." He reported McDonald's chief marketing officer as saying, "We know we need to be more modern and more relevant in how we communicate to today's consumers." Charlie Bell, the company chief operating officer, added that, besides appealing to young consumers, the campaign would "be fun, it'll be relevant, it'll be hip, it'll be compelling, and it will connect with people of all ages."

Rance Crain, writing in *Advertising Age,* said that McDonald's "all-or-nothing bet on the youth market" was a risk. Referring to an ad featuring a cameo by singer Timberlake, Crain wrote, "I think I can say without fear of contradiction that the commercial is off-putting to most of the non-target market…If it doesn't register with kids, the corporate campaign could have a negative impact overall, and McDonald's will have spent $100 million for the privilege of alienating vast swatches of its customers."

COMPETITION

As the *Evansville [IN] Courier & Press* reported, "McDonald's and Burger King have been going burger-to-burger for more than 30 years, with Wendy's and smaller companies also fighting for consumers' hearts and appetites." Faced with its own declining sales and with competitor McDonald's increasing sales, explained in part by its "I'm Lovin' It" campaign, number-two Burger King launched a counterattack in the burger wars with the reintroduction of its popular "Have It Your Way" slogan and with its "Lunch Break Gang" television ads, which featured a group of 20-something coworkers ordering lunch their way.

The Burger King campaign did not have strong positive results with consumers, however, with *USA Today* reporting that only 14 percent of those familiar with the ads liked them and thought they were effective, while 30 percent of the people polled said that they did not like the ads. Nevertheless, the Burger King campaign won the Silver Award at the 2004 Cannes Lions and a Bronze Award at the Clios. More importantly, the campaign had a positive effect on Burger King's sales, with increases reported for 10 consecutive months following its launch in February 2004.

Number-three Wendy's responded to declining sales and the 2002 death of company founder and spokesman Dave Thomas by launching a marketing campaign in 2005 that AdAge.com reported was created to help the company "shed its folksy image and one-size-fits-all message." The new theme, "Do What Tastes Right," also was designed to appeal to the chain's core customers—baby boomers—as well as to attract young adults and those in their early teens, Wendy's customers of the future. The marketing budget was increased, and for the first time the company ventured into Internet advertising.

MARKETING STRATEGY

As *PR Newswire* observed, the "I'm Lovin' It" campaign was "a key part of McDonald's business strategy to connect with customers in highly relevant, culturally significant ways around the world." Part of that strategy was to shoot the "I'm Lovin' It" commercials in various locations worldwide. Jim Kirk reported in the *Chicago*

NOT EVERYONE LOVED MCDONALD'S "I'M LOVIN' IT"

In markets where McDonald's had earned a reputation for bad service or where the stigma of junk food hung over the company's restaurants, its "I'm Lovin' It" campaign was not necessarily loved by consumers. According to Kate MacArthur, writing in *Crain's Chicago Business,* England was one of those markets. "To win over skeptical Britons," MacArthur said, McDonald's launched a new campaign with the theme "Changes": "The campaign replaces the famous Golden Arches logo with a yellow question mark and carries the line, 'McDonald's. But not as you know it.'" The new campaign, created by the London office of Leo Burnett, McDonald's Chicago-based agency, was designed to replace the negative image British consumers had of the fast-food giant. It was followed by a direct-mail campaign informing people of the chain's new healthful menu choices and smaller portions. Larry Light, McDonald's executive vice president and chief global marketing officer, told MacArthur that the "Changes" campaign was designed "to encourage people to think of us differently and make them aware of new products. There's no intention to abandon either the Arches or 'I'm lovin' it.'"

Tribune that filming was done in Prague in the Czech Republic, Rio de Janeiro in Brazil, Johannesburg in South Africa, Singapore, and other international locations. Larry Light, executive vice president and chief global marketing officer for McDonald's, told the *New York Beacon,* "The high energy launch in the U.S. is further proof that this global campaign is far more than just advertising or a new theme line. It is a multidimensional approach to customers around the world that goes from television sets and computers to our restaurants... and everything in between."

Mike Roberts, president of McDonald's USA, told *PR Newswire* that the "theme and attitude of this full-scale campaign is being integrated into every aspect of the business... from crew training and the overall restaurant experience to national sponsorships, promotions and all new local street marketing." He added that the company was "focused on bringing the 'I'm lovin' it' theme to life not only in our advertising but also for every customer who visits our restaurant. This world-class marketing strategy is the latest element of our overall plan to continue revitalizing McDonald's."

In an interview reported by *PR Newswire,* Timberlake commented on his role in the McDonald's advertising campaign: "I love what McDonald's is doing with this new campaign and it's cool to be part of it. We share the same crowd... people who like to have fun...and that's what this new partnership is all about." In addition to the television spots featuring Timberlake, appearances by the singer were scheduled in selected markets in the United States and Europe, and he performed in a U.S. concert tour titled "McDonald's Presents Justin Timberlake Lovin' It Live." Dean Barrett, McDonald's senior vice president for global brand business, told *Advertising Age,* "Surprise is a key part of this campaign. The idea is to take 'I'm Lovin' It' to new heights." Writing in *AP Worldstream,* Carpenter said, "Once packaged with music, video and other creative aspects, McDonald's executives promised that the new campaign will generate a 'wow' effect with consumers and restaurant operators. The intent, they said, is not only to attract more customers but to persuade them to come more often and to build brand loyalty."

OUTCOME

If success can be measured by awards, recognition, and increased sales, McDonald's "I'm Lovin' It" campaign hit the jackpot. In 2004 *Advertising Age* named the company Marketer of the Year for its achievements. In response to the award Jim Skinner, McDonald's new CEO, said, "I'm lovin' it! We're honored to be recognized with one of the most coveted awards in the advertising and marketing world."

McDonald's Light said that awareness of the "I'm Lovin' It" campaign reached 86 percent of consumers in the top 10 countries tagged by the company. The success of the campaign was "another sign that we're connecting with customers like never before," he said. Noting the international success of the campaign, the *Scottish Daily Record & Sunday* in Glasgow reported that "McDonald's advertising slogan 'I'm lovin' it' has been crowned king of the catchphrases. The fast-food giant's jingle is being repeated in 43 percent of workplaces, says a new survey."

The *Cincinnati Post* wrote in November 2003, "The biggest single-month increase at its U.S. restaurants in more than five years lifted McDonald's Corp. to an impressive 8.4 percent gain in comparable sales last month... [The company] attributed the increased business in part to benefits of the first full month of its exhaustive new advertising campaign, featuring the tag line 'I'm lovin' it.'" In addition, the newspaper noted that sales in France, Germany, and Britain, the company's three biggest European markets, also showed increases over the previous year.

FURTHER READING

Carpenter, Dave. "McDonald's New Advertising Tag Line: 'I'm Lovin' It.'" *AP Worldstream,* June 11, 2003.

Crain, Rance. "Does McD's Need 'Lovin' It'? Wary Kids the Big Unknown." *Advertising Age,* September 22, 2003.

Eisenberg, Daniel. "Can McDonald's Shape Up? The Fast-Food King Thinks Better Service, Nicer Décor and Bigger Bargains Will Get Business Cooking Again." *Time,* September 30, 2002.

"'I'm Lovin' It' Pays Off for McDonald's." *Cincinnati Post,* November 8, 2003.

MacArthur, Kate. "McD's Taps Timberlake for 'I'm Lovin' It' Tie-In: Fast-Feeder to Pay Pop Star $6 Mil." *Advertising Age,* August 4, 2003.

———. "No Love for McD's Tagline in U.K.: 'I'm Lovin' It' Tough Sell Overseas; Takes Fortnight Off, New Spots Filling In." *Crain's Chicago Business,* November 1, 2004.

———. "Wendy's Overhauls Marketing Strategy." May 19, 2005. Available from <http://www.AdAge.com>.

McCarthy, Michael. "Burger King Tries Old Slogan Again: 'Have It Your Way' Returns to Some Mixed Reviews in Kitschy New Ads." *USA Today,* May 23, 2005.

"McDonald's and Justin Timberlake Team Up for U.S. and European Concert Tour: 'McDonald's Presents Justin Timberlake Lovin' It Live' Latest Extension of McDonald's Global 'I'm Lovin' It' Brand Campaign." *PR Newswire,* October 10, 2003.

"McDonald's Named 'Marketer of the Year.'" *PR Newswire,* December 13, 2004.

"McDonald's USA Launches 'I'm Lovin' It' Brand Campaign: New Partnerships...New Commercials... Relevant to Today's Consumers." *PR Newswire,* September 23, 2003.

"McDonald's Widens Gap over Burger King in Fast-Food Wars." *Evansville [IN] Courier & Press,* January 28, 2004.

McHugh, David. "McDonald's Hopes Young Customers Are 'Lovin' It.'" *Bergen County [NJ] Record,* September 3, 2003.

"Not Lovin' It That Much." *Delaney Report,* October 27, 2003.

"Office Staff Are 'Lovin' It.'" *Scottish Daily Record & Sunday,* August 28, 2004.

Rayna Bailey

WE LOVE TO SEE YOU SMILE CAMPAIGN

OVERVIEW

McDonald's Corporation, with more than 26,000 restaurants serving 43 million customers every day in 2000, was the world's number one fast-food burger chain and also the best known. But despite its brand recognition and international reach, the nearly 50-year-old chain was struggling through an inexplicable sales slump that had industry experts scratching their heads and wondering what the problem was. In an effort to revive its image and boost sales, McDonald's upgraded its restaurants. The overhaul included upgrading the interiors, repainting the exteriors, introducing new menu items and a new food-cooking system, and dressing employees in trendy new uniforms.

To promote the reinvented McDonald's brand and drive consumers into the chain's restaurants, the company had advertising agency DDB Chicago develop a new marketing campaign. Themed "We Love to See You Smile," the $500 million campaign began in June 2000 with a series of eight television spots that emphasized how McDonald's fit into consumers' lives. The first spot featured the chain's famous spokescharacter, Ronald McDonald, interacting with people in various settings. Subsequent spots focused on people going about their lives, but with visits to McDonald's playing a role in their day-to-day activities. Other commercials emphasized different aspects of McDonald's restaurants, such as their drive-through windows or customer service.

Although there were high expectations for the new campaign, it failed to achieve its goals. One year after it began, sales at the chain's restaurants remained stagnant. Further, negative comments about the campaign included the *Delaney Report* deeming it "ineffective" and *Advertising Age* noting that it was irrelevant to consumers. In 2001 DDB modified the campaign and introduced a companion tagline, "Variety Is the Smile of Life," which ran along with the original "We Love to See You Smile." The campaign was revised again in 2002, and the tagline was shortened to "Smile." As the chain's sales slump continued, McDonald's charged its two key agencies, DDB Chicago and Leo Burnett, to develop a new campaign. In 2003 Leo Burnett's effort, "I'm Lovin' It," replaced DDB's "Smile" campaign.

HISTORICAL CONTEXT

Ray Kroc opened his first McDonald's restaurant in Des Plaines, Illinois, in 1955 and rang up just over $360 in sales the first day. From those beginnings McDonald's evolved into a chain of fast-food restaurants with a reputation for providing a family-friendly dining environment and for quickly serving a selection of good food. By 2000 the McDonald's chain had grown to become the number one fast-food burger chain, with 26,800 restaurants in 119 countries, serving some 43 million people each day. The chain's iconic spokescharacter, Ronald

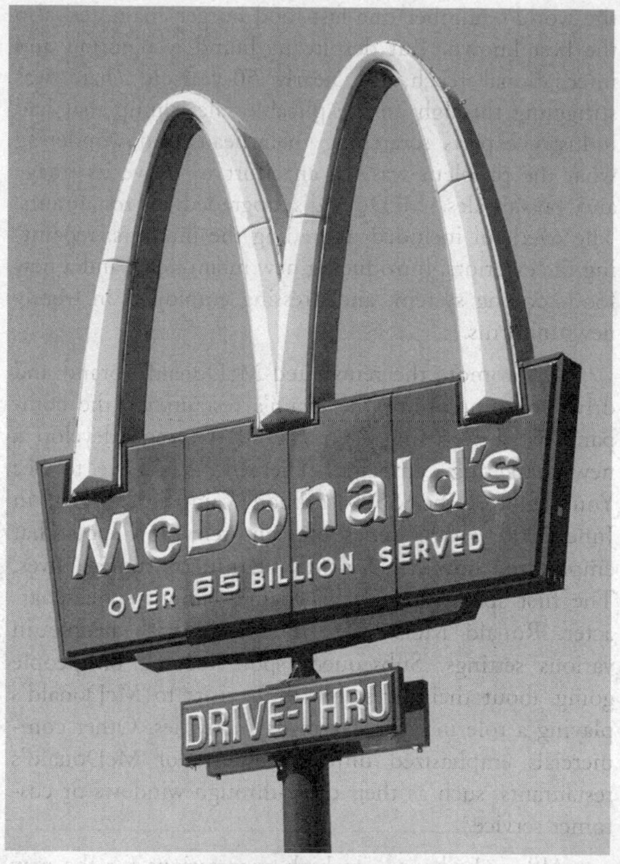

© BO ZAUNDERS/CORBIS.

McDonald, was recognized by 96 percent of children, falling in second behind Santa Claus.

Despite the numbers and worldwide brand recognition, in 2000 McDonald's was suffering through another year of stagnant sales—both in the United States and its international markets—that had industry analysts asking what was going wrong. For July and August 2000 McDonald's reported that sales averages were up 1.5 percent, an increase that was attributable to the higher prices being charged for menu items. But the chain's overall sales transactions for that period were down 6 percent. The company cited a variety of reasons for its below-market sales performance, including currency fluctuations in foreign markets and unsuccessful marketing and advertising in the United States.

To reestablish its brand, to stand out in the over-saturated fast-food arena, and to win back its fleeing customers, McDonald's initiated a makeover of its restaurants. Included in the revamp was repainting the chain's restaurant exteriors in bright, eye-catching colors, upgrading restaurant interiors, installing a new cooking system, adding new menu items, and updating employee uniforms. To promote the changes and assure consumer awareness of the new McDonald's, the company replaced its nearly three-year-old advertising campaign and tagline, "Did Somebody Say McDonald's?" with a campaign created by its agency DDB Chicago. The new campaign, with the theme and tagline "We Love to See You Smile," was released in June 2000.

TARGET MARKET

When planning its campaign, McDonald's identified three specific target markets: mothers, young adults, and families with children. The campaign's goal was to reach each of these demographics and show them that when it was mealtime, McDonald's had a place in their lives. Also targeted by the campaign, with special television spots, were Hispanic and African-American consumers of all ages. Additionally, "We Love to See You Smile" was designed to reach what the company described as "veto-voters," women who did not typically eat at McDonald's and usually made the decisions about where their families would eat when they dined out. Always remembering that primary among its core customers were kids—preteens and teens—the campaign featured spots that would appeal to that age group as well.

COMPETITION

The number two burger chain, Burger King, was founded in 1954 with its first restaurant in Miami. By 2000 it had grown into a chain of more than 11,180 restaurants. But also by 2000 the company had fallen into a sales slump in the United States. Although Burger King reported that overall sales increased 5 percent in 2000, the growth was driven by its international business (which was up 2 percent in the United Kingdom, 8 percent in Spain, and 4 percent in Latin American). In North America sales were stagnant, up just one-tenth a percentage point. After several failed U.S. marketing campaigns—including "Going the Distance," which was released in 1999, and "Got the Urge?" which began in early 2000 and featured the voice of actress Kathleen Turner—the chain noted that it was time for a change. In a *Knight Ridder/Tribune Business News* report Burger King president Mikel Durham was quoted as saying that the company "didn't feel like the advertising was moving the needle enough. We're not confident that we're driving sales and getting across the key brand message."

To try and reverse its downward sales trend, Burger King put its $400 million advertising account up for review in 2000. Its creative agency at the time was Lowe Lintas & Partners (previously Ammirati & Puris). The agency had created the successful "It Just Tastes Better" campaign, which began in 1996 and ran through 1998. Following the review Burger King awarded McCann-Erickson its U.S. adult general advertising account. In early 2001 Burger King released a new national advertising campaign created by McCann-Erickson. Themed "The Whopper Says," the effort targeted burger lovers of all ages and included two television spots. It gave the chain's Whopper sandwich a personality that the company described in a press release as "entertaining, fun, and confident." Its new tagline was "In the land of burgers, Whopper is king."

In 2000 Wendy's International, founded in 1969 in Columbus, Ohio, was the number three fast-food burger chain with some 6,000 restaurants. While competing fast-food restaurants were reporting sales declines in 2000, Wendy's had the distinction of increasing sales. The chain reported same-store sales increases of 3 percent in its U.S. restaurants in November 2000. For 2001 the chain's same-store U.S. sales continued to increase, inching up a reported 1.6 percent. Helping drive the upward sales trend was the company's marketing program, created by ad agency Bates USA New York. For 11 years its advertising efforts featured Wendy's founder and chairman-CEO, Dave Thomas, and he had become one of the nation's most recognized corporate spokesmen. His affable approach to promoting his company's burgers and other menu items encouraged hungry, time-strapped consumers to stop in for a quick, tasty meal. Things took a sudden turn in 2002, when Thomas died of liver cancer. What followed was an effort described by the company as "Life after Dave," which included boosting the media budget 30 percent to about $308 million in an effort to keep the sales and earnings growth momentum going. Don Calhoon, Wendy's executive vice president of marketing, told *Advertising Age* that the chain stood out with consumers either with or without the presence of founder and spokesman Dave Thomas. He added that the chain's new advertising would have the "continuity, brand recognition, and emotional ties that Dave has brought us over these years. The perfect replacement for Dave is the Wendy's brand."

MCDONALD'S FLASHY RETRO COLORS GET ATTENTION AND COMPLAINTS

In an effort to stand out in the crowd of fast-food chains cluttering the landscape, McDonald's returned to its roots with a new paint scheme for its restaurants. While McDonald's may have considered nostalgic the bright red, yellow, and white colors that began appearing on the exterior walls of the restaurants, some people considered the colors to be garish or tacky. Many communities that were more comfortable with the muted colors the chain had previously used on its buildings took a stand against the new paint. Planning and zoning officials in some smaller cities turned to their ordinances and refused to allow the chain to repaint the restaurants in the new colors. McDonald's restaurants located in the busy commercial areas of bigger cities met with few complaints about the new colors, however. McDonald's executives agreed that in some places the new color scheme may not have been appropriate and left the old colors in place. In a *Crain's Chicago Business* report a company spokesman was quoted as saying, "We want to make sure we're good neighbors wherever we are."

MARKETING STRATEGY

McDonald's moved into 2000 looking for a new marketing campaign and slogan to replace its nearly three-year-old theme and tagline, "Did Somebody Say McDonald's?" Although according to McDonald's executives the long-running campaign was a success, the chain's earnings and sales had been slipping for several years. The company hoped that a new marketing effort would boost its sagging sales numbers in the second half of 2000. A new campaign was also necessary to promote the changes that McDonald's had made to its restaurants over several years, from a new cooking system and new menu items to updated uniforms for employees and revamped restaurant interiors and exteriors. To help achieve the company's goals, ad agency DDB Chicago created the campaign and tagline "We Love to See You Smile." The campaign, with a reported $500 million budget, included radio spots and eight television commercials that began airing in June 2000. More than 80 different versions of the original spots were also planned to follow the initial ones.

Each television spot portrayed the different ways that McDonald's connected with a variety of consumers in their daily lives. The kick-off spot was described by *Advertising Age* as a "slice-of-life commercial" that featured a dancing Ronald McDonald in a parade, then at an outdoor wedding, and finally with a construction crew (one burly member of which was about to enjoy a Happy Meal). The chain's mascot did not appear in subsequent spots, but each maintained the slice-of-life format. In one spot a doctor was shown leaving home to complete her morning rounds at a hospital. When she reached her car, she noticed a message from her children reminding her about breakfast: an *M* drawn in the condensation that had formed on the car window overnight. Another spot showed a mother and a father preparing to go out for the evening and discussing with their preteen kids which babysitter they should call. When the kids' preferred sitter arrived, she was still dressed in her McDonald's uniform. Other spots featured a McDonald's drive-through; in one, for instance, a teenage couple pulled into the drive-through and placed their order. The girl ordered a Big Mac without onions. Her date followed her lead, looking forward nervously to what not eating onions could mean. Another commercial showed a father sitting at a McDonald's drive-up window in his car while taking dinner orders from his kids on a cell phone. A spot developed for the Hispanic market emphasized the chain's service by following a customer from the time he entered the restaurant until his order was delivered to his table by a McDonald's staffer. Throughout the spot everyone was smiling, emphasizing the "We Love to See You Smile" tagline.

OUTCOME

The 2000 introduction of the much-anticipated "We Love to See You Smile" McDonald's campaign did little to help restore momentum to the chain's earnings. The campaign also only boosted sales slightly. According McDonald's, in the year following the campaign's launch, third-quarter earnings dropped 1 percent, while sales increased just 3 percent. The chain also noted that sales and earnings were expected to remain flat through the end of 2001. "We Love to See You Smile" also led to negative comments from industry insiders as well as from some McDonald's officials and franchisees. The *Delaney Report,* an ad-industry newsletter, described the campaign as "ineffective," while an unidentified McDonald's source stated that the chain's advertising was "a sad situation." Kate MacArthur of *Advertising Age* reported in 2000 that responses to the television spots by some of the chain's franchisees were "lukewarm"; in a 2002 article she pointed out that many observers had criticized the campaign, along with past efforts, for being "too milquetoast and conservative to be relevant to contemporary consumers."

In 2001 DDB revamped the McDonald's campaign to help promote additional changes to the chain's menu and again attempt to drive sales. Included in the effort were three new television spots. The spots concluded with two taglines: "Variety Is the Smile of Life" was followed by the original "We Love to See You Smile." Another makeover followed in 2002 with 13 new spots that had an edgier tone and a shortened tagline, "Smile." Despite the revised marketing efforts, by 2003 the chain was still struggling to boost sales and earnings. McDonald's began testing different advertising approaches created by its two key agencies: DDB, which had developed the "We Love to See You Smile" and "Smile" campaigns, and Leo Burnett USA. Later that year the campaign developed by Leo Burnett, "I'm Lovin' It," replaced the "Smile" campaign.

FURTHER READING

Galloro, Vince. "McDonald's Debuts New Commercials." *Arlington Heights (IL) Daily Herald,* July 1, 2000.

Gallun, Alby F. "McD's Splashy Look; Some Towns Cringe at the Chain's New Color Scheme." *Crain's Chicago Business,* August 21, 2000.

Kirk, Jim. "2 Agencies Battle to Set McDonald's New Theme." *Chicago Tribune,* April 14, 2003.

"Let's Try It This Way." *Delaney Report,* October 29, 2001.

MacArthur, Kate. "McDonald's Varies Menu, Promos." *Advertising Age,* January 22, 2001.

———. "McD's Poised to Launch New Attack Strategy; Recruits Military-Style Consultancy to Battle Slump." *Crain's Chicago Business,* September 4, 2000.

———. "McD's Serves Up $500 Mil Smile with a New Logo; Slice-of-Life Commercial Kicks Off Long-Awaited Campaign This Week." *Advertising Age,* June 26, 2000.

———. "McMakeover; Ad Age's Kate MacArthur Reports on McDonald's Recent Media Road Show Staged to Trumpet the Fast-Food Giant's 'Brand Reinvention' Efforts." *Advertising Age,* July 17, 2000.

———. "New Tone at McD's." *Advertising Age,* February 2, 2002.

Walker, Elaine. "With Sales Slumping, Burger King Seeks New Ads, Puts Out Account for Review." *Knight Ridder/Tribune Business News,* September 13, 2000.

Rayna Bailey

MCI LLC

22001 Loudoun County Pkwy.
Ashburn, Virginia 20147
USA
Telephone: (703) 886-5600
Web site: www.mci.com

■■■

1-800-COLLECT CAMPAIGN

OVERVIEW

Before the 1980s the telecommunications giant American Telephone & Telegraph Corp. (AT&T) dominated the collect-call market by simply owning the majority of America's pay phones. After pressing "0" to make a collect call, consumers were automatically routed to AT&T operators. In 1993 MCI Communications Corporation changed the landscape with its 1-800-COLLECT program. By dialing MCI's toll-free number, callers were routed to MCI operators and bypassed AT&T's inflated rates. Hoping to undermine further AT&T's stronghold on the collect-call business, MCI released its "1-800-COLLECT" campaign, which targeted college students, military personnel, and the parents of both groups.

Created by the ad agency Messner Vetere Berger McNamee & Schmetterer (MVBMS), the "1-800-COLLECT" campaign included television, radio, and print mediums. Spots for the $112 million campaign first aired on May 19, 1993. Most collect calls were being made by young people calling home, and MCI hoped to encourage their families to pressure them into choosing the most affordable carrier. One print ad featured the headline "What's Out" above an earring in a pierced ear, a torso clothed in leopard-skin briefs, and an "OPER 0" telephone button. Below the headline "What's In" was a ring in a pierced nose, a torso clothed in stylish boxer shorts, and the slogan "1-800-COLLECT. America's inexpensive way to call someone collect." The text added, "Dial it instead of '0' and save up to 44 percent." MVBMS filmed commercials with celebrities such as the former talk-show host Arsenio Hall, actor David Spade, sitcom actress Alyssa Milano, and basketball legend Michael Jordan—all pitching the low cost of 1-800-COLLECT. Later spots did not even mention MCI, because the company believed that its brand was not needed to advertise the service. "1-800-COLLECT" spots aired until the end of 2001.

The *USA Today* Ad Track survey revealed that the first "1-800-COLLECT" spots were most popular among consumers 25 to 29 years old. The company reported a 50 percent increase in annual revenues between 1994 and the late 1990s. Even though collect calls were losing ground throughout the telecommunications industry in 2001, MCI still generated profits with its collect-calling service.

HISTORICAL CONTEXT

Microwave Communications, Inc., later known as MCI Communications Corporation, was founded in 1963 to provide microwave communications to a limited service area. The company later installed a nationwide network of fiber-optic telephone cables and invested in other types of communications equipment. After years of legal disputes, MCI gained the right to compete with AT&T, a government-regulated public utility that had essentially monopolized the long-distance telephone industry since 1913. MCI began offering long-distance services in 1980 and launched a series of advertisements that spoofed AT&T's poignant "Reach Out and Touch Someone" campaign. MCI's low prices were the focus of these and subsequent humorous advertisements during the 1980s. "Sure, reach out and touch someone. Just do it for up to 30, 40, even 50 percent less," said one television commercial. In an era when negative and comparative advertising was not common, MCI brashly compared its prices and services to those of its primary rival. AT&T frequently responded with similar tactics.

MCI's irreverent, wisecracking ad campaigns increased revenues substantially and helped generate a corporate image, but by 1991 the public was growing tired of negative advertisements from telephone companies. MCI softened its image that year with the warmhearted "Friends & Family" campaign, which offered significantly discounted prices for consumers who persuaded their acquaintances to designate MCI as their long-distance carrier. The campaign established such a strong brand identity for the Friends & Family calling plan that long-distance calling plans were thereafter marketed with more emphasis on brands and less on prices. In the $3 billion market for collect calls, however, price continued to be an important consideration, because those calls were often among the most expensive. Although most collect calls were made through AT&T, MCI conducted market research and devised a way to persuade consumers to use its new 1-800-COLLECT service.

TARGET MARKET

Collect calls, placed 300 million times annually, could be up to twice as expensive as calls dialed directly. MCI's research revealed that consumers under the age of 30 placed 70 percent of collect calls. Consumers 18 to 24 years old were most likely to make collect calls. College students and other young people contacting their parents accounted for 33 percent of collect calls, and military personnel calling home accounted for 24 percent. Although it was generally believed that price was not a concern to people who made collect calls, since the bill would be paid by someone else, MCI reasoned that pressure from family members could persuade callers to choose a less-expensive carrier. The "1-800-COLLECT" campaign emphasized price with the slogan "Save the people you call up to 44%." Its contemporary, offbeat style was intended to appeal to young people and to convince them that dialing 1-800-COLLECT was a shrewd choice that demonstrated their knowledge of current culture.

LOW PROFILE

People who initiated a collect call by dialing 1-800-COLLECT reached an operator who made the connection without mentioning that the carrier was MCI Communications Corporation. To ensure that consumers would not assume the service was available only to MCI's long-distance customers, the "1-800-COLLECT" advertising campaign avoided direct mention of the firm's name. Angela Dunlap, president of MCI's consumer markets unit, said that the MCI name was not included in the campaign because the name had nothing to do with the way people made collect calls. Rival company American Telephone & Telegraph Corp. (AT&T) contended that MCI was deliberately confusing people who assumed that when they made a collect call it would be routed through AT&T. According to AT&T's research, more than 50 percent of consumers had no idea who owned 1-800-COLLECT, almost 40 percent thought it was operated by AT&T, and only 5 percent realized it was an MCI enterprise.

COMPETITION

The procedure for placing a collect telephone call had not changed much since the invention of the telephone during the 1870s. Consumers had traditionally dialed "0" on their telephones, and an operator had reversed the charges for them. Most collect calls were routed through AT&T, including many calls made from pay phones. In contrast, MCI's 1-800-COLLECT service allowed people to connect directly with MCI and circumvent the carrier that normally handled collect calls from any given phone. When MCI launched its "1-800-COLLECT" advertising campaign in 1993, AT&T first responded by criticizing the service, but it then introduced its own 1-800-OPERATOR service, which was discontinued in 1994. At the same time AT&T responded to MCI's Friends & Family residential calling plan by introducing its own "i" plan (which was also discontinued in 1994) and by running advertisements saying that "Friends & Family" invaded the privacy of MCI's customers. AT&T had revenues of $37 billion in 1990 and $80 billion in 1995. *Advertising Age* reported that in 1994 AT&T spent about $259 million on advertising. Of that amount, $174 million went to television commercials, $10 million to radio commercials, $40 million to magazine ads, and $35 million to newspaper ads. By 1995 AT&T had

60 percent of the overall long-distance market (down from 63 percent in 1991), MCI was in second place with 20 percent (up from 16 percent in 1991), and Sprint Corporation was third with 10 percent (up from 9.5 percent in 1991). AT&T's advertising budget that year was $700 million.

Instead of using negative and comparative advertising, Sprint usually focused on cultivating a consistent, pleasant corporate image. During most of the 1990s its promotions featured actress Candice Bergen as spokesperson. Bergen became known as the Dime Lady when she starred in advertisements for Sprint Sense, a calling plan that offered a simple, flat rate of 10 cents a minute. Many consumers switched to Sprint Sense because they had never been sure of the price of calls they made through other carriers that used complex rate schedules and confusing calling plans. Another of Sprint's residential long-distance plans, The Most, resembled MCI's Friends & Family plan, but instead of recruiting customers to help sell the service, it offered half-price calls to the person each customer called most frequently. In 1997 Sprint introduced a collect-calling service named 1-800-ONE-DIME, which charged a flat rate of 10 cents a minute plus a $1.59 set-up charge during certain hours, in contrast to the various rates used by MCI and AT&T. One television commercial showed a family locking their son in a room and confronting him about his habit of using MCI's 1-800-COLLECT instead of Sprint's 1-800-ONE-DIME to call them. Another showed two teenage boys stopping their car on a dark street and rushing to catch their younger brother at a pay phone, dialing 1-800-COLLECT instead of 1-800-ONE-DIME. *Advertising Age* reported that Sprint spent about $63 million on advertising in 1994, with $44 million going for television commercials, $12 million for magazine ads, and $6 million for newspaper ads. By 1995 Sprint's advertising budget was $189 million.

MARKETING STRATEGY

MCI executives Angela Dunlap, Patricia Proferes, and Paul Erickson spearheaded the development of the 1-800-COLLECT plan in 1993. After brainstorming sessions that included MCI employees from departments such as finance and operations, the service was launched 11 weeks later, on May 19, 1993. To ensure that AT&T would not learn the details of the plan prematurely, MCI did not train its operators to handle the incoming calls until just two days before the new service was announced. Instead of using telemarketers or sales representatives, MCI promoted 1-800-COLLECT entirely through advertising handled by MVBMS. Fun, interesting advertisements for print media, radio, and television were designed to command attention and generate a personality for the brand. Each spot featured the 1-800-COLLECT number prominently, often repeating it several times to help consumers memorize it for future use.

One visually arresting advertisement in *People* consisted primarily of a bold headline in a hodgepodge of typestyles and sizes, as if someone had cut individual letters from various printed sources, jumbled them together to make words, and glued them to the page beside an old-fashioned rotary telephone (to indicate outdated thinking) and an alarm clock (to indicate an awakening and the passage of time). The words seemed to bounce up and down instead of resting on evenly spaced, horizontal lines. "You still dialing," it began, and a graphic image was inserted to depict the telephone button marked with the letters "OPER 0" for dialing the operator. The headline continued, "To call people collect? Time to retrain your finger." The size of the last two words was much larger than the rest of the headline, making them seem to leap out at the reader. Numerous graphic lines radiating from the headline at all angles emphasized this effect. Below, a drawing of a hand pointed at the words, "Dial 1-800-COLLECT instead. Save the people you call up to 44%." Small type added, "Use it every time you make a long distance collect call." Tiny type aligned vertically in an upper corner said, "Savings based on a 3 min. AT&T operator dialed interstate call."

Another magazine advertisement showed a woman carrying an armload of laundry. Her clothing and hairstyle suggested that the photograph had been taken decades earlier, when she was a young mother. The headline read, "She gave you life. She gave you clean underwear. The least you can do is give her a call." The text urged consumers to commemorate Mother's Day by purchasing savings certificates that would give their mothers $9 worth of 1-800-COLLECT calls. In reverse type against a dark box, the 1-800-COLLECT logo was positioned in a lower corner. Text below said, "Save the people you call up to 44%. Use it every time you make a long distance collect call." The ad concluded in tiny type, "Savings based on a 3 min. AT&T operator-dialed interstate call." Television commercials in the campaign starred celebrities such as actor Wayne Knight (who played Newman on the situation comedy *Seinfeld*) courting beautiful women, actor Ed O'Neill (who played Al Bundy on the sitcom *Married with Children*) as a sort of telephone policeman chastising strangers for not using 1-800-COLLECT, and New Orleans Saints football coach Mike Ditka.

MCI spent about $112 million on advertising in 1994, up from $56 million in 1990. Of that amount, $98 million went to television commercials, $6 million to radio commercials, $4 million to magazine ads, and

$4 million to newspaper ads. In 1995 MCI's total advertising budget was $325 million. According to *USA Today,* the company spent about $70 million in 1996 and $148 million in 1997 to advertise 1-800-COLLECT. Celebrities continued to surface as 1-800-COLLECT pitchmen. Arsenio Hall and comedic actor David Spade were featured in 2000 explaining how much consumers could save by dialing 1-800-COLLECT. The next year new celebrities were featured with pseudonyms. The *Who's the Boss?* actress Alyssa Milano starred as "Eva Savealot" in four spots, and Mr. T of *A-Team* fame took on the name "Inspecta Collect" to let people know that they could "save a buck or two" with 1-800-COLLECT. The final celebrities for the campaign were the six-feet-five basketball star Michael Jordan beside the two-feet-eight actor Verne Troyer (best known for playing Mini-Me in the *Austin Powers* movies). Both touted the "Big Savings" of 1-800-COLLECT. Spots for the campaign stopped airing in the fall of 2001.

OUTCOME

MCI's annual revenues from 1-800-COLLECT amounted to $200 million by 1994 and $300 million by the late 1990s. At that time consumers were using the service for almost a third of their collect calls. According to *Fortune* magazine, MCI sales rose from $11.9 billion in 1993 to more than $18 billion by 1996. MCI's share of all long-distance calls increased from 17 percent in 1993 to 20 percent in 1995, but by 1997 it had slipped back to 18 percent. MCI merged with WorldCom that year to form one of the nation's largest communications companies, MCI WorldCom.

A 1998 survey by *USA Today* found that the "1-800-COLLECT" campaign was most popular among consumers 25 to 29 years old. The primary target group of consumers 18 to 24 years old liked the ads less, but 18 percent said that the campaign was "very effective." Of the ads that MCI ran concurrently to promote its other services, the musing, surreal "Defining the Future" campaign of 1994 and 1995 won widespread acclaim and positioned MCI as a capable, knowledgeable corporation that could help its customers make the best use of the Internet and other technological innovations.

Although the long-distance industry was collectively slipping in 2001, MCI reported that its 1-800-COLLECT service still generated substantial revenues. The campaign's later spots starring Michael Jordan and Verne Troyer, however, were generally disliked, according to *USA Today*'s Ad Track survey. Nevertheless, MCI representatives claimed that the final spots bolstered 1-800-COLLECT's growth. "Effectiveness relative to the collect-caller marketplace is what's important for us," Jeff Grosman, director of 1-800-COLLECT, said, explaining that those surveyed by *USA Today* were not in the campaign's selected target. "When you're polling a broader audience, [Ad Track results] may not be as relevant," Grosman explained. The campaign ended in late 2001. A few months later MCI awarded its $100 million ad budget to the agency Deutsch Advertising, a unit of the Interpublic Group of Companies.

FURTHER READING

"Cable Makes the Connection." *Brandweek,* April 25, 1994, p. S4.

Carlson, Tracy. "The Race Is On." *Brandweek,* May 9, 1994, p. 22.

Fass, Allison. "AT&T and Sprint Try to Lure Business from MCI Customers by Emphasizing Their Longevity." *New York Times,* July 23, 2002, p. 7.

Howard, Theresa. "Jordan's Ad Star Flickers." *USA Today,* January 25, 2002, p. B02.

Lazare, Lewis. "MCI Calls on Jordan for 'Collect' Spots." *Chicago Sun-Times,* July 23, 2001, p. 59.

Lefton, Terry. "800 Ways to Call Long-Distance." *Mediaweek,* October 18, 1993, p. S106.

———. "The Future Is Now: MCI: Warm and Fuzzy Technology." *Brandweek,* November 29, 1993, p. 18.

"Ma Bell's Rival." *Time,* February 23, 1981, p. 99.

Sellers, Patricia. "Yes, Brands Can Still Work Magic." *Fortune,* February 7, 1994, p. 133.

Spurge, Lorraine. *MCI: Failure Is Not an Option,* Encino, California: Spurge Ink!, 1998.

Weil, Ulric. "MCI Strives to Win on Services, Not Prices." *Government Computer News,* September 14, 1992, p. 23.

Vranica, Suzanne. "AT&T Collect-Call Ads Reach Out to Teens." *Wall Street Journal,* February 28, 2001, p. B13.

Susan Risland
Kevin Teague

DENNIS MILLER ADS CAMPAIGN

OVERVIEW

NOTE: Since the initial appearance of this essay in the 1999 edition of *Major Marketing Campaigns Annual,* MCI WorldCom changed its name to MCI LLC. The essay continues to refer to the company's former name, as that was the official name of the organization when the campaign was launched.

To promote its 10-10-220 "dial-around" plan in television and print ads, MCI WorldCom Inc. enlisted comedian and former *Saturday Night Live* cast member Dennis Miller. The sneering funnyman appeared in a series of commercials beginning in 1998 in which he extolled the virtues of the company's dial-around service to dubious consumers. The Miller ads, created by

Messner Vetere Berger McNamee Schmetterer/Euro RSCG, New York, were in keeping with the emerging practice of using celebrity spokespersons to endorse dial-around services. Television fixtures Miller, Tony Danza, and John Lithgow were just a few of the stars who agreed to lend their genial personas to the cause of long-distance savings in the 1990s.

Through its subsidiary Telecom USA, MCI WorldCom was one of the pioneers of the lucrative dial-around market in the 1990s. Dial-around numbers were access codes that allowed users to bypass their primary long-distance carrier for an alternative firm on a call-by-call basis. Ironically, many dial-arounds were operated by the same carriers, although their ads generally did not say so. By the late 1990s MCI WorldCom had established two popular dial-around numbers—10-10-321and 10-10-220—which helped it achieve a dominant position in this growing market.

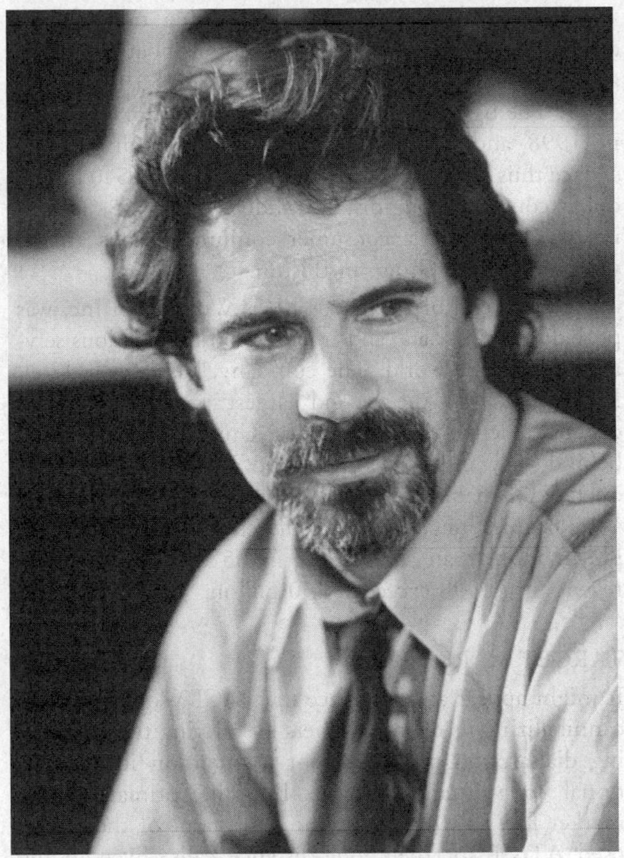

Comedian Dennis Miller. **THE KOBAL COLLECTION. REPRODUCED BY PERMISSION.**

HISTORICAL CONTEXT

America's long-distance telephone rates began declining in 1984 with the government- mandated breakup of the Bell System. Suddenly the once monolithic "phone company" was subject to the same vicissitudes of competition as other businesses. A host of smaller companies, such as MCI and Sprint, emerged to pose a challenge to "Ma Bell's" hegemony.

MCI Communications Inc., as it was then known, was the first to gain a foothold in the market when it managed to snag millions of AT&T residential customers through the clever marketing of its Friends and Family calling plan, a long-distance scheme that provided discounts for frequently dialed numbers. A series of feel-good television ads spelled out the virtues of the service and established the equity of the MCI brand.

MCI's success prompted Sprint and other small carriers to develop a wide range of calling plans, all with low monthly fees and sharp reductions in basic per-minute long-distance rates. In time some carriers came out with plans that offered a single discounted rate 24 hours a day. Despite all of the price slashing, however, by the 1990s the majority of America's residential phone customers—upward of 60 million households—had not signed up for a low-cost calling plan. In most instances these customers made few long-distance calls, less than $20 worth per month.

This unfilled niche created an opportunity for the emergence of dial-around carriers. Hoping to attract infrequent callers without a strong allegiance to a long-distance carrier, small phone companies jumped into the dial-around market on a regional basis beginning in 1990. The dial-around, or "10-10," phenomenon did not fully bloom, however, until MCI began to expend its resources in order to promote the idea and its own brand. The company unveiled its 10-10-321 program (originally known as 10-321) in January 1997, supported by a large-scale ad campaign starring movie and television actor Lithgow.

In October 1998 MCI WorldCom debuted a second dial-around program—10-10-220—this time with Miller as its spokesman. MCI officials believed that the two numbers could coexist and even complement each other. "10-10-321 took off like a rocket," said MCI WorldCom spokesman Brad Burns. "After charting very healthy growth with 3-2-1, we launched a second product [10-10-220], which is aimed at a younger, edgier audience."

Dial-around business provided a tremendous boost to MCI WorldCom's bottom line, enabling the company to report revenues of $30.4 billion for 1998, a 15 percent increase over 1997. "We're in front of a parade that's got tremendous momentum and accelerating power. It's literally unstoppable," said Tim Price, MCI WorldCom's chief executive officer for U.S. operations.

Indeed, in the late 1990s the rising tide of dial-around service appeared to be lifting all boats. Industry analysts forecast dial-around revenues at $3 billion for 1999. The figure represented an increase from $2 billion in 1998 and $1.5 billion in 1997. The dial-around service thus represented a sizable chunk of the $40 billion dollar consumer long-distance industry in 1998, according to Fred Voit, a consumer communications analyst with the Yankee Group in Boston.

By the end of the 1990s MCI WorldCom Inc. was providing voice, data, and Internet communications services around the world. The company, based in Jackson, Mississippi, was the second largest provider of long-distance telephone service in the United States, ranking behind only industry leader AT&T. MCI WorldCom operated a nationwide fiber-optic network more than 45,000 miles long. The company employed 75,000 people in more than 300 offices in 65 countries, and its revenues in 1998 exceeded $30 billion.

TARGET MARKET

It might appear at first glance that MCI WorldCom was cannibalizing its own customers by offering two competing dial-around programs, not to mention its conventional long-distance service. But the primary target market for 10-10-220 was the large pool of those who used AT&T for their long-distance calls. Even in the highly competitive long-distance industry, AT&T still commanded the allegiance of more than 70 percent of customers. As a minority player in the long-distance game, MCI WorldCom had everything to gain by picking off AT&T customers, even if it was only on a once-a-month or once-a-year basis.

Marketing officials at MCI WorldCom placed a special emphasis on targeting the substantial number of AT&T customers who, for whatever reason, had stuck with standard long-distance service. These consumers tended to pay higher rates for long-distance calls than those who had chosen plans customized to their individual calling habits. "There's no question we're targeting AT&T's standard rate customers," said MCI WorldCom spokesman Burns. "When we make our promise of significant savings, they are the callers we're reaching out to. We can and do save them a lot of money."

How much of a savings did 10-10-220 offer? According to MCI WorldCom figures, it cost an AT&T standard-rate customer $2.80 to make a 10-minute call from Los Angeles to New York during peak hours. The same call would cost $1.41 if the customer bypassed AT&T and dialed 10-10-321. The longer the call, the greater the savings, claimed MCI WorldCom ads. With the 10-10-220 program, for example, the AT&T customer calling from Los Angeles to New York would pay 99 cents for a 20-minute call, compared to $3.20 with AT&T.

NUMBERS GAME

Confused about the savings claims made by dial-around services? You were not alone, said some long-distance industry observers. But the array of calling plans on the market—and the attendant parade of celebrity endorsers—also could be bewildering. Herewith a handy guide to some of the more prominent players in this vibrant segment of the telecommunications industry:

Access Code: 10-10-220 Owned by: Telecom USA (a wholly owned subsidiary of MCI WorldCom Inc.) Celebrity Endorsers: Dennis Miller, Doug Flutie, George Carlin

Access Code: 10-10-321 Owned by: Telecom USA (a wholly owned subsidiary of MCI WorldCom Inc.) Celebrity Endorsers: John Lithgow, Tony Danza

Access Code: 10-10-345 Owned by: AT&T Corp. Celebrity Endorsers: None; used Lucky Dog mascot

Access Code: 10-10-457Owned by: Telco Communications Group Inc. Celebrity Endorsers: None; relied on a no-frills theme embodied in the tag line "No fine print. No bull"

Access Code: 10-10-502Owned by: WorldxChange Communications Celebrity Endorsers: None; used the tag line "Talk Cents"

Access Code: 10-10-811Owned by: VarTec Telecom Inc. Celebrity Endorsers: Sugar Ray Leonard

How large was the market being targeted by MCI WorldCom? Potentially enormous, said industry analysts. Nearly 50 percent of long-distance users were under no rate plan at all. Instead, they simply signed up with a long-distance carrier without specifying a plan. One study put the number of U.S. households without rate plans as high as 56 percent and estimated the added cost to consumers at $2 billion annually. "I think we make it clear that these are programs designed for people who plan to spend a lot of time on the phone. They save money and they are very satisfied," Burns said.

COMPETITION

The $85 billion domestic long-distance market was largely divided among three companies—AT&T, MCI, and Sprint—which among them controlled between 85 percent and 90 percent of the business. MCI

WorldCom was the first of the three to sense the market potential of dial-around services, something that smaller regional players in the long-distance industry were already exploiting in the early 1990s. "The major long-distance companies were losing minutes of usage to smaller carriers, some offering dial-around, others with prepaid calling cards, and realized they had to respond," remarked Robert Fox, a telecommunications analyst with Mercer Management Consulting.

MCI's success with 10-10-321 prompted AT&T, which had once dismissed the dial-around business, to belatedly enter the fray with the introduction of its Lucky Dog 10-10-345service. Lucky Dog was an AT&T subsidiary whose 10-10 rates were low enough to siphon customers from the company's established calling plans. "We just did not think customers would spend the time to dial the extra digits," said Howard McNally, president of Lucky Dog. "We were simply late," conceded AT&T chairman C. Michael Armstrong.

MARKETING STRATEGY

With the advent of dial-around service, long-distance companies switched their marketing efforts from signing up permanent subscribers to selling service one phone call at a time. And consumers, attracted by the novelty, responded to the marketing efforts, even though the major phone companies offered calling plans that in many cases were cheaper than their 10-10 services.

The first selling point of MCI WorldCom's 10-10-220 was the savings, as comedian Miller repeatedly pointed out in commercials for the service. Under the dial-around arrangement, customers paid a flat 99 cents for all calls under 20 minutes and 10 cents a minute thereafter. There were a number of caveats to this seemingly simple equation, however. For example, although a 20-minute call cost an inexpensive 5 cents a minute, a 1-minute call to the same recipient was an exorbitant 99 cents a minute. But the use of celebrities such as Miller and Lithgow in dial-around ads was designed to cut through the clutter of normal long-distance advertisements—not to mention the fine print of the plans themselves—and to plant the numbers themselves in the forefront of consumers' minds. "The brand name is the product name," said Kelly Seacrist, a spokeswoman for MCI WorldCom, in explaining the approach.

One of the reasons dial-arounds became prominent in the 1990s was that consumers were increasingly tuning out the traditional ads for telephone service. "The industry found out that residential customers believe very little of what they hear any more," said Robert Self, publisher of *Dr. Bob's Long Distance for Less,* an industry newsletter. "You about have to take a 2-by-4 and hit people over the head to get new customers."

The celebrities in the ads invariably extolled the simplicity of the plan's savings features while avoiding discussion of details that might confuse consumers or dissuade them from using the dial- around service. When an inquisitive long-distance caller asked in one of the ads how exactly dialing around could save him money, the sardonic Miller quipped, "How does popcorn pop?" His "What am I, a genie?" pose helped put viewers at ease and made them feel that they were not merely being tricked into entering into an arrangement so labyrinthine in its restrictions that they could have no idea whether or not they were saving money. In another MCI WorldCom ad Buffalo Bills quarterback Doug Flutie sounded a similar tone when contrasting 10-10-220's dialing restrictions to his offensive playbook. "If only football were this easy," a grinning Flutie pronounced.

OUTCOME

According to MCI WorldCom spokeswoman Seacrist, consumer response to the proliferation of dial-around ads in the 1990s was "huge." Even impartial observers of the long- distance industry tended to agree with this assessment. Dial-arounds "seem to be popular with consumers because they can use a different phone company on a call-by-call basis—they don't have to commit to leaving their own carrier," said Becky Sachs, a spokeswoman for Telecommunications Research and Action Center, a consumer advocacy group that monitored the industry. "Also, there is very aggressive advertising that intrigues people."

Sachs pointed out, however, that there was also a lot about the ads featuring Miller and other celebrities that confused consumers. "It is very difficult for the average consumer to really decipher what is going on in these ads," she cautioned. Among the many catches that Miller and his fellow spokespersons failed to point out, according to critics, was that, while some ads referred to a "50 percent" savings, they failed to specify the base on which the savings were calculated. In addition, some dial-arounds charged a service fee in any month a user made a call, with some fees as high as $4.50, so that a single 99-cent call could cost as much as $5.49, or upwards of 27 cents a minute.

Despite these complaints MCI WorldCom claimed that its customers were well served by the dial-around service. An internal customer survey conducted in 1998 revealed that 88 percent of MCI WorldCom's clients rated themselves as "satisfied to very satisfied" with the 10-10-321 and 10-10-220 programs. A similar poll conducted by the independent group J.D. Power & Associates, however, found that only 36 percent of those dialing around were "extremely or very satisfied." The most satisfied dial-around customers tended to be those who took the time to review their calling habits and acquaint themselves with the rules of the calling programs before they picked up the phone. "MCI is not the Salvation Army," cracked industry watchdog Voit. "They are a publicly traded company that operates to make money for the stockholders. They can't do that if they are giving away long distance services."

Satisfied or not, more and more people were trying the dial-around alternative. According to the Yankee Group, as of 1999 about 11 percent of U.S. households were using one or another 10-10 number. Of these about 47 percent said that they had saved money with the service; about 29 percent said that they were not sure if they had saved money; and 20 percent said that they had not saved money. The future looked even brighter for the dial-around market. "There's no question it's growing, and as long as the providers keep hammering away with promises of big savings, the trend should continue," Voit said.

FURTHER READING

Hall, Jason. "Dial-Around Market Confusing for Consumers: Phone Companies Often Lure Customers with Promises of Big Savings—Savings That Sometimes Aren't Delivered." *Sarasota Herald-Tribune,* February 21, 1999.

Tahmincioglu, Eve. "Dial Around Plans: The 411 on 10-10 Plans." *St. Petersburg Times,* May 30, 1999.

Van Bakel, Rogier. "No Funny Business." *Advertising Age,* April 1, 1998.

Robert Schnakenberg

McIlhenny Company

601 Poydras St., Ste. 1815
New Orleans, Louisiana 70130-6037
USA
Telephone: (337) 365-8173
Fax: (504) 596-6444
Web site: www.tabasco.com

■■■

MOSQUITO CAMPAIGN

OVERVIEW

NOTE: Since the initial appearance of this essay in the 1998 edition of *Major Marketing Campaigns Annual,* the E. McIlhenny and Sons Corp. changed its name to McIlhenny Company. The essay continues to refer to the company's former name, as that was the official name of the organization when the campaign was launched.

Although its Tabasco brand hot pepper sauce had been around since 1868, E. McIlhenny and Sons Corp. had never before used national, high-profile television advertising to promote the product. Instead, its strategy had been to build the hot sauce category, of which Tabasco owned by far the largest share, primarily through recipe-driven marketing. By the mid-1990s, however, research conducted by McIlhenny's advertising agency revealed a widening gap between existing users, for whom Tabasco was the only hot sauce, and the younger generation of potential users, who were more open to the marketing efforts of competing brands.

This younger market, famously sought after by advertisers of products like soft drinks and sports shoes, was made up of consumers raised on television and television advertising, with its emphasis on humor, irony, and visual sophistication. It could not be expected to respond to, or even see, recipe ads. With an 18-34 age group in mind, the agency developed a single 30-second television spot in which a young man was seen eating a pizza that had been liberally doused with Tabasco sauce. He watched as a mosquito landed on his leg, drew blood, and flew away into the night only to explode in midair, presumably from the Tabasco. The man gave a smug smile of satisfaction. The whole campaign consisted of the single commercial plus one billboard that shared the same attitude and focus toward the younger consumer, if not the mosquito.

The spot tested well in several local media markets during 1997 and then was aired during the 1998 Super Bowl, traditionally a showplace for new advertising. Despite a favorable response by the huge audience and numerous prestigious awards for excellence, the "Mosquito" spot was not aired again nationally, nor was it followed up with similar spots, although it could continue to be seen at the company's website. Instead, McIlhenny chose to put its marketing budget into NASCAR racing promotions.

HISTORICAL CONTEXT

Tabasco brand hot sauce was a classic American product in a way that many similar packaged goods would like to be but few actually were. It had a long and colorful history, it was made the same way it was 130 years ago, and it dominated the category it had created. Edmund McIlhenny, whose descendants still owned the company along with all of Avery Island in Louisiana, where the sauce was bottled, began brewing the savory condiment

DDB/NEEDHAM, DALLAS. REPRODUCED BY PERMISSION.

to give to friends. Company legend maintained that the peppers were grown from seeds originally given to McIlhenny by a guest on the island before the Civil War. Although the war took a heavy toll on the plants, leaving only a single surviving pepper, by 1868 they had rebounded to the extent that McIlhenny could produce enough sauce to fill a hundred discarded cologne bottles. (Their shape, it was said, closely resembled the distinctive glass bottles still in use.) The only other ingredients besides the peppers were vinegar and salt, mined from an enormous salt dome that underlay Avery Island.

Demand for the sauce soon turned it from a novelty to a local industry. The family-owned company was mostly content to let demand dictate supply, during most of its history avoiding aggressive marketing strategies. This was a viable approach for much of its 130 years because, unlike other home recipes made good, such as Coca-Cola, there was no pressing competition, and sales continued to support the company's operations. In 1986, however, McIlhenny hired DDB/Needham, Dallas, to work with the company's in-house marketing department based in New Orleans. Nonetheless, the company's overall approach to marketing remained conservative, being mostly recipe driven. This strategy attempted to increase sales of the product by increasing its consumption among existing buyers through ads that offered tempting new ways to use it. Thus, the familiar bottle of Tabasco that sat in the kitchen cabinet and was gradually used up over the course of a year, say, would now get replaced every six months thanks to all of the new uses to which it was put. In this way sales could be doubled without adding any new consumers. With such a low-profile marketing history, it was perhaps surprising that the company was willing to make a radical departure from its usual style, but that it did highlighted the role of the modern ad agency as an instigator of change for established companies.

TARGET MARKET

The "Mosquito" campaign arose largely out of the realization that the average age of Tabasco users was rising, indicating that younger consumers were not buying it as frequently as their parents did. Such a trend was always worrisome to the makers of consumer products and their advertising agencies, for in the long term it forecast diminishing sales and in the short term left the door open to competitors. According to Stephanie Dieste, account supervisor on the McIlhenny account at DDB/Needham, "The younger generation needed to be brought into our franchise, but without alienating current users." Rick Dunn, vice president of sales and marketing at McIlhenny, described the consumer his company was looking for as the 18 to 34 age group, a much more finely tuned demographic profile than the 18- to 49-year-old category the company had previously targeted. The sharper focus allowed the agency to craft a message likely to appeal to this mediawise cohort.

COMPETITION

Tabasco's 30 percent share of the $100 million dollar hot sauce market made it by far the largest brand in the category. Indeed, asserted DDB/Needham's Dieste, "Tabasco is the only national hot pepper sauce." It was distributed in more than 100 countries and marketed in 18 languages. Even such brands as Red Hot, Tabasco's main competitor, and Cholula, marketed in conjunction with its tequila, were far behind, and some brands were regional sauces that had come into existence only in the previous decade as the national taste for salsa and spicy food in general took firm root. Yet so firmly established was Tabasco's name that, although fiercely protected by the company as a trademark, it was close to entering the language. The *American Heritage Dictionary of the English Language,* for example, offered "a trademark for a pungent sauce made from the fruit of a pepper" as its first definition of the word "Tabasco." No other hot sauce came anywhere near this kind of universal recognition. Its dominance of both the category and the culture clearly put McIlhenny in a rare position from which to launch its marketing initiatives.

NO MOSQUITOES WERE HARMED

In E. McIlhenny and Sons Corp.'s "Mosquito" commercial, the pizza-eating man, played by actor Steve Monroe, watched amused as the hungry insect hovered and then landed on his leg. It was no doubt an uncomfortable moment for many viewers when the camera zoomed in for a tight close-up of the mosquito among the man's leg hairs, preparing to plunge its proboscis into his vulnerable flesh. But never fear, for neither Monroe nor any mosquitoes suffered during the filming, at least not from bites or angry slaps. In fact, the agency obtained a still photo of a mosquito and then animated it. Galen Greenwood, writer and creative director of the spot, described the process at McIlhenny's website: "No mosquitoes were harmed during the production of this commercial. We ended up recycling the same mosquito from a print ad, but it had to be reconstructed so its legs could move for the shoot."

MARKETING STRATEGY

The new campaign signaled a departure from McIlhenny's strategy of enlarging the hot sauce category through its recipe-centered ads and promotions. It now set about building its image within that category. And with the target market redefined as 18- to 34-year-olds, the team at DDB/Needham knew that they would have to present a hip image, yet one that did not appear to be self-consciously striving for hipness. In the words of DDB/Needham's Dieste, "You can't tell them it's cool. They have to decide that for themselves." With several potential candidates—for example, company history, a secret recipe, the special enhancement of food that Tabasco provided—the agency settled on the sauce's hotness as its unique selling point. Heat in peppers was measured in Scoville units, and Tabasco peppers fell somewhere between the familiar jalapeno and the scorching hot habaneros and scotch bonnets. Tabasco sauce already had the reputation of being hot—too hot for some consumers—and the agency decided that this reputation for extreme heat was exactly the right key for appealing to a generation known for its extreme pastimes, from bungee jumping to sky surfing.

Yet the agency's creative team of writer Galen Greenwood and art director Tom Moudry avoided making the only human in the spot into a glamorous character. Indeed, as played by actor Steve Monroe, he had a simple backwoods persona. Likewise, they cut against the prevailing trends of quick edits, recycled rock and roll, and clever dialogue to create a commercial that had no spoken words, no music, minimal sound effects, and only a small, tasteful logo at the end. All of this understatement served to make the spot's climax—a small but fierce fireball and accompanying bang when the mosquito exploded—all the funnier and more memorable. The message that Tabasco sauce was hot, though unmistakable to any viewer of the spot, had become secondary to the real message—that Tabasco was smart, funny, cool, just like the audience it was seeking to reach. The commercial tested well with both the target audience and with Tabasco's traditional consumers, which satisfied the company's stipulation that any new advertising not alienate its older users. Although somewhat nervous about the commercial's radical departure from the its traditional marketing style, the executives at McIlhenny were pleased, and the spot was rolled out in selected regional markets during 1997. Then, on January 25, 1998, it received its first and only national airing during the Super Bowl.

OUTCOME

The public's response to the "Mosquito" spot was immediate and overwhelmingly positive. Because of the Super Bowl's huge audience—133 million Americans tuned in, making it the third most heavily watched television show in history—and reputation as an advertising showcase, it was, as always, heavily polled to find out which commercials were most effective in terms of such factors as impact, memorability, and likability. *USA Today*'s Ad Track poll, one of the most closely watched, gave the spot a fourth place ranking out of 52 national commercials aired during the broadcast. Various other regional and national rankings placed it as high as first among viewers. Advertising pundit Bob Garfield, reviewing the Super Bowl's crop of commercials in the industry journal *Advertising Age,* gave it three and a half stars and said of the spot, "Simple. Visual. Splendid."

In addition to public acclaim, the spot also won many of the industry's most prestigious awards for creativity, including an Addy, a New York Art Director's Club Award, and a Gold Lion at the International Advertising Festival in Cannes, France, generally held to be the pinnacle of peer recognition in advertising. According to McIlhenny spokesmen, the spot continued to draw nearly universally favorable comments at the company's website, where it could be seen in its entirety. According to DDB/Needham's Dieste, the campaign achieved all of its goals. Domestic sales of Tabasco sauce rose, along with usage by younger consumers. Thus, the impact of the campaign was enormous, especially considering the fact that the marketing budget was tiny—estimated at 10 percent of annual sales of $30 million—compared to typical national advertising budgets that could run into the hundreds of millions of dollars.

Considering the positive response, the company's next move was puzzling from a marketing point of view. Instead of putting what was by national standards a fairly limited budget to work supporting what had been achieved with a single, brilliantly conceived, perfectly placed commercial, it chose to pull all of its marketing dollars out of advertising and put them into NASCAR racing promotions. In doing so, it abandoned a campaign that had already achieved what other companies routinely spent many times as much to achieve but never did—widespread, positive recognition for its product among the target audience as well as with the wider market.

FURTHER READING

"The Best Awards: Grocery Products: 'Mosquito' Shows Tabasco Bite." *Advertising Age,* May 26, 1997.

"Broncos & Packers." *Government Press Releases,* February 6, 1998.

Elbert, David. "'Net Poll Shows Iowans Hot for Tabasco Spot." *Des Moines Register,* January 29, 1998.

Garfield, Bob "Bob Garfield's Ad Review: Bud Lizards Electrify Super Bowl Ads." *Advertising Age,* January 26, 1998.

"InterVU Heats Up Online Advertising Campaign for McIlhenny Company, Makers of Tabasco Brand Pepper Sauce." *PR Newswire,* March 24, 1998.

Krajewski, Steve. "DDB Dallas Southwest Agency of the Year." *Adweek* (Eastern Edition), February 9, 1998.

———. "DDB Heats Up Tabasco in Spot TV Hot Shots." *Adweek Southwest,* January 20, 1997.

Neilan, Edward. "Hottest Story in Marketing (Success of American Tabasco Pepper Sauce in Japan)." *Tokyo Business Today,* March 1994, p. 48.

Wentz, Laurel. "Swedish Spots for Diesel Jeans Take Grand Prix." *Advertising Age,* June 30, 1997.

Patrick Hutchins

Mercedes-Benz USA, LLC

1 Mercedes Dr.
Montvale, New Jersey 07645-0350
USA
Telephone: (201) 573-0600
Fax: (201) 573-0117
E-mail: mailmaster@mbusa.com
Web site: www.mbusa.com

MERCEDES-BENZ CORPORATE BRANDING CAMPAIGN

OVERVIEW

Mercedes-Benz of North America was at the peak of its game in 1997 when it launched a comprehensive print and television brand campaign. Its sales were generally strong, its products were highly rated by industry analysts, and its market was loyal. This last point, though, held the seed of trouble; Mercedes knew enough not to remain complacent about its market. The plateau was illusory, because markets are dynamic: if Mercedes did not expand its market, and at the same time continually romance its existing market, eventually the market would be lured elsewhere. That year, Mercedes introduced its largest product line ever. New offerings included the M-class sport utility vehicle, the SLK roadster, the CLK coupe, and the E-Class station wagon. These joined the Mercedes classics, the S-, E-, and C-Class cars.

One unique aspect of the new brand campaign, created by Lowe & Partners/SMS, New York, was that it had no tag line. "One of the reasons we don't use a tag line is to bring new attributes to the [Mercedes] star," explained Michael Jackson, executive vice president of marketing for Mercedes, in *Advertising Age.* "The star is already one of the most admired logos in the marketplace.... This is going to be a remarkable defining of brand Mercedes in new ways." That assertion was no overstatement; the ads targeted a new younger market, emphasized visuals and sometimes music over dialogue, dispensed almost completely with product descriptions, and incorporated such elements as humor, whimsy, and even raciness.

The brand campaign, Mercedes' first since the early 1990s, was intended to lay the foundation for specific product launches later in the year. It broke in mid-February 1997 with a 30-second commercial on prime-time network and cable television. The television component was accompanied by six print ads, as well as outdoor, transit, and airport ads. It comprised five ad spots: "Symbols," "Press Conference," "Mercury," "Falling in Love," and "Don't Fence Me In." The spots ran initially for nine weeks and then reappeared later in the year. Each of the print ads featured an object that incorporated the Mercedes star, with one descriptive word, such as "fun," that related to the brand. Not once was the word "Mercedes" used.

HISTORICAL CONTEXT

By the end of the 1980s, U.S. sales had dropped for most European luxury car makers, including Mercedes. The economic recession, the luxury tax, and the dollar/mark valuation were part of the problem. In addition, Honda,

Mercedes is one of the most recognized luxury brands in the world. © FREDERIC PITCHAL/CORBIS SYGMA.

Toyota, and Nissan were launching their first luxury lines in the United States, a move that split the luxury market three ways—American, European, and Japanese—instead of the previous two. A June 1991 report by the automotive market research firm J.D. Powers & Associates revealed that luxury owners appreciated status and prestige but "bought reliability." Reliability was the area in which Japanese cars excelled, even though Mercedes used about six times as much labor per car as did Toyota. The Powers study found that luxury buyers ranked Mercedes (and archrival BMW) higher for status than as cars they actually wanted to own. Among the reasons was that Mercedes were harder to maintain than the Japanese brands—the result of their being crafted more than manufactured.

The mind-set behind Mercedes' approach to production and its markets was expressed by Edzard Reuter, then chairman of Daimler-Benz: "We constantly study our position and we always come to the conclusion that we should stay away from mass production. The economies of scale wouldn't help us. Besides, we have a culture of engineering and product differentiation that would make it difficult." The cars were expected to last at least ten years, and some models could travel smoothly at 150 m.p.h. Although Germans and other Europeans were willing to pay for this hyperengineering, Americans increasingly were viewing it as irrelevant. By 1991, Mercedes was only beginning to pay attention to what the customer, and the American customer in particular, wanted. Before that, reports Alex Taylor in *Fortune,* Mercedes' motto was "The best or nothing." In 1990, the company changed it to "The best for our customers." This rewording coincided with a move to start improving production efficiency.

Turning some the focus from engineering to the customers prompted the recognition by Mercedes of North America that the future lay with the baby boomers. This group had a vastly different sensibility than did the traditional Mercedes customer base. Mercedes made its first deliberate attempt to reach this boomer audience in 1994 with a TV ad by Lowe & Partners/SMS using Janis Joplin's song about a Mercedes, with the famous line, "Lord, won't you buy me a Mercedes-Benz?" The ad received mixed reviews from industry watchers: Bob Garfield of *Advertising Age* considered this ad to be "an unspeakable misappropriation of '60s iconography… in support of the bourgeois trappings [Joplin] soulfully rejected." *The Dallas Morning News* noted that "while a risky departure from Mercedes' staid image," the ad "turned out to be wildly popular with the baby boomers the company was targeting." Cordell Koland of the *Business Journal Serving San Jose & Silicon Valley* called it "a breath of fresh air" and said "it was almost like seeing an ad for the Vatican featuring the Dallas Cheerleaders."

Mercedes continued in the same general direction with its 1995 campaign, also by Lowe. In the midst of a "demographic and cultural transformation," as Garfield described it, Mercedes still was not entirely natural with a hip stance. One commercial, set in New York, featured cameos of the designers Donna Karan, Bill Blass, and

Isaac Mizrahi admiring a new Mercedes. However, the spot was full of inside jokes that would mystify most non-New Yorkers. Another commercial in the campaign depicted three cupids trying to help the owner of a Mercedes fall in love with his car. The message, presumably, was that it is okay to have a passion for your car. A third spot showed a Mercedes driving down the road, passing supermodel Paulina Porizkova, then space aliens, then Ed McMahon beckoning with a $10 million check. The voice-over says, "The new E-Class is so much fun to drive, what would you possibly want to stop for?" Particularly surprising for Mercedes, given its staid image, was the TV spot "Paradise Woman," featuring actor Michael Richards, who played Kramer on *Seinfeld,* in a racy bedroom scene. The final spot in the series takes place during an unusual rush hour; a Mercedes is surrounded by a herd of computer-generated rhinos. When one rhino kicks the door, the side air bag inflates. "Heaven knows," the voice-over muses, "there are animals on these roads."

Albert Weiss, director of national marketing communications for Mercedes-Benz of North America, stated to Koland that the goal of the campaign was to reconnect with the marketplace and establish relevancy with it. "The common thread throughout all these TV spots is relevancy—the things that our buyers relate to." In less than 10 years, Mercedes had gone from telling its buyers what they should value and presenting the product to them as a given, to trying to address their lifestyles and needs through the style as well as the content of its ads.

TARGET MARKET

When Weiss discussed the 1994 and 1995 ad campaigns with Koland, he explained the need to communicate to a "broader, more diverse universe of customers." Those ads therefore targeted "a new generation of buyers—the baby-boom generation who are now entering our demographic segment." He further noted that the ads also reinforced the attributes that appealed to the current Mercedes-Benz owners. The 1997 brand campaign by Lowe continued to target these two groups, with growing emphasis on the baby boomers. The continuity among the various campaigns indicated that Mercedes recognized the need for persistence and steadfastness in communication, as well as ongoing efforts to understand the baby boomers. With those campaigns Mercedes was in essence building a relationship almost from scratch.

These "younger buyers" were people in their 40s. Most of Mercedes' current customers were in their 50s—in 1997 the average age of a Mercedes buyer was 52. The company expected the age of those who would buy the newer models, such as the SLK, the CLK, and the M-Class, to be in the 40-to-45 age range. If they had made enough money to purchase a Mercedes, these boomers could be considered part of the "establishment"—executives and professionals, but they did not necessarily start out that way. Often their path to financial security wound through the cultural upheavals that began in the 1960s. Even though on the outside the boomers may have resembled the more established customers, their perspective would always be a little "outside" and irreverent; Mercedes could not sell them with status and tradition alone. Connecting with the baby boomers took a slightly offbeat approach. Mercedes got it.

TV SPOTS AND ASSOCIATED EMOTIONS OR EXPERIENCES, FROM THE MERCEDES-BENZ 1997 "CORPORATE BRANDING" CAMPAIGN

"Symbols": Brings together the many positive aspects of Mercedes ownership, including *performance, excellence, fun, power, prestige, beauty, safety, innovation, value.*

"Press Conference": *fun.*

"Mercury": *performance.*

"Falling in Love Again": *passion.*

"Don't Fence Me In": *joy.*

COMPETITION

On one level any luxury car marketed in the United States could be considered competition for Mercedes—the American makes, such as Cadillac and Lincoln, and the Japanese makes, such as Lexus (Toyota) and Infiniti (Nissan). Certainly their markets overlapped with Mercedes, especially those of the Japanese, who entered the fray in the late 1980s.

Mercedes' most significant competition, however, came from BMW. Headquartered only 120 miles apart from each other, the two German companies were known for their rivalry. Eberhard von Kuenheim, BMW's chairman for 21 years, said in 1991, "When we take a global view of our competitors, in Los Angeles, Tokyo, and Rome, we always see Mercedes-Benz." In 1996, the two rivals moved in opposite directions. Mercedes was trying to shed its stuffy image and "appear hip with new designs, new models, and new advertising," noted Alex Taylor in *Fortune.* He quoted chairman Helmut Werner, "We had to understand that the world had changed, and that the philosophy Mercedes had pursued so successfully had come to an end." At that time BMW, which already had a younger market than Mercedes did, was turning more conservative.

In the United States, the two German luxury car makers had not been competing for exactly the same customers. Mercedes' buyers tended to be wealthier, older, and more conservative. According to Taylor, they were interested primarily in "engineering, prestige, and safety." BMW buyers were "less often married and . . . more often female." Taylor quoted Susan Jacobs, a luxury car marketing consultant in New Jersey: "BMW had the image everybody wants—performance, handling, fun to drive." In 1995, BMW surpassed Mercedes in worldwide unit sales for the first time, although Mercedes continued to lead in revenue due to the higher price of its cars.

Mercedes' ad efforts through 1994 and 1995 therefore took aim at a segment of BMW's market. In 1995, BMW produced an ad introducing its Z3 roadster that starred Pierce Brosnan as James Bond. In November the movie "Goldeneye" opened, and in it Bond drove a Z3 instead of his usual Aston Martin. The two television spots were created by Fallon McElligott, Minneapolis, using film footage. Dealers were sent "BMW 007 kits," and their customers were given an opportunity to preview both the movie and the car before they were released. The media exposure was unprecedented: more than 16 million Americans saw the Z3 roadster on the screen within four weeks of the movie's opening. By the end of 1995 more than 9,000 Z3s had been ordered, exceeding the target of 5,000. The goal, according to Jim McDowell, was to "establish the Z3 as an icon in the American cultural landscape."

The approach was so successful that BMW did the same thing in 1997 with the James Bond movie "Tomorrow Never Dies." The agency incorporated movie footage into three spots, four print spreads, and a newspaper ad. Secret agent Bond drove BMW's 750iLsedan and R 1200 Cruiser motorcycle.

MARKETING STRATEGY

Mercedes' brand campaign of 1997, at $45 million, represented the most expensive marketing initiative Mercedes had ever undertaken in the United States. The campaign aired on such top-10-rated network TV shows as *Seinfeld, Friends,* and *ER,* as well as prime-time cable. Mercedes saw the campaign as an investment in the relationship with baby boomers that it had been nurturing over the previous three years. In some ways it was not a typical brand campaign, however. "Mercedes is using its brand equity to create an umbrella over the new models," explained Frank S. Washington of *Automotive News.* Doing a separate launch for each new product would have led to confusion, noted Mercedes-Benz president Michael Basserman.

To entertain the target audience while informing them, Mercedes took a two-layered approach with the ads. The campaign was intended to highlight the attributes of the various models and the emotions they inspired in drivers. Basserman explained that Mercedes wanted to "tell the story about the vehicles, their value, performance and quality. But we want to add the dimension of emotion, passion and fun." Such qualities were essential to capture the attention of baby boomers, for whom status and self-importance would not be compelling—indeed, could possibly be a negative. Conversely, it was important, while conveying a new, youthful image, to "be respectful of our 100-year-old heritage," as marketing executive vice president Michael Jackson put it. To achieve this goal, the ads did not talk about quality but tried to embody it through elegance and wit.

Four of the five television spots focused on a specific emotion that expressed an aspect of ownership of a Mercedes. The fifth, "Symbols," illustrated how Mercedes embodied a breadth of fundamental qualities. In "Press Conference," engineers in white coats act as backup singers. Lyrics at the bottom of the screen are followed by a bouncing Mercedes star logo. In "Mercury," the god Mercury chases a cannonball; both are overtaken by a Mercedes driven by two women, one of whom snaps a photo of Mercury as they pass. The god is perplexed. In "Passion," historical footage of Mercedes cars, owners, and employees is digitally enhanced to mouth the words "falling in love again," sung by Marlene Dietrich. In "Don't Fence Me In," a couple in the Southwest views a smiling moon from an SLK convertible while animals sway to the Gene Autry song. In "Symbols," familiar images, some nostalgic, flash onto the screen: Superman, the game Twister, a bald eagle, a pyramid, a light bulb, and a smiley face. They represent performance, excellence, fun, safety, innovation, and value. "Can a symbol stand for all of these things?" a voice-over asks. "It depends on the symbol," comes the reply, as the Mercedes star comes on the screen.

Each of the six print ads showed an object that incorporated the Mercedes star logo. A single word tied it to the Mercedes brand. For example, a yellow rubber duck, with the logo in it eyes, was paired with the word "fun." A monarch butterfly had the logo in its wings and was connected with the word "beauty."

The Mercedes logo, ubiquitous throughout the campaign, represented masterful use of brand equity. For those who cared most about status and prestige, there it was. For those who cared most about quality, there it was. For those who cared most about performance, there it was. In this campaign the Mercedes star was not just a symbol; it became a mirror as well.

OUTCOME

"The finest car campaign on the air and the best Mercedes advertising ever done," wrote Bob Garfield in *Automotive News.* He concluded his piece, "You take the high road. I'll take the Lowe road. And I'll be in the showroom before you." Praise for the campaign was practically universal. Lee Clow, chairman and chief creative officer of Lowe competitor TBWA Chiat/Day, wrote in *Advertising Age* regarding the "Falling in Love" spot, "This is one of those commercials where you say, 'Damn, I wish I'd done that.' The brilliant recreation of historic film, combined with the song… is elegantly irreverent. It's good, it's smart, it's entertaining. It captures so much of the soul of the brand in a very special way."

Mercedes' sales continued to increase through 1997—14.4 percent by August. In March 1998, almost exactly one year after the branding campaign was launched, sales were up 69 percent from the previous March. The multiyear advertising strategy for reaching the baby boomers, which started tentatively and achieved maturity with the 1997 branding campaign, made a major impact on those sales and on the willingness of baby boomers first to consider and then to buy Mercedes.

FURTHER READING

Garfield, Bob. "Mercedes Ads Find Their Voice, Their Style." *Automotive News,* March 3, 1997, p. 13.

———. "Mercedes Bends, Uses Quirky Humor to Lure Baby Boomers." *Advertising Age,* December 11, 1995.

Halliday, Jean. "Ads Focus on Star Logo with No Tagline, Few Voice-Overs." *Advertising Age,* February 10, 1997, p. 16.

Kazenoff, Ivy. "In a High Performance Pursuit of Youth, Mercedes-Benz Gets Slightly Undignified." *Advertising Age,* March 1997, p. 27.

Koland, Cordell. "Coming Down to Earth." *Business Journal Serving San Jose & Silicon Valley,* December 30, 1996-January 5, 1997, pp. 18-19.

"Road Show for Mercedes: German Automaker Livens up Advertising Campaign in the U.S." *Dallas Morning News,* February 5, 1997, p. 2D.

Taylor, Alex. "Autos: BMW and Mercedes Make Their Move." *Fortune,* August 12, 1991, p. 56.

———. "Speed! Power! Status! Mercedes and BMW Race Ahead with a New Generation of Cars to Lust For." *Fortune,* June 10, 1996, pp. 46-49.

Cynthia Tokumitsu

PASSION CAMPAIGN

OVERVIEW

Mercedes-Benz, whose cars were known for precise design and an elite image, felt the market shifting. Growth lay in the lower end of the luxury car market, as a strong economy put large numbers of people in a close-to Mercedes price range. Also, luxury features formerly available only on cars like Mercedes began appearing in other, lower-priced automobiles. In reaction to these trends Mercedes broadened its market by offering more models, some at lower prices, and an updated image. The accompanying advertising campaign was unconventional enough that it met substantial skepticism within the industry when it first appeared.

Lowe & Partners/SMS's award-winning national brand campaign for Mercedes, "Passion," was introduced early in 1997. The agency added to the campaign on Sunday, September 14, 1997, when ads introduced four new models. It was the company's largest retail launch in history. The 60-second "Falling in Love Again" television spot opened with documentary-style footage of Mercedes-Benz's earliest years. Throughout the spot Marlene Dietrichsang the song, "Falling in Love." The spot continued to visually walk through the car company's history with more and more people joining the singing. Lines included: "Never wanted to," "I can't help it," "Love's always been my game," "Play it out I say," and "I was made that way." The film quality of each shot reflected the era shown, with the spot changing to color in the scene set in the 1940s. At the close the viewer saw a 1997 convertible with the top going down. A couple leaned toward each other and kissed, as Dietrich sang the last line of the song and one word appeared on the screen, "Passion."

One of two 30-second television spots that ran for four weeks in November 1997 featured singer Robert Goulet spoofing himself while touting the great value Mercedes offered. A woman stopped her Mercedes at a toll barrier. When Goulet, as the toll taker, saw the car, he broke into singing "It's Impossible." In other scenes Goulet played a biker, a mop man at a car wash, and a meter maid, always running into the same woman and her Mercedes, always reacting with the song "It's Impossible."

The fall 1997 60-second "Big Show" spot featured archival and digitally enhanced footage from a popular 1960s television variety show hosted by Ed Sullivan. Amid scenes of acrobats, contortionists, ballet dancers, and others, the Mercedes ML320performed its own driving, handling, and traction feats.

Mercedes advertised on such shows as *NFL Football, Frasier, Nightline, The Tonight Show With Jay Leno,* and *Late Show With David Letterman.* Print ads appeared in the *New Yorker, Fortune, Car & Driver, Wall Street Journal, USA Today,* and many other magazines and newspapers. Mercedes spent an estimated $100-110 million on ads in the U.S. market in 1998.

HISTORICAL CONTEXT

Independently of each other two German engineers, Carl Benz and Gottlieb Daimler, began working on the

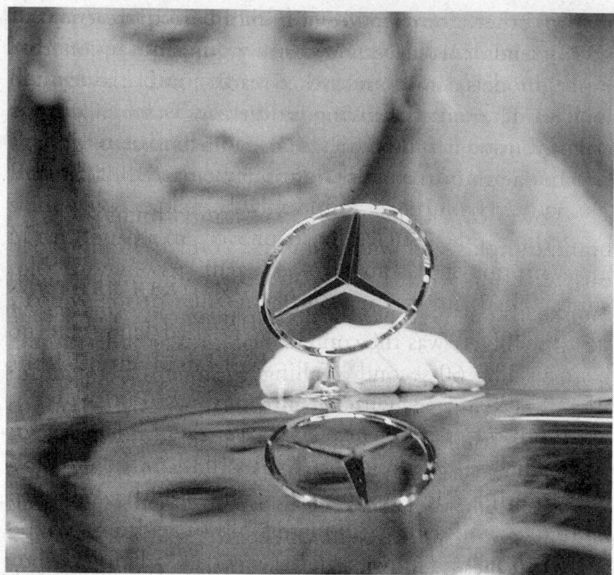

© BERND WEISSBROD/EPA/CORBIS

internal combustion engine in the mid-1880s. Although they lived only about 60 miles apart, it seems that they never met. By 1885 Benz had built a three-wheeled car that could circle a track at 10 m.p.h. Daimler set up a workshop in 1882, testing his first engine on a wooden bicycle. In 1900 a member of the Daimler company board outlined a type of racer he wanted built. He promised to buy 36 of the racers but asked that the car be named after his one-year-old daughter, Mercedes. The car's top speed of 30 miles per hour made it one of the fastest on the road in 1900.

The companies began coordinating some design and production work by 1924, and in 1926 they merged to form Daimler-Benz AG. The three-pointed star became the corporate symbol, reportedly to represent the three arenas where its engines dominated—air, land, and sea. The company served the Nazi regime during World War II, but in the 1950s it established itself as a luxury car manufacturer. Its appeal as a car for the wealthy, status-conscious buyer grew steadily. On January 1, 1965, Mercedes-Benz of North America opened its doors.

The 1980s brought tough times for European car makers in the United States. Japanese competition, a weak dollar, and quality problems drove Renault, Peugeot, and Fiat from the U.S. market. Volkswagen lost market share with its rust-prone Rabbit and closed its Pennsylvania factory. Then in 1989 Lexus and Infiniti, luxury brands from Japanese car makers, hit showrooms. Lexus, in particular, delivered a level of quality and comfort unmatched by any other comparably priced high-end vehicle. The global marriage of Daimler-Benz AG and Chrysler Corporation in 1998 created DaimlerChrysler, the world's second largest corporation.

TARGET MARKET

By 1994 Mercedes began reacting to a shift in the market for luxury cars. Previously, luxury cars were bought by a small number of the wealthy—often lawyers, doctors, and highly successful businessmen. A strong U.S. economy, plus the aging and growing affluence of the baby boomers, brought the prospect of buying a luxury car to the doorstep of many more, and much younger, people. Product features that had been available only in luxury cars were now being offered by manufacturers like Honda and Subaru. Many boomers passed up the Cadillac DeVilles favored by the previous two generations in favor of smaller, leaner, sportier cars like the Cadillac Catera.

Among the luxury car market a subcategory began to grow. Marketers called this segment near-luxury or entry-luxury cars. Examples included the BMW 3-Series, the Lexus ES 300and the Mercedes C280. The fall 1997 introduction of Mercedes' American-made sport-utility vehicle, the M-Class, was another example.

In 1998 Lindsay Chappell reported in *Advertising Age* that Mercedes had early jitters about how its brand equity might be diluted by reaching for this new, younger customer base. The early answer in 1998, based on the demand for the M-Class, was an overwhelmingly positive one. Demand outstripped supply. The *New York Times* wrote in December of 1997 that "Mercedes advertising has become clever—cool, even—and cars such as the C-Class sedan, the SLK roadster and the new CLK coupe are putting the three-pointed star within the grasp of younger buyers." Mercedes pegged the median age of the M-Class target buyer at 40, while the target for its high-end E-Class was age 52.

COMPETITION

BMW and Mercedes appealed to similar markets and attracted almost identical sales in the U.S. in 1997. BMW sales rose more than 15 percent in 1997 to about 122,500 while Mercedes sales rose about 35 percent to 122,265 vehicles that year. One 1997 BMW print ad was a close-up of a gear shift. Instead of the familiar lines and numbers showing the shifting pattern, the lines led to the letters "YEEEHA." A single line of copy across the bottom of the ad read "Nothing is so blissful as driving a manual transmission. That's why we offer 11 models so equipped. All of which have the ability to leave you impressed beyond words. The Ultimate Driving Machine. It's far more than a slogan." Another ad shown a car about to broadside a BMW and a headline that read "Other head protection systems may be available in

MERCEDES-BENZ U.S. SALES

1993—61,899; 1994—73,002; 1995—76,752; 1996—90,844; 1997—122,265; 1998—170,245

12 months. Ours is available in the next .0025 seconds." An ad for BMW's M Roadster used the tag line "The wax can barely hang on."

Toyota Motor Corporation founded its Lexus division in 1989 largely to compete with the likes of Mercedes and BMW. It succeeded. Lexus quickly gained a reputation for high quality and successful products. Although Mercedes remained a more popular brand name than Lexus in the United States, consumers bought 98,000 Lexus vehicles in 1997. Lexus ran a campaign with a tag line from Shakespeare's Macbeth, "Something wicked this way comes." Three spots that ran on the Fox Network's *The X-Files* and *Millennium* in early October of 1997 all ended with this line. Lexus sought to attract what it called expressive buyers in their 40s. The campaign aimed to connect the Lexus GS 300and GS 400sedans with performance, fun, and excitement.

By the late 1990s Mercedes and its competition had taken their marketing efforts far beyond the traditional venues. Several car manufacturers began dueling in marketing arenas like concert sponsorships, literary events, and films. Lexus sponsored a 32-city world tour by rock musician Eric Clapton. Mercedes teamed up with the publishing company, Conde Nast, to lure magazine subscribers into fine restaurants to meet author Gay Talese. Inside the restaurants Mercedes parked one of its CLK coupes. BMW and Lexus sponsored a variety of events for subscribers of *Harper's Magazine* and *Bon Appetit*, respectively. The James Bond films *Goldeneye* and *Tomorrow Never Dies* featured BMWs, while the Mercedes sport-utility vehicle later starred in Steven Spielberg's *The Lost World: Jurassic Park.*

MARKETING STRATEGY

"Passion" and other late 1990s Mercedes advertising campaigns reflected a shift away from an elite and exclusive image toward a keen, clever, and humorous approach. In the past, advertising for Mercedes seemed to imply that people should not even think about buying one unless they did not have to consider price. Television viewers got used to seeing Mercedes ads featuring German engineers in starched white lab coats talking about how well built and safe the car was. Other typical spots focused on beautiful mansions as the car pulled up front.

In 1994 this strategy changed. Since then, Mercedes ads have featured a singing baby, Johnny Carson's television sidekick Ed McMahon, former rock singer Janis Joplin, and Michael Richards, the actor who played Jerry Seinfeld's crazy television neighbor.

The company's rejection of elitism and embrace of contemporary smartness continued with "Falling In Love Again." Creative director/art director Andy Hirsch said that spot was intended to get people thinking, "Wait a minute, how did all these people sing this song before [the advent of] talking film?"

The president of Mercedes-Benz North America, Mike Jackson, said the seminal moment came in 1993 when the company decided to go for a total brand approach and deep-six all tactical activities like rebating and subsidized leases. Mercedes moved toward innovative and emotional products and toward creating aspiration rather than admiration. "We had to define the brand in new ways that made more sense to the people we were after, which was, and is, people within our income demographic, but somewhat younger than the 50- to 52-year-old average age buyer we had at the time," Jackson said.

In the late 1980s Mercedes and other European auto makers had been trounced by Japanese manufacturers of less expensive, better-built cars. The *Wall Street Journal Europe* said Mercedes and the other European companies renewed their focus on quality and value and learned to give customers what they wanted. What they wanted were vehicles like the Mercedes M-Class sport-utility. Mercedes also equipped its cars with features the consumer wanted, even mundane features like coffee cup holders. "Before, we were convinced we had to educate U.S. customers not to drink coffee when they drove," said Juergen Hubbert, a Daimler-Benz board member. "They responded by buying the other guys' cars." In 1998 the $33,950 Mercedes M-Class had five cup holders.

Mercedes also decided to build a car for Americans in America. It opened its Tuscaloosa, Alabama, plant to produce the sport-utility vehicle that would compete directly with Ford Explorer and Jeep Grand Cherokee. The Alabama plant eliminated the exchange-rate risk and saved 10-20 percent in labor costs.

Another key to the strategy was a focus on building customer relationships. For example, two years before releasing its first sport-utility vehicle, Mercedes built a customer base through an eight-piece direct-mail campaign. The campaign yielded a database of more than 100,000 names of people who said they were interested in buying the new car. With each mailing Mercedes included a survey, and it dropped every prospect who did not return it. Ranging from 5 to 50 percent, the response rate "blew us away" said Al Weiss, director of marketing communications. Weiss called the campaign a litmus test to see if the company could maintain a dialogue with customers.

Mercedes said its relationship building extended to its Internet site, where it created an S-class preview in November of 1998. Prospective buyers were sent only information they requested. If they asked only about performance, and not about safety or features, they were sent only performance information via E-mail or regular mail. "The more we tailor the communication to the prospect based on their feedback, the more excited the customer gets at a faster pace," said Bill Hurley, manager of new media and relationship marketing.

"Before 1994, the company was communicating 'the best car,'" Jackson told *Brandweek.* "Since the plan was put in place, we have been trying to inspire the consumer to feel 'the best car for me.' There is a big difference... You have to have a certain connection. You can't sit up there on a pedestal as an icon."

OUTCOME

On Wednesday, January 7, 1998, one of the "Passion" spots, "Falling in Love Again," was named the year's best television commercial at the third annual International Automotive Advertising Awards. The spot also won an ADDY as the best single ad for automotive advertising at the 13th annual Best of New York American Advertising Awards.

In the February 9, 1999, issue of the *New York Times,* Stuart Elliott said Lowe's campaigns for Mercedes had been among the most honored in advertising, and sales increased substantially after the agency gained the account in November of 1993. The fall 1997 launch of the M-Class provoked a buying frenzy. Showrooms across the country reported huge crowds. Total company sales, which had increased more than 35 percent from 1996 to 1997, jumped another 39 percent in 1998.

"What was very effective was the dialogue of listening to the concerns of the people we invited to the relationship marketing, responding in a meaningful, knowledgeable way, and keeping that dialogue going through the whole process. The success of the relationship marketing program led to the situation where we have extraordinary demand for M-Class, which has been a sales success," said Jackson.

FURTHER READING

"Benz in the Road." *Brandweek,* October 26, 1998.

Chappell, Lindsay. "Shift in Viewing: Mercedes Scores with Hot M-Class." *Advertising Age,* April 6, 1998, p. S27.

Henry, Jim. "ML320 Launch Taught Mercedes a New Way To Attract Customers." *Automotive News,* October 13, 1997, p. 13M.

Mitchener, Brandon. "In Overdrive: German Car Makers Stage a Comeback in North America." *Wall Street Journal Europe,* January 6, 1998.

Chris John Amorosino

SMOOTH RIDE CAMPAIGN

OVERVIEW

The launch of the sport utility vehicle Mercedes M-Class ML320 represented how far Mercedes-Benz of North America had traveled in recent years from its staid, conservative base and the depth of the cultural change it was undergoing. The ML320 was a midsize luxury sport utility vehicle (SUV) targeted to compete on price, as well as on features and attributes. Its September 1997 launch was an important component of Mercedes' three-year effort to expand its U.S. market to a younger group of buyers. This multifaceted effort involved new product development and line expansion, comprehensive brand advertising, product-specific campaigns, and even the construction of Mercedes' first U.S.-based manufacturing facility. It ultimately meant, as articulated by Mercedes-Benz chairman Michael Bassermann in *Automotive News,* "turning from an engineer-driven to a market-driven company."

The M-Class introduction was part of an $80 million advertising initiative running from September through December for four new products, the most Mercedes had ever brought out at one time. The other three were the SLK roadster, the CLK coupe, and the E-Class E320 station wagon. Lowe & Partners/SMS of New York, Mercedes' agency of record, generated the three spots for the M-Class products.

The development of the ML320 was well orchestrated, as was the overall marketing and advertising strategy. The project took four years, cost $300 million, plus an additional $350 million for dealer upgrades, involved a million test miles, and spurred the building of a new plant in Tuscaloosa, Alabama. In fact, the product represented a number of "firsts" for Mercedes: its first U.S. manufacturing facility, its first noncar vehicle, and its first price-based targeting. The vehicle was listed at about $34,000, making it a midrange rather than a high-end SUV.

Industry response to the design and handling of the vehicle was generally positive. Sue Zesiger of *Fortune* summed up her response after test-driving a new ML320 for three days in the Rockies: "It is classy, classic, and... wholly understated. It will tirelessly protect you and tend to your needs.... It will chauffeur you with the

The M Class SUV by Mercedes. © FREDERIC PITCHAL/CORBIS SYGMA

elegance and smoothness to which you should be accustomed. It will schlep all your sports equipment and wine cases and kids, and still fit into a normal-sized parking place."

Lowe had been involved in most of the marketing activities and campaigns that composed the major branding drive. For the M-Class product introduction, they produced three spots: "Big Show," "My Dad," and "Smooth Ride." The spots incorporated humor, nostalgia with pointed cultural references, and conceptual sophistication—by that time, Mercedes had come to understand well the baby boomer target market. Mercedes' brand equity and several years of strong sales and marketing had created an ideal context in which to run these ads and undertake the launch.

HISTORICAL CONTEXT

From 1991 through 1996, sales growth for sports utility vehicles averaged 9.8 percent. The 1997 SUV sales through August were up 15 percent; however, the midsize models were not experiencing the stunning growth of the previous years. Ford and Chrysler both put incentives on their midsize entries, a notable shift from the year before, when the products had been selling at full price. Trucks accounted for 31.7 percent of the passenger-vehicle market in 1987; by 1997 their share had climbed to 44.5 percent. Promising as this trend seemed to SUV makers, some industry analysts predicted that it would top off at 46 percent. Nextrend, a market research group in California, reported that the proportion of buyers switching from cars to trucks dropped to 28.6 percent in 1997 from about 33 percent in 1994. Mercedes clearly was entering a maturing market. Yet with about one-quarter of Mercedes owners also owning an SUV, the company felt compelled to leverage its name and grab some of those high-profit sales—SUVs were often laden with options, making them a high-margin product and a profit center for auto makers. These factors, along with an estimated SUV market value of $42 billion, meant Mercedes could not afford to stay out of the market.

The SUV market was also getting crowded with new entrants, as Lincoln and other car manufacturers launched new sport utility vehicles. Mercedes thus needed an innovative platform for reaching the best potential customers. The company settled on selling vehicles by mail order, something it had never done before. The goal was to have the entire first year's allotment of 35,000 vehicles presold. Mike Jackson, executive vice president of marketing at Mercedes-Benz of North America, explained, "We knew we were the more admired brand, but we needed to inspire more yearning. Besides, the world is not exactly waiting for a new sports utility vehicle from Mercedes-Benz." Mercedes would also use the direct mail campaign to get closer to potential buyers. The company, with direct marketing agency Rapp Collins Worldwide, obtained about 500,000 names from Mercedes' own and other, related lists. The mail campaign yielded much more than sales: it yielded valuable customer data and nurtured a relationship with customers and potential customers.

The people on the lists were asked if they would be willing to engage in a "two-year dialogue-by-mail," as *Forbes* described it, leading up to the introduction of the M-Class. Interested potential buyers received two bulk mailings, each of which contained a detailed survey questionnaire asking about a range of preferences, including styling, conveniences, and safety features. The responses would prompt a letter from the company describing the vehicle features in which the person had expressed an interest. Respondents also had an impact on the vehicle design. This direct mail campaign exemplified the transformation underway at Mercedes toward becoming "market-driven."

TARGET MARKET

Sport utility vehicles have largely appealed to upper-income people who seldom use the vehicles' off-road capabilities but like their powerful presence on the road, their rugged styling, and their purported safety. Often, the owners have families with older children. Families with younger children tend to buy minivans, according to Takahashi of the *Wall Street Journal.* As the youngsters grow up, the family may switch to "a more powerful, more stylish sport utility vehicle such as a Chevrolet Suburban or Jeep." After the kids leave home, the parents are ready for a luxury car. Takahashi quoted one 36-year-old owner of a Jeep Cherokee: "Frankly, this is the age when you get a sport-utility vehicle." He added that he planned to buy a BMW when he hit his "midlife crisis," which he projected would occur around age 45. These people were younger than Mercedes' traditional customers; they were even on the younger side for baby boomers. The ML320 is Mercedes' "most significant attempt to attract a younger, less moneyed buyer," explained Zesiger of *Fortune.* By targeting the baby boomers, and even those slightly younger, with the relatively low price of the M-Class vehicle, Mercedes was laying the groundwork for securing the next generation of luxury car owners. If the Jeep Cherokee owner quoted above had instead owned an ML320, most likely he'd be planning to purchase a Benz rather than a BMW to soothe his anticipated midlife angst.

COMPETITION

Throughout the early 1990s, a few producers battled for the sport utility market. Ford Motor Company's Explorer held the lead; Chrysler Corp.'s Jeep Grand Cherokee, with the second-largest market share, and Cherokee, with the third, each took significant percentages. Numerous other entrants, such as the Chevrolet Suburban and Blazer, had smaller but loyal market slices. In the mid-1990s, consumer interest shifted virtually en masse from minivans to SUVs. As the sports utility market fragmented, great success for new entrants would be an "uphill battle," according to Michael Davis of Gannett News Service. For example, Ford Motor Company's Lincoln-Mercury Division introduced the high-end Mercury Mountaineer in 1996. That same year, Japanese makers rushed to grab more of the hot market by putting their names on SUVs made by others: Honda Acura sold a version of the Isuzu Trooper as the Acura SLX, Toyota sold a version of the Toyota Land Cruiser as Lexus LX 450, and Nissan's Infiniti offered a version of the Nissan Pathfinder as Infiniti QX4.

By late 1997, the SUV segment was showing signs of vulnerability. Sales rose slightly from the same period in 1996, but sales for market leaders Jeep Cherokee and Grand Cherokee, Ford Explorer, and Chevy Blazer were down. The Explorer suffered the greatest loss, dropping over 4 percent from 1995 to 1996. Both Jeep and Ford put price incentives on their midsize entries, the Cherokee and Explorer, further evidence of the sales slowdown. Meanwhile, Toyota Motor Corp., which previously had never made enough of its sports utilities to meet demand, began advertising in the summer of 1997 new availability of its Land Cruisers, 4Runners, and RAV4s.

Into this fray jumped the M-Class. To the surprise of many, it targeted not so much the high-end SUVs, such as the Land Rover, but the Jeep Grand Cherokee and Ford Explorer. Mercedes was willing to sacrifice a little profit margin for volume and, more important, longer-term customer relationships. The ML320 was intended as the introductory Mercedes product for younger buyers who would eventually buy more expensive Mercedes cars. Zesiger described the move: "The final flourish: the German haute manufacturer announced . . . that the ML320 would list for $33,950. In other words, Mercedes comfort, safety, and reliability at a middle-of-the-pack price? Move over, Jeep Grand

THE MERCEDES ML320 IN A CROWDED MARKET

The ML320 ($33,950-$39,520 in 1998) competed on two fronts: the midsize, midprice SUVs, which it challenged on value, and luxury SUVs, which it challenged on price: Midsize, about $30,000 Ford Explorer Limited Jeep Grand Cherokee Toyota 4Runner Luxury Lexus LX450 ($48,700-$53,400 in 1997) Lincoln Navigator ($43,300 in 1998) Range Rover 4.6HSE ($63,625 in 1997).

MERCEDES ML320 WILD DEBUT

In early 1997, Mercedes used the movie "Lost World: Jurassic Park" to launch the ML320. Prominent product placement in the film was leveraged with ads and retail promotions from Lowe & Partners. This promotion, along with the direct mail campaign, worked better than expected. One example was a party in September for the introduction of the M-Class. At a Silicon Valley dealership, 3,200 customers showed up. According to the *Wall Street Journal,* "The gridlock outside got so bad that a nearby freeway exit had to be shut down." The dealership manager said that when the demonstrator models arrived "it was like a World Wrestling Federation match. People were screaming, 'It's mine!' 'I've got it next!'" Near-frenzy occurred at many showrooms. The M-Class had sold out in many areas, and some prospective buyers were forced to wait until spring for delivery.

Cherokee. Take that, Land Rover Discovery. Heck, the analysts are even mentioning the ML320 in the same breath as the best-selling 4x4, Ford Explorer."

An advertising campaign by Ford to boost Explorer sales in late 1996 proved popular with consumers but only moderately successful in boosting sales. In the effort to woo affluent baby boomers, it relied on nostalgia, with a takeoff on the old television show *Green Acres* in one spot and the use of the cartoon *Rocky and Bullwinkle* in another. The spot was most effective among 30- to-49 year olds, roughly the same age group, the early forties, that Mercedes was targeting for the ML320.

MARKETING STRATEGY

The three-spot M-Class campaign created by Lowe & Partners/SMS that Mercedes launched in the fall of 1997 also made use of nostalgia to target the baby boomers with the "Big Show" spot featuring Ed Sullivan footage. Sullivan was part of the cultural underpinning of that generation, having introduced such groups as the Beatles and the Supremes to the baby boomers during their formative years. The "Big Daddy" spot spoke to the boomers' role as parents and their concern about safety, albeit in a spoofing manner.

The third spot, "Smooth Ride," gently mocked the whole "have your cake and eat it too" mind-set of this market. While baby boomers liked to think of themselves as young and outdoorsy and vigorous, hence the image value of the SUV, they also preferred not to have their comfort disturbed. The ad spot shows the ML320 tearing across demanding terrain. Inside the car, a woman painted her nails in the front seat. In back, her daughter built a house of cards. Her son offered his grandmother a cup of fresh tea, saying "Here's your scalding hot cup of tea." The family dog, a terrier, balanced a ball on its nose and several china cups on its paw. These feats were a humorous overstatement of the smooth ride. The message: don't worry, you are not overreaching; you can have it all—your swagger and your comfort.

In developing the spot, Lowe aimed to put the focus on the situation, not the characters. Thus, "straight-looking" people were used, which also enhanced the "mirror value" of the spot for the viewers. The humor, nostalgia, and whimsy in the ads were a continuation of Mercedes' ongoing strategy as enacted in its earlier 1997 brand campaign. Although presenting and marketing a specific product, these three ad spots also worked synergistically with the broader brand campaign to advance the overall brand-building initiative.

Mercedes bought ad time during the Emmy Awards for the spots and also ran the ads on its usual prime time schedule, which included *Seinfeld* and *ER,* as well as on cable, including A&E and ESPN. Print ads broke in the fall issues of *Outside, The New Yorker, Forbes,* and other publications.

OUTCOME

Buyers continued to pour into the showrooms after the three ad spots, "Smooth Ride," "Big Show," and "Big Daddy," broke in the fall of 1997. Many factors may have contributed to this interest, however, including the direct mail campaign and the branding initiative. The buyers, however, were exactly the group that the ads had targeted. Along with the broader branding campaign initiated earlier in the year, these ads continued to affect the cultural shift at Mercedes from being "engineer-driven" to "customer-driven." Part of that process was leaving behind the snob-appeal aspect of the brand while keeping—indeed strengthening—the sense of quality and substance. Certainly these ad spots treaded that fine line. No one could accuse these ads of portraying Mercedes' products as elitist or exclusive. The final answer to the question of whether the ad campaign succeeded would only come when enough time has passed to determine how many young, forty-something M-Class buyers traded up to Mercedes' luxury car models.

FURTHER READING

Giardina, Carolyn. "Dir. Simon West Takes a 'Smooth Ride' in a Mercedes." *Shoot,* September 19, 1997.

Halliday, Jean. "Mercedes-Benz Widens Media Buys for M-Class Intro." *Advertising Age,* September 1997.

Levine, Joshua. "Give Me One of Those." *Forbes,* June 3, 1996, p. 134.

Reitman, Valerie. "Autos: With Mercedes' New M-Class, Make That M for Mania." *Wall Street Journal,* October 9, 1997, p. B1.

Takahashi, Corey. "Autos: Midlife Crisis? Trucks, Vans Start to Lose Their Luster." *Wall Street Journal,* August 14, 1997, p. B1.

Zesiger, Susan. "Spending the Big Ticket: It's a Car. It's a 4x4. It's a Benz." *Fortune,* September 29, 1997, pp. 310.

Cynthia Tokumitsu

UNLIKE ANY OTHER CAMPAIGN

OVERVIEW

With the arrival of the brand-new SL500, Mercedes-Benz USA (MBUSA) wished to gain the number one spot in the U.S. luxury-automobile market. At the time it sat in third place, behind BMW and Lexus. MBUSA and Merkley Newman Harty & Partners (later renamed Merkley and Partners), an ad agency based in New York, believed that by simply revealing the SL500 as "Mercedes at its finest," Mercedes's goal could be achieved. Thus, the 2002 "Unlike Any Other" campaign was launched. As it was promoting an $85,000 automobile, the campaign was not intended to appeal to the masses. Instead the goal was to remind Mercedes's customers of the SL500's automotive excellence, style, and tradition.

Debuting the week of March 11, 2002, on major network television, "Unlike Any Other" was seen on both local and national cable networks as well as during the Academy Awards ceremony and the NCAA basketball tournament. Print advertising, present in major newspapers and magazines, was also big-budget. Further support came through radio, outdoor, and interactive advertising, relationship marketing (in which emphasis was placed on building long-term relationships with customers), and collateral materials (such as sales brochures). The campaign's strategy involved enhancing an emotional connection consumers had with their Mercedes cars. Although MBUSA did not disclose the campaign's budget, it was known that the luxury-automobile company had spent $164 million on advertising in 2001.

The campaign's advertisements won few awards, perhaps because the focus was less on creativity than on confirming authenticity. And while the SL line of vehicles experienced a brief jump in sales in 2002, success was limited. Soon afterward sales of the SL began to weaken, and from 2003 to 2004 the number of SL-class vehicles sold in the United States declined 3.3 percent. Overall, MBUSA's sales did not fare much better, with a mere 1.3 percent increase in auto sales from 2003 to 2004. In the end MBUSA was not able to move into first place in U.S. luxury-car sales. Still, the advertisements benefited Mercedes-Benz, as they clearly demonstrated the undeniable beauty and excellence of the SL500.

HISTORICAL CONTEXT

Since it was established in 1965 Mercedes-Benz USA, LLC, a subsidiary of DaimlerChrysler AG, had been considered the standard in automotive luxury and excellence. As a result marketing efforts for the automobile were most often targeted at a wealthy, elite group. Such was the case for the 2002 "Unlike Any Other" advertising campaign. Yet since its beginnings, Mercedes had grown to include more affordable automobiles in its lineup. In particular, the introduction of the C-Class in 1994 made Mercedes more accessible to some who sat outside of the elite class.

In 1995 Mercedes-Benz broke from a tradition of marketing to a mostly (older) male elite crowd with its use of the Janis Joplin song "Lord, Won't You Buy Me a Mercedes-Benz" in its advertising. The goal was to appeal to a generation raised on rock music in a more approachable, less sedate, manner. The new advertising strategy largely promoted the lower-priced C-Class, which then sold for as low as $30,000. It worked, and the cars sold. The marketing approach continued beyond the Joplin commercials, including those promoting the new E-Class, with a $40,000 price tag, in 1996. The promotions included extensive Mercedes catalogues spreads. With such titles as "Inspiration," "Imagine," and "Dreams," the catalogues spread a message of approachability, value, and fun. This type of marketing approach, which focused on value, continued for Mercedes-Benz but was different from that of the 2002 "Unlike Any Other" campaign. The latter campaign focused less on value and more on the automobile's tradition of engineering excellence.

TARGET MARKET

Because the SL500 had a price tag of $85,000, Mercedes's target market for the car was not all that diverse. Actually, it was rather insular, especially with its focus on people's emotional connection with their Mercedeses. Such television spots as "Reincarnation"—in which an aged Mercedes car was about to be crushed, and its "life" flashed before its eyes—established an emotional connection to the brand. This marketing was

RIGHT OVER THEIR HEADS

Michael McClure, the renowned Beat Generation poet, wrote "Mercedes Benz," which was released as a Janis Joplin song in 1971. With the lyrics "Oh lord, won't you buy me a Mercedes Benz? My friends all drive Porsches, I must make amends," the song was intended as a satire of materialism.

directed toward long-term Mercedes owners, who historically had been a loyal bunch, often sentimentally so.

Mercedes-Benz would not always target such a small market, as was later seen in the 2004 "Portraits" campaign. That campaign, which used approximately 25 percent of MBUSA's $140 million advertising budget, announced the arrival of products for just about everyone, not simply the wealthy, with products' prices ranging from $25,000 to $450,000. But this was not the case with the "Unlike Any Other" campaign, because the SL-Class models obviously could not be attained by everyone. With this campaign Mercedes simply wished to remind those already familiar with Mercedes, and in particular the SL Class, that, because of the car's construction, power, beauty (everything that made a Mercedes a Mercedes), it was well worth the price.

COMPETITION

While Mercedes was debuting "Unlike Any Other," Audi AG, a top competitor with DaimlerChrysler (the parent company of Mercedes), launched one of the biggest ad campaigns in its history. As with "Unlike Any Other," Audi's "A8" campaign banked on people's emotional attachment to their cars. In the campaign's prelaunch phase the Audi brand, and in particular its sporty and progressive image, was portrayed emotionally through its history. Using approximately 600 people—including Audi employees, advertising specialists, producers, photographers, a symphony orchestra, composers, directors, and actors—Audi packed its entire history into a series of television commercials, while at the same time introducing a new product. At the campaign's start Audi AG's sales were about $23 billion. In the year following the campaign's debut, sales jumped to over $29 billion. By 2004 the number had exceeded $33 billion. But at the same time Audi of America, a more direct competitor with Mercedes-Benz USA, was experiencing serious declines in sales. In 2004 it sold under 78,000 cars, reflecting a 9.8 percent decrease from 2003.

A relative newcomer in the industry, Lexus (owned by Toyota) was launched in 1989 and quickly became the best-selling line of U.S. luxury cars. In 2003, however, BMW took the lead, and Lexus fell to second. But at the same time, the consulting firm Automotive Consultants Incorporated published results from a year-long study, claiming: "The Lexus LS 430 is the finest luxury sedan in America." Lexus used this data in a 2002 advertising campaign, challenging customers to think of Lexus in the same (or even higher) category as other leading luxury-car manufacturers, such as Mercedes and BMW. But any success this brought, including record sales in 2002, was not long lasting. From 2004 to 2005 Lexus sales in the U.S. dropped by 4.4 percent.

Also during the debut of "Unlike Any Other," another Mercedes competitor, BMW, was making advertising history with its release of "The Hire" short-film series. Created by top Hollywood directors such as John Woo and Guy Ritchie, the eight Internet-broadcast films starred BMW cars and actor Clive Owen, who played the driver. BMW's original goal was to have two million consumers view the eight-minute online commercials. Within a year this was very much surpassed, with more than 45 million viewers. Following the debut of the advertising films, BMW's worldwide sales grew more than steadily, from $44 billion in 2002, to $52 billion in 2003, up to $60 billion in 2004. U.S. sales also increased each year from 2002 to 2005. In 2003 BMW became the best-selling luxury car in the U.S.

MARKETING STRATEGY

In conjunction with the arrival of the newest model of Mercedes-Benz automobiles, the SL500, Mercedes-Benz USA (MBUSA) launched a major marketing campaign under the tagline "Unlike any other." The campaign launch featured four national and seven regional television spots as well as an extensive print-media campaign. Led by ad agency Merkley Newman Harty & Partners, New York, it represented the largest U.S. marketing campaign for Mercedes since the 1990s.

The SL500 represented Mercedes at its best, often inducing an emotional response from customers. According to one *Road and Travel Magazine* writer: "Just when you thought it couldn't get any sexier . . . Mercedes-Benz rolls out the unforgettable new 2003 SL500. . . . And once you take a look, you'll take a second one. Soon thereafter is when your jaw hits the ground, rendering you a blubbering mess of drool. Trust us. We've spent time in this car. It has that effect on people. It's simply arresting.?"

This was what MBUSA and Merkley were banking on when it launched the "Unlike Any Other" campaign. The tagline, which adorned all ads in the new campaign, was supposed to be met with nods of agreement among consumers, who would know exactly what Mercedes was talking about. Further, the campaign was intended to regain Mercedes-Benz's leadership position in the U.S. luxury-automobile industry. In 2001 Mercedes had slipped to third, behind BMW and Toyota's Lexus.

Meanwhile, the first television spot, "Timeless Ride," which aired nationally, represented an attempt to draw on people's long-standing affection for the SL model. The ad featured a woman driving different generations of the SL, in conjunction with the time period each existed. Beginning in the 1960s and ending post-2000, such images as oversized Jackie Onassis-style sunglasses, a disco ball, punk hairstyles, and so forth, coincided with those of the car's various models. With a similar theme of sentimentality, three other nationally run spots debuted: "Reincarnation," during which an old Mercedes-Benz"s" life "flashed before its eyes;" Sanctuary, "a flashback to 1950s black-and-white dramas; and" Crash Test, "which focused on Mercedes's legendary strength. Each of the four national spots ended with various twists on the tagline:" Timeless. Unlike any other,"" Soul. Unlike any other,"" Security. "Unlike any other," and last, "Built. Unlike any other."

The regional ads went a step further than the national ads. Even as they kept the strong commitment to the Mercedes brand and the "Unlike any other" tagline, the seven regional executions moved the focus into three specific areas: value, safety, and customer service. And this was done with a backdrop of humor. In "Woman," for instance, a man riding a bus used the panorama roof of the C-Class Coupe to his advantage, when he passed on his phone number to the attractive woman driver. It wound up in the glove compartment, along with many others. The spot ended with the tagline "Value. Unlike any other." In "Baby" parents out shopping for baby-proofing items realized that had they left the baby in the car. A voice-over stated, "If everything was as safe as an M-Class, you'd have a lot less to worry about," and the commercial ended with "Security. Unlike any other."

The 2002 television spots were debuted the week of March 11 on major network TV, appearing during such popular shows as *The West Wing, ER,* and *The Tonight Show,* as well on as such national cable networks as ESPN, A&E, CNN, and MSNBC. More significantly, the ads were run during that year's Academy Awards and NCAA Conference Finals, Championship, and Final Four basketball tournaments. Beyond TV, the print advertising was displayed in major papers and magazines, including the *Wall Street Journal, Vogue, Fortune,* and the *New Yorker.* The campaign's other efforts, including radio spots, outdoor and interactive ads, relationship marketing, and collateral materials, further spread Mercedes's message.

OUTCOME

While the "Unlike Any Other" campaign did not cause a sensation in the advertising world, it did win a few awards. The television commercial "Reincarnation," during which a classic Mercedes was about to be crushed, for instance, garnered an AdForum Creative Hits award (determined by users of the *AdForum* website) in 2002 and was shortlisted at the International Advertising Festival in Cannes, France in 2003. The campaign was more successful in terms of financial payoff for the company, but the SL class that was specifically promoted in "Unlike Any Other" experienced only brief and limited success.

The months following the launch of "Unlike Any Other" reflected an increase in MBUSA's sales, which peaked in July 2002, when 14,937 new vehicles were sold (causing a seven-month year-to-date sales record for MBUSA, of nearly 118,000 cars sold). Further, the SL class posted a 78.5 percent increase for the month and more than double its year-to-date volume of the same period during 2001. But by the following year the numbers were dwindling. From 2003 to 2004 the number of SL-class automobiles sold in the United States declined 3.3 percent, even as MBUSA's total sales improved 1.3 percent during the same time period. And this increase would not be enough for MBUSA to meet its goal. In the end Mercedes was not able to come close to becoming the leader in U.S. luxury-car sales.

FURTHER READING

Green, Jeff. "Mercedes Ad Campaign to Push Luxury Image." *Chicago Sun-Times,* March 12, 2002, p. 50.

Hamilton, Andrew. "The Most Desirable of a Very Desirable Lot." *Irish Times,* March 20, 2002, p. 63.

Hepworth, Kevin. "Million-Dollar Babies." *Daily Telegraph* (Sydney), March 16, 2002, p. G01.

Holloway, Nigel. "The Best-Driven Brand." *Forbes.com,* July 22, 2002. Available from <http://www.forbes.com/global/2002/0722/024.html>

Jedlicka, Dan. "Mercedes Didn't Play by Numbers on SL Series." *Chicago Sun-Times,* November 16, 2003, p. 58.

Kiley, David. "Mercedes Takes Risk by Trying for Mass Appeal." *USA Today,* March 24, 2004, p. 5B.

Maynard, Micheline. "Foreign Automakers Unleash a New Wave of Luxury." *New York Times,* September 27, 2003, p. C1.

McMains, Andrew. "Merkley Touts Mercedes." *Adweek,* March 22, 2004.

"Mercedes Sales Rise." *Atlanta Journal-Constitution,* May 7, 2005.

Reinan, John. "Ad Agency Fallon Wins Top Award at Cannes." *Minneapolis Star Tribune,* June 26, 2003, p. 1D.

Siler, Steve. "'Mercedes-Benz SL500'—Uber-Sexy." *Road and Travel Magazine,* 2002.

Williams, G. Chambers, III. "Mercedes SL Near Perfection; For Those with $90,000 to Spare, This Roadster Is a Dream Come True." *San Antonio (TX) Express-News,* February 24, 2002, p. 1F.

Candice L. Mancini

MetLife, Inc.

200 Park Avenue
New York, New York 10166
USA
Telephone: (212) 578-2211
Fax: (212) 578-2211
Web site: www.metlife.com

METLIFE HELPS YOU MAKE SENSE OF IT ALL CAMPAIGN

OVERVIEW

Between 1985 and 1995 consumers came to associate Metropolitan Life Insurance Co. (later renamed MetLife, Inc.) with its animated mascots, Charles Schulz's "Peanuts" characters and especially Charlie Brown's resourceful beagle, Snoopy. MetLife, as the company was commonly called, wanted to retain this strong brand identity while adapting to societal transformation and spreading awareness of the company's changing nature (namely the fact that it offered a full range of financial services in addition to its life-insurance products). These efforts were complicated, moreover, by a wave of insurance-industry scandals headlined by an alleged MetLife scheme to swindle consumers. The company met these substantial challenges with large-scale internal restructuring efforts, and it communicated the notion of a new and updated MetLife through an advertising campaign themed "MetLife Helps You Make Sense of It All."

Crafted by the New York agency Young & Rubicam and released in September 1995, the campaign marked a strategic shift in MetLife's branding even as it continued to employ the familiar cartoon beagle with which the company was so closely identified. Whereas previous MetLife campaigns had featured Snoopy and the other Peanuts characters in fully animated commercials, the new campaign wedded the animated Snoopy to live-action scenarios featuring real people and backdrops. This conceptual shift was meant to suggest that MetLife was evolving with the times, a notion that was underlined by the content of the spots, each of which used Snoopy as a symbol for MetLife itself. One spot, for instance, illustrated MetLife's ability to rescue consumers from figurative financial jungles by showing Snoopy taming an actual tiger; another showed Snoopy dancing with a bride whose wedding had been financed with the proceeds of her parents' MetLife mutual fund. MetLife's typical annual media budget during the late 1990s was between $20 and $30 million.

After posting record profits in 1997, MetLife seemed to have emerged from its mid-1990s difficulties. Young & Rubicam's research indicated that consumer awareness of the brand increased during the campaign. Although MetLife continued to rely on the Peanuts characters to differentiate its brand from competitors, Snoopy ceased playing a starring role in the company's advertising when a new campaign was unveiled in 1999.

HISTORICAL CONTEXT

In August 1993 an investigation by the Florida Department of Insurance revealed that MetLife agents had sold life-insurance policies disguised as the Nurses Guaranteed Retirement Program, a tax-deferred retirement plan. One victim of this scheme, Sherry Horton, reluctantly bought a policy from MetLife agent Mark Moser, mainly on the strength of MetLife's good name: "After all, who hasn't heard of Metropolitan Life and Snoopy?" Horton told *Money* magazine's Walter L. Updegrave. More than a thousand policyholders filed claims against MetLife as a result of this investigation; at the same time, Moser filed a lawsuit against MetLife claiming that MetLife had scripted the scheme. MetLife settled these suits out of court for between $40 million and $50 million. This settlement was only the beginning of a wave of revelations of market misconduct that plagued the entire insurance industry. In light of the estimated $100 million that MetLife paid in settlements and fines, the tagline "Get Met. It pays" took on new and unwelcome meaning for the company.

In 1994 the MetLife Express program was implemented, reengineering the company by strengthening its internal structure and technological capabilities in the face of stiffer competition and industry consolidations. As part of this initiative MetLife spent several million dollars to revamp the mechanisms it used for ensuring compliance with federal and state regulations; the company established an ethics and compliance committee and expanded the role of the single compliance ombudsman to an entire compliance department that answered directly to the company's president. Creative directors at Young & Rubicam developed the new platform, "MetLife Helps You Make Sense of It All," to highlight how these changes were initiated with the consumer in mind. A stronger compliance network functioned not only to explain confusing policies to clients but also to ensure against further misconduct on the agents' or the company's part.

A MAP OF THE INTERNET—YOU CAN'T GET HERE FROM THERE

United Media, which owned the copyright for the Peanuts characters, licensed the use of Snoopy and the gang to MetLife—but only for the countries where MetLife sold financial services. This became a stumbling block when MetLife and its Internet ad agency, Agency.com, wanted to feature Snoopy and other Peanuts characters on the MetLife Online website. Because computer users in countries such as Japan and Australia (where MetLife did not do business and thus did not have licensing) could access the World Wide Web, Agency.com had to devise a way to block them from viewing copyrighted characters. United Media allowed MetLife and Agency.com to try this blockout system with a 5 percent margin of error. But according to Agency.com's Chan Suh, "We tried to find a map of the Internet and, of course, we discovered there is no such thing." The companies spent two months mapping out a system to locate computers trying to connect to their site in order to block out those from restricted areas with a 99 percent degree of accuracy. Frances Katz reported in *Direct* magazine the relative success of this system: "Of the 18,000 hits [to the MetLife Online website] recorded on March 5, [1996,] only 60 were rejected and only two of those were from users who should have been granted access (including this reporter)."

TARGET MARKET

The market goals of the new campaign were to attract new customers and to retain current policyholders who might be tempted to seek the financial services of other companies. Both markets required the same tactic: to restore faith in MetLife's reputation through improved customer service and reinvigorated compliance with insurance regulations. Loyal MetLife customers needed to see a new face suggestive of a change in the body of the company. Because the scandal rocked the entire insurance industry, consumers could not migrate from corruption to purity. Although none of the major insurance companies had consciously conspired to deceive policyholders, all of them shared some degree of guilt, so they all had to rebuild consumer confidence. Ironically, the lawsuits ended up adversely affecting all policyholders more than the companies themselves, as the financial performance of insurance policies suffered from the scandal. MetLife's new campaign attempted to convey the message that the company was committed to shielding its policyholders from the kind of confusion that had led to the scandal in the first place.

COMPETITION

The three major players in the insurance industry—MetLife, Prudential, and New York Life—outperformed the rest of the industry in the late 1980s and early 1990s, a time when new sales throughout the industry were flat. MetLife generated growth at an astounding rate, with a peak sales increase in 1989 of 60.92 percent. Prudential crested that same year with a 41.84 percent gain, while New York Life peaked two years earlier, in 1987, with a 59.9 percent increase in sales. Combined, the three companies gained market share steadily in this time period, climbing from 7.32 percent in 1985 to peak at 16.46 per-

DOING THINGS THAT SEEM IMPOSSIBLE

A visual-effects supervisor from Sight Effects of Venice, California, was on the sets for the shooting of the live-action sequences of the "MetLife Helps Make Sense of It All" commercials to help the director leave room in the frame for post-production animation. This advisor could help the director film in a way that anticipated the bluescreening and compositing that would happen later. This technique represented a whole new approach to commercial production: "Nowadays, agency creatives are designing their ads without having to think about the limitations of technology, and that's how it should be," said Sight Effects founder Alan Barnett. "Ultimately, you have to find ways of doing things that seem to be impossible."

cent in 1992. With the revelations of market misconduct in 1993, the three descended collectively in market share and individually in sales. By 1995 their combined market share had fallen to 11.12 percent. MetLife suffered the most individually, with sales plummeting 38.33 percent in 1994 as compared with 1993. Prudential's sales decreased 11.56 percent in 1994 and then another 22.58 percent in 1995. New York Life's sales fell 31.49 percent in 1994 but rebounded in 1995 with an increase of 36.82 percent. While the mid-1990s reversed many of the trends of the late 1980s and early 1990s, MetLife, Prudential, and New York Life competed on a level playing field—all three experienced unprecedented gains simultaneously, and all three fell from grace as dramatically.

By 1995 insurance companies had reconciled themselves to the shock of a greatly changed marketplace and were prepared to rebound by redefining their positions in that new atmosphere. In some ways the scandal helped the insurance industry by forcing them out of a comfort zone that had allowed them to fall behind the times in terms of consumers' needs and expectations.

Many of the new ad campaigns that broke in the wake of the scandal were more attuned to the contemporary advertising atmosphere that acknowledged more concrete realities. The tagline for the new ad campaign of Boston-based John Hancock Mutual Life Insurance Co. exemplified this attitude perfectly: "Real Life, Real Answers." Prudential took a riskier approach, but one that even more accurately reflected consumers' attitudes: the "Be Your Own Rock" campaign acknowledged the shift from corporate dependence to self-reliance on the consumer's part while still asserting a role for the insurance company in helping consumers to discover their own best financial solutions. These two campaigns as well as MetLife's shifted emphasis from the institution to the individual in an attempt to redefine insurers' roles and recapture the imaginations of consumers.

MARKETING STRATEGY

Over the previous 10 years MetLife had created tremendous brand identity and equity through its relationship with the Peanuts characters. During that time period, especially just prior to the new campaign, American culture at large and MetLife specifically underwent major changes, so the company wanted to redefine its relationship with the Peanuts characters to reflect those changes. Artist Bill Melendez brought Charles Schultz's characters to life through animation, but their cartoon quality put them at a remove from reality. MetLife sought to introduce the characters into reality. "We decided to refresh our advertising campaign to reflect the changing world in which we live," explained MetLife chairman and CEO Harry P. Kamen. "People are overwhelmed by the growing number of financial decisions they must face every day. Placing Snoopy in a real world setting personifies our commitment to provide solutions to help consumers adapt to this changing world."

Combining animation with live action was not new technologically (after all, Dick Van Dyke had danced with animated penguins in Walt Disney's 1964 movie *Mary Poppins*), but it was new strategically to MetLife. The combination of live-action with animation derived its marketing strength from its power to suggest metaphorical connections: Snoopy, personifying MetLife, helped real people overcome huge obstacles, such as jungles and cliffs, which symbolized the real financial dilemmas that policyholders found themselves confronting. Young & Rubicam's chairman and CEO, Peter Georgescu, maintained that the new approach of this campaign held more relevance for consumers; MetLife president and chief operating officer Ted Athanassiades echoed this sentiment, adding that MetLife was "re-energized and refocused to be an institution which manages relationships with consumers."

The first two commercials, scripted by Young & Rubicam and directed by Eric Saarinen from Plum Productions of Santa Monica, California, debuted in September 1995 during prime-time shows such as the *CBS Tuesday Night Movie,* ABC's *Dateline,* and NBC's *Wings.* In the first spot, "Tiger," Snoopy rescued a man from a financial jungle by taming a real-life tiger; at the end of the commercial a voice-over announced, "What you need is MetLife... to help you make sense of it all." In "Rock Climber" Snoopy scaled a cliff to save a climber who realized in her predicament that she needed help to overcome her financial challenges; concluding this commercial, the voice-over announced that MetLife "helps you to get a grip on things and helps you make sense of it all." Both 30-second commercials, which together cost $1.5 million to produce, fused live action with animation, metaphorically suggesting that MetLife (represented by Snoopy) confronted real-life situations with real-life solutions.

After these two introductory spots Young & Rubicam followed up periodically with commercials based on similar themes and also featuring live action with animation. In mid-1996 Snoopy's ears transformed into helicopter blades as he swooped down to save canoeists from tumbling over a waterfall in "River." In "Wedding," which debuted in early 1997, Snoopy danced with a real bride at her wedding, which had been financed by her parents' mutual-funds investments with MetLife. In "Floating Man," also run in early 1997, Snoopy the lifeguard saved a retired man whose raft had deflated, suggesting that MetLife could help retirees guard against the air being let out of their retirement benefits. In early 1998 "Jargon" found Snoopy sitting in front of a television, mesmerized by a show on retirement planning and befuddled by the terminology it used; in contrast, the commercial assured viewers that MetLife explained finances in understandable language. These TV spots, along with the MetLife Online website, advertised the diversity of MetLife financial services and made the company seem accessible and helpful.

OUTCOME

By 1997 MetLife had reversed its downward sales trend of the mid-1990s. In March 1998 MetLife announced record earnings for the 1997 fiscal year. Consolidated pre-tax earnings from operations totaled $1.7 billion, representing a 21 percent increase over 1996. Consolidated net income (after paying taxes and $1.7 billion in dividends to policyholders) amounted to $1.2 billion, up 41 percent from 1996. Both of these results broke company records. Additionally, MetLife increased the amount of assets it managed along with its affiliates, from $298 billion in 1996 to over $330 billion in 1997. Young & Rubicam's proprietary research showed that consumer awareness of MetLife advertising increased with the new campaign. All of these numbers painted a picture of a healthy financial-services company that had regained consumer confidence.

MetLife continued to evolve in the late 1990s, increasingly seeking to emphasize the full range of its financial services as it announced plans to make an initial public offering, a move that would change its status from that of a mutual insurance company to that of a stock company. MetLife's use of the Peanuts characters in its marketing evolved in concert with these institutional changes but also because the company had to guard against the risks inherent in its close association with a cartoon franchise that, no matter how effective it had been in establishing a unique brand identity, was beginning to show its age at the close of the twentieth century. Snoopy ceased playing a starring role in MetLife's advertising in 1999, appearing instead as a brand icon at the end of TV spots and in other company communications. MetLife went public in April 2000. Its subsequent marketing efforts were characterized by the ongoing attempt to craft an updated identity without sacrificing the brand equity it had accumulated through its long association with the Peanuts characters.

FURTHER READING

Champagne, Christine. "Sights Now Seen: Through Confidence and a Personal Touch, Sight Effects Keeps Pace with the Big Boys." *Shoot,* May 3, 1996.

Katz, Frances. "It's a Big World, Charlie Brown; All's Well Now, but MetLife Found Net Life Can Be as Messy as Pigpen." *Direct,* April 1, 1996.

"MetLife Reinvents Its Identity with Launch of Ad Campaign." *Best's Review,* June 2001.

"More than 'Peanuts' at Stake with MetLife Branding." *Bank Advertising News,* March 6, 2000.

Panko, Ron. "Fallout from the Market Conduct Bomb Penetrates Life Industry (Allegedly Deceptive Sales Practices)." *Best's Review,* Life-Health Insurance Edition, December 1, 1996.

Updegrave, Walter L. "Life Insurance Mess: Don't Be Suckered into the Life Insurance Mess; the Embarrassing Scandals Involving Major Life Insurers Illustrate that the Industry Badly Needs Reform. Here's How to Protect Yourself." *Money,* January 1, 1995.

William D. Baue
Mark Lane

Microsoft Corp.

1 Microsoft Way
Redmond, Washington 98052-6399
USA
Telephone: (425) 882-8080
Fax: (425) 936-7329
Web site: www.microsoft.com

IT'S GOOD TO PLAY TOGETHER CAMPAIGN

OVERVIEW

Xbox, a video-game unit of the Microsoft Corp., was introduced in 2001, and within two years it had established its brand as a high-end video-game manufacturer. After passing Nintendo Company, Ltd., in 2003 to become the second-largest video-game manufacturer in the world, Xbox set its sights on outstripping PlayStation 2, the number one video-game manufacturer. Sony Corp. was the developer of PlayStation 2, which consisted of both the game-processing hardware referred to as the "console" and video-game software. In order to overtake PlayStation 2's 54 percent share of a $10.4 billion industry, Xbox released a campaign titled "It's Good to Play Together" that touted the "sociability" benefits of its new online gaming service, Xbox Live.

The estimated $100 million campaign, developed by advertising agency McCann-Erickson, involved print, television, radio, and Internet elements. Print ads first appeared on August 4, 2003, and television spots began airing on August 25. Initially the campaign advertised Xbox's "NFL Fever 2004," a football video game that allowed gamers to play anyone in the world by connecting their television to the Xbox console, which was connected to Xbox Live's Internet service. The first print ads appeared in gaming and lifestyle publications and featured the tagline "Nothing unites a group of strangers like pure contempt for the guy in first place." The campaign continued with a series of commercials featuring rapper Sean "Puffy" Combs, promotional events on Viacom Inc.'s Music Television, and high-stakes competitions that took place on Xbox Live.

Not only did the campaign win a Gold EFFIE Award in the Entertainment category, but it helped Xbox to increase its market share 10 percent by 2005. The campaign continued to emphasize that with Xbox Live gamers could challenge remote friends and family who subscribed to the service. "Xbox games have always had the ability to draw people in due to their looks, but increasingly it's the social elements our gamers crave, and we're giving in to them," Peter Moore, the corporate vice president for retail sales and marketing at Xbox, stated in *Media and Marketing Europe.*

HISTORICAL CONTEXT

When Xbox entered the video-game market in November 2001, gamers held misconceptions, based on the Microsoft association, about the performance of its processing hardware, commonly referred to as the console. "They (jokingly) wanted to know how long Xbox took to boot and where the control-alt-delete keys were," Robbie Bach, a chief officer for Xbox, told the *Financial Times.* Xbox hired McCann-Erickson to develop a campaign that positioned Xbox as a serious, powerful gaming

Microsoft Xbox chief XNA architect J. Allard. © FRED PROUSER/REUTERS/CORBIS.

brand. In 2002, with a marketing launch budget of $500 million—more than the remaining industry's combined budget—Xbox released its "Life Is Short, Play More" campaign, which increased the brand's market share from 0 percent to 27 percent by 2003. One television spot, which was eventually banned in the United Kingdom, began with a woman giving birth. Like a cannonball, her baby soared from the birth canal and burst through the hospital's window. Flying through the air, the newborn began aging rapidly while circling the globe at what appeared to be supersonic speeds. At the commercial's end the newborn had aged into an old man and crashed into a grave. The spot ended with the tagline "Life is short, play more."

By 2003 Xbox had shifted its efforts from increasing brand credibility to heralding the online feature, Xbox Live, as the next generation of video game. Xbox gamers could now play with or against anyone who also subscribed to the service. "Before, our theme was more focused on power and the unique capabilities of the Xbox technology," Don Hall, director of Xbox brand strategy and Xbox.com, told the *Seattle Post-Intelligencer.* "As we go to reach a broader audience, we're shifting our focus more to the consumer benefits, the experiences of playing Xbox with your friends and family." Xbox created games that were not only for multiple players but also compatible with Xbox Live. "We're actually consciously evolving our brand on the idea of gaming as a social experience—people playing together whether it's through Live, or sitting next to each other on the couch. And it also turns out to be a much broader concept," Bach explained to the *Financial Times.*

TARGET MARKET

"It's Good to Play Together" targeted males between the ages of 14 and 34 who enjoyed social gaming. Not only did print ads and television spots exhibit Xbox's state-of-the-art graphics, but to also attract the social gamer, they explained features such as music sharing, photo storage, buddy lists, and live chats. Print ads ran in magazines with strong male readerships, such as *FHM, Playboy,* and *Maxim.* The campaign also advertised Xbox's family-oriented products, such as Music Mixer, software that turned the Xbox console and the gamer's television into a karaoke machine. One microphone was included in every Music Mixer package.

After realizing that a high percentage of consumers who subscribed to movie channels were also likely to purchase video games, Xbox and the movie-oriented Showtime Networks partnered for a 2005 marketing tie-in. Every new Showtime subscriber received free Xbox games and an Xbox Live starter kit. By 2005 more than half of U.S. households reportedly had some type of video-game console. Analysts noted that many of the consumers who had already bought PlayStation 2 were also purchasing Xbox.

COMPETITION

In 2003 Sony's PlayStation 2 dominated more than 50 percent of the video-game market. With a yearly advertising budget of $250 million, Sony released television spots for PlayStation and promotional events with the tagline "Fun, anyone?" Original television commercials featured sample footage from PlayStation 2 games that were edited to resemble movie trailers. Eventually Sony's ad agency switched to using animated commercials to differentiate the brand from Xbox, which had begun airing similar commercials. PlayStation 2 also sponsored weekend activities, titled "PlayStation Freedom," which

XBOX LIVE

First released in November 2002, Xbox Live was a service created for the video-game console Xbox and allowed gamers to challenge each other from remote locations over the Internet. When Xbox released "Tom Clancy's Rainbow Six 3," new records were set for Xbox Live. In a single 24-hour period gamers spent more than 250,000 hours playing the game. That was equivalent to one person playing the game incessantly for 30 years.

included musical performances from bands such as Kasabian, Jamiroquai, and Babyshambles. In London Sony allowed 40,000 gamers to sample upcoming PlayStation 2 games at a four-day event called "PlayStation Experience." After the Xbox Live service grew increasingly popular, PlayStation 2 released its own online service and began focusing on gaming sociability.

While PlayStation 2 and Xbox targeted the 14- to 34-year-old market, the world's third-largest console manufacturer, Nintendo, released games for younger gamers. Many games created for Nintendo's console, GameCube, were priced lower than PlayStation 2 or Xbox games and delivered content more suitable for the 8- to 12-year-old demographic. Industry insider Alex Seropian told *Xbox Nation,* "Nintendo has such a different character than Microsoft or Sony. They seem to be much more of a gaming company—or even a toy company—than an electronics manufacturer or a giant software house."

MARKETING STRATEGY

With print debuting on August 4, 2003, and television spots appearing on August 26, "It's Good to Play Together" first advertised Xbox's "NFL Fever 2004" football game. Print ads featured the tagline "Nothing unites a group of strangers like pure contempt for the guy in first place." Multiple gamers in remote lactations could play the same football game. Later that year television, print, and radio advertisements announced the Xbox warfare game "Tom Clancy's Rainbow Six 3." One 30-second commercial began with a man sitting in a darkened living room. Next, video-game scenes played while someone said, "I thought we were ready. The chopper came in hard and safe. The target was in our sights." When a woman turned on a light, the man from the spot's beginning was revealed to be playing Xbox Live and crying before his television. A final voice-over stated, "Rainbow Six 3: their lives in your hands. It's good to play together." The TV commercial was written and art-directed by Gary Marjoram and Rob Brown. It was directed by Christophe Williams of the production company Igloo Films. Print ads appeared in gaming magazines and in men's lifestyle magazines such as *FHM* and *Maxim.*

The rapper and music producer Sean "Puffy" Combs, also known as "P. Diddy," was paid more than $50 million to endorse Xbox games such as "NFL Fever 2004" and "Grabbed by the Ghoulies." Spots featured footage from the games, separated by scenes of gamers playing. All spots included voice-overs from Combs, such as "It's good to make the entire league beg for mercy together." Some industry experts considered it a bold move to use a music celebrity to endorse sports games. Referring to Xbox's contract with Combs, Eli Friedman, the group marketing and communications manager at Xbox, told *Advertising Age,* "We look at his voice as the right voice for Xbox." All spots ended with the campaign's tagline, "It's good to play together."

Xbox orchestrated other nationwide promotional events. More than 50 "A" icons were hidden inside the game "Advent Rising." Gamers who found the hidden icons were eligible for hundreds of prizes, including one grand prize of $1 million. In 2005 Electronics Boutique Holdings Corp., a video-game retailer, allowed more than 25 of its kiosks in retail locations to feature games with Xbox Live. New subscribers to the movie channel Showtime were also given free Xbox games and Xbox Live starter kits. Other promotional events were spearheaded by MTV, which released a half-hour program titled "MTV Presents: The Next Generation Xbox Revealed." During the program the actor Elijah Wood from the *Lord of the Rings* trilogy explored new Xbox games on-camera while rock band the Killers performed. In its monthly technology feature *Playboy* magazine displayed the Xbox RX2 Media Chair, designed with built-in surround-sound speakers.

OUTCOME

Despite some analysts criticizing McCann-Erickson for a lackluster campaign with an uninspired title, the campaign earned a Gold EFFIE Award in the Entertainment category in 2005. More importantly, however, the campaign helped Xbox's market share continually grow between September 2003 and January 2005. By 2005 Xbox had increased its market share by 11 points, more than any other console manufacturer. Cameron Ferroni, general manager of Xbox Live, explained in a 2004 issue of *Xbox Nation,* "With 20-plus million consoles sold and more than 1.5 million Xbox Live members targeted by the end of this fiscal year, Xbox is clearly resonating on a cultural level."

Besides the brand's success with console sales, three of its video games, "Halo 2," "Need for Speed: Underground 2," and "Star Wars: Knights of the Old Republic 2," were among the 10 best-selling video games of 2004. Microsoft was confident that the campaign had positioned Xbox at the forefront of online gaming, which analysts believed was the future of video gaming.

FURTHER READING

Bishop, Todd. "New Ad Aims to Draw More into Xbox Play." *Seattle Post-Intelligencer,* August 11, 2003, p. C3.

Chandiramani, Ravi. "Brand Health Check—Nintendo." *Marketing,* April 17, 2003, p. 15.

———. "Xbox Develops 40m 'Sociable' Ad Strategy." *Marketing,* September 18, 2003, p. 1.

Clifford, Lee. "This Game's Not Over Yet: Xbox vs. PlayStation." *Fortune,* July 9, 2001, p. 164.

Cuneo, Alice Z. "Microsoft Plots Global Xbox Push; Drafts AKQA as Online Agency." *Advertising Age,* August 11, 2003, p. 3.

———. "Microsoft Taps 'Puffy' for Xbox." *Advertising Age,* October 20, 2003, p. 4.

Doan, Viet. "Gamers Doing Double Takes." *Houston Chronicle,* November 20, 2004, p. 3.

Gaudiosi, John. "Nintendo Nuts about Squirrel." *Video Business,* January 29, 2001, p. 35.

Hein, Kenneth. "Let the Games Begin." *Brandweek,* July 30, 2001, p. 1.

Kent, Steven L. "Nintendo May Top PlayStation 2, Xbox GameCube Fires Up Analysts." *Seattle Times,* April 11, 2001, p. C1.

Lau, Alex. "Hype Builds for Nintendo's New Game Boy." *San Francisco Chronicle,* March 22, 2001, p. 53.

Nuttall, Chris. "Marketing—The New Social Service." *Financial Times* (London), November 18, 2003, p. 6.

Rumsey, Angela. "Xbox Targets Sociability." *Media and Marketing Europe,* October 31, 2003, p. 5.

Tran, Khanh T.L. "As Microsoft's Xbox Debut Nears, Fan Sites Get Cocky, Rivals Wary." *Wall Street Journal,* April 12, 2001, p. B1.

Zito, Kelly. "Clash of the Consoles." *San Francisco Chronicle,* May 17, 2001, p. B.1.

Kevin Teague

WHERE DO YOU WANT TO GO TODAY? CAMPAIGN

OVERVIEW

Microsoft Corporation, the world's largest software company, signaled a new direction for its massive branding campaign "Where Do You Want to Go Today?" in the fall of 1998, when it launched the first of three series of ads designed to burnish the company's image. Although Microsoft had used been using "Where Do You Want to Go Today?" since 1994, the company wanted to ensure that it was perceived as approachable and inspirational. Some of Microsoft's previous advertising efforts had been criticized for being cold. More significantly, an ongoing antitrust investigation by the United States Justice Department had the potential to brand Microsoft as a high-tech thug—a bloodthirsty corporation using its tremendous size to squeeze its competitors out of existence. With these new ad packages, which all explored Microsoft's role in building and strengthening various types of communities, the company sought to demonstrate its kinder and gentler side. "We want to make sure that we're communicating our values, and the benefits of our products to consumers," a Microsoft spokesperson told the *Seattle Post-Intelligencer.*

The three sets of ads all depicted how Microsoft technology enhanced the lives, work, dreams, and futures of everyday Americans. The first series of six television spots debuted on September 6, 1998, and focused on Microsoft employees talking candidly about their work at the company. These ads portrayed the gigantic corporation as a community committed to making software for both the present and the future. The initial commercial, called "Inside Microsoft Anthem," was a montage of diverse Microsoft employees, while the five subsequent ads featured one employee in each spot. The commercials connected to Microsoft's "Where Do Want to Go Today?" slogan by having each of the spotlighted Microsoft workers answer that question. "Why is our company's tag line a question?" queried the voice-over. "Well you can't make a software better till you know what people want to do with it."

In December 1998 Microsoft next rolled out a sequence of five ads set in remote Lusk, Wyoming, where—as one spot noted—"cows outnumber people 100 to 1." This speck of a town had thoroughly wired itself for future high-speed Internet connections in a fashion disproportionate to its diminutive size. Microsoft's ads included such vignettes as that of 13-year-old Dan Hanson using the Internet to research a school paper on dung beetles, and Margy Brown relying on Microsoft software to manage her beeswax hand-cream business efficiently. Again, Microsoft presented itself not as the predatory purveyor of bug-laden software but as a force for fostering communities—for helping outposts like dusty Lusk survive and indeed thrive.

A third group of community-oriented ads, which used the Maxwell Middle School in Tucson, Arizona, as a backdrop, was inaugurated in March 1999. Two commercials related how devoted teachers at the school used Microsoft products to draw their students more fully into the lessons, while a third portrayed a Mexican American boy who learned about Mexican history on the Internet. "Technology is giving Jose a way to study his heroes, and maybe someday he can be one himself," intoned the voice-over provided by actor Jeff Daniels. "We are creating tools that help people do amazing things," Eric Koivisto, Microsoft's director of advertising, told the March 8, 1999, *Advertising Age,* as he explained the impetus behind these new "Community" facets of the broader "Where Do You Want to Go Today?" branding campaign.

Microsoft ran these "Community" ads in heavy rotation on network and cable television. Each contained the "Where Do You Want to Go Today?" tag line. Like

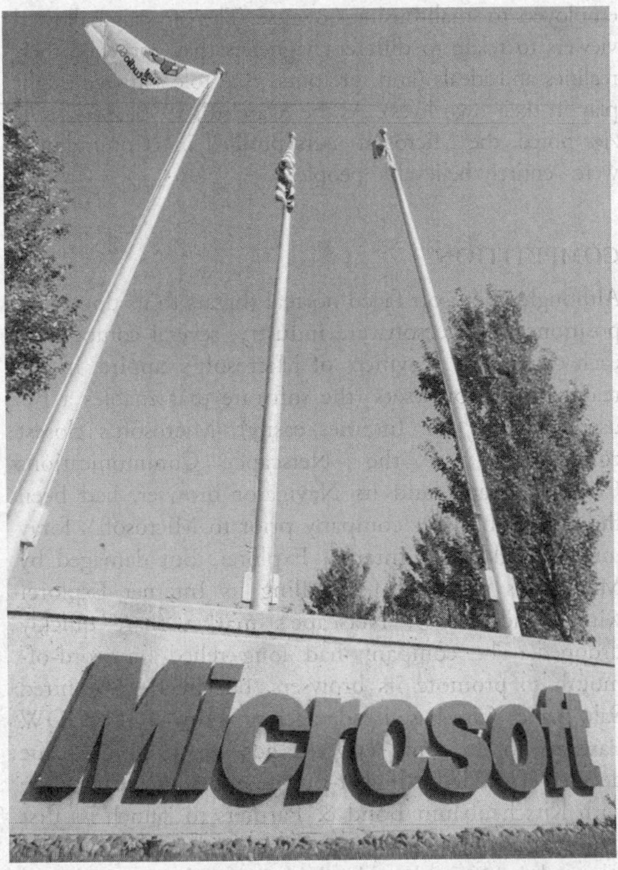

Entrance to Microsoft Corporation, in Redmond, Washington. AP IMAGES.

most of its branding efforts at the time, these spots were conceived by Wieden+Kennedy, the Portland-based firm that had inaugurated Microsoft's questioning slogan. Although Microsoft professed complete satisfaction with this latest branding installment, in 1999 the company severed its ties with Wieden+Kennedy and instead hired McCann-Erickson (which owned Anderson & Lembke, which, in conjunction with Wieden+Kennedy, had created past ads for Microsoft). The company expressed its desire to better integrate its product and branding campaigns.

HISTORICAL CONTEXT

Founded in 1975, Microsoft came to control the global software market. In 1998 the company's annual sales had reached $14.5 billion, and 9 out of 10 personal computers ran on its Windows operating system. (Operating systems are the software that controls all the computer's functions.) Microsoft's founder, Bill Gates, had achieved iconic status, both as one of the world's richest men and as a maverick techie who had eschewed conventional business models and flourished. Beginning in 1994, Microsoft used "Where Do You Want to Go Today?" as a way to "make consumers comfortable with the personal computer and its plethora of applications," according to the *Wall Street Journal* on November 11, 1994. The first commercial of the campaign, which stylishly melded an array of scenes, proposed that Microsoft's products "make you powerful," as the voice-over put it. The *Wall Street Journal* noted in its June 27, 1994, edition, "Where Do You Want to Go Today?" was designed to "reinforce the Microsoft brand," while specific product ads (which appeared on television, in mainstream and computer trade magazines, in newspapers, and on the Internet) touted individual technologies. For example, Microsoft's much anticipated release of a new version of Windows—Windows 95—was supported by a high-profile Wieden+Kennedy campaign that used the Rolling Stones's song "Start Me Up." After an initial blizzard of advertising, the branding campaign began to impress itself into consumers' minds. Microsoft then decided to scale back the intensity of the effort and devoted more of its 1997 marketing budget to its Internet and print ads than to its flashier television spots.

The Justice Department's ongoing investigation of Microsoft's business practices, and particularly its decision to file suit against the software titan in 1998, made it imperative for Microsoft to refocus attention on managing its brand image. The antitrust trial, which began in November 1998, had the potential to damage Microsoft's reputation and therefore hurt its sales. The suit centered around Microsoft's policy of "bundling" its Internet browser, called Internet Explorer, into its Windows 95 operating system. The government alleged that Microsoft improperly required computer makers to ship Internet Explorer on personal computers loaded with Windows 95. Compaq Computer testified that Microsoft had threatened to cancel its Windows 95 license if Compaq sold computers with the operating system, but not the Internet browser. Since Microsoft had a virtual stranglehold on the operating systems market, critics claimed that the company's policies regarding Internet Explorer were intended to eradicate rival Internet browsers and effectively give Microsoft a monopoly in that sector. "This isn't about the browser. It's about trying to monopolize electronic commerce," said Ken Wasch, president of the Software Publisher Association. Although the filing of the suit had no discernable impact on consumers' attitudes toward the company—surveys taken at the time the company launched its "Community" ads indicated that consumers perceived neither Microsoft nor Bill Gates differently than before the lawsuit—Microsoft wanted to ensure that "regardless of what happen[ed] in the courts of law, the company

NOT SO WIRED

Perhaps the ultimate irony of the Lusk, Wyoming, spots was that the town's vaunted high-speed fiber-optic and coaxial cable networks remained unnetworked. Instead, the lines ended 100 feet from town, unconnected to any other source. A funding shortage and the election of a less technology-friendly mayor had caused the project to be suspended. Many of Lusk's residents hooked up to the Internet anyway, although through slower phone lines. But Microsoft's ads were not lying about Lusk. The commercials were carefully worded to express that the town wired itself "for the future of the Internet," omitting the fact that it was not presently wired. Nevertheless, after the ads ran, Lusk was bombarded with telephone calls and E-mails from urban dwellers longing to move to a small town and still stay connected.

[would] not be hurt in the court of public opinion," the *Seattle Post-Intelligencer* observed.

TARGET MARKET

With its "Community" ads, Microsoft attempted to reach a broad consumer audience. While computers and software had been pitched almost solely to technology-savvy users in the early 1990s, the market for personal computers was expanding every year. By 1994 one-third of all American households owned a PC. "Software buyers have evolved from a small community of technical decision makers to everyone," Microsoft's director of corporate marketing told the *Wall Street Journal* on November 11, 1994. "We want to encourage people to become more involved with the technology."

By casting its net so widely, Microsoft had to devise advertising that could connect with consumers of all sorts across the demographic divides. To appeal to as wide a group as possible, Microsoft presented computer users of different races, ethnicities, and lifestyles. The Microsoft employees showcased in the first installment of the "Community" ads were a friendly collection of Asian Americans, African Americans, men, and women. The Lusk, Wyoming, spots portrayed a small farming town where traditional values and hard work were still the norm. The Maxwell Middle School commercials featured a Mexican American boy connecting with his heritage. The occupations of "Community" characters ranged from an agricultural worker to a student to corporate employees to small-business owners. The campaign allowed viewers to relate to different vignettes that portrayed their realities and ideals (and, of course, the role software might play in their own lives). As the March 8, 1998, *Advertising Age* noted, the Microsoft users profiled in "Community" were "entirely believable people."

COMPETITION

Although Microsoft faced no real threats to its dominant position atop the software industry, several competitors each challenged provinces of Microsoft's empire. In the realm of web browsers (the software that enables a PC user to access the Internet easily), Microsoft's closest competitor was the Netscape Communications Corp. Netscape, and its Navigator browser, had been the leading browser company prior to Microsoft's foray into the field with Internet Explorer. But damaged by Microsoft's practice of bundling its Internet Explorer with Windows 95, Netscape's market share quickly dropped. The company had long relied on word-of-mouth to promote its browsers, but in 1997 it hired Salt Lake City-based ad agency Euro RSCG DW Partners to do some targeted ads. In 1998 Netscape decided it needed a higher-profile effort and teamed up with Kirschenbaum Bond & Partners to launch its first major consumer campaign. "We need to get people where they are, and to do that, we need to use a broad mix of media," Netscape's marketing director, Judy Logan, told *Advertising Age* on June 1, 1998. In its bid to survive Microsoft's advances in the web browser market, Netscape opted to start giving away its browser for free and to generate revenue from web-based advertising rather than product sales. With the print component of its new campaign, which consisted of eight separate pieces running in business and computer magazines, Netscape particularly wanted to reach business users.

Apple Computer, Inc. and International Business Machines Inc. (IBM) provided the most visible competition in terms of rival operating systems. Apple's Mac OS operating platform, although far behind Windows in its number of users, had a committed core of adherents. In 1997 Apple broke an image campaign called "Think Different," which was designed to reinforce Apple's reputation as a creative alternative to the scores of PC clones. This print and television campaign, which ran through 1999 (in conjunction with product ads), used striking black-and-white photos of revolutionary thinkers, leaders, and artists, to demonstrate that Apple was no mere computer company. "Think Different" proposed that Apple created the tools that enabled geniuses and rebels to work. IBM's OS/2 Warp operating system also received ad support in IBM's massive "Solutions for a Small Planet" branding campaign, conceived by Ogilvy & Mather.

Midas, Inc.

1300 Arlington Heights Road
Itasca, Illinois 60143
USA
Telephone: (630) 438-3000
Fax: (630) 438-3880
Web site: www.midas.com

TRUST THE MIDAS TOUCH CAMPAIGN

OVERVIEW

In January 2003 a new chief executive officer, Alan Feldman, took over Midas, Inc. Though possessing a well-respected brand, the company was in disarray. For years Midas had focused on muffler manufacturing and used its franchised shops as a way to move inventory. But with the introduction of longer-lasting mufflers in the 1990s, Midas's old business model showed cracks. In addition to recasting Midas as a pure franchisor, Feldman wanted to move the company farther away from its muffler heritage to make Midas muffler shops into general car-maintenance centers. But just as better mufflers had hurt specialty shops, improved quality in cars in general during the 1990s hurt everyone in the auto-repair industry, making the field extremely competitive. Midas, however, had one significant advantage in the marketplace: its well-recognized brand. Feldman awarded the $40 million-plus Midas advertising account to the Chicago office of DDB Worldwide Communications Group Inc. to help in rebranding Midas as a general car-care center that consumers could trust. Midas brought back a slogan first developed in the early 1980s, "Trust the Midas Touch," to anchor the new marketing campaign.

Relying on humor to convey their message, the campaign's television spots, in both English and Spanish, featured the honesty of Midas technicians being questioned by customers, who were assured that Midas personnel were both knowledgeable and trustworthy. The first wave of commercials helped to establish Midas's brake business, while the second promoted the chain's other services.

The "Trust the Midas Touch" campaign played a key role in Feldman's success in turning Midas around. Franchisees were pleased with the increase in business, as was Wall Street, which bid up the price of Midas stock.

HISTORICAL CONTEXT

Midas grew out of a muffler-manufacturing company founded in Chicago in 1938 by Nate Sherman. Believing he could make more money by selling mufflers directly to the public in repair shops, he formed Midas in 1956. He soon began franchising his muffler-shop concept, and within the first year the chain had 100 stores in 40 states. By the late 1980s the number of units totaled about 2,000, and Midas had manufactured more than 100 million mufflers. Much of the growth during this period was due to a successful marketing campaign that relied on the slogan "Trust the Midas Touch," introduced in the early 1980s. The chain enjoyed tremendous brand recognition and was the undisputed leader in the muffler-repair field. In addition Midas had branched out beyond mufflers, adding to the mix shock absorbers in

1960, brakes in 1979, and alignment in 1988. Changes in the 1990s, however, jeopardized the future of the company.

Midas had always enjoyed a steady business selling mufflers that could be expected to last about two years, resulting in regular visits from customers. But in the 1990s stainless-steel exhaust systems with a life span of 10 years or more were introduced, completely altering the muffler-repair business. Moreover automobiles were better built in the 1990s and in less need of repair, putting a crimp on Midas's other business segments. To offset declining sales Midas tried to increase the inventory flow of its franchisees by building a network of strategically located distribution centers in the late 1990s. But the cost to set up the network was great and the payoff meager. Midas also tried to expand what most of its shops had to offer, adding air-conditioning services, oil changes, and other basic maintenance and repair services. Along the way the company lost the Midas touch in terms of its marketing as well. In the mid-1990s it severed its ties with the Chicago office of Wells Rich Greene, which had held the advertising account for more than 25 years and was responsible for coining the slogan "Trust the Midas Touch." TV spots by the new agency, Euro RSCG McConnaughy Tatham, were uninspiring, prompting management to seek a more dynamic, attention-getting approach. Instead Midas reached its nadir in advertising in 2002 when it approved a television spot created by its new ad agency, Cliff Freeman & Partners. In it a Midas manager told an elderly female customer about the company's lifetime guarantee on shocks and struts. "Lifetime guarantee?" she replied. "That's great. What can you do with these?" With her back to the camera the customer then opened her shirt to the befuddled manager, who looked away and said, "There are limits to what we can do." After fielding a number of complaints from customers, the company pulled the offensive commercial. Unhappy with management on any number of fronts, the franchisees were ready to revolt.

On the brink of bankruptcy Midas in January 2003 brought in a new CEO, one well familiar with forging strong relationships with franchisees: Alan Feldman, former president and chief operating officer of McDonald's Americas. He quickly moved to exit the distribution business, which he outsourced to auto-parts retailer AutoZone, and began to convert Midas into a pure franchising operation. The plan was to retain only a handful of company-owned stores, where new prototypes and procedures could enjoy a dry run before being rolled out to the franchisees. Feldman also wasted little time in dumping Cliff Freeman and turning over the advertising to the Chicago office of DDB, with whom he had enjoyed a good working relationship during his days at McDonald's. The agency's task was nothing less than rebranding Midas, to play up the brake business rather than mufflers and to position Midas as more of a general repair shop than just a specialist.

> ## WHAT'S IN A NAME?
>
> "Midas" was an acronym for the Muffler Installation Dealers' Association, formed in 1956 by Chicago muffler manufacturer Nate Sherman to create a chain of franchised muffler shops. In that same year the first Midas franchise opened in Macon, Georgia.

TARGET MARKET

As Midas broadened its auto-maintenance offerings, it in turn expanded its target market. In 1993 the average age of a car in the United States was 6.5 years, but by 2003 that number had increased to 8.6 years, due to higher quality cars. With so many more cars on the road operating beyond their warranties, Midas eyed an increasing amount of potential business. In fact it was estimated that drivers neglected some $60 billion worth of car maintenance each year. Midas hoped to capture a significant share of that business and regular maintenance. Its greatest advantage in entering other areas of automobile repair was its brand, which enjoyed a 90 percent awareness. In addition an estimated 40 percent of Americans had visited a Midas shop in their lifetimes. Perhaps the greatest strength of the brand, aside from sheer recognition, was its association with the word "trust." Given that the automotive-repair industry had been long tied in the minds of consumers with dishonesty and the belief that drivers with little mechanical knowledge were taken advantage of, trust would be a key element in selling Midas. The target market consisted of average drivers, especially women, who did not maintain their own cars and who, after years of feeling cheated by disreputable mechanics, would prefer a national chain that staked its reputation on honesty. Another part of the Midas target market would be the Latino community, not because they were any more vulnerable to deceitful auto-repair shops than the average person but as a testament to their growing numbers in the United States.

COMPETITION

The aftermarket repair industry was huge, valued at about $110 billion. Midas, one of only a handful of national players, was well positioned in the marketplace.

A WOMAN'S TOUCH

The slogan "Trust the Midas Touch" was coined in the early 1980s by the ad agency Wells Rich Greene, which was founded in 1966 by advertising pioneer Mary Wells. After her boss at Jack Tinker & Partners offered to pay her as president of the firm but refused to give her the title, Wells quit and, joining forces with two colleagues, became president of her own firm, Wells Rich and Greene. The agency went on to create a number of memorable catchphrases in addition to "Trust the Midas Touch," including "At Ford, Quality Is Job 1," "I Can't Believe I Ate the Whole Thing," "Try It, You'll Like It," "Flick My Bic," "Raise Your Hand if You're Sure," "The Citi Never Sleeps," and "Friends Don't Let Friends Drive Drunk."

The closest comparable competitors were Meineke Discount Mufflers (which in January 2003 changed its name to Meineke Car Care Center), operating about 900 stores in Canada and the Americas, and Monro Muffler and Brake, with about 600 stores in the United States. Midas had 1,700 domestic units. But Midas also had to contend with local competition, the mom-and-pop repair shops, as well as a different set of national players. For example, there were auto-parts retailers, including Pep Boys nationally and Strauss Discount Auto in the Northeast, that were opening supercenter formats to offer auto-repair services in very much the same way that Sears had been doing for years.

Automobile dealers' service centers, a key profit center, were also adversely impacted by improved quality in vehicles. Most of their work had been related to warranty repairs, but as they diminished in the 1990s, dealers found themselves in a difficult spot. Diminished repair sales limited the amount of money dealers were able to invest in mechanic training and service facilities. Potentially this situation could lead to a downward spiral: poor service quality leading to poor reputation, resulting in an even further erosion of sales. General Motors responded by requiring all of its 7,400 dealerships to participate in the Mr. Goodwrench program, which was revamped in 2003. A well-financed marketing campaign was then launched to drum up nonwarranty repair work. Ford Motor Co.'s Quality Care service centers provided Midas with competition from this quarter as well.

MARKETING STRATEGY

Although Midas had long been associated with mufflers, DDB and the Midas marketers elected to use the chain's brake services (which accounted for 42 percent of sales) as a wedge to expand its business into other areas of auto repair. After winning the account in July 2003, DDB put together an interim campaign while it developed a more comprehensive approach to rebranding Midas. The television spots that ran in the fall of 2003 featured everyday people completing the sentence "I brake for..." The team agreed that in the first quarter of 2004 Midas would center its advertising on a promotional price point of $89.99 for brake work. DDB was tasked with both ensuring the success of this promotion and building the Midas brand through 15-second and 30-second TV spots (60 percent of which were of the shorter variety).

In January 2004 DDB made a creative presentation to Midas, first offering a brand-positioning statement out of which everything flowed: "Your neighborhood Midas owner is restoring trust to auto service by providing expertise, responsiveness, and the best value to every customer, every time." Storyboards for possible spots were then presented on three themes: "Popular Mechanics," "See You Down the Road," and the venerable "Trust the Midas Touch." After the meeting the themes were tested on focus groups, and after the first round of testing it was obvious that "Trust the Midas Touch," albeit long in the tooth, retained a great deal of power. According to a DDB memo reporting on the findings, "The other two themes did not play well to the test group."

In March 2004 the first commercial in the new "Trust the Midas Touch" campaign broke. (Auto-repair sales typically spiked around April in the Northeast and Midwest.) As with the other spots to follow, it emphasized brakes and portrayed Midas as trustworthy. In it a Midas repairman was hooked up to a polygraph machine and being questioned by a customer, who asked, "Will you sell me something I don't need?" "Do you do more brake jobs than anyone else?" and "Are your brake pads and shoes really guaranteed for as long as I own my car?" The first wave of these humorous spots ran for a month on prime-time and late-night television, including such sporting events as the NCAA basketball tournament.

Midas was pleased with the results of the initial thrust of the "Trust the Midas Touch" campaign. In March 2005 it launched a second phase, which continued to emphasize trust while building on the company's success with brakes to include other maintenance services. The monthlong advertising effort promoted the $29.95 "Midas Touch" maintenance package, which included an oil change, tire rotation, and a check of battery, tires, belts, hoses, fluid levels, coolant, and air filter, as well as a visual brake check. Once more taking a humorous tack, the commercials featured customers grilling mechanics with questions about the services Midas had to offer and about the chain's trustworthiness. In the spot titled "Polygraph Backrub," a mechanic was tricked into saying "yes" when asked if Midas did back rubs. The spot closed with the mechanic alternately working on a car and massaging the customer's back. In "Young Voyagers," a mechanic proved he was "one of us" to a group of Boy Scout–like Young Voyagers. In "Sworn In," Midas personnel, with hands placed on a thick parts manual, testified about the Midas lifetime guarantee of its brake work. The spots again played during the NCAA basketball tournament as well as other network and cable programming.

In addition this second phase of commercials included the first that Midas made for the Latino community. These spots aired on Univision, Telemundo, Galavision, and Telefutura. The "Trust the Midas Touch" promotion was also supported by point-of-purchase materials produced in both English and Spanish. At the same time, the Midas website (also available in Spanish) was beefed up and relaunched to support the campaign.

OUTCOME

The "Trust the Midas Touch" campaign was a key element in Feldman's effort to turn around the fortunes of Midas and shift its focus from distribution to growing the franchise system. Even as the company's commercials were selling trust to customers, Feldman and his management team were rebuilding trust with the franchisees. Due in large part to the marketing campaign, consumers responded positively to Midas shops selling tires and adding other maintenance services. The result was increasing business for franchisees and renewed confidence from Wall Street. When Feldman took over in January 2003, Midas stock was priced below $7, but during the summer of 2005 it approached $25. Although there remained more work to be done, Midas, supported by the strength of the "Trust the Midas Touch" campaign, was clearly on the right track.

FURTHER READING

Alcock, Joseph. "Midas Inc." *University of Oregon Investment Group Monitor,* January 7, 2004.

Baar, Aaron. "'Midas Touch' Reappears in DDB Campaign." *Adweek,* March 4, 2004.

Barboza, David. "Midas Is Looking for a New Agency." *New York Times,* July 14, 1995, p. D4.

Garfield, Bob. "Innocence Lost: Midas Sags to a Low with Geriatric Nudity Spot." *Advertising Age,* April 1, 2002, p. 57.

Halliday, Jean. "Midas Repositioning Shows It's More than Just a Muffler Shop." *Advertising Age,* May 15, 2000, p. 87.

Heist, Lauren. "Midas Gets Its Groove Back." *Arlington Heights (IL) Daily Herald,* July 24, 2005.

Jacobs, Daniel G. "Fine-Tuning the Midas Touch." *Smart Business Columbus,* October 1, 2004, p. 24.

Levere, Jane L. "Midas Picks DDB to Replace Freeman." *New York Times,* July 17, 2003, p. C7.

Murphy, H. Lee. "Mufflers Dragging, Midas Retools Shops." *Crain's Chicago Business,* May 30, 2005, p. 7.

———. "Refocused Midas Out to Fuel Profits." *Crain's Chicago Business,* May 31, 2004, p. 12.

Ed Dinger

Mike's Hard Lemonade Company

159 S. Jackson St., 4th Fl.
Seattle, Washington 98104
USA
Telephone: (206) 267-4400
Fax: (866) 350-4095
Web site: www.mikeshardlemonade.com

HARD DAY CAMPAIGN

OVERVIEW

Mike's Hard Lemonade Company, a Lakewood, Colorado–based subsidiary of Vancouver's the Mark Anthony Group Inc., in 1999 introduced Mike's Hard Lemonade, a sweet, malt-based alcoholic beverage vying for a place among an emerging group of products commonly called "malternatives." Malternatives, or ready-to-drink alcoholic beverages reminiscent of sodas and other sweet nonalcoholic drinks, were aimed at young people who wanted the experience and cachet of drinking alcohol but who did not care for the taste of beer, wine, or hard liquor. In an effort to establish a clear brand image in the face of increased competition, Mike's Hard Lemonade enlisted Cliff Freeman and Partners, a New York–based ad agency known for producing edgy, offbeat work, and in 2001 launched a campaign called "Hard Day."

The "Hard Day" campaign, whose two-year budget was estimated at $30 million, consisted of three television commercials in 2001 and three more in 2002. It established a distinctly beer-like, masculine product image while simultaneously sending up classic notions of masculinity as presented in beer commercials of an earlier era. The first year's spots featured blue-collar workers who, after being impaled by construction materials or losing limbs, cared more about their after-work Mike's Hard Lemonade than their injuries. In the second year the slapstick execution continued but was applied to horror-movie scenarios and was used to support an additional product, Mike's Hard Iced Tea.

Amid a flurry of new malternative products, Mike's Hard Lemonade positioned itself, thanks in large part to the "Hard Day" campaign, as one of the few brands in the category with a clear identity. As such, it outlasted the category's initial rush of increased competition and maintained its position as the number two malternative while other brands floundered.

HISTORICAL CONTEXT

In the late 1990s a new category of beer-like beverages hit the U.S. market. Called "malternatives" by their partisans and "alcopops" by detractors who believed that they appealed principally to underage drinkers, the beverages were malt-based (like beer and whiskey) but much sweeter than traditional alcoholic drinks. Among the first wave of these products was a lemonade-like drink called Hooper's Hooch, popular in Australia, which arrived in America in 1996. Several competing citrus-flavored brands appeared in quick succession, among them Mike's Hard Lemonade, which was launched in 1999.

As more and more companies entered the malternatives arena, widespread industry speculation began about the future of the category. Many predicted that the new wave of products would go the way of wine coolers, which, in the 1980s, similarly relied on sweetness to appeal to drinkers who did not like the taste of traditional alcoholic beverages. After generating big-budget advertising campaigns and scores of new brands, the wine-cooler category faded dramatically in the latter part of that decade. Another noteworthy beer-like alternative, the Adolph Coors Co.'s Zima, had seen sporadic market success since its 1993 launch but had in general failed to live up to expectations, despite significant marketing and promotion efforts.

TARGET MARKET

Mike's Hard Lemonade, like other malternatives, projected a beer-like image to appeal to twentysomething young adults, especially newly legal drinkers who did not have a taste for beer or other alcoholic beverages. The sweetness of the product's flavor promised a natural transition for young people used to drinking soda, and Mike's strove to create a bold, exciting sensibility in its marketing. The spots in the first year of the "Hard Day" campaign each focused on masculine toughness, thereby distancing the drink from potential charges that it might be insufficiently manly—an image problem that had haunted malternative predecessor Zima—while simultaneously sending up that very idea to appeal to irony-savvy young people. Whereas a previous generation's beer commercials had sincerely extolled hard work and endurance and had positioned particular beer brands as a man's natural reward at the end of a long day, "Hard Day" offered scenarios in which workingmen were severely maimed on the job but still looked forward, absurdly, to their end-of-day Mike's Hard Lemonade.

Critics contended that both the sweet taste and the bold image of drinks like Mike's Hard Lemonade were evidence that the true target market for the malternative category was 14- to 18-year-olds. As George Hacker of the Center for Science in the Public Interest told the *New York Times,* "these products are designed to disguise the taste of alcohol and are jazzed up to more resemble nonalcoholic beverages... Forty-year-olds don't drink this, nor do they respond to the advertising." Another advocacy group, the National Consumers League, in 2000 filed a complaint with the Federal Trade Commission (FTC) regarding Mike's Hard Lemonade, claiming that it was "the perfect introductory drink for teenagers raised on soda and other sweet beverages." The FTC took no action on the complaint.

OUTRAGEOUS?

Cliff Freeman and Partners, the advertising agency behind "Hard Day," was known for its edgy, outrageous ideas. In addition to its Mike's Hard Lemonade work, the agency had made waves in the industry for using cannon-fired gerbils in a spot for online superstore Outpost.com. Notable flops, too, were blamed on the agency's penchant for the extreme. For instance, a commercial for Midas Mufflers that used a topless elderly woman lost Freeman the Midas account. Despite its reputation, however, the agency's résumé included some of the most prominent mainstream American advertising in recent decades, including the Wendy's "Where's the Beef?" and the Little Caesars "Pizza Pizza" campaigns.

COMPETITION

After leading the malternative category in 2000, Mike's Hard Lemonade saw its competition increase dramatically in 2001, the year that "Hard Day" was launched. Its most noteworthy competitor, and the category leader for that year and subsequent years, was Diageo's Smirnoff Ice. With the rapid growth of the top-two malternatives, domestic beer giants began teaming with hard-alcohol brands to offer numerous new product entries, flooding the category in 2002. Industry estimates put malternative-related ad spending at $300–$450 million for that year.

In the first six months of 2001 Smirnoff Ice—which, despite its association with the Smirnoff Vodka brand, was malt-based, like Mike's Hard Lemonade—was the beneficiary of a national, $50 million ad campaign. Similar in tone to "Hard Day," the campaign was called "Smooth Move" and showed drinkers of the beverage going to outlandish extremes to secure their Smirnoff Ice. In one spot a young man was shown putting honey on his friend while on a wilderness fishing trip, so that the friend would be busy fending off bear attacks and therefore would be unable to drink any of the Smirnoff Ice they had brought. Not only did Smirnoff Ice benefit from its association with its hard-liquor namesake, but it was believed that advertising for the malternative lifted brand awareness and sales of Smirnoff Vodka. Smirnoff Ice sales reached $615 million in 2001; the brand sold almost twice as many cases as Mike's, its nearest competitor. Diageo anted up $100 million for a 2002 advertising campaign, and the company purchased and refurbished an old Pabst beer brewery to accommodate increased production of Smirnoff Ice.

America's leading domestic beer makers, Anheuser-Busch and Miller, were slow to enter the malternative category, presumably believing, along with many in the industry, that the beverage type represented a fad unworthy of the enormous expenditures associated with product launches. As the category grew, however, the brewing giants changed course dramatically, rushing to find branding partners and introduce liquor-associated malternatives. Anheuser-Busch and Bacardi introduced Bacardi Silver with an estimated $60 million ad campaign in 2002, using the tagline "Your night just got more interesting." Miller partnered with Skyy Vodka to promote Skyy Blue, earmarking more than $40 million for the product's marketing while preparing to unveil additional malternative lines Sauza Diablo, Stolichnaya Citrona, and Jack Daniel's Original Hard Cola. Coors, which had long had a malternative product in Zima, rebranded the ailing beverage with a 2002 campaign intended to appeal to young men and launched a fruit-flavored extension of the brand called Vibe.

MARKETING STRATEGY

"Hard Day" was launched in the spring of 2001 with three 30-second television spots and an estimated budget of $15 million. The 2002 installment of the campaign ran with an equal budget and number of spots. In keeping with the brand's attempt to connect to young males in particular, the commercials aired on such cable stations as Fox Sports Net, ESPN, and Comedy Central.

In 2001 the "Hard Day" spots took the form and principles of classic beer advertising to absurd extremes, showing workers getting horrifically maimed but shrugging off their injuries at the prospect of an after-work Mike's Hard Lemonade. In one spot a construction worker was shown falling 20 stories and being impaled on a steel bar. Noticing the bar protruding from the man's chest, his foreman suggested that the injury might warrant a trip to the doctor. "Or maybe," the injured man answered, "we should get a delicious Mike's Hard Lemonade instead." As the scene shifted to a barroom, a drinking buddy was shown casually using the steel bar, still implanted in the man's chest, as a bottle opener, while a voice-over proclaimed, "A hard day calls for a hard lemonade. Make it Mike's." In another spot the same concept was applied to a lumberjack who accidentally chopped off his lower leg with an axe. Noting sadly, "My wife just bought me them boots yesterday," he retired to a bar, where he and his coworkers jovially clinked bottles, one playfully using the amputated (and still booted) foot instead of a bottle, as the voice-over delivered the "Hard Day" tagline. The third commercial, meanwhile, featured an aquarium worker who lost a hand while offering a snack to a killer whale.

As *Adweek* 's Barbara Lippert noted, the extreme violence of the commercials was not offensive "because the spots are so aggressively and unabashedly dumb, fake and deadpan." In addition to the obvious appeal of slapstick humor, in parodying not only traditional beer advertising but the more widespread advertising tactic of suggesting that a product could cure what ailed the consumer, the commercials appealed to the young target audience's desire to be among an exclusive, knowing group who considered themselves superior to such outdated pitches. As Bob Garfield wrote in *Advertising Age,* "the blue-collar-reward storylines provide perfect cover for the real message—which is not 'Yo, Joe Sixpack, here's an alternative to beer,' but instead, 'Hey, look at us! We're funny and cool, and if you get our jokes, so are you!'"

The campaign's second season marked an extension of this brand of ironic humor with a similarly deadpan treatment of outrageous storylines as well as a continuation of the "Hard Day" tagline. Rather than continuing to parody classic beer ads, however, the three spots that appeared in 2002 focused on horror-movie scenarios. In one an affectionate couple was seen loading groceries into their car, when suddenly a pack of monkey-like aliens parachuted from the sky and abducted the wife. "Wow, that sucks," a bystander said to the husband. "Looks like you could use a refreshing Mike's Hard Lemonade." After a short pause the man turned to the bystander and said, "You're on!" In the standard closing bar scene one of the aliens was shown stealing the husband's Mike's Hard Lemonade.

The other two 2002 commercials were used to promote a new product, Mike's Hard Iced Tea. In one spot a female coworker approached a downcast man at his cubicle. "What's wrong?" she asked. "I think I've grown a second evil head," he answered. Coolly surveying the evil head protruding from his collar, the woman said, "Sorry. What if we go out to get a refreshing Mike's Hard Iced Tea. Would that help?" The evil head, while ogling the woman's breasts, added, "I didn't know Mike's made a hard iced tea." In the other Hard Iced Tea spot, a man getting an ultrasound found that the stomach pains he had been experiencing were caused by a nest of snakelike fetuses. Told that he did not have long to live, the man asked the doctor if he had time enough to go out and get a Mike's Hard Iced Tea, and the doctor answered that he did not know there was such a product. "You bet!" the patient answered.

OUTCOME

Mike's Hard Lemonade managed to establish and maintain its distinct brand image in a flooded market while spending, on "Hard Day," a fraction of the amount allotted to brands backed by bigger companies. Mike's sold 13 million cases in 2001 (up from its 1999 total of

1.1 million cases) and, with Smirnoff Ice, pushed the category's share of the overall beer market to 2.5 percent, a level of success that predecessors Zima and Hooper's Hooch never approached. In 2002 Mike's sold 11.5 million cases in the face of proliferating competition, establishing itself as one of the few malternative brands with staying power. As of 2005 Mike's and Smirnoff Ice remained the top-two malternative brands, together accounting for 74 percent of the category's sales. That year Mike's Hard Lemonade Company left its Denver-area home for Seattle, a move intended to increase the company's ability to attract creative talent while bringing it geographically closer to its Vancouver-based parent, the Mark Anthony Group. The company planned to expand its operations after completing the move.

FURTHER READING

Beirne, Mike. "Beer." *Adweek,* April 21, 2003.

———. "Beer." *Mediaweek,* April 22, 2002.

Beirne, Mike, and Kenneth Hein. "Care for Some Booze with Your Beer?" *Brandweek,* June 17, 2002.

Ebenkamp, Becky. "The Thing with Two Heads Is Thirsty." *Brandweek,* April 29, 2002.

Elliott, Stuart. "Slightly Sweet Malt Beverages Get Some Heavy Marketing, with Young Drinkers the Targets." *New York Times,* March 6, 2002.

Garfield, Bob. "Cheesy Approach Works for Mike's Hard Lemonade." *Advertising Age,* May 7, 2001.

Keane, Bob. "Malternative Maelstrom: Love 'Em or Hate 'Em, Operators Have Come to Accept that to Some Degree Flavored Malt Beverages Appear Here to Stay." *Cheers,* July/August 2003.

Khermouch, Gerry. "Grown-Up Drinks for Tender Taste Buds." *BusinessWeek,* March 5, 2001.

Lippert, Barbara. "Head Trip." *Adweek,* May 13, 2002.

———. "Lemon Sent." *Adweek,* May 7, 2001.

Melillo, Wendy. "Marketing of Sweet Alcoholic Beverages Under Fire." *Adweek,* May 7, 2001.

Price, Stephen. "Rocky & Mike's Hard Day." *Boards,* May 1, 2002.

Sampey, Kathleen. "Monsters Run Amok for Mike's." *Adweek,* April 29, 2002.

Svaldi, Aldo. "Mike's Hard Lemonade to Move from Colorado to Seattle." *Knight Ridder/Tribune Business News,* February 16, 2005.

Vranica, Suzanne, and Brian Steinberg. "Media & Marketing—The Advertising Report: After Some Recent Turmoil, He's Ready for a Comeback." *Wall Street Journal,* November 26, 2003.

Mark Lane

Miller Brewing Company

3939 W Highland Blvd.
Milwaukee, Wisconsin 53208-2688
USA
Telephone: (414) 931-2000
Fax: (414) 931-3735
Web site: www.millerbrewing.com

MILLER HIGH LIFE MAN CAMPAIGN

OVERVIEW

NOTE: Also see essay for SABMiller.

The Miller Brewing Company, a subsidiary of cigarette maker Philip Morris, was the second largest beer maker in the United States behind Anheuser-Busch. The Milwaukee-based company brewed about 44 million barrels of beer a year and controlled approximately 20 percent of U.S. sales. Popular Miller Brewing brands included Miller Genuine Draft, Miller High Life, and Icehouse, as well as Red Dog, Meister Brau, Milwaukee's Best, and the nonalcoholic brew Sharp's. Miller Brewing owned eight breweries in seven states, including California, Texas, and its home state of Wisconsin.

In 1998, in an effort to revive interest in its flagging High Life brand (once the company's flagship brew but now its third biggest selling brand behind Miller Lite and Miller Genuine Draft), Miller introduced High Life's first national ads in seven years. The ad campaign, "Miller High Life Man," was created by ad agency Weiden & Kennedy, based in Portland, Oregon, and launched on April 12 during professional basketball and baseball telecasts. The tongue-in-cheek commercials, aimed at young male beer drinkers, offered bombastic salutes to duct tape, donuts, diner food, and America's debt to the French for having invented mayonnaise. Miller Brewing Company spent an estimated $5-10 million on the campaign. The well-received television ads were reinforced by new packaging featuring sleek, tall bottles and incorporating the long-retired "Girl on the Moon" symbol and the brand's erstwhile catchphrase "The Champagne of Beers."

HISTORICAL CONTEXT

Brewed since the beginning of the twentieth century, Miller High Life was the foundation brand for the Milwaukee-based Miller Brewing Company, which emerged as the industry's principal challenger to Anheuser-Busch. Beginning in 1906 High Life was touted in ads as the "Champagne of Bottled Beer," in an attempt to appeal to more affluent and status-conscious consumers. By the time the Philip Morris Company acquired Miller in 1969, however, the tag line had contributed to a widespread perception of High Life as a rich man's brew. One typical print ad from then-agency Mathisson & Company of Milwaukee, featured a needlepoint rendition of the bottle with the tag line "Home Is Where the Miller Is."

The brewing giant's new owners immediately ordered a change in direction. The ad slogan was shortened to "Champagne of Beers," and the decision was made to position High Life as a working man's brew. McCann-Erickson, a New York-based agency, was enlisted to create new ads for the brand. Their campaign, using the tag line "Miller Time," helped quadruple sales

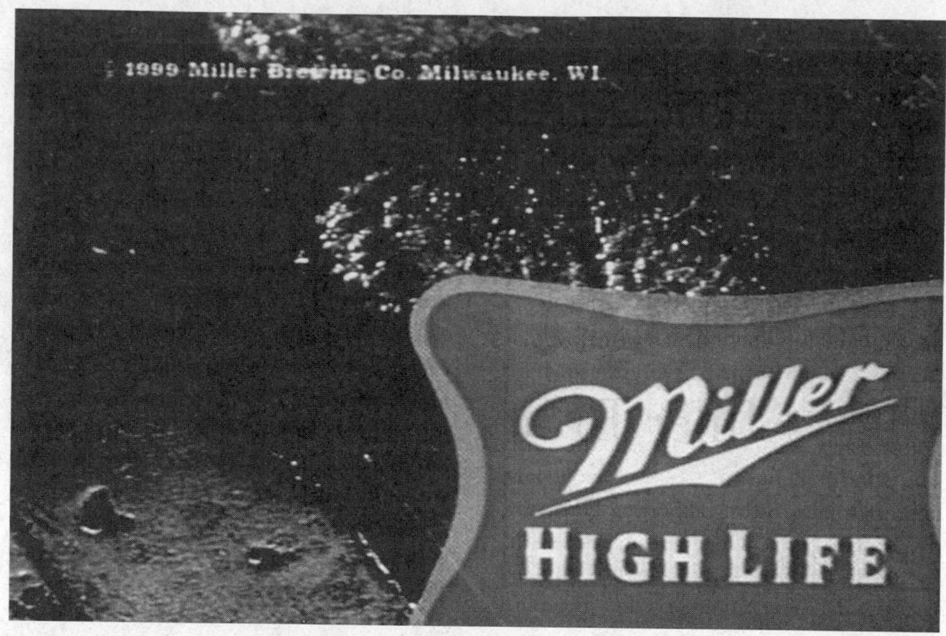

MILLER BREWING COMPANY. REPRODUCED BY PERMISSION.

of High Life between 1970 and 1978. At 21.7 million barrels annually, it ranked just behind Anheuser-Busch' s flagship brew, Budweiser.

In 1979 Miller shipped nearly 24 million barrels of Miller High Life to distributors. That proved to be the high water mark for the brand, however. A precipitous sales decline ensued, attributable to several factors. The rising popularity of imported beer, together with the emergence of the "light" category (a trail blazed by Miller itself with its revolutionary Miller Lite brand) helped erode sales of High Life during the 1980s. Budweiser found it could gain market share by imitating High Life's strategy of pitching the brand as the workers' reward. The 1985 introduction of Miller Genuine Draft also cut significantly into High Life's business.

In 1988, in an attempt to revive High Life's sales performance, Miller changed its packaging, abandoned the "Champagne of Beers" slogan, and developed new ad campaigns. Its last national ad push for the brand came in 1991 and employed the tag line "Buy that Man a Miller." Sales continued to decline, however, and in 1993 the brewer cut the brand's price and slashed its marketing budget. Once a major force in the premium category, where it competed with the likes of Budweiser and Coors, High Life now occupied a lower-priced segment dominated by brands like Busch.

By 1996 High Life shipments had sunk below 5 million barrels. The following year, extensive tactical discounting by the brewer helped spur sales 6.8 percent to 4.7 million barrels, making it the eighth largest selling beer in the country. The surprising reversal of fortunes prompted Miller to embark on a major new marketing push for 1998. Nostalgia-driven campaigns reviving the "Miller Time" tag line had already been created for Miller Lite and Miller Genuine Draft, so a back-to-basics approach was adopted for High Life as well.

While Miller executives did not expect High Life to reclaim its former prominence, it was expected to play an important role in making Miller competitive against lower-priced rivals. "[Miller High Life] has a loyal base of consumers, and we want to articulate what it stands for to people who don't know," said Bruce Winterton, Miller's brand manager for High Life and Miller Genuine Draft, in announcing the new campaign.

TARGET MARKET

Miller High Life's "High Life Man" ads were targeted primarily at males aged 21 to 27. Historically the United States's most prolific beer drinkers, this group represented both a demographic challenge and an opportunity for America's brewers. While their numbers declined by about 3 million between 1990 and 1998, experts expected the population of "entry-level drinkers," as they were known, to begin growing around the year 2000 and to increase 14 percent over the first five years of the new millennium.

Studies showed these youthful beer drinkers to be both highly brand conscious and notoriously lacking in brand loyalty, making them an attractive challenge for

A still from the "Miller High Life Man" campaign. MILLER BREWING COMPANY. REPRODUCED BY PERMISSION.

advertising professionals. "Studies have indicated that is where we have the greatest opportunity to influence brand choices," commented Jeff Waalkes, Miller Brewing sales communications manager. "Although the over-30 market comprises a large segment by volume, the fact is that brand choice is pretty well set by the time a person turns 30. Rather than attempting to get such consumers to switch at that point, we believe it's more effective to try to make Miller their first choice at an earlier period."

People in their twenties were also known to be very ad-resistant, making them a hard group to reach with traditional sales approaches. "They look at advertising and marketing as almost a spectator sport," said Steven Grasse, chief executive of Gyro Worldwide, a Philadelphia advertising agency that specialized in marketing to people ages 18 to 30. "This is a savvy audience," noted Mike Johnson, brand director for Miller Lite. "They started shopping earlier; they've had candy marketed to them; they've had Channel One in their classrooms. They've been there; they've done that; they've bought the T-shirt."

To reach these jaded young consumers, beer companies often tried out offbeat marketing and promotion ideas. Miller's strategy was to have constantly changing television ads, to promote the theme of "fun, fresh, unexpected, entertaining." Other companies relied on the kind of "twisted childish humor" that these consumers grew up on. According to Janine Misdom, a partner at Sputnik, a New York marketing firm, males under the age of 30 responded most favorably to the Budweiser commercials in which a talking lizard hatches a murder plot against a group of frogs. "It's funny, it's a little bit nostalgic, and there is a little bit of the bad-boy thing," Misdom said. "They've all grown up on this offbeat humor."

COMPETITION

The beer industry remained highly competitive in 1998, with little change from the previous year in terms of market position among the major brewers. Anheuser-Busch set the pace overall in 1997, with 47.5 percent of the U.S. beer market, the same figure as 1996, according to the Maxwell Consumer Report published by analyst Jack Maxwell of Davenport & Company. Its flagship brand Budweiser was off 2 percent, which in the sluggish premium segment represented "the best performance by the brand in six years," according to Anheuser-Busch officials. Miller Brewing ended the year with a total market share of 21.4 percent. Shipments were up in double-digits for Foster's, Icehouse, and Red Dog, while Miller High Life and Milwaukee's Best also showed strong increases. Bringing up the rear of the market were Coors Brewing, at 10.9 percent, and Stroh Brewery (including former Heileman products) at 7.4 percent.

After being outspent by Miller Brewing Company in 1997, Anheuser-Busch announced plans to invest more than $300 million in brand ads in both 1998 and 1999. True to its word, the St. Louis-based brewer increased ad spending 54.7 percent to $187.2 million during the first six months of 1998, according to Competitive Media Reporting. Much of the new spending went to the

TURNING BACK THE CLOCK

The Miller Brewing Company was not the only marketer looking to boost its profits by reviving a once popular brand. In fact, it was one of many companies following a growing nostalgia trend in 1998. German automaker Volkswagen, for example, hoped to tap into baby-boomer nostalgia by rolling out a redesigned version of its Beetle, a cheap compact car favored by college-age drivers in the 1960s and 1970s. And the Pepsi-Cola Company reformulated its orange Slice brand, redesigned its container, and launched commercials designed to revive interest among teens and young adults. Like High Life, Slice, introduced amid much fanfare in the mid-1980s, had not been advertised nationally in a decade.

Why revive a fading brand rather than create a new one? Because "we know something about those old brands," said Ned Levine, a marketing consultant based in Providence, Rhode Island. "You have people out there who think of something when they think of Miller High Life. If you can take the evocative nostalgic elements out of one of those brands, it's more efficient than starting from zero."

Budweiser and Bud Light brands, while Anheuser-Busch retrenched in the specialty, ice, and dry beer segments. In early 1998 Anheuser-Busch also announced plans to launch a new, contemporary campaign directed at adult drinkers. The spots featured humans, rather than the brewer's popular animated lizards and frogs. While the reptiles remained a part of the company's creative mix, ads with people allowed Anheuser-Busch to portray consumers having a good time with beer, according to Bob Lachky, vice president of brand management for Anheuser-Busch.

MARKETING STRATEGY

Miller High Life's "High Life Man" ad campaign was designed to remain faithful to the blue-collar roots of the brand, even as its humorous style attracted younger beer drinkers. The ads, directed by Errol Morris of @radical.media, all featured a shadowy figure known as "High Life Man," whose activities are commented upon by an unseen narrator. "We are trying to emphasize the simplicity, pride, and common sense that are valued by Miller High Life drinkers of all ages," said Winterton. "The High Life guy wants to eat what he wants, fix things himself, and do his own thing."

The "High Life Man" campaign blended populist themes from the 1970s "Miller Time" spots with the ironic humor popular in the 1990s. In one new commercial, "Duct Tape," a Miller High Life drinker demonstrates the power of the versatile adhesive as he places a swatch of duct tape on the door of an old refrigerator filled with bottles of High Life. "The High Life man knows that if the Pharaohs had duct tape, the Sphinx would still have a nose," a voice-over intoned.

In another ad, "Boat," a man leans on a rake as he watches his hapless neighbor attempt to back a car with a boat trailer into his driveway. "Time was a man knew how to command his own vehicle," says the narrator. "Just how far are we willing to fall? Better reacquaint yourself with the High Life, soldier, before someone tries to take away your Miller Time."

In a third ad, "Burger," viewers look on as several greasy hunks of ground beef are fried on a diner stove. "Something's not quite right," however, the voice-over informs us. Then the waitress tops a burger off with a generous dollop of butter, which elicits a pleased response: "There, now that's a sandwich... That's living the High Life. That's Miller Time." Another ad, "Deviled Egg," shows a disheveled man alone in his kitchen after a party, pondering the advisability of eating the last deviled egg left on the party platter. "Mmmm, that last egg's looking real good," says the unseen narrator. "You've had quite a few though. Maybe you shouldn't." Ultimately, however, the man decides to go for it. The narrator approves. "See there," he says. "When you have the High Life, you can live it both ways."

One ad in the campaign, "Doughnut," shows a close-up of grease on a mechanic's hand, as he flicks around a powdered doughnut. The narrator says it's not a problem if the man can't wash his hands properly, since the grease provides a "semiprotective barrier between your fingerprint and your nutrition." Grease, the voice-over concludes, is nothing but added flavor "to a High Life man."

OUTCOME

Reaction to Miller's "High Life Man" ad campaign was largely positive, although there were a few brickbats. One beer industry rival dismissed the High Life effort, calling it "too little too late" and claiming that the new ads made fun of High Life drinkers "rather than giving them joy." Perhaps echoing this sentiment, almost a quarter of respondents polled by *USA Today* disliked the campaign, a high disapproval rate given that the average in all *USA Today* polls for respondents who disliked a campaign was 13 percent. Of some consolation to High Life's marketing team was the fact that men liked the new ads more than women did. Eighteen percent of men said they liked the "High Life Man" campaign "a lot," while only 8 percent of women did.

Most advertising critics, by contrast, found the ads witty and inventive. "The direction . . . is priceless," raved the reviewer for *Advertising Age* magazine. "Even the subtle nuance of the off-kilter logos at the end of each spot makes the work feel at once old-fashioned yet completely contemporary." "The spots seem real," added the critics at *Adweek Western Advertising News.* "They feel like beer tastes. If you like beer, that's a good thing."

Wieden & Kennedy's "Miller High Life Man" campaign won a number of advertising industry awards, including three Addy Awards. At the annual One Show Awards, the agency picked up two gold, two silver, and one bronze medals. "Mayonnaise" won the Gold Pencil in the 20-second or less, single ad category and "Sally," another spot in the campaign, took the Silver Pencil in that category. The campaign's "Sally," "Donut," and "Fridge" took the Gold Pencil in the varying lengths campaign category, while "Boat," "Mayonnaise" and "Router" earned the Silver Pencil in that category. In addition, Wieden & Kennedy took the Bronze Pencil in the 30-second campaign category for "Boat," "Duct Tape" and "Deviled Egg."

FURTHER READING

Arndorfer, James B. "Miller Restages High Life Brand with Nod to Past." *Advertising Age,* May 18, 1998, p. 27.

Canfora, Jack. "Manly Men Doing Manly Things: Direction, Execution Star at Miller." *Advertising Age,* May 31, 1999, p. S8.

Khermouch, Gerry. "Miller Litens Up." *Brandweek,* April 6, 1998.

Wells, Melanie. "Miller High Life Ads Get Low Grades." *USA Today,* March 22, 1999.

Robert Schnakenberg

MILLER LITE'S MILLER TIME CAMPAIGN

OVERVIEW

On January 12, 1997, during championship games of the American and National Football Conferences and on the Fox Network's *The X-Files,* the Miller Brewing Company introduced Dick as its new spokesperson for Miller Lite. The series of four commercials all began in the same way, with a campy 1950s beer can logo bearing the slogan "Miller Time," a familiar tag line that had not been used since the mid-1980s, followed by a picture of Dick, apparently straight out of his 1975 high school yearbook, complete with long hair and sideburns. Each spot ended with a coda to the "Miller Time" logo, Dick's signature of approval and his statement "Thank you for your time," a la Bartles and Jaymes. In between the logos Dick told viewers, "Anything can happen."

The four scenarios lived up to this promise. In "Adios, Amigos," several cowboys stood at the bar of a saloon and drained their bottles of Miller Lite, after which they filed into the bathroom, sadly serenading their beers with the title song. In "Magician" the title character played a shell game with mice and Miller Lite, making one disappear and the other appear in its place, except that the mice ended up under the armpits of his blond assistant. "Man in the Field" showed the upper half of a walking man, his bowler hat bobbing above a field of wheat, but when he stepped past the end of a row, his naked bottom half was revealed. (Dick maintained modesty with a strategically positioned bottle cap.) "Product Tester" followed the adventures of Dick's friend Jimmy, who could not seem to let go of his bottle of Miller Lite as he tested it by tossing it off high buildings and throwing it down staircases. More scenarios in the $140 million campaign followed throughout 1997.

The initial critical response to the ads tended to be negative. Bob Garfield panned the ads in *Advertising Age,* calling them "a smug, masturbatory sort of advertising." Rance Crain, the magazine's editor, proclaimed, "Miller Lite's new agency, Fallon McElligott, has invoked the" Miller Time" heritage—which is nothing less than sacrilege—but has come up with ads so horrendously bad that I'm ready to revoke their 1996 Ad Agency of the Year award." Not all of the publication's readers shared this response, however. One reader wrote in to say that the ads amused him, as did the critical reaction.

Miller, of course, was more concerned with the reaction of its target audience. In the decade since the "Miller Lite All Stars" had last argued the "Great Taste/Less Filling" debate, Miller Lite's market share had fallen, and Anheuser-Busch's Bud Light, the main competition, had replaced Miller Lite as the best-selling light beer. To turn the situation around, Miller Lite reduced the age at the upper end of its target market, from 30- to 38-year olds, while simultaneously adopting a more hip tone that would resonate with a younger audience. According to Mike Johnson, Miller Lite's brand director, the basic element of the new strategy was to "create a lot of talk with contemporary adult beer drinkers." Even negative reactions to the advertisements worked in favor of this goal, for people talked more about Miller Lite. People not only talked, however; they also began to buy more Miller Lite.

HISTORICAL CONTEXT

In 1975 Miller Brewing introduced a new concept when it established the low-calorie, or "light," beer category, brewed to appeal to the taste buds as well as the paunches of beer drinkers. During the previous year filming had begun on commercials for the new "Miller Lite All Stars" campaign, created by the Chicago advertising agency Leo Burnett USA. The ads featured former athletes and coaches arguing whether it was better that the new beer "Tastes Great" or was "Less Filling." The "Tastes Great/ Less Filling" tag line tattooed itself on the psyche of American popular culture through a sustained advertising campaign that ran until the cost of hiring ex-athletes became prohibitively expensive. The campaign eventually became a victim of its own success, explained Gina Shaffer, Miller's marketing communications manager, for as other advertisers followed the precedent set by Miller Lite, it drove the value of appearances by ex-athletes through the roof.

After Miller abandoned this tag line, it decided to revive "Miller Time," which had once been the slogan of its flagship brand, Miller High Life, and which had become a cultural icon. Although Miller had laid the slogan to rest in 1985, "Miller Time" maintained its currency in American culture. Jack MacDonough, Miller's chairman and CEO, spoke about the resurrection of the slogan: "We [hadn't] been talking Miller Time for the last fifteen years... But this society did. It's never gone away. In the sports pages, somebody named Miller [basketball player Reggie Miller] would do well and they'd say it was 'Miller Time' last night. The phrase continued in the popular culture, which is why it was so much fun to pick it up again."

While Miller executives made the task sound easy, executives at Fallon McElligott, the Minneapolis advertising agency that had wooed the Miller account away from Leo Burnett, approached the job with a more realistic perspective. Mary Van Note, Fallon McElligott's group planning director, recalled that "fear struck [her] heart" when she first heard of the assignment. "It's one thing to discuss how to jumpstart a brand," she said, "it's quite another to turn around one of the biggest beers in America." Such a transformation required innovation, risk, and self-confidence, all trademarks of Fallon McElligott.

TARGET MARKET

Miller wanted to redefine Miller Lite by narrowing the age span of the target audience. The lower end would remain at 21, the legal drinking age, but at the upper end the campaign would focus on those age 30, rather than extending to 38, which had been the strategy for many years. Beer drinkers typically establish their brand preference in their 20s and maintain steadfast allegiance into their 30s and beyond, thus making it very difficult for advertising to effect a switch. Fallon McElligott thus formulated the Dick campaign to appeal to those under 30 without alienating older beer drinkers.

The campaign used the character of Dick to reach Generation Xers through various media, including commercials aired during *The X Files,* promotional tie-ins with MTV's *Singled Out,* contests to win a behind-the-scenes look at the shooting of *Sports Illustrated*'s swimsuit issue along with print ads in the magazine, and even a Miller Lite World Wide Web page, where computer users could play "Dick-tac-toe." Miller Lite had traditionally geared its advertising toward sports, and the new campaign continued to do so as a way of maintaining its over-30 base while simultaneously reaching its younger target market.

As was typical of Fallon McElligott's self-reflexive tendencies, this age division became the topic of a commercial in which Dick solicited the opinions of Miller plant workers about his ad campaign. In one commercial father and son Jimmy and Clint Nelson disagreed over Dick's campaign. Predictably, Jimmy, who had worked at Miller's Fort Worth plant for 18 years, did not like the bizarre commercials, while Clint, his bearded, longhaired, tie-dyed son, did. Critics labeled this tactic a postmodern spoof on advertising, but Fallon McElligott copywriter Linus Karlsson called it honest. "It's not spoofy... It's straightforward. This is Dick; this is what he does."

Leslie Savan of the *Village Voice* doubted such a simplistic formulation. Rather, she claimed, the slick postmodernism of the ads veiled their objectionable content. Savan pointed out that Dick's friend Jimmy in the "Product Tester" spot happened to be black, concluding that "commercials designed to appeal to white guys who drink beer by using a black man doing slapstick and looking stupid are in dangerous territory," bordering on blaxploitation. Miller seemed to be in safer territory when it appealed to diversity directly. It hired the Dallas-based firms Lucero Bentz and Square One to create a Spanish-language spot on the soccer rivalry between Spain and Argentina and hired Frazier Smith, a New York agency specializing in urban advertising, for a pair of rap commercials featuring Ice-T and Dr. Dre.

A still from the "Miller Time" campaign. MILLER BREWING COMPANY. REPRODUCED BY PERMISSION.

Miller's Shaffer defended Fallon McElligott's tactics. "We don't expect people to like every ad," Shaffer said. "You can't be meaningful to everyone at once. It's the recall. People can repeat to us, frame by frame, what the commercial is about." In order for recall to translate into retail, however, the consumer must remember the brand as well as the message. Ken Gutwillig, manager of the Press Box Sports Emporium in Tampa, said that customers found the ads "clever and interesting." But he reported that less than a third of them remembered that the commercials advertised Miller Lite.

COMPETITION

Until Bud Light introduced competition in 1982, Miller Lite dominated the low-calorie beer market it had created. In the 1990s, however, the market shares of Miller Lite and Bud Light practically flip-flopped. Miller Lite began the decade controlling 33 percent of the light-beer market, compared with Bud Light's 19 percent. By 1997, however, Miller Lite's share of the light-beer market had fallen to 22 percent, while Bud Light's had risen to 30 percent. "In the flattest of beer decades, Bud Light has been such an exception to the no-growth rule that you wonder whether it's actually a beer," stated Greg Prince in *Beverage World.* "For five consecutive years, the brand has added volume on an annual double-digit basis. That figure has actually increased from 1994 (10 percent) to '95 (11.5 percent) to '96 (13.9 percent)."

Bud Light overtook Miller Lite in 1995 on the strength of a series of successful ad campaigns that dated to the late 1980s when Spuds Mackenzie, the cool dog with the black eye, became a cultural phenomenon. Bud Light carried this momentum into the 1990s with the catchphrases "Yes I am" and "I love you, man." According to Bob Scarpelli of DDB Needham Chicago, Budweiser's advertising agency, these phrases "established the brand as hip, and that translates into sales." Bud Light's success stemmed largely from its strategy of targeting 21- to 30-year-old men, many of whom saw themselves mirrored in Mr. Insincerity, a character who at any opportunity that might reward him with a Bud Light would utter, "I love you, man."

In 1997 Bud Light competed against "Miller Lite's Miller Time" campaign with a new campaign—"What Do We Have Here?"—in which Bud Light drinkers discovered seemingly endless supplies of their favorite beer. The competition played itself out not only in advertising but also in ad budgets. According to Competitive Media Reporting, which tracked ad expenditures, Miller Lite outspent Bud Light by $54 million to $31 million in the first half of 1997. Notwithstanding this advantage, Miller's

THE REAL DICK

Dick was, of course, a fictional character, but the man pictured in the "Miller Lite's Miller Time" advertisements really did exist. In fact, he tended bar in Seattle and played guitar in a garage band. When asked, Gina Shaffer, Miller's marketing communications manager, would not reveal the true identity of Dick—"He wants a personal life" —but she did reveal that the photo was not a 1970s vintage shot but rather a current portrait—"That's how he looks."

Johnson maintained that "the concept is outthinking, not outspending, the competition."

MARKETING STRATEGY

Fallon McElligott's real challenge in taking on the Miller Lite account was to create a strategy for making an old brand seem new. Breweries, including Miller, had spent the previous few years introducing new products, but the failure of these new items to expand the market forced a retreat to core brands. To change the perception of a product without changing the product required sleight of hand. The creative staff at Fallon McElligott dreamed up Dick to solve this problem, with the solution amounting to the simplest of ideas—advertise the advertising. Nike had already diverted attention from its products to its message, and now Fallon McElligott took the technique a further step, circling back to draw attention to the advertising itself.

Adweek pointed out the risk of this tactic: "With armpit mice and urinating cowboys, Miller Lite advertising displayed signs of going off the deep end. What some viewed as strategic bravery, others saw as advertising suicide. What you've got is a fairly desperate client and an agency that thinks it can do no wrong. That is a recipe for either brilliance or disaster." As with all advertising, Fallon McElligott's campaign, since it could not control the audience's perception, involved a calculated risk. Through calculation, however, the agency attempted to mitigate the degree of risk. "Nothing we do is reckless," said Rob White, Fallon McElligott's director of account planning. "We know exactly what we are doing. Everything is carefully researched."

In the process of exhuming its "Miller Time" slogan, Miller decided to apply the tag line of its Miller High Life brand to its other core brands, Miller Genuine Draft and Miller Lite. The concept of "Miller Time" was also revised to fit the times. Formerly, Miller High Life advertising had defined "Miller Time" for its audience as an afterwork panacea. Miller Lite advertising allowed consumers to define "Miller Time" themselves. "Miller Time" was no longer defined by the positions of the hands on a clock, for Dick redefined "Miller Time" to describe any attitude that lent itself to the enjoyment of Miller Lite.

OUTCOME

Dick continued to create controversy, but he also continued to boost beer sales, prompting Miller to extend its "Miller Time" campaign into 1998. (In mid-1997, however, it quietly dropped Dick as its spokesperson.) The campaign won the inauspicious distinction of being named the "Most Self-Conscious Attempt to be Postmodern" in *Entertainment Weekly*'s yearly survey of advertising. Fallon McElligott swept the awards at the competition sponsored by the Advertising Federation of Minnesota and Minnesota Art Directors/Copywriters Club, including the best of show honors for the "Product Tester" spot.

In terms of sales the numbers went up slowly but steadily for Miller Lite throughout 1997. A Nielsen Scan Track following retail sales of light beer reported an increase of 0.8 percent for Miller Lite during January 1997, while Bud Light fell by 0.1 percent. From January to June Miller Lite's supermarket sales rose 12 percent. Statistics at the end of the year showed that these trends had continued, with Beverage Marketing Corporation reporting a 1.7 percent increase in domestic shipments of Miller Lite, a healthy increase considering the competitive climate of the brewing industry.

The increases in sales did not come without a price. According to Competitive Media Reporting, Miller Lite increased its first-quarter advertising budget by $16.2 million, from $22.5 million in 1996 to $38.7 million in 1997. On the whole, however, Miller Brewing still managed to raise its volume, share, and profits in 1997, a year noted for price wars. Miller's MacDonough attributed much of the company's success in 1997 to the "Miller Time" campaigns, despite, or perhaps because of, the controversy surrounding them: "We had taken a number of calculated risks in changing our advertising and our advertising agencies and changing our strategy from introducing new products every year to let's grow what we already have to rearranging what brands we're supporting. . . . You would think that with all those calculated risks we would have something that didn't work. What was unusual is everything worked better than we expected. We like that."

FURTHER READING

Lippert, Barbara. "See Dick Drink: A Look at Miller Lite's 'This Is Dick' Advertising Campaign." *Adweek* (Eastern Edition), January 20, 1997.

"Of Beer and Brain Candy." *Adweek Western Advertising News,* March 16, 1998.

Prince, Greg W. "Time and Again: Miller Goes Straight to the Core and Likes the Results." *Beverage World,* February 15, 1998.

Savan, Leslie. "Mock and Shock: The Ad Agency That Moons You." *Village Voice,* March 4, 1997.

Wollenberg, Skip. "New Beer Ads Redefine Miller Time: Will They Sell Beer?" Associated Press, February 21, 1997.

William D. Baue

Minnesota Partnership for Action against Tobacco

Two Appletree Square
8011 34th Ave. S, Ste. 400
Minneapolis, Minnesota 55425
USA
Telephone: (952) 767-1400
Fax: (952) 767-1422
Web site: www.mpaat.org

MINNESOTA PARTNERSHIP FOR ACTION AGAINST TOBACCO CAMPAIGN

OVERVIEW

The Minnesota Partnership for Action against Tobacco (MPAAT) was created in 1998 with funding from that state's individual out-of-court settlement of its suit against tobacco companies. Charged with a mission of encouraging adults to stop smoking, the organization supplemented counseling, support, and education services with a statewide marketing campaign. In its early years of operation, MPAAT used ads developed for similar campaigns in other states, but in 2000 it began an agency search preparatory to launching its own original antismoking advertisements. The result was a multiyear campaign, crafted by Minneapolis agency Clarity Coverdale Fury (CCF), integrating messages about secondhand smoke with the promotion of a toll-free hotline.

The MPAAT campaign, budgeted at an estimated $5 to $6 million a year, took as its starting point the notion that adult smokers were already aware of the health risks of their habit and that an advertising message capable of encouraging smokers to quit had to provide motivation beyond the effects on the individual, no matter how dramatic. The campaign thus focused on smokers' loved ones, both by making direct reference to the relatively underappreciated perils of secondhand smoke and by showing what smokers had to lose were they to die prematurely as a result of smoking. Noteworthy TV spots included one in which secondhand smoke took the form of a ghostly hand strangling an infant; one in which a grandfather bent down to catch his newly toddling infant grandson in his arms, only to have the infant walk through him, revealing that the grandfather was a ghost; and one in which a dying woman held her infant and recorded herself singing "You Are My Sunshine" as a keepsake for the child to have after the mother's imminent smoking-related death.

MPAAT claimed immediate gains in the number of smokers who had stopped smoking in front of children, and thousands of people called the toll-free helpline established to provide support for smokers making the attempt to quit. The spot featuring the dying mother and her infant was one of the only regional commercials named among *Adweek*'s Best Spots of 2002. CCF continued to refine and develop its secondhand smoke and helpline pitches in subsequent years.

HISTORICAL CONTEXT

Antitobacco advertising first became effective in the late 1960s, when the Federal Communications Commission ruled that TV broadcasters must donate airtime to one antitobacco advertiser for every four commercial slots sold to tobacco companies. Organizations such as the American Cancer Society, whose marketing resources were minimal compared with those of tobacco corporations, were able to push their messages, for the first time, in front of a prime-time television audience. This era of prominent antismoking messages lasted only until 1971, however, when a congressional ban on the TV advertising of tobacco products was passed. The new law meant that donated airtime became dramatically harder to come by, and the 1970s and 1980s saw a corresponding dearth of antitobacco advertising during peak viewing hours.

This situation began to change in 1988, with the passage of a California referendum calling for a tax hike on cigarettes to be used in part to fund an ambitious media campaign aimed at denormalizing tobacco use. The campaign won wide acclaim and helped reduce California's smoking rates. Several other states followed the California model of taxpayer-funded antismoking campaigns in the 1990s, and many more states went on to launch campaigns with money from the historic 1998 settlement of tobacco lawsuits filed by 46 state attorneys general.

Minnesota reached an individual out-of-court settlement with the tobacco companies in 1998 and earmarked $202 million of its $6.6 billion total payout for the endowment of a nonprofit public interest group, the Minnesota Partnership for Action against Tobacco. MPAAT's mission was to encourage current smokers to give up the habit and make it easier for them to do so. The organization used advertising to motivate smokers to quit, and it provided counseling and information to help them see the decision through. In its first years of existence, MPAAT ran advertising originally crafted for campaigns in other states, but in 2000 the organization began planning for an original media campaign. MPAAT underwrote focus groups to arrive at the strategic outlines of the campaign and in early 2001 selected CCF to helm the effort.

TARGET MARKET

The MPAAT campaign targeted all Minnesota residents who were smokers. Focus-group preparation for the campaign had led MPAAT to the conclusion that the campaign needed to communicate more than the health risks of smoking if it were to be effective with this audience.

FIGHTING TOBACCO ON TWO FRONTS

The Minnesota Partnership for Action against Tobacco (MPAAT) was funded by that state's 1998 settlement with tobacco companies for the specific purpose of persuading current smokers to quit. All of the organization's advertising, therefore, targeted adult smokers. MPAAT was not the only state-sponsored antitobacco advertiser in Minnesota, however. The Minnesota Department of Health launched its own campaign, "Target Market," which was, like the MPAAT work, crafted by Minneapolis agency Clarity Coverdale Fury. "Target Market" was aimed at teenagers and encouraged them to avoid tobacco use in part by pointing out the ways in which tobacco companies manipulatively targeted underage groups.

Smokers were aware of the health risks to themselves, the agency believed, but were in need of a message that would motivate them by other means to take on the arduous task of overcoming their physical addiction. Research conducted by the Centers for Disease Control had revealed, however, that smokers had divergent attitudes toward the habit and that no single approach could be trusted to speak to the whole group. CCF thus strove to "do a comprehensive campaign," creative director Jac Coverdale told *Adweek,* "so that everywhere people look there's lots of different messages." Each of these messages, moreover, had to avoid belittling smokers or seeming to take the moral high ground on the issue of tobacco. Though the antismoking message had to be dramatic enough to motivate people to quit smoking, CCF recognized the difficulty smokers had in quitting and sought to honor that truth in the campaign, while placing a complementary priority on transmitting respect for smokers as people.

COMPETITION

The California Department of Health Services (CDHS) continued, during this time, to devote cigarette-tax revenues to one of the nation's most ambitious antismoking efforts, typically budgeted at more than $20 million a year. One of the most well-known CDHS marketing efforts was a 1997 billboard campaign featuring cowboys on horseback overtly reminiscent of the famous Marlboro Man imagery. CDHS put new words in the cowboys' mouths, however. Copy running with one ad read,

"I miss my lung, Bob." In 2000 CDHS changed course somewhat by launching a newly aggressive assault on the integrity of tobacco companies themselves. Commercials featuring fictional tobacco executive Ken Lane began appearing in 2001 and garnered notice not just from the advertising industry and consumers but from the tobacco industry as well. The fly-on-the-wall, documentary-like TV spots showed Lane, in discussions with his colleagues, explaining with relish the insidious business practices of tobacco companies. Two real-life tobacco companies filed a lawsuit against CDHS alleging that the Lane commercials infringed on their rights and biased potential jurors in ongoing tobacco litigation. The lawsuit was eventually dismissed, and CDHS remained committed to a large-scale media campaign.

Two other states, Massachusetts and Florida, preceded Minnesota with high-profile media campaigns meant to reduce the influence of tobacco companies and limit teen smoking. The campaigns, both called "Truth," were aimed at pointing out the supposed dishonesty of the tobacco industry. One of the early Massachusetts TV spots featured Patrick Reynolds, a grandson of tobacco-company founder R.J. Reynolds, who informed viewers about the numerous harmful chemicals added to cigarettes. Noteworthy work in the Florida campaign paired images of tobacco executives giving congressional testimony with a sitcom laugh track and showed teenagers phoning tobacco companies to ask pointed questions.

The 1998 master settlement of tobacco litigation between four companies and 46 state attorneys general resulted in the creation of a public interest group called the American Legacy Foundation (ALF), among many other changes. Funded by money from the settlement, ALF supported a nationwide antismoking media campaign of unprecedented scope and budget resources. Crafted by the agencies responsible for the Massachusetts and Florida campaigns, the ALF campaign (also called "Truth") confronted tobacco companies perhaps more vigorously than any advertising that preceded it. An early series of spots focused on the filming of teenagers leaving body bags outside the corporate headquarters of Philip Morris, but the major TV networks pulled the commercials following protests by the tobacco companies.

MARKETING STRATEGY

After the results of four Minnesota focus groups revealed that both smokers and nonsmokers in the state felt that antismoking advertising needed to go beyond warnings about the personal health risks of smoking, MPAAT presented these findings to the eight Minnesota ad agencies it was considering for the account. CCF, more than the others, successfully integrated the focus-group findings with its proposed creative work. It was CCF's belief that, while individuals might not quit smoking because of health risks to themselves, the knowledge that they were harming loved ones to an extent still widely unrecognized could provide them with the necessary motivation to kick the habit. Illustrations of the dangers of secondhand smoke and of the kinds of heartbreak resulting from early death caused by smoking thus formed the basis of the emotional appeals in the campaign. CCF and MPAAT also recognized the need to provide smokers with hope in their battle with the addiction, so a 24-hour helpline was established.

Budgeted at an estimated $5 to $6 million annually, the CCF-crafted MPAAT advertising was launched in early 2001 and continued to run through 2005 with different taglines but without significant alteration in concept, with TV, radio, outdoor, and print elements, all of which conformed to the same overall strategy. Early on CCF negotiated with TV broadcasters, radio stations, newspapers, and owners of outdoor advertising spaces, securing additional placement time for no additional charge by asking these outlets to consider the ads part of their commitment to public service initiatives. CCF thereby gained access, in the campaign's first year, to 34 percent more TV time than it paid for, as well as 76 percent more time to run outdoor ads.

Many individual executions were intended to jolt smokers unpleasantly, while others used humor to illustrate the dangers of secondhand smoke or to promote the helpline. In all of the campaign advertising, CCF took pains to avoid any hint of insult or condescension. An early TV spot portrayed secondhand smoke as a phantom hand reaching out to choke a baby, and a poster showed a pet bird killed in its cage by secondhand smoke. Another TV spot from the campaign's first year showed a grandfather crouching delightedly to hug his toddling grandson, who had just learned to walk, but the child walked through the grandfather, revealing that the grandfather was a ghost. A similarly direct radio spot featured a helpline caller whose unpleasantly coarse, croaking voice was the result of having her larynx and vocal cords removed because of throat cancer.

"Sunshine," perhaps the MPAAT effort's most arresting TV spot, appeared as the centerpiece of the 2002 installment of the campaign. The commercial showed a young woman, bald and wearing a knitted cap, setting up a home-movie camera while holding her infant daughter. Speaking to the camera, the mother said, "Hi, Emma. It's Mommy, and this is you. Emma, Mommy's really sick." Going on to explain that she wanted to give her daughter something to remember her by, the mother, all the while trying to suppress her palpable torment at the situation, sang "You Are My

Sunshine" to the obliviously curious infant. At the end of the plaintive song, text appeared onscreen reading, "Be there tomorrow. Stop smoking today." The toll-free helpline number then appeared.

Other spots conveyed their antismoking message with more humor. One spot showed a man in the passenger seat of a car silently lighting a cigarette. The woman driving responded by jerking the car's wheel so that the car sped through a meadow and narrowly missed an enormous tree as the smoking passenger screamed for his life. When the driver casually returned the car to the road, she informed the man, "You're endangering my life. I'm just returning the favor." Another showed a man at a dinner party being pulled out of his seat, pinned against the wall, and dragged outside of the house by an unseen force. The man then lit a cigarette and a voice-over explained, "It's tough to fight the urge to smoke. With help, you're seven times more likely to quit." The helpline number then appeared onscreen.

OUTCOME

Three months after the campaign's launch, MPAAT sponsored a survey whose findings indicated that more than 70 percent of Minnesota's smokers had curtailed their smoking around children because of MPAAT's advertising. Another survey indicated that 60 to 70 percent of those surveyed recalled the advertising, and a large number of respondents had extremely specific memories of the advertising. During the campaign's first year more than 5,000 people called the MPAAT helpline to ask for help in quitting smoking. In 2002, after the TV spot featuring the grandfather who turned out to be a ghost was picked up for airing in California, a reference to the commercial as "chilling" appeared on the popular prime-time sitcom *Friends,* testifying to the spot's power and talk value, and the commercial "Sunshine" was chosen as one of *Adweek* 's Best Spots of 2002. As of 2003 more than 10,000 Minnesota smokers had called the MPAAT helpline, and more than 7,800 had sought counseling. The campaign continued to evolve in 2004 and 2005.

FURTHER READING

Baar, Aaron. "Anti-Smoking Group That Targets Adults Talks with 4 Shops." *Adweek* (midwest ed.), December 4, 2000.

———. "CCF Ads Urge Smokers to Quit." *Adweek* (midwest ed.), June 18, 2001.

———. "Prime-Time Smokeout." *Adweek* (midwest ed.), November 11, 2002.

Cooper, Ann. "Clearing the Smoke." *Print,* May/June 2001.

"Creative Best Spots 2002." *Adweek,* January 27, 2003.

Dolliver, Mark. "Portfolio." *Adweek,* November 25, 2002.

Goldrich, Robert. "Super Resolution." *Shoot,* February 6, 2004.

Jarvis, Steve. "Minn. Campaign Grabs Smokers by Throat." *Marketing News,* April 15, 2002.

Takaki, Millie. "Dir. De Cercio Throws a 'Dinner Party.'" *Shoot,* April 11, 2003.

———. "Quitting Is No Longer a Remote Possibility." *Shoot,* February 6, 2004.

———. "Wolf." *Shoot,* January 30, 2004.

Mark Lane

Mitsubishi Motors North America, Inc.

6400 Katella Avenue
Cypress, California 90630-0064
USA
Telephone: (714) 372-6000
Fax: (714) 372-6000
Web site: www.mitsucars.com

WAKE UP AND DRIVE CAMPAIGN

OVERVIEW

Mired in a slump caused by sinking sales, a dwindling market share, an anonymous image, and an ill-defined marketing drive, Mitsubishi Motors North America, Inc., (then called Mitsubishi Motor Sales of America) introduced an updated version of its midsize sedan, the Galant, in August 1998. Mitsubishi saw this redesign as an opportunity to reinvigorate the company's brand image, and it selected the advertising agency Deutsch, Inc., of New York and Marina del Ray, California, to craft a campaign that would not only distinguish the Galant from its more established rivals but that would also prove strong enough to apply to the entire line of Mitsubishi automobiles.

The resulting $50 million campaign, tagged "Wake Up and Drive," focused on TV, with supporting print, outdoor, and Internet elements. The commercials positioned the Galant as an alternative to the staid family sedan through the use of a pulsing sound track, quick-cutting footage of the Galant barreling down rural and urban streets, and flashes of text messages designed to appear as though they were emerging from the road. The text transmitted the campaign's controlling theme: that responsible adults could remain youthful at heart and choose their automobiles accordingly. As Mitsubishi began to find success with this style-focused pitch, it awarded its entire $180 million-plus U.S. advertising account to Deutsch, which set about applying the theme to the full range of Mitsubishi automobiles. When paired with its affordable compact and sports cars—the Lancer and Eclipse—in particular, the "Wake Up and Drive" pitch more openly courted younger buyers.

Mitsubishi successfully created a youthful and energetic brand identity, surpassing Volkswagen as the automaker with the largest portion of under-35 drivers. North American sales grew by roughly 80 percent over the campaign's five-year run, and in 2002 Mitsubishi predicted further growth of an additional 70 percent or more in the following five years. These predictions proved drastically off the mark, however, as it became apparent that Mitsubishi's sales gains were partly attributable to untenable lending practices. Many of the young people who had bought Mitsubishi vehicles as a result of the brand's newly youthful image began to default on their loans, and when Mitsubishi tightened its lending regulations, sales plummeted back to their pre-1999 levels.

HISTORICAL CONTEXT

Mitsubishi began operating in the United States in 1982. In 1994 the company sold 230,279 cars in that market and anticipated setting sales records well into the future. None followed, however, and Mitsubishi instead failed to break the 200,000-car mark again. In fact, its share of the U.S. car market dropped from 1.5 percent in 1994 to 1.2 percent in 1997. Sales for 1997 were 12.2 percent lower than in 1996, and even more disturbing was the Galant's performance, which was down 35.1 percent from the prior year. Likely contributing to the free fall was the fact that the company was rated below average in several customer-satisfaction surveys. "Mitsubishi Motor Sales of America has just about hit bottom," *AutoWeek* pronounced.

Mitsubishi's woes were significantly exacerbated by its image—or lack thereof. "As the market gets more cluttered, it is incredibly important for a manufacturer to have a distinct image that is easy for consumers to understand," an industry analyst told the *Los Angeles Times.* But when Mitsubishi quizzed customer focus groups about its brand image, they had difficulty associating the name with any of its vehicles. The campaign that its ad agency, G2 Advertising, had created, called "Built for Living," with its scenes of Mitsubishi vehicles being used in everyday situations, had done little to correct this problem. Moreover, since the company often used rebates and price cuts to drive sales for the Galant, the sedan tended to draw a customer base of bargain hunters rather than Mitsubishi enthusiasts. The company's newly appointed executive vice president and chief operating officer, Pierre Gagnon, summed up "Built for Living" as a better "corporate philosophy" than "brand statement," according to *Automotive News.* With the debut of the Galant looming large, a change was needed. Mitsubishi had hired Deutsch to conceive a dealer-oriented campaign in April 1998 and was pleased with the irreverent tone of the spots. Deutsch was therefore assigned the new Galant campaign as well.

COPYCAT?

After the successful release of the "Wake Up and Drive" campaign, two ad agencies representing other car companies accused Deutsch of stealing ideas from their earlier auto campaigns. Ron Lawner of Arnold Communications and Pat Fallon of Fallon McElligott scoffed that pieces of "Wake Up and Drive" were wholly derived from their creative work for Volkswagen and BMW. "That's so comical I can't even dignify it with a response," retorted Donny Deutsch of Deutsch to *Adweek.* "The children should go back to their crayons."

TARGET MARKET

"Wake Up and Drive" sought to remedy the errors of earlier campaigns. After determining its initial target audience to be consumers under the age of 45, typically married, and with an annual household income above $55,000, Mitsubishi strategized about the best ways to reach this demographic group. The company's solution was to pitch the Galant as an antidote to the drab routines and responsibilities of adulthood. Recognizing that its chief competitors, the Honda Motor Co. and Toyota Motor Corp., were unassailable in their reputations for quality and reliability, Mitsubishi opted to present the Galant as an exciting alternative to bland family sedans. "Wake Up and Drive" delivered "a sharp jab into the restless heart of the carpool driver," the *Wall Street Journal* opined, and "pull[ed] hard on the last youthful cravings for excitement in sedan buyers." While its target audience shouldered the duties of marriage and parenthood, they chafed at the notion of getting old and dull. "We're talking to that youthful spirit that lives in all of us—the one that wants to look attractive, to have fun, to stay young," a company spokesperson told the *Bloomington Pantagraph.*

As the "Wake Up and Drive" tagline and high-energy approach was extended to other Mitsubishi models, including the Eclipse sports car and the Lancer compact—neither of which were aimed primarily at a family market—the youth-oriented nature of Mitsubishi's brand image became more and more pronounced, tailored to the literally young rather than to the merely young at heart. The company paired its energized brand personality with financing offers that made it strikingly easy for younger consumers to qualify for loans. By late 2002, at the apex of the marketing campaign's success, Mitsubishi had bested Volkswagen as the American auto industry's leading youth brand: 42 percent of Mitsubishi buyers were under 35, compared with 41 percent for Volkswagen.

COMPETITION

As the ninth-biggest car company in the United States, Mitsubishi's decision to avoid fighting its giant rivals on their own turf was a logical one. The midsize sedan category of cars to which the Galant belonged was the largest-selling segment of the American auto market. Three of the seven best-selling cars were midsize sedans. "The segment is brutal," an industry analyst told the *Orange County Business Journal.* Mitsubishi faced fierce opposition from the Honda Accord, the Toyota Camry, and the Ford Taurus in its bid to gain a greater share of this sector with the updated Galant. Those vehicles perennially vied for the rank of the best-selling car in the United States. Moreover, each of these three companies had introduced updated versions of their sedans since 1996.

The Camry had topped U.S. sales charts in both 1997 and 1998. Toyota had released a redesigned Camry in 1996, supporting it with a $50 million television, magazine, outdoor, and direct-mail campaign, using the simple slogan "The New Camry. Better Than Ever." According to the June 30, 1997, *Advertising Age,* the ads were "as understated as the car." With the debut of its brandwide "Everyday" campaign in the fall of 1997, Toyota incorporated Camry spots into this umbrella effort. Quite the opposite of "Wake Up and Drive," Saatchi & Saatchi's campaign for Toyota glorified the mundane. Instead of presenting the Camry as an escape route, "Everyday" showcased the multiple meanings of everyday: not only was the Camry ideal for "everyday" use, it would also be there "every day." This stolid and reliable image helped Toyota control an impressive 8.1 percent of the U.S. car market.

Honda debuted a redesigned Accord in 1997 and inaugurated a campaign touting the car's new advances that same year. Created by Honda's longtime ad agency Rubin Postaer & Associates, this massive "An Accord like No Other" campaign evoked the Accord's long legacy in the United States. Like Toyota, Honda highlighted its conservative side in these sedan ads. As the *Washington Times* noted, "never have its cars been the most stylish or the most powerful, but always competent and with no vices. They just deliver all the features with a high degree of satisfaction, and seldom is there any item to complain about." Later Accord campaigns continued to underscore this reputation with simple, clean ads that always made the car the hero. One 1998 commercial depicted a stressed traveler finding sanctuary in her Accord. "It's not just a car. It's a state of mind," declared the tagline.

When it introduced its all-new Taurus in 1996, Ford repositioned the car as affordable and family-friendly. But over the next two years Ford changed directions in its Taurus advertising, particularly in 1997 ads created by J. Walter Thompson USA, which used NASCAR themes to emphasize that the Taurus had recently entered the racing circuit. But during the Winter Olympic Games in February 1998, Ford returned to the basics with a new brandwide campaign. These commercials, which told stories centered on various Ford products, were narrated by actor John Corbett. One spot portrayed a Taurus owner reconciling with her father. By November 1998 Ford had committed to continuing its efforts to emphasize primarily brands over individual models.

MARKETING STRATEGY

By presenting the Galant in a different light from the more traditional Camry, Accord, and Taurus, Mitsubishi strove to forge a unique brand image for its sedan. At the opposite end of the spectrum from Toyota's paean to everyday life, Mitsubishi "show[ed] itself as making its drivers look cool," explained the *Orange County Business Journal.* The aggressive rock songs chosen for the commercials' sound tracks implied that the Galant was no stolid "family-mobile" but rather that it was rebellious and sporty. The spots were filmed in rapidly shifting spurts, which conveyed a sense of speed and made the spots look more like music videos than traditional commercials. The accompanying captions, however, were the heart of "Wake Up and Drive." One commercial, which depicted the Galant zooming around urban streets illuminated only by a neon glow, proclaimed, "You have a family / You have a house / You have a dog / You have a pulse." Another commercial delivered an additional wry commentary: "The other soccer moms will talk." At its core, "Wake Up and Drive" poked at the raw nerve of insecurity lurking within family-oriented consumers who were not ready to declare themselves "middle-aged" or "terminally responsible." According to the *Wall Street Journal,* "the idea [wa]s to lure . . . soccer moms and baseball dads who don't really see themselves in a Toyota Camry or a Honda Accord."

Although the new brand personality was initially tied to the August 1998 Galant launch, Mitsubishi hoped, from the outset, that "Wake Up and Drive" would resonate among consumers to a degree that would justify adapting the platform to other models. It was "an opportunity for us to re-launch this franchise," Gagnon told the *Bloomington Pantagraph.* Satisfied with the initial buzz surrounding the Galant introduction, the company applied the campaign tagline and concept in November of that year to commercials for its Montero SUV. Set to heavy-metal legend Ozzy Osbourne's song "Crazy Train," the commercial was even aired during the 1999 Super Bowl—a first for Mitsubishi.

Mitsubishi expressed delight with Deutsch amid growing signs of the campaign's success, and in 1999 it awarded the agency the entire ad account for its U.S. operations, at an estimated total budget of more than $180 million. "Wake Up and Drive" subsequently became the rallying cry for the whole Mitsubishi line, and the agency continued to produce corporate-image advertising notable for its evocations of youthful energy and overt appeals to vanity. This branding strategy was particularly apparent in a 1999 installment of the campaign announcing a new redesign of the Eclipse sports car. Crafted to appeal to both young people and older men having midlife crises, as Deutsch's executive vice president and creative director Eric Hirshberg told *Advertising Age,* the new Eclipse commercials were characterized by an emphasis on sex appeal. For instance, the voice-over in one spot posed the following set of questions: "If you had to be stranded on a deserted island with just one other person, who would it be? A boat builder? Or a survival expert? Perhaps a fisherman? Or would it just be someone who looks really good in a swimsuit?" The redesigned Eclipse was then shown speeding into view, and the voice-over continued, "There are more sensible choices, but who cares?"

With sales of the Galant and Eclipse surging, in 2000 "Wake Up and Drive" focused on the 2001 models of the Eclipse Spyder, a new convertible, and the Montero, as Mitsubishi upped its overall advertising budget by roughly 20 percent over 1999, to an estimated $223 million. In 2001 the company again boosted spending, devoting a large portion of its budget to the U.S. launch of its Lancer compact car, which was then popular in Europe. The affordable Lancer was seen as a way of enhancing Mitsubishi's allure among young and first-time car buyers, and the spots in which it was featured incorporated music from youth-oriented rock bands such as the Barenaked Ladies. Mitsubishi's focus on the music of lesser-known and younger artists during these years made practical as well as strategic sense. The licensing fees for such songs were, of course, substantially smaller than those for mainstream hits, but also, as Hirshberg told the *New York Times,* "It gives street cred to Mitsubishi and shows that they are not just a corporation with a big budget, but a brand cool enough to tell you what's new." Prominent Mitsubishi spots in 2001–02 focused on young people inside cars, moving to the music that had become increasingly central to the campaign.

OUTCOME

"The... ads are bringing people into the dealerships," Mitsubishi's Gagnon said in the November 2, 1998, issue of *Advertising Age.* "We're getting Accord and Camry buyers, who never shopped us before." By September 1998 Mitsubishi had sold 4,691 Galants (compared to 2,366 the prior year), and by year's end the number had shot up to 44,202. The company's total American car sales edged closer to the 200,000 mark for 1998, thanks in no small part to the Galant launch. The 2000 Eclipse redesign, introduced in the summer of 1999, was equally successful, and surging sales of these two models helped the company achieve record-breaking sales in late 1999 and a full-year total of 261,254 cars sold in the United States. By 2002, despite the intervening difficulties presented by the economic recession and geopolitical turmoil, Mitsubishi sales in North America—the overwhelming majority of which were in the United States—approached 350,000. Mitsubishi seemed well on the road to recovery in the United States. Gagnon predicted that the automaker would annually sell 600,000 cars in North America by 2007.

In 2003, however, it became apparent that in pairing its "Wake Up and Drive" brand identity with easy credit deals, Mitsubishi had pushed sales among an untenable target market. So-called "zero-zero-zero" loan packages specifically created with young buyers in mind allowed customers to take possession of new Mitsubishi cars with no down payment, no monthly payments for an introductory period of time (often six months), and with zero percent financing once payment became due. Many of the 20-somethings who bought Mitsubishis under these terms were unable to make payments after the introductory phase of ownership passed, and as the *Wall Street Journal* reported, the result was "an avalanche of defaults." When Mitsubishi responded by increasing its loan requirements, sales plummeted. In 2003 the company posted full-year U.S. sales losses of 25.6 percent. The following year was even worse for Mitsubishi in America: sales declined by an additional 37 percent.

FURTHER READING

Goo, Sara Kehaulani. "Mitsubishi Launches Galant Drive Aimed at Rebels." *Wall Street Journal,* July 28, 1998.

Halliday, Jean. "Deutsch-Created Galant Ads Grab First-Time Buyers." *Advertising Age,* November 2, 1998.

———. "Mitsubishi Kicks Off 2001 Campaigns." *Advertising Age,* March 13, 2000.

Keenan, Tim. "Galant Gallops Away from the Deal." *Ward's Dealer Business,* August 1, 1998.

McKinney, Kathy. "Mitsubishi Ads Aim to Wake Up Spirit." *Bloomington (IL) Pantagraph,* July 27, 1998.

"Mitsubishi Bets $60 Million on Spirited New Image." *Brandweek,* July 6, 1998.

O'Dell, John. "Mitsubishi Repairs Planning, Marketing Autos." *Los Angeles Times,* April 15, 1998.

Patton, Phil. "Like the Song, Love the Car." *New York Times,* September 15, 2002.

Rechtin, Mark. "Moving Mountains at Mitsubishi." *Automotive News,* December 15, 1997.

Sanders, Lisa. "Deutsch Dominates." *Advertising Age,* January 13, 2003.

Storck, Bob. "Auto Show." *Washington (DC) Times,* December 26, 1997.

"Strategy 2001: Steve Gough/Mitsubishi." *Automotive News,* January 15, 2001.

Vaughn, Mark. "Change Is Gonna Do You Good: A Whole New Car from a Whole New Company." *AutoWeek,* July 6, 1998.

White, Joseph B.. "Mitsubishi's Eclipse Ads Appeal to the Ego." *Wall Street Journal,* August 31, 1999.

Zaun, Todd. "Bad Loans Bump Mitsubishi Motors off Road to Recovery." *Wall Street Journal,* November 12, 2003.

Rebecca Stanfel
Mark Lane

Monsanto Company

800 N Lindbergh Blvd.
St. Louis, Missouri 63167
USA
Telephone: (314) 694-1000
Fax: (314) 694-8394
Web site: www.monsanto.com

MONSANTO IMAGE CAMPAIGNS

OVERVIEW

In 1994 St. Louis-based agribusiness giant Monsanto introduced Posilac, a drug designed to raise cows' milk production. Sold through the company's dairy division, formerly known as Protiva, the product was marketed to dairy farmers; yet in order to gain larger acceptance for Posilac, it became necessary to sell the public on the drug, which contained the genetically engineered chemical BST, or bovine somatotropin. The company began a limited image campaign for the product in 1994, and it used methods that by 1998 gained much wider exposure for its genetically modified (GM) food products, primarily in Europe. Concerns over GM foods both at home and abroad, where one of Monsanto's outspoken critics was England's Prince Charles, motivated the company to invest $1.6 million in its European campaign in 1998, along with an undisclosed amount on U.S. advertising. British ads were created by the firm of Bartle Bogle Hegarty and in the United States by the St. Louis office of the Sargent & Potratz advertising agency. Monsanto spent $80 million overall on consumer advertising in 1998.

Monsanto made a variety of chemical products, including Roundup, one of the world's leading herbicides; and NutraSweet, the leading artificial sweetener; and a number of pharmaceuticals, marketed through its Searle line. Monsanto products had not been without controversy, however, and that was particularly true of Posilac and GM foods. From a financial standpoint and in terms of distribution, Posilac had proven a success by the end of 1998, with Monsanto reporting that 100 million doses of the drug had been distributed since it began marketing more than four years before. But image concerns remained, suggesting an uncertain future for consumer advertising on the part of the company. Trade advertising, on the other hand, seemed relatively stable.

HISTORICAL CONTEXT

Despite the fact that its products were as much a part of daily life as the areas they addressed, Monsanto itself was hardly a household name. Founded in 1901 by John Queeny in St. Louis, the company's first product was saccharin, a popular sugar substitute until the advent of Monsanto's own NutraSweet. The company went public in 1927, by which time its products included caffeine, aspirin, and other chemical goods. During World War II, it supplied the first synthetic tires used by the U.S. Army.

In the 1960s and 1970s the company introduced several herbicides, the most successful being Roundup, which debuted in 1973. In the preceding year, Monsanto discontinued saccharin production, and later bought the licensing rights to NutraSweet, the brand name for the artificial sweetener aspartame. This occurred in 1985, the same year the company acquired the G.D. Searle pharmaceuticals firm.

In 1993 it enhanced its already large lawn-care line with the purchase of Ortho from Chevron.

In the mid-1990s, under the leadership of former Searle executive Robert Shapiro, the company expanded its pharmaceutical offerings, and in 1996 purchased a minority interest in DEKALB Genetics. In collaboration with DEKALB, Monsanto introduced a strain of soybean which could withstand herbicides such as Roundup. During this period, it also greatly expanded its agribusiness area, moving more and more into GM foods.

In 1994 Monsanto introduced Posilac, and after winning Food and Drug Administration (FDA) approval for the use of the bovine somatotropin product, it was required to undertake a thorough post-approval study. The company presented the results to the FDA's Veterinary Medicine Advisory Committee (VMAC) in November 1996. In a hearing to assess the study, VMAC addressed two questions, according to *Food Chemical News*: "whether the proposed revised label for Posilac provided adequate directions for farmers [on the use of the product] and whether the results of Monsanto's Post-Approval Monitoring Program adequately addressed the safety of the milk supply. After daylong presentations, the Food and Drug Administration's advisory committee answered yes to both questions."

TARGET MARKET

The FDA and VMAC were hardly the only barriers Monsanto had to face in gaining approval for Posilac, however; there was public opinion to consider. Technically, the consumers of Posilac had no opinion, since they were cows, not humans. As for the cows' owners, dairy farmers in the United States and Europe, a large portion were enthusiastic about a product that would enhance profitability on their farms. But there were the consumers of dairy products to consider; and as with other twentieth-century technological innovations, such as nuclear power or experiments in cloning, chemical enhancement of food production frightened many people.

Almost from the beginning, Posilac encountered criticism from consumer groups concerned about the potential side effects of using drugs to enhance milk production. The company's first response in the form of advertising came with a 30-second television commercial run exclusively in the key dairy state of Wisconsin. The company targeted the February 1994 spot for that state, a Monsanto spokesman told Robert Steyer of the *St. Louis Post-Dispatch,* "because it's been the hotbed of activity. We thought it might get our message out better."

By 1998 Monsanto had come to increasingly position itself as a so-called life sciences company rather than as a chemical manufacturer. In so doing, it keyed in on the growing interest among the baby-boomer population in enhancing their lifestyles or, to use a variation on an old DuPont advertising slogan that fell into disfavor during the 1960s, "better living through chemistry." Stephanie Thompson reported in *Brandweek* in 1998 that "nutraceuticals," scientifically developed food products, were gaining acceptance among baby boomers, and Monsanto developed much of its marketing around this trend. Its food and nutrition businesses, Thompson wrote, were "all newly repositioned under the banner of 'Food, Health, Hope.'" Thus a company spokesman told her that Monsanto was well-positioned to "take the best of all areas and identify the consumer market and consumer needs that other companies aren't qualified to do."

COMPETITION

Chemicals to increase food production, or a drug that could enhance milk production by 10 to 20 percent, were bound to have their adherents, and not just among farmers. Central to the 1994 Wisconsin television spots was Dr. Ronald E. Kleinman, associate professor of pediatrics at Harvard Medical School and former chairman of the American Academy of Pediatrics's nutrition committee. In the commercials Kleinman, who reportedly received no payment for his endorsement, announced that Posilac was every bit as "safe, nutritious, and wholesome" as the milk produced by cows who had not used it. He also warned viewers, "Don't let anyone scare you into reducing milk consumption."

The primary competition for Posilac or GM foods came not from other agribusiness companies such as Archer Daniels Midland or ConAgra, but from consumer groups and others who were just as likely to oppose the efforts of those companies to create better living—and better food production—through chemistry. Taking a sardonic tone, Kirkpatrick Sale wrote in the *Nation* in early 1999, "The old Monsanto was a chemical company, and had been since 1901, but its chemical division was spun off into a separate company in 1997. The new Monsanto is, as it puts it, 'a life sciences company,' which means that it is interested in creating, controlling, patenting, and profiting from life." Sale went on to note that "bovine growth hormone, though it has been adopted by enough dairy farmers in the United States to make it a profitable line, is still resisted by many farmers and consumers." Much of the opposition came from the same baby-boomer population segment that, according to Thompson's 1998 *Brandweek* report, had become increasingly more open to the idea of scientifically enhanced food products. If ever there was a baby-

GETTING THE MESSAGE ACROSS—INSIDE THE COMPANY

Julekha Dash in *Software Magazine* compared the corporate culture at Monsanto's dairy division, formerly known as Protiva, to that of an Ivy League university. "Okay," Dash admitted, "so the St. Louis-based provider of agricultural and pharmaceutical goods isn't exactly Harvard University." But consultants with Renaissance, an information technologies firm, "say the atmosphere of the 150-person [division] . . . was similar to the one you find in the academic world. Employees are highly trained scientists with PhDs and specialties in areas such as biology, chemistry, and genetics. And they guard their knowledge carefully."

Naturally they guard that knowledge from Monsanto's competitors—but what happens when members of a company's brain trust keep information from each other? "That was the problem," Dash wrote. "The fiercely independent culture of this group conflicted with Monsanto's knowledge management program, a company-wide strategic initiative whose objectives necessitated that employees share information using collaborative tools." Renaissance attacked the problem by arranging regular sessions in which management explained decisions to employees and stressed the contributions of individuals to overall performance. Under the guidance of Renaissance consultants, software developers at Protiva engaged in workshops and training sessions that offered an opportunity for various professionals to gather and discuss collaboration methods. Using these and other measures, Renaissance ran a pilot phase of its new program with the objective of involving three project teams in the process. Results exceeded expectations, with a total of eight teams involved by the end of the four-week pilot phase in January 1998. "What we managed to convince" the group, a Renaissance executive told Dash, "is [that] it is their collective knowledge that brings power. That was a major milestone."

boomer-style company, it was Ben & Jerry's ice cream, which according to Sale won a lawsuit that allowed it to label its ice cream as being free of all recombinant bovine growth hormones.

In fact, Ben & Jerry's home state of Vermont passed a bill requiring that suppliers of bovine growth hormones be licensed by the state agricultural commissioner. In January 1998 Monsanto challenged the legislation with a letter to Governor Howard Dean, state agriculture commissioner Leon Graves, and members of the Vermont dairy industry. Governor Dean later indicated that he would veto the bill, but only because an apparent majority of Vermont farmers opposed it.

Monsanto faced similar challenges over genetically modified foods in Europe in 1997 and 1998. When the company hired British ad agency Bartle Bogle Hegarty to create an image campaign in 1997, the agency's Soho office was besieged by a group of naked protesters. No less a figure than Charles, the Prince of Wales, weighed in against GM foods in June 1998, saying, "We don't know the long-term consequences for human health and the wider environment of releasing plants bred in this way."

MARKETING STRATEGY

Monsanto's 1998 image efforts for Posilac in the United States were muted compared to the campaign it ran simultaneously in Britain to counter fears concerning GM foods, and indeed the latter effort illustrates much about Monsanto image advertising on either side of the Atlantic. The Bartle Bogle Hegarty ads, launched in June 1998, were "designed to be objective and considered [that is, thoughtful] rather than 'adsy' or gimmicky," according to Ruth Nicholas in *Marketing,* "and to provide information and present the strengths of GM foods in a measured way." A Monsanto representative told Nicholas, "We want to give people information, and we are quite comfortable with the coverage."

As part of the three-month campaign, Monsanto urged customers to call a toll-free information line, visit its website—and even obtain the views of opposing organizations. Advertising warned that in the future, foods without genetically modified ingredients would become increasingly expensive. This led to a backlash from many groups, despite the company's apparent efforts at openness. A representative of the environmental activist organization Greenpeace told Alex Scott of *Chemical Week,* "If you compare [Monsanto's] campaign with any previous ones, it tells an interesting story—that of ignoring consumer concern. Consumers don't need a fancy advertising campaign. They need better labeling."

Greenpeace and other activist groups were not the only forces arrayed against Monsanto's efforts to enhance the company image and educate the public concerning its scientific innovations in food production. When Monsanto's international government affairs director Marcia Hale said that "it will become very expensive for the manufacturer and the consumer" not to use GM foods in the future, a representative of the British supermarket chain Iceland referred to this as a "frightening" sign of things to come. Iceland became the first retail chain in Britain to refuse to market foods with GM ingredients.

OUTCOME

In March 1999 the United Kingdom Advertising Standards Authority (ASA) upheld 6 of 13 complaints filed by the Green Party, the Royal Society for the Protection of Birds, and other groups of environmentalists against Monsanto. The ASA report claimed that the company had provided "misleading" information in the campaign. During the same month, Sale's lengthy article in the *Nation* noted that the image campaign had arrived in the United States, using the slogan "Biodiversity... matters to Monsanto."

In response to criticisms, the company produced and distributed a "Report on Sustainable Development" in late 1998. The report acknowledged that "some of what we're doing—especially in agricultural biotechnology—raises questions in the minds of many people." It also promised that "we'll continue to listen to all points of view... and to engage in honest and respectful communications." In line with the strategy of openness that Monsanto had used in its European campaign, the report even included statements from detractors such as the German Friends of the Earth, another environmental group.

Monsanto switched its U.S. advertising account in January 1999 from Sargent & Potratz, which thereupon closed its St. Louis office, to Osborne & Barr. According to the *Delaney Report,* the company "is finding that its problems in areas such as pharmaceuticals and biotechnology are having a spill-over impact on how it markets its products to consumers." As a result, it planned to drastically cut its $80 million global consumer advertising budget. A source told the *Delaney Report,* "There is a 'tomorrow' mentality at [Monsanto] right now. Marketing money for today is being put on hold while management regathers itself for the future."

Although the company had faced a number of challenges in its image marketing to consumers, products such as Posilac continued to thrive. In December 1998 Monsanto reported that 100 million doses of the drug had been sold since its introduction four and a half years before. Furthermore, a company representative told *Food Chemical News,* "Sales [of Posilac] are increasing. Our sales this year are 30 percent higher than in 1997, and sales in 1997 were up 30 percent over 1996."

FURTHER READING

Bentley, Stephanie. "Monsanto Warns of High Prices for 'Natural' Foods." *Marketing Week,* June 11, 1998, p. 8.

Dash, Julekha. "Cultivating Collaboration." *Software Magazine,* March 1, 1998, p. 94.

Fox, Harriot Lane. "Who Needs Corporate Brands?" *Marketing,* August 13, 1998, pp. 22-23.

"Monsanto Muddle." *Delaney Report,* June 14, 1999, p. 2.

Nicholas, Ruth. "Test-Tube Food Ads Stir Up Row." *Marketing,* June 11, 1998, p. 3.

"100 Million Doses of Posilac Sold in U.S., Monsanto Says." *Food Chemical News,* December 21, 1998.

Sale, Kirkpatrick. "Monsanto: Playing God." *Nation,* March 8, 1999, p. 14.

Scott, Alex. "Monsanto Begins Campaign." *Chemical Week,* June 17, 1998, p. 16.

Scott, Alex. "Advertising Board Slams Monsanto Publicity." *Chemical Week,* March 10, 1999, p. 16.

Steyer, Robert. "Monsanto Hopes Ads Counteract Critics." *St. Louis Post-Dispatch,* February 10, 1994, p. C-3.

Thompson, Stephanie. "Food for What Ails You." *Brandweek,* May 4, 1998, pp. 36-42.

"VMAC Praises Monsanto's Post-Approval Study for Posilac." *Food Chemical News,* November 25, 1996.

Judson Knight

Monster

5 Clock Tower Place
Maynard, Massachusetts 01754
USA
Telephone: (978) 461-8000
Fax: (978) 461-8100
Web site: www.monster.com

TODAY'S THE DAY CAMPAIGN

OVERVIEW

Monster, formerly known as Monster.com, persevered through the tech industry downturn of early 2001 by maintaining its position as the most used job website in the world. In 2004, besides being the top online recruitment company for Germany and India, Monster held half of America's online job-recruitment market and 10 percent of America's combined online and print market. Monster offered ads for employers that were cheaper and more visible than newspaper ads. For job seekers Monster offered a free résumé-building service and job-opening alert tools, and it allowed employees to post their résumés for free. This bundle of features, along with Monster's marketing strategy, helped the company's database of résumés rise from 26 million in 2003 to 34 million by 2005. In that year Monster.com boasted 800,000 unique monthly visitors.

Often criticized for overspending on marketing expenditures, Monster's founder and CEO, Andrew J. McKelvey, spent $125 million on worldwide advertising in 2004, launching campaigns across television, radio, print, and the Internet. One $50 million campaign, "Today's the Day," originated with New-York based ad agency Deutsch, which handled Monster's creative efforts until 2005. The first 30-second spot in the "Today's the Day" campaign aired on December 26, 2003, during the College Bowl Championship Series. Two others spots were aired on February 1, 2004, during Super Bowl XXXVIII. The three spots ran in rotation on network television and national cable until the campaign ended on April 12, 2004. Targeting a wide range of skilled, salaried, and hourly job seekers as well as both national and local employers, the first spot began with a voice-over asking, "Will today be the day...?" It then showed ordinary people, including a man and woman lying in bed, a woman showering, a young woman applying makeup while riding the bus, and a man adjusting his tie. Unlike Monster's 1999 "When I Grow Up" campaign, which had facetiously depicted children yearning for the banal qualities of corporate America, "Today's the Day" was meant to inspire employees to further their careers and their lives.

"Over the past ten years, Monster has become one of the most recognizable global brands," Jeff Taylor, Monster.com's global director, told *Adweek*. "Our 2004 plan, defined by continuous advertising, a multi-faceted online marketing strategy and ongoing sponsorships, is designed to further maximize our brand recognition as the online recruitment leader." Ten months after the first spot aired Monster reported $618.1 million in revenue, far surpassing the $499.2 million earned in the same period during 2003. The campaign helped Monster to continue its domination of the online job-recruitment market over competitors such as CareerBuilder and HotJobs.com, the latter a unit of Yahoo! Inc.

HISTORICAL CONTEXT

Monster Worldwide, Inc., the parent company of Monster, was founded by McKelvey in 1967 as TMP Worldwide. It grew to be one of the world's largest recruitment agency networks. Monster.com, which was launched in 1994, achieved industry renown in 1999 by being the first dot-com to air ads during the Super Bowl. Created by the Mullen agency in Wenham, Massachusetts, the campaign "When I Grow Up" included three 30-second spots that aired during Super Bowl XXXIII. Costing $4 million, the ads featured children saying such things as "When I grow up, I want to file all day" or "I want to climb my way up to middle management." By late 2003 Monster had awarded advertising responsibilities to Deutsch, an agency based in New York. Bryan Black, senior vice president of Deutsch, told *Shoot,* "Monster felt like they had grown up a bit, and they wanted the voice to be a little bit more mature and also a bit more appropriate for the day and age we live in right now." In 2003 Monster.com was renamed Monster.

Using the inexpensive advertising capabilities and worldwide visibility of the Internet, Monster tried overtaking newspapers' market share of help-wanted advertising. The concept fanned excitement during the 1990s tech boom and helped Monster Worldwide's stock peak at $10 billion. The company, and McKelvey especially, were criticized, however, for spending too much on advertising and not enough on the development of technology. Nonetheless, Monster saw its shares skyrocket from $10 in 1998 to $85 in 2000. Monster also increased its partnerships by sponsoring the 2004 U.S. Olympic team and joining with WeightWatchers.com after 19 percent of Monster's users listed "losing weight" as their top resolution for 2004. By 2005 Monster had shifted the creative responsibilities for its advertising from Deutsch to Boston-based agency Brand Content.

TARGET MARKET

In December 2003 Taylor told *Adweek,* "The 'Today's the Day' campaign is alive, encouraging and hopeful. As we embark on the new year, it is these inspirational qualities that empower job seekers everywhere to take control of their careers and realize their dreams and aspirations." The campaign's broad target, according to Scott Lahde of Deutsch, consisted of "salaried, hourly and skilled, national and local job seekers and employers." The campaign also targeted the growing population of young workers who were more inclined to use a computer than a newspaper when looking for help-wanted ads. "Monster's Website reportedly has become obligatory viewing among college-grad job seekers, and others hip to the online job-hunting scene," wrote Andrew Bary in *Barron's.* Television spots featured mostly white-collar urbanites wearing business attire and looking hopeful about finding new jobs.

Monster wanted the "Today's the Day" campaign to be different from the deadpan nature of its 1999 "When I Grow Up" ads and to inspire viewers to achieve greater things. " 'Today's the Day' is the perfect encouragement to get people to do something to change their lives right now. Right this second," Kathy Delaney, managing partner and executive creative director at Deutsch, told *Business Wire.* During the campaign Monster increased its sales staff and marketing expenditures to attract blue-collar workers and small-business employers. The initial effort hurt Monster's margins, but McKelvey believed that it would pay off for the company in years to come.

In the first month of the "Today's the Day" campaign Monster released findings that 93 percent of Americans would look for a new job during 2004. By the end of 2004 Monster's self-assessment index, called the Monster Employment Index, showed that the demand for employees had risen from 134 points in July to 151 points by September. According to the index, the health-care industry reflected the largest growth throughout 2004.

COMPETITION

Monster's closest competitor was CareerBuilder, founded in 1995 and based in Chicago. It sold advertisements to employers at $100 below Monster's baseline price. In 2003 visitors to the CareerBuilder website could peruse more than 600,000 jobs and 10 million résumés. That same year CareerBuilder's sales reached $31 million. Although this was only a small fraction of Monster's $424 million, CareerBuilder posted greater sales growth during 2003, 17 percent as opposed to only 1.9 percent for Monster. Cramer-Krasselt, an agency headquartered in Chicago, launched a national ad campaign for the company in 2003, coinciding with Monster's "Today's the Day" campaign. It was reported that CareerBuilder spent $20 million on the ads, which included television spots featuring employees trying to escape the monotony of their jobs. In one commercial, for example, a bank teller pretended to rob a bank and then meekly tiptoed away. Another 30-second spot featured a blue-collar worker escaping from his factory by crawling inside an enormous teddy bear. The ads were followed by the tagline "The smarter way to find a better job," a subtle jab at market leader Monster.

In 2004 HotJobs.com, which had been acquired by Yahoo! in 2002, ranked third in the online recruitment industry, with 10 percent of the market. HotJobs promoted itself primarily through HotJobs Career Expo job fairs and directly through Yahoo!.com, the world's second most used search engine. In 2003 HotJobs expanded

TRUMP DANCES FOR MONSTER

Monster's signature mascot, Trump, the animated green monster that resembled a prehistoric toad, was redesigned for the "Today's the Day" campaign. Ad agency Deutsch hired the animation director John Kricfalusi, who had also developed the television hit *The Ren & Stimpy Show,* to reconstruct the mascot. The airing of the 30-second spot "Today" on December 26, 2003, was Trump's first appearance in cel animation, as opposed to his previous appearances in computer-generated animation (CGI). "He looks great in CGI, and I always thought that was an amazing piece of animation," Scott Schindler, Deutsch's vice president/associate creative director/art director, told *Shoot.* "But we felt this was a new campaign, and also when people do interact with Trump on the Monster site or see him in print, he is flat. He is a 2-D cartoon. So we wanted to capitalize on that and animate him so that he looked like what he does in print and on the Website."

its ad efforts with the release in the top 10 markets of 30- and 60-second television spots created by the New York–based agency Bouchez & Kent. In addition, there were print ads, and Internet ads were released across Yahoo!'s related websites. In 2004 HotJobs recruited applicants for *The Apprentice,* NBC's number one program, in return for brand placement, including HotJobs ads on the doors of the taxis carrying "fired" contestants leaving the show.

MARKETING STRATEGY

The initial 30-second spot in the "Today's the Day" campaign was "Today," first aired on December 26, 2003, during the College Bowl Championship Series. Edited by Hank Corwin of the film-editing company Lost Planet, "Today" featured a montage of 20- to 30-something urbanites getting ready for work. The commercial quickly moved through scenes that included a man and woman waking up in bed, a woman showering, a man exercising, and a woman applying makeup as she rode a city bus. During the montage a female voice-over asked various questions: "Will today be the day that starts the rest of the days?" "Will it be the day you put on your suit?" "Will it be the day you don't hit snooze?" The questions sometimes directly addressed the images. The spot ended with Monster's signature mascot, a bright-green and purple cartoon monster named Trump dancing beneath the words "Today's the day."

Jeff Preiss of production company Epoch Films directed "Today" in an apartment building overlooking downtown Los Angeles, along with nearby locations in Echo Park and Van Nuys, California. He strove to make the spots feel improvised by having actors repeat their lines in rehearsal before filming. He also wanted the spot to have vision and not just be "an anthem in the abstract." "We all felt like Jeff was the guy to go to," Scott Schindler, Deutsch's vice president/associate creative director/art director told *Shoot.* "He's amazing with casting, and we wanted something that wasn't overly designed and art directed." Preiss had worked previously with Deutsch on ads for MCI.

The format was changed slightly in the next two spots, which were aired during the 2004 Super Bowl. "Soulmates," airing during the first quarter of the game, used Robert Smith's "I Dig You," which repeated the lines "I dig you / you dig me." The spot began by showing the similar morning routines of a middle-aged executive and a young job applicant, for example, struggling over crossword puzzles and feeding their fish just before walking out their doors. The spot suggested that the two, although they were separated by age and by job positions, were compatible. The commercial ended with the two soul mates shaking hands at the start of a job interview and with the Trump mascot and the tagline "Find the one you dig." The third spot, "I Feel Love," featured a number of employees who were enthusiastic about beginning their workday and used the Blue Man Group's rendition of Donna Summer's song "I Feel Love." It ended with the tagline "Get ready for a job you love," again beneath Trump, the dancing Monster mascot.

Internet ads for "Today's the Day" appeared on websites such as Weather.com, Lycos, and About.com. Efforts also went into improving Monster's Web indexing on major search engines so that geographical and vocational keywords were more succinctly correlated with the content of Monster.com. Print ads, using "Today's the day" as the tagline, were also launched in 2004. One ad featured photographs of nine PC monitors, all sitting inside office cubicles and all decorated differently. Soon after the Super Bowl spots, Monster aired a campaign called "Portraits," which was derived from "Today's the Day." The spots featured real job seekers and recruiters explaining what they wanted out of employment. The spots aired throughout February on both network and cable television, including NBC, ABC, ESPN, VH-1, and USA.

OUTCOME

Not surprisingly, Monster saw the greatest spike of success on the days after the two ads aired during Super

Bowl XXXVIII, thus reaching 143.6 million viewers. On February 2, the day after the game, 62,007 résumés were submitted on Monster.com, surpassing the 53,510 submitted the Monday after Monster's 2003 Super Bowl ads. On February 3, the second day after the 2004 Super Bowl, another 59,126 résumés were uploaded. "Once again, the Super Bowl has proven to be a rewarding venue to propel our brand and new message to millions of viewers all over the country and in almost every demographic," Taylor told *Business Wire.* "We're excited to build upon this momentum with the launch of a new series of ads featuring real users, the face and voice of Monster."

By October 2004 the Monster division's deferred revenue had reached a new high of $195.4 million, a 52 percent increase over the previous year. Despite the success of the "Today's the Day" campaign, however, by mid-2005 Monster had reassigned its creative responsibilities to a different ad agency, Brand Content. Explaining the shift from Deutsch, Brad Baker, chief product and marketing officer at Monster, told *Adweek,* "The new Monster voice celebrates the individual, their talents and aspirations. . .for employers, this means a more qualified candidate to meet their needs." *Adweek* suggested that the changeover resulted from disputes over fees and issues of "chemistry" in Monster and Deutsch's relationship during the 2003–2005 period. Deutsch retained Monster's media buying and planning duties, however.

FURTHER READING

Barker, Robert. "Monster's Monstrous Appetite for Cash." *Business Week,* May 17, 2004, p. 138.

Bary, Andrew. "Work in Progress: Monster's Job Website Has Huge Potential." *Barron's,* August 23, 2004, p. 17.

Capell, Perri. "Career Journal: Executive's Job Hunt Proves Pricey and Tough . . . but Worth It." *Wall Street Journal,* June 21, 2005, p. B4.

Champagne, Christine. "Monster Employs Dir. Preiss for 'Today': Deutsch-Created Commercial Encourages Jobseekers to Seize the Day." *Shoot,* January 23, 2004, p. 10.

Gianatasio, David, and Lisa Van der Pool. "Monster Names Brand Content Lead Agency." *Adweek,* June 1, 2005.

Kahlenberg, Rebecca. "Dad-Friendly Benefits Must Be Nurtured: Corporate Culture, Not Official Policy, Still Governs at Work." *Washington Post,* June 12, 2005, p. K1.

Kirby, Carrie. "Online Resumes Turn Risky: Job Seekers Post Data that Can Be Used by Identity Thieves." *San Francisco Chronicle,* July 4, 2005, p. E1.

Konrad, Rachel. "Tech Job Outlook on the Decline in United States." *Baton Rouge (LA) Advocate,* June 26, 2005, p. I2.

Lazare, Lewis. "Blue Demon Pitch Taps Coach's Star Power." *Chicago Sun-Times,* January 6, 2004, p. 51.

Magill, Ken. "Monster.com to Spend $125M on Ads." *New York Sun,* December 18, 2003.

Reidy, Chris. "Monster.com Founder Planning to Step Down to Launch Venture." *Boston Globe,* June 15, 2005, p. D3.

Steinberg, Brian. "Advertising: Monster to Get Jump on Ad Season—Web Jobs Finder to Increase TV Spending on Dec. 26; Rivals Plan Own Campaigns." *Wall Street Journal,* December 17, 2003, p. B4.

Kevin Teague

Montres Rolex SA

3, rue Francois-Dussaud
Geneva 24, CH-1211
Switzerland
Telephone: 41 22 3022200
Fax: 41 22 3002255
Web site: www.rolex.com

CELEBRITY ENDORSEMENT CAMPAIGN

OVERVIEW

Rolex, the Geneva-based maker of ultra-high-quality and high-priced timepieces, had at one time or another sponsored the Wimbledon tennis tournament as well as the PGA and LPGA golf circuits, and its advertising made heavy use of athletes. Thus in 1997 it signed a deal with young golfing sensation Tiger Woods for a campaign that ran through 1998 and beyond, adding his name to a roster that included golfer Arnold Palmer, Olympic skier Picabo Street, and mountain climber Ed Viesturs. Rolex advertising in 1998 featured Woods, Street, and others, including quite a different category of celebrity—classical musicians. J. Walter Thompson of New York handled the account, which was valued at $9.3 million in 1996. Spending for 1998 was well over $10 million and focused primarily on magazine advertisements.

Rolex historically had tended to take a low-key approach to marketing, as befit a company whose customer base was in the top fraction of all income earners. Nonetheless, given the fact that it was known for the accuracy of its timepieces, Rolex began to market itself in connection with athletic events at least as early as the 1970s. It also established itself as the timekeeper of record for a number of international competitions. Certainly athletics was a "great leveler," bringing together people of different backgrounds, and with its 1998 advertising Rolex sent a clear message that it intended to reach a somewhat wider market with its products, particularly the lower-priced Tudor line.

HISTORICAL CONTEXT

Rolex was founded in 1905 by Hans Wilsdorf, a Swiss watchmaker. Central Europe, of course, had a reputation for producing some of the finest timepieces in the world, and the company quickly established a reputation as one of the best. As the Australian watch retailer Greg Alexander told Dugald Jellie of the *Sydney Morning Herald,* however, "It's a sales and promotion and public perception phenomenon. They're good-quality watches, but they're no better quality than any number of other brands that sell for much less."

Whether or not this was so, Rolex quickly made—and kept—a name for itself as one of the premier watch manufacturers in the world. It was the first to popularize the wristwatch. Up until the early twentieth century, timepieces had typically been worn in the pocket, attached to a man's waistcoat with a chain. But as times changed, so did watch buyers, and by the mid-twentieth century women were at least as likely to purchase watches as men, which opened up new markets for Rolex.

In addition to its men's and women's wristwatches, Rolex produced stopwatches, clocks, and old-fashioned

Picabo Street during the 1998 Winter Olympic Games in Nagano, Japan. GETTY IMAGES.

pocket watches. With its image of precision timekeeping, the simplest Rolex retailed for hundreds or even thousands of dollars even in the 1970s, but Rolex also offered models in bronze or gold as well as its "plain" stainless steel line. Buyers with an urge to add even greater status to their wrists could also purchase varieties of Rolex encrusted with diamonds or other gemstones.

The corporate culture of Rolex was secretive, as befit its image as the maker of high-tech products for a small portion of buyers. It maintained no website, nor did its name pop up in news stories with anything like the frequency of lower-priced competitors. In an effort to gain greater control of its production, in the 1990s the company acquired Gay Freres, a European company that supplied watch straps.

As Rolex became more widely known in the 1970s and thereafter, the company had to deal with a number of imitators, counterfeit Rolexes that carried a price tag thousands of dollars lower than the real item. One way buyers could know a real Rolex from an imitator was by watching the dial: if the second hand "ticked" perceptibly as it moved between numbers, it was not a true Rolex. The genuine article, like time itself, moved smoothly, without breaks.

TARGET MARKET

There was a time when few people questioned status symbols, along with the right of a very small minority to own what was beyond the reaches of the masses. By the end of the twentieth century, however, egalitarian sensibilities had taken over in western Europe and the United States, and a product such as Rolex might have become marginalized as an expensive bauble available only to the elite. But coupled with this change in political direction was a change in the direction of marketing, and Rolex moved with the times.

The Swiss watchmaker's strategy in the late 1990s could be likened to that of another precision instrument that emerged from central Europe to capture the sensibilities of American buyers—the Mercedes-Benz. Built by Daimler Benz AG of Stuttgart, the Mercedes had long been viewed as a car available only to the upper crust, but in the 1990s Mercedes introduced new lines that would place its product within the reach of middle-class buyers. Of course this strategy came about not as the result of a newfound democratic impulse; rather, it was a sound marketing decision that greatly increased Mercedes's market share.

Rolex applied a similar idea with its Tudor line. Whereas the price tag on a typical Rolex started at $2,000 and could go as high as $180,000 or more, according to Terry Lefton in *Adweek,* a buyer could put a Tudor around his or her wrist for as little as $850. The high end of the Tudor line ran to $4,000, a meager price compared to that of the most expensive Rolex. Regarding Woods's endorsement for Tudor, Left on wrote that the young golfing sensation would "take the lead role in Rolex's repositioning of its Tudor line as the more youthful, accessible brand in a tiered brand-family system."

Woods's multiracial background was surely no accident either. The golfer raised eyebrows in 1997 when he declared himself a "Cablinasian," an acronym that referred to his mixed heritage: Caucasian, black, Indian, Asian. His image in Rolex ads sent the message that the watchmaker wanted to extend its appeal beyond white buyers, and the use of Yo-Yo Ma and Kiri Te Kanawa, classical musicians of Asian heritage, in Rolex advertising sent a similar message.

COMPETITION

In November 1997, Wendy Hessen of *Women's Wear Daily,* one of the foremost publications of the fashion accessories industries, presented the magazine's list of the top 10 brands of jewelry and watches. As Hessen noted,

WATCHING THE STATUS SYMBOL

"On a first date," wrote Dugald Jellie in the *Sydney Morning Herald,* "a girl once told me you could tell the quality of a man by the quality of his shoes and watch. At the time, I was wearing black R.M. Williams boots. And a Rolex on my wrist. Mind you, it was a 100 per cent *faux* Rolex, picked up in Hong Kong for about $7. That's the sort of bloke I am; a fake, a phony who straps on a $7 watch. But hey, it told the time. Which is what a watch is all about, plus a whole lot more."

As Jellie went on to observe, a watch was at least as much a status symbol as it was a timepiece. On the question of watches as an investment, Jellie cautioned readers never to buy a new watch, a much better strategy being to invest in a used model of proven quality. His second rule was "never invest in a woman's watch. Women buy their watches for function and because they look good. Men buy their watches as objects of mechanical design and engineering, and because they can wear them underwater to 100 metres."

Jellie also advised his readers not even to consider investing in a digital watch. These, he wrote, "remain nothing more than a flashing footnote in the history of time and keeping it. For a brief second there, it appeared they would supersede traditional timepieces with hour and minute hands, until dateline 1982, when a worldwide oversupply caused the market to crash. Digital watches—some priced at $2,000 when introduced—were being sold for $3."

"With the exception of Cartier and Rolex, most of the names on the list are broader-based or even mass-distributed brands that are more familiar to the mainstream consumer than the luxury patron." The other eight brands on the list were indeed, with one exception, familiar to most American buyers: Timex, Seiko, Bulova, Citizen, Casio, Swatch, Monet, and Swiss Army.

Although the latter was, like Rolex, a Swiss product, it appealed to buyers with far less disposable income than the typical Rolex customer. Given the high prices of Rolex, however, there was a broad market available to potential competitors such as Swatch, which had run ads with supermodel Tyra Banks to promote its new ultrathin Skin line of watches. The headline said it all: "Am I naked? Or am I not?"

In July 1998 *Jewelers Circular Keystone* conducted what it called an "informal survey" of independent jewel-

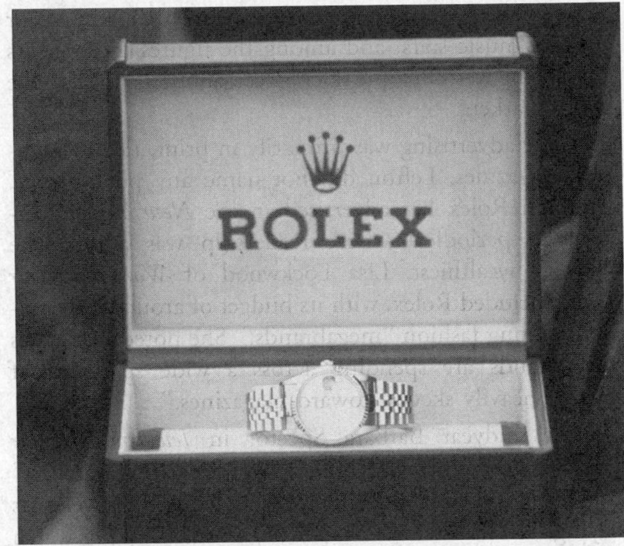

© KEVIN R. MORRIS/CORBIS.

ers around the United States. It found that Seiko was the brand carried by the greatest number of respondents—31 percent. This was not nearly as surprising as the fact that Rolex came in second, with 24 percent. Rolex was followed by Bulova, at 19 percent; Pulsar, with 18.5 percent, and Cyma, at 17 percent.

Inasmuch as it tied its marketing to sports and was also a Swiss company, TAG Heuer was a competitor to Rolex, although its products sold for much lower prices. The company had fallen on hard times, but it had set the pace for other watchmakers with an aggressive program of marketing, launching campaigns such as "Don't Crack under Pressure" and "Inner Strength" in both Britain and the United States.

More direct competition for Rolex came from Movado Group, the producer of Concord watches. The latter carried a price tag between $2,000 and $15,000. In October 1998, Stuart Elliott of the *New York Times* reported that Movado Group had assigned its $8 million advertising budget to Arnell Group, known for campaigns it had undertaken for Tommy Hilfiger, Donna Karan, and others.

MARKETING STRATEGY

Elliott noted that Movado Group's advertising choice was "an example of how marketers of premium-priced products are stepping up efforts to peddle their wares to consumers." This was certainly Rolex's strategy when, in May 1997, it signed Woods to a five-year deal that included endorsement fees and royalty payments. An advertising source told Lefton of *Brandweek,* "The idea is to get people in the Rolex family earlier. [Rolex] felt that Tudor will be legitimized and made more youthful by

Tiger." Rolex continued to focus on either athletic or classical music stars, and among the figures included its advertising was Olympic skier Street, another appeal to the youth market.

The advertising was primarily in print, tied to high-end magazines. Lefton did not name any publications, although Rolex has advertised in the *New Yorker,* certainly a periodical whose readership was among the nation's wealthiest. Lisa Lockwood of *Women's Wear Daily* included Rolex, with its budget of around $10 million, among fashion "megabrands." She noted, "Today's megabrands are spending across a wide spectrum of media, heavily skewed toward magazines."

At midyear Barbara Spector in *Jewelers Circular Keystone* wrote that "the time is right for selling watches," and she quoted a prominent Massachusetts jeweler as saying, "We do seem to be in the middle of a big watch boom." In this climate Rolex enhanced its position through careful marketing methods. Wrote Spector, "Many jewelers say that high-end watch companies have helped them compete by limiting distribution of their products. Several specifically mention Rolex's stricter policy, adopted by the company a few years ago." One retailer told her, "We increased the number of Rolex products [in our store], they reduced the number of Rolex dealers, and we sold more Rolexes. Since then, we've been very happy." With the new policy, the retailer continued, "We have a totally different relationship with the salesman; he's extremely supportive and helpful."

OUTCOME

The boom market in watches continued into 1999, and companies scrambled to make the most of it. European watchmakers, as Keith Flamer of *Jewelers Circular Keystone* observed, had discovered a new country, the United States, one that offered a huge potential market along with a number of obstacles. An Italian watch company executive contrasted buying patterns in the United States with those in his homeland: "Spending $400 on a watch is a major investment here, compared to Italy, where it is an afterthought." Indeed, as Flamer noted, "Watch executives say the United States is the most difficult country in which to market watches because it's heavily populated, regionally fragmented, constantly changing, and price-conscious." In such a challenging, yet potentially quite lucrative, market, "consumers must be bombarded with brand messages from all directions."

Of most watch marketing during 1998 and 1999, Flamer wrote that "subtlety is out . . . Like a kid acting up in class, the unconventional advertising [of watch companies] is commanding attention, especially among the young." A Rolex ad that appeared on the back of the May 31, 1999, issue of the *New Yorker,* however, showed that the Swiss company's idea of letting it all hang out was still fairly conservative. The ad showed Ma, his arms spread wide, one hand on his cello. "Yo-Yo Ma favors Italian instruments made in the early eighteenth century," the headline announced. "Occasionally, however, he makes an exception." According to the copy, "Yo-Yo Ma says his 1712 Stradivarius is 'like a great Bordeaux,' while his 1783 Mantagnana is 'earthier, like a Burgundy.' About a third instrument, his Rolex, he says, 'I just love it. You can use it for any occasion.' "

Precisely because of its low-key approach, Flamer referred to Rolex—along with competitors Cartier, TAG Heuer, Movado, Omega, Raymond Weil, and Swatch—as one of "a handful of companies whose marketing efforts stand out. They've built brand awareness with specific niches, creativity, consistency, distinctive product, appeals to the emotions, and yes, multimillion-dollar advertising campaigns."

In April 1999 Rolex chose Olympic champion Ekaterina Gordeeva as the first figure skater to appear in one of its ads. Two other things set the Gordeeva ad apart from others. First, the photograph was staged, not a candid action shot, as was typical of Rolex advertising using athletes. And the watch on Gordeeva's wrist was her own, a gift from Sergei Grinkov, her late husband and skating partner.

FURTHER READING

Banoo, Sreerema. "TAG Heuer Sticks to Its Momentum." *Business Times* (Malaysia), February 10, 1999, p. 15.

Elliott, Stuart. "Movado Group Hires an Outside Agency to Reset the Luxury Face of Its Concord Watch." *New York Times,* October 27, 1998, p. 7.

Flamer, Keith. "Watch Marketing Hits Fever Pitch." *Jewelers Circular Keystone,* April 1, 1999.

Gann, Kyle. "Classical Sleaze: Who Killed Classical Music?" *Village Voice,* August 19, 1997, p. 75.

Hessen, Wendy. "Rich Heritage Scores High." *Women's Wear Daily,* November 19, 1997, p. S52.

Jellie, Dugald. "A Timely Investment." *Sydney Morning Herald,* July 8, 1998, p. 4.

Lefton, Terry. "Tiger to Pitch for Tudor." *Brandweek,* May 26, 1997, p. 3.

Lockwood, Lisa. "Fashion's Deep Pockets." *Women's Wear Daily,* May 15, 1998, p. B4.

Nisse, Jason. "Swiss Watchmaker Feels the Force of an Untimely Curse." *Times* (London), June 30, 1998, p. 31.

Parr, Karen. "A Season for Silver and Gold." *Women's Wear Daily,* July 21, 1997, p. S50.

"Rolex on Ice." *Women's Wear Daily,* April 26, 1999.

Spector, Barbara. "Good Times Are Ticking for Watches." *Jewelers Circular Keystone,* July 1998, pp. 86-88.

Judson Knight

Morgan Stanley

1585 Broadway
New York, New York 10036
USA
Telephone: (212) 761-4000
Fax: (212) 733-2307
Web site: www.morganstanley.com

AT YOUR SIDE CAMPAIGN

OVERVIEW

NOTE: Since the initial writing of this essay Morgan Stanley Dean Witter & Co. shortened its name to Morgan Stanley. The essay continues to refer to the company's former name, as that was the official name of the organization when the campaign was launched.

After Morgan Stanley Group Inc. merged with Dean Witter, Discover & Company in 1997, the resulting company retained Dean Witter's well-established tagline "We measure success one investor at a time." With the advent of the twenty-first century, the firm toyed with new taglines, eventually settling on "One client at a time." Although sounding similar in nature, the new tagline reflected a transition in the firm's marketing approach, which now emphasized a commitment to long-lasting client relationships. In 2004 Morgan Stanley and its longtime advertising agency, Leo Burnett, launched the "At Your Side" advertising campaign, which took the concept further, showing Morgan Stanley financial advisers acting like close family members in a series of humorous television spots. The goal was to address everyday financial needs with which the audience could relate, such as paying for a child's college education or wedding or funding early retirement.

The television spots in the "At Your Side" campaign, accounting for the bulk of Morgan Stanley's $80 million budget in 2004, continued to be shown in 2005. Each relied on an attention-grabbing trick: leading the viewer to believe that a Morgan Stanley adviser was a close family member. One commercial, for example, showed a couple sitting on a beach. The man—who thought he knew how to tweak the couple's investment portfolio so that a dream house could be bought—turned out to be a Morgan Stanley adviser. The real husband was napping on his wife's lap and popped his head up when he learned the good news.

The "At Your Side" campaign won awards and helped Morgan Stanley elevate itself above a crowded media landscape. Its success did not, however, ensure that Leo Burnett would keep the business. With the installation of new leadership at Morgan Stanley in 2005, the advertising account was put into review, and rather than participate, Leo Burnett severed a 17-year relationship with the client.

HISTORICAL CONTEXT

For old-line firms like Morgan Stanley, involved in selling security brokerage services to the public, the conventional marketing approach for many years had been to emphasize knowledge and competency—essentially conveying the message "We're the experts"—while projecting a sense of trust. For many years Salomon Smith Barney employed actor John Houseman, who intoned, "They make money the old-fashioned way. They earn it." Another (now defunct) firm coined, "When E.F. Hutton talks, people listen." During the 1980s Dean Witter, before merging with Morgan Stanley, used the advertising slogan "You look like you just heard from Dean Witter." During the 1990s it proclaimed, "We measure success one investor at a time." When Dean Witter and Morgan Stanley merged in 1997, the tagline continued to be used by the combined retail business.

With the rise of Internet brokers in the 1990s, financial advertising took a dramatic turn. Newcomers like E*Trade Group and Ameritrade Holding Corporation spent heavily to establish their brands using irreverent humor and by treating stock trading as a game and mocking traditional stockbrokers. They appealed to a young, broader demographic, leaving the old guard like Morgan Stanley to appear stodgy and only interested in already wealthy customers.

In the 2000s Morgan Stanley began to adjust its approach. It tried to skew to a young demographic in the retail business while promoting its electronic capabilities, as evidenced by new advertising campaigns developed in 2000 by Leo Burnett that eschewed the "one investor at a time" tagline to center around a new tagline, "Well Connected." The implication was that Morgan Stanley combined electronic connectivity with the insider relationships of a well-established firm. Likewise an institutional campaign launched in 2001 relied on the tagline "Network the World."

The bull market of the 1990s gave way to a recession, exacerbated by the terrorist attacks of September 11, 2001. For the past 20 years Morgan Stanley and other firms offering investment services had spent a great deal of money appealing to small investors, but that strategy no longer made sense. Cheap online transactions had taken all of the profit out of the transaction side of the industry, eliminating the executional advantage that financial firms had long held. Now the likes of Morgan Stanley found that their profits were in dispensing advice—independent, trustworthy advice.

In 2002, after five years of integrating the Dean Witter operations, Morgan Stanley decided to consolidate its advertising account at Leo Burnett, which was charged with creating a campaign that sought to present a unified message behind all of Morgan Stanley's products and strengthen the Morgan Stanley brand. A new tagline was crafted, one that would provide resonance with the firm's past while continuing to develop a new approach to reaching out to potential customers: "One client at a time." The goal was to portray Morgan Stanley as a firm that despite its size cared about customers on an individual basis. The initial television spots showed Morgan Stanley advisers talking emotionally about how they helped their clients. In one commercial a couple was helped to retire to Paris, while in a second a daughter's tuition to the Julliard School was the subject. In 2004 Leo Burnett pursued similar themes using humor in the "At Your Side" campaign, which continued to use the "One client at a time" tagline.

WHAT'S IN A NAME?

The "Morgan" in Morgan Stanley Dean Witter & Company refers to the legendary banker J.P. Morgan, who in the late 1800s and early 1900s was one of the most powerful men in the world. In 1935, 20 years after his death, J.P. Morgan & Company spun off its securities and investment banking businesses as Morgan Stanley & Company.

TARGET MARKET

Morgan Stanley's "At Your Side" campaign targeted retail customers, the focus on partnering with baby boomer parents (roughly 40 to 55 years of age), the kind of people who might be dealing with early retirement or their children's weddings. The younger investors that the TV spots of the previous two years had hoped to reach were not the primary concern, nor were people past retirement age. The new campaign, rather, centered on the needs of upper-middle-class parents, either married or single, or empty nesters looking to take the next step in their lives. These people had no illusions of becoming day traders and wanted the kind of asset-management services that a website or their local bank was unable to offer. Although Morgan Stanley no longer courted small investors, there were still plenty of potential customers. At the start of the twenty-first century, some 11 million households used professional financial advisers. That number was expected to grow to 60 million within 15 years.

COMPETITION

There was no shortage of entities hoping to carve out a share of that huge market of potential customers. Electronic brokers like E*Trade and Ameritrade remained competitors for Morgan Stanley, primarily because they spent a great deal of money on advertising, their ads were attention getting, and their marketing at the very least created a great deal of clutter in the marketplace for investment products and services. But given the kind of people the "At Your Side" campaign hoped to appeal to, Internet rivals were not primary concerns. Competition instead came from other quarters.

A CAST OF THOUSANDS

Morgan Stanley Dean Witter & Company's longtime advertising agency, Leo Burnett, was responsible for some of the most recognizable product characters in advertising history. These included the Jolly Green Giant, Morris the Cat, Charlie the Tuna, Tony the Tiger, the Maytag repairman, the Marlboro Man, and the Pillsbury Doughboy.

Increasingly insurance companies and banks encroached on Morgan Stanley's turf, all of them attempting to provide customers with a one-stop shopping center of financial services. Mutual fund companies, such as the Fidelity Group and the Vanguard Group, also provided competition. In addition Morgan Stanley had to contend with competition from rivals in the retail/wholesale financial-management sector. They included longtime king Merrill Lynch as well as Goldman Sachs, Citigroup subsidiary Salomon Smith Barney, and Charles Schwab.

MARKETING STRATEGY

The strategy behind the "At Your Side" campaign on the consumer side was to continue the "One client at a time" theme and further position Morgan Stanley not just as a firm interested in helping clients build wealth, but as a firm whose advisers cared about customers' lives and were as committed as a member of the family in helping them realize their cherished dreams. Morgan Stanley was not alone in pursuing the partnership theme, however. Writing for *U.S. Banker,* Matthew de Paula quoted Bill Wreaks, publisher and chief analyst of the *Journal of Financial Advertising & Marketing,* who commented, "This whole notion of partnership is very evident in a lot of financial advertising.... What makes that different from the past, is that before it was like 'We're the experts, we know what we're doing and you should have confidence in what we're doing. But back off.' And now it's about what we can do together." According to Wreaks, "This trend came about partly because financial firms are finally clueing into what advertisers in other sectors have realized for a long time: everything starts with people." It was a lesson learned a long time ago by consumer brands, which predicated their marketing approach with people in mind, seeking to show how the product or service fit into customers' everyday lives.

To make the point that Morgan Stanley could be a partner and play a role in everyday aspects of clients' lives, Leo Burnett decided to employ humor, "not crazy or ridiculous like the E*Trade ads from years past," Wreaks told de Paula. Rather, Morgan Stanley opted for "light humor, fun and subtle." The creative team also adopted a misdirection ploy, coaxing the audience to believe one thing, then pulling a surprise to get their attention. The Morgan Stanley television spots led the audience to believe that a friendly Morgan Stanley financial adviser was a family member. For example, in one commercial a woman was shown cheering wildly for a child in a soccer game, berating the referee, and urging other players to pass the ball to "her" kid—leading the viewer to see her as a typical soccer mom. A bystander then asked her which child was hers, only to learn that she was in fact the financial adviser of the child's parent. The implication was that she cared as much about the child as the client, that she shared the client's dreams. Another spot showed a couple sitting on the beach. The man said that if some adjustments were made to their investment portfolio, they could afford their dream home. The wife then asked her husband what he thought, at which point another man (her husband) sat up. He had been hidden all this time because his head was on his wife's lap. Once again the viewer was tricked into thinking a Morgan Stanley adviser was a close family member. In another spot an adviser at a ribbon-cutting ceremony was confused with a CEO, and in a fourth an adviser shared personal stories of a child at a graduation party as if he were the father of the honored child.

The "At Your Side" spots were clearly not attempting to be believable. Rather, they were intended to be symbolic. Some viewers accepted the commercials' premise and played along with the humor, while others took a more literal approach and regarded the fictional advisers as little more than disturbed stalkers. The spots—loved, hated, or merely tolerated—were at the very least memorable.

OUTCOME

From Morgan Stanley's perspective the "At Your Side" commercials were very successful. According to Scott Spry, executive vice president of brand advertising and brand analytics for Phoenix Marketing International, quoted in a May 2005 *Investment News* article, "The campaign generates extremely high recall, and it breaks through the clutter." Unlike advertising that talked about the company, which fared poorly in the Phoenix survey, the Morgan Stanley spots were the top rated among both "general" and "affluent" investors. Beth Allan, president of Phoenix's advertising and brand analytics division, explained that "people like the relevant scenario. They can see themselves in the situations that the Morgan ads portray, like a wedding and early retirement. People want to know what a company can do to help you do well. The core notion is that the consumer is in charge, not the company."

Leo Burnett's work on the "At Your Side" campaign was also recognized by the advertising industry. It won the Corporate Image award in the annual Financial Communications Society Portfolio Awards. In addition "At Your Side" garnered a Silver in the Financial Services/Image category of the 2005 Effies, presented by the New York American Marketing Association to honor the year's most effective advertising campaigns.

Neither awards nor a 17-year relationship guaranteed that Leo Burnett would retain the Morgan Stanley account, however. In June 2005 Morgan Stanley changed chief executive officers, unseating Philip Purcell, whose connection with Leo Burnett dated back to his days with Dean Witter well before the 1997 merger. As part of the changes that came with the installation of new leadership, Morgan Stanley's $80 million account was put into review. Leo Burnett was invited to participate, but in August 2005 it decided to resign as the advertising agency of record.

FURTHER READING

Baar, Aaron. "Morgan Stanley Bows Campaign." *Adweek,* March 25, 2002, p. 8.

———. "Morgan Stanley to Sum It Up." *Adweek,* February 18, 2002, p. 5.

Cardona, Mercedes M. "Morgan Stanley Pursues Younger, Well-Heeled Investors." *Advertising Age,* August 28, 2000, p. 3.

Curtis, Carol E. "The Next Hot Products: Advice." *U.S. Banker,* May 1999.

de Paula, Matthew. "In '04, Bank Ads Scored Big. Message Delivers." *U.S. Banker,* January 2005, p. 38.

McGeehan, Patrick. "Morgan Stanley Dean Witter Drops a Familiar Image to Take Aim at Electronic Brokerage Firms." *New York Times,* August 28, 2000, p. C1.

Paikert, Charles. "Majors Firms Increase Advertising Spending." *Investment News,* May 16, 2005, p. 3.

Ed Dinger

IT PAYS TO DISCOVER REVISITED CAMPAIGN

OVERVIEW

NOTE: Since the initial writing of this essay Morgan Stanley Dean Witter & Co, shortened its name to Morgan Stanley. The essay continues to refer to the company's former name, as that was the official name of the organization when the campaign was launched.

In 1999 the San Francisco ad agency Goodby, Silverstein & Partners won the $90 million account of Discover Financial Services Inc. and its Discover credit card operation, which was owned by the investment bank Morgan Stanley Dean Witter & Co. Although it was the fourth-leading credit-card brand—trailing only Visa, MasterCard, and American Express—and boasted the largest independent card network in the United States, the Discover credit card was regarded as an also-ran in the industry. Its primary competitive advantage over the years had been what was called the "Cashback Bonus." This program was the focal point of the company's marketing for more than a decade, as reflected in the tagline "It pays to Discover." As the Discover card tried to move beyond its one-note advertising pitch, Goodby dropped the tagline. Two years later, however, the agency brought back the venerable tagline and once again concentrated on the Cashback Bonus feature.

The new campaign featured both television and print advertising, along with other elements that included the sponsorship of a NASCAR race car. In addition to pursuing the rebate theme, the campaign also promoted a new product, the Discover 2GO card, a minicard encapsulated in a protective coding that was suitable for attachment to a key chain.

The campaign, which began in June 2002, ran through 2004, at which point Discover asked for new ideas from Goodby and competing ad agencies to move away from its cash-back program. The campaign had succeeded in growing the Discover card business but not enough to take it to the next level and establish the card as a serious competitor to the top three brands. Nevertheless, Goodby's work was well received, and the agency retained the account.

HISTORICAL CONTEXT

The Discover card was launched by Sears, Roebuck & Company in the 1980s and soon established itself in the credit-card industry. Although it would become a cash cow for its eventual owner, Morgan Stanley, the Discover card was very much an also-ran compared to rivals American Express, MasterCard, and Visa. Its only significant advantage was the Cashback Bonus rebate offered to cardholders based on how much they used their cards. This facet was the keystone of the tagline "It pays to Discover," coined in 1988. A major obstacle preventing the growth of the Discover card was its inability to issue cards through banks, which had become the exclusive preserve of MasterCard and Visa. The task of going it alone became even more difficult in the 1990s following a wave of bank mergers, which resulted in ever-larger entities issuing MasterCard and Visa cards. Large banks were capable of using economies of scale to offer better terms and services and, in turn, to attract more customers.

Led by a new management team, the Discover card tried to fight back in the late 1990s. It issued a platinum card, which was backed by the bulk of the company's marketing budget, in hopes of gaining business in new market segments, while the Bravo and Private Option cards were dropped. But the creative approach was muddled, and in late 1998 the advertising account was put up for review. Considered something of a long shot, Goodby emerged the winner in early 1999, despite having developed only one minor campaign in the financial-services area in its history. Nevertheless, Discover was banking on the San Francisco agency's sterling reputation for producing award-winning advertising for clients across a wide range of industries. The Discover card's vice president of advertising and communications, Catherine Davis, told the press, "We are confident that Goodby will provide a new perspective and fresh approach that will help Discover Card reposition itself."

The company particularly wanted to dispel the notion among consumers that the Discover card had a low merchant-acceptance rate and offered nothing more than rebates, a feature the company believed had lost some of its luster since the industry had begun to copy the idea of cash-back bonuses. Discover did not necessarily want to drop its longtime tagline, "It pays to Discover," but it did want to change its message. "It the past we had focused on 'no annual fee' and 'cash-back bonus,' but the industry over the last five to seven years has copied that, so it's not as unique as it used to be," Davis told Miriam Kreinin Souccar, writing for *American Banker.* When the first Goodby campaign opened in the fall of 1999, it featured a new tagline, "There's always something more to Discover," the card's first marketing effort to focus on something other than the cash-back feature. Instead, the ads promoted a broader spectrum of card benefits. After two years, however, further research revealed that the "It pays to Discover" tagline retained resonance with consumers. In a *Credit Card Management* article Kate Fitzgerald wrote, "According to an insider at Discover, the vast majority of consumers still immediately recalled that line, inked in 1988, while employees at the company struggled to remember the credit card's more recent themes." Deciding to take advantage of the lingering power of the discarded tagline, Discover reprised the "It pays to Discover" theme in a broad new campaign launched in June 2002 in which, once again, the card's cash-back program was front and center. In addition, the company also promoted its new 2GO card, the first card in the industry small enough to attach to a key chain.

TARGET MARKET

The Discover card's core market was described by David Robertson, publisher of the credit-card industry newsletter *Nilson Report,* as "meat-and-potatoes, blue-collar, middle of the road." The new "It Pays to Discover" campaign not only wanted to maintain a connection with this middle-market audience but wanted to reach out to other consumers as well. Edgy humor would be used to promote the new 2GO minicard to the highly coveted segment of adults between the ages of 18 and 40, people who were cost-conscious but who led active lifestyles. Moreover, research indicated that these consumers were likely to use the minicard in fast-food and convenience stores, venues that generally experienced a low volume of credit-card use. It was also thought that the 2GO card, a technological innovation in the staid credit-card landscape, would be an advantage in pitching Discover to a new generation of users entering the marketplace.

> ### IT PAYS TO REMEMBER
>
> The Discover card grew out of a diversification effort of Sears, Roebuck & Company, which in 1981 acquired the securities firm Dean Witter Reynolds Inc. In 1985 Sears launched the Discover card as a combined credit and financial services card that also offered savings accounts through Greenwood Trust Company, a bank that had been acquired by a Sears subsidiary. Financial difficulties forced Sears to spin off Dean Witter and the Discover card in the early 1990s. Then, in 1997, Dean Witter, Discover & Co. merged with Morgan Stanley Group Inc. to create the Discover card's corporate parent, Morgan Stanley Dean Witter & Co.

COMPETITION

When the new campaign was launched in June 2002, Discover was firmly entrenched as the number four brand among credit cards. According to *Credit Card Management* and research conducted by *Brandweek,* its $93.3 billion in total sales in 2001 was well ahead of the $12.4 billion generated by number five Diners Club, making Discover the largest independent credit card network in the United States. But the Discover card also trailed the top three brands by a considerable margin: American Express recorded total sales in 2001 of $224.5 billion, followed by MasterCard's $518 billion and category leader Visa's $916 billion. The amount of money the top brands spent on advertising in 2001 also reflected their standing. Discover spent $82.1 million in advertising, compared to $251.3 million for Visa, $197.3 million for MasterCard, and $153.9 billion for American Express. Diners Club spent a mere $8.8 million.

Aside from the hefty budgets they had at their disposal, the Discover card's larger rivals had either carved out clear niches or had honed highly effective marketing appeals. Historically American Express played on its exclusivity, as reflected by the memorable tagline "Membership has its privileges," which was dropped in the 1990s as the culture changed. Nevertheless, American Express was able to continue to pursue a successful niche strategy of appealing to high-end consumers. MasterCard and Visa fought it out to gain business in a much broader market, and both were able to develop effective ad campaigns. Visa scored with its "Everywhere you want to be" tagline, while MasterCard effectively exploited its "Priceless" campaign.

One of the disadvantages of the Discover card was that it could be used only in the United States, and even there it was not as widely accepted as its three larger competitors. For many consumers the card was thus relegated to second-class status. Part of the problem was not being able to distribute the cards through banks, although that provided a competitive advantage as well; since Visa and MasterCard could not make specific claims on their products or services, they could not guarantee that the banks would honor them. In addition, according to a 2002 *Brandweek* article, "Discover Card edged out MasterCard, Visa and American Express on the category's most crucial driver. Fees and rates used to be a point of differentiation. But not these days, when interest rates are down low enough to make them meaningless. Discover indexed higher than the ideal and competitors because it gives money back."

MARKETING STRATEGY

Given the results of market research, Discover decided to play to its strengths in the new campaign, reviving the "It pays to Discover" tagline and once again emphasizing its rebate program. At the same time it promoted the new 2GO card, along with merchant alliances, exclusive sponsorships, and other perks and privileges available to card members. The broad campaign included television spots and print ads as well as other elements.

The first phase in the new "It Pays to Discover" campaign featured three television spots, two of which highlighted the Cashback Bonus program, with the third focusing on the 2GO card. The most memorable was titled "First Date," a 30-second spot that recorded a series of first-date experiences by a young, single male lawyer, each one starting out promising but ending up a disaster. One of his dates hated lawyers, another asked if he liked to shop, and a third thought that he was "kind of boring," while yet another woman was quick to ask, "Where do you think this thing is going between us? Because my clock's kind of ticking." The silver lining in this dark cloud was that, by using his Discover card to pay for his bad dates, the man accrued a Cashback Bonus award of $160. A final date with another lawyer offered some hope, as a voice-over commented that the man might someday use his Cashback Bonus to help pay for an engagement ring. This was followed by the tagline "Discover Card's New Cashback Bonus Program, where you get paid for the things you buy anyway." The ads began airing on June 2, 2002, during a NASCAR telecast, and they continued throughout the rest of the year during early morning news programs and prime-time shows as well as on syndicated programs and on cable networks.

To provide continuity with the new television commercials, the ongoing print campaign in magazines, which focused on the Discover card's many merchant relationships and its growing acceptance among retailers across the United States, also adopted the "It pays to Discover" tagline. A $5,000 shopping spree promotion was launched with *Lucky*, a magazine devoted to shopping. Furthermore, the company promoted itself in other novel ways. It sponsored a NASCAR car for six races, including the race on which the new television spots had their debut. Discover acquired the naming rights to an Atlanta-area shopping mall, which became Discover Mills and where card members could take advantage of exclusive offers and promotions. The Discover card also beefed up its website, where card members could redeem Cashback Bonus awards as well as pay their bills and take advantage of other customer-service activities.

The Discover card continued to pursue the "It Pays to Discover" campaign in 2003 and 2004, releasing a new wave of television commercials. One 2003 effort, titled "Sporting Goods," featured a father who spent a great deal of money buying sporting equipment for a son who was not athletic. In the end he used his Cashback Bonus to help the boy pursue success with chess. Other 2003 television spots used off-the-wall humor to promote the 2GO card. In one a man used the card to pay for lunch, but as he left the restaurant, he was assaulted by ninjas. The man tried to fend them off with his 2GO card, prompting the comment from a voice-over "Discover 2GO. Convenient. Innovative. Not good for ninja fights." Other spots featured a woman trying to use her 2GO card as a paddle in a ping-pong tournament and a man attempting to use the card to cut a tangled fishing line. In 2004 Discover offered a 10 percent Cashback Bonus in a two-month push to encourage members to buy groceries with their cards. One television spot in this effort, titled "10," used a variety of everyday items that appeared side by side to form the numeral 10, such as a long package and a wreath, a baguette and a hat, and a quart of milk and a melon. The idea was successful with both merchants and card members, leading to a similar campaign with restaurants in the fall of 2004. By then, however, Discover had decided once again to move away from its cash-back program and, as the account was put up for review, asked Goodby and other ad agencies to present new ideas.

OUTCOME

The marketing campaign revisiting the "It pays to Discover" tagline was successful on several levels. According to an October 2004 article in *Credit Card Management,* Discover, because of its marketing and other initiatives, was at the top of the list of "comeback of the year" stories in the credit-card industry. "But competitors have adopted both rewards and minicards, making Discover a seeming also-ran." Indeed, the landscape was experiencing a significant change. In October 2004 a U.S. Supreme Court ruling allowed Discover to form partnerships with banks as well as with other companies, such as Wal-Mart and General Electric Consumer Finance.

In addition, although the prospects appeared to be improving for the Discover card, Morgan Stanley came under pressure from investors to spin off the business. Investors argued that the card's middle-market clientele was a poor fit with Morgan Stanley, failing to offer synergy with a corporate parent whose core investment-banking business targeted far wealthier consumers and corporations. After initially indicating, during a period of internal dissent, that it would unload Discover, Morgan Stanley announced in August 2005 that it would keep the business. Goodby also prevailed in the account review for the Discover card and looked to build on the work accomplished in the "It Pays to Discover" campaign.

FURTHER READING

"Card-Carrying Members Share Perks, Pet Peeves about Plastic." *Brandweek,* February 25, 2002, p. 18.

Cardona, Mercedes M. "Small Credit Cards Get Big Ad Pushes." *Advertising Age,* September 8, 2003, p. 3.

Cassidy, Hilary. "Sports Provides Value for Card Collectors." *Brandweek,* June 17, 2002, p. S42.

———. "Top Cards Still Hold Solid Hands." *Brandweek,* June 23, 2003, p. S36.

Davis, Ann, and Robin Sidel. "Morgan Stanley Reassesses Plan to Pursue Spinoff of Discover Card." *Wall Street Journal,* June 17, 2005, p. A1.

De Paula, Matthew. "Ad Beat: Moving beyond Merely Wallet-Size." *U.S. Banker,* May 2003, p. 35.

"Discover Rediscovers Discover." *Credit Card Management,* October 2004, p. 6.

Fitzgerald, Kate. "No Fads in These Ads." *Credit Card Management,* December 2002, p. 18.

Purcell, Philip J. "Sizing Up a Credit Card That's Out on Its Own." *New York Times,* April 5, 2005, p. C20.

Souccar, Miriam Kreinin. "Discover Seeks Broader Appear with New Ads." *American Banker,* September 17, 1999, p. 9.

Ed Dinger

MAKE A STATEMENT CAMPAIGN

OVERVIEW

NOTE: Since the initial appearance of this essay in the 1998 edition of *Major Marketing Campaigns Annual,* Dean Witter, Discover & Company became a unit of Morgan Stanley. The essay continues to refer to the company's former name, as that was the official name of the organization when the campaign was launched.

The Discover card burst onto the scene in 1986 with something no other card offered—a year-end cash bonus equal to 1 percent of purchases. The cash-back feature, coupled with no annual fee, made a lot of sense to value-conscious consumers who were accustomed to paying for the convenience of using a credit card. In its first six years alone, Discover had already put $355 million back into the pockets of its cardholders. It was not long, however, before competitors began issuing their own rebate and no-fee cards, which eroded Discover's once sure hold on the "value" market. Convincing consumers to use one card over another became an increasingly tough sell. In addition, most credit card companies issued multiple, targeted cards for different market segments. An American Express spokeswoman explained the trend to *American Banker* by saying, "If we have fifteen different products we can offer you, if you call in and don't qualify for one card, we can give you a different one instead." Despite the industry shift toward specialized cards, Discover held to the notion of being the card for everybody. William Hodges, Discover executive vice president and general manager, told *Brandweek,* "When everyone else is offering every flavor, maybe it's better just to have the best vanilla anybody is selling."

Over the years the company had built up a respectable merchant network that was nearly on a par with the Visa/MasterCard duopoly. Doubt about Discover's acceptance, however, remained a thorn in the company's side. While its merchant network had grown and the card was accepted at some 90 percent of U.S. locations that took bankcards, public perception remained that it was not as well received as other cards. Consumers were particularly reluctant to use Discover at upscale retail stores and restaurants. The "Make a Statement" campaign, which showed celebrities using their Discover cards in trendy places, was developed to remedy this image problem. The campaign was a departure from past campaigns, which had driven home the message of value and functionality. Debuting in August 1996, the commercials downplayed the cash-back rebate and implied that Discover was hipper than consumers might have previously thought.

HISTORICAL CONTEXT

When Sears, Roebuck launched the Discover card in 1986, it offered value-conscious consumers a revolutionary combination of features: no annual fee and a cash award of up to 1 percent of yearly purchases. At a time when other cards charged annual fees of $20 or more and interest rates of 19.8 percent, Discover's introduction made a newsworthy splash in the industry. Naysayers, however, claimed that there was no way Discover could make a profit and said that retailers would not want to go through the process of setting up a payment system with Discover.

Discover proved the critics wrong by flourishing. A consumer survey in 1989 showed that 27 percent of those households whose members carried credit cards named Discover as their favorite. In 1991 Discover cards were in the wallets of almost 40 million consumers. By charging retailers lower fees than its competitors, Discover also readily gained merchant acceptance. *Business Week* heralded the card's growing success with the headline "The Discover Card Is No Longer a Joker," and a headline in *American Banker* proclaimed, "Sears' Discover Card a Weakling No More."

But during the 1990s Discover's once unique features became widely imitated by other credit card companies. Some cards actually beat Discover's rebate, offering a 5 percent rebate toward airline tickets or purchases of automobiles. Meanwhile, Discover did not alter its offerings. Industry experts criticized Discover for its reluctance to develop new products and services, such as platinum or affinity cards. "You could either say that they have been slow to respond to the leading trends or have chosen not to follow," said Shelly Porges, a credit card consultant. In 1995 Discover's new parent company, Dean Witter, recognized that the Discover card alone did not have the breadth to capture a vast market share. It chose not to dilute the Discover card brand image and instead launched a series of niche cards under the Novus Services brand. While Discover successfully continued expanding its merchant network under the Novus label, the card still lagged in the travel and entertainment sector and was not accepted internationally. By 1997 the card had not wholly shed its underdog status. Among the four major credit cards in the United States, Discover still finished in fourth place.

TARGET MARKET

During Discover's early years it was marketed as a card for the masses. In 1991 Thomas R. Butler, Discover's president, told *American Banker* that the company was "targeting every creditworthy cardholder in the whole damn U.S. marketplace. We are really going after the broad cross section of everyone." This initial marketing thrust had been effective in getting the card into as many people's wallets as possible, but times had changed, and most consumers now had multiple cards to choose from. While plenty of people had maintained their Discover card accounts, only one-half to two-thirds of those people regularly used the card. The emphasis in 1997 shifted to getting Discover cardholders actually to pull the card out and use it.

"People don't always think of Discover as a card they can use at an upscale merchant; we want to uplift that image," Robert E. Wood II, executive vice president of Discover-Novus marketing, told *Credit Card Management.* With the "Make a Statement" campaign the target market for Discover changed from everyman and everywoman to a slightly more upscale audience, including younger cardholders who were less concerned with counting their pennies. The campaign capitalized on the public interest in celebrities' lives, as evident in the success of magazines like *People* and *In Style* and television shows like *Entertainment Tonight.*

COMPETITION

According to *Credit Card News,* Discover's 1996 charge volume in the United States was $53.6 billion, compared to $131 billion for American Express, $220.6 billion for MasterCard, and $393.1 billion for Visa. One of the things that hurt Discover's ability to expand was its lack of international presence. The U.S. market was already flooded with cards. Within the United States, Discover had issued 40 million cards, and 29.6 million American Express cards, 164.5 million MasterCards, and 240.7 million Visa cards were in circulation. While other issuers put out a variety of cards for the segmented marketplace, Discover offered only one. It did not have a platinum card, for instance, one popular way that other cards were competing for upscale consumers. Discover was also late to market another niche product, cobranded cards. In 1997 the company finally decided to move into cobranding, issuing cards linked to the Smithsonian Institution, Universal Studios, and the game show *Wheel of Fortune.* "The long-term perspective is characteristic of our company," Hodges explained in *Promo* magazine. "We think a lot about what we're getting into, because we're in it for the long haul."

Because of saturation, the U.S. credit card market was not expected to grow significantly. "All you have to do is open your mailbox to see that the marketplace is much more competitive and fragmented than it has been historically," Gail Wasserman, an American Express spokeswoman, told *American Banker.* Advertising proved a key weapon in the battle for companies hoping to get consumers to choose their card over another. Of the four major cards, according to Competitive Media Reporting, Visa topped the chart for spending on advertising in 1997, with an estimated $242 million, followed by

American Express at $195.9 million. MasterCard spent $109.3 million, and Dean Witter, Discover came in fourth at $99.2 million.

Visa's "Everywhere You Want to Be" campaign was still going strong after 13 years and continued to generate new business. Meanwhile, American Express fanned the flames of its longtime rivalry with Visa by running ads during the Visa-sponsored Olympic Games to make consumers aware that other cards were accepted in the city hosting the games. American Express also ran its stylish "Do More" campaign, which gave consumers a broad look at the company's product line of credit cards, travel services, and financial planning. In 1997 MasterCard hired a new advertising agency to embark on a repositioning of its card. Over an eight-year span the company had tried three different ad themes—"Master the Moment," "Smart Money," and "The Future of Money"—all of which had fallen flat with consumers. "Priceless" was the theme of the new campaign that emerged late in 1997. It positioned MasterCard as the credit card that made life's precious moments happen. One spot, for instance, put a dollar value on the tickets and snacks at a baseball game that opened the door for a father to have a priceless real conversation with his 11-year-old son.

MARKETING STRATEGY

Discover card's earliest advertising campaigns drove home the message of value. Commercials showed money pouring from the sky or dropping in bags and used the tag line "It pays to Discover." But with so many other cards coming to tout the same attributes of no annual fee and a cash rebate, Discover needed to find a way to distinguish itself from the pack. It needed to shake the blue-collar image inherited from its former parent company, Sears, Roebuck, without alienating loyal users. Discover's Hodges told *American Banker,* "I think we're shifting emphasis a little bit more toward a focus on the brand and the brand name, and a little bit less in terms of delivering the functional features of the cards. The emphasis is a slight change—it's not like we're abandoning what we do."

The campaign, which focused on notable people using their Discover cards, was created by DDB Needham Chicago. One of the celebrities featured in the first group of television commercials was John Lithgow, star of the popular prime-time comedy *3rd Rock from the Sun.* The spot showed Lithgow using his Discover card to buy camping equipment, flowers for his wife, and a wet suit for himself. "The toughest thing about buying a wet suit," he said, "is trying it on." Liz Torres, singer, stand-up comedienne, and actress, was shown in another commercial using her card for purchases at antique shops, at a Cuban restaurant, and "little things that make a girl sing." Tennis pro Michael Chang's Discover card statement included "tons of tennis balls" as well as charges for groceries, travel, tropical fish, and a cash advance for recreation. Bill Nye, star of *The Science Guy,* talked in one commercial about Discover card's partnership with the Smithsonian Institution. According to *Brandweek,* the campaign's eclectic mix of personalities were chosen to help upgrade Discover's down-market image to a middle-tier position. DDB Needham managing partner Ray Gillette said, "We had the card in a lot of wallets, but we wanted to make people feel better about pulling it out. 'If John Lithgow used it, then it is certainly good enough for me.'"

Creatively produced with quick-cut editing and interesting camera angles, the spots deftly sidestepped some of Discover card's weaknesses: the fact that many restaurants did not accept it and its lack of an international network. Stephen Drees of Strategic Marketing Services commented in *Brandweek,* "The positioning is sort of 'everywhere you want to be' for the middle class, which is smart because they will never be a travel and entertainment card, and only a very small percentage of people leave the country and have to deal with the fact they aren't accepted outside the U.S."

The television campaign began on August 13, 1996, on both prime-time network and cable programs. Network radio advertising began in late September. Print advertising appeared in October issues of magazines such as *Rolling Stone, People, Sports Illustrated, Entertainment Weekly, Glamour, Hispanic Business,* and *Hispanic Magazine* and in various college newspapers. A second group of television commercials featuring other notable people began on February 16, 1997. This group featured Gregory Hines, tap dancer on Broadway and in motion pictures; Paula Poundstone, stand-up comedienne; Sheryl Swoopes, basketball player in the professional women's league; Kurt Vonnegut, author of *Slaughterhouse Five;* and Trisha Yearwood, country singer. These spots ran through the remainder of 1997 and into 1998 and were complemented by radio and print ads.

OUTCOME

Discover's marketing strategy did not help the company gain ground, as overall market share slipped from 7.9 percent in 1996 to 6.7 percent in 1997. The company's Hodges told *Brandweek,* however, that a better measure of the campaign's effectiveness was Discover's direct-mail response rates, which were more than twice the industry average.

According to *USA Today* 's Ad Track, the "Make a Statement" campaign was somewhat effective among consumers but was not popular. With only 7 percent of those questioned saying that they liked the campaign a lot, it ranked among the 10 least popular ads ever measured by Ad Track. In contrast, other credit card campaigns ranked among the 20 most popular. Of those asked about a Visa campaign starring basketball stars Hakeem Olajuwon and Scottie Pippen, 30 percent liked the ads a lot, and 32 percent asked about American Express ads with comedian Jerry Seinfeld said the same. Discover card's choice of racially diverse stars and its media placements paid off with minorities, however. Compared with 19 percent of all consumers, 30 percent of black consumers found the ads very effective.

Reception of the campaign among industry insiders was also lukewarm. In an April 1997 critique in the trade publication *Card Marketing,* the panel questioned Discover's decision to downplay its cash rebate, one of the card's most recognizable features. It noted that the campaign was "not terribly original." In February 1998 *Card Marketing* again took the series of celebrity spots to task. The panel criticized Discover's decision to continue running the campaign, saying that, while there was little to fault with the "solid and workman-like" commercial, there was little "sizzle" or reason to pay attention. The campaign, the panel said, paled in comparison to other celebrity commercials for credit cards, such as the American Express spots featuring Seinfeld.

Some marketing experts commented that the campaign, while a departure from the benefits-driven approach of the past, was still too familiar. Consumers were looking for newer benefits than the tried-and-true cash-back bonus. "It may be time for Discover to come up with some breakthrough offers for existing users," wrote Lisa Holton in *Card Marketing.* "This also might help them attract new ones."

FURTHER READING

Berry, Jon. "Shuffling the Cards." *Adweek's Marketing Week,* October 7, 1991.

Coulton, Antoinette. "Universal Deal May Help Dean Witter Catch Up." *American Banker,* April 4, 1997.

D'Orio, Wayne. "Partners in Discovery." *Promo,* October 1997.

Enrico, Dottie. "Discover Ads Pale despite Celebrity Cast." *USA Today,* August 11, 1997.

Fickenscher, Lisa. "Dean Witter Shedding Its Contrarian Image: It's Producing Specialized Cards, Cobranding to Supplement Discover." *American Banker,* January 30, 1997.

Greising, David. "The Discover Card Is No Longer a Joker." *Business Week,* October 9, 1989.

Jensen, Trevor. "Celebrities Take Center Stage for Discover Card." *Adweek* (Midwest Edition), August 19, 1996.

Kingson Bloom, Jennifer. "Card Advertising War Intensifies: Firms Spend $700M on Stars, Mud." *American Banker,* July 7, 1997.

Lefton, Terry. "New Cards in Discover's Hand." *Brandweek,* September 15, 1997.

Kim Kazemi

TOW TRUCK CAMPAIGN

OVERVIEW

Known as Lombard Brokerage, Inc., until Morgan Stanley Dean Witter (later shortened to Morgan Stanley) purchased and renamed it in 1996, the discount brokerage firm Discover Brokerage Direct, Inc., was a direct competitor with other online brokerages, such as Ameritrade and E*TRADE Financial Corp. In the late 1990s online trading flourished; E*TRADE, for instance, reported a profit increase of 300 percent a year. The worldwide access of the Internet allowed any consumer, for a minimal fee, to profit from the seemingly unstoppable stock market surge during the latter half of the decade. Hoping to target responsible, self-directed American investors—not the very wealthy or the risk-taking speculator—Discover Brokerage released its "Tow Truck" marketing campaign.

In 1997 Discover Brokerage Direct, Inc., hired Black Rocket, a young advertising agency in San Francisco, to handle its $20 million advertising account. Black Rocket created a print and television campaign that used humor and atypical characters and settings to make the point that investing was not just for the rich or the reckless but was for everyone. The first commercial in the campaign, aired on television beginning in September 1998, was "Tow Truck." In this 30-second spot a businessman whose BMW was being towed commented on a copy of *Barron's* lying on the seat of the truck. It turned out that the tow-truck driver read the magazine and that he invested online with Discover Brokerage. As the conversation unfolded, viewers found out that the driver not only had made enough from online investing to retire but that he also owned his own island. "Tow Truck" ran until March 1999, after which five more television spots in the same vein were introduced, all featuring regular-looking people who turned out to be successful online investors.

Discover Brokerage's parent company, Morgan Stanley, reported a 14 percent sales increase in 1999. From an ad-industry perspective, the "Tow Truck" spot was a success, having been nominated for several Emmys. According to *USA Today* 's survey Ad Track, "Tow Truck" was the most liked commercial released by any online company in 1999.

HISTORICAL CONTEXT

Investors had traditionally paid a commission to brokers for financial advice and to have brokers conduct transactions on their behalf. Online investing through the Internet was a phenomenon of the 1990s, and although it started out small, within a few years it had created waves in the financial-services industry.

In late 1996 Dean Witter, Discover & Co. bought Lombard Brokerage, Inc., a small but well-respected San Francisco firm. Dean Witter renamed the unit Discover Brokerage Direct, Inc. (In May 1997 Dean Witter merged with Morgan Stanley Group Inc. to create Morgan Stanley Dean Witter & Co.) Discover Brokerage claimed to be one of the first to offer online investing, which it began to do in August 1995. According to Dow Jones News Service, it was planned that Discover Brokerage would offer Discover cardholders a variety of online financial services, such as balance lookups, portfolio evaluations, and consolidated financial statements, in order to draw them in as clients. In addition, the Web-based unit could be used to generate additional business for its more traditional parent company.

In the late 1990s the Internet brokerage business mushroomed. In February 1999 *BusinessWeek* called it an "exploding phenomenon," reporting that in 1996 online trading "was an almost invisible blip. Two years later, it was hard to miss." The magazine went on to report, "The Net poses the most serious threat to the established industry's economics and primacy since the unfixing of commissions on May Day, 1975, when deregulation created the discount-brokerage business, threatening, but not vanquishing, a cozy oligopoly."

TARGET MARKET

Discover Brokerage's advertising, starting with "Tow Truck," was targeted toward the everyday, hardworking Joe or Jane. According to Glenn Tom, senior vice president of marketing, it was an attempt to "reach the responsible self-directed investor through humor." *Advertising Age* described Discover Brokerage's target market as "middle Americans." Liz Seade, an account supervisor at Black Rocket, said in a June 1999 interview that Discover Brokerage sought "to open up the power of Wall Street to Main Street," aiming for business among those somewhere in between the rich guys with the big cigars and the "riverboat gambler" type of investors.

COMPETITION

A plethora of Web-based brokerage companies emerged during the late 1990s. In February 1999 *BusinessWeek* reported that, since 1996, online firms had gone from "'an insignificant technological curiosity'... to a band of more than a hundred online brokers." Discover Brokerage was a relatively small player and, according to Credit Suisse First Boston Corp., ranked ninth among its competitors, with 3.8 percent of the market (based on trades per day) in the second quarter of 1998. The rest of the top nine split the market as follows: Charles Schwab & Co. had 29.7 percent; E*TRADE Securities LLC, 11.5 percent; Fidelity Personal Investments and Services Group, 9.2 percent; Waterhouse Securities Inc., 9.2 percent; Datek, 8.5 percent; Ameritrade Holding Corp., including Accutrade Inc. and Ameritrade Inc., 6.9 percent; DLJdirect Inc., 4.3 percent; and Fleet Financial Group Inc., including Quick Sz Reilly Inc. and Suretrade Inc., 4.2 percent.

Nonetheless, Discover Brokerage was rated number three among online brokerage services by Gomez Advisors, a research outfit founded in 1996 that provided information to banks, brokerages, and other financial institutions wanting to offer Web-based financial services. *Wall Street & Technology* said of Discover Brokerage that users were "particularly impressed" with its customer service, which one user believed would help distinguish it from the competition. According to the article, "Given that the online brokerage market is

SEC CRITICISM OF ONLINE ADS

It was reported in May 1999 that the Securities and Exchange Commission (SEC) was concerned about the advertising of online brokerages. In fact, SEC chairman Arthur Levitt remarked in a speech before the National Press Club that some of the advertising resembled commercials for the lottery. Two of the spots he mentioned were "Tow Truck" and a spot for Ameritrade. In the latter, two mothers discussed their differing fortunes, with one elated because she had made $1,700 from online investing while the other bemoaned her decision to put her money into a mutual fund.

David Eckstein, speaking on behalf of Discover Brokerage Direct, Inc., said that the company fully supported the idea of "an informed investing public who are aware of the risk and rewards of investing." But the idea of including detailed disclaimers with the ads was resisted by John Yost of Black Rocket, who said that consumers deserved credit for being intelligent: "They realize that just because you suggest one guy's been wildly successful, they understand risks inherent in investing. They understand the joke."

Critic Barbara Lippert put it a bit more bluntly when she wrote in the May 1999 issue of *Adweek,* "Hello? It's known as advertising, which exaggerates reality in a comedic and entertaining way to make an impression, to get your attention. Did the Man from Glad really arrive from the sky by pontoon?... I find [Levitt's] criticism amazing, if not downright ironic."

already maturing and becoming a 'commodity' market, two factors—price and value-added customer service—will become critical. The big Wall Street players have the resources, but the race will favor the creative."

MARKETING STRATEGY

The decision by Morgan Stanley Dean Witter to choose Black Rocket to handle the Discover Brokerage advertising was reportedly made without a review and in the wake of the resignation of the company's previous agency, J. Walter Thompson USA, which gave up the account because of a conflict with new client Merrill Lynch & Co. The decision represented a coup for Black Rocket, which only a month before had landed a $2 million account with *Wired* and which could boast billings of more than $50 million after getting the Discover Brokerage account.

When the ad agency first advanced the idea for the "Tow Truck" commercial, Discover Brokerage executive vice president Tom O'Connell had reservations. After Black Rocket executives presented the script, O'Connell "wasn't sure if it was good or not... I went back to them the next week and said, 'We need a couple more ideas, so we can choose one.' They said, 'We've looked at all our ideas, and that's the best we have.'" O'Connell noted, however, that by the time the commercial was being filmed "it was pure trust and total magic."

The campaign was part of a general trend in the financial-services industry toward changing the traditionally stodgy tone of its advertising. "Shots of suspender-clad brokers and white-columned edifices are fading from view," reported the *Dallas Morning News.* "In their place are Lily Tomlin, Don Rickles and Peter Lynch for Fidelity Investments. On-line broker E-Trade tells potential customers it 'kicks butt.' Discount broker Charles Schwab features the top stock picks of real customers."

The "Tow Truck" spot, which was filmed in the California desert, opened with a burly workingman named Al towing a BMW, its businessman owner riding with him in the truck. The businessman spied a copy of *Barron's* on the seat and asked, "You, uh... read *Barron's*?" "Oh yeah, all the time," Al replied. He went on to tell the businessman that he invested money online through Discover Brokerage, mentioning that it had been *Barron's* top-rated online broker for the previous three years. He said that he had retired but continued to drive a tow truck anyway because he liked helping people. When the dumbfounded businessman noticed a photograph of an island attached to the visor, he asked if it was a vacation spot. Al sheepishly admitted, "Actually, it's a picture of my house." "That's a... that's an island," the businessman stammered. "Well," Al said affably, "technically, it's a country."

AWARD-WINNING PRINT ADS

In addition to the television campaign, Discover Brokerage Direct, Inc., and Black Rocket received acclaim for their print advertising. "You Are the CEO of Your Life," "Look Out Wall Street. Here Comes Main Street," and "Filthy Stinking Rich" won awards for best print campaign in the area of consumer retail given by the Financial Communications Society. The ads, all making the point that Discover Brokerage was for the middle-class investor, were done in black and white with eye-catching headlines. In "Look Out Wall Street. Here Comes Main Street," for example, the headline was placed next to a picture of a lower-middle-class neighborhood. "You Are the CEO of Your Life" showed a young woman holding her baby. Black Rocket partner Bob Kerstetter said, "We wanted to make a bold and simple look for these ads. We wanted the ads to have some craft and credibility to them, especially because the strategy is bigger than just a price/value message."

The campaign used humor and irony to make the point that online investing was for everyone, not just businesspeople. Bob Garfield of *Advertising Age* noted that the last example of humorous ads for investment companies he could think of went all the way back to the E.F. Hutton commercials of the late 1970s ("When E.F. Hutton talks, people listen"). Garfield thought that the Discover Brokerage ads were "straight to the point. It's just a jokey way of saying 'Discover's about making money.'"

The commercial also challenged the stereotype of the successful investor, presenting him as a regular person. As John Yost, a principal with Black Rocket, put it, "The ad is saying, 'This is the online brokerage for the rest of us.' It's humor that touches an honest emotion in people." Ken Harris, a marketing consultant with Cannondale Associates, said that the spot "appeals to the workaday guy who feels he doesn't get respect from people who are condescending to him. But it doesn't offend the people who might be more affluent."

Bob Kerstetter, another partner of Black Rocket, contrasted Discover Brokerage's approach with those of other online trading companies: "E-Trade's positioning is 'Screw your broker.' Charles Schwab is safe but boring. Discover believes everyone should be empowered to trade on line. They want to demystify it."

The campaign continued with five more spots, titled "Airplane," "Bartender," "Cab," "Waiting," and "Teenager." They featured middle-class people who had become millionaires by trading with Discover Brokerage. "Teenager," which was the most praised spot second to "Tow Truck," featured two parents waiting for their 18-year-old son to return home. When the stern parents asked where he had been, he pleaded, "I had to drop Jenny off in Cleveland, and Steve lives in Miami." His unappeased father restricted his son's use of Discover Brokerage for one week. The punch line of the spot came when the father told his son not to park his helicopter in the front yard. The helicopter had apparently been earned from investing with Discover Brokerage. The campaign ended on February 9, 2000, after Discover Brokerage changed its name to Morgan Stanley Dean Witter Online and released its "Know Your Source" campaign. The brokerage would shorten its name to Morgan Stanley in 2002.

OUTCOME

According to *USA Today,* "Tow Truck" was one of the most popular commercials tested in its Ad Track poll. Of 165 adults who saw the spot, 46 percent said that they liked it "a lot," with only 9 percent of respondents indicating that they disliked it.

In May 1999 Discover Brokerage and Black Rocket won Best of Show for "Tow Truck" at the annual Portfolio Awards of the Financial Communications Society, a nonprofit organization dedicated to improving professional standards in financial communications. The commercial was selected from more than 300 entries from banks, securities firms, exchanges, mutual funds, investment advisers, and accounting and insurance firms throughout North America and Europe. Black Rocket also received a San Francisco Ad Club Cable Car Award for the commercial. In addition, the campaign was named the best off-line campaign by "Adweek IQ," the interactive portion of *Adweek* magazine, and it won an ADDY. Further, *Advertising Age* gave its Bobby Award for Best Actor to the hapless businessman, played by Larry Cedar. Travis McKenna, who played the good-natured tow-truck driver/millionaire, was also nominated.

According to the *Dallas Morning News,* it was not clear exactly what effect the spots had on Discover Brokerage's business. "While I may enjoy the ad, I have not received any compelling reason to move my business," said Charlene Stern, head of Stern Marketing Group, a company that helped financial-services firms such as Discover's rival Ameritrade compete in the market. Black Rocket disagreed, calling humor in advertising a "time-tested" way to get business. Discover Brokerage's market share continued to hover between 3 and 4 percent, according to the *Wall Street Journal,* although Black Rocket's Seade indicated in June 1999 that since the campaign's launch new accounts had grown fivefold. There was no doubt, however, that the company's commercials had made a favorable impression on the industry and on television viewers.

FURTHER READING

Arndorfer, James B.. "Discover Online Acc't to Black Rocket." *Advertising Age,* July 20, 1998, p. 2.

———. "Online Brokerages Face New Marketing Challenge." *Advertising Age,* September 7, 1998, p. 43.

Buckman, Rebecca. "Morgan Stanley's On-Line Experiment Is Test for Traditional Brokerage Firms." *Wall Street Journal* (Eastern ed.), September 8, 1998, p. C1.

———. "Renamed Discover Brokerage Ready to Take On Bigger Rivals." Dow Jones News Service, July 25, 1997.

"Discover Brokerage TV Advertisement Wins 'Best of Show' at Financial Communications Society Portfolio Awards." Business Wire, May 7, 1999.

Hill, Miriam. "Brokerages Put Smiles Back into Ads." *Dallas Morning News,* April 5, 1999, p. D2.

Hoffman, Thomas. "Major Brokerages Play Catch-Up with Online Trading Upstarts." *Computerworld,* June 30, 1997, p. 14.

Lippert, Barbara. "E-Trade and Discover Traffic in Hyperbole and Fantasy to Sell Their Web Services." *Adweek* (eastern ed.), May 17, 1999.

O'Connell, Vanessa, and Suzanne Vranica. "No More Bull." *Wall Street Journal,* March 28, 2001, p. C1.

"Online Investing Jumps in Last 3 Months." *Journal Record,* December 22, 1998.

Poniewozik, James. "Online Broker Ads: 'The Slow Die First,'" *Fortune,* June 7, 1999, p. 30.

Spiro, Leah Nathans, and Edward C. Baig. "Who Needs a Broker?" *BusinessWeek,* February 22, 1999, p. 113.

Wells, Melanie. "Viewers Love Discover's Tow Truck Driver." *USA Today,* March 29, 1999, p. B5.

Debbi Mack
Kevin Teague

Mothers Against Drunk Driving, Connecticut Chapter

565 Washington Ave.
North Haven, Connecticut 06523
USA
Telephone: (203) 234-6521
Fax: (203) 234-6523
Web site: www.madd.org

■■■

DRUNK DRIVING'S A SERIOUS CRIME. LET'S TREAT IT THAT WAY. CAMPAIGN

OVERVIEW

The campaign "Drunk Driving's a Serious Crime. Let's Treat It That Way" was originally created in 1997 for the Connecticut chapter of Mothers Against Drunk Driving (MADD). It was deemed so effective, however, that it was later adopted by chapters around the United States. At no charge, advertising agency Pagano Schenck & Kay of Boston created a television commercial and four posters, approximately 13 by 16 inches, designed to look like warning or safety signs. Each poster compared the lenient sentences drunk drivers sometimes received with the tougher sentences handed out for much less serious offenses. All of the incidents cited in the campaign were true. In a nutshell, the campaign argued that the punishment for drunk driving did not fit the crime, that, in fact, the absurdly light sentences often given to drunk drivers trivialized the crime.

"Warning," a silent, stark 30-second television spot, showed white text rolling against a black screen. "Warning[,] this program is intended for public viewing," it began. "Unauthorized reproduction and exhibition many result in up to five years in prison and a $250,000 fine. Which is a far greater punishment than what a drunk driver got after his car rammed into 18-year-old Mary Sanders[,] crushing her. The drunk driver spent three months in jail. Mary Sanders went into a coma. And died. Mothers Against Drunk Driving. It's a serious crime. Let's treat it that way."

Under the headline "NO GRAFFITI," one of the posters read, "Convicted persons may serve six months in jail. That's two months more than what a drunk driver served after smashing her car into 14-year-old Eric Zimmerman. Eric's head was pierced by a chain-link fence, which killed him." At the bottom appeared the line "Mothers Against Drunk Driving. It's a serious crime. Let's treat it that way."

A second poster used the headline "Keep Off the Grass." The copy read, "Punishable by a fine of up to $99. That's $99 more than what a drunk driver paid after crashing into the car carrying 15-year-old Kerry Dunlop. The drunk driver got off scot-free. Kerry's neck broke and she died." Another poster pointed out that a $50 fine for not curbing a dog was more severe than the punishment given to a drunk driver who smashed into Julia Coppola and her two daughters. The final poster said that shoplifters could be imprisoned for up to one year, which exceeded the time served by a drunk driver who slammed into Russ Gordon and Michael Albert, both 26 years old. The drunk driver received eight months, while "Russ and Michael received death."

There was an initial printing of 5,000, with MADD distributing the posters to all Connecticut police and state trooper departments. They also were sent to high schools and colleges, as well as to shopping malls. To introduce the campaign, MADD held an event on the state capitol steps to acknowledge Crime Victims Rights Week (April 13-19, 1997). Family members of each victim mentioned presented oversized posters to MADD representatives.

HISTORICAL CONTEXT

Candy Lightner founded Mothers Against Drunk Driving in California in 1980 after a drunken man with multiple convictions for driving while intoxicated ran down and killed her 13-year-old daughter. The man had been released from jail two days earlier for another hit-and-run drunk driving crash. By 1998 the national organization had an annual budget of $50 million and 600 chapters.

MADD worked to stop drunk driving and prevent underage drinking through new legislation, stronger enforcement of current laws, increased public awareness, and assistance to victims. The organization considered one of its major accomplishments to be the raising of the national drinking age from 18 to 21 in 1984. As a non-profit organization, MADD did not produce paid advertising, but the national headquarters and its chapters sometimes produced public service announcements (PSAs) for print, radio, and television. One of its most widely known programs was the "Tie One On for Safety" red ribbon project.

Pam Bingman, the assistant traffic manager at the Pagano Schenck & Kay advertising agency, had lost her brother to a drunk driver, and she and her family found out firsthand how lenient the sentence for drunk driving could be. When Bingman encouraged her employer to become involved, the agency agreed to offer its services to MADD's Connecticut chapter, of which Bingman was a member. "Our pro bono efforts have tended to revolve around education and youth and this seemed to fall nicely into that area," said Woody Kay, the agency's chairman and executive creative director. Thus was born the "Drunk Driving's a Serious Crime" campaign.

TARGET MARKET

Every person who could drive, drink, and vote was considered part of the potential audience for the "Drunk Driving's a Serious Crime" campaign. Otherwise, the campaign did not seek out any particular demographic groups. Janice Heggie, executive director of the Connecticut chapter, said that the people most likely to read the posters were social drinkers, community leaders, responsible parents, and young people just beginning to understand the relationship between alcohol and driving. But Mothers Against Drunk Driving also hoped to reach people of influence, those in the state legislature or those who would contact state legislators with its message.

MADD MARKS FIRST ANNIVERSARY OF PRINCESS DIANA'S DEATH

In 1998 the national headquarters of Mothers Against Drunk Driving distributed a public service announcement to the media and its chapters with the headline "On August 31, 1997 the world was victimized by another drunk driver." The copy continued, "Mothers Against Drunk Driving mourns the loss of Princess Diana as well as the other estimated 250 victims killed in our country over the Labor Day weekend. Isn't it time we say enough is enough?"

COMPETITION

Organizations with messages similar to that of Mothers Against Drunk Driving, such as Students Against Driving Drunk (SADD), were allies, not competitors. "The most important work that we have learned to do is to partner with as many in the community as we can to stop drunk driving. I don't chose to promote competition against anybody," said Heggie. "We are trying to educate the liquor lobbyists. We are trying to educate our state legislators. There are many legislators who work with us to toughen the drunk driving laws that we have."

The beer and alcohol industry and the establishments that sold alcohol were not considered to be competitors. "Beer and alcohol distributors don't make people drive and drink. There isn't one beer company that wants people to drink their product and then drive," Heggie said. MADD also sought to assure people that it was not against the consumption of alcohol by those 21 and older. Thus, the competition was not any particular group of people or organizations but rather what could best be described as irresponsible drinking or ignorance of the effects of drinking and driving.

MARKETING STRATEGY

The charge of the Connecticut chapter of Mothers Against Drunk Driving to the ad agency was a general one: to increase awareness of the problem of drunk driving. What the "Drunk Driving's a Serious Crime" campaign ultimately attempted to do was to change attitudes and to make people aware of drunk driving and of the lenient sentences that were often handed down in drunk driving cases. "Drunk drivers are literally getting away with murder," said Amy Swearingen of Pagano Schenck & Kay. "Too often, the sentences given convicted drunk drivers are more suited to people who have torn labels off mattresses than to criminals who have killed innocent victims or destroyed their lives."

As the agency became involved in building the campaign, it was shocked by the lack of punishment for drunk driving. Staff members spent many hours talking to the families of the victims of drunk drivers. What always came up in these conversations was the fact that the families had a loved one who had either been killed or maimed while the perpetrator had received a minor sentence or none at all.

Talking to the victims' families was a natural move for the agency. To advertise a product, the agency would talk to the people who bought that product. To create advertising for MADD, the agency talked to the people the organization sought to serve. Dylan Lee, the copywriter for the campaign, and Carla Mooney, the art director, both spent many hours interviewing victims' families, whose names had been supplied by MADD. In addition, since Bingman had brought MADD to the agency's attention because she was the member of a victimized family, it was natural that the agency would look at the project through the eyes of the victims' families. "We were really trying to burst some bubbles," Kay said. "So many of us, including many of us here at the agency, are sort of living in a bubble when it comes to this. We don't realize that people are literally getting away with murder when it comes to drinking and driving." The depth of the commitment of the employees of Pagano Schenck & Kay to the campaign was significant. Lee, for example, came to feel so strongly about MADD and the campaign that he donated his annual bonus to the Connecticut chapter.

Pagano Schenck & Kay hoped that the campaign would motivate people to put pressure on their state legislators to increase the penalties for drunk driving violations. Although there was an ongoing debate about whether or not severe punishment helped to reduce crime, in this case MADD was pointing out that the issue was often a matter of not punishing lawbreakers at all. The campaign did not promote any specific punishment or even harsh punishment; rather, it used facts to demonstrate the disparity between the crime and the punishment.

One conversation Lee had with a mother inspired the direction the campaign eventually took. The mother, whose daughter had been killed by a drunk driver, had just returned from court. She was extremely upset because the driver had gotten off with a light sentence. To take her mind off her anger and frustration, she put a video into her VCR. When the standard warning about the punishment for illegal use of the video came on the screen, the mother was overcome. She realized that by copying the video she could receive a much heavier sentence than the person who had caused the death of her daughter.

There were a number of reasons the agency chose to make posters the main component of the campaign. Public service announcements tended to receive airtime on television in the early morning hours or at other times when viewership was low. In addition, it was difficult to get any radio time for PSAs or to get them placed in print media. MADD told the agency that, if it produced a series of posters, the organization would make certain they were distributed.

This led Pagano Schenck & Kay to think about the many signs that were displayed in schools and in businesses and other workplaces. Office walls, for example, were often covered with signs on safety, government regulations, or company policies for employees and visitors. The signs were sometimes required by the government or were a part of company training. The agency concluded that, because employers displayed such signs, they might be willing to display a strong message about an issue as important as drunk driving.

OUTCOME

The television spot and four posters garnered the top prize in the 1997 Hatch Awards, New England's largest advertising show, and first place in the 1998 John O'Toole Public Service Advertising Awards, hosted by the American Association of Advertising Agencies. The campaign also won a Clio and awards at the One Show and from Communications Arts. The Connecticut chapter's campaign was so well received that the national headquarters sold the posters for use across the United States.

Boston Business Journal reported that for every 1,000 arrests of people driving while they were intoxicated, 347 offenders were put in jail or placed on probation in 1997, compared to 151 in 1986. The treatment of offenders appeared to have changed, although there was no firm evidence of the role the campaign had played in this development.

FURTHER READING

Hanrahan, William. "Ads Are MADD about Law's Inequities." *Waterbury (Connecticut) Republican American,* April 24, 1997.

Jones, Sarah, and Gianatasio, David. "A Hatch with No Single Winner: Arnold, Pagano Share Top Prize." *Adweek New England Advertising Week,* September 29, 1997.

"What's New Portfolio." *Adweek New England Advertising Week,* Monday, May 12, 1997.

Chris John Amorosino

Motorola, Inc.

1303 E. Algonquin Road
Schaumburg, Illinois 60196
USA
Telephone: (847) 576-5000
Web site: www.motorola.com

INTELLIGENCE EVERYWHERE CAMPAIGN

OVERVIEW

Motorola, Inc., began by selling radio accessories in the 1920s, but by 2000 mobile phones were Motorola's highest-grossing product. Even though Motorola was the world's second-largest mobile-phone company behind Nokia, Inc., it was brutally affected by the tech industry's downturn in 2001. Motorola's stock price had plummeted nearly 70 percent in just 12 months. The company also announced thousands of layoffs during the same year. Executives at Motorola believed that the best way to prevail in the new decade was to lead the telecommunications industry with innovative products. In 2001 the company released its "Intelligence Everywhere" campaign, which hinted at what the future would look like with Motorola products.

Motorola awarded its advertising account to the ad agency Ogilvy & Mather New York in 2000. After debuting Motorola print ads at trade shows during March 2001, Ogilvy & Mather launched its estimated $150–$200 million print campaign nationwide in May of that year. The first nationwide advertisement was an eight-page spread that appeared in the *Wall Street Journal.* Each ad featured different appliances communicating to each other with products not yet invented. One ad showed a parking meter sending a message to a Motorola customer whose meter was about to expire. Another featured a refrigerator sending its milk order to a supermarket. One print ad showed an image of a Chihuahua with the copy "I'M LOST." The image of a personal digital assistant (PDA) adjacent to the Chihuahua announced, "I'LL FIND YOU." The ad suggested that Motorola would locate lost pets by using Global Positioning System (GPS) technology.

Motorola reported $30 billion in sales for 2001, a disappointing drop from the $37 billion it had posted in 2000. Other mobile-phone companies experienced a similar decline. Motorola sales dipped to $26 billion in 2002. The company did not post a sales increase until 2003. Advertising critics still praised the "Intelligence Everywhere" campaign for revitalizing Motorola's antiquated image. Others criticized it for catering to "dreamers" and advertising a product that did not yet exist.

HISTORICAL CONTEXT

In 1928 Paul Galvin founded Galvin Manufacturing, which sold components that allowed radios to use household electrical currents instead of batteries. After the success of the company's motorcar radios, in the 1940s Galvin changed the company name to Motorola. By the 1990s Motorola had begun focusing primarily on the production of semiconductors, telecommunication infra-

Motorola phone with Windows Mobile Software. © ANTHONY BOLANTE/REUTERS/CORBIS.

structure hardware, and mobile phones. The company's advertising account was spread across several ad agencies, and its phones were advertised with an array of taglines, including "W/O Wires," "The Heart of Smart," and "Digital DNA."

Hoping to reproduce the success that International Business Machines Corporation (IBM) had experienced after it consolidated its advertising account to one agency, Motorola awarded its entire account in 2000 to Ogilvy & Mather, which had been creating IBM's advertisements since 1994. "I am impressed by the way IBM was able to reposition its company," Motorola CMO Jocelyn Carter-Miller said to *Brandweek.* She added that Motorola's future positioning would center on "making things smarter and people's lives better." Because of waning sales, Motorola slashed its advertising budget by 70 percent just six months after signing it over to Ogilvy & Mather.

Between 2000 and 2001 Motorola was forced to reduce its workforce by tens of thousands. Corporate executives believed that the most effective way to increase sales was to release innovative products. As Ogilvy & Mather prepared to launch the "Intelligence Everywhere" campaign, Motorola was planning the release of its A830 mobile phone, which would be the world's first wireless phone to browse the Internet at speeds comparable to that of a cable modem.

Ogilvy & Mather dropped Motorola's "W/O Wires" and "The Heart of Smart" taglines in order to replace them with something more innovative. Also, Motorola did not want the upcoming campaign to contain the word "wireless," which the company considered outdated. As Motorola chief brand officer Geoffrey Frost explained to Steven Burke, a reporter for *CRN,* "We don't refer to the [early] auto industry as 'horselessness.' Eventually, wireless networking will be second nature."

TARGET MARKET

"Intelligence Everywhere" targeted a demographic of consumers who were interested in how future technologies would affect their daily lives. The ads implied that Motorola would provide the product-to-product communication hardware for futuristic appliances. Discussing the ads with the *New York Post,* Milosz Skrzypczak, an analyst with the market research firm the Yankee Group, said, "We're talking sci-fi here." Skrzypczak, who was 28 years old, explained that the products featured in the campaign probably would not be available in his lifetime.

The campaign was released simultaneously with premium Motorola phones that were loaded with state-of-the-art features. The Motorola A760 was equipped with Bluetooth wireless technology that could send images and even small multimedia files from phone to phone. "Today, there are more than 1.2 billion mobile handset users—and there is plenty of opportunity for more growth through both new users and those who want to replace or upgrade their handsets. We are focused on building momentum," Tom Lynch, president of Motorola's Personal Communications Sector, said to *PR Newswire.* "This means winning across all price points by working with wireless operators to innovate, create, and deliver 'must have' products and 'gotta-do' mobile experiences."

Other advertising analysts, such as Mary Huhn of the *New York Post,* criticized the campaign for limiting itself to "dreamers." The print ads suggested that Motorola products could help appliances such as washing machines read the handling labels on clothes. Unfortunately, the availability of such appliances was not expected for decades, and critics were skeptical about whether consumers would pay a premium price to save a few seconds of their time even if such technologies did become available.

LITIGATION EVERYWHERE

When the mobile-phone division of Motorola began using the tagline "Intelligence Everywhere" for a 2001 advertising campaign, database-software company MicroStrategy filed a complaint with the U.S. District Court. The Virginia-based MicroStrategy claimed that it had been using the tagline "Intelligence Everywhere" in advertising since 1998. A federal judge later decided to allow Motorola use of the tagline.

COMPETITION

Just before "Intelligence Everywhere" was released, Nokia held 30 percent of the global mobile-phone market, which was twice the amount that Motorola held. The Finland-based Nokia attributed success to its stylish phones that were easy to use and to its straightforward brand campaigns. The market researcher Interbrand rated Nokia as one of the top five brands of 2000. In Europe Nokia was rated highest in *Reader's Digest* 's "Trusted Brands" survey. "They built their business on great design and an excellent interface which made the phones very easy to use. They combined that with the brand and I think the brand itself is associated with and perceived as providing the best products," Ben Wood, senior analyst for the research and analysis firm Gartner Europe, told *Ad Age Global.*

Nokia had been using the tagline "Connecting People" since 1993. By 2001 advertising accounts for Nokia were spread across several different advertising agencies. Grey Worldwide EMEA was responsible for Nokia's advertising for Europe, the Middle East, and Africa. Advertising in the United States was created by the ad agency the Richards Group. TBWA\Chiat\Day Canada handled Nokia's Canadian account. Most of the campaigns released for Nokia were straightforward and direct. One of the brand's most repeated images was that of two hands reaching for each other. The ad featured Nokia's logo and the tagline "Connecting People." Referring to Nokia's advertising strategy, Caroline Carter, the president of Grey Worldwide EMEA, explained in *Ad Age Global,* "They have a clear view that it's not about the technology, it's about what the technology does for people."

MARKETING STRATEGY

At the start of 2001 the first print ads for the "Intelligence Everywhere" campaign appeared at the CeBIT trade show in Hanover, Germany. They surfaced again at the Cellular Telecommunications Industry Association trade show in Las Vegas. With an estimated $150–$200 million budget, the campaign was released nationwide in May 2001 and first appeared as an eight-page spread in the *Wall Street Journal.*

The campaign was Ogilvy & Mather's first execution for Motorola since winning its advertising account in September 2000. The agency developed the tagline "Intelligence Everywhere" to suggest that future appliances and objects everywhere would use Motorola technology to benefit people's lives. "It is about capturing the knowledge that's around us and using it wisely to develop products that offer real solutions to the challenges faced by real people," Bob Growney, Motorola's president and chief operating officer, was quoted in *Business Wire.*

The campaign's ads depicted future technologies at work in home, office, car, and personal-life situations. Each ad was separated into two panels. The left panel featured a single object communicating to an object in the right panel. For one of the campaign's most remarked-upon ads, the left panel featured a carton of milk with the copy "I'M SPOILED." The refrigerator on its right responded, "I KNOW." The ad implied that refrigerators of the future would automatically sense milk's expiration date. Another print featured a sweater beside the copy "BE GENTLE." The washing machine in the right panel replied, "I WILL." Other print ads featured mobile phones communicating with vending machines, computers talking to PDAs (personal digital assistants), and televisions talking to schools.

"Sometimes technology is on a faster curve than the market is ready for," Rachelle Franklin, director of corporate brands at Motorola, said to the *New York Post.* "What we're trying to express is, 'We'll be ready with relevant technology when you're ready for it.' That's key. It's all about timing."

Another print ad featured a Chihuahua beneath the copy "I'M LOST." On the ad's right panel a PDA resembling a Palm Pilot answered, "I'LL FIND YOU." The ad suggested that future Motorola products could find lost pets using GPS technology. Criticizing the ad, Nancy Gohring, a senior writer with *Interactive Week,* wrote, "Personally, I think it's kind of weird. How much of a monthly fee will people pay to track pets?"

Motorola executives wanted "Intelligence Everywhere" to convey Motorola's dedication to a future of seamless mobility, meaning that consumers would be connected wirelessly to conventional objects. Motorola's CEO, Ed Zander, explained the concept of seamless mobility to investors at the company's Merrill Lynch Global Communications Investor Conference in 2004. As a theoretical example, Zander explained that if someone was wakened by a song on his or her radio alarm clock,

MOTOROLA MUSIC

In 2004 the mobile-phone division of the company Motorola unveiled a technology that allowed automobiles to connect wirelessly with home Internet connections. The technology transferred digital music that resided inside a home computer to a car's stereo.

the song could follow the consumer throughout his or her house on a home stereo system. The music would eventually be transferred "seamlessly" to the customer's car stereo.

Without giving specifics, Dan Burrier, executive creative director at Ogilvy & Mather, explained to *Brandweek* how Motorola contributed to seamless mobility. "If Motorola becomes the leader of Intelligence Everywhere, then things like Motorola phones become your key into it," Burrier said. "If phones become part of a larger dialogue, then that is an honorable, smarter place to be."

OUTCOME

The "Intelligence Everywhere" campaign enjoyed some advertising success, including a 2002 One Show award, but many advertising critics lambasted the campaign for advertising a technology that did not yet exist. Sales for Motorola in 2001 plummeted $7 billion below its sales figure for 2000. Instead of blaming the "Intelligence Everywhere" campaign, critics cited other factors, such as a widespread slump in the technology sector, Motorola's reduced advertising budget, and the Motorola brand falling out of favor with consumers. Motorola's sales did not improve until Ogilvy & Mather released a subsequent campaign that abbreviated the company's name to "Moto." That campaign would resonate so well with younger consumers that competitor Nokia would be forced to alter its time-tested advertising strategy.

Some ad critics commended "Intelligence Everywhere" for initiating Motorola's transformation into a more stylish and contemporized brand. Creatives at Ogilvy & Mather would use the simplistic messaging of "Intelligence Everywhere" in later Motorola campaigns. "Technology is in a panic mode," Chris Wall, co-chief creative officer for Ogilvy & Mather, said to *MC Technology Marketing Intelligence*. "People got fat and happy in the late '90s [from the Internet], but now they've written off technology as being a leprosy. Ultimately, what technology has to have is real value. I think simplicity wins."

FURTHER READING

Barns, Emma. "Motorola to Review $100m Ad Account." *Campaign,* March 18, 2005, p. 1.

———. "O&M On Alert as Motorola Reviews $100m Global Ad Account." *Campaign,* March 18, 2005, p. 1.

Bernstein, Roberta. "2003 Ad Agency of the Year." *MC Technology Marketing Intelligence,* May 1, 2003, p. 24.

Callahan, Sean. "Embattled Motorola Maps Out New Focus with Digital DNA Ads." *B to B,* February 11, 2002, p. 3.

———. "Motorola Dials Down Marketing Strategy." *Crain's Chicago Business,* February 18, 2002, p. 21.

Elkin, Tobi. "Motorola Cuts Global Budget $250 Million." *Advertising Age,* March 26, 2001, p. 1.

Huhn, Mary. "Ready for a Talking Fridge?" *New York Post,* July 12, 2001, p. 48.

Iezzi, Teressa. "Fight to the Finnish." *Ad Age Global,* June 1, 2002, p. 14.

Mawhorr, S.A. "Motorola's Logo Back on TVs." *Arlington Heights (IL) Daily Herald,* October 15, 2003, p. 1.

Pinkerton, Janet. "Mindshare." *Dealerscope,* April 1, 2001, p. 3.

Wasserman, Todd. "Ailing Motorola Puts Big Campaign on Hold." *Brandweek,* March 26, 2001, p. 4.

———. "Motorola's New Groove." *Brandweek,* May 7, 2001, p. 1.

Kevin Teague

MOTO CAMPAIGN

OVERVIEW

In 1995 Motorola, Inc., dominated the mobile-phone market with 54 percent of the global market share. Over the next few years, however, Motorola was accused of losing sight of its customers' needs and designing unsightly phones with overly complex features. By 2000 Motorola had surrendered much of its business to Nokia, Inc., a company renowned for creating stylish mobile phones with an easy-to-use functionality. To salvage its brand Motorola hired Tim Parsey, who had worked previously at Apple Computer, to head a team to design a new line of premium, stylish Motorola phones. Once the new phones were completed, Motorola released its "Moto" campaign to rebrand Motorola as a fun, creative company with a cutting-edge product line.

In 2000 Motorola had selected the ad agency Ogilvy & Mather New York to handle its advertising. Creatives at the agency's Taiwan office noticed that the local youth, who were unaccustomed to the *r* and *l* syllables, referred to their Motorola phones simply as "Moto." Ogilvy & Mather used the moniker to construct the brand's new quip, "Hello Moto," which first appeared in January 2002 for the campaign's Asian debut. The campaign continued in more than 200 countries and included outdoor ads, print ads, and television spots. Spending for the campaign was estimated at $100 million. Initially it targeted 20-something trendsetters. Later the target was expanded to include a much younger demographic. Instead of touting phone features, the "Moto" spots blended contemporary music with fashion to build Motorola's new stylish image. More than 80 print ads were created. Each featured a different "Moto-ism," such as "BANGBANGMOTO," "METALMOTO," and "DIVAMOTO," to convey a new attitude that was surrounding Motorola. The campaign continued until 2005.

Advertising and technology critics praised the campaign for giving Motorola's brand a much-needed revitalization. During the fourth quarter of 2002, "Moto" and the contemporized Motorola phones helped Motorola sales outperform Nokia sales for the first time in four years. In 2005 Motorola's market share had grown more than 5 percent over its market share in 2000.

HISTORICAL CONTEXT

In the 1990s Motorola products consisted primarily of semiconductors, telecommunication infrastructure hardware, and mobile phones. The latter, the company's most lucrative product, was derided by technology critics for being overly focused on engineering and not attending to the needs of customers. Motorola phones between 1995 and 2000 were criticized for their bulky, unattractive design. "Motorola is a company that listens more to its engineers, while Nokia listens more to its customers," Stefan Daiberl, the director of brand valuation at the consultancy group Interbrand, was quoted in *Reuters News*.

Motorola executives made decisions between 1999 and 2001 that would eventually improve the company's market share and resurrect the Motorola brand. In 1999 Motorola hired Nike Inc.'s global director of advertising, Geoffrey Frost, to lead Motorola's marketing department. Frost formulated a two-year plan that involved hiring designer Tim Parsey, who had previously served as design chief at Apple Computer, to create a stylish line of Motorola phones. Taking its cue from International Business Machines Corporation (IBM), which had met with success after consolidating its advertising account with Ogilvy & Mather in 1994, Motorola awarded its entire account to that agency.

Ogilvy & Mather first released a print campaign in May 2001 titled "Intelligence Everywhere," which featured objects of the future communicating to each other with the help of Motorola. One ad featured an image of a milk carton below the copy "I'M SPOILED." The refrigerator appearing on the adjacent page responded with the copy "I KNOW." The particular ad implied that refrigerators of the future would automatically sense milk's expiration date. Even though "Intelligence Everywhere" received little praise from the advertising community, critics cited the campaign as a turning point for Motorola. In early 2002 Tim Parsey's line of Motorola phones were ready for market. Motorola needed a campaign that not only matched the stylish look of Parsey's phones but also updated the corporation's antiquated image.

TARGET MARKET

The "Moto" campaign initially targeted trendsetters in their mid-20s who, as the creatives at Ogilvy & Mather explained, were always searching for the best phone. The ad agency hoped that if the initial spots resonated with such trendsetters, the perception of Motorola as a young, hip brand would spread into other demographics. Before they were available to the public, new Motorola phones were given to celebrities such as British actress Helen Mirren and *Lord of the Rings* director Peter Jackson. The new V70 Motorola phone was also released when the "Moto" campaign began. Ogilvy & Mather assumed that the $400–$500 price tag for the V70 would deter younger mobile-phone users. After V70 sales tripled Motorola's original expectations, the campaign's target expanded to include younger consumers, businesspeople, and even the young sales associates in phone retail outlets.

"Until last year [2002], Motorola had no brand image," Chris Ambrosio, an analyst for the telecommunications research firm Strategy Analytics, explained to *Brandweek*. "It was a mom's handset or a dad's handset. In 2002, they corrected that. They solidified their core offerings and 'Moto' really took off in the U.S.," Ambrosio concluded. The campaign targeted younger consumers by airing commercials with popular electronic music artists, such as Paul Van Dyke and Felix da Housecat. Commercials ran across networks popular among youths, such as MTV. Promotional material was given to the young sales associates working in phone retail stores. Expanding the campaign's target proved effective. The consultancy company Gartner Group noted in 2003 that, within retail outlets, Motorola phones were two of the top three most recommended handsets.

COMPETITION

Motorola's two major competitors were Nokia, a company based in Finland, and Samsung, a South Korean mobile-phone company. In 2001 Nokia's market share was 30 percent—twice that of Motorola. Nokia was known for its stylish and user-friendly phones, and it

GEOFFREY FROST

In 1999 Geoffrey Frost left his position as global director of advertising at Nike to help the electronics company Motorola improve its archaic image. Frost soon hired a former design chief of Apple Computer, Tim Parsey, to design a new line of Motorola phones. Many considered Frost to be the mastermind of Motorola's rebound during the successful 2002 "Moto" campaign. Just after his promotion to executive vice president and chief marketing officer for Motorola, Frost died of natural causes on November 17, 2005. Although he remained elusive about his actual age in interviews, it was later reported he was 55 years old at the time of death. Remembered for his booming laugh and love for pop culture, Frost told *Advertising Age* just before he died, "I'm 17 forever."

relied on straightforward ad campaigns with the tagline "Connecting People," which it had used since 1993. In an interview with *Ad Age Global,* Caroline Carter, president of Grey Worldwide EMEA, one of Nokia's ad agencies, explained, "[Nokia has] a clear view that it's not about the technology, it's about what the technology does for people."

Samsung Electronics North America, the North American branch of the South Korean company Samsung Group, spent $200 million on marketing its product range with a global campaign titled "DigitAll Experience." In 2002 Samsung was the world's third-largest mobile-phone manufacturer, behind Nokia and Motorola. "DigitAll Experience" used Internet ads, print ads, and television spots to promote Samsung products that included personal digital assistants (PDAs), flat-screen computer monitors, plasma-screen televisions, DVD players, and even Samsung's Homepad Internet Refrigerator. The latter featured an embedded computer that recorded and displayed digital photos, browsed the Internet, and even captured digital video.

Marketing executives at Samsung hoped that, by promoting all of the premium products at once, Samsung's entire brand would be bolstered. "If you see ads for our DVDs [players], [the ads] will help us sell refrigerators, and the refrigerator ads will help us sell other product. We want to reach anyone who has ever purchased a Samsung product before," Peter Weedfald, vice president of North America strategic marketing and new media at Samsung, said to the *Delaney Report.* The campaign was developed by the ad agencies Foote Cone & Belding and Chiel Communications America.

Print ads displayed sleek product images with the tagline "DigitAll" and Samsung's logo. Television spots showed consumers enjoying a wide range of Samsung brand electronics. Internet advertising consumed the brunt of the campaign's resources. In early 2002 the price per Internet ad impression—also known as the single display of an Internet ad—was estimated at $2.50, a historical low for online advertising. Samsung took advantage of the bargain prices and released ads across 57 of the Internet's most popular websites, including Forbes.com, Yahoo.com, Fortune.com, BusinessWeek.com, and CRN.com. Several online ads included a sweepstakes offering a $5,000 shopping spree at Sears, which was also one of Samsung's retailers.

MARKETING STRATEGY

Creatives at the Taiwan office of Ogilvy & Mather first took notice of Taiwanese youth, who were unversed in the English *r* and *l* syllables, referring to their Motorola phones as "Moto." The agency's New York office liked the abbreviation so much that it constructed Motorola's estimated $100 million campaign around it. The campaign first surfaced in January 2002, when Ogilvy & Mather hired a graffiti artist to leave keyhole-shaped designs on the pavement within Hong Kong's trendy Lan Kwai Fong nightspot area. The shapes resembled Motorola's new V70 phone. TV commercials aired across Asia during the same month. In March print ads and television spots were released in North America and Europe. The campaign's lead spot, "Hello Moto," was backed by electronic music and copy that conjoined the word "MOTO" with words that reflected Motorola's new image. In the spot businessmen were shown talking on phones, and the word "MEETINGMOTO" appeared. The phrase "MOTOHIP/MOTOHOP" was then juxtaposed over an image of a club scene; and the spot ended with a male voice-over stating, "Hello Moto." The phrase referred to the website www.HelloMoto.com, which provided Motorola phones and accessories.

The campaign's print ads featured varying "Moto-isms" superimposed over images of individuals that represented the "Moto-isms." "GIZMOMOTO," "ALPHAMOTO," "BANGIN'MOTO," "BANGBANGMOTO," and more than 80 other words were created for the ads. One of the most commented-upon print ads, "DIVAMOTO," featured a beautiful 20-something woman wearing a black feather stole and holding a Motorola clamshell phone. "We're trying to create a new culture around our products," Jacquie Amacher, director of brand communication for Motorola North America, said to the *Chicago Sun-Times.*

During the campaign's initial weeks, advertising critics considered the strategy a gamble because it excluded information about the phones' features. Instead the ads relied entirely on stylish and fashion-conscious content to attract customers. Ad critic Lewis Lazare of the *Chicago Sun-Times* wrote, "This startlingly different ad campaign could backfire badly if Motorola doesn't prove at heart to be the kind of company the advertising so dramatically suggests it is in the process of becoming."

As the campaign proved to resonate not only with 25-year-old trendsetters but also with the youth culture, Motorola extended the campaign's life span past its initial November 2002 completion date. The campaign's target was also expanded to include a younger crowd. During the 2003 MTV Video Music Awards, three television spots featured different electronic-music artists and the new mixable ring tones (which allowed users to assign different sounds to specific callers) for the Motorola C350 phone. One spot began with DJ Felix da Housecat, who received a phone call inside a bar. DJ Felix began humming the phone's catchy ring tone, which was later hummed by everyone who came in contact with the jingle. The spot ended with the previous campaign's tagline, "Intelligence Everywhere," followed by a voice-over saying "Hello Moto." Another spot featured cars that started bouncing up and down after a phone rang with a song by DJ Colette. The third spot depicted city lights pulsing to the beat of a ring tone created by DJ Paul Van Dyke. The campaign ended in 2005.

OUTCOME

Advertising analysts attributed the revitalization of the Motorola brand largely to the "Moto" campaign, along with Tim Parsey's new design for Motorola. But strong advertising and sleek design were not the only contributors. In order to improve sales and distribution, Motorola had also strengthened relationships with carriers such as the Sprint PCS Group. Matt Baker, Motorola's senior director of North American marketing, explained to *Brandweek,* "We started to leverage relationships we hadn't in the past. There was growth in the Verizon business and deeper conversations with the Best Buys and Circuit Citys of the world."

Motorola outperformed Nokia in sales for the first time in four years during the fourth quarter of 2002. For 2003 Motorola posted its first annual sales increase in three years. Two years later Motorola's global market share was estimated at 16.8 percent, a substantial improvement from the company's 11 percent in 2000. *Adweek Magazine's Technology Marketing* gave Ogilvy & Mather its 2003 Ad Agency of the Year award for creating the "Moto" campaign and other high-profile campaigns, such as IBM's "Gizmo." The head of Motorola's global marketing, Geoffrey Frost, was named one of *Brandweek* magazine's Marketers of the Year in 2005. The October 10 *Brandweek* article praised Frost by stating, "Once known for unfashionable phones and clunky advertising, Motorola now has probably the hottest phone on the market [RAZR], a deal with Apple's iTunes, and a hipper image thanks to its catchy 'Moto' ads."

FURTHER READING

Barns, Emma. "Motorola to Review $100m Ad Account." *Campaign,* March 18, 2005, p. 1.

———. "O&M On Alert as Motorola Reviews $100m Global Ad Account." *Campaign,* March 18, 2005, p. 1.

Bernstein, Roberta. "2003 Ad Agency of the Year." *MC Technology Marketing Intelligence,* May 1, 2003, p. 24.

Callahan, Sean. "Embattled Motorola Maps Out New Focus with Digital DNA Ads." *B to B,* February 11, 2002, p. 3.

———. "Motorola Dials Down Marketing Strategy." *Crain's Chicago Business,* February 18, 2002, p. 21.

Elkin, Tobi. "Motorola Cuts Global Budget $250 Million." *Advertising Age,* March 26, 2001, p. 1.

Huhn, Mary. "Ready for a Talking Fridge?" *New York Post,* July 12, 2001, p. 48.

Iezzi, Teressa. "Fight to the Finnish." *Ad Age Global,* June 1, 2002, p. 14.

Mawhorr, S.A. "Motorola's Logo Back on TVs." *Arlington Heights (IL) Daily Herald,* October 15, 2003, p. 1.

Pinkerton, Janet. "Mindshare." *Dealerscope,* April 1, 2001, p. 3.

Wasserman, Todd. "Ailing Motorola Puts Big Campaign on Hold." *Brandweek,* March 26, 2001, p. 4.

———. "Motorola's New Groove." *Brandweek,* May 7, 2001, p. 1.

Kevin Teague

MoveOn.org

336 Bon Air Center, No. 331
Greenbrae, California 94904
USA
Telephone: (510) 524-6100
Fax: (360) 397-2645
Web site: www.moveon.org

REAL PEOPLE CAMPAIGN

OVERVIEW

Founded in 1998 by a pair of California-based software entrepreneurs as a way to mobilize like-minded liberal activists for political causes, MoveOn.org became a driving force in funding, organizing, and promoting Democratic platforms and candidates during the 2004 U.S. presidential election, and it was the most successful independent political-action group to do so exclusively through the Internet. In the summer of 2004 MoveOn hired the Academy Award-winning documentary filmmaker Errol Morris to produce a series of television and print ads of his own devising. Morris proposed to film "real people" speaking directly to the viewer about why they were planning to vote for Senator John Kerry and not President George W. Bush. The hope was that this direct, one-to-one approach would help to convince the influential demographic of undecided voters to follow suit.

With MoveOn's backing, Morris set out to film interviews with ordinary citizens speaking in their own words, completely unscripted and unprompted, which he then edited into individual 30-second television spots. MoveOn initially earmarked $3 million for the campaign, with plans to run both TV and print advertising in late August to coincide with the Republican National Convention. Filmed against a plain white background with soft, even lighting, each person spoke frankly into the camera. In one ad, for example, a 26-year-old business analyst from New Jersey said, "We don't have, you know, universal health care, we've cut benefits for veterans, No Child Left Behind is a joke—we can't afford another four years of George Bush. It would be disastrous."

While the ads won critical accolades from industry insiders, incumbent Bush was reelected by a narrow margin. On the whole, however, MoveOn played an influential role in mobilizing both liberal donors and volunteers in the year leading up to the election. And while it did not achieve its goal of preventing a second term for President Bush, it continued to use the Internet to raise money and mobilize its members to promote liberal causes at both the local and federal levels.

HISTORICAL CONTEXT

Historically, because presidential candidates were often reluctant to have negative, biting, or derisive ads directly associated with their own campaigns, few "person-on-the-street" advertisements proved to be decisive factors in elections. Notable exceptions were the "Confessions of a Republican" spot run by the Lyndon Johnson campaign in 1964 and the Gerald Ford commercials attacking Jimmy Carter in 1976. Both of these spots featured people on the street, or supposedly real people, talking honestly of their concerns about the rival candidate. The

Founders of MoveOn.org, Wes Boyd (L) and Joan Blades (R), May 11, 2004. © CHIP EAST/REUTERS/CORBIS.

Johnson spot actually used an actor in a studio and was scripted, although it was meant to appear authentic, while the Ford attack ads used street interviews with residents of Georgia, Carter's home state, explaining why they were not going to vote for their own governor as president. Both of these spots and others like them were in the category of "common people talking common sense," advertising aimed not directly from the candidate to the voter but from peer to peer in an attempt to convince people on either side to vote accordingly.

While political ads on television, from hard-hitting attack ads to feel-good slices of Americana, had changed little in tone and approach since the medium's inception in the 1950s, what did change dramatically in 2004 was how such ads were funded and targeted. MoveOn.org, more so than any other group inside or outside the political mainstream, embraced the relatively new technology of the Internet as both a fund-raising tool and a sounding board for its creative ideas. It even used its member base to help create ads, through calls for entries on its website. MoveOn repeatedly sent E-mails to its more than 2 million members and in many cases was able to raise hundreds of thousands of dollars literally overnight. And in the case of the spots directed by Morris, MoveOn was able to ask its members to vote for their favorites. This participatory process not only kept MoveOn's support base engaged but also shaped the group's decisions about which ads to air, based on popularity and efficacy.

TARGET MARKET

The 2004 presidential election may be remembered as the election that cemented the term "swing voter" in the minds of the American public. In this case swing voters were those undecided or uncommitted citizens capable of "swinging" their votes either from Republican to Democrat or vice versa, regardless of their traditional party affiliation. The poll numbers suggested that these voters represented the largest block of undecided voters and that they could decide the election. It was no surprise, then, that both the Bush and Kerry campaigns searched for ways to attract this demographic, as did an increasing number of independent political-action groups, MoveOn.org chief among them.

MoveOn's own base of supporters and volunteers was hardly undecided. The group did not shy away from taking risks or unabashedly wearing its liberalism on its sleeve. In fact, in late 2003 MoveOn sponsored a series of political ads attacking both President Bush and his policies. Its most widely known ad, "Child's Play," was never actually aired. The ad, the winner of a "Bush in 30 Seconds" contest sponsored by MoveOn, featured a series of images of young children working in menial jobs with the tagline "Guess who's going to pay off President Bush's $1 trillion deficit?" CBS refused to air the ad during the 2004 Super Bowl, but the ensuing media coverage of the controversy helped promote MoveOn's cause to a wider audience.

THE RISE OF 527 GROUPS

So-called 527 groups had been around for decades, but they came to prominence only after the McCain-Feingold campaign-finance reform bill was signed into law in 2002. The law banned unlimited donations to candidates, political parties, or campaigns, limiting contributions to $2,000 from any individual or group. The law did not, however, restrict donations to nonprofit political groups that operated independently of a candidate's campaign. The number "527" referred to section 527 of the Internal Revenue Code, under which these organizations filed for their status as independent political groups. As such, the groups were able to receive unlimited donations so long as they were not in direct contact and did not coordinate their efforts with any political party or campaign. MoveOn.org, Swift Boat Veterans for Truth, America Coming Together, and the Media Fund were the largest and best funded of these groups during the 2004 election.

As the election neared, MoveOn realized that galvanizing its liberal support base was one thing, while influencing the outcome of the election was another. In enlisting the work of Morris, the group hoped to change the minds of undecided voters with a more mannered, heartfelt approach.

COMPETITION

While no other piece of political advertising used such a direct, one-on-one approach to target undecided voters, the ad campaign run by the Swift Boat Veterans for Truth, a 527 group (or independent political organization), was effective in directing voters' attention away from the MoveOn.org ads and their message. This group, spearheaded and funded in part by John O'Neill, a longtime critic of Kerry and himself a Vietnam veteran and former Swift Boat commander from the same unit, moved quickly to produce a series of ads directly calling into question the legitimacy of Kerry's war record. The ads specifically cast doubt on the circumstances in which Kerry had received his war medals, notably one of his Purple Hearts and his Bronze and Silver Stars. In addition, the Swift Boat Veterans used testimony given by Kerry in 1971 before the Senate Foreign Relations Committee as fodder for the attack ads. In his testimony, given shortly after his tour of duty, Kerry adopted an antiwar stance and described atrocities committed by U.S. soldiers against Vietnamese citizens, atrocities that he claimed were perpetrated with the full knowledge of the commanders in the field. While the Swift Boat Veterans ads were initially poorly funded and aired in smaller markets, the media attention they received gave them instant notoriety and national publicity, which led to additional financial backing from a number of wealthy Texas conservatives.

The commercials from the Swift Boat Veterans featured overlapping snippets of a series of vets talking about Kerry's conduct in Vietnam. In just one ad alone, titled "Any Questions?" veterans appearing in the ad collectively used the words "lied" or "lying" in relation to Kerry four times, the word "betrayed" twice, and the phrase "not been honest" twice. While much of the media coverage of the ads called into question their veracity—many of the men who spoke in the ads had not served with or been on active duty concurrently with Kerry—the damage was done. While the impact of a single campaign was difficult to measure, it was widely accepted that the Swift Boat Veterans ads, which ran for most of August and up until the election, had the greatest effect of any political ad campaign during the period.

MARKETING STRATEGY

Morris approached the Kerry campaign in the spring of 2004 with his idea for "switchers" ads, that is, ads designed to persuade those who were undecided to vote for Kerry. The Kerry campaign was interested in the concept but in the end felt that the ads would be too controversial to bear the imprimatur of the candidate. It was at this point that MoveOn.org became involved. Morris took the idea for the ads directly to Wes Boyd, the cofounder of MoveOn. Boyd was immediately supportive, and he agreed to fund the production and to buy the television time and the newspaper space for the ads. Morris had conceived of ads featuring real people, notably Republicans who had voted for Bush in 2000 but who intended to vote for Kerry in 2004, talking in their own words about why they were making the switch. This was in the wake of producing the "Switchers" campaign for Apple Computer, Inc., in which Morris had filmed people explaining their decision to switch from Windows PCs to Macintosh computers.

Morris felt that his political ads would be a powerful way to talk directly to swing voters in an unmitigated fashion. As he told the *New Yorker,* "It isn't pollsters talking through actors. It isn't longtime Democrats talking to themselves. It's thoughtful Republicans . . . saying it's not us who are abandoning Bush; he's abandoned us." The ads were designed to be as simple and unadorned as possible. Each featured a single person against a plain white background talking directly into the camera in his or her own unscripted words. Morris used a device of his own invention, the Interrotron, to record the interviews; through a series of two-way mirrors Morris's face was projected across the camera lens as he talked with the subjects. This kept the subjects relaxed and comfortable while they looked and spoke directly into the camera. In essence the interviewees were looking a virtual Morris in the eye as they responded to his questions.

The subjects were culled from an E-mail questionnaire sent to MoveOn's more than 2 million members. Of the more than 20,000 people who responded to the E-mail, at least 500 fit the profile. In the end 41 were selected to be interviewed. The final group was diverse. It included military personnel, housewives, a financial advisor, a former U.S. ambassador, a medical transcriptionist, a college professor, warehouse workers, and Christian evangelicals. Morris interviewed each person for nearly an hour, eventually cutting the footage from each session to fill a 30-second television spot. He did not prepare the subjects for the interviews or ask them warm-up questions; he wanted the interviews to be open-ended and as uninfluenced by the process as possible.

As diverse as the participants were, they were united in one thing: they had voted for Bush in 2000 but were voting for Kerry in 2004. "The underlying idea is that the election is going to be decided by a very small group of voters," Morris told the *Boston Phoenix*. "What about these so-called undecideds? How do you reach them? I'm not particularly interested in just simply creating ads that make Democrats feel better. I'm interested in creating ads that will have some influence on that group." That influence, Morris decided, would come best from ordinary people talking directly to others without any motive other than explaining their own decisions to switch.

Morris and MoveOn's plan was to begin to air the ads—both as television spots and as full-page newspaper ads featuring photos of the interviewees with quotations from their testimonies as captions—during the Republican National Convention in New York City at the end of August. This would give the ads the greatest exposure to Republican voters in the hope that some, like the people featured in the ads, were not yet cemented in their voting positions. A full-page ad featuring nine of the people ran in the *New York Times* on the day the convention began.

OUTCOME

In the end MoveOn.org did not spend the full $3 million budgeted for the ads or follow through with its plans to air them in all of the "battleground" markets, as originally intended. According to Barbara Lippert in *Brandweek,* "MoveOn.org funded production, but in the end, for reasons unclear, three ran only once on Fox, and one ran in Ohio. That effectively neutered them." Perhaps because the competition stepped up the viciousness of its own ads in the three months leading up to the election, MoveOn chose to go with harder-hitting negative ads rather than milder ads produced by Morris.

"MoveOn didn't, ultimately, help the Democrats capture the White House or even pick up any Congressional seats," wrote Todd Wasserman in *Brandweek,* "but it used the Internet in a way that had eluded other nonprofits and major political parties." Measured in terms of achieving its political goals, MoveOn's success was limited. But in terms of using a relatively new medium to maximum effect, MoveOn was a force to be reckoned with. As Amanda Griscom noted in *Rolling Stone* magazine, "MoveOn is the 800-pound gorilla left of center. There's no competing organization right of center that can exercise the same leverage, influence and muscle." Most importantly MoveOn tapped directly into a vast liberal base of supporters through the Internet, "galvanizing grass-roots activists in a way that hasn't been seen since the 1970s," according to Tara McKelvey in the *American Prospect.*

FURTHER READING

Ansolabehere, Stephen, and Shanto Iyengar. *Going Negative: How Political Advertisements Shrink and Polarize the Electorate.* New York: Free Press, 1995.

Burdman, Pamela. "MoveOn.org." *California Journal,* August 1, 2004, p. 46.

Gourevitch, Philip. "Swingtime." *New Yorker,* August 23, 2004, pp. 34–40.

Huck, Peter. "Moving the Masses." *Age* (Melbourne), August 26, 2004, p. A3.

Justice, Glen. "Political Groups Reflect on a Rewarding Year." *New York Times,* p. F12.

Lazaroff, Leon. "Activist Group Softens Anti-Bush Ads in Effort to Reach Swing Voters." *Chicago Tribune,* August 25, 2004.

Lewis, Charles. *The Buying of the President 2004.* New York: Perennial, 2004.

Lippert, Barbara. "Kerry Is So Very." *Adweek,* November 1, 2004.

Reilly, Adam. "Ad Value: Acclaimed Documentarian and Advertising Pro Errol Morris Had a Plan for Reaching Swing Voters. Too Bad John Kerry Wasn't Interested." *Boston Phoenix,* October 8, 2004.

Richardson, Glenn W., Jr. *Pulp Politics: How Political Advertising Tells the Stories of American Politics.* Lanham, MD: Rowman & Littlefield, 2003.

Sidoti, Liz. "Ordinary People Testify in Political Ads." *Associated Press,* September 4, 2004.

York, Byron. *The Vast Left Wing Conspiracy.* New York: Crown Forum, 2005.

Jonathan Kolstad

MTV Networks Company

1515 Broadway
New York, New York 10036
USA
Telephone: (212) 258-8000
Fax: (212) 258-6175
Web site: www.mtv.com

■■■

WATCH AND LEARN CAMPAIGN

OVERVIEW

In the 1990s and early 2000s MTV Networks Company's MTV was the leading trendsetter among American youth. Though initially it solely aired music videos, MTV had evolved into a network focused on the projection of a stylish, youth-oriented brand identity rather than on the exclusive promotion of music. The tone of its programming was established primarily by a stable of popular reality shows. Additionally, part of the network's branding had always been accomplished through distinctive on-air promotional material that typically appeared between programs. Starting with the universally famous "I want my MTV" slogan and continuing through the bizarre, critically lauded "Jukka Brothers" campaign, MTV's commitment to unconventional branding work was already well established by 2003, when the network became aware of an independent art project then running in art galleries and on the Internet. The project, called "Instructoart," was created by Matt Vescovo, an advertising freelancer and graphic artist, and it used the format of airline safety pamphlets to offer facetious visual instruction in a variety of mundane daily rituals and behaviors.

MTV contracted Vescovo to produce animated versions of his "Instructoart" illustrations for an on-air station-identification campaign named "Watch and Learn." Using a minimal budget, Vescovo worked with design shop Hornet to create an initial series of eight spots. All were under 20 seconds long and premiered during the August 2003 MTV Video Music Awards. The spots, which adopted Vescovo's "Instructoart" concept exactly, enlightened viewers about such matters as the three-second rule regarding dropped food and the relative sex appeal of a range of musical instruments. They used minimal movement and music. With their quietness, the "Watch and Learn" spots stood out from MTV's boisterous programming, and the offbeat social commentary they offered meshed well with the network's desire to maintain a unique, unpredictable image.

"Watch and Learn" won numerous awards in 2004, and MTV commissioned another series of the spots that began running that year. Vescovo likewise extended the "Instructoart" franchise with further art-gallery shows and with book versions of the pieces. MTV remained one of the world's most distinct and envied consumer brands as well as the top forum for advertisers seeking to connect with America's youth.

HISTORICAL CONTEXT

MTV's name, Music Television, was a literal description of its programming upon its launch in 1981 and for its first several years on the air. MTV was a 24-hour music video network, the world's first, with blocks of videos hosted by so-called VJs (video jockeys) but with minimal original content otherwise. The format caught on quickly, but as the network matured, it increasingly sought to offer long-form programming. Such shows, which kept audiences' attention for a half-hour or more, appealed to advertisers, whereas three- and four-minute videos made it difficult to know when a particular audience would be tuning in or out. In the mid-1980s MTV began offering long-form programming such as the original game show *Remote Control* and the style-conscious dance show *Club MTV.*

In the 1990s the network further developed its programming with notable shows that included the cartoon *Beavis and Butthead* and TV's first reality show, *The Real World.* By the turn of the millennium MTV rarely played music videos at all, and it relied on a heavy rotation of reality shows, the most successful of which included *The Osbournes,* featuring former Black Sabbath singer Ozzy Osbourne and his family, and *Newlyweds,* which followed the lives of just-married musical celebrities Jessica Simpson and Nick Lachey. By the early 2000s MTV had long been regarded as perhaps the single most influential force in American youth culture and as the premier forum for advertisers seeking to connect with adolescents and young adults.

Throughout MTV's evolution its own on-air promotions played a significant role in shaping the brand image. Most of this work ran on the network itself and was generated by in-house creative personnel. The early "I want my MTV" slogan permeated pop culture in the 1980s. To maintain the network's edgy image, subsequent branding work used odd, unpredictable content, including spots featuring hippie spokesman Randee of the Redwoods and, later, rants delivered by the then-little-known comedian Denis Leary. In 1999 the network turned to advertising agency Fallon McElligott (later called Fallon Worldwide) for its award-winning "Jukka Brothers" campaign. It featured four Finnish brothers whose only contact with the world beyond their homestead in the Scandinavian backcountry was MTV, which they watched in an outhouse.

MTV: LIVING THE DREAM

Matt Vescovo, the freelance creator of the MTV "Watch and Learn" spots, had spent more than a decade in the advertising industry, working full-time for such agencies as Fallon Worldwide and Cliff Freeman and Partners in addition to freelancing for numerous other top agencies. In an *Adweek* interview, Mae Anderson asked Vescovo about his dream assignment, and he replied that the MTV "Watch and Learn" project was it. "I feel like they just let people do what they know how to do," Vescovo said. "They don't really meddle. I've shown them 15 promos, and they haven't changed a frame yet. I'm waiting for something to go wrong, because it doesn't seem like it should be like this."

TARGET MARKET

MTV's target audience was 12- to 34-year-olds, with a particular emphasis on teens and young adults. MTV was also television's number one destination for viewers aged 18 to 34, a prime demographic for advertisers. The network's clear focus on its target audience had always been integral to its success. By staying in touch with the lifestyles and desires of teens and young adults and crafting its network personality accordingly, MTV had become much more than a simple source of entertainment for young people. Members of the so-called "MTV generation" presumably consulted the network for ideas on music, fashion, and social behavior. Further, pop-cultural literacy mandated a working knowledge of each season's MTV program offerings.

While the debate over the exact nature and extent of the network's influence on young people proved insoluble and ongoing, it was generally accepted that MTV powerfully informed the lives of many young people. "Watch and Learn" thus made implicit reference to the network's reputation for mind control. The trivial nature of the lessons presented in the "Watch and Learn" spots poked fun at the idea that young people turned to MTV for life instruction. At the same time the spots were intended to be entertaining in their own right, and their peculiarity served the purpose, in the network's view, of communicating MTV's consistently adventurous and unorthodox personality, a key attribute in its enduring appeal among young people.

COMPETITION

Because the average TV viewer in the 2000s had access to hundreds of channels, brand definition had become particularly important for cable networks. In many ways MTV, with its clear brand identity and focused target audience, was the model for cable networks, positioned as it was to survive in an increasingly specialized and competitive cable marketplace. Among cable networks, ESPN, which focused on sports, had similar strengths and was, during this time, attempting to bolster its brand image further with a major television advertising campaign. Networks whose programming had traditionally been aimed at more general audiences, such as TBS Superstation, were meanwhile trying to sharpen their brand images through a combination of new programming strategies and advertising.

ESPN, an all-sports network launched two years before MTV, had similarly grown into a television giant as a result of its successful targeting of a specific audience. In the first two decades of its existence ESPN built a dedicated base of 18- to 34-year-old male viewers, for whom the sports network was an essential component of everyday life. In 2002 the network sought to reinforce the idea that it was virtually synonymous with sports through a TV campaign that asked viewers to consider a world without sports. "Without Sports" focused on everyday scenarios that showed the many ways in which sports and life were intimately and often humorously bound together. During the course of its multiyear run the campaign became a critically acclaimed award winner.

TBS Superstation, whose roots also extended to the early days of cable TV, was primarily known among consumers for rebroadcasts of movies and for live coverage of Atlanta Braves baseball games. Amid the proliferation of cable channels, however, in 2004 the network began to brand itself more rigorously, with a focus on comedy. After buying the rights to syndicated reruns of sitcom hits, including *Sex and the City, Friends, Seinfeld,* and *Everybody Loves Raymond,* TBS launched a campaign positioning the network as an arbiter of what was funny. Called "TBS. Very Funny," the campaign centered on a fictional hotline phone desk, where TBS representatives advised callers as to whether events they had witnessed were funny or not.

MARKETING STRATEGY

The "Watch and Learn" concept originated as the art project of an advertising freelancer, Matt Vescovo. A former creative director at high-profile ad agencies Fallon Worldwide and Cliff Freeman and Partners, Vescovo began focusing, in his spare time, on simple codes and rituals that shaped daily life. Borrowing the visual style of airline safety manuals, he created an initial set of 11 graphic-design images that would purportedly "teach" people about a variety of commonplace subjects. The project, collectively called "Instructoart," advised people, for example, on the appropriate techniques for removing hair from a bar of soap, doing the hokey pokey, and pretending to hold an elevator door for someone while letting it shut in his face. The "Instructoart" pieces were shown at art galleries in Asbury Park, New Jersey, and in New York in 2003, and Vescovo posted the so-called lessons on a website, http://www.instructoart.com. The website included tongue-in-cheek personal information and an artist's statement in which Vescovo jokingly expressed an interest in adapting "Instructoart" for MTV station-identification spots. As it happened, MTV liked the idea and contracted Vescovo to adapt several of his pieces for television. Vescovo enlisted design shop Hornet to assist with the job, and the still illustrations were turned into live animation lessons.

Running under the tagline "Watch and Learn," and with a budget described only as minimal by MTV, an initial group of eight animated "Instructoart" pieces premiered during the MTV Video Music Awards on August 28, 2003. The Video Music Awards, presented as a brash alternative to conventional awards shows, typically drew the network's biggest yearly viewing audience. The first eight spots ran in programming breaks that night and through the next year, at lengths of 15 to 20 seconds, and they served as calm interludes amid the network's typically noisy and high-energy programming. The animation was intentionally flat, maintaining the look of airline-safety pamphlets. With figures that moved only minimally, the spots were free of dialogue and generally quiet. Kitschy music ran at the conclusion of each spot along with the MTV logo and the "Watch and Learn" tag.

Individual spots in the campaign included "Three-Second Rule," an illustration of the child's rule for eating food that had been dropped on the floor. One woman was shown picking up her food within the three-second span, eating it, and then continuing on her way. A second woman hesitated after dropping her food and thus violated the three-second rule; after she popped the bite in her mouth, she collapsed in pain with her hands on her stomach. "Musical Instruments" ranked, in descending order, various instruments—the electric guitar, the drums, the trumpet, the flute, the accordion, and the tuba—according to a meter labeled "sex" that appeared on one side of the screen while figures playing the instruments appeared on the other side. "Gay/Straight" showed one man patting another's buttocks while wearing normal clothing; the scenario was labeled "Gay." Then the same act was repeated, only the participants were wearing baseball uniforms; this time the scenario was labeled "Straight." Other memorable spots showed viewers how to produce impolite bodily noises with the underarm and how to hide male-pattern baldness with the universal "comb-over" technique.

OUTCOME

"Watch and Learn" won numerous advertising-industry honors during the 2004 awards season. These included a Golden Pencil at the One Show Awards in the Consumer TV Campaign (Under:20) category, a Silver ANDY for media campaign, a Bronze ANDY in the interactive category (for the instructoart.com website, which continued to run throughout the MTV campaign and incorporated the MTV spots), and the "Best Low Budget Campaign" honor at the London International Advertising and Design Awards. The campaign was also awarded top honors in the "Best Use of Humor" category of the 2005 Viral Awards, and it was a runner-up for that competition's grand prize, the "Most Infectious North American Viral Campaign."

MTV enlisted Vescovo to craft another round of "Watch and Learn" spots in 2004, and Vescovo continued to expand the "Instructoart" franchise beyond the network. In February 2004 *Instructoart: The Book* was released, and the "Instructoart" pieces made the rounds of international art galleries in subsequent years. Two more book versions of "Instructoart" were published in 2004 and 2005. MTV remained one of the world's strongest brands and the top TV destination for young people.

FURTHER READING

Anderson, Mae. "On the Spot: Matt Vescovo." *Adweek,* July 26, 2004.

"Conquering the Universe with Big Hair, Beavis and the Backstreet Boys." *Newsweek,* July 23, 2001.

Dover, Caitlin. "Life: A User's Manual." *Print,* March/April 2004.

Fera, Rae Ann. "How to Live, MTV Style." *Boards Online,* August 27, 2003. Available from <http://www.boardsmag.com/articles/online/20030827/mtv.html>

"Hornet's MTV How-To Guide." *Creativity,* September 2003.

"MTV 'Watch and Learn.'" *Creativity,* April 2005.

Nudd, Tim. "MTV Hooked on 'Instructoart.'" *Adweek,* September 15, 2003.

Shortman, Melanie. "Hornet." *Creativity,* March 2004.

Vescovo, Matt. *Instructoart.* <http://www.instructoart.com>

Mark Lane

The Museum of Contemporary Art, Los Angeles

250 S. Grand Avenue
Los Angeles, California 90012
USA
Telephone: (213) 621-1750
Fax: (213) 620-8674
Web site: www.moca.org

■■■

LABELS CAMPAIGN

OVERVIEW

Even with a $13.5 million operating budget and one of the largest contemporary art collections in the United States, the Museum of Contemporary Art, Los Angeles (MOCA), toiled to draw crowds in 2001. Competing against a variety of entertainment destinations in Los Angeles County that ranged from beaches to baseball games, along with other museums, MOCA's recently appointed director Jeremy Strick wanted to surpass the previous year's 500,000 MOCA visitor count. Hoping to boost awareness of the museum throughout Los Angeles County, MOCA released "Labels," the largest advertising campaign in its 21-year history.

The $1 million campaign, created by the Los Angeles office of ad agency TBWA\Chiat\Day, first appeared on January 1, 2001. The core of the campaign consisted of 61 billboards across Los Angeles County that featured black copy on white backgrounds. The billboards' copy parodied the description labels that appeared beside artworks in museums. Each billboard featured a message relevant to its surroundings. Above a restaurant's valet parking service, for instance, one billboard's title read, "Men Running with Keys, 2001." Below the title it listed the "medium" as "Restaurants, thick-soled shoes, paper tickets with red ink / Collection of the Museum of Contemporary Art." Similar advertisements appeared across Los Angeles newspapers, outdoor posters, dry-cleaning hangers, and radio spots. The campaign's three television spots featured titles such as "Husband and Wife on a Sofa, A Study of Still Life, 2001," "Remote Control, 2001," and "The Demise of Culture, 2001." The campaign lasted for six months.

Some critics felt that the billboards' message was misunderstood and required too much reading; others disliked them completely. As *Los Angeles Times* writer Christopher Knight explained, "Artists tell me that they hate the MOCA campaign." Nonetheless, the advertising community showered it with praise. *Advertising Age's Creativity* awarded "Labels" with one of the magazine's annual Creativity Awards in 2001. The campaign was one of the most awarded entrants for the 2001 annual International ANDY Awards, where it collected a Gold ANDY and 10 Silver ANDYs.

HISTORICAL CONTEXT

In 1999 Jeremy Strick was appointed the director of MOCA, one of America's largest contemporary-art museums, with a staff of 130 people, 13,000 paying members, and an annual attendance of 450,000. Because Strick had only been a curator at his previous post at the Art Institute of Chicago, many critics denunciated the new director for his lack of administrative experience.

To establish himself as an apt leader, in 1999 Strick opened a MOCA retrospective exhibition of the

Museum of Contemporary Art (MOCA), Los Angeles, California. © KEVIN BURKE/CORBIS.

commercial artist Barbara Kruger's work. Kruger was famous for printing pithy comments such as "I shop therefore I am" upon images of women. Not only did the Kruger exhibition generate wide acclaim, but Los Angeles critics were also impressed by the show's attendance. The show also led to the addition of 1,700 new MOCA members. Strick strategically asked Kruger, whose résumé included working as head designer for *Mademoiselle* magazine, to create the show's advertising. "She developed print ads with us and also radio ads," Strick was quoted by the *Los Angeles Business Journal:* "We see this as a way of both getting the word out about MOCA and the exhibition and bringing art into new and different public spheres... The show's been well attended and people seem very aware of the campaign. It's stirred up some interest and a little controversy, too. That's great."

According to the *Washington Post,* in late 2000 Strick approved the allocation of $1 million to brand the museum as "something new, something fresh" to do in Los Angeles County. Just six days before "Labels" was released, the *Los Angeles Business Journal* quoted Strick explaining, "MOCA is all about creativity and inspiration. The unique gift we bring to Los Angeles is to showcase the creativity of cutting-edge artists from throughout the world, in the hope that it will in turn inspire our visitors."

TARGET MARKET

The "Labels" campaign targeted creatively minded 25- to 34-year-old Angelenos, the nickname for inhabitants of Los Angeles County. Suzanne Evans, a writer for the *Los Angeles Business Journal,* described the campaign's target as a "wary, advertising-bombarded youthful audience that is sometimes difficult to reach." Strick explained in the *New York Times* that Angelenos were often more leery of blatant advertising than the residents of cities such as Chicago and New York City. Instead of merely advertising the museum's logo or full name on billboards, "Labels" hoped to recreate the contemporary-art-museum experience within Los Angeles so that the target could engage with the community as an outdoor museum. Billboards suggested that the audience reflect on normally mundane objects such as restaurants, stoplights, and freeways in the same way that museum visitors reflected on art inside MOCA.

Some Los Angeles art critics pointed out that the campaign not only alienated its target market, including longstanding MOCA members, but also actually embittered the museum's featured artists. Doug Harvey, an art critic for *LA Weekly,* described the billboards as "unfathomable condescension" and "second-rate '60s conceptual art." *Los Angeles Times* critic Christopher Knight wrote, "The museum, with its conceptual commercials, appears to be usurping the role of artist, and bad artist at that."

COMPETITION

Not only was MOCA competing against two other contemporary-art museums within Los Angeles city limits, but it was also contending for visitors to larger art museums such as the Los Angeles County Museum of Art and

CAMPAIGN, 2001

In 2001 the Museum of Contemporary Art, Los Angeles (MOCA), released 61 billboard ads throughout Los Angeles that mimicked the description tags commonly found beside its works of art. To increase awareness about MOCA in the Los Angeles community, the campaign attempted to recreate the same reflective thinking needed to understand contemporary art. One billboard ad above a street crowded with car washes and tiny Mexican restaurants read, "Car Washes and a Couple of Taquerias, 2000." Courtesy of the Museum of Contemporary Art. Drawing its pithy campaign back to the museum, MOCA sold coffee cups in its museum gift shop that read, "Habit, 2001: Coffee in glazed ceramic. On loan from the Museum of Contemporary Art, Los Angeles."

the wildly successful J. Paul Getty Museum. With the exception of the latter, most of Los Angeles's museums were struggling financially. Having to compete against the city's other attractions, such as beaches, concert halls, theater houses, sporting events, and movie theaters, the museums struggled to remain profitable. The Latino Museum of History, Art, and Culture was forced to shut down in August 2000 after sinking $500,000 in debt. According to the *Washington Post,* Maya Rao, the TBWA\Chiat\Day copywriter for the "Labels" campaign, explained, "Why do museums need to advertise? Well, there is a lot of competition for eyeballs in this town."

With small advertising budgets, museum directors had to market their museums creatively in 2001. In Chicago the Museum of Contemporary Art's (MCA) director, Robert Fitzpatrick, began his new position by getting the museum's guards "out of those awful paramilitary costumes," Fitzpatrick was quoted in the *Chicago Sun-Times.* The MCA spent $17,500 on new uniforms that Fitzpatrick had ordered from the Banana Republic retail store. Fitzpatrick also commissioned Chicago artist Dan Peterman to construct benches outside of the MCA to provide seats for businesspeople to eat their lunches. Different farmers' markets were brought to the MCA plaza as well. Free admission days were increased from once a month to once a week; and Fitzpatrick decreased the price of the museum's self-guided tour AcoustiGuides from $3.50 to $1. "It's not just advertising, but it's about being accessible," Fitzpatrick further explained in the *Chicago Sun-Times.* "Are you going to spend $7 here, as opposed to a movie? It's not a choice you force them to make, it's a choice that you invite them to make, by being inviting."

MARKETING STRATEGY

For the months prior to January 2001, TBWA\Chiat\Day copywriter Maya Rao and art director Moe Vergrugge traversed Los Angeles in search for billboard locations that they could use for their upcoming MOCA campaign. What resulted was Los Angeles's largest site-specific billboard campaign in history. After writing more than 80 possible executions, 61 billboards were chosen. All of them advertised MOCA for at least six months. In addition to appearing on the billboards, the campaign's copy was placed on dry-cleaning hangers, paper coffee-cup bands, buses, free postcards distributed at bars, newspaper ads, and gas-pump handles. Radio and television spots were released as well. With more than 150 media placements, the "Labels" campaign was, according to the *Los Angeles Business Journal,* one of the largest ever released by a Los Angeles museum.

Every advertisement appeared as a label, similar to those describing artwork in a museum. One of the more provocative billboard titles, which was placed above a strip club, read, "Nudes 2001." Below the title the copy explained, "Bodies, dimensions variable. A study of First Amendment rights, entertainment, and business, all acting in concert to provide a debate among lawyers, politicians, and the general public. On loan from the Museum of Contemporary Art, Los Angeles."

TBWA\Chiat\Day took a risk with the amount of copy used on each billboard. According to Melanie Axtman, the group media director at TBWA\Chiat\Day, an advertising-industry guideline for outdoor advertising was that billboard copy should be limited to eight words or less. The ad agency justified breaking the guideline because the "Labels" billboards were placed in heavily congested areas where people were afforded more time to read the message. Some critics disagreed. The senior editor for National Public Radio, Andy Bowers, joked on the radio program *All Things Considered* that the billboard above a shopping plaza that read "People in designer labels buying more designer labels" should have instead read "People in designer labels ignoring billboard." Bowers later added, however, that once onlookers understood that the billboard was commenting on their surrounding environment, they became instantly fascinated by the advertisement.

Although the campaign's copy required more reading comprehension than most billboards, MOCA officials believed the campaign still befit Angelenos. According to the *Washington Post,* Strick explained, "People are used to seeing labels in museums and we liked the idea of labeling the city—extending out to the city the museum experience... Billboards are an L.A. institution. It's the way people communicate here, driving as much as we do, and so we asked what happens if you look at the city with the same attentiveness you look at art in a museum?"

Three television spots aired as public-service announcements across local TV stations in Los Angeles. The commercials featured titles similar to the billboards, such as "Husband and Wife on a Sofa, A Study of Still Life, 2001," "Remote Control, 2001," and "The Demise of Culture, 2001." The campaign included screensavers and computer-desktop wallpaper that could be downloaded from MOCA's website, www.Moca.org.

OUTCOME

The "Labels" campaign collected some of the advertising industry's most coveted awards. In 2002 it garnered a Gold EFFIE Award in the "Culture and the Arts/National or Regional" category. *Advertising Age's Creativity* magazine awarded the campaign one of its 2001 Creativity Awards. "Labels" also earned one Gold ANDY and 10 Silver ANDYs at the 2001 annual International ANDY Awards, making TBWA\Chiat\Day the most-decorated advertising agency of the ANDYs that year.

Despite the campaign's positive fanfare at awards shows, MOCA only attracted 315,000 visitors during 2001, a major reduction from the 500,000 visitors it recorded in 2000. Some analysts attributed the decline to the museum's dwindling donations and to budget cuts made by the California Arts Council, which provided a large portion of the museum's funding. MOCA's operations budget dropped from $20 million in 1999 to $13.5 million in 2001. Besides reduced funding, the nationwide recession and the terrorist attacks of September 11, 2001, had affected all of Los Angeles County's museums. Jay Aldrich, director of tourism and publications at the Autry Museum of Western Heritage, explained in the *Los Angeles Business Journal*, "Attendance was in decline in every Southern California attraction in 2001 due to 9/11."

FURTHER READING

Anderton, Frances. "Traffic Jam: Harried Drivers, Seduced by Museum Come-Ons." *New York Times*, February 8, 2001, p. 3.

Bensinger, Ken. "Art & Money." *Wall Street Journal*, December 22, 2000, p. W8.

Bodey, Michael. "Inside Tinseltown." *Daily Telegraph* (Surry Hills, Australia), August 26, 2000, p. 24.

Booth, William. "'L.A. Ads' 2001, Mixed Media, Message; Art Museum's Eye-Catching Billboards Put the City in the Picture." *Washington Post*, June 26, 2001, p. C01.

Bowles, Johnson K. "Taking A Long, Hard Look." *Afterimage*, May 1, 2000, p. 12.

Campbell, Duncan. "Saturday Review: The State They're In." *Guardian* (London), February 10, 2001, p. 3.

Elliott, Stuart. "Two Groups Give Creativity Awards." *New York Times*, April 25, 2001, p. 6.

Farr, Sheila. "Get a Creative Tuneup while Idling at the Intersection." *Seattle Times*, October 13, 2000, p. I26.

Hayt, Elizabeth. "If You Wow Them, They Will Come." *New York Times*, February 18, 2001, p. 33.

Heartney, Eleanor. "A Catholic Controversy?" *Art in America*, December 1, 1999, p. 39.

Muschamp, Herbert. "Tributes to the Stage, Steel Mills and Rock Star Style." *New York Times*, September 12, 1999, p. 103.

———. "When Getting to It Is Part of a Museum's Aesthetic." *New York Times*, November 26, 2000, p. 34.

Purdum, Todd S. "Up on a Hill: The Getty Learns to Weather the Crowds." *New York Times*, May 2, 2001, p. 12.

Wilkinson-Ryan, Tess. "The Work," *Advertising Age's Creativity*, February 1, 2001, p. 13.

Kevin Teague

Napster, Inc.

9044 Melrose Avenue
Los Angeles, California 90069
USA
Telephone: (310) 281-5000
Web site: www.napster.com

IT'S COMING BACK CAMPAIGN

OVERVIEW

In 1999, 19-year-old Shawn Fanning achieved celebrity status as the file-sharing industry's founder when he created www.Napster.com, a website that facilitated the sharing of music across the Internet. Napster's members could freely download other members' songs onto their own computers, an innovation that sent the music industry into a panic. As other file-sharing applications surfaced, the music industry singled out Napster and forced it to shut down by 2001. Two years later digital music firm Roxio, Inc., purchased Napster's assets, formed licensing agreements with recording studios, repackaged Napster as a Web space from which to legally download music, and renamed Roxio "Napster, Inc." The "It's Coming Back" campaign was launched in 2003 to attract older, paying customers without alienating the former Napster members.

Roxio spent $6.4 million to relaunch Napster in 2003 and awarded its advertising budget to agency Venables, Bell, and Partners (VB&P). The "It's Coming Back" campaign surfaced on June 30, 2003, when VB&P changed the website www.Napster.com to www.NapsterBits.com, a title hinting at Napster's rebirth. Four months later nine short Internet-based films, three of which became television spots, aired with a character that VB&P had created from Napster's "kitty" logo. The films, if watched consecutively, formed a loosely connected storyline that metaphorically told Napster's fall and hopeful rise. The first Internet spot showed the Napster "kitty" repelling from a prison window, only to be sniped on his way down. Next, the "kitty" recovered inside a hospital until he was strong enough to approach a skyscraper filled with cutthroat music moguls. After collecting the signature of a music-industry executive, the "kitty" left to promote hip-hop, metal, reggae, blues, techno, country, folk, and indie music genres. All Internet spots, as well as a 15-second television-only spot titled "Old School," were constructed with Flash, a software language that animated images similar to cartoons.

Sales between March 2004 and March 2005 grew 53 percent, reaping $46 million for Napster. The campaign gave Napster a second chance in the industry it had once created. "It's Coming Back" also snagged two Gold Cyber Lions at the International Advertising Festival in Cannes, France, the Bronze Pencil at the One Show Interactive Awards, and a Silver Cube at the Art Directors Club Awards.

HISTORICAL CONTEXT

Using only word of mouth at its conception, Napster maintained its title as the world's top file-sharing application until 2001, when the Recording Industry Association of America and other music-industry giants forced Napster to shut down on grounds of copyright infringement. Soon afterward Bertelsmann AG (a book, movie, and music retailer) purchased Napster's brand, which was later purchased by Roxio. Roxio then acquired Pressplay, a service similar to Napster, and changed its name to Napster, Inc. Hoping to imitate the success Apple Computer had had with iTunes, an application that allowed the legal download of music at 99 cents per song, the revived Napster surfaced in 2003 with more than one million songs available, all accessible to subscribers who paid a monthly service fee. As with iTunes, Napster members could also pay per song.

In 2003 Venables, Bell, and Partners (VB&P), an agency based in San Francisco, pitched its advertising concept to Napster, believing that Napster should be branded in conjunction with music, but not free music. "We're going to pitch business with them as appropriate," agency partner Paul Venables told *Adweek.* "We like to have them in from the get-go, figuring out how digital work can play a role." After winning the account the agency set out to build the campaign around Napster's previous brand awareness. "It's the only pure music brand in that space," a VB&P agency representative told the *San Francisco Chronicle,* "and the brand still has ninety percent-plus awareness. It still resonates with people in a big way."

In 2003, before the official "It's Coming Back" campaign launched, VB&P released what they called "teasers." Napster placed its logo, usually without copy, in print and outdoor advertisements. "The idea is to tease, period. Not as part of the bigger campaign, not as a glimpse of what's to come. That, we feel, would be too perfect a communication, therefore too corporate," Venables told *Advertising Age's Creativity.*

TARGET MARKET

According to VB&P, the campaign targeted "the music-loving 30-something corporate overachiever who holds down a $75,000 job by day, and goes to see live music at night. In short, we wanted the real music lovers and those who had more money than time." This target deviated from Napster's earlier member base. Referring to the Napster users between 1999 to 2001, Scott Steinberg, senior vice president of marketing for Napster, told the *Asian Wall Street Journal,* "The youth-pirate university culture definitely has more time than money." The "It's Coming Back" campaign refocused on an older demographic with an inverse time-money relationship.

When the campaign first appeared, Napster walked a fine line to maintain its hip image while not appearing as a sellout for negotiating music-licensing agreements. "We wanted to stay cool with the cool crowd," Venables told the *Asian Wall Street Journal.* To maintain its antiestablishment tone, VB&P played up Napster's outlaw image with ten funny and occasionally graphic short films to be played on the Internet and on TV. The Napster "kitty" was shown breaking out of jail and then recovering from a gunshot wound. The "kitty" later weathered the bloodbath of a music-industry business meeting, complete with caricaturized executives attacking each other with paperclips, ink pens, and staplers. Next, the Napster "kitty" performed for an indie-music crowd, grooved to hip-hop music, rocked out to blues music, danced with Rastafarians, and postured with a heavy-metal band. The spots sometimes poked fun at the music genres, but they always maintained, according to analysts, a strong connection to contemporary music. Except for the spots focusing on blues, indie, metal, and reggae music, the films were primarily scored with hip-hop music.

Bob Garfield, an ad critic for *Advertising Age,* wrote, "Unlike much of the rich media that passes for online creativity, these ads don't overtake your screen and grab your attention by force. Instead, they rely on wit and storytelling to seduce you, suck you in and cultivate whatever dormant seed of Napster affection is still buried within you."

COMPETITION

At the dawn of legally downloadable music, Apple's iTunes Music Store dominated with a 70 percent market share and 125 million downloads in less than two years after appearing in 2003. Early iTunes advertising stood on the shoulders of Apple's iPod "Silhouette" campaign, which showed black silhouettes dancing to the music of pop groups such as the rock band Jet and the hip-hop group Black Eyed Peas. The spots, designed by TBWA\Chiat\Day, Los Angeles, ended with copy

NAPPY SHAWN FANNING

Shawn Fanning created the first version of Napster when he was a Massachusetts college freshman in 1999. Amazed at how many hours his roommates spent searching the Internet for obscure rap music, Shawn set out to create a program that allowed the sharing of music between computers connected online. Shawn released his own beta version of Napster on June 1, 1999. The name "Napster" was taken from Shawn's own nickname, a title he earned in college for his nappy hair.

THE EFFICIENCY OF MP3S

MP3s were substantially smaller music files than the CD-DA audio tracks burned into store-bought compact discs. MP3s saved room by ignoring the sound waves that the human brain could not perceive and by compressing the remaining sound data.

directing people to the iTunes website. Convincing users to pay 99 cents per song was initially difficult for iTunes Music Store, since music fans could download songs for free, although illegally, from peer-to-peer file sharing applications such as Altnet, Inc.'s KaZaA. Sales, however, steadily grew for iTunes, which made it easy to download music onto an iPod, Apple's digital music player.

iTunes' success spurred competitors to release a surge of other legally downloadable music applications. For $160 million Yahoo! Inc. purchased Musicmatch, an online music store and Internet-radio service provider. The site allowed users to purchase and download single songs or entire albums. RealNetworks, Inc., the creator of RealPlayer, a digital music and video player, would occasionally sell songs at 49 cents apiece to undercut iTunes. Microsoft Corp. also joined in by creating MSN Music, an application that started with half the song selection of Napster and iTunes. "Every time there's a new technology, it starts at its broadest base, but eventually must narrow down to be segmented based on consumer needs," Steven Flanders, president of Icon Entertainment, an entertainment-marketing firm, told the *Asian Wall Street Journal.*

Napster attempted to capture the iTunes market by offering an unlimited song subscription. After the "It's Coming Back" campaign ended, Napster created in-house ads with the tagline "Do the math." It claimed that a user could fill the iPod's 10,000-song capacity with Napster's $9.95 monthly subscription fee, a thrifty alternative to iTunes' 99-cents-per-song pricing.

MARKETING STRATEGY

Before the "It's Coming Back" television spots appeared on October 15, 2003, VB&P released what it called "teasers" in outdoor and print ads. One teaser involved dividing Napster's logo, the "kitty" head, into three different billboards and displaying them along L.A.'s Sunset Strip. Venables explained to *Advertising Age's Creativity* that the spots were "complete teasers for the 'influencer' music consumer," referring to trendsetting music consumers. In major cities VB&P also pasted fake sappy poster ads with stickers depicting the Napster "kitty" slapped over the ads' faces. "The fact that the stickers were a separate element and that they looked like guerrilla Xeroxes—not perfect, colorful logos—was key," Venables continued in *Advertising Age's Creativity.*

For the ensuing "It's Coming Back" campaign VB&P built on Napster's headphone-wearing, white cat-face logo by furnishing it with a body as well as a personality. Faced with the challenge of preserving Napster's hip image, the campaign's Internet and television spots were designed with Flash, a cutting-edge software language that animated images much like a cartoon. Commenting on the use of Flash, Venables told *Advertising Age's Creativity,* "I don't think there's ever been another company that's created something using the tools of the web, and then exported it to their mainstream broadcast campaign." VB&P continued giving Napster's brand a never-before-seen, stylized look. "If we went out with the mechanics of a traditional packaged-goods campaign, we would have put the brand back in the grave," Steinberg explained to the *Asian Wall Street Journal.*

The short Internet films first appeared on Napster.com and NapsterBits.com in the summer of 2003. On October 15 one 15-second television spot, "Old School," aired across cable channels such as Comedy Central, MTV, and ESPN. "Old School" featured the Napster "kitty" break-dancing to hip-hop music, followed by text stating, "Old School" and then, "Get it at Napster.com." Varying from the colorful Flash commercials, one charcoal-colored print ad showed the Napster icon carved into a tombstone above a recently vacated grave. The ad's only copy stated, "Go to Napster.com." It appeared in magazines such as *Entertainment Weekly.*

Continuing with the feline metaphor, the campaign's short Internet films told the story of Napster's transition from a file-sharing lawbreaker to a legitimate downloadable-music service. The first Internet spot, "Jailbreak," showed the Napster "kitty" escaping through the window of his jail cell only to be sniped on the way down by a guard. Next the "kitty" was shown recovering with a weakened pulse in the spot titled "EKG." After recovering, the "kitty" collected a needed signature from a music-industry executive that enabled him to promote different genres, including heavy metal, reggae, hip-hop, blues, and indie music. The final spot, "Reunion," rushed through a montage of more musical tastes, such as trance, country, and folk. The story climaxed when the Napster "kitty" bounced off a diving board and soared above a swimming pool surrounded by onlookers. The text "Napster.com" flashed just before the "kitty" sank into the pool. Three of the Internet spots eventually aired as television commercials.

OUTCOME

The "It's Coming Back" campaign helped Napster successfully bounce from a two-year remission period into an industry that was blossoming. A month after the television spots first aired, www.Napster.com registered 3.2 million visitors, surpassing iTunes' 2.7 million. During the last quarter of 2003 Napster had more Web traffic than any other music-shopping website. By crafting a campaign that told the story of Napster's struggle against the music industry, VB&P helped Napster rebrand itself with music rather than the free music for which it had previously been known. "Napster has incredible name recognition," Lee Black, a music-industry analyst with Jupiter Research in Connecticut, told *Adweek*. "Everybody knows what it was. It was the classic David and Goliath anti-establishment case."

By following the music industry's rules and paying for permissions, the new, legal Napster achieved more profit than its earlier version ever did. Sales between 2004 and 2005 jumped 53 percent and collected $46 million, an impressive figure considering Roxio only spent $6.4 million to launch the service. Besides bottom-line success, the "It's Coming Back" campaign also earned two Gold Cyber Lions (awards that recognized an advertisement's excellent use of the Internet) at the International Advertising Festival in Cannes, the Bronze Pencil at the One Show Interactive Awards, and a Silver Cube at the Art Directors Club Awards.

FURTHER READING

Gaither, Chris. "Once Again, the 'Net Is the Next Big Thing." *Calgary Herald,* July 3, 2005, p. D3.

Garfield, Bob. "Garfield's AdReview; Cool Jailbird Cat Helps Napster Go Straight, but Keep Its Edge." *Advertising Age,* September 27, 2004, p. 83.

Garfield, Bob. "10 Ads I Loved." *Advertising Age,* December 20, 2004, p. 14.

Garrity, Brian. "IPod Rivals Square Off against Apple." *Billboard,* September 25, 2004, p. 59.

Graham, Jefferson. "Beatles Record Label Sues Apple Computer—Again." *USA Today,* September 20, 2004, p. B4.

Hastings, Michael, and Rana Foroohar. "Changing Channels." *Newsweek International,* June 6, 2005, p. 42.

Hays, Constance. "Agency Is Selected for Napster Revival." *New York Times,* June 26, 2003, p. 10.

Jeffers, Michelle. "Venables' Hipster Mission: 'Keep It Cool' for Napster." *Adweek,* June 30, 2003, p. 12.

Kinnes, Sally. "1 in 3 Rejects Technology." *Sunday Times* (London), July 10, 2005, p. 12.

Norton, Justin. "VB&P Uses Mekanism for Digital." *Adweek* (western ed.), January 14, 2002, p. 5.

Parpis, Eleftheria, and Mae Anderson. "The Best Creatives You Don't Know 2004." *Adweek,* September 27, 2004, p. 22.

Pender, Kathleen. "Grokster Decision Has Industry Listening." *San Francisco Chronicle,* June 28, 2005, p. D1.

Raine, George, Carolyn Said, and Todd Wallack. "Business Digest." *San Francisco Chronicle,* June 26, 2003, p. B2.

Steinberg, Brian, and Nick Wingfield. "Ad Campaigns Try to Sell That Tune." *Asian Wall Street Journal,* November 11, 2003, p. A7.

Kevin Teague

The Nasdaq Stock Market, Inc.

1 Liberty Plaza
New York, New York 10006
USA
Telephone: (212) 401-8700
Fax: (212) 401-1024
Web site: www.nasdaq.com

LISTED ON NASDAQ CAMPAIGN

OVERVIEW

Nasdaq, the world's first electronic stock market, was flying high in the late 1990s, its advertising proclaiming it to be "The stock market for the next 100 years." All but synonymous with the Internet-focused "New Economy" and heavy with technology companies, the Nasdaq was dealt a severe blow when the tech sector collapsed in 2000, compounded a year later by an economy in recession. The Nasdaq's image was severely tarnished, leading to a change in advertising agencies in 2001. McKinney & Silver, an agency based in Durham, North Carolina, was hired to restore some luster to the brand. The resulting "Listed on Nasdaq" campaign was intended to reassure the investment community, especially high-level corporate executives, that Nasdaq was still a great place to be listed for both tech and non-tech companies alike.

The Nasdaq spent approximately $30 million a year on the campaign, which broke in August 2002. The campaign's television and print ads featured CEOs from prominent companies listed on the Nasdaq, including Microsoft's Steve Ballmer, Staples's Tom Sternberg, and Starbucks's Howard Schultz. In the television spots their inspiring comments were intercut to portray the Nasdaq as a progressive and innovative stock market.

The "Listed on Nasdaq" campaign won a 2005 EFFIE Award. It also succeeded in restoring confidence in the brand without also driving up the ratings of the New York Stock Exchange (NYSE), a first in Nasdaq advertising history. In addition, the campaign helped to stem the flow of company defections to the NYSE as Nasdaq regained dominance in initial public offerings of stock. The campaign ran into 2005.

HISTORICAL CONTEXT

When Nasdaq was launched in 1971 as the world's first electronic stock market, it was considered a "bridge" exchange, a stepping stone for companies looking to eventually gain a listing on the American Stock Exchange or the New York Stock Exchange. Later major corporations, including Microsoft and Dell, opted to stay on the Nasdaq because they preferred its electronic market-making concept (matching buyers and sellers using computers instead of specialist brokerage firms), and in the 1990s Nasdaq become the natural home for high-tech companies, most of which, when they grew large enough to qualify for a listing on an old-guard exchange, preferred to stick with the Nasdaq. As a result the Nasdaq enjoyed tremendous growth during the economic boom of the late 1990s, prompting its marketers to craft the tagline "The stock market for the next 100 years." It appeared to be an accurate statement at the time, given that between 1990 and 1995 the index grew from 416 to

755, and that in the second half of the decade it soared to an incredible peak of 5049 in March 2000.

As the Internet companies (the so-called New Economy) that had fueled much of the Nasdaq's growth began to fail in what was dubbed the bursting of the "dot-com bubble," the Nasdaq saw the bottom fall out of its market in 2000. All but equated with the New Economy, the Nasdaq's reputation was tainted, and the exchange found itself besieged from all angles, from the NYSE on one side and the electronic communications networks (ECNs)—which eliminated third parties in the trading of stocks in a purely electronic environment—on the other. To make matters worse, the economy slipped into a recession in 2001. According to Paula Dwyer and Amy Borrus writing in *BusinessWeek,* a poor economy created a vicious circle for the Nasdaq: "Wall Street firms retrench, leasing few NASDAQ trading terminals. As companies falter, their stocks are delisted, cutting NASDAQ's fee revenue. When listings decline, the market receives fewer quotes from market-makers and ECNs and can't collect as much from reselling the data. As fewer shares trade, transaction fees shrink." In essence, Nasdaq was soon fighting for its very survival, far from certain that it would be around in one year, let alone 100.

After a shake-up at the top ranks of management, in April 2001 Nasdaq brought in a new marketing head, Denise Benou Stires, who expressed confidence in the exchange's chances of rebuilding its image with investors and the public in general. "I feel like I've inherited one of the most extraordinary brands in the world," she told Mercedes M. Cardona of *Advertising Age.* "I'm not sure you could find a reasonably affluent Mongolian shopkeeper who doesn't know Nasdaq." She quickly put the $30 million advertising account into review, looking for a fresh approach after 12 years with the New York ad agency Messner Vetere Berge McNamee Schmetterer/Euro RSCG. The agencies that participated all had Nasdaq-listed corporate parents, an intentional consideration. In August the winner emerged: North Carolina–based McKinney & Silver of the Havas Group.

TARGET MARKET

Although the "Listed on Nasdaq" campaign would reach the general public, especially through television spots, the target audience was really the investment community, particularly corporate chief executives and other top-level officers who played key roles in deciding where a public company chose to be listed. The campaign sought to assure these executives that Nasdaq was more than the market for failed Internet companies and was a suitable home for both tech and non-tech companies alike. More important than attracting new listings, however, was the need to prevent defections. Stires admitted to Alicia Griswold of *Adweek* that "Our messaging has to appeal to the chief officers of our listed companies so that they feel re-affirmed by choosing us." Only on a secondary level did the "Listed on Nasdaq" campaign target investors.

> ### A MOUTHFUL
>
> NASDAQ is an acronym for National Association of Securities Dealers Automated Quotations.

COMPETITION

Having merged with the American Stock Exchange in 1998, Nasdaq's only major exchange competitor was the New York Stock Exchange (NYSE). While Nasdaq may have harbored dreams of luring away NYSE companies with the "Listed on Nasdaq" campaign, in truth only one company in 30 years had ever made the switch. A more realistic goal was to stem the flow of defections from the Nasdaq to the NYSE and regain its share of IPOs (initial public offering of stock). Should the Nasdaq lose sufficient strength, it also faced the loss of business to small regional exchanges, such as the ones in Boston, Cincinnati, Chicago, Los Angeles and San Francisco (the Pacific Exchange), and Philadelphia.

A more immediate threat was the ECNs (electronic communications networks), which, unlike the Nasdaq, did not rely on market makers (specialist firms that bought stock and for a commission matched up sellers and buyers). Rather, ECNs merely coordinated buy and sell orders electronically for a fee, acting more as matchmakers than market makers. Arguably, Nasdaq only had itself to blame for the rise of ECNs, which had grown out of a Nasdaq price-fixing scandal in the mid-1990s. The Securities and Exchange Commission (SEC) responded by encouraging the growth of ECNs, some of which were backed by Wall Street firms. By the time the new campaign broke, ECNs had captured nearly half of the trading volume in Nasdaq-listed stocks, roughly two-and-a-half times as much as Nasdaq was able to do through its own trading system. Competing against the ECNs was no easy task, because they were also Nasdaq's customers, and should Nasdaq create its own ECN it would also compete against other customers, the dealers. Nasdaq tried to launch its own ECN, SuperMontage, in 2001, but ECN complaints to the SEC forced a two-year delay in the rollout of the system. What was eventually unveiled suffered from so many compromises along the way that it was no match for the ECNs on their own turf.

THE BUTTONWOOD AGREEMENT

The auction system for selling stock dates back to 1792, when two dozen brokers, who often met informally under a buttonwood tree at 68 Wall Street in Manhattan, signed an agreement to trade only with one another. This two-sentence document, signed under the tree, became known as the Buttonwood Agreement and would lead to the creation of the New York Stock Exchange in 1863.

MARKETING STRATEGY

In preparation for the "Listed on Nasdaq" campaign, McKinney & Silver conducted research with a number of people in the target group. The agency asked them where the computer companies Microsoft, Apple, and Intel were listed, and invariably the answer was the NYSE, the assumption being that any companies that large and successful were out of place on the Nasdaq. The subjects were then presented with list of three Nasdaq-listed companies—Costco, PETsMART, and Starbucks—and once again the subjects believed that they were listed on the NYSE because they were not technology companies. As a result of this research, it was clear that even highly knowledgeable people like top corporate executives harbored misperceptions about the Nasdaq that the campaign would have to address.

The goal of the "Listed on Nasdaq" campaign was to restore credibility to the brand while making some subtle changes to common views about the Nasdaq. Instead of "high tech" Nasdaq wanted to be seen as "progressive," and rather than "high risk" it preferred to be known as "innovative." The Nasdaq also wanted to draw a distinction between itself and the NYSE by making the point that a large percentage of Nasdaq-listed companies were led by their founders, who McKinney & Silver would portray as visionaries. To accomplish these ends the agency decided that, rather than promote Nasdaq the institution, the advertisements would feature some of the visionary CEOs of Nasdaq-listed companies, including both tech companies and other kinds of companies. It would be in this context the Nasdaq was to be positioned as progressive and innovative.

McKinney & Silver filmed interviews with 20 CEOs for the "Listed on Nasdaq" campaign and then put together commercials that each featured three of the executives. The media strategy for airing these spots centered on the tendency of the investment community to be voracious and particular consumers of news as well as to be highly literate. Hence, commercial time was mostly bought on select cable news channels, including CNN, MSNBC, and Bloomberg. The print component of the campaign was focused on mainstream business and finance publications, including *Forbes* and *Fortune,* as well as more highbrow fare such as the *New Yorker.*

The "Listed on Nasdaq" campaign broke in August 2002 with four television spots. The CEOs profiled included high-tech stars, such as Steve Ballmer of Microsoft, John Chambers of Cisco, Michael Dell of Dell Inc., and Craig Barrett of Intel, as well as heads of non-tech successes, including Staples' Tom Sternberg and Starbucks' Howard Schultz. Excerpts of their comments were intercut with each other to fashion the spots. Highlights included Chambers's comment: "I would hope that people would think about Cisco in terms of changing the way the world works, lives, plays and learns"; Dell revealing, "At first my parents were pretty upset with me when I dropped out of college, but after a while they got over it"; and Ballmer recalling, "When I first came to Microsoft, my father asked what software was. My mother asked a more interesting question: why would a person ever need a computer." The tagline for the spots was "Visionaries. Listed on Nasdaq," followed by the featured CEOs announcing the name of their companies and one of them proclaiming, "Listed on Nasdaq." A second round of spots premiered in December 2002, and the CEO interviews were also used to create a long-form video that Nasdaq used when meeting with prospective listed companies.

In the print portion of the campaign Starbucks was also featured along with such companies as eBay and Nasdaq's largest banking company, Fifth Third Bank. The ad for Fifth Third Bank, as an example, showed a signed Post-It note from CEO George Schaefer. His message: "There are 86,400 seconds in a day. On your mark, get set, go."

OUTCOME

The "Listed on Nasdaq" campaign was successful on many levels. In 2005 it garnered McKinney & Silver a Gold EFFIE Award (Financial Services/Image category), given out annually by the New York American Marketing Association in recognition of the year's most effective advertising campaigns. More importantly, the campaign, according to McKinney & Silver, helped to restore confidence in the Nasdaq brand. In a write-up for the EFFIE Awards, the agency maintained that measures of confidence in the brand and its positioning had improved dramatically, "driven by proven recall of the campaign." It added, "This is the first time that advertising improved perceptions of NASDAQ without improving

NYSE ratings." McKinney & Silver also claimed that the campaign helped to stem the flow of defections to the NYSE and that Nasdaq had regained its dominant share of IPOs. The agency noted that, 16 months after the campaign had begun, the Nasdaq grew 76 percent, or twice the rate of the Dow Jones Industrial Average (an market index that tracked the growth of high-cap companies), which grew 38 percent during the same period. The agency then commented, "It would be foolish to take credit for this rise. Then again, traders will tell you that psychology moves markets . . ."

FURTHER READING

Cardona, Mercedes M. "Denise Benou Stires, Nasdaq; Perception is Redefined." *Advertising Age,* June 3, 2002, p. S8.

Dwyer, Paula, and Amy Borrus. "NASDAQ: The Fight of Its Life." *BusinessWeek,* August 11, 2003, p. 64.

Garfield, Bob. "Nasdaq Taps Heavy Hitters to Shore Up Battered Image." *Advertising Age,* September 9, 2002, p. 29.

Griswold, Alicia. "Nasdaq Taps McKinney & Silver." *Adweek,* August 13, 2001, p. 3.

McMains, Andrew, and Ann M. Mack. "McKinney Contends for Nasdaq." *Adweek,* May 28, 2001, p. 5.

"Nasdaq Ads Spotlight CEOs." *Adweek* (eastern ed.), August 19, 2002, p. 28.

Nilson, Kim. "Ad Shop Facing Gauntlet of Pillowtex Failure, Nasdaq Woes." *Raleigh (NC) Triangle Business Journal,* August 15, 2003, p. 12.

"Overcoming NASDAQ's Crisis." *BusinessWeek,* August 11, 2003, p. 108.

Smith, Samantha Thompson. "Raleigh, N.C., Ad Agency Wins Nasdaq Account." *Raleigh (NC) News & Observer,* August 8, 2001.

Traugot, Catherine Liden. "Crafting Campaigns." *Raleigh (NC) Triangle Business Journal,* September 6, 2002, p. 19.

Ed Dinger

National Association for Stock Car Auto Racing

1801 W. International Speedway Boulevard
Daytona Beach, Florida 32114
USA
Telephone: (386) 253-0611
Fax: (386) 252-8804
Web site: www.nascar.com

■■■

HOW BAD HAVE YOU GOT IT? CAMPAIGN

OVERVIEW

The National Association for Stock Car Auto Racing (NASCAR) saw its popularity dramatically increase between the 1970s and the 1990s. Long considered a sport followed chiefly by blue-collar males in the southern United States, NASCAR's audience had in reality evolved considerably since its early days. With a growing base of middle- and upper-income fans of all ages and both genders scattered across all parts of the country, NASCAR set out in 2001 to expand its audience even further. Explicitly targeting families and departing from previous campaigns in which intense racing footage was used to appeal to hardcore fans, NASCAR's ad agency, Young & Rubicam of Chicago, crafted a campaign meant to inspire new fans to greater devotional heights without alienating the faithful.

"How Bad Have You Got It?" was budgeted at an estimated $25 to $30 million a year, and it was launched in February 2001 to coincide with that year's 10-month racing season. The TV spots depicted a seemingly ordinary family—the same one in all eight executions—whose ordinary activities were dramatically colored by an obvious obsession with NASCAR. For instance, one commercial showed the family station wagon parking in front of a diner, whereupon all four members exited the car via the windows, after the fashion of NASCAR drivers. Another spot showed the husband and wife unable to sleep, presumably because of the revving engine noise outside. The husband rose and opened the window, and, soothed by the louder engine sound, the couple quickly fell into a peaceful slumber. The campaign's run was extended through the 2002 racing season, with new content and slight alterations in strategy.

The campaign received favorable critical attention on its way to winning a Bronze Lion at the Cannes International Advertising Festival and a Gold EFFIE from the New York American Marketing Association. NASCAR's television audience and fan base both continued to grow rapidly in subsequent years.

HISTORICAL CONTEXT

NASCAR was formed in 1948 by William France, Sr., and Ed Otto as a means of formalizing rules and procedures for the racing of "stock" cars, or cars that had not been modified outside of the factories that produced them. The first NASCAR race was held at the Charlotte Speedway in North Carolina on June 19, 1949. By the mid-1960s the cars were no longer true stock cars; they

© SAM SHARPE/THE SHARPE IMAGE/CORBIS.

had bodies similar to ordinary factory-produced cars but were actually built specifically for racing. NASCAR expanded throughout the next several decades, but its fan base remained localized in the southeastern region of the country, where, prior to 1970, all tracks but one (Riverside Raceway in Riverside, California) were located.

The year 1972 marked the beginning of the modern era of NASCAR, characterized by a new competitive structure that included a point system and a series of races called the Winston Cup, sponsored by the R.J. Reynolds cigarette brand of the same name. In the mid-1970s portions of NASCAR races began to appear on television, and the first full telecast of a race from beginning to end was the 1979 Daytona 500. This race proved effective in introducing mainstream America to the drama of stock car racing: the lead cars, driven by Cale Yarborough and Donnie Allison, crashed during the final lap, and Richard Petty won. The excitement continued after the race, when Yarborough, Allison, and Allison's brother immediately engaged in a fistfight on national television.

By the early 2000s NASCAR had grown well beyond its home base in the Southeast. Its regular-season television ratings were second only to the National Football League among pro sports, with weekly telecasts attracting more than 20 million viewers. A 2001 brand study conducted by market-research firm Ipsos-Reid put the number of devoted NASCAR fans at 40 million. Corporate branding played an integral role in NASCAR races—cars as well as drivers were closely identified with, and decorated with the logos of, their sponsoring brands. Because of this and the related perception that NASCAR fans were the most brand-loyal of any sports fans, the sport was an increasingly attractive venue for Fortune 500 sponsorship. A 2001 deal with television networks NBC, TNT, FOX, and FX regularized the broadcasting of NASCAR races and allowed for further expansion of the sport's audience.

NASCAR did not do any national advertising until 1998, when it introduced the "This Is NASCAR" tagline. Primedia of Atlanta served as NASCAR's marketing agency during the late 1990s, handling licensing, media buying, and other strategic matters while subcontracting the creative work for national advertising. TV spots typically focused on dramatic race footage and the personalities of drivers, in a style described by freelance creative director Cleve Wilcoxon in *Adweek* as "a fastball down the middle." The campaign's yearly budget was estimated at $7.5 million in 2000.

TARGET MARKET

"How Bad Have You Got It?" coincided with a change in demographics among NASCAR's fan base. NASCAR's appeal had transcended its regional beginnings, though the largest and arguably most dedicated group of fans was still to be found in the South; and stereotypical notions holding that the sport was the province strictly of blue-collar men were likewise outdated. NASCAR increasingly drew fans from middle- and upper-income brackets, and in preparing for the campaign, Young & Rubicam uncovered an important but largely unrecognized aspect of stock-car racing: its appeal to families. "Families travel together for weekends to see the sport," Young &

DEADLY THRILLS

For NASCAR fans part of the thrill came from the risk that drivers took in traveling at such speeds and in such dangerous proximity to one another. Many fans openly acknowledged that they attended races hoping to witness car crashes. In 2001, however, just as the "How Bad Have You Got It?" campaign was getting underway, one of the sport's most traumatic accidents occurred. Dale Earnhardt, sometimes referred to as the Michael Jordan of NASCAR, was killed in the final lap of the Daytona 500 on February 18, 2001. The violent end to his career, which spanned more than 25 years, led many in the media to call for stricter safety standards for NASCAR races, but fans, observers noted, considered death an inevitable part of the drama that drew them to the sport. Perhaps supporting this notion was the fact that NASCAR saw significant ratings jumps for the 2001 races following Earnhardt's death.

Rubicam creative director/art director Jon Wyville told *Shoot.* "It's not just dad going to the races . . . whole families are into it."

While the agency had no choice but to take the changing nature of NASCAR fandom into account, its creative team recognized the necessity of appealing to the sport's longtime core fans as well. These fans tended to be extremely knowledgeable about the intricacies of the season-long points system and rules governing individual races, and they could be more clearly associated with NASCAR's regional past. Many newer fans, however, had little concern for NASCAR's regional affiliation and little knowledge of the sport's procedural details. They were drawn simply by the excitement and drama of the races.

Young & Rubicam thus had to calibrate its message so that it would speak to both kinds of NASCAR fans. "How Bad Have You Got It?" attempted to do so by focusing on the fans themselves, featuring intentionally ordinary-looking families in suburban neighborhoods with no regional or geographic markers. These families were defined by the one characteristic uniting NASCAR fans across cultural boundaries: their obsession with the sport.

COMPETITION

The National Football League (NFL) was the dominant sports league at this time, far outranking other pro sports in terms of U.S. popularity. The NFL, however, was not immune from the effects of the 2000–01 economic downturn, which decreased ad revenues during game broadcasts. In an effort to combat this trend as well as declines in ratings, in 2001 the NFL enlisted an outside advertising agency for the first time, choosing the New York office of the same agency NASCAR had recently engaged, Young & Rubicam. The resulting campaign, released in the fall of 2001, was meant to encourage casual NFL fans to become more devoted followers of the sport. Whereas previous campaigns had used the tagline "Feel the power" along with high-energy, collision-focused game footage to appeal to ardent fans, the new campaign, tagged "This Is What It's All About," was built upon the idea that casual fans had less appreciation for the collisions and athletic feats that thrilled devotees of the sport. The NFL and Young & Rubicam believed that these casual fans watched NFL games for social reasons, enjoying the camaraderie surrounding the broadcasts and the conversations about games at work each Monday during football season. In a move that was similar to NASCAR's new marketing strategy, the campaign's TV spots thus focused on fans rather than game footage. One commercial juxtaposed a fan's pregame activities with those of star Tennessee Titans running back Eddie George, while another depicted a fan's game-time backyard barbecue as a high-stakes "NFL experience" in its own right.

In 2001 the National Basketball Association (NBA) was struggling to generate the ratings it had enjoyed prior to the 1999 retirement of Michael Jordan, arguably the greatest basketball player in the league's history. This was Jordan's second retirement. As a means of countering sagging U.S. viewership, the NBA emphasized international markets in a campaign that was launched contemporaneously with "How Bad Have You Got It?" The campaign's TV commercials featured still photographs that transformed into live action, and they showcased a new generation of NBA stars, including Shaquille O'Neal, Vince Carter, and Tim Duncan. Producer Joe Chodosh of NBA Entertainment (the in-house department responsible for the campaign) told *Adweek,* "Because of the beauty of the moment captured in still photos, viewers are able to see a lot more in these images than when they normally watch basketball." The campaign aired in 207 countries. In the fall of 2001 Jordan announced that he would once again return from retirement. This complicated the league's marketing of younger stars but promised dramatic ratings increases. Jordan retired for the last time after the 2002–03 season.

MARKETING STRATEGY

NASCAR budgeted an estimated $25 to $30 million for marketing in the 2001 racing season, a dramatic increase over previous years that was in keeping with the sport's growing popularity and the new network-broadcast arrangements. "How Bad Have You Got It?" consisted of eight different TV spots, each of which focused on the same NASCAR-obsessed family. The spots aired on the stations with newly minted broadcast rights to NASCAR races: NBC, TNT, FOX, and FX. Print ads echoed the theme of a family's obsession with the sport and ran in NASCAR race programs and other in-house publications as well as in *USA Today.* The campaign's launch on February 18, 2001, was timed to coincide with the start of that year's 10-month racing season.

The campaign had its genesis in the advertising review NASCAR had conducted in 2000. As part of its pitch to win the NASCAR account, Young & Rubicam had sent to the organization's executives a video depicting agency employees who could not contain their enthusiasm for racing. One segment, for instance, showed an employee using a toilet lever as though it were a gearshift while making revving sounds. The agency's pitch for the account also included the family-oriented strategy, which resonated with the organization's sense of its changing audience. The move away from the focus on racing footage that had grounded the previous three years' TV spots was also partly determined by the nature of the other advertising that appeared during NASCAR telecasts. Because sponsors typically included racing footage in their advertising, NASCAR needed a different formula if it hoped to build further brand equity within that environment.

The "How Bad Have You Got It?" TV spots each revealed the intensity of the subject family's NASCAR addiction by showing how it altered otherwise ordinary situations. For instance, "Tire Swing" showed the father changing out his daughter's tire swing as though he was the member of a racing team's pit crew. "Diner," meanwhile, focused on the family's wood-paneled station wagon as it pulled into a restaurant parking space; rather than exiting through the car doors, the family members simultaneously climbed out through the windows, mimicking stock-car drivers' mode of entry and exit. "Badminton" opened with a shot of the family's children playing badminton; the camera then cut to a shot of the father replacing the car windows with netting from the badminton set to duplicate the look of stock-car windows. "Neighbor" introduced the commonplace scene of a husband and wife in bed, unable to sleep because of a noisy neighbor—a neighbor who was, significantly, revving an engine. When the husband rose from bed, viewers were meant to anticipate a verbal confrontation or an attempt to mute the sound; instead, the husband opened the window wide. The commercial then cut to a scene of husband and wife sleeping peacefully, lulled by the roaring engine in the background.

Print ads used imagery in keeping with the family-focused NASCAR obsession dramatized in the TV spots. For instance, a man was shown on a riding mower with an image of a racetrack scored into the lawn beneath him. Another print ad showed a child's crayon portraits of racetracks affixed to a refrigerator.

"How Bad Have You Got It?" was extended into the 2002 racing season, but the concept was tweaked to avoid repetition, which had become a slight problem the year before because the same eight spots had continued to run for the entire 10 months of the season. "We needed to throw a new element into the campaign," Roger Vandersnick, NASCAR's director of brand and series marketing, explained to *Adweek.* This included an expansion of the cast of characters to include not just racing fans but also NASCAR stars. The overall concept, as well as the avoidance of extensive racing footage, remained in place. Young & Rubicam provided viewers with further variety in the middle of the 2002 season by unveiling a subcampaign in which a news anchor opened spots by asking fans to compare their own NASCAR fever to that of other comically devoted fans.

OUTCOME

"How Bad Have You Got It?" won a Gold EFFIE Award and garnered a Bronze Lion at the Cannes International Advertising Festival in 2002. The NASCAR television audience increased substantially during the campaign's run, though the streamlined TV broadcasting arrangement brokered in 2001 was also a significant factor in these increases. NASCAR's fan base continued to grow. In 2002 NASCAR initiated an ad-agency review, soliciting ideas from DDB Chicago and the Martin Agency of Richmond, Virginia, but the organization decided that its interests would be best served by continuing to work with Young & Rubicam. "We have been impressed by the quality of work we have seen [from the contending agencies]," Vandersnick told *Adweek,* "but believe wholeheartedly that Y & R remains the agency for us."

FURTHER READING

Elliott, Stuart. "In a Soft Economy, the National Football League Changes Direction and Tries to Woo Casual Fans." *New York Times,* September 7, 2001.

Gross, Matt. "Start Your Engines." *Shoot,* April 6, 2001.

Jensen, Trevor. "Y & R Gets in Gear for NASCAR." *Adweek* (midwest ed.), July 31, 2000.

Lang, Mark. "An NBA Slam Dunk." *Adweek* (southeast ed.), January 22, 2001.

Lazare, Lewis. "NASCAR Spots Shift into Passion Gear." *Chicago Sun-Times,* February 12, 2001.

Panczyk, Tania D. "NASCAR Ads Focus on Fans." *Adweek* (midwest ed.), February 12, 2001.

———. "NASCAR Sets Midseason Shift." *Adweek* (midwest ed.), February 4, 2002.

———. "Y & R Tops Nascar Challengers." *Adweek* (midwest ed.), September 16, 2002.

Siebert, T.W. "'This Is Nascar' Gets Green Flag." *Adweek* (southeast ed.), February 14, 2000.

"Stock Footage." *Creativity,* March 2002.

Thompson, Stephanie, Jean Halliday, and Alice Z. Cuneo. "Crash Affects Campaigns." *Advertising Age,* February 26, 2001.

Mark Lane

National Football League

280 Park Avenue
New York, New York 10017
USA
Telephone: (212) 450-2000
Fax: (212) 681-7573
Web site: www.nfl.com

NFL PLAYOFFS CAMPAIGN

OVERVIEW

In the late 1990s and early 2000s the National Football League (NFL) began to visualize itself as an entertainment megabrand along the lines of Viacom and Disney, with an imperative to compete not just with other sports leagues but with all other entertainment options on television. In addition to launching a magazine and cable TV station, the league began to market itself more aggressively during telecasts of its games. It partnered with New York agency Young & Rubicam (Y & R) for a successful joint NFL/United Way public-service campaign, and then it enlisted the agency for a branding campaign called "This Is What It's All About," designed to strengthen the league's image among casual fans. In 2002 the league further commissioned Y & R to craft a campaign promoting its slate of postseason playoff games.

The "NFL Playoffs" campaign, launched to coincide with the 2002–03 postseason, used the "This Is What It's All About" tagline and attempted to create excitement around the series of games leading up to the Super Bowl. Having seen ratings for playoff games decline during the 1990s, the league particularly targeted fans of specific teams that had not made it to the playoffs. The individual spots featured the acclaimed actor Don Cheadle speaking of NFL players and past postseason games in passionate, reverent monologues typically paired with dramatic game footage. Cheadle's monologues frequently focused on individual words, phrases, or proper nouns whose meaning had allegedly been changed by events in NFL playoff games. The mythologizing tone of the spots suggested that viewers would miss out on defining cultural events if they did not watch the NFL playoffs.

The campaign was well received by NFL fans and advertising-industry observers, and it won numerous awards, including a Silver Lion at the Cannes International Advertising Festival and a Gold EFFIE. In subsequent years it was reintroduced without significant alteration in preparation for the NFL postseason.

HISTORICAL CONTEXT

After its launch in 1920 the National Football League (NFL), America's premier organization of professional football teams, struggled to attain the cultural prominence of college football or professional baseball, then the country's most popular sports. But in the 1950s the NFL became increasingly popular, thanks in large part to the fact that games began to be televised. The 1960 introduction of a rival organization, the American Football League (AFL), was a measure of the sport's burgeoning popularity, and after several years of heated competition for star players and the attention of fans, the NFL and the AFL merged in 1966, paving the way for the modern NFL, in which AFL teams played in the

American Football Conference (AFC) and teams from the original NFL played in the National Football Conference (NFC), with the champions of each to meet in the NFL championship, otherwise known as the Super Bowl. The Super Bowl was the culmination of each conference's playoff system, in which teams that had been successful during the regular season faced off against one another to qualify as their conference's representative in the big game. In the latter decades of the twentieth century NFL football became far and away the country's most popular spectator sport, and the Super Bowl was the equivalent of a national holiday.

Beginning in the late 1990s the NFL began to focus its marketing and other communications programs on the development of the league not simply as an organization of teams but as a brand competing in the wider entertainment world for an audience and advertisers. Setting its sights on such heavyweight media brands as Viacom and Disney, the NFL devoted more resources to branding advertisement and for the first time began to work with an outside advertising agency. The NFL's first involvement with New York agency Young & Rubicam came in the form of cobranded public-service commercials for the United Way, one of America's leading charity organizations, with whom the league had long maintained a high-profile partnership. The new United Way campaign, released in 2000, poked gentle fun at prominent NFL players, marking the first substantial use of humor in either a United Way or NFL advertisement. The campaign's warm reception led the NFL to tap Y & R to craft an additional branding campaign on the league's behalf. Called "This Is What It's All About," the campaign began in 2001 with the intention of extending the NFL's appeal beyond its core fans.

Given the drop-off in viewership and advertising revenue in the late 1990s and early 2000s, the branding imperative made further sense for the NFL. This decline was attributable to a number of factors, including a softening U.S. economy and the fragmentation of TV audiences caused by the proliferation of cable programming options. Within the larger context of shrinking audiences and ad revenues, the NFL had seen marked declines, dating from 1992, in TV ratings for its postseason playoff games. Because postseason games regularly generated the drama that drew fans to football in the first place, telecasts of these games served as an ideal forum for NFL branding. In 2002 the NFL charged Y & R with the task of developing a campaign on behalf of playoff game broadcasts.

TARGET MARKET

Like other professional sports leagues, the NFL drew its most consistent fans from the over-34 male population. At the same time the NFL routinely made special efforts to reach out to males 18 to 34, one of the most coveted and difficult-to-reach demographics for marketers. In the late 1990s and early 2000s the league had put a particular emphasis on marketing to women and casual fans. The 2001 introduction of "This Is What It's All About," for instance, saw NFL branding take a newly inclusive turn, as that season's commercials were designed to appeal not to hard-core loyalists of the sport but to those who watched football for social reasons.

The "NFL Playoffs" campaign had the specific goal of appealing to fans across demographic borders who had lost or were likely to lose interest in the playoff games because their favorite teams had been eliminated from competition. The campaign emphasized the drama of the playoffs, attempting to remind these fans of the momentousness of past playoff games and to suggest that they were likely to miss similarly unforgettable occurrences if they failed to tune in to the current series of playoff games.

DON CHEADLE

The star of the "NFL Playoffs" campaign, Don Cheadle, rose to prominence thanks to his roles in films such as *Devil in a Blue Dress, Boogie Nights, Traffic, Ocean's Eleven,* and *Hotel Rwanda.* After the warm reception afforded the first season of the "NFL Playoffs" campaign, Cheadle was tapped to direct spots in the campaign's second and third seasons.

COMPETITION

TV ratings for National Basketball Association (NBA) games during the 1990s and early 2000s were strongly tied to the on-again, off-again approach to retirement of Michael Jordan, commonly considered the greatest player in the game's history. Jordan first retired at the peak of his career in 1993 and then returned in 1995. When Jordan retired again in 1999, presumably for the last time, the NBA began focusing its marketing efforts on a new generation of marquee players—including Tim Duncan, Shaquille O'Neal, and Vince Carter—and on an expanded international target market. TV commercials featuring these young stars aired in 207 countries in 2001 before Jordan announced, shortly after the September 11 terrorist attacks of that year, that he would return to basketball yet again and donate his 2001–02 salary to victims of the atrocity. Though Jordan's return promised improved ratings for the league, the effort to market a new generation of basketball greats was complicated by his return. After Jordan's final retirement in 2003, the league again found itself faced with declining fan enthusiasm and no clear marketing answers to this dilemma.

During the 1990s and early 2000s the National Association of Stock Car Auto Racing (NASCAR) experienced a surge in viewership and saw its fan base consequently evolve. Some estimates as of 2001 placed the sport second behind the NFL in its total fan base and in its TV audience numbers. Having transcended its roots as a blue-collar sport enjoyed primarily by men in the southeastern United States, NASCAR released the most substantial marketing effort in its history in 2001, timed to coincide with that year's 10-month racing season. Tagged "How Bad Have You Got It," the campaign focused on a suburban, NASCAR-obsessed family whose everyday behavior was comically influenced by their love of stock-car racing. A lack of geographical specificity in the commercials as well as a focus on the commonality uniting all NASCAR fans—their love of the sport—allowed the campaign to speak both to core NASCAR fans and to newer fans. The family-oriented commercials also reflected a little-known fact about NASCAR: families frequently attended or watched telecasts of races together.

MARKETING STRATEGY

The "NFL Playoffs" campaign was introduced in late 2002 to build enthusiasm preparatory to and during the 2002–03 postseason, culminating with the Super Bowl. In following years the campaign was likewise timed to coincide with the unfolding of the postseason. The commercials ran during network telecasts of NFL games and on sports-focused cable outlets such as ESPN and the NFL Network.

The spots, created by Y & R and produced by NFL Films, attributed mythological weight to events that had happened and would presumably continue to happen in NFL playoff games, as a means of convincing viewers that missing the broadcast of a playoff game might mean missing a defining cultural and historic moment. Representative commercials featured the acclaimed actor Don Cheadle performing this mythologizing function via spirited monologues. He argued that the meaning of a common word or phrase had been changed by postseason events in years past or by the players who would be competing in the current year's playoff games. Cinematic, often slow-motion footage of dramatic football plays was intercut with the monologue to aid Cheadle in his argument.

In "Crazy," for instance, Cheadle began by saying, "'Crazy.' The word defines itself. 'Crazy' knits a sweater for a hamster. 'Crazy' spends 10 minutes yelling at a plant for not growing... But that was before football, before this season, before 'crazy' became an art form." A succession of noteworthy plays from the preceding football season ran on-screen as Cheadle continued to talk, pointing out the superlative "craziness" of each play or player shown as a means of supporting his concluding contention that "Only football can turn 'crazy' into 'crazy.'" Similarly, in the commercial "Joe," Cheadle argued, "The phrase 'average Joe' was coined for a reason. 'Joe' is the guy who wears a shirt that says 'Joe' on it. 'Joe' doesn't steal the girl, he's the guy you pal around with. But not since the playoffs." Footage from football legend Joe Namath's career then appeared onscreen, and Cheadle narrated the ways in which Namath's playoff performances changed "everything." In Namath's wake, Cheadle argued, "Fathers expect more from a kid named Joe. That's how big the playoffs are. They took the name 'Joe' and made it 'Joe.' " Cheadle subtly made the second "Joe" sound more substantial.

Other spots altered the premise slightly. In "The Catch," for instance, Cheadle mused on an alternate course of football history that might have taken shape had "The Catch," one of the most famous touchdown receptions in football history (made by San Francisco's Dwight Clark in the 1982 NFC playoffs) not taken place. "Dante Hall," meanwhile, pitted the Kansas City Chiefs wide receiver of that name against Cheadle in a footrace. Cheadle noted at the commercial's outset that he and Hall were very similar in physical size, and the two appeared side by side onscreen in football gear. As soon as the race began, however, the supposedly equitable matchup became a rout, with Hall leaving Cheadle far behind. "And I'm kind of fast," Cheadle said at the end of the race. Each spot closed with an NFL playoff logo and the tagline "This Is What It's All About."

OUTCOME

The campaign was greeted with substantial enthusiasm by NFL fans and the advertising industry. *Creativity* said of the commercials, "These make dedicated followers proud to be so, while inspiring lackadaisical sideliners to get their asses back in the game." The spot "Crazy" won a Silver Lion at the Cannes International Advertising Festival in 2003, and "Joe" won a Silver ADDY that same year. The campaign as a whole won numerous awards in 2003, including a Gold ADDY and a silver award for best copywriting at the New York Festivals. The campaign also won a 2004 Silver EFFIE Award. The 2002–03 playoff telecasts posted ratings numbers that were among the best the league had enjoyed in the preceding five years, including an overall 16 percent ratings increase among men 18 to 34. That year's Super Bowl became the most watched television program of all time.

FURTHER READING

"Campaign: NFL Playoffs." *Creativity,* January 2004.

Canfield, Kevin. "Who Watches NFL, by the #s." *Media Life,* September 13, 2002.

Elliott, Stuart. "In a Soft Economy, the National Football League Tries to Woo Casual Fans." *New York Times,* September 7, 2001.

Fatsis, Stefan. "NFL's Marketing Thrust Goes on Display." *Wall Street Journal,* November 21, 2001.

Janoff, Barry. "NFL Keeps Motoring to Detroit; SI for Kids Kicks It Up a Notch." *Brandweek,* January 9, 2006.

McMains, Andrew. "Pro Football Is a Funny Game." *Adweek,* September 2, 2002.

Melillo, Wendy. "Humor Pitch Uplifts 'Stodgy' United Way." *Brandweek,* September 4, 2000.

Thomaselli, Rich. "National Football League: John Collins." *Advertising Age,* November 17, 2003.

———. "Sports Star in Marketing Game." *Advertising Age,* May 10, 2004.

"The Week." *Advertising Age,* December 8, 2003.

Mark Lane

National Railroad Passenger Corporation

60 Massachusetts Avenue NE
Washington, D.C. 20002
USA
Telephone: (202) 906-3000
Fax: (202) 906-3306
Web site: www.amtrak.com

LIFE ON ACELA CAMPAIGN

OVERVIEW

By the late 1990s the National Railroad Passenger Corporation, popularly known as Amtrak, was ready to embrace high-speed rail transportation. High-speed trains had been in operation for years in Europe and Japan, and Amtrak had come off poorly in comparison with those systems. The initial Amtrak high-speed trainsets (consisting of high-speed engines and redesigned coaches) were to run in the Northeast Corridor, between Boston and Washington, D.C., the area in the United States where train usage was heaviest. The new trains, named Acela (pronounced a-cell-a), were to replace the diesel and electric Metroliners, which had served customers for years. In 1998 Amtrak chose the ad agency DDB Needham to handle the rebranding and market the new trains to the public.

The rebranding campaign had an initial annual advertising budget of $20 million. The Acela rebrand actually encompassed all of the Northeast rail service, not just the high-speed trains. The initial advertising campaign for the new trains, dubbed "Life on Acela," emphasized the comfort and amenities on the new passenger cars in addition to the convenience of shorter traveling times on the express and regional trains. The first four spots began appearing in Northeast movie theaters on June 4, 1999; they were run prior to feature films with the purpose of familiarizing the public with the Acela name. Those initial spots were coupled with *Star Wars: Episode I—The Phantom Menace.* One of the commercials, titled "Unwind," featured a man suddenly relaxing amidst the rush-hour crush. The tagline was "Find a better place. Life on Acela." The theater spots were followed by posters placed at heavily trafficked sites—including airports—in Boston, Manhattan, and Washington, D.C.

Because of a number of delays in rolling out the trainsets themselves, gauging the effectiveness of the "Life on Acela" campaign proved difficult. By the time the Acela trains did begin running (the Regional in January 2000 and the Express the following December), passengers were aware of the new brand, though it often caused confusion because the Acela name, which many associated with high-speed rail travel, was used for the entire spectrum of Northeast rail service.

HISTORICAL CONTEXT

There were a number of factors that influenced Amtrak's decision to adopt the Acela service. First and foremost was the success of the European and Japanese high-speed trains, which reached speeds in excess of 150 miles per hour. Because railway stations tended to be more conveniently located than airports, these bullet trains had been trumpeted as the modern, comfortable mode of travel for the savvy customer. Americans had endured slower trains for years with a resultant falloff in ridership.

Amtrak's Acela high speed train at Boston's South Station, December 11, 2000. © REUTERS/CORBIS.

BREAKING THE RECORD

On October 11, 1999, during testing in Rhode Island, a high-speed Acela train set a new U.S. train-speed record of 168 miles per hour. Back in March 1999 an earlier version of the Acela also reached a speed of 168 mph, but that was on a closed test track. The October record was reached on a stretch of track between Warwick and Kingston, Rhode Island. The previous record, set by a Metroliner during testing decades earlier, was 160 mph.

The second reason for Amtrak's decision to convert to Acela was far more quotidian: finances. Since its establishment on May 1, 1971, Amtrak had never achieved the ideal of financial self-sufficiency. In fact, despite receiving ever-increasing annual federal subsidies, it continued to lose money. After U.S. Congress passed a law in 1997 that would end the federal operating subsidies by 2003, Amtrak hoped to win back riders with a new, improved service—at a higher cost for travelers.

Huge investments were made to upgrade not only the trains but also the tracks themselves, especially the stretch of tracks from New Haven, Connecticut, through Providence, Rhode Island, to Boston, where diesel engines had previously been running. The tracks were electrified as part of the changeover to Acela service. Tracks along the less popular routes in the Northeast remained unelectrified, however.

TARGET MARKET

The target market consisted of travelers in the northeastern United States. The Northeast was chosen because it had the highest daily train ridership in the country and thus was potentially the most profitable. This market was divided into three segments. The primary segment consisted of business travelers going back and forth between Boston, New York, and Washington, D.C. As Judith Schoolman reported in the New York *Daily News,* Amtrak's share of business travelers between Washington and New York was already competitive with airlines. It lagged far behind the airlines, however, in transporting business travelers between Boston and New York. In October 1999 Amtrak also announced tentative plans to extend the express service to Richmond, Virginia.

The second segment of Acela's target market was regional travelers—those traveling within a given region of the Northeast, such as southern New England or the mid-Atlantic states. Regional ridership in the Northeast had been increasing throughout the 1990s, a trend that was expected to continue once Acela was installed. The final segment of the Acela target market consisted of daily commuters. Because Acela ticket prices would not be competitive with prices for existing commuter trains, this was the least profitable and most problematic group.

COMPETITION

Amtrak faced stiff competition from airlines, interstate bus companies, regional train companies, and another important in the compact Northeast, America's car culture. Each of these modes of transportation posed a different stumbling block to Amtrak's goal of financial independence. Though more expensive than trains, airlines cut traveling time greatly between the major cities along the Northeast Corridor. Interstate bus companies and local and regional train services (such as Metro North and New Jersey Transit) offered lower rates than Amtrak. In the case of the latter, the trains often ran on the same tracks as Amtrak trains. Automobiles offered the double bonus of less expense and the convenience of door-to-door service.

WHAT'S IN A NAME?

The name Acela was developed by the design company IDEO in conjunction with Amtrak managers. According to Brent Oppenheimer, creative director of IDEO, the word was a combination of the words "acceleration" and "excellence." The name "Acela" was one of 400 original possibilities, but the short list came down to three. Of the other two words, one retained the "metro" prefix—already in use for Amtrak's Metroliner—while the other suggested relaxation. Before it was chosen as the new rebrand, "Acela" passed three hurdles: focus-group tests, Amtrak officials, and whether or not it had negative connotations in other languages. As to the latter, some pointed out that, though it was simply a neologism, "Acela" seemed etymologically related to the Spanish verb *acelerar* (to accelerate).

Airlines lured customers—business travelers in particular—with short hops between Boston and New York City. A person could conceivably fly to a business meeting in one city in the morning, a second meeting in another city in the afternoon, and return home by evening. Not even the fastest train could match that.

MARKETING STRATEGY

To counteract the competition's various selling points, DDB devised the "Life on Acela" campaign. The first task for DDB and Amtrak was to overcome customer unfamiliarity with the brand. This was done initially through movie-theater spots, which began airing in June 1999, and the subsequent poster campaign. The idea was to familiarize people with the new brand name, Acela, which played off the word "accelerate."

The campaign also needed to make consumers aware that Acela was actually two different services that served three segments of travelers. Acela Express, with a top speed of 150 miles per hour, had all-new cars and amenities and catered primarily to business travelers, while the Acela Regional, which also ran on the electrified tracks at a top speed of 125 miles per hour, was intended to serve commuters and occasional travelers.

In a 1999 article in the *New York Times* Stuart Elliott interviewed Barbara Richardson, who was then Amtrak's executive vice president for marketing. Describing the philosophy behind the campaign, she said, "It's not just about a train ride. Acela is a big departure for us, representing a really new change in direction. . . . The campaign is meant to signal to people who have not considered us previously that we offer a service they perhaps had not expected from us previously."

In that same article Abigail Kolodny, an account planner at DDB, explained the campaign's approach vis-à-vis the competition, noting, "Travelers for the most part said that travel by car or plane interrupts their lives. But Acela lets you continue your life while traveling, working, eating, meeting." The "Life on Acela" campaign thus argued that Acela trains met the traveler's needs better than other modes of transportation. The Acela Express trainsets featured redesigned coaches. The new amenities included larger windows, chairs that swiveled, conference tables for conducting business, bistro-like café cars with improved menus, and a quiet car where cell phones were not allowed.

The posters, which appeared in June 1999, employed what Elliott described in his article as "surreal imagery" coupled with pithy slogans that alluded to Acela travel for businesspeople. These included "Arrive at a decision," "Be productive. Do nothing," "Brainchild on board," "Find lost time," "Return your mind to its upright position," and "Transfer between left and right brain." Discussing the posters, Ken Shuldman, group creative director at DDB, explained to Elliott, "What we intentionally tried to do was to create an Acela 'language,' visual and verbal, to interpret this new mindset of traveling. It's very optimistic, reflecting the feeling of what the train means to Amtrak." He further commented, "At the heart of the campaign is the human benefit of travel . . . You can walk into a meeting and say something intelligent because the ride didn't dehumanize you."

In late summer 1999, because of delays in starting up the Acela service, the campaign's emphasis shifted slightly. Amtrak had originally scheduled to begin the yearlong phase-in of Acela before Christmas 1999, but during tests in Colorado it was discovered that there was a problem with the suspension system, which caused the wheels to wear down quicker on curves. The initial Express service was rescheduled for spring 2000. As reported by Russell Garland in the *Providence Journal-Bulletin,* Amtrak officials themselves were taking to the road to promote the delayed Acela service, reinforcing the Acela brand to 40 major corporations in Providence alone. Among those officials was then-president of Amtrak's Northeast Corridor, Stan Bagley, who declared that the Acela Express would sell itself once regular service began between Boston and Washington, D.C.

In an article by Sharon Klahr in *Advertising Age's Creativity,* Steven Landsberg of DDB pointed out that the campaign's "real focus is on creating anticipation of

Acela's arrival. Rather than taking a more conventional approach and talking about speed and how it minimizes the time, we wanted to talk about how Acela maximizes time. It's a really smart, subversive way to look at it."

OUTCOME

Not everyone responded positively to the Acela advertising campaign, especially the posters. Some thought the message was lost in the strangeness, prompting Joseph T. DiVincenzo, a senior vice president for marketing at Amtrak, to come to ads' defense. "We want people to stare at it and question it and scratch their heads and say, 'What is this?'" he told Chip Jones of the *Richmond Times-Dispatch.*

In fact, public awareness and anticipation (though some of it was cynical) grew in the months during the delay of the first Acela trains. Thus, when the Acela Regional made its debut on January 31, 2000, there was much fanfare. The train departed from Boston's South Station heading for New York City by way of Providence and New Haven. Because of the electrification of the lines between New Haven and Boston, the trip was "seamless"; there was no change of locomotives in New Haven from diesel to electric. Furthermore, the electric train ran faster than the diesel, cutting travel time between New York and Boston from about five hours to slightly less than four.

In mid-March Amtrak reported that 43,028 riders had boarded the four Acela Regional trains in operation during the first month of service. This represented an approximately 50 percent increase in ridership compared to February 1999. Amtrak also noted that Acela's on-time rate was 85 percent during its first month. Once the bloom was off the Acela Regional, the percentage increase shrank. Nevertheless, by October 2000 ridership was up 11 percent, and revenues had increased by 22 percent.

Meanwhile, the much-anticipated, $1.7 billion Acela Express was delayed yet again. And despite the effort of the "Life on Acela" campaign, the focus of the Express was still on the high-speed aspect. As Amtrak lobbied Congress for $10 billion for high-speed rail improvement, critics began to question whether the high-speed aspect would be enough to make rail service competitive with air travel.

An inaugural run of the Acela Express took place on November 16, 2000, and regular service began on December 11, 2000. The first regular Acela Express left Washington, D.C., at 5 a.m. and arrived at New York City's Penn Station at 7:47 a.m., just three minutes behind schedule. The run from New York to Boston was 12 minutes behind schedule.

Even before the terrorist attacks in New York and Washington, D.C., on September 11, 2001, which briefly grounded and then extensively crippled airlines, Amtrak ridership in the Northeast was on the increase. For the third quarter of 2001 Amtrak's share of the Washington–to–New York market was 53 percent. The company also saw its share of the New York–to–Boston market increase to 35 percent. Amtrak as a whole fared worse. By the end of 2004 it still had not reached self-sufficiency and in fact posted a net loss of $1.3 billion for the year, with sales and employee growth each down more than 10 percent. Furthermore, Amtrak was never able to resolve the confusion engendered by the Acela rebrand for Regional as well as Express services and dropped the Acela name from the Regional service in 2003.

FURTHER READING

"Amtrak Trumpets Ridership on New Acela Regional Train." Associated Press State & Local Wire, March 16, 2000.

Cassedy, Kathleen. "Case Study: Amtrak." ATME (Association of Travel Marketing Executives) 2002 Travel Marketing Conference Report. Available from <http://www.atme.org/pubs/members/PF_75_307_1302.cfm>

Elliott, Stuart. "An Offbeat Campaign for Amtrak Introduces a New Rail Service." *New York Times,* June 4, 1999.

Garland, Russell. "Amtrak Earmarks $20 to Promote High-Speed Service in Northeast." *Providence Journal-Bulletin,* September 22, 1999.

———. "Amtrak Seeks New Image with New Name, High-Speed Train." *Providence Journal-Bulletin,* March 12, 1999.

Holcomb, Henry J. "Delivery of High-Speed Trains for Amtrak's Northeast routes Delayed." *Philadelphia Inquirer,* September 2, 1999.

Johnson, Greg. "Amtrak Train Hits 168 mph, but Service Still Stuck at Station." Associated Press State & Local Wire

Jones, Chip. "Amtrak Welcomes Attention to New Ads." *Richmond (VA) Times-Dispatch,* November 15, 1999.

Klahr, Sharon. "The Little Campaign that Could." *Advertising Age's Creativity,* November 1, 1999.

Lewis, Raphael. "Amtrak Announces Start Date for High-Speed Train between Boston, Washington." *Boston Globe,* October 19, 2000.

Machalaba, Daniel. "Amtrak to Begin Movie-Theater Ads to Promote Acela." *Wall Street Journal,* June 4, 1999.

Schoolman, Judith. "Amtrak Up to High-Speed: Train Zooms Along as Fog Zaps Airport." *New York Daily News,* December 12, 2000.

Sharkey, Joe. "The Acela Express May Not Be as Competitive with Airlines as Was First Thought by Many." *New York Times,* September 27, 2000.

Frank Caso

Negro Leagues Baseball Museum

1616 E 18th St.
Kansas City, Missouri 64108-1610
USA
Telephone: (816) 221-1920
Fax: (816) 221-8424
Web site: www.nlbm.com

■■■

1998 PRINT CAMPAIGN

OVERVIEW

Billing itself as "the centerpiece of the historical renaissance of Negro Leagues baseball throughout the nation," the Negro Leagues Baseball Museum (NLBM) opened in Kansas City, Missouri, in January 1991. The museum was housed in small quarters in the Lincoln Building in the 18th and Vine Historic District but in the fall of 1997 moved into a new facility nearby. The museum's collection covered the leagues' entire history—from the earliest days of organized baseball after the Civil War through the final days of all-black baseball in the 1960s, preserving the history of the Negro Leagues for both baseball fans and social historians.

In 1998 the NLBM commissioned the Martin Agency, a Richmond, Virginia, ad agency, to create a print campaign. Hal Tench served as creative director for the campaign, with a creative team consisting of art director Christopher Gyorgy, copywriter Chris Jacobs, and print producer Paul Martin. Photographs for the print ads were culled from the museum's archives.

HISTORICAL CONTEXT

When organized baseball began in the middle of the nineteenth century, whites and blacks played the game together. After the Reconstruction period that followed the Civil War, however, segregation permeated most aspects of American life, including baseball, and by the turn of the century, blacks had been effectively banned from the game. They joined together and formed teams and, eventually, leagues of their own. At a meeting at Kansas City's Paseo YMCA in 1920, Rube Foster, then owner of the all-black Chicago American Giants, founded the Negro National League with other independent black professional organizations. Three years later the Eastern Colored League was formed. Both leagues operated successfully until 1932 when financial difficulties during the Great Depression caused their collapse. A second Negro National League was formed the next season, followed by the Negro American League in 1937. Both thrived until baseball's color barrier was broken when Jackie Robinson, a former Negro Leaguer, joined the Brooklyn Dodgers in 1947.

The re-integration of baseball was a major civil-rights victory for African Americans, but it spelled doom for the Negro Leagues. Stars such as Willie Mays, Hank Aaron, Ernie Banks, Roy Campanella, and Satchel Paige followed Robinson into the majors and left the Negro Leagues without any marquee players. Other great performers of the Negro Leagues era included Ted "Double Duty" Radcliffe, Josh Gibson, Buck O'Neil, Buck Leonard, and James "Cool Papa" Bell.

In its early days the Negro Leagues Baseball Museum was short on both space and money. Much of the memorabilia remained in boxes because a lack of display space in the cramped, 2,500-square-foot Lincoln Building facility. The responsibility for the rent was passed each month among the museum's founding members. Eventually enough money was raised to allow the NLBM to move into a larger, state-of-the-art facility.

The museum's opening gallery exhibited uniforms, caps, and other paraphernalia of notable Negro Leagues teams such as the Kansas City Monarchs, the Cuban X-Giants, the Baltimore Elite Giants, and the Indianapolis Clowns. The walls were covered with posters, broadsides, pennants, photos, and other ephemera documenting the excitement of the games and the grind of the barnstorming road shows. A mock locker room featured uniforms and other memorabilia of the dozen Negro Leaguers enshrined in the Hall of Fame at the National Baseball Museum and Hall of Fame in Cooperstown, New York.

Once established, the Negro Leagues Baseball Museum began to actively market itself to the public through special events and promotions. In 1995, to celebrate the 75th Anniversary of the founding of the Negro Leagues, the museum held a reunion, bringing more than 200 veterans of the Negro Leagues to Kansas City. In 1997 the museum unveiled a new logo commemorating the 50th anniversary of the breaking of the color barrier in Major League Baseball.

That same year the Coors Brewing Companybecame the first official sponsor of the Negro Leagues Baseball Museum. Coors and the museum embarked on a three-year partnership to enhance the national exposure opportunities for the museum and to assist in its membership campaign. Program elements included a national Black History Month advertising and merchandising program, support of a Black Entertainment Television (BET) classroom cable program featuring Negro Leagues baseball history, and other fundraising elements to assist with the museum's overall efforts. Another tactic that the NLBM used to promote the story of the Negro Leagues was through the sale of apparel and other merchandise through its own licensing program. These specialty items—sold in the museum's gift shop—proved very successful in drawing people into the mission of the museum. "People can come and buy active wear and historically based items, learn about the history and look good as well," said Raymond Doswell, curator of the NLBM. "But the main focus for us is to really use those items to draw people into the larger story, the larger issue of black entrepreneurship, freedom in an oppressive society for African Americans. That's what the story is all about."

The museum relied on cooperative initiatives with educational institutions to promote its mission of raising public awareness of the Negro Leagues. In 1999 the NLBM announced a partnership with Kansas State University's College of Education and the a local school district. Specific projects covered under this joint effort included the creation of websites allowing the museum to connect and interact with students, researchers, and fans worldwide; creation of a book series dealing with the established themes of the museum (leadership, economic self-sufficiency, race relations, and preservation of local cultural heritage); the development of a curriculum series; and the establishment of virtual and traveling museums.

A PLACE FOR THEIR STUFF

Acquiring materials for the Negro Leagues Baseball Museum's collection was both "easy and difficult," according to curator Raymond Doswell. The history of the Negro Leagues was well-chronicled through photographs, and pictures made up a majority of the exhibit. Other memorabilia proved more difficult to collect; much of it was squirreled away in basements or attics and later thrown away. Some items of immense historical value were lost in this fashion, including the last set of uniforms worn by the Kansas City Monarchs. Stored in the basement of the team's former owner, the uniforms were discarded after a flood.The museum expanded its collection through the generosity of the surviving players and the families of others. "A lot of people had things in the basements or attics that their grandfather or great-grandfather had," said the museum's honorary chairman, former Negro Leagues player Buck O'Neil. "We started advertising, and people started looking around and recalling things they had." A number of key artifacts were in the hands of private collectors, many of whom made donations to the museum. Some items were on auction markets, however, and the museum lacked the necessary funds to compete in that area.

TARGET MARKET

Print ads in the 1998 Negro Leagues Baseball Museum campaign appeared in a number of national and local publications, including the *Missourian, Chicago* magazine, the *Sporting News,* and *Baseball America.* The campaign was targeted toward adult baseball enthusiasts and presented the NLBM as a potential vacation destination. Special emphasis was placed on the African-American community, with ads placed in such prominent black publications as *Jet, Ebony,* and *Vibe.* The aim was to fulfill the museum's continuing mission to raise awareness of the contributions blacks made to America's national pastime—even before the days of integrated baseball. Don Motley, the museum's executive director, explained the need to target this audience during a 1998 interview: "A few months ago, a group of black high school kids visited our museum, and I asked them who was the first black ballplayer in the major leagues. They said Babe Ruth! So do you see why our facility is necessary?"

COMPETITION

The Negro Leagues Baseball Museum was one of many baseball museums across the United States and Canada. Many of these institutions appealed to visitors on a regional basis; for example, the Indiana Baseball Hall of Fame commemorated the heritage of baseball in the state of Indiana. The Negro Leagues Baseball Museum was one of two baseball museums that attempted to serve a more national or societal educational mission. The other was the National Baseball Hall of Fame and Museum. Established in 1935 by Major League Baseball, the National Baseball Hall of Fame and Museum sought to honor the game's great players, owners, managers, umpires, and innovators—including Negro Leaguers. Like the Negro Leagues Baseball Museum, the National Baseball Hall of Fame and Museum collected, through donation, baseball artifacts, works of art, literature, photographs, memorabilia, and related materials that focused on the history of the game and its players.

MARKETING STRATEGY

The Martin Agency agreed to create the 1998 Negro Leagues Baseball Museum print campaign on a pro bono basis owing to the lack of funds available to the nonprofit museum. The project captured the look and feel of filmmaker Ken Burns's 1994 PBS documentary *Baseball.* The deliberate echo of Burns' style was no coincidence; Burns served on the Negro Leagues Baseball Museum's board.

The Martin Agency produced three full-page newspaper ads and a television spot for the campaign. Burns granted the Martin Agency permission to use a rendition of "Take Me Out To the Ball Game" from the *Baseball* soundtrack. Many of the same rare photographs and film footage Burns used of Gibson, Paige, and other Negro League stars from the 1920s and 1930s also were employed. "We knew we didn't have the money for new photography, so that was out of the question," Gyorgy said. "But it really wasn't needed, as there was a wealth of existing photos to draw from. This is a real piece of Americana."

In developing the print campaign, Gyorgy and Jacobs drew on their own sense of wonder upon discovering the depth of the subject. "[The museum] provides a wonderful glimpse of how the leagues provided something for the communities to rally around," Gyorgy said. "Since little is known about Negro Leagues baseball our ads feature a lot of copy and are designed to educate people about the importance of the leagues and the impressive caliber of the players."

The print portion of the campaign consisted of mock newspaper ads and three fundraising posters. The copy pointed out that the quality of play in the Negro Leagues was as good, maybe better, than that of Major League Baseball during the time the sport was segregated. One headline read: "Just Because They Weren't in the Same League as Babe Ruth and Ty Cobb, Doesn't Mean They Weren't in the Same League as Babe Ruth and Ty Cobb." Another, highlighting great long-ball hitters, asserted: "420 Feet is 420 Feet, No Matter What the Color of Your Skin Is." A third mock newspaper ad posed the question "Was Josh Gibson the Black Babe Ruth?" with the subhead reading, "Or Was Babe Ruth the White Josh Gibson?" "The campaign really captures the essence of what we are about an what we are working to achieve," Doswell said.

OUTCOME

For 1998 the Negro Leagues Baseball Museum saw attendance increase by 12 percent. Its membership rolls also received a boost from the ad campaign, swelling by 15 percent for the year. Merchandise sales remained brisk, with preliminary figures indicating an increase over the previous year, according to official museum figures.

The campaign captured numerous awards. At the annual Richmond Show, a production of the Advertising Club of Richmond, the Martin Agency snared six golds, including four from its work for the NLBM. The agency also scored significant wins at the annual Art Director's Club of New York awards. The NLBM campaign was awarded the prize for Distinctive Merit in the category of advertising posters and billboards, public service or nonprofit/educational. The campaign also received an award in the category of newspaper, public service/nonprofit, full page or spread.

FURTHER READING

Giancaterino, Randy (with Paul Debono and Barbara Gregorich). "A Pitch for Black History." *American Visions,* June-July 1993, p. 22.

Gutierrez, Paul. "Up to Date in Kansas City." *Sports Illustrated,* January 12, 1998, p. 101.

Ratliff, Tamara. "A League of Their Own." *Nashville Commercial Appeal,* June 10, 1994.

Rayner, Bob. "Martin Agency Sparkles At Bash: Big Not Always Best At Annual Richmond Awards Presentation." *Richmond Times-Dispatch,* March 28, 1998.

Robert Schnakenberg

Nestlé Purina PetCare Co.

Checkerboard Sq.
St. Louis, Missouri 63164
USA
Telephone: (314) 982-1000
Fax: (314) 982-2134
Web site: www.purina.com

INCREDIBLE DOGS CAMPAIGN

OVERVIEW

NOTE: Since the initial appearance of this essay in the 1999 edition of *Major Marketing Campaigns Annual,* Ralston Purina was acquired by Nestle USA. The essay continues to refer to the company's former name, as that was the official name of the organization when the campaign was launched.

With the "Incredible Dogs" marketing campaign—a broad effort that included advertisements, an essay competition, and canine athletic events—Ralston Purina Company encouraged consumers to purchase Purina Dog Chow and Purina Puppy Chow to help their pets attain an exceptional level of health and energy. An advertisement in *Reader's Digest* in November 1998 showed a man in a business suit prone on the sidewalk in front of his house. A large puppy stood on the man's chest, regarding him inquisitively. In the door of the house was a hole shaped like the outline of a puppy, implying that the dog had burst through and tackled his owner outside. The headline read, "It's gotta be the Puppy Chow." The text said that Purina Puppy Chow offered appealing taste and the perfect nutritional formulation—including calcium and protein but no artificial colors—for puppies to develop strong bones and muscles. The ad included the slogan "Incredible puppy food. Incredible puppies" beside a picture of the product. The "Incredible Dogs" campaign was developed by the Fallon McElligott advertising agency. It ran through 1998 and into 1999 in print and broadcast media.

HISTORICAL CONTEXT

Ralston Purina was founded as the Robinson-Danforth Commission Company in St. Louis, Missouri, in 1894 by William H. Danforth, George Robinson, and William Andrews. The enterprise began by marketing feed for horses and mules and expanded into hot breakfast cereals, including Purina Whole Wheat Cereal. The name was derived from the company's slogan, "Where purity is paramount." The product was later called Ralston Whole Wheat Cereal when it was endorsed by Dr. Albert Wester Edgerly, a widely recognized health advocate commonly known as "Dr. Ralston." In 1902 the business was renamed Ralston Purina Company. During World War I Danforth served as YMCA secretary for troops in France, where he noticed that soldiers responded eagerly to the word "chow." After the war he changed the word "feed" to "chow" on all of his company's livestock and poultry feeds. In 1986 Ralston sold its animal feed business, Purina Mills. The divestiture allowed Ralston Purina to concentrate on pet food and other consumer packaged goods.

In 1998 Ralston Purina was the world's largest maker of dry dog food and dry and soft-moist cat foods.

Its dog food brands included Dog Chow, Puppy Chow, Fit & Trim, Grrravy, Mainstay, Butcher's Blend, and a premium product named Purina O.N.E. The company also made Purina Biscuits, Beggin' Strips, and T Bonzpet treats; Cat Chow and Meow Mixcat foods; Tidy Cats cat litter; and Eveready and Energizer batteries. Rural Purina dealers had been selling food for hunting dogs and working farm dogs since 1926, but the company's dog food was not available at grocery stores until 1957. Purina spent five years researching and formulating pressure-cooked Purina Dog Chow, a nutritious and palatable brand designed specifically for grocery outlets. The product gained popularity so quickly that for a time the company could not manufacture enough to keep up with demand. By January 1958 Purina had 14.8 percent of the dry dog food market, and by the following August Dog Chow was the most popular brand in the nation, a position it held for the next 40 years.

Dog Chow was first advertised with an "eager eater" theme that focused on its appealing flavor. An advertisement in *Good Housekeeping* in 1990 continued that tradition by showing a dog with its head and front end buried in a sack of Purina Dog Chow as it ate food straight from the bag. The text said that, although they were unaware that the product contained real meat, bone meal, whole grains, and 43 nutrients, dogs loved it because it tasted good. The ad included the slogan "All you add is" and a heart-shaped graphic to represent the word "love." That slogan had been in use since the 1960s, but it was replaced during the 1990s as the company worked to revive interest in the brand. An advertisement that ran in *Country Living* in 1997 showed a dog trotting up to a sack of Purina Dog Chow and crawling inside to eat from the bag. The ad said that dogs could not resist the product's taste. "It's packed with quality ingredients for the unsurpassed, scientifically balanced nutrition you expect from Dog Chow," said the text. The tag line was: "Purina. Bring out the champion in your dog."

UNDERSTANDING THE TARGET MARKET

In 1996 Fallon McElligott won a Grand Effie Award, a top honor in the advertising industry, for the "Purina Dog Chow Every Day" campaign, which advised consumers to buy only Purina Dog Chow to provide their pets with a consistent, nutritious diet. Fallon McElligott developed the campaign after research indicated that consumers who usually purchased Dog Chow realized that dogs did not need variety in their diets. In contrast, consumers who frequently switched brands thought that dogs, like humans, needed various types of food. The advertising campaign emphasized the fact that dogs tended to develop stomach problems or become finicky eaters when they were given assorted brands of dog food.

TARGET MARKET

In 1996 there were at least 54 million dogs and 59 million cats in the United States. More than half of the nation's households owned pets. One survey in the late 1980s indicated that most dogs lived with people who owned homes in small communities. Households with dogs—especially those with purebreds—were usually larger and had more money than those without dogs. Dog owners tended to be 35 to 54 years old, and their children were most likely to be 6 to 17 years old. People considered their dogs to be part of their families, often treating them as if they were children or regarding them as best friends. About 6 percent of the average dog owner's grocery bill went for dog food. In 1996, with sales of $7.5 billion, the pet food market was larger than the market for juice, baby food, and pasta. Since people felt strong affection for their dogs and wanted them to live as long as possible, they usually shopped for the best pet food they could buy. They wanted manufacturers to consult with veterinarians and breeders to develop highly nutritious pet food.

The "Incredible Dogs" campaign emphasized that Ralston Purina used scientific research to formulate healthful products. Since it included athletic competitions, the marketing effort appealed to consumers who enjoyed extreme dog games, one of the fastest growing activities for people and their pets. In these sports competitions dogs performed spectacular feats such as leaping off ramps into water, executing acrobatic routines, and racing through obstacle courses. Some participants in events sponsored by Purina had first qualified by winning competitions hosted by regional chapters of organizations such as the North American Flyball Association, a group that promoted the popular sport of dog flyball.

COMPETITION

Purina Dog Chow had remained the nation's top brand of dry dog food since 1958, although its market share had slipped to about 10 percent by the early 1990s. According to *Pet Food Industry* magazine, Purina Dog Chow led the category in 1993 with sales of $245 million. Purina Puppy Chow was second with sales of $140 million, and Meal Time (made by Kal Kan, the pet food division of Mars, Inc.) was third with sales of

DISTINCTIVE TRADEMARK

The red-and-white "checkerboard" logo of Ralston Purina Company was based on a textile pattern that one of the company's founders, William H. Danforth, remembered from his childhood. He had noticed that it was easy to identify the children of a certain family in his hometown because their mother made all their garments from one bolt of cloth. One year she used gingham with alternating red and white squares, a design that Ralston Purina later incorporated into its trademark to give its products a distinctive, unified look. In 1921 the company introduced one of the first animal feeds in pellet form, a product line known as "Checkers." In 1933 Admiral Richard Byrd brought Ralston Purina Dog Chow Checkers along to feed the sled dogs that accompanied him on his expedition to the South Pole, a celebrity endorsement that helped publicize the brand.

$100.5 million. By the end of 1998 Ralston Purina had 15.4 percent of the U.S. pet food market, according to *Feedstuffs* magazine. The Friskies PetCare division of Nestlé S.A. was second with 12.4 percent, and the Heinz Pet Food division of H.J. Heinz Company was third with 12.3 percent.

In 1998 Mars continued its effort to achieve global consistency among its products by changing the name of Pedigree Select premium dog food to Cesar Select Dinners. The Cesar name had been used in Europe and Asia but was new to the United States. Aimed at small dogs, the product was promoted with print ads that showed a diminutive pet dragging its owner out of bed by the leg of his pajamas. The tag line was: "What do you feed the head of the household? Only the best." Meanwhile, Friskies PetCare advertised its Alpo brand with the tag line, "A great dog deserves Alpo." Other primary rivals included premium brands such as Iams Natural, made by Iams Company, and Hill's Science Diet, made by Hill's Pet Nutrition, Inc. "What vets feed their pets," said the headline in an ad for Hill's Science Diet. The text added, "There's nothing better for your best friend."

MARKETING STRATEGY

The "Incredible Dogs" campaign was a broad marketing effort that included advertisements, contests, and performances by canine athletes. Designed around the theme "Incredible dog food. Incredible dogs," the Internet site for Purina Dog Chow featured information about events related to the campaign. The Fallon McElligott agency developed advertisements to emphasize that with nutritious food and proper care, any dog had the potential to show exceptional qualities and live a long, healthy life. According to *Advertising Age,* Purina spent $89.9 million to advertise all its pet foods in 1998, up 19 percent from $75.6 million in 1997. Of that amount, $58.6 million went for television commercials and $30.6 million for print advertisements.

One magazine advertisement showed a boy in a basketball uniform watching a small dog balance a spinning basketball on its nose. The headline said, "It's gotta be the Dog Chow." The text added that Purina had used advanced scientific knowledge to develop a product with the perfect amount of omega fatty acids to make a dog's coat grow thick and lustrous and to ensure proper immune function. The ad concluded with the tag line "Incredible dog food. Incredible dogs" beside a picture of a bag of Purina Dog Chow. Another magazine advertisement showed an airborne boy gripping a stick. Below, a puppy holding the other end of the stick was apparently lifting the boy high off the ground. The text explained that the highly digestible product had been reformulated to help puppies build strong bones, muscles, and immune systems. The ad included the headline "It's gotta be the Puppy Chow" and the tag line "Incredible puppy food. Incredible puppies."

Early in 1998 Purina became the sponsor of Lou "Mack" McCammon's traveling animal act, which had been touring the country for a decade. The act was renamed the Dog Chow Incredible Dog Team. Dressed in spangled costumes that featured the Purina logo, the energetic canine stars of the show performed impressive acrobatic feats such as jumping over obstacles, leaping into the air, and catching flying Frisbee disks. McCammon wore a costume that featured the Purina logo, and the insignia was displayed on signs, on a piece of artificial turf where the animals performed, and on coupons and flying disks that were given to spectators. The dogs performed on television programs and at state fairs, amusements parks, sporting events, and corporate gatherings, primarily in the West. The dogs were of assorted breeds, and some had been adopted from animal shelters. One of them, Scooter the Wonder Dog, was the official mascot of the San Francisco 49ers sports team. Purina's sponsorship of the show was intended to demonstrate that any dog had the potential for incredible achievements if its owner gave it good care, exercise, and proper nutrition.

In 1998 the company also sponsored the first Purina Dog Chow Incredible Dog Challenge, an extreme sports event for canine athletes. The competition was publicized via a national public relations campaign, local radio advertising, point-of-purchase promotions at supermarkets, and coverage on the ESPNcable television network. Several thousand spectators and more than a thousand dogs attended the competition, which was part of the annual Purina Pet-Pourrievent at Purina Farmsin St. Louis. Participants included a beagle that had learned to jump hurdles by watching a team of Labradors in training, a dog that won a diving competition by leaping into water from a height of 20 feet, the River City Flyers team of border collies and one terrier, and a formerly homeless dog that had been adopted by a stranger and eventually toured with Ringling Brothers Barnum and Bailey Circus.

Another contest, the Purina Dog Chow Search for America's Most Incredible Dog, was in its third year in 1998. Competitors submitted photographs of their dogs along with brief essays describing the qualities that made each animal incredible. Contestants were not judged on appearance or breeding but on endearing qualities such as loyalty, companionship, and playfulness. The winner in 1998 was Keisha, an abused German shepherd that had survived two euthanasia attempts, was rescued, and blossomed into such a lovable companion that she inspired the friends of her new owner to adopt other pets from rescue organizations. The dog and her owner, Melissa Osburn, received a $10,000 cash prize, a lifetime supply of Purina Dog Chow, a medallion, a tour of Washington, D.C., and a stay at the luxurious Willard Hotel. Senator Bob Dole was the master of ceremonies at a celebration in honor of the winner and four other finalists in the contest.

OUTCOME

Advertisements in the "Incredible Dog" campaign continued to run during 1999 as other facets of the marketing effort attracted large numbers of participants and spectators. In 1999 the winner of the fourth annual Purina Dog Chow Search for America's Most Incredible Dog was Harley, a Jack Russell terrier from Bridgeport, Connecticut. Events in the second annual Purina Dog Chow Incredible Dog Challenge were conducted at locations throughout the United States. Participants competed for $75,000 in prize money in contests that included sled dog sprinting, racing through agility courses, diving, catching flying disks, high jumping, cross-country racing with human partners on skis, and rescuing avalanche victims. The promotion received 12 hours of national coverage on ESPN.

Advertising Age reported that while the U.S. market for canned dog food was flat to declining in 1997 and the first quarter of 1998, sales of dry dog food in food, drug, and mass merchandise outlets increased by 8.4 percent to $2.38 billion. Ralston Purina had sales of $4.7 billion in fiscal year 1998, up from $4.5 billion in 1997. Sales in its Pet Products division increased 12 percent to $2.58 billion. In 1999 Ralston Purina announced that it would spin off its Eveready Battery Company, Inc., subsidiary into a separate business to enable the parent company to concentrate on dog food and other core products.

FURTHER READING

"Animal House: Is Your Dog the Best?" *San Diego Union-Tribune* (Lifestyle section), May 7, 1998.

"Bob Dole Announces Winner of 1998 Search for the Great American Dog: Star-Spangled Salute to America's Most Incredible Dog." *PR Newswire,* July 3, 1998.

Cohen, Joyce. "Purina Gets Naming Rights on McCammon's Dog Team." *Amusement Business,* December 14, 1998, p. 4.

Dickinson, Rachel. "Why True Love is Like Puppy Chow: Nutrition-Conscious Pet 'Parents' Pay Attention to the Labels on Dog and Cat Food." *American Demographics,* January 1996, p. 14.

"Dog Chow Contest Has $10,000 Prize." *Tulsa World* (Living section), January 31, 1999.

Fitzgerald, Kate. "Dog-Beat-Dog World: Purina Gives Canines Their Own Version of 'Extreme Games,'" *Advertising Age,* June 22, 1998.

Fucini, Suzy. "Dog Fight!" *U.S. Distribution Journal,* May 15, 1994, p. 26.

"Ralston Remakes Its Successful Dog Chow." *St. Louis Post-Dispatch,* February 15, 1998.

Susan Risland

MULTIPLE STRENGTH FOR MULTIPLE CATS CAMPAIGN

OVERVIEW

Tidy Cat was the established U.S. leader among cat-litter brands in the 1990s, but a new wave of product innovations claiming to enhance the odor-controlling properties of cat litter resulted in market gains for competitors while leaving Tidy Cat without any defined product advantages beyond its low price. Aiming to position the brand for sustained dominance, a project that required changing consumers' perceptions about its odor-controlling power, owner Ralston Purina (which was acquired by Nestlé S.A. in 2001 and grouped with that company's pet-related product lines under the Nestlé Purina PetCare Company banner) decided to relaunch Tidy Cat as a litter specifically designed for households with multiple cats. This was partly accomplished through alterations in packaging and product variety as well as through a change in name from Tidy Cat to Tidy Cats. The company enlisted agency Berlin Cameron & Partners (later renamed Berlin Cameron/Red Cell and then Berlin Cameron United) to communicate the newly branded product's image in a campaign that was launched in July 1998.

Budgeted at $10 to $15 million a year and running for many years, the Tidy Cats campaign was called "Multiple Strength for Multiple Cats." Most of the campaign's spending was on TV spots, and the controlling idea behind the commercials did not change over the course of the campaign's long run. Building on a research-driven understanding of multiple-cat owners' views of their pets, the spots showed groups of talking cats with distinct personalities who commented on the attributes of Tidy Cats while fooling humans into believing that they were just cats. The cats were aided in a variety of misdeeds and corresponding cover-ups by the odor-controlling power of Tidy Cats, which enhanced the cats' innocence in the minds of their owners.

According to a 2004 study conducted by marketing-research firm Millward Brown, the Tidy Cats relaunch successfully convinced consumers that the brand was synonymous with multiple-cat litter-box effectiveness, and it dramatically rehabilitated perceptions of Tidy Cats' odor-controlling capabilities. Tidy Cats sales grew each year during the campaign without any investment in new technologies or the development of product advantages beyond the brand's newly crafted image.

HISTORICAL CONTEXT

Tidy Cat, first introduced in the 1960s, had been the longtime market leader among cat-litter brands in the United States when, in the 1990s, its market share began to erode. This was primarily a function of the arrival of new products claiming innovations, such as litter varieties that clumped for easy scooping or that boasted odor-control features activated by the cat's movements. The promise of even slight relief from what was usually an unpleasant household chore drove consumers to embrace the brands that had supposedly improved upon the standard formula for basic clay cat litter. As the uncontested category leader, Tidy Cat had invested neither in research that might allow it to unveil its own technological breakthroughs nor in marketing meant to differentiate the brand by virtue of any product advantages. Tidy Cat's main brand attribute was its low price; consumers did not perceive it as the most effective litter for controlling odor.

This situation threatened to make the erosion of Tidy Cat's market share an ongoing phenomenon, and Ralston Purina solicited ideas for a new marketing campaign that would remake the product's image among consumers. As of 1997 Tidy Cat's advertising, featuring the tagline "If it's anything less than Tidy Cat, you'll know," was handled by Fallon McElligott Berlin (FMB), the New York office of the Minneapolis-based agency Fallon McElligott (which later became Fallon Worldwide). FMB principal Andy Berlin, however, had recently enlisted that agency branch's core creative personnel in the establishment of a new entity, Berlin Cameron & Partners. After a review of multiple agencies in 1998, Ralston Purina selected Berlin Cameron to craft the new Tidy Cat campaign.

Among various Tidy Cat litter varieties, sales of its product intended for multiple cats had been growing throughout the 1990s at double-digit rates, while sales of the brand's other formulas remained flat. It became apparent that consumers believed that Tidy Cat Multiple Cat Formula offered greater odor control. This facet of a cat-litter brand's image being far and away the most important one, Ralston Purina decided to pitch Tidy Cat as a litter specializing in multiple-cat-strength odor control, thereby creating a distinct identity that no other cat-litter brand could claim. Ralston Purina thus staked the brand's future on a risky move: a product relaunch of a brand that was already number one in its category. This consisted of a package redesign, a realigning of product offerings, and even a renaming of the brand (albeit a slight one). Each of the product variants was now marketed as intended for multiple cats. That fact was prominently showcased on the new packaging, and the product's name was changed from Tidy Cat to Tidy Cats.

TARGET MARKET

Owners of multiple cats composed the target market for the "Multiple Strength for Multiple Cats" campaign. Half of cat owners owned more than one cat, and these owners bought 70 percent of all cat litter. If Tidy Cats could recast itself as the only brand formulated to satisfy this portion of the cat-owning public, all other competitors would be left with a target market consisting only of single-cat owners, who purchased less litter per capita. Meanwhile Tidy Cats would not necessarily be losing the business of single-cat owners, because multiple-cat strength was equivalent, in the eyes of many consumers, with greater odor-controlling power. This, of course, was what all cat-owners wanted in a cat-litter brand.

There were no key demographic factors that unified multiple-cat owners, but Berlin Cameron had found, over the course of intensive research into the cat/owner relationships in such households, that these consumers had a different attitude toward their cats than did owners of only one cat. Because cats' idiosyncrasies stood out by contrast with one another, multiple-cat owners usually valued the unique personalities of their cats more intensely than single-cat owners did. A lone cat in a household often established a relatively calm atmosphere. In contrast, a multiple-cat home was more likely to

MULTIPLE-STRENGTH DIATRIBE

Not everyone was sold on the Tidy Cats relaunch strategy. Writing critically of the decision to recast the brand through packaging, changing the product lineup, and altering the name of the product—previously called Tidy Cat—Laura Shanahan remarked in *Brandweek,* "Yeah, babe, very necessary, that 's' on the end... but anyway, that's not the problem. See, there's three—count 'em, three—new formulas under the new 'n' improved pluralized name and I don't see a dime's worth of difference between 'em." Noting that the Tidy Cats stable included formulas for "Immediate Odor Control," "Long Lasting Odor Control," and "Antibacterial Odor Control," Shanahan wondered why one litter could not provide all three forms of odor control, as she had assumed was the case with the original Tidy Cat product. "If you were a betting man, which would you choose?" she asked. "I chose another brand."

produce entertaining and dramatic scenes resulting from the interaction of cat personalities. The people who presided over these households tended to relish the eventful tableaux enacted by their cats, even when the result was disorder or slight property damage. Many multiple-cat owners, Berlin Cameron further found, suspected that their cats communicated with one another.

"Multiple Strength for Multiple Cats" built on this understanding of multiple-cat owners and attempted to show them that Tidy Cats alone understood their relationship with and appreciation of their pets, while also convincing them of the rational benefits of the brand.

COMPETITION

At the time of the "Multiple Strength" launch, Tidy Cats' leading competitors were First Brands' Scoop Away and Clorox's Fresh Step. First Brands had recently introduced the industry's first cat-activated charcoal litter, one of the technologies that threatened Tidy Cats' market share. A new arrival on the industry scene also brought a category-wide threat. In 1997 Church & Dwight, the corporate parent of universally known freshness product Arm & Hammer Baking Soda, introduced Arm & Hammer Super Scoop, a litter that included baking soda and thereby leveraged consumer trust in the older, extremely well-established product.

In a category not known for its use of humor in marketing, Fresh Step had meanwhile launched a campaign that, like "Multiple Strength for Multiple Cats," was noteworthy for its reliance on a comic concept. Tagged "Fresher with Every Step" and budgeted at an estimated $8 million, the campaign broke at the same time as "Multiple Strength" and attempted to showcase Fresh Step's supposed superiority over less expensive cat-litter brands, presumably including Tidy Cat(s). "Fresher with Every Step" showed cats discarding packages of cheaper litter when their owners were not looking, so that the owners might be more readily encouraged to buy Fresh Step.

MARKETING STRATEGY

The "Multiple Strength" campaign was launched in July 1998 and ran for a number of years. Its annual budget was estimated at $10 to $15 million, the overwhelming majority of which was allocated to TV spots. The campaign was meant to work with the package redesign, the product lineup changes, and the alteration in product name to establish Tidy Cats as the one and only litter for multiple-cat households. The chief obstacles to the campaign's success included the inherent limitations of the cat-litter industry. Unlike other pet products, cat litter had little emotional resonance for pet owners. Associated with a chore that most people dreaded, cat-litter brands had a difficult time inciting consumer affection. Berlin Cameron needed to demonstrate the brand's knowledge of the multiple-cat owner's bond with his or her pets, and it needed to enliven the product's image to make emotional connections with consumers. At the same time the agency had to transmit the practical, odor-control message that would provide a rational basis for purchasing Tidy Cats.

The agency set out to accomplish these tasks with a humor-based narrative concept that remained the same throughout the campaign's multiyear run. Each of the TV spots employed the conceit of talking cats in multiple-cat households. Litter naturally found a place in the cats' conversations, and the supposed effectiveness of Tidy Cats, making for a decrease in litter-box odor, gave the cats increased credibility with their owners and with other cats. This translated into increased freedom to misbehave and live fully. In general the cats in the commercials were shown to have exaggerated versions of the communicative resources and distinctive personalities that multiple-cat owners, according to Berlin Cameron's research, believed their cats to possess.

The campaign's first TV spot, for instance, featured a pair of cats discussing the new Tidy Cats litter that had been put into their litter box. One cat said, "It is specially designed for multiple cat households," and the other retorted, "Or one cat with a very large bladder." When humans approached, one cat said to the other, "Quick, act like cats!" and the cats darted off in different directions. As the campaign progressed, the conceit of cats living sophisticated lives behind their owners' backs was extended and made more elaborate. For instance, a 2004 spot showed cats behaving like secretive teenagers and throwing a wild party when their "parents" were away from home. The spot's backdrop was a richly detailed, decadent cat party, featuring cats leaping on and off furniture, cats swatting at aquarium fish, a cat "scratching" a record on a turntable, and a generalized cat-party roar of laughs, exclamations, catcall whistling, and even a belch on the sound track. The instigator of the party, a cat named Max, was shown talking with an impressed, naive female cat. "Great party," the female cat told Max, "but won't you get caught?" "Nah," Max said coolly, "I have them all the time." "How do you get away with it?" "Tidy Cats," Max answered. The sound of his owners arriving home led Max to shout, "Everyone out!" A human couple walked through the door to find the house silent except for the sound of Max and his two compatriots purring together in a pet bed on the floor.

OUTCOME

A tracking study undertaken by marketing-research firm Millward Brown indicated that Tidy Cats had accomplished its goal, between 1998 and 2004, of building the consumer perception that it was the single brand of cat litter "specially formulated for multiple cats." By fall of 2004 Tidy Cats was recognized by more than 60 percent of consumers as owning this brand attribute, up from 30 percent before the brand relaunch in 1998. The Millward Brown study discovered a corresponding rise in the consumer perception that Tidy Cats was an effective odor-controlling litter. Overall, Millward Brown ranked Tidy Cats as the top-scoring product in 18 key areas that the firm used for rating consumer perceptions of cat-litter brands. Tidy Cats' sales increased every year between 1998 and 2004, even though the Tidy Cats formula offered no new technologies or innovative chemical advantages to compare with other growing brands. The repositioning of the brand, entirely a work of image crafting rather than product substance, seemed the only explanation for such sales growth.

FURTHER READING

Brody, Barbara. "Ralston, Clorox Trying New Tactic in Pet Market." *Advertising Age,* July 20, 1998.

Comiteau, Jennifer. "Berlin Cameron Wins Ralston Brand after a Review." *Adweek,* February 2, 1998.

———. "Ralston Purina Pet Brand in Play." *Adweek,* January 5, 1998.

Dini, Justin. "Chatty Kitties Relaunch Tidy Cats." *Adweek,* July 20, 1998.

Mehegan, Sean. "Arm & Hammer, the Cat Litter." *Brandweek,* September 8, 1997.

Sanders, Lisa. "Berlin Cameron Stands On Its Own." *Advertising Age,* January 12, 2004.

Shanahan, Laura. "Designated Shopper." *Brandweek,* July 26, 1999.

Mark Lane

Nestlé S.A.

Avenue Nestlé 55
Vevey, CH-1800
Switzerland
Telephone: 41 21 9242111
Web site: www.nestle.com

MADE LIKE NO OTHER CAMPAIGN

OVERVIEW

Given a European-sounding name by its American creator, Reuben Mattus, Häagen-Dazs reigned as the United States' top-selling superpremium ice cream during the 1980s. The ice cream's success partially resulted from its pure, unaltered ingredients and also from its decadent reputation. In the 1990s Häagen-Dazs's popularity waned as consumers identified it as an antiquated brand from the previous decade. Häagen-Dazs's fastest-growing competitor, Ben & Jerry's Homemade, marketed its superpremium ice cream as a product for everyone. Nestlé S.A., the owner of Häagen-Dazs, purchased 67 percent of Dreyer's Grand Ice Cream Holdings in 2003 and then allowed Dryer's to manage the Häagen-Dazs brand. To shed the ice cream's 1980s stigma of elitism and tout the product's all-natural ingredients, Dryer's released the "Made Like No Other" campaign.

The $5 to $10 million Häagen-Dazs advertising account was awarded to the ad agency Goodby, Silverstein & Partners in 2003. The agency broke the "Made Like No Other" campaign's first 60-second TV spot, "Anthem," in May 2004. The commercial displayed copy such as "There is a school of thought that less is more" upon minimalist images of landscapes. Further copy read, "Elegance is simplicity. This is how we make our ice cream." Two 30-second commercials, "Strawberry" and "Vanilla," aired in June 2004 with similar copy and imagery. All three spots featured the same soothing piano music and ended with the Häagen-Dazs logo above the campaign's "Made Like No Other" tagline.

The "Made Like No Other" campaign won a Gold EFFIE Award in 2005 in the Snacks/Desserts/Confections category. The campaign's debut spot, "Anthem," also collected a 2005 Bronze Clio Award for the Original Music category. The campaign's success was not limited to the advertising industry. According to the campaign brief written by a Goodby, Silverstein & Partners representative, "the advertising spurred a dramatic turnaround: sales and market share swelled as old and new audiences were won over—reminded why they loved Häagen-Dazs once more."

HISTORICAL CONTEXT

With his parents already in the ice-cream business, Reuben Mattus spent his youth formulating an ice cream made from premium, all-natural ingredients. After creating his first three flavors, vanilla, chocolate, and coffee, in 1961, Mattus named his new ice-cream brand Häagen-Dazs, a fabricated word adorned with a Germanic umlaut. Even though Häagen-Dazs's ownership shifted from the Mattus family to the Pillsbury Company during the 1980s, Häagen-Dazs sales soared and eventually spearheaded the new superpremium-ice-cream category.

In the 1990s, to fuel the brand's notoriety as a luxury item, advertisements for Häagen-Dazs employed such taglines as "Just perfect." The ad agency Bartle Bogle Hegarty created three-dimensional bus-shelter advertisements to introduce new flavors such as the Häagen-Dazs Malibu flavor. In 1999 Nestlé Ice Cream Company was created as a joint venture between food company Nestlé and Pillsbury, the latter being the primary owner of Häagen-Dazs. In 2002 Häagen-Dazs's advertising account was awarded to the ad agency J. Walter Thompson.

Propagating Häagen-Dazs as an ice cream reserved for the rich, in 2002 J. Walter Thompson released the "Pure Pleasure" campaign, which included the 30-second commercials "Brownies" and "Cookie Dough." Nestlé purchased 67 percent of Dreyer's stock the following year, making itself into a $1.4 billion ice-cream titan. After the stock purchase Dreyer's was still allowed to manage products with the Dreyer's name. Nestlé also relinquished Häagen-Dazs's management duties to Dreyer's. To gain back market share that Häagen-Dazs had been losing to Ben & Jerry's for more than 10 years, Dreyer's awarded the Häagen-Dazs advertising account to its own longtime ad agency, Goodby, Silverstein & Partners. The agency began crafting a campaign that ignored Häagen-Dazs's posh reputation and focused solely on the ice cream's pure ingredients.

In an interview with *Adweek,* Albert Kelly, the associate creative director at Goodby, Silverstein & Partners, explained the pretension that was associated with the Häagen-Dazs brand two decades earlier. "The name brought up cheesy luxury, and [people] thought of snobby hedonism in the '80s, like the guy in the ascot leaning against the Bentley. The image had become outdated."

TARGET MARKET

Goodby, Silverstein & Partners tailored the "Made Like No Other" campaign for an expansive demographic of ice-cream enthusiasts. In 2005 the campaign partnered with cable TV network Showtime for a promotion in which new Showtime subscribers would receive 12 free pints of Häagen-Dazs ice cream. Rick King, Showtime Networks' vice president of promotions and partnership marketing, explained the campaign's target market to the *PR Newswire.* "Almost everyone loves ice cream, so we felt this campaign would appeal to even the most difficult to reach consumer."

During the 1980s middle-class consumers were more likely to purchase cheaper ice cream from brands such as Breyers Ice Cream, owned by Kraft, or Edy's Grand Ice Cream, owned by Dreyer's. With a marketing strategy that greatly differed from that of Häagen-Dazs, the superpremium ice-cream brand Ben & Jerry's began expanding its presence to middle-class consumers in the 1990s. "It's hard to find two competitive brands neck-and-neck that are so very different in consumers' minds," Walt Freese, chief marketing officer for Ben & Jerry's, said to *Advertising Age.* He stated that Häagen-Dazs was assumed to be "for the chosen few" but that Ben & Jerry's was generally identified as a "super-premium for the people."

"The everyday consumer has morphed into a connoisseur in the pursuit of affordable indulgence," Joan Steuer, one of America's foremost authorities on chocolate and a leading expert on new products and food trends, explained to *PR Newswire.* "It is the attention to detail, the fine craftsmanship and all natural ingredients that allow Häagen-Dazs to turn a treat like ice cream into the everyday luxury consumers are demanding."

ICE CREAM SOCIOLOGY

Dreyer's Grand Ice Cream Holdings, Inc., the company that managed the superpremium ice cream brand Häagen-Dazs, conducted research to gain a better understanding of its core customer. One of Dreyer's surveys revealed that men preferred to eat four or more scoops of ice cream, while most women enjoyed only two. After eating the scoops, men also preferred to lick the bowl more than women did.

COMPETITION

Ben & Jerry's, which became Häagen-Dazs's most threatening competitor in the 1990s, branded its superpremium ice cream around fun and irreverence. It also used a large percentage of its advertising budget to sponsor socially conscious events. The strategy proved effective. From April 2003 to April 2004, Ben & Jerry's boosted its sales by 15.9 percent, while sales for Häagen-Dazs dropped 16.5 percent. Ben & Jerry's brand manager Dave Stever explained to *Advertising Age* that the brand's television spots had proven "inconclusive" during the 1990s. "The amount of lift or volume increases necessary to make those [TV] buys pay off is quite substantial," he said.

Instead of using TV commercials, Ben & Jerry's sponsored events such as the Rock the Vote bus tour in 2004. The tour involved musical artists performing across America and encouraging 18 to 24 year olds to vote. Ben & Jerry's also released an ice cream flavor called One Sweet Whirled, which referenced the song "One Sweet World" by the popular Dave Matthews Band. On April 27, 2004, Ben & Jerry's distributed free ice cream at Rock the Vote events in hope of increasing voter registration. In 2004 the ad agency

ROCKY ROAD

With its beginnings in a California ice-cream parlor, Dreyer's Grand Ice Cream was the brainchild business of William Dreyer and Joseph Edy. The two men created the world's first Rocky Road ice cream flavor during the Great Depression. The flavor's name commented on the financial troubles of the time.

Amalgamated, New York, created print advertisements for Ben & Jerry's that included cartoonish illustrations of the ice cream's ingredients.

MARKETING STRATEGY

Goodby, Silverstein & Partners focused on the quality of Häagen-Dazs ice cream rather than on its upper-class connotation or falsely assumed foreign heritage. The brunt of the campaign's $5 to $10 million budget went toward airing three television spots. This strategy intentionally capitalized on Ben & Jerry's resistance to making television spots. Burt Flickinger, managing director at the business consultancy Strategic Resource Group, validated the approach in *Advertising Age.* "Häagen-Dazs is taking the correct strategy by going to TV," Flickinger explained, "where the category has been uncharacteristically dark, especially in premium [ice cream] positioning."

The campaign's first 60-second television spot, "Anthem," first aired in May 2004. The commercial began with a white square floating before an off-white background. Dreamy piano music played while the copy, "There is a school of thought that less is more," appeared across the square image. Eleven orange umbrellas on a beach were then shown; all opened at the same time as the copy read, "that elegance is simplicity." Further tranquil images followed: one of rain falling in a puddle and another of a perfectly still pond. The copy continued, "and simple can be beautiful." The commercial then showed a shiny spoon slowly scooping into vanilla Häagen-Dazs ice cream. Text reading "This is how we make our ice cream" appeared, and the image changed to that of green plants growing beside a field of red dirt. "A composition in cream and vanilla," the spot continued, "a blueberry haiku." Similar images continued with copy that stated, "The beauty of Häagen-Dazs is what we put in but also what we leave out." The commercial did not feature any voice-overs, only the melodic piano score. It ended with the Häagen-Dazs logo appearing above the tagline "Made Like No Other."

Häagen-Dazs had originally asked its new ad agency to contemporize the brand. Jeff Goodby, the principal and co–creative director at Goodby, Silverstein & Partners, explained to *Adweek* that his agency's goal was to update Häagen-Dazs's past image. Previously campaigns had, he said, a "Donald Trumpish, golden-brown boudoir feeling to it. And the advertising reinforced it. Our job was to reestablish it as a terrific product."

The campaign's three spots were filmed in Spain and Malaysia. The later two 30-second spots, "Strawberry" and "Vanilla," started airing in June 2004. The first began with black-and-white images of a strawberry farm. As rain began falling upon the strawberry plants, the plant's colors began to appear. As more colors replaced the black-and-white imagery, copy read, "flavor enhanced by nature alone." The spot ended with Häagen-Dazs's logo above the campaign's tagline. The "Vanilla" spot featured a woman harvesting vanilla beans in a rainforest. The spot's copy stated, "start with the finest vanilla add nothing but cold."

OUTCOME

Prior to the campaign, according to *Advertising Age,* ad executives outside of Goodby, Silverstein & Partners were skeptical about the resurrection of the Häagen-Dazs brand. The magazine quoted an undisclosed executive as claiming, "Like Porsche, Häagen-Dazs has become associated with those who use the product and not the product itself." Goodby, Silverstein & Partners believed that the "Made Like No Other" campaign did in fact revitalize the Häagen-Dazs brand. Sales for Häagen-Dazs began to increase compared to the previous year. The campaign also won a Gold EFFIE Award in 2005 in the Snacks/Desserts/Confections category. The 60-second commercial "Anthem" was awarded a Bronze Clio in 2005 for the Music-Original category.

After "Made Like No Other" helped the sales of Häagen-Dazs to increase, members of the advertising industry began to view the ice-cream brand more optimistically. In mid-2004 Gary Koepke, a cofounder of the Boston ad agency Modernista!, praised the campaign in the *Boston Globe.* "I like the new Häagen-Dazs ad with the tagline 'made like no other.' It shows umbrellas opening on an empty beach and rain falling on a pond. It takes me by surprise. They're not showing the typical scoop of ice cream. The ad makes ice cream precious like a reward or a setting sun. It's just nice. It's different."

FURTHER READING

Anderson, Mae. "May." *Adweek,* June 14, 2004, p. 28.

Aoki, Naomi. "Q&A Modernista Pair Discuss Messages, New Media." *Boston Globe,* July 11, 2004, p. C2.

DePass, Dee. "Pillsbury Vet Named to Succeed Dolan at Tennant." *Minneapolis Star-Tribune,* October 7, 2005, p. 1D.

Elliott, Stuart. "Accounts." *New York Times,* November 3, 2003, p. 13.

Emert, Carol. "Dreyer's Enters the Cold War," *San Francisco Chronicle,* August 28, 1999, p. D1.

Evangelista, Benny, Benjamin Pimentel, and George Raine. "Daily Digest." *San Francisco Chronicle,* June 8, 2005, p. C2.

Harper, Scott. "Band Funds Its Green Message." *Roanoke (VA) Times* & *World News,* April 26, 2004, p. B1.

Parpis, Eleftheria. "June." *Adweek,* July 19, 2004, p. 16.

Sampey, Kathleen. "Jason Gaboriau On the Spot." *Adweek,* April 5, 2004, p. 24.

Sarasohn, David. "Oregon's Vanishing Strawberry." *Portland Oregonian,* October 2, 2005, p. D1.

Solley, Sam. "Brand Health Check: Häagen-Dazs." *Marketing,* June 16, 2004, p. 22.

Thompson, Stephanie. "Summer Forecast: Ice Cream Marketers Chilly on Ad Spending." *Advertising Age,* June 10, 2002, p. 6.

———. "Symbol of Yuppie Greed? Häagen-Dazs Goes for Mass, Not Class." *Advertising Age,* March 22, 2004, p. 4.

Van Dusen, Lisa. "Keep Some 'Old' in New New York." *Calgary Herald,* October 9, 2005, p. A13.

Ward, Celeste. "Goodby Pulls Häagen-Dazs Back from 1980s Limbo." *Adweek,* June 14, 2004, p. 11.

Kevin Teague

New Balance Athletic Shoe, Inc.

Brighton Landing
20 Guest Street
Boston, Massachusetts 02135-2040
USA
Telephone: (800) 343-1395
Fax: (617) 787-9355
Web site: www.newbalance.com

NEW BALANCE THUNDERSTORM, STAIRS CAMPAIGN

OVERVIEW

Founded in 1906, the Boston-based company New Balance Athletic Shoe, Inc., had become the third-largest manufacturer of athletic shoes in the United States by 2003. Long catering to the serious athlete, New Balance prided itself on creating a quality product in a wide range of specialty sizes—a rarity in the athletic-footwear world. In 2002 New Balance launched two television commercials: "Thunderstorm" and "Stairs." Running under the larger, long-running "Achieve New Balance" umbrella campaign, both spots focused on products for female athletes—the former on women's running shoes and the latter on women's cross-training shoes. Both commercials were developed by New Balance's longtime ad agency, Messner, Vetere, Berger, McNamee, Schmetterer (MVBMS).

The commercials, a central feature of the company's $19 million marketing effort for 2002, premiered in March on several cable networks and continued throughout the year. They were aimed at 21- to 55-year-olds, a slightly broader demographic than New Balance's traditional target of 35- to 50-year-olds. The campaign also included magazine ads in such publications as *Shape, Cooking Light, Condé Nast Traveler, Runner's World,* and *Fitness.* A companion set of spots for men's running and cross-training shoes debuted at about the same time. John Donovan, New Balance's marketing services manager, explained to Chris Reidy of the *Boston Globe* that the commercials were about "how important exercise is for citizen athletes trying to balance the stresses of life."

Both spots were widely acclaimed by the advertising industry; "Stairs" was applauded for its dead-on depiction of what made a female athlete tick, and "Thunderstorm" won praise for its witty special effects. "Thunderstorm" was named one of the best commercials of 2002 by *Adweek* magazine.

HISTORICAL CONTEXT

For fiscal year 2003 New Balance's sales topped $910 million; they were down from $1.16 billion in 2001 but were enough to maintain the company's third-place rank, between Reebok and adidas. In a market dominated by Nike, New Balance had deliberately steered clear of high-profile advertising campaigns that targeted the urban-youth market by featuring superstar athletes and musicians. Additionally, New Balance's strongest category had always been running shoes, which made running a natural choice for its new television campaign.

New Balance had never advertised heavily on television. For years the company had preferred a more grassroots approach that allowed it to zero in on its best customers. To this end, most of its advertising budget went toward sports magazines and sponsorship of semiprofessional sporting events. Since 1989 New Balance had been a major sponsor of the Susan G. Komen Race for the Cure, a national event dedicated to raising funds to fight breast cancer, and since 1995 the company had been a major sponsor of the International Modern Pentathlon, an Olympic sport consisting of a single day of competition in five events: shooting, fencing, swimming, equestrian jumping, and running. The company's choice to sponsor these events highlighted its dedication to serving both female athletes and sports events that rewarded personal excellence.

TARGET MARKET

In a market dominated by youth, New Balance was a rarity: a footwear manufacturer that catered to middle-aged runners. "They have been after me for years to make more shoes for 14- to 15-year-olds. I don't want to do it," CEO Jim Davis told Daren Fonda of *Time* magazine. Unusual also was the fact that the company manufactured much of its product in the United States, years after most companies had outsourced that work to Asia. These factors worked to the company's advantage. Older consumers were very brand-loyal, and New Balance's U.S. facilities allowed the company to "respond more quickly to fashion cycles and requests from retail customers than overseas sneaker factories with long lead times," wrote Reidy in the *Boston Globe.*

Despite its satisfaction with its market niche, New Balance had always sought growth. By 2002 the company had enjoyed double-digit growth for several years, in part because of its acquisitions of Dunham boots, a "brown shoe" competitor to Timberland, and P.F. Flyers, a vintage brand with nostalgic appeal to baby boomers. In addition, New Balance "trail shoes" enjoyed a brief vogue among 20-somethings in the late 1990s, which further propelled sales figures. By 2001 the company's sales had topped $1 billion. But Davis, a runner himself who bought the company on the day of the Boston Marathon in 1972, had no intention to shift his main focus away from top-end athletic shoes. "We're going to continue to do what we know how to do, and we'll be gaining little bits of market share on an annual basis," he told Mark Sullivan of *Sporting Goods Business.*

In 2001 New Balance's $20 million advertising budget concentrated on television spots targeted at runners over the age of 45—a narrow demographic, but one easily reached through magazines such as *Working Mother, Men's Journal, Prevention,* and *Outside.* Though not as glitzy an approach as that of their competitors, targeting this niche made great business sense, according to New Balance marketing vice president Paul Heffernan. He told Hilary Cassidy of *Brandweek,* "We keep seeing studies that show the largest segment of the population is over 50, so we're spending some money there, and we don't think our competition is thinking about that group."

> **THE CHALLENGE OF FILMING IN ICELAND**
>
> New Balance's "Thunderstorm" spot was filmed in Iceland by director Agust Baldersson, though the storm that taunted the runner was computer-generated and on-site props consisted of rice and polystyrene. Real rain, in fact, preempted filming several times during the weeklong shoot. Fortunately, August in Iceland meant nearly 24 hours of daylight—plenty of time to get it right.

COMPETITION

New Balance also faced competition from industry leaders Nike and Reebok, mainstays adidas and Puma, and "boutique" brands such as Saucony and Brooks. In 2001 adidas announced plans to increase its marketing budget by 25 percent in a direct bid to leap over New Balance and take the number three spot behind Reebok. Adidas's ads highlighted a new technology called ClimaCool, which was used in its cross-training and basketball shoes to increase air circulation through the shoe.

In addition, adidas launched T-MAC, a new basketball shoe endorsed and named for Orlando Magic star Tracy McGrady. In response New Balance also introduced a new line of basketball shoes, endorsed by no one and aimed at the 15- to 21-year-old market. "Play to Live" was the tagline, and its grassroots "Hoop Troop" campaign included company appearances at local basketball courts to introduce the product directly to consumers. New Balance also sponsored the NBA's Hoop-It-Up tour, which featured 3-on-3 tournaments in 40 cities.

Whereas Nike dominated the field of high-tech shoe cushioning field with its tremendously popular Shox shoes, New Balance promoted its own Abzorb cushioning as the centerpiece of its superior technology. In 2004 adidas attempted to gain ground on New Balance with the $300 Adidas 1, which boasted a computer chip that automatically adjusted the shoe's cushioning level for maximized performance.

MARKETING STRATEGY

Unlike its primary competitors, Nike and Reebok, New Balance had long practiced an advertising strategy defined as "endorsed by no one," meaning it did not build marketing campaigns around top-name athletes. Likewise, "Thunderstorm" and "Stairs" were designed to appeal to goal-driven athletes who valued personal achievement over trendiness. "We don't want to be perceived as doing anything gimmicky," Stuart Babb, head of the company's running division, told Reidy of the *Boston Globe.*

New Balance's 2002 television spots deftly illustrated two modes of athletic perseverance with which its potential customers could identify. In "Thunderstorm" a runner made her way down a deserted highway as ominous storm clouds closed in on her. When the storm unleashed heavy rains, she took cover beneath a freeway overpass. As soon as she did, however, the rain stopped, taunting her with the suggestion that it was waiting for her to try to outrun it again. The voice-over asked, "What keeps you going?" and the tagline "Achieve New Balance" appeared. Shot in a similarly artistic black-and-white style, "Stairs" followed a woman as she ran up a stairway on a seaside cliff. At the top she rewarded herself with a treat—a single piece of chocolate. She continued again, down the stairs and up, to win another.

"'Conspicuous' is not in the New Balance dictionary; 'low profile' is," wrote Davis in an editorial for the *Boston Globe.* Indeed, not only were the athletes in these commercials "low profile" (they were exercising alone), but they also demonstrated discipline and fortitude, qualities that typified the ideal New Balance customer.

"New Balance sneakers are still basically known for their technical aspects, comfort, stability—and dowdiness," Fonda commented in *Time.* That did not seem to bother Davis. "If we hit on fashion, that's fine... but our shoes are really designed to run up hills." Indeed, New Balance's reputation for creating a quality product, particularly for people with hard-to-fit feet, had won it many influential customers, among them podiatrists, chiropractors, and serious runners. Nevertheless, market analyst Matt Powell told Natalie Zmuda of *Footwear News,* "I think the consumer still sees them as the noncorporate brand." That seemed to suit the company just fine. "Technical customers are consistent, even in difficult times, and that makes them more predictable," Nick Richino, global apparel operations manager for New Balance, explained to Rosemary Feitelberg of *Women's Wear Daily.*

OUTCOME

Writing in *Fast Company,* Randall Rothenberg named "Thunderstorm" the ad of the month for September 2002, calling it "gorgeous to look at" and praising its high production value, which he said brought to mind both *The Wizard of Oz* and the cult film *Run, Lola, Run.* Rothenberg also applauded the commercial's "subtle playfulness" as a refreshing antidote to the "humorlessness" of many athletic-shoe commercials aimed at women.

The "Achieve New Balance" campaign, of which the spots were a part, was revised in 2003 into the "N Is for Fit... N Is for Performance" campaign, which featured new print ads and television spots and emphasized the technical construction of New Balance shoes more than the previous years' advertising had. Also, subsequent campaigns focused on promoting New Balance's basketball shoes; despite Nike's dominance in that area, New Balance officials believed that it was a big enough market that the company could grab a slice of market share without a splashy star-driven campaign.

As Ann Davis, the company's executive vice president and the wife of CEO Jim Davis, told Katie Abel of *Footwear News,* the "spirit of perseverance has been one of the company's defining characteristics throughout the past 30 years." The commercials "Thunderstorm" and "Stairs" epitomized that spirit, which was verified by the attention the spots garnered from the advertising world. "New Balance chooses to celebrate everyday athletes who set their own performance goals," wrote Jim Davis in the *Boston Globe.* "We don't pay celebrities to sell our product. We believe our product sells itself."

FURTHER READING

Abel, Katie. "A Balancing Act: Jim and Anne Davis Have Always Had More on Their Minds, and Hearts, than Athletic Shoes." *Footwear News,* December 9, 2002, p. 44.

Cassidy, Hilary. "A Balanced Foothold." *Brandweek,* March 25, 2002, p. 19.

———. "New Balance Ages Up." *Brandweek,* January 8, 2001, p. 8.

Davis, Jim. "New Balance Maintains 'Low Profile.'" *Boston Globe,* February 10, 2002.

Dill, Mallorre. "Rain and Shine." *Adweek,* March 18, 2002.

Feitelberg, Rosemary. "Brands on the Move." *Women's Wear Daily,* April 5, 2001, p. 7.

Fonda, Daren. "Sole Survivor: Making Sneakers in America Is So Yesterday. How Can New Balance Do It—and Still Thrive?" *Time,* November 8, 2005, p. 48.

"On a Roll: Joyce Minkoff." *Advertising Age,* May 21, 2001, p. 29.

Reidy, Chris. "New Balance Dons High-Tech Addition to Keep Strong Position in Runners' Market." *Boston Globe,* October 23, 2001.

———. "New Balance Plots Independent Strategy." *Boston Globe,* August 4, 2005.

———. "No-Name Kid Dazzles in New Balance's Basketball-Sneaker Advertising Launch." *Boston Globe,* August 10, 2002.

———. "TV Advertisements for New Balance Athletic Shoes Target Younger Audience." *Boston Globe,* March 1, 2002.

Rothenberg, Randall. "Ad of the Month: New Balance 'Thunderstorm.'" *Fast Company,* September 1, 2002.

Sullivan, Mark. "Marathon Man: Thirty Years after Buying New Balance, Jim Davis Is Still Running—All the Way Past the $1 Billion Mark." *Sporting Goods Business,* April, 2002, p. 36.

Zmuda, Natalie. "Rising Athletic Fortunes." *Footwear News,* May 17, 2004, p. 8.

Kathy Wilson Peacock

New York State Lottery

1 Broadway Center
Schenectady, New York 12301-7500
USA
Telephone: (518) 388-3300
Fax: (518) 388-3368
Web site: www.nylottery.org

■■■

IF I HAD A MILLION DOLLARS CAMPAIGN

OVERVIEW

In October 2001 the New York State Lottery unveiled a new advertising campaign promoting its flagship Lotto game. The campaign embodied a sense of fun and community and was embraced by the state's residents. The new television and radio spots featured everyday New Yorkers singing along with the bubbly pop song "If I Had a Million Dollars." The fact that the participants were consistently off-key only added to the charm of the spots. A second part of the campaign used real New Yorkers musing on camera about what they would do with a million dollars, while the jingle played in the background.

Conceived by the New York branch of ad agency DDB Worldwide Communications Group, the campaign was intended to reacquaint people with Lotto and encourage those who had stopped playing to give the game another try. By promoting Lotto, the New York State Lottery also hoped to increase the sales of its instant and other jackpot games. In addition to the television and radio spots that relied on real people singing, there were print ads under the headline "If I Had a Million Dollars" that included pictures of people with text saying what they would do with the money.

While it was difficult to determine if Lotto sales had increased because of the "If I Had a Million Dollars" campaign, there was an abundance of anecdotal evidence that indicated the ads were effective. And though the spots won no major awards, the New York State Lottery was pleased with the work done by the agency. The campaign continued until the spring of 2003.

HISTORICAL CONTEXT

With profits earmarked for the state's education fund, the New York State Lottery was launched in 1967 as a raffle-style game. At the time, other than racetrack betting and church bingo, there was no legal gambling on the East Coast, leaving the New York State Lottery to compete against illegal numbers games and bookies. Then in 1971 the New York City Off-Track Betting Corporation, billing itself as the "New Game in Town," launched operations to allow people to bet on horse races at off-track betting shops. Casino gambling arrived in Atlantic City later in the 1970s, followed by gaming run by Native Americans in Connecticut. With the increase in competition, the New York State Lottery introduced its flagship product, the twice-weekly pick-six Lotto, in 1978. After a slow start it gained in popularity during the 1980s when large jackpots, in New York as well as in other states, received a great deal of news coverage. But state lotto games were increasingly jackpot driven, and without a large payout at stake the game became stale to players. Moreover, big jackpots became

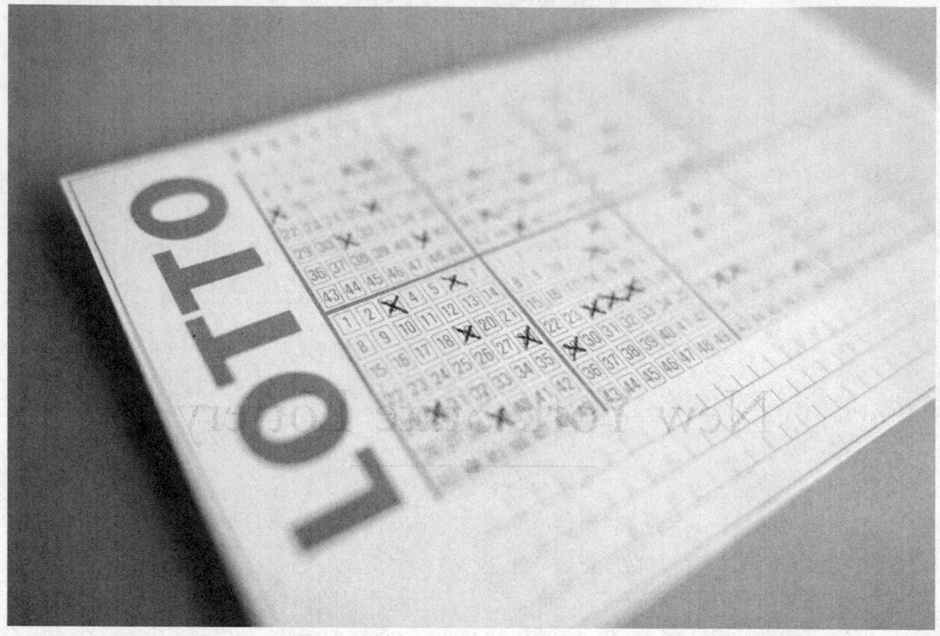

© G. SCHUSTER/ZEFA/CORBIS.

less newsworthy over time, eliminating much of the free publicity the games had previously enjoyed.

In response the New York State Lottery introduced a number of other games, including instant scratch-off and daily games and even one, Quick Draw, that held a drawing every four minutes. New York did a better job than most states at holding the line on diminishing Lotto sales and more than made up for the drop in Lotto revenues with increased sales from new games. While smaller states banded together to create a super lotto game, Powerball, in New York Lotto remained very much the key product, with its promotion benefiting the other games. The success of the New York State Lottery during a time when many businesses were chasing scarce entertainment dollars was to a large extent explained by the efforts of its ad agency, DDB, as well as its large marketing budget. In 1995 the state spent about $42 million on television commercials alone, and with $3 billion in sales New York's lottery was the largest in the country.

DDB won the New York State Lottery account in 1988. As mandated by state law, the contract ran for three years, with the possibility of three one-year renewals. DDB held the account for the next decade, during which time the agency coined several memorable themes, including "All You Need Is a Dollar and a Dream." Even more successful was the award-winning "Hey, You Never Know" campaign. Humorous spots showing how people would change their lives if they won the Lotto included a tollbooth operator who paid everyone's fare. In the opinion of some, however, the ads fostered false expectations and did not deal frankly with the true odds of winning an instant fortune. Also coming under fire was the introduction of Quick Draw, a fast-paced game that many thought was open to abuse by problem gamblers. In a move that critics called hypocritical and an effort to gain a political advantage, Governor George E. Pataki insisted that the New York State Lottery amend its approach because "[it] fostered false expectations with bold promises of easy money," according to Raymond Hernandez in a *New York Times* article from August 21, 1996. "Hey, You Never Know" was shelved in favor of "New York Lottery, It Makes Us All a Little Richer," which was more in the line of a public-service announcement. Fantasies were replaced by depictions of modest winners and praise for the Lottery's contributions to the state's education system.

As required by law, in 1998 the New York State Lottery account was put up for review. DDB lost out to Grey Worldwide, an agency headquartered in New York, not because the Lottery was disappointed with the work DDB had done over the previous decade but because of Grey's low bid. Grey continued to focus on the more modest aspirations of winners in its "Will You Be Ready If It Happens to You?" campaign. At the time DDB lost the business, art director John Staffen had proposed the idea of using an upbeat song by the Canadian rock group Barenaked Ladies, "If I Had a Million Dollars," in an

A LONG WAY TO THE TOP

The song that anchored the "If I Had a Million Dollars" campaign for the New York State Lottery was written by the rock band Barenaked Ladies in the 1980s. Not until it had built a following through incessant touring was the Canadian group signed by a major record label, Reprise Records, in the mid-1990s. "If I Had a Million Dollars" was their first single released by Reprise.

advertising campaign. He had to file the plan away for three years, until 2001, when the New York State Lottery account was again put up for review. In DDB's pitch the "If I Had a Million Dollars" idea was one of three submitted in the agency's successful effort to regain the lottery business. The two parties then agreed to pursue a campaign promoting Lotto based on the song.

TARGET MARKET

The finalists for the New York State Lottery account were asked to demonstrate how they would "increase awareness and consideration of the lottery among lapsed players." Thus, according to DDB management supervisor Mary Collopy in a 2005 interview, the intention of the "If I Had a Million Dollars" campaign was not necessarily to drum up new players. Rather, the hope was either to motivate people to play more often or to encourage people who had formerly played Lotto to try it again.

COMPETITION

The New York State Lottery faced direct competition for people's gambling dollars from a number of sources, including the lotteries of neighboring states; off-track betting; casinos in Atlantic City, Connecticut, and upstate New York; and unregulated gambling on the Internet. But indirectly the New York State Lottery was vying against all forms of entertainment, with everyone trying to gain a share of the limited amount of money consumers were able to spend to amuse themselves. As a result, the state was forced to spend huge amounts of money to promote Lotto and its other games to remain competitive.

MARKETING STRATEGY

The "If I Had a Million Dollars" campaign was designed to appeal to people on a number of levels. It tapped into what had made earlier DDB campaigns successful, encouraging people to daydream about what they would do if they won the Lotto jackpot while steering clear of the excesses of previous campaigns. As Staffen explained to Stuart Elliott in the *New York Times,* the song had "such simple charm and innocence, begging you to dream, without getting to the rational side: 'How much would that new house really cost? How much would the maintenance be?' " Just as important, wrote Elliott, "the trappings of wealth described in the lyrics are far more down-to-earth than evocative of 'Lifestyles of the Rich and Famous' . . . 'It's about what you'd do for others, not for yourself,' [worldwide account director Leo J.] Mamorsky said, which helps diffuse any perceptions of the song—and the campaign—as paeans to greed . . . For instance, the singers proclaim that the windfall would enable them to 'buy you furniture for your house (maybe a nice chesterfield or an ottoman)'; or 'build a tree fort in our yard.' " It was expected that the marketing of Lotto, the flagship product, would then drive sales of the state's other games of chance.

More than the charm of the catchy pop song was the use DDB made of it, filming everyday New York residents, from upstate to the streets of the Bronx, singing the lyrics delightfully off-key. Once the right to use the song on television and radio and on the Internet was acquired from Reprise Records, Barenaked Ladies' record label, DDB hired the New York production company @radical.media to travel across the state to film anyone willing to sing. Elliott wrote in the *New York Times,* "People were stopped without notice at sites ranging from barbershops and town squares to diners and farms. The film of the resulting spontaneous performances—some accompanied by dancing, hand gestures and even a warbling dog—was edited as it was shot in a mobile facility on a laptop computer." According to Collopy, DDB made minor changes to the song: "It was basically the 'needle drop.'" A few of the volunteer singers, however, offered up their own lyrics, which found their way into the spots.

As the "If I Had a Million Dollars" campaign neared its launch date, the terrorist attacks occurred on September 11, 2001, forcing a postponement. Like all marketers, DDB and officials at the New York State Lottery had to reassess how to advertise in the new climate. In the first week of October the campaign was presented to focus groups, asking people to sing along with the song as if they were going to appear in the commercials. The results were highly positive according to lottery officials, who said that to the participants the campaign suggested community, fun, and entertainment. As Mamorsky explained to Elliott, "The Lottery is part of the fabric of New York . . . To me, this campaign really

TALK OF THE TOWN

Dana Fisher, one of participants in the "If I Had a Million Dollars" print ads, became the subject of a "Talk of the Town" piece in the *New Yorker*. A visiting scholar at Columbia University studying global climate change, she firmly believed that automobiles were the main cause of global warming. When she stopped at a Lottery table while shopping, she wrote down that if she had a million dollars she would start a foundation to deal with global environmental issues. Weeks later Fisher was told by a number of people at Columbia that her first name and picture were displayed on a bus shelter ad exclaiming that if she had a million dollars she would "buy a car and a cute driver to go with it." Given that she was about to sign a contract at Columbia and receive a grant from the Earth Institute, she was dismayed that her appearance in the ad was being spread by E-mail throughout the school. Fisher complained to DDB, which then made a sticker with her actual quote to paste over the offending line.

helps reinforce that the spirit of New Yorkers, from Buffalo to Montauk, is strong and alive."

The "If I Had a Million Dollars" campaign was introduced on October 30, 2001. In addition to the television spots, DDB produced radio commercials, billboards, and signs for use in bus shelters and subways. The print ads that appeared in New York City were developed by stopping people on the street with the offer of a free lottery ticket and a drink. Their pictures were taken, and they were asked to write down what they would do if they had a million dollars. Participants signed waivers and were promised that, if they appeared in a Lotto ad, they would be paid $200.

The campaign was well received on all fronts. At worst New Yorkers perceived the jingle as a pleasant annoyance in their lives. Several weeks later DDB built on the campaign's success by working in a second phase, which was introduced on February 25, 2002. Instead of singing along, people were asked in impromptu interviews what they would do if they had a million dollars. The music to "If I Had a Million Dollars" played in the background, providing continuity with the first phase of the campaign. Because they were not asked to sing, more people were willing to participate, resulting in a great deal of material. The agency ultimately had 17 rough cuts to choose from in crafting what were mostly 15-second TV commercials.

OUTCOME

The "If I Had a Million Dollars" campaign ran for 18 months. According to Collopy, DDB believed that Lotto enjoyed an increase in sales as a result of its effort, but this could not be firmly established. In 2002 the New York State Lottery became part of the multistate Mega Millions game, and as a result sales were combined, making it virtually impossible to determine what part the campaign played in growing lottery sales. The ads did not win awards, but at the very least the agency's reputation was enhanced. In reviewing the year in advertising for the *Wall Street Journal* in 2001, Suzanne Vranica and Vanessa O'Connell wrote that the campaign catapulted the New York office of DDB "into the same league as DDB's gifted Chicago branch that masterminded the original 'Whassup' commercials on behalf of Anheuser-Busch Cos."

FURTHER READING

Elliott, Stuart. "A Winsome Campaign for the Lottery." *New York Times,* October 29, 2001, p. C10.

Hernandez, Raymond. "Benefits to Education Stressed over Wealth." *New York Times,* August 21, 1996, p. 1.

Lentz, Phillip. "Lott O' Options Hurt Lottery Flagship." *Crain's New York Business,* August 29, 1994, p. 3.

"New York Lottery Has New Ad Agency." *New York Times,* August 1, 1998, p. D14.

Sampley, Kathleen. "DDB Gambles Pays Off." *Adweek,* June 25, 2001, p. 6.

———. "You Never Know." *Adweek,* December 17, 2001, p. 16.

Thomaselli, Rich. "NY Lottery Breaks Second Ad Wave." *Advertising Age,* February 25, 2002, p. 6.

Vranica, Suzanne, and Vanessa O'Connell. "2001: Year of the Hard Sell—Struggling Ad Agencies Fought to Grasp Nation's Psyche through Toughest of Times." *Wall Street Journal,* December 20, 2001, p. B1.

Ed Dinger

Nike, Inc.

1 Bowerman Drive
Beaverton, Oregon 97005
USA
Telephone: (800) 344-6453
Fax: (503) 671-6300
Web site: www.nike.com

■■■

9,000 SHOTS CAMPAIGN

OVERVIEW

Of all of the commercials Michael Jordan had done for Nike, Inc., he was most proud of the 1997 spot that took a glimpse at his humanness. The commercial, filmed in a nine-hour shoot at Soldier Field in Chicago, showed a well-dressed Jordan exiting his limousine and strolling past banks of fans, humbly acknowledging the custodians and security workers along the way. Amid these outward signs of success, Jordan's voice-over revealed his inner thoughts: "I've missed more than 9,000 shots in my career. I've lost almost 300 games. Twenty-six times I've been trusted to take the game-winning shot—and missed. I've failed over and over and over again in my life." Such self-doubt seemed unthinkable from perhaps the greatest basketball player ever, until the camera showed Jordan heading into the locker room and the voice-over added one last thought: "And that is why I succeed."

Jordan began his relationship with Nike in 1985, his rookie season with the Chicago Bulls in the National Basketball Association. He carried with him extraordinary fame dating to "the shot," his game winner as a freshman when the University of North Carolina captured the 1982 National Collegiate Athletic Association (NCAA) title against Georgetown. David Falk, Jordan's agent, invited shoe companies to court his client. Nike was struggling at the time, but Jordan fit the strategy on which Philip Knight had founded his company—to market products in the glow of the limelight surrounding maverick sports stars. Nike offered the 22-year-old Jordan the largest basketball endorsement to that time, $2.5 million plus royalties over five years. In a compromise over the brand name, Nike fused the company's new technology with the player's high-flying reputation, resulting in Air Jordan. The investment proved to be a wise one, as the Air Jordan line of athletic shoes and apparel garnered $130 million in revenues within its first year, stabilizing Nike and in fact turning the company around to take back the lead from Reebok in the sporting shoes market by 1990.

Nike's marketing of Jordan became legendary and transformed the mechanics of advertising. The creative directors and writers at Wieden & Kennedy in Portland, Oregon, redefined advertising techniques with several risky but ultimately successful strategies. They experimented with black-and-white commercials; they diverted attention from the product itself, focusing instead on the image the product could create for its owner; and they employed renowned and expensive directors like Spike Lee. They even created such widespread brand recognition that they eventually removed the company name from the ads, replacing it with one of their trademarks—the Nike swoosh, an air-bound silhouette of Jordan, or the Nike credo "Just Do It."

Jordan's inaugural commercial for Nike featured a slow-motion shot of a jump from the foul line for a dunk, accompanied by a sound track of a jet taking off.

Nike also advertised in this heroic vein with its "Frozen Moment" spot, which shifted back and forth between stills of Jordan in flight toward the basket and stills of faces in the crowd, their jaws agape in awe at his apparently superhuman skill. Jordan admired the "9,000 Shots" spot because it humanized him, sending the message that his fallibility was an inherent component of his success. Air Jordans could not endow their wearers with Jordan's abilities, but "9,000 Shots" pointed out that anyone could achieve success by accepting failure.

HISTORICAL CONTEXT

Knight had founded Nike on the vision of a Michael Jordan. In a 1998 speech Knight traced the company's genesis to the trunk of his Plymouth Valiant, from which he had distributed imported track shoes made by the Onitsuka Company of Kobe, Japan, for a $254 profit in 1964. Even then, Knight imagined that the magical aura surrounding star athletes could be transferred to the equipment they wore. Of the factors that made athletes great—talent, skill, timing, dedication, hard work—equipment alone was a commodity. Consumers could access sports greatness by outfitting themselves as their heroes did.

Knight had hit upon a version of what psychologists called "spontaneous trait transference." When a speaker discussed the traits of a thing or a person, in an act of transference the listener attributed the traits to the speaker. Knight shifted this equation, relying on the transference of the spokesperson's traits onto what was being described, namely, Nike shoes. University of Oregon track star Steve Prefontaine acted as Nike's first sports star spokesperson, handing the torch to other Jordan precursors, including tennis stars John McEnroe and Andre Agassi and basketball star Charles Barkley.

In Jordan, Knight discovered the embodiment of his dreams. He was a sports icon who combined exemplary play with extraordinary character, who established his individualism without resorting to radicalism—an "outlaw with morals," to quote the formula that consultant Watts Wacker helped Knight to hone. By 1990 Jordan's unbelievable abilities, including a penchant for flight and a quick wit, helped catapult Nike, with revenues of $2.24 billion, over Reebok, with revenues of $2.16 billion. At the same time, Nike spent several million dollars promoting Air Jordan within the first years of the line's existence, creating unlimited exposure for Jordan. The situation created a positive feedback loop, what economist Tyler Cowen called the "mutualism of endorsements," whereby the more Nike promoted Jordan, the more famous he became, enabling him to sell ever more products while simultaneously enhancing his own image, visibility, and worth.

STATS

Wieden & Kennedy's Jamie Barrett wrote the script for "9,000 Shots" from his personal knowledge of Michael Jordan's career. Off the top of his head he knew Jordan's career points and his approximate shooting percentage, and, applying simple math, he estimated about 8,000-9,000 shots missed. When he later researched the numbers, his guesstimate turned out to be on target. He took more liberty with the number of times Jordan had missed game-winning shots, since such statistics were not recorded. Barrett had to choose between watching every game in Jordan's 13-year career or simply surmising that Jordan had failed to shoot the game winner about twice a season. He opted for the latter. In a press conference a few days after "9,000 Shots" first aired, a reporter pressed Jordan on the statistic. Jordan admitted that he could not be sure, but in typical fashion he confidently responded, "It sounds about right to me."

TARGET MARKET

Males under 18 years of age accounted for a quarter of all athletic footwear sales in the United States, and the "9,000 Shots" campaign involved the effect on young people's self-esteem of advertising Jordan's inimitable success. Jordan explained the concept of the commercial to Henry Louis Gates, Jr., for a profile published in the June 1, 1998, *New Yorker:* "The idea [was] to tell young kids, 'Don't be afraid to fail, because a lot of people have to fail to be successful—these are the many times that I've failed but yet I've been successful.'" Wieden & Kennedy's Jamie Barrett wrote the commercial without a specific target market in mind. He trusted his gut instinct instead of allowing demographics to determine his angle. The idea he hit on happened to resonate particularly with teens, those in the throes of defining themselves and their personal definitions of success and failure.

Nike avoided targeting specific markets, preferring to broaden its appeal across boundaries of age and social status. In this instance Nike realized that insecurity over success continued past the age of 18. Most adults considered their lives less successful than Jordan's, and so this commercial spoke to them too. Jordan specifically wanted the commercial to turn introspective, revealing his motivations and moods. Barrett responded by comparing Jordan's accomplishments to his defeats, thus urging viewers not to compare their failures to Jordan's successes but rather to consider their failures in light of their own successes.

While "9,000 Shots" implicitly targeted the adult market, its companion commercial, "Challenge Me," targeted adults more directly. This spot also humanized Jordan, addressing aging, an issue absent from his commercials but foremost in the minds of the majority of his audience. "Challenge me. Doubt me. Disrespect me. Tell me I'm older. Tell me I'm slower. Tell me I can no longer fly. Go ahead, I want you to," Jordan narrated. Although the audience varied slightly between these two spots, the message was consistent. Jordan was indeed human. What made him seem superhuman was his determination.

COMPETITION

Nike's late 1970s climb to control the U.S. market in athletic shoes was fueled by the jogging craze, which slowed in the mid-1980s. Reebok, a British line of white leather women's shoes, took advantage of the next craze in athletics—women's aerobics. By 1987, with $1.4 billion in revenue, Reebok had catapulted past Nike. Nike rebounded by diversifying into new markets, specifically confronting Reebok in the women's market. At the same time, Reebok diversified into Nike's traditional markets of men's sports. By the 1990s the two companies competed head-to-head for control of the market in sports shoes. In 1994 Nike earned $299 million on $3.79 billion in revenue as compared to Reebok's $254 million on $3.28 billion in revenue. That year the two companies combined controlled 50 percent of the U.S. market and 40 percent of the global market, with Adidas having 10 percent.

In an attempt to regain market dominance in the early 1990s, Reebok duplicated Knight's marketing strategy by assembling a team of superstars to endorse its products: Michael Chang in tennis, Frank Thomas of the Chicago White Sox in baseball, and Emmitt Smith of the Dallas Cowboys in football, to name a few. It was not until 1992, however, that Reebok entered the endorsement competition in earnest, signing Jordan's counterpart, the Orlando Magic's seven-foot rookie Shaquille O'Neal, to a five-year, $15 million contract. "It was the signing of Shaq, really, that marked the start of the war between Nike and Reebok for the hearts, minds, and feet of the American public," commented Kenneth Labich in the September 15, 1995, issue of *Fortune.*

Both Jordan and O'Neal were called "human billboards," in part because of the excessive number of endorsements each maintained but also because their every action carried the potential to support (or mar) their endorsements. In this highest level of corporate endorsements, competition entered every imaginable arena. The actions of the so-called dream team, the U.S. basketball squad in the 1992 Olympics, illustrated this point well. Reebok sponsored the team, supplying warm-up suits for the medal ceremony. As the team climbed the podium to receive their gold medals, Nike endorsers obscured their Reebok logos, with Jordan and Barkley going so far as to wrap themselves in American flags in allegiance to their country and their brand.

MARKETING STRATEGY

Wieden & Kennedy originally conceived the "9,000 Shots" commercial as a follow-up to the Air Jordan commercials directed by Lee, and for it they planned to use another famous Hollywood director, Oliver Stone. Jordan balked. "I had to fight the agency about it, because they had wanted to have me work with Oliver Stone," Jordan revealed to Gates in the *New Yorker,* "... and Oliver Stone was going to go through that process of trying to figure out why my game is my game. And I said, 'Oliver Stone don't know shit about basketball. Why don't you just show the actual situation? Let the people see exactly what's happened over the twelve years of my career.'" Jordan retained this degree of creative control over the marketing of his image. Just as Nike and Jordan mutually bolstered each other's success, so, too, Jordan had put Wieden & Kennedy on the map of ad agencies. Jim Riswold, Wieden & Kennedy's creative director, respected Jordan's input and responded by streamlining the campaign.

In an interview with Elliot Harris of the *Chicago Sun-Times,* Erin Patton, Nike's director of product marketing for Jordan basketball, revealed the intentions of the "9,000 Shots" commercial. "I think the objective was to take an introspective look at Jordan's passion for the game of basketball and how he prepares himself emotionally and physically to continue to raise his level of performance.... It's almost like we wanted to peel down all the layers and just give you Michael and get inside of his mentality. You turn on the TV and you see Michael score 55 points against the Washington Bullets, but the part that you don't see is what we're trying to deliver in this ad." "A glimpse into Jordan's soul?" Harris asked. Patton replied, "It's a soul that thrives on challenges and constantly challenges himself to get better."

Rarely did commercials attempt to examine the soul, but Jordan's persona belonged to the public domain in that so much of his life was devoted to public performance. The subject of his commercials was not so much Air Jordan as Michael Jordan. His personage earned so much revenue for corporations that the value of his image increased exponentially. Strangely, this became its own kind of endorsement. Simply combining Jordan with a product suggested to the consumer that such a vast expenditure on the manufacturer's part must mean that the product was worth such an investment. In this sense Nike marketed its marketing in order to sell its products.

OUTCOME

Others besides Jordan appreciated the "9,000 Shots" commercial. *USA Today* voted it, along with ads for HBO and Altoids, the best campaign of 1997. "No marketer spins perspiration into ad inspiration like Nike," judge Dottie Enrico explained. The campaign also gained international attention as the first foreign-produced commercial to win the grand prize in the All Japan CM Festival, which was sponsored by the All Japan Radio & Television Commercial Council.

The ad, however, also coincided with further accusations of human rights abuses in Nike's international labor practices. Because much of Jordan's value derived from the unfathomably high wages he was paid and from his integrity, he became the lightning rod for criticism of Nike. Both Frederick L. McKissack, Jr., of *Progressive Media Project* and Kevin Clarke of *U.S. Catholic* magazine wrote scathing critiques. Ironically, Jordan found his least likely defender in Jesse Jackson, whose Operation PUSH had been boycotting Nike since 1990. Jackson supported Jordan's apolitical stance and lent it credence. "Why is it expected of a ballplayer or a boxer to be an astute sociopolitical analyst?" Jackson asked. "The issue of trading with Indonesia without regard to human rights or child labor is fundamentally a matter that United States trade policy must address. It isn't right to shift the burden to him because he's a high-profile salesman."

Chris Zimmerman, Nike's U.S. director of advertising, confirmed this division of responsibility, with the role of Nike's marketing being to develop advertisements that promoted products in the most creative ways possible. While some in the media placed blame on Jordan for Nike's reported dehumanization of its overseas workers, the commercial itself represented a maturation in the marketing of Jordan's image, humanizing him and grounding his myth in the realities of sweat and disappointment. The controversy and praise surrounding the "9,000 Shots" campaign demonstrated the influence Jordan wielded in his culture.

FURTHER READING

Gates, Henry Louis, Jr. "Net Worth: How the Greatest Player in the History of Basketball Became the Greatest Brand in the History of Sports." *New Yorker,* June 1, 1998.

Katz, Donald. *Just Do It: The Nike Spirit in the Corporate World,* New York: Random House, 1994.

Labich, Kenneth. "Competition: Nike vs. Reebok. A Battle for Hearts, Minds & Feet. Agassi and Sampras? Intense. Shaq and Jordan? Spectacular. But for Murderous Rivalry, Few Contests in Sports Can Match the War of the Sneakers." *Fortune,* September 18, 1995.

McKissack, Frederick L., Jr. "His Airness Should Not Accept the Wages of Nike's Sins." *Progressive Media Project,* Knight Ridder/Tribune News Service, June 12, 1996.

William D. Baue

HELLO WORLD AND "I AM TIGER WOODS" CAMPAIGNS

OVERVIEW

Tiger Woods was one of the most acclaimed golfers in the world before he ever took a single swing as a professional. Nike, Inc., the footwear and apparel giant known for its industry-defining advertising campaigns featuring superstar athletes, bet the future of its golf product lines on this emerging star in 1996, signing the young phenom to a five-year, $40 million endorsement deal just after he announced that he would be turning pro. Woods's appeal to advertisers was manifold: he was said to be the most gifted golfer in the sport's history, he was handsome and articulate, he was young, and he was multiracial. The initial Woods-centered campaign and its immediate successor, both developed by ad agency Wieden+Kennedy, proved to be among the most noteworthy Nike advertising efforts in recent memory.

"Hello World," released to coincide with Woods's turning professional, combined a three-page spread in the *Wall Street Journal* with a commercial aired on ABC's *Monday Night Football* as well as on other networks. The TV spot offered a provocative message contrasting Woods's unprecedented accomplishments as an amateur golfer with the fact that there were still golf courses in the United States where he would not be allowed to play because of his skin color. This introductory campaign was immediately followed up by a more affirmative nod to Woods's ethnicity, the "I Am Tiger Woods" campaign. TV spots showed people from a wide range of ethnic backgrounds saying, "I Am Tiger Woods," a statement that, thus repeated, suggested the inspirational nature of Woods's entry into a sport previously assumed closed to nonwhite Americans.

Woods attracted legions of new fans to golf, and the grandstands at tournaments in which he competed began to appear more youthful and ethnically diverse. This, of course, created vast new markets for a sport that had traditionally appealed to a select audience, and Nike benefited greatly from its association with Woods. Sales of Nike golf shoes and apparel skyrocketed, and Woods quickly became the most sought-after product endorser in the world.

Golfer Tiger Woods. AP IMAGES.

HISTORICAL CONTEXT

Nike entered the golf market in 1983, four years before that market exploded, with a line of footwear (it later added a line of shirts). The move took Nike outside its traditional realm of running and beyond the sports of basketball, baseball, and football. Nike maintained consistency, however, with its core marketing strategy being to sign well-known athletes to endorsement contracts that would raise the visibility of the company name within the sport as well as with a more general audience. Among golfers Nike first signed Peter Jacobson, and it then gained marketing strength with the names of Curtis Strange and Nick Price. In 1994 Nike's "Golf Is an Invitation" campaign with Price won numerous ad-industry awards, helping to solidify the brand's positioning amid a category boom. According to the National Sporting Goods Association, consumer expenditures on golf equipment rose by 113 percent between 1987 and 1997, from $1.8 billion to $3.9 billion.

In August 1996 Tiger Woods won his third straight U.S. Amateur Championship at Pumpkin Ridge Golf Club in Cornelius, Oregon, just 15 miles away from Nike headquarters. Three days later Woods announced that he was turning professional. Three days after that he signed a $40 million, five-year agreement with Nike to endorse its Nike Golf line of footwear and apparel. Neither Nike nor Woods's agent, Hughes Norton of Cleveland-based International Management Group (IMG), had ever heard of an athlete landing such a lucrative contract, much less a 20-year-old who had yet to earn a single dollar in his sport. Woods represented a unique marketing opportunity, however, because the visibility of his extraordinary talent was compounded by his appearance, for he was a young, handsome multiracial man breaking into the ranks of a nearly all-white sport. Woods called himself Cablinasian, an acronym he had invented to describe his Caucasian, black, American-Indian, and Asian heritages.

TARGET MARKET

Chris Zimmerman, Nike's director of U.S. advertising, explained the highly effective marketing style developed by the company. Traditionally, demographics determined target markets, with advertisements created to appeal to specific age and social brackets. Nike altered this formula by determining its target markets by what Zimmerman called psychographics. The company developed a psychological profile of consumers who appreciated Nike's philosophy, thus targeting a mind-set rather than a certain age or social status. Furthermore, according to Zimmerman, Nike's advertising promoted gender and racial equity within the world of sports. Woods's image fit perfectly into this psychographic formula, while simultaneously taking advantage of demographic shifts that were occurring in golf in response to his popularity.

Nike's existing classic line of golf apparel and footwear catered to a traditional market, those in their mid-20s to mid-40s. The "Hello World" and "I Am Tiger Woods" campaigns introduced a new line geared toward a younger consumer, with less conservative styling and bolder colors, such as Woods's signature black and red. This younger orientation coincided with one of the fastest-growing demographic groups in golf, those under 18 years of age. Nike thus retained its traditional positioning while actively attracting this new, growing market.

Just as Woods developed an affinity for golf because of his early exposure to the game (Earl, his father, had placed a putter in his hands at 10 months), so, too, did children develop brand loyalty. Nike was not blind to this trend. One spot featured kids chanting "I Am Tiger Woods," and children who saw the commercial in Saint Louis, for example, responded by swamping a local chain specializing in children's athletic footwear with requests for Woods's shoes. Nike also was not blind to the appeal of Wood's multiculturalism, and the company targeted specific markets on this basis. "In Asia, the next great sports market, he is thought of as one of their own,"

"GOLF'S NOT HARD, WITH TIGER WOODS"

With its subsequent campaign, "Golf's Not Hard, with Tiger Woods," Nike lightened up on the player's image. In all four spots Woods offered seemingly simple advice, with the punch line hinging on the impossibility of even the best golfer re-creating his feats. In "Golf Swing" Woods first gave three easy-to-follow tips but then added a barrage of technical jargon accompanied by sophisticated computer graphics. In "Bunker Shot" he told golfers to hit the ball 300 yards, no more and no less, from a sand trap and then demonstrated with ease: "Next week, basic tips on difficult shots." In "Slice" Woods demonstrated his practice technique of lining the gallery with spectators, preferably women and children, leaving only a narrow strip of daylight through which to tee off, but when Joe, the less-than-average golfer, attempted the technique, he overcompensated for his slice and hooked the ball into the cardboard heads of an old lady and man. Finally, in "The Drive/Revised," Woods revealed his secret for long drives; he teed the ball just above the head of his driver, swung, and then waited the remaining 25 seconds of the spot for the ball to land. Simple as that!

observed James F. Sweeney in the *Cleveland Plain Dealer.* In response to his popularity, Nike ran a subtitled version of the "I Am Tiger Woods" campaign in Thailand, homeland of his mother Kultida. In the same vein, to grace Woods's own official line of clothing, Nike designed a multicolored jewel symbol as a logo representing his ethnic blending.

COMPETITION

Nike's foremost competitor was Reebok, a company that emulated Nike's strategy of signing highly visible sports stars to endorse its products. In golf the charismatic Australian player Greg Norman had signed a lifetime agreement with Reebok, a commitment that was rare in endorsements. The company was so confident of Norman's value that it had deleted the Reebok logo from his line of clothing, thus highlighting Norman's shark logo. When Nike dedicated a line of golf clothing to Woods in 1998, it thus competed directly with Reebok and Norman's Shark brand.

Although endorsements remained a key to success, the golf market differed significantly from other markets. Robin Carr-Locke, Nike Golf's director of marketing, explained that competition varied according to the sales venue. Sales of golf clothing and equipment occurred in four distinct places: at department stores, in sporting-goods stores, in off-course golf stores, and on the grass at golf courses. The main difficulty in determining the competition in this market was that, depending on the venue, Nike competed with different brands. On the course, for example, Nike footwear competed against Etonic and Foot-Joy golfing shoes, whereas in department stores Nike apparel competed with brands like Ralph Lauren's Polo collection.

This diversity of competition made it almost impossible to develop specific competitive strategies. Historically, however, Nike had focused less on keeping up with the competition and more on developing its own strategies in anticipation of market shifts. Nike sought to define its markets, not react to the competition. In 1992, for example, Nike had recognized the vast potential of the golf market it had yet to tap, but at the time there were no rising golf stars who fit the mold of maverick Nike endorsers, the formula that had created such success for the company in other sports. Hence, Nike diverted its strategy from endorsements by individual golfers to a tour endorsement, buying out the flagging Ben Hogan Tour and renaming it the Nike Tour. This kind of ingenuity had become a trademark of Nike.

MARKETING STRATEGY

When Jim Riswold, creative director and partner at Wieden+Kennedy, first conceived the Woods campaigns, he immediately decided against focusing on what he called "shoeness." He decided instead to use the advertising as an opportunity to expose and crystallize what was on everyone's mind—the issue of color. Woods was a sensation regardless of his race, but the very color of his skin called into question the degree of racial prejudice that persisted in golf and, by extension, in American society in general. Rather than divert attention away from this issue, Riswold harnessed its power to Nike's advantage.

"We obviously had to tell [Woods] what we were thinking," Riswold said, "and he felt it was time to talk about that issue." Contrary to suggestions that Nike exploited him, Woods had creative input. "Golf has shied away from [racism] for too long," said Woods. "Some clubs have brought in tokens, but nothing has really changed. I hope what I'm doing can change that." Woods envisioned himself as an "ambassador of change" for golf, opening the way for minorities and young people. His father went further, suggesting that Woods would "transcend the boundaries of golf [by] using golf as a vehicle to do that," in the same way that Muhammad Ali had transcended boxing and Michael Jordan basketball.

The TV spot that headlined the effort accordingly featured captions alongside retrospective clips from Woods's career as an amateur: "I shot in the 70s when I was 8. / I shot in the 60s when I was 12. / I won the U.S. Junior Amateur when I was 15. / I played in the Nissan Open when I was 16. / I won the U.S. Amateur when I was 18. / I played in the Masters when I was 19. / I am the only man to win three consecutive U.S. Amateur titles." The last captions read, "There are still courses in the U.S. I am not allowed to play—because of the color of my skin," and "I've heard I'm not ready for you. Are you ready for me?" The print ads used the same provocative concept.

Critics pointed out that earlier athletes who had been civil rights activists, such as Jackie Robinson and Arthur Ashe, had become agents of change through their achievements, not through campaigns to change their sports. Further, they had to maintain their integrity and conviction in the face of intense opposition. Nike's Merle Marting responded by pointing out that Woods already had significant achievements, thus qualifying him to comment on issues that concerned him. "If you look at the ad, it's basically a celebration of what Tiger has accomplished and what he's about," said Marting. Woods also stood in a different position than Robinson or Ashe, partly because they and others had already made significant progress toward racial equity that Woods could build on and also because society had changed in the intervening years.

The "I Am Tiger Woods" campaign replaced the "Hello World" campaign after its initial weekend run. This second campaign broadened Nike's message to celebrate multiculturalism with commercials depicting people of all races and ages declaring, "I Am Tiger Woods." Whereas "Hello World" focused on Woods's personal achievements and challenges, "I Am Tiger Woods" focused on how others related to him, both through his diverse racial background and through the quality of his character and play. In conjunction with the spots Nike sold T-shirts emblazoned with the words "I Am Tiger Woods." In April 1997 Nike relaunched the "I Am Tiger Woods" campaign on the momentum he had created with his Masters victory, and in June Charlie Sifford and Lee Elder joined Woods to pay homage to African-American golfers in a commercial titled "I Won't Forget."

OUTCOME

The "Hello World" and "I Am Tiger Woods" campaigns created sales increases in almost every section of the golf market. Carr-Locke's expectation of a 60 percent increase in Nike Golf sales was exceeded, as sales of the clothing line doubled after Woods signed on. In fact, because of the backlog of orders, some stores could not get Woods's official line of clothing when it came out in the spring of 1998, while others could not restock the line on their quickly depleted shelves. As it turned out, the genius of the "I Am Tiger Woods" campaign was that everyone wanted to be Woods. He quickly became the most successful Nike representative, proving the wisdom of the company's formula of advertising successful sports stars in a way that made consumers want to own a piece of the person.

Comparative statistics provided a sense of the phenomenon created by Woods. Nike Golf generated $43 million in 1994; in 1996, when Woods joined Nike two-thirds of the way through the year, sales increased to $120 million. Sales for 1997 rose to $210 million. Woods also created spikes in sales. In response to Woods's Masters victory, for example, sales of Nike footwear jumped 80 percent in the second quarter of 1997 as compared to the second quarter of 1996. Woods's successes—winning four tournaments, including the Masters, in his first year as a pro, being named *Sports Illustrated* 's Sportsman of the Year for 1996 and the Rookie of the Year and Player of the Year on the PGA Tour in 1997, and being selected as one of *Time* magazine's 25 most influential Americans in 1997—further bolstered Nike's success, with sales increasing 177 percent in the U.S. market, 67 percent in Asia, and 25 percent in Europe after his signing.

In the first year that the National Academy of Television Arts and Sciences gave an Emmy for the best commercial, the "Hello World" spot was nominated. The success of the campaigns helped draw attention to the Tiger Woods Foundation, an initiative to help inner-city kids to learn golf as a means of opening up their lives to broader opportunities. Nike's PLAY (Participate in the Lives of America's Youth) foundation cosponsored Woods's workshops, in part to advance a worthy cause but also to develop brand loyalty in this growing market.

Woods became the advertising world's most sought-after brand endorser. In subsequent years his endorsement deals included, among many others, contracts with Buick, Rolex, American Express, Wheaties, Tag Heuer, Titleist golf equipment, *Golf Digest* magazine, and Electronic Arts video games. Nike, however, remained the brand most closely associated with Woods, thanks to his initial connection to the brand as well as his ongoing appearances in Nike advertising. One of the most talked-about TV commercials of 1999, for instance, was a Nike spot in which Woods was shown effortlessly bouncing a golf ball on the face of his club, keeping it aloft for a full 28 seconds—sending it behind his back and between his legs, and even catching it on his club twice—before striking it, while it was still in the air, with the calm confidence of an ordinary golf shot.

In late 2000 Woods extended his endorsement deal with Nike for another five years, effective in September 2001. A possible measure of Woods's value to Nike was that the company more than doubled the record-breaking amount it had paid him for his first five-year deal, agreeing to a compensation package worth $85 million. As the *New York Times* noted, however, each of the companies then paying Woods to endorse their products was getting a bargain: "He's now . . . the most recognizable sports figure on the planet. And when it's time to renegotiate the contracts, all those companies will find, as Nike did, that he'll be more expensive next time. Much more expensive."

FURTHER READING

Ahrens, Frank. "Ad Doesn't Subtract from Legend of Tiger." *Washington Post,* July 10, 1999.

Anderson, Dave. "Endorsements Help Woods Become the World's Best Conglomerate." *New York Times* September 17, 2000.

Jensen, Jeff. "Nike, Adidas Ads Target Younger Golfwear Buyers." *Advertising Age* (midwest ed.), January 26, 1998.

———. "Woods Hits Golf Jackpot." *Advertising Age* (midwest ed.), September 2, 1996.

"Jordan, Woods Really Know How to Sell It; Economics: Retired NBA Star Has Few Rivals when It Comes to Endorsements, but Young Golfer Is Ready to Take the Torch." *Los Angeles Times,* December 31, 1999.

Mason, Bruce. "Commotions, Promotions and a New Superstar." *Advertising Age* (midwest ed.), December 23, 1996.

Mitchell, Doug. "Tiger Woods Nike Ad a Big Disappointment." *Wall Street Journal,* September 17, 1996.

Smallwood, John. "Ad Campaign Won't Allow Woods to Be Known Simply as a Golfer." Knight Ridder/Tribune News Service, September 5, 1996.

Smith, Eric L.,"Eye of the Tiger." *Black Enterprise,* September 1997.

Sweeney, James F.. "The Care and Feeding of Tiger: How Cleveland Agents Make Sure Tiger Woods Is One Very Fat Cat: IMG Keeps Tiger Woods Very, Very Happy: How Long Will It Last?" *Cleveland Plain Dealer,* March 30, 1997.

William D. Baue
Mark Lane

MEET THE LEBRONS CAMPAIGN

OVERVIEW

In 2002, before ever playing an NBA game, basketball prodigy LeBron James had secured a $90 million endorsement deal with the world's largest athletic company, Nike, Inc. The Zoom LeBron basketball shoe was born at Nike's Beaverton, Oregon, headquarters in the hope that LeBron could pick up the marketing mantle of retired superstar Michael Jordan and his industry-changing Nike Air Jordan shoes. By 2005 James had been named Rookie of the Year, thus living up to expectations. Nike featured him in introductory print and TV advertisements that played off the nickname "King James" that was often used in the press. James as a personality still had not broken through to the greater public. With that goal in mind Nike released a new TV-centered campaign called "Meet the LeBrons" in late 2005.

Using a portion of Nike's $170 million that was allotted for advertising that year, Portland, Oregon, agency Wieden + Kennedy was responsible for the off-beat television commercials that depicted James as four different versions of himself, all living in the same upscale household. Each spot was meant to be a spontaneous look at the family. Wise LeBron, an old-timer, bickered with the slick All Business LeBron. Kid LeBron bounced around with earphones on, while Athlete LeBron practiced his athletic moves. A tag at the end of each spot directed viewers to www.nikebasketball.com, an elaborate "Meet the LeBrons" section of the Nike website.

The "Meet the LeBrons" campaign generated plenty of buzz in the press and online, even spawning action figures of the four characters. In 2005 Nike footwear sales were up a healthy 11 percent over the previous year, and the company's annual report for 2005 stated that it had been a record year for sales and profits. James flourished on the court, being named to the All-Star team for that season, and off the court endorsement money from a variety of companies continued to flow in his direction.

HISTORICAL CONTEXT

Nike, Inc., began as Blue Ribbon Sports, a modest joint venture by accounting student Phil Knight and his former University of Oregon running coach, Bill Bowerman. In 1962 Knight had the idea to bring low-priced, high-quality Japanese athletic shoes to the U.S. market to compete against an industry dominated by German footwear. He and Bowerman became partners that year and began importing Onitsuka Tiger shoes from Japan. Soon Knight and Bowerman started producing their own shoe under the Nike moniker. Within 30 years Nike developed into the largest sports and fitness company in the world.

Nike initially set itself apart through innovation. In 1979, for instance, former NASA employee Frank Rudy invented the air cushioning that would rock the world of athletic shoes. Technical innovation came first, but athlete endorsements and savvy advertising promotion ultimately set Nike up to conquer the world. The

Cleveland Cavaliers's LeBron James. © JOE GIZA/REUTERS/CORBIS.

record-setting runner Steve Prefontaine was the first world-class athlete to wear Nikes and consult on their design. Nike joined forces with Michael Jordan in the mid-1980s. The promising Chicago Bulls basketball rookie endorsed a line of shoes and apparel called Air Jordan, consulting on shoe design and ultimately catapulting Nike into dominance in basketball. Other apparel collections followed, including a John McEnroe line for tennis and a Bo Jackson line for football. Nike built campaigns around the personalities of athletes. In 1987 its groundbreaking "Revolution" television spot broke in support of the Air Max shoe. The black-and-white commercial, set to the Beatles' song "Revolution," showed quick cuts of regular athletes interspersed with the likes of Michael Jordan and John McEnroe in play. There was an outcry from rock purists, and the Beatles band members themselves sued. The spot was a huge attention-getter for Nike and put it on the cutting edge of advertising.

In 1988 Nike made a lasting impression on American culture with the first "Just Do It" commercial, created by Portland agency Wieden + Kennedy. The slogan spoke to personal as well as athletic goals. In a huge television and print blitz consumers were encouraged to disregard their excuses for not exercising and "Just Do It." The slogan worked its way thoroughly into the national lexicon. Air Jordan's "Jumpman" logo and the Nike "swoosh" logo also became apparel must-haves in the urban and youth markets as well as essential wear among the growing hip-hop music scene.

By the year 2000 Nike was nearing its 30-year anniversary. The legendary Michael Jordan line continued on after his retirement, but Nike was on the lookout for a next-generation athlete. In 2003 the company gave high-school phenom LeBron James, frequently referred to as just LeBron, a $90 million shoe contract before he had stepped on an NBA court. Nike was banking on James to replace Jordan as the next great professional-basketball juggernaut. His first television commercial was understated, showing him nervous under the pressure of expectations before his first NBA game and then smiling as he blended into the rhythm of the game. A later TV spot included comedian Bernie Mac turning the court into a church revival meeting of sorts. The spot played on the idea of James as the "chosen one," or "King James," as he was sometimes called in the press, but then asserted that the young rookie just wanted to be a team player. Posters and billboards were less humble in nature: one image showed James seated on a throne with lions at his feet. In 2004 a campaign titled "The Chamber of Fear" made James the star of a highly stylized commercial spoofing kung fu movies. In battling multiple enemies with names like "Complacency," "Self-Doubt," and "Haters," his only weapons were his athletic ability and his new Nike shoes. The spot, banned in China because censors deemed it offensive to the state, was memorable, but it still did not do enough to advance the LeBron persona in the United States. A new campaign, "Meet the LeBrons," followed in 2005.

TARGET MARKET

In the late 1980s and 1990s sports attire became increasingly acceptable among Americans as casual wear. At the same time NBA basketball was reaching an all-time high in popularity. Also during this period urban hip-hop music culture was growing fast, and recording artists wore basketball apparel in their videos and during other appearances. These influences combined to make Nike athletic gear, especially shoes, the thing to wear for the trend-conscious city-dwelling consumer. Teenage boys and men in their early 20s, who made up the vast majority of recreational and amateur basketball players, were a particular focus for shoes. These young men tended to be loyal consumers, aligning themselves with a player and sportswear brand. Sports attire had become a status symbol in youth culture. LeBron James himself was

KNIGHT HANDS OVER NIKE REIGNS

In 2005 Phil Knight, the visionary leader and cofounder of Nike, Inc., stepped down as CEO but retained his position as chairman of the board. Knight handpicked William Perez, president and CEO of consumer-products company S.C. Johnson, to be his successor. Perez was viewed as a surprising choice. He had overseen S.C. Johnson's $6.5 billion stable of worldwide brands, but aside from an enthusiasm for running, he had no footwear experience. Perez immediately slashed the Nike advertising budget, a move that clashed irrevocably with Knight's marketing philosophy, and in January 2006 Perez resigned.

barely out of his teen years. An all-around player who was able to execute from any position on court, he was living up to the pre-NBA hype, which would ensure that the Zoom LeBron shoe series would appeal to the coveted market of young males from high-population centers.

In addition to courting the core male youth audience, Nike was looking to be more inclusive with its "Meet the LeBrons" commercials, which showed four versions of the athlete at different stages of life. Peter Stern of Strategic, a sports and entertainment consulting firm, evaluated the spots in the January 10, 2006, edition of the *Wall Street Journal,* saying that Nike was "showing the athlete in a different light that might appeal to someone who's more fashion-conscious or image-conscious versus someone who wants to wear the shoe to jump higher or score more."

COMPETITION

Founders Knight and Bowerman created their shoe company in response to a German stronghold on the athletic-shoe market. Within 30 years of its inception Nike had surpassed German company adidas as the largest athletic-shoe maker in the world. Still, Nike continued to take adidas very seriously. In 2003 Nike spent $153 million on advertising, compared to adidas's $34.3 million. Much of that ad money was directed toward Nike's new star, LeBron James. Ironically, adidas had a relationship with James first and was considered the likely sponsor for the NBA-bound high schooler before Nike swooped in with a $90 million, seven-year deal.

Adidas won a few battles in the ensuing years. The German company beat out Nike for sponsorship of the 2008 Olympics in Beijing, China. This was a particularly harsh blow given the LeBron James "Chamber of Fear" commercial debacle, which had weakened Nike's position in the immense Chinese market. The spot depicted James vanquishing a dragon, a traditional symbol of the Chinese state, and it was banned by the government. Nike lost NBA player Yao Ming, also hugely popular in China, to Reebok, which was soon acquired by adidas for nearly $4 billion. The sale of Reebok to adidas prompted Nike to spend more time looking over its shoulder. Once combined, adidas and Reebok captured about 20 percent of the U.S. market, making inroads to Nike's enviable 36 percent. As 2005 came to a close, adidas released a campaign featuring basketball star Kevin Garnett of the Minnesota Timberwolves that was remarkably similar in tone and purpose to "Meet the LeBrons." It centered on a television spot that depicted Garnett in a five vignettes to represent the many sides of his personality: a general on a battlefield, a superhero, a kid playing tag, a gladiator, and even a comic.

MARKETING STRATEGY

By the time LeBron James was signed as a Nike spokesman, Wieden + Kennedy had been creating advertising for Nike for many years. James was an unknown quantity when his first Nike advertisements appeared in 2003. He won NBA Rookie of the Year his first season, and in two short years the Cleveland Cavaliers player had proven himself a major force in basketball. Nevertheless, by 2005 the public at large was just getting to know James, and Nike needed to help that process along. Its agency devised a campaign called "Meet the Lebrons," which included television commercials, cinema spots, and online banners as well as an extensive website, all introduced in December 2005. The cornerstone of the campaign was composed of four quirky TV spots featuring James as different characterizations of himself. The four characters were Wise LeBron, the cranky old-timer; All Business LeBron, slick and self-absorbed; Kid LeBron, a headphone-wearing, basketball-obsessed youth; and finally the serious but good-natured Athlete LeBron, who barely spoke. This oddly constructed family inhabited a sleek and expansive modern residence, with Wise LeBron's tiny, ancient-looking TV set occasionally featured in the background showing on-court footage of LeBron James. In one commercial the LeBrons danced to Rick James's funk anthem "Superfreak." In two others they bickered at the dinner table, and in the one called "New Shoes" they finally referred to the actual product when Wise LeBron told All Business LeBron, "It's not about you. It's about the shoes." The spots had no tagline except a modest "nikebasketball.com" at the bottom of the screen.

The website destination listed in the spots was an interactive trip to the LeBrons' house, where visitors could explore their home to get a better view of the pineapple on the kitchen counter or zoom in on the luxury car in the driveway. There were bios for each character, ads to view, wallpaper to download, and Zoom LeBron shoes for sale. Nike wanted to make fans comfortable in the LeBron James pseudoworld. Ralph Green, the U.S. basketball brand director for Nike, described the purpose of the campaign to the *Wall Street Journal.* "We were aware of elements of LeBron's personality that had not been seen by most of our consumers.... So our goal was to give consumers a peek at these varied elements of the LeBron persona but to do so in a subtle, figurative, and humorous manner." The actual budget for the costly campaign was not revealed, but according to research firm TNS Media Intelligence, it probably took up a significant portion of the $170 million that Nike spent on advertising from January through November 2005.

OUTCOME

The "Meet the LeBrons" campaign resonated with consumers. As a result of the popularity of the campaign, action figures of the characters were created for sale by Upper Deck, a sports-memorabilia company. Nike, ever confident in James, planned a special edition Zoom LeBron shoe specifically for the 2006 NBA All-Star Game. More importantly Nike's annual report for 2005 reflected healthy footwear sales, with revenues up by 11 percent over the previous year, making fiscal 2005 a record year for sales and profits. Wieden + Kennedy's reputation was enhanced as well, perhaps contributing to its growing client list in 2005 that included new accounts from mega-advertisers Coca-Cola Company and Procter & Gamble. James himself continued to reap the rewards of widening positive exposure; by the end of 2005 he had five corporate sponsorships in addition to Nike, including Powerade and Sprite.

FURTHER READING

Areddy, James T. "Nike Switches China Ad Account to Wieden in Blow to WPP Unit." *Wall Street Journal,* November 23, 2005, p. B4.

"The FN List: Ad It Up; Top 10 Athletic Shoe Brand Advertisers." *Footwear News,* April 19, 2004, p. 22.

Goldman, Robert, and Stephen Papson. *Nike Culture: The Sign of the Swoosh.* London: SAGE Publications, 1998.

Kang, Stephanie. "Nike, Adidas Aim to Look 'Cool' in Sneaker Ads." *Wall Street Journal,* January 10, 2006, p. B2.

Kang, Stephanie, and Matthew Karnitschnig. "Leap Forward: For Adidas, Reebok Deal Caps Push to Broaden Urban Appeal." *Wall Street Journal,* August 4, 2005, p. A1.

Lebovich, Jennifer. "Shoe Fans Hurry Up and Wait to Get LeBron James Sneaker." *Knight Ridder/Tribune Business News,* April 1, 2005, p. 1.

Lippert, Barbara. "Hyping the Hype." *Adweek,* January 12, 2004, p. 30.

Roth, Daniel. "Can Nike Still Do It without Phil Knight?" *Fortune,* April 4, 2005, p. 59.

Russak, Brian. "LeBron James Shoe Set to Debut Dec. 20." *Footwear News,* December 15, 2003, p. 18.

Stevenson, Seth. "LeBron James, Thespian." *Slate,* January 2, 2006. Available from <http://img.slate.com/id/2133494/>

Thomaselli, Rich. "Deal Sets Stage for Full-Scale War with Nike." *Advertising Age,* August 8, 2005, p. 5.

Williams, Christopher C. "In the Game." *Barron's,* June 9, 2003, p. 16.

Simone Samano

MOVE CAMPAIGN

OVERVIEW

Nike Inc., based in Beaverton, Oregon, and the world's leading manufacturer of athletic footwear, premiered its "Move" television spot in early 2002 during the Winter Olympics in Salt Lake City, Utah. A lyrical homage to physical activity, the 90-second sequence featured athletes and nonathletes alike, all engaged in the actions of their sports. From swimming to skateboarding, to video golf and gymnastics, each person's movements were coordinated with the next person's, creating a seamless paean to physical activity. Though passing images of Nike's famous "swoosh" logo appeared in the spot, the commercial did not promote a specific product. Instead, it capitalized on the emotional nature of the Olympic Games and equated the Nike brand with the same feeling of goodwill.

The "Move" commercial was created by Nike's longtime advertising agency, Wieden+Kennedy (W+K), and directed by filmmaker Jake Scott. Although the 90-second spot had its premiere during NBC's coverage of the Olympics, 60-second and 30-second versions later ran briefly on other television networks. The games, with their huge ratings over a two-week period, offered advertisers a rare opportunity every two years to launch new products or to redefine brands by creating commercials that capitalized on the games. In the case of "Move," the tie-in was represented by cameo shots of famous Olympic athletes, including skier Picabo Street and speed skater Apolo Anton Ohno. Shots of these stars were intercut with shots of "ordinary" people, beginning with a boy running down a suburban street and ranging from the simple (a toddler playing on a bed) to the thrill seeking (a BASE jumper

Speed skater Apolo Anton Ohno during the 2002 Olympic Winter Games in Salt Lake City, Utah, February 16, 2002. © TIM DE WAELE/ISOSPORT/CORBIS.

leaping from a bridge). The commercial's message was clear: No matter how you do it, just move.

Nike did not make the cost of the commercial public, and by the spring of 2002 the company had moved on to other, more product-focused campaigns. "Move" continued to attract notice, however, and it won the 2002 Emmy Award as the outstanding commercial from the Academy of Television Arts and Sciences and a Gold Lion at the 2003 Clio Awards.

HISTORICAL CONTEXT

At the time of the 2002 Winter Olympics, Nike's annual revenues totaled well over $9 billion, more than triple that of its nearest competitor, Reebok. The company's advertising prowess, guided for years by W+K, was legendary. Nike's swoosh logo and its indelible motto, "Just Do It," had long since joined the pantheon of advertising's greatest campaigns. In 1993 Nike became one of the first three companies, along with Coca-Cola and Absolute Vodka, inducted into the American Marketing Association Hall of Fame.

Over the years many individual Nike television commercials, including the Michael Jordan spots directed by Spike Lee and the "Bo Knows" campaign featuring Bo Jackson, had garnered attention, spawned catchphrases, and won awards. "Move" continued in that tradition. But with such fame came an equal amount of notoriety. Partly because of the company's position as the industry leader, by the 1990s Nike had become embroiled in controversies regarding its overseas labor practices and its marketing tactics in the United States. The company was accused of underpaying foreign workers and of indulging in "ambush" marketing, whereby it co-opted publicity during sporting events it did not sponsor.

Nike's so-called ambush marketing tactics had angered sponsors of previous Olympic Games, who had each paid a hefty sum for the privilege of using the Olympic logo in its advertising and of associating itself with the games. Nike had never paid such a sponsorship fee but had circumvented the official rules so effectively that polls showed many people erroneously identifying Nike as an Olympic sponsor. Most famously, in 1992 Nike pitchman and "Dream Team" member Jordan accepted the gold medal for basketball in Barcelona, Spain, after covering up the Reebok logo on his uniform. In the 2002 Boston Marathon, sponsored by adidas, Nike stole its rival's thunder by blanketing area subway stops with advertisements and by spray painting swooshes on the pavement at the finish line. Nike defended its tactics, however. Simon Pestridge, Nike's brand manager, told a reporter for MSNBC that "Nike likes to come at things from a different angle... We play inside the rules and we bring a different point of view that's true and authentic to sport."

Nike always retained its high advertising profile no matter what public relations fiasco might be playing out at the time. Running spots that aimed to increase brand identification rather than promote specific products had been part of that strategy for years. With "Move," Nike sought to improve its global image by identifying itself with the type of international fellowship featured at the Olympics, even though the company was not an official sponsor.

TARGET MARKET

The 2002 Winter Olympics were broadcast on NBC, which struggled to attract the 18- to 45-year-old demographic that was coveted by advertisers. Prior to 2002, the Olympics had tended to attract older audiences, but the introduction of newer sports, such as snowboarding and the skeleton, helped NBC reverse the trend by appealing to younger viewers, such as those who had made ESPN's X Games so popular. Nike even aided in the endeavor by producing a 30-minute promotional show that aired on January 26 and that featured lesser-known Olympic athletes teaching NBA star Charles Barkley and Olympic champion runner Marion Jones about winter sports. This cross-pollination effort sought to attract Nike's customer base—both Barkley and Jones had recently been featured in high-profile Nike campaigns—in addition to the Olympics' traditional audience, which included hefty numbers of viewers who were more interested in the athletes' personal stories than in the sports themselves. The "Move" spot also catered to this demographic by concentrating on everyday people "just doing something" as well as featuring professional athletes who epitomized the "Just Do It" ethos.

The Winter Olympics aired a week after Super Bowl XXXVI, the year's other high-profile television advertising event. The Super Bowl had the distinction of offering the most expensive airtime of the television year, roughly $2 million for a 30-second commercial. The Winter Games were less expensive, about $600,000 per 30 seconds, and had the advantage of airing over a two-week period. Nike elected not to advertise during the Super Bowl, instead concentrating its efforts on the Olympics. Ironically, Nike had no major competition. As with the Super Bowl, the biggest advertisers at the Olympics tended to have nothing to do with sports or sporting goods. Xerox, Bank of America, and AT&T all had a sizable presence, with Nike being the only sports-related advertiser to air commercials.

One explanation for this was that Nike was primarily a retail company, and the Olympics often catered to business-to-business advertisers. "Advertisers believe that the size of the audience, the global exposure and the duration of the event combine to provide a powerful opportunity to reach their target audience," wrote Kate Maddox in *B to B* magazine. In this light Nike's "Move" commercial was nontraditional in that it was aimed squarely at the consumer. Yet in terms of not promoting a specific product, Nike was right in line with the trend. "Twenty to 30 years ago, it would have been branding advertising. Advertising today has probably become more strategic in use," Rick Burton, the executive director of the Warsaw Sports Marketing Center, told Jane L. Levere of Salt Lake City's *Deseret News.*

A 10-DAY SHOOT FOR 90 SECONDS OF FILM

Nike's Emmy-winning "Move" spot was shot over a period of 10 days by director Jake Scott, the son of Oscar-nominated film director Ridley Scott. Finding a skateboarder to launch himself off the roof of a building onto a ramp proved difficult. The first two candidates refused to attempt the stunt, and the task finally fell to a young local volunteer. The most harrowing part of the shoot took place in Auburn, California, where professional BASE jumper Lottie Aston and a cameraman repeatedly hurled themselves off the Foresthill Bridge. Despite the inherent danger in the jump, Nike spokesman Scott Reames said, "It's young, it's edgy . . . You can't deny the coolness factor."

COMPETITION

The Olympics were "a bellwether for advertisers," wrote Michael Dumiak of *Financial Services Marketing.* Toward that end many advertisers created special campaigns that capitalized on the emotions the games engendered in their viewers. Bank of America, McDonald's, and Visa all produced spots specifically for the games. "The Olympics represent what is pure and good about sports," Mark Vogel, executive vice president of brand management for the Osborn & Barr consulting firm, told Thomas Lee of the *St. Louis Post-Dispatch,* "and these companies want their brands associated with that." Nike was the only major sporting goods company to buy substantial airtime. Though the company did not release budget figures for the commercial, Monster.com, another major Olympic Games advertiser, spent more than $10 million on nearly 200 spots for the games, and Samsung spent more than $15 million. Nike's nearest competitor, Reebok, did not advertise during the games but did garner publicity for its Reebok Human Rights Award, which was given in a ceremony in conjunction with the Olympic festivities.

MARKETING STRATEGY

"Move" opened with a long shot of a boy running down a suburban street. As he looked over his shoulder, the scene cut to a matching shot of a hockey player. In turn others were shown moving as well—a man rotated his legs around a pommel horse, a basketball player shot to score, a jogger ran in place at a red light, a tennis player swung a backhand. Shots of professional athletes Street, Vince Carter, Lindsay Davenport, and Landon Donovan were intercut with shots of everyday athletes engaged in their pursuits. The sports varied in intensity, from the speed of the hockey player and the long-distance jumper to the more languorous underwater splash of the high diver and the gentle descent of the parachuting BASE jumper, resulting in a rhythm that rose and fell with the music and the pace of the editing. Three-quarters through, the words "just do it" were superimposed on an underwater shot of a high-diver plunging into the blue swimming pool. The commercial eventually ended with a continuation of the scene of the boy running down the street, and it concluded with an understated swoosh in the center of the screen. All of the action was presented in real time, "lovingly choreographed," according to *Advertising Age,* without the slow-motion effect so common in sports advertising.

The spot proved inspiring, both visually and musically. With the variety of people and activities—from children to seniors, basketball players, swimmers, golfers, and skiers—chances were that every viewer found an image with which he or she could identify. Nike even reached beyond its own interests in athletic footwear to include athletes in bare feet and ice skates. As W+K's Hal Curtis explained to the Web-based *Boards* magazine, "Nike is perceived as a core sport brand for football, basketball, baseball and soccer. Showing other sports and stretching that is a good thing strategically."

Critics applauded the understated elegance of the spot. "'Move' quietly breaks through the clutter due to its refreshing realness," wrote Christine Champagne in *Shoot,* and a writer for *Creative Review* called it a "luscious" expression of "how movement can translate from one sport to the next." Adam Bonislawski of *Shoot* praised the way in which "each detail flows naturally from the ones that precede it."

Many people singled out the music as a major factor in the spot's appeal. While Nike commercials often included rap or techno music with a strong, fast beat, "Move" was different. A gentle piano score composed by Jonathan Elias especially for the spot accompanied the real-time images, creating an uplifting, inspiring mood as opposed to a hard-driving, competitive feel.

OUTCOME

Curtis told Champagne that with "Move," "we wanted to show that sport is a shared experience, whether you're a kid on a skateboard or a pro like Vince Carter playing an NBA game." It worked, Champagne declared. "The mix of professional and amateur athletes, the real and natural production, and the music combined helped to create an ad that would appeal to anyone who watched the Winter Olympics—not just to hard-core athletes and thrill-seeking teens," she wrote.

"Move" won several awards, including a Gold Lion at the annual Clio Awards in South Beach, Miami, Florida, and a 2002 Emmy Award from the Academy of Television Arts and Sciences for outstanding commercial. Apart from the recognition of the advertising industry, the spot also pleased filmmakers. "The commercial attains that great aesthetic Holy Grail," wrote Adam Bonislawski in *Shoot,* "the seamless integration of form and content." A writer for *Adweek* called it a "visual and aural masterpiece."

FURTHER READING

Bonislawski, Adam. "Jake Scott: On the 'Move' for Nike." *Shoot,* March 22, 2002, p. 54.

Champagne, Christine. "Dir. Jake Scott Puts the 'Move' on Nike." *Shoot,* March 1, 2002, p. 10.

Dumiak, Michael. "Ad Spending: Bellwether or Blitz; Will Olympics and Super Bowl Boost Spending?" *Financial Services Marketing,* January/February 2002, p. 5.

Lee, Thomas. "High Olympics Ratings Bring Good News to Corporate Sponsors." *St. Louis Post-Dispatch,* February 14, 2002.

Levere, Jane L. "Advertisers Try New Games Campaigns." *Deseret News,* December 31, 2001.

Maddox, Kate. "XIX Winter Olympics: Marketing Hot Spot." *B to B,* February 11, 2002, p. 1.

"Move—New Nike Ad Celebrates Shared Movements and Emotions of Sports." *PR Newswire,* February 8, 2002.

"Nike Move." *Adweek* (eastern ed.), January 27, 2003, p. 18.

"Nike—Move." *Boards,* November 2005. Available from <http://www.boardsmag.com/screeningroom/commercials/250>

"Nike Move Campaign." *Creative Review,* April, 2002, p. 17.

"Nike Spot Wins an Emmy Award." *New York Times,* September 20, 2002, p. C4.

"Nike, Wieden + Kennedy, Portland, Ore. 'Move.'" *Advertising Age,* May 26, 2003.

Sauer, Abram. "Ambush Marketing Steals the Show." May 27, 2002. Available from <http://www.brandchannel.com/>

Kathy Wilson Peacock

PLAY CAMPAIGN

OVERVIEW

"Just Do It" became one of the most recognizable catchphrases in advertising. It belonged to Nike Inc., the Oregon-based company that dominated the athletic footwear and sports apparel industry beginning in the 1980s. Long known for its television and print ads featuring superstar athletes who personified the "just do it" ethos, Nike conceived its "Play" campaign to appeal to the opposite demographic—those who preferred a more lighthearted, less strenuous approach to fitness. Toward this end the advertising agency Wieden + Kennedy, based in Portland, Oregon, created a series of television spots to promote Nike shoes as being ideal for everyday life. The soft-sell strategy focused on the brand rather than a specific product, as witnessed by the subtle placement of the Nike "swoosh" logo above the word "Play" at the end of the spots.

Consisting of a series of three television spots, the $25 million "Play" campaign was launched in August 2001 with "Tag," "Shade Running," and "Tailgating." In "Tag," for example, a man dressed for work emerged from a subway staircase, coffee in hand, and was tapped on the shoulder by a stranger. With a slight sigh the man understood that he had just been tagged "it." People on the street scattered in all directions as he looked around for someone to pursue. Everyone abandoned their commute in favor of playing the game.

The "Play" campaign was a success on all fronts. "Tag" won the Grand Prix for television commercials at the 49th International Advertising Festival in Cannes, France, in 2002, with "Shade Running" taking a Gold Lion and "Tailgating" a Bronze Lion. Nike's profits for the quarter following the campaign rose 8.3 percent, despite the fact that sales in the United States fell 2 percent, likely because of the economic fallout following the terrorist attacks of September 11, 2001. Because the campaign was not product specific, however, and because Nike ran many campaigns simultaneously, it was hard to pinpoint exactly how the "Play" ads affected sales. The short-lived campaign ran through Labor Day 2001.

HISTORICAL CONTEXT

With sales figures in 2001 more than triple that of Reebok, its nearest competitor, the biggest hurdle Nike had to overcome was its own reputation. The success of "Just Do It," a phrase dreamed up by Dan Wieden, founder of Wieden + Kennedy, in the early 1980s, represented a "tough love" approach to fitness and sports. Recognizing that not everyone appreciated the no-excuses sentiment, however, Nike officials decided to soften its image by portraying working people dispensing with obligation in order to enjoy a moment of frivolity. "'Just Do It' is supremely motivating, no question about that," wrote Bob Garfield in *Advertising Age*, "because it brooks no excuse for sitting on your fat ass a moment longer. But that campaign is also a bit on the, um . . . harsh side. A little grim, you know?" Focusing on a more lighthearted nature of play, which harked back to the school playground, Nike wanted to reach out to potential customers who were not athletic in the traditional sense.

Previous legendary Nike advertising campaigns had featured the biggest sports celebrities of the day, from Jimmy Connors to Michael Jordan to Lance Armstrong, a tactic that usually lured young people, teenagers in particular, to the brand. With the "Play" campaign the focus was on the urban world of work and the fantasy of escaping from it for a moment. The strategy seemed to signify an attempt to attract slightly older consumers and those who had not been previously influenced by Nike's strong alliance with world-class athletes.

TARGET MARKET

Historically most Nike commercials were fairly transparent when it came to their target audiences. Ads featuring star athletes attracted fans of that athlete, particularly young people. The bigger the star—Tiger Woods or Lance Armstrong, for example—the bigger the target. The "Play" campaign, however, strayed from that strategy, instead focusing on "everyday" people going about their business. The message was clear: Nike shoes were not just for the basketball court or the track or any other sport. They were perfect for the street or for the office. A person did not even have to like sports; he or she just had to like a good challenge.

Nike coyly denied, however, that it targeted a specific demographic with the "Play" campaign or, for that matter, with any of its other campaigns. Andy Mooney, Nike's vice president of global brand management, told

PLAYING TAG IN TORONTO

The Nike "Tag" commercial, which featured an urban rush-hour crowd spontaneously breaking into a childlike game of tag, was filmed in Toronto, Ontario, with 400 extras. The city's locations were available only during weekend mornings. Director Frank Budgen's careful planning fell by the wayside when the weather failed to cooperate, forcing crews to shoot in three locations simultaneously. The award-winning result relied as much on happenstance as on the script. For instance, the man chased in the subway by the person designated "it," after everyone else had safely escaped onto a train, was recruited off the street right before shooting began.

Dick Silverman of *Footwear News* that "people . . . get way too focused on age and demographic segmentation. Sports fans are sports fans, no matter what." Tom Clarke, president of Nike, agreed with Mooney. "If we were trying to sell computers or something else, I think maybe a more fine-tuned demographic focus would be in play," he told Silverman. "But I think sports as an inspiration point gives you a lot of access into individuals and a pretty broad array of ages." Dave Larson, Nike's director of brand initiatives, told Sarah J. Heim of *Adweek,* however, that the "Play" campaign targeted teens but that it also aimed "to reach a psychodemographic: anyone who is youthful in attitude and spirit." The idea worked. "Nike has shown a softer, more engaging side," wrote the editors of *Campaign* magazine in a review of the ads.

COMPETITION

Nike's nearest rival was Reebok, based in the United Kingdom, whose annual sales in 2001 were dwarfed by Nike's. Nike also outspent Reebok on marketing efforts, however, dedicating $130 million for the year as opposed to Reebok's $52 million. But in the summer of 2001, after years of taking a beating from Nike, Reebok announced the launch of its RBK line of shoes and sportswear with two aggressive marketing campaigns. In an effort to reach women, Reebok advertised heavily during the reality show *Survivor,* the year's top-rated program among female viewers of all age groups. The commercials featured notable female athletes, such as Venus Williams, as well as several *Survivor* cast members. Concurrently RBK's urban credentials were established with a series of ads featuring NBA star Alan Iverson; musicians Jadakiss, R. Kelly, and Missy Elliott; and street basketball players from Harlem, the likes of which Nike had just featured in its "Freestyle" campaign. Richard Linnett of *Advertising Age* called Reebok's new RBK campaign "a bold move onto Nike's turf."

Nike lost further ground to Reebok when the British company signed a 10-year deal to provide uniforms and warm-up apparel for the NBA, a commission Nike had held for years. The turnabout attracted much media attention. "For one thing," wrote Ron Stodghill II in *Time* magazine, "it means that if Michael Jordan returns to the game, no matter what he wears on his feet, he'll be wearing a Reebok logo on his back." Adam Helfant, Nike's director of global sports marketing, was not concerned. Reebok's $50 million NBA deal, he told Stodghill, amounted to "two months' worth of Jordan business for us." Stodghill concurred with Helfant. "Nike's path to the future has shifted from building brand awareness . . . to gaining a stronger foothold in growth markets like soccer and golf," he wrote.

Adidas, the number three athletic-shoe manufacturer in 2001, was never much of a threat to Nike but vowed to increase its share of the U.S. market from 10 to 20 percent, according to David Goetzl of *Advertising Age.* New Balance, a company that specialized in running shoes, showed substantial market growth during the year, however, up more than two 2 percentage points, to 9.6 percent. Also encroaching on the athletic-shoe market were makers of "brown shoes," such as Timberland hiking boots, which continued to increase in popularity in the early years of the decade.

MARKETING STRATEGY

Along with the "Tag" spot, the "Play" campaign featured two other commercials, "Shade Running" and "Tailgating." In "Shade Running" a woman went for a run through the streets of Manhattan, making sure to stay in the shade at all times. Viewers saw her cross the street in the shadow of a moving crane and use the shade of other moving targets, such as a truck, to guard her path through the crowded city. "Tailgating" showed a businessman with a briefcase being followed down the street by a man dressed for a game of basketball. He dribbled the ball ominously close to the businessman, who tried to ignore him. Finally the businessman flung his briefcase aside and pivoted to confront his "tailgater." The pair faced off in a game of one-on-one in a city alley. What all three spots had in common was a distinctly urban feel, with crowded city streets and acres of pavement that were transformed from infrastructure into a playing field. In essence the world became a playground.

Though the campaign was a departure from Nike's heralded "Just Do It" slogan, "Play" was not a rejection of it. As Larson told Heim of *Adweek,* "play" was just a different aspect of "doing it." "Play emphasized why you should just do it," he told her. Coincidently the campaign tapped into an idea that other companies were exploring for themselves. Jennifer Carofano of *Footwear News* noted that the "Play" campaign, along with the "Champagne" spot for Microsoft's Xbox, which featured the tagline "Life is short. Play more," represented a new trend in advertising. "The newest batch of print and television ads promote childhood games and pre-adolescent innocence as the ultimate goal for consumers of all ages," she wrote.

According to Monica Rigali, a Nike spokesperson, the campaign was a matter of art imitating life. "We are seeing people, especially young people, doing sports in a totally new way, just kids hanging out in their neighborhood playing games," she told Carofano. Mike Byrne, copywriter for Wieden + Kennedy told a writer for *Adweek* that "play is the mother of all sports . . . A kid gets interested because he falls in love with the movement: throwing, running, catching." In addition, Hal Curtis, creative director for Wieden + Kennedy, told *Adweek* that "it doesn't matter if a person's big or small" when playing tag. Such was the message imparted to viewers. As Curtis said, "We wanted to . . . bring people back to their youth and garner an emotional reaction."

Emotions aside, the campaign was convincing in its message that Nike made shoes for everyone. Jeff Goodby, the Cannes jury president, told Eleftheria Parpis of *Adweek* that "Tag" was subtly persuasive in conveying the point that Nike shoes "weren't just [an] athlete's shoes, but something you can use in everyday life." It was meant to convey this idea even if a person's morning commute did not break out into a four-block game of tag.

OUTCOME

The "Play" campaign was launched on August 1, 2001, with "Summer of Play," a star-studded party held at the Niketown store in Beverly Hills, California. The party was essentially a promotional event for a promotional campaign, an illustration of the synergy between Hollywood and Nike. The attendance list, which included Snoop Dogg, Leonardo di Caprio, and Tobey Maguire, helped Nike maintain its image as the go-to company for footwear for the rich and famous. Even though the commercials aired for less than a month, as had been the plan, they were yet another stellar addition to Nike's considerable repertoire of advertising, one that had made it the overwhelming industry leader for years. While most U.S. retailers saw their profits suffer after September 11, 2001, Nike's sales slumped only 2 percent, and the company ended the fiscal year with sales up by 5.5 percent.

"Play" was deemed one of the most creative and successful campaigns of the year by leaders in the advertising industry. In addition to winning the top awards at Cannes, Nike was named Advertiser of the Year at the 2002 Clio Awards, based on Wieden + Kennedy's work for the company. As for peer reviews of the spots, Laurel Wentz and Stefano Hatfield, writing in *Advertising Age,* called the "Tag" spot "a beautifully directed TV commercial with perfect timing." Garfield was similarly impressed. He called the "Tag" commercial "breathtaking in its conception, its choreography, its wry sensibility, and—beneath its exceedingly complex production—its sheer simplicity."

FURTHER READING

Carofano, Jennifer. "Fountain of Youth." *Footwear News,* July 16, 2001, p. 12.

Garcia, Sandra. "You're It! Nike's Summer Play Initiative Kicks Off." *Shoot,* July 6, 2001, p. 12.

Garfield, Bob. "Cannes Grand Prix Winner, Nike's 'Tag' Is It in Every Way." *Advertising Age,* June 24, 2002, p. 77.

Heim, Sarah J. "Nike Exhorts the Public to 'Play' in $25 Mil. Campaign." *Adweek,* July 2, 2001, p. 5.

Linnett, Richard. "Repositioning: Reebok Re-brands for Hip-Hop Crowd." *Advertising Age,* January 28, 2002, p. 3.

Marshall, Caroline. "I've Only Done Great Work for Nike." *Campaign,* June 22, 2001, p. 22.

Mills, Dominic. "Mills on . . . Nike." *Campaign,* November 15, 2002.

"Nike Commercial." *Creative Review,* December 2002, p. 23.

"Nike Wins Clio's Advertiser of Year Honor." *Adweek,* April 15, 2002, p. 72.

Parpis, Eleftheria. "Nike's 'Play' Pays Off for Wieden." *Adweek,* June 24, 2002, p. 2.

Parpis, Eleftheria, Barbara Lippert, and Ann M. Mack. "Why Nike's 'Freestyle' Fell Flat at Cannes." *Adweek,* June 25, 2001, p. 5.

"Reebok Launches Its Most Aggressive Women's Initiative Ever." *PR Newswire,* October 9, 2001.

Silverman, Dick. "Demographics Subject to Rules of Style." *Footwear News,* April 5, 1999, p. 20.

Wentz, Laurel, and Stefano Hatfield. "Nike 'Tag' Bags Grand Prix." *Advertising Age,* June 24, 2002, p. 1.

Kathy Wilson Peacock

PRODUCT ASSAULT CAMPAIGN

OVERVIEW

Going into the summer of 1997, Nike gave its advertising firm, Portland, Oregon-based Wieden & Kennedy, an "emergency assignment," according to Jimmy Smith, a copywriter for the agency. The "Product Assault" campaign "wasn't even budgeted for the summer, and we had to turn it around quickly," explained Smith in Kathy DeSalvo's August 1997 *Shoot* article. "Nike wanted to do something to let people know that these cool shoes are out there. After we received all the background information on them, we looked at them and [decided] that they're really cool-looking shoes, so why not just show them?" Nike advertising director for North America Chris Zimmerman expounded further on the strategy behind the campaign: "These ads are really about showing that the product speaks for itself," Zimmerman explained after asserting in Andrew Ross Sorkin's July 1997 *Portland Oregonian* article that "every shoe has a story to tell."

The resulting print and outdoor advertisements focused visually on the sneakers themselves, but the ads also included minimal copy that promised more to the story. For example, the ad for the Air Foamposit

I featured what most people would recognize as an E-mail address—in this instance, penny@breakudown.com. Sports-savvy consumers could decipher the references embedded in the address: "penny" referred to the guard for basketball's Orlando Magic, Anfernee "Penny" Hardaway, and "breakudown" referred to his speed in wearing out his opponents.

By suggestion, the ads prompted Internet users to send E-mail messages to the given address; Nike's computer server then bounced automated responses back to the sender. For an E-mail sent to penny@breakudown.com, the response read, "Hey, thanks for the email. So you've seen the new Air Foamposit I, also known as Penny's new space boot. Pretty cool, huh? You probably haven't had a chance to really study 'em cuz Penny's always moving so fast, so check out http://www.breakudown.com." This address led Internet surfers to the World Wide Web, where Nike had devoted a website to telling the more complete story of the new shoe. "We don't think of them as Web sites so much as we think of them as 'sitelets,' all linking back to Nike" through the corporate home page, http://www.nike.com, explained Nike's Zimmerman in Sorkin's article. "This is really the first time we have ever done anything like this," continued Zimmerman, summarizing the overall strategy of this integrated campaign.

HISTORICAL CONTEXT

Outdoor advertising, since it was an oversized medium that amplified the visual spectacle of the new shoes, served as the centerpiece of the campaign that also included print advertising as well as television and radio spots, though these latter two media were lacking the E-mail component of the campaign. Besides directing the television spots, photographer Dan Winters of bicoastal X-Ray Productions also shot the pictures for the campaign, ensuring that the photos would retain their quality when enlarged. At the time, outdoor advertising, which included billboards, phone kiosks, and bus shelters, was experiencing a resurgence in popularity. For example, the billboard company Outdoor Systems Inc. went public on the New York Stock Exchange at about the same time Nike launched this campaign, in 1997. Over the next two years the price of this stock rose about 1,500 percent, putting its growth on par with rapid-growth Internet stocks such as Yahoo! and Amazon.com and enticing Infinity Broadcasting, a subsidiary of media giant CBS Corp., to buy out Outdoor Systems for $8.3 billion in stock and assumed debt. "We seem to be in a golden age with the world's oldest medium, even in the Internet age," said Brian McLean, president and chief executive of Canadian-based Mediacom Inc., a subsidiary of Outdoor Systems, in John Mahler's *Toronto Star* article on billboard advertising.

Doug Linton of the Toronto-based ad agency Ambrose Carr Linton & Carroll sang the praises of outdoor advertising in the same article: "It's the ultimate precis. You have to have it down in eight words or less . . . It's like working without a net. You're not surrounded by editorial copy or competing with a TV program. You're out there on your own." Whereas McLean and Linton suggested that outdoor advertising gained its strength as a medium isolated from other media, Nike sought to enhance this singular strength by integrating other media into the mix. In essence, Nike walked the high wire of outdoor advertising while also unfurling a net—specifically, the Internet.

Nike had used a similar interactive strategy in a campaign dating back two years, except instead of featuring E-mail addresses superimposed over the photographs focusing on the sneakers, the shoe-centered ads listed toll-free telephone numbers. Those who called simply listened to prerecorded conversations between celebrity athlete endorsers and Nike employees talking about that particular shoe model. This strategy relegated the caller to a passive role in that, after dialing, the caller merely listened. The new campaign forced more active interaction, though the Internet user remained essentially a recipient of information as opposed to engaging in a dialogue about the shoe. A fully interactive campaign would require more human intervention—this campaign utilized technology to draw the consumer into as much of an interactive experience as possible.

TARGET MARKET

Mediacom's McLean continued to discuss in Mahler's article how outdoor advertising reached target audiences more efficiently than other media did: "People aren't home all night on the Internet, despite what some might think. They're driving, shopping, going to arenas, travelling on subways, waiting for buses . . . And we want to catch them when they're out and about, when they're making the choice to purchase." Instead of separating these targeting techniques, Nike combined them to target consumers on the go while simultaneously enticing computer-proficient consumers to extend their interaction with the advertising on the Internet. Nike's youth-oriented targeting dovetailed perfectly with this strategy, as the younger generation grew up with computer technology. If anything, Nike used the print advertising as a gateway to reach this core target market of youths. "The cool thing is when grownups look at the ads, and don't know what it means," explained Wieden & Kennedy's Smith. "They aren't supposed to know. If they were getting it, then we'd be in trouble."

COMPETITION

In May 1998 a print advertisement appeared on the back cover of *ESPN Magazine* featuring a picture of an athlete

LIKE THOSE RAVE UNDERGROUND PARTIES

When asked why Nike's "Product Assault" campaign forced consumers to take the extra step of sending E-mail to receive the World Wide Web addresses for each shoe model instead of simply including those URLs in the ads, Nike advertising director for North America Chris Zimmerman explained that this more involved process was "more interactive." Wieden & Kennedy copywriter Jimmy Smith expounded further on this strategy in Kathy DeSalvo's *Shoot* article. "As far as the e-mail addresses, we just wanted a fully integrated campaign," Smith said. "We kind of thought of it as being like those rave underground parties, where you have a number that you call and then that takes you somewhere else. So you send e-mail to these addresses, and then it sends you back a message where to go to get to these other Nike web pages."

in running gear replicated 6,000 times. The advertiser went unidentified except for what appeared to be the address for a website, http://www.97005.com. Most consumers would not recognize the number as the zip code of Nike's corporate campus in Beaverton, Oregon. The website itself featured the same picture as the print ad, accompanied by a window containing the message "Learn," in addition to a box prompting viewers to enter their own E-mail addresses. Seemingly, this integrated ad extended Nike's existing campaign. But as it turned out, this was a teaser ad created for Nike's archrival, Reebok International, by Mindseye Technology. The campaign launched in earnest by sending announcements revealing the identity of the advertiser as Reebok to all of the E-mail addresses gathered by the teaser ad. The teaser website then transformed into a full-fledged ad for Reebok urging runners to "break out" of the mold that had become generic through overproliferation, a swipe at Nike's ubiquitous marketing, and instead to express individuality by wearing Reebok gear.

Nike's other main competitor, Fila USA, which doubled its sales between 1993 and 1997 to enter third place in the athletic shoe category behind Nike and Reebok, consolidated its $20 million advertising account under Arnell Group Brand Consultancy, New York, which had held $7 million of Fila's account. Despite award-winning creative work from Foote, Cone & Belding, New York, Fila awarded the entire account to Arnell for its expertise in building "corporate identity, branding and image development," according to Fila's vice president for advertising Howe Burch in Jeff Jensen's August 1997 *Advertising Age* article. Specifically, Fila was attempting to reposition itself as more of a performance brand without losing its identity as a fashion brand. Arnell's first assignment involved the November 1, 1997, launch of the Hill IV, a basketball sneaker named after professional player Grant Hill, which would retail for $90 after the previous model, the $100 Hill III, underperformed sales-wise. The campaign would appear in print, outdoor, and television advertising, as well as being pushed at the point of purchase, and ran into 1998.

MARKETING STRATEGY

Besides Hardaway, Nike's "Product Assault" campaign featured numerous other prominent athlete-celebrities with self-descriptive E-mail addresses endorsing specific shoe models: Alonzo Mourning of the Miami Heat (zo@bangonu.com) endorsed the Air Metal Force; boxer Roy Jones, Jr. (rjones@ringyobell.com), cross-trained in the Air Ubiquitous Max; Seattle Supersonic Gary Payton (gpayton@dyoazzup.com) flew in the Air Hawk Flight; Green Bay Packer Reggie White (rwhite@goodgawd) posed for the Air Cover Max; Detroit Lion Barry Sanders (bsanders@madeumiss.com) endorsed the Air Super Zoom; Olympic decathlete Dan O'Brien (dobrien@trynkeepup.com) ran in the Air Max; and Indiana Pacer Reggie Miller (rmiller@makeitrain.com) jumped in the Air Total Max. E-mail sent to these addresses received messages back from the address Email@webmail.nike.com.

Copywriter Tina Hall, in conjunction with the rest of the Wieden & Kennedy team—art director Gary Koepke, creative directors John Jay and Dan Wieden, and management supervisor Karen Brown—used spoken language in the reply messages, employing sports slang and everyday vernacular to make the messages sound authentic. For example, messages sent to O'Brien received the reply "Bet you were out running and you saw the new Air Max, right? Probably didn't get a real good look at it, though, because you just whizzed right by it, clipping off those sub-five-minute miles, huh? That's what we thought, so take your time checking out Dan O'Brien's new Air Max at http://www.trynkeepup.com." A message sent to Miller's address received the reply "So you've seen Reggie Miller's new Air Total Max, huh? Now when you finish practicing your jumpers, go check out http://www.makeitrain.com and witness the ultimate ride for sinkin' threes."

While the print ads ran on billboards as well as in consumer magazines such as *Sports Illustrated* and *Rolling Stone,* the campaign also included radio and television spots that ran on ESPN and MTV. In one television commercial the camera centered on a Nike Air Hawk Flight basketball sneaker resting on the dashboard of a car passing through a tollbooth while a radio broadcast of a Seattle Supersonics basketball game featuring the shoe's endorser Payton played on the car radio. Director Winters synchronized the play-by-play announcements to correspond with the car's progress through the tollbooth. As Payton "drives down the lane" of the basketball court, so too did the car with the shoe ornament drive down the tollbooth lane; when the car driver tossed the coin into the hopper to open the tollgate, the radio announced excitedly, "He's got it! Nothing but the bottom of the cup!" as if announcing the driver's coin toss instead of Payton's layup.

OUTCOME

Sorkin reported in his *Portland Oregonian* article that "interacting with the ads can be tedious." Indeed, the ads required much more patience than consumers were accustomed to in an age of instant gratification. Nike and Wieden & Kennedy, a team that had defined many of the marketing trends of the 1990s, trusted that consumers were oversaturated with advertising that did all the work for them and instead yearned for interactive advertising, especially as consumers became more and more adept at traversing the Internet. In fact, the technical knowledge required by the ads amounted to the most simple of Internet activities—sending E-mail and accessing websites. Furthermore, most advertising did not require any commitment from consumers, as they remained passive recipients of stimuli urging them to purchase the advertised products. This traditional form of advertising left a gap between the viewing of the ad and the purchasing of the product. Nike and Wieden & Kennedy sought to fill in this gap with interaction. If potential buyers entered the gateway of sending the E-mail message, then they had started the process of interaction with the product. This kind of commitment was more likely to lead to a purchase than passive viewing of the product.

Nike's Zimmerman summed up the campaign's strategy with his assessment in DeSalvo's *Shoot* article: "We're always looking for new and interesting ways to present our product... I think that as much as anything else, we thought that this was a very simple, honest and hopefully intriguing approach. In our marketing, we're passionate about a lot of things—sports, athletes." Zimmerman continued, "We want to show consumers how passionate we are about our products. I think [the 'Product Assault' campaign] was a fairly arresting approach visually."

FURTHER READING

Carmichael, Matt. "Mystery E-Mail." *Advertising Age,* May 18, 1998.

DeSalvo, Kathy. "Interactive Nike Ads Send Users to Internet for Sneaker Info: Print and Outdoor Campaign Features E-Mail." *Shoot,* August 8, 1997.

Jensen, Jeff. "Fila Unifies $20 Mil Acc't at Arnell Group: Late '97 Ad Push Planned for New Grant Hill Shoe." *Advertising Age,* August 25, 1997.

Sorkin, Andrew Ross. "Nike Tries to Get Consumers to Jog on Net." *Portland Oregonian,* July 23, 1997.

Wright, Lisa. "Forget All the New Technology—Outdoor Ads Are Booming." *The Toronto Star,* May 19, 1999.

William D. Baue

WHAT IF WE TREATED ALL ATHLETES THE WAY WE TREAT SKATEBOARDERS? CAMPAIGN

OVERVIEW

Nike, Inc. launched its first national advertising campaign portraying skateboarders in 1997. The three television ads that made up the effort used a pseudo-documentary style to depict the tribulations skateboarders suffered when they tried to practice their sport. "Running," "Golf," and "Tennis" showed participants in these three mainstream sports being derided and harassed simply for engaging in their chosen activities. Each spot closed with the tag line that served as the campaign's title: "What if we treated all athletes the way we treat skateboarders?" Created by San Francisco-based advertising agency Goodby, Silverstein & Partners, the campaign sought to "develop a relationship between the brand and the skaters, and change how [skaters] view[ed] Nike in skateboarding," a Goodby representative told *Adweek.*

Revamping its image among skateboarders would be no easy task for Nike. Nor was it an unimportant one. Nike's sales were falling, and the brand had lost some of its popularity with teenage consumers—the most profitable segment of the market for athletic footwear and apparel. Once the paragon of hip in youth footwear, the company had fallen into the ranks of the hopelessly uncool and could only watch as smaller rivals captured an ever greater share of the market. Nike had introduced a line of skateboarding shoes and clothing, but consumer reaction had been tepid. Nike hoped "Skateboarders" would boost the popularity of its offerings and drive sales, but the underlying purpose of the campaign was to change perceptions of the company within the youth market. Therefore, "Skateboarders" was conceived less to push a specific product than to gain the respect of the trendy skateboarding community and with it the loyalty of a new generation of consumers.

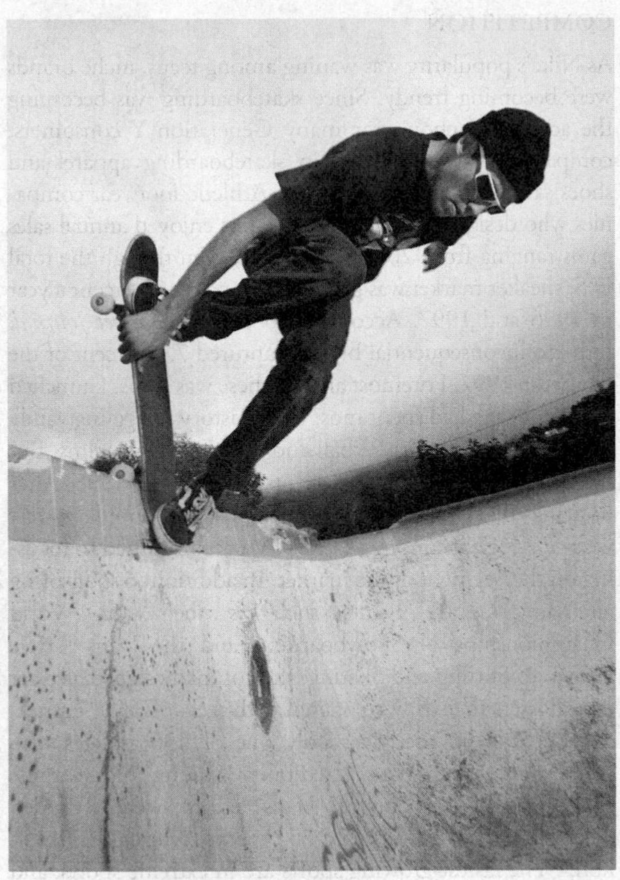

© TIM TADDER/CORBIS.

HISTORICAL CONTEXT

When former track athlete Phillip Knight founded Blue Ribbon Sports in 1964 and began selling shoes out of his car, few would have believed he was laying the foundation for the rise of one of the world's great mega-brands. But in 1972 Knight rechristened his company Nike, after the Greek goddess of victory, and set out to take the athletic shoe industry by storm. Before that time most firms just offered simple and inexpensive sneakers designed for multipurpose use. Nike, by contrast, began to make shoes for specific athletic endeavors and heavily touted the technological advances of its products. This strategy, coupled with Nike's development of a stable of superstar athlete endorsers, catapulted the Oregon-based firm to the top of the industry. In the 1990s alone athletes ranging from Michael Jordan to Tiger Woods donned the Nike swoosh and helped reinforce its association with elite athleticism and excellence. Despite the fact that market research showed that the vast majority of Nike consumers were more likely to hit the mall than the playing field in their new shoes, the brand's advertising drenched itself in sweat and athletic prowess and the company thrived. "We're in the sports business, not the shoe business," a Nike vice president told *Time* magazine. Between 1995 and 1998 Nike's average annual growth rate was 39 percent, and by 1998 it had seized nearly half the U.S. athletic shoe market.

By the late 1990s, however, cracks began to show in the seemingly impregnable Nike facade. Its footwear sales had dropped 18 percent in 1998, forcing the company to lay off 250 employees at its Beaverton, Oregon, headquarters. Most troubling for Nike was its poor image. While it had once cultivated an outsider image, Nike was increasingly lambasted in the media as a corporate marauder. Critics cited its labor practices in Asia as especially galling. In an effort to change these negative opinions, Nike dropped its famous "Just Do It" campaign in January 1998 in favor of the gentler "I Can," which celebrated everyday athletes more than the superstar professionals. The company also diversified into sports equipment, designing products ranging from baseball cleats to snowboards. As *Time* explained, "Nike is reassessing everything, from the way it sells to retailers to the number of times the famous swoosh appears in products and in advertising."

TARGET MARKET

Nike's efforts to shake its slump were hindered by a generational changing of the guard. While its athletic shoes had captivated both baby boomer and Generation X consumers, Nike proved to be less popular with the so-called Generation Y, or "echo-boom," generation—those consumers born between 1979 and 1994. It was this demographic group that Nike courted with the "Skateboarders" campaign. Generation Y was an essential market for Nike to reach. These children of the baby boomers numbered 60 million, three times the size of Generation X. They commanded an estimated total annual disposable income of between \$82.1 and \$108 billion, according to the *New York Daily News,* and exerted considerable influence over family purchases ranging from electronics to groceries. Since "Nike's best customers" were teens, as *Time* explained, the brand's sinking image was an obstacle to the company's continued success. *Business Week* confirmed that "Nike's sneaker sales are tumbling as the brand sinks in teen popularity polls."

In its effort to shore up its status among young people, Nike turned to skateboarding. According to the *Wall Street Journal,* 6.5 million skateboarders rolled across America's streets in 1998 alone. That number was expected to triple by 2001. Even more important was the fact that skateboarding was a tremendously popular sport among teens. As the *Journal* noted, extreme sports—which included snowboarding, skateboarding, and street luge, among others—"appeal to Generation

THEY DID IT

The resistance Nike initially faced in the skateboarding community was quite strong. Prior to the campaign many skaters had taken to wearing "Don't Do It" buttons, an unflattering reference to Nike's long-running "Just Do It" campaign.

Y . . . because they aren't the [sports] their parents grew up playing." Moreover, "boarding tend[ed] to have a dangerous edge parents view as rebellious, which is just fine by teenagers."

This was not the first time Nike had tried to get out on the cutting edge of youth fashion. In its basketball shoe advertising of the early 1990s, the company had stylishly portrayed the gritty culture of inner-city basketball and featured spokespeople such as outspoken bad boy Charles Barkley. These ads were designed to appeal particularly to the urban youths who acted as trendsetters for the rest of the teen and 20-something market. The strategy worked, as the popularity of Nikes among urban youth quickly translated to suburban success for the company. In the late 1990s skateboarders—much maligned by authority figures for their clothes, hair and piercing styles, and perceived rebelliousness—had partially taken over this fashion-setting role and played a large part in shaping the shoe buying patterns of the youth market. Nike hoped to repeat its earlier success by improving its cachet among this group.

Nike had some heavy baggage to overcome, however, before skateboard aficionados would accept the company. Nike's traditional formula of slick national advertising laden with superstar athletes was ineffective with echo-boomers, who were less prone to worship basketball, football, and baseball icons than previous generations. Although skateboarding was an Olympic exhibition sport in 1996, many potential participants—the heroes of Generation Y—spurned the competition because of the Games' burgeoning corporatism. Moreover, as a gigantic global conglomerate, Nike was loathed by many professional skateboarders who "regard[ed] corporations and organized communications as evils," explained the *San Francisco Examiner.* While the flashiness of a Jordan spot might not win over a teen consumer, that group did respond to "humor, irony, and the (apparently) unvarnished truth," reported *Business Week.* Nike made sure that its "Skateboarders" spots were imbued with these attributes.

COMPETITION

As Nike's popularity was waning among teens, niche brands were becoming trendy. Since skateboarding was becoming the activity of choice for many Generation Y consumers, companies that produced hip skateboarding apparel and shoes saw their market share rise. Athletic footwear companies who designed products for skaters enjoyed annual sales gains ranging from 20 to 50 percent, even though the total U.S. sneaker market was growing at a paltry 2 percent a year in 1996 and 1997. According to the *Wall Street Journal,* hitherto inconsequential brands captured 7.3 percent of the market in 1997. Foremost among these was Vans. Launched in 1966, Vans had spent most of its history struggling vainly against Nike in the basketball and running shoe realms. But the company radically changed its approach in 1995. After noticing that its clothes and shoes were popular street wear—especially among skaters—Vans committed to focusing on this segment of the market. In addition to sponsoring alternative sports events such as the Vans World Championships of Snowboarding and the Vans Triple Crown of Surfing and Skating, the company signed a roster of endorsers that truly resonated with teens. Daniel Franck, an elite snowboarder, was only one of 236 athletes who further enhanced Vans' credibility among the extreme sport-crazed echo-boomers. Vans' efforts were rewarded when its 1997 sales increased 26 percent to reach $159 million. "The fastest-growing sports are in extreme sports, and our target market, some 78 million strong, plays them," Vans' vice president of marketing told *Advertising Age.*

Another hip skating brand was Airwalk, which tripled its television ad budget in 1998 when it launched the "Airwalk: The Musical" campaign. With ad agency Lambesis, Airwalk created two commercials that ran on MTV and ESPN, as well as during Comedy Central's popular animated show *South Park.* The spots spoofed *The Sound of Music* in their portrayal of extreme athletes engaged in daring stunts. Airwalk also attempted to make its products more mainstream. To reach a broader audience, it expanded its print campaign to include general interest magazines, along with more youth-oriented mountain biking, snowboarding, and skateboarding publications.

Nike's effort to reinvigorate its brand image also confronted more familiar challengers, as Nike was not the only established athletic shoe company to covet the Generation Y market. Adidas, Nike's German rival, met with great success in 1998, when its sales increased 94 percent, making it the third best-selling brand in the United States. Perhaps because Adidas was viewed as less of a behemoth than Nike, it found greater acceptance in the youth segment of the market. In 1999 Adidas introduced its "Forever Sport" campaign, which presented both elite and everyday athletes. In one commercial 18-year-old tennis phenomenon Anna Kournikova hit a tennis ball as the words "Take Control of the Stadium" appeared on the screen. In another "Take Control of the Streets" flashed across the screen while a skateboarder jumped over various obstacles. Adidas also signed on as an official sponsor of the X Games, an annual extreme sport competition that was tremendously popular with echo-boomers.

MARKETING STRATEGY

As predominantly an image-rather than a product-driven campaign, the component ads of "Skateboarders" did not need to focus particularly on the actual business of buying and selling. Nike, therefore, was able to avoid the pitfalls of other youth-oriented campaigns that tried (and generally failed) to portray images of Generation Yers to themselves in a way that would actually resonate with those consumers. Instead, Nike strove to connect with its audience emotionally. Mindful that echo-boomers were highly skeptical of glossy marketing efforts, Nike sought to instill "Skateboarders" with as much authenticity as possible.

Goodby, which employed two veteran skateboarders on the campaign's creative team, used firsthand interviews with skaters to map its strategy. They discovered that skaters were often harassed by passersby, hounded by the police, and derided as being nonathletic. Goodby opted to turn "skaters' experience inside out" and use this concept as the campaign's foundation, an agency spokesperson told *Adweek*. Through a clever inversion, the three commercials vividly refracted the experiences of skaters. In "Running" two joggers were abused in the street. A women screamed at them, and an elderly man denounced them as crazy while drivers hurled garbage at the hapless pair. In "Golf" two players were arrested on the green simply for trying to play, while "Tennis" depicted the obstacles tennis players might encounter: after meeting stealthily for a midnight game, a security guard interrupted them and chased them away. In all these ads the implications of Nike's message were clear: skaters should be taken as seriously as other athletes, rather than treated as loitering delinquents.

Goodby realized that the spots' visuals would be as important as their message in reaching echo-boomers. Therefore, the spots were shot to look grainy and "low-budget." "[A] lot of skateboarders film themselves," *Shoot* noted, so the homemade feel contributed to the aura of authenticity Nike hoped to project. Moreover, the popularity of television programs featuring home videos had skyrocketed, especially among Nike's target audience. Shows ranging from *When Animals Attack* to *Scariest Police Chases* garnered a considerable audience on network television. Movie directors even adopted the faux-realist technique. "Kids," a bleak tale of alienation and despair among Generation Yers, used this same style to powerful effect. Nike designed its spots to be at home in this milieu.

Nike ran the campaign on a broad array of programs in order to connect with as wide a swath of its target audience as possible. But a cornerstone of the media strategy was the campaign's heavy rotation on ESPN and ESPN 2 during those networks' coverage of the X Games, which captured the exact demographic group Nike sought to reach. "The X Games has done a virtual full court press around males aged 12-to-34," the *Washington Post* reported. "According to ESPN, the Summer X Games delivered more viewers in that age group than any other sporting event, including the Super Bowl."

OUTCOME

Nike declared that "Skateboarders" succeeded in its attempt to reach younger consumers. The company told the *San Francisco Examiner* that it received scores of favorable letters, one of which praised Nike in the language of Generation Y: "Right on, dude." A Goodby spokesperson explained to *Adweek* a more subtle positive outcome of the campaign. Prior to the debut of the three commercials, Nike's massive size was its chief liability in the eyes of skating culture. They "viewed Nike as the ultimate big company—a corporation that, they suspected, didn't know anything about skateboarding." The "Skateboarders" ads made Nike's size seem beneficial. The spots "actually became a PR campaign for skateboarders with the general public, rendering Nike's 'bigness' a good thing," the Goodby spokesperson noted. Skateboarders played the ads in court as a defense against anti-skateboarding tickets. One skating magazine told the story of a cop who told skaters, "I agree with the Nike ads," and decided not to fine them. A skater wrote to the company that "Nike brought skateboarding something no one else could."

The campaign also won critical acclaim. "Skateboarders" was awarded the Grand Prix (the top prize) at the renowned International Advertising Festival in Cannes, France. Agency head Jeff Goodby expressed his theory about the campaign's true achievement to the *San Francisco Examiner:* "It was about something that is true. The best advertising, like the best of anything, resonates as something that is true."

FURTHER READING

Bourgeois, David. "Lowest Common Denominator: Are These Popular Low-Down, Cheap-Looking Shots Actually Low Budget?" *Shoot,* August 21, 1998.

"A Grassroots Plan to Bring Together Two Unlikely Allies: Nike and Skateboarders." *Adweek,* July 13, 1998.

Kelly, Keith. "The Wonder Years." *New York Daily News,* January 22, 1998.

Neuborne, Ellen, and Kathleen Kerwin. "Today's Teens—the Biggest Bulge Since the Boomers—May Force Marketers to Toss Their Old Tricks." *Business Week,* February 15, 1999.

Pereira, Joseph. "Going to Extremes: Board-Riding Youths Take Sneaker Maker on Fast Ride Uphill." *Wall Street Journal,* April 16, 1998.

Raine, George. "Bay Area Agencies." *San Francisco Examiner,* November 27, 1998.

Saporito, Bill. "Can Nike Get Unstuck?" *Time,* March 30, 1998.

Tuttle, Dennis. "On the Cutting Edge: Radical Sports Find a Foothold." *Washington Post,* January 11, 1998.

Rebecca Stanfel

WOMEN'S CAMPAIGN

OVERVIEW

Nike, Inc., the sports-shoe manufacturer whose use of celebrity athletes as endorsers had helped it become the dominant American brand in its category, began focusing an increasing amount of its marketing resources on women in the 1990s. By the mid-1990s Nike's women's shoes and apparel accounted for over a quarter of its total U.S. sales, and in 1995 the company released its highest-profile women's commercials to date. These early spots were among the first examples of what became known as "empowerment advertising." Nike experimented with other approaches in its women's-products advertising, and at times the brand's paeans to female athleticism were greeted with skepticism, but regardless of Nike's motives, in these campaigns the company consistently sought to address issues that were important to American women.

Among the early empowerment spots—created by longtime Nike advertising agency Wieden+Kennedy of Portland, Oregon—was one that pointed out the dramatic social, health, and psychological benefits that girls derived from participation in sports. Another equated a girls' sports team with a pack of wolves. In 1997–98 Nike, with spots created by San Francisco's Goodby, Silverstein & Partners, moved away from the empowerment message to focus on the emotional drama of a fictional high-school girls' basketball team during a championship season. Spots featuring female Olympic athletes also ran in 1998, and a similar focus on the U.S. women's soccer team prevailed in 1999, before Goodby was relieved of its duties.

Nike lost market share during this period, but it effectively laid the groundwork for a sustained emphasis on women's products, which promised more possibilities for future growth than any of its other lines. Wieden+Kennedy's work for Nike at the start of the new century included a return to empowerment-themed advertising.

HISTORICAL CONTEXT

As early as the 1980s Nike began to extend its marketing specifically to women, but these efforts were not especially effective since most of the company's energy was directed to its high-profile men's advertising. By 1990, however, the company, under prodding from some of its own women executives, woke up to the potential of the women's market and began to address it seriously in its advertising. By 1992 Nike was seeing substantial sales gains in the category. Having started by redesigning the shoes for women's different bodies and patterns of use, the company recognized that its advertising, too, might need to take a different approach if it was to have a positive impact on women. Following a series of women-centered campaigns created largely by women at Wieden+Kennedy, Nike was widely praised for its progressive, proactive stance.

The changes in Nike's marketing of women's sports products came after 20 years of changes in the way U.S. educational institutions treated girls' sports programs in general. The passage of Title IX in 1972—the same year Nike was founded—marked a turning point for women's athletics because it barred sex discrimination by any institution receiving federal funding. Furthermore, the new law required schools to offer sports programs for males and females based on their proportional enrollment numbers. The result was a steady increase in the number of girls participating in school sports, from 1 in 27 at the high-school level in 1972 to 1 in 3 in the 1990s, according to the Women's Sports Foundation. Nike spokeswoman Kathryn Reith saw the changes that had overtaken the category of women's athletic footwear as cumulative. "From my perspective," she observed, "there's been evolution, not revolution. Most of the greatest growth probably occurred in the '70s."

During the 1980s Nike stuck to building its reputation as the premier maker of high-performance men's shoes and apparel. The bulk of the women's market was left to Reebok, L.A. Gear, Avia, and others, all of whom tended to downplay technical features in favor of the more traditional appeal of fashion. It was not until the 1990s that Nike began to see women as a vast, largely untapped market for high-tech, high-performance footwear and apparel. Many pointed to the generation that came of age under Title IX as the most significant factor in this development. Suddenly girls who had grown up playing team sports like basketball, volleyball, and soccer were reaching the national stage. Nowhere was this more apparent than at the 1996 Olympic Games in Atlanta, Georgia, where many of the biggest winners for Team U.S.A. were women. Nike signed basketball player Lisa Leslie and soccer player Mia Hamm to endorsement contracts. With more than a quarter of its sales coming

NIKE ACCUSED OF EXPLOITING WOMEN

In 1997 Nike's positive reputation as a leader in advertising to women was undermined by the revelation that it used cheap labor—most of it women and young girls—in the Asian factories it contracted with to make many of the company's products. A coalition of women that included Congresswoman Maxine Waters of California, author Alice Walker, and the National Organization of Women (NOW) wrote to Nike's CEO, Phil Knight, to say, "While the women who wear Nike shoes in the U.S. are encouraged to perform their best, the Indonesian, Vietnamese and Chinese women making the shoes often suffer from inadequate wages, corporal punishment, forced overtime and/or sexual harassment." Ironically, the message and tone of the company's earlier commercials seemed to inflame the situation even more. Elizabeth Toledo, vice president of NOW, commented, "when companies try to make their products into a feminist statement, they had better back it up by corporate policies."

from women's products, the company was now convinced of the financial wisdom of marketing to women.

TARGET MARKET

Nike's natural demographic profile for the campaign was young women ages 18 to 34 who had an interest in athletics. This was the Title IX generation, those who had grown up participating in team sports at their schools and who found athletic activity a natural part of their lives. It was also an age group that was actively concerned with brands in defining its identity and that had disposable income to spend on premium-priced athletic shoes. In Nike's early print advertising to women, the messages spoke directly to women living on their own for the first time and addressed the issue of separating their own identity from that of their families. One headline typical of the campaign said, "You do not have to be your mother," with the ad going on to address its audience in the intimate, conversational manner of a close friend. As a corollary, the market also included teenage girls who would be entering the primary group within five years, the girls specifically featured in Nike's "If You Let Me Play" commercial. Yet the spot spoke to their parents as much as to the girls themselves. Empowerment in this case had to include the financial decision makers. In 1996 Nike sponsored *Sports Illustrated*'s special *Sports Illustrated for Kids* editions as a way of getting in front of this important demographic segment during the years when children were first forming brand loyalties.

COMPETITION

Nike had long dominated the athletic-shoe industry it had helped to shape. In 1996 *Sporting Goods Intelligence* estimated Nike's share of the market at 37 percent, with second-place Reebok trailing at 21 percent. Nike was three times as big as number three Fila and number four adidas combined. Yet in the women's segment of the market the situation was quite different. Nike had long seemed locked into its male-oriented market position and even appeared uncomfortable when attempting to reach out to women. One ad during the late 1980s sounded as if Nike's agency, Wieden+Kennedy, were trying to talk to women in the same way it talked to men. "It wouldn't hurt to stop eating like a pig, either," accused a copy line. During the 1980s Nike had been beaten by rival Reebok in the marketing of women's aerobic shoes. Misjudging the potential size of the market for comfortable exercise footwear for women, Nike had stayed out, allowing Reebok to gain a dominant share. Other rivals, including Keds, L.A. Gear, and Avia, also took advantage of Nike's absence to establish their own sizable market shares. Therefore, when Nike began to take the women's market seriously in the 1990s, it faced the prospect of competing against companies that had been talking to women for years. As it launched its first serious campaigns aimed at women, most of the company's competitors immediately stepped up their own marketing efforts as well.

MARKETING STRATEGY

The empowerment advertising exemplified by "If You Let Me Play" and the other spots in Wieden+Kennedy's 1995 television work for Nike's women's division was addressed at least as much to parents as to the girls themselves. It recognized that the parents of Title IX girls were themselves of a generation that had grown up accepting social change. Now they were the parent coaches, the school-board members, and the teachers who were making many of the key decisions concerning girls' sports programs. Nike spokeswoman Vizhier Corpus noted, "Our message, which is directed to parents, is that sports [are] no less valuable to girls than to boys. If you are a parent interested in raising a girl who is physically and emotionally strong, then look to sports as a means to that end."

One often-noted spot presented young girls speaking over a montage of powerful women athletes. In somber yet unsentimental tones, they spoke of the advantages to their physical and psychological health of being allowed to play sports: "If you let me play I will be 60 percent less likely to get breast cancer"; "I will suffer less depression if you let me play sports"; "I will be more likely to leave a man who beats me." Such statements were typical of the messages. Although some critics thought that the spot did not empower girls so much as put them back into the supplicant's role, the commercial was received mostly positively by its target market, the parents of young girls as well as the girls themselves. Another spot in the series compared a girls' sports team to a pack of wolves ready to pounce, breaking with the stereotype of girls as less aggressive athletes.

Despite mostly positive response to the spots, Nike reassigned its women's advertising early in 1997 to the San Francisco agency Goodby, Silverstein & Partners, which changed the tone of the advertising from empowerment to a more performance-oriented message. (Nike retained its long-term affiliation with Wieden+Kennedy, its marketing partner since 1982, but announced that the agency had been reduced to equal status with Goodby.) Goodby, a more research-friendly agency than Wieden+Kennedy, discovered that the empowerment message was beginning to wear thin with the market, and Nike, in the midst of corporate soul-searching brought on by public criticism of its labor practices as well as by falling profits, decided that it was time to address the market directly. The result was a documentary-style series of nine spots focusing on a fictitious high-school girls' basketball team, the Charleston Cougars. Called "A Championship Season," the campaign was introduced in late 1997 and ran through the first half of 1998. Individual spots captured specific moments in the Cougars' march toward their championship, and as a whole the series was meant to transmit an insider's sense of the ups and downs, anguish, joy, and drama inherent in school sports. Avoiding even a tagline or logo, much less a direct sales pitch, the commercials lingered only long enough on the girls' shoes to identify the Nike brand. A company representative noted, "The Wieden spot was aimed more at parents, while this work talks to the girls themselves." Goodby also crafted a series of Nike commercials that aired during the 1998 Winter Olympics; they featured poems written at Nike's request to celebrate female U.S. Olympic athletes.

In 1999 Goodby focused on the U.S. national women's soccer team, favorites to win that summer's Women's World Cup. The campaign, tagged "We Will Take On the World as a Team," used humorous exaggeration of the superstar players' devotion to their teammates. For instance, one spot showed a young man arriving for a date with one of the team's players, Tisha Venturini, only to find that her teammates Mia Hamm, Brandi Chastain, Briana Scurry, and Tiffney Milbrett would be joining them for the evening. Another spot showed a group of uniformed players in a dentist's office, kicking a ball around aimlessly to the off-camera sound of a dentist's drill. Brandi Chastain then emerged into the waiting room and told her teammates that she had just gotten two fillings. Mia Hamm stood and requested two fillings. "But Mia," the dentist said. "I just examined your teeth. They're perfect." Hamm insisted on submitting to the same treatment as her teammate, and the rest of the players followed her lead, each insisting that she would have two fillings as well. The spirit of teamwork proved so potent and contagious that the dentist's receptionist stood and announced that she, too, wanted two fillings.

Chastain went on to provide Nike with an unexpected boost when, upon kicking the penalty shot that gave the U.S. team the World Cup championship, she celebrated by removing her shirt on live TV. Underneath her uniform Chastain was wearing a Nike Inner Actives sports bra, a product that the company was then readying for launch. Though presumably unrelated to Chastain's act, the Inner Actives print campaign mounted soon after the World Cup similarly tweaked societal conventions regarding the female body. One noteworthy ad featured a frontal view of a woman's bare upper body with text reading, "Exercise and tone every muscle in your body, except the one in your breast."

OUTCOME

The print campaign for the Inner Actives line would be Goodby's last for Nike; in late 1999 the company consolidated its entire advertising account once again with Wieden+Kennedy. "We were hired during hard times for the client in order to offer a different perspective and shake things up," Goodby creative director and cochairman Rich Silverstein told *Adweek*. "I think we did our job." Similarly, Nike maintained that the move had more to do with streamlining its brand advertising than any dissatisfaction with the Goodby work.

Ironically, Nike's past successes made it vulnerable to a backlash from those who saw the company's very dominance as reason to choose other brands that spoke more directly to a woman's individuality. In that case, the company would have to look beyond marketing to its own corporate philosophy. An *Adweek* editorial in January 1998 questioned, "Has the brand become so big that sporting a baseball cap with a swoosh now says more about the power of Nike than it does about the person wearing it? If so, Nike is vulnerable. . . . Cutting-edge advertising may not be enough to keep Nike on the cutting edge." Even as the company consolidated its advertising at Wieden+Kennedy again, it remained unclear how the megabrand would deal with this challenge in the years to come.

Wieden+Kennedy's first women's effort after resuming responsibility for this portion of the Nike account came during the 2000 Summer Olympics, and it did not resonate in the way the agency had hoped it would. The spot showed Olympic runner Suzy Hamilton being pursued through her house and into a forest by a masked, chainsaw-wielding man. Hamilton's speed and endurance were too much for the villain, who was shown dropping his chainsaw and walking away, as onscreen text appeared, reading, "Why sport? Because you'll live longer." Although the commercial was meant to spoof horror-film conventions, many felt that it made light of violence against women, and NBC, the network broadcasting the Olympics, pulled it from the programming schedule after the first few days of its intended run.

In 2001 Wieden+Kennedy changed tactics in its work for Nike's women's lines, relying on depictions of ordinary women for whom fitness was a way of life, rather than using celebrity athletes with whom female athletes were expected to identify. This shift marked a partial return to the focus on empowerment that had initially raised Nike's profile among women. Nike increasingly pinned its hopes for future growth on the women's market for sports apparel and footwear, which was then growing much more rapidly than the men's market for such products.

FURTHER READING

Adamsak, Phil. "Nike Maps Growth Plan in Women's Activewear." *Women's Wear Daily,* September 23, 1997, p. 2.

Dawson, Angela, and Joan Voight. "The Party's Over." *Adweek* (western ed.), November 29, 1999.

Elliott, Stuart. "Television Campaigns Are Creating Some Controversy during the Summer Games." *New York Times,* September 19, 2000.

Grimm, Matthew. "The Sneaker Warriors Gun for Women." *Adweek's Marketing Week,* March 23, 1992, p. 12.

Hartlein, Robert. "Nike: Women's Push Pays Off." *Women's Wear Daily,* February 5, 1992, p. S6.

Jenson, Jeff, and Alice Z. Cuneo. "Goodby's 1st Nike Ads Back Biking, Boarding: Agency Also Preparing Women's Campaign for Later This Summer." *Advertising Age,* June 16, 1997, p. 2.

Lippert, Barbara. "Power Positions." *Adweek* (eastern ed.), February 12, 2001.

———. "Team Mia." *Adweek* (western ed.), June 21, 1999.

LoRusso, Maryann. "Women from Mars: Through New Marketing Strategies, Athletic Companies Are Reinforcing the Importance of Female Consumers." *Footwear News,* February 16, 1998, p. 30.

Magiera, Marcy. "Nike Has Women in Mind." *Advertising Age,* January 4, 1993, p. 36.

Melville, Greg. "Touting the Line." *Footwear News,* July 7, 1997, p. 22.

"That Can-Do Spirit." *Adweek* (midwest ed.), January 12, 1998.

Voight, Joan. "Change of Tack on Nike Spots." *Adweek,* December 22, 1997.

Voight, Joan, and Eleftheria Parpis. "Adweek Feature." *Adweek,* June 22, 1998.

Williams, Christopher. "Girl Talk." *Barron's,* October 15, 2001.

Patrick Hutchins
Mark Lane

Nikon Corporation

1300 Walt Whitman Road
Melville, New York 11747
USA
Telephone: (631) 547-4200
Fax: (631) 547-0299
Web site: www.nikonusa.com

MASS MARKET INITIATIVE CAMPAIGN

OVERVIEW

Nikon Corporation, well known for its high-end cameras embraced by professional photographers and advanced amateurs, faced an increasingly challenging marketplace in the final years of the twentieth century. The market for film cameras was saturated, and the emerging digital-camera market was crowded with competition. In addition to such old-line rivals as Canon, Minolta, and Olympus, Nikon had to contend with well-heeled newcomers, including Hewlett-Packard and Sony. Starting in 2000 Nikon and its ad agency, Minneapolis-based Fallon Worldwide, made a concerted effort to extend the Nikon brand to the mass market.

Nikon introduced a number of new products geared toward the general consumer, and the company scored a hit in 2001 with the Coolpix 775, a best-selling camera during that year's holiday season. The campaign reached a peak in 2002 with the airing of the first Nikon television spot in eight years. The spot, titled "The Search," supported the launch of the Coolpix 2500, the first camera to feature a swivel lens. Although there was no announced budget for the campaign, Nikon had steadily ratcheted up its advertising budget, which grew from \$11.7 million in 2000 to \$18.2 million in 2001 and to almost \$20 million in 2002.

While Fallon made some progress in positioning Nikon in the mass market, the two parties experienced creative differences. In October 2002 Nikon severed its business with Fallon, and the mass-market campaign came to an end.

HISTORICAL CONTEXT

Founded as an optical glass company in 1917, Nikon did not make its first camera until 1946, following the lead of two other Japanese companies, Canon and Minolta. Japan at the time was occupied by U.S. forces, who bought the Japanese cameras in post exchanges and brought them home. The Nikon cameras were especially well regarded because of their high quality. During the Korean War, U.S. combat photographers asked Nikon to produce lenses that would fit their German Leica cameras, and soon professional photographers of all types were singing the praises of Nikon lenses and cameras. By the mid-1960s photographers for such major magazines as *Life* and *National Geographic* relied on Nikon cameras, which had become accepted as professional-grade while also attracting the interest of advanced amateurs. While Canon and Minolta branched off into making office equipment such as copiers and printers, Nikon remained focused on high-end cameras. In 1983 it gained a foothold in the low end of the market with the introduction of its successful One-Touch camera. But by then the camera business was mature and offered few opportunities for sustained growth.

In the 1980s Nikon placed more emphasis on other optical equipment—such as binoculars, eyeglass lenses, and sunglasses—and diversified into consumer electronics, developing scanners and printers. During the 1990s the camera industry underwent a major upheaval, as digital-camera technology came into its own and quickly surpassed traditional film cameras. The digital revolution also brought with it a new batch of competitors, including Hewlett-Packard, Nokia, and Samsung, electronics companies with no reputation in the photography field but with the advertising muscle to carve out shares in the digital-photography market. In 1997 Nikon introduced the Coolpix line of consumer-priced digital cameras. The first product, the Coolpix 300, was a disappointment. Despite a sleek design it produced poor pictures. Nikon made steady progress on the Coolpix line, albeit enjoying more success on the high end of the market.

As the 1990s came to a close, Nikon possessed a brand with an excellent reputation among professionals and camera enthusiasts, but it still faced a challenge in extending the brand to the mass market. Ever since Nikon hired Minneapolis-based ad agency Fallon McElligott in 1994, the mandate had been to extend the brand. In 2000 the agency (renamed Fallon Worldwide that year) at last launched an intense effort to establish Nikon in the mass market and to promote the company's new line of less-expensive digital cameras. To become more accessible Nikon also moved beyond its traditional channels of specialty photo stores and catalogs and added mass-market retailers such as Target to its distribution network.

TARGET MARKET

Most digital-camera makers concentrated on the huge family market, targeting women in particular. According to studies roughly three-quarters of all family pictures were taken by women. Wives and mothers were also the stewards of family memories and the maintainers of the photo albums. It was understandable that the likes of Kodak and Fuji Film would focus on this large slice of the market. Nikon opted instead to target a different demographic of the amateur-photography market: younger people—25 to 35 years of age, 45 at the outside—who were more technologically savvy and likely to be impressed by Nikon's innovations. The company further reasoned that these consumers would also be attracted to Nikon's reputation for quality.

COMPETITION

Nikon continued to compete on the high end of the photography market with longtime rivals Minolta, Canon, Olympus, and Kodak. It fought for market share on the lower end with these companies plus a range of newcomers who had arrived on the camera scene as a result of the switch from film to digital technology. These companies included Hewlett-Packard, Nokia, Samsung, and Sony. Because they all possessed other successful product lines in consumer electronics, they had already established the distribution channels needed to sell digital cameras at a mass-merchandising level. Moreover the digital entrants all had the kind of financial backing needed to launch aggressive advertising campaigns and to essentially buy credibility in the market. Their combined marketing heft was also instrumental in the rapid rise of digital technology, which supplanted film cameras at a faster-than-expected pace. Two traditional camera companies, Kodak and Fuji, were especially caught off guard because they had been reluctant to give up the highly profitable sale of film and fully embrace digital photography.

Cameras, which were not especially profitable, were actually of secondary importance to many of Nikon's competitors. Most of the companies instead jockeyed to control the output side of the business: the print market. While the competition was developing home printers and self-service kiosks, Nikon remained focused on cameras, but it was not certain that its cachet with professionals would carry over to the mass market, where price was a key factor. In 2000 about two-thirds of digital cameras sold for $69 or less, placing a heavy burden on Nikon's marketers to convince customers to spend the extra money on a Nikon camera, the least expensive of which, the One-Touch, cost $129.

MARKETING STRATEGY

In 2000 Nikon introduced a number of new 35-millimeter digital cameras geared toward the mass market, including the One-Touch Zoom 90QD and the Light-Touch Zoom 120ED/QD. In May of that year Nikon ran the

CREATIVE DIFFERENCES

Nikon's "The Search" was the first U.S. television spot for its South African director, Kim Geldenhuys, who had to cut both 30- and 60-second versions. "I found it very frustrating to have to do a 30-second spot and put so much into it," he told Adam Remson of *Shoot* magazine. "It is a new discipline for me because we've always been able to do sixty-second spots [in South Africa]. And if not a sixty, we could do a fifty or a fifty-five or a forty-five. We have got these really strange lengths that we can make commercials over here."

first ads for these products in consumer magazines, making the point that Nikon cameras were not just for professionals. But Nikon also did not neglect the high-end digital market, introducing the $1,000 Coolpix 990, which was promoted in photo and computer magazines with ads aimed at the "discriminating digital camera user," according to a Fallon spokesperson.

All told Nikon spent $11.7 million on advertising in 2000, but as the company made a greater push to enter the mass market, its ad budget rose to $18.2 million in 2001. The primary digital camera it promoted was the Coolpix 775, listed at $399, a price at which consumers were willing to stretch to buy a Nikon product and one that afforded a profit in a low-margin field. Todd Wasserman of *Brandweek* quoted market research analyst Michelle Slaughter as saying the Coolpix "was a very strong product for [Nikon] at a very competitive price point." It was one of the best-selling digital cameras during the 2001 holiday season. The supporting advertising campaign featured actress Kim Cattrall (from *Sex and the City*) as a spokesperson. Her endorsements consisted of hosting promotional events and appearing with the Coolpix 775 during interviews. Nikon also conducted a guerilla-marketing van tour across the United States to offer consumers a chance to try out the Coolpix 775.

In 2002 Nikon launched another product in the Coolpix line, the Coolpix 2500, priced on store shelves at $379.99. It was in support of this product that Nikon's mass-market push reached its culmination and resulted in the production of Nikon's first television commercial in eight years. The spot, called "The Search," evolved from the experience of Fallon's creative team with the camera. "It's not like picking up a normal camera," Fallon's group creative director Bruce Bildsten told Aaron Baar of *Adweek*. "It has a quality to it. You just want to pick it up and play with it." The defining feature of the Coolpix 2500 was an inner swivel lens, which allowed the user to take a self-portrait or a picture of the sky, among other things, without tilting the camera. According to Baar, "as Bildsten and his team worked on ways to target young, digitally aware consumers, curious passersby took a fancy to a prototype of the camera.... That idea, coupled with Nikon's target of 25- to 35-year-olds, suggested a party where the camera gets passed around the crowd."

For the commercial "The Search," Fallon chose the award-winning South African director Kim Geldenhuys, who had directed spots for BMW in European markets. Fallon was BMW North America's ad agency, so it was already familiar with the director's work. Because it was much less expensive to work in South Africa, the spot was filmed there. It was done in 18-hour days, during which Geldenhuys attempted to create a nonstop party, hiring a DJ and urging the actors to mingle during their downtime. As a result several improvised moments made their way into the commercial.

In "The Search" a gawky 20-something man at a party took a picture of himself against a sunset, drawing the attention of two attractive women, who asked to look at the camera and then took it inside. The young man chased the camera throughout the crowded party. When he finally caught up to it, it was in the possession of two different women. To determine if the camera really was his, the women scrolled through the camera's memory of pictures, finally coming across an embarrassing one of him. Highly amused by what they saw, they handed over the camera and left him to offer the awkward defense, "It's just a hobby." The spot's concluding line was "The one that swivels." The nature of the embarrassing picture and the man's "hobby" were left to the audience's imagination. "For all we know, it could be him wearing an engineer's hat, just playing with model trains," Bildsten told Baar. "The Search" was aired for the first time in late April 2002 during *The Late Show with David Letterman.* Afterward it was shown on a variety of network shows and national cable channels. For 2002 Nikon increased its advertising budget to nearly $20 million, most of which supported the company's strategy of gaining a foothold in the mass market.

OUTCOME

While Fallon's mass-market initiative met with some success, especially with the Coolpix 775 in 2001, it was not enough to overcome the creative differences that had developed between the agency and client. Six months after the "The Search" premiered, Nikon and Fallon terminated their relationship, the client stating in a press release that "the time was right to explore new creative options in our advertising activities." For its part Fallon was tight-lipped, merely saying, "We've been proud to represent this highly revered brand, and we wish them every success in the future." According to *Adweek* 's Baar, however, "Nikon's conservative, retail-oriented ad approach clashed with Fallon's desire to craft brand-image ads. The client wanted to use an actor in its ads; the agency didn't." Shortly after the split, in fact, Nokia turned to its retail-marketing agency, Source Communications, and created a spot that featured actor Val Kilmer.

FURTHER READING

Baar, Aaron. "The Inside Pitch: Nikon—Melville, N.Y." *Adweek,* February 3, 2003, p. 20.

———. "Popular Photography." *Adweek,* April 29, 2002, p. 20.

Beardi, Cara. "Nikon Extends Brand to Mass Market." *Advertising Age,* April 3, 2000, p. 26.

Kawamoto, Wayne. "Nikon Coolpix 300." *Presentations,* December 1997, p. 13.

Lauro, Patricia. "Nikon and Fallon End Relationship." *New York Times,* October 30, 2002, p. C8.

"Nikon Returns to TV with Fallon Spot." *Adweek* (Midwest ed.), April 15, 2002, p. 9.

Remson, Adam. "Kim Geldenhuys: The American Dream Visits South Africa." *Shoot,* October 18, 2002, p. 42.

Wasserman, Todd. "Nikon Focuses on Mass Market with TV." *Brandweek,* April 22, 2002, p. 4.

Ed Dinger

THE NIKON SCHOOL CAMPAIGN

OVERVIEW

Nikon Corporation, one of the leading manufacturers of professional photography equipment, ran an advertising campaign in 1997 to invite photographers of all skill levels to participate in the Nikon School, a seminar that traveled to cities across the United States. The advertisements ran exclusively in print media, including numerous photography magazines. One spot, "Tip #5," featured a close-up photograph of a cat and a small dog looking at each other. Below them, a mouse crouched on a dinner plate and nibbled at a piece of food as if oblivious to the larger animals looming over it. The caption read, "Tip #5: Some photo opportunities only last a second." A block of smaller text continued, "For some reason, we feel compelled to open by mentioning the lunch that comes with our 8-hour class. But more importantly, our expert instructors will teach you everything from basic composition to advanced exposure techniques. You also get the 157-page Nikon School Handbook, all for a mere $95." Nikon's tracking studies revealed that inquiries about the school increased sharply after the ads ran, and in many cases attendance at the seminars was higher than the company had anticipated. The campaign was developed by Fallon McElligott, which had been named advertising agency of the year in 1995 by *Advertising Age.*

HISTORICAL CONTEXT

Nikon, a global company based in Japan, was established in 1917 when three optical manufacturers merged. By 1997 the company was making many types of optical equipment, including cameras and other photography products, microscopes, binoculars, electronic imaging equipment, eyeglasses, and surveying instruments. It was one of the few companies that handled all the steps in the manufacturing of optical equipment, from making glass to shaping, polishing, and assembling lenses. Optical technology by Nikon was used in the radiometer with an optical sensor that produced visible, near-infrared light for the Advanced Earth Observing Satellite called Midori, which had been launched in 1996. The company also produced a large objective mirror for astronomical telescopes, and its research into the properties of the spectrum was being applied to fields such as astronomy, biotechnology, and the making of semiconductors. In response to demand for high-quality equipment for professional photographers, the company began manufacturing camera lenses in 1932, selling more than 24 million by 1997. It made 35mm format cameras since the 1940s and was one of five companies that cooperated to develop the Advanced Photo System (APS), an alternative to 35mm cameras and film that was introduced in 1996. Nikon's share of the worldwide photographic products market had varied over a five-year period, with 6.8 percent of the market in 1997, 3.6 percent in 1996, 1.3 percent in 1995, 8.5 percent in 1994, and 4.1 percent in 1993.

Because Nikon photographic equipment was used extensively by professionals, the company's advertising had frequently used technical language to describe the quality and versatility of the products. One ad in a photography magazine in 1993 consisted of an impressive landscape photograph and a picture of a Nikon camera surrounded by fourteen paragraphs of text full of highly technical information such as: "By adding the Nikon SB-24 AF Speedlight, you can automatically balance the flash illumination with ambient background light without calculating fill-flash ratios." The ad featured the tag line Nikon had used for years, "We Take the World's Greatest Pictures." In 1994, at the suggestion of ad agency Fallon McElligott, the tag line was expanded to "We Take the World's Greatest Pictures. Yours." The addition of the one word made the company's products seem more relevant and accessible to the average consumer without alienating the professional photographers who had been Nikon's biggest customers.

The Nikon School was established in 1993 to help amateurs, semi-professionals, and professionals improve their skills in 35mm photography. Its intensive, one-day sessions replaced a similar program that had featured two-day sessions. Each year the courses were offered on weekends in cities across the United States. Using lectures and slide shows, the school's instructors covered topics such as composition, flash photography, and photographing natural phenomena such as rainbows and sunsets. Because students had a broad range of skill levels, the Nikon School had to be interesting enough for advanced students but not too difficult for novices.

TARGET MARKET

Many of Nikon's advertisements in 1997 targeted the general public. In that year the company ran the "Nikon School" campaign and also a series of simple, uncluttered

PROMOTIONAL VIDEOTAPES

The Nikon School was also publicized through the "Nikon Masters Series," a video collection of some of the world's best photographers working in their fields of expertise. The series featured interviews, documentary footage, and photography on location. Along with an inside perspective on professionals at work, the videos showed how accomplished photographers used Nikon equipment. The series covered photojournalism, wildlife photography, portraits, action shots, and the use of light to make exceptional pictures. Beginning in August 1997 the videotapes were available from Nikon dealers and directly from Nikon Corporation.

spots for its photographic equipment. Ads from two or more of the company's campaigns frequently appeared in the same issue of magazines such as *Popular Photography.* One camera advertisement featured a snapshot of a young man swimming beneath the words, "You point it. You shoot it. You frame the sucker." Smaller text added, "When we say the N50 is easy to use, we don't mean 'easy for people who've won Pulitzers for Photography.' We mean seriously simple, as in, hand it to an average dad and say, 'push here.' In Simple Mode, you can literally point the N50, shoot it, and capture frame-worthy, SLR-quality images like this. The camera is positively foolproof. Or more to the point, dad-proof." The ad concluded with the new tag line "We Take the World's Greatest Pictures. Yours."

Although Nikon had broadened its marketing efforts to appeal to the average consumer, the company had not abandoned the professionals who had always been its core customers. One magazine advertisement in 1997 invited photographers to visit Montana with their cameras. Positioned next to spectacular pictures of mountains in Glacier National Park was text explaining why a professional photographer had used Nikon equipment to make the images, how he had composed them, the type of lenses he had chosen, the aperture settings, and the shutter speeds he used. The language was simple enough for an amateur to understand, but it provided details of interest to more advanced photographers.

By explaining the basics of photography along with advanced techniques, the Nikon School appealed to consumers with a broad range of skill levels, but most considered themselves amateurs or advanced amateurs. Some had recently purchased a sophisticated, single-lens-reflex camera, and they wanted to learn how to use it effectively. Some simply wanted a better understanding of photography in general. Others had studied photography in the past but needed a refresher course that would inform them about the latest equipment and techniques. Some had attended previous sessions of the school and knew how valuable the classes could be. "Repeat visitors to the school treat the experience as if it were a pilgrimage. They are seeking inspiration and renewal for their craft. And they know from prior experience that they will get it," said Tom McEnery, management supervisor with Fallon McElligott.

COMPETITION

In 1997 some of Nikon's competitors also ran magazine advertisements that featured photography tips for readers. A two-page spread for Fuji Photo Film U.S.A. (commonly known as Fujifilm) in the March issue of *Popular Photography* was timed to coincide with the airing of the magazine's cable television program *Freeze Frame: Switzerland.* A team of still photographers using Fujifilm products had traveled throughout Switzerland with cinematographers from the Travel Channel, taking pictures on assignment for *Popular Photography* and providing tips for viewers who wanted to improve their travel shots. The magazine advertisement featured a large background photograph of Europe's largest glacier filling a valley between jagged mountains. Smaller photographs of Swiss scenery and the television program's participants were superimposed over the large picture, along with explanatory text. The captions outlined the content of the program, listed the dates and times at which it could be seen on television, provided tips for taking photographs like those in the ad, and told which film and equipment made by Fujifilm had been used to make each image.

Another competitor, Sigma Corporation of America, ran a series of magazine advertisements that showed how professional photographers used the company's products to take spectacular pictures. One ad featured a large photograph that had been shot through the railing of a bridge on the Thames River in England. The caption read, "For this assignment, I went back to this familiar bridge on the Thames and made some fresh discoveries. The Sigma lens I chose is light, compact, and easy to operate." The text went on to explain some of the advantages of that lens, along with the aperture and shutter speed used to make the photograph. Another advertisement was dominated by a photograph of an unusual, rounded structure with a metallic exterior. The caption read, "Amid buildings and sites stamped in history, at the south bank of the Thames, you suddenly come upon futuristic scenes. The Sigma lens I chose to photograph this scene responded accurately to my design."

Another series of advertisements promoted the New York Institute of Photography's correspondence course. A two-page ad in *Popular Photography* called the institute the "world's oldest and largest photography school" and said, "We guarantee you'll be a better photographer! Send for free booklet to learn how NYI will bring out your hidden talent. For well over 80 years NYI has helped promising amateurs become successful photographers. Now our new 'Century 2000' Method makes learning at home easier and more enjoyable than ever." The ad explained that the course included lessons on videotape and audiotape, an illustrated textbook, and audiotaped critiques of each student's work. It included a coupon that the reader could fill out and mail for more information, along with the company's Internet address.

In contrast, much of the advertising by several of Nikon's other competitors in 1997 promoted the Advanced Photo System (APS), a new type of equipment and film that made photography easier for consumers. These ads typically focused on the products instead of featuring how-to tips. APS had been developed jointly by Nikon, Canon U.S.A., Minolta Corporation, Eastman Kodak Company, and Fujifilm. All five companies made their own brands of APS cameras, but only Kodak and Fujifilm made APS film. Although each company had advertised the launch of the new system in 1996, Kodak had spent by far the most—about $80 million worldwide—to publicize its Advantix brand. According to *Advertising Age,* the total spent by all advertisers to promote APS products in 1996 was $115 million. In 1997 Kodak's worldwide advertising budget for Advantix was about $100 million, with about $60 million allocated for advertising in the United States. Kodak's new advertisements for 1997 explained what APS was and familiarized the public with the Advantix brand name. Each spot featured Kodak's general corporate signature "Take Pictures. Further." Canon promoted its ELPH brand of APS products with the tag lines "It's So Advanced . . . It's Simple" and "ELPH: The Big Name in the Advanced Photo System." The tag line for Fujifilm's advertising was "Isn't It About Time Taking Pictures Made Everyone Smile?" Minolta marketed its Vectis brand with the catch phrase "Big Bang Technology." The five companies ran some co-op advertisements, including one that read, "The Nikon Pronea 6i Advanced Photo System camera takes many different lenses. And Kodak Advantix film." In addition to the Pronea brand, Nikon offered the Nuvis brand of APS compact cameras.

MARKETING STRATEGY

By featuring Nikon equipment at the seminars and offering expert instruction in the latest photographic techniques, the Nikon School helped the company convey an image of professionalism without blatantly promoting the brand. Likewise, the advertising campaign took a low-key approach to publicizing the company's products. Although the Nikon name was prominently displayed in the ads, the company's logo and general tag line, "We Take the World's Greatest Pictures. Yours," were not included. Each advertisement caught the reader's eye with a large photograph above two rectangles, one solid gold and one black. The gold block framed a caption, and the black one framed the words "The Nikon School" in reverse type.

In one advertisement a group of firefighters posed in front of a building with flames and smoke billowing out the windows. The caption said, "Tip #34: Remember to compensate for backlighting." The accompanying text added, "Before snapping a photo, it's a good idea to take a gander at what's happening in the background. Just one of the topics covered in our eight-hour class, where you'll learn everything from basic composition to advanced exposure techniques. You also get the 157-page Nikon School Handbook and a lovely lunch, all for $95." Another advertisement showed a tiny dog looking intimidated by the unusually tall fire hydrant towering over it. The caption read, "Tip #44: To get animals to hold still, give them something to focus on." The smaller text said, "We can all feel a tad overwhelmed now and then, and photographers are certainly no exception. Which is exactly why we recommend taking our eight-hour class, where you'll learn everything from basic composition to advanced exposure techniques." A third ad featured a photograph of two tombstones with the names "Knock" and "Knock." The caption said, "Tip #52: Try a slower film for motionless objects."

Because each ad focused on one aspect of photography, the campaign helped show that the school offered instruction in many subjects, such as how to choose the best lens for each picture; how to measure light; how to choose the best film speed, shutter speed, and aperture; how to use flash lighting; how to recognize and compose an effective photograph; and how to master close-up photography. The advertisements addressed problems that photographers of all skill levels commonly encountered, and they promised that students would find answers and access to knowledgeable professionals at the Nikon School. Each ad included a telephone number to call for more information, and some provided the company's Internet address and a list of cities where the school was scheduled to be offered that year. The advertisements ran only in print media, particularly photography magazines.

OUTCOME

One of the "Nikon School" campaign's primary objectives was to boost attendance by reaching out to creative amateur photographers who wanted to improve their craft. According to McEnery of Fallon McElligott, the advertisements succeeded in generating enthusiasm for the school and conveying the key message that the classes could help photographers who wanted to be better than "good enough." Another objective was to encourage consumers to call for more information. McEnery said the campaign clearly achieved those goals. "The 1997 Nikon School season has been one of the most successful ever. Anticipated ticket sales were exceeded on a regular basis. Given our limited schedule of insertions, Nikon was able to track the spike in mail and phone calls following each ad. And we had concrete proof of those conversations; approximately a third of attendees in several sites stated in their exit survey that they learned about the Nikon School through advertising," McEnery noted.

FURTHER READING

Bounds, Wendy. "Don't Blink: Photo Industry Launches Global Blitz to Tout New Cameras, Film." *Wall Street Journal,* February 1, 1996.

Fannin, Rebecca A. "APS Camera Brands Make Picture-Imperfect Debut: Kodak, Fuji Lead Marketers Who Are Banking on New System." *Advertising Age International,* January 13, 1997.

Gleason, Mark. "Advertising Age's Agency of the Year: Fallon McElligott." *Advertising Age,* April 15, 1996.

"The New Nikon School of Photography." *Petersen's Photographic,* February 1993, p. 29.

"The Nikon School Photo Contest Winners." *Petersen's Photographic,* June 1996, p. 16.

Wilke, Michael. "Kodak Tries Humorous Tack in $60 Mil Advantix Effort: Ads Strive to Create Human Attachment to New Tech." *Advertising Age,* June 9, 1997.

Susan Risland

Nissan Motor Company, Ltd.

17-1, Ginza 6-chome
Chuo-ku
Tokyo, 104-8023
Japan
Telephone: 81 3 35435523
Fax: 81 3 55652228
Web site: www.nissan-global.com

■■■

DO YOU SPEAK MICRA? CAMPAIGN

OVERVIEW

In the late 1990s, after nearly a decade of declining sales, Japan's Nissan Motor Company, Ltd., flirted with bankruptcy. The 1999 arrival of Carlos Ghosn as Nissan's CEO, however, marked the beginning of one of the automotive industry's most striking turnarounds. Within a few years Ghosn moved Nissan out of debt and into a new era of profitability, thanks to dramatic cost-cutting measures and a renewed emphasis on innovation in car design. The European automotive market remained a tough one for Japanese brands, but Nissan was counting on a 2003 redesign of its subcompact Micra model to drive growth across the continent. To announce the redesign, Nissan and its agency, TBWA\G1 Europe, created an integrated advertising campaign called "Do You Speak Micra?" which suggested that the supposedly groundbreaking Micra redesign required the invention of a new descriptive language.

"Do You Speak Micra?" combined TV, cinema, print, outdoor, and online elements, among other assorted marketing platforms, and it spanned 19 European countries and multiple languages, at a price tag of more than 20 million euros. The idea of "speaking Micra" was first circulated by a January 2003 television and cinema spot in which a set of mysteriously disembodied blue lips intoned invented words, such as "modtro" (a combination of "modern" and "retro"), to describe the new Micra. This spot also ran online courtesy of an arrangement between Nissan and Yahoo!, and print and outdoor ads used the same concept and imagery. As the 12-month campaign matured, individual country-specific variants of the "Do You Speak Micra?" message were implemented.

In 2003 Micra sales grew by 70 percent compared to 2002, outperforming Nissan's ambitious precampaign goals. Unaided, spontaneous awareness of the Micra model grew considerably, as did consumers' willingness to consider purchasing a Micra. The campaign won a French EFFIE in 2003 and a bronze Euro EFFIE in 2004 in the automotive category.

HISTORICAL CONTEXT

After a production peak in 1989, Japan's Nissan Motor Company saw its sales decline steadily throughout the 1990s, so that by 1999 the automaker was on the verge of bankruptcy. That year, however, France's second-largest automobile manufacturer, Renault, purchased nearly 37 percent of Nissan's public shares and set the Japanese company on the road back to solvency by providing a much-needed infusion of cash and by installing Carlos Ghosn as CEO. Ghosn instituted the Nissan Revival Plan, mandating a return to profitability by 2001, an increase in operating margin (the percentage of revenue remaining after a company had fully paid its production costs but before it paid interest or taxes), and a dramatic reduction of its debt load in the coming years. Ghosn was able to meet these benchmarks ahead of schedule, thanks to measures that included an aggressive diet of job cuts and a streamlining of the company's supply chain. By early 2002 Nissan had officially recovered from its near-death experience and could focus again on future growth. At the same time Renault increased its Nissan holdings to 44 percent, paving the way for an increasingly vital partnership.

In the European market Nissan was particularly counting on a 2003 update of its subcompact-class Micra, which had not been redesigned since 1992. Not only did the Micra redesign offer aesthetic value and new technological features, but it was also priced lower than the Micra had been in previous years. Nissan was able to offer the Micra at a lower price partly because of its alliance with Renault—the new Micra and a Japanese version of the same car, the March, shared a chassis codesigned by Nissan and Renault, which allowed the companies to purchase parts in greater volume at substantial savings—and partly because Nissan changed its parts-buying patterns for the Micra, purchasing outside of the United Kingdom (where the Micra was built) when necessary in order to cope with fluctuating exchange rates.

Historically, Europeans had been much more hesitant to embrace Japanese auto brands than Americans had, vastly preferring cars produced in Europe. As of 2002 Japanese brands accounted for only 11.5 percent of the 15 million cars sold annually in Europe; in contrast, 30 percent of autos sold in the United States were Japanese.

TARGET MARKET

"Do You Speak Micra?" targeted European professionals between the ages of 25 and 34 and with moderate to high incomes. The small size of the Micra made it a selection that was most natural for those who did not yet have children and for those who lived in urban areas. The campaign ran in Austria, Cyprus, the Czech Republic, Finland, France, Germany, Greece, Iceland, Ireland, Italy, the Netherlands, Poland, Portugal, the Slovak Republic, Spain, Sweden, Switzerland, Turkey, and the United Kingdom.

Nissan and TBWA set campaign goals of generating a 2003 Micra sales increase of 60 percent compared to 2002, which necessitated an appeal that would draw consumers who were previously loyal to other automotive brands. Additionally, Nissan hoped to establish an iconic, enduring market presence for the Micra among young people. Although the Micra had an established reputation in Europe, TBWA and Nissan used the dramatic redesign as an opportunity to relaunch the model and imbue it with a new, captivating personality. The campaign's various executions were accordingly bold, positing the idea that an effective description of the radically redesigned Micra required the invention of a new language.

CORPORATE HERO

Carlos Ghosn, the CEO who orchestrated Nissan's dramatic turnaround beginning in 1999, became a folk hero of sorts in Japan because of what he did for the company. "The Japanese public sees in Nissan a company that is representative of problems that many Japanese corporations face," Ghosn told *Forbes.* "The fact of turning Nissan around in a clear, neat way is a strong message of hope in Japanese society. People stop me in the street and say gambatte [go for it!] and wish me luck."

COMPETITION

Among Europeans, Japanese cars historically had a reputation for lackluster styling and handling, and as of 2000, according to *BusinessWeek,* Toyota alone had managed to crack this stereotype. The model with which Toyota had done so, the Yaris, was a subcompact positioned directly against the Micra. Designed with European tastes in mind, the Yaris's "distinctive grill and curvaceous dashboard," as *BusinessWeek* put it, displayed "the sort of pizzazz Europeans expect from Volkswagen, Fiat, or Renault." The Yaris was the best-selling Japanese car in Europe, and among Japanese automakers in Europe, Toyota was the top seller by a comfortable margin, with 800,000 vehicles sold in 2002, a far cry from the 470,000 that second-place Nissan sold in Europe that year. Toyota's sales grew by 14 percent in Europe in 2002, even though the European automobile market as a whole was down 4 percent. Sales were again down industry-wide in Europe in 2003, but that year Toyota sales increased by more than 10 percent. By early April 2004 Toyota's market share in Europe was 5.4 percent, greater than that of such stalwart European brands as Audi and BMW and approaching that of the Italian carmaker Fiat.

Honda Motor Company was the third-best-selling Japanese brand in Europe. Although it had been losing market share regularly since the late 1990s, Honda rallied in 2002. The recent introduction of a redesigned Civic hatchback and a new subcompact, the Jazz, drove a European sales increase of 17 percent that year. The

Jazz, positioned to compete with the Micra and the Yaris for young consumers, was Honda's first subcompact car to be sold in Europe since the discontinuation of the Logo in the 1990s, and it represented Honda's most promising appeal to younger Europeans in recent memory.

Foremost among European subcompacts was the Volkswagen Golf. The Golf accounted for 15 percent of all cars manufactured by Volkswagen, but Golf sales were in decline worldwide and in Europe. The first new Golf redesign in seven years was unveiled in late 2003, threatening the renewed strength of the Micra's market positioning in the wake of the "Do You Speak Micra?" campaign. Golf sales in 2004 did not meet Volkswagen's expectations, however, forcing the company to offer incentive programs that undercut its profits. In light of the increasing European success of Japanese brands such as Toyota and Nissan, many analysts saw Volkswagen's difficulties as symptomatic of a larger shift in the European automotive market.

MARKETING STRATEGY

"Do You Speak Micra?" was created by TBWA\G1 Europe and then adapted by various European branches of the TBWA Worldwide network, depending on the country and language used, as the campaign evolved over its January–December 2003 run. TV, cinema, outdoor, print, online, and interactive placements were used to build consistent mainstream awareness across the campaign's geographic range, and supplementary executions were developed according to each country's individual demands. The campaign's total budget was in excess of 20 million euros.

The campaign was defined by suitably unordinary imagery, most prominently a single striking image of surreally disembodied, shiny, blue, female lips. This image was introduced in a TV and cinema commercial directed by the famously offbeat American film director David Lynch, known for cult classics such as *Eraserhead* and *Blue Velvet* and the TV series *Twin Peaks.* The English-language version of the spot showed the glistening blue lips hovering mysteriously over a noir-inflected nighttime cityscape, intoning the words "modtro," "simpology," and "spafe" against visuals of the redesigned Micra in motion on the streets below. After the lips pronounced each word, onscreen text informed viewers of its meaning: "modtro" was a combination of "modern" and "retro," "simpology" an amalgamation of "simple" and "technology," and "spafe" a fusion of "spontaneous" and "safe." Although the imagery remained consistent in non-English-language versions of the spot, the neologisms and their root words varied depending on the language used. The spot concluded with the paired images of the blue lips and the new Micra, as the lips asked, "Do you speak Micra?"

Print and outdoor ads recycled the image of the lips as well as images of the Micra itself, and each ad typically focused on one particular neologism. Nissan also partnered prominently with the online company Yahoo! to extend the buzz surrounding the TV and cinema spots, presenting the Lynch-directed commercial for online viewing at the Yahoo! music channel LAUNCH (http://launch.yahoo.com). Free Micra-related gifts were also offered to those Yahoo! users who, having previously opted to receive promotional information from the company, responded to an E-mail offer to test-drive the new Micra.

Country-specific advertisements included a print series in France that was more explicitly geared toward female members of the target market. One such ad showed images of the new Micra paired, according to color, in mathematical equations with images of various outfits of female clothing; each combination of Micra color and outfit was said to equal one of the French neologisms used in the campaign. For instance, a dark-gray Micra, when paired with a red halter top, black jeans, and high heels, was said to equal "aggressuelle," a combination of the French words for "aggressive" and "sensual." One of the more noteworthy U.K.-specific elements of the campaign was a guerilla effort targeting those who drove competitors' cars. Informational packets about the Micra, including a reply mailing to request a test drive as well as a questionnaire to be returned for a chance to win a free vacation, were attached to the side mirrors of parked cars manufactured by Nissan's competitors.

OUTCOME

Nissan surpassed its precampaign goal of increasing Micra sales in 2003 by 60 percent over the preceding year; the 2003 sales increase reached 70 percent in Europe. Micra sales accounted for 42 percent of Nissan's total European sales that year, and Micra's market share in the small-car segment increased by 62 percent during the campaign's run. The campaign also substantially increased awareness of the model. According to a tracking study, spontaneous awareness of the Micra model increased by 69 percent as a result of the relaunch campaign, and the number of consumers willing to consider purchasing a Micra increased by 88 percent. The campaign won a 2003 EFFIE Award in France and a bronze 2004 Euro EFFIE. The Euro EFFIEs were the European counterpart to the prestigious EFFIE Awards that were sponsored by the New York American Marketing Association.

Despite the fact that European auto sales were down overall, 2003 was a growth year for Nissan as well as other Japanese brands in Europe. By the end of 2004

Europe's resistance to Japanese cars began to seem a relic of history, as Nissan and Toyota, among other Asian automakers, continued to increase their market shares at the expense of their European counterparts.

FURTHER READING

"David Lynch Speaks Micra." *Carpages,* January 8, 2003. Available from <http://www.carpages.Companyuk/nissan/nissan_david_lynch_speaks_micra_part_1_08_01_03.asp>

Dawson, Chester, Christine Tierney, and Anna Bawden. "A Pileup in Europe for Japan's Carmakers." *BusinessWeek,* December 18, 2000.

Diem, William. "Supplier Switch Saves Nissan $1,800 on Micra." *Ward's Auto World,* January 2003.

Fulford, Benjamin. "Gambatte!" *Forbes,* July 22, 2002.

"Nissan Launches 'Intriguing' Micra Campaign to Lure Younger Drivers." *Precision Marketing,* June 20, 2003.

"Nissan Turns a 180." *Ward's Auto World,* February 2002.

Sweney, Mark. "David Lynch Directs TV Spots for Nissan Micra." *Campaign,* January 17, 2003.

Tierney, Christine, and Chester Dawson. "Negotiating Europe's Curves." *BusinessWeek,* December 16, 2002.

Treece, James B. "Nissan Ends Era of Revival." *Automotive News,* February 11, 2002.

Wentz, Laurel. "Lynch Directs Micra Teaser." *Advertising Age,* January 13, 2003.

Mark Lane

Nissan North America, Inc.

18501 S. Figueroa St.
Gardena, California 90248
USA
Telephone: (310) 532-3111
Fax: (310) 771-3343
Web site: www.nissan-usa.com

ENJOY THE RIDE CAMPAIGN

OVERVIEW

Nissan launched the biggest marketing effort in its history, the "Enjoy the Ride" campaign, in August 1996. The $200 million budget was four times the previous budget and placed Nissan behind only General Motors in spending on advertising. "Enjoy the Ride" was designed as a brand identity campaign. Its intent was to remind consumers of Nissan's deep heritage and love of cars and to convince potential customers that the company's cars were fun to buy and drive. Nissan also wanted to persuade customers that their feedback and car-buying experiences were important.

The campaign encompassed the gamut of marketing. Spots appeared on network as well as cable television, on syndicated shows, and on televised sporting events. An extensive outdoor and print campaign ran in tandem with the television ads, with advertisements appearing on buses, billboards, benches, and other places. The campaign, which ended in late 1997, boasted more than a dozen television spots with various Nissan automobiles and included the unveiling of the 1998 Nissan Altima.

Each ad starred an elderly Japanese man with a Jack Russell terrier. The character, intended to symbolize Nissan's heritage, was inspired by Yutaka Katayama, president of Nissan from 1965 to 1975 and known as Mr. K. Katayama's personal philosophy was "Love people. Love cars. Love life," and this was the philosophy behind the "Enjoy the Ride" campaign.

HISTORICAL CONTEXT

Historically, automobile advertising in the United States was not innovative. Most television commercials showed a new car driving down a scenic road, with a narrator describing the car's features. Research indicated that many viewers disliked the typical car ads, which motivated Bob Thomas, at the time the president and CEO of Nissan's U.S. operations, to strive for something unconventional and different. Rob Siltanen, a creative director at TBWA Chiat/Day, Nissan's advertising agency, told *Adweek,* "We discovered that consumers hate car advertising... They said it's all the same—shiny cars driving down roads. They could smell them coming. As soon as they saw the car, they flipped the channel." In *USA Today,* Tom Orbe, Nissan's vice president of marketing, agreed, "If you asked someone if they'd rather see a car ad or get a root canal, they'd say they'd rather get a root canal."

Nissan decided to gamble on its brand identity rather than on individual models of cars and hoped to present its brand image in an innovative fashion. Thomas asserted that, because many automobile manufacturers produced good cars, "a good product is no longer good enough" in the industry. He stated, "We at Nissan are on a mission to put sales prospects and Nissan owners first. Ultimately, this will increase sales retention rates and generate potential owners who actively seek out our brand, not our lowest sale price." The brand image Nissan hoped to convey was the love of life, cars, and driving.

The campaign was launched in August 1996 with the two-minute spot "Dream Garage," which appeared during the closing ceremonies of the Olympics. The spot introduced the Mr. K. character in a dreamlike garage filled with classic Datsun and Nissan models. It ended with the tag line "Life is a journey. Enjoy the ride." The spot was designed to cement Nissan's brand identity in viewers' minds and to evoke the thrill of car ownership.

Nissan followed up "Dream Garage" with "Toys" in November 1996. This animated spot featured a GI Joe-type character who drove off in a Nissan convertible with a Barbie character, leaving a Ken look-alike pouting in the background. The ad was set to the song "You Really Got Me" by Van Halen. The spot was immensely popular and received awards as the best commercial of the year from *USA Today, Rolling Stone, Adweek,* and other publications.

Encouraged by the positive response, Nissan continued the "Enjoy the Ride" campaign into 1997 and hoped that sales would follow. Although 1996 sales fell 2.7 percent from 1995, Thomas told the *Los Angeles Times* that a Nissan survey revealed that brand awareness had risen by 30 percent and that the brand's likability had gone up by 100 percent.

TARGET MARKET

According to Nissan, its primary target market included college-educated, upscale individuals who typically purchased new import automobiles. Because this consumer group invariably disliked car commercials, Nissan sought to connect with potential buyers by presenting a fun and quirky marketing campaign. Chiat/Day's Siltanen told the *New York Times,* "… auto advertising is No. 1 least liked. So you give them [viewers] things that delight them, that reward them, for watching a commercial and treat them as if they have brains." Nissan's Orbe elaborated on the idea behind the campaign by saying, "No running footage. No performance specs. In order to reach our audience and effectively invite it to like us, as a car company, we had to create commercials that were 'bigger' than that." Nissan bet that the campaign would convey the message that Nissan cars were both reliable and unique, built for people who embraced life and loved cars and driving. If the viewers liked Nissan, it was thought, they would then visit a Nissan dealer.

One of the hurdles Nissan needed to overcome in its marketing campaign was to convince the target market that its cars were on a par with those of rivals Toyota and Honda. In *USA Today* Ron Pinnelli, an auto analyst with AutoData, stated, "People's perception is that [Nissan's] quality is not up to the level of Toyota and Honda… They have really not gotten their quality message across." In fact, there was evidence confirming the quality and reliability of Nissan's cars. A 1997 study by the research firm J.D. Power and Associates indicated that in the first 90 days of ownership the Nissan Altima had the fewest number of reported complaints among midsize sedans. Nissan needed a method for conveying this information to would-be consumers in a convincing, effective manner.

MR. K.

Some observers questioned the decision to use a Japanese character to convey the spirit of Nissan. Japanese corporations were generally wary of promoting their cultural heritage, partly because of the 1992 "Buy America" campaign that had promoted the big three U.S. automakers—General Motors, Ford, and Chrysler.

COMPETITION

The 1990s were a difficult period in the U.S. automobile market as U.S. manufacturers became more competitive and Japanese makers introduced strong models. Although Nissan held steady with its popular Altima and surpassed Honda in 1993, the company was not as competitive as it wished to be, and Nissan's market share began to dwindle. According to *Business Week,* in 1996, the year the "Enjoy the Ride" campaign began, Nissan's market share dropped from 5.2 percent to 5 percent. The *Los Angeles Times* reported that Nissan's sales had risen 8.4 percent in January 1997, but competitors Toyota and Honda enjoyed increases of 52.8 percent and 21.7 percent, respectively. In comparison, Nissan's increase seemed insignificant.

Some observers attributed Nissan's slip in market share to the fact that the company was not manufacturing new models or offering popular styles, such as sports utility vehicles. Toyota and Honda both had new sports utility vehicles on the market, but Nissan's newest model lagged more than a year behind. While Toyota and Honda's midsize sedans had become roomier in order to compete with the popular Ford Taurus, the Nissan Altima had not. In addition, Nissan did not introduce a new car for an entire year after it launched the "Enjoy the Ride" campaign.

Nissan's main competitors in the U.S. market were fellow Japanese companies Honda and Toyota. The Nissan Altima was in the same class as the Toyota Camry and Honda Accord, and each had a luxury line to cater to the high-end consumer. Also prominent in the car market were American manufacturers General Motors, Ford, and Chrysler. According to *Market Share Reporter,* in 1996 these three U.S. automakers had market shares of 32.1, 25.1, and 15.9 percent, respectively. Other Japanese companies with U.S. models included Mazda, Subaru-Isuzu, Mitsubishi, and Suzuki, but because their market shares were considerably less, they were not considered as serious competition to Nissan.

MARKETING STRATEGY

Despite declining sales in 1996 that, in part, led to the announcement in early 1997 that Nissan would reduce its workforce by 450 jobs in sales and marketing, the company forged ahead with the "Enjoy the Ride" campaign. In *Advertising Age* Nissan's Thomas affirmed, "Our research confirms that our brand campaign has had a huge impact on the awareness and imagery of the Nissan brand... It's inarguably a huge success." It was believed that because "Enjoy the Ride" was a long-term brand-building campaign, it would take time for sales to follow.

Nissan yielded, however, to dealer complaints that the spots were unsuccessful in generating sales and dealership traffic by adding regional spots that focused more on the product than the brand. These ads ran in tandem with the "Enjoy the Ride" spots and featured a cameo appearance by the Mr. K. character. Nissan spokesperson Gerry Spahn told *Newsday,* "They're going to focus more on the product, on the technical specifications and on the pricing... Basically, they're going to be more traditional ads."

"Enjoy the Ride" started out 1997 with two spots that premiered during the telecast of Super Bowl XXXI, assuring an estimated 140 million viewers. Nissan's Orbe stated, "We've worked hard to break through the commercial clutter, giving consumers innovative advertising that not only entertains, but also reinforces Nissan's image as a creative company offering cars that are fun to drive." The first spot, "Doggie Mind Control," showcased the Nissan Pathfinder and featured a dog and its entranced owner cruising the neighborhood in the middle of the night. The dog drove and picked up dog friends until there was no more room in the car. They then left the owner standing in the street. The song "Low Rider" by War played in the background. The second spot, "Pigeons," showed a flock of pigeons in bomber jackets chasing and "attacking" a just washed Nissan Maxima.

In mid-July 1997, Nissan unveiled its 1998 Altima with three new spots that featured the tag line "Have you seen it?" Prior to the Altima's launch, Nissan initiated an introductory campaign that included advertising on billboards, posters, and bus wraps and shelters, all with the Mr. K. character asking, "Have you seen it?" It was the first new product to be introduced since the "Enjoy the Ride" campaign started, and Nissan had high hopes for the Altima. "People have told us how much they love our campaign and its character," said Orbe. "And as everyone has come to know, wherever the magical man is, wonderful things happen. Now, with the launch of a new Altima, we're telling everyone we have something special worth checking out." One of the spots, "Farmer," showed the transformation of a grim-faced farmer when he traded in his old pickup truck for an Altima. He returned from the dealership singing to the Monkees' "I'm a Believer" and speedily driving in circles. "Witness Protection" portrayed a man getting ready to start his new life in a witness protection program. He was issued an Altima, which then attracted the attention of passersby, a far cry from the low-key image he wished to adopt.

The final spots in the "Enjoy the Ride" campaign debuted in November 1997 and featured the 1998 Frontier pickup truck with the motto "Dogs love trucks." As Chiat/Day's Siltanen explained, "People trust their dogs, and because the majority of truck owners are dog owners, we used dogs to call attention to the Frontier's features." One of the spots, entitled "Chair," showed a dog taking its slumbering owner on a joyride through the city streets on a recliner. They overcame obstacles such as cars and pedestrians, and at one point they went under a semi truck in the reclined position. The chair stopped in front of a Nissan agency, the owner woke up, and the two drove home in a new Frontier.

OUTCOME

Many of the 1997 "Enjoy the Ride" spots earned accolades equal to the prizewinning 1996 ads "Dream Garage" and "Toys." *Advertising Age* voted "Chair" the third best television spot for 1997 in the automotive category and named TBWA Chiat/Day the 1997 U.S. agency of the year, in large part because of its innovative work on the "Enjoy the Ride" campaign. Ad Track, *USA Today*'s poll that tabulated the popularity and effectiveness of ad campaigns, ranked "Enjoy the Ride" as the third most popular campaign it reviewed in 1997. Of those surveyed, 35 percent stated that they liked the ads. The effectiveness rating was just above average.

Advertising Age published results from CNW Marketing/Research that reported the awareness of Nissan increasing from 15 percent before the campaign to 42 percent in January 1997. And while Nissan made it onto only 4.2 percent of the shopping lists of potential buyers before "Enjoy the Ride," in January 1997, 11.8 percent stated that they were considering purchasing a Nissan. The Mr. K. character was also well known, with 78 percent of those in one survey recognizing him as the Nissan spokesperson.

Despite positive affirmations from Nissan's Thomas regarding the effectiveness of the brand campaign, sales failed to reach expectations, with *USA Today* reporting that Nissan's U.S. sales had fallen by $580 million in 1997. Chiat/Day's Siltanen confessed to the *New York Times,* "The backlash to the 'Enjoy the ride' campaign kind of caught us by surprise, . . . because everybody said, 'This is great advertising.' We were riding and smiling all the way, then people said it wasn't working." As a result Thomas left the company in October 1997. Michael Seergy, who was promoted to vice president and general manager of Nissan's U.S. division, indicated that the company would alter its marketing strategies, and he told *USA Today,* "We were focused on the brand. Everything was the brand. We didn't tell people anything about the product. Now we will."

FURTHER READING

Armstrong, Larry. "In Reverse at Nissan." *Business Week,* March 9, 1998, p. 42.

Eldridge, Earle. "Struggling Nissan Changes Focus: Carmaker Rolls Out New Models, New Sales Tactics." *USA Today,* May 28, 1998, p. B6.

Elliott, Stuart. "Nissan Exults Over an Offbeat Campaign, Despite Flat Sales and a Debate on Ads That 'Entertain.'" *New York Times,* August 14, 1997, p. D5.

Enrico, Dottie. "Nissan's Ads Take High Road: Sales Stall." *USA Today,* November 24, 1997.

———. "Nissan Ads Take Viewers on Joy Ride." *USA Today,* November 11, 1996, p. B5.

Garfield, Bob. "Nissan's Gentle Mr. K Holds Too Many Cards." *Advertising Age,* August 12, 1996.

Gellene, Denise. "Nissan Will Give an Overhaul to Its TV Campaign." *Los Angeles Times,* February 19, 1997, p. D1.

———. "A Return to Their Roots: Campaigns Trumpet Companies' Japanese Side." *Los Angeles Times,* November 13, 1996, p. D2.

Incantalupo, Tom. "Automakers Launch Recall of Offbeat TV Commercials." *Newsday,* February 20, 1997, p. A49.

Johnson, Bradley, and Mark Rechtin. "Nissan Wants Sales to Enjoy the Ride, Too." *Advertising Age,* February 24, 1997, p. 1F.

Parpis, Eleftheria. "New Directions." *Adweek,* January 27, 1997, p. 27.

Wells, Melanie. "Nissan Stays on Offbeat Track with Latest Altima Ads." *USA Today,* August 14, 1997, p. B2.

Mariko Fujinaka

NISSAN QUEST MINIVAN LAUNCH CAMPAIGN

OVERVIEW

In 2004 Nissan North America, the North American subsidiary of Japanese automaker Nissan Motor Co., Ltd., introduced a redesign of its Quest minivan. Originally a joint project with the Ford Motor Company, the Quest was selling only about 30,000 units per year by that time, and it was felt that the vehicle needed to be radically reconceived in order to compete with other minivans. Imports had risen to 34 percent of all minivan sales, meaning there was a solid market for the Quest to tap into. In an effort to make gains in this market, Nissan introduced the redesigned Quest in 2003 and 2004.

Since the new Quest was a bold, sleek-looking minivan, it was decided to market the vehicle as the minivan of choice for what Nissan termed "Sexy Moms"—younger, hipper, financially successful suburban mothers and families that wanted the interior space of a minivan but were uncomfortable with the segment's dowdy image. The ad agency TBWA\Chiat\Day Los Angeles was brought in to handle the $20 million campaign, which featured a major television spot, print ads, and billboards. The TV spot featured young, hip women going out at night in the city or loading musical instruments and surfboards into their Quests. It closed with the tagline "Moms have changed, shouldn't the minivan?" The message was that the Quest was a car for independent, image-conscious drivers. Nissan also sponsored events, such as a fashion show during New York's fashion week, in an effort to reach an audience that might not have been familiar with the earlier version of the Quest.

The campaign succeeded in attracting a younger, wealthier consumer than the original Quest and received a 2005 Gold EFFIE Award from the New York American Marketing Association. The median age for Quest drivers during the relaunch was 47, the youngest in the minivan segment, and the typical Quest buyer had an income of approximately $98,000. Sales of the new Quest were, however, below expectations overall. This was blamed more on the minivan's radical design than on the marketing strategy.

HISTORICAL CONTEXT

The Nissan Quest began as a joint project between Nissan and Ford's Mercury division. Initial models of the car were all but indistinguishable from the Mercury Villager. Both were smaller minivans meant to serve as an entry into the lucrative minivan market for each company. The vehicles were designed by Nissan and built around Nissan engines but were actually constructed by the Ford Motor Company. The collaboration was not a particularly successful one. In 1998 Nissan only moved about 30,000 units of the Quest, while competitors such as the Dodge Caravan sold more than 300,000 units.

The Quest's failures were emblematic of company-wide shortcomings. By 1999 Nissan was nearly $22.9 billion in debt. A new CEO, Carlos Ghosn, was brought in to stem the tide of red ink that year. Ghosn immediately instituted the Nissan Revival Plan, requesting a $5.2 billion cash infusion from French company Renault, which owned more than 36 percent of Nissan stock in 2004, to help the brand revitalize its fleet. The plan also included a new emphasis on deficit reduction, improved vehicle performance, increasing the company's revenue flow, and working closely with parent company Renault. A key part of this plan was the decision to focus on building a smaller number of vehicle lines. Model quality, not quantity, would be the order of the day.

During the revitalization, Nissan and Ford agreed to discontinue the Quest/Villager project, ending with the 2002 model, even though the program was originally slated to continue for another three years. Ford decided to cancel the Villager line altogether after the 2002 model. Nissan, however, had other plans. In the short term the line was to be suspended for one year so that its design could be reworked.

The new Quest had an aggressive style, likened by some to the Renault's Scénic, a sleek, compact European multipurpose vehicle, similar to an American minivan. To give it a sleeker look than its competitors, it featured a longer wheelbase (the distance between the front and rear axle) than most minivans. The minivan's central control stack, located in front of the driver, was designed to look like a table, giving the interior a unique appearance. Nissan also emphasized performance. The car's second and third rows of seats both folded flat into the base of the vehicle, allowing for extra storage space, and side-impact airbags were meant to appeal to safety-conscious drivers.

The relaunch was planned for model year 2004.When he became CEO in 1999, Ghosn vowed to make sure every Nissan automobile would be redesigned by 2004. As a result Nissan had a number of major new projects emerging in the mid-2000s, including a redesign of its popular Maxima, Xterra, and Altima lines. The company was also introducing a new sport-utility vehicle (SUV) line, the Murano. The Quest would be Nissan's major effort to break into the minivan market. From 1997 to 2004 imports had risen from 9 percent of the minivan market to 34 percent. Nissan hoped the Quest would be able to capitalize on this trend.

SUPERHERO CEO

In 1999 Nissan Motor Company, Ltd., was struggling financially. It was $22.9 billion in debt and was widely viewed as a company in decline. That year Nissan entered into an alliance with French company Renault. Renault gained more than one-third of voting stock in Nissan and worked to strengthen its partner almost immediately. The most visible part of this strengthening was the appointment of Renault's Carlos Ghosn as Nissan's chief operating officer later that year. Within two years Ghosn would become the global CEO of Nissan. Born in Brazil to Lebanese parents and later educated in France, Ghosn had an international outlook that had served him well during previous stints with Michelin and Renault.

Upon joining Nissan, Ghosn instituted a major initiative called the Nissan Revitalization Plan. He put the company's survival first and bypassed the keiretsu system (a Japanese practice in which certain established suppliers received special treatment) in favor of pursuing the lowest-priced supplies and materials. Ghosn also pledged to have every vehicle in the Nissan fleet redesigned by 2004. To foster better cooperation among Nissan's divisions, he instituted Cross-Functional Teams, groups put together from different divisions of the company.

The Nissan Revitalization Plan was wildly successful, and within five years the company was out of debt and turning a $7 billion profit. Ghosn's success gave him a high profile internationally. In Japan he was memorialized in an anime comic book that presented the businessman as a kind of superhero. He was even encouraged by some to run for president of Lebanon.

TARGET MARKET

With a sticker price of about $25,500, the Quest was geared toward middle-class car buyers. Like previous Quest models, the new version was particularly aimed at young suburban families interested in a sportier minivan. Nissan saw the introduction of the new Quest as an opportunity to redefine the minivan market with a bold new design. This separated Quest from the pack in the minds of image-conscious consumers. As with all minivans, interior space was key, and the new Quest featured three rows of seating to accommodate larger families. But the rise of SUVs had created a demand for a larger exterior as well.

In particular, Nissan aimed the new Quest at female suburban mothers whom they called "Sexy Moms," more affluent, image-conscious car buyers. Nissan was looking for individualistic mothers who would be enticed by its splashy new look.

COMPETITION

With competitors building ever-more-spacious minivans, such as Honda and its Odyssey model, Nissan decided that the Quest's relatively compact size was a liability. The Quest had traditionally matched up against smaller minivans such as the Dodge Caravan, but the Quest had never been able to cut into Dodge's market share, with the Caravan posting a 10 to 1 sales advantage in 1998 alone.

In an effort to revitalize the Quest line, Nissan made it bigger. The Quest became a midsize minivan, sized about halfway between the old Quest and large minivans like the Dodge Grand Caravan and the Toyota Windstar. Now the Quest's primary competition would be the Honda Odyssey and the Toyota Sienna.

The minivan market was rife with already successful vehicle lines, such as the Toyota Caravan, with strong name recognition and loyal drivers. Nissan saw an opening, however, in the relative blandness of many of these competitors. Unlike SUVs or sports cars, minivans were seen by many as a more practical automobile, and as a result few vehicles in the class were designed as boldly as the Quest. In a way the Quest would be an avant-garde minivan, attracting younger, hipper buyers.

MARKETING STRATEGY

Nissan hoped drivers would see the Quest as a "sexy" minivan. This was a departure, because minivans were almost always sold on their practicality and utility, not their design. In an effort to show off this sexiness, the company put a major push behind the North American relaunch. There was a major television campaign orchestrated by TBWA\Chiat\Day Los Angeles, along with magazine and newspaper ads and billboards, also designed by TBWA. The total budget exceeded $20 million.

Nissan's goals included tripling pre-launch sales volume, attracting newer and more affluent consumers, and making design a key motivation for purchasing the vehicle. Because so many minivans emphasized reliability and safety in their commercials, it was felt that this strategy was no longer effective at reaching consumers. Therefore a focus on the design advantages of the new Quest had practical value as well. Nissan was aiming the Quest at drivers who might not own a minivan, people who may have been put off by the segment's conservative image. Nissan and TBWA\Chiat\Day called these drivers "Sexy Moms," a play on the "Soccer Moms" who were widely seen as the minivan's usual target market.

To reach "Sexy Moms" print ads ran in such progressive publications as *Organic Style* and *Yoga Journal.* In addition Nissan sponsored a number of untraditional events to reach new customers. One of the most notable of these was a fashion show at the Altman Building in New York City during Fashion Week 2003. The company also sponsored the National Women's Show in Toronto, Canada, in November 2003, to coincide with the launch of the 2004 model. The show functioned as a kind of public trade exhibit for various health and beauty companies.

The center of the campaign was a 30-second television commercial. Set in a trendy urban environment, it showed a group of young women piling into a Quest for a fun night out in the city. The spot also featured women loading musical instruments and surfboards into their Quest, with a voice-over that asked, "Moms have changed, shouldn't the minivan?"

OUTCOME

Results of the campaign were mixed. Critics loved the commercials. In 2005 the campaign won the prestigious Gold EFFIE Award in the Automotive and Vehicles category. Presented by the New York American Marketing Association, the EFFIE honored the strong progress the campaign had made in increasing consumer awareness of the vehicle among targeted demographics. The campaign was credited with helping the Quest achieve a median buyer age of 47, the lowest in the minivan segment. Nissan also reached its goal of tapping into the affluent-driver market: the average annual household income for Quest buyers was approximately $98,000. Efforts to promote the look of the Quest also appeared to have succeeded, because customers who bought the Quest listed "exterior styling" among the top five reasons for their purchase, a rarity in the minivan segment.

Overall, however, sales of the new Quest were disappointing. Nissan had hoped to move 80,000 to 85,000 units annually. First-year sales topped out at 30,448, well below what was anticipated. The numbers were barely better than pre-launch sales and were significantly behind the old Quest's 1995 sales peak of 54,050 units. Fortunately for Nissan, this disappointment came amid other success: the Nissan Revival Plan produced a $7 billion profit by 2004, with the company clearing itself of debt. The automaker remained positive about the Quest, though some blamed its restyling for the lower-than-anticipated sales numbers.

The automaker itself admitted that the style might have been too forward looking. Shiro Nakamura, Nissan's design director, told reporters that the new Quest was just "too cutting edge." The company believed the basic design would still work in the long run and planned to tweak the model a little to get sales back on track. It was considering dropping some of the Quest's bolder innovations, such as the vehicle's centrally located instrument gauges, in an effort to make the car more "warm."

FURTHER READING

Flaherty, Julie. "Guys Mod Up to Solve Their Midlife Minivan Minicrisis." *New York Times,* October 22, 2003.

Hakim, Danny, and Fara Warner. "Sure, It's Pragmatic. But Stylish? The Minivan Is Getting a Makeover." *New York Times,* August 27, 2004.

Howard, Theresa. "Nissan Adds 'Stylish Flair' to Minivan." *USA Today,* November 30, 2003.

Mandel, Dutch. "Here Today, Ghosn Tomorrow: Thirty Hours Shadowing the World's Most Extraordinary Car Executive." *AutoWeek,* January 3, 2005.

Maynard, Micheline. "Chic? Sexy? Is Japan Really Talking Minivans?" *New York Times,* May 25, 2003.

Patton, Phil. "Inspired by Japan, the Copycats Are Now the Copied." *New York Times,* October 25, 2004.

Rechtin, Mark. "Nissan Design Chief Says Quest Minivan Styling Went Too Far." *AutoWeek,* August 23, 2004.

———. "Nissan Unveils a Redesigned Quest and Maxima." *AutoWeek,* January 6, 2003.

Tadesse, Luladey B., and Cori Bolger. "Women Have Become Car-Buying Force." *Detroit News,* June 19, 2005.

Zaun, Todd. "Nissan Profit Up as Luxury Models Sell Well." *New York Times,* April 27, 2004.

Guy Patrick Cunningham

OWN ONE AND YOU'LL UNDERSTAND CAMPAIGN

OVERVIEW

In the 1970s and 1980s the luxury component of the U.S. auto market stayed relatively immune from the threats of Japanese competition, which was able to zero in on the budget and mid-priced segments of the market because of complacency in the American auto industry. The high-end segment remained divided between American and European auto producers, both with their own loyal customers and identity, as had been the case for years.

Honda introduced its high-end Acura, the first Japanese luxury line, to the U.S. market in 1986. Then Nissan introduced the Infiniti line in 1989, the same year that Toyota presented the Lexus. These Japanese luxury cars swiftly gained market share as well as acclaim for their quality and reliability. The widespread belief that no one would pay more than $20,000 (where the "luxury" segment began at that time; this baseline rose to about $35,000 by 1997) for a Japanese car was decisively put to rest.

Nissan created a separate division with its own showrooms, the Infiniti Division, to market and sell the Infiniti line. Its flagship sedan, the V-8 powered Q45, was one of the biggest, most powerful, and most expensive—priced at around $38,400—Japanese cars sold in the United States when it was introduced. The smaller M30, with a price tag of $23,500, was introduced at the same time.

The early 1990s were ripe for the new entrants into the luxury auto market. Baby boomers were hitting their prime earning years, and many of them were new luxury car buyers. They did not necessarily have allegiance to the entrenched American and European brands. Moreover, they had positive experiences with lower-end Japanese cars, making them more receptive to the new Japanese luxury models.

It took a long time for Infiniti to get its advertising footing. Since its early minimalist campaign that featured rocks and trees, Infiniti struggled to communicate a clear brand message and information about its product. At the end of 1996 Infiniti turned to the agency TBWA Chiat/Day, of Venice, California, to "start from scratch and do another breakthrough campaign," explained agency chairman and chief creative officer Lee Clow to *AdWeek*; the mandate was to "push luxury car advertising to a new level the way we did for Nissan." The result was the $80 million "Own One and You'll Understand" campaign, which featured an ongoing series of television spots illustrating Infiniti owners' unwavering devotion to their cars. One, called "Half," showed a man having second thoughts about his impending divorce when he realizes he might have to give up his Infiniti. The ads brought Infiniti renewed media and consumer attention and played a part in the brand finally turning the corner to strong sales.

HISTORICAL CONTEXT

In the late 1980s the luxury car market experienced change and expansion. "Mystique and ostentation" were "no longer the main attraction," according to Alex Taylor III of *Fortune* magazine. Even status-conscious shoppers sought value, quality, and durability, in part because the one luxury they did not have was time. For many of the newly affluent baby boomers, these were fundamental values—part of the way they defined themselves.

By early 1989 Honda had already sold more than 70,000 Acura Legends. On the other hand, the European car makers were being hurt by the weak dollar; their sales had fallen 26 percent in two years. It was largely the buyers of European luxury cars that Infiniti targeted—for about $40,000, the Q45 was designed to offer comfort, performance, and technology equal to that of European cars costing far more. Cadillac-long considered the premiere American luxury car—generally stayed away from this sophisticated younger market; after flirting with it briefly with the short-lived Cimarron and the Italian-made Allante, Cadillac returned to targeting the male, 60-something crowd. The typical Lincoln purchaser also was male and in his 60s. On the other hand, the typical Acura buyer was 45, earned $88,000 annually (in 1989 dollars), and had already owned Japanese cars. These were exactly the consumers the European auto makers had been targeting and winning.

Infiniti employed a $60 million new-age-flavored campaign to introduce its cars. The 1989 campaign, from Hill, Holliday, Connors, Cosmopulos, featured rocks, meadows, gulls, trees, and water, but no cars—no product shots whatsoever. Although the campaign won praise from some marketing consultants, other analysts such as Taylor of *Fortune* considered it "perplexing." Others ridiculed it; *Time* magazine dubbed Infiniti "Most Mysterious New Car." The campaign did not give the Infiniti line the needed lift among consumers. Other factors also contributed to the slow start, however, including 15 fewer showrooms opened by the target date than planned. In 1990 Nissan sold only 7,161 Infinitis in the United States.

A new, more elegant and stylish series of commercials turned the camera on the product. TBWA Chiat/Day used British actor Jonathan Pryce to demonstrate features of the car with simple props against a stark white background. Pryce would become the spokesman for Infiniti for the next five years.

By 1994 Infiniti, along with Lexus and Saturn, ranked as top-scoring brands the third year in a row in a survey of quality and design engineering by market researchers J. D. Power and Associates. That year Infiniti began a concerted effort to reach more women consumers. Forty-three dealers participated in an event in which speakers addressed women—mostly executives and professionals—about topics related to business or lifestyle but not directly related to cars. The aim was to get women into dealerships in a non-sales atmosphere and increase their familiarity with the product. *Newsday* reported that Infiniti ended up selling cars to 12 percent of the women who attended a forum.

Infiniti developed a new tag line, "Thinking of You," which aired in 1996 with a campaign designed to evoke emotional response. But concrete news about price cuts was drowned out by the emotional impact of the spots. Infiniti abandoned the campaign after several months. Through 1996 Pryce continued to speak for Infiniti. One spot, "That Jazz," had him in a jazz club where Nancy Wilson was singing. As he leaves the club he extols the virtues of Infiniti over a soundtrack of Dave Brubeck and Paul Desmond's rendition of "Take Five."

The advertisements had gotten more down to earth than the initial approach, and they directly addressed the car's features, but they retained an esoteric edge that shortchanged Infiniti's potential to become a truly popular luxury car. Sales remained below their targets and potential as well, and in late 1996 Infiniti marketing vice president Tom Orbe gave Chiat-Day a clean slate to create a campaign that would break new advertising ground for Infiniti.

TARGET MARKET

Roughly 8 percent of the car-buying population could afford to buy an Infiniti in the mid-1990s. Of this population, Infiniti targeted baby boomers. This group was both expanding the market for luxury cars and bringing new characteristics to the luxury auto market. They had been buying their first cars when the American auto industry was making some of its worst cars ever. Thus, their relationship with the American industry was soured by their formative experiences with cars of questionable quality. Moreover, being a post-World War II generation, they did not shy away from buying Japanese and German products as the previous generation had. Given their ingrained suspicion of American car quality, they were far more likely to turn to European and Japanese brands when they purchased their first luxury car. Here the Japanese had an edge because many boomers had owned lower-priced Japanese cars at least once and experienced their quality and dependability. Known as the "have it all" generation, baby boomers found these attributes particularly attractive because they simply had very little time for tasks like car maintenance.

COMPETITION

Infiniti's competition fell into three main categories, decided largely by geographical location: American producers, European producers, and Japanese producers. The Americans, primarily Cadillac and Lincoln, targeted consumers in their later 50s and 60s. The Europeans, primarily BMW and Mercedes-Benz, targeted the traditional middle-aged, high-end consumers but also started

CRITICISM AND PRAISE FOR "HALF"

Criticism . . .

Garfield from *Advertising Age*: "An anticlimactic ending to a broad, obvious, and derivative commercial."

Los Angeles Times: "If you don't own one, the ad doesn't steer you to why you should."

. . . and Praise.

Bruce Shulman, general manager of Pray Infiniti, Greenwich, Connecticut: "The direction and message of the advertising are much better and appropriate than they were before."

Entertainment Weekly: Named "Half" as one of the 10 best television commercials of 1997.

to go after the aging boomers, many of whom were just entering the high-end market. Among the Japanese producers, Lexus presented the most direct and daunting challenge. Its tag line, "The relentless pursuit of perfection," initiated in 1989 and used throughout the 1990s, was no exaggeration. Toyota had already achieved the largest market share among baby boomers, so a large portion of potential consumers was open to the appeal of trading up from a Toyota to a Lexus.

A particular challenge for Infiniti in relation to Lexus was product differentiation. In 1997 the Lexus LS 400 was priced at $46,225; the Infiniti Q45 at $44,241. They both featured state-of-the-art technology, superior dealer service, and dependability. They were often mentioned in the same breath to represent Japanese technical or corporate prowess—for example, Bob Garfield's 1995 comment in *Advertising Age,* "Lexus and Infiniti have changed perceptions of what constitutes automotive luxury and prestige." Although Lexus had been on top in sales volume and customer surveys, in 1996 Infiniti surpassed Lexus in J. D. Powers & Associates' annual customer satisfaction report. It was the first time Lexus fell to number two on the much-watched index. Shortly after that, Lexus shifted its advertising style to a less pretentious, more "funky" approach that was exemplified by Infiniti's "Own One and You'll Understand" campaign. During the 1990s Lexus ads had presented a sophisticated voice. In the fall of 1997 (about four months after the new Infiniti campaign was launched), Lexus introduced a campaign from Team One in El Segundo, California, that unabashedly celebrated the slightly wicked pleasures of its 300-horsepower V-8 GS, "the fastest automatic sedan in the world." The imagery, inspired by the grotesque and eerie work of cartoonist Charles Adams, was accompanied in each spot by the tag line "Something wicked this way comes." While the commercials were visually arresting and fun to watch, the tag line ultimately failed to communicate a substantive message about Lexus.

MARKETING STRATEGY

Although the number of Infiniti owners was not as large as Nissan might have wanted, those owners nevertheless had voiced vigorous appreciation for the vehicles since the inception of the division in 1989. This customer feedback was the origin of the "Own One and You'll Understand" campaign. It reflected the devotion Infiniti owners felt to the brand. The challenge for Nissan was to get those who had never driven an Infiniti, or even a Toyota, to want to experience this satisfying ownership.

Nissan had performed market research that revealed that consumers of luxury vehicles in the 1990s were not as self-consciously highbrow in their tastes as traditional luxury-item consumers; rather, they were "regular people" who happened to have high annual incomes. "There is a myth out there that upscale consumers only enjoy upscale media and entertainment," explained Infiniti marketing vice president Orbe, "but the reality is, they enjoy shows like *ER* and *Seinfeld.* Baby boomers are the first generation to grow up in mass entertainment culture. If we want to reach them, we've got to entertain and engage them."

The consumer of luxury products in the 1980s had been far more status-conscious and ostentatious than those in the 1990s. While the boomers of the 1990s appreciated excellence and "the finer things," they were less interested in status symbols. Trying to balance professional lives, family, and recreation, boomers had little spare time for television viewing, making them selective about what they did watch; they tended to do less channel surfing. Advertising had to be highly engaging to hold their attention and avoid being "muted" with the remote. Orbe described the unique Infiniti personality as "youthful, smart, innovative," not coincidentally the core attributes baby boomers seemed to value in themselves and others.

When the new campaign was assigned to Chiat-Day at the end of 1996, there was much speculation about whether Pryce would continue to serve as Infiniti spokesman. "There's no mandate for Pryce to be in or out," said agency chairman Clow. "If we think there's a fun twist, we'll do it." But rumors proved correct; Pryce was out, definitive proof that the snob factor was dropped.

"Own One and You'll Understand" was a brand promise of sorts. It reached beyond entertaining the viewers to engaging them in a potentially meaningful experience. The campaign had a two-pronged goal: to arouse non-owners' curiosity about the Infiniti, and to reinforce current owners' pride of ownership. In achieving these two goals, the campaign also would provide Infiniti its own strong identity and differentiate it more strongly from Lexus.

The various television spots, directed by Joe Pytka (his first for Chiat-Day in 20 years), used dark humor. One was set at a funeral and showed an elderly man being buried with his Infiniti. In another a man scrambles through an airport for a set of keys to his Infiniti. In the third spot, "Half," a man is served divorce papers. He is informed that his wife wants half of everything, and he goes into a rage. "She gets half? I'll give her half," he snaps. Then he maniacally takes a chain-saw and cuts in half all his possessions, including a piano, furniture, pool table, and artwork. Next, he grabs an acetylene torch and moves to the garage. But he stops when he comes to his Infiniti. "On second thought, maybe we can work this out," he mutters. The viewers did not learn much about Infinitis, but the message at least was clear: Infiniti owners had a real passion for their cars.

The television campaign covered all geographic areas where Infiniti retailers were located and ran on top prime time and cable network programs. It continued to run through 1997 and into 1998.

OUTCOME

In mid-1996 Infiniti dealers were less than happy with the franchise. A significant part of this displeasure was caused by confusion in the advertising message. But by the end of 1997 sales had climbed 17.1 percent to 65,552 units, a record. Dealer profits were higher than ever before. The division overall finally became profitable and recouped its original investment in the United States. The "Own One and You'll Understand" campaign could be credited with a major role in the turnaround.

Indeed, Infiniti saw the campaign as key to its new success; the company extended the campaign into the summer of 1998, with the plan to shift some of the focus from story lines to product features. The lack of such focus had drawn complaints from some critics. "If you don't own one, the ad doesn't steer you to why you should," commented the *Los Angeles Times.* Bob Garfield of *Advertising Age* criticized "Half," saying that it had "an anticlimactic ending to a broad, obvious, and derivative commercial."

Nevertheless, simplifying seemed to have worked for Infiniti. Gone were the stuffy English accents and tuxedos. Given the sales data after the campaign began running, the company had successfully leveraged the simple fact that Infiniti owners loved their cars.

FURTHER READING

Garfield, Bob. "Actor Takes Infiniti on a Tour de Force." *Advertising Age,* June 9, 1997, p. 53.

Johnson, Bradley and Mark Rechtin. "Nissan Packs $200 Mil into Yearlong Drive for Brand." *Advertising Age,* August 5, 1996.

Rechtin, Mark. "Turnaround Puts Infiniti on Road to Strong Sales." *Automotive News,* January 26, 1998, pp. 3-4.

———. "Infiniti Alters Ad Strategy." *Automotive News,* January 20, 1997, p. 6.

Taylor, Alex III. "Nissan's Bold Bid for Market Share." *Fortune,* January 1, 1990, p. 99.

Cynthia Tokumitsu

Nordstrom, Inc.

1617 Sixth Avenue
Seattle, Washington 98101-1742
USA
Telephone: (206) 628-2111
Fax: (206) 628-1795
Web site: www.nordstrom.com

MAKE ROOM FOR SHOES CAMPAIGN

OVERVIEW

According to *Forbes* magazine, Internet and catalog shoe shopping was a $2 billion business in 1999. Clothing retailer Nordstrom, Inc., which had launched an Internet subsidiary—Nordstrom.com—in 1998, quickly discovered that selling shoes online could be big business. By the end of that year shoes accounted for 30 percent of all Nordstrom's online sales. In response to growing consumer interest in shopping online for shoes, and armed with its history as a shoe store and its reputation for offering a wide selection of footwear, Nordstrom.com spun off a new website, Nordstromshoes.com. The site's inventory included 20 million pairs of shoes from some of Nordstrom's most popular brands and promised consumers that it was the world's biggest online shoe store.

Nordstrom enlisted ad agency Fallon McElligott Minneapolis to create a marketing campaign, estimated to have a budget between $15 million and $17 million, to support the launch of the shoes-only website. Although the new site offered a selection of shoes for women, men, and children, the campaign, titled "Make Room for Shoes," targeted women, who were most likely to be passionate about footwear. It began in November 1999, ran for 60 days, and included television spots, billboards in selected markets, and print ads in fashion, business, and entertainment magazines.

"Make Room for Shoes" was well received by the advertising industry and consumers. Among the awards presented to Fallon for its efforts were two Bronze Clios and multiple Cannes Lion awards for the print ads and an MPA/Kelly Award for the fact that the campaign exceeded all expectations and drove consumer traffic to the new website. In addition, *Fortune* magazine rated the shopping experience on the Nordstromshoes.com website above par compared with other Internet shopping sites. *The Gunn Report,* which listed results of all the major advertising award contests each year to establish a worldwide guide of top-winning ads for the advertising industry, ranked the Nordstromshoes.com print ads among the year's most awarded. Nordstrom also reported that its July 2000 online sales increased 700 percent compared to the same period the previous year.

HISTORICAL CONTEXT

When John W. Nordstrom opened his first store in 1901 in Seattle, Washington, the only merchandise he offered was shoes. The business grew, becoming the largest independent shoe-store chain in the United States by 1960. In the mid-1960s the retailer expanded its offerings to include women's clothing. Men's and children's apparel were added to the product mix in 1966. The chain eventually grew to 103 stores in 23 states. For people who were unable to shop in one of its stores, Nordstrom offered a mail-order-catalog business. In 1998, responding to growing consumer interest in Internet and online shopping, Nordstrom launched Nordstrom.com as a subsidiary of the company. The company's new e-commerce presence was focused on expanding its retail business both online and in catalog sales.

Nordstrom.com and its merchandise selection appealed to consumers. Following the launch of its website in 1998 the company reported that Internet sales, along with catalog purchases, accounted for $200 million of the company's $5 billion in overall sales. And shoes were a big seller. According to company records, 30 percent of its Internet sales were shoes, with footwear accounting for 7 of the top 20 best-selling items online. Based on the success of shoe sales through its website, in 1999 the company launched Nordstromshoes.com. The new site was a subsidiary of Nordstrom.com and focused entirely on shoes. It offered a selection of 20 million pairs of shoes and featured products from 40 of Nordstrom's top shoe brands for everyone in the family, including Cole-Haan, Dr. Martens, and Stride Rite, as well as its private-label brands Classique and Preview. Nordstromshoes.com also returned to the retailer's roots as the largest independent shoe-store chain in the United States, but now Nordstrom tagged its new website as the largest shoe store in the world. At the time of Nordstromshoes.com's launch, company copresident Dan Nordstrom told *Business Wire* that Nordstrom's 100-year history as a shoe retailer combined with the technological skills of the team behind Nordstrom.com would help develop "one of the most exciting fashion destinations on the Internet."

TARGET MARKET

Fallon's research prior to the creation of its "Make Room for Shoes" campaign indicated that, while not all women were passionate about shoes, many women considered it impossible to own too many pairs of them. That idea became the basis for the campaign to introduce Nordstromshoes.com. Although the site offered shoes for men and children as well as women, the campaign took a humorous approach to the passion that a large cross section of the female population had for shoes. It targeted busy professional women who wanted to buy shoes but who had little time to shop in traditional brick-and-mortar stores. It was also aimed at younger, hipper consumers who perceived Nordstrom as a store for more mature shoppers. In addition, Fallon hoped to convince consumers that it was possible to purchase shoes without trying them on first and that buying them online was a good alternative to buying them in a traditional store.

> ### WIN SHOES FOR LIFE CONTEST INTRODUCES SHOPPERS TO NEW NORDSTROM WEBSITE
>
> To attract shoppers to its new website, Nordstromshoes.com, Nordstrom launched its Make Room for Shoes contest, in which five grand-prize winners would receive new shoes for life. The prize had an estimated retail value of $15,000. In addition, 25 first-prize winners would each receive new shoes for one year, with a retail value of up to $1,000. The contest ran from November 1 through November 30, 1999, with a winner drawn weekly beginning November 7. Winners selected their prizes from the Nordstromshoes.com inventory of more than 20 million pairs of men's, women's, and children's shoes.

COMPETITION

In 1999 Nordstrom was not the only company venturing into the online shoe business. A long list of retailers—both brick-and-mortar ones such as Nordstrom as well as businesses specifically created for the Internet—were selling shoes on their websites. Among the sites were bluefly.com, which offered discounts on Prada stilettos, Dr. Scholl's sandals, and everything in between; candies.com, which sold its own brand of footwear for teens; 81shoes.com for kids or preteens; MVP.com, offering athletic shoes for everyone; magnumboots.com, with a selection of work boots designed for men and women with jobs in construction, law enforcement, and the postal service; and kennethcole.com for fashion-minded women. Two online stores that went head-to-head with Nordstromshoes.com were Zappos.com and onlineshoes.com.

Zappos.com shared two things in common with Nordstromshoes.com: it was launched in 1999, and it billed itself at the world's largest online shoe store. The company competed with Nordstromshoes.com by allowing consumers to shop for shoes using a variety of criteria, such style, size, and price, and it offered a selection of shoes from 125 brand names as well as a personal-shopper service. It also reportedly had 90,000 styles and 2 million pairs of shoes in stock. By July 2000, one year after its launch, Zappos.com was named the highest-ranking footwear e-tailer by *PC Data Online,* ahead of Nordstromshoes.com.

Onlineshoes.com was an old-timer by Internet retailer standards. The company had been selling shoes online since 1996, and like Nordstromshoes.com, it was an Internet spin-off of its brick-and-mortar parent company, the shoe-store chain Gerler & Son, based in Seattle, Washington. Its website promised, "All the Shoes, All the Sizes, All the Time." According to the company, its Internet business plan followed the model of a traditional retail company. It also stated that it planned to promote its business primarily through advertising on the Internet, supplemented by ads in magazines and newspapers. To encourage consumers to shop for shoes at its site, onlineshoes.com offered a 30-day money-back guarantee on all of its merchandise.

MARKETING STRATEGY

When Nordstrom decided to launch an online shoe store, the company enlisted Fallon McElligott Minneapolis to create a marketing campaign that would introduce the new website to consumers. According to Peter McHugh, Fallon's group creative director, consumer research—which included interviews with women who seemed to agree that a woman could never have too many shoes—led to the idea for the campaign's theme, "Make Room for Shoes." Working from the original idea, Fallon developed three television spots that showed women making room for their shoes. The $15 to $17 million, 60-day campaign also included print and outdoor advertisements.

The "Make Room for Shoes" television spots, titled "Moving Van," "Crush," and "Doorstep," used humor to portray the passion many women had for shoes and the extremes they might go to in their attempt to make sure they had plenty of room for new additions to their footwear. Spots appeared during prime time on network and cable channels and aired during some of television's most popular programs aimed at women, including *Ally McBeal, The Practice,* and *Frasier.* In "Moving Van" a young couple was shown driving down a highway in a moving van loaded with their possessions. Suddenly struck by the need to make room for more shoes, the woman began throwing their belongings from the van. Lamps, a sofa, and her husband's motorcycle were all tossed out onto the highway. "Crush" depicted a middle-aged woman arriving at a junkyard in a shiny, fully restored 1957 red Cadillac. After a brief conversation with the junkyard's owner, the woman watched as the car was lifted onto a crushing machine and flattened. A scene shift then showed the woman's husband at home opening the garage, ready to wash his prized Cadillac, only to find the flat car propped against the wall. His wife, too, had made room for more shoes. The final spot, "Doorstep," pictured a woman stopping her car in front of a moonlit home. She got out of the car and struggled to carry her sleeping husband, dressed only in his boxers, to the home's front door. She quietly set the still-sleeping man down on the porch and attached a note to him that read, "Please take care of my husband." This woman had thus also made more room for her shoes.

Print ads appeared in newspapers that were typically read by women professionals, such as the *Los Angeles Times, USA Today,* and the *Wall Street Journal.* Print ads also ran in fashion, entertainment, and business magazines, including *Allure, W, InStyle, Entertainment Weekly,* and *Fast Company.* Billboard ads were strategically placed in Chicago, New York, and San Francisco to target women commuting to and from work. One print ad showed a picture of a smiling couple in which the man had been ripped out. Another pictured a child's bedroom with everything removed except the curtains and a pink mylar balloon floating near the ceiling in one corner. The text read, "Make room for shoes. Get rid of everything else. Nordstrom has the world's biggest shoe store."

OUTCOME

Fallon's "Make Room for Shoes" campaign was well received by both the advertising industry and consumers. Following the campaign's 1999 launch, the 2000 *Gunn Report,* an annual industry publication that listed the award-winning campaigns from the top international and national creative competitions, named Fallon the third-most-awarded advertising agency in the world. The report also placed Nordstromshoes.com at number 18 on the list of most-awarded print ads.

Among the awards given in 2000 that led to Fallon's ranking in *The Gunn Report* were two Clios for the Nordstromshoes.com print ads "Public Transportation" and "Kid's Room," Bronze Cannes Lions awards for the print ads "Kid's Room," "Closet," and "Screw Cooking," and a Magazine Publishers of America (MPA) Kelly Award for the entire campaign. The MPA/Kelly Award noted that the campaign exceeded expectations in encouraging consumers to visit the Nordstromshoes.com website and in showing that the retailer understood women's passion for shoes. In addition, the Advertising Women of New York, which recognized agencies and clients for their positive or negative portrayals of women in advertising, honored the campaign. During the organization's annual "The Good, the Bad, and the Ugly" awards event Fallon received several Good awards, including the Grand Good for the Nordstromshoes.com television spot "Moving Van."

As consumers faced the hectic holiday season, one of the websites they turned to for shopping was Nordstromshoes.com, which opened for business in November 1999. A review of 50 shopping websites conducted during the holidays for *Fortune* magazine by Columbus, Ohio–based Resource Marketing rated the shopping experience at Nordstromshoes.com above par. Rating criteria included the ease with which orders were placed, on-time delivery of orders, and the helpfulness of each site's customer-service staff. Further, according to Nordstrom officials, July 2000 sales at the company's online sites Nordstrom.com and subsidiary Nordstromshoes.com increased 700 percent over July 1999 sales.

FURTHER READING

Bernard, Sharyn. "Webbed Feet." *Footwear News,* February 4, 2000.

Champagne, Christine. "Getting the Job Done: Fallon's Production Dept. Benefits from Early Creative Involvement." *Shoot,* December 7, 2001, p. 28.

Cuneo, Alice Z. "Nordstrom Moves Women's Footwear to Own Online Rack." *Advertising Age,* October 11, 1999.

DeSalvo, Kathy. "In-Step." *Shoot,* January 21, 2000, p. 24.

Kuchinskas, Susan. "Attention, Please." *Brandweek,* January 17, 2000, p. 56.

Lohrer, Robert. "Nordstrom Announces Major Online Initiative." *Daily News Record,* August 25, 1999.

Michaelson, Elizabeth. "The Good, the Bad and the Ugly Strike Again." *Shoot,* October 6, 2000, p. 7.

Mullins, David P. "Full Service; With a New Website Devoted Solely to Footwear, Nordstrom is Extending Its Image as an Accommodating Retailer with a Vast Array of Hot Product." *Footwear News,* March 6, 2000.

———. "Shoe Bytes; Footwear Websites Are Popping Up on the Internet at a Breakneck Pace." *Footwear News,* March 6, 2000.

Mullins, David W., Jr. "Mouse Trap; As Many of Their Competitors Go Bust, Footwear Web Sites Try to Avoid the Pitfalls through Focused Business Plans, Comprehensive Marketing and Supreme Customer Service." *Footwear News,* February 26, 2001.

"Nordstrom.com Launches World's Biggest Shoe Store with Make Room for Shoes Sweepstakes." *Business Wire,* November 1, 1999.

"Nordstrom.com Unveils First-Ever National Advertising Campaign for Nordstromshoes.com." *Business Wire,* October 29, 1999.

Parpis, Eleftheria. "Creative Awards: Budding Genius." *Adweek,* May 29, 2000.

Plotkin, Amanda. "Nordstrom Seeks Lion's Share of Online Shoe Biz." *Footwear News,* August 30, 1999.

"Zappos.com Offers the Largest Selection of Men's and Women's Shoes On-Line." *PR Newswire,* April 4, 2000.

Rayna Bailey

REINVENT YOURSELF CAMPAIGN

OVERVIEW

In 2000 Nordstrom was an aging retailer with an identity crisis. Its core customers—baby boomers—continued to rely on the chain's classic merchandise and top-of-the-line customer service that often included employees writing thank-you notes following a purchase and staffers willing to carry an overloaded customer's packages to her car. Younger consumers, however, considered the department store, which typically served as an anchor in a suburban mall, as a place where their grandmothers shopped. In 1998 Nordstrom undertook a series of surveys and focus-group studies of customers and noncustomers, employees, and stockholders. The results indicated that Nordstrom's steadily declining sales, particularly in women's apparel, were due in part to the perception that its stores were stuffy and its fashions boring and outdated.

In 2000 Nordstrom began the process of reinventing itself, including opening new stores with more contemporary decor—such as one on Chicago's Michigan Avenue—remodeling existing stores, and stocking trendier merchandise. At the same time, with the help of its Minneapolis-based advertising agency, Fallon Worldwide, Nordstrom launched a national marketing campaign encouraging customers to reinvent themselves as well. The $40 million campaign, appropriately themed "Reinvent Yourself," began in early 2000 and included spots aired during hit television shows such as *Friends* and *Ally McBeal.* Print ads appeared in major magazines, and billboards ads were placed in key markets, including New York City's Times Square. The print ads depicted new takes on traditional stereotypes; for instance, the girl next door, who was expected to be dressed in a dotted dress and pigtails, was instead showed dressed in non-stereotypical orange spike-heeled boots paired with red slacks.

Despite earning accolades and awards from the Advertising Women of New York for the campaign's positive portrayal of women, and although the campaign resonated with younger consumers, it alienated the baby boomers that made up Nordstrom's core customer base. Nordstrom's sales continued to drop following the campaign's launch, slipping 24 percent in the first quarter of 2001. In response, the chain pulled the campaign and backpedaled on its merchandising strategy.

HISTORICAL CONTEXT

Nordstrom opened for business in 1901 in Seattle, Washington, as a shoe store. Over the years the company built a devoted customer base on its business philosophy of providing exceptional service, selection, quality, and value. Eventually the company grew to eight stores, and by 1960 it was the largest independent shoe-store chain in the United States. Its offerings gradually expanded to include apparel. The company went public in 1971 and by 1973 had passed the $100 million sales mark.

© GREG SMITH/CORBIS.

In 1998 Nordstrom expanded its six-year-old catalog business and ventured onto the Internet. It launched Nordstrom.com with the goal of building its flagship business and focusing on what had given the chain its start: selling shoes. Breaking from its tradition of using regional marketing with a focus on newspaper print ads, in 1999 the chain launched its first-ever national advertising campaign. The $15 million campaign, developed by Fallon McElligott, was designed to promote Nordstrom's subsidiary, www.Nordstrom.com, and it especially emphasized the company's wide selection of high-quality shoes, sold on the new site www.NordstromShoes.com, which was touted as the "world's biggest shoe store." Tagged "Make Room for Shoes," the campaign included print and television advertising as well as a national sweepstakes with a grand prize of a lifetime supply of shoes (valued at $15,000). But despite shifting to a national approach for its marketing, in 2000 the aging retailer found itself on a downward slide. To try and reverse the trend and to entice younger consumers away from the middle-of-the-mall boutique-style shops and into its department stores, Nordstrom decided to run another national marketing campaign and enlisted Fallon to develop it. The resulting "Reinvent Yourself" campaign was launched in 2000.

TARGET MARKET

With its high-quality, classic clothing offerings and reputation for catering to customers' needs, Nordstrom was a shopping haven for baby boomers, both men and women. But in an effort to shake its stodgy image and lure younger customers into its stores, Nordstrom updated its merchandise and aimed its advertising at younger urban consumers. Not wanting to alienate the older suburban shoppers who were used to the chain's informal, easygoing approach to customer service, Nordstrom also wanted to aim the advertising at middle-aged, middle-income, suburban women. Additionally, the company hoped to shatter cultural stereotypes such as soccer moms, women who shuttled their kids from one activity to another, the girl-next-door, and high-energy career women. All women were encouraged to reinvent themselves and their way of thinking about how they expressed their individuality. Nordstrom did not neglect men with the "Reinvent Yourself" campaign, either. The campaign encouraged men—from recent college graduates starting their careers to experienced professionals—to rethink everything from business suits to casual wear.

COMPETITION

While Nordstrom worked to reinvent its stores and update its merchandise to attract new, younger customers while keeping its core customers, Federated Department Stores, Inc., the largest upscale department-store retailer in the United States, was facing similar challenges. Although Federated, which owned the department-store chains Bloomingdale's and Macy's, reported record-high profits in 1999, in 2000 its goal was to attract younger customers, who perceived department stores as places

TEENS ON NORDSTROM'S MARKETING RADAR

Using computers and software technology, Nordstrom launched a marketing campaign in 2000 designed to attract teen shoppers. The retailer partnered with *Teen People* magazine to produce an interactive CD, called "BP-ROM," that promoted Nordstrom's junior department, the Brass Plum. Featured on the CD were spring fashions, accessories, and beauty products, clips from music videos, and select scenes from WB Network television shows. *Selling to Kids* magazine stated that the campaign fit with the high-tech lives most teens lived and that the promotion meshed perfectly with Nordstrom's "Reinvent Yourself" campaign, which was developed to dispel common stereotypes about the high-end retail department store, including that the store was out of sync with contemporary shoppers.

where their grandmothers shopped. With a reported annual employee turnover rate of 60 percent in some stores, another concern for Federated was hiring and keeping staff. Federated's strategy included testing several revamped junior departments in its California and Florida stores, introducing a private-label brand of apparel and accessory items for kids and teens, and increasing efforts to hire young talent through its recruitment website for college students, www.retailology.com.

The number three department-store chain in the United States—behind Federated and Saint Louis, Missouri–based May Department Stores Company—was Dillard's, headquartered in Little Rock, Arkansas. It faced its own unique problems in 2000. Dillard's reported that earnings for its second quarter in 2000 were down 74 percent from 1999, and adding insult to injury was an article published in *Forbes* magazine that questioned every aspect of the company's management, from the Dillard family's iron-fisted rule to its refusal to provide business-related information to investors, analysts, and the media. The article stated that, while Dillard's had once been a first-class retailer, it had fallen to perhaps the nation's worst. Looking for ways to improve its profit margins, Dillard's turned to one of Federated's tactics: private label brands. But problems, including negative press, continued to hinder Dillard's. In 2001 the company pulled its commercials from CBS television affiliates following a *60 Minutes* segment alleging that Dillard's practiced racial profiling to target shoplifters. According to a report in *Advertising Age,* Dillard's stated that *60 Minutes* had treated the chain unfairly in its broadcast, allowing it only a few seconds of a 13-minute story for a response.

MARKETING STRATEGY

Nordstrom's $40 million national marketing campaign, "Reinvent Yourself," was reportedly the biggest ever undertaken by the company. The campaign was based on extensive consumer research conducted by Nordstrom that made it clear that Nordstrom's reputation for offering classic clothing in a prim and proper shopping environment no longer resonated with shoppers. Instead there was a strong preference for searching for trendy merchandise in a hip environment. In addition, customers perceived the stores as outdated and difficult to shop in. Nordstrom took the surveys to heart and began a major remodeling project at its stores and revamped its merchandise offerings. To support the effort Nordstrom launched its "Reinvent Yourself" campaign. Developed by Minneapolis-based agency Fallon Worldwide, it featured ads in print and on billboards as well as television spots. The campaign was designed to convince consumers that Nordstrom was listening to what customers were saying and that the company was determined to meet their needs by updating its stores and restructuring its women's apparel divisions, among other efforts.

"Reinvent Yourself" kicked off in February 2000 with TV spots that ran during network shows, including *Friends, Ally McBeal,* and *The Practice,* as well as on cable channels such as VH-1 and A&E. The spots suggested a variety of ways that viewers could reinvent themselves or aspects of their lives, much as Nordstrom was reinventing itself. One black-and-white TV spot, titled "Doorway," portrayed a young man standing outside a closed door under an umbrella in the rain, waiting to meet his date. When the beautiful woman opened the door, it was clear from the man's expression that he was impressed. The spot closed with the tagline "Reinvent the compliment."

In a break from Nordstrom's tradition of running its ads in newspapers, print ads for the campaign appeared in glossy national magazines, including *Elle* and *Vanity Fair.* Ads published in the magazines *Essence* and *Latina* reached out to minority shoppers. The marketing also encouraged consumers to think outside of the box and used humor to address cultural stereotypes. One print ad portrayed a middle-aged woman dressed in glittery red slacks and a black cardigan along with the slogan "Reinvent soccer mom," and another suggested "Reinventing the heirloom" and pictured a shapely young woman's abdomen with a diamond stud in her navel. Ads aimed at men included one that pictured a businessman lounging in a reclining chair with a legal pad and pencil in hand but dressed in an unbuttoned oxford shirt and khaki shorts. The slogan exclaimed, "Reinvent the power suit."

OUTCOME

Evidence that the company seemed to be reaching its target audience of younger consumers was revealed in comments made by shoppers in a Detroit-area Nordstrom. A 30-year-old, stay-at-home mother referred to the store's designer fashions department when she told the *Detroit Free Press,* "This section used to be so grandmothery, and now it's fun." A 23-year-old college student said of the updated store and merchandise, "I love it. I've noticed there's a lot better selection for my age group. The prices appealed to me, too." The "Reinvent Yourself" campaign was also recognized by the Advertising Women of New York for its positive portrayal of women in its television spots. During its "The Good, the Bad, and the Ugly" awards ceremony the organization presented two of the spots with "Good" honors.

Despite the company's "Reinvent Yourself" campaign and Nordstrom's efforts to update stores and push more trendy merchandise, many customers and industry insiders still perceived the aging department store as old fashioned and dull. An unidentified retailer told *Women's Wear Daily,* "Generally the merchandise has become boring. They've been flat for too long." Others noted that the campaign seemed to cater to 20-something consumers, resulting in the loss of the store's core customers: baby boomers.

Further, while Nordstrom's "Reinvent Yourself" campaign achieved some of its goals, it was not enough to produce positive results. In the first quarter of 2001 Nordstrom reported that its profits had dipped 24 percent and that same-store sales had fallen 3.7 percent. Following the continued drop in sales, a complete shakeup at the upper levels of the chain—including pushing out company chairman and chief executive Jack Whitacer—eventually returned full control of the business to Nordstrom family members. Additionally, because the "Reinvent Yourself" campaign had alienated the company's core customers, Nordstrom reversed itself and pulled the campaign. By July 2001 Nordstrom appeared to be back on track, reporting that sales were up 1.8 percent from the same month in 2000. The company also reported that sales in the women's category, the one that attracted baby-boomer shoppers and that accounted for 36 percent of total sales, had shown increases for the previous six months.

FURTHER READING

Allen, Angela. "Nordstrom Reinvents Vitamin C—and Its Looks." *Vancouver Columbian,* March 18, 2000.

Baeb, Eddie. "Nordstrom Gets Hip; Mag Mile Store Tests Retailer's Urban Chic Strategy." *Crain's Chicago Business,* May 22, 2000.

"Breakfast Briefing: Weekend." *Chicago Sun-Times,* February 12, 2000.

"Can the Nordstroms Find the Right Style?" *BusinessWeek,* July 30, 2001.

Chaney, Don. "Stinging Forbes Article Adds Insult to Dillard's Injury." *Arkansas Business,* September 11, 2000.

Cuneo, Alice Z. "Nordstrom Breaks with Traditional Media Plan; Retail Chain Applies $40 Mil to Reviving Sales." *Advertising Age,* February 14, 2000.

DeSimone, Elaine. "Nordstrom Reinvents Itself." *Shopping Center World,* June 1, 2000.

Hanson, Holly. "Nordstrom Has Brighter Ideas: Hipper Clothes, Sharper Stores." *Detroit Free Press,* March 16, 2000.

Kossen, Bill. "Sales Climb in July for Seattle-Based Nordstrom." *Seattle Times,* August 7, 2001.

Lillo, Andrea. "Dillard's to Shift Focus to Private-Label Goods." *Home Textiles Today,* December 4, 2000.

Lindeman, Teresa F. "Federated, May, Penney's Setting Out to Capture a Younger Market." *Women's Wear Daily,* May 22, 2000.

Moin, David. "Shakeup in Seattle: CEO Out, Family Back at Nordstrom Helm." *Women's Wear Daily,* September 1, 2000.

"One Size Doesn't Fit All: Today's Working Mothers Defy the Label 'Soccer Mom.'" *American Demographics,* May 2000.

Rayna Bailey

Norelco Consumer Products Company

1010 Washington Blvd.
Stamford, Connecticut 06912-0015
USA
Telephone: (203) 973-0200
Web site: www.norelco.com

NORELCO REFLEX ACTION RAZOR CAMPAIGN

OVERVIEW

Norelco Consumer Products Company introduced the Reflex Action Razor in 1996. The product launch, backed by an unusually large advertising budget and an aggressive marketing campaign, helped revitalize the stagnating electric shaver category. A strategy of wooing wet-shaver users, especially young men, led Norelco's advertising agency, D'Arcy Masius Benton & Bowles (DMB&B) of New York, to create several animated ads that made shaving with a wet razor look about as safe and soothing as using a hungry crocodile to perform the same task. Electric shavers, however, typically required a period of adjustment before they did not irritate the skin, so the Gillette Company, far and away the leader in the wet-shaving market, sued Norelco and won an injunction that prevented Norelco from claiming that its electric shavers were less irritating than wet-shaving systems.

To meet the legal requirements DMB&B created a series of ads in which young men were asked to shave with the Reflex Action Razor for 21 days and then decide whether to toss their conventional wet razors. The series included the popular "Hockey" spot, which featured players from the Hartford Wolfpack minor league hockey team who were initially skeptical about the electric shaver. The players were eventually won over, however, and their clean-shaven faces garnered comments such as the following from an opposing team's mascot: "Look at you, pretty boys. So smoooooth." The mascot was then slammed into the boards by the beard-free Wolfpack players. The campaign was a success, and the electric shaver category saw growth in its aftermath.

HISTORICAL CONTEXT

The Philips Company was founded in 1891 as a lightbulb company in the Dutch town of Eindhoven by a young engineer, Gerard Philips. Gerard's brother Anton joined the company in 1895, and it was he who encouraged Professor Alexandre Horowitz to develop the company's rotary electric shaver. During the Great Depression Philips sales lagged, and the company began searching for products to expand its market reach beyond the lightbulbs and radios for which it had become known. A Philips executive traveling in the United States collected a number of electric shavers, which had been developed by American Jacob Schick in the 1920s. Horowitz showed interest in the electric shavers and created his own shaving system, which, unlike Schick's reciprocating-cut shavers, used rotating cutters. The Philishave was first sold in 1939 in Europe, just as World War II was breaking out. American GIs returning home from the war in Europe who had used the Philishave created a demand for the product in the United States. Philips began marketing shavers in the United States under the Norelco name in 1948. Norelco's first product was a man's rotary razor, which was an immediate success. Norelco led the electric razor category from that time forward.

The company expanded over the next several decades and increased its product line to include hundreds of household items. In the late 1980s, however, Norelco scaled back and cut by 50 percent the number of products it was selling, leaving some markets altogether in order to focus on shavers, coffeemakers, steam irons, and air-filtering machines. Norelco also decided to focus its marketing efforts on high-end products for which consumers would be willing to pay a premium. For years the company's razors were advertised with special Christmastime ads that showed an animated Santa Claus sledding over snowy hills on a Norelco shaver and the tag line "Norelco—even our name says 'Merry Christmas.'" The ads, although long-running, neither boosted electric razor sales nor converted blade users; instead, they promoted the notion that Norelco was a toy company. The ads were dropped in 1986, and Norelco began a high-tech campaign with DMB&B emphasizing models with features such as the company's patented lift-and-cut system, rechargeable batteries and charge meters, and ergonomic design. "We made close comfortable" was the tag line.

From 1986 to 1989 sales of Norelco's razors soared from $100 to $160 million annually, as did the company's advertising budget. When DMB&B signed on with Norelco in 1987, the ad budget was reported at $10 million annually. Over two years the budget grew to $30 million, enabling the company to buy year-round advertising, rather than its traditional limitation to fourth-quarter ads.

By the mid-1990s sales in the industry had flattened out. Research showed that users of electric razors tended to stick with them, but that wet-razor users—younger men in particular—rarely switched over to electric systems. In the mid-1990s Norelco began an aggressive marketing campaign for its razors. Norelco's Reflex Action Razor enjoyed a historically large advertising budget and was joined in competition by Braun, Remington, and other razor companies trying to reinvigorate the category.

TARGET MARKET

Loyal male electric razor users, most in the 35-plus age range, were known to update their products occasionally. With the launch of the Reflex Action Razor, however, Norelco looked to broaden the market for its electric systems by appealing to younger men and expanding the target consumers to include 18-to-34 year olds. Norelco president Pat Dinley told *Advertising Age* in 1996, "Long-term, the big opportunity is in converting people who use blades to electric." DMB&B account director Robert Easley explained to the same *Advertising Age* reporter the correlation between blade users and youth: "Blades are more heavily developed in the younger segments. They view conventional blade shaving as the norm."

COMPETITION

Norelco dominated the men's electric shaving category, with a reported 50-plus percent market share throughout the 1990s. Remington Products Corporation held the number two spot, and Gillette's Braun was third in sales of electric shavers. Competition among these companies heated up after Norelco introduced the Reflex Action Razor in 1996. Remington launched the Dual Microscreen in 1997, with a sleek design, a beefy advertising budget (up 40 percent from the year before), and the tag line "Built to shave incredibly close." In 1998 Remington rolled out the Microscreen 3. At the same time Braun was pushing its Flex Integral electric shaver to young men and women. All three companies backed up their campaigns with promotions and flashy new packaging.

Perhaps more intense than the competition among electric shaver manufacturers was the war between Norelco and Gillette, the overwhelming leader in the wet-shaving category. Among the first ads for Norelco's Reflex Action Razor was a series of animated spots with names such as "Fire Breathing Razor" and "Twin Blade

SURPRISE PLAY

The hockey players and cadets who eventually starred in Norelco ads did not know at first that they might wind up doing them; they were simply given a free shaver and asked to test it for three weeks. Some of those who liked the shavers were asked to work in the ads, and after the ads had run, a number of the men expressed surprise at their newfound fame. "We didn't think it would be that big," a Wolfpack member told the *New York Daily News.* "So many people have called the house and said, 'I can't believe it, but I just saw you on TV.' It came out great. It's on all the time. It's unbelievable. The whole team was out at dinner the other night and there was a game on and the commercial came on and everybody starting hooting and hollering."

Serpent" that depicted wet razors as nasty creatures, biting, stinging and burning men's faces. The ads carried the tag line, "Anything closer would be too close for comfort." Although the ads did not name a specific brand of wet razor, Gillette sued Norelco for maligning wet shaving and for falsely advertising that electric systems were pain-free. Norelco asserted that its ads were not intended to impugn a specific brand or product, but Gillette spokespeople were widely quoted as saying, "When you disparage wet shaving, you are disparaging Gillette because we are the clear leader in the industry."

Gillette was on somewhat shaky legal ground when it took the Norelco ads personally. But it had a stronger case on its allegation of misleading advertising. It was not common knowledge that electric shavers could irritate skin for up to three weeks on first use and that there was usually a period of adjustment before they provided a thoroughly comfortable shave. Gillette charged that Norelco did not adequately warn consumers about this risk and that the ads showing wet razors as greater irritants were thus deceptive. In December 1996 a judge ruled that Norelco could not claim its own product was less irritating than wet-razor systems, but the judge did not bar the company from portraying wet razors as vicious, and the lawsuit continued. In 1998 a federal court rejected a majority of Gillette's claims (a few points continued in litigation), although by then Norelco had adjusted its advertising to make clear the fact that electric razors might not provide the best shave before a three-week acclimation period.

MARKETING STRATEGY

In 1997 a DMB&B executive was quoted in *Advertising Age,* "You've got to fish where the fish are, and wet razors have great penetration among 18-to-34-year-olds. We're trying to change the perception of electric razors as old-fashioned." To lure younger consumers Norelco designed the Reflex Action Razor to include cutting-edge razor technology that allowed for various shaving angles, an LCD display, and an appealing choice of colors. In its advertising Norelco positioned wet razors as harsh and irritating and showed electric shavers as a less fraught alternative. The ads were intended to reach young men—a group in which about half self-identified as having sensitive skin—and the tag line for the launch campaign of the Reflex Action Razor was, "Anything closer would be too close for comfort." Ads were bought in publications such as *Men's Fitness, GQ,* and *Men's Health* and on both network and cable television.

To back up its ads Norelco invested in direct mail to about three million consumers, in-store displays, and various promotions including a sweepstakes with a car as one of the prizes. Don Imus, a nationally syndicated radio show host, was convinced to take the "21-day test drive" on the air, and consumers were offered a money-back guarantee if they took the test and found the Reflex Action Razor did not satisfy their needs. Norelco also bought a sponsorship with the National Hockey League, whose viewers were predominantly young and male. For Norelco's sponsorship the NHL created a "Face Off" award, tracking individual and team face off statistics. While shaving sponsorships were not new to the world of professional sports, the NHL sponsorship was particularly notable because Norelco had not invested much in such promotions previously.

Norelco spent more on its launch of the Reflex Action Razor than it had on any previous campaign. According to *Brandweek,* "[Norelco] normally outspends the rest of its competitors combined on advertising and spent $30 million on the intro of its Reflex Action Razor."

OUTCOME

The electric shaver market grew a modest 3 to 4 percent per year during the mid- and late 1990s. Retailers attributed the growth both to advertising and to improved packaging that made the shopping experience easier for the consumer. The ads themselves were a hit, and the "Hockey" commercial garnered an *Adweek* award for one of the top spots of 1998. Sportswriters favorably compared the ads to the NHL's own marketing, and Sherry Ross of the *New York Daily News* noted that "one of the most amusing sports-themed advertisements on television [portrayed] hockey players as personable and human, something the NHL has failed to do."

Following on the success of the Reflex Action Razor ads, Norelco continued its use of the 21-day trial period concept with new products such as the Advantage Razor, attempting to further penetrate the blade-users market. The Advantage was a hybrid electric unit, dispensing shaving lotion and intended for use with water. Advertising for the Advantage challenged consumers to take the 21-day test drive, at the end of which they could get their money back if they had not made the razor part of their daily routine. In one ad for the Advantage, a gritty Hartford Wolfpack player likened the action of Norelco's newest product to that of an ice-smoothing Zamboni machine.

Another set of 21-day-trial ads for the Advantage Razor employed Virginia Military Institute (VMI) cadets. The *Roanoke Times* reported that the "inspection-dreading cadets" of America's military schools were chosen because they must "have a close shave all of the time." Four of the cadets who tried the Advantage were chosen to star in the spot, which was a campy send-up of military life. For instance, after using the Norelco razor for three weeks, one cadet was seen smearing camouflage makeup on his face for woods maneuvers when he had the revelation that he had gotten a really close shave from the Advantage. The stars were paid $450 per day during the three-day filming of the ad, and VMI was paid $12,500 for use of the site. Although VMI accepts women, none were asked to participate in the exercise.

FURTHER READING

Chittum, Matt. "Razor Ad Whets Cadets' Interest; Norelco Plays on Need to 'Have a Close Shave All of the Time,'" *Roanoke Times* & *World News,* July 31, 1998, p. B1.

Eckhouse, Kim. "Men's Shaver Makers Try for a Greater Edge." *HFN: The Weekly Newspaper for the Home Furnishing Network,* October 12, 1998.

"Federal Court Rejects Vast Majority of Gillette Claims that Norelco's 1996 Advertisements for the Reflex Action Were False or Misleading." *Business Wire,* October 16, 1998.

King, Thomas R. "Norelco Fires Santa from Ads; Sales Gain." *Wall Street Journal,* December 29, 1989.

Lefton, Terry. "NHL Nets Norelco as Official Blade." *Brandweek,* January 6, 1997, p. 1.

Martinez, Matthew. "Norelco Revives Campaign that Sparked Suit: Electric Shaver Marketer Budgets $17 Mil for Ads Blasting Wet Razors." *Advertising Age,* October 13, 1997, p. 3.

Mehegan, Sean. "New Remington Regime Re-enters Media Pipeline with $10M in Ads." *Brandweek,* November 10, 1997, p. 8.

Millstein, Marc. "Norelco Looks to the 90's: Banks on Strategy of Consolidation, Innovation." *HFN: The Weekly Home Furnishings Newspaper,* December 4, 1989, p. 64.

"Norelco's New Reflex Action Men's Electric Razor Features Innovative Engineering; Delivers Less Irritation than Blades." *PR Newswire,* September 20, 1996.

Petrecca, Laura. "Norelco Courts Younger Crowd; Reflex Action Razor Gets $30 Million Campaign to Appeal to the Hip." *Advertising Age,* September 30, 1996, p. 64.

———. "Norelco Puts New Shaver to the Test: Trial Is Key Component of Estimated $35 Mil Ad Push for Advantage." *Advertising Age,* August 31, 1998, p. 10.

Ross, Sherry. "League Is Missing Promotional Boat." *New York Daily News,* November 29, 1998, p. 109.

Sarah Milstein

Normark Corporation

10395 Yellow Circle Dr.
Minnetonka, Minnesota 55345-9101
USA
Telephone: (612) 933-7060
Fax: (612) 933-0046
Web site: www.rapala.com

■■■

CUSTOM LURES CAMPAIGN

OVERVIEW

Based in Minnetonka, Minnesota, Normark Corporation was the exclusive U.S. distributor for Rapala, a Finnish-made fishing lure that was the leader in its market segment. Normark had long worked with Carmichael Lynch, a Minneapolis-based advertising agency noted for its many accounts with makers and distributors of sports-related merchandise. Over the years Carmichael Lynch turned out a number of significant print and television ads for Normark, but the company's 1998 advertising was much more limited. By far the most prominent piece was a small—but highly effective—ad that ran in *World Traveler,* the in-flight magazine of Northwest Airlines, late in the year. Budget for the ad, or that of Normark's overall 1998 advertising, was not disclosed.

Rapala was a family-owned business whose founder developed a unique lure in the 1930s. It entered the U.S. market in the early 1960s with the founding of the company that would become Normark and gained great exposure thanks to a 1962 article in *Life* magazine. Rapala lures became so popular with U.S. anglers that competition was not a significant factor.

The 1998 promotion marked a new and interesting strategic direction for Normark, whose *World Traveler* ad offered businesspeople the opportunity to purchase custom lures engraved with their corporate logo. The latter, Normark suggested, would make great promotional gifts. "What we found," a company executive stated in a news release, "is many of these companies looked at our fishing lures as a unique way to bond with their customers or show their sales force a sign of appreciation, rather than giving them another golf ball or paperweight."

HISTORICAL CONTEXT

Rapala founder Lauri Saarinen, better known as Lauri Rapala, was born in central Finland in 1905. While working as a commercial fisherman, Rapala hit upon the idea of developing a lure that imitated the movement of minnows, which were eaten by larger fish. In 1935 he fashioned his first lure from cork. Because he did not have much money, Rapala had to use common materials that he could find in the village where he lived. He used tinfoil from cheese packets and chocolate bars to make the lure shiny, and he melted used photographic negatives to coat the surface. Rapala's first lure is still on display at the company's Vaaksy, Finland, headquarters: black on the top, gold along the sides, and white on the bottom, it is the same color as the minnows that swam in Lake Paijanne, where Rapala fished.

The lure proved enormously successful, and with it Rapala was able to catch 600 pounds of fish a day. While serving in the Finnish army during World War II he began to interest his comrades in the lure. They were using a much cruder method to catch fish, dynamiting a lake, and Rapala proved to them that he could catch more fish with his lure than they could with their dynamite. After the war, the Rapala family—Lauri, his four sons, and his wife Elma, who worked as bookkeeper—founded the Rapala company and began manufacturing the lures.

TARGET MARKET

Rapala had a huge business among U.S. anglers through Normark, the company that held exclusive distribution rights to Rapala lures in the United States. That company was founded by Ron Weber and Ray Ostrom, two Minnesotans impressed by the quality of Rapala lures. Weber discovered the product by chance in 1959 when a friend received a Rapala lure from a relative who worked at the U.S. embassy in Helsinki. Enthusiastic over his new find, Weber wrote to the company requesting 500 lures, and Rapala's international business was born. A year later the company that would become Normark set up shop in the basement of Ostrom's Marine & Sporting Goods Store.

The Rapala product held instant appeal for fishermen seeking more lightweight lures, and its ability to catch fish made it an instant winner despite its relatively high price. When Weber and Ostrom first went into business—they initially called their enterprise the Rapala Company and later Nordic Enterprises before settling on Normark in 1965—typical lures sold for 99 cents, and many anglers balked at Rapala's $1.95 price tag. When they saw what it could do, however, they quickly began buying the lures in large quantities.

The name Normark was meant to symbolize the northern United States, and indeed Normark did much of its business among anglers—a group that is largely, though not exclusively, male—fishing in that area. Minnesota itself was known as the "Land of 10,000 Lakes," and many small bodies of water surrounded the Great Lakes region. But the appeal of Normark equipment extended throughout the nation, and its lures became as much a part of fishing in other areas as they were in the north.

COMPETITION

Another Minnesota company, Lindy-Little Joe, made lures in the 1990s, and indeed, Dennis Anderson of the *Minneapolis-St. Paul Star-Tribune* lamented the fact that large companies such as it and Normark dominated the field. "Long gone are the times when small, independent firms could hand-stamp a few lures a day and expect to make a profit," he wrote. "Onetime notable manufacturers such as National Bait Company of Minneapolis and the Paul Bunyan Bait Company of the Twin Cities

A SPORTING AGENCY

Carmichael Lynch, the Minneapolis advertising agency that handled Normark's Rapala lure and Blue Fox tackle accounts, was "unofficially known as the master of pastimes," wrote Kathy DeSalvo in *SHOOT,* "due to its fishing, boating, biking, and in-line skating related accounts." In addition to Normark, Carmichael Lynch's other sporting clients included Stren Fishing Lines, Polaris snowmobiles and watercraft (Polaris moved to Martin/Williams in 1998), Schwinn Cycling & Fitness, Rollerblade, and Harley-Davidson Motor Company. "In fact," DeSalvo noted, "it's probably the only agency with Harleys parked in its lobby." President and executive creative director Jack Supple told her, "For a long time, people thought it was, like, a motorcycle gang here."

DeSalvo described a Rollerblade spot by Carmichael Lynch, directed by Eric Young of Young & Company: "A beautiful young woman, 'Colette,' walks down her front steps and chucks a bouquet of roses. The footage is intercut with shots of a letter written by a suitor, explaining he'd wanted to 'stop by' but couldn't because 'the hill's too steep.' We learn that the unrequited lover's skates lacked the patented AVT brakes, 'the easiest way to stop from the company that got it all started.'" Supple explained his agency's appeal: "It isn't just fishing or hobby accounts; it's any 'enthusiast' account—even if that's stretched as far as a bank or a turkey. It can be 'enthusiasm' as well; that's what you should feel in the work."

It was perhaps no accident that Supple himself was a fishing enthusiast, as reported by Doug Smith in the *Minneapolis-St. Paul Star-Tribune.* "I mix business and pleasure," he told Smith. "You see, Rapala is one of our accounts. What better way to develop ideas for lure advertisements than by going fishing?" To judge from Supple's easy handling of fishing lingo, he spent plenty of time on the lakes: describing one fishing adventure, he said, "It was bluebird sky and lots of sun, and you don't really want that. We were throwing black Vibrax bucktails out . . . . On the next cast, I was figure-eighting (swirling the lure in a figure-eight at the side of the boat), hoping [the fish] would come back, when all of a sudden, this 51-incher came out of nowhere. It was cool."

are now absent from the scene. So is the Preston, Minn., firm that once produced the Lazy Ike. Actually, the Lazy Ike—which today is produced by Pradcoin Fort Smith, Ark.—was once manufactured by two companies, one in Decorah, Iowa, and one in Preston, Minn. As one might expect, a court battle ensued over rights to the name, and the Iowa firm . . . ultimately prevailed."

Clearly a great many of Rapala's would-be competitors had been consigned to oblivion, their names known only to enthusiasts and scholars of fishing arcana such as Anderson. Though it was certainly not the only maker of lures and other fishing equipment, Rapala did not face any stiff competition. Noting the 60th anniversary of Rapala lures in 1996, *Outdoor Life* magazine called them "the most popular lure of all time." By that point Rapala was turning out some 15 million lures a year, with plants in Finland and Iceland, and selling its product in more than 120 countries. Revenues had reached $100 million, with annual growth at a staggering 15 percent. It was an impressive achievement for a company that had started with a penniless fisherman, and many years after Lauri Rapala's death in 1975, the company remained in the hands of his family.

MARKETING STRATEGY

Rapala's U.S. advertising perhaps had its beginning with an August 17, 1962, story in *Life* magazine. The cover featured Marilyn Monroe, who had just died, and inside was a small article entitle "A Lure Fish Can't Pass Up." This, of course, was the best kind of advertising—unpaid and unrequested—and it had phenomenal results. Lauri Rapala's grandson, who became the firm's CEO in 1989, told John Steinbreder of *Outdoor Life,* "People wanted my grandfather's plugs so badly they were renting them from tackle shops for $5 a day. With a $25 deposit! And that was at a time when the lures were selling for only a dollar apiece."

With Carmichael Lynch in the 1980s and 1990s, Rapala pursued a much more scientific advertising strategy, using print ads and carefully targeted spots on cable television. "I don't think there is anything more targeted than the fishing category," Rapala's Tom Mackin told William Spain of *Advertising Age.* "We can buy a saltwater fishing show or a walleye fishing show or a bass-fishing show" on networks such as ESPN and TNN. Such networks, Mackin said, "are a very targeted and efficient way to reach [Rapala's] audience. There is no waste involved. It is buying TV with the same strategy we would buy print."

Among notable earlier print advertising Carmichael Lynch did for Normark's Blue Fox line was a television and print campaign in the 1980s, "One Drop Is Powerful Magic," to promote its Dr. Juiceline of scents, which were designed to draw fish to a lure. A low-cost 1988 spot for the Foxee Jig proved highly effective, as did an August 1995 print ad. Of the latter, Lambeth Hochwald in *Sales & Marketing Management* wrote: "To achieve Normark's goal, using large type that nearly filled a two-page spread, the ad 'shouted' that if the product didn't reap a reward, customers [should] stop fishing and find a new hobby—in this case, golf." Hochwald singled out this ad, along with four others by other agencies, as an example of exciting advertising.

Carmichael Lynch's work for Normark in 1998, by contrast, was much less prominent. Only one piece gained notice, and then only some time later, but it was worth the wait. Described in a Normark news release as "a little, half-page ad," the advertisement ran in *World Traveler,* Northwest Airlines' in-flight magazine, late in the year and promoted the idea of fishing lures as unique promotional gifts for use by businesspeople. Rapala offered to print a corporate logo on the side of the lure, thus making it an unusual and memorable gift to exchange as a means of sealing deals between businesses.

OUTCOME

It was a simple idea, but it caught on, according both to Rapala's own news release and to a small article that appeared in the *Arizona Republic* in May 1999. Mackin, Rapala's vice president of marketing, said that within days of the ad's publication, the company received requests from an array of large corporations, including Coca-Cola, Merrill Lynch, 3M, Volkswagen North America, Cargill, Michelin/Uniroyal, and Northwest Airlines itself. As of May 1999, Normark had sold more than 60,000 of the specially imprinted lures.

"I think we really tapped into something," Mackin said. "We initially placed the ads as a test. We saw it as a way to extend our business to a new segment of the market, selling direct business-to-business." The Normark news release also quoted Barbara May, executive director of Sales and Marketing Executives International in Alexandria, Virginia. "As business becomes more cutthroat, sales and marketing executives are exploring opportunities that help them bond better with their clients," May said. "The response to the Rapala fishing lure doesn't surprise me. Companies are focusing harder than ever on one-to-one relationships with customers. To do that, they sometimes need to give mementoes with meaning." Though it planned "to move forward with other marketing tools to fuel this promotion," at the time of the news release, Rapala had no plans for any follow-up advertising to support the lure offer.

FURTHER READING

Anderson, Dennis. "Inventiveness Is Minnesota's Angling Legacy." *Minneapolis-St. Paul Star-Tribune,* April 11, 1999, p. 5-S.

———. "One Man's Passion: Without Lauri Rapala's Lures, Anglers Are Like Fish Out of Water." *Minneapolis-St. Paul Star-Tribune,* May 9, 1999, p. 18-C.

———. "Big Fish Don't Lie: Minnesota Angler Larry Dahlberg 'Hunts for Big Fish' Every Week on His Popular ESPN Show." *Minneapolis-St. Paul Star-Tribune,* May 14, 1999, p. 1-C.

"The Arizona Republic Business Buzz Column." *Arizona Republic,* May 21, 1999.

"Catch a Bass, Seal the Deal." *Business Wire,* May 11, 1999.

DeSalvo, Kathy. "Serious Sports." *SHOOT,* July 14, 1995, p. 34.

Ecker, Don. "Casting About for Right Tackle." *Bergen County (New Jersey) Record,* January 14, 1998, p. S-8.

Hochwald, Lambeth. "It's the Sizzle That Sells." *Sales & Marketing Management,* April 1, 1997, p. 50.

Obolensky, Kira. "Carmichael Lynch: Turning Admen into Enthusiasts." *Graphis,* May-June 1998, p. 48.

Smith, Doug. "Legends You Don't Know: Jack Supple, Muskie Man." *Minneapolis-St. Paul Star-Tribune,* April 11, 1999, p. 4-S.

Spain, William. "Fishing for Sales Through Cable." *Advertising Age,* March 27, 1995, p. S-6.

Steinbreder, John. "The Value of a Plug: Lauri Rapala's Hand-Carved Cork Plug, the Most Popular Lure of All Time, Celebrates Its Diamond Jubilee." *Outdoor Life,* November 1996, p. 10.

Judson Knight

North American Coffee Partnership (Starbucks Corp.)

2401 Utah Avenue South
Seattle, Washington 98134
USA
Telephone: (206) 447-1575
Fax: (206) 447-0828
Web site: www.starbucks.com

■■■

BRING ON THE DAY CAMPAIGN

OVERVIEW

Pepsi and Starbucks joined forces in 1994 to create the North American Coffee Partnership (NACP) to market cold ready-to-drink coffee products under the Starbucks name and using the Pepsi distribution network. The joint venture's first product, Frappuccino, quickly dominated the category. It was positioned as an afternoon drink, but research indicated that there was also a market for a cold coffee drink in the morning, leading to the introduction in 2002 of a second product called DoubleShot, an espresso drink. NACP provided some advertising dollars to launch the new brand, but after two years DoubleShot had failed to achieve much brand recognition. The 2004 "Bring On the Day" campaign, developed by ad agency Fallon of New York, sought to rectify this problem, create a buzz around the brand, and build sales.

While the campaign included some radio spots and DoubleShot giveaways at ski resorts and music events, the entire success of the campaign hinged on a single television spot, "Glen." It featured a young man drinking DoubleShot and getting ready for work. While he did so, he was serenaded live by the 1980s rock band Survivor singing their hit song "Eye of the Tiger," but with lyrics that commented on Glen's workaday world. The campaign was budgeted at $5 million to $10 million.

"Glen" was a hit with the target audience and was widely acclaimed, garnering an Emmy nomination and a Bronze EFFIE Award in 2005. It was also pirated on the Internet and became a subject of conversation on blogs and online forums. More importantly, the campaign, which ended in September 2004, dramatically increased brand awareness, increased the conversion rate from mere awareness to actually trying the product, and increased sales in DoubleShots' main distribution channels, supermarkets and convenience stores.

HISTORICAL CONTEXT

In 1994 Starbucks Coffee Company and PepsiCo, Inc., forged a joint venture, the North American Coffee Partnership (NACP), its goal to marry the Starbucks brand with Pepsi's massive distribution system to produce and market cold, ready-to-drink coffee products for grocery and convenience stores and other outlets. Two years later NACP introduced Frappuccino, a bottled version of Starbucks's popular combination of ice, milk, and coffee, available in half a dozen flavors. Frappuccino became so dominant that it achieved generic name status for all ready-to-drink (RTD) coffees, in a manner similar to the way Kleenex was associated with facial tissues. By the early 2000 this 800-pound gorilla in the RTD coffee category controlled 82 percent of the grocery channel and 75 percent of the convenience channel. In truth, Frappuccino had no serious rival.

NACP positioned Frappuccino as an afternoon drink, essentially a reward or pick-me-up drink. Overall, the RTD category represented a tiny percentage of coffee consumption, the vast majority of which took place in the morning. Research revealed that consumers would be receptive to a cold Starbucks' morning product, albeit one a bit lighter in milk. Sensing a opportunity to carve out morning sales in the RTD market, NACP introduced a new product in 2002: DoubleShot, a single-serve, 6.5 ounce can of espresso blended with nonfat milk, cream, sugar, and caramel color. The name was a reference to the way customers at Starbucks phrased their orders. The spring rollout was supported by an introductory advertising campaign, developed by Fallon Worldwide's New York office, featuring a pair of television spots as well as print and outdoor advertising that positioned DoubleShot as an invigorating drink "to get you going" in the morning. In-store merchandising and targeted sampling efforts were also included. The 2003 campaign introduced the tagline "Bring on the day" and featured a television spot in which a man who did not want to go to work was chased around his apartment by his business suit until a drink of DoubleShot braced him for the day ahead and he finally prepared for work.

After two years in the marketplace, DoubleShot had not succeeded as well as NACP had hoped. According to a write-up on the 2004 "Bring On the Day" campaign that Fallon produced for the EFFIE Awards, as of 2003 DoubleShot had still "never quite made it into the front ranks of on-the-go morning beverages." It went on to explain that this was because "not enough people have heard of DoubleShot, and not enough people get that it can really change how you experience your morning.... So our plan was to tap into the 'pain of mornings' and make Starbucks DoubleShot famous as Liquid Motivation for the day ahead."

TARGET MARKET

Greg W. Prince of *Beverage World* explained that NACP viewed the target market for DoubleShot to be different from the one for Frappuccino. Whereas the latter appealed to a broad age range of 18 to 49 years old, DoubleShot was aimed at the younger side of that spectrum. But the target market was characterized more importantly by something that cut across age: a certain attitude toward life assumed by a type of person that the marketers dubbed an "Intensity Hunter." These were described as passionate people who sought out new and exciting experiences; they were consumers of sports drinks, specialty coffees, and energy bars. "But two things really stood out for us about Intensity Hunters," wrote Fallon in its brief of effectiveness for the EFFIE Awards. "They index highly for listening to music (they're the iPod crew) and they're desensitized to 'marketing'—they know a shill when they see one, and they run a mile to avoid it."

CALL ME ISHMAEL . . . AND NO FOAM, PLEASE

When friends Gordon Bowker, Jerry Baldwin, and Zev Siegl founded Starbucks in Seattle in the late 1960s as a single shop, they mined Herman Melville's great American novel, *Moby Dick,* for a name. They found it in the coffee-loving first mate of the Pequod: Starbuck. For a logo the partners devised a two-tailed mermaid-siren. The image, appropriate for the 1960s, was modified over the years, becoming less sexy and more stylized.

COMPETITION

DoubleShot faced limited competition in the RTD coffee category that its sister brand, Frappuccino, dominated so thoroughly. Because of the backing of Pepsi's distribution network, both brands operated from a position of strength that only Coca-Cola could challenge. Coke acquired Planet Java, a bottled coffee, to test the waters, but after a few months it pulled the product, concluding that the size and scale of the market did not meet Coke's financial criteria. Nestlé also made a stab at the market, only to make a hasty withdrawal.

While Coke remained interested and waited for the market to grow—and risked allowing its rival Pepsi to gain an insurmountable foothold in RTD coffee—other players stepped forward. A distant second in the category was the Arizona brand of iced coffee. Folgers, backed by parent company Dean Foods Company, introduced Jakada, the first chilled coffee beverage to be sold in single-serve HDPE (high-density polyethylene) plastic bottles. But NACP did not view Jakada as a threat, believing that it would actually grow the category to the benefit of Frappuccino and DoubleShot Another newcomer was Wolfgang Puck Gourmet Lattes, and while it benefited from the name of the famous chef, it had limited distribution and did not seek to challenge Frappuccino and DoubleShot. Rather, it too wanted to grow the category and carve out its own slice. Other small players in the category included private-label iced coffees and regional brands such as New Jersey's Cappuccino Havana; California's Espresso Coffee Soda; Brooklyn, New York's Espresso Coffee Soda produced by Manhattan Special; and Extreme Coffee's Shock brand, marketed in California, Arizona, Alaska, Minnesota, and Wisconsin.

MARKETING STRATEGY

The 2004 "Bring On the Day" campaign had four goals: to increase brand awareness; to create brand fame through entertaining ads; to push consumers actually to try DoubleShot; and to increase sales by at least 10 percent. Reaching a target market that was jaded by a lifetime of exposure to advertising was a daunting challenge, however. In essence the creative team wanted to demonstrate to that audience how to drink the product (i.e., as a morning jump-start), but in an amusing fashion. Because the target audience included hard-core music fans, it made sense to lean heavily on music. According to the EFFIE write-up, "A music-based approach would allow the advertising to act as a metaphor for the drinking experience... After all, what's more motivational than a pumped-up, charging piece of music?"

Out of this strategic thinking came the idea to made use of one of the best known motivational songs, "Eye of the Tiger," by the band Survivor. The song had been used in the 1982 film *Rocky III,* helping to motivate boxer Rocky Balboa to become a champion again. The idea of the resulting television spot called "Glen" was to rewrite the lyrics of "Eye of the Tiger" and apply it to an everyday member of the target demographic as he began his day, in effect turning the pop song into a mock-heroic ballad. To take the idea to the next level, the creative team enlisted the services of Survivor itself not only to help rewrite the song but also to actually sing it to Glen in the commercial.

The 30-second spot opened with Glen drinking a can of DoubleShot in his apartment kitchen, with the sound of traffic in the background. Survivor was then heard singing "Glen! Glen, Glen, Glen" to the power chords that launched "Eye of the Tiger." The band itself was shown serenading Glen in his living room. As he shaved, the band crowded into his bathroom to continue the song: "Glen's the man. Goin' to work. Got his tie, got ambition." Next, Glen walked to the bus stop with Survivor tagging along, the drummer and his kit towed on a platform. The group continued to sing to him on the bus: "Middle management is right in his grasp. It's a dream he will never let die. Glen's the man of the hour, he's the king of his cube! Status quo reports have finally met their rival." They rode up the elevator with him and kept singing until the door opened and he walked off to his cubicle: "Burning the candle at both ends on his way to the top, he knows one day he just could become... Supervisor!" A picture of the Starbucks logo was accompanied by a voice-over: "Starbucks' DoubleShot espresso drink. Bring on the day." As a final twist, a young man walked past the open elevator door and Survivor began to follow him, starting the song over again: "Roy! Roy, Roy, Roy."

Modestly budgeted between $5 and $10 million, the campaign aired "Glen" on national cable television channels that offered what the target audience liked: music, pop culture, and sport. Hence, spots appeared on MTV, MTV2, Fuse, ESPN, ESPN2, and Spike. The 2004 campaign also included radio spots and sponsored regional sampling events at a number of ski resorts and music venues, but the centerpiece of the campaign was "Glen."

OUTCOME

The "Glen" spot was a hit from the very beginning, achieving the marketers' goal of creating buzz about the DoubleShot brand. A wide variety of newspapers and magazines—including the *New York Times, USA Today, Creativity,* and *Adweek* —published articles that praised the commercial. Moreover, "Glen" developed a grassroots following on the Internet, where the video was pirated and viewed by countless people. It was also widely discussed on websites, blogs, and forums. Starbucks posted the spot on its website, where it was viewed 3,000 times a week for the next few months. "Glen" received a nomination for an Emmy Award, and the "Bring On the Day" campaign was awarded a Bronze EFFIE in 2005 at the prestigious EFFIE Awards, presented by the New York American Marketing Association.

More important than accolades was the fact that the 2004 "Bring On the Day" campaign increased brand awareness by nearly 50 percent. Furthermore, the number of people who went from becoming aware of the brand to actually trying the product more than doubled. During the time that "Glen" aired on television, from May 2004 to September 2004, gross volume sales increased nearly 60 percent in convenience stores and almost 40 percent in grocery stores, with no distribution gains that could account for the change other than the advertising.

FURTHER READING

Berk, Christina Cheddar. "Makers of Ready-to-Drink Coffee Are Searching for Broader Appeal." *Wall Street Journal,* May 12, 2004, p. B9D.

Berry, Donna. "Milk and Sugar, Please." *Prepared Foods,* January 2003, p. 95.

Brown, Suzanne J. "Iced Coffee Is Now Ready-to-Drink." *Tea & Coffee,* May/June, 2002.

———. "Ready-to-Drink Coffee & Tea: A Bottleneck of Opportunity." *Tea & Coffee Trade Journal,* August 20, 2003, p. 36.

"Fallon Sets Musical Mood for Starbucks." *Adweek,* May 7, 2004.

Hein, Kenneth. "Starbucks Adds Buzz to DoubleShot, Frappuccino Drinks with New Push." *Brandweek,* May 12, 2003, p. 9.

Howard, Theresa. "Starbucks TV Ads Hit the Spot." *USA Today,* October 3, 2004.

Prince, Greg W. "Pepsi Espressos Itself." *Beverage World,* March 15, 2002, p. 76.

Schoenholt, Donald N. "The State of the Rage." *Tea & Coffee Trade Journal,* March 2004, p. 56.

"Starbucks, Pepsi Introduce New Ready-to-Drink Espresso." *Packaging Digest,* May 2002, p. 2.

Wilcha, Kristin. "Starbucks 'Glen' Receives Emmy Nod." *Shoot,* August 19, 2005, p. 12.

Ed Dinger

North Carolina Division of Tourism, Film and Sports Development

301 N Wilmington St.
Raleigh, North Carolina 27601
USA
Telephone: (919) 733-8372
Fax: (919) 715-3097
Web site: www.visitnc.com

HERITAGE CAMPAIGN

OVERVIEW

In 1998 the North Carolina Division of Tourism, Film and Sports Development, previously known as the North Carolina Division of Travel and Tourism, continued an advertising campaign ("Heritage") undertaken in 1997 by Loeffler Ketchum Mountjoy (LKM) of Charlotte. The campaign's primary focus was the state's heritage, and it stressed historic events that had occurred in North Carolina, as well as natural resources and cultural sites of interest in the state. Prominent among the advertising was a print ad celebrating the Civil Rights movement with a black-and-white photograph of a formerly segregated lunch counter and the caption "Here, four brave people refused to move. What they did moved an entire nation." Television advertising, along with some radio and public relations work, accompanied the print ads. The tourism division's annual advertising budget was estimated to be between $2.5 million and $3 million.

Advertising played up North Carolina's varied heritage, and a number of ads focused on its significance in African American history. The state made a strong push for overseas visitors, particularly business travelers from Great Britain, and under the leadership of Gordon Clapp, the tourism division greatly expanded its offerings. In July 1998 North Carolina's efforts paid off with a prestigious award from the nation's tourism directors. "When 50 people in the advertising community recognize your work," LKM creative director Jim Mountjoy said in a press release, "it tells you that your work has hit the mark creatively. But when the top 50 people in the tourism industry single you out, it tells you that strategically you are dead-on."

HISTORICAL CONTEXT

Outsiders have been coming to North Carolina since a group of settlers sent by Sir Walter Raleigh established the first English colony in North America on Roanoke Island in 1585. That first settlement ended after just 10 months and was replaced by a second colony in 1587. But this colony, where Virginia Dare became the first child of English parents born in the New World, was ill-supplied: when reinforcements arrived from England in 1590, they found Roanoke deserted. Thus began the legend of the famous "Lost Colony."

Of course the English were not the first people in North Carolina. For centuries the state had been inhabited by a number of Native American tribes, most notably the Cherokee and Catawba. Thus when twentieth-century novelist Thomas Wolfe set out to create a fictionalized version of North and South Carolina, he called them Old and New Catawba. Carolina was named after King Charles II in 1663 and officially separated into North and South Carolina in 1712.

The Revolutionary War added new legends to North Carolina history. There was the so-called Mecklenburg Declaration, a statement of rights and independence from Great Britain supposedly created by the citizens of Mecklenburg County in May 1775, though its authenticity was doubtful. North Carolina was the site of a battle on February 27, 1776, at Moore's Creek Bridge, which has been dubbed the "Lexington and Concord of the South." On April 12 of that momentous year, North Carolina's Provincial Congress adopted the Halifax Resolution, authorizing its delegates to the Continental Congress in Philadelphia "to concur with the delegates of the other colonies in declaring independency." Thus North Carolina became the first of the 13 colonies to issue an explicit directive calling for independence.

In 1861 North Carolina threw its lot in with a less successful independence effort, and though the Civil War left it much less battle-scarred than neighboring Virginia, slavery and segregation created scars of their own. By the mid-twentieth century, however, North Carolina had emerged as one of the more cosmopolitan southern states, and television's popular *Andy Griffith Show*—not to mention its many spin-offs—celebrated the state's easygoing way of life. The late twentieth century saw an increase of business, education, and scientific interest in the state, particularly in the "Research Triangle" formed by the capital at Raleigh and the neighboring cities of Durham and Chapel Hill.

North Carolina also had a growing film industry, placing it third in the nation after California and Florida. Partly for this reason, the North Carolina Division of Travel and Tourism changed its name in 1998 to the North Carolina Division of Tourism, Film and Sports Development. By then, the tourism division had worked with several advertising agencies. In July 1976 a relationship with the firm of Loucheim, Eng and People, Inc., had ended badly, with a legal action in which the state attempted to recover $145,000 in damages. According to its claim, the state had been overcharged for costly print ads and television spots that barely mentioned North Carolina. McKinney & Silver of Raleigh won the account later in 1976 and held it for 15 years, until LKM became the agency of record.

TARGET MARKET

The state of North Carolina and its tourism division made a number of efforts targeted to specific market segments; for instance, in 1994 the state spent some $8 million to attract British visitors. American Airlines had recently established direct service between Raleigh/Durham and London's Gatwick Airport, and this, combined with British Airways' service to Charlotte, spurred on the campaign. Cellet Travel Services in Great Britain handled the marketing initiative.

Harry Hoover, vice president of public relations for LKM, told Barbara J. Mays of *Travel Weekly* in March 1997, "Our new research shows that our visitors expect a restful, relaxing vacation and beautiful natural scenery." Hence tag lines such as this one, promoting the barrier islands along the coast: "Out here, we haven't burned our bridges with the 20th century. We just never built them." Another ad, promoting remote retreats in the mountains of western North Carolina, asked, "Remember how, when you were a child, you had your own secret hiding place?"

The principal thrust of North Carolina's 1998 tourism marketing was heritage. Along with its "four brave people" ad, celebrating four black Greensboro Colleges students who in 1960 refused to leave a segregated lunch counter, the state drew attention to its rich African American history. Advertising promoted sites such as the Mattye Reed African Heritage Museum, the Hayti Heritage Center in Durham, and that city's Parrish Street. The latter was known as "the Black Wall Street" because of the many successful African American businesses that started there during the 1920s, among them the largest black-owned enterprise in the United States, the North Carolina Mutual Life Insurance Company.

COMPETITION

Clapp told Jim Osterman and Katy Eckmann of *Adweek* in 1996 that North Carolina faced "stiff competition right in our own region." A number of neighboring states, in particular Tennessee and Virginia, had much larger tourism budgets, and indeed Virginia was the home of what was undoubtedly the most successful state tourism campaign of the twentieth century: "Virginia Is for Lovers." Created by Martin & Woltz of Richmond in 1969, the campaign proved to be enormously popular during the 1970s, and though Virginia later tried to replace it with other efforts, the classic slogan kept coming to the fore. In 1999 Virginia celebrated the campaign's 30th anniversary with renewed promotion.

North Carolina's advertising budget of $2.5 to $3 million was certainly a modest one, given the fact that a single North Carolina county devoted about as much—$2.5 million—to its own tourism advertising. This was Buncombe County, site of Asheville, a city in the mountains of western North Carolina with a thriving arts community and tourist attractions such as Biltmore Estates, the Thomas Wolfe house, and the luxurious Grove Park Inn. Of course promotion for Buncombe County and other areas within the state could only

PEN PALS ACROSS NORTH CAROLINA

In October 1998 the North Carolina Division of Tourism, Film and Sports Development launched a program to match up young pen pals across the state of North Carolina. Formed in cooperation with the state's Department of Public Instruction, the program began with some 1,400 fourth-graders, and organizers planned for greater expansion in coming months.

According to a press release accompanying the launch, Division of Tourism, Film and Sports Development director Gordon Clapp said, "This program encourages students to learn about their home state and what is has to offer. By sharing . . . experiences across the state, young people can gain fresh perspectives while reinforcing what they learn in the classroom."

North Carolina elementary schools received a "Pen Pal package," complete with recommendations on how to best implement the program. The packet included a brochure on North Carolina, suggestions of topics on which youngsters might correspond, a list of related websites, and other material. "We have already matched up several fourth-grade classes," Clapp said, "and will continue to do so as we receive more information from interested teachers."

benefit North Carolina, and for that matter, competition between states often gave way to cooperation. Thus in 1999 Clapp told *Travel Trade Gazette UK* & *Ireland* that the state was working with South Carolina and Virginia to set up a network of "heritage trails."

Clapp organized the January 1999 Travel South Marketplace, a convention that brought together the tourism divisions of 12 southern states, along with buyers from all over the world. Included were Alabama, which in the late 1990s had a $5 billion-a-year travel industry; Arkansas, which had devoted considerable sums to the renovation of sites in Little Rock and Hot Springs; Florida, always one of the nation's top vacation spots; Georgia, then in the process of adopting recommendations from a study called "A Vision for Georgia Tourism 2000 and Beyond"; Kentucky, which offered visitors a *Great Kentucky Getaway Guide;* Louisiana, which celebrated its 300th birthday in 1999; Mississippi, where tourism was growing on the strength of gambling and riverboat tours; South Carolina, which had recently published a guide called *South Carolina Adventures—Nature-Based Packages;* Tennessee, a state with an $8 billion-a-year tourism budget; Virginia, where the commemoration of the 200th anniversary of George Washington's death coincided with the "Virginia Is for Lovers" anniversary; and West Virginia, which had recently launched its "West Virginia: Full of Wonder—Plenty of Wild" advertising campaign.

MARKETING STRATEGY

One of the complaints North Carolina lodged against Loucheim, Eng in 1976 was the fact that the firm's advertising for the state was loosely targeted. The legal action cited, for instance, a four-page ad in *Glamour* magazine featuring models in expensive designs from Sax Fifth Avenue, with only peripheral mention of North Carolina. The agency had also spent $22,000 on two 30-second spots and a billboard during the 1975 Peach Bowl football game—more wasted money, in the state's view.

Efforts by McKinney & Silver and its successor, Loeffler Ketchum Mountjoy, were much more successful. In fact, agency president John Ketchum started with McKinney & Silver, where he had worked on the state account before leaving the firm in 1988. In the five years between the time North Carolina hired LKM in 1991 and the time of an agency review in 1996—state law required a review after five years—LKM's advertising had earned several Addy Awards, along with recognition from the Kelly Awards and The One Show.

In April 1996, after LKM bested three other agencies to retain the account, Clapp announced that the advertising effort in coming years would address two major areas, in the words of Osterman and Eckmann in *Adweek:* " 'heritage' tourism, which promotes the state's history and its natural and cultural resources; and stepped-up tourism awareness programs, particularly in public relations."

Though the 1998 tourism campaign included electronic media, the primary thrust was print, with black-and-white artwork. In fall 1985 a pair of studies reported by Gilbert R. Yochum in the *Journal of Travel Research* found that black-and-white newspaper advertising was more effective than the same sort of advertising in magazines. Both studies showed that newspaper ads tended to draw tourists who spent more money than those attracted by magazine ads; by comparison, a radio campaign in Virginia Beach, Virginia, proved to be less effective than either variety of print advertising. Nonetheless, North Carolina's 1998 campaign included ads in the magazines *Southern Living, American Heritage,* and *Smithsonian,* as well as spots on the Arts & Entertainment network (A&E) and Cable News Network (CNN). These moves, according to Mark Harrison of LKM, were targeted to potential tourists who would spend the most money in the state.

Print ads, most of which LKM introduced in 1997 and continued in 1998, stressed both the historical and the natural heritage of the state. One ad, referring to the famous Lost Colony, was headlined "The first English settlers vanished into the mists of history here. We've been looking for them ever since." Other advertising promoted Kitty Hawk, where Wilbur and Orville Wright launched the first airplane in 1903; and Fort Macon, site of an important Civil War battle. One of LKM's most prominent print ads noted that "according to geologists, North Carolina was once connected to Africa"—thus promoting the many exotic species at the North Carolina Zoo in Asheboro.

OUTCOME

Clapp won praise from Susan J. Young of *Travel Agent* in mid-1998 for "significantly enhanc[ing] the look and feel of the state's tourism product." Among his most notable undertakings was the adoption of the "Heritage" theme, complete with a network of historic sites linked by "heritage trails"—some actual hiking trails, some driving routes—between Virginia, North Carolina, and South Carolina. The heritage trails program, Young noted, would be fully operational by 2000.

"It's a whole new way of promoting North Carolina," Clapp told her. "One of the gratifying rewards is bringing together diverse groups of people who thought they had nothing in common, such as environmentalists, economic development representatives, and cultural resource people. It's exciting." Later in 1999 the state would introduce garden tours throughout North Carolina, and Clapp expressed an interest in creating African American and Native American trails as well.

Meanwhile, LKM promoted North Carolina's hiking trails with an ad headlined "Colossal upheavals, landslides, and brutal glaciers make for darned fine hiking trails." Seven of its ads, which "focused on North Carolina's scenic beauty and relaxing atmosphere," according to a July 1998 press release, won the agency and the state the "best print advertising campaign" and "best individual print ad" at the annual conference of the National Council of State Tourism Directors in Palm Springs, California.

FURTHER READING

Barile, Suzy. "State Struggles to Maintain History." *Triangle Business Journal,* August 21, 1998, p. 27.

Koonce, Burke III. "State Travel Unit Reviews Ad Shops." *Triangle Business Journal* (Raleigh-Durham-Chapel Hill, North Carolina), March 22, 1996, p. 6.

Mays, Barbara J. "Officials Hope New Ads Provide Tourism Boost." *Travel Weekly,* March 31, 1997, p. M21.

"North Carolina Advertising Wins Top Tourism Awards." *PR Newswire,* July 16, 1998.

Osterman, Jim. "15 Years of Travel Ends." *Adweek* (Southeast edition), May 4, 1998, p. 8.

Osterman, Jim, and Katy Eckmann. "Loeffler Ketchum to Defend N.C. Tourism Turf 'n' Surf." *Adweek* (Southeast edition), March 4, 1996, p. 2.

———. "N.C. Tourism Renews Contract." *Adweek* (Southeast edition), April 22, 1996, p. 2.

"Pen Pals Begin Exchanging Lessons in NC History, Culture." *PR Newswire,* October 1, 1998.

"Visitors Relive the Past." *Travel Trade Gazette UK & Ireland,* March 15, 1999, p. 53.

Yochum, Gilbert R. "The Economics of Travel Advertising Revisited." *Journal of Travel Research,* fall 1985, pp. 9-12.

Young, Susan J. "Blazing Tourism Trails." *Travel Agent,* May 18, 1998, p. 12.

———. "On to Greensboro." *Travel Agent,* December 14, 1998, p. 126.

Judson Knight

Northwest Airlines Corporation

2700 Lone Oak Pkwy.
Eagan, Minnesota 55121-3034
USA
Telephone: (612) 726-2111
Fax: (612) 726-7123
Web site: www.nwa.com

E-TICKET CAMPAIGN

OVERVIEW

With the "E-Ticket" advertising campaign Northwest Airlines, Inc., the largest subsidiary of Northwest Airlines Corporation, encouraged consumers to try its electronic ticketing system on the Internet instead of purchasing paper tickets via telephone or at an office such as a travel agency. The new service streamlined the process of booking a flight, checking in at the airport, and boarding the plane, and it eliminated the possibility that the ticket would be lost or stolen. Advertisements for Northwest E-Ticket began running in print media soon after the service was introduced in 1996 and continued into 1999. The campaign was developed by two Minneapolis agencies, Hunt Adkins and Valentine McCormick Ligabel.

An advertisement in *Fortune* magazine in 1998 illustrated the connection between a customer's computer and an airplane flight with three graphic elements: a man using a computer mouse, a binary pattern that formed an image of a Northwest jet's tail fin, and an ascending airplane. The headline read, "The Information Runway." The text read: "Select a flight and purchase a ticket from your computer with Northwest Airlines. We've taken travel planning to new heights of ease and convenience. Just hop on the Internet and jet over to WorldWeb, the Northwest Airlines web site at www.nwa.com. You can review flight schedules, check availabilities, book a seat and even purchase a Northwest E-Ticket, the convenient and paperless way to travel. With a few clicks of the mouse, you're ready to fly. It's that simple. But don't stop there. Discover all the great ways in which WorldWeb can make your travel planning a breeze. Explore vacation ideas. Save money with exclusive CyberSaver fares. Book your car rental and make hotel reservations. Verify departure and arrival times. Check your WorldPerks account and more." The ad concluded with the company's red-and-white logo above the slogan "Some People Just Know How to Fly" and a toll-free telephone number to call for more information.

HISTORICAL CONTEXT

Northwest Airlines was created by mergers among numerous airlines. The first was Northwest Airways, founded by Colonel Lewis Brittin in 1926 at Speedway Flying Field, which later became Minneapolis/St. Paul International Airport. The company initially delivered mail to Chicago and the Twin Cities but soon began carrying passengers and expanding its service regionally. Its name was changed to Northwest Airlines, Inc., in 1934. Other carriers that eventually became part of Northwest were Wisconsin Central Airlines (later known as North Central Airlines), Southern Airways, Hughes Airwest (formed by the merger of Hughes Air Corporation and Air West), Pacific Airlines, Bonanza Airlines, and West Coast Airlines (formed by the merger of Zimmerly Airlines and Empire Airlines). Through a later merger Northwest and KLM Royal Dutch Airlines became subsidiaries of a holding company named Northwest Airlines Corporation. By 1998 Northwest was one of the largest airlines in the world, serving 21 countries and transporting more than 51 million passengers.

Northwest began using computers to keep track of tickets and reservations in 1973, but consumers were not able to make travel arrangements via the Internet until two decades later. Instead the customer telephoned the airline or booked the flight through a travel agent. A paper ticket was issued and, if the reservation was made by telephone, the ticket usually had to be delivered to the buyer. Without a ticket in hand the traveler could not board the airplane. In the mid-1990s airlines began offering electronic tickets. This innovation could save a company $25 million annually in recordkeeping expenses, since the cost of handling an electronic ticket was $1 compared to $8 for a paper ticket. An electronic ticket could be purchased through a travel agent, but typically the consumer used a computer to visit an airline's home page on the World Wide Web, booked a flight there, and paid by credit card. Northwest designed its Internet site to explain the advantages of electronic ticketing and other programs, to show customers how to use the services, and to offer discounts and perks. Advertisements to publicize E-Ticket also encouraged consumers to spend time exploring the company's home page.

CYBERSAVERS

Consumers often saved 20 percent to 30 percent by shopping for discounted airline fares on the Internet. In 1998 Northwest Airlines stimulated interest in on-line reservations with a program called "CyberSavers." Every Wednesday the company announced substantially reduced fares to specific destinations. The offers expired on the following Saturday. Consumers could request weekly E-mails that listed the latest special offers. After booking a flight on-line the customer received confirmation of the reservation by E-mail and then received an itinerary receipt by U.S. mail. The flights could also be booked by telephone, but customers who purchased these fares over the Internet received an additional $20 discount.

TARGET MARKET

Northwest E-Ticket was a popular option because paper tickets could be lost or stolen, and they were not always delivered in time for the customer to depart on schedule. In addition, people with electronic tickets were usually able to board the plane faster than other passengers. Those who booked an E-Ticket received customer itinerary receipts via E-mail and U.S. mail. At the airport these customers needed only photo identification along with either their itinerary receipts or their last names and flight numbers. Travelers with E-Ticket could check in at the ticket counter, the gate, or at one of Northwest's Electronic Service Centers. The service was particularly popular among business travelers because it eliminated the cost of overnight delivery services and the expense of replacing lost tickets. Northwest's Internet site included a search engine that could quickly find the lowest coach fares available for any round trip. Customers could also use the site to reserve hotel rooms and car rentals and to redeem frequent-flyer miles. The computer system stored data to build a profile of each customer, making note of details such as whether the person liked to sit near the aisle or a window and which individuals would require a vegetarian or kosher meal. Frequently customers could pick the exact seats they preferred for their flights. Advertisements for E-Ticket explained these advantages and emphasized that the service was quick and easy to use, a modern convenience that made air travel more pleasant.

COMPETITION

According to *Aviation Week & Space Technology,* United Airlines, Inc., led the U.S. segment of the industry in 1998; American Airlines was second; Delta Air Lines, Inc. was third; Continental Airlines, Inc., was fourth; Northwest was fifth; and US Airways Group, Inc., was sixth. One of the first airlines to use electronic ticketing was ValuJet, a regional carrier based in Atlanta that began operations in 1993. In January 1995 Southwest Airlines Company began offering the service, and within eight months nearly a third of its customers were making reservations electronically. Delta also began testing electronic tickets on a few flights in April 1995. Vying with Continental to be the first carrier to feature the option throughout the country, United tried electronic ticketing in selected markets in the spring of 1995 and began offering it nationwide in September. Promotions for United and Southwest discussed electronic ticketing that year, with United's ads promising "ease of use and ease of mind."

In 1997 United discontinued its long-running "Come Fly Our Friendly Skies" slogan and introduced the straightforward "Rising" campaign, which ran through 1998. The new ads acknowledged that traveling by plane was not always pleasant, and they promised that

United would rise to the challenge of improving its services. In a print advertisement the words "Your Flight is Delayed" were spelled out in a bowl of cereal. "Does the truth really need to be sugarcoated?" the text asked. The ad promised that customers would receive an honest explanation when there was a problem with a flight. Another advertisement in *Travel & Leisure* in 1998 simply showed a Hawaiian beach and palm trees below the headline "Fly United Airlines to Kapalua." The ad displayed the United logo above the word "RISING" in a lower corner. According to *Advertising Age,* United spent $63.6 million on total measured advertising in 1998 (down from $67.2 million in 1997 and $75.2 million in 1991) with $27.8 million going for television commercials and $33.6 million for print advertisements.

In second place, American Airlines advertised its electronic ticketing, "AAccess," by emphasizing that the service allowed customers to know all the details about their flights and to make better choices based on that information. An advertisement in *Newsweek* showed one traveler who knew nothing about his flight to Los Angeles except that he would be aboard the airplane. Another traveler profiled beside him knew the flight number, the type of plane, when and where the flight originated, its arrival time, his seat assignment, which in-flight movie he would see, and how many frequent-flyer miles he would earn from the trip. *Advertising Age* reported that American spent $70.7 million on measured advertising in 1998 (compared to $64.6 million in 1997 and $115.9 million in 1991), with $20.4 million going for television commercials and $47.7 million for print advertisements.

Meanwhile, Delta's surreal "On Top of the World" campaign noted that travelers had "millions of reasons to fly today; only one that matters to you." The fantasy advertisements showed Delta employees striving to meet the individual needs of passengers and to show the comfortable conditions in Delta's new transatlantic business class of seats. In January 1999 Delta added a $2 surcharge for all tickets that were not purchased electronically through the company's Internet site. Beset by angry telephone calls from consumers, Delta withdrew the fee.

In 1998 Delta and United discussed but ultimately abandoned a marketing and code-sharing alliance that would have given them nearly 39 percent of U.S. air traffic. American and US Airways considered a similar alliance to control 25 percent of the market but reduced the proposal to a reciprocal frequent-flyer plan. During 1998 Northwest and Continental began forming a partnership that would have about 16 percent of the market, a slightly smaller share than the percentage held by each of the three leading airlines. Delta had considered merging with Continental in 1997, and early in 1998 Continental received takeover proposals from both Delta and Northwest, but no agreement was reached by the end of the year.

TRADEMARK DESIGN

Since 1948 Northwest had been known for the red tail fins on its airplanes, a design that was often included in advertisements near the company's red-and-white logo.

MARKETING STRATEGY

Since electronic ticketing was a new service, the E-Ticket campaign cited the advantages of paperless tickets, explained how to buy them, and invited consumers to visit Northwest's Internet site for more information. An advertisement called "Planet Zortron," which was developed by Hunt Adkins and ran in travel agent publications throughout 1997, showed a UFO hovering against a cloudy, purple sky. The ad described "Plan A," in which tickets were booked through a travel agent who gave them to a delivery driver. En route to the customer, the driver stopped to repair a flat tire, had to escape from an evil clown who commandeered the truck, was abducted by aliens and taken to the planet Zortron, and finally delivered the tickets one minute after the customer's flight had departed. In "Plan B," the travel agent booked a Northwest E-Ticket, and the customer boarded the flight without incident. The text explained: "With Northwest Airlines' E-Ticket, there are no flight coupons to print or tickets to deliver, and you can change reservations quickly and easily without having to reissue a ticket. All of which saves you a considerable amount of both time and money. E-Ticket is now available throughout the U.S. and to Canada (sorry, not yet available to planet Zortron)."

Advertisements created by Valentine McCormick Ligabel promoted E-Ticket and Northwest's Internet site during 1997 and 1998. One magazine ad showed a sailboat, a blue-green ocean, and a sandy beach below the headline, "You're Virtually There." The text read: "On-line Vacation Planning With Northwest Airlines. Explore a whole new world of vacation planning. Fly across the Internet to WorldWeb, the Northwest Airlines web site at www.nwa.com. You can explore exciting destinations, browse the WorldVacations specials and review flight schedules. Once you pick a vacation spot, you can book your flights on-line and even purchase a Northwest E-Ticket, the convenient and paperless way to travel. While you're touring WorldWeb, take in all the other great ways in which our web site can make your travel planning a day at the beach. Verify departure and arrival times. Cruise our exclusive, money-saving CyberSaver fares. Book your car rental and make hotel reservations. Check your WorldPerks account and more." The ad showed a computer pointer clicking on the word "Vacation" in large type. It concluded with the slogan "Some People Just Know How to Fly" below Northwest's red-and-white logo.

Several times during 1998 Northwest awarded free WorldPerks Bonus Miles (frequent-flyer credits) to customers who booked E-Ticket flights. In October consumers who purchased a ticket on-line at regular rates were invited to bring a companion on a subsequent trip for only $99. Advertisements for E-Ticket ran in trade publications for travel agents, in business magazines, and in other print media. *Advertising Age* reported that Northwest spent $66.7 million on total measured advertising in 1998, up from $48.2 million in 1997, $49.1 million in 1992, and $35.5 million in 1991. The company budgeted $9.2 million for television commercials in 1998 (up 135.9 percent from $3.9 million in 1997) and $52.5 million for print advertisements (up 32.6 percent from $39.6 million).

OUTCOME

In 1997 about 10 percent of airline reservations were booked electronically. By March 1998 almost 30 percent of travelers used electronic tickets, and by June 1998 about 40 percent of Northwest's passengers were using them. By October 1998 more than 2 million consumers were visiting WorldWeb Reservation each day. "E-Ticket has been one of the most popular and rapidly adopted programs ever offered by Northwest. People appreciate E-Ticket's convenience and speed," said Al Lenza, the company's vice president of distribution planning. By the spring of 1999 Northwest's site on the World Wide Web was generating approximately $220 million in annual revenues, which amounted to 2 percent of its total sales, compared with $275 million in revenues (2 percent of sales) for United and $225 million (3 percent of sales) for Delta. In 1999 *Business 2.0 Magazine* listed Northwest Airlines among the top 100 companies making the best use of the Internet. In 1997 Northwest's WorldWeb site was named Best Airline Web Site by *Internet World* magazine, and Northwest ranked second on *Fortune* magazine's list of the world's most admired companies. The Northwest website received awards from *Advertising Age, Internet World, Inside Flyer International,* and other publications and organizations. In 1998 the airline generated more than 95 percent of its parent company's operating revenues, but the corporation lost $224 million during the third quarter because of a pilot strike that lasted from June to September. The corporation had revenues of $10.2 billion in 1997 and more than $9 billion in 1998.

FURTHER READING

"Choose a Winner for Your Airline Travel Needs." *Association Management,* September 1998, p. A34.

"Flying in Formation." *Economist,* January 31, 1998, p. 67.

Grimes, Paul. "The On-Line Traveler." *Chicago Tribune,* July 12, 1998.

Levere, Jane. "Internet Pursuit Heats Up." *Airline Business,* December 1998, p. 2.

"Northwest Airlines: Acclaimed nwa.com Serves as Model for Other Online Sites." *M2 Presswire,* June 17, 1998.

Perman, Stacy. "Allied Air Force." *Time,* February 9, 1998, p. 76.

Rosato, Donna. "Fliers Flock to Airlines' E-Tickets." *USA Today,* March 17, 1998.

Sacharow, Anya. "Here, There, Anywhere: Best Use of Newspapers." *Mediaweek,* May 20, 1996, p. 64.

Susan Risland

Novartis AG

Lichtstrasse 35
Basel, CH-4056
Switzerland
Telephone: 41 61 3241111
Fax: 41 61 3248001
Web site: www.novartis.com

TUMMIES CAMPAIGN

OVERVIEW

At the turn of the millennium pharmaceutical giant Novartis AG of Switzerland boasted a wide range of products, including one of the industry's most promising stables of prescription drugs awaiting government approval. The drug Zelnorm, indicated for women suffering from Irritable Bowel Syndrome (IBS) with constipation, was poised to become one of the company's biggest sellers upon winning the approval of the U.S. Food and Drug Administration (FDA), but amidst controversy surrounding another IBS medication, Zelnorm's application for approval was denied in 2001. A surprise FDA reversal in 2002 brought Zelnorm to the U.S. market, and Novartis enlisted New York–based agency Deutsch, Inc., to craft a direct-to-consumer ad campaign on the drug's behalf.

Called "Tummies," the campaign broke in late 2003, following up Zelnorm's 2002 introduction to the market. The direct-to-consumer spots were meant to help women identify their symptoms as components of the little-understood condition of IBS and to encourage them to ask their doctors about Zelnorm. Superimposing symptom lists over images of female abdomens in television, print, and online advertisements, "Tummies" offered a memorable tutorial on IBS while indicating that Zelnorm offered relief. The slim female bellies likewise helped downplay the stigma associated with intestinal distress while clearly identifying the drug's target market.

The "Tummies" campaign swept the first annual Medical Marketing & Media Awards in 2004 and won a Gold EFFIE Award in 2005. Novartis reported that growing numbers of women were asking their doctors about Zelnorm and that awareness about both IBS and the Zelnorm brand were dramatically increasing. Although the FDA offered new warnings about side effects in 2004, it also approved Zelnorm for a second condition, chronic constipation, broadening the drug's market considerably. At a European conference of gastroenterology professionals, a Novartis executive projected that Zelnorm would, with the opening of European markets and the approval of further uses, eventually reach $1 billion in annual sales.

HISTORICAL CONTEXT

At the turn of the millennium Swiss pharmaceutical giant Novartis AG's portfolio included wide-ranging generic-drug, over-the-counter, and consumer-products divisions, and the company had one of the industry's most enviable pipelines of prescription drugs awaiting government approval. Novartis had especially high hopes for Zelmac, a pill designed to treat Irritable Bowel Syndrome. Only one other prescription drug was approved to treat the condition in the United States, and it was believed that the unmet need for an IBS treatment could translate into

$400 million to $1 billion a year in sales for Novartis, should Zelmac be approved. As part of the approval process Novartis was asked to rename Zelmac in order to avoid confusion with the drugs Zantac and Zyrtec, and the company settled on the revised name Zelnorm, believing FDA approval to be imminent. Novartis geared up for a blockbuster launch, enlisting another multinational pharmaceutical company, New York–based Bristol Myers-Squibb, as Zelnorm's co-marketer.

Novartis, like other drug companies at the time, had been capitalizing on a 1997 relaxation of FDA policy regarding the advertising of prescription drugs. The policy shift immediately changed the nature of prescription-drug advertising, as pharmaceutical companies, long reliant on the almost exclusive marketing of prescription drugs to physicians and other medical professionals, now began to advertise their products directly to consumers, much as other consumer goods had always been advertised. Though restrictions remained regarding the disclosure of side effects, and though most companies continued to submit their advertisements for FDA approval before airing them, direct-to-consumer pharmaceutical advertising quickly became ubiquitous in America, increasingly putting patients, rather than their doctors, in the position of deciding which drugs might best satisfy their needs.

In late 2000 the existing available Irritable Bowel Syndrome drug in the United States, Glaxo Wellcome's Lotronex, was pulled from the market by its manufacturer after safety concerns prompted the FDA to order prohibitively strict guidelines for its prescription. This initially seemed to bode well for Zelnorm, in that it left the IBS market uncontested, but in June 2001 the FDA officially denied Zelnorm approval, citing concerns over the drug's links to an increased incidence of abdominal surgery. Bristol Myers-Squibb dropped out of the agreement to co-market Zelnorm, and Novartis faced the prospect of staging new clinical trials, which would have delayed the approval process for several years. The company launched a creative review for a future Zelnorm campaign in the summer of 2002. Then, in June 2002, the FDA reapproved Lotronex (with restrictions on its marketing and prescription) after sustained appeals from patients; and in July of the same year patient pleas likewise resulted in a surprise FDA about-face regarding Zelnorm. In November of that year Novartis hired New York–based ad agency Deutsch, Inc., to helm the estimated $80 million dollar Zelnorm account.

TARGET MARKET

Up to 45 million Americans, according to some estimates, suffered from IBS, and two-thirds of those were women. Because of the variance in symptoms from one patient to another—and because there was neither a single identifiable cause nor, in the past, a single effective treatment—the condition had not always been recognized as a specific, treatable ailment. IBS patients usually suffered from either constipation or diarrhea, but some complained of an alternation between the two. Other symptoms included abdominal pain and bloating; a variety of psychological and emotional complaints, such as sleeping problems and tension, were also common.

Because doctors could find no physical source for IBS, the condition had, in the past, been attributed to stress or other psychosomatic causes. As the *New York Times* reported, however, recent studies had found that the interaction of the brain and the colon might be responsible for the syndrome. "The brain and bowels are wired with a series of nerves," gastroenterologist Brennan M.R. Spiegel told the *New York Times.* "If you have IBS, you're wired up in a slightly different way, and that can cause diarrhea, constipation or pain." Serotonin, which in the brain was thought to influence mood, in the colon worked to regulate the contractions called peristalsis. Irregularities in colon serotonin levels were believed to be at least partially responsible for IBS, and Zelnorm worked on serotonin receptors, stimulating them in order to spur peristalsis and relieve constipation. Lotronex, Zelnorm's main competitor in the IBS market, worked in the opposite fashion, relieving diarrhea by blocking serotonin receptors.

Zelnorm was thus approved to treat IBS with constipation, whereas Lotronex was intended to treat IBS with diarrhea. Zelnorm clinical studies had used women as subjects, and the FDA's approval of the drug specified women as candidates for treatment. The "Tummies" campaign accordingly targeted women suffering from IBS with constipation as a primary symptom. The Deutsch-created ads catered to this target market by spreading awareness of IBS and helping to destigmatize it, making it possible for the large number of women suffering from the condition to ask doctors about Zelnorm.

COMPETITION

While Lotronex was still in clinical trials, its manufacturer, Glaxo Wellcome, began trying to spread awareness of IBS. Glaxo helped fund an international conference designed to establish protocols for the diagnosis of the condition, and it backed a survey that gauged the breadth of IBS's reach among the population as well as the degree to which it was misunderstood. Glaxo also partnered with Nancy Norton, an IBS sufferer who had started the International Foundation for Functional Gastrointestinal

DIFFERING PERSPECTIVES

Controversy surrounded the introduction of both Lotronex and Zelnorm as treatments for Irritable Bowel Syndrome (IBS). Consumer groups accused Glaxo Wellcome and Novartis, the drugs' respective manufacturers, of downplaying side effects and overselling the drugs' effectiveness relative to placebos, as discovered in clinical trials. Some doctors, meanwhile, wondered whether IBS, which was not life threatening, should be treated by drugs whose potential side effects included life-threatening conditions. Women who suffered from IBS, however, often had a different perspective. As IBS sufferer Cynthia Huschle told *U.S. News & World Report* in a story about Lotronex's volatile introduction to the market, the form of diarrhea-based IBS with which she was afflicted had forced her to quit her job of classroom teaching and become a home-based reading specialist, and it made her incapable of doing simple things like shopping for groceries, because she had to have constant access to a restroom. During Lotronex's short-lived initial period on the market, Huschle said, she "had begun to dream again."

Disorders, an organization that offered reliable information for those afflicted and that sought to attract more attention to the condition.

Lotronex first went on sale in March 2000 as the first prescription treatment specifically approved to treat IBS. Limited in its approval to women suffering IBS with diarrhea, Lotronex was used by an estimated 300,000 women in the United States before being taken off the market less than a year after its launch. The move was prompted by FDA-ordered restrictions stemming from at least 70 reported cases of severe side effects. In clinical trials Lotronex's use had resulted in extreme constipation among a quarter of participants and in potentially fatal intestinal ulcers for four participants. Consumer advocates accused Glaxo of downplaying these numbers, while patients' groups and Glaxo emphasized the large number of suffering women who had, because of Lotronex, been able to resume the normal lives that they had believed lost to IBS. In June 2002 Lotronex went back on sale after the FDA placed new conditions on its marketing and prescription.

MARKETING STRATEGY

Many doctors were still hesitant about IBS medications after the highly publicized problems with Lotronex, and consumer watchdog groups raised similar questions about Zelnorm, contending that the possible side effects outweighed potential benefits. Sidney Wolfe, director of the Health Research Group at the Washington, D.C.–based advocacy organization Public Citizen, for instance, told the *Wall Street Journal,* "There's no evidence to show it works better than Metamucil." Many test subjects had experienced extreme diarrhea as a result of taking Zelnorm, and there was a less frequent incidence of more dangerous intestinal problems.

This measure of negative attention notwithstanding, one of Novartis's other primary obstacles in the marketing of Zelnorm was the mainstream public's lack of knowledge about IBS. The "Tummies" campaign, which broke in 2003, was meant to help people understand that the symptoms they were experiencing were indications of IBS and then to encourage them to ask their doctors about Zelnorm as a treatment for the condition.

Beginning with an onscreen list of the common symptoms of the variety of IBS treatable with Zelnorm—abdominal pain, bloating, and constipation—the campaign's 60-second television spot then superimposed the words "abdominal pain," "bloating," and "constipation" onto trim, attractive female stomachs. Not only did the attractiveness of the "tummies" serve to counteract the stigma associated with the symptoms listed while simultaneously specifying the medication's target market, but the visual technique of combining symptoms with stomachs also provided an efficient and memorable description of IBS. The spot likewise indicated that Zelnorm offered relief from those symptoms and directed viewers to an informational website.

Print ads used the same concept, featuring the text of symptoms written in black marker on women's stomachs, together with the copy, "If you are one of the millions of women living with these symptoms, you may have IBS with constipation. And now there's help." Print insets provided more detail about the condition by using the "tummies" imagery with diagrams of normal and abnormal intestinal functioning. The tagline was "Be yourself again." Online ads likewise used the Zelnorm name, together with the image of symptoms written on female stomachs. A clickable button labeled "Learn about relief" directed consumers to an informational page about IBS and Zelnorm.

OUTCOME

According to the magazine *Medical Marketing & Media,* prescriptions for Zelnorm increased by 68 percent in the campaign's first year; unaided awareness of IBS as a condition rose to 38 percent of consumers; and the Zelnorm brand was recognized by 53 percent of consumers, up from a figure of 3 percent prior to the campaign. At the 2004 United European Gastroenterology Week conference in Prague, Czech Republic, a Novartis executive predicted that Zelnorm was on its way to being a billion-dollar-a-year earner for the company. Deutsch and Novartis swept the first-ever Medical Marketing & Media Awards, held in 2004, with the "Tummies" campaign winning Best Total Integration Program, Best TV Campaign, and Best Product Launch Ad in Consumer Press. The campaign also went on to win Gold at the 2005 EFFIE Awards, given out by the New York American Marketing Association.

The Zelnorm launch was not without its setbacks, however. In April 2004 the FDA added new warnings for Zelnorm users, publicizing the drug's links with severe diarrhea and more dangerous problems whose initial symptoms included fainting, rectal bleeding, bloody diarrhea, or worsened pain. The "Tummies" ads were revised accordingly, offering additional information about these side effects.

In 2004 Zelnorm was granted FDA approval as a treatment for a second condition, chronic constipation, which increased the drug's target market to include both men and women, and the "Tummies" concept was adapted accordingly in 2005, with script superimposed on both male and female stomachs. Novartis was trying to win European approval for Zelnorm and was engaged in research that it hoped would establish the drug as a treatment for upper gastrointestinal disorders, which would open up an additional, extremely large market for the drug.

FURTHER READING

"Best Product Launch Advertisement in Consumer Press." *Medical Marketing & Media,* November 2004.

"Best Total Integration Program (for Companies above $5 Billion in Sales)." *Medical Marketing & Media,* November 2004.

"Best TV Campaign." *Medical Marketing & Media,* November 2004.

Duenwald, Mary. "New Remedies for a Frustrating Illness. But Do They Work?" *New York Times,* December 7, 2004.

"FDA Approves Restricted Marketing of Lotronex." *FDA Consumer* 34, issue 3 (July/August 2002).

Fuhrmans, Vanessa. "Novartis Drug Receives Approval by FDA for Sale—Prior Decision Is Reversed for Zelnorm, which Treats Irritable-Bowel Syndrome." *Wall Street Journal,* July 25, 2002.

———. "Novartis Posts Drop of 8% in Earnings, Hastens Drug Launch." *Wall Street Journal,* July 23, 2002.

Fuhrmans, Vanessa, and Gardiner Harris. "Novartis Posts 2% Drop in Sales, Outlines New Pipeline of Drugs." *Wall Street Journal,* October 18, 2002.

Goetzl, David. "A Bitter Pill." *Advertising Age,* August 6, 2001.

"Novartis Looks to IBS Drug Zelnorm as Its Next Blockbuster Drug." *Pharma Marketletter,* September 29, 2004.

"Safer Alternatives to Zelnorm." *Consumer Reports,* September 2004.

Sampey, Kathleen. "New Drug to Get $100 Mil. Push." *Adweek,* June 10, 2002.

Shapiro, Joseph P. "A Pill Turned Bitter." *U.S. News & World Report.* December 11, 2000.

Mark Lane

Office Depot, Inc.

2200 Old Germantown Road
Delray Beach, Florida 33445
USA
Telephone: (561) 438-4800
Web site: www.officedepot.com

WHAT YOU NEED. WHAT YOU NEED TO KNOW. CAMPAIGN

OVERVIEW

In 2001 Office Depot, Inc., prided itself as the world's largest seller of office furniture and second-largest supplier of office supplies after Staples, Inc. In addition to having a stronghold on the office-furniture market, the retailer sold art and engineering supplies, computer hardware and software, and printing and copying services. Except for the fact that it touted its office furniture slightly more than the competition, Office Depot's marketing strategy paralleled the rest of the office-supply industry. Office Depot, Staples, and OfficeMax relied heavily on back-to-school sales. To first attract parents who needed school supplies for their children and later to draw in small businesses, Office Depot released a campaign titled "What You Need. What You Need to Know."

The "What You Need. What You Need to Know" television, radio, and print campaign was created by BBDO New York in 2001. The campaign's budget was undisclosed, but according to the market research firm Nielsen Monitor-Plus, Office Depot spent $25 million on advertisement for the fourth quarter of 2002. The campaign initially aired television commercials suggesting that parents could improve their children's school success with the proper back-to-school supplies. After research showed that 80 percent of Office Depot's customers were purchasing supplies for small businesses, the campaign shifted in September 2003. Four new television spots told the stories of office workers whose work lives improved thanks to Office Depot. Near the end of 2003 the campaign also advertised Office Depot's exclusive line of Christopher Lowell office furniture. The campaign ended in December 2004.

Although some within the advertising community criticized it for not differentiating the Office Depot brand from its competition, the campaign helped Office Depot's sales outperform Staples in 2002, during which it posted $11.4 billion in sales. By 2004 Office Depot had again slipped behind Staples, which had become the world's largest supplier of office supplies. Although other campaigns contributed to the ad agency's success, "What You Need. What You Need to Know" helped BBDO earn "Agency of the Year" in 2002 from *Shoot* magazine.

HISTORICAL CONTEXT

The first Office Depot opened in Lauderdale Lakes, Florida, in 1986. By the end of 1987 the office-supply store had opened nine more stores. After growing at breakneck speeds, the Florida-based chain had a nationwide presence in the early 1990s. Created by the ad agency Gold Coast Advertising, one of Office Depot's first campaigns was titled "Takin' Care of Business." The tagline was taken from the title of a 1974 song by the rock band Bachman-Turner Overdrive. In 1996 Office Depot awarded its estimated $67 million account to the Chicago office of J. Walter Thompson USA, a unit of the WPP Group. J. Walter Thompson elaborated on the previous campaign's theme with the tagline "This is where I take care of business." The campaign was intended to make Office Depot every business' first choice for office furniture and office supplies.

In 1996 Staples tried to purchase Office Depot for $3.4 billion, but the government stopped the acquisition on antitrust grounds the following year. Undaunted by the decision, Office Depot moved forward with store expansion and a nationwide advertising campaign. The cartoon-strip character Dilbert was used for a $30 million campaign that first aired on Thanksgiving Day in 1997. The following year Office Depot released a campaign targeting parents of schoolchildren and starring Dilbert's canine sidekick, Dogbert. The cartoon dog appeared in two 30-second television spots that aired in August 1998. In the commercials the bespectacled Dogbert touted Office Depot as the best place for school supplies. The $10 million campaign included a sweepstakes in which 40 different people were eligible to win a $5,000 Office Depot shopping spree. The campaign included a Supporting School Values program that provided discounts for PTA members and teachers.

TARGET MARKET

When the campaign broke in 2001, it targeted the parents of children returning to school in the fall. Commercials suggested that if parents truly wanted their children to succeed, they should outfit them with the proper school supplies, which could be found at Office Depot. That same year Staples conducted a survey that two years later would affect how Office Depot defined its target market. Staples discovered that business customers accounted for 90 percent of its profits. Following Staples' example, in 2003 Office Depot shifted the campaign's target from parents to small businesses. During the second half of 2003 Office Depot still held large back-to-school sales, but it spent much of its 2003 budget on four commercials aired in September 2003. The spots featured office workers trying to improve their work environments with Office Depot products. More than 40 percent of Office Depot's sales were also generated by the company's business-services group, which delivered office products to medium and large businesses.

The shift of the campaign's target market led to a two-pronged strategy that involved not only the advertising campaign but also the Office Depot store interiors. Whether shopping as executives or employees, women made up 60 percent of Office Depot's customer base, according to a *New York Times* interview with Bruce Nelson, Office Depot's CEO. To cater to the female majority, store interiors were decorated in pastel colors, which supposedly resonated more with women than men. In order to shed the warehouse stigma of a typical office-supply store, Office Depot also began selling premium office furniture and displaying products in a way that modeled non-warehouse retailers.

Executives at Office Depot believed that if small businesses and entrepreneurs were more prosperous, Office Depot sales would subsequently improve. Part of the campaign involved a partnership between Office Depot and Florida Atlantic University's Small Business Development Center (SBDC). SBDC business analysts spoke at two-hour seminars at Office Depot stores that could be attended free of charge by Florida's local business leaders. "For years, we provided small businesses with the tools they needed to run their business," Monica Luechtefeld, the executive vice president who headed Office Depot's online business, said to the *Palm Beach Post.* "Today those tools tend to be information as much as products. A large part of our customer base is small business and the small business entrepreneur. As they become healthy, that obviously creates a healthy customer for us."

DESKS, CHAIRS, AND FILE CABINETS

Between 2001 and 2003 the office-supply company Office Depot ran an advertising campaign titled "What You Need. What You Need to Know." During the campaign Office Depot reigned as the leading retailer of office furniture. Desks, chairs, and file cabinets were Office Depot's best-selling furniture items.

COMPETITION

In 2001 Staples reigned as the world's largest office-supply store. Starting in the mid-1990s Staples advertised under the slogan "Yeah, we've got that." The campaign ended in 2003, when Staples severed its eight-year relationship with the ad agency Cliff Freeman & Partners and gave its account to Martin/Williams of Minneapolis. Martin/Williams's first campaign for Staples, which was released with an estimated $50–$70 million budget, featured the tagline "That Was Easy" to emphasize the ease of shopping at Staples. The office-supply store also shifted from advertising in Sunday circulars to mailing ads directly to businesses. The first of two TV spots for

OFFICE DEPOT RETAIL GIANT

In 2003 the office-supply company Office Depot was the world's second-largest online retailer. It was also the sixth-largest furniture retailer in the United States.

"That Was Easy" featured two executives trying to lead a business meeting with ridiculously misprinted handouts. The second spot featured an office-supply store calling out printer cartridge numbers as if they were number-letter combinations in Bingo. At the spots' conclusions a voice-over explained how the shopping experience at Staples was less stressful than at the competition. "Our job is getting people to drive by Office Depot and OfficeMax and go to Staples instead," John Karlson, senior vice president for strategic development at Martin/Williams, said to the *New York Times.* "The way to do that is by making it easier to get through the store, within the format of the large superstore."

In conjunction with the "That Was Easy" campaign's theme of convenience, Staples also began advertising products unique to its stores. Staplers that allowed consumers to staple giant stacks of paper with one finger were featured in direct mailers. Combination locks that used scrambled words instead of numbers were pushed with the "That Was Easy" campaign. "We want our brand to stand for ease and innovation," Ronald L. Sargent, the chief executive of Staples, told the *New York Times.*

MARKETING STRATEGY

The "What You Need. What You Need to Know" television, radio, and print campaign was created by BBDO in 2001. Over its four-year lifespan, the campaign's strategy morphed as its target market changed. The first TV spots targeted the parents of children returning to school in the fall of 2001. These commercials suggested that if parents wanted their children to succeed, the children should be equipped with the proper school supplies. Several months later, in 2002 Office Depot aired one 30-second spot to announce its sponsorship of the Winter Olympics. In a $2 million Super Bowl spot titled "Don Barcome, Curling Expert," a man watching the Olympic sport of curling on television wondered aloud, "What is that?" No one answered. Then the copy "But, if life was like Office Depot..." appeared. Now, with a life "like Office Depot," the same man asked, "What is that?" The ice curling champion Don Barcome suddenly appeared and explained, "Curling, an ancient Scottish ice sport, played with a 42-pound stone." The same man who had asked, "What is that?" next appeared shopping inside an Office Depot. The spot ended with the Office Depot logo, the Olympics logo, and the tagline "What you need. What you need to know." During the same week a similar spot featured the figure skater Tara Lipinski explaining the lutz ice-skating jump.

The campaign also partnered Office Depot with Florida's SBDC. Executives at the office-supply company believed that if small businesses and entrepreneurs improved their businesses, the success would equate to higher sales for Office Depot. Throughout 2002 speakers from SBDC were hired by Office Depot to speak at stores in Miami and Coral Springs, Florida.

In 2003 the campaign stopped airing commercials related to the Olympics and created spots that targeted small businesses. The change came after an Office Depot survey discovered that 80 percent of the store's customers were buying for their small businesses. Office Depot's largest competitor, Staples, had successfully targeted small businesses earlier. From September until the end of November, four spots suggested that Office Depot products could improve the lives of small-business employees. "The strategy builds on what we did for back-to-school about owning your kids' success," explained BBDO senior creative director Adam Goldstein in *Adweek.* "This is about owning the success of your small business." The first spot featured a worker who received a raise after Office Depot helped her choose an ink cartridge. The next spot, "JoAnn," lampooned reality television shows with a small-business owner who needed to "update her look" with Office Depot products. The third featured adults running after an Office Depot van as if it were an ice-cream truck. The final spot showed an Office Depot "ringer" helping a business win its corporate softball game.

Near the end of 2003 Office Depot advertised its exclusive Christopher Lowell line of office furniture. Executives at Office Depot hoped that the furniture would differentiate Office Depot more from its competitors. The tagline "What you need. What you need to know" was used until December 2004.

OUTCOME

The campaign's first full year helped Office Depot outperform Staples. When Staples posted $10.7 billion in global sales for 2002, Office Depot led the industry with $11.4 billion. The following year, however, Staples became the leader with $11.6 billion in sales. Analysts within the office-supply sector explained that Staples had surpassed Office Depot by placing stores in more preferred locations. Office Depot CEO Bruce Nelson also attributed the change in supremacy to international currency exchange rates. With 16 percent of Office Depot's locations existing outside of North America in 2002, the deflated U.S. dollar sent Office Depot's operational costs skyrocketing.

The "What You Need. What You Need to Know" campaign was one of many campaigns that earned BBDO "Agency of the Year" from *Shoot* magazine (an ad-industry publication focusing on commercial production) in 2002. In regards to Office Depot's future advertising campaigns, ad critics pointed out that "What You Need. What You Need to Know" successfully defined a preferred target market of small-business owners and entrepreneurs for Office Depot. The retailer's exclusive Christopher Lowell office furniture further promoted Office Depot as an office-furniture leader. With the inside of its stores decorated to appeal to women, Office Depot separated itself even more from the warehouse-style interiors of OfficeMax and Staples. Advertising critics agreed that, after struggling to define its brand throughout the 1990s, Office Depot had finally differentiated itself during the span of "What You Need. What You Need to Know."

FURTHER READING

Albright, Mark. "Office Supply Shoppers." *St. Petersburg (FL) Times,* June 25, 2001, p. 3E.

Charry, Tamar. "Office Depot Prepares to Revitalize Its Campaign after Merger Plans with Staples Are Undone." *New York Times,* July 28, 1997, p. 9.

Deutsch, Claudia H. "Big Office Supply Retailers Try to Build a Smaller Box." *New York Times,* August 12, 2004, p. 1.

Elliott, Stuart. "Staples Is Changing Its Slogan to Stress the Ease of Shopping for Office Supplies in Its Stores." *New York Times,* February 27, 2003, p. 6.

Howard, Theresa. "Advertisers Turn to Bowl Pregame." *USA Today,* January 24, 2002, p. B16.

Lowes, Robert. "Office Design and Supplies." *Medical Economics,* June 18, 2004, p. 38.

Masters, Greg. "Office Superstores Tidy Up." *Retail Merchandiser,* November 1, 2002, p. S5.

Sampey, Kathleen. "Office Depot Talks to Small Business: It's the Client to the Rescue in 4 Playful BBDO Spots." *Adweek,* September 29, 2003, p. 9.

Sataline, Suzanne. "Office Depot Sues Staples over Ads Placed on Google." *Wall Street Journal,* October 21, 2005, p. B2.

Troy, Mike. "Rebounding Office Superstore Rivals Pose New Challenge for Staples." *DSN Retailing Today,* November 5, 2001, p. 25.

Waresh, Julie. "Office Depot's New Campaign Enlists a Well-Known Dogface." *Palm Beach (FL) Post,* August 3, 1998, p. 3.

———. "Still in Print." *Palm Beach (FL) Post,* October 21, 2002, p. 1D.

Kevin Teague

Office of National Drug Control Policy

PO Box 6000
Rockville, Maryland 20849-6000
USA
Telephone: (800) 666-3332
Fax: (301) 519-5212
E-mail: ondcp@ncjrs.gov
Web site: www.whitehousedrugpolicy.gov

EARLY INTERVENTION YOUTH CAMPAIGN

OVERVIEW

In late 1998 advertising agency Ogilvy & Mather was put in charge of the "National Youth Anti-Drug Media" campaign, charged with curbing drug use in teenagers. The original emphasis was on prevention, aimed at 12 and 13 year olds, but some research indicated that the advertising was counterproductive, kindling a curiosity about drugs in young people and actually leading to increased usage. The campaign raised the target age to 14 to 16 year olds, and a new effort was developed, the "Early Intervention Youth" campaign, which sought to convince teens to urge friends with alcohol and drug problems to seek help.

The $37 million campaign broke in early 2004 and ran through the rest of the year. The primary media vehicle was television spots on network and cable TV, although radio also played a major role. To a lesser extent print, Internet, and out-of-the home advertising where teens gathered was also used. In addition the advertising sought to drive traffic to the freevibe.com website, where teens could learn more about the deleterious effects of drinking and drugs and the importance of intervention, as well as ways to accomplish it.

Ogilvy statistics indicated that the "Early Intervention Youth" campaign met its primary objectives of increasing awareness of the intervention concept with the target market, convincing teens that intervention was a good thing, and stimulating an increase in the number of visits to the website. Nevertheless, it was difficult to determine the effect the campaign had on the ultimate goal, curbing alcohol and drug use among the target audience. What was certain was that the "National Youth Anti-Drug Media" campaign soon changed direction and crafted a new message rather than build on the "Early Intervention Youth" effort.

HISTORICAL CONTEXT

The White House Office of National Drug Control Policy (ONDCP) was established in 1988 by the Anti-Drug Abuse Act, the goal of which was to create a "drug-free" America. One component of that effort was the use of advertising. Hired in late 1998, advertising agency Ogilvy & Mather was put in charge of the "National Youth Anti-Drug Media" campaign, responsible for evaluating ads produced by several ad agencies and buying media. According to Vanessa O'Connell, writing in the *Wall Street Journal* in 2002, the campaign included more than 212 TV commercials featuring such performers as the Dixie Chicks and hip-hop singer Mary J. Blige, as well as actors posing as drug users. The campaign, developed by some of the best-known agencies on Madison Avenue, was "considered a novel step in public health advertising because it was aimed directly at children." But in 2002, as the campaign was up for reauthorization for five more years, the anti-drug effort and Ogilvy came under fire. The new U.S. "drug czar," John P. Walters, claimed that not only had recent anti-drug advertising failed but it might have actually inspired young people to experiment with marijuana. O'Connell wrote, "Mr. Walters suggested that the ads' messages were 'too indirect' to have an impact, and speculated that the commercials might be doing more harm than good. 'If an ad answers a question that a child doesn't have, there's a chance you'll incite his or her curiosity,' he said." According to *Advertising Age*'s Rance Crain, Walters believed that eliminating the source of drugs was a more effective approach: "Before he became drug czar, Mr. Walters said an anti-drug campaign aimed at teens is a 'lazy man's way of trying to appear that they're doing something.' "

To complicate matters further, Ogilvy had come under fire for its billing practices, including allegations that agency employees altered time sheets and billed ONDCP for items not permitted under government contracts, leading to criminal and civil fraud probes. Early in 2002 Ogilvy settled the civil claims, and eventually five Ogilvy executives would either plead guilty or be convicted of fraud charges. To the surprise of most observers, Ogilvy was retained in 2002 as the lead ad agency in the "National Youth Anti-Drug Media" campaign. ONDCP maintained that it would work with Ogilvy to refine the campaign and make it more "hard-hitting."

One problem all public-health advertising aimed at teens had to contend with was the natural rebelliousness of youth. The "National Youth Anti-Drug Media" campaign tried to promote the concept of the "anti-drug," natural ways to get high, such as hang gliding or kayaking. The advertisers tried yet another new approach in its 2004 campaign, called "Early Intervention Youth," which sought to keep the anti-drug motif alive yet move the campaign from prevention to intervention, to leverage peer pressure and convince teens to convince other teens that their drug use was a problem that required attention.

TARGET MARKET

In the first few years of the "National Youth Anti-Drug Media" campaign, the target audience was 12 to 13 year olds. After Ogilvy retained the contract with ONDCP, the focus shifted to 14 to 16 year olds. The "Early Intervention Youth" campaign targeted youths in this age group who had close friends who used drugs (primarily marijuana) or alcohol. These teens tended to be tolerant of the choices their friends made and were reluctant to urge them to change their behavior. While they believed that they should intervene only if the drug or alcohol use became a problem, what constituted a problem was open to interpretation. Some teens considered experimentation itself to be a problem, while others only viewed drug and alcohol use as a problem if it became dependency or, worse yet, grew self-destructive or destructive of their friendship. In order to address the widest segment of 14 to 16 year olds with close friends who used drugs, the campaign elected not to define when use became a problem. Instead it hoped to allow teens to receive the intervention message on their own terms.

> **ANY ANSWERS?**
>
> Perhaps the most famous anti-drug television commercial ever produced showed a man frying an egg in a sizzling pan. He commented, "This is your brain on drugs. Any questions?" Sponsored by the nonprofit organization Partnership for a Drug-Free America, the scare-tactic spot became the fodder for comedians. It became an object lesson for advertisers on how not to influence a target audience about drug usage.

COMPETITION

No other group was encouraging teens to intervene with friends who had problems with drugs or alcohol. And if there had been such a group, it would not have constituted relevant competition but rather would have been viewed as an ally in the effort. The opposition, in this case, would be the forces encouraging drug use among teens.

There was no competing advertising urging 14 to 16 year olds to take drugs, although some would argue that the media glamorized the activity. The real competition came from other teens. Just as the "Early Intervention Youth" campaign planned to use peer pressure to urge teens to stop using drugs and alcohol, other teens of their own volition were urging their friends to start drinking and using drugs and to continue using them. Popular teens who drank and did drugs offered the same message on an indirect level, serving as peer role models. Moreover, the campaign had to contend with sheer curiosity and the rebelliousness of the age group.

MARKETING STRATEGY

The strategy behind the "Early Intervention Youth" campaign was to motivate the teen who would serve as the person intervening with a friend who had a drug or alcohol problem. First a case had to be made about the negative consequences of a friend's drug or alcohol use, whether it related to health concerns or the harmful impact on their friendship. Second the messenger had to be motivated to act. This was to be accomplished by portraying the situation as a moral obligation, bolstered by examples of teens taking the step—or not—to intervene with friends. But fulfilling this strategy remained a tricky transaction. In a write-up of the campaign for the EFFIE Awards, a prestigious advertising industry competition, Ogilvy explained, "While this campaign intended to instill in youth a sense of moral responsibility for intervening with friends who are developing patterns of use, it was imperative that executions guide youth to this conclusion, without dictating their 'responsibilities' to them directly. It was vital that teens feel their decision to intervene is one they have come to themselves, and not one being forced on them to accept, otherwise they will disregard the message."

The "Early Intervention Youth" campaign established three objectives. It sought to increase awareness in teens that they had a responsibility and an ability to help friends with alcohol and drug problems. Second the campaign wanted to educate youths about the dangers of drug and alcohol abuse, thus empowering them when they intervened. The final objective was to drive traffic to the campaign's website, freevibe.com, where teens could find more information on the importance of intervention and ways to achieve it.

The campaign used a mix of media in order to reach the largest percentage of the teen population. Television was the primary media vehicle, accounting for nearly half of the $37 million budget, almost all of which was spent on network and cable TV. Spot television, time bought on local stations as it became available at attractive rates, was also used in the top 25 markets where drug use was concentrated. Another 9 percent of the budget was spent on the Channel One daily television newscast shown to middle, junior high, and senior high school students. Network radio was the next most important media component, representing nearly a third of the budget. Spot radio was also purchased on top teen stations. In addition the campaign spent about 4 percent of the budget on ads in teen magazines and 2 percent on out-of-home advertising, such as signage at malls where teen congregated.

Typical of the campaign's television spots was "Lake," which first aired on the hit television show *Survivor* following the Super Bowl telecast in early 2004. In the spot a teenage girl cried for help as she was drowning in a lake, while on a nearby wharf another girl watched, hands in her pockets, doing nothing to help. The voice-over of a young woman then said, "If your friend was in trouble, you'd help them. Wouldn't you?" The girl on the wharf turned her back on the drowning friend, then the commercial cut to title cards that read, "If a friend has a problem with drugs or drinking, do something. Friendship. The anti-drug. freevibe.com."

OUTCOME

According to Ogilvy's EFFIE summary, the "Early Intervention Youth" campaign succeeded on a number of levels. Regarding the first objective the agency claimed that after just one month the campaign achieved 68 percent awareness among the target audience, an impressive showing given that new product introductions that last as long as six months reach comparable awareness levels. In terms of educating and empowering youths, according to Ogilvy data, teens exposed to the advertising were significantly more likely than other teens to say that they should get involved if a friend was having a problem with drinking or marijuana or that they would feel good about intervening in such a situation. Finally traffic to freevibe.com increased by an average of 108 percent each month after the launch of the campaign, a significant increase over same-month traffic from the prior year.

FURTHER READING

Crain, Rance. "Drug Czar, Partnership Feud Over Ad Direction and Tactics." *Advertising Age,* August 12, 2002, p. 15.

Day, Sherri. "Antidrug Campaign Keeps Ogilvy & Mather." *New York Times,* July 5, 2002, p. C2.

Melillo, Wendy. "Cold Turkey for White House?" *Brandweek,* November 10, 2003, p. 8.

———. "ONDCP Introduces New 'Influence' Tag." *Adweek,* September 19, 2005, p. 8.

———. "ONDCP Links Drugs, Drinking in New Ads." *Adweek,* January 26, 2004.

———. "ONDCP's PR Review Draws a Few Unusual Suspects." *Adweek,* May 24, 2004, p. 10.

Melillo, Wendy, and Kathleen Sampey. "ONDCP Sees a Brand New Day with FCB." *Adweek,* October 4, 2004, p. 6.

O'Connell, Vanessa. "Drug Czar Says Ad Campaign Has Flopped." *Wall Street Journal,* May 14, 2002, p. B1.

———. "Ogilvy Retains U.S. Antidrug Pact." *Wall Street Journal,* July 5, 2002, p. A10.

Teinowitz, Ira. "Drug Office Kicks Old Ad Habits." *Advertising Age,* October 31, 2005, p. 1.

———. "Drug Office to Yank Terror Ads in About-Face." *Advertising Age,* March 31, 2003, p. 1.

———. "Ogilvy Cut Off from Anti-Drug Account." *Advertising Age,* December 1, 2003, p. 3.

———. "White House Drug Office in Feud over Failed Ad Campaign," *Advertising Age,* May 20, 2002, p. 3.

Ed Dinger

OfficeMax Inc.

150 East Pierce Road
Itasca, Illinois 61043
USA
Telephone: (630) 438-7800
Fax: (800) 572-6473
Web site: www.officemax.com

WHAT'S YOUR THING? CAMPAIGN

OVERVIEW

OfficeMax Inc., the third largest chain in the office supplies superstore category, faced the difficult task of differentiating itself from larger rivals Staples, Inc., and Office Depot, Inc. In late 2003 OfficeMax and its new advertising agency, DDB Chicago, launched the "What's Your Thing?" campaign to help mold a distinct image.

The campaign was mostly driven by television spots. One of the three spots in the initial phase featured an Afro-sporting African-American, the Rubberband Man, who delivered supplies from a souped-up pushcart to his office colleagues while dancing to the Spinners' 1970s hit song "The Rubberband Man." The character became a hit with consumers and led to a back-to-school television spot, as well as a commercial that parodied a vintage stop-motion holiday special. More Rubberband Man spots followed in 2005.

The first Rubberband Man spot won an Emmy Award nomination, and all of the spots featuring the character were repeatedly downloaded from the OfficeMax website. Sales improved dramatically, and the company was so convinced that the Rubberband Man provided the point of difference it was looking for that it built its marketing around the popular character.

HISTORICAL CONTEXT

In 1986 three office supplies superstores were launched in different corners of the United States: Staples in Massachusetts, Office Depot in Florida, and Office Club in California. Two years later another chain, called OfficeMax, Inc., was established (in Cleveland, Ohio). Along with Staples and Office Depot, OfficeMax became one of the fastest growing companies in the rapidly consolidating office supplies category that had been revolutionized by the superstore concept. By virtue of their size these retailers could leverage their buying power and eliminate traditional middlemen in the industry to offer small businesses and general consumers a wide variety of items at lower prices. Although it started late, OfficeMax emerged as the second largest player (trailing Office Depot) by 1995. At that point OfficeMax was larger than Staples. In the second half of the 1990s, Staples surged, however, taking over the top spot, leaving OfficeMax as the third largest office supplies chain.

At the start of the 2000s OfficeMax was challenged on a number of fronts. As the U.S. economy lapsed into recession, sales sagged, leading to losses and the closing of stores. OfficeMax also faced an image problem. The company's vice president of marketing, Scott Williams, told Suzanne Vranica of the *Wall Street Journal* in an August 2004 interview, "We found customers had difficulty in differentiating the office supply brands. They saw similarities between colors and the name. They didn't see differences in messaging. There was a lot of confusion with the brands . . . We wanted to break out. There was a lot of awareness, but we wanted to make sure OfficeMax was known for a unique and different experience." The pressure to hone the OfficeMax identity was further intensified after the Boise Cascade Corp. agreed to pay $1.3 billion for the chain in a deal that closed in December 2003. At the end of the month, the company and its new advertising agency, DDB Chicago, unveiled the "What's Your Thing?" campaign to address the image problem.

INSPIRATION CLOSE TO HOME

The popular Rubberband Man character in the OfficeMax television spots was conceived by DDB Chicago creative director Don Pogany. He didn't have to look far for inspiration; he modeled the character after the ad agency's service center coordinator.

TARGET MARKET

The target market shifted as the "What's Your Thing?" campaign evolved. Initially the audience was the small business customer, which back in the 1980s had made the office supplies superstore concept viable. Many major corporations at that time had slashed their workforces, and a rising number of small businesses emerged to take up the slack in the economy. The distribution of office supplies was controlled by six major wholesalers, which then sold the goods to office supply dealers and stationery stores. In turn the dealers supplied large corporations and the stationers sold to small businesses and individuals. Superstores were able to eliminate these middlemen and offer much lower prices than the stationers could. As a result small business customers became a mainstay for OfficeMax. With the rise of home computers and home offices, the number of individuals buying paper, ink and toner, and other supplies also increased. After the initial phase of the "What's Your Thing?" campaign was completed, and the Rubberband Man character had connected with the general public, OfficeMax focused on these individuals. It launched a back-to-school campaign targeting parents and teachers shopping for school supplies. This mass market was next targeted in a holiday campaign that positioned OfficeMax as a place to buy gifts.

COMPETITION

When OfficeMax appealed to a wider market in its back-to-school push and holiday gift-buying pitch, it encountered competition from the likes of Wal-Mart and other retailers, but at its core the company's competition was Staples and Office Depot, both larger in size. According to an analysis conducted by Credit Suisse First Boston, Staples led the way in sales, posting $7.8 billion in 2003, followed by Office Depot's $5.7 billion, and OfficeMax's $4.7 billion. OfficeMax also trailed its larger rivals in the amount of money it could spend on advertising. In terms of measured media, in 2003, according to TNS Media Intelligences/CMR, Office Depot outspent Staples $89 million to $73 million, while OfficeMax spent $49 million. Other competition in the office supplies arena were mom-and-pop stationers and retailers that carried offices suppliesmdash;Wal-Mart, drugstore chains, and larger supermarkets. There were also warehouse clubs like Sam's Club and Costco to contend with, as well as companies that sold by catalog or online, such as Quill Corp., which operated as an independent Staples subsidiary.

MARKETING STRATEGY

The initial three television spots developed for the "What's Your Thing?" campaign tried to spice up the office supplies category, the advertising for which was not known for its creativity. OfficeMax commercials in the past had shown people shopping for a single product in a store setting. "Ads in stores set up certain limits to what you can do creatively," Tom Russell, director of marketing for OfficeMax, told Theresa Howard of *USA Today.* "People know OfficeMax has stores. We said, 'Let's get out of the store.' That opens up a world of possibility for you." And while the category might be mundane, Russell also noted that the marketers learned that consumers were actually passionate about office supplies: "We found whether it's a notebook, pen, highlighter or organizing system, they have to have a certain one."

In one of the new offbeat television spots, two office friends plotted to get out of work by faking an illness. They colored their faces with highlighters to affect a sickly hue, which worked well for the one who chose yellow but aroused the suspicion of the boss for the one using pink. A second spot featured a pair of mountain climbers in a fight over who forgot to bring the food. A candid still photograph of the tussle made it seem as if they were actually helping each other up. The picture then appeared as part of a poster positioned behind a motivational speaker rallying a group of employees.

It was the third commercial, called "Rubberband Man," that caught the attention of the public and overshadowed the other two spots. The Rubberband Man

SEXY IS AS SEXY DOES

Actor Eddie Steeples, who had never done a commercial and rarely worked before landing the part as the Rubberband Man, became something of a minor celebrity. His rise to prominence culminated in him being named one of *People* magazine's Sexiest Men of 2004. "It's very flattering," he told *Adweek.* "At the same time, I just don't understand who decided that."

character, a lanky African-American with a large Afro hairstyle, was identified by a large spinning disco ball of multicolored rubber bands on his pushcart, which itself was replete with fat tires and side mirrors. He danced and grooved and thoroughly enjoyed his job dispensing office supplies to his coworkers while in the background played "The Rubberband Man," the 1976 hit song by the Spinners.

The song was selected first, and then the creative team held a Los Angeles casting call and auditioned about 100 people of all types, both whites and African-Americans, goofballs and hipsters. One actor stood out—Eddie Steeples, a 30-year-old actor who had never done a commercial and only auditioned at the urging of a friend. "He had the right combination of looks and maneuvers, and the key thing for us was he grasped how varied the character could be," DDB's creative director, Don Pogany, told Mae Anderson, writing for *Adweek.* "The random items in the cart, he was thinking about each and every one. The other guys were a bit more superficial with it." Steeples described his character to Anderson as "kind of a happy guy going along, doing his thing. In my eyes, he's sharper than most people, especially more than most people give him credit for being. At the same time, he makes everybody happy." In the commercial the character was seen issuing supplies even before people realized they needed them. For example, a new desk chair was slipped under an employee to replace a broken one, and a woman with a messy office received a new desk organizer.

The upbeat "Rubberband Man" spot with its catchy feel-good tune first aired shortly after Christmas 2003. Soon the OfficeMax website began receiving E-mails from people raving about the commercial. The company made the spot available on its website, and within two days it was downloaded 15,000 times. The marketers realized that the Rubberband Man had touched a chord with consumers and began making plans to exploit the character and center the marketing around him. A website was developed for him, offering outtakes from the TV spot and downloadable images. In-store signs featuring the Rubberband Man were designed, and he would also play a prominent role in catalogs and direct marketing. In June 2004 the Rubberband Man was featured in three half-page ads in the issue of *Rolling Stone* that celebrated the 50th anniversary of rock and roll. Moreover OfficeMax received a great deal of free publicity, as the spot was parodied on the *Tonight Show,* and Katie Couric and Matt Lauer of the *Today* show raved about it.

The follow-up to the original "Rubberband Man" spot was a back-to-school effort called "The Party's Over," which began airing in July 2004. The 60-second spot showed the Rubberband Man out of the office, merrily delivering school supplies from his pushcart to children (who were less than enthusiastic about going back to school) at summertime venues, like a beach and a ballpark. This spot continued to use the "What's Your Thing?" tag.

The creative team then began brainstorming about a Rubberband Man ad for the upcoming holiday season. They recalled the stop-motion holiday specials they watched as children and decided to turn the Rubberband Man into a clay figure in a spot with the style and look of an old stop-motion show. Since the character, like Santa, enjoyed giving out things, he was in his element giving out the kind of items OfficeMax sold that were suitable as gifts, such as a glue stick to keep Santa's beard in place, a new paper cutter to carve a roast, and a stepladder to help a short man kiss a woman beneath some mistletoe. Steeples, although not appearing in person, was filmed as part of the animation process.

The "What's Your Thing?" campaign and its star continued to flourish in 2005. A pair of Rubberband Man ads called "Lost" and "Found" were developed. The first promoted OfficeMax color ink and toner supplies as the character plastered an office with flyers and handed out other copies, announcing that his brightly colored ball of rubber bands was missing. The "Rubberband Man" song, minus the lyrics, played in the background. The "Found" spot opened with more somber music as the character glumly made his rounds, dumping products haphazardly. A "found" poster then caught his eye. After being reunited with his ball, the Rubberband Man was once again strutting down the hallway as the Spinners' song kicked in.

OUTCOME

The "What's Your Thing" campaign was a success on all levels. The Rubberband Man spots were highly popular and were downloaded repeatedly from the Office-Max website, and the character helped to distinguish

OfficeMax from Office Depot and Staples. Increasingly the company built its marketing around the Rubberband Man. Writing in *Advertising Age,* James B. Arndorfer noted, "Some question whether OfficeMax should pour marketing resources into a character that might be phased out after a couple years or so. Unlike some marketers who need to constantly change tactics to reach a changing customer base—brewers, athletic-wear marketers—OfficeMax is targeting a stable market." The strategy appeared to be working, as reflected by increasing sales for OfficeMax. In 2004 sales grew by more than 60 percent to $13.3 billion and net income soared to $173 million. While it was difficult to determine how much credit for the success was due to the advertising, there was no doubt that the campaign played a significant role. The Rubberband Man also reached iconic status, providing a boost for OfficeMax that money simply could not buy. Rather than avoid the spots, consumers actually sought out the Rubberband Man commercials. Although the campaign did not win any major advertising industry awards, the first Rubberband Man ad received a highly coveted nomination in the Emmy Award competition for commercials in 2004.

FURTHER READING

Anderson, Mae. "Rubberband Man' Makes OfficeMax Deliveries." *Adweek,* November 24, 2004.

———. "Supplies and Demand." *Adweek,* September 13, 2004, p. 30.

Arndorfer, James B. "Stretching into an Icon." *Advertising Age,* May 31, 2004, p. 3.

Baar, Aaron. "DDB, OfficeMax Bounce Back to School." *Adweek,* July 22, 2004.

Cardona, Mercedes M. "Taps McCann—Staples' Holiday Wish List: Humor." *Advertising Age,* July 19, 2004, p. 8.

Champagne, Christine. "Dr. Chel White Stretches to Create Rubberband Man." *Shoot,* December 17, 2004, p. 10.

Howard, Theresa. "OfficeMax Turns to Own Office Supply Guy for Inspiration." *USA Today,* May 10, 2004, p. 8B.

"Office Depot, Inc." *International Directory of Company Histories,* vol. 65. Farmington Hills, Michigan: St. James Press, 2004.

"OfficeMax, Inc." *International Directory of Company Histories,* vol. 43. Farmington Hills, Michigan: St. James Press, 2002.

"The Office Max Rubberband Man Appears in Stop-Motion Spot." *Computer Graphics World,* December 2, 2004.

"Staples, Inc." *International Directory of Company Histories,* vol. 55. Farmington Hills, Michigan: St. James Press, 2003.

Vranica, Suzanne. "'RubberBand Man' Breathes New Life into OfficeMax." *Wall Street Journal,* August 11, 2004.

Ed Dinger

Old Navy, Inc.

2 Folsom St.
San Francisco, California 94105
USA
Telephone: (650) 952-4400
Fax: (415) 427-2553
Web site: www.oldnavy.com

■■■

'70S RETRO TV CAMPAIGN

OVERVIEW

The valued-focused Old Navy apparel brand was an immediate hit when it was introduced in 1994 by San Francisco parent company and national clothing retailer Gap, Inc. Old Navy made a name for itself with eccentric television commercials that featured an array of offbeat celebrities extolling the virtues of Old Navy products on campy artificial sets. The kitschy look and tongue-in-cheek humor, which remained a component of all the company's ad campaigns, reached a climax in 2002 with a series of spots parodying the 1970s TV shows *The Brady Bunch* and *Green Acres.*

Two similar commercials spoofing *The Brady Bunch* and titled "The Rugby Bunch" began airing in the summer of 2002. They showed an imitation Brady family wearing colorful Old Navy rugby shirts. To emphasize a cross-generational appeal, the spots recreated the nine-square divided screen that had become the iconic image from the opening credits of *The Brady Bunch.* The words "The Rugby Bunch" were superimposed over Brady-like actors of all ages. These commercials were followed in the fall by a spot that referenced the show *Green Acres* and highlighted painter pants. Both spots featured longtime Old Navy pitchwoman Morgan Fairchild, a distinctive blond television actress famous in the 1980s. The shows' theme songs were adapted with lyrics celebrating rugby shirts, painter pants, and Old Navy in general and were sung, sometimes quite badly, by the commercials' actors. The cost of these three spots was included in Old Navy's media budget of $133 million in 2002.

The spots aired from August until the end of October. They were the first in what would become for the next two years a recurring retro-television motif used by Old Navy Marketing, the company's in-house advertising unit. The impact of the '70s retro TV commercials was reflected in fiscal 2003 sales numbers, which revealed that Old Navy was responsible for $6.4 billon in sales, nearly 40 percent of the $15.8 billion taken in by Gap, Inc., that year.

HISTORICAL CONTEXT

Retail giant Gap, Inc., began in 1969 with one San Francisco store. Doris and Don Fisher wanted to make it easier for young customers to find a hugely popular clothing item: jeans. It eventually expanded into one of the world's largest apparel chains. The San Francisco–based company introduced a new brand to the retail world with the opening the first Old Navy store, in Colma, California, in 1994. The mission was, according to one of Old Navy's most successful past taglines, to make "shopping fun again" with low prices for trendy clothes. Old Navy quickly made money—and history—becoming the first retailer to achieve $1 billion in sales in fewer than four years.

Actress Morgan Fairchild. © FRANK TRAPPER/CORBIS.

From Old Navy's inception, advertising was an inside job. Its in-house ad agency, Old Navy Marketing, set about creating commercials that would stand out from the rest of the pack. It recruited 1970s–80s television vixen Morgan Fairchild to tout hip clothing to a generation that may not have even known who she was. The highly stylized Old Navy look continued in the fall of 1997 with commercials that featured a legendary fashion writer, Carrie Donovan, then in her late 60s. She was a figure certainly unfamiliar to the teen audience, but celebrity identification was not the objective. The spots were bright and campy, with a low-budget feel. The aforementioned celebrities were attention-getters because of their unforgettable and sometimes over-the-top looks. Donovan did not even wear Old Navy clothes. Her signature look was that of a midcentury New York professional woman. In the commercials she donned her usual black suit, white pearls, and thick, round-rimmed glasses and extolled the virtues of the latest Old Navy clothing or accessories. She became known as the "Old Navy Lady" and appeared in 42 spots, including one that featured her piloting an airplane with another frequent Old Navy commercial cast member, a dog named Magic. Other celebrities, including quirky actress Fran Drescher and rapper Lil' Kim, lined up through the years to help sell the hip but value-priced merchandise.

The often-wacky Old Navy commercials were either loved or hated by media watchers, but no one could deny their effectiveness. The in-house advertising team, helmed by creative director Dennis Leggett, was responsible for these memorable nostalgia-oriented campaigns until Leggett's retirement in 2004. That year Old Navy hired Deutsch Los Angeles, making it the first outside agency to handle the company's advertising.

TARGET MARKET

While it offered clothing for all ages and both sexes, Old Navy's most reliable consumers had always been girls ranging in age from 8 to 18. In a successful attempt to better serve the retail needs of the mothers of those core customers, the retailer expanded to offer baby, maternity, and plus sizes. The summer 2002 television push for the coming school year took into account a broader spectrum of potential customers—both kids and parents. The commercials spoofing 1970s television classics were meant to create good feelings on the part of adults, who would remember the shows from their childhoods. As an acknowledgement of the ever-present generation gap, the spots were also campy enough to provide a requisite mocking of the past, a quality that appealed to teens. These kids thus might be willing to shop at the same store as their parents, but for very different reasons.

Painter pants, which first gained popularity in the 1970s, were the central product in the "Green Acres" commercial. This product was an ideal crossover from generation to generation. The aim of the spot was to make moms and dads take notice when the unmistakable melody of the *Green Acres* theme song began. The spot featured Old Navy mainstay Morgan Fairchild singing, "Old Navy you're the pants for me . . ." to the tune of the original song. The desired result was that parents would make the trip to Old Navy brimming with nostalgia for the pants they loved as teens—and of course bring their kids along as well. Once in the store the whole family would have plenty of fresh, trendy products to chose from.

COMPETITION

When Gap, Inc., created the value-oriented Old Navy brand, it may have also generated more competition than it bargained for. "Over the past 10 years, Old Navy's concept quickly became part of how America shops," said Old Navy president Jenny Ming in a 2004 *PR Newswire* press release. "We brought something to

OLD NAVY GETS A STYLISH NEW SISTER

Over the decades since it was founded, Gap, Inc., grew to include a stable of retail specialty stores that were among the world's most recognizable brands: Gap, Banana Republic, and Old Navy. In August 2005 a long-awaited Gap, Inc., expansion occurred with the introduction of a new chain, Forth & Towne. A women's store designed to combine department-store variety with the service and intimacy of a boutique, Forth & Towne made its debut in West Nyack, New York, and was the antithesis of Old Navy. Forth & Towne promised a figure-friendly fit in high-end clothes at more reasonable prices. Four more stores followed in the Chicago area that same year. The company hoped to entice women over the age of 35, a group responsible at the time for 39 percent of women's-apparel spending.

shoppers that didn't exist when we started—affordable fashion." Old Navy's successful strategy of emphasizing the look of low-cost clothes as more desirable than a designer label resulted in a glut of surprising competitors for the chain. Department stores Sears and J.C. Penney, as well as mass retailers such as Target, took advantage of a trend—largely attributed to Old Navy—that made discount shopping cool. These companies' ad campaigns began to focus on the teen market, specifically teenage girls, who had long been the core of Old Navy's customer base.

Old Navy had to hold its own against the growing popularity of the Kohl's chain, which by 2003 was reporting $10.2 billion in sales, according to *Adweek.* To attract the fashion-savvy consumer, chains such as Kohl's produced, under their own labels, affordable knock-offs of trendier, more expensive clothing lines. As the stigma of value shopping continued to fade through the end of the twentieth century, low-budget megastores K-Mart, Meijer, and Wal-Mart began to pursue a wider audience for their apparel departments. One common tactic that emerged was to make deals with reputable designer brands to manufacture a more value-conscious clothing line to be carried only in their stores. Target was successful in partnering with such designers as Isaac Mizrahi, Liz Lange, and Mossimo to increase sales. To keep consumer dollars away from competitors, Old Navy had to strengthen and constantly renew its brand presence in the national consciousness.

MARKETING STRATEGY

In 2002 Old Navy's answer to the increasing number of entrants into the cool-clothes-for-less territory it had once ruled was a new television campaign that sought to bring a wider variety of shoppers into the fold. Old Navy Marketing creative head Dennis Leggett shepherded in three parody commercials of retro television shows from the 1970s. The spots saturated the airwaves in the summer and fall of 2002. Hyperglamorous blond actress Morgan Fairchild was once again front and center as the mom in the two spots titled "The Rugby Bunch," a *Brady Bunch* spoof. These were the first retro-TV-flavored commercials, which would become a running advertising device for the next two years. The 30-second spots, directed by Gap and Old Navy veteran Matthew Rolston, used a replica of the original show's set and a reworded theme song—"Here's the story of a shirt named rugby . . . ,"—to bring the Brady Bunch's good natured naïveté into the service of selling striped shirts for the whole family.

Old Navy's take on *Green Acres* focused on painter pants (an updated version of the multipocket work pants once worn only in the painting trade), with Fairchild as a pseudo-replacement for the series' original female lead, Eva Gabor. This spot aired through the end of October 2002 on a wide variety of cable channels as well as during television-ratings giants such as *Friends, Everybody Loves Raymond,* and *The West Wing.* The comedy of *Everybody Loves Raymond* was firmly rooted in exploring parental and marital struggle. An hour-long political drama, *The West Wing* had a decidedly adult audience demographic. A commitment to the expensive advertising sponsorship of these two shows reflected how intent Old Navy was on capturing the interest of an older consumer.

To promote new products, Old Navy used mass-mail flyers and print inserts, but concentrating on television spots for greatest exposure had been an Old Navy tactic from the outset, and thus the lion's share of the advertising budget went toward TV spots. Old Navy's media spending in the period between January and November 2002 was reported to be $133 million by TNS Intelligence/CMR, a leading provider of marketing and advertising information. Parodies of *The Love Boat* and *The Dating Game* continued through the company's 10th-anniversary commercial, as did the use of 1970s TV actors, including Sherman Hemsely of *The Jeffersons.* Dennis Leggett reflected on the retro TV campaigns in a March 2003 issue of *Brandweek,* saying, "The challenge is to create something memorable that drives customers to the stores." He added, "We're doing that."

OUTCOME

The result of the 2002 retro TV campaign was a sales increase in fiscal 2003. Old Navy was responsible for generating $6.4 billion in sales in 2003, leading a rebound for parent company Gap, Inc., which boasted a second-quarter profit in 2003 of more than three times that of the previous year. The Old Navy retro TV commercials in particular were credited with spurring an 11 percent increase overall for Gap, Inc., in same-store sales, which took into account store openings and closings. The TV-spoof spots also appeared consistently in high positions on the Ad Age/IAG Top Spots list. This top-10 list, assembled by Intermedia Advertising Group and *Advertising Age* magazine, measured viewer recall and thus the success of new ad campaigns. Other companies even followed suit. Chevy, ING, and American Express Blue all launched commercials using retro TV show themes or parodies to sell their own products. In the 10 years since its first store opened in 1994, Old Navy played a significant role in the success of Gap, Inc., contributing to revenues listed in 2004 as $16.3 billion.

FURTHER READING

"Gap Hopes to Woo Boomers Back with New Store." *MSNBC.com,* August 26, 2005. Available from <http://www.msnbc.msn.com/id/9054063/>

Greene, Joshua. "Mass Appeal; Stores Such as Target, J.C. Penny and Sears Try to Grab the Teen Customer with Creative Marketing and Plenty of Sponsored Events." *Women's Wear Daily,* May 30, 2002, p. 16B.

Horyn, Cathy. "Carrie Donovan: One-of-a-Kind Fashion Editor and TV's 'Old Navy Lady.'" *New York Times,* November 13, 2001

Howard, Theresa. "1970s-Inspired Shtick Propels Sales for Old Navy." *USA Today,* July 21, 2003, p. B4.

"Inside the Pitch." *Adweek,* April 12, 2004, p. 15.

Janoff, Barry. "Old Navy Sets a Date to Renavigate the Channels of Classic TV Land." *Brandweek,* March 10, 2003, p. 8.

"Old Navy Invokes Retro 'Family' Theme for the Holidays." *Brandweek,* November 18, 2002, p. 8.

"Old Navy Stays Retro with Green Acres Ad Rollout." *Brandweek,* September 30, 2002, p. 5.

Tate, Ryan. "Gap Sales Pull Out of Lengthy Tailspin." *San Francisco Business Times,* February 21, 2003, p. 3.

"Usual Suspects Top IAG Ad-Recall Survey." *Broadcasting & Cable,* June 23, 2003, p. 23.

Walker, Rob. "Generation Gap: Old Navy's Fondness for Even Older TV." *Slate.com,* October 28, 2002. Available from <http://www.slate.com/id/2073190/>

Ward, Celeste. "Old Navy Debuts Final In-House TV Spots." *Adweek,* May 12, 2004.

Wiles, Greg. "Profits More than Tripled, Gap Inc. Says." *San Diego Union-Tribune,* August 22, 2003, p. C-4.

Simone Samano

DESTINATION CAMPAIGN

OVERVIEW

In only its second year of national television advertising and its fourth year in existence, Old Navy clearly announced its arrival as a major marketer by securing a spot on the final episode of the decade-defining sitcom *Seinfeld.* The 30-second spot, entitled "Woof," featured some of the many stars experiencing career revivals thanks to Old Navy, including Joan Collins and Morgan Fairchild, as well as Old Navy ad staples Magic the Dog, the company's mascot, and Carrie Donovan, the 70-year-old former *New York Times* fashion editor who donned her signature oversized black-rimmed glasses and classic Chanel cuffs. The departure of *Seinfeld* from prime time on May 14, 1998, amounted to a Super Bowl of advertising, as NBC charged $1.7 million per 30-second slot, surpassing the NFL Super Bowl with its airtime rates of $1.3 million per 30-second slot. The campy atmosphere of Old Navy advertising dovetailed well with the quirkiness of the sitcom. "The retro-ness and Dada-esque quality of the commercials has an off-the-wall camp component, one 'that maybe a fifth of the audience may understand as camp,'" said Old Navy public relations director Joe Enos in Cynthia Robins's 1998 *San Francisco Examiner* article. "But like the brand, these spots are approachable, fun and friendly," Enos continued.

"Woof" was one of a trilogy of ads in Old Navy's "Destination" campaign, which set all three spots on a vintage 1970s-era airplane. The *Seinfeld* slot represented a departure from the norm, as Old Navy concentrated the majority of its media buy on cable television, a scheme that allowed the company to marry its commercials to complimentary programming. In fact Old Navy, which produced the spots not through an ad agency but rather in-house, tied into programming that it sponsored and placed its products on personalities appearing on shows during which Old Navy ads ran. Strategies such as these created a brand image that remained consistent across the board, as explained by advertising critic Barbara Lippert in her *Adweek* column: "The tone of the ads, the look of the store, the merchandising and design of the clothing, even the shopping experience itself is consistent with the whole."

HISTORICAL CONTEXT

Donald G. and Doris F. Fisher founded Old Navy's parent company, the Gap, in 1969, naming the store after the generational schism prevalent at the time. They sold discount records and tapes to woo in customers to buy the uniform of the counterculture, Levi's jeans. At the time Levi Strauss did not allow discounting of its products, so the Gap's profit margins soared until 1976, when the Federal Trade Commission ruled against this monopolizing practice, forcing the Gap to discount Levi's and shift to private-label apparel. In 1983 Don Fisher hired Mickey Drexler to vertically integrate the Gap, and Drexler promptly whittled down the private labels to one—the Gap. Drexler repositioned the Gap from a chain store into a brand, and in the 1990s Drexler further revamped the Gap formula to mimic the ubiquitous success of Coca-Cola. It was Drexler's vision to dominate consumers' wardrobes by simplifying the shopping experience.

Drexler, president of Gap Inc. since 1987 and CEO since 1997, happened upon the name "Old Navy" on the marquee of a bar in Paris in the early 1980s. A decade later he was on the verge of opening a new venture under the name Gap Warehouse when he remembered passing that bar in Paris. Just before the 1994 opening of the new enterprise, Gap lawyers bought the rights to the name from the French bar owner. Old Navy would fill out the Gap's portfolio of retail apparel stores, with Banana Republic, purchased in 1983, catering to high-end consumers, the Gap appealing to mid-level shoppers, and Old Navy representing the bottom rung, reaching the mainstream, mass market through discounting. Drexler, however, could not afford to jeopardize the Gap's reputation for quality by replicating the formula of most discounters selling cheap goods at a cheap price. He and his colleagues sought to distinguish Old Navy.

"When we started Old Navy, we sat around and we talked about what we didn't like about discount stores—poor quality, colors that are always just a hair off. We really thought, 'What do we not want to be?' and just took it from there," recalled Jenny Ming, Old Navy's executive vice president for merchandising, in Nina Munk's *Fortune* magazine article. By maintaining quality standards and injecting whimsy into the discount shopping experience, Old Navy managed to grow extremely quickly. The company boasted that it was the first apparel retailer to reach sales of $1 billion in just four years, with about 300 stores. "This is a feat that's unmatched in the history of specialty apparel retailing," said analyst Marcia Aaron of BT Alex. Brown Inc. in Michael J. Pachuta's *Investor's Business Daily* article.

At first Old Navy relied on advertising in newspapers, magazines, and spot television and radio. Old Navy commenced its national television advertising in 1997, spending the majority of its $160 million advertising budget, which represented 2.5 percent of sales, on cable television. That year's fall back-to-school campaign demonstrated the potential success of Old Navy's marketing techniques. Advertising in support of a sale on cargo pants was scheduled to run three weeks, but near "the end of the second week, we were asked to turn off national cable, because cargo pants were no longer available in stores," recounted Pam Marcus, vice president and director of national broadcast at Deutsch Inc., which executed the campaign alongside the Old Navy's internal production company. "We effectively sold out their merchandise," Marcus continued in the 1998 *Brandweek* article.

TARGET MARKET

Old Navy's success stemmed in part from its broad appeal. In a narrow sense it targeted middle-income families, but its appeal eclipsed this categorization. The timing of Old Navy's inception coincided with a pervasive trend back to bargain shopping and away from the ostentation of the 1980s. "There was a time, not so long ago, when people who shopped at department stores wouldn't shop at Wal-Mart—that was declass,," said Kurt Barnard of Barnard's Retail Trend Report in Munk's 1998 *Fortune* magazine article. "Then it became chic to shop downscale, to shop for a bargain. People used to pay $10 and they said they paid $20. Now they pay $20 and say they paid $10." Munk then continued, "Old Navy captures this trend brilliantly. It's discount shopping with an edge, discount shopping that appeals to people who can afford Gucci."

Old Navy bridged the gap between bargain and brand shopping by creating a trustworthy brand backed by the reputation of the Gap. As with its parent company, Old Navy appealed to consumers transgenerationally. Low prices particularly appealed to parents, while their kids appreciated the fashionable styling of Old Navy clothes. The challenge for Old Navy advertising consisted of reaching these diverse demographic segments. Old Navy solved this problem by concentrating its media buys on cable television, where the brand could deliver its message to different constituents on different networks that targeted specific segments. "The beauty of cable TV was that we could get younger target prospects to find us on MTV, males on Comedy Central and moms on Lifetime," said Walter Coyle, vice president and associate media director at Deutsch Inc., in a 1998 *Brandweek* article.

COMPETITION

Whereas the Fishers founded the Gap on sales of Levi's, after the 1976 FTC intervention led to private labeling the Gap competed fiercely against the company it previously supported. The inception of Old Navy opened up another front to attack the original American outfitter, from below in terms of price. Old Navy benefited from the vertical integration of the Gap Inc., which controlled every aspect of the business, from production to

I'D BE AWFULLY GOOD ON TV

In 1994 Old Navy hired fashion doyenne Carrie Donovan to write a 45-word mock columnette that appeared every Friday on page A-4 of the *New York Times,* the newspaper from which she retired in 1990 as fashion editor. The ad appeared to be a memo from Donovan reporting on the "merch," as she called it, or merchandise about to hit the shelves at Old Navy stores. When Donovan still worked for the *Times,* she appeared on *Good Morning America,* the *Today Show,* and *CBS This Morning.* Tom Brokaw once commented that she was a natural for television, and years later, when Donovan was talking with Old Navy executives, she joked, "Oh, I'd be awfully good on TV." Old Navy took the joke seriously and began featuring her in its television commercials. They did not take her too seriously, though, as her gogglelike glasses lent levity to the spots.

distribution to inventory to retail sales. Levi's, on the other hand, was primarily a manufacturer. It entered the retail business on the coattails of the Gap but could not translate the success of the Gap's cohesive retail execution. Nevertheless, Levi Strauss sales soared throughout the 1990s, mostly on the strength of the cool image it promoted as the quintessential jean.

Levi sales plummeted 13 percent in 1998, however, down to $6 billion. Peter Arnell, chairman and executive creative director of Arnell Group Brand Consulting, ascribed this decrease to Levi's redirection away from brand building on the strength of its own heritage, as Levi's positioned itself in contrast to its competition. "The moment they start trying to compete with other brands, they don't do very well," Arnell commented in Miles Socha's *WWD* 1999 article on Levi's. 1998 Levi's campaigns included the tag lines "Tommy Wore Them," "Ralph Wore Them," and "Calvin Wore Them," referring to designers Hilfiger, Lauren, and Klein respectively, as well as the tag line "Our Models Can Beat Up Their Models," featuring Marilyn Monroe and James Dean in Levi's. Besides referring to the competition, these ads copied the Gap's successful "Who Wore Khakis?" campaign that featured famous personalities such as Dizzy Gillespie, Miles Davis, Ernest Hemingway, and Pablo Picasso in everyday, Gap-like clothes.

Gap Inc. risked competing with itself in opening Old Navy, though surprisingly little cannibalization of sales occurred, according to a report on the World Wide Web site "The Motley Fool." Old Navy proved to be the tier with the broadest appeal, however, as evidenced by fourth quarter comparable-store sales, which increased more than 30 percent at Old Navy while increasing more than 20 percent at Banana Republic. The Gap experienced an increase in the high single-digit percentage and GapKids in the low single-digit percentage. Old Navy grew by shifting sales away from discount department stores such as JC Penney, Target, and Kmart, which could not match the hip styling and atmosphere of Old Navy.

MARKETING STRATEGY

By focusing on campaigns around specific items such as cargo pants, drawstring pants, and fleece jackets, Old Navy advertising created demand, as these very items became hip in the youth culture. Old Navy created and then supported these trends by enlisting television personalities to wear Old Navy clothing during programming that featured Old Navy advertising. MTV's Mike Davis appeared on "Winter Lodge" dressed in Old Navy clothing, and MTV devoted a segment called "Magic Moments" to the musical taste of Old Navy's mascot, Magic. Fashion model Markus Schenkenburg, outfitted in Old Navy garb, hosted *MTV Jam,* which segued into an Old Navy commercial featuring Schenkenburg at a mock fashion show presided over by Magic and Donovan and featuring a shunned Jerry Hall, the fashion model.

"In each case the program acted as a wrap-around for the ads," said Walter Coyle, vice president and associate media director at Deutsch Inc., in a 1998 *Brandweek* article. "There is tremendous value in having regular commercials subtly supported by visual and verbal in-program reminders. You simply won't—or can't afford to—match that degree of flexibility on conventional network television," Coyle continued. Old Navy also made itself visible as a sponsor of program blocks on *Comedy Central,* a top 10 countdown on *VH1,* and a Christmas party on *Nick-at-Nite,* as well as making an appearance during a fashion segment on *E! Entertainment TV.*

Besides outfitting personalities familiar to the youth culture, Old Navy revived the careers of stars from the 1960s, '70s, and '80s. Old Navy commercials featured the likes of the Smothers Brothers, Dr. Joyce Brothers, and Isabelle Sanford and Sherman Helmsley from the television show *The Jeffersons.* These appearances generated the retro feeling that Old Navy supported in-store with vintage 1952 navy Chevy pickups parked in the middle of the warehouse retail space and utilized as product displays. These appeals to a glorious past both generated and drove the retro trend.

OUTCOME

Adweek advertising critic Lippert noted the extremity of Old Navy advertising, pointing out that "anything that extreme is polarizing—people tend to love it or hate it." In a *Los Angeles Times* survey of viewers' reactions to commercials, Courtney Evans stated that the spots "actually made me swear never to buy the product." Critical response in the advertising community, however, was much more positive. "Gap and sister company Old Navy have been responsible for some of the most innovative retail advertising to come down the aisle in recent years," said Holly Haber and Sharon Edelson in their *WWD* article. Lippert echoed this admiration for Gap Inc. advertising of its three chains. She singled out Old Navy advertising as particularly noteworthy and effective with her interpretation of how it functioned: "Old Navy advertising imposes a superstructure of hip superiority—graphically riotous, in-the-know fun—that overrides any residual feelings of being a loser at a bargain basement."

FURTHER READING

Duff, Mike. "The Answer to Branded Value." *Discount Store News,* December 14, 1998.

Haber, Holly, and Sharon Edelson. "Retail Ads: Upping the Ante." *WWD,* May 15, 1998.

Lippert, Barbara. "Tailor-Made." *Adweek,* May 10, 1999.

Munk, Nina, with Michelle McGowan. "Gap Gets It: Mickey Drexler Is Turning His Apparel Chain into a Global Brand." *Fortune,* August 3, 1998.

"Old Navy Shakes Up Key Retail Seasons." *Brandweek,* April 13, 1998.

Pachuta, Michael J.. "With Old Navy's Strong Sales, Gap Inc. Regains Momentum." *Investor's Business Daily,* September 4, 1998.

Robins, Cynthia. "Old Navy's Old Lady the Former Fashion Editor Is Featured in a $1.7 Million Commercial on the Final 'Seinfeld,'" *San Francisco Examiner,* May 14, 1998.

William D. Baue

Orange S.A.

50 George St.
London, W1U 7DZ
United Kingdom
Telephone: 44 207 9841600
Web site: www.orange.com

■■■

GOLDSPOT CAMPAIGN

OVERVIEW

In 1994 a new British mobile-phone operator, Orange S.A., debuted in the wake of Britain's more established operators, such as Vodafone Group and BT Cellnet. Orange grew quickly by offering the United Kingdom's first mobile-phone service that billed according to the seconds of talk time instead of rounding up to the next minute. Nine years after Orange's debut, telecommunications analysts predicted that the maturing U.K. mobile-phone industry was reaching a saturation point. Realizing that the population of new subscribers was dwindling, in 2003 Orange released its "Goldspot" cinema campaign to draw customers away from the competition.

"Goldspot" was created by the ad agency Mother Ltd., which had won Orange's estimated $75 million account in 2002. The campaign claimed its title from the nature of its placement: the commercials appeared during the 60 seconds after movie trailers but before the start of the main feature. This advertising slot was commonly referred to as the "goldspot" in the United Kingdom. Nearly every campaign spot featured a real-life Hollywood figure pitching his or her film idea to actors playing Orange executives. In one spot featuring the director Spike Lee, the director asked Orange to finance a movie about the baseball legend Jackie Robinson, the first African-American to play Major League Baseball. After listening to Lee's heartfelt pitch, the executives audaciously suggested that Robinson's story be altered to advertise Orange's services. One executive suggested that in the movie Robinson should play instead for the San Francisco Giants, whose team colors were orange, unlike the colors from Robinson's actual team, the Brooklyn Dodgers. Similar suggestions prompted Spike Lee to leave the meeting prematurely. "Goldspot" commercials ended with the text "Don't let a mobile phone ruin your movie. Please switch it off." The campaign continued into 2004.

"Goldspot" helped Orange retain its position as one of the largest mobile-phone providers within Europe. The ad-industry publication *Campaign* named three "Goldspot" commercials as the best Cinema Ads of 2004. The campaign also collected a Gold Lion for Commercial Public Services at the 2004 Cannes Lions International Advertising Festival.

HISTORICAL CONTEXT

Orange was founded in 1994 by the Hong Kong company Hutchison Whampoa Limited, through its Hutchison Telecommunications subsidiary. It was the fourth mobile-service provider to appear in the United Kingdom and was considered an underdog by telecommunications analysts. By not imposing fees that were unnecessarily enforced by the larger providers, Orange outgrew most of its competition. In 1994 Orange's network only covered 50 percent of the United Kingdom.

Two years later it covered 90 percent of the United Kingdom and claimed 25 percent of the nation's digital-mobile-phone subscribers.

The London ad agency WCRS Group helped launch Orange in 1994 with one-word posters featuring the words "laugh," "cry," or "listen" printed in orange letters on a black background. The agency also released an estimated $1.6 million television spot titled "Better Place," directed by Ridley Scott, whose film-directing credits included the *Blade Runner* (1982) and *Gladiator* (2000). Other advertisements featured the tagline "pay for what you say" to tout Orange as the first British mobile-phone company to charge customers by the second instead of by the minute. After claiming that its ad work had increased Orange's market value by an estimated $480 million, WCRS was awarded an IPA Effectiveness Award. WCRS's later work for Orange included an approximately $20 million campaign that broke in mid-2000. One spot, titled "Hold Up," featured a man sitting inside a bar and listening to the sound of a siren outside. The outside police chase then materialized into small miniature cars racing along the bar's countertop. A voice-over explained that Orange subscribers could use their phones to receive current news regardless of their location.

After partnering with the mobile-service provider through strong subscriber growth and a series of award-winning Orange campaigns, WCRS executives were shocked when Orange awarded its advertising account to the ad agency Lowe & Partners in 2000. According to *Campaign* contributor John Tylee, after the Orange brand was acquired by France Telecom SA in 2000, Orange needed an agency with a larger scope. Lowe's relationship with Orange was short-lived. After a string of high-level resignations within Lowe and a release of what Orange executives considered to be weak advertisement, Orange's new marketing director, Jeremy Dale, awarded Mother Ltd. the advertising account in 2002. The agency began formulating a humorous campaign to lure customers away from the competition.

TARGET MARKET

"Goldspot" targeted the competitions' customers. Research conducted by Orange before the campaign revealed that two-thirds of British mobile-phone subscribers felt confused and apathetic about their service contracts and never reviewed their mobile-phone plans. The cinema-themed spots also aimed to encourage existing Orange customers to use their text and voice features more often. The campaign released a minimal amount of information about Orange's services and focused more on Orange's brand image than its features.

> ### CELEBRITY FAMILY
>
> Carrie Fisher, the actress who played Princess Leia in *Star Wars,* was featured in a commercial for the U.K. mobile-phone operator Orange in 2003. Even though she first became widely known for her 1975 performance as Lorna in *Shampoo,* fame was not foreign to the young actress. Her parents were the singers Debbie Reynolds and Eddie Fisher, both of whom were pop icons in the 1950s. Eddie Fisher married the actress Elizabeth Taylor in 1959.

Advertisers historically regarded cinema spots as the best medium for targeting 15- to 34-year-olds, but the medium had expanded its scope during the 10 years preceding the launch of "Goldspot." According to *Campaign,* the surge of period films, comedy dramas, and remakes of Hollywood classics were attracting older and more mature audiences to movie theaters. In 2004 *Campaign* reported that 71 percent of the U.K. population over the age of 45 went to the cinema, which was 300 percent greater than the same age group's attendance in 1994.

"Goldspot" targeted U.K. movie audiences with cinema-themed humor. Not only were the Orange executives featured in the spots made out to be buffoons, but the actors chosen for the spots were also parodied for their previous movie work. In one spot the actress Carrie Fisher, who played Princess Leia in *Star Wars,* pitched her film idea for a nineteenth-century romance. The Orange executives stated that they would only finance the film if she could somehow incorporate text messaging into the movie. Steve Davies, chief executive for the British Producers Association, explained to *Brand Republic* that British audiences enjoyed watching celebrities be self-deprecating. "The British public doesn't like big-headed celebrities," he said.

COMPETITION

Vodafone, which outperformed Orange in revenue but not in quantity of subscribers, released a campaign in 2004 that featured billboard and bus-shelter ads with the mobile-phone text message "FAN C A" followed by an image of a shag carpet. If read aloud, the message asked, "Fancy a shag?" which in the United Kingdom meant "would you like sexual intercourse?" This advertisement, along with a billboard that featured the word "NICE" above two watermelons, was stopped by the U.K.

SPIKE

Spike Lee, the director of controversial movies such as *Malcolm X* and *Bamboozled,* was featured in an advertising campaign for the mobile-phone operator Orange in 2003. The award-winning director was actually born Shelton Lee in 1957. His mother gave him the nickname "Spike" because of his tough nature at an early age.

advertising watchdog the Advertising Standards Authority (ASA). Vodafone released a television spot in 2004 that was also criticized. It featured a teenage boy clothed in nothing but fruit and whipped cream. He used a mobile phone to photograph himself and sent the image to his girlfriend. Some of the commercial's harshest critics accused Vodafone of encouraging pedophilia. After a review the ASA deemed the spot suitable for mature audiences.

The prominent British entrepreneur Richard Branson, founder of Virgin Records and Virgin Atlantic Airways, introduced the mobile-service operator Virgin Mobile Telecoms in 1999. Although it was dwarfed by its competition, much as Orange had been five years earlier, Virgin Mobile grew quickly by emphasizing prepaid mobile phones and airing provocative television commercials. To warn against the competition's long-term contracts, Virgin Mobile released its estimated $9 million "Be Careful What You Sign" campaign in late 2002. The campaign was created by the London ad agency Rainey Kelly Campbell Roalfe/Y&R. One spot featured the rapper Wyclef Jean, who thought he was signing an autograph but instead signed a contract that condemned him to a mobile-home park. Jean escaped the park but was soon arrested and placed in prison. Inside the prison's group-shower area, Jean stood beside a giant man who dubiously told Jean, "Hey Superstar, pass the soap." The spot ended with the tagline "Be careful what you sign," Virgin Mobile's logo, and a voice-over explaining the freedom of prepaid calling plans.

MARKETING STRATEGY

The "Goldspot" cinema commercials first appeared in spring 2003 during movie theaters' "goldspot," a U.K. advertising term that referred to the 60 seconds just before the beginning of the featured film. Each of the campaign's first four spots featured a different Hollywood celebrity pitching his or her film idea to the Orange Film Commission, a fictional panel of executives that decided what movies Orange would finance. The spots featured Carrie Fisher from *Star Wars,* the *X-Men 2* star Alan Cumming, the *Jaws* star Roy Scheider, and the director Spike Lee. After each celebrity pitched his or her film concept, the executives adulterated the pitch with possible opportunities for Orange advertisement. In one spot Lee explained the relevance of his movie idea about Jackie Robinson, the first African-American to play for a Major League Baseball team, the Brooklyn Dodgers. Lee believed that the movie should "tell the world" that some causes were worth the fight. The director was interrupted by an Orange executive who suggested that Jackie Robinson should, instead, "text the world." In the spot starring Alan Cumming, the Scottish actor explained that his film would be "a rites-of-passage movie," at which point the head Orange executive yawned, "Seen it."

Leon Jaume, an executive creative director for WCRS, anatomized the campaign's humor in the business publication *Marketing.* "The glaze on the cherry is the unbelievable stroke of casting the clients as Philistines, regarded with contempt by their expensively hired stars," wrote Jaume. "Let's just pause to consider the implications. First, you invest heavily in a campaign reminding people how annoying your product can be, then you agree to be portrayed as a character so crass it makes [British director] Michael Winner look humble and gifted." Each spot ended with the text "Don't let a mobile phone ruin your movie. Please switch it off."

The campaign continued into 2004 with spots featuring Sean Astin, who had starred in *Rudy* and the trilogy *The Lord of the Rings.* Other spots featured Verne Troyer, who played Mini Me in *Austin Powers: The Spy Who Shagged Me.* One spot even included the character Darth Vader from the *Star Wars* trilogies. After Darth Vader entered the Orange Film Commission boardroom, the head executive asked, "Darth, thought you were dead, what can I do for you?" Vader pitched his concept for another film about fellow "Sith lords and their dominance over the universe." The executives ridiculed Vader's pitch by suggesting that he join the "Orange side" instead of the "Dark side"—a reference to the *Star Wars* trilogies.

The commercials sometimes mentioned mobile features such as text messaging, but they relied more on their self-deprecating humor, which the British enjoyed, according to some advertising analysts. "The marketing strategy [of Orange] has always been to put the customer at the heart of everything we do," Orange's Jeremy Dale explained in *Marketing.* "It's always been about being straightforward and honest and friendly. One of the challenges we are solving at the moment is making sure the services we bring to the market are what customers genuinely want. It's about changing consumers' behavior; helping them understand the benefits of the technology, not shouting at them about technology."

OUTCOME

The "Goldspot" campaign helped Orange remain competitive with other U.K. mobile-phone operators. Determining which of the top five U.K. operators dominated the industry varied by what statistics were evaluated. Although Orange led with the most U.K. subscribers in 2003, Vodafone reported slightly higher revenue by charging more per customer. Other competitors, such as Virgin Mobile, T-Mobile International AG, and O2 plc, trailed closely behind. In the campaign's first three years, sales for Orange leapt from $17.9 billion to $26.8 billion.

From an advertising standpoint, "Goldspot" collected some of the industry's greatest awards. At the 2004 Cannes Lions International Advertising Festival the campaign won a Gold Lion for the Commercial Public Services category. *Campaign* rated the spots starring Alan Cumming, Sean Astin, and Verne Troyer as the best cinema commercials for 2004. The commercial starring Spike Lee earned a silver award at the 2004 British Television Advertising Awards in the category of spots that were made specifically for the cinema. Advertising critics praised the campaign not only for its self-deprecating humor but also for creating a cinema-themed message in the 60 seconds before movies started. Drawing more praise from advertising critics was the fact that the spots ended with a public service announcement requesting that mobile-phone ringers be silenced before the start of the movie.

FURTHER READING

Bold, Ben. "Mother Proves It Is More than Just a Creative Hotshop to Top Financial League." *Brand Republic,* September 7, 2005, p. 1.

Chalet, Debbie. "The Annual 2004." *Campaign,* December 17, 2004, p. 32.

Gray, Robert. "Orange—A Bright Future?" *Marketing* (London), October 24, 2002, p. 22.

Hicks, Robin. "WCRS Faces Orange-less Future." *Media and Marketing Europe,* September 1, 2000, p. 6.

Inge, Charles. "The BTAA Awards 2004." *Campaign,* March 12, 2004, p. 3.

Jaume, Leon. "Cinemawatch—Orange—'Goldspot.'" *Marketing* (London), May 6, 2004, p. 30.

Palmer, Camilla. "Orange Cinema Spots Use Hollywood Names." *Campaign,* May 23, 2003, p. 4.

Tylee, John. "Changing the Guardians." *Campaign,* August 1, 2003, p. 20.

Watts, Jenny. "Close-Up—Live Issue—Orange." *Campaign,* October 25, 2002, p. 17.

Weinraub, Bernard. "For Hollywood Misery, an Alter Ego Helps." *New York Times,* February 11, 2004, p. 1.

Whitehead, Jennifer. "'Austin Powers' Star Gives the Finger in Orange Spot." *Brand Republic,* August 19, 2004, p. 1.

———. "Controversial UK Ads Make Cannes Lions Film Shortlist." *Brand Republic,* June 28, 2004, p. 1.

———. "Humour Dominates in 50 Best British Ads of the Year." *Brand Republic,* September 22, 2003, p. 1.

———. "WCRS Makes Shortlist for Orange Account." *Brand Republic,* September 18, 2002, p. 1.

Kevin Teague

Outward Bound USA

100 Mystery Point Rd.
Garrison, New York 10524-9757
USA
Telephone: (845) 424-4000
Fax: (845) 424-4121
Web site: www.outwardbound.org

OCEANS, MOUNTAINS, FORESTS, FEAR. WHICH DO YOU CONQUER FIRST? CAMPAIGN

OVERVIEW

The originator and once undisputed leader of outdoor wilderness courses, Outward Bound USA saw enrollments plunge and its visibility dim in the early 1990s. The nonprofit corporation reacted slowly to the need to battle its ever-increasing number of competitors. It struggled to update its image and set a clear marketing direction. Too many people thought of Outward Bound (OB) as a once-in-a-lifetime training and educational experience in wilderness survival when what they wanted was an exciting adventure where they could meet like-minded friends.

Ogilvy & Mather (O&M) earned the task of increasing awareness of OB as a challenging outdoor adventure and generating inquiries to its toll-free phone number and website. The New York agency responded with a national public service announcement campaign that first appeared in October 1998. Consumer print publications and websites carried the ads. Since Outward Bound was nonprofit and did not pay for advertising, the ads ran whenever a publication or site had available space.

The first ad in the series, "Rock Climber," placed a shopping-mall-style "You Are Here" sign next to climber's ropes dangling down a vertical rock wall. A black piece of climbing equipment at the bottom of the ad contained the Outward Bound compass logo next to the tag line, "Oceans, Mountains, Forests, Fear. Which Do You Conquer First?" The only other copy was Outward Bound's toll-free number and website address.

The campaign evolved away from the tag line but continued the same visual approach and theme. An April 1999 ad showed a climber upside down crossing a deep ravine on ropes. A sign on a rock ledge above the climber read, "Pay Toll Ahead." The new tag line, "Same World. Different Place." was supported by a small line of additional copy, "Backpacking, Rafting, Mountaineering, Dog Sledding—Adventures That Take You Someplace Different." White-water rafters in a third ad passed a warning sign: "Caution: Management Not Responsible for Lost or Stolen Articles."

HISTORICAL CONTEXT

The name "Outward Bound" derived from a nautical term for leaving home port for the adventure of the open seas. In 1941 educator Kurt Hahn, a German refugee in Britain during World War II, developed a program in Wales for young sailors. Its mission was to help British merchant seamen learn how to survive on the high seas after German submarines torpedoed their vessels. The men learned how to dangle from ropes, a must for sailors being transferred from sinking ships to lifeboats. They learned how to climb up and down their ships' 40-foot-high smooth steel walls. Acquiring these and other skills also instilled a "can-do" spirit in the men and, most importantly, increased their survival rates. A ropes course and a wall course later became staples of every OB program. The courses became known for "solos," 24- to 72-hour periods at the end of each course when participants had to survive on their own in the wilderness.

The first Outward Bound school in the United States opened in Colorado in 1961. By then OB had adapted to peacetime conditions, placing its emphasis on wilderness survival. The philosophy and activities of OB meshed fashionably with the 1960s and 1970s emphasis on personal growth. People wanted to be more self-reliant and prove to themselves that they could survive outdoors under difficult conditions. In the 1980s the nonprofit hit full stride, buoyed by a spirit of egocentricity in the country. This was the wilderness organization's heyday.

Growth in the 1980s was also fueled by many corporations jumping on board. Xerox, General Foods, Burger King, and other high-profile companies sent their managers and executives to Outward Bound to learn teamwork, confidence, and self-reliance through tasks such as building rafts without tools, pulling each other up vertical walls, and walking across rope bridges while blindfolded. Celebrities added to OB's allure and visibility. NBC news anchor Tom Brokaw and former President Jimmy Carter were among the personalities who participated in Outward Bound treks.

After consistent U.S. growth throughout the 1970s and most of the 1980s, the nonprofit organization's enrollments began declining. Annual enrollment in its 750 wilderness treks and outings plunged from 13,325 in 1986 to about 9,000 in 1997, according to the *Wall Street Journal.* Young people chose more extreme experiences. Revenues remained flat at about $38 million from 1995 to 1997. One of the nonprofit's own internal surveys showed that many young people, its core customers, did not know the Outward Bound name.

Even among its own participants, Outward Bound faced criticism. One 19-year-old, a two-time OB course participant and the daughter of one of the organization's instructors, announced in a front-page national newspaper article in July 1997 that she preferred the National Outdoor Leadership School (NOLS). She claimed that NOLS offered more practical survival skills while Outward Bound emphasized personal growth.

During this period the wilderness organization's advertising sometimes emphasized the toughness or the rite of passage aspects of its courses. One 1996 ad showed a variety of leaves with one-word labels for each: "single-ply," "quilted," and "2-ply." A pine cone was labeled "extra strength." Another 1996 ad featured a silhouetted backpacker on top of a mountain with an asterisk next to him. Down below, the explanation of the asterisk read, "May Be Subject To Change." Body copy continued: "When you return from an Outward Bound Wilderness Experience, you'll look the same. But you just might be a different person."

By 1998 the nonprofit outdoor wilderness education group offered hundreds of annual courses in sailing, canoeing, sea kayaking, dog sledding, rock climbing, desert backpacking, and other activities at five U.S. wilderness schools. OB also had two urban education centers and 25 base camps in the United States. Courses were designed to inspire self-esteem, self-reliance, concern for others, and caring for the environment. The cover of OB's 1999 catalog carried the statement, "To Serve To Strive And Not To Yield." That catalog listed five core Outward Bound values: (1) adventure and challenge, (2) compassion and service, (3) learning through experience, (4) personal development, and (5) social and environmental responsibility. The nonprofit operated in more than 24 countries, but the United States remained the source of more than half the organization's business.

TARGET MARKET

Historically Outward Bound programs targeted young adults. About 75 percent of OB's open-enrollment students were young people between the ages of 14 and 21. But by 1998 the company had expanded into specific programs for college age, adult, educators, and instructors. A few courses targeted other groups such as women, couples, families, and parent/child pairings. College-age courses were longer and more technical. Adult courses were built to provide more renewal and reflection. People interested in a career in wilderness education could take the instructor courses.

Still, "Oceans, Mountains, Forests, Fear. Which Do You Conquer First?" sought first to reach moderately fit and athletic young people ages 16 to 24 in middle- to high-income households. Adults age 25 and older were a secondary target. Not only might adults want to go on an Outward Bound expedition themselves, they might be paying for one or more children to take one.

COMPETITION

Although Outward Bound was the oldest and largest outdoor wildness education group, by the 1990s it found itself in a crowded, competitive marketplace. Several regional companies began offering a range of outdoor courses similar to those provided by OB. Other

OTHER APPROACHES

One print ad in a series used previously to the "Oceans, Mountains, Forests, Fear: Which Do You Conquer First?" campaign had readers looking nearly straight up at a rock climber. The headline read: "Our Instructors Teach You. You Test Yourself." Body copy continued, "Instead of a grade, you'll earn respect for yourself, others and the environment through courses in dogsledding, canoeing, and more." The tag line was, "The Adventure Lasts A Lifetime."

competitors specialized in one area—white-water rafting, canoeing, backpacking, or another.

Calling itself "The Leader in Wilderness Education," the National Outdoor Leadership School of Lander, Wyoming, offered 50 courses that attracted more than 2,800 students a year by 1998. Other competitors included Northern Wilderness Adventures of Ontario, Canada; Trails Wilderness School in Kelly, Wyoming; and the Team Leadership Center of Door County, Wisconsin.

Another set of competitors included the specialty camps where young people spent a week or two learning a sport, doing community service, participating in the arts, or doing one of numerous other activities. Soccer, tennis, basketball, baseball, and football camps all had gained followers. A 1997 *Los Angeles Times* article listed Outward Bound as one choice among 39 summer programs ranging from exploring architecture to classes at a police academy to enhancing study skills. Ogilvy & Mather also saw the entertainment industry as a competitor. Amusement and theme parks, resorts, and vacation destinations provided alternatives to the OB experience.

MARKETING STRATEGY

"Outward Bound provides outstanding expeditions in spectacular wilderness settings for thousands of everyday teens and young adults across the country," said Rolf Linder, vice president of marketing for OB in a news release. That wasn't the message the organization's key markets were hearing. "Outward Bound is suffering from a lack of punch," said John Green, admissions dean at St. Paul's School in Concord, New Hampshire, in an article in the *Denver Post.* In the same article the dean of admissions at the University of Pennsylvania added, "We're more impressed with someone who went off to help rebuild a village somewhere than with someone who climbed a mountain to find himself."

Before developing its marketing strategy Ogilvy & Mather decided to conducted some research. The agency delved particularly into the opinions of young people between the ages of 14 and 21. It discovered a low awareness of OB. Only 5 percent of those surveyed knew and understood what OB offered. The study groups had a negative impression of Outward Bound as a place for problem kids. They did not hear much about the organization, they did not really know what it was, and what they did hear came by word of mouth. Overall Ogilvy & Mather's research showed little enthusiasm for OB and a general feeling that "it's not for me."

The perception that OB was for people with problems seemed fed by communications emphasizing self improvement and leadership skills. O&M said those attributes had little relevance or appeal to the young audience OB strove to attract. The self-improvement message caused many of those surveyed to think of OB as a program for the underconfident and weak. Losers took an Outward Bound course to get a sense of achievement. The antisocial went there to learn how to get along with other people. Some OB prospects felt the wilderness course was a way for people from the city to experience nature. Other young people thought of it as "survival courses for kooks and weirdoes," O&M said. They assumed OB taught how to live off the land through exhausting, unnecessary hardship and pain.

A second portion of O&M's research identified the types of communications that would appeal to young people. What the study groups found appealing were: trying things for the first time; doing something completely different; thrill and excitement; friendships; remote, unspoiled locations; and challenges. O&M said people interested in Outward Bound wanted to step outside their normal lives. They wanted to do something that would put a stamp on their individuality, something other people only talked about. They did not want an experience that seemed "manufactured" or "glossy," but one that would be a lasting memory.

The research further asked how OB should be described. Expedition was a good word to use, according to the survey responders, because it had credibility and implied heritage. The study groups warned against words like "course" or "program" because they made OB sound too much like sitting in a classroom and had a zero thrill or excitement factor. Likewise, research indicated that OB should not talk about introspection, nor should it tell people what they will get out of participating in a course.

Most people responded with surprise when they learned about the places they could go with Outward

Bound. They liked the fact that OB could take them to remote, unspoiled places like Nepal, the Utah desert, Costa Rica, and Alaska. "This audience is looking for exciting things to do during summer break or summer vacations," said Kevin Scully, account executive at Ogilvy & Mather. "They aren't motivated by the educational aspects of Outward Bound, but rather the sense of adventure, the opportunity to meet new people, and the chance to do something different, something unique in their peer group."

With people over age 24, Ogilvy & Mather wanted to change old perceptions. Agency research indicated that many people in this secondary target market had a 1960s or a 1970s perception of Outward Bound. The campaign needed to update what was often a perception of OB as a purely educational survival skills course to one of a challenging adventure.

Outward Bound also identified the perception of its courses as a once-in-a-lifetime experience as a concern. Alumni did not come back in large numbers. The marketing strategy included tailoring more expeditions to specific age groups and promoting them as ongoing education, not single-event rites of passage. "Essentially, the campaign was designed to suggest that OB will take you outside the boundaries of your everyday life," Scully said. "Rather than put forth the rational argument that OB is an educational encounter, we believed that the emotional approach is of greater interest and a more powerful motivator to get people to contact OB for more information."

Besides changing perceptions the campaign sought to enlarge Outward Bound's media reach and presence. Previously the nonprofit's ads had only appeared in print publications. Creating versions of the ads for websites opened a new marketing channel rich with people in Outward Bound's target market.

OUTCOME

FURTHER READING

Shaw, John. "The Duke of Edinburgh's Award: Building Character by Stretching Endurance to the Limit." *Daily Telegraph* London, March 3, 1995, p. 1.

Pereira, Joseph. "Outward Bound's Enrollment Plunges: Wilderness-Trek Competitors Gaining On Pioneer in Outdoor-Adventure Field." *Denver Post,* July 27, 1997, p. B7.

Chris John Amorosino

Oxygen Media

75 Ninth Avenue
New York, New York 10011
USA
Telephone: (212) 651-2000
Fax: (212) 651-2099
Web site: www.oxygen.com

FRESH TELEVISION FOR WOMEN CAMPAIGN

OVERVIEW

The Oxygen Network was the centerpiece of Oxygen Media, an entertainment company that catered to an exclusively female audience via television and the Internet. The network's 2000 introduction had not been as successful as the company had hoped, and by 2002 it was languishing behind industry leader Lifetime, the most popular network in all of cable TV, with a 2.0 rating share and access to more than 80 million households. Oxygen hoped that 2002 would be the start of a major turnaround. That year the company partnered with AOL Time Warner to integrate Oxygen's Web content with that of AOL. The deal also helped Oxygen break into Time Warner Cable's coveted market of New York subscribers, which would give Oxygen access to an additional 10 million households.

To help attract viewers in this new market, Oxygen contacted the Wenham, Massachusetts, agency Mullen, which had developed a critically acclaimed spot for the network's initial launch. Mullen's new campaign for 2002 consisted of a television spot that was cut into 30- and 60-second versions. The spot started at a beauty pageant in midcentury America in which a contestant was asked what she would do to make the world a better place. The spot cut into her answer to jump forward though other beauty pageants, each one taking place in an ensuing decade, such as the 1960s and the 1970s, until the final "answer" to the question, given in the present, was a call for more accurate depictions of women in the media. The satirical spot closed with the tagline "Fresh Television for Women."

While Oxygen was too far behind Lifetime to entirely close the gap, the spot did help the network acquire some forward momentum. By 2005 it had gained access to more than 55 million households, and Oxygen Media was generating advertising revenue in excess of $46 million per year.

HISTORICAL CONTEXT

The Oxygen Network was an independent cable station owned by Oxygen Media, a company founded by former Nickelodeon CEO Geraldine Laybourne and a group of highly successful partners, including TV personality Oprah Winfrey and Microsoft cofounder Paul Allen. The network was introduced in 2000 with a highly praised spot aired during Super Bowl XXXIV. At the time Oxygen was only available in about 6 million homes. The cable network was designed to be integrated closely with the company's website, oxygen.com. The website was intended to serve as the lynchpin of Oxygen Media's e-commerce business. Unfortunately, the telecommunications industry crash in 2000 and 2001 damaged Oxygen Media's Internet business, and it quickly had to drop its e-commerce operations.

Oprah Winfrey, February 27, 2005. © LUCY NICHOLSON/ REUTERS/CORBIS.

The Oxygen network also fell on tough times, a result in part of its odd mix of programming. It featured talk shows, syndicated reruns, animation, fashion programming, and game shows. This hurt its efforts to forge an identity against specialized cable stations such as the Game Show Network, the Cartoon Network, and more established female-oriented networks, such as Lifetime. Oxygen Media also experienced a financial crunch after spending $75 million to develop original programming for the network, only to see most of those programs, like the critically reviled magazine show *Pure Oxygen,* fail to find an audience.

Oxygen Media hoped that 2002 would signal a turnaround. In September of that year the Oxygen Network was scheduled to begin broadcasting reruns of the popular *Oprah Winfrey Show.* The program, hosted by one of the network's key supporters, was the most popular daytime talk show in the United States and had helped make Oprah Winfrey one of the most famous people in the world.

More importantly, the network was able to access new markets. Oxygen Media partnered with AOL Time Warner in 2002, allowing AOL to handle advertising sales on oxygen.com. This helped the network break into Time Warner Cable's New York market. By April 2001 the network was still only available in 13 million homes, not enough to compete with Lifetime or WE, the other two major women's networks. The addition of 10 million households via Time Warner Cable, including more than 1 million viewers in New York City itself, meant that by the end of 2002 Oxygen would be available in 30 million homes. The network wanted to hit the ground running with a new national campaign. In effect Oxygen would be relaunching itself for its new viewers.

TARGET MARKET

Oxygen's core demographic was 18- to 49-year-old women, especially those who were career-oriented. Some of the company's detractors felt that this demographic was too broad for the world of cable television. Many cable stations were narrower in focus; for example, MTV zeroed in on 13- to-18-year-olds. Oxygen's wide reach was blamed for its occasionally scattered programming.

The network's biggest draw in the early 2000s was reruns of the syndicated program *Xena: Warrior Princess,* a campy show that attracted teenagers and gay men in addition to women. This audience differed greatly from the middle-aged women who tuned in to watch reruns of the 1980s and 1990s sitcoms, such as *Cybill* and *Kate and Allie,* that the network also aired.

To help find its voice, Oxygen started including more original programming. Its morning exercise program *Inhale* featured yoga; in contrast, competitors such as Lifetime offered more traditional aerobics fare. It was hoped that this would help the network draw a younger audience than Lifetime and other competitors. After focus groups indicated that the network was too "preachy," Oxygen made an effort to infuse its programming with wit and flare. It introduced a fashion talk show hosted by the comedian Tracey Ullman and another talk show starring the well-known (and colorful) fashion designer Isaac Mizrahi. Such light and irreverent fare was part of the attempt to forge the identity of the Oxygen Network.

The network also wanted people in the ad-buying industry to see that Oxygen was a company on the rise and a potentially strong partner for advertisers. Thus, the network's new availability in New York City gave it the opportunity to connect with another audience: the ad buyers who lived and worked in Manhattan. Oxygen's presence in the United States' largest television market was seen as a major step in becoming an industry player.

OPRAH WINFREY

In 2000 Oxygen Media introduced the Oxygen Network, a television network dedicated to women-centered programming. Though Oxygen was faced with strong competition from Lifetime, an established women-centered cable network known for its original movies, the network felt that it had a secret weapon: the support from talk show host Oprah Winfrey.

The Mississippi native first rose to prominence in 1984 when she became host of the struggling *AM Chicago,* a local program in Chicago. In 1985 the show was renamed *The Oprah Winfrey Show* and began to be syndicated nationally. Within a year it was the most popular daytime talk show, besting such established stars as Phil Donahue. Oprah achieved even more fame after her successful acting performance in the 1985 film *The Color Purple.*

By the early 2000s Winfrey was one of the most famous people in the world, prompting *Time* magazine to name her one of the 100 most influential people of the twentieth century. Her talk show's "book club" was highly influential, introducing wide audiences to the work of authors such as Toni Morrison. She owned a successful production company, Harpo, and was a partner in Oxygen Media. In 2003 *Forbes* magazine disclosed that she was the first African-American woman to become a billionaire.

COMPETITION

Oxygen was faced with a crowded marketplace. Several additional networks were aimed at the same female audience. The most important competitors were the Lifetime and WE (Women's Entertainment) networks. Access to the New York market was essential, because it boosted Oxygen's availability to 30 million homes. This brought it closer to WE, which was available to 44 million households by the early 2000s. Neither network, however, was able to match the availability of Lifetime, which had access to more than 80 million homes.

Lifetime was introduced in 1984, and by 2002 it had become the gold standard for women's television. The network had a good pedigree, as it was a joint venture by two successful entertainment conglomerates, the Walt Disney Company and the Hearst Corporation. In fact, with a 2.0 average daily Nielsen rating, Lifetime had been the most-watched cable network in the entire United States since 2001. Lifetime's ratings were still climbing by up to 18 percent per year. It had even managed to spin off a successful sister network, the Lifetime Movie Network. Lifetime's calling card was its original films that focused on women's issues, some of which drew praise from such organizations as the women's-rights advocate NOW (National Organization for Women).

In contrast to Oxygen, Lifetime had a specific focus on families and sensational "victim" stories (movies about, for example, women in abusive relationships or fighting breast cancer). This helped it form a cohesive identity for viewers. Lifetime also had the advantage of being the first female-oriented network. As a result it was earning more than $500 million per year in advertising by 2002; in comparison, Oxygen had about $20 million in ad sales. This had the effect of making Lifetime's Web portal more successful as well, enabling lifetimetv.com to draw major advertisers, including General Motors.

Meanwhile, WE, which had previously shunned advertising, was looking to offer up-front commercial time to advertisers for the first time in 2002. Although commercials would be limited to about eight minutes every hour, this would still dilute the potential advertising base for Oxygen.

MARKETING STRATEGY

Oxygen hired the Mullen advertising agency to develop a new commercial that would help the network reach new viewers. Mullen, based in Wenham, Massachusetts, had also handled the company's first television spot. That original spot had featured a maternity ward where the newborn girls rejected the pink caps that the hospital had placed on their heads. This was meant to show that Oxygen would not cater to female stereotypes.

Mullen's new spot would convey a similar message, but because the network was now more mature, it would require new imagery to do so. The new commercial focused the action on a beauty pageant. Such pageants, with their strict codes of traditional femininity, were an obvious foil for Oxygen, which wanted to appeal to career-oriented women. The spot would subvert this beauty-pageant femininity with a more feminist message designed to bolster the network's image.

The commercial began at a pageant in post–World War II America. A young contestant was asked what she would do to make the world a better place. After she began to answer, the spot cut to a pageant set in the 1960s. After allowing that contestant to expand on the answer, the spot cut again to a 1970s pageant, and again to the 1980s, and then the 1990s. The final answer, after each decade's contestant had added to it, was: "I'd do my very best to make sure that every time you ever witness a woman in the media it would be sure to reveal her true complexities, not just the same old stereotypes that do an incredible disservice to all humanity." The spot closed with the tagline "Fresh Media for Women." Both 30- and 60-second versions of the spot were developed.

The spot underscored several points Oxygen wanted to make about itself. The first and most important was that Oxygen was a network for women, free from the stereotypes found on other networks. This somewhat feminist message would help the network reach out to the career-oriented young women that Oxygen wanted as viewers. It also showed some of the network's humor: the spot was clearly a satire on the traditional "femininity" put forth by beauty pageants, which often reduced women's worth to their appearance. Finally, the spot's passage through time gave the impression that Oxygen was a hip, modern network—not one stuck in the past like its competition. This was also important in attracting the younger demographic that Oxygen sought.

OUTCOME

The "Fresh Media for Women" campaign was on balance a success. Critics loved the spots, and Oxygen's ratings continued to improve. While Lifetime remained the top network on cable, Oxygen began to draw more of an audience. In the wake of its access to the New York market, the network experienced an increase in its number of subscribers, and by 2005 the network was available in more than 55 million households nationwide.

Though none of Oxygen's shows became a breakout hit in the way that Lifetime's original movies were, combined advertising sales from the Internet and network were a healthy $46.5 million by 2004. The network broadened its talk-show offering to include the Emmy-winning program *The Ellen DeGeneres Show,* the *The Tyra Banks Show,* as well as a call-in show about sex and sexuality, *Talk Sex.* The partnership with AOL Time Warner paid especially big dividends for the website, which by 2003 had more than 200 advertisers and generated greater revenue than the network itself.

FURTHER READING

Carter, Bill. "Gambling Heavily on the Tried and the True; New Channel for Women Is Moving Ahead." *New York Times,* January 3, 2000.

———. "Oxygen Media to Eliminate 10 Percent of Its Jobs." *New York Times,* December 6, 2000.

Gates, Anita. "A Sly Assault Launched from Inside Oxygen's Tent." *New York Times,* October 6, 2002.

Hall, Ann C., ed. *Delights, Desires, and Dilemmas: Essays on Women and the Media.* Westport, CT: Praeger, 1998.

Macdonald, Myra. *Representing Women: Myths of Femininity in the Popular Media.* New York: E. Arnold, 1995.

Prose, Francine. "A Wasteland of One's Own." *New York Times,* February 13, 2000.

Rutenberg, Jim. "Poor Showing for Oxygen in Ratings." *New York Times,* April 22, 2002.

Stanley, Alessandra. "The Oxygen TV Channel Is Bowing to Tastes." *New York Times,* February 25, 2002.

Whelehan, Imelda. *Overloaded: Popular Culture and the Future of Feminism.* London: Women's Press, 2000.

Wilson, Sheryl. *Oprah, Celebrity, and Formations of Self.* New York: Palgrave Macmillan, 2003.

Guy Patrick Cunningham

Pabst Brewing Company

121 Interpark Blvd., Ste. 300
San Antonio, Texas 78216-1852
USA
Telephone: (210) 226-0231
Fax: (210) 299-6807
Web site: www.pabst.com

■■■

REMEMBER RAINIER CAMPAIGN

OVERVIEW

Rainier beer, a longtime staple in the Pacific Northwest, had, like many local beer brands in America, seen its fortunes decline substantially in the 1970s and 1980s as giant national brewers flattened smaller competitors. In the late 1990s and early 2000s, however, a new niche-marketing trend emerged in the beer industry. A number of local and national blue-collar beer brands found a new consumer base among authenticity-seeking young people. Rainier owner Pabst Brewing Company enlisted Seattle agency Cole & Weber/Red Cell to craft a 2004 campaign thus reestablishing the brand among young people in its regional market.

"Remember Rainier," with a campaign budget of a mere $400,000, made direct use of Rainier's heritage in the Northwest while pushing brand awareness in unorthodox ways. The re-airing of vintage Rainier commercials from the 1970s and 1980s was embedded within a larger fictional framework developed in an 11-episode series of 30-minute comic talk shows called *RainierVision.* The shows, featuring a pair of fictional Rainier fanatics (Tim and Chuck), ran Sundays at 1 a.m. on the Seattle affiliate of a major cable network. Supplementary online campaign material worked to further fill in the larger Rainier storyline while also providing product information, and guerilla-marketing stunts featuring Tim and Chuck took the "Remember Rainier" story directly to Seattle residents. The campaign's buzz-generating power was further heightened by a bizarre turn of events involving a real black bear found passed out in a resort area after clawing his way into three dozen cans of Rainier.

The campaign helped Rainier to its first sales gains in nearly two decades, and it won numerous industry awards, including a Gold Clio and a Best of Show ADDY honor. Tim and Chuck were featured in a short film that premiered in 2005, and the integrated marketing effort continued to evolve.

HISTORICAL CONTEXT

The Rainier beer brand was first introduced to Pacific Northwest consumers in the 1880s, when the Sweeney Brewery in the Georgetown area of Seattle, Washington, opened for business. After a merger with two other local brewers, the company became the Seattle Brewing and Malting Company, and its leading product, Rainier, was popular across the West and in Alaska. Prohibition came to Washington state in 1916, four years before it was a federal mandate, and the Rainier brand was bought in the meantime by a California brewery. After the law's 1933 repeal Fritz Sick and his son Emil bought the rights to the Rainier name in the Northwest. The Sicks eventually took full control of the Rainier brand and enlarged the original Georgetown brewery, leading Rainier beer back to the top of the regional market. A giant red *R* perched atop the brewery became a Seattle landmark.

The 1970s and 1980s, however, saw the rise of megabreweries like Anheuser-Busch, Miller, and Coors, which pushed most local American beer makers out of business. Rainier survived but suffered consistent sales declines during these decades, despite a popular, offbeat TV advertising campaign that ran regionally in the 1970s and 1980s. The 1990s presented Rainier with yet another obstacle, as the trend toward craft and microbrewed beers, which was particularly pronounced in the Pacific Northwest, left little market space for low-priced, unassuming brands like Rainier. During these decades Rainier had been bought and sold by a succession of corporate parents, none of which could revive the brand.

In the late 1990s, though, marketers of Pabst Blue Ribbon (whose corporate parent, Pabst Brewing Company, became Rainier's owner in 2000) noticed that sales of its similarly outdated classic brand had begun picking up among authenticity-seeking young people. Other national brands with a similar down-market profile, like Miller High Life, also experienced a measured resurgence after being adopted by urban hipsters who valued the beer's simple and straightforward image. The trend seemed at least partly a backlash as well, not only against mainstream beers and their blockbuster marketing campaigns but also against the high prices and pretensions of microbrews.

TARGET MARKET

Rainier was thus naturally positioned, among consumers in the Northwest, as an alternative to these two groups of competitors, and its history in the region served as its chief marketable attribute. By asking beer drinkers in and around Seattle to "Remember Rainier," Cole & Weber's creative team was establishing the brand's authenticity and appealing to consumers' nostalgia in ways specific to the region. Neither mainstream brands nor microbrews could compete with Rainier on these terms.

Rainier's successful relaunch depended, like the sustained success of most alcohol products, on winning the loyalty of young men aged 21 to 34. Though men in this age group obviously had not been Rainier drinkers in the 1970s and 1980s, Cole & Weber expected many of them to recall family members drinking Rainier and to remember the zany Rainier TV commercials that ran during those decades. The old commercials, which Cole & Weber re-aired as a key component of the new campaign, capitalized on widespread nostalgia for the Pacific Northwest of yesteryear, as contrasted with a new, gentrified Northwest of upscale coffee shops and computer-industry professionals. The *RainierVision* series of TV shows, meanwhile, took the campaign beyond the simple rehashing of retro commercials. By embedding the commercials within the larger storyline of a Rainier-centric talk show hosted by two young, over-the-top brand loyalists, Cole & Weber was able to leaven the overt appeal to nostalgia with ironic humor suitable to the target market's sensibilities. The "Remember Rainier" website further tied the effort together, while partnerships with Seattle bars and the circulation around town of a pickup truck towing the locally famous red *R* further spread brand awareness, in unique and unpredictable ways, among the local target.

LOCAL?

Though the "Remember Rainier" campaign was a direct appeal to nostalgia surrounding the brand's Seattle roots and Northwest heritage, Rainier was no longer brewed in or near Seattle. It was, in fact, brewed by Miller Brewing (owned by SABMiller plc), one of the corporate giants from which Rainier was attempting to differentiate itself by rebuilding a homegrown image. Miller brewed most of the beers for Rainier's owner, Pabst Brewing Company, which had become a holding company rather than a brewer—an owner of various beer brands but a brewer of none. Pabst, closely associated with its hometown of Milwaukee, had in 1996 moved its company headquarters to San Antonio, Texas.

COMPETITION

Rainier was part of the so-called subpremium category, which comprised beers costing less than mainstream brands like Budweiser, Bud Light, Miller Lite, and Coors Light. The surprising resurgence of several beers in this category in recent years had created a new marketing niche, in which seemingly out-of-date products like Miller High Life, Pabst Blue Ribbon, and blue-collar local beers similar to Rainier found themselves able to capitalize on the perception that they were more authentic than mainstream beers, whose success seemed largely fueled by slick, expensive ad campaigns. As these newly desirable brands began trying to spread their individual messages of authenticity, however, they had to take pains to avoid marketing styles that would call that authenticity into question.

In 1998, after seeing modestly encouraging sales spikes in isolated markets, Miller High Life unveiled its first national TV campaign since the mid-1980s.

Directed by acclaimed documentary filmmaker Errol Morris, the High Life campaign successfully delivered the same message for many years: America was suffering an epidemic shortage of masculinity, and it was up to those select few diehards, the "High Life men," to reinvigorate the country. Intentionally over-the-top without ridiculing the High Life men, the campaign managed to appeal simultaneously to young hipsters and Miller High Life's long-established blue-collar market. The campaign won many awards and was credited with significantly raising the profile of a nearly defunct brand.

Pabst Blue Ribbon (a corporate sibling of Rainier's) had, like High Life, the aura of an unpretentious, workingman's beer and had similarly fallen on hard times in recent decades. When PBR executives noticed inexplicable sales spikes in the Portland, Oregon, area in the 1990s, they investigated the phenomenon and came to the surprising discovery that, unaided by any advertising, an urban subculture of bicycle messengers and their peers had become champions of the PBR brand. Seeing an opportunity for a PBR comeback but recognizing that traditional marketing tactics might alienate a young audience craving the authentic aura surrounding the brand, PBR's marketers dispatched on-the-ground brand representatives to selected urban markets. These people were charged with building buzz about the brand in ways that were unobtrusive; therefore they spent time appearing simply to hang out in locales frequented by its young, antiestablishment target.

Rheingold beer, a regional brand sold primarily in New York City, was not, for geographic reasons, a competitor with Rainier at this time, but it was in the midst of a resurgence thanks to a marketing strategy strikingly similar to Rainier's. Having noticed a desire for simple, authentic products among hip, downtown New Yorkers, and having further observed that there was no New York–centric beer that satisfied such a product profile, a group of investors relaunched Rheingold, which was once New York's most popular beer, to fill this niche and, ultimately, to reclaim its spot at the top of the city's beer market. Utilizing the same miniscule budget as Rainier ($400,000), and mindful of its target audience's aversion to mainstream marketing, Rheingold staged an unconventional guerilla marketing effort combining in-bar promotions with cryptic billboard placements and the revival of the Miss Rheingold beauty pageant, which had been extremely popular in the 1950s and 1960s.

MARKETING STRATEGY

Given the $400,000 budget available for advertising, Cole & Weber by necessity had to stage an unconventional campaign for Rainier. The fact that Rainier's biggest asset was its regional heritage dovetailed with the limited budget, as the re-airing of old advertisements proved an economical way of pitching the "Remember Rainier" message. The old ads themselves, created by Seattle agency Heckler and Bowker in the 1970s and 1980s, proved suitable for contemporary tastes. Whereas Budweiser and Miller advertising of that era focused on sincere appeals to hard work, Rainier ran ads that relied on humor and quirky premises. In "Motorcycle" a biker voiced the words "Rainier beer" in a way that mimicked the simultaneous revving and gear-shifting sounds of his motorcycle's engine as he accelerated on an open highway. In "Crossing" a family on a rural road slowed down at a "Beer Crossing" sign; their caution was rewarded with the sighting of two giant bottles and a can of Rainier walking across the road.

Cole & Weber felt that the re-aired ads alone, however, would not be enough to reignite Northwesterners' interest in Rainier. "We needed something bigger," the agency's executive creative director Guy Seese told *Creativity.* "We needed a talk show." The talk-show idea became *RainierVision,* an 11-episode series of half-hour talk shows devoted to the beer. Hosted by Tim and Chuck, two fictional Rainier-obsessed, 20-something Seattle residents, and modeled after *Wayne's World* (the *Saturday Night Live* spoof of a public-access cable show that became a successful movie), *RainierVision* ran Sundays on a local UPN affiliate at 1 a.m. Taking as its premise the idea that Tim had come across videotapes of old Rainier commercials in a thrift shop and decided, with Chuck, that the world needed to see them, the talk show integrated the vintage spots with sketch-comedy adventures featuring recurring characters and Rainier-related ephemera.

The cross-platform integration of the "Remember Rainier" campaign did not stop with *RainierVision,* however. A website, http://www.rememberrainier.com, further established the overarching story behind Tim and Chuck's television mission, while filling in gaps in viewers' knowledge of the show's content and providing other campaign- and product-related information. Additionally, as Tim and Chuck became known commodities in Seattle, the actors who played them were dispatched to selected bars in the city, where, in character, they further spread the word about their passion for Rainier. They also drove a pickup around Seattle, towing the giant red-neon letter *R,* a mock-up of the one that had stood on top of the Rainier Brewery and been a Seattle landmark in decades past.

As *RainierVision* ran a freak occurrence that made local headlines gave the campaign an unexpected boost. A two-year-old black bear, having wandered into a campground at the Baker Lake Resort area in Washington state, was found unconscious next to a group of 36 empty Rainier beer cans, which he had clawed open and consumed. Further investigation by wildlife agents revealed, moreover, that the bear had first raided a stash of Busch beer but had drunk only two before moving on to the brand that was presumably better suited to his palate. The astounding event was given a further marketing-friendly twist when the wildlife agents attempted to capture the bear, which had returned to the campground after his initial binge, by using a trap set with doughnuts, honey, and two open cans of Rainier. A delighted Cole & Weber immediately incorporated the incident into the campaign, first by running an online contest to name their new "spokesanimal" (the winning name was Brewtus) and then by incorporating a beer-drinking, bear-suit-wearing character into four original 30-second spots that also featured Tim and Chuck.

OUTCOME

"Remember Rainier" was credited with spurring the brand's first sales gains in 17 years, at a time when the beer market overall was flat. The campaign was likewise a big winner on the 2005 advertising-industry awards circuit. It won a Gold Clio, a Gold ADDY, and the ADDY Best of Show award, and it was a Gold winner at the New York Art Directors Club awards. It was named the Yahoo! Big Idea Chair winner, and it won the Grand Prize at the first annual ANA/AICP Battle of the Brands event, besting much larger contest entrants like Burger King, Sega, and ESPN.

The success of "Remember Rainier" led to the continuation of Tim and Chuck's adventures in 2005. The Rainier fanatics were featured in a short film that included many of the recurring characters from the previous year's *RainierVision* shows, and new episodes of *RainierVision* entered production. The cross-platform nature of the campaign remained in place, as the online, film, TV, and print executions all worked together as parts of an integrated Rainier storyline.

FURTHER READING

Anderson, Mae. "Guy Seese on the Spot." *Adweek,* May 30, 2005.

———. "Strange Brew." *Adweek,* July 25, 2005.

Cuneo, Alice Z. "Brands Battle." *Advertising Age,* February 21, 2005.

Dougherty, Sheila. "Rainier Beer: Operation Liberation." *Advertising Age,* July 18, 2005.

Goldrich, Robert. "Rainier Beer Tops ANA/AICP Battle of the Brands." *Shoot,* February 25, 2005.

"Guy Seese, Executive Creative Director, Cole & Weber/Red Cell." *Creativity,* August 2005.

Kaplan, Andrew. "What's Old Is New Again." *Beverage World,* October 15, 2004.

Nudd, Tim. "Rainier's Party Animal." *Adweek,* August 23, 2004.

"Rainier Fires Retro Rockets." *Creativity,* June 2004.

Wilcha, Kristin. "Winning Ways." *Shoot,* June 10, 2005.

Mark Lane

Pacific Cycle, Inc.

4902 Hammersley Rd.
Madison, Wisconsin 53711
USA
Telephone: (608) 628-2468
Web site: www.schwinnbike.com

■■■

FAST. IT'S CORPORATE POLICY. CAMPAIGN

OVERVIEW

Hoping to capitalize on the tail end of the mountain bike and bicycle motocross (BMX) craze of the late 1990s, Schwinn Cycling & Fitness purchased GT Bicycles for $170 million in 1998. The resulting company was named Schwinn/GT Corp and was later purchased by Pacific Cycle, Inc., which now operates Shwinn as a brand. Relying on word of mouth and a century-old brand name, Schwinn typically partitioned only a small amount of its budget for advertising, usually executed by Carmichael Lynch, Inc. By 1999, however, the $5 billion American bicycle industry was waning. Schwinn was rapidly losing market share from its antiquated mode of selling bicycles through independent dealerships. In a last-ditch effort to keep from filing bankruptcy, Schwinn launched the "Fast. It's Corporate Policy." campaign to tout the speed of its new GT Bicycles. Prior to its acquisition by Schwinn in 1998, GT Bicycles handled all advertising internally.

Executed with the help of Carmichael Lynch, "Fast. It's Corporate Policy." was primarily spearheaded by Miami-based Crispin Porter + Bogusky, which named the campaign and designed its print ads, the campaign's sole medium. With a budget of $1 million, the campaign hoped to depict GT Bicycles as the "most advanced, fastest, human-powered vehicles on the planet." Within an industry that typically ran print ads of sponsored riders, Crispin Porter + Bogusky tailored the campaign around GT Bicycles employees and their obsession with speed. Print ads showed employees injuring themselves from running too fast through the office. One of the campaign's more risqué ads, "Sex Bicycles," showed an employee triumphantly raising his arms beside his girlfriend. Reclining in the back of a company van, both were covered in blankets. The ad suggested they had just finished having sex. The employee's girlfriend, looking much less satisfied, lay beside him. The tagline "Fast. It's Corporate Policy." appeared below the photograph.

Continuing through 2000 the campaign garnered two Clios along with seven Gold Lions at the Cannes Lions International Advertising Festival. GT Bicycles was also the only industry brand to report a market share gain (up 6 percent) in 2000. Because of Schwinn/GT's unwillingness to branch outside of its 1,900 independent dealerships, however, the corporation filed for Chapter 11 bankruptcy protection in mid-2001.

HISTORICAL CONTEXT

For more than half of the twentieth century, Schwinn dominated America's bicycle industry. The first major sign of the company's inability to change with consumer trends occurred during the 1970s when Americans gravitated toward light-framed European road bikes. Schwinn continued manufacturing its larger, bulkier models.

Schwinn again dismissed the 1980s popularity of the BMX and mountain bike. After losing considerable market share, the family-owned Schwinn business filed for bankruptcy protection in 1992 and was later purchased by an investment firm. Even with new owners Schwinn continued relying on its brand identity and exclusive bicycle retail stores to rally back. Around the time "Fast. It's Corporate Policy." appeared, about 250 individual retailers still had "Schwinn" in their name. Industry analyst Ray Keener told *Hoover's,* "That doesn't sound like a lot, except that Trek is second with one dealer—the Trek factory store—and no one is in third."

Previous to its relationship with Crispin Porter + Bogusky, Schwinn outsourced advertising to Carmichael Lynch, which developed successful television spots such as "The Ride." *Adweek* deemed this Schwinn commercial a "top spot" in 1993. Schwinn's advertising budget was small, only reaching $1.3 million in 1998, even though the company's overall expenditures reached $37.3 million. To ward off its second bankruptcy of the 1990s, Schwinn bought the popular BMX and mountain bike brand GT Bicycles for $170 million. Previous to the acquisition GT Bicycles executed all advertising in-house and sponsored professional BMX riders such as Stephen Murray, who held the record for the longest jump.

After acquiring GT Bicycles in 1998, Schwinn/GT wanted to aggressively market the brand to overtake competitors like Cannondale Bicycle Corp., Specialized Bicycle Components Inc., and Trek Bicycle Corp. In regard to previous GT Bicycles ads, Gregg Bagni, Schwinn/GT's marketing vice president, told *Adweek,* "The GT ads were funny... [but] Schwinn is about escape and freedom. We're constantly looking for new ways..., to look at biking from a fun standpoint." Even though Crispin Porter + Bogusky was named agency of record for the "Fast. It's Corporate Policy." campaign, Carmichael Lynch contributed as well to position GT Bicycles as the fastest bike in the industry.

TARGET MARKET

"Fast. It's Corporate Policy." created humorous and sometimes salacious print ads to attract younger extreme sports enthusiasts. Ads portrayed young GT Bicycles employees engaging in day-to-day life events with the same speed and vigor of a BMX rider. Bill Smith, Huffy's vice president of marketing, told *SportStyle,* "Unlike the adult bike market which continues to soften as baby boomers mature and buy fewer mountain bikes, there is an uptick in kids' and BMX bikes which derives from the popularity of extreme sports."

The campaign's print ads deviated outside of traditional BMX advertising, which typically displayed photographs of sponsored riders performing stunts with the brand's product. Crispin Porter + Bogusky strove to brand GT Bicycles with speed and humor by making every employee at GT Bicycles appear obsessed with doing things fast. Focusing on the product instead of the brand was something the bicycle industry was often criticized for, especially inside the actual IBDs (individual bicycle dealers). "Many IBDs come from an enthusiast background—they're bike geeks and it's hard for them to let go of that," Marshall Hannum, manager of Poison Spider Bicycles, told *SportStyle.* "The result is that we get businesses that look more like car garages than like Nordstrom's, and most people would rather shop at Nordstrom's."

CANYON GANG

A group called the Canyon Gang is commonly credited for inventing the mountain bike. The group's four members—Robert and Kim Kraft, John York, and Tom Slifka—began riding heavy-framed Schwinn bicycles down mountain trails within California's Marin County. The members would take the wide-tired bikes, which they called "ballooners," to the peak of 2,600-foot Mount Tam and ride down trails, braking as little as possible. Schwinn, ironically, dismissed mountain bicycles as a passing fad and never designed mountain bikes during the 1970s or '80s.

COMPETITION

During the late 1990s three brands—Huffy, Roadmaster, and Murray—reigned over 65 percent of the American bicycle market by manufacturing bikes in China and retailing them through Wal-Mart Stores, Inc. and the Kmart Corporation. The faster-growing high-end bicycles accounted for the market's other 35 percent and retailed primarily through individual bicycle dealers.

The Texas-based Trek Bicycle Corporation, America's largest manufacturer of high-performance bicycles, first sponsored three-time Tour de France winner Greg Lemond and then later seven-time Tour de France champion Lance Armstrong. Besides making road bikes Trek also produced mountain, BMX, children's, recumbent, and police bikes. Brand promotion was accomplished through the sponsorship of athletes and races. Much of Trek's success inside a struggling industry was attributed to the corporation's savvy sponsorships, great customer service, greater affordability, and sleek design. "It's easy to make a few missteps in this business but you can't argue

> **GT**
>
> Robert Long and Gary Turner first designed the light-framed GT Bicycles in 1979. Gary Turner was a bike aficionado, and the company's name came from his initials.

with the quality of their bikes," Mark Sani, editor of *Bicycle Retailer,* an industry trade journal, told *Capital Times.* "They're basically blowing everybody else out in terms of lower cost, customer service and great delivery."

Unlike many of its competitors, Trek also manufactured its bicycles in America, finding the cost comparable to Asian manufacturing. "Our growth is even more amazing when you consider the fact that the bike business itself hasn't been growing," Tom Albers, Trek president and CEO, told *Capital Times.* "We've been growing because we've been taking market share from our competitors."

Cannondale Bicycle Corp., another high-end American bicycle manufacturer, advertised by cosponsoring bike racing teams. The company struggled much as Schwinn/GT did in the late 1990s and eventually sold assets to the private equity firm Pegasus Capital Advisors. "It's a price game. It's a commodity market. And it's very difficult to make a profit," Jay Townley, a former Schwinn vice president, remarked on the bicycle industry to the *Milwaukee Journal Sentinel.* "Ask anybody who's done business with Wal-Mart."

MARKETING STRATEGY

To slow the diminishing of its market share, Schwinn in the 1990s made restructuring decisions like purchasing GT Bicycles in 1998 and focusing advertising on the newly acquired brand's BMX and mountain bikes. "We've come back, hit the mountain bike market, dropped down into BMX, and are looking at pushing the road bike market," Schwinn BMX market manager Geoff Hannen told *SportStyle.* "But we will continue efforts in BMX because we've already seen amazing growth there and [the category] holds tomorrow's mountain bike buyers."

In 1999 Schwinn awarded Crispin Porter + Bogusky a majority of its $1 million advertising budget. Creatives from the agency then met with Schwinn/GT Bicycles representatives to discuss the campaign. "We did a planning exercise with them to get to what their core attributes were," Jeff Steinhour, partner and director of account service at Crispin Porter + Bogusky, told *Adweek Southeast.* "They'd never been through something like that, and by the end of the second day, we were down to seven to ten words. The one that kept coming up most often was 'fast.' " The agency then went on to produce humorous print above the tagline "Fast. It's Corporate Policy."

Crispin Porter + Bogusky's Ari Merkin wrote the print's copy. Alex Burnard was responsible for the campaign's art direction. Until the end of 2000 the campaign's sole medium, print ads, appeared in popular bicycling magazines, the magazine *Outside,* and the *Men's Journal.* One print ad, titled "Sex Bicycles," showed a young, blanket-covered couple lying in the back of a GT Bicycles company van. The young man raised his arms in victory above the tagline "Fast. It's Corporate Policy." His less-than satisfied girlfriend was rolling her eyes beside him. Below the ad was a small picture of a GT Bicycle. Another ad showed GT Bicycles employees who accidentally knocked each other unconscious after running through their office. "We felt we needed to leverage 'fast' into a compelling consumer message that invites people in," Steinhour told *Adweek Southeast.* Another ad, titled "Speeding Tickets Bicycles," showed a parking lot filled with GT Bicycles employees, each receiving a speeding ticket from a different highway patrol officer.

Erik Proulx of the agency Brokaw explained in *Advertising Age's Creativity* that Crispin Porter + Bogusky's strategy was to simply exaggerate "the bejeezus" out of the product's benefit. The same could be applied to, as Proulx stated, dish detergent. The tagline would be "Maybe we make dishes a little too sparkly." The ad critic continued to say, "After all, what is 'Fast. It's Corporate Policy,' for GT bikes other than 'Maybe we make bikes a little too fast' by another name?"

OUTCOME

The "Fast. It's Corporate Policy." campaign saw Schwinn/GT Bicycles maintain $400 million in sales for both 1999 and 2000. During the campaign's last 12 months, GT Bicycles also gained 6 percent market share, the largest gain within the entire bicycle industry. The campaign collected two Clios and later seven Gold Lions at the Cannes Lions International Advertising Festival.

Despite its success in 2000 Schwinn/GT Bicycles filed for Chapter 11 bankruptcy protection in July 2001. Analysts cited the corporation's neglect of the 1970s road bike trends, along with the 1980s BMX and mountain bike trends. Also Schwinn was criticized for its insistence on selling bikes exclusively through Schwinn's 1,900 independent dealerships. Others cited flaws in the pricing mind-set of the entire industry's retailers. "A bike is the only product with 100-plus parts that can be bought for under $100. There's something wrong with that picture," bike industry consultant Bill Fields of Fields Associates told *SportStyle.* Schwinn/GT Bicycles' assets were eventually divided and sold to competitors.

FURTHER READING

Delaney, Ben. "Loyal Schwinn Dealers Are Facing an Identity Crisis." *Bicycle Retailer,* August 15, 2001, p. 20.

———. "Out & About: Why China Is Attractive to Makers of Outdoor Gear." *Santa Fe New Mexican,* March 24, 2005, p. C1.

———. "Performance Splits with Giant, Specialized." *Bicycle Retailer,* August 15, 2005, p. 1.

Dollivers, Mark. "The Trouble with Movies, a Man and His Passions, Paging Dr. Internet, Etc." *Adweek* (eastern ed.), July 12, 1999, p. 36.

Ivey, Mike. "Trek Cycles to the Top: Wisconsin Bicycle-Maker Pedals over Competition." *Capital Times,* March 29, 1996, p. 1C.

Lesser, Chris. "IBDs Combat Growing Threat of Sporting Goods Retailers: Variety of Channels Grab Market Share." *Bicycle Retailer,* March 1, 2005, p. 50.

McClenahen, John S. "Supplier Scenarios: The Experiences of Three Wal-Mart Suppliers—Jack Link's, HP and Pacific Bicycle—Illustrate How Manufacturers, Sometimes in Very Different Ways, Are Working with Wal-Mart's RFID Mandate." *Industry Week,* April 1, 2005, p. 47.

Proulx, Erik. "POV: Copywriter Erik Proulx of Cleveland Agency Brokaw Helpfully Outlines the Essential Building Blocks of Ad Appropriation." *Advertising Age's Creativity,* September 1, 2003, p. 10.

Siebert, T.W. "Split Shift for Crispin." *Adweek* (southeastern ed.), October 18, 1999, p. 12.

Tompkins, Megan. "*Outside* Magazine Lures Advertisers with Lower Rates." *Bicycle Retailer,* July 1, 2005, p. 1.

Vernon, Felton. "Retailers, Suppliers Find Freeriding in Odd Places." *Bicycle Retailer,* September 1, 2005, p. 49.

Wang, Li. "A Smelly Classic Highlights Festival." *Patriot-News,* May 27, 2005, p. D01.

Wiebe, Matt. "Huffy Bets on Chopper Sales as Bankruptcy Hearing Looms." *Bicycle Retailer,* December 1, 2004, p. 1.

Kevin Teague

WHAT A RIDE CAMPAIGN

OVERVIEW

NOTE: Since the initial appearance of this essay in the 1998 edition of *Major Marketing Campaigns Annual,* Schwinn Cycling & Fitness was acquired by Pacific Cycle Inc. The essay continues to refer to the company's former name, as that was the official name of the organization when the campaign was launched.

In 1997 Schwinn Cycling & Fitness Inc. launched a print campaign designed to entice the masses of mountain bike enthusiasts while altering the company's image as an out-of-touch dinosaur. Schwinn dominated the U.S. bicycle market from the 1950s to the 1970s but hit the financial skids in the 1980s, in part due to the company's dismissal of the mountain bike craze of the late 1970s and early 1980s as nothing more than a passing trend. Sales of mountain bikes climbed and by 1992 amounted to nearly two-thirds of all bicycle sales. Schwinn was left in the dust and lost $25 million in 1992. The company's market share plummeted, and Schwinn was more than $80 million in debt when it finally limped into bankruptcy court in October 1992. The Schwinn brand, once a revered American icon, teetered on the edge of extinction.

Scott Sports Group purchased Schwinn in early 1993 and implemented some major changes, including moving Chicago-based Schwinn to Boulder, Colorado, the mecca of outdoor enthusiasts. Scott cut the headquarters' workforce by more than half, hired new management familiar with the cycling industry, infused money into the company, and introduced new and redesigned models of bicycles. Also on the priority list was the task of pumping new life into the brand image. The Schwinn brand had become passé and to zealous mountain bikers was considered sedate and "uncool." A marketing executive with mountain bike manufacturer Cannondale told *USA Today* in 1995: "When I was a kid, if you had a Schwinn you were the luckiest kid in the world.... Ask a college kid now and they'll say, 'Oh, Schwinn? They're toast.' "

To remedy the image problem, Schwinn engaged the help of Minneapolis-based advertising agency Carmichael Lynch. Early advertising campaigns were aimed at the high-end mountain biking crowd, including biking fanatics and bike shop employees who influenced many customer purchases. Schwinn hoped for a trickle-down effect; but the trickle was slow, so Schwinn kicked off the "What a Ride" campaign to chase down the masses, namely midrange consumers. Eye-catching color print ads relating the postride musings of mountain bikers appeared in national magazines. Careful not to neglect the high-end riders, "What a Ride" also included a black-and-white print effort geared toward specialized cycling magazines. All the ads boasted a hip, slightly irreverent attitude and spoke specifically to mountain bike enthusiasts. As Gregg Bagni, Schwinn's vice president of marketing,

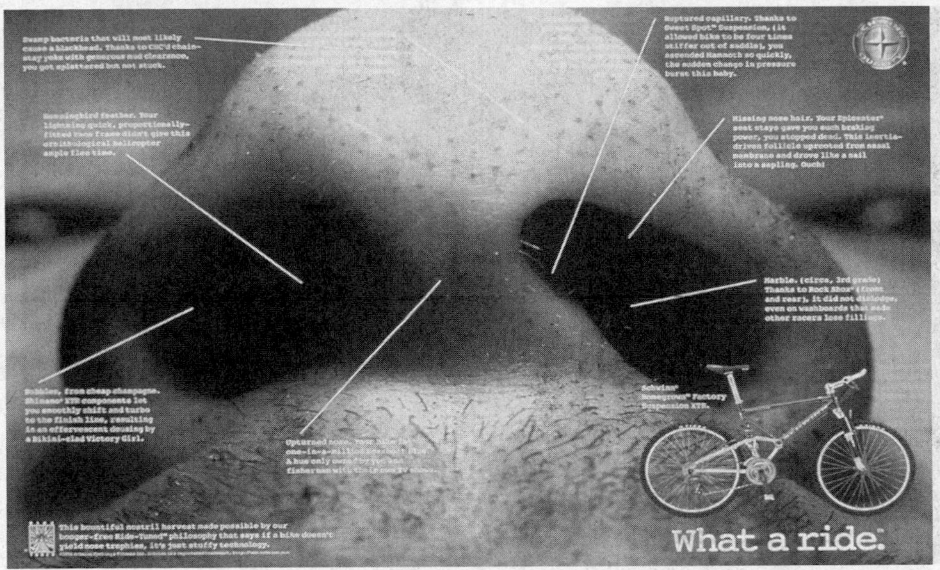

The "Nose" print advertisement from Schwinn's "What A Ride" campaign. CARMICHAEL LYNCH. REPRODUCED BY PERMISSION.

told *Advertising Age,* "We're trying to stop readers dead in their tracks."

HISTORICAL CONTEXT

Before its downfall, family-owned Schwinn ruled the bicycle realm, commanding as much as 25 percent of the U.S. market. By 1995, the year Schwinn celebrated its 100th anniversary, Schwinn's market share had dropped to 5 percent of the $2.5 billion annual market, according to *USA Today.* Despite the company's struggles, however, its sales, attitude, and brand image were much improved since the Scott buyout, and by 1996 Schwinn was back near the top: in terms of units sold, Schwinn ranked second in U.S. bicycles sold through the independent-dealer marketplace.

Advertising forays following the company's resurrection sought to change Schwinn's tarnished image. Carmichael Lynch, which had a good track record of working with companies returning from the brink of death, suggested a campaign showing a new side of Schwinn, one with an attitude and an edge that would appeal to biking zealots. Most considered Schwinn products archaic and associated them with an older generation, and thus Schwinn desperately needed to convince consumers that the company knew and understood the customer and the product, that it was "cool," and that it was capable of manufacturing technologically progressive bicycles. To accomplish these goals, Schwinn targeted the crowd that lived to ride—bicycle shop employees, professional racers, and fanatics obsessed with mountain biking. Schwinn found that this group influenced more than 60 percent of all mountain bike purchases and thus hoped to win their approval.

The first campaign included a print ad of a bicycle messenger riding down a busy urban street. The copy stated, "Read Poetry. Make Peace with All but the Motor Car," and continued, "Schwinn is red, Schwinn is blue, Schwinn is light and agile too. Cars suck." The ad was a far cry from the polite, traditional Schwinn of old, and Bagni met with resistance when he sought the go-ahead from management left over from the prebankruptcy Schwinn days, specifically the former chief operating officer Ralph Murray. Murray found the ad offensive and nixed the campaign, but Bagni ignored Murray's complaints and ran the ad. Bagni explained his tactics to *Reputation Management,* saying that "once you're in this business you have to get to know the customer, you have to understand the culture. This was a guy who'd never been on a bike in his life." Bagni also asserted that the old Schwinn "was a marketing-driven company, not a market-driven company. A marketing-driven company will try to sell a warehouse full of yellow bikes. A market-driven company will determine what the customer wants first." Schwinn's plans paid off—the company's high-end bicycle sales per units sold increased 10.4 percent since the campaign began.

TARGET MARKET

Schwinn critically needed to win over the high-end mountain biking crowd to begin rebuilding its image,

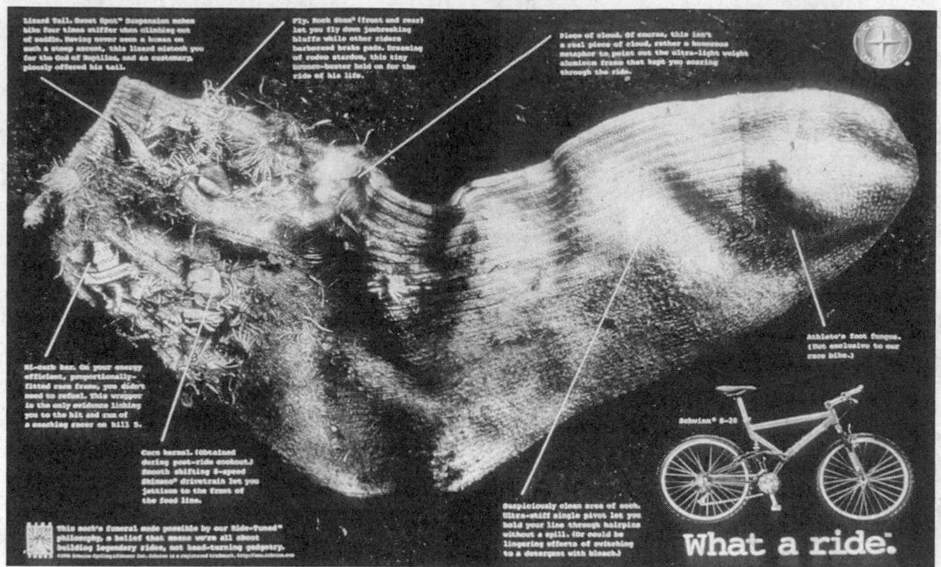

The "Sock" print advertisement from Schwinn's "What A Ride" campaign. CARMICHAEL LYNCH. REPRODUCED BY PERMISSION.

and the company was not shy about its intent. Tom Stendahl, Scott and Schwinn's CEO following the buyout, told *Industry Week*: "Our objective was to go after the top notch and make sure that the high-end consumer of mountain bikes would realize that we made a damn good product and could be proud to own a Schwinn again. Our second stage was to go after the whole middle market." The "What a Ride" campaign represented this second stage.

To become relevant to the high-end group, Schwinn produced cutting-edge bicycles in the $1,500 to $5,000 range. As a result, Schwinn exceeded its high-end bicycle sales goals in the mid-1990s. Low-end products that sold for less than $500 also fared well, but buyers who sought bicycles in the $500 to $1,500 range, who constituted a large percentage of the market, felt Schwinn did not offer products appropriate for their lifestyles or budgets. Schwinn's hope was to dispel these opinions and increase sales among midpriced mountain bikes with the "What a Ride" campaign. Specifically, Schwinn's target group consisted of affluent male bicyclists ranging in age from 28 to 42 who rode habitually but were not obsessed with bicycling. These active males desired reliable, technologically sound products and enjoyed the challenges of mountain biking. These consumers had seen Schwinn jump from manufacturing no mountain bikes to producing top-of-the-line bikes and were unconvinced that Schwinn could cater to, or even understand, their needs.

While Schwinn hoped to sway the masses buying in the midpriced bicycle range with "What a Ride," the company did not abandon its preliminary target—serious bicyclists. These high-end riders continued to have an impact on purchase decisions, and Schwinn felt it was important to maintain a strong brand identity among this group to help increase awareness and sales in the midrange market.

COMPETITION

When Schwinn entered the mountain bike market, the company faced an uphill struggle. Companies including Trek Bicycle, Specialized Bicycle Components, Cannondale, and Giant had established themselves as mountain biking leaders, enjoying tremendous growth through the 1980s and early 1990s as mountain biking surged in popularity. Trek, the market leader, sold 950,000 units in 1995 to earn approximately $300 million in revenue, according to *USA Today*. Schwinn, in contrast, reportedly sold about 480,000 units in 1995, up from U.S. annual sales of around 300,000 during the time of Scott's takeover, as noted in *Industry Week*. Schwinn's market share sagged under the 5 percent mark in 1995, but by 1996 the company had worked its way into the number-two position in terms of units sold and was striving to improve. Bagni summed up Schwinn's turnaround in *Rocky Mountain News*: "Considering that the patient was bleeding to death and having a heart attack simultaneously when we [new management] came on board, we've come a long way, and now we want to go to the next level. . . . We're not comfortable with No. 2."

Schwinn may have chosen a challenging time to launch its growth campaign, since the bicycle market

SCHWINN DEALERSHIPS

In Schwinn's heyday independent dealers across the country sold Schwinn bicycles exclusively. This lock on the market began to crumble in the late 1980s as dealers began to stock several brands. Suddenly customers faced choices, and Schwinn products did not always win the sale. When bankruptcy hit, many dealers were stuck with unwanted inventories of Schwinn products, and thus they were reluctant to reestablish relationships with Schwinn after the Scott takeover. Schwinn found itself convincing dealers, as well as consumers, of how much the company had changed.

had begun to shrink, dropping 5 percent in 1996. Mountain bikes continued to dominate the market, selling 68 percent of the total units sold through the independent dealer network, but sales fell 9 percent from 1995 and had been declining since mountain bike sales peaked in 1993.

MARKETING STRATEGY

Considering that the bicycle market was in decline and Schwinn's image among the target group was shaky, Schwinn's goals for the "What a Ride" campaign were high. Schwinn chose to produce ads that spoke directly to mountain biking enthusiasts, using appropriate terminology and focusing on specific product features and components to prove Schwinn's understanding of mountain biking. The campaign consisted of two print efforts—one geared toward the mass audience and one targeted toward the high-end crowd. The first included several color ads and appeared in mainstream publications such as *Outside, Rolling Stone,* and *Men's Health* for maximum exposure. Black-and-white ads aimed for the serious cyclists were published in specialty magazines, including *Velo News, Bike,* and *Mountain Bike.* Mountain biking conveyed an image of adventure and individuality, and the ads incorporated these traits to spark the attention of readers.

Schwinn's provocative color ads included "Nose," "Sock," and "Shower," and each features a close-up view of the subject of its title, accompanied by comments regarding various parts of the close-up. For instance, "Shower" provides a shot of a shower drain. Various objects—remnants of a postride shower—lay scattered by the drain, each coupled with commentary. Human hair, a bloated tick, a leaf, toxic sewage, and candy corn are among the objects. The text for the toxic sewage reads: "Toxic sewage. Thanks to your lightweight butted Cro-Moly frame, you hydroplaned through this glowing, putrid cesspool before your legs were melted to stumps." The text is humorous yet demonstrates Schwinn's knowledge of technology and components specifically of interest to the target group.

"Sock" displays a dirty sock that has just been worn on a ride. A fly, lizard tail, corn kernel, and some athlete's foot fungus are among the debris stuck to it. The text for the fly reads: "Fly. Rock Shox (front and rear) let you fly down jawbreaking bluffs while other riders barbecued brake pads. Dreaming of rodeo stardom, this tiny bronco-buster held on for the ride of his life." Again, the elements of humor, irreverence, and technological insight sought to convince consumers of Schwinn's shared passion for riding. "Nose" shows a close-up shot straight up a pair of nostrils. The ad points out a missing nose hair, a ruptured capillary, a hummingbird feather, swamp bacteria, and more. The caption for the missing nose hair states: "Your Epicenter seat stays gave you such braking power, you stopped dead. This inertia-driven follicle uprooted from nasal membrane and drove like a nail into a sapling. Ouch!" A shot of a Schwinn mountain bike along with the tag line, "What a ride," appears in the lower right-hand corner of each ad.

The black-and-white ads are simpler and subtler than the color ads, but the messages are just as strong. The minimalist design of the ads and their antimainstream attitude conveys the target group's single focus on mountain biking as a way of life. "Veal Stall" shows two identical diagrams of a stall-like room. The first diagram is labeled, "Veal Stall," and the second, "Office Cubicle." The message to biking enthusiasts is clear—having an office job provides as much freedom as being a calf confined to a veal stall. Another ad displays a peace sign labeled "Peace" and underneath a diagram of a bicycle wheel with spokes labeled "Love." A third ad shows two triangles. One states, "Hierarchy of Needs," and within the triangle "Food," "Clothing," and "Shelter" are listed. The second triangle depicts a snow-capped mountain. The label reads "Hierarchy Revised." This ad cleverly illustrate the priorities of mountain bike zealots who live not for the basic necessities but for riding.

OUTCOME

Schwinn exceeded its goals for the "What a Ride" campaign and continued to produce ads with the "What a ride" tag line through 1998 based on the success of the campaign. The company's market share, according to *Rocky Mountain News,* increased to 14 percent in 1997, while competitor Trek's share dropped to 19 percent. Schwinn continued to fare well with the high-end group, selling out of all high-end mountain bike models and increasing sales by 25 percent. Schwinn also sold out of all models of Moab mountain bikes, Schwinn's mid-priced line, and sales jumped 50 percent over 1996. Overall, Schwinn's unit sales increased 16 percent in 1997 from 1996, successfully tripling Schwinn's original sales goal of 5 percent, an impressive feat considering the mountain bike market declined 9 percent during the same period. Charles Carlson, general manager of Boulder's University Bicycles, explained to *Rocky Mountain News*: "Schwinn is kicking butt right now. They have an awesome bike. Two years ago we said 'There is no way we would ever sell a Schwinn mountain bike.' Now they're responsible for about one-third of our annual sales." Schwinn hoped to continue gaining momentum in the mountain bike industry to once again become the brand coveted by everyone.

FURTHER READING

Jesitus, John. "On the Road Again: New Top Management Uses a Teamwork Approach to Put Schwinn Back into the Bicycle-Industry Race." *Industry Week,* November 11, 1996, p. 28.

McGeehan, Patrick. "Resurrected Schwinn Rolls into Mountain Territory." *USA Today,* August 5, 1995.

"We Fell. We Got Up. End of Apology." *Reputation Management,* September/October 1996.

Mariko Fujinaka

Palace Sports & Entertainment

2 Championship Drive
Auburn Hills, Michigan 48326
USA
Telephone: (248) 377-0100
Fax: (248) 377-3260
Web site: www.palacenet.com

GOIN' TO WORK. EVERY NIGHT. CAMPAIGN

OVERVIEW

After their run of two consecutive championships in 1989 and 1990, the Detroit Pistons of the National Basketball Association began a decline that lasted into the early years of the twenty-first century. The team suffered through numerous losing seasons, and attendance fell drastically. To reverse at least the latter trend, Palace Sports & Entertainment, the parent company of the Pistons, enlisted Minneapolis-based agency Olson & Company to create an advertising campaign that would stir up fan interest throughout the region. The campaign, titled "Goin' to Work. Every Night," began with the 2001–02 season and was designed to identify the team with the hard-working culture of Detroit.

The campaign sprang from an earlier one titled "Every Night," which emphasized the team's commitment to playing hard. But "Goin' to Work. Every Night" broadened the focus to include the fans. It consisted of television, radio, direct mail, print, outdoor signage, and an online interactive component. This was accomplished on an initial budget of less than $500,000. The players themselves and even workers at the Palace of Auburn Hills (where the Pistons played their home games) reinforced the ad campaign. In its early stages two local entertainers were hired to appear in humorous television spots that emphasized the role of the fan in helping the Pistons turn things around. The spots were popular enough that the entertainers themselves gained minor celebrity status in the Pistons' television-viewing area as the "Pistons Lady" and the "O Guy." As the campaign progressed through the years, the fans' involvement continued to be reinforced.

Because of the effectiveness of the "Goin' to Work. Every Night" campaign in surpassing its three major goals for the 2001–02 basketball season—increase the rate of season ticket renewals, increase attendance, and double the number of sellouts—it was recognized with a 2003 Gold EFFIE Award. The campaign became the pivotal theme of all Pistons activities. Indeed, after Detroit captured its third NBA championship by defeating the Los Angeles Lakers in the 2004 NBA Finals, one of the team's stars, Richard Hamilton, proclaimed to the fans, "We've been goin' to work. Every night." This certainly resonated with the local audience.

HISTORICAL CONTEXT

The Detroit Pistons joined the National Basketball Association (NBA) during the 1957–58 season and after years of struggle became the league's premier team, winning consecutive championships in 1989 and 1990. Those championship teams were branded the "Bad Boys" because of the no-nonsense, hardscrabble style of play that contrasted with the rival Los Angeles Lakers'

Guard Richard Hamilton (L) goes to work, every night, as a member of the Detroit Pistons.
© REBECCA COOK/REUTERS/CORBIS.

"showtime" style. In the years following the championships, however, the Pistons fell in the standings, which accelerated the erosion of its fan base. The faltering economy of the early years of the twenty-first century also affected season-ticket sales. Because of corporate cutbacks, season-ticket sales for the 2000–01 season fell to about 7,000. These figures were poor enough to rank Detroit 22nd in attendance in the NBA.

Two other problems that team officials faced were the lack of team identity and the fact that team outreach to the community had declined. The Pistons no longer projected the gritty image that had defined them in their championship years and that the city of Detroit had taken to heart. Nor were players as accessible in promoting the team or community affairs. Both of these factors had an impact on the decline in fan support and the apathy of many of those who did show up.

The Pistons made the first step in correcting the situation in 2000, when the team named Joe Dumars as director of player personnel (later promoted to team president). Dumars had been a star of Detroit's 1989 and 1990 championship teams and had been known for bringing a solid work ethic to the game. In his administrative capacity he began drafting and trading for players who shared his work philosophy. Dumars was also astute in choosing coaches for the Pistons. The next step was to get the word out to the community that the Detroit Pistons were serious about turning the team around and reconnecting with their fans.

TARGET MARKET

The target market for the "Goin' to Work. Every Night" campaign was divided into two segments. The primary segment consisted of the season-ticket holders. During the 2000–01 season the number of season tickets sold was approximately one-third of the capacity of the Palace of Auburn Hills. The second segment consisted of those fans who attended games on a more casual basis. In the "Brief of Effectiveness" it submitted for the 2003 EFFIE Awards, Olson & Company stated that the focus within these two groups was males aged 18 to 54 but that "we were still cognizant of others and avoided alienating other groups."

COMPETITION

Over the years the competition for sports dollars had gotten stiff, especially in a working-class city like Detroit. The economic downturn of the early years of the twenty-first century exacerbated the problem, and, of course, the team's poor on-court performance also placed the Pistons at a disadvantage. The Pistons' main competition came

TWO CHAMPIONS

The Pistons' 2004 NBA championship marked the second championship in two years for Detroit and Michigan basketball fans. The Pistons brought the Larry O'Brien Trophy—emblematic of the NBA championship—to the Palace of Auburn Hills, and in 2003 their counterparts in the Women's National Basketball Association (WNBA), the Detroit Shock, were the WNBA champions. The Shock's motto was "Bring It." To show the teams' appreciation of their fans throughout the state, both trophies were on display at various locations in Michigan from early July to mid-September 2004. While the 2003–04 Pistons were coached by the legendarily peripatetic Larry Brown, the Shock's championship team was coached by local favorite and former Pistons "Bad Boy" Bill Laimbeer.

from the Detroit Red Wings of the National Hockey League—the professional basketball and hockey seasons were practically concurrent. The Red Wings were riding a wave of success in which they had won the Stanley Cup (awarded to the league champion) in 1997, 1998, and 2002, and they had been highly competitive during the years between championships. The basketball season also overlapped with the baseball and football seasons, so the Pistons also competed for viewers with the baseball team the Detroit Tigers and football team the Detroit Lions. Further competition for fans came from the University of Michigan and Michigan State University. With myriad nonsports entertainment choices—ranging from hundreds of television channels to movies, theater, concerts, and clubs—the Pistons and Olson & Company clearly had a tough job ahead.

MARKETING STRATEGY

Despite a small budget, Olson & Company devised an inventive campaign. In the "Brief of Effectiveness" it submitted for the EFFIE Awards the agency stated, "We couldn't promise what we couldn't deliver, wins or All-Stars, so we established an idea that made fans a part of the NBA grind." The brief also described the "social contract with the players and fans. The players promised to go to work if the fans went to work [going to the games and cheering]." This last sentence echoed the sentiments of Joe Dumars, who had major input into the campaign's message. It also showed that the hard-work philosophy went beyond the players on the court to encompass the entire organization, right down to the arena staff—ushers even wore work shirts.

In a 2004 *Brandweek* article by Hilary Cassidy, Pistons CEO Tom Wilson pointed out, "In Detroit, we're so blue-collar, even white-collar people from here think they're blue-collar." Cassidy quoted John Olson, CEO of Olson & Company, as explaining, "No matter where you are on the [income] spectrum, you consider yourself a member of this hardworking, gritty town . . . We can take that idea and leverage it for the team." Part of that leverage, Cassidy noted, was that "the team stepped up promotions with more than 30 gift nights . . . Previous high-tech laser shows were scrapped for player intros in the form of low-key video showing the guys at home leaving for the Palace."

Both traditional and new advertising media were employed to get the word out. In the campaign's first season, which won an EFFIE Award, two new television stars were born: local blues singer Thornetta Davis as the grouchy "Pistons Lady" who would not stand for any slacking off, and actor and college instructor Greg Trzaskoma as a zealous fan dubbed the "O Man" because of the *o* in the word "Pistons" painted on his stomach. One of the signs of the success of the spots was that it was viewers who gave these characters their names. Julie Hinds of the *Detroit Free Press* wrote, "Although their combined point average for the season is zero, Davis and Trzaskoma scored big in other ways. Their efforts have spread the word on the team's new work ethic. Fans love them."

Because of budgetary constraints Olson & Company had to be innovative when it came to promoting the campaign. In addition to using conventional advertising, the agency reinforced the hard-working approach and fan involvement in four unique ways. The first involved the actual season tickets, which were designed to look like time cards. Ticket holders punched in, so to speak, every time they attended a game. The second tactic involved the season-ticket renewal program, one of the ad campaign's key goals. The renewal brochure itself was in the form of a Detroit Department of Labor annual report that, according to the agency's EFFIE "Brief of Effectiveness," "reviewed fans' 'work statistics' in a solemn yet humorous manner." The other two tactics involved six metal "help wanted" signs positioned in the arena and a dedicated website for an online contest in which fans voted for Detroit's hardest-working fan.

In her article Hinds also quoted Craig Turnbull, vice president for brand management for Palace Sports & Entertainment, who pointed out that the campaign was not designed to be quickly replaced by another. "This isn't a one-hit, one-year campaign," he said. "It's our promise as an organization." The Pistons carried through on that promise. They not only rolled the campaign over each year but also found new ways to include the fans. In August 2003 the team announced a casting call to hire 75 fans to serve as extras for television spots for the 2003–04 version of the campaign.

OUTCOME

The "Goin' to Work. Every Night" campaign was a success by any measure. It reinforced throughout the entire Pistons organization the hard-work ethic that culminated in another championship in 2004. Also, from the very beginning it connected on a deep level with the fans. The 2003 EFFIE Award was recognition for the campaign's success, but statistics revealed the full story; the team exceeded all three of the goals set for the ad campaign during the 2001–02 season. One of the goals was to increase attendance by 15 percent to an average of approximately 16,000 per game. The actual average Pistons attendance for the 2001–02 season was 18,556; this amounted to a 32 percent increase over the previous season, when attendance was 14,070 per game. Another challenge was to increase the renewal rate for season-ticket holders; it had been 60 percent during the 2000–01 season, and the objective was to reach 80 percent for 2001–02. That season the renewal rate for season-ticket holders exceeded expectations by jumping to 90 percent. The final goal was to double the number of sellouts from the 2000–01 season, going from three to six. Instead the Pistons recorded 15 sellouts for the 2001–02 season. Building on the 2004 championship and 2005 NBA Eastern Conference Championship, by January 2006 the Pistons had recorded more than 100 consecutive sellouts.

The success of the Pistons on the court attracted sponsors and increased attendance and merchandise sales, but Pistons CEO Tom Wilson emphasized the value of marketing. In the *Brandweek* article Hilary Cassidy quoted Wilson's summation of the campaign: "We systematically created a belief in our fans in our approach to the game and they got caught up in it. . . . They became the hardest-working fans in sports, showing up in hard hats, carrying signs. It all went together. You can win more games when you have 20,000 people going crazy than when you have 14,000 people sitting there staring."

FURTHER READING

Cassidy, Hilary. "Lunch Pail Set: Nothing but Net." *Brandweek,* October 11, 2004.

"Detroit Pistons and Detroit Shock Send Championship Trophies on Tour of Michigan." *PR Newswire,* July 1, 2004.

"Detroit Pistons, Olson & Company Win Gold at EFFIE Awards." *PR Newswire,* June 6, 2003.

DuPree, David. "Dumars Has Pistons Hitting on All Cylinders." *USA Today,* April 26, 2002.

"Extra! Extra! The Detroit Pistons Are Looking for Extras." *PR Newswire,* August 20, 2003.

Hinds, Julie. "Pistons Lady and the O Guy." *Detroit Free Press,* April 19, 2002.

Walsh, Tom. "Success Story Goes to Work at the Palace." *Detroit Free Press,* October 28, 2003.

Frank Caso

Peace Corps

1111 20th Street NW
Washington, D.C. 20526
USA
Telephone: (202) 692-2000
Fax: (202) 692-2901
Web site: www.peacecorps.gov

■■■

LIFE IS CALLING. HOW FAR WILL YOU GO? CAMPAIGN

OVERVIEW

The Peace Corps was signed into existence by President John F. Kennedy in 1961 as a federal organization designed to improve education, community development, health care, and environmental services in undeveloped countries. The organization received a steady flow of recruits throughout the 1960s and '70s, but by 2002 the number of new Peace Corps volunteers was dwindling. According to the ad agency BBDO Atlanta, the Peace Corps' image had grown outdated. Also, it had become increasingly difficult to convince recent college graduates, who were eager to begin their careers, to volunteer for a 27-month, low-paid Peace Corps commitment. To increase by 20 percent the number of applications it received over a one-year period, the Peace Corps released its "Life Is Calling. How Far Will You Go?" campaign.

The campaign began on September 25, 2003, after the business-development firm Threespot Media released a new Peace Corps website that included online applications and a plethora of information about the Peace Corps. Soon afterward BBDO released television spots with the tagline "Life Is Calling. How Far Will You Go?" Some commercials featured an English voice-over from the American actor Matthew McConaughey; others used a Spanish voice-over by the Latino actor Eduardo Verástegui. Print, billboard, and radio advertising ensued. Before the campaign's release, BBDO updated the Peace Corps' target demographic, which had previously consisted of recent college graduates. The new campaign targeted personality types that BBDO dubbed "Unfulfilled Idealists," abstract-thinking optimists who believed life was to be lived as a constant search for fulfillment.

In 2005 the campaign won a Gold EFFIE Award in the Recruitment Advertising category. It also helped catapult the rate of submitted Peace Corps applications by 20 percent in just nine months. The Peace Corps' website traffic increased by 73 percent over the previous year, and total website, E-mail, phone, and mail inquiries increased 47 percent. By 2004 the total number of Peace Corps volunteers had reached 7,733, more than the agency had reported in 29 years.

HISTORICAL CONTEXT

In 1960, while John F. Kennedy was still a U.S. senator, he spoke to students at the University of Michigan who would eventually become the first Peace Corps advocates. Kennedy suggested that if Americans volunteered in underdeveloped countries, they might encourage international peacekeeping in conjunction with enhancing

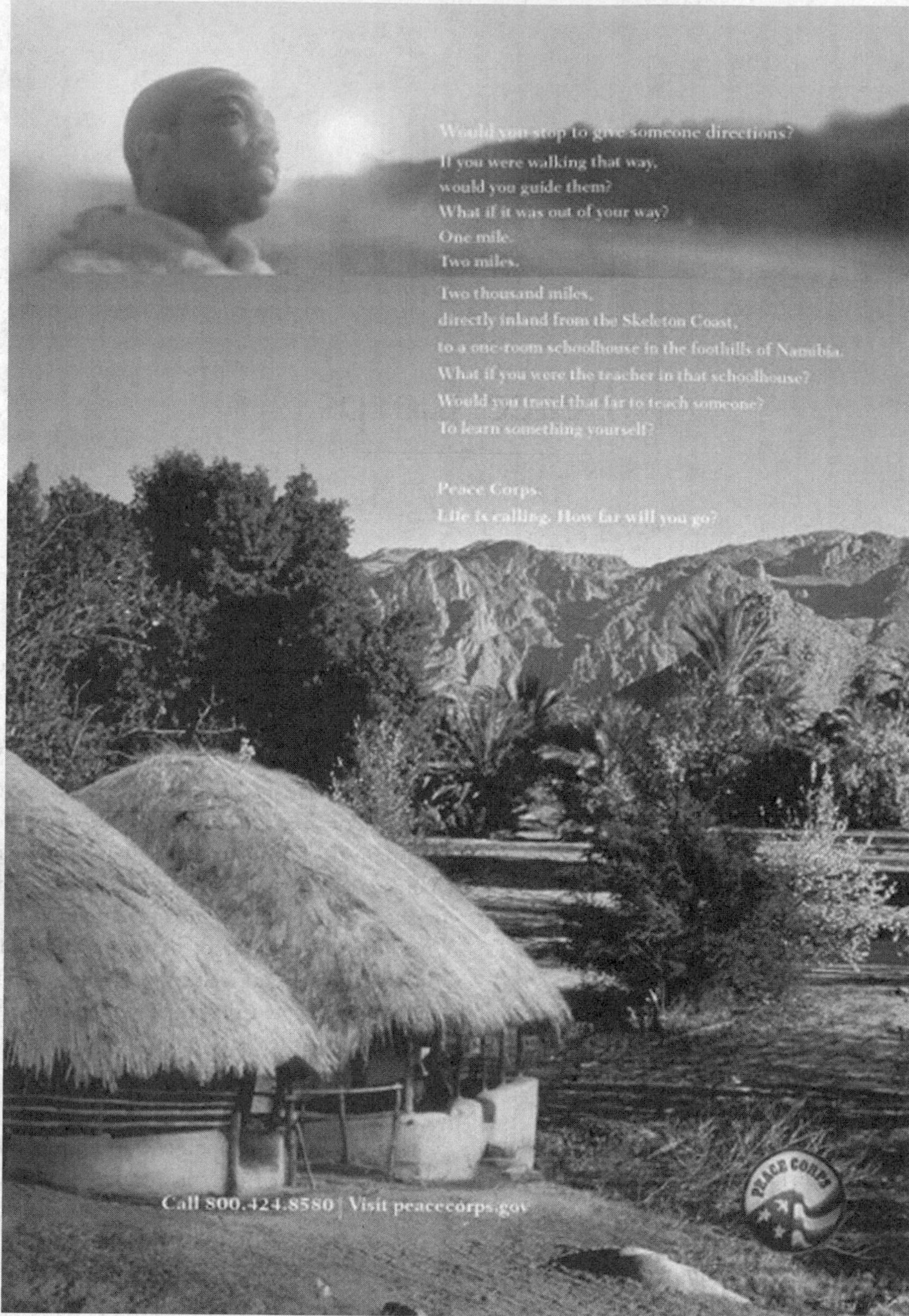

A still from the Peace Corps's "Life Is Calling. How Far Will You Go?" campaign.
PHOTOGRAPHY BY MAGNUM PHOTOS AND SCOTT LOWDEN. COURTESY OF THE PEACE CORPS. REPRODUCED BY PERMISSION.

America's image. After Kennedy was elected president of the United States, he created the Peace Corps on March 1, 1961. The new agency required volunteers to submit to an intense three-month training period that was followed by two years of service in an underdeveloped country. Six months after the Peace Corps was created, the first group of its volunteers arrived in Ghana, West Africa, to start their mission.

Before the "Life Is Calling. How Far Will You Go?" campaign, much of the Peace Corps' advertising used facts to attract volunteers. In 2000 the Peace Corps released advertising under the tagline "How far are you willing to go to make a difference?" Copy from a print ad stated, "No 401k, no profit sharing, no stock options, yet you won't find a better place—better benefits anywhere: the Peace Corps." The ads targeted all college-educated adults.

Despite the Peace Corps' attempts to empower college-educated Americans to volunteer for the 27-month commitment, Peace Corps application submissions were in decline. Peace Corps director Gaddi Vasquez explained his organization's antiquated image to the *Orange County Register*. "We have found anecdotally and through our research that people have high regard for the Peace Corps," Vasquez said, "but in many instances they talk about it in the past tense. A lot of people think it ceased to exist some years ago because it's kept such a low profile." In 2003 the Peace Corps hoped to rebrand itself as a viable organization and to increase its application submissions by 20 percent. President George W. Bush had also encouraged the Peace Corps to double its volunteers between 2004 and 2008.

TARGET MARKET

Instead of targeting a demographic of college-educated young adults, as the Peace Corps had been doing for more than 40 years, "Life Is Calling. How Far Will You Go?" targeted a personality type. It consisted of what ad agency BBDO referred to as "Unfulfilled Idealists," or optimists with an expansive worldview and a belief that life was a constant search for fulfillment. BBDO redefined the Peace Corps' target audience after the agency's own research revealed that "Unfulfilled Idealists" composed more than 80 percent of Peace Corps volunteers. By targeting a personality type, the campaign's scope could expand past the education limitations placed on the previous target.

In 2003 Vasquez also pledged to diversify the Peace Corps by targeting older Americans, couples, community-college students, and more ethnic minorities than the agency had reached in the past. "We are definitely emphasizing greater diversity from retirees to ethnic [groups]," Vasquez told the *Washington Times*. "We want the volunteers to represent a cross section of America." Later in the article Vasquez stated, "We want to break the stereotype that [the] only people who serve in the Peace Corps are younger." The campaign also fostered partnerships with Historically Black Colleges and Universities (HBCU) and Hispanic Serving Institutions (an association of American colleges and universities committed to Hispanic higher education). Spanish voice-overs for some television spots were provided by the Latino actor Eduardo Verástegui. To reach older "Unfulfilled Idealists," the Peace Corps also partnered with the Retired Teachers Association and the American Association of Retired Persons. Although a minimum age of 18 was required to join the Peace Corps, the organization did not post an age maximum. The Peace Corps had historically recruited individuals as old as 85 years of age.

DANGER OF PEACE

Serving the Peace Corps, a government organization that sent volunteering Americans to underdeveloped countries for humanitarian assistance, was considered dangerous business. During the Peace Corps's first 43 years, an average of one Peace Corps volunteer was killed every two months. Out of the total killed, 20 were murdered. Seventy percent of all Peace Corps assault victims were women.

COMPETITION

After the invasion of Iraq began on March 19, 2003, the United States Army spent the majority of its $200 million advertising budget on its "Army of One" campaign, developed by the ad agency Leo Burnett. In order to attract new enlistees the campaign touted the Army's range of combat technology. Television spots resembled video-game advertisements and attempted to lure new recruits by showing off the Army's war gadgetry. When the campaign yielded few results and the Army needed to quickly increase its active duty population from 482,400 to 512,400, a series of reality-based television spots were released under the new tagline "2400/7." The updated commercials featured the real-life situations of new recruits and the Army infantry. "All of our advertising is based on real-life stories," explained Colonel Thomas Nickerson, director of strategic outreach for the U.S. Army, to *Advertising Age*. "If you look at our '2400/7' series, it demonstrates what soldiers are doing in their jobs. It's reality TV. We don't use actors. Our research tells us that these kids want to know what the deal is. They want to know what the experience is before they purchase it."

In 2004 the U.S. Marine Corps, notorious for attracting thrill seekers, continued its longtime advertising message about the Marines' commitment to courage, honor, and pride. The WPP Group's ad agency J. Walter Thompson, Atlanta, had created advertising for the Marine Corps since World War II. "The Marines have always been the warrior class of all the services," Jay Cronin, managing director of J. Walter Thompson, explained to *Advertising Age*. "All its advertising has

PEACE WAGES

The Peace Corps, a U.S. government agency dedicated to assisting underdeveloped countries, paid its American volunteers the wages earned by a native working in the same profession. The volunteers' vaccinations, immunizations, and travel tickets were paid for. During his or her 27 months of service, each American volunteer in 2004 also received a stipend of $225 per month.

always been true to that message. We have tweaked it, but we have not altered it." In 2004 the Marines Corps aired television spots with the tagline "The Few. The Proud. The Marines."

MARKETING STRATEGY

The "Life Is Calling. How Far Will You Go?" campaign began with the release of a new Peace Corps website on September 25, 2003. Designed by communications firm Threespot Media, the new site not only allowed the Peace Corps to measure increased Web traffic during the campaign, but it also added a plethora of new features, including an online application form. According to *PR Newswire,* David Belman, one of Threespot Media's founders, explained, "With the new site, prospective applicants, current applicants, former Peace Corps volunteers, educators, students, donors, and members of the media, among other groups, can all find precisely what they're looking for quickly and easily."

BBDO tailored the campaign's television, print, radio, and billboard advertisements to target "Unfulfilled Idealists." Prior to launching the campaign in September, the ad agency analyzed the communication styles and decision-making processes of "Unfulfilled Idealists." Then, hoping to package the 27-month-long commitment with the Peace Corps as an opportunity for personal growth, BBDO released advertising that mimicked the target audience's communication style. The actor Matthew McConaughey provided the voice-over for a television spot titled "Life Is Calling," which first showed images specific to a prospering society, such as freeways and commercial jets in flight. The spot ended with images such as people pulling fishing nets onto a beach and other scenes from underdeveloped countries. During the 60-second commercial McConaughey asked, "How far would you go to help someone? Would you go to the end of your driveway? Would you cross a street? Would you cross an ocean? To a place 6,000 miles from home? And how long would you go . . . Would you go for a week? A month? A year? Would you go for two years? Would you go if you could use your knowledge to teach someone and, in the process, maybe learn something yourself? Life is calling. How far will you go? Peace Corps."

The campaign tried to deliver its message as if from a kindred spirit of the "Unfulfilled Idealist." Commercial dialogue and ad copy mimicked the metaphoric language that BBDO had observed among "Unfulfilled Idealists." Print ads featured the Peace Corps logo above the image of a sunrise and the copy "Never have to start sentences with 'I should've . . ." Print ads targeting an older audience included the copy, "Do people tell you you're over the hill? What if you were? Over the hill, over a stream, and over an ocean. To another continent." The Emmy-winning actor Forest Whitaker was featured in a radio advertisement titled "Paths," during which Whitaker suggested that listeners should take the path less traveled by joining the Peace Corps. "Could you explain that helping the people of Peru improve their community would also have an effect on your own?" he asked. "Or assisting an entrepreneur in Ukraine to launch her small business? Or creating a support group in Malawi for children orphaned by AIDS?"

The campaign appeared in 27 American advertising markets, including Washington, D.C., Philadelphia, San Francisco, Detroit, and Atlanta. The campaign's TV spots aired across cable networks on donated media. Outdoor posters also appeared on Metrorail and Metrobus signs in the Washington, D.C., area.

OUTCOME

Not only did "Life Is Calling. How Far Will You Go?" earn a Gold EFFIE Award in the Recruitment Advertising category in 2005, but the campaign also helped increase the number of submitted Peace Corps applications by 20 percent in nine months. The Peace Corps' retrofitted website, which started accepting online applications at the beginning of the campaign, saw a 73 percent surge in activity over the previous year.

Even though the campaign's application submissions increased 20 percent, the number of volunteers accepted into the Peace Corps increased very little. As a result of limited funding, the organization only expanded by 277 volunteers between 2003 and 2005. When the Peace Corps requested an annual budget of $359 million from Congress at the start of the campaign, the organization was only granted a little over $300 million. The *U-Wire* quoted Anne-Michelle Reilly, an advocacy intern for the Peace Corps, as explaining, "the Peace Corps is a great organization that is grossly under-funded. They are one of the few U.S. Government organizations that is respected worldwide, mostly because the goal of the program is to present to the world a positive view of America." Reilly continued, "[President George W.] Bush promised to double the number of volunteers to 14,000 and he proposed a budget increase of 20 percent last year, but Congress reduced that significantly."

FURTHER READING

Bruce, Jeff. "Commentary; Peace Corps Series Prompts Invitations." *Dayton (OH) Daily News,* March 25, 2004, p. A14.

Bunis, Dena. "Putting a New Face on the Peace Corps." *Santa Ana (CA) Orange County Register,* September 26, 2003, p. 1.

Carper, Kandis. "Peace Corps Recruiter to Answer Questions." *Spokane (WA) Spokesman-Review,* October 7, 2004, p. N12

De Marco, Donna, "Peace Corps Wants Diversity." *Washington Times,* October 6, 2003, p. C15.

Dignam, John. "Peace Corps Volunteer Sees Pride in Ukraine." *Worcester (MA) Telegram & Gazette,* December 9, 2004, p. B1.

Dingmann, Tracy. "Book Revisits Peace Corps Volunteer's Killing." *Albuquerque (NM) Journal,* October 17, 2004, p. E8.

Jervis, Rick. "Army, Marine Recruiters Shift Focus to Wary Parents." *USA Today,* April 5, 2005, p. A.1

Lamothe, Ernst. "Peace Corps Representatives Look for Recruits on Campus." *Champaign (IL) News-Gazette,* November 11, 2004, pp. B1–B2.

Lazare, Lewis. "Business Week Putting Fresh Face Forward Today." *Chicago Sun-Times,* September 29, 2003, p. 55.

Linnett, Richard. "Reaching 'Generation Kill': Army Fails to Battle New Recruit Reality." *Advertising Age,* July 26, 2004, p. 3.

Markley, Melanie. "Peace Corps Has High-Tech Goals in Mexico." *Houston Chronicle,* October 11, 2004, p. 5.

Mergian, Gwen. "Peace Corps Benefits from a Bit of Maturity." *Albany (NY) Times Union,* November 28, 2004, p. G1.

Paine, Danielle. "Peace Corps Worker Back from Paraguay." *Springfield (MA) Republican,* December 8, 2004, p. NP20.

Kevin Teague

PepsiCo, Inc.

700 Anderson Hill Road
Purchase, New York 10577-1444
USA
Telephone: (914) 253-2000
Fax: (914) 253-2070
Web site: www.pepsico.com

CODE RED CAMPAIGN

OVERVIEW

In 2001 PepsiCo's Mountain Dew was the fourth-best-selling soft drink on the U.S. market. Even so, since the 1990s soft-drink sales overall had been seriously declining. While Mountain Dew's sales growth had often been in the double digits since the 1970s, by the turn of the century, growth had trickled to around 2 percent. To revive sales Pepsi introduced a bright-red version of the original called Mountain Dew Code Red. The new cherry-flavored beverage was to be marketed in a different direction than the original Dew. While Mountain Dew's target market had long been young, white males interested in extreme sports, Code Red's market was to be ethnically diverse and urban.

Working with ad agency BBDO New York, Pepsi introduced Code Red slowly, beginning within the target market of the original Dew instead of the new target market. Prior to placing the product onto store shelves, PepsiCo offered samples to extreme-sports enthusiasts at the February 2001 X Games and established a Code Red game on the Mountain Dew website in April 2001. A month later Code Red was finally distributed to stores.

A "teaser campaign" accompanying the launch consisted of print ads and radio spots with an urban, multicultural focus. Television commercials were added in October 2001. The initial spots featured NBA stars Tracy McGrady and Chris Webber as well as singer and actress Macy Gray. These spots ran through 2003, when two new television commercials, "Mascot" and "Football Court," were introduced.

By September 2001 Code Red had become the fifth-best-selling soft drink in convenience stores. PepsiCo's overall third-quarter 2001 net income jumped an astonishing 22 percent, largely because of Code Red. Advertising awards for the campaign included a Gold EFFIE Award, one of the most prestigious honors in the ad industry. But the success did not last. By 2002 Code Red sales numbers had begun to dwindle, and in 2003 its sales volume dropped 37 percent. The problem was that sales of soft drinks were declining as consumers chose healthier beverages such as bottled water and juice.

HISTORICAL CONTEXT

Tennessee's Tri-City Beverage became the first Mountain Dew franchise in 1954, and by 1958 it had adorned the bottle with Mountain Dew's first logo. The old red-and-white labels featured a hillbilly shooting at a government agent fleeing an outhouse. The agent represented a revenuer, one whose job was to stop bootlegging. Slang for moonshine, and invented in the Tennessee hills in the 1940s, Mountain Dew was originally used as a mixer with whiskey. The label, as well as the drink itself, embodied the moonshiner days of 1920 through 1933, when Prohibition made the use of alcohol illegal in the United States.

In 1964 PepsiCo bought the franchise, bringing Mountain Dew into the national marketplace. Two years later Pepsi introduced its first nationwide Mountain Dew advertising campaign, "Ya-Hoo, Mountain Dew!" The catchy phrase helped Pepsi establish recognition of its new soft drink. In 1973, when advertising agency BBDO took over the Mountain Dew account, advertising for the brand began to focus on a target market of young, active people who enjoyed the outdoors. It also emphasized Mountain Dew's high caffeine content. The 1973 and 1974 advertising campaigns, "Put a Little Ya-Hoo in Your Life" and "Hello, Sunshine, Hello, Mountain Dew," represented early shifts toward this focus. By the 1980s, although Mountain Dew sales were climbing, a trend toward healthier eating and drinking habits was emerging. In response PepsiCo introduced Diet Mountain Dew in 1986. By this time Mountain Dew had become the industry's sixth-biggest brand, and the growth continued. From 1984 through 1993 Mountain Dew's volume doubled, bringing in $2.2 billion in sales in 1993. But meanwhile the healthy-eating trend had spread. Mountain Dew's reaction was aggressive.

The 1993 "Do the Dew" campaign was enormous, accounting for a 44 percent increase in ad spending from 1992 to 1993. The "Do the Dew" debut included 28 TV spots, which appeared on nine television networks. During the campaign's launch the ad schedule involved an astonishing 14 minutes of advertising per night. With "Do the Dew" Mountain Dew's sales continued to grow, even when soft-drink sales were in serious decline. In 1999 Mountain Dew's sales, while not matching the double-digit growth of the past, grew by 7.1 percent. In an attempt to reclaim the huge sales growth of years prior, PepsiCo created a new product in 2001: Mountain Dew Code Red.

CAFFEINE JOLT

Pepsi and other soft-drink distributors long claimed that the caffeine added to soft drinks provided a bitter taste that was needed to balance the predominant sweetness. But in a study conducted by Johns Hopkins University in 2001, four out of five tasters could not tell the difference between a cola with an average amount of caffeine (35 mg) and one without any caffeine. When the researchers doubled the amount to 70 mg, however, more than half the tasters could detect it. A 20-ounce bottle of Mountain Dew (containing 55 mg of caffeine) contained about the same amount of caffeine as a strong cup of brewed coffee.

TARGET MARKET

When ad agency BBDO took over the Mountain Dew account in 1973, the brand's target market was defined as the young and active. Since then the focus had zeroed in on extreme sports. With the "Do the Dew" campaign that began in 1993, this focus was obvious. The commercials featured four adventurous young men performing such thrilling stunts as jumping from a cliff and boogie-board waterfall diving. As noted in a 1993 *PR Newswire* article, Mountain Dew's focus was on young, energetic males. In particular, Mountain Dew sought 20-somethings who represented a "vibrant, adventure-seeking group that is 40 million strong and spends $125 billion each year." Mountain Dew's well-known high caffeine content helped to retain these customers.

Code Red's target market differed in two ways from the original drink. The target age was younger, and the target socioeconomic group was more diverse. Code Red, with the same 55 mg of caffeine as its predecessor, targeted teens. Still, this teen was similar to the 20-something targeted by the original Mountain Dew. He was a male, thrill-seeking adrenaline addict. As Gary Rodkin, then PepsiCo CEO, told the *New York Times,* the target consumer was "a kid with his hair on end, his eyes bugging out. He's a little bit on edge." Next, while Mountain Dew appealed most directly to nonurban white males, Code Red was marketed to urban, minority populations. In its research Mountain Dew concluded that a large percentage of people from minority groups had historically chosen soft drinks with sweet, fruity flavors. Code Red, with its red color and cherry flavor, fit the bill.

COMPETITION

In response to Pepsi's success with Mountain Dew, top Pepsi competitor Coca-Cola introduced citrus-flavored Mello Yello in 1964. Like Mountain Dew, Mello Yello boasted higher than normal caffeine amounts, 53 mg per serving. In marketing the product Coke first connected the drink with urbane jazz, thus portraying its "mellowness." But once Mountain Dew became the drink for extreme-sports enthusiasts, Mello Yello followed suit, introducing the tagline "There is nothing mellow about it." To reinforce the point, Coke plastered Mello Yello packaging with images of people engaging in extreme sports. Nevertheless, by the 1990s Mello Yello was still far behind Mountain Dew in sales and popularity. While Mountain Dew had climbed to the number four spot in total U.S. soft-drink sales, Mello Yello, with only 0.5 percent of the market in 1996, was nowhere near the top-10 list. In 1997 Coke introduced Surge, which sold 69 million cases in the first year but flopped soon afterward. But Coke was far from quitting the game.

With a plan to phase out Surge, Coca-Cola returned its focus to Mello Yello, introducing a big-budget advertising campaign, "Mello Yello: It's Smooth," in 1999. The campaign's target audience closely resembled that of Mountain Dew: boys in their late teens. With heavy advertising on TV stations Fox and WB as well as a saturation of the evening and late-night radio waves, the campaign was an enormous hit. "Mello Yello: It's Smooth" won a plethora of advertising awards, including an EFFIE, an award that was among the most prestigious in its category. Even more substantial were the financial results. For two years following the campaign's start, Mello Yello experienced double-digit growth in the United States. But the success did not last. Mountain Dew's introduction of Code Red helped to burst the Mello Yello bubble. In 2004 Mello Yello launched its own red version: Cherry Mello Yello. But the beverage flopped so badly, Coke began pulling it off shelves within a year.

Mello Yello never made it to the top-10 list, but another Coca-Cola product, Sprite, did. By 2003 Sprite sales, at $57 million, had surpassed Mountain Dew's $54 million. But this followed two consecutive years of losses for both soft drinks. The sales decrease may have been connected to Code Red sales, which reportedly stole market share from the others. As such, in 2003 Coke introduced Sprite Remix, which added tropical flavors to the original drink. The new Sprite, however, could not fully compete with Code Red for two reasons. With zero caffeine, Sprite Remix's market was different than Mountain Dew's. Further, Sprite, unlike Code Red, did not focus on the inner-city market.

MARKETING STRATEGY

By 2000 Mountain Dew, one of the soda industry's fastest-growing brands ever, was slowing in sales. In 2001, in an attempt to revive sales, Pepsi released Mountain Dew Code Red, a wild-cherry version of Mountain Dew. Code Red, unlike regular Mountain Dew, was to be aimed at a minority, urban population. Hiring ad agency BBDO New York to handle the account, Pepsi was in no hurry to start a big television campaign for the new product. Instead, largely in response to the challenge of pursuing a new target market, Pepsi wanted to first spread word of the product slowly and steadily. It began marketing the new drink with subtlety and within the core Mountain Dew target market.

The unveiling of Code Red occurred in February 2001, at the X Games in Mount Snow, Vermont, an event focused on young extreme-sports enthusiasts. Next Pepsi sent Code Red bottles to approximately 3,000 core Mountain Dew users, including extreme-sports athletes, disc jockeys, and musicians. In April 2001 an online Code Red car-racing game was introduced on the Mountain Dew website; approximately 1,500 winners of the online game won samples of Code Red. At this time advertising of the product was made more evident, and posters with the headline "Prepare to Get Your Swirl On" were hung in urban centers. Mountain Dew Code Red entered the marketplace on May 2001, but only in single-serve 20-ounce and one-liter plastic bottles. A television campaign was still months off. Instead, a "teaser campaign" was launched, with print ads appearing in *Vibe, Source, XXL,* and *Slam,* magazines with large ethnic readerships. In addition, a billboard appeared in May 2001 in New York City's Times Square; it featured the headline "Crack the Code." A radio spot, "On the One Twos," in which rappers Busta Rhymes and Fatman Scoop offered a Code Red jingle, was also introduced at this time.

In October 2001 Code Red aired its first television spot, "Hoops." The commercial, which portrayed an inner-city basketball game, was far from ordinary. For the spot BBDO sent NBA stars Tracy McGrady and Chris Webber to an outdoor court to initiate a pickup basketball game without revealing their identities. Within seconds a crowd gathered, oohing and aahing over the jumping, the swishing, the incredible ball-handling skills, a dunk. One spectator gave a play-by-play of the action over his cell phone. To create the commercial, 10 hidden cameras captured the action. With this spot BBDO seemed to accomplish Mountain Dew's goal perfectly. Or, as *Advertising Age* critic Bob Garfield put it, "So comes now this brand extension of Mountain Dew, the caffeine-spiked Code Red, and—lo and behold—the scene is an inner city playground where large numbers of Target-Audience Americans are shooting hoops and spectating." Another television spot, "Macy," starring female African-American singer/actor Macy Gray, also appeared in 2001. When Pepsi was trying to regain momentum for Code Red in 2003, it aired two new television spots, "Mascot" and "Football Court," as well as a new radio spot, "High Noon." Print advertising also expanded at this time. The 2003 advertising budget for Code Red was reportedly $6.3 million (in comparison, $18 million was allotted for advertising the core Mountain Dew brand). Between 2004 and 2005 no new TV commercials were introduced for Code Red, although one radio spot, "Street Legends," as well as a print ad called "Legends," appeared in 2004.

OUTCOME

While the marketing of Mountain Dew Code Red began slowly, momentum for the product was immediate and massive. Even before Code Red hit the shelves, the press wrote about it, and consumers could not wait to have a taste. Thus, Pepsi was optimistic about the product. As Dave Burwick, then Pepsi's vice president for marketing, told the *New York Times,* "Today's marketing environment is so hypersaturated it's hard to get noticed. But this one will float seamlessly above the noise." And from the start, Code Red did exactly that. Within five weeks of its May launch, Code Red reached its initial 34-week sales goal of 17 million cases. Further, within three months of entering the market, without even a television campaign, Code Red became the fifth-best-selling soft drink in convenience stores. These figures were good news for PepsiCo, which had been suffering from a lag in soft-drink sales for the past decade. In October 2001 PepsiCo's third-quarter net income jumped 22 percent; Pepsi granted Code Red half the credit for this feat (its Aquafina bottled water was credited for the other half). Advertising awards also followed. Most notably, in 2003 the Code Red campaign as a whole won a Gold EFFIE Award (Carbonated Soft Drink category) from the New York American Marketing Association. The EFFIEs were among the most prestigious in advertising awards.

Sales, meanwhile, began to drop. In 2003 Code Red's sales volume declined 37 percent. In response to slowing sales Mountain Dew introduced the orange-flavored Mountain Dew LiveWire around Memorial Day 2003. But within months it became clear that the new flavor was not going to repeat the instant success of Code Red. It also seemed that Code Red may have hit its performance peak in a market of consumers seeking beverages that were healthier than soft drinks. Further, Mountain Dew's high caffeine content was losing its edge in a market that was becoming saturated with relatively new energy drinks (which offered even more caffeine than Mountain Dew as well as other ingredients—such as B vitamins and ginkgo—that had energizing properties). In 2004 PepsiCo introduced the grape-flavored Mountain Dew Pitch Black. But this time Mountain Dew recognized trends from the past. Pitch Black was thus available only during a 10-week period surrounding Halloween. Meanwhile, although Pepsi continued to sell Code Red, it returned its focus to the original Dew. In 2004 it initiated a "Dew U" continuity program, a major push in the long-standing "Do the Dew" advertising campaign. "Dew U" included three television spots as well as radio and online advertisements; these were Mountain Dew's only major advertising focus that year.

FURTHER READING

"Breaking News: Code Red; Dunking with the Big Boys." *Advertising Age,* October 1, 2001, p. 58.

Chura, Hillary. "Pepsi-Cola's Code Red Is White Hot." *Advertising Age,* August 27, 2001, p. 1.

Garfield, Bob. "Code Red's Ads Present a New, Riveting Take on Reality." *Advertising Age,* October 22, 2001, p. 61.

Ives, Nat. "Mountain Dew Double-Dose for Times Square Passers-By." *New York Times,* April 8, 2004, p. C1.

McKay, Betsy. "Advertising: Pepsi's Code Red May Score with Subtlety." *Wall Street Journal,* September 28, 2001, p. B9.

"Mountain Dew's 1993 Ad Campaign Debuts with 14-Minute Single-Night Advertising Schedules." *PR Newswire,* March 17, 1993.

Unger, Henry, and Scott Leith. "Code Red Making Waves since Debut." *Atlanta Journal-Constitution,* July 8, 2001, p. 1F.

Wilder, Shannon. "Mountain Dew's Formula for Cool: Code Red." *Point of Purchase,* November 2001, p. 16.

Winter, Greg. "Red to the Rescue; PepsiCo Looks to a New Drink to Jolt Soda Sales." *New York Times,* May 1, 2001, p. C1.

Candice L. Mancini

DO THE DEW CAMPAIGN

OVERVIEW

Mountain Dew, a lemon-lime flavored, highly caffeinated soft drink, became a prominent national brand for PepsiCo, Inc., in the 1980s, posting double-digit annual sales increases. Many observers expected the brand's growth to level off in the next decade, but Mountain Dew continued to grow. Its annual volume increased at least 10 percent every year between 1993 and 1995, surpassing even Diet Pepsi as the parent company's second-highest seller. By 1996 the citrus drink had displaced Dr Pepper as the top-selling noncola product in the United States. In 1997 the brand released a campaign with the tagline "Do the Dew" to solidify the youth-focused marketing strategy that had so effectively driven sales since the early 1990s.

"Do the Dew," budgeted at \$30–\$40 million annually in the late 1990s and at \$50–\$70 million between 2000 and 2005, was able to establish and maintain a Mountain Dew brand identity while remaining on the cutting edge of an ever-changing youth culture. One of the hallmarks of the campaign was a close association of the brand with extreme sports. As exemplified by the X Games (the "X" stood for extreme)—an alternative Olympics consisting of daredevil events such as sky surfing and street luge—this trend appealed to young people's high energy and sense of adventure. Mountain Dew commercials featured "Dew Dudes" participating in extreme sports as well as celebrity endorsers who, either through tongue-in-cheek humor or athletic prowess, could be effectively associated with the "extreme" brand image that the drink was nurturing.

Mountain Dew sales outpaced those of all other full-calorie soft drinks during most of the time that "Do the Dew" ran. The brand did not grow at the double-digit rates that it had known in the 1980s and early 1990s, but the campaign firmly established the product as the number four soft drink in the United States, behind Coke, Pepsi, and Diet Coke, while managing to retain Mountain Dew's aura of daring, youthful edginess. Although its formula of appealing to young men through an association with extreme sports and similarly bold brand imagery was frequently imitated, few marketers in the United States were as effective in making their brands synonymous with youthful exuberance as Mountain Dew was between 1997 and 2005.

HISTORICAL CONTEXT

Mountain Dew in its earliest incarnation was developed in the 1940s by A.A. "Ollie" Hartman, a Tennessee bar owner, to serve as a mixer with whiskey. The product was named after the illegal moonshine that was said to be as plentiful as early morning dew on the mountain. The original marketing of Mountain Dew failed, but the product stayed alive in one form or another until Bill Jones, a manager at the soft-drink company Tip Corporation developed the drink's now-famous high caffeine formula in order, he said, to help people combat the fatigue that generally occurred at around 2:30 in the afternoon. Jones began selling the product in 1961 using a simple marketing campaign that attempted to put the drink in as many hands as possible. Mountain Dew was a huge success (Tip Corporation was selling more than 10 million cases annually), and by March 1964 a number of national corporations, including PepsiCo, were contacting Jones asking to purchase the formula.

In August 1964 the board of directors of PepsiCo approved a plan negotiated with Jones to acquire the rights to Mountain Dew. The sale made news around the world. Mountain Dew swiftly became PepsiCo's second-best-selling drink, providing the soft-drink giant with a tool to compete successfully in the so-called flavor market. In 1965 PepsiCo launched its inaugural ad campaign for Mountain Dew with the tagline "Yahoo Mountain Dew . . . It'll Tickle Your Innards." That tagline was used for five years until it was replaced by "Get That Barefoot Feelin' Drinkin' Mountain Dew" in 1969.

PepsiCo stuck with a hillbilly theme for the product until 1972, when it shifted its advertising and graphics package toward action-oriented scenes. This switch was exemplified by the soft drink's new slogan for 1973, "Put a Little Yahoo in Your Life." Sales jumped appreciably. Two years later the "Hello Sunshine" campaign was launched. This campaign remained intact for almost six years, although the tagline was modified in 1979 to "Reach for the Sun, Reach for Mountain Dew." In 1981 it was succeeded by "Give Me a Dew," which gave way to "Dew It to It" in 1983.

The rustic theme that had marked the early years of the brand's marketing was reintroduced in 1986 with the slogan "Dew It Country Cool." This remained in place for almost a decade, at which point a move was made toward more youth-oriented marketing. In 1995 Mountain Dew sponsored the Grammy Awards and used the jaded tagline "Been There, Done That, Tried That." That same year tennis superstar Andre Agassi signed a deal to promote Mountain Dew in the United States.

Piggybacking on the cultural trend toward extreme sports and activities, the brand's innovative commercials featured an actor dressed as James Bond snowboarding, Agassi bungee jumping, and pop vocalist Mel Tormé (known as "The Velvet Fog") free-falling from the roof of a Las Vegas hotel. In 1996 Mountain Dew launched a massive beeper network called "The Mountain Dew Extreme Network." The "Do the Dew" tagline was unveiled the following year.

TARGET MARKET

With its youth-oriented campaign, the Mountain Dew brand was aimed at 13- to 29-year-old consumers and became the most popular soft drink among teenagers. More than any other Pepsi brand, Mountain Dew was directly targeted at young people, or what the company called "Generation Nexters with more edge." To nurture this relationship, the brand relied on focus groups of young consumers and conducted extensive sampling.

The youth market was targeted increasingly in the 1990s as youth spending skyrocketed. According to a study conducted by Texas A&M University, in 1997 consumers under the age of 18 spent $172 billion. In addition, young people were indirectly responsible for $300 billion in spending by their parents.

Research had shown that brand preferences were formed at an early age. With teenagers making up the largest segment of soft-drink consumers, appealing to this market became critical for brand success. Mountain Dew was one of the best-selling soft drinks at convenience stores, which, according to industry analysts, were the most popular point of sale for younger consumers.

COMPETITION

Mountain Dew's principal challenge in the carbonated-citrus-soft-drink sector came from industry giant Coca-Cola. But Coca-Cola had mixed results trying to

AN EXTREME SACRIFICE

Commercials that appealed to extreme-sports enthusiasts of necessity demanded extreme risks on the part of their participants. In 1996 one skydiver paid the ultimate price when he died filming a spot for Mountain Dew.

Rob Harris, a 28-year-old stunt diver and veteran of ESPN's X Games competition, plummeted to his death during the filming of a Mountain Dew commercial spoofing James Bond movies. The shoot called for Harris to dive from an exploding plane at 5,000 feet, the kind of daring stunt he had performed in a dozen TV spots since 1993. This time, however, his parachute lines got tangled, and his reserve chute failed to open in time.

PepsiCo officials considered scrapping the spot but ultimately decided to ask Harris's parents for permission to use footage of their son taken before the fatal jump. The grieving family reluctantly agreed, and Harris's friends and fellow skydivers were treated to the eerie spectacle of watching commercials featuring their late friend. In perhaps a more fitting tribute, one of Harris's best friends later released a sachet of his ashes into the sky during a sky-surfing competition.

overshadow the success of Mountain Dew. Coca-Cola's first foray into the so-called heavy citrus market was in 1979, when it introduced Mello Yello, a drink named after a song by the 1960s pop star Donovan. In 1994 the brand was marketed with a NASCAR racing tie-in and featured the slogan "Make Some Noise." But it failed to generate more than a whimper with consumers, and the product was retired in all but a few markets.

In 1996 Coca-Cola introduced a new citrus product, Surge, with a mandate to take a chunk out of Mountain Dew's market share. "The Coke system has been looking for a Dew killer for quite some time," Michael Bellas of Beverage Marketing Corp. told the *Atlanta Journal-Constitution.* "This is the most direct attack against Dew, a head-on offensive with some massive advertising behind it." With the tagline "Feed the Rush," Surge spots debuted during the telecast of the Super Bowl on January 26, 1997. The company spent a total of $60 million on an advertising blitz to promote the product. By contrast, PepsiCo spent only $27.5 million to advertise Mountain Dew in the first nine months of 1996.

By the end of 1997 the new drink was available in 90 percent of the U.S. market and had achieved a loyal teen following. But the increased competition seemed to spur Mountain Dew on to more sales, as the market leader continued to enjoy vigorous growth of its own. "There have been a wide array of wannabes that have tried and failed to put a dent in Dew," commented PepsiCo spokesman Brad Shaw.

MARKETING STRATEGY

Mountain Dew's "Do the Dew" campaign was not a radical departure from what had gone before it. "It's always been an outdoor, active drink," Bill Bruce, a copywriter on the account, told *Beverage World* magazine. "We wanted to bring it up to date and try to do things people hadn't seen before."

One of the new elements the campaign introduced was the "Dew Dude" persona, a young person with a passion for extreme sports like street luge and in-line skating. Mountain Dew deemed these commercials "aspirational," meaning that even those who did not participate in these dangerous sports could relate to the spirit of adventure behind them. Expanded to encompass "Dewdettes" in 1997, the characters represented a natural evolution from previous campaigns that had featured young people engaged in outdoor activities. The consistency of its message helped Mountain Dew maintain a strong brand identity despite changes in youth culture. "When you have a basic consistent core selling proposition for a brand," remarked PepsiCo's vice president of flavors Dave Burwick to *Beverage World,* "no matter how you dress it up and how you communicate it and how you execute it to your consumer, it needs to vary over time, because your consumers change over time, particularly when you're talking about teens whose tastes change less than yearly."

As the campaign progressed, the "Dew Dude" persona remained consistent even as it evolved to refer more to a daring state of mind than to literal participation in extreme activities, and later "Do the Dew" commercials used comedy to convey the brand's essence. A 2000 Super Bowl spot, for instance, illustrated a young man's fearless athleticism as well as his attachment to the product by showing him chasing down a cheetah that had stolen his Mountain Dew. Similarly, a 2001 commercial featured the same young man engaging in a head-butting match with a ram in order to retrieve a Mountain Dew that the animal was guarding.

Another component of the "Do the Dew" campaign was the judicious use of celebrity endorsers. Humor was employed in some of these television spots, such as a commercial in which crooner Mel Tormé was shown falling from the top of a Las Vegas hotel. Another spot, produced by the agency BBDO, featured martial-arts superstar Jackie Chan performing a series of death-defying stunts. At the end of the spot Chan encountered the spirits of the "Dew Dudes," who encouraged him to "see the Dew, be the Dew, do the Dew." The ironic humor was part of a strategy to appeal to teens who might ordinarily be turned off by big-name spokespersons. "If you talk down to teens," observed senior brand manager Ron Coughlin to *Beverage World,* "they'll see it right away and they'll punish you." Not all of Mountain Dew's celebrity endorsers were subject to such tongue-in-cheek treatment, however. Star athletes such as the professional football quarterback Brett Favre and the Olympic runner Michael Johnson were used in spots that tied the bold nature of their athletic talent with the "extreme" brand image.

Among the most effective ongoing components of the "Do the Dew" campaign was Mountain Dew's sponsorship of the X Games, the annual extreme-sports competition telecast by the cable sports network ESPN. The sports featured in the games often figured prominently in Mountain Dew commercials. "There's no better stamp of authenticity for the X Games than Mountain Dew," ESPN's Judy Fearing told *Beverage World.*

Mountain Dew, like other soft-drink brands looking for renewed energy during what became a protracted industry downturn (a result of growing consumer preference for bottled water, teas, and other alternative beverages), pursued brand growth via new products beginning in 2001. That year's introduction of Code Red, a cherry-flavored version of Mountain Dew aimed chiefly at urban African-American and Hispanic youth, was the most successful of the new products. Advertisements in Code Red's first year included a teaser launch campaign tagged "Do the New Do," a rap jingle called "Crack the Code" (performed by Busta Rhymes and Fatman Scoop), and graffiti-cartoon print ads in hip-hop-influenced magazines such as *Vibe* and the *Source.*

In 2004, after four years of sliding sales, PepsiCo shifted most of its Mountain Dew marketing resources back to the core brand. In addition to the ongoing weakness of the soft-drink market as a whole, Mountain Dew also had to contend with the aging of its initial Generation X target. PepsiCo continued to emphasize a mix of extreme sports, celebrity endorsers, and humor in its Mountain Dew advertising, but the company was also aware of changing behaviors and tastes among the rising generation of prospective Dew Dudes. Among the new extensions of the highly durable "Do the Dew" positioning, therefore, was an effort to increase the brand's visibility among "gamers," or video-game players, who spent more time engaged in that activity than watching extreme sports on TV.

OUTCOME

Mountain Dew's consistently distinct brand identity, as communicated through "Do the Dew," was widely credited with sales growth that—though it slowed from the double-digit gains of the mid-1990s—outpaced virtually all other soft-drink products during the last several years of the twentieth century. In 1999 *Beverage Digest* publisher John Sicher told the *Los Angeles Times* that the drink was "one of the two or three strongest brands in the beverage industry today"—in sales volume it ranked fourth behind Coke, Pepsi, and Diet Coke—and that "Pepsi has done a masterful job of marketing Mountain Dew." Every year from 2000 to 2003 the core Mountain Dew brand posted modest sales declines of between 0.5 and 4 percent, but these were attributed primarily to the changing beverage marketplace, as bottled water, teas, and blended-juice beverages gained in popularity. The Mountain Dew spin-off brand Code Red performed well between 2001 and 2003, but its success was believed to have come at least partially at the expense of the core brand. In 2004 Mountain Dew returned to form, outpacing all other full-calorie soft drinks with sales volume growth of 1.5 percent.

"Do the Dew" remained vital and effective at maintaining Mountain Dew's brand image regardless of the vicissitudes of the beverage industry. In 2003 *Adweek* columnist Barbara Lippert reflected on the cultural significance of the preceding 10 years of Mountain Dew advertising, noting that the brand had debuted its "dude-centric" approach "before the *Dumb and Dumber* guys and a half-generation pre-*Jackass*... when Ashton Kutcher was learning cursive and the Dell dude was wearing a night brace... And the campaign has remained fresh and imaginative through all those wild, nature-defying executions." Although numerous marketers attempted to replicate the Mountain Dew formula for appealing to youth, none was able to make itself as synonymous with an enduring set of youth values as Mountain Dew did through its seemingly timeless "extreme" positioning.

FURTHER READING

Chura, Hillary. "Pepsi Tests More Dew." *Advertising Age* (midwest ed.), December 18, 2000.

Enrico, Dottie. "Mountain Dew's Hip Ads Refresh Viewers." *USA Today,* May 18, 1998, p. 4B.

"Fatal Pursuit: Behind a Zany Mountain Dew Ad Lies the Sad Saga of the Death of Pro Skydiver Rob Harris." *People Weekly,* July 15, 1996, p. 154.

Hein, Kenneth. "Dew unto Others." *Brandweek,* April 8, 2002.

Horovitz, Bruce. "Marketers Get in Line for Extreme Sports." *USA Today,* June 2, 1997, p. 10B.

Johnson, Greg. "Advertising & Marketing; Mountain Dew Hits New Heights to Help Pepsi Grab a New Generation; No. 4 Soft Drink Has Succeeded by Taking Extreme Measures Since

Its Hillbilly Days and Its 'Tickle-Your-Innards' Slogan." *Los Angeles Times,* October 6, 1999.

Lippert, Barbara. "Long Live the Dudes." *Adweek,* June 2, 2003.

Prince, Greg W. "Give Them Their Dew: Credit Pepsi for Marketing a Mountain of a Brand." *Beverage World,* January 15, 1998.

Roush, Chris. "Coca-Cola's New Surge Taking Different Tack." *Atlanta Journal-Constitution,* December 17, 1996.

Robert Schnakenberg
Mark Lane

DRINK MORE WATER CAMPAIGN

OVERVIEW

In 2004, when PepsiCo and advertising agency BBDO New York released the Aquafina "Drink More Water" campaign, Aquafina was the best-selling bottled water in the United States. With "Drink More Water," Aquafina highlighted the pure fun of water, straying slightly from its long-established focus on the young athlete. Still, the campaign embodied Aquafina's dismissal of the pretentious bottled-water image of the past. It was also intended as a means to maintain Aquafina's number-one position in the U.S. bottled-water market. Since its 1999 launch, Coca-Cola's Dasani water in particular had been infringing upon Aquafina's market.

The campaign debuted to 30 million viewers on July 13, 2004, during the broadcast of Major League Baseball's 75th All-Star Game. The initial spot, "Drink Up," helped to create a connection between water (in particular, Aquafina water) and happy fun. It depicted a barroom scene with an unusual twist: the happy, singing crowd, all gathered in a Bavarian-style beer garden, was not, in fact, guzzling beer. Instead, all were toasting with water. "Make your body happy," said a voice-over, "Drink more water!" BBDO released another television commercial, "I Feel Pretty," for the campaign in 2004 as well as two more in 2005. All the spots followed the happy and fun theme of "Drink Up." Print ads that ran in major magazines as well as on billboards also hyped up water's pure fun. PepsiCo did not disclose the campaign's budget.

The "Drink More Water" campaign found widespread success. A number of advertising awards and recognitions rolled in, including a WIN (Women's Image Network) Ad Award, a bronze New York Festivals Advertising Award, and a nomination for an Emmy Award for best commercial. There were also financial benefits. In 2004 Aquafina sales grew in the double digits. In the first quarter of 2005 the bottled water experienced a 25 percent growth in sales. For PepsiCo, whose cola sales had been dwindling for more than a decade, this was good news. In the summer of 2005, one year after the start of "Drink More Water," PepsiCo reported its biggest quarterly gain in sales in more than three years. Aquafina (along with Gatorade sports drinks and Lipton tea) were credited for this growth.

HISTORICAL CONTEXT

By the 1990s consumers nationwide were increasingly purchasing healthier beverages, such as teas, fruit drinks, sports drinks, diet colas, and bottled waters. In response soda companies rushed to diversify their beverage varieties. Bottled water, for one, caught the attention of such companies. From 1976 to 1986 U.S. bottled-water consumption rose by more than one billion gallons (from 354 million gallons to 1.366 billion gallons) per year. Within the following decade the number increased dramatically, to nearly 3.5 billion gallons a year. In 1994 PepsiCo jumped on board, launching its first bottled-water brand, Aquafina.

The 1994 release of Aquafina was small and local, beginning in Wichita, Kansas. Though full national distribution of the product did not occur until 1997, larger marketing efforts soon evolved. In May 1995 Aquafina cosponsored the third All-Star Benefit Concert, a charity concert and auction to benefit the Pediatric AIDS Foundation. The event's auction took place online, becoming accessible to 30 million subscribers worldwide. This, plus the large celebrity presence at the event, generated the first widespread recognition of the Aquafina name. Further promotional efforts followed, and in July 1997 Aquafina began its first national print and radio ad campaign under the tagline "Take Me to the Water." The campaign, which cost Pepsi $8 to $10 million in the first year alone, was intended to change bottled water's image as stuffy and overpriced. It initiated Aquafina's long-term association of its water with healthy young adults, in particular athletes. As such, "Take Me to the Water" centered on a trio of sports sponsorships: the Association of Volleyball Professionals, U.S. Soccer, and the Professional Golfers' Association.

In 1999 Aquafina reaffirmed its connection with athletes when it became the lead sponsor of the All-American Soccer Stars Victory Tour. Aquafina's first national television campaign, which had the tagline "Every part of your body needs pure water," was introduced in 2000. The campaign continued Aquafina's focus on a young-adult target market. Success followed, as sales of Aquafina jumped by an astonishing 59.4 percent from 2000 to 2001. In 2003 Aquafina launched what was then its biggest national campaign, "Aquafina

Pure Luck." The campaign doubled as a rewards program, offering consumers a chance to win cash prizes for being spotted with Aquafina products. By 2004, when "Drink More Water" was released, Aquafina had become the U.S. bottled-water business's first billion-dollar brand as well as the nation's top-selling bottled water.

TARGET MARKET

"It wasn't long ago [that] bottled water was considered an oddity, an affectation, a pretentious luxury good. Who drank only bottle water? Snobs... effetes... Hollywood phonies." So said BevNet.com writer Greg Prince. For a long time this had been the predominant image of bottled water. Over the course of the 1990s the image began to change. The shift coincided with the growth of an active and health-conscious population, especially among those in the young-adult age group. Full-calorie soft drinks were going out of style; healthy, low-sugar, low-calorie beverages were in. And what could be lower in calories, and more beneficial to health, than water? The problem was that tap water could contain contaminants, and more often simply did not pass the taste test among drinkers. Thus, a lucrative bottled-water market emerged.

Right away Aquafina identified its target drinkers: healthy, active adults aged 25 to 39. By 1997, the year it began national distribution, Aquafina had become the official sponsor of three professional athletic organizations: the Association of Volleyball Professionals, U.S. Soccer, and the Professional Golfers' Association. Thus, its image and its target market were immediately carved into consumers' minds. And it was a very different target market from that of the luxury bottled water of years prior. Aquafina did not hesitate to point this out. In television spots that aired in 1998, Aquafina, alluding to Evian's pricey brand and pretentiousness, mockingly referred to its competitor's water as "Envie." Aquafina's then-tagline, "Pure water. No additives. No attitude," along with a lower price, further reinforced its unpretentious image, thus directly appealing to the young-adult market. By focusing on the all-inclusive fun of water, the "Drink More Water" campaign diverted slightly from the young athlete. Still, Aquafina's target market remained the same.

COMPETITION

Coca-Cola entered the U.S. bottled-water scene a little late, in 1999, with the introduction of Dasani. Coca-Cola, like PepsiCo, was well aware of the consumer trend toward healthier drinks, including water. Yet Coke was hesitant to jump into the bottled-water market, as it continued to hold optimism that the trend would reverse and that consumers would return to their beloved sodas. But in 1998, a year prior to Dasani's launch, the bottled-water industry was up to $4.3 billion, reflecting a nearly 10 percent increase from the previous year. As such, Pepsi's main rival was drawn in. Though late to the game, Dasani found immediate success. In 1999, with only a half a year of distribution, Dasani jumped to the number-five spot in U.S. bottled-water sales.

In 2000 Coca-Cola released a $15 million national ad campaign for Dasani. "Life Simplified" focused on the busy and stressed-out woman, revealing how her life could be simplified by drinking Dasani. Dasani's target market consisted of women ages 25 to 49. The marketing approach worked. Soon after "Life Simplified" was presented to the public, Dasani climbed its way to the number-two U.S. bottled-water distributor spot, with nearly $150 million in sales. That number, however, lagged far behind Aquafina's $203 million. In response Coca-Cola switched marketing gears. While Aquafina was promoting "Drink More Water" in 2004, Dasani was infringing upon the athletic market with its "Go for Six" campaign. The latter campaign teamed up with Tour de France bicycling champion Lance Armstrong as a way to reinforce Dasani's tagline, "Can't Live without Dasani."

Food giant Nestlé found tremendous success in the U.S. bottled-water market. Nestlé's water offerings had grown to include 10 separate brands, which, when accumulated, made Nestlé the top-selling bottled-water distributor in the United States. In 2003 Nestlé had three of the top-five-selling U.S. bottled-water brands (Poland Spring, Arrowhead, and Deer Park) as well as six among the top ten. That year Poland Spring, holding 7.8 percent of market share and $649 million in sales, sat at number three. In its marketing Poland Spring reminded customers that its water was true "spring water," from deep in the Maine woods (as opposed to the top-two

DIRTY WATER

In 1999 the Natural Resources Defense Council (NRDC), a top U.S. environmental-action organization, completed a comprehensive four-year study on the quality of bottled water. After testing more than 1,000 bottles of 103 brands of bottled water, the NRDC disclosed that approximately one-third of waters tested contained levels of contamination. The NRDC's findings did not seem to affect bottled-water sales. By 2002 wholesale U.S. bottled-water sales had reached 7.8 billion. By 2003 the number had increased to 8.3 billion.

brands, Aquafina and Dasani, which both used filtered municipal water). Or, as Poland Spring's longtime slogan claimed, its water represented "What it means to be from Maine."

MARKETING STRATEGY

Aquafina, with ad agency BBDO New York, debuted its "Drink More Water" campaign on July 13, 2004, during the broadcast of Major League Baseball's 75th All-Star Game. To the 30 million viewers who tuned in, Aquafina revealed an entirely new kind of "watering hole." The "Drink Up" TV spot opened at a city intersection, empty except for a lone male accordion player and his dog. The reason that the streets were empty was quickly revealed: everyone was at a local Bavarian-style beer garden, singing and carousing. "Drink! Drink! Drink!" they sang. "To eyes that are bright as stars when they're shining on me!" Then came the final twist. The patrons were not toasting beer, as one might expect. Instead, each and every glass, bottle, and jug was filled with (Aquafina) water. The spot concluded with a voice-over stating, "Drink to your health; because the more water you drink, the better you'll feel. So make your body happy. Drink more water!" For 60 seconds the viewer was transported to pure fun. Or, as ad critic Lewis Lazare of the *Chicago Sun-Times* put it, the commercial hit the viewer "like a giant burst of energy unlike any we've experienced in television advertising in quite some time." The spot ran through the end of 2004 and continued in 2005.

A theme of pure musical fun continued with the release of the "I Feel Pretty" television commercial in 2004. In this fast-moving spot various ordinary-looking people—from an old man on a lawn mower to a city cabdriver to a pig farmer—flashed on the screen, smiling and drinking Aquafina, while the *West Side Story* tune "I Feel Pretty" played in the background. The commercial's voice-over said, "Drinking water. Makes you feel better, look better, and your whole body more beautiful. Make your body happy. Drink more water. Aquafina." The spot continued to air into 2005. Also in 2005, two additional television commercials were added to the campaign: "On Top of the World" (which used the Carpenters' tune of the same name) and "Man and Woman."

In addition to the television spots, Aquafina's "Drink More Water" involved large-scale print and billboard advertising. The print campaign ran in the 2004 year-end issues of *People, Sports Illustrated,* and *Time* magazines. To celebrate the 2005 New Year, Aquafina put up its first-ever billboard in New York City's Times Square. In a spirit much like that of the "Drink Up" television commercial, the billboard urged consumers to drink water in order to celebrate and have a good time. "Make your body happy, drink more water," the sign read. A similar billboard appeared at the New Year's 2005 celebration at the intersection of Hollywood and Vine in Los Angeles. Last, to further reinforce a connection between Pepsi's bottled water and New Year's celebrations, Aquafina became the official water of MTV's "Iced Out New Year's 2005."

OUTCOME

Aquafina and BBDO's "Drink Up" television commercial gained widespread recognition in the advertising world. Advertising critic Lewis Lazare said, "Aquafina has decided just to hit hard on the fact that water makes your body happy, so it's smart to drink lots of it. The message is smart. But more importantly, it's being delivered in a commercial that engulfs us with bliss... How refreshing." Others also took notice. In 2004 "Drink Up" was given a WIN (Women's Image Network) Ad Award. The award honored creatively excellent advertising that portrayed women as empowered. The winning of this award suggested that Aquafina, indeed, had reached its female target market. The commercial was also nominated in 2005 for an Emmy for best commercial and was a finalist for a Clio Award. The Emmy and Clio had come to represent the epitome of positive advertising recognition. "I Feel Pretty" was also admired and won a bronze at the New York Festivals Advertising Awards.

Consumers liked the advertisements as well. In a poll that Pepsi conducted about the Aquafina brand, most respondents stated that they found the campaign effective in communicating a memorable message. Aquafina's 2004 sales grew in the double digits; in the first quarter of 2005 sales grew by 25 percent. In the larger picture, Aquafina's success helped to improve PepsiCo's sales, even at a time when sales of the company's signature cola had been slipping. In the summer of 2005, for instance, PepsiCo reported its biggest quarterly gain sales in three and a half years. This increase was attributed to three of Pepsi's noncarbonated beverages: Gatorade sports drinks, Lipton tea, and Aquafina water.

FURTHER READING

"Aquafina Plays Up Pure Water Necessities in First National TV Advertising Campaign." *PR Newswire,* May 15, 2000.

Benezra, Karen. "Real Money: Advertising Activity in the Media Marketplace." *Mediaweek,* June 2, 1997.

"Bottled Water Is Almost the Real Thing." *Sunday Star Times* (Wellington, New Zealand), February 21, 1999, p. 13.

"Bottled Water: Pure Drink or Pure Hype?" *Natural Resources Defense Council,* March 1999. Available from <http://www.nrdc.org/water/drinking/nbw.asp>

Furman, Phyllis. "Watered Down." *New York Daily News,* December 23, 2004.

Lazare, Lewis. "Ad Makes Beer Garden Truly a Watering Hole." *Chicago Sun-Times,* July 28, 2004, p. 75.

Leith, Scott. "Coke, Pepsi Unleash Flood of Ad Muscle for Branding Water." *Atlanta Journal-Constitution,* July 12, 2001.

"102.7 KIIS-FM and Aquafina Unite for the 3rd All-Star Benefit Concert." *Business Wire,* May 25, 1995.

Prince, Greg W. "It's the Little Differences." *BevNet.com,* July 25, 2004. Available from <http://www.bevnet.com/news/2004/07-25-2004-prince_the_little_differences.asp>.

"Profit Slips at PepsiCo, but Big Sales Lift Shares." *New York Times,* September 30, 2005, p. 5.

Turcsik, Richard. "Pepsi Expecting to Get Big Bang From Pop." *Business and Industry,* January 15, 1996, p. 20.

Unger, Henry. "Coke Launches Advertising Campaign to Boost Bottled-Water Line." *Atlanta Journal-Constitution,* June 3, 2000.

Vranica, Suzanne. "Advertising: Partyers Knock Back a Few ... Aquafinas." *Wall Street Journal,* July 13, 2004, p. B4.

Candice L.Mancini

GENERATION NEXT CAMPAIGN

OVERVIEW

For more than 30 years PepsiCo, Inc. has been courting younger consumers, and youthful cola drinkers have formed a major battleground for Pepsi and its number one rival, Coca-Cola. The struggle for this demographic was especially contentious because teenagers made up the largest group of soft drink consumers in the United States.

The PepsiCo Inc.'s 1997 advertising campaign, featuring the theme slogan "Generation Next," was unveiled during the national telecast of professional football's championship game between the Green Bay Packers and the New England Patriots. The new commercials were created by Pepsi's longtime agency BBDO. A new Pepsi "globe" logo was introduced at that time as well. For the far-reaching "Generation Next" campaign, PepsiCo Inc. forged powerful marketing alliances with Major League Baseball and the international pop group the Spice Girls. These complex promotions were touted by the soda maker's marketing officials as vital forms of outreach to the global youth culture. By and large, consumers responded favorably to these initiatives. By 1998, however, PepsiCo's executives and bottlers were beginning to rethink a strategy that was focused on only one segment of a large and diverse soft drink market.

HISTORICAL CONTEXT

PepsiCo Inc. was founded in 1965 through the merger of Pepsi-Cola Company and Frito-Lay, Inc. By the 1990s it was the second-largest maker of soft drinks in the United States and among the most successful consumer products companies in the world, with annual revenues of more than $20 billion and about 140,000 employees. PepsiCo had achieved a leadership position in each of its two major packaged goods businesses: beverages and snack foods. The company was a world leader in soft drink bottling and the world's largest producer of snack chips. PepsiCo's brand names were some of the best known and most respected in the world.

Pepsi-Cola provided advertising, marketing, sales, and promotional support to Pepsi-Cola bottlers and food service customers, and its advertising was among the world's most recognized. Traditional features of Pepsi advertising included humor, an emphasis on youth, and the use of storylines.

As early as the 1960s Pepsi signaled its intention to win over young consumers with its tag line "Pepsi—For Those Who Think Young." In 1963 the soda giant unveiled its "Pepsi Generation" tag line, created by agency BBDO. This long-running campaign was replaced by "The Choice of a New Generation" in the 1980s and revised in 1997 as "Generation Next."

On January 21, 1997, PepsiCo Inc. launched a new advertising campaign designed to stake the company's claim to the global youth culture. "Generation Next" commercials began airing in markets worldwide shortly thereafter. Pepsi, which had purchased ad time during the previous 12 Super Bowls, secured a total of four commercial minutes before, during, and after the 1997 Super Bowl. A total of six Pepsi spots were aired during the championship contest, three of which can be summarized as follows. "Shaq/Shaft" featured gargantuan NBA superstar Shaquille O'Neal in a takeoff on the 1970s blaxploitation classic *Shaft* starring Richard Roundtree. New music was recorded for the spot by Oscar-winning *Shaft* composer Isaac Hayes. In "Bears" a computer animated gaggle of grizzlies called the "Village Bears" danced to the Village People chestnut "YMCA." In perhaps the most enduring ad, supermodels Cindy Crawford, Tyra Banks, and Bridget Hall blew kisses to "Norman Pheeny," an infant fresh out of the maternity ward, while they were drinking Pepsi. The accompanying voice-over dubbed Pheeny a "Pepsi drinker for life."

In March 1997 PepsiCo, Inc. and Major League Baseball announced a broad five-year marketing alliance that sought to expand the bonds between Pepsi's youthful "Generation Next" consumers and America's national pastime. As part of this deal, PepsiCo Inc. agreed to advertise heavily on national television broadcasts of baseball games. The soft drink giant also agreed to produce a series of baseball-oriented television ads for airing during the 1998 season. The deal also made Pepsi the official soft drink of Major League Baseball and gave the soft drink giant exclusive rights to use Major League Baseball's trademarks, including postseason event logos (such as the World Series), the All-Star Game logo, and collective use of Major League Baseball team marks, in advertising, packaging, merchandising, and promotions.

The Spice Girls, an international all-female pop music combo, forged their own alliance with the soda maker in May 1997. The first details of this relationship were leaked to the press via *London Music Week* magazine. The massive promotional relationship easily eclipsed Pepsi's previous music sponsorship deals with such artists as Michael Jackson, Tina Turner, Madonna, and Lionel Richie.

TARGET MARKET

Pepsi officials repeatedly defined the target market for "Generation Next" in one word: youth. "There is an identity at Pepsi which is timeless," observed Brian Swette, executive vice president and chief marketing officer for Pepsi-Cola North America. "Essentially, it's about being eternally youthful. Youth means innovation and optimism—with a sense of humor and just a little cynicism. That's what being youthful is about, and that's the character of the brand."

Young consumers, who form their brand preferences early in life, responded favorably to Pepsi's efforts to gear its advertising toward them. According to one market study, Pepsi ads ranked number two in popularity with children aged 6 to 17. The soda maker's shrewd use of rock music performers, sports stars, and whiz-bang special effects have often been cited as the reasons for this strong showing.

An emphasis on youth and youth culture informed many of the marketing initiatives undertaken by Pepsi with its "Generation Next" campaign. High-profile promotional deals with the Spice Girls and Major League Baseball seemed designed to enhance Pepsi's image with the youth demographic. By and large Pepsi's marketing partners benefited from the newly forged relationships as well. "This association is great for baseball," crowed Allan H. "Bud" Selig, chairman of the Major League Baseball executive council. "Pepsi is uniquely qualified to infuse the game with contemporary youthfulness and help reconnect baseball with America's kids and teens, one of our key goals."

COMPETITION

In the competitive soft drink market, Pepsi's volume gains lagged behind Coca-Cola's through much of the 1990s. From 1994 through 1997 Coke's share of the U.S. soft drink market grew from 41 percent to 43.9 percent, while Pepsi's slipped from 31.2 percent to 30.9 percent, according to Beverage Digest/Maxwell data.

To stem this tide, PepsiCo Inc. decided on a new advertising and marketing strategy. In mid-January 1997 PepsiCo Inc. executives huddled with the company's bottlers in New Orleans, where top officials—including CEO Roger Enrico—outlined Pepsi's "Generation Next" initiative. Insiders expected the number two ranked soft drink giant to introduce global themes designed to improve the performance of its overseas divisions. A more aggressive approach on pricing and store displays, in response to successful Coke initiatives in these areas, was forecast as well.

MARKETING STRATEGY

The tag line for PepsiCo's 1997 campaign, "Generation Next," represented something of a return to the company's roots. Replacing the two-year-old theme "Nothing Else Is a Pepsi," the new theme echoed one of Pepsi's most memorable campaigns of previous years, which featured the tag line "Choice of a New Generation." Both themes were concocted by the New

"GENERATION LESS"

The "Generation Next" campaign is considered a failure by most industry analysts, but another of the cola giant's moves of 1997 won instant accolades from its shareholders. In January of that year PepsiCo Inc. announced that it was spinning off its restaurant subsidiaries into a separate company. The decision was taken to allow Pepsi to concentrate on its core packaged food businesses.

The restaurant unit—comprising the popular chains KFC (formerly Kentucky Fried Chicken), Pizza Hut, and Taco Bell—would thereafter have its own management and corporate structure. PepsiCo retained direct control over its other two units, Pepsi (soft drinks) and Frito Lay (snack foods), businesses it believed were of a distinctly different dynamic than fast food.

Wall Street responded enthusiastically to the change. When the news came down, PepsiCo Inc. stock surged by 11 percent in the first day alone. Market analysts believed that investors would respond favorably to the spin-off in the long term as well.

York ad agency BBDO. The "Generation Next" campaign was designed to leverage Pepsi's "generation" equities of humor and humanity while positioning Pepsi and its drinkers as looking in anticipation to the future. The new spots encompassed a diverse swath of themes and characters but retained traditional Pepsi features like the storyline approach.

One of the spots, entitled "Move Over," employed original music and images to depict how "Generation Next" reflected the lives of contemporary youth—their likes, their language, and their attitude. A series of other storyline spots offered a mix of Pepsi-style humor, irreverence, and attitude. The humor this time was a bit edgier than in past campaigns, with a more concerted focus on youth. The entire campaign was linked together with a new brand icon: a spiraling Pepsi globe bearing the legend "Generation Next." "Generation Next is an ageless, borderless idea that defines Pepsi and its drinkers with style, wit, and attitude," remarked Brain Swette, PepsiCo's executive vice president of global marketing. "And in today's global youth culture—where styles and attitudes aren't limited by languages or boundaries—the time is right to unleash this idea on the world."

The campaign relied heavily on big-name celebrity endorsers like gargantuan NBA star Shaquille O'Neal and supermodel Cindy Crawford. In addition, Pepsi unveiled a massive promotion tied to Lucasfilm's re-release of the popular *Star Wars* movie trilogy. But the most far-reaching marketing partnerships were those forged with Major League Baseball and the Spice Girls, respectively.

The baseball partnership included a number of innovative marketing initiatives. For starters, the new relationship gave Pepsi exclusive rights to Major League Baseball's All-Star balloting program. The soft drink purveyor then used the balloting effort to execute a nationwide promotion tying together 6,000 7-Eleven stores and a Fox TV watch-and-win sweepstakes program. Baseball fans were able to vote online via the Pepsi Internet web site. As part of the All-Star Game festivities, PepsiCo Inc. participated at the annual All-Star Fanfest, held in 1997 at the Cleveland Convention Center. The synergy here was fortuitous because Pepsi served as the official soft drink of the Cleveland Indians and Jacobs Field, the park where the 1997 All-Star Game was played.

A baseball component was also added to PepsiCo Inc.'s popular "Pepsi Stuff" giveaway program, which provided free youth-oriented merchandise to loyal Pepsi consumers. The 1997 edition of Pepsi Stuff featured New York Yankee shortstop Derek Jeter in more than 100 million catalogs distributed across the United States. A new wrinkle to Pepsi Stuff was the inclusion of a special "fantasy prize" in which a lucky fan was awarded the opportunity to throw out the ceremonial first pitch at Game Two of the 1997 World Series between the Cleveland Indians and the Florida Marlins.

Pepsi's effort to reach out to young baseball fans was not limited to the traditional marketing avenues, however. Nontraditional initiatives included the placing of postings on Major League Baseball's official World Wide Web site. Pepsi also pledged to sponsor the MTV cable network's "Rock 'n' Jock" and "Pepsi All-Star Softball Games," as well as activity on the Channel One educational classroom network.

The partnership with Major League Baseball cemented PepsiCo Inc.'s longtime involvement in America's national pastime. In the late 1990s the soft drink maker also served as the official soft drink of the Chicago Cubs, Seattle Mariners, and Kansas City Royals, as well as the 1998 expansion teams, the Arizona Diamondbacks, and Tampa Bay Devil Rays. Pepsi also maintained relationships with almost half of America's minor league franchises.

With the Spice Girls, a Europop supergroup, Pepsi was sailing into uncharted waters, establishing a relationship with an up-and-coming entity in the hopes of tapping into the worldwide youth market. The cornerstone of this partnership was the release of a new Spice Girls song, "Step to Me," to be made available only through a Pepsi promotion and not through traditional record retailers. Tickets to the only Spice Girls concert of the year, in Istanbul, Turkey, were made available solely through a Pepsi offer as well.

The Spice Girls also agreed to appear in commercials for Pepsi. The first of these, a 30-second spot featuring the group wailing the Pepsi theme "Move Over," was screened on television and in movie theaters during the summer of 1997. A second commercial promoted the Spice Girls single and concert offers. The promotions were made available to consumers in 78 countries in Europe and Africa, and the spots were screened worldwide, including in North America, the Far East, and Australia.

Pepsi also hooked up with other bands, like 3T and Shaggy, featuring them in promotional advertising offering prizes of concert tickets and merchandise. The soda maker limited the use of these musical groups to the countries in which they were popular. In another bid to capture the youth market, Pepsi contracted with MTV to offer tickets to the cable channel's Video Music Awards in September.

OUTCOME

Public reaction to Pepsi's first batch of "Generation Next" commercials was largely favorable. *USA Today*'s instant Ad Meter found that both the dancing bears and the Norman Pheeny spots won over consumers as their favorite commercials aired during the Super Bowl telecast. A second survey taken the next day found the Pepsi commercials were recalled by more than half of the respondents polled. Anheuser-Busch was a distant second with only a 36 percent recall score.

Industry analysts were split in their judgment on the new commercials, however. *Advertising Age* magazine rated the Pepsi Super Bowl spots "profoundly disappointing," claiming the spots fell "flatter than a two-liter bottle left uncapped overnight." The *Florida Times-Union* took the opposite tack, placing the Pepsi commercials as a group among its Super Bowl "hits." The *Milwaukee Journal Sentinel* seemed to call it both ways, declaring that Pepsi's "lame 'Generation Next' slogan didn't do it" but conceding victory in the ad wars to the soda maker on the strength of its commercials.

Ultimately, "Generation Next" failed to win favor with the most important audience of all: PepsiCo itself. The campaign's commercials elicited sharp criticism from Pepsi bottlers and top brass at the company's annual convention in January 1998. The spots were lambasted for failing to address a wide enough audience and not effectively showcasing Pepsi's new globe icon. Increasingly bottlers complained that the edgier, more youth-oriented spots were alienating important audience segments. In 1998 its lead agency was asked to retool a portion of the campaign, which retained the "Generation Next" tag line. The soda giant was also reportedly examining a possible consolidation of its $170 million U.S. media planning and buying efforts for Pepsi and Frito Lay.

FURTHER READING

Ashton, Robert. "Spice Girls Add Fizz to Pepsi Power." *Music Week*, May 10, 1997.

Benezra, Karen. "Pepsi Again Talkin' 'bout Generation." *Brandweek*, January 20, 1997.

———. "Strategy: NEXT!" *Brandweek*, April 13, 1998.

Fahey, Alison. "It's a Pepsi Generation, Again." *Adweek*, January 20, 1997.

Robert Schnakenberg

THE JOY OF PEPSI CAMPAIGN

OVERVIEW

By 2001 PepsiCo, Inc., had long been suffering the effects of consumers' quest for healthier beverages. Though the company's offerings of Gatorade, Aquafina, Propel, and Tropicana Orange Juice, as well as its diet sodas, were experiencing growth, PepsiCo's signature cola sales had been on a steady decline. Yet PepsiCo was far from giving up on its star drink. The company turned to a multimillion dollar campaign, "The Joy of Pepsi," that enlisted megastars Britney Spears, Beyoncé Knowles, and Shakira. Replacing "The Joy of Cola," the new campaign, which was created by advertising agency BBDO New York, represented a major attempt to appeal to customers' tastes, especially those in the younger age brackets.

"The Joy of Pepsi" had its premier with a television spot, "Testimonial," that ran during the 2001 Super Bowl. The intention of the spot, which starred former U.S. Senator Bob Dole, was to represent youthfulness despite age. Nearly 80 at the time, Dole claimed that Pepsi helped keep him young. Later in the campaign a younger and hipper group of spokespeople were used to persuade consumers of the youthful side of Pepsi. Spears, as seen in her debut Pepsi ad, "Britney Rooftop," embodied this approach. In the television spot, which was first aired during the 2001 Academy Awards ceremonies, she performed what was billed as her new "hit," titled "The Joy of Pepsi." Before its debut on television, the spot was given a major buildup, which included online viewing. In all, 14 television spots, as well as extensive print and online advertisements, were included in "The Joy of Pepsi."

"The Joy of Pepsi" was extraordinarily popular, especially among its target market of teens and young adults. For example, an incredible 2 million viewers saw "Britney Rooftop" online before it appeared on television. The campaign also won a number of honors from the advertising industry. But all this did not mean that it succeeded in increasing the sales of Pepsi. During 2003 Pepsi actually suffered a drop in sales of more than 5 percent. Over the longer term, from 2000 to 2003, sales of Pepsi dropped approximately 12 percent. PepsiCo did not throw in the towel, however, although it did change its advertising strategy. The "Pepsi. It's the Cola" campaign, which replaced "The Joy of Pepsi" in 2003, took a more direct and practical approach to selling the drink. Instead of relying on celebrities, who were expensive and who sometimes stole the show from the product, the new campaign highlighted the various foods that tasted good with Pepsi.

HISTORICAL CONTEXT

Pepsi was first introduced in 1893 under the name "Brad's drink." Created by Caleb Bradham, a pharmacist, the beverage was made of carbonated water, sugar, vanilla, various oils, pepsin, and flavoring from cola nuts. It quickly became the most popular drink in the pharmacy. In 1898 Bradham renamed the beverage Pepsi Cola, for the pepsin and cola nuts used in the recipe, and further success followed. But the company manufacturing the drink suffered a series of bankruptcies, including one in which Bradham lost control of the firm, before it finally became stable. Under the ownership of the Loft Candy Company, beginning in 1931, Pepsi had huge success when it introduced a 12-ounce bottle for five cents, which had formerly been the price of a 6-ounce bottle. "Nickel Nickel," the first advertising jingle ever broadcast nationwide on radio, was introduced in 1940 and was later recorded in 55 languages. The firm's stability was established, and in the following year it became a public company.

Early Pepsi advertising campaigns played off the "Nickel Nickel" jingle with such slogans as "Twice as Much" and "Why Take Less When Pepsi's Best?" Then, with a 1953 campaign called "The Light Refreshment," Pepsi shifted its focus from lower prices to a lower caloric content. Soon thereafter, however, teens and young adults began to emerge as Pepsi's main consumers, and the marketing focus shifted once again. The 1958 tagline "Be Sociable. Have a Pepsi" represented the first major targeting of youth. During the 1960s the "Now It's Pepsi, for Those Who Think Young" and "Pepsi Generation" campaigns continued the company's concentration on young consumers. The latter campaign went a step further, however, focusing not only on youth but on their lifestyle as well. For a number of years the company maintained this marketing approach. At the same time it never lost enthusiasm for advertising jingles, thus setting the stage for later campaigns that relied on music.

TARGET MARKET

The 2001 campaign "The Joy of Pepsi" was the latest in a long line of advertising efforts from PepsiCo, beginning with "Be Sociable. Have a Pepsi" in 1958, that targeted young people. The previous campaign, "The Joy of Cola," which dated to 1999, had strayed somewhat from this focus by attempting to reach both younger and older consumers. In this campaign spokespeople like Marlon Brando and Aretha Franklin, as well as the 1970s heavy metal band KISS, had turned the focus toward an older customer base. Even so, PepsiCo did not neglect younger consumers with "The Joy of Cola." The company, for example, undertook a promotional tie-in with the film *Star Wars: Episode 1,* which was extremely popular with teens.

Thus, "The Joy of Pepsi" was in a sense an updated return to the focus on a youthful lifestyle. The company wanted young consumers to identify personally with Pepsi, as they had done in the past with the help of campaigns that used such celebrities as Kirk Cameron, Michael Jackson, and Gloria Estefan. It was with this in mind that Spears was chosen to promote the product. The effort was reinforced in 2002 when Pepsi signed on Knowles, another illustrious pop star, as part of "The Joy of Pepsi." But the new campaign did not entirely neglect those in older age brackets, especially consumers who longed for a return to youth. Thus, the television premier of "The Joy of Pepsi" starred the far-from-young Dole, who was approaching 80, as its spokesperson. In the spot, which was titled "Testimonial," the World War II hero and former U.S. senator from Kansas who had run for president in 1996, touted Pepsi as a fountain of youth, even ending the spot with a back flip on a beach.

COKE'S LOST OPPORTUNITY?

In 1931 Charles Guth, president of the Loft Candy Company, asked the Coca-Cola Company to give him a discount on the soda he bought in huge quantities for the approximately 200 stores he operated. After Coca-Cola had refused, he purchased the firm manufacturing Pepsi. Later, however, when sales of Pepsi remained flat, Guth was desperate enough to approach his old rival with an offer to sell. But Coca-Cola would not even make a bid. Then Guth began selling 12-ounce bottles of Pepsi for the 6-ounce price, sales skyrocketed, and Pepsi became a longstanding competitor of Coke.

COMPETITION

The rivalry between Pepsi and Coke had begun in 1931 when Charles Guth, head of a chain of candy stores, became angry with the Coca-Cola Company for what he felt was their overcharging for syrup. To get even, Guth purchased Pepsi, setting the stage for what was to develop into one of the biggest corporate rivalries in history. The rivalry pitted an image of heritage (Coke) against one of taste (Pepsi). In blind taste tests among consumers Pepsi repeatedly beat Coke. Nonetheless, in worldwide sales Coke remained number one among carbonated soft drinks. Largely in response to a consumer base that continued to become more conscious of health issues, the two companies eventually moved well beyond colas to include additional types of soft drinks, as well as orange juice, bottled water, other beverages, and various snack foods. Sales of PepsiCo's soft drinks, which included Mountain Dew and Slice, fell behind Coca-Cola's, but at the same time the company's Tropicana Orange Juice, Frito-Lay snacks, and Aquafina bottled water were at the top in their respective categories.

While Spears was promoting Pepsi in the campaign "The Joy of Pepsi," such celebrities as Penelope Cruz and

Courtney Cox were advocating the "real" side of Coke. Other competitors were also using celebrities to help sell their products. Cadbury Schweppes, for instance, used the actor and comedian Orlando Jones as "the 7 UP guy." There were significant differences in the fortunes of these companies, however. In 2002, for example, Cadbury Schweppes, which offered a long line of beverages and chocolate products, had sales of $8.5 billion. On the other hand, Coca-Cola's sales in 2002 were $19.5 billion, while PepsiCo's topped the group at $25 billion. Two years later sales for Cadbury Schweppes had increased to $13 billion, for Coca-Cola to $22 billion, and for PepsiCo to $29 billion.

MARKETING STRATEGY

In the 1990s sales of Pepsi, like the colas of other companies, began a steady decline. In response PepsiCo tried a number of things to improve the image of its beverage, including the signing of a variety of celebrities for its advertising campaigns. Thus, the 2001 campaign, "The Joy of Pepsi," used celebrities that appealed to young people, including Spears, Knowles, and Shakira. The campaign represented a return to a focus on youth, something the company had begun a half century earlier. But the campaign did not entirely exclude older generations, for "The Joy of Pepsi" also wanted to remind older consumers that they, too, could feel young.

Under the guidance of the BBDO agency in New York, "The Joy of Pepsi" made its debut during the telecast of the 2001 Super Bowl and did so with someone who was not a persona of youthfulness. In the television spot "Testimonial" former politician Dole offered a spoof of his earlier commercial for Viagra, a drug used to treat erectile disfunction, which claimed that the little blue pill had returned him to a feeling of youth. In the "Testimonial" spot Dole once again made the connection between a feeling of youthfulness and a "faithful little blue friend," this time referring to Pepsi. The 60-second spot ended with Dole doing a back flip on a beach.

In all, PepsiCo aired eight television spots during the first year of the campaign. These included the "Britney Rooftop" spot, which had its premier during the telecast of the 2001 Academy Awards ceremonies. It was the first in a series of spots starring the teen idol Spears, and the build-up to its debut was extensive. In conjunction with Yahoo!, online viewing of the full commercial was allowed for two hours before it had its debut on television. More than 2 million viewers watched Spears perform the song "The Joy of Pepsi" online. In addition, PepsiCo purchased all of the advertising space available on the Yahoo! home page for the entire weekend of the 2001 Academy Awards. It was the first time that Yahoo! had sold all of its ad space to a single company.

"The Joy of Pepsi" maintained its momentum throughout 2002. In an extended spot, the 90-second "Now & Then," Spears gave consumers a brief tour of the history of Pepsi advertising while performing an updated version of her song "The Joy of Pepsi." This blockbuster spot, which had its premier during the telecast of the 2002 Super Bowl, reached millions of viewers. In addition, BBDO created three shorter versions of "Now & Then." Titled "Diner," "Beach," and "Modern Day," all starred Spears. Later that year the new pop sensation Knowles replaced Spears in the campaign. Knowles appeared in four television spots for "The Joy of Pepsi," including one in 2003 titled "Tango" in which the ardent singer danced with the nerdy employee of a convenience store. This commercial was one of three aired in 2003 that marked the end of the campaign. In addition to the television spots "The Joy of Pepsi" was supported by an extensive print and online advertising campaign. In 2003 "Pepsi. It's the Cola" replaced "The Joy of Pepsi." Like its predecessor, this new campaign stressed youth, but it took a more practical approach to advertising the cola. Instead of starring celebrities, the ads in the new campaign emphasized all of the foods that would go with a Pepsi.

OUTCOME

Both among the public and in the advertising industry "The Joy of Pepsi" was an incredibly popular campaign. Millions of fans watched Spears perform "The Joy of Pepsi" online and on television. The premier of the Spears spot on Yahoo! was chosen by *Adweek* as the Best Online Event of 2001. In 2002 "The Joy of Pepsi" won an EFFIE, and in 2003 Spears's Super Bowl spot won adage.com's Bobby Award as the best performance by a celebrity. In addition, the campaign added to Pepsi's status as a leader in multicultural advertising, and in 2002 PepsiCo received its second Corporate Mosaic Award from the American Advertising Foundation Center on Multiculturalism. "The Joy of Pepsi" also contributed to PepsiCo's overall reputation for advertising success. In 2003 PepsiCo and BBDO New York won the American Advertising Federation's first-ever Grand Addy Award for their outstanding creative endeavors over the previous two decades, and in the same year PepsiCo was honored for continuous advertising excellence at the International Advertising Festival in Cannes, France.

The popularity of "The Joy of Pepsi" and its success in the world of advertising did not mean, however, that the sales of Pepsi grew. During each year the campaign ran sales of Pepsi actually declined. In 2003, for example, sales dropped by more than 5 percent. During the period 2000 through 2003, sales of Pepsi dropped by approximately 12 percent. Some critics claimed that stars like Spears and Knowles may have overshadowed the product, creating greater recognition for the performers than for the cola. It was thought to be more likely, however, that the cause of the decline lay in the decade-long trend away from high-calorie sodas. For example, rival Coca-Cola, the leader in the cola business, was also suffering. From 2000 through 2003 sales of Coke dropped by approximately 9 percent.

As a result of falling sales and the continuing trend away from colas, PepsiCo increasingly invested in healthier beverages. In 2003, while "The Joy of Pepsi" campaign was ending on a financially unhealthy note for the cola, PepsiCo enjoyed double-digit growth in its lines of healthier beverages, which included Gatorade, Aquafina, and Propel. The company's Tropicana Orange Juice also experienced growth and maintained its number one spot in the market. But this did not mean that PepsiCo planned to abandon its signature cola. In 2005 the "Pepsi. It's the Cola" campaign was going strong, with humorous new commercials highlighting Pepsi and the foods that could accompany it. In one, for example, two "sumo chickens" wrestled each other for the honor of going home with the guy who had the Pepsi. The commercial was a hit, especially among young consumers, although it was not known whether it made them run out and buy a Pepsi.

FURTHER READING

Day, Sherri. "Pepsi Looks to Pop Stars to Reach Minorities and Mainstream." *New York Times,* August 27, 2002.

Elliot, Stuart. "In a Quest for Youth, an Old Pepsi Theme." *New York Times,* March 21, 2002, p. C8.

Fass, Allison. "Most Wanted: Drilling Down/Commercials; Pop Goes the Ad." *New York Times,* June 3, 2002, p. C10.

Horovitz, Bruce. "Marketers Aim Britney Spears to Appeal to Wider Audience." *USA Today,* February 16, 2001, p. B12.

Leith, Scott. "Ditching Divas: Pepsi Dumps Celebrities for Simpler Ads." *Atlanta Journal-Constitution,* November 20, 2003, p. F1.

Michaelson, Elizabeth. "Bob Dole Owes Joy of... to Pepsi-Cola." *Shoot,* February 9, 2001.

"Pepsi Ads Aim at More Fizz: Campaign Uncaps Multi-Talented Beyoncé Knowles." *Ottawa Citizen,* December 19, 2002, p. D4.

"Pepsi Bottlers Praise New 'Joy of Cola' Ads." *Beverage Digest,* March 12, 1999.

"Pepsi Bounces Britney for Beyoncé." *USA Today,* December 18, 2002.

"Pepsi Cans Ludacris Ads." *Houston Chronicle,* August 30, 2002, p. 2.

"Pepsi Picks Pink to Promote Drinks Campaign." *Glasgow Herald,* December 24, 2003, p. 2.

Stein, Andrew. "Hot or Not? Coca-Cola." *CNN/Money,* June 17, 2004.

Taylor, Catharine P. "Britney Leads Super Bowl Ad Lineup." *E Online,* January 31, 2002.

Terhune, Chad. "Pepsi Unveils Ad Campaign Emphasizing Food and Cola." *Wall Street Journal,* November 20, 2003.

Candice Mancini

THE NOT-SO-VANILLA VANILLA CAMPAIGN

OVERVIEW

For beverage manufacturer PepsiCo, Inc., the second half of 2003 was a time of transition for the brand identity of its signature soft drink, Pepsi. Not only did it unveil a new slogan for its core beverage, Pepsi-Cola, but a new product was also in the offing. Pepsi Vanilla was created in direct response to the successful introduction of Vanilla Coke by Pepsi's longtime rival Coca-Cola the year before. Cola volume, which had peaked in 1988 with 68 percent of the carbonated-soft-drink market, was down to 60 percent by 2002. In reaction, cola companies were expanding their soft-drink varieties to keep appealing to increasingly choice-driven consumers. *BusinessWeek* quoted David Burwick, chief marketing officer of Pepsi-Cola North America, as saying, "The era of the mass brand has been over a long time... It took our category longer than most to accept that." Within six months of that statement, Pepsi was set to go head-to-head against Coca-Cola in the battle for vanilla market share.

The "The Not-So-Vanilla Vanilla" campaign, created by advertising agency BBDO New York, led the charge as Pepsi Vanilla and its low-calorie counterpart, Diet Pepsi Vanilla, hit store shelves in August 2003. It had an estimated budget of $25 million. The campaign, which implied that Vanilla Coke's taste was overbearing and behind the times, was wide-reaching. The Pepsi Vanilla brand sponsored the National Football League's season-kickoff event. Ads directed at the younger population or those seeking variety were everywhere, from print to outdoor to online. Unlike in previous personality-driven Pepsi campaigns, the product was front and center. Television spots such as "Trucks," which featured a musical duel of sorts between a hip, hyper-customized Pepsi Vanilla truck and a mundane, older Vanilla Coke vehicle, succeeded in capturing critical and consumer attention.

The bulk of Pepsi's "The Not-So-Vanilla Vanilla" campaign was concentrated in the first two months of the product's introduction. Immediately following the campaign launch, Pepsi Vanilla enjoyed increased sales and dug into Vanilla Coke's market share, thereby accomplishing one of its primary goals. The campaign also won a number of ad-industry honors, including a Gold EFFIE Award.

HISTORICAL CONTEXT

The name Pepsi-Cola, coined by its creator, a druggist named Caleb Bradham, was meant to suggest a relationship to pepsin, which was used for medicinal purposes. Bradham patented his drink and founded the Pepsi-Cola Company in 1902, and Pepsi began to find its way into the marketplace as a health-promoting refreshment. Bradham sold the company under threat of bankruptcy in 1923 to Craven Holding Company, which did not fare much better. Growth stagnated further under the guidance of the next owner, the Loft Candy Store chain. Loft's acquisition of Pepsi in 1931 was the cola company's first jab at Coca-Cola. Sales were deathly slow until president Charles Guth made one bold last-ditch effort. He decided to offer his Depression-era consumers 12-ounce bottles, instead of the 6-ounce units sold by competitors, for the bargain price of a nickel each. Sales took off, and within a few years Pepsi was working its way into the national market.

Pepsi proved to be a cutting-edge self-promoter early on in the company's history, always with a youthful consumer in mind. The late 1930s and early 1940s saw the advent of popular cartoon characters Pepsi and Pete, a pair of Keystone Kop imitators who promoted Pepsi with the slogan "Cost small! Liked by all! Bottle tall!" in Sunday comic strip form and an animated short film. In this era, with Walter Mack at the helm of Pepsi, media usage was becoming a key tool. It was then that Pepsi became a radio-jingle pioneer with the hugely successful "Pepsi-Cola Hits the Spot," which soared to the top of the popular-music charts.

Many memorable slogans and campaigns carried the Pepsi banner since then, all with a similar mission to make each new generation a "Pepsi generation." In the sixties, under Pepsi marketing chief Alan Pottasch, the decision to acknowledge the widening gap between old and young consumers was made, and the BBDO agency won the Pepsi account. Lifestyle had always been a component in Pepsi ads, but under BBDO creative director Phil Dusenberry youth beach culture and fun-centered activities were featured. These sentiments were put forth in the slogan "for those who think young" and folk jingles such as "You've got a lot to live, and Pepsi's got a lot to give." In the 1970s "Join the Pepsi People, Feelin' Free" was an even more obvious reference to the political mood of America's youth. The 1980s and 1990s saw the rise of celebrity-focused campaigns. Pepsi spent millions to align its self with the music and media stars of each decade, most notably pop icon Michael Jackson, actor Michael J. Fox, and later, supermodel Cindy Crawford and teen sensation and singer Britney Spears.

The year 2003 marked an advertising shift for Pepsi's signature brand, Pepsi-Cola, which adopted a fresh slogan, "Pepsi, It's the Cola." Pepsi Vanilla would follow suit with its "The Not-So-Vanilla Vanilla" campaign. Youth was still king, but the celebrity-driven ads of the previous two decades were scaled back to reflect a new product-centered advertising philosophy. Catchy jingles would not play a primary part in the Pepsi Vanilla campaign either. Music was a background element or part of a storyline. In a November 2003 *Wall Street Journal* article Dave Burwick, chief marketing officer of Pepsi-Cola North America, said, "It's time we shined the light on the product itself."

TARGET MARKET

By early 2000 variety-seeking consumers had caught the attention of cola companies. Market share lost to bottled water and non-cola soft drinks was threatening the strength of flagship colas such as Pepsi. Product spin-offs were seen as an opportunity to regain fading cola sales volume, bolster signature brand identity, and retain traditionally loyal consumers whose diverse tastes might lure them in a competitor's direction. Pepsi Vanilla was created to address all these concerns.

Pepsi traditionally aimed its marketing at the youth demographic, with 25 year olds as the center of the age range, and its target audience for "The Not-So-Vanilla Vanilla" was no different. This young consumer would, Pepsi surmised, have a taste for variety and might even have a Vanilla Coke in the refrigerator. Pepsi wanted to convince these consumers to become loyal Pepsi Vanilla drinkers. Pepsi also hoped to encourage existing Pepsi drinkers to diversify their tastes and give Pepsi Vanilla a try.

COMPETITION

Throughout both their histories Pepsi-Cola and Coca-Cola were locked in a battle dubbed "the cola wars" for the hearts, minds, and dollars of beverage consumers. In 2003 the market-share leader was still Coke, with Pepsi trailing in second place. Pepsi was also facing competition from the third-largest beverage maker, Cadbury Schweppes, whose Dr Pepper was cited in *Beverage Digest* as the number one performing brand in its 2002 Top 10 listing. Dr Pepper's success was yet another indicator to Pepsi that consumers were willing to stray from the century-old mainstays and choose from a wider array of beverages.

In May 2002 the beverage industry witnessed the successful introduction of Vanilla Coke and Diet Vanilla Coke into the marketplace. It was Coca-Cola's first major successful new drink since it introduced Diet Coke some 20 years earlier. Coca-Cola's hope for its vanilla offerings was to gain market share among the teen market. The company implemented a major marketing push to promote the products, including television spots featuring actor Chazz Palminteri. In the commercials Palminteri's

PEPSI BLUE

One day prior to the introduction of Vanilla Coke in 2002, a surprise announcement came out of the Pepsi camp. It would launch a line extension of its own called Pepsi Blue, a berry-flavored cola with a strong bluish tint. While Vanilla Coke sales soared, Pepsi Blue proved to be a misstep. Pepsi Blue, developed with significant input by teens, may have been too narrowly focused and soon went the way of such ill-fated spin-offs as Crystal Pepsi, Pepsi AM, and Pepsi Max from a decade before.

imposing, tough-guy character caught teens in somewhat mischievous situations, such as sneaking looks through peepholes, and rather than punishing the teens, he commended them on their "youthful curiosity" and rewarded them with Vanilla Cokes. The launch and the campaign were successful, and Vanilla Coke quickly gained recognition and market share. Within half a year Vanilla Coke was among the top 10 brands in the highly competitive convenience-store arena.

MARKETING STRATEGY

Pepsi sought to emulate Coca-Cola's success with Vanilla Coke. It used the fact that it was the second vanilla-flavored cola to its advantage by seizing on some critiques that Vanilla Coke was too sweet and heavy tasting. The product and the "The Not-So-Vanilla Vanilla" campaign were designed to take on Vanilla Coke directly and exploit a perceived weakness. Pepsi Vanilla wanted everyone to know that its product was lighter and more refreshing, an improvement in taste and a younger approach to flavored cola. *CNN/Money* writer Parija Bhatnagar reported that the number two beverage maker was confident at launch time, quoting Pepsi marketing chief Dave DeCecco as saying, "We're doing vanilla our way. If consumers want Pepsi Vanilla, they can have it now, and we want a share of the market."

Coke may have created the vanilla-cola category, but Pepsi was determined that it not only could do vanilla better but also could woo the variety seekers by equating Pepsi Vanilla with youth culture. Youthful appeal had always been a Pepsi advertising hallmark. BBDO devised "The Not-So-Vanilla Vanilla" to acknowledge that Coke's product was first while disparaging it as old-fashioned and too sweet. To specifically address this, a two-part television commercial made its debut during the MTV Video Music Awards, a highly youth-oriented program. In both ads two young men were stymied in their quest to buy a Pepsi Vanilla when the vending machine kept going on and off, preventing them from making a purchase. There was a Vanilla Coke machine nearby, but the men made it clear that the other brand was not an option. Later it was revealed that two mischievous shop workers across the street were causing the machine's malfunction. The spot's focus played to a youthful audience, referring in part to popular prank shows of the time while also positioning Vanilla Coke as an unthinkable beverage choice.

An approximately $25 million dollar advertising budget was allotted for the introduction of Pepsi Vanilla, matching in spending the Vanilla Coke launch budget from the previous year. Pepsi Vanilla's comprehensive campaign featured print, outdoor, and online advertising as well as product placement, but the highest visibility came from four television spots, only one of which featured a celebrity, singer Beyoncé Knowles. The real standout of the four was called "Trucks" and debuted in mid-August. The commercial began with a Vanilla Coke truck stopped at an intersection alongside a Pepsi Vanilla truck. The Vanilla Coke driver challenged the Pepsi driver by cranking up a 1970s rock classic by REO Speedwagon on his radio. The confident but cool Pepsi driver was then shown flicking a switch, which converted his truck into the ultimate low-rider, blasting hip-hop music, to the delight of the young New York City onlookers. The bested Vanilla Coke driver said, "That was awesome." The voice-over that followed said, "There's a new vanilla in town. Introducing Pepsi Vanilla. The perfect blend of cola and vanilla . . . that's not so vanilla." The "Trucks" spot represented the kind of good-natured swipe against Coke that Pepsi had worked to refine over the years.

At launch time media saturation was key. A concentration of print ads appeared daily in *USA Today* four weeks running, while inserts were placed in carefully selected magazines, such as *Rolling Stone* and *Sports Illustrated.* Television spots appeared during season premieres of such highly rated shows as *ER, Law & Order,* and *Third Watch.* Outdoor ads were installed in densely populated urban areas, and online efforts included a large presence on Yahoo! as well as E-mails sent to Pepsi loyalists. Sponsorship of the one-hour National Football League Kickoff festival on September 4, 2003, was also key; the phrase "presented by Pepsi Vanilla" was even included in the title of the event. It was broadcast live on ABC, prior to the season's opening game, and featured a variety of musical acts, including Aerosmith, Britney Spears, Mary J. Blige, and Aretha Franklin. The event, conceived in coordination with the U.S. Department of Defense as a tribute to troops abroad and those in public service at home, also aired on the American Armed Forces Radio and Television Service. A sweepstakes was another part of this promotion.

OUTCOME

Pepsi's attempt to steal the thunder of the slightly older brand Vanilla Coke was successful. *USA Today*'s Ad Track weekly survey confirmed that the television spots had done their job; it reported that 25 percent of consumers polled liked the Pepsi Vanilla spots "a lot," which was above the Ad Track average of 21 percent. Ad agency BBDO also reaped the benefits of the campaign's success by winning a Gold EFFIE Award, an industry award for marketing efficacy.

Within the first two months of the campaign's introduction, sales of Pepsi Vanilla were brisk, and the product earned a market share of 1.4 percent in the convenience-store category and 1.6 percent in the mass-market channel, surpassing the company's goal of 1 percent. To Pepsi's delight, Vanilla Coke's market share dropped by approximately 1 percent immediately following the launch of Pepsi Vanilla. Sales remained strong the following year. In April 2004 the *New York Times* cited a new quarterly report by the Pepsi Bottling Group stating a 28 percent profit increase, specifically attributing a portion of that growth to Pepsi Vanilla.

FURTHER READING

"BBDO Strikes Gold at the EFFIEs; Wins More Gold than Any Other Agency." *PR Newswire,* June 8, 2005.

Bhatnagar, Parija. "Coke vs. Pepsi: What's Your Flavor?" *CNN/Money.com,* April 17, 2003. Available from <http://money.cnn.com/2003/04/17/news/companies/coke_pepsi/index.htm>

Christy, Nick. "100 Years of Advertising Innovation." *Beverage World New York,* January 1998, pp. 188–94.

Gaylin, Alison Sloane. "Truck Wars: Pepsi Vanilla Takes on Vanilla Coke." *Shoot,* September 5, 2003, p. 16.

Howard, Theresa. "Pepsi Takes Some Fizz off Vanilla Rival." *USA Today,* November 17, 2003, p. 6.

Khermouch, Gerry. "Call It the Pepsi Blue Generation." *BusinessWeek,* February 3, 2003.

Leith, Scott. "Pepsis Uses Contests, New Flavor to Put Charge Back into Sales." *Atlanta Journal-Constitution,* April 10, 2003.

Lippert, Barbara. "Pepsi Gets Peevish." *Adweek,* September 8, 2003, p. 36.

McDonough, John. "Pepsi Turns 100: One of the World's Great Brands Has Been Shaped in Large Measure by Its Advertising." *Advertising Age,* July 20, 1998.

Sfiligoj, Eric. "The Birthright Stuff." *Beverage World New York,* January 1998, pp. 237–42.

Steinberg, Brian. "Pepsi Is Planning Promotions to Put Some Fizz into Summer." *Wall Street Journal,* May 1, 2003, p. B5.

Steinberg, Brian, and Chad Terhune. "Media & Marketing—Advertising: Cola Rivals' Over-the-Top Ads Yield to Down-to-Earth Spots." *Wall Street Journal,* November 7, 2003, p. B6.

Simone Samano

ORIGINS CAMPAIGN

OVERVIEW

In 2001 PepsiCo merged with the Quaker Oats Company, giving the soda king rights to the $1.5 billion-a-year brand Gatorade. Pepsi already had its own sports drink, All Sport, but it had become clear that Gatorade's 35-year history in the market made it a formidable opponent. As such, Pepsi sold All Sport and invested heavily in the marketing of Gatorade. In 2002, after polls concluded that 60 percent of consumers had no idea where the name "Gatorade" originally came from, Pepsi had advertising agency Element 79 Partners create the Gatorade "Origins" campaign.

In 2002 Pepsi launched the first "Origins" television commercial with the straightforward desire to educate consumers about Gatorade's humble beginnings. In a style resembling a documentary, the spot showed the 1965 football field at the University of Florida, where Gatorade was invented to help the college's football team, the Florida Gators, combat dehydration. The commercial also featured a player who was on the team, the inventors of the drink, an announcer, and a sportswriter, each of whom confirmed the drink's role in the Gators' success. In 2003, with a spot called "Origins 2," the campaign moved to the NFL field, where Gatorade had also proved an early hit. In a 2005 television spot, "Testimonial," triathlete Chris Legh provided a personal account of the drink's benefits. The "Origins" campaign, which carried the ongoing "Is it in you" tagline, also included print ads with the Gator mascot, Albert, as well as retired Gator players. Throughout the "Origins" campaign, Pepsi also continued to run Gatorade's splashier campaigns featuring big-name athletes such as Michael Jordan.

While "Origins" was underway, Gatorade increased its market share from 78 to 81 percent in a sports-drink market that was rapidly growing. Gatorade's multitiered marketing approach spread the credit for such success in various directions, but "Origins" was acknowledged as an important factor. Additionally, whereas the famous-athlete ads gained more immediate attention, "Origins" offered greater long-term possibilities. It directly added authority and sincerity to the Gatorade name. "Origins" also gained attention in the advertising world, winning "Best Spots" awards from *Adweek* magazine in both 2002 and 2003.

HISTORICAL CONTEXT

Gatorade was invented in 1965 by a University of Florida professor of medicine, Robert Cade, to aid the university's football team. The mixture of water, salt, sugar, and lemon juice immediately helped to reduce dehydration in, and improve the endurance of, the athletes. The team's performance improved dramatically that season, even helping the Florida Gators to make it to their first-ever Orange Bowl. The overnight success drew little attention from the business world, and in 1967 the Indianapolis-based food-processing company Stokely-Van Camp bought the rights to Gatorade for just $30,000.

Gatorade's first nationwide advertising campaign was released in 1969, costing Stokely-Van Camp $4 million. At the time Gatorade's sales were in the hundreds of thousands. But sales soon rose dramatically, attracting the interest of several U.S. food giants. In 1982, with Gatorade's annual revenues at $90 million, Stokely-Van Camp became the target of an aggressive bidding war. The following year the Quaker Oats Company acquired the company for $269 million, winning full rights to the Gatorade brand. Quaker further immersed Gatorade in the sports world; in 1984 it launched the Gatorade "Thirst Aid" advertising campaign and in the meantime connected the drink brand to several professional sporting leagues, including Major League Baseball, NASCAR, the NBA, and the Olympics.

By 1990, with an approximate 90 percent share of the $635 million annual U.S. sports-drink market (which had been worth $220 million in 1985), Gatorade's advertising media budget was up to $31 million a year. Soon a significant amount of this exorbitant budget was thrown in one direction: Michael Jordan. In 1991 Gatorade signed a $13.5 million, 10-year contract with the basketball superstar, creating the "Be Like Mike" advertising campaign. Meanwhile, the U.S. sports-drink market continued to expand rapidly, to $800 million in 1992 and to $940 million in 1994. Of the latter figure, Gatorade claimed nearly $800 million. By 2000, when the U.S. sports-drink market was up to an incredible $1.9 billion—of which Gatorade accounted for 78 percent—another aggressive bidding war for Gatorade was underway. In the end, PepsiCo's $13.4 billion bid to merge with Quaker won it the rights to Gatorade. Within a year Pepsi, with its 2002 Gatorade "Origins" advertising campaign, helped the 35-year-old sports drink make its history known.

WHAT IS DEHYDRATION?

Before Gatorade was invented, it was widely believed that athletes should abstain from drinking anything, even water, during games, because drinking might have caused cramps and nausea. The 1965 assistant Gator football coach, Dwayne Douglas, helped to change this perception when he asked a University of Florida professor of medicine, Robert Cade, why his players never had to urinate during games. Cade concluded that the players were sweating so much they had no fluids left to urinate. And in that moment, the idea of Gatorade was created.

TARGET MARKET

Gatorade had been used for a variety of purposes, including hydration for athletes; relief for women in labor; a cure for the common cold, menstrual cramps, diarrhea, and hangovers; and roach-trap bait. This made Gatorade's target market incredibly diverse. Nonetheless, since its 1965 beginnings, in which Gatorade was invented to help the University of Florida's football team, Gatorade's primary focus had been on athletes.

After Quaker Oats acquired Gatorade in 1983, the drink's connection to professional athletes was fixed. In 1984 and 1985 Gatorade became a corporate sponsor of several high-profile sporting organizations, including Major League Baseball, the Olympic Track & Field Trials, NASCAR, and the NBA. The 1991 "Be Like Mike" television commercials, in which NBA superstar Michael Jordan promoted Gatorade, provided final confirmation of Gatorade's connection with serious athletes. By the time PepsiCo merged with Quaker in 2001, Gatorade had become the most-recognized drink of athletes. Gatorade's 2002 "Origins" advertising campaign reflected this focus by taking the consumer through Gatorade's history, and in particular, through its long-time connection with sports.

COMPETITION

When Quaker Oats bought Stokely-Van Camp Co. for an astounding $269 million in 1983, it was clear that Gatorade brought the possibility of big earnings. Skeptics were omnipresent, but Gatorade sales rose dramatically. Within a decade the sports drink was bringing in $700 million a year. By that time big beverage distributors wanted in on the lucrative sports-drink market, and by 1992 both PepsiCo and Coca-Cola had introduced their own lines of sports drinks. PepsiCo's All Sport fell into the number three spot in the market, where it became stuck. Even its initial big-budget national advertising campaign, featuring the immensely popular basketball superstar Shaquille O'Neal, could not move the product up the ranks. For the next decade, while All Sport sales improved, it became clear to Pepsi that, while it might be possible to overcome Coca-Cola's Powerade, it would be nearly impossible to surpass Gatorade, which controlled approximately 80 percent of the market.

In a 2001 deal costing $13.4 billion, PepsiCo merged with Quaker, allowing the soda company to take control of Gatorade. And in a strange twist to the deal, Pepsi's All Sport was sold to the root-beer distributor Monarch Beverage Company, thus turning All Sport into a Pepsi competitor. It proved to be an insignificant opponent, however. At the time of its sale All Sport held 4.4 percent of the sports-drink market. By April 2002, no longer under Pepsi ownership, All Sport's market share had dropped to 1.3 percent. In response to the slump, Monarch announced a major sponsorship with the United States Postal Service Pro Cycling Team, the only American cycling team to have won the Tour de France. Consumer promotions of the sponsorship included a grand prize trip for two to the 100th Tour de France in 2003. In a further attempt to gain market share, in 2004 Monarch introduced two low-carbohydrate versions of its sports drink. But by that year All Sport's market share had decreased to under 1 percent, making it clear that the sports-drink market, at least for the moment, would be dominated by two main competitors: Pepsi and Coke.

Coca-Cola had also attempted to acquire Gatorade, offering a bid for Quaker in 2000. But the deal did not pan out. With 15 percent of the $1.9 billion sports-drink market, Coca-Cola was far from out of the game, however. After Pepsi secured the Quaker deal, Coca-Cola was ready for battle. In 2001, while Pepsi was preparing to launch the Gatorade "Origins" campaign, Coca-Cola was aggressively marketing Powerade. First it slashed prices of the drink, making Gatorade the more expensive choice. Next Coca-Cola secured a Powerade promotional deal with the cable sports network ESPN. At the same time Coke completely overhauled Powerade's packaging and promotional materials. The total marketing push reportedly came at a $60 million price tag. In 2001 Powerade gained 2.5 percent market share. The following year Powerade achieved another feat, becoming the new official sports drink of NASCAR, a promotional position that Gatorade had previously held. Coke kept up the momentum in 2003. While Pepsi was promoting its "Origins 2" advertising campaign (a sequel to its 2001 "Origins"), Coke's sports drink, too, was involved in a sequel. Powerade became a major sponsor of the 2003 movie *The Matrix Reloaded,* a sequel to the 1999 box-office hit *The Matrix.* Still, none of Powerade's efforts were enough to hurt Gatorade's dominant market share. By 2004, when the sports-drink market grew to an astonishing $5 billion, Powerade controlled just 14 percent of the market, compared to Gatorade's 81 percent.

MARKETING STRATEGY

After it acquired Gatorade in 2001, PepsiCo conducted a poll that revealed that few consumers knew anything about Gatorade's origins. Some thought, for instance, that it was an invention of someone named Mr. Gator, while others believed it to be a concoction of alligator juice. In response, Pepsi hired ad agency Element 79 Partners of Chicago to develop a marketing campaign that would paint Gatorade's history. In June 2002 the 60-second "Origins" television commercial disclosed Gatorade's University of Florida football roots. The spot opened with a Florida Gator football player standing before a row of urinals and telling the camera that, before Gatorade, the team's coach had no idea why none of the players urinated during games. A Florida newspaper sportswriter followed, providing first-hand testimony of the team's dramatic improvement after the players started drinking Gatorade. Last, veteran sportscaster Keith Jackson was featured to add credibility to the success story. The campaign included print ads with the Gator mascot, Albert, and 54-year-old former Gators linebacker, Chip Hilton, who also appeared in the "Origins" commercial. The campaign, which incorporated the existing "Is it in you?" Gatorade tagline, was also used to celebrate Gatorade's 35-year anniversary.

In July 2003 Pepsi and Element 79 Partners followed up "Origins" with a sequel named "Origins 2." Whereas the first "Origins" concentrated on Gatorade's Tallahassee roots, the "Origins 2" TV spot took the viewer to the NFL playing field, and in particular, to the field of the Kansas City Chiefs. The Chiefs, as the commercial pointed out, was the first NFL team to use Gatorade. The 60-second spot illustrated how the journey from Gators to Chiefs helped to secure Gatorade's position as the beverage choice of athletes. The "Is it in you?" tagline continued, as it would in the next installment of the campaign, which arrived in January 2005. As the entire history of Gatorade had already been disclosed in the first two commercials, a new angle had to be explored. This time Gatorade zoomed the lens in on one particular athlete, Australian triathlete Chris Legh. Legh seemed a perfect candidate to make an argument for Gatorade, as he had collapsed from severe dehydration, just yards from the finish line, at the 1997 Ironman Triathlon World Championship. The "Testimonial" commercial revealed how Gatorade came to the rescue, helping Legh to win the 2004 Ironman competition.

Although the campaign's budget was not disclosed, PepsiCo reportedly spent nearly $130 million on Gatorade advertising from 2001 through October 2004. But during this time, the "Origins" campaign was not the only Gatorade advertising endeavor. Other big-budget campaigns coincided with "Origins," including the New Year's Day 2003 launch of the Michael Jordan tribute television commercial, in which cutting-edge technology allowed the basketball legend to compete against himself on the court.

OUTCOME

Except for a couple of *Adweek* "Best Spots" awards, the "Origins" advertising campaign did not win advertising awards. Ad critic Lewis Lazare wrote negatively of the campaign, stating, "As an infomercial, 'Origins' works OK. But as a compelling and entertaining sales tool, it falls short of the mark." Perhaps the commercials were overshadowed by splashier Gatorade ads starring such athletic greats as Mia Hamm, Derek Jeter, and Michael Jordan.

Besides educating consumers, "Origins" contributed to the tremendous sales growth Gatorade experienced during the campaign. From 2002 through 2005 Gatorade increased its market share from 78 to 81 percent; in a sports-drink market worth $2 billion in 2002 and $5 billion by 2005, the earnings proved incredible. Such numbers generated fierce competition in the market. In particular, longtime Pepsi rival Coca-Cola aggressively marketed its Powerade against Gatorade. Although it was the second-best-selling sports drink in the United States, Powerade was a far distant number two (holding 14 percent of the market in 2005). Gatorade and Powerade both boasted nearly identical benefits for athletes, including reducing dehydration and improving endurance, and both were promoted by huge-budget corporations. Yet Powerade was unable to catch up with Gatorade, largely because the latter had the longer history, not only in the marketplace, but also—and more importantly—on the athletic field. The "Origins" campaign successfully reinforced Gatorade's strongest advantage by establishing the brand's history in the minds of consumers.

FURTHER READING

Bonkowski, Jerry. "Gatorade Adds Jordan to Team." *USA Today,* August 9, 1991, p. 2C.

Chura, Hillary. "PepsiCo vs. Coca-Cola." *Advertising Age,* February 18, 2002, p. 5.

"Is Stokely Worth Quaker's Lofty Bid?" *BusinessWeek,* August 1, 1983, p. 25.

Lazare, Lewis. "Ad Tells Gatorade's Origins." *Chicago Sun-Times,* June 13, 2002, p. 65.

———. "Element 79 Scores for Gatorade." *Chicago Sun-Times,* July 15, 2003, p. 49.

Leith, Scott. "Atlanta-Based Owner of Sports Drink Thirsts for Larger Market Share." *Atlantic Journal-Constitution,* April 5, 2002.

———. "Pepsico Merger Positions Its Gatorade vs. Coke's Powerade." *Atlanta Journal-Constitution,* August 2, 2001.

Liesse, Julie, and Patricia Winters. "Gatorade Set to Bench New Rivals." *Advertising Age,* March 19, 1990, p. 4.

"Quaker Sees New Markets for Gatorade." *New York Times,* August 8, 1983, p. D4.

Rice, Justin. "Legend of UF's Link to Gatorade Grows." *Palm Beach (FL) Post,* June 25, 2002, p. 1C.

Rovell, Darren. *First in Thirst: How Gatorade Turned the Science of Sweat into a Cultural Phenomenon.* New York: AMACOM, 2005.

Candice L.Mancini

PEPSI. IT'S THE COLA CAMPAIGN

OVERVIEW

In the early 2000s the cola wars were as hot as ever with number two brand Pepsi-Cola battling to catch up with the top brand, Coca-Cola. But things were not going well for any of the cola brands, including Pepsi. In 1999 Pepsi Cola's market share fell 0.03 percent to 14.2 percent, while Coca-Cola Classic remained flat with 20.8 percent, as consumers turned to other beverage choices. Sales continued on a downward spiral, and during the first nine months of 2003 sales of regular Pepsi Cola dropped 5.5 percent, and Diet Pepsi's sales fell 3.6 percent. Pepsi's mission became reversing the slip of its brands in the marketplace.

Pepsi closed out 2003 by launching a new marketing campaign, "Pepsi. It's the Cola." The new theme replaced the slogan "The Joy of Pepsi," which the company had used since 2000. The new campaign also shifted the company's advertising focus from the brand and back to the product. Pepsi's longtime advertising agency BBDO New York created the campaign, which kicked off with a series of three television commercials followed by outdoor ads displayed on billboards and bus shelters located near restaurants and fast-food establishments. Radio, print, and online advertising was also part of the campaign. The ads were humorous and drove home the campaign's message that Pepsi and food go together. One television spot featured comedian Dave Chappelle being attacked by a robotic vacuum cleaner determined to grab his Pepsi to go along with the Doritos chip it had just sucked up off the floor. A billboard ad showed a veggie wrap sandwich hugging a glass of Pepsi.

The campaign resonated well with consumers, particularly young adults, and based on sales it was a success. At the end of 2003, following the campaign's launch, Pepsi reported that sales of all its beverage brands had increased 0.4 percent to 31.8 percent. The company also morphed the successful campaign into one for Diet Pepsi: "Diet Pepsi. It's the Diet Cola."

HISTORICAL CONTEXT

When Pepsi turned 100 years old in 1998, John McDonough, writing for *Advertising Age,* said that Pepsi defined itself against its rival, Coke, "through the wizardry of the slogan, the jingle and the storyboard." Describing the cola wars as having little to do with cola, McDonough wrote that for Pepsi the cola wars were about "beating Coke, and the weaponry [was] not cola but advertising."

Throughout the highs and lows of Pepsi's early years, concerns focused more on the company's survival than advertising, but McDonough wrote that by 1936 Pepsi had an ad budget of $500,000, and by 1938 that budget had doubled, with most money earmarked for newspaper ads and signage. (Radio advertising was still too costly.) During the 1939 New York World's Fair, Pepsi took its marketing to the sky with a skywriting campaign over the fair's grounds.

From a comic-strip format that ran in newspapers and featured Keystone Kop–like characters named Pepsi and Pete to radio spots that featured the famous "Pepsi-Cola Hits the Spot" jingle, the company's advertising continued to evolve and its budget to grow. McDonough said that following World War II Pepsi had an advertising budget that approached $4 million. Pepsi pushed for a more glamorous image in the 1950s with themes such as "More Bounce to the Ounce," which McDonough said was a veiled reference to a well-known television actress of the time who favored low-cut necklines and plenty of exposed cleavage, and "Reduced Calories," before diet drinks were the rage. The tagline "Say Pepsi Please" was introduced in 1957 and lasted through the end of the decade. In 1960 BBDO took over Pepsi's advertising.

Under BBDO's creative direction the tagline "For Those Who Think Young" became Pepsi's theme. The "Pepsi Generation" and the "Come Alive . . . You're in the Pepsi Generation" campaigns followed. Other campaigns, including "Taste That Beats the Others Cold, Pepsi Pours It On" and "Join the Pepsi People, Feelin' Free," were designed to maintain the original "Pepsi Generation" idea. Shifting its focus from the baby boomer "Pepsi Generation" to younger consumers, the marketing theme in 1984 became "The Choice of a New Generation," followed by the long-running "Generation Next" campaign. According to *Advertising Age* the "Generation Next" theme was scrapped in 1998 as too narrowly focused for mass appeal and was replaced with "The Joy of Cola." The new campaign was well received by consumers when it was unveiled in 1999, but in 2000 the theme morphed into "The Joy of Pepsi." The company dropped its "Joy of Pepsi" theme with the introduction of "Pepsi. It's the Cola" in 2003.

TARGET MARKET

Pepsi's target market was "so broad it's hard to narrow it down, but the focus is teens and young adults," said company spokesman Dave DeCecco. He added, "Consumer research showed people were drinking Pepsi with foods anyway," so the new campaign was a way to remind them to enjoy a Pepsi with their meal. Katie Lacey, Pepsi's vice president for colas and media, told the *Atlanta Journal-Constitution* that research revealed people drink colas but not as often as they did in the past. The variety of other beverage choices was cited as one of the reasons for declining cola sales. The "Pepsi. It's the Cola" campaign hoped to convince consumers of all ages that Pepsi is the perfect beverage to drink with meals or anytime food is being eaten and enjoyed.

WHAT COLA WARS? NEW BATTLEFRONT IS LEMON-LIME

Pepsi-Cola and Coca-Cola drew a new line in the so-called cola wars in 2003, and the new front had nothing to do with cola and everything to do with citrus fruit—lemon-lime, to be exact. Reporting for *Advertising Age,* Hillary Chura wrote, "Two new lemon-lime soft drinks are hitting the market, including the first extension of [Coke's] Sprite, called Sprite Remix, and PepsiCo's national rollout of Sierra Mist." With the introduction of the two new products, Cadbury Schweppes jumped into the fray with its noncola beverage 7 UP. John Sicher, editor of *Beverage Digest,* told Chura, "The three-way face-off this year among Sprite, 7UP and Sierra Mist is going to be a very heated battle." Charlee Taylor-Hines, PepsiCo's brand manager for Sierra Mist, told Chura, "I see this summer as the lemon-lime wars . . . We'll see each brand try to create a niche for itself in marketing."

COMPETITION

In the ongoing cola wars the brand to beat was number one Coca-Cola, and in 2003 the company consolidated its $350 million media planning and buying account to maintain its competitive edge. Reporting for *Advertising Age,* Kate MacArthur wrote that Coke's consolidation was "another step toward enabling its plan to create the 'experienced-based, access-driven marketing'" the company's president and chief operation officer had mandated. MacArthur continued, "With the cola wars officially escalated, [Coke's] under intense pressure to connect with consumers." Coke attempted to connect with consumers when it launched its new "Real" campaign, which relied on consumers' nostalgia for the company's 1970s "The Real Thing" theme, according to Bob Garfield in *Advertising Age.* He noted that Coke's new campaign was more contemporary and hip than many of the company's previous campaigns, most of which had lacked a youthful flair. Garfield stated that despite its hipper appeal the new campaign repeated the mistake of earlier efforts and failed to focus on the product. And like Pepsi's "It's the Cola" campaign, Coke's campaign was created to convince consumers its beverage was great with food. Garfield commented that Coke also was great with food, "which, if we're not mistaken, is the real reason people buy the stuff."

Rather than a cola the number three soft drink behind Coke and Pepsi was 7 UP, owned by Cadbury Schweppes Americas Beverages. Instead of following the lead of Coke and Pepsi and launching a new ad campaign, Cadbury Schweppes chose to stay with its successful, award-winning "Make 7 UP Yours" campaign. John Clarke, chief advertising officer for Dr Pepper/Seven Up, told *PR Newswire,* "Entering into its fifth year, the 'Make 7 UP Yours' campaign continues to be a favorite among consumers, positively impacting both advertising and brand awareness." The company reported that product awareness had more than doubled since the "Make 7 UP Yours" campaign was introduced in 1999. In addition the campaign resonated particularly well with 12- to 24-year-olds, 7 UP's target audience.

MARKETING STRATEGY

Although past campaigns had been high on star power, the "Pepsi. It's the Cola" campaign took a different approach: keep it simple. The *Atlanta Journal-Constitution*'s Scott Leith wrote, "Pepsi will dispense with the kind of flashy ads it has used in the recent past—think Britney Spears—and instead pitch itself as a food-friendly cola." Pepsi's chief marketing officer and senior vice president Dave Burwick said of the campaign, "This is a different approach for us. It's not the diva-of-the-year kind of thing." Besides a simpler theme the campaign took a different approach with its launch date. Pepsi typically released new campaigns in January, but "Pepsi. It's the Cola" debuted in November to take advantage of the upcoming holiday season, a time when people typically celebrate with family and friends and good food.

Working with the food and fun theme, Pepsi's agency, BBDO, created a series of commercials designed to showcase the product. The campaign launched with three television spots aired during NFL games and other programming that attracted a large viewing audience, such as the Macy's Thanksgiving Day Parade. Radio, print, online, and outdoor advertising was also part of the campaign.

The first television spot, titled "Summer Job," showed a young woman dressed as a giant hot dog handing out flyers to passersby, inviting them to visit a nearby restaurant. Following repeated rejections by people who didn't want the flyers, the woman, alone and dejected, moved down the sidewalk, where she encountered a soul mate—a young man dressed as a can of Pepsi. The two walked away hand in hand as a voice-over stated, "Hot dogs love Pepsi. Pepsi loves hot dogs. It's the cola." A second television spot featured Chappelle, who had gone to his girlfriend's apartment to pick her up for a date. While waiting Chappelle was attacked by the girl's robotic vacuum cleaner, which was after his can of Pepsi. The last in the series of three TV commercials was set during a pre–football game tailgate party in which a can of Pepsi was sent sailing through the air in slow motion. Outdoor ads, which were posted on billboards and bus stop shelters, included pictures of a veggie wrap sandwich hugging a glass of Pepsi and a strand of spaghetti roping a Pepsi cowboy style.

OUTCOME

During the first nine months of 2003, Pepsi's U.S. sales dropped 5.5 percent. Following the launch of the "Pepsi. It's the Cola" campaign in November, Pepsi's market share began a slow climb. In March 2004 the company reported an increase of 0.4 percent to 31.8 percent as it took away business from its competitors, including Coke. In addition the new campaign seemed to resonate with at least one consumer group: young adults. From the perspective of college students in Boston, Pepsi was a hit. One student quoted in the *Boston Herald* said, "Pepsi's advertising is probably attracting more of the population. The only Coke ads I can think of are the polar bears ads around the holidays." Another student added, "I think Pepsi is aimed more toward a younger crowd. Coke seems more old-fashioned." As further evidence that Pepsi was pleased with the campaign's results, for the 2004 Academy Awards the company launched a modified version of the campaign for another of its brands, Diet Pepsi. The new campaign was themed "Diet Pepsi. It's the Diet Cola." Burwick said, "People drink both Pepsi and Diet Pepsi with food and while they're having fun, so the same strategy applies to both brands."

FURTHER READING

Chura, Hillary. "Coke, Pepsi Launches: Lemon-Lime the Battle Front in This Summer's Cola Wars." *Advertising Age,* March 10, 2003.

Garfield, Bob. "Garfield's AdReview: Misguided Nostalgia Obscures What's Really 'Real' about Coke." *Advertising Age,* January 13, 2003.

———. "Garfield's AdReview: Pepsi Finally Acknowledges Real Point of Cola in New Ads." *Advertising Age,* December 1, 2003.

Kramer, Louise. "Coke, Pepsi: Don't Look for Shifts in Ad Strategy." *Advertising Age,* May 18, 1998.

Leith, Scott. "In Cola Wars, No Coke—Pepsi!" *Boston Herald,* September 29, 2004.

Manuse, Andrew. "Coke Launches New Ad Campaign." *Atlanta Journal-Constitution,* January 9, 2003.

———. "Pepsi Adds U.S. Market Share; No. 1 Coca-Cola Loses Ground." *Atlanta Journal-Constitution,* March 5, 2004.

———. "Pepsi Dumps Celebrities for Simpler Ads." *Atlanta Journal-Constitution,* November 20, 2003.

MacArthur, Kate. "Coke Consolidation in Line with Strategy." *Advertising Age,* December 1, 2003.

McDonough, John. "Pepsi Turns 100: One of the World's Great Brands Has Been Shaped in Large Measure by Its Advertising." *Advertising Age,* July 20, 1998.

"Pepsi-Cola Adds New Player to Super Bowl XXXVIII Commercial Roster; Spike DDB Joins the Pepsi Super Bowl Lineup." *PR Newswire,* January 29, 2004.

"Pepsi-Cola to Scrap 'Generation Next' Theme." *Advertising Age,* November 2, 1998.

"Pepsi Launches Holiday Effort." *Advertising Age,* November 24, 2003.

"Pepsi Unveils New Advertising Campaign: 'Pepsi. It's the Cola'; Brand's First Major Campaign Shift since 1999." *PR Newswire,* November 19, 2003.

"7 Up Marks the New Year with Four New Commercials from Its Award-Winning 'Make 7 Up Yours' Advertising Campaign; Comedian Godfrey Returns as the Well-Intentioned, Yet Hapless, 7 Up Marketing Executive." *PR Newswire,* December 29, 2003.

Rayna Bailey

QUAKER–WARMS YOU, HEART AND SOUL CAMPAIGN

OVERVIEW

NOTE: Since the initial appearance of this essay in the 1999 edition of *Major Marketing Campaigns Annual,* Quaker Oats Company was acquired by PepsiCo and functions as a unit of its parent company. The essay continues to refer to the company's former name, as that was the official name of the organization when the campaign was launched.

For years the Quaker Oats Company had promoted the health-related benefits of its oatmeal products, and so its 1998 "Warms You, Heart and Soul" campaign was not a departure from established strategy. Indeed, a 1997 federal ruling gave increased strength to the claim, but along with this ruling came a rising firestorm of criticism from public-interest groups, such as the Center for Science in the Public Interest (CSPI). The television spots, created by Foote, Cone & Belding (FCB), showed residents of a Colorado town who took Quaker's "Smart Heart Challenge": 98 out of 100 participants, the commercials indicated, lowered their cholesterol levels by eating one bowl of Quaker Oatmeal a day. In 1997 Quaker Oats spent $35 million on advertising its oatmeal, and the figures for 1998 were reportedly much higher. The campaign included print advertising and promotion on Quaker's packaging, but the primary thrust was on television.

"Spotlighting a town and the voices of its everyday people is unprecedented in Quaker's advertising campaigns," Sally Kroha, director of oatmeal advertising for the company, told Judann Pollack of *Advertising Age* in 1998. As Pollack noted, however, other companies had used similar themes in recent years. Campbell Soup Company, for one, had used the tag line "Good for the Body, Good for the Soul." Nor was it new for Quaker to cite the health benefits of its cereal, a strategy it had applied as early as 1899, with an advertisement in the *Saturday Evening Post* that stated "How foolish to keep on eating meat to the exclusion of Quaker Oats when dietary experts agree that Quaker Oats is more nourishing and wholesome."

But while Quaker remained the nation's leading brand of hot cereal, with a 60 percent share of a $618 million industry in 1996, much else had changed in a century. Quaker had grown into a vast corporation with $4.8 billion in annual sales during 1998, a total which included such significant brands as Gatorade and Cap'n Crunch cereal, as well as its hot cereals. And while consumer interest in healthy eating had increased, so had consumer skepticism about advertising claims, an attitude that was reinforced by the work of CSPI and other groups.

HISTORICAL CONTEXT

The Quaker Oats trademark, depicting a smiling Quaker gentleman, was born in 1877. Two of the four men who organized the Quaker Mill Company in Ravenna, Ohio, claimed credit for the trademark, one of the world's most famous. William Heston later said that he got the idea from a picture of Pennsylvania founder William Penn; on the other hand, Henry O. Seymour asserted that he came upon the idea after seeing an entry on Quakers in an encyclopedia, which inspired him with "the purity of the lives of the people, their sterling honesty, their strength and manliness." In any case, the trademark has nothing to do with the actual Quaker religious sect, formally known as the Society of Friends, although in fact Heston was a Quaker.

The company underwent a series of changes, assuming its present name in 1901. Along the way, it established itself as a seminal entity in what were then almost entirely new and undiscovered fields: packaging, advertising, and marketing. Quaker was, quite simply, the first nationally advertised food brand, but its historical significance goes deeper than that: it was one of the first brands, period, and proved to be one of the most enduring.

When Quaker Oats first went on the market in the late 1800s, grocers typically sold their products unpackaged, from large barrels, which often was unsanitary. By selling its product in cardboard packages, Quaker could promote the advantage of safety. The use of cardboard packages decorated with the Quaker logo had the further advantage, of course, of making the brand highly recognizable. Then there was advertising, which at the time was considered an unseemly activity for businesses, since most advertising promoted patent medicines and other so-called miracle cures. By the 1890s, however, Quaker was advertising its name on billboards and streetcars.

By the time other companies caught on to the idea of advertising in the twentieth century, Quaker was already an established master of the art, employing leading celebrities of the 1930s and 1940s, such as Roy Rogers and Babe Ruth, to make endorsements. The midcentury also saw a rising interest in the health benefits of oatmeal. So when scientists in the 1930s discovered that oats contained a significant dose of the vitamin B-1, Quaker's sales increased by 35 percent almost overnight.

TARGET MARKET

Since its early days Quaker had claimed health benefits for its products, and it was a combination of public interest in the advantages of oats, along with the company's savvy marketing, that transformed oatmeal from a niche product to a staple of American households. Originally, Quaker's principal consumers were German, Irish, or Scottish immigrants; by contrast, mainstream Americans considered oats a food fit only for animals. By the early twentieth century, however, most people in the United States considered oatmeal a good, solid breakfast. Of course, oatmeal was far from fashionable—until the 1980s. By that time, Quaker's sales had been in a long decline, which began with the widespread introduction of ready-to-eat cereals following World War II. But revenues soared again as studies showed a link between oatmeal consumption and lowered cholesterol. During the 1980s Quaker promoted its product with the tag line "It's the Right Thing to Do" in ads featuring actor Wilford Brimley. Later, the tag line became "Every Day Should Feel This Good."

Until 1997, however, the Food and Drug Administration's (FDA) regulations prohibited companies from making specific claims about a link between their products and a reduction in heart disease. Stephen Ink, director of nutrition at Quaker's research laboratories, had been working to establish such a link for his brand since 1975, and late in 1996, as Quaker prepared for a favorable ruling, he told Stephanie Thompson of *Brandweek,* "In the past, health claims have required generic language like, 'fruits, grains and vegetables carrying dietary fiber may limit the risk of heart disease,' but we couldn't specifically say oatmeal"—much less Quaker Oatmeal. According to Thompson, "Quaker Oats hopes to start a new oatmeal and oat bran craze, pending a much-anticipated FDA ruling on Quaker research regarding the benefits of its core products. The firm plans to make the health pitch a major focus of new packaging and advertising by year-end."

Late in January 1997 the ruling came down, and as Janet Raloff reported in *Science News,* "even Quaker was surprised by the scope of the FDA's ruling." Ink admitted that although research had shown a possible link between oat bran and lowered cholesterol, this had not been proven conclusively. Nonetheless, on the heels of the ruling, the company ran a full-page ad in the *Washington Post* that showed the famous Quaker man portrayed in the logo along with the headline "Now he has another reason to smile. The FDA confirms the first food-specific health claim: Soluble fiber from oatmeal, as part of a low saturated fat, low cholesterol diet, may reduce the risk of heart disease."

COMPETITION

Quaker was not the only company that benefited from the FDA ruling. Raloff noted that, for instance, General Mills' Cheerios, a ready-to-eat cereal, was also covered, and indeed General Mills ran its own newspaper ads, accompanied by a television spot, which appeared before a Quaker commercial with a voice-over reporting the results of the FDA ruling. The FDA's ruling was welcome news to cereal giant Kellogg as well: earlier, the company had been required to change the name of its Heartwise cereal to Fiberwise because the FDA held that the brand name could be deceptive.

Technically, the only major competitor for Quaker as a hot cereal was Nabisco Foods Group's Cream of Wheat; but with its strong position in the category—and its offerings in other areas—Quaker was prepared to take on larger game. In January 1998 it launched a $20 million campaign, primarily on television, with spots created by FCB touting its Quaker Fruit & Oatmeal Cereal Bars as superior to Kellogg's Nutri-Grain Bars. In terms of the cholesterol claims in advertising for Quaker Oatmeal, however, the true competition came in the form of CSPI and other critics outside the industry.

In November 1996, just before the FDA ruling, Bruce Silverglade of CSPI told Thompson, "Instead of permitting claims for single foods, we have urged the [FDA] to include information on the benefit of oats within the existing claim on all foods high in soluble fiber." CSPI would become much more vocal about Quaker's advertising in 1998, but consumer groups were not the only critics. In December 1998 the *Wall Street*

THE LEMON AWARDS

On January 14, 1999, representatives of a coalition of public-interest groups, led by the Washington, D.C.-based Center for Science in the Public Interest (CSPI), gathered to present the 14th annual Harlan Page Hubbard Lemon Awards, which were presented each year to companies that, in the coalition's opinion, ran misleading ads. CSPI nominated Quaker Oats for its 1998 commercials about the link between lowered cholesterol levels and consumption of Quaker Oats, but Quaker did not "win". That honor went to Telecom, USA, which advertised the 10-10-321 and 10-10-220 long-distance services. According to Becky Sachs of the Telecommunications Research & Action Center, "Commercials tell consumers that 10-10-321 can save them money, but what they don't tell consumers is that a call has to last at least 10 minutes for the discounts to kick in."

Other candidates for the "Lemmie" award included Miller Beer, which according to United Press International ran a commercial "showing a young man playing with a puppy, then a can of beer, and the graphic 'man's other best friend'"; the Brown & Williamson Tobacco Company, "which promot[ed] the cool, menthol taste [of an unnamed cigarette brand] without mentioning that the numbing effect of menthol in cigarettes has not been fully studied"; and the First USA credit card, which "offer[ed] low-interest checks to consumers . . . while closer inspection of fine print reveals buried 'transaction finance charges'." Several other brands and companies were cited; it should be noted, however, that the statements represent the opinions of the public-interest groups who participated and do not necessarily reflect the views of consumers or advertisers.

Journal speculated that although advertising by Quaker and other companies might initially draw in more consumers, the higher costs of heart-smart products—not to mention people's tendency to lose interest in a healthy eating regimen—might limit the chances of success.

MARKETING STRATEGY

In 1997 Quaker dropped longtime advertising agency Jordan, McGrath, Case & Taylor, which had handled its campaigns during the 1980s, in favor of FCB. A distinguished agency of long standing, FCB had fallen on hard times in the early 1990s, but with the Quaker account and others, analysts predicted renewed strength for the firm. Its first ads for Quaker, in 1997, used the song "Heart and Soul." During most of 1998, FCB and Quaker concentrated on Quaker Oats Fruit & Oatmeal, as well as Quaker's Dino Eggs. The Dino Eggs, a brand extension for children whose introduction was tied to Universal Pictures's release of a new film in the popular *Land Before Time* series, were marketed in the shape of eggs. When hot water was added to them, they "hatched" into brightly colored dinosaurs.

In the late summer and early fall, however, FCB and Quaker presented the "Warms You, Heart and Soul" campaign. Television ads included a 30-second spot and six 15-second spots, and the company supplemented these with a single print ad, as well as packaging changes. The campaign centered around the town of Lafayette, Colorado, where 100 residents were recruited to take the Quaker "Smart Heart Challenge," eating a bowl of Quaker oatmeal every day for 30 days. They were monitored by the Boulder, Colorado, Community Hospital, which reported that at the end of the month-long trial, 98 of the 100 participants had lowered their cholesterol levels by an average of 24 points.

Eleven of the participants appeared in the television spots, and pictures of six of the participating residents were on special packages of Quaker Toasted Oatmeal, Quaker Toasted Oatmeal Squares, and Quaker Instant Oatmeal. One television spot, for instance, showed Dan, a Lafayette police officer, standing in front of a sign showing a 30-mile-per-hour speed limit; as Dan explained, he had lowered his cholesterol by one less point, 29. In other spots, Lafayette residents appeared with a variety of numbers, including bingo signs and price markers that signified the amount of points by which they had lowered their cholesterol. The print ad showed the entire group seated on bleachers at Lafayette's high school.

OUTCOME

The "Warms You" campaign, Pollack reported in *Advertising Age,* was to be the "baseline effort supporting all Quaker's other hot cereals," beginning with its introduction in August 1998. Pollack noted that sales had not increased in the two years following the favorable FDA ruling. It remained to be seen whether the cheerful, folksy ads would activate Quaker's sales; in the meantime, the company faced renewed attacks from CSPI in 1999.

CSPI nominated the Quaker spot for the Harlan Page Hubbard Lemon Award, given annually for advertising that the consumer advocacy group and other public-interest lobbyists deemed the most "misleading, unfair, and irresponsible ads." Bonnie Liebman of CSPI pointed out that on the Quaker Web site, consumers would learn that the Lafayette study participants had combined their consumption of Quaker Oats with a program of exercise and fat reduction, but "the ads never mention [that], just the 'powerful oatmeal'." In late January 1999 CSPI demanded that the Federal Trade Commission (FTC) force Quaker to take the commercials off the air. "Quaker's ad implies that oatmeal is a 'magic bullet' that can cause impressive drops in blood cholesterol with little effort," CSPI stated in its petition. Margaret Kirch Cohen, a spokesperson for Quaker, told *Food Labeling News* that "the results of the Smart Heart Challenge were completely consistent with nearly 40 years of scientific studies that have demonstrated the cholesterol-lowering benefits of oatmeal." She added, "I think we took a very conservative approach to our advertising campaign and selected a wide range of individuals whose experiences varied."

FURTHER READING

"CSPI Asks FTC to Prohibit Cholesterol Claims in Quaker Oatmeal TV Commercial." *Food Labeling News,* February 3, 1999.

"Feeling Their Oats." *Supermarket News,* February 3, 1997, p. 10.

"Full-Page Quaker Oats Advertisement." *Food Labeling News,* January 30, 1997.

"Lemon Awards Given for Worst Ads." United Press International, January 15, 1999.

Hume, Scott. "Passing the Oatmeal Challenge." *Adweek* (Midwest Edition), August 17, 1998, p. 4.

O'Connell, Vanessa. "New Pitches Set for Anti-Cholesterol Foods." *Wall Street Journal,* December 11, 1998, p. B-8.

Pollack, Judann. "Ordinary People Star in New Fall Quaker Effort: Ads Document Cholesterol Drop among Residents of Colo. Town." *Advertising Age,* August 17, 1998, p. 42.

"Quaker Goes Prehistoric." *Promo,* December 1998.

Raloff, Janet. "FDA Allows Heart Health Claims for Oats." *Science News,* February 1, 1997, p. 71.

Thompson, Stephanie. "New Wave of Grain?" *Brandweek,* November 11, 1996, p. 1.

———. "Quaker: $20M Push to Disbar Kellogg." *Brandweek,* January 12, 1998, p. 1.

———. "Very Big Push for Very Berry." *Mediaweek,* June 22, 1998, p. 48.

Judson Knight

SECURITY CAMERA CAMPAIGN

OVERVIEW

From humble beginnings in a North Carolina pharmacy a century ago, Pepsi-Cola grew to become one of the best-known products throughout the world. The company behind it grew as well, to become one of the top marketers of beverages in the world. In 1965 Pepsi-Cola and Frito-Lay merged to form PepsiCo, Inc. In the years since then PepsiCo has become one of the world's largest consumer product companies. Remarkable for a company of its size, PepsiCo has also remained a growth company, increasing its sales and its return to investors every year since its founding. Pepsi-Cola beverages were available in more than 190 countries and territories, and the company used its advertising and high-energy promotions to maintain the brand's "young" image.

"Security Camera" was the second in a series of story line spots created for Pepsi by its longtime ad agency BBDO. In the first spot in the series, which debuted during the telecast of Super Bowl XXIX in 1995, actor Joe Bays played a Coca-Cola deliveryman who refused to give back a Pepsi to a driver in a diner. The second spot, "Security Camera," was aired during NBC's telecast of Super Bowl XXX in 1996. Shot in black and white to resemble the video feed from a surveillance camera, the commercial continued the saga, as the same Coca-Cola driver was shown loading up a convenience store cooler with his product. Then, glancing up and down the aisle to make sure that no one was watching, he slipped his hand into the nearby Pepsi shelves to filch a can of the competitor's soda. Complications ensued when the shelf collapsed, sending dozens of Pepsi cans crashing to the floor around him. As a crowd of gawkers arrived, the sound track played Hank Williams's country chestnut "Your Cheatin' Heart."

"Security Camera" was consistently rated by viewers as one of the most effective and memorable spots shown during the Super Bowl telecast. It went on to win numerous industry awards and was considered one of the most successful commercials of the 1990s. Observers gave it high marks for its humor, refreshingly low-tech approach, and use of old-time music.

HISTORICAL CONTEXT

The Pepsi story began at the turn of the century, a time when the drugstore soda fountain was a popular place for people to gather for a refreshing drink. Pharmacists experimented with various mixtures of coca leaf and kola nut—thought to have extraordinary health benefits—in making their drinks. The soft drink industry was born when some of these "cola" drinks became so popular that their recipes were patented and trademarked for mass distribution to other drugstores.

During the 1890s Caleb Bradham concocted a new fountain drink in his drugstore in New Bern, North Carolina. His creation was a unique mixture of kola nut extract, vanilla, and rare oils that he named Pepsi-Cola.

He advertised it as being "exhilarating" and "invigorating" and claimed that it aided digestion. Sales began to grow, and in 1902 Bradham launched the Pepsi-Cola Company in the back room of his pharmacy and applied to the U.S. Patent Office for a trademark. At first he mixed the syrup himself and sold it exclusively through soda fountains. But he soon realized that there was a greater opportunity in bottling Pepsi-Cola so that people could drink it anywhere. Business boomed until the postwar years of 1917–18, when sugar jumped from 5.5 cents a pound to 22.5 cents a pound. For Pepsi-Cola, which was retailing at a nickel per bottle, this development spelled disaster. After collapsing into bankruptcy, the company changed hands four times before winding up in 1931 as a subsidiary of Loft Incorporated, a large chain of candy stores and soda fountains.

By the mid-1950s Pepsi was enjoying an extended period of growth and expansion. Product innovation continued, and in 1958 a distinctive new "swirl" bottle was introduced. That same year, a new advertising campaign, "Be Sociable, Have a Pepsi," was launched. It was the first Pepsi-Cola campaign to focus on young people as the brand's major target and was soon followed by another youth-oriented campaign, "Now It's Pepsi, for Those Who Think Young."

In 1965 the Pepsi-Cola Company merged with the successful Dallas marketer of salty snacks, Frito-Lay, to form PepsiCo, one of the largest consumer products companies in the United States. Industry analysts began to observe that Pepsi, an upstart, aggressive company, was challenging the dominant soft drink company, Coca-Cola, with increasing success, and the media dubbed the competition the "cola wars." In the 1970s "The Pepsi Challenge," a landmark marketing strategy, was born when consumer tests confirmed that many people found Pepsi's taste to be superior to Coke's. "The Pepsi Challenge" used filmed taste tests to translate the results into advertising. The campaign was periodically reintroduced to new generations of consumers.

Throughout the 1980s a long list of stars lent their endorsement weight to Pepsi, including pop music icons Lionel Richie, Tina Turner, and Gloria Estefan and sports greats Joe Montana and Dan Marino. The actor Michael J. Fox appeared in a series of Pepsi and Diet Pepsi commercials, including the classic "Apartment 10G." Michael Jackson starred in the first ever episodic commercial, "Chase," which became the most watched commercial in history.

The 1990s ushered in a new generation of award-winning Pepsi advertising. Supermodel Cindy Crawford helped introduce a new package design, and Pepsi reminded people to "Be young, have fun, drink Pepsi." Basketball star Shaquille O'Neal carried on Pepsi's tradition of youth-oriented ads, and by the middle of the decade Pepsi advertising was pointing out that "Nothing Else Is a Pepsi." The period was an era of high-tech, effects-driven commercials, with the use of big-name celebrity endorsers de rigueur for spots aired during Super Bowl telecasts. It thus came as something of a surprise when Pepsi scored its biggest splash in years with the decidedly low-tech, celebrity-free "Security Camera."

TARGET MARKET

The Super Bowl, the annual National Football League championship game, was a chance for major U.S. advertisers to reach the largest captive audiences ever assembled. The telecast, which attracted an audience of more than 138 million viewers worldwide in 1996, was one of the few times a television set was watched by dozens of people in the same room.

Fortunes were sometimes spent on producing a single spot for the Super Bowl, and vast sums went toward buying time on the telecast. In 1998 the rate for a 30-second spot was about $1.3 million, up from $1.2 million in the previous year. The ultimate cost of airing a failed Super Bowl spot could be much more than the amount spent for air time or the millions spent to produce it. A flop could cost an ad agency business, force a marketing overhaul, and—at least temporarily—destroy a marketer's image.

On the other hand, well-done spots could be an effective way to get consumers to remember a product. This was especially true for young consumers, who in the 1990s showed an increased willingness to spend money on products like soda, chips, and candy. Thus, it was not surprising that teenagers were the target of many Super Bowl pitches from, among other products, Pepsi and Frito-Lay.

COMPETITION

Pepsi was often cited for the consistency of its message, and in the 1990s its advertising profited from the example of its closest competitor. In the 1980s Coca-Cola, stung by Pepsi's growth and prominence, had abandoned its century-old Coke recipe in favor of a new product formulated to taste more like Pepsi. Consumers, however, quickly rejected the new Coke, and in short order Coca-Cola was forced to reinstate the original product under a new name, Coca-Cola Classic.

After that debacle Coca-Cola concentrated on nurturing its brand identity. Introduced in 1994, its "Always Coca-Cola" theme succeeded by hammering its image-building message home to consumers. Clearly learning from the example of its rival, Pepsi strove for a similar consistency in its "Nothing Else Is a Pepsi" campaign. "Security Camera" was one in the second generation of Pepsi ads to end with this tag line. The ad effectively

BIRTHDAY BASH

Nowhere was the birthday of Pepsi-Cola more festively celebrated than in its birthplace of North Carolina. The state's celebration began on New Year's Day in 1998, 100 years after the pharmacist in New Bern had put the finishing touches on his unique concoction. The company sponsored special events and projects throughout both North and South Carolina as a way of acknowledging the region's support of the brand from its beginning.

"Generation Next" was given a special part in the anniversary. Pepsi bottlers in the two states gave one share of company stock to the first baby born at participating hospitals on New Year's Day. In addition, special packages containing such items as Pepsi baseball caps, bibs, and refrigerator memo boards were delivered to all New Year's Day babies and their parents. Nearly 135 hospitals participated in the project. Other activities included a commemorative poster contest, an art competition, a parade, a flotilla, a fireworks display, historical tours, and the exhibit of memorabilia called *100 Years of Pepsi.*

blended humor with image building to contrast the styles of the two brands. "The campaign helps Pepsi's trademark, because Pepsi's trying to stay young and paint Coke as gray," said Tom Pirko, an industry consultant.

In 1995 Coca-Cola spent $125.7 million to advertise its regular and diet colas. By contrast, Pepsi's ad spending that year topped out at $122.9 million. Marketing experts were divided over which company was getting the most bang for its buck. Some pointed to above average sales increases by both regular brands and declared a stalemate. Others felt that Pepsi was winning the marketing battle in the United States, with Coke edging ahead in foreign markets.

MARKETING STRATEGY

Pepsi and Anheuser-Busch were the biggest advertisers for Super Bowl XXX, with four minutes of spots each. For Pepsi the telecast was the kickoff for its 1996 ad campaigns. Pepsi spent $5 million to create its ads and another $11 million or so to air them. The outlay represented 10 percent of Pepsi's 1996 television ad budget for its flagship brand.

"Security Camera" was the fruit of an unusual brainstorming session at BBDO. Michael Patti, executive creative director, and Don Schneider, senior creative director/art director, were conceptualizing a new Pepsi campaign when chief creative officer Ted Sann poked his head into the office and said, "Security camera." It was not the first time that, in the middle of creative discussions, Sann had thrown out a word or phrase that later came to form the essence of a campaign. "Ted will always come up with something valuable," Schneider told *Shoot* magazine, "whether it's the germ of an idea, adding to the idea or killing an idea that doesn't make sense."

As originally presented to Pepsi, the commercial had a different ending. In the original the Coca-Cola driver found himself caught by an old woman in his attempt to snatch a Pepsi from the display case. The gag ended with the guilty-faced deliveryman sneaking back later to retrieve the can. After shooting the commercial in this form, Patti and Schneider decided to go in a different direction. The new slapstick ending had the driver accidentally bringing down a torrent of Pepsi cans in his effort to steal a beverage for himself. Instead of having the driver slink back to grab a Pepsi, the new denouement, improvised by actor Bays, had the deliveryman putting a lone Pepsi back on the empty shelf before fleeing the scene of the incident. According to Sann, the success of the commercial lay in its use of showing, rather than telling, its story line. "Ads that depend on visual puns tend to be more successful," he observed.

"Security Camera" was the latest in a long line of quirky, humorous Pepsi ads, most of them created by BBDO. Pepsi's traditional reliance on humor dovetailed nicely with a growing trend in advertising. The increasing complexity of contemporary society was often cited as the reason viewers wanted to be amused by television commercials. During the first eight years that *USA Today*'s Ad Track survey measured viewer response to Super Bowl ads, only one nonhumorous spot made it into the annual list of five top-rated ads. The success of commercials like "Security Camera" represented a victory of the new thinking in advertising over what had been the conventional wisdom in past decades. "For years, Madison Avenue was deathly afraid that humor would reflect badly on their products," observed comedian Marty Ingels. "But today, you have automatic product acceptance if you can make people laugh."

OUTCOME

USA Today's Ad Track rated "Security Camera" the number one commercial of the 1996 Super Bowl telecast. In fact, the Pepsi spot came within 2 percentage points of topping the Budweiser frogs as the most popular of all campaigns rated by Ad Track since 1995. About 45 percent of respondents reported that they liked the new campaign a lot. There was, however, a difference in the response of women and men, with 51 percent of women as opposed to 39 percent of men reporting high favorability.

"It's great because Pepsi confronts Coke," said 24-year-old Erich Peters, one of 60 randomly selected volunteers who used handheld meters to chart their second-by-second reactions to the commercials. "They acknowledge that Coke is there, but Pepsi shows why they are better." Perhaps more importantly, the spot was remembered by a majority of those who watched it. Creative Marketing Consultants of Southfield, Michigan, called 493 Super Bowl viewers after the game and asked them which companies or products they remembered being advertised during the telecast. Pepsi's "Security Camera" came out ahead, with almost 60 percent of survey participants saying that they recalled the spot.

Newsday assembled a panel of seven advertising and marketing executives to review the more than four dozen commercials aired during the Super Bowl telecast. Four of them chose "Security Camera" as their favorite spot. "It was simple and it wasn't overproduced," said David Angelo, executive vice president of Cliff Freeman & Partners.

Ad reviewers responded favorably to the spot as well. "It was true and it was good," *Adweek* magazine's critic wrote of the use of Williams's "Your Cheatin' Heart." Another reviewer dubbed the spot "comic genius," saying that it offered a "precious glimpse of humanity in black and white, reminiscent of Candid Camera." *Advertising Age* magazine named the "Security Camera" spot a category winner in its annual awards. "Coca-Cola better can that guy before BBDO and Joe Pytka strike again," the magazine's editors wrote.

BBDO was awarded a 1996 gold Clio for "Security Camera." At the 1997 New York Festivals, which honored television and cinema advertising and public-service announcements, BBDO won the award for best campaign for its work on "Security Camera" and two other Pepsi spots, "Frozen Tundra" and "Goldfish." The campaign was also honored as the best soft drink series. "Security Camera" took the gold as the best soft drink commercial, for best art direction, and as the best humorous spot.

FURTHER READING

Christy, Nick. "100 Years of Advertising Innovation." *Beverage World,* January 1, 1998.

Goldrich, Robert. "Theory of Evolution." *Shoot,* September 26, 1997.

Lippert, Barbara. "The Big Game's Big Three." *Adweek,* February 12, 1996.

"Madison Avenue's Super Bowl Lesson Is a Knee Slapper." *USA Today,* January 30, 1996.

Robert Schnakenberg

THAT'S BRISK, BABY! CAMPAIGN

OVERVIEW

PepsiCo, Inc., entered the ready-to-drink tea market in 1991 when it joined with the Thomas J. Lipton Company (which later became part of Unilever) to form the Pepsi-Lipton Tea Partnership to market, produce, and develop tea-based drinks. Two ready-to-drink Lipton brands defined the partnership: Lipton's Brew (later renamed Lipton's Iced Tea), a bottled, hot-brewed tea; and Lipton Brisk, a lower-priced tea manufactured after the fashion of soft drinks and sold in aluminum cans. In 1996 Pepsi began backing the latter product with a high-profile campaign dubbed "That's Brisk, Baby!" Created by ad agency J. Walter Thompson, it featured model-animated versions of pop-culture icons.

Each of the TV spots hewed closely, throughout most of the campaign's seven-year-run, to a simple story line in which a downtrodden or exhausted celebrity (living or dead) was able to revive himself dramatically by drinking Lipton Brisk. Those figures made into latex-covered puppets for Pepsi's benefit included Frank Sinatra, Sylvester Stallone, Bruce Willis, Elvis Presley, James Brown, Willie Nelson, and Coolio, among others. In 2000 integrated print and online components each assumed a substantial role in the campaign, but the surreal TV spots were the centerpiece. The budget ranged between $7 million in 1996 and $21 million in 2002.

"That's Brisk, Baby!" was a hit among consumers—especially young adults—and among ad-industry critics. Lipton Brisk increasingly dominated in the ready-to-drink tea market through 2000, but its market share and sales volume began to erode in that year. Although PepsiCo allotted more advertising money to the brand in 2002 than in any previous year, Lipton Brisk posted a record 14 percent sales volume decline. The campaign was phased out, and the brand did little advertising in 2003 and 2004.

HISTORICAL CONTEXT

The 1990s cola slump was attributed partly to the health consciousness of the decade. Baby boomers, now in their 40s and 50s, were rejecting traditional colas for more wholesome concoctions. Snapple Beverage Corporation pioneered a new kind of soft drink and inspired both Pepsi and Coke to improve the taste of ready-to-drink tea. According to an article in *Marketing* by Joshua Levine, the "so-called new age sodas" were expensive, with no preservatives or additives. In the 1990s, wrote Levine, "That's the highest kind of praise." The ready-to-drink tea market increased by 50 percent in 1991, and experts predicted that it would increase at least that much more over the following

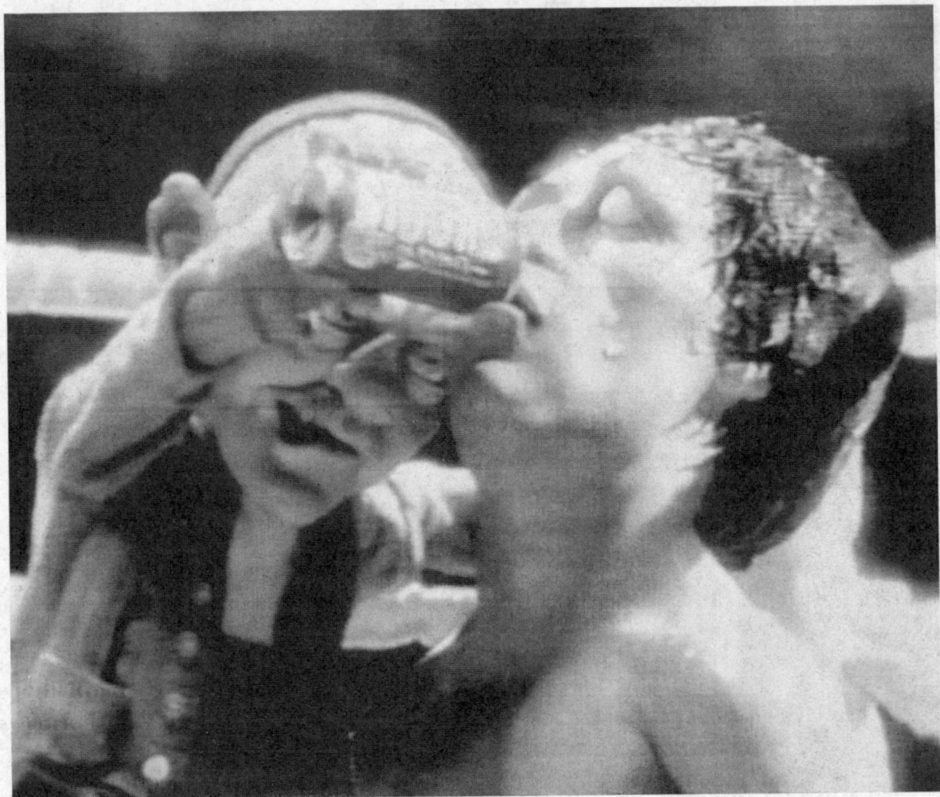

The clay-mation figure of Rocky Balboa from Lipton's "That's Brisk, Baby!" campaign.
PEPSI-COLA COMPANY. REPRODUCED BY PERMISSION.

several years. In comparison cola sales increased just 1.5 percent in the same year. The market value for cola, however, was $34 billion, compared to a modest $600 million for tea. Still, both Pepsi and Coke were looking to the future when they began marketing tea in 1992.

Within a few years the tea market had exceeded expectations. By 1994 sales of ready-to-drink tea had reached the $1 billion mark, and on February 1, 1994, PepsiCo announced that earnings from its U.S. beverage division had risen by 17 percent to more than $900 million. Part of the increase was credited to the streamlining of packaging and to a cost-effective restructuring in which Pepsi eliminated 1,800 people from middle management and shifted them into sales. But according to analysts, the increase had more to do with PepsiCo's quest for new products.

According to a December 1992 article in *Fortune,* this hunger, nothing new for Pepsi, stemmed in part from a "pressure to catch up." In addition to Frito-Lay products, PepsiCo operated three profitable fast-food chains: Pizza Hut, KFC (formerly Kentucky Fried Chicken), and Taco Bell. CEO Wayne Calloway, who headed Pepsi from 1984 until 1996, regularly pushed managers to "rethink business." Under Calloway's leadership Pepsi started marketing All Sport in 1993 and testing a carbonated juice drink, Splash, in 1994. According to *BusinessWeek,* approximately two-thirds of Pepsi's volume growth in 1993 came from noncarbonated beverages. By 1997 Pepsi was marketing other alternative drinks, including Aquafina, a bottled water, and Frappuccino, a ready-to-drink coffee beverage created in partnership with Starbucks Coffee.

By the mid-1990s marketing experts feared that Pepsi had overextended itself with so many products that it could not concentrate on marketing its soft-drink syrup, which still constituted the bulk of its sales and profits. In 1997 PepsiCo made a decision to spin off its restaurant chains into a separate business entity so that, as *BusinessWeek* said, it could "focus on its core beverage and snack food business."

TARGET MARKET

In the "That's Brisk, Baby!" campaign the Pepsi-Lipton Tea Partnership targeted consumers between the ages of 18 and 39. This was the age bracket that drank the most iced tea, said Jon Harris, public relations manager for the

The clay-mation figure of Reggie Jackson in "The Babe," the third television commercial in the campaign. PEPSI-COLA COMPANY. REPRODUCED BY PERMISSION.

Pepsi-Lipton Tea Partnership. "However, when we do spots, we're appealing to all," he added. Mickey Paxton of the J. Walter Thompson agency described the campaign as having a lot of what he called "breadth." "We threw out a huge net," Paxton said. "Tea is not what you drink when you're 14, 15, 16 years old. You're not as concerned about health at that age. When you're 20 to 25, though, it's totally different."

The campaign was designed to appeal to those 20- and 30-somethings that Paxton believed were looking for truthfulness. "They are very sophisticated and cynical, and you need to put it in a package they can appreciate. 'Don't treat me like an idiot' is their message," he said. "At the same time, the campaign needed to be universal. Sinatra's music is appreciated by everyone, even the 20-somethings." Harris agreed: "The Lipton Brisk campaign matched the intelligence of today's young adult. It's about talking with them, not down to them."

The campaign was, in fact, especially popular and effective with younger consumers. In a poll of 356 adults conducted by *Advertising & Marketing* and *USA Today*'s Ad Track, close to 40 percent of consumers aged 18 to 29 said that they liked the ads a lot, and 21 percent called them very effective. In contrast, 23 percent of consumers age 30 to 49 said that they liked the ads a lot, while 15 percent in that age bracket rated them as very effective. No one at the Pepsi-Lipton Tea Partnership was surprised by the success of the campaign. They had expected the target audience to react "very well," said Harris, "and we exceeded our expectations."

COMPETITION

Lipton Brisk's major competition was Coca-Cola's Nestea Cool, produced by Coca-Cola Nestlé Refreshment. While PepsiCo led the market in sales of ready-to-drink ice tea, Coke commanded the beverage industry overall, outselling Pepsi both in the United States and elsewhere. According to *BusinessWeek,* in North America in 1997 Coke had about 45 percent of the market share compared to Pepsi's 30 percent. In other countries Coke's lead was even greater. In Europe Coke had 45 percent of the market compared to PepsiCo's 15 percent, and in Latin America 55 percent to 18 percent. While Coke earned $3.9 billion on $18.5 billion in sales in 1996, PepsiCo's beverage department reported earnings of $582 million on $10.5 billion in sales during the same year.

I HEAR VOICES

Joe Piscopo, actor and stand-up comic, provided the voice for Frank Sinatra in the "Backstage" TV commercial. Piscopo's Sinatra imitation had been part of the performer's stand-up act for several years and was seen periodically on NBC's *Saturday Night Live.* Billy West played the part of Sinatra's rather eccentric agent. Sinatra's wife, Tina Sinatra, approved both the script and the voice for the commercial.

The following year, when Sylvester Stallone continued the campaign, he did his own voice. "Once we got Sinatra, Stallone was interested," said the campaign's creator, Mickey Paxton of the ad agency J. Walter Thompson. According to Paxton, being in the same category as Sinatra carried a certain amount of respect, and Stallone wanted to be a part of the series and the reputation it was earning. In "The Babe," the campaign's third commercial, Reggie Jackson and Yankees owner George Steinbrenner did their own voices.

By 1997 marketing experts believed that PepsiCo had renewed a commitment to give Coca-Cola a run for its money, much as it did during the 1970s with its "New Generation" campaign. The decision to spin off its fast-food operations indicated one step in that direction. "Shedding its restaurants will . . . give PepsiCo an opportunity to boost sales of its soft-drink syrups to other restaurant chains, which have been reluctant to sell Pepsi products because it . . . put money in their competitor's pockets," wrote Ken Sheets in *Kiplinger's Personal Finance Magazine.* In 1997 PepsiCo introduced a new logo (a globe) and color (blue), evident on the Lipton Brisk can. Both were part of PepsiCo's efforts to create "a corporate icon that's as powerful as Coke's script," wrote Nicole Harris in *BusinessWeek.*

MARKETING STRATEGY

By 1996 Lipton Brisk commanded the number one spot in the ready-to-drink tea market. "We had the number one tea and we wanted to identify with the number one pop culture icons," Jon Harris, public relations manager for the Pepsi-Lipton Tea Partnership, said. "The biggest challenge of the campaign was deciding which icon to go with." Because Lipton Brisk was sold and distributed as a soda, the partnership felt that it needed a campaign that would appeal to the soda crowd. Marketing experts, in fact, felt that the campaign was successful because Lipton Brisk was marketed as a soda, not a tea. Tea was usually marketed for taste, quality, and processing. "Because we're competing in the soda-drinking category, we needed something that was fun and breakthrough," Paxton said. "People watching and being entertained and liking it." He added that "the whole idea was to go beyond cool, all the way to brisk. Cool people are flawed. People identify with them. And Frank Sinatra was the coolest person we could think of."

Paxton's belief that the younger consumers of the late 1990s were intelligent and high-tech led him to choose the sophisticated technology of stop-frame model animation, a method used in the feature-length films *James and the Giant Peach* and *The Nightmare before Christmas.* Each frame of the film was shot separately, with 24 frames every second. The actors were miniature latex figures. The only thing in color in the commercials was the blue Lipton Brisk can. "The black-and-white technology adds a bit of class," Paxton said.

The campaign's first spot, which debuted on June 17, 1996, showed the miniature animated Sinatra figure performing to a packed house of screaming fans, only to be too tired to do an encore. After a backstage swig of Lipton Brisk, the crooner burst out with "Ahhhh, that's brisk, baby!" and was ready to sing all night. A year later, in the week of May 8, 1997, a second commercial aired during the National Basketball Association Playoffs. This spot featured a model-animated figure of Rocky Balboa, the boxing hero of the 1976 film *Rocky* starring Sylvester Stallone. In the spot Rocky came up a winner because he drank Lipton Brisk tea at the 11th hour, which gave him the edge he needed to knock out his opponent.

In the spring of 1998 the campaign focused on legendary New York Yankees players and coaches of different eras, as an exhausted Babe Ruth was given an ice-cold Brisk by Reggie Jackson. Invigorated, Ruth hit the winning run. Yankees Billy Martin, Mickey Mantle, and George Steinbrenner made appearances in the spot.

The parody of pop-culture figures in a 1999 update of "That's Brisk, Baby!" was somewhat more pointed. One spot, released during that year's Oscar Awards broadcast, showed model-animated versions of the characters George and Louise Jefferson from the 1970s sitcom *The Jeffersons* accosting the actor Bruce Willis at a Planet Hollywood (a chain of celebrity-themed restaurants that the real-life Willis co-owned). "Willis," George Jefferson said, "you gonna put a George Jefferson display at Planet Hollywood, or what?" "Sorry, pal," Willis replied. "Stopped movin' on up in the '70s." The Jeffersons attacked Willis, and the action-movie star was able to vanquish them, after downing a Brisk, by causing a model whale to fall from the ceiling on top of them. Another 1999 spot showed the martial-arts movie star

Bruce Lee facing off with the fictional martial-arts hero the Karate Kid from the 1984 movie of the same name.

In 2000 Pepsi and J. Walter Thompson turned their attention once again, as in the campaign's introductory Sinatra spot, to the world of popular music. In the new commercial figures from different eras and genres—Elvis Presley, James Brown, Willie Nelson, and Coolio—sang and danced to a hip-hop version of the Presley hit "Jail House Rock." A series of four print ads, one devoted to each of the musical stars featured in the TV commercial, also ran that year, marking the campaign's first significant extension into print media. Internet became an increasingly important part of the "That's Brisk, Baby!" campaign in 2000 as well, as J. Walter Thompson's interactive unit, Digital@JWT, won the campaign's Web duties away from online specialists Agency.com, whom Pepsi had initially chosen for the work. Banner ads on popular websites were used, while TV spots and print ads directed consumers to a Lipton Brisk website where the TV spot as well as behind-the-scenes features were available for viewing.

The most significant 2001 addition to "That's Brisk, Baby!" was an online trivia contest targeting 18- to 24-year-olds, in which the model-animated James Brown and Rocky figures served as hosts of a "Total Refresh Tour." The virtual tour consisted of pop-up ads placed on five websites popular among the target group; consumers had to answer trivia questions on each of the five sites in order to qualify for the promotion's grand prize, a Ford Focus automobile. In 2002 Pepsi phased out the model-animated concept by means of an elaborate in-joke. A spot that aired during that year's Super Bowl featured an animated model of the actor Danny DeVito leading a protest of Lipton Brisk's decision to fire its puppet-spokespersons because a reformulated version of the drink "tastes so good it sells itself." A second 2002 spot showed DeVito and James Brown revenging themselves on the brand by vandalizing a parked Lipton Brisk truck, destroying boxes and cans of the product with crowbars and bats.

OUTCOME

The campaign was well received by consumers and highly lauded within the advertising industry. It won several prizes in the creative category, including Clio, British Design and Art Direction, and ADDY awards. J.J. Jordon, executive vice president of J. Walter Thompson, said, "It's different than anything on the tube." The campaign was seen by its creators as honoring things that America's heroes stood for, and they hoped to align Lipton Brisk with that kind of image. "These are forever icons," said Jon Harris, "and so is Lipton tea." The puppets became celebrities in their own right. For instance, the NBC show *Dateline* commemorated Sinatra's 1998 death with footage of the model-animated Sinatra from the Lipton Brisk commercials, and Sylvester Stallone appeared on *The Tonight Show* with the puppet version of himself in hand.

"That's Brisk, Baby!" also played a substantial role in Lipton Brisk's sales success during these years, though that success slowed substantially toward the end of the campaign's run. During the seven-year life of the campaign, Lipton Brisk helped redefine the ready-to-drink tea market, which had previously been dominated by premium-priced, hot-brewed, bottled teas such as Snapple and Arizona. By 1999 the brand was firmly at the top of the ready-to-drink tea market, and many analysts credited the youth appeal of "That's Brisk, Baby!" for spurring consistent growth. In 2000, however, Lipton Brisk's sales volume began to decline, and these declines continued in subsequent years. In 2002, when Pepsi spent more to market Lipton Brisk than it had in any previous year—an estimated $21 million—the brand's sales volume declined by 14 percent. In 2003 and 2004 Lipton Brisk's marketing profile plummeted dramatically; aside from small-scale promotions targeting urban teens, Pepsi did little to advertise the brand.

FURTHER READING

Butler, Simon. "Puppet Tea Party." *Adweek* (eastern ed.), June 24, 2002.

DeLory, Cherie. "The King Rocks with Lipton Brisk Iced Tea." *Boards Online,* March 9, 2000. Available from <http://www.boardsmag.com/articles/online/20000309/brisk.html>

Enrico, Dottie. " 'Ol Blue Eyes,' Sly Give Lipton Brisk a Taste of Success." *USA Today,* October 6, 1997.

Garfield, Bob. "While Brand Is Brisk, the Ads Are Baffling." *Advertising Age,* March 22, 1999.

Harris, Nicole. "If You Can't Beat 'Em, Copy 'Em." *BusinessWeek,* November 17, 1997, p. 50.

Levine, Joshua. "Watch Out, Snapple!" *Forbes,* May 10, 1993, pp. 142, 146.

McKay, Betsy, and Suzanne Vranica. "Selling Iced Tea in February: Inside One Campaign." *Wall Street Journal,* January 28, 2002.

Owens, Jennifer. "Digital@JWT Unveils Online Promo for Lipton Brisk." *Brandweek,* April 23, 2001.

Prince, Greg W. "Power Couple." *Beverage World,* March 15, 1999.

Sellers, Patricia. "Can Coke and Pepsi Make Quaker Sweat?" *Fortune,* July 10, 1995, p. 20.

———. "If It Ain't Broke, Fix It Anyway." *Fortune,* December 28, 1992, pp. 49–50.

Sheets, Ken. "PepsiCo Goes in Search of Its Next Pepsi Generation." *Kiplinger's Personal Finance Magazine,* April 1997, pp. 32, 34.

Streisand, Betsy, Eva Pomice, and Dana Hawkins. "Mixed-Up Media Messages." *U.S. News & World Report,* December 9, 1991, pp. 61, 64.

Zinn, Laura. "Does Pepsi Have Too Many Products?" *BusinessWeek,* February 14, 1994, pp. 64–66.

Anita Coryell
Mark Lane

THIS IS DIET? CAMPAIGN

OVERVIEW

Since the first diet soft drink was introduced in the 1960s, the diet category has been a vital part of the beverage industry worldwide. Diet Pepsi is PepsiCo's second-biggest trademark, a $3 billion brand. Yet this important brand has been at the mercy of cultural trends that have seen low-calorie sodas go in and out of style as Americans think and rethink the merits of a healthy lifestyle.

Throughout the 1980s diet soft drinks enjoyed robust sales, with the explosion of the exercise and health food industries. Diet sodas eventually cornered some 30 percent of the soft drink business. The biggest players in this category were the two giants, Diet Pepsi and Diet Coke, which together controlled about 75 percent of the soft drink business. Diet Coke invariably vied for market share on the basis of taste. Its signature slogan, "Just For the Taste of It," began running in 1982. The idea was to convince consumers that they did not have to sacrifice full cola enjoyment in their pursuit of a low-calorie soft drink. By contrast, Pepsi ads appealed to the confidence and self-image of the consumer, in what has been termed a "lifestyle" approach. The benefits of drinking Diet Pepsi were stressed with little mention of its taste. In the 1990s, however, those marketing strategies, and the fortunes of the diet category as a whole, changed dramatically.

By the middle of the decade, the diet category had been dealt a blow by the rising popularity of bottled waters and alternative soft drink flavors. Soft drink manufacturers also had lagged in their efforts to promote diet brands, perhaps in anticipation of the Food and Drug Administration's pending approval of new artificial sweeteners. Some cultural observers even blamed the declining sales on the emergence of a new hedonist ethic in American society, as abstinence, asceticism, and calorie counting went out and cigar smoking and sensual gratification came back in. The major players in the diet soda category had to rethink their marketing approaches with this new cultural move toward self-indulgence.

In April 1997 PepsiCo launched a massive creative campaign for Diet Pepsi, complete with a new tag line, packaging, and a co-promotion with Pepsi-owned snack chip manufacturer Frito-Lay. The new slogan, "This Is Diet?," heralded a national repositioning of the brand's look and image. The company introduced a colorful new bottle, which it termed "sophisticated and assertive, with classic good looks."

For the first time PepsiCo was selling its diet brand on the basis of its taste. A major confrontation with rival Coca-Cola was avoided only because Coca-Cola changed to a more lifestyle-oriented advertising strategy. This curious switch amused many industry observers, who wondered aloud whether consumers would even notice the change. As Diet Pepsi's sales continued to fall through 1998, it became increasingly clear that consumers had not noticed and that the "This Is Diet?" campaign alone would not suffice to turn around Diet Pepsi's market fortunes.

HISTORICAL CONTEXT

During its first 65 years the Pepsi-Cola Company sold only one product—Pepsi. With the post-World War II baby boom, however, the way the nation thought of soft drinks changed along with other changes in the population. For many people, soft drinks had to be not just refreshing but also a complement to diet habits. So in 1963 the company developed a new low-calorie drink that carried the Pepsi-Cola name: Diet Pepsi.

First advertised alongside Pepsi, Diet Pepsi later took on an identity of its own. One of its earliest campaigns, "Girlwatchers," was built around a catchy jingle that became so popular it was released as a commercial record and hit the Top 40 list. The diet craze soon spawned other beverages as well. In 1975 Pepsi Light, with a distinctive lemon taste, was introduced as an alternative to traditional diet colas. In 1982 Pepsi Free and Diet Pepsi Free, the first major brand caffeine-free colas, were introduced.

In 1984 Diet Pepsi was reformulated with a new artificial sweetener, aspartame, which was marketed under the trade name NutraSweet. PepsiCo also ran a series of popular television spots to advertise the new formulation. Geraldine Ferraro, the first woman to run for the office of vice president of the United States, starred in a Diet Pepsi spot following her election defeat in 1984. In 1986 Diet Pepsi's television commercial "Apartment 10G," featuring actor Michael J. Fox, was widely hailed as the commercial of the year and became an instant classic. This superbly edited commercial forced Fox to defy rain, traffic, and a menacing gang to fetch a soda for his beautiful female neighbor. Pepsi was so thrilled with the response that the *Family Ties* star got a reported $2 million a year deal to star in three more spots. The same year saw the unveiling of a new Diet Pepsi logo.

In 1987 another Diet Pepsi commercial, "Mustang," became the first advertisement ever to appear on a movie video. In 1990 the singer Ray Charles joined Diet Pepsi campaign veterans Billy Crystal and Michael J. Fox in a new campaign called "The Right Ones." In 1991 the slogan for Diet Pepsi was modified as Ray Charles—backed up by the Uh-Huh Girls—starred in one of the most popular advertising campaigns of the time, "You got the right one baby, uh-huh!" That catch phrase remained in place until the launch of "This Is Diet?" in 1997.

Diet Pepsi sales remained stable despite fluctuations in the diet cola market. But market share sluggishness forced PepsiCo to reexamine its marketing strategy. In 1996 Diet Pepsi sales rose by 1.6 percent while overall volume in the soft drink market rose by 3.6 percent. Diet Pepsi's market share dropped from 5.8 to 5.7 percent, and the brand plummeted from fourth to seventh in brand rankings.

TARGET MARKET

Market research conducted by Coca-Cola in 1997 in preparation for its revamp of Diet Coke advertising shed light on the types of market groups targeted by both Diet Coke and Diet Pepsi. The three "attitudinal groups" of consumers were identified as "Fit and Confidents," "Reluctant Dieters," and "Aggressive Dieters." According to Coca-Cola company documents, "Fit and Confidents" were men and women in their 20s who kept their weight down but drank diet colas anyway to stave off unwanted weight gain. "Reluctant Dieters" were men and women in their 30s who were also known as the "Big Mac and Diet Coke" group because they watched their weight but valued taste as well. Finally, the "Aggressive Dieters" group was comprised of women over 35 who put a high value on staying in shape.

But diet cola drinkers who fit into those categories formed only part of the target market for Diet Pepsi. With dieting declining in importance on Americans' list of priorities, and with many more beverage options open for those who do prefer a low-calorie alternative, Diet Pepsi's marketing strategists faced the difficult task of persuading new consumers to try their drink. They decided that the best way to appeal to these consumers was on the basis of taste. The phrase "This Is Diet?" was crafted to appeal primarily to those who would not normally opt for a diet cola but who might do so if pleasantly surprised by its taste.

Not that PepsiCo gave up on dieters entirely. It hoped to win over health-conscious consumers by convincing them to drink Diet Pepsi rather than a competing beverage, whether that beverage was another diet soda, fruit juice, or bottled water. But in a climate of declining diet sales, the battle for new customers had become even more imperative than usual. Advertising, merchandising, and giveaways were all ways in which Diet Pepsi fought to persuade more Americans to start drinking its diet cola.

THIS IS SKUNKY?

One of the reasons PepsiCo was in such a rush to win FDA approval for its new artificial sweetener acesulfame potassium (also known as Ace K) was to provide an alternative for consumers turned off by aspartame, the sweetener used in Diet Pepsi. For years Diet Pepsi drinkers have complained about a certain "skunky" quality in the beverage when it has been left on the shelf for a while.

Some dismissed the skunkiness as a figment of peoples' imaginations. But studies have indicated that NutraSweet—the trade name of aspartame—can begin to taste bad in a relatively short period of time. Apparently, diet soda made with NutraSweet does not age well. In fact, as time goes by, the sweetener decomposes, allowing the other "flavor notes" in cola—mostly sour acids and bitter caffeine—to become more pronounced because they are no longer balanced by the sweetness.

Some health experts also have claimed that aspartame breaks down into chemicals that may be harmful to humans. They cite studies by the National Cancer Institute and the Washington University School of Medicine. But both the U.S. government and the manufacturer maintain that aspartame is safe and say there is no scientific evidence that it causes any health problems, even when it breaks down.

To deflect public criticism until Ace K could be introduced, Diet Pepsi began putting freshness dates on its cans. Consumers were informed that the quality of aspartame-sweetened products deteriorates within 60 to 90 days. The warmer the temperature, the quicker the deterioration. Consequently, experts recommend that diet sodas containing aspartame be stored in a cool place.

COMPETITION

While Diet Pepsi's market share slipped from 5.8 percent to 5.7 percent in 1995, Diet Coke was having its own problems. It too lost a percentage point off its share, though it remained fixed atop the market at 8.7 percent.

With the launch of the "This Is Diet?" campaign in April 1997, Diet Pepsi focused on the taste of the drink in a marketing campaign for the first time. A week later Coca-Cola announced that Diet Coke was dropping its 15-year-old tag line "Just For the Taste of It" in favor of the lifestyle-based "You Are What You Drink." A number of industry observers pointed out the irony of the two soft drink giants essentially flip-flopping their marketing positions in the course of a month.

MARKETING STRATEGY

"This Is Diet?" represented the biggest new campaign for Diet Pepsi since its "You've Got the Right One Baby, Uh-Huh" campaign in the early 1990s. PepsiCo's national repositioning of its Diet Pepsi brand was designed to emphasize what the company called Diet Pepsi's "refreshing great taste." The national ad campaign kicked off with two new commercials, "Interrogation" and "Wedding," that began running the week of April 15, 1997. Both spots were created by longtime PepsiCo Inc. ad agency BBDO Worldwide, New York, and were aired in 30- and 60-second versions.

In "Interrogation" *NYPD Blue* actor Dennis Franz played a tough cop questioning a suspect who is tied to a chair. He holds a cup of Diet Pepsi while he tries to intimidate the suspect, and eventually he tosses it in the man's face. The second spot, "Wedding," featured a young bride who had been left at the altar on her wedding day. In an effort to comfort his tearful daughter, the bride's father offers her a can of Diet Pepsi. Both commercials close with a moment of ironic humor as the refreshing taste of Diet Pepsi surprises the recipients, who then pose the brand's tag line question, "This Is Diet?"

In Great Britain the ads were given a distinctly British gloss. Three spots were created by Abbott Mead Vickers BBDO, doing creative work for Diet Pepsi in the United Kingdom for the first time since 1993. The spots featured a girl so swept away by the taste of her Diet Pepsi that she remains oblivious to all sorts of disasters taking place around her. The ads, which retained the "This Is Diet?" tag line, were an attempt to win over cynical British audiences who might not have related to the "Americanized" versions airing across the pond.

To further support its repositioning efforts, PepsiCo designed new packaging and logos for both Diet Pepsi and Caffeine-Free Diet Pepsi. The word "Diet" appeared in script in red and silver on Diet Pepsi cans, which had previously listed both words in blue block letters. The new logo was intended to be more contemporary and eye-catching, with new graphics that built on the brand's former look, adding depth to the design and creating a three-dimensional effect.

A Frito-Lay co-promotion was also part of the marketing effort. Beginning in late April 1997, Pepsi offered consumers savings on what it termed its "better for you" beverages and snacks. On specially-marked Diet Pepsi 12- and 24-pack cases, consumers received coupons for savings on low-fat snacks from Frito-Lay. Likewise, Frito-Lay also featured coupons on specially-marked packaging, offering savings on two-liter bottles of Diet Pepsi and on 12- and 24-pack cases. The campaign was supported with "This Is Diet?" point-of-purchase materials.

OUTCOME

"This Is Diet?" failed to stem the tide of declining sales for Diet Pepsi. As a sign of what has been called "cola fatigue," Coca-Cola Classic, Diet Coke, Pepsi-Cola, and Diet Pepsi all lost share to flavored drinks in 1997. Although Diet Pepsi's sales fell 1 percent, the other colas did post modest volume gains. Coca-Cola Classic's sales rose 2.5 percent, and Diet Coke's sales increased 0.9 percent, while Pepsi sales inched up 0.5 percent.

The "This Is Diet?" campaign also brought PepsiCo and the brand some unwanted publicity. The Dennis Franz "Interrogation" spot created controversy when the NBC network refused to air it on the grounds that it promoted rival ABC's series *NYPD Blue.* The commercials failed to win any industry awards and were generally deemed below the standards met by Pepsi and BBDO in previous campaigns.

A long-term solution for Pepsi's diet cola problems may have finally come in 1998 with the Food and Drug Administration's approval of acesulfame potassium, an artificial sweetener known more commonly as Ace K. The new sweetener, which has a longer shelf life than aspartame, was rushed quickly to market in a new low-calorie cola product, Pepsi One. The new drink scored higher among consumers than any new product PepsiCo had ever launched. Industry response was swift and favorable. "The diet segment has long needed a healthy dose of news and excitement," commented John D. Sicher, publisher of *Beverage Digest.* "I'm sure Coke is going to take a long, hard look at this."

FURTHER READING

"Cola Wars Produce New Ads for Diet Pepsi, Sprite." *Tampa Tribune,* April 19, 1997.

"Diet Pepsi Gets New Look, New Ads." *Sentinel Orlando,* April 20, 1997.

Elliott, Stuart. "Coca-Cola Will Take a New Tack To Appeal to Diet Soda Drinkers." *New York Times,* May 14, 1997.

"Hot Spot: Diet Pepsi: Low-Cal Relief for Stressful Situations." *Advertising Age,* April 21, 1997.

Robert Schnakenberg

Perdue Farms Inc.

■

31149 Old Ocean City Rd.
Salisbury, Maryland 21801
USA
Telephone: (410) 543-3000
Fax: (410) 543-3292
Web site: www.perdue.com

■■■

NOW ARRIVING CAMPAIGN

OVERVIEW

For many years chicken has been a staple of the American dinner table. And one of the leading companies to produce and market poultry has been Perdue Farms Inc. of Salisbury, Maryland. The beak-like visage of its chairman and chief spokesman, Frank Perdue, had come to symbolize freshness and quality in the minds of many poultry consumers. In the 1990s, however, increased public awareness of food safety—spurred on by highly publicized outbreaks of food poisoning—threatened to erode the image of Perdue chickens as wholesome, healthful foods. Changes in federal food safety regulations enacted in 1996 were only part of the solution to this problem. Perdue took the health scare as an opportunity to reinforce the core image of its brand as one of "golden yellow" freshness. A series of print and television ads hammered home this message in whimsical, then alarmist fashion.

The television commercial "Now Arriving" was crafted in May 1997 by Perdue's longtime agency Lowe & Partners/SMS. It shows company president Jim Perdue—Frank's son and new company spokesman—being greeted in an airport by a Hare Krishna who offers him a marigold. Marigolds being an integral part of a chicken's diet, Perdue harangues the mendicant at length about the healthy feed regimen of Perdue's poultry.

Then in August 1997 Perdue took out full-page ads in major newspapers questioning the safety of its competitors' poultry products. "Warning! Before You Buy Another Chicken, Read This!" announced the banner headlines on the ads, which touted the chicken giant's policy of requiring its birds to "pass 65 quality inspections, 22 more than the government's so-called Grade A standards." The attention-grabbing print ads were designed by R. C. Auletta & Company and signed by Jim Perdue. This and the Hare Krishna ad both addressed a specific market problem—the food safety concern. They also attempted to build brand value in a manner consistent with two decades of Perdue advertising. Most industry observers rated them a success on both fronts.

HISTORICAL CONTEXT

In the late 1990s Perdue Farms was the second-largest poultry producer in the United States. Its branded chicken and turkey products were sold in retail supermarkets, grocery stores, and butcher shops in a market area comprising almost 40 percent of the nation's population. Perdue's food service chicken and turkey products were sold nationwide, and the company's products were exported to more than 30 countries. Sales for all operations exceeded $2 billion annually.

Founded as a table-egg poultry farm in Salisbury, Maryland, by Arthur W. Perdue in 1920, Perdue did not hire a second associate until 1930. In 1939 Arthur Perdue's 19-year-old son, Frank, joined the company as its third employee. In 1950 Frank assumed control of the company. Incorporated in 1953, the company began the process of vertically integrating its operations by constructing hatcheries, feed mills, and storage facilities. By the late 1960s this process was complete. Perdue Farms now had complete quality control of its poultry products.

In 1968 the Perdue brand was born as the company entered the highly competitive New York City broiler market. A limited radio ad campaign was launched, emphasizing the quality of the Perdue brand of broilers. That same year Frank Perdue assumed the role of lead company spokesman. Three years later Perdue Farms embarked on its first national advertising campaign, commissioning the fledgling New York ad agency of Scaly, McCabe, and Solves. Relying on the tag line "It Takes a Tough Man to Make a Tender Chicken," the print and television ads played off Frank Perdue's owlish persona. Scaly, McCabe, and Solves would oversee the Perdue account for the next 15 years.

The following year Perdue ads introduced another of the signature themes that would come to define the brand. In commercials that debuted in the Philadelphia, Providence, and Boston markets, the company compared its own fresh chickens to competitors' frozen birds in order to emphasize Perdue's trademark "yellow" freshness. A decade later the freshness and healthfulness was still front and center in the minds of company marketers. In 1983 Perdue became the first poultry processor to provide nutritional labels on its products. That same year Jim Perdue, son of Frank, joined the family business as a management trainee in quality control at the Salisbury plant.

In its pursuit of quality control Perdue initiated the Quality Improvement Process in 1985. An official Quality Process was also adopted at that time. Responding to the needs of health-conscious consumers, Perdue's feed researchers in 1986 implemented a new diet that substantially reduced fat in chickens. And a 1990 television commercial had Frank Perdue driving a nail into a birdhouse with a competitor's frozen chicken to highlight Perdue's freshness.

In 1991 Jim Perdue took over from his father. He was named chairman of the board of Perdue Farms, with Frank Perdue designated chairman of the board's executive committee. In one of his first moves, Jim Perdue green-lighted the launch of the "Fit 'n' Easy" line of skinless, boneless chicken and turkey products. Additional nutrition initiatives included expanded nutritional labels and a series of "Guides to Nutrition" for consumers. And when a drive to enhance safety capabilities was spurred by outbreaks of E. coli and salmonella in various parts of the United States, Perdue Farms capped its efforts in this arena with the establishment of a new microbiology laboratory in 1993.

The mid-1990s proved to be a period of important changes at Perdue. In 1993 ad agency Scaly, McCabe, and Solves merged with The Lowe Group to form Lowe & Partners/SMS. A concerned Frank Perdue expressed reservations about such a large agency paying sufficient attention to his account. After assurances from Lowe & Partners/SMS executives, the poultry scion agreed to stick with the reconfigured ad house.

In 1994 Perdue did some reconfiguring of its own. The poultry giant acquired Howell Farms, purveyors of the Cooking' Good chicken brand, as well as a processing plant in Milford, Delaware. Perdue Farms was now the second-largest poultry farm in the United States. That same year Jim Perdue made his commercial debut in a series of local television spots with his father Frank. The "Third Generation" spots eased the transition for Perdue to take over the role of company spokesman.

In the late 1990s Perdue's television spots continued to emphasize freshness and food safety. A 1996 spot showed Jim Perdue scolding one of his chickens for eating pizza instead of Perdue's own premium feed. These advertising initiatives were backed up by a highly publicized food safety information campaign. In 1996 Perdue began to implement the HACCP (Hazard Analysis Critical Control Point) program. The company also introduced a free educational booklet for consumers, "Perdue Guide to Safe Handling of Chicken and Turkey Products," and invited members of the press on food safety tours.

TARGET MARKET

"I think about germs," Terri Savage of Oklahoma City told *USA Today* in 1997. "I'm very aware of them. There are all kinds of little buggies you can get that get misdiagnosed as flu and what you've got is food poisoning." Savage was part of a growing number of American consumers who worried as much about food safety as good taste when they cooked. With the increased incidence of food poisoning in the 1990s, this group became a market that Perdue Farms wanted to sell itself to.

Accordingly the poultry giant's 1997 ads addressed the American consumer's legitimate fears about food safety. Polls showed that more than 65 percent of American consumers had some trepidation over food safety, with chicken one of the major areas of concern. Poultry sold in supermarkets is safe to eat if properly handled once it departs the production facility. But the birds must be thoroughly cooked, and any surface or utensil that comes in contact with the uncooked poultry should be washed with soap and hot water. With the

LIKE FATHER LIKE SON

Perdue Farms marked a milestone in 1994 when chairman Frank Perdue introduced his successor as chief company spokesman—his son Jim. In the initial television spot Frank described Jim as "a little project I've been working on for the past 45 years."

It was not the first time that two generations had crossed paths in the world of advertising. Bespectacled popcorn patriarch Orville Redenbacher began appearing in commercials with his grandson shortly before his death in 1995. And Frank Perdue himself once appeared in a print ad with his own father, company founder Arthur Perdue. But there are always risks when the baton is passed from a successful spokesperson to an unknown quantity.

Initially reluctant to try to replace his father, Jim Perdue was swayed by company research showing that consumers liked the idea of knowing who is behind a product. "It turned out it was very important," said the younger Perdue. "It's certainly the heritage of our company. And it's something that the consumer's having a harder time finding today. So that's why we decided to go ahead and try it."

In making the switch from father to son, Perdue's ad partners wisely decided not to try to transplant Frank's personality. "Jim is a little bit softer than Frank," said Sam Scaly, deputy chairman of Lowe & Partners/SMS. "He's not as hard-nosed." So out went the tag line "It Takes a Tough Man to Make a Tender Chicken." And in came the Hare Krishna's. The torch had most assuredly been passed.

overwhelming balance of its business in chicken, Perdue looked to reassure these customers about the freshness and safety of its products.

COMPETITION

The year 1996 was one of record growth for Perdue Farms. The company's acquisition of Howell Farms in January was the second-largest merger in poultry industry history, and the purchase of ConAgra's Milford, Delaware, processing plant vaulted the company to number two in the poultry sector behind Tyson Foods. The two industry leaders had always competed on chicken quality. But the food safety concerns of the mid-1990s gave Perdue a unique opportunity to exploit its advantage on freshness. Emphasizing this point of difference between the two brands was given further impetus due to a series of health scandals that bedeviled Tyson in 1997.

Just days before July 4th—one of the biggest barbecuing days of the year—U.S. Department of Agriculture inspectors found severe problems with chicken heading to consumers from the Tyson slaughtering and processing plant in Cumming, Georgia. Some birds had black machine grease on them, according to reports filed by inspectors. Others had infections under their skin or had been stored in temperatures favorable for bacterial growth. In what one Tyson employee contended was "an act of God," chickens spewed from a machine onto a broken conveyor belt too quickly for workers to handle, and birds were falling onto the floor and piling up. The birds that fell into the plant's drain water were destroyed. The others were reportedly cleaned up and sold. Inspectors classified those deficiencies as "critical," meaning the meat heading to the market was contaminated and, if eaten, would be certain to harm the consumer. The previous year Tyson Foods had accumulated 311 "critical" citations at its Cumming plant, which processes about 1.3 million birds a week.

MARKETING STRATEGY

The "Now Arriving" television ad, in concert with the surrounding print campaign, was what industry analysts considered the rarest of advertising creatures: a brand value spot that also addressed a specific market concern in an effort to build sales. The ads emphasized the traditional Perdue brand themes of freshness and nutrition while countering a growing public perception that commercial chickens may pose a health hazard. In an era when many creative shops seemed to opt for the offbeat and surprising in order to grab the attention of the public, the long-term, big picture thinking implicit in a brand value strategy sometimes got short shrift. As a result companies saw growth in short-term sales without adding any long-term value to their brand.

Novel or dramatic approaches in advertising often can be effective, but usually only if there is some element that reminds consumers what the brand is and what it represents. Often this is a long-term process in which a brand message is hammered into public consciousness repeatedly until the market gets the message. Marketing professors often explain this approach to students by asking them to explain their brand in a single word or phrase. In this way American consumers have come to understand that the Nike brand translates into athletic achievement, BMW is "the ultimate driving machine," and, in this case, Perdue stands for freshness and safety. If the ultimate goal is to get the customers to call up this word or phrase when asked what a brand represents, the first goal is get everyone in the marketing department to agree on this proposition. Unfortunately many creative shops never even bother to ask the question; consequently, a sense of continuity from one campaign to the next may be lost, and that which made the brand famous to begin with is the first casualty.

Every brand has a history—a personality profile in a sense. All brands also possess certain practical advantages that can be used as selling points to the consumer. But most analysts agree that advertising, if it is to be effective in the long as well as the short term, must do more than just lay out the product's pros and cons. A whimsical or offbeat ad is fine as long as its message is drawn from the brand's core identity in order to build the value of the brand.

Brand identity carries with it all sorts of benefits, attributes, and emotional associations. The brand's identity in the final analysis is what sets it apart from all other brands in its category; often called the sustainable point of difference, it is the one thing that customers seem to desire most. Companies that have isolated this "one thing"—in Perdue's case, freshness—and stick to it in their ads usually enjoy a long and healthy life. They can then use whatever gewgaws their creative agencies come up with to attract consumer attention and address specific market concerns, like food safety.

Perdue's print ad, which ran in newspapers in every major city east of the Mississippi, was designed to address consumer concerns (some apparently fostered by other poultry companies) that commercial chickens such as Perdue's were not safe. The testimonial, signed by Jim Perdue, read in part: "Every chicken we sell is raised on a strict, all-natural diet, full of things like corn, soybeans, and marigolds. And no hormones. Our fresh birds have always been fresh, never frozen." The ad failed to mention the fact that many supermarkets froze Perdue chickens once they arrived at the store, but this was tangential to the purpose of the ad, which was to reassure the public that Perdue meat was fresh.

In the television spot entitled "Now Arriving," the same message is relayed in a more humorous manner. Genial Jim Perdue—clearly helped by his physical resemblance to his father—reminds viewers of the healthiness of his poultry products by detailing their macrobiotic diet to an airport Hare Krishna. The fact that the Hindu mendicant flees Perdue and his accordion of chicken snapshots only reinforces the notion that Perdue is almost obsessive about the health of his chickens. The birds' golden yellow color is mentioned three times as a visual cue for consumers who will associate yellow Perdue packaging with healthiness and nutrition the next time they go shopping.

OUTCOME

Perdue's print and television ads of 1997 retained two essential elements from previous Perdue advertising: the use of the company spokesman and the emphasis on freshness, specifically the all-natural diet. In this way the ads remained consistent with the brand identity already established through years of successful advertising. "Perdue is fresh," the ads essentially said, and, concomitant with that, "Perdue is run by a nice man who would not allow you to eat anything that was not good for you." At the same time, however, the ads reacted to a specific consumer concern that threatened to affect chicken sales. In this rare case building long-term brand value and addressing short-term sales concerns went hand in hand.

FURTHER READING

Cavetto, Neil. "Retired Perdue Farms Chairman." *The Cavuto Business Report,* June 19, 1998.

Manning, Anita. "Cooking Up Ways to Safeguard against Food Poisoning." *USA Today,* March 31, 1997.

Moore, Martha T. "New Perdue Onstage—Son Jim Rules Roost and Takes the Spotlight." *USA Today,* April 27, 1994, p. 4.

Nelton, Sharon. "Crowing Over Leadership Succession." *Nation's Business,* May 1, 1995, p. 52.

Yee, Laura. "Perdue Playing Off Fears of Consumers." *The Cleveland Plain Dealer,* August 13, 1997.

Robert Schnakenberg

Pfizer Inc.

235 E 42nd St.
New York, New York 10017-5755
USA
Telephone: (212) 573-2323
Web site: www.pfizer.com

■■■

THE POWER OF ZYRTEC CAMPAIGN

OVERVIEW

Pfizer Inc. emphasized the strength of Zyrtec, a prescription antihistamine, with surreal advertisements that showed people fleeing from allergy-inducing animals and flowers, then taking Zyrtec and resuming their normal routines. "When allergies are a nightmare, remember Zyrtec for fast relief," said one print ad. Since its U.S. launch in 1996, Zyrtec had experienced dynamic growth. This was due in large part to changes in the way that prescription drugs were marketed. After the U.S. Food and Drug Administration began allowing pharmaceutical companies to advertise prescription medications directly to consumers, demand for allergy drugs increased dramatically. Early promotions for Zyrtec and its rivals had mystified consumers, because marketers were not allowed to name a drug and specify what ailment it was designed to treat in the same ad. In August 1997 the guidelines for television commercials were revised, and drug companies began airing spots that described their products, their purposes, and possible side effects in more detail. "The Power of Zyrtec" campaign was developed by the Lyons Lavey Nickel Swift advertising agency and the New York office of Health Medical Consumer Advertising & Marketing. The campaign ran in print and broadcast media throughout 1998 and into 1999.

HISTORICAL CONTEXT

Pfizer was founded in Brooklyn, New York, in 1849 when Charles Pfizer began producing chemicals such as citric acid to add flavor to food. Because the company had difficulty obtaining limes and lemons from Italy during World War I, a way was invented to extract citric acid from molasses. The spacious vats used in that process were perfect for making large quantities of penicillin to treat the ill and wounded during World War II. By 1998 Pfizer was manufacturing dozens of drugs, which accounted for 85 percent of its sales. Its prescription medications included Norvasc for hypertension, Zoloft for depression, Zithromax for infection, Viagra for erectile dysfunction, Lipitor for elevated blood cholesterol, and Aricept for Alzheimer's disease. Pfizer also made nonprescription products such as Visine and OcuHist eyedrops, Unisom sleep aids, BenGay muscle rub, Plax mouthwash, Bain de Soleil sunscreens, and medicines for animals.

Zyrtec, first marketed in the United States in 1996, had been sold in other countries since 1987. Available in tablet form and as a fruity syrup, it was designed to be taken only once a day to provide relief from allergies for 24 hours. Ads for Zyrtec emphasized that the product was easy to use and caused only "mild to moderate" side effects, but because of restrictions imposed by the Food and Drug Administration, the brand's first television commercials did not state that Zyrtec was an allergy medication. One spot that aired early in 1997 featured a businessman scaling a rock wall. The camera rose to provide a bird's-eye view, revealing that the wall spelled out the brand name. A three-page print advertisement published in the spring of 1997 was equally surreal but less mystifying. It showed a man in a business suit using a rope to climb a giant sunflower. A headline on the second page said, "Big Allergies. Big Relief." The text promised "BIG relief" and "BIG value—lowest cost/day of widely prescribed branded antihistamines." The third page listed the drug's potential side effects in smaller print. "The Power of Zyrtec" campaign continued to emphasize the product's strength, but it focused on the word "power" instead of using size to convey that message.

PRODUCT DEVELOPMENT

Pharmaceutical companies often spent hundreds of millions of dollars to bring a drug to market, but only 30 percent of drugs approved by the federal government generated sufficient sales to make a profit. To increase the probability that a product would be successful, Pfizer's marketing team had an unusual amount of influence over which drugs the company would develop. When a new product was under consideration, the marketing staff ran complex cash flow models to predict how factors such as the drug's side effects might increase or decrease sales. If the analysis indicated that the company was unlikely to recoup its development costs, the drug was seldom placed on the market. Pfizer also employed more than 5,000 sales representatives to distribute free samples of its products and to discuss a drug's efficacy with doctors.

TARGET MARKET

Demand for pharmaceuticals in general increased dramatically after drug manufacturers were allowed to advertise their prescription products directly to consumers. The advertisements were part of a larger marketing effort in which sales representatives visited doctors and pharmacists to deliver free samples and discuss the results of clinical trials that measured the performance of each drug. Although doctors and pharmacists were targets of the advertisements, another primary audience was patients who would see the ads, realize that medication appropriate for their health problems might be available, and ask their health care professionals about the drugs. Of 40 million to 50 million U.S. consumers who suffered from seasonal allergies, an estimated 12 percent consulted doctors to alleviate their misery. About 18 percent endured the symptoms without taking any medication, while others relied on over-the-counter remedies available without a prescription.

Seasonal allergy attacks were the body's response to outdoor irritants such as mold spores and pollen from trees and weeds, which caused problems only during certain times of the year. Perennial allergy attacks were typically caused by dust mites, house pets, and other indoor irritants. The body produced a chemical called histamine to counteract the irritants, which caused sneezing, itching, watery eyes, swelling, and other unpleasant symptoms. Market research indicated that people with allergies were most interested in a strong product that would quickly relieve their symptoms. Zyrtec and other remedies known as antihistamines worked by blocking the release of histamine, but the drugs sometimes led to side effects such as rapid heartbeat, headache, or fatigue. Most advertisements for antihistamines explained briefly how the drugs worked, then mentioned the possible side effects as required by law. Ads for Zyrtec and its two major competitors emphasized that they were less likely than many other antihistamines to cause drowsiness. Zyrtec was effective against both indoor and outdoor allergens and could also be used to treat chronic itching and hives. In May 1998 Zyrtec became the first leading prescription antihistamine approved by the U.S. Food and Drug Administration for use by children two to six years old.

COMPETITION

In 1998 the leading brand in the $2 billion U.S. market for allergy drugs was Claritin, made by Schering-Plough Corporation, with U.S. sales of $1.1 billion. Claritin's sales of $908 million in 1997 were more than twice its 1995 revenues. Zyrtec was second with U.S. sales of $355 million in 1998 and $250 million in 1997. Allegra (made by a German company, Hoescht AG) was third in 1998 with U.S. sales of $324 million, up from $201 million in 1997 and $22 million in 1996. Flonase (an antiallergy nasal spray manufactured by a British company, Glaxo Wellcome PLC) had U.S. sales of $207 million in 1997. As sales skyrocketed, companies significantly increased their advertising budgets. The industry's direct-to-consumer advertising totaled $595.5 million in 1996, $843.9 million in 1997, and more than $1 billion in 1998, according to Competitive Media Reporting.

Schering-Plough spent $69 million to advertise Claritin in 1997, up 21 percent since 1996, with $31.2 million going for network television commercials.

Launched in the United States in 1993, Claritin had worldwide sales of $1.73 billion in 1997 and was the most popular antihistamine in the world by 1998. At that time it controlled more than 50 percent of the U.S. market. Schering-Plough was one of the first pharmaceutical companies to run advertising campaigns aimed at consumers, and Claritin was the first prescription product advertised on prime-time television after the Food and Drug Administration revised its direct-to-consumer advertising guidelines in 1997. Some of the brand's advertising in 1998 included appearances by Joan Lunden, host of the television program *Good Morning America*. These were the first direct-to-consumer advertisements in which a celebrity was allowed to endorse a prescription product.

Claritin's extensive promotional program included the "Blue Skies" campaign of print advertisements and television commercials, introduced in August 1997. An advertisement in *Money* magazine in March 1998 showed a profile of a woman's face gazing serenely at a powder-blue sky where a Claritin tablet hovered like the sun, complete with a pink and blue halo and white rays radiating outward. The headline read, "Escape the limitations of seasonal allergies." The ad urged consumers to ask their doctors about Claritin, a drug that would not make them drowsy and could be taken just once a day. The text emphasized that Claritin was the leading prescription antihistamine, that it caused few side effects, and that it was available only by prescription. The ad included the company's Internet address, a toll-free number to call for more information, and the tag line, "Nothing but blue skies from now on."

The third most popular prescription antihistamine, Allegra, was promoted with television commercials in which people exclaimed, "Ah, Allegra!" Ads for Allegra emphasized that the medication could enable allergy sufferers to experience outdoor adventures even during allergy season. Whimsical television commercials showed people wind surfing through a wheat field, snorkeling through a field of flowers, and skiing through a meadow in the summertime. Like Zyrtec, Allegra was introduced to the United States in 1996, three years after Claritin's launch. In 1997 Hoechst spent $64 million to advertise Allegra, a 220 percent increase since 1996, with $17.2 million going for network television commercials. Allegra had worldwide sales of $215.1 million in 1997, up from $17.3 million in 1996.

Hoechst also made Seldane but voluntarily discontinued that popular allergy medication early in 1998 because it caused serious heart problems if consumers took it with certain other drugs. Seldane had been launched in 1985 and was one of the first major prescription drugs promoted with direct-to-consumer advertising. After the Food and Drug Administration proposed in 1997 to remove Seldane from the market, Hoechst spent more than $20 million on advertisements that invited consumers to try its other antihistamine, Allegra, "a seasonal allergy medicine with the relief of Seldane but with more freedom." Meanwhile, the makers of Claritin ran two-page newspaper advertisements that said, "Seldane may no longer be an option. Claritin is a clear choice."

Zyrtec also competed with numerous nonprescription allergy drugs such as Nasalcrom, made by Pharmacia & Upjohn, Inc. A headline in a 1998 magazine advertisement said, "The best way to stop suffering is don't start!" The ad explained in detail that Nasalcrom could "flat-out prevent allergies" within a week of continual use, and the product caused no drowsiness or other unpleasant side effects. The text added, "It's so safe you can buy it without a prescription, at full prescription strength, and use it through the whole allergy season." The tag line was "Allergy prevention pure and simple."

MARKETING STRATEGY

In August 1997, when the Food and Drug Administration revised the guidelines that governed television commercials for prescription drugs, pharmaceutical companies were allowed to expand the content of their advertisements. Pfizer could move beyond its vague references to Zyrtec's "big relief" and discuss in some detail the product's effectiveness as an antihistamine. The Food and Drug Administration dictated that television commercials for prescription drugs had to explain some of the major risks that could result from taking the drugs. In addition, the commercials had to inform consumers where they could obtain more information regarding who should take the medication, how it would affect them, and what side effects it might cause. Because of the complexity of the regulations and the brevity of television commercials, most spots promoting prescription drugs were so-called "reminder" ads that did not go into much detail. Instead, they were designed to familiarize the public with the brand and encourage consumers to ask for it by name when they visited their health-care providers. Print advertisements were required to describe the uses, benefits, and risks of each drug in much more detail. They often included a second page of small type that provided much of the same information typically inserted into the drug's package for use by doctors and pharmacists.

Like earlier ads for the brand, "The Power of Zyrtec" campaign featured intriguing, surreal images. One television commercial used special effects and computer graphics to show a man opening his front door and facing the "nightmare of allergies." Pollen-producing vines and flowers grew in seconds from the cracks in his brick walkway. Dogs and cats joined the looming, threatening plants as they chased the man through his house. He ran into his bathroom and found a package of Zyrtec. The nightmarish plants and animals ran back outside, and the man went on with his day, protected by "the power of Zyrtec." The campaign included extensive print advertisements. One magazine ad featured a photograph of a man fleeing through his house, pursued by a dog, cat, flowers, and a vacuum cleaner. The headline read, "When allergies are a nightmare, once-a-day Zyrtec starts working fast." A smaller photograph showed the man hugging the same dog after taking Zyrtec. Another television commercial showed a woman encountering a poodle and then sneezing. A mob of animals came running from numerous doorways as she fled down a corridor. She rushed into a room, slammed the door behind her, and swallowed a Zyrtec tablet. In great relief, she went outside and met a woman carrying a poodle. The poodle sneezed, and the allergy sufferer smiled.

Direct-to-consumer advertising and other promotions for Zyrtec were handled jointly by Lyons Lavey Nickel Swift (a unit of Omnicom Group) and the New York office of Health Medical Consumer Advertising & Marketing. In 1997 Pfizer spent $103 million to advertise its prescription drugs directly to consumers, according to Competitive Media Reporting. Its advertising budget for Zyrtec was $53.5 million that year, with $4.5 million going for network television commercials. During the first five months of 1998, Pfizer spent more than $12.3 million to advertise Zyrtec, Schering-Plough spent $11.1 million to advertise Claritin, and Glaxo Wellcome spent $7.3 million to advertise Flonase, according to Scott-Levin's Direct-to-Consumer Advertising Audit.

OUTCOME

In February 1999 "The Power of Zyrtec" campaign won Health Medical Consumer Advertising & Marketing first place in the International Mobius Competition's pharmaceutical category. In September 1998 a nationwide survey of 2,000 physicians found that when patients asked for a drug by its brand name, they most often requested an allergy medication. Zyrtec, Claritin, and Allegra were among the four brand-name drugs requested most often. Three years after its introduction to the United States, Zyrtec was the second most popular prescription antihistamine in the United States. It had worldwide revenues of $416 million in 1998, up from $265 million in 1997 and $146 million in 1996. *Forbes* magazine reported that the wholesale drug market in the United States generated record revenues of $81 billion in 1998, an increase of more than 60 percent since 1994. Pfizer's pharmaceutical sales increased three times faster than the industry average. In 1998 the company had overall revenues of $13.5 billion, including $12 billion in drug sales, an increase of 26 percent since 1997. For the second consecutive year *Fortune* magazine included Pfizer on its list of the world's most admired companies. *Forbes* magazine named Pfizer the "Company of the Year" in January 1999. *Chief Executive* magazine listed the board of directors at Pfizer among the top five in the nation. At the end of 1998 Pfizer was the third largest pharmaceutical enterprise in the world, up from thirteenth in 1990.

FURTHER READING

"Allergy Drugs Wage a Bitter War of the Noses." *Wall Street Journal,* May 23, 1996.

"Are Drug Ads a Cure-All?" *Business Week,* March 30, 1998.

"Claritin Sets DTC Spending Record." *Advertising Age,* June 7, 1999.

"Drug Makers Try to Win Over Seldane Users." *Wall Street Journal,* January 31, 1997.

Engel, Styli. "Claritin: Nothing but Blue Skies for Schering-Plough." *Med Ad News,* May 1, 1998.

Galewitz, Phil. "Drugmakers Turn to Stars to Tout Their Medications." *Philadelphia Inquirer,* February 20, 1999.

"Pfizer Media Review Keys on Three Specific Brands." *Advertising Age,* November 30, 1998.

Seo, Diane. "Drug Makers Aiming Straight for Consumers' Watery Eyes." *Los Angeles Times* (Business/Financial Desk Section), April 2, 1998.

Woolley, Scott. "The Forbes Platinum 400: Our Company of the Year Decision Was Fairly Easy: Pfizer—and No Viagra Jokes, Please." *Forbes,* January 11, 1999, p. 1.

Susan Risland

SCHICK TRACER FX ADS CAMPAIGN

OVERVIEW

NOTE: Since the initial appearance of this essay in the 1999 edition of *Major Marketing Campaigns Annual,* Warner-Lambert was acquired by Pfizer Inc. The essay continues to refer to the company's former name, as that was the official name of the organization when the campaign was launched.

In 1995 Schick, a unit of the Warner-Lambert Company since 1970, introduced the Tracer FX, a permanent razor that was designed to alleviate shaving irritation. The product was targeted at young men with sensitive skin and was positioned against the Gillette Company's Sensor Excel, which incorporated a number of high-tech safety and comfort features. To launch the

Tracer FX, the J. Walter Thompson advertising agency created a campaign that showed the model Magali shaving her face and flirting with male viewers. The ads were a hit, but the Tracer FX itself did not live up to consumers' expectations, and once the launch campaign had run its course, Schick shifted its marketing focus to other products.

By mid-1997, however, the Tracer FX was back in the spotlight as Warner-Lambert launched a $100 million global campaign to burnish the overall Schick image among younger consumers. J. Walter Thompson developed the new campaign, highlighted by slick television spots relaunching the Tracer FX with the tag line "The Feel of Smart Design." The spots featured hard-hitting sound tracks and male athletes using high-performance equipment—a pitch to the consumer who it was hoped would choose the Tracer FX. Schick also continued its ongoing association with the National Basketball Association (NBA), focusing particularly on rookie players. By 1998, in an intensely competitive and growing shaving market, the Tracer FX was enjoying a significant increase in sales worldwide.

HISTORICAL CONTEXT

From 1923 on, the Gillette Company was the leading manufacturer of razors, holding steady at about 65 percent of the wet-shaving market throughout the twentieth century. Schick was consistently a distant second to Gillette in razor sales, historically with about 15 percent of the overall market. And while Gillette was a product innovator, Schick was a follower, albeit a fast one.

In the mid-1970s the Bic Corporation shook up the shaving market with its introduction of the disposable razor. Gillette quickly developed its own disposable razor, a move that Schick followed. By the late 1980s disposables represented 60 percent of all razors sold, and because the profit margin on these units was low, shaving product companies began looking to create alternative sales with permanent razors. In 1990 Gillette introduced the Sensor, a high-tech, premium-priced razor with two independently suspended blades that were designed to give a "contoured" shave. The company took a risk by spending large sums to develop the product. It then increased its marketing budget by more than 40 over the previous year, throwing nearly all of its advertising behind the Sensor and abandoning its advertising for disposable razors. The strategy worked as men picked a closer shave and a higher price over cheaper convenience. As Lawrence Ingrassia reported in the *Wall Street Journal* in 1990, "Gillette says it sold 20 million Sensor razors in its first eight months on the market, which was its original goal for the entire year." The shaving wars of the 1990s had begun.

Schick saw the wisdom of selling an appealing, premium permanent razor, and in 1991 the company came out with the Tracer, a variation on the Sensor and an attempt to capture some of Gillette's market. The Tracer was described as a razor with blades that adjusted "to follow the unique contours of your face"—terms that essentially paraphrased the description of the Sensor—and it was aimed at what Schick called "young, active, risk-takers." Schick put a reported $12 million toward advertising for the Tracer and an additional $17 million into waves of hard-hitting promotions that included product samples, coupons, and rebates. Bruce Cleverly, a marketing vice president for Gillette, told the *Wall Street Journal* that his company was "delighted" that Schick was introducing a new permanent razor system, as it "reinforces the success of our business strategy." Meanwhile, Gillette countered Schick's move with coupons of its own and stepped up its ad campaign with the tag line "Gillette: the best a man can get."

By late 1993 *Chain Drug Review* was stating that "retailers say that in general men are demonstrating heightened interest in their appearance and a greater willingness to broaden the range of grooming products they buy. Manufacturers have responded with line extensions and a slew of value-added promotions." Manufacturers did indeed respond. In 1994 Gillette introduced the Sensor Excel, which had a rubber strip and other innovations that promised a closer, safer shave. The item was a tremendous success and was often credited with driving an overall boost in sales of shaving products during the 1990s. Schick's Tracer FX followed in 1995. Like the Sensor Excel, the Tracer FX also represented a product upgrade with advanced technology. But rather than focus on technological superiority and safety as the Sensor advertising did, Schick chose to pursue the niche of men with sensitive skin. *Mediaweek* quoted a Schick senior product manager as saying that the improvements on the Tracer answered "an important consumer need."

The razors themselves featured flexible blades, a skin-conditioning strip with aloe and vitamin E, a rubber skin guard, and an ergonomically designed handle. These attributes, while similar to the Sensor's, were used to distinguish the Tracer FX as the only razor designed specifically for sensitive skin. At the same time the brand's high-tech name and special packaging put it in direct competition with the design advancements of the Sensor Excel. In addition to capitalizing on a niche market and competing with the Sensor Excel, the Tracer FX also afforded Schick more shelf space in retail outlets. Too, the Tracer FX's packaging and marketing were used to distinguish the brand from other, less expensive Schick products.

For the Tracer FX launch in 1995, Schick ran the Magali ads. After an initial surge, sales dropped off, however, and Schick discontinued the campaign. Then, in 1997 the Tracer FX was relaunched (with a slightly revised design) as part of an overall master branding effort, this time carrying the tag line "The Feel of Smart Design." The $100 million Schick put toward its overall campaign in 1997 and 1998 represented a tremendous increase in spending on advertising, which in the previous year had been estimated at approximately $70 million.

TARGET MARKET

The same brand of razors was typically not marketed to both men and women, and the initial target for the Tracer FX was men with sensitive skin. Men in general accounted for about 70 percent of razor sales in the United States, and Schick's research found that more than 50 percent of men felt that they had sensitive skin. Those identifying themselves as having sensitive skin skewed slightly younger than average—18 to 34.

For its branding campaign Schick used the relaunch of the Tracer FX to position itself as hipper and trendier than the broad-based Gillette and to draw in younger men. In 1997 a Warner-Lambert vice president explained to Stuart Elliott of the *New York Times,* "Our target has been more of a general audience of males 18 to 54. Now we are focusing on a younger target audience, 18 to 24."

COMPETITION

In the world of razors Gillette was the name marketers had to contend with. In fact, Gillette's preeminence in the market was so complete that in some countries the very name had become synonymous with "razor." Gillette built its dominance by aggressively anticipating trends and constantly developing high-quality products in all niches of the shaving market. The company's research and development of products was a model for the industry, and Gillette often spent many years and millions of dollars before introducing a new item. In the 1970s Gillette shrewdly began protecting its ideas by designing products that required complicated machinery for their production and thus were difficult for competitors to copy.

When the Sensor—with its independently suspended blades—was introduced in 1990, it had gone through a decade of development and had cost Gillette $200 million, including the equipment needed to manufacture it. Schick later won rights to the Sensor patent but was unable to replicate the product because the company did not have the laser-welding machinery needed to reproduce the Sensor technology. Although Schick captured some market share with the Tracer and Tracer FX, its premium-priced products never caught up with Gillette's Sensor and Sensor Excel.

> ### BETTER ADVERTISING THAN TECHNOLOGY
>
> When the Tracer FX was originally launched in 1995, it was positioned to appeal to shavers on the basis of skin sensitivity rather than on the technological advancements around which the rival Gillette Company touted its Sensor products. The television spots showed 19-year-old French fashion model Magali lathering up her face and shaving it as she teased male viewers about their shaving woes. Magali purred lines like "You guys are so sensitive." Or, as she shaved under her chin, she asked, "Is this the sensitive part, right here?" The voice-over interspersed bits of information about the razor's design "for a smooth shave with less irritation." Magali finished the ads by wiping water from her upper lip and saying, "Are you the sensitive type? I like that."
>
> The Magali campaign was considered a success in launching the Tracer FX. The ads generated media attention, and trial sales of the handle and initial blade were good. Manufacturers realized their greatest profits in repeat sales of blades, however, and because the product did not perform especially well, the Tracer FX failed to win over long-term customers. A J. Walter Thompson executive said, "The advertising worked, but the technology didn't."

MARKETING STRATEGY

Following the Magali campaign, Schick conducted extensive research and found that younger men were dissatisfied with the shaving products available to them. These men were more than willing to try alternatives and were even seeking new products. With the opportunity open to build brand loyalty among a group still forming its shaving habits—men 18 to 24—Schick relaunched the Tracer FX with an image campaign. "The Feel of Smart Design" was reflected in the ads, which dispensed with the traditional man-at-the-sink shaving spots. Instead, a high-performance sports image was employed to appeal to the target audience and to draw a link to the improved control offered by the new product.

Sports popular with younger men formed the motif for the campaign. The artistic, stylized television ads, which showed athletes windsurfing, skateboarding, skiing, golfing, and performing other feats, were fast paced. They had techno-rhythm music in the background and a dark contemporary look. J.J. Jordan, a J. Walter Thompson vice president, told the *New York Times,* "There are hallmarks of great, functional design, especially for men, in the world of sports," and the Schick ads "clearly communicate" that spirit. For instance, a diver bouncing off a board into a pool paralleled the "flexing action" of the Tracer FX. Jordan also explained that the ads conveyed the idea that the product was "distinctive, [looked] cool and [had] a smart reason for being that way." Since good design was a central concept of the campaign, it was thought that older customers would not be put off by the spots and might even find them appealing.

In tandem with the advertisements, Schick continued its ongoing sponsorship of the NBA Rookie Game and recruited spokesmen from among the players. The company also became the premier sponsor of the NBA's website and launched a website for Schick separate from the Warner-Lambert site. Special promotions, such as a package of Tracer FX razors and a free can of another company's shaving gel, helped sales in 1998 as well.

OUTCOME

Schick's overall branding campaign was considered to be a success, with the Tracer FX in particular catching consumers' attention. In a review of shaving products, a writer for the *Los Angeles Times* said that the "smooth Tracer FX handles like a Porsche on the Grande Corniche." Throughout 1998 sales of Schick's Tracer FX system and refills grew. In addition, the introduction of the Schick Protector bolstered the brand's market share. The Protector, with a new technology of wire-wrapped razors and a striking, curvy red handle, was touted as a product for sensitive skin and was intended to compete with Gillette's forthcoming MACH3. By 1999 *Drug Store News* was reporting that "though Gillette dominated the refill razor category, Warner-Lambert's Schick showed strong increases for 1998, a performance attributed to relaunches and strong ad support." Shaving systems generally were Warner-Lambert's best-performing category for 1998.

Despite these successes, however, Gillette's 1998 introduction of the MACH3 overshadowed all other developments in the shaving category. Gillette spent a reported $750 million to develop the MACH3's ultra-thin, diamond-carbon-coated blades. The investment paid off. Launched in mid-1998, the MACH3, which was more expensive than the Sensor or Tracer lines, ranked third in sales for the year.

FURTHER READING

Elliott, Stuart. "Warner-Lambert Campaign Targets Younger Customers." *Journal Record* (*New York Times* News Service), June 5, 1997.

Ingrassia, Lawrence. "Schick Razor to Try for Edge against Gillette." *Wall Street Journal,* October 8, 1990, p. B1.

———. "Taming the Monster: How Big Companies Can Change." *Wall Street Journal,* December 10, 1992, p. A1.

Malbin, Peter. "Systems Get Big Push in Shaving Category." *Drug Store News,* September 22, 1997.

Mehegan, Sean. "Schick's $13M Techie 'Protector' Aims at Gillette." *Brandweek,* September 22, 1997.

"Men's Grooming Emerges." *Chain Drug Review,* October 6, 1997.

"New Entries in Shaving Shake Up Market." *Drug Store News,* May 17, 1999.

"New Items Bring Higher Margins to Shaving Arena." *Chain Drug Review,* January 20, 1997.

Rubin, Chris. "Stubble Jeopardy: The Newest Disposable Razors and Electric Shavers Make That Morning Ritual a Kinder, Gentler Experience." *Los Angeles Times,* February 18, 1997.

"Smooth Operator." *Adweek,* November 20, 1995.

"Warner-Lambert's First Schick Master Brand Image Campaign Breaking in June." *Rose Sheet,* June 23, 1997.

Weis, Pam. "Schick Ups Razor Ante via $23M on Tracer FX." *Brandweek,* July 24, 1995.

Sarah Milstein

SEE YOU LATER, ALLIGATOR CAMPAIGN

OVERVIEW

NOTE: Since the initial appearance of this essay in the 1998 edition of *Major Marketing Campaigns Annual,* Warner-Lambert was acquired by Pfizer Inc. The essay continues to refer to the company's former name, as that was the official name of the organization when the campaign was launched.

In 1990 the Warner-Lambert Company began an advertising campaign that starred eye-catching alligators to illustrate the beneficial properties of its product, Lubriderm Hand and Body Lotion. The campaign, which continued throughout the 1990s, featured the reptiles walking or swimming near beautiful women who had soft, moisturized skin. To emphasize that the alligators were metaphors, the J. Walter Thompson ad agency used stark settings with white backgrounds that symbolized the clean feeling of Lubriderm lotion. Because most other advertisements for hand and body lotion centered on women applying the product to their skin, the unusual alligator campaign set Lubriderm apart from its many competitors. The ads emphasized the therapeutic and cosmetic properties of the brand by contrasting the scaly skin of alligators with the smooth skin of the women using Lubriderm, and they created an icon that would make consumers think of

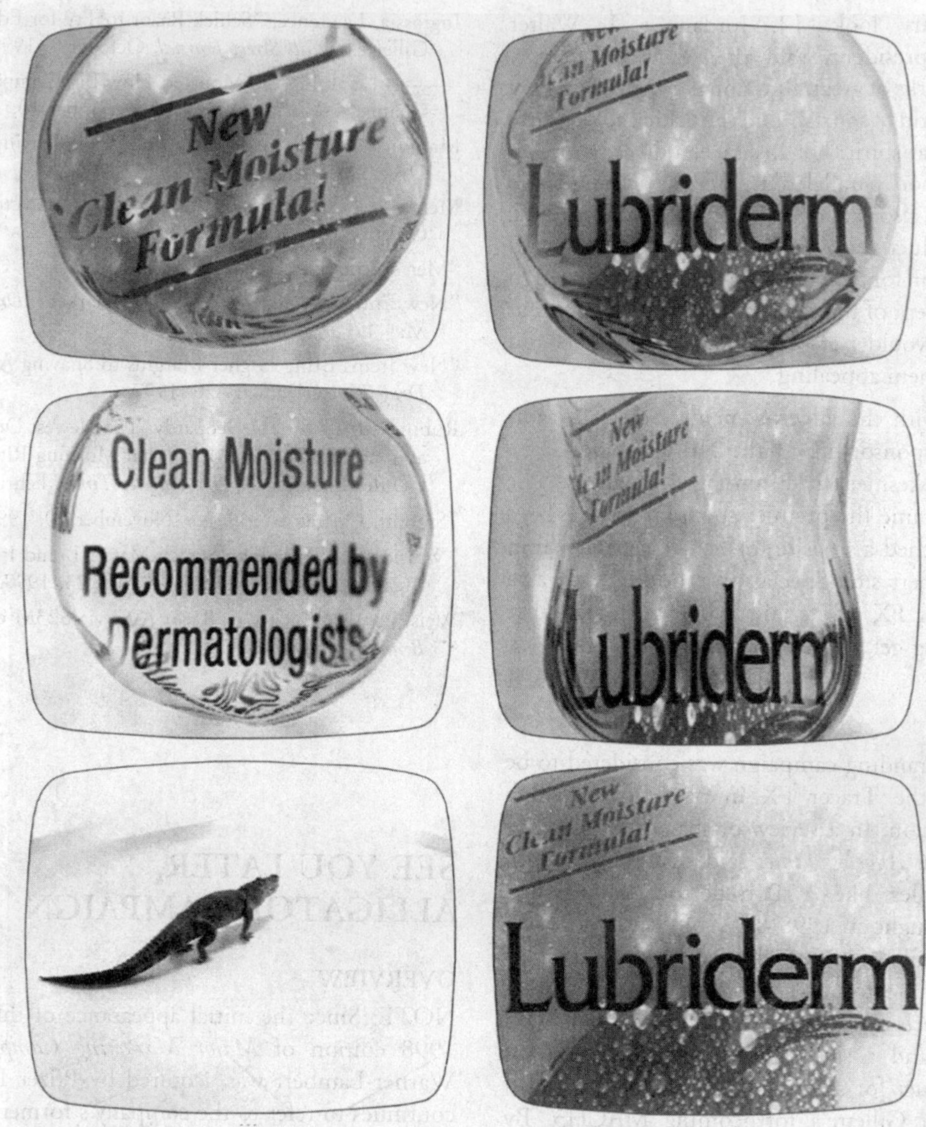

Six stills from the "Big Drop" television spot for Lubriderm's "See You Later, Alligator" campaign. J. WALTER THOMPSON. REPRODUCED BY PERMISSION OF PFIZER CONSUMER HEALTHCARE, PFIZER INC.

Lubriderm when they needed a moisturizer. The company credited the ad campaign with helping to heighten customer awareness of the brand and increase sales.

HISTORICAL CONTEXT

Lambert Pharmaceutical Company had been established in 1881, and Warner Drug Company had been founded in 1886. The two companies merged in 1955. Warner-Lambert became one of the world's largest marketers of prescription drugs, consumer health products, and confectionery. In 1997 the company's products included Listerine mouthwash, Trident and Dentyne gum, Certs breath mints, Benadryl antihistamine, Sudafed nasal decongestant, and Schick shavers. The original Lubriderm hand and body lotion had been developed in 1946 as a compounding base for dermatologists, and in 1950 Warner-Lambert began marketing the product to pharmacists in the United States. Lubriderm was first marketed to the general public in 1980. During the next two decades, the company introduced several line extensions including a body bar, a loofah bar, a bath and shower oil, a moisturizing gel cream, and a lotion for sensitive skin. Some of those products were subsequently discontinued.

A still from Lubriderm's "See You Later, Alligator" campaign. J. WALTER THOMPSON. REPRODUCED BY PERMISSION OF PFIZER CONSUMER HEALTHCARE, PFIZER INC.

Because the first ads for Lubriderm had been aimed at dermatologists, they had focused on its therapeutic value as a remedy for dry skin. Later, when the product was sold directly to consumers, advertisements mentioned its cosmetic value as a lotion that could improve the appearance of skin, but the fact that it was recommended by dermatologists was still an important element in the marketing strategy. Advertising campaigns helped publicize each line extension as it was introduced. The basic Lubriderm formula was upgraded in 1996, new graphics were designed for the product's packaging, and new advertisements were developed in 1997 to promote the reformulated base lotion.

TARGET MARKET

Lubriderm was sold primarily to women 18 to 49 years old, but a line extension was being developed for launch in 1998 for women slightly older who were concerned about the aging effects of the sun's ultraviolet rays. A large percentage of the general population suffered from some degree of dry skin, and more than 80 percent of women in the United States used hand and body lotion once or twice daily. Consumers wanted a long-lasting product that would soothe and moisturize without leaving a greasy residue that would rub off on their clothing.

PHARMACEUTICAL INNOVATION

During the 1800s William R. Warner, one of the founders of Warner-Lambert Company, invented sugar-coated pills to mask the bitter taste of medicines. In 1879 the company's other founder, Jordan Lambert, developed the first surgical antiseptic, which saved the lives of many patients undergoing medical operations. By 1997 the product had become the world's most popular mouthwash, Listerine Antiseptic.

By emphasizing that Lubriderm was the brand of skin and body lotion most often recommended by dermatologists, Warner-Lambert called attention to the product's therapeutic, healing qualities. The ads also pointed out Lubriderm's cosmetic benefits by showcasing beautiful models with smooth, radiant skin. The campaign assured women that the lotion would feel clean, not greasy or clammy, and many of the ads mentioned water or showed photographs of it to emphasize Lubriderm's ability to hydrate the skin.

COMPETITION

Traditionally, mass-marketed lotions had been advertised with an emphasis on their cosmetic benefits—such as making skin soft and attractive-while premium lotions that sold for a somewhat higher price had stressed their therapeutic, healing properties. Lubriderm products had 5.6 percent of the premium market in the United States, putting the brand in third place in the hand and body lotion category. The top-selling lotion was Vaseline Intensive Care, made by Chesebrough-Pond, a division of Unilever. In second place was Jergens, made by Andrew Jergens Company, a subsidiary of Kao Corporation. Other major competitors included Suave Skin Therapy Lotion, made by Helene Curtis, Inc., another division of Unilever; Curel, made by Bausch & Lomb, Inc.; and Nivea, made by the Beiersdorf Company. Annual revenues in the hand and body lotion category totaled $808 million.

The Procter & Gamble Company's Oil of Olay brand led a related category, facial skin care, with a market share of 24.5 percent. L'Oreal's Plenitude brand had 17.1 percent, and Unilever's Pond's brand had 14.7 percent, according to Information Resources, Inc. The world's best-selling brand of skin care products was Nivea, but in the United States the brand's top line extension, Nivea Visage, was ranked sixth with only 4.5 percent of the facial skin care market. In 1997 Beiersdorf ran a $20 million campaign on television and in print media with the tag line "Nivea Brings Your Face to Life. Nivea Brings Your Skin to Life." Samples of the product were distributed in conjunction with the ad campaign. After the ads ran, Nivea's annual sales were $21.5 million, an increase of 5.2 percent.

Another facial skin care brand, Revitalift, was promoted in 1997 by a $25 million ad campaign. The antiaging cream, which was part of L'Oreal's Plenitude line, had led the category in 1996. The corrective, antiwrinkle cream category had been pioneered during the early 1990s and was the most rapidly expanding segment of the skin care market. It served primarily women who were at least 40 years old. Also in 1997 L'Oreal Plenitude FUTUR.e, a moisturizer that contained vitamin E, was launched with a $20 million advertising campaign on television and in print media.

The top-selling hand and body lotion, Vaseline Intensive Care, was publicized in March 1997 with Chesebrough-Pond's sixth annual "Skin Awareness Month." The $6 million promotion featured advertisements in the magazines *Better Homes & Gardens, Woman's Day, Family Circle, Good Housekeeping, Reader's Digest,* and *TV Guide.* A toll-free consumer hotline, referrals to dermatologists, and displays at retail outlets were also included. Other advertisements for the brand used sandpaper to represent the feeling of dry skin. Products in the Vaseline Intensive Care line had been reformulated in 1995, the brand's packaging had been redesigned, and its advertising budget had been increased to $25 million, up from about $8 million previously. In addition to hand and body lotion, Chesebrough-Pond offered a line extension called Vaseline Intensive Care Moisturizing Body Wash.

Commercials for the second-place brand in the hand and body lotion market, Jergens, focused on the touchably soft skin of a mother and her daughter. The company also offered line extensions in closely related market categories. The company had invigorated the $158 million liquid body cleanser market with the introduction of Jergens Refreshing Body Shampoo in 1994. The next year it launched Jergens Naturals with Baking Soda Deodorant Skin Care Bar. For consumers who preferred products that cleansed and moisturized at the same time, Jergens had introduced a water-activated gel called Shower-Active Moisturizer. The company had also restaged Jergens Aloe & Lanolin and Vitamin E body wash bars.

Another competitor, Procter & Gamble, led the body wash category in 1996 with a market share of nearly 30 percent, thanks largely to its Oil of Olay 2-in-1 Moisturizing Body Wash. Its $50 million marketing plan revolved around the tag lines "You May Never Need a Body Lotion Again" and "Moisturized Skin No Bath Bar

PROFESSIONAL RECOGNITION

In 1997 the advertising industry bestowed an ADDY Award for excellence on "Smart Woman," a print advertisement in the "See You Later, Alligator" campaign for Lubriderm hand and body lotion.

Can Touch." During 1997 Procter & Gamble continued its Marketing Breakthrough 2000 program, which had been launched in 1995 in an attempt to lower marketing costs from 25 percent to 20 percent of net sales. For the fiscal year ended June 1997, the company's marketing costs were 24.3 percent, up from 24.1 percent in the previous year. By the end of 1997 Procter & Gamble had abandoned the program, but it was still cutting costs, including its advertising budget.

MARKETING STRATEGY

Like many of its competitors, Warner-Lambert had developed line extensions of its original hand and body moisturizer over the years. But in 1997 the Lubriderm bath and shower oil, body bar, and loofah bar were discontinued, and marketing efforts concentrated on the basic skin therapy lotion, which had been upgraded in the previous year. A campaign budget of $16 million was allocated for television and print advertisements in the United States. "Big Drop," the only television spot that aired during 1997, began with a woman's face reflected in a drop of water while she asked, "What exactly is clean moisture? Well, it's what you'll find in a new, even better Lubriderm." The drop of water reflected the words "New, Clean Moisture Formula" and the Lubriderm logo on a bottle of lotion. The camera panned across the woman running her hands over her arms, legs, and shoulders while she continued, "And it's best defined by a feeling. A feeling that's almost invisible on your skin. One that feels distinctly less greasy, even though it's working every bit as hard as always. So it's recommended by dermatologists even more than before. New cleaner-feeling Lubriderm." The drop of water reflected more words from the Lubriderm bottle and the woman's face, and finally the drop fell into an alligator's eye. As the reptile strolled away, the woman's voice concluded, "See you later, alligator. Hello, clean moisture." The commercial aired primarily on network television during the day and during prime time, but it also ran on cable and syndicated television.

During 1997 several print ads also ran in magazines with large female readerships, such as *Better Homes & Gardens* and *Cosmopolitan.* One ad featured a model in a pose that emphasized her bare arms and legs as she lounged beneath the words, "Moisturizers and dieting. Live by the same rules. If it's greasy, stay away." Another ad read, "Your moisturizer shouldn't make you feel clammy all over. That's what first dates are for." A third said, "Some moisturizers act like your ex-boyfriend. A little too clingy." In each ad smaller type at the bottom read, "Lubriderm's clean moisture formula is a hardworking, fast-absorbing lotion that helps get rid of dry, ashy skin without feeling greasy or clingy. That must be why it's the #1 leading moisturizer recommended by dermatologists." Each print ad featured a picture of a bottle of Lubriderm lotion next to the tag line "See you later, alligator," but none actually showed the alligator.

The company developed at least one new spot each year in the "See You Later, Alligator" campaign, and there had been variations on the central theme since the advertisements were introduced in 1990. One of the first television commercials had featured attractive women swimming underwater with live alligators. Another showed models and alligators in surroundings that looked like glamorous bedrooms. All the spots referred to the alligator in some way, but by 1997 the creature had become a signature at the end of some television spots instead of the central figure it had played in earlier commercials. In some spots the alligator made only a brief appearance, walking away as the tag line "See You Later, Alligator" was spoken. Other spots featured the alligator throughout.

The idea of using alligators as an eye-catching visualization for rough, scaly skin had originally been suggested by a copywriter at J. Walter Thompson. Alligators are frequently thought of as being dry, rough, and scaly. In addition, "See you later, alligator" is a familiar phrase, an informal way of saying good-bye. Therefore, the tag line invited the consumer to say good-bye to dry skin by using Lubriderm. In developing the advertisements, the challenge was to achieve a highly stylized tone yet deliver a message to which consumers could relate. The simple white backgrounds of the ads helped emphasize the clean, nongreasy nature of Lubriderm lotion, and the campaign emphasized that Lubriderm was the brand most often recommended by dermatologists. "Lubriderm always tries to stand for the highest standard of therapeutic moisturization. We're not the housewife in the kitchen talking about dry elbows," said Wendy Trees, an account executive with J. Walter Thompson. Because the ads were strikingly different from those of Lubriderm's numerous competitors, they helped the brand stand out and created a memorable image that would make consumers think of Lubriderm when they thought of relieving dry skin.

OUTCOME

It took time for consumers to become accustomed to the alligator ads and to associate them with Lubriderm after the campaign was launched in 1990. But the company stayed with the same advertising theme, and eventually the alligator became Lubriderm's signature. "Consumers love the alligator. Our sales have increased since we've been using it. It's highly effective," said Trees. In a 1997 survey by *USA Today*'s Ad Track, 22 percent of respondents said the ads were effective, although only 11 percent said they "liked the ads a lot." Respondents 18 to 24 years old gave the campaign higher scores; 36 percent said it was effective, and 26 percent said they liked the ads. Only 8 percent of men liked the ads, compared to 13 percent of women. Nearly half of the 1,002 respondents recalled seeing the ads at least three times.

Warner-Lambert reported record income in 1997, including a 1 percent increase in its $1.4-billion U.S. consumer health care operations. That segment of the company had grown 3 percent in 1996. The company's worldwide sales were $8.2 billion.

FURTHER READING

Enrico, Dottie. "Popularity Scores Low, but Lubriderm's Sales Grow." *USA Today* Ad Track, August 18, 1997.

"Jergens Introduces Shower Lotion." *Advertising Age,* November 15, 1995.

"Jergens Plans Drive." *Advertising Age,* November 16, 1995.

"Jergens Restages Skin Care Bar." *Advertising Age,* May 17, 1995.

"Lubriderm Gator Is Back." *Advertising Age,* October 18, 1995.

"March Campaign for Vaseline." *Advertising Age,* February 19, 1997.

"Pond's Launching New Facial Treatment." *Advertising Age,* July 31, 1995.

Sloan, Pat. "$48 Mil Effort for Nivea as Revlon Readies Rival." *Advertising Age,* June 16, 1997.

"Vaseline Intensive Care Will Be Backed by $25M." *Advertising Age,* June 5, 1995.

"Warner-Lambert Reports Fourth Quarter, Full-Year Sales and Earnings." *PRNewswire,* January 28, 1997.

"Warner-Lambert Reports Record Fourth Quarter Sales and Records Sales and Earnings for 1997." *PRNewswire,* January 27, 1998.

Susan Risland

SUPER FANS CAMPAIGN

OVERVIEW

NOTE: Since the initial appearance of this essay in the 1999 edition of *Major Marketing Campaigns Annual,* Warner-Lambert was acquired by Pfizer Inc. The essay continues to refer to the company's former name, as that was the official name of the organization when the campaign was launched.

With a budget estimated at $20 million and a campaign overseen by J. Walter Thompson USA of New York, the Warner-Lambert Company in mid-1998 launched a series of television spots for its Rolaids brand antacid tablets. The campaign, Rolaids' first since 1996, focused entirely on television as opposed to print, and it represented a return to traditional themes for the brand, including an emphasis on sports. Hence the title "Super Fans."

Recent years had seen a number of changes in the highly segmented category of digestives, including an increased emphasis on the calcium content of antacids. Much more portentous for antacids, however, had been the introduction of histamine 2, or H2, acid blockers. Whereas antacids neutralized acids in the stomach, H2 blockers actually stopped the production of stomach acid. According to *Advertising Age* in 1996, industry experts believed that sales of H2 blockers alone would reach nearly $2 billion by 1998.

With the advent of this innovative over-the-counter treatment for heartburn, Rolaids and its traditional competitors had struggled to keep up with a changing market. "Rolaids is such a classic brand," Christina Villante of J. Walter Thompson told Michael Wilke in *Advertising Age* at the outset of the 1998 campaign, "but got lost in the last couple of years with the H2 blockers, which really changed the game. Everyone in the category was re-evaluating their advertising, and that cost them equities. But if you ask consumers about Rolaids, they remember the spelling and the sports, so it's a natural to go back to that."

HISTORICAL CONTEXT

The word "spelling" was a reference to Rolaids' classic advertising campaign from the 1970s, "How do you spell relief?" As millions of TV viewers during that decade learned, the proper spelling was "R-o-l-a-i-d-s." Spots dramatized this in numerous ways, for instance with a waitress scrawling the seven-letter name on an order pad or a coach in a locker room spelling it out on a chalkboard. Indeed, the themes of food, sports, and tension repeatedly came together in the heyday of Rolaids advertising, as they would again with the 1998 "Super Fans" campaign.

Warner-Lambert introduced Rolaids in 1954 with a single flavor, peppermint. In 1988 it extended its line to include assorted fruit flavors, but from the beginning its emphasis was on scientific claims rather than on taste. Hence the much-touted promise that "Rolaids consumes 47 times its weight in stomach acid," illustrated in television ads with a dramatization using a simulated Rolaids tablet and a bucket of colored water. The company backed up the claim with detailed information regarding clinical testing and research.

In the mid-1980s, as competitors touted the calcium content in their products, Warner-Lambert let it be known that Rolaids had always contained limestone, which included calcium. The company also touted other health factors in its product, including the fact that Rolaids was aspirin-, cholesterol-, and fat-free.

TARGET MARKET

Assessing the market for H2 blockers and antacids in 1997, Al Heller of *Drug Store News* could as easily have been citing the potential for the resurgence of antacids when he noted "the ongoing high-stress lifestyle of Americans, which makes stomach remedies as essential a personal accessory as a pen, pager, or credit card. Digestive diseases impair more than 2 million Americans and result in 200,000 absences from work each day, according to the Glaxo Institute for Digestive Health, Digestive Disease National Coalition. As a nation, we experience 32 million new cases of frequent heartburn each year, another 20 million of irritable bowel syndrome and gallstones, and 4 million ulcers."

Warner-Lambert itself conducted a study, the results of which it reported in October 1998. In line with its use of sports imagery in the "Super Fans" campaign, the company undertook what it called the "Rolaids Fanatical Fan Sports Ritual" survey, which found that one of every six sports fans had at some time experienced acid indigestion, heartburn, or sour stomach. The survey found that, of some 100 million sports fans in the United States, one in five described themselves as "fanatical fans" who would "do practically anything to support their favorite teams."

To an extent the survey was tongue-in-cheek, but it also presented a number of realities that served to indicate the target market for Rolaids. A press release announcing the survey results indicated that "fanatical fans" typically experienced the worst indigestion when their teams lost, of course, but win or lose, "the foods that baseball fans traditionally enjoy in large quantities—such as hot dogs and other fatty foods—are also associated with heartburn. During the 1998 baseball season, it was predicted that a record 26 million hot dogs would be eaten in the nation's 30 stadiums."

The somewhat humorous portrayal of sports fans called to mind a popular *Saturday Night Live* skit from the early 1990s in which comedian Chris Farley and others conducted a talk show devoted exclusively to the Chicago Bears football team and the Chicago Bulls basketball team. In the midst of talking about "Da Bearce" and "Da Bullce," as they called them, Farley and company consumed vast amounts of fatty foods and alcohol, which led to regular "heart attacks" in the middle of the talk show. Ironically, the 33-year-old Farley's own unhealthy lifestyle caught up with him in December 1997, when he was found dead in his Chicago apartment.

HOW DO YOU SPELL ACCOUNT?

In October 1998 former advertising sales representatives of Turner Broadcasting held a 20-year reunion. Among them were Larry Diveny of Comedy Central, Lou LaTorre of Fox Sports Net, and Harvey Ganot and John Popkowski of MTV. Because of another commitment, Ted Turner himself could not attend the reunion, which was held at Denim & Diamonds in New York City, but as Bradley Johnson speculated in *Advertising Age,* "Ted stories no doubt will abound." Johnson relayed a particularly popular anecdote concerning Turner and Warner-Lambert, makers of Rolaids.

At the time the many sales alums had gone to work for Turner Broadcasting in the late 1970s, Turner was already a well-known millionaire man-about-town in Atlanta, but he was far from the billionaire he would become. There was no Jane Fonda, no CNN, no Turner Classic Movies; indeed, there were few of the fixtures that would come to characterize the Turner legend. Turner's broadcast "empire" consisted of little more than flagship station WTCG (later WTBS) in Atlanta, and cable TV itself was struggling at the fringes. Nor could the industry count on Turner's magnetism to increase its exposure, since Turner himself was not the national celebrity he would later become. But he was well on his way.

WTCG desperately needed the advertising dollars of consumer products giant Warner-Lambert, and Turner managed to get a meeting with the top brass at the company. On the date of the appointment, however, he showed up looking ill, holding his stomach and moaning. He did this until one of the Warner-Lambert executives asked him what was wrong, whereupon Turner—no doubt with a sly smile—said, "I need a Rolaids." He got the account.

The participants in the putative talk show looked like a portrait of Rolaids' target market: middle-aged men who lived a high-tension lifestyle. Of course, Rolaids was also marketed to women, but the greater presence of male figures in commercials suggested a heightened focus on men. Age was also a factor, for as Heller noted, future increases in the digestives market would "be fueled by the continued aging of baby boomers, who have greater needs for the products as they cross the 50-year threshold."

COMPETITION

Perhaps it was fitting that in a market in which sales were motivated in part by physical and mental tension among users, competition itself was tense. Among Rolaids' many competitors were the liquid antacids Maalox, produced by Ciba-Geigy, and Procter & Gamble's Pepto-Bismol. Even more direct competition came from SmithKline Beecham's Tums, like Rolaids a chewable antacid.

When the calcium craze hit during the 1980s, Tums took advantage of the new trend not by changing its product—which already contained calcium—but by touting that fact aggressively in its marketing efforts. This led to a staggering 50 percent increase in sales during 1985, knocking Rolaids out of first place among antacids. Warner-Lambert responded by producing a sodium-free version of Rolaids and by introducing calcium supplements, but its marketing placed much less emphasis on calcium content than did the advertising for Tums.

A decade later, not only Rolaids but all traditional antacids were reeling from the introduction of entirely new competitors: H2 blockers, led by SmithKline Beecham's Tagamet HB. As Leon Jaroff of *Time* wrote in 1995 in describing Tagamet's forceful marketing, "Suddenly a roar issues from the TV set. On the screen, a giant tongue of flaming gases erupts from the sun, and one bold statement after another is superimposed on the solar surface: 'The idea behind it led to the Nobel Prize in Medicine,' reads the first, followed by, 'It's the most prescribed medication of its kind.' . . . Then, against the glowing corona of a totally eclipsed sun, 'And now it's available without a prescription.' "

Introduced in 1977, Tagamet enjoyed patent protection for 17 years, and during the 1980s it became the first drug ever to earn $1 billion in a single year. But as the end of the patent approached in the early 1990s, SmithKline Beecham applied for and received federal approval for an over-the-counter version. Around the same time Johnson & Johnson/Merck presented Pepcid AC, and British pharmaceutical company Glaxo Wellcome introduced Zantac 75. Warner-Lambert held U.S. marketing rights for the latter, but at the same time it also began to market Rolaids more aggressively.

By 1996, when Warner-Lambert launched a new advertising campaign for Rolaids, the fortunes of the once-powerful brand had fallen greatly. Having fallen from first place a decade before, it now held just 4.6 percent of the $1.45 billion digestives market, placing it 10th after Pepcid AC, Tums, Mylanta (McNeil Pharmaceuticals), Tagamet, Imodium (McNeil), Pepto-Bismol, Zantac 75, Maalox, and Alka-Seltzer (Bayer). Of the growth in H2 blockers, a Warner-Lambert executive told *Chain Drug Review,* "I can't think of any one category that has grown like this."

MARKETING STRATEGY

During the late 1990s still more H2 brands entered the market, and antacid manufacturers in 1996 spent a total of $55 million in advertising to shore up their brands by "setting them apart from the many acid blockers," as Wilke wrote in *Advertising Age.* A brand manager for Maalox told him, "It's self-preservation from the OTCs [over-the-counters] against the H2s." Of that $55 million, Warner-Lambert devoted a hefty portion—$14 million—to a new Rolaids campaign orchestrated by J. Walter Thompson.

Rolaids, which had recently added magnesium to its product, used advertising to highlight quick relief and acid absorption. Still sales declined, and by early 1997 Rolaids had less than a 4.4 percent market share. Worse news appeared on the horizon in early 1998 when Pepcid introduced chewable H2 tablets, thus "targeting loyalists of roll antacids such as Tums and Rolaids," according to *Tan Sheet.*

Hence the change of advertising strategy by Warner-Lambert in mid-1998. The company increased media spending for Rolaids by $6 million, to $20 million, and as Wilke reported, "look[ed] to the brand's past for its first new campaign since 1996." Once again, Rolaids advertising would contain the tag line "R-o-l-a-i-d-s spells relief" and would emphasize sports. The thrust of the advertising would be different, however. The 1970s spots for Rolaids had included sports figures such as then Los Angeles Dodgers manager Tommy Lasorda, whereas the 1998 campaign would poke gentle fun at sports fans themselves. As always, the focus would be on television, with no print ads planned.

Thus in October 1998, when Warner-Lambert reported the results of its "Rolaids Fanatical Fan Sports Ritual" survey, the company noted that "'fanatical [sports] fans' seem to already be fans of Rolaids, as represented in the current Rolaids ad campaign that personifies the fan in action—body painted, cheering, and finding relief from acid indigestion in Rolaids."

OUTCOME

At the time of Rolaids' return to the roots of its classic campaign, Paul Kelly of Silvermine Consulting told Wilke in *Advertising Age,* "I'm surprised they're abandoning the quick relief message already, since from a marketing standpoint that's how everyone is dividing out." The last phrase presumably referred to the fact that, just as the growth in H2 blockers had tapered off, the decline in antacid sales had leveled off as well. In spite of this settling in the market, however, Rolaids sales had dropped still further by the middle of 1998, when the company adopted its new campaign.

The results of the campaign had not materialized by mid-1999, and the lack of reporting on the subject made it difficult to discern the future direction of Rolaids. As early as mid-1997, when the market was still decidedly bullish on H2 blockers, one industry analyst had suggested to Heller that Rolaids still had a well-defined and assured niche: "There is still a place for conventional antacids in the convenience part of the [digestives] market. It's easier to carry with you a roll of Tums or Rolaids in that form than it is to carry individual doses of Tagamet, which are tablets but not chewables. This is still an important aspect."

Although the advent of chewable Pepcid AC had placed even that aspect of Rolaids' appeal in jeopardy, the time-honored brand enjoyed the support of a company with a long history of marketing consumer products and substantial resources to devote to that marketing. The $20 million Warner-Lambert put into Rolaids in 1998 said volumes concerning how the company felt about its 42-year-old chewable antacid brand.

FURTHER READING

"Acid Blockers on Way to Etching Out a $2 Billion Segment." *Advertising Age,* September 30, 1996, p. S13.

"Antacid Sales Take Off in Wake of Major Rx-to-OTC Switches." *Chain Drug Review,* January 6, 1997, p. 56.

"Fanatical Fans Take to the Stands: Rolaids Survey Reveals How Obsessive Fans Suffer Physical Consequences." *PR Newswire,* October 20, 1998.

Heller, Al. "H2 Blocker Sales Continue to Surge, but Warning Signs Appear." *Drug Store News,* July 14, 1997, p. CP23.

"H2 Blockers' US Sales Boom Set to Slow?" *Marketletter,* October 21, 1996.

"J&J/Merck Pepcid AC First Chewable H2 Is Latest Twist in Stomach Remedy Market." *Tan Sheet,* January 12, 1998.

Jaroff, Leon, et al. "Fire in the Belly, Money in the Bank: Get Ready for Door-to-Door Combat As Drug Companies Get Their Brand Names Ready for a (Stomach) Acid Test in the Nonprescription Market." *Time,* November 6, 1995, p. 56.

Johnson, Bradley. "The Absolut in Frustration." *Advertising Age,* October 19, 1998, p. 8.

Rogers, Michael. "A Lot of Hoopla over Plain Old Calcium: The Moral of the Latest Health Craze: If Your Product Contains Calcium, Flaunt It. If It Doesn't Add It—And Flaunt That." *Fortune,* May 26, 1986, p. 62.

Shaheen, Carol Ann. "Over-the-Counterpunches." *Men's Health,* November 1996, p. 92.

Wilke, Michael. "Antacids Seek Relief with $55 Mil in Ads." *Advertising Age,* July 1, 1996, p. 3.

———. "Rolaids Seeks Boost with $20 Mil Drive: Warner-Lambert Brand Goes Back to Sports, Spelling." *Advertising Age,* July 6, 1998, p. 29.

Judson Knight

VIAGRA LAUNCH CAMPAIGN

OVERVIEW

In March 1998 Pfizer Inc., the world's largest research-based pharmaceutical company, won FDA approval of its anti-impotency drug, Viagra. Because of the nature of the condition it was meant to treat, Viagra came to market that April amid a frenzy of publicity, much of which mocked impotency and its treatment. Though the publicity helped Viagra to reach record-setting sales figures before any advertising appeared on behalf of the drug, Pfizer wanted to exert control over the Viagra image. After waiting for the media buzz to wane, the company, along with health-care advertising agency Cline, Davis & Mann of New York, broke its first ads supporting the drug's launch in late June 1998.

The first series of ads, having an estimated price tag of $25 million, were branded print spots featuring older dancing couples and the tagline "Let the Dance Begin." These were followed, in the spring of 1999, by a television commercial featuring former senator and presidential candidate Bob Dole speaking frankly about his experience with erectile dysfunction, as impotence came to be known. The Dole spot, which did not mention Viagra, was complemented by TV versions of the "Let the Dance Begin" ads, which, though they used the Viagra name, included no dialogue or explanation of the product's use. By sidestepping a full explanation and identification of Viagra in these two different ways, Pfizer was able to avoid an FDA-ordered listing of the drug's side effects. The cost of the 1999 television campaign was estimated at $35 million, and the TV spots were supported by the ongoing print segment of the campaign.

Viagra sold extremely well both before and after the advertising campaign's debut, and its introduction, along with the initial advertising behind it, was credited with helping to destigmatize impotency. The focus on elderly people in both the dancing spots and the Dole spots, however, risked alienating younger men. In following years Pfizer attempted to appeal to a broader age range of men by enlisting younger sports celebrities as Viagra spokesmen.

HISTORICAL CONTEXT

Started by immigrant cousins Charles Pfizer and Charles Erhart in 1849, Pfizer helped usher in the age of modern medicine by answering the U.S. government's call, during World War II, to devise a process for mass-producing penicillin. During the early 1960s Pfizer was the primary North American manufacturer of the Salk polio vaccine, and during the 1970s and 1980s an increased commitment to research and development led to the discovery of major medicines and fueled the company's global expansion. During the 1990s the pharmaceutical giant launched blockbuster drugs Zoloft, Lipitor, and Norvasc, among others.

In 1997 the U.S. Food and Drug Administration relaxed its policies regarding the television and radio advertising of prescription drugs, and drug company advertising expenditures increased dramatically as a consequence. Long reliant on marketing drugs primarily to physicians and other medical professionals, pharmaceutical manufacturers now began to advertise their products directly to consumers, much as other consumer goods had always been advertised. Though restrictions remained regarding the disclosure of side effects, and though most companies continued to submit their advertisements for FDA approval before airing them, direct-to-consumer pharmaceutical advertising quickly became ubiquitous in America, putting patients, rather than their doctors, increasingly in the position of deciding which drugs might best satisfy their needs.

In March 1998 the FDA approved Pfizer's anti-impotency drug Viagra, the first easily administered treatment for an affliction widely assumed, until then, to be essentially untreatable. Viagra's groundbreaking and controversial nature, unaided by any consumer advertising, made it an immediate pop-culture phenomenon upon its April launch.

TARGET MARKET

Pfizer allowed the initial media buzz to abate somewhat before launching its first advertisements on behalf of Viagra in late June 1998, a delay which likewise allowed for FDA approval of the ads. Some questioned the necessity of advertising a drug that seemed fully able to sell itself, but Pfizer, enlisting agency Cline, Davis & Mann, wanted to exert control over the Viagra image in the face of widespread, often uncomplimentary commentary about the drug. The primary audience in the campaign's early stages was older males. Among males over 65, the incidence of impotence ranged from 15 to 25 percent.

Pfizer's use of focus groups to prepare for the first Viagra campaign led to the conclusion that, as company executive David Brinkley told *Advertising Age,* "people want a positive message, they don't want to be reminded of their dysfunction and already know how devastated they are by it." Individuals in the focus group likewise "responded to the 'connectedness' the drug helped them feel with their partners." The first branded print ads, using the tagline "Let the Dance Begin," conveyed this positive, dignified message of connectedness, positioning Viagra as the answer to the romantic problems impotence can cause, through photos of mature couples dancing cheek to cheek alongside an image of the distinctive diamond-shaped blue pill.

The campaign's television launch, in the spring of 1999, brought to center stage, through the figure of former senator Dole, the message that erectile dysfunction was a condition to be taken seriously rather than dismissed or stigmatized. The unbranded Dole spot, which had a print counterpart, took the form of a public-service announcement and did not even mention Viagra, with the elderly senator speaking frankly about his own erectile-dysfunction experience and urging afflicted men to seek treatment. Branded 15-second TV spots, again featuring the dancing couples and using no dialogue or voice-over, broke soon after, reinforcing the image of Viagra as a path back toward romantic union.

DOLE'S OTHER "LITTLE BLUE FRIEND"

For the 2001 Super Bowl, Pepsi and BBDO New York used Bob Dole in an ad that directly parodied Dole's work for Viagra. The spot showed Dole on a beach with a golden retriever, mimicking imagery associated with pharmaceutical ads. Dole said, "I'm eager to tell you about a product that put real joy back into my life... What is this amazing product?" The product was Dole's "faithful little blue friend" Pepsi, of course. After cutting to a store interior in which a man told viewers to "ask your local convenience-store clerk" if Pepsi was right for them, the camera returned to Dole, who was shown doing backflips on the beach and saying, "I feel like a kid again."

COMPETITION

Viagra was preceded to the anti-impotency treatment market by a variety of less effective therapies and drugs that could be delivered only via injection. The first treatment not requiring injection—a urethral suppository named Muse, manufactured by VIVUS, Inc.—debuted in January 1997 and generated 17,000 prescriptions a week as well as a rapid increase in the price of VIVUS stock in its first year. The 1998 Viagra launch, however, proved devastating for VIVUS. Muse prescriptions dropped to 3,000 a week, the company lost $80 million, and VIVUS stock fell from its peak price of $40 per share to $2.

For five years Viagra remained the only impotence treatment available in pill form. As such it established a virtual sales monopoly in its category beginning at the time of its launch, but in late 2003 two new rivals touting advantages over Viagra entered the market behind high-profile launch campaigns.

Bayer AG and GlaxoSmithKline plc teamed up to market Levitra, which was touted as a faster-acting alternative to Viagra and which could be, unlike Viagra, taken with food. The partner drug companies anted up $6 million a year for a three-year Levitra sponsorship of NFL football, as well as an additional $10 to $15 million in media buys, and enlisted former Chicago Bears and then-current New Orleans Saints coach Mike Ditka as Levitra's spokesman. The resulting TV, print, outdoor, and promotional campaign, dubbed "Tackling Men's Health," broke in time for the fall 2004 football season. Within four months of its launch, Levitra had amassed a 14.4 percent market share.

After winning FDA approval for Cialis in late 2003, Eli Lilly and Company partnered with ICOS Corp. to comarket the drug. The Cialis launch campaign cost an estimated $100 million and broke during the broadcasts of the two NFL conference championships on January 18, 2004, before Cialis joined Levitra as an advertiser on that year's Super Bowl broadcast. Cialis distinguished itself from competitors by touting its 36-hour window of effectiveness, compared with the four or five hours promised by Viagra and Levitra. In order to make this claim in its "Bathtubs" television ads, Cialis broke with Viagra and Levitra to run spots featuring not only the product name but also an explicit explanation of its use. This was seen as a risky move because of FDA requirements calling for a corresponding focus on a long list of side effects, which could negatively affect viewers' perceptions of the drug. Cialis likewise targeted a key portion of its target market with a 2004 sponsorship of the PGA Tour. By October of 2004, Cialis was the number two anti-impotency drug, with an estimated 17.8 percent market share, compared with Viagra's 68.9 percent and Levitra's 10 percent.

MARKETING STRATEGY

The unprecedented media attention generated by Viagra's April 1998 launch was both a help and a hindrance to Pfizer as it set out to define the brand on its own terms in July of that year. On the one hand, as Pfizer executive Brinkley said, "It became OK overnight to talk about erectile dysfunction." Moreover, as consultant Al Ries of Ries & Ries told *Advertising Age,* "Publicity created the credentials for the brand before the advertising ran, so when you saw the ad you were already convinced that if you took one of the pills, you'd see a bodily reaction." On the other hand, much of the publicity was negative. Viagra and impotency became prime material for late-night monologue jokes, making Pfizer worry that many men, seeing that the condition had been dismissed as trivial, might yet remain unwilling to seek treatment.

A month after Viagra's launch, while Pfizer and Cline, Davis were still planning the drug's first advertisements, former senator Dole, as a guest on CNN's *Larry King Live,* revealed that he had participated in clinical trials for Viagra after prostate surgery and that he considered it "a great drug." Pfizer and Cline, Davis were surprised by the conservative icon's readiness to speak about such a sensitive matter, and they approached the former senator about doing an awareness campaign to supplement the ads then in production. He agreed to the proposal.

The consumer campaign broke in late June 1998 with the reserved, relationship-centered "Let the Dance Begin" print ads as well as educational spots, which appeared in magazines including *Newsweek, Time, Life,* and *U.S. News & World Report.* Then in March 1999 the Dole spot marked Viagra's television launch. It was supported by branded 15-second Viagra advertisements as well as the ongoing print portion of the campaign. The branded TV spots used the concept of dancing couples from the initial print campaign and included no dialogue, voice-over, or text explaining Viagra's function. Because of the early publicity Pfizer could count on consumers knowing the Viagra name and its intended use, so the branded spots needed no explanation and therefore could forego any FDA-mandated listing of side effects.

The Dole commercial likewise was informed by the early publicity and was, in a different way, able to steer consumers toward Viagra without having to mention any side effects. Though Dole directly addressed the condition of erectile dysfunction, there was no mention of the Viagra brand. The spot was framed, instead, as a public-service announcement in which Dole, against a stately senatorial-looking office backdrop, urged men suffering from erectile dysfunction to learn about all available treatment options. Viagra was, however, the only treatment then available in pill form, and its universal brand recognition made it the logical beneficiary of the pitch.

Dole opened with the word "courage" and then explained, "When I was diagnosed with prostate cancer, I was primarily concerned with ridding myself of the cancer. But secondly, I was concerned about postoperative side effects." Dole acknowledged, after introducing the previously little-known term "erectile dysfunction" in place of the less palatable "impotence," that "it's a little embarrassing to talk about E.D., but so important to millions of men and their partners . . . and there are many treatments available." Dole also referred viewers to an 800 number for the American Federation of Urological Disorders hotline.

OUTCOME

Before the advertising campaign broke, Viagra had already set a prescription-drug launch record by amassing $182.2 million in sales in its first two months on the market. In its nine months on the market in 1998, Viagra's total sales reached $788 million, and in following years its sales topped $1.5 billion. It became one of the most well-known brand names in the world, changing "pharmaceuticals as a business by virtue of the rapidity and degree to which it was absorbed into popular culture," according to Pfizer marketing executive Pat Kelly.

The advertising that supported Viagra's launch, particularly the Dole commercial, was credited with helping to destigmatize the condition of impotence, but both the branded spots and the Dole spot were blamed for attaching an "elderly" image to the medical condition and brand, thereby threatening to alienate younger men. In 2000 Pfizer began to phase out the Dole work as well as the branded spots, in favor of a "Faces of ED" theme, which featured men from a range of age groups. In 2001 Pfizer enlisted NASCAR driver Mark Martin, then in his early 40s, as a Viagra spokesman. A TV spot showing Martin's Viagra-sponsored car making laps around a track ended with Martin, on-screen, taking off his helmet and asking, "Who'd you expect? Bob Dole?" In 2002 Pfizer continued to run advertising that appealed to a broader range of men than the initial campaign had, using then-38-year-old baseball player Rafael Palmeiro in TV spots for the drug.

FURTHER READING

"Does Viagra Need Bob Dole? Or, Does Bob Dole Need Viagra?" *Medical Marketing and Media,* January 1999.

Fellman, Michelle Wirth. "Preventing Viagra's Fall." *Marketing News,* August 31, 1998.

Freeman, Laurie. "Pfizer Shifts Conversation on Viagra in a New Direction." *Advertising Age,* March 15, 1999.

Goetzl, David. "Pfizer Aces Its Advertising Test." *Advertising Age,* December 10, 2001.

———. "Viagra." *Advertising Age,* June 28, 1999.

———. "Vivus Targets Viagra-averse to Rebuild Share." *Advertising Age,* May 3, 1999.

Goldman, Debra. "Rising to the Occasion." *Adweek,* May 4, 1998.

Langreth, Robert. "Hard Sell." *Forbes,* October 16, 2000.

Lippert, Barbara. "Guise and Dolls." *Adweek,* September 28, 1998.

———. "On the Rise." *Adweek* March 8, 1999.

"Rx for DTC: Creativity." *Advertising Age,* March 15, 1999.

Wilke, Michael. "Pfizer Breaks 1st Ads for Viagra as Rivals Mull Own Campaigns." *Advertising Age,* July 6, 1998.

Mark Lane

Pharmavite LLC

8510 Balboa Blvd.
Northridge, California 91345
USA
Telephone: (818) 221-6200
Fax: (818) 221-6644
Web site: www.vitamin.com

TRUSTED BY THE ONES YOU TRUST CAMPAIGN

OVERVIEW

In January 1998, Pharmavite launched a $17 million national television, print, and radio campaign for its Nature Madeline of vitamins and nutritional supplements. Created by Leo Burnett, the campaign featured the tag line "Trusted by the ones you trust" in order to highlight the brand's endorsement by the American Medical Women's Association (AMWA), an organization of female doctors and medical students that lobbied for women's health issues. The "Trusted by the Ones You Trust" campaign was Pharmavite's largest marketing effort ever, necessitated by the increasingly crowded field in the natural care market of vitamin and herbal supplements.

Although Nature Made was the leading supplement brand in terms of retail sales, several major pharmaceutical companies announced their entry into the sector in 1997 and 1998. Private-label brands produced by chain stores such as Wal-Mart were also growing in popularity and profitability. Moreover, as aging consumers became more interested in using herbs and vitamins as alternatives to conventional therapies for the treatment and prevention of disease, the vitamin industry underwent significant changes. The most popular products previously had been multivitamin supplements designed to boost overall health. By the late 1990s, however, consumers began to seek out individually packaged vitamins and minerals that were believed to address specific ailments or body systems. Pharmavite hoped that the "Trusted by the Ones You Trust" campaign would defend Nature Made's position in this lucrative but shifting market.

In two television spots Pharmavite set out to make sure that consumers were aware that the AMWA had conferred its seal of approval upon the company's offerings. Since the natural care market was still struggling for legitimacy, a medical endorsement such as this was a major boon for Pharmavite. Both spots depicted the AMWA helping underprivileged people. One spot was set in the period after World War I, while the other used an Appalachian mining town in the 1930s as a backdrop. By linking its image to the AMWA's "emphasis on patient self-care," Pharmavite sought to strengthen the brand, according to the *Tan Sheet.* The company felt that the campaign helped increase both sales and consumers' awareness of the Nature Made line.

HISTORICAL CONTEXT

The supplement industry had once been predominantly a niche market, embraced more by a minority of so-called health nuts than by mainstream consumers. But a number of political, scientific, and social developments during the 1990s served to broaden the market tremendously. After much heated debate, the U.S. Congress passed a law in October 1994 that granted makers of dietary supplements greater freedom to make claims about their products' health benefits. Prior to this legislation, the Food and Drug Administration had forbidden supplement manufacturers from asserting that a vitamin or herb acted on a specific body part. In the wake of the loosening of supplement labeling laws, however, companies could correlate their products specifically with the health and well-being of consumers. For instance, Nature Made was able to tout its chromium tablets as "help[ing] regulate glucose metabolism," its lycopene supplement "as a key antioxidant," and its vitamin E products as "essential for normal growth and development . . . [and] protect[ing] tissues (cells) against damage caused by free radicals." At the same time that supplement companies were making more medical claims on their product packaging, several key studies about the efficacy of vitamins and herbal products received a great deal of attention in the media. Consumer magazines such as *Newsweek* and *Time* devoted feature articles to such remedies as DHEA (a hormone that some claimed could slow the aging process) and melatonin (which was praised by some for regulating sleep cycles). This sort of coverage enhanced the perceived legitimacy and efficacy of nutritional supplements.

According to *Time,* sales of natural foods and supplements grew 20 percent each year between 1990 and 1997. By 1997 total vitamin sales had reached $2.35 billion, up almost 15 percent from the year before. Pharmavite was in an ideal position to capitalize on this explosion. Founded in 1971 by two young entrepreneurs, the company introduced its Nature Made vitamin line the following year. Although Pharmavite initially sold its wares mostly at independently owned drugstores, it quickly built a sophisticated distribution network that incorporated chain drugstores and food stores. After being acquired by Otsuka Pharmaceutical Company, Ltd., in 1989, Pharmavite had the backing of a major corporation, which afforded it the resources to grow further. Fortuitously, just as Pharmavite expanded its distribution network, supermarkets and mass retailers like Wal-Mart and Kmart began to recognize the profits to be made from supplement sales and therefore gave the products more shelf space and more in-store promotional support. Nature Made quickly became a leading supplement product at these stores.

Pharmavite was aware of the important role brand building and marketing could play in the industry. In 1996 the company inaugurated a $10 million campaign for Nature Made conceived by the San Francisco-based agency Hal Riney & Partners. Like the ads in the "Trusted by the Ones You Trust" campaign, these earlier ads strove to play up the brand's medical legitimacy. Each spot claimed that Nature Made supplements were "recommended by pharmacists more than a thousand times everyday." Although the campaign did well, Pharmavite opted to change ad agencies in 1997, and it teamed up with Leo Burnett in an effort to bolster its national consumer advertising presence.

TARGET MARKET

A key factor fueling the growth of the supplement industry was the aging of baby boomer consumers. It was this main audience that Nature Made sought to reach with the "Trusted by the Ones You Trust" campaign. In their quest for a "natural alternative to prescription drugs," baby boomers ingested the largest quantity of supplements of any demographic group in the United States, explained *Chain Drug Review.* This population was interested not only in treating an illness after its onset but also in preventing disease in the first place and in counteracting the natural effects of aging. "Consumers are searching for the elusive fountain of youth, and certainly vitamins are a very big part of this," an industry analyst told *Discount Merchandiser.* This new trend was fueled in part by changes in the health care industry. As price-conscious health maintenance organizations limited patients' access to physicians, consumers looked for new ways to remedy medical complaints. "The comfortable paternalistic relationship—the doctor has all the answers, the patient obediently follows directions—is slowly disappearing," the *Wall Street Journal* averred on October 19, 1998. In fact, noted the paper on November 23, 1998, "Older Americans—long members of the 'see your doctor club'—are seizing upon nontraditional remedies."

Baby boomers were an ideal market to target. Not only were they massive in their sheer size, but they were also growing wealthier as they reached the peaks of their careers and earning power. As *Discount Merchandiser* succinctly concluded, "Vitamins cater to the aging, yet very affluent, older generation." Moreover, as baby boomers continued to age, "the incidence of chronic conditions [would] increase correspondingly," *Chain Drug Review* observed on February 3, 1997. Pharmavite anticipated that these consumers would seek supplements to treat such conditions. All indications were that vitamin usage was on the rise among older adults. By 1997, 43 percent of all households had at least one adult taking vitamins, up from 40 percent in 1996.

Women of the baby boomer generation were an especially important group for supplement sales. Women over 35 were drawn to natural products in search of "healthy" ways of dealing with menopause. In fact, according to *Chain Drug Review,* women bought approximately two-thirds of all natural care products. The "Trusted by the Ones You Trust" ads therefore particularly targeted women between the ages of 35 and

WAS IT A MAN'S WORLD?

Although companies such as Pharmavite had long ago introduced soy-based supplements designed for women, it was only with the sector's explosion in the last 1990s that male-specific herbal and vitamin remedies (such as one intended to keep the prostate in good working order) entered the marketplace.

64, explained the June 23, 1997, issue of *Chain Drug Review.* The emphasis on the AMWA's endorsement was the primary method by which the "Trusted by the Ones You Trust" campaign sought to reach this audience. As Pharmavite said in a company press release, "To educate women on the value of supplementation, Nature Made's campaign [focused on] AMWA's commitment to improving women's health and in support of its Nature Made products." The AMWA had established itself as a respected advocate for women's health issues, such as breast and cervical cancer. The spots not only mentioned the AMWA's approval, but they also were linked to the organization's history and activism.

COMPETITION

Nature Made was not the only company to take note of the money-making opportunities afforded by the natural care market. By 1998 the industry was experiencing "a growing trend toward bigger, more aggressive marketing efforts," according to the *Tan Sheet.* Although it was already a competitive market, large pharmaceutical companies entered the fray in 1997 and 1998. Warner-Lambert launched its Hails Zinc Defense in 1997 and backed it with a substantial marketing effort featuring actress Lauren Hutton. Within a few weeks SmithKline Beecham introduced a line of German herbals dubbed Abtei, and American Home Products prepared to debut an array of herbal products that would be marketed under the well-known Centrum brand name. In February 1998 the Feeling Fine Company also released a line of vitamin and nutritional supplements. To distinguish itself in the increasingly crowded arena, the brand commissioned Dr. Art Ulene of NBC's *Today* show fame to market and promote the company's Nutrition Boost multivitamin and mineral formula.

Established industry participants were not willing to let new market entrants poach unopposed on their turf. In 1999 Bayer introduced a campaign for its One-A-Day Specialized Blends. The commercials featured actress Annie Potts and portrayed her facing everyday challenges such as keeping up with an energetic toddler. Each spot closed with the tag line "Help your body help itself with One-A-Day Specialized Blends . . . just what you need to feel your best." One-A-Day also offered specialized multivitamins that targeted distinct audiences, such as One-A-Day 50-Plus and One-A-Day Men's Formula. In 1997 White-Hall Robbins also expanded its efforts to reach aging consumers by spending nearly $33 million to advertise Centrum Silver, which the company had originally introduced in 1990. This campaign, which pictured glowingly healthy older folks engaging in active pastimes such as canoeing, used the tag line "Life is an adventure because you're over 50 and still exploring." Centrum Silver became the second best-selling vitamin brand in 1998. Nature Made's other close competitor, Rexall Sundown Inc., tried to differentiate its supplements from its numerous competitors by incorporating "high-potency" formulas into its Sundown line. For a part of 1997 Sundown became the top-selling retail vitamin brand, but Nature Made reclaimed the distinction in 1998.

Private-label brands were another growing threat to Nature Made. Many retail chains, such as Safeway and Long's, produced their own versions of natural care products. In 1998 these brands controlled 15 percent of the market, but they were expected to continue to grow. Unlike their branded competitors, the private-label products incurred few marketing expenses and were therefore able to draw consumers by their lower prices as well as in-store support.

MARKETING STRATEGY

Television was the essential element of Pharmavite's strategy for Nature Made. Prior to the early 1990s, most single-element vitamins and almost all herbal supplements were sold at health food stores rather than major retailers. The suddenness of the supplement sector's boom and its arrival in the mainstream meant that most consumers had not yet formed strong brand allegiances. Before pharmaceutical corporations entered the market in 1997, most of the companies fighting for market share operated on low advertising budgets, but this was soon to change. Pharmavite used the "Trusted by the Ones You Trust" ads not only to increase vitamin sales during the campaign's tenure but also to build the Nature Made brand, so that consumers would specifically seek it out at retail stores. To bring the message of the "Trusted by the Ones You Trust" campaign to its target audience, Pharmavite ran the ads on a range of network and cable television programs. Among these were *Good Morning America, Today, Inside Edition, American Journal, World News Tonight,* and daytime CNN shows, and the ads ran on CNN Headline News, Discovery, Lifetime, and USA, all venues that were popular with the baby boomers the company wanted to reach. Advertising on news programs was an especially important component of Nature Made's strategy. "We have found that single vitamin consumers are very focused on news and information programming," a company spokesperson told the June 23, 1997, issue of *Chain Drug Review.* "They respond to clinical studies; they respond to press reports." Print ads, which also prominently displayed the brand's affiliation with the AMWA, ran in major consumer magazines as well.

Trust was the core theme of the campaign, and it was also the basis upon which Pharmavite intended to bolster the Nature Made brand. While the supplement industry was growing exponentially each year, only about half of the adult population were regular supplement users by 1998. Market research revealed that those consumers who eschewed natural care products often did so because they lacked crucial information about items, had safety concerns, or did not have "a recognizable brand name they knew and trusted," explained *Chain Drug Review.* By highlighting Nature Made's relationship with the AMWA, Pharmavite hoped to assuage consumers' concerns. Moreover, a majority of consumers polled by the magazine stated that "they would be most likely to consider [a supplement] purchase after receiving information from pharmacists, nutritionists, friends, or relatives." Nature Made hoped that by trumpeting the AMWA endorsement it could imbue its products with this aura of authority.

The company also aimed to get pharmacists—a crucial link between consumers and products—more involved in the supplement category. In addition to circulating *Nutrition Report,* the company's bimonthly publication detailing the latest clinical information about supplements, to many pharmacists, Pharmavite provided them with product information to give consumers. Even more innovative was the company's Drug Induced Nutritional Deficiency Program, which strove to inform pharmacists about nutritional deficiencies that resulted from the use of certain prescription medications. Upon filling such a prescription, the pharmacist could then recommend the appropriate supplement—which the company hoped would be the Nature Made brand—to address the problem.

Pharmavite augmented this multifaceted strategy with sophisticated in-store advertising. Instead of adding Nature Made bottles to the slew of brands already crowding shelves, Nature Made often opted for a dedicated display to create a more eye-catching effect for its products. This "wall of yellow labels," reflecting the company's packaging design, would "take advantage of [Nature Made's] strong brand recognition and the popularity of individual products," Marshall Fong, the company's brand manager, told *Chain Drug Review* on June 29, 1998.

OUTCOME

Pharmavite expressed satisfaction with its advertising efforts. A phone survey completed shortly after the "Trusted by the Ones You Trust" campaign broke indicated that 82 percent of consumers who regularly took supplements were aware of the Nature Made brand. "That's about 50 points higher than any other broad line supplement line," Nature Made's Fong proclaimed to *Chain Drug Review.* "People recognize Nature Made as a credible brand name." In the spring of 1998 Pharmavite continued to expand Nature Made's product line with the addition of nine new supplements.

Sales figures in 1998 reflected a positive year for Nature Made. The company had an 18 percent share of the vitamin E market, compared to its rivals' shares of about 3 percent each. "Our sales are growing faster than the category because of our advertising and contact with customers," Fong crowed to the *Chain Drug Review.* Content with what the campaign had accomplished, Pharmavite dedicated most of its advertising budget in late 1998 and early 1999 to promoting its Nature's Resource line of herbal remedies.

FURTHER READING

Eder, Rob. "Natural Care Will Create Most OTC New in '98." *Drug Store News,* January 12, 1998.

"Healthy Outlook." *Supermarket Business,* April 1, 1998.

Hume, Scott. "Burnett Lands Vitamin Client." *Adweek,* May 26, 1997.

Kadlec, Daniel. "How to Invest in the Herbal Remedy Boom." *Time,* November 23, 1998.

Mendelson, Seth. "Mass Retailers Seem to Be Taking Full Advantage of the Excitement Surrounding the Vitamin and Herbal Supplements Categories." *Discount Merchandiser,* May 1, 1998.

"Pharmavite Extends Nature Made Line." *Tan Sheet,* June 29, 1998.

"Pharmavite Nature Made Supplements Ads Break January 5." *Tan Sheet,* January 5, 1998.

"Science Fuels Boom in Herbal Products." *Chain Drug Review,* February 3, 1997.

Sullivan, Ben. "Growth Spurt; Herbs Able To Rack Up Big Sales." *Los Angeles Daily News,* May 3, 1998.

"Suppliers Scramble to Capitalize on Herbs." *Chain Drug Review,* October 12, 1998.

Rebecca Stanfel

Philips Electronics North America Corp.

1251 Avenue of the Americas
New York, New York 10020
USA
Telephone: (212) 536-0500
Fax: (212) 536-0500
Web site: www.philipsusa.com

■■■

GETTING BETTER CAMPAIGN

OVERVIEW

The third-largest manufacturer of consumer electronics, the Dutch company Koninklijke Philips Electronics N.V. was a well-known and respected firm in many parts of the world. The maker of such diverse products as televisions, telephones, compact disc (CD) players, medical imaging systems, semiconductors, appliances, and light bulbs—the company was the global leader in the lighting industry—Philips marketed its goods in 150 countries in the late 1990s. Unlike other electronics companies, such as Sony and Panasonic, Philips did not have a brand name that was easily recognized in the United States, where Philips Electronics North America Corp., the U.S. branch of the Dutch company, developed and sold products under such brand names as Philips, Philips Magnavox, Marantz, and Norelco. To increase Philips's worldwide brand recognition, the electronics company released its "Getting Better" campaign.

The print and television effort was released in September 1998 and became the largest advertising campaign in the history of the 107-year-old company. Although the campaign was designed to elevate the brand's image around the world, the company hoped especially to penetrate the U.S. market. With an estimated $100 million to spend on U.S. advertising alone, the New York–based ad agency Messner Vetere Berger McNamee Schmetterer/Euro RSCG developed the "Getting Better" campaign to position Philips as a cutting-edge company offering the most technically progressive and advanced products. Commercials featured young, hip individuals whose lives were "made better" by Philips's products and featured a cover version of "Getting Better," a song written by Paul McCartney and John Lennon of the Beatles. The campaign concluded on June 20, 2001.

Ed Volkwein, executive vice president of global brand management for Philips in the United States, announced in a prepared statement, "We are focused on generating high levels of brand awareness and preference for Philips in the U.S. We are determined to make Philips a well-recognized U.S. brand." Four months after the campaign began, Philips's brand recognition within the United States leapt from 39 to 56 percent, according to *American Demographics*.

HISTORICAL CONTEXT

Founded in the Netherlands in 1891 as a lamp factory, Philips soon diversified into other categories and became a powerful authority in the European business world. Hoping to increase its presence in the United States, the company made a number of acquisitions in the 1970s and 1980s, notably Magnavox in 1974 and Westinghouse in 1983. Despite such key gains, however,

Philips made a series of marketing and business errors in the late 1980s and early 1990s that signaled a loss of direction. Although Philips developed such innovative breakthrough products as the audiocassette, the videocassette recorder (VCR), and the CD, the company allowed others, namely Japanese electronics firms, to mass-produce the items and make enormous profits. Philips also miscalculated consumer desires; the company neglected to grasp the importance of new technologies such as mobile telephones yet heavily promoted such items as the compact disc-interactive and the digital audiotape, which failed to ignite interest or sales.

In order to survive in the quickly changing consumer-electronics industry, Philips underwent major restructuring during the first seven years of the 1990s. In 1996 a new chairman, Cor Boonstra, was brought on board to stave off further losses. Boonstra recognized the importance of elevating the Philips brand and began injecting additional funds into the marketing budget. Boonstra also intended to position Philips as a technology innovator and to increase brand awareness in the United States, a crucial market for new high-tech products and an area in which the Philips image was weak. In 1996 Philips combined its well-known Magnavox name, which was the third-best-selling brand of television in the United States, with its lesser-known Philips name to create Philips Magnavox. It then spent more than $40 million to sear the new brand name into the memories of consumers. The campaign, Euro RSCG's first U.S. effort for Philips, promoted budding technologies such as the Internet and combined the corporate tagline, "Let's Make Things Better," with the phrase "Philips Magnavox. No matter how you say it, it will change the way you see and hear forever." Philips continued its push in the United States in 1997 with a $50 million campaign for DVD players. According to Philips's Volkwein, the efforts paid off. "[Ninety] percent of our target customers in North America on an aided basis recognize the Philips-Magnavox brand," Volkwein said in *HFN: The Weekly Newspaper for the Home Furnishing Network.* "The goal," Volkwein continued, "is to have consumers associate the Philips name with digital products." Philips seemed to be moving closer to its goal. Volkwein indicated that brand awareness jumped 50 percent in 1997, compared to 1996, with 20 percent of its global sales in 1997 (about $8 billion) attributed to the United States.

TARGET MARKET

To position itself as an innovative and a high-tech leader, Philips targeted those most accepting and aware of new technology—young adults aged 25 to 35. Philips selected this rather narrow audience through a detailed study conducted at the end of 1997. A total of 14,000 individuals aged 13 to 65 and representing 17 countries were asked about their feelings toward and expectations of technology, as well as about their lifestyles and values. The results of the study showed that those familiar with the Philips brand considered it reliable and trustworthy but that they were often not aware of the brand's high-end products. The research also indicated that, while many were fearful of technology, those in their late 20s embraced innovation. Philips's director of global consumer and market intelligence, Elissa Moses, explained to *American Demographics* that this age group was considered by the general public to be the most knowledgeable about technology because "they take it for granted . . . It's almost an extension of their arms and legs."

To appeal to this particular group, labeled by Philips as "the Philips Generation," the company felt the need to focus its advertising efforts on state-of-the-art, high-end products, which the firm chose to call "star products." These items, which included the flat-screen television, the audio CD recorder, and the DVD player, would particularly appeal to the 20-something audience of well-educated, confident, and motivated consumers who kept current with the latest innovations. A prepared statement by Philips explained that, although the advertising would be geared toward the so-called Philips Generation, the campaign's appeal would spread to others through that group. "The group represents what many people see as 'the best years of our lives,' when we're most independent and carefree. Through the attitudes and lifestyle of this group, Philips aims to develop a brand personality that's 'human, imaginative . . . and somehow seductive.'"

COMPETITION

Since the 1950s Japanese companies, along with the European players Philips and Thomson S.A., had led the consumer electronics market. In the 1990s Matsushita Electric Industrial Co. Ltd., maker of such brands as Panasonic, Technics, and Quasar, dominated the fiercely competitive $385 billion global consumer-electronics category, followed by Sony Corp. and Philips, respectively. In the realm of color televisions, Philips dominated the market, while Matsushita, France-based Thomson S.A., and Sony followed. As these companies entered the 1990s, however, they faced an entirely new battle—that of the digital revolution—and all clamored for top status in the mind of the consumer. Joseph Clayton, executive vice president of Thomson Consumer Electronics, Inc., the U.S. subsidiary of Thomson S.A., declared in *Electronic Engineering Times* in 1996, "I believe now is the time to declare this . . . year the true beginning of an age that will change the direction of the consumer-electronics industry."

BUILDING THE BRAND

In addition to the large-scale "Getting Better" campaign, Philips undertook numerous promotional activities to elevate brand awareness in the United States. The company sponsored *Motown Live,* a musical variety program, was a promotional partner for the major motion picture *Austin Powers,* sponsored a NASCAR racing team, and managed to get an athletic stadium named for the company—Philips Arena became the home for the Atlanta Hawks basketball team.

Much of the campaign for digital dominance was played out in the United States through intensive marketing. As DVD players began to trickle onto the marketplace in late 1996 and early 1997, companies readied their advertising assaults. Philips promoted DVD extensively as "technology for the heart, spirit and imagination," targeting a broad audience. Other companies focused primarily on print advertising and on those most interested in new technology. Panasonic Corp., for instance, released a high-tech television commercial that pushed DVD as "the next thing in home entertainment," and Sony limited its efforts to magazines geared toward high-end users of audiovisual equipment. Beginning in 1998 electronics companies shifted focus to spotlight digital television, or high-definition television (HDTV), sets. Mitsubishi Consumer Electronics America, a division of Mitsubishi Electric of Japan and the maker of the best-sellers among large-screen televisions, used the theme "True HDTV" and emphasized the technical advantages of Mitsubishi HDTV sets. Panasonic, in its biggest U.S. campaign in eight years, focused on the spectacular features of HDTV. In the *Wall Street Journal* in late 1998 Panasonic's Bill Mannion explained the importance of promoting the new technology aggressively and of setting up early leadership: "In the next two years, the industry is redefining who will be the leaders for the next 10 years."

MARKETING STRATEGY

The goal of the "Getting Better" campaign was to reach 95 percent of Philips's target consumer an average of 55 times during the first year. Philips's senior director of marketing, Gérard Dufour, who was responsible for global brand management, explained in a prepared statement the strategy of spotlighting the high-end, so-called star, products that many would find unattainable. "The result [of the advertising] is that the Philips name is linked with leading edge, sophisticated products, whose 'halo' extends to the company's mainstream products," he said. "Although many consumers might not buy the 'stars,'" Dufour continued, "they'll be eager to own other Philips products to get some of the reflected star attraction."

The branding campaign was described by the company as featuring "wry, humorous ads that portray young, clever, motivated consumers finding ways to improve their everyday lives with the help of Philips's products." The print ads appeared in a wide variety of magazines, including those in such categories as sports, science, entertainment, travel, business, lifestyle, and food. The television spots, which starred members of what Messner called the Philips's "tribe," 20-something individuals comfortable with technology and aware of how it enhanced their lives, aired on prime-time network TV during entertainment and sports programs as well as on cable channels such as MTV, USA Network, and E! Entertainment Network. The television commercials featured a cover version of "Getting Better" performed by the up-and-coming British band Gomez. Philips's Moses explained in *American Demographics* that Gomez was selected to give the three-year-old corporate tagline, "Let's Make Things Better," a new life. "It really brought to life what we felt our products were going to do for people in a way that was both comforting—because you've heard the song before—but contemporary, because it's somebody new singing it," Moses said.

In the spot "Everything Fits" three young people prepared to furnish a modern-looking beach house. The house was oddly shaped and extremely narrow. The friends first brought in a narrow orange sofa, followed by a 42-inch flat-screen television, which they hung on the wall. The three plopped onto the couch, pointed the remote control, and the television show *Flipper* appeared, much to their delight. The music, "Getting Better," then played briefly as the screen read, "Presenting Flat TV from Philips." The spot finished with the Philips logo and tagline. Another spot, "The Gift," showcased the Halogena, a halogen light bulb that came with a two-year guarantee. The first commercial in 10 years for the lighting division, it made its debut in November during the telecast of a National Football League game. In the spot a young man arrived home at his apartment only to discover that his light bulb was out. With a groan, the man began piling up pieces of furniture to reach the bulb in the high-ceilinged room. As he climbed on his furniture with a replacement bulb in his mouth, a neighbor caught sight of his plight through a window. He rushed to the man's apartment with a Halogena bulb, stating, "Check this out." The man mumbled, "But I've got a bulb," to which the neighbor replied, "But this'll last you two years. Guaranteed." The man then compared the two and replied, "Cool." The spot ended with "Getting Better" and the Philips tagline.

Philips began 1999 with invigorated sales and a new television spot that debuted during the Super Bowl. It was the company's first time advertising in that high-profile venue. The commercial, which showcased the new Philip. 64-inch high-definition projection television, retained the "Let's Make Things Better" theme. Three of the campaign's final 2001 spots featured young adults furbishing their high-ceilinged lofts with a selection of Philips's premium electronics. In one spot a woman passed on the opportunity to take home a puppy in favor of a Philips flat-panel television. Although the final three commercials appeared to take place inside an apartment building, they were actually filmed in an abandoned mental hospital in Cape Town, South Africa.

In late 2000 Philips announced that it was parting ways with Euro RSCG, and it assigned its global account to two agencies. DUB Worldwide was given duties for Philips's consumer-electronics and corporate accounts, and the roster shop D'Arcy Masius Benton & Bowles was chosen to advertise Philips's lighting and medical systems. "Getting Better" ended in June 2001.

OUTCOME

Philips considered the "Getting Better" campaign a success. Volkwein told *USA Today,* "We've seen a tremendous upsurge in awareness... We feel the campaign is working extremely well." Immediately following the 1998 release of "Getting Better," Philips enjoyed a brief sales increase and even longer-lasting brand awareness in the United States. According to *American Demographics,* Philips's brand-recognition rating in the United States jumped from 39 to 56 percent four months after the campaign began.

According to Ad Track, the *USA Today* poll designed to determine a campaign's popularity and effectiveness, 23 percent of consumers surveyed indicated that they liked the campaign "a lot." Those in Philips's target audience especially enjoyed the campaign, with 38 percent of people aged 18 to 24 saying that they enjoyed the commercials. *Brandweek* writer Tobi Elkin praised the campaign as well and stated, "[It] scored strong results and raised the firm's profile in less than a year. Philips's focused campaign is a model for its competitors." "Getting Better" shifted Philips's focus away from product advertising and toward brand advertising. In a prepared statement, Dufour explained, "A product is replaceable; a brand is what consumers buy and keep on buying." Citing creative differences, Philips ended its 10-year relationship with Euro RSCG in early 2001. "Getting Better" officially concluded on June 20, 2001.

FURTHER READING

du Bois, Martin. "Philips Electronics Aims to Boost Its Brand." *Wall Street Journal,* May 15, 1998, p. B7A.

Edy, Carolyn. "The Olympics of Marketing." *American Demographics,* June 1, 1999, p. 47.

Elkin, Tobi, and Kate MacArthur. "Why Philips Left Messner." *Advertising Age,* January 15, 2001, p. 4.

Hall, Lee,"Philips Puts On $100 Million Digital Push: Massive TV Blitz Targets Young Adults." *Electronic Media,* September 21, 1998, p. 35.

McCarthy, Michael. "Philips Can't Lose with Puppies, Beatles." *USA Today,* January 15, 2001, p. 7B.

Silberg, Lurie. "Goal of Big Ad Push: Propel Philips Brand." *HFN: The Weekly Newspaper for the Home Furnishing Network,* January 26, 1998, p. 38.

Takaki, Millie. "Dir. Jim Byrkit Plugs in Philips." *Shoot,* February 8, 2002, p. 1.

Mariko Fujinaka
Kevin Teague

Piaggio USA, Inc.

140 E. 45th St., 17th Fl.
New York, New York
USA
Telephone: (212) 380-4400
Fax: (212) 380-4459
Web site: www.piaggiousa.com

■■■

VESPA REINTRODUCTION CAMPAIGN

OVERVIEW

The Vespa motor scooter gained worldwide fame when one was ridden by actress Audrey Hepburn in the 1950s film *Roman Holiday.* Manufactured by Italian company Piaggio & C. SpA, the Vespa became an international cultural icon, known primarily for its style. By the mid-1980s, however, the scooter had failed to keep up with engine design and failed to meet more stringent U.S. emissions standards. Rather than update the engine, Piaggio simply pulled out of the market. Fifteen years later Vespa was able to meet emissions levels and once again eyed the United States, where scooters were enjoying a resurgence. In 2000 the scooter was brought back to the United States, and Piaggio USA launched a marketing campaign to reintroduce Vespa to the country.

The Vespa reintroduction was a free-form effort in many ways. Dealers were allowed to develop their own ads and sell to whatever market looked most promising to them. The first advertisements began running in 2002. Regardless of region, however, the ads were often sexual in nature, playing off of the scooter's Italian image. At the national level Piaggio mostly worked cross-marketing deals with other companies and succeeded in placing the Vespa in many of these companies' advertisements. There was no announced budget for the campaign, much of which was funded locally with contributions from Piaggio.

The reintroduction of Vespa came to a close at the end of 2004, when Piaggio began seeking an advertising agency to implement a national branding strategy. Vespa had staked out its claim in the marketplace, distinguishing itself from the competition on the grounds that it was more than a scooter and instead represented a lifestyle that many people found appealing. Some of the ads also received recognition from the advertising industry. The newspaper ads that Mullen Advertising created for the campaign won a bronze at the 2003 One Show awards, hosted by the One Club in New York City.

HISTORICAL CONTEXT

Launched in Italy shortly after World War II by Piaggio, the stylish Vespa motor scooter soon became a cultural icon. It was immortalized in the 1950s when Audrey Hepburn rode one in the film *Roman Holiday,* and its stylish reputation spread when it appeared in the Italian movie *La Dolce Vita* (1960) and was taken up by the Mods in Britain in the 1960s. An entire subculture developed around the Vespa in Europe and North America. In the mid-1980s, however, the Vespa faced new, more stringent air-emissions standards in the United States. While always a fashion leader, the Vespa still relied on 30-year-old technology: a two-stroke engine that spewed liberal amounts of pollutants into the air. Rather than reengineer the bike and refit its Italian factories, Piaggio opted to abandon the North American market and to continue to sell its high-emission scooters in Europe and Asia.

Piaggio's strategy worked well for about a decade, but eventually other countries began tightening their emissions standards as well, and Piaggio was forced to install a cleaner, modern engine in the Vespa. As the century came to a close, there was no longer a reason to avoid the U.S. market. In fact, America presented an excellent opportunity for Piaggio, as scooters were regaining favor in that market. According to the Motorcycle Industry Council, about 12,000 scooters were sold in the United States in 1997, but that number had begun to grow at a 20 percent clip each year. In addition, the successful launch of the new Volkswagen Beetle in the late 1990s—as well as general nostalgia for the 1960s—bode well for the Vespa's return to the United States. Piaggio also discovered that the Vespa had been anything but forgotten. "In the mid- to late-1990s, when the Internet exploded, the most amazing thing happened," wrote Doug Sarti in Vancouver's weekly newspaper *Georgia Straight.* "Scooterists reconnected, and it became clear that although Vespa culture had gone underground in North America, it was alive and well."

In 2000 Piaggio began exporting new Vespas to the United States, after which Piaggio USA began a long-term marketing campaign to reintroduce the Vespa to America. It relied a great deal on the initiative of dealers but also included the use of national promotional tie-ins with other companies' products.

THE WASP TAKES WING

The company that manufactured the Vespa, Piaggio & C. SpA, started out in the 1880s outfitting ocean liners. Over the years it became involved in trains and cars, but prior to World War II the family business made the mistake of adding passenger airplanes and bombers to its expertise. Because it manufactured planes for the Axis war effort, Allied forces bombed its factories, eventually destroying them completely. After the war the founder's son, Enrico Piaggio, revitalized the company by looking to serve the transportation needs of everyday Italians. The result of the company's engineering efforts was a scooter that relied on airplane technology. It featured a front fork reminiscent of an airplane's landing gear and a sleek steel chassis. When Piaggio saw the prototype, he exclaimed, "Sembra una vespa!" (It looks like a wasp). The name "Vespa" stuck, and a cultural icon was born.

TARGET MARKET

According to Christopher Montgomery of the *Dayton Daily News,* Piaggio sought to market Vespas to two main demographic groups: "twenty-somethings that want to zip around college campuses and big cities; and middle-aged consumers nostalgic for the scooter heyday of the 1950s and '60s." Hence, the age demographic ranged from 16 to 70.

But there were other potential customers aside from students and retirees. Given the high costs of automobiles and the rising price of gasoline, many people began to consider the scooter an economical mode of basic transportation. Wealthier people, on the other hand, viewed the Vespa as a weekend toy. Unlike motorcycles, which were overwhelmingly marketed to men almost to the exclusion of women, scooters—especially style-conscious ones like Vespa—found a receptive market among women. Almost 40 percent of the new scooter buyers were women, and they were more likely than men to pay extra to personalize and accessorize their scooters. Because this meant extra profits for Piaggio, the company catered to the female customer. There was one other market for scooters, one that was less interested in fashion and that Vespa did not aggressively pursue: people who had lost their driver's license after a DUI (driving under the influence) conviction. In some states residents did not have to register a scooter that had a 50cc engine, nor did they need to possess a license to drive one. In such circumstances a scooter became known as a "liquorcycle."

COMPETITION

As Americans' interest in scooters was rekindled, so too was competition between scooter manufacturers. Piaggio had an Italian rival in Aprilia Group, the second-largest seller of scooters in Europe behind Piaggio. During the course of the Vespa reintroduction campaign, that threat was removed in 2004, when Piaggio acquired Aprilia.

Vespa's most serious challengers in the U.S. market were three Japanese companies: Honda, Yamaha, and Suzuki. Until the mid-1980s Vespa, along with another Italian scooter, the Lanbretta, had dominated the world scooter market. Then Honda introduced the Elite, and Yamaha created the Riva; these plastic upstarts offended the sensibilities of scooter purists but were reliable and inexpensive and found a mass audience. Once Piaggio left the U.S. market, the Japanese were able to build up their dealer networks and dominate the scooter business. Honda became the dominant force, because it was able to leverage its 1,200 dealerships to control the U.S. scooter market. In cases where the company believed dealership sales would not be adversely impacted, Honda also sold its scooters through multiline scooter shops. Yamaha, the second largest in terms of U.S. market share, carved out its own niche primarily based on price. Yamaha would also attempt to take on Vespa directly by introducing its Vino Classic, a bike that not only mimicked Vespa's look but also was positioned as having Italian flair with the slogan "Can you say ciao bella?"

Heading the list of secondary competitors was Suzuki, which branched into scooters in 2003 and found its own niche by focusing on the increasingly popular category of maxi-scooters, which offered greater comfort and a more powerful engine. There was also a pair of Taiwanese-made scooters with which to contend: Kymco, a former Honda licensee, and MZ, an offshoot of Germany's MZ Motorcycle Company. China offered the TN'G, establishing a beachhead in the U.S. market through a distribution deal with the warehouse-club chain Costco and later setting up its own dealer network. A pair of scooter manufacturers in India, LML and Bajaj, also offered competition. In addition Vespa was anticipating the entrance into the U.S. scooter market of two French rivals, Peugeot and MBK.

MARKETING STRATEGY

Shortly after Vespa was reintroduced to the United States in November 2000, Piaggio's president, Giancarlo Fantappie, told *BusinessWeek,* "We're selling a lifestyle, not just a scooter." The Vespa mystique alone was able to generate sales; a seven-month wait for the bikes soon developed. Hence, at this stage there no need to push sales aggressively, and marketing was kept low-key. Vespas were awarded to the winners of the New York City Marathon, but no major media blitz ensued. According to *BusinessWeek,* Piaggio was content to "sell its 'recreational toys' through the Neiman Marcus Christmas catalogue, as well as in 'Vespa boutiques' in trendy spots like East Hampton, [New York], and Palm Beach, [Florida]." More than 40 more of the boutiques, which also sold Vespa clothing and accessories such as helmets and riding gloves, were slated to be opened within the next year.

Piaggio gave the dealer groups a great deal of latitude in handling Vespa's marketing, and the first wave of advertising began appearing in 2002. Wenham, Massachusetts–based Mullen Advertising produced a series of three newspaper ads. An example of the shop's humorous take was the headline used in one ad: "A hog for you temporary-tattoo types." The agency Kirshenbaum Bond + Partners created three billboards in San Francisco employing a sexy approach to promoting the Vespa. Each execution showed a woman grasping a male driver, either with her hands, arms, or legs. In Denver in 2002 the first TV spot was aired for the Vespa. Created by the agency Viewpoint Studios (later renamed Viewpoint Creative), it combined humor and sex to make its point. A young man apparently addressed a woman reclining in a lawn chair. In an Italian accent, he praised her curves and figure, saying, "Your petite but powerful body will purr with excitement when we are together." As he said, "I will mount you now," the camera panned to reveal that he was talking to a Vespa scooter.

Writing for *Dealernews,* Shay Moftakhar explained Piaggio's national marketing strategy; it devised "an ingenious marketing program that incorporates 'viral' advertising in many major campaigns. Scooters are seen in ads for products ranging from Washington State apples to cell phones to laptop computers, all serving to ingrain scooters in the consumer subconscious." Moftakhar also pointed out that Piaggio had increased Vespa awareness in retail venues through cross-promotions with Target and the Sharper Image. In addition, Piaggio succeeded in placing Vespa in ads for the likes of American Express, McDonald's, Starbucks, and JetBlue Airways. Hearkening back to its motion-picture heritage, Vespa was featured in a remake of *Alfie,* starring Jude Law. The Vespa had also appeared in the original 1966 film.

In 2003 Piaggio introduced a more powerful scooter, the Vespa Grand Turismo, and to help with the launch the company hired R.C. Auletta & Company to handle national public-relations responsibilities for what was to be Vespa's top-of-the-line model and an important money maker. National coordination began to take on greater importance, because Vespa seemed to be marketed to a different audience depending on the region. Amanda Schupak wrote in *Forbes,* "In Denver the gay crowd has embraced the brand. In Boston Vespa is coveted by coeds. Celebs and hipsters ride the scooters in Los Angeles and New York. And in San Francisco Vespa dealer Walter Dawydiak is pushing the fashionable bikes, which get 70 miles to the gallon and run up to 70 miles per hour, on the San Francisco Police Department." The reintroduction of Vespa had succeeded by the end of 2004, at which point Piaggio began searching for an advertising agency to develop a national branding strategy and take Vespa to the next level.

OUTCOME

Although uncoordinated in many ways, the marketing campaign to reintroduce Vespa to the United States succeeded. Sales in 2004 reached $25 million, an 80 percent increase over the previous year that was largely a result of sales of the Grand Turismo. The brand also reconnected with its legions of fans after a 15-year absence from the U.S. market, and in addition to selling scooters, Piaggio succeeded in selling Vespa apparel and other items; as of May 2003 there were 62 Vespa boutiques in the United States. Rising gas prices made scooters appealing to an even wider market, and Vespa's winning lifestyle image, which made it stand out from the competition, promised to attract a new and broader set of customers.

What little advertising that was done in support of Vespa was also well received. In 2003 the newspaper ads created by Mullen Advertising won a bronze at the One Show, the annual advertising awards sponsored by the One Club, a New York–based nonprofit organization established to promote excellence in advertising.

FURTHER READING

Fillion, Kate. "So Very Vespa." *Maclean's,* November 18, 2005.

Gomez, Henry. "Scooter Sales Riding Upward." *Crain's Cleveland Business,* October 11, 2004, p. 6.

Greenberg, Karl. "Vespa Scooters in Hunt for Shop." *Adweek,* December 13, 2004, p. 9.

Heim, Sarah J. "Vespa's Sex Appeal Promoted in KBP West Ads." *Adweek* (western ed.), April 22, 2002, p. 2.

Kline, Maureen. "Vespa Is Really Starting to Scoot." *BusinessWeek,* March 28, 2005, p. 28.

Montgomery, Christopher. "Will Boomers Take to Scooters?" *Dayton (OH) Daily News,* May 30, 2002, p 1E.

Rountree, Kristen. "Viewpoint Studios Intros Racy TV Work for Vespa." *Adweek* (New England ed.), July 1, 2002, p. 2.

Sarti, Doug. "Vespa Scoots Sexily Back to Vancouver." *Georgia Straight* (Vancouver, BC), June 3, 2004.

Schupak, Amanda. "Calling Audrey Hepburn." *Forbes,* April 11, 2005, p. 60.

Scully, James. "Hot Wheels: Inspired by Aeronautics and Adapted by the Dolce Vita Set, the Vespa Is Still the Quickest Way to Get Around." *Time,* November 29, 2005, p 20.

"The Ultimate Scooter Returns." *BusinessWeek,* November 27, 2000, p. 14.

Zammit, Deanna. "R.C. Auletta Rides Away with Vespa." *Adweek* (eastern ed.), July 25, 2003.

Ed Dinger

Piedmont Federal Savings and Loan Association

16 W. 3rd Street
Winston-Salem, North Carolina 27101
USA
Telephone: (336) 770-1000
Fax: (336) 770-1055
Web site: www.piedmontfederal.com

IT'S YOUR MORTGAGE. KEEP IT HERE. CAMPAIGN

OVERVIEW

In 2003 Piedmont Federal Savings and Loan Association was composed of 10 branches, making it the third-largest financial institution in North Carolina. Piedmont Federal operated as a "portfolio lender," meaning it lent only its money and kept all mortgages in-house. This time-tested method of financing provided greater security for homebuyers but usually resulted in higher interest rates. In order to unbind their capital, Piedmont Federal's competition usually sold mortgages to third-party institutions. Though the interest rates were cheaper, the competition's customers were usually unaware of who actually carried their mortgages. Between 2000 and 2002, 29 percent of Piedmont Federal's customers left for banks, credit unions, and mortgage brokers offering lower interest rates. To restore Piedmont Federal's customer base and accentuate its safer method of financing, the bank released a campaign titled "It's Your Mortgage. Keep It Here."

Based in Winston-Salem, which was also home to Piedmont Federal's headquarters, the advertising firm the Woodbine Agency launched the "It's Your Mortgage. Keep It Here." campaign in January 2003. Costing less than $500,000, the campaign used television and radio spots as well as print, direct-mail, and online ads. The advertisements never mentioned interest rates, something Piedmont Federal's competition focused on, but instead touted Piedmont Federal's safer mortgaging. One of the print ads featured the copy "Separation anxiety shouldn't apply to your mortgage." Hoping that realtors would recommend Piedmont Federal as a preferred lender to homebuyers, the bank's loan officers distributed house-hunting kits to local realtors. After running for 18 months, the campaign ended in June 2004.

"It's Your Mortgage. Keep It Here." claimed a Silver EFFIE Award in 2005 for the Financial Services/Products category. It also helped Piedmont Federal rebuild its customer base. The bank originated 21 percent more mortgages during the campaign than during the 18 months prior. According to Market Perspectives, a marketing research and consulting firm, 49 percent of those surveyed in the Winston-Salem area said that they were "more likely to use Piedmont Financial Services because of advertising."

HISTORICAL CONTEXT

Ever since Piedmont Federal opened in 1903, it had been relying on quality customer service and mutual trust to attract customers. It was one of the few institutions during the Great Depression that not only retained all of its depositors' cash, but also continued paying interest on depositors' investments. "We have been committed to being a hometown savings and loan throughout our history, and that has been our biggest strength and competitive advantage," Nick Mitchell, Jr., the president and chief executive of Piedmont Federal, told the *Winston-Salem Journal.* "Our average employee has been here 17 years, which provides a consistent face to the community. We've had a branch presence in most of the communities we've served for three or four decades."

With little advertising Piedmont Federal grew from one branch to ten over the course of a century. By 2000, however, Piedmont Federal's customer base had begun to wane. Many of its older customers were paying off their mortgages. Other home owners were switching to outside lenders that could refinance their homes at lower interest rates. The competition also increased their marketing expenditures 39 percent in 2002, while Piedmont Federal's advertising remained relatively miniscule. Between 2000 and 2002 its customer base dropped 29 percent. Piedmont Federal also financed all of its own mortgages, while the competition was quickly selling mortgages to institutions outside of Winston-Salem's Forsyth County. Jim Lambie, the former cochairman of the Downtown Winston-Salem Partnership, an economic-development organization, stated to the *Winston-Salem Journal,* "[Piedmont Federal] has always been a source of community admiration because of its commitment to remaining local when there were opportunities to expand in a major way outside Forsyth." Because Piedmont Federal could not compete with the competition's interest rates, its ad agency, Woodbine, decided to advertise from an emotional platform that boasted of the bank's familiarity and loyalty to the Winston-Salem area.

CATERING TO THE ELDERLY

In 2002 Michael Sullivan, cofounder of the marketing consulting firm 50-Plus Communications Consulting, offered suggestions for marketing to the elderly in *America's Community Banker.* First, he recommended that when bankers greeted individuals over 60 years old, they should gently shake their hands. Most senior citizens suffered from arthritis, making a firm handshake uncomfortable. Second, he suggested that bankers display patriotic symbols such as American flag pins, because the older demographic tended to be more patriotic. Third, because 80 percent of Americans over 60 years old had grandchildren, bankers should display pictures of their children around the office. Pictures would suggest to the elderly that the banker shared their values. Finally, Sullivan suggested that bankers not use the term "senior citizen." People over 60 generally admitted to feeling 15 years younger than they actually were and preferred not to be reminded of their actual age.

TARGET MARKET

"It's Your Mortgage. Keep It Here." targeted two separate demographics. Woodbine named the first the "Cul-de-Sac Crowd," which consisted of 25- to 39-year-olds outgrowing their starter homes. The second target, "New Affluents," was composed of 35- to 49-year-old professionals looking to refinance their current home and possibly purchase a second. Although these two groups shared little in common, the campaign catered to the targets' similar hopes for the Winston-Salem area. According to Woodbine, which was also based in Winston-Salem, both groups had gone to school in the area and planned to stay there. Also, both were classified as cautious spenders who preferred to keep their money within the local economy. The "Cul-de-Sac Crowd" and the "New Affluents" also wanted to preserve hometown traditions and improve the area for future Forsyth County generations.

According to the *Winston-Salem Journal,* Thad Woodard, the president of the North Carolina Bankers Association, remarked early on in the 2003 campaign that Piedmont Federal's customers were "probably a little more gray-haired" than those at commercial banks. To shed its stigma as a bank just for the elderly, Piedmont Federal retrofitted its system to include online banking before the 2003 campaign was released. The "Cul de Sac Crowd" and the "New Affluents" included consumers that fell within Generation X, the generation of Americans born between approximately 1965 and 1976. According to Karen Ritchie, author of *Marketing to Generation X,* the Generation X banker "goes into branches the least often of any generation, but they actually interact with the bank the most often, either through phone, ATM or online." Ritchie also wrote, "Gen Xers are worrying about their retirement plans at the age when baby boomers were worrying about Bob Dylan going electronic."

COMPETITION

Southern Community Financial, another community bank in Winston-Salem, released a newspaper and billboard campaign in 2003 that featured images of a Great Dane looming over a Chihuahua. In an approach that was similar to that of Piedmont Federal, Southern Community boasted that its smaller size afforded the bank more flexibility and friendlier service than larger institutions. Southern Community's campaign was an obvious jab at the Wachovia Corporation, a North

Carolina–based bank that was acquired by the much-larger First Union Corporation. Suggesting that larger banks had a one-sided relationship with their customers, one ad's copy read, "They bark. You roll over. Not a very healthy relationship." Another print ad asked, "How much bank is too much bank?" The Bloom Agency created the campaign for Southern Community, which in 2003 had eight branch locations.

Doug Lebda founded LendingTree, LLC, in 1997 after his own attempt to secure a mortgage proved "dis-empowering, hard to sort through and difficult to understand," according to *Mortgage Banking* magazine. LendingTree, based in Charlotte, North Carolina, allowed future homeowners to visit its website to request mortgage quotes, which were usually available within 10 minutes. The service submitted a customer's loan request to a plethora of lenders, who competed for the lowest interest rate. Between 1997 and 2004 LendingTree facilitated more than $74 billion in loan funding. Lenders used the service because it generated leads cheaper than anyone else. According to *Mortgage Banking,* home owners enjoyed the service because it turned the mortgage process upside down. No longer were consumers pleading with banks to be approved for mortgages. Lenders had to compete with each other to provide consumers the best possible lending rates. In 2004 the company spent $70 million on advertising, which included television spots and print ads.

MARKETING STRATEGY

Prior to the campaign's January 2003 release, Woodbine interviewed existing and possible Piedmont Federal customers, who said that they would take loans with higher interest rates if it meant keeping their mortgages within Forsyth County. Those interviewed said that not only did they prefer to have their money benefit the local economy, but they were also frustrated with the amount of paperwork that ensued after their mortgage was sold to an outside institution. Based on this feedback, Woodbine developed a campaign with two different phases. The first part would create uneasiness amongst Winston-Salem home owners about their mortgages being sold to outside institutions. The second part would assure the community that Piedmont Federal would never sell their mortgages. The message was summed up in the tagline, "It's Your Mortgage. Keep It Here."

For the campaign's first phase, one radio commercial simulated a call between a frustrated North Carolina resident on the phone with an out-of-state bank. During the commercial an out-of-state customer service representative mocked the North Carolina customer for using the Southern word "y'all." Print ads suggested that large cities such as New York, Chicago, and San Francisco were a "great place to visit, but are they really where you want to send your home mortgage payments?" Billboard ads featured the copy "Separation Anxiety Shouldn't Apply to Your Mortgage." One Winston-Salem billboard read, "You live here in Boone, NC. So why is your mortgage in Boonesville, TX?"

The second phase of the campaign featured print and radio advertisements that used "hometown pride," as a Woodbine representative put it, to attract Winston-Salem customers. "It's your hometown. It's your home mortgage. Keep It Here." was the copy for one newspaper advertisement. Woodbine was aware that Piedmont Federal would fail if it entered the price wars between competing lenders, so none of the advertisements mentioned interest rates. Instead the advertising targeted areas that Woodbine perceived as "points of pride" among the "Cul de Sac Crowd" and the "New Affluents." Promotions during local high school football games included Piedmont Federal posters, ads in program books, and radio spots. In 2003 Piedmont Federal purchased newspaper ads that celebrated the bank's 100-year anniversary in the Winston-Salem community. Radio spots were aired during University of North Carolina and Wake Forest University football and basketball games. Full-page newspaper ads that warned of mortgages being sold to out-of-state institutions were placed adjacent to the competitions' ads.

The campaign hoped to stoke Piedmont Federal's reputation as a supporter of the Winston-Salem community. As suffering tobacco, furniture, and textile businesses were forced to lay off local residents, Piedmont Federal wanted to reinforce its dedication to Winston-Salem's prosperity. "We don't sell off our loans to create extra revenue because we remain prudent and fiscally conservative with our portfolio," Mitchell explained to the *Winston-Salem Journal.* "Those loans stay at home, and customers who have a question about their loan or want to purchase or move up in housing can talk directly to us."

Understanding that realtors heavily influenced which lender a homebuyer selected, Piedmont Federal created 1,200 house-hunting kits for Winston-Salem realtors in the hopes of being recommended as a lender. The bank inserted maps, a mortgage calculator, a notepad, and a pen into a Piedmont Federal–branded binder. The kits were then used as "handshake pieces" by Piedmont Federal loan officers who met with local realtors. "It's Your Mortgage. Keep It Here." ran for 18 months, ending in June 2004.

OUTCOME

In 2005 "It's Your Mortgage. Keep It Here." earned a Silver EFFIE Award (Financial Services/Products category) from the New York American Marketing Association. The award also made Woodbine one of only two North Carolina advertising agencies ever to place in the EFFIE Awards. During the campaign's 18-month run Piedmont Federal originated 1,688 mortgages, which was 21 percent more than during the 18 months before the campaign. Market Perspectives, a marketing research and consulting firm, also concluded that 36 percent more consumers would choose Piedmont Federal to finance a loan after they viewed the campaign's advertisements than if they had not viewed them. Woodbine asserted that the campaign transformed Piedmont Federal's reluctance to sell mortgages to outside institutions from a weakness into a strength. As "It's Your Mortgage. Keep It Here." drove the message that Piedmont Federal strongly supported the local economy, Winston-Salem's lenders were forced to rethink loans as more than just a commodity sold at the lowest price. Forsyth County residents were beginning to choose lenders based on the lender's commitment to the local economy, which was suffering from recession.

FURTHER READING

Cherrie, Victoria. "Group Has Big Project in Its Sights." *Winston-Salem (NC) Journal,* March 15, 2005, p. 1.

———. "Planning Again; Old, New Ideas Combined for Downtown Design." *Winston-Salem (NC) Journal,* March 22, 2005, p. 1.

Craver, Richard. "FDIC Plan Alters Rules; Banks' Low-Income Investing Involved." *Winston-Salem (NC) Journal,* October 26, 2004, p. 1.

———. "Safe and Sound; Piedmont Federal Stays Steady as It Builds on a Century of Helping People Buy Homes." *Winston-Salem (NC) Journal,* June 8, 2003, p. 1.

———. "A Waggish Ad Blitz; Southern Community Bank Plays on Its Size to Attract Customers." *Winston-Salem (NC) Journal,* April 11, 2003, p. 1.

Harwood, Melanie. "Talking to the Generations: How to Market to Different Age Groups." *America's Community Banker,* July 1, 2002, p. 28.

Milligan, Jack. "A Household Name." *Mortgage Banking,* May 1, 2004, p. 22.

Norton, Frank. "Banks Respond to Data Loss." *Raleigh (NC) News & Observer,* July 2, 2005, p. D2.

Roush, Chris, and Dail Willis. "Banks on It." *Business North Carolina,* August 1, 2005, p. 26.

Schmid, Barbara Beal. "Making Waves; Outer Banks of North Carolina the Mecca of Kiteboarding." *Grand Rapids (MI) Press,* April 1, 2005, p. E11.

Sturiale, Jeanne. "Ad Agency Woos Clients with Homey Touch." *Winston-Salem (NC) Journal,* April 12, 2003, p. 1.

———. "Ad Industry Prepares for War's Effects; Commercial- and Ad-Free Coverage Expected to Disrupt Advertising Plans." *Winston-Salem (NC) Journal,* March 18, 2003, p. 1.

Kevin Teague

Pizza Hut, Inc.

14841 Dallas Pkwy.
Dallas, Texas 75254
USA
Telephone: (972) 338-7700
Fax: (972) 338-6869
Web site: www.pizzahut.com

■■■

BIG NEW YORKER PIZZA CAMPAIGN

OVERVIEW

Pizza Hut distinguished itself from its competitors in part because of its proactive approach to product development and marketing. Beginning with the original thin-crust pizza first served in 1958, Pizza Hut made continuing efforts to refine its products and to develop new products suited to every consumer's taste. In January 1999 the Dallas-based chain introduced the Big New Yorker Pizza. The new pizza was hand-stretched to 16 inches and featured a more savory, sweeter sauce and toppings baked on top of 100 percent real cheese. The Big New Yorker was cut into eight foldable slices and was priced starting at $9.99 for one topping.

The Big New Yorker Pizza was the largest new product introduction in Pizza Hut history and was backed by an $80 million advertising and marketing campaign created by BBDO Worldwide. The campaign included television, radio and print ads as well as in-store promotional materials such as counter cards, window clings, banners, and pennants. The Big New Yorker was also featured on the newly designed Pizza Hut website. Ads for the Big New Yorker debuted on January 28, 1999, during NBC's Thursday "Must See TV" lineup, and they continued on ABC's "T.G.I.F." lineup. Celebrity ads featuring New Yorkers Spike Lee, Fran Drescher, and Donald Trump debuted on the Fox network on January 31 during the Super Bowl telecast.

HISTORICAL CONTEXT

Pizza was introduced to Americans on a wide scale in the 1940s, when returning World War II servicemen who had served in Italy began opening pizzerias serving the traditional tomato pie. Pizza Hut began in 1958 when two college students from Wichita, Frank and Dan Carney, were approached by a family friend with the idea of opening a pizza parlor. The brothers quickly saw the potential of such an enterprise, and after borrowing $600 from their mother, they purchased secondhand equipment and rented a small building at a busy intersection in their hometown. The results of their entrepreneurial efforts were the first Pizza Hut restaurant and the foundation for what would become the largest and most successful pizza chain in the world.

In 1965 Pizza Hut unveiled its first television commercial, with the musical jingle "Putt-Putt to Pizza Hut." Three years later the chain entered the international market by opening its first restaurant in Canada. In 1969 the first Pizza Hut restaurant was opened in Mexico, and construction also began on outlets in Germany and in Australia. In that same year the distinctive red roof was adopted for all of its restaurants.

By 1971 Pizza Hut had become the number one pizza chain in the world in both sales and number of

© JAMES MARSHALL/CORBIS.

restaurants, and expansion continued throughout the decade. Within two years the company had opened units in Costa Rica, Japan, and England. Product innovation proceeded apace, and in 1975 a new variety, Thick 'N Chewy, was introduced. A Super Supreme pizza was introduced in the United States in 1977. In the same year Pizza Hut stockholders overwhelmingly approved a merger with PepsiCo, Inc., for an undisclosed sum.

The Sicilian Pan Pizza was introduced in 1979, and it proved so popular that by 1983 the Personal Pan Pizza, guaranteed to be ready in five minutes, was introduced throughout the system. Two less successful menu items, Priazza and Calizza, were rolled out in 1985. Perhaps reflecting the end of consumers' fascination with pan pizza, the Hand-Tossed Traditional Pizza was introduced throughout the system in time e for Pizza Hut's 30th anniversary in 1988.

By the beginning of the 1990s Pizza Hut sales had reached $4 billion, and the chain continued to develop new products. A lunch buffet was introduced in 1,800 units in 1992, and the next year the chain rolled out its Bigfoot Pizza—two square feet of pizza cut into 21 slices—as well as the Chunky Style Pizza. By the end of the year Pizza Hut was leading the entire restaurant industry in growth and was setting new company records for sales and profits. Continued robust growth attracted celebrity endorsers to the brand, with soccer legend Pelé becoming one of the first when he kicked a ball through the door of Pizza Hut restaurant number 10,000, in Sao Paulo on April 13, 1994.

In 1995 Pizza Hut launched a new ad campaign featuring the tag line "You'll Love the Stuff We're Made Of." That same year, Buffalo Wings—spicy chicken wings served with dipping sauce—were added to the menu. And in one of the most successful product introductions in the chain's history, Pizzeria Stuffed Crust Pizza immediately set company sales records. The following January, Pizza Hut aired its first-ever ad during the Super Bowl. In May 1996 the chain introduced two varieties of chicken-topped pizza, Italian Chicken and Chicken Supreme.

In 1997 Pizza Hut unveiled "Totally New Pizzas," a quality initiative that put fresh sliced vegetables and meatier meats on its pizzas. Later that year The Edge, a specialty pizza without a crust, was crafted to appeal to what were called "extreme" tastes among consumers. There were more product introductions in 1998 to mark Pizza Hut's 40th anniversary year. The Sicilian Pizza, which had garlic, basil, and oregano baked into the crust, was a precursor of the back-to-basics approach later embodied by the Big New Yorker. The new pizza was accompanied by an ad campaign that used the tag line "The Best Pizzas under One Roof." As of 1999, Pizza Hut offered its customers five major products: Pan, Thin 'N Crispy, Hand-Tossed, Stuffed Crust, and Big New Yorker.

TARGET MARKET

"We are targeting this toward the heavy pizza user," explained Mike Rawlings, chief concept officer of Pizza Hut, of the Big New Yorker Pizza. "That may be a large

YO SOY BIG NEW YORKER!

In February 1999, shortly after the national rollout of the Big New Yorker Pizza, Pizza Hut announced plans to expand the campaign into Latin America as well as to target the large and growing Latino community in the United States. To help in this effort, the Dallas-based pizza giant joined forces with the recently crowned Miss Venezuela, Carolina Indriago. The curvaceous Indriago was tapped to star in Spanish-language television spots to be aired throughout the United States and Latin America. The spots, which costarred actor David Norono, were designed to give millions of Spanish-speaking Americans their first opportunity to see and hear the beauty pageant winner and to learn about Pizza Hut's New York-style pizza.

"This is a tremendous honor to be a part of Pizza Hut's largest ever new product introduction effort," said Indriago. "I enjoyed the opportunity to be a part of the campaign, [and] as a Latina I am pleased to see such a large company address the Hispanic community as a consumer and a viable resource."

family that is looking for a great value, or it may be teen-agers or young adults who need money to spend on other things."

In fact, the term "heavy pizza user" could be applied to many Americans. According to a survey conducted by the National Association of Pizza Operators, Americans ate 100 acres of the food every day. The appetite for pizza made it a $30 billion industry. As of 1999, about 17 percent of all restaurants were pizzerias, and the industry was continuing to grow. Pizza was especially popular with young consumers, and a Gallup poll conducted in 1996 discovered that among children aged 8 to 11 pizza was the most popular thing to eat.

COMPETITION

Pizza Hut, a division of the multinational PepsiCo, Inc., was the dominant player among pizza chains. As of 1999, Pizza Hut, with 7,132 stores, controlled 22 percent of the market, while its main competitor, Papa John's, had only one-fourth as many stores and controlled less than 5 percent of the market. Nonetheless, competition between the two chains remained fierce, largely because, between 1993 and 1999, for every point Pizza Hut lost in market share Papa John's gained a point. The battle was especially pitched since, during the same period, pizza sales rose just 3.6 percent a year. Analysts did not forecast that sales would grow much faster in the future, and thus Pizza Hut and Papa John's had no choice but to try to win over each other's customers.

During the 1990's Pizza Hut tried numerous strategies to slow Papa John's growth. It revamped its pizzas by using better ingredients. It increased its advertising budget to an estimated $150 million. And it rolled out a veritable arsenal of designer pizzas: the Triple Deckeroni Pizza, with 90 pieces of pepperoni and a six-cheese blend; the Bigfoot, with two square feet of pizza; the chicken-topped line, which promised to deliver "the uniqueness and unexpectedly great taste of chicken-topped pizza to Americans everywhere;" and the Fiesta Taco Pizza, with a bean sauce and chopped lettuce toppings. Papa John's, by contrast, maintained just two items in its arsenal: a thin-crust pizza and a regular-crust pizza. Its ad slogan was commensurately simple: "Better ingredients. Better pizza."

Complicating the marketplace battle was the presence of a third major pizza delivery chain, Domino's, which, in the words of Pizza Hut's Rawlings, "has more tenure and saliency in the consumer's minds than any of the rest of our competition." Nevertheless, since 1993, while Papa John's was steadily growing, Domino's could not manage to grab even one additional point of market share. In 1998, however, Domino's did make a dent in consumer consciousness with the introduction of heat-retaining delivery bags known as HeatWave pouches, which allowed pizzas to be delivered with the cheese still hot and the crust still crisp. Sparked by the success of the pouches, Domino's in 1999 revamped the recipe for its hand-tossed pizza. For the first time in nearly a decade, taste rather than delivery was made the central theme of the chain's advertising.

Prompted in part by this initiative and by the inroads made by Papa John's, Pizza Hut responded with the introduction of the Big New Yorker in 1999. The competitors reacted with predictable aplomb to the rollout. "We view this as another phase of Pizza Hut's constant new-product strategy—pizza of the month if you will," observed Papa John's vice president of communications Chris Sternberg. "Their strategy is to do new product rollouts that are supported by heavy marketing spending with the goal of creating trial. Certainly, when you spend $70 [million] to $80 million on a new product rollout, you will get the phone to ring. But while they will probably have some trial in the short term, we don't expect it to have a long-term impact on our sales."

MARKETING STRATEGY

The marketing campaign introducing the Big New Yorker Pizza was designed to build on Pizza Hut's competitive strategy of providing "variety, value and quality for consumers." The product itself was crafted to attract consumers seeking a traditional-style pizza similar to those found in local mom-and-pop pizzerias. Market research conducted by the chain indicated a desire on the part of consumers for a bigger, more savory pizza. "America associates great pizza with New York-style pizza, in fact, they crave it," said Pizza Hut's Rawlings. "However, until [the] introduction of The Big New Yorker Pizza, only one-third of the population actually ever tried a true New York-style pizza. The Big New Yorker Pizza gives consumers a slice of New York right in their own home."

In order to illustrate the fact that its new product was an authentic New York-style pizza, Pizza Hut enlisted three archetypal New York celebrities to appear in its television commercials. Filmmaker Lee, actress Drescher, and real estate developer Trump were defined in company press releases as "big New Yorkers." Each of the 30-second commercials highlighted one of the celebrities in an environment that fit the person's personality. The commercials were the celebrities' tongue-in-cheek presentation of their personalities and of the grand personality of New York. The spots debuted during the pregame segment of the most-watched television event of the year, the Super Bowl, a placement designed to influence the halftime meal decisions of the sports fans assembled.

The first commercial, directed by Lee and produced by his company, 40 Acres and a Mule, starred the filmmaker and other New York residents, including an artist, street performers, basketball players, and a police officer, in real-life roles. The Drescher spot put the whining comedienne in a variety of New York locations, including Fifth Avenue and the skating rink in Central Park and atop a skyscraper. The Trump ad highlighted his role as a business tycoon by showing footage of the developer in Times Square, riding in a limousine, and meeting with an architect on a new building project.

The rollout of the Big New Yorker Pizza was supported by a national marketing campaign designed to promote the city of New York. Mayor Rudolph Giuliani attended the press conference launching the new pizza. "We needed to introduce this New York-style pizza in a big way," quipped Pizza Hut's Rawlings. "What is bigger and better than having the mayor of New York City help us launch the pizza?" Rawlings added that, while New York made no financial contributions to the campaign, the city allowed the chain to put its apple logo on the pizza boxes. The new boxes also included New York's official website address, and Pizza Hut agreed to link its website, which received at least 30,000 visits per month, to the New York City site. The cross-promotional campaign helped to generate 100 million website impressions for New York tourism per month.

OUTCOME

Critical response to the Big New Yorker Pizza television ad campaign was largely favorable. When the *Los Angeles Times* asked three advertising employees to critique commercials shown during the Super Bowl telecast, the Big New Yorker spots were singled out for high praise. "Not only are these spots funny and beautifully produced," the panelists concluded, "they wisely take advantage of what only a Super Bowl telecast can do—make 200 million customers instantly aware of your product."

Despite generating high interest in a new product, the Big New Yorker campaign seemed to be doing little to help Pizza Hut in its battle against Papa John's. Comparable store sales for the challenger continued in the high single-digit range in the first quarter of 1999 despite bad weather and the fact that Pizza Hut was spending $80 million on its Big New Yorker.

FURTHER READING

Donnelly, Frank. "Pizza Ads Another Success for Chambers Hill Native." *Harrisburg Patriot,* February 1, 1999.

Roth, Daniel. "This Ain't No Pizza Party." *Fortune,* November 9, 1998, p. 158.

Zuber, Amy. "Pizza Hut Serves a Saucy Slice: The Big New Yorker." *Nation's Restaurant News,* February 8, 1999.

Robert Schnakenberg

Polaris Industries, Inc.

2100 Highway 55
Medina, Minnesota 55340
USA
Telephone: (763) 542-0500
Fax: (763) 542-0599
Web site: www.polarisindustries.com

THE NEW AMERICAN MOTORCYCLE CAMPAIGN

OVERVIEW

In 1998 Polaris Industries, Inc., best known as a manufacturer of snowmobiles, introduced the Victory Motorcycle, the first new American motorcycle to be introduced in 60 years. Although it was part of the cruiser category dominated by Harley-Davidson, Victory was not intended to challenge the icon of the industry. Rather, Polaris looked to find its own niche in a large and growing category, hoping to play off its American roots to take sales away from Japanese companies Honda, Yamaha, Kawasaki, and Suzuki. To help establish Victory in the marketplace, Minneapolis-based advertising agency Martin/Williams launched a major marketing campaign in the summer of 2000.

The campaign, estimated at $2–4 million, centered on print ads that appeared mostly in the leading motorcycle magazines. To a lesser degree Polaris spent money on television spots that ran on national cable channels and in some local markets on a spot basis. Some local radio advertising was also done. The main objective was to convince potential customers to visit their local Victory dealer, where they could pick up promotion materials but more importantly could take a Victory motorcycle for a test-ride. The motorcycle itself was expected to close the sale.

"The New American Motorcycle" campaign ran until Martin/Williams gave up the account in the spring of 2004. By that time Victory had enjoyed a steady increase in sales, had established a niche in the marketplace, and was well positioned to enjoy strong growth in an expanding category.

HISTORICAL CONTEXT

The manufacturer of Victory Motorcycles, Polaris Industries, Inc., was best known for its snowmobiles, a vehicle the Minnesota-based company had pioneered in the 1950s and popularized in the 1960s. Over the years Polaris suffered through some tough times and looked to diversify, moving into producing all-terrain vehicles in the 1980s and personal watercraft, such as jet skis, in the 1990s. Later in the decade Polaris sensed an opportunity in heavy-cruiser motorcycles (the largest bikes on the market), a category that competitor Harley-Davidson ruled.

Harley-Davidson had reached cult status that extended beyond motorcycles. The owners of its "hogs" would tattoo the name on their bodies, and people who had never ridden a motorcycle in their lives would wear a Harley-Davidson leather jacket as a fashion statement. A number of companies like Polaris in the mid- to late 1990s sensed there was room in the heavy-cruiser class for a new American bike. The famous Indian brand, last

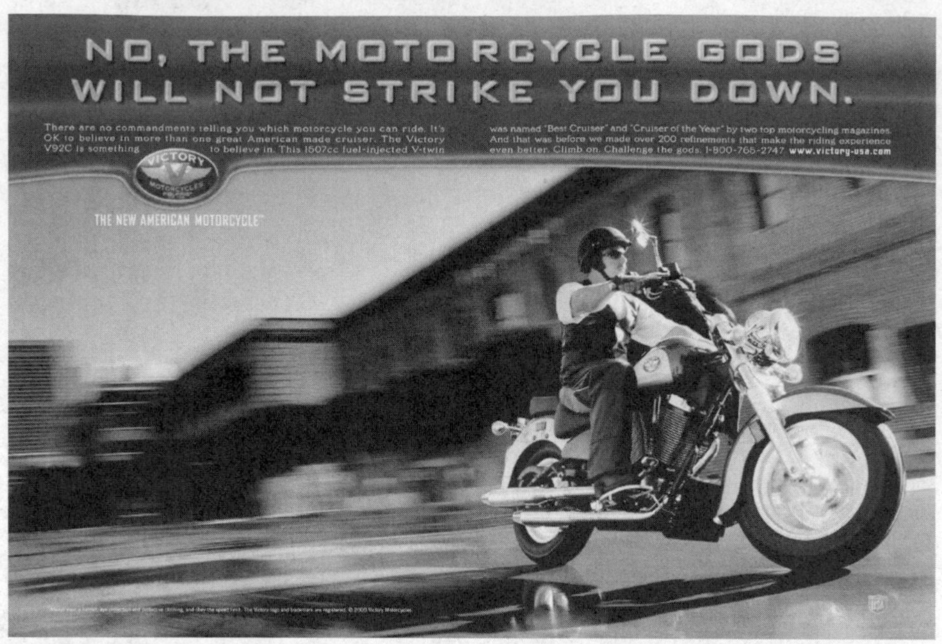

Polaris Industries's Victory motorcycle. PHOTO BY HUNTER FREEMAN. COURTESY OF MARTIN WILLIAMS, INC. REPRODUCED BY PERMISSION.

seen in 1953, returned with the newly formed Indian Motorcycle Company, as did Excelsior-Henderson Motorcycle Manufacturing Company of Minnesota. They were joined by startups such as Big Dog Motorcycles of Sun Valley and a number of smaller shops. Many of them made the fatal error of trying to challenge Harley-Davidson head-on. Polaris, on the other hand, sought to offer something different than Harley: more contemporary styling along with advanced technology, such as electronic fuel injection, overhead camshafts, and premium brakes. The result was the Victory motorcycle, which first rolled off the line in July 1998, becoming the first new American cruiser-class motorcycle to be introduced in 60 years. It was positioned as more of a compatriot of Harley-Davidson than a threat.

Two years after its introduction Victory had enjoyed only modest success, ranking a distant sixth in sales, behind Harley-Davidson and the Japanese imports. In December 1999 Polaris awarded the reported $2 to $4 million Victory Motorcycles advertising account to Martin/Williams, a Minneapolis agency that was already handling the company's snowmobiles and personal watercraft. In July 2000 Victory Motorcycles launched a new marketing campaign under the banner of "The New American Motorcycle."

TARGET MARKET

In general the campaign targeted men between the ages of 35 and 54 with annual incomes of at least $65,000. More specifically, the marketers hoped to appeal to former motorcycle owners who had given up their bikes for family life or other reasons and now had the time, money, and inclination to resume their interest in motorcycles. Some of them, hopefully, would opt for a forward-looking American-made cruiser instead of the Harley or Japanese models. Polaris also wanted to appeal to consumers who already owned a Harley, had a passion for riding, and would buy a Victory as a second bike. Harley referred to many of these consumers as "Rolex" riders, a clientele wealthy enough to indulge their interest in motorcycles by buying more than one brand. To a lesser degree Polaris also wanted to appeal to younger, first-time buyers who might prefer the Victory style and technology over what Harley had to offer. Built lower to the ground than a Harley, the Victory also became an option for women interested in buying an American cruiser-class motorcycle.

COMPETITION

Founded in the early 1900s, Harley-Davidson was a survivor, outlasting scores of other motorcycle companies to emerge in the 1950s as the "king of the road." The bike also gained an outlaw image, due in no small measure to the Marlon Brando movie *The Wild One,* in which Harley-riding renegades terrorized a community. While the company was not entirely pleased with the motorcycle-gang connection, it benefited from the subculture

DUE NORTH

The parent company of Victory Motorcycles, Polaris Industries, Inc., was founded in 1945 in Roseau, Minnesota, closer to Manitoba, Canada, than to Minneapolis. It started out producing custom-made farm machinery under the name Hetteen Hoist & Derrick, and it was not until the 1950s that it sold its first snow-going vehicle. The company began making the transition from fabricating farm equipment to snowmobiles, in the process changing its name. Drawing on the Latin name for "north star," it became Polaris Industries in 1954. At the time, several years before Alaska became a state, Polaris was one of the northernmost companies in the United States.

that developed around the brand. The introduction of the larger, throaty superbikes in the form of the Sportster model in 1957 only added to the Harley mystique. Although the company had long ago vanquished its American competition, during the 1960s it received a fresh challenge from Japanese companies such as Honda, Suzuki, Yamaha, and Kawasaki, which offered bikes in all categories, including heavyweight. Harley suffered through the recession of the early 1980s but made a strong comeback later in the decade, and by 1990 it held a 62.3 percent share of the U.S. heavyweight-motorcycle market.

Although the Victory Motorcycle campaign poked good-natured fun at Harley-Davidson in some of its advertising, Polaris did not want to directly compete against the icon of the class. Moreover, Harley-Davidson continued to bring out a good product and could match anyone in spending on development and marketing. Instead Polaris wanted to play up the Victory's combination of nostalgia and technology in order to compete with Harley while emphasizing its American roots in order to take on the Japanese bike makers Honda, Kawasaki, Suzuki, and Yamaha. All of them were well-established brands with the financial resources necessary to maintain market share. In addition, Victory had to contend with a number of domestic upstarts also trying to establish themselves as the American alternative to Harley-Davidson: the likes of the legendary Indian brand, Excelsior-Henderson, and Big Dog Motorcycles. There were also scores of local shops offering custom-built cruisers that competed for the disposable income of motorcycle aficionados.

MARKETING STRATEGY

The marketing team attended bike rallies, such as the major events held at Sturgis, South Dakota, and Daytona Beach, Florida, and talked with people in the target demographic. They learned that indeed there was an opening for an American-made alternative in the cruiser-motorcycle category. Consumers said that they would be interested in a bike that was modern yet had classic lines. The original Victory, however, lacked curb appeal, that aesthetic quality that provoked an emotional purchase.

Out of the conversations with the target market, Victory and Martin/Williams settled on "The New American Motorcycle" positioning. To make the case for Victory Motorcycles, the agency focused on the print medium. The core market was comprised of extreme motorcycle enthusiasts who wanted to know what was new. Hence, in July 2000 Victory Motorcycle ads began to appear in leading motorcycle magazines, including *American Motorcycle, Cycle World, American Iron,* and *American Rider.* In addition the company advertised in other publications that reached the right audience, such as *Popular Mechanics* and *North American Hunter.*

Despite the intention not to compete directly with Harley-Davidson, one of the first ads made an amusing allusion to Harley-Davidson, the copy reading, "No, the motorcycles gods will not strike you down." In many ways "The New American Motorcycle" campaign helped the marketers to refine their approach, the allusions to Harley giving way to a pure focus on Victory.

The later ads gave the audience what it wanted to see: the bike itself. To emphasize the positioning of the brand, its American essence, the bike was photographed in iconic American settings such as the West. But to connect it to its hardworking audience, the motorcycle was also displayed in industrial scenes. In other ads the bike was set in urban nightlife scenes to suggest that the Victory was a motorcycle for the city as well as the open road. The text was spare, with the print ads mostly relying on the tag "The new American motorcycle." Victory later redesigned its catalog to include new images of the bikes, a lesson it learned from this initial campaign.

Because the campaign's budget Polaris only did a limited amount of television advertising for the Victory, but it was an important medium because it provided potential customers with the sound of the bike—and the roar of a heavyweight bike was a major part of its appeal—while showing the lines of the Victory in motion. The company produced one or two 30-second TV spots a year over the next four years. They were shown on select national cable channels, such as the Speed Channel, ESPN, and TNN. The company also did some limited local radio advertising.

The goal of all the advertisements was to persuade potential customers to visit their area Victory dealership. There the company provided brochures and posters, and most importantly people were able to test-ride a Victory Motorcycle. The company believed that if it succeeded in getting someone in the saddle of a Victory, it had a good chance of selling one.

Gradually customers began to accept the Victory brand. In 2002 the company launched a new set of print ads that played with the tagline "That is my Victory" and featured testimonial letters from customers expressing what the Victory motorcycle meant to them. Although the advertising played a key role in growing the brand, perhaps of more importance were changes that company made on other fronts. In 2002 Victory introduced the Freedom engine to greatly improve performance. Another significant development was the introduction of the Vegas model, the styling of which finally gave Victory a distinctive look, one that met with approval from motorcycle enthusiasts. Four of the major motorcycle magazines named the Vegas the "best cruiser of the year" in 2003. Victory also enjoyed success with a limited-time Custom Order Program that allowed customers to design their dream bike online. As a result Victory Web traffic increased sevenfold in 2003.

OUTCOME

During the time it ran its "The New American Motorcycle" campaign, Victory experienced a steady gain in sales. Although Victory had a small market share (about 2 percent) in the cruiser category, the company was confident that it had successfully established itself in the marketplace. Much of that success, granted, was based on anecdotal evidence, such as the sight of a Victory motorcycle riding side-by-side with a Harley through the streets of Sturgis and reports of bikers with Victory tattoos. "Victory is very, very strong," Mark Blackwell, general manager of Polaris's Victory division, told *Powersports Business* in 2004. "We've reached critical mass. Three years ago, people were asking, 'Who is Victory? Are you the guys from Minnesota who are bankrupt?' Last year, people were asking about the Vegas and now people are pretty well informed; they know we're part of Polaris." According to Motorcycle Industry Council data reported in September 2005, Victory Motorcycle was the fastest-growing brand in the industry, with retail sales increasing at a rate of about 50 percent. Although difficult to quantify, the spadework done by Martin/Williams's "The New American Motorcycle" campaign played a significant role in that growth.

FURTHER READING

Blackwell, Mark. "Victory Motorcycle Comes of Age." *Powersports Business,* June 28, 2004, p. S46.

Carney, Daniel F. "Chrome, Sweet Chrome." *Popular Science,* July 2000.

Chura, Hilary. "Victory Kicks Off Effort to Catch Up with Harley." *Advertising Age,* July 24, 2000, p. 8.

Frank, Aaron P. "Victory Vegas: The New American Motorcycle Company Rolls the Dice on a Radical New Cruiser." *Motorcyclist,* October 2002, p. 54.

Geiger, Bob. "Minneapolis-Based Martin/Williams Drops $15 Million Polaris Account." *Minneapolis (MN) Finance and Commerce,* March 6, 2004.

Greenberg, Karl. "Victory Motorcycles Powers into Hollywood." *Brandweek,* April 25, 2005.

Hallinan, Joseph T. "Polaris Expects to Ride Out Speed Bumps in Economy." *Wall Street Journal,* December 29, 2000.

Kiley, David. "E-Z Rider." *Brandweek,* August 18, 1997.

Klebnikov, Paul. "Clear the Roads, Here Comes the Victory." *Forbes,* October 20, 1997.

Miller, James P. "Polaris Set to Challenge Harley in Motorcycle Market." *Wall Street Journal,* March 11, 1998.

Panczyk, Tania D. "Victory Takes Testimonial Tack." *Adweek,* February 25, 2002, p. 4.

Roderick, Thomas. "Ace in the Hole: This Vegas Is a Sure Bet." *Dealernews* 39, no. 8 (August 2003).

Ed Dinger

RIDE THE BEST CAMPAIGN

OVERVIEW

Minneapolis, Minnesota-based Polaris Industries Inc. continued "Ride the Best," a long-standing campaign, to promote its personal watercraft (PWC) in 1998. The campaign, handled by Carmichael Lynch of Minneapolis, had been in effect for much of the time since Polaris introduced its PWC in 1993 and was used primarily in magazine advertising. During 1998 Polaris spent an estimated $7 million on advertising, $5 million on snowmobiles and watercraft, both handled by Carmichael Lynch until October 1998. At that point the company was the world's leading snowmobile maker and one of the leading producers of personal watercraft.

The big story regarding Polaris's watercraft advertising during 1998 was not so much the advertising itself as it was the swirl of events surrounding that advertising. After a 15-year relationship with Carmichael Lynch, Polaris undertook an agency review in September 1998, and after considering a number of agencies and raising much speculation regarding what its ultimate choice would be, the company selected Martin/Williams of Minneapolis. Accompanying the change of agencies

A print ad from Polaris's "Ride the Best" campaign. POLARIS INDUSTRIES, INC. REPRODUCED BY PERMISSION.

would be a change of focus, with a greater emphasis on television advertising as opposed to magazines.

As to what prompted the switch, Polaris did not make any explicit statements, and the suddenness of the review seemed to catch Carmichael Lynch off guard. In any case, by early 1999 Polaris and Martin/Williams were ready for a new push and some fine tuning of strategy—though the "Ride the Best" campaign would stay. Polaris also made all-terrain vehicles (ATVs) and the Victory motorcycle; advertising for both was handled by Associates and Stahl of Minneapolis and was not affected by the review.

Coupled with the changes in Polaris's advertising lineup was a continued choppiness in the world of maritime recreational equipment. On the one hand, a strong economy and the lower prices of personal watercraft compared with boats gave Polaris an advantage over boat manufacturers; on the other hand, PWC sales had not been explosive either. But things were looking up for Polaris as 1998 went on, and by the end of the year profits were looking up as well.

HISTORICAL CONTEXT

Around the end of World War II, Edgar Hetteen and David Johnson earned a living doing welding and repair work for neighbors and by making custom machinery for farmers in rural Minnesota. Hetteen and Johnson formed Hetteen Hoist & Derrick in Rousea, Minnesota, in 1945, and a few years later Johnson developed a gas-powered sled. The latter evolved into the snowmobile, which Hetteen Hoist & Derrick began producing under the Polaris brand name in 1954.

By the late 1950s the company—now named Polaris Industries Inc.—was selling some 300 snowmobiles a year. Eventually Hetteen left after a dispute with some of the company's investors and went on to form Arctic Enterprises (later Arctic Cat Inc.), maker of the Arctic Cat snowmobile. The latter would prove to be one of Polaris snowmobiles' most significant competitors in years to come. Meanwhile, Hetteen's brother Allan became Polaris's president, and in 1968 the company was acquired by Textron, which also owned Bell helicopters, Schaefer pens, and Talon zippers. Also in 1968 Polaris began what would turn out to be a long relationship with Fuji Heavy Industries of Japan, with an agreement whereby Fuji became the exclusive manufacturer of the engines used in Polaris snowmobiles.

Initially, Polaris had sold its snowmobiles purely as utility vehicles, which meant that its customer base was confined to persons in extremely cold northern states who could justify the expense for their work. If the company wanted to expand its customer base, it would have to begin marketing snowmobiles as recreational vehicles, which it did in the 1960s. By 1971, however, recreational snowmobile purchases had risen as high as they ever would, with Polaris selling almost 500,000 units in that year. A decade later Textron was ready to close the doors at Polaris, but company president Hal Wendel led a buyout by management.

One of Wendel's greatest contributions to the company was in the area of diversification. For a number of reasons—not least of which was the fact that people in most places could only use snowmobiles for part of the year—Wendel recognized the need to develop a supplementary product line. This appeared in 1985 in the form of the ATV, and again Polaris approached the product as a utility rather than a recreational vehicle. Soon it had become the world's No. 2 ATV maker, after Honda, and in 1991 it emerged as the leading snowmobile company.

With the introduction of personal watercraft in 1993, Polaris extended its offerings even further, and in 1994 it made an initial public offering of its stock. Three years later Polaris announced an extraordinary initiative: it would become the first American company in half a century to enter the motorcycle market. By that point all American motorcycle manufacturers with the exception of Harley-Davidson had shut down, forced out of business by cheaper and more efficient Japanese models. Nineteen ninety-eight saw the rollout of the first Victory motorcycles.

TARGET MARKET

"In less than a decade," wrote Susan Feyder in the *Minneapolis-St. Paul Star-Tribune,* "personal watercraft have established a beachhead on the water sports scene." According to research conducted by the National Marine Manufacturers Association, unit sales of personal watercraft more than tripled between 1991 and 1996. By 1996, when 191,000 units were sold in the United States, PWCs made up 37 percent of all powered watercraft sold in the nation—as opposed to just 20 percent five years before.

Personal watercraft typically drew a younger buyer than did boats. This was true for several reasons, one of which was price. As Feyder noted, personal watercraft ranged from $4,000 to $8,000, whereas a boat buyer most likely would have to spend more than $10,000 to acquire a good powerboat. "With personal watercraft, you're appealing to a different kind of buyer," an industry analyst told her. "This is either someone who wouldn't buy a boat, or an existing boat owner who buys [a personal watercraft] to have one more toy."

Feyder noted the contrast between the image of the boating industry as opposed to that of personal watercraft as reflected in advertising: An ad for Genmar Wellcraft powerboats featured in the Saks Fifth Avenue Christmas catalog showed a well-heeled couple enjoying the pleasures of boating with a headline announcing "The Gift of Style." "Compare that to the way personal watercraft makers promote their products with ads picturing daredevils recklessly churning up spray and jumping waves," Feyder said. "There's the ad for the Arctic Cat Tigershark that reads, 'There's powerful. And then there's staple-the-sunglasses-to-your-head powerful.' " She went on to cite a Carmichael Lynch print ad for Polaris "featuring a rotund buyer sitting on his Polaris SL650offering this testimonial: 'Take my word for it, this thing hauls some serious butt.' "

RIDING HIGH ON LAKE TAHOE

Primarily because of the reportedly higher rate of danger associated with personal watercraft, a number of lawmakers in the United States during the 1990s sought to restrict if not ban the use of personal watercraft on public waterways. This effort reached all the way to Capitol Hill, where the House of Representatives reviewed a number of ultimately unsuccessful initiatives intended to put brakes on what some perceived as careless use of personal watercraft. Then in May 1999 the Tahoe Regional Planning Agency (TRPA) at Lake Tahoe, Nevada, achieved what Washington seemingly could not: as a means of protecting the lake's environment, if not for the purposes of safety, it established regulations prohibiting virtually all personal watercraft from the Lake Tahoe area.

So why would Polaris Watercraft want to announce this fact, in triumphant tones, in a May 28, 1999, news release? The TRPA prohibited virtually all models of watercraft—"except one," as Polaris proudly noted: "The new direct fuel injection system of the Polaris Genesis FFI is the only technology available that has unrestricted permanent usage rights on Lake Tahoe." According to Jim Baegte, TRPA executive director: "Lake Tahoe is a unique natural resource and national treasure. Because it is also a popular recreational destination, we must constantly search for balance so people can continue to enjoy activities such as boating without causing further harm to the sensitive environment. We are pleased that manufacturers like Polaris have responded in such a timely fashion to the call for finding that balance by developing cleaner watercraft engine technology."

COMPETITION

Irwin Jacobs would not have found this the least bit funny. Jacobs was the owner of Genmar Holdings, makers of the Wellcraft and other boats, from the $850 Crestliner fishing boat to the $9.2 million Hatteras yacht. Typical Genmar offerings carried a five-figure price tag. "In Jacobs's mind," Feyder wrote, "the interests of the boating and personal watercraft industries are so at odds that he doesn't consider personal watercraft to be boats at all."

Quite aside from boat manufacturers such as Jacobs, Polaris had to compete with the other leaders in the personal watercraft market. Leading the pack was Bombardier Inc., a Canadian company that produced the ultra-popular Sea-Doo and enjoyed a 49 percent market share. At a distant second came Yamaha with 18 percent, followed closely by another Japanese company, Kawasaki, which held 14 percent of the market. Fourth in line, and top among American manufacturers, was Polaris, holding a 13 percent share. Far below it was its only American competitor, Arctic Cat Inc., with just 5 percent of the market. All remaining personal watercraft manufacturers made up the last 1 percent of sales.

All was not rosy in the personal watercraft category. Brunswick, a Chicago company with a $2 billion marine division that produced powerboats and engines, had flirted with the personal watercraft market in 1996 before deciding to make a retreat. "In our view, it is not a growth market," a company spokesperson told Feyder. More significant was the fact that industry leader Bombardier had been forced to make cutbacks. But Polaris and Arctic planned to maintain their production force at about the same levels as they had been the previous year.

Discussing the move by Brunswick into yachts and away from personal watercraft, investment analyst Jill Krutick of Smith Barney told Feyder: "Given the crowded field in personal watercraft and slower growth there, it's turned out to be a savvy move. You've got a potentially big market from baby boomers with wealth they've accumulated in the strong stock market." This did not stop Jacobs from sounding a sour note with regard to personal watercraft: "Through glitz and marketing they've created a glorified environment over something that is a nuisance and dangerous," he said. And Phil Keeter of the Marine Retailers Association of America, Feyder noted, was not convinced by watercraft manufacturers' claims that they were not hurting boat sales. He had seen a jump in the number of personal watercraft at the lake where he did his boating, and said, "I think they're keeping people from trading up to another boat."

MARKETING STRATEGY

In July 1999, when new agency Martin/Williams unveiled its first campaign for Polaris, Aaron Baar in *Adweek* described the work of Carmichael Lynch, which had lost out in the fall 1998 agency review: "Carmichael's last work for Polaris showcased its watercraft with humorous artwork and copy that stressed the benefits of the vehicle's engine." Typical of this advertising was the ad showing the overweight man and the "serious butt" caption. On the other hand, Baar wrote that Martin/Williams's campaign "addresses the bond between man and machine." In contrast to Carmichael Lynch's humorous approach, that of Martin/Williams was much more tongue-in-cheek. One constant remained, however: the tag line "Ride the Best."

In September 1998 Polaris inaugurated the agency review that led to the switch. Naomi Teske, the company's marketing communications manager, told *Adweek* that Polaris was undertaking the review in order to "make sure we're with the right agency." Along with the review came a change in leadership at Polaris, with Wendel stepping down to be replaced by Thomas Tiller as CEO.

According to Baar in *Adweek,* Polaris had sent out feelers to about a dozen agencies before cutting the number in half by late September. As for incumbent Carmichael Lynch, agency spokesman Stephen Dupont told Tim J. Johnson of *Minneapolis-St. Paul City Business* in early October that the agency had not been invited to take part in the review. "Until we got the word a couple days ago, we didn't know ourselves," he said regarding Polaris's final choice. As for why the company had decided to switch agencies, he said: "We're really disappointed in the decision, but we know that a lot of companies, especially ones that have worked with an agency for a long time, simply want a change. We understand that."

OUTCOME

Perhaps another possible cause for Polaris's decision to conduct an agency review may be found in an April 6, 1998, story by Baar in *Adweek.* According to Baar, Carmichael Lynch was "working on undisclosed projects for Outboard Marine Corp.," a Waukegan, Illinois, company that produced boats, engines, and boating accessories. Two weeks later a Polaris news release indicated that the company had reduced its personal watercraft production as a response to a decrease in demand across the industry. In such an environment, it may have considered Carmichael Lynch's work for Outboard Marine an indication of divided loyalties.

Whatever the case, Polaris announced the choice of Martin/Williams in October 1998, and later that month Baar reported that the new agency's "first task will be to develop a campaign and collateral materials for the company's 2000 model year snowmobiles." Mike Gray of Martin/Williams told Baar, "Over the longer term, [Polaris] wants to look at what [its] brand means across all categories."

By June 1999 *Delaney Report* announced that "Agencies should keep an eye on Minneapolis-based Polaris Industries, which is gearing up for a big marketing offensive." The following month Polaris and Martin/Williams launched a campaign for snowmobiles and personal watercraft. Headlines of print ads read: "It's only engineering until you get on. Then it's all chemistry." The company also prepared, for the first time in several years, to run television spots.

FURTHER READING

"Agency Rumblings. . . ." *Delaney Report,* June 7, 1999, p. 4.

Alper, Mila. "Playing Around." *Forbes,* August 9, 1999, p. 148.

Baar, Aaron. "Carmichael Lynch Back in Drink with Outboard Marine Projects." *Adweek* (Midwest edition), April 6, 1998, p. 5.

———. "Polaris Narrows List." *Adweek* (Midwest edition), September 28, 1998, p. 3.

———. "Polaris Selects M/W to Handle Its Account." *Adweek* (Midwest edition), October 19, 1998, p. 7.

———. "Man, Machine Meld for Polaris." *Adweek* (Midwest edition), July 12, 1999, p. 8.

Feyder, Susan. "Making Waves." *Minneapolis-St. Paul Star-Tribune,* January 5, 1998, p. 1-D.

Johnson, Tim J. "Firms Pitch for Polaris Snowmobiles." *Minneapolis-St. Paul City Business,* October 9, 1998, p. 4.

"Most Personal Watercraft Restricted from Lake Tahoe Beginning June 1; Polaris Genesis FFI Is the First Personal Watercraft Permanently Allowed on Lake." *Business Wire,* May 28, 1999.

Peterson, Susan E. "Revving Up Polaris: With Ambitious Plans in Store, New CEO Tom Tiller Intends to Set a Fast Face for the Company." *Minneapolis-St. Paul Star-Tribune,* May 18, 1999, p. 1-D.

"Polaris Reports First Quarter Results: Company Says Outlook for Full Year Sales and Earnings Growth Is Unchanged." *Business Wire,* April 21, 1998.

"Polaris Reports Record Sales and EPS for Second Quarter." *Business Wire,* July 21, 1999.

Judson Knight

Polaroid Corporation

1265 Main Street
Waltham, Massachusetts 02451
USA
Telephone: (781) 386-2000
Fax: (781) 386-8588
Web site: www.polaroid.com

I-ZONE/JOYCAM/ STICKY FILM TEEN CAMPAIGN

OVERVIEW

Polaroid Corporation, manufacturer of one of the premiere brands of cameras for more than 50 years, faced a crisis in the 1990s as the rise of new technologies, in particular digital cameras, negated the company's edge in the instant delivery of prints. After putting its account in review in 2000, Polaroid selected a new advertising agency, Leo Burnett Worldwide, to help rekindle the brand's sagging fortunes. The focus over the next three years was on taking advantage of the successful launch of the small I-Zone and JoyCam cameras and the small adhesive-backed "sticky film" they used. The company's target was teens, in particular 15- to 17-year-old girls.

Because the marketers were playing to an audience that normally rejected typical hard-sell appeals, they attempted to be innovative and engaging while subtly urging teens in both television spots and print ads to buy the cameras and apply the "sticky pics" to whatever surface struck their fancy. For example, one television spot featured a young woman jumping up and down on her bed, slapping Polaroid pictures on the ceiling. A print effort included an insert of pictures that could be applied as a form of commentary to an accompanying fake advertisement, and teens were encouraged to "hijack" real ads with their own sticky pics.

Over the course of three years Leo Burnett succeeded in many ways. Much of the work received industry awards, and Polaroid enjoyed sales spikes. The added revenue did not, however, stave off bankruptcy for the company, which never approached spending the $150 million the account was worth when Leo Burnett took over. Instead it was estimated that Polaroid, short on cash, spent only about $70 million a year. When the account was again put up for review in 2003, Leo Burnett opted not to participate, leaving the task of rebuilding one of the great brands in American history to others.

HISTORICAL CONTEXT

Polaroid Corporation grew out of the polarization research conducted by Edwin Land beginning in the 1920s. After developing a polarizing material he struggled to find a commercial application, initially finding success with the sale of sunglasses. On Christmas Day 1943, in a flash of inspiration, Land conceived of a camera and self-developing film utilizing his polarizing material. With Polaroid on the verge of financial ruin by 1946, Land placed all his hopes on the development of his instant camera. It was introduced into the market a year later with a great deal of fanfare and was an immediate hit.

During the 1950s the company grew rapidly and became a marketing success story. In the camera industry

Polaroid played Pepsi to Kodak's Coca-Cola. Much of Polaroid's success was due to its creative approach to advertising. It was quick to take advantage of the rising popularity of television, enlisting early stars of the medium, like *Tonight Show* hosts Steve Allen and Jack Paar, to demonstrate Polaroid cameras in live television commercials. According to Stuart Elliott, writing for the *New York Times,* in the 1970s Polaroid introduced "a series of popular spots featuring James Garner and Mariette Hartley, whose relaxed, playful banter led millions of viewers to think they were married. As recently as the late 1990s, a comic Polaroid campaign carrying the theme 'See what develops' won numerous awards."

The proliferation of one-hour photography developing shops and the increasing popularity of digital photography dramatically changed the landscape for Polaroid during the 1990s. To counteract declining revenues in its core instant film business, Polaroid cut costs while attempting to diversify into such areas as medical imaging (a major failure), flashlights and batteries, and graphic arts. By the end of the decade, however, Polaroid decided to once again turn to the consumer market, this time focusing on a younger demographic market with the I-Zone Instant Pocket Camera, a slim camera producing small instant pictures, and the JoyCam, a smaller, lower-priced version of the company's standard instant camera. Both were introduced in the second half of 1999. Polaroid also looked to expand its business in Europe and the Pacific and as a result dropped its advertising agency, Goodby, Silverstein & Partners, in favor of Leo Burnett, which had global reach as a part of the Publicis Groupe. After taking over the Polaroid account, at the time worth about $150 million, in the spring of 2000, Leo Burnett launched a marketing campaign to promote the I-Zone and JoyCam following their successful introduction.

TARGET MARKET

While the I-Zone and JoyCam were aimed at the 18-to-25 demographic, the cameras' core users were girls aged 15 to 17, and it was this audience that the ensuing campaign targeted. But it was a tricky population to address, given the marketing savvy possessed by contemporary teens, who from the cradle had been bombarded by advertising. They knew when they were being marketed to and were especially resistant to corporate, hard-sell approaches. Polaroid knew its advertising would have to be innovative, witty, and engaging if it were to reach the mark. The goal was to make the I-Zone and JoyCam must-have items for teenage girls. Moreover the marketers wanted to establish I-Zone and JoyCam as enduring brands in the market, rather than mere fads soon to be abandoned by fickle teens. On all levels it was a tall order for Polaroid's marketers.

ON SECOND THOUGHT

Polaroid Corporation was established to produce polarizing material, which it initially attempted to sell to automakers for nonglare car headlights and windshields, but Detroit showed no interest. At the 1939 New York World's Fair, Polaroid wowed the public with a three-dimensional film that required special filtering glasses. This time it was Hollywood's turn to pass on Polaroid's innovative technology.

COMPETITION

Historically Polaroid's strength in the photography field was the instant delivery of photographs. That edge eroded with the emergence of new technologies, however. Conveniently located photo shops and counters in mass retailers offering one-hour development cut into Polaroid's market share, as consumers proved willing to trade off instant development of a single shot for the quick delivery of prints plus the film's negatives in order to make multiple copies of favorite shots. Even more devastating to Polaroid was the introduction of digital photography and its rapid acceptance with mainstream consumers. Not only did digital cameras offer instant gratification, but poor shots could be immediately discarded and favorite ones transferred to home computers, from where they could be printed on ink-jet printers or sent by E-mail to friends and family.

The players in the new digital photography field included old-guard rivals Canon, Olympus, Fuji, Minolta, and Kodak, although the latter, like Polaroid, was not as nimble as the other companies to embrace digital photography. In addition Polaroid had to contend with a new breed of entrants in the field, including corporate giants like Hewlett-Packard, Nokia, and Samsung. What they may have lacked in track record in photography, they made up in large advertising budgets. Their combined marketing heft promoted digital photography, superseding traditional photography at a pace that took the likes of Polaroid and Kodak by surprise. Kodak was much larger and better diversified than Polaroid and had at least been a pioneer in digital photography, holding a number of key patents. It could always change its focus to digital technology, a step the company took in the 2000s. But Polaroid faced a far more serious crisis: how to survive in a marketplace that seemed to have passed it by.

MARKETING STRATEGY

When Leo Burnett launched a marketing campaign in the spring of 2000 to promote the I-Zone and JoyCam to

WAIT UNTIL THE PRICE COMES DOWN

When Polaroid Corporation introduced the first instant-developing camera in 1947, it was priced at $89.75. The sepia-toned film cost $1.75 for eight exposures.

younger consumers, in particular 15- to 17-year-old girls, the objectives were clear but difficult to achieve. The marketers wanted to increase sales of both the cameras and the film they used, but at the same time they hoped to establish the brands and avoid the trap of becoming a passing fancy. The goal wasn't to be on teens' must-have list for just this year but rather for many years to come. The strategy of the campaign was to appeal to the target audience's sense of fun, to encourage them to take pictures with I-Zone and JoyCam cameras and to play with the images. A key feature of the new cameras was their sticky film, which allowed users to apply the small pictures they took to any surface.

Both television spots and print ads in the campaign followed the same game plan. According to *Shoot* magazine's Fred Cisterna, "the high-energy ads show hip young adults having fun with the new cameras and with the Sticky Film." For example, the television spot titled "Ceiling" opened with the tease of a young woman jumping up and down out of the frame. Next the audience saw that she was jumping on her bed and with each leap was sticking a small Polaroid picture on her bedroom ceiling. In another ad, "Pasties," featuring a teen boy, the audience first saw two photos moving back and forth in time to a techno track of drums and bass. The payoff, as revealed in a widening shot, was that the pictures were stuck to the chest of a young man watching himself in a mirror and moving to the music.

Polaroid attempted to build on the campaign in 2001. The JoyCam was positioned as a social lubricant to consumers in their 20s in an adverting effort themed "It Only Comes Out at Night." Unlike the typical ads selling cameras or film that showed only appealing pictures, this series featured unflattering candid shots of partying young people. Again the marketers hoped to nudge the target audience not only to buy Polaroid's small cameras but to take more pictures, thereby generating increased revenues. In 2001 Polaroid also launched an advertising campaign to promote its core product, introducing a new tagline, "Click, Instantly," which suggested that Polaroid pictures had the ability to bring people together in such a way that they clicked, helping to transform a boring party or mend fences between feuding couples. The company's attempt on the one hand to forge a relationship with teens and on the other to remind an older demographic audience that it still had emotional relevance could not overcome the financial hole Polaroid had slipped into, however. In October 2001 Polaroid filed for Chapter 11 bankruptcy protection. The company had no choice but to continue to spend money to promote its products or risk becoming virtually irrelevant in the marketplace, but because of its debts Polaroid would only be able to budget a fraction of the $150 million global account Leo Burnett thought it had won in 2000.

The campaign to pitch the I-Zone and JoyCam to the teen market continued in 2002. The most innovative work during the year came in the second half when Leo Burnett developed the concept of "hijacking." The inspiration came from copywriter Eric Routenberg, who one day spotted a Polaroid photo stuck on a bumper of a parked car. He told Aaron Baar of *Adweek,* "That car stopped being a car, and it was an ad for an I-Zone." Out of that experience grew a somewhat subversive, interactive print campaign that the agency hoped would appeal to teens. In several teen magazines Polaroid placed an insert of 32 sticky pics, of a scuba diver, a monkey face, and a man's hairy chest, among others. On the next page was a fake print ad, which the users could comment on by affixing some of the stickers. The goal of these ads was to reengage the core market, to reacquaint people with the I-Zone product and urge them to use their own imagination in finding ways to make a statement using sticky pics—to in essence hijack ads and other images for their own purposes. A more practical objective for Polaroid was to simply increase much-needed sales in the fourth quarter of the year.

OUTCOME

The work Leo Burnett did for Polaroid promoting the I-Zone, the JoyCam, and sticky film was successful in a number of ways. When the campaign broke in 2000 Polaroid experienced an immediate jump in sales, and research indicated that the target market liked the products a great deal, suggesting that they would not fade away like many fads. Leo Burnett also received industry recognition for some of the work it did over the course of two years. It received a 2001 Effie Award from the New York American Marketing Association. In 2002 the agency was a finalist for a Magazine Publishers of America Kelly Award and, among other distinctions, received the Best of Show and Award of Excellence in the Chicago Windy Awards, the Art Director's Club of New York 2002 Merit, and Gold and Silver ADDY Awards, given out by the American Advertising Federation. Leo Burnett's hijacking work in 2003 was also an MPA Kelly finalist.

Despite the success of the marketers, Polaroid continued to struggle. In July 2002 the company was bought out of bankruptcy and taken private. Polaroid simply did not have the cash it had once budgeted for advertising. According to press accounts the company was now spending about $70 million a year, less than half of the $150 million the account was estimated to be worth in 2000. When the account was put up for review in 2003, Leo Burnett opted not to participate. Euro RSCG Worldwide then took over the task of reviving the fortunes of one of the truly great brands of the second half of the twentieth century.

FURTHER READING

Baar, Aaron. "Burnett Declines to Defend Polaroid." *Adweek,* July 21, 2003.

———. "JoyCam Positioned as Social Tool." *Adweek,* May 21, 2001, p. 5.

———. "Leo Stuck on I-Zone." *Adweek,* October 28, 2002, p. 6.

Baar, Aaron, and David Gianatasio. "Goodby at Risk in Polaroid Consolidation." *Adweek,* April 17, 2000.

———. "Polaroid Face-Off." *Adweek,* April 17, 2000, p. 9.

Cisterna, Fred. "Hank Smith Music Livens Up the San Francisco Music Scene." *Shoot,* May 19, 2000.

Elliott, Stuart. "Polaroid Hopes the Flash of a New Campaign Wins Back Its Image of Being on the Cutting Edge." *New York Times,* October 6, 2003, p. C5.

Gatlin, Greg. "Polaroid, Healing, Puts $20M into Ads." *Boston Herald,* March 19, 2002, p. 30.

Levere, Jane L. "Polaroid's New Campaign Moves Away from the Family and Toward the Young and the Hip." *New York Times,* March 18, 2002, p. C8.

"Polaroid Files Chapter 11." *Adweek* (western ed.), October 15, 2001, p. 6.

"Polaroid Will Launch Print Ads for I-Zone Instant Camera." *Advertising Age,* October 28, 2002, p. 45.

"Sticky Business Clicks with Teens." *MediaWeek,* September 22, 2003, p. 16.

Ed Dinger

SEE WHAT DEVELOPS CAMPAIGN

OVERVIEW

By 1995 Polaroid Corporation was perceived as a brand and a company whose time had passed. Disposable and 35mm cameras were less expensive than instant ones, their film was much cheaper and could be developed in an hour, and they produced better-quality photos. Polaroid sales had been declining steadily over the years, and the brand had largely faded from view. Although the company had no new products to tout, it began attempting to rebuild its brand in the United States through marketing. Polaroid tapped the San Francisco advertising agency Goodby, Silverstein & Partners to craft a campaign that would create positive buzz around the brand while reminding consumers of the unique characteristics of instant photography.

"See What Develops" ran from 1996 through 1998. The campaign leveraged an estimated annual budget of between $30 million and $35 million and included TV as well as print components. The campaign's first series of executions specifically touted the advantages of instant photography, whereas the second installment, unveiled in 1998, focused on human behavior peculiar to the instant-photography experience. For instance, an early TV spot showed a businessman who opened his briefcase to find a surprise photo placed there by his wife as an incitement to come home for lunch, and a later TV spot gently pointed out the absurdity of consumers' insistence on shaking or blowing on Polaroid photos as though to help them develop.

The campaign was well received within the advertising industry, and it initially drove substantial sales increases in Polaroid cameras and film. Polaroid's long-term outlook for recovering its spot atop the U.S. camera industry remained bleak, however, and 1998 saw the company post a 16 percent sales decline versus 1997.

HISTORICAL CONTEXT

On February 21, 1947, Edwin H. Land announced his invention of one-step photography at a meeting of the Optical Society of America. Since that time the Polaroid Corporation, Land's company, had been synonymous with instant photography. There was an explosion of popularity in the 1970s, when instant cameras became simple to use and the shooter did not have to wait weeks for 110 or 35mm film to be developed. By the 1990s, however, instant photography was perceived as a relic of the past, and so was Polaroid.

TARGET MARKET

There was a broad target audience for the "See What Develops" campaign. Polaroid wanted to reach out to current users, lapsed owners, and those who had never owned an instant camera. According to a Goodby report, this included "men, women, parents, single adults, African Americans, Latinos and Caucasians, people in their 20s and people in their 40s." They also knew that groups such as realtors, contractors, and insurance agents used the cameras in business. Goodby wanted to influence those users while they were away from their jobs—watching TV at home—to reinforce the need for instant pictures and Polaroid.

NO ACROSS-THE-BOARD INTEGRATION PLAN DEVELOPED

Goodby did not plan an extensive integration effort in the "See What Develops" campaign. There were few direct-mail and in-store promotions. There was, however, a successful seasonal camera promotion that was publicized during the holidays in late 1996 and spring 1997 to encourage buyers of the basic One Step camera to mail in a $10 rebate form. This promotion was tied in with 15- and 30-second TV spots that ran during that time. The "See What Develops" campaign themes also were used by Polaroid's public relations department on the company website and on a promotional van tour.

COMPETITION

Increased competition from disposable and easy "point-and-shoot" 35mm cameras, along with one-hour film-processing centers, had made Polaroid's instant photography increasingly irrelevant, and the company had lost its positioning in the market over the years. There was no perceived need to take a Polaroid picture when 35mm photography produced images that were cheaper, could be developed quickly, and had better quality.

Since 1990 the company's retail sales had decreased approximately 3 percent a year. The public was not using Polaroids anymore. The cameras were in the backs of closets in many households. Owners used the past tense if they talked about the brand at all. According to Goodby research, people felt like " 'it was state-of-the-art twenty years ago . . . my dad had one . . . we used to use it all the time for parties . . . it was so clunky . . .' And the only advertising they seemed to recall clearly for this 'cultural relic' was the old James Garner and Mariette Hartley campaign from the 1970s."

In addition to the brand's image problem, Polaroid's chief rival, Kodak, planned to buy $108.8 million in advertising time in 1996. Polaroid's ad budget of $33.7 million for the same period was less than a third of Kodak's.

MARKETING STRATEGY

In 1995 Polaroid did not have a new product to release. Goodby, Silverstein & Partners and its client decided that "the advertising would have to bear the responsibility for changing perceptions and attitudes about the Polaroid brand," according to one agency report. They had three objectives—to get people thinking and talking about Polaroid, to make instant photography relevant again and reestablish the uniqueness of Polaroid, and to increase sales of Polaroid cameras and film.

Goodby consumer research indicated high negatives when Polaroid was compared to 35mm cameras and when it was perceived as an ordinary camera for taking pictures for photo albums. Those questioned repeatedly mentioned the poor quality of Polaroid pictures compared to 35mm and that the film was expensive. The ad agency knew it needed to avoid direct comparisons with other cameras. Focus-group participants were given Polaroid cameras and film, and they were asked to bring the pictures they shot to the next meeting. Goodby wanted to discover how instant cameras could become attractive again to camera buyers. As expected, most of the returned photos were of friends, pets, and family—typical photo album pictures. But the agency discovered in the focus groups that the shots that made the price of a camera and film worth it were the shots that would not be put in albums. For example, one man reported that he had taken a picture to send to his insurance agent of his car's damage from an accident. A woman had used the camera when she was trying on sunglasses to show her husband at home how the glasses looked on her.

The research that drove the creative team was the concept that taking a Polaroid picture was only the first step. Goodby determined that the photo should be used as "an instant solution to a problem, an instant tool to make something happen. There should always be a purpose, the picture should always set off a chain reaction . . . something should always happen next." From that concept the "See What Develops" campaign was born.

The agency produced a series of print ads for magazines as diverse as *People, Rolling Stone,* and *Time.* Most of the print ads it designed were very simple, consisting of a Polaroid photo, a comment, the Polaroid logo, and the tagline "See What Develops." For instance, one ad featured a photo of the front of a business with a neon sign above it saying MOM. A letter was next to the photo on WOW Productions letterhead, addressed to the Hung-Rite Sign Company. The text simply read "You moron." The picture, the letterhead, and the logo and tagline made the point succinctly. Another print ad featured four shots of a toilet with the seat up. Below each picture was handwritten the day of the week and the time. The text read, "Honey, you always do that. No, I don't. Yes you do. No, I don't. Wanna bet?" followed by the logo and tagline.

The media plan included television spots on shows such as *NYPD Blue, Seinfeld, Melrose Place,* and *ER,* which were characterized by Goodby as "hip, high 'talk-value' programming." The aim was to get people talking about Polaroid, to create some "buzz." Because Polaroid had less money to spend than Kodak, the creative team decided to employ a—that is, focus placement entirely in the 6:00 to 9:30 p.m. time slots and run the commercials for a shorter number of weeks than usual to have more impact. The strategy resulted in an average of 133 gross rating points each week for 14 weeks, according to the Competitive Media Report.

Almost $3 million in additional media time was obtained by working with the major TV networks to link upcoming shows with Polaroid and "See What Develops." For instance, a typical program teaser was "See What Develops next week on Melrose Place." *Mediaweek* honored Polaroid for the best media plan for a campaign spending more than $25 million.

The new television spots, while complicated visually, still conveyed the simple message that sometimes a Polaroid photo was the only thing that would work. "The Architect" was a 30-second spot that featured a group of people in a meeting, heatedly discussing solutions to a crisis. The phone rang, and a man with architectural drawings on his desk indicated to his wife on the line that he was too busy to go home for lunch. She asked him to check his briefcase. The man took out a Polaroid picture and with a delighted and surprised intake of breath, involuntarily said, "Ooohh." He then said he would be home in 10 minutes. A shot of the logo and tagline ended the commercial. The image he saw was left to the viewer's imagination. In "Dog and Cat," another 30-second spot, there were quick shots of a spilled kitchen trash can, a woman scolding a dog as a cat looked on, the dog later watching as the cat approached the trash container, the dog thinking back to the scolding, then picturing his options—a rolling pin, a cleaver, a Polaroid camera. Cut to the logo and tagline. The dog, with a picture in its mouth of the cat in the trash, then greeted the owner at the door, who said, "Oh, dear."

As the campaign matured, Polaroid and Goodby focused on documenting humorous Polaroid-influenced human behavior rather than on explicitly pointing out situations in which instant cameras might be necessary. For instance, in 1998 one documentary-style spot focused on three different adults at a party, each of whom detailed the trademark poses that he or she relied on when instant photos were taken at such events. Another spot poked fun at the unnecessary rituals, such as blowing and shaking the photo, that Polaroid users frequently engaged in as a way of "helping" the image emerge. The season's third TV spot focused on the embarrassment that an otherwise dignified bank manager felt about a Polaroid taken of him at a party.

OUTCOME

Campaign objectives were initially met and exceeded. Three months after the release of "See What Develops," a tracking study showed that there was a "buzz" about Polaroid. Goodby cited tracking study data when it explained, "unaided brand awareness among ou[r] 18–49-year-old target increased from 31 to 39 percent. Unaided ad awareness rose from 11 percent to 22 percent."

The campaign also got attention from publications besides the advertising press—"something Polaroid's advertising hasn't gotten since the days of the well-liked Garner-Hartley campaign," one Goodby report stated. The report cited articles in *Newsweek, USA Today, Time,* and the *Los Angeles Times Magazine* and added that one of the print ads had been talked about by Tom Snyder on the *Late Late Show.*

The objective of redefining the relevancy and uniqueness of Polaroid instant photography was also exceeded in the early stages of the campaign. Prelaunch Goodby and Polaroid qualitative research in 1995 and 1996 had found that focus-group members who had negative attitudes about Polaroid before the meeting would leave the session feeling enthusiastic after having viewed the campaign. Goodby reported that the group members said that "they now wanted to buy a Polaroid camera, how they saw all these new ways of using it, how it could still do things no other camera could do." According to the ad agency, copy tests had revealed that 60 percent of Polaroid owners said that they would buy film after seeing the spots, versus 30 percent for the control group.

The qualitative research done before the campaign began was proven correct. The tracking study determined that consumer intent to purchase a Polaroid camera rose from 9 percent before the campaign to 13 percent three months later. Goodby explained, "we had given consumers a new way of looking at 'old Polaroid,' and it made them reconsider buying Polaroid cameras and film."

The objective of increasing Polaroid camera and film sales was also met. Partial year A.C. Nielsen data for 1996 indicated that camera sales increased by 13 percent. Film sales, which had been declining 3 percent a year for a long time, increased 1 percent—a turnaround of 4 percent.

In addition to the *Mediaweek* award, Goodby and Polaroid received a Silver EFFIE. Polaroid's long-term prospects, however, failed to improve significantly after the campaign's initial effects wore off. "See What Develops" continued to win accolades within the advertising industry, but Polaroid's total sales for 1998 declined 16 percent, dropping to $1.8 billion from a 1997 total of $2.1 billion.

In 1999, although Goodby had unveiled a new theme, "Right Now," for its Polaroid branding work, the company abruptly pulled that tag, reportedly in response to high-level executives' displeasure about the fact that the same slogan had been used on behalf of a Pepsi product a few years earlier. "See What Develops" was thus resurrected to serve as the tagline for a set of three TV spots that ran in the spring and summer of that year. In the fall of 1999 Polaroid introduced a line of products already popular in Japan and China rather than any that had been developed specifically for the United States, a move that some analysts considered a desperate tactic to spur growth by any means necessary. These products—a pocket-sized camera that produced passport-sized instant photos with adhesive backs and a disposable instant camera—were marketed in the United States as the Polaroid I-Zone line and targeted a previously untapped market of 6- to 17-year-olds. A Goodby-helmed I-Zone launch campaign resulted in fourth-quarter sales gains of 20 percent, boosting Polaroid's total 1999 sales by 7 percent, to $1.97 billion.

In 2000, however, Polaroid reshuffled its advertising duties to reflect its need for global rather than U.S.-specific marketing platforms, awarding the U.S. account to Chicago's Leo Burnett, an affiliate of Polaroid's European agency Bartle Bogle Hegarty of London and of the Japanese agency Dentsu, which had been simultaneously enlisted to take over the brand's advertising in that country. This reorganization did little to forestall the continued decline of Polaroid's fortunes. Yet another photographic innovation, the digital camera, was becoming increasingly popular among consumers, and its numerous advantages over previous technologies included precisely the capability to offer instant gratification that had been Polaroid's chief marketable advantage over other camera brands. Polaroid filed for Chapter 11 bankruptcy protection on October 12, 2000.

FURTHER READING

Burgi, Michael. "GS&P: High Exposure." *Mediaweek,* June 23, 1997, p. 30.

Dietrich, Joy, and Jon Herskovitz. "Polaroid Imports Ideas from Japan." *Advertising Age International,* April 12, 1999.

Garfield, Bob. "Polaroid Ads Show Flash of Brilliance." *Advertising Age,* March 11, 1996, p. 37.

Gellene, Denise. "Advertising and Marketing; Ad Reviews; Polaroid Spots Provide Instant Gratification." *Los Angeles Times,* February 12, 1998.

McGinn, Daniel. "A Camera for a New Generation?" *Newsweek,* April 29, 1996, p. 46.

Parpis, Eleftheria. "Polaroids Don't Lie." *Adweek* (eastern ed.), February 10, 1997, p. 38.

"Polaroid Spot an Eye-Opener." *Advertising Age,* May 26, 1997, p. 4.

"See What Develops." *Adweek* (eastern ed.), August 5, 1996, p. 10.

Voight, Joan. "Polaroid Corp." *Mediaweek,* March 4, 1996, p. 34.

———. "Polaroid Yuks Up with $40M Push." *Brandweek,* February 26, 1996, p. 6.

Wells, Melanie. "Agency's Trouble-Shooters Click with Polaroid." *USA Today,* June 17, 1996, p. B3.

Wilke, Michael. "Polaroid Advertising Push Targets Younger Consumers." *Advertising Age,* February 2, 1998.

Wilke, Michael, and Alice Z. Cuneo. "Polaroid Plans $30 Mil in Ads as Sales Decline." *Advertising Age,* February 12, 1996, p. 2.

Allison I. Porter
Mark Lane

Porsche Cars North America Inc.

980 Hammond Dr. NE, Ste. 1000
Atlanta, Georgia 30328-5313
USA
Telephone: (770) 290-3500
Fax: (770) 290-3700
Web site: www.porsche.com

CAYENNE LAUNCH CAMPAIGN

OVERVIEW

Well known for its pricey sports cars, German automaker Porsche AG and its American subsidiary, Porsche Cars North America Inc., began to change directions following a sales slump in the early 1990s. It successfully launched a less expensive two-seater, the Boxster, and in 1998 announced that it would enter the luxury SUV market early in the next century. To many it seemed a questionable decision, one that threatened the exclusive nature of the Porsche brand. But the company correctly surmised that the luxury market was moving toward SUVs and the timing for the launch of its SUV entry, the Cayenne, proved fortuitous. In 1999 the company hired a new advertising agency, Minneapolis-based Carmichael Lynch, well known for its work on Harley-Davidson motorcycles, to begin the spadework necessary to promote the new vehicle.

For three consecutive autumns Porsche launched advertising campaigns that attempted to expand on the brand's audience. The TV spots and print ads emphasized the fun and thrill of a Porsche and showed a wide variety of people enjoying Porsche cars. In the background the company also began conducting a direct-mail program to build a database of potential customers, which was also augmented by Web elements and a dedicated website. By the time actual spots for the Cayenne ran on television and ads appeared in magazines, three months before the vehicle went on sale, Cayenne was already enjoying a brisk pace of orders.

When the $15 million main campaign came to a close in the fall of 2003, it had been clearly successful. Porsche enjoyed record sales and profits despite a significant drop in the sale of its sports cars. Also of importance was that only one in five Cayenne buyers were already Porsche owners, meaning that the campaign had succeeded in creating a wider audience for Porsche.

HISTORICAL CONTEXT

Long dependent on the U.S. market to buy its expensive sports cars, Porsche was severely wounded by the recession of the early 1990s. Car sales bottomed out around 14,000 cars in 1993, a far cry from the 50,000 cars Porsche had sold seven years earlier, of which two-thirds were sold in the United States. New leadership was installed, Japanese manufacturing techniques were introduced to improve efficiency and cut costs, and in 1996 Porsche introduced a new sports car, the Boxster, which found a receptive market for its $40,000 price tag. It was a move that made the brand available to a wider number of potential customers, especially younger buyers. Two years later the German automaker decided to venture even more mainstream, announcing that it would join forces with Volkswagen to jointly develop a new sports

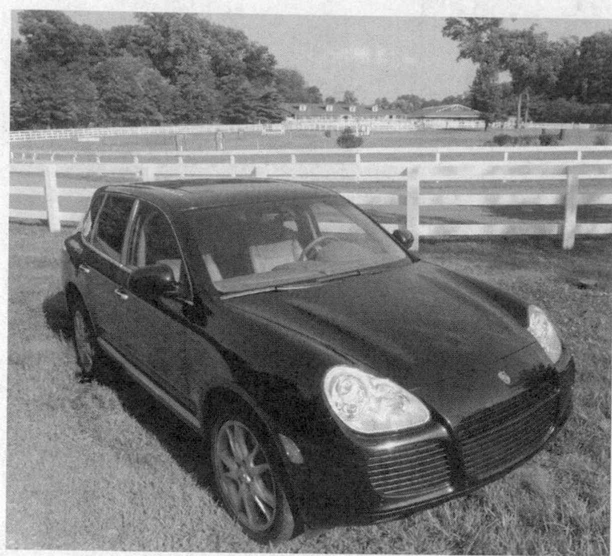

A 2003 Porsche Cayenne Sport Utility Vehicle. © **NAJLAH FEANNY/CORBIS.**

utility vehicle, which would be called the Cayenne, scheduled to go on sale by the year 2002. Although research indicated that 45 percent of Porsche owners also owned an SUV, it was a risky decision. According to Gail Edmondson, writing for *BusinessWeek,* "Porsche aficionados cringed. Even the Porsche family shareholders balked, fearing the company's sports-car tradition and exclusive brand name didn't befit bulky off-roaders." Because the SUV market was most mature in the United States, the marketing effort to launch the Cayenne would primarily fall on the shoulders of Atlanta-based Porsche Cars North America.

In years just preceding the Cayenne's launch, Porsche had spent most of its advertising budget on print ads in car-enthusiast magazines, while television was mostly limited to spots run on regional TV in the top eight markets for the brand. In order to prepare the ground for the Cayenne launch, Porsche hired a new advertising agency in 1999, turning over the $15 million account to Minneapolis-based Carmichael Lynch, which had earned a solid reputation for the work it did for Harley-Davidson motorcycles over the previous 20 years. The agency would develop a pair of interim campaigns to promote Porsche while broadening the brand's appeal in advance of the Cayenne launch. In particular the company wanted to expand its advertising in lifestyle magazines and also increase its direct-mail efforts. Porsche's chief operating officer Richard Ford explained the greater challenge to Jean Halliday of *Automotive News:* "The key is maintaining our core business and expand without disrupting our core buyers and without losing our brand image."

TARGET MARKET

Porsche, because of its price tag and emphasis on performance, had always appealed to an older, monied male market. That changed somewhat with the introduction of the Boxster, but the target driver, aged 34 to 54, still had an annual income of at least $150,000. And about 80 percent of Boxster buyers were men. The interim campaigns did little to change these sales numbers, but the marketing brought the brand to a wider audience and made it more appealing to them. For the campaign that directly promoted the Cayenne launch, the target market was 42- to 47-year-olds, and because the price range was $52,000 to $75,000, the income of the target market was again high, at least $225,000 a year. Because the SUV was more utilitarian than a two-seat sports car, it was expected to appeal to more women, who could accept it as a family vehicle. Nevertheless Porsche expected that about 70 percent of Cayenne owners would be men.

COMPETITION

The Cayenne competed in the luxury SUV category, which boasted a deep and varied field. The first luxury SUV, the Acura SLX, was introduced by Honda Motor Company in late 1995 and was soon emulated by other automakers, and the concept was embraced by car buyers. Many of the luxury models were simply upgrades of an existing SUV platform: the Cadillac Escalade was a luxury version of the Chevrolet Tahoe; the GMC Yukon Denali depended on the GMC Yukon; the Lincoln Navigator was beholden to the Ford Expedition, as was the Lexus GX 470 to the Toyota 4Runner and the Infiniti QX56 to the Nissan Pathfinder Armada. A pair of vehicles with military roots, the Hummer H1 and the Mercedes-Benz G-Class, also entered the already crowded field. The Cayenne was one of a group of vehicles designed from the start as luxury SUVs, including the Mercedes-Benz M-Class, the Lexus RX 330, and the BMW X5.

By the time of the Cayenne launch, the luxury SUV category was a key to the growth of all luxury brands, with only Rolls Royce and Jaguar electing to remain on the sidelines. According to Chris Isidore, *CNN/Money* senior writer, "Luxury car executives say that their SUVs are a choice for both traditional SUV buyers moving up in brand and traditional luxury car buyers looking for more room. But data from CarsDirect.com shows that most luxury SUV buyers are comparing those vehicles to other SUVs, including the lower-priced models. Most are not shopping among luxury cars. Thus the SUV is becoming the key to bringing new customers to

A PAST NOT BY DESIGN

Porsche AG was founded in 1931 as an engineering and design consulting firm by Dr. Ferdinand Porsche, who had previously served as technical director for German automaker Daimler. Porsche's work in designing high-quality cars soon caught the attention of a rising politician: Adolf Hitler. When he came to power Hitler enlisted Porsche to develop the Volkswagen and fulfill his vision of an inexpensive car that the average German could own. Later in the 1930s, with Hitler's blessing, Porsche designed a sports car to compete in Grand Prix races. Because of his ties to Hitler and the Nazi party, Dr. Porsche was briefly incarcerated following World War II.

the luxury dealerships." The decision by Porsche to develop its own entrant, therefore, proved prescient.

Porsche touted Cayenne's superior performance as a point of difference. Able to reach a top speed of 165 miles per hour, it became the fastest luxury SUV on the market. The vehicle also boasted a suspension with six settings for driving on and off roads and was capable of towing as much as 7,700 pounds. Porsche considered its primary competition to be the BMW X5, the Mercedes-Benz M-Class, and Ford Motor Company's new Land Rover SUVs.

MARKETING STRATEGY

In the fall of 1999 Carmichael Lynch unveiled its first campaign for Porsche, which continued to appeal to sports-car enthusiasts and essentially positioned Porsche as a brand to covet. In one TV spot, for example, a suspicious woman learned that a phone number in a man's pocket was actually for a Porsche dealer. While Porsche owners, research indicated, were quick to grasp the brand message, others were not. A year later the agency crafted a campaign that was less cerebral, extended to a broader market, and better suited to the task of setting the stage for the Cayenne launch. The television spots took more of a storytelling approach, featuring characters who did not look like fashion models. The premise of the two spots, fleshing out the theme "It's a thrill like no other," was the length that people would go in order to drive or ride in a Porsche. In one spot set in Ireland two older men argued in a pub about which one of them should be the designated driver that night, while in the other spot a girl intentionally missed the school bus in order to catch a ride in her father's Porsche. The campaign also included five new print ads that attempted to associate fun with the brand. In one ad, for example, a yellow Boxster was shown driving through a field of sunflowers. The headline read, "What a dog feels like when the leash breaks."

The fall 2001 TV and print campaign continued to build on the "It's a thrill like no other" theme. In one of the two new spots, three traffic controllers caused a Porsche driver to stop at three straight traffic lights just so they could check out the car from every angle using their surveillance cameras. In addition to this brand-building work, Porsche also began to directly promote the Cayenne. In 2001 the company made a direct-mail pitch for the vehicle to approximately 70,000 owners of luxury SUVs and sedans. The response rate was in the 8 to 9 percent range, significantly better than the response Porsche had received in previous direct-mail efforts. Part of the success was due to the vehicle, but a great deal of credit was due to improved targeting techniques, model econometrics, which allowed Porsche to better target people similar to its existing buyers. All told, half a dozen mailings would be made before the Cayenne went on the market. Porsche also made use of its website to build up its database of prospects, as Web banner ads and print ads drove people to the site. People were also added to the database by calling a toll-free telephone number.

More groundwork was done in the Cayenne launch in the fall of 2002, again emphasizing the fun and thrill of driving a Porsche. In one TV spot a man at a business lunch and a woman at a meeting took cell-phone calls that apparently brought bad news and forced them to leave. The man, behind the wheel of a Boxster, was then seen waiting for the woman as they sped off and a voice-over suggested that Porsche was "perhaps the perfect getaway car."

The Cayenne promotion began in earnest in January 2003 when TV spots and print ads were run for three weeks and then returned in March when the vehicle went on sale. The advertising introduced the line "Pure Porsche in an unexpected form." Two TV spots, which premiered during NFL football telecasts, anchored this phase of the Cayenne launch. In one a man had a cab follow a Cayenne off the highway and into rough terrain. By the end of the journey the cab was all but wrecked while the Cayenne was unscratched. In the second spot a man driving a motor home passed a Cayenne waiting to enter the highway. He left the wheel and ran to the back of the motor home while his wife slept in order to get a better look at the Porsche. He then watched it through the side windows as he worked his way to the front, took up the wheel again, and longed for the Cayenne, now out of sight. A second pair of 30-second spots began running in August 2003. In one a man revved the engine of his Cayenne in his driveway to the confusion of his neighbors, then stepped out of the car, picked up a cell phone on the ground, and said to a listener, "Is that cool or what?" In the second spot a young boy pretended he was driving a car with his green beans and mashed potatoes, only to have his father explain how to accelerate through a corner. A representative print ad showed a Cayenne at night. The text read, "Do you really need 450 HP to pick up diapers? You ever run out of diapers?"

OUTCOME

The buildup to the Cayenne launch was so successful that the vehicle was selling well through orders before the direct advertising even began. In a year that saw Boxster sales fall off 40 percent and the more expensive 911 model dip 14 percent, Porsche was able to post record sales in fiscal 2003 and a 22 percent increase in net profits to $684 million, all due to sales of Cayenne. Moreover, only about a fifth of Cayenne buyers were already Porsche owners, reflecting the campaign's success in broadening the automaker's customer base. Sales of the luxury SUV continued to grow in 2004, when Porsche introduced a less expensive V6 version of the Cayenne (capable of exceeding 130 miles per hour), a move that opened up the brand to an even wider audience.

FURTHER READING

Baar, Aaron. "CL Brings Back Driving Excitement to Porsche Ads." *Adweek* (midwest ed.), September 16, 2002, p. 2.

———. "The Driver's Seat." *Adweek* (eastern ed.), October 2, 2000, p. 34.

———. "Porsche Seeks Wider Audience." *Adweek* (midwest ed.), September 25, 2000, p. 6.

———. "Porsche Steers Marketing Message to Thrill of Driving in Prep for SUV." *Brandweek,* September 16, 2002, p. 4.

———. "Porsche SUV Entry Teases with Web, Print Effort." *Adweek* (midwest ed.), April 29, 2002, p. 3.

Cantwell, Julie. "Porsche Boosts Ad Spending for Cayenne's Launch." *Automotive News,* March 25, 2002, p. 6.

Edmondson, Gail. "This SUV Can Tow an Entire Carmaker." *BusinessWeek,* December 22, 2003, p. 22.

Halliday, Jean. "Porsche Goal: Add Prospects." *Automotive News,* August 16, 1999, p. 18.

———. "Porsche Puts Laughter Back in New Ad Pitch." *Advertising Age,* September 25, 2000, p. 4.

———. "Research, Econometrics Hone Auto's Direct Touch." *Advertising Age,* November 11, 2002, p. 24.

Meiners, Jens. "Porsche Moves Further from Its Sports Car Roots." *Automotive News,* December 1, 2003, p. 32j.

Ed Dinger

priceline.com Incorporated

800 Connecticut Avenue
Norwalk, Connecticut 06854-9998
USA
Telephone: (203) 299-8000
Web site: www.priceline.com

TROUBADOUR CAMPAIGN

OVERVIEW

In 1996 entrepreneur Jay Walker came upon a startling statistic: every day airlines flew with an average of 500,000 empty seats. The revelation spurred Walker to create priceline.com, a website that encouraged travelers to set their own price for airfare. If the customer's bid on an unused ticket was at least 70 percent of the ticket price, the customer usually received the discounted ticket. Priceline.com's concept of "name-your-own-price" was different from that of the competition. Travelocity.com and expedia.com, for instance, allowed consumers to compare prices from competing airlines. By 2000 priceline.com had expanded its services to include purchasing cars, financing homes, booking hotels, and even buying groceries. To increase consumer awareness about its growing spectrum of services, priceline.com released its "Troubadour" campaign in 2000.

"Troubadour" starred William Shatner, the actor who had played Captain James T. Kirk on the popular *Star Trek* series. The ad agency Hill, Holliday, Connors, Cosmopulos (often called Hill Holliday) created more than 20 "Troubadour" commercials that used priceline.com's $60 million advertising budget. First airing on January 1, 2000, the campaign also included print and radio spots. The commercials featured Shatner crooning off-key to songs such as "The Age of Aquarius," "Freebird," and "I Want You to Want Me." Lyrics were modified to advertise airfare and other services from priceline.com. Although Shatner later admitted that his performance was meant to be a self-parody, some critics mistook Shatner's deadpan delivery for earnestness. The campaign ended in late 2000.

The campaign's "We Gotta Get Out of This Place" spot was awarded one of *Adweek* magazine's "Best Spot" rankings in 2000. During the first quarter of 2000, priceline.com sold 43 percent more airline tickets than in the same quarter in 1999. Just days after the campaign debuted, priceline.com set a one-day sales record of $3 million.

HISTORICAL CONTEXT

In 1997, one year after Jay Walker discovered that airlines flew with more than 500,000 empty seats daily, the entrepreneur started the website priceline.com so that customers could bid on unused seats. Walker assumed that airlines would be eager to reduce their losses and that consumers would appreciate the discounted tickets. The ad agency Heater of Boston first created advertisements (radio spots and print ads) for priceline.com in 1998. The agency's creative director, Bill Heater, explained to the *Boston Globe* that the first priceline.com advertisements did not follow a particular strategy. Later the agency wanted a celebrity spokesperson that would "get cheap awareness for a new and complex service." Two actors were suggested: Bill Cosby and William Shatner. Priceline.com chose Shatner, hoping that his *Star Trek* fame would add a futuristic quality. After weeks of negotiations, Shatner agreed to the role in exchange for future company stock.

The first Shatner advertisement broke in 1998 and only used radio spots and print ads. Not only did Shatner star in the radio spots, but he also helped edit some of the dialogue. "I wrote the line about how Priceline was going to be 'big—really big,' and Shatner put his own spin on it," Heater recalled in an interview with the *Boston Globe.* "It sounded so good it became the tagline."

In a decision that was considered controversial in the late 1990s, priceline.com's chief marketing officer, Paul Breitenbach, refused to advertise his Web-based company with banner ads on websites. He said to *Advertising Age,* "Online advertising's got a long way to go before it's a part of the [media] mix for me." After priceline.com announced its 1999 public offering, the company outgrew the scope of Heater. That year priceline.com awarded its advertising account to a larger agency, Hill Holliday. The new agency kept using the 68-year-old Shatner and released a campaign to herald the website's expanded features.

SHATNER THE SINGER

In 1968, when the television series *Star Trek* was at its zenith, William Shatner recorded an album titled *The Transformed Man.* He created unlikely medleys, such as combining Bob Dylan's folk hit "Mr. Tambourine Man" with recitations of lines from the play *Cyrano de Bergerac.* Shatner believed that both sources shared themes of personal loss. Even though he could not carry a tune "beyond three notes," according to *Adweek,* he crooned for the travel website priceline.com's 2000 "Troubadour" campaign. In the commercials, as on his debut album, Shatner sang with a distinctive stop-and-go delivery that was similar to his performance as Captain Kirk on *Star Trek.*

TARGET MARKET

When priceline.com emerged in 1997, executives believed that its core customer would consist of low-income consumers who could not afford to travel without discounted airfare. Instead the website attracted a demographic of price-conscious consumers from multiple income brackets. According to a company spokesperson, when "Troubadour" was released, most priceline.com customers were Web-savvy, college-educated, upper-income travelers. Also, Breitenbach explained to *Advertising Age,* "We really see ourselves as serving two markets, the marketers who have unsold inventory and the consumer who wants to save money... We're not going to serve one at the expense of the other."

"Troubadour" ran throughout 2000, a tumultuous year for the technology industry. Nearly 50 percent of the 2000 Super Bowl advertisers were dot-coms, companies that existed mostly on the Internet. Ad critics praised the humor of most dot-com commercials but condemned them for rarely connecting the message to what was being sold. Hill Holliday hoped that its "Troubadour" target market would remember priceline.com because of Shatner's campy rendition of songs that referenced priceline.com services. The target consisted of various age groups. Hill Holliday selected Shatner partially for what was considered a multigenerational appeal. In some of the campaign spots Shatner was accompanied by contemporary rock musicians popular with college-age and 20-something consumers, such as Lisa Loeb, Ben Folds Five, and members of Fishbone. To target baby boomers the songs that Shatner sang were hits from the 1960s and 1970s.

Speaking with *Internet World,* Barbara Callihan, senior vice president and group account director at Hill Holliday, explained the campaign's effect on the target: "They break through the clutter," she said. "And not in an over-the-edge way to shock or turn people off. They make people talk—'Have you seen the new Shatner stuff?'—but it entertains more than the first time you see it. People enjoy seeing them again and again, and enjoying new nuances. It makes you tune in more."

COMPETITION

Priceline.com was one of the first websites that allowed consumers to choose an airfare from among competing airlines. One year before priceline.com was available, expedia.com was created as a joint venture between the Microsoft Corporation and American Express Company. A similar site, travelocity.com, which became another leader in online travel, was created by American Airlines, a subsidiary of the AMR Corporation. Priceline's competitors refrained from letting consumers set their own airfare. When one company, expedia.com, attempted to do so in 1999, allowing consumers to "name-their-own" hotel prices, priceline.com sued Microsoft for patent violation. Thus, competitors instead listed the discounted prices of all competing airlines.

Travelocity.com released two television spots in 2001 that were created by the Richards Group ad agency.

TREK-OR-TREAT

William Shatner, who played Captain James T. Kirk on the popular *Star Trek* series, starred in a series of television commercials for priceline.com, a travel website that allowed visitors to set their own price for various services. With a sense of humor that surfaced during the commercials, Shatner described to the *Washington Post* a joke he had played one Halloween. When he took his children trick-or-treating, he dressed as Captain Kirk and wore not one, but two masks of his *Star Trek* character. "They'd open the door, and there I was," Shatner explained. "I'd take off the first mask, and it was Captain Kirk! And I'd take off the second mask—and it was Captain Kirk!"

Both spots focused on the pleasure of travel rather than touting Travelocity.com as a low-price leader. "In the early days we concentrated on the control we offer our customers of shopping and buying," Jason Pruismann, Travelocity director of advertising and promotions, said to *Adweek*. "But we learned people are more into the experience of traveling rather than going from point A to point B. We wanted to take the high ground with this campaign, show that we can offer the experiences that are most special to people." One 30-second spot featured a couple bicycling up a volcano on Maui. Another showed a couple watching the tribal dance of Native Americans near Vancouver, British Columbia.

In the United Kingdom Travelocity.com released a print and television campaign that was created by the London ad agency St. Luke's. The campaign emerged after one study revealed that British employees worked harder than those in any other European country. One spot exaggerated a worker's hectic, overworked lifestyle. It concluded with the copy "YOU WORK TOO HARD" and then "YOU NEED A HOLIDAY." The spot's final image was of a tropical beach.

MARKETING STRATEGY

William Shatner starred in more than 20 spots for priceline.com's "Troubadour" campaign. Hill Holliday hired the crew from the music network VH1 to create a lounge stage similar to the one used on the performance program *VH1 Storytellers.* In each commercial Shatner covered a popular song from the 1960s or 1970s, such as Lynyrd Skynyrd's "Freebird" and Cheap Trick's "I Want You to Want Me." Occasionally he referenced more recent material, such as the rapper Young M.C.'s 1990 hit "Bust A Move." One spot featured Shatner rapping in a taupe suite about "fly" rental cars and "dope" airfares. "You want some of this?" he asked an audience of 20-somethings. "Bust a move!" During another television spot Shatner shouted, "If saving money is wrong, I don't want to be right." In an unscripted move the *Star Trek* icon grabbed a band member's guitar and smashed it on the stage. In another spot he gave a deadpan monologue: "Everybody knows somebody who's saved money using Priceline.com. A grandmother, a nephew . . . a lover."

Shatner's straight-faced delivery of campy dialogue was so convincing that ad critics debated whether they were laughing with Shatner or at him. Shatner later revealed that he had purposely blended parody and realism to keep his audience guessing. Explaining to *Adweek* why this technique was more appealing, Shatner said that if his performance was exaggerated, "You would say, 'He's not serious.' That would be easy. But this is more interesting."

Ten spots were filmed for the January 1, 2000, campaign launch. Thirteen more were shot in a day and a half at New York's Sony Studios in April. Hill Holliday cast contemporary musicians to play onstage with Shatner, such as guitarist/singer Carrie Brownstein of Sleater-Kinney and guitarist/singer Mary Timony of Helium. Real musicians were used to make the humor more subtle. The director of the "Troubadour" spots, Phil Morrison, explained to *Shoot,* "We didn't want, 'Oh, isn't that funny that he's got an eighteen-year-old guy with green hair playing with him?' "

The campaign, created using priceline.com's annual $60 million advertising budget, lasted throughout 2000. Some spots announced new services offered by priceline.-com, such as home financing and a long-distance phone service. Jackie Stern, director of advertising for priceline.-com, told *Brandweek* that the company was in the midst of figuring out how specifically it needed to market each of the services it was adding. "If it's mortgages, then which TV and radio stations profile high for mortgage customers, or is that product an E-mail strategy or an online strategy? It comes down to juggling all these products and making ourselves heard on each one of them."

To advertise priceline.com's new long-distance phone service, print ads appeared in 10 university newspapers. One headline read, "Rental Car, Ski Jump, Lake," above the copy "With one hour free long distance, now you can tell the whole story." Radio spots, which typically cost less to air than television spots, featured Shatner's exact audio from the commercials. Stern believed that this technique would make consumers feel like they had seen the commercials more.

OUTCOME

Adweek selected the campaign's commercial "We Gotta Get Out of This Place" as one of its "Best Spots" of 2000. While many ad critics praised the campaign for its quirkiness, others considered Shatner's off-key crooning to be little more than buffoonery. Nonetheless, even those lambasting the campaign acknowledged that the spots were memorable. Hill Holliday president Fred Bertino noted to the *Boston Globe,* "In every [newspaper] story about Priceline.com, Shatner is always mentioned somewhere in the first three paragraphs."

The NBC program*Saturday Night Live* lampooned Shatner's onstage "Troubadour" performances. Other network shows, such as *The Today Show* and *Entertainment Tonight* covered the campaign as well, earning what *USA Today* estimated to be $40 million of free publicity. Total sales for priceline.com were $1.2 billion in 2000, a significant amount over the $482 million posted in 1999. Once priceline.com allowed digital versions of the "Troubadour" spots to be downloaded from its website, traffic on the site increased 4,000 percent. Unfortunately, priceline.com's high expenses caused the company to post an overall loss for 2000. It was not until the next year that priceline.com would report its first annual profit. In 2002, when priceline.com's stock had greatly depreciated, it ended its relationship with Hill Holliday and drastically reduced ad spending.

FURTHER READING

Anthony, Ted. "For Shatner, Priceline's Right." *Albany (NY) Times Union,* June 2, 2000, p. D8.

———. "William Shatner Goes from Rags to Pitches." *Toronto Star,* June 4, 2000, p. 1.

Beirne, Mike. "Calling Captain Kirk." *Brandweek,* October 16, 2000, p. M76.

Champagne, Christine. "Phil Morrison." *Shoot,* March 24, 2000, p. 52.

Cuneo, Alice Z. "Fresh Priceline Spots Take Flight." *Advertising Age,* May 29, 2000, p. 70.

Freeman, Laurie. "Let's Make a Deal." *Advertising Age,* November 1, 1999, p. S24.

Gilbert, Jennifer. "Star Attraction." *Advertising Age,* November 8, 1999, p. 100.

Howard, Theresa. "A New Way of Measuring the Best, Worst Ads of 2000." *USA Today,* December 29, 2000, p. 08B.

Lippert, Barbara. "Shop Around." *Adweek* (eastern ed.), November 22, 1999, p. 36.

McCarthy, Michael. "Priceline's Campy Ads Polarize Audience." *USA Today,* March 13, 2000, p. 05B.

———. "Self-Parody Pays Off for Shatner; Priceline Actor's Deals Envied, but Not Those Songs." *USA Today,* June 21, 2000, p 01B.

Reidy, Chris. "Beam Us Up, Scotty, Kirk's Singing Again." *Boston Globe,* January 21, 2000, p. C09.

———. "Captain of This Domain; Shatner Pitches Priceline.com into Spotlight." *Boston Globe,* January 15, 2000, p. C1.

Warner, Judy. "Hill, Holliday Lands Priceline." *Adweek* (New England ed.), July 12, 1999, p. 8.

———. "Kirk Sings." *Adweek* (eastern ed.), January 17, 2000, p. 3.

Kevin Teague

The Procter & Gamble Company

One Procter & Gamble Plaza
Cincinnati, Ohio 45202
USA
Telephone: (513) 983-1100
Fax: (513) 983-9369
Web site: www.pg.com

THE BEST PART OF WAKIN' UP IS FOLGERS IN YOUR CUP CAMPAIGN

OVERVIEW

During the 1970s Procter & Gamble (P&G) helped establish its Folgers line as one of the two leading ground-coffee brands in the United States, along with General Foods' Maxwell House. By 1998 Folgers held the lead over Maxwell House in the $3.1 billion instant- and ground-coffee industry. For ground coffees, a $2.0 billion segment, Folgers held a 29.4 percent share in 1997, compared to 21.1 percent for Maxwell House. As the coffee market expanded, fueled by emerging competitors such as Starbucks, both companies faced new challenges.

To build its Folgers brand and drive business, in the 1960s Procter & Gamble turned to strong television advertising with a campaign created by the New York firm of Cunningham & Walsh that featured the advice-dispensing Mrs. Olson. In the mid-1980s Cunningham & Walsh introduced a new campaign built around the theme "Wakin' Up." By 1987 P&G had moved its Folgers account to N.W. Ayer. In 1998 Folgers continued to use the jingle "The Best Part of Wakin' Up Is Folgers in Your Cup" in its radio and television advertising, which was supplemented with print ads. Although P&G kept a close watch on company information, the fact that it spent $136.1 million on Folgers's advertising in a 20-month period during 1996 and 1997 suggested that the budget for the 1998 campaign was high.

The success of its "Wakin' Up" campaign led P&G to keep both the theme and its familiar jingle into the first years of the new millennium, despite changes in its advertising agencies. In 1999 the Folgers account was moved from Ayer to the agency's sister, D'Arcy Masius Benton & Bowles. That agency was closed in 2002 by its new owner, Publicis Groupe, and the Folgers account was shifted to Publicis shop Saatchi & Saatchi. The campaign was updated by Saatchi & Saatchi to introduce each Folgers line extension, including the launch of its Folgers Café Latte, an instant coffee designed to appeal to latte-drinking younger consumers and to take on upscale coffeeshops such as Starbucks.

HISTORICAL CONTEXT

In 1850, during the California gold rush, James A. Folger began selling coffee beans to miners. Eventually he established J.A. Folger & Company, which during the next century began to spread eastward throughout the United States. With the 1960 merger of its San Francisco and Kansas City divisions, each of which had operated almost as separate companies, Folgers began to take the Midwest by storm. By 1963, when it became a subsidiary of Procter & Gamble, it had annual sales of $160 million.

During the mid-1960s P&G battled with the Federal Trade Commission (FTC), which questioned its purchase of Folgers as a possible antitrust violation. P&G eventually obtained FTC approval of the purchase, but as early as 1962 it was clear that a few large companies were becoming dominant in the industry; in that year the top five coffee producers controlled a combined 62.9 percent share of the market.

Folgers began to expand into large Eastern markets, aided by the Mrs. Olson commercials, which ran from the mid-1960s to the mid-1980s. These spots featured an attractive elderly woman played by actress Virginia Christine, who appeared with a seemingly endless array of young couples. Although the commercials never developed much of a backstory for Mrs. Olson, her name and accent suggested she was Swedish American, and her role was that of an advisor to the almost interchangeable newlyweds under her tutelage. The solution to all problems, to judge from Mrs. Olson's advice at least, was Folgers.

The Mrs. Olson years saw numerous changes in the coffee industry, among them a sharp increase in prices brought on by poor Brazilian harvests and other world events during the mid-1970s and the rise of decaffeinated coffee during the late 1970s and early 1980s. Although Folgers responded to these changes, its market share slipped somewhat, from 27.3 percent in 1979 to 24.9 percent in 1983. By the mid-1980s P&G had adopted a new strategy with the "Wakin' Up" campaign.

TARGET MARKET

The switch to "Wakin' Up" arose from a realization among P&G executives that, despite the effectiveness of Mrs. Olson at one stage, that campaign was no longer effective in reaching younger consumers. The youth market, although it was the segment least inclined to drink coffee, also represented the best area for future sales. During the mid-1980s, as consumers increasingly moved away from coffee and toward soft drinks and other beverages, P&G made the switch to ad agency NW Ayer and developed the "Wakin' Up" theme, which centered on images of morning and newness. Eventually this evolved into the "Best Part of Wakin' Up" jingle, which started to get heavy exposure during the early 1990s.

At the same time a surprising thing happened in the marketplace. Suddenly, coffee, long considered the drink of one's parents or even grandparents, was perceived as a fashionable beverage. It had appeared for a time that coffee would go the way of its old companion, cigarettes—marginalized as an unhealthy, antisocial product—but by the early 1990s coffee had emerged as a new favorite among consumers under 35. Leading the trend were coffee bars, a phenomenon that first sprouted on the West Coast and then, like Folgers itself, spread eastward. In contrast to cigarettes, coffee now seemed decidedly healthy, part of an active lifestyle, and coffee bars appeared as a positive alternative to old-fashioned alcohol bars.

This new trend offered great promise for established brands like Folgers, but it also presented new challenges. It was true that the much-sought-after youth market was drinking coffee in great numbers, but they were buying it from retail chains such as Starbucks. In response to the trend, P&G in the mid-1990s stepped up promotion of Millstone, a specialty blend sold in stores. Millstone offered buyers the opportunity to make the kind of coffee they would normally buy at coffee bars, but to do so at home. As for Folgers, in 1998 it introduced its own whole-bean coffee line alongside a heavy advertising campaign orchestrated by NW Ayer.

COMPETITION

In 1990, before the coffee-bar phenomenon exploded, Bill Saporito in *Fortune* described the fierce competition between Folgers and Maxwell House in these terms: "Think of two large men competing to see who can keep his hand in a pot of scalding brew the longest. For more than ten years," Saporito wrote, the nation's two leading brands had been "locked in an often profitless struggle to dominate the market, warring with blasts of advertising, perpetual rounds of price cutting, and millions upon millions of cents-off coupons." Although Folgers held the lead among all brands, Saporito reported, General Foods had a larger overall share through its control of the Yuban and Sanka brands, along with Maxwell House.

Taster's Choice was a brand produced by the Nestlé Beverage Corporation that exceeded both Folgers and Maxwell House in the instant-coffee category, a segment accounting for nearly $600 million in annual sales by 1994. Since 1991 Taster's Choice had been running commercials that created more buzz than those of either of its large competitors. These spots revolved around the "Taster's Choice Couple" as their romance built over cups of Taster's Choice. Successive installments in this saga offered ever more intriguing details, "from their first meeting as neighbors to the surprise visit of a young man calling the woman 'Mom,' " as Leah Rickard wrote in *Advertising Age.* At the end of the next spot, which aired during the highly popular CBS program *Northern Exposure* on June 13, 1994, Rickard reported, "Viewers will find out the young man is [the woman's] son, Jeremy, who is home from college. Later that evening after meeting with her son, the woman calls her suitor on the phone to tell him how much Jeremy liked him. He asks, 'Is there anything else you forgot to tell me?' The spot ends with her answer: 'Volumes.' " Industry analyst

WE SUBSTITUTED INSTANT FOLGERS. . .

During the 1980s Folgers ran a television spot that, although it never attained the notoriety of the famous "Mrs. Olson" spots, nonetheless proved memorable. The commercial, for Folgers instant, showed diners at a fine restaurant being served coffee at the conclusion of the meal. As a voice-over informed viewers, the restaurant's patrons did not know it, but the staff had substituted Folgers instant for their regular brand. The climactic point of the commercial came when several of the restaurant customers, informed that they had been drinking Folgers instant, proclaimed it every bit as good as the restaurant's usual brew.

"If you're at all skeptical," wrote Caroline Knapp in *Boston Business Journal,* "you probably assumed the whole thing was a scam . . . Well, food snobs and cynics, guess again." In fact the responses were real, although the diners themselves had been carefully selected during five months of marketing research. It was an elaborate process, but one to which Folgers's parent company Procter & Gamble had become well accustomed in its many years as a leading marketer of consumer brands.

With the help of New York–based Tom Dale Market Research Company, P&G had carefully whittled down a large sample of survey respondents in the Boston area. The interview subjects had no idea that coffee was the focus of the study. According to P&G spokesman Don Tasone, in order to "throw respondents off, we ask[ed] them about everything—what airline they fly, how often they go to movies, that kind of thing." Eventually the group of respondents had been narrowed to just 50, who in exchange for their time were invited to dinner at one of Boston's most upscale restaurants, Maison Robert. On the appointed night, 36 of them showed up in a restaurant that—unbeknownst to them—had been equipped with a one-way mirror, microphones, and hidden cameras. After the dinner, the maitre d' went from guest to guest, serving them chocolate truffles and coffee and chatting with them. Ultimately he worked the conversation around to the subject of the coffee they were drinking, and from a series of discussions, the company pulled three particularly glowing appraisals for the commercial. Participants who signed interview release forms were given gratuities of $50 each.

Ronald Morrow told Rickard, "It's a very effective advertising campaign. The campaign is part of the reason why Taster's Choice has increased market share."

By 1997 all traditional coffee brands faced a new and fierce competitor: Starbucks, which began test-marketing specialty coffees in supermarkets. The retail chain, Alice Z. Cuneo reported in *Advertising Age,* "expects to surpass P&G's category-leading Folgers in [supermarket] sales. Indeed, Starbucks—which predicts it will have $1 billion in coffee revenue this fiscal year—already claims to be the leading brand, thanks to its retail outlets and alliances with United Airlines, Nordstrom, and other partners. But the new thrust is intended to tap the store shelves from which 80 percent of the nation's coffee is purchased, a venue now dominated by Folgers and Kraft's [General Foods' parent company] Maxwell House."

MARKETING STRATEGY

Folgers had much to fear from new competitors in the late 1990s, but it also had plenty of advantages on its side, thanks to its parent company. A survey conducted by *Shopper Report* in early 1997 revealed that "a very high number of P&G brands"—including Folgers—"popped up in response to our request to name the best value products on the market this year." These results suggested "that advertising, coupled with high performance, continues to play a major role in brand value perception." Folgers's advertising had long won acclaim. In 1998 advertising executive Harry Beckwith cited a 1980 spot for Folgers freeze-dried coffee as an example of what Walter J. Schruntek in *Foodservice Director* called "a study in superior brand positioning . . . and a lesson for today's 'brand-reinventors.' "

To an extent, Folgers's "Best Part of Wakin' Up" commercials had reinvented coffee advertising with the contributions of French-born medical anthropologist G. Clotaire Rapaille, whose work with autistic children in Europe had resulted in a concept he dubbed the "mental imprint." Applying this principle to Folgers marketing, Rapaille had urged that the company emphasize aroma over taste, because, in the words of the *Wall Street Journal*'s Jeffrey Ball, "aroma invokes feelings of home." Thus many variations of the "Best Part" jingle mentioned aroma, as in "the aroma wakes him up." An example was a spot in which a young soldier, home from the army, entered the family kitchen and put on a pot of Folgers. As Ball noted, "Its aroma wakes up his mother, who senses immediately that her son has returned."

To compete more directly with Starbucks and other premium lines, in late 1997 Folgers introduced Folgers Select Whole Bean coffee to test markets in Massachusetts and Wisconsin. This was accompanied by an N.W. Ayer campaign that offered a variation on the "Wakin' Up" theme: "Wake Up to a Whole New Folgers—Folgers New Whole Bean." The campaign continued to evolve each year. One 1998 spot used the singing talents of the a cappella group Rockapella for the Folgers jingle, while another capitalized on interest at the time in Gaelic dancing as popularized by the *Riverdance* Broadway show.

By the middle of 1999 Folgers was introducing its Whole Bean brand extension throughout the nation. A massive campaign involving print, broadcast, coupons, direct mail, shelf takers, and in-store sampling accompanied the launch. Folgers also moved into the new field of high-definition television (HDTV) with a spot titled "Crew Morning," first broadcast on July 15, 1999. In late 1999 P&G introduced another Folgers brand extension, instant Folgers Café Latte, which, like its whole-bean variety, also sought to compete with coffeeshops such as Starbucks and to target young, hip consumers who patronized coffee bars. Additionally, new spots for traditional ground Folgers were released on network television. While continuing to use the long-running "Best Part of Wakin' Up" theme, the commercials were more contemporary. One holiday spot featured a group of friends who were prepared to cut down a Christmas tree, only to change their minds when they saw how beautiful the tree looked in the snowy forest.

To celebrate the 150th birthday of Folgers, Procter & Gamble sponsored a competition in 2000 for which the prize was a chance to sing the familiar "Wakin' Up" jingle in a new television commercial. The winning group, Indiana-based funk hip-hop band Zambow, joined the ranks of other music stars who had performed the song in commercials since 1984, including Aretha Franklin, who starred in a Folgers commercial in 1988.

OUTCOME

Throughout the late 1990s P&G concentrated on gaining market share in the growing areas of specialty and whole-bean coffees. This it did in part through Millstone, to which it devoted increasing advertising dollars, and through Folgers Whole Bean. Folgers extended advertising to the Internet and continued to wage war with Maxwell House. The two brands still dominated the market, with one or the other assuming first place, only to be overtaken by its competitor.

Clearly changes were afoot in the world of coffee marketing, and Folgers—thanks to heavy advertising campaigns built around the "Wakin' Up" theme—continued to weather the changes and hold its place at or near the top end of the segment. In 1999 the brand's marketing was moved from N.W. Ayer to sister shop D'Arcy Masius Benton & Bowles (DMB&B). Another agency change happened in 2002 when DMB&B was closed by its new owner, Publicis Groupe. At that time the Folgers account was moved to Publicis shop Saatchi & Saatchi. Despite agency changes, shifts in the industry, and evolving consumer tastes, the "Wakin' Up" campaign followed the path of the long-running "Mrs. Olson" campaign and remained a constant. Twenty years after its 1985 introduction the campaign was still going strong, as evidenced by a visit to the Folgers website (www.folgers.com), where the promise "The best part of wakin' up is Folgers in your cup" was still prevalent in 2005.

FURTHER READING

Ball, Jeffrey. "But How Does It Make You Feel?" *Wall Street Journal,* May 3, 1999, p. B1.

Chura, Hillary. "D'Arcy Fallout: P&G Centers $3.8 Billion at Publicis and Grey Global; Havas Loses Out as McGrath Is Cut from Roster." *Advertising Age,* November 18, 2002.

Cuneo, Alice Z. "Starbucks Readies Supermarket Invasion." *Advertising Age,* June 9, 1997, p. 1.

Knapp, Caroline. "How Folgers Finds Its Tasters: Random but Precise." *Boston Business Journal,* March 17, 1986, p. 1.

Kramer, Louise. "Folgers' New Instant Shoots from the Hip; P&G's Coffee Brand Aims Ads Younger, Tests Café Latte Line." *Advertising Age,* November 15, 1999.

"Multi-Media Pitch behind Folgers Whole Bean Debut." *Brandweek,* April 19, 1999, p. 25.

Neff, Jack. "P&G Takes Millstone Coffee into Mail-Order: Test Moves Brand to High-Profit Arena Already Inhabited by Kraft." *Advertising Age,* March 31, 1997, p. 33.

"Pinpointing Items Strengthens Brands." *Shopper Report,* February 1, 1997.

Reynolds, Rhonda. "Ann M. Fudge: Brewing Success; The Newest Chief Executive at General Foods USA Is on a Mission: To Persuade Young Coffee Drinkers to Add the Maxwell House Brand to Their Grocery Lists." *Black Enterprise,* August 1994, pp. 68–70.

Rickard, Leah. "Taster's Choice Rolls Love Potion No. 9." *Advertising Age,* June 13, 1994, p. 70.

Saporito, Bill, and Mark D. Fefer. "Can Anyone Win the Coffee War? The Lesson from the Endless, Almost Comic, Battle between Philip Morris's Maxwell House and P&G's Folgers: Market Share Isn't Always What It's Cracked Up to Be." *Fortune,* May 21, 1990, p. 97.

Schruntek, Walter J. "Today's Brands." *Foodservice Director,* July 15, 1998, p. 42.

Thompson, Stephanie. "Whole Beans Percolating at Folgers." *Brandweek,* December 15, 1997, p. 8.

Turcsik, Richard. "Chock Full o' Nuts Seeks Retailer Tie-Ins." *Supermarket News,* June 3, 1996, p. S10.

Judson Knight
Rayna Bailey

CLEANER CLOSE CAMPAIGN

OVERVIEW

In 2003 the Procter & Gamble Company felt that its Daz laundry detergent, the number four brand in its category in the United Kingdom, had become outdated, thanks in no small part to a long-running advertising campaign perceived as artificial and old-fashioned. Procter & Gamble (P & G) thus charged advertising agency Leo Burnett's London office with the task of dramatically redefining the Daz brand in the United Kingdom and Ireland. With an eye toward attracting a younger generation of homemakers, Leo Burnett crafted "Cleaner Close," a series of commercials that was modeled after, and that openly spoofed, a television soap opera.

The TV spots began appearing in March 2003 during the top U.K. soap operas of the time, mimicking the conventions of the genre with a cast of recurring one-dimensional characters interconnected chiefly by sexual infidelity and intrigue. Each commercial, however, hinged on the cleaning capability of Daz. For instance, an adulterous husband hiding in a closet was, in one episode, literally sniffed out by his wife because of the "beautiful ... citrus ... unmistakable" smell of his underpants, the only article of clothing he was wearing. In another commercial a mother reprimanded her son's "grubby" taste in women after finding a dingy white bra in his room; she exhorted his girlfriend to use Daz, only to find out that the bra in question was not the girlfriend's. Storylines involving these and other characters evolved in characteristically absurd fashion over the campaign's subsequent years. Supporting print ads featured characters from the TV spots, and Daz packaging provided ministories related to the ongoing melodrama. Consumers could likewise visit the Daz website to view all of the "Cleaner Close" episodes and to fill in their knowledge about the series as well as the brand.

Conflicting data about Daz sales during this time obscured the campaign's practical impact on the laundry-detergent industry, but the campaign won two Gold Euro EFFIEs in 2004, suggesting that P & G had achieved its primary goal of reinvigorating the Daz image.

HISTORICAL CONTEXT

Cincinnati-based Procter & Gamble was founded by brothers-in-law William Procter and James Gamble in 1837 as a candle and soap company. Though the market for candles declined precipitously with the invention of the lightbulb, P & G did extremely well in the soap business, introducing the iconic Ivory brand in the 1870s while selling numerous other varieties of soap in smaller numbers. Branching out in the early twentieth century, P & G launched another American product that became a household name, Crisco vegetable shortening, and 1930 saw the company expand geographically, making its first entry into Europe with the acquisition of England's Thomas Hedley & Sons, the makers of the Fairy Soap brand. In the following decades P & G continued to expand its range of products and move into new product categories, while progressively establishing its global network of companies. Tide detergent, Prell shampoo, and Crest toothpaste were among P & G's top new products at midcentury. The company also acquired Charmin Paper Mills and entered the market of toilet tissue, napkin, and paper towel products. P & G continued to build a stable of products central to modern life—Downy fabric softener, Pampers diapers, Folgers coffee—and to expand at a rapid pace across product categories and national borders. In 1980 the company's annual sales topped $10 billion; by 1993 sales had reached the $30 billion mark. In 2002 P & G owned 12 brands that generated more than $1 billion apiece in annual revenue; with the 2005 acquisition of Gillette, P & G added five more billion-dollar brands to its portfolio.

A familiar brand in the United Kingdom since its midcentury debut, P & G's Daz, that country's number four brand of laundry detergent, had an outdated image by the start of the twenty-first century. This was at least partly the result of a decade-long advertising campaign that was seen as anachronistic and artificial. Known as the "Doorstep Challenge" campaign, the effort depicted lower-tier celebrities arriving, as if randomly, at the homes of ordinary housewives and then demonstrating the superior cleaning attributes of Daz. At the campaign's close in 2003, the *Sunday Times* noted that the doorstep challenge commercials had once been voted the most annoying spots on TV and asked sardonically, "If a week is a long time in politics, what's 10 years in commercials? Answer: about eight years too long." P & G acknowledged that younger consumers in particular were unmoved by the doorstep-challenge scenario, perceiving it as an overtly fake, old-fashioned marketing stunt. The company asked Daz's agency, the London office of Leo Burnett, to rethink the brand's advertising dramatically.

TARGET MARKET

Daz's traditional target in the United Kingdom was value-conscious homemakers, but the brand's image, as communicated with the "doorstep challenge" commercials, had alienated women at the younger end of this target group's age range. The "Cleaner Close" campaign was meant to correct this problem and endow the brand with an energized personality while still transmitting

Daz's traditionally down-to-earth image and attributes such as good value, whitening capability, and honesty. Because Leo Burnett believed that younger women had been alienated by Daz's image, it specifically targeted 25- to 34-year-old homemakers who used competing brands of detergent.

Leo Burnett determined that TV soap operas were extremely popular among this target group, and the agency accordingly created a series of mini soap-opera spoofs set in an area dubbed "Cleaner Close." Using the "soap" television format for commercials on behalf of actual soap was, in Leo Burnett's view, a fun and offbeat way of communicating the populist values of the Daz brand. The agency felt that the concept had the potential to energize the target group's interest in the product; the campaign thus had the feel of a brand relaunch.

IMITATING THE IMITATION

Although Daz's "Cleaner Close" series of mini–soap operas overtly poked fun at actual soap operas, its creators in the London office of advertising agency Leo Burnett apparently mastered the conventions they set out to parody. The first episode of "Cleaner Close," in which a mother confronted her son and his girlfriend in a local pub after finding a dingy white bra in his room, appeared in March 2003, and approximately two months later the popular BBC soap opera *EastEnders,* set in a working-class London suburb, recycled the commercial's plot almost exactly. In the actual soap opera the mother-son relationship was changed into a half-sibling relationship, and the bra in the Daz commercial became a pair of "knickers" in the *EastEnders* episode. But the half sister's encounter with her half brother took place in a pub, as in the commercial; the girlfriend with whom the half brother was sharing a drink responded to the half sister's comments by saying that the knickers were not hers, as in the commercial; and the actual owner of the knickers, present in the pub at the time of the confrontation, dropped her glass in response to the girlfriend's admission, as in the commercial.

COMPETITION

The United Kingdom's leading laundry detergent brand during this time was Persil, owned, in an uncommon corporate arrangement, by Lever Faberge (which took the Unilever name in late 2004) in the U.K. and Henkel in Germany. (Each company had, over the years, tried unsuccessfully to buy the brand outright from the other. To complicate matters further, the detergent formula branded as Persil in the U.K. was sold by Unilever as Omo, Skip, and Ala in other markets.) Despite these brand anomalies, Persil's U.K. roots ran particularly deep: launched in 1908, the brand became in 1955 the country's first laundry detergent to advertise on TV in the U.K., and it had maintained a consistent marketing profile in the years since, balancing an appeal to young people with more traditional messages relating to cleaning power and maternal caring. Persil shifted marketing tactics significantly in 2005, when it adopted a "Dirt Is Good" theme. The message that children should be encouraged to get dirty, and that Persil could handle the fallout of such a parental attitude, was uncommon in an industry whose advertising tended to focus on dirt as a problem to be solved.

P & G's own Ariel was the United Kingdom's second-best-selling laundry detergent. One of the brand's defining advertising campaigns focused, in the late 1970s, on the testing of Ariel versus a competitor's brand in the cleaning of two fishmongers' soiled aprons; the person judging whose apron was cleaner was their mother, an archetypal motherly perfectionist in the matter of laundry. This maternal-themed, product-attribute pitch gave way in the 1990s and the decade that followed to messages that reflected changing gender roles while acknowledging that women remained the primary target market for Persil. For instance, a 1997 TV spot showed another mother-son relationship, but this time the teenage son, returning from a rock festival with a soiled shirt, was told by his mother that in her day they did not wear clothes at such events. A 2002 spot was likewise irreverent, showing a man in his underwear who, while attempting to do his own laundry, was forced to ask his wife, "What load do I put it on?" The wife, who was sitting and talking to a female friend at that moment, said, as though making reference to her husband in his underwear, "Small load." The two women laughed, while the man remained oblivious to the comic substance of the exchange.

MARKETING STRATEGY

"Cleaner Close" referred, in a British usage uncommon in the United States, to a housing development that served as the mini–soap opera's setting. The British pronunciation of the word "close," used in this sense, rendered the soap opera's title a homonym of "cleaner clothes." As in a real soap opera, the "Cleaner Close" series of commercials featured recurring characters whose schemes and love affairs brought them into absurdly melodramatic conflict with one another. In "Cleaner

Close," however, each episode ultimately hinged on Daz detergent. The openly unrealistic nature of "Cleaner Close" and the soap genre as a whole was acknowledged not just in the tone and staging of the commercials but in the campaign tagline, which appeared at the end of each episode: "Daz: the soap you can believe in."

The first "Cleaner Close" spot, which appeared in March 2003, opened with a scene of a mother, Maureen McGrath, cleaning her young-adult son's room. Finding a bra under his bed, Maureen marched indignantly outdoors and through the streets with it and then entered a pub where her son was sharing a drink with his girlfriend. "If you're going to play around in my house, Sean McGrath," Maureen said, waving the bra in front of her son, "don't play around with a grubby girl." Maureen then proceeded to lecture her son's girlfriend about the cleaning properties of Daz, which would render the "grubby" bra as white as Maureen's own blouse. Maureen handed the bra to the young woman, who said, "But that's...not my bra." A barmaid in the corner dropped the glass she had been holding, and the camera focused on her nervous expression as she backed away into another room, implying that the bra was hers.

The series, as in an actual soap opera, relentlessly focused on infidelity, and Episode 3 introduced another set of characters whose sexual lives uncomfortably intersected. The voice-over informed viewers, "Pat's convinced she's finally caught [her husband] Mick with Jackie Strong," and showed Pat bursting into Jackie's bedroom and asking, "Where's Mick?" Pat then pulled a box of detergent from her shoulder bag and said, "Have you heard of new Limited Edition Daz Citrus Blast?" As Pat described the "beautiful... fresh... unmistakable citrus fragrance" of the product, it became clear that she smelled that very fragrance in Jackie's apartment. Pat then said, authoritatively, "Out you come, Mick," and Mick emerged from a closet wearing nothing but white underwear. "Brilliant white, aren't they, Jackie?" Pat asked. "Or hadn't you noticed?"

The series continued to evolve over the course of 2004, 2005, and 2006. Episode 8 showed Pat, having left Mick, at the altar with Steve Grey. Mick interrupted the wedding, however, to point out how much whiter his own shirt was than Steve's, effectively reestablishing himself as the right man for Pat. Maureen McGrath's death, meanwhile, yielded new plot developments in Episode 9. At the reading of her will, it emerged that she was a multimillionaire, but to her son Sean's frustration, she had left her fortune to "her beloved Daz," and the money had been converted into Daz coupons. Another plotline focused on Jackie Strong's husband, Vince, recently released from prison, and his relationships with former lover Pandora Packer, with his current (male) lover Rick Daniels, and with DC Strange, the police detective determined to catch him in a criminal act. When Vince was "blasted" by lemon and lime in Episode 13, consumers were directed to consult packages of Daz to determine who was responsible for the misdeed.

The commercials ran primarily during major U.K. soap operas—in keeping with the insights about the target market that dictated the creative strategy—and were supported by print ads that focused on the characters introduced in the TV spots. "Cleaner Close" story snippets appeared on Daz packaging, and the Daz website, www.dazwhite.co.uk/, was also integrated into the campaign. Consumers could visit the site to view the TV commercials, read biographies of the "Cleaner Close" characters, and find a variety of campaign- and product-related information.

OUTCOME

According to P & G, as a result of the "Cleaner Close" campaign Daz's market share increased for the first time since 1996, growing from a precampaign figure of 6.5 percent to 8.2 percent after the campaign's first year. *Marketing,* however, reported that Daz sales declined 15 percent between 2002 and 2004. Leo Burnett pointed to research indicating that "Cleaner Close" was the best-known laundry-detergent campaign of its time in the United Kingdom and Ireland and that the new advertising approach had effectively updated the Daz brand. The campaign won two Gold Euro EFFIE Awards in 2004, one in the "Household" category and one in the "Brand Revitalisation" category.

FURTHER READING

"Brandfame Ariel." *Marketing* (London), September 21, 2005.

"Brandfame Persil." *Marketing* (London), September 21, 2005.

Chandiramani, Ravi. "Daz Adds Web Offering to Support 'Dogs' Work." *Marketing* (London), October 4, 2001.

Costello, Rose. "Dated and Annoying Daz Moves into Soapland." *Sunday Times* (London), March 23, 2003.

"EastEnders Gives Daz Dirty Laundry Surprise Second Public Airing." *Campaign,* May 30, 2003.

Lee, Jeremy. "Leo Burnett Introduces Daz Soap Opera Theme." *Campaign,* March 21, 2003.

Mills, Dominic. "Ad of the Week." *Daily Telegraph* (London), April 8, 2003.

"P & G to Relaunch Daz Detergents." *Marketing* (London), March 31, 2005.

Solley, Sam. "Daz Uses 'Soap Opera' Cliffhanger to Back Citrus Debut." *Marketing* (London), June 12, 2003.

Sweney, Mark. "Daz Dishes the Dirt with a Sex-and-Soap Strategy." *Campaign,* March 28, 2003.

Mark Lane

GOT THE POWER CAMPAIGN

OVERVIEW

Procter & Gamble created the disposable-diaper market in 1961 when it introduced its Pampers brand. Despite being the first successful disposable diaper, by 1985 Pampers was falling behind competitor Kimberly-Clark's Huggies brand, which was introduced in 1968 but was not rolled out nationally until 1977. The Pampers brand continued to slip in the market, and by 2001 Pampers' market share had fallen to more than 14 percentage points behind Huggies. The relaunch of Pampers in 2002 with the introduction of Baby Stages of Development disposable products, which included a line of training pants for toddlers, helped narrow the gap between Pampers and Huggies. To help push Pampers further ahead, the company introduced a new disposable training pant for toddlers, called Feel 'n Learn Advanced Trainers, that was designed to help make toilet training easier.

To rebuild consumer awareness of the Pampers brand and to support the introduction of the Feel 'n Learn Advanced Trainers, the company contracted advertising agency Saatchi & Saatchi New York for the creation of a marketing campaign. The new campaign, themed "Got the Power," began in August 2004, at a time when many parents were trying to get their toddlers toilet trained before entering preschool. No specific amount for the campaign's cost was available, but estimates placed it at more than $20 million. "Got the Power" included television spots set to the 1990 hit song "The Power" by Snap. The campaign also employed print ads that appeared in national consumer magazines and "Potty Power" training kits that were sold through national retail outlets.

Within weeks of the campaign's launch it became clear that both it and the new training pants were a hit with parents of toddlers. According to a report in *Advertising Age,* Procter & Gamble's market share in training pants jumped to 30 percent in September, and by October 2004 Pampers had closed the gap, with Huggies falling behind by three points. The campaign won a Bronze EFFIE Award in 2005 for successfully increasing awareness of the Pampers brand and for encouraging consumers to try the Feel 'n Learn Advanced Trainers with their toddlers.

HISTORICAL CONTEXT

The Procter & Gamble Company was founded in 1837 by William Procter, a candle maker, and James Gamble, a soap maker. By 1859 the company was thriving; it reached $1 million in sales that year. During the Civil War it had a contract to supply candles and soap to the Union Army. Procter & Gamble introduced Ivory Soap to consumers in the 1880s. As electricity became more common, in the 1920s the company stopped making candles and focused its attention on a diverse variety of consumer products, including Crisco shortening, Prell shampoo, and Tide laundry detergent. In the 1950s chemical engineer Victor Mills, a Procter & Gamble employee, took an idea developed in 1946 by Marion Donovan—a mother tired of leaky cloth diapers and the rashes her babies often got from wearing wet diapers—and built on it. The idea, disposable diapers, evolved into Procter & Gamble's Pampers brand.

The new product was introduced to consumers in Peoria, Illinois, in 1961, followed by launches the next year in Sacramento, California, and two years later in Saint Louis, Missouri. Pampers diapers went on sale nationally in 1970. Busy parents appreciated the convenience of the disposable diapers, and as demand grew, Procter & Gamble kept improving on the product. Changes included adding tape fasteners, switching from creped tissue to fluff pulp for the diaper's base, and adding new products to the diaper line, such as Luvs, which had a better fit for older babies, and smaller diapers for newborns. The line continued its growth with the addition of diapers specifically designed for girls (extra padding in the back) and boys (extra padding in the front).

Although Pampers had created the disposable diaper and built a market for the product, by the 1990s the brand had fallen behind Kimberly-Clark's Huggies brand, which was launched in limited markets in 1968, some seven years after Pampers. Kimberly-Clark expanded the Huggies line to include Pull-Up disposable training pants for toddlers in 1989. Pampers did not introduce its own disposable training pant for toddlers until 1993, four years after competitor Huggies, leading Pampers' market share to drop further behind its competitor. Getting the jump on Huggies, in 2002 Pampers introduced its Toddlers Transition line of products, which included First Steps disposable absorbent pants, designed for pulling on while a child was standing, and Easy Ups for toddlers who were not fully potty trained but ready to pull their underwear on by themselves. The new products helped improve Pampers' standing in the market. In 2004 Feel 'n Learn Advanced Trainers, designed to assist in the potty-training process by letting the toddler feel wet and learn to stay dry by going to the bathroom, was added to the line. To promote the new product and increase brand awareness, the company launched its "Got the Power" campaign.

TARGET MARKET

"Got the Power" had two target audiences: the toddler who was going through toilet training, and the parents, typically mothers, who were helping with the process.

Based on research by potty-training coaches, parents thought that potty training a child would take about five months, when in fact the process usually took eight to ten months. It was also found that during that time the toddler would have accidents and parents could not always prevent them. Parents could not make their children learn to use the toilet or master the skill faster; rather, the toddler was best off if he or she was allowed to move through the process at his or her own pace, with encouragement and support from parents.

The marketing challenge was to reach both working and stay-at-home mothers 25 to 34 years old and to convince them that Pampers' new Feel 'n Learn Advanced Trainers could help them and their children in the toilet-training process. The campaign targeted mothers on an emotional and intellectual level. Emotionally, moms could see that the trainers enabled them to be cheerleaders for their toddlers' successes. Intellectually, moms could recognize that the trainers allowed them to empower and motivate their toddlers to go to the bathroom and use the toilet on their own. A side target market was day-care centers and preschools, which were believed to have a strong influence on parents and their decisions about child training.

PAMPERS BRAND INTRODUCES KANDOO PERSONAL HYGIENE LINE FOR TODDLERS

After giving kids the power to master the potty with its line of training pants, Pampers took toilet training to the next level by introducing a line of personal-hygiene products just for kids. The new products—flushable wipes and hand soap—were designed for kids aged two to seven. To ensure that the products helped youngsters learn bathroom basics, the Kandoo wipes and soap came in fun scents and easy-to-use, kid-friendly packages. The new product line was the first venture by Pampers' parent Procter & Gamble into toiletries for kids. Kandoo's launch was supported by a national marketing campaign with a cartoon spokescharacter called the Kandoo Frog and a new website, www.kidskandoo.com.

COMPETITION

In 1968 Kimberly-Clark Corp., best known for its paper products, such as bathroom tissue, paper towels, and feminine-hygiene products, introduced Huggies disposable diapers. The product put the 125-year-old paper company in direct competition with Procter & Gamble's Pampers. By 1985 Huggies had passed Pampers to become the number one disposable diaper in the United States. In 1989 Huggies introduced the first disposable training pants for toddlers, called Pull-Ups. From the mid-1990s and throughout that decade Huggies was the market leader in disposable diapers and training pants, pushing ahead of Pampers by more than 14 points in the third quarter of 2001. Kimberly-Clark also took on Johnson & Johnson, the leading maker of toiletries for babies, when it introduced its own 20-item baby-care product line under the Huggies brand in 2004. Prior to the new line, Huggies had only offered two baby-care products, a basic wash and disposable washcloths. The new toiletries included shampoo, lavender-and-chamomile and shea-butter lotions and baby washes, diaper-rash cream, and liquid baby powder. To promote the new product line the company employed direct mailings, promotions attached to packs of Huggies diapers and Pull-Ups training pants, and television spots and print ads produced by the ad agency Ogilvy & Mather New York.

F. Carlyle Harmon, who joined Johnson & Johnson in 1947 and soon thereafter became head of the company's fabric-research department, developed the nonwoven, highly absorbent material used to make disposable diapers. Johnson & Johnson produced Chux disposable diapers in 1948; eventually, however, the company discontinued the diaper and shifted its focus to what went on the baby's skin before the diaper. The company was best known for introducing Johnson's Toilet and Baby Powder in 1890. While the company never expanded into the disposable-diaper market like its competitors Kimberly-Clark and Procter & Gamble, it slowly evolved into the market leader for baby-care toiletries. In the 1920s it introduced baby cream. Johnson & Johnson's baby powder held 60 percent of the market share in 2004, and its baby shampoo held a 70 percent share. To promote its products and show consumers that the company understood the needs of new parents, Johnson & Johnson launched its "Having a Baby Changes Everything" campaign, developed by Lowe & Partners Worldwide New York. In 2004 the campaign, which included print ads and television spots, won a Gold EFFIE Award for strengthening the company's already strong brand image.

MARKETING STRATEGY

When Pampers introduced its training-pants product Feel 'n Learn Advanced Trainers in 2004, it charged its advertising agency, Saatchi & Saatchi New York, with the job of creating a marketing campaign that would achieve several goals. Besides the primary challenge of quickly building brand awareness for the new product, the campaign was also expected to increase market share for the new training pants and to support Pampers' overall product brand. Timing of the campaign's release was crucial. It had to reach parents whose toddlers were getting ready to start preschool and who faced the dreaded no-diaper rule enforced in most preschools (which meant that children who were not toilet trained could not be enrolled in classes). The "Got the Power" campaign began in August, toilet-training crunch time for millions of parents and toddlers.

The campaign, estimated to cost at least $20 million, was a multifaceted marketing blitz that included Pampers naming August as "national toddler 'We Can Do It' month." Saatchi & Saatchi created television spots with "The Power," an upbeat 1990 hit by the dance-music group Snap, playing in the background. The TV spots kicked off in August. Print ads ran in publications beginning in September to coincide with back-to-school activities. The ads featured cute toddlers at play in various situations, but with surprised looks on their faces. The copy read: "Uh-oh, here comes that gotta go feeling again."

Also supporting the campaign were "Potty Power" training kits, sold at national retailers such as Wal-Mart, Target, and Safeway, that included toilet-training tips and suggestions for parents, reward stickers for kids who made it to the toilet in time, and a CD of potty songs based on traditional children's songs such as "Twinkle, Twinkle Little Star." It also included the theme song from the television spots, "The Power." For parents who were anxious to motivate their toddlers, press-and-play sound chips were available that could be attached to the toilet lid. When the little one did his or her job, he or she could press the chip and hear words of praise from cartoon characters Dora the Explorer or Spider Man. The characters also embellished the training pants: Dora on girls' pants and Spider Man on boys'.

OUTCOME

Signs that the campaign resonated with its target market, parents of toddlers, included studies that indicated a 52 percent brand recall among consumers who were surveyed following the launch of "Got the Power." In addition, the campaign helped Feel 'n Learn Advanced Trainers capture 10 percent of the training-pants market, and within nine weeks of its launch the product shipped 31 percent of the planned one-year goal, far surpassing shipment expectations. In addition to consumer recognition, the campaign earned honors from the advertising industry. In 2005 "Got the Power" was awarded a Bronze EFFIE from the New York American Marketing Association for achieving the goal of increasing consumer awareness of the new training-pants product.

FURTHER READING

"As Birth Rate Rises, Sales Follow." *MMR,* November 15, 2004.

"Beyond Potty Training: Pampers Now Helps Kids Master the 'Bathroom Basics.' " *PR Newswire,* December 13, 2004.

Bittar, Christine. "Pampers Gives Trainees 'Power' to Hit Bull's-Eye." *Adweek,* March 7, 2005.

"Brands, Specialty Items Create the Excitement." *Chain Drug Review,* October 11, 2004.

"Disposable Diapers (A Brief History of Disposable Diapers)." *Newsweek,* December 22, 1997.

Ellison, Sarah. "Parents of Preschoolers Face No-Diaper Deadline." *Chicago Sun-Times,* August 20, 2004.

Kirk, Jim. "Procter & Gamble Launches Media Spending Consolidation." *Chicago Tribune,* July 15, 2004.

Neff, Jack. "Huggies Extends: K-C Pampers Tots with Toiletries." *Advertising Age,* December 13, 2004.

———. "P&G Diaper Demand Surges on Turnaround." *Advertising Age,* November 15, 2004.

———. "Procter & Gamble; 2004 Heavy Hitter." *Advertising Age,* December 13, 2004.

"A New Way to Help Potty Train? OK, Show Me, Smarty Pants." *PR Newswire,* August 4, 2004.

"Procter & Gamble Boost Sales and Profits in Current Financial Year." *Medical Textiles,* October 1, 2004.

Rayna Bailey

HABITS CAMPAIGN

OVERVIEW

According to a survey by *National Clothesline,* a trade publication for garment-care professionals, approximately two billion items were cleaned each year by dry cleaners. In an effort to offer a cleaning alternative for nonwashable items and garments, Procter & Gamble (P&G) created a new product and a new market category: home dry-cleaning kits. In 1997 the company began test-marketing the kits in a limited area, and in 1999 it introduced its home dry-cleaning kit, Dryel, nationwide.

To support Dryel's launch, help build the brand's newly created category, and quickly establish the product as the category leader, Procter & Gamble's ad agency, Leo Burnett USA, Chicago, created a marketing campaign with a budget estimated at more than $20 million and themed "Habits." The campaign embraced its challenge: changing consumers' long-standing habits by convincing them that they could turn their home clothes dryer into a dry cleaner without damaging their clothes or other dry-clean-only items. Included in the campaign were teaser ads that appeared in newspapers and on billboards beginning in late 1999. Ads included the tagline

"Suddenly, 'Dry Clean Only' Isn't." In 2000 television and radio spots began airing. Another part of the campaign was a $15 million field-marketing effort called the Dryel National Mall Tour, which hit the road in September 2000.

The "Habits" campaign produced mixed results. Consumers were willing to try Dryel, resulting in $45.7 million in sales in the first six months that it was on the market. The product also earned a *Good Housekeeping* "Good Buy" endorsement. The campaign was named one of *Promo* magazine's 50 Best Promoted Brands of 2000, and it won a 2000 Silver EFFIE Award. On the downside, the International Fabricare Institute, which represented dry cleaners, filed a complaint against Procter & Gamble with the Federal Trade Commission alleging the campaign made "false and misleading" claims about Dryel. Sales of Dryel failed to meet P&G's first-year goals of selling more than $100 million, and as sales began to slip further at the end of 2000, a new series of television spots and print ads was released.

HISTORICAL CONTEXT

Since the introduction of Dreft laundry detergent in 1933, which was followed by industry-leading Tide laundry detergent in 1946, Procter & Gamble had built a reputation for helping consumers take care of their washable clothes in their own homes. But there was an untapped niche in the home-laundry market: dry-clean-only garments. Those articles of clothing, such as wool sweaters, silk blouses, and satin dresses, among others, could not be cleaned in the home washing machine without risk of fading or shrinkage or colors running. To fill the gap in the home-laundry market and offer consumers the option of eliminating regular trips to the dry cleaners, Procter & Gamble developed the Dryel Fabric Care System. Not only was Dryel a new concept in the home care of clothing, but it also created a new product category.

P&G began test-marketing Dryel in 1997 in Columbus, Ohio. In July 1999 the product hit stores nationwide, and six months later the product had recorded $45.7 million in sales. The national launch was supported by a marketing campaign created by ad agency Leo Burnett USA, Chicago; it consisted of print ads and billboards with the tagline "Suddenly, 'Dry Clean Only' Isn't." Despite the early sales success, consumers were intimidated by the new alternative to dry cleaning and worried about tossing their expensive garments into the home clothes dryer. Further, competitors such as the Clorox Company quickly jumped into the market, releasing their own versions of home dry-cleaning kits. In 2000 Dryel's marketing effort was expanded to include television and radio spots. The campaign also included a shopping-mall tour to give consumers an opportunity to see Dryel at work firsthand. The expanded campaign was themed "Habits," based on its idea of changing consumers' deeply entrenched dry-cleaning habits.

TARGET MARKET

According to the information provided by Leo Burnett in the brief it submitted for the EFFIE Awards outlining the Dryel "Habits" campaign, more than any other demographic, professional career women were the most likely to buy and wear dry-clean-only clothes, from sweaters and slacks to dresses and suits. Additionally, because of their busy schedules working women were usually inconvenienced when forced to fit into their hectic days trips to the dry cleaners to drop off or pick up clothes. With working women accounting for some 60 percent of those using dry-cleaning services, Leo Burnett created the Dryel "Habits" campaign to appeal to women. More specifically, the campaign targeted working women aged 18 to 54. Leo Burnett further described the campaign's target consumer as "the clothes lover that's inconvenienced by the dry cleaner."

COMPETITION

In March 2000 the Clorox Company, best known for its bleach products, introduced its own home dry-cleaning kit, called FreshCare. To promote its new product and entry into the emerging home dry-cleaning category, Clorox turned to advertising agency DDB Worldwide, San Francisco. FreshCare's national marketing campaign, estimated to cost between $15 million and $20 million, included television and radio spots and print ads that ran in consumer magazine such as *People* and *Good Housekeeping*. Despite heavy promotion, in September 2001 Clorox reported that it was discontinuing FreshCare. According to *Advertising Age*, a Clorox spokeswoman stated that one reason for the decision was that the home dry-cleaning category "wasn't as big as projected." The company reported that FreshCare registered sales of $11.6 million for the 52 weeks ending July 15, 2001, compared to Dryel's $50.6 million in sales during the same period.

Also jumping into the home dry-cleaning market was the Dial Corporation (producer of, among other things, Dial and Coast soaps) with its 1999 purchase of the Custom Cleaner home dry-cleaning section of Creative Products Resource, Inc., a company based in Fairfield, New Jersey. Creative Products had introduced Custom Cleaner in 1996 as its main product offering. Partnered with Dial in the purchase was the German consumer-products company Henkel. At the time that Dial/Henkel acquired Custom Cleaner, the product's annual sales amounted to $10 million. In

PROCTER & GAMBLE'S LAUNDRY SPA

Despite being known for its home laundering products, including Tide and Cheer detergents, Febreze fabric freshener, and Dryel home dry-cleaning kits, in 2001 Procter & Gamble began test-marketing a home-laundry valet service dubbed the "Laundry Spa." The service's actual name, Juvian, was being offered in suburbs in and around Atlanta, Georgia, and included picking up dirty laundry at the customer's home, cleaning the items, and returning them to the customer. The service cost $17 per bag, which was the equivalent of two loads of dirty laundry. Extras included "aromatherapy" treatments for $5 per bag and "hue and tone preservation," also $5 per bag. The service was not limited to dirty clothes. Customers could also send their shoes in for repairs and shining or draperies, bedding, and rugs for cleaning.

2001 Dial/Henkel reported that sales of Custom Cleaner had reached just $12 million for the 52 weeks ending July 15 and that the company was discontinuing the dry-cleaning kits.

With both Clorox's FreshCare and Dial/Henkel's Custom Cleaner home dry-cleaning kits off the market, the only competition remaining for Procter & Gamble's Dryel brand was Dry Cleaner's Secret, which was introduced by Dry, Inc., of Portland, Oregon, in 2000. The start-up company was headed by Scott Heim, a former executive for Kimberly-Clark Corp. and DowBrands. Supporting the new product's launch were television and radio spots created by ad agency Bates Southwest of Houston, Texas. The campaign targeted consumers in 17 U.S. markets and touted the benefits of the product compared to the competition, such as a lower cleaning cost per garment and not requiring that clothes be placed in a bag before tossing them into the dryer. Although Dry Cleaner's Secret reported sales of just $2.5 million in the 52 weeks ending July 15, 2001, Dry, Inc. was not ready to throw in the towel. The company anticipated increased growth in its sales with the exit of FreshCare and Custom Cleaner from the market.

MARKETING STRATEGY

When Leo Burnett began planning its marketing campaign for Procter & Gamble's new product, Dryel home dry-cleaning kits, the challenges included changing the long-standing habits of consumers specific to how they cared for their dry-clean-only clothing. The campaign also had to help consumers overcome their reluctance to try a unique new product, and it had to respond to their skepticism about the product's effectiveness. Additionally, the campaign's goals were to help create a new product category and assure that Dryel would establish itself as the brand of choice, because it was assumed that competitors in the category would soon follow Dryel's lead.

With those goals and challenges in mind, Leo Burnett developed the "Habits" campaign. It included teaser ads prior to the product's launch as well as traditional advertising methods, including television and radio spots and print ads in consumer magazines and newspapers. No specific budget was available, but the agency noted that it was more than $20 million. Teaser ads appeared in print and outdoor executions such as on billboards and included the tagline "Suddenly, 'Dry Clean Only' Isn't." Another ad showed a "Dry Clean Only" label with a slash mark through it. Television spots that followed explained to consumers that they could clean dry-clean-only clothes at home with Dryel rather than taking them to a dry cleaner. The first TV spot in the campaign was released in 2000 and featured a woman frustrated when she arrived at her dry cleaner after hours and so was unable to pick up her clothes. A follow-up spot showed a woman who tried to wash her sweater rather than take it to the dry cleaner. The result was a sweater shrunken to doll size. In early 2001 a new series of print ads was introduced that portrayed women dressed in professional business attire doing atypical jobs, such chopping down trees. Another ad showed a woman wearing an evening gown while milking a cow.

Based on research indicating that 85 percent of all dry-clean-only clothing was purchased at shopping malls, the campaign included a tour of malls to demonstrate the product directly to consumers and give them hands-on experience with Dryel. The field-marketing effort, called the Dryel National Mall Tour, began at the Mall of America in Minneapolis, Minnesota, in September 2000. The tour was planned to continue through March 2001 and appear at 275 malls in the United States and Canada. Included were demonstrations that featured working clothes dryers and Procter & Gamble representatives showing consumers how Dryel worked to clean and freshen clothes. Also appearing were guest speakers helping to promote the product, including actress Alison Cuffe from the daytime soap opera *General Hospital* and Cathy Turner, an Olympic-gold-medal-winning speed skater.

OUTCOME

Although Procter & Gamble's Dryel home dry-cleaning kits were met with mixed reviews from consumers and industry watchdogs, its marketing efforts were well received. Within one year of the start of the campaign, Dryel sales had reached $115 million, and *Good Housekeeping* magazine named Dryel one of seven new products to win its "Good Buy" award in 2000. The award was based on the product's ingenuity, value, and exceptional performance. On the flip side of the consumer coin, following the introduction of the new product CBS television consumer reporter Herb Weisbaum stated during a *CBS This Morning* broadcast that, while Dryel had its uses in "limited circumstances," he would not give up his dry cleaner. In addition the International Fabricare Institute (IFI), a dry-cleaning trade organization based in Silver Spring, Maryland, ran Dryel through a series of scientific tests at the request of Procter & Gamble and found that the product came up short of its advertised promises. In December 1999, based on its test results and Dryel's teaser advertising, the IFI filed complaints with the Federal Trade Commission and the National Advertising Council of Better Business Bureaus against Procter & Gamble, alleging that the Dryel campaign made "false and misleading" claims about the product.

The campaign received accolades from *Promo* magazine, which listed Dryel as one of its 50 Best-Promoted Brands in 2000. As further recognition, in 2001 the "Habits" campaign earned a Silver EFFIE Award (in the New Product or Service Introductions category) for successfully educating consumers about the product and helping change entrenched habits about how to clean dry-clean-only clothes. Procter & Gamble reported that the Mall Tour effort reached more than 1.5 million consumers in malls. An additional five million consumers requested product information.

FURTHER READING

Bidlake, Suzanne. "P&G, Unilever Aim to Take Consumers to the Cleaners; Detergent Makers Tackle Tasks of Door-to-Door Pickups and Deliveries." *Advertising Age,* February 12, 2001.

"CBS's 'This Morning' Strips away Misinformation about Dryel, According to IFI." *PR Newswire,* September 2, 1999.

"Event Marketing; Clean Sweeps: P&G Puts Dryel through Its Paces for Mall Visitors." *Promo,* March 1, 2000.

Gilbertson, Dawn. "Scottsdale, Ariz-Based Dial Corp. Acquires Home Dry-Cleaning Product." *Knight Ridder/Tribune Business News,* July 21, 1999.

"IFI Pushes for FTC Action against P&G's Dryel." *American Drycleaner,* December 1, 1999.

Larkin, Patrick. "Dial Soap Is among Top U.S. Brands." *Cincinnati Post,* February 28, 2000.

Neff, Jack. "Clorox Adds an Entry in Home Dry-Cleaning; March FreshCare Intro Planned; TV, Radio Spots to Break April 17." *Advertising Age,* January 3, 2000.

———. "Clorox, Dial Exit Dry Cleaning Biz; At-Home Kits Are Discontinued." *Advertising Age,* September 10, 2001.

———. "Dryel; Noel Geoffrey." *Advertising Age,* June 26, 2000.

———. "P&G Shifts Strategy for Dryel; Dry-Cleaning Kits Fail to Meet Company's Ambitious Sales Goals." *Advertising Age,* January 24, 2000.

———. "Upstart Dry Clean Brand Targets Dryel, FreshCare; Dry's Product Makes No Secret of Superiority over Rival Lines." *Advertising Age,* July 17, 2000.

"P&G Launches National Marketing Campaign, Wins 'Good Buy' Award." *Nonwovens Industry,* January 1, 2000.

"P&G's Dryel Has Competitor." *Cincinnati Post,* February 22, 2000.

"Promo's 50 Best Promoted Brands." *Promo,* October 1, 2000.

Rayna Bailey

INGENIOUS PROTECTION FOR INGENIOUS WOMEN CAMPAIGN

OVERVIEW

The Procter & Gamble Company (P&G) acquired the Tampax tampon brand in 1997 when it purchased the parent company, Tambrands Inc., of White Plains, New York, in a deal valued at nearly $2 billion. Tampax tampons had been sold to women since the mid-1930s, and at the time of the acquisition by P&G they were the number one brand in the tampon segment of the U.S. market for feminine hygiene products. But by 2002 the Tampax brand was losing market share to other brands, including its closest competitor, Gentle Glide tampons, made by Playtex Products. In an effort to reverse the decline, P&G introduced Tampax Pearl tampons. The new product featured a plastic rather than a cardboard applicator and thus was in direct competition with Playtex's Gentle Glide tampon, the number one selling plastic applicator tampon.

To support the introduction of the Tampax Pearl tampon, an aggressive marketing campaign was created by the brand's agency, Leo Burnett USA. The campaign, with an estimated budget of between $30 and $40 million, included television spots and print ads that used the tagline "Are you a Pearl girl?" It also raised the ire of Playtex, which quickly filed two lawsuits against P&G. One lawsuit, based on the design of the Tampax Pearl plastic applicator, cited patent infringement. The second lawsuit alleged false advertising for P&G's claims that the "Pearl girl" product was superior to Playtex's Gentle Glide tampon. In 2003, ruling that there were enough differences between the Tampax Pearl and the Gentle

Glide plastic applicators that no patent infringement had occurred, a court dismissed the first lawsuit. P&G lost the battle in the false advertising lawsuit, however, and was ordered to pay $2.96 million in damages to Playtex and to cancel all Tampax Pearl advertising that claimed it was a better product than the Gentle Glide tampon. Complying with the ruling, the "Pearl girl" ads were pulled, and Leo Burnett revamped the campaign. In 2004 the campaign was relaunched as "Ingenious Protection for Ingenious Women."

The new campaign appeared to have success in achieving its goals of increasing awareness of the new Tampax brand product and of expanding the sales of Tampax Pearl tampons. In addition, the campaign was honored with a 2005 Silver EFFIE, and Tampax Pearl was named one of *Advertising Age*'s 2005 Marketing 50 for product creativity and marketing innovation.

HISTORICAL CONTEXT

P&G entered the tampon market in 1975 with the introduction of its Rely brand. The company recalled Rely tampons and discontinued their production in 1980, however, after use of the product was linked to toxic-shock syndrome, a sometimes fatal disease that usually affected women using tampons. P&G reentered the tampon market in 1997 when the company acquired Tambrands Inc. and its Tampax brand. At the time of the acquisition, Tampax had been sold to consumers for more than 60 years and was the number one tampon brand in the United States. Following completion of the $1.85 billion purchase, P&G assigned the Tampax account to the Chicago advertising agency Leo Burnett. By 2002, although Tampax was still the brand leader, its market share had dropped from 45 to 40 percent of the overall tampon segment. In an effort to reverse the brand's declining sales, P&G introduced Tampax Pearl, the first Tampax product to use a plastic applicator rather than the standard cardboard, in 2002. A marketing campaign, estimated to cost between $30 and $40 million, supported the new product. Created by Leo Burnett, the campaign used the tagline "Are you a Pearl girl?" and included television spots and print ads.

Before Tampax Pearl tampons ever reached retail stores, however, rival Playtex filed a lawsuit against P&G, alleging that the new tampon's design infringed on the patent Playtex held for the plastic applicator used in Gentle Glide tampons. Despite the lawsuit, in September 2002 P&G proceeded with the introduction of Tampax Pearl tampons and the supporting advertising campaign. Soon after the new campaign was launched Playtex was back in court, claiming that the P&G Tampax Pearl ads made false claims about Playtex's Gentle Glide tampons.

In 2003 the court dismissed Playtex's claim of patent infringement against P&G, ruling that the Tampax Pearl did not violate the patent because its plastic applicator had rounded surfaces as opposed to the flat surfaces of the Playtex plastic applicator. In the same year, however, a judge ruled against P&G in the suit alleging that its advertising made false claims about rival Playtex and its Gentle Glide tampons. P&G was ordered to pay Playtex $2.96 million in damages and to withdraw its advertising campaign for Tampax Pearl. A P&G statement published in *USA Today* said that the company had begun to comply with the judge's orders to stop making advertising claims that Tampax Pearl offered "superior wearing comfort and superior protection versus Playtex Gentle Glide." In response to the court's orders, Leo Burnett revised its campaign for Tampax Pearl tampons, and in 2004 the "Ingenious Protection for Ingenious Women" campaign was launched.

TARGET MARKET

The average woman experienced 12 to 13 monthly periods annually for 35 to 40 years, or until she reached the beginning of menopause in her early 50s. This created a large and ongoing market for feminine hygiene products. According to the industry, the market was also divided by three specific categories of use: age, personal needs, and financial resources. Research by P&G indicated that women made up 80 percent of the customers for the company's range of products. Further, young women in their 20s and 30s were the largest market for tampons. Thus, when P&G added Pearl tampons to its Tampax line, the product's design and packaging were created with the 20- to 30-something age group in mind. A strand of pearls was pictured on the box, and a window in the front allowed consumers to see the product inside. Tampax Pearl also targeted girls in their teens, those just entering the feminine hygiene market. Efforts included wrapping individual tampons in noncrinkle plastic so that teenage girls could discreetly use the product in public bathrooms. Also targeted were women with the resources to buy higher-end feminine hygiene products with a higher price point, which included Tampax Pearl tampons. The new tampon was about 30 percent more expensive than other brands, including traditional Tampax with cardboard applicators.

COMPETITION

Playtex Products, Inc., based in Westport, Connecticut, had introduced the first tampon with a plastic applicator, the Gentle Glide tampon, in 1968. In 2001 Playtex's Gentle Glide brand was the leading seller in the plastic applicator tampon segment. The brand was also entrenched in the number two spot in the overall tampon

PROCTER & GAMBLE USES INTERNET TO EDUCATE WOMEN ABOUT FEMININE HYGIENE

The Procter & Gamble Company used two websites to educate women about the firm's feminine hygiene products and how to choose the correct products for their individual needs. The Tampax.com site included a section on frequently asked questions about tampon use. Through an "Ask Iris" link women were able to address personal questions about menstruation, reproduction, and health to Iris Prager, the North American education manager for Tampax. Another link, "Help Me Choose," helped women decide which feminine hygiene products were best for them. The BeingGirl.com website targeted younger girls and offered lifestyle advice for teens (for example, on the importance of cliques and on inappropriate crushes), health advice (on preparing for a first visit to a gynecologist), and other information, as well as articles on popular celebrities and an "Ask Iris" link.

segment and was winning market share from the number one brand, P&G's Tampax, which had been the tampon segment leader for years. At the end of 2001 the market share for Playtex's Gentle Glide tampons had climbed to 21.7 percent. The situation changed in 2002, however, when P&G added a tampon with a plastic applicator to its Tampax line. This new product, Tampax Pearl, went head to head with the Playtex Gentle Glide tampon. Following the introduction of the Tampax Pearl, sales of Playtex's Gentle Glide tampons dropped 7.4 percent, while the sales of the Tampax brand grew 9.4 percent. In response to the new product and its marketing, Playtex filed two lawsuits against P&G, one for patent infringement and the other for false advertising. In 2003 Playtex's patent infringement lawsuit against P&G was dismissed, but its false advertising claim was upheld in court. Despite winning a battle, Playtex appeared to be losing the war. Playtex reported that its feminine care segment posted a drop in net sales to $48.8 million in the first quarter of 2003, compared to $61.1 million for the same period during the previous year. According to an article in *Nonwovens Industry,* "Playtex executives attributed the income decline, in part, to the extensive spending in the tampon category, in response to the launch of Procter & Gamble's Tampax Pearl plastic applicator tampon." At the end of 2003, however, the company reported that its tampon segment had stabilized, with 26 percent of the market share, and a new product—Beyond tampons—was set to be introduced in January 2004.

Although Kotex, made by the Kimberly-Clark Corp. of Irving, Texas, was the number one feminine care brand in the United States, its Security tampons were a distant third in the tampon segment, with a market share of 12.7 percent in 2001. To reach younger women and to update its brand image, the company launched its "Red Dot" advertising campaign in 2000. Created by Ogilvy & Mather Chicago, the campaign took an approach to advertising feminine care products that was more honest than usual, with the red dot symbolizing women's periods. It was described in *PR Newswire* as taking a "frank, you-go-girl tone." Kotex was the only brand that offered products in all three feminine care sectors—sanitary pads, pantiliners, and tampons—and the campaign emphasized that the products and packaging made women feel special. In 2003, responding to the changing tastes of women, Kotex introduced an improved line of products and packaging, including updated packaging for its Security tampons that was designed specifically to appeal to younger women. At the end of 2003, the sales of Security tampons, while still in the number three spot, had inched up 2.8 percent, to $74.2 million, compared to sales during the previous year. Kotex's "Red Dot" campaign evolved in 2004 to give a better portrait of the world of young women, encompassing all major aspects of their lives and not just the times of their monthly periods.

MARKETING STRATEGY

When P&G introduced its new Tampax product, Pearl tampons, in 2002, the brand's agency, Leo Burnett USA, created an aggressive marketing campaign using the tagline "Are you a Pearl girl?" to support the product. In 2004, responding to a 2003 court order requiring P&G to pull all of its Tampax Pearl advertising that included claims of the product's superiority to competitor Playtex's Gentle Glide tampon, Leo Burnett revamped the campaign. The new campaign, "Ingenious Protection for Ingenious Women," included television spots and print ads. Similar to the original campaign, the new ads had a fashion look and were designed to resonate with contemporary women. Using humor, the ads also helped remove the stigma often associated with women's monthly periods, while encouraging them to be proud of their intelligence and ingenuity.

The television spots were aired on cable channels, including MTV, and on national networks during programming that typically attracted a female audience, such as *Law and Order.* In one spot, titled *Leak,* a happy looking couple were shown drifting on a lake in a small boat. When the boat suddenly began to leak, the man panicked, uncertain about what to do. His ingenious female companion saved the day when she pulled a Tampax Pearl tampon out of her day pack and quickly plugged the leak. The spot used the new tagline, "The one. The only." In another spot, "Embarrassment," an attractive woman dressed in white caused the heads of passengers in a passing bus to turn as she walked down the street. As she continued to walk, a man sitting in a café turned to look at her. The attention was not because she was beautiful but because, as she noticed when she checked herself in a mirror, the hem of her skirt was caught in her panties. The tagline was "Embarrassment happens. Leaks shouldn't."

Print ads appeared in national publications that were read by young women, including *Seventeen.* The ads were heavily shaded in blue, the color of the Tampax Pearl box. One full-page ad, for example, featured a woman skin diving in the depths of a deep blue ocean while a shark swam toward her. The text read, "A leak can attract unwanted attention." In the bottom right-hand corner of the page was a picture of a Tampax Pearl box with the tagline "The one. The only." Another ad pictured a young woman, dressed in blue slacks and sweater and wearing a pearl bracelet and ring, cuddling a pudgy puppy in her lap. The puppy looked guilty, and the text read, "Certain leaks can be forgiven." Again, the Tampax Pearl box appeared at the bottom of the ad, with the tagline "The one. The only."

OUTCOME

The "Ingenious Protection for Ingenious Women" campaign achieved or surpassed its goals of building buzz about P&G's Tampax Pearl tampons and of increasing product share within the feminine hygiene market. The company reported that following the launch of the campaign in 2004, shipments of Tampax Pearl tampons to retailers increased 74 percent and that market share increased six points over the same period in 2003. The campaign won a Silver EFFIE in 2005 for its unique advertising that connected with young women. The TV spot portraying a woman with the hem of her skirt caught in her underwear was included on *Advertising Age*'s Top 20 list for likability. In addition, *Advertising Age* recognized Tampax Pearl as one of its 2005 Marketing 50, cited for attracting consumer interest in the product through the use of innovative marketing, creative product design, and other outreach efforts.

FURTHER READING

Alexander, Antoinette. "Kotex Gets Flourishing Makeover." *Drug Store News,* June 6, 2005.

Casabona, Liza. "Forgotten Frontiers? More Retail Attention May Boost Feminine Hygiene." *Supermarket News,* February 2, 2004.

Ellison, Sarah. "P&G Chief's Turnaround Recipe: Find Out What Women Want." *Wall Street Journal,* June 1, 2005.

"Innovation May Shake Up Tampon Segment." *Chain Drug Review,* June 10, 2002.

"Judge Bars P&G from Claiming Tampon Superiority." *USA Today,* May 30, 2003.

"Judge Rules in Favour of Procter & Gamble in Playtex Tampon Suit." *Medical Textiles,* January 1, 2004.

Kane, Courtney. "Marketing a New Feminine Hygiene Product." *New York Times,* May 11, 2004.

"Kimberly-Clark Introduces New, Improved Kotex Products." *PR Newswire,* July 2, 2003.

"Kotex Brand Launches Evolution of Iconic 'Red Dot' Campaign." *PR Newswire,* October 20, 2004.

"Late News: Playtex Files Lawsuit as P&G Launches Pearl." *Advertising Age,* July 29, 2002.

Neff, Jack. "P&G Finds Aggression Has a Price: More Ad Challenges Than Usual." *Advertising Age,* June 2, 2003.

"Playtex Reports Sales Drop." *Nonwovens Industry,* June 1, 2003.

Rivkin, Jill. "Finding the Feminine Approach: Changing Demographics and Baby Boomers Keep the Feminine Hygiene Category Looking for the Right Strategy." *Private Label Buyer,* August 1, 2005.

"Targeted Marketing Now a Must." *Chain Drug Review,* June 7, 2004.

"Tyson's 'Power' Wins Top Spot." *Advertising Age,* November 8, 2004.

Rayna Bailey

SHARING AND CONNECTING CAMPAIGN

OVERVIEW

In 1995, after two years of testing, the Procter & Gamble Company of Cincinnati, Ohio, was ready to introduce a new product: Febreze, which eliminated odors in fabrics. Not only was Febreze a new product, it was also the pioneer brand of an entirely new category for Procter & Gamble and the marketplace in general. Because of that the launch campaign was more difficult than most. In addition, there was a natural skepticism on the part of consumers that Febreze would bear out the advertising claims. Procter & Gamble's advertising agency, Grey Advertising of New York City, created a campaign whose two primary objectives were to educate consumers about the new product and to drive purchases of it.

The campaign, which began in July 1998, was titled "Sharing and Connecting." It cost approximately $65 million and included television spots and print ads.

Each of the initial spots was 45 seconds long and consisted of a montage of people discussing Febreze's uses. The product's identity was reinforced with the tagline "Febreze cleans bad smells out of fabrics. For good."

The "Sharing and Connecting" campaign was successful all around. Not only did sales of Febreze exceed Procter & Gamble's expectations, but Febreze was also one of the top 10 best-selling new consumer packaged goods of 1998, even though it hit stores in midyear. The campaign ended in 1999 and won a 2000 Silver EFFIE Award in the New Product category.

HISTORICAL CONTEXT

Founded in 1837 by two Cincinnati businessmen, candle maker William Procter and soap maker James Gamble, the Procter & Gamble Company by the end of the twentieth century had become a global leader in home-cleaning products. Nevertheless, many (as much as 75 percent) of the household surfaces that needed regular cleaning were fabrics, and most of the dry-cleaning of these fabrics was done to remove odors, which odor-fighting products had at best only been able to mask.

In the mid-1990s Procter & Gamble began testing a product that the company hoped would capture an as-yet-unidentified market. In fact the new product, which was named Febreze, created a whole new category for the company: fabric refresher. Quoted in a 1998 Proctor & Gamble press release published by *PR Newswire* was R. Kerry Clark, president of North American laundry and cleaning products at Procter & Gamble: "With Febreze, we're expanding beyond our core franchise of laundry and cleaning products. Now we can offer a broader range of home fabric and textile care... [Consumers] will be able to permanently eliminate odors from a wide variety of fabrics, including upholstery, carpet, and clothing." It was not the first time that Procter & Gamble had broken new ground, but in an age when consumers had become savvy and hence skeptical, the introduction of a new product required careful preparation. Thus, Febreze had gone through testing and test-marketing well in advance of its national release.

TARGET MARKET

Initially Grey Advertising and Procter & Gamble had pinpointed the primary target market for Febreze as specifically as possible. In the Brief of Effectiveness that the agency submitted in consideration for an EFFIE Award, this target consumer was described as a woman between the ages of 18 and 49 and who had children. Furthermore, because Febreze was expected to be an ideal low-cost alternative to dry-cleaning, the average income of individuals in this group was less than $30,000 per year. Test-marketing and in-store sampling broadened the target market. Also, brand and advertising commentators saw the product as appealing to young professionals whose after-work club hopping would of course make their clothing smoky.

THE SCIENCE BEHIND FEBREZE

The basic hows and whys of Febreze were revealed by Rachel Ross in an October 2003 *Toronto Star* article. Breaking the science down into simple terms, she discussed the main active ingredient in Febreze, cyclodextrins. Cyclodextrin molecules, which contained a minimum of six dextrose units, were ring-shaped. As the water from the spray solution evaporated, cyclodextrin became molecular crystals, and the odor molecules bound to the inside of the ring, which neutralized the smell. There were various types of cyclodextrins, Ross further explained, some of which were allowed in food, while others were "used in a wide variety of products, including AIDS drugs and lipsticks."

COMPETITION

Almost from the beginning competing companies jumped into the fray, bringing out their own products within a year of Febreze's introduction. In fact, before the "Sharing and Connecting" campaign had ended, companies such as Reckitt & Colman, Clorox, and Bioshield Technologies were preparing to launch their own brands: Resolve Fabric Freshener, Fresh Care, and OdorFree, respectively. Meanwhile Unilever and S.C. Johnson were also readying their own fabric-refresher products. Christine Bittar noted in a March 1999 *Brandweek* article, "Priced in the same range as Febreze, the new products are expected to perform similarly by 'lifting' odors out of fabrics rather than merely masking odors." Earlier that year the car-care products company Turtle Wax had introduced Odor-X, an odor eliminator and deodorizer for the upholstery and carpets in cars.

In the second half of 1999 Reckitt & Colman released an approximately $15 million advertising campaign for Resolve, while Clorox spent about $25 million on advertising for Fresh Care in early 2000. Bioshield Technologies began with a regional campaign to promote OdorFree in Texas in April 1999 but had enlarged the campaign to a national one by the end of the year. The cost of the OdorFree campaign was approximately $20 million.

MARKETING STRATEGY

For two years prior to its national launch in 1998, Febreze went through a series of marketing trials in Phoenix, Salt Lake City, and Boise, Idaho. These early trials did not go as well as expected, forcing Procter & Gamble and Grey Advertising to refocus the marketing of the product. Early on the product was described as an odor neutralizer, which may have caused some consumers to think that it merely masked odors. Also, during the early testing it was marketed solely as a way of removing cigarette-smoke odors. After conducting extensive interviews with people who liked Febreze but were putting it to different uses, Grey Advertising devised a series of 45-second television spots in which satisfied consumers discussed Febreze and the various ways they used it. Later in the campaign 30-second spots were employed. Procter & Gamble also redesigned the packaging of Febreze. By the time of the national release in July 1998 more than half a million people were familiar with the product.

After the launch Procter & Gamble also used in-store sampling to broaden consumer awareness of Febreze. Richard Turcsik, in a 1998 article published in the *Brand Marketing Supplement* to *Supermarket News,* quoted Drake Stimson, who at the time was Febreze brand manager. "What we have learned with these 'new-to-the-world' categories," Stimson said, "is that there are two critical objectives: educating consumers and creating an in-store presence." Stimson also mentioned that Febreze had to overcome heavy consumer skepticism and that live presentations were the best way to do that. Turcsik clarified that, because Febreze was a new product, shoppers had not yet made it a regular item on their shopping lists. He also noted that in-store sampling of Febreze had occurred at every retail level, including club stores, drugstores, supercenters, and supermarkets.

Although Febreze was made available in stores in the United States in March 1998, the actual national launch of the product, with the supporting advertising campaign, came in July of that year. The 52-week "Sharing and Connecting" campaign began with television spots and introduced print advertising in consumer magazines six months later. As Grey Advertising explained in its EFFIE Brief of Effectiveness, this approach was used in order to create a maximum awareness of the new product.

In their depiction of common household conditions for which Febreze would be needed, the television spots were intended to inform the public about the product and make it seem excitingly relevant. The choice of actors for the spots was considered crucial, since they had to be able to impart the new information and at the same time connect with consumers. The agency believed that the latter trait would play an important part in overcoming consumers' initial skepticism. In order to emphasize that the product was not just another masking spray, the campaign used the tagline "Febreze cleans bad smells out of fabrics. For good."

The campaign received a boost before it had even begun when Febreze was awarded the Good Housekeeping Seal of Approval. Toward the end of its run the campaign was further bolstered by a June 1999 *Consumer Reports* article that gave Febreze good performance marks. The unsigned article stated, "In our tests, it [Febreze] got rid of heavy cigarette odors and the smell of sautéed onions and garlic from lightweight draperies, nylon carpeting, and wool sweaters in a matter of hours."

There was one glitch during the campaign, and that was an Internet rumor that claimed that Febreze was harmful to pets. The *Consumer Reports* article touched on this issue by mentioning that the National Animal Poison Control Center was investigating the allegations and had not found any problems by the time the magazine had gone to press. Nevertheless the rumors persisted. *Good Dog! Magazine* also decided to investigate the rumors. The magazine contacted both Procter & Gamble and the National Animal Poison Control Center. Spokespeople for the former related the chronology of the rumors as they knew them, while an official statement from the National Animal Poison Control Center contradicted the rumors. Still, they remained, causing more of a public-relations headache than an advertising problem.

OUTCOME

Febreze was a success from the start. The campaign achieved both of its objectives: informing consumers about the new product and driving trial and consumption of it. This was borne out by statistics that the agency supplied for the EFFIE Brief of Effectiveness, in which it noted that Grey Advertising and Procter & Gamble had set a benchmark of getting 4 percent of consumers to make a trial (i.e., first) purchase in the first three months of the national launch, but in fact Febreze achieved 9 percent. The agency also noted that, by the end of one year on the market, the product had achieved a 40 percent trial-purchase rate and a 30 percent repurchase rate. The "Sharing and Connecting" campaign was awarded a 2000 Silver EFFIE from the New York American Marketing Association; the EFFIE Awards was one of the most prestigious award programs in the advertising industry.

Six months after the campaign began, Procter & Gamble was claiming that Febreze had become one of the country's top 10 laundry and cleaning brands. Quoted in a March 1999 issue of *MMR,* Mike Jensen, Procter & Gamble's director of research and development, said, "People are really impressed with the product's versatility. We have found that once people use Febreze, they find more and more uses for it."

By the time the "Sharing and Connecting" campaign ended in July 1999, a number of competitors had entered the fabric-refresher category. Febreze, however, was the category leader by late summer 1999. In fact, with approximately $107 million in sales for 1998, Febreze ranked seventh on the list of top-selling new consumer packaged goods for that year. Because of its later release the product was only on the market for 36 weeks in 1998. For comparison purposes Febreze was placed in the rug/upholstery-cleaner category, where it was the best-selling brand for the 52-week period ending January 31, 1999. The number two brand was category competitor Resolve. Procter & Gamble noted that Febreze was the most successful product launch in the company's history (and that included such venerable name brands as Ivory soap, Tide detergent, Crest toothpaste, and Mr. Clean floor cleaner).

Because the "Sharing and Connecting" campaign and its product were so successful, Procter & Gamble did not hesitate to make Febreze available in other markets worldwide. It was introduced into the United Kingdom in February 1999. By the end of 1999 Febreze was available in 18 markets in Latin America, Europe, Australia, New Zealand, and Asia.

Febreze not only created a category that other manufacturers rushed to fill but also became a successful Procter & Gamble product line of its own. By 2006 the original fabric refresher was available in five different scents, and there were an additional four specific solutions. There was also Febreze Air Effects, which used the same technique to eliminate odor molecules in the air. A second Febreze air-freshener product was Febreze NOTICEables. Plugged into a wall socket, each Febreze NOTICEable had two scents that alternated. There were five different pairs of Febreze NOTICEables on the market by 2006. The final Febreze product was by far the most technologically advanced and a natural progression from the plug-in. Febreze Scentstories were disks that gave off scents when played on a special player. Marketed as being similar to a scented candle, though longer lasting, Scentstories was available in six scents.

FURTHER READING

Bittar, Christine. "Category Wars: Febreze Can't Breeze in '99 as Challenger Set Deep Warchests to Dislodge P&G Pioneer." *Brandweek,* April 19, 1999.

———. "Category Wars: Febreze Sniffs Odor of Competition." *Brandweek,* March 22, 1999.

Mehegan, Sean. "Febreze." *Mediaweek,* October 27, 1997.

Neff, Jack. "P&G Shifts Ad Focus for Rollout of Febreze: Deodorizer for Fabrics Will Go National with $65 Mil Effort." *Advertising Age,* April 6, 1998.

"P&G's Febreze Finds a Niche of Its Own." *MMR,* March 22, 1999.

Parker-Pope, Tara. "P&G Targets Textiles Tide Can't Clean." *Wall Street Journal,* April 29, 1998.

"Procter & Gamble Creates New Product Category with the National Introduction of Febreze." *MMR,* March 31, 1998.

"Product Test: When You Can't Air It Out, Spray This On." *Consumer Reports,* June 1999.

Ross, Rachel. "How Science Engineers Unwanted Odors Out." *Toronto (ON) Star,* October 27, 2003.

"Rug/Upholstery Cleaner." *MMR,* May 17, 1999.

"Survey Cites Top 10 New Items." *MMR,* June 14, 1999.

Tatum, Christine. "Procter & Gamble to Expand Fledgling Hotel-Cleaning Service." *Denver Post,* January 21, 2005.

Turcsik, Richard. "Try It, You'll Like It." *Brand Marketing Supplement* to *Supermarket News,* November 1998.

Frank Caso

SINK BOY CAMPAIGN

OVERVIEW

Pert Plus, a combined shampoo and conditioner, was a major seller for the Procter & Gamble Company in the 1980s and early 1990s and prompted other companies to produce competing brands. Later in the 1990s, however, the convenience of two-in-one products was apparently offset by the problem, real or perceived, of residues these products left in one's hair. Usage had reportedly dropped off among women in particular, though the company maintained that the product still had a strong following among men.

Procter & Gamble reformulated Pert Plus to include a water-based conditioner, eliminating any oils or waxes. In order to inform consumers (particularly women) about the change, the company decided to use an advertising campaign that would evoke the product's lightness without overwhelming users with detailed information. Leo Burnett USA of Chicago created the Sink Boy character based on the established man- (or woman-) on-the-street concept that had been used successfully in previous Procter & Gamble advertising in the United Kingdom and the United States. In the first television spot, run in late fall 1998, Sink Boy roamed the streets of South Beach, Florida, with a portable sink, scoping out volunteers to demonstrate the new Pert Plus. While the general concept of the campaign was old, it incorporated elements of flippant humor and took the nontraditional turn of directly criticizing the old product and describing why the new product was better. The campaign ran on television, in print, outdoors, and on the Internet. Sink

Boy went on to appear in other commercials at locations around the country.

The campaign was a hit with consumers. A Sink Boy fan club (composed mostly of women) sprang up, and members urged the traveling hair-care demonstrator to come to their towns. Sink Boy's website also appealed to consumers. Procter & Gamble reported that, in the week's following its launch, an average user visited the site 1.9 times and lingered about six minutes each visit. Sink Boy was put on hiatus in December 2000. In 2002 Sink Boy was shelved for good, and plans for a new Pert Plus campaign were announced.

HISTORICAL CONTEXT

Pert Plus was reportedly created almost as an afterthought. Procter & Gamble scientists spent years developing the formula for a new two-in-one shampoo and conditioner, only to get a cool reception from top executives, who were more focused on other brands in the mid-1980s. When they got around to figuring out what to do with the new formula, company managers were cautious. Because the shampoo market was so competitive and consumers could be fickle, the company decided not to launch a new brand but to incorporate the formula into an existing product. Pert, a brand introduced in 1981, was practically washed up, with barely 2 percent of the U.S. shampoo market. The company reformulated the product and called it Pert Plus. The company test-marketed the product with relatively low expectations, but it quickly realized it had a hit when results came in. Within a year Pert Plus was made available throughout the United States and then expanded into overseas markets. The product was reported to be one of the fastest-growing hair-care brands in the country during the late-1980s, and in January 1991 Pert Plus was the best-selling shampoo worldwide. The product's phenomenal success prompted other companies to develop and market competing two-in-one brands.

During the 1990s, however, shampoo/conditioner combos fell out of favor, and sales of Pert and similar competing products dropped. One explanation offered by Bob Garfield of *Advertising Age* was that the "convenience of 2-in-1s sent the category skyrocketing … but the heavy, gummy residue eventually turned consumers, especially female consumers, way off." In a bid to revive the brand, Procter & Gamble changed the formula to eliminate waxes and oils, but the company still faced the task of communicating the change to consumers, particularly women. In late 1998 Procter & Gamble ran a television campaign developed by advertising agency Leo Burnett USA in Chicago geared toward changing people's minds about Pert Plus.

A SHAMPOO BY ANY OTHER NAME …

When Procter & Gamble was planning to launch Pert Plus in the mid-1980s, one problem the company had to deal with was the name. While Pert Plus was acceptable in the United States, in some other countries it was too similar to other products already on the market or it violated trademarks. So Procter & Gamble departed from its usual strategy of using one name for a product around the world and sold it under various names in different countries.

According to the December 6, 1990, issue of the *Wall Street Journal*, the shampoo was known as Rejoy in Japan and Rejoice in Singapore. It was also sold under a Vidal Sassoon label in Germany and Britain. The *Journal* reported that marketing one brand under different names would not necessarily hurt its sales. One observer noted that the two-in-one product's launch might have been faster if the company had used one brand name, but that by using different names Procter & Gamble ended up with many successful lines instead of just one.

TARGET MARKET

Although the new advertising campaign was targeted at both men and women, the company had a particular interest in persuading women to reconsider using Pert Plus. A company spokeswoman said that Pert Plus still had a strong following among men. In May 1999 *Brandweek* reported that 55 percent of Pert Plus users were men. The company sought to reach consumers through print media, television, outdoor advertising, and the Internet.

COMPETITION

Drug & Cosmetic Industry reported in September 1998 that the hair-care market had been declining steadily since 1994 and that this was a result in part of a saturated consumer base. The market was highly competitive, with products being deeply discounted to increase market share. The shampoo segment was reported to be the largest category worldwide, however, and shampoos had $1.83 billion in retail sales in the United States in 1997.

Procter & Gamble held almost one-third of the mass-market shampoo category, based in large part on the success of Pantene, according to the February 1,

1999, issue of *Advertising Age.* Pantene held the top spot among shampoos with 14.3 percent of the market. Procter & Gamble products made up 30.6 percent of the market during the quarter that ended September 30, 1998, while Unilever held 18.5 percent with its Suave and Finesse brands. Bristol-Myers Squibb Co. held a 14.4 percent share, buoyed by the continued success of Clairol Herbal Essences and the launch of the Daily Defense line.

The intense competition prompted shampoo marketers to revamp existing brands or issue new ones, often aimed at niche markets or highly specialized needs. Bristol-Myers Squibb's Daily Defense brand was being pitched as a shampoo with ingredients that helped protect hair from pollution, excess heat, and other environmental stress factors. Revlon Inc. expanded its ColorStay line of shampoos and conditioners for tinted hair to include color-specific products. The Pantene Pro-V line was expanded with four new products: heat-activated conditioner, antidandruff shampoo, and eight formulations of two different brands of hairspray. In October 1998 Procter & Gamble announced that it was "restaging" Pantene Pro-V with a new name (Pantene Ultra-V), new formula, and new package. In addition, *Chain Drug Review* reported in March 1999 that Procter & Gamble planned an overhaul of the Vidal Sasson line to include a texturizing shampoo, conditioner, and a two-in-one product called Ultra Care, and intended that each product be offered in one of four versions: voluminizing, body building, moisturizing, and for color-treated hair. Alberto-Culver Co., in an ambitious move, was budgeting $300 million for reviving its decades-old VO5 line.

Amid this vast and ever-changing array of specialized hair-care products, Pert Plus occupied the middle of the pack among the top 10 best-selling shampoo brands, ranking fifth in dollar sales and sixth in unit sales, as reported by *Chain Drug Review* in March 1999. Two of the brands that beat it out, Pantene and Head & Shoulders, were owned by Procter & Gamble.

MARKETING STRATEGY

Leo Burnett developed an advertising campaign based on an old idea from its London office, which had done advertising for Procter & Gamble's Daz detergent. In those commercials a mock television news team would go door-to-door, offering to do the household wash with Daz. This approach was later used in Gain detergent commercials in the United States. According to the *Rose Sheet,* the strategy was also similar to one Procter & Gamble used to sell Sure antiperspirant, in which people on the street were asked to use Sure and compare it with their current brand. Leo Burnett once again used the man-and woman-on-the-street approach and developed the campaign around Sink Boy or Sink Guy, who walked the streets with a portable sink offering to wash people's hair. Sink Boy was described by the company as a "goofy, offbeat" character who did the "unpredictable." The campaign invoked quirky humor and, in a departure from the norm, dealt candidly with the perceived shortcomings of old Pert Plus. Actor Michael Collins was hired to play Sink Boy in the television commercial, which was filmed in South Beach, Florida.

The 60-second spot opened with Sink Boy saying, "Hi! We're in Miami. We've got a sink, new Pert Plus with 'clean conditioning.' We're washin' hair and we're changin' minds." The commercial then proceeded, by way of on-the-street interviews, to discuss the problems with the old product. Sink Boy asked passersby, "Have you ever used one of those shampoo and conditioners in one?" and they responded with remarks like "Didn't like it," "I hated them," "Kinda... uhhgh," "Limp and

PUTTING SPARK IN THE DULL, LIFELESS SHAMPOO COMMERCIAL

Procter & Gamble was not the only company trying to liven up its shampoo commercials. The *Globe and Mail* in March 1999 noted a number of brands that were getting away from the old formulaic approach, in which a model bemoaned some problem with her hair, used the shampoo, and ended the spot by triumphantly flipping her tresses.

In particular, companies favored edgy humor, usually geared toward female viewers. A Lever Pond's commercial for Salon Selectives showed a young woman reading a magazine article titled "Is he right for you?" In a brief fantasy, her boyfriend transformed into a hunk, but the dream ended when he belched. The voice-over said, "If only you could customize a man like you customize with Salon Selectives." Clairol Herbal Essences was relaunched with a campaign that drew inspiration from Meg Ryan's fake orgasm in *When Harry Met Sally.* It featured women using the product and exclaiming, "Yes, yes!" after which sex therapist Dr. Ruth Westheimer showed up and added, "If you think that's great, the new conditioner is really intensive." While some thought it was "a different approach" that seemed to work, other industry observers though it was "kind of in poor taste."

dead," and "Weighs your hair down." Sink Boy said, "We're 0-for-4, my friend," then offered to wash their hair with new Pert Plus, explaining that the company "redid it, it's been revolutionarily, like, redesigned with a water-based conditioner. There's no oil, no wax, so your hair's gonna feel clean, clean." When he was finished, the participants' comments were "Wow!" "It feels light," and "It does seem lighter." The lightness of the commercial's tone was meant to reflect the lightness of the product. The spot ended with the tagline "If we can wash your hair, we can change your mind."

After the original South Beach spot aired, Sink Boy commercials were filmed in other locations, including Las Vegas, New Orleans, and Chicago. According to *Brandweek* in May 1999, the television commercials were "all ad hoc, based on real customer reactions, without reliance on storyboards or scripts." The new campaign was supported with in-store displays, point-of-entry marketing, and a toll-free number. In accordance with the trend toward offering specialized products, the reformulated Pert Plus was launched in four different versions—normal, dry/damaged, fine, and oily.

The concept behind the campaign was the desire to "get people to rethink and retry" the product, according to Kevin Burke, Pert Plus brand manager. To do this, Burke said, the company needed to overcome "a predisposition against 2-in-1 products," but to do so without inundating consumers with information. The "Sink Boy" campaign attempted to reach people with tongue-in-cheek humor, as well as its upfront discussion of the old product versus the new and a kind of in-your-face spunkiness in the character of Sink Boy. Although Procter & Gamble had generally favored conservative advertising, it tried a different approach with this campaign. According to Procter & Gamble spokeswoman Stefani Valkonen, "What we wanted was to really establish a new image . . . we wanted it to be looked at as more contemporary and more fun."

OUTCOME

As *Brandweek* reported in May 1999, the Sink Boy television spots became "the cornerstone of an integrated marketing effort, one component of which was the introduction of Sink Boy into on-line society." The Sink Boy website, developed by Giant Step, a Leo Burnett-owned interactive agency, was considered a "natural extension" of the more traditional forms of advertising. According to Pert Plus brand manager Burke, a "light bulb went off" when the company and the advertising agency saw how "adaptable" Sink Boy was on television, and "we challenged Leo Burnett to turn it into more than TV." Giant Step reportedly intended to "further explore the [Sink Boy] character, building on the TV commercials." Mark Rattin, director of creative development at Giant Step, said, "We'll probably extend the understanding of [Sink Boy] . . . allowing some interesting personality facets to come out online and using those humor instances to allow users to interact with some relationship components."

The Sink Boy website reportedly drew substantial interest, with the average user visiting the site 1.9 times during the six weeks following the site's launch and spending an average of six minutes viewing the site. *Brandweek* reported that Sink Boy "is apparently warming some hearts. Providing users the chance to write back has created a devoted Sink Boy fan club made up mostly of women, according to Burke, who says they seem to want to get to know the character. Some have even invited them to set up a hair-washing stall in their hometowns." *Brandweek* noted that, since the.

Burke said in May 1999 that Procter & Gamble was looking at other places to send Sink Boy, based on the mail that was coming in for him. The company did not plan at that time to set up chat rooms or bulletin boards, relying instead on consumer-to-consumer contact to promote Web traffic. The company did intend to include occasional product news updates on the website. *Brandweek* also reported, "The site will . . . be updated to reflect the evolution of the traditional advertising campaign, incorporating some new Burnett ads that Rattin says are 'even crazier.' "

Despite the Sink Boy campaign's success, in December 2000 it was put on temporary hold. As competition from other brands, such as Unilever's discount-priced Suave shampoo, began chipping away at Pert Plus sales, in 2002 Procter & Gamble announced a complete makeover of the product. Rather than revise the Sink Boy campaign, it left it on the shelf permanently and planned a new campaign that was also developed by Leo Burnett.

FURTHER READING

Bani, Eirmalasare. "A Rejoice-ful End to Bad Hair Days." *New Straits Times Press,* January 20, 1999, p. 10.

Chura, Hillary. "Leo Group Posts Stunning Turnaround; Global Agency Network of the Year: Starcom Mushrooms, Worldwide Billings Soar and a Closed Culture Opens Up." *Advertising Age,* January 31, 2000.

Gallagher, Patricia. "Globalization Pushed Pert Plus to No. 1." *Cincinnati Enquirer,* January 6, 1991, p. I01.

Garfield, Bob. "Man-on-the-Street Is a Big Plus for Pert." *Advertising Age,* October 26, 1998, p. 55.

Heinzl, John. "Shampoo Ads Don a New Hairdo." *Toronto (ON) Globe and Mail,* March 10, 1999, p. B27.

Neff, Jack. "Hair-Care Offensive: P&G Cuts In on Suave Price." *Advertising Age,* May 13, 2002.

———. " 'Sink Boy' to Lead Ad Push for Pert: P&G Kicks Off $20 Mil Campaign to Revive Shampoo." *Advertising Age,* October 12, 1998, p. 3.

Omelia, Johanna. "News on the US Mass Market Hair Care Front." *Drug & Cosmetic Industry,* September 1998, pp. 50–53.

"Pert Plus Opens Web Site." *Cincinnati Post,* March 8, 1999, p. 10B.

"Pert Plus Water-Based Reformulation Addresses Build-Up Complaints." *Rose Sheet,* October 19, 1998.

"Sinkboy Soars." *Brandweek,* May 3, 1999, p. IQ/38.

Stewart, Al. "Hair Care Has Momentum." *Chain Drug Review,* March 15, 1999.

Swasy, Alecia. "How Innovation at P&G Restored Luster to Washed-Up Pert and Made It No. 1." *Wall Street Journal,* December 6, 1990, p. B1.

Williamson, Debra Aho. "P&G's Reformulated Pert Plus Builds Consumer Relationships." *Advertising Age,* June 28, 1999, p. 52.

Debbi Mack
Rayna Bailey

STRANGE BUT TRUE CAMPAIGN

OVERVIEW

By 2004 the Procter & Gamble Company's Gain detergent brand had been available to consumers for nearly 38 years. Gain was best known for its distinctive citrus scent, which many consumers embraced but which was considered a generic fragrance by others. Although Gain was the number-two brand of powdered laundry detergent in 2004, its sales had dropped 4 percent from the same period in 2003. That slip came after an 11.9 percent drop from the same period in 2002. With Gain's sales on a steady decline, Procter & Gamble charged ad agency Leo Burnett Canada with pushing Gain ahead of the competition, increasing sales, and turning Gain's fragrance into an important element of the brand experience.

Leo Burnett approached the challenge from the aspect of Gain's fragrance. But rather than tell consumers what they already knew—how the detergent smelled—the agency asked them to consider how the fragrance made them feel when they smelled it on their freshly laundered clothes. From that idea the "Strange but True" campaign evolved. The campaign, released in 2004, entailed television spots based on the "strange but true" love stories told by Gain users.

The campaign achieved its goals of increasing market share, improving brand identity, and driving consumer awareness of the product. Six months after it began, Gain's share had jumped 10 percent. The campaign also succeeded in increasing consumer awareness as people logged on to the product's website to share their own Gain detergent "love stories." In addition, the campaign's television spots earned praise from the ad industry. *Adweek* described one of the spots as "sophisticated." The campaign also won a 2005 Bronze EFFIE Award.

HISTORICAL CONTEXT

Procter & Gamble built a reputation for getting laundry clean, first with its Dreft detergent, introduced in 1933 as an improvement over the washing-machine-clogging, fabric-dulling soap flakes that consumers had used since the 1920s. Tide brand, introduced in 1946, took laundering another step forward, cleaning not just lightly soiled laundry as Dreft did, but tackling heavily soiled clothes. By 1964 Tide laundry detergent had been through 22 transformations, with each change improving the product. In 1966 Procter & Gamble started selling a new detergent brand, Gain, which featured a distinctive green color and a unique citrus scent. In response to changing consumer preferences Gain liquid was introduced in 1993.

Ten years after its initial introduction Gain had acquired a loyal following of consumers, who loved its cleaning power and fresh scent. The powdered variety of Gain was the number-two powdered laundry detergent in 2003 with a 13.8 percent market share, but it trailed far behind the number-one powdered detergent, its big brother Tide, which claimed a 46.9 percent share of all powdered detergents sold. In the liquid detergent category liquid Gain came in even further down the list, ranking fifth. As Gain's unique qualities—especially its fragrance—were gradually getting lost in a market saturated with laundry-detergent choices, in 2004 Procter & Gamble's ad agency Leo Burnett Canada created a new marketing campaign designed to help boost brand identity, increase sales, and push Gain ahead of the competition.

TARGET MARKET

Although the EFFIE Awards website summarized the "Strange but True" campaign as the stories of all fanatics who loved the scent of Gain, the typical user of laundry detergents was women. Women were also the ones usually found in supermarkets buying the product. But Procter & Gamble also targeted another market with its Gain detergent: Hispanic consumers. According to a report in the *Cincinnati Enquirer,* "Gain is a symbol of the company's success in targeting certain brands to consumers in certain ethnic groups." In the United States the text on each box of Gain appeared in both English and Spanish. Further, consumers in target communities received direct-mail offers printed in Spanish. The report in the *Cincinnati Enquirer* also noted that in 2003 Procter & Gamble spent $80 million on marketing that targeted Hispanics, an increase of 15 percent from

PROCTER & GAMBLE'S ACQUISITION OF COLGATE-PALMOLIVE EUROPEAN DETERGENT BRANDS

With its U.S. laundry-detergent market reaching saturation and sales leveling off, Procter & Gamble in 2003 announced plans to acquire Colgate-Palmolive's European detergent business. Included in the acquisition were Colgate's Axion and Gama, sold in France; Dynamo, sold in Denmark; Ajax, sold in Sweden; and Dinamo, sold in Italy. According to a report in *Chemical Week,* combined European sales of the Colgate-Palmolive products was $100 million. Prior to its acquisition of the Colgate-Palmolive detergent line, Procter & Gamble was the number-three detergent producer in the European market, falling in behind number one Unilever and number two Henkel.

the previous year. As a result of such targeted efforts, sales of Gain to the Hispanic market increased notably, surpassing the brand's U.S. sales in general. And although Gain's scent was described in the EFFIE summary as a "hedonistic experience" for all consumers, the fragrances were particularly important to Hispanic consumers. A *BusinessWeek Online* article noted that Procter & Gamble had added a new scent to its Gain line after a study found that 57 percent of Hispanics liked to smell their product purchases before buying.

COMPETITION

The company name Church & Dwight Co., Inc., may not have been familiar to consumers, but one of its brand was: Arm & Hammer. The Princeton, New Jersey–based company, founded in 1846, was the number-one producer of baking soda, but it also offered a variety of products with the Arm & Hammer label, including laundry detergents in both powder and liquid forms. Instead of relying on advertising, Church & Dwight strengthened its detergent brands through acquisitions. In 2001 the company acquired USA Detergents for $120 million. The addition of USA Detergent's brand Xtra—which was ranked the number-six liquid laundry detergent in the United States that year—was expected to boost Church & Dwight's sales. The acquisition also pushed Church & Dwight into the number three laundry-detergent spot, with sales of powdered and liquid brands combined hitting $400 million (an 8.8 percent market share). Unlike its competitors, including Procter & Gamble, Church & Dwight reportedly had no immediate plans to gain customers by expanding into foreign markets. In 2004 Arm & Hammer detergents were given a new fragrance and redesigned packaging. Despite such efforts, for the 52 weeks ending October 31, 2004, Arm & Hammer brand's powdered-detergent sales slipped 13.6 percent to about $55.2 million, and it was ranked number four in the U.S. powdered-detergent category. During the same period the brand's liquid-detergent sales dropped 2.3 percent to about $107.6 million, putting it in eighth place among liquid detergents.

Unilever, based in London, England, offered U.S. consumers a variety of laundry detergents, including All and Wisk, but its market share was as varied as its products. With $246 million in U.S. sales (a 10.1 percent share) for the 52 weeks ending October 31, 2004, the company's All brand liquid detergent claimed the number-two spot in the liquid-detergent category in the United States. This meant that it ranked just behind Procter & Gamble's giant seller, Tide, and well ahead of Procter & Gamble's Gain. But with $15.3 million in sales, the powdered version of All ranked near the bottom of its category for the same period, claiming just a 1.8 percent share. Also during that period Unilever's Wisk liquid laundry detergent fell in at number six among liquid detergents, with sales of $124.7 million (a 5.1 percent share).

To give its brands a boost in the U.S. market, in 2004 Unilever switched creative responsibilities for its All brand from Lowe Worldwide to Bartle Bogle Hegarty. Creative for the Wisk brand remained with Lowe. Both brands also launched marketing efforts in 2004. The All brand released two campaigns, "Look on the Bright Side" and "Small Chef—Big Mess Challenge." The "Look on the Bright Side" effort encouraged consumers to find the humor in life's small mishaps, such as red wine spilling or freshly washed clothes being dropped on the ground. The "Small Chef—Big Mess" campaign featured a cooking contest for children in which the winner would receive a $25,000 scholarship and a chance to cook with Food Network chef Rachel Ray, known for her cooking program *30 Minutes Meals.* Both campaigns also promoted All's promise that it could get 99 top food stains out of clothes.

Unilever's fading Wisk brand was best known to consumers for its 1960s advertising that portrayed an embarrassed housewife whose husband had "ring around the collar." The first stage of the 2004 campaign featured television spots with the theme "Go Ahead, Get Dirty." Subsequent ads appeared on billboards, and a website was created that allowed moms to chat online about dirt and getting it out with Wisk. Signed on as spokesperson was Baltimore Orioles shortstop Cal Ripken, Jr., famous for his get-dirty style of play.

MARKETING STRATEGY

When Leo Burnett Canada created the "Strange but True" campaign for Procter & Gamble's Gain laundry detergent, the challenge was to push a product identified with its fragrance to the forefront of a market crowded with laundry products that were promoted by their scents. According to the campaign summary that the agency submitted for the 2005 EFFIE Awards, its goal was to turn Gain's "generic scent into a unique brand experience." In developing television spots for the campaign, Leo Burnett used true stories about consumers' individual experiences with Gain detergent.

One spot that first aired in early 2004 told the true story of a 20-something man, Adam, whose girlfriend left one of her freshly laundered dresses at his apartment when she went on a two-week vacation. The woman's little white dress had been washed in Gain, and based on the young man's response to the garment, its smell was irresistible. Consoling himself in the absence of his love, Adam was shown talking to his girlfriend's little white dress, napping with it, and eating dinner with it. Eventually Adam put the dress on a life-size cardboard cutout of Sylvester Stallone in his Rocky persona. With the Patsy Cline song "Crazy" playing in the background, Adam took the Stallone cutout in his arms and danced around the living room. The spot ended with Adam's girlfriend returning home and seeing in the apartment window the silhouettes of her boyfriend and the cutout dancing. A voice-over stated: "Adam, yeah, I hope your relationship lasts as long as the fresh scent of Gain."

In a follow-up spot, a group of five guys were shown watching a sports event on television. The man hosting the get-together said in a voice-over, "Recently my wife started using Gain detergent. I really like the fresh scent, but I didn't believe her when she said even the guys would notice the difference." When the group's favored team scored, the guys jumped up, cheering, slapping high fives, and hugging each other. In an awkward moment, one of the guys clung to the host in a bear hug, burying his nose in his friend's Gain-fresh T-shirt. The voice-over said, "Now I believe her. Gain. Making believers out of everyone, even the guys." During the spot text appeared on the screen noting that the commercial was "based on an actual letter from a Gain lover."

Each of the campaign's spots ended with a shot of a bottle of liquid Gain and the tagline "The smell says clean." On-screen text also directed viewers to a website, www.ilovegain.com, that enabled consumers to post their own personal Gain-related "love stories" or to read stories posted by other Gain lovers. Those who posted personal stories on the site included one consumer who told of putting powdered Gain in the vacuum-cleaner bag so that the smell would fill the house. The author of the anecdote stated, "Now I love to do laundry and to vacuum." Another wrote, "Gain gets rid of any stink on my clothes, and it makes my bionic nose happy." One woman said that she was so entranced by the Gain smell that she no longer cuddled with her husband, preferring to hug his freshly laundered shirts. Kids were not excluded from the Gain lovefest. A youngster wrote that when his mom bought Gain, she worried about him because he disappeared for hours. But she worried needlessly, because the child was "in the laundry room smelling."

OUTCOME

Leo Burnett's "Strange but True" marketing effort for Gain detergent was a success on several levels. In the six months following its launch, the campaign resulted in a 10 percent growth in market share for Gain. Overall, Gain powder claimed a 14.9 percent market share, or $126.2 million in U.S. sales for the 52 weeks ending October 31, 2004. Gain liquid sales climbed 24.5 percent to $167.7 million for the same period. Consumers, driven to the ilovegain.com website by the campaign, logged on to read the stories of others who had shared their experiences with Gain detergent or to post their own Gain "love stories." The campaign earned praise from *Adweek* when its critic Barbara Lippert described one television spot as a "breakthrough" and "sophisticated." She wrote that the spot "motivates the viewer to buy the stuff, if only to figure out just how 'dirty' clean can get." Further recognition came when the campaign was honored with a 2005 Bronze EFFIE Award for surpassing the campaign's share-growth goals by 263 percent and for successfully encouraging consumers to take part in the brand experience.

FURTHER READING

"Church & Dwight (the Top 50)." *Household & Personal Products Industry,* July 1, 2004.

Grow, Brian. "Hispanic Nation: Hispanics Are an Immigrant Group Like No Other; Their Huge Numbers Are Challenging Old Assumptions about Assimilation. Is America Ready?" *Business Week,* March 15, 2004.

"Kids Get Cookin' in All Laundry Detergent's 'Small Chef-Big Mess' Challenge." *PR Newswire,* June 14, 2004.

Lippert, Barbara. "Barbara Lippert's Critique: A Whole Lotta Sniffin'." *Adweek,* April 12, 2004.

Mack, Ann M. "Clients Share Global Marketing Insights." *Adweek,* June 24, 2005.

McArdle, Nanci. "Laundry Daze: Manufacturers Search for Ways to Entice Consumers by Adding New Benefits to Existing Brands." *Household & Personal Products Industry,* January 1, 2005.

McMains, Andrew. "Unilever Moves Detergent Brand to BBH." *Adweek,* March 18, 2004.

Neff, Jack. "Laundry Lines Find New 'Touch' Points." *Advertising Age,* June 27, 2005.

———. "Making Soil a Selling Point." *Advertising Age,* June 14, 2004.

Peale, Cliff. "Gain Detergent an Ethnic Winner." *Cincinnati Enquirer,* January 23, 2004.

"P&G Delivers 16 Percent Earnings per Share Growth for June Quarter and 14 Percent for Fiscal Year." *PR Newswire,* August 2, 2004.

Walsh, Kerri. "Church & Dwight Bags USA Detergents." *Chemical Week,* April 11, 2001.

———. "Soaps and Detergents: Crossing the Atlantic to Find New Customers." *Chemical Week,* January 28, 2004.

Rayna Bailey

TASTING IS BELIEVING CAMPAIGN

OVERVIEW

The 1998 advertising campaign for Fat-Free Pringles potato chips, involving an investment of $30 to $40 million in television, radio, print, and in-store promotions, was actually part of a much larger effort by Procter & Gamble (P&G) to market a fat substitute called Olean. The latter was its brand name for olestra, developed at a cost of some $500 million and 30 years of research, which promised fat-free eating without the fat-free taste. Fat-Free Pringles contained Olean; hence, the principal tag line of Pringles 1998 campaign, created by Grey Advertising in New York, was "Tasting Is Believing."

P&G also had an advertising campaign for Olean, handled by another agency, with the tag line "Fat-free Olean. A good place to start." In fact Olean, though not yet marketed directly to consumers (P&G certainly hoped to do so in the future), was a product unto itself and placed P&G in the unusual position of selling to a competitor. Thus Fat-Free Pringles in 1998 went up against a chip manufactured by competitor Frito-Lay, owned by PepsiCo, which also contained Olean.

The idea behind Olean was an intriguing one: a substitute that contained all the taste and richness of fat but that, because of its chemical makeup, would not be absorbed by the body. Instead, it would be expelled—and that fact created a problem, because many participants in Olean studies complained of diarrhea.

HISTORICAL CONTEXT

If ever there was a company with the resources for the kind of extensive and in-depth research required to develop a product such as Olean, it was Procter & Gamble. Founded in Cincinnati, Ohio, in 1837 by candle maker William Procter and soap maker James Gamble, the company's growth over the next 161 years had been explosive. By 1998 it had worldwide sales of $37.15 billion, with profits of $3.78 billion.

Equally impressive was the array of P&G products lining grocery store shelves: Crest toothpaste, Tide laundry detergent, Pampers disposable diapers, Scope mouthwash, Cascade automatic dishwasher detergent, Charmin bathroom tissue, Clorox bleach, Head & Shoulders shampoo, NyQuil cough formula . . . the list went on and on and was not limited to nonedible consumables. Although P&G was not typically associated with food in the popular mindset, the consumer products giant manufactured a wide variety of foods and food-related items. Topping the list was Crisco shortening, which in 1911 became its first food-related product. The 1956 purchase of Duncan Hines greatly added to P&G's food offerings, and although the company sold Duncan Hines in 1998, its food lineup was impressive, including Folgers coffee, Jif peanut butter, Eagle Snacks, and Pringles.

Pringles, of course, were perhaps best known for their packaging, a cylindrical can about the same size as the ones in which tennis balls were sold. Pringles cans contained a neat stack of potato chips, seemingly so precise in their placement that it was almost as though the grooves of one chip fit neatly into those of the chip below it. For years P&G sold Pringles on the basis of taste; but with the advent of Olean, a new and intriguing idea presented itself: what if Pringles could offer the same flavor, without any of the fat? Hence Pringles ran an ad campaign, which ended in February 1998, whose tag line played on the famous Pringles packaging: "Can you get great taste in a fat-free chip? Yes, you can."

TARGET MARKET

In 1968, when P&G researchers began the experiments that would ultimately yield olestra and Olean, Americans—motivated both by concerns over appearance and health—were just beginning to turn to low-fat and fat-free products. Some of the first low-fat and fat-free products, of course, tasted awful by almost everyone's standards, but with time it appeared that consumers did not have to sacrifice taste for low calories. Yet for all the efforts of science to enhance the flavor of low-fat and no-fat foods, it was easy enough to taste the difference. A September 1997 report by Laurie Freeman in *Advertising Age* spoke volumes concerning feelings about fat and flavor. "It's not that Americans have lost their taste for no-fat, low-fat, reduced-fat foods," Freeman wrote. "After all, retail sales of reduced-fat foods in the U.S. totaled $23.8 billion in 1996, and will grow at a compounded annual rate of 5.8 percent through 2001, reports [consumer research firm] Find/SVP. What is emerging is a growing sense that consumers are beginning to balk at reduced-fat foods because of texture or the lack of flavor. Consumers may as well be saying: if the products don't taste like the real thing but still deliver high calories, then hand over the rich food."

It was up to P&G, then, to reinvigorate interest in fat-free eating. In a February 1998 press release announcing the rollout of fat-free snacks with Olean, the company noted that the average American ate 21 pounds of salted snacks, containing 6 pounds of fat and more than 22,800 calories, each year. "If only 10 percent of these people ate Olean snacks instead of full-fat snacks," the P&G press release went on, "Americans would avoid 77,400 tons of fat and more than 600 billion calories a year. If a person who eats one ounce of full-fat potato chips every day were to substitute chips fried with Olean, he or she would avoid eating eight pounds of fat a year."

COMPETITION

Those were some impressive *ifs*, but P&G faced some equally impressive challenges over Olean, challenges that threatened the success of Fat-Free Pringles. That threat did not come from traditional competitors, since in fact Pringles' fiercest competition bought its Olean from P&G. In mid-1998 Frito-Lay introduced olestra versions of its Doritos tortilla chips and Ruffles and Lays potato chips under the Wow! label. Frito-Lay projected $900 million in retail sales; thus, its management had every reason to wish for the success of Olean, if not the success of Fat-Free Pringles.

Instead, leading the charge against Olean was the Center for Science in the Public Interest (CSPI), a Washington, D.C., advocacy group known by detractors as "the food police." In 1996 Dr. Michael Jackobson of the CSPI held a press conference to introduce a new anti-olestra commercial. The spot featured a close-up of a slowly revolving dog food can. "As the can rotated," wrote Alicia Mundy in *Mediaweek,* "it revealed the contents, including Olean, and the possible side-effects of that oil: loose stools, cramps. 'If this were a can of dog food, would you feed it to your dog?' queried a voice-over. 'Then why would you eat it yourself?' the voice asked."

Jacobson held another press conference in 1997, claiming that test-marketing of Olean in Columbus, Ohio, and other areas had caused massive outbreaks of diarrhea. Indeed, some 300 persons who tried Olean products filed complaints with the CSPI, which had in turn demanded that the Food and Drug Administration (FDA) and Federal Trade Commission (FTC) require P&G to add a stern warning on products—including Fat-Free Pringles—that contained Olean. The CSPI's recommended wording would have a notice that the product "may cause abdominal cramping and loose stools." According to Terry Kinney in *Fort Worth Star-Telegram,* P&G had "asked the FDA to rewrite the label, suggesting this phrase: 'Because it is not digested, olestra may cause discomfort or a laxative effect.' The FDA rejected the idea."

SCARCE AS HENS' TEETH

Fortune had been good to Procter & Gamble. Indeed, in the Cincinnati-based consumer products giant's repertoire, failed products were scarce. On that short list was an item called Crush, a soft-drink line purchased by P&G in 1980 and sold nine years later after it had failed to perform. Of course P&G did not create Crush, but it did create some other questionable products, including Fit, a wash designed specifically for fruits and vegetables. As of mid-1998 the company was still trying to figure out how to market it.

A product of much earlier provenance was Radar, a men's hair dressing that included a plastic scalp stimulator. Then there was Abound, like Radar developed at some point in the past decades: the hair conditioner never caught on with women, perhaps because it was sold in the form of coated sheets to be rubbed on the hair, rather than in the usual liquid form. More notorious were Rely tampons, which P&G removed from store shelves in 1980 after researchers found that use of Rely was linked to toxic shock syndrome.

MARKETING STRATEGY

On the one hand P&G ran a standard promotional campaign for Fat-Free Pringles; on the other hand it also had to undertake a defensive campaign for Olean as olestra came under attack from the CSPI and others. This it did with the tag line "Fat-free Olean. A good place to start," created by Grey Advertising, and with commercials that aired on February 21, during the Winter Olympic Games.

A key strategy in the Olean campaign was the identification of olestra with P&G's first food-related product, Crisco. In the words of Tara Parker-Pope in the *Wall Street Journal,* the Olean Winter Olympics commercial "shows wholesome scenes from an American farm to remind consumers that olestra is made with soybeans.... Amid scenes of golden fields, tractors, and a family gathering on the farm, a soybean farmer tells viewers that 'the folks who make Crisco' are now using soybeans to make a 'new kind of cooking oil.'" In P&G's February 10, 1998, press release announcing the introduction of fat-free snacks, chairman and CEO John E. Pepper stated that "At the start of this century, Crisco was a good idea for healthier eating. On the eve of the next century, a fat-free, calorie-free cooking oil from the makers of Crisco is an even better idea, and snacks are a great place to start."

The first thrust in the Fat-Free Pringles campaign came on the heels of its test marketing efforts and used many of the same methods—primarily distribution of free samples at lunch hour in many large cities. On February 2, Judann Pollack and Chuck Ross reported in *Advertising Age* that P&G expected to roll out the actual product nationally on October 1, but by late February stores in selected Ohio cities were already selling the new Pringles. P&G gave away some 3,000 samples of Pringles to lunchtime crowds in Cincinnati on February 27, a date Mayor Roxanne Qualls had proclaimed "Fat Free Pringles Day." It did the same in other Ohio cities. In early March P&G hung out a 100-by-32-foot banner, covering nine stories on one of the twin towers of its Cincinnati headquarters, to advertise Fat-Free Pringles.

Using the tag line "Yes I can!," P&G introduced Fat-Free Pringles nationally starting on June 15. TV spots showed adults in a variety of locations—a party, a sporting event, in their homes—holding cans of Fat Free Pringles in one hand and regular Pringles in the other. In addition, P&G ran commercials for Pringles featuring young adults and targeted to that market. New Pringles packaging proclaimed its "amazing taste," but also contained a warning concerning abdominal cramping.

Parker-Pope in the *Wall Street Journal* reported in June that lunchtime sampling, conducted in 20 major cities such as New York, Minneapolis, and Atlanta, was a major part of the new "Tasting Is Believing" campaign. New commercials, which began appearing in July, according to Parker-Pope, "Focus on the fact that consumers will be pleasantly surprised by the taste of Fat-Free Pringles. A second execution will target consumers who have stopped eating snacks to avoid fat." Pringles marketing manager Casey Keller told Parker-Pope that the latter ads would send the message that "You can have fun again, and you can get back into snacking."

OUTCOME

As the "Tasting Is Believing" campaign continued into the second half of 1998, so did advertising for Olean, this time featuring a young woman in jeans walking around what she claimed was the family farm and again referring to Olean as a product in the Crisco tradition. The commercial promised, "You know a good thing when you see it." By mid-1999, however, many industry observers had begun to have doubts concerning the success of olestra from a business standpoint. P&G had produced only 35 percent of the Olean it had projected to manufacture during the first fiscal year of the product's sale, and purchases were down accordingly.

In May 1999 Pamela Sherrid reported in *U.S. News & World Report* that "olestra is a long way from achieving mainstream status." Ironically, one of olestra's most impressive success stories was Pringles competitor Frito-Lay, which sold $350 million of Wow! brand snacks in its first year of sales. Sales for Pringles, by contrast, had not captured a great deal of attention. "But P&G has staying power," Sherrid observed. "It stuck with languishing Pringles for 20 years before the brand finally took off in the early 1990s." P&G and Pringles had enjoyed less than glowing results in one round of the olestra battle, but the fight was far from over.

FURTHER READING

"Fat-Free Snacks Coming Soon from Procter & Gamble." PR Newswire, February 10, 1998.

Freeman, Laurie. "Leading National Advertisers: Backsliding Consumers Losing Interest in Low-Fat: Texture, Taste Problems Soften Figures; Olestra Fights Trend, Stomach Upset." *Advertising Age,* September 29, 1997, p. S-30.

Kinney, Terry. "Fat-Free, Label-Heavy Procter & Gamble Defends Food Substitute with Ad Campaign." *Fort Worth Star-Telegram,* January 25, 1997, p. 2.

Larkin, Patrick. "Olean's Last Test: Attracting Consumers; P&G Starts Ad Campaign As Olestra Goes National." *Cincinnati Post,* February 11, 1998, p. 6-B.

"Media Blitz Aims at Trust in Olestra; Procter & Gamble Ads Called Bid to Drown Out Food Additive's Critics; Health Risks at Issue; Analysts Say Revenues Could Hit $3 Billion with Broad FDA Approval." *Baltimore Sun,* July 20, 1998, p. 5-D.

Mundy, Alicia. "From Bubba to Fat-Free: The People Who Got Bill Clinton Elected Have Now Taken Up the Cause of Procter & Gamble's Olestra." *Mediaweek,* February 10, 1997, p. 22.

O'Hanlon, Kevin. "P&G Goes National with Fat Substitute." Associated Press, February 10, 1998.

Parker-Pope, Tara. "P&G Dresses High-Tech Olestra in Down-Home Image in New Ads." *Wall Street Journal,* February 11, 1998, p. B-6.

———. "P&G Puts Lots of Chips on Plan to Give Away Fat-Free Pringles." *Wall Street Journal,* June 23, 1998, p. B-14.

Parker-Pope, Tara, and Nikhil Deogun. "Frito-Lay to Begin Selling Wow! Chips Made with Olestra Later This Month." *Wall Street Journal,* February 10, 1998, p. B2.

Pollack, Judann, and Chuck Ross. "Frito, P&G Ready National Launch of Olean Chips." *Advertising Age,* February 2, 1998, p. 1.

Sherrid, Pamela. "It's Crunch Time for P&G's Olestra." *U.S. News & World Report,* May 31, 1999, p. 57.

Judson Knight

WHEN YOU'RE STRONG, YOU SPARKLE CAMPAIGN

OVERVIEW

At the beginning of the twenty-first century, Procter & Gamble's Secret deodorant had been a leading product among women consumers for nearly 50 years. Through years of improvements of the product and extensions of the brand, Secret had remained the number one deodorant for women. But by 2003 sales were slipping for all established brands in the antiperspirant and deodorant categories, including Secret. The only products experiencing growth were newcomers to the category. To reverse the negative trend, the company introduced its own new product, Secret Sparkle, a deodorant designed to appeal to women 16 to 24 years old, who had been abandoning the aging brand in large numbers.

To increase brand awareness among its target audience and to support the launch of Secret Sparkle deodorant in 2004, Procter & Gamble's Chicago-based ad agency, Leo Burnett USA, created a campaign themed "When You're Strong, You Sparkle." The campaign included animated television spots and print ads in national magazines typically read by girls in the target demographic. In addition, Procter & Gamble turned to the Internet for part of its marketing. A brand-themed website, SecretSparkle.com, was created by imc2, a Dallas-based interactive advertising agency. A test promotion on MySpace.com, a social-networking website heavily used by young women, ran for one month. In 2005 the company expanded Secret Sparkle to include a body spray for girls 7 to 12 years old. The marketing was expanded as well with the launch of an Internet blog site, SparkleBodySpray.com.

Following the campaign's launch, overall dollar and volume shares of the Secret brand increased 4 percent and 3 percent, respectively. Teen dollar shares jumped 40 percent. "When You're Strong, You Sparkle" also received a 2005 EFFIE Award for successfully turning around the Secret brand's business. The campaign experienced negative consequences, however, regarding the body-spray marketing that targeted girls under age 12. According to the Children's Advertising Review Unit (CARU) of the Council of Better Business Bureaus, the program violated CARU's guidelines, so Procter & Gamble agreed to cancel that portion of the campaign.

HISTORICAL CONTEXT

When Procter & Gamble introduced Secret deodorant in 1956, the product was a cream that women applied with their fingertips. In 1958 Secret became available as a roll-on; the spray version was introduced in 1964, followed by the solid in 1978. Besides innovations in the product's application methods, Secret was offered in a changing variety of scents that reflected women's lifestyles of the time, from Powder Fresh and Spring Breeze in the 1980s to Ambition, Genuine, and Optimism in 2001. The company was also working to improve its Secret deodorant formulas to provide better protection from perspiration and odor for longer periods of time. By 2002 the antiperspirant and deodorant category had become enormous, with some national retailers such as the Walgreen's drugstore chain offering a selection of as many as 300 varieties. According to the retail-business-tracking company Information Resources, in 2002 Americans spent more than $1 billion on antiperspirants and deodorants. Procter & Gamble's Secret brand held the number one spot that year, with sales of $389 million.

Despite holding the top position in its category, the Secret brand was aging along with its core consumers, women who had begun using the product in their late teens and early 20s and who were loyal to the brand. By the 2003–2004 fiscal year Procter & Gamble had reported three straight years of declining sales. To reverse the slip, it introduced several new products in the Secret line, including Secret Platinum in invisible solid and clear gel forms. In 2004 the company introduced Secret Sparkle, a new Secret deodorant line designed to appeal to young women. A marketing campaign themed "When You're Strong, You Sparkle" was created to support the launch of the new product.

TARGET MARKET

According to Procter & Gamble, 80 percent of its products were purchased by women, and based on that information the company's marketing for most of its products specifically targeted women. The age of the women targeted varied based on the item being promoted. When Procter & Gamble introduced its Secret Sparkle deodorant in 2004, the product and its marketing were designed to reach young women 16 to 24 years old. Dave Knox, Procter & Gamble assistant brand manager, explained during an interview with *Advertising Age,* "If you don't target the consumer during her formative years, you're not going to be relevant through the rest of her life." Knox further noted that girls were beginning to use deodorant products at a younger age than in the past. With that in mind, in 2005 Procter & Gamble expanded its Secret Sparkle line to include body sprays and increased its marketing to target girls 7 to 12 years old. Because the younger girls had experienced body sprays at chain stores such as Bath & Body Works, they were familiar with the products, making them the ideal target market for the new Secret body spray.

NEW PROCTER & GAMBLE DEODORANT TARGETS YOUNG MEN

As the men's grooming category expanded to include body deodorant sprays similar to those used by teen and 20-something women, Procter & Gamble expanded its Old Spice brand in 2003 to appeal to younger men. The new product, Old Spice Red Zone, offered new fragrances (Glacial Falls and Aqua Reef), contemporary packaging, and a formula that was designed to stop odors before they started. Besides both invisible and soft solid deodorants, the line included a body spray and a body wash. Signed on as spokesman for the Red Zone line was Chicago Bears football linebacker Brian Urlacher.

COMPETITION

Unilever, based in the Netherlands, offered a variety of personal-cleansing products under the Dove brand, including a beauty bar introduced in the 1950s. The brand was eventually expanded to include skin moisturizers and hair-care products such as shampoos and conditioners, and in 1999 Dove deodorant was added to the mix. In 2004 Unilever added Radiant Silk antiperspirant to the Dove deodorant line and became the first brand to combine underarm odor and wetness control with skin care. Dove deodorant's popularity with its target market, women aged 18 to 34, was evident in the sales numbers. Within four years of its introduction Dove deodorant had grown to the number five brand based on sales. From January 2003 to January 2004 Dove reported a sales gain of 11.9 percent, to $58.5 million. In October 2004 a new global branding campaign was launched with the theme "Dove's Campaign for Real Beauty." It included all products with the Dove label and was designed to broaden the definition of beauty beyond physical attractiveness. Print ads featured women who were not models and who ranged from a plus-sized woman to a 96-year-old proudly showing off her wrinkles.

Andrew Jergens Company's market share for all of its personal-care products was on a downward spiral in 2002. At the end of that year the company reported a 3.5 percent drop in retail sales of its products, to $102 million. The report did not include sales at retail giant Wal-Mart, which were expected to give the sales numbers a 20 percent boost. To help execute a business turnaround, in 2003 Jergens began updating its existing products and added several new items, including skin-care products specifically designed for African-American women. In addition, to support its product efforts the company boosted its advertising budget 20 percent for 2003. Among existing products getting an update was Ban deodorant. In 2000 Jergens acquired the 50-year-old Ban brand from Chattanooga, Tennessee–based Chattom, Inc., which produced over-the-counter medications and skin-care products. After three years of work by Jergens scientists to improve Ban's formula, the deodorant got new packaging with a more contemporary and feminine look. A marketing campaign to support the new and improved Ban was launched in 2004 with a target market of young women aged 17 to 24. The campaign's target market put Ban in direct competition with category leaders Dove and Secret. It had the tagline "We'll take care of sweat and odor. The rest is up to you."

MARKETING STRATEGY

In 2004 Procter & Gamble's Secret deodorant brand had been on a three-year decline, with most of the volume and dollar share losses reported in the teen and college-aged-women market. In an effort to generate renewed interest in the brand among younger consumers, the company introduced a new Secret line, the Secret Sparkle collection, which was geared toward teens and young women. To support the launch of the new product line, Procter & Gamble's longtime advertising agency, Leo Burnett USA, created the "When You're Strong, You Sparkle" campaign. It included national television spots aired during programming that attracted an audience of teens and young women, such as MTV's *Laguna Beach* and Fox network's *The O.C.* Print ads also appeared in magazines read by the teen-to-24-year-old demographic, including *Teen People* and *Cosmo Girl.*

Each print ad highlighted one of the new product's four fragrances: Pear Illusion, Peach Shimmer, Violet Dazzle, and Moonlit Rose. The tagline, "When you're strong, you sparkle," was printed across the top of the ads. The ads were heavily illustrated and featured a beautiful woman in the center of a fairy-tale setting with images of twinkling stars, birds in flight, unicorns, flowers, and sparkling gems. The print ads were so appealing to young women that many visited the brand's website, where copies of the ads could be downloaded and printed as posters. Television spots were animated and used a magical theme similar to that of the print ads.

Recognizing that its target audience typically spent as much time online as it did watching television or reading magazines, Procter & Gamble also pursued a new approach to market its Secret Sparkle brand by turning to the Internet. Besides launching a website for the brand, SecretSparkle.com, Procter & Gamble arranged a promotional deal with MySpace.com, a social-networking website favored by young women. The MySpace.com home page featured a profile of singer Hilary Duff and included logos for Secret Sparkle deodorant. Internet surfers who viewed the singer's profile could enter Secret's contest "Discover the Secret Strength of Today's Hottest Rising Music Stars." The MySpace.com promotion ran for the month of December 2004 and included ads for Sparkle as well as links to other musicians popular with the target age group, such as the Donnas and Bonnie McKee.

In 2005, when Secret Sparkle Body Spray was added to the Sparkle product line to appeal to an even younger group of girls, those aged 7 to 12, Procter & Gamble again turned to the Internet for its marketing. The company released its first Web log marketing program for the Secret brand: SparkleBodySpray.com. Set up to look like the Web logs (or blogs) of each of the Secret Sparkle Body Spray characters (such as Rose and Peach), the site was interactive, with games and downloads. Dallas-based interactive advertising agency imc2, which had created the SecretSparkle.com website, also developed the body spray's blog site. The new site was designed to appeal to preteen girls as well as to enhance the television and print campaign created by Leo Burnett.

OUTCOME

The campaign was well received by the teens and young women who composed its target audience. Following the launch of "When You're Strong, You Sparkle," Procter & Gamble reported that the Secret brand, overall, increased in both dollar and volume sales share. Increases were especially notable in the teen market, with dollar share growing 40 percent. The campaign also won a 2005 Silver EFFIE Award in the Beauty Aids category.

On a negative note, although the advertising was a success, in 2005 Procter & Gamble agreed to stop advertising its Secret Sparkle Body Spray to girls 12 years old and younger. According to a report in *Advertising Age,* a ruling by the Children's Advertising Review Unit (CARU) stated that Procter & Gamble's marketing program violated the agency's guidelines. CARU, a division of the Council of Better Business Bureaus, was the children's unit of the advertising industry's self-regulation program. Its guidelines read, "Products inappropriate for use by children should not be advertised directly to children." The Secret Sparkle Body Spray carried the warning "Keep Out of Reach of Children." After pulling the advertising, Procter & Gamble said that it believed the program had adhered to CARU's guidelines and noted that the company had not received any reports of misuse of the product by children.

FURTHER READING

Alexander, Antoinette. "The Andrew Jergens Co. Recently Changed Its Name to Kao Brands Co. in an Effort to Reflect the Expansion of the Scope of Its Global Business Portfolio." *Drug Store News,* October 11, 2004.

"Broadband Ads' Speedy Progress." *BusinessWeek,* April 4, 2005.

Hevrdejs, Judy. "The Science of Sweat." *Chicago Tribune,* June 11, 2004.

"Intros Tout Value-Added Features, Packaging." *MMR,* April 19, 2004.

Ives, Nat. "The Media Business: Advertising; A New Type of Pitch to the Online Crowd Mixes Pop Stars and Personals." *New York Times,* December 3, 2004.

Nagel, Andrea M.G. "Andrew Jergens Polishes Image." *Women's Wear Daily,* January 1, 2003.

Neff, Jack. "P&G Pulls Children's Body Spray Advertising." *Advertising Age,* June 10, 2005.

———. "Strong Enough for a Man but Made for a Tween." *Advertising Age,* April 25, 2005.

Prior, Molly. "Dove's Great Expansion." *Women's Wear Daily,* December 10, 2004.

"The Secret Is Out: Secret Sparkle Body Spray Launches New Website." *Market Wire,* May 16, 2005.

Williamson, Richard. "Imc2 Creates Secret Sparkle Site." *Adweek,* May 17, 2005.

Zammit, Deanna. "Ban's New Message to Young Ladies: Don't Sweat It." *Adweek,* March 29, 2004.

Rayna Bailey

The Prudential Insurance Company of America

751 Broad St.
Newark, New Jersey 07102-2992
USA
Telephone: (800) 778-2255
Web site: www.prudential.com

BE YOUR OWN ROCK CAMPAIGN

OVERVIEW

When Elizabeth Krupnick arrived at Prudential Insurance Company of America in June 1994 to take over as chief communications officer, she inherited advertising that she called "mediocre at best." She also inherited one of the most identifiable icons in advertising: the rock. Her mission, as she conceived it, was to modernize Prudential's advertising without abandoning the equity it had invested in the rock. "Only an idiot would give up one of the world's most powerful icons," she said. She intended to distinguish Prudential from typical insurance advertising, which she thought tended to be "staid, corny, and jingoistic."

In 1995 Prudential chose an ad agency whose reputation was the antithesis of typical insurance advertising. Fallon McElligott of Minneapolis had established a name for itself on the success of its calculated risk taking. Insurance companies generally wanted to reduce risk to a minimum, but Krupnick wanted to push the envelope with advertising that was riveting and attention getting. With its renowned creativity, Fallon McElligott was perhaps the most appropriate choice to fulfill this goal. Bill Westbrook, Fallon's creative director and president, fulfilled Krupnick's mission of updating Prudential's image without losing its heritage by transforming the tired tag line, "Get a piece of the rock," into "Live well; make a plan; be your own rock." Krupnick called the transformation a piece of genius.

In another bold move, Westbrook and his associates sought out real Prudential clients who illustrated the new tag line instead of using actors in the commercials. After a lengthy nationwide search, they ended up with a handful of mavericks over 50 years old who had lived according to the principles of the new campaign. The finished spots, which began running during the 1996 Super Bowl, were six commercials featuring, among others, a former prima ballerina with the Israeli Ballet, a retired jazz musician from Connecticut, a former senator from South Carolina, and a holistic doctor from Colorado who mused in the commercial, "Somehow, on some deeper level, we're responsible for what happens to us."

The campaign, however, suffered a premature demise when Prudential hired Roger Lawson as executive vice president of marketing. As a result of Lawson's decision to create an in-house agency to handle advertising, Krupnick resigned her post, and Fallon resigned its account. Both Krupnick and Fallon regretted the lost opportunity to witness the "Be Your Own Rock" campaign run its course, but observers respected their decisions to maintain their professional integrity and creative independence.

HISTORICAL CONTEXT

Prudential had devised its traditional tag line "Get a piece of the rock" to be an assurance of stability and security for its customers. Prudential's vice president of corporate advertising Mary Lou Sack explained the history behind the tag line switch: "Our stance was always: lean on us, rely on us. We're still there for people, but people are really wanting to take more control for themselves of their finances, their life choices, of everything." In the 1990s a pervasive distrust of large institutions developed, especially the insurance industry. In the mid-1990s the insurance industry was the target of major lawsuits by several companies charging market misconduct, which affected not only their bottom lines but their entire corporate culture, including their advertising.

At Prudential the scandal had its origins in three distinct arenas. At the center was the Direct Investment Group of Prudential Bache Securities, which had been selling billions of dollars worth of dubious investments. More peripheral was a churning scandal, whereby Prudential agents convinced policyholders to refinance smaller policies into larger policies for higher dividends without informing them of the inherent glass ceiling. Finally, whistle blowers within Prudential filed suits charging that they were disciplined and even fired when they tried to point out Prudential's wrongdoings—such as churning—to their supervisors. In October 1994 Prudential Securities avoided criminal indictment by admitting fraud. Lawyers representing approximately 10.7 million policyholders claimed more than $1 billion in damages and in the end negotiated an open-ended settlement wherein Prudential agreed to pay the policyholders more than $410 million. The three largest life and health insurers—Prudential, Metropolitan Life Insurance Company, and New York Life Insurance Company, or the "Big Three," as they were called—paid a combined $575 million in settlements. Lost business due to flagging consumer confidence cost these companies even more money than the price of the settlements; they fell short of their projected sales of $198.57 billion by approximately $72.46 billion in 1995.

Prior to this scandal, insurance companies could safely assume that people would seek their services as a matter of course, and thus they could afford mediocre advertising. Traditionally, in fact, insurance advertising used two strategies that relied on negation instead of affirmation: it either patronized consumers or made them feel guilty. After the scandal, insurers scrambled to recover from the impact of the suits, both internally by restructuring their businesses and externally by redefining public perception through more aggressive and memorable marketing. At Prudential Krupnick decided to redirect consumers' distrust by focusing on how the company could help them achieve their own financial goals.

TARGET MARKET

Prudential's spot entitled "The Grandfather" depicted the 78-year-old former South Carolina senator looking out of place on the beach in a business suit while his grandchildren buried him in sand up to his neck. The joyousness of the kids' actions contrasted with the somberness of the mock act of burial. The soundtrack heightened this sense of contrast, as the senator's serious contemplations on his financial philosophy were accompanied by a lighthearted reggae beat, trumpeter Baba Brooks' 1965 recording of "Teenage Ska." These contrasts helped bridge the gap between the message—securing a retirement, which one associates with old age, and the target market, thirty- to fifty-year olds still young enough to plan for their future. Fallon McElligott's senior producer Bruce Wellington defined the challenge of the "Be Your Own Rock" campaign: to get "thirtysomethings to think that planning for their future can be cool." Fallon capitalized on the mood of ska music—a precursor to reggae with a much faster beat—by saddling its hip, upbeat sounds onto what otherwise would have been a very morbid theme. This music would have fallen on deaf ears if it had been targeted at an older audience, but most 30- and 40-somethings appreciated the ska style, even if they didn't recognize the song itself.

Krupnick explained the efficacy of this strategy of portraying happily fulfilled and successful older people as a means of appealing to those younger in life. "The surprising thing was that these ads tested exceptionally well among young people, better than they did among old people. They looked at these older people as rocks, as role models. They are people who have survived into retirement and are living fun, joyful lives." With life expectancy rising, insurance consumers in their middle years worried less about dying too soon and more about outliving their own assets and Social Security. Scare tactics thus seemed less effective to Westbrook than a more positive approach to financial planning. "Let's make it a joyful campaign," Westbrook suggested.

While fear of death spoke primarily to those actively contemplating their advancing years, the idea of enjoying life spoke to a much broader audience. Krupnick defined Prudential's target market much more broadly than Wellington's "thirtysomethings." Since Prudential maintained over 50 million clients—which amounted to one in five Americans—Krupnick half joked that Prudential targeted "anyone with a pulse." This comment seemed less of a jest taking into account that the commercials were not life insurance ads but rather brand advertising meant to raise the visibility of Prudential as a whole, with all of its services that covered financial concerns "from the cradle to the grave."

COMPETITION

The other two members of the so-called Big Three—Met Life and New York Life-were Prudential's main competition.

DIRTY SCOTCH

Fallon McElligott's president and creative director Bill Westbrook personally interviewed the people who were profiled in the six "Be Your Own Rock" commercials. Since the interviews involved a lot of reflection and retrospection, emotions ran high and stories frequently ended in tears. Having developed a deep level of intimacy with his subjects, Westbrook cried along with them as they recounted moments with pride or regret. One man described his main vice—"dirty scotch," a combination of milk and scotch whiskey. When this conversation got too emotional, the man suggested that he and Westbrook take time out for a dirty scotch.

Between 1987 and 1990 all three posted significant increases in sales: New York Life peaked in 1987 with a 59.9 percent increase in sales, while both Met Life and Prudential peaked in 1989 with sales increases of 60.92 percent and 41.84 percent, respectively. The market misconduct scandal, which first surfaced in August 1993 when a group of Florida nurses charged that Met Life agents sold them life insurance in the guise of retirement plans, hit all of the Big Three in 1994. That year Met Life's sales plummeted 38.33 percent compared with the previous year, while New York Life's sales fell 31.49 percent and Prudential's dropped 11.56 percent. These decreases continued in 1995 for Met Life and Prudential (which fell another 22.58 percent); New York Life, which did not admit any wrongdoing as Prudential and Met Life did, recouped its lost ground with a 36.82 percent gain in 1995.

Insurance companies reacted to the scandal by setting up new departments devoted to complying with stricter regulations. At the same time, their marketing strategies reflected a transformed approach in response to a transformed marketplace. Advertising campaigns exited the realm of the abstract and firmly grounded themselves in the pragmatic. Met Life's new tag line promised to help in "making sense of it all," while John Hancock Life Insurance Company grounded its approach in "real life" with "real answers." While the scandal created hardship for both the insurers and the insured, one positive outcome was the reevaluation and revitalization of an industry where changes were long overdue, especially in terms of marketing.

MARKETING STRATEGY

Krupnick decided to take a considered approach to revising Prudential's faltering image after the scandal. Internally she implemented a sweeping campaign to simplify the language and look of the company, from reducing the use of jargon to clarifying the names and functions of subsidiary arms of the company to consistent use of an updated rock logo on company literature. This simplification and updating carried over into the advertising. Before brainstorming for new marketing ideas, Prudential and Fallon McElligott conducted extensive market research to assess both the damage done by the scandal and the attitude toward insurance companies. Surprisingly the research suggested that the scandal had done far less damage to Prudential's name than suspected; however, the scandal did solidify consumer's attitudes, which had been shifting away from reliance on external support such as insurance policies and toward self-reliance. Consumers no longer wanted to lean on institutions that they felt they could not fully trust, but they did realize that they could not be fully self-sufficient—they would still require the services of institutions such as the insurance industry, but on their own terms, not the industry's.

Westbrook captured the spirit of the self-reliance trend with the transformation of the tag line into "Be your own rock." This move alone could not reestablish consumer trust; all aspects of the campaign would have to reflect a commitment to integrity. Hence, the decision to cast actual customers instead of actors. "Insurance agencies in the past have used actors and passed them off as real people, but you know they're actors," Bill Westbrook explained. "And historically when using real people, concepts in this category have been intimidating and scary." Westbrook tried a different approach, taking a chance on finding older people who illustrated his tag line. Several casting directors interviewed over 200 candidates nationwide, narrowing the field down to 12 before making the final decision on the six youthful older people to be profiled in the commercials.

Fallon enlisted the services of director Jeffery Plansker of bicoastal/international Propaganda Films, who supported the use of nonactors to stress Prudential's integrity. Using nonactors represented more risk, but that risk paid off. Westbrook explained, "We wanted a chance for magic and were willing to take the risk in order to create some chill bumps, and something we'd never seen before." Plansker echoed Westbrook, adding that their strategy allowed for "unexpected surprises." This unpredictability enhanced the sense of candor in the spots, which supported Prudential's goal of creating trust through truth telling.

OUTCOME

The "Be your own rock" campaign did not live long enough to produce quantifiable results. Krupnick was prepared to follow multiple indicators to track the success or failure of the ads, but she didn't have the opportunity to gather sufficient data. In the absence of quantitative research results, Krupnick reported "fabulous" qualitative and anecdotal evidence; Prudential executives and agents alike reportedly loved the campaign. In 1997 two spots from the campaign were chosen as television finalists by the One Show. A group of advertising and marketing executives chosen by *Newsday* to evaluate ads broadcast during the 1996 Super Bowl were divided over the Prudential spots—some found them "refreshing," while others found them "confusing." When asked what work he was most proud of, Fallon McElligott cofounder Pat Fallon replied, "The work we did for Prudential. When you think of how difficult that was to sell through the process and how strategically brilliant it was and how well it was executed, that's awesome." Walking away from the Prudential account in 1996 was a devastating experience for Fallon, but the assertion of creative integrity may have compensated for the loss in revenues in the long run. Largely on the strength of the "Be your own rock" campaign, Fallon McElligott was named agency of the year in 1996 by *Adweek* and *Shoot,* two of the major advertising trade magazines.

FURTHER READING

Albo, Amy. "Open Door Policy (How Commercials are Produced at Fallon McElligott)." *Shoot,* December 13, 1996.

DeSalvo, Kathy. "Fallon McElligott." *Shoot,* December 13, 1996.

Fadden, James. "Real Work: Capturing the Truth Is an Exhaustive Process." *Shoot,* August 30, 1996.

William D.Baue

Public Broadcasting Service

1320 Braddock Place
Alexandria, Virginia 22314
USA
Telephone: (703) 739-5000
Fax: (703) 739-0775
Web site: www.pbs.org

BE MORE CAMPAIGN

OVERVIEW

In 2002 the Public Broadcasting Service (PBS), the nonprofit U.S. media organization, was owned by 349 member television stations with an audience of more than 100 million viewers per week. Despite the efforts of CEO Pat Mitchell to "reinvent" PBS with newer, updated shows, including segments directed by Martin Scorsese, Clint Eastwood, and Robert Redford, the broadcaster was reeling from a 23 percent drop in ratings over the previous 10 years. To continue branding PBS as a resource that educated, inspired, and empowered its viewers, the organization released its "Be More" campaign in 2002.

PBS awarded its $15 million advertising budget to longtime partner Fallon Minneapolis, a division of Fallon Worldwide. On July 22 Fallon launched the first four television spots of the "Be More" campaign. Two of the spots were directed by Alfonso Cuarón, the director of such films as *Y tu mamá también* and *Harry Potter and the Prisoner of Azkaban.* The other two spots were directed by François Girard, director of the film *The Red Violin.* Cuarón's "Fish" spot, which won the greatest number of awards for the campaign, featured a computer-generated image (CGI) of a goldfish watching salmon swim on television. Inspired by the salmon, the goldfish leaped from its bowl and then flopped, jumped, and free-fell its way into a river. The spot ended with the goldfish migrating upstream with the salmon. The spot's tagline was "Be More Empowered." Other variations on "Be More" continued into 2005, with all of the spots airing exclusively on PBS.

Despite garnering an Emmy Award as the best commercial, a Bronze Clio, and two AICP Show honors, the "Be More" campaign was not accompanied by increasing PBS income, which came from underwriting, member fees, grants, product sales, royalties, and license fees. Between 2002 and 2003 total income slipped $35 million. Further, the audience base for PBS continued to migrate to higher-end programs on cable networks like the Discovery Channel and the History Channel. Although the broadcaster was losing viewers, its website (www.pbs.org) remained the most popular dot-org website in existence, with an average of 12 million visitors a month. In addition, PBS's TeacherSource website (www.pbs.org/teachersource/) was used by 250,000 teachers every month.

HISTORICAL CONTEXT

PBS was created in 1969 as a government-subsidized organization to provide cultural and educational programming for the public. Because PBS was intended to be noncommercial, the U.S. Federal Communications Commission (FCC) prohibited the use of commercials. What was called "underwriting" became the only advertising allowed on PBS. Underwriters were allowed to mention their corporations or brand names between programs but were not allowed to promote products or services. In the 1980s, because of dwindling funds for PBS, the FCC allowed some underwriters to purchase what were called "enhanced underwriting acknowledgments," which to critics appeared to be the same as advertisements on commercial networks. The acknowledgments were restricted by the FCC, however, and underwriters did not have the greater freedom offered to sponsors by the commercial networks.

In 2000 PBS hired Fallon to launch a $25 million ad campaign titled "Stay Curious" that attempted to reshape the perception that the broadcaster catered to an "elite" audience. The campaign won several honors, including an Andy and an Emmy Award. Besides the campaign there was another significant development in 2000. Pat Mitchell, who had worked as a cable executive, was hired as the CEO of PBS. The organization was already floundering when she took on the job, however. As A.J. Frutkin expressed it in *Media Week,* "Viewers often equate PBS programming with spinach. It may be good for them, but they don't want to eat it."

Mitchell approached her job at PBS with the mantra "keep the best, reinvent the rest." Major changes included an updated version of *The Forsyte Saga,* the BBC series based on the novels of John Galsworthy, and Ken Burns's documentary series on the Civil War. In 2003 she engaged Martin Scorsese to produce *The Blues* and Robert Redford to produce *Skinwalkers,* the latter a series based on Tony Hillerman's mystery novels. In one of her most controversial moves, she replaced Louis Rukeyser, who for 32 years had been the popular host of *Wall Street Week.* Among other daring moves were including a lesbian couple in an episode of a children's television show and creating the Latino drama *American Family.*

Despite Mitchell's innovations in programming, financial problems continued to haunt PBS. The perpetual catch-22 was that to attract the talent PBS wanted the broadcaster needed corporate sponsorship, but corporate sponsors expected 30- to 60-second commercial spots. Lack of funds hindered PBS from selecting from the talent pool it wanted. John Wilson, senior PBS vice president, told *Media Week,* "When we say yes to something, we say, 'Yes, and here's a third of your money. So now let's spend the next 18 months looking for the other two-thirds.' "

TARGET MARKET

The target market for PBS included the 18- to 49-year-old viewer who craved literate, informative, high-quality programming. Preferring to target a psychographic, a group with specific attitudes and values, rather than a strict age demographic, PBS was successful during its first decades in capturing an audience. The aim of the "Be More" campaign was to retain the PBS audience, especially between programming segments. Because PBS did not air commercials, the credits and station breaks between programs ran from two and a half to three minutes. This was the time, research showed, that PBS viewers changed over to networks like TLC, Animal Planet, and the Travel Channel. Frutkin wrote in *Media Week,* "Whereas PBS's often heady subject matter can intimidate the average viewer, cable programs like the Discovery Channel's Walking with Dinosaurs have made dry topics viewer-friendly. Call it PBS Lite."

Some advertisers saw the value of underwriting PBS's "upscale" programming. In addition, compared to commercial broadcasters, there was less clutter on the PBS airwaves. "The maximum number of messages you'll compete with is two," Guy McCarter, senior vice president and director of entertainment marketing at OMD USA, told *Media Week.*

"We are not ratings-driven. That's not the mandate of PBS. But we do want to expose our programming to the widest possible audience," Jacoba Atlas, a senior vice president, told the *Washington Times.* One market segment that remained loyal to PBS, especially with the onslaught of satellite television, was made up of those viewers who relished local shows. Other than local news, the commercial networks tended not to air community programming except for the "occasional once-a-week, low-budget, no-resources program in an undesirable time period," wrote Bob Sirott of the *Chicago Sun-Times.* PBS often satisfied this need. Nonetheless, although PBS claimed more than 100 million viewers per week in 2002, the audience had dropped to 90 million by 2005.

FRANK ZAPPA

"Puppets," the spot Scott Hicks directed for the Public Broadcasting Service in 2003, was filmed in Melbourne, Australia, over a period of two days. The spot featured two marionettes, one a hero and the other a villain, fencing inside a puppet tent until the hero liberated himself by cutting off his strings. Australian puppeteers, not actors, were featured in the spot. Fallon's art director, Gerard Caputo, told *Shoot* that the villain marionette was whimsically named Frank: "We called him Frank because he looked like Frank Zappa."

HIV-POSITIVE MUPPET

The decision of the Public Broadcasting Service (PBS) to create a HIV-positive Muppet character for the South African version of *Sesame Street* incited a U.S. congressman, Billy Tauzin of Louisiana, to warn PBS not to re-create the character for American programming. Mitchell complied, saying that *Sesame Street* and PBS did not plan to release the character in the United States. Executives at PBS and *Sesame Street* felt, however, that the Muppet was an appropriate character for South Africa, where, in 2003, 21.5 percent of the population was living with AIDS.

COMPETITION

"In many ways, PBS is competing for the same dollars that a cable network like A&E wants. But it can't deliver what A&E can," Laura Caraccioli, vice president/director of Starcom Entertainment, told *Media Week.* Arts and Entertainment Television Networks (A&E), which was established in 1984, claimed 85 million subscribers by 2003. In 1995 A&E launched the History Channel with a million subscribers, a number that steadily rose to 85 million by 2003. Quality programming, such as the flagship *Biography* and *Law and Order* series, even though the latter was subsequently acquired by Turner Network Television (TNT), greatly attributed to A&E's success. A&E also forged shrewd advertising partnerships, especially with Barnes & Noble, which featured A&E's *Biography* videos in its stores in exchange for on-air promotions. In comparison with PBS, which relied on a composite of ratings, reviews, and Internet responses, which were dubbed its "point of impact," A&E could dazzle advertisers with its ability to quote hard data on the numbers of people who viewed particular ads. In 2002 A&E posted $550 million in sales.

In the mid-1980s John Hendricks, the founder and CEO of Discovery Communications, Inc. (DCI), was struggling against bankruptcy, with only $5,000 in cash and with $1 million owed to the BBC. By 2003, however, he had turned DCI around with the Discovery Channel and claimed subscriptions in more than 85 million households. In that same year DCI also operated 170 retail stores. DCI launched its successful Discover.com website in 2000 to sell games and science and nature videos. Subsequent channels launched by DCI included the Travel Channel, TLC, and Animal Planet, all of which helped the company earn a whopping $1.7 billion in sales by 2003. DCI's market had swelled to 1.2 million subscribers worldwide by 2005, overshadowing both A&E and PBS, and it had $605 million in revenue.

MARKETING STRATEGY

Cuarón filmed the first 60-second PBS spots, "Fish" and "Naked Emperor," in Prague over a period of 10 days. "The shoot itself was radically under-funded and considerably ambitious, given the number of scenes we had to do, and [the fact that we had] to make them work exactly in time," Mark Sitley, the producer, told *Shoot.* "Fish," the campaign's most ambitious spot and an award winner, featured a CGI goldfish that, after being inspired by a program on salmons, escaped from its fishbowl. "Naked Emperor," playing on Hans Christian Andersen's "The Emperor's New Clothes," featured an eastern European-type dictator marching through his bleak, repressed empire. Except for black boots and socks, and momentarily a hard hat, the emperor was stark naked. After passing legions of saluting soldiers and admiring adults, the emperor reached a hallway full of children. "Hey, you're naked," one of the boys blurted out to laughter and the emperor's embarrassment. The tagline "Be More Honest" then appeared.

Because of his Harry Potter commitment, Cuarón declined to work on project when Fallon initially approached him. After reading some of the scripts, however, Cuarón reconsidered the offer. "It was not about selling or convincing anybody to buy anything," he told *Shoot.* "It was about two beautiful concepts done in an amazing storytelling kind of way. The moment I received them I said, 'I have to do these.' "

After Fallon had approached Girard to direct "Birds" and "Orchestra," the agency met with him in Montreal for 10 days to discuss the project. "As soon as I looked at the boards, I knew I wanted to do them," Girard told *Shoot.* He filmed both spots in Santa Monica, California. "Birds" featured the well-known Canadian composer Walter Boudreau struggling at the piano with "writer's block" until he looked out a window, where he found inspiration in five telephone wires populated by birds, a scene resembling sheet music. The spot ended with the tagline "Be More Inspired." "Orchestra" featured a sextet interpreting a work by Johannes Brahms, with one cellist performing with Jimi Hendrix-style bravado. It closed with the tagline "Be More Passionate." Girard commented to *Shoot,* "The spots were perfect for a director. They're such smart ideas. Plus it's a noble cause; everyone wants to support PBS because of the brilliance of its programming."

In 2003 Girard filmed two more spots for the "Be More" campaign, "Aura" and "Hot Potato." Two later spots, "Skunk" and "Puppets," were directed by the Oscar-nominated Scott Hicks, the director of the films *Shine* and *Snow Falling on Cedars.* Fallon staff members met with Hicks in Australia, where he preferred to work, and filmed the two spots with the Academy Award-winning cinematographer Dion Beebe.

Particular attention was given to the word that would follow "Be More" in each spot. Mike Gibbs, the Fallon art director, told *Adweek,* "Picking the right words was a considerable struggle. We were trying to find things that fit the best, that feel like they come from PBS."

OUTCOME

By the third year of the "Be More" campaign, it seemed clear that the efforts of PBS to hold on to its viewers were not working. Although more than 100 million people watched PBS weekly in 2002, the number had dropped to 90 million by 2004. CEO Mitchell tried making program changes to coincide with the launch of the "Be More" campaign, for example, introducing reality shows like *The 1900 House* and *Frontier House,* but audience numbers continued to decline. In addition, PBS continued to suffer financially. Between 2002 and 2003, for example, the broadcaster's income dropped from $533 million to $498 million.

Some analysts pointed fingers at the confusing sales process at PBS, whereby the broadcaster's top producers, such as WNET in New York and WGBH in Boston, approached sponsors who were then later also solicited by local stations and producers. Other analysts attributed the decline of PBS to the restrictions on corporate commercials. The resulting lack of funding caused talent that PBS would have had to drift during the 1980s to toward wealthy cable networks like DCI and A&E. Despite the continued drift of PBS, Mitchell remained steadfast on the matter of maintaining the broadcaster's policy on sponsorship. She told *Media Week,* "If we stay the course as the only one not pandering to the lowest common denominator, it's going to pay off."

The "Be More" campaign did strike gold within the ad industry, however. It won a number of awards, including a Bronze Clio, two AICP Show honors (including one in the category of visual effects), and an Emmy for best commercial, the second Emmy for the Fallon-PBS collaboration.

FURTHER READING

Anderson, Mae. "Fallon Evolves PBS Makeover: 'Be More' Theme Extended in 4 New Commercials." *Adweek,* September, 8, 2003, p. 34.

Baar, Aaron. "Fallon 'Does More' for PBS." *Adweek* (eastern ed.), July 29, 2002, p. 6.

Champagne, Christine. "Alfonso Cuarón:" Fish" Reels in the Emmy for Best Primetime Commercial." *Shoot,* October 17, 2003, p. 36.

———. "Dir. Scott Hicks Puts On a Puppet Show for PBS: Fallon, Minneapolis-Created Commercial Illustrates the Beauty of Being Independent." *Shoot,* October 3, 2003, p. 10.

Day, Sherri. "PBS Ad by Fallon Picks Up an Emmy." *New York Times,* September, 18, 2003, p. 6.

Dunlap, Bill. "Winning Techniques: Agency Producers behind the Emmy-Nominated Spots Speak Out." *Shoot,* August 15, 2003, p. 23.

Eastwood, Alison. "Top Spots." *Boards,* October 1, 2003, p. 16.

Frutkin, A.J. "Reinventing PBS." *Media Week,* November 4, 2002.

Garcia, Sandra. "Two Hats: DP Dion Beebe Pulls Strings for PBS." *Shoot,* October, 31, 2003, p. 18.

Goldrich, Robert. "Fallon's Primetime Catch: Spot Emmy for PBS 'Fish'; Dir. Cuarón Reflects on the Honor and on Working with Agency Creatives." *Shoot,* September, 19, 2003, p. 1.

———. "Hungry Man, BBDO Top Emmy Noms." *Shoot,* August 1, 2003, p. 1.

Grossman, Andrew. " 'Colonial House' on PBS Schedule: Pubcaster's Strategy Includes New Independent Focus." *Hollywood Reporter,* July 29, 2002, p. 3.

Lazare, Lewis. "New PBS Spots Take Classy Tack: But High-End Approach May Not Be Enough." *Chicago Sun-Times,* July 31, 2002, p. 65.

Kevin Teague

The Quiznos Master LLC

1475 Lawrence St., Ste. 400
Denver, Colorado 80202
USA
Telephone: (720) 359-3300
Fax: (720) 359-3399
Web site: www.quiznos.com

BABY BOB CAMPAIGN

OVERVIEW

By the end of 2004, Quiznos, a chain of sub sandwich shops run by parent company Quiznos Master LLC, had grown to more than 2,500 restaurants and had hit the $1 billion sales mark. In addition, Quiznos had established a brand identity through a four-year run of over-the-top advertising campaigns, featuring everything from the company's cofounder making sandwiches in his underwear to guitar-strumming, singing rodents. But the company wanted to move in a new direction by distancing itself from the fast-food label of other sub sandwich shops and joining the ranks of the rapidly expanding niche of fast-casual restaurants, which were associated with higher-quality food. Quiznos also hoped to increase consumer awareness of its products—fresh, made-to-order sandwiches on toasted breads—by introducing a new tagline, "Mmmm . . . Toasty."

In 2005 Quiznos launched a new marketing campaign created by Los Angeles-based ad agency Siltanen & Partners that featured the talking infant "Baby Bob" (former star of a 2002 sitcom of the same name) as spokesman. The eight-month-old genius spoke in an adult voice, lip-synching via computer animation. Estimated, according to *Adweek,* to be worth as much as $60 million, the campaign kicked off with a spot in which Baby Bob told viewers that he would love to eat a Quiznos sandwich but that he had no teeth. While his mother enjoyed the sub, Bob was fed strained peas. "I love the gal, but that's just wrong," Baby Bob said. The campaign was expanded to include the Internet and radio along with additional television spots.

"Baby Bob" was a hit with most consumers, with the ads rating in the top 10 for recall and likeability four out of the five months following its launch, according to *Advertising Age.* Further, by using a spokesman described as a 40-year-old man trapped in a baby's body, the ads maintained the edginess that Quiznos had created with its earlier campaigns, albeit toned down to appeal to an older, more sophisticated audience. By the third week into the "Baby Bob" campaign, Quiznos had reported a 9 percent increase in same-store sales.

HISTORICAL CONTEXT

In 1981 Quiznos was a single restaurant serving sub sandwiches in Denver, Colorado. By 2000 the chain had grown to 1,000 restaurants and was secure in the number three spot behind Subway (number one) and Blimpie International, Inc. Hoping to attract consumers looking for more than a traditional cold sandwich, Quiznos began making efforts to distinguish itself in the submarine sandwich shop arena and to convince consumers it was no ordinary fast-food restaurant. Instead, Quiznos planned to position its restaurants in the growing field of fast-casual foods, alongside chains such as Boston Market and Noodles & Co. John Hamburger, president of Franchise Times Corp. (publisher of news for the franchising industry), told the *Denver Post,* "Fast-casual has been winning customers because of food quality, not price. If Quiznos is going down that route, they're going to distinguish themselves from the Subways, Blimpies and about 50 other sub chains out there."

To create name recognition for its expanding chain, beginning in 2000 Quiznos launched a series of sometimes controversial or bizarre marketing campaigns depicting quirky characters in unconventional situations. One spot featured a man grabbing a sandwich from his dog, which had pulled it off the kitchen counter. The man was then shown on the floor eating the sandwich. In another spot a man and a woman were walking down the street when the woman spotted an empty Quiznos sandwich wrapper in the trash. She pulled the wrapper out of the garbage, then licked the wrapper clean. Those spots were followed three years later by commercials featuring Quiznos cofounder Jimmy Lambatos, nicknamed "Chef Jimmy," who was so obsessed with making the perfect sandwich that he forgot to put on his pants. In another TV spot a woman was shown comparing sub sandwiches in a competitor's test kitchen. When she chose a toasted Quiznos sub rather than the untoasted sandwich the tester was pushing, she was stuck in the neck with a dart by the tester. Another featured a businessman eating an untoasted sub; he was asked if he "was raised by wolves," the implication being that to eat such a sandwich was uncivilized. He was then shown in a flashback nursing from a female wolf. In 2004 came the "Spongemonkeys," strange, rodent-like, guitar-playing creatures screeching the praises of Quiznos subs.

The ad campaigns worked. While not all comments were positive, awareness of the brand had been created; people were talking about Quiznos. It was time to shift focus from branding to the product itself. The company began airing food-focused television spots and introduced the theme "Mmmm...Toasty." In 2005 the company started using a new spokesman, Baby Bob, described by the company as "a 40-year-old man trapped in a baby's body" who would love to eat the subs but lacked the molars. Baby Bob had been created in 1997 by Siltanen & Partners as spokesperson for a series of commercials directing consumers to a website, freeinternet.com (which later went off-line). In 2002 the child prodigy appeared in a short-lived television show, "Baby Bob," that aired on CBS.

TARGET MARKET

Early marketing campaigns for Quiznos were aimed at men between the ages of 18 and 24—typical fast-food customers—and were designed to make the brand seem cool to that audience. While still slightly offbeat, the "Baby Bob" campaign focused on the quality of the chain's product to attract older, more sophisticated consumers as well as families.

To further connect with families, Quiznos introduced a special Mother's Day promotion through its website that enabled people to E-mail personalized greetings from Baby Bob to their moms. Trey Hall, chief marketing officer for Quiznos, said to *Business Wire,* "Due to the popularity of the Quiznos ads that feature Baby Bob, we developed a fun, easy way for people—young and old—to send Mom a special, personalized message from her favorite 'spokesbaby.'"

COMPETITION

In 2005 Subway sandwich shops boasted 18,000 locations, significantly more than the 3,000 restaurants owned by Quiznos. Subway was, however, feeling the pressure of competition from Quiznos. Technomics, a restaurant consulting firm based in Chicago, noted that

OFFBEAT ADS CREATE BUZZ FOR QUIZNOS

Quiznos was known for its quirky, sometimes over-the-top advertising, from "Chef Jimmy," who was so excited about his Quiznos sub that he failed to notice that his pet parakeet had died, to a woman getting stuck in the neck with a dart when she chose a toasted Quiznos sub over a cold sandwich offered by the competition. The ads drew plenty of attention, not all of it good. "Chef Jimmy" raised the ire of animal lovers, including one who complained in a letter to the chain's ad agency, "Do you realize that the sight of a dead bird can be very traumatic to bird lovers?"

Despite the buzz created by the offbeat ads, none of the chain's marketing efforts attracted attention equal to its television spots featuring the computer-generated "Spongemonkeys." Response to the tone-deaf, rodent-like creatures was phenomenal; Quiznos received 30,000 E-mails, phone calls, and messages during the month following the launch of the campaign, most of them complaints about the use of rat-like creatures to sell food. After a seven-month run, the company canceled the "Spongemonkeys" and shifted its focus to its products.

in 2004 Subway's sales grew 10 percent, while those of Quiznos grew 37 percent. In what Thuy-Doan Le, writing for the *Sacramento Bee,* described as the "battle of the buns," Subway responded to upstart Quiznos's push for market share by introducing its own line of toasted subs. Le wrote, "While burgers and fries have long been the staple of America's carryout lunch, their dominance is waning. And scrambling to lure those bored or bothered by burgers are sandwich chains." A Subway spokesman told Le that it considered its key competitors to be large chains such as McDonald's and Burger King. Subway stated further that it did not consider itself to be in direct competition with Quiznos, but rather that when a Quiznos opened a shop near a Subway, it was in fact an advantage because it helped direct consumers' attention away from typical fast-food fare. "If someone starts thinking sandwiches, instead of burgers and fries, they eventually could be our customer," the spokesman explained.

While Subway and Quiznos battled the submarine wars, Blimpie International, Inc., founded in 1964, recognized that trouble had arrived when Quiznos overtook Blimpie to claim the number two spot in the sub sandwich market. In 2005 Blimpie announced plans to reinvigorate its brand with redesigned restaurants, an updated logo, and new menu offerings such as panini-grilled sandwiches. The chain also unveiled a new slogan, "It's not just a sandwich—it's a BLIMPIE." According to *PR Newswire,* Mark Mears, the company's chief marketing officer, said, "We have always been an innovator in menu concepts . . . Now our brand reflects this forward thinking positioning, transforming Blimpie from its heritage as a traditional neighborhood sub shop to a more consumer-driven, contemporary deli."

MARKETING STRATEGY

Quiznos was aggressively gaining ground in the submarine sandwich wars. With its warm, crispy rolls and television and radio spots that proclaimed, "Mmmm . . . Toasty," consumers were increasingly aware of the chain and what it had to offer. The aggression carried over into Quiznos marketing with advertising that included offbeat humor to capture the attention of consumers. According to Quiznos, the "Baby Bob" campaign was created to stand out from other advertising on television. But the company had shifted from push-the-envelope marketing, such as its short-lived and sometimes controversial "Spongemonkeys" campaign, which was designed to create name recognition, to entertaining but less edgy product-focused advertising. Company executives explained that the goal in the new marketing was to make consumers be more aware of the food it offered than of the spokescreatures promoting the product. Having a cuddly, eight-month-old baby genius talking about Quiznos sandwiches, his mouth moving in time with the words by way of computer animation, achieved the company's goals of maintaining quirky humor in its ads while focusing on the food.

Television spots, which debuted during the hit shows *Desperate Housewives* and *24,* had Baby Bob in a variety of situations involving a tasty Quiznos sub that was just out of his reach; but given his lack of molars he could not have eaten the sandwich anyway. In one spot to promote the chain's line of Real Deal sandwiches (which offered prices comparable to other chains' value menus), Baby Bob was perched on a director's chair talking to the camera about how much he would love to eat a Quiznos sandwich but that he had no teeth. "But, when my molars grow in, I'm all over the stuff," he announced in the deep voice of a 40-year-old man. In another spot, which promoted the Chicken Milano Chicken Sub, the precocious infant was in Italy being driven around in a motorcycle sidecar by a gorgeous model. Of the sandwich, he stated, "It's not quite like riding around Milan with an Italian supermodel, but it's close." For another spot Bob took a seat on a park bench to talk about the great Angus steak subs his dad was always bringing home from Quiznos. He concluded, "One day when the old man's not looking, Sayonara." All the ads end with the tagline, "Mmmm . . . Toasty."

OUTCOME

In a press release the company described "Baby Bob" as "a genius . . . his brains and infinite knowledge are both a blessing and a curse." The clever child who started talking at three months old turned out to be a blessing for Quiznos's marketing. While many of the chain's earlier campaigns resulted in negative feedback, following its launch "Baby Bob" consistently ranked among the top 10 commercials for likeability and consumer recall in four of its first five months, and it ranked first in January, according to *Advertising Age.* In addition, Quiznos reported a 9 percent increase in same-store sales within three weeks of the first "Baby Bob" television spots. The company also reported that the number of visits to the Quiznos website reached record numbers, and E-mails from fans who loved the "Baby Bob" commercials poured into company headquarters. The campaign was so successful that it continued into 2005 with a new batch of television spots.

FURTHER READING

Apuzzo, Matt. "Subway, Quiznos Fight, but Often on Same Side." *Houston Chronicle,* August 1, 2005.

"Blimpie Brand Repositioning Becomes Reality." *PR Newswire,* March 23, 2005.

Brand, Rachel. "Feathers Fly over Quiznos Ad: 'Dead' Parakeet in Super Bowl Segment Sparks Angry E-mails." *Denver Rocky Mountain News,* January 28, 2003.

Cebrzynski, Greg. "Verdict In on Three New TV Campaigns." *Nation's Restaurant News,* February 18, 2002.

Forgrieve, Janet. "Quiznos Quietly Quits Quirky Ads: Chain's New Spots Focus on the Food, Not Offbeat Setups." *Denver Rocky Mountain News,* July 30, 2004.

Hopkins, Brent. "Sandwich Shops Are Stacking Up against Hamburger Chains." *Los Angeles Daily News,* July 11, 2003.

Keen, Russ. "Aberdeen, S.D., Residents Continue to Eat at Quizno's despite Annoying Ads." *Aberdeen (SD) American News,* March 3, 2004.

Le, Thuy-Doan. "Sandwich Wars." *Sacramento Bee,* August 6, 2005.

MacArthur, Kate. "Quizno's Axes Spongemonkey Spokesthings; Franchisees Welcome Decision." *Advertising Age,* August 2, 2004.

———. "Subway Heats Up in Fighting Off Underdog Quiznos." *Advertising Age,* June 14, 2004.

Pate, Kelly. "Owners Hope to Distinguish Quizno's Sub Shops with Fast-Casual Approach." *Denver Post,* February 2, 2003.

Pennington, April Y. "Neck and Neck: Being No. 1 in the Franchise Race Has Its Advantages, but There Will Always Be Others Nipping at Your Heels." *Entrepreneur,* January 1, 2004.

Schmelzer, Randi. "Baby Bob Is Back for Quiznos." *Adweek,* January 7, 2005.

Walker, Andrea. "U.S. Advertisers Use New Tactics of Cutting 'Clutter' to Reach Target Audience." *Baltimore Sun,* May 12, 2004.

Rayna Bailey

Reebok International Ltd.

1895 J.W. Foster Boulevard
Canton, Massachusetts 02021-1099
USA
Telephone: (781) 401-5000
Fax: (781) 401-7402
Web site: www.reebok.com

TERRY TATE, OFFICE LINEBACKER CAMPAIGN

OVERVIEW

In 2003 Reebok International Ltd. was the second-largest maker of athletic shoes and fitness apparel in the United States. With profits approaching $1.5 billion, the Canton, Massachusetts–based company enjoyed a small lead over competitors New Balance, adidas, and Puma, although it was well behind market leader Nike, Inc. Several years of steady growth had, however, put Reebok in a good position to launch its most successful television campaign ever, the award-winning "Terry Tate, Office Linebacker."

Developed in conjunction with Reebok's ad agency, the Arnell Group, the first "Terry Tate, Office Linebacker" commercial premiered in February 2003, as a 60-second, $4 million spot aired during Super Bowl XXXVII. It introduced fictional retired National Football League (NFL) linebacker Terrible Terry Tate (played by actor Lester Speight, also known as the Mighty Rasta), sporting shoulder pads and a Reebok football jersey, as an employee of Felcher & Sons, a typical bustling corporate office. Tate's job as "office linebacker" was to tackle and reprimand employees who violated company protocol, or at the very least threaten that his "pain train" was heading their way. Tate's action sequences were intercut with the staid Ron Felcher—the fictional company's CEO and appointed talking head—explaining how Terry had made a positive impact on the company's bottom line. The slapstick humor of a hulking football player diving on top of defenseless coworkers crosscut with Felcher's dry irony proved irresistible to fans, who rated "Terry Tate, Office Linebacker" the most popular Super Bowl commercial of 2003. In the week following the commercial's premiere, it was downloaded from the Reebok website more than 1.2 million times.

The spots ran through 2003 and 2004, but by 2005 Reebok had announced Terry Tate's "retirement." The unusual campaign boosted awareness of the Reebok brand and earned the Arnell Group a Gold Lion at the Cannes International Advertising Festival in 2003. In addition, in 2003 *Adweek* magazine named Reebok the Interactive Marketer of the Year.

HISTORICAL CONTEXT

Beginning in 2000 Reebok awoke from a decade-long slump in sales and market share with the return of Paul Fireman as the company's CEO. Throughout the 1990s Nike had dominated the athletic-shoe market with its high-profile product launches and multimillion-dollar deals with the biggest names in sports. Reebok responded in 2002 with the launch of RBK, a line of hip-hop-inspired shoes and clothing. The line quickly gained prominence through Reebok's exclusive licensing deals with the NFL and the NBA, territory that had once been Nike's domain. Further good luck followed when Nike severed much of its business with Foot Locker, the world's largest athletic-footwear retailer, over a retailing dispute. Reebok quickly filled the void with its "Above the Rim" displays of RBK merchandise at Foot Locker stores throughout the country.

With these bold moves Reebok was determined to take a substantial portion of market share away from Nike. The launch of the "Terry Tate, Office Linebacker" campaign was the company's coup de grâce—a commercial as memorable as any of Nike's most celebrated campaigns from the 1980s and 1990s. Better still was the fact that "Terry Tate" did not limit its appeal to fans of a particular sport. Though "Terrible Terry" was an NFL player, the spots' humor transcended sports altogether through its deft send-up of both professional sports and the business world.

TERRY TATE, CALIFORNIA GOVERNOR?

"Save Our State—Vote Terry Tate" was the rallying cry in 2003, when Reebok sought extra publicity for its "Terry Tate, Office Linebacker" campaign by filing papers to declare Tate a candidate for governor of California during the state's recall election. Unfortunately, the actor who played Terry Tate, Lester Speight (also known as the Mighty Rasta), did not qualify to run for office, which put an end to a campaign that promised to "tackle white-collar crime" and "end partisan gridlock by knocking some fiscal sense" into government officials.

TARGET MARKET

Reebok's decision to premiere the "Terry Tate" spot during the Super Bowl was telling. With a 60-second spot costing $4 million, it was the most expensive air time of the year. In return for their investment, advertisers were guaranteed a huge audience and post-game buzz in many major media outlets. Not only would they attract sports fans—obviously Reebok's choice customers—but they would also attract a wider audience of those who tuned in to the game because others were watching it, or for the half-time entertainment, or simply for the commercials themselves.

After the initial launch Reebok became more selective in airing the spots. Millions in their target market—young, sports-minded people who liked to think of themselves as part of the cutting edge—had already found the longer Terry Tate films on Reebok's website and signed up for a mailing list, which enabled the company to engage in a form of direct Internet marketing virtually for free. In essence, the television spots became a promotion for the website, which offered long-format films, Terry Tate screen savers, and bobble-head dolls. "The Web allows for a more intimate and more seductive and longer-lasting relationship with our consumers," Peter Arnell of the Arnell Group told Ann Mack of *Adweek,* "So we use the Web to manage relationships, as well as portray the brand and product."

COMPETITION

In 2003 Nike held 39.1 percent of the athletic-shoe market, compared with Reebok at 12 percent, which was followed closely by New Balance at 11.6 percent and adidas at 9.6 percent. With Reebok's sales rising 70 percent over the previous year, however, the company seemed poised to close the gap with Nike. Yet Fireman acknowledged that the increase had less to do with the "Terry Tate" campaign and more to do with Reebok's introduction of signature shoes endorsed by rappers Jay-Z and 50 Cent and NBA star Allen Iverson. Fireman stated that his goal was to increase the company's market share from 12 percent to 20 percent within a few years. "I view this as a renaissance, a complete regrouping, a complete rebirth," he told Tracie Rozhon of the *New York Times* about the business turnaround fueled by the "Terry Tate" spots.

Yet Reebok was aware that "Terry Tate" alone could not close the gap with Nike. The company needed other elements, such as a logo as indelible as Nike's "swoosh" and a tagline as unforgettable as "Just Do It." To that end Reebok had recently launched other campaigns to highlight its vector logo and to promote the tagline "Wear the Vector, Outperform." "Reebok is still looking for a logo that rivals that of Nike," wrote Rozhon. "We need our own swoosh," Fireman told her. "We need a recognizable symbol, something that gives the kid at the gym an emotional attachment."

MARKETING STRATEGY

"Terry Tate" began as a short film written and directed by independent filmmaker Rawson Thurber in 2000. Later it was picked up by the film company Hypnotic, which showed it to Peter Arnell, head of the Arnell Group, Reebok's advertising agency, who thought it would make a great commercial. Reebok executives agreed and gave Thurber additional millions to produce more short films.

Four long-format "Terry Tate" films were produced for Reebok's website: "Terry's World," "Terry Tate,

> ### THE "PAIN TRAIN" RUMBLES THROUGH THE BOSTON MARATHON
>
> Reebok took its "Terry Tate, Office Linebacker" campaign to the Boston Marathon in April 2003, when 500 college students were hired to wear temporary tattoos on their foreheads that read "Reebok . . . the pain train is coming." Many of the students, who were placed at strategic points throughout the route, also wore red Reebok jerseys with Tate's number, 56, on them. The actor who played Terry Tate, Lester Speight (also known as the Mighty Rasta), appeared at the event. The official sponsor of the marathon was Reebok's rival, adidas.

Sensitivity Training," "Draft Day," and "Office Athlete of the Century." Each four-minute film was also condensed into 30-second edits, which ran as television spots. In addition, two other short spots were filmed: "Terry Tate, Vacation" (a 30-second spot promoting the Scrimmage shoe) and "Terry Tate, On the Field" (the spoof of Nike's "Streaker" commercial). All incarnations featured the overzealous Tate, clad in his red jersey, tackling unsuspecting coworkers and dressing them down with his rhyming, shame-inducing couplets ("You kill the joe, you make some mo'"; "You can't cut the cheese wherever you please"). No infraction was too small to escape his notice: long-distance phone calls on company time, playing solitaire on the computer, and walking away from a paper jam in the copier. All resulted in reprimands of a physical nature, culminating in his trademark battle cry, a victorious "Whooooo."

Throughout the spots, the boss, Ron Felcher, defended Tate to the harassed employees, declaring that profits were up 47 percent since Tate was hired. Felcher pointed out that Tate was a team player, and subsequent shots showed Tate wearing a party hat and presenting a birthday cake to a coworker, giving a multimedia boardroom presentation, and waving a friendly greeting to a coworker in the middle of pummeling another. Another sequence dramatized a knee injury Tate sustained from an accident with an office mail cart. Coworkers rooted for him as he underwent physical therapy and returned to work.

With the exception of the sole spot for the Scrimmage shoe, the "Terry Tate, Office Linebacker" campaign did not promote a specific product. Indeed, the Reebok name was not even noticeable in the spots. The most obvious connection was that Tate's red jersey sported the vector logo. "The ultimate thing we are striving for is not brand recognition," Fireman told Jennifer Carofano of *Footwear News,* "but how people perceive us. Our goal here is not only to reinvent the brand, but to counter a lot of the staleness in the industry." The tactic paid off in terms of increased Web traffic. "It caused a huge pop culture tremor, and the Web is the best place to manage pop culture tremors," Arnell told Mack.

This "pop culture tremor" was extended by other inexpensive but highly effective guerilla marketing tactics that garnered Reebok additional—and invaluable—publicity. Hundreds of college students sporting Terry Tate temporary tattoos on their foreheads were hired to infiltrate the adidas-sponsored Boston Marathon, and in August 2003 Terry Tate filed papers to run for governor of California. Arnell told Stuart Elliott of the *New York Times* that these "tactic[s] [are] known as borrowed interest, marketers seeking to gain attention by associating themselves with news events that consumers are following closely." In addition, Reebok sponsored a "Take Terry to Work" sweepstakes that offered entrants the chance to see Terrible Terry Tate in action on their home turf.

The campaign went head-to-head with rival Nike when Reebok officials commissioned Thurber to star in a spoof of Nike's January 2003 "Streaker" spot. The Nike commercial was itself a humorous vignette based on the British phenomenon of streaking at soccer matches. Filmed to look like real news footage, a naked man wearing Nike shoes eluded capture on a soccer field. In Reebok's "Terry Tate" streaker spot the same scenario was recreated, with the added twist of Tate appearing seemingly out of nowhere to tackle the streaker to the ground. Reebok officials lauded the commercial not only for its timeliness but also for its symbolic pummeling of Nike.

In July 2003 Tate was back on cable television promoting Reebok's Scrimmage shoe in a spot called "Training Camp," which showed the office linebacker fending off office-worker dummies and dodging filing cabinets. By the end of the year downloads of the Terry Tate spots from Reebok's website had surpassed 20 million. For the 2004 Super Bowl, however, Reebok pulled out of the high-stakes television game and premiered a new short film on its website, which was promoted on MTV in 15-second spots and in E-mails to more than a million registered users of the website TerryTate.com.

OUTCOME

According to some, even though Reebok's sales increased 70 percent in the fourth quarter of 2003, those gains were attributable more to the company's rap- and sports-star endorsements than to Terry Tate's "Pain Train." "As a sales catalyst," wrote Rich Thomaselli in *Advertising Age,* "Terry Tate seems to be as flat as the office workers he leaves in his wake." Others agreed. Stuart Elliot, writing in the *New York Times,* reported that "some critics have said the ads ought to make a more direct link between Reebok and the character to make a better case for the performance credentials of Reebok sportswear and footwear."

Nevertheless, the "Terry Tate" spot garnered the most buzz of all the Super Bowl commercials, which added a priceless word-of-mouth component to the campaign. In addition to becoming one of the cultural touchstones of 2003, "Terry Tate, Office Linebacker" was voted the third-most-liked commercial in the *Advertising Age* Top Spot poll, and the spots were downloaded more than 20 million times from Reebok's website. The spot won a Golden Lion at the Cannes Lions International Advertising Festival and was voted "Most Likable Ad of 2003" by *USA Today. Adweek* named Reebok the Interactive Marketer of the Year for using the Internet "to build upon—rather than merely maintain the momentum of—an offline campaign, and for its recognition that the Internet should play a significant part in an integrated campaign," according to *Adweek* writer Ann Mack.

FURTHER READING

Adams, Steve. "Reebok Passes on Super Ads." *Quincy (MA) Patriot Ledger,* February 1, 2005.

———. "Taking Aim: With Nike Exposed, Reebok Sends in a Hitman." *Quincy (MA) Patriot Ledger,* February 5, 2005.

Carofano, Jennifer. "The Turnaround Gunning for the No. 1 Spot in Athletic Footwear, Reebok Cranked up the Heat in 2003." *Footwear News,* December 8, 2003.

Elliott, Stuart. "Reebok Ad Tackles Nike Commercial." *New York Times,* February 5, 2003.

———. "The Reebok Campaign Joins the California Campaign." *New York Times,* August 12, 2003.

Linnett, Richard. "Reebok Re-Brands for Hip-Hop Crowd." *Advertising Age,* January 28, 2002.

Mack, Ann M. "Grabbing Market Share." *Adweek,* November 24, 2003.

Oser, Kris. "Reebok, Encouraged by 'Terry Tate,' Expands Its Definition of I-Marketing." *Advertising Age,* April 25, 2005.

Rozhon, Tracie. "Former King of Sneakers Is Coming Back." *New York Times,* March 6, 2003.

Thomaselli, Rich. "Reebok's Terry Tate Set to Play Dirty Ball." *Advertising Age,* April 21, 2003, p. 4.

———. "Terry Tate Builds Buzz for Reebok, But Not Shoe Sales." *Advertising Age,* February 2, 2004.

Wilonsky, Robert. "The Pain Train." *Miami New Times,* February 6, 2003.

Kathy Wilson Peacock

The Rheingold Brewing Company

130 W. 42nd Street
New York, New York 10036
USA
Telephone: (212) 481-1018
Fax: (212) 481-0233
Web site: www.rheingoldbeer.com

RHEINGOLD BEER CAMPAIGN

OVERVIEW

Rheingold beer, originally produced by the Liebman Brewery of Brooklyn, New York, had enjoyed a several-decades' stint at the top of New York City's beer market in the middle of the twentieth century. It had also earned a place in the minds and hearts of multiple generations of New Yorkers, thanks to ubiquitous advertising slogans and jingles and to the "Miss Rheingold" competition, an enormously popular, citywide beauty pageant staged in the 1950s and 1960s. The rise of national brewing powerhouses Anheuser-Busch, Miller, and Coors, however, pushed countless local brands, including Rheingold, out of business in the late 1960s and 1970s. After more than two decades of dormancy, Rheingold was brought back to the New York market by a group of investors, and the new enterprise was called the Rheingold Brewing Company. Initial attempts to reintroduce the beer in the late 1990s were unsuccessful, but in 2002–2003 the branding agency Powell of New York unveiled a guerilla campaign that was intended to make Rheingold the beer of choice among denizens of the city's hippest neighborhoods.

Limited by a campaign budget of $400,000, Powell had no choice but to eschew traditional strategies of mass-media messaging, but its target group of authenticity-craving hipsters was notoriously resistant to such marketing tactics anyway. The Rheingold beer campaign instead chose 15 key bars in select New York neighborhoods to serve as staging grounds for the brand's rejuvenation. A series of promotional events, including an updated version of the "Miss Rheingold" pageant, supported the word-of-mouth buzz created by cryptic billboard placements, a sales force drawn from the hipster target market, and other untraditional means of spreading awareness.

The campaign ran through the end of 2003 and was considered an enormous success. Rheingold, initially available in only seven New York City bars, spread to 2,000 locations within a year. The campaign won two Gold EFFIE Awards in 2004. Rheingold and Powell continued to seek out untraditional means of winning back its place at the top of the New York beer market.

HISTORICAL CONTEXT

The Rheingold brand was introduced in 1883 by Joseph, Henry, and Charles Liebman, whose father, Samuel, a German immigrant, had successfully established the Liebman Brewery in Brooklyn, New York, a generation earlier. Prior to the outbreak of World War I more than 700,000 barrels of Rheingold were being produced annually, but the company's success was hindered by the anti-German prejudice surrounding the war effort as well as by the onset of Prohibition in 1920. After surviving Prohibition by producing nonalcoholic products, including "near beer," Rheingold enjoyed monumental success in its primary market of New York City during the subsequent decades. For nearly 30 years, beginning in the mid-1930s, Rheingold was New York's best-selling beer, and the brand's advertising slogan ("Rheingold Extra Dry") and radio jingle ("Rheingold, the dry beer—think of Rheingold whenever you buy beer") became midcentury cultural touchstones for millions in the city. Additionally, the "Miss Rheingold" beauty pageant, whose winner was selected by bar patrons citywide each year, was an enormously popular local event. At its peak in the 1950s and early 1960s, the promotional contest was decided by more than 20 million ballots, a number almost equal to the turnout of U.S. presidential elections of the time.

In the mid-1960s, however, Rheingold's fortunes declined along with those of other local beer brands across the United States, who could not compete with emerging megabreweries such as Anheuser-Busch, Miller, and Coors. The Liebman brewery was shuttered, and the Rheingold brand seemed to have become part of history by the late 1970s. In the late 1990s, however, a team of investors enlisted a member of the Liebman family and embarked on a plan to reestablish the Rheingold brand. An initial strategy of targeting suburban grocery stores, traditional area restaurants, and sports fans did not effectively rejuvenate the Rheingold brand. During this time, though, a surprising beer-drinking trend emerged, particularly in urban centers across the country: so-called sub-premium brands such as Pabst Blue Ribbon and Miller High Life were being reclaimed by 20-something hipsters, as were other nearly defunct local brands similar to Rheingold. Rheingold executives decided on a change of course for the brand's relaunch.

HE WENT THAT WAY

Among the many unpredictable ideas developed by advertising agency Powell of New York for the Rheingold beer campaign was a strange flier that began appearing on lampposts in the city during the summer of 2003. The flier, printed on fuchsia paper and lettered in black marker, said, "Help! Have you seen this beer?" and offered an extremely specific description of the Rheingold that had been "lost." A working Manhattan phone number was provided as a contact. When staff members of the magazine *Adweek* called the number, they got an answering machine. The voice on the recording was that of a desperate woman who was not home because she was looking for her Rheingold.

The woman was, in reality, a marketing director from Powell, Sarah Riddler, and she told *Adweek* that the flier generated upward of 130 phone calls within a week. Among the responses were calls informing Riddler that her Rheingold had been seen fleeing by bus and others claiming that they were holding the beer for ransom.

TARGET MARKET

Powell's Rheingold Beer campaign centered on a particular group of New Yorkers that the agency identified as "downtown culture drivers," residents of Manhattan's Lower East Side and East Village as well as of Williamsburg, Brooklyn. These neighborhoods harbored a high concentration of the city's most self-consciously hip, creative young people, "young Lou Reeds and Patty Smiths," as Powell phrased it, whose tastes frequently defined tastes throughout the city and, by extension, in large portions of the United States. Not coincidentally, this audience was roughly the same age as the overall beer industry's prime target market, 21- to 27-year-olds, who consumed far more beer per capita than other Americans. Rheingold's downtown target drank more than a quarter of New York's beer and tended to stay out later than other residents of the city.

These consumers favored presumably authentic and simple brands like Levi's jeans, Marlboro cigarettes, and Converse shoes, and Powell observed that they had rejected high-end microbrews, which had been extremely popular in the 1990s, as part of a larger rejection of "all things fancy and pretentious." In the beer world this attitude had translated into a return to such nationally distributed beers as Pabst Blue Ribbon and Miller High Life, but Rheingold and Powell saw that their target market might be susceptible—especially in the climate of affection for the city following the terrorist attacks of September 11, 2001—to a New York beer that measured up to the approved standards of simplicity and authenticity.

Rheingold thus attempted to position itself as "100% New York by Volume," a "macro-brew" that shared the city's "bold, dirty, electric, up-till-dawn, bad-ass independent" spirit. It could not, however, communicate this message using traditional advertising tactics, for two reasons: its target was notoriously skeptical of all overt marketing appeals, and the minimal campaign budget would not allow for such an approach. Powell accordingly crafted a guerilla-marketing effort that depended largely on word-of-mouth buzz and the participation of owners of neighborhood bars.

COMPETITION

Miller High Life was, during this time, one of the national brands that had experienced a revival partly driven by consumers similar to those Rheingold was targeting. Beginning in 1998 Miller unveiled the first national TV campaign on behalf of High Life since the mid-1980s. The campaign both celebrated and poked fun at retro notions of manhood by defining the "High Life man" as someone who solemnly trusted the power of duct tape, ate hamburgers topped with hunks of butter, and scorned neighbors who could not effectively handle their motorized vehicles. The commercials' combination of nostalgia and irony allowed them to appeal not only to High Life's traditional market of older, blue-collar males but also to its newly minted hipster consumer base, who presumably prized the aura of authenticity conjured by the brand and its emphasis on old-school values. The TV campaign won numerous awards and ran for many years.

Pabst Blue Ribbon, similarly, had long been considered an affordable workingman's beer. In the 1990s, though, the brew's marketers noticed a spike in sales in the Portland, Oregon, area. The Pabst Blue Ribbon team found that the beer had been adopted among the city's bicycle-messenger subculture and that the brand's authentic image was fueling word-of-mouth buzz among young, hip drinkers. Believing that such an audience might be alienated from the brand by a traditional marketing approach, Pabst hired on-the-ground marketers, who traveled to several U.S. cities in order to stoke further interest in Pabst Blue Ribbon simply through conversation. These representatives not only spoke to wholesalers and bar owners but also frequented the gathering places of its target consumers, such as tattoo shops, local music clubs, and bike-messenger races, dropping off cases of Pabst Blue Ribbon and talking to those present. Print ads, which were carefully calibrated not to offend the Pabst Blue Ribbon target's antimarketing sensibility, ran in music magazines and alternative publications.

There was no single leading candidate for the title of New York's favorite beer, a designation that summed up Rheingold's long-term goal beyond its relaunch. The sheer number of retail outlets and bars made for enormous fragmentation of the beer market, and the United States' leading beers—Bud Light, Budweiser, Miller Light, and Coors Light—had less traction among the city's fickle consumers than among America's beer drinkers at large. Local brands, such as those produced by the Brooklyn Brewery, founded in the mid-1980s, had identified themselves as quintessentially New York beers, but Brooklyn Brewery and its local competitors were upscale microbrews with limited marketing resources.

MARKETING STRATEGY

Rheingold and its investors charged Powell, a boutique agency, with the tasks of creating instant sales results and building long-term brand equity, all on a miniscule budget of $400,000. Powell thus focused narrowly on its target of so-called "downtown culture drivers" and selected 15 bars to serve as staging grounds for the brand's revitalization. Rather than hire conventional beer reps to talk the brand up among bar owners, Rheingold and Powell assembled a sales force drawn from its target demographic and trained them to be billboards not just among proprietors but also among customers themselves. The agency signed Rheingold on as a sponsor of the CMJ Music Marathon, an indie-rock festival frequented by large numbers of the target audience, and distributed free Rheingold beer to the press, the bands, and festival attendees.

Rheingold promotional events in the 15 core bars continued to spread word-of-mouth awareness, and Powell bought placements on two billboards at Houston Street and Avenue B, "the gates of the Lower East Side," to run photographs that were in keeping with the brand's desire to associate itself with the mystique of rock music. The grainy black-and-white photographs, which were taken at the CMJ festival, were placed side by side; one showed a rock musician, and the other an audience. No Rheingold logo or any other advertising cues ran with the images. "We wanted to go up 'naked,' with no branding," Powell chief Neil Powell told *Adweek,* "to sort of tease the images and also just to sort of give the Lower East Side some beautiful pieces of art."

As buzz began to build, Powell brought back the "Miss Rheingold" pageant but updated the spectacle to suit its downtown market's sensibilities. Powell selected the winner from among the bartenders at the 15 drinking establishments that had been so central to the campaign thus far. The winner was photographed, during a shoot at the classic bohemian haunt the Chelsea Hotel, revealing her beauty secret: she was shown lounging in a bathtub filled with Rheingold, empty bottles littering the floor around her. This image appeared on the Houston Street billboard space as promotional events surrounding the pageant began.

Meanwhile, a concurrent Powell strategy of sending cases of Rheingold to various prominent New York organizations and institutions, and even to a pair of squatters on the Lower East Side who had recently made headlines, paid off when a reference to the beer was made on *Saturday Night Live.* The plug came as a surprise to Rheingold and Powell and was both a boon to the ongoing marketing effort and a measure of how successful it had been.

OUTCOME

Between the end of 2002, when the guerilla campaign began, and the end of 2003, Rheingold's distribution base went from 7 New York City bars to more than 2,000, and the company claimed a one-year sales increase of 2,500 percent The campaign attracted a significant amount of admiring national and international press coverage, was included in a Marketing Concepts class at NYU's Stern School of Business, and won two Gold EFFIE Awards in 2004.

Rheingold and Powell continued to use untraditional methods of communication in the attempt to recapture the title of New York's favorite beer. In 2004 the "Don't Sleep" campaign included paintings by edgy local artists; they were done on the aluminum security nightshades covering storefronts after business hours in Rheingold's target neighborhoods, the first-ever known use of the nightshades as advertising billboards. The guerilla marketers also flirted with the mainstream that year, running TV spots on local stations, but these commercials managed to generate antiestablishment buzz despite their format. In ridiculing facets of contemporary life in New York that interfered with its downtown consumers' lifestyles, such as a newly enacted ban on smoking in bars, Rheingold attracted an immediate critical response from Mayor Michael Bloomberg, who publicly questioned the brewer's authority to speak on behalf of the city.

FURTHER READING

Anderson, Mae. "Beauty and the Beer." *Adweek,* March 17, 2003.

———. "Rheingold's Night Shift." *Adweek,* November 8, 2004.

Butler, Simon. "In the Sightlines." *Adweek,* January 6, 2003.

"The Case of the Missing Beer." *Adweek,* June 30, 2003.

Kaplan, Andrew. "What's Old Is New Again." *Beverage World,* October 15, 2004.

Moynihan, Colin. "After Brewer Unveils Ads, Mugs Aren't All that's Frosty." *New York Times,* April 19, 2004.

Neuborne, Ellen. "Beauty Is in the Eye of the Beer Holder." *Business 2.0,* June 2003.

Nudd, Tim. "Rheingold Earns Twice the Buzz." *Adweek,* March 17, 2003.

"Rheingold." *Creativity,* April 2005.

Scarpa, James. "Canned Nostalgia." *Restaurant Business,* September 15, 2003.

Thomson, Patricia, and Lisa Trollback. "Hipster Hops." *Print,* July/August 2003.

Todd, Heather. "Packaging that Speaks for Itself." *Beverage World,* November 15, 2003.

Wadler, Joyce, with Campbell Robertson and Paula Schwartz. "Boldface Names." *New York Times,* September 25, 2003.

Mark Lane

Rock the Vote

10635 Santa Monica Blvd., Ste. 150
Los Angeles, California 90025
USA
Telephone: (310) 234-0665
Fax: (310) 234-0666
E-mail: info@rockthevote.com
Web site: www.rockthevote.com

YES/NO BALLOT BOX CAMPAIGN

OVERVIEW

Rock the Vote, a nonprofit, nonpartisan organization, encouraged the young electorate to vote since its founding in 1990. Two years after its conception, Rock the Vote was credited for the second largest 18- to 24-year-old turnout in America's voting history. For the next few years, however, the young electorate steadily decreased. To engage America's youth in political topics they might otherwise show no interest in, Rock the Vote launched its "Yes/No Ballot Box" campaign before the 2000 presidential election.

Launched across various media, including print, radio, outdoor billboards, television, Internet, and even E-mail, "Yes/No Ballot Box" did not use typical partisan rhetoric but presented provocative issues that would appeal more to youth. One ad displayed a chilling photo that looked down a revolver's gun barrel. The young, out-of-focus child holding the gun seemed barely strong enough to take aim at the camera. To the right of the photo, a short paragraph explained both sides of the contemporary gun-control issue. "Yes" and "No" check boxes rested at the bottom of most Internet ads. Whichever box was clicked, the selection's opposite stance opened up. "Yes" or "No" boxes appeared at the bottom of other key-issue images, such as an electric chair, a clear-cut forest, a fetus, and a gay couple, all attempting to spark interest within young voters. Mario Velasquez, executive director of Rock the Vote, told *Business Wire,* "Rather than using just words and images, we are using innovative new media to engage young people in the political process." With a budget of $35,000 to $40,000 per television spot, the campaign was conceived by the advertising agency Collaborate.

Despite the campaign's ad industry success, only 28.7 percent of 18- to 24-year-olds voted in the 2000 election, which was considered to be one of the closest elections in history. This was a significant drop from the 32.4 percent who voted in 1996. According to analysts youth were interested in key issues but not necessarily in who was elected president. Also according to analysts, as well as Rock the Vote organizers, 2000's presidential candidates did not invest much interest in the youth vote as compared with President Bill Clinton's campaigns during the 1990s.

HISTORICAL CONTEXT

Concerned that politicians would censor some of their best-selling music, members of the recording industry started the nonprofit organization Rock the Vote in 1990 to protect freedom of speech and artistic expression rights. "Censorship Is UnAmerican" was the tagline for the first campaign, which featured a series of public service announcements from Woody Harrelson, the Red Hot Chili Peppers, and Iggy Pop. In 1991 Madonna, draped in an American flag, urged young people to vote on MTV but was later criticized for not even being registered at the time. Despite some early criticism Rock the Vote and MTV's 1992 "Choose or Lose" campaign saw a 38 percent voter turnout for 18- to 24-year-olds, the highest turnout since the voting age was lowered in 1972. Rock the Vote also helped pass the National Voter Registration Reform Act, or "Motor Voter Bill," which in 1993 gave voters more rights and retrofitted the voting system.

During nonpresidential election years Rock the Vote used celebrity endorsements and MTV's free donation of airtime to address other political issues. In 1993 President Clinton signed another Rock the Vote–sponsored bill, the National and Community Service Trust Act, which encouraged political volunteerism. In 1995 Rock the Vote helmed "Out of Order: Rock the Vote Targets Health," a series of award-winning short films, which starred Giovanni Ribisi, Cuba Gooding, Jr., Joey Lauren Adams, and Amy Smart. The films focused on health-care issues and won Rock the Vote a Peabody Award.

Despite the organization's awards, young voter turnout decreased every year after the incredible 38 percent turnout in 1992. Rock the Vote organizers believed the decrease resulted from a mutual apathy between presidential candidates and the younger electorate. Robin Raj, Collaborate's creative director, explained to *Adweek* that the "Yes/No Ballot Box" campaign was an attempt to "provoke and confront kids with issues that might ordinarily turn them off."

TARGET MARKET

"Yes/No Ballot Box" targeted the 18- to 24-year-old unregistered electorate who were not interested in politics but were intrigued by provocative social issues. Democrat and Republican candidates in 2000 were accused by many journalists of demonizing young voters in order to win points with the larger, older electorate. Joe Lieberman, Al Gore's running mate and selection for vice president, was criticized for pandering to religious groups by moralizing the "vulgarity" in pop culture, such as Eminem's music and even the television show *Friends.* In the wake of the Monica Lewinsky scandal, Democrats, according to analysts, steered away from anything young, hip, or provocative. Henry Bindbeutel, the twenty-one-year-old heading Libertarian J. Fred Staples' campaign for the U.S. House of Representatives, told the *Portland Press Herald,* "They talk about drugs and teen smoking and violence in schools. It is all targeted at this vision of the young being in some way corrupt."

MOTOR VOTER BILL

In 1991 Rock the Vote supported the National Voter Registration Reform Act, also called the "Motor Voter Bill." Vetoed in 1991 by President George Bush, the bill forced all voting jurisdictions to use the latest technology to maintain a statewide voting database. The Election Review Commission was also created by the bill to educate voting officials about updated voting technologies. The Voter's Bill of Rights, to which voting officials had to comply, was designed for the entire electorate. Among the rights included were "If you make a mistake or spoil your ballot before it is submitted, you have the right to receive a replacement ballot and vote" and "If you are in line at your polling place any time between 7:00 a.m. and 8:00 p.m., you have the right to vote." President Bill Clinton later approved the bill in 1993.

To draw younger voters to the polls in 2000, "Yes/No Ballot Box" avoided political banter and focused on youth-centric issues. "Young people have their own set of priorities and it's important for them to see how the candidates respond to them," said Stephen Koepp, executive editor of *Time,* to *PR Newswire.* "They care particularly about higher education, about civil rights and personal privacy, about violence they encounter in real life, not in the movies. They know a thing or two about these issues because they affect their lives right now."

The Garin Hart Yang Research Group polled 600 people aged 17 to 24 in October 1999. The survey showed that only 30 percent would vote in the 2000 election. The top issues for that same demographic, according to MTV, were education (58 percent), violence and crime (50 percent), jobs and the economy (46 percent), drugs (44 percent), and health care (38 percent).

COMPETITION

"Youth Vote 2000," launched by Youth Vote Coalition, was the largest nonpartisan campaign urging young people to vote in 2000. It was composed of organizations such as Campus Green Vote, Black Youth Vote, League of Women Voters, and Rock the Vote. Volunteers placed phone calls and went door-to-door, targeting the electorate under age 30 in college communities of New York, Colorado, and Oregon. Post-analysis showed that the young voters called were 5 percent more likely to vote than voters not called. And the individuals targeted by the face-to-face campaign were more likely to vote by 8 percent. A comparison of the campaign's cost with the final youth-voter turnout showed the cost per vote averaged between $10 and $12.

The World Wrestling Federation (WWF) launched its "Smackdown Your Vote" campaign in 2000. Also partnered with "Youth Vote 2000," "Smackdown Your Vote" featured guest appearances by wrestling personalities such as the Rock and Chyna at the National Republican and National Democratic conventions. "We wanted to find a way that we could use our popularity to highlight activities which affect our fans and our communities," Gary Davis, WWF vice president of communications, said in the *Grand Rapids Press.* "We've already registered close to 120,000 new voters in the past two months and the response has been great." This number was significantly fewer than the 565,000 of "Yes/No Ballot Box." "Smackdown Your Vote" also focused on familiarizing children under the age of 18 with the election process. Thomas Patterson, an investigator with the Vanishing Voter Project at Harvard University, told the *Sunday Patriot-News Harrisburg* that people between the ages of 18 and 19 were three times more likely to know who won the Super Bowl than the Republican primaries. Paula Case, a Kids Voting USA project manager, remarked, "The reason to start so young is so the voting place becomes a familiar place, not a scary place, so voting becomes a habit."

MARKETING STRATEGY

"Yes/No Ballot Box" in 2000 marked a new turn in Rock the Vote's 10-year-old approach to enticing youth to the polls. In the past the organization had focused its main efforts on approaching celebrities to make public appearances or television public service announcements. Collaborate wanted to market the 2000 campaign differently. "Our feeling was kids had been there, done that. Rock stars presenting the message of 'vote' is important, but it is only one tactic and wasn't enough to break through the cynicism," Raj told *Adweek.* The online portion of the campaign launched September 25, 2000, and the broadcasts began October 7. The entire campaign continued until Election Day (November 7).

"Yes/No Ballot Box" pooled work from several different agencies. Collaborate oversaw the creative aspect, while Pandemonium and Western Images supplied the resources. "Yes/No Ballot Box" also partnered with MTV's "Choose or Lose" campaign, along with the Youth Vote Coalition. Because more than 10 media agencies were involved, one challenge was to make "Yes/No Ballot Box" execute seamlessly. "The team worked together to facilitate a convergent production that ensures that concepts not only look the same, but also act the same as people interact with them," Tommy Means, Pandemonium's director of convergent production, told *Business Wire.*

Collaborate designed the Internet advertisements, which played something like an interactive television commercial. Powered by Unicast's proprietary technology, the Web ads preloaded into the viewer's browser so that when the ads were clicked they played immediately. Each Web ad lasted an estimated 20 seconds and took the form of an interactive debate. Advertising space was donated by websites like AltaVista.com, BlackVoices.com, and E!Online.com. Different issues were conveyed by different images, such as an overflowing ashtray appearing beneath the copy "Ashes to ashes" for the smoking issue. Viewers could click on either "Yes" or "No" depending on their stance regarding the smoking issue. Whatever choice was clicked, the opposing argument was then displayed on the website. Eventually the ad directed the audience back to Rock the Vote's website, where they could register to vote, read more information about key issues, or send the ad's content by E-mail to a friend.

Other key issues were abortion (conveyed by the image of a fetus), capital punishment (an electric chair), hate crimes (a burning cross), and the legalization of marijuana (cannabis leaves). Five different 15-second television spots broadcast the same "Yes" or "No" ballot boxes transposed over similar images. Also 8 million E-mails were sent. "This effort is based on confrontation. Confrontation to create interaction. Maybe that will get more kids to register and vote," Raj told *Business Wire.* "Contrary to the conventional wisdom that people don't care about issues, we find people, and especially young people, are more engaged on issues than rhetoric."

OUTCOME

The "Yes/No Ballot Box" campaign, even though it did not draw more young voters in 2000 than voted in 1996, was still successful from an ad industry and Web marketing standpoint. The overall campaign registered 168,000 voters online; Rock the Vote registered 565,000 total. The campaign reached 20 million viewers and earned Collaborate the Interactive Media Andy Award in 2001, along with a Silver Effie in 2002. Hilary Fadner, Unicast's director of corporate communications, said in *Electronic Advertising & Marketplace Report* that the ad's "click-through rate [was] six times the current average for banners."

Most analysts did not attribute the decrease in young voters to a weakness in campaigning but to the youth's disinterest in the 2000 election. Some journalists speculated that both parties assumed the youth would not vote and therefore simply ignored them. The youth, in turn, ignored the election. "George W. Bush and Al Gore may be the human equivalent of Sominex to most young people," Bruce Horovitz wrote in *USA Today.* "But one thing appears to have cut through teen boredom with the presidential contest: Rock the Vote."

FURTHER READING

Bernstein, Roberta. "Picture This." *Adweek* (eastern ed.), December 4, 2000, p. 26.

DePledge, Derrick. "Even in War Times, Voter Apathy Persists among Young Americans." *Gannett News Service,* October 9, 2002.

Dill, Mallorre. "Click the Vote." *Adweek* (eastern ed.), October 9, 2000, p. 34.

Elliott, Stuart. "Campaign to Use E-Mail to Promote Youth Vote." *New York Times,* September 25, 2000, p. 19.

Goldberg, Danny. "Papa, Don't Preach." *American Prospect,* January 1, 2001, pp. 17–19.

Holzwarth, Dean. "WWF Invades the Political Arena." *Grand Rapids Press,* October 14, 2000, p. C8.

Horovitz, Bruce. "Rock the Vote Aims to Click with Young Electorate." *USA Today,* October 23, 2000, p. 5B.

Jacobs, Heather. "Propaganda and Satellite Try to Rock the Vote." *Shoot,* November 10, 2000, p. 7.

Johnson, Mark. "Youth-Voter Push Seen as Flop." *Richmond Times-Dispatch,* February 14, 1997, p. A2.

Kattleman, Terry. "All's Not Quiet on the Western Front." *Advertising Age's Creativity,* December 1, 2000, p. 46.

Raine, George. "Local Ad Agency a Big Winner in N.Y. Competition." *San Francisco Chronicle,* April 25, 2001, p. C4.

Weichselbaum, Simone. "American U.: Youth Vote Rate up in 2000." *Eagle,* November 20, 2000.

Weinstein, Joshua L. "Youths Speak Out: 'Nobody's Rocking the Vote This Year' Series: Campaign 2000." *Portland Press Herald,* November 6, 2000, p. 1A.

Kevin Teague

Round Table Pizza

1320 Willow Pass Rd., Ste. 600
Concord, California 94520
USA
Telephone: (925) 969-3900
Fax: (925) 969-3978
Web site: www.roundtablepizza.com

THE LAST HONEST PIZZA CAMPAIGN

OVERVIEW

By 1998 Round Table, an employee-owned chain based in Walnut Creek, California, that offered an upscale line of gourmet pizzas, had used the same advertising tag line, "The last honest pizza," for 15 years. The campaign continued throughout much of the year, enhanced by television commercials such as a series called "The Adventures of Gary Garlic," created by Butler, Shines & Stern of Sausalito, California. But by the fall of 1998 Round Table Pizza, with an advertising budget estimated between $8 and $10 million annually, had canceled the campaign, which also included radio and magazine advertising, the latter handled by Tom Geary & Associates. It also ended its two-year relationship with its advertising agency and signed with Wieden & Kennedy of Portland, Oregon. By the spring of 1999 a new campaign was under way.

Round Table Pizza had already changed advertising agencies twice in eight years before abandoning Butler for Wieden late in 1998. Throughout that time, however, and for many years preceding, the chain had maintained its tongue-in-cheek "Last Honest Pizza" campaign. The advertising featured an intrepid character named Bill, who challenged fate in a variety of ways, and later spots included a sidekick called Gary Garlic, created by Butler. But as Jeff Manning and Cesar Diaz reported in the *Portland Oregonian* in September 1998, "After two years of sales as flat as a cheese pizza," the company was ready to consider a new strategy.

The change in advertising agencies and campaigns mirrored larger strategic changes in the chain, which in 1998 had some 530 franchised operating units and $365 million in sales. Although the company intended to stick with—and indeed enhance—its gourmet-style menu, it had begun to look at new ways of serving customers, in part through "delco" (delivery and carry-out only) establishments. Furthermore, with facilities in eight western states, Round Table had begun to look eastward, toward a much larger share of the more than $22 billion U.S. pizza industry.

HISTORICAL CONTEXT

In 1959 businessman William Larson borrowed $2,500 to establish the first Round Table Pizza restaurant in his hometown of Menlo Park, California. At that time pizza, which had first gained popularity in the United States after World War II, was starting to take hold among the U.S. population, and by 1962 Larson was in a position to begin selling franchises.

Despite the fact that gourmet-style pizza would not really come into vogue until the late 1980s and thereafter, from that early stage Larson had determined to build a better pizza, and he developed strict standards for franchisees to follow. Among the facets that made Round Table unique was the fact that all of its ingredients were fresh, including dough made daily from scratch, freshly grated cheeses, and fresh sauces.

The chain grew rapidly on the West Coast, an area where consumers were inclined to look for and accept extraordinary culinary ideas. In 1979, 17 years after Larson began franchising, Round Table had expanded to include more than 150 units. It was in 1979 that an investment group purchased Larson's company, and four years later the new owners launched "The Last Honest Pizza" campaign, which focused on the quality ingredients and pizza-making methods used at Round Table.

The first of several advertising agencies hired by Round Table Pizza in the 1990s was San Francisco-based Goldberg Moser O'Neill. This relationship lasted from 1990 until late 1993, when the firm was replaced by California ad agency Bertram Wooster. By February 1996, Round Table was ready for another change, at which point it took on Butler, Shines & Stern. At that point its advertising budget was valued at $7 to $8 million, with 50 percent dedicated to television and the remainder to a mix of radio, magazines, and other formats. The changes in agencies primarily affected electronic media, as Round Table had continued throughout much of this time with the firm of Tom Geary & Associates for its print advertising, while EH&Y Media Services of Santa Barbara took care of media buying.

As of mid-1992, Round Table ownership passed to its employees, who on June 1 of that year purchased the company. In later years there would be disputes over advertising between the Round Table Owners Association and franchisees who refused to contribute to its cooperative advertising fund. An agreement between the Owners Association and some 120 renegade franchisees in February 1998, in fact, helped open the way for the chain's planned expansion into the eastern United States and a variety of marketing venues.

TARGET MARKET

By the late 1990s Round Table had franchise locations in seven western states besides its home base of California: Oregon, Washington, Idaho, Nevada, Utah, Alaska, and Hawaii. It also had facilities in six nations in the Middle East and in East Asia. With well over 500 locations and more than $300 million in annual sales, the company prepared for a massive expansion intended to carry it into new geographical areas and new operating venues, where it would serve new products to a widening range of buyers.

Joan Voight of *Adweek* noted in April 1996 that the company was "looking to zero in on the health-conscious [baby] boomer market by 'making our product line more upscale,'" the latter according to vice president of marketing Diane Waitkus. This would, in Voight's words, "give the restaurant a more contemporary feel and set it apart from its rivals peddling inexpensive, high-fat products." Yet like some of those more down-to-earth competitors, Round Table had begun by mid-1998 to move increasingly toward delivery and carryout facilities, in addition to its sit-down units.

Hand in hand with the growth of these delco units—and with a broader-based strategy of expanding into unusual venues—was a move in the direction of eastward growth. John Klacking, one of Round Table's leading franchisees, told Amy Zuber of *Nation's Restaurant News* in June 1998 that the company's new corporate team "has more of a mind to expand eastward and be more aggressive." Nonetheless, the company had a long-standing regional identity. "If you grew up on the West Coast, you ate Round Table Pizza," Klacking said. "It is a tradition." Because of his own western

(COMMUNITY) SERVICE WITH A SMILE

In June 1999, Round Table Pizza honored 11 franchisees who had provided outstanding service to their communities. Among those cited for their record of community service was a franchisee that organized local resources to raise $20,000 for a woman and her children after the husband and father had been killed in an automobile accident. Another Round Table operator was recognized for assisting special-needs students with vocational training, and promotion of community service on a website earned kudos for yet another franchisee.

According to company president Jim Fletcher, in 1998 Round Table franchisees supported some 1,000 youth sports teams, either by purchasing uniforms, assisting in fund-raising, or helping in some other way. Estimated giving to community needs by Round Table restaurant owners reached $2 million in 1998, with efforts including companywide sponsorship of a summer reading program that involved some 100,000 students in the San Francisco Bay Area. "Our operators look for the best ways to make a difference in their communities," Fletcher told *Nation's Restaurant News*. "In emergencies and on a daily basis, Round Table franchisees are there, lending a hand."

background, Klacking suggested, "I didn't have an interest in opening a Pizza Hut or a Domino's."

The eastward expansion was still in its opening stages in 1998, but much further along was a move to place Round Table franchises in unusual locations, at least one of which would aid the geographical expansion in an innovative way. Ontario International Airport in California might not be the first place one would think of for pizza, but for hungry travelers the airport Round Table was a welcome addition. "One of the terminals where we are located," Round Table chief financial officer Rob McCourt told Zuber in November 1998, "has flights coming in and out from all over the country. That gives us a unique opportunity for national exposure, and it will help us support our expansion."

COMPETITION

By 1998 the U.S. pizza industry accounted for $22 billion in sales, meaning that Americans spent more on pizza than the entire gross domestic product for the nation of Bolivia during that same year. It was an impressive figure, and Round Table began to aggressively go after a larger portion of this growing industry.

At the top in terms of sales was Pizza Hut, a Dallas-based chain owned by the gigantic foods conglomerate PepsiCo. Second in total sales, and first in delivery sales, was Domino's, a chain whose facilities were entirely delco units. Next was Little Caesars, followed by Papa John's, based in Louisville. Round Table stood just outside the big four of the industry, above other chains such as the upscale California Pizza Kitchen and the much more utilitarian Pizza Inn.

Many of the larger pizza lines had begun to take an interest in gourmet-style pizzas at least as early as the mid-1990s. Thus Pizza Hut, which in 1995 had sales of $7.9 billion, in 1996 introduced a number of specialty items such as Italian Chicken pizza, which included a garlic-flavored white sauce rather than the traditional tomato-based sauce. Papa John's, which advertised with the tag line "Better ingredients, better pizza," created by the Richards Group of Dallas, had begun to emphasize thin-crust pizzas. Even Pizza Inn, a chain that had begun expanding through express stores in gas stations, began offering a flavored crust in the mid-1990s.

MARKETING STRATEGY

When Round Table hired Butler, Shines & Stern in February 1996, Voight suggested in *Adweek* that, although "Butler is expected to put its own imprint" on Round Table advertising and its character of Bill, advertising would nonetheless "focus on the chain's gourmet pizza selections and a fresh line of healthful menu offerings." This was in line with established strategy, since "Round Table has maintained its position . . . over the years by concentrating on the quality of its food and sticking to a steady diet of attitude and humor in advertising."

The first series of Butler ads, which appeared in the late spring of 1996, consisted of about a dozen TV spots built around the tag line "Round Table. The last honest pizza." One ad, for instance, promoted specialty pizzas with unusual ingredients such as Chinese chili sauce or cashews and showed the pudgy pizza guy Bill taunting a biker at a stoplight. The intimidating biker reacted not by throttling Bill but simply by shaking his head in consternation. "Some days you just feel more adventurous," the voice-over suggested. According to Round Table's Waitkus, "We decided to show Bill in familiar, humorous, very '90s situations. By portraying the frailties of Everyman, Bill can defend the brand in a fun way."

In March 1998, Butler unveiled a 30-second TV spot featuring Bill along with the time-honored tag line and a new sidekick, Gary Garlic. The latter was the creation of M-5 Industries in San Francisco, the firm also responsible for the Penny Hardaway puppet used in Nike commercials. In "The Adventures of Gary Garlic," one of more than a half-dozen Round Table commercials undertaken by Butler over the course of the year, Gary Garlic and Bill—a.k.a. Bill Bonham—promoted Round Table's new Roastin' Toastin' Garlic Pizza.

Jane Irene Kelly in *Adweek* compared Gary Garlic to Mr. Bill, the hapless claymation character featured on *Saturday Night Live* in the late 1970s and early 1980s. "Naive, but dedicated to his dream," wrote Kelly, "Gary is roasted with a blowtorch, thrown in a food chopper, crushed by a falling artichoke and cleaved in half—all at the hands of [Bill] Bonham." Butler, Shines & Stern principal and creative director John Butler told Kelly that Bill was glad to have a cohort, since for many years he had been the one "endur[ing] all the stunts. This time it's Gary . . . but he always bounces back."

"In typical cartoon fashion," Kelly observed, "Gary's deadly encounters leave him undaunted. Each spot ends with him flying away on an angel's wings, cheerfully calling, 'Bye, everybody!'" Then, of course, there was the tag line "The last honest pizza," intended to signify the quality of Round Table's product. Although Gary was a new addition, the high-spirited style of the ads featuring him was not significantly different from that of the "Some Days You Just Feel More Adventurous" spot two years earlier.

OUTCOME

After 15 years of "The Last Honest Pizza," Manning and Diaz reported in the *Portland Oregonian* in late September 1998, "Neither the company nor the ad campaign had much of a hold on the public imagination." Their observation was the result of research conducted by Wieden & Kennedy, the company's new advertising agency. Round Table had recently dismissed Butler, Shines & Stern in favor of the Oregon agency, best known for its Nike "Just Do It" ads.

Manning and Diaz indicated that the first new Round Table ads would appear in March or April, and on March 8, 1999, the company issued a press release in which it proclaimed the "Round Table Pizza Bill of Rights." The latter, the press released noted, "is the foundation for the campaign developed by Wieden & Kennedy." Five new television spots, along with radio ads, would "feature various animated characters [designed by underground cartoonist Peter Bagge] celebrating the Bill of Rights." One of these was "Steam Dance," a 15-second spot illustrating Article 7 of the 33 articles in the Bill of Rights: "The right to size up your fourth slice while you're still working on your third."

Another spot featured a sleepy rooster trying to wake up in the morning. A cold slice of Round Table pizza brought him to life, thus giving a visual image to Article 16: "The right to eat pizza for breakfast." In addition to the "Bill of Rights" campaign, which featured the tag line "If you love pizza, we love you," Round Table in mid-1999 ran a promotion in which it offered to host block parties—including 15 large pizzas, a large salad, and soft drinks for 50 people—for 33 winners of a random drawing. The promotion and the new ad campaign made note of Round Table's 40th anniversary, which the company celebrated throughout 1999.

FURTHER READING

Bertagnoli, Lisa. "Just Dough It: Flavored Crusts Top Pizza Chains' Menu Rollouts in Last Six Months." *Restaurants & Institutions,* July 15, 1996, pp. 34-36.

Dawson, Angela. "We the Pizza People." *Adweek* (Western Edition), March 15, 1999, p. 4.

Kelly, Jane Irene. "Butler, Shines & Stern Introduces Round Table's 'Gary Garlic' Puppet." *Adweek* (Western Edition), March 16, 1998, p. 4.

Manning, Jeff, and Cesar Diaz. "Round Table Signs with Wieden." *Portland Oregonian,* September 30, 1998, p. C3.

"'Pizza Eaters Have Their Rights!' Proclaim Round Table Revelers." Business Wire, March 8, 1999.

"Round Table Pizza Awards Franchisees for Community Outreach Programs." *Nation's Restaurant News,* June 21, 1999, p. 22.

"Round Table Pizza Proclaims 'Rights' for Pizza Lovers." *Nation's Restaurant News,* March 22, 1999, p. 14.

"This Summer's Going to Be a Pizzapalooza! How about a Block Party for 50—Free from Round Table?" Business Wire, June 2, 1999.

Voight, Joan. "Butler Swipes Round Table's Pizza Business." *Adweek* (Western Edition), February 5, 1996, p. 4.

———. "Round Table's Slice of Life." *Adweek* (Western Edition), April 1, 1996, p. 6.

Zuber, Amy. "Round Table Pizza Looks to Nontraditional Venues for Expansion." *Nation's Restaurant News,* November 30, 1998, p. 3.

———. "Round Table Plans Aggressive Expansion Eastward." *Nation's Restaurant News,* June 15, 1998, p. 6.

Judson Knight

Royal Appliance Manufacturing Company

7005 Cochran Rd.
Glenwillow, Ohio 44139
USA
Telephone: (440) 996-2000
Fax: (440) 996-2027
Web site: www.dirtdevil.com

■■■

DARIN' CAMPAIGN

OVERVIEW

NOTE: Royal Appliance Manufacturing Company is the parent company of Dirt Devil. The essay refers to the Dirt Devil division, as that company was responsible for the campaign profiled.

In September 1998 Dirt Devil, Inc., a subsidiary of Royal Appliance Manufacturing Company, introduced the Swivel Glide Vision, a bagless upright vacuum with a unique see-through container. A new television campaign was created for the launch, the product of a collaboration between Bennett, Kuhn & Varner of Atlanta and the Wolf Group of Cleveland. Inspired by the movie *Toy Story,* the six commercials featured a child's toy that came to life in the form of a computer-generated daredevil character called Darin'. They were directed and produced by Strom Magallon Entertainment of Los Angeles, which used technical wizardry to showcase the vacuum's features and capabilities in a way that was thought to be more compelling for viewers than a typical product demonstration.

On August 10, a month before the launch of the product, the company aired two direct-response television spots that showed Darin' being sucked into the vacuum and taking a thrill ride inside it. The viewer saw the inner workings of the Vision vacuum through Darin's eyes. Thanks to the product's see-through canister, Darin' was eventually found and rescued. On September 14 the direct-response ads were replaced with a 15-second and a 30-second retail spot that showed Darin' playing cat-and-mouse games with the vacuum. These two ads, titled "Thrill Ride," were intended to demonstrate the product's power, bagless design, and ease of use. Again, the daredevil was swept inside the vacuum but later retrieved and returned to the toy box. The campaign continued into 1999 when a second set of two retail spots, titled "Thrill Seeker," were unveiled, in which Darin' tried to outdo the Vision vacuum on a toy motorcycle, giving a visual display of the product's maneuverability.

HISTORICAL CONTEXT

The parent of Dirt Devil, Inc., was Royal Appliance Manufacturing Company, said to be the oldest maker of vacuums in the world. Royal began in 1905 as the P.A. Geier Company, named for the man who founded the business in a backyard garage in Cleveland. Geier started out making metal cleaners by hand. The business grew, moved into a four-story building, and began to diversify into other consumer goods, including mixers, hair dryers, and washing machines. Vacuum cleaners continued to be its main product, however, and the first handheld vacuum, the Royal Prince, was introduced in 1937.

In 1953 the Walter E. Schott Organization bought the company and renamed it the Royal Appliance Manufacturing Company but quickly lost interest in the business. In 1954 Royal was acquired by Stan Erbor

Seven stills from the "Thrill Ride" television commercial for Dirt Devil's "Darin'" campaign. THE WOLF GROUP. REPRODUCED BY PERMISSION.

and a group of employees. The company began to grow again, relocated to new headquarters in 1969, and expanded its operations. Erbor remained active in the company until his death in 1981. In that year the company changed hands once more, this time going to a group of Cleveland investors headed by John Balch. The new regime came in with a fresh sales and marketing approach that transformed Royal into a major contender in the vacuum cleaner market. According to the company, Royal's sales grew from just under $5 million in 1981 to about $286 million in 1996.

One of the most significant developments was the redesign of Royal's handheld metal vacuum. In 1984 the product began coming out in red plastic, which was both cheaper and flashier than the old model, and it was renamed the Dirt Devil. The new hand vacuum not only had eye-catching styling, but it also featured a revolving brush, a large capacity, and a power cord for plugging into an electrical outlet. Further, at $30 it was relatively inexpensive. The new ownership began an aggressive marketing strategy. Whereas Royal had traditionally relied upon small mom-and-pop outfits to sell its products, the company now began marketing through national retail chains such as Kmart, Wal-Mart, and Target. To assure that purchasers were satisfied, Royal established an unconditional 30-day return policy, set up a customer satisfaction computer network, and printed its toll-free telephone number on each vacuum, prompting thousands of customers to call each month. The company also began to advertise more heavily. Previously, as more and more domestic cleaning came to be done by household members rather than hired help, sales had risen without advertising. When the steady growth of the market tapered off, however, Royal looked for ways to boost sales, including the use of consumer advertising on television beginning in the early 1990s.

The Dirt Devil soon became a leader in the market for handheld vacuums, and by 1992 the company had sold more than 4 million. Royal used its dominance in the handheld market to work its way into other market segments, and it relied heavily on outside sources to make product components, giving it flexibility to meet consumer demands more quickly. Royal brought out the Dirt Devil Broom Vac in 1987 and a canister model in 1988. In 1990 the company introduced its first upright vacuum, going head to head with competitors like the Hoover Company, Eureka Company, and the Regina line made by Philips Electronics. Despite the competition, Dirt Devil increased its market share from 2 percent in 1990 to 7 percent in 1992.

Royal ran into various problems in getting its uprights on the market, however. In the early 1990s one upright model failed to pick up dirt because of a design flaw. Although the company fixed the problem, the damage was reflected in a steep drop in its market share in upright vacuums, from 24.3 percent in 1992 to 17.2 in 1993. Royal also became embroiled in litigation with upright vacuum leader Hoover, alleging that the latter's use of a so-called Cleaning Efficiency Rating was "misleading advertising" and asking the court to force Hoover to recall all advertising and promotional material related to the rating and to take it off its products. Hoover claimed that Royal was the false advertiser and accused it of defamation and interference with business relations. Royal was also named in at least four class-action lawsuits brought by shareholders. Despite these difficulties, the company continued to dominate the handheld market and managed to work its way into the upright segment.

TARGET MARKET

The traditional target market for housecleaning products was women in the 25- to 54-year-old age bracket. As in previous years, Dirt Devil products in 1998 were targeted to the mass market and were sold primarily through

AN ADVERTISER'S BEST FRIEND

RCA, Polaroid, Kodak, Nissan, and Dirt Devil had at least one thing in common on the marketing front: at one time or other all had used dogs or puppies to sell products.

Dirt Devil started using golden retriever puppies in its advertising in 1991. The long-haired pets turned out to be effective mascots for the company's marketing effort. *USA Today* reported in December 1996 that its Ad Track poll found Dirt Devil's holiday advertising, featuring three mischievous but cuddly pups, to be "very popular and very effective with consumers." Of those polled, 37 percent thought that the ads were "very effective," and 31 percent said that they "liked the ads a lot." Further, out of 46 ads measured in the previous 12 months, the Dirt Devil campaign made the top 10 for popularity and effectiveness.

Apart from the puppies' cuteness, Dirt Devil had a practical reason for using man's best friend in its advertising: it illustrated the product's ability to suck up pesky dog hair. "Dogs are always popular in ads, but any company that can use them to show a product's practical uses is at an advantage," according to Diane Cook Tench, director of the Ad Center at Virginia Commonwealth University.

major retailers (for example, Kmart, Wal-Mart, and Target), electronic chains (Best Buy, Circuit City, and Service Merchandise), warehouse clubs (Sam's Club), regional chains, and department stores. Royal reported in its annual filing with the U.S. Securities and Exchange Commission (SEC) that in 1998 Wal-Mart (including Sam's Club), Target, and Kmart made up 31.6 percent, 14.1 percent, and 13.4 percent, respectively, of its net sales and that these were the only retailers who accounted for 10 percent or more of its sales in 1997 and 1998.

Royal continued to use television, print, and cooperative advertising to market its Dirt Devil products and to obtain shelf space from major retailers. Some of the advertising and promotion was tied to holidays and to specific promotional activities of retailers. Royal indicated in its SEC filing that its business was highly seasonal and that it believed many of its products were given as gifts and therefore sold in higher volumes during the Christmas shopping season.

COMPETITION

In the market for handheld vacuums Royal's principal competitors were Hoover and Eureka, along with Black & Decker Corp. In fact, Black & Decker created the handheld vacuum market when it introduced its cordless DustBuster in 1979. The Dirt Devil came out five years later, allowing Royal to take advantage of the booming replacement market for hand vacuums. With its low price and attractive features, the Dirt Devil sold 50,000 units in 1984 and soon became the market leader. A couple of years later, Dirt Devil held two-thirds of the handheld vacuum market and was selling more than all of its competitors combined.

By the early 1990s the competition had begun to challenge Dirt Devil on features and price. In 1991 Black & Decker introduced a revolving brush, corded model. At the same time Dirt Devil's market share in the handheld segment was slipping, and it continued to decline during the next two years. Meanwhile, third-place Hoover began to capture more business from Dirt Devil and Black & Decker. Dirt Devil remained dominant, however, and it began advertising on television in 1991, putting pressure on its rivals to develop new products and to increase their own advertising. By 1998 Royal held the number two share of the upright vacuum cleaner market, with uprights constituting about 55 percent of the company's business. In 1999 Royal maintained that the Dirt Devil was the largest selling handheld vacuum in the United States.

MARKETING STRATEGY

According to Deborah Holtkamp, Dirt Devil's director of advertising and sales promotion, the first two ads were aired before the product was available in stores in order to "raise awareness and generate excitement around the Vision's introduction; and to educate the consumer on the product's unique features and benefits." Holtkamp said that "it's in these spots that Darin' has his first encounter with the new Vision and unexpectedly gets the ride of his *life.*" In the ads, after a child had left Darin' lying outside the toy box, he was accidentally scooped up by the vacuum. Viewers rode along with Darin' to get a firsthand look at the inside of the new product. "This story is not only relevant to our target consumer, but also sends a powerful message about the product design," Holtkamp said. "Darin' would have been lost forever if he had been swept into a traditional vacuum that uses a bag, but thanks to the Vision's clear, removable dirt container, he is able to go on to future adventures."

In the first retail commercials Darin' played a cat-and-mouse game with the vacuum. As he attempted to outdo the Vision's power, he was foiled each time and got sucked into the vacuum, but he was spotted through the clear container and safely returned to the toy box. Holtkamp said that the ads not only showed the product's power and unique bagless design but also how easy it was to empty the vacuum.

OUTCOME

In March 1999 Royal ran a second round of retail commercials in which Darin' attempted even greater feats of daring on a toy motorcycle. Along with the vacuum's other features, these ads emphasized its maneuverability. According to Holtkamp, as Darin' zoomed around the floor, "his swift moves on the bike mirror those of the vacuum as it maneuvers around furniture. He's in effect showing the consumer how easy it is to push and turn the Vision with its unique swivel caster wheel design." As in the previous set of commercials, Darin' ended up inside the Vision but was rescued.

The company used focus groups in Cleveland, Atlanta, and Chicago to get feedback about the new product and its advertising campaign. Holtkamp said that, "based on feedback from consumers, we believe that bagless uprights are a huge opportunity in the marketplace. We're very excited about the Vision introduction and its sales potential."

FURTHER READING

Chanil, Debra. "Vacuums Clean Up." *Discount Merchandiser,* January 1992, pp. 48-51, 61.

Gerdel, Thomas W. "Investor Says Royal Overstated." *Cleveland Plain Dealer,* August 15, 1992, pp. F1-2.

"Here Are Some of the Deadliest Ads on TV." *Toronto Star,* November 14, 1998, p. M14.

Holstein, William J. "Little Companies, Big Exports." *Business Week,* April 13, 1992, pp. 70-72.

King, Eileen M. "Next Step for Dirt Devil: Full Ad Blitz for Its First Cyclonic Vacuum." *HFN,* August 17, 1998, p. 61.

Mallory, Maria. "The Dirt Devil Made Royal Do It." *Business Week,* August 26, 1991, pp. 30-31.

———. "Royal Is Having a Devil of a Time." *Business Week,* August 10, 1992, p. 28.

Pledger, Marcia. "Dirt Devil Debuts Sweeper: Ad Introduces Bagless, Upright Vacuum Cleaner." *Cleveland Plain Dealer,* September 3, 1998, p. C1.

———. "Dirt Devil Maker Sees Sales Drop." *Cleveland Plain Dealer,* February 16, 1999, p. C1.

Ringer, Richard. "Dirt Devil Disappoints Investors." *New York Times,* August 12, 1993, p. D1.

"They're at It Again . . . Dirt Devil Launches Innovative, New Product with Another Groundbreaking Advertising Campaign." Dirt Devil, Inc., February 1999.

Wollenberg, Skip. "Super Bowl Ads Yield Fumbles, Scores." *Sacramento Bee,* January 20, 1998, p. E1.

Debbi Mack

FRED ASTAIRE CAMPAIGN

OVERVIEW

NOTE: Royal Appliance Manufacturing Company is the parent company of Dirt Devil. The essay refers to the Dirt Devil division, as that company was responsible for the campaign profiled.

Dirt Devil, Inc., a subsidiary of Royal Appliance Manufacturing Company, generated free publicity for itself with its innovative and controversial "Fred Astaire" advertising campaign. In the mid-1990s Jim Holcomb, vice president of marketing and strategic planning at Royal Appliance, successfully created product awareness and informed the consumer public about Dirt Devil products even before they hit the retail market by using direct response television advertisements. Using the direct response ad strategy boosted sales of several Dirt Devil products, but the company saw even more impressive results after the 1997 Super Bowl, the "stage" where the newest and most innovative ads are seen. Holcomb aired three 15-second spots featuring Fred Astaire dancing with three of Dirt Devil's newest products: the Broom Vac, the Ultra Hand Vac, and an upright vacuum called the Ultra MVP.

Manufacturers pay top dollar to air their product advertisements during the Super Bowl. For the Super Bowl 1997, Fox Network received an average of $1.2 million dollars from each of approximately 25 advertisers. Advertisers are willing to pay such large sums of money because the Super Bowl has the highest viewer ratings of any television program. Super Bowl Sunday is also a widely studied phenomenon—the information obtained, such as the ratio of male/female viewership, the age of viewers, the socioeconomic status of viewers, and which commercials are the most favored, provide useful data for marketing specialists.

The ads for the "Fred Astaire" campaign that aired during the 1997 Super Bowl took more than one year to create and contained film footage from two of Astaire's best-known movies, *Royal Wedding* and *Easter Parade.* To produce the ads, identical movie sets needed to be reconstructed "down to the screw heads." An experienced dancer, dressed in a special green suit, copied Astaire's original dance steps while holding a Dirt Devil appliance. The dancer needed to perform specific routines from the

FRED ASTAIRE: WHISKING YOU AWAY

Before Darin' was created, Dirt Devil had another highly innovative, and controversial, marketing effort in a 1997 campaign that featured the late Fred Astaire. The 15-second spots, created by Meldrum & Fewsmith Communications (later acquired by the Wolf Group) and produced by Strom Magallon Entertainment, included re-creations of dance scenes from the Astaire movies *Easter Parade* and *Royal Wedding.* The commercials, which took more than a year to make, required a painstaking reconstruction of the movie sets "down to the screw heads." A dancer was hired to re-create Astaire's original dance steps while holding a Dirt Devil. The dancer wore a green suit and performed on a matching green set. With the magic of computers the Dirt Devil images from the green set were combined with original footage so that the finished commercials showed Astaire dancing with various Dirt Devil vacuums.

Although the actor's daughter, Ava McKenzie, was upset over the ads, Astaire's widow approved the use of the images. In a January 1997 interview aired on National Public Radio's *All Things Considered,* Robyn Astaire admitted that her role in creating the ads had made her the focus of criticism. Her response was that "the fact is that Fred danced with a mop in the '30s, swabbing the deck of some ship. A prop is a prop. The bottom line is I know Fred would have approved this, and that is my only concern."

movies in a special set that matched his green suit. The Dirt Devil images were then lifted from the green film footage by an advanced computer hardware/software program called Inferno, and another type of electronic technology called Animotion placed the Dirt Devils into the original footage. The new film footage was adjusted in several ways to match the old footage, and the end result was Astaire holding a Broom Vac instead of a coat rack in the *Royal Wedding* footage. In the other ads Astaire danced up a wall and on the ceiling while holding an Ultra Hand Vac to demonstrate the ease of reaching ceiling fixtures, and he danced up the stairs with an Ultra MVP to demonstrate the key feature of the appliance: an extra long cord.

The "Fred Astaire" ads, created by the Cleveland advertising agency Meldrum & Fewsmith Communications, were covered as news by such major publications as the *New York Times, USA Today,* and *Entertainment Weekly.* The "Fred Astaire" ads were also covered by *CNN Headline News, CBS Evening News,* and ABC's *Good Morning America* television programs. The ads received this publicity for several reasons. The ads were a departure from Royal's past campaign ads, which featured Golden Retriever dogs, and the technology used to produce the "Fred Astaire" ads was extremely time consuming and complex. Fred Astaire's daughter was critical of using his image and tried to prohibit their use, whereas his widow, Robyn, supported their use as long as she had significant input and Royal would donate money to the Arthritis Foundation.

The "Fred Astaire" campaign for Dirt Devil was the first time Robyn Astaire allowed advertisers to use her husband's image since his death in 1987. She agreed because, as she said, "he was always receptive to new proposals. He would have used a vacuum cleaner in a minute. Why, he used a mop in the 1930s." In a quote included in a press release from Royal Appliance, Mrs. Astaire stated, "My husband was often trying innovative things in his movies—dancing with props, in unusual settings, or up a wall and onto the ceiling. In considering Dirt Devil's concept, it was important to me that Fred's original performances remain intact, without alteration." Mrs. Astaire continued, "From the beginning, Dirt Devil maintained the integrity of his work, and at the same time, used new technology in a way Fred would have approved. I'm happy with what we've achieved because I know his wishes have been respected."

Fred Astaire in 1941. © BETTMANN/CORBIS.

HISTORICAL CONTEXT

The first Royal vacuum was made in 1905 by the P.A. Geier Company in Geier's garage, making Royal Appliance, the direct descendent of the P.A. Geier Company, the oldest vacuum cleaner manufacturer in the world. In 1937 the P.A. Geier Company made the first handheld vacuum cleaner. The company was purchased in 1953 by an investment group called the Walter E. Schott Organization and was renamed Royal Appliance Manufacturing Company. Soon after, in 1954, Royal was sold to a group of employees headed by Stan Erbar. Under Erbar's leadership the company thrived and was able to expand its operations during the late 1960s. Erbar remained very active in the company until 1981, when he was 80 years old. The company was then sold to a small group of investors who were eager to use new and innovative marketing strategies to increase sales. Advertising in the industry had been minimal because vacuum cleaner sales over several decades had risen without it. As more households installed wall-to-wall carpeting (which replaced area rugs that were taken outdoors, hung over the fence or on a clothesline, and cleaned with a rug beater), more vacuums were being sold. As society and the economy changed, more households were performing the housecleaning tasks themselves instead of hiring others to do the job. Vacuum cleaners, especially those with attachments, made housecleaning easier, and they practically sold themselves. As this steady growth in the market tapered off, however, Royal looked for ways to increase sales. It became one of the first floor care companies to bring consumer advertising to television in the early 1990s.

Since 1981 Royal had distributed its products into such mass retail outlets as Kmart and Wal-Mart. By the time Fred Astaire appeared during the 1997 Super Bowl, dancing across the screen with a Dirt Devil, consumers already knew about several Dirt Devil Products.

TARGET MARKET

Traditionally, the target market for housecleaning products is women between the ages of 25 and 54—the ages that parents or caregivers, particularly women, are actively raising children and are subsequently more active in keeping the home clean and organized. The "Fred Astaire" ad campaign attempted to expand the traditional market by appealing to a larger consumer market, including both males and females and consumers of a greater age range. According to Denise Gellene of the *Los Angeles Times,* "Dead celebrities allow advertisers to tap into feelings of nostalgia about times spent gathered around the television watching classic shows—an emotion that reverberates with baby boomers in particular." A large part of the U.S. population, baby boomers were in their prime money-earning years; also, the number of aging Americans was growing rapidly. In addition, during the 1990s, the "cocooning decade," more households were focusing on the home environment. The combination of these factors presented the perfect marketing climate for an ambitious ad campaign. The "Fred Astaire" campaign was indeed timely. Michael Merriman, president and CEO of Royal Appliance, commented, "Fred Astaire lit up the silver screen with his elegant dance steps and made the impossible look easy. His performances were amazing yet appeared effortless and fun, qualities we aspire to at Dirt Devil."

When Dirt Devil launched what *HFN,* the weekly newspaper for the Home Furnishing Network, called "the most aggressive campaign to date," Robyn Astaire and Royal also entered into a long-term partnership with the Arthritis Foundation. Together they sponsored "quality of life" programs and funded arthritis research. Dirt Devil also made a commitment to provide ongoing fund-raising efforts for the Arthritis Foundation. Royal strove to design lightweight, portable, and easy-to-use cleaning appliances that would be easier to use for those who are physically challenged. For example, the Broom-Vac is a rechargeable, cordless broom that sucks up the dirt, eliminating the need for a dustpan. Because it is easy to use, one does not have to bend over to plug it in or pick up the dirt. The Dirt Devil Ultra Hand Vac has a powerful motor, a built-in stretchy hose, and an extra-long cord—one can have all the cleaning power of a full-sized vacuum without the heaviness or inconvenience. The Ultra MVP also has an extra-long cord and a built-in stretchy hose.

SUCCESS FOR MELDRUM & FEWSMITH

Meldrum & Fewsmith, the advertising agency that was involved in making the "Fred Astaire" ads, received a lot of favorable attention after the ads appeared—so much so, that soon after the 1997 Super Bowl, the firm was acquired by The Wolf Group, the parent company of Wolf Winterkorn Lillis Advertising, Inc. The acquisition made The Wolf Group one of the largest advertising firms in the Great Lakes area.

COMPETITION

Royal's oldest competitors were Hoover, which became a division of Maytag, and Eureka, which was bought by Electrolux. By 1927 Eureka was supplying one-third of all vacuums cleaners in the United States. Other rivals in the 1990s included Oreck and companies mainly associated with the electronics industry, such as Panasonic and Sanyo. Early vacuum cleaners could be purchased at department stores, through catalogues, or from door-to-door sales representatives, and ads for vacuum cleaners were typically seen in newspapers or heard on the radio. After Royal began advertising on television in 1991, it held the most market share, but the competition developed new products and increased their advertising efforts.

Royal did not drastically increase its advertising budget to produce the "Fred Astaire" campaign. The ads cost $1.8 million for 45 seconds of air time—each spot cost $250,000 to produce. Only 16 percent of Dirt Devil's annual $16 million advertising budget was used for the "Fred Astaire" ads. Hoover and Eureka spent approximately $20 million per year on advertising. According to Jim Holcomb, the "Fred Astaire" campaign was developed "to make our core line advertising dollars work harder."

MARKETING STRATEGY

Using celebrities, alive or dead, to sell products was not new and had shown variable results. The "Fred Astaire" ads appeared during a time when Jackie Gleason was seen with a hand mixer made by Braun Appliance Company and John Wayne was seen popping into the local saloon to swill some Coor's beer. The "Fred Astaire" campaign was multilayered and caused many issues to be addressed.

Many people were bothered by the "Fred Astaire" ads. Obviously, the film footage used for the commercials was used without his consent, which raised the question of who, in an instance such as the "Fred Astaire" spots, is the primary artist of the old film footage? Was it the dancer Fred Astaire, the director of *Royal Wedding* and *Easter Parade,* the producer, or the studio who provided the finances?

Before the 1997 Super Bowl the public relations firm Robert Falls and Company launched a public relations campaign in conjunction with the ad campaign created by Meldrum & Fewsmith. DWJ Television shot behind-the-scenes footage of the commercials being edited and demonstrated the technology used to create the commercials. DWJ also videotaped interviews with Robyn Astaire, the CEO of Royal Appliance, and the creative team who made the commercial. It then combined these pieces with excerpts from the "Fred Astaire" commercials, from some of Astaire's films, and from a press conference to make a video news package. Placement specialists from DWJ "pitched" the story to news producers and "fed" the news package to stations across the country three times: just before a press conference, the day of the press conference, and the day of the 1997 Super Bowl. The campaign package was seen by an estimated 53 million viewers and was aired a total of 164 times. Of all the segments included in the video package, the behind-the-scenes footage was used the most.

In addition to the three Super Bowl spots and the partnership with the Arthritis Foundation, Royal also developed a "Scratch & Win-Match & Win" contest, in which consumers could win five dollars, ten dollars, or one million dollars by matching numbers from a newspaper insert with the UPC code on a newly purchased Broom Vac.

OUTCOME

To determine the popularity of commercials run during the Super Bowl, a national polling organization, Gordon S. Black, chose 139 adult volunteers in two cities. The volunteers used handheld meters to register how much or how little they liked a particular spot. The "Fred Astaire" commercials did not make the top ten or the bottom five, and they did not qualify as favorites according to gender, age (under 40), or income (under $40,000). The top-scoring commercial during the 1997 Super Bowl was a Pepsi ad of bears dancing to a tune by The Village People, which scored 8.22 points out of a possible 10 points. The lowest score went to Janus Funds at 4.84 points. The "Fred Astaire" spots ranked as follows: Broom Vac with fancy footwork scored 6.05 points, Ultra Hand Vac with Astaire dancing on the walls and ceiling measured 5.51 points, and Astaire dancing on the stairs with an Ultra MVP also measured 5.51 points.

Although the "Fred Astaire" commercials were not among the most popular, in the three weeks that the spots ran, starting with Super Bowl Sunday, the volume of Dirt Devils sold tripled. Sales went up 4 percent, while industry sales were down 6 percent. In comparison, sales during the first quarter of 1998 showed a net loss, a decrease of 11.5 percent compared with the first quarter in 1997. Of course, these numbers were influenced by several factors. CEO Michael Merriman stated, "Although sales of Dirt Devil products to consumers, through our major retailers, increased in the first quarter over last year, retail ordering patterns and inventory reduction by certain of these large retailers negatively affected our shipments in the first quarter 1998. Additionally, January shipments related to last year's successful Super Bowl advertising campaign were not duplicated in January 1998 . . . The company's gross margin in the first quarter of 1998 declined due to this lower sales volume coupled with higher consumer returns following much higher fourth quarter shipments than in recent years. I view these issues as principally timing in nature. We fully expect to be profitable in 1998. We are encouraged by the higher retail point-of-sale sell-through in the first quarter, especially where we have gained marker share."

FURTHER READING

"Announces for First Quarter of 1998 and New Financing Commitment." PR Newswire, April 17, 1998.

Arthritis Foundation "Arthritis Foundation Teams with Mrs. Fred Astaire and Dirt Devil." *News from the Arthritis Foundation,* January 8, 1997.

"Astaire to Dance with Dirt Devils." *The Fort Worth Star-Telegram,* January 9, 1997.

"The Best and Worst of Super Bowls Ads." *USA Today,* January 28, 1997.

Enrico, Dottie, and Melanie Wells. "Money." *USA Today,* January 27, 1997.

Gellene, Denise. "Advertisers Look to Dead Celebrities." *Los Angeles Times,* September 13, 1997.

Gromer, Cliff. "New Hope for the Dead." *Popular Mechanics,* July 1997.

Hill, Dawn. "Dancing with Vacs." *HFN: The Weekly Newspaper for the Home Furnishing Network,* January 13, 1997.

"Nostalgic Super Bowl Ad Campaign Puts Dirt Devil in the National News." Business Wire, January 31, 1997.

Pledger, Marcia. "A Devil of a Time: Fred Astaire and Dancing Dustpans." *The Plain Dealer,* January 9, 1997.

Smith, Dana. "In a Virtual World, Who Owns the Virtual You?" *Orlando Sentinel,* Friday, January31, 1997.

Whalen, Jeanne. "The Marketing 100: Dirt Devil: Jim Holcomb." *Advertising Age,* June 30, 1997.

Christine MinerMinderovic

Royal Caribbean Cruises Ltd.

1050 Caribbean Way
Miami, Florida 33132
USA
Telephone: (305) 539-6000
Fax: (305) 374-7354
Web site: www.royalcaribbean.com

GET OUT THERE CAMPAIGN

OVERVIEW

In the late 1990s Miami-based Royal Caribbean Cruises Ltd. began repositioning its namesake brand, Royal Caribbean International. After campaigns meant to market the brand as an alternative to resort vacations as well as to other cruise companies, in 2000 Royal Caribbean undertook a more ambitious recasting of its image. Amid industry-wide increases in fleet size, Royal Caribbean attempted to attract new customers by appealing to baby boomers and Generation Xers, in addition to the industry standby market of retirees. To accomplish this goal, Royal Caribbean charged the Boston-based agency Arnold Worldwide with the task of changing consumers' stereotypical notions of the cruise ship experience.

The resulting multiyear integrated campaign, called "Get Out There," drew on an estimated $80 million annual budget and included television and print as well as online and promotional components. Television commercials depicted cruise vacations as action-packed avenues for acquiring exotic life experiences, with dramatic, fast-moving imagery synchronized to the high-energy rhythms of the Iggy Pop song "Lust for Life." Print ads supported the message of the cruise as an adventure, and innovations in the Royal Caribbean website played an important role in the brand's desire to appeal to a younger market.

The campaign substantially increased Royal Caribbean's awareness relative to other cruise lines, and the "Get Out There" tagline as well as the song "Lust for Life" became closely associated with the brand. The campaign won a Gold EFFIE Award in 2002 and a Silver EFFIE Award in 2003.

HISTORICAL CONTEXT

The Royal Caribbean Cruise Line came into being in 1968 as a partnership between three Norwegian shipping companies: Anders Wilhelmsen & Company, I.M. Skauge & Company, and Gotaas Larsen. The line's first vessel, *Song of Norway,* made its maiden voyage in 1970, and the company added two more ships in the early 1970s. The late 1970s and 1980s saw cruise ships and the industry as a whole grow in size, and in the 1990s Royal Caribbean expanded beyond the tropical destinations referred to in its brand name, offering trips to various parts of Europe, including Scandinavia and Russia. The company went public in 1993 and continued to expand its fleet and its geographic range. In 1997 the brand name was changed from Royal Caribbean Cruise Line to Royal Caribbean International, a reflection of its increasingly global reach and aspirations.

At around this time Royal Caribbean also began repositioning itself to compete not just against other cruise lines but against vacation resorts as well.

Radiance of the Sea on the Campbell River, September 13, 2003. © ORJAN F. ELLINGVAG/ELLINGVÅG/ØRJAN/CORBIS.

Television and print advertising, running under the tagline "Like no vacation on earth," began to focus increasingly on off-ship possibilities for adventure at the various destinations frequented by Royal Caribbean vessels. In the late 1990s the company added new ships almost yearly, steadily increasing its passenger capacity and planning further such increases well beyond the new millennium.

Spurred by a booming U.S. economy, Royal Caribbean's competitors were likewise dramatically increasing their carrying capacity during these years. Still, only about 10 percent of Americans had been on a cruise vacation. Though the expanded occupancy numbers mandated that Royal Caribbean and its competitors correspondingly expand their consumer base, the industry's most consistent customers were older and retired couples, and Americans tended to associate cruise vacations with inactive forms of sightseeing and unexciting onboard activities like shuffleboard and all-you-can-eat buffet dinners. In 1999 Royal Caribbean entrusted its mainstream advertising duties to Arnold Worldwide of Boston and charged the agency with expanding its appeal beyond the traditional cruise market.

TARGET MARKET

Building on the findings of the market research firm Yankelovich Partners, Arnold pinpointed a target market for the "Get Out There" campaign that was united by a mind-set more than age or other demographic divisions. Arnold dubbed this group "Explorers," adults of all ages with a thirst for adventure. As Pam Hamlin, the agency's executive vice president and group account director, told *American Demographics,* the so-called Explorers "might be 30 or 70, but [they] . . . don't want to be sightseers or lounge-chair potatoes. Sure, they want a pina colada at the pool at some point, but they also want to go bike riding in Copenhagen or swimming with dolphins."

Though portions of this group fell into the traditional 50-plus age bracket that had long made up the industry's core consumers, the fact remained that adults looking for excitement and adventure on their vacations were naturally clustered in younger portions of the American population. On average, therefore, Arnold and Royal Caribbean were targeting a significantly younger crowd than any cruise line had in the past. Baby boomers, aged 36 to 54 at the time of the launch of "Get Out There," were a particularly important part of the newly envisioned Royal Caribbean target. In Arnold's view baby boomers tended to approach aging with a different attitude than had previous generations of mature adults, placing a high priority on continuing to experience new things and enrich themselves personally through travel and adventure. "They are going to be much younger—in their minds—than the elderly population has ever been," Arnold group creative director Pete Favat told *Advertising Age.* "This generation is trying to stay as young as possible as long as they can." Members of Generation X, too, were as old as 35 at this time, and Royal Caribbean hoped that its pitch would resonate with them as well.

"LUST FOR LIFE"

The energetic beat and affirmative message of Iggy Pop's "Lust for Life" no doubt seemed to many consumers a good fit for the "Get Out There" campaign, which sought to encourage the perception that cruise vacations were stimulating and adventure oriented, and indeed over the years the song became closely associated with the Royal Caribbean brand. Not surprisingly, only a selected portion of the song was played during the TV spots, so that consumers might not have been aware of any disconnect between the song and its commercial use. As many observers noted, however, Pop was an unlikely spokesperson for a cruise line. Often called the "Godfather of Punk," he was a key influence on the notoriously misanthropic practitioners of 1990s Seattle grunge. "Lust for Life" was itself a song about one of Pop's several recoveries from heroin addiction and was prominently featured, a few years before the debut of the Royal Caribbean campaign, on the sound track to the movie *Trainspotting,* a dark comedy about Scottish heroin addicts.

COMPETITION

The industry's leading company, Carnival Cruise Lines, was, like Royal Caribbean, headquartered in Miami, associated primarily with Caribbean cruises, and, beginning in the late 1990s, actively expanding its fleet. After retiring a long-running ad strategy of using celebrity spokesperson Kathy Lee Gifford in campaigns positioning itself as the company of "fun ships," Carnival tried markedly different approaches in two campaigns, both directed by Cooper HMS Partners (later Cooper and Hayes). A campaign launched in early 2000 took a reality-based approach. Amateur actors were sent on Carnival cruises and then interviewed after the fact. The results of the interviews were culled to create spots focusing on the highlights of the onboard cruise experience, which the interviewees in general claimed they had not expected to enjoy as much as they ultimately did. The campaign targeted a traditional cruise industry audience and hoped to dispel cruise vacation stereotypes by having the actors address such matters in the spots. As agency chief executive and copywriter Ric Cooper told *Adweek,* "We wanted people with preconceived ideas about this kind of vacation . . . Fifty percent of this business is repeat customers." A 2002 campaign, by contrast, resurrected the company's positioning as the "fun" cruise line in spots that evoked the romance of cruising and used lively pop music in the hope of enticing first-time cruisers.

The third largest cruise company during this time was Princess Cruise Lines, whose Southern California–based fleet had built its reputation on cruises to Mexico and Alaska and on one of its ship's role as the setting for the popular 1970s and '80s TV drama *The Love Boat.* A significantly smaller line than either Carnival or Royal Caribbean, Princess had in the late 1990s positioned itself as a cruise brand offering a more personal, customized experience than its better-known competitors. After the turn of the century Princess began pursuing fleet expansions, in keeping with the rest of the industry, and both Carnival and Royal Caribbean competed to purchase the smaller line. In 2002 Carnival prevailed, adding Princess to its increasingly diverse roster of cruise brands.

MARKETING STRATEGY

"Get Out There," which was launched on January 16, 2000, was an integrated TV, print, direct-mail, and promotional campaign, with important tie-ins to the company's website beginning in late 2000. The budget for the complete effort was an estimated $80 million annually, roughly half of which was allotted to the media campaign. Though "Get Out There" was the campaign theme from its inception, the phrase did not become the official tagline until 2002.

The campaign's goals were ambitious: to change consumer perceptions of an entire industry as a means of expanding Royal Caribbean's market. Rather than focus on the onboard experience—associated in the popular consciousness with passive recreational options deemed suitable for the elderly—the new 30- and 60-second TV spots featured fast-moving imagery of, for instance, the Egyptian pyramids, Italy's Amalfi Coast, rock climbers, and vacationers on bicycles in Copenhagen. The quick editing of the commercials was synchronized with the propulsive, up-tempo Iggy Pop song "Lust for Life," which became the brand's theme song over the course of the long-running life of the campaign.

The print portion of the campaign, which ran in national magazines and in newspapers in selected markets, kicked off in February 2000. Dramatic natural and architectural scenery was used in concert with questions and statements meant to stimulate the desire for travel and adventure. The copy for one ad read, "Yeah, you've seen ice sculptures made by a chef. Ever seen the ones made by God?" Another ad informed consumers, "Among the things you'll learn biking in Sardinia: In Italian, even 'my cuff is caught in the chain' sounds romantic."

In May 2000 Royal Caribbean unveiled a redesigned website (www.royalcaribbean.com), which for the first time allowed consumers to make cruise reservations online. This was a significant step toward the brand's goal of attracting younger consumers, who tended to be more Internet-savvy than their elders, and another addition to the website prior to the 2001 installment of "Get Out There"—the creation of an online "virtual" cruise experience—further positioned Royal Caribbean to grow its market among the increasing number of Americans who made travel reservations online. The "Get Out There" TV spots in 2001 were little different from their predecessors the year before, except that they directed viewers to royalcaribbean.com, where Web users could experience the activities shown in the commercials as though test-driving the vacation. For instance, users could see the streets of Copenhagen from the vantage point of the cyclists who appeared in one popular TV spot, or they could duplicate the experience of swimming underwater with stingrays.

In late 2001 the "Get Out There" concept was adapted to an Alaska-specific pitch. One noteworthy TV spot in this portion of the campaign opened on what appeared to be a dramatic mountain-climbing scene. Two men struggled as though barely able to continue an attempt at the summit, but a female voice then interjected, "If you guys don't quit it, I'm going to miss my massage." The opening chords of "Lust for Life" began playing, followed by quickly intercut images of action-oriented adventure, the trademark of the campaign, before a voice-over proclaimed, "Somewhere between the glacier hiking, the dogsledding, the train tours, and the rock wall, it hits you: this is way more than a cruise. See for yourself at royalcaribbean.com, and get out there."

A 2002 print portion of the campaign likewise adapted the larger advertising strategy to pitch a specific branch of Royal Caribbean's offerings, using images of the Sistine Chapel and the Louvre, among other marquee European destinations. Copy promoted the complementary benefits of tourist activities and cruise ship luxury. Otherwise, in subsequent years the campaign retained its signature visual look and sound track on TV spots.

OUTCOME

The first several years of the "Get Out There" campaign were marred by the steep declines in tourism related to depressed economic conditions and a widespread fear of traveling following the terrorist attacks in the United States on September 11, 2001. Nevertheless, Royal Caribbean managed to significantly affect consumers' perceptions of cruise vacations and build a brand image that was directly associated with the new, more dynamic idea of such travel. As of 2005, Royal Caribbean's unaided brand awareness had climbed 33 percent above its 2000 level, and it had become the cruise line most often recommended by travel agents. Royal Caribbean's online bookings increased dramatically in the years following the debut of the website, and the company's stock price had increased more than 100 percent by 2005. The campaign's effectiveness was honored twice with EFFIE awards. The overall campaign won a Gold EFFIE in 2002, and the Alaska portion of the campaign won a Silver EFFIE in 2003.

FURTHER READING

Beirne, Mike. "Exploring New Waters." *Brandweek,* January 1, 2001.

———. "Royal Caribbean Primes U.S. Cruisers to Set Sail for Overseas Destinations." *Brandweek,* November 4, 2002.

Chura, Hillary, and David Goetzl. "Royal Caribbean Christens New Baby Boomer Effort." *Advertising Age,* January 17, 2000.

Gianatasio, David. "Royal Caribbean Breaks TV Ads." *Adweek,* January 8, 2001.

Goetzl, David. "Cruising to Nowhere." *Advertising Age,* November 12, 2001.

———. "Luxury Cruise Lines Woo Boomers to Sea." *Advertising Age,* March 15, 1999.

Grimm, Matthew. "Anchors Aweigh." *American Demographics,* March 2001.

Pool, Lisa van der. "Arnold, Royal Caribbean Go Cruising in Alaska." *Adweek,* November 5, 2001.

Warner, Judy. "Like No Vacation on Earth." *Adweek,* April 3, 2000.

Zbar, Jeffrey D. "Royal Caribbean." *Advertising Age,* June 26, 1998.

Mark Lane

Saab Cars USA, Inc.

4405-A International Boulevard
Norcross, Georgia 30093
USA
Telephone: 770-279-0100
Fax: 770-279-6499
Web site: www.saabusa.com

■■■

LIFE IS NOT A SPECTATOR SPORT CAMPAIGN

OVERVIEW

Saab Cars USA, Inc., was the American affiliate of the Swedish company Saab Automobile AB, which was in turn owned by the General Motors Corporation, a Detroit-based corporation that was the largest automaker in the world. Saab was in a difficult financial situation in 2002; it lost $504 million worldwide that year alone. This came on the heels of mediocre sales throughout the early 2000s, both worldwide and in the United States, Saab's biggest market. Saab hoped that the introduction of its new 9-3 Sport Sedan would help it turn things around. The company was prepared to spend $70 million on marketing all of its lines in the United States, with the desire of sparking a rise in sales that could help the company become profitable again.

Boosting sales would be a significant challenge for the Lowe Group, whose Swedish affiliate Lowe Brindfors (Saab's longtime European agency) was assigned Saab's U.S. portfolio in 2001, giving the Lowe Group full responsibility for all of Saab's marketing. Lowe introduced the new 9-3 Sport Sedan to the U.S. market with a commercial that had already run in Europe. Set during the World Cup, it featured a young man joyriding through Barcelona, and it closed with the tagline "Life Is Not a Spectator Sport." This was followed by a series of other television, print, and radio initiatives that ran throughout 2003.

The 9-3 Sport Sedan helped Saab post its best sales year in 47 years of doing business in the U.S. market. The company moved 47,914 units of its automobile line, up from only 35,062 units sold the year before. This took Saab closer to its stated goal of doubling its U.S. sales within five years.

HISTORICAL CONTEXT

Saab's name began as an acronym, SAAB, for Svenska Aeroplan Aktiebolaget (Swedish Aircraft Company). As the name indicated, the company began by manufacturing aircraft. In 1946 it started exploring the possibility of manufacturing cars as well. In 1949 the Saab 92 became the first Saab automobile available to the public. The aircraft portion of Saab, Saab AB, later separated from the automotive manufacturer to form a second, fully independent company.

On December 15, 1989, Saab-Scania AB and General Motors announced an agreement to form Saab Automobile AB as a joint venture. This led to the creation of Saab Cars USA, Inc. Prior to GM's investment the brand had spent little on marketing in the United States, leading Saab to develop a reputation as a niche brand. Following the agreement Saab achieved modest but consistent U.S. sales. By the late 1990s, however, sales seemed to be picking up. In 1999 Saab sold 39,366 units in the United States, making that country the company's largest single market, even larger than that of its native Sweden. This was a significant improvement from the 30,516 units the automaker sold in the U.S. in 1998. In 2000 GM took complete control of the Swedish automaker, hoping to build on those gains.

In 2002, however, Saab's development costs were getting out of hand, and a weak dollar kept Saab prices (which were pegged to the stronger Swedish kronor currency) high in the United States, creating a drag on sales. The company was expected to lose $504 million in 2002 alone. One problem was the decision to construct expensive brand centers, owned outright by Saab, which would serve as high-class showrooms for its vehicles. These showrooms, designated for major cities such as San Francisco and Chicago, had to be canceled by Saab's parent, GM, after costs spiraled out of control.

Saab's international sales division was organized into two regions: one was Europe and the Americas, and the other handled Asian/Pacific markets. The company saw itself as an international organization. And internationally, sales were weak. By November 2002 the company was only on pace to move about 125,000 units for the year, well short of the 140,000-unit goal set by the automaker.

Saab CEO Peter Augustsson began to design an 18-month recovery plan to pare down costs and boost sales. Despite the major gains seen in 1999, U.S. sales in the first couple years of the 2000s were flat, with only about 37,000 units sold for 2001. The company wanted to turn things around in a hurry. Much of its hopes were pinned on the new 9-3 Sport Sedan, a high-performance vehicle that featured a smaller engine. The 9-3 had a sleeker, more "American" look than many other Saab vehicles. The company hoped that the 9-3 Sport Sedan would help lead the way to a doubling of U.S. sales within only five years.

TARGET MARKET

Saab's cars were high-performance luxury vehicles, and the 9-3 Sport Sedan was no exception. Although the car was priced competitively at about $30,000, it was aimed at young premium-car buyers. The driver's seat had a cockpit feel to appeal to these consumers. The company viewed its cosmopolitan, European reputation—which was enhanced in part by the fact that the company was not ubiquitous in the United States—as an important asset. With such features as Saab Active Head Restraints (seat-based restraints that protected the driver in a crash) and side airbags, Saab also appealed to safety-conscious consumers.

THE (ADVERTISING) PROFESSIONAL

Saab Cars USA, Inc., had a lot riding on the introduction of its 2003 9-3 Sport Sedan. The company's advertising agency, Lowe Brindfors, had a secret weapon to help the vehicle crack the U.S. market, however: a Saab spot called "Big Match" that had already aired to acclaim in Europe. Befitting an international campaign, the spot was directed by international director Luc Besson.

Besson was a French director who had made the rare transition from the French film industry to blockbuster Hollywood action films. He achieved success in his homeland with the international hit *La Femme Nikita,* which eventually inspired a U.S. television series. He came to the attention of American cinephiles with his first English-language film, *The Professional* (1994; also known outside the United States as *Léon*), which featured the debut of Natalie Portman.

Later he directed the major science-fiction picture *The Fifth Element* (1997). The film starred Bruce Willis and Chris Tucker and was admired for its unique visual palette. After his ambitious 1999 film *The Messenger: The Story of Joan of Arc* failed to find a wide audience, Besson stepped away from directing films for a time, turning his attention to writing and producing movies and directing commercials such as "Big Match."

COMPETITION

Saab's primary competition came from other European automakers, including Mercedes-Benz, BMW, and Audi. Its biggest competitor was Volkswagen. Volkswagen was Europe's largest automaker and was the parent of Audi. There were several other sport sedans on the market in 2003. The entry-level luxury sport sedan segment was crowded with established stars, such as the BMW 3-Series and the Mercedes C-Class. These fellow European automakers were making vehicles that offered a similarly high-performance ride. Saab needed to distinguish itself in order to succeed. The Acura 3.2 TL was another strong contender in this segment.

One thing that helped Saab stand out from these competitors was its customer service. Saab's customer-service record also attracted buyers. In 2003 the influential marketing-information firm JD Power and Associates ranked Saab seventh in its Customer Service Index, making it the highest-ranking European automaker, ahead of competitors BMW (number 10) and Volvo (number 11).

MARKETING STRATEGY

In May 2001, not long before the 9-3 Sport Sedan campaign began, Saab hired a new advertising agency, Sweden's Lowe Brindfors, part of the Lowe Group, to develop and implement its marketing campaigns. Lowe also operated a U.S. division based in New York, which would handle the U.S. component of Saab's campaigns. The Martin Agency, Saab's previous U.S. advertising agency, was retained to handle direct advertising in that country. Saab consolidated its worldwide advertising with one organization as part of an effort to make its marketing efforts more efficient. Lowe was already handling Saab's non-American campaigns, and it was becoming too complicated and costly to coordinate the efforts of two different agencies.

Saab was having trouble in the U.S. market, in part because of the Swedish krona's strong standing against the dollar, which raised Saab prices in the United States. To help shore up its sagging prospect, Saab earmarked a massive $70 million dollars for media advertising, nearly doubling its previous expenditures. The 9-3 would be a major focus of this advertising. In January 2002 Saab kicked off the year by introducing the new vehicle. It would close the year by touting the 9-3 to American car buyers in a new advertising campaign.

It was decided to import a successful Lowe Brindfors spot from Europe to be the center of the campaign, which began in the fall of 2002 to coincide with the introduction of the 2003 9-3 Sport Sedan. Called "Big Match," the spot had premiered in Europe in the summer of 2002, during the World Cup soccer tournament, the world's biggest sporting event. It was directed by Luc Besson, a French director known to American audiences for Hollywood films such as *The Fifth Element.* The commercial was set in Barcelona, Spain, during the World Cup. While everyone was at home watching the day's big soccer match on TV, a man snuck out and took his Saab 9-3 on a joyride through the city's empty streets. But he still got back in time to see the game's big goal. The spot closed with the tagline "Life is Not a Spectator Sport," before urging viewers to "Experience the All New Saab 9-3 Sport Sedan."

"Big Match" was a vivid demonstration of why Saab wanted to consolidate its worldwide marketing effort. The commercial had already been well received in Europe, so it was less of a risk bringing it into the United States. While the spot was edited for the U.S. market, most of the work was already done on the original spot, meaning that it cost far less than developing an all-new television campaign. For a company struggling with costs, this was especially appealing. Also, the European streetscape reinforced the company's sophisticated, cosmopolitan image.

Throughout 2003 Saab built on the "Big Match" spot through a print campaign geared at upscale readers, using publications such as *GQ, Gourmet,* and *Condé Nast Traveler.* Ads also ran in major newspapers, including the *Wall Street Journal* and the *New York Times.* Finally, the company reached out to its target market by becoming an official sponsor of National Public Radio.

Lowe developed a series of television campaigns to run throughout 2003. They mainly aired on national cable stations such as ESPN, Bravo, A&E, and CNN. Beginning in May 2003 Saab ran five spots featuring the tagline "Welcome to the State of Independence." These spots also primarily focused on the 9-3, though some featured other vehicles as well. One spot purported to show the behind-the-scenes process of designing new Saabs. As the 2003 line of Saab cars was shown, a series of rhetorical questions was asked, such as "What if innovation were the official currency?" Each spot closed with the new tagline. The idea was to capitalize on Scandinavia's reputation as a freethinking, open-minded society, implying that the Saab 9-3 was a car for freethinking, open-minded drivers.

OUTCOME

The campaign to launch the 9-3 Sport Sedan was a success. By January 2003 sales were increasing across the board at Saab. Saab USA moved 2,551 units that month, up 62 percent from January 2002. The 9-3 Sport Sedan was a major component of that success, selling 1,427 units. That meant that more than half of all Saabs sold in January 2003 were 9-3 Sport Sedans. As the campaign continued, Saab's sales numbers kept growing. Saab Cars USA's first quarter in 2003 saw the company move 10,885 units. This was the best sales quarter in Saab's 47 years selling vehicles in the United States and constituted a 19 percent sales increase over the previous year's first quarter.

Saab moved 4,967 units in April 2003, for the best single month to that point in terms of U.S. sales. Once again, the 9-3 Sport Sedan was primarily responsible, selling 2,768 units that month. The previous monthly sales record had held since 1986. Saab's momentum continued after the second phase of the campaign—featuring the "Welcome to the State of Independence" spots—began in May. By November Saab had already posted its best yearly sales record in 16 years. The company had broken the 40,000-unit threshold, something it had not done since 1987. By the time the year was over, Saab had broken its yearly sales record by moving a total of 47,914 units, a significant improvement over the 35,062 units the company sold in 2002.

FURTHER READING

"Best Spots: Saab, 'Big Match.'" *Adweek,* December 16, 2002. Available from <http://www.adweek.com/aw/creative/best_spots_02/021216_16.jsp>

Cantwell, Julie. "GM Says It Remains Committed to Saab, Pushing Brand into New Segments." *Automotive News,* February 11, 2003.

Ceppos, Rich. "Still Too Many Brands and Not Enough Difference between Them." *AutoWeek,* November 19, 2002.

Cobb, James G. "A Suave, Smooth Operator." *New York Times,* September 15, 2002.

Eldridge, Earle. "Saab Hoping to Leave 'Nutty Professor' Image in Dust." *USA Today,* May 20, 2002.

Elliott, Stuart. "3 Big Advertisers Shift Their Accounts." *New York Times,* October 22, 2002.

Hamilton, Anita. "Detroit's Hot Pursuit." *Time,* January 12, 2004.

Keebler, Jack. "2003 Saab 93: Still Quirky—and Newly Affordable." *Motor Trend,* September 2002.

Krebs, Michael. "Saab's Wish List: More Models." *New York Times,* February 9, 2003.

Stoll, John D. "Japanese Shine, Europeans Sputter, Domestics Surprise in J.D. Power Durability Study." *AutoWeek,* July 9, 2003.

Guy Patrick Cunningham

SABMiller plc

1 Stanhope Gate
London, W1K1AF
United Kingdom
Telephone: 44 20 76590100
Fax: 44 20 76590111
Web site: www.sabmiller.com

LOW CARB CAMPAIGN

OVERVIEW

NOTE: Also see essay for Miller Brewing Company.

In 2002 South African Breweries bought the ailing Miller Brewing Company from the Phillip Morris Companies, took the name SABMiller, and set about trying to bring America's second-largest beer maker out of a decade-long slump. The brewer's leading product, Miller Lite, had been struggling to regain its spot at the top of its category since 1994, when Anheuser-Busch's Bud Light first overtook it, but its recent advertising campaigns had, without exception, failed to move product. A diet craze then sweeping the United States, however, provided Miller Lite the opening it needed to challenge its competitors and reverse the market-share losses of the past years.

Capitalizing on a variety of diets calling for drastic reductions in carbohydrate intake, and taking its cue from Anheuser-Busch's own low-carb offering, Michelob Ultra, Miller Lite launched an advertising campaign (whose price tag was estimated at more than $20 million) comparing its carbohydrate count to that of mainstream rivals Bud Light, Coors Light, and Michelob Light. Pairing the numerical carbohydrate comparison with the simple image of beer being poured into a glass, the brewer and its agency, Ogilvy & Mather, at long last established a clear reason for consumers to prefer Miller Lite to its competitors.

The campaign not only arrested the seemingly permanent slide in Miller Lite's market share, but it resulted in the beer's first sales gains in nearly five years, gains that outpaced Coors Light as well as Bud Light, a brand that had been accustomed to double-digit percentage increases. Building on the success of its direct challenge to competitors, Miller Lite took aim at Bud Light in future campaigns, and the brand's revival continued.

HISTORICAL CONTEXT

Introduced in 1975, Miller Lite was America's first light beer. The low-calorie product was initially seen as a risk in a beer-marketing era defined by overtly macho appeals to hard work, such as the classic "Miller Time" and "This Bud's for You" campaigns. To offset any unmanly associations with the idea of light beer, Miller and its agency at the time, McCann-Erickson, enlisted retired professional football players for its advertising and had them engage in heated debates over whether Miller Lite's chief attribute was that it "Tastes Great" or was "Less Filling." The campaign was a huge success, and the product category Miller Lite created irrevocably changed the beer industry in America.

Anheuser-Busch, maker of Budweiser beer, ventured into the low-calorie category with Bud Light in 1982, and in the mid-1980s Bud Light hit its marketing stride, leveraging its parent's deep pockets to churn out consistently strong advertising amid a growing consumer preference for reduced-calorie beer. Bud Light's market share increased exponentially, while Miller Lite sales peaked in 1990. Bud Light surpassed its older rival in 1994 on its way to becoming, by 2001, not simply the top reduced-calorie beer but the most popular beer in America, knocking its sibling Budweiser, "The King of Beers," off its pedestal. Meanwhile, Miller Lite was surpassed by Coors Light and fell to number three in the category it had pioneered. Miller Lite's woes greatly compounded the declining fortunes of Miller's other main brands, Miller High Life and Miller Genuine Draft. The brewer saw its market share fall from 23 percent in 1995 to 19.4 percent in 2002. South Africa Breweries in 2002 bought the ailing Miller portfolio from Phillip Morris with the intent of turning the ailing American powerhouse around. The new company was called SABMiller.

A significant factor in Miller's sharp declines, according to industry observers, was inept advertising behind its leading product. From the mid-1990s through the early years of the new millennium, Miller Lite struggled to establish any clear brand identity. A high-profile, offbeat campaign called "Dick," featuring absurdist vignettes dreamed up by a fictional advertising copywriter, was lauded for its creativity but harshly criticized for its failure to connect to the product's virtues and thereby translate into increased sales. Later attempts to mix humorous advertising with a focus on product quality faltered, and as sales continued to slump, Miller Lite in 2003 unveiled an intentionally sensational advertising campaign, via agency Ogilvy & Mather, called "Catfight." Resurrecting the "Tastes great, less filling" debate but using a wrestling match between nearly nude women to decide the outcome, the campaign generated a high volume of mostly negative publicity while scoring well with 21- to 34-year-old males. As with other recent Miller Lite campaigns, however, "Catfight" had no effect on sales.

At this time, additionally, a developing diet trend was cutting into beer sales industry-wide. Diets such as the Atkins and South Beach programs, in which carbohydrate intake was drastically curtailed while protein and fat sources were recommended, increasingly became the preferred weight-loss method for Americans. The demand for pasta and bread products declined sharply, and food manufacturers of all types developed low-carb lines or relabeled existing products to capitalize on the trend. In 2002 Anheuser-Busch made the beer industry's first direct play for the low-carb dollar, introducing Michelob Ultra, a brew boasting a mere 2.6 grams of carbohydrates per 12-ounce serving.

TARGET MARKET

In touting Miller Lite's own low 3.2 grams of carbs per serving, SABMiller displayed its awareness of the extensive mainstream and cross-generational appeal of the low-carb diet programs. Among the beer industry's core audience of men aged 21 to 34, Ogilvy & Mather and SABMiller described their ideal target, according to a brief filed for the 2005 EFFIE Awards, in the following way: "[The] consumer is confident, growing and dynamic . . . Single, possibly in his first job, he's optimistic, diverse but mainstream in background and interests . . . He's much more concerned with staying fit for physical appearances than necessarily for health reasons." The brewer and its agency likewise expected the "Low Carb" spots to register with the over-35 drinker who was "Much like the pack, but a bit older . . . As he enters mid-life he has put on a few pounds, the spare tire, and is looking for ways to watch what he eats without giving up the things he loves."

COMPETITION

Bud Light's advertising prior to the launch of Miller Lite's "Low Carb" campaign had been characteristically noteworthy. One of the brand's most lauded marketing efforts ever, a radio campaign called "Real Men of

BEERS IN COURT

During the intensifying beer wars of the summer of 2004, a rallying Miller made light of Budweiser's "King of Beers" slogan, as well as its trademark Clydesdale horses, in the "President of Beers" campaign. In response, Anheuser-Busch ran a print ad reiterating its status as "King of Beers" and calling Miller Lite the "Queen of Carbs," while pointing out that Miller was (in contrast to the patriotic theme of its "President of Beers" campaign) owned by South African Breweries.

SABMiller took America's top brewer to court, claiming that the "Queen of Carbs" insult was misleading and that the South African Breweries claim was untrue: although SABMiller's roots were in South Africa, its headquarters were now in London; moreover, there was no longer any entity called South African Breweries (the name had been retired when the merger with Miller took place). A U.S. district judge issued a preliminary injunction stating that Anheuser-Busch could no longer refer to Miller as "owned by South African Breweries" but that it could call Miller "South African–owned." A decision on the "Queen of Carbs" issue was postponed until a later hearing.

Genius," had made the leap to television, and three of the TV spots won Gold Lions at the 2004 Cannes International Advertising Festival. The campaign poked fun at classic beer advertising with mock paeans to such "men of genius" as "Mr. Really Really Really Bad Dancer."

As the Miller "Low Carb" campaign began running, however, it became clear that the direct comparison of Miller Lite's carbohydrate count with Bud Light's was causing a negative impact on the latter's sales. Anheuser-Busch reacted by making the rare move of using its advertising to respond to a competitor. Anheuser-Busch used the "Real Men of Genius" concept to mock "Mr. Over-the-Top Carb Watcher," and it ran "Bud Light Institute" spots in which the fictional scientific group created devices "to burn off the ridiculously low carbs" in Bud Light. The devices included a treadmill for fingers and a workout machine for toes. Another series of Bud Light spots argued that all light beers were low in carbs and advised consumers to "choose on taste." Miller Lite retorted to this advertisement with a spot thanking Bud Light for the endorsement, the obvious implication being that Miller Lite was the better-tasting beer. Thus began one of the more bitter installments in the "beer wars."

One complexity in Anheuser-Busch's position relative to the low-carb craze was the fact that its own brand, Michelob Ultra, had been responsible for the carb comparison among beers in the first place, and, indeed, for part of the fall-off in Bud Light's growth. Anheuser-Busch estimated that up to 50 percent of Bud Light's sales were lost to Michelob Ultra during the new brew's popularity peak. Also, as Anheuser-Busch tried to argue that Bud Light's slightly higher carbohydrate count relative to Miller Lite was no cause for concern, it risked decreasing demand for Michelob Ultra, whose primary appeal was that it had an even lower carb count than Miller Lite.

The Adolph Coors Company, a distant third in the American beer wars, increased its market share in the late 1990s, and its leading product, Coors Light, had by 2001 surpassed Miller Light to become the country's third most popular beer (and second most popular light beer). Recent Coors Light branding work included spots featuring doctored footage of legendary actor John Wayne as well as youth-targeted ads featuring musician Kid Rock. Like Bud Light, Coors Light found itself forced to respond to the Miller Lite "Low Carb" commercials. One spot asserted that the carbohydrate difference between Miller Lite and Coors Light was so miniscule that the amount could be burned off during a slow dance. Coors also introduced a low-carb beer, Aspen Edge, in 2003.

MARKETING STRATEGY

An assumption driving domestic light-beer advertising had long been that, since consumers recognized no significant difference in product quality among the mainstream brands, the focus of marketing campaigns should be on establishing an approachable and fun brand identity. Anheuser-Busch's Bud Light had successfully done this since the 1980s, whereas Miller Lite had, since the product-quality emphasis of its early "Tastes Great, Less Filling" campaign, struggled to rival its much-larger competitor's branding work. Anheuser-Busch, in confronting the low-carb diet craze directly with the introduction of Michelob Ultra in 2002, simultaneously exposed a weakness in the positioning of its other brand, Bud Light. As carb-conscious drinkers abandoned Bud Light for Michelob Ultra, Miller Lite saw an opening that would allow it to challenge Bud Light by returning to a product-quality focus.

The Miller Lite "Low Carb" ads were extremely simple. As Bob Garfield of *Advertising Age* put it in an approving review of the campaign, "The creative concept is... well, there is no creative concept." Instead, the campaign's spots put the focus entirely on the product and its comparative carbohydrate content. A close-up of beer being poured into a glass was the sole visual element in TV spots, aside from on-screen type that followed the lead of a voice-over as it revealed that Miller Lite had half the carbs of Bud Light, 1/3 fewer carbs than Coors Light, and 70 percent fewer carbs than Michelob Light. As the campaign continued, only one other idea was added to the low-carb message: that Miller Lite tasted great, too.

The phrasing in the 15-second spots was subject to minor adjustments as the campaign evolved. Most notably, after Bud Light responded to Miller Lite's "Low Carb" spots with its own commercials claiming that consumers should "choose on taste," Miller Lite aired "Endorsement," in which the voice-over thanked its competitor for suggesting Miller Lite. Holiday versions of the commercials added to the low-carb/rich taste message with lines like, "the turkey will be the only thing that's stuffed." Radio, print, and outdoor advertising similarly focused directly on the message of Miller Lite's carbohydrate count and taste relative to the competition. After the low-carb theme had been clearly established, taste became the campaign's central focus, positioning the brand for further growth beyond the inevitable waning of the dieting trend.

The "Low Carb" campaign broke in August 2003, and the TV spots targeted high-profile programming that appealed to its male target, relying especially on broadcasts of National Football League and Major League Baseball games. The campaign ran heavily on cable networks such as FoxSports, ESPN, and VH-1, with supporting buys on TBS and TNT. In addition to airing with sports and music programming, the spots ran during male-oriented movie broadcasts. Print ads ran in national sports and lifestyle magazines with a large male audience, including *Maxim, ESPN,* and *Rolling Stone,* and outdoor ads targeted important urban centers. The radio spots ran primarily on rock, contemporary hit radio, urban, R&B, and album-oriented rock stations. The campaign cost more than $20 million and ran into 2004.

OUTCOME

The "Low Carb" campaign exceeded Miller Lite's goal of the preceding decade: to reverse the seemingly unstoppable erosion of the brand's market share. Thirteen weeks into the campaign's run Miller Lite had already seen its first sales gains in nearly five years. For the first eight weeks of 2004 Miller Lite sales were up 15 percent compared with the same period of the previous year, while both Bud Light and Coors Light lost market share. In-house as well as external media analysis of Miller Lite's turnaround attributed the success almost solely to the brand's low-carb positioning. The campaign won a Bronze EFFIE Award in the Beverages/Alcohol category from the New York American Marketing Association in 2005.

As the peak summer selling season approached, SABMiller remained on the offensive, continuing its attacks on Anheuser-Busch with an election-themed campaign (coinciding with the 2004 U.S. Presidential election) created by Portland (Oregon) ad agency Wieden+Kennedy, in which a candidate-like spokesman argued from a podium that there was no place for monarchy in the United States (a reference to the longstanding Budweiser slogan, "King of Beers") and that beer drinkers should elect Miller "President of Beers." Anheuser-Busch fought back with print ads that called Miller Lite "The Queen of Carbs" (presumably suggesting that carb-counting was not a masculine activity) and that drew attention to its South African ownership (the implication being that Miller's patriotic stance was fraudulent). Miller Lite continued to take aim at Bud Light with a campaign centered on blind taste tests in bars, the results of which allegedly indicated an overwhelming preference for Miller Lite. Miller Lite's market share continued to grow at higher levels than Bud Light's, and the brew's advertisements kept boasting about its supposedly superior taste. In 2005 Miller Lite outsold Coors Light to reclaim the number two spot in its category. By this point the low-carb diet craze had begun to wane.

FURTHER READING

Beirne, Mike. "About Time: Miller Lite's Turnaround Is Igniting the Beer Category." *Brandweek,* September 12, 2005.

———. "Beermakers Set the Stage for Summer Barrel Brawl." *Brandweek,* April 19, 2004.

Elliott, Stuart. "Miller Brewing Finds that Women Wrestling in Wet Concrete Get Attention but Don't Help It Sell Beer." *New York Times,* June 4, 2003.

Garfield, Bob. "This Time Miller Lite Gets It Right by Forgoing 'Creativity.'" *Advertising Age,* September 22, 2003.

Kirk, Jim. "Chicago Tribune Marketing Column." *Knight Ridder/Tribune Business News,* March 16, 2004.

MacArthur, Kate. "Miller Surge Goads Coors." *Advertising Age,* December 8, 2003.

Simon, Bernard. "Defying Conventional Beer Wisdom, Miller Lite Is Making a Comeback." *New York Times,* March 18, 2004.

Steinberg, Brian. "Miller Pokes Fun at Budweiser Icons." *Wall Street Journal,* April 20, 2004.

Steinberg, Brian, and Christopher Lawton. "Anheuser Is Told to Pull Ads Targeting Competitor Miller." *Wall Street Journal,* June 1, 2004.

Mark Lane

MILLER HIGH LIFE CAMPAIGN

OVERVIEW

For much of the twentieth century Miller High Life had been the flagship brand of the Miller Brewing Company (which became SABMiller plc in 2002) and one of America's best-selling beers, but during the 1980s, as light beers exponentially gained in popularity, High Life's sales declined sharply. Miller stopped supporting the brand with national advertising, focusing its attention instead on its leading products, Miller Lite and Miller Genuine Draft, and in 1993 the company downgraded High Life's pricing to subpremium, taking it out of competition with leading full-calorie beers like Budweiser. In 1998, as Miller struggled to make up market share against industry-dominating Anheuser-Busch, it repackaged Miller High Life in bottles with a retro look and labeling and initiated a national television campaign positioning the beer as the embodiment of no-nonsense American masculinity.

The "Miller High Life" campaign, created by Wieden+Kennedy (W+K) of Portland, Oregon, and directed by documentary filmmaker Errol Morris, played on nostalgia for an earlier era while employing 1990s irony. The TV spots featured men with straightforward appetites and values and used deadpan voice-overs to bemoan the state of present-day manhood while celebrating the virtues of such throwback staples as buttered hamburgers and duct tape. The combination of blue-collar values and postmodern irony allowed High Life to appeal not just to its traditional audience of older

© JERRY ARCIERI/CORBIS.

drinkers but also to a niche group of hip, younger consumers. Launched with a first-year budget of approximately $5 million, the campaign's price tag grew, as a result of increasing sales, to more than double that amount in later years.

A clear sales boost was attributed to the campaign, exceeding Miller's initially modest expectations. The campaign also attracted significant critical acclaim and numerous awards during its long run, during which time Miller raised the brew's profile among its stable of beers.

HISTORICAL CONTEXT

Miller Brewing Company started in 1855 as the Plank Road Brewery in Milwaukee. In 1903 the company introduced Miller High Life, and in 1906 the slogan "Champagne of Bottled Beers" was attached to the brew. By the 1960s the slogan had given the brand the aura of a rich man's beer, but the rich alone did not provide Miller with the consumer base it needed to increase its market share. Philip Morris bought the brewery in 1969, edited the slogan to "Champagne of Beers," and hired McCann-Erickson of New York to market Miller. The agency helmed the classic "Miller Time" campaign of the 1970s, which positioned High Life as a workingman's beer and paved the way for booming sales in the 1970s. By 1978 Miller High Life, with sales of 21.7 million barrels, was a close second to Budweiser.

Soon thereafter, however, the light-beer category, which was invented by Miller with Miller Lite, began to cut into High Life's sales, and during the 1980s Miller's flagship beer rapidly lost market share. In 1985 Miller introduced Miller Genuine Draft, which eventually replaced Miller High Life as the company's leading full-calorie beer, and in 1988 Miller High Life's packaging was updated and the "Champagne of Beers" slogan dropped entirely. New advertising campaigns did nothing to halt the brand's free fall, and in 1993 Miller discounted High Life to subpremium pricing and drastically cut advertising on its behalf. Miller had meanwhile been allocating most of its marketing resources to Miller Lite and Miller Genuine Draft.

Miller lost market share across all categories in the mid- to late 1990s, however, as Bud Light outpaced Miller Lite and Miller Genuine Draft failed to keep pace with Budweiser in an increasingly tough full-calorie beer market. In 1997 strategic discounting led to improved sales of High Life, and Miller decided to try to bolster the sales of its once-leading product with more aggressive branding. The company repackaged the beer in tall bottles with retro labels that resurrected the "Champagne of Beers" slogan and hired W+K to mount the first national television campaign behind High Life since the mid-1980s.

TARGET MARKET

The "Miller High Life" campaign targeted male baby boomers and young adults simultaneously, using nostalgia as well as irony. The beer's new packaging hearkened back to Miller's 1970s heyday, and the campaign saluted traditional masculinity. But the subject matter and the tone of the paeans in the commercials were intentionally exaggerated to appeal to a knowing audience. As Paul Lukas noted in *American Demographics,* both the beer's packaging and the new ads made reference to the past without glorifying it, "sidestepping both the heavy kitsch factor inherent in the current spate of retro appeals and the bop-on-the-head ironies of postmodern ads." *Advertising Age*'s Jonah Bloom noted that "it was the rare example of a campaign that appealed to young hipsters, and even some frat boys, without alienating the more-mature drinker."

The commercials set out to define manhood via the concept of a High Life man who embodied waning all-American values that Miller sought to connect with the brand. A "Miller High Life Manifesto," conceived by W+K creative director Jeff Kling, announced that "only a large-scale decline in American manhood can account for the near disappearance of Miller High Life Beer," and the ensuing TV spots drove home this point by

ERROL MORRIS

Errol Morris, who directed the Miller High Life ads for the duration of the multiyear campaign, was an award winner in both the advertising and the documentary film worlds. With a well-regarded film catalog already behind him, including *A Thin Blue Line; A Brief History of Time; Fast, Cheap & Out of Control;* and *Mr. Death,* Morris won an Oscar for Best Documentary in 2004 for his film *The Fog of War: Eleven Lessons from the Life of Robert S. McNamara.* That same year he won the Directors Guild of America Award for Best Commercial Director based on his work for Miller High Life, Nike, and Cisco. "It's almost like I have these two separate careers," he told *Adweek.* "I have a career as a documentary filmmaker, and I have a career as a commercial director, and oddly enough, there are people who know me for one and not the other."

illustrating acceptable and unacceptable behaviors from the point of view of a High Life Man. Kling told *Shoot,* "We are appealing to that masculine sensibility, the way men are always imparting undue significance to whatever it is we're doing, like a guy saying if I can't drive that 16-penny nail in three strokes I'll quit right now . . . It's like it's a matter of pride, as if the very fabric of our democracy is being woven here with the shifting gears of backing up a trailer . . . It's an absurd way of thinking that's pretty particular to guys." But at the same time, as Barbara Lippert noted in *Adweek,* the commercials, with their emphasis on nostalgia, did not alienate viewers with different belief systems: "We're all invited in—hetero, homo, male, female, young, old, redneck, hipster, micro or imported beer drinker."

COMPETITION

Anheuser-Busch's share of the domestic beer market approached 50 percent during this time, while Miller had less than a quarter and the Adolph Coors Company roughly 10 percent of the market. Full-calorie brew sales were waning for each company. Budweiser, the country's top beer for decades and formerly Miller High Life's direct rival, had been losing ground to sibling Bud Light for years. Coors Light, meanwhile, had long ago surpassed full-calorie Coors Original.

In the late 1990s and early 2000s, Anheuser-Busch advertising consistently set the standard for the beer industry, and despite declining sales of Budweiser, the brewer continued to support the "King of Beers" with blockbuster ad campaigns. Budweiser ads featuring talking frogs who croaked "Budweiser" in combination with one another gave way to a competing cast of lizards and an evolving swamp creatures story line, and then Budweiser made an even bigger splash with "Whassup?!" which featured a group of friends who greeted one another using the idiosyncratic slang question that gave the campaign its name. Among Bud Light's campaigns during these years was a radio effort called "Real American Heroes" that, similar to the "Miller High Life" campaign, updated the values associated with 1970s beer advertising. In contrast to the everyday heroes showcased in the classic "Miller Time" and "This Bud's for You" campaigns, "Real American Heroes" used 1990s-style irony in mock salutes to such "heroes" as the inventor of foot-long hotdogs.

The attempt by Coors to resuscitate sales of Coors Original by touting its rich taste—and, implicitly, its alcohol content—met with mixed results in the declining market for full-calorie domestic beers. Like Miller, Coors allocated the lion's share of its advertising budget to its light beer, which was by far its top seller and was threatening to overtake Miller Lite in sales. Coors Light campaigns of the time included the "Beer Man" commercials, which focused on ballpark beer vendors, and ads featuring doctored footage of legendary actor John Wayne.

Anheuser-Busch brands Natural Light, Busch, and Busch Light each consistently outsold High Life in the subpremium category. Among these brands only Busch received substantial advertising support, however.

MARKETING STRATEGY

W+K's Kling and Jeff Williams, the creative director and art director, respectively, for the "Miller High Life" campaign, generated the controlling concept and drafted the initial scripts for the television spots. They "wanted the spots to have the authority of looking older, and lavishing these arcane and absurd subjects with a lot of attention," Kling told *Shoot.* "But we also didn't want them to look irrelevant and retro." Based on these priorities, Kling and Williams contacted the acclaimed documentary filmmaker Morris, whose movie *Fast, Cheap & Out of Control* had convinced them that he might have the sensibility to match their vision. Once Morris agreed to work on the commercials, the three of them collaborated to define the visual elements of the campaign. Doug Jeffers was hired to do the deep-toned, calm, authoritative voice-over work that Kling and Williams had envisioned.

Taken together, the 15- and 30-second spots, which ran primarily on sports programming, were meant to construct a coherent world in which, according to

Morris, "values have been correctly readjusted." In "Hamburger," for instance, a greasy burger was served to a diner patron as a voice-over stated, "Something's not quite right." Then the waitress added a large scoop of butter to the patty, and the voice-over proclaimed, "There, now that's a sandwich. And there's only one beer that can stand up to a man's meal. Right again. That's living the High Life. That's Miller Time." "Duct Tape" showed a man repairing his garage refrigerator, which held High Life, baking soda, and pickles, with duct tape, as Jeffers intoned, "The High Life man knows that if the pharaohs had duct tape, the Sphinx would still have a nose. We salute you, duct tape. You help a man get to Miller Time." "Boat," on the other hand, distinguished the High Life man's values by using the negative example of a neighbor incompetently backing a boat trailer into his driveway with an SUV. "This is enough to put a High Life man off his lunch," proclaimed the voice-over. "Time was a man knew how to command his own vehicle. Just how far are we willing to fall? Better reacquaint yourself with the High Life, soldier, before someone tries to take away your Miller Time." As the campaign continued, both the concept and the execution stayed the same, with Morris continuing to direct all of the spots.

OUTCOME

The campaign was immediately applauded by critics and advertising industry insiders. Upon its launch *Adweek*'s Barbara Lippert compared it favorably to virtually all other beer advertising: "It's so original and charming, it's as if Miller has finally found its way out of the image desert. There isn't a beer ad cliché in sight. This work reaches way beyond male bonding, bikinis and sports, as well as their second-generation replacements: anxious men, cross-dressers and talking frogs." *Advertising Age* named Morris's work on the campaign the Best Effort in Direction in 1998 and named the overall campaign its runner-up for Best of 1998 honors. W+K won a campaign gold award from the Art Directors Club in 2003 on the basis of its "Miller High Life" work, and Morris was nominated as Best Commercial Director by the Directors Guild of America in 2004, based in part on his work on "Miller High Life." In the campaign's sixth year *Creativity* said, "As other brewers assume all manner of unbecoming poses in efforts to get with the cool kids, the Miller High Life campaign keeps on keeping its pants on and is, as a result, cooler than just about any work out there."

Originally allotted only $5 million of Miller's budget on an experimental basis, the campaign grew in stature both within and without the company during its nearly 7-year run, and it was credited with stopping a 20-year slide in High Life sales. Miller never expected High Life to challenge the likes of Budweiser, but by 2002 the subpremium brand had overtaken its premium sibling, Miller Genuine Draft, even though the latter's advertising budget of $25.3 million was nearly double that of the "Miller High Life" campaign at the time. Despite the fact that 21- to 27-year-olds, the primary target for most beer advertising, were only part of the target market for the "Miller High Life" ads, the percentage of sales among that segment more than doubled in the years 2001–03. When SABMiller decided in 2005 to phase out the High Life man, Bloom of *Advertising Age* lamented, "The High Life man deserves a promotion, not retirement."

FURTHER READING

Arndorfer, James B. "Miller May Move High Life to Wieden." *Advertising Age,* September 1, 1997.

———. "Miller Restages High Life Brand with Nod to Past." *Advertising Age,* May 18, 1998.

Beirne, Mike. "SABMiller Taps High Life for Higher Profile." *Brandweek,* May 5, 2003.

Bloom, Jonah. "Memo to Miller: High Life Man Is the Beer Drinker's Everyman." *Advertising Age,* April 18, 2005.

"Campaign: Miller High Life." *Creativity,* January 2004.

Champagne, Christine. "Director: Errol Morris." *Adweek,* January 24, 2005.

"Harry Cocciolo and Sean Ehringer." *Adweek,* May 11, 1998.

Lippert, Barbara. "High on Life." *Adweek,* September 14, 1998.

Lukas, Paul. "I Like Ike and . . ." *American Demographics,* October 1998.

Middlekauff, Tracey. "A Man's Life." *Shoot,* December 8, 2000.

Oberlag, Reginald. "It's Guts & Glory Time for Miller High Life." *Shoot,* May 29, 1998.

Wilcha, Kristin. "W+K Mines Gold at Art Dirs. Club." *Shoot,* April 11, 2003.

Mark Lane

Sanford, L.P.

2707 Butterfield Road
Oakbrook, Illinois 60523
USA
Telephone: (708) 547-6650
Fax: (708) 547-6719
Web site: www.sanfordcorp.com

WRITE OUT LOUD CAMPAIGN

OVERVIEW

Sanford, L.P., a fixture among ink companies since the mid-nineteenth century, introduced the Sharpie permanent marker in 1964. In subsequent decades the Fine Point black Sharpie became the world's most popular permanent marker, and the Sharpie brand experienced sustained growth at the expense of its competitors. With market dominance assured in the near term, Sharpie began looking for further brand growth via the introduction of new tip designs and ink colors. By 2002, however, the brand was still almost exclusively associated with its most successful product, the black Sharpie Fine Point. Sanford enlisted the New York office of ad agency McCann-Erickson Worldwide to helm a 2003 marketing campaign intended to spur sales of the other Sharpie lines and position the overall brand for sustained market growth.

The campaign, called "Write Out Loud," leveraged an initial budget of $7 million in the attempt to build a brand to which consumers could become emotionally attached, thereby driving sales of newer Sharpie models. McCann-Erickson's messaging strategy was built on the notion that, since marks made with a Sharpie were permanent, those who used the product were making a bold statement that was the equivalent of "writing out loud." One TV spot, for instance, showed a young husband preparing to record over a videotape marked "Our Wedding" in metallic silver Sharpie ink. While looking at the silver print, the husband saw an image of his wife's face and imagined her saying, "Don't even think about it." Point-of-sale tie-ins supported the media portion of the campaign, as did a series of promotions benefiting educational organizations in various American cities. The campaign began in June 2003.

During the campaign's 2003 run sales of Sharpie varieties that were showcased in the TV spots—the Chisel Tip, Fine Point Color, and Metallic lines—increased substantially. Sales of all Sharpie products likewise ballooned, helping the brand reach its sales goals for the entire year several months ahead of schedule. The campaign was extended in 2004 to pitch another new Sharpie line, a retractable-tip version of the marker that could be used with one hand, and in 2005 the "Write Out Loud" concept was once again reprised behind the new Sharpie Mini product, a smaller version of the standard marker.

HISTORICAL CONTEXT

In 1857 Frederick W. Redington and William H. Sanford, Jr., started the Sanford Manufacturing Company, a maker of ink and glue based in Worcester, Massachusetts. The company relocated to Chicago in the following decade and continued to grow through the late nineteenth and early twentieth centuries. It managed to expand even during the Great Depression, thanks primarily to the quality of its products and its distribution network. Early Sanford marketing included a Norman Rockwell print with copy reading, "It's lucky for you, child, your Gran'dad wrote this will with Sanford's Ink!" Renamed the Sanford Ink Company in 1940, the company moved its headquarters in 1947 to the suburban Chicago location that it would occupy for the rest of the century and beyond. The company moved into the emerging permanent-marker field in the 1960s, introducing the world's first pen-style permanent marker, the Sharpie. Among the initial marketing on behalf of the new product were celebrity endorsements by talk-show hosts Jack Parr and Johnny Carson. In subsequent decades the Sharpie Fine Point black marker became America's most popular permanent marker and the brand's iconic product.

In the 1970s and 1980s Sanford introduced Sharpie Extra Fine Point and Ultra Fine Point markers, and in the 1990s the company began to offer its range of Sharpie models in a variety of different colors. Although the brand grew during the 1990s, partly as a result of the growth of the memorabilia industry—virtually all sports and celebrity autographs were signed using Sharpies—sales of the new Sharpie colors and models did not meet expectations. The number of Sharpie colors and models continued to increase through the early 2000s, but the brand remained almost entirely connected, in consumers' minds, with the stalwart Fine Point black model. To push the full range of the brand's products, Sharpie used its largest marketing campaign to date, a 2002 integrated effort tagged "How Do You Use Your Sharpie?" A TV spot used man-on-the-street testimonials meant to demonstrate the multiple important uses to which various Sharpie markers were put. Though the campaign reinforced consumers' positive opinions of Sharpie's functionality, it did little to build emotional resonance around the brand.

TARGET MARKET

Because Sharpie users did not fit into any specific demographic group or groups, McCann-Erickson targeted a diverse market with "Write Out Loud." Though the disparate ways in which Sharpies were used would seem to complicate the brand's messaging tactics, McCann-Erickson found, through qualitative research, that individual Sharpie users were united by their desire to leave a permanent impression. When using a Sharpie, as opposed to a pencil or pen, the consumer wanted whatever he or she was writing to attract attention. This insight was translated into the idea that those who used Sharpies were bold and assertive—and into a target market unified by a mindset rather than a cultural or generational identity.

THE SHARPIE 500

Among Sharpie's marketing efforts outside of the "Write Out Loud" campaign was its ongoing partnership with the National Association of Stock Car Auto Racing (NASCAR). In 2001 the permanent-marker brand became the sponsor of the Bristol Night Race, a nighttime NASCAR event held at the Bristol Motor Speedway in Tennessee, and the race was accordingly renamed the Sharpie 500. The sponsorship deal was renewed in 2003, guaranteeing that the race would continue to be called the Sharpie 500 at least through 2008.

McCann-Erickson dubbed this target market "Impression Makers" and described them, in a 2004 EFFIE Award entry brief, in the following way: "['Impression Makers'] wanted to impose their will on their environment. They wanted to express themselves strongly with confidence and creativity and leave an imprint on their world (and every surface in that world). And they wanted a specific marker for a specific job that would allow them to leave that imprint and make that impact." By speaking to such qualities as boldness of personality and creativity despite the obviously down-to-earth nature of the product being marketed, McCann-Erickson hoped to build emotional resonance around the Sharpie brand. The agency and its client believed that an increase in the emotional ties to the Sharpie brand would boost consumers' interest in the specific new products highlighted in the campaign.

COMPETITION

The Sharpie brand accounted for an estimated 50 percent of permanent markers sold in the United States. Competing brands included Marks-A-Lot, owned by adhesives and office-supply maker Avery Dennison, and a line of permanent markers made by Eberhard Faber, a company known primarily for its pencils. Bic, the well-known pen company, also produced a line of Sharpie look-alike markers called "Mark-It." None of these competing brands had an advertising presence comparable to Sharpie's.

MARKETING STRATEGY

Budgeted at $7 million in its first year, "Write Out Loud" showcased fine-point colored and chisel-tip varieties of the Sharpie line, in addition to the new Sharpie Metallic product, which was designed to show up on dark surfaces. Though Sanford wanted to move Sharpie's brand image beyond its well-established reputation for functionality, the resulting emotional message, which focused on consumers' ability to make an imprint on the world with Sharpies, was naturally rooted in a key functional aspect of the product: the ink's boldness and permanence. Consumers, McCann-Erickson postulated, were mindful that the mark they were making with a Sharpie was permanent; therefore, their choice to make that mark was a bold and forceful one. As Greg Stoner, vice president and general manager of the Sharpie brand, announced in a press release, "If you want to make a bold statement—when you want to write out loud—you do it with a Sharpie marker." Sanford hoped that this more emotional brand positioning would drive sales of the specific advertised products, but the company also hoped that it would provide fuel for longer-term growth of the brand as a whole.

The campaign was released on June 23, 2003, with the first of three spots that aired on national network and cable TV in both 15- and 30-second versions. The initial spot, "Videotape," was also the campaign's most prominent one, showcasing the Sharpie Metallic marker by casting it in a humorous real-life situation involving a young married couple. The spot opened on a shot of a 20-something man searching in a frenzy for a blank videotape on which he could record a TV program that was about to begin. The only tape available was labeled "Our Wedding" in bold silver Sharpie Metallic ink; as it became clear that he was considering using the tape anyway, the Sharpie ink morphed onscreen into an image of his wife's face as she warned him, "Don't even think about it." The spot closed on an image of the married couple cozily watching their videotaped wedding together. The campaign's other two spots were "Party Cup," which focused on the subtleties of plastic-cup labeling, and "Moving Day," which communicated the impact that a Sharpie-labeled notice, such as "Fragile," had on professional movers. These spots showcased the fine-point colored and chisel-tip Sharpie varieties.

Point-of-purchase displays also communicated the "Write Out Loud" message, as did a series of promotional events prominently featuring Terrell Owens, a wide receiver for the San Francisco 49ers professional football team. Owens had become a de facto Sharpie endorser the previous season when he famously celebrated a touchdown by autographing the football he had been carrying, on the spot, with a Sharpie marker. Beginning in July 2003, after the "Write Out Loud" TV spots had begun airing, Owens participated in a program called "AUTOgraphs for Education," in which he and other professional football players visited Boys & Girls Clubs, schools, and other educational organizations, arriving in special-edition Sharpie Metallic Hummer H2 trucks to collect signatures from community members (signed using Sharpie markers, of course). Based on the number of signatures collected, Sharpie donated funds to the participating educational organization.

OUTCOME

During the campaign's 2003 run Sharpie Chisel Tip marker sales climbed by 7.3 percent, and Fine Point Color sales increased by 18.6 percent, according to McCann-Erickson. The launch of Sharpie Metallic was considered a success as well. Overall Sharpie sales grew by 27.5 percent during the 2003 portion of the campaign, with the brand meeting its sales goals for all of 2003 by September of that year, an acceleration of sales that Sanford attributed to the new campaign.

In 2004 the "Write Out Loud" campaign was extended on behalf of another new Sharpie line, Sharpie Retractable markers, which had writing tips that could be clicked into position using one hand, as with retractable pens. One TV spot focused on a mother whose baby began howling as soon as she put him down, leaving her only one hand with which to complete a time-sensitive Sharpie-labeling task. The retractable model, of course, allowed her to accomplish the task with her one free hand. The "AUTOgraphs for Education" series of promotions was continued in 2004 as well.

In 2005 Sanford and McCann-Erickson adapted the "Write Out Loud" tag to suit the launch of yet another suite of Sharpie products, the Sharpie Mini markers, which were about half the size of a standard Sharpie and thus more portable. Sanford increased the campaign budget to $10 million—a record high for the Sharpie brand—and added online and print advertisements to the continuing emphasis on television. The Mini TV spots were split into two vignettes, as in "Moon/Helmet": the first half of the spot showed an astronaut who, after landing on the moon, used a Sharpie Mini (attached to a lanyard around his neck) to sign "Doug Was Here" on the flag he planted into the moon's surface; the scene then shifted to a youth football game, where a coach drew a game-winning play on the back of the center's helmet so that the quarterback would remember how to execute it. Once again, the autograph promotion benefiting educational institutions provided grassroots support for Sharpie's mainstream marketing efforts, though the 2005 installment focused on professional golfers.

FURTHER READING

Daly, Sean. "Sharpie Nation." *St. Petersburg (FL) Times,* October 20, 2005, p. 1E.

Garfield, Bob. "Tribute to Contrarians: Selling Brand Benefits." *Advertising Age,* January 25, 1999.

Hein, Kenneth. "Sharpie 'Mini' Draws a Crowd." *Brandweek,* May 9, 2005.

Lazare, Lewis. "M&Ms Fade Out B&W to Sound of 'Color My World' Pitch." *Chicago Sun-Times,* March 22, 2004, p. 59.

Rhoden, William C. "The N.F.L.'s New Twist on Fun." *New York Times,* October 17, 2002.

"Sharpie Produces Signature Football Ad." *USA Today,* November 8, 2002.

Weisz, Pam. "Sanford Taps McD to Reach Kids." *Brandweek,* March 6, 1995.

Mark Lane

Sanofi-Aventis

174, ave. de France
Paris, F-75013
France
Telephone: 33 1 53774000
Fax: 33 1 53774296
Web site: www.sanofi-aventis.com

SPIRIT OF FREEDOM CAMPAIGN

OVERVIEW

NOTE: Since the initial appearance of this essay in the 1998 edition of *Major Marketing Campaigns Annual,* Hoechst Marion Roussel became a part of Sanofi-Aventis. The essay continues to refer to the company's former name, as that was the official name of the organization when the campaign was launched.

On August 8, 1997, the United States Food and Drug Administration (FDA) announced new guidelines regulating direct-to-consumer (DTC) advertising of prescription drugs. The following Monday Hoechst Marion Roussel of Kansas City, Missouri, aired a revised version of its "Wheat-surfer" commercial for Allegra, its non-sedating prescription antihistamine. The previous version of the spot mentioned the brand name but not the condition it treated, in compliance with the old FDA rules that prohibited the mention of both the brand and the condition. The new commercial, which was the first television spot to take advantage of the updated rules, complied with the new standards by stating the brand, purpose, and benefits of the drug, while also mentioning possible risks or side effects and indicating a toll-free telephone number and a website for further information about the product.

The commercial itself fused high technology with symbolic imagery suggesting the freedom Allegra offered its users from their allergies. In the commercial a windsurfer sailed across a sea of wheat, suggesting both the ability to coexist with allergens and the liberty to remain active and have fun during the allergy season. Hoechst's advertising agency, the Medicus Consumer division of DMB&B New York, enlisted the services of Industrial Light & Magic Commercial Productions, the outfit that revolutionized special effects with the *Star Wars* movies, to create the illusion of windsurfing on dry land. Industrial Light & Magic subsequently produced follow-up commercials depicting a snorkler swimming through a flower field and a skier traversing a meadow. Competitor Claritin used similar imagery—a brightly-colored hot-air balloon that rose high above allergy-producing plants.

Traditionally pharmaceutical companies had targeted physicians with their prescription-drug advertising, since doctors by law controlled the consumption of these medicines. Patients, however, were the final consumers of the products, so in the mid-1980s companies began to target consumers directly, first with print ads and then with television commercials. The FDA's loosening of restrictions was intended to lessen the confusion created by the previous policies, though some critics questioned the wisdom of over-commercializing medicines since the consumer had no direct control over the accessibility of these drugs; doctors remained the gatekeepers.

HISTORICAL CONTEXT

In 1985 Hoechst Marion Roussel introduced Seldane, the first nonsedating antihistamine. Seldane dominated the prescription market almost immediately, forcing antihistamines containing sedatives such as Schering-Plough's CTM and Parke-Davis' Benadryl to be sold over the counter. The prescription antihistamine market expanded markedly as consumers responded to this new remedy that produced significantly less drowsiness. Other pharmaceutical companies developed nonsedating antihistamines to take advantage of this new market, but none could challenge Seldane's market control. Johnson & Johnson's Hismanal came closest, with sales of more than $200 million in 1992; that same year Seldane's still dominated the market, with sales of more than $500 million.

Also in 1992 researchers discovered that Seldane could be hazardous in certain circumstances. If patients also suffered from liver disease, or if they were also taking a common antibiotic (erythromycin) or antifungal drug (ketaconozole), Seldane could build up in their bodies, possibly causing heart problems such as cardiotoxicity and arrhythmia that could threaten their lives. Although these circumstances were rare, the "black box" warning on the label required by the FDA branded Seldane as dangerous, eroding its control of the market. The subsequent year, Schering-Plough rebounded from its departure from the prescription antihistamine market by introducing Claritin. Claritin was marketed on the strength of its easy, once-a-day dosage and on the weakness of Seldane's perceived dangers. With the addition of Zyrtec from Pfizer, Seldane's control of the prescription antihistamine market dwindled, while Claritin's control increased until it gained dominance of the prescription antihistamine market in 1995.

In August 1996 Hoechst introduced Allegra, a prescription antihistamine that was a metabolite-meaning that it entered the bloodstream pharmacologically active instead of having to be metabolized to be activated. Allegra thus avoided the hazardous problems associated with its parent drug, Seldane. Furthermore, FDA regulations prevented television advertising of Seldane because of its "black box" status, so the advent of Allegra allowed Hoechst to recommence its television advertising. Although it was tempting to market Allegra on the equity created by Seldane, Hoechst realized that the negative publicity surrounding Seldane's hazards damaged the integrity of this equity, so Hoechst set out to create Allegra's own brand identity among the four other non- or low-sedating antihistamines on the prescription market.

TARGET MARKET

The marketing of Allegra represented a challenge to Medicus, as the advertising had to reach two distinct camps: physicians and consumers. Since physicians alone could prescribe medications, they needed to be informed of what Medicus' executive vice president and management director Lorraine Pastore called Allegra's "constellation of benefits": speed of action, power, efficacy, convenience of dosage, and all-around safety. "The diversity of preferences [that doctors mentioned in Medicus' research] led us to a collage presentation," Pastore said. Resembling a *Monty Python* cartoon, the collage featured 19th medical engravings as part of a six-page print ad that ran in prominent medical journals such as the *Journal of the American Medical Association, Diversion, Medical Economics, Postgraduate Medicine, New England Journal of Medicine, American Family Physician, Cortland Forum,* and *Family Practice News,* as well as publications geared toward allergy specialists and internists.

Simultaneously (and equally important), Medicus initiated a consumer print campaign in August 1996, featuring stills of the wheat-surfer in such mainstream publications as *USA Today,* the *New York Times,* the *Washington Post,* and weekly and monthly magazines. A television commercial featuring action shots of the wheat-surfer appeared two months later, in October 1996. Television's far-reaching influence was a key to marketing Allegra, with the potential to directly access those who suffered from allergy symptoms, the majority of whom did not seek prescription relief. A 1997 study by the American Pharmaceutical Association and *Prevention* magazine revealed that almost two-thirds of all consumers had seen DTC advertising, and 60 percent of those saw commercials on television. This exposure prompted almost a third of those who had seen DTC ads to ask their doctors about the advertised prescription products, and 29 percent of that third asked their doctors to write a prescription for the product. Doctors heeded these requests three-quarters of the time. So DTC advertising created a funneling effect whereby vast media exposure prompted a moderate number of

ALLEGRA FREEDOM FORECAST

In order to offer consumers (especially those not currently prescribed Allegra) more information about allergic reactions, Hoechst Marion Roussel set up the Allegra Freedom Forecast via a toll-free number and the Allegra website. The forecasts—devised by the aeroallergen research firm Multidata, Inc., of St. Paul, Minnesota—automatically fed variables such as past pollen records, variations of temperature, humidity, and rainfall, and percent of sunshine into a mathematical formula that predicted allergen counts with 85 percent accuracy in 50 U.S. cities on a daily basis.

inquiries, some of which translated into prescriptions and purchases.

Allegra's marketing targeted not only those who suffered from allergies regularly but also those who experienced allergic reactions sporadically. The revised "Wheat-surfer" spot specifically mentioned seasonal allergic rhinitis (SAR), an allergic reaction triggered by unseasonal changes in the weather or travel to new places that caused chronic flu-like symptoms. Since SAR could strike even those unaccustomed to allergies, and since its symptoms resembled those of a cold or flu, informing consumers of SAR was a means of establishing new markets.

COMPETITION

Schering-Plough's Claritin led the prescription antihistamine market in both revenues and market share. Claritin's North American sales amounted to $1.7 billion dollars in 1997, as compared to second-place Zyrtec's $265 million and third-place Allegra's $214 million. In the United States 67 percent of all antihistamine prescriptions written were for Claritin; Allegra was the second most-prescribed antihistamine, at 16 percent, followed by Zyrtec at 14 percent. Although Allegra was prescribed more often than Zyrtec, Allegra was the lowest-priced prescription antihistamine on the market, thus earning less in revenues. But Hoechst priced Allegra lower to attract customers from Claritin, which cost approximately 18 percent more. Each company spent roughly the same amount in 1997 advertising for these products, according to Competitive Media Reporting: Schering-Plough spent $68.4 million on Claritin, Hoechst spent $64.2 million on Allegra, and Pfizer spent $53.5 million on Zyrtec. Comparing these expenditures to revenues, Claritin was clearly the profit leader.

Claritin's commercials used imagery similar to Allegra's. Claritin's "Blue-Skies Balloon" spot featured a bright-colored, logo-branded hot-air balloon flying above the earth and then depositing its riders on the ground, unaffected by floating allergens. But the spot did not fully comply with the new FDA regulations; the benefits of the antihistamine pill overshadowed the risks and safety information, which were presented faster and in colors that did not distinguish the print from the background. The commercial had been in production when the FDA changed its rules, forcing Power Post Production to revise the spot quickly. An updated version that complied with new FDA regulations broke a few weeks later, in late August 1997.

Claritin ran into trouble earlier when it tried to capitalize on Seldane's hazards. On January 13, 1997, the FDA announced that it was considering banning Seldane because its benefits "no longer outweigh[ed] the risks of potentially fatal cardiac side effects"; Claritin immediately mounted a print campaign that quoted this FDA statement, then added, "Claritin. A safe choice." Hoechst filed a false-advertising lawsuit against Schering-Plough on the grounds that the FDA's announcement was based upon the availability of Allegra as an alternative to Seldane, a fact that the Claritin ad overlooked. The U.S. District Court in Kansas City, Missouri, granted a temporary restraining order blocking the Claritin ad. This had little effect, however, as the ad had already run its course. Hoechst and Schering settled the suit out of court in mid-February 1997, though the terms were not made public.

MARKETING STRATEGY

The strategies Hoechst developed for marketing Seldane's principal active metabolite, fexofenadine HCL, spread wide, extending as far as the choice of name: Allegra. Ads headlined, "Ahhh! Allegra!," followed by a lead-in line reading, "This allergy season, go far ahhhfield." The alliterative invocation of the "a" sound not only echoed the brand name but also reminded the consumer of respiratory relief. The first four letters of the name mirrored the condition it corrected, allergies, but the middle passage of the name also sounded like another important allergy-related term, alleviate. In its logo the swirling "e" was meant to suggest the spirit of freedom.

The "Spirit of Freedom" motto underpinned the entire Allegra campaign. Allegra offered physicians "prescribing freedom" with Allegra's "constellation of benefits"—the fact that Allegra responded to so many different symptoms freed doctors to prescribe Allegra with confidence that it would address their patients' needs and be safe for use. Researchers did testing of the collage ad on the toughest professional audience, New York City doctors, renowned as ad skeptics who did not typify national attitudes. The underlying humor of the collage ads struck a chord with the cynical crowd, and—much to the surprise of the marketing team—the test results from New York City matched the positive feedback from doctors around the country. Defending the seeming irreverence of the *Monty Python* approach, Hoechst's product manager Jan Creidenberg commented, "It's provocative. We want it that way so that you can't turn the page without looking at it. It will stop M.D.s. Research shows that."

Creidenberg applied a similar spin to the consumer audience for Allegra: "We've done a lot of in-depth research with the consumer on this. We think we've captured allergy sufferers' deepest needs—wanting to be free of the limitations of allergies. We think we've expressed the consumers' spirit of yearning for the freedom to enjoy life to the fullest." The actions of the windsurfer were intended to emphasize this spirit—not only did the windsurfer sail across the wheat, she also did flips and twists, accentuating her freedom. Medicus creative director Jerry Weinstein explained, "We wanted the right body language in the surfer. It's freedom with ability and confidence." Weinstein further explained that the marketing of Allegra attempted to move beyond surface reasons for using this antihistamine and delve into the internal motivations for taking allergy medications—a longing for freedom from the effects of allergies.

This approach was "unexpected," according to Weinstein. Traditionally, noted Medicus creative director Richard Norman, antihistamine advertising relied on "conventional allergy icons—smiling patients, pills, flowers, fields, allergens, clear skies for clear breathing, sunrises for day-long effects." He continued, "We decided we could work against this background to create a strong Allegra brand identity. Allegra is a brand with a mind of its own." Hoechst and Medicus could have marketed Allegra using the usual imagery for antihistamines, or as Seldane's offspring, but neither method would have garnered as much attention as the bold move they made in striking out into unchartered territory to redefine the way antihistamines were advertised and marketed.

OUTCOME

Allegra outpaced most drugs in terms of its research, development, and submission for FDA approval, completing these steps in 2.8 years as compared with the average 14 years it took most drugs to reach the market. But Hoechst needed a product to replace Seldane quickly. When Allegra entered the market alongside Seldane, approximately half of Seldane's consumers switched to Allegra, maintaining company loyalty; at the same time, approximately a third of consumers new to the prescription antihistamine market chose Allegra, according to Hoechst public relations spokesperson Julie Gladman. On December 24, 1997, the FDA approved Allegra-D, which reached pharmacies in January 1998. On February 1, 1998, Hoechst removed Seldane and Seldane-D from the market altogether. The speed with which the two Allegra products replaced the two Seldane products minimized any damage done to public perception by the hazards associated with Seldane and maximized the transfer of market shares from Seldane to Allegra as much as possible.

The efficiency and efficacy of Hoechst's introduction of Allegra was too successful in one sense: since the "Wheat-surfer" spot was the first to take advantage of the relaxed FDA regulations, and since its technological wizardry made it so memorable, it became a lightning rod for criticism of the commercialization of prescription drugs. Two newspaper reporters, Daniel J. Vargas of the *San Antonio Express-News* and Erik Parens of the *Cincinnati Enquirer,* wrote articles criticizing FDA regulations of DTC advertising using examples from the "Wheat-surfer" spot. Neither article focused exclusively on prescription antihistamines, so Allegra bore the brunt of criticism for the entire prescription drug market.

Parens' editorial encapsulated others' arguments against DTC advertising, stating that "when advertisers aim their products at patients rather than physicians, they are changing the dynamic of the way drugs are prescribed. They are suggesting that consumers diagnose themselves—and present that diagnosis to their doctor." Diane Seo of the *Los Angeles Times* quoted doctors' pronouncements that "medicine should not be a commodity" and that the "role of the physician is being displaced by the push of consumerism." There was concern that some patients would fixate on the brand name advertised and remain deaf to doctors' advice that cheaper alternatives existed.

But doctors admitted that DTC advertising sometimes benefited patients, educating them about certain medical conditions and the drugs available to treat them. Hoechst's Julie Gladman pointed out that consumers "still can't get the product on their own," since doctors alone could write prescriptions. The makers of Allegra, according to Gladman, wanted "to increase the dialogue between consumer and doctor." Unlike most advertising, prescription drug advertising had a filter built in between the consumer and the product in the person of the doctor, thus necessitating greater saturation of the market with the brand's message, and even this did not guarantee a return on advertising expenditures.

The most noticeable outcome of the FDA's relaxation of DTC advertising regulations was the predictable increase in advertising spending: the American Association of Advertising Agencies reported a leap in DTC ad spending from $250 million in 1995 to $1 billion in 1997 (Allegra's ad expenditures jumped from $19.9 million in 1996, when it was introduced to the market, to $64.2 million in 1997). In the battle for shares of this $2-billion-a-year market, which promised to grow since the majority of those who suffered from allergic reactions did not seek prescription relief, Allegra continued to spin out new versions of its "Spirit of Freedom" message.

FURTHER READING

Castagnoli, William G. "HMR Stresses Creativity for Allegra Introduction." *Medical Marketing and Media,* October 1, 1996.

Seo, Diane. "Drug Makers Aiming Straight for Consumers' Watery Eyes Pharmaceuticals: As Regulations Have Eased, the Allergy Pitches Have Increased. El Nino Hasn't Hurt, Either." *Los Angeles Times,* April 2, 1998.

Vargas, Daniel J. "A Bitter Pill? Are Drug Ads Helping or Misleading Consumers?." *San Antonio Express-News,* June 19, 1998.

William D.Baue

Saturn Corporation

100 Saturn Parkway
Spring Hill, Tennessee 37174
USA
Telephone: (931) 486-5000
Fax: (931) 486-5059
Web site: www.saturn.com

SATURN RELAUNCH CAMPAIGN

OVERVIEW

After establishing a clear identity as a customer-friendly carmaker in the 1980s, Saturn Corporation, a subsidiary of General Motors Corporation (GM), lost its way in the late 1990s. To regain its footing, Saturn designed a new automobile, the Ion, in the early 2000s. Instead of turning over the marketing of the car to its longtime advertising agency, Publicis & Hal Riney, the company opened up the account to the bids of other shops. The winner, in early 2002, was Goodby, Silverstein & Partners, based in San Francisco.

Soon after hiring Goodby for the Ion account, worth approximately $30 to $50 million, Saturn decided to make a complete break with the past and relaunch the Saturn brand. It expanded Goodby's deal into a $300 million account that would encompass all of Saturn's advertising. The Saturn relaunch campaign, which stretched from 2002 until the spring of 2004, was supported by grassroots marketing efforts that involved dealers and included concert sponsorships and promotions at minor league baseball games.

The campaign culminated in the introduction in 2004 of a new tagline, "People first," replacing Saturn's first slogan, "A different kind of company. A different kind of car." While one of the television spots, "Sheet Metal," won prestigious awards, the campaign did not succeed in preventing the erosion of Saturn's sales.

HISTORICAL CONTEXT

Saturn Corporation was created in the early 1980s as GM's answer to the Japanese automakers that had been successfully selling small cars in the United States. Saturn's approach was unique for U.S. carmakers on a number of levels. Most notably the company replaced the traditional assembly line with flexible work teams and gave its employees extensive training in teamwork, self-direction, and responsibility. In addition Saturn established a "no-haggle" sticker price to appeal to customers who disliked the high-pressure sales tactics of traditional dealers. Years before the first car rolled off the production line, Saturn settled on its customer profile, which was similar to that of the imported-car buyer: people under 40 years of age with an average salary of $51,000, half of whom were college graduates. Because a major part of its market would be on the West Coast, Saturn in 1988 hired San Francisco–based ad agency Hal Riney & Partners (later called Publicis & Hal Riney).

Riney's goal was to build a charismatic brand. Thus all car models were to be called Saturns and distinguished only by numbers. The agency then crafted emotional advertising that focused not on the cars themselves but on the Tennessee town in which the cars were made, the people who built them, and the dealers who sold them.

The idea was to get people to root for the company because they related to it. This approach was embodied in the tagline "A different kind of company. A different kind of car." Saturn's advertisements were pure Americana, warm and generous soft sells that told human stories.

Although Saturn was able to develop a mystique through its marketing, the company struggled to sell enough cars to make the venture a true success. By the late 1990s sales had become stagnant. In response Saturn introduced the L-Series midsize sedans and wagons in 1999. The advertising, however, failed to drive sales of these new models, leading some to question whether Riney's low-key approach had lost its edge and if a more traditional tactic might not work better. While Riney developed the advertising campaign for the Vue (Saturn's entry in the sport-utility-vehicle market), a new model called the Ion was in the works.

In 2001 Saturn invited competing ad agencies to bid on the Ion account, estimated to be worth $30 to $50 million, and it was won in 2002 by another San Francisco shop, Goodby, Silverstein & Partners. The agency's founders, Jeff Goodby and Rich Silverstein, were former protégés of Hal Riney who had left his firm in 1983 to start their own shop. Immediately after winning the Ion business Goodby inherited the entire Saturn account. Saturn's management had concluded that it was not wise to split responsibilities between the two agencies. Hence Goodby's task grew from promoting the Ion into relaunching the Saturn brand.

TARGET MARKET

Writing for *Advertising Age* in 2002, Bob Garfield maintained that Riney's "long-cultivated folksiness" approach to advertising the Saturn "attracted certain buyers but repelled many others. The same values that made Saturn appealing to middle-aged, female *Consumer Reports* subscribers made it uninteresting, even emasculating to men." In a separate *Advertising Age* article, Garfield described Saturn owners as "utilitarian souls who proudly wore their plodding not-quite-Nissans as badges of inconspicuous consumption." Aside from attracting more female than male buyers, the Saturn also appealed to an older market, with a median age of 44 for its owners. By not offering a version of the L-Series with both a six-cylinder engine and a five-speed manual transmission, the carmaker lost the business of younger drivers who wanted a more robust, fun-to-drive vehicle. A major reason Goodby won the Ion account was that its pitch appealed to these buyers. In its effort to promote the new Ion and to relaunch the Saturn brand, Goodby targeted small-car buyers aged 18 to 34 and attempted to reach a larger percentage of men than had previously chosen a Saturn.

THE NAME GAME

At the time Saturn was founded, Japanese imports were luring large numbers of customers away from American cars. It was with a pro-American message in mind that GM chose the name "Saturn," a reference to the Saturn rocket that propelled U.S. astronauts to the moon, arguably the greatest technological feat ever accomplished by Americans.

COMPETITION

Saturn originally sought to compete with the Toyota Corolla and the Honda Civic in the subcompact sedan and coupé market, and during the mid-1990s it succeeded in luring a large number of buyers who had previously bought foreign cars. But when the brand was hot, cash-strapped GM failed to invest in bringing out new Saturn models, opting instead to put money into its Oldsmobile brand. While Saturn stood still, Japanese carmakers added features that it was unable to match. Moreover Saturn faced increased competition from South Korea's Hyundai Motor Co. and from U.S. automakers such as Chrysler, which introduced the Plymouth/Dodge Neon subcompact model in 1994. The L-Series, aimed at the midsize-car market, was supposed to be Saturn's salvation, but it proved a major disappointment, selling in far smaller numbers than expected. To make matters worse the company did not keep pace with changing consumer tastes as an increasing number of buyers opted for SUVs and luxury cars.

MARKETING STRATEGY

Once the decision was made to move the entire Saturn account from Riney to Goodby, the two agencies shortened the usual three-month transition, and Goodby set to work. Its immediate task was to promote Saturn's newly redesigned small car, the introduction of which would be followed by the launch of the Ion and the redesign of the midsize cars. Instead of discarding the work done by Riney over the years, Goodby elected to build upon it and in some cases play off of it, as evidenced by the new tagline "It's different in a Saturn," which echoed Riney's "A different kind of company. A different kind of car." Nor did Goodby wish to abandon Riney's work in establishing Saturn's core values of honesty and integrity in the minds of consumers. Rather, the shop wanted to make the same points but with a little humor. The most significant departure from the Riney approach was to be an increased emphasis on the car;

"MORNING AGAIN IN AMERICA"

Hal Riney, the man behind Saturn's original soft-selling, folksy advertising approach, was also responsible for one of the most memorable television commercials in the history of politics, the "Morning Again in America" spot for Ronald Reagan's 1984 reelection campaign. The spot featured positive images of everyday people, portraying their lives as having greatly improved since Reagan had become president.

Goodby had concluded that, after a decade of advertising, the audience had already learned enough about the company. It was ironic, therefore, that the first major television advertisement Goodby developed for Saturn did not even focus on the car.

Jamie Barrett, a Goodby creative director, told *Automotive News*'s Julie Cantwell how his team approached its task. After initial discussions about the car company and what it represented, the team began to focus on Saturn customers and generated concepts such as "people first" and "people before sheet metal." The latter idea became the inspiration for a television spot called "Sheet Metal," which set the stage for the commercials that followed. The concept was to show people pretending to be cars, punctuated by a voice-over at the end: "When we design cars, we don't see sheet metal. We see the people who may someday drive them." Saturn's marketing department instantly embraced the "big idea" nature of the spot, as did director Noam Murro of Biscuit Filmworks in Los Angeles.

Goodby developed four more ideas and then presented "Sheet Metal" before focus groups, where it "effectively bombed," in the words of Barrett, who wrote the script. Nevertheless neither Saturn nor the agency lost faith in the idea, although the reaction of the focus groups led the agency to add 9 seconds of footage of an L-Series car to the end of the 60-second commercial. In a review for *Advertising Age,* Garfield praised the spot: "The automotive body language of our car nation—from backing out of the driveway to sitting in traffic, to yielding at intersections, to riding the school bus—was reproduced, dead on, in actual body language... It was also beautiful. The choreography, cinematography, direction, and editing were crafted as if there were no joke afoot, and the accompanying piano etude by the Polish/French musician/composer Gregory Czerkinsky is a gentle and irresistible counterpoint."

Many television viewers found the "Sheet Metal" spot captivating, but it was important for other reasons. According to Garfield, "It was also a declaration that the old, clunky, homespun Saturn image was (if the advertising worked) about to change." Barrett told Alison Sloane Gaylin of *Shoot* that the spot "helped all of us understand what we were trying to do with Saturn. It created a reference point for us."

After creating the first spot, the intention of which was to shape the brand's image, Goodby fashioned product-focused TV commercials that built on the underlying concept of putting "people first" while also targeting younger car buyers. According to Jeff Goodby, the agency wanted to avoid the typical approach of selling cars to young people as "badges of cool." Rather, Barrett explained, the agency conceived of its target market as "young adults who are at an intersection—they are nostalgic about what they are leaving behind, but eager to make the move to full-fledged adulthood." Each of the four spots supporting the Ion launch in January 2003 showed four young adults driving in a car together through a town where everyone was experiencing the same life stages. For instance, in the spot called "Childhood" the passengers encountered an entire town of children playing on rocking horses, swing sets, and slides. Everybody was involved in the prom in one commercial, another portrayed a town devoted to college antics, and in the fourth everyone in town was getting married. Each spot closed with a voice-over that declared, "The all-new Saturn Ion. Specifically designed and engineered for whatever's next." Saturn hoped that the commercials would also appeal to older buyers, who could look back with fondness on their own passage through these stages of life.

OUTCOME

Goodby's rebranding campaign, which employed the tagline "It's different in a Saturn," came to a close in 2004, when the agency introduced a new series of television commercials that used a streamlined tag: "People first." Research had shown that many people did not understand the line "It's different in a Saturn." As Barrett told *Adweek,* "We thought, 'Why get cryptic? Let's just tell people about it. Saturn is not about being overtly tricky or clever. We can get this done in two words.'" Although the agency was able to hone the Saturn message, it was not successful in selling more cars. After an uptick in 2002, sales in 2003 dropped 3.2 percent to 271,157 vehicles delivered, a far cry from the more than 1 million comparable entry-level sedans that Honda and Toyota each sold. "Sheet Metal" received a number of accolades, however. Primarily on the strength of the spot, Murro was nominated for the Directors Guild of America award for best commercial director. The spot also garnered the prestigious Gold Lion award for Goodby at the 2003 International Advertising Festival in Cannes, France.

FURTHER READING

Cantwell, Julie. "Saturn Ads Try to Update Image." *Automotive News,* August 18, 2002, p. 4.

Freeman, Sholnn. "Saturn Spots Put Emphasis on People, Not Cars." *Wall Street Journal,* August 12, 2002, p. B7.

Garfield, Bob. "Aiming for a Wider Audience, Saturn Ads Make a Right Turn." *Advertising Age,* August 19, 2002, p. 33.

———. "Walking the Walk." *Advertising Age,* May 26, 2003, p. S1.

Gaylin, Alison Sloane. "Different Kinds of Ads: Goodby, Silverstein & Partners and Saturn Bring Cars to Life." *Shoot,* May 2, 2003, p. 17.

Nauman, Matt. "Saturn to Sign On Different Ad Agency." *San Jose Mercury News,* February 2, 2002.

Norton, Justin M. "Goodby's First Saturn Ads Will Tout Spring Sale." *Adweek,* April 1, 2002, p. 5.

Raine, George. "Rites of Passage Focus of Goodby's Saturn Campaign." *San Francisco Chronicle,* January 9, 2003, p. B3.

———. "Saturn Corp. Switching Ad Agencies." *San Francisco Chronicle,* February 2, 2002, p. B1.

Ward, Celeste. "Saturn Comes Out and Says It: 'People First.'" *Adweek,* March 8, 2004, p. 16.

Ed Dinger

WHY DIDN'T ANYONE THINK OF THIS BEFORE? CAMPAIGN

OVERVIEW

On November 1, 1998, the Saturn Corporation, a subsidiary of General Motors (GM), became the first car company to offer a three-door coupe when it introduced an updated model of its SC coupe. The third door, a rear access door, made it more convenient to load passengers and cargo into the back seat. Saturn hoped the innovation would shore up its flagging sales and carve out a niche for itself in the shrinking and highly competitive small-car market. Falling fuel prices and a vibrant U.S. economy had led many consumers to eschew smaller, more fuel-efficient cars like those offered by Saturn in favor of pickup trucks, sport-utility vehicles (SUVs), and minivans (vehicles collectively classified as "light trucks"). Saturn turned to its longtime San Francisco-based ad agency, Publicis & Hal Riney, to craft a campaign that would not only announce the coupe's arrival but also send a powerful positive message about the overall Saturn brand. The ensuing $40 million "Why Didn't Anyone Think of This Before?" television, radio, print, and outdoor campaign, which focused specifically on the utility of the third door, used the same quirky humor that had come to define Saturn's marketing.

The primary purpose of "Why Didn't Anyone Think of This Before?" was to highlight the practical elements of the coupe and to underscore Saturn's longstanding marketing position as a "different kind of company." Saturn had been receiving criticism for failing to expand or update its original line of small cars. In "Why Didn't Anyone Think of This Before," the company presented itself as the maker of innovative automobiles designed for the needs—from the utilitarian to the unusual—of innovative drivers. In one of the three commercials, for instance, a child stands alone in a vast, flat field playing "When The Saints Go Marching In" on a tuba. At the end of the spot, his mother arrives in a sporty red Saturn coupe. The third door clicks opens, and the boy climbs into the back seat with his tuba in tow. The message was clear: a Saturn three-door coupe could carry cumbersome items, offered easy access to the back seat, and was suitable for children. The commercial closed with a voice-over. "Arriving at last, from Saturn. The world's first three-door coupe. Why didn't anyone think of this before?" Two print ads that focused on the uniqueness of the third door accompanied the television spots.

Saturn planned to use the three-door coupe as a launching pad for additional new products. It expected to release its first midsize sedan (the LS) in 1999 and first SUV in 2001. Saturn wanted the coupe ultimately to be viewed as merely one facet of an innovative company. In any event, the three-door coupe and its supporting ad campaign proved to be unequivocal successes. Coupe sales rose immediately to unexpected levels, providing "one of the few positive notes in the small-car market," said the *Sunday Gazette-Mail.* Saturn continued to run "Why Didn't Anyone Think of This Before?" through the spring of 1999. "It was a launch campaign with enough life to last eight months," said Lisa Hutchinson, Saturn's marketing director.

HISTORICAL CONTEXT

Saturn was founded by GM in 1985 to convince young consumers to return to the flock of domestic car buyers. Years of bland products and bad press had convinced many U.S. consumers that American cars were inferior to Japanese imports, such as those made by Toyota Motor Corp. and Honda Motor Company. GM took care not to associate itself too closely with the Saturn name, and gave Saturn management free reign to institute more customer-oriented policies. When the first Saturns rolled off the production line in 1990, they managed to attract consumers who would not ordinarily even consider purchasing a GM vehicle. Saturn also revolutionized the often exasperating process of buying a car. Its dealerships were devoid of the high-pressure sales tactics and

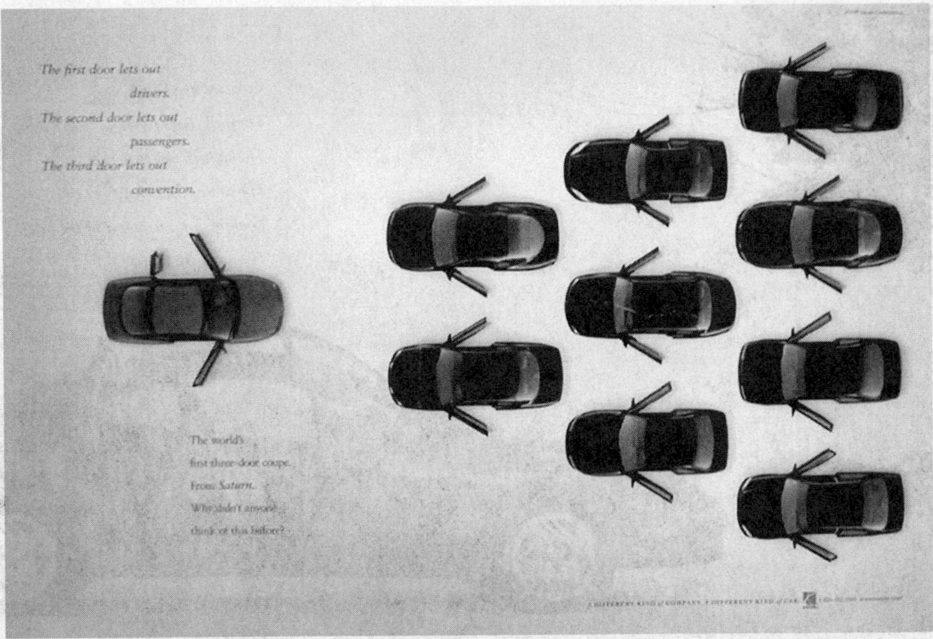

Print ad from Saturn's "Why Didn't Anyone Think of This Before?" campaign. PUBLICIS & HAL RINEY PARTNERS. REPRODUCED BY PERMISSION.

horse-trading that were so common in the automobile industry. Instead, Saturn used low-key sales representatives and set-pricing packages. Moreover, the company took pains to inculcate consumers with the notion that purchasing a Saturn was more like joining a community of Saturn owners and employees than simply engaging in a depersonalized financial transaction. Events such as the Saturn Reunion, a gathering at the company's plant in Tennessee to which all Saturn owners were invited, reinforced this image.

Saturn's advertising also stressed its distinctiveness among car companies. Since its inception, Saturn had used the tag line "A Different Kind Of Company. A Different Kind Of Car" in unusual ads conceived by Publicis & Hal Riney. The commercials were slice-of-life vignettes that featured actual Saturn employees and owners. Spots such as one that depicted a security guard who logged 100,000 miles on his Saturn without ever leaving his small town were "unexpected, understated, and unsurpassed in [their] ability to carve out a brand image," according to *Advertising Age.* "[They] had the most brilliant marketing campaign of any car in the last decade," a marketing analyst told the *The Tennessean.*

Although Saturn's small cars and unique brand image proved popular, rival companies were quick to imitate Saturn's friendly sales process and excellent service. In addition, the American small-car market grew more competitive, and U.S. gas prices were falling to new lows, undercutting consumers' interest in seeking out fuel-efficient cars like Saturn. Moreover, the booming economy produced more people willing to spend $30,000 or more for trendy SUVs. By 1998 the light truck market accounted for 51 percent of new car sales, while small car sales had plummeted 20 percent between 1997 and 1999. Saturn's troubles were compounded by its limited product line. With only one subcompact car—offered in sedan, coupe, and wagon versions—Saturn did not provide consumers with as many options as did competitors like Toyota. "Their life is dependent on how small cars are selling, and small cars have been tough to sell," an industry expert told *AP Online.* In the first nine months of 1998, Saturn's sales were 9.6 percent lower than in the same period of 1997, which themselves had been 10 percent less than 1996.

TARGET MARKET

Saturn's strength had traditionally been its appeal to young consumers. The two-door coupe was especially attractive to unmarried drivers who often traveled alone and liked its sports car-like style. The typical coupe was not, however, the most practical of vehicles. It was difficult for passengers to maneuver into the back seat through one of the two front doors, and it was also hard to access the space to stow even such cargo as groceries or laundry. As Saturn's core market of first-time car buyers began to start families, own pets, and grow a bit older, they came to favor roomier cars. Consumers with children were especially prone to disregard the coupe as a car

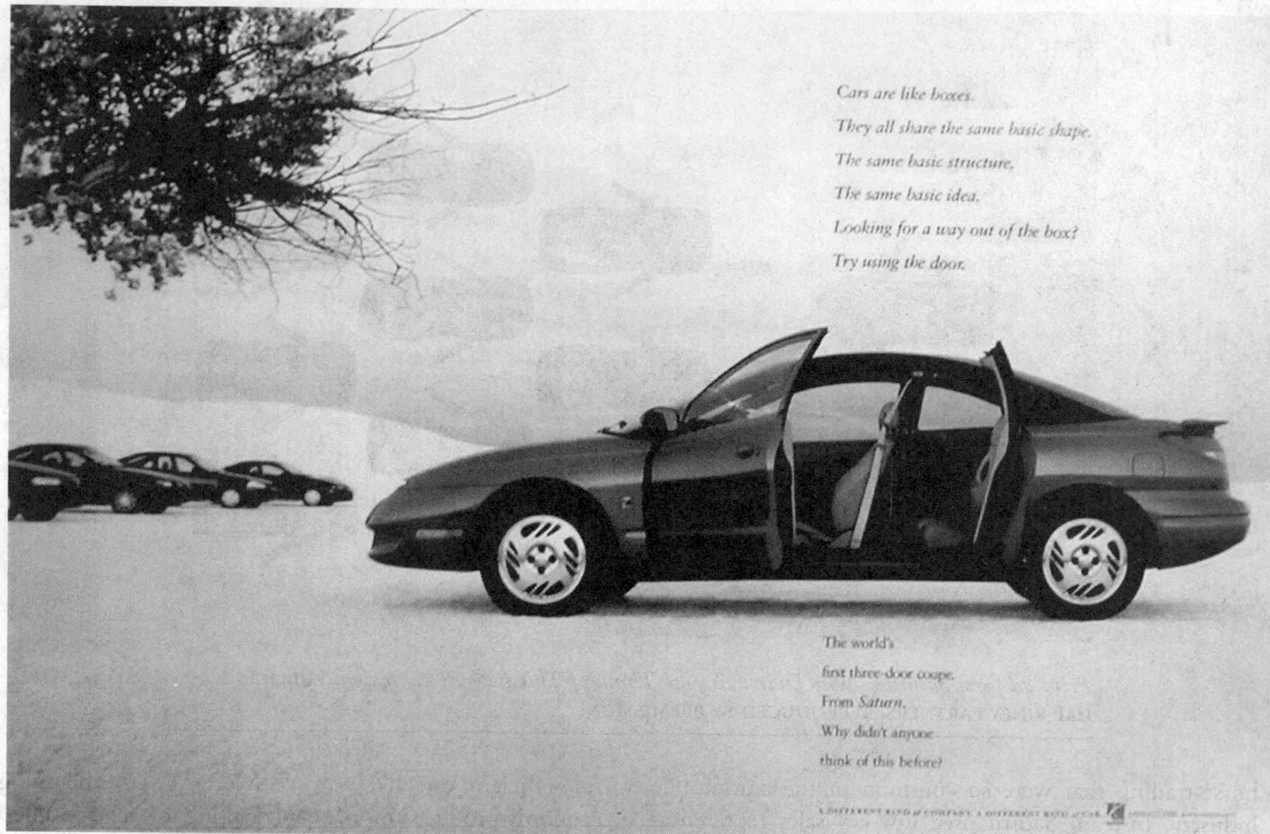
Cars are like boxes.
They all share the same basic shape.
The same basic structure.
The same basic idea.
Looking for a way out of the box?
Try using the door.
The world's
first three-door coupe.
From Saturn.
Why didn't anyone
think of this before?

Print ad from the "Why Didn't Anyone Think of This Before?" campaign for Saturn Corporation. **PUBLICIS & HAL RINEY PARTNERS. REPRODUCED BY PERMISSION.**

choice. "Well, we've had a child now, so we'll have to go on to another product," said Dennis Aman, a member of the SC launch team. The debut of the three-door SC coupe was intended to address this problem. "We think the access door will... pull in some people who bought sedans before," Jim Ulrich, Saturn's chief engineer.

"Why Didn't Anyone Think of This Before?" reinforced this message by making children central to the campaign. In addition to the "Tuba" spot, Saturn also ran "Pick-Up," an ad that featured a father and a Little League team. After the coupe pulls into the driveway of a model suburban home and disgorges its passengers, a small boy dashes back to close the third door left open. These two commercials touted the utility of the three-door coupe by emphasizing the car's capacity to be a family car—with style.

While the campaign encouraged family-car owners to consider the coupe as a viable car option, Saturn recognized that the primary market for the coupe would still be its base of young, single consumers, who might not appreciate the car's ability to tow tykes and their tubas. A third commercial, "Mannequin," addressed these consumers. The spot opened with the scene of a young man waiting outside a restaurant as a woman leans on his shoulder. A Saturn coupe pulls up, and he proceeds to load the "woman"—now recognizable as a mannequin—through the rear door into the back seat. By stressing that the three-door coupe could carry any item, no matter how unusual, Saturn made its point to childless viewers. Moreover, even the commercials that did use kids as the focus did not resort to sentimentality. The edgy humor and quirky scenarios would draw in all viewers, with or without families.

COMPETITION

Saturn wanted to broaden the coupe's appeal because of the severe contraction in the small-car market. According to the *Wall Street Journal*, by 1998 "sales of conventional passenger cars have slumped to levels not seen since the early 1980s recession." As companies jostled to maintain market share in a shrinking pool of consumers, competition grew ever more fierce. In its bid to boost sales, Saturn was confronted by several rivals. In January of 1999, DaimlerChrysler AG debuted its model-year 2000 Neon, which it sold under both its Dodge and Plymouth nameplates. When the Neon was first launched it 1994, the company (then Chrysler) attempted to imbue the car with a likable personality.

FROM THE MOUTHS OF BABES

The concept of the three-door coupe came from neither the company's design team nor from marketing planning sessions. Instead, Stuart Lasser, a Saturn dealer, suggested the idea at a meeting. His eight-year-old son had complained loudly about climbing into the rear seat of the family's two-door model. "Everybody just kind of stopped dead in their tracks and wondered why this hadn't been thought of before," a company representative told the *Northern New Jersey Record.*

This "Hi" campaign anthropomorphized the small Neon. Although "Hi" was critically-acclaimed, DaimlerChrysler devoted $40 million to a new television, print, outdoor, and web banner campaign by BBDO Worldwide that began in March of 1999. "We tried to get away from cute, so the ads are more sophisticated," Arthur Liebler, a senior vice president at DaimlerChrysler told *Advertising Age.* The initial commercials were set to familiar song melodies, to which comedian George Carlin provided voice-overs of Neon-praising lyrics. In one ad, a Neon was shown in a field of sunflowers while Carlin intoned lines like "When your foot hits the gas and you're off in a flash—that's amore" to the strains of the Dean Martin classic. The Ford Motor Company's Escort was another challenger. In February 1998 Ford launched a new campaign created by ad agency J. Walter Thompson that encompassed the entire Ford division. These spots, which featured actor John Corbett, incorporated the tag line "Built to Last" into stories about Ford cars and their owners.

Saturn would also need to fend off imports to prosper. Toyota's Corolla received considerable media spending in the brand-wide "Everyday" campaign created by Saatchi & Saatchi, which debuted in the fall of 1997 and continued to run through 1999. The television ads incorporated the song "Everyday People" by Sly and the Family Stone and stressed Toyota's reliability. In March 1998 eight-page "Everyday" spreads appeared in major magazines like *Life, People,* and *Time.* In the summer of 1998 Toyota debuted the Solara, a coupe that directly challenged Saturn's SC. Honda's Civic also vied for the consumers Saturn desired. Although the model-year 1999 Civic was redesigned, Honda continued to use agency Rubin Postaer & Associates, which had crafted the company's advertising since the Civic was introduced in 1974. Spots for the Civic remained product-focused. Moreover, in March of 1998, Volkswagen AG launched its New Beetle into what the *Wall Street Journal* termed "a cutthroat market" and captured the bulk of the attention aimed at the small-car sector. To support the New Beetle, agency Arnold Communications conceived clever print and television ads that not only conjured up memories of the iconic original Beetle, but also proved popular among younger consumers.

MARKETING STRATEGY

"Why Didn't Anyone Think of This Before?" sought to carve out a distinct niche for the three-door Saturn SC coupe. To succeed in this venture, the campaign needed to make consumers take note of the coupe and its most unique aspect—the rear access door. This was, of course, no easy task since viewers were inundated with a virtual tidal wave of car advertising. But Publicis and Hal Riney strove to create ads that were intensely engaging and that captivated the viewer. One crucial aspect of this strategy was the initial teaser (or bookend) spot. Without revealing the brand or the product, Saturn aired a commercial that simply showed a child playing a tuba. During the next commercial break, the final version played, which showed the three-door Saturn coupe arriving and picking up the young tuba player. The goal was to entice viewers to wait for the follow-up ad and watch closely to see what product was being hawked with such an odd commercial.

Since Saturn hoped to reach a wide array of viewers, the company used national television as its primary venue. The campaign aired on an assortment of programs, ranging from *60 Minutes* to shows that captured a younger audience, such as *The X-Files* and *The Simpsons.* This initial blitz was supported with print ads in both regional newspapers and national lifestyle magazines, such as *Sports Illustrated,* and newsweeklies. These print pieces broke new ground for Saturn. Rather than relying on its usual print method of presenting stories describing Saturn owners or employees, the company ran two mostly graphic ads ("Convention" and "Fox") that focused on the coupe itself. The copy was spare, the visual images striking and simple. Billboard versions of these spots were erected in major markets and made available to local Saturn dealers. Radio ads and point-of-sale material in Saturn dealerships provided the final elements of the campaign.

OUTCOME

Despite the pessimism of some commentators who predicted the failure of both the three-door SC coupe and the campaign to support it, Saturn was so convinced of the coupe's potential that it made the three-door design standard. "It's going to bring a different customer into our coupes, a broader market," an SC launch team member told *The Tennessean.* After one month, Saturn's optimism was justified as sales rose. In December 1998 Saturn reported "its first month-over-month increase since April," according to the *Sunday Gazette-Mail.* Sales continued to increase through January. In fact, coupe sales were 28 percent higher than in 1997. Moreover, the portion of Saturn's overall sales composed of coupe sales rose from 15 percent to 20 percent. This double digit growth continued during the months after the campaign's inauguration. Even more striking was the fact that Saturn's coupe sales soared during winter months, normally a slow sales period for the sporty model.

The "Why Didn't Anyone Think of This Before?" campaign itself was also well-received. *Advertising Age* pronounced the commercials to be "marvelous." Marketing director Hutchinson told the February 8, 1999, edition of *Advertising Age* that the spots "broke through clutter and helped Saturn's coupe sales." The company continued to run the campaign through the spring of 1999, at which point it was shelved in favor of new ads touting the LS, Saturn's forthcoming midsize sedan.

FURTHER READING

Akre, Brian. "Saturn Hopes For Coupe Revival." *AP Online,* October 29, 1998.

"CMR Top 50." *Mediaweek,* March 15, 1999.

Fann, Gina. "Saturn Springs First Three-Door Sports Car." *The Tennessean,* October 30, 1998.

Garfield, Bob. "Saturn Ad Inscrutable but Entirely Irresistible." *Advertising Age,* November 9, 1998.

"GM's Saturn Division To Cut Production 14% over Six Months." *Wall Street Journal,* January 22, 1998.

Gowrie, David. "Dealer Sells Saturn on Idea." *Northern New Jersey Record,* January 5, 1999.

Halliday, Jean. "Campaign Urges Drivers To Say Hello to New Neon." *Advertising Age,* March 8, 1999.

———. "Three-Door Coupe Cuts through Clutter." *Advertising Age,* February 8, 1999.

Krebs, Michelle. "Saturn Hits Jackpot with Door No. 3." *Sunday Gazette-Mail,* February 14, 1999.

Mateja, Jim. "Saturn Open-Door Policy a Breakthrough." *Chicago Tribune,* October 30, 1998.

Newman, Heather. "Saturn on the Line." *The Tennessean,* May 28, 1995.

Stein, Beth. "Saturn's Odd Little Number." *The Tennessean,* April 19, 1999.

Warner, Fara. "US Truck Sales Reach Minor Milestone." *Wall Street Journal,* December 3, 1998.

Rebecca Stanfel

SBC Communications Inc.

175 East Houston
San Antonio, Texas 78205-2233
USA
Telephone: (210) 821-4105
Fax: (210) 351-2071
Web site: www.sbc.com

■■■

LAUREL LANE CAMPAIGN

OVERVIEW

In the late 1990s broadband Internet service was becoming a much sought-after commodity in suburban areas. To expand its phone and Internet service to California, SBC Communications Inc. purchased California-based Pacific Bell in 1997 and then spent $6 billion retrofitting existing phone lines to support DSL (digital subscriber line) high-speed Internet by 2001. Soon SBC Pacific Bell became a leading DSL provider for California. Instead of using preexisting phone lines to provide Internet service (as done by DSL providers), cable Internet providers, such as Road Runner Holdco LLC, provided high-speed Internet through television coaxial cable. Because of utility regulations cable and DSL Internet services performed at relatively similar speeds. After encouragement from its advertising agency, SBC Pacific Bell released the "Laurel Lane" campaign, which suggested that cable slowed down if too many people used it at once.

Awarded SBC Pacific Bell's estimated $100 million advertising account, Omnicom Group's Goodby, Silverstein & Partners created three 60-second television spots—"COPS," "Neighborhood," and "Mailman"—that aired in March 2000. All three spots took place on the fictional Laurel Lane, which was supposedly wired with cable Internet. Presuming that high Internet usage reduced the Internet speed for everyone on Laurel Lane, the spots humorously depicted the street's residents calling each other "Web hogs" and spray painting messages such as "Log off" on the back of an ice cream truck. The spots ended with the tagline "Don't share a cable line. Get Pacific Bell DSL. Always fast. Never shared."

The spots swept advertising awards shows, such as winning Best of Show from *Advertising Age*'s 2001 Best Awards and a Gold Lion at the Cannes Lions International Advertising Festival, and assisted the agency in winning the Bellringer award at San Francisco Advertising Association's 15th annual show. In 2000 the entire SBC Communications' sales climbed $2 billion over the previous year. So many SBC Pacific Bell customers were added during the campaign that the DSL network had to be expanded. Later in the campaign SBC Pacific Bell's "never shared" claim was proven false, and a disclaimer was added to the commercials. DSL users actually did share the connection at the nearest telephone switching office.

HISTORICAL CONTEXT

Pacific Bell had first awarded Goodby, Silverstein & Partners its advertising account in 1996. The following year SBC purchased Pacific Telesis, the parent company of Pacific Bell, to expand coverage into California. Initial SBC Pacific Bell spots focused on features such as caller ID and voice mail. In one television spot, "The

Message," a seven-year-old boy struggled to retell his mother a phone message he had accidentally erased from the answering machine. He began, "The meeting has been changed because, um...we're not going to have the meeting today. We're going to go to the zoo to get ice cream, um, whatever." By 1999 Goodby, Silverstein & Partners changed strategies after polling consumers and discovering that most disliked phone use at home after talking on a phone at work all day. As reported in *Adweek*, a 1999 campaign strove to "make the phone a friend again."

Also in 1999 SBC Pacific Bell budgeted $6 billion for the next three years to provide DSL broadband service to 80 percent of its customers. Originally SBC Pacific Bell asked Goodby, Silverstein & Partners to brand the company as the status quo for broadband service. Because of DSL pricing plans and technology limitations, DSL and cable services performed almost identically. SBC Pacific Bell had no intention of positioning itself as a competitive company. "It took a while to convince them it was the right thing to do," Bob Molineaux, account executive for Goodby, Silverstein & Partners, told *Adweek*, "because they were going from a non-competitive mindset to an open market where they go directly after the competition."

Several concepts depicting consumers' frustration with slow cable Internet services were pitched to SBC Pacific Bell. In one a boy grew a snail shell while waiting for his cable modem to connect to the Internet. SBC Pacific Bell finally chose the "Laurel Lane" campaign for its portrayal of connectivity frustrations in a suburban environment.

TARGET MARKET

"Laurel Lane" targeted residential Internet users who preferred a quicker Internet connection than the 56Kb-per-second speed offered by dial-up services like EarthLink and America Online (AOL). SBC Pacific Bell planned on providing DSL broadband by 2001 to 80 percent of its preexisting phone subscribers. Broadband, although a relatively new residential service, had already reached 3.8 million subscribers the year "Laurel Lane" appeared. The Yankee Group predicted that 18 million homes would use broadband by 2004 even in the midst of a nationwide recession.

The campaign also targeted consumers wavering between DSL and cable. Even though connection speed was nearly identical between the two services, "Laurel Lane" took advantage of consumers unaware of their similarities. "Broadband providers should move away from attacking each other and move to educate consumers," Fritz McCormick, a Yankee Group analyst, suggested to the *Wall Street Journal*. Instead Goodby, Silverstein & Partners misinformed its target audience. The commercials erroneously suggested that customers restricted to only using cable Internet service would be frustrated by their lack of bandwidth (the amount of data one connection can handle). The campaign also incorrectly stated that DSL never slowed down, and no matter how many people in one area used DSL, the connection remained unaffected.

CHRIS SMITH

Chris Smith, who directed all three SBC Pacific Bell "Laurel Lane" commercials, won the Grand Jury Prize at the Sundance Film Festival in 1999 for his documentary *American Movie: The Making of Northwestern*. The documentary followed moviemaker Mark Borchardt, who ran out of funds while making his independent film *Northwestern*. The financial predicament forced him to return to a previously unfinished horror-movie project titled *Coven*.

COMPETITION

The advertising climate among broadband providers was relatively mild before the "Laurel Lane" campaign. Immediately after, however, the cable Internet provider Road Runner, a joint venture between Time Warner Inc. and AT&T Corp., released radio and television spots to attack DSL and phone service providers. One spot featured a DSL technician entangled with phone wires as he installed a DSL modem. Installation took so long that a new mother living in the house actually named her baby Walter after the technician. The spot's ending voice-over stated, "Get DSL and you may be more acquainted with the technicians than the services. Get Road Runner and find out how simple going online can be." The spots were created from reports that some DSL customers complained about installation complications. The spots were created by Shepardson Stern & Kaminsky and aired across San Diego, Cincinnati, and Austin markets. In 2000 it was estimated that 2.4 million consumers used cable while only 1.4 million used DSL.

The largest cable Internet provider in California's Bay Area, AT&T, attacked DSL for having a limited range covering an area of only a few miles around its telephone switching office. The limitation even forced SBC Pacific Bell to snake extra fiber-optic lines from remote neighborhoods to switching offices. In an AT&T spot titled "Marathon," a sprinter became

DSL VERSUS CABLE

Theoretically cable actually outperformed DSL in raw performance speed. Cable peaked at speeds of 30Mbps, whereas most DSL only reached speeds of 10Mbps. The numbers were misleading, however, because most service providers offered residential service plans that started around 1Mbps. Data throughput speed in 2000 was not so much dependent on the type of connection as on the service plan the consumer paid for.

exhausted immediately after starting a race. The commercial tried to expose DSL's limited range.

Dial-up service providers, which could offer a cheaper but much slower Internet connection, released advertisements that boasted of improved features such as pop-up blockers, spam guards, and more secure connections. In 2002 EarthLink released its "In Your Face" campaign to counter AOL's claims of a better pop-up blocker.

MARKETING STRATEGY

Colin Nissan and Sean Farrell, the Goodby, Silverstein & Partners creative directors who collaborated on "Laurel Lane," designed the campaign to show limitations with cable Internet service. Although the depicted limitations later proved incorrect, the agency's associate partner, Paul Venables, told *Advertising Age* that the attack was "more theoretically [correct] than in reality. The more people in your neighborhood that get on [cable] slow it down a little bit, because they're sharing the bandwidth. But there's probably no neighborhood in America where cable Internet use is so dense that it would make a difference right now."

Three 60-second television spots—"COPS," "Neighborhood," and "Mailman"—first aired in March 2000 and showed clips of residents bickering over the neighborhood's bandwidth use. The spot "Neighborhood," directed by Chris Smith, was narrated by a resident of the fictional Laurel Lane. Explained during the character's voice-over, the neighborhood was peaceful until "everyone started sharing the same cable line for the Internet. That's when things online got slower and people started acting, well, downright un-neighborly." First an impatient woman started smacking her desk while waiting for her computer to download. Then a girl sitting before a computer shouted, "Come on!"

The sharing of cable caused so much neighborhood tension that when a child's balloon floated into an older woman's yard, she popped it with her gardening tool. Beside a garage door spray painted with the words "Web Hog," neighbors were shouting at each other, "You're a Web hog!" "No, you're a Web hog!" When a delivery boy lobbed a newspaper onto a house's doorstep, the paper came flying back to smack him off his bicycle. Similar exchanges occurred back and forth, revealing Laurel Lane as a complete donnybrook. One man attacked his neighbor's flower bed with a hedger. Another neighbor snipped the next-door cable coaxial line. The spots ended with the tagline "Don't share a cable line. Get Pacific Bell DSL. Always fast. Never shared." It was later revealed that DSL was in fact shared and its speed sometimes slowed during high Internet traffic periods.

"DSL is a critical product to us, and one way to achieve greater advertising advantage is to point out the differences between your product and the consumer's other choices," Charlene Lake, SBC's vice president of advertising, told *Advertising Age.* "It's just Advertising 101." The three spots were aired just long enough to sweep award ceremonies and bump DSL sales so high that SBC Pacific Bell was forced to install more Internet hubs within some neighborhoods. After the cable provider Excite At Home Corp. proved to a U.S. district court judge that "Laurel Lane" claims were untrue, a disclaimer was added to the spots: "Guaranteed speed is from your home to central office." Undaunted by the backlash from cable service providers, Venables told *Advertising Age,* "We're dealing with a public utility, a monolithic beast. And we take a small point and make a human story around it. We were kind of planting a seed of doubt. I think it's kind of deep. It's smart. And it worked like hell. I'm real proud of it."

OUTCOME

The premise of "Laurel Lane" was considered such a lucid, humorous portrayal of its competition that it collected a Gold Effie from the American Marketing Association, the Best of Show award from *Advertising Age*'s 2001 Best Awards, and a Gold Lion at the Cannes Lions International Advertising Festival. It reaped so many awards at the San Francisco Advertising Association's 15th annual show that the campaign helped Goodby, Silverstein & Partners win the prestigious Bellringer award, given to the agency with the most awards. In regard to the spot "Neighborhood," Bob Garfield from *Advertising Age* wrote, "Seldom has a commercial better framed a supposed problem and a clear-cut solution, while simultaneously turning a widely loathed institution into a protagonist." Although initially praised, the campaign's premise, suggesting that DSL never lagged during high traffic times, later proved to be untrue.

Despite the fact that the spots later posted a disclaimer and the entire campaign disappeared after a few months, the campaign's financial success nearly rivaled its ad industry success. Sales in 2000 for SBC Communications climbed $2 billion over the previous year's sales. Venables told *Advertising Age,* "The orders they got just overloaded their ability to fill them. It was really, really effective. By the end of the campaign running its course, Pac Bell itself was forced to install a few hubs."

FURTHER READING

Anderson, Mae. "Festival Honors Comic Spots." *Adweek* (eastern ed.), February 5, 2001, p. 30.

Cuneo, Alice Z. "Creative That Endures." *Advertising Age,* January 29, 2001, p. 1.

———. "Pacific Bell: Charlene Lake." *Advertising Age,* October 8, 2001, p. S24.

DeSalvo, Kathy. "Bryan Buckley." *Shoot,* March 23, 2001, p. 20.

Dill, Mallorre. "Story Selling." *Adweek* (eastern ed.), July 30, 2001, p. 20.

Garfield, Bob. "Cannes-do's, Cannes-don'ts." *Advertising Age,* June 18, 2001, p. 1.

———. "There Goes the 'Neighborhood': *Ad Age* 's Best Commercial, Goodby Silverstein's Spot for Pac Bell, Shows Ugly Side of Sharing." *Advertising Age,* May 28, 2001, p. S2.

Lazare, Lewis. "Spotting Winners? Exec Picks Ads for Burnett's Cannes Prediction Reel." *Chicago Sun-Times,* June 13, 2001, p. 63.

Michaelson, Elizabeth. "DDB, Goodby, FCB Top N.Y. Fest Ad Field." *Shoot,* February 9, 2001, p. 1.

Parpis, Eleftheria. "The Best Creatives You Don't Know: You've Admired the Work. Now Meet the Rising Stars behind It." *Adweek,* September 22, 2003, p. 20.

Raine, George. "Goodby Loses SBC Ad Account/Telecom Giant Says It Will Divide Business among Different Agencies." *San Francisco Chronicle,* February 7, 2003, p. B1.

Vranica, Suzanne. "Broadband Brouhaha Heats Up Offline." *Wall Street Journal,* September 12, 2000, p. B8.

———. "Hard Sell: In 2000, Good Taste Was Optional—Fewer Dot-Coms, but Wackiness Ruled." *Wall Street Journal,* December 22, 2000, p. B3.

Wilkinson-Ryan, Tess. "The Buzz." *Advertising Age's Creativity,* June 1, 2001, p. 10.

Kevin Teague

Schick-Wilkinson Sword

10 Leighton Road
Milford, Connecticut 06460-3552
USA
Telephone: (203) 882-2100
Fax: (203) 882-2415
Web site: www.schickintuition.com

SHAVING MADE SIMPLE CAMPAIGN

OVERVIEW

For many years Schick-Wilkinson Sword was a distant second to Gillette Company in all categories of the global market for shaving products, but in the late 1990s Schick recognized an opening in the women's grooming category. Shaving razors specifically marketed to women was a relatively new category. Previously women had used men's razors to shave their legs, and even women's products were nothing more than a men's product in a feminine package. But then Schick decided to develop a shaving product specifically intended for women. The result was Intuition, a three-blade pivoting razor with a conditioning soap that provided its own lather, ideal for use in the shower.

The $120 million "Shaving Made Simple" campaign to introduce Intuition was launched in April 2003 and ran through the rest of the year. It featured television, radio, and print elements, all of which took a humorous approach to the problems women had shaving the traditional way. The song "Intuition," released by popular music star Jewel, was also licensed at the cost of $500,000.

The "Shaving Made Simple" campaign succeeded in doubling Schick's share of the women's shaving market and was an important step in Schick becoming a greater challenge to Gillette in the global shaving market. The campaign also won a prestigious award, a 2005 bronze EFFIE in the Beauty Ads category of the annual EFFIE Awards sponsored by the New York American Marketing Association.

HISTORICAL CONTEXT

For years women used men's shaving razors, and even as razor companies recognized that women's shaving products was a distinct category, the products made for women were little more than variations of men's products. As Charles Forelle wrote in the *Wall Street Journal,* "Women's razors weren't much more than men's versions with a pink handle." Schick, which was looking to make inroads against its larger rival and industry leader Gillette Company, recognized in the late 1990s that there was an opening to exploit in the women's shaving category. In 1999 Schick convened worldwide conferences where employees brainstormed about the way women shaved their legs. The primary conclusion was that they shaved in the shower, where they often fumbled with shaving gel. According to Forelle, "Back in her room one evening after a session in Greenwich, Connecticut, Glennis Orloff, a Schick razor engineer, saw a small bar of hotel soap on the edge of the tub and wondered if she could figure out a way to lather up and shave at the same time. Ms. Orloff took the bar back to the lab, carved a hole in it, and stuck a razor cartridge in the hole. 'It worked really well considering how crude it was,' she said."

Orloff's idea was put into development along with a number of other projects, but it soon received greater attention in 2000 after Pfizer Inc. acquired Schick's owner, Warner-Lambert. Executive Joe Lynch, who subsequently became Schick's president, was dispatched along with a colleague to take stock of the blade company. Lynch told Forelle that he found a company with world-class capabilities but little direction. According to Forelle, "It lagged sorely in high-end replacement razors and had missed two opportunities to capitalize on Gillette's delays in releasing women's razors—a two-year gap between Sensor and Sensor for Women, and a three-year gap between Mach3 and Venus . . . So Mr. Lynch put the brakes on scores of research projects and told engineers to start building prototypes of the two ideas he considered most promising: a four-bladed men's razor and the Intuition concept."

Orloff's crude idea was developed into a new Schick women's shaver called Intuition, a one-step product that featured a cartridge with a pivoting triple-blade razor surrounded by a skin-conditioning solid that contained aloe, cocoa butter, and vitamin E to produce a soft, smooth finish. The skin was lubricated with each pass, and the shower washed away the hair. Initially the skin-conditioning solid came in two varieties: fresh-scented Normal to Dry formula and a fragrance-free Sensitive Skin formula. In addition a razor kit was developed that included a refillable handle, a pair of cartridges, a protective travel cap, and a shower hanger for storing the shaver.

Intuition was ready for market in the spring of 2003, timed to launch in the middle of a Gillette product cycle, at a time when the latest Gillette offering was beginning to look old and a new product could not be quickly launched to counter Schick's move. In this way Schick avoided going head-to-head with its more powerful competitor. In the spring of 2003, with J. Walter Thompson handling the advertising, Schick launched the $120 million "Shaving Made Simple" campaign to introduce Intuition, the largest marketing launch in the company's history.

ABOUT FACE

The man behind the Schick name was Jack Schick, a U.S. Army lieutenant colonel who retired from the military in 1910 and staked mining claims in Alaska and Canada. With a lot of free time on his hands during the long, cold winter nights, he conceived of a dry razor that did not need water or lather. He found no backers for the idea but had more success with the magazine repeating razor, inspired by his military training. Like a rifle that used a clip of bullets, Schick's razor stored replacement blades in a clip in the handle that could be fed into position as needed. His idea led to the highly popular Schick Injector Razor, which featured a separate clip of blades that could be slipped into the razor, the forefather of all razor systems.

TARGET MARKET

In general, Intuition targeted a mass audience: women who shaved their legs in the bath or shower, a group that ranged widely in terms of age and income. Because the potential Intuition customer had to be willing to fundamentally change her shaving behavior, the focus of the advertising was on younger women, whose habits were not as longstanding and who were by nature more open to try a new product and were willing to pay extra for the added benefits. They were also generally more interested in beauty, and increasingly shaving products were being marketed as part of a greater beauty category, which appealed to the younger demographic. According to Intuition brand manager Lynne Macchiarulo in an interview with Stephanie Loughran and Dan Alaimo for *Supermarket News,* the Intuition target market was "looking for products that make their lifestyle easier and products that take care of their skin better. Women look for products with multiple benefits, while men are interested in the technology in shaving."

COMPETITION

Schick's Intuition product competed against all methods used by women to remove leg hair, including depilatories, like Nair, which used chemicals to disintegrate hair; waxes, which caused pain when peeled off but lasted four to six weeks; and epilators, essentially wax-free waxing machines that gently plucked out the hair. Schick's direct competition, however, came from Gillette and Société BIC. Gillette had dominated the women's shaving category, first with Sensor for Women and later with its top-selling Venus product, a woman's three-blade system akin to the men's Mach3 product introduced in 2000. In 2002 Gillette generated $37 million in sales of Venus razors and another $86.9 million in refill razor blades, compared to Schick and Intuition's predecessor, Silk Effects Plus, which accounted for $7.2 million in razor sales and $13.5 million in refill blades. It was from Venus that Schick hoped to take away considerable business and begin to make inroads against Gillette on the world stage, where Gillette controlled about 70 percent of the men's and women's razor market and Schick just 18 percent. The only answer to Intuition that Gillette had available was Pink Passion Venus, which offered more of a fashion statement than an innovative concept like Intuition. But Gillette had plenty of money to promote Pink Passion and developed a campaign using the tagline "Passion for Life" and even sponsored a fashion show in which pop star Christina Aguilera modeled a hot pink gown inscribed with the words "Venus Passion." It would take another year, however, before Gillette would be able to take on Schick directly by launching a new product, called Venus Divine, which included an aloe-enriched moisture strip.

Flying somewhat under the radar was BIC, which had not advertised much in recent years and concentrated on disposable razors. Both Gillette and Schick were reluctant to promote their disposable products, afraid to take away sales from their more profitable systems business. In 2003 BIC finally launched its own three-bladed model, BIC Comfort 3, for men and women. As a value-priced product, it did not figure to offer serious competition for Intuition, which was aimed at target customers willing to pay a premium for additional benefits.

MARKETING STRATEGY

The goals of the "Shaving Made Simple" campaign were to introduce the Intuition product, educate women about how it worked, and motivate them to change their shaving behavior and try the product. According to Suzanne Vranica, writing for the *Wall Street Journal,* "Schick took the advice of a creative team composed entirely of young women—and embraced a campaign that uses humor to make its points ... [it] pokes fun at the mishaps that women experience when trying to shave, such as continuously losing the soap in the tub. The tagline for the effort is 'Trust Your Intuition.' "

To ready the market for the introduction of Intuition, Schick first launched a teaser campaign to familiarize consumers with the product. Before the April 2003 launch of the main campaign, the company also sponsored an overnight event at a New York hotel for magazine beauty editors, who were able to try out the razor themselves. The product was officially unveiled in Central Park, where musical artist Jewel gave a free concert and sang her newly released song "Intuition," and free product samples were given out to 5,000 attendees. Schick also paid about $500,000 to license the Jewel song for use in commercials.

The "Shaving Made Simple" campaign included television, radio, print, Internet, and outdoor elements, such as renting Times Square signage. Intuition would also become an official sponsor of the LGPA, participating at every women's golf tournament, offering product demonstrations, samples, and interactive games. In addition four LGPA golfers became "ambassadors" for the product. Another aspect of the campaign would be the sponsorship of Speaking of Women's Health, an organization dedicated to educating women to make informed decisions about their health, well-being, and personal safety.

The campaign's television spots began airing on such shows as ABC's *All American Girl* and NBC's *ER.* An example of the TV spots was "Soap Slip." It showed a woman in a bathtub, with a plastic razor in her mouth, attempting to lather her legs with a bar of soap, only to have the soap slip from her grasp and fall to the floor. The voice-over asked, "Shouldn't shaving be simpler? It is with Schick Intuition." Another woman was then shown using the product in the shower. A second spot, "Shaving Follies," included the same woman in the tub as she fumbled for the soap on the floor, along with another woman struggling to shave her legs with a foot in the sink and eventually losing her balance and kicking the shaving can across the room, and a third who tried to lather her legs with shaving cream but sprayed her face instead. The voice-over asked, "Why shave the old way? When millions of women have already found a simpler way with Schick Intuition." Images of some of the same women were also used in print ads. "Soap Slip" featured the woman in the tub with the headline "Now there's a solution to the soap opera of shaving," while "Wobbler" showed the young lady attempting to shave her legs over the bathroom sink with the headline "Now you can kick the shaving cream can ... permanently." A representative radio spot from the campaign used the sound of a sputtering, near-empty can of shaving cream to make the point that Intuition offered greater convenience than the traditional shaving method.

OUTCOME

The "Shaving Made Simple" campaign won a 2005 bronze EFFIE in the Beauty Ads category in the annual competition sponsored by the New York American Marketing Association, one of the most prestigious awards in the advertising industry. More importantly Intuition enjoyed strong sales, resulting in Schick doubling its share of the women's shaving market. Gillette fought back, as was to be expected, and launched Venus Divine in the spring of 2005 along with a Venus disposable, supported by an abundance of marketing muscle to win back lost business. Schick countered by adding a new Intuition skin-conditioning solid, cucumber melon, and Quattro for Women, a four-blade shaver based on the successful men's product. Gillette increased the stakes even higher with the introduction of Venus Vibrance, a battery-powered shaver using the technology developed for the men's M3Power product, which sent out vibrations to the skin to raise hairs for a closer shave. The razor wars were still tilted in Gillette's favor, but Schick had established itself as a more formidable opponent with the introduction of Intuition.

FURTHER READING

Feldstein, Mary Jo. "Razor Wars Shave Profits at Energizer Holdings." *St. Louis-Post Dispatch,* November 16, 2004.

Forelle, Charles. "Schick Puts a Nick in Gillette's Razor Cycle." *Wall Street Journal,* October 3, 2003, p. B7.

Howard, Theresa. "Gillette Hopes to Power Shaver Sales to Women with Vibrance." *USA Today,* October 22, 2005.

Loughran, Stephanie, and Dan Alaimo. "Getting the Edge." *Supermarket News,* April 21, 2003, p. 41.

McTaggart, Jenny. "Three-in-One Shaver: Schick's Triple-Blade Wet Shaver for Women Cuts Out the Need to Lather Up." *Progressive Grocer,* May 15, 2003, p. 58.

Neff, Jeff. "Gillette Flexes Its Muscle." *Advertising Age,* August 2, 2004, p. 1.

———. "$120 Mil in Spending: Gillette, Schick, BIC Launch Blades." *Advertising Age,* February 24, 2003, p. 8.

Prior, Molly. "Fighting for the Edge in Shaving." *DSN Retailing Today,* March 8, 2004, p. 21.

"PR Plays Prominent Role as Schick Introduces Intuition." *PR Week,* May 19, 2003, p. 5.

Tritto, Christopher. "Energizer Gets Boost from Razor Unit." *St. Louis Business Journal,* May 14, 2004, p. 1.

Vranica, Suzanne. "Schick Challenges Gillette with $120 Million Campaign." *Wall Street Journal,* April 7, 2003, p. A18.

Wasserman, Todd. "Schick's Intuition Prompts New Quattro." *Brandweek,* March 21, 2005, p. 8.

Ed Dinger

Scotts Miracle-Gro Company

14111 Scottslawn Road
Marysville, Ohio 43041
USA
Telephone: (937) 644-0011
Fax: (937) 644-0011
Web site: www.scotts.com

NEIGHBOR TO NEIGHBOR CAMPAIGN

OVERVIEW

The Scotts Company, later to be named Scotts Miracle-Gro Company, had been a leading manufacturer of lawn- and garden-care products since 1868. It sold grass seed, fertilizers, herbicides, and potting soils from its family of brands, which included Ortho, Miracle-Gro, Hyponex, and Turf Builder. Even though it was one of the largest garden and indoor plant-care companies in America, Scotts's marketing efforts floundered during the early 1990s. After Scotts acquired Miracle-Gro in 1995, the founder of Miracle-Gro, Horace Hagerdon, helped solidify the Scotts brand and orchestrated the removal of Scotts CEO Theodore J. Host, whom Hagerdon considered ineffective. Hoping to improve sales and further build the Scotts brand, Scotts released its "Neighbor to Neighbor" campaign.

Created by the ad agencies Wolf Group and Partners & Shevack, the $2 million campaign began in 1996. The budget was soon increased to $20 million. The campaign initially entailed television and radio spots, but in 2003 it expanded with print executions. "Neighbor to Neighbor" featured real customers who raved about their successes in attaining a lush, green yard by using different Scotts products. Each of the television commercials focused on a specific Scotts lawn-care product, and they incorporated humor to make the often intimidating task of lawn care seem less threatening. The advertisements also all included Scotts's formal guarantee of its products' efficacy. The company viewed the guarantee as "more of a promise than a traditional tag line," as Gordon Hecker, Scotts's vice president of advertising, told *Adweek.* Scotts recognized that "consumers depend on the company for advice on lawns and gardening, as well as for the product." In 2003 the Wolf Group, by then the sole agency handling the Scotts account, closed its doors, and the campaign continued under the ML Rogers Agency.

Although the campaign scored unusually low on *USA Today*'s Ad Track consumer survey, "Neighbor to Neighbor" was deemed a success by Scotts and its agencies. The campaign garnered some ad-industry awards and helped Scotts increase its sales by double digits throughout a majority of the campaign.

HISTORICAL CONTEXT

By the time Scotts inaugurated "Neighbor to Neighbor," it was already the market leader in the consumer lawn-care industry. Founded in 1868 by O.M. Scott, the company had initially introduced its Turf Builder fertilizer in 1928. Despite this long history, however, Scotts's marketing efforts had been chaotic before it teamed up with ad agency Partners & Shevack. Although it was a national brand, for many years Scotts poured most of its

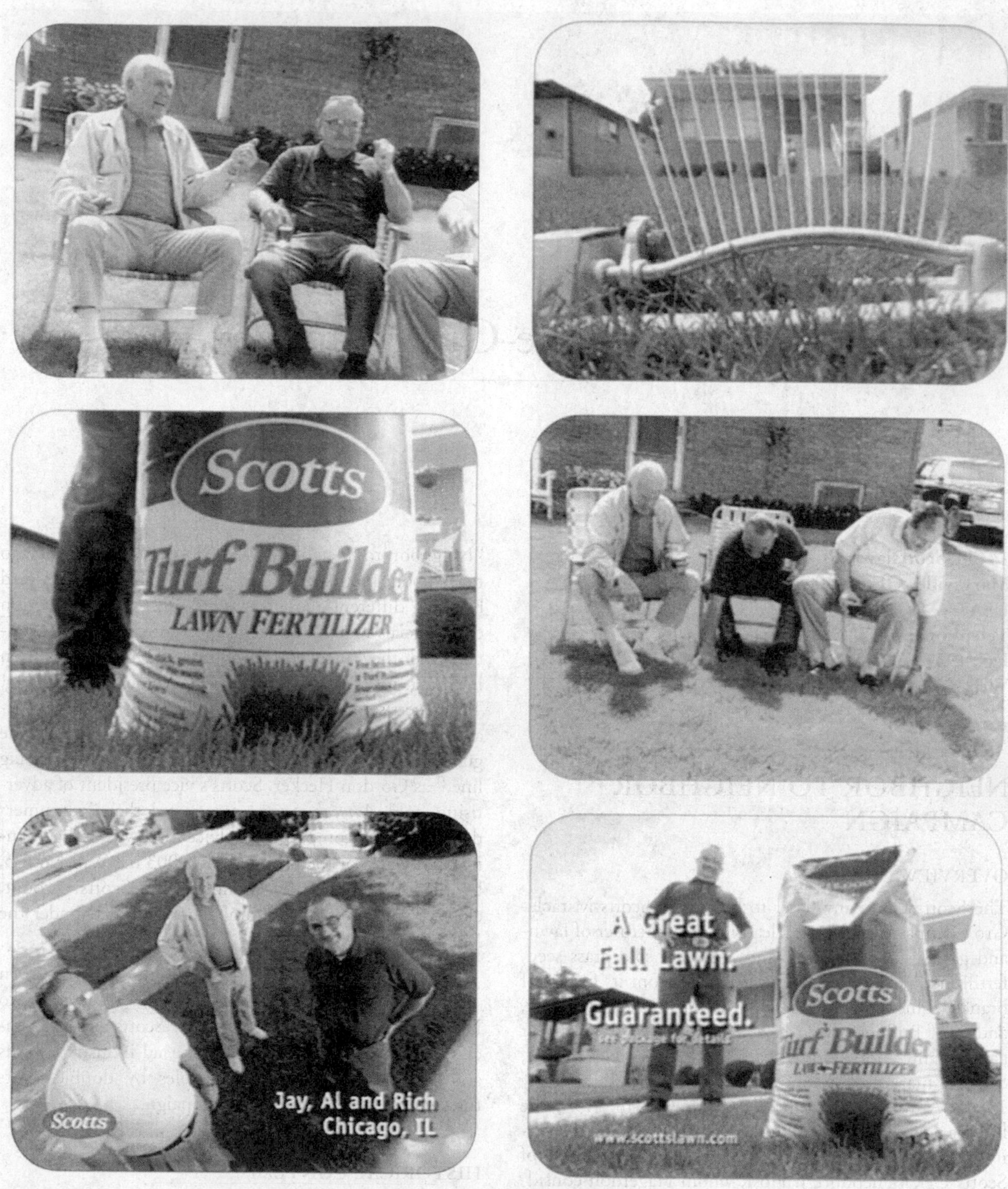

Six stills from the "Three Amigos" television spot from Scott's "Neighbor to Neighbor" campaign. PARTNERS & SHEVACK INC. REPRODUCED BY PERMISSION.

Six stills from the "Looby Lawn" television spot from Scott's "Neighbor to Neighbor" campaign. **PARTNERS & SHEVACK INC. REPRODUCED BY PERMISSION.**

media dollars into scattershot local and regional ads. Using taglines such as "The Scotts Difference," the company often stressed the science behind its products rather than their uses in everyday life. People were absent from most of the commercials, which relied heavily on animated drawings that depicted the nitrogen of Scotts's fertilizers nourishing a lawn. The company's efforts to connect directly with consumers were also thwarted by its tendency to rely on a network of retailers to market its products and by its slim profit margins.

Scotts's fate changed in 1995, however, when the company acquired Miracle-Gro, a flourishing plant-food company that had used savvy marketing to its advantage. "It was a classic case of a lean entrepreneurial company indirectly taking over a sluggish old tortoise company," explained *Forbes* magazine. Miracle-Gro's enthusiastic founder and chief, Horace Hagerdon, exerted a powerful influence over his new parent company. "The truth of the matter is, Scotts didn't buy Miracle-Gro . . . we bought Scotts," he proudly told the *Wall Street Journal.* After Theodore J. Host, then Scotts's CEO, implemented a disastrous marketing scheme that resulted in the company having to restate its 1996 earnings (which promptly led to a 16 percent drop in its stock price), Hagerdon engineered to have him replaced by Charles Berger, a former H.G. Heinz executive. Berger had big plans for the company, which included expanding its presence in the marketplace. "I'd like to create the Procter & Gamble of law and garden," he revealed to the *Columbus Dispatch.* Thus, 1996 was a rebuilding year ("a memorable year we'd like to forget," as Berger told the *Dispatch*), in which the company reported a loss of $2.5 million. One of Berger's first steps was to restructure Scotts and its marketing program. He chose to emphasize the consumer lawn business, which then accounted for about one-third of Scotts's revenues, and it was during this transition period that "Neighbor to Neighbor" was initiated.

TARGET MARKET

Another of Berger's innovations was to target Scotts's lawn-care advertising at the people who actually bought the products. "I restored a consumer orientation to the company," he told the *Columbus Dispatch.* The primary vehicle for this change was the "Neighbor to Neighbor" campaign. It had a wide audience to reach. The company wanted to persuade homeowners across racial and demographic lines to try Turf Builder and its siblings. In addition to capturing consumers from other brands, Scotts sought to bring lawn-care novices into the Scotts fold. The profit potential for this strategy was considerable. According to *Forbes,* Americans spent an astonishing $2.7 billion on lawn and garden products each year. The consumers of such products were skewed slightly toward males, according to Partners & Shevack's Tim Roan. Instead of hiring actors, Partners & Shevack commissioned genuine Scotts's customers, whom it discovered on scouting trips through leafy residential neighborhoods. Out went the drawings of nitrogen molecules. In their place were impassioned, and often quirky, Scotts users who conveyed the benefits the company's products had brought them. The "Neighbor to Neighbor" stars were excited about their lawns and even more excited about the Scotts products that made their grass greener and thicker. The commercials showcased an array of lawn aficionados that included people of different ages and races and both men and women. In the spots Scotts's impromptu spokespeople were interviewed standing on lawns in front of everyday houses in everyday neighborhoods. The "Neighbor to Neighbor" theme expressed the idea that these folks with impossibly green grass were "just like you" and "just like your neighbor."

ALL SCOTTS, ALL THE TIME

According to Partners & Shevack's Tim Roan, Scotts's marketing efforts made up 80 percent of the lawn-care industry's total 1998 advertising. This dominance played a major part in helping Scott expand its lead in the lucrative industry and ensured that the company outpaced its rivals.

In addition to encouraging viewers to relate to the spokespeople, "Neighbor to Neighbor" strove to make lawn care less intimidating. Many people limited their lawn-care activities to mowing and watering because anything more extensive was often perceived as requiring arcane knowledge possessed only by a few. Much of the advice available to would-be homeowners seemed designed to perpetuate this myth. A lawn-care article published in the *Des Moines Register,* for instance, discussed such seemingly complicated concepts as "fertilization regimes that vary for different types of grasses and lawn use" and suggested that people's lawns would benefit if they raked "about one-quarter inch of compost or aged manure onto the lawn each spring and fall." Assuming that anyone had made it that far, the article went on to discuss raking, mulching, and aerating techniques. "Neighbor to Neighbor" was the antithesis of this sort of approach. In the spots Scotts's products were depicted as easy to use and effective. "In late spring, I put [Turf Builder with Plus 2 Weed Control] in my spreader, [and] a couple of days later the weeds are looking sick and the lawn's looking green," one satisfied Scotts's customer related in a television spot.

COMPETITION

Scotts's efforts to build its brand met with little concerted resistance. For the most part the lawn-care business was a "regionalized, fragmented industry," according to the *Columbus Dispatch.* Scotts's closest competitor was

Vigoro, which was acquired in 1998 by Alabama-based Pursell Industries. Once a more powerful brand, Vigoro's market share had fallen far behind Scotts's. In 1997 Vigoro sought to return to the national stage and challenge Scotts. As part of this strategy, Vigoro entered into a relationship with the popular Home Depot chain, which had more than 500 stores across the United States and which attracted the sort of consumers most likely to lavish time and energy (and money) on their lawns. As a part of the arrangement, Home Depot obtained the exclusive right to sell Vigoro's line of lawn-care products. The deal proved to be a boon for Vigoro, as Scotts quickly discovered that its high-profile advertising—which motivated customers to think about lawn care and drove them into megastores like Home Depot—could actually run the risk of boosting the sales of its competitors. Although Vigoro did not pursue the same sort of national and regional marketing efforts as Scotts did, it did have considerable support from the staff at Home Depot. Because Vigoro was Home Depot's private-label brand, the chain's employees were more apt to recommend the slightly less expensive Vigoro over Scotts. In-store displays and shelf arrangements also aided Vigoro's Home Depot sales.

Pursell produced a number of other lawn-care products as well. In addition to manufacturing private-label brands for Kmart and Lowe's, Pursell produced Sam's Choice Lawn Food for Wal-Mart and a line of six organic garden fertilizers sold in the Martha Stewart Everyday gardening line at Kmart. In 1996 Pursell achieved $100 million in sales. To support is flagship product, the Sta-Green brand, Pursell ran 60-second commercials on the Home and Garden cable television network in 1996. Its primary target was aging baby boomers, who were apt to spend more time on lawn maintenance and gardening.

MARKETING STRATEGY

Scotts had two overarching goals for the "Neighbor to Neighbor" campaign. The company wanted to drive sales of its Turf Builder line and to strengthen the entire Scotts brand. Before it launched its barrage of consumer-centered advertisements, Scotts was perceived primarily as a "fertilizer company," Hecker told the *Columbus Dispatch*. The impetus behind "Neighbor to Neighbor" was to transform Scotts into a "consumer branded company." The television spots did much to further this goal. With their almost paternalistic tones, the spots presented the company as a knowledgeable neighbor offering advice not only about which brand to use but also about how to care for a lawn. Furthermore, by airing "Neighbor to Neighbor" nationally during prime-time shows and sports telecasts and on a variety of cable programs, Scotts strove to make more consumers aware of the brand. In the commercials Scotts positioned itself not just as a fertilizer company but also as a "lawn educator." Of course, this kind of saturation strategy required considerable expenditures. Although "Neighbor to Neighbor" was initially budgeted at only $2 million, by 1998 Scotts, which recognized that brand building required expensive, high-exposure media buys, was dedicating $20 million to the campaign.

Scotts complemented the brand-oriented television commercials with radio spots that were geared more toward stimulating the sales of specific products. Ashton Ritchey, the voice behind the radio commercials, advised listeners on which Scotts product was ideal for lawn care "this weekend." The spots, which ran in 78 markets, allowed Scotts to focus its message and closely tie its product recommendations to season and climate, since different products were obviously needed to care for a lawn in Maine in September as opposed to a lawn in Florida in June. According to Tim Roan of Partners & Shevack, the radio component of the campaign was especially effective because it "created urgency" and sent listeners into stores intent on buying specific products.

In 1998 Scotts coordinated its television and radio components in an innovative move to increase its fertilizer sales. Most homeowners typically fertilized their lawns in the spring, which resulted in a 10-week buying period for the company's fertilizer offerings each year. In an effort to increase its Turf Builder sales, Scotts promoted its products from Labor Day until October, a strategy "which hardly anyone had done before," noted *Forbes*. The "Three Amigos" TV commercial was part of this effort. In it, real-life customers named Jay, Al, and Rich advocated fertilizing with Scotts Turf Builder Lawn Fertilizer in autumn. The spot closed as the words "A Great Fall Lawn. Guaranteed" appeared on the screen. The maneuver was only one example of Scotts's foray into new territories. As the uncontested market leader, its growth potential was limited if it aimed only to cannibalize consumers from its rivals. Through user-friendly commercials played in heavy rotation, the company sought to bring new consumers into the lawn-care industry and to encourage existing consumers to think about their lawn-care needs in new ways. As Berger told *Forbes*, Scotts's underlying agenda was to "grow the total market dynamically and then take all the growth."

In 1999 Scotts executives feared that the branding campaign was not explaining enough about the product. "We had to develop new informative packaging to help consumers better identify the right product for their own lawns," Scotts senior vice president Gordon Hecker said in *Advertising Age*. To solve the problem without loading the television spots down with product information, tear-off fliers were distributed at selling points.

Ashton Ritchie, the voice behind Scotts radio spots for six years, began appearing in television spots in 2002. Scotts executives and even Ritchie were not sure if he was the right choice. "I think the TV commercial is a surprise to some people," Ritchie said in the *Columbus Dispatch.* "After all, it's common knowledge here I have the face for radio." Jeff Williamson, the senior vice president and associate creative director for the Wolf Group, insisted that Ritchie's approachable deposition was perfect for the brand.

Because of the American military invasion of Iraq in 2003, advertisers reduced their ad spending, especially during news time. In contrast Scotts increased marketing expenditures by 20 percent and, because of discounted advertising rates, was able to purchase more airtime than it could have before the war. The campaign also expanded with inspirational print ads that read, "Green is part of the dream" to celebrate the fertilizer Turf Builder's 75-year anniversary. The campaign continued into 2006.

OUTCOME

The company achieved its 1998 goal of convincing customers to shift from the traditional spring-only pattern to year-round lawn fertilization. According to *Discount Store News,* Scotts's sales of fertilizer during the fall of 1998 "went through the roof," growing 50 percent. Hecker explained to *Adweek* how these outstanding gains had come about. "We've been able to experience these double-digit increases really without a lot of new products. It's come through more marketing." Partners & Shevack's accomplishments in conceiving the "Neighbor to Neighbor" campaign were recognized by the advertising industry, with the firm receiving a 1998 EFFIE Award for its work.

Even though the campaign bolstered sales for Scotts, the commercials were not necessarily popular with the general public. Only 13 percent of those surveyed by *USA Today's* Ad Track consumer poll liked the spots "a lot," versus the poll average of 21 percent. Lee Reichart, vice president of advertising for Scotts, explained to *USA Today* that the company did not consider the low score to be extremely important. "For people who aren't involved in caring for lawns, this has no relevance," he stated. Scotts's sales for lawn products had increased from $280 million in 1996 to $525 million in 2002.

In January 2004 the Wolf Group, by then the only agency creating advertising for the $80 million Scotts account, closed its doors because of financial problems at its Toronto headquarters. Mike Rogers, who was once president of the Wolf Group's New York office, quickly founded the new ad agency ML Rogers. He then recruited most of his previous Wolf Group employees and continued the "Neighbor to Neighbor" campaign. "We were informed that Wolf was shutting down on a Friday morning, and by Monday morning, Mike was up and running," Bill Burke, Scotts vice president of marketing services, told *Adweek.* "Mike really made the transition seamless for us." The campaign continued into 2006.

FURTHER READING

Dini, Justin. "Homeowners: Scotts Co.'s Advertisement for Its Fertilizer." *Adweek,* August 24, 1998.

Fowler, Veronica. "Grow the Perfect Lawn." *Des Moines Register,* April 18, 1999.

Freeman, Laurie. "Scotts." *Advertising Age,* June 28, 1999, p. S28.

Gomez, Henry. "Wolf Trio Pitches Buyout." *Crain's Cleveland Business,* March, 15, 2004, p. 3.

Howell, Debbie. "Savvy Marketing Feeds Fertilizer Sales." *Discount Store News,* April 5, 1999.

Jaffe, Thomas. "Lean Green Machine: A Few Years Ago, Scotts Co. Was a Slow Moving Company." *Forbes,* November 16, 1998.

McCarthy, Michael. "Scotts 'Lawn Envy' Spots Get Mixed Reaction." *USA Today,* May 19, 2003, p. B7.

Murray, Matt. "Turning the Tables: Miracle-Gro Family Seeds Ranks of Firm that Bought It Out." *Wall Street Journal,* July 23, 1996.

Williams, Brian. "A Blooming Success." *Columbus Dispatch,* July 27, 1997.

Wolf, Barnet D. "Visibility to Grow for Scotts Pitchman." *Columbus (OH) Dispatch,* May 29, 2002, p. 1G.

Zammit, Deanna. "Amid Crowds and Chaos, ML Rogers Sees 'Fresh Air.'" *Adweek,* May 24, 2004, p. 15.

Rebecca Stanfel
Kevin Teague

Sears, Roebuck & Co.

3333 Beverly Road
Hoffman Estates, Illinois 60179
USA
Telephone: (847) 286-2500
Fax: (847) 286-7829
Web site: www.sears.com

COME SEE THE SOFTER SIDE OF SEARS CAMPAIGN

OVERVIEW

The impressive comeback of Sears, Roebuck and Co. was one of the major success stories of the 1990s. Sears was losing billions of dollars a year in the early 1990s but recovered to become one of the top retailers in the nation by 1997. Under the leadership of Arthur C. Martinez, its new chief executive officer, Sears had divested itself of various peripheral businesses, focused on its strengths, updated its stores and merchandise, and publicized the changes by releasing one of the largest advertising campaigns in its history: "Come See the Softer Side of Sears."

The campaign, which began in 1993 and ran until the summer of 1999, featured print ads and an appealing, memorable jingle on television that invited consumers to "Come See the Softer Side of Sears." This helped the floundering, 109-year-old department-store chain emphasize that it offered more than the Kenmore appliances, DieHard car batteries, Craftsman tools, and other "hard" merchandise for which it was best known. The advertising contrasted "softer side" clothing and accessories with the store's "hardline" products. For example, a two-page print ad showed a car battery against a simple white background and under the words "I came in for a DieHard." The other half of the ad concluded with the line "And left with something drop dead," which was superimposed over a warm, color photograph of a woman in an elegant cocktail gown.

For a while the store's transformation and marketing efforts paid off handsomely as women responded well to the "Come See the Softer Side of Sears" campaign. A study by *Fortune* magazine found that from September 1992 to April 1997, the total return to investors from Sears was 300 percent. Competitors J.C. Penney and Wal-Mart returned closer to 75 percent and 10 percent, respectively. In addition, apparel sales at Sears tripled over the course of the campaign. But Sears faced a host of challenges in the late 1990s, including a younger market with which it failed to connect and competition from upscale department stores, specialty stores, and discounters. As a result, the venerable retailer was once again struggling to remain relevant.

HISTORICAL CONTEXT

Sears's advertising slogans in the past had not been particularly memorable. "Where America shops" and "Everyday low prices" had not caught the public's fancy in the way that the "Come See the Softer Side of Sears" campaign did. After a hundred years in business, the company fell into a worsening sales slump for two decades while many of its competitors quickly gained market share.

Sears hit its peak in 1972 and was in a steep decline when Martinez took the helm in 1992. He promptly closed more than a hundred stores that were not performing well, laid off 50 thousand workers, and discontinued the famous Sears Catalog. "Those were very, very difficult decisions, but they were necessary," said Paula Davis, a public-affairs specialist with Sears. If Martinez had not made those tough choices, she added, more employees probably would have lost their jobs as the company continued to flounder. Further, Martinez tightened the company's focus by selling the Allstate insurance company, the Discover credit card, and other financial-service businesses. He also hired John H. Costello to head Sears's marketing efforts.

Information about millions of households was compiled from the company's credit database, consumer research contacts, and sales personnel at Sears stores. The data was analyzed to identify the company's strengths, primary customers, and main competitors. This research revealed that Sears had a solid reputation for trustworthiness. Its brands, including Kenmore, Craftsman, and DieHard, were known for their quality and affordable prices. Unfortunately, however, women were not particularly enthusiastic about the store's clothing, shoes, and accessories. In general, Sears was perceived as an old, reputable company with stores that looked somewhat outdated in comparison to the Home Depots and Wal-Marts that had sprung up to challenge it.

TARGET MARKET

One of the basic problems was that Sears had no profile of its key customers. Identifying primary consumers was not easy for a company with hundreds of individual stores selling a wide range of merchandise to many types of people. For years Sears had assumed that its key customers were men, about 45 years old, who needed items such as power tools and car tires. As the company reevaluated its operations, however, research showed that its core customers were actually working mothers 25 to 54 years old with household incomes of $25,000 to $60,000. Most of them were already making some purchases at Sears, and they often made most of the buying decisions for their families. For example, it was noted that women bought more than 70 percent of men's clothing.

Therefore, Young & Rubicam designed an advertising campaign that appealed specifically to women by emphasizing the "softer side" of the store, in contrast to its hardware. Some of the early spots added, "We're not who you think we are." The advertising focused on stylish, affordable, comfortable clothing of good quality that women could wear at work, at home, or at social events. At the same time Sears had softer lighting installed in its stores, modernized apparel departments, and moved them near the stores' doorways in shopping malls, where women could spot the clothing, shoes, cosmetics, and related items as they walked past. "Sears apparel has been our best-kept secret," said Robert L. Mettler, president of Sears Apparel Group. "We've taken dramatic steps to improve our apparel quality, value, selection, price, and fashion levels. This campaign is aimed at communicating those changes and inviting women into our departments to see our progress first hand."

"Our new campaign is designed to close the perception gap between what our customers expect to find in our stores and what we actually have in our stores in fashionable and affordable apparel," said John Costello, senior executive vice president and general manager of the marketing division for Sears. "Based on extensive customer research, we expect our women customers to react very favorably to the new campaign."

COMPETITION

Sears was not the only long-established department store struggling to change with the times. At least one rival followed Sears's lead and began an attempt to change its image in 1997. While under the protection of Chapter 11 bankruptcy, Montgomery Ward launched a $50 million advertising campaign with the tagline "Shop Smart, Live Well. Ward's." The commercials, which ran on radio and on prime-time television during programs such

OTHER MARKETING APPROACHES

Sears did not depend entirely on advertising to attract customers and cultivate a positive image for itself in 1997. As part of its marketing efforts during 1996 and 1997, the company was the exclusive sponsor of a concert tour by pop singer Gloria Estefan. Sears was also a sponsor of the Women's National Basketball Association, the Trans-Am Championship, and the Ringling Brothers and Barnum & Bailey Circus.

In addition, Sears was the only retail outlet selling ties and scarves for Gilda's Club, a nonprofit organization for people with cancer. The club—named for Gilda Radner, a well-known comic who died of cancer—received 10 percent of the proceeds from Gilda's Club neckwear. Sears also contributed funds from other promotions to Gilda's Club.

as *Friends,* resembled the Sears campaign in many ways. The characters were mainly women who discussed their reasons for purchasing apparel, household goods, and other products from Ward's. In a move away from its previous advertising, which had tended to emphasize attractive prices, the company called attention to its wide selection of quality merchandise.

Another old competitor, the J.C. Penney Co., ran a holiday promotion intended to offer "convenience, speed, and hassle-free" shopping for "time-starved women." Penney's called its sales associates "gift experts" and ran television commercials encouraging customers to use the store's suggestion lists for purchasing gifts.

In contrast, Gap's stylishly stark television spots during 1997 featured celebrities performing music that always concluded with the jingle "Fall into the Gap." For example, during the holiday season the clothing store's commercials included performances by Lena Horne singing "Winter Wonderland" and pop stars singing other Christmas carols.

The message was different at Kmart Corporation, where holiday advertising included humorous television spots with celebrities Penny Marshall and Rosie O'Donnell as average American friends shopping together at the North Pole and other unlikely locations. The ads were part of a popular campaign, launched in 1995, that conveyed the message that Kmart understood who its customers were and how they shopped. In that year Kmart had, like Sears, begun to overhaul its image and change its marketing tactics.

Marshall directed another campaign in 1997 to promote the company's new Big K retail centers. It featured celebrities such as model Kathy Ireland and home improvement guru Martha Stewart running, walking, and riding to the stores. At the same time the company launched a separate campaign that targeted minority customers for its Big K outlets in certain locations.

Early in the year Kmart also formed an alliance with Martha Stewart Living Omnimedia LLC to design, promote, and sell Martha Stewart Everyday bed and bath products. "Customers trust Martha Stewart to inspire a sense of style that they can confidently and comfortably bring to life in their own homes," said Floyd Hall, chairman, president, and chief executive officer of Kmart. The marketing campaign for the products, which underscored their mix-and-match styles, included television spots and advertising in women's magazines and home-and-garden publications.

OTHER ADVERTISING

Sears's multifaceted approach to advertising included a campaign called "Todo para ti" ("everything for you") that targeted Hispanic consumers. In addition, the company circulated 800,000 copies of its magazine, *Nuestra Gente,* which featured articles along with ads and other promotional material. *Nuestra Gente,* in its fifth year of publication, was one of the largest Spanish-language magazines in the nation. In 1997 Sears also launched its first advertising campaign promoting apparel for African-Americans. The campaign included ads in magazines and spots on television and radio. The company also used direct marketing to place promotional materials in consumers' households. Sears mailed more than 150 million catalogs, including millions of Wish Book catalogs during the holidays. Another 90 million advertising preprints were inserted in newspapers, and 180 million mailers were sent directly to households. Finally, Sears began marketing its products via the Internet. Customers could order Craftsman tools and other merchandise from the Sears website.

MARKETING STRATEGY

The "Come See the Softer Side of Sears" campaign ran on television and in major publications, including women's magazines and general interest publications, to reach the women who were the campaign's primary target. "The company really needed to get the woman back into the store," Davis explained. "We wanted an advertising campaign that would speak to her." The thinking was that once women had been persuaded to shop in the apparel department the advertising slogan could be expanded to publicize other attractions at Sears.

Young & Rubicam had designed other campaigns for Sears and was chosen from a field of other agencies that submitted ideas for campaigns that could help change Sears's image. Young & Rubicam was known for creating focused, uncomplicated ads that hinged on "inspired simplicity" and clearly distinguished the agency's clients from competitors.

For its part, Sears made a financial commitment that helped make the venture a success. The company increased its total spending on marketing apparel to more than $200 million a year, invested about $4 billion in store renovations, and allocated about $40 million annually to advertise the changes. "Through our 'softer side' campaign, we want to tell American women that we have upgraded our apparel assortments and that we have what they are looking for," Martinez said. "We want the campaign to disarm the skeptics and pleasantly surprise our customers and feature the kind of merchandise that's on our sales floor right now."

By 1997 the campaign had been running successfully for four years without deviating from the primary message that women should come in and see the modernized apparel department and home furnishings at Sears. The initial phases of the commercials had focused mainly on women's apparel and related merchandise. As the years passed, the focus expanded to include apparel for men and children, footwear, holiday purchases, and other aspects of the store. One big-budget campaign publicized "the service side of Sears," a new division that provided appliance repair and other services in customers' homes.

A companion campaign, "The Many Sides of Sears," was launched in 1993 and also was incorporated through the years as a slogan within the "Come See the Softer Side of Sears" campaign, in other advertisements, on the company's Internet site, and in Sears outlets nationwide. It depicted Sears as a store that met the needs of everyone in the family, with a broad range of merchandise and a new image. The women who were Sears's new target market had busy schedules, and Sears thought they would appreciate a store that offered the opportunity to purchase everything from makeup to a new washing machine to gifts for their husbands. "We are one of the last traditional department stores," Davis noted. With the "many sides" campaign the company was also reaching out to the men who had always been an important part of its customer base.

In August 1997 Sears expanded both the "Many Sides of Sears" and "Come See the Softer Side of Sears" campaigns with simultaneous television debuts in Canada as part of a $300 million capital investment undertaking. The Canadian marketing effort included radio spots and print advertisements.

In the fall of 1998 the "Come See the Softer Side of Sears" campaign turned to humor to get its message across. In print ads that appeared in women's magazines and three 30-second television spots, outdated fashions were compared to the modern look of Sears's apparel. Women were urged to "take another look" at Sears.

By 1999, however, it was becoming clear that the message "Come See the Softer Side of Sears" was losing its effectiveness. A new marketing chief was hired and a major creative overhaul was begun, but not before one last execution of the campaign, albeit muted, was introduced in spring 1999 and ran through August. The slogan was never spoken in these television spots and was instead relegated to a graphic at the end. Furthermore, the "softer side" jingle was modified and only made a token appearance in the closing moments of the dozen or so 15-second fashion spots released in the effort. The emphasis was now on price, in keeping with a Sears's announcement that it would attempt to bolster apparel sales by cutting prices by 15 percent on average. Hence, each of the new spots promoted a specific sale, such as 25 percent off swimsuits. Attempting to compete on price with discounters such as Wal-Mart was not a winning strategy, however, and Sears struggled in the new century to settle on a new marketing theme that provided the traction that "Come See the Softer Side of Sears" had given the company through much of the 1990s.

OUTCOME

Response to the "Come See the Softer Side of Sears" campaign at its height was so positive that it became part of the company's overall image. It provided a much-needed morale boost to Sears's employees, many of whom had become despondent after seeing 50 thousand of their coworkers laid off and many Sears stores closed. Davis explained, "This was the rallying cry that things were changing at Sears. It was a signal that Sears was in touch with who our customer was; we were upgrading; things were changing. Also, we had a new management team coming in, people who were the best at what they did. Increasing employee morale was extremely important." Employee attitude improved, which led to an improvement in customer service, which in turn led to additional sales.

The campaign also increased profits more directly by convincing consumers to visit Sears and see the changes for themselves. "The campaign increased traffic, increased sales, and increased market share," Davis said. The ads were particularly popular with the women customers who were their main target. According to a 1997 survey conducted by *USA Today*, 24 percent of all respondents and 30 percent of women gave the "Come See the Softer Side of Sears" ads the highest popularity rating, and 32 percent said the campaign was very effective. Only 4 percent disliked the campaign, well below the survey average of 13 percent.

According to Ad Track, "Store revenues for the 43 weeks ended November 29 were $32.2 billion, up 6.9 percent from the same period in 1996." The *Advertiser* reported that Sears had lost $2.9 billion in 1992 but was operating at a profit of $890 million within two years, just after the campaign was first launched in 1993. Earnings peaked in 1995, when Sears posted a record $1.8 billion. But this would prove the high-water mark, as income began to tail off.

The "Come See the Softer Side of Sears" campaign and its spin-offs received various honors for excellence in advertising, including the Ogilvy Award in 1996 and EFFIE Awards in 1994, 1997, and 1998. And if imitation was a reflection of success as well as the sincerest form of flattery, Wal-Mart appeared to pay Sears the ultimate compliment in 2006 when it began its "Look Beyond the Basics" campaign, which was eerily similar to "Come See the Softer Side of Sears." Not only did Wal-Mart target women and try to convince them to consider Wal-Mart apparel and not merely shop there for household staples, but also, the execution of some ads were all but identical to the Sears effort. For example, a two-page print Sears ad stating, "We were looking for a refrigerator. But I found something much cooler," was matched by a similar two-page Wal-Mart testimonial with the text "I went in for eye drops and found something eye-opening."

In the end "Come See the Softer Side of Sears" was somewhat memorable but proved not to be the turning point in the history of Sears that many had thought. The message, however well delivered, could not overcome the reality that once women were lured into the apparel aisles, they were generally disappointed with the fashions. This was especially true of younger consumers. Moreover, Sears had to contend with increasing competition from all sides: from specialty stores such as Gap, from more upscale department stores such as Nordstrom and Neiman Marcus, from discounters such as Wal-Mart and Target, and from category-killers Circuit City, Best Buy, Home Depot, and Lowe's. In 2001 Sears tried out the theme "Sears. Where else?" Unfortunately for Sears, consumers could think of a number of alternatives.

FURTHER READING

Altaner, David. "Sears Remains a Factor, after All These Years." *Sun-Sentinel Fort Lauderdale,* December 7, 1995.

"Ample Dollar Support Has Five Retailing Powerhouses Heading in Different Directions." *Advertising Age,* 1995.

Barbaro, Michael. "Wal-Mart Shows a Similar Side to Sears." *New York Times,* March 31, 2006, p. C2.

"Clothing Comeback: Sears' Softer Side Strengthens Sales." *Apparel Merchandising,* December 5, 1994.

Cuneo, Alice Z.. "Penney's, Others Pitching Gift Ideas for Busy Shoppers." *Advertising Age,* November 1997.

———. "Sears Breaks 'Interim' Spring Ads." *Advertising Age,* March 15, 2006, p. 56.

Dobrzynski, Judith. "Reinventing the Sears Corporation." *Ottawa Citizen,* April 20, 1996.

Dolbow, Sandra. "Mid-Tier Muddle." *Brandweek,* April 10, 20006, p. 36.

Elliott, Stuart. "Sears to Focus on Variety Not Price." *New York Times,* August 21, 2001, p. C1.

Enrico, Dottie. "Sears' Softer Approach: Consumers, Especially Women, Take to Ads." *USA Today,* December 15, 1997.

Evans, Keith. "Use One-Shot, One-Idea Approach to Advertising." *Angus Journal,* December 1996.

Kirk, Jim. "Success of 'Softer Side' May Tilt Sears Budget to Broadcast." *Adweek* (midwest ed.), September 4, 1995.

Malmo, John. "First, Truly Change; Then Advertise." *Commercial Appeal,* January 7, 1996.

McMurray, Scott. "Sears Fashions a New Future for Itself." *U.S. News & World Report,* May 13, 1996, p. 61.

Podmolik, Mary Ellen. "Ward's Airs New Ad Pitch." *Chicago Sun-Times,* August 29, 1997.

"Sears Finds Success with 'Softer Side,'" *USA Today,* 1996.

"Sears Unveils Its Many Sides." *Canada NewsWire,* August 29, 1997.

Sellers, Patricia. "Sears: The Turnaround Is Ending: The Revolution Has Begun." *Fortune,* April 28, 1997, p. 106.

"The Transformation of Sears: A Marketing Perspective." *Advertiser,* Fall 1995.

Susan Risland
Ed Dinger

SEARS. WHERE ELSE? CAMPAIGN

OVERVIEW

By the 1990s Sears, Roebuck & Co.Company, a massive retail chain selling thousands of products, was in serious trouble from the loss of market share to big-box stores such as Wal-Mart, Target, and Home Depot. In response Sears spent large amounts of money on advertising campaigns that touted what was special about its stores. Through various campaigns involving hundreds of television commercials, print ads, and newspaper circulars, Sears hoped to overcome the increasing threat to its business. From the "Softer Side of Sears" (1993) to the "Good Life at a Great Price" (1999) and the "Sears. Where Else?" campaign (2001), the company advertised many things about itself: its affordable prices, vast range of merchandise, heritage, and strong family values. Especially with the "Sears. Where Else?" campaign, which spoke to all the above, Sears attempted to set itself apart from competitors by portraying the company as a place that simply could not be matched.

The "Sears. Where Else?" campaign made its debut in September 2001, the same month in which terrorist attacks took place in the United States. Thus, the campaign was introduced at a time of economic distress. Nonetheless, during the four years it ran Sears spent between $600 million to $1 billion annually on the campaign. During the 2001 holiday season alone, 40 different television spots were released. For the television commercials Sears and its ad agency, Young & Rubicam Chicago, used humor to convey its message: that for many generations Sears had been dependably providing families with everything they needed to run a home. The target market was the "mission-focused" woman, the household shopper who was under time constraints. In

Sears store in the Woodbridge Mall, Woodbridge, New Jersey. © NAJLAH FEANNY/CORBIS.

the ads Sears called attention to its diverse selection of merchandise, which included clothing for the entire family, jewelry, electronics, appliances, tools, auto supplies, and much more. While some previous campaigns had showed only snippets of what the store offered, the "Sears. Where Else?" campaign portrayed Sears in its entirety. Although newspaper circulars were the main medium for the print ads, the campaign also appeared in a number of magazines oriented toward families and women. It was the first time in many years that Sears had advertised in magazines.

Early numbers seemed to confirm that the "Sears. Where Else?" campaign was having some success. The 2001 holiday season ended a tough economic year for most American retailers. Although Wall Street analysts predicted a decline of up to 5 percent for same-store holiday sales, Sears's decline was just under half that. In addition, the local advertising industry liked the campaign. The use of humor in the ads, a new approach for Sears, won several Windy Awards, given to Chicago-area agencies. In the end, however, it was difficult to know whether or not the ads helped Sears long-term. While Sears's 2002 sales increased $1 billion over the previous year, from $40 to $41 billion, by 2004 its sales had fallen to $36 billion. Competition from big-box bargain stores continued to increase during the "Sears. Where Else?" campaign. Then, in March 2005 Sears was acquired by Kmart Holding Corp., one of its big-box competitors.

HISTORICAL CONTEXT

From its beginnings in the nineteenth century, Sears marketed to average American consumers. Early 500-page catalogs that sold such items as women's garments, shoes, watches, baby carriages, stoves, wagons, and firearms were directed toward farmers. These catalogs, which offered farmers a cheaper alternative to rural stores, where the markup on goods was often as much as 100 percent, served as highly effective advertising for Sears. Still, the company undertook additional advertising efforts. In 1905, for instance, Sears wrote to its most loyal customers in Iowa to ask that each person distribute 24 catalogs to friends and neighbors. In return, when each of the recipients sent in an order, the original customer received premiums, including such items as stoves or bicycles. The marketing program in Iowa was successful and was later repeated in other states.

Although Sears stopped enlisting customers to distribute catalogs, its campaigns in the twentieth century carried similar themes. For one, the focus on prices remained at the core of its advertising. As well, Sears ads continued to be directed primarily toward ordinary Americans. A 1976 campaign tagline claiming that Sears was "Where America shops" captured this focus. Over the following decade, however, it became clear that Sears benefited more from the loyalty of seniors than from other age groups. By the 1980s Sears had begun to shift its focus to entire families, in particular to women as heads of households. Advertising portrayed Sears as a place where a woman could find all of her family's needs. The introduction of the KidVantage WearOut Warranty and Frequent Purchase programs, both of which reduced the cost of children's clothes, appealed directly to mothers. Soon afterward, however, the focus shifted again, this time to the woman herself.

The "Softer Side of Sears," a campaign introduced in 1993, epitomized this change. The ads invited women to "come see the softer side of Sears," referring to women's clothing and accessories. The campaign told women that, although they could still find clothing for their kids and power tools for the men in their lives, they should not neglect their own needs and wants. From then on the emphasis in marketing was balanced among families, prices, diversity of merchandise, and Sears's heritage, but always with a female target market. The campaign ran until 1999, when it was replaced by "Good Life at a Great Price," which returned full circle to the company's heritage but which continued to focus on the American woman. In another two years this campaign was replaced by "Sears. Where Else?" which, once again, shifted the focus by highlighting Sears's ability to offer customers virtually all of their household needs.

TARGET MARKET

Beginning in the 1980s, Sears's advertising began to center on families, with ads heavily promoting its ability to meet the needs of entire households. In 1993, however, with the "Softer Side of Sears" campaign, the focus shifted from the family to the woman of the household. These ads asked customers to take another look at Sears's apparel for women. Because women had long been the primary shoppers for families, the shift was seen as being a shrewd one. The campaign "Good Life at a Great Price," which in 1999 replaced "Softer Side of Sears," continued to target women but focused more on affordability. The campaign clearly was an attempt to compete with such successful discount giants as Wal-Mart and Target.

By the time the "Sears. Where Else?" campaign was launched in 2001, women accounted for more than 70 percent of Sears's sales. The company had come to refer to its core customer as the woman who was a "mission shopper." According to Sears, time constraints brought a woman to its stores, where she could find anything she needed for herself and her family. While the focus remained on the woman as shopper, products for the whole family once again came to be emphasized. Sears wanted to appeal to customers who might be more concerned with saving time than money. "Where else," asked Sears, could a woman find all of the products she and her family needed?

MASSIVE CONSTRUCTION

In 1973 the completion of the Sears Tower gave the big chain store a brand new headquarters in downtown Chicago. The 110-story tower, then the world's tallest building at 1,456 feet, required a massive amount of materials in its construction. Included were 76,000 tons of steel, 2 million cubic feet of concrete, 16,000 tinted windows, 80 miles of elevator cable, and 1,500 miles of electrical wiring, which was longer than the entire western coast of the United States.

COMPETITION

Sears was not the only retailer trying to convince women that they could find all of their needs under one roof. Advertising for JC Penney stores, for example, took a similar approach. By the time Sears introduced the "Sears. Where Else?" campaign, the J. C. Penney Company, Inc., had been running the campaign "It's All Inside" for a year. This campaign focused on women and on the many roles they played in their daily lives. Nonetheless, even as JC Penney stores took some market share from Sears, the company's own numbers began to dwindle. In 2002 J. C. Penney had more than $30 billion in sales, with net profits of $405 million. In the following year, however, the company's sales plunged almost by half, and it suffered a loss of nearly $1 billion in net profits.

Like JC Penney, Sears was being squeezed on both sides, on one hand by higher-end department stores such as Macy's and on the other by deep discounters such as Wal-Mart. Sears's net profits began to fluctuate dramatically. In 2001, when the "Sears. Where Else?" campaign was launched, the company's net profits were $735 million, down from more than $1.3 billion the year before. In 2002 the number rose to almost $1.4 billion, and in 2003 it rose again, to nearly $3.4 billion. At the same time, however, Sears's sales had remained virtually stagnant, at about $40 billion from 1997 to 2003.

Other retailers, especially deep discounters such as Wal-Mart, Target, and Kohl's, were meeting with greater success. A shift had occurred in U.S. spending, reflecting shoppers' high priority on low prices. Wal-Mart seemed to embody this trend best, as was confirmed by its sales numbers. In 2002 Wal-Mart's sales exceeded $217 billion, representing a 16 percent increase from the year before, and this was followed by a 14 percent increase in 2003. The company's annual net profits, both in 2001 and 2002, exceeded $6 billion. In 2003 its profits jumped to more than $8 billion.

In the category of household appliances, Sears suffered from the success of other big-box stores. Such discounters as Best Buy and Home Depot, for example, were experiencing healthy growth. In 2002 sales for Best Buy, at nearly $18 billion, showed an increase of almost $3 billion over 2001. The retailer had even greater success in 2003 and 2004, with sales at $21 billion and $24.5 billion, respectively. Thus, with deeply discounted appliances in its more than 700 store in the United States, Best Buy was giving other appliance retailers serious competition. Home Depot's numbers during the same time period were even more impressive. From 2002 to 2004 its net sales grew from $58 billion to $73 billion. Both retailers were dominant in marketing, with their ads focusing on the many products offered in their stories at affordable prices.

MARKETING STRATEGY

In September 2001 Sears returned to its heritage with the "Sears. Where Else?" campaign. Led by Mark Figliulo, the chief creative officer at Young & Rubicam Chicago, the campaign also involved seven other agencies, including Ogilvy & Mather, Chicago, and Burrell Communications Group, Chicago. With an advertising budget that ranged between $600 million and $1 billion a year, Sears set out to remind customers of everything it had to offer. As Figliulo put it, the campaign simply let "Sears be Sears." The television campaign, which included 40 spots that ran during the 2001 holiday season alone, was concentrated in prime-time and early morning slots. Although newspaper circulars represented the heart of the print campaign, ads also appeared in magazines catering to families and women. These included *People* and *TV Guide,* as well as *O,*, the magazine published by Oprah Winfrey.

To spread its message, Sears and Young & Rubicam used humor that had a slight edge to it. For example, the 2001 holiday ads, which played on women's fantasies, were sexy in a humorous way, representing a strategy that was different from any previous Sears campaign. In the ads women were shown fantasizing about various men: a sexy lumberjack or a man in Levi's helping repair a woman's car with Craftsman tools. The women's fantasies helped them decide what to buy their own men for Christmas. Other ads in the campaign were more centered on reality, but they still used a touch of humor. For example, in "Everything for Baby," an ad for a video camera, a mother was trying to soothe her crying child when the father tripped over the baby gate, which made the baby laugh.

A year later, under the same "Sears. Where Else?" theme, the campaign shifted gears in order to convey the company's long heritage more strongly. These new commercials, which debuted in August 2002, were augmented by what was called "now and then" spots. As Figliulo said, "We're not changing our voice as much as adding a new tone of voice. There's still humor in it, but it's a little more emotional." In the ads black-and-white images of customers from earlier years were interspersed with color images of contemporary customers. The customers of the past were seen using vintage products from different periods, bought at Sears, of course, while their contemporaries asked for such things as video games. The aim was to remind people how reliable Sears had been throughout the years for all of the needs of the family. The "Sears. Where Else?" ads continued throughout 2004, when they began to be replaced by a new campaign that featured Ty Pennington, the host of ABC's *Extreme Makeover: Home Edition.*

OUTCOME

Numbers seemed to confirm that the "Sears. Where Else?" campaign had some initial success. The 2001 holiday season, which followed the terrorist attacks on the United States in the previous September, was a tough period for most department stores. Nonetheless, same-store holiday sales for Sears declined only 2.4 percent, less than the 3 to 5 percent that financial analysts had predicted for department stores generally. Overall the 2001 holiday season accounted for approximately 40 percent of Sears's annual profits.

Ad Track surveys showed that the new ads gained recognition with the public, especially among the target market. When asked if they liked the ads "a lot," 21 percent of the respondents said yes, just below the average of 22 percent for all ads. Among women, who represented Sears's primary target, 28 percent claimed that they liked the ads. Of all respondents, however, only 12 percent thought that the ads were "very effective," much lower than the average of 23 percent. Judges for advertising awards, on the other hand, thought that the ads were effective in using humor. In 2002 the early "Sears. Where Else?" television ads won several Windy Awards, which recognized the top advertising efforts from Chicago-area agencies.

Whether or not the ads were finally effective for Sears was hard to determine. In a market that increasingly favored discount stores like Wal-Mart, such department stores as Sears struggled. In 2001 sales at Sears were at $40 billion, and in 2002 they grew to exceed $41 billion, an increase that may have been partly a product of the "Sears. Where Else" campaign. In 2003, however, after the campaign had shifted its focus to the Sears heritage, the company's sales were virtually unchanged. In 2004, it dropped dramatically, to $36 billion. Perhaps the "Sears. Where Else?" ads were effective enough to keep the company afloat for a while. In March 2005, however, Sears was acquired by Kmart and a new parent company, Sears Holding, was formed. The merger directly connected Sears to the discount-store world that had provided its greatest competition.

FURTHER READING

Carpenter, Dave. "Dowdy Sears Tries on Makeover, Lands End." *Seattle Post-Intelligence,* November 30, 2002.

Elliot, Stuart. "Sears, Riding Wave of Nostalgia, Emphasizes Heritage in Campaign." *New York Times,* August 23, 2002.

Guy, Sandra. "Sears Readies More Cost Cuts." *Chicago Sun-Times,* October 21, 2002, p. 53.

Howard, Theresa. "Sears Marketing Strategy Goes Back to Basics." *USA Today,* January 1, 2002.

———. "Sears Sees Shopping Rise with Ty Pennington Ads." *USA Today,* November 15, 2004.

Hutchinson, Katherine. "Sears Launches Comic Campaign Positioning as One-Stop Destination." *DSN Retailing Today,* September 3, 2001.

Lazare, Lewis. "Sears Ads Play for Cheap Laughs." *Chicago Sun-Times,* August 27, 2001, p. 45.

———. "Sears Sticking with Humor for Holidays." *Chicago Sun-Times,* November 15, 2002, p. 71.

———. "Sears to Start Campaign." *Chicago Sun-Times,* August 22, 2001, p. 71.

Monks, Robert A.G., and Minow, Nell. "Sears Case Study." Available from <http://www.lens-library.com/info/sstan.html>

"New Sears Ad Campaign to Feature Ty Pennington: Celebrates Renewed Energy, Excitement of Stores." *PR Newswire,* September 20, 2004.

Candice Mancini

Sega of America, Inc. & Take-Two Interactive Software, Inc.

Contact information for Sega of America, Inc.:
650 Townsend St., Ste. 650
San Francisco, California 94103-4908
USA
Telephone: (415) 701-6000
Web site: www.sega.com

■■■

Contact information for Take-Two Interactive Software, Inc.
622 Broadway
New York, New York 10012
USA
Telephone: (646) 536-2842
Web site: www.take2games.com

■■■

BETA-7 CAMPAIGN

OVERVIEW

When Electronic Arts (EA) held the position as the world's largest independent video game publisher in 2003, a bilateral effort was made by Take-Two Interactive Software and Sega of America to overtake EA's number one selling football game with their own *ESPN NFL 2K5.* Created by Take-Two and distributed by Sega, the football game could be played on two video game consoles, Xbox and PlayStation. Besides gaining ground on *Madden NFL 2005* (EA's football game), *ESPN NFL 2K5* sold at the unusually low price of $19.99 and was also marketed with an unprecedented campaign titled "Beta-7."

Portland-based Wieden+Kennedy named the "Beta-7" campaign after a fictitious game tester who, W+K claimed, once tested games for Sega. W+K hired an actor to play the Beta-7 character, who supposedly became so traumatized while testing *ESPN NFL 2K5* that he suffered frequent blackouts and uncontrollably tackled bystanders. Crusading fiercely against Sega, the Beta-7 character posted an anti-Sega website and blog in an attempt to prevent the game's release. Other fictional game testers created by W+K surfaced to support Beta-7's claims, while Sega pretended to refute the game's malefic effects. Speculation fanned across the Internet, with gamers attempting to decipher Beta-7's authenticity.

The four-month-long campaign helped Sega and Take-Two surpass the sales forecast of *ESPN NFL 2K5* by 20 percent. Although "Beta-7" assisted Sega's immediate need in 2004, EA retaliated in 2005 by purchasing exclusive five-year rights to NFL logos and player names and 15-year rights to ESPN's programming and personalities. By capitalizing on the gaming community's need for current team content, EA would monopolize all football video games, according to analysts, for the next five years.

HISTORICAL CONTEXT

Sega's ongoing hot-or-cold video game success began in the late 1970s groundbreaking console game hits like

Turbo, Frogger, and *Zaxxon* followed by a lackluster string of arcade games. In the latter part of the 1980s, Sega had hits like *Out Run* and *After Burner.* The games' success spurred Sega to develop its first home console, the Sega Master System, a U.S. commercial flop. Determined to capture some of the Nintendo Entertainment System's (NES's) market, Sega released its second home console, Sega Genesis, which Sega promoted as being "far superior to the NES." Within the home console market, Sega Genesis was Sega's only commercial success throughout the 1990s. The company developed the Sega Saturn to compete with PlayStation in 1995 and then the 128-bit Sega Dreamcast in 1998. Both consoles yielded meager sales, forcing Sega to focus primarily on software game development.

Take-Two was founded in 1993 by Ryan Brant, who was chairman for the company until litigation forced him to step down in 2004. *Grand Theft Auto: San Andreas,* a game launched under Take-Two's subsidiary Rockstar Games, was the top-selling video game for 2004. To counter EA's five-year NFL rights procurement, Take-Two purchased its own two-year license to use Major League Baseball team likenesses, a harsh blow to EA's successful *MVP Baseball.*

As one video game industry source told the *Delaney Report* in 2005, "Like a lot of other video-game marketers, advertising has become formulaic. A lot of the video-game advertising now looks like movie theatrical trailers, 30 seconds of game play. Advertising is visible, but it's not very compelling and it has no edge." Sega and Take-Two wanted W+K to create a campaign that stepped outside of traditional video game advertising and generated its own buzz within the gaming community.

TARGET MARKET

Ty Montague, a creative director for W+K, told the *Financial Times,* "The campaign worked because its target audience of video-game enthusiasts was hip enough to get the jokes but playful enough to keep on reading what Beta-7 wrote." The campaign was aimed toward the broadening age of video game players—or gamers, as they were called—which was quickly diversifying at the time of launch. In 2005 an Entertainment Software Association survey showed that the average gamer's age was 30, while the average game purchaser was 37 years old. "Computer games aren't relegated to 12-year-old boys who are playing in their parents' basement," Dan Hewitt of the Entertainment Software Association told the *Arkansas Democrat Gazette.*

"Beta-7" did not specifically target demographics within the gaming community as much as two subgroups: gamers susceptible to Internet hoaxes and gamers impervious to them. Conflicting believability between these two subgroups spurred the campaign's success across the Internet. "Gamers are predisposed to stories that they can actually participate in," Montague explained to *Advertising Age's Creativity.* "It's also important to remember that it's only a hoax in retrospect. While the experience unfolded the goal was to make it feel plausible, at least to part of the target. We also wanted some people to dismiss it immediately. It was the argument between those two groups that powered the campaign."

After the event some judges for the 2004 Grand Clio explained that their partial impetus for awarding "Beta-7" the Grand Clio was because of the campaign's ability to successfully target gamers. Nick Brien, Grand Clio judge and CEO of Arc Worldwide Chicago, told *Creative Review,* "The gaming community is highly cynical and media savvy, they don't want to be marketed to. The campaign really was an experience and the agency went out of their way to completely fuse content and contact thinking and pulled it off brilliantly. They never forgot about the gamer."

> **IT'S NOT ONLY YOUNG BOYS**
>
> According to statistics released by Entertainment Software Association in 2005, 74 percent of U.S. heads of households were game players. Surprisingly enough women over the age of 18 represented a greater portion of the game-playing population than boys ages 6 to 17. To further debunk the assumption that all gamers are young boys, the average age of a game player was 30, while the average age of a game buyer was 37.

COMPETITION

EA, despite criticism for producing fairly mediocre games, sold more video games than any other competitor in 2004. From 1995 to 2005 EA relied on San Francisco–based See Advertising to market most of its titles. In 2004 EA's best-selling *Madden NFL 2005,* the third highest-selling video game of the year, was seriously threatened by Sega and Take-Two's *ESPN NFL 2K5.* To reduce future competition EA signed an exclusive five-year license (to begin in 2006) with the NFL, giving EA exclusivity on using NFL stadiums, players, teams, and colors in its games. EA also signed a 15-year private contract with ESPN to exclusive use of ESPN's name, programming, and personalities, just like Sega and Take-Two had done previously with *ESPN NFL 2K5.* Recognizing the advantage that "Beta-7" gave *ESPN NFL 2K5,* EA also ended its 10-year contract with See Advertising and signed all marketing over to W+K in 2005.

Microsoft's *Halo 2,* designed exclusively for Xbox, was the second highest-selling video game of 2004. *Halo 2* launched with its "I Love Bees" campaign, created by Microsoft's Elan Lee and Steven Spielberg. "I Love Bees" utilized normal, educational websites about bees and through manipulation made them appear hijacked by an artificial intelligence. The campaign required participants to work collectively and answer random pay phone calls, which eventually revealed the involvement of artificial intelligence.

Many analysts judged a video game's success by the quantity purchased by America's second-largest video game retailer, Electronics Boutique Holdings Corp. (EB). Despite Take-Two's release of *Grand Theft Auto: San Andreas,* the top-selling game of 2004, the company accounted for only 7 percent of EB's games at the start of 2005. With 31 games to its name, EA accounted for 14 percent of EB's games in 2004, according to *Warren's Consumer Electronics Daily.* Nintendo came in second with 12 percent, followed by Microsoft at 10.3 percent. The future of *ESPN NFL 2K5* was not hindered so much by the competition's advertisement but by EA's savvy NFL and ESPN licensing agreements.

MARKETING STRATEGY

Beta-7, a fictional former game tester, surfaced on www.Beta-7.com during the summer of 2003. W+K, Haxan Films (producers of *The Blair Witch Project*), and Chelsea Pictures cast actors to play parts for the campaign's four-month duration. Each actor, including Jim Gunshanan (who played Beta-7), replied to blogs, sent E-mails, left voice mails, posted messages on independent gaming sites, and even conducted interviews with the gaming press to authenticate Beta-7's existence.

The website served as the campaign's hub. Beta-7 claimed to have suffered so much duress from testing the football game that he regularly blacked out and tackled people. To prove it Beta-7 set up cameras at the beach and at an office where he delivered mail that hilariously showed him exhibiting "symptoms." Throughout the website Beta-7 ceaselessly called out for *ESPN NFL 2K5* testers who also suffered from the same conditions to come forward and testify on his website. He claimed too that Sega was threatening to shut him up. The "threats" grew so malevolent that Sega eventually razed his tiny, frumpy apartment. Photos to prove it were published on the website. At one point Beta-7 even mailed unauthorized, prereleased versions of the game to gamers so they could experience the effects themselves.

Authenticity became a major constituent of the campaign. Instead of making them in-house, W+K paid a Kinko's clerk to design Beta-7's flyers (warning of the psychological trauma inflicted by the game), which were passed around San Francisco. The project's art director, Robert Rasmussen, told *Adweek,* "It was more work than any project I'd done before. It was eight hours a day for four months while we were doing a million other jobs at the same time. You never knew if things were going to work. We were taking a lot of chances."

To fuel the conspiracy W+K had Sega play Beta-7's antagonist. Immediately after Beta-7 mailed unauthorized games, Sega sent letters demanding them back. On ESPN W+K broke an *ESPN NFL 2K5* spot starring Tracy Morgan. At the commercial's end Sega posted a disclaimer saying that excessive playing of the game would not lead to violent or erratic behavior.

The gaming community's debate over the legitimacy of Beta-7 became integral to the campaign's success. "The idea for the campaign was to create an experience for gamers that would cause them to debate its accuracy," Montague told the *Financial Times.* "We never said it was true or not true." In the "FAQ" section of www.Beta-7.com, the fictional youth wrote, "I don't work for Sega, or anyone for that matter. This is not a marketing campaign, it is a campaign to make a deceitful and dangerous corporation be held accountable for its actions. I'm sure Sega would like you to believe it's a marketing campaign or a hoax, because then they will not have to take responsibility for what they have done."

OUTCOME

"Beta-7" yielded substantial success with *ESPN NFL 2K5* sales and struck a positive chord within the advertising industry. W+K earned a Yahoo! Big Idea Chair and Silver at the Andy Awards, a Gold Pencil at both the One Show and the One Show Interactive, a gold medal from the Art Directors Club, and a Grand Clio. Others in the advertising industry were outraged by the disingenuousness of "Beta-7." Gary Ruskin, director of Commercial Alert, told the *Oregonian* that "Beta-7" was "deeply sleazy and part of the creep of advertising into every nook and cranny of our lives and culture." W+K shrugged off the condemnation, stating that the actual "engine of the campaign" was the contention between praise and criticism, between belief and disbelief.

Quantifying the campaign's effectiveness outside the advertising community was more difficult. Steve Raab, senior vice president of marketing for Sega's ESPN Videogames, told *Adweek,* "I think it's really tough to tie it back to the ultimate objective, which is sales and getting people to sample the games. Other measurements, however, what kind of traffic Web sites are getting, how much time people are spending with this, those are very successful. The average person who checked out 'Beta-7' during its first month or two spent more than 10 hours on the site." According to *Creative Review,* www.Beta-7.com received 2.25 million hits by August 2004.

According to Sega even though the game's launch came inadvertently after *Madden NFL 2005,* sales of *ESPN NFL 2K5* exceeded projection by 20 percent. The game was the fourth highest-selling video game for 2004. Unfortunately, with the gamer's demand for current sports game content, *ESPN NFL 2K5* was crushed under EA's five-year exclusive license agreement with the NFL and 15-year procurement of ESPN content.

FURTHER READING

Anderson, Mae. "Tall Tales: Advertising Steps into Interactive Fiction, Where the Buzz Is Real—Even When the Stories Aren't." *Adweek,* October 11, 2004, p. 28.

Arango, Tim. "Electronic Arts Reaches 15-Year Deal with ESPN." *New York Post,* January 18, 2005, p. 31.

Buchanan, Matt. "Commentary: EA Corrupting Game Industry." *U-Wire,* February 2, 2005.

Cooper, Ann. "One Show Divides the Judges on Quality of Traditional Work." *Campaign,* May 21, 2004, p. 22.

Eastwood, Alison. "Special Report: Festival Report Card—Tonight We're Gonna Party like It's 1984." *Boards,* August 1, 2004, p. 23.

Hanas, Jim. "Cannes Predictions: Will 2004 Be the Year of the Hoax?" *Advertising Age's Creativity,* June 1, 2004, p. 22.

Lippert, Barbara. "Wieden's Great Hoax: Award-Show Fave 'Beta-7' Turns Advertising on Its Head." *Adweek,* May 24, 2004, p. 25.

Read, Richard. "Guerrilla Marketing Raises Questions about Deception." *Oregonian,* September 13, 2004, p. A09.

Sherman, Gabriel. "End of the 30-Second Spot." *New York Observer,* December 20, 2004, p. 20.

Silverman, Gary. "After the Break: The 'Wild West' Quest to Bring the Consumers to the Advertising—Companies Are Moving Closer to the Entertainment Industry as They Try to Promote Their Products to Jaded Customers." *Financial Times,* May 18, 2005, p. 17.

Wahl, Andrew. "My Pick: EA, By about a Billion." *Canadian Business,* January 31, 2005, p. 17.

Woolmington, Paul. "Unbundled Bundling: P&G Again Sends the Media-Agency Business a Wake-Up Call." *Adweek,* July 26, 2004, p. 23.

Kevin Teague

Serta International

5401 Trillium Boulevard
Hoffman Estates, Illinois 60192-3411
USA
Telephone: (847) 645-0200
Fax: (847) 645-0205
Web site: www.serta.com

■■■

COUNTING SHEEP CAMPAIGN

OVERVIEW

At the beginning of 2000 mattress maker Serta International had three advertising goals in mind: increase brand awareness, win consumer loyalty, and entice retailers to stock more of the company's products. Traditionally an unexciting category, mattress advertising did not generate much consumer passion. Buyers tended to feel that there was little difference between the companies that manufactured mattresses. This was not helped by the fact that Serta's biggest competitors, Sealy and Simmons, also had names beginning with *S.* Michigan advertising agency W.B. Doner & Company (known as Doner) sought to remedy Serta's image and advertising problems with the "Counting Sheep" campaign.

Claymation company Aardman Animations was enlisted to create original and lovable sheep characters to inhabit TV commercials that would tout the comfort and quality of Serta mattresses. In the launch spot of July 2000, sheep with numbers on their sides arrived at the home of an insomniac couple so that they could "count sheep" to fall asleep. The couple informed the bewildered sheep that they were so comfortable on their new Serta bed that the sheep's counting services were no longer required. This and similar television commercials ran nationally at bedtime and on the weekends, when most mattresses were purchased. The campaign's budget of $24 million primarily bought television time on networks and cable channels. Print ads, in-store displays, and Internet elements were also included in the budget.

Results of the campaign were immediately measurable. In 2001 a survey by polling-services company Roper Starch Worldwide showed that more women who had a mattress brand in mind had settled on Serta than on industry leader Sealy (58 percent to 18 percent respectively) for their next mattress purchase. This was a significant change from a precampaign Roper survey that put both companies at an even 39 percent. The campaign itself garnered a Gold EFFIE Award in 2002 for the ad agency, and the spots themselves won other industry recognition.

HISTORICAL CONTEXT

Serta International, headquartered in the Chicago suburb of Hoffman Estates, Illinois, was founded in 1931 by 13 mattress makers who joined together to license the Serta name. The privately owned company expanded, reconfiguring many times through the years. By 1997 Serta had become a private mattress-licensing entity with 28 factories in the United States and 20 internationally. The company's Perfect Sleeper mattress was listed then as the one most purchased by American hotels, and it was third in the country for mattress market share. In 1990 Serta had achieved an industry coup when Ed Lilly, formerly of the number one mattress maker, Sealy, joined the company as president and CEO. During the 1990s, under Lilly's guidance, advertising on a national level included television, print, and support of National Public Radio. The "We Make the World's Best Mattress" campaign began in 1993 and continued for the rest of the decade. It was designed to heighten brand awareness by creating emotional connections with the mattress-buying audience (in contrast to the product-focused ads of its top competitors). In 1997 the company spent $17 million on national campaigns.

By the year 2000 Serta had reached $729 million in mattress sales. It had for the moment pushed past Simmons. The Atlanta-based Simmons had been accustomed to the number two spot in the field, but it recorded $2 million less than Serta in sales that year. Slipping into second place by a narrow margin, Serta was looking to put some distance between itself and Simmons while gaining on the other "Big S," Sealy. Doner, which was headquartered in a Detroit suburb and was the country's largest independent advertising agency, was given the task of refreshing the company's national presence. It met the challenge by creating the hugely successful "Counting Sheep" campaign.

TARGET MARKET

As the 1990s came to a close, the consensus in the mattress industry was that women were either more likely to buy new mattresses for themselves or were responsible for initiating the purchase of a new mattress for their family. Thus Serta aimed its "Counting Sheep" campaign at women aged 25 to 54. Satirical humor was combined with an approachable cute factor in an attempt to win women's dollars and brand loyalty. Because a mattress was not a frequent purchase for most customers, Serta needed to make a lasting impression in women's minds. A sensitivity toward women was reflected in the company's website. For instance, a "Pillow Talk" section described the various stages of life and sleeping patterns, singling out children's as well as pregnant and menopausal women's sleeping needs. Men's sleeping needs were not specifically mentioned at all but rather were covered under the umbrella of stages for adolescents, adults, and seniors.

In the industry as a whole a new trend toward catering to the female audience began to emerge in mattress marketing and design. Furniture designer and former supermodel Kathy Ireland launched her own mattress line that was made by Lady Americana. Actress Lindsay Wagner (perhaps best known for playing the title character of the 1970s TV show *The Bionic Woman*) was made spokeswoman for Select Comfort, while Simmons tapped designer Karen Neuberger for a top-of-the-line mattress tie-in. Not to be outdone, Serta designed a mattress specifically for women, called Perfect Day, which made its debut in 2005. This product not only featured attractive embroidered details but also, and more importantly, promised to help address the energy deficit that busy women so often experienced. The Serta ad pitch toward women was maintained by the "Counting Sheep" commercials through the early 2000s, and it seemed to hit the target. A 2002 survey by polling firm Roper Starch Worldwide indicated that 75 percent of women in the 25-to-54 age group said that they had seen or heard of the sheep commercials.

LESS FIREPOWER FROM SERTA

Serta received national attention in spring 2004, when it introduced FireBlocker, a flame-dampening material, on all Serta mattresses. The launch of the flame-resistant products had come well ahead of the January 2005 deadline for a new bedding standard mandated by law in California and was expected to be an effective selling point for retailers.

COMPETITION

Sealy had long been the number one company among the top three mattress producers: Sealy, Serta, and Simmons. Throughout the period of 2000 to 2005 Serta and Simmons had been trading the second and third spots back and forth. In 2000, when Serta's "Counting Sheep" first hit the national scene, the North Carolina–based Sealy pulled in a hefty $1.102 billion compared to Serta's $729 million and Simmon's $727 million. Sealy, in business since 1906, was the first mattress maker to focus on back support, introducing its Posturepedic line of mattresses in the 1950s. Advertising in the mattress industry had always been notoriously dull, but with the success of the "Counting Sheep" campaign, even Sealy took notice. By 2002 it had released its own creative ad campaign using the tagline "It's made for sleep. It's a Sealy." The premise of the TV commercials for this campaign was that if Sealy made other products, they would be so comfortable that buyers would fall asleep in the showroom. One TV spot featured a car buyer who could not stay awake once he sat in a "Sealy" car at the dealership. The voice-over that followed stated, "This is why we don't make cars."

At this time Simmons, the perennial thorn in Serta's sales side, focused advertising on its longtime message "Better Sleep through Science." Always positioning itself as an innovator, Simmons touted the "no-flip" mattress design of its flagship brand, Beautyrest, as well as the advent of the Olympic Queen, which fit on a queen-size frame but allowed 10 percent more sleeping space than the traditional queen-size mattress.

MARKETING STRATEGY

In 2000 the ad agency Doner devised the Serta "Counting Sheep" campaign to do three things: measurably increase brand awareness by communicating an identifiable image for Serta; achieve preference on the part of female buyers so that they would go into a store intending to buy a Serta; and make sure more retailers were stocking Serta's product lines. The campaign was a full-scale integration of television, industry publications, point-of-sale, and online media. Most of the $24 million advertising dollars that Serta budgeted for 2000 went toward buying airtime for its newly crafted television spots. Created by Aardman Animation, the Claymation company behind the hit animated feature *Chicken Run* (2000), the spots featured adorable sheep that arrived to provide their counting services for a couple who was usually sleep-challenged, only to be turned away because of the superior comfort provided by the couple's new Serta mattress. The commercials were a mix of animated characters and live actors. The sheep themselves had the familiar widemouthed look of the animals from the popular film, which conveyed the kind of charm and appeal that every advertiser hoped for. The personality-driven "Counting Sheep" campaign was a deliberate move away from previous Serta advertising imagery of anonymous people sleeping on clouds or awakening from a restful, refreshing sleep.

Released in July of 2000, the spots aired on cable channels and national network hit shows, such as the female-oriented comedy *Ally McBeal,* the family-focused game show *Who Wants to Be a Millionaire,* and the late-night comedy staple *Saturday Night Live.* Airing at nine o'clock p.m. or later, Wednesday through Saturday, these shows were chosen because of their proximity to bedtime and weekend mattress shopping. The company's old tagline, "We Make the World's Best Mattress," gave way to a new message, "So Comfortable, You'll Feel the Difference the Moment You Lie Down." Rather than emphasize the long-term benefits of back health or good sleep, Serta wanted to convince potential buyers that they would experience immediate satisfaction if they tested a Serta out at a retailer.

The counting sheep were well received and came back for more pitching duties in subsequent years. They became the face of Serta and were used on all advertising materials. In an August 2002 issue of *Furniture Today,* Susan Ebaugh, Serta chief brand officer, expressed her confidence in the campaign: "Based on the outstanding results we're getting, the Counting Sheep campaign will be around for a long time. . . . There is virtually no limit to the story extensions that can be developed." The campaign continued in 2002 with a $21 million dollar budget for national advertisements, which Serta intended to reach nearly all U.S. adults. The new spots showed the numbered sheep becoming increasingly frustrated by the fact that Serta's comfort and quality caused their employment prospects to dwindle. One fed-up sheep committed the unlawful act of ripping a mattress tag off with his teeth. Another spot featured the sheep attempting to sue Serta for emotional distress. More TV spots were introduced in 2003 and 2004. In each of the 2004 spots a voice-over at the end announced Serta's Web address and mentioned that "counting sheep" merchandise was available at the site. In a September 2004 issue of *Furniture Today,* Serta's Ebaugh restated the company's commitment to the effort, saying, "Each year, Serta's Counting Sheep campaign continues to expand consumer awareness of and preference for the Serta brand."

OUTCOME

Serta's goals of gaining more favorable brand recognition, creating a higher percentage of buyer preference, and increasing retail demand were beginning to be met by "Counting Sheep" in the first two years of the effort. In 2001 *HFN,* a publication for the home-products industry, listed Serta in the number 12 spot on its survey of the 100 most recognizable home brands, a dramatic rise from its position as 17th in 1999. Also in 2001 Roper Starch Worldwide, a polling-services company, released results of a survey showing that, among women who expressed a brand choice for their next mattress purchase, more intended to buy a Serta (58 percent) than a Sealy (18 percent). A similar Roper study prior to the campaign had put intent to purchase for the two brands at an equal 39 percent.

Retailers responded to the campaign by readily using sheep-themed support items, such as Serta Sheep poster displays in the showrooms and a giant sheep balloons floating over the stores. In 2002 Doner won a Gold EFFIE Award—an esteemed advertising prize rewarding campaign efficacy—for the campaign in the Household Furnishings category. Other awards included a first-place award for one sheep commercial in the London International Advertising Festival in 2001. Serta looked healthy as 2005 approached, registering a 5.5 percent increase in shipments, which had totaled $783 million the previous year.

FURTHER READING

Buchanan, Lee, and Nancy Meyer. "That Peaked Feeling." *HFN,* March 12, 2001, p. 55.

"Conveying the Message—with Feeling." *HFN,* July 14, 2003, p. 50.

Ebenkamp, Becky. "The Flock Gets Fleeced." *Brandweek,* July 10, 2000, p. 60.

Kunkel, Karl. "The Brands Play On: Companies Continue to Explore Methods of Getting Their Name Out to the Masses." *HFN,* July 12, 2004, p. 46.

———. "Commercial Success." *HFN,* August 19, 2002, p. 46.

———. "An Industry Awakens: Sales in the Category Rise as More Retailers Realize the Benefits of Bedding." *HFN,* July 12, 2004, p. 42.

"National 2001 Agency Report Cards." *Adweek,* April 15, 2002, p. 20.

Perry, David. "Big 'S' Brands Still Top List of Bedding Majors." *Furniture Today,* November 28, 2005 p. 3.

———. "More Counting Sheep Are B-a-a-a-ck." *Furniture Today,* August 5, 2002, p. 47.

———. "Sheep Take Another Prize." *Furniture Today,* June 17, 2002, p. 26.

———. "Sherman: Serta Committed to FR." *Furniture Today,* October 25, 2004, p. 53.

Simone Samano

Sharp Corp.

22-22 Nagaike-cho
Abeno-ku
Osaka, 545-8522
Japan
Telephone: 81 6 66211221
Fax: 81 6 66271759
Web site: www.sharp.co.jp

MORE TO SEE CAMPAIGN

OVERVIEW

Japanese electronics company Sharp Corp. had experienced limited success in television manufacturing and was a lackluster brand in the United States until a change in leadership in the late 1990s resulted in the company focusing on liquid crystal display (LCD) technology, in which it had been a leader for more than 25 years. In 2001 Sharp introduced the Aquos line of flat-panel LCD TVs. To improve brand perception in the United States and drive sales globally, the company, with ad agency Wieden & Kennedy, launched the "More to See" campaign in September 2004.

Not only did the campaign consist of television, print, and Internet components, it was integrated with an "alternate reality game" sweepstakes called "Legend of the Sacred Urns." Consumers were invited to solve a mystery: the location of the urns hidden by a game fanatic. The television spots and print ads were teases, urging the audience to visit a network of websites to unearth clues and learn more about the Aquos line of flat-panel TVs along the way.

The "More to See" campaign, which ran through the holiday season of 2004, won a Clio Award in 2005 and was also instrumental in increasing brand awareness for Sharp in the United States and in improving Aquos sales around the world. But the mystery element proved frustrating to many consumers and in some ways overshadowed the brand itself. Sharp elected in subsequent campaigns to return to a more traditional marketing approach.

HISTORICAL CONTEXT

For many years Sharp was an also-ran in television manufacturing, limited because it did not produce the most important component, the cathode-ray tube (CRT). "Forced to cobble together parts bought from competitors," wrote Jim Frederick in a *Time International* article. "Sharp was essentially an assembler, cranking out televisions that were always a little too expensive and too poorly engineered to attract many customers." But Sharp was a pioneer in liquid crystal display (LCD) technology, which it introduced in 1973 as part of a mass-produced calculator. The technology was later used in computer monitors, handheld computers, portable game systems, and wireless phones. In 1987 the company offered it first flat-panel LCD televisions, but it did not make a commitment to the technology until Katsuhiko Machida took over as president of Sharp in 1998. The former head of Sharp's television unit, Machida concentrated the company's resources on a new LCD television design called Aquos, introduced in January 2001. It was priced lower than Sharp's earlier LCD TVs and was the first to be sold by big-box retailers (large, warehouse-type stores) such as Best Buy.

Sharp quickly established itself as the leader in the LCD TV category and increased its U.S. sales in 2002 with the "Be Sharp" brand campaign, which included in-store displays and print advertisements. Despite Sharp's status, however, Sony was, according to marketing surveys, the only LCD TV brand that American consumers could name. In fact, Sony, the longtime leader in overall television sales, was slower than the competition to embrace LCD and plasma technologies. It was clear that Sharp needed to improve its image in the U.S. market, but it was also facing a global challenge from both major and small electronic companies and even from computer makers Dell and Gateway, all eager to grab market share in the fast-growing LCD TV sector.

Sharp looked for a new agency to create a global marketing campaign that would both promote the Aquos line of LCD televisions and protect its leading position. To satisfy the increasing demand for larger televisions, Sharp planned to introduce a 45-inch Aquos, which would be the largest LCD TV on the market at the time. Moreover, the company wanted to improve the perception of its brand in the key U.S. market, where Sharp was perceived as a value brand rather than a high-end one (as it was considered elsewhere in the world). Rather than turning to the large Japanese agencies it had worked with in the past, in January 2004 Sharp looked to the United States, and without conducting a review it hired advertising agency Wieden & Kennedy. Although it was an independent firm based in Portland, Oregon, Wieden & Kennedy was well positioned to launch a global effort because it maintained operations in New York, London, Amsterdam, Shanghai, and Tokyo. Nine months after winning the Sharp account the agency was ready to unveil the "More to See" campaign.

TARGET MARKET

In general the "More to See" campaign was geared toward the mass market in hopes of educating people about the benefits of LCD technology. Given that the new 45-inch set cost $10,000, however, the campaign targeted affluent consumers between the ages of 25 and 54. Within this group the marketers tried to appeal to sports fans, who had proven over the years that they were willing to pay top dollar for televisions offering a more vivid experience of sporting events; to entertainment "junkies," who liked the experience of watching movies and other television fare on a large set; to design aesthetes, who would appreciate the sleek look of the Aquos models; and to technology aficionados, who would not only be interested in the advanced LCD technology used in the Aquos sets but also would be attracted to the interactive aspect of the "More to See" campaign.

TECHNICALLY SPEAKING

The Aquos line of flat-panel televisions relied on liquid crystal display (LCD) technology. Behind an LCD screen was a light, and the liquid crystal cells on the display either allowed the light to pass through or blocked it to form an image on the screen. LCD's greatest rival in flat-panel TVs was plasma technology, which worked much the same way as neon lighting. Plasma screens consisted of rows of pixels, each of which contained xenon and neon gases and were capable of shining red, green, or blue (the basic elements of color television), depending on the electric charge delivered to it.

COMPETITION

Sharp faced competition on any number of fronts. LCD TVs still competed with CRT-based products, although as consumers increasingly opted for wide-screen high-definition TVs, the size and weight of CRT televisions became problematic. A 40-inch widescreen CRT TV could easily weigh more than 300 pounds and measure 26 inches deep. Rear-projection TVs, another type of television, were thinner and lighter than CRT TVs but were still much heavier and thicker than comparable LCD models. But rear-projection TVs challenged LCD TVs because they were much cheaper and provided good quality. Offering even more competition were flat-panel plasma TVs, which could be made in larger sizes than LCD TVs. Plasma technology had its drawbacks, however: it was buggy, subject to "burn in" (the creation of a ghost image if a graphic, such as a network logo, remained on the screen for too long a period of time), and the picture had a tendency to degrade more quickly than with televisions employing other technologies.

In the LCD sector itself, Sharp was not lacking in rivals. There were computer manufacturers Dell and Gateway in the United States, Dutch giant Philips Electronics, Samsung Electronics of South Korea, and Japanese companies Hitachi, Sony, and Toshiba. In addition Sharp had not been as willing as the competition to spend on advertising; the company tended to emphasize product development over brand building. The "More to See" campaign was a first step in shifting that focus while warding off the advances of Sharp's many rivals.

MARKETING STRATEGY

The premise of the "More to See" theme was that, just as television was the most powerful storytelling device (with perhaps a tip of the hat to cinema), Sharp's Aquos product line offered the most advanced televisions, providing viewers with a more vivid experience through its superior color, detail, and sound. One of the campaign's five television spots showed people—a mother dressing her daughter, a man cooking, an audience at a movie theater—going about their lives with their eyes closed. Finally a woman opened her eyes in an art museum in front of Victor Meirelles's painting *Battle of Guararapes.* A voice-over then said, "The Sharp Aquos liquid crystal television. Suddenly there's more to see." Some critics took exception to the underlying concept. Writing in *Brandweek,* Barry Janoff commented, "Taking the spot's premise literally means to imply that people can't really see or appreciate their lives unless television is there to help them. And, more so, they won't truly value their own lives unless they trade in their ordinary TVs for an Aquos. Of course, Sharp can't tell people to get out and enjoy life by turning off their TVs."

The message of "More to See" may have been simplistic and even illogical, but the method by which the centerpiece of the campaign was delivered was as innovative as Sharp's LCD technology. The campaign was more than multifaceted; it was in many ways an example of interactive fiction, using the different elements—television spots, print ads, websites, and an "alternate reality game" contest—to engage the audience and keep it involved in the campaign for months on end. Such an approach was intended to counteract the resistance that consumers had built up to 30-second commercials after years of being bombarded by them, not to mention the ability of digital-video-recorder owners to skip over commercials. The pioneering effort in this type of promotion was the independent film *The Blair Witch Project,* which created a buzz by dropping hints in the media that the film was a student documentary project that went horribly awry. The curious were led to the producer's website, and a large number of people began to debate among themselves whether the "found footage" of the student filmmakers was real or fake. When the low-budget film opened, it became the surprise hit of the summer of 1999, generating an impressive $150 million in domestic box-office sales.

Sharp engaged the services of the *Blair Witch* producers, Haxan Films, to help create the mystery story around which the "More to See" marketing campaign and contest would revolve. The resulting tale was called "Legend of the Sacred Urns," and consumers were invited to solve the mystery of where an eccentric millionaire had hidden three prized urns. The three television commercials that developed the storyline—"The Key," "The Pool," and "The Tooth"—weaved a "cinematic mystery," in the words of *Shoot* magazine's Bill Dunlap, "set in a country estate, involving a beautiful woman, an older man in a swimming pool and a careless driver in a Volkswagen Karmann Ghia." Marcus Robinson, writing for *Boards Magazine,* offered his own summary of the setup: "A guy, Peter Lindeman, is swimming in the pool of his big French chateau, and his babe girlfriend wanders out on the road to meet her lover. Unfortunately, he's massaging a toothache and had his eyes on the rearview, which forces him to swerve to avoid hitting her. He ends up launching his red sports car into the pool."

All three spots showed the same incident from a different point of view. In "The Pool," for example, a woman from a bedroom window watched Lindeman swimming in the pool when a car suddenly flew through the air and landed in the water. A Sharp television was then shown, and on its screen viewers were directed to the campaign's website, Moretosee.com. The site provided audio and visual clues, and featured blogs, purportedly written by the three characters engaged in the hunt for the three mystery urns. Chat rooms were also available for people to ponder the mystery together. Once viewers were at the website, they had to opportunity to learn more about LCD technology and Sharp's Aquos line of televisions. Participants were also directed to other websites to uncover clues. The spots were directed by award-winning documentary filmmaker Errol Morris, whose credits included *Gates of Heaven, The Thin Blue Line,* and *Fast, Cheap, and Out of Control.*

The television spots began airing in September 2004 and were shown on a variety of network and cable programming, including ABC's *Monday Night Football* and CBS's *60 Minutes.* The "More to See" campaign also included print ads, executed by Wieden & Kennedy's Amsterdam office, that also attempted to drive people to the website. After starting in the United States, "More to See" was rolled out to 18 other countries. In an ancillary component of the campaign, Sharp opened a storefront in New York City, where consumers could experience the Aquos product line and where further clues were made available. The campaign ran for four months, through the critical holiday season, with bits of the mystery parceled out over time. In the end, Ken Floss of Ohio solved the puzzle and won the grand prize, an Aquos television and other home theater equipment.

OUTCOME

"More to See" was successful in a number of ways. Advertising awareness in the United States increased from 30 percent to 57 percent, according to market-research surveys conducted by Sharp. The advertising industry also recognized the campaign's creativity; it won a Bronze in the Television/Cinema category of the prestigious Clio Awards in 2005. The contest was also successful in that it attracted more than one million website visitors over a four-month period, but the marketers were disappointed because it failed to engage all segments of the target audience. Bob Scaglione, senior vice president of marketing for Sharp, told Mae Anderson of *Adweek,* "We really focused on the techno-geek portion and alienated the other three [target markets] to some extent." He added, "Along the way, I think we confused a lot of people."

In a follow-up campaign launched in 2005 Sharp elected to go with a more traditional approach, relying on television spots and print ads without the extra elements. "You run the risk of alienating consumers with a more creative campaign," Scaglione explained. "We think the complexity of the creative last time may have overpowered the brand message."

FURTHER READING

Anderson, Mae. "The Age of Engagement." *Adweek,* August 22, 2005, p. 18.

———. "Tall Tales." *Adweek,* October 11, 2004, p. 28.

Dunlap, Bill. "Errol Morris: Reel Life." *Shoot,* March 25, 2005, p. 27.

Dvorak, Phred. "Sharp Pursues Big-Screen Ambitions." *Wall Street Journal,* June 9, 2005, p. B10.

Frederick, Jim. "A Sharper Focus." *Time International* (Asia ed.), May 9, 2005, p. 36.

Janoff, Barry. "What You Really See Is What You Should Get." *Brandweek,* October 4, 2004, p. 34.

Oser, Kris. "Sharp Touts TV in Net Mystery Adver-Blog." *Advertising Age,* November 1, 2004, p. 54.

———. "Web Wizards Take the Lead in Creative Process." *Advertising Age,* December 6, 2004.

Parry, Caroline. "Turning Viewers On to LCD Technology." *Marketing Week,* September 16, 2004, p. 24.

Robinson, Marcus. "Sharp Puzzles Up Global Brain Teaser." *Boards Magazine,* November 1, 2004, p. 19.

Roha, Ronaleen R. "Thin Is In." *Kiplinger's Personal Finance,* September 2004, p. 92.

Sampey, Kathleen. "Sharp Hands Aquos Work to Wieden." *Adweek,* January 21, 2004.

"Sharp Rolls Out Global Branding Campaign." *Wireless News,* September 10, 2004.

Vranica, Suzanne. "Sharp Aims to Enhance Aquos Brand." *Wall Street Journal,* September 10, 2004, p. B3.

Ed Dinger

Sierra Club

85 Second St., 2nd Fl.
San Francisco, California 94105
USA
Telephone: (415) 977-5500
Fax: (415) 977-5799
Web site: www.sierraclub.org

HYBRID EVOLUTION CAMPAIGN

OVERVIEW

By the early twenty-first century, the Sierra Club, one of the oldest and largest environmental advocacy groups in the United States, boasted a membership of more than 700,000. One of the principal concerns of the organization was the low gas mileage of U.S. automobiles. The popularity of inefficient sport-utility vehicles (SUVs) meant that U.S. cars averaged only 21 miles per gallon. Because fossil fuels were believed to be the number-one cause of global warming, this had serious consequences for the environment. Hybrid cars, which got up to 47 miles per gallon and thus burned less gasoline, could help alleviate the problem. It was for this reason that the Sierra Club acted as an advocate for hybrid cars, encouraging more automakers to sell them and trying to convince the U.S. government to promote their use.

The Sierra Club worked with the Change, an advertising agency based in Raleigh, North Carolina, to promote energy conservation. On Memorial Day in 2004 the organization launched the "Hybrid Evolution" campaign. The Sierra Club often undertook campaigns designed to influence behavior, as opposed to self-promotion, and "Hybrid Evolution" was one such effort. The campaign featured print and Web-based advertisements targeted at young trendsetters, encouraging them to drive hybrid cars. The key element in the campaign, however, was three long-distance tours on which Sierra Club members drove hybrid vehicles across interstate routes in the United States, stopping for rallies and posting updates about the trips on the campaign's website. The campaign also spotlighted the organization's opposition to the energy policies of George W. Bush, the incumbent U.S. president who was running for reelection in 2004.

Since the campaign was geared toward changing behavior, not promoting the Sierra Club, its success was difficult to gauge. Bush was reelected in November 2004, but the fuel efficiency of automobiles was not a significant issue in the campaign. The number of hybrid models offered by automakers continued to rise, however, and the cars gained in popularity. While only 47,000 hybrid vehicles were sold in the United States in 2003, by 2004 the number had risen to more than 88,000, and in 2005 it rose to 200,000.

HISTORICAL CONTEXT

The Sierra Club was founded on May 28, 1892, by a group of 182 conservationists. The environmental pioneer John Muir was the club's first president. Its first major undertaking was an effort to defend the borders of Yosemite National Park. Over the ensuing decades the Sierra Club became one of the most prominent and successful environmental organizations in the United States, with approximately 700,000 members by the first decade of the twenty-first century. Its stated purposes were to explore and protect wilderness land, to educate the public about conservation, and to promote conservation generally. Previous advertising campaigns had spotlighted the group's key role in promoting environmental conservation over the years.

One of the Sierra Club's most important goals in the early twenty-first century was to promote energy efficiency. Because of the increasing demand for energy from developing nations like China and India, the international market for oil and gasoline was steadily rising. In addition, the United States was in the midst of a protracted military engagement in the oil-rich Middle Eastern nation of Iraq. The conflict put additional pressures on oil markets, and as a result, by 2004 gasoline prices in the United States were higher than they had been for several years. More important from the Sierra Club's point of view was the impact on the environment of the burning of fossil fuels like gasoline. The organization was particularly concerned about global warming. Most scientists agreed that when fossil fuels like oil and coal were burned they released so-called greenhouse gasses, which trapped heat inside the Earth's atmosphere, causing temperatures to rise.

The United States, however, was noted for its "car culture." With the rise in popularity of SUVs in the 1990s, the average fuel efficiency of American cars had fallen to only about 21 miles per gallon. The more gasoline used, the more greenhouse gasses emitted into the air. The Sierra Club considered this to be a major issue and argued that hybrid vehicles, especially hybrid cars that could get upwards of 47 miles per gallon of gasoline, were the best way to reduce this figure. Hybrid cars combined elements of gas-powered and electrical engines. It was the electrical engine that handled most of the work when the car was moving at a constant speed, with the gasoline engine coming into play to help the car accelerate. When the driver stepped on the brake pedal, the energy thus created charged the electrical engine. By 2004 three hybrid models were available in the United States: the Toyota Prius, the Honda Insight, and the Honda Civic. Both Toyota and Honda were Japanese-based companies. The Prius proved particularly popular, with a six-month waiting list for the vehicle, but this was in part because Toyota limited itself to making 47,000 units of the vehicle in 2004.

THE KYOTO PROTOCOL

During the 2004 presidential campaign, the Sierra Club and other environmental groups voiced strong opposition to the policies of U.S. President George W. Bush on climate change. Relations between Bush and such groups had been severely strained since his decision in March 2001 to withdraw the U.S. signature from the Kyoto Protocol. This agreement, named for the Japanese city in which it had been negotiated, was a UN-sanctioned effort to create a general international protocol for addressing global warming. It committed all of its signatories, especially the 39 industrialized nations that ratified it, to reduce the levels of greenhouse gases they were emitting to about 5 percent below the levels of 1990. After objections from Russia, the reduction was renegotiated downward to about 2 percent. The agreement would be toughest on the United States, since at the time of the protocol's inception in 1990 it was producing 36 percent of all such emissions. Bush objected to the agreement on the grounds that it would harm the U.S. economy. Environmentalist countered, however, that Bush was merely protecting large companies in the energy industry, especially oil companies. These critics pointed out that Bush and his vice president, Dick Cheney, had both previously worked in the oil industry.

TARGET MARKET

The "Hybrid Evolution" campaign was geared mostly toward young people, particularly college students and people in their 20s. In an effort to convince young people to buy hybrids, one of the Sierra Club's goals was to help make the cars seem cool and trendy. To this end, each of the print ads in the campaign featured a hip young person, someone who represented a likely hybrid driver.

The campaign was also aimed at auto manufacturers. At the time the campaign was introduced, none of the so-called Big Three automakers in the United States—General Motors, Ford, and DaimlerChrysler—offered hybrid automobiles. In addition, the companies that offered hybrids did so only in limited quantities. As a result, by 2004 the Toyota Prius, for example, had a six-month waiting list. The Sierra Club wanted to pressure automakers to offer more hybrid models and to increase the production of the lines that were already available. Though the "Hybrid Evolution" campaign featured the Toyota Prius and the Honda Civic hybrids, the automakers were not involved in the campaign in any capacity.

The fact that 2004 was a presidential election year in the United States was also a factor in the Sierra Club's campaign. Though the "Hybrid Evolution" campaign did not overtly endorse particular candidates, it was meant to encourage both young people and undecided voters to focus on issues of fuel efficiency in the midst of the campaign and to encourage politicians to take fuel efficiency seriously.

COMPETITION

The Sierra Club's primary goal for the "Hybrid Evolution" campaign was to promote the energy efficiency of hybrid cars, not the organization itself. Since Bush, the incumbent president, was seen as hostile to the position of the Sierra Club on environmental matters in general and not supportive of efforts to improve the efficiency of motor vehicles through public policy, the "Hybrid Evolution" campaign also served to counter the administration's environmental policies. Though the campaign did not attempt to promote the candidacy of Massachusetts Senator John Kerry, who challenged Bush in the 2004 election, the Sierra Club was open in saying that the "Hybrid Evolution" campaign was opposed to the environmental policies of the incumbent administration. Some ads, in fact, questioned the president's policies by name.

The Bush administration had withdrawn from the Kyoto Protocol, which required signatories to reduce the use of fossil fuels. Further, Vice President Dick Cheney had gone on record as saying that energy conservation was a matter of private choice, a position that many people felt implied that the administration had no interest in promoting energy conservation in general or hybrid cars in particular. The Bush administration was not inclined to provide subsidies or other types of government support for the development of hybrid vehicles.

In a sense, therefore, the campaign's main competition was the Bush administration, which the Sierra Club saw as unresponsive to conservation issues. The organization was also seeking to counter certain members of Congress, including Representative Bill Thomas of California. Thomas, the chairman of the Means and Ways Committee of the U.S. House of Representatives, was seen as opposed to providing tax incentives to consumers who bought hybrid vehicles.

MARKETING STRATEGY

The Sierra Club developed the "Hybrid Evolution" campaign in conjunction with the advertising agency the Change, which was based in Raleigh, North Carolina. The Change was experienced in working with nonprofit organizations like the Sierra Club. The campaign was built around print and online ads, but the focus was on a series of tours across the United States that featured hybrid cars. Members of the Sierra Club drove hybrid vehicles on three separate tours along different routes. One route extended from Key West, Florida, to Portland, Maine, with stops for rallies in 25 major metropolitan areas along the way. The second followed U.S. Route 66 from Chicago, Illinois, to Los Angeles, California, with more than 15 stops. The final route extended from Seattle, Washington, to San Diego, California, with 9 stops.

The tours featured only two of the three hybrid cars on the market, the Toyota Prius and the Honda Civic hybrid. The club decided not to use the Honda Insight, which offered only two seats, feeling that a larger car would be better for the tours. The club also used the West Coast tour to promote the new Ford Escape, a hybrid SUV that was to be introduced in 2005. The Escape would be the first American-made hybrid vehicle. None of the automakers were directly involved in the campaign. In fact, one of the campaign's goals was to pressure the automakers into manufacturing greater numbers of hybrid cars. The campaign did, however, benefit the automakers by giving them free publicity.

In conjunction with the campaign, on May 28, 2004, the Sierra Club launched the I Will Evolve website (www.iwillevolve.org). The site gave reports on the three tours, and it had ads and banners that could be downloaded free of charge. This served as a low-cost way of distributing campaign material among Web users. All of the Web ads featured young people wearing campaign T-shirts, part of the effort to appeal especially to a young demographic. In addition, the campaign had a print component, which also appeared on the I Will Evolve website. Each print ad included a shot of a young person wearing a T-shirt with the slogan "I Will Evolve." The ads also featured text that highlighted the benefits of hybrid cars. They focused on the environmental advantages of hybrids and, in addition, touched on economic concerns. One ad, for example, forecast that an energy-efficient economy built around hybrid cars would create 3.3 million jobs. The forecast was meant to rebut claims by opponents that greater fuel efficiency would hurt the U.S. economy. The ads also encouraged consumers to test-drive a hybrid car so that they could experience the technology in action.

Each ad specifically criticized the Bush administration for its policies. One ad, for example, accused the White House of wanting to give $23.3 billion in subsidies to the fossil fuel industry while earmarking only $5.9 billion to promote the further development of energy-efficient technologies. Each ad closed with the tagline "Is the Bush administration for evolution OR AGAINST IT?" The tagline was an attempt to ensure that energy issues were not lost amid the election year campaigning. While the ads did not mention Kerry by name and did not openly advocate his election, they did echo one of his campaign themes. Kerry supported greater investment in hybrid vehicles and energy efficiency, and he had supported legislation in the U.S. Senate that would offer incentives to drive hybrid vehicles. Environmental policy was thus a key point of difference between the two candidates, and this was something the campaign made note of.

OUTCOME

Since the intent of the "Hybrid Evolution" campaign was to change people's lifestyle, its success was not easy to measure. Bush was reelected in November 2004 by more than 3 million votes, but environmental issues were not particularly important for many voters. Nonetheless, hybrid vehicles were selling in ever-increasing numbers in the United States. Although only about 47,000 units of hybrid vehicles had been sold in 2003, some 88,000 units were sold in 2004, with more than 200,000 the following year.

More important, additional automakers began manufacturing hybrids. Toyota's Lexus brand unveiled the RX 400H, an SUV hybrid, and Honda introduced a hybrid Accord as well. By 2005 more than 1 percent of all new cars sold in the United States were hybrids. ExxonMobil, the world's largest oil company, forecast that by 2030 as much as 30 percent of the U.S. auto market could consist of hybrid vehicles.

FURTHER READING

Aldershot, Ulf Hjelmar. *The Political Practice of Environmental Organizations.* Brookfield, VT: Ashgate, 1996.

Fonda, Daren. "Make Vroom for the Hybrids." *Time,* April 9, 2004.

Gross, Jane. "From Guilt Trip to Hot Wheels." *New York Times,* June 13, 2004.

Hakim, Danny. "Energy-Saving Spots Give Cars Short Shrift." *New York Times,* June 25, 2004.

———. "A Fuel-Saving Proposal from Your Automaker: Tax the Gas." *New York Times,* April 18, 2004.

Justice, Glen, and Jim Rutenberg. "Senators Say Political Groups Are Circumventing Finance Law." *New York Times,* March 11, 2004.

Lemonick, Michael D. "Life in the Greenhouse." *Time,* April 9, 2001.

Motavalli, Jim. "Speaking Up for Cleaner Air." *New York Times,* April 26, 2004.

Turner, Tom. *Sierra Club: 100 Years of Protecting Nature.* New York: HN Abrams, 1991.

Westbrook, Michael H. *The Electric Car: Development and Future of Battery, Hybrid, and Fuel-Cell Cars.* Warrendale, PA: Society of Automotive Engineers, 2001.

Guy Patrick Cunningham

Sims Sports, Inc.

22105 23rd Dr. SE
Bothell, Washington 98021
USA
Telephone: (425) 951-2700
Web site: www.simsnow.com

BE FREE CAMPAIGN

OVERVIEW

Sims Sports, Inc., maker of Sims Snowboards, asked its advertising firm, Seattle-based Hammerquist & Halverson, to create a campaign for the 1997-98 winter season that would "return to the roots of snowboarding," according to agency copywriter Ian Cohen in *Advertising Age's Creativity.* "Sims wanted to shake up the market," explained Cohen in an article by Margaret Richardson in *Print.* Cohen said that Sims "had run ads for years on the back cover of snowboard magazines and were coming in dead last in reader-recall surveys. We wanted a different perspective than the typical jumping snowboarder ad. So we created a mantra: 'Be Free.' We didn't want to say a lot, but we wanted to say it up front."

The centerpiece of the "Be Free" campaign, even though it ran only in niche magazines such as *Snowboarder* and *Transworld Snowboard,* was a print execution that played off the famous photo of the standoff between a Chinese student protesting for democracy and military tanks in Tiananmen Square. Hammerquist & Halverson hired photojournalist Bob Peterson of Streetsmart, who had worked as a staff photographer for *Life* magazine, to give the shot an air of authenticity. Creative director Fred Hammerquist and art directors Matt Peterson and Mike Proctor then mocked-up the ad to make it appear as if it were a newspaper clipping, complete with a half-ripped caption extolling the "courageous act" of a single snowboarder standing off a lineup of Snowcat grooming machines.

On the one hand it was a soft-sell ad in the sense that the product name, Sims Snowboards, appeared only as a half-ripped headline, with the Sims logo just discernable on the bottom of the renegade's snowboard. On the other hand it was a hard-sell ad in the sense that it politicized the struggle of snowboarders. Whereas the Chinese student had stood up for freedom of political expression, the snowboarder was standing up for the freedom to have powder snow. Snowboarders were renowned for the lengths they would go to for fresh, ungroomed powder snow, which they could ride as a surfer rode a wave. The ad walked a tight line—gaining from the symbolic power of Tiananmen Square while retaining an edge of sarcasm—in comparing the struggle for political freedom with the struggle of a recreational sport. It had an air of absurdity that rang through the execution. The rest of the ads in the campaign similarly walked the line between the serious and the humorous.

HISTORICAL CONTEXT

The Colorado Snowboard and Ski Museum in Vail had on permanent display the first snowboard, made in 1963 by Tom Sims in his high school woodworking class in Haddonfield, New Jersey. It measured 34 by 8 inches, with carpet covering the top and aluminum the bottom.

The first snowboard like device to be marketed, however, dated to 1965, when Sherman Poppen, a businessman based in Muskegon, Michigan, fastened together two snow skis to form a single wide board for his children to slide on as they held on to a rope tied to the front for balance and steering. Recognizing the potential marketability of such a piece of equipment, Poppen licensed what he called the Snurfer (from "snow surfer") to the Brunswick Corporation. Brunswick marketed Snurfers for $10 apiece until the middle of the 1970s, when the company discontinued production. Brunswick never capitalized on the concept by improving the design and technology of the snow board, and it almost died from undermarketing.

As the Snurfer was dying out as a toylike fad, concerted efforts were being made to establish snowboarding as a more serious sport. Sims marketed his first snowboard in 1976. Jake Burton, the other major snowboard pioneer, who founded Burton Snowboards in 1977, built prototypes in the woodworking shop of his friend Emo Henrich, the director of the ski school at Stratton Mountain in Vermont. Burton tested more than 100 designs before he happened upon the combination of shape, wood laminates, and binding style that worked best. Burton, who got a Snurfer when he was 14 years old, spoke of the aborted beginnings of snowboard history in an article by Michael Finkel in *Sports Illustrated:* "I always felt there was an opportunity for [the Snurfer] to be better marketed . . . for serious technology to be applied to it, so Snurfing could become a legitimate sport instead of a cheap toy. I knew there was an opportunity there. I couldn't believe Brunswick never took advantage of it."

At the beginning of the 1980s most ski resorts banned the use of snowboards, claiming that snowboarders created an insurance liability. The ski resorts, which catered to those who could afford expensive lift tickets and ski equipment, remained reluctant to open up their slopes to the reputed counterculture associated with snowboarding. When the insurance excuse proved flimsy and snowboarders persisted in their demands that they be allowed on the slopes, ski areas acquiesced and opened their snow up to the sport. According to Finkel's article in *Sports Illustrated,* Paul Johnston, the manager at Stratton Mountain, reportedly stated that "nobody wants [snowboarders] on our mountain, but nobody has a good reason why [snowboarders] shouldn't be allowed on."

The trend toward banning snowboarding was reversed in the late 1980s, and as of 1997, 95 percent of ski areas in the United States allowed snowboarding. According to the National Sporting Goods Association, over the prior decade, since 1988, the number of snowboarders had risen 77 percent, while the number of skiers had fallen 25 percent. Clearly, snowboarding was filling its ranks at the expense of the skiing population. As of 1997, snowboarders numbered 2.3 million in the United States, accounting for 20 percent of the traffic at ski resorts. The final legitimization of the sport came in 1998 when the Winter Olympics in Nagano, Japan, included two snowboarding events—the halfpipe freestyle event and the giant slalom racing event—reflecting a decision made in 1995 by officials of the International Olympic Committee.

TARGET MARKET

Snowboarding had its roots in the maverick sports of surfing and skateboarding. The Alpine skiing community viewed these as illegitimate sports and consequently looked down on snowboarding as an bastardization. In addition, snowboarders were seen as punks. For their part, snowboarders embraced the image as rebellious outsiders, and when ski resorts banned snowboarding, this reinforced the image of snowboarders as outlaws. Ironically, the stereotype benefited snowboarders. If they were banned, they became martyrs (at least in their own eyes) for the freedom of athletic expression, and if they were not banned, they got to ride on the slopes, which was their ultimate goal. Snowboard manufacturers played up this maverick image as a means of paying tribute to snowboarders who fought the system while also enticing nonparticipants into the counterculture of snowboarding.

"This audience is so sensitive," said Hammerquist & Halverson's Cohen in Richardson's article, a statement that seemed counterintuitive to snowboarders' tough image. What these 14-to-28-year-olds were sensitive to was the nuanced representation of their sport and themselves. They greeted mainstream advertising with the same enthusiasm they would have for spending a gondola ride with a dozen mediocre skiers from New York City. The "Be Free" campaign from Sims and Hammerquist & Halverson spoke to snowboarders on their own terms, capturing the irreverent spirit of the sport.

COMPETITION

The snowboard market began with two companies based on either coast—Sims Snowboards in the Northwest and Burton Snowboards in the Northeast. Although Sims started making and marketing snowboards well before Burton, the latter managed to gain a commanding lead in the snowboard market early on. As of 1997, Burton Snowboards dominated with a 45 percent share of the market and with sales of more than 100,000 boards per year. Nonetheless, this represented a decline from earlier in the 1990s, when Burton owned the majority of the market. This kind of domination, however, risked the appearance of the mainstream commercialism that snowboarders avoided. Burton's lead proved unsustainable

NOT AVAILABLE ANYWHERE—PLEASE SEND NO MONEY NOW

Hammerquist & Halverson poked fun at mainstream marketing techniques with two mock product offers. One print ad, which urged viewers to "collect all three today," featured three plastic cups like those fast-food restaurants gave away to promote Hollywood megahits. Instead of picturing Batman or characters from the latest *Star Wars* epic, the cups pictured endorsers Allan Clark, Noah Salasnek, and Tina Basich in action shots riding their Sims Snowboards, with short blurbs on the opposite side of the cups describing the snowboard models they had designed. Fine print in the corner revealed the ad to be a sham: "Sorry, these cups are not available anywhere."

A second execution went further over the top by promoting a porcelain plate like the ones featuring puppy dogs and furry cats that were advertised in supermarket tabloids. The headline of the ad read, "The Sims Mint Proudly Presents the Mark Fawcett Commemorative China Plate," with the copy reading, "The front of this beautiful plate features Mark Fawcett engaged in big air on his beloved T. Sims board." A candle cast glowing light on the plate. Hammerquist & Halverson captured all of the tacky elements of this genre of advertising, which was conspicuously at odds with the elements of snowboarding culture. The cutout order form revealed the ad to be a farce: "Please Send No Money Now. If you want to order the Mark Fawcett commemorative plate, you can't. They will never ever be sold, in order to protect the as-yet-untarnished image of Mark Fawcett."

anyway, as the number of entries into the snowboard market multiplied. Ski manufacturers such as American-based K2and French-based Rossignol entered the market, increasing the competition with advertising budgets that dwarfed those of most snowboard manufacturers. As of 1997, approximately 250 companies competed in the snowboard market, which boasted more than 2,500 individual models.

MARKETING STRATEGY

Hammerquist &Halverson's "Be Free" campaign sought to recapture the original spirit of snowboarding and its culture of the outsider. In the print ad entitled "Mantra," Hammerquist & Halverson stated the snowboarder's philosophy: "The time has come to slash the jugular of mainstream mentality. To dismantle the notion of boundaries. To reclaim the mountains bastardized by conformity. The time has come to be free." The motto appeared to be handwritten on a poster bearing a cartoon silhouette of a figure who, having cut himself free from a ball and chain that had shackled his ankle, held a Sims snowbird above his head. To add to the political dimension of the ad, Bob Peterson used a curved lens to shoot a wide-angle photograph that revealed the man who had been plastering the message over other posters on Seattle's Pioneer Square and who was fleeing the scene with squeegee and glue bucket in hand, as if he were a fugitive. The execution created a sense of political urgency to the message, as if holding the tenets central to snowboarders' beliefs carried a risk.

A similar execution featured a snowboarder dressed in signature knee-length shorts and skateboarding sneakers who was fleeing the scene of a prank to an awaiting car with snowboards strapped on the roof rack. His crime was that he had rearranged the lettering on a restaurant sign that had read, it could be surmised through reconstruction, "Welcome Skiers Egg and Bacon Breakfast $2.99" to read "Sims Be Free." He had also slapped a Sims sticker on a telephone pole during his flight. Another print ad advanced a less subtle message. It featured five snowboards of differing lengths arranged to resemble fingers folded into a fist, with the middle snowboard longer than the rest, like an extended finger sending the universally understood message. The copy, which seemed haphazardly glued onto the picture, which was itself haphazardly stapled at the corners, read, "Tell your inhibitions, insecurities and fears where to go." The gesture suggested by the ad epitomized snowboarders' philosophy.

A television spot went in the opposite direction by playing off the familiar plot twist of a popular Saturday morning cartoon program. The commercial began unassumingly at a ski resort on a beautiful day, when the calm was suddenly broken by the appearance on-screen of a huge six-foot rabbit sporting giant fangs and seeking snowboarder blood. In slapstick fashion a snowboarder knocked the bunny over, revealing it to be the resort owner Mr. Jenkins. In the familiar words repeated at the end of every episode of *Scooby Doo,* the villain boasted that he would have gotten away with his crime "if it weren't for you meddling kids!" The ads thus returned to the history of the sport, pitting snowboarders against the establishment. The humor of the spot, however, arose from the fact that snowboarders could now joke about the past enmity of resort officials, whom the snowboarders had essentially defeated in reality as they had in the mock commercial.

OUTCOME

Advertising critics appreciated the "Be Free" campaign and showered it with laurels. The Hammerquist & Halverson team, which in addition to art directors Peterson and Proctor, included copywriters Cohen and Grant Holland and creative directors Hugh Saffel and Hammerquist, won a Gold Pencil at the One Show in New York for the Sims campaign. The agency as a whole won 22 awards at the 1998 Seattle Show, including the best of show commendation for its print work for Sims. In addition, the campaign won a silver ADDY in the print category, and *Graphis* magazine included the campaign in its annual edition surveying the best in graphic advertising for the year. But it was Hammerquist & Halverson's Cohen who, in Richardson's article, summed up the most important result of the campaign: "The outcome was that the consumers were digging it."

FURTHER READING

Atkin, Ross. "A Man Who Helped Skiers Get on the Snowboard." *Christian Science Monitor,* February 11, 1998.

Finkel, Michael. "Chairman of the Board Jake Burton Took a Childhood Toy and Launched an International Craze." *Sports Illustrated,* January 13, 1997.

Kim, Nancy J. "Marketing and Media." *Puget Sound Business Journal,* December 18, 1998.

Richardson, Margaret. "Snow Business." *Print* 53, no. 3.

"Upfront." *Advertising Age's Creativity,* December 1, 1997.

"The Works This Month: Amateur Hour 5." *Advertising Age's Creativity,* June 1, 1998.

William D.Baue

Six Flags, Inc.

11501 Northeast Expressway
Oklahoma City, Oklahoma 73131
USA
Telephone: (405) 475-2500
Fax: (405) 475-2555
Web site: www.sixflags.com

IT'S PLAYTIME CAMPAIGN

OVERVIEW

With 30 theme parks in North America and 8 in Europe in 2004, Six Flags, Inc., was the world's second-largest operator of theme parks, surpassed only by Walt Disney Parks and Resorts. But the company's parks were showing their age, attendance was on a downhill slide (falling 2.7 percent in the first nine months of 2003), and Six Flags was mired in a $2.3 billion debt. Six Flags announced that, to help pay down its debt, it would sell its European parks for $345 million and its park in Cleveland, Ohio, for $145 million. To help rebuild brand identity and drive up attendance, the company planned a national marketing campaign, its first such effort in seven years.

The first step in Six Flags' marketing strategy was to replace its agency, Ackerman McQueen, based in Oklahoma City, with independent agency W.B. Doner & Company (which did business as Doner) of Southfield, Michigan. Doner's new campaign for Six Flags, "It's Playtime," began in March 2004 with a television spot that featured an elderly, balding, bespectacled, and extremely vigorous spokesman referred to as Mr. Six. No specific budget for the campaign was available, but *Adweek* estimated the amount to be $70 million.

The "It's Playtime" campaign met with mixed results. In the months following its launch the campaign's spots repeatedly were included among *Advertising Age* magazine's list of top spots. Further, curiosity about Mr. Six fueled an onslaught of customer calls to the Six Flags offices. Although the campaign generated buzz, it failed to drive up park attendance. By June 2004 attendance at the parks had dropped 4 percent from the same period the previous year. Also, some people had begun to take a second look at Mr. Six and were finding him creepy rather than humorous. Standing by their man, Six Flags introduced new spots featuring Mr. Six in early 2005, but a proxy takeover of Six Flags later that year resulted in the company's new executive team putting Doner in review and ceasing use of the Mr. Six character.

HISTORICAL CONTEXT

Angus Wynne, a Texas oil baron, opened the first Six Flags park in 1961 in Arlington, Texas. At the time Wynne's goal was to develop large regional amusement parks in close proximity to where people lived. Just over 40 years later Six Flags counted 30 parks in the United States that served people living in or visiting 34 of the country's 50 largest metropolitan areas. By 2004 Six Flags was the second-biggest theme-park organization in the world, based on attendance, falling in just behind Walt Disney Parks and Resorts.

Prior to 1995 Six Flags' marketing efforts were handled by more than 10 different agencies. In December

Six Flags. © LARRY LEE PHOTOGRAPHY/CORBIS.

1995 the company announced plans for a national expansion, and in conjunction with that effort its media buying and advertising were consolidated, with McCann-Erickson New York named the agency of record. McCann-Erickson created a new advertising campaign that began in 1996 and targeted teens and young adults in addition to parents and kids. In 1998 Premier Parks, then the world's second-largest theme-park company based on attendance, acquired the Six Flags theme parks for $1.8 billion. Following the acquisition Six Flags' advertising duties shifted to Premier's longtime agency, the independent firm Ackerman McQueen, based in Oklahoma City. Premier's marketing technique was oriented toward promotions, and as a result traditional advertising for Six Flags dwindled. Recognizing the value of the Six Flags brand and name recognition, in 2000 Premier Parks changed its name to Six Flags, Inc. Four years later, as it planned to resume national advertising, Six Flags announced a review of its advertising agency. Soon afterward it replaced Ackerman McQueen with the Michigan agency Doner, and development of the "It's Playtime" campaign was underway.

TARGET MARKET

Family entertainment was big business, and Six Flags promoted itself as a destination for families in search of a good time. When Six Flags released the campaign "It's Playtime," its goal was to reach families and assure them that Six Flags theme parks were the place to go for family fun and entertainment for all ages. According to the company 70 percent of its annual media spending targeted women aged 25 to 49 years old, many of them mothers who made the plans for their children's entertainment. Teens and young adults were also in the company's marketing sights. In a press release Six Flags executives stated that the company's new marketing effort was intended to make families aware that Six Flags could provide the "ultimate release" for parents with busy home and work schedules as well as for kids, who felt the pressures of their school-related responsibilities and chores at home. In the same press release Charles Salemi, the company's vice president of marketing, said, "Our new campaign shares the excitement of a day at Six Flags, giving everyone, parents included, the freedom to let loose and enjoy the benefits of playtime."

COMPETITION

Walt Disney Parks and Resorts' Disneyland theme park, located in Anaheim, California, opened its doors to visitors in 1955. Despite shaky beginnings—on opening day the public toilets clogged, restaurants ran out of food, and the spike heels on women's shoes sank in the still-wet asphalt on the walks and streets—within 10 years of that first day 49 million people had made the trip to Anaheim for a visit to Disneyland. It became the gold standard for family theme parks and attracted a growing number of visitors. In 2004 Disneyland was the world's second-most-popular theme park based on attendance. That year 13.4 million people strolled through its gates. The number one theme park in the world was also a Disney facility: the Magic Kingdom at Disney World in Orlando, Florida, which had 15.2 million visitors in 2004. As Disney prepared to celebrate the 50th birthday of its first theme park in 2005, the company embarked on a year of planning that included a marketing campaign to invite the world to its party. Billed as the "Happiest Celebration on Earth" (a play on Disney's familiar slogan "The Happiest Place on Earth"), the campaign began on New Year's Day 2005. Developed by Disney's longtime agency, Leo Burnett, it was Disney's first global advertising effort and expanded on its traditional advertising.

The company Universal Parks & Resorts got its start in the 1960s by providing tourists with tours of the facilities of Universal Studios Hollywood, near Los Angeles. From those first trolley rides around the back

The Titan at Six Flags Over Texas, Arlington, Texas, August 5, 2001. AP IMAGES.

lots where movies and television programs were filmed evolved an international company with theme parks in Osaka, Japan; Salou, Spain; Orlando, Florida; and the original park in Universal City, Los Angeles County (though surrounded by the city of Los Angeles, Universal City remained unincorporated). In 2003 the combined attendance for the four parks was 23.25 million, a 12 percent drop from the previous year. That year the NBC Television Network merged with Universal Studios to become NBC Universal. The company, 80 percent of which was owned by General Electric and the rest by Vivendi Universal France, included the struggling Universal Studios theme parks. By 2004 NBC was contemplating selling the money-losing theme parks, but instead it created a separate division under the name Universal Studios Partnerships to help integrate the parks into the NBC structure. Although one year later it was still uncertain whether or not General Electric would eventually sell the theme parks, at least one of the facilities, Universal Orlando, reported that in 2004 attendance had jumped 14 percent to 12.1 million visitors. To help draw even more visitors Universal Orlando released a national advertising campaign in 2005 that broke the rules usually applied to theme-park advertisements: the spots did not depict families having fun on the park's rides, and they did not include a phone number or website address for people wanting additional information before visiting the park. Described by the company as "un-branded" advertising, the "Have a Life" campaign was created by Los Angeles–based independent agency davidandgoliath. It was aimed at people who, according to a Gallup poll, skipped vacations because they often felt guilty if they took time off from work, encouraging them to take back their vacation time and to visit specially designed websites such as www.iwantmycacation.com. The site provided data about the importance of vacations and described options offered by Universal Orlando.

MARKETING STRATEGY

In 2004, when Six Flags planned to improve attendance at its theme parks and rebuild its brand through a new marketing campaign, its first since 1996, the company hired independent agency W.B. Doner & Company (Doner). The Southfield, Michigan–based agency created an unusual spokesman, known first as a "dancing ambassador of fun," then as Mr. Six, to star in television spots promoting Six Flags. Mr. Six was a strange little senior citizen with a bald head and a gaping, toothless grin, who wore oversized black-framed glasses, a bow tie, and a tuxedo with the trousers hiked up high above his waist.

The "It's Playtime" campaign's initial spot hit the air in March 2004, running during popular prime-time programs such as Fox television's *American Idol,* ABC's *Hope & Faith,* and NBC's *Law & Order SVU.* During the spot Mr. Six slowly shuffled out of a colorful vintage bus that had stopped in front of a house where a tired-looking family was doing yard work. With the strains of the 1998 hit song *We Like to Party* by the Latin band Vengaboys reverberating in the background, Mr. Six suddenly began dancing with an energy and enthusiasm unexpected in an octogenarian, enticing the family, in true Pied Piper style, to drop their rake and garden hose, turn off the lawn mower, and join Mr. Six for a day of fun at Six Flags. The spot ended with Mr. Six leading a conga line into the theme park as the tagline "It's playtime" appeared on the screen. A subsequent spot portrayed the wildly dancing Mr. Six convincing two caddies, who were schlepping heavy golf bags at a busy course, to drop the bags and run off with him for a little fun. The tagline said, "There's time for work and time for play. It's playtime."

In 2005 a new national TV spot kicked off that gave viewers a peek at where Mr. Six spent the winter and how he was helping prep the theme parks for a new season. Titled "Retirement Home," the spot opened with a shot of a retirement home; a staff nurse opened the curtains to let in the sunshine. Mr. Six was shown getting dressed in his tuxedo and bow tie, climbing into his signature bus, and driving to Six Flags, where he began preparing the park for its opening-day visitors. With the entrance turnstiles oiled, windows washed, roller coaster polished, and the grounds pruned, Mr. Six turned on the lights, and his theme song, "We Like to Party," began playing. The voice-over stated, "There's a new level of excitement throughout the park."

OUTCOME

The "It's Playtime" campaign quickly generated buzz, most of it related to Mr. Six. Two months after the first television spot aired, Six Flags reported being inundated with calls to their offices by fans of the mysterious Mr. Six who wanted to know who or what the character was. Speculations about the spry octogenarian ranged from whether he was actually a young man or a woman to rumors that he was really actor Martin Short or Jaleel White, best known for playing the nerdy character "Urkel" on the 1990s television comedy *Family Matters.* Debbie Nauser, a Six Flags spokeswoman, told the *Baltimore Sun,* "It was just amazing. In all the time I've been at this company, we've never gotten letters and calls like the ones coming in for this spot."

Several of the campaign's commercials were named "Top Spots" by *Advertising Age* in 2004, including in April, May, and July. The distinction was based on brand-recall studies conducted by the marketing-research firm IAG. The publication's 2004 quarterly survey also rated the Six Flags spots number one for likability. *USA Today* rated the spots number two for effectiveness in its year-end Ad Track consumer poll. As Mr. Six's popularity soared, he was discussed on radio talk shows and television news broadcasts. The Mr. Six character also appeared as a guest on *Good Morning America.*

Despite the success of the campaign, it failed to achieve its goal of increasing visits to the Six Flags theme parks. In the six months following the introduction of the campaign, combined attendance at the parks dropped 4 percent. For all of 2004 attendance dropped 3.4 percent to 33.5 million. Further, while Mr. Six resonated with some consumers, he irritated—or worse, alienated—others. The *Chicago Tribune* called Mr. Six "a fascinating figure," but the *Columbia Daily Tribune* described him as "a major blight on society." Additional bad news came from a survey conducted by the Los Angeles–based teen-marketing company StreetWise Concepts & Culture. In 2004 the company asked 700 teens to rate recent commercials, including those for Six Flags, as either "totally great" or "really terrible." The kids deemed the entire Six Flags campaign terrible and commented that it "really needs to die." And although Six Flags dubbed Mr. Six as a "dancing ambassador of fun" and a pop-culture icon, he also was referred to in the media, including a report in *Advertising Age,* as creepy, unwholesome, and not to be trusted.

In late 2005 a corporate battle arose within Six Flags. Washington Redskins owner Daniel Snyder—whose investment firm Red Zone LLC was the largest Six Flags shareholder—announced plans to take over the company. The board of directors tried to prevent the takeover by putting the company up for auction, but the effort failed when there were no bidders. Amidst charges of mismanagement and poor marketing, and with a new president and chief operating officer at the helm, the company announced the creation of an entertainment and marketing department, and its advertising account was put up for review, with the incumbent agency, Doner, invited to defend. As part of the change Mr. Six danced off into history.

SIX FLAGS PARKS INSTALLS "NO SMOKING" SIGNS

In late 2005 the Six Flags theme parks chain was under new ownership, and with that came new policies, including banning smoking in all 32 of its facilities. The smoking ban was intended to make the parks more family friendly. The *Washington Post* reported that, according to Six Flags' new owner, Daniel M. Snyder (also owner of the Washington Redskins football team), parents waiting in line with their kids to get on a ride were not the smokers: "It's the young adults who hang out in packs, puffing," Snyder said, adding that this was the element he wanted removed from the parks.

FURTHER READING

Baar, Aaron. "Doner's Mr. Six Earns Return Engagement." *Adweek,* March 24, 2005.

Feuer, Jack. "The Kids Have Spoken." *Adweek,* September 13, 2004.

Haberkorn, Jen. "Six Flags Offers Icon; Dancing Pitchman Rises in Recognition Via TV Ads." *Washington (D.C.) Times,* July 6, 2004.

Himmelberg, Michele. "First Advertisement for Disneyland's 50th Birthday Party to Air New Year's Day." *Santa Ana (CA) Orange County Register,* December 31, 2004.

Ho, Rodney. "Commercial's Buzz Is a Boon for Six Flags." *Atlanta Journal-Constitution,* July 15, 2004, p. NW10.

Klaasen, Abbey. "Six Flags Takeover Duo Could Deep-Six Mr. Six; Snyder's RedZone Enlists Shapiro to Control Board and Revamp Marketing." *Advertising Age,* August 22, 2005.

Knight, Jerry. "Six Flags Gains Ground under Redskins' Snyder." *Washington Post,* January 23, 2006.

MacArthur, Kate, and T.L. Stanley. "Does Six Sell? Despite the Ubiquity of Its Mr. Six Ad Icon, Six Flags Attendance Has Dropped 4% This Year." *Advertising Age,* July 26, 2004.

Simons, Andrew. "Thrill Ride? NBC to Take Control of Universal as Revenues Freefall at Theme Parks." *Los Angeles Business Journal,* May 3, 2004.

"Six Flags Launches First National Ad Campaign in Seven Years; New Brand Character Transports Overscheduled, Stressed-Out Families to a Day of Ultimate Fun!" *PR Newswire,* March 19, 2004.

"Six Flags Launches Year Two of National Ad Campaign Featuring Mr. Six; The Be-Spectacled, Dancing, Nationwide Phenomenon Is Back—New TV Spot Reveals His Winter Home." *PR Newswire,* March 24, 2005.

Stafford, Leon. "Six Flags Ad Draws Calls from All Over." *Atlanta Journal-Constitution,* May 8, 2004, p. F2.

"Universal Orlando Takes Radical Approach to New National Ad Campaign; 'Have a Life' Television Campaign Combines Blunt Messages, Humor and Un-Branded Ads to Urge Americans to Take Back Their Vacations." *PR Newswire,* February 14, 2005.

"U.S. Advertisers Use New Tactics of Cutting 'Clutter' to Reach Target Audience." *Baltimore Sun,* May 12, 2004.

Yoshino, Kimi, and Dave McKibben. "The Kingdom Was His Glory." *Bergen County (NJ) Record,* July 31, 2005.

Rayna Bailey

Sony Corporation

6-7-35 Kitashinagawa
Shinagawa-ku
Tokyo, 141-0001
Japan
Telephone: 81 3 54482111
Fax: 81 3 54482244
Web site: www.sony.com

FUN, ANYONE? CAMPAIGN

OVERVIEW

Games consoles, the electronic devices that play video games, became big business after their introduction in the 1970s. Originating with Nintendo and Sega, the gaming industry was lucrative from the start, and it grew dramatically. In 1988 Sony Corporation entered the field, although the company was slow to make a name for itself. By the time Sony had introduced its state-of-the-art PlayStation console in 1994, however, success was snowballing for the company. By 2004 more than 100 million units of PlayStation had been shipped worldwide, making it the biggest selling games console in history. When Sony introduced PlayStation 2 in 2000, customers lined up outside stores to buy it. By 2003, largely owing to the success of PlayStation 2, Sony held 74 percent of a market worth nearly $13 billion. But with Nintendo and Microsoft, Sony's biggest competitors, spending huge amounts of money on marketing and research, Sony could not be complacent. To further promote the PlayStation 2 and its software and to help maintain its position in the market, Sony launched the "Fun, Anyone?" campaign in 2003, and it ran through 2004.

The highlight of the "Fun, Anyone?" campaign was the "Mountain" television commercial. Shot in Brazil, "Mountain" showed an excited mob of people climbing on top of one another, with Shirley Temple's recording of "Get on Board, Lil' Children" on the sound track. The human "mountain" was meant to symbolize a highly social experience. Other "Fun, Anyone?" ads, such as the silly cartoon spots "Dancing Robot," "Laughing Mouths," "Winners and Losers," and "Wobble," helped to create a new image for Sony. They were an effort to replace the image of gaming as an insular, aggressive, largely male adolescent activity with a focus on sociability.

The campaign, created by TBWA\London, was highly successful. The "Mountain" television commercial in particular gained international praise. With the new focus on sociability, Sony widened its consumer base, from primarily 18- to 39-year-old-males to a larger family demographic. By making PlayStation more appealing to a wider public, Sony exceeded its sales targets and dramatically reinforced its position in the market for games consoles. A year after "Fun, Anyone?" began, Sony's share in the market had increased from 74 to 77 percent.

HISTORICAL CONTEXT

The introduction of the Sony PlayStation 2 in 2000 had caused a sensation in the gaming world. Sony could not get the consoles onto shelves quickly enough, and stores could not keep them in stock. Consumers virtually staked out stores that announced a shipment. According to *Kiplinger's Personal Finance Magazine,* no retailer was taking back orders, and even Amazon.com could offer little hope to wold-be buyers. All of Amazon.com's allocation of PlayStation 2 for 2000 apparently sold out in less than 10 minutes. A one-day record of $150 million in sales was an indication of the success of PlayStation 2.

To market PlayStation 2, Sony used advertisements that were dark and mysterious. They appealed to a largely male audience, especially to those who preferred to spend time alone with their games consoles. The focus was not on social activities or on the real world but rather on exclusion and on the shadowy world created by PlayStation. This focus could be seen, for example, in the "Signs" trailer, part of a $250 million marketing promotion in 2002 that was included in the campaign "Live in your World. Play in Ours." Appearing on more than 5,000 cinema screens, "Signs" showed a young man walking the streets of a city alone. As Andrew House, Sony's executive vice president for marketing, explained in *Advertising Age,* "The lead character is almost like he's in the midst of his own role-playing game. He needs to follow clues to save the heroine. There is a sense that he's being drawn into our world."

This marketing approach was enormously successful. Barely three years after the introduction of PlayStation 2, Sony had shipped 50 million units worldwide, and sales numbers continued to rise. During November and December 2002, for example, sales were up 42 percent over the same months in the previous year. By 2004, 70 million units had been shipped worldwide. Given this level of success, straying from its marketing approach was risky, but by 2003 Sony decided that it was time to make a shift. One of the factors in making a change was the increasing wariness about antisocial behavior, especially among the young.

TARGET MARKET

The gaming industry traditionally focused its primary marketing toward 18- to 39-year-old males. Sales numbers supported this approach. In 1999, for example, males accounted for an estimated 89 percent of the market for games consoles and 94 percent of the market for gaming magazines. As a result games almost exclusively featured male protagonists, with females playing more subservient roles, for example, being saved from an enemy by a male hero. In addition, the themes of games—including sports, action, and violence—reflected society's view of male interests. Thus, the gaming industry displayed a significant gender gap.

Sony's "Fun, Anyone?" campaign, and especially the "Mountain" television spot that embodied it, represented the beginning of an effort to lessen this gap. Although the campaign did not focus on female gamers in particular, neither was it exclusively focused on males. Rather, it was much more gender-neutral than previous PlayStation campaigns had been. Although achieving gender-neutrality may not have been Sony's main concern, it was part of the change of focus to sociability and community.

Thus, the new marketing approach for PlayStation targeted a different gamer than in the past. *Marketing* magazine reflected on this change, stating that consumers had begun to identify less with solitary pursuits and more with activities that involved socializing. It was becoming out of fashion, for instance, to lock oneself up in a room with a video game. Recognizing this trend, Sony shifted its attention from a target market of solitary young men to a more general, and a more sociable, public. Not only were women now part of the PlayStation market, but so were entire families. 'Mountain' particularly was focused on broadening the gaming market. TBWA\London representative Sue Ellen Craig was quoted in *Game Planet,* a New Zealand publication, as saying, "'Mountain' reflects and acknowledges the current PlayStation 2 audience as well as inviting the new and emerging customer markets to 'get on board'. It brings out the player in everyone, and hooks strongly into the idea of simple, permissible fun."

A "MOUNTAIN" OF AWARDS

"The Mountain" television commercial won more than 40 awards and nominations in advertising, most notably the 2004 Grand Prix at the Annual International Advertising Festival in Cannes, France. By 2005 PlayStation had won 26 Cannes Lions, including three Grands Prix, the most prestigious award bestowed by the organization. In recognition of its overall contribution to advertising, Sony's PlayStation was named Advertiser of the Year at the 2005 Cannes festival. As Terry Savage, CEO of the festival, noted, "When one brand wins so many Cannes Lions honours, it's not a difficult process to select them for this prestigious award. We honour a client who honours us with great creative executions over a number of years."

COMPETITION

Driven by a highly lucrative market, the competition between games consoles, sometimes called the "console wars," was fierce. At the beginning of gaming, in the 1970s, only two companies, Nintendo and Sega, were in the market. Sony entered the business in 1988, ironically in a partnership with Nintendo. At the time the two worked together on the development of the Super Disc, a CD-ROM attachment. Eventually, however, they ended their partnership, and Sony moved on to use a modified version of the Super Disc as part of its newly developed games console. By the time Sony had released its first PlayStation, in 1994, it had made a clean break with Nintendo. Sega, meanwhile, had fallen behind. For a short time, the company rebounded, with huge earnings from the introduction of the Dreamcast console in 1998–99. By 2001, however, Sega had discontinued production of the Dreamcast and had left the console market altogether.

By this time Microsoft had entered the business with its own games console, while Nintendo and Sony were preparing to introduce new consoles of their own. At the 2001 Electronic Entertainment Expo, the gaming industry's major convention, there were three undisputed participants in the console wars: Sony PlayStation 2, Nintendo Game Cube, and Microsoft Xbox. Sony left the 2001 exposition as the clear champion and continued to hold its lead. By 2003 Nintendo, who a few years earlier had held more than 70 percent of the market, was suffering disastrous results with its Game Cube and had a mere 13 percent share. Microsoft's share also was at 13 percent, even though it had just entered the market. This left Sony with an astonishing 74 percent of the market in 2003. Nonetheless, Nintendo and Microsoft did not leave the business. Given the size of the games console market, approximately $13 billion in 2004, there were profits to be made even if a company held only a small percentage of the business.

MARKETING STRATEGY

The "Mountain" advertisement embodied the message of the "Fun, Anyone?" campaign. Asking consumers to "get on board," the commercial represented fun that was accessible to everyone. Shot over six days in Rio de Janeiro, the big-budget ad involved more than 500 extras, 50 stunt people, and a 300-person production team. With cinematography suitable for a high-budget feature film, "Mountain" followed a crowd of excited people through town, while Shirley Temple sang "Get on Board, Lil' Children" in the background. Following this opening scene, the throng of people began clambering on top of one another. In the end they formed a human "mountain," creating a symbol of cooperation in society. In the words of Sony, "even as countries fight each other, people from around the world are finding new ways to come together by playing online digital games on systems such as PlayStation 2." The commercial, which was referred to as "art" by many viewers, won more than 40 awards and nominations in the field of advertising.

"Mountain" was produced by Trevor Beattie, the creative director of TBWA\London, the advertising agency for Sony Computer Entertainment Europe, and Liz Browne, producer for the Mill, one of the world's leading visual-effects company. The 60-second television commercial originally aired in 30 countries throughout Europe and Asia in November 2003, and it ran through 2004. The commercial could also be viewed on various websites long after its original airing.

Before launching "Mountain," TBWA\London, aired four ads that served as a opening for the "Fun, Anyone?" campaign. These 30-second spots—titled "Dancing Robot," "Laughing Mouths," "Winners and Losers," and "Wobble"—featured line-drawn cartoon characters. The opening ads won honors of their own, with "Laughing Mouths," for example, taking three awards, including an Advertising Creative Circle Memorial Award for Best Use of Humor. With their focus on fun, the four spots thus marked the beginning of the shift by Sony from dark, enigmatic ads to ones that were lighter and more amusing. The message of the new ads was endorsed in August 2003 at the PlayStation Experience in London. This four-day event provided Sony with the opportunity to promote its new campaign and slogan, not simply by telling consumers but also by showing them. For this purpose Sony created areas in which gamers could play one other, thus creating a sense of gaming as a social activity. The event was covered by local television and print news, which helped to spread PlayStation's new image.

The British trade magazine *MCV* reported that during the 2003 Christmas season Sony spent 5 million pounds (more than U.S.$8 million) on advertising. This included a six-week television campaign featuring the "Fun, Anyone?" ads. The campaign ran during 2004, with promotions made through cinema, television, print, merchandise, and public events. Even after the promotional period for the "Fun, Anyone?" campaign had ended, the slogan continued to represent the Sony PlayStation console.

OUTCOME

Sony's decision to transform the image of its PlayStation console and of gaming, from one that was dark and mysterious to one that was light and fun, turned out to be successful. The "Fun, Anyone?" campaign, particularly the "Mountain" television spot, achieved success on all levels. Not only did the ad win a number of awards in advertising, but it also gained popularity for PlayStation and helped increase sales, thus helping to confirm the logic behind the "Fun, Anyone?" slogan.

By promoting the idea that gaming could be a social, as well as a solitary, experience, the "Fun, Anyone?" campaign was successful in expanding the market for gaming. Without abandoning its edginess and "cool" status, PlayStation was appealing to a much broader audience. As a result the Sony PlayStation further established its number-one position in game consoles, boasting 77 percent of the market share after the campaign. The "Fun, Anyone?" tagline appeared to work its magic on consumers, and in 2004 Sony celebrated the milestone of more than 70 million PlayStation 2 units shipped. With the sales of consoles, hardware, and software combined, PlayStation 2 brought in an astounding $2 billion in revenue during the 2003 holiday season alone.

FURTHER READING

Deok-hyun, Kim. "Microsoft Faces Tough Challenge on Video Game Market." *Korea Times,* June 25, 2003.

Elkin, Toby. "'Signs' Trailer Is Part of $250 Million Effort for PlayStation2 Line." *Advertising Age,* September 2, 2002, p. 4.

Elliot, Stuart. "The Media Business: Advertising—Addenda; Campaign Disqualified at 'Advertising Festival.'" *New York Times,* June 19, 2003, p. 4.

"Fun, Anyone?" *Game Planet,* December 8, 2003. Available from <http://www.gameplanet.co.nz/mag.dyn/Features/2156.html>

"Girls Got (Video) Game." Available from <http://www.abcnews.go.com>, March 27, 2005.

Hall, Emma. "Spotlight: Sony PlayStation." *Advertising Age,* November 17, 2003, p. 14.

Lankford, Kimberly. "How to Get Game." *Kiplinger's Personal Finance Magazine,* April 2001, p.123.

"The Mill Builds a People Mountain for Playstation." *Mill Publicity,* May 20, 2004. Available from <http://features.cgsociety.org/cgfilms/cgfilm.php?story_id=2097>

"PlayStation Mountain Spot Takes British Ad Craft Awards." *Animation World Network,* November 3, 2004. Available from http://news.awn.com/index.php?ltype=top&newsitem_no=12350>

"PlayStation Promotes the Experience." *Revolution,* September 4, 2003, p. 9.

Price, Amy L. "The 'Battle of the Boxes.'" *Point Of Purchase Magazine,* April 2001, p. 38.

Sanchanta, Mariko. "PlayStation 2 Sales Hit 50m Worldwide." *Financial Times,* January 17, 2003, p. 29.

Sweney, Mark. "Budgen Directs Latest PlayStation Campaign." *Campaign,* November 7, 2003, p. 7.

———. "TBWA Uses Humorous Tone in Its New PlayStation Campaign." *Campaign,* July 18, 2003, p. 2.

Veldre, Danielle. "PlayStation Warms Up." *B&T Weekly (Australia),* November 27, 2003.

Candice Mancini

SONY BRAVIA CAMPAIGN

OVERVIEW

During the second half of the twentieth century the Tokyo-based Sony Corporation developed a reputation as a global leader in consumer electronics, thanks to its numerous iconic products, such as the Trinitron color television, the Walkman portable cassette player, and the Betamax videocassette recorder. In the early years of the twenty-first century, however, the company misjudged the speed at which consumers were ready to adopt liquid crystal display (LCD) and other flat-panel TV technologies, and its TV sales, strongly tied to its formerly cutting-edge cathode-ray-tube (CRT) technology, began eroding steadily. Sony attempted to rectify its product-development oversight by partnering with rival Samsung to produce the next generation of LCD TVs, and in fall 2005 Sony introduced what it hoped would be the industry's leading LCD product and a new Sony icon: the BRAVIA line. Among the campaigns supporting the BRAVIA line's global launch, the European effort, crafted by the London office of ad agency Fallon Worldwide, was the most noteworthy.

The European campaign ran not only on the continent and in the United Kingdom but also in Australia and New Zealand. It centered on one commercial (edited to three different lengths) that cost several million dollars to produce. It debuted in the United Kingdom in November 2005 as part of an estimated $30 million marketing push to drive BRAVIA sales during the holidays. The spot dramatized the BRAVIA theme "Colour like.no.other" by showing 250,000 brightly colored rubber balls bouncing hypnotically down a steep San Francisco street.

The worldwide BRAVIA launch was a success, although U.S. sales overshadowed those in Europe. This was at least partly a function of the fact that Sony Europe was unable to keep pace with demand for BRAVIA TVs.

HISTORICAL CONTEXT

Sony was founded as Tokyo Tsushin Kogyo (Tokyo Telecommunications Engineering Corporation) in 1946 by Masaru Ibuka and Akio Morita, an engineer and a physicist, respectively. When, in the early 1950s, the company won a license to build products using the newly invented transistor (an electronic device that allowed for amplification, switching, and voltage regulation, among many other functions, but that occupied far less space than the vacuum-tube technology that had driven consumer electronics in previous years), Tokyo Tsushin Kogyo's founders saw the opportunity to attract a global consumer base. Because the original company name had no resonance outside of Japan, Ibuka and Morita renamed their enterprise Sony, an invented word meant to transcend nationality (the name came from *sonus,* the Latin word for "sound," and was meant to evoke the American expression "sonny boy," which was then a slang term used in Japan to mean "whiz kid"). While other companies focused on the military and computing applications of the transistor, Sony found great success in applying the technology to mass-produced pocket radios. Later entertainment-based applications of new technologies—such as the Trinitron color television (first sold in 1968), the Betamax videocassette recorder (1975), the Walkman portable cassette player (1979), and the world's first compact-disc player (1982)—made the Sony brand synonymous with high-quality, cutting-edge electronics.

The company made high-profile entries into new economic sectors (including, most prominently, film production and music recording) in the 1980s and 1990s, but consumer electronics remained Sony's core business and the source of its brand identity. At the start of the new century, however, Sony hesitated to enter both the flat-panel-television market and the digital-music market, betting instead on its mainstay CRT television products and its traditional line of portable music devices. (The company also resisted the digital-music zeitgeist in part because of the threat it posed to recording artists in Sony's music division.) Meanwhile other electronic brands invested more quickly and heavily than Sony in LCD and plasma TV technology, and a host of new competitors emerged in this market, complicating Sony's efforts to defend its brand positioning. As sales began to slide, Sony was further eclipsed, in the minds of many consumers, by Apple Computers as the industry's foremost maker of cutting-edge electronics. Apple's introduction of the enormously successful iPod, a handheld digital-music player, quickly made traditional equivalents all but obsolete.

Sony's declining consumer-electronic sales were accompanied by a series of upheavals at the corporate level, and Sony struggled to regain its footing, depending for a disproportionate amount of its revenues on its Sony PlayStation video-game console as well as the studio movies it produced. Having fallen behind in LCD technology, Sony entered into a partnership with its rival Samsung, according to which Samsung would manufacture the flat-panel displays for a new line of Sony televisions. In early 2005, as Sony recalibrated its global marketing to address its ongoing sales and image problems, the company unveiled a new long-term positioning for its European electronics markets, tagged "like.no. other." In September 2005 Sony conducted the global introduction of its next-generation LCD TVs, called BRAVIA (an acronym standing for "best resolution audio visual integrated architecture"), a line that included the first products to emerge from the Samsung partnership. Of the simultaneously running global campaigns in support of the BRAVIA line, the most ambitious, in creative terms, was one designed to run in the European market (as well as in Australia and New Zealand) under the "like.no.other" tagline from November 2005 through the holiday season.

TARGET MARKET

Sony consumer electronics traditionally cost more than other mainstream brands worldwide, giving the company a brand positioning at the high end of the mass market. The BRAVIA line of LCD TVs was no exception. Sony had always depended on its industry-defining models, such as the Trinitron and, later, the Trinitron WEGA, together with its overall reputation for engineering excellence, to encourage mainstream consumers to spend the extra amount of money necessary to purchase a Sony TV. The WEGA line, however, was predominantly associated with the CRT technology to which Sony had remained committed in spite of the growing consumer preference for flat-panel TVs, and the company understood the need, in 2005, to reinforce Sony's reputation as a forward-looking brand. The introduction of the BRAVIA line was thus an attempt to create a new and enduring icon product for Sony, after the fashion of the Trinitron or the Walkman. The European BRAVIA campaign, headlined by the high-profile commercial "Balls," was accordingly meant to send the mass-market message that Sony was, as Sony Europe senior vice president for communications David Patton told the *International Herald Tribune*, "a committed and powerful brand," while simultaneously serving as "a statement to the investment community that we will continue to develop and market innovative products." "Balls" and the campaign's accompanying print ads ran in European countries and in Australia and New Zealand as well.

COMPETITION

The fact that Sony had not kept pace with LCD technology and manufacturing in the first few years of the twenty-first century left it reliant on exterior suppliers for its LCD screens. As a result Sony had to pay higher prices, and its profit margins were thinner than would have been the case if it manufactured its own screens, an especially undesirable position in a climate of falling prices for LCD TVs. This arrangement also fostered a perception among consumers (putatively abetted by salespeople) that the higher prices Sony commanded could not be justified if the company itself did not manufacture the most important part of the TV. Sony entered into a partnership with one of its leading rivals in the flat-panel sector, South Korea's Samsung, thus substantially lowering production costs for its LCD TVs, effective with the BRAVIA launch in September 2005. This was a striking partnership given the fact that Samsung was Sony's top global rival in the wider electronics industry. Samsung was, moreover, the best-selling LCD TV brand in Europe prior to and during Sony's BRAVIA campaign.

IN THE UNITED STATES

The U.S. launch of Sony's new BRAVIA line of LCD TVs was not accompanied by an advertising campaign as visually exciting or as critically lauded as the one simultaneously mounted by Sony Europe in late 2005, but the product launch itself was far more successful. While the U.S. BRAVIA campaign was less conceptually ambitious than its European counterpart, it was credited with driving sales by pointing out the quality differences between Sony's BRAVIA and competitors' LCD offerings. Also, the far larger amount of revenue generated by the BRAVIA line in the United States was a function of a more mature LCD market: Europeans were, on the whole, slower than their American counterparts to make the switch from cathode-ray-tube to flat-panel TVs. Additionally, Sony was able to keep pace with demand in the United States, as it was not able to do in Europe.

One area in which Samsung had not begun to rival Sony, however, was advertising. Samsung attempted to integrate its global advertising and to position itself as an increasingly upscale brand during these years, but it failed to settle on a consistent strategy or creative direction in Europe and elsewhere, as reflected by its searches for new global agencies in both 2004 and 2005.

The Philips brand of LCD TVs also outsold Sony in Europe during this time. Beginning in 2003 Philips consolidated its global advertising, budgeted at $600 million, with the agency DDB Worldwide, which already held approximately half of that business. In addition to consumer electronics, Philips sold medical equipment and lightbulbs, among other product categories. Like Sony and other consumer-electronics brands, Philips had to deal with the difficulty of successfully advertising its diverse range of products without resorting to bland imagery and rhetoric. The company's long-running European brand message, "Let's make things better," was often derided for its dullness and lack of specificity.

MARKETING STRATEGY

All Sony communications in Europe during this time were to be organized around the "like.no.other" theme, setting Fallon London the challenge of creating a campaign that was literally unlike anything else in the advertising industry. In its research Fallon had found that the primary idea in consumers' minds when they considered buying a TV was the quality and vibrancy of the colors delivered by the set. For the BRAVIA campaign Fallon thus settled on the theme "Colour like.no.other" and centered its communications on a single commercial titled "Balls," which was edited to run in a 180-second flagship version, a 60-second version, and a 30-second version. This spot indeed broke with all contemporaneous advertising on behalf of TV brands, dramatizing the "Colour like.no.other" idea with an image never before captured on film: that of 250,000 brightly colored "superballs" bouncing en masse down the hilly streets of San Francisco.

Fallon negotiated for months with San Francisco city officials and the police department in order to secure approval for the three-day shoot, which required closing 12 of the city's hilliest streets. The balls were dropped by the thousands from bins lifted high into the air by heavy machinery, while smaller batches were shot from cannons. Twenty-three camerapersons were positioned along the balls' paths (in comparison, only four were required for a standard commercial shoot), and each time a set of balls was released into the streets, the camerapersons had only one take to capture the resulting images. Fallon had set itself the goal of using only live footage, avoiding any digitized manipulation of the images in an attempt to endow the spectacle with more "soul."

The finished spots opened with a panoramic view of San Francisco and then cut to a cloudlike mass of bright rubber balls filling the entire width of a city street at the crest of an enormous hill. The commercial then tracked the balls as they bounced, in slow motion, all the way down the road and pooled in the streets below. Individual shots at times focused on the hypnotic movements of the vivid mass of balls making its way down the hill and at times singled out particular balls and subgroups of balls, emphasizing the unique coloring and bouncing behavior of each. There was no dialogue or narrative element beyond the balls' bouncing and their resultant interaction with the characteristically San Franciscan surroundings (including Victorian homes, vintage automobiles, street gutters, and sidewalks). Each version of the commercial used the José González song "Heartbeat," an emotionally resonant, lullaby-like song featuring hushed singing and acoustic guitar. The spots closed with the "Colour like.no.other" tagline and an image of the flat-panel BRAVIA television.

"Balls" was filmed in July 2005, in preparation for a November U.K. launch. The pronounced interest on the part of San Francisco spectators, however, resulted in a productive level of viral buzz dating from the commercial's filming. Many advertising-focused bloggers took photographs or videos of the shoot itself and posted them on their websites, so that before the commercial had even officially premiered, ad-industry observers in the United States were already predicting that "Balls" would be an award-winning commercial. The spot premiered in the United Kingdom in its 180-minute version, occupying an entire commercial break just prior to a high-profile soccer game between Manchester United and Chelsea. Although the commercial never aired in the United States, Sony made it available on the Internet at www.bravia-advert.com, which allowed it to further circulate beyond its target regions. Additional online material included a behind-the-scenes featurette focusing on the film shoot, information about the Swedish singer-songwriter José González, and photographs and downloadable images. After the initial long version ran in the United Kingdom, the shorter versions aired through the holiday season across the campaign's entire geographic range. According to Sony Europe's Patton, "Balls" alone cost several million dollars to produce, and Sony's budget for the BRAVIA campaign during fall 2005 approached $30 million. Print, outdoor, and in-store executions maintained the "Colour like.no.other" theme.

OUTCOME

Sony leapfrogged competitors to become the best-selling brand of LCD TVs globally in early 2006, up from the fourth-place spot prior to the BRAVIA launch. In Europe Sony increased its share of the LCD market to 14 percent from 10 percent, but it did not surpass Samsung and Philips in sales. This was at least partly a function of lack of inventory; Sony was unable to keep pace with product demand and was still filling December 2005 back orders in March 2006. Sony predicted that it would double European LCD sales in 2006 amid a projected 60–70 percent expansion of that continent's market for LCD TVs, and the company set a goal of reaching a 20 percent market share by the end of the year. Though the European BRAVIA launch was considered successful, it was overshadowed by the line's overwhelmingly successful reception in the United States, which led many analysts to predict that Sony was poised to reclaim its spot as the world's preeminent consumer-electronics brand.

FURTHER READING

Brook, Stephen. "Sony Bounces Back for New Campaign." *Guardian Unlimited,* October 25, 2005. Available from <http://media.guardian.co.uk/advertising/story/0,,1600198,00.html>

Dvorak, Phred. "Sony Plans Ad Blitz to Boost Ailing TV Unit." *Wall Street Journal,* August 29, 2005.

Hall, Emma, and Laurel Wentz. "Spotlight." *Advertising Age,* October 31, 2005.

Lippert, Barbara. "The Old Ball Game." *Adweek,* November 7, 2005.

Nicholson, Kate. "Fuglsig Lets the Balls Fly for Sony Bravia TV Ad." *Campaign,* November 4, 2005.

Palmer, Jay. "Sony's Brighter Picture." *Barron's,* January 23, 2006.

Pfanner, Eric. "On Advertising: Sony Tries to Show It Has 'Bounce.'" *International Herald Tribune,* October 30, 2005.

Shannon, Victoria. "Sony Looking to Add Glitter in Europe." *International Herald Tribune,* April 15, 2005.

"Sony Announcing Turnaround Strategy." *Associated Press,* September 21, 2005.

Van Grinsven, Lucas. "Reuters Summit—Sony Targets 20 Pct of European LCD TV Market." *Reuters,* March 1, 2006.

Mark Lane

Sony Corporation of America

550 Madison Ave.
New York, New York 10022
USA
Telephone: (212) 833-6800
Fax: (212) 833-6956
Web site: www.sony.com

WHAT'S NEXT? CAMPAIGN

OVERVIEW

At least four factors converged to make April 1997 the time for Sony Corporation of America to introduce a new brand-advertising campaign. Sony knew that as electronic technology continued its rapid pace of change the importance of a strong brand name would increase. Companies built around a product today might be unknown tomorrow if technology made that product or its category obsolete. A second factor was that Sony stood poised to unleash several major new digital products. This change would bring Sony into competition with new, powerful Internet and computer companies with high name recognition and vast resources of their own. Thirdly, Sony was better known among baby boomers than with younger generations. It wanted to groom its future customers for a lifetime relationship with Sony. A fourth factor was the desire to capitalize on a Sony strength while humanizing it. For 50 years Sony was a leading innovator in consumer electronics—a history of accomplishment worthy of being touted—but not without stressing the importance of people.

The "What's Next?" campaign broke in the April 14, 1997, issue of *U.S. News and World Report.* Lowe & Partners/SMS of New York created the print campaign, its first major effort for Sony after winning the $50 million account two years earlier. The six double-page print ads all featured black-and-white photography of children. Copy was minimal. Each ad closed with a chronological list of four electronics products followed by the phrase "What's next?" and the Sony name. Industry sources listed the budget as $10 to $15 million.

One ad featured a young child, wading in waist-high water, peering down into the water. Six short lines of small copy read: "He doesn't know what a phonograph is. He's never heard of 8-track. The only time he saw an LP was in his grandparents' attic. CDs and diskettes are his parents' toys. What will be his?" In one small line below were the words "Walkman Home VCR CD Digital Satellite System What's next? Sony." A second ad showed two bare-chested boys standing back to back as they glared out at the reader. The four lines of copy read: "Their grandfathers fought over toy trucks. Their fathers fought over electric trains. They fight over the remote. What will their kids fight over?" Small type below continued, "Transistor Radio Trinitron Home VCR Digital Satellite System What's Next? Sony." A third in the series showed three girls sitting on a stone wall with their backs to the viewer and their arms around each other. Among the banks of billowing clouds that composed most of the ad, the copy read: "Their grandparents used letters to share a funny story. Their parents used a wire to confess an intimate thought. They use a cell phone to reveal a piece of gossip. What will their kids use to make each other smile?"

"What's Next?" was unusual in that most Sony advertising was product-specific. It also was the first time Sony tied brand and product advertising together. Each double-page ad led into a third full-page, product-specific ad. According to Patrick Flaherty, Sony Electronics senior vice president of marketing services, this technique allowed Sony to not only raise an important question but also to supply the answer. The third product page was continually updated with new products like Sony's WebTV Internet terminal. Gary Goldsmith led the creative team, while Dean Hacohen wrote the copy.

HISTORICAL CONTEXT

The company founders combined two words to come up with the word "Sony," which means a very small group of people with the energy and passion for unlimited creation. Sony Corporation of America was a subsidiary of Sony Corporation of Tokyo. Engineer Masaru Ibuka and physicist Akio Morita formed Sony on May 7, 1946, to develop and produce communications equipment. Soon the company began a history of making electronic breakthroughs. In 1950 it introduced Japan's first tape recorder. Five years later the company brought Japan's first transistor radio to market. The world's first transistor TV was a 1960 Sony breakthrough. Other innovations have included the 3/4-inch U-matic VCR, 1974; the Walkman headphone stereo, 1979; compact-disc player and Watchman television, 1982; 36-inch color HDTV for home use, 1990; and the MiniDisc system, 1992.

Few other companies metamorphosed as often as Sony. The company frequently transformed itself through one of its new, instantly popular products. Examples included the transistor radio, the Walkman, the camcorder, and the PlayStation. Part of the reason for the changes at Sony was the markets it served. Consumer electronics advanced quickly. To stay a viable business, manufacturers had to keep pace with the technology or die. In the 1960s the company's main product was the transistor radio. The next profit driver for Sony became the small television. After that came tape recorders, then VCRs, and compact discs. Every five to seven years Sony had a new core product. By 1998 the PlayStation had taken center stage at Sony. In one week of December 1998 Sony sold 4 million PlayStations in the United States. From 1995 through 1998 Sony sold more than 50 million PlayStations. The product was so key to company success that Sony announced a $100 million marketing campaign to tout PlayStation and its software in June 1997. It was the largest marketing campaign ever for both Sony and the video-game industry.

Along with its success Sony did hit some bumps in the road. Some innovations, like the Betamax VCR, never delivered on their promise. When Nobuyuki Idei took the reins as Sony president in 1995 times were difficult. Sony had recently made the strategically sensible but badly executed purchase of the Hollywood movie studios Columbia and Tristar Pictures. Sony's music division, by then the world's fourth largest record company, fell out of the music industry's good graces after a public battle with one of its leading artists, George Michael. Idei himself was an unusual choice for Sony's top spot. He had worked for Sony since 1960, but he ascended through the ranks on the marketing side, not the technological side, which had always been the pride of the company. Idei recognized the importance of the U.S. market and set about westernizing the company. He hired outsiders for several key spots. He also changed the company mindset and focus. Previously Sony described itself as a consumer electronics company or an entertainment company. In 1998 Idei said the company would be a digital entertainment company supplying both technology and software.

Sony was now one of the world's largest entertainment and electronics companies and the world's thirtieth largest corporation. Sony Electronics, the division "What's Next?" was created for, generated more than a fifth of the Sony Corporation's global sales. In fiscal year 1996 Sony Electronics had revenues of $9.6 billion, while total Sony revenues reached $43.0 billion. The company had divisions focused on music, movies, computer entertainment, electronics, and online entertainment. It also entered into the life insurance business.

TARGET MARKET

"What's Next?" was designed with opinion leaders, early adopters, and technologically advanced families in mind. Sony wanted to hit consumers age 25 to 54 through publications including *Time, Forbes, Scientific American,* the *Smithsonian,* the *New York Times Magazine,* the *New Yorker, U.S. News & World Report,* and *Wired.* The company wanted high recognition among those consumers most likely to enthusiastically embrace new developments in digital convergence technologies like WebTV and digital cameras. Part of the rationale was that many of these consumers also made technology-buying decisions in the workplace.

COMPETITION

Although Sony was the largest consumer electronics company in U.S. sales and market share, it ranked second worldwide behind Matsushita, a $60.0 billion revenue company in 1998. An important part of Matsushita's empire in America, Panasonic, was one of the most recognized names in consumer electronics and a leader in VCRs, color televisions, and personal stereos. Toshiba America, a $6.2 billion diversified electronics and

WHAT ELSE IS NEXT?

About the same time that "What's Next?" ran, Sony Corporation of America conducted several other major advertising campaigns. On February 5, 1998, during NBC's top-rated Thursday night prime-time lineup the company launched "Make It With MD," a $35 million campaign for MiniDisc, a tool that made digital personal recordings. The campaign targeted adult music enthusiasts age 20 to 35. In June of that year Sony announced an advertising and marketing campaign for Metal Gear Solid, a product made by its strategic partner, Konami of America, and available exclusively on Sony PlayStations. Young & Rubicam developed a 60-second television spot in the fall of 1998 that tried to develop an image for Sony that would unify its electronics and entertainment business segments. That spot showed an egg that falls off a truck and picks up colors as it rolls across a sidewalk chalk drawing, a road's yellow lines, and flower petals. Now with a Faberge-like look, the egg is discovered outside Christie's auction house by a young girl who auctions it and reaps millions. A tagline at the spot's end read, "Do you dream in Sony?"

high-technology company with 10,000 U.S. employees, was a leader in the retail notebook-computer market and part of the worldwide Toshiba Corporation, a $54.0 billion revenue, 190,000 employee giant. Electronics rival Pioneer could closely match Sony's history of innovation. It offered products that often led their categories in the 1970s and early 1980s. Then Pioneer fell behind Sony with less-than-average marketing efforts. In 1998 Pioneer announced a seven-year goal to use digital technology to double the company's size. It updated its 30-year-old logo and said advertising and sponsorship spending would be greatly increased.

But "What's Next?" viewed companies other than those traditional rivals as the main competition. Sony saw its core consumer electronics industry blending into other industries. Traditional consumer electronics companies began bumping into companies in the computer, communications, or entertainment businesses. For example, Sony's then up-and-coming PlayStation II was billed as a new kind of computer. "As we're moving into this digital world you've got companies like Microsoft already ingrained as your top of mind, high-technology companies. Companies like Sony that used to occupy that space are drifting into the past," said Gary Goldsmith, vice chairman and executive creative director at Lowe & Partners.

So once again in 1997 Sony shifted its product focus. It announced cutbacks in some traditional businesses such as TVs, video players, and hi-fis and high concentration in the new digital markets for products like DVD audiovisual systems. Sony also set the stage to market its Emotion Engine chip, a computer chip it claimed was three times faster than Intel's Pentium III processor. The Emotion Engine chip would serve as the foundation for Sony's next generation of products.

MARKETING STRATEGY

Although baby boomers fondly thought of Sony as an innovative producer of quality products like the Walkman, younger people did not have the same attachment. The oldest baby boomers were in their early 50s by 1998, and Sony did not want its image to age along with them. Many in the younger crowd did not remember the days before compact discs or other recent innovations. Sony was ready to introduce new products like digital video and audio disc players, more advanced video games, and high-definition televisions. The company wanted to capture the attention of these up-and-coming consumers. Sony also wanted to build on its strength—a long history of electronic product innovation. To meet these objectives each "What's Next?" execution carefully blended nostalgia with a glimpse of the future.

Beyond the advertising, Sony learned marketing lessons from the eyebrow-raising successes of several new high-flying technology and Internet companies. Idei became convinced that his company had to change and adapt to the merging worlds of consumer electronics, computing, and the Internet. He wanted the company to behave more like a Silicon Valley company—quick, aggressive, and prominent on the Internet. Some of the growth and success these companies achieved came from good marketing and advertising. The "Intel Inside" brand-marketing campaign helped Intel move from 20 percent name recognition among home computer buyers in 1992 to 80 percent by 1996.

Idei believed breakthrough technology alone was not enough. A strong brand name had always helped retain customers and boost credibility when a company introduced a new product or entered a new market. Idei also saw how strong brand names helped build America Online and Yahoo! Sony, a company that had shunned image campaigns for many years, recognized that with the ever-increasing speed of product obsolescence, a strong brand would be one of the company's most vital attributes.

Lowe & Partners built "What's Next?" to not only popularize the Sony brand name, but also to humanize the company. It wanted to package the technology and innovation Sony was known for with a human, emotional face. Sony's competition tended to focus on "bits and bytes and zip and zap aspects of technology," according to Goldsmith. "We really wanted to find shots that captured the emotion," he told *Advertising Age.* "The idea was to . . . really go in the opposite direction and not talk about technology but bring the human aspect into it." The campaign aimed to demonstrate Sony's 50-year history of innovation while focusing on how that innovation affected people's lives. Showcasing children was seen as a good way to represent the future.

OUTCOME

Communication Arts selected "What's Next?" as one of the best consumer magazine ad series of the year. Other honors bestowed on ads in the campaign included a Gold Pencil at the One Show; a 1998 Andy Award for magazine advertising; Best of New York 1998 Addy Awards for print, posters, and a magazine campaign; and two 1998 Addy Citations. The print ads got such a strong reaction that Lowe & Partners created a television spot on spec that test-marketed well in Wisconsin. However, by 1999 Sony had switched advertising agencies so the campaign ended after about a 12-month run.

As with any brand-image campaign, Sony's internal audience was important. The company did embrace "What's Next?" In November 1997 giant versions of the ads were wrapped around Sony's 550 Madison Avenue building in Manhattan. And Sony turned the ads into posters and other types of collateral.

In a large global company like Sony, the effect of a single campaign running in one country for less than a year was difficult to measure. Fiscal-year sales for Sony's electronics business declined worldwide about 3 percent in 1998–99, but Sony attributed the decline to intensified price competition and sluggish non-U.S. sales. In the video category revenues jumped 11.3 percent as sales of home-use camcorders, digital still cameras, and DVD players grew mainly in the United States and western Europe.

FURTHER READING

Comiteau, Jennifer. "Sony Says Bye to 'Bits and Bytes'; Lowe's New Print Ads Give the Technology an Emotional Content." *Adweek* (Eastern Edition), April 7, 1997.

Nakache, Patricia. "Secrets of the New Brand Builders." *Fortune,* June 22, 1998, p. 167.

Nisse, Jason. "Sony Enters Next Generation." *The Times* (London) (Business Section), March 13, 1999.

Ono, Yumiko,"Sony, in Bid to Woo the Young, Launches Global Image Campaign." *Wall Street Journal,* August 14, 1997, p. B8.

Schlender, Brent. "Sony's New Game: Idei's Silicon Valley Makeover." *Fortune,* April 12, 1999, p. 30.

Chris John Amorosino

Southwest Airlines Company

2702 Love Field Drive
Dallas, Texas 75235
USA
Telephone: (214) 792-4000
Fax: (214) 792-5015
Web site: www.southwest.com

MUST BE FOOTBALL SEASON CAMPAIGN

OVERVIEW

Southwest Airlines Company began as a carrier connecting the Texas cities of Dallas, Houston, and San Antonio and remained a regional airline for nearly two decades before taking its short-haul, small-airport, ticketless model across the country. In doing so it changed the airline industry, forcing full-service carriers to match its low fares even though they could not afford to do so. As Southwest expanded in the 1990s, so did its advertising budget. Having begun full-scale national branding work in 1996, Southwest became a National Football League (NFL) sponsor in 1997. Always known for its offbeat, down-to-earth brand image, Southwest and its agency, GSD&M of Austin, Texas, crafted a series of humorous football-themed ads to be aired during national telecasts of NFL games.

The campaign, the first-year budget of which was estimated at $30 million, was called "Must Be Football Season." It ran for three football seasons, starting in the fall of 1998. Four new 15-second spots were created in the first two seasons, and the third season consisted of a best-of selection of the previous eight spots. Taking the idea of fanaticism to comic extremes, the spots featured fans, usually women, whose enthusiasm for the sport led them to reproduce football behavior in everyday settings. One spot, for instance, showed women piling on an errant watermelon in a grocery store, while another featured a woman crouching in a quarterback's stance behind a man bent over to retrieve something from the floor of a movie-theater lobby.

"Must Be Football Season" was highly popular with football fans, generating more talk value, according to GSD&M, than any campaign the agency had produced in its 18-year relationship with Southwest. After discontinuing the campaign Southwest expanded its strategy of sports sponsorships and related advertising with a similar National Hockey League agreement. As the rest of the airline industry struggled, Southwest continued to expand, remaining profitable through some of the toughest times the industry had ever seen.

HISTORICAL CONTEXT

Started by Texas businessman Rollin King and his lawyer Herb Kelleher as a carrier linking the cities of Dallas, Houston, and San Antonio, Southwest Airlines began flying out of Dallas's Love Field in 1971. "Love" became the centerpiece of the company's initial ad campaigns, and the airline continued to fly out of Love Field even as most of its competitors moved to the Dallas/Fort Worth International Airport. Southwest remained a regional carrier throughout its first two decades, but it expanded rapidly in the 1990s. By focusing on short flights and small airports, reducing turnaround time on the ground,

Two women pounce on a fumbled watermelon in Southwest Airlines's "Must Be Football Season" television campaign. PHOTO COURTESY OF GSD & M.

flying only one type of plane (the Boeing 737), and offering a single class of unassigned seats, Southwest was able to keep its overheard lower than other airlines. Southwest was known among consumers for its friendly service, its casual atmosphere, and, especially, its low fares. As it established nationwide service, it transformed the airline industry, spawning a host of low-fare imitators and forcing the major full-service carriers to match Southwest fare prices despite their much higher operational costs.

In 1996 Southwest, then the country's seventh-largest carrier, began diverting a significant portion of its advertising resources away from its bread-and-butter strategy—running local advertisements about fares—and into national branding campaigns. Consolidating its accounts with GSD&M of Austin, Texas, its primary agency since 1980, Southwest launched the "Symbol of Freedom" campaign, intended to build brand loyalty over time while fare ads helped to keep seats full in the short term. Because of Southwest's rapid expansion in the 1990s, a rare feat among airlines at that time, its advertising budget grew accordingly, surpassing that of any carrier in the industry. Midway through the 1997 NFL football season Southwest enhanced its marketing profile by signing a sponsorship agreement with the league. In the fall of 1998, in concert not only with fare-oriented marketing but also with its other ongoing branding spots, Southwest prepared a major advertising push, leveraging its status as an NFL sponsor and the "Official Airline of the Super Bowl."

TARGET MARKET

Southwest had always prided itself on its divergence from industry norms and on its friendly, no-frills image. As a GSD&M spokesman put it, "They take their business, but not themselves, seriously." Southwest advertising had historically supported this fun, quirky brand image, and "It Must Be Football Season" extended this message to a new national audience, relying on comedy to forge a connection with viewers. Each spot featured fans, most of whom were women, going to humorous extremes of football-related excitement in incongruous everyday settings.

Southwest's heavy commitment to sports sponsorships and sports-programming ad buys was a means, in the airline's view, of establishing a personal connection with consumers. "Generally, people are passionate about sports, and we hope they transfer some of that passion to us because we're associated with something that they love," Christy Hall, senior manager for sports and licensing at Southwest, told *Advertising Age.* With its NFL sponsorship Southwest was able to target a predominantly adult-male audience and hence to communicate its brand message to a large number of business travelers. The fact that the commercials featured women allowed for a greater sense of comic surprise given the

HOCKEY IN TEXAS, SOUTHWEST IN THE NORTHEAST

Southwest had long been a sponsor of sports teams in the local markets it serviced, and its National Football League sponsorship was several years old in 2000, when the airline inked a deal with the National Hockey League (NHL). The agreement gave Southwest the chance to spread brand recognition by running commercials during NHL games, by occupying billboard space around rinks in prime camera-coverage spots, and by linking the Southwest name with the "GoalCam" responsible for rink-level shots during telecasts. Odd though it may have sounded for a Texas-based company to establish a relationship with the most northern of North American sports, it made sense for at least two reasons. First, Southwest was in the process of expanding into lucrative Northeastern markets; and second, the NHL was expanding into the Southern states. In fact, at the time of the sponsorship agreement, 7 of Southwest's 10 biggest markets had NHL teams.

football-oriented antics on display, but Southwest also believed that the airline potentially served 5 percent to 7 percent more women than other airlines. Further, national sports sponsorships and advertising made sense for a growing airline like Southwest because they reinforced brand recognition in current markets while laying the groundwork for entry into new markets.

COMPETITION

UAL Corp.'s United Airlines, the number two carrier during this time, had recently changed advertising agencies, as well as its long-running tagline "Fly the Friendly Skies." In May 1997 United launched a major new branding campaign called "Rising," conceived by its new agency, Fallon McElligot. Breaking with industry tradition, "Rising" acknowledged many of the complaints consumers had about air travel and indicated that United, alone among carriers, was intent on correcting these problems and moving in a new direction. In one spot, for instance, recreated footage of the Wright brothers' first flight was shown, while on the soundtrack a contemporary airport's public-address system informed travelers of flight cancellations. "If Orville and Wilbur had to go through what you do just to fly," the voice-over intones, "they would have stayed in the bicycle business." In 1998 United extended "Rising" beyond a critique of current problems and began to use it to show evidence of the changes the airline was making to improve the flying experience.

Delta Air Lines, Inc., was number three in the airline wars, and it used the tagline "On Top of the World" in a branding campaign that broke almost simultaneously with the United "Rising" ads. In stark contrast to United's admission of difficulties, Delta and its agency, Saatchi & Saatchi, used dream scenarios in which passengers had a whole jetliner to themselves and were being extravagantly pampered by a staff of professionals. When the dreamers awoke to find themselves in business class on a Delta transatlantic flight, they were not disappointed by the reality of their comfort level.

AMR Corp.'s American Airlines, the world's number one airline and Southwest's hometown rival, in 1997 ran a local advertising campaign criticizing a change in federal law that, by allowing more flights at Love Field (and thereby benefiting Southwest), threatened to weaken Dallas/Fort Worth airport, American's hub. The campaign was pulled in 1998 over fears that it might be hurting the airline's image. In 1998 American spent an estimated $10 million on advertising in the New York area, offering itself as "New York's bridge to the world." The campaign was quickly answered by a New York–focused Delta campaign. In 2000 American unveiled national branding work touting its additional room in coach and business class.

MARKETING STRATEGY

Created by GSD&M, the "Must Be Football Season" commercials ran during the 1998–1999, 1999–2000, and 2000–2001 NFL football seasons on national television broadcasts of games on CBS, ABC, Fox, and ESPN. An NFL sponsor and the "Official Airline of the Super Bowl," Southwest wanted the spots to be "on every game people see," according to company executive Joyce Rogge. GSD&M produced four 15-second spots in each of the first two seasons of the campaign's run. In the second season the new creative was supplemented by two reruns from the season before, and in the third season, rather than budget for new creative, Southwest reran selected spots from the previous two seasons.

"Must Be Football Season" was built on the common notion of people becoming fanatical about football with the season's arrival each fall. By acknowledging this experience, GSD&M's Brian Brooker told *Advertising Age,* "[We] hope that we've tapped into the mindset of the fan and that would rub off on Southwest." The agency appealed to the fan's frame of mind by taking the phenomenon to comic extremes, by playing against stereotypes through the use of female characters, and by using ordinary life as a springboard for the overt absurdity of the characters' behavior. "We tried to find everyday situations that would not telegraph the football scenario that was coming," Brooker explained to *Adweek,* "so it would be a real rewarding surprise for the viewer."

Using "Must Be Football Season" as a tagline, the campaign's first season, with an estimated $30 million price tag, included spots featuring female grocery shoppers piling onto a dropped watermelon, two businesswomen head-butting each other in preparation for an office conference, and two wedding ushers emptying the contents of a punch bowl over the heads of a just-married couple. The concept and execution of the spots remained the same in the campaign's second season, with spots including one in which a woman leaving a crowded shop ran and spiked a crystal vase; one in which a woman in a movie-theater line assumed the quarterback stance behind a man who had bent over to pick something up off the floor; and one in which a woman in a shoe store, seeing a salesman holding a shoe for another customer, dashed up and kicked it, as though for a field goal. An additional element appeared during the campaign's second season as well. At the end of games, 15-second commercials with the tag "The game is now over" ran, offering advice such as, "The game is over. Wipe the buffalo wings off your chin," and "The game is over. You can stop yelling at the TV." Because Southwest believed that the first two seasons' spots still resonated with viewers, and because of cost considerations stemming from rising jet-fuel prices and an actors' strike, the third season consisted of a mix of spots from seasons one and two. Southwest renewed its NFL sponsorship prior to the campaign's third season.

OUTCOME

"Must Be Football Season" was an immediate hit with viewers. Audrey Moss, GSD&M account supervisor for Southwest, told *Adweek,* "We've had this account for 18 years and we've never had anything this successful in terms of talk value. The reaction was just phenomenal." Some commentators, however, such as *Advertising Age* columnist Bob Garfield, questioned the value of a campaign that, while entertaining, had little to do with the airline itself. Southwest continued to emphasize sports sponsorships on both the local and the national level, bolstering its NFL deal with a similar NHL agreement and a corresponding media buy.

Southwest continued to expand its fleet and geographical range during the years that "Must Be Football Season" ran. It initiated transcontinental flights in 1998 and continued to expand its East Coast presence in 1999. It placed its largest-ever order for jets in 2000. Southwest remained profitable and even expanded its operations during the years following the terrorist attacks of September 11, 2001, which decimated the industry and forced other airlines to file for bankruptcy.

FURTHER READING

Beirne, Mike. "American Air Stretches Its Legs, Seats." *Brandweek,* June 26, 2000.

Ebenkamp, Becky. "Southwest Airlines." *Brandweek,* March 24, 1997.

Garfield, Bob. "New Delta Ads Can't Stay Aloft; United 'Rising' Hinges on Service." *Advertising Age,* May 26, 1997.

———. "Punting Brand Mention a Funny Waste of Money." *Advertising Age,* October 4, 1999.

Goetzl, David. "Southwest Works Up NHL Ad Effort." *Advertising Age,* August 28, 2000.

Goetzl, David, and Laura Petrecca. "Southwest Airlines Signs Up for 3-Year NFL Sponsorship." *Advertising Age,* July 17, 2000.

Hill, J. Dee. "Southwest Looks for More Grid Fame." *Adweek,* September 13, 1999.

Krajewski, Steve. "Account Tree." *Adweek* (western ed.), March 17, 1997.

Martin, Ellen Rooney, and Michael McCarthy. "New Delta and United Ads Take Flight, Target Business Travelers." *Adweek,* May 5, 1997.

"NFL Signs Southwest for Airline Sponsorship." *Advertising Age,* November 3, 1997.

Wilke, Michael. "Southwest May Shift More Spending to Nat'l." *Advertising Age,* March 10, 1997.

———. "Southwest Ties $30 Mil Effort to NFL." *Advertising Age,* August 31, 1998.

Mark Lane

Specialized Bicycle Components Inc.

15130 Concord Circle
Morgan Hill, California 95037-5428
USA
Telephone: (408) 779-6229
Fax: (408) 779-1631
Web site: www.specialized.com

■■■

SPECIALIZED CAMPAIGN

OVERVIEW

One of the originators of the mountain bike, Specialized Bicycle Components Inc. continued to excel in that bike niche with a combination of frequent innovation, deep devotion to biking, and award-winning advertising. The "Specialized" campaign reflected the frenzied dedication that its target market exhibited for the sport of mountain biking. With a stylized clean look and humor, the ads showcased the benefits of Specialized products and sounded as if the bikers themselves had written them.

One ad introducing a full-suspension bicycle featured an image of a biker navigating a steep mountain grade, and that was accompanied by a single line of small copy: "Mountains should take millions of years to form. Not climb." The name "Specialized" appeared on the bike but only the company's stylized "S" logo served as a signature. In another ad an intense biker sped down a steep S-curved hill. The copy read: "The unmatched cornering, durability and speed of the 1998 Turbo Tire. It'll make the hair on the back of your neck stand up, unless you've already shaved that too." A third ad looked ancient and stained. The headline dominated: "In 1974, Mountain Biking Was in Our Blood. Along with a Lot of Other Crap." The ad included dated photos, an old schematic drawing of a bike, and the body copy: "We started building mountain bikes over 20 years ago. Back when all we had was a love for riding, a desire to build a better bike, and, well, a lot of other stuff we can't seem to remember."

Creators of the 1996–98 campaign, Butler, Shine & Stern of Sausalito, California, placed the bulk of this all-print campaign in bike-enthusiast magazines like *Bicycling, Mountain Bike,* and *Bike.* Some ads ran in active lifestyle publications like *Men's Journal.*

HISTORICAL CONTEXT

In the early 1970s an unreliable van caused Specialized founder Mike Sinyard to start commuting by bike from his trailer home to San Jose State University. After graduation Sinyard sold the van for $1,500 and took a bike tour of Europe. He bought bike components from several manufacturers of Italy's classic touring and racing bikes. Sinyard reasoned that his $1,100 investment in chains, handlebars, stems, and other components would sell fast back home because parts for high-end 10-speed bikes were in short supply. With a handwritten catalog he did sell out quickly to local bike shop owners, but then he wanted to continue along the same business path.

Sinyard got dealers and customers to pay upfront for their next order and he restocked. In 1974 he officially founded Specialized. A few years later, when he became uneasy about only selling other manufacturers' wares, he began designing his own bike components. The first, born in 1978, was a durable, high-performance tire Sinyard named the Turbo. Specialized sales jumped. But the company's biggest early breakthrough came in 1981 when it introduced the "Stumpjumper," the world's first production mountain bike. This hybrid of the lightweight 10-speed and the durable, wide-tire, no-frills bikes of Sinyard's childhood later swept the country. By 1994 mountain bikes made up 64 percent of all bike sales. An original Stumpjumper was enshrined in the Smithsonian Institution in Washington, D.C.

In 1985 the company created the first professional mountain-bike racing team. In a joint venture with DuPont, Specialized introduced the three-spoke composite wheel in 1989. Other innovations like metal-matrix composite technology for bikes, lighter helmets, advanced full suspension, and extruded-frame technology followed.

TARGET MARKET

Buying a bike changed in the 1970s. Consumers used to have three or four choices, much like buying a major appliance. The number of different makes, models, designs, and companies exploded in the late 1970s and 1980s. By the 1990s serious bikers had a wide array of expensive high-performing alternatives. Many bikers started with a good off-the-rack model from Trek, GT, or Specialized. The serious rider would then purchase new parts so that after a while the entire bike might be different from the one originally purchased. Hundreds of bike component manufacturers lifted technology and manpower from defense contractors and learned to use exotic materials and $100,000 milling machines to design parts. In this environment Specialized appealed to the most serious of bikers.

Specialized promoted itself as a company full of bike fanatics and a company for bike fanatics. Its advertising targeted mountain-bike enthusiasts and opinion leaders. The company wanted to reach those people most likely to buy new mountain bike products and those who set the stage for trends. To some degree the campaign targeted bike dealers because they often made recommendations to potential bike buyers.

The profile of the Specialized target market was at least as psychographic as it was demographic. Specialized aimed to attract people who biked three to four days a week and spent a lot of their free time immersed in the sport of mountain biking. Often they were experienced mountain bikers between 20 and 40 years old. The average age of Specialized's buyers in 1998 was about 35. The profile skewed toward males and toward people in the Western states where mountain biking was more popular.

Although Specialized priced bikes as low as $400 to $500, its advertising and marketing efforts went more into its higher-end $3,000 bikes. That's where the influencers or enthusiasts bought. "If we sell to them they will spread the word about the Specialized brand," said Chip Smith, Specialized's advertising manager.

THE ANGLE ON BODY GEOMETRY

Sales of Specialized's impotence-fighting Body Geometry seat were boosted by an eye-catching poster featuring President Bill Clinton. The poster showed the president's head superimposed on the body of a muscular, much younger cyclist carrying a bicycle equipped with the seat. The copy read: "The new Body Geometry saddle was medically designed and tested to eliminate numbness while still providing support. You go all day.... And you go all night." Earlier in the 1990s a Specialized ad put Mikhail Gorbachev, then leader of the U.S.S.R., on a Specialized road bike and stylized the birthmark on his forehead to resemble the Specialized logo.

COMPETITION

Specialized competed with companies like Trek, Cannondale, and GT in the mountain-bike category. Cannondale began in 1971 when it introduced the cycling industry's first bicycle trailer. The company produced its first bike in 1983, an aluminum model in an industry then dominated by steel. In 1998 Cannondale, with a reputation for innovation, was the leading manufacturer of aluminum bicycles and tallied $171 million in total sales. Trek often used the line, "your source for the ultimate cycling experience." Begun in a Wisconsin barn in 1976 the company grew into a mountain-bike leader and boasted of its own advanced technology and innovation. In June of 1998 the makers of Schwinn bikes bought GT Bicycles of Santa Ana, California, for $78.6 million, instantly creating one of the world's largest bike manufacturers. The company boasted annual sales of $400 million. In an article in the *Los Angeles Times* the executive director of the National Bicycle Association called it a powerful combination that Trek, the number-one company selling through bicycle shops, would not have an easy time overcoming. GT led the industry in BMX bikes with 40 percent of the market. Schwinn had long-term brand awareness and a strong share of sales in the $200 to $400 range.

MARKETING STRATEGY

When Butler, Shine & Stern reviewed the competition it concluded that everyone was claiming authenticity. Authenticity in the mountain-bike category should belong to Specialized, the agency felt, because Specialized's roots went back to the foundation of the sport, and the company was still a leader and innovator. Many of the company's ads pointed to its role in founding the mountain-bike category and its technological innovations, like the Body Geometry saddle. "We wanted to take advantage of their heritage and proclaim loudly that this is the originator; they're still on top as an innovator in terms of technology and bike design and therefore this is the bike you should consider," said Greg Stern, an agency principal.

To demonstrate serious dedication to mountain biking, Specialized took an active stand in resolving trail disputes among bikers, hikers, and equestrians. It contributed financially to the International Mountain Biking Association, an advocacy group, and for several years was one of only two companies with a full-time advocacy coordinator on staff. Specialized also supported the Bikes Belong Coalition, a national lobbying group.

Another important component of the marketing strategy was the professional bike team. The company felt that unique personalities like cyclist Shawn Palmer added allure to the Mountain Dew/Specialized bike team and to the company. Palmer was a five-time world snowboard champion who decided to take up downhill mountain biking and earned the world's second ranking in his first full year in the sport. *People, GQ* and *USA Today* all published features on Palmer. "He's a real character, a real personality with a lot of tattoos and he gets a lot of attention," Smith said. Another Specialized team member, Bart Brentjens, won the first gold medal for mountain biking at the 1996 summer Olympic Games in Atlanta. The media exposure Specialized received from such big-name professional bike athletes, in addition to the cyclists' input on product innovations, contributed substantially to the company's success.

When Brentjens and Palmer joined the team a full-page print ad fashioned to look like a birth announcement appeared in trade journals. The copy proudly announced the bikers' weight and length while directing readers to go to the Specialized website to see for themselves "how our sweaty little bundles of joy are doing." A teddy bear riding a tricycle with "Specialized" on the frame and wearing a bib with the company logo smiled and waved at the reader.

Specialized also fostered a quality look and image in its advertising by using a visually rich, copy-sparse approach. Ads were designed to be clean and stylized. For the 1998–99 ads Specialized took this concept one step further. The ads showed the company's website address, often directing readers to a specific address relating to the particular bike or other product being promoted. Readers who typed in the address in the ad for the Specialized helmet found themselves not at a home page but at a page devoted to that helmet.

Certain touches to the ads—such as not signing off with a large company name, address, and logo—kept the layouts clean. Some ads did not use the company name, relying instead on the simple logo to communicate the company's identity. Phone numbers and addresses did not appear. When the website address appeared it was always in tiny type. The visual, often a bike and rider in the heat of action, dominated. Sometimes the word "Specialized," while not in the copy, appeared in the visual—on a tire or another bike part. Smith also said that within the mountain-bike community the stylized "S" logo had recognition similar to the Nike "swoosh" logo. Repeating the company name was not deemed necessary in the United States while it did appear in the ads used in Europe.

The ads tried to capture a humorous, fanatical attitude—the same 110 percent-devoted attitude that the target audience expressed for its sport. "After all, when you've been riding as long as we have, you tend to have something to show for it. Besides missing teeth," read copy in one ad. For a Specialized helmet the copy read, "Good News: The New Air Cobra Lets You Crash Into Stuff With Less Wind Resistance, Lighter Weight, And A Cooler Scalp."

The "Specialized" campaign served a dual purpose, Stern said. It was used to introduce new products (bikes and bike equipment such as helmets and shoes) and to build the company's image. "We tried to create a brand image that took advantage of their history and authenticity within the sport," Stern said. One example of brand building was a 1997 ad announcing the fact that a Specialized bike was part of the Smithsonian collection: "Some Bikes Are Stored In the Garage. Some Bikes Are Stored In The Smithsonian." Another image ads featured one of the company's professional riders. An ad picturing Ned Overend used this headline: "Now You Too Can Wear Ned's Shoe. A New One, We Mean. Not An Old One. (That Would Be Gross.)"

To portray the right personality and style in the ads, Butler, Shine & Stern went directly to the target audience: The agency attended bike races. Staffers would travel up a local mountain with a video camera, ads, and water. They would stop bikers to ask for feedback on the ads, Specialized, and mountain biking.

OUTCOME

The Butler, Shine & Stern campaign won several awards, including several merit awards in the One Show. Ads were also finalists for the Prints Sports and Entertainment Award and the Kelly Award.

In the 1996-97 bike-sales season, Specialized sales went down, partially because of a recall that hurt the brand image. In 1998 the company had a stronger product, the FSR XC, the lightest dual-suspension cross-country bike. *USA Today* named it one of the hottest models of the year. The FSR XC and the new advertising both contributed to a substantial sales increase, according to Smith. "In a declining market we've taken market share away from the competition in 1999," he said in July 1999. "For this year we're ahead a little over 20 percent."

FURTHER READING

Holzinger, Albert G. "A Cyclist Who's Riding High," *Nation's Business,* August 1992, p. 16.

Ruibal, Sal. "Happy Trails: New Bikes Enflame Passions." *USA Today,* September 25, 1998, p. 20C.

———. "Bike Seat Offers Help For Unspoken Problem." *USA Today,* December 10, 1998, p. 9C.

Chris John Amorosino

Sprint Nextel Corporation

2001 Edmund Halley Dr.
Reston, Virginia 20191
USA
Telephone: (703) 433-4000
Web site: www.sprint.com

■■■

DIME ZONE CAMPAIGN

OVERVIEW

NOTE: Since the initial appearance of this essay in the 1998 edition of *Major Marketing Campaigns Annual,* the Sprint Corporation merged with Nextel to become Sprint Nextel. The essay continues to refer to the company's former name, as that was the official name of the organization when the campaign was launched.

It was in 1995 that Sprint Corporation launched its national "Sprint Sense," an advertising and marketing campaign to sell long-distance phone service. The idea behind "Sprint Sense" was simplicity for the customer: give consumers one flat long-distance rate to anyplace they called during evenings and weekends. This flat rate—one dime for one minute—became known as "Sprint Sense," an umbrella term for the company's flat-rate long-distance calling product and used the tag line "It All Makes Sense." According to Sprint, the flat rate revolutionized long-distance calling with an easy-to-understand pricing system that people loved. The 1995 "Sprint Sense" campaign, handled by J. Walter Thompson of San Francisco, introduced Candice Bergen as Sprint's spokesperson. The following year, in 1996, the "Dime Lady" campaign featured Bergen assuring consumers that it was indeed "one minute, one dime, no kidding."

Selling long-distance phone service to the public with flat-rate pricing paid off for Sprint. A customer satisfaction survey released by J. D. Power & Associates in August 1996 showed Sprint to be number one in customer satisfaction, with AT&T second and MCI third. In 1995, the first year of the survey, Sprint had been number one with high-volume users, but it trailed AT&T with the 80 percent who spent less than $50 a month on calls. In the second year of the poll, however, Sprint beat AT&T, its main competitor, and MCI in all categories.

"Sprint Sense" introduced a new campaign in 1997, the "Dime Zone," which premiered on May 5. This campaign promoted the dime zone as the time people called long distance the most—nights and weekends—and featured three new commercials. The first two spots advertised Sprint's dime-a-minute rate for long-distance calling, and the third added another product, Sprint's $10-a-month pager. The campaign, which showed people finding a dime and then being whisked away to a place where everything went their way, did not, however, prove to be popular with consumers in *USA Today* 's 1997 Ad Track survey. Only 9 percent of those polled liked the "Dime Zone" ads "a lot," while 23 percent disliked them. Nonetheless, the same poll showed that people remembered the ads even though they may not have liked them. Those polled in 1997 tended to favor ads that "were laden with reality and light on fancy," wrote Dottie Enrico in *USA Today.* "The most effective campaign was a social commentary starring golf phenomenon Tiger Woods for Nike."

"Dime Zone" was created as an answer to competitors who were offering their own flat-rate long-distance calling systems. "The competition realized Sprint had struck an emotional chord with consumers," said the creators at J. Walter Thompson, "and followed suit with their own flat-rate product." According to Sprint, this left them to defend the "position of the dime," which resulted in the "Dime Zone" campaign.

HISTORICAL CONTEXT

In 1984 United Telecommunications (United Telecom), which later became Sprint, announced that it would build the first nationwide fiber-optic long-distance system. Transmitting messages via light pulses, fiber-optic networks were more durable and could carry greater amounts of information than conventional cables. They were used especially for delicate and intricate systems like computers and the Internet. At the same time, AT&T had billions of dollars invested in copper wire, putting the company that would become Sprint on the cutting edge of telecommunications technology. In a 1995 *Forbes* article by Subrata N. Chakravarty, Sprint chief executive William Esrey was quoted as saying, "We were starting with a clean piece of paper, and we could build a nationwide network that would give superior quality to the product we were selling." According to Chakravarty, however, it was a big risk for a small rural telephone company to invest in new technology. For this reason United Telecom teamed up with GTE-Sprint to build its fiber-optic network, and in 1990 United Telecom purchased Sprint from GTE and took its name. Since then, Sprint has continued to build its long-distance calling business while taking the lead in telecommunications technology.

In January 1997, four months before "Dime Zone," Sprint began a campaign advertising its Internet service, Sprint Passport. Then in May the company introduced the "Dime Zone" campaign, featuring Sprint's long-distance "dime sense" flat calling rate as well as its $10 flat-fee offer for a numeric pager, a product that displayed only the number of the person who called. "Within the consumer services group that Sprint offers is long-distance calling, paging, and Sprint's Internet service Passport," said Daniel Gallagher, senior partner and associate planning director at J. Walter Thompson. "We're trying to establish that Sprint is more than just a long-distance company."

By 1998 Sprint's local calling business, still its main enterprise, had 7.5 million customers in 19 states, and it had 10 percent of the yearly $85 billion U.S. long-distance calling market. According to *Fortune* magazine, in the third quarter of 1997 Sprint's calling volume climbed 14 percent, and profits increased 8.1 percent, outdistancing both AT&T and MCI.

HUMBLE ORIGINS

In the rural Midwestern and Plains states telephone service by the Bell Telephone Company proved expensive and was often slow to arrive. Many independent companies sprang up to provide local service, and these states came to have the highest percentage of non-Bell telephone companies in the United States. What eventually came to be Sprint was started in 1899 by Cleyson L. Brown as the Brown Telephone Company, a small local business in Abilene, Kansas. In 1900 Brown Telephone connected its first long-distance circuit. In 1903, in order to provide long-distance service to Kansas City, 14 independent phone companies in the state joined with Brown to form the Union Telephone and Telegraph Company, and in 1911 Brown merged his company with three others. The merged companies, which took the name United Telephone Company, became the second largest telephone company in Kansas. By 1976 United Telephone had become United Telecommunications, a system that served more than 3.5 million local telephone customers coast to coast, and in 1990 it became Sprint.

TARGET MARKET

The "Sprint Sense" strategy, which included the "Dime Zone" campaign, targeted an audience of well-educated, high-income adults between the ages of 18 and 49. "The flat rate appeals to a higher spender," said Gallagher, "and we don't target people who are much over 50." According to Gallagher, people over the age of 50 tended to buy long-distance service from AT&T, a company they had been with for a long time. For these consumers, Gallagher said, switching companies was too much trouble, and people would stay where they were comfortable.

Younger consumers, however, were more apt to shop around and to look for what made sense to them, which was why Sprint appealed to this particular audience with its flat-rate marketing. According to J. Walter Thompson, the targeted consumers "know the dime rate is good [but] they have not switched because they are uncertain about the peak/off-peak pricing. They need to be reassured that the dime rate is available when they call the most."

COMPETITION

Sprint's main competition, according to Gallagher, was AT&T. "All the apples tend to fall off the tree into one of our baskets. We don't share too many baskets with MCI." Marketing analysts, however, usually discussed the so-called big three telecommunications companies—AT&T, Sprint, and MCI—together when talking about market shares for long-distance calling. By 1996, one year after introducing "Sprint Sense," the market share for long-distance calling was growing faster for Sprint than for the competition. According to *Business Week*, Sprint's net income in 1996 rose 29 percent to $317 million, while profits grew 12 percent to $3.5 billion. The magazine further said: "Long-distance calling volume rose a stellar 19% over the year-ago period, compared with 15% for MCI and a dismal 5% for AT&T…. Sprint was the only one of the Big Three whose calling volumes grew more in the second quarter than in the first."

In 1997 WorldCom acquired MCI. But an even more important development occurred the year before with the Telecommunications Act of 1996. Under the new law Baby Bell companies would be able to offer long-distance services in their regions, making it likely that both AT&T and WorldCom/MCI would lose more of their declining long-distance market. "Sprint may be in a better position than AT&T and MCI," wrote Peter Elstrom in *Business Week*. "The Bells are focusing on residential customers who account for only a third of Sprint's business. And Sprint has cut deals with Nynex, Bell Atlantic, SBC Communications, and Pacific Bell—which are loath to give business to giant AT&T—to carry their long-distance calls."

In 1998 Sprint remained number three in the long-distance business, with about 10 percent of the market, behind AT&T, with 52.6 percent, and WorldCom/MCI, with 18 percent. According to a 1998 *Forbes* article, however, Sprint continued to grow faster than both of these competitors.

MARKETING STRATEGY

A 1997 *Fortune* article by Henry Goldblatt characterized Sprint's marketing as the best in the business. "Its innovations, like flat-rate pricing plans, are aped by everyone else," wrote Goldblatt. "Sprint just has a way of getting its name out there." According to Sprint, it recognized long ago that customers wanted easy-to-understand long-distance rates, which was what led to the "Sprint Sense" strategy in 1995.

In late 1996 Sprint faced new challenges. In September AT&T introduced a flat rate of 15 cents that was available seven days a week and 24 hours a day. The company's spokesperson was television star Paul Reiser from the 1990s hit *Mad About You*. AT&T eventually withdrew the offer in its advertising campaigns, but Sprint felt that the ads had created doubts in the minds of customers about its own peak/off-peak pricing for evenings and weekends. Sprint believed that, even though its competitor's pricing was more expensive, people perceived it as being simpler. The "Dime Zone" campaign was created to defend Sprint's flat calling rates on evenings and weekends and to assure customers that there was nothing complicated about it.

The creators at J. Walter Thompson felt that they needed to find a new way to make "Sprint Sense" relevant to people's lives. "We had been doing dime sense for a while," said Gallagher, "and wanted to find another way to make the dime relevant." The real genesis of the campaign, according to Gallagher, was learning the time of day most people made long-distance calls. After studying the consumer base, it became clear that 70 percent of Sprint's customers called long-distance in the evenings after work and during weekends. "That statistic inspired the team," said Gallagher. They came up with the concept that "dime time" was one's own time. "We tried to link up dime time with leisure time and being in the dime zone," said Gallagher. "If you went with Sprint's 10 cents a minute, things would just go your way. At work time things don't always go your way, but during dime time things go right."

The "Dime Zone" campaign included three 30-second spots and two 30-second direct-response ads for national cable television. In the first ad a man finds a dime in his car. "I'm heading home from work, and suddenly I'm in the dime zone," he proclaims. When he arrives home, everything is perfect: dogs stop barking, and blowing leaves miss his yard. Lying on a diving board at a swimming pool, he reiterates the Sprint dime-a-minute rate: "Best of all, my calls are just 10 cents a minute." Just then Candice Bergen appears with a cordless phone. "You'll probably need one of these," she says.

The second spot was similar to the first, with a woman finding the magic dime and heading into the dime zone, where everything miraculously goes her way. "Best of all," she says while talking on her deck, overlooking a beach, "my calls are just 10 cents a minute all weekend long." In the third commercial a man finds a dime and is transported to a lovely mountain stream where he can fly-fish. Bergen appears out of nowhere and hands the man a Sprint pager. "So now when I'm out, I'm always in touch," the man exclaims. A raccoon hands him his bill. "Unlimited paging for just $10 a month," he says, "a rate that's as easy to understand as my long distance."

The emphasis was on placing the "Dime Zone" ads in prime-time slots and on highly rated programs. They premiered on the *Today* show and ran on such programs as *Melrose Place*, *48 Hours*, and *Chicago Hope*. They also appeared on ESPN SportsCenter and on the final episode of *Married with Children.* Sprint's strategy was to reach as many viewers as possible in order to produce high sales and call volume.

The creators linked the "Dime Zone" campaign with other promotional efforts. On April 3, 1,000 gold-plated dimes, minted by the U.S. Treasury, were circulated throughout the United States. In the "Amazing Sprint Sense Dime Find" the 24-karat dimes were placed in locations where consumers made phone calls, and those lucky enough to find the dimes won money. One of the dimes was worth $25,000 and a year's worth of long-distance calling. "It was all part of the strategy of the dime zone," said Gallagher. "Find the dime, and you'll enter the dime zone, where good things happen." Viewers of the direct-response ads who called in to switch their long-distance service to Sprint received 100 free minutes of calling. Sprint spent $20 million for the entire campaign, including the promotional efforts.

OUTCOME

In the period May through August 1977, following the introduction of the "Dime Zone" campaign, calls placed through Sprint increased 34 percent over calls placed during the first four months of the year, exceeding the company's forecast by 17 percent. In comparison, calls increased 67 percent over the same period in 1996. According to a study by the international research firm Millward-Brown, brand recognition for Sprint was equal to AT&T's at the end of the campaign and was clearly higher than MCI's. In the months following the campaign, Sprint's churn figures—the number of customers it lost—was better than AT&T's and the industry in general. According to an analysis by NPD Study, a company that researches new products, in the last quarter of 1996 and the first quarter of 1997 Sprint's churn decreased 10 percent, while AT&T's increased 16 percent and the overall industry's increased 13 percent. In the first half of 1996 AT&T's churn was 117 percent, MCI's was 79 percent, and Sprint's was a low 27 percent.

The advertising industry recognized J. Walter Thompson twice for its Sprint campaigns. The agency won silver Effie Awards for effectiveness in 1996 and 1997 for the "Sprint Sense" and "Dime Lady" campaigns, respectively. The agency submitted "Dime Zone" for the 1998 Effie.

FURTHER READING

Chakravarty, Subrata N. "Nimble Upstart." *Forbes,* May 8, 1995, pp. 96–99.

Elstrom, Peter. "Did You Say Sprint Was No. 1?" *Business Week,* September 2, 1996, pp. 72–73.

Enrico, Dottie. "Consumers Bought into Real-World Ads in '97." *USA Today,* December 29, 1997.

Goldblatt, Henry. "Why Sprint's on the Block." *Fortune,* February 2, 1998, pp. 106–7.

Kupfer, Andrew. "The Telecom Wars: For Long-Distance Companies, Going Local Is a Grind." *Fortune,* March 3, 1997, pp. 136, 138, 141–42.

"The Quiet Comer." *Forbes,* February 23, 1998, pp. 76–77.

Anita Coryell

MONDAY NIGHTS FREE AND CLEAR CAMPAIGN

OVERVIEW

NOTE: Since the initial appearance of this essay in the 1998 edition of *Major Marketing Campaigns Annual,* the Sprint Corporation merged with Nextel to become Sprint Nextel. The essay continues to refer to the company's former name, as that was the official name of the organization when the campaign was launched.

Sprint Corporation's "Monday Nights Free and Clear" campaign publicized free long-distance calling services that the telecommunications company offered during the last four months of 1997. Each month customers could make up to 500 minutes of telephone calls on Monday evenings at no charge. The two-part campaign began with a phase tied to the company's sponsorship of the National Football League (NFL); these commercials featured professional football players. The second phase featured a commercial called "Speak Freely on Monday Nights" in which people misunderstood Sprint's invitation to "speak freely" and ruined relationships with friends and families by voicing opinions they would not normally have shared. For example, in one segment a man said to a friend wearing a toupee, "Bob, you're not fooling anyone. It doesn't even look like hair." The two-part campaign was intended to persuade consumers to try Sprint's long-distance service and to publicize the company's flat rate of 10 cents a minute in the evenings and on weekends. Sprint's straightforward calling plan had helped increase the company's sales at a time when its primary competitors were alienating some consumers by airing ads that were perceived to be attacks on other telecommunications companies. Most advertisements for telecommunications services were not very popular with the public, but surveys showed that consumers liked the "Monday Nights Free and Clear" campaign more than Sprint's previous commercials.

HISTORICAL CONTEXT

Sprint Corporation began as the Brown Telephone Company, founded in Abilene, Kansas, in 1899. By

1976 it had become the United Telephone system and served more than 3.5 million local telephone lines nationwide. In 1986 the company began offering long distance services under the Sprint brand name. By 1997 the organization was known as Sprint Corporation, a global communications company that carried the world's largest volume of Internet traffic. It provided long-distance and local telephone services, telecommunications equipment, security and alarm systems, and telephone directories. Together with Deutsche Telekom and France Telecom, Sprint offered a service called Global One for multinational corporations and travelers. Sprint Personal Communication Services (PCS) was a joint venture with Comcast Corporation, Tele-Communications, Inc. (TCI), and Cox Communications, Inc.—all cable television companies—to provide personal communications services across the United States. Sprint had an average of $14 billion in annual revenues and served more than 16 million businesses and residential customers. In 1997 Sprint was the highest rated telecommunications company in customer satisfaction surveys by J. D. Power and Associates and by the Yankee Group.

In 1988 Sprint had been the first company to provide a nationwide, digital, fiber-optic telephone network. Previously calls had been carried over copper wires or via microwave radio and satellite transmissions that used analog signals, and callers had frequently heard background noise and distortions in the sound. One of Sprint's early commercials showed a straight pin falling in slow motion and landing with an audible sound, demonstrating that the company's state-of-the-art technology provided calls with such clarity that customers could hear a pin drop over the telephone. The company's customer service number, 1-800-PIN-DROP, reminded consumers of that well-known campaign, and the falling pin was featured at the end of all Sprint commercials.

Sprint's next major campaign featured the actress Candice Bergen, who became known as the "Dime Lady" after she starred in commercials that promoted the company's dime-a-minute calling plan. Early in 1997 Bergen made cameo appearances in other campaigns publicizing Sprint's dime-a-minute plan. "The Power of a Dime" campaign followed a dime as it was passed from one person to another and magically improved their lives. In one spot a man found the dime on a subway platform. The train arrived on time, he found that someone had saved a seat for him, and, when he snapped his fingers, the train became an express that stopped at the best destination for him. When he arrived home, Candice Bergen was there to hand him a phone bill that was easy to understand because of Sprint's simple calling plan. The tag line was "Sprint. It All Makes Sense." A subsequent campaign with similar scenarios and the same tag line referred to the "Dime Zone," the evening hours when Sprint's dime-a-minute rate went into effect. In April 1997 the company also ran a promotional contest in which gold-plated dimes were placed in circulation nationwide, and consumers who turned them in had a chance to win up to $25,000.

In the autumn of 1997, at the same time that Sprint was offering free calls on Monday evenings, it ran another campaign called "1-800-ONE-DIME" to publicize its flat rates for collect calling services. Surveys had revealed that three out of four consumers had no idea what a collect call would cost since other carriers figured their long-distance charges from complex rate tables and discount systems. By contrast, Sprint's rates were simply 10 cents a minute for night and weekend calls and 25 cents a minute for daytime calls Monday through Friday, plus a low connection fee of $1.59 for state-to-state collect calls.

THE MONDAY NIGHT MADNESS MOBILE

The "Monday Nights Free and Clear" campaign was supported by related promotions during the National Football League season. When the first game aired on *Monday Night Football,* Sprint introduced two fans, nicknamed "Free" and "Clear," who traveled the country and searched out other football fans in a vehicle called the Monday Night Madness Mobile. The traveling promotion provided a chance for the public to participate in Sprint Most Outlandish Fan contests and Monday Night FREE Frenzy events to sample Sprint products and services and to take home memorabilia. In addition, the Sprint PCS NFL Skills Pavilion was set up in malls before Monday night games. Fans were invited to sample Sprint PCS telephones and to participate in simulated football drills. Proceeds were donated to the charity United Way.

TARGET MARKET

The "Monday Nights Free and Clear" campaign was designed to attract new customers to Sprint's dime-a-minute calling plan. The primary target group was consumers 20 to 45 years old, and the campaign was skewed somewhat toward women, who were more likely than men to make decisions regarding long-distance services. The company had conducted a national survey in which consumers named Monday as their least favorite day of the week because it marked the end of a fun-filled weekend without stress and the beginning of a new work week. When asked what would make them feel better about Mondays, many consumers mentioned free or discounted services.

In addition, surveys showed that many football fans made phone calls during the television show *Monday Night Football,* which featured highlights of NFL games. Fans would rush to the telephone to gloat or celebrate with friends when the players scored touchdowns, fumbled or intercepted the ball, were injured, or performed so well or so badly that the score became lopsided. Since Sprint was a sponsor of the NFL, its decision to offer free calls on Monday nights meshed perfectly with *Monday Night Football* and helped generate interest in NFL games. According to Tom Weigman, president of Sprint Consumer Services Group, "First, we always want to provide top-quality products and services while fulfilling our customers' telecommunications needs. Second, with the excitement of *Monday Night Football,* Sprint wants to make sure Monday nights will never be the same by not only bringing you closer to family and friends, but closer to live NFL action."

THE JETSONS CONNECTION

Sprint's "Monday Nights Free and Clear" campaign helped publicize Sprint stores located within the 6,000 U.S. outlets of RadioShack, a division of Tandy Corporation. Some ads with the theme "Welcome to the 21st Century" featured characters from *The Jetsons,* an animated science-fiction series. Part of the promotion featured actors in Jetsons costumes making a simulated spaceship landing in front of the Sprint Store at RadioShack in New York City's Times Square amid a cloud of smoke and a blaze of lights.

COMPETITION

Among long-distance telephone carriers in the United States, AT&T Corp. was in first place with 52.6 percent of the U.S. long-distance market in November 1997. MCI Communications Corporation was second with 18 percent, and Sprint was third with 10 percent, according to *USA Today.* In a time of rapidly expanding Internet services, AT&T had about 60 percent of the business communications market. AT&T estimated that there were 30 million Internet users in 1997, and it expected the number to increase to 13 billion within three years. AT&T spent about $300 million annually to advertise to consumers. Competitive Media Reporting calculated that in 1995 AT&T spent a total of $607 million for advertising, MCI spent $308 million, and Sprint spent $209 million.

For several years AT&T and MCI had been running campaigns that compared their prices and services. MCI had promoted its Friends & Family "calling circle," which provided reduced rates to the telephone numbers that members called most often. AT&T had responded with ads featuring people who said "I hate the circle!" and went on to cite details of AT&T's long-distance plans. MCI ran a campaign in which psychologist Dr. Joyce Brothers and fictitious consumers explained why they liked MCI better than AT&T. Although surveys showed that some of the commercials were effective, they were also perceived as mean-spirited mudslinging, and the barrage of information about complex calling plans had confused consumers. When Sprint introduced its "dime-a-minute" Sprint Sense calling plan in 1995, the company experienced record sales as consumers signed up for the simple, flat-rate service from a company that had not become so involved in talking about its competitors. In 1996 AT&T began airing ads that disparaged Sprint's calling plan.

By 1997 AT&T and MCI were airing more polite commercials that appealed to the emotions of consumers instead of focusing on competitors. Beginning in May AT&T spent between $90 million and $100 million on a popular series of advertisements that focused on life in the high-tech 1990s. The "It's All within Your Reach" campaign showed consumers how the company's products and services could improve their lives. One spot featured a mother who put her professional obligations aside for a while so that she could spend time with her daughters at the beach. In another commercial teenagers chatted via their home computers after an evening out together. The advertisements included well-known rock and roll songs and country music, such as Elton John's "Rocket Man" and Patsy Cline's "Walking after Midnight." Critics called the commercials some of the best for AT&T since the company's warm-hearted "Reach Out and Touch Someone" campaign, which had run years before.

Throughout 1997 AT&T also ran a campaign in which comedian Paul Reiser explained the company's new one-rate calling plan without attacking its direct competition, Sprint's dime-a-minute plan. Nearly one in five consumers in a *USA Today* survey said they liked the spots. In addition, AT&T aired a campaign during the spring that used the theme song from the old television series *Hawaii Five-0* to promote its Internet services. The ads, which featured smartly dressed business people, drew a connection between the famous ocean surf of Hawaii and the slang term for on-line exploration, "surfing the Net." Fifteen percent of respondents in a

USA Today survey said they "liked the ads a lot," but the commercials were popular with 29 percent of respondents 18 to 24 years old.

MARKETING STRATEGY

Sprint hoped to attract consumers to its Sprint Sense calling plan by offering them significant savings on their first few long-distance bills and by pointing out that Sprint Sense offered low prices and a simple rate schedule. New customers were allowed 500 free minutes each month for long-distance calls on Monday evenings for a limited time. Existing customers could also request the free calls. The company had estimated that the average long-distance bill for a household in the United States was about $25 a month. Sprint's offer of 500 free minutes was worth twice that amount, $50 at the Sprint Sense rate of 10 cents a minute. In addition, the campaign promoted the digital, wireless telephone technology available through an affiliated company, Sprint Personal Communications Services (PCS). New subscribers after September 1 received free local calls on Monday evenings until the end of the year, and their rates were as low as 10 cents a minute at other times. "By making local Sprint PCS calls free on Monday nights, we are giving new customers another reason to experience the clarity and benefits of Sprint PCS service," said Chuck Levine, chief marketing officer for Sprint PCS. "Whether people are at home watching the game, at a friend's house, or in their car, they can enjoy clarity virtually as good as their home phone." The spots that promoted Sprint PCS emphasized the word "clear" since clarity of sound was a selling point for digital communications equipment.

The "Monday Nights Free and Clear" campaign was rolled out in two phases. The first, also called "Monday Nights Free and Clear," was developed by Hal Riney & Partners/Heartland in Chicago in conjunction with NFL Films. The three advertisements in this part of the campaign featured professional football players promoting Sprint long-distance services and Sprint PCS wireless communications. In one spot Marcus Allen, a football star with the Kansas City Chiefs team, had not been playing well and had been pulled from the game when his wife called to tell him that his mother-in-law would not be moving in with them after all. Allen smiled broadly, went back into the game, and began making spectacular plays. The second stage of the campaign, "Speak Freely on Monday Nights," was created by the J. Walter Thompson ad agency. It consisted of a single commercial that showed people having telephone conversations in which they said more than they should have because they misunderstood Sprint's invitation to "speak freely." A young man told his mother, "It's not the dress that makes you look big. It's your hips." A girl told a friend, "Sure she thinks you're cute. You're rich." A woman looked at a photograph of a child and commented, "Yeah, I have seen cuter babies." The camera cut to Sprint spokesperson Candice Bergen, who remarked, "When they said speak freely, I don't think that's what they had in mind." Like all Sprint ads, each spot ended with the company's signature image of a pin dropping. The NFL spots aired only on the ABC and ESPN television networks, but the "Speak Freely on Monday Nights" commercial aired during a wide variety of network and cable television programs.

MOTION PICTURE TIE-INS

To publicize its long-distance calling rates, Sprint ran promotions tied to two adventure movies in 1997. In connection with the release of *Dante's Peak,* starring Pierce Brosnan and Linda Hamilton as people trying to survive the eruption of a volcano, contests on the radio awarded prepaid telephone cards worth 10 minutes of free calls from Sprint. (Sprint had sold more prepaid phone cards than any other company and had a 30 percent share of the prepaid card market in 1997.) Later in the year a Sprint campaign promised free tickets to the science-fiction comedy *Men in Black,* starring Tommy Lee Jones and Will Smith, for consumers who signed up for the Sprint Sense long-distance calling plan.

OUTCOME

According to Jerry Gramaglia, vice president of marketing for Sprint's consumer services, the "Monday Nights Free and Clear" campaign boosted sales. The company's call volume during the third quarter rose 34 percent higher than the volume for that quarter in 1996, and Sprint's tracking strategies revealed that many consumers called throughout the remainder of 1997 in response to the advertisements. The "Speak Freely on Monday Nights" campaign was more popular than previous Sprint advertisements, according to a consumer poll by *USA Today*'s Ad Track. The ads were liked by 17 percent of respondents, compared to a survey average of 22 percent, and 17 percent said the campaign was very effective, slightly better than the survey average of 16 percent. The ads were more popular with consumers 18 to 24 years old, with 22 percent saying they "liked the ads a lot."

Fifteen percent of respondents said they disliked the campaign. Previous Sprint ads had scored no higher than 10 percent for popularity and 15 percent for effectiveness, and 28 percent of respondents had said they disliked the "Dime Lady" campaign.

But the Sprint campaign was not popular with many consumer awareness groups. The Consumer Federation of America criticized the campaign for misleading consumers because it failed to explain that customers would have to "jump through numerous hoops" to receive the free calls. The public interest group the Center for Science in the Public Interest agreed and gave a "lemon" award to Sprint. A Sprint spokesperson answered that those limitations applied primarily to existing Sprint customers and that the campaign had been intended mainly for people who had not yet signed on with Sprint.

FURTHER READING

"An Ad Blitz for the 21st Century; Sprint Store at RadioShack Launches Massive Ad Campaign with Over 2.3 Billion TV Impressions." *PRNewswire,* September 24, 1997.

Cleland, Kim. "Bergen Leaves Spotlight in Sprint's New 'Dime' Ads." *Advertising Age,* January 13, 1997.

Cleland, Kim. "Sprint Moving Beyond Product Ads." *Advertising Age,* May 12, 1997.

Enrico, Dottie. "AT&T's 'One-Rate' Ads Ring True with Viewers." *USA Today Ad Track,* February 10, 1997.

———. "MCI Ads Raise Hackles But Seem to Work." *USA Today Ad Track,* June 5, 1995.

———. "Sprint Leaps Forward with New Ad Campaign." *USA Today,* November 10, 1997.

———. "Sprint Sees Success in Dime Campaign." *USA Today Ad Track,* August 4, 1997.

———. "Viewers Give No Quarter to Sprint's 'Dime Lady.'" *USA Today Ad Track,* June 17, 1996.

Enrico, Dottie, and Lydia Gibson. "AT&T Makes Connection with Ad Campaign." *USA Today Ad Track,* May 19, 1997.

"Great Rates: Sprint Offers Free Calls Monday Nights and a New Collect Calling Service." *PRNewswire,* September 8, 1997.

Jensen, Jeff, and Kim Cleland. "Sprint Nears Connection with NFL." *Advertising Age,* April 29, 1996.

"Sprint Launches NFL Season Campaign to Boost Monday's 'Likeability' Index." *PRNewswire,* August 25, 1997.

"Sprint Ranking High on All Fronts, Say Three New Studies." *PRNewswire,* August 20, 1997.

"Sprint Unveils New Advertising; Campaign Goes Beyond Long Distance." *PRNewswire,* January 13, 1997.

Tanouye, Erik. "Advertisers Get 'Lemon' Awards; Public Interest Groups Knock Nine Ads They Claim Mislead Consumers." *San Antonio Express News,* December 6, 1997.

Susan Risland

NEXTEL. DONE. CAMPAIGN

OVERVIEW

NOTE: Since this essay was first written, Nextel Communications, Inc. merged with Sprint Corporation to form Sprint Nextel Corporation. The essay continues to refer to the company's former name, as that was the official name of the organization when the campaign was launched.

The telecommunications industry underwent such fierce competition during 2003 that many analysts were comparing its advertising climate to the "cola wars" of the previous decade. The fifth-largest wireless-service provider, Nextel Communications, Inc., held 10.5 percent of the industry's market share and achieved revenues reaching $10 billion. The cumulative advertising budget from the top six providers (with Verizon Communications leading the pack) had reached a whopping $3.5 billion by 2004. To keep pace with one another, corporations catered to specific niches. Verizon tailored advertising around its large coverage footprint, while the Sprint PCS Group touted its wide range of features. Nextel, distinguished by its walkie-talkie feature called Push-to-talk, was used by construction crews, technicians, and government agencies that relied on Push-to-talk's quick capabilities. To continue within this niche, Nextel launched its "Nextel. Done." campaign to position itself as the most efficient work-related provider, one that allowed communication without interference.

With a starting budget of $200 million, the New York branch of ad agency TBWA\Chiat\Day orchestrated "Nextel. Done." using television, print, radio, Web and outdoor advertising. In September 2003 bright-yellow outdoor ads with the word "Do" were posted in cities nationwide. Newspaper ads featured copy such as "Stop believing that whoever talks most in the meeting wins." Also, nine television spots humorously showed people using Nextel's Push-to-talk feature to accelerate their jobs and other life events, such as weddings. With the campaign's tagline, "Nextel. Done," TBWA\Chiat\Day hoped to communicate the speed and pragmatism of Nextel's service. The campaign continued into 2004.

By the end of 2004 Nextel had posted more than $13 billion in sales, a 23.5 percent increase over 2003. "Dance Party," the campaign's most acclaimed television spot, earned a Bronze Lion at the Cannes Lions International Advertising Festival and a Silver Award at the D&AD (Design and Art Direction) Awards.

HISTORICAL CONTEXT

Mullen Advertising, part of the Interpublic Group of Companies, provided Nextel's advertising until 2003.

The agency's last Nextel campaign, "Coast to Coast Walkie Talkie," exaggerated the mechanics of Nextel's nationwide Push-to-talk technology with television spots showing Nextel repeaters (devices that amplified the range of a radio signal) fastened to the antlers of antelopes and clamped to the legs of pigeons. One spot, "Giant Antenna," suggested that Nextel provided service with the help of a 400,000-foot radio antenna that could transmit coast-to-coast. Mullen also bolstered Nextel's brand in an advertising war with Verizon. Verizon first discredited Nextel's inferior coverage area, which prompted Mullen to release copy such as "We have push-to-talk. They have push-to-wait." The last television spot Mullen created for Nextel was released in June 2003.

A Nextel spokeswoman, Audrey Schaefer, explained to the *Boston Globe* that Nextel changed ad agencies simply because it had outgrown Mullen. Nextel's revenue rose from $333 million in 1996 to $8.72 billion by 2002. "We're looking to take it to the next level," she said, referring to Nextel awarding TBWA\Chiat\Day the advertising account in 2003.

TBWA\Chiat\Day formulated a campaign that contrasted with the format that both Verizon and Sprint employed: using the same actor as a spokesman in every commercial. As Barbara Lippert wrote for *Adweek,* "I'm so glad that in this first campaign for Nextel from TBWA\Chiat\Day, the agency avoids all the usual telecom suspects: no obsessive guys in trench coats, no repetitive catchphrases, no B-list celeb endorsers or once-proud A-listers interrupting and/or hang gliding and break dancing." Instead, TBWA\Chiat\Day wanted "Nextel. Done." to continue Nextel's popularity within working environments that relied on quick, effortless communication. A spokesperson for the ad agency told *Adweek,* "The whole category is about talk, but Nextel is going to be about doing."

TARGET MARKET

"Nextel. Done." focused on branding Nextel as a business-to-business service provider that targeted working adults such as construction workers, technicians, and government agencies. Jobholders who valued efficiency and work speed were targeted as well. "Our customers put a premium [on] getting things done," Mark Schweitzer, senior vice president of Nextel, was quoted in *Total Telecom.* The tagline "Nextel. Done." attempted to capture Nextel's startup, accelerated attitude.

Push-to-talk, a service only offered by Nextel until Verizon released its own version in August 2003, allowed mobile-phone users to contact other Nextel subscribers cheaply and quickly with the push of a button. The service ranged nationwide and worked like a long-ranged walkie-talkie service. Many of the campaign's television spots featured white- or blue-collar workers using their Push-to-talk feature in job interviews and business meetings and accomplishing other tasks with their Nextel phones. "Nextel is positioned as a tool for people who need to get things done instantly," one Nextel executive was quoted as saying in *Adweek.* Another executive added, "It's not about empowerment, it's about accomplishment." During the campaign's first week, bright yellow posters with "Do" in thick, black copy appeared around New York and other cities.

PUSH-TO-TALK

Nextel was the first major wireless service to provide Push-to-talk, a technology borrowed largely from the walkie-talkie. In addition to making wireless calls that allowed both parties to talk and hear simultaneously (a mode termed "full-duplex calling"), Nextel phones were also capable of Push-to-talk, allowing only one party to talk at once. The feature made calls cheaper and faster to place than traditional full-duplex calling. A Nextel subscriber could simply push a button or buttons that corresponded to another Nextel subscriber's phone number. The subscriber receiving the call would immediately hear a chirp on his or her phone and could then choose to answer, queue, or clear the call alert. If it was answered, the two subscribers alternated between using the microphone with a speak-button. Depending on how callers toggled the button, Nextel's infrastructure knew in which direction the signal should be traveling.

COMPETITION

Verizon reigned as America's largest wireless-service provider in 2003. Besides ranking highest in service quality, Verizon also scored higher in customer satisfaction than any of its six closest competitors. To reinforce its positioning Verizon spent $1 billion every three months just to improve its network. In 2003 Verizon was spending $300 to $400 million on its "Can You Hear Me Now?" campaign, which featured actor Paul Marcarelli as the brand's "Testman," who was shown, in more than 100 television spots, testing Verizon coverage across America. Verizon spent an additional $700 to $800 million on direct-mail and in-store promotions, making it the largest advertising spender out of all American brands. Verizon led the industry until February 2004, when Cingular

> **JOE PYTKA**
>
> Joe Pytka, who directed the first four television spots of "Nextel. Done," was credited with directing more than 5,000 commercials. His influence encompassed Ray Charles's "Uh-huh" campaign for Diet Pepsi along with the McDonald's campaign "Nothing But Net," which featured basketball greats Larry Bird and Michael Jordan.

Wireless LLC purchased AT&T Wireless Services for $41 billion.

Before Cingular acquired AT&T, it stood as the second-largest wireless service provider and spent an estimated $500 million on advertising in 2003. The company launched its enigmatic "mLife" campaign, which ran into trouble after consumers confused it with MetLife Insurance. When Cingular later acquired AT&T, Cingular's coverage area enlarged, and the company initiated a campaign called "Raising the Bar," a phrase that referred to the phone's signal-strength meter. Despite the fact that the acquisition gave Cingular more subscribers than any other competitor, the provider only ranked fourth in customer satisfaction, and it received four times as many service complaints as Verizon.

Similar to Verizon with its "Testman," Sprint PCS created more than 100 television spots with its own spokesman, "Sprint guy," who explained various Sprint features and service plans to consumers. In 2003 Sprint spent an estimated $550 million on advertising and posted $1 billion in revenues. In December 2004 Sprint and Nextel announced plans for a $36 billion merger to challenge their two larger rivals. "Even with the combined resources of Sprint and Nextel, we are up against two Goliaths in Cingular and Verizon," Mark Schweitzer, Nextel's senior vice president, told *Advertising Age.*

MARKETING STRATEGY

In September 2003, during the campaign's first week, bright-yellow posters with the word "Do" began appearing in cities. The posters served as teasers for the upcoming campaign, which would continue across print, radio, television, and the Internet. Four 30-second television spots, all directed by seasoned commercial director Joe Pytka, aired during September. Print and Internet ads and radio spots also began appearing. New television spots were released at the beginning of 2004.

The campaign's most-awarded commercial, "Dance Party," aired in January 2004. The 30-second spot, directed by Jim Jenkins, featured three tie-wearing office workers grooving to hip-hop's Salt-N-Pepa playing on a portable stereo. When their boss walked in to discover all three not working, he snapped, "What's going on? We don't know how many converters we have in stock. We don't know where our trucks are. No one knows where Mackler is." Despite their boss' irritation, the three did not turn off the music or stop dancing until he finished his scolding. Then, with the quick flip of a Nextel phone and keystroke of a laptop, the three answered the boss' questions within three seconds, after which they restarted the music and continued dancing. Deviating from its competitors, Nextel focused on "the concept of 'done' rather than talk," TBWA\Chiat\Day group creative director John Hunt told *Campaign.*

Continuing within the same vein, another 30-second spot, "Meeting," appeared in September 2003. The commercial began with an elderly boss entering an office and everyone around the table flipping open their Nextel phones. Throughout the short meeting, attendees communicated rapidly with Nextel's Push-to-talk feature. To amplify the spot's absurd humor, it was scripted with tongue-twisting dialogue such as the boss saying, "Pittsburgh? Pursue the potential pitch for property pronto."

One television spot without a work-related storyline, "Wedding," featured a bride and groom rushing through wedding vows using Nextel's Push-to-talk feature. The spot attempted to exemplify humorously the speed of Nextel's service. Another 30-second spot, "Romeo and Juliet," showed teens rushing through a Nextel rendition of the Shakespeare play while their phones flipped open and closed.

Ads appeared in print publications such as *USA Today,* with copy conveying a similar theme of efficiency. One ad stated, "Stop believing that whoever talks most in the meeting wins." Other ads only featured Nextel's "finish line" symbol, a straight vertical line placed upon a yellow background. The symbol notified Nextel subscribers of a message's end. Other ads, using the same yellow background, featured short copy such as, "Cancel dance class," "Call dog walker," and "Book a flight," to convey Nextel's get-it-done positioning. "Nextel. Done." commercials continued into 2004.

OUTCOME

Nextel's sales increased 23.5 percent (to $13 billion) during a majority of the campaign's lifespan. Some analysts criticized the campaign for not explaining the Push-to-talk service, which most wireless customers did not use. As *Adweek*'s critic Barbara Lippert wrote, "Unless you already know about Nextel's 'Push-to-talk' service... it's hard to figure out what benefit is being sold, since the p-t-t phrase is never mentioned." Other critics accused TBWA\Chiat\Day of dehumanizing face-to-face communication in the campaign's television spots. Nevertheless, the campaign, overall, garnered a fair amount of ad-industry praise. It earned TBWA\Chiat\Day a gold award at the American Association of Advertising Agencies' account planning conference in New Orleans. "Dance Party" was considered one of *Adweek* magazine's "best spots" during October 2004. "Dance Party" also earned a Bronze Lion at the Cannes Lions International Advertising Festival and a Silver Award at the D&AS Awards, given out by Design & Art Direction, a London-based professional association and charity.

In an ad review for *Advertising Age's Creativity,* Kevin Moehlenkamp, cochief creative officer at McCann-Erickson San Francisco, remarked on the first four television spots. "They're beautifully shot and hard not to watch. Using the phones in ordinary situations like a wedding to get across the idea that 'these little suckers just work and get the job done' is a nice, memorable device." Reviewing the campaign for *Adweek,* Mae Anderson stated that "Dance Party" was "one of the best positioning/tags that I've seen in a long time. This spot is well directed, cast, written and shot. And it builds off of a positioning that is relevant and different."

FURTHER READING

Anderson, Mae. "September." *Adweek,* October 25, 2004, p. 22.

Bischoff, Glenn. "Nextel, Zetron Intro Interop Solution." *Mobile Radio Technology,* January 1, 2005, p. 38.

Charski, Mindy. "Ad Exec by Day... for Some Agency Staffers, Two Careers Are Better than One." *Adweek,* September, 22, 2003, p. 30.

Cuneo, Alice. "CMO Merges Conflicting Cultures into One $35B Wireless Behemoth." *Advertising Age,* July 11, 2005, p. 32.

Cuneo, Alice, and Lisa Sanders. "Street Cred for Prepay: Nextel's Boost Dials Up Rappers to Pump Sales." *Advertising Age,* September 6, 2004, p. 10.

Donker, Anne "Sprint-Nextel Merger: Cellular Change." *Optimize,* January 1, 2005, p. 58.

Elliott, Stuart. "Forecasts of an Ad Blitz by Wireless Services Providers ahead of a Key Rule Change May Prove Wrong." *New York Times,* November 7, 2003, p. 3.

Jackson, Donnny. "FCC Lowers Nextel's Rebanding Cash." *Mobile Radio Technology,* January 1, 2005, p. 10.

Lippert, Barbara. "Nextel's Cell Block: 'Done' Campaign Takes a New Tack—but to What End?" *Adweek,* September 22, 2003, p. 26.

McMains, Andrew. "Nextel Bets It 'Done' in 1st Campaign from TBWA\C\D." *Adweek,* September 8, 2003, p. 9.

Moehlenkamp, Kevin. "The Work." *Advertising Age's Creativity,* November 1, 2003, p. 36.

Reidy, Chris. "Ad Shop Mullen to Lose Nextel, Its Biggest Client." *Boston Globe,* May 2, 2003, p. E1.

Sabatini, Patricia. "Nextel Television Commercial Singles Out Pittsburgh." *Pittsburgh Post-Gazette,* September 24, 2003, p. B1.

Steinberg, Brian. "The Advertising Report: Spurning Ad-Company Throne for a Comfortable TBWA Home." *Wall Street Journal,* August 3, 2005, p. B3B.

Kevin Teague

SPRINT PCS CAMPAIGN

OVERVIEW

NOTE: Since the time of this campaign's launch, the Sprint Corporation merged with Nextel to become Sprint Nextel. The essay refers to the company's former name, as that was the official name of the organization when the campaign was launched.

During 2002 competition between wireless-telecommunication providers grew so fierce that the top four were spending $1.5 billion on media outlays, a leap above the $435 million spent in 1999. With more subscribers than AT&T Wireless Services, Inc., Cingular Wireless LLC, or the Sprint PCS Group, Cellco Partnership's Verizon Wireless spent more on advertising than any other American brand. Analysts feared that the industry's competitive pricing and excessive advertising would cripple profitability. Hoping to remain the fourth-largest provider, Sprint PCS retrofitted its network with high-speed data capabilities in 2002 and heralded their improved network with a campaign titled "Sprint PCS Campaign."

On June 24, 2002, the San Francisco–based ad agency Publicis & Hal Riney (PHR), a longtime collaborator with Sprint PCS, released the campaign on an estimated $400 million budget across television, radio, print, and in-store promotions. In 1999 PHR had conceived "Sprint Guy," the trench coat–clad actor that became Sprint PCS's widely recognizable spokesperson. "Sprint PCS Campaign" continued with the same handsome, witty character played by actor Brian Baker. Cross-promotion with Hollywood served as a major constituent for the campaign. In the movie *Men in Black II,* released by Sony Pictures Entertainment in July of 2002, Sprint PCS phones were used by the on-screen heroes. In turn, Sprint PCS's 30-second television spot "MIBII" showed the Sprint Guy clarifying the words "trampoline" and "tangerines" for alien worms that had been featured in the movie.

The campaign helped Sprint PCS remain America's fourth-largest wireless provider throughout 2002. Sales for the Sprint Corporation, of which Sprint PCS made up almost half, increased $563 million between 2001 and 2002. Sprint PCS's high "customer churn rate," the industry term referring to customers frequently changing providers, forced the company to cut back 6 percent of its employees and to require nonrefundable deposits for certain wireless customers. Some of the campaign's television spots earned Gold and Silver ADDYs at the American Advertising Awards. The campaign also earned a Silver award at the Design & Art Direction Awards.

HISTORICAL CONTEXT

Sprint PCS created the nation's first all-digital, fiber-optic network that was void of analog-only calls. Most wireless providers mixed their digital infrastructure with an antiquated analog infrastructure. The older technology was notorious for quickly draining phone batteries, increasing electromagnetic radiation, lacking call security, and usually emitting high static during phone calls. Since 1999 Sprint Guy had served as Sprint PCS's spokesperson, who explained the network's clarity in typically zany commercials. Publicis & Hal Riney (PHR), the agency that created the character, filmed one spot in which Sprint Guy helped a small town where everybody spoke with garbled analog static. In another commercial Sprint Guy aided a woman who, after rushing through long-distance calls on her expensive calling plan, habitually rushed everything else in life.

"It's always had a certain level of absurdity, so over time you always have to look for fresh ways to attack the same problem," Mike Mazza, creative director at PHR, told *Advertising Age's Creativity.* "Originally, the campaign had a different type of humor. A lot of it was parody; a lot of it was underplayed, and with the exception of one or two spots, it wasn't all that broad. What we've done over time is broaden out the humor, and the more we've done that, the more people are talking about the spots." In addition to emphasizing Sprint's clarity, Sprint Guy also explained features such as text messaging and voice mail.

In the summer of 2002 Sprint PCS rolled out its PCS Vision network, which was similar to Verizon's updated broadband network. The retrofitted PCS Vision increased Sprint PCS's bandwidth to allow more callers on its network and 10 times the amount of data throughout it. The updates were necessary for phone features like photo messaging, high-graphic games, sending and receiving E-mail, and downloading music. PHR crafted the "Sprint PCS Campaign" to announce the new features, which many executives hoped would bolster Sprint's subscriber base. "It's a precursor to our upcoming launch of our third-generation network," Chip Novick, Sprint PCS's vice president of consumer marketing, explained to *Reuters News* in regard to the campaign. "It's really helping people to see that wireless is not just about phone calls anymore and the next trend in wireless is wireless for your eyes as well as for your ears."

WIRELESS INTERNET

Sprint PCS's improved Third Generation (3G) network that rolled out in 2002 allowed subscribers to access wireless broadband Internet service in most areas that had previously only supported wireless phone service. PC wireless-connection cards were released by Sprint PCS to allow customers to use their laptops to surf the Web faster than the 56 KB-per-second speed of a dial-up connection. Subscribers could also connect to the Internet using Sprint PCS phone Web browsers.

TARGET MARKET

The "Sprint PCS Campaign" involved television spots that blended absurd situations and the Sprint Guy's deadpan humor to capture the target market, which, depending on sources, ranged from 18 to 24 years old. In a quarterly survey conducted by Intermedia Advertising Group (an advertising-performance-assessment firm) after the campaign, a spot in which Sprint Guy consoled a group of disgruntled mobile-phone users ranked as the wireless-provider commercial that television watchers found most memorable.

During the campaign, research conducted by Sprint PCS's largest affiliate, Alamosa PCS, discovered that the 18- to 24-year-old age range only constituted 6 percent of the overall market share. The largest consumer base had a median range of 44 years old. During the campaign Alamosa PCS expanded its target market to include 25 to 54 year olds by reducing "Spring PCS Campaign" radio spots in the top six youth radio stations and refocusing on talk radio.

With just over 18 million subscribers, Sprint PCS was recognized worldwide as the foremost provider to develop, manage, and implement a nationwide, all-digital wireless network. Sprint PCS appealed to technology enthusiasts looking for mobile phones loaded with extra features. "We are focusing our marketing on innovation to differentiate from the pack," Sprint spokesman Dan Wilinsky stated in a press release. "You can do more things with your Sprint PCS phone than with any other network." The June 2002 campaign aired commercials

THE "CELL PHONE" MISNOMER

As mobile telephones grew popular during the 1990s, it became common to call any such phone a "cell phone." This was a misnomer; the word "cell" actually referred to the cellular band of radio frequencies partitioned by the Federal Communications Commission. About half of the nation's mobile phones resided within this radio band, whereas the other half operated on the personal communication services (PCS) band. The analogy between FM and AM radio waves was commonly used to explain the PCS and cellular relationship. In 2002 Verizon Wireless was the largest provider operating within the cellular band. Sprint was one of the largest operating within the PCS band.

that featured Sprint PCS phones performing photo messaging and other cutting-edge capabilities. Many of the features were also used by Will Smith and Tommy Lee Jones's characters in *Men in Black II,* which featured Sprint PCS phones.

COMPETITION

Verizon reigned as America's largest wireless provider in 2002. Besides ranking highest in service quality, Verizon also scored higher in customer satisfaction than any of its six closest competitors. Similar to Sprint PCS, Verizon used C.D.M.A. (Code Division Multiple Access), a technology developed by Qualcomm Incorporated, to increase network bandwidth and subsequently handle more phone traffic in 2002. Verizon network updates rolled out months before Sprint's PCS Vision did, so Verizon preceded Sprint PCS to the market with such services as high-speed wireless Internet. To maintain its lead in service quality, Verizon spent $1 billion every three months just to improve its network. The expensive network meant higher prices for Verizon calling plans, so the provider targeted consumers who would pay for the better service. Verizon also used actor Paul Marcarelli to play Test Man, a nerdy version of the Sprint Guy, in more than 100 television spots. By 2003 Verizon was spending $700 to $800 million on direct-mail and in-store promotions, making it the greatest advertising spender out of all American brands.

In contrast to Verizon's pitch to higher-paying consumers, AT&T, the third-largest wireless-service provider, advertised its lower-cost calling plans with features such as rollover minutes and anytime minutes. In 2002 the corporation launched its enigmatic "mLife" campaign, which ran into early trouble after consumers confused it with MetLife Insurance.

Fifth largest in the nation, Nextel Communications, Inc., was distinguished by its walkie-talkie feature called "push-to-talk," which was widely used by construction crews, technicians, and government agencies. "Push-to-talk" worked nationwide and allowed callers to communicate faster and cheaper than with traditional wireless calls, but it only permitted one caller to talk at a time. To promote the service's efficiency, Nextel spent $200 million on its "Nextel. Done." campaign in 2003.

MARKETING STRATEGY

During the rush in 2002 to bring broadband features to wireless-phone subscribers, Sprint PCS placed a large portion of its operating budget into transforming its Second Generation (2G) network—which supported digital voice calls, text messaging, and voice mail—into a Third Generation (3G) network that boasted photo messaging, music downloads, rapid Web browsing, and color-graphic games. "Our customers tell us they're ready for a wireless device that does more than make a phone call," William T. Esrey, chairman and chief executive officer of Sprint, told the *PR Newswire.* On June 24, 2004, Sprint PCS released the "Sprint PCS Campaign" across television, radio, print, and in-store promotions to herald its network's upcoming features.

Sprint Guy starred in the television spots just as in previous commercials, but PHR broadened the humor. Past spots had used humor specific to phone technology, such as a town whose speech was troubled with analog static or people confused by roaming fees. The newer "Sprint PCS campaign" usually depicted characters misunderstanding words over the phone, resulting in ridiculous scenarios such as cowboys herding dachshunds and a soap-opera star invading suburban homes.

The campaign also tied in with the summer blockbuster *Men in Black II,* starring Tommy Lee Jones and Will Smith. Sprint PCS subscribers could enter contests for free tickets, and their phones were capable of downloading images and songs from the movie. In turn, Sprint PCS phones assisted the movie's protagonists, two government agents who monitored aliens living on earth. "The agents use many wireless applications—digital imaging, voice command, wireless Internet access, phone calls and more to accomplish their mission," Novick told the *Kansas City Star.* "The wireless applications . . . form a bit of a precursor to how people will be able to do more with the launch of 3G."

Men in Black II attracted more than $35 million from other brands hoping to tie their product in, including Burger King, Mercedes-Benz, Mountain Dew, RayBan, and Hamilton Watches. The original *Men in Black* movie grossed more than any other movie in 1997. The saturation of product placement in its sequel, however, drew criticism from movie critics. Novick of Sprint PCS disagreed. "It's a naturally organic integration and not one directed by the company, rather one that fit with the story line and the plot of the movie," he told the *Kansas City Star.* "The last thing we'd want... is for the interaction to be forced."

PHR also created a spot, "MIBII," in which Sprint Guy clarified the words "trampoline" and "tangerines" for alien worms from the movie. One campaign spot that deviated from the themes of *Men in Black II* and word confusion was titled "Microwaveable Burrito." It featured a woman standing inside a mini-mart, who said into her Sprint PCS phone, "You're not going to believe what I'm looking at. I can't even tell you." Sprint Guy appeared to explain, "You don't have to tell her, you can show her." Sprint Guy then photo-messaged what the woman found so astonishing: the Las Vegas entertainers Siegfried and Roy microwaving a burrito.

Some analysts criticized the lackluster quality of the campaign's print ads. A critic for *Adweek* stated, "The idea behind humorous Sprint PCS work—trench-coated spokesman clarifies absurd miscommunications caused by static—may be four years old, but writing keeps jokes fresh. Sprint print [is] surprisingly bland by comparison."

OUTCOME

Sprint PCS composed almost 50 percent of its parent company, Sprint Corp., which posted a $563 million sales increase for 2002. Unfortunately, Sprint PCS's high customer churn rate during 2002 forced a 6 percent cutback in workforce and a reduction of early subscriber growth forecasts. For many providers fervent competition became the industry's most destructive force. "The competition is out of control. Irrational competition in the industry will almost preclude anybody from operating profitably," Gary Stibel, founder and principal of the marketing-consulting firm New England Consulting Group, told *Advertising Age.*

Sprint did maintain its position as the fourth-largest wireless provider, and the campaign continued branding the service in conjunction with voice clarity and a broad set of features. Besides the campaign's bottom-line success, more than one television spot earned a Gold and Silver ADDY at the American Advertising Awards. Jim Hanas of *Advertising Age's Creativity* wrote, "One of the more unexpected successes of the season has been Publicis & Hal Riney's Sprint PCS campaign... The campaign isn't so well respected domestically, because, frankly, it started out so bad. But it's gotten better as the misunderstandings that Sprint claims to prevent have gotten more absurd." The campaign also earned a Silver Award at the Design & Art Direction Awards, an international competition based in the United Kingdom.

FURTHER READING

Brune Mathis, Karen. "In the Pipeline." *(Jacksonville) Florida Times-Union,* March 11, 2002, p. FB-14.

Cox, Jonathan. "Have We Got a Deal for You." *Raleigh (NC) News & Observer,* November 22, 2002, p. D1.

Cuneo, Alice. "Cell Giants Plot $1.5B Ad Bonanza; New FCC Rules Spark Battle to Entice Rivals' Customers." *Advertising Age* October 6, 2003, p. 1.

———. "Sprint Consolidates." *Advertising Age,* March 8, 2004, p. 49.

Davies, Jennifer. "Where Do Films Start, Ads Stop?" *San Diego Union-Tribune,* August 3, 2002, p. C1.

Hanas, Jim. "Other Spots to Watch." *Advertising Age's Creativity,* June 1, 2003, p. 24.

Laughlin, Kirk. "Desperate to Be Different." *America's Network,* December 1, 2002, p. 26.

Mazza, Mike. "Special Report: Creative Directors." *Advertising Age's Creativity,* March 1, 2002, p. 38.

Meyer, Dan. "Carriers Wary of Wi-Fi Hype, but Invest Nevertheless." *RCR Wireless News,* November 25, 2002, p. 8.

Muraskin, Ellen. "Multimodality Starts Walking and Talking." *Communications Convergence,* December 1, 2002, p. 18.

Myers, George, Jr. "Tech the Halls for the Holidays." *Columbus (OH) Dispatch,* November 15, 2002, p. 16.

Noguchi, Yuki. "Cell Phone Carrier Switches May Encounter Hang-Ups." *Washington Post,* November 19, 2003, p. E01.

Parpis, Eleftheria. "Riney's Rebounder: Can Kirk Souder 'Rediscover the Greatness' of the San Francisco Shop?" *Adweek,* August 18, 2003, p. 20.

Rose, Marla Matzer. " 'MiB2' Lines Up Promo Partners." *Hollywood Reporter,* February 4, 2002, p. 1.

Kevin Teague

Stanley Steemer International, Inc.

5500 Stanley Steemer Parkway
Dublin, Ohio 43016
USA
Telephone: (614) 764-2007
Fax: (614) 764-1506
Web site: www.stanleysteemer.com

■■■

LIVING BRINGS IT IN. WE TAKE IT OUT. CAMPAIGN

OVERVIEW

Stanley Steemer International, Inc., a carpet-cleaning service with franchises across the United States, began seeing sales declines in 2002. Wanting to change its marketing profile to address these declines as well as to integrate messages about new services beyond its carpet-cleaning business, the company asked agencies to submit pitches for a new campaign. Young & Laramore, based in Indianapolis, won the account with a proposal to move Stanley Steemer away from its previous positioning as a service to be used only when carpet was visibly stained. The resulting campaign, "Living Brings It In. We Take It Out," aimed to stimulate more frequent use of professional carpet-cleaning services.

With an estimated $20 million budget in its first year, the "Living Brings It In. We Take It Out" campaign targeted working women who were homeowners and parents and encouraged them to think about the overwhelming amount of hidden dirt in their homes. Television spots and print ads used humor and imagery that suggested the innocent ways in which adults, their children, and their pets routinely brought dirt from the outside world into their homes. Copy read by voice-over in the TV spots and appearing on the page in the print ads suggested, "Maybe cleaning your carpets once a year isn't enough." The campaign's tagline likewise underscored the ideas of blameless accumulation of dirt and the corresponding need for professional service.

Stanley Steemer not only reversed its sales decline during the first 16 months of the campaign but also saw an 11 percent increase, which many observers attributed to the repositioning accomplished by "Living Brings It In. We Take It Out." The campaign won a Gold EFFIE and was extended and adapted to additional Stanley Steemer service offerings in subsequent years.

HISTORICAL CONTEXT

Founded in 1947, Stanley Steemer grew consistently throughout the second half of the twentieth century to become America's leading professional carpet-cleaning service, with 270 franchises across the country and the best-established brand name in its business category. In 2002, while experiencing some of the first sales declines in its history, Stanley Steemer bolstered its core carpet-cleaning business with new services that included duct cleaning, tile and grout cleaning, and water removal. In July of that year, with an eye toward reviving sales and incorporating these new capabilities into its brand image, Stanley Steemer formally initiated a review of its advertising account. The company invited new agencies as well

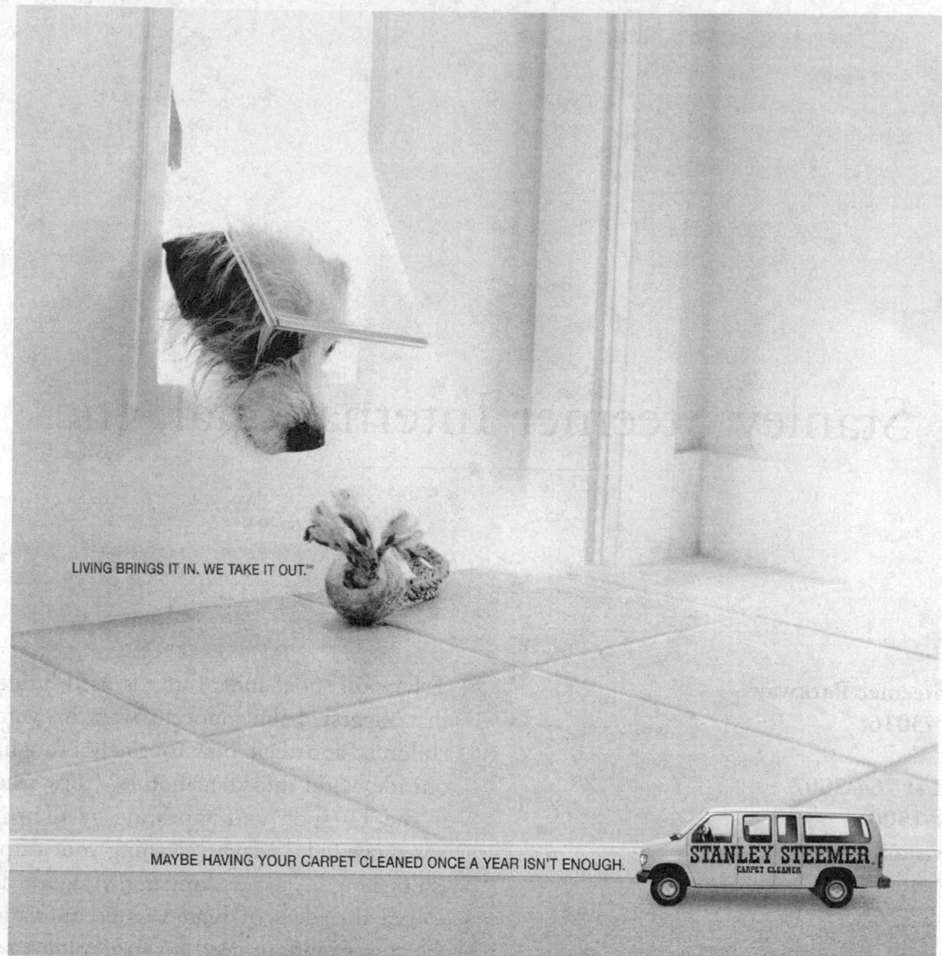
LIVING BRINGS IT IN. WE TAKE IT OUT.℠
MAYBE HAVING YOUR CARPET CLEANED ONCE A YEAR ISN'T ENOUGH.
STANLEY STEEMER
CARPET CLEANER

A still from Stanley Steemer's "Living Brings It In. We Take It Out." campaign. CAMPAIGN CREATED BY YOUNG & LARAMORE. REPRODUCED BY PERMISSION.

as its current national and franchise agencies to submit creative and strategic marketing ideas.

Stanley Steemer's advertising at both the national and the franchise levels, using the long-running tagline "Tough on dirt, gentle on carpet," had traditionally focused on images of dramatic stains and their removal. At the time of the account review, for instance, a national TV spot featured a young boy jumping on a plastic bottle of chocolate syrup atop a white carpet. Though images of Stanley Steemer employees and equipment easily vanquishing such stains positioned the company as an effective cleaning service, these images also gave the impression that such cleaning was only occasionally and in extreme circumstances truly necessary. The Indianapolis agency Young & Laramore won the Stanley Steemer account in August 2002 thanks to a strategy that effectively challenged this stain-based model for driving business.

TARGET MARKET

Stanley Steemer had long understood that its most consistent customers were women aged 35 to 65 who were married, owned their own homes, and were parents as well as pet owners. In crafting the new campaign, "Living Brings It In. We Take It Out," Young & Laramore used this target market as the starting point, but the agency found in its research that an overlapping group of women served as the most likely pool for generating new and consistent Stanley Steemer business. This group consisted of working women between the ages of 25 and 49 who were homeowners and parents.

These women were extremely busy, Young & Laramore observed, but cared deeply about keeping their homes clean for their families. They had become accustomed, however, perhaps partly because of the carpet-cleaning industry's reliance on stain-based advertising, to presume that they did not need to have their carpets

MAYBE HAVING YOUR CARPET CLEANED
ONCE A YEAR ISN'T ENOUGH.

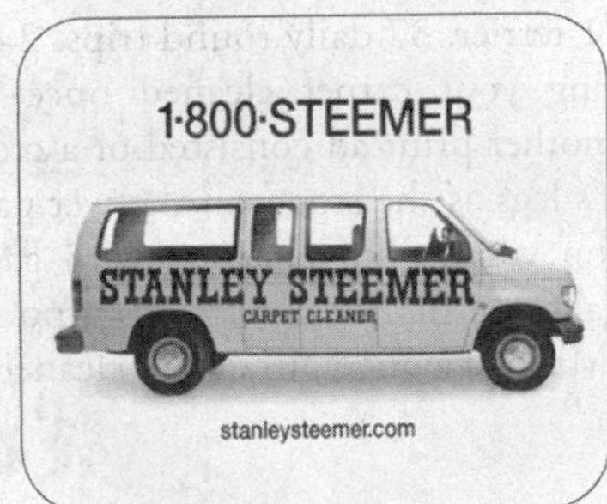
1·800·STEEMER
STANLEY STEEMER
CARPET CLEANER
stanleysteemer.com

LIVING BRINGS IT IN. WE TAKE IT OUT.

Five stills from Stanley Steemer's "Living Brings It In. We Take It Out." campaign. CAMPAIGN CREATED BY YOUNG & LARAMORE. REPRODUCED BY PERMISSION.

professionally cleaned more than once a year or when there were visible stains. Young & Laramore thus set out to convince these women that their carpets needed regular cleaning, rather than only sporadic cleaning to remove stains. Young & Laramore found that, while 33 percent of its target claimed they had their carpets professionally cleaned once a year, the true figure was actually closer to 9 percent. This figure of 9 percent, however, well eclipsed the percentage of people in the population at large who were conscious of carpet cleaning.

COMPETITION

Among Stanley Steemer's national rivals during this time were ServiceMaster Clean and Chem-Dry. These companies operated with the same franchise-based model as Stanley Steemer, but unlike Stanley Steemer they typically advertised primarily on the local and regional levels. Stanley Steemer's national marketing profile, as engineered by its corporate office, was unique in the industry.

ServiceMaster Clean was part of a larger ServiceMaster family of brands that included Terminix, Merry Maids, TruGreen ChemLawn, and a range of other residential and commercial services. The parent company, ServiceMaster, had helped create the practice of outsourcing, the contracting out of labor-intensive services by companies and institutions, when it began partnering with health care and educational facilities to perform janitorial duties in the 1960s. ServiceMaster Clean offered commercial janitorial as well as commercial and residential carpet-cleaning and disaster-recovery services. Though it did not match Stanley Steemer's carpet-cleaning sales volume, it was a larger entity overall, operating a worldwide network of more than 4,500 franchises. While not typically an advertiser on national television, ServiceMaster Clean provided franchisees with already developed ad content ready for placement in local media or for use in a wide range of promotional contexts.

Chem-Dry Cleaning was founded in the 1970s on the strength of a new carbonated solution that allowed carpet to be cleaned by using significantly less water than steam-based systems like those employed by Stanley Steemer and ServiceMaster. The Chem-Dry slogan, "Drier. Cleaner. Healthier," made direct, comparative reference to its competitors, as did virtually all of the company's promotional materials.

MARKETING STRATEGY

"Living Brings It In. We Take It Out" was a national television campaign initially consisting of three spots, and there were supporting print, direct-mail, and promotional components. The estimated first-year budget of $20 million represented no significant increase over Stanley Steemer's spending on advertising in a typical year.

In an attempt to motivate more frequent use of the service, however, the new campaign, unlike typical Stanley Steemer advertising, moved away from a stain-centered pitch. Young & Laramore thus sought to convince people that the everyday accumulation of dirt was reason enough to have carpets professionally cleaned and that keeping carpets clean required more than the once-a-year treatment that had been traditionally recommended. As the campaign's creative director, Carolyn Hadlock, told *Shoot,* "It's really not about seeing dirt on the carpet... It's more the Hitchcock approach of letting somebody imagine what's there." While trying to persuade consumers that their homes were dirtier than popularly acknowledged, Young & Laramore wanted to avoid turning its Stanley Steemer pitch into a guilt trip. It was necessary therefore to introduce humor and sympathy into the individual ads of the campaign and to make the central issue one of raising awareness rather than suggesting that the target market's cleaning practices were deficient. Though the pitch did not specify reasons for choosing Stanley Steemer over its competitors, Young & Laramore was counting on the logic that, as the market leader, Stanley Steemer would be the principal beneficiary of an industry-wide increase in sales volume.

The TV spots thus used everyday scenarios that humorously emphasized the impossibility of living without accumulating unseen dirt in a home. In one spot, for instance, a woman speed walking in a normal suburban neighborhood was shown to be unconsciously traversing a veritable obstacle course of filth; she traveled through water, packed dirt, and a steaming construction area and along a trash-strewn commercial strip before entering her otherwise well-maintained house without wiping her feet. In another spot a young boy was shown pulling his backpack through a milk-splattered school cafeteria and across long stretches of puddle-dotted asphalt and billowing dirt and then using the bag as a footstool to help him reach a drinking fountain before casually dragging it into his house and up the carpeted stairs to his room. The third spot in the first year of the campaign compressed a small house dog's daily routine into 30 seconds, showing its numerous and varied missions outdoors from a vantage point at eye level with the home's dog door. The action in each spot ran against a sound track of lighthearted, propulsive music, with the only commentary coming at the end when a gentle female voice-over suggested, "Maybe having your carpet cleaned once a year isn't enough." The voice-over then intoned the tagline, "Living Brings It In. We Take It Out," which also appeared as text on the screen.

The direct-mail and newspaper components of the "Living Brings It In. We Take It Out" campaign, which appeared in all Stanley Steemer markets in 2003, typically included coupons for special rates on multiple room cleanings. Print ads in targeted consumer magazines conformed to the message and imagery of the TV spots. The "Dog Door" spot, for example, had a print companion that showed a still of the terrier's head poking through the dog door to inspect a soiled toy, with the text spelling out the message that had been dramatized in real time on television: "1 terrier. 37 daily round trips. 2 dozen 'gifts.' Maybe having your carpet cleaned once a year isn't enough." Another print ad consisted of a cropped photo of a woman's legs as she stood on the wet pavement of a service station while filling her car with gas. The copy read, "1/2 gallon of gas. 44 ounces of slurpo. 3/4 quart of anti-freeze. Maybe having your carpet cleaned once a year isn't enough."

STEAMER/STEEMER

The Stanley Steamer was a steam-powered automobile invented by Francis Edgar Stanley and variously called "the locomotive of the highway" and "the flying teapot." First manufactured in 1897, the Stanley Steamer was the fastest automobile of its time, setting a land speed record of 127.7 mph in 1906. Production boomed in the early 1900s, but as improvements in the design of the internal-combustion engine made it a far more practical machine, steam automobiles became obsolete, and the last Stanley Steamers were produced in the mid-1920s. When, in 1947, Jack Bates, the founder of Stanley Steemer International, Inc., began using steam-powered vacuums to clean carpets, he was reminded of the Stanley Steamer automobile. He liked the name and made it his company's own with a strange, albeit slight, alteration in spelling.

OUTCOME

Without increasing its advertising budget, Stanley Steemer saw an 11 percent increase in sales over the first 16 months of the "Living Brings It In. We Take It Out" campaign. Young & Laramore, as well as industry analysts, took this as clear evidence of the effectiveness of the strategy and the message of the advertising. In recognition of the campaign's perceived effect on sales, the New York American Marketing Association presented "Living Brings It In. We Take It Out" with a Gold EFFIE Award in 2005 in the Household Supplies and Services category.

The success of the campaign during its first year translated into an extension of the tagline and theme in

2004, as print ads continued to push the notion that daily life itself was enough to warrant the intervention of cleaning professionals. For instance, one ad showing a young girl with dirty bare feet on a park swing featured copy that read, "1 certified tomboy, 10 little piggies, 93 days of summer," along with the tagline and the exhortation to more frequent carpet cleaning: "Maybe having your carpet cleaned once a year isn't enough." Another ad showed a foot-level, under-the-table view of two parents' shoes amid the food-strewn tile floor below an infant's high chair. Pitching one of the new Stanley Steemer services that the company had begun introducing in 2002, the copy read, "Life goes on. Most days it goes on your tile and grout," while also including the "Living Brings It In. We Take It Out" tagline. Meanwhile, television spots in 2004 applied the campaign's theme to the company's Emergency Water Damage Service. Among the most popular spots that year was "Dishwasher," which followed the second-by-second progress of an overflowing dishwasher and of the water inching its way toward the carpet in an adjacent room. Text reading "Not all floods make the national news" appeared on the screen, followed by the "Living Brings It In. We Take It Out" tagline.

The Stanley Steemer campaign was credited with hastening the death of stain-based advertising in the carpet-cleaning industry and for thereby altering the playing field within the business category as a whole. The strategy of encouraging target consumers to think of Stanley Steemer as part of a regular household cleaning routine remained in place in subsequent advertising.

FURTHER READING

Bittar, Christine. "Stanley Steemer Comes Clean about Life's Dirt." *Brandweek,* March 17, 2003.

Gaylin, Alison Sloane. "Young and Laramore." *Shoot,* July 5, 2004.

O'Loughlin, Sandra. "Stanley Steemer Digs Up Dirt." *Brandweek,* May 3, 2004.

Panczyk, Tania D. "Dirt Bedevils Homes in Stanley Steemer Ads." *Adweek,* March 17, 2003.

———. "Stanley Steemer Kicks Off $35 Mil. Review." *Adweek,* July 15, 2002.

———. "Y & L Sweeps Up Stanley Steemer." *Adweek* (Midwest ed.), September 23, 2002.

"Y & L Calls Stanley Steemer." *Shoot,* June 4, 2004.

Mark Lane

Staples, Inc.

500 Staples Drive
Framingham, Massachusetts 01702
USA
Telephone: (508) 253-5000
Web site: www.staples.com

■■■

THAT WAS EASY CAMPAIGN

OVERVIEW

In 2002 three retailers, Office Depot, Inc., Staples, Inc., and OfficeMax, Inc., were America's largest office-supply superstores, with Staples trailing closely behind Office Depot, the industry leader. Advertising analysts criticized the trio for not differentiating their brands. Each offered an abundance of office products, furniture, computers, and printing services at competitive prices. All three used humorous ad campaigns during the back-to-school season and targeted small businesses throughout the year. In February 2002 Ron Sargent was appointed as Staples' new chief executive officer. After research revealed that consumers did not want just low prices but also an effortless shopping experience, Sargent had the store layouts changed so that every aisle could be viewed from the main entrance. Printer cartridges were made more accessible. Unpopular items were removed from Staples' inventory to reduce clutter. To herald its more convenient in-store environment, Staples released the "That Was Easy" campaign in 2003.

The $73 million print, online, radio, and television campaign was created by Omnicom's ad agency Martin/Williams of Minneapolis. The first two commercials ran during the CBS program *60 Minutes* on March 2, 2003. Both spots exaggerated the frustration some customers experienced at office-supply stores. In one spot, titled "Ink Cartridge Bingo," a frazzled office-supply worker called out printer cartridges as if they were Bingo letter-number combinations. Later spots aired during programs that included the Major League Baseball playoffs, prime-time premieres, *Monday Night Football,* NFL football games on CBS, and the 2004 Super Bowl. Staples ended its relationship with Martin/Williams in July 2004 but continued using the "That was easy" tagline for later campaigns.

Just days after "That Was Easy" began, Staples posted 2002 fourth-quarter earnings that repositioned Staples as the new industry leader over Office Depot. The campaign's spot "Ink Cartridge Bingo" was awarded *Adweek* magazine's Best Spot honor in April 2003. The campaign was also credited with boosting sales for Staples' printer cartridges by 14 percent. Additionally, sales for printing services more than doubled during the campaign.

HISTORICAL CONTEXT

Thomas Stemberg was credited with starting the first office-supply superstore, Staples, in 1986 after realizing that small businesses paid too much for office supplies. Before Staples existed, large businesses could buy discounted office supplies in bulk, but smaller businesses purchased their supplies from small, expensive retailers. The average price for one case of copy paper in 1986 was $65. As a result of the emergence of office-supply superstores, 20 years later the price had dropped to $23.

In 1994 Staples awarded its advertising budget to Cliff Freeman and Partners, an ad agency based in New

© NAJLAH FEANNY/CORBIS.

York. The agency's long-running campaign, "Yeah, We've Got That," which promoted the breadth of Staples' merchandise selection, became insignificant after OfficeMax and Office Depot boasted a similar selection. Staples' sales slowed from 2000 to 2001. Not only had the waning economy affected the retailer, but customers were also complaining about the stores' confusing merchandise layouts.

When longtime Staples executive Ron Sargent replaced founder Stemberg as CEO in 2002, employees were already aware of the new CEO's modesty. Even after the promotion, Sargent commuted to work every day in an older Toyota Corolla. Two months later the company's advertising account was reassigned to Martin/Williams. Hoping to take the industry's lead position away from Office Depot, Staples conducted a survey to identify what its own stores were lacking. The survey revealed that the main reason customers chose an office-supply store was not price or selection but in-store convenience.

Staples replaced 700 of its low-end items, such as $9 paper shredders and vegetable-shaped pens, with products more suitable for small businesses. After the survey revealed that convenience outweighed selection in the minds of consumers, newer Staples outlets were opened with less space and fewer items. The aisles were repositioned so that customers could view the entire store from the entrance. In early 2003 Martin/Williams developed the tagline "That was easy" to herald the new store format.

TARGET MARKET

Prior to the "That Was Easy" campaign, marketing analysts criticized Staples for catering to the "casual customer" with cheap, eccentric items such as glitter markers and glow-in-the-dark magnets. "Casual customers" were infrequent buyers who added little to Staples' bottom line. After the 2002 Staples survey revealed that small businesses spending at least $500 annually on office supplies accounted for 90 percent of Staple's profits, Martin/Williams created "That Was Easy" to target small business customers. The survey also revealed that price was not the main impetus behind what office-supply stores small businesses chose; customers simply expected Staples, OfficeMax, and Office Depot to offer the same low prices. In a 2002 earnings conference call Sargent explained the needs of small businesses to investors. "... [W]e asked the customer[s] what they thought and what they needed. What we found out ... is that customers wanted us to be in stock," he said. "They wanted to us have helpful associates. They wanted to us have quick checkout. If they had a problem, they wanted it fixed easily."

One of the campaign's first commercials, "Ink Cartridge Bingo," showed small-business customers waiting impatiently for printer cartridges. The spot was derived from customer feedback. "Based on customer research, 84 percent of small businesses surveyed said a critical aspect of shopping for office products is having the toner or ink cartridge they need in stock," Shira Goodman, executive vice president of marketing at Staples, said in a *Business Wire* press release.

NOT THAT EASY

One month after the office-supply chain Staples released its "That Was Easy" campaign in 2003, the Idaho-based office-supply company Boise Cascade filed a lawsuit against Staples. Executives at Boise Cascade claimed that Staples was unfairly capitalizing on its older slogan, "Boise. It couldn't be easier."

In August 2003 and again in July 2004, the campaign's target market was expanded to include the parents of children returning to school. One humorous spot featured a father interacting with a cardboard cutout of his wife at his daughter's soccer game. The mother's absence was attributed to her having to wade through school supplies at a non-Staples office-supply store. Goodman explained in the press release, "Our customers have told us they are time starved. We've responded this back-to-school season by making it easy for them to get the supplies they need quickly."

COMPETITION

OfficeMax's successful "What's Your Thing?" campaign, which began in December 2003 with a 60-second commercial sharing the campaign's title, featured a lively character called Rubberband Man delivering office supplies inside an office building. In the spot the Afro-sporting character danced to the 1970s Spinners hit "Rubberband Man" while tossing office supplies to employees and pushing an OfficeMax cart. The spot proved so successful that it was parodied on NBC's *The Tonight Show* and was even nominated for a 2004 Emmy within the "Outstanding Commercial" category. Omnicom Group's ad agency DDB Chicago created the campaign with an annual budget of $49 million, helping OfficeMax remain third-largest in the office-supply industry. OfficeMax posted $4.7 billion in sales for 2003. In comparison, Staples posted $11.6 billion in sales that year.

The campaign initially targeted businesses, but after the Rubberband Man character, played by Eddie Steeples, resonated so well with other demographics, further spots promoted back-to-school supplies. "The first 'Rubberband Man' ad established OfficeMax as the best source for business office supplies. These new spots show that OfficeMax is the best place to go for back-to-school shopping because we have a large selection year-round," Dave Goudge, executive vice president of marketing at OfficeMax, said in a *PR Newswire* press release. "The 'Rubberband Man' appeals to kids, teens, college students and parents, giving us a perfect opportunity to make our point in a highly memorable way."

MARKETING STRATEGY

The $73 million Staples campaign's first two commercials aired during the CBS program *60 Minutes* on March 2, 2003. Both spots depicted customers who were frustrated with non-Staples office-supply stores. "Our new work for Staples takes an experience that every small business person can relate to and exaggerates it," John Karlson, senior vice president of strategic development for Martin/Williams, said in a *Business Wire* press release. "It's humorous and memorable, and it differentiates Staples as a brand that makes life easier, saves time, and delivers products consumers need and trust."

One of the first commercials, "Meeting Paper Shuffle," touted Staple's improved three-step printing and photocopying service. The spot began with a business presentation that suddenly went awry due to grossly misprinted handouts. "Before we start, if everyone could move page 15 up two pages," one executive apologetically said. "And if your page 5 in the deck is fuzzy, just pass it down." The camera revealed page 8 to be a misplaced invitation to a luau. "Page 8 . . . just remove it," the executive said. The commercials' voice-over explained, "Unprofessional documents lead to messy meetings. But at Staples, you'll get professional copying and printing."

The campaign's commercials dropped Staples' previous closer, in which a stapler stapled around the corporate logo. Instead Martin/Williams ended "That Was Easy" spots with images pertinent to the service advertised. "Meeting Paper Shuffle" concluded with the Staples logo being scanned inside a photocopier. The campaign's other debut spot, "Ink Cartridge Bingo," which promoted Staples' commitment to a wide selection of printer cartridges, ended with the Staples logo emerging from a printer.

The campaign suggested that Staples did not offer just office supplies but also competent service and advice. "Our new tagline, 'Staples. That was easy' goes far beyond an advertising campaign," Goodman said in the *Business Wire*. "It represents a fundamental shift in our approach to selling office products. It is evolving the Staples brand and guiding every business decision that takes place at the company."

In August 2003 Staples modified the display of its school supplies much as it had done its office products. "Grab and Go" bins with essential school supplies were placed near the stores' entrances. Each store was stocked with ample amounts of filler paper, pencils, and folders to ensure that parents could get everything they needed in one trip. One back-to-school commercial featured a

A PAPER CLIP IS A PAPER CLIP

Competitive pricing between America's largest office-supply chains, Staples, OfficeMax, and Office Depot, was credited with lowering the nationwide cost of office supplies. Kurt Barnard, president of Barnard's Retail Consulting Group, explained to the *Providence Journal Bulletin* that the stores did this by treating office supplies as commodities. "A paper clip is a paper clip is a paper clip is a paper clip," Bernard said. "It doesn't matter where you buy it. It doesn't come with aroma. It doesn't come in flavors. It's like selling pork bellies."

father interacting with a cutout version of his wife at their daughter's soccer game. It ended with the tagline "Back to school shopping at Staples. That was easy." The spot implied that, by shopping for school supplies at Staples, parents could spend more time with their children.

In 2004 Staples also spent $2.25 million to air its first Super Bowl spot. The commercial featured a mean-spirited distributor of office-supplies making his employees provide him candy before he would issue supplies. The commercial concluded with the modified tagline "Staples. That was easy," and targeted a broader audience of consumers that did not typically watch television.

OUTCOME

In July 2004 Staples ended its relationship with Martin/Williams, citing "creative differences," and instead awarded its advertising account to McCann-Erickson New York. The new agency continued using "That was easy" as a tagline but introduced the "Easy Button" campaign, which referred to a device that solved life's problem in the same way that Staples solved office-supply problems. Despite the fact that the Martin/Williams campaign had lasted for only two years, it helped Staples outpace Office Depot from late 2002 to 2004. *Adweek* magazine named the commercial "Ink Cartridge Bingo" a Best Spot of April 2003, commenting, "It's a clever way to promote a dull and frustrating product." Sales of Staples' printer cartridges increased by 14 percent during the breadth of the campaign, and the company's printing-services business more than doubled.

Advertising critics and Staples executives, including Staples' CEO Ron Sargent, initially praised Martin/Williams for reflecting in-store changes so succinctly in the campaign's message. The tagline "That was easy," however, was soon criticized. In late 2003 the Dow Jones News Service released results from a survey that determined which corporate slogans were most recognized by the American public. Out of the survey's 1,021 respondents, not one correctly identified Staples with "That was easy." Nonetheless, Staples executives considered the slogan worthwhile and continued using it after parting with Martin/Williams.

FURTHER READING

Adams, Steve. "Easy Does It: Staples Sued over Phrase." *Quincy (MA) Patriot Ledger,* April 16, 2003, p. 36.

Arndorfer, James B. "Stretching into an Icon." *Advertising Age,* May 31, 2004, p. 3.

Bulik, Beth Snyder. "Martin/Williams 'Easy' Approach to Ads Pays Off." *B to B,* March 8, 2004, p. 28.

Cardona, Mercedes M. "Staples' Holiday Wish List: Humor." *Advertising Age,* July 19, 2004, p. 8.

Conklin, Melanie. "Pressing People's Buttons." *Madison (WI) Capital Times/Wisconsin State Journal,* November 20, 2005, p. A2.

Deutsch, Claudia H. "Big Office Supply Retailers Try to Build a Smaller Box." *New York Times,* August 12, 2004, p. 1.

Eckelbecker, Lisa. "Staples Is Now World Leader." *Worcester (MA) Telegram & Gazette,* March 6, 2003, p. E1.

Elliott, Stuart. "ING Retires Fresh Thinking to Focus on the Simpler Life." *New York Times,* January 12, 2006, p. 4.

———. "Staples Is Changing Its Slogan to Stress the Ease of Shopping for Office Supplies in Its Stores." *New York Times,* February 27, 2003, p. 6.

———. "Staples Plans to Replace Martin/Williams." *New York Times,* May 3, 2004, p. 8.

Gatlin, Greg. "Staples Rethinks, then Resurges." *Boston Herald,* April 24, 2003, p. H13.

Hanrahan, Tim. "When Worlds Collide." *Wall Street Journal,* April 28, 2003, p. R1.

Lee, Thomas. "It's An Ad, Ad, Ad, Ad World." *St. Louis Post-Dispatch,* January 26, 2004, p. A1.

Randy, Ray. "Is It Mainly Because of the Tag Line?" *Toronto (Ontario) Globe and Mail,* November 7, 2003, p. B11.

Vranica, Suzanne. "The Advertising Report: 'RubberBand Man' Breathes New Life into OfficeMax." *Wall Street Journal,* August 11, 2004, p. B5.

Williams, Helaine R. "Let's Talk Wanted: Big Button to Make Life Easier." *Arkansas Democrat-Gazette,* October 16, 2005, p. 61.

Kevin Teague

YEAH, WE'VE GOT THAT CAMPAIGN

OVERVIEW

Staples, Inc., was one of three office-supply-superstore chains to emerge in the 1980s, each vying to differentiate itself from the others. In 1994 Staples launched its first full-fledged television campaign, airing a pair of 30-second spots produced by its new ad agency, Cliff Freeman & Partners, New York. Targeting people who worked at home, the spots used the tagline "Yeah, We've Got That," a phrase that expressed the breadth of products a Staples superstore had to offer. In 1997 Staples would use the tagline as an anchor for a national campaign.

The "Yeah, We've Got That" campaign targeted small-business owners but also hoped to appeal to general consumers, such as parents shopping for school supplies. While the campaign included radio spots, it was primarily a television campaign. The humorous TV spots attempted to use real-life situations to appeal to their audience. Perhaps the most popular of all the commercials was the back-to-school spot that featured upbeat parents, dour children, and the song "It's the Most Wonderful Time of the Year" playing in the background.

The "Yeah, We've Got That" campaign ran for eight years. It won several advertising awards and played a major role in driving Staples' sales beyond the $10 billion mark. A change in management and a desire to reposition the brand led to the departure of Cliff Freeman and the introduction of a fresh marketing campaign in 2002.

HISTORICAL CONTEXT

Staples was the original office-supply superstore in the United States. It opened its first store in 1986 and grew rapidly, by the end of 1996 operating about 600 stores throughout the United States and Canada. It also had 40 stores in the United Kingdom and 16 in Germany. Depending on the location and the services they offered, the North American stores were called Staples, Staples Express, Business Depot, or Bureau En Gros. In 1997 Staples had the second-largest market share in the United States, behind Office Depot but ahead of OfficeMax, and was the largest operator of office superstores in the world.

Staples filled a market need by providing office supplies, furniture, computer hardware and software, and related items for small businesses at the same substantial discounts previously available only to large corporations. In addition, it offered Staples Direct delivery service, a mail-order business, and contract stationer operations called Staples Business Advantage and Staples National Advantage, which mainly served large companies.

TARGET MARKET

Most people who shopped at Staples fell into one of three categories. The company's primary customers were from 27 to 54 years old and owned small businesses, with many having home offices. Staples estimated that it had 3.5 million customers in this category. "We mostly target the small-business customer, because that's really what Staples is all about. We're sort of the champion of the small-business person," said Dwight Garland,vice president of retail advertising. Staples calculated that small businesses were growing at four times the rate of large businesses and that half the households in the United States would have home offices by the year 2000. Other people shopped at Staples for items such as school supplies for their children. These customers created a strong seasonal market for certain products. In addition, the company's contract and commercial division served large regional and national businesses. These three categories left ample room for growth in the office-supply business. The company noted in its annual report that the U.S. office-products market was estimated at $205 billion and was increasing by 10 percent each year.

The primary target of the "Yeah, We've Got That" campaign was small businesses and individual consumers. "The idea is to engage these targeted customers by touching on real-life situations," Garland explained. The commercials conveyed the message that Staples understood its

HUMOR SELLS

Cliff Freeman & Partners, the ad agency that developed the "Yeah, We've Got That" campaign for Staples, was known for its use of offbeat humor. The agency had done a campaign for the Little Caesar pizza chain in which a cartoon Caesar cheerfully said, "Pizza! Pizza!" According to a survey by the *Wall Street Journal,* that campaign was the best remembered and most popular in the United States in 1992. The agency also created a well-known campaign for Wendy's in which a woman examining a competitor's hamburger demanded, "Where's the beef?" In addition, the agency developed the "Sometimes You Feel like a Nut, Sometimes You Don't" campaign for Mounds and Almond Joy candy bars and the "Get the Sensation" campaign for York peppermint patties. The agency's chairman and chief creative officer, Cliff Freeman, had won 22 Clio Awards for excellence in advertising, including three awards for the best campaign of the year.

customers, and the use of gentle humor worked to create a friendly, helpful image for the company. The stores offered a wide variety of products to help customers organize and streamline their businesses and work, and the prices were typically lower than those of most competitors, an important selling point for owners of small enterprises. Some Staples locations also featured Federal Express shipping stations, photocopy centers with printing capabilities, and bindery equipment, thus providing one-stop convenience. "It comes back to the mission of finding ways to cut the prices and hassles for our customers," said Garland.

COMPETITION

According to *Time* magazine, when the "Yeah, We've Got That" campaign began, Office Depot was the number one office-supply superstore in North America, with about 6 percent of the market, and OfficeMax was third, with about 3 percent. Staples was second, with 4 percent of the $92 billion retail market and 2 percent of the $63 billion contract and commercial market. There also were numerous independent office-supply stores and retail outlets that sold computers and other office machines. In addition, large chains such as Wal-Mart sold office supplies, business machines, furniture, and related products.

During 1997 Office Depot ran a marketing campaign that featured the popular comic-strip character Dilbert, known for his wry observations on the absurdities of office life. The tagline was "Business Is Crazy, but Office Depot Makes Sense." *USA Today*'s Ad Track found that the ads were slightly less popular than the average campaign surveyed, with 7 percent of women and 14 percent of men saying that they disliked the commercials. Office Depot maintained that its research indicated that the Dilbert commercials were popular with its target market and that they had increased brand awareness for the company. Nevertheless, in 1999 it shelved Dilbert, concluding that the popular cartoon character overshadowed the brand and did not produce the desired results.

OfficeMax was founded later than Staples and Office Depot, but it enjoyed a strong run in the first half of the 1990s. Although by 1995 it ranked second behind Office Depot, it was soon eclipsed by Staples and relegated to the number three position in the office-superstore category. Not until the first decade of the new millennium did OfficeMax begin to develop its own brand identity, aided in large part by the creation of its Rubberband Man character, who served to anchor its marketing efforts.

MARKETING STRATEGY

With its "Yeah, We've Got That" campaign, Staples focused on customers who owned small businesses. During 1997 the commercials placed new emphasis on the fact that Staples offered low prices as part of its basic mission. Since the campaign's inception in 1994, there had been slight variations in the message and target audience for some of the advertisements, but the general concept had remained the same. Garland explained that the commercials were developed with a clear goal—to create an image for the company. When customers laughed at an advertisement, they would be apt to make an association with Staples and expect to find a friendly attitude there. The slogan "Yeah, We've Got That" at the end of each commercial referred especially to the company's wide selection of merchandise and attention to customer service. "Cliff Freeman came up with that tag line, and we still use it today," Garland said. "We've done research in many markets, and people remember it." The tagline was mentioned at the end of every broadcast spot but was used in only a few print ads, because its effectiveness depended to a large extent on voice inflection and facial expression. Garland said that customers also tended to comment on the sequence at the end of the commercials, in which a "kchink, kchink, kchink" sound accompanied the visual of a stapler spelling out "Staples."

The company's broader marketing plan included circulars, direct mailings, catalogs sent to customers, and other promotions in print media, but the "Yeah, We've Got That" campaign was developed for television. In addition, a few of the spots with the most focused messages were broadcast via radio. The promotions in print media gave details about the company's products, services, and prices. In contrast, the television commercials were intended to make the public aware of Staples in general. "TV is the best vehicle to generate awareness, and awareness is a key component of growth," Garland noted. The television commercials supported the print promotions by calling attention to various aspects of Staples. For example, the Staples mail-order catalog figured prominently in the "Intern" spot.

There had been about 40 spots in the campaign since 1994, and a quarter of them ran in 1997, the first year the commercials were seen on national network television. Some spots in the campaign targeted a broad audience, while others, such as "Intern," were aimed at a narrower market. In the "Intern" spot an ambitious office administrator asked a young woman what she was doing. She held up a Staples catalog and explained, "A cost analysis. I think we're spending too much on office supplies." He sent her to polish a refrigerator while he hurried to show the catalog to his boss and underhandedly take credit for the intern's work. As the two men walked past the intern, the boss said, "Oh, I see you've met my daughter." At the end of the commercial appeared the campaign's tagline, "Yeah, We've Got That." Of the 122 advertisements featured in *USA Today*'s Ad Track consumer polls in 1997, the "Intern" spot scored among the most popular.

The first spot developed for the back-to-school season won a Clio Award and was so popular that the company subsequently ran it at the end of every summer. It featured a father, son, and daughter shopping for school supplies at Staples while "It's the Most Wonderful Time of the Year" played in the background. Although the song actually referred to Christmas, the sentiment reflected the father's elation at seeing his children going back to school. The children, however, were glum because their summer vacation was ending. "It touches an emotion everybody feels," said Garland. "This spot really strikes a chord." He added that the commercial was so popular that customers frequently called Staples at other times of the year to find out when it would be aired again. Even as new back-to-school spots were created for the campaign later in the 1990s, Staples continued to mix in this perennially popular commercial.

Later in the "Yeah, We've Got That" campaign, Staples targeted entrepreneurs with a television spot that featured a businessman standing on a mountain peak. A voice-over declared, "There is a new breed of businessperson who had decided to go it alone." The man then threw his briefcase, tie, jacket, and shoes into the valley below before stepping into an SUV stuffed with Staples office supplies and driving away. Next, a hiker with a shoe imprint on his forehead was shown. "What hit me?" he asked a friend, who replied, "Wingtip." As usual, the spot concluded with the "Yeah, We've Got That" tagline.

OUTCOME

In addition to the Clio and EFFIE awards, over the years the Staples commercials won numerous other advertising honors, including several ADDYs, an ANDY, and a Mercury Award for a radio spot. The "Yeah, We've Got That" campaign was among the five most popular surveyed by *USA Today*'s Ad Track from June 1996 to June 1997. In another *USA Today* survey in December 1997, the campaign's "Intern" spot received an effectiveness score of 32 percent and a popularity score of 37 percent, the highest of the 122 advertisements studied that year. Only 7 percent of respondents said that they disliked the ads. Almost 45 percent of respondents 30 to 49 years old and 33 percent of respondents 18 to 29 said that they "liked the ads a lot." The campaign was most popular with women, with 35 percent giving it high scores for effectiveness, compared to 28 percent of the men surveyed. "It's been a very successful campaign. On the whole, it's run very smoothly. We know people like the work, because we do a great deal of research," said Garland.

While the "Yeah, We've Got That" campaign drove sales, Staples continued to trail Office Depot. In 2001 Office Depot generated $11 billion in sales, compared to $10.7 billion for Staples. Believing that "Yeah, We've Got That" had run its course, Staples, which had also undergone a change in management, put its advertising account up for review with the intent of repositioning the brand. Cliff Freeman & Partners was invited to defend but chose not to participate in the process. The Minneapolis ad agency Martin/Williams won the business in 2002, and that year it released the first Staples campaign in eight years that did not rely on the "Yeah, We've Got That" tagline.

FURTHER READING

Baar, Aaron. "Staples Issues 'Apologies' in New TV Campaign." *Adweek* (New England ed.), October 7, 2002, p. 3.

Baumohl, Bernard, John Greenwald, Joseph R. Szczesny, and Adam Zagorin. "March of the Superstores." *Time,* September 16, 1996.

"The Best Awards: Family Affair Highlights Humor Ploy for Staples." *Advertising Age,* May 27, 1996.

Brown, Ed. "Why the FTC Needs to Chill." *Fortune,* April 14, 1997.

Enrico, Dottie. "Staples Nails Office Images." *USA Today,* June 9, 1997.

Garfield, Bob. "Ad Review: Office Depot." *Advertising Age,* August 19, 1996.

"How the Ad Track Ads of 1997 Stack Up." *USA Today,* December 29, 1997.

Sampey, Kathleen, and Ann M. Mack. "Staples Shifts Gears." *Adweek* (western ed.), April 15, 2002, p. 4.

Taylor, Cathy. "For Office Homebodies: Staples TV Spots Target At-Home Workers." *Adweek* (eastern ed.), April 11, 1994, p. 4.

Susan Risland
Ed Dinger

State Farm Mutual Automobile Insurance Company

One State Farm Plaza
Bloomington, Illinois 61710-0001
USA
Telephone: (309) 766-2311
Fax: (309) 766-3621
Web site: www.statefarm.com

TRUE STORIES CAMPAIGN

OVERVIEW

The leading automobile insurer since World War II, State Farm Mutual Automobile Insurance Company had relied for many years on advertising that took a serious tone and was anchored by its longtime slogan, "Like a good neighbor, State Farm is there." But in the 1990s the industry was turned upside down by direct marketer GEICO, which emerged from obscurity to blanket the television airways with a bevy of humorous commercials promoting the low price of its car insurance, which it was able to offer largely because it did not maintain the extensive agent network of a company such as State Farm. The Progressive Corporation also beefed up its marketing budget to make its own price pitch. State Farm and its closest competitor, Allstate, shied away from the insurance price war that developed, but by the first decade of the new millennium, price had become paramount in the mind of consumers, and State Farm, which had always promoted customer service over price, found itself losing market share. In 2004 State Farm released a new advertising campaign created by ad agency DDB Chicago. Called "True Stories," it made the case that an agent-client relationship was important.

The "True Stories" television spots were humorous depictions of unusual ways that actual State Farm agents helped their customers. The agents played themselves, while the customers and supporting cast were portrayed by actors. One spot, for example, concerned a Wisconsin State Farm agent who was also the local diver. When an out-of-town driver accidentally drove his car into a lake, the agent simultaneously settled the claim and salvaged the car. The budget for "True Stories" was not made public.

State Farm was pleased enough with the campaign to continue producing new television spots, including one that first aired during the pregame show for the 2006 Super Bowl. State Farm began to reverse the trend of losing market share, and in 2005 the company exceeded its sales quota by a large margin.

HISTORICAL CONTEXT

Since 1971 State Farm had centered its marketing around the slogan "Like a good neighbor, State Farm is there." The advertisements of State Farm and such rivals as Allstate and Nationwide touted their networks of agents and the customer service they provided, while avoiding any mention of price. In the 1990s GEICO, a direct marketer with no agents at all, began to upset the balance of the industry. The broad humor it employed in its commercials was a complete departure from the warm and serious tone adopted by State Farm and the old-guard insurers. More importantly, GEICO and the Progressive Corporation began bombarding the media with advertising that focused solely on price. They had everything to gain by such an approach, and both added market share during the 1990s and into the new century. State Farm, on the other hand, refused to contend for business on those terms, fearful that auto insurance would be reduced to commodity status: a low-profit item, only the cheapest of which customers bought. Instead the company continued to emphasize the level of customer service that its agents provided, maintaining that it warranted the higher costs of its premiums.

Although State Farm maintained it top position in the auto-insurance market, it began to experience erosion in the first years of the new millennium. It enjoyed a 19.3 percent share of the private-passenger auto-insurance market in 2002, but that number dipped to 19 percent in 2003 and continued to decline in 2004. Through their constant advertising GEICO and Progressive had changed the terms of the debate about shopping for auto insurance: price had become paramount, and the value of having a relationship with a agent was relegated to secondary status. In many ways the auto-insurance field was engaged in a battle of business models. Writing for *Advertising Age,* Mya Frazier reported that the fight was "pitting the call-center row of headset-wearing operators taking claims and signing on new customers against neighborhood agents who know a customer's kids and may even be a neighbor. It's pitting Internet price quotes vs. in-office consultations and the yearly search for a best price vs. a lifetime relationship with an agent." The direct model was enjoying faster growth than the agent-based approach. In an effort to return the focus to service and differentiate between price and value, State Farm in 2004 released its "True Stories" campaign, a lighthearted depiction of the lengths to which actual State Farm agents would go in service of their customers. While State Farm did not give in to GEICO and adopt a price message, it did drop its usual serious tone in favor of humor.

TARGET MARKET

Auto insurers had to contend with one of the broadest target audiences in all of marketing. The law required every driver to be insured, creating a massive pool of potential clients that encompassed all genders, races, and ages. The younger demographic, however, was more price-conscious and had not grown up with the assumption that one did business with an agent. In fact, many of them preferred not to have a relationship with an agent and were more than willing to switch insurance companies if the price was right. It was the older, less price-sensitive driver who was a more appropriate target for State Farm's "True Stories." Many of these people were already State Farm customers, and the company was eager to keep their business by reminding them of the value of an agent relationship. The campaign also sought to persuade other older drivers of the importance of what State Farm had to offer. At the same time the company was not writing off younger customers. One of the television commercials focused on a young woman who had two accidents within her first hour of having a driver's license. The spot appealed to both young people and parents.

> ### A SPECIALIST IN TRUE STORIES
>
> The first television spots in State Farm's "True Stories" campaign were directed by Academy Award–winning documentary filmmaker Errol Morris. He received his Oscar in 2004 for *The Fog of War,* concerning the life of Robert S. McNamara, U.S. secretary of defense during the Vietnam War. Morris's other documentaries included *Gates of Heaven, The Thin Blue Line, A Brief History of Time,* and *Fast, Cheap, and Out of Control.*

COMPETITION

State Farm's closest rival was Allstate, which had about 10 percent of the auto-insurance market in 2004. Next came Progressive with 7.1 percent and GEICO with 5.5 percent, followed by Farmers Insurance Group, Nationwide Group, United Services Automobile Association Group, American International Group, Liberty Mutual Group, and American Family Insurance Group. Because of GEICO's attention-grabbing advertising and Progressive's willingness to spend exorbitant amounts of money on television advertising, every company in the industry was forced to follow suit. The bulk of the advertisements were price appeals, and even Allstate, which, like State Farm, had always avoided such a message, made a concession to the prevailing trend. Its "Our Stand" campaign, featuring actor Dennis Haysbert, who played the U.S. president in the hit television series *24,* began in November 2003. It promoted Allstate's good-driver discount and touted statistics showing that people who switched to Allstate saved $200 a year on average.

There was another compelling reason that insurers were padding their marketing budgets in an effort to poach customers from one another: the car-insurance business had become more profitable than ever. Cars were better built and safer. There were fewer accidents caused by mechanical problems, and as a result insurers paid out fewer claims. The U.S. population was also growing older. Older drivers tended to drive slower and more cautiously, again resulting in fewer accidents and claims and greater profits for insurers. Hence, State Farm's eroding market share was costing it a great deal of money. The company wanted not only to hold the line but also to build on its number one position and post even greater profits in the years to come.

MARKETING STRATEGY

The purpose of the "True Stories" campaign was to demonstrate the personal care that State Farm agents offered their customers. The company's advertising agency, DDB Chicago, said that to develop the campaign it had contacted State Farm's 13 regional zones, asking agents to submit actual customer experiences that revealed exceptional and highly unusual service. About 250 agents responded; 15 were determined to be of interest, and of them 6 were chosen to be dramatized. While actors would play most of the roles, the State Farm agents played themselves.

How the agents appeared on film, however, may have played a major part of the selection process. According to *About Business,* published by the city of Edina, Minnesota, one of the State Farm agents featured in "True Stories," local woman Joan Roisum, was nominated by a State Farm regional vice president. Next she was videotaped to determine if she was photogenic enough for the commercial. According to writer Cheryl Anderson, "She then needed to have a 'true story' to capture the interest of both State Farm and its advertising agency. They called her periodically for a year to ask if she had a story about a particular topic, but her stories had not interested them." Roisum finally caught the agency's attention when she was asked if she had any stories about people who switched from another insurer to State Farm. She told them about a newly married couple with whom she had worked: they had two of everything, including dogs, but the wife was a GEICO customer and the husband a State Farm customer. In the end they kept State Farm. A few weeks later Roisum was in Hollywood to shoot her commercial.

The 30-second television spots were first shown during baseball's World Series, which was telecast on the Fox network on October 23, 2004. Subsequently the commercials aired on major network shows and cable programming. In addition to the general-market spots, the campaign included the creation of single spots aimed at the African-American, Hispanic, and Chinese-American markets (for the latter separate spots were filmed in Cantonese and Mandarin). The spot called "Diver" featured Wisconsin State Farm agent Larry Bitterman, who served an out-of-town State Farm driver whose car had somehow fallen into a lake as a result of a faulty map. Not only did Bitterman settle the claim, but he also helped raise the car from the lake in his capacity as local diver. The "New Driver" spot showed a State Farm agent providing counsel for a San Jose, California, teenager who crashed her car twice in 10 seconds, within 45 minutes of receiving her driver's license. Her tale was interwoven with commentary from her parents and brothers. Other spots included Roisum's newlyweds as well as twin sisters who had accidents in the same intersection. The six agent stories were also fleshed out on the Internet as interactive ads. Radio versions of the television spots were created, and the campaign included a handful of print ads, but television was far and away the main messenger. Although one spot touted State Farm's financial services, the campaign focused on car insurance.

OUTCOME

State Farm considered the "True Stories" campaign a success and continued to air the television spots, along with new executions, into 2006. One of the new spots made its debut during the pregame ceremony of the 2006 Super Bowl. In 2004 State Farm's market share fell further, to 18.2 percent. In the company's annual report chairman and chief executive officer Edward B. Rust, Jr., made note of the poor showing of State Farm's auto division, writing, "Although we wrote 5.6 million auto applications and added more than 375,000 policies and accounts to our total book of business, we fell short of our growth goals in our core auto business. Our toughest competitors increased their share of the auto market—we did not." The situation improved in 2005, however, when State Farm made great strides in reversing the trend. The company set a goal of 400,000 new policies and exceeded that number by 225,000. Consumers surveys conducted after the start of the campaign also revealed significant improvement concerning positive brand image and likelihood for a non–State Farm customer to consider State Farm as an insurer.

FURTHER READING

Anderson, Cheryl. "National Television Ad Features True Story of Edina Insurance Agent." *About Business,* Winter 2006, p. 14.

Cavanaugh, Bonnie Brewer. "Price Wars." *Best's Review,* October 2005, p. 37.

Dunlap, Bill. "Errol Morris: Reel Life." *Shoot,* March 25, 2005, p. 27.

Frazier, Mya. "Progressive, Geico Prod Auto Rivals into Price War." *Advertising Age,* February 28, 2005, p. 4.

Goch, Lynna. "State Farm's Commercials Feature Agents on the Job." *Best's Review,* December 2004, p. 69.

Lazare, Lewis. "Stunt to Sell Taste if Tasteless." *Chicago Sun-Times* October 22, 2004.

"State Farm Spots Tell 'True Stories.'" *Adweek* (midwest ed.), October 22, 2004.

Waggoner, Judy. "Appleton Insurance Man Stars in TV Ad." *Appleton (WI) Post-Crescent,* June 13, 2005.

Wasserman, Todd. "Risky Business." *Brandweek,* November 15, 2004, p. 6.

Ed Dinger

Steelcase, Inc.

901 44th Street, SE
Grand Rapids, Michigan 49508
USA
Telephone: (616) 247-2710
Fax: (616) 475-2270
Web site: www.steelcase.com

WORK EFFECTIVENESS CAMPAIGN

OVERVIEW

The world's leading contract seller of office furniture at the end of the twentieth century, Steelcase, Inc., was closely associated with one of its pioneering products, the Series 9000 Systems Furniture line. Introduced in the 1970s, it became the building block of the modern-day corporate cubicle environment. Steelcase was so closely tied to the cube and its often dehumanizing deployment that the company was stigmatized as being uncreative. Aside from that image, considered unfair by the company, Steelcase had to contend with a corporate mind-set that viewed office furniture as a cost to contain, a necessary but not imperative expense that could be put off during bad times. As a result of this thinking, office furniture competed mostly on the basis of price, and profit margins were trimmed. As the economy stalled at the start of the new century, Steelcase launched the "Work Effectiveness" campaign to recast itself not only as an innovative company offering stylish furniture but also as a corporate partner who could help customers improve the work conditions of employees, thereby increasing productivity and having a positive impact on the bottom line.

The "Work Effectiveness" campaign, developed by Minneapolis-based advertising agency Martin/Williams, focused on two audiences: the traditional target of designers and facility managers along with corporate executives, the decision makers to whom Steelcase wanted to make the pitch that top-of-the-line office furniture not only paid for itself but could make the company money and help in attracting workers. This notion was backed by research Steelcase conducted showing that a good work environment improved employee productivity and could be even more effective in improving profitability than a comparable investment in technology or even research and development. To make its case the campaign offered three ads. To target the conventional audience the ads ran in trade publications, but to reach the corporate suites Steelcase turned to more mainstream business and technology publications, the likes of *Forbes* and *Fortune*.

The "Work Effectiveness" campaign succeeded in improving Steelcase's image with designers and facility managers but failed to register with corporate executives. After the tech bubble collapsed and the marketplace was glutted with used furniture, executives, who were themselves tightening their belts, had little incentive to buy new furniture, no matter how good it was. The contract office furniture industry slipped into its worst slump in 50 years. Steelcase was able to maintain its dominant market share, however. The "Work Effectiveness" campaign was honored with a major award, the 2002 Grand CEBA.

HISTORICAL CONTEXT

A pioneer in office furniture since 1912, Steelcase was the undisputed global leader in the contract office furniture business at the start of the 2000s, but in some ways it was a victim of its own success. In the early 1970s Steelcase unveiled the Series 9000 Systems Furniture line, introducing white-collar workers around the world to cubes. The functional but hardly aesthetic furniture became ubiquitous in the corporate workplace and made a lot of money for Steelcase over the next 30 years but led to perception problems for the company at the dawn of the new century.

The image of the contract furniture industry was closely tied to cubicles, which as they were assembled into endless bays became a dehumanizing environment that did not engender positive associations. Rather, they became fodder for the *Dilbert* comic strip, which chronicled the foibles of the modern corporate workaday world. As a result Steelcase, the father of "Dilbertville," was seen as anything but an innovative company. Perhaps of more importance was that office furniture in general had been reduced in the eyes of corporate executives as a mere cost center, an expense to reduce as much as possible, and something that did not make any positive contribution to a business. As long as the economy was strong, companies paid out money for new furniture, but during slumps costs were contained and office furnishings became a vulnerable line in the budget. After a 20-year boom in office furniture sales, Steelcase experienced a slump in the early 1990s. Business picked up as the economy rebounded, then as the economy again faltered in the early 2000s Steelcase once more had to contend with companies cutting back on the purchase of new office furniture. The debate about office furniture rarely ventured beyond the questions of price and efficiency.

In the fall of 2000 Steelcase hired Minneapolis-based advertising agency Martin/Williams, which soon concluded that executives at corporate customers were being shortsighted, a thought supported by extensive studies Steelcase commissioned on the importance of the work environment on white-collar workers. The research indicated that a comfortable, efficient work environment could have a profound effect on productivity and in turn make as great an impact on the bottom line as investments in information technology, research and development, or human capital. In a nutshell people could not concentrate on their work if they were forever adjusting their chair or their lamp, and an uncomfortable setup could tire workers and hinder their effectiveness. Martin/Williams and Steelcase then developed the "Work Effectiveness" campaign as a way to change the image of Steelcase and reframe the debate about the importance of office furniture—from cost containment to an investment in productivity.

FURNITURE CITY

Grand Rapids, Michigan, the home of Steelcase, Inc., was founded in 1850. The city became a major lumbering center, so it was no surprise that some of that wood ended up being used to make furniture. The furniture-making industry thrived in Grand Rapids, which would be dubbed Furniture City.

TARGET MARKET

"Work Effectiveness" was a business-to-business campaign that focused on two audiences. The first was Steelcase's traditional target reached through trade publications: facilities managers, designers, and architects. To these people Steelcase wanted to make the case that it was more than a provider of cubes, that it also sold stylish products that were ergonomic and offered enhanced technology capabilities (such as a computer desk that offered an innovative sheath to house the many computer and telecom cables that created a tangle and bedeviled the modern worker). The second target audience resided in the corporate suites: CEOs, COOs, CFOs, and the like. While the first audience might recommend that a Steelcase product be purchased, it was the second audience that had to be convinced that the corporation would get enough bang for its buck to justify signing off on the request. To them style was nice, but productivity that impacted the balance sheet was what mattered.

COMPETITION

Steelcase was the global leader in its field. Its largest competitors were HNI Corp.; Haworth, Inc.; and Herman Miller, Inc. All of them had traditionally relied on a network of dealers to move their products and limited their advertising budgets to trade publications, but now retailers like OfficeMax and Staples were spending millions on advertising to reach a general audience. According to Rob Kirkbride, writing for the *Grand Rapids Press* in 2001, this new competition was "forcing the [contract furniture] companies to reach out to mass markets." Steelcase's director of corporate communications, Allan Smith, told Kirkbride that the company recognized that advertising was an incredibly important tool to show corporate decision makers that Steelcase could help them work more effectively. Steelcase was not alone in spending money on more general publications. Herman Miller had recently placed ads in the *Wall Street Journal* and *Adweek.* And Haworth had in previous years launched a campaign that included ads in *Forbes*

WOULD THAT IT WERE METAL

Steelcase, Inc., was founded in 1912 in Grand Rapids, Michigan, as the Metal Office Furniture Company. It fabricated furniture out of sheet metal, the main advantage of which was that it was not flammable. At the time offices were cluttered with wooden furniture and still heated and lit by open flame appliances.

and *Fortune* as well as television spots. In fact, in 1995 Steelcase had funded a print and television campaign. But times were different now. The economy had slipped into a recession, and although Steelcase maintained that the "Work Effectiveness" campaign was not designed to combat difficult times, it was important that Steelcase stake its claim as a vibrant and innovative company to at least fend off the competition from making inroads into its dominant share of the market.

MARKETING STRATEGY

The "Work Effectiveness" campaign sought to change what the marketers called a category debate, to shift the focus from price and depth of product line to how furniture and workplace design helped people improve their productivity. And as long as corporate decision makers considered office furniture as a cost center, furniture would be lumped into the same category, almost reduced to the status of a commodity, and with that attitude came greater price competition in the marketplace and lower profit margins for Steelcase. Instead the marketers wanted to position Steelcase as a partner, someone who brought more value to a customer than just selling them a desk and chair. Steelcase wanted to portray itself as providing workplace solutions, helping to create environments in which employees could flourish—and ultimately make more money.

The "Work Effectiveness" campaign, limited to the print medium, was launched with a series of three ads. To reach the architects, designers, and facilities managers, the ads were run in trade publications: *Architectural Record, Interior Design,* and *Facility Manager.* To catch the attention of corporate executives, Steelcase also advertised in mainstream business publications, including *Forbes, Fortune,* and the *Wall Street Journal* as well as *Harvard Business Review.* In addition it bought ad space in technology-oriented publications, such as *Wired, Fast Company,* and *Metropolis.*

The three print ads focused on a particular product design element, and the copy made the case that the product made life easier and improved an employee's overall effectiveness. One of the ads featured a close-up picture of the curved back of the Steelcase Leap Chair. The headline read, "Ergonomic chic." A second ad featured a trash can that hooked beneath the desk surface. The copy read, "Furniture design to make you think better. A built-in trash can in case you don't." The final ad showed a picture of a computer desk that used an S-shaped "spine" that organized computer cables. "It has a spine," read the copy. "Therefore, it must have a brain."

The ads directed readers to the Steelcase website, where more information could be found. For the most part the ads were lean, but in some publications additional information was adjacent to the ad. An example of a page-and-a-third ad, a relatively new concept in print advertising, was the trash can ad supplemented with a sidebar titled "Can a piece of office furniture raise your IQ?" The copy then offered the results of a work environment research study that emphasized the need for a good work environment and made the case that Steelcase designed products with the users' needs and desires in mind, "even with clever details like the trash can attached to the side of the desk."

OUTCOME

Research indicated that the two-year "Work Effectiveness" campaign succeeded in changing the perception of Steelcase among architects, designers, and facility managers, which began to view the company as more innovative than previously thought. But the campaign failed to have any kind of impact on the other target, the executives residing in the corporate suites. The advertising budget was simply too small to have the kind of impact that would dent the perception of this audience, and the ad buys shifted entirely to the trade publications. It was unlikely that given economic conditions any amount of advertising was going to convince executives to buy new office furniture, no matter how stylish and technically advanced. Following the bursting of the technology bubble, a lot of companies folded and their unneeded furniture, churned out by furniture manufacturers during the heady days of the late 1990s, now created a huge aftermarket for office furniture. The question for executives was simple: why buy new when you could buy used—and cheap? As a result the bottom fell out of the contract furniture industry, which experienced the worst slump in half a century, losing about two-thirds of its market. One of the few positives for Steelcase was that its "Work Effectiveness" campaign was effective enough that the company maintained market share under these difficult conditions. Moreover it was able to successfully introduce two new products and a workplace-planning tool.

The "Work Effectiveness" campaign was also a success creatively and was honored by the advertising industry. In 2002 the campaign, beating out 420 competing campaigns, was recognized as the best business-to-business advertising in the United States for that year by the American Business Media when it awarded Martin/Williams the Grand CEBA (Creative Excellence in Business Advertising).

FURTHER READING

Baar, Aaron. "Martin/Williams Wins Grand CEBA Award." *Adweek,* October 31, 2003.

———. "M/W Kicks Off Steelcase Work." *Adweek,* May 28, 2001.

Bulik, Beth Snyder. "Martin/Williams 'Easy' Approach to Ads Pays Off." *B to B,* March 8, 2004, p. 28.

Jensen, Trevor. "Steelcase Seats Martin/Williams." *Adweek,* August 28, 2000, p. 8.

Kirkbride, Rob. "Office Furniture Firms Using More Mass Market Ads." *Grand Rapids Press,* July 13, 2001, p. A13.

"Martin/Williams Wins Grand CEBA." *B to B,* November 11, 2002, p. 2.

"Steelcase, Inc." *International Directory of Company Histories,* vol. 27. Farmington Hills, Michigan: St. James Press, 1999.

"Steelcase Survey: Comfort + Collaboration = Productivity." *Facilities Design & Management,* February 2003, p. 13.

Ed Dinger

Suburban Auto Group

36936 Highway 26
Sandy, Oregon 97055
USA
Telephone: (800) 691-4204
Web site: www.suburbanautogroup.com

TRUNK MONKEY CAMPAIGN

OVERVIEW

In 2003 Carlson Chevrolet Co., Inc., a Chevrolet car dealership located in Sandy, Oregon, just a few miles southeast of Portland, represented the Chevrolet-selling half of the Suburban Auto Group. On the other side of U.S. Highway 26 the car dealership Suburban Ford, Inc., represented the Ford-selling half. Nancy Jaksich controlled the Chevrolet dealership, and her husband, Jerry Jaksich, managed Suburban Ford. Compared to other dealerships in Oregon, the Suburban Auto Group was "not even in the top 10 in terms of money spent on advertising by car dealers in the Portland area," reported the *Portland Business Journal.* Hoping to stand out amongst the clutter of local car dealership advertising, the Suburban Auto Group launched its "Trunk Monkey" campaign.

"Trunk Monkey" was created by the ad agency R/West for less than $50,000. The campaign's first spot, "Road Rage," cost only $3,000 and debuted during the 2003 Super Bowl in the Portland region. The 30-second spot featured a timid man cowering inside his Ford sedan while another man berated him from outside the sedan's driver-side window. When apologies did not placate the raging man outside, the man inside the car pressed a button labeled "Trunk Monkey." Suddenly a chimpanzee wielding a tire iron emerged from his trunk and clobbered the road-raging loudmouth. The Suburban Auto Group's logo then appeared while a voice-over explained, "The Trunk Monkey. A revolutionary idea you'll find only at Suburban Auto Group—pending approval by the attorney general." The campaign featured five more "Trunk Monkey" spots and one radio advertisement.

According to one Suburban Auto Group representative, gauging the "Trunk Monkey" campaign's effect on car sales was difficult. It received recognition from the ad industry: the campaign earned a silver award at the One Club's 2003 One Show awards in the category of commercials made with less than $50,000. In one period of seven days the Suburban Auto Group's website recorded 3 million downloads of the first commercial.

HISTORICAL CONTEXT

Nancy Jaksich got into the auto-retail business by selling cars for her father, Pete Carlson, who first owned a Portland used-car lot and later the Carlson's Chevrolet dealership in Sandy, Oregon. Nancy's husband, Jerry Jaksich, had a similar background, having been raised around his uncle's car dealership in Sacramento, California. Nancy and Jerry later worked for Nancy's father at the Carlson's Chevrolet dealership until they opened a Ford dealership in 1984. Sixteen years later Nancy and Jerry purchased her father's Chevy dealership. Nancy ran the dealership, which conducted business as Suburban Chevy, and worked side by side with Jerry's

Suburban Ford dealership, located on the other side of Highway 26. Together they functioned as the Suburban Auto Group.

In 2000 the husband-and-wife partnership hired the Portland ad agency Big Ads, which later changed its name to R/West, to create two television commercials: "Return Buyer" and "Beep Beep." The president of Big Ads, Sean Bilxseth, contracted Derek Barnes, a copywriter for the ad agency Wieden + Kennedy, to direct the spots. "The client was very accommodating creatively," Barnes said to *Shoot* magazine. "It was a great learning experience."

In December 2002 the Suburban Auto Group asked R/West "go out on the edge" for the next campaign. Jerry and Nancy Jaksich believed that, to compete with the larger advertising budgets of Portland's car dealerships, their commercials needed to be outrageously creative. R/West first proposed a commercial that featured a man about to jump to his death. The suicide would be thwarted by a second man who would feign compassion merely to protect his car parked below. According to the *Oregonian,* Jerry Jaksich passed on the concept and asked R/West for a wackier and edgier commercial.

The idea for "Trunk Monkey" was conceived after R/West creatives pondered the many features available on most new cars. The *Oregonian* quoted the R/West creative director Hart Rusen, who remembered thinking, "Wouldn't it be funny to have a feature that addressed some of the other problems of the road?" The "Trunk Monkey" became an all-purpose feature that assisted with "other problems," such as chaperoning, roadside baby delivery, and even road rage.

TARGET MARKET

The campaign targeted potential Oregon car buyers with a healthy sense of humor and a penchant for offbeat comedy. Neither R/West nor the Suburban Auto Group foresaw the campaign's later success. Several months after the "Road Rage" spot debuted in Oregon, an out-of-state company, the Byers group of auto dealerships, paid $10,000 to use the spot for six months in the central Ohio region. Reporting for the *Columbus Dispatch,* Barnet D. Wolf wrote that the spot was extremely popular with young professionals. The journalist described his experience of being at a tavern in Easton, Ohio, when the "Road Rage" spot played on the bar's television set: the audience grew attentive, and people in the bar stopped talking.

The Chevy and Ford duality of the Suburban Auto Group catered to the loyalties of two distinct customers. The rivalry between Chevy and Ford owners had persisted for decades. For instance, in the mid-1980s an argument about which was better, Ford or Chevy, took place inside a bar in Scio, Oregon. After a man was slapped because of the truck he drove, he walked home and returned with a hunting rifle to murder the man who had struck him. Nancy Jaksich explained to the *Oregonian* that this rivalry between Ford and Chevy owners had always been good for business.

According to R/West, the humor in the campaign relied on storylines that the audience could readily connect with. "We've all seen people out there like that," Rusen said to the *Oregonian.* "We've all seen the guy in the beat-up pickup truck, driving around looking like he wants to kill someone." R/West executives believed that if the target found the spots funny, the audience would be more inclined to trust the Suburban Auto Group brand.

COMPETITION

Thomason Auto Group, Portland's largest car dealership, was created by the charismatic Scott Thomason. The company began as one dealership in 1983 and by 1998 had expanded into a chain posting revenues of $550 million. Its founder was credited with changing dealership advertising in the Portland area during the 1990s. Advertising analysts observed that, before the success of Thomason Auto Group, most Portland dealerships advertised low prices and let their car manufacturers advertise the car brands. Thomason Auto Group was the first to advertise the dealership's brand and car prices simultaneously. Until he left Thomason Auto Group in 2003, Scott Thomason starred as the brand's bespectacled mouthpiece in most of the chain's print ads and television spots. He typically made wisecracks such as "We finance anyone the law allows" or "If you don't come see me today, I can't save you any money." Explaining his strategy, Scott Thomason said to the *Oregonian,* "When customers in my market thought of buying a car, I wanted them to think of Thomason first."

FAMOUS CHIMP

In 2003 the Suburban Auto Group, which was composed of two Oregon car dealerships, released an advertising campaign titled "Trunk Monkey." The campaign featured a helpful chimpanzee that lived inside the trunks of cars and could be released at the touch of a button. The chimpanzee that played "Trunk Monkey" in the first few spots was named Jonah. Jonah, who was paid union wages, was also featured in the 2001 remake of the film *Planet of the Apes.*

DOUGHNUT

In a humorous commercial for an advertising campaign titled "Trunk Monkey," a chimpanzee emerged from a car trunk after its owner was pulled over for speeding. When the highway patrol officer asked the driver for "license and registration," the chimpanzee tried bribing the officer with a doughnut. According to the *Oregonian,* the chimpanzee kept eating the doughnut he was supposed to use for bribing the officer. Handlers for the monkey solved the problem by substituting a plastic doughnut for the real one.

The chain of car dealerships known as Lithia Motors, Inc., based in Medford, Oregon, attributed its success not so much to advertising as to making its dealerships conform to similar standards. Standardizing all Lithia dealerships proved wildly successful. Lithia grew from one dealership in 1946 into a chain of 84 dealerships nationwide that collectively posted revenues of $2.51 billion in 2003. That same year Lithia was acquiring outside dealerships at an average rate of two per month. After an acquisition Lithia typically closed its new dealership for 24 to 48 hours so that a team of 25 to 30 people could redesign it to reflect Lithia's image.

MARKETING STRATEGY

The first "Trunk Monkey" commercial, titled "Road Rage," cost less than $3,000 and was filmed in one day. It debuted in the Portland region during the 2003 Super Bowl. The spot featured a man trapped inside his car with another man screaming at him from the street. "Who do you think you're honking at, huh?" the antagonist yelled. Insults continued until the man inside the car pressed a button labeled "Trunk Monkey" that was located next to the rearview mirror. The car's trunk opened to reveal a chimpanzee armed with a tire iron, who struck the antagonist in the head. The Suburban Auto Group's logo was then displayed while a voice-over explained, "The Trunk Monkey. A revolutionary idea you'll find only at Suburban Auto Group—pending approval by the attorney general."

Speaking with *Shoot* magazine, Barnes said, "['Road Rage'] was a great script.... We shot on the shortest day of the year, sundown was at 4:02 p.m., and we felt under-the-gun. But the chimp, Jonah, was money every time." The spot's greatest expense was hiring the chimpanzee. According to an R/West spokesperson, Jonah required transporting fees, and his handlers needed to be flown from Los Angeles to Portland to film the commercial. To reduce costs some spots were later filmed in Los Angeles. A female chimpanzee named Bella was also used in other spots.

One of the campaign's less violent spots, "Throwing Eggs," began with three boys tossing eggs at a man's car. After the assaulted driver pressed his "Trunk Money" button, a chimpanzee leaped from the trunk and chased the boys. Two of the perpetrators successfully jumped over a fence, but the "Trunk Money" grabbed the third boy by his legs. The spot ended with the Suburban Auto Group's logo and a final shot of the boys cleaning eggs off the man's car. "Two endings were done for that one," Erinn Sowle, the general manager at Suburban Auto Group, said to *Ward's Dealer Business.* "The one we didn't use simply ended with the kid being dragged down off the fence."

Later commercials included "Pediatric Edition." This 30-second spot featured a pregnant woman in the backseat of a Ford sedan while her husband sped toward a hospital. When the woman screamed that she would not make it to the hospital, the "Trunk Monkey" appeared to help her deliver the baby. Another commercial featured the "Trunk Monkey" theft-retrieval system. After a car thief shattered the passenger-side window of a car, the "Trunk Monkey" emerged from the trunk, accosted the robber, and heaved his body off of a bridge. A less violent spot, titled "Chaperone," began with a teenage girl and her boyfriend parked at a scenic overlook. The girl said, "I can't believe my dad even let us touch his new car." Just as she leaned in for a kiss, a "Trunk Monkey" hiding in the backseat threw a banana peel at the teenage boy's face. Then, after hearing the chimpanzee loudly cock a shotgun, the frightened boy hurried out of car and ran away screaming.

Speaking with the *Oregonian,* Marian Friestad, a marketing professor at University of Oregon's Lundquist College of Business, explained the risk of using humorous advertising. "Nothing's more irritating or uncomfortable than a bad joke," Friestad said. Also according to Friestad, humor was not a unanimous phenomenon. What one person found funny could be considered offensive by others. "The ads are a big hit here," Sowle of Suburban Auto Group boasted to *Ward's Dealer Business,* referring to the spot's success in Sandy, Oregon. "People love them. We've had only a couple of complaints. Some thought 'Road Rage' was too violent."

OUTCOME

Many other car dealerships paid for syndicated use of the spots, and some advertising analysts noted that this fact alone was a measure of the success of the "Trunk

Monkey" campaign. The commercials aired just as they were used originally, but with other dealerships' logos and voice-overs at the end. By 2004 "Trunk Monkey" spots were syndicated across 31 markets in the United States, Great Britain, Australia, and New Zealand. R/West and the Suburban Auto Group divided the syndication profits, helping the Suburban Auto Group offset the original cost of the campaign. The campaign's effect on car sales, however, was more difficult to measure. "It's hard to quantify how many actual sales are a result of the ads," Sowle told *Ward's Dealer Business.* "They're not your standard call-to-action dealership ads. But they've given us a lot of name recognition."

The ad industry first took notice of "Trunk Monkey" after *Shoot,* a publication focused on advertising, listed "Road Rage" in its February 2003 gallery of "The Best Work You May Never See." Months later the One Club, a nonprofit organization that sponsored annual advertising competitions, honored "Trunk Monkey" with a silver award in the category of commercials made with less than $50,000. So many "Trunk Monkey" video files were downloaded from the Suburban Auto Group's website the day after the commercial appeared, the website had to be taken off-line. Later the commercials were placed on their own website. In one seven-day period the new site recorded 3 million downloads. Advertising critics praised the campaign for its "viral" success, or ability to be spread through word of mouth. Many consumers forwarded the commercials via E-mail to friends, colleagues, and family. "It did go past where we thought it would go, in a good way," R/West art director Chris Sauer, who worked on the campaign, said to the *Oregonian.* "You get lucky once in a while."

FURTHER READING

Champagne, Christine. "Laugh Factory." *Adweek,* April 4, 2005.

Finlay, Steve. "Monkey Shines in Ads." *Ward's Dealer Business,* May 1, 2004, p. 5.

Fitting, Beth. "Local Economy Makes Small Gains in 2004." *Central New York Business Journal,* December 24, 2004, p. 14.

Goldrich, Robert. "Out of the 'Trunk.'" *Shoot,* May 16, 2003, p. 4.

———. "Recognition." *Shoot,* June 13, 2003, p. 4.

Goodale, Gloria. "Youth Powers TV, but Is That Smart Business?" *Christian Science Monitor,* September 13, 2002, p. 18.

Mortenson, Eric. "More Proof Opposites Attract." *Portland Oregonian,* October 6, 2004, p. B02.

———. "Monkeyshines." *Portland Oregonian,* October 26, 2004, p. C01.

Muldoon, Katie. "Customer Bait." *Direct,* August 1, 2004, p. 65.

Wilcha, Kristin. "Mini Cooper Scores Major Coup at the One Show." *Shoot,* May 16, 2003, p. 1.

———. "RSA USA Reaches 'Hire' Ground at the AICP Show." *Shoot,* June 13, 2003, p. 1.

Williams, Chambers G., III. "Ford, General Motors Introduce Luxury Pickup Truck Models." *San Antonio (TX) Express-News,* August 24, 2001.

Wolf, Barnet D. "A Little Trunk Monkey Business Is Paying Off." *Columbus (OH) Dispatch,* July 18, 2003, p. 01A.

Kevin Teague

Swift Boat Veterans for Truth

PO Box 26184
Alexandria, Virginia 22313
USA
E-mail: media@swiftvets.com
Web site: www.swiftvets.com

SWIFT BOAT VETERANS FOR TRUTH CAMPAIGN

OVERVIEW

It was generally acknowledged that the ad campaign having the greatest impact on the 2004 U.S. presidential election was that run by the political action group Swift Boat Veterans for Truth. The group, which counted 275 Vietnam War veterans among its ranks, strongly opposed Senator John Kerry's presidential bid, charging him with being unfit to lead America as its commander in chief. To that end they created, with the help of the Virginia-based advertising agency Stevens Reed Curcio & Potholm, a series of damning television ads calling into question Kerry's war record, the medals he had been awarded, and even his patriotism. The attacks were direct, personal, and highly effective.

Over the course of six months, from May through October 2004, the Swift Boat Veterans, led by fellow Vietnam veteran John O'Neill, raised $6.7 million, all but $800,000 of which was spent producing and airing its television spots. The ads were simple in design and clear in purpose. Each featured a number of real veterans, all members of the Swift Boat Veterans organization, explaining in their own words why they felt that Kerry was ill-equipped to be president. In one ad the veterans repeatedly used words and phrases such as "not been honest," "lied," "lying," "dishonored," "cannot be trusted," and "betrayed" in reference to Kerry. While most major news outlets debunked or refuted the claims of the Swift Boat Veterans, and although only a very few of their ranks had ever actually served with Kerry in combat, their message was played and replayed throughout the national media, garnering them far more exposure than their limited budget ever could have allowed. Indeed, this was part of their overall strategy.

Regardless of the accuracy of their claims, or perhaps because of their inflammatory nature, the Swift Boat Veterans were successful in casting doubt on one of the cornerstones of Kerry's campaign: his war record. President George W. Bush was reelected for a second term, but more importantly for the Swift Boat Veterans, Kerry was defeated. The group all but disbanded once the election was over and chose to use what little money remained from their fundraising to help disabled veterans and the families of soldiers killed in action.

HISTORICAL CONTEXT

Both Kerry and O'Neill served in Vietnam in the late 1960s, both served on small river patrol craft, or "swift boats" (O'Neill took over the command of Kerry's boat once Kerry had completed his tour of duty), and both were decorated for valor and service in combat. Soon after Kerry returned to the United States, however, he became vocal in his opposition to the war. Despite having served in Vietnam—or perhaps because of what he had witnessed there—he came to feel that the war was both immoral and unwinnable. After meeting with a group of Vietnam veterans in early 1971 to hear their eyewitness accounts firsthand, Kerry testified in April of that year before the Senate Foreign Relations Committee as an outspoken member of Vietnam Veterans against the War. His testimony detailed atrocities, war crimes and violations of the Geneva Convention that had taken place during the conflict. Many veterans felt that Kerry was betraying and dishonoring them by making sweeping accusations about the conduct of soldiers in the field. In truth, Kerry's primary goal was not to denigrate the actions of his fellow soldiers but rather to condemn those of higher rank who, he felt, either sanctioned or turned a blind eye to crimes being committed against the civilians of Vietnam. U.S. soldiers, Kerry testified, "personally raped, cut off ears, cut off heads, cut off limbs, [and] randomly shot at civilians." He claimed that these acts "were not isolated incidents but crimes committed on a day-to-day basis with the full awareness of officers at all levels of command."

In support of those who opposed Kerry's position, O'Neill joined the group Vietnam Veterans for a Just Peace, and in June 1971 he and Kerry appeared in a one-on-one televised debate on *The Dick Cavett Show.* Kerry defended his Senate testimony, while O'Neill blasted him for turning his back on the very men with whom he had served. "Never have so many been libeled by so few," said O'Neill, referring to Kerry and other former soldiers who had spoken out against the war.

O'Neill's ire was rekindled in February 2004 when it became clear that Senator Kerry was poised to win the Democratic nomination for U.S. president. "It was important for me to be involved in this because everything is not just politics," O'Neill told the *Washington Times.* "Kerry is a guy who deeply lied about what happened and that has been demeaning to those of us who were really there." Soon thereafter he became one of the prime architects of the Swift Boat Veterans for Truth. O'Neill succinctly summed up the group's guiding principle in the *Wall Street Journal:* "We formed Swift Boat Veterans for Truth for one purpose: to present to the American public our conclusion that John Kerry is not fit to be commander in chief."

A "SWIFT BOAT" PRIMER

The term "swift boat" referred to a type of 50-foot aluminum-hulled craft used to patrol rivers and deltas throughout Vietnam during the war. The official Navy term for the boat was PCF, or Patrol Craft, Fast. The origin of the nickname remained in doubt, however. Some claimed that it came from the manufacturer of the boats, Sewart Seacraft, which named its products after seabirds, in this case a swift. Others said that SWIFT was an acronym for Shallow Water Inshore Fast Tactical Craft. Still others claimed that it was a nickname applied after a Navy admiral had watched a demonstration of the boats and offhandedly called them "swift."

TARGET MARKET

The 2004 presidential election was extraordinarily close; in any given poll either candidate's lead often was within the margin of error. On one hand this meant that even the slightest gain from any single demographic could influence the outcome of the election; on the other it meant that the majority of voters had already made up their minds.

In order to differentiate himself from President Bush, who served in the Air National Guard during the Vietnam War but was never called up for active duty, Senator Kerry made his Vietnam service and decorated heroism a cornerstone of his political campaign. He drew as much attention as he could to his wartime conduct, often appearing with fellow veterans at campaign stops and even saluting the audience as he walked onstage at the Democratic National Convention. Unfortunately for Kerry, this served to make the attack of the Swift Boat Veterans for Truth on his honor and character all the more potent. By casting doubt on Kerry's war record and by bringing attention to his own antiwar protests in the early 1970s, the Swift Boat Veterans successfully targeted those Kerry supporters for whom his war record and numerous medals were decisive factors in their support.

COMPETITION

The Swift Boat Veterans for Truth was not the only independent political group on the offensive in 2004. In fact, so-called 527 groups—named for the section of the Internal Revenue Code that governed their operations as nonprofit groups without political affiliation—proliferated after the McCain-Feingold campaign finance reform law was enacted in 2002. The law capped donations to political candidates and their campaigns at $2,000; it also capped donations in the same manner for any political group directly affiliated with a candidate or campaign. The 527 groups circumvented this rule by remaining independent of the candidates, even though groups on both sides pulled no punches when it came to divisive politics. On the liberal side MoveOn.org, the Media Fund, and America Coming Together all funded or produced TV ads blatantly in support of Kerry or against Bush, while conservative groups such as the Club for Growth and Progress for America spent millions of dollars in support of Bush's reelection.

Once the ads of the Swift Boat Veterans had begun to appear, both MoveOn and the Kerry campaign itself were quick to produce ads in response. MoveOn's spot featured one of the Swift Boat Veterans' ads in the background, with a voice-over calling its allegations into question and ending with a call to President Bush to "take that ad off the air." The trouble with this approach was that, as much as the Swift Boat Veterans' ads were helping Bush by harming Kerry, the Bush campaign was not responsible for them. MoveOn was trying to establish a tenuous link between the Swift Boat Veterans' ads and Bush, but there was no such verifiable connection.

MARKETING STRATEGY

The Swift Boat Veterans for Truth had set out to host a single press conference to voice their opposition to Kerry and his bid for the White House. Nearly 200 veterans met in Washington, D.C., on May 4, 2004, to issue a press release outlining their concerns about Kerry's war record and his ability to lead. The veterans did not expect to make a big splash as a result of the press conference, but they were surprised by the complete lack of coverage by the mainstream media. Not surprisingly, some smaller cable shows and news networks ran their story, but the major media paid little attention to it.

"The mainstream media can ignore a press conference," Chris LaCivita, one of the lead creatives behind the Swift Boat Veterans' ad campaign, told the *National Review,* "but they can't ignore an ad." With Rick Reed, LaCivita subsequently developed the first ad of the campaign in conjunction with the Stevens Reed Curcio & Potholm agency. The ad itself was straightforward. It featured overlapping testimony by numerous swift boat veterans that impugned Kerry's heroism and cast doubt on the actions that led to his being awarded the Silver Star and the Bronze Star as well as one of his three Purple Hearts. As Reed told *Brandweek,* "The key was to let these guys talk. What made the campaign work was that these were credible men, telling credible stories, with no agenda outside the truth."

The first ad was inexpensive to produce, but the Swift Boat Veterans had little funding to put it on the air where it would count. At the time their advertising coffers contained only $500,000. Instead of buying airtime in major markets, something they could ill afford anyway, they chose to release the ad at the beginning of August in minor television markets in only three states: Wisconsin, West Virginia, and Ohio. To help ensure that the ad received the media attention the original press conference on May 4 had not, the group worked with the conservative political consulting firm Creative Response Concepts, which sent press releases and extensive background material to conservative radio talk shows, cable news programs, and journalists, hoping that the controversial content of the ad would become a story that the mainstream media would subsequently pick up and disseminate. The plan worked. "By the time the ad made its debut," wrote Jason Zengerle of the *New Republic,* "the conservative media was primed, and the group's allegations against Kerry spread like wildfire through it."

OUTCOME

The upshot of the media attention was not just that the message of the Swift Boat Veterans for Truth got out to a wider audience but that it also brought in scores of new donations. By the time the group rolled out its second television spot, titled "Ravaged," it had $2.5 million to spend. And for the final ad, called "Questions," it had over $3 million at its disposal.

Through the creative leveraging of conservative media channels, the group was also able to turn its controversial political advertisements from simple television spots into a national news phenomenon. No other group received the same media attention for its ads. Even MoveOn.org, which at one point had two member-created ads posted to its website likening President Bush to Adolf Hitler, failed to generate a comparable buzz among journalists.

As for achieving its goal of defeating Kerry's presidential aspirations, the Swift Boat Veterans played a significant role in the election's outcome, although a precise measure of the group's impact was difficult to determine. While media analysts and political observers gave the group a good deal of the credit for helping to erode support for Kerry, O'Neill remained modest. When asked by Fox News if he thought that his group had contributed to Kerry's defeat, he replied, "No, not really. I think we had two significant effects. First, I think John Kerry was unable to run simply as a war hero. And second, I think that we reclaimed, I believe, the honor of our guys living or dead who served in Vietnam. I don't think anybody will claim again that we're war criminals."

Having seen its goal fulfilled on November 2, 2004, the Swift Boat Veterans for Truth used the remaining $800,000 worth of donations to help both the families of soldiers killed in action and wounded veterans through a charitable foundation.

FURTHER READING

Cummings, Jeanne, and Joe Flint. "Small Ads Win Big Uproar in New Political Media Game." *Wall Street Journal,* September 17, 2004, p. B1.

Gizzi, John. "Swift Boat TV Ads Packing Punch, Says Leading Pollster." *Human Events,* August 23, 2004, p. 5.

Graber, Doris A. *Media Power in Politics.* Washington, D.C.: CQ Press, 2000.

Justice, Geln, and Eric Lichtblau. "Windfall for Anti-Kerry Veterans' Group, with Texans among Those Giving Most." *New York Times,* September 11, 2004, p. A13.

Kaid, Lynda Lee, and Anne Johnston. *Videostyle in Presidential Campaigns: Style and Content of Televised Political Advertising.* Westport, Conn.: Praeger, 2001.

Miller, John J. "What the Swifties Wrought." *National Review,* November 29, 2004, pp. 18–22.

O'Neill, John. "We're Not GOP Shills." *Wall Street Journal,* August 27, 2004, p. A12.

O'Neill, John, and Jerome R. Corsi. *Unfit for Command.* Washington, D.C.: Regnery Publishing, 2004.

Rutenberg, Jim, and Kate Zernike. "Going Negative: When It Works." *New York Times,* August 22, 2004, sec. 4, p. 1.

Seper, Jerry. "O'Neill Leads Charge against Kerry's 'Lies.'" *Washington Times,* August 27, 2004, p. A1.

Teinowitz, Ira. "Ubiquitous Anti-Kerry Ad Proves PR as Political Tool." *Advertising Age,* August 23, 2004, p. 3.

Thomas, Evan. *Election 2004: How Bush Won and What You Can Expect in the Future.* New York: PublicAffairs, 2004.

York, Byron. "Vietnam Veterans against Kerry." *National Review,* May 31, 2004, pp. 32–34.

Zernike, Kate, and Jim Rutenberg. "Friendly Fire: The Birth of an Attack on Kerry." *New York Times,* August 20, 2004, p. A1.

Jonathan Kolstad

Swiss Army Brands, Inc.

1 Research Dr.
Shelton, Connecticut 06484
USA
Telephone: (203) 929-6391
Fax: (203) 929-3786
Web site: www.swissarmy.com

SWISS ARMY EQUIPPED CAMPAIGN

OVERVIEW

The "Swiss Army Equipped" campaign, created by Mullen Advertising for Swiss Army Brands, Inc., established a single brand image that unified advertisements for an assortment of merchandise. The company marketed watches, sunglasses, pens, and other items, but its best-known product was the Original Swiss Army Knife, a multiblade pocketknife that included implements such as a fish scaler, a nail file, a wood saw, a screwdriver, a bottle opener, a wire stripper, and a corkscrew. One advertisement for the Original Swiss Army Knife pointed out the product's many uses with the headline "The Swiss never begin sentences with 'If only I had a . . .'" The "Swiss Army Equipped" campaign used the popularity of Swiss Army knives to promote other products. In addition, its military tone and references to Switzerland called attention to the company's name and stressed the idea that the products were built to precision standards, suitable for use by the Swiss Army. The "Swiss Army Equipped" campaign was launched in print media in April 1998 and continued running into 1999.

HISTORICAL CONTEXT

Swiss Army Brands began as a firm that sold butcher scales in New Britain, Connecticut. When the company's founder, Charles Forschner, died in 1877, his son Richard moved the business to New York City and named it R.H. Forschner. During the 1920s the company imported high-quality cutlery from Germany, but supply problems in the years shortly before the outbreak of World War II prompted Forschner to begin buying cutlery and what was later called the Victorinox Original Swiss Army Knife from a Swiss company named Victorinox. During World War II thousands of American soldiers were stationed in Europe, where they observed that the Swiss Army was equipped with multipurpose pocketknives that the Americans called Swiss Army knives. After World War II there was great demand for Swiss Army knives in the United States, and R.H. Forschner marketed the product through hunting and camping stores and a few specialty retailers. The Forschner family sold the business in 1957, and it changed hands again in 1974. At that point pocketknives accounted for $800,000 (about 20 percent) of the company's annual sales of nearly $4 million.

The new owner, Louis Marx, Jr., began marketing Swiss Army knives through Wal-Mart, Target, and other mass merchandise outlets. In 1983 the company moved back to Connecticut and was renamed the Forschner Group, Inc. In 1989 it introduced the Swiss Army Brand Watch. By 1994 the firm's watches were selling for $75 to $500 each for a total of about $30 million a year, but pocketknives accounted for half of the company's annual sales of $125 million. In 1996 the firm changed its name to Swiss Army Brands, Inc., and began marketing Swiss Army brand sunglasses and writing instruments imported from Switzerland. It also marketed Victorinox Watches, Swiss Air Force Watches, and R.H. Forschner cutlery for commercial food operations. Late in 1997 the company introduced Victorinox multi-tools, which resembled Swiss Army knives but were built around a primary implement such as pliers or scissors instead of a knife blade. Unlike competing brands, the Victorinox SwissTool, was designed with individual springs to move each implement, locking devices to hold the implements securely as customers used them, and housing for the implements on the outside of the handle so the consumer did not need to open the entire unit to use one part.

As the company expanded its product line, its image became less clearly defined. Some advertisements used the popularity of Swiss Army knives to promote other merchandise, but the campaigns were not unified, and at times they used three different logos. The company was designing some of its own advertisements and hiring various agencies to develop campaigns for specific products. In the fall of 1997 Mullen Advertising was hired to create a strong, sharp brand image that would harmonize all the company's marketing efforts.

TRADEMARK DISPUTE

The term "Swiss Army knife" was not trademarked in the United States and was not clearly defined. To further complicate matters, in the early 1900s the Swiss Armed Forces had split the contract for its military knives between a Swiss company named Victorinox (which eventually called its product the Victorinox Original Swiss Army Knife) and a French company named Wenger (which called its product the Genuine Swiss Army Knife). The rival firms operated under a gentleman's agreement regarding the use of the name until 1992, when Arrow Trading Company began marketing an inferior Swiss Army knife that looked almost the same as theirs but was made in China. Swiss Army Brands, the U.S. marketer of Victorinox products, sued Arrow, but the court ruled that "Swiss Army knife" was a generic term that could be used by anyone. The Swiss Federal Defense Department registered a trademark containing the words "Swiss Army" and in 1996 granted Swiss Army Brands the right to its use outside the United States and its territories, Canada, and the Caribbean. The company continued to press for exclusive rights to the term "Swiss Army" in U.S. courts during 1996 and 1997.

TARGET MARKET

Swiss Army Brands referred to itself as the company that could equip people for life's adventures, and it described its target market as "people with a live-on-the-edge attitude at work and play" and "people who define themselves by their avocation, are passionate about what they do, and love strong brands." Its products were used by sports enthusiasts who participated in hiking, snowboarding, golf, and other outdoor adventures. The multipurpose knives were popular among backpackers and travelers who wanted equipment that took up little space but could be used for everything from opening cans to sawing small pieces of wood. Workers in specific trades, such as plumbers and electricians, also used the company's tools and other multipurpose products. The firm's merchandise was sold at outdoor, sport specialty, and hunting outlets, in addition to some department stores.

The firm's rugged military image tended to appeal more to men than to women. The Swiss Army name carried a certain mystique, and the company's products were noted for being durable and functional. Corporations frequently had their names and logos imprinted on Swiss Army knives to be distributed as promotional gifts. (This was a particularly common practice among pharmaceutical sales representatives, who gave the knives to doctors as they discussed the latest information regarding prescription drugs.) In general, the company's customers liked to view themselves as people who could cope with any situation. With tongue-in-cheek humor the "Swiss Army Equipped" campaign acknowledged that consumers tended to fantasize that they could depend on the products to survive a dangerous adventure, but in fact the items would often be put to more mundane use such as tightening the screws in a pair of eyeglasses, removing the cork from a bottle of wine, or slicing cheese.

COMPETITION

Original Swiss Army Knives controlled about 75 percent of their category, but the company's other products faced strong competition. In the $300 million market for multi-tools—a relatively new segment that had great potential for sales to industrial customers—Leatherman Company was a major contender. Leatherman had begun making innovative multi-tools in 1983, long before Swiss Army Brands entered the category. Another primary rival, Wenger, was based in Switzerland, but its products were marketed in the United States through a New York company named Precise International. In 1998 Wenger announced that it would spend $40 million over a five-year period to develop a global brand image and marketing strategy for its Genuine Swiss Army Knives and Wenger Swiss Military Watches.

Some advertisements for watches focused on their rugged construction. A campaign from the Magellan Group, Inc., featured the headline "The watch issued to U.S. troops during Desert Storm." The text cited the durability and functional features of the products, particularly their luminous dials, which glowed in the dark because they contained phosphorous. The "Irony" campaign for watches made by Swatch Group showed timepieces being lifted out of liquid mercury. Advertisements for Timex Corporation's Ironman watches maintained that they could withstand extreme conditions. Bulova Corporation emphasized the fine Swiss craftsmanship of its Accutron Swiss watches by superimposing a close-up photograph of two timepieces over a panoramic view of majestic mountains and cabins covered in deep snow.

Other campaigns revolved around the use of watches in sporting events and outdoor adventures. The Timex Expedition was advertised with the slogan, "The watch you wear out there," below vivid color photographs of average people exploring in wide open spaces. Each ad showed a selection of watches strapped to items such as canoe handles and large rocks. A black-and-white magazine ad for Timex's stainless steel watches included a snapshot of five smiling young people on a boat above a selection of five watches and the headline "So much about a family is revealed in its faces." In 1998 TAG Heuer International SA ran a $10 million print campaign called "Inner Strength," which showed the company's watches beside portraits of famous athletes such as tennis star Boris Becker. Each included a quote that revealed the celebrity's attitude about winning. "I drew my strength from fear. Fear of losing. I don't remember the games I won, only the ones I lost," said the quote from Becker. A *National Geographic* ad for watches made by the Swiss company Montres Rolex SA featured a photograph of a diver above the headline "Deep beneath the ocean, Dr. Sylvia Earle's Rolex is an indispensable piece of oceanographic equipment. Back on dry land, it's an indispensable piece of jewelry." The text explained that the watch was an "officially certified Swiss chronometer" used to time each dive, crafted for precision performance but also nice looking.

In the market for sunglasses Swiss Army competed with established brands such as Ray-Ban, made by Luxottica Group S.p.A. Oakley, Inc., marketed a wide assortment of high-tech sunglasses and goggles that were popular among tennis players, skiers, basketball players, and other sports enthusiasts. AAi. FosterGrant ran an advertising campaign that showed celebrities wearing sunglasses above the headline "Who's that behind those FosterGrants?" The text in one magazine advertisement answered, "Someone who wants a wide range of styles for a diverse, active lifestyle. Someone who's as smart about how much they spend as how they look."

MARKETING STRATEGY

Mullen Advertising created the "Swiss Army Equipped" campaign to define an identity for Swiss Army Brands and to promote the company's various product lines, including its pocketknives, multi-tools, watches, sunglasses, and writing instruments. The advertising budget for Swiss Army Brands was estimated at $10.0 million in 1998, up from $4.9 million in 1997, according to *Adweek*. Replacing the three insignias that Swiss Army Brands had used previously, Mullen created a new logo with a white cross on a red background, a design that resembled the silver cross on the red handles of Original Swiss Army Knives. Advertisements in the "Swiss Army Equipped" campaign featured a dark red background that contrasted with the white cross in the new logo. The campaign emphasized the company's long, reputable history of marketing Original Swiss Army Knives and other merchandise imported from Switzerland, a country known for its fine workmanship. The ads had a military look, with the company logo and tag line in separate compartments.

The campaign used sly humor to point out that Swiss Army Brands products could be invaluable during grand adventures but could also be applied to less dramatic, everyday problems. One magazine advertisement showed light glowing inside a ski hut at night. The headline read, "A Swiss patrol is prepared to overcome any situation. A fallen bridge, a crushing avalanche, a stubborn cork." The text added that Swiss Army products were useful "whether you need to battle a perilous blizzard or a tightly sealed bottle of vintage Pinot Noir." An ad for watches suggested, "The luminous hands and hour markers are ideal for timing midnight maneuvers during a blizzard in perilous terrain. Handy at the movies too." Another advertisement said, "Tightening a screw. Slicing a well-aged cheese to accompany wine. In Switzerland, it's natural to be equipped for the task at hand. And if someone here is found to be lacking the right tool, it only means he's a tourist."

The ads ran in magazines for outdoor enthusiasts and general consumers, including *Outside, Backpacker, Conde Nast Sports for Women, Vogue, Rolling Stone,* and *Men's Journal.* The company designed its Internet site around the "Swiss Army Equipped" theme and sponsored sporting events such as the U.S. Open Snowboarding Championship, the Crested Butte Extreme Skiing Championship, and the Franklin Templeton Tennis Classic. Swiss Army products were placed conspicuously throughout *Armageddon,* a blockbuster science fiction film released in the summer of 1998. Actor Bruce Willis and other stars in the motion picture wore space suits with built-in Swiss Army sunglasses, and the Swiss Army logo was displayed on helmets and lunar-landing vehicles used in the production. Swiss Army Brands advertised extensively and sponsored consumer contests to publicize its connection to the film. In 1998 the "Swiss Army Equipped" campaign supported the launch of two new products: the SwissTool, a multipurpose item that featured an assortment of blades and instruments, and the SwissCard, a slim variation of the Swiss Army knife that could fit inside a purse. Swiss Army Brands also became the worldwide licensee for St. John Timepieces, a product line with prices ranging from $50 to $18,000, which targeted sophisticated women.

OUTCOME

In September 1998 the "Swiss Army Equipped" campaign won 24 awards, including best of show honors, at the thirty-eighth annual Francis W. Hatch Awards, sponsored by the Ad Club of Greater Boston. In May 1999 at One Show, a gathering to recognize excellence in advertising, Mullen won a print advertising award for the "Swiss Army Equipped" campaign. To publicize its many products, Swiss Army Brands dispatched two promotional trailers on a mobile marketing odyssey, the Equipped Tour, which crisscrossed the United States and sent back reports that were posted on the company's Internet site. Each trailer was outfitted with a giant Victorinox Original Swiss Army Knife on its roof. The promotion included the inauguration of the Swiss Army Equipped Awards, a national program that recognized the achievements of people who exhibited the resolve and leadership to complete difficult tasks.

Field and Stream magazine nominated the new SwissTool as the "best of the best" multi-tool on the market. In April 1999 Swiss Army Brands acquired the assets of Bear MGC Cutlery, Inc., an Alabama company that made knives and multi-tools. New Swiss Army Brands multi-tools introduced that year were designed for consumers with specific interests. The board sport tool featured components that could be used to adjust snowboards, skateboards, and in-line skates. The business tool featured a flashlight and a travel alarm clock. The auto tool included a tire gauge and an ice scraper. New sunglasses that the company introduced in 1999 had names such as Hurricane, Squall, Windstorm, and Tornado.

Swiss Army Brands had net sales of $127.0 million and profits of $1.5 million in 1998, compared to sales of $119 million and a loss of $4 million in 1997. The company attributed the growth primarily to sales of its new products. By December 1998 the Swiss Army brand of watches, sunglasses, and writing instruments accounted for about 50 percent of the company's sales. Revenues from the Victorinox brand, including Swiss Army knives and multi-tools, amounted to about 35 percent of sales, and R.H. Forschner commercial cutlery items amounted to about 15 percent.

FURTHER READING

Dimock, Christina. "Traveling Light: Manufacturers Offer Young Travelers More Bang for Their Buck with Multipurpose Travel Gear." *Daily News Record,* July 9, 1999, p. 10.

"Finding Riches in Business Niches." *Money,* August 1994, p. 38.

Flamer, Keith. "Swiss Army Brands Fights Back." *Jewelers Circular Keystone,* April 1998, p. 52.

———. "Watch Brands Face Off with Creative Ads." *Jewelers Circular Keystone,* October 1998, p. 132.

Kauffman, Matthew. "Business Rivals Take Stab at Market for Swiss Army Knife." *Hartford Courant,* November 13, 1998.

"Making a Lunge for Swiss Army." *Business Week,* July 12, 1999, p. 155.

Meeks, Fleming. "Blade Runner." *Forbes,* October 15, 1990, p. 164.

Shannon, Thomas. "Sharp Colors." *Sporting Goods Business,* November 1993, p. 51.

Susan Risland

Taco Bell Corp.

17901 Von Karman Avenue
Irvine, California 92614
USA
Telephone: (949) 863-4500
Fax: (949) 863-2252
Web site: www.tacobell.com

■■■

THINK OUTSIDE THE BUN CAMPAIGN

OVERVIEW

Despite being the number one fast-food chain serving up Mexican-style items like tacos and burritos, Taco Bell Corp. in 2001 had an image in need of a boost and sales that were in a steady decline. A former Taco Bell customer who had been eating at the fast-food chain for 10 years told Andrew Bluth of the *Tribune Business News,* "About six months ago, we just got fed up with Taco Bell… I'm not sure what's contributing to the problem, but I won't be back until they make some changes." In addition, Taco Bell in 2000 had canceled its long-running ad campaign featuring a Spanish-speaking dog described by Bluth as a "tired marketing strategy epitomized by an overused Chihuahua." To regain a marketing identity and win back customers, Taco Bell in September 2001 launched a campaign that featured the slogan "Think outside the Bun."

Created by Taco Bell's agency, Foote, Cone & Belding San Francisco, the $200 million advertising campaign was designed to encourage consumers to do what the slogan suggested and "rethink their eating habits and demand bold, innovative menu items like those found at Taco Bell… not to just settle for another burger or sandwich,'" reported *Business Wire.* The first ad in the campaign, a television spot, highlighted the technology popular with Taco Bell's core customers, young men. It featured Jeff Bezos, Amazon.com's chief executive officer, joined by other staffers discussing Taco Bell's newest "handheld," a chicken quesadilla. Continuing with the tech theme other TV spots included descriptions such as "three-cheese upgrade," "gooey interface," and "ergonomic design." Subsequent advertising, which included a multilevel sweepstake for gamers as well as television and print ads, featured tie-ins to Microsoft Corp.'s Xbox.

At the launch of the campaign, Taco Bell reported that same-store sales had dropped 24 of the previous 35 months, including a 2 percent drop for the quarter ending September 8. In May 2002, about eight months after the campaign's launch, Taco Bell reported an 8 percent increase in same-store sales for the first quarter of the year. The company cited the "Think outside the Bun" campaign as one of the reasons for the increase in sales.

HISTORICAL CONTEXT

Taco Bell founder Glen Bell's first effort at selling fast food was in the early 1950s when he opened a stand offering hot dogs and burgers. Perhaps seeing the success of the McDonald brothers on the horizon, Bell turned his attention to alternative menu items and his personal favorite: tacos. He opened Taco Tia in 1954 and sold it in 1956 when he acquired El Tacos, which grew to 100 units by 1958. Preferring independent ownership—Bell said, "It's tough to share a dream"—he sold his share of

El Tacos to his partners and built the first Taco Bell in 1962. After 13 years at Taco Bell's helm, Bell resigned as chairman of the board, and in 1978 he sold the 868-restaurant chain to PepsiCo, Inc.

Under PepsiCo's ownership Taco Bell went head-to-head with big burger chains, like McDonald's and Burger King, and developed both a marketing niche and a national presence by attracting its core customers, college students, with affordable menu items. Some analysts, however, believed Taco Bell's problems could be traced back to its time as a division of PepsiCo. Bluth reported in the *Tribune Business News,* "Sales hit record levels, and the chain found a niche. Then came Pepsi's attempt to have Taco Bell run a hamburger chain, Hot n' Now, and some sit-down restaurant concepts. Then the big mistake: 'Border Lights,' an attempt at a healthier Taco Bell menu. The dramatic 1995 food addition was a total flop."

Bluth wrote in 2000 that Taco Bell's sales suffered a two-year decline under "Border Lights" and did not experience a slight increase until the strategy was eliminated in 1997 and the talking Chihuahua was introduced with the "Yo Quiero Taco Bell" theme. But, he said, "sales were flat [in 1999] and by all accounts 2000 is even uglier." To turn around its falling sales and compete in a market saturated with fast-food and casual-dining chains, Taco Bell dropped the Chihuahua and "Yo Quiero" theme, upgraded the quality of its menu items, and introduced "Think outside the Bun."

TARGET MARKET

Taco Bell defined its core customers as young men who typically went out for fast food at least a dozen times each month. Bob Sandleman, of the market research firm Sandleman & Associates, said in an interview with the *Orange County Register* that the chain's new "Think outside the Bun" advertising efforts seemed perfectly planned to resonate with its target audience and the chain's core customers, young men. In an effort to further boost sales, company president Emil Brolick broadened Taco Bell's target audience to also include older consumers with more expendable income and with higher expectations that the food they purchased would be good quality.

Some analysts believed that Taco Bell's shift in marketing focus from its core customer to a broader audience could fail to achieve its intended goal of increased sales. Douglas Christopher, an analyst with Crowell, Weedon & Co., told the *Orange County Register,* "Targeting too many audiences at once might prove difficult. Becoming all things to all people never works." Other analysts, however, including Technomic Inc., believed that Taco Bell had the financial resources to pull off the strategy as long as the marketing included advertising that would resonate with the separate audiences.

ONLINE MUSEUM PAYS TRIBUTE TO FOOD IMAGE SIGHTINGS

You never know what you will see looking back at you when you sit down with a slice of pizza, a piece of toast, or a bowl of nachos, but diners have been spotting images of everything from butterflies to the Liberty Bell to the Virgin Mary and Jesus in their food. To pay tribute to this unusual phenomenon, Taco Bell "launched a home for these edible 'visions' via the first online Food Sightings Museum at Tacobell.com," Amy Johannes reported in *Promo.* According to Johannes, the website was launched after consumers reported seeing images in the chalupa shells they purchased at Taco Bell. The website encouraged customers to submit photos of their food images online. Any food, not just Taco Bell's menu items, was admissible. People were also able to vote for their favorite image as well as whether the images were real, altered, or unrecognizable as anything other than the food pictured. "People are finding visions in many things," said a company spokesperson. "A customer a few years ago said he found Jesus in his Chalupa. We're playing off the phenomenon. We hope we get a lot of fun submissions."

COMPETITION

In 2000, as Taco Bell dumped its talking Chihuahua and was rethinking its marketing strategy, Del Taco, Inc., Taco Bell's number two competitor, was also restructuring its marketing and preparing to launch a new advertising campaign. Tim Hackbardt, Del Taco's vice president of marketing, told *Nation's Restaurant News* that the company would continue to target consumers 18 to 34 years of age, but the new advertising would be more focused on the chain's menu offerings. Hackbardt added that the Del Taco character, which, because if its resemblance to Zorro, had gotten the chain into legal trouble, had been eliminated. Additionally, although the company had traditionally turned to radio for its advertising, the new campaign would be focused on television spots with some radio support.

Del Taco replaced its Zorro-like spokescharacter and launched its new ad campaign using another spokesman, Dan the Product Guy, for its new TV spots. By featuring the self-effacing product-development character Dan, Del Taco hoped to reach fast foodies, usually 18- to

34-year-old men, but not to alienate women. The marketing also was designed to focus on what Taco Bell did not offer and to clearly communicate the differences between the two chains.

In 1998 McDonald's Corp. entered the quick-service Mexican food competition when it acquired a minority interest in the Denver-based gourmet-burrito chain Chipotle Mexican Grill, Inc. With financial backing from McDonald's, Chipotle nearly tripled its size, growing to 100 units by the end of 2000 and claiming the number three spot in Mexican fast-food eateries, behind Taco Bell and Del Taco. The difference with Chipotle was it offered food that was not only spicy but freshly prepared daily. In addition, every restaurant had a unique design, and there were no children's menus. Chipotle's founder, Steve Ells, told *BusinessWeek,* "This is not the typical fast-food experience. This is something grown-up."

As part of its plan to develop branding and a corporate identity, Chipotle executives visited its different restaurants to talk with customers and created a website allowing consumers to submit comments about the chain. Based on the information gathered, Chipotle planned to increase the advertising promoting the freshness of its ingredients and to continue its "Food with Integrity" theme.

MARKETING STRATEGY

Taco Bell's "Think outside the Bun" theme was more than an ad campaign. It was also a brand repositioning effort that covered everything from marketing to food quality to how the company was run. It was designed to assure that consumers were aware of how Taco Bell differed from chains serving up burgers and sandwiches. In a move to further differentiate Taco Bell from other chains, its stores began offering a 98-cent value menu with a crunchy taco and a bean burrito, while burger chains were charging 99 cents for their value menu items. Another part of the new marketing strategy was that Taco Bell installed grills in its restaurants, enabling it to upgrade the menu and compete more effectively against "fresh Mex" chains, such as Chipotle. In addition, Taco Bell used tie-ins to high-tech products like Microsoft's Xbox to appeal to its core customers.

Moving the brand away from a campaign based on a chatty Chihuahua to a campaign that was food focused was also part of the strategy. San Francisco–based Foote, Cone & Belding Worldwide created Taco Bell's campaign, which connected fast food with the Internet and dot-coms and was designed to appeal to tech-savvy young men. The $200 million campaign launched with a television spot that featured two computer geeks eating lunch outside their office building and using computer-operating letter code to discuss their meals. In another spot the chain's chicken quesadilla was described as a hand-held device with an ergonomic design and gooey interface. Maintaining the technology theme, a print ad for the introduction of the chain's steak quesadilla tied it to the release of Microsoft's Xbox. The ad read, "The Xbox era begins at Taco Bell, 10.18.01."

OUTCOME

Taco Bell's "Think outside the Bun" campaign was a hit. The slogan and advertising received positive reaction from both frequent and casual customers of the chain. The success of the campaign was reflected in Taco Bell's sales numbers as well. After nearly three years of slipping sales, Taco Bell reported sales were up five straight months following the campaign's launch. Tricon Global Restaurants, the parent company of Taco Bell, said that fourth-quarter sales at Taco Bell stores open for more than one year rose 8 percent in 2001 over the same period in 2000. The company's marketing chief, Greg Creed, told the *Orange County Register* that "Think outside the Bun" was more than a clever slogan. Rather, he explained, the slogan was the "phrase that company leaders decided defines the brand. It's another reinforcement that we're not like the other guys." Based on the success of the campaign's youth-oriented and technology-based theme, Taco Bell expanded it through sponsorships such as the MTV 2002 Video Music and 2003 Movie awards.

FURTHER READING

"Better Beans, Tastier Tortillas and Meatier Marketing for Taco Bell." *Business Wire,* January 9, 2002.

Bluth, Andrew. "Analysts Say Chihuahua Ad Campaign Not Sole Cause of Taco Bell Slump." *Tribune Business News,* August 1, 2000.

Cebrzynski, Gregg. "Chipotle Airs New Radio Spots, Plans More Ads under 'Integrity' Theme." *Nation's Restaurant News,* December 2, 2002.

———. "Del Taco Restructures Marketing Duties, Plans More TV Advertising," *Nation's Restaurant News,* May 8, 2000.

———. "Taco Bell TV Spots Push Envelope—If This Were 1985." *Nation's Restaurant News,* October 15, 2001.

Hamstra, Mark. "McD's Buys Stake in Chipotle Mexican Grill." *Nation's Restaurant News,* February 23, 1998.

Johannes, Amy. "Taco Bell Launches Online Food Sightings Museum." *Promo,* June 6, 2005.

Kramer, Louise. "Del Taco Barks Back with Its Own Spokescharacter: Eponymous Pitchman Uses Western Theme to Tout Value." *Advertising Age,* June 21, 1999.

Leonhardt, David. "The Corporation: Strategies: Mickey D Wakes Up and Smells the Cilantro." *BusinessWeek,* February 22, 1999.

MacArthur, Kate. "Chipotle Mexican Grill." *Advertising Age,* June 26, 2000.

———. "Games People Play: Looking for Lift, Taco Bell Stakes $70 Mil on Xbox." *Advertising Age,* October 1, 2001.

———. "Taco Bell: Brands in Demand; After Ditching the Dog, Taco Bell Becomes Yum's Strongest Chain by Focusing on the Food." *Advertising Age,* March 24, 2003.

———. "Underdog vs. Chihuahua in Mexican Chain Battle: Del Taco Effort Pits Chicken Taco against Rival Taco Bell's Gorditas Line." *Advertising Age,* June 26, 2000.

Montgomery, Tiffany. "Taco Bell Debuts $200 Million Ad Campaign." *Orange County Register,* September 22, 2001.

———. "Taco Bell Notes 8 Percent Jump in Fourth Quarter Sales." *Orange County Register,* February 12, 2002.

Zuber, Amy. "Tricon on Rise: BK Not in Picture; Sees Italian, Asian and Sandwiches on Multibranding Horizon." *Nation's Restaurant News,* May 13, 2002.

Rayna Bailey

WANT SOME? CAMPAIGN

OVERVIEW

In 1997 Taco Bell Corp. was the sixth-largest fast-food chain in the United States and the only Mexican-style fast-food restaurant operating nationwide. But in the previous two years the chain had experienced declining revenues. To repopularize itself and cement its brand image as a fun, appealing quick-service restaurant, in mid-1997 Taco Bell released a new marketing campaign created by ad agency TBWA\Chiat\Day of Venice, California.

The $200 million campaign included a number of television commercials, several of which were set in a pink room intended to depict the inside of a hungry person's stomach. Each spot ended with the tagline "Want some?" and displayed the Taco Bell logo. The final spot in the initial campaign, "Chihuahua," starred a talking dog. Because it was not expected to be popular, it was televised only in the northeastern United States in September 1997. In the spot a male Chihuahua named Dinky sniffed his way down a street, seemingly in search of a female companion. Instead he passed by a female Chihuahua to approach a human eating food from Taco Bell. Dinky then said in Spanish, "Yo quiero Taco Bell" (I want Taco Bell).

Public reaction to the "pink room" spots was lukewarm, and they were short-lived. Because of the excitement surrounding the regional spot featuring the Chihuahua, however, Taco Bell chose to air it nationally in October. The company followed it up in late December 1997 with a campaign that focused exclusively on the hungry little dog. The spots promoted the value pricing of certain Taco Bell items while solidifying the Chihuahua's role as Taco Bell's brand icon and marketing mascot. In

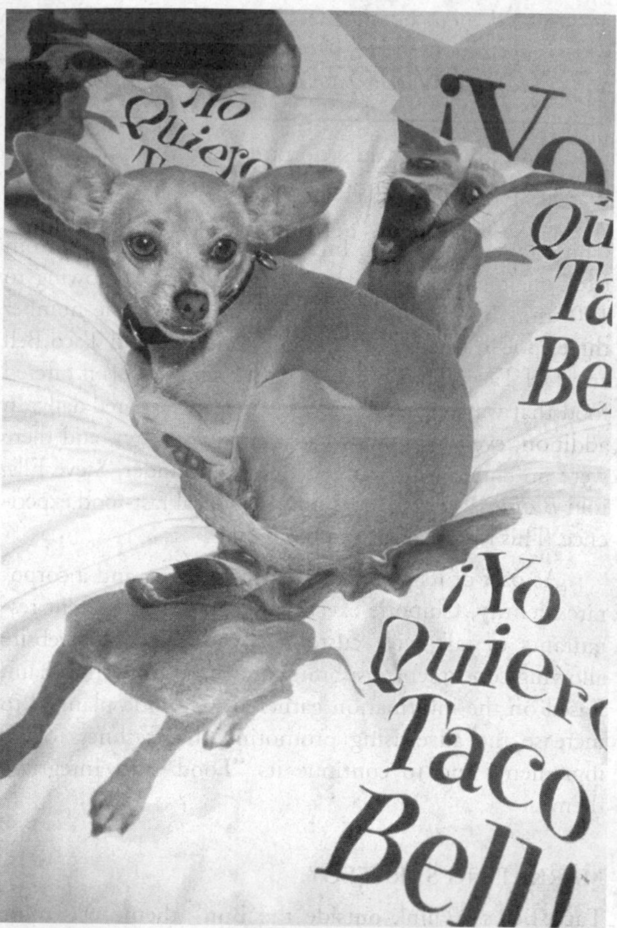

The Taco Bell Chihuahua. © MITCHELL GERBER/CORBIS

May 1998 Dinky returned as part of a $60 million campaign to promote Taco Bell's Gorditas, a new menu item. Dinky's position as top dog began to fade in 1999, when he was reduced to a supporting character in the chain's commercials, and in 2000 insiders were calling Dinky "overused." Later that year Taco Bell dropped the Chihuahua along with TBWA\Chiat\Day.

HISTORICAL CONTEXT

Although it was the only nationwide Mexican-style fast-food restaurant in the United States, in 1995 and 1996 Taco Bell suffered declining revenues, which was largely attributed to increased competition in the industry. In addition, the company's marketing campaigns were not successful in increasing sales or meeting company expectations. In an article in *USA Today* Taco Bell president Peter Waller stated, "We spend $200 million a year on advertising, and I really want that investment to pay off." He added, "We had a strong campaign in the late '80s, but since then, we haven't made a connection with the consumers." Analysts in the fast- food industry concurred, indicating that Taco Bell's image needed updating. A PaineWebber analyst remarked that "Taco Bell ha[d] gotten stale" and lacked new ideas.

In 1997 Taco Bell sought to reverse the drop in sales and give its image a face-lift. In March 1997 Taco Bell awarded advertising agency TBW\Chiat\Day of Venice, California, the creative portion of its marketing account. Industry executives shared with the *Wall Street Journal* their belief that "the biggest problem facing Taco Bell is its image, and it's one the people at TBWA Chiat/Day will need to work hard at." The Costa Mesa, California, office of the agency that had represented Taco Bell from 1994 to 1997, Bozell Worldwide, maintained media-buying responsibilities, and its managing partner, Peter Stranger, stated, "We lost the creative portion because Taco Bell is looking for magic in the creative areas which we have not struck with them to date. If they can find magic, we support that."

TARGET MARKET

TBWA\Chiat\Day chose to focus its marketing efforts on men between the ages of 18 and 34, the group that accounted for the majority of fast-food sales. According to an article in the *Los Angeles Times,* Taco Bell's "advertising and marketing gradually shifted toward a more general audience—and away from its most important customers, the hungry young males who drive fast-food sales." Taco Bell had hoped to expand its consumer base, but when the strategy proved ineffective, the company chose to focus again on its core consumer group. The new campaign by TBWA\Chiat\Day aimed to use offbeat, catchy commercials to gain the attention of Taco Bell's core market of young males.

The chain reported that its target market consisted of consumers aged 18 to 34 who were loyal customers of Taco Bell. Vada Hill, Taco Bell's chief marketing officer, stated, "Our consumers have an intense emotional tie with the Taco Bell brand and associate great memories and experiences with eating our food." TBWA\Chiat\Day's research revealed that Taco Bell's consumers were "incredibly savvy, individualistic and pragmatic," and thus the agency sought to create a campaign that would be appreciated by this target group. Lee Clow, TBWA\Chiat\Day's chief creative officer, said, "Taco Bell's consumers have grown up in a media-saturated environment and respond to brand messages that are direct, honest and funny . . . We wanted to create a campaign that incorporates those key elements and breaks through the clutter by speaking directly to our audience about the desire for Taco Bell in a fun, humorous and memorable way."

HISPANIC REACTION

Not everyone was thrilled by Taco Bell's "Chihuahua" campaign. Many in the Hispanic community found the Dinky commercials insulting and inappropriate. Gabriel Cezares, the president of the Tampa Bay, Florida, chapter of the League of United Latin American Citizens (LULAC), was quoted in the *Tampa Tribune* as saying, "They have a little Mexican dog to represent Mexican people who work like dogs and are treated like dogs and don't even get a burrito from Taco Bell to put on their tables." Cezares proposed a boycott of Taco Bell and urged Hispanics to write protest letters to the company's headquarters. Others in the Hispanic community, however, disagreed. Belen Robles, LULAC's national president, told the *Tampa Tribune,* "LULAC has a good working relationship with Taco Bell. I seriously doubt they would intentionally air something that is offensive to the Hispanic community."

Peter Stack, Taco Bell's vice president of public affairs, stated that precautions had been taken and that Hispanic focus groups had responded positively to the spots. He said, "This research is done to ensure that our ads are received in the manner that they are intended: to entertain and inform, never to offend." Campaign creators Chuck Bennett and Clay Williams explained that they tried to be careful not to offend anyone, that the Chihuahua was portrayed as smart and heroic, and that Hispanic actors were used to provide the dog's voice.

In an effort to appeal to a broader audience and include potential customers outside the target group, Taco Bell also began to offer a 100 percent guarantee on its food items and service: "You'll love it, or we'll eat it." The guarantee was incorporated into commercials and was designed to lure new customers by informing them that the quality of Taco Bell's food had improved.

COMPETITION

With more than 6,500 units in the United States, Taco Bell had no national competitors in the Mexican fast-food category. In 1997 it dominated the market, claiming more than two-thirds of all sales in Mexican quick-service food. Independent restaurants, with a share of 19 percent, followed Taco Bell. Regional chains such as Taco John's, Del Taco, Taco Time, and Taco Bueno made up less than 10 percent of Mexican quick-service sales.

In the overall fast-food market, Taco Bell held 2.1 percent of the national share in 1996 and ranked fourth, following McDonald's, Burger King, and Pizza Hut. Rounding out the top 10 fast-food restaurants were Wendy's, KFC, Hardee's, Subway, Dairy Queen, and Domino's Pizza. Thus, three divisions of Tricon Global Restaurants—Pizza Hut, Taco Bell, and KFC—were in the top 10, and their combined market share of 6.2 percent placed them second after McDonald's, which in 1996 had a market share of 7.7 percent.

Some of Taco Bell's competitors capitalized on the Chihuahua spot by creating marketing campaigns that included a Chihuahua. El Pollo Loco, a regional Mexican-style fast-food chain in southern California, aired a spot that mocked the talking Chihuahua by indicating that its growth might be stunted if it continued to feast on tacos. The spot was part of a series of spoof advertisements by El Pollo Loco. Jack in the Box also created a parody that featured a talking Chihuahua. The spot pitted the dog, visibly pudgier than Taco Bell's, against Jack in the Box's ball-headed Styrofoam Jack character and attempted to direct attention to Jack in the Box's specialty items.

MARKETING STRATEGY

In the late 1980s and early 1990s Taco Bell enjoyed growth in sales and continued to expand its locations. In 1995, however, earnings began to suffer. Same-store sales fell by 4 percent in 1995 and by 2 percent in 1996. Taco Bell appeared ready for change when it gave TBWA\Chiat\Day, an agency known for its innovative work, creative responsibilities for advertising in March 1997.

In planning the $200 million marketing campaign, Taco Bell hoped to update and build its brand image and to solidify its rank as one of the top fast-food chains in the country. It also wanted to boost store traffic and reverse the two-year sales slump. In the *Los Angeles Times* Hill discussed Taco Bell's goals by explaining, "The challenge isn't getting this core group to eat fast-food ... The challenge is getting them to turn right into a Taco Bell as they drive down fast-food row instead of McDonald's or Burger King." Hill also noted, "It's not that they're not coming to our restaurants ... It's just that we want them to come more often."

The new campaign was released in July 1997 on prime-time network television with several of the "pink room" spots, which were intended to convey the message "There's something inside you that's hungry for Taco Bell." The first commercial that appeared on network television showed two young men in an apartment who were awakened by their growling stomachs. Another spot featured a throng of youths dancing and thrashing about in a pink room, with the chaotic activity meant to symbolize the rumblings of an empty stomach. The final spot in the initial campaign, developed by the TBWA\Chiat\Day creative team of Clay Williams and Chuck Bennett, featured Dinky the male Chihuahua. Bennett explained the development of the spot in *PR Newswire*: "We wanted the Chihuahua's character to be perceived as a 19-year-old guy in a dog's body who primarily thinks about food and girls. We were able to craft the spots in such a way as to bring this character out and convey the message that the dog was on an undying quest for Taco Bell."

Williams and Bennett had come up with the Chihuahua concept while eating together at a Mexican restaurant in Venice, California. They spotted a determined-looking Chihuahua walking down the street by itself. Bennett explained, "He was a little dog totally on a mission, on full cruise mode to something only it saw ... He appeared to have no concept that he was a [three]-pound dog in a giant world." Bennett and Williams decided that the Chihuahua could play an entertaining and effective role in the Taco Bell campaign.

In May 1998 new television spots starring Dinky began airing to promote Taco Bell's new food offering, Gorditas. The spots were tied to the release of the new *Godzilla* movie; one featured the feisty Chihuahua trying to trap the giant monster with a cardboard box and a few Gorditas while he beckoned, "Heeere, LEE-zard LEE-zard." The little dog also starred in a music video to promote a new rap/urban-pop album by Los Angeles Lakers basketball star Shaquille O'Neal.

The campaign was modified in 1999, with Dinky still playing a part but in a supporting role rather than as the star. A new tagline also replaced the popular "Yo quiero Taco Bell." Television spots that began airing in December 1999 used the tagline "Grande taste. Loco price. Only at Taco Bell," and in them the chain's food upstaged Dinky. One spot, titled "Bus," showed Dinky taking over a public bus in hot pursuit of a working mom on her way home in a minivan with a Taco Bell Grande Meal beside her on the front seat. The meal was meant to feed the mom's hungry family, but the Chihuahua had other plans for the dinner: claiming it for himself.

OUTCOME

Although the public did not embrace the original spots featuring the pink room, Taco Bell had a winner with the talking Chihuahua. The *Licensing Letter* quoted Peter Stack, Taco Bell's vice president of public affairs, as saying, "This is a phenomenon; it's safe to say it happens once in a brand's lifetime." "Yo quiero Taco Bell" became the mantra of the masses, the Chihuahua breed grew in popularity, and Taco Bell's two-year sales decline ended. In 1997 the chain enjoyed a 2 percent increase in same-store sales.

Taco Bell's Hill stated, "These ads are just the kind of break-through advertising that we challenged TBWA Chiat/Day to create." The Chihuahua spot was so successful that Dinky became the star of subsequent Taco Bell ads. Hill explained, "The original commercial captured the imagination and excitement of our consumers and the catch phrase 'Yo Quiero Taco Bell' is also becoming part of our target market's vernacular. The response has been so overwhelming that we had no choice but to bring back the Chihuahua." TBWA\Chiat\Day's Williams commented on the spot's effectiveness. "After the launch of the first Chihuahua commercial," Williams recalled, "it became apparent that this spot was creatively right on the mark. It was able to connect with our target market while at the same time being broad based enough to speak with the entire market as a whole."

The Chihuahua spots ranked among the top three most popular campaigns ever analyzed by Ad Track, *USA Today* 's weekly poll designed to measure a campaign's popularity and effectiveness. Ad Track had covered more than 140 marketing campaigns since 1995. Only 8 percent of the poll's 566 respondents stated that they disliked the Dinky commercials, while 47 percent said that they liked them. Among the target group of 18- to 24-year-old consumers, 53 percent of the females and 40 percent of the males polled stated that they liked the spots. Minority groups surveyed also enjoyed the Chihuahua spots. Among Hispanic consumers 55 percent said that they liked the commercials, and 57 percent of black respondents gave their approval. When polled regarding the campaign's effectiveness, 36 percent considered the commercials to be effective. *Entertainment Weekly* rated a Chihuahua spot as one of the top 10 television commercials of 1997.

Billboards emblazoned with the Chihuahua's image appeared across the United States, and Taco Bell implemented a toll-free telephone number for customers who wanted to order Dinky T-shirts. Posters and cardboard cutouts of Dinky were displayed at Taco Bell restaurants, but Dinky proved so popular that the posters were frequently stolen. Taco Bell reaped the benefits of the Chihuahua craze with increased revenues and immense recognition in 1997 and intended to ride the Dinky wave as long as possible. According to the *Virginian-Pilot and Ledger-Star,* Taco Bell public relations manager Laurie Gannon stated, "When the commercials run their course, we'll move on to something else."

Despite earning accolades as one of the "most memorable ad campaigns in recent history," according to *Knight Ridder/Tribune Business News,* by 2000 Dinky the Chihuahua had worn out his welcome. The *Knight Ridder/Tribune Business News* article described the campaign as a "tired marketing strategy" and Dinky as an "overused Chihuahua." In mid-2000 Taco Bell reported that same-store sales had dipped 6 percent for the second quarter compared to the previous year. In response, the chain replaced its president, Peter Waller, and fired its ad agency and Dinky's creators, TBWA\Chiat\Day. In 2001 Taco Bell released a new marketing campaign, "Think Outside the Bun," created by the chain's new agency, San Francisco–based Foote Cone & Belding.

FURTHER READING

Bluth, Andrew. "Analysts Say Chihuahua Ad Campaign Not Sole Cause of Taco Bell Slump." *Knight Ridder/Tribune Business News,* August 1, 2000.

Bonko, Larry. "Yo Quiero Chihuahua! Taco Bell Commercials Boost Breed's Popularity." *Virginian-Pilot and Ledger-Star,* March 30, 1998, p. E1.

Brownfield, Paul. "Where's the Pitch." *Los Angeles Times,* May 3, 1998.

Enrico, Dottie. "Viewers Sit Up and Notice Taco Bell Ads." *USA Today,* March 30, 1998.

Garfield, Bob. "Perspicacious Pooch Scores for Taco Bell." *Advertising Age,* March 9, 1998.

Hardesty, Greg. "El Pollo Loco Parody Ads Are Skewering the Competition." *Santa Ana (CA) Orange County Register,* February 27, 1998, p. C2.

Montgomery, Tiffany. "Taco Bell Debuts $200 Million Ad Campaign." *Knight Ridder/Tribune Business News,* September 22, 2001.

———. "Taco Bell Refocuses on Hungry Young Males." *Los Angeles Times,* July 24, 1997, p. D7.

———. "Taco Bell Rehires Talky Chihuahua." *Santa Ana (CA) Orange County Register,* December 30, 1997, p. C1.

Reddick, Tracie. "Dinky Strikes a Sour Note." *Tampa Tribune,* March 7, 1998, p. 1.

———. "Hispanic League's National Leader Says 'Si' to Taco Bell's Dinky." *Tampa Tribune,* March 11, 1998, p. 1.

"Taco Bell Consumers Say 'Yo Quiero More Chihuahua!" *PR Newswire,* December 29, 1997.

Weiner, Jennifer. "Biting Image? Taco Bell's Chihuahua Is One Hot Dog." *Philadelphia Inquirer,* April 23, 1998, p. A1.

Wells, Melanie. "Taco Bell Cooks Up $200M Ad Campaign." *USA Today,* July 23, 1997, p. B8.

Mariko Fujinaka
Rayna Bailey

Target Corporation

1000 Nicollet Mall
Minneapolis, Minnesota 55403
USA
Telephone: (612) 304-6073
Fax: (612) 696-3731
Web site: www.target.com

NEW YORKER MAGAZINE SPONSORSHIP CAMPAIGN

OVERVIEW

In a bold move designed to attract an upscale clientele and garner widespread media attention, the Target Corporation purchased all of the advertising space in the August 22, 2005, issue of the *New Yorker* magazine. Target had always aimed for a more affluent demographic than its main competitors, Wal-Mart and Kmart, but in grabbing the attention of the *New Yorker's* readership, Target was seeking to lure an even higher-end consumer to its stores.

The campaign, created by Peterson Milla Hooks, was limited to the single issue of the *New Yorker* and consisted of 21 different illustrations created by as many artists. The ad space alone cost in excess of $1 million. Each ad used only the colors black, red, and white, and each featured the Target bull's-eye logo incorporated into a New York scene or theme. The ads ranged from loose, hand-drawn sketches to computer-generated geometric cityscapes. One ad featured a low-angle view of a leather-clad female motorcycle rider in the foreground with a giant bull's-eye rising behind the Brooklyn Bridge in the background, while another depicted a crowd of martini-sipping gallery-goers crowded into a room whose paintings were pop art versions of the Target logo. Not a single line of text or image of a specific product appeared in any of the ads. Instead of selling its wares, Target was selling an urbane, artistic impression of itself to a sophisticated audience it had not reached quite so directly in previous campaigns.

The single greatest success of the campaign was its ability to generate media coverage and to create controversy far beyond the readership of the magazine itself. Almost every national newspaper covered the story of Target as the sole advertiser in the magazine—the first time in its history the magazine had been sponsored by one advertiser—and National Public Radio ran two spots about the phenomenon. And while the American Society of Magazine Editors issued a reprimand to the *New Yorker* for not following its guidelines for single-sponsor issues, this merely led to additional press coverage and sparked a debate in industry circles about the merits of such an undertaking.

HISTORICAL CONTEXT

Founded in 1962 as a subsidiary of the Dayton Company, Target quickly became the most profitable of the parent company's retail chains. From the beginning the idea behind Target stores was to appeal to customers on the basis of the style of its merchandise and the design of its stores rather than low prices alone. As Bryan Curtis wrote in the online magazine *Slate,* the founders decided that Target would

PHOTOGRAPH BY KELLY A. QUIN. THOMSON GALE.

"exude the mild pretension of a low-end department store rather than the folksiness of a high-end dime store."

By the mid-1980s Target executives were referring to the company's positioning in the marketplace as "upscale discount." Creating this market niche was a way to differentiate Target from its main rivals, Wal-Mart and Kmart, whose sole emphasis was on having the lowest prices in the industry. In keeping with this slightly upscale approach, Target stores were designed with brighter lighting, wider aisles, and more available checkout lines than the competition.

Additional reinforcement of the "discount luxury" concept came in 2000 when Target hired the noted architect and designer Michael Graves to create a line of exclusive household goods for its stores. Graves had previously won an industry award for a tea kettle he designed in 1985 for the Italian firm Alessi, which retailed for $140. The tea kettle he designed for Target, which subsequently became a top seller for the chain, bore a passing resemblance to his previous piece but sold for only $40.

The combination of national branding and upscale designer housewares propelled both Target's sales and its reputation to such heights that in 2000 the company that had founded it (by then Dayton-Hudson Corporation) formally changed its name to Target Corporation. Within a year the company had sold off its other, less-profitable retail divisions.

TARGET MARKET

For Target's "upscale chic" approach to translate into increased revenue, it needed to attract a similarly upscale clientele to its stores. Target had high consumer awareness and strong customer loyalty among lower- and middle-income shoppers, but what the company yearned for was to turn its "more-stylish-than-the-competition" image into a shopping reality for upper-income consumers. To that end, in 1997 Target began to advertise heavily in New York City, mainly through billboards and outdoor signage, even though at the time there were no Target stores in the city or the surrounding metropolitan area. The company was expanding its presence in the northeastern United States, however, and believed that building brand awareness well before the stores were actually open would pay off in the end. In addition, Target hoped to attract a more hip, urban, and wealthy group of customers to its stores, banking on the idea that once trendy New Yorkers were seen wearing Target's clothing lines or using its household goods this would up its cachet among other urbanites nationwide.

It was this that led Target to advertise in the *New Yorker*. Generally regarded as one of the most prestigious magazines in the United States, this weekly publication was filled with extraordinarily literate journalism mixed with topically relevant New York–themed articles and current events. (It should be noted, however, that despite the magazine's New York area bias, it had more subscribers in California than in New York State.) A casual glance through other issues in August 2005 revealed ads for Jaguar, NetJets, Chanel, Level vodka, BMW, Mercedes, Hartford mutual funds, and Rolex watches, among various high-end products. The average *New Yorker* reader was hardly a demographic match for the average Target shopper, which was exactly the point. It was among those consumers who could afford to purchase such high-end merchandise that Target hoped to position itself.

The monopolizing of advertising space in the *New Yorker* made Target's presence in the magazine almost impossible to ignore, but in order to appeal to the tastes and desires of the *New Yorker* readership the ads themselves did not hawk any particular product or service but instead reinforced Target's branded bull's-eye logo in a variety of subtle and creative ways. Through the Minneapolis-based agency Peterson Milla Hooks, 21 artists were hired to create the full- and partial-page ads for the magazine. No two were alike, and each artist had extraordinary creative license in illustrating the ads. The hope was that the ads, some drawn by the same artists whose work had appeared previously in the editorial portion of the magazine, would attract attention not because of their content but because of their look and style. In short, Target's tastefully creative ads were designed to impress a refined, rather than a bargain-hunting, consumer.

SINGLE-SPONSOR ADVERTISING

In the early days of both radio and television entire shows were run under the banner of a single advertiser. Ford Theater, General Electric Theater, General Mills Radio Adventure Theater, and Kraft Music Hall were just a few of the programs whose entire content was "brought to you" by one company. As television increased in popularity beginning in the 1960s and as broadcasters became more powerful, the price of advertising on television skyrocketed, and eventually sales of single 30-second spots became the norm. In the fall of 2005, however, despite the enormous costs involved, a number of companies gambled on the relative "newness" of the idea and bought all of the ad spots during a number of shows, including CBS's *60 Minutes* (Philips Electronics), NBC's *The Tonight Show* (Chevrolet), and FX's *Nip/Tuck* (Sony Pictures). At upwards of $2 million for a complete program, these companies were betting that saturating the airwaves with their products would catch the attention of viewers in a way not seen for two generations.

COMPETITION

In 2005 Target was the number-two discount retailer in the United States, behind Wal-Mart and with Kmart number three on the list. Target's overall strategy of emphasizing style and not just price had helped to propel it to the number-two spot, but Wal-Mart's size and ruthless determination to slash prices by every available means meant that Target could hardly hope to compete on price alone.

While Wal-Mart's advertising strategy simply reinforced its low-price approach, with ads and television spots literally showing "falling prices," Target chose to promote style and youthful attitude in its marketing efforts, in large part to differentiate itself from its rival. Thus, while Wal-Mart was Target's number one competitor, Target's strategy was not to lure shoppers away from Wal-Mart but rather to lure shoppers away from even higher-end stores than its own.

MARKETING STRATEGY

In 1999 Target decided to launch an ambitious ad campaign to capitalize on its success as a stylish retail chain by solidly branding the company with its simple red and white bull's-eye logo. The hope was to increase consumer awareness of the logo, thereby creating national iconographic recognition for the company. Target aimed to have the bull's-eye join the ranks of McDonald's "golden arches" or Nike's "swoosh" logos, and it succeeded. The campaign ended up yielding a 96 percent awareness of the bull's-eye logo among consumers. The company continued to make the logo a feature of all of its campaigns in all media, reinforcing the connection between the logo and the store.

The success of this campaign, and of others in the interim, allowed Target to feature only its logo, without its name or any other identifying text, in the ads it placed in the *New Yorker*. The criteria for the illustrations were simple: each ad could consist of only the three colors black, white and red; each was to feature a New York theme or location of some kind; and each needed to feature the Target logo somewhere in the ad. Beyond that the 21 illustrators were allowed to pursue their creative impulses in designing the content of each ad. In what was an unusual move, the agency did not contribute to the look or feel of any of the ads but was responsible only for hiring the illustrators and thereby shaping the overall stylistic mode.

No single ad looked like any other. The ad by Andre Dubois, for example, featured a drawing of a giant high-heeled red shoe, decorated with white Target bull's-eyes, that was positioned over the water as a bridge or gateway into lower Manhattan. Another, by Milton Glaser, depicted a series of flying red bull's-eyes emerging from the distant night sky and leading up to and encircling the spire of a skyscraper in a cosmic version of the game of ringtoss. The first 19 pages of the magazine featured 10 pages of Target ads, 7 of them a full page, and within these 10 pages the Target logo was featured more than 200 times. In all there were 21 pages of ads in the magazine's 90 pages.

Some of the artists chosen, most notably the illustrator Robert Risko, were regularly featured in the *New Yorker* as part of the editorial content rather than the advertising. This fact alone generated controversy among industry insiders who felt that Target, with the tacit approval of the *New Yorker,* was blurring the line between advertising and content. None of the ads was labeled as such, and there was no explanation of the single-sponsorship phenomenon anywhere in the magazine. In fact, the only text devoted to the ads at all came in a sidebar on page 87 that stated, "Our thanks to all the talented illustrators who brought this project to life," followed by a complete list of the illustrators and the pages in the magazine on which their work could be found. Referring to the advertising blitz as a "project" contributed to the outcry from the likes of Lewis Lazare, who wrote in the *Chicago Sun-Times* that the advertising ploy was "the most jaw-dropping collapse of the so-called sacred wall between editorial and advertising in modern magazine history." Despite his distaste, Lazar could not help but give a nod to the actual efficacy of the ads: "Target... has had its image immeasurably burnished by the practically seamless blending of its ads into *The New Yorker* editorial product."

OUTCOME

Industry experts estimate that Target spent between $1.1 and $1.3 million for the ad space alone, and according to most analysts Target got its money's worth. "On a simple, immediate level, the campaign worked because it [was] sufficiently unusual to have the disruptive, first-mover advantage that is central to many of today's best campaigns," wrote Jonah Bloom in *Advertising Age.* By attaching itself to a "high-brow" magazine such as the *New Yorker* and by creating ads that were promoting nothing but an artistic sensibility and a logo, Target created a whirlwind of media attention. Overall, the reaction in the national press was positive. The ads themselves were praised for their tasteful imagery, understated message, and creative diversity. Barbara Lippert wrote in *Adweek* that Target's sponsorship of the *New Yorker* was "the most exciting example of branded entertainment I've ever seen." The *New York Times,* the *Boston Globe,* and the *San Francisco Chronicle* joined the chorus of supporters. At the other end of the spectrum, although much in the minority, was Edward Wasserman, who held that "the bottom line is that *The New Yorker* 's deal with Target transformed the look and feel of the country's most highly regarded magazine into a promotional vehicle for a retail chain." This last comment betrayed the double-sided nature of Target's sponsorship of the *New Yorker.* Many of those who held the magazine in high regard found the ad buyout by a discount retail chain a sullying move for a literary icon, while those who viewed the retailer positively to begin with were more likely to find the ads both provocative and tasteful. In either case both readers of the magazine and readers of the national press were treated to what every advertiser hoped for—a heavy dose of media attention.

By the time of the publication of the *New Yorker* issue, Target had 5 stores in New York City, although none in Manhattan, and 53 in the New York metropolitan area, plenty to choose from for those consumers whose curiosity was piqued by the ads. Beyond New York, however, the ads contributed to an increased, albeit enigmatic, awareness of Target among the magazine's mostly affluent, urban readers and sparked a months-long debate in the media over the artistry and ethics of such an approach.

FURTHER READING

Abelson, Jenn. "And Now, a Few (More) Words from Our (One) Sponsor." *Boston Globe,* October 24, 2005, p. E1.

Bloom, Jonah. "On Target: Why Presenting Sponsorship's Time Has Come." *Advertising Age,* August 22, 2005, p. 18.

Curtis, Bryan. "Target: Discount Retailer Goes to the New Yorker." *Slate,* August 17, 2005. Available from <http://www.slate.com>

Denitto, Emily. "Target Stores Gun for NYC Market." *Crain's New York Business,* May 26, 1997, p. 3.

Elliott, Stuart. "And What Would Thurber Say? A Single-Sponsor *New Yorker.*" *New York Times,* August 12, 2005, p. C5.

Gladwell, Malcolm. *The Tipping Point: How Little Things Can Make a Big Difference.* New York: Little, Brown and Company, 2000.

Lazare, Lewis. "Target, New Yorker Cross Line." *Chicago Sun-Times,* August 19, 2005, p. 69.

Lippert, Barbara. "Barbara Lippert's Critique: Hitting the Bull's-eye." *Adweek,*, August 22, 2005.

New Yorker 81, no. 24 (August 22, 2005).

Rowley, Laura. *On Target: How the World's Hottest Retailer Hit a Bull's-eye.* Hoboken, NJ: John Wiley, 2003.

Wasserman, Edward. "Turning an Esteemed Magazine into an Ad Tract." Journalism and Mass Communications, Washington and Lee University, September 9, 2005. Available from <http://journalism.wlu.edu/knightcom/09-19-05.html>

Jonathan Kolstad

TAKE CHARGE OF EDUCATION CAMPAIGN

OVERVIEW

With more than 860 stores and sales of $20.4 billion, Minneapolis, Minnesota–based Target in 1998 pursued a broad-based advertising and marketing effort designed to further an upscale image and bring in wealthier consumers. Thus it sought to distinguish itself from other companies in the discount-retail niche, and, in fact, its overall advertising strategy made it a standout: in line with the policies of parent company Dayton Hudson of Minneapolis (since renamed Target Corporation), the retailer had not had an agency of record. Rather, it had pursued a number of campaigns, the most prominent of which was its "Take Charge of Education" program, a television effort largely overseen by Martin/Williams of Minneapolis. Total spending for television, radio, print, and other forms of advertising by Target in 1998 was estimated at $50 million.

With "Take Charge of Education," the company promoted the fact that it would donate 1 percent of all purchases that customers made using its charge card, the Target Guest Card, directly to customer-designated schools, kindergarten through high school, as well as to a variety of other educational initiatives, including scholarships and arts programs. One of the principal offerings of the campaign was a 30-second spot in which a hapless boy played by child actor Alan James Morgan made a mess of customers' cars at a school-sponsored car wash. The humorous commercial promoted the Target program as a more efficient way to give money to schools.

The "Take Charge of Education" program successfully launched Target's school-funding initiative, which benefited local communities while also enhancing Target's brand equity by associating the brand with a relevant cause. The company expanded the program to include a Target Visa card that also made contributions on purchases made outside of Target stores. By 2006 the "Take Charge of Education" program had donated about $155 million to more than 108,000 schools.

HISTORICAL CONTEXT

In 1962 Dayton's, a Minneapolis-based department store chain, opened its first Target store in Roseville, Minnesota. It was a good year for discount chains: Wal-Mart and Kmart, Target's leading competitors, also began business in 1962. From the beginning, however, Target pursued a strategy that set it apart from other discounters, emphasizing an image of high quality alongside its low prices.

Dayton's in 1969 merged with another retailer, Hudson, to create Dayton Hudson. Meanwhile, Target grew rapidly, from four stores at the end of 1962 to a chain of 24 stores eight years later. In the 1970s and 1980s growth accelerated rapidly through acquisitions. With the purchase of a 16-store chain in the western United States, Target in 1971 moved into Colorado, Iowa, and Oklahoma, and purchases in 1980 and 1983 expanded it throughout the Midwest and West Coast, respectively.

In 1990, with 420 stores nationwide, the company opened the first of its Target Greatland stores, which were half again as large as regular Target facilities up to that time. Target stores became even bigger in 1995, with the introduction of the first SuperTargets, 175,000-square-foot units that offered groceries in addition to the items traditionally available in a department store. By the late 1990s, as it expanded rapidly along the East Coast, Target had begun to position itself as a fashionable discount chain, one that appealed to customers whose purchases were driven as much by a sense of style and quality as by price.

The founder of Target's parent company, George Draper Dayton, set the tone for Target's philanthropy. In 1918 he founded the Dayton Foundation, and his family would later commit the predecessor of Target Corporation to donating 5 percent of profits to charity. In fact, his grandsons, Bruce and Kenneth Dayton, who ran the family business in the 1960s and 1970s, were veritable zealots when it came to urging other companies to give back to their communities. Thus, it was no mere marketing ploy for Target in the 1990s to establish the "Take Charge of Education" program, in which the company pledged to donate 1 percent of all consumer purchases on a Target Guest Card to any school (kindergarten through 12th grade) of the customers' choice. In 1998 Target began a marketing effort to promote the program.

TARGET MARKET

From the beginning, Target's image was that of a high-end discounter, with an appeal somewhere between that of dollar stores and bargain basements on the one hand and pricey chains such as Bloomingdale's or Marshall Field's on the other. Certainly a niche existed between these two extremes, and Target sought to fill it by offering customers a pleasant shopping environment. Stores were designed so as to be well lit, with broader aisles than those of a typical discount chain. During the 1990s the company increasingly offered more fashionable lines of housewares and clothing, designed to appeal to a younger, wealthier clientele.

Company surveys had found that the typical Target shopper was about 40 years old and enjoyed a household annual income of just under $50,000. Hence the thrust of its "Grab Your Own Style" marketing in 1998, which, in the words of Lisa Vincenti in *HFN: The Weekly Newspaper for the Home Furnishing Network,* "downplays [the company's] hallmark bull's eye," a logo associated in many minds with low prices. Instead, Sunday newspaper inserts in May 1998 "sent a new message to American households: contemporary, sophisticated, and coordinated home decorating ideas." As Vincenti noted, customers had come to jokingly refer to Target as "Tar-jay" or "Tar-zhay," with a French-style pronunciation to indicate its newer upscale image.

According to Jeffrey Arlen in *Discount Store News,* Target was at the front end of an industry-wide move "to change the long-time retailing mantra from 'location, location, location' to 'image, image, image.'" As Arlen observed, "No mass merchant has taken this concept to heart with more sincerity than Target Stores. By coupling clever, sophisticated advertising with sharp on-trend merchandising in a mutually beneficial way, it can be argued that the store has successfully created a niche of its own." An industry executive told Arlen that Target "truly understands the importance not just of merchandising . . . but of combining the merchandise with marketing for their customers . . . No matter what your income demographic, there is no negative to shopping in the Target stores."

COMPETITION

The largest retail chain in America, and the largest retailer of any kind, was Wal-Mart Stores, which in 1998 had an annual budget of $172 million in measured media—more than three times Target's advertising budget. Far behind the massive Arkansas retailer was Kmart, putting Target in third place, well ahead of J.C. Penney and the ailing giant Sears Roebuck. Significantly, in December 1997 Sears hired Robert Thacker, former vice president of marketing for Target, to run its strategic marketing and promotion.

According to Bob Geiger of the Minneapolis–Saint Paul *Star Tribune,* Thacker was responsible for the "seamless" look of Target's marketing, a feat in itself since the company had accounts with more than a dozen advertising agencies and other creative sources. Thacker's move to Sears came at a critical time for that company, which sought in part to imitate Target's winning strategy: as with Target, Geiger wrote, "image is an equally critical issue for Sears, which has attempted in recent years to lure more upper-middle-class shoppers to its stores."

Target pursued a strategy of keeping prices lower than those of Sears or Kohl's Department Stores, another strong competitor, but higher than Wal-Mart's or Kmart's. It also increasingly pursued a strategy of providing a whole range of furnishings, just as Sears, Montgomery Ward, and J.C. Penney had once done. Target, with its line of housewares designed by architect Michael Graves, went head to head with Kmart's Martha Stewart collection—and with the offerings of high-end retailers such as Pottery Barn, Crate & Barrel, and Bed Bath & Beyond. Hence a retail consultant's appraisal of the last-named retailer's reaction to Target's massive "Grab Your Own Style" promotion, as quoted by Vincenti in *HFN*: it "runs right into their underwear."

TARGET ON THE WASHINGTON MONUMENT

In January 1999 Target ran a full-page ad in *USA Today* showing the Washington Monument alongside the company's well-known bull's-eye logo. This followed advertising for American Airlines using photos of natural wonders in Utah as well as scenes from the Great Smoky Mountains National Park, all of which prompted Mark Johnson of the *Seattle Times* to write, "Corporate advertisers have cut deals to use national monuments in ads that, at first glance, look like Smokey the Bear has sold his soul."

In fact both ads promoted preservation of monuments, and indeed both Target and American Airlines—along with other companies using similar advertising—had donated millions of dollars to the nonprofit National Park Foundation. Target, for instance, had made a gift of $6.5 million for the restoration of the Washington Monument. "It's kind of a two-pronged win for us," Target spokeswoman Carolyn Brookter told Johnson, "being able to help a good cause and get the visibility." This type of "cause-related marketing" began in 1984 with advertisements for American Express that noted that for every time consumers used their American Express cards, the company would donate a small percentage of their purchases to the restoration of the Statue of Liberty.

Foundation rules, along with federal guidelines, dictated that tobacco manufacturers, liquor companies, and corporations involved in litigation with the Department of the Interior were not allowed to use national monuments in their advertising; furthermore, use of corporate logos should be limited. These rules, Johnson wrote, "may seem a little silly given the commercials that already exist, such as the Statue of Liberty picking up and admiring an Oldsmobile or the United Airlines ad depicting a Thomas Jefferson statue pulling a carry-on suitcase."

MARKETING STRATEGY

In the late 1990s Target's marketing seemed to be everywhere. Thus the company in 1997 moved increasingly into a relatively new field, running a 90-second commercial aired in movie theaters nationwide. Such advertising was much less expensive than airing a traditional television spot, and with the increasing segmentation of the television market, it helped the company reach sometimes elusive consumers. Yet even Rod Eaton, Target's national director of sales promotion, professed surprise when a Target spot actually drew cheers from a movie audience. After all, audiences who had paid as much as $8 for a movie ticket might be inclined to consider commercials an intrusion. The spot, created by HMS partners, featured "a blonde woman in a 'North African' bazaar," according to Diane Richard of *Minneapolis–St. Paul CityBusiness,* "who exchanges a mysterious note for a package that, lo and behold, contains chocolate chip cookies, a note from Mom, and a Target Sunday circular."

Target also pursued joint advertising with other companies, a strategy already adopted in 1997. Thus it teamed with Revlon and Hachette Filipacchi Magazines, Inc., for an advertising supplement to the December 1998 issue of *Elle* magazine. The nine-page section, entitled "C'est Target," showed models wearing Revlon cosmetics and clothing from Target. In November 1998 Target joined Columbia TriStar Television Distribution (CTTD) in a $10 million cross-promotional deal tied to the variety talk show *Donny & Marie,* starring singers Donny and Marie Osmond. In part through *Target the Family,* its in-store publication, the company heavily promoted the *Donny & Marie* tie-in.

December 1997 had seen Target's first-ever network television special, *Snowden on Ice,* which aired on CBS. The show was built around a snowman character, and throughout 1998 Target promoted Snowden spin-offs such as a $15 plush toy. More Snowden marketing followed at Christmas of 1998, along with a 30-second Christmas spot created by Peterson Milla Hooks of Minneapolis, the latter featuring the Rosemary Clooney song "Come On-a My House."

A number of these campaigns were tied in some way to Target's community-service efforts on behalf of schools. The latter was most forcefully promoted in "Take Charge of Education," for which Martin/Williams had created a spot called "Ding Dong" in 1997. "Ding Dong" starred Morgan, who went from door to door selling products that ranged from candy bars to birdseed in order to raise money for his school. Morgan had "charmed viewers with his nervous sales pitches," Aaron Baar wrote in *Adweek,* and in a 1998 spot the boy was shown to be "up to the same old tricks . . . working at a school car wash, backing one car into another and soaking everything." According to Baar, "His bumbling antics and commentary . . . are intended to remind viewers that Target's Guest Card . . . is an easier way to support education."

"Take Charge of Education" became a mainstay of Target's community-outreach programs. It was expanded to include a school-uniform program in which Target credit-card holders received 10 percent off, and in 1999 the company worked with Golden Books Entertainment on the "Read-In" literacy program, which provided books for children to read in Target stores while their parents shopped. For its part, Target produced nearly 100,000 flyers about the program, which were distributed to elementary-school teachers. In 2001 Target introduced a Target Visa card, aimed at customers who preferred not to carry several charge cards. Target took advantage of the new card to benefit the "Take Charge of Education" program. As with the Target Guest Card, by using the Target Visa for purchases at Target stores, customers donated 1 percent of the total to the school of their choice, but in addition, purchases on the card outside of the store also resulted in a one-half percent donation to the school. Target sweetened the pot even more in 2005 with the "Twice as Nice for Your School" promotion. All program donations were doubled on purchases made from July 24 through September 10, 2005. The concept was also extended to another Target charity. All health-related or pharmacy purchases resulted in a donation to St. Jude Children's Research Hospital, the United States' largest center for treating children with pediatric cancer and other serious illnesses.

OUTCOME

The "Take Charge of Education" program and the marketing effort behind it were successful on a number of levels. From the time the program began, in 1997, through 2006, Target donated in excess of $154 million to schools and other educational programs. All told, 9 million Target customers enrolled in the "Take Charge" program, and more than 108,000 schools received twice-yearly checks from Target to be used in any way they chose, whether it be for books, basic supplies, computers, or grants. Not only was the program worthwhile philanthropy, but it also served Target's business interests. Target officials were, however, generally reluctant to boast about the program, and it was clear that charitable giving had been part of the corporate culture for decades. Frank Clancy of the *New York Times* reported, "Internal research showed that customers enrolled in this program spent significantly more at Target than other charge card customers." Moreover, Target's commitment to education and other charitable causes helped to elevate its brand, creating value that was likely worth far more than what the company donated. Finally, the "Take Charge of Education" marketing campaign succeeded on a creative level. In October 1998 ad agency OptionOne was recognized in *Promo* magazine's annual World PRO Awards of Excellence for its "School Fundraising Made Simple" and "School Connection" programs, both tied to "Take Charge of Education."

FURTHER READING

Arlen, Jeffrey. "Target: Aiming for a Niche of Its Own." *Discount Store News,* April 19, 1999.

Baar, Aaron. "Target Stores." *Adweek* (midwest ed.), January 5, 1998, p. 25.

———. "Target's New Style." *Adweek* (midwest ed.), April 13, 1998, p. 8.

"Brand Building." *Chain Drug Review,* February 15, 1999.

Clancy, Frank. "Concern in Minneapolis as Target Remakes an Icon." *New York Times,* November 20, 2000, p. F14.

Cuneo, Alice Z.. "Retailers Put Extra Polish on Their Brand Image, Retail: TV Ads More Important than Ever for Target Stores." *Advertising Age,* October 5, 1998, p. S22.

Friedman, Wayne. "'Donny & Marie' Gets Targeted." *Hollywood Reporter,* November 19, 1998, p. 40.

Geiger, Bob. "Target Vice President Robert Thacker Moves to Sears." *Minneapolis–St. Paul Star Tribune,* December 29, 1997, p. D2.

Halkias, Maria. "Penney Brings in Da Noise: Retailer's Magazine Aimed at Teen Market." *Dallas Morning News,* April 6, 1999, p. D1.

Johnson, Mark. "Ads Feature National Parks, Landmarks in Dual Publicity." *Seattle Times,* February 14, 1999, p. A18.

Richard, Diane. "Target Debuts Ad Campaign on the Big Screen." *Minneapolis–St. Paul CityBusiness,* May 30, 1997, p. 1.

"Target Takes Charge of Education." *Science Activities,* Winter 2006, p. 42.

Tellijohn, Andrew. "Target Visa Tested in 3 Markets." *Minneapolis–St. Paul CityBusiness,* May 25, 2001, p. 1.

Vincenti, Lisa. "Aggressive Target Launches a Marketing 'Glitzkrieg,'" *HFN: The Weekly Newspaper for the Home Furnishing Network,* May 18, 1998, p. 1.

Warner, Fara, and Joseph B. Cahill. "Republic Industries Names an Executive from Sears, John Costello, as President." *Wall Street Journal,* December 7, 1998, p. B9.

Judson Knight
Ed Dinger

Thomas Cook Tour Operations Ltd

The Thomas Cook Business Park
Coningsby Road
Peterborough, PE3 8SB
United Kingdom
Telephone: 44 8702 430416
Web site: www.flythomascook.com

PERSPECTIVES CAMPAIGN

OVERVIEW

In 2001 approximately 120,000 young European vacationers, mostly British, booked their vacations through Thomas Cook Tour Operations Ltd's Club 18-30, the United Kingdom's largest booking agency for 18- to 30-year-olds. The service offered Britons more than 14 sun-drenched destinations, including Spain, Greece, the Canary Islands, Ibiza, and Turkey. The company had previously gained notoriety for its risqué advertising. In 1995 the British Advertising Standards Authority (ASA) forced a Club 18-30 campaign, created by ad agency Saatchi & Saatchi and titled "Beaver España," to cease after hundreds of complaints were made regarding the campaign's sexual implications. Undeterred, in 2002 Club 18-30 released a similarly suggestive campaign titled "Perspectives" that attempted, as its executives explained, to present an "honest reflection" of what young people did on vacation.

Created in late 2001 by Saatchi & Saatchi with an estimated $1 million budget, "Perspectives" consisted of three print spots, "Pool," "Beach," and "Bar." At first look, each print ad portrayed beautiful young people engaged in normal resort activities such as throwing a Frisbee at the beach, sunbathing poolside, or socializing inside a bar. Upon closer inspection the youth in each photograph were juxtaposed to suggest various sexual acts. To avoid the backlash "Beaver España" had received from older consumers, "Perspectives" appeared only in magazines targeting young males.

The campaign helped Club 18-30 maintain its position as industry leader, but its sexual content elicited a range of negative responses from critics and advertising judges. Nancy Vonk, a judge for the International Advertising Festival in Cannes, France, said that she hated the ads. Enough festival judges in 2002 favored the ads, however, to award "Perspectives" the Grand Prix award and a Gold Lion in the poster category. Another festival judge, Olivier Altmann, told *Brand Republic,* "They were fresh, enjoyable and enthusiastic. You can stay in front of them for 10 minutes and have a deep relationship with each ad."

HISTORICAL CONTEXT

Club 18-30 had been targeting partygoers long before "Perspectives" came to fruition. Founded by David Heard in 1965, Club 18-30 first booked 580 vacationers to Costa Brava, Spain, under the tagline "Your granny wouldn't like it." In 1994 Saatchi & Saatchi won Club 18-30's advertising account and released a campaign with the tagline "Holidays your mother wouldn't like." Moray MacLennan, Saatchi & Saatchi's joint managing director, told *Campaign* in 1994, "Our task is to build the profile of Club 18-30, which has been out of the market for some time. The company has to make a lot of noise."

The next year Club 18-30 released its highly controversial "Beaver España" campaign, which used print and outdoor mediums. One image featured a close-up of boxer shorts with the tagline "Girls, can we interest you in a package holiday?" Another ad's copy stated, "It's not all sex, sex, sex. There's a bit of sun and sea as well." After the ASA received more than 500 complaints regarding the campaign's indecency, the advertising watchdog banned "Beaver España" billboards and posters. Much to Club 18-30's delight, the order was carried out on the exact day the campaign was scheduled to end. Saatchi & Saatchi continued to handle the company's advertising. In a 1995 television spot it created for Club 18-30, titled "Mosquito," a mosquito drank the blood from a young man's buttock. After drinking its fill of alcohol-rich blood, the intoxicated insect buzzed off and smacked into a window.

Leading up to "Perspectives," Saatchi & Saatchi wanted to release a campaign that, in the ad agency's opinion, honestly depicted what young partygoers did on vacation. James Griffiths, a director at Saatchi & Saatchi, explained to the *Sunday Telegraph,* "If you get a lot of young people on holiday, sex happens. It's just that nobody talks about it, and Club 18-30 are not afraid of being honest and saying, 'This is what happens; this is what we're about.'"

JUXTAPOSED

In late 2001 eight young women and eight young men were photographed on the Mediterranean island of Ibiza for the controversial "Perspectives" campaign. After photographing the models on the beach, beside a pool, and inside a bar, the ad agency Saatchi & Saatchi flew the models back to London. Their photographs were later juxtaposed for three print ads titled "Pool," "Beach," and "Bar."

At first glance, the young people shown in the three ads seemed to be participating in wholesome activities. For the print ad "Pool," two young men tossed a beach ball back and forth. Upon closer inspection, however, one of the men seemed to be groping a girl standing poolside. The 16 models chosen for the shoot did not know how their images would later be used. One of the models, Mark Kavanagh, told the *Liverpool Echo* in October 2001, "I still haven't seen the photos and they won't tell us what the adverts will be like, so I won't see them until everyone else does."

TARGET MARKET

"Perspectives" targeted vacationing partygoers over the age of 18. Saatchi & Saatchi purposely photographed 16 models with whom its audience would hopefully identify. Club 18-30 marketing manager Clare Burns explained to the *Liverpool Echo* why Mark Kavanagh, one of the models featured in "Perspectives," was chosen. "He's got lovely eyes which twinkle and he's good looking with a decent body. But not so good looking that lads looking for a holiday would think he's a model, rather than someone like themselves."

The campaign's cheeky, sexual humor was something Saatchi & Saatchi believed its target would appreciate. *Reuters News* quoted Griffiths as explaining, "The intention was to present an honest reflection of Club 18-30 in a humorous way. People go on these holidays to have fun. And when you talk about fun for people of that age group, sex and getting drunk tend to coincide." Using sexually suggestive imagery may have effectively resonated with young consumers, but it also incited a backlash from older audiences, including advertising-festival judges and international ad critics. Kirk Carr of *Advertising Age* wrote, "It's been argued these ads are not offensive in the context of the media in which they ran or to the audience to which they were directed. Even so, honoring these ads as among the best that advertising has to offer is an embarrassment to the global advertising community."

Pre-campaign research conducted by Saatchi & Saatchi suggested that Britain's youth was comfortable with sexual topics that had previously been considered taboo. A Club 18-30 spokesman explained in the *Sunday Telegraph,* "Girls in particular are more liberated than boys were, even 20 years ago. Without a doubt the girls are more confident than before." Despite the spokesman's observation about liberated youth, much of the United Kingdom's general population was offended by such advertisements. According to a survey conducted by the ASA in July 2002, 19 percent of those surveyed were personally offended by ads they had viewed during the previous year, and 32 percent believed that ads they had witnessed would be offensive to someone they knew.

COMPETITION

Style Holidays, a U.K.-based vacation-booking agent, tried capturing Club 18-30's market with stylish brochures and low-priced vacation packages. Its sales for the Spanish beach areas of Costa Blanca grew 57 percent in 2001, and its bookings for Spain's island of Majorca rose 42 percent. Style Holidays' marketing manager, John Heyes, commented on the company's success in *Travel Trade Gazette UK & Ireland*: "It is because of the quality of our product and because we're not greedy in terms of prices. There has been very little movement—less than two percent increases." Analysts believed that the increased number of bookings may have also resulted from the strengthening British currency and a spike in youth travel.

In 2002 British travel company First Choice's youth travel brand, 2wentys, rebranded its booking service to attract the "sophisticated partygoer who wants a higher level of flexibility on holiday." The brand hired ad agency Main Artery to revamp its direct mailers, brochures, and website. Clare Tobin, the head of 2wentys, told *Travel Trade Gazette UK* & *Ireland,* "We will highlight things that differentiate us from other brands, such as our customer service." The booking service devised a three-year strategy to grow 20 percent and overtake Club 18-30's industry lead. In 2001 the booking service's sales rose 15 percent over the previous year. The company also heavily promoted its November reunion parties, which attempted to re-create the party atmosphere of summer getaways.

MARKETING STRATEGY

In late 2001 Saatchi & Saatchi selected eight females and eight males to fly to Ibiza, a Spanish island and popular vacation destination located along the Mediterranean Sea. The 16 models, chosen for their modest attractiveness, were then photographed in different island locations. Three print images, "Beach," "Pool," and "Bar," were chosen for the campaign. In the print ad "Beach" the models appeared on a sunny beach along the Mediterranean Sea. At first glance the bikini- and swim-trunk-wearing models were engaged in wholesome beach fun, such as throwing a Frisbee, playing paddleball, and lying out to sunbathe. Upon closer inspection the posture of each model intimated a different sexual act. A man preparing to swat an incoming paddleball also appeared to be spanking a bikini-clad girl. One man innocently gazed into the horizon, but his face was juxtaposed between the legs of a woman sunbathing. "Usually photographs in ads have a single point of focus," Donald Gunn, creator of the Gunn Report, an ad-industry publication, told *Advertising Age.* "These are like murals, or tableaux. You're likely to spend a minute with them rather than 10 seconds."

In another spot, titled "Bar," six young men and eight women were shown at a bar. The models seemed to be participating in typical bar behaviors, such as dancing, talking, and drinking beer. The models' expressions conveyed a relaxed and gregarious demeanor. When the ad was viewed more carefully, those featured could also be perceived as engaging in sexual acts ranging from groping to oral intercourse. Even though the ads' content was considered obscene by many, the ASA did not entirely ban them, allowing them to appear in magazines that targeted young males, such as *Maxim* and *FHM.* A Club 18-30 spokesman told the *News of the World,* "There was no intention to offend. They are tongue in cheek." The ASA did register some complaints about the campaign, but not enough to warrant its cessation. Despite criticism, Club 18-30 and its agency stood behind the campaign's message. Griffiths of Saatchi & Saatchi told the *Globe and Mail,* "It's honest. It doesn't try to pull the wool over anyone's eyes."

In the third print ad, "Pool," a mixture of 15 males and females were shown socializing around a luxurious swimming pool. Two males played pool at a nearby table. Everyone's expressions appeared innocent. As in the other two ads, the models' actions took on double meanings. One young man reaching for a beach ball also appeared to be groping a bikini-clad woman. Other images implied oral sex and masturbation.

OUTCOME

Not only did "Perspectives" help Club 18-30 maintain its position as Britain's leading vacation-booking company for partygoers, it also managed to be controversial enough to generate publicity for the brand yet tame enough to escape reprimand by advertising watchdogs. At the 2002 International Advertising Festival in Cannes, France, several judges criticized the campaign for its provocative material and later lambasted the judges who awarded it the Grand Prix award. Cannes judge Nancy Vonk, cocreative director at ad agency Ogilvy & Mather in Toronto, told the *Globe and Mail* that she hated the campaign. She criticized her fellow judges who gave it the Grand Prix, stating, "It's like giving Austin Powers an Oscar. It's a cheap pee-pee joke." Mike Hughes, another of the festival's judges, told *Adweek,* "It's easy sex jokes. I'm not a PC type of guy, but I think a club that sells itself as a place to go for sex is coarse and rude." Judges who appreciated the print ads included Olivier Altmann, who explained to *Adweek,* "It was the most fresh and the most enjoyable. They know the purpose [of such vacations] is to have sex. It's very honest advertising."

FURTHER READING

Aaronovitch, David. "It's People, Not Dogs, Who Are Being Demeaned." *Independent* (London), May 7, 2002, p. 15.

Burrell, Ian. "The Ten Most Controversial Billboards." *Independent* (London), July 27, 2005, pp. 12–13.

Byrne, Ciar. "It's No Longer 'Sex, Sex, Sex' as Club 18-30 Goes Upmarket." *Independent* (London), April 2, 2005, p. 15.

Faulkner, Scott. "Mark's the Face of Fun in the Sun for 18-30 Jetsetters." *Liverpool Echo,* October 12, 2001, p. 3.

Hall, Emma. "Club 18-30 Switches to Grown-Up Approach." *Advertising Age,* April 18, 2005, p. 22.

Heinzl, John. "Beautiful Bodies and British Cheek Catch Cannes Prize." *Globe and Mail* (Toronto, Ontario), June 21, 2002, p. B9.

McIntyre, Paul. "Furore over Sexy Ads." *Ad News,* June 21, 2002, p. 3.

Michael, Neil. "It's Club 18-Dirty." *News of the World* (London), April 28, 2002, p. 30.

Miller, Phil. "It's Sun, Sea, Sex, Sand and Celluloid for 18-30." *Scotsman* (Edinburgh), March 4, 2000, p. 3.

Milner, Catherine. "News: Club 18-30's 'Dog Porn' Advert Condemned." *Sunday Telegraph* (London), May 5, 2002, p. 6.

———. "Saatchi's Grand Prix Win a Close-Run Thing." *Brand Republic,* June 20, 2002, p. 1.

Parpis, Eleftheria. "Sex, Studs and Deadly Sins." *Adweek* (eastern ed.), June 24, 2002, p. 28.

Pearlman, Julia. "Less 'Aggressive' Image Scores Results for Club 18-30 as Sales Climb." *Brand Republic,* March 16, 2005, p. 1.

Wentz, Laurel. "Sex Sells and Wins." *Advertising Age,* June 24, 2002, p. 76.

Kevin Teague

Time Warner, Inc.

1 Time Warner Center
New York, New York 10019-8016
USA
Telephone: (212) 484-8000
Web site: www.timewarner.com

CARTOON NETWORK PROMOTIONAL AND BRANDING CAMPAIGN

OVERVIEW

In 1998 Time Warner Inc.'s Cartoon Network, second in children's programming to Viacom Inc.'s Nickelodeon Network, was a 24-hour basic-cable service offering nonstop animated entertainment. Cartoon Network created and showcased original programming such as *Dexter's Laboratory, Johnny Bravo,* and *Space Ghost Coast to Coast.* Drawing from the world's largest cartoon library, it also relied heavily on reruns of such classic cartoon series as *The Flintstones* and *Scooby-Doo* along with the entire Warner Brothers cartoon archive. Time Warner and vice chairman Ted Turner hoped that Warner Brothers' material and its own ad campaigns would make Cartoon Network a top channel, with 60 million-plus subscribers, by the first years of the twenty-first century.

For the first time in the Cartoon Network's six-year history, advertisements for the network appeared outside of the channel's own programming, in the form of small television campaigns and cross-promotions with other brands. March 31, 1998, marked the debut of "Get Tooned," a campaign that resulted from the partnership between the Cartoon Network and food company Kraft Foods, Inc. Cartoon characters appeared on Kraft packaging. Several "Get Tooned" spots were created with the Cartoon Network's $53 million on-air budget. The network's senior vice president of on-air promotions, Michael Ouweleen, developed the fictional Cartoon Crisis Center for the spots, in which phone counselors humorously guided cartoon characters through the stress of cartoon stunts. The tagline for all the spots was "Screwy, Ain't It?" The next year the Cartoon Network released a nationwide promotion titled "Coaster 2 Coaster" in conjunction with Six Flags theme parks. In 1999 the network formed a cross-branding campaign with the snack maker Pepperidge Farms titled "Ultimate Cartoon Hangout." Similar promotions and branding campaigns continued into 2006.

In November 2000 the Cartoon Network met its goal with 67.5 million U.S. subscribers and 145 million subscribers worldwide. The campaigns also earned several ad-industry awards, including a 2002 Gold One Show award in the category of Consumer TV (Various Lengths). In 2004 one spot garnered a gold medal for media promotion at the Golden Award of Montreux, an advertising festival held in Switzerland.

HISTORICAL CONTEXT

Cartoon Network was launched in 1992 when Turner Broadcasting, Inc., acquired the 8,500-cartoon Hanna-Barbera and MGM cartoon libraries. After a tough start, Cartoon Network began to grow rapidly during the mid-1990s. The network was able to challenge the cable children's channel Nickelodeon, in markets where they competed, with little more than reruns of old Hanna-Barbera cartoons like *Scooby-Doo* and *The Jetsons.* Early in 1994 the burgeoning cable channel finally broke even thanks to high ratings. Limited channel capacity and reregulation, however, meant its subscriber base faced a challenge in moving much past 11 million homes.

In 1995 Turner Broadcasting merged with international media conglomerate Time Warner. That alliance brought additional material from the vast Warner Brothers library, including a complete set of Bugs Bunny and Daffy Duck cartoons. The merger, with its influx of new programming, helped propel Cartoon Network to even more robust growth. "Cartoon Network may have just turned 4 years old, but it's not acting like a toddler," announced network president Betty Cohen in 1996. "Where we aren't on yet, we're usually either first or second in line. You're never happy [with your subscriber count], but at least those 30 million homes are real homes that haven't been acquired through cash payments or retransmission-consent deals."

The network added 16 million subscribers between December 1996 and December 1997 alone. By the end of 1997 the channel was available in nearly 50 million homes nationwide. Viewership grew correspondingly, according to Nielsen Media Research; by February 1998 it was in seventh place in prime-time ratings among the top 20 cable channels. That growth enabled Cartoon Network to embark upon an aggressive promotional push for 1998, many aspects of which involved cartoon characters in lieu of flesh-and-blood stars.

TARGET MARKET

Cartoon Network saw its marketing mission as selling "the cartoon spirit, its zaniness," according to Cohen. "That way we appeal to the kid in everyone, even the adult market, which is crazy for cartoons." While the principal market for cartoons was children ages 2 to 11, the network was able to broaden its base considerably by playing on the nostalgia of adult viewers as well. Worldwide, more than 35 percent of Cartoon Network's audience were adults, a fact that made it especially attractive to advertisers. Besides such traditional children's show advertisers as Nestlé and Procter & Gamble, companies that focused on adults, such as Max Factor, bought time on the Cartoon Network.

As an illustration of this trend, one of the Cartoon Network's top-rated shows was *Scooby-Doo,* a 1970s Hanna-Barbera series about a group of teenage sleuths and a dim-witted Great Dane who drove around in a psychedelic van solving mysteries. Children ages 2 to 11 made up 68 percent of the audience for *Scooby-Doo,* while adults comprised 25 percent. Nostalgia for the animated characters of their youth explained the show's appeal to adults. "From 1969 to 1991, Scooby was never out of production," explained Fred Seibert, Hanna-Barbera's president. "You have 22 years of audiences with fresh *Scooby-Doo* episodes in their minds. All those people are now at the age where they have enough time, enough memory, and enough money to capture the parts of their lives they enjoyed the most."

FLIGHT OF THE BOOMERANG

How many cartoon networks could one market sustain? In July 1999 Turner Broadcasting decided to try answering that question when it announced plans to introduce a second cable television channel featuring all-day and all-night cartoons. The new channel, to be called Boomerang, was scheduled to begin airing on April Fools' Day, 2000.

The launch of Boomerang marked a shift in strategy for Cartoon Network. The first network would now focus on airing original cartoons, while Boomerang featured cartoons from the company's Hanna-Barbera library. "Boomerang would serve baby boomers and kids ages 2 to 7," explained Cartoon Network president Betty Cohen. "These people have told us they want more of the old Hanna-Barbera cartoons." In contrast, Cartoon Network would be marketed more to middle-graders, teenagers, and young adults who, studies showed, favored contemporary animation. To boost original production, Turner Broadcasting planned to create a separate animation studio for Cartoon Network. The Atlanta-based cable giant hoped to lease a building and renovate it into a state-of-the-art facility in Los Angeles.

Boomerang's creation reminded many cable industry analysts of a strategy Turner Broadcasting followed with its TNT and Turner Classic Movies channels. At first, TNT featured old movies from Turner Broadcasting's vast film library. Then the channel switched to airing films made in the 1970s and 1980s and live sports programming. The company then moved its old movies to a new channel, Turner Classic Movies.

COMPETITION

Nickelodeon was the reigning king of cable television children's programming in the 1990s, capturing over

50 percent of the children's television market. As of 1999 Nickelodeon's *Rugrats* was entrenched as the most popular cartoon program on television (most weeks the show was among the top 15 basic cable programs, with a typical audience of more than 3 million). Several channels posed a challenge to Nickelodeon's dominance, however, including Walt Disney, Fox, the Cartoon Network, and the three major networks.

Historically, Cartoon Network provided the stiffest competition for Nickelodeon. As early as 1996 independent research showed that, in homes that got both Nickelodeon and Cartoon Network, Nickelodeon's ratings were lower among viewers ages 2 to 11 than in homes that did not have Cartoon Network. The two cable networks employed similar methods in competing for the same audience. Like Nickelodeon, Cartoon Network worked extremely hard to market itself as a safe and fun television haven for children. "It's like the reruns that do better on [Nickelodeon spin-off] Nick at Nite than they would somewhere else—the network has created a destination," said Cohen. "A cartoon that runs on our network and that also runs on another Turner network, like TBS or TNT, will do better with us, because we're a destination."

On the other hand, there were also some salient differences in the ways Nickelodeon and Cartoon Network pursued their viewers. "If Nickelodeon is about empowering kids, Cartoon Network is about freedom to be wacky and zany," explained Joe Uva, president of sales and marketing for Turner Broadcasting. Cartoon Network also gained a competitive advantage against Nickelodeon because it was the only network devoted to full-time children's programming.

MARKETING STRATEGY

"We are the champions of all things 'cartoony,'" Craig McAnsh, Cartoon Network's senior vice president of marketing, said in explaining the cable channel's personality. "If something can come from the world of cartoons, smash through the glass of a TV set, and somehow penetrate a kid's life, then we've achieved that personality. We are cranky, surprising, and a little irreverent. Our tonality tries to reinforce all those things."

Cartoon Network's 1998 television advertising campaign was designed to reflect that iconoclastic "tonality." In one series of spots, "Cartoon Crisis Center," created in-house by Michael Ouweleen, creative director and senior vice president of on-air promotions for the network, telephone counselors manned emergency hotlines in a Cartoon Crisis Center. In one representative spot, "Ledge," a crisis counselor was depicted talking to a cartoon character who had walked off a ledge. He told the animated creation what to expect: first his legs would run in place while funny music played, then he would fall to the ground, creating a hole in his exact outline, and finally, he would walk off making accordion noises. The tagline for all the spots was "Screwy, Ain't It?" "That campaign went a long way to helping define our personality," said McAnsh.

In addition to these commercials, Cartoon Network ran $53 million worth of on-air sponsored promotions in 1998. That year the network completed its on-air promotional calendar by mid-April, achieving its earliest and most profitable yearlong schedule of corporate-sponsored on-air events to date. In one such promotion, Cartoon Network and Kraft Foods—a major children's advertiser that had been a mainstay partner with Nickelodeon—struck a $10 million deal to feature the Cartoon Network logo and animated characters on some 80 million boxes of macaroni and cheese, cereals, and other foods popular with children. Cartoon Network characters appeared on Kraft products through March 31, 1998, as part of a publicity campaign called "Get Tooned." Among those products were Post brand cereals, Hand-Snacks, Kool-Aid, and Kraft Singles. Cartoon Network also conducted a contest that awarded one lucky child a free trip to Hollywood. The winner was featured in an original two-minute cartoon produced by the channel's animators. "This helps us plant our brand name in areas where we're not always visible," said Jodi Tull, the channel's director of promotion marketing. "We're also partnering with a brand that is already powerful with kids."

The "Get Tooned" promotion was a breakthrough in several ways for Cartoon Network. It was the first time the channel had promoted itself outside of television advertising. The Kraft deal also represented the first time Cartoon Network used characters from both its Hanna-Barbera and Warner Brothers Looney Tunes libraries in a promotion campaign. Daffy Duck, the Tasmanian Devil, and Marvin the Martian were among the Looney Tunes characters. The Hanna-Barbera characters included Scooby-Doo, Yogi Bear, and a new one called Dexter.

Dexter was also featured in a giveaway featuring Dexter-related toys and a Dexter Laboratory built in the winning child's bedroom as the grand prize. Cartoons tied in with Discovery Zone for on-air spots in this promotion, which also featured the zany Dexter Mobile, a specially equipped bus that toured 25 cities and 64 stops in 90 days, including Discovery Zone locations, Six Flags theme parks, and various malls. The Dexter Mobile events were organized in conjunction with Beyond DDB, Chicago, a division of the ad agency DDB Needham Worldwide. Additional tour sponsors included Schering-Plough Corp.'s Coppertone, Gardetto's, and Nestlé Foods. The Dexter tour provided another example of the way in which Cartoon Network branded itself.

"The promotion was very much about treating our characters as stars," said Cohen.

Cartoon Network's other on-air sponsored promotions in 1998 included Coaster 2 Coaster, a spring contest to send children on a roller coaster journey across the United States sponsored by Six Flags Theme Parks, got milk?, and Zoinks!; an October celebration of the ever-popular *Scooby-Doo* and the 25th anniversary of Lego; and Say When!, an annual toy-driven holiday fantasy from Hasbro Toys and Games. Finally, *Toonami,* Cartoon Network's afternoon adventure programming block, provided a launching ground for instant on-air giveaways for premiere toy manufacturers Nintendo, Bandai America, and Hasbro Toys and Games. "We could not ask for a more prominent list of sponsors to be involved in Cartoon Network integrated promotions," declared McAnsh. "It's a compliment to us that recognized industry leaders such as these choose to align themselves with our emerging brand of cartoon entertainment."

To supplement the on-air promotional spots, Cartoon Network's Cartoon Branding Group created a number of major brand extensions in 1998, including retail, music, theme parks, and publishing. On the retail side, the network partnered with Six Flags Over Georgia in Atlanta for the 31,000-square-foot Cartoon Network Superstore. There was also a Camp Cartoon Network section at Six Flags Great America park in Gurnee, Illinois, featuring a number of rides tied to cartoon characters. On the music side, Cartoon produced character-titled music CDs in a partnership with Kid Rhino Records.

Time Warner connections also played a key part in Cartoon Network's 1998 marketing strategies. The network experimented with stand-alone, branded sections inside some Warner Brothers Studio stores. Publishing partner DC Comics, also owned by parent Time Warner, produced comics and activity books featuring Cartoon Network characters. And in a major Warner Brothers children's direct-to-home video release, *Scooby-Doo on Zombie Island,* Cartoon Network inserted a trailer hyping its upcoming new series *The Powerpuff Girls* and *Ed, Edd n Eddy.*

In 1999 Cartoon Network partnered with another provider of children's snacks, Pepperidge Farm, for the "Ultimate Cartoon Hangout" campaign. Characters from cartoons were placed on two million packages of Pepperidge Farm Flavor Blasted Goldfish Crackers. A 60-second commercial that mixed cartoons with computer-animated Pepperidge Farm Goldfish also aired on the network. To promote its popular *Powerpuff Girls* cartoon, Cartoon Network joined with Nintendo in 2000 to create a Game Boy video game featuring Powerpuff characters. Cartoon Network then gave away 500 Game Boy Color systems and *Powerpuff Girls* games via an on-air promotion.

In early 2002 Cartoon Network serviced 77.7 million subscribers and was about to campaign for one of the highest-grossing movies of the year. Movie critics predicted failure for the feature-length film *Scooby-Doo,* which was based on one of the Cartoon Network's most popular cartoons. The movie lacked A-list actors and was financed by AOL Time Warner, one of the smaller studios in the movie industry. Nonetheless, on its opening weekend the movie earned $56.4 million, more than any other movie that month, according to the *Wall Street Journal.* The film's success was partially credited to its heavy promotion on Cartoon Network. *Scooby-Doo* advertisements targeted not only children but also adults who had watched the show during the 1970s and 1980s. Time Warner specifically advertised *Scooby-Doo* to adults by featuring ads on AOL's website.

OUTCOME

Cartoon Network's advertisements and its on-air and off-air promotions helped it achieve exceptional ratings and delivery gains in 1998. The campaigns helped propel Cartoon Network to second place among basic-cable networks in the 6- to 11-year-old demographic group in total day Nielsen ratings during the summer, right after Nickelodeon. One successful campaign, "Dexter's Duplication Summer," promoting the network's original animated series *Dexter's Laboratory,* drew 35 million phone calls over eight weeks—despite the fact that the toll-free phone number was only flashed on the screen once a day.

The strong performance of Cartoon Network's marketing programs and brand campaign earned the cable channel widespread industry recognition, including several awards. *Advertising Age* magazine named Cartoon Network its 1998 Cable TV Marketer of the Year. At the 22nd annual One Show Awards in New York, sponsored by the One Club for Art & Copy, Cartoon Network won gold in the 30-second campaign category for its internally created image campaign and took a silver in the 30-second single-spot category for "Ledge." The network also won several Golden Marble Awards at the first annual Advertising to Kids Conference, hosted by Brunico Marketing of Los Angeles. The judges consisted of a panel of senior creative professionals from ad agencies and from the children's entertainment industry. The campaign later won two Gold One Show awards, one in the Consumer TV (Various Lengths) category and one in the Consumer TV (Under $50,000 Budget) category. In 2004 one spot, titled "Duck vs. Rabbit," which was created by the animation studio Cuppa Coffee, collected a gold medal at the Golden Award of Montreux, an international advertising competition held in Switzerland. The spot promoted a 12-hour marathon of Bugs Bunny and Daffy Duck cartoons.

The terrorist attacks of September 11, 2001, negatively affected ratings for both Nickelodeon and the Cartoon Network. One year later, however, Cartoon Network's ratings bounced back; from the fourth quarter of 2002 to the first quarter of 2003, the daytime delivery for Cartoon Network rose 8 percent for children between 2 and 11 years old, according to the data analysts Nielsen Media Research.

As much as the Cartoon Network increased its subscriber base, Nickelodeon increased its own even more and continued to dominate the children's television market. In 2002 Nickelodeon reported its best year ever. With hit shows such as *Blue's Clues, Little Bear, Dora the Explorer, Bill Cosby's Little Bill,* and *Franklin,* Nickelodeon remained the leader in 2003 and ranked number one for children ages 2 to 5. Its share of the 2- to 11-year-old market grew 3 points in 2003.

FURTHER READING

Ault, Susanne. "Mattel Motors to Warner to Distrib Hot Wheels Titles." *Video Business,* February 14, 2005, p. 5.

Carvell, Tim, and Joe McGowan. "Showdown in Toontown." *Fortune,* October 28, 1996, p.100.

Curry, Sheree. "A Seller's Market." *Television Week,* April 14, 2003, p. 22.

Lippman, John, and Bruce Orwall. "'Scooby-Doo,' Where Are You?" *Wall Street Journal,* June 17, 2002, p. B5.

Ross, Chuck. "Cartoon Network: Cable TV Marketer of the Year." *Advertising Age,* November 30, 1998, p. S1.

Robert Schnakenberg
Kevin Teague

THE WORLD'S MOST INTERESTING MAGAZINE CAMPAIGN

OVERVIEW

In the early 1990s media watchers predicted the death of the weekly news magazines, yet *Time* magazine seemed as strong or stronger than ever in 1997. To succeed in changing times, the magazine adapted by emphasizing the depth, interest, and insight it brought to a wide span of subjects.

Introduced in 1996, *Time*'s "The World's Most Interesting Magazine" campaign grew to include more than 50 color print ads. The series, from the advertising agency Fallon McElligott, featured large, compelling photographs with a key section boxed by the *Time* icon—the magazine's name within a red border. The mostly print campaign ran first and foremost in *Time* but also appeared in several other Time Warner publications-*Sports Illustrated, Money,* and *Fortune* —as well as some trade journals.

One ad featured an aerial shot of a forest and road engulfed in smoke. A stream of emergency vehicles headed into what looked like a major forest fire. With the *Time* icon partially hidden by the smoke, the copy read, "If there's a story in there, we'll find it." Another ad showed X Game competitors in helmets and bright colored leathers whisking around a race track corner. The leader's helmet was boxed by the *Time* icon, and the copy read "824 words on the X Games. (And only two of them were 'dude.')" A sports ad used the *Time* icon to frame boxer Evander Holyfield's ear just after Mike Tyson had bitten it. The copy read, "What kind of bandage can boxing possibly put on this?" When a gorilla nurtured and protected a three-year-old boy who had fallen into her enclosure at a zoo, *Time* used the photograph in the campaign with the line, "A weekly reminder that the world is a pretty amazing place." The only ad in the campaign that did not use copy showed a heavily perspiring President Bill Clinton framed by a red box. It ran early in 1998 during the height of speculation about the President's relationship with former White House intern Monica Lewinsky.

Time used this series to stress the depth and breath of its coverage. The magazine wanted to move beyond the usual assumptions about weekly news magazines and broaden people's view of what they could find within *Time.* Building brand affinity was another campaign goal. The campaign demonstrated that the 75-year-old magazine covered not only hard news and major world events but also technology, business, sports, lifestyle, and entertainment.

HISTORICAL CONTEXT

For several years the three major weekly news magazines—*Time, Newsweek,* and *U.S. News* & *World Report*—had been called dinosaurs. The theory was that with so many up-and-coming news sources (cable news stations like CNN and MSNBC, television talk shows, national editions of newspapers, the Internet, week-in-review sections) the weekly news magazines were not needed. But instead of disappearing, the magazines gained strength while some competitors—newspapers and network TV—struggled to stay afloat.

Critics claimed the weekly news magazines were losing their hard news edge and pampering readers by featuring pop culture stories. They pointed out that during a week when India and Pakistan were testing nuclear bombs, *Time* devoted its cover to the death of entertainer Frank Sinatra. While in 1987 *Time*'s cover featured government or foreign affairs 23 times, by 1997 that number dwindled to five. The number of celebrity covers changed little over this 10-year span—from seven in 1987 to eight in 1997.

Time began stressing elements such as human interest stories, entertainment, health and science, and women's issues and lifestyle that had formerly been associated with other types of magazines, such as *Reader's Digest, People, Prevention,* and *Ladies Home Journal.* The magazine also changed format, going for a more graphic look, shorter articles, and more photographs and charts. And it produced more special issues covering colleges, personal finance, health, business, and technology. These changes needed to be communicated and explained to the *Time* audience.

"The World's Most Interesting Magazine" campaign grew directly out of *Time*'s 1995 campaign, "Understanding Comes with *Time.*" To deal with the "dinosaur issue," the 1995 campaign reasserted the value of the weekly news magazine. The campaign sought to emphasize that while there were many different outlets through which to receive news, many of them provided headline news without the depth, perspective, and insight *Time* could provide. "Understanding Comes with *Time*" focused on the magazine's coverage of big news stories and its commitment to giving readers a fuller understanding of them. "The World's Most Interesting Magazine" carried on much of the look and feel of the earlier campaign but focused on the wide variety of subject matter and interests *Time* covered.

TARGET MARKET

Because *Time* strove not to increase circulation but to increase the quality of the audience within that circulation, the campaign targeted current *Time* subscribers. Historically the magazine has kept a close watch on the demographics of its readership and has kept its advertisers informed of the type of readers it has.

According to Pew Research Center, about 15 percent of all adult Americans regularly read *Time, Newsweek,* or *U.S. News & World Report.* Compared with the general population, this audience is older with a strong upscale orientation. In 1997 Pew Research found 13 percent of readers were under age 30 while 40 percent were age 50 or older. The same study found that 44 percent of regular news weekly adult readers had an annual household income of at least $50,000; 27 percent had incomes of more than $75,000.

Compared with other adults, these readers followed some subjects, like international affairs and national politics, more closely. *Time, Newsweek,* and *U.S. News & World Report* readers were 80 percent more likely than the total adult population to be very close followers of international events.

CLIENT IDEAS STRENGTHENED *TIME* CAMPAIGN

"Usually when they [*Time*] push us it's to get us to look at an issue from *Time* 's perspective," said the art director on the campaign, Bob Barry. For example, the agency proposed an ad about a bombing in Northern Ireland that killed three children. The photograph showed a crowd mourning at the funeral as three tiny caskets were carried in. The proposed headline illustrated more about the situation in Ireland than about the perspective that *Time* brought to the story: "What Will It Take To Achieve Peace in Ireland?" The magazine asked for a rewrite. Copy writer Dean Buckhorn wrote another headline that won quick approval: "We'll Let You Know If Ireland Can Also Wage Peace." "The client has been great," said Barry, "they have their opinions and they're usually right."

COMPETITION

In 1997 *Time* was the clear leader in its category. Its 4.2 million subscriber base was 1 million more than *Newsweek* 's and about 2 million more than *U.S. News & World Report* 's. These competitors were not an influential factor in *Time*'s campaign. During the year both *Newsweek* and *U.S. News* concentrated on advertising directed toward the industry or advertisers.

In response to increasing competition beyond the other two weekly news magazines, *Time* no longer sought to be the sole all-encompassing source for news. Instead, the magazine assumed its readers got the news headlines from television, radio, and other sources. *Time*'s role became explaining the news and providing insight into headline stories.

MARKETING STRATEGY

When Walter Isaacson took over as managing editor in 1996, he instituted a high-profile, high-interest strategy that helped restore the magazine's authority. "We've brought more storytelling to *Time,* to try to get at great issues through interesting tales, and to create high impact journalism that makes a difference," he said. Isaacson raised awareness of the magazine by being a frequent social and talk show presence. He also redefined *Time*'s role away from hard news toward lifestyle and high interest topics.

In 1997 *Time*'s cover featured, among others, comedian Ellen DeGeneres, film director Steven Spielberg, pop singer Jewel, actor Brad Pitt, and comedian Bill Cosby on the death of his son. Also making the cover were features such as "What's Cool This Summer," "Turning Fifty," and "The Most Fascinating People in America." Hard news cover stories included "Big Tobacco Takes a Hit," "Does Gore Have What It Takes?," "What's Wrong at the FBI?" and "Echoes of the Holocaust."

Editor-in-chief Norman Pearlstine told the *Columbia Journalism Review* that the switch from hard news to lifestyle subjects was attributable to two factors. One was the healthy economy. People felt secure and comfortable and were less concerned with hard news than they had been during a tense period such as the Cold War or a bad economy. The other factor was the readers' search for stories focusing on self-interest topics. "It's not surprising that the country has turned more inward. There's always been a balance between educating your reader and serving your reader, but we're not getting a lot of demand for international coverage these days," Pearlstine said.

Time wanted to be viewed less as a studious read and more as an engaging read. While maintaining a hard news element, *Time* sought to broaden the base of reasons to get involved with the magazine. "This campaign was an attempt to say what people enjoy about the magazine is very personal. Just as the concept of 'interesting' is a self-defined idea, what you take from the magazine is self-defined as well, so that gave us an umbrella so we could say we are different things to different people. There's surprise along with what you expect every week," said Fallon McElligott's Amy Frisch.

Time also decided to concentrate on its long-term relationship with readers. Subscribers to weekly news magazines are among the most attractive targets for advertisers. They are well educated with high incomes and in job positions where they often control significant expenditures. *Time* studied its core readers and looked for ways to retain them and improve the quality of its readership. Creating a campaign with high interest visuals and provocative copy seemed right.

Nearly all the images used in the campaign first appeared in *Time* stories. When looking for ideas, the Fallon McElligott team targeted those stories in which *Time* had both captured strong visuals and delivered a unique written perspective or analysis. An earlier proposed campaign that emphasized the visuals was rejected because the magazine also wanted to convey the importance of its writing.

Senior management had an usually deep involvement in designing the campaign. Each ad was approved by *Time* managing editor Walter Isaacson and president Bruce Hallett. *Time* often improved the campaign through its suggestions to the agency's creative team. The campaign ads were instantly identifiable as *Time*'s. With the traditional icon prominent in every ad, readers quickly recognized which magazine was being advertised. The campaign ran mostly—about 70 percent—in consumer magazines, with some trade magazines and a few TV spots on CNN and elsewhere.

The campaign's creators intended for its more than 50 different ads to flow together but also to be distinct from one another. Rather than creating a few ads and running them frequently, the strategy was to continually change the running ad to emphasize the many different aspects of the magazine's contents and to keep the campaign fresh and timely.

OUTCOME

In 1997 key demographics of *Time*'s readership improved. The magazine held and increased its subscriber base and made the type of quality gains in audience that advertisers seek. The goal of renewed brand affinity was also met to the magazine's satisfaction. *Time*'s 1997 financial results were among the best in the business. Newsstand sales increased 40 percent. Reported ad revenue increased 21 percent (an additional $94 million). Ad pages jumped 16 percent. The gain in ad revenue was nearly three times that posted by the two other major weekly news magazines combined.

Adweek listed *Time* number one on its list of the 10 hottest magazines in 1997. The campaign itself garnered many awards, including several Addy Awards at the American Advertising Federation Awards.

FURTHER READING

Hickey, Neil. "Money Lust: How Pressure for Profit Is Perverting Journalism." *Columbia Journalism Review* July/August 1998, p. 28.

Pogrebin, Robin. "At Work and at Play, Time's Editor Seeks to Keep Magazine Vigorous at 75." *New York Times* March 9, 1998, Business Section, Page C6.

Sheets, Ken. "Time Warner Confounds The Skeptics." *Kiplinger's Personal Finance Magazine* May 1998, p. 32.

"Who Reads The Newsweeklies?." *Research Alert* November 21, 1997, p. 7.

Chris Amorosino

TiVo Inc.

2160 Sold Street
Alviso, California 95002
USA
Telephone: (408) 519-9100
Fax: (408) 519-5330
Web site: www.tivo.com

■■■

TIVO, TV YOUR WAY CAMPAIGN

OVERVIEW

A year after introducing its digital video recorder (DVR), which was able to record and store television programs on a hard drive, TiVo Inc. hired Goodby, Silverstein & Partners, an advertising agency based in San Francisco. The firm's tasks were to build brand awareness for the difficult-to-describe device and to begin transforming TiVo from something reserved for technophiles into a consumer product with mass appeal. TiVo was also keen to establish a dominant market share to gain leverage over its chief rival, ReplayTV, and to thwart the aspirations of potential future competitors. Goodby's $50 million campaign, called "TiVo, TV Your Way," began in early July 2000.

The campaign, which cost $50 million and continued well into 2001, included television spots, print ads, and an updated website that provided detailed information such as price, features, and technical specifications. It had three waves of television commercials. In the first Goodby employed quirky humor to make the claim that having TiVo allowed subscribers to act as their own network television programmers. The second set of spots built on this concept; one, featuring ex-football stars Joe Montana and Ronnie Lott, was a parody of an annoying commercial. In the final phase of the campaign, the spots attempted to show the everyday benefits of owning TiVo.

TiVo became the dominant brand in its market, but sales failed to meet the expectations of investors. Because of its depressed stock price, the company slashed its advertising budget to control costs and looked for other ways to build its business. When the account was put up for review (opened to bids from competing ad agencies), Goodby declined to participate.

HISTORICAL CONTEXT

When TiVo Inc. introduced its DVR in March 1999, it faced the task of selling a product that defied simple description. The device stored TV programs on a computer hard drive instead of cassette tapes or discs, but wary that the word "digital" might prompt consumers to fear their televisions would crash like their personal computers, the company did not want to call its product a digital video recorder. Nor did it want to compare the product to a VCR, since many people were frustrated by their inability to program VCRs. As a result TiVo initially called the product a personal video recorder (PVR). Writing in the *Wall Street Journal,* David P. Hamilton elaborated on the challenge of selling a product that crossed over from the computer realm to that of living-room electronics: "While earlier generations of consumer electronics were basically extensions of existing products—DVD players, for instance, essentially crossed compact-disk players with the playback capability of

Michael Ramsay, co-founder of TiVo. AP IMAGES.

VCRs—the PVRs don't fit neatly into any category." TiVo's chief executive, Michael Ramsay, explained to Hamilton that the product was also different from other electronic components in that it was difficult for people to understand how it worked until they actually used it.

For the product launch TiVo hired the Los Angeles agency Campbell-Ewald West to develop television and radio commercials as well as in-store ads. Using the tagline "You run the show," the 30-second television spots attempted to explain the features of TiVo in an entertaining fashion. In one spot a man watching television was abducted by aliens, but because TiVo had been digitally recording his show, after escaping, he returned to watching it where he had left off. The device was capable of performing a wide range of programming tasks, and pausing live television was actually one of its less compelling features, but it was one of the few that could be easily addressed in a 30-second commercial. Only a few months later, TiVo decided to change its approach, intending to shy away from explaining how its product worked and to concentrate instead on building brand awareness and its customer base. It put up its business for review by other ad agencies, and in February 2000 Goodby, Silverstein & Partners won the account.

TARGET MARKET

TiVo was readily embraced by the early adopters of technology, but to become profitable the company needed to appeal to a broader audience, despite the high price of the product and the subscription fees (either lifetime or monthly) that went with it. The goal of the "TiVo, TV Your Way" campaign was to extend the brand beyond technophiles to TV viewers who were willing to pay for digital control over programming. Ultimately the company wanted to reach an even broader market: the kind of consumers who bought VCRs, DVD players, and personal computers. TiVo hoped to stake its claim in the market and to establish brand awareness by the time these late-arriving customers were ready to buy a DVR.

COMPETITION

TiVo was in essence a glorified VCR, but because of its far more advanced capabilities, it did not really compete against VCRs or even DVD recorders. Its primary competitor in the "personal television market" was ReplayTV, another company that featured a product with a hard drive and similar programming functions. The two companies differed most significantly in their business models; ReplayTV opted to sell its unit and service for a single price, while TiVo, in response to marketing research, kept down the price of the unit itself by charging a monthly subscription fee or a one-time lifetime fee. On the horizon competition was also taking shape in the form of Microsoft's UltimateTV, intended for use with satellite provider DirecTV, and the DVR in development for DirecTV's rival, EchoStar. Large cable companies were also interested in incorporating DVR functions into their set-top cable boxes.

MARKETING STRATEGY

The $50 million "TiVo, TV Your Way" campaign started in July 2000. Its primary purpose was to establish the brand, building on the company's base of some 30,000 subscribers. Rather than talking about the price or explaining TiVo's capabilities in detail, Goodby kept the focus on the brand, using edgy humor to portray the DVR as a useful home-entertainment product and making the claim that owning TiVo was like having one's own TV network. The facts about the product were relegated to the company's website, which was updated to provide consumers with information about TiVo, such as its capabilities, its cost, and where to buy it. The TV spots ran on network programming and national cable channels as well as on local stations in certain areas, including Atlanta, Chicago, Dallas, Los Angeles, New York, and San Francisco. In addition the campaign featured print ads in regional newspapers and in such

> ## "BOY HOWDY!"
>
> Perhaps the funniest moment in the TiVo television spot that featured ex-football players Joe Montana and Ronnie Lott—a spoof of over-the-counter drug ads—was Lott's delivery of the phrase "Boy Howdy!" He made the exclamation after Montana explained how bacteria could cause "masculine itching" and "unsightly discomfort." According to Susan Fornoff, writing in the *San Francisco Chronicle,* "Lott never heard 'Boy Howdy' growing up in Southern California. But ad agency copy writer Chris Ford, who is from Reno, swears he might have heard a cowboy or two utter the phrase." Ford commented that, as a substitute for an expletive, the phrase was more memorable than "you're kidding."

national magazines as *Rolling Stone, People,* and *Sports Illustrated.*

TiVo's first ad in the campaign, a 30-second spot called "Network Executive," generated controversy. Set to air during the hit show *Survivor,* the spot was unexpectedly rejected by CBS. It portrayed callous network executives scheduling and canceling TV shows. "Look at these guys: network TV programmers," declared an off-screen voice with obvious disdain. "They decide what we watch and when we watch it." At that point a pair of bouncers appeared and tossed one of the executives out a window. "Who needs them?" asked the announcer, followed by text that read, "Program your own network. TiVo, TV your way." CBS said that it rejected the commercial because it was not an accurate reflection of the way a network operated and that it would not accept advertising that disparaged its business. Another TiVo spot was accepted by CBS, however.

Goodby produced two more 30-second TV spots for the initial phase of the campaign. One of them portrayed an inept, overweight police officer tumbling over a chain-link fence while chasing a suspect. He finally caught and cuffed the man, only to be kicked in the groin by the suspect, who then escaped. The policeman explained to an unseen interviewer, "TiVo's been a godsend for me . . . When I get home, TiVo is my salvation." While fixing a sandwich, he was asked what he liked to watch and replied, "Mostly cop shows." The other spot featured a father using TiVo to explain ice-skating moves to his daughter, only to have his son emulate them instead. Clearly concerned about his son's masculinity, the father shouted, "Bobby, stop that! Bobby!" The edginess of the campaign also extended to the print ads that centered on bodily functions. One character extolled the virtues of TiVo's ability to pause live TV for bathroom breaks.

Another set of three television spots, which built on the earlier ones, was filmed. They aired during the first week of November 2000 as part of a holiday push. The centerpiece was a spot spoofing drug ads and featuring football greats and close friends Joe Montana and Ronnie Lott. The spot had been written for unknown actors and only became a vehicle for Montana and Lott when TiVo suggested them to Goodby, an agency not known for using celebrities in its advertising. Despite Goodby's initial skepticism, the commercial proved popular, and the former athletes' involvement brought added attention to TiVo. In the spot, while the two were playing golf, Lott made a poor swing. Montana commented, "What's the matter, Ronnie—masculine itching?" The spot closed with Montana approaching Lott with a glob of "Extra Strength Itch Stopper Plus" on his fingers. The action was abruptly stopped by an unseen TiVo user while an announcer said, "Get TiVo and skip the stuff you don't want to see." Another spot in this phase of the campaign portrayed a hospital emergency room filled with frustrated television viewers who had injured themselves smashing their television sets. The third spot featured a TiVo user who felt so liberated by TiVo that, in the spirit of doing whatever he wanted, he drove the wrong way down a one-way street and sawed a parking meter in half.

In the campaign's final phase, which began in May 2001, TiVo and Goodby applied lessons learned from their earlier advertising attempts. Brodie Keast, TiVo's senior vice president of marketing, told *Brandweek* 's Todd Wasserman that the company had gained a greater sense of the underlying consumer issues, in particular the "inertia about how people watch TV." To address these issues, the three new spots suggested how consumers could take advantage of TiVo in real-life situations. They showed a family racing through dinner to avoid missing the season finale of their favorite show, a couple staying up to snuggle to a late-night movie but falling asleep, and a husband who had to run an errand during *The Sopranos* and became frustrated in his attempt to find out from his wife what he had missed.

OUTCOME

At the very least the "TiVo, TV Your Way" campaign played a role in establishing TiVo as the dominant brand in its category. The DVR was also helped, however, by its passionate base of customers, who expounded to their friends on the virtues of TiVo. Even before the close of 2000, the company's main rival, ReplayTV—which trailed in the number of users by a four-to-one margin—had conceded the consumer-electronics field.

It elected instead to pursue a business-to-business model, licensing its technology to cable providers and electronics companies (such as Panasonic, which licensed ReplayTV technology to develop a television with an integrated DVR). TiVo's brand was so strong that it gained currency as a verb in popular culture, as in "Did you TiVo that show?"

The campaign also helped to drive up traffic to the company's website and contributed significantly to increasing sales, but the numbers were still disappointing to the company and its investors. TiVo's losses since its founding mounted to more than $400 million, and the price of its stock, which had peaked at $79, dipped as low as $3. In an effort to cut costs and placate shareholders, TiVo dramatically cut the amount of money it spent on television advertising, spending $40 million in 2001, $8 million in 2002, and just $115,000 in 2003, according to Nielsen Monitor-Plus. Because TiVo customers demonstrating the DVR to their friends had always proven effective in selling the device, TiVo looked to make better use of its strong word-of-mouth recommendations, encouraging TiVo owners to host "TiVo-ware parties," similar to Tupperware parties, for their acquaintances. This approach left little for a traditional ad agency to do. When the account went into review, Goodby elected not to put in a bid to renew its deal.

FURTHER READING

Elliott, Stuart. "TiVo Teams Up with Omnicom Group to Tell the World about Digital Video Recorders." *New York Times,* October 13, 2000, p. 1.

Fornoff, Susan. "Itching to Be Funny." *San Francisco Chronicle,* December 5, 2000, p. C4.

Garfield, Bob. "Boy Howdy! TiVo Send-Up Isn't Heinous; It's Hilarious." *Advertising Age,* November 13, 2000, p. E1.

Hamilton, David P. "TiVo, ReplayTV Fail to Take Off despite Big Fans." *Wall Street Journal,* February 7, 2001, p. 109.

Kirsner, Scott. "Can TiVo Go Prime Time?" *Fast Company,* August 2002, p. 82.

Kranhold, Kathryn. "TiVo Ad Campaign's Sly Humor Isn't a Hit with CBS Executives." *Wall Street Journal,* July 5, 2000, p. 36.

Lippert, Barbara. "TV Interruptus." *Adweek,* July 17, 2000, p. 5.

Wasserman, Todd. "As TiVo, MS Square Off, No Time to Hit Pause." *Brandweek,* May 21, 2001, p. 5.

———. "TiVo Team Goes for Gooey Laughs in Zapper's Zany World of 'Bad TV.'" *Brandweek,* November 6, 2000, p. 8.

Ed Dinger

T-Mobile International AG & Company KG

Landgrabenweg 151
Bonn, 53227
Germany
Telephone: 49 228 93631717
Fax: 49 228 93631719
Web site: www.t-mobile-international.com

GET MORE CAMPAIGN

OVERVIEW

As the telecommunication industry spent $5.8 billion on consumer advertising in 2003, top competitors formulated brand identities that would gain them footholds in the industry. The Sprint PCS Group created advertising to boast its all-digital, nationwide service loaded with features, whereas Cellco Partnership's Verizon Wireless, the biggest advertising spender and wireless provider in the United States, branded Verizon Wireless as a high-quality service with its "Can You Hear Me Now?" campaign. When Europe's largest telecommunications company, Deutsche Telekom AG, acquired the U.S. telecommunications companies VoiceStream Wireless and Powertel, Inc., in 2001, it combined the two under the name T-Mobile International AG & Company KG, which then stood as the sixth-largest provider in the United States. The next year T-Mobile used VoiceStream's 1998 "Get more" tagline for a campaign intended to brand T-Mobile as a service that offered more minutes, features, and service than its competitors.

For the new campaign T-Mobile chose not to renew its contract with spokesperson and actress Jamie Lee Curtis, who had appeared in VoiceStream commercials since 1998. To attract younger subscribers, in 2002 T-mobile hired the 11-years-younger actress Catherine Zeta-Jones as the brand's spokesperson and awarded ad agency Publicis West a $100 million ad budget to release "Get More." Using television, print, outdoor, and radio mediums, the campaign first appeared on September 3, 2002. The first 30-second commercials, which aired on network and cable TV, featured Zeta-Jones improving people's romantic predicaments with a T-Mobile phone. In the spot "Czech" a disappointed young man on vacation told a Czech woman that he could not join her in Venice because of his dog-sitting responsibilities back home. Zeta-Jones appeared with a T-Mobile phone so that he could ask his friend in New York to watch the dog.

Six months into the campaign T-Mobile was the fastest-growing wireless provider in United States. It added 2.9 million subscribers in 2002, a 41 percent increase over 2001. During the campaign's first three months 4 out of 10 new mobile phone customers chose T-Mobile over its competitors. By 2004 T-Mobile had overtaken Nextel Communications to become the nation's fifth-largest wireless provider. The campaign continued into 2005 and also won a Bronze EFFIE Award from the New York American Marketing Association.

HISTORICAL CONTEXT

Although Deutsche Telekom acquired both Powertel (based in Atlanta) and VoiceStream (based in Washington state) in 2001, VoiceStream provided the majority of T-Mobile's U.S. subscriber base. Besides being the nation's sixth-largest wireless-service provider, VoiceStream was the first to offer two-way text messaging and high-speed wireless data services to the U.S. marketplace. In 1998 Curtis starred in most of VoiceStream's "Get More" campaign commercials to reinforce the provider's tagline, "One phone, one number, one service." VoiceStream's infrastructure used GSM (Global Systems for Mobile Communications), the world's most recognized wireless technology, which allowed T-Mobile subscribers to place calls in more than 90 different countries for as low as 99 cents per minute. The campaign hoped to target globe-trotting businesses that roamed from one country's network to another. Curtis was chosen for her sassy, versatile image. "Her active lifestyle runs the gamut—wife, mother, actress, author—she epitomizes who can use it to get more from life," Kim Thompson, a spokeswoman for VoiceStream, explained to the *Associated Press.*

In hindsight VoiceStream recognized that its original "Get More" campaign targeted a narrow demographic. "What portion of the population actually travels between Europe and America on any kind of regular basis? You have to look at it as a stand-alone business with its own ability to generate cash rather than as some kind of strategic global initiative," Charles Golvin, senior analyst at Forrester Research (a firm specializing in researching technology trends) told the *International Herald Tribune.*

In 2001 Deutsche Telekom purchased VoiceStream and Powertel for $30 billion. After acquiring additional smaller companies, Deutsche Telekom unified its telecommunications conglomerate under the name T-Mobile in 2002. In the United States T-Mobile repositioned its brand to capture the burgeoning youth market. "The T-Mobile debut in California and Nevada continues several things that the company did well as VoiceStream—namely building upon its 'get more' philosophy, offering competitive pricing and including features like AOL Instant Messenger that appeal to younger consumers. The teen youth segment presents an immediate opportunity for growth as they begin to aggressively add new subscribers," Knox Bricken, senior analyst with the Yankee Group (a research and consulting firm specializing in the technology market), told *Business Wire.* To further entice youth, T-Mobile offered calling plans as low as 8.2 cents a minute, undercutting its competitor Verizon's 14.8 cents a minute.

TARGET MARKET

Once VoiceStream was rebranded as T-Mobile, the international-traveler target became secondary, and the youth demographic was made primary. The target market became 18- to 34-year-olds as opposed to 18- to 49-year-olds. "VoiceStream historically has had a younger subscriber type," John Clelland, senior vice president for marketing and communications at T-Mobile, told the *International Herald Tribune.* "With the merger and the brand conversion, we are better equipped to go after those accounts." While competitors such as Nextel and Sprint targeted adults by featuring businesspeople using phones to solve business problems, "Get More" commercials featured young people using phones to improve romantic predicaments. The content was considered more appropriate for youth.

To continue marketing the service's continued global versatility, the first three commercials starred Czech, British, Italian, and American actors benefiting from T-Mobile's service. To attract the younger target T-Mobile also replaced Jamie Lee Curtis with 32-year-old Catherine Zeta-Jones (who had starred in *Chicago* and *The Mask of Zorro*) as the brand's spokesperson. "So the new Dona T-Mobile is younger, more sassy, and darn intercontinental. And if you're going global, who could possibly do better in that arena than a Welsh woman who pretends she's Spanish: Catherine Zeta-Jones?" jabbed *Adweek*'s Barbara Lippert.

COMPETITION

During the Jamie Lee Curtis portion of the campaign, expensive advertising and competitive pricing within the mobile-phone industry threatened to cripple the top providers' profitability. "The industry has hit an inflection point where it's not just about trying to lure new customers," Weston Henderek, an analyst at telecom-research firm Current Analysis, said to *RCR Wireless News.* "Carriers are having to go after their competitors' customers with advertisements explaining why they are a better choice." Sprint PCS used its trench coat–wearing spokesman, "Sprint Guy," to tout the provider's all-digital, nationwide network loaded with cutting-edge features. Verizon's "Can You Hear Me Now?" campaign demonstrated the network's strong coverage. In 2003

PARIS HILTON'S SIDEKICK

The Sidekick, a device developed by T-Mobile to allow subscribers to check E-mail, surf the Internet, and place voice calls, was one of the T-Mobile's highest-end handset options. T-Mobile received attention when hotel heiress Paris Hilton's Sidekick was hacked into and her entire contact list posted on the Internet. Within hours celebrities such as tennis player Anna Kournikova and teen actress Lindsay Lohan were receiving phone calls from hundreds of strangers.

PHONE GAMES

Seamus McAteer, a senior analyst at M*Metrics (a telecommunications-industry-analysis company), told *Wireless Week* that although most PC and console gamers were male, the majority of mobile-phone gamers were young females.

Verizon spent an estimated $300 million to $400 million on that campaign with an additional $700 to $800 on direct-mail and in-store promotions. Another provider, Cingular, spent $873 million on advertising in 2004.

According to analysts and consumer polls, providers were not distinguishing themselves from one another by establishing clear brand identities. AT&T Wireless Services and Cingular, for instance, simultaneously branded themselves as low-cost providers with personalized calling plans in 2002. Also, using service features to entice customers was not working. Industry terms such as "rollover minutes" and "anytime minutes" did not mean much to consumers. "Carriers will need to explain to customers what their more-advanced networks can provide," Henderek explained to *RCR Wireless News.* "You can't just launch these services and expect consumers to understand why they should be spending more money for higher-speed networks. You have to explain the nitty-gritty details so they can see the value of advanced services." Verizon, the largest advertising spender out of all American brands in 2003, led the competition with 37.5 million subscribers. When the second largest, Cingular, acquired the third largest, AT&T, in early 2004, the combined subscriber base boosted Cingular to the number one position.

MARKETING STRATEGY

In 1998 VoiceStream used the tagline "Get More" to showcase its service's ability to operate in over 90 different countries. Once VoiceStream was rebranded as T-Mobile, the tagline "Get More" was changed to mean "more minutes, more features, and more service." Robert Dotson, president of T-Mobile's U.S. headquarters, told *Business Wire,* "Mobile communications have exploded in the past two years, extending way beyond voice-only services to give customers constant access to their E-mail, the Internet and other information virtually whenever and wherever. The T-Mobile global brand reflects the whole spectrum of mobile services we provide on a worldwide basis, while maintaining our 'Get more' promise to provide customers with the best overall value and service in their wireless communications."

The campaign's first spots were directed by Tarsem Singh, who had directed the psychological thriller *The Cell.* The first 60-second commercial, "Anthem," used a mélange of dazzling images and had actors repeating the lines, "More minutes, more features, more service." Catherine Zeta-Jones also appeared in the spot to explain, "more asking, more getting." The spot ended with the tagline "Get more from life."

Three additional 30-second spots directed by Singh appeared during the campaign's first month. All featured Zeta-Jones solving communication problems for young people with a T-Mobile phone. In "Czech," a spot that appeared to take place in Prague, a beautiful Czech girl asked an American man, "You stay and we go to Venice?" He passed on the invitation by stating he needed to watch his dog at home. Zeta-Jones then appeared to say, "Stop, stop, stop—is he kidding?" She handed him a T-Mobile phone so he could call his friend back home, who agreed to watch the dog another week. Another spot featured an English woman attempting to attract the attention of a nearby Italian man. Zeta-Jones saved the day again with a T-Mobile phone, helping the woman call a language institute and learn an Italian phrase. In the fourth spot Zeta-Jones provided a phone for a bored postal clerk to invite a friend to a martial-arts movie.

Critics praised the initial spots for their youthful, global positioning but criticized the campaign's muddled message. *Adweek*'s Barbara Lippert wrote, "Is T-Mobile a phone and a service? We don't find out. And while aiming at Gen X-ers is an interesting idea, low-energy slackers like the post office guy aren't exactly the kind of hard-driving businessmen who rely on having the same phone and number when traveling."

Between 2002 and 2005 Publicis used "Get More" to advertise T-Mobile's photo messaging, downloadable HiFi ringers, and its popular Sidekick II, a device that combined E-mail, phone, and wireless-browser capabilities. Throughout the campaign Zeta-Jones starred as the brand's spokesperson. The actress "totally connected with our vision, which is a cross between the fun 'girl next door' and a magical catalyst for spontaneous communication," Publicis executive creative director Bob Moore told *Entertainment Weekly.*

OUTCOME

The ad-industry high-water mark for "Get More" was winning a Bronze EFFIE Award (Telecom Services category) from the New York American Marketing Association in 2004. More significantly, the campaign helped T-Mobile unify its brand and become one of the biggest challengers within a cutthroat industry. In 2003 telecom analyst Jeff Kagan told the *Seattle Times,* "T-Mobile is a patchwork quilt of so many different companies that it's a big challenge to run and operate. The wireless industry is going through a major transition. T-Mobile is definitely a player, but they're a very small player." The "small player" was the year's fastest-growing wireless provider and increased its subscribers by 41 percent, totaling almost 10 million by 2004. During the campaign's first three months, 4 out of every 10 new subscribers were choosing T-Mobile.

T-Mobile's domestic success was primarily attributed to three factors: the appointment of Robert Dotson as president of T-Mobile's American base, the brand's average service price of 8.2 cents a minute, and Publicis's effective marketing campaign. "We have grown a fabulous business and team at T-Mobile built around the compelling philosophy of 'Get more' for our customers. [Dotson] is the author of that philosophy and it's through his relentless focus on making it a reality for our customers that he has lead our team to become the fastest growing company in the U.S. wireless industry," T-Mobile's domestic chairman, John Stanton, told *Business Wire.*

FURTHER READING

Carter, Ben. "ANALYSIS: McDonald's and BT Go After the Wi-Fi Diners." *Marketing,* January 15, 2004, p. 14.

Cuneo, Alice. "Cell Giants Plot $1.5B Ad Bonanza; New FCC Rules Spark Battle to Entice Rivals' Customers." *Advertising Age,* October 6, 2003, p. 1.

Duryee, Tricia. "VoiceStream Gives Curtis a Dial Tone." *Seattle Times,* November 11, 2004, p. E1.

Garner, Heather. "R-JENERATION: It's For You." *Las Vegas Review-Journal,* December 17, 2002, p. 4E.

Howard, Theresa. "'Can You Hear Me Now?' a Hit; Simple 'Test Man' Ads Help Verizon Wireless Stay Strong." *USA Today,* February 23, 2004, p. B08.

Luke, Robert. "Rivals Smell Blood in AT&T-Cingular Waters." *Atlanta Journal-Constitution,* March 26, 2004, p. E3.

Marek, Sue. "Mobile Game Standouts; Wireless Operators Weigh In on What It Takes to Make a Top-Selling Mobile Game." *Wireless Week,* January 1, 2005, p. 24.

Meyer, Dan. "Dotson to Take Over Top Reins at T-Mobile USA." *RCR Wireless News,* March 31, 2003, p. 3.

———. "Operators Spend Big to Get Message Across." *RCR Wireless News,* April 25, 2005, p. 12.

Norris, Gary. "Nortel Rebuilds Image with Ad Campaign." *Toronto Star,* November 9, 2004, p. D02.

Vinakmens, Kristen. "Wireless Wars: Carriers Strive for Identity as Cell Market Matures." *Strategy,* September 8, 2003, p. 2.

Wallace, Brice. "Making Connections." *Salt Lake City (UT) Deseret News,* August 3, 2003, p. M01.

Kevin Teague

Tommy Hilfiger U.S.A., Inc.

25 W 39th St.
New York, New York 10018
USA
Telephone: (212) 548-1000
Web site: www.tommy.com/

AMERICAN TARTANS CAMPAIGN

OVERVIEW

In September 1997 Toth Design and Advertising introduced a Tommy Hilfiger U.S.A., Inc. ad campaign for men's tartan-style polo shirts. The polos were usual enough, typical plaids in green, reds, blues, and blacks. The men in the ads, however, were all wearing skirts, Scottish kilts to be exact, and frolicking about like schoolboys, kicking up their feet and having a glorious time. The images expressed in the "American Tartans" campaign were typical for Tommy, a men's, women's, and children's clothing and accessory business that was founded in 1984 by Tommy Hilfiger, the company's director and principle designer.

Among Tommy's more visible products was a line of baggy, well-worn street clothes marketed to what is called the hip-hop generation, a term characterized by 1990s inner-city youth, rap music, and MTV rock videos. The clothes were often produced in red, white, and blue colors that sported the Tommy logo—a white, red, and blue flaglike rectangle with the names "Tommy" and "Hilfiger" boldly embossed across the top and bottom. Tommy also produced a wide array of men's casual sports clothes that managed to attract the 20-something buyer to high-end sportswear in department stores. It was to this latter audience that the "American Tartans" campaign was partly aimed.

Toth handled Tommy's advertising from 1992 to 1997. Their strategy was to create a brand image for Tommy that could compete with its main rivals, Polo Ralph Lauren and Nautica. Both of these brands of men's clothing embraced particular images that the "American Tartans" campaign wanted to counteract. "We looked closely at both Polo and Nautica and the lifestyles portrayed in their fashion," said Tyrone Sayers, an account supervisor at Toth. "Their image was highly affluent, something the common man will not identify with." When Toth advertising began its work for Tommy, it wanted to describe a lifestyle that someone could see themselves in. Tommy "is more relaxed and open, goofing around and smiling. We wanted something that was more approachable," said Sayers. "We wanted to present a product that was youthful, relaxed, informal." The "American Tartans" campaign reflected this principal image.

HISTORICAL CONTEXT

When Toth began to create advertising campaigns for Tommy in 1992, the business was still small and growing. "We were virtually unknown when we started," said Sayers, "and the name—Hilfiger—was easy to trip over. We needed a brand image that would reinforce who we were, and that took precedence over any particular product." That image turned out to be what Sayers described as the "Peter Pan syndrome," which, according to him, was present in just about every man. "The image of men in their 20s is actually all men. Men grow up and acquire families and mortgages and responsibilities, but they still see themselves in their 20s, laughing with their friends and having a good time. This is the Peter Pan syndrome."

Playing on this concept, Toth placed men in ads that turned the fashion world on its head. They smiled, they laughed, they hugged each other, and they had fun. "What we did was position Tommy as somebody who really is aspiring to be *happy,* " said Michael Toth of Toth Design and Advertising in a 1996 *Vogue* article. In the early 1990s leading men's fashion campaigns used images that were glum and stoic. "People were ready to see a guy *smiling in an ad*—which was like a no-no at the time—doing something that felt real and honest. People inspire to happiness because everyone wants to be happy, and that's what Tommy projects. It's not something we invented. The suit fit." One Toth ad campaign portrayed a group of young men playing football, covered in mud from head to toe. Their clothes, which happened to be the product, were also covered with mud. Hilfiger liked the fun that was taking place in the ad, although he admitted that it might be difficult to sell clothes covered in mud. The article quoted Hilfiger as saying that such an ad was one "Ralph [Lauren] definitely wouldn't do and some of the other competitors wouldn't even consider, which is what I like about it."

Tommy's ads also sought to reach different nationalities and socioeconomic groups, setting another trend in the fashion world. "Tommy described the life he saw around him—blacks, Hispanics, Asians, men, and women," said Sayers. "Two and a half years ago," said Hilfiger in a 1997 *US* article, "you may not have found too many black models in advertising campaigns with top designers. Today, most top designers use them. I believe I was a part of that." A typical Tommy campaign often incorporated models of different ethnic backgrounds, walking and talking together, their arms wrapped around each other, playing ball and having fun. It was an approach that spoke to Hilfiger's vision of a more diversified world. "The young people of America today, or the world today, have very open minds," said Hilfiger. "They're not looking at minorities as being negative. They're just looking at it at face value, that this is America today, this is the world today. We're all a part of it. We should be enjoying it, we should be understanding it, we should be living it; we're all part of the dream."

Living life and enjoying it to the fullest became the image that characterized Tommy products. Toth's campaigns for Tommy showed healthy, happy, diverse people in a carefree atmosphere. "It was a lifestyle picture that we were after," said Sayers, "and we always tried to tell a consistent story."

TARGET MARKET

The "American Tartans" campaign was designed to appeal to men between the ages of 18 and 40. Part of what Hilfiger called his "American Classics," the long-sleeve tartan polo shirt was marketed to men who felt and acted as if they were 20, which, according to Sayers, was just about all men. Part of the inspiration for the campaign was The Mighty Mighty Bostons, a rock group that wore kilts when performing. The rock band's image helped attract men in their late teens and early 20s to the product, said Sayers.

In addition, 30- and 40-year-olds who worked during the week and dressed casually on the weekends—men who fell into the Peter Pan syndrome—were also targeted. Sayers said, "When these men come home from work, they feel as though they are dressing and acting far different than their fathers did. People's chronological age and the way they act are very different today. A youthful spirit and lifestyle appeal to these men, and we took that approach."

COMPETITION

Tommy's main competition, Polo Ralph Lauren and Nautica, both marketed upscale men's fashions and a wide array of additional products, everything from cologne to home furnishings. Polo Ralph Lauren, which also carried the brand names Polo Sport and Chaps, designed and marketed menswear and women's wear sold in department stores. The Polo Home Collection sold products ranging from linens to giftware, much of it manufactured by such companies as Reed and Barton, makers of flatware, and WestPoint Stevens, which made bedding. In February 1998 Polo's net worth was put at $147.6 million, with 5,800 employees. Nautica's subsidiaries, Nautica International and Nautica Furnishings, offered men's sportswear, outerwear, dress shirts, robes, loungewear, and swimwear. Nautica's net worth in February 1998 was $56.4 million, and the company employed 1,700 people.

A company somewhere between Polo Ralph Lauren and Nautica in size, Tommy netted $113.2 million and employed 1,820 workers at the end of fiscal year 1998. In order to compete, Tommy had branched out considerably since the company's first signature collection of men's clothing was introduced in 1984. In 1996 Tommy launched a line of women's clothing and fragrance under the name "tommy's girl" and a line of children's clothing. The company was scheduled to introduce a collection of home furnishing products in 1998. All of this was in addition to Tommy's extensive line of fashions, which had grown to include athletic wear, dress and business clothing, men's cologne, and accessories such as belts, bags, and sunglasses.

FROM HIPPIE TO HIP-HOP

A product of the late 1960s hippie counterculture, Tommy Hilfiger grew his hair long and sported bell-bottoms in high school. He was the first kid in Elmira, a town in upstate New York, to dress like a hippie. He and a few friends spent the summer of 1969 on Cape Cod working in a boutique—called a head shop back then—selling posters, incense, and other paraphernalia. At the end of the summer, they used their earnings to buy out the store, added some bell-bottom jeans and velvet tops, and went back to Elmira to open their own shop. They called it People's Place and housed it in a tiny basement they painted black. By 1975 People's Place had stores throughout upstate New York, usually near college campuses.

Instead of buying clothes for his stores, Hilfiger wanted to become a designer. People told him that with only a high school diploma he could not be successful at designing clothes or at breaking into business. But Hilfiger was not deterred, and he went to New York City to pursue his dream. In New York Hilfiger worked for various companies, all the time waiting until he could start his own. In 1984 Calvin Klein offered him a job for $100,000 a year, but Hilfiger turned it down. Soon afterward Mohan Murjani, an apparel manufacture, invested in Hilfiger, and in 1986 his first ad campaign hit the streets.

Initially Hilfiger's fashions were designed for the preppy-minded consumer. Then in March 1994 something unforeseen happened: Snoop Doggy Dogg wore an oversize Tommy T-shirt on *Saturday Night Live.* The hip-hop generation went wild buying Tommy clothes, and Hilfiger was smart enough to capitalize on the association. He began to cater to hip-hop consumers, designing just for them. Other designers "thought it was the plague," Hilfiger was quoted as saying in a 1997 article in *US* magazine. But the strategy paid off, and Hilfiger's fashions set the trend for street clothes in the 1990s.

Like its major competitors, Tommy opened its own retail stores, both in the United States and elsewhere. In November 1997 Tommy's first flagship store debuted on Rodeo Drive in Beverly Hills, and in September of that year the company opened a London store on Salone Street that featured men's sportswear. By February 1998 Tommy had 55 retail outlet stores in the United States, compared to Polo's 100 and Nautica's 50.

There were other competitors for Tommy in the higher end of fashion and accessories. Perry Ellis, Gap, Donna Karan, and Calvin Klein all vied with Tommy in the fashion world. Tommy's more universal marketing strategy, however, attracted the businessman as well as the hip-hop generation and the campus crowd. Michael Callahan, writing in a 1995 *America West Airlines Magazine* article, described Tommy's marketing strategy: "A tanned Wall Street banker carrying a Coach leather attache stands one aisle over from the hip-hop youth in headphones, both picking through tartan Oxfords that sell for $95, tennis shirts for $52, and hunter-green cardigans for $82. The banker is too young, too current for Lauren; the hip-hopper too fresh, too streetwise for The Gap or Structure. But they're both perfect for Tommy Hilfiger, the man who is revolutionizing how the younger generation is wearing clothes—*his* clothes."

MARKETING STRATEGY

According to Sayers, tartan plaids had been a repeated theme in the fashion world. "Tartans come and go," said Sayers. "It's a ubiquitous design and everyone uses them. We had to find a way to distinguish from everyone else's tartan shirt. We took the plaid story and turned it on its ear." The decision to develop the tartan theme for the 1997 fall men's campaign came out of a product meeting, Sayers said. Tartans were usually a part of the fall line, and Tommy had featured plaid boxers and skirts for women in the past. "This fall, we saw tartan reoccurring across all deliveries [new shipments], and it was the biggest single theme," Sayers said. "So we developed a tartan focus instead of the usual brand message. We had to decide how we were going to deliver it."

"But we still had to present our consistent lifestyle message and brand statement that's an umbrella over everything Tommy," said Sayers. Toth decided to dress the models in Scottish kilts—tartan plaids were Scottish, after all—and show the men "jumping and cavorting and having a ball." The men were relaxed, open, and goofing around in what Sayers described as a "strong American identity: active, slightly irreverent, and diverse." This was keeping with the brand image Toth had developed for Tommy, including the Peter Pan syndrome.

The "American Tartans" campaign was mainly a print campaign, with ads appearing in such men's magazines as *GQ, Men's Health,* and *Esquire.* Print ads also appeared in the *New York Times* and on billboards in Atlanta, Boston, and Los Angeles. In addition, some public telephone kiosks in New York ran images of the campaign.

OUTCOME

The "American Tartans" campaign did not noticeably increase sales of Tommy's long-sleeve woven plaid jerseys. But it did invoke smiles from the advertising industry, Sayers said, "whenever we showed it." In May 1998 Toth ended its relationship with Tommy, whose image, according to Sayers, was shifting. "Tommy has become more well known and successful, and what Tommy wants the brand to be has changed," said Sayers. "It's now upscale and sophisticated. It's a great company with great potential, and we watched it grow from $70-odd million to a company worth $1.5 billion."

From 1994 to 1998 the company's sales increased from $321 million to $847 million. Compared to Polo and Nautica, Tommy's net growth from 1997 to 1998 was the largest, 31 percent, as compared to 25.8 percent for Polo and 28.2 percent for Nautica. Hilfiger himself had won several awards for his fashion images and marketing strategies. In 1995 he was named Menswear Designer of the Year by the Council of Fashion Designers of America. That same year he received rock video station VH1's From the Catwalk to the Sidewalk Award at its annual Fashion and Music Awards.

FURTHER READING

Avins, Mimi. "Take a Spin inside Tommy Hilfiger's Fashion Cuisinart." *Los Angeles Times Magazine,* August 25, 1996, p. 19.

Callahan, Michael. "The Rise and Rise of Tommy Hilfiger." *American West Airlines Magazine,* October 1995, p. 36.

Tavee, Tom. "The People's Choice." *US,* November 1997, p. 111.

Van Meter, Jonathan. "Hip, Hot Hilfiger." *Vogue,* November 1996, pp. 306-9.

Anita Coryell

Toyota Motor Sales, U.S.A., Inc.

19001 S. Western Avenue
Torrance, California 90509
USA
Telephone: (310) 468-4000
Fax: (310) 381-7800
Web site: www.toyota.com

A CAR TO BE PROUD OF CAMPAIGN

OVERVIEW

Toyota Motor Sales, U.S.A., Inc., was the subsidiary of Toyota Motor Corp. charged with selling, marketing, and distributing the Toyota, Lexus, and Scion brands in the United States. The Toyota Corolla was the first line of cars Toyota ever introduced in the United States, and it had long been one of the most successful lines in the world. In 2002 Toyota launched the ninth generation of the Corolla with a campaign titled "A Car to Be Proud Of." This campaign came on the heels of a disappointing year for Corolla sales; in 2002 sales declined by nearly 50,000 units from the previous year.

Saatchi & Saatchi, an ad agency with long-standing ties to Toyota, developed and administered the $30 million–plus campaign. Conill Advertising and the Burrell Communications Group were also enlisted to conduct campaigns targeting the Latino and African-American communities, respectively. The campaign was designed to appeal to younger consumers, particularly those aged 25 to 35. This image-conscious group often saw the Corolla as a staid, overly practical automobile. To change that perception Saatchi & Saatchi released daring commercials such as "Key Party." In this spot a roomful of men at a swingers' key party looked on anxiously as a heavyset woman took her turn choosing a set of keys that would determine with whom she would go home. Despite the men's reluctance to be matched up with her, when she picked the keys to a Corolla, everyone rose to claim them. The spot closed with the tagline "A Car to Be Proud Of."

The campaign was a hit with critics, and it won a Silver Lion (Cars category) at the 2002 Cannes International Advertising Festival and a 2004 Silver Clio Award. It also led to a sales boost: 262,064 Toyota Corolla units were sold in 2003, versus only 195,767 units the previous year.

HISTORICAL CONTEXT

By the end of the twentieth century Japanese car company Toyota was producing more than 5.5 million units per year, making it one of the largest auto manufacturers in the world. The Corolla was originally introduced to the Japanese market in 1966. Two years later it became the first Toyota car launched in the United States. The original Corolla was small, affordable, and dependable. Because Americans in the 1960s often had a negative view of the performance of Japanese-made vehicles, establishing a reputation for quality was important for Toyota.

Once Toyota had established the Corolla as a quality automobile, it worked on making it more attractive to consumers. In the 1970s it made the car larger and added horsepower to the engine. These improvements appealed to car buyers, and the Corolla became one of the most successful cars in the world. By the late 1970s and early 1980s Toyota had added sport coupé, hatchback, and liftback versions to the Corolla line. The Corolla underwent a major redesign in 1988, with the liftback being phased out in favor of a new front-wheel-drive coupé. In an effort to keep the car fresh Toyota redesigned the Corolla several more times over the years. The Corolla's reputation only grew, and by 1997 it was the best-selling car in the world.

By 2003 it was time for Toyota to reimagine the Corolla once more. Sales in 2002 had been disappointing. In contrast to a successful 2001, during which Toyota moved 242,750 units of the Corolla line, sales in 2002 sagged to 195,767 units. Because the Corolla was among the most visible automobiles in its fleet, Toyota viewed this nearly 50,000-unit decline as cause for concern.

In terms of units sold, Corolla was still one of the most popular cars in the world, a result in large part of a reputation for being a long-lasting, high-performing machine. It was, however, viewed by younger buyers as an unglamorous, uncool car. Toyota's traditional marketing approach played into this image. The company had focused on its vehicles' performance instead of on the design. One of Toyota's best-known campaigns, "Oh, What a Feeling," was sometimes parodied because each spot closed with a scene in which the Toyota driver jumped up, overcome with excitement after driving his Toyota. The spots were earnest and unflashy, just like the Corolla itself.

OOBEYA

The new Corolla was designed according to the Japanese principle of *oobeya,* which roughly translated to English as "big, open office." Rather than adhering to a rigid, hierarchical system to conceive and build the new Corolla, the entire design team, from engineers to marketers, worked together to make the Corolla succeed. That meant that sales, engineering, marketing, and other departments all had input on how the new Corolla looked and what kind of special features it had. From sales and marketing professionals, designers learned what consumers liked about previous editions of the Corolla and what features drivers did and did not respond to. That feedback led to the introduction of a CD-player option for the Corolla.

The most important aspect of *oobeya,* however, was the way it improved communication. Logistical problems were caught early, saving money for the company. For example, the only North American plant that made Corollas with sunroofs was in Canada, even though far more consumers in the United States purchased that option. Engineers pointed out that making the sunroofed Corollas in California would save transportation costs. This helped Toyota keep the Corolla's price below $20,000.

TARGET MARKET

Toyota set a goal of selling 230,000 units for model year 2003. It wanted to expand Corolla's market share further by attracting a new population of drivers. The car had always performed well with middle-class drivers, especially families, but among the automaker's biggest challenges was a perception that the steady, reliable Corolla was also a dull car. To address this problem Toyota decided on a two-pronged approach. First, Toyota redesigned the Corolla with an eye toward making the car more aesthetically pleasing to consumers. It had been several years since the Corolla had been significantly redesigned, and some consumers were growing bored with the older look. Next, the company introduced the Toyota Matrix, a new line built on the Corolla platform. The Matrix featured a sleeker design to appeal to single car buyers in their 20s.

This approach kept Toyota from spreading the Corolla too thin. Rather than expecting the Corolla to be all things to all people, Toyota used the Matrix to take pressure off the older vehicle line. While the Corolla would have a sleeker look, the Matrix could push that even further because there was no risk of alienating an existing audience. Toyota could go forward with its efforts to reach young compact-car buyers without worrying that the existing Toyota compact-car audience was being overlooked. Between the two vehicles, Toyota hoped to have the entire compact segment covered.

While the Matrix was aimed at image-conscious singles who ordinarily might not buy a subcompact car, the Corolla was still geared toward the traditional subcompact market. But the company also wanted to attract more buyers in the 25- to 35-year-old range. Often Corolla buyers were in their 40s, and the company felt that younger car buyers were an untapped market. Therefore, the "Car to Be Proud Of" campaign's concentration was on consumers aged 20 to 29.

COMPETITION

Toyota's primary rivals were two other Asia-based automobile manufacturers: Honda Motor Company and

Nissan Motor Corp. Both were expanding their North American manufacturing in the early 2000s, which many observers felt would help the companies to build customer loyalty in the American market. The Honda Civic and Nissan Sentra were particularly strong competitors against the Corolla, since both were imported cars in the compact segment. Other major imports that competed with the Corolla were the Mitsubishi Lancer and the Mazda Protegé. Because of its sleek exterior the Protegé in particular attracted a younger, hipper consumer than the Corolla. The Ford Focus also provided the Toyota Corolla with some competition.

Toyota had been making serious inroads against these competitors in the late 1990s and early 2000s. While the automaker had an 8.8 percent share of the U.S. market in 1998, that had risen to more than 9 percent by 2000. By October 2003 Toyota controlled 11.2 percent of the U.S. market.

MARKETING STRATEGY

Toyota earmarked upwards of $30 million for the campaign. It designated Saatchi & Saatchi Los Angeles to implement it. Saatchi & Saatchi was a major worldwide advertising agency whose parent company, the Publicis Groupe, was Europe's largest communications company. The agency had handled a number of campaigns for Toyota Motor Sales, U.S.A., Inc., including the U.S. launch of the entire Lexus brand. Saatchi & Saatchi's approach was to turn brands into "lovemarks," brands that inspired devotion in consumers that endured "beyond reason." Because Corolla was a well-known brand with a lot of visibility, it was a good example of a potential "lovemark."

One component of the campaign was to make the entire Toyota brand a highly visible sponsor at both the Florida and California branches of Universal Studios. Another component was the company's outreach program to Latinos and African-Americans. Conill Advertising in Torrance, California, was retained to create new print ads and television commercials specifically for the Latino community and to adapt the current Corolla campaign for that market. The Chicago-based Burrell Communications Group was retained to handle outreach to African-Americans.

The campaign featured a variety of posters and print advertisements, but the key to the campaign was a series of television spots. The theme of the campaign was that the Toyota Corolla was "A Car to Be Proud Of." This tagline evoked the car's reputation for quality. In order to grab the attention of younger consumers, however, the television spots themselves were irreverent, even controversial.

The spots ran on youth-oriented programs on the WB, Fox, and NBC networks. In keeping with Toyota's efforts to reach out to young consumers, the commercials used humor to give the car a cooler, edgier image. The two central spots were "Key Party" and "Party Dress." "Key Party" featured a group of couples sitting around at a swingers-style key party, picking car keys as a way to pair up for the evening. As a heavyset woman walked forward to choose a set of keys, all the men in the room grew tense. When she pulled out the keys to a Corolla, all that changed. One by one, every man in the room claimed the keys were his, implying that every man wanted to claim he owned a Corolla. The spot closed with the tagline "A Car to Be Proud Of." The spot's sexual innuendo—key parties were usually associated with the swingers scene of the 1970s—drew some criticism, however.

"Party Dress" was a 40-second spot that also used humor to show the lengths to which people would go in order to claim a Corolla. The commercial began with a man and his daughter walking on a sidewalk. The daughter was ready for a party in a new dress until a Corolla drove by and splashed water on the two pedestrians, ruining the dress. The father searched for the perpetrator and came across an innocent bystander. When the father asked the bystander if he knew who was driving the car, however, the bystander took responsibility himself. Off-camera the father was then heard to strike the man. The joke was that the bystander was willing to be assaulted just to claim that he owned a Corolla. "A Car to Be Proud Of" appeared at the end of the commercial.

OUTCOME

Critics applauded the Toyota campaign. While some found the sexual and violent undertones of the "Key Party" and "Party Dress" spots to be unpleasant, the typical response was one of unqualified enthusiasm. Saatchi & Saatchi's work won the Silver Lion in the Cars category at the International Advertising Festival in Cannes, France, in 2002. This ceremony, dubbed "the Olympics of Advertising," was considered to be the most prestigious award in the industry. The campaign also garnered a Silver Clio Award in 2004 for "Party Dress."

More importantly, sales of the Corolla rebounded strongly. With 262,064 units sold in 2003, the Corolla not only outperformed its disappointing 2002 sales of 195,767 units, but it also surpassed the stronger 2001 sales period, during which 242,750 units were sold. The Corolla had returned as a major force in the industry and helped Toyota post strong company-wide sales in 2003.

FURTHER READING

Belson, Ken. "Slowdown? Don't Tell Toyota Motor." *New York Times,* October 31, 2002.

———. "Toyota Bucks the Economy and Posts Record Earnings." *New York Times,* November 9, 2001.

Chappell, Lindsay. "Toyota Envisions U.S. as Future Vehicle Development and Export Base." *AutoWeek,* August 7, 2002.

Knoll, Bob. "A Touch of Luxury for Old Reliable." *New York Times,* August 11, 2002.

Kohn, Joe. "Toyota Chases Youth with Corolla, Its Oldest Car." *AutoWeek,* December 31, 2001.

Liker, Jeffrey. *The Toyota Way: 14 Management Principles from the World's Greatest Manufacturer.* New York: McGraw-Hill, 2003.

Maynard, Micheline. "Even Cars Need to Make a Good First Impression." *New York Times,* March 8, 2002.

Roberts, Kevin. *Lovemarks: The Future beyond Brands.* New York: powerHouse, 2004.

Yamaguchi, Yuzo. "Toyota, Honda Predicting Bigger Share of U.S. Sales in 2002." *AutoWeek,* December 27, 2001.

Zaccai, Gianfranco. "Designed for Loving." *BusinessWeek,* July 21, 2005.

Guy Patrick Cunningham

EVERYDAY CAMPAIGN

OVERVIEW

During the late 1990s Japan's largest carmaker, Toyota Motor Corporation, was edging its way into the American car industry's top triumvirate. The "Big Three" U.S. automakers were General Motors Corporation, DaimlerChrysler Corporation, and Ford Motor Company; but Toyota's reputation as a modest, reliable car yielded record-breaking sales nearly every year throughout the 1990s. Despite their reputation as Japanese imports, most Toyota cars sold in America were also made in America. Toyota Motor Sales, U.S.A., (TMS) was the American sales, distribution, and marketing subsidiary of Toyota and employed more than 30,000 Americans. Hoping to continue its success with a first-time branding campaign for Toyota, the automaker released a campaign called "Everyday."

Instead of advertising its cars' details, like many American automakers, TMS wanted to advertise the Toyota brand and its appeal to everyday people. An overarching slogan, "Everyday," was introduced across print media and television. The campaign was developed by the ad agency Saatchi & Saatchi Pacific of Torrance, California, and was used to market nearly every model manufactured by the company. Created from TMS's $350 million ad budget, these advertisements, which portrayed real people in real-life situations, first aired on September 12, 1997. The late-1960s hit "Everyday People" by Sly and the Family Stone was the emblem song for the campaign. One of the less celebrated spots featured a couple debating whether or not to roll up the windows on their Toyota Corolla. After smelling their baby in the backseat, they decided to keep the windows lowered. In the middle of the campaign the tagline changed to "Every Day" until the effort concluded in late 2000.

The spots were ridiculed by critics for being tedious or sanctimonious. Polls conducted by *USA Today* found that other ad agencies rated "Everyday" the fifth-worst campaign of 1998. Only 23 percent of the consumers surveyed liked the ads a lot. Saatchi & Saatchi explained that it initially used the word "everyday," meaning commonplace, instead of "every day," which suggested reliability, because visually one word looked better in print ads. Ad critics lambasted the decision. Nonetheless, in terms of sales growth TMS outperformed nearly every large automaker in America.

HISTORICAL CONTEXT

In September 1997 Toyota released its new "Everyday" ad campaign with 30- and 60-second commercials on network television and print ads in *USA Today* and the *Wall Street Journal.* The advertisements, developed by Saatchi & Saatchi, were set in commonplace environments and showed people in routine situations. Previous Toyota slogans, such as "You asked for it, you got it," "Who could ask for anything more?" and "I love what you do for me" (initiated in 1990), focused on the object being sold. The "Everyday" ads, in contrast, focused on people more than products. Initial ads centered on a series of lifestyle affirmations—regular people were shown responding to the challenge "All you have is today. How will you make it count?" This reflected a strategic switch from the advertising of specific product details to storytelling—creating a world for the product to exist in.

TARGET MARKET

The target market for the "Everyday" campaign consisted of baby-boomer consumers—those who came of age in the 1960s. "Everyday People," the song by Sly and the Family Stone that was used in the campaign's television commercials, hit the charts in 1969. "Music marks our lives, and 'Everyday People' is just one of those songs that people associate with a meaningful time in their lives," said Joe McDonagh, executive creative director at Saatchi & Saatchi. The song was used as an anthem evoking a lifestyle and an attitude more than as an overt theme song to be associated with a particular product. The emotional weight of the song came through its associations with baby-boomer nostalgia (other songs considered were "Day Tripper," "Yesterday," and

"Daydream Believer"). But it was also hoped that it would be given a contemporary hearing as well, with its message of diversity.

Both ends of the baby-boomer spectrum were targeted, but in particular the ads were directed at parents. Some ads targeted parents of young children, with posters for the campaign distributed to 1,250 child care centers and an additional 3 million brochures sent to these centers as well as to the parents of newborns at hospitals.

Other ads, specifically those for Toyota's sporty Camry Solara, were directed at older parents—active empty nesters with a median age of 40–45. Toyota researchers found that about 1.5 million empty-nest baby boomers entered the market each year. Thirty-second spots developed by Saatchi & Saatchi for this group carried the "Everyday" tagline but said, "There are times when life is full of responsibilities. There are vehicles for those times. This is not one of those vehicles."

Targeting baby boomers also meant targeting a population saturated with years of television advertising. The challenge for an ad agency marketing any product, whether hamburgers, tennis shoes, or cars, was to reach television viewers who had learned to tune out hard-sell, product-oriented commercials and connect with these viewers emotionally—hit them, so to speak, where they lived.

EVERYDAY OR EVERY DAY

The incorrect use of "everyday"—meaning common, ordinary—to connote reliability ("every day") was a conscious choice made by Saatchi & Saatchi. "Grammatically, it should be two words," Sally Reinman, an executive with the ad agency, conceded to the *Wall Street Journal.* But after six months of intense discussion, Saatchi & Saatchi decided to go with one word. It looked friendlier and zippier, Reinman said. "It's more than just a word. It's how the word looks. It's how you deconstruct the language." Reinman said she herself preferred the one-word slogan because it looked as if it came from real consumers, not a big car manufacturer. Art directors wanted it too, because two words looked awkward as a signature. By retaining the two-word variant in the body of its ads, Saatchi & Saatchi showed that it knew what it was doing. "I will always speak my mind. Every day," said a man wearing sunglasses in one commercial. Then the slogan appeared: "Toyota. Everyday."

COMPETITION

As reported by Frank S. Washington in *Automotive News,* the 1990s brought parity to the U.S. automotive market. "Other Asian manufacturers as well as the Big 3 and European automakers are building products of comparable quality, and currency valuations have led to competitive pricing. The bottom line: quality alone is no longer the primary reason to buy any vehicle," he wrote. While Japan's "Big Three"—Toyota, Honda, and Nissan Motor Corporation—traditionally had gained market share in the United States through the quality of their cars, the challenge now was to achieve an identity in the American cultural landscape. Toyota's "Everyday" campaign, which presented the company as an interpreter and promoter of family values, stressed a company-wide identity for Toyota; other car manufacturers responded with umbrella campaigns of their own.

By June 1996 Nissan had a brand familiarity of 69 percent, according to marketing research conducted by the Allison-Fisher firm of Southfield, Michigan. This trailed Honda's 74 percent. Toyota led, with 81 percent. To give Nissan a sense of personality, a $200 million "Life Is a Journey—Enjoy the Ride" brand campaign was released. The ads were popular with consumers, hundreds of whom requested copies to download onto their personal computers, and the number of car shoppers who said they intended to buy a Nissan rose 21 percent. Honda, however, remained Toyota's toughest competitor. Toyota's Camry was the best-selling U.S. car in 1997, but Honda's Accord outsold Camry as of August 1998, selling 266,280 units compared to Camry's 176,577.

Of the smaller competitors, Mitsubishi initially emphasized a theme similar to Toyota's "Everyday" with its own "Built for Living" campaign. As in the Toyota ads, individual Mitsubishi models were shown in everyday situations with unexpected, humorous outcomes. At the end of each commercial an assortment of car models was then displayed, with the purpose of extending the spot's impact to the full Mitsubishi line. These spots were credited with increasing Mitsubishi sales in 1997. But a subsequent "Wake Up and Drive" campaign by Mitsubishi had a slightly different emphasis that contrasted with this celebration of the quotidian. It highlighted the exceptional in the everyday, with spots showing a car racing through a tunnel accompanied by the words "No one will ever notice the baby seat." Mazda Motor Corporation took a similar tack with its "Get In. Be Moved." ad theme. Mazda was not trying to simplify lives, sell cars for everyday people, or make vehicles popular with dogs, Richard Beattie, president and chief executive of Mazda North American Operations, told the Associated Press. "We appeal to people who love to drive," he said, "drivers who take the long way home. We are not a brand for everybody."

The "Everyday" theme appeared to have more success. In 1998 Toyota sales in the United States were up 6.4 percent. Toyota Motor Corporation and Honda Motor Co., the biggest Japanese automakers, both gained in the United States that year, while the smaller Japanese competitors, Nissan, Mitsubishi, and Mazda, after promising starts (Mazda sales were up 6.8 percent early in the year) fell further behind.

MARKETING STRATEGY

By 1997 auto marketers spent more on advertising than any other industry, but they were one of the last categories to initiate brand campaigns. To get more mileage out of their advertising dollars, car companies in 1998 took their cue from other industries, especially the fashion industry, and made the move to establish brand campaigns. Toyota planned to increase its 1998 ad budget by at least 10 percent, from an estimated $350 million in 1997, but all products were to fall under the "Everyday" branding campaign.

"We feel it's our first brand campaign," Dave Illingworth, senior vice president and general manager of the Toyota Division of Toyota Motor Sales, U.S.A., told *Advertising Age.* He said he considered the previous "Oh, what a feeling" tagline to be "more of an advertising line." "'Everyday' reminds customers that Toyota is more than a car, or a truck," Illingworth elaborated to *PR Newswire.* "It is a company with integrity, dedicated to enabling consumers to meet their life needs, whatever they may be. It is a company that places the consumer first—everyday. Central to the [branding] strategy is the need to enable the consumer to find a way into the brand, in general, and the product, in particular. Connecting with the consumer is key."

This branding campaign coincided with breakthrough advertising that focused on the consumer and the buying experience more than on the actual product. Ads had to be both soft sell and sophisticated, connecting with consumers who likely viewed about 36,000 television commercials each year. A *USA Today* survey ranked automotive commercials last in likability. Auto marketers realized that they had to learn to talk with consumers, not at them. "Consumers today possess a highly sophisticated filtering system," said Illingworth. "Our message must talk with, not at the consumer. It must show how our products contribute positively to the consumer's life. And it must show that we are serious about winning customers for life—everyday."

The "Everyday" campaign fit into a new school of marketing that saw ads as road maps for consumers, showing them how real people, spanning a variety of ages, races, and environments, actually used a product and how it fit their lives. Gimmicky commercials—such as the kind featuring a 175-pound man suspended high above a city, attached to a beam with Super Glue—were out. "Today we've got to show the customer how our product is an elemental part of their lives," said Joe Cronin, president and chief executive of Saatchi & Saatchi Pacific, Toyota Motor Corporation's advertising agency for 22 years.

This so-called show-me approach to marketing did not mean, however, that ads had to be humorless or devoid of whimsy. A television spot for the Toyota Sienna minivan showed the minivan emerging from a garage accompanied by the voices and sounds of a baby being born ("Take a breath now. Push. Here it comes."). The tagline—"Your life will never be the same"—appeared, followed by the brand slogan, "Toyota. Everyday."

Babies, in fact, were a favorite topic in the ads. An older couple in one spot wrangled over the window controls—up or down? The question was settled by a suspicious odor emanating from the infant in the backseat. Another spot showed a mother expertly and easily flipping up the backseats to look for a lost pacifier. Some commercials were everyday to the point of being charmingly laconic, as detailed by Bob Garfield in *Advertising Age*: "the best shows two working stiffs waking from a lunch-break snooze. 'We gotta go,' says one, sprawled on the far-reclining passenger seat of his buddy's Corolla. 'You're ruining my nap,' says his buddy, still sacked out on the driver's side. 'You don't understand. I can't get back late.' 'I do understand. We work for the same people,' says his friend, as we watch them in fast motion performing a series of post-nap ablutions and speeding back to work just in time. 'Technically we're an entire minute early.' 'I'll note this on my time sheet,' says the passenger dryly. Then the inimitable Sly Stone begins crooning, 'I . . . I . . . I . . . am everyday pe-o-ple.' This spot, in Garfield's opinion, said that Toyota did not merely set the standard; it was the norm. 'Everyone looks [every day] for those they can count on whether it's in a person or a brand," said Saatchi & Saatchi's McDonagh. "We believe we've found, and will demonstrate, Toyota's rightful place in people's lives—nothing more and nothing less."

When TMS released its first full-size pickup truck, the 2000 Tundra, Saatchi & Saatchi did not believe that "Everyday" advertised the truck's uniqueness. Instead, the Tundra was promoted with the inquisitive tagline "Have we gone too far? Or have others not gone far enough?" In September 1999 the "Everyday" tagline was split into two words after the one-word slogan was relentlessly criticized for suggesting that Toyotas were mediocre. To herald Toyota's year-2000 vehicles, eight new spots were created with TMS's $150 million budget. One spot featured a city suffering a power blackout while an unaffected Corolla remained powered. The tagline, "Always there. Every day," appeared on the screen. Further spots were created for the new Sienna, Camry, and Tacoma. Another 1999 commercial featured computer-animated ants crossing a road to advertise the diligence of Corolla's new VVTi engine. The spot ended with the copy "Charging ahead. Every day."

The campaign also splintered in September 1999. Realizing that baby boomers were no longer the majority of America's consumers, Saatchi & Saatchi adjusted the campaign to target consumers under the age of 35. TMS executives feared that the Toyota brand might succumb to the fate of Oldsmobile and Buick—both antiquated brands in the late 1990s. Sly and the Family Stone's "Everyday People" jingle was replaced with contemporary hip-hop and heavy-metal music. Spots ending with the tagline "Everyday People" featured 20-somethings enjoying Toyota's new subcompact car the Echo, which started at $9,995. Print and television spots for "Every Day" ran through the end of 2000.

OUTCOME

In a December 21, 1998, *USA Today* article in which advertising experts reviewed the best and worst ads of 1998, Richard Kirshenbaum of the ad agency Kirshenbaum, Bond and Partners in New York called the "Everyday" campaign a bust, saying, "Even everyday people don't want to be everyday people." The campaign "irritates most everyday people I know," added Gary Goldsmith, vice chairman and executive creative director of Lowe and Partners/SMS.

But as the article made clear, a campaign's popularity—or unpopularity—did not necessarily guarantee its longevity or sales. While the effectiveness ratings in the *USA Today* survey for the Toyota campaign were even lower than those for popularity, Toyota sales in the United States rose 6.4 percent in the calendar year 1998, compared with a 2.9 percent industry-wide increase. Toyota's sales, awareness, and consideration among car buyers had increased since the campaign was initiated, said Toyota ad manager Michael Bevan. David Pelliccioni, Toyota Division vice president of marketing, concurred that the "Everyday" campaign had succeeded in increasing customer awareness of Toyota.

"Toyota's one of the few companies that can afford to get away with running creative ads that emphasize image more than features," said Jim Wangers, a consultant with Automotive Marketing Consultants. Nevertheless, as reported in *Automotive News* in January 1999, a Toyota source said that the company wanted to return to more product-specific advertising and eliminate storytelling, which it accomplished with its subsequent "Get the Feeling" campaign, released in 2001.

Despite poor response to the campaign—which included consumer polls discrediting the campaign's effectiveness, critics accusing the campaign of mediocrity, and competing agencies pronouncing "Everyday" one of the worst campaigns of 1998—sales for TMS soared. December 2000 vehicle sales rose 14.2 percent above the previous year. Reflecting on TMS's success, the *Advertising Age* ad critic Bob Garfield wrote in 2005 that Toyota's slogans, such as "Everyday," were "a statement of the generic obvious" but were still effective for selling cars. The slogan's humdrum tone only skirted Toyota's main quality, which Garfield believed was safety. "Not the crash-test kind [of safety]; that positioning belongs to Volvo," he wrote. "The safety that defines Toyota is the certain knowledge you can buy one and not make a mistake. It's safely within the styling standards of contemporary good taste. It's safely within the boundaries of reasonable power and performance." Garfield then criticized campaigns such as "Everyday" for only advertising Toyota's reliability. He suggested that Toyota's future campaigns advertise the quality he first defined as "safety" and later as owner "satisfaction"—the real reason Toyota excelled worldwide.

FURTHER READING

Enrico, Dottie. "Toyota Ads Dote on Family, Appeal to 'Everyday People,'" *USA Today,* February 16, 1998.

Garfield, Bob. "Bob Garfield's Ad Review: Toyota's 'Everyday' Has Excellent Feeling." *Advertising Age,* November 17, 1997.

———. "Moving Forward or Step Backward?" *Advertising Age,* February 21, 2005, p. 40.

Halliday, Jean. "Brand Management Builds on Image Making: Every Carmaker Has Heightened Need to Craft a Champion; Execution Varies." *Advertising Age,* April 6, 1998.

———. "Saatchi Breaks Ads for $40 Mil Intro." *Advertising Age,* October 13, 1997.

———. "Toyota Boosts Ad Budget at Least 10% for 1998: New Products Fuel Increase in Spending." *Advertising Age,* February 16, 1998, p. 39.

———. "Toyota's Solara Ad Muscle to Hit with New TV Season: Coupe's Debut Targets Boomers with Empty Nests." *Advertising Age,* September 7, 1998.

Henry, Him. "Toyota Soars as Industry Falters." *Automotive News,* September 10, 2001, p. 43.

Kiley, David. "New Day for Toyota Will Launch a New Tagline 'Toyota. Every Day.' To Replace Its 'I Love What You Do for Me,'" *Brandweek,* August 18, 1997.

Ono, Yumiko. "Sometimes Ad Agencies Mangle English Deliberately." *Wall Street Journal,* November 4, 1997.

Pollack, Judann. "Carpe Diem: Toyota, Carvel, Dixie Ads Making the Day-to-Day Special." *Advertising Age* June 1, 1998.

Rechtin, Mark. "Toyota: Few Tomorrows for 'Everyday' Ad Theme?" *Automotive News,* January 18, 1999.

Reidy, Chris. "This Is a Car Ad? What Else Are They Selling?" *Boston Globe,* September 28, 1997.

"'Toyota/Everyday' Launched as Core Strategy in All-New Brand Advertising Campaign." *PR Newswire,* September 12, 1997.

Washington, Frank S.. "Japanese Adopt 'Image' Ad Strategy: Stressing Quality Isn't Enough." *Automotive News,* January 6, 1997.

Megan McNamer
Kevin Teague

FUEL FOR THOUGHT CAMPAIGN

OVERVIEW

Toyota Motor Sales U.S.A., Inc., was responsible for the distribution, marketing, and sales of all Toyota vehicles in the United States. It was owned by the Toyota Motor Corporation, a Japanese company that by 2004 had become the second largest automaker in the world. Toyota's advertising efforts were organized on three levels: national, regional, and local. Regional campaigns were run with dealer associations, which were cooperative marketing groups made up of Toyota dealers operating within key metropolitan areas. The Chicago Region Toyota Dealer Association, centered on Chicago, Illinois, but including areas in three surrounding states, was one such co-op. At the time domestic competitors like the General Motors Corporation and the Ford Motor Company were using major incentives to promote their vehicles. These included cash rebates for buyers of new cars, which were designed to convince consumers that that they were getting a good value from those brands. One of the consequences for Toyota was that in 2003 its sales dipped 8.9 percent in the Chicago region.

Toyota and the Chicago Region Toyota Dealer Association charged Saatchi & Saatchi Chicago, the local office of Toyota's primary advertising agency, with developing a campaign to boost sales and increase dealer profitability. The campaign, which was titled "Fuel for Thought" and which had a budget of more than $20 million, included television and radio spots built around consumer testimonials on the quality, reliability, and safety of Toyota vehicles. It ran for nine months, from January through September 2004. The campaign strategy was to redefine "value" so that it meant not simply low price but also included the buyer's getting a reliable, safe vehicle for the money. Some spots depicted two or more drivers discussing the value of a Toyota, while others featured testimonials from drivers. Print ads featured copy that emphasized similar themes. This approach harkened back to earlier Toyota campaigns that also had focused on the company's reputation for well-built, dependable cars. Key vehicles in the campaign were the Camry, the best-selling car in the United States in 2003; the Corolla, a compact car; the RAV4, a compact sport-utility vehicle (SUV); the Highlander, a conventional SUV; and the Tundra pickup truck.

The "Fuel for Thought" campaign succeeded with both advertising critics and consumers. It won a 2005 Bronze EFFIE Award, and it also helped Toyota's market share climb from 7.5 percent to 8.7 percent in the Chicago region. One vehicle, the RAV4 compact SUV, saw its sales jump by more than 10 percent in the area. The Toyota Camry, which remained the top-selling car in the United States in 2004, saw unit sales improve by 4.8 percent. In fact, the Chicago Region Toyota Dealer Association posted higher sales increases than any other Toyota region in the United States and exceeded its sales expectations in seven of the nine months during which the campaign was running.

HISTORICAL CONTEXT

In 1957 the Toyota Motor Corporation founded Toyota Motor Sales U.S.A. to handle all distribution, marketing, and sales of Toyota automobiles in the United States. The American company was based in Torrance, California. By January 2004 Toyota had become the second largest automobile manufacturer in the world, behind only the American company General Motors. By that time Toyota was selling more than 5.5 million units worldwide every year.

In order to increase the effectiveness of its advertising, Toyota Motor Sales U.S.A. organized its marketing efforts on three distinct levels. The first was made up of the company's national advertising campaigns. The second consisted of campaigns undertaken for the regional dealer associations that were centered around major metropolitan areas, as, for example, Portland, Oregon; Denver, Colorado; or Chicago, Illinois. Finally, individual dealers advertised locally. In the Chicago region 2003 was a difficult year for automotive sales. By September the sales of light passenger vehicles were down 8.9 percent from the previous year. To remedy this, Toyota dealers in the area decided to create a campaign tailored to the needs of their region.

Such regional advertising was always created in conjunction with local dealers. Thus, while each dealer ran its own local advertising, dealers from across a metropolitan area banded together to form associations. In this sense a dealer association was a marketing co-op made up of dealerships operating within a given area. The Chicago

Region Toyota Dealer Association consisted of 112 separate dealerships across parts of four states.

Most of the advertising for Toyota in the early 2000s had been developed by Saatchi & Saatchi, an international agency owned by the French communications corporation the Publicis Groupe. In the United States most national Toyota campaigns were handled by Saatchi & Saatchi LA. The agency had become known particularly for its belief that brands should be turned into "lovemarks," that is, as something that inspired a deep loyalty from consumers. Advertising for the Chicago region was done by Saatchi & Saatchi Chicago, the agency's regional office.

Toyota's key passenger cars in 2004 included the Camry, the top-selling vehicle in the North American automobile market in both 2002 and 2003, selling more than 420,000 units each year. Also important was the Toyota Corolla, one of the best-selling compact cars in the United States, which sold more than 300,000 units in 2003. Because between these two vehicles accounted for such large sales, their continued success was a vital element in Toyota's goals for 2004.

CAMRY: TOYOTA'S KEY VEHICLE

In 2004, at the time Toyota Motor Sales U.S.A., Inc., and the Chicago Region Toyota Dealer Association were developing the "Fuel for Thought" campaign, the Camry was one of the company's key vehicles. Introduced in 1980, the Toyota Camry was the best-selling car in the U.S. market in seven of eight years between 1997 and 2004 (1997–2000 and 2002–04). In 2004 Toyota Motor Sales U.S.A. sold 426,990 units of the vehicle. The car began life, however, as an offshoot of the Toyota Celica. It was originally called the Toyota Celica Camry, but by model year 1983 it had become an independent line.

The Toyota Camry was a midsize car, not known for a flashy exterior or souped-up engine. The vehicle's appeal rested on its reputation as a steady, reliable, safe car. The 2004 Camry came in three different versions: the LE, SE, and XLE. The LE was the most basic model, retailing for about $19,000 with a four-cylinder engine (the model cost $22,000 with a V-6.). The SE sold for almost $20,000 ($23,000 with a V-6) and featured a power moon roof along with bigger wheels and tires for a sportier drive. The XLE was the high-end model, with power seats, wood-grain trim, a CD player, and an alarm system, among other amenities. The sticker price ranged from $22,295 to $25,405, depending on the engine.

COMPETITION

One factor that Toyota had to contend with was its competitors' use of incentives to lure new car buyers. In effect, such incentives put vehicles on sale, since they reduced the prices consumers paid to dealers. At the time the three large U.S.-based automakers, Ford, General Motors, and DaimlerChrysler, were offering generous incentives, which included cash rebates and favorable lease terms, on many of their vehicles. These automakers developed their advertising campaigns around the incentives, thus helping to bring their lower prices to the attention of consumers. Such developments put pressure on Toyota dealers, who were forced to compete without the benefit of similar incentives.

A number of other automakers produced vehicles that were comparable to key Toyota cars and trucks. These included the Honda Accord and Nissan Altima, which competed with Toyota's best-selling passenger car, the Camry. Competition for the Corolla included the Honda Civic, the Nissan Sentra, and such domestic cars as the Ford Focus. The RAV4 competed with other compact crossover SUVs like the Honda CR-V and the Ford Escape, while the Highlander SUV appealed to drivers who might also consider the Nissan Murano or the Honda Pilot. The Tundra pickup competed with imported trucks like the Nissan Titan.

TARGET MARKET

Toyota was interested in attracting a fairly broad range of consumers, hoping to boost sales for all of its key vehicles. The campaign, however, was geared mostly at adults between the ages of 25 and 49, especially those with a household income of more than $50,000. The advertising also targeted people who were most likely to explore buying a new car, by visiting a dealership for example, sometime within a month of coming in contact with the campaign. Beyond that, Toyota wanted a campaign that focused on a diverse group of buyers from different ethnic backgrounds and educational levels.

MARKETING STRATEGY

The "Fuel for Thought" campaign was developed by Saatchi & Saatchi Chicago, the regional office of Toyota's principal advertising agency. In developing the campaign, the agency worked with both Toyota Motors Sales and the Chicago Region Toyota Dealer Association.

Traditionally Toyota and their dealers had not spent as much on advertising in the Chicago area as had General Motors or Ford, automakers that were based in the region. The "Fuel for Thought" campaign was expensive, however, costing more than $20 million. Toyota attempted to use its resources efficiently by saturating a particular medium like television, for example, before introducing the campaign to another medium. The company also tried to reach the largest market possible with each spot or ad. As a result, 80 percent of the campaign consisted of advertising on television, 14 percent involved radio, and the rest was made up of print ads. The campaign ran for the first nine months of 2004

Toyota had high expectations for its Chicago-area dealerships. It was hoped that the "Fuel for Thought" campaign would boost sales in 2004, improve the company's share of the Chicago-area automotive market, boost profits for local dealers, and improve the penetration of the company's key vehicles into the Chicago market. To accomplish this, Saatchi & Saatchi decided that it was important to highlight the value of Toyota vehicles. This approach was not entirely new, for earlier national Toyota campaigns had focused on value, specifically on the quality and reliability of the company's cars and trucks. The "Fuel for Thought" campaign was centered around the company's key vehicles, the Camry and Corolla cars, the RAV4 and Highlander SUVs, and the Tundra pickup.

While Toyota offered some price incentives as well, these were not major elements in the campaign. In fact, Toyota's month-to-month incentives remained largely unchanged from 2003. Instead, the copy in all of the advertising used testimonials from drivers and straightforward product descriptions to focus on the value offered by a Toyota vehicle. Both television and radio spots used a slice-of-life format, depicting consumers talking to other consumers about the advantages of owning a Toyota. One definition of "value"—the idea that was at the center of the incentive programs of the three major U.S. automakers—was the value of a low price. The "Fuel for Thought" campaign, however, promoted the idea that value in a motor vehicle also included such things as quality, safety, innovation, and the cost of ownership. By these standards the ads promoted the idea that Toyota buyers were getting a good value for their purchase.

OUTCOME

The "Fuel for Thought" campaign was considered to be successful. Critics liked it, and the campaign won a 2005 Bronze EFFIE Award. Further, in 2004 the Chicago area had the largest sales growth for Toyota of any region in the United States. By the end of 2004 the Chicago Region Toyota Dealer Association had posted its best sales numbers since its creation more than 25 years earlier. Sales were up 17 percent over 2003, and they exceeded expectations in seven of the nine months the campaign was running. During three of those months the Chicago region posted better sales numbers than any other Toyota region in the country.

As a result, dealers in the Chicago region had higher profitability growth as a group than did dealers in any of the other Toyota regions. This achievement occurred as Toyota posted its best sales ever in 2004, selling a total of 2,060,049 units. It was the first time that Toyota Motor Sales U.S.A. had sold more than 2 million units in North America. In January 2004 the Toyota Motor Corporation passed the Ford Motor Company to become the world's second largest automobile manufacturer in terms of sales, behind only Detroit-based General Motors.

Toyota's success occurred despite an industry-wide decline in sales of motor vehicles of 2.6 percent across the Chicago region. One result was that from 2003 to 2004 Toyota's market share in the region grew from 7.5 percent to 8.7 percent. In addition, its share of the light vehicle market rose from 9.5 percent to 10.9 percent, and its share of the light truck market rose from 5.8 percent to 7.0 percent. Each key vehicle in the campaign saw an increase in sales, with Camry increasing 4.8 percent in units sold, as it became the best-selling car in the Chicago area for 2004. The RAV4 saw its sales volume jump more than 13 percent, sales of the Corolla and Highlander both grew by more than 6 percent, and the Tundra saw sales rise by about 2.5 percent.

FURTHER READING

Gordon, Jane. "Wheel Is Turning against S.U.V.'s." *New York Times,* October 24, 2004.

Hakim, Danny. "3 Japanese Carmakers Gain against Big 3 in the U.S." *New York Times,* January 5, 2005.

———. "Toyota Overtakes Ford as World's No. 2 Automaker." *New York Times,* January 27, 2004.

Liker, Jeffrey. *The Toyota Way: 14 Management Principles from the World's Greatest Manufacturer.* New York: McGraw-Hill, 2003.

Popely, Rick. "GM, Ford Plan to Boost Incentives." *Chicago Tribune,* July 2, 2004.

Roberts, Kevin. *Lovemarks: The Future beyond Brands.* New York: powerHouse, 2004.

Schweitzer, Kevin. "Just Who's Buying the New Cars?" *Chicago Tribune,* April 25, 2004.

Warner, Fara. "Toyota Begins a National Campaign to Highlight More Than a Vehicle's Mere 'Rational Attributes.'" *New York Times,* September 28, 2004.

Zaccai, Gianfranco. "Designed for Loving." *BusinessWeek,* July 21, 2005.

Zaun, Todd. "Expansion Costs at Toyota Limit Its Earnings Growth." *New York Times,* February 4, 2005.

Guy Patrick Cunningham

GET THE FEELING CAMPAIGN

OVERVIEW

Toyota Motor Sales, U.S.A., Inc., the American subsidiary of Toyota Motor Corporation, was responsible for the marketing and sales of the company's products in the United States, including the Toyota, Lexus, and Scion brands. In 2001 Toyota redesigned the Celica in honor of the model's 30th anniversary. At one time the Celica had been a premier line for Toyota, and the Camry, which was spun off from it, became one of the most popular cars in the entire U.S. market. Nonetheless, in the face of competition, especially from Honda and Acura, the Celica had come to need revitalization. In 2000, while the Camry sold 422,961 units in the United States alone, the Celica lagged far behind, at only 52,112 units. Geared toward buyers between the ages of 18 and 35, the redesigned Celica had a look that was inspired in part by Indy 500 race cars. Among other sporty highlights, it featured an adjustable rear wing. Toyota wanted to capitalize on the dramatic redesign of the car with a new marketing campaign.

The "Get the Feeling" campaign, developed by Saatchi & Saatchi Los Angeles, located in Torrance, California, emphasized the car's appearance. This was a departure for Toyota, which had previously highlighted the performance and reliability of its automobiles. The centerpiece of the campaign, which began in 2001 and ran for a year, was a series of three 15-second television spots with the tagline "Looks Fast." All three spots began with a single camera shot of a red Celica parked on a suburban street. The shot was held in silence for several seconds, giving the viewer the chance to ogle the car. Each spot then ended with a humorous event, in which the parked car was mistakenly believed to be moving quickly, based on its sleek appearance alone. In the spot "Dog," for example, a dog was shown running onto the screen, trying to chase what looked to be a moving Celica. The dog then crashed into the back of the car, leading to the "Looks Fast" tagline.

The spots were successful with critics and won a number of awards, including the prestigious Cannes Gold Lion for "Dog." The campaign was not, however, able to revitalize the Celica. Sales of the car dropped substantially in both 2001 and 2002, and they continued to fall until the entire Celica line was finally canceled in 2004.

HISTORICAL CONTEXT

Toyota Motor Sales, U.S.A., Inc., was founded in 1957 to handle the marketing, distribution, and sales of Toyota vehicles in the United States. The company was based in Torrance, California. By the beginning of the twenty-first century, the parent company, which was based in Japan, had become the world's third largest automaker in unit and net sales, producing more than 5.5 million vehicles every year. Toyota's advertising traditionally had been conservative, emphasizing the company's reputation for well-made, fuel-efficient vehicles. This was embodied in the advertising of the "We're Quality Oriented" campaign, used by the company in the 1970s. Toyota then introduced the "Oh, What a Feeling" campaign in the 1980s. This campaign and its slogan became widely associated with the brand, though some criticized it for being dull. In fact, dealers in Ontario, Canada, produced a parody of the ad, tweaking what came to be known as the "jump," the shot of a Toyota driver leaping in excitement that often closed the spots. Nonetheless, the conservative advertisements were consistent with Toyota's image as a maker of dependable cars that got good gas mileage.

The Toyota Celica was introduced to the U.S. market in 1971. Conceived of as Toyota's answer to the Ford Mustang, the Celica was intended to be an affordable sports car. It was successful with both critics and customers and was named *Motor Trend* 's Import Car of the Year in both 1976 and 1978. The Celica was eventually eclipsed by another Toyota product, however, its offshoot, the Camry. Launched in 1980 as the Toyota Celica Camry, the new line was spun off on its own in the 1983 model year, and it became Toyota's best-known automobile. Soon most of the company's general advertising, particularly on television, was devoted to the top-selling Camry, which in sales was consistently one of the most popular midsize cars in the United States.

By the late 1990s there were rumors that Toyota was considering discontinuing the Celica. The car had been available in the U.S. market for more than two decades, which was a long time for a model to be in circulation. Further, for several years after 1993 the car had not undergone a significant redesign, which some people took as a sign of Toyota's flagging interest in the vehicle. In 1999 the Celica Coupe was eliminated, leaving only the GT Liftback and GT Convertible models. For the 2000 model year, however, Toyota redesigned the Celica, using Calty Design Research, Inc., to reconceive the styling of the car. The new Celica featured a cab-forward design and a distinctive spoiler, which gave it more of a racing look. In fact, the Celica's new appearance was partially inspired by Indy 500 cars. In honor of its 30th anniversary, the car was given an aggressive promotion at the 2001 New York International Auto Show.

COMPETITION

Toyota's closest competitor was Honda. Both were Japanese-based automakers that had penetrated deep into

ADVERTISING AUTEUR

The award-winning television spots of the "Get the Feeling" campaign were produced by Independent Media, in Santa Monica, California, and directed by Chris Smith. The respected filmmaker, who had also directed ads on behalf of other major brands, such as TiVo and Lee jeans, had an ongoing relationship with Independent Media. He was especially known in the film industry, however, for his award-winning documentary *American Movie.* The film, which followed the efforts of the failed filmmaker Mark Borchardt, connected with audiences at the 1999 Sundance Film Festival, where it won the Grand Jury Prize for Best Documentary. The work was praised for the way it mixed the comedy of its subject's eccentricities with a real affection for his determination. Smith's 1995 comic documentary *American Job* had also been screened at the festival.

the North American automobile market by earning respect for their performance and reliability. In 2000 Honda sold 1,158,860 total units, up more than 7.5 percent over the previous year. The company went on to have an even better year in 2001, selling 1,207,629 units. Honda's Acura division made particularly big gains in 2001, with sales jumping 19.5 percent over 2000, to 170,469 units. Toyota, however, sold 1,741,254 units in 2000, buoyed by the ever-popular Camry, which that year sold 422,961. While the Celica sold a respectable 52,112 units, it was about to feel the pressure from new Honda models, such as the Acura RSX.

Celica's traditional competitor, however, was the Ford Mustang. Both were relatively inexpensive sports cars geared toward young buyers. But in popular culture the Celica had never achieved the status of the Mustang, at least partly because the latter, with its powerful, high-performance engine, was seen as more of a muscle car. Still, by 2001 the primary competition for the Celica was coming from Honda and its subsidiary Acura. In 2001 Acura replaced the Acura Integra Coupe, which had previously competed with the Celica, with the RSX. The Acura RSX was an immediate hit with critics and in 2002 and 2003 was named one of the 10 best cars of the year by *Car and Driver* magazine. The car shared a platform with the Honda Civic. Though the Civic traditionally was seen more as an economy car, it also eventually came to compete with the Celica. In 2001 the Civic Type-R was introduced, featuring a sportier look than previous models, another development that put pressure on Toyota.

TARGET MARKET

With the advent of the "Get the Feeling" campaign in 2001, Toyota began a new drive to sell the Celica. Once again the company turned to Saatchi & Saatchi, which handled almost all of its advertising. Toyota charged the Los Angeles office of Saatchi & Saatchi with the development of advertising that would attract a younger audience. While an understated advertising approach worked for the Camry, a four-door car popular with families, it had been less effective for the sporty two-door Celica. Toyota was also concerned that its customer base for the vehicle was becoming too old. In addition, the Celica was underperforming among male car buyers, and there was concern that it did not project the kind of macho image a sports car should have.

The "Get the Feeling" campaign was directed at both males and females between the ages of 18 and 35 who were in the market for a new car. Toyota wanted to build on its reputation for quality by highlighting the stylistic elements of the car. To accomplish this, Saatchi & Saatchi developed a series of three 15-second television spots—"Dog," "Old Man," and "Motorcycle Cop"—all with the tagline "Look Fast."

MARKETING STRATEGY

Saatchi & Saatchi stated that its purpose in the "Get the Feeling" campaign was to turn Toyota into a "lovemark," as opposed to simply a trademark. The thinking was that Toyota had achieved a high level of respect but that in a competitive automobile market respect alone was not enough. Many manufacturers of automobiles, such as Honda and Volkswagen, had achieved a high level of regard for the performance of their vehicles, and Toyota needed to distinguish itself from its competitors. The company needed an entertaining campaign that made an emotional connection with consumers. The concept of the lovemark, which was unique to Saatchi & Saatchi, was used by the agency to describe a brand that inspired "loyalty without reason." To build this kind of loyalty, Saatchi & Saatchi wanted to burnish Toyota's image by showing that its automobiles were not only reliable but aesthetically pleasing as well. The Celica was a good candidate for this approach, since it had a sporty look and competed with visually striking cars like the Acura Integra.

Key agency players in the development of the ads were the creative directors Neal Ford and Doug van Andel, copywriter Sherry Hawkins, and art director Verner Soler. The spots were produced by Independent

Media, of Santa Monica, California, and were directed by Chris Smith. Rather than developing the traditional 30-second spot, they were kept short, at 15 seconds each. The spots were designed so that two could run back-to-back. "Dog," the anchor spot, featured a single shot of a red Celica parked on a suburban street. After a few seconds a dog was shown running across the screen and crashing into the car. The implication, of course, was that the sporty new Celica looked fast even when it was standing still.

The other two spots used the same setup as "Dog": a single shot of a red Celica parked on the street. In the "Old Man" spot an elderly gentleman walking past the car stopped to yell that the driver should "slow down." The joke, of course, was that not only was the car parked but that no one was behind the wheel to hear him. In "Motorcycle Cop" a police officer pulled up behind the parked Celica to give it a speeding ticket. As with the "Old Man" spot, there was no driver to give a ticket to. All three spots closed with the "Looks Fast" tagline.

The point of the three spots was to demonstrate that the new Celica looked fast even when it was standing still. In all three the long single-camera shot put the focus on the car, inviting the viewer to admire its sleek design. Instead of an emphasis on Toyota's reputation for quality and performance, which is what might have been expected, the "Get the Feeling" campaign highlighted visual style in the most direct way possible. The humor of the campaign was meant to underscore the car's main selling point, its sporty new look. Since all three spots relied on a sustained single camera shot, the costs were kept at a minimum.

OUTCOME

Saatchi & Saatchi claimed that the "Get the Feeling" campaign helped lower the average age of Celica buyers by eight years. In 2001 and 2002 the median age of new Celica buyers was 29, well within Toyota's target range. Overall, however, sales of the Celica began to flag in the face of pressure from the Honda Civic and Acura Integra. While the Celica sold 52,112 cars in 2000, only 35,508 units were sold in 2001, and by 2002 the number of sales was down to just 22,676. On July 16, 2004, Toyota decided to discontinue the car altogether, citing increased competition.

Within the advertising industry, however, the campaign was highly successful, and the ads won numerous awards. Both the campaign as a whole and the "Dog" spot won prestigious Clio awards. The campaign also received a Silver Effie, among other accolades. The International Advertising Association gave individual Silver awards to both the "Dog" and "Old Man" spots. *Ad Age* named the "Dog" spot the Best Automotive Commercial of the Year. "Dog" also took home the 2002 Cannes Lions Grand Prix in Film, the Gold Lion, considered the most prestigious award in television advertising. The spot defeated 411 finalists, which had been whittled down from 5,059 entries. The "Old Man" spot won a Bronze Lion in the same competition.

FURTHER READING

Allen, Leslie. "Toyota Targets Hopes, Dreams in New Marketing." *Detroit Free Press,* September 28, 2004.

Elliott, Stuart. "Music Is at the Center of New Toyota Campaign." *New York Times,* August 28, 2001.

———. "Toyota Snubs Its Main Ad Agency." *New York Times,* July 15, 2002.

Garfield, Bob. "Toyota Touts an Ugly Celica in Compact Spots That Hum." *Advertising Age,* September 3, 2001.

Kiley, David. "A New Season for Car Slogans." *Business Week,* September 28, 2004.

Liker, Jeffrey. *The Toyota Way: 14 Management Principles from the World's Greatest Manufacturer.* New York: McGraw-Hill, 2003.

McCarthy, Michael. "USA Stays in Running for TV Ad Award." *USA Today,* June 21, 2002.

Roberts, Kevin. *Lovemarks: The Future Beyond Brands.* New York: powerhouse Books, 2004.

Saatchi & Saatchi. "Dog." Available from <http://www.saatchikevin.com/workingit/Saatchi_TVCS.html>

Zaccai, Gianfranco. "Designed for Loving." *Business Week,* July 21, 2005.

Guy Patrick Cunningham

KIDS RULE CAMPAIGN

OVERVIEW

Toyota Motor Sales, U.S.A., Inc., was the distributor of Toyota Motor Corp.'s Toyota, Lexus, and Scion brands in the United States. In model year 2004 the company released a new version of its Sienna minivan. This launch was a top priority for the automaker, because the minivan segment featured strong competition from the new Honda Odyssey and Nissan Quest as well as from established domestic brands such as the Chrysler Town & Country. A segment-wide decline in sales throughout the 2000s made it imperative that the Sienna improve its meager 41 percent awareness rate among consumers, especially when the segment average stood at 48 percent.

To establish the Sienna in the minds of car buyers, Toyota turned to the Los Angeles office of ad agency Saatchi & Saatchi for a new kind of advertising campaign. In addition to using print ads, the Sienna would be marketed through a series of television commercials aimed at kids. Surveys indicated that more and more families were allowing their children to contribute to the decision about what automobile to purchase. To capitalize on this trend Sienna commercials featured child actors talking up kid-friendly features of the newly redesigned vehicle. For example, one spot featured a crash-test teddy bear, while another plugged the car's roomy interior by having a young boy explain that the car offered enough space for him to avoid his little sister. Each spot featured the tagline "Kids Rule." Toyota also sponsored Yahoo!'s family-friendly Yahooligans! Book Club and capitalized on other unorthodox advertising venues. The campaign's budget exceeded $20 million.

The 13-month launch was an unqualified success. In addition to winning a Silver EFFIE Award in 2005, the campaign led to a 99 percent jump in brand awareness among consumers, and this in turn fueled solid sales increases throughout the year. These gains came despite a slowdown for other vehicle sales in the segment, especially among the Sienna's key competitors.

HISTORICAL CONTEXT

Based in Torrance, California, Toyota Motor Sales, U.S.A., Inc., was founded in 1957 by the Japanese company Toyota Motor Corp. to handle U.S. sales, marketing, and distribution of Toyota automobiles. By the early 2000s Toyota was among the world's largest auto manufacturers, responsible for the production of more than 5.5 million units per year.

The Sienna first appeared in 1998 as a replacement for the unsuccessful Toyota Previa minivan line. While the vehicle was lauded for its safety and performance, it was not as successful as competitors such as the Honda Odyssey. By 2003, in anticipation of relaunching the line, Toyota had decided to redesign the Sienna. The car would be priced from $23,000 to $35,000 and would feature a sporty look and a more powerful 3.3-liter V-6 engine. The car was a success from the beginning with car critics, and *Car and Driver* named it one of 2004's Five Best Trucks in the "van" category.

TARGET MARKET

Toyota's primary focus for the Sienna was on consumers in the 30- to 39-year-old age range. The Sienna's target market was the same that most minivans shot for, namely professionals, retirees, couples, and families. With the Sienna launch Toyota made the innovative move of targeting not only the parents in those families but also the children. According to a 1999 survey conducted by marketing-information firm J.D. Power and Associates on behalf of the Nickelodeon television network, 62 percent of parents claimed that their children participated actively in the family's decision on what car to buy. Toyota planned to target those children directly with kids-centered advertising and the introduction of the "Kids Rule" tagline.

INTERNET OUTREACH

In April 2004 Toyota became the first automaker to host a Chinese-language website in the United States on behalf of a new automobile. The site was produced as part of the 2004 relaunch of the Sienna minivan. By the early 2000s Asian-Americans were the third-largest minority group in the United States, after Latinos and African-Americans. At the beginning of the decade Toyota began a companywide outreach program aimed specifically at these demographic groups. In some cases advertising agencies were enlisted to provide marketing campaigns specifically tailored for Latino and African-American consumers. Toyota decided to approach the Asian-American market, however, through the Internet.

Toyota chose to conduct a Web-based campaign after internal research revealed that, when looking to purchase an automobile, Asian-American Toyota buyers relied more heavily on the Internet than any other Toyota customer group. Because Chinese-Americans were the largest Asian-American group, the company focused primarily on them. Chinese speakers were also the largest group among Asian immigrants to the United States. The Chinese-language site featured information about the Sienna similar to that available on the English-language Toyota website. By June 2004 approximately 1.1 percent of visitors to Toyota's main site were choosing to read the Chinese-language Sienna page over the English one, well within the company's projections.

Toyota also identified new markets for the Sienna and pinpointed demographic groups that were more inclined to buy a Toyota minivan. As a result of company research, Toyota specifically marketed the Sienna to Asian-Americans. It released a Chinese-language website to help sell the Sienna—the first time an automaker had done so to promote one of its vehicles in the American market. Toyota's research indicated that 14 percent of all Sienna buyers were Asian-American and that the Sienna was more popular in the Asian-American community than any other Toyota vehicle. Because 70 percent of Chinese-Americans had Internet access, versus a national access rate of 60 percent, the Web was seen as the ideal forum for reaching these buyers. The Internet campaign, which featured pictures of and information about the Sienna, was also a way to reach these consumers that was more cost-effective than TV advertising.

COMPETITION

By 2004 the minivan market was a crowded one, and to make matters worse the segment had seen sales decline since 2000. Adding to the pressure on Toyota was the fact that Ford introduced its new minivan, the Freestar, almost simultaneously with the new Sienna. That vehicle replaced Ford's fading Windstar line. The Chrysler Town & Country was a comparable unit already on the market. Toyota was even more concerned about the Nissan Quest, which was another Japanese-made minivan debuting at the same time and gunning for the same buyers as the Sienna. The Quest launch would be backed by a campaign that cost more than $20 million, and the vehicle was poised to be one of the Sienna's primary competitors.

Because Honda and Toyota often competed for the attention of the import-car buyer, Toyota was also concerned about the threat that Honda's Odyssey minivan posed to the Sienna. Toyota decided to give the Sienna a 3.3-liter V-6 engine to make the vehicle more powerful than the Odyssey, which used a 3.0-liter V-6. Toyota knew that it was at a disadvantage in consumer awareness. While the segment average was a healthy 48 percent, the Sienna only managed a 41 percent awareness rate prior to the "Kids Rule" campaign. In addition, many of Toyota's competitors offered incentives—for example, Chrysler offered several thousand dollars back through dealers—and Toyota had chosen not to go that route with the Sienna.

MARKETING STRATEGY

Toyota commissioned Saatchi & Saatchi Los Angeles to conduct the campaign, which cost more than $20 million to produce. The company had a long relationship with Saatchi & Saatchi, which had helped launch the entire Lexus brand in the United States in the late 1980s and early 1990s. The agency had also handled the advertising for the redesigned Toyota Celica, creating a campaign that garnered a Gold Lion at the International Advertising Festival in Cannes, France, in 2002. Saatchi & Saatchi's approach was to turn brands into "lovemarks," meaning that they inspired customer devotion that endured "beyond reason."

This approach stood in contrast to Toyota's traditionally more conservative campaigns. In the 1970s and 1980s the company's primary concern was reinforcing its image as a maker of safe, dependable vehicles. This led it to feature campaigns that many saw as uninspired, or at least unadventurous. Now, however, Toyota wanted more sophisticated campaigns that showed consumers that Toyota cars could be fun to drive and stylish to look at. The light touch of the "Kids Rule" campaign, which relied on humor to attract kids and families, was an example of this.

While the campaign was focused on a series of television spots, it also featured a number of unorthodox efforts. The Sienna became the official sponsor of Yahoo!'s Yahooligans! Book Club, which was geared toward kids and families, precisely the audience Toyota was after. Sienna ad banners ran on the Book Club's website as well as on the Yahoo! homepage. Additionally, advertisements for the Sienna were included in the "wish list" E-mails that kids using the site were encouraged to send their parents. Toyota sponsored "Live Your Best Life," a tour of self-help speeches and seminars organized by television personality Oprah Winfrey and aimed at women, especially mothers. Another innovative idea was Toyota's sponsorship of a series of *Time for Kids Extra!* magazines. These publications, an offshoot of Time Warner's *Time,* were distributed to a large audience of some 3 million students and their parents. Each eight-page issue was packed with interesting bits of information about the world. These advertising tactics helped Toyota reach new customers, which was important because the minivan segment was so competitive, with several new vehicles launching in a short period despite sagging sales across the segment.

The key to the campaign was a series of television spots centered on children. These commercials ran on kid-oriented networks such as Nickelodeon and the Discovery Channel. In one spot a group of young girls invaded a Sienna design session, demanding extra cupholders and other kid-friendly features for the vehicle. Another depicted a young boy acting as a "salesman" for the car, paying special attention to the vehicle's roominess, which made it easier for passengers to avoid their little sisters. In yet another spot a little girl strapped her doll and teddy bear into the Sienna for a crash test. After each emerged unscathed, the girl sat them down for a tea party. Other spots repeated the formula of young actors talking up child-friendly aspects of the car.

Each spot closed with the tagline "Kids Rule." The commercials walked a fine line, mixing humor but still underscoring Toyota's reputation for safety. While kids might want a fun car, parents were interested in keeping their children safe. Because the minivan segment was primarily aimed at families with children, any campaign would have to reassure parents that their children would be protected. Toyota's playful spot featuring the teddy bear and doll crash-test team was a good example of how Toyota was able to use a light touch to reinforce the brand's strong record for quality.

OUTCOME

The campaign was wildly successful. Sienna's sales went up 119 percent after the launch, while its competitors took a tumble. The Quest underperformed in its debut, selling 30,448 units, well below Nissan's target of 80,000 to 85,000. Meanwhile, Chrysler's Town & Country saw sales decline 7.5 percent, and Ford's Freestar sold 17.5 percent less than its predecessor, the Windstar, had. Many observers gave direct credit for the Sienna's success to the "Kids Rule" campaign. The campaign was also a hit with critics, and it won a Silver EFFIE Award from the New York American Marketing Association in 2005.

Toyota addressed the Sienna's awareness problem; from the prelaunch period to June 2004 its ad awareness jumped 99 percent. Total sales for 2004 reached 157,587 units, a significant rise from the previous year's 104,378 units sold. *USA Today* also reported that, based on the results of its Ad Track surveys, the "Kids Rule" campaign was among the 10 most likeable ads of 2003.

FURTHER READING

Blumberg, George P. "To Sell a Car that Women Love, It Helps if Women Sell It." *New York Times,* October 26, 2005.

Broder, John. "A Family Cocoon with Frills." *New York Times,* October 23, 2005.

Howard, Theresa. "Ads Put Kids in Minivan Spotlight." *USA Today,* June 29, 2003.

Jackson, Kathy. "Toyota Counts on Kids in Sienna Campaign." *Automotive News,* April 28, 2003.

Liker, Jeffrey. *The Toyota Way: 14 Management Principles from the World's Greatest Manufacturer.* New York: McGraw-Hill, 2003.

Rechtin, Mark. "Toyota's New Sienna Minivan Incorporates the Best from All Comers." *Auto Week,* January 20, 2003.

Roberts, Kevin. *Lovemarks: The Future beyond Brands.* New York: powerHouse, 2004.

Vaughn, Mark. "Bigger Is Better: There's More Sienna Almost Anywhere You Measure." *Auto Week,* February 24, 2003.

Zaccai, Gianfranco. "Designed for Loving." *BusinessWeek,* July 21, 2005.

Guy Patrick Cunningham

THE ROAD IS CALLING CAMPAIGN

OVERVIEW

In 1989 Toyota Motor Sales, U.S.A., Inc., boldly placed itself in direct competition with such automakers as Bayerische Motoren Werke AG (BMW) and Mercedes Benz when it launched Lexus, a new division of near-luxury cars. A precedent was set, and fellow Japanese automakers Honda and Nissan would soon follow with their own divisions to compete in the lucrative over-$35,000 car market. Among the Lexus lines, the ES proved immensely popular, providing for approximately 50 percent of all Lexus sales by 1996. Hoping to increase sales for the already popular ES 300, Toyota released a campaign titled "The Road Is Calling."

The campaign debuted on October 10, 1996, across television, print, outdoor, interactive, and direct-marketing mediums. The ad agency Team One Advertising created the $60 million campaign to shake the cold, unemotional image that some had associated with the ES 300. For the campaign Team One put a captivating new spin on the typical car-zipping-along-a-scenic-landscape approach to car ads. In TV spots for "The Road Is Calling," celebrity actors, including Demi Moore and John Cleese, uttered voice-over lines scripted for such roads as the Autobahn and Fifth Avenue. By craftily choosing stars whose voices corresponded with a given aspect of the Lexus image, Team One portrayed the ES 300 as a tantalizing entity, one that even a road could fall in love with. The tagline was "The road is calling. Answer it." Bold, aggressive, and provocative, the enticing spots increased consumer awareness of the ES 300 as a car that represented luxury, performance, and value. The campaign concluded in 1998.

Not only did ad critics praise "The Road Is Calling," but also, more than 1,100 advance orders for the new ES 300 were placed before the car was made available at dealerships. Two months after the campaign began, Lexus's segment share increased 5 percent and sales were 32 percent greater than expected by Toyota's executives. Company representatives and Team One deemed the campaign a triumph.

HISTORICAL CONTEXT

When Toyota introduced its Lexus division in 1989, it faced an uphill challenge toward an upscale image. Toyota had earned a long-standing reputation for producing reliable, dependable, and unassuming cars. After investing $500 million in research and development to create the Lexus division, Toyota had to create an image that would not be regarded as the Toyota in emperor's clothes. In addition, the company had to press to stay ahead of its traditional competitors, Honda and Nissan, who were quick on the heels of Toyota in launching their own near-luxury divisions, Acura and Infiniti.

Toyota did not allow its conservative, unpretentious reputation or the slowing of the go-go 1980s economy to dispel a dream of developing a car that could go tire-to-tire with such European luxury cars as Mercedes Benz, BMW, and Porsche. Undaunted by a marked slow down in conspicuous consumption in the United States, Toyota chairman Eiji Toyoda told *Fortune* magazine, "The people who have been buying our cars were moving up in life. We wanted to meet their heightened needs."

To introduce a near-luxury car at a dramatically lower price than its German competitors, Lexus had to shape a compelling new image. Research had shown that the older-age market for luxury cars in the United States would not be easily seduced away from their love affair with Cadillacs and Lincolns. Existing owners of high-end German cars, a market deeply tied to established status symbols, would be no less difficult to convert. There was, however, that little niche acknowledged by Toyota chairman Toyoda: the younger buyer moving up in life who wanted a true luxury car but who could not yet afford it.

In an utterly self-confident move, Lexus staged its debut to the press in Germany, the homeland of its targeted competition. U.S. industry journalists from such publications as *Car and Driver* and *Road & Track* were flown into Frankfurt for an exhilarating, heady five days of competitive driving in cars by Lexus, BMW, Jaguar, and Mercedes. From slow cruising along the Rhine to testing mettle on the Autobahn, the newborn Lexus captured attention for its serene quiet and stability at blinding speeds.

An aura of anticipation was generated for Lexus's American debut. A massive direct-mailing targeted 250,000 prospective consumers. In August dealers were given the nod to sell the new cars as soon as they rolled onto the lot, one month before the official introduction. Creating image lust was paramount for Lexus. Team One's objective was to bathe the Lexus in an image of quality, luxury, and dependability. They put together a tagline that would epitomize what Lexus had to offer: "The relentless pursuit of perfection."

By 1997 Team One's image for the ES 300 had shifted, adding style and performance to an earlier emphasis on safety and style. Through evocative narration from the road's perspective, "The Road Is Calling" spots deftly rolled a message of luxury, performance, safety, and value into one desirable car.

TARGET MARKET

Team One's primary goal with its "The Road Is Calling" campaign was to keep existing Lexus owners coming back for more, with a secondary goal of luring new owners away from competitive luxury cars like the Mercedes-Benz C-Class, Volvo 850, Infiniti I30, Acura TL, and Cadillac Catera. Surveying had shown Team One that buyers owning or considering these brands were demographically similar and that they were open to trading across the segment.

Affluence and image were key components in pinpointing demographics. The primary target average was a 49-year-old, college-educated, professional, married male with a median household income of $104,000. Psychologically, this audience was colored by a young mindset, a love of travel, and an active lifestyle. They were already driving a near-luxury, midluxury, or Japanese midsize car and were confident and comfortable about their professional and personal life.

To attract this attitude-demanding audience, Team One set out to fashion a new air of excitement about the tried and true ES. They had to portray the ES 300 as a multifaceted car, one promising a sporty performance wrapped in a luxurious package while offering a good value. A look at the Nielsen ratings suggested "The Road Is Calling" would reach this audience with spots on NBC's Thursday night lineup of *Friends, Seinfeld,* and *ER.* Print ads were widely targeted at various segments of this market in business, sports, travel, food and wine, and home magazines.

Although the target market had been pinpointed as primarily male, Lexus aimed at women buyers as well, sponsoring such promotional events as *Bon Appétit* 's seventh annual Wine & Spirits Focus tours and a retrospective of fashion photography. Steve Sturm, Lexus's corporate marketing manager, told *Advertising Age,* "Traditionally, buyers of luxury cars are men, but we're reaching out now specifically to women who have their own income, their own sense of style for luxury cars."

In targeting a younger, hipper audience, Team One began to de-emphasize the Lexus as a sophisticated, mature product. In a 1997 spot entitled "Video Noise," a montage of futuristic imagery and alternative music were used to attract younger buyers to Lexus GS, LS, and RX models. Tom Cordner, cochairman and executive creative director for Team One, explained to *Adweek,* "The market is a little fickle now. People are in search of a brand of car, and they're experimenting more, and you want to grab their attention. At one point, they had an impression of Lexus, and we're a totally different company in terms of attitude. This was an opportunity to say to the world, 'Here is a new Lexus.' We are reaching down to a younger, hipper audience in an attempt to attract buyers we previously had not connected with."

COMPETITION

Lexus was not alone in recognizing and targeting the spending power of a more youthful audience in 1997. In *Crain's Detroit Business,* Lexus's Steve Sturm said, "The higher in price you go, the more competitive it gets. All of us are participating in a changing marketplace, and we have more changes in [model year] 1998 than any year in history. We are broadening our image to be younger, more energetic in approach."

Lexus's major competitors had their sights aimed at just this market in both ads and promotional sponsorship. In spots energized by racing camera angles and spirited music, BMW simulated the feel of being behind

A ROAD LESS TRAVELED

"Come closer. Come closer. There. I'm the road and I'm so bored. It's been so long since someone new came into my life and hugged me, caressed me, and excited me." Such were the sad, lonely longings uttered by Demi Moore as the famous Monterey, California, byway in the "17-Mile Drive" segment of "The Road Is Calling." Alas, although the 17-mile stretch of road was amply sated when the ES 300 slipped along its asphalt, it would be but a brief encounter. Lexus had to pull the "17-Mile Drive" spot soon after its original airing, when Cadillac bought all filming rights to 17-Mile Drive.

the wheel, nudging a new generation into Beemer lust. In a spin on a sophisticated wine tasting, the car company sponsored a "BMW Tasting" in a cooperative effort with *Food* & *Wine.* For the price of a test-drive, prospective buyers received free cooking pans from the magazine. Nordstrom department stores and upscale gadget retailer Hammacher Schlemmer were also the scene of BMW's special promotions. "These events don't attract huge crowds, but that's not our goal," said Rich Brooks, BMW's marketing and events communications manager, to *Advertising Age.* "The intimate setting lets us talk to high-end buyers in unique settings that suit their outlooks and lifestyles."

Mercedes underscored its reputation for elegance by sponsoring a series of co-op literary events with Condé Nast. Groups of subscribers to *Allure, Architectural Digest, Condé Nast Traveler, Gourmet, Vanity Fair,* and *Vogue* were invited to exclusive restaurants to rub elbows with author Gay Talese.

The near-luxury marketplace in 1997 was the most competitive segment among luxury manufacturers. Lexus had to contend with the emergence of the sport-utility vehicle as the new vehicle of privilege, in addition to vying for market share with their traditional competitors. Infiniti's I30 was a major competitor in the value-oriented market; Acura's TL, Audi's A4, and Volvo's 850 were gaining in visibility; BMW and Mercedes were both gaining market share after a five-year decline; and Cadillac's Catera was rumored to be lobbing a direct hit at Lexus.

MARKETING STRATEGY

Lexus and Team One pulled out all the stops in marketing the ES 300 in what would be the most integrated launch campaign in Lexus's history. The approximately $60 million campaign, which included television, print, outdoor, interactive, event, and direct-marketing mediums, was developed to express ES 300's well-rounded qualities of luxury, performance, safety, and value. It was released on October 10, 1996.

Team One's challenge was to dramatize these qualities and increase awareness of the brand. Their approach in "The Road Is Calling" was innovative. The list of car ads that featured sleek, out-of-focus, mysterious vehicles gliding down a curvaceous highway was endless, but when had the road had a say about the sexy stuff going on its blacktop? In a series of spots, Team One handed the stage to famous roads. Through the voice-overs of equally well-known celebrities, the featured roads responded passionately to playing host to the ES 300.

Via the posh voice of *Frasier* star Kelsey Grammer, Fifth Avenue was the essence of elegance. Grammer's patrician voice lent dignity to the Avenue's boredom with its day-to-day life... until the new ES 300 rolled its way. Finally, it encountered something "worthy of its asphalt." The car's performance was praised in spots featuring the Autobahn (Jeremy Irons) and the Brooklyn Bridge (Joe Pesci). Irons/Autobahn taunted, "Do you think you have what it takes to tame me?" and closed the spot by laughing, "Come back. I let you win this time." The Brooklyn Bridge, aka Joe Pesci, challenged the ES's ability to maintain a smooth ride with a tough-guy brashness and a surface pocked with potholes. "You want a piece a' me?... I got your suspension right here!" Valencia Gayles, Team One account supervisor, spoke with *Entertainment Weekly* about the Pesci spot. "He has the quintessential tough-guy voice. We look for celebrity voices that correspond to the personality of the road." One of the campaign's final spots, "Canterbury," featured John Cleese extolling the ES's safety under pressure, whereas "Wall Street" had a bullish response to the model's value. Each spot ended with the tagline "The Road Is Calling. Answer It," enticing consumers to identify not only with the car's image, but also with that of the accommodating (or challenging) road traversed. Enticement was the theme of "The Road Is Calling" print ads as well, with the road beckoning the ES in such come-hither catchphrases as "Pick Me," "Feed Me," "Yoo-Hoo," and "Take Me, I'm Yours."

Brand ads for the Lexus LS 400 depicted the ultimate intimate relationship between driver and car. In "Running Man" and "Seamless," the driver literally blended right in, visually becoming one with his Lexus. The work of makeup artist Joanne Gall, who had painted actress Demi Moore's body for an infamous *Vanity Fair* cover, was matched by the tagline, "You've never felt this connected to a car." Sturm told *Adweek,* "We have an all-new car from the inside out, and we wanted to make a dramatic and dynamic statement."

Commercials for the Lexus GS sport sedan were equally bewitching. In *Automotive News,* Bob Garfield described the haunting spots as "Edward Gorey meets William Shakespeare meets Charles Addams meets Tim Burton." An ominous female voice warned, "Ill winds mark its fearsome flight, and autumn branches creak with fright. The landscape turns to ashen crumbs, when something wicked this way comes." Then came a tagline that could give the highway patrol something to worry about: "Introducing the 300 horsepower V-8 Lexus GS. The fastest automatic sedan in the world."

The highly integrated campaign had been inaugurated by what Team One believed to be a first-ever advance E-mailing to consumers. Targeted were owners of rival cars who had stopped by Lexus's website, where a virtual test-drive was being offered. At the same time, Lexus mailed product brochures and interactive promotional videos to existing owners in advance of the ad launch.

Considered together, Team One's 1997 Lexus advertisements were tinged with a beguiling brand identity. Lexus and its major competitors were following an emerging trend in automotive advertising, that of brand building. With Lexus and its competitors all offering dazzling performance and style, the key to registering in consumer consciousness was to align the brand name with desirability. Lexus's 1998 decision to "relaunch" its original tagline, "The Relentless Pursuit of Perfection" was a direct effort to reestablish a brand identity that had held the test of time. "The Road Is Calling" ended in 1998.

OUTCOME

With the beckon "The Road Is Calling. Answer it," Lexus's ES 300 was introduced with an attitude of energetic enticement. The campaign positioned the ES 300 as the most successful launch in Lexus's history. Amid an arena crowded with competitors, the ES moved up the scale of consumer awareness thanks to the marketing efforts of the campaign. Dealership traffic was brisk, and all sales goals were exceeded during the launch time frame. The ES 300 continued to surpass monthly sales goals well beyond the initial push of the launch.

The ES 300 introduction generated an impressive level of consumer demand. Direct E-mailing and interactive promotions resulted in more than 1,100 advance orders before the ES even reached the showroom. During the first two months segment share increased from 7 percent to 12 percent, and the first six months' sales objective was exceeded by an average of 32 percent. In fact, consumer demand dramatically outpaced supply, necessitating a scaling back of advertising to allow for the limited supply.

Results of the Allison Fisher Awareness and Purchase Intention Data Study were equally decisive. The study found that demand for the ES was generated immediately upon launch, with shopping intentions moving up for four consecutive months. The ES was successful in attracting existing ES owners while also gaining share from the competition's Infiniti I30, Acura TL, Mercedes C-Class, and Volvo 850. The campaign's goal of increasing an image of good value scored high, with the ES's "reasonably priced" rating elevated to an all-time high. The performance image was also enhanced, with the model receiving its highest-ever rating for "excellent acceleration." The ES 300 gained a marked lead in the near-luxury segment in both awareness and familiarity, 10 points higher than the nearest competitor. Lexus's ad recall increased for 1997, primarily as a result of the ES 300's "The Road Is Calling" campaign.

Across the board, Team One's ads for Lexus models met with critical success. The agency's ads were seen as stylishly provocative, and Team One received the most awards from the 1997 International Automotive Advertising Awards.

Team One Advertising and Lexus had set out to inject the company's image of elegance, safety, and dependability with a fresh shot of youthful energy. "The Road Is Calling" hit this mark in spades by targeting a younger market and repainting Lexus as a near-luxury car that could deliver performance and pleasure. After the campaign's second year U.S. sales for Lexus were 60 percent higher in 1998 than they had been in 1997. December sales for the ES 300 during the campaign's final year were 2.7 percent greater than the previous December's ES 300 sales.

FURTHER READING

Caro, Mark. "Advertisers Sold on Using Major Stars for TV Voice-Overs." *Chicago Tribune,* April 10, 1998.

Enrico, Dottie. "Automakers Switch Gears on Ads." *USA Today,* October 1, 1997.

Feuer, Jack. "For Carmakers, Image Is Everything." *Crain's Detroit Business,* October 27, 1997.

Fitzgerald, Kate. "In Upscale Traffic: Magazines Offer Affluent Events for Carmakers." *Advertising Age,* January 12, 1998.

———. "Taking Tony Route: Carmakers Have Eye on Women as Autos Park at Stylish Events." *Advertising Age,* November 25, 1996.

Garfield, Bob. "Rating the Ads: Lexus Wins, Toyota Loses." *Automotive News,* October 13, 1997.

Guildford, Dave. "Lexus' New Safety Ads Depict Risky Drivers." *Advertising Age,* October 18, 1999, p. 26.

Halliday, Jean. "'99 Lexus Ads Shine Spotlight on Quality." *Automotive News,* June 29, 1998.

Johnson, Bradley. "Lexus Tries E-Mail for Auto Intro." *Advertising Age,* October 7, 1996.

Laine, Tricia. "Talk of Fame." *Entertainment Weekly,* May 8, 1998.

McCarthy, Michael. "Lexus Promotes Sportier Attitude." *Adweek,* October 7, 1996.

Taylor, Alex, and William E. Sheeline. "Competition: Here Comes Japan's New Luxury Cars." *Fortune,* August 14, 1989.

"Team One Lives up to Its Name at Awards Show." *Los Angeles Times,* January 15, 1998.

Tyrer, Kathy. "Lexus Makes an Emotional Appeal." *Adweek,* September 8, 1997.

———. "New Team One Spot Helps Lexus Let Down Its Hair." *Adweek,* September 22, 1997.

Barbra Brady
Kevin Teague

Travelocity

3150 Sabre Drive
Southlake, Texas 76092
USA
Telephone: (682) 605-1000
Fax: (817) 785-8004
E-mail: travelocity@travelocity.com
Web site: www.travelocity.com

■■■

ROAMING GNOME CAMPAIGN

OVERVIEW

The pioneering online travel-booking company known as Travelocity had enjoyed a leadership position since its launch in 1996, but it eventually lost significant market share to Expedia.com, its most aggressive competitor. Orbitz, third in market share, was also gaining ground. Travelocity was owned by Texas-based Sabre Holdings Corp., a world leader in travel commerce. To provide an emotional connection and to differentiate itself from competing online travel-booking services with similar user experiences, Travelocity launched a high-profile television, print, public relations, radio, and outdoor advertising campaign in January 2004. The campaign began with a clever premise: the "kidnapping" of a two-foot-tall gnome lawn statue who unwittingly traveled the world with his captors.

The $80 million multimedia campaign was conceived by Raleigh, North Carolina–based ad agency McKinney & Silver, an independent operating unit of worldwide communications group Havas. A three-week guerilla public relations campaign spearheaded the initiative with a poster reading, "Wanted: My garden gnome. Have you seen him?" These posters, which were distributed and posted around the United States in key media and consumer markets, featured the gnome's photo, a toll-free tip line, and the Web address www.whereismygnome.com. Corresponding print ads showed a two-foot-tall garden gnome with a ruddy complexion and pointy red cap and used the identical poster copy, purportedly written by the gnome's desperate owner, "Bill." Next the TV campaign broke on January 1, 2004, during the Rose Bowl.

Once the gnome's peripatetic premise was established, the roaming continued with vigor. In 2005 the campaign won a Gold EFFIE Award, which gave international recognition to ad campaigns for their measured marketing effectiveness. The gnome even had his own merchandise Web page on the Travelocity.com site, physical proof of the power of the campaign's effective branding to invigorate sales. Midway through the campaign an updated tagline, "You'll never roam alone," was added to showcase the new "Travelocity Guarantee" and "Customer Bill of Rights."

HISTORICAL CONTEXT

Before the widespread use of the Internet by consumers, only travel professionals used computer systems to find itineraries and prices of travel offerings. In 1996 Sabre Holdings opened a new business called Travelocity, a website at which the consumer user could find on his own the same transportation, hotel, and related travel offerings. Competitors Expedia and Orbitz joined the fray, but all three websites functioned similarly, and consumer differentiation was nonexistent.

In the two years prior to the "Roaming Gnome" campaign Travelocity had struggled, losing its industry-leading status to rival Expedia, and it had faced increased competition from Orbitz, which was funded by airlines. Travelocity had never recorded a profit and found itself playing catch-up as competitors unveiled new features and vacation packages. The company thus beefed up its promotional efforts in mid-2002 with "Travelocity Can," a $40 million branding campaign consisting of TV, radio, print, and online advertising that highlighted travel possibilities available both through the website and by calling the phone number 888-Travelocity. The campaign presented Travelocity.com as a "travel dream factory" that served as the ultimate consumer resource for all travel needs. TV advertising consisted of two 30-second spots, which were supported by corresponding print and online ads. "Wedding," one of the TV spots, highlighted the resources available through the site by featuring travelers in places all over the world. The second spot, "Elephant," showed people experiencing things that they had never dreamed possible, such as renting an elephant, because of the help they had received via Travelocity.com's travel tools. David Hall, principal for the Richards Group, the agency that created the campaign, said, "we feature real-life people describing how Travelocity helped them plan their entire trip."

In 2003 Travelocity's revenue grew 16.5 percent to $394.5 million, although the company reported a $100 million operating loss. Of the 64 million travelers who planned trips online in 2004, 45 million booked on the Internet, which reflected an increase of 6 percent over 2003, according to the Travel Industry Association of Washington, D.C.

In October 2003 Travelocity hired the Raleigh-based firm McKinney & Silver to create new marketing ideas. The gnome idea was one of proposals the agency had made during its bid for the Travelocity ad contract. "We thought the gnome was really lovable, someone who has a sense of the fun of travel," Susan McLaughlin, vice president of marketing for Travelocity, told the *News & Observer*.

GNOME, COME HOME: HOW TRAVELOCITY'S MASCOT WAS BORN

In a 2004 *Christian Science Monitor* article, Susan McLaughlin, vice president of marketing and merchandising at Travelocity, was quoted as attributing the gnome inspiration to a curious custom in Europe, where gnomes that decorated lawns and gardens were stolen and then taken on trips by pranksters, who sent the gnome owners amusing "ransom" notes with photographs of their missing gnomes on vacation.

The custom gained worldwide appeal via the 2001 French film *Amelie,* in which the protagonist, in an effort to inspire her father to travel, conspired with a flight attendant to send her father's gnome on a photo-documented tour of foreign landmarks. Years before *Amelie* the long-running British soap opera *Coronation Street* featured a similar plot in which a man stole his neighbor's gnome and then taunted him with ransom letters.

According to David Emery, a writer and specialist in urban legends, gnome-napping was an international phenomenon with at least a 20-year history that started in Australia when a Sydney family's gnome disappeared. In France the Front de Libération des Nains de Jardin (Garden Gnome Liberation Front) had reportedly "liberated" more than 6,000 gnomes since 1997. Several French websites were devoted to this cause.

TARGET MARKET

Traditionally women were responsible for purchasing leisure travel in most U.S. households, said Henry Harteveldt, an analyst at Forrester Research, a market-research firm. Travelocity's research indicated that there was a subset of high-value online travel purchasers who appeared to be potentially more loyal to Travelocity than others. Further analysis showed an attitudinal profile of these people, which resulted in the identification of an opportunity segment that Travelocity marketing executives called "The Insiders." This group of 44 million people (33 percent of leisure travelers) loved to travel and was active, self-directed, resourceful, information-hungry, and Internet-savvy. The so-called "Insiders" loved to discover new things and liked to feel that they were "in the know." They also enjoyed passing their "Insider" knowledge on to others.

Additional markets the company identified included affluent, middle-aged, career-driven professionals; comfortable retirees (both couples and singles); young singles and newlyweds who worked hard and played hard; affluent, educated couples, with or without children, who led active cultural and recreational lives; and 40-something, middle-income families whose teen-dominated households kept them busy.

COMPETITION

Expedia, Travelocity, and Orbitz all ranked among the top 10 in sales, but traditional travel agencies American Express Travel and Minneapolis-based Carlson Wagonlit

Travel still claimed the top two positions in 2005. Travelocity struggled with losing share to Expedia and facing increasing competition from Orbitz. In 2002 Expedia held a 36 percent market share, with Travelocity at 24 percent and Orbitz at 13 percent. Expedia spent $95 million on media in 2002, compared with $70 million for Orbitz and $59 million for Travelocity, according to TNS Media Intelligence/CMR.

In 2001 Expedia launched a television, print, and outdoor campaign, devised by the Los Angeles office of ad agency Deutsch, that used travel humor as its selling point. The TV spots showed unhappy but amusing travel scenarios played as flash-forward vignettes. The protagonist rethought and then rebooked his or her trip, precluding the potential ill-fated excursion. For example, in the spot "Business Trip," a woman reconfigured her trip in order to avoid an obnoxious male colleague who would have otherwise sat next to her throughout it. "House Party" showed a couple rethinking the wisdom of leaving their teenage son home during a vacation as they imagined a wild teen party. The couple then booked a trip to include the teen. "The campaign attempts to own better travel planning, which equals better travel experience," Eric Hirshberg, executive creative director at Deutsch, told *USA Today.* "These spots demonstrate the breadth and depth of Expedia's travel tools and how easy they are to use to plan and book your trip." Realistic casting added appeal to the target consumer, described as regular folk instead of "aspirational" travelers.

Competitor Orbitz aimed to put the romance and fun back into travel with its "Visit Planet Earth" print campaign, which was released in mid-2001, prior to the corresponding TV campaign. To inspire the kind of warmth and excitement that it asserted that consumers ought to feel in traveling, Orbitz's agency, New York–based TBWA\Chiat\Day, tapped the original artists behind the fun, mod travel posters of the 1960s and '70s.

MARKETING STRATEGY

"We did a lot of consumer research, and they told us all the websites look alike. They're all visually cluttered," said Jeff Glueck, Travelocity's chief marketing officer, in an interview with the Fort Worth *Star-Telegram.* Once McKinney & Silver signed on, it tackled the problem of how to explore new directions and regain Travelocity's market share in the online travel business. Glueck explained that the idea for the traveling gnome originated with agency group creative directors Philip Marchington and Lisa Shimotakahara. They had noticed a news story about a group calling itself the Gnome Liberation Front, which kidnapped garden gnomes in France and ran a website about it. "We thought, what a great spokesman for a travel brand," Glueck said.

"Tour Guide," a 30-second spot, showed the gnome, obviously enjoying his kidnapping, driving a double-decker bus through the streets of London. Speaking with a slight British accent, he narrated postcards meant for his owner Bill. They were snapshots of his adventures and showed him on a ski lift, in a spa, and almost fully submerged in a hot tub. The campaign tagline, "Book with Travelocity. Don't Forget Your Hat," was meant to convey the idea that the brand took care of its customers' needs.

Travelocity strove to set itself apart from the competition by positioning the company as one that gave customers the best possible travel experiences, with a range of choices from the beginning of the booking process to the completion of the trip. Travelocity developed a strategy based on initially creating "pre-buzz" through grassroots efforts; once a real "buzz" had been created among consumers, the roaming gnome was connected to Travelocity as the website's new face. This strategy guided the tactics and the overall timing and implementation of the campaign.

To pique consumer and media interest prior to revealing the gnome's connection with Travelocity, the company and ad agency McKinney & Silver designed a "Missing Gnome" poster, describing the gnome's kidnapping from his fictional owner, Bill. The posters featured the gnome's photo, a toll-free tip line, and the Web address www.whereismygnome.com. Posters were distributed and posted around the country in key media and consumer markets. Additionally, more than 2,500 handwritten letters were mailed on Bill's behalf, soliciting help from reporters for the gnome's safe return. Efforts surrounding the gnome's pre-buzz included outreach to key travel industry analysts; to crime, lifestyle, and metro reporters at community, daily, and national newspapers; and to on-air personalities and news-assignment editors at radio and TV stations in the top 25 U.S. media markets.

OUTCOME

"We think this is the only time in history when the spending went up after the pitch," McKinney & Silver CEO Brad Brinegar said to the *News & Observer,* referring to the tendency of some clients to cut back their spending plans after awarding an account to an ad agency. Campaign results included successfully generating brand awareness. The effectiveness of the three-week teaser, which ran from December 2003 to January 2004, was demonstrated by the 1,554,000 hits received at the wheresmygnome.com website and by the 3,180 E-mails sent to Bill, the gnome's fictitious owner. Brand momentum led to increased visits to the Travelocity website, and after just one month of the new campaign, site hits were

250 percent over the original goal; through July 2004 hits were 108 percent over the goal. The campaign won a 2005 Gold EFFIE Award for campaign efficacy in the specialized Retail/E-tail category.

FURTHER READING

Ahles, Andrea. "New Chief Executive for Travelocity Faces Uphill Road to Profitability." *Fort Worth (TX) Star-Telegram,* February 2, 2004.

———. "Travelocity Hopes Gnome Ad Campaign Will Relaunch Brand." *Fort Worth (TX) Star-Telegram,* January 6, 2004.

Anderson, Mae. "Behind the Scenes." *Adweek,* January, 24,2005, p. 26.

Fuquay, Jim. "Travelocity Posts First Profit Ever in Second Quarter." *Fort Worth (TX) Star-Telegram,* July 23, 2004.

———. "Travelocity to Unveil New Website Design." *Fort Worth (TX) Star-Telegram,* March 25, 2004.

Garfield, Bob. "Garfield's AdReview: Travelocity Vagabond Gnome Talks, but to Wrong Audience." *Advertising Age,* January 26, 2004, p. 33.

Howard, Theresa. "Expedia Ads Focus on Vacation Experience, Not Just Fares." *USA Today,* March 21, 2004.

Lazare, Lewis. "Travelocity's 'Roaming Gnome' Idea Came from European Custom." *Chicago Sun-Times,* January 9, 2004, p. 51.

Lovel, Jim. "David Baldwin On the Spot." *Adweek,* January 24, 2005, pp. 28–28.

Pierceall, Kimberly. "Industry Refines Services as Competition from Web Grows." *Riverside (CA) Press-Enterprise,* August 28, 2005.

Rajewski, Genevieve. "Roaming Gnomes in the News Again." *Christian Science Monitor,* January 30, 2004, p. 14.

Ranii, David. "Travelocity Books $80 Million with North Carolina Marketing Firm for Gnome Ads." *Raleigh (NC) News & Observer,* January 7, 2004.

Thomaselli, Rich. "Travelocity Hands McKinney $30M Biz." *Advertising Age,* October 27, 2003.

Trickett, Eleanor. "The Mix: Travelocity Pulls Off Hard Task of Sustaining Simultaneous Memorable Branding Efforts." *PR Week,* January 17, 2005.

Jan Arrigo

Triarc Companies, Inc.

280 Park Ave.
New York, New York 10017
USA
Telephone: (212) 451-3000
Fax: (212) 451-3134
Web site: www.snapple.com

RETURN OF THE SNAPPLE LADY CAMPAIGN

OVERVIEW

On June 5, 1997, Wendy Kaufman, known to millions of consumers as "the Snapple Lady," was welcomed back as a brand spokesperson after an almost two-year hiatus. The move completed a circle of sorts for Snapple, a brewer of iced teas and fruit flavored beverages that just three months earlier had been purchased by the Triarc Beverage Group. A stormy period of declining sales as a subsidiary of the Quaker Oats Company—during which the highly popular Snapple Lady was ushered out of the spotlight—was now over, and Snapple was in a mood to celebrate.

The Kaufman announcement was made in midtown Manhattan in New York City with style, flair, and a healthy dose of kitsch, all trademarks of the Snapple brand. Triarc retooled an empty storefront at 319 Fifth Avenue (at the corner of 32nd Street) to resemble an old-fashioned New York deli. Mike Weinstein, chief executive officer of the Triarc Beverage Group, stood up to welcome the media, distributors, and invited guests. Then Kaufman, escorted by several Snapple trucks, drove up to the "deli" on a parade float modeled to replicate the label of Snapple Orange Tropic, the new drink the company had formulated to commemorate her return. Kaufman then burst into the press conference to announce that she was, in fact, reunited with Snapple. A video of her latest Snapple television commercial was then played for the invited guests.

The commercial and the campaign were designed to return Snapple to its roots. This was an important strategy for a brand that had seen its sales decline by 21 percent during two years of Quaker Oats management. Triarc executives hoped the return of the Snapple Lady would energize the brand and once again put it in the forefront of American consumer consciousness.

The stakes were high for the new campaign. Triarc Companies, a holding company whose subsidiaries were engaged in beverages, restaurants, and propane distribution, spent $300 million in March 1997 to secure control of Snapple from Quaker Oats Company, the maker of Gatorade, Cap'n Crunch, and Rice-a-Roni brands. The acquisition added to the company's beverage interests, which also included subsidiaries Mistic Beverages and Stewart's. The company was also the franchiser for more than 3,000 Arby's fast-food restaurants. In addition, Triarc owned 43 percent of National Propane Partners.

HISTORICAL CONTEXT

Founded in 1972 in Brooklyn, New York, Snapple began as a natural soda sold in health food stores. By the early 1980s the line had expanded to include fruit flavors with evocative names like Mango Madness and Tropical

Fantasy. Later the company added a line of bottled teas as well. On its packaging Snapple emphasized the "natural" aspects of its beverages. The brand attracted a loyal following, particularly among college students and hip young professionals. Other companies soon moved to market similar products. By the end of the 1980s the so-called "New Age drink" market was growing briskly at 50 to 100 percent a year.

Kaufman became known as the Snapple Lady, answering mail for the Long Island-based beverage company. Majoring in film and sociology at Syracuse University, Kaufman spent eight years of dispatching trucks at her father's metal warehouse before getting a job in Snapple's order department in 1991. Having learned the workings of the beverage business, Kaufman started personally to answer consumers' letters to Snapple headquarters. Her oft-stated sentiment was that if people cared enough about Snapple to take time to write to the company, the company owed it to the consumers to respond. The company, which traded on a folksy image, decided to incorporate Kaufman into its ad campaign in 1993, and 36 award-winning television commercials between 1993 and early 1996 would ensue.

The spots were decidedly low-concept. In most of them Kaufman simply sat behind a desk and answered letters from Snapple consumers. "Hi and hello from Snapple," she predictably announced in her Long Island accent. Yet something about her authenticity and sense of humor struck a chord with audiences across the country. "I don't play the part, I *am* the part," she once observed, and Snapple drinkers embraced her as a company spokesperson they could relate to. As Snapple's "ambassador of goodwill," Kaufman did more than just appear in television commercials. She traveled the country performing promotional activities for the company, such as attending a prom with a New Jersey fan and dancing with the Los Angeles Classical Ballet. She even took a whirlpool bath in kiwi strawberry flavored Snapple in order to promote that new drink.

The "Snapple Lady" campaign came during a time of enormous growth for the brand. Between 1989 and 1993 Snapple sales rose from $23.6 million to $516 million. The ads and promotional activities made Kaufman a minor celebrity. She appeared on television talk shows like *Oprah, Regis and Kathy Lee,* and *The Rosie O'Donnell Show.* But her time in the national spotlight would run out when cereal giant Quaker Oats bought Snapple for $1.7 billion in December 1994.

There were ominous portents almost as soon as the Quaker Oats acquisition was completed. Some analysts noted that the allure of the so-called New Age beverages, which had gained popularity across the country, was fading at the time. Quaker Oats then compounded its troubles by trying to meld the Snapple distribution network into its top-selling Gatorade network, which did not go over well with distributors.

Quaker Oats then gave the green light to a series of new television commercials, dismissing Snapple Lady Kaufman just months before the expiration of her contract. The new spots, launched in April 1996, followed a four-month television advertising blackout, during which time Quaker Oats worked intensely to develop a new strategy for the struggling brand. For the first commercials of this campaign, created by agency Kirshenbaum, Bond & Partners, the iced tea and juice marketer tapped filmmaker Spike Lee to helm one of five new television spots. Echoing the old "We Try Harder" campaign for Avis Rent-a-Car, the new Snapple spots trumpeted the fact that while Snapple was not in the same league as soft-drink giants Coca-Cola or Pepsi-Cola, it would be happy as a high-ranking also-ran. "Threedom Equals Freedom" and "We Want to Be No. 3" were the tag lines for the spots. Some viewers were confused by the abruptness of the Snapple Lady's departure from the scene. Neither Quaker Oats nor Spike Lee offered any explanation for the change. "She had her run," said Lee.

While being proud to be third might have sufficed as a quirky campaign mantra, it proved unsuccessful as a market proposition. The campaign left consumers confused about the brand's identity, and Snapple took a beating from competitors who saw its problems as an opportunity to pour new products onto the market. The high-priced ads did nothing to slow the erosion in Snapple sales. Quaker Oats executives ultimately were forced to try giving the drink away in a $40 million summer campaign to try to lure skeptical consumers back to the brand. Despite these efforts, Snapple endured a $100 million loss in 1996.

In March 1997 Quaker Oats sold Snapple to Triarc Companies, Inc,. for less than one-fourth of what it had paid for the brand. The diminution was a result of losses that totaled $160 million in 1995 and 1996 alone and sales that dropped 21 percent in two years to $550 million. Triarc Companies, Inc., was perhaps ideally suited to try to revive the sagging fortunes of Snapple. Best known for its RC Cola brand, subsidiary Royal Crown Company made flavor concentrates for private-label soft drinks. The company was run by financiers Nelson Peltz and Peter May, who profited from several large investments in the 1980s. The pair eventually bought a controlling stake in Triarc, an industrial conglomerate then known as DWG Corp., from financier Victor Posner in 1993 for $71.8 million. In the 1990s Triarc began to focus on beverages and restaurants, purchasing the Mistic teas and juice drinks and the T. J. Cinnamons restaurant chain. It operated almost 3,000 restaurants, including Arby's and P. T. Noodles.

One of Triarc's first orders of business was to renew its association with Kaufman, and the beloved Snapple Lady was soon appearing in Snapple ads once again. In addition, a new Snapple flavor, Snapple Orange Tropic, was developed as part of a new line dubbed Wendy's Tropical Inspiration. Calling Kaufman "the embodiment of Snapple's lovable, offbeat nature," company officials appointed her to the newly created post of Snapple Ambassador for Community Relations.

TARGET MARKET

The New Age segment of the beverage category began as an alternative to highly carbonated soft drinks, offering iced teas, fruit-based beverages, and flavored waters in the 1980s. In the 1990s new New Age alternatives included caffeinated waters, herbal concoctions, and "premium" sodas with less sweetness and carbonation. By this time non-colas had grown to command more than 60 percent of the soft-drink market.

Snapple was created by a trio of marketers from Long Island: Leonard Marsh and Hyman Golden, brothers-in-law who owned a window-washing company; and Arnold Greenberg, who had a health food store. Because the three did not have the financial clout of the big soft-drink makers, they marketed mainly to small stores. Along the way their beverage developed a cachet among the young and trendy. This sought-after cachet was encouraged with clever advertising and the constant introduction of new, offbeat flavors. In the late 1990s Snapple continued to market its products to those young and health-conscious consumers who preferred an alternative to colas.

COMPETITION

Beverage industry giants Coca-Cola and Pepsi were to a large degree responsible for the slump in sales in the New Age beverage category that betokened the sale of Snapple to Triarc and the return of the Snapple Lady. Their glitzy marketing campaigns and big-budget commercials helped depress Snapple sales to the point where Quaker Oats found it necessary to sell the brand. Triarc's only recourse seemed to be a "back to the roots" strategy designed to recapture Snapple's lost consumers.

Snapple's overall success emboldened the giant soda makers to develop fruit and tea products to compete in this market. Coca-Cola spent an estimated $15-20 million to promote its Fruitopia brand of juices. Pepsi also embarked on an expensive relaunch of its Lipton's Brew brand of ready-to-drink teas.

FIFTEEN MINUTES AND COUNTING

"I never left Snapple. Snapple left me," Wendy Kaufman observed following her re-hiring by the beverage maker in 1997. "When Quaker came into the picture they decided I was no longer the image they wanted to project, that I had had my time, and that they wanted to go mainstream." That was the extent of the public bitterness expressed by Kaufman (although she did make a point of saying, "I'll never eat oatmeal again"—a not-so-veiled jab at Quaker Oats, Snapple's erstwhile parent company—at her reintroduction extravaganza). The happy-go-lucky Long Island native seemed to have accepted her so-called fifteen minutes of fame with an equanimity that other celebrities could learn from.

While away from Snapple Kaufman tried a few other show business gigs. She held a job hosting a radio call-in advice segment called "Ask Wendy" and appeared briefly in the Chevy Chase film *National Lampoon's Vegas Vacation.* But she could not escape the image that she had built for herself as a heartfelt iced-tea pitchwoman—especially after a Colorado disc jockey launched a "Bring Back Wendy" campaign. Kaufman even turned down an offer to promote Mistic soft drinks because her heart reportedly remained with Snapple. "I was heartbroken," she said of her dismissal. "All I wanted to be was the Snapple Lady." In March 1997 she got her wish—and so did her legions of fans worldwide.

MARKETING STRATEGY

Before Quaker Oats purchased Snapple in 1994, growth in the New Age beverage category had slowed to about 20 percent from the highs of the 1980s. By the end of 1995 Snapple sales had fallen 9 percent, and the brand lost $100 million including charges and write-offs. "What the hell is Snapple?" groused corporate brand consultant Alan Brew in March 1997. "No one knows what it means anymore." Indeed, the single greatest challenge faced by Triarc marketers in the wake of the beverage company's acquisition of Snapple was to rebuild the brand's identity. "It's not edgy anymore, but we can bring that edginess back," declared Triarc Beverage Group CEO Weinstein. He immediately entered into negotiations with Kaufman to discuss her future role with Snapple.

"Time is of the essence because summer is coming," Kaufman remarked after their initial meeting. "One more year of bad Snapple advertising would be devastating for the brand." Heeding Kaufman's advice, Triarc in May 1997 announced that it had hired the New York-based ad agency Deutsch to create advertising for Snapple. The $40 million account had been in the hands of Chicago agency Foote, Cone, and Belding. Kirshenbaum, Bond & Partners, Snapple's original agency, was contacted by Triarc but declined to offer a pitch for the account.

With Deutsch now in charge of the creative side, Kaufman was once again tapped to star in a Snapple television commercial. This spot, however, finds her venturing far afield from her previous role as a company ombudsman responding to consumer letters. The new spot traces the efforts of a search party that has set out to find the missing Snapple Lady. The searchers eventually trace her steps to an island near Bora Bora, where the rotund New Yorker is being worshiped as a god by the natives. Kaufman is ultimately located and returned to Snapple headquarters. "They need me!" she says as a rowboat whisks her away from the island paradise. The commercial ends with a humorous twist as one of the islanders mistranslates her parting words as "we can eat you" and looks menacingly on the team of rescuers. The ad plays humorously off of Kaufman's oft-repeated public pronouncement that she spends her time away from Snapple touring the tropics.

Snapple Orange Tropic, the product commemorating Kaufman's renewed association with the company, blended fruit juices and purees to conjure up "the tastes and scents of the tropics," according to a company press release. The all-natural beverage contained 12 percent juice. It also featured Kaufman on its packaging. The 16-ounce bottles of the new product were wrapped by a whimsical drawing of the Snapple Lady relaxing in her island getaway. Reclining on a chaise lounge and outfitted in a floral dress with a lei and a fruit-topped hat, Kaufman is shown surrounded by lobsters, fish, and tropical birds. Palm trees and tropical plants and flowers serve as a backdrop. The new drink was distributed for a limited time starting in June 1997.

Weinstein stressed that Kaufman's return would not be a one-time proposition. While she would not be asked to fulfill her previous role answering letters and would no longer serve as company spokesperson, the Snapple Lady would be deployed to make personal appearances and aid the brand in other ways. Although Kaufman's potency as a pitchwoman was said to be strongest on the East Coast, due to her pronounced New York accent, Weinstein also emphasized Snapple's commitment to remain a national brand.

OUTCOME

The return of the Snapple Lady seemed to generate the kind of energy around the Snapple brand that its marketing executives had hoped for. Kaufman's coming-out party was heralded with a blitz of free publicity in Snapple's core East Coast markets, as local newscasts scrambled to cover the return of the prodigal pitchwoman. The commercials themselves evaded the usual critical scrutiny as reviewers preferred to remark on the new aspects of Kaufman's reemergence.

Kaufman soon settled into her role as spokesperson emeritus for Snapple brands. She rode the Snapple Orange Tropic Float in the 24th Annual New York City Halloween Parade on October 31, 1997. Meanwhile, Triarc went about the business of crafting a long-term marketing and advertising strategy for the brand. During this period sales rebounded. For the year ending March 1, 1998, dollar sales of refrigerated teas grew 4.8 percent, with Snapple leading the market. Triarc stewardship halted a three-year sales decline and actually increased Snapple case volume slightly in the second half of 1997 compared to the second half of the previous year. The return of the Snapple Lady—along with improved distributor relationships, targeted advertising, and product innovation—was credited with the upswing.

In the spring of 1998 Snapple introduced a new tag line, "The Best Stuff Is in Here," in commercials that retained the quirkiness of previous ads but without the Snapple Lady. The product-focused spots were designed to illustrate the wide variety of Snapple flavors and were again created by Deutsch New York. Industry analysts were undecided about whether the brand's turnaround was permanent or temporary.

FURTHER READING

Beatty, Sally Goll. "Quaker Wants Snapple to Be No. 3, But Will the Strategy Bear Fruit?" *The Wall Street Journal,* April 2, 1996, p. B6.

Petrecca, Laura, and Judann Pollack. "Snapple's Wendy Returns via Deutsch." *Advertising Age,* May 19, 1997, p. 1.

"Snapple Lady Gets Her Job Back." *The Baltimore Sun,* June 26, 1997, p. 3E.

Wells, Melanie. "She May Be Back in a Snapple." *USA Today,* April 28, 1997, p. 2B.

Robert Schnakenberg

Turner Broadcasting System, Inc.

One CNN Center
100 International Boulevard
Atlanta, Georgia 30303
USA
Telephone: (404) 827-1700
Fax: (404) 827-2437
Web site: www.turner.com

31 DAYS OF OSCAR CAMPAIGN

OVERVIEW

In 1994 Turner Classic Movies (TCM) was a small start-up cable network with a collection of 4,000 movies, 21 employees, an operating budget of between $13 and $15 million, and 1 million subscribers. TCM also had the backing of television giant Turner Broadcasting System (TBS). Within a year of its launch TCM had increased its subscriptions to include 4.3 million homes, and its classic movie library had grown to 5,600 films. But the new network had a goal of being the leading classic movie brand. To help achieve this goal, the network in 1995 introduced its "31 Days of Oscar" marketing campaign, which every year ran during March, the month of the Academy Awards.

By 2002, "31 Days of Oscar" had become a staple of advertising for the commercial-free, all-movies network, but to broaden its appeal to a younger audience while not alienating its core viewers—middle-aged Americans—the network reevaluated the campaign. For the updated version of "31 Days of Oscar," TCM partnered with the New York-based agency nicebigbrain and creative Jim Jenkins to produce a series of three ads that spoofed classic movies. The ads were shown as trailers in theaters and also as television spots. The first ad was a takeoff on the film *Rocky* that featured senior citizens in the starring roles. This was followed by a rendition of *Ben-Hur* performed by second and third graders, and the third was a remake of *The Dirty Dozen* that was set in an ice rink, with skaters taking the roles. While the company did not release budget figures for the campaign, previous budgets reportedly had ranged from $1 to several millions.

TCM's decision to shift its marketing strategy was a success. The "Rocky" ad earned a Bronze Lion at Cannes, and the overall campaign as well as the individual ads earned gold awards in several categories from Promax. In addition, the campaign appeared to achieve the goal of attracting younger viewers to the network.

HISTORICAL CONTEXT

In 1994 Turner Network Television (TNT) launched the commercial-free, all-movies cable channel TCM. The new channel went head-to-head with the long-running cable network American Movie Classics (AMC). TCM's enticement to persuade cable providers to include the new network in its channel listings was its library of 4,000 movies, which dated from the 1930s to modern classics such as *Chinatown* and *Ordinary People.* The network's broader movie offerings were also expected to draw younger viewers than those who typically tuned in to AMC.

Within a year the TCM library had grown to 5,600 movies, which included 2,300 films obtained in licensing deals with Paramount and Columbia Pictures, Warner Bros., and MGM/UA. Its subscriptions had increased from 1 million to 4.3 million homes. Fueling the new channel's growth was its ability to advertise on other Turner-owned networks, including TNT, Cable News Network (CNN), and TBS Superstation.

In 1995, to promote its commercial-free programming, TCM launched the marketing campaign "31 Days of Oscar." As part of the campaign TNT ran a special program titled *Inside the Academy Awards.* The TNT promotion kicked off the campaign, which included showing only films that had won or been nominated for Academy Awards during the month of March. TCM's "31 Days of Oscar" campaign became an annual marketing event for the network, with a budget by 1999 that was reported to be "several million dollars," according to *Multichannel News.* As well as print ads and cross-channel television spots, the campaign included movie trivia contests. In 2000 TCM's director of marketing, Katherine Evans, told *Multichannel News* that the annual "31 Days of Oscar" campaign was the network's highest profile event, with a budget of about $1 million. According to Evans, the company devoted about six months annually to planning for the campaign. "31 Days of Oscar is something we never stop thinking about. As soon as this [year] is over, we'll do a postmortem and start working on the next year," she said.

ATTRACTING YOUNGER VIEWERS

Turner Classic Movies (TCM) has traditionally appealed to an older audience. In 2003 the average age of its viewers was 56. That year TCM, hoping to attract younger television watchers, launched a series titled *Under the Influence.* According to the network, the new series reached out to viewers who were between 18 and 34 and who might not be familiar with movies from the 1930s to the 1960s. "A lot of our audiences are older Americans who have a built-in relevance to our movies, but our challenge is to create that relevance among younger viewers," Tom Karsch, TCM's senior vice president and general manager, told *Multichannel News.* The series featured contemporary stars talking about classic movies they had been inspired by, as well as screenings of more recent films that would resonate with the target audience, such as *Ferris Bueller's Day Off* and *Austin Powers: International Man of Mystery.*

TARGET MARKET

From its inception TCM had aimed the "31 Days of Oscar" campaign at serious film buffs of all ages. In 2002, in an effort to attract younger viewers, TCM shifted its marketing focus by sending the message that classic films had an impact on current culture. TCM hoped to show younger audiences that the events from the past portrayed in classic movies had relevance to contemporary life. In an discussion in *Broadcasting & Cable,* a quote attributed to actress Elizabeth Taylor—"The only difference from movies and real life is better lighting and music"—was used to explain the inspiration for reaching out to young viewers: The network was careful, however, not to abandon traditional viewers, those in the 55-and-older demographic. Many of TCM's core viewers had seen the movies in the network's line-up as original releases in theaters, and they tuned in to watch once again those movies they had enjoyed when they first appeared on the big screen.

COMPETITION

In 1984, when AMC joined the list of cable television networks, it was the premier choice for viewers in search of commercial-free, all-movies programming. AMC held that position for 10 years, until in 1994 TNT launched TCM. The race for viewers was then on. At the time industry experts questioned whether there were enough viewers to support two all-movie channels and whether cable operators were interested in offering subscribers both networks. But when TCM was launched, AMC executives commented that they expected their new competitor to be a great channel.

By 1995 AMC counted 54 million subscribers, compared to 4.3 million for TCM, but the new network was positioning itself to take over the classic movie brand. Hurting AMC was the fact that it did not own the movies it showed. Rather, the network depended on licensing agreements with studios such as RKO, which was owned by TBS, the parent of TCM. Predictions that within 10 years AMC would be driven out of business by TCM pushed Kate McEnroe, AMC's executive vice president and general manager, to ask, "If AMC is going out of business in 10 years, does that mean that A&E, ESPN and HBO are going out of business?" She noted that those cable networks also did not own their products.

AMC responded to pressures from TCM with aggressive advertising and consumer marketing campaigns that began in 1994. The network also shifted from its all-movies format to develop original programming that appealed to a broader audience. In 2002 AMC was still in business and tackling TCM's successful "31 Days of Oscar" campaign with its own event, the 10th annual *Film Preservation Festival.* Programming included documentaries of highlights from 1970s movies, as well as screenings of movies like *The Last Waltz, This Is Spinal Tap,* and *Saturday Night Fever.*

While AMC and TCM were battling for classic movie viewers, A&E Television Networks in 2002 was updating its 14-year-old flagship program, *Biography.* According to a report in *Crain's New York Business,* the program had "become somewhat stodgy and plodding." The show had lost its appeal to younger viewers as well as to older audiences who preferred faster-paced, edgier cable programming. The network reported that the viewership of *Biography* had slipped from 1.6 million in 2000 to 1.1 million by 2002, and the audience of 18- to 49-year-old viewers had dropped from 494,000 to 288,000.

To revitalize its floundering network, A&E updated its programming and launched a campaign designed to lure back viewers. To increase its appeal to younger viewers, the network updated the movie celebrities and other people it profiled. Included were such contemporary actors as Tom Hanks and Jerry Seinfeld, rather than performers from the past like actress Judy Garland or actor and former president Ronald Reagan, who typically attracted an older audience. A television spot promoting a *Biography* segment on soccer player Pelé featured a close-up of Bill Clinton with a voice-over saying, "You've scored more than any player in history." Other changes included a program titled *TVography,* which profiled a television program rather than a person, and man-on-the-street interviews on *Biography* subjects. To promote *Biography* further and to celebrate the program's 15th anniversary, A&E launched a 10-city tour in 2002 that included stops in Los Angeles, Denver, and Chicago.

MARKETING STRATEGY

In 2002, for the eighth year, TCM used the "31 Days of Oscar" campaign as a marketing strategy to promote its library of Academy-winning or -nominated films and to attract viewers. It was the first year, however, the network had taken a tongue-in-cheek approach. The three ads of the campaign were spoofs of the classic movies *Rocky, Ben-Hur,* and *The Dirty Dozen.* The ads, which were laced with humor, were designed to appeal to young adults as well as to older film afficionados. Tom Karsch, TCM's executive vice president and general manager, said in an interview with *Multichannel News* that, while "31 Days of Oscar" had always been the gem in the network's crown, it was time to make the campaign more entertaining. "It was time to have some fun with it, and do something a little different, and call attention to the festival in a nontraditional way," he said. TCM executives declined to provide the cost of the campaign, but Karsch told *Multichannel News* that the eighth edition of "31 Days of Oscar" was the network's biggest promotion to date. In terms of marketing support from affiliates, he put the value overall to be "in the millions."

TCM devoted almost its entire 2002 marketing budget to production of the "Rocky" ad, which featured residents of a retirement home starring in a remake of the classic movie. During the ad senior citizens duked it out in a boxing ring, throwing knockout punches and reciting memorable lines from the movie, including "Rocky, you're breaking the ribs" and "Can you take off you're hat? I always knew you was pretty." A voice-over at the end of the ad stated, "31 straight days of Oscar-nominated movies. It's bound to have an effect. Watch *Rocky* and 300 other commercial-free classics ... all March long."

The hilarious remake of *Rocky* was such a hit with audiences that TCM ordered additional ads focusing on two other classic films. TCM's agency, nicebigbrain, staged the second ad as an elementary school version of *Ben-Hur,* with second- and third-graders playing the parts. Hearing a seven-year-old recite the classic line "Your eyes are filled with hate, Ben-Hur. That's good, hate keeps a man alive," followed by a cough that steamed up the child's glasses, or seeing a child throw himself under the hooves of a hobbyhorse generated laughs and more praise for the campaign.

"Dirty Dozen on Ice," a spoof on the film *The Dirty Dozen,* was the third ad in the campaign. Described as "laugh-out-loud funny" by *Adweek,* it was set in an ice arena, with the prisoners training for their suicide mission while executing all of the jumps and moves of seasoned figure skaters. The skaters shouted, "Let's go kill some Nazis," before crashing through a picture of Adolf Hitler. Then came the order "Blow it, Jefferson," and with the skills of a hockey star the character tossed hand grenades into the vents. Both the "Ben-Hur" and "Dirty Dozen on Ice" ads used the tagline "When every great movie is a classic, it's bound to have an effect."

The ads were shown as trailers in theaters in New York, Los Angeles, Atlanta, and Denver, and they were aired as television spots on affiliated stations in New York and Los Angeles, on the Turner networks, and on radio stations. TCM also partnered with sister network Home Box Office (HBO) to generate consumer awareness and increase the ratings for the "31 Days of Oscar" programming.

OUTCOME

Although TCM's "31 Days of Oscar" had long been considered successful, the campaign hit a high note with its 2002 effort. "Rocky" and "Dirty Dozen on Ice" won recognition from *Adweek* as Best Spots, and "Rocky" also won a 2003 Cannes Lions Bronze Award. Promax recognized campaign and the ads with a list of gold awards in several categories; the overall campaign won in the category Program Campaign Using More Than One Media, and "Rocky" and "Dirty Dozen on Ice" won in the categories Funniest Promo and Branding/Image Campaign, respectively. In addition, "Rocky" won in the Out-of-House Program Promotion category.

As further evidence of the success of the campaign, a report in *Electronic Media* noted that "31 Days of Oscar" resonated with younger viewers. This was the target audience TCM was hoping to reach.

FURTHER READING

"A&E Tour Salutes 'Biography.'" *Multichannel News,* April 15, 2002.

Chunovic, Louis. "Rules for Winning TV Ad Campaigns: Sessions at CTAM Touts Simplicity, Single-Mindedness." *Electronic Media,* July 22, 2002, p. 20.

Cox, Ted. "A Rockumentary Built on Sand: AMC Tries to Give '70s Music Movies Their Due, but It Can't Be Bothered with Anything of Substance." *Arlington Heights (IL) Daily Herald,* August 30, 2002.

Dill, Mallorre. "The Ice Brigades." *Adweek,* July 15, 2002, p. 22.

Donohue, Steve. "AMC's Golden Go-To Guy: Net Keys Promo Campaign around Upcoming Oscars." *Multichannel News,* January 1, 2005.

Forkan, Jim. "Oscar Fever Heats Up for TCM, E!" *Multichannel News,* February 25, 2002.

Goetzl, David. "Aging 'Biography' Goes for Hipper Memoirs: A&E Revamps Show for Younger Viewers." *Crains's New York Business,* September 9, 2002.

Haugsted, Linda. "Mini Cinema." *Multichannel News,* July 8, 2002.

Hogan, Monica. "TCM Draws On Oscar Star Power." *Multichannel News,* February 21, 2000.

Karrfalt, Wayne. "The Fine Art of Allure: Every Screen Legend Requires Special Promo Care—and So Does the Channel That Spotlights Them." *Broadcasting & Cable,* April 12, 2004.

Katz, Richard. "TCM Demonstrates Turner's Muscle." *Multichannel News,* April 17, 1995.

Lippert, Barbara. "Two Thumbs Up: TCM Takes Clever Aim at the Failings of Modern Movies." *Adweek,* April 21, 2003, p. 30.

Mitchell, Kim. "New Rate Card in Mail for New Turner Network." *Multichannel News,* February 21, 1994.

"TNT and Turner Classic Movies Announce the Ultimate Academy Award Television Tribute." *Business Wire,* February 15, 1995.

Umstead, R. Thomas. "TCM Courts Younger Viewers with Series." *Multichannel News,* January 20, 2003.

Rayna Bailey

TBS VERY FUNNY CAMPAIGN

OVERVIEW

Although it reached 88 million households in 2003, the daily average viewership of the cable Turner Broadcasting System (TBS) Superstation had dropped to 979,000, down 6 percent over the previous year. Viewers tuning in each day during prime time had slipped 5 percent, to 1.7 million. Further, the average age of viewers was skewing older, rather than the younger adult demographic craved by advertisers. In addition, with programming that included reruns of old black-and-white sitcoms, action movies, and Atlanta Braves baseball games, the TBS offerings in general entertainment and the station's lack of focus were becoming liabilities in the huge cable television arena.

To focus its programming, establish a clear identity with viewers, and attract a younger audience, TBS in 2004 reinvented itself by borrowing a strategy that, three years earlier, had been successful for sister station Turner Network Television (TNT). While TNT had positioned itself as the network for drama, TBS claimed the flip side of the coin and relaunched itself as the place for comedy. To support the makeover, the network dropped its "Superstation" moniker and adopted the tagline "TBS very funny." Working with Publicis New York, it also launched a rebranding campaign that included television spots set in a TBS call center, with operators responding to callers' descriptions of funny situations. One spot, for example, showed a caller asking if a boss's verbal abuse of a coworker was funny. The operator listened to the description of the situation and then told the caller that it was "very funny" and that the caller could laugh. The campaign also included print, online, and outdoor ads. Although network executives did not release the cost of the campaign, the *New York Times,* estimated the budget at $50 million.

Based on industry and viewer response, the campaign appeared to accomplish its goals of making people laugh, helping to establish TBS as the network for comedy and attracting a younger viewing audience. The campaign won awards, and critics in such publications as *Adweek* and *Advertising Age's Creativity* described the television spots as "inspired," "verbally adroit," "outrageously funny," and "one of the best TV promo campaigns in the history of the genre." While the network's number of daily viewers in 2004 averaged 940,000, similar to the number in 2003, TBS reported that in 2005, one year after the launch of the campaign, the average age of prime-time viewers had dropped from 40 to 37 and that the age of daytime viewers had dropped to 31.

HISTORICAL CONTEXT

In 1970 the Atlanta-based outdoor advertising executive Ted Turner bought a struggling television station and renamed it WTCG, for Turner Communications Group. Turner created the "superstation" concept in 1976 and began broadcasting the station's programming to cable systems via satellite. The fledgling network attracted viewers with reruns of old black-and-white television favorites, such as *The Andy Griffith Show* and *Leave It to Beaver,* Atlanta Braves baseball games, and championship wrestling. In 1979 the network was renamed the Turner Broadcasting System (TBS) and went on a growth binge. Among the channels added to the TBS family were Cable News Network (CNN), Turner Classic Movies (TCM), Turner Network Television (TNT), and TBS Superstation. When the network was acquired by Time Warner in 1996, changes were not far behind. While broadcasts of the Atlanta Braves games and old sitcoms were sacred and remained in place, Time Warner gave wrestling the ax. The original programming was combined with sitcoms and old movies to further enhance TBS's position as a general-entertainment network.

As the clutter of cable networks grew, increasing by some estimates to more than 500 channels, the number of viewer options that originally had made cable programming a success became a handicap. Robert Thompson, of Syracuse University, said that "the whole business model had to change. Now you have to play by a whole different set of rules." To stand out in the crowd, networks were forced to begin establishing brand identities. The Lifetime channel became known as the network for women, MTV was the channel for music, and TBS sister station TNT redefined itself as the place for drama. These changes were the impetus behind the move by TBS in 2004 to establish its own identity in order to create a niche, find an audience, and rebuild sagging viewership. Armed with research indicating that 25 percent of viewers considered themselves comedy fans who believed in the old cliché that "laughter is the best medicine" and with a library that included some of the best sitcoms and comedic movies ever produced, TBS was positioned to establish itself as the network for comedy. In 2004 TBS dropped "Superstation" from its name and embraced the moniker "Very Funny," and the change from a general- to a focused-entertainment network was under way.

TARGET MARKET

With programming that ran the gamut from baseball and professional wrestling to reruns of old movies and TV sitcoms, TBS had always considered itself a "general-entertainment" cable network, but it lacked a clearly defined identity and target audience. Throughout the 1980s and 1990s the TBS audience was slightly older than the ideal, with viewers typically in their mid-40s. In addition, the network was gradually losing its audience. In 2003 the network's average daily viewership was 979,000, down 6 percent from 2002. Further, the slip in prime-time viewers was 5 percent, to 1.7 million, from the previous year. Thus, TBS had an audience that was both older than the optimum and one that was declining.

The "TBS Very Funny" campaign was specific not only about programming lineup but also about the audience it intended to reach. As TBS prepared to launch the campaign, company executives explained during a meeting with advertisers that its target audience consisted of well-educated, upscale young adults in the 20- to 30-something age group. Steven Koonin, the TBS executive vice president and chief operating officer, told the *New York Times,* "In cable, unless you stand for something, you're doomed. TBS will be for young adults who want television to make them laugh."

COMPETITION

At the end of 2003 A&E Television Networks was in the midst of change. Faced with ratings problems, the network had earlier begun to revamp its programming, and by November 2003 A&E reported that its efforts to turn the numbers around were working. In the first two weeks of that month viewers had increased to 1 million, 11 percent over the same period during the previous year. Viewers in the 25- to 54-year-old age group, A&E's target market, were up 22 percent, to 422,000. To keep the momentum going, A&E launched a new branding campaign "The Art of Entertainment," which was adapted for its three main programming genres: "The Art of Biography," "The Art of Documentary," and "The Art of Drama." As part of its rebranding efforts, A&E embraced reality television in the vein of *Survivor* and *Queer Eye for the Straight Guy* by introducing its own reality show, *Airline.* The network also updated its programming on *Biography,* with episodes on such contemporary celebrities as Pierce Brosnan and The Rock. In 2004 A&E was losing some of its former core audience, viewers in their 60s, and compared to 2003, its total viewership had dropped about 13 percent, to 1.15 million. The network, however, reported double-digit increases in viewers of its target audience, those between the ages of 25 and 54. Abbe Raven, A&E executive vice president and general manager, said during an interview with *Variety,* "As the interests of our core audience broadens, so will we. We're reaching to newer audiences but continue to satisfy our loyal viewers."

As TBS and A&E took aim at young adults and baby boomers with their marketing and programming,

SANITIZED SEX PLAYS ON TBS

In 2004, as part of its prime-time programming, Turner Broadcasting System (TBS) entered into an eight-year agreement with Home Box Office (HBO) to buy and show in reruns the pay channel's hit series *Sex and the City.* Before launching the reruns, however, TBS editors cleaned up the steamier dialogue and scenes so that the program fit the strict guidelines of basic cable standards. The network also created a marketing campaign that used print ads and television spots featuring young actors who portrayed the show's adult female characters as teens. Other ads used the trendy new forum of Web logs, or blogs. These ads, introduced during the 2004 national elections, appeared on 50 political blogs with the theme "Vote Carrie," highlighting the character played by Sarah Jessica Parker. Web users who clicked on the ad were taken to VoteCarrie.org, a blog spoof that described her political platform and encouraged users to E-mail their comments. Including *Sex and the City* in its programming and the new campaign promoting it were designed to appeal to TBS's target audience—affluent, well-educated, computer-savvy young adults.

ABC focused on a different audience, namely, families. To interconnect its cable networks—ABC Family, Disney Channel, and Toon Disney—ABC Cable introduced the tagline "Imagination is part of the deal" and a campaign to support it. Ben Pyne, ABC Cable's senior vice president of affiliate sales and marketing, said of the new strategy, "It defines what we've always tried to do, but now we're coming out and saying it." As part of the attempt to build brand identity, ABC Cable introduced a redesigned website and a public-affairs effort under the theme "Learn Together" that encouraged parents to be more involved with their children and their activities. An increase in viewership among adults was taken as evidence that the strategy was working. In the first quarter of 2004 the Disney Channel, with a target audience of children under the age of 17, reported an average prime-time audience of 406,000 adults between 18 and 49, indicating that parents were spending time watching television with their kids. Rich Ross, the president of Disney Channel Worldwide, said that the network was making an effort to reach out to parents: "We have families in our shows, so we think it makes a difference because kids and families can see themselves."

MARKETING STRATEGY

The "TBS Very Funny" rebranding campaign used a series of five television spots to answer the question of what was funny while at the same time tickling viewers' funny bones. The campaign, with a budget estimated at $50 million according to the *New York Times,* was created for the network by its agency, Publicis New York. In addition to television spots that ran on the Turner networks and on other Time Warner affiliates, the campaign included trailers that ran in movie theaters, print and billboard ads, and special promotions that ran on the updated TBS website.

Created with the intent of strengthening the image of TBS as a place for comedy, the television spots were set in a call center, with operators responding to viewers who dialed an 800 number (800-TBS-FUNNY) to tell their funny stories and to have them rated. In one spot a factory worker called to ask if her sloppy boss's continuing verbal abuse of a coworker was funny. After listening to the worker's detailed explanation of the abuse, the operator told the caller that the situation was "really quite funny" and that she could laugh. Another spot featured an office worker calling to find out how funny it was that her boss repeatedly called a coworker by the wrong name. After listening to the details, the TBS operator decided that the situation was only "mildly funny." One spot, titled "Strange Fruit," took place in an art gallery. After listening to the caller's description of a woman telling her older male companion that she wanted to buy something "really big and really expensive," the operator concluded, "Fake fruit, pompous jerk and arm candy."

In the background of each spot were brief glimpses of scenes from some of TBS's most popular comedy programming, such as *Seinfeld.* Also featured were cameo appearances by supporting cast members from various programs shown on TBS, including Marcel the monkey from *Friends;* Estelle Harris, who played Mrs. Costanza on *Seinfeld;* and Mario Cantone and Willie Garson, who appeared as Anthony and Stanford, respectively, on *Sex and the City.* Working with the New York-based agency Cliff Freeman & Partners, TBS created additional campaigns to promote individual television programs, including *Sex and the City.*

Although TBS already had been using its full roster of comedy programming for several years, the "TBS Very Funny" campaign was designed to rebrand the network as the authority on television comedy. The effort also was intended to shift TBS from its reputation as a general-entertainment superstation toward a more focused, clearly defined image as a place for entertainment. The strategy was borrowed from sister network TNT, which had successfully reinvented itself with the "We Know

Drama" campaign as the network to turn to for drama. Koonin called the TBS rebranding effort "a full-fledged media push. We're literally changing everything on the network, the look and the lineup." Changes to the program lineup included reruns of contemporary sitcoms the network already owned, such as *Friends, Home Improvement,* and *Seinfeld,* as well as the addition of reruns of the Home Box Office (HBO) hit *Sex and the City.* The network also announced plans to develop original comedy programming, such as a reality show based on the original *Gilligan's Island* television series. The popular TBS series *Dinner and a Movie* remained on the schedule, but comedy movies were to dominate prime-time programming on weekends.

OUTCOME

If getting a laugh from viewers, driving home the message that TBS was, as Koonin put it to *Broadcasting & Cable,* the "epicenter of funny," and reaching the target audience were the desired results, then the "TBS Very Funny" campaign was a success. Following its launch, a report in *Advertising Age's Creativity* praised the television spots as "outrageously funny." The campaign also appeared to resonate with the target audience of young adults. In 2005, following the launch of "TBS Very Funny," the network reported that the average age of viewers tuning in during prime time had dropped from 40 to 37.

In addition, the "TBS Very Funny" campaign was honored by the advertising industry. It received a 2005 Gold EFFIE, as well as a Silver CLIO for the spots "Name," "Wings," and "Strange Fruit."

FURTHER READING

Colford, Paul D. "Publishing Column." *New York Daily News,* October 5, 2004.

Elliott, Stuart. "TBS Puts Serious Money into Promoting Itself as a Place for Laughs." *New York Times,* April 22, 2004, p. 3.

Hill, Lee Alan. "'Sex and the City' Special Report: Promax & BDA." *TelevisionWeek,* June 20, 2005.

"License to Laugh." *Advertising Age's Creativity,* June 1, 2004, p. 14.

Lippert, Barbara. "TBS' New 'Very Funny' Campaign Lives Up to Its Name." *Adweek,* July 12, 2004, p. 26.

Martin, Denise. "Young at Art: In a Demo Sea Change, Cultured Cabler Embraces Celebs and Reality." *Variety,* February 2, 2004.

Miller, Stuart. "ABC Cable: A Four-Network Initiative Involves Parents and Kids." *Broadcasting & Cable,* June 28, 2004.

Moss, Linda. "ADC Cable Touts Imagination." *Multichannel News,* May 3, 2004.

"A New Look at TBS." *United Press International,* May 15, 2004.

"Ready for Takeoff: A New Programming Strategy and Branding Campaigns Aim for Some Bigger Audience Numbers Next Year." *Multichannel News,* December 8, 2003.

Romano, Allison. "Comedy Tonight: TBS Brands Itself the 'Very Funny' Network." *Broadcasting & Cable,* April 26, 2004.

Umstead, R. Thomas. "The Parent Trap: Kids Programming Is Getting a Lift from a Silent Minority of the Viewership Base, and Advertisers Are Taking Note." *Multichannel News,* May 17, 2004.

———. "TBS Says Joke's on Us: Net; Our Sitcoms, Reality Shows Will Skew Younger." *Multichannel News,* April 26, 2004.

Wilbert, Caroline. "TBS Fashions a Makeover: Image Is Geared to Younger Viewers." *Atlanta Journal-Constitution,* February 21, 2004.

"The Work." *Advertising Age's Creativity,* June 1, 2004, p. 27.

Rayna Bailey

TV Guide, Inc.

7140 S. Lewis Avenue
Tulsa, Oklahoma 74136-5422
USA
Telephone: (918) 488-4000
Fax: (918) 488-4979
Web site: www.tvguide.com

ON THE INSIDE CAMPAIGN

OVERVIEW

Although *TV Guide,* with a circulation of 9 million and a total readership of 28 million, was ranked in the top three major magazines in 2003, its circulation had dropped 30 percent since 1998. Adding to the aging iconic publication's woes was its loss of advertisers. According to the Publisher Information Bureau/CMR, the number of ad pages sold by the publication had decreased 11 percent in 2002. Reversing the trend of fleeing readers and, subsequently, fleeing advertisers was the goal set by *TV Guide* 's new executive team, which included John Loughlin, president of TV Guide Publishing Group, and Michael Lafavore, the magazine's editor-in-chief.

As part of the revitalization effort the magazine was completely redesigned based on extensive consumer research, and its website was upgraded to better integrate with the publication. To promote its new look *TV Guide* partnered with Dallas-based ad agency the Richards Group and launched a two-phase marketing campaign aimed at both media buyers and consumers. The "On the Inside" campaign, which began in 2003, had the tagline "We see everything" and an estimated budget of between $20 million and $30 million. Phase one of the campaign was created to alert media buyers of the magazine's new format and included print and outdoor ads. Phase two, targeted at consumers, included three television spots, each portraying a day in the life of a *TV Guide* reporter on the prowl for a scoop to print in the magazine.

Within two months of the campaign's launch, it was evident it had resonated with the target audiences. The first phase, aimed at media buyers, won a 2004 EFFIE Award and reversed a three-year decline in advertising sales. Phase two's message reached readers and led to a 40 percent jump in newsstand sales in September compared to the prior three months. The upgraded website was also attracting new subscribers, nearly 10,000 each week compared to only several hundred new subscribers a week before the campaign began.

HISTORICAL CONTEXT

In 1953 half of the homes in the United States had television sets providing family entertainment with programs that included *I Love Lucy, Dragnet, The Adventures of Superman, Candid Camera,* and *Kraft Television Theatre.* To help keep viewers informed of what was on at what time, *TV Guide* was introduced in April 1953. The magazine quickly became the television viewer's bible, with a circulation of 1.7 million in September of that year. By the mid-1970s *TV Guide* 's circulation had reached more than 19 million.

In 1988 the owner of *TV Guide,* Walter Annenberg, sold the publication to media conglomerate News Corp., which eventually entered a partnership with Gemstar, a company that made electronic TV-program guides. But the new CEO, Henry Yuen, neglected the aging magazine, focusing the company's energies on technologies such as interactive program guides and *TV Guide's* website. For five years the magazine did not mail out subscriber solicitation notices, and for 18 months it operated without a publisher. Compounding the magazine's problems were the facts that television was evolving, viewers' needs had changed, and other ways to learn what was on television became available—from newspapers publishing daily or weekly TV listings to TV remote controls that enabled viewers to surf through the channels from the comfort of their chairs. By 2003 the magazine's circulation had dropped to about nine million.

Yuen was forced out in 2002, and changes at the magazine began. John Loughlin, TV Guide Publishing Group's president, brought on board Scott Crystal as executive vice president and publisher and Michael Lafavore as editor-in-chief. The team set to work reinventing *TV Guide* with completely reworked editorial content. Loughlin said that the goal was to create a magazine that was more than a list of television programs. He told *Adweek* that the revamped magazine would be "the guide and trusted voice of helping people make decisions about in-home, on-screen entertainment." As *TV Guide* was undergoing its transformation, the Richards Group was creating the supporting "On the Inside" marketing campaign with the tagline "We see everything."

TARGET MARKET

From 1953, when it was founded, through 1988 *TV Guide* was successful, reaching a circulation peak of 19 million. But as times and readers' needs changed, the iconic magazine went into a slump. As the publication lost subscribers, dropping to a circulation of 9 million in 2003, it also lost advertisers. When *TV Guide* began its "On the Inside" marketing campaign in 2003, it had two target audiences: media buyers and consumers.

Phase one of the campaign was aimed directly at media buyers, who purchased advertising space for their clients and had redirected their spending to other publications that included television listings and viewing information in their editorial content. The second phase of the campaign was directed at consumers in an effort to convince them that *TV Guide* was the magazine to read for all things TV, from program listings to inside scoops on small-screen stars. Lynda Hodge, the Richards Group's art director, said that people had come to believe that only old people read *TV Guide,* and the consumer portion of the campaign was designed to change that stodgy image. She added that the goal was to show consumers that they could read the magazine for entertainment as well as for TV program listings.

CLASSIC TV PROGRAMMING NOW OFFERED ON DVD

With a 50-year history of covering television, *TV Guide* in 2004 began using its authority on television shows to release favorite programming on DVD. *TV Guide* –branded DVDs began to be sold that year by Genius Products, Inc. DVD titles would be released in collections with six hours of programming. Categories included comedies, Westerns, and detectives. Besides the television episodes, each DVD featured related trivia questions, commentary by the *TV Guide* editors who had selected the specific episodes, and a subscription offer to *TV Guide* magazine.

COMPETITION

For years *TV Guide* had defined TV remotes as its primary competition—because when viewers had remote controls they could more easily find out what shows were on merely by flipping through the channels while seated—but when the magazine reinvented itself, it also was forced to redefine the competition. Clear rivals for ad dollars and readers were other publications that offered entertainment news; other competitors were websites, on-screen listings, and newspapers that ran daily or weekly television program listings. Among the top print rivals were Gannett Company Inc.'s *USA Weekend* and Wenner Media LLC's *Us Weekly.*

USA Weekend was an entertainment and lifestyle magazine that was distributed through newspapers. In 2003 the publication reported a circulation of more than 23 million. Also in 2003, however, advertising agency executives and other publications, including *TV Guide,* were questioning the accuracy of those huge circulation numbers. Under debate was whether research methods credited the total circulation of the newspapers carrying *USA Weekend* as the total circulation of the magazine itself. It was also questioned whether or not *USA Weekend* was a true magazine or simply a weekly newspaper supplement. To answer the question a poll of readers was conducted through an industry-wide initiative led by *Parade* magazine, with the results showing that most people perceived *USA Weekend* as a magazine rather than a newspaper supplement.

As advertisers and other publications debated the accuracy of *USA Weekend* 's circulation numbers and whether it was a magazine or newspaper supplement, *Us Weekly* was named the 2004 Magazine of the Year by *Advertising Age.* In announcing its award, *Advertising*

Age described *Us Weekly* as a "cultural reference point" that had connected with younger, affluent women readers and in the process attracted advertisers. The first six months of 2004 saw *Us Weekly* 's newsstand sales climb 47.3 percent, and its ad pages increased 25.2 percent from the same period the previous year. Mediamark Research reported that the median household income of the magazine's female readers was higher than readers of both *Vanity Fair* and *In Style.*

MARKETING STRATEGY

The 2003 "On the Inside" campaign was *TV Guide* 's first consumer marketing effort in more than 10 years. With an overall budget of between $20 million and $30 million, it far surpassed the $250,000 the publication had budgeted in 2002 for advertising. Loughlin told *Adweek,* "It's a fair characterization to say that for several years, there's been virtually no media spend." In addition, for the previous two years the publication had no advertising agency. The first step in *TV Guide* 's reinvention was making changes to the magazine itself. It added more pages of editorial content, which featured up-to-the minute stories about television celebrities, behind-the-scenes reports, and detailed recommendations about programming. Lafavore said that the magazine's editorial content had been adjusted to reflect the changing attitudes of viewers and the cultural role of television. The new campaign was designed to inform media buyers and consumers of the changes and lure them back to the magazine.

For the first phase of the campaign the Richards Group designed outdoor and print ads as teasers for media buyers. Signs that appeared in magazines and on billboards, buses, and buildings featured slogans that made tongue-in-cheek references to the television industry in general, such as "Like everyone else, we're having a little work done," "New look, new style, new attitude. Soon we'll be dating models half our age," and "We're back from rehab and ready to party." In addition, the magazine flew 250 advertisers to Los Angeles for a post–Emmy Awards party, the first ever hosted by the magazine.

Phase two of the campaign targeted consumers with the tagline "You miss nothing, because we see everything," which was shortened to "We see everything." The campaign included television spots, radio commercials, and print ads that emphasized the point that readers would not miss anything if they read *TV Guide,* because the publication's team of reporters were always working to get the inside story for its readers. The advertisements used humor to send their message. One spot, titled "Make Up Artist," showed a male reporter dressed in drag and posing as *Average Joe* star Kathy Griffin's makeup artist to get the scoop on a script she was working on. Griffin caught on to the scheme, and the reporter was kicked out the door. Another spot, "Wired," showed an aggressive reporter slipping a bug onto *NYPD Blue* actor Gordon Clapp just before he filmed a scene of the show. The bug trashed the film equipment and, once again, the sly reporter was caught and given the boot.

Rod Underhill of the Richards Group said that the publication's marketing push was more than a campaign; rather, it was helping *TV Guide* recreate itself as a brand. "The world is confused about what is TV Guide," he told *Adweek.* "The brand itself doesn't carry any baggage, it doesn't have a lot of negatives. It's just suffering from neglect."

OUTCOME

In September, six weeks after the launch of its redesigned publication and the accompanying "On the Inside" campaign, *TV Guide* reported a 40 percent jump in newsstand sales. That month's sales averaged 850,000, which included a 250,000 increase over the number of issues sold in each of the previous three months. In addition the publication's website, which had been redesigned in conjunction with the magazine, was adding as many as 10,000 new subscribers each week, compared with only hundreds per week previously. The new subscribers also tended to be younger—31-years-old on average versus 41—and more affluent. During an interview with *Media Industry Newsletter,* Loughlin said, "In a magazine used to seeing year-over-year newsstand drops of 20 percent to 30 percent this is progress."

Media buyers responded favorably to the campaign as well. According to *Business Wire,* ad pages in *TV Guide* 's feature-well—the center of a magazine where the longer articles were published—jumped 71 percent in September compared with September of the previous year, and all available ad space had been sold. A report in the *Wall Street Journal* stated that the magazine's September issue had 102.4 ad pages, the most it had sold since 1996, and that for the first time in six consecutive years ad revenue inched up rather than declined.

Further indication of the campaign's success was its win of a 2004 Bronze EFFIE from the New York American Marketing Association. The award was presented for the "TV Guide Color Bar" print ad that was used in phase one of the campaign, which was directed at media buyers.

FURTHER READING

"At 'TV Guide,' the 'Eye' Had It in 1957—And Has It in 2003." *Media Industry Newsletter,* September 15, 2003, p. 1.

Charski, Mindy. "Aiming to Revitalize Brand, 'TV Guide' Turns to Richards." *Adweek,* March 24, 2003, p. 14.

Fine, Jon. "Magazine of the Year: 'Us Weekly.'" *Advertising Age,* October 25, 2004.

———. "TV Guide Updates Image." *Advertising Age,* July 14, 2003, p. 4.

Howard, Brendan. "TV Guide Makes a Genius Move in TV DVD Distribution." *Video Store,* September 19, 2004.

Lazare, Lewis. "Ads Mislead on What's in New TV Guide." *Chicago Sun-Times,* September 11, 2003, p. 51.

Mandese, Joe. "No Rain on This Parade." *Folio: the Magazine for Magazine Management,* April 1, 2003.

Myerhoff, Matt. "How's That? The LABJ's L.A. Stories—$5 MN Ad Campaign for TV Guide Magazine." *Los Angeles Business Journal,* December 1, 2003.

"Redesigned 'TV Guide' Is Off to a Good Newsstand Start." *Media Industry Newsletter,* October 20, 2003, p. 1.

Rose, Matthew. "TV Guide: New Logo, New Strategy." *Wall Street Journal,* September 8, 2003, p. B3.

"TV Guide Launches New Design." *Oakland (CA) Tribune,* September 9, 2003.

"TV Guide Unveils New Look, New Attitude and New Editorial." *Business Wire,* September 8, 2003.

Rayna Bailey

Tyson Foods, Inc.

2210 W. Oaklawn Drive
Springdale, Arkansas 72762-6999
USA
Telephone: (479) 290-4000
Web site: www.TysonFoodsInc.com

POWERED BY TYSON CAMPAIGN

OVERVIEW

After the Arkansas poultry farmer John Tyson developed a method of transporting live chickens during the Great Depression, he sparked a legacy that would be passed down for three generations. When John Tyson's grandson, who shared his grandfather's first name, became CEO in 2000, Tyson Foods, Inc., was the largest chicken producer in the United States. The new CEO soon expanded the company's role in the packaged foods and meats market. One year after assuming leadership John Tyson agreed to buy IBP, Inc., America's largest beef processor and second-largest pork processor. The acquisition transformed Tyson into the world's largest meat producer. Subsequently executives needed to rebrand Tyson to include beef and pork. After 18 months of research Tyson discovered that the public considered protein to be the main quality that beef, pork, and chicken shared. To herald Tyson as a leading provider of protein, the corporation released "Powered by Tyson," the largest advertising campaign in Tyson's history.

The Boston ad agency Arnold Worldwide released the $75 million campaign on August 30, 2004. The campaign's television spots humorously featured individuals performing amazing feats simply because they were "Powered by Tyson." In one commercial a parasailing man was lifted into the air by a Tyson-fueled woman rowing a boat. The campaign's high-protein message was embraced by those following the popular Atkins Diet, a weight-loss program that involved eating high-protein foods. In addition to television spots the campaign included radio spots, print advertising, and outside promotions. Tyson products were also strategically placed on network programs, including the popular Monday night CBS sitcom *Still Standing,* which starred Mark Addy and Jami Gertz.

According to a 2004 Ad Age / IAG Quarterly Ad Performance Report (an ongoing study conducted by research firm IAG and published in *Advertising Age*), one "Powered by Tyson" commercial, which featured a mother running up a wall to catch her child's balloons, was rated the quarter's "best-liked spot." Tyson's fourth-quarter sales for 2004 were $500 million above those of the same quarter of 2003.

HISTORICAL CONTEXT

Arkansas farmer John Tyson, who supported his family during the Great Depression by selling produce and chicken, devised in 1935 an unprecedented method to transport chickens from Arkansas to Chicago. He attached food-and-water troughs inside a trailer that kept the birds alive long enough to be sold in Chicago. The business of transporting and selling chickens proved to be a lucrative trade for the Tyson family. John's son Don became manager in 1960 and took the corporation

© RAMIN TALAIE/CORBIS.

public in 1963. Although packaged chicken was Tyson's mainstay, the company expanded into other meat products. In 1992 Tyson purchased Arctic Alaska Fisheries and Louis Kemp Seafood, and two years later it acquired the frozen-foods company Culinary Foods. Its foray into the seafood business was short-lived, however; the company sold the division in 1999. The ad agency DDB Chicago had been creating advertising for Tyson since 1995. According to the Associated Press news service, Tyson chief marketing officer Bob Corscadden described the company's marketing during this period as "warm and fuzzy." In 2001 DDB introduced a $20 million print campaign for Tyson titled "It's What Your Family Deserves."

Tyson's best-selling food line, Tyson Country Fresh Chicken, reinforced Tyson's position as America's leading chicken producer. The titan was 60 percent larger than its closest competitor, Pilgrim's Pride. After the third-generation CEO, John Tyson, took control in 2000, he instigated the purchase of IBP, America's largest beef producer and second-largest pork producer. After the IBP acquisition the Tyson brand was hard-pressed to reposition itself as something other than a producer of chicken. Many Tyson investors, worried about the company's newly acquired debt of approximately $1.5 billion (which it had taken on from IBP as part of the deal), considered John Tyson too inexperienced and doubted his ability to salvage the corporation. John Tyson responded by recruiting apt executives for Tyson, including the former president of IBP, Richard L. Bond. John Tyson also oversaw 18 months of comprehensive research, which included holding 90 focus groups to determine how the Tyson brand should move forward. The research determined that consumers identified one shared quality between all meat products: high protein content. In addition, the strategic brand consultant Faith Popcorn's BrainReserve helped Tyson conduct an ad-agency review that resulted in the selection of Arnold Worldwide, an agency headquartered in Boston.

According to advertising analysts, building a brand for packaged meat was somewhat unprecedented. Beginning in the 1970s the poultry company Perdue Farms had branded its product around its founder Frank Perdue, but most consumers continued to consider meat a commodity. Pork and beef especially were selected because of how it looked behind its plastic wrapping. Price, according to one Tyson survey, was not the deciding factor. "This is virgin territory for branded manufacturers," John M. McMillin, a food analyst at the Prudential Equity Group, said to the *New York Times.* "Beef and pork have largely been commodity areas, and what Perdue and Tyson did to chicken 10 to 20 years ago is what Tyson is now trying to do to beef and pork."

TARGET MARKET

The campaign targeted several demographics, including consumers who enjoyed cooking meals from scratch and busy consumers who preferred cooking food that was already prepared. Advertising critics believed that the campaign successfully targeted dieters subscribing to the Atkins Diet, a low-carbohydrate weight-loss plan that had become highly popular by 2004. The marketing

HURRICANE RELIEF

In the aftermath of America's devastating 2005 hurricane season, Tyson Foods, the world's largest producer of meat, offered victims displaced by Hurricane Katrina jobs through its Houston and Dallas employment offices. During the previous year's hurricane season Tyson had donated more than 110,000 pounds of precooked chicken to feed those affected by hurricanes.

agency Lopez-Negrete Communications in Houston created TV spots for the campaign that targeted Latino consumers. In one TV commercial with a Spanish voice-over, two "powered" dancers outlasted the competition in a salsa dance contest as a result of eating Tyson meat.

"Powered by Tyson" also sought to reach the African-American market. A Tyson press release that appeared in *Market News Publishing* stated, "The foundation of African-American food preferences is soulfood ... A major part of soulfood is protein, which gives families strength and energy to accomplish the many challenges of their busy days. Nobody brings quality, branded chicken, beef and pork protein to this consumer in more ways than Tyson Foods." Tyson hired the Chicago marketing agency E. Morris Communications to create television and print advertising that targeted African-American consumers.

During the campaign Tyson provided scholarships through the Tom Joyner Foundation, an organization dedicated to helping African-Americans afford higher learning. Recipe books titled *Powered by Tyson* were issued at football games and other events hosted by Historically Black Colleges and Universities (a category of institutions that were recognized as being founded for the education of African-Americans).

COMPETITION

With its beginnings dating to 1945, Pilgrim's Pride became America's second-largest poultry producer under the longtime leadership of Lonnie (Bo) Pilgrim. The company was also credited with treating chicken as more than just a commodity. In 1983 the Texas-based company first offered boneless and low-fat chicken products. In 1997 it targeted health-conscious baby boomers with Eggs Plus, a line of eggs enriched with fatty acids that aided in human cell growth and fat metabolism.

In mid-2004 Pilgrim's Pride released a commercial that featured the company's founder, Bo Pilgrim, dressed as a cook for a group of roughneck cowboys. According to Dan Emery, Pilgrim's Pride vice president of marketing, using the founder and chairman as an actor in the spot was a natural choice. "Bo's health, vitality and sense of fun testify to the kind of diet he espouses and enjoys—low in fat, cholesterol, carbohydrates, and triglycerides. He remains ahead of his time. Today, millions agree that chicken is the best choice for any healthy diet," Emery was quoted by the PR Newswire news service.

When Bo Pilgrim's character offered herb-roasted chicken and cooked vegetables in the 2004 commercial, the beef-loving cowboys became visibly peeved. The chicken was appreciated, however, when the cowhands remembered that they all had high cholesterol. The spot was created by the Wolf Agency. Initial spots were aired in states with the largest Pilgrim's Pride presence, such as Texas, Oklahoma, Louisiana, New Mexico, and Michigan. Later the commercial was extended to other U.S. regions.

MARKETING STRATEGY

Arnold and several other contributing agencies released the $75 million campaign on August 30, 2004. The campaign's original seven 30-second commercials all featured individuals "powered" by Tyson meats. Their shaky filming suggested that the content had been captured with a camcorder and was unintended for professional use. One spot showed a small child kicking a football across the street and over the power lines. Another spot featured a fun-loving family "Powered by Tyson" and sledding their way past a high-altitude base camp on what appeared to be Mount Everest. The spot "Parasailing" began with shaky camera footage of a man parasailing. It was then revealed that he was being pulled by his wife, who was merely rowing a boat. Each spot ended with the question "Have you had your protein today?"

When the campaign began in 2004, many consumers were eating meat for its high-protein, low-carbohydrate sustenance. This dietary craze was pioneered by the popular Atkins Diet, which advised the consumption of meat. Tyson, however, wanted "Powered by Tyson" to brand meat as an excellent energy source, not a weight-loss product. Corscadden explained to *Nation's Restaurant News* that Arnold Worldwide's strategy stressed the sustenance of Tyson products by using the formula "protein = energy = power," which suggested that pork, chicken, and beef provided consumers with more power. The strategy worked in Tyson's favor. In 2005 many American who had previously subscribed to the Atkins Diet were beginning to consider it an incomplete regimen.

CORPORATE RELIGION

John Tyson, the third-generation president and CEO of the world's largest meat producer, Tyson Foods, had taken control of Tyson in 2000. He soon integrated his religious beliefs into the corporate structure. One addition to Tyson's core values stated, "We strive to be a faith-friendly company." Another explained, "We strive to honor God and be respectful of each other, our customers, and other stakeholders." To provide support for employees John Tyson oversaw the hiring of 87 chaplains who would offer counseling in the business's 58 processing plants.

Print ads for "Powered by Tyson" appeared in popular consumer magazines such as *People* and *Redbook.* One ad featured a child performing world-class gymnastics on her school playground. The ad's copy asked, "Have you had your protein today?" In addition to appearing in print ads and television spots, the "Powered by" message was used at Tyson-sponsored USA Gymnastics and Crew Chief Club (an association of NASCAR head mechanics) competitions. To reach African-American communities Tyson sponsored events for Alpha Kappa Alpha Sorority (AKA), America's first Greek-letter organization founded by and for African-American women. Tyson also contributed to Historically Black Colleges and Universities. In return for Tyson's scholarships, recipe books titled *Powered by Tyson* were distributed at college and university events.

Tyson paid the media conglomerate Viacom to place Tyson products on network and cable programming. Tyson foods appeared on CBS's popular sitcom *Still Standing* and on the soap opera *As the World Turns.* Short vignettes for Tyson were also filmed with actresses from the soap opera. The PR Newswire quoted Corscadden commenting about Tyson's product placement, "We're very excited about being part of this innovative effort ... One of the primary components of our new 'Powered by Tyson' communications strategy states that we'll be seen in expected and unexpected places. This is new. It's unexpected. It dovetails nicely with our new strategy."

OUTCOME

According to advertising critics, "Powered by Tyson" helped Tyson expand beyond its chicken-only stigma and move forward as America's largest meat producer. An Ad Age / IAG Quarterly Ad Performance Report determined that the "best-liked spot" of the final quarter of 2004 was the Tyson commercial in which a mother ran up a wall to catch her child's helium balloons. One month after the campaign debuted, *Fortune* magazine ranked Tyson 44th out of the "100 Fastest-Growing Companies." During the 2004 quarter that the campaign was released, Tyson's sales were $500 million above the same quarter of 2003.

In February 2005 *Fortune* 's "Most Admired" list rated Tyson as America's "most admired company in food production." The PR Newswire quoted John Tyson's response to the accolade. "It's an honor to be recognized for the progress we've been making since our acquisition of IBP three years ago," the chairman and CEO said. "We're continuing our aggressive campaign to increase our value-added product sales over the next three to five years and believe our recently unveiled 'Powered by Tyson' marketing campaign will boost our efforts." In late 2005 Tyson was added to the S&P 500, an influential index of America's most prestigious blue-chip stocks.

FURTHER READING

Clayton, Chris. "Tyson Hunts for Next Chicken Wing." *Omaha World-Herald,* July 7, 2005, p. 01D.

Clubb, Deborah M. "Tyson Foods Donates Chicken to Food Bank." *Memphis Commercial Appeal,* November 14, 2002, B6.

Cody, Cristal. "Tyson Sales Up, Earnings Down; Chicken Sales Rising, but Mad Cow Slices into Beef Income." *Arkansas Democrat-Gazette,* May 3, 2005, p. 21.

Deogun, Nikhil, and Scott Kilman. "Tyson Makes a Move for Meat-Packer." *Wall Street Journal,* December 5, 2000, p. A3.

Harrison, Eric E. "Tyson Markets Organic Chicken Outside Arkansas." *Arkansas Democrat-Gazette,* July 24, 2003, p. 42.

Ives, Nat. "Tyson Is Counting on Protein to Bulk Up Its Image in a Campaign to Push Its Chicken, Beef and Pork." *New York Times,* August 4, 2004, p. 2.

Kilman, Scott. "Can Tyson Fight 'Chicken Fatigue' with Pork, Beef?" *Wall Street Journal,* January 10, 2001, p. B1.

Lazare, Lewis. "Humor Feeble in Toilet Paper Spots with Angels Larry, David." *Chicago Sun-Times,* August 16, 2004, p. 67.

Liskey, Tom Darin. "Tyson Earnings Shoot Up 75 Percent on Strength of Its Beef, Chicken Sales." *Arkansas Democrat-Gazette,* November 11, 2003, p. 27.

Lucas, John. "Poultry Odor Issues Are Many, Varied." *Evansville (IN) Courier & Press,* April 22, 2002, p. B1.

Reyes, Sonia. "Tyson Raises Heat on Hormone-Free Chicken Claim in $20M Print Splash." *Brandweek,* December 11, 2000, p. 4.

Riell, Howard. "Meat Makes a Comeback." *Frozen Food Age,* October 1, 2004, p. 24.

Weiss, Michael. "Pilgrim's Pride to Enter Cold-Cut, Deli Market." *Dallas Morning News,* May 13, 1986, p. 16d.

Zellner, Wendy. "The Wal-Mart of Meat; Tyson Foods Produces One of Every Four Pounds of U.S. Beef, Chicken, and Pork. Is That a Problem?" *BusinessWeek,* September 20, 2004, p. 90.

Kevin Teague

UBS Financial Services Inc.

1285 Avenue of the Americas
New York, New York 10019
USA
Telephone: (212) 713-2000
Fax: (212) 713-9818
Web site: financialservicesinc.ubs.com

THANK YOU, PAINE WEBBER CAMPAIGN

OVERVIEW

NOTE: Since the initial appearance of this essay in the 1999 edition of *Major Marketing Campaigns Annual,* Paine Webber became a part of the UBS Financial Services organization. The essay continues to refer to the company's former name, as that was the official name of the organization when the campaign was launched.

In November 1998 retail investment brokerage Paine Webber, a unit of Paine Webber Group Inc., launched an ambitious $20 million print and television campaign, the largest in the company's history. Overseeing the account was Saatchi & Saatchi, which had handled Paine Webber's advertising since 1981. The tag line, however, was much older than Paine Webber's relationship with its advertising agency: it had first used "Thank you, Paine Webber" in 1975 and had maintained the tag line until 1987. Now Paine Webber revived it in an effort to reinforce the company's identity.

Paine Webber was an old firm that had weathered a number of difficulties in recent years. In a business increasingly perceived as a commodity rather than a service, identity was an all-important factor if Paine Webber hoped to attract more business, and the firm's 1996 campaign—with the tag line "Invest with more intelligence"—had not proven particularly memorable. "Thank you, Paine Webber" was its first advertising effort since then, but this campaign retained at least one theme from the 1996 campaign: the idea that a customer who invested his or her money through Paine Webber could rest assured.

HISTORICAL CONTEXT

In 1879 Boston bank clerks William Payne and Wallace Webber formed their own brokerage house. They joined the New York Stock Exchange in 1890, and in 1899 they opened their first branch in Houghton, Michigan, where Paine Webber had a substantial interest in copper mines. Except for an understandable slump during the Great Depression, the company experienced many years of growth and in 1963 relocated from Boston to New York City. After incorporating in 1970 and going public two years later, Paine Webber created a holding company, the Paine Webber Group, which controlled all its properties. The 1970s saw expansion into Britain and Japan and the purchases of several U.S. companies involved in the investment industry.

Paine Webber hit on its first truly significant challenges in the 1980s. Soon after purchasing Blyth Eastman Dillon, an investment banking firm, in 1979, many of Blyth's executives left, and with them went some of the many lucrative accounts Paine Webber had hoped to acquire with the buyout. By the time Paine Webber had managed to get the bank fully operational, a number of other brokerages had outpaced it in taking advantage of the 1980s boom in mergers and acquisitions. The 1987 stock market crash proved another significant blow, and in the following year Paine Webber made a problematic loan to the faltering Federated Department Stores chain.

Just as Paine Webber was getting on its feet again in the early 1990s, again it hit upon a series of troubles. Once more it lost a number of important personnel, this time from its Mitchell Hutchins Institutional Investors in 1993. The next year saw a crash in the bond market that hit Paine Webber hard; significant layoffs ensued. This followed the acquisition of Kidder, Peabody, an investment banking firm that had fallen on hard times, from General Electric, and the expenditure further hurt Paine Webber's bottom line. By the end of 1994 the company had suffered a staggering 87 percent drop in earnings.

Nineteen ninety-six brought more challenges to Paine Webber. In 1989 it had run an advertising campaign to support its Provider line, a life-insurance policy. The campaign had included a direct-mail effort involving some 1 million pieces, along with the purchase of 800,000 consumer leads and a television spot featuring Paine Webber president Joseph J. Grano. Paine Webber discontinued the product in 1993 after selling 7,200 policies, but in 1996 buyers of the Provider policy initiated a class-action lawsuit, charging that Paine Webber's brokers had led clients to believe that Provider was not a life-insurance policy but a retirement investment. The company agreed to pay more than $332 million in fines as well as restitution. Also in 1996 it was ordered to pay $2.5 million for charges of illegal hiring practices stemming from an action in which it had lured a number of employees from a Prudential Insurance office.

Nonetheless, earnings in 1996 were higher than they had ever been, and in 1997 Paine Webber launched a new investment product, the Paine Webber EDGE. In 1998 German financial institution Dresdner Bank AG expressed an interest in buying Paine Webber, but as of fall 1999, no further move had been made.

TARGET MARKET

In 1999 Paine Webber purchased an interest in an Internet software company and launched on-line trading services targeted to clients at relatively lower income levels. "Lower income levels" was a relative term, since persons who required the services of an investment brokerage had to have something to invest in the first place. (An equally appropriate term would be "younger investors," since Paine Webber, like all marketers, tried to keep one eye on the future.)

In the main, however, Paine Webber's target market could be described as mature, both in terms of years and of assets. Thus a November 1998 news release accompanying the launch of the "Thank you, Paine Webber" campaign included this statement from Mark B. Sutton, president of the Paine Webber Private Client Group: "Paine Webber has enormous opportunities for growth, particularly as millions of affluent baby boomers seek guidance in managing their assets and transferring wealth to the next generation. This campaign emphasizes that in the age of the Internet, financial information has become a commodity, causing information overload and further complicating investment decisions. Now more than ever, excellent investment advice tailored to investors' needs is highly valued."

Placement of campaign spots and print ads was broad, with inclusion in more than 40 news, consumer, and trade publications and media placement on network and cable television programs including National Football League and college bowl games, as well as the popular *60 Minutes* news magazine program on CBS. Again, the latter tended to attract older viewers than many offerings on television.

Paine Webber's news release went on to note that quarterly research conducted in cooperation with the Gallup Organization had shown that "while many investors have ambitious plans for their futures, most underestimate the resources required to accomplish their goals, and few have considered wealth preservation planning." Simply put, this meant that many investors in their late 30s, 40s, and even 50s had not begun making adequate preparations for retirement, and Paine Webber sought to present itself as the solution to their problems.

COMPETITION

In 1998 Paine Webber ranked fifth among investment brokerages, with Merrill Lynch & Company in first place. It struggled to develop a position for itself as a brokerage offering strong individual service along with an aggressive institutional strategy. Meanwhile, as it launched "Thank you, Paine Webber," Stuart Elliott of the *New York Times* reported that both Merrill Lynch and John Nuveen & Company, another competitor, were in the process of changing advertising agencies.

Thanks in part to advertising that prominently featured its bull logo, thus carrying the image of an investor-friendly "bull market," Merrill Lynch had established strong name recognition with consumers. So had Fidelity Investments, a unit of the FMR Corporation whose highly personalized television advertising had also made its offerings a standout. Elliott reported that Fidelity and other brokerages were in the process of increasing their advertising presence in late 1998.

PAINE WEBBER'S MEDIA CONFERENCE

From December 7 to 11, 1998, Paine Webber held its 26th annual media conference at the McGraw-Hill Building in New York City. The five-day conference, as a company news release stated, was "designed to inform investors about the changes that have occurred within the [media] industry during the last year." It brought together representatives from a number of large media concerns, including Viacom, Time Warner, CBS, the *Washington Post,* the *New York Times,* Times Mirror, Knight-Ridder newspapers, Saatchi & Saatchi advertising, and many more.

Media Industry Newsletter commented on the absence of a major, if troubled, participant: *Reader's Digest,* still one of the nation's most widely circulated magazines. Tom Ryder of the Reader's Digest Association (RDA) had originally been scheduled to present "Phase 3" of the company's planned restructuring, but as it turned out, RDA was not ready for the presentation. Nonetheless, as *Media Industry Newsletter* conceded, Paine Webber media/entertainment managing director Chris Dixon and others managed to produce an impressive lineup. The conference, Dixon promised, would present a refreshing approach: instead of yet another discussion on the Internet and other new media, this one would place its greatest emphasis on the role of traditional media in the twenty-first century.

Paine Webber also had to contend with the somewhat troubled reputation it had acquired as the result of hardships during the 1980s and 1990s. Indeed, its choice of "Thank you, Paine Webber," a campaign first run in 1975, harkened back to a simpler time—or at least to what many perceived as a simpler time in hindsight. Meanwhile, Paine Webber kept a close watch on the competition. When Saatchi & Saatchi was invited to take part in a $50 million review for Chase Manhattan Bank in March 1998, it initially accepted, then pulled out, according to *Adweek,* for fear that a relationship with Chase Manhattan might be perceived as a conflict of interest.

MARKETING STRATEGY

The pullout from the Chase Manhattan bid may have been the event that sparked a rumor in *Adweek* that Paine Webber itself was on the hunt for a new agency. According to the April 13, 1998, report, the company had requested proposals from more than a dozen agencies. "Sources said Paine Webber needs a shop to take on creative and media chores for its corporate identity account," *Adweek* reported, "and would narrow the field to 12 this week. Two more cuts will be made before the company picks an agency in late June." Tony Dalton of Saatchi & Saatchi told *Adweek,* "I would be surprised if it [the Paine Webber account] were in play, and I would wait to see what the client had to say before deciding whether to defend."

It is no wonder that Dalton professed to be surprised by the rumor, which turned out to be just that—a rumor. Saatchi & Saatchi had maintained the account since 1981 and would continue to do so into 1999. It had launched its last campaign for Paine Webber in 1996, using the tag line "Invest with more intelligence." In one spot a 50-ish man was shown on a sailboat while a voice-over speculated as to how he had managed to achieve the sort of lifestyle that would allow him to go sailing while others his age were still working—and worrying about retirement. "How's he doing it?" the voice-over asked. The answer: "More research, insight, understanding."

In 1996 Paine Webber had devoted $19 million to its advertising, but in the following year the budget dropped to $8 million. By August 1998 the company had spent only $3.5 million; that would change with the launch of the new $20 million "Thank you, Paine Webber" campaign in November. The latter slogan had first appeared in 1975, created by Marshall Karp and Andrew Langer. It had run until 1987, when it was dropped in favor of successive campaigns, including "Invest with more intelligence." Elliott wrote in the *New York Times* that with the re-launch of the near-classic tag line, "Fans of advertising slogans that develop into catch phrases and enter the vernacular can gratefully start saying 'Thank you, Paine Webber' again" as Paine Webber "reviv[ed] the gratitude attitude."

Included in the initial launch were six print ads and two television spots that, in the words of the Paine Webber news release, "support[ed] its strategy to differentiate the firm by offering customized advice to high net-worth investors through highly trained investment professionals. The multi-million dollar print and television campaign capitalizes on Paine Webber's strong name recognition and its most memorable tag line, 'Thank you, Paine Webber.' " Launched just prior to Thanksgiving 1998, the campaign would continue well into 1999.

The print ads, with a heavy concentration on upscale publications, marked Paine Webber's first venture into print advertising in five years. As for the television spots, these juxtaposed images of worried investors—who presumably had not invested with Paine Webber—against those of satisfied-looking Paine Webber clients. One commercial showed parents and grandparents watching a children's soccer game as the thoughts of various spectators were projected in voice-overs. One mother said to herself, "It'd be great if money would grow as fast as these kids," while a father thought, "College in four years, costs up ... someone do the math here." By contrast, the thoughts of a happy Paine Webber investor were much simpler: "Thank you, Paine Webber." As the campaign progressed other spots depicted similar scenes on a commuter train and in an airport terminal.

OUTCOME

In January 1999 Denise Gellene of the *Los Angeles Times* gave a less than glowing appraisal of Paine Webber's television advertising. "The gratitude of these customers seems excessive," she wrote. "There's no evidence in these commercials that Paine Webber has performed remarkably; none of its customers are boarding Lear jets. And let's not forget that Paine Webber's customers are paying full-service commissions for investment advice. Maybe Paine Webber should be thanking them."

Also in January *Wall Street Letter* noted that "Though the firm dug up its old 'Thank you, Paine Webber,' slogan ... institutional salespeople reportedly had different feelings upon receiving their 1997 bonus checks" in February 1998. Investment earnings had been down, and *Wall Street Letter* attributed the cause to changes in key personnel, in particular sales director John Kelleher. According to the publication, "The jury apparently is still out" on whether the company would make the changes necessary to better compensate its sales force.

Likewise the jury was still out on the continuing "Thank you, Paine Webber" campaign. Certainly Paine Webber had weathered greater difficulties and come out on top. Like an investment, the campaign needed time to mature as it proceeded throughout 1999.

FURTHER READING

"ADVISORY/Paine Webber 26th Annual Media Conference." *Business Wire,* November 23, 1998.

"Corrections." *New York Times,* November 25, 1998, p. 2.

Dupree, Scotty. "Paine Webber Last Week Signed a Multi-Year Deal as the Executive Title Sponsor of ABC/Raycom College Football." *Mediaweek,* November 20, 1995, p. 9.

Elliott, Stuart. "Paine Webber Finds There's No Time Like the Present to Bring Back a Classic Catch Phrase" *New York Times,* November 20, 1998, p. 6.

Gellene, Denise. "For Paine Webber, Does Performance Count?" *Los Angeles Times,* January 14, 1999, p. C-6.

"Paine Webber." *Wall Street Letter,* January 4, 1999, p. 9.

"Paine Webber Account in Play: Seeks Advertising Agency for Creative and Corporate Image Work." *Adweek* (Western edition), April 13, 1998, p. 46.

"Paine Webber Could Have a Peck of Trouble." *Business Week,* October 7, 1996, p. 140.

"Paine Webber Introduces Advertising Campaign; Focuses on Investment Advice for High Net Worth Individuals." *Business Wire,* November 20, 1998.

"Paine Webber Reprises Familiar Tag in New Ad Thrust." *Brandweek,* November 23, 1998, p. 5.

"Paine Webber to Resume Advertising in Print." *Advertising Age,* October 5, 1998, p. 56.

"Paine Webber's 'Back to Basics' Media Conf. Leaves Out 'Most Basic' RDA." *Media Industry Newsletter,* November 30, 1998.

Judson Knight

Unilever PLC

Unilever House
Blackfriars
London, EC4P 4BQ
United Kingdom
Telephone: 44 20 78225252
Fax: 44 20 78226191
Web site: www.unilever.com

CAMPAIGN FOR REAL BEAUTY CAMPAIGN

OVERVIEW

In the most sweeping and ambitious advertising effort in the company's history, Unilever PLC launched a global ad campaign in 2003 that aimed not just to sell its new line of Dove brand products but also, in the words of Dove's U.S. marketing director, Philippe Harousseau, to "broaden the narrow and stereotypical view of beauty." Unilever was significantly expanding its Dove line from simple cleansing solutions (soaps, facial cleaners, and shower gels) to include deodorants, hair-care products, and more importantly, a whole new product category for the company: skin firming and lifting creams. To promote both the new products and the new idea of beauty, Dove and its ad agency, Ogilvy & Mather of Chicago, chose to use real women in the advertisements instead of models, and they selected women whose looks or weight were not typical for beauty-industry advertisements.

Dubbed the "Campaign for Real Beauty," it began as an outdoor campaign with billboards and mass-transit ads but eventually expanded to include print ads and TV spots, culminating in a 45-second spot that aired during the 2006 Super Bowl—all at an estimated total cost of over $100 million worldwide. The initial billboards in the United States showed six women, sizes 6–14, dressed only in white undergarments against a plain white background. (The rollout in each of the more than 10 countries where the campaign appeared followed a parallel course, with six women scouted locally and featured on billboards.) Equally important to the success of the campaign was Dove's interactive website, which offered descriptions of the product line and live discussion forums where women could discuss their feelings about the campaign.

By any standard the campaign was a smashing success. Not only did it help to increase Dove's global sales by 13 to 25 percent, but it also generated a phenomenal amount of media coverage. There was some backlash in the press, but the majority of critics found little fault with the campaign, and most lauded its willingness to use real women instead of idealized (and practically unattainable) icons of beauty. Industry awards were plentiful as well, making the campaign well worth the company's significant investment.

HISTORICAL CONTEXT

Dove soap emerged from product development research into ways of treating burn victims during World War II, and in the 1950s it was originally launched by Unilever in the United States as a moisturizing soap. The simple Dove soap bar was repositioned as early as 1957 as a "beauty bar" aimed at women with the spin that regular soaps would dry out their skin during bathing, while the Dove bar would not. From that point on such market differentiation and exclusive targeting of female consumers

Real women in Dove's Campaign for Real Beauty. IMAGE COURTESY OF THE ADVERTISING ARCHIVE LTD. REPRODUCED BY PERMISSION.

became the sole focus of the Dove brand. In addition, Dove set out to use clinical research to bolster its moisturizing claims, peppering its early ads with "dermatological studies" touting Dove as being milder on the skin than all other leading brands and using the tagline "Soap dries your skin, but Dove *creams* your skin while you wash."

It was not until 2001 that the Dove brand began to expand beyond skin cleansers into other personal-care categories, namely hair care, antiperspirants and deodorants, and finally, in 2004, "firming" lotions to tighten and smooth the skin. Unilever never abandoned its use of the term "Beauty Bar" for the Dove product, and the concept of beauty was the thread that connected its advertising for more than 50 years. It came as no surprise, then, that the conventional definition of beauty and the issue of a woman's self-image would become the thrust of Unilever's global campaign to introduce its new line of products aimed at women. Having spent half a century trying to associate its products with an abstract concept, Dove chose to take the bold step of redefining the historical notion of beauty (as depicted in advertising) by featuring women in its advertisements who looked radically different from the models traditionally used to promote beauty products.

TARGET MARKET

The Dove brand of products had always been aimed exclusively at women. (Unilever had other lines of grooming products specifically for men.) The "Campaign for Real Beauty" did not try to appeal to a group beyond that which was already in the company's sights, but it did set out to attract even more women between the ages of 18 and 45 in a new way. With the introduction in 2004 of a new line of skin-care products, the company moved beyond mere cleansers and entered a new product category aimed at women who were dissatisfied with the appearance of their skin, whether it was too saggy, blemished, wrinkled, or just not firm enough. Such products were typically the domain of more upscale cosmetics companies, such as Clinique, Lancôme, and Chanel. Dove was not seeking to lure high-end customers away from these boutique brands (a stretch-mark cream from Clinique, for instance, sold for $95 in 2005, while Dove's Intensive Firming Cream sold for only $7.99); instead, Dove sought to reach its established customer demographic with a new product line and chose a controversial ad campaign to garner as much media and consumer attention as possible.

The new line of skin creams was aimed squarely at women whose assessment of their own skin's appearance was less than optimal—which, in practical terms, meant just about all women. To verify this assumption Dove, in conjunction with the research consulting firm the Downing Street Group, commissioned a study that surveyed some 3,000 women in more than ten countries to find out just how they felt about their own appearance. The extensive results, published as *The Dove Report:*

BEAUTY ACROSS THE GLOBE

As Dove expanded its "Campaign for Real Beauty" to more than 10 countries, it found through its research that the issues of beauty and self-image among women were nearly universal. The percentages of women in Japan, Korea, Vietnam, France, Germany, and elsewhere who rated themselves either "beautiful" or "attractive" were as low as those in the United States. Interestingly, however, the company had to modify its advertising approach to fit the social mores of each country. In Brazil, for instance, the group of six women photographed in plain white undergarments was found to be overly prudish by testing groups, and so the final ads pictured women in lacier and more stylishly colorful bras and panties. In China, where partial nudity was considered scandalous, the models were photographed in less revealing outfits and were not touching or depicted quite as playfully as their U.S. counterparts.

Challenging Beauty, stated that, among other things, only 2 percent of women considered themselves "beautiful," while only 9 percent felt comfortable describing themselves as "attractive." The report's introduction said, "our vision is that a new definition of beauty will free women from self-doubt and encourage them to embrace their real beauty." Armed with this database of information about the self-images of women worldwide, Dove worked with Ogilvy to create an ad campaign that strove to subvert the expectations the public had about beauty in both advertising and daily life.

COMPETITION

Dove's main brand competitors for skin and body-care products worldwide were Nivea (made by Beiersdorf AG) and Neutrogena (made by Johnson & Johnson). In 2005 Nivea's European market share was 20 percent; Dove's was 5.5 percent. U.S. market shares were more balanced among the three rivals. In the same year Nivea launched a pan-European media campaign, complete with a theme song, "New Days," by the up-and-coming German band Asher Lane. The song became a hit in Europe and was released as a CD single that was available for purchase from Nivea's website as well as at music stores; the packaging sported a sticker with the Nivea logo. The campaign's main TV spot depicted a wide cross section of people—young and old, male and female—in myriad situations (for instance, bathing, shaving, running, exercising, playing, or relaxing) casually using a range of Nivea products while "New Days" played. The approach was far more typical than Unilever's and far less controversial. With its established lead in European product sales, Nivea had no stake in rocking the boat. Dove, on the other hand, had little to lose.

MARKETING STRATEGY

In fall 2003, armed with the exhaustive information from *The Dove Report,* Ogilvy and Unilever began what would become a worldwide media campaign, starting with a series of billboards in the United Kingdom. The ads featured an unretouched photograph of six women of varying sizes and ages, wearing nothing but plain white bras and panties, standing together against a white background. Each woman in the ad was scouted from the general British populace; no modeling agencies were used. The ad boasted the tagline "New Dove Firming. As tested on real curves." The notion of "reality" suffused the entire campaign, and Dove made sure to emphasize the fact that the women in its ads were everyday citizens and not idealized beauties. Of course, the company selected rather attractive, healthy-looking women for its ads, even if they were a larger size or not as young as expected. The initial billboards caused a stir in the British press, eliciting praise from those who lauded Dove's use of real women as models and derision from those who either felt that the ads promoted an unhealthy body weight or thought the women were simply unattractive. Either way, U.K. sales of the featured firming cream doubled within a month of the ads' appearance.

The campaign moved to the United States in 2004 with a similar use of billboards and outdoor signage, although in America the initial intent was not to sell a particular product but first to position Dove as a company whose main concern was breaking the molds of established "fashion beauty" imagery. Each billboard in this first phase featured an unretouched photograph of a woman whose looks or age were atypical for the beauty industry. The first woman selected to appear in an ad, scouted from a home for the elderly, was 96 years old. The text in the ad consisted of two words adjacent to two check boxes marked "Wrinkled?" or "Wonderful?" and was designed to prompt the viewer to think about the image and the concept of beauty. A 96-year-old woman was indeed wrinkled, but could she be beautiful too? Clearly Dove was sending the message that it thought so. Another billboard featured a plus-size model with the words "Oversized?" or "Outstanding?" Each ad in the initial series followed the same template, showing a woman who was either older, less thin, or less typically attractive than expected alongside a pair of words that viewers could mull over. The ads directed viewers to the

> **BEAUTY, BODY SIZE, AND WEALTH**
>
> Historically, what was considered beautiful or attractive had more to do with scarcity of resources than any other factor. In times past, when rich foods were less plentiful, being overweight was a sign of high status—it meant a person was not only eating well but could afford to do so; it was the poor who were underfed and thin. By the second half of the twentieth century, with the advent of corporate farming and cheaply made, fattening foods, anyone could "afford" to be fat, and thinness became a sign of status. The new ideal, one difficult to attain even for the wealthy, was to be ultrathin. Signaled in 1966 by the supplanting of robust icons of beauty such as Marilyn Monroe by the supermodel Twiggy—who stood 5 feet 7 and weighed only 91 pounds—beautiful came to be synonymous with unnaturally thin and free of body fat. In 2005 the average American model was 5 feet 11 inches tall and weighed 117 pounds, while the average American woman was 5 feet 4 inches and 140 pounds. Obesity had transformed from a sign of status to a social stigma, signifying a lack of self-control and the inability to afford high-quality, healthy foods.

company's website, where they could register their votes for either adjective; the subsequent poll results were tabulated on the site. This interactive component served to introduce people to the website and its various sections, which were aimed at stimulating discussion about the concept of beauty. The website was designed from the outset to be a cornerstone of the campaign, containing, along with information and images from the campaign, various forums for users to post their own feelings about their bodies, their lives, or the campaign itself. It was eventually expanded to include live discussion groups where visitors could share their thoughts with each other in real time.

Phase two of the U.S. campaign mirrored the British rollout, with six women scouted from locations ranging from a coffee shop to a college campus. Again, all six women were sizes 6–14 and were pictured standing together in plain white undergarments against a white background. Each was smiling, some were leaning on one another, and all appeared to be having a good time. Each was in her 20s. The image of all six women appeared simultaneously on billboards and mass-transit ads in most major U.S. markets, including Chicago, Miami, Boston, Atlanta, New York, Dallas, Los Angeles, San Francisco, and Washington, D.C. The image eventually appeared as a print ad in national magazines with the same "tested on real curves" tagline as well as text that stated, "Let's face it, firming the thighs of a size 2 supermodel is no challenge." The ads caused an even bigger sensation in the media in the United States than they had in Great Britain. Naysayers were few, although some found fault with the firming product itself, debunking its effectiveness. Others took issue with Unilever's mixed messages. While it used its Dove brand as a vehicle for transformative change in the ways that women and beauty were regarded in advertising, one of its other product lines, Axe deodorant, was being promoted with ads whose theme was sexually provocative and featured thin, attractive, scantily clad models fawning seductively over men who were presumably wearing the Axe product. In any case, the enthusiasm about the use of real women in the Dove ads led the six women to be interviewed on high-profile TV programs such as *The Today Show* and to appear on the cover of *People* magazine.

Dove continued its crusade to examine, redefine, and boost women's self-image in relation to beauty and body shape through its website and through its philanthropic efforts. To this end, in conjunction with the Girl Scouts of America, Dove helped fund (with an initial donation of $3 million) a program called "Uniquely Me!" that was designed to foster self-esteem in girls aged 8–17. In addition it created its own Dove Self-Esteem Fund for the same purpose. During the 2005 Super Bowl Dove ran a commercial not for its products but for this program, spending $2.5 million for the spot, hoping that it would both encourage support for the Self-Esteem Fund and continue to bolster the understanding of Dove's commitment to improving the self-images of women. Of the decision to promote the Dove Self-Esteem Fund rather than a particular product during the most expensive advertising time on television, Philippe Harousseau, U.S. marketing director for Dove, said, "It's time to free the next generation from these [beauty] stereotypes and give girls the tools they need to discover their own definition of beauty."

OUTCOME

Dove's gamble to create controversy by attempting to redefine the concept of beauty paid off in spades, and the value of the resulting media coverage far outweighed the financial costs associated with the campaign itself. According to Unilever's internal research, the media coverage generated by the campaign was worth 30 times more than the paid-for media space. Dove's global sales rose 25 percent in 2005, thanks in large part to its advertising blitz. In Asia sales increased 26 percent, while

Dove's U.S. sales increased by a total of 13 percent in 2005 over the previous year. Based on this success, Dove planned to roll out three new product platforms in 2006, including new skin-toning creams, advanced hair-care products, and an expanded line of its skin-firming lotions, all advertised with the same paradigm-inverting use of real women instead of models.

The campaign picked up numerous ad-industry awards, including the Grand Prix at the 2005 European EFFIE Awards (a prestigious advertising-awards program hosted by the European Association of Communication Agencies), a Gold Euro EFFIE in the Toiletries and Beauty category, the Best of Show award at the 2005 Canadian Media Innovation Awards, and the Rethink Pink! Best Marketing Award for 2005. (The Rethink Pink! Conference, held annually in the United Kingdom, focused on marketing to women.) In addition, the advertising-news magazine *Campaign* named Dove its International Advertiser of the Year.

The impact of Dove's "Campaign for Real Beauty" could be seen in the trail of imitators it left in its wake. In 2005 the sportswear company Nike released a series of print ads featuring real women by using photographs of body parts (thighs, buttocks, arms, shoulders, legs, etc.) with accompanying text in which the woman in the photograph frankly discussed her features. A sample tagline: "My shoulders aren't dainty or proportional to my hips. Some say they are like a man's. I say, leave men out of it." Also in 2005, cosmetics giant Revlon chose 58-year-old actress Susan Sarandon as a model and spokesperson. Both Nike and Revlon followed Dove's lead, using either real women or atypical women to help sell their products. While the trend was never destined to catch on industry-wide, there was no doubt that Unilever and Ogilvy steered Dove into advertising territory worth emulating.

FURTHER READING

Brothers, Joyce. "Beauty Is No Longer Exclusive Domain of Magazines and Films; Dove's 'Campaign' Ads Are Raging Success because They Are Aspirational, but 'Doable.'" *Advertising Age,* August 1, 2005, p. 14.

Garfield, Bob. "Garfield's Ad Review: Women May Be 'Real' but Product Is Baloney." *Advertising Age,* July 25, 2005, p. 53.

Howard, Theresa. "Dove Ad Gets Serious for Super Bowl; 'True Colors' of Real Beauty Part of Self-Esteem Message." *USA Today,* January 12, 2006, p. B1.

Mills, Dominic. "Dove's Commitment to 'Real Beauty' Is Only Skin Deep." *Daily Telegraph* (London), January 18, 2005, p. 34.

Orbach, Susie. "Fat Is an Advertising Issue." *Campaign,* June 17, 2005, p. 26.

Prior, Molly. "Dove Ad Campaign Aims to Redefine Beauty." *Women's Wear Daily,* October 8, 2004, p. 18.

Vranica, Suzanne. "The Advertising Report: Dove's Curvaceous Campaign Tries to Renew Brand's Passion." *Wall Street Journal,* October 5, 2005, p. B3.

Wolf, Naomi. *The Beauty Myth: How Images of Beauty Are Used against Women.* New York: Anchor Books, 1992.

Jonathan Kolstad

DO IT ONCE. DO IT RIGHT. CAMPAIGN

OVERVIEW

In 1998 Unilever PLC subsidiary Lever Brothers, makers of Wisk laundry detergent, launched a new advertising campaign with the tag line "Do It Once. Do It Right." The primary element in the campaign, created by J. Walter Thompson (JWT) USA in New York, was television commercials. In one spot a woman's voice announced "Wisk presents the ten thousand million things we have to do." There followed a series of hilarious scenes with laconic titles, provided by the voice-over, such as "Locate stuff," "Prevent osteoporosis," and "Save the planet." After this litany, the voice-over presented yet another thing women had to deal with in the course of their busy workday: "Then we still have to do the laundry. Really well. Good thing Wisk has a targeted cleaning system. Now everything you wash gets done right the first time. Do it once. Do it right."

Bob Garfield of *Advertising Age* lauded the new spot, which he called "witty, refreshing, thoughtful." The commercial was particularly impressive, Garfield wrote, in light of Wisk's past history as a brand name that "evokes painful memories of unbearable shrillness, obnoxious and demeaningly stereotyped gender roles." He was referring to Wisk's "Ring-around-the-Collar" commercials from the 1970s.

Despite—or rather, precisely because of—the fact that many viewers found the "Ring-around-the-Collar" ads irritating, the earlier campaign proved one of the most successful in history. It had earned a place among *Advertising Age*'s top 100 campaigns of the twentieth century and helped Wisk become one of the leading brands of laundry detergent. This in turn helped pave the way for the triumph of liquid brands, such as Wisk, over old-fashioned powdered detergents. The 1998 spots helped maintain Wisk's position among leaders, and assisted in Unilever's resurgence against its primary competitor, Procter & Gamble (P&G), whose Tide brand had long held the top spot.

HISTORICAL CONTEXT

In the early 1950s Lever Brothers introduced Surf as a detergent to compete with Tide, which debuted in 1946. Although Surf established a strong market position, it did little to shake Tide's hold, so in 1956 Lever Brothers brought out Wisk, the first heavy-duty liquid detergent. Its uniqueness made Wisk a significant contender almost from the start and quickly earned it a market share of 4.2 percent, despite the fact that the new brand cost nearly twice as much as most powdered detergents. But by the mid-1960s, as the novelty of liquid detergents began to fade, so did Wisk's position. With less than 3 percent of the market in 1967, the company decided on a new strategy. Thus was born "Ring-around-the-Collar," the creation of James Jordan.

In 1968 Jordan, who went on to establish Jordan, McGrath, Case & Taylor, was a copywriter with Batten, Barton, Durstine & Osborn (BBDO). "It took about a minute and a half to write that commercial," he later told *Advertising Age.* "And the rest was history." Originally, Lever Brothers had not been enthusiastic about the spots, which focused on the dirty rings left on shirt collars by less-than-effective brands of laundry detergent. But the commercials, involving embarrassing situations in which homemakers were shamed by public exposure of "ring around the collar" on the clothes of family members, gained huge exposure for Wisk.

"It was the first time a liquid detergent dramatized the product's cleaning benefit," wrote Robyn Griggs in *Advertising Age,* and largely as a result of the spots, Wisk became the first Lever Brothers brand to sell 1 million cases a year. It emerged as the leading liquid detergent in the United States, and with an 8 percent share of a highly segmented market, it occupied the number two slot overall, behind Tide. Yet in 1987, the year Wisk dropped "Ring-around-the-Collar," new Liquid Tide knocked Wisk out of second place.

In 1989 Lever Brothers moved its advertising account to JWT, which assigned copywriter J. J. Jordan—ironically, the son of James Jordan—to the account. Although the campaign was new, the approach proved much the same as that of "Ring-around-the-Collar," using concepts of shame and embarrassment, albeit presented in a humorous light. In one spot, an actor was splashed with mud while those around chided him with "tisk, tisk, tisk." A voice-over then responded with "Wisk, Wisk, Wisk."

TARGET MARKET

Despite the many changes that had occurred in the social fabric of American life since the introduction of Wisk in the mid-1950s, the focus of its marketing remained on women. Even though a large portion of America's female population worked outside the home, typically it was still women—whether married women with outside jobs, homemakers, single mothers, or single women—who were responsible for the laundry in their households.

Feminists might have considered the old "Ring-around-the-Collar" approach demeaning, as Garfield suggested; by contrast, the "Do It Once. Do It Right" campaign two decades later paid tribute to the many roles women are required to perform. In place of shame, a staple of advertising geared toward women from the earliest days of modern marketing, the new campaign offered an attitude of pride, encouraging women to feel good about their ability to succeed at a wide variety of tasks.

Discussing the change in Wisk's approach, Garfield asked, "What if [shock TV talk show host] Jerry Springer hosted a civil, witty round-table discussion that commenced the end of gratuitous sex and violence on TV?... What if the ghost of [ineffectual 1930s British prime minister] Neville Chamberlain appeared at the United Nations, admonishing the world to stop the Serbs before it is too late? It would be ironic, that's what, because these people are too identified with ugly events to be imagined transforming from monster or coward or scapegoat to hero." Yet Wisk had effected precisely such a transformation with "a striking new spot that speaks to busy launderers with candor and charm."

RING AROUND THE RACETRACK

Detergents and racing may not seem like an obvious combination, but Wisk managed to bring the two together for a 1999 promotional campaign in the southeast. During the period from March 16 to April 30, some 600,000 specially marked boxes of Wisk contained in-box premiums—die-cast replicas of historic race cars. Whereas typically 50 percent of Wisk retailers in an area participate in a promotion, the race-car campaign, supported by sales incentives, radio, print ads, direct mail, and in-store displays, enjoyed 85 percent participation. The campaign, spearheaded by Championship Group in Atlanta, doubled or tripled Wisk market share in the area during the period of its run. Total cost of the promotion was less than $500,000.

COMPETITION

The market for laundry detergents was divided not only among many brands, but also among several types of

THIRTY OUT OF THIRTY UNILEVER EXECUTIVES

In early 1999 *Forbes* reported on the resurgence of Unilever's soap division, thanks in part to the efforts of executive Niall FitzGerald. One of FitzGerald's most trying experiences, according to Deborah Orr of *Forbes,* was a 1994 scandal surrounding the company's Persil Power. The problem with the detergent, marketed in Britain, was not its inability to clean but rather its tendency to clean too well. Hence as Orr noted, "the British press had a field day—'It's Official! Persil Can Rot Your Knickers'."

During this difficult time, FitzGerald had a pivotal experience when he gathered 30 Unilever executives in a board room and asked how many did their own laundry. " 'Not one person raised a hand,' he says with amazement. 'There we were, trying to figure out why customers wouldn't buy our soap—and we didn't know the first thing about how it was used' That taught FitzGerald a lesson he heeds to this day: Never lose touch with your customer." In the end, FitzGerald elected to discontinue Persil Power, a move that meant a loss of several hundred million dollars in the short run but that ultimately served Unilever's long-term aim of gaining market share against Procter & Gamble and others.

detergent. As Tide was the first significant powdered brand in 1946, so Wisk a decade later became the first major liquid detergent. With the introduction of Liquid Tide in the mid-1980s, Lever Brothers responded by bringing out Advanced Action Wisk, and the company continued to create newer varieties of the brand to compete with P&G's market leader.

But the early days of laundry detergent's history also saw the introduction of what was then a much more obscure phenomenon: concentrated powders. The first brand in this category was probably SA-8, a creation of the Amway Corporation marketed primarily by direct sales in the late 1950s and early 1960s. The first mass-market concentrate, however, appeared in 1980, when Colgate-Palmolive introduced Fresh Start.

Fresh Start proved to be ahead of its time, but a decade later, in the early 1990s, concentrated powders began to take away market share both from regular powders and from liquids. In response, Lever Brothers introduced Wisk Power Scoop, using advertising built around the sort of scientific claims typical of the 1950s. The company promoted the new product as "an entirely new class of enzymes specifically designed to dislodge and dissolve oily dirt and stains." Power Scoop was "concentrated to the theoretical limit of density," advertising claimed. Yet then-Lever Brothers president David F. Webb, discussing the concentrated quality of the product with *Advertising Age,* used language familiar from the 1960s or early 1970s: "Small is beautiful," he announced, referring to the reduced packaging required for Power Scoop.

Tide and other powdered brands moved to concentrates, but overall there was a trend in favor not only of concentrates over traditional powders, but also of liquid over powder. By 1999 liquid detergents, despite their higher prices, for the first time exceeded sales of powders. The key players remained Unilever and P&G—with the latter still in the lead. P&G, with Tide, Cheer, Gain, and Era, controlled almost 54 percent of the U.S. market, while Unilever, with Wisk, Surf, and All, held a 19 percent share.

MARKETING STRATEGY

In June 1998 Lever Brothers presented the "Do It Once. Do It Right" campaign, which primarily centered around a single television spot. At the opening of the commercial, a woman's voice announces "Wisk presents the ten thousand million things we have to do every day." First among these is "Locate stuff," accompanied by a shot of a woman reaching under a bed, searching for something. There follow a series of other tasks, each with an accompanying dramatization—all of them decidedly tongue-in-cheek. "Prevent osteoporosis" shows a woman sitting astride a cow and balancing a glass of milk on her head. Under the spoken heading "Conquer flab," another woman is shown jogging furiously behind an ice-cream truck. Next, the voice-over announces "Train dog," and this time no woman appears, only a Labrador retriever balancing a model train on its head. Another segment, "Control frizz," is a shot of a woman with birds nesting in her hair.

The duties become ever more lofty as the spot progresses. The next one is "Remind kids of family infrastructure," which features a scene of a child playing before a portrait of the parents dressed in the uniforms of dictators. Next to last is "Save the planet," a serene tableau with a woman standing before a sky filled with stars. Finally the commercial comes to its central theme. "Then," the voice-over announces, as though to say "After all this", "we still have to do the laundry. Really well. Good thing Wisk has a targeted cleaning system. Now everything you wash gets done right the first time. Do it once. Do it right." During the week of

September 7 to 13, 1998, Lever Brothers and Wisk held a position among the top 50 brands advertising on network prime-time television, with 11 spots on ABC, CBS, NBC, FOX, UPN, and WB.

OUTCOME

"What's so marvelous about this ad," wrote Garfield, "is how it recognizes the responsibilities, concerns, and vanities of the busy 1998 woman without pandering or idealizing—or going into an angry tirade." He declared the spot "endearing, self-deprecating, and above all, knowing about the semi-liberated American mom." As Garfield noted, Wisk had come a long way from the days of its famously irritating "Ring-around-the-Collar" spot, and although the new ad proved a critical success, it came at a time when Unilever faced ever more stiff competition from P&G. So even though Unilever experienced gains in sales of its liquid detergents—not only Wisk but All and Surf—during 1998, they did not offset losses in sales of powdered All and Surf. For the 52-week-period ending November 28, 1998, the company posted gains of 14.8 percent in its liquid detergents but losses of 19.6 in powders. P&G, by contrast, lost 10.9 percent in powders and gained 23.6 percent in liquids.

As Pamela Sauer related in *Chemical Market Reporter,* "the issue in 1999 for the U.S. laundry detergent industry will again be the battle of liquid versus powder." According to a March 1999 report in *Brandweek,* P&G was about to launch a new effort to "revitalize the slowly dying powder laundry detergent category" with the introduction of new Tide and Cheer product extensions, priced low to contend with Wisk and Surf. This would be accompanied by a $30 million advertising budget. At the same time, industry publications hailed the resurgence of Lever Brothers as P&G's leading competitor—an indication that the fierce ongoing battle between the two companies would continue into a new century.

FURTHER READING

Bittar, Christine. "P&G Sets Anti-Fade Plan for Ailing Powder Detergents: New SKUs." *Brandweek,* March 22, 1999, p. 4.

"Breaking: Wisk: Nobody Knows the Trouble." *Advertising Age,* June 1, 1998, p. 10.

Freeman, Laurie. "Wisk Rings in New Ad Generation." *Advertising Age,* September 18, 1989, p. 1.

Garfield, Bob. "Wisk Blots Out Stain of 'Ring Around the Collar,' " *Advertising Age,* June 8, 1998, p. 53.

Griggs, Robyn. "Irritation Tagline Rings True for Wisk." *Advertising Age,* March 29, 1999, p. C41.

"Lever Intros Whisk HE for High-Efficiency Front-Loaders." *Brandweek,* April 27, 1998, p. 8.

Orr, Deborah. "A Giant Reawakens." *Forbes,* January 25, 1999, p. 52.

"Reggie Bronze." *Brandweek,* March 29, 1999, p. R22.

Sauer, Pamela. "Finding the Profit in Liquids." *Chemical Market Reporter,* February 1, 1999, p. FR-3.

Thurm, Samuel. "Ten Who Helped Build N.Y.'s Sold Foundation: Creating a Washday Legacy Via 'Ring Around the Collar,'" *Advertising Age,* January 27, 1997, p. C12.

Walsh, Kerri et al. "Soaps and Detergents: Sharing the Risks and Rewards." *Chemical Week,* January 27, 1999.

"A Weekly Ranking of the Top 50 Brands' Advertising in Network Prime Time." *Mediaweek,* September 28, 1998.

Judson Knight

Unilever United States

700 Sylvan Avenue
Englewood Cliffs, New Jersey 07632-9976
USA
Telephone: (201) 894-2104
Fax: (201) 871-8257
Web site: www.unileverusa.com

REAL COOKING CAMPAIGN

OVERVIEW

Although dry mix meals had been available since 1937, when Kraft introduced its packaged Kraft Macaroni and Cheese dinner, the category did not begin to expand until 1970, when General Mills launched its Betty Crocker brand of dry dinner mixes called Hamburger Helper. The consumer-goods giant Unilever jumped into selling dry dinner mixes (food kits that usually required only the addition of meat for a complete meal) with its Lipton Sizzle & Stir in 1999. By then the total category accounted for $450 million in annual sales. In 2000 Lipton Sizzle & Stir claimed $30 million in sales in the category, which had grown to $500 million in total sales. The number one brand that year, with $405 million in sales, was Hamburger Helper. Kraft Foods' Stove Top Oven Creations captured $65 million in sales.

Despite the successful introduction of its new product, which had been supported by a $15 million marketing campaign created by the New York office of ad agency Bartle Bogle Hegarty, Unilever hoped to increase sales of its Lipton Sizzle & Stir brand to $40 million in 2001. As part of the growth effort, Bartle Bogle Hegarty developed a new ad campaign for the brand. Called "Real Cooking," the campaign put a unique twist on the traditional family gathered for dinner, using celebrities in the roles of parents and kids. It had a budget of $25 million and, like the initial campaign, included television spots and print ads.

"Real Cooking" was a hit, earning praise from *Adweek,* which named one of the television commercials a Best Spot of 2001. Also recognizing the TV spots for their humor and creativity were *Entertainment Weekly, Time,* and *USA Today.* But while the campaign was a success, the product was not. Sales of Lipton Sizzle & Stir failed to meet Unilever's expectations, and in 2002 the company canceled the campaign and shifted its marketing focus to its more popular Lipton Side Dishes brand.

HISTORICAL CONTEXT

When Unilever United States made the decision in 1999 to venture into the rapidly growing category of dry dinner mixes, the company did so by expanding its Lipton brand. At the time Lipton was best known for its variety of teas, dry soup mixes (especially Lipton Onion Soup), and dry side-dish mixes (such as Lipton Noodles & Sauce). The new product, Lipton Sizzle & Stir, was launched in January 2000 with the support of a $15 million marketing campaign that included television spots and print ads. The campaign, which was created by Bartle Bogle Hegarty, New York, targeted women ages 25 to 44 years old and had the tagline "Surprisingly Real." TV spots used supposedly real situations to highlight the idea that Sizzle & Stir was a more substantial or "real" product than competing dry dinner mixes. In one spot a teenage boy dropped a fork on the floor, picked it up, wiped it off on his shirt, then placed the fork on the table beside his mother's dinner plate as the words "Real teenager. Would rather be someplace else," scrolled across the screen.

The campaign helped push sales of Lipton Sizzle & Stir to $30 million during its first year on the market. Although the "Surprisingly Real" campaign was a success, Unilever hoped to attain annual sales of $40 million the following year. Bartle Bogle Hegarty was charged with creating a new campaign for the product. The new campaign took the idea of traditional family dinner settings and replaced the standard cute kids and patient parents with not-so-typical characters played by an unusual mix of celebrities. Themed "Real Cooking," the campaign began in early 2001.

TARGET MARKET

The goal of the Lipton Sizzle & Stir "Real Cooking" campaign was to reach all busy families, and in particular mothers who may have been working outside of the home but were also responsible for serving healthy meals at the end of the day. A report in *Advertising Age* cited studies revealing that mothers, regardless of how hectic their schedules were, wanted to mother the way that their own moms had done. Studies also found that many women were frustrated or felt guilty about their inability to emulate the cultural definition of traditional moms in the style of June Cleaver, the ideal mother in the 1950s sitcom *Leave It to Beaver.* "Real Cooking" was designed to convince these women that it was possible to serve a home-cooked meal without spending hours chopping, stirring, and sautéing.

The campaign further enhanced its message by using celebrities easily recognized by women 30 to 45 years old, the main purchasers of meal kits. Reaching a younger demographic was an alternate aspect of the campaign. According to *Supermarket News,* in 2001 consumers ages 15 to 24 ate out three or more times each week. Bringing these young people back to the family kitchen to enjoy a home-cooked dinner was a potential benefit of the campaign, but more importantly, it could help establish brand identity with young consumers who would be the purchasers of meal kits in the future.

COMPETITION

Kraft Foods got its start in 1903, when James L. Kraft began a wholesale cheese business in Chicago. In 1937 Kraft introduced the granddaddy of convenience foods, Kraft Macaroni and Cheese. It did not take busy housewives long to appreciate that the new convenience foods could help them make a good meal with less time in the kitchen. Other convenience foods followed. Stove Top Stuffing mix became available in 1972 (at the time the brand was owned by General Foods). Kraft's Stove Top brand was revamped in 1998 as Stove Top Oven Classics, boxed meals that included everything but the meat. It was reintroduced to consumers with a $15.5 million marketing campaign. Stove Top Oven Classics quickly caught on, and by 2000 sales had jumped 51 percent to $65 million. In 2001 Kraft added three new flavor varieties to the brand. But with ever increasing, and less expensive, meal kit options available to consumers—110 such products were offered in 2002—Kraft's Stove Top brand sales were slipping, achieving just $40 million in sales in 2002. Kraft discontinued its Stove Top Oven Classics meal kits in 2003.

General Mills may have been best known for its brand icon Betty Crocker. The mythological homemaker got her start in 1921 as a pen name that consumers wrote to for baking advice. Betty Crocker began offering consumers convenience foods with the 1931 introduction of Bisquick baking mix. In 1950 General Mills published the first Betty Crocker cookbook, and in 1970 the company launched Hamburger Helper under the Betty Crocker brand. Although Kraft's Macaroni and Cheese mix had been on the market for close to 40 years when Hamburger Helper was introduced, Hamburger Helper fueled the popularity of dinner meal kits. Eventually the brand was expanded to include Chicken Helper and Tuna Helper. Despite growing competition from brands such as Kraft's Stove Top Oven Classics and Lipton's Sizzle & Stir, Hamburger Helper maintained its number

UNILEVER PROGRAM HELPS KIDS VISIT NATIONAL PARKS

The America's Best Classroom program was part of an ongoing, multimillion-dollar effort by Unilever to help preserve and protect the United States' national parks. In 2002 the program, through a partnership with the National Park Foundation and the Albertsons grocery-store chain, provided $190,000 in scholarships to kids from 18 communities. The scholarships helped fund trips to national parks for more than 2,500 kids from Boys and Girls Clubs in participating communities throughout the United States. Scholarships were awarded based on the number of purchases made of Unilever products at Albertsons stores in each community. Participating communities included Dallas, Chicago, Phoenix, Denver, and Orlando.

one spot, with a 75 percent market share of the dry-dinner-mixes category in 2001. To help maintain its top spot and ward off competitors, General Mills reintroduced its "Helping Hand" spokescharacter, first used in advertising for the Hamburger Helper brand in 1977. Beginning in September 2001 television spots appeared that featured an updated version of the disembodied, four-fingered hand with eyes, a red nose, and a mouth; the accompanying voice-over stated, "Helping you make a great dinner tonight."

MARKETING STRATEGY

To help Lipton Sizzle & Stir break through the cacophony of typical food advertising, Bartle Bogle Hegarty took a nontraditional approach to traditional families and dinnertime. The "Real Cooking" campaign began in February 2001 and included television spots and print ads. The TV spots portrayed a traditional family dinner scenario of parents stirring a hot pan on the stove and kids arguing about who would set the table, but with what could only be described as a nontraditional family preparing the meal.

Kicking off the campaign was a television spot titled "The Woolerys," which was followed by a spot titled "The Ts." Both spots featured an oddball cast of characters—a who's who of former A-list celebrities—filling the roles of parents and kids. Starring as the parents in "The Woolerys" were game-show host Chuck Woolery and talk-show host Sally Jesse Raphael, and actor Pat Morita (of the *Karate Kid* films) and singer Little Richard played the argumentative siblings. The spot opened with Sally chopping a carrot into a skillet on a stove while Chuck read instructions to her from the back of a box of Sizzle & Stir. Chuck stated that the serving instructions suggested adding broccoli, to which Sally responded, "That's just a suggestion. I grew this carrot and, so help me, I'm going to use it." In the midst of the discussion over what vegetable to use, Pat was busy setting the table. Sally called Little Richard to "see if Pat needs help setting the table," to which Little Richard, in typical annoyed-kid fashion, tossed a spoon onto the table and said, "There. I helped." A battle between the two "brothers" was stopped when Chuck, in his sternest dad voice, said simply, "Boys." Sally added, "Come on, boys. Can't we have one nice meal together?"

"The Ts" followed a similar format but with actor Mr. T, complete with gold necklaces and Mohawk haircut, as the dad and actress Lonnie Anderson as the mom. Taking on the roles of brother and sister were actor George Hamilton and gymnast Mary Lou Retton. In the spot Mr. T was standing over the sizzling pan of food on the stove while Lonnie called, "George. Set the table." George, engrossed in a program on television, responded, "In a minute." On the sidelines was Mary Lou, who answered the ringing telephone and said in a teasing voice, "George. It's a girl." George took the call, saying to Mary Lou, "At least I get calls." With the inquisitive family looking on, George looked uncomfortable and said into the phone that he couldn't talk. After hanging up the phone he said to his "parents" and "sister," "She's not my girlfriend." Mary Lou tauntingly responded, "Is too." At which point George took a big-brotherly swipe at her. Mr. T scolded in his coarse voice, "Knock it off."

Each television spots had the tagline "When you cook, you're a family" and sent the message that the definition of family as well as family cooking had changed over the years and that Sizzle & Stir was ready to meet the changing needs of both. Print ads showed the pseudo-families gathered in their respective kitchens while mom cooked dinner. Included in the bottom right portion of the ads was the tagline "When you cook, you're a family," a menu stating "Dinner at the Woolerys" or "Dinner at the Ts," and a list of ingredients: a package of Sizzle & Stir, and appropriate meat and vegetables.

OUTCOME

The "Real Cooking" campaign was recognized for its humorous and creative approach toward families gathered around the table for dinner. An article in the *New York Times* described the campaign as "offbeat" and stated further that it seemed to have "captured the public's imagination." In addition, *Adweek* named the "Woolerys" television commercial as one of its Best Spots. *Entertainment Weekly, USA Today,* and *Time* also each named "The Woolerys" as one of the best TV commercials of 2001. Writing for *Advertising Age,* Bob Garfield stated that the campaign created by Bartle Bogle Hegarty was "fabulous." He added that the use of nontraditional families in a traditional setting coupled with good food photography almost assured that the campaign would not fail.

Fail it did, however. In January 2002 Unilever canceled its "Real Cooking" campaign citing the failure of Lipton's Sizzle & Stir meal kits to live up to the company's sales expectations of an estimated $40 million annually. Although the company spent about $38 million in advertising for the brand from 2000 through September 2001, it reported just $30 million in sales. Recognizing that the brand was floundering with consumers, the company refocused its marketing on its Lipton Side Dishes, which accounted for $250 million in sales in 2000. Unilever charged Bartle Bogle Hegarty with creating a campaign as edgy as the Sizzle & Stir effort for that product line. The new $15 million campaign for Lipton Side Dishes, which began in May 2002 with the theme "Dinner Games," replaced the Sizzle & Stir campaign.

FURTHER READING

Carpenter, Dave. "Kraft Puts Big Effort into Making Food More Convenient." *Chicago Sun-Times,* June 17, 2002.

Crook, Laura. "Hamburger Helper Offers Generous, Tasty Portions." *Spokane (WA) Spokesman-Review,* October 17, 2001.

Dornblaser, Lynn. "Meal Kits—The Next Generation? Kraft Foods Introduces Freshmade Creations Line." *Prepared Foods,* March 1, 2001.

"Editorial: Why Unilever Is a Smart Client." *Advertising Age,* January 21, 2002.

Garfield, Bob. "New Spots for Sizzle & Stir Let Real Family Values Ring True." *Advertising Age,* February 12, 2001.

"Kids Trek to National Parks for Enriching Experience in 'Living' Classrooms." *PR Newswire,* June 17, 2002.

Lauro, Patricia Winters. "Advertising: Lipton Shakes Up a Stodgy Image." *New York Times,* May 8, 2001.

Mills, Karren. "General Mills to Buy Pillsbury." *Oklahoma City Journal Record,* July 18, 2000.

Neff, Jack. "Lipton Sizzle & Stir: Alicia Rockmore." *Advertising Age,* October 8, 2001.

Thompson, Stephanie. "Bartle Bogle Ads Deliver Real Thing for Sizzle & Stir." *Advertising Age,* April 24, 2000.

———. "Lipton Stirs Up 'Family' Effort; Familiar Faces Gather around Table in $25 Million Marketing Campaign." *Advertising Age,* February 5, 2001.

———. "Prepared Dinners: Oven Meals Challenge Microwave." *Advertising Age,* June 24, 2002.

———. "Raising the Hand; Hamburger Helper Revives Its Familiar Spokescharacter." *Advertising Age,* September 3, 2001.

———. "Strategies: Sizzle & Stir's Hot Spots Get Shelved; Unilever Shifts Focus and Funds to Better Sellers." *Advertising Age,* January 14, 2002.

Zwieback, Elliot. "Sell Young Shoppers on Home Eating." *Supermarket News,* May 14, 2001.

Rayna Bailey

SOOTHING CUCUMBER EYE TREATMENTS ADS CAMPAIGN

OVERVIEW

In July 1998 Chesebrough-Pond's, a division of Unilever United States, introduced a new item—Soothing Cucumber Eye Treatments—to its Pond's line of facial care products. These were pliable, premoistened eye pads that were designed to look and smell like real cucumbers and that Pond's claimed would "relax and relieve tired eyes." Using cucumber slices over the eyes had long been a staple treatment in spas and salons. Pond's hoped that its synthetic version of this age-old remedy for swollen eyes would captivate consumers who wanted an indulgent beauty regime that also provided concrete benefits. Soothing Cucumber Eye Treatments, which contained cucumber extract, aloe, vitamin E, chamomile, and green tea, promised to reduce eye area puffiness and lighten dark under-eye circles.

To promote the new product, Pond's turned to its advertising agency, Ogilvy & Mather, to create a campaign that would not only fuel the sales of Soothing Cucumber Eye Treatments but also continue to modernize the company's image. The resulting print campaign was a visually stunning effort that incorporated Soothing Cucumber Eye Treatments into simple, uncluttered ads. The ads bore only the tag line "Feast Your Eyes," the Pond's name, and small-print copy listing the product's ingredients and extolling its virtues in short, declarative sentences ("Better than real cucumber"; "Relax away puffiness in 10 blissful minutes"), thus making the product itself the focal point of the executions. The pads were depicted tumbling out of a glistening glass jar, looking like nothing so much as thinly sliced cucumbers—right down to the seed patch in the middle. The effect was intentional. "We made face care have appetite appeal," Mike Indursky, the category director at Pond's, told *Advertising Age.*

Soothing Cucumber Eye Treatments performed far above expectations. The product had a profound effect on the company's image, helping Pond's in its quest to position itself as an innovative company capable of meeting its powerful competitors head-on. Moreover, Soothing Cucumber Eye Treatments and its supporting campaign helped bring younger consumers to the Pond's facial care line, an important accomplishment for the brand.

HISTORICAL CONTEXT

Pond's was one of the original participants in the birth of the facial care industry, and it had gone on to become an "institution in a jar," as the April 26, 1999, issue of *Advertising Age* quipped. But while its cold cream could claim the distinction of being one of the oldest cleaners still in existence, the storied history of Pond's alone could not ensure the continued success of the company as the skin care market modernized and high-tech formulations came to be preferred by consumers. With the debut of over-the-counter products containing alpha-hydroxy acids in early 1990s, a premium was increasingly placed on laboratory-engineered offerings over the old-fashioned products made by Pond's. The company did make efforts to keep up with these changes, and in 1993 it created the

Pond's Institute, a research and development facility dedicated to formulating cutting-edge products. Despite its best efforts, however, Pond's continued to struggle with image problems. According to the October 13, 1997, issue of *Advertising Age,* Pond's was "having a rough time in facial care," with its sales of both moisturizers and cleansers steadily decreasing.

It was interesting that the opportunity for a turnaround by Pond's was provided, although unintentionally, by a competitor. In 1997 the Andrew Jergen's Company released its Biore line of facial cleansing products. Among the new offerings was Biore's Pore Perfectstrip, which adhered to the face and removed blackheads. The cosmetic was an instant success. That same year, following Biore's lead, Pond's introduced its own pore strip. This, too, met with an enthusiastic response, especially from younger consumers concerned more with acne than with the wrinkles that so exercised the company's traditional base. As an industry analyst told the December 21, 1998, issue of *Advertising Age,* "The experience with pore strips showed Pond's there is an opportunity in the 18-to-34 market."

TARGET MARKET

With the debut of its Soothing Cucumber Eye Treatments, Pond's hoped to continue to attract younger consumers to its facial care brand. "The challenge is to show young women that 'This Pond's is for me, [it's] not just my mother's Pond's,'" a cosmetic consultant explained in *Advertising Age.* The desire of Pond's to court younger women was grounded in impeccable business logic. Not only would women under the age of 35 add valuable immediate sales for the company, but as they matured, they would also be more likely to remain loyal to the products. Market research in other fields had consistently demonstrated that brand allegiances were formed at a young age and that the bonds were strong, often remaining with consumers for their whole lives. This dynamic held true in the facial care industry as well. "If [a company] can get them into the line," an analyst told *Advertising Age,* "[it] can get them to trade up to [its] other products later." The primary way in which both Soothing Cucumber Eye Treatments and Ogilvy & Mather's supporting campaign targeted these younger women was to stress the product's natural ingredients. "Natural ingredients are broadening facial skin care's appeal to a young generation of consumers," proclaimed *Chain Drug Review.* In addition to touting Soothing Cucumber Eye Treatments' virtual garden of botanical extracts, the print ads portrayed the eye pads as realistic, even as edible.

At the same time that Pond's wanted to expand its presence among younger women, the company did not want to alienate it core base of consumers, who were typically 35 and older. The company therefore sought to make its new product speak to women of different ages. Pond's targeted more mature women by emphasizing the product's soothing properties. A company spokesperson reported to the *Rose Sheet* that 60 percent of women experienced daily stress and said that they needed "magic moments" of private time to relax. Often they used baths or other beauty regimes as ways to diffuse their tension. "We were looking at quality-of-life issues and how difficult it is for women to balance things like work and family," Indursky told the June 28, 1999, issue of *Advertising Age,* as the Pond's category director explained the impetus behind Soothing Cucumber Eye Treatments. To reach these women, Pond's pitched the product with the line "Relieve Your Tired Eyes and Renew Your Spirit."

TOO NATURAL?

Pond's put a great deal of effort into making its Soothing Cucumber Eye Treatments resemble actual cucumbers. The company was almost too successful. One beauty columnist jokingly reminded her readers not to eat Soothing Cucumber Eye Treatments by mistake.

COMPETITION

The chief competitor of Pond's in the facial care market was Biore, the Jergen's brand that had breathed new life into the entire category. "Cleaners before Biore were dead," an industry consultant said in the June 29, 1998, issue of *Advertising Age.* "Biore showed that technology could bring them back." When the company launched its five-item skin treatment line, it immediately set its sights on women between the ages of 18 and 34, a group that had generally been ignored by facial care companies. The Pore Perfect strip was the centerpiece of this strategy. The company recognized that it was "a new brand in a world of giant manufacturers serving a very skeptical group of consumers," as Biore's marketing director, Jeff McCurrach, confessed to *Brandweek.* For this reason Biore adopted an innovative marketing approach to distinguish itself from its competitors.

Biore's Pore Perfect strip campaign eschewed glamorous models and avoided making sweeping claims. Instead, the component spots focused on the workings of the strip—showing it resting on a model's nose—and often portrayed the results of the product—blackheads adhering to the strip's surface. "We weren't just giving hope in a bottle," McCurrach stressed in the June 29, 1998, issue of *Advertising Age.* "We had a state-of-the-art product and we demonstrated the results," he added. "The first reaction is 'Oh, that's gross.' Then people realize they can really get their faces clean."

In addition to its print and television ads, Biore tried unconventional strategies that paid off handsomely. It signed up as a sponsor of Lilith Fair, a traveling music tour featuring all female performers that garnered a huge following among Biore's target audience. The company then deployed a battalion of company employees at every Lilith Fair event. Armed with spritz bottles and Pore Perfect, Biore's staff convinced a sizable number of women to try the product, and sales skyrocketed. In its first full year after the strip's introduction in the United States, Biore commanded an impressive 22.5 percent of the facial care market.

The rest of the industry recognized Biore's phenomenal debut and began to introduce more products designed to appeal to younger female consumers. Neutrogena Corp., a subsidiary of Johnson & Johnson, was already a category leader when it released its Neutrogena Deep Clean cream cleanser to augment it full line of facial cleansers and moisturizers. Johnson & Johnson also produced its own full skin care line, called Clean & Clear. In addition, Procter & Gamble sought to reinvigorate its classic but tired Noxzema facial cleanser in 1999, especially by drawing consumers between the ages of 18 and 30 to the brand. The company launched the new line Noxzema Skin Fitness and supported it with a massive advertising campaign conceived by Leo Burnett. Aware that many of the young women it wanted to reach were athletic, Procter & Gamble used fitness themes to market the items. The campaign adopted the tag line "Feel Fitness within Every Inch of Your Skin," which was incorporated into television ads featuring personal trainer Kathy Kaehler as a spokesperson.

MARKETING STRATEGY

Despite the venerable pedigree of Pond's, Soothing Cucumber Eye Treatments were a "latecomer to the category," noted *Advertising Age.* To break through the numerous advertisements of its competitors, Pond's counted on Ogilvy & Mather to formulate a campaign that would catch consumers' attention and carve out a niche for Soothing Cucumber Eye Treatments, particularly among the coveted younger demographic group. To accomplish this goal, the company opted for visually arresting ads. As *Women's Wear Daily* remarked, the print executions had a "cleaner, more sophisticated look than [had] been associated with the brand in the past." Soothing Cucumber Eye Treatments, looking more like a snack than a beauty product, were the center of the ads. The presentation was calculated to make consumers more receptive to the pads. "Food is the ultimate comfort area," a Pond's spokesperson told the *Syracuse Post-Standard.* "People always return to that."

The recurring image of cucumber slices was intended to resonate with consumers in other ways as well. "The sight of a woman relaxing with cucumber slices over her eyes has become a visual cliche of sorts, the image of the pampered spa guest," explained the *Newark Star-Ledger* in its October 18, 1998, edition. By tapping into this trend, Pond's could accomplish two goals. First, the pictures of cucumbers allowed the company to tap into an idyllic imagery that crossed generational lines. Consequently, it did not have to risk alienating one age group by keying the ads to the concerns of the other, for example, by focusing on wrinkles rather than acne. Second, the ambience of affluent luxury projected by the spa association could polish the entire Pond's brand, not just boost sales for an individual product.

To reach all segments of its target audience, the company placed the ads for Soothing Cucumber Eye Treatments in a diverse array of magazines. Ads appeared in such cosmetic industry staples as *Cosmopolitan, Elle, Glamour,* and *New Woman.* In addition, Pond's recognized that many of the women it wanted to connect with were interested in health and fitness. Accordingly, the ads appeared in publications such as *American Health, Shape,* and *Fitness.* Pond's also wanted to be sure that it did not overlook its traditional consumers and therefore ran ads in *Ladies' Home Journal, Good Housekeeping, McCall's,* and *Family Circle.*

OUTCOME

For Pond's, Soothing Cucumber Eye Treatments reinvigorated both its sales and image. Almost immediately, Soothing Cucumber Eye Treatments became one of the 15 best-selling items in the skin care industry. The company's 1998 retail sales soared 169.9 percent over the year before, to reach a volume nearly four times its 1991 sales. The company's share of the facial care market in 1998 rose to 16.7 percent. Even more impressive was *Advertising Age*'s assessment of June 28, 1999, that Pond's had captured the number two spot in the facial cleanser category (behind Biore but comfortably ahead of Noxzema) because of the blistering sales of Soothing Cucumber Eye Treatments. Pond's reported that the product generated tremendous repeat business. In fact, retailers complained about being swamped with requests for Soothing Cucumber Eye Treatments. Moreover, beauty magazine columnists lauded the product, both for its ability to diminish eye puffiness and because the process of applying the pads themselves was so relaxing.

The annual Cosmetic Executive Women Awards named Soothing Cucumber Eye Treatments as the best mass-market skin care product of 1998.

Especially promising was the fact that the product had attracted consumers from a wide age range. Category director Indursky crowed to *Women's Wear Daily* that for the first time in eight years his company could claim that "no matter how old you are, Pond's has the skin care product for you." The company professed such delight with the results of the Soothing Cucumber Eye Treatments campaign that it dedicated its largest marketing budget ever to the Pond's brand in 1999. With this allocation the company aimed to use Soothing Cucumber Eye Treatments to make further inroads into the younger market. One month after the product hit retailers' shelves, Pond's debuted another new item, Cleansing and Make-Up Remover Towlettes, to follow in the pads' wake. Pond's also announced plans to introduce Clear Solutions, a skin care line specifically designed for younger women, in 1999.

FURTHER READING

"Biore: The Nose Knew at Lilith Fair." *Chain Drug Review,* September 28, 1998.

Brookman, Faye. "The Marketing 100: Biore Pore Perfect." *Advertising Age,* June 29, 1998.

———. "Soothing Cucumber Eye Treatments." *Advertising Age,* June 28, 1999.

Cardona, Mercedes. "P&G Reclaims Noxzema Franchise with Fitness." *Advertising Age,* April 26, 1999.

———. "Pond's Courts Younger Women with New Line." *Advertising Age,* December 21, 1998.

"Facial Care Products." *Brandweek,* September 15, 1997.

Sloan, Pat, and Laura Petrecca. "Unilever Extends Pond's to Bodycare." *Advertising Age,* October 13, 1997.

Stith, Barbara. "Food for Your Face." *Syracuse Post-Standard,* November 10, 1998.

Tode, Chantal. "Pond's Finds Life after Cold Creams." *Women's Wear Daily,* November 6, 1999.

Rebecca Stanfel

United Airlines Corp.

1200 E. Algonquin Road
Elk Grove Township, Illinois 60007
USA
Telephone: (847) 700-4000
Fax: (847) 700-4081
Web site: www.united.com

IT'S TIME TO FLY CAMPAIGN

OVERVIEW

The September 11, 2001, terrorist attacks crippled the airline industry in general and UAL Corporation's United Airlines in particular, forcing the company to file for bankruptcy in 2002. Though United was still the world's number two carrier in 2004, substantial obstacles lay along the airline's path back to profitability. Trying to reorganize and emerge from bankruptcy, United launched "It's Time to Fly," the airline's first branding campaign since 1999.

Conceived by United's agency of record, Fallon Worldwide of Minneapolis, "It's Time to Fly" targeted business travelers with animated TV commercials set to United's signature sound track, George Gershwin's *Rhapsody in Blue.* Print, outdoor, and online advertising likewise used distinctive illustrations to communicate the campaign's key message: that United understood the lives of businesspeople. Focused primarily on hub cities Chicago, Denver, Los Angeles, San Francisco, and Washington, D.C., "It's Time to Fly" likewise included innovative international components in London and Hong Kong.

One of the campaign's TV spots was nominated both for an Emmy Award and an Annie Award from the International Animated Film Society, and the stylishness of the campaign as a whole was a bright spot and a potentially significant step in the company's arduous struggle to remake itself for the future.

HISTORICAL CONTEXT

The early years of the new millennium were extremely difficult ones for airlines, and United had it tougher than most. In 2001 a proposed merger with U.S. Airways was blocked by antitrust regulators, and then two United jets were involved in the September 11, 2001, terrorist attacks that both changed global politics and left the airline industry in shambles. During the decline in air travel that followed the attacks, United had to lay off more than 20 percent of its employees and eliminate a substantial number of its flights. The airline lost $2.1 billion in 2001 and filed for Chapter 11 bankruptcy protection in late 2002. UAL progressively cut its workforce and instituted pay and benefit decreases during bankruptcy reorganization, and in late 2003 it launched a low-fare carrier, Ted (a shortened version of the brand name United), to compete with discount airlines such as Jet Blue and Southwest, whose lower fares had long spelled trouble for full-service airlines like United.

The airline's last branding campaign, "Rising," which ran in 1999, had been an ill-timed and poorly received attempt to convince consumers that the airline's best days were in front of it. The difficulties facing full-service airlines were at that time all too apparent, and UAL's growing operational and labor troubles—problems that contributed significantly to the company's eventual bankruptcy—already loomed on the horizon. After it filed for bankruptcy the company had an understandably modest advertising budget. Since 2002 United's advertising had been largely restricted to promotional and fare-sale efforts.

TARGET MARKET

"It's Time to Fly" was a global campaign that primarily targeted frequent business travelers, attempting to show them that United understood its role as a facilitator of their success. The tagline itself implicitly referred to the airline industry's recent troubles and emphasized the benefits of traveling for business purposes. As a company spokesperson told the *Wall Street Journal,* "It's Time to Fly" was "a call to action for our own employees and a call to action for our customers... it's time to get back to meeting face to face... we are ready when you are."

TV ads paired George Gershwin's *Rhapsody in Blue,* which had been United's theme music since the 1980s, with animated storylines (free of dialogue) dramatizing the role that air travel played in the lives of businesspeople. "Interview," for instance, showed the importance of face-to-face meetings by dealing with the ups and downs of the job-interview process. In the commercial a man woke up early, fussed over his appearance, and caught a United flight to an out-of-town interview, only to realize, on the elevator just before meeting his prospective employers, that he was wearing one brown shoe and one black shoe. He was dejected after the interview until he got a call on his cell phone informing him that the job was his. On the United flight home he napped with a smile on his face, and a flight attendant thoughtfully pulled down the window shade. Meanwhile, "A Life" traced the life and retirement of a business traveler in 60 seconds, during the course of which he traveled for both business and pleasure. This illustrated not only the business traveler's dependence on United but the seamless integration of all phases of his life, made possible by the airline's worldwide presence. The music in each commercial mirrored the ups and downs of the lives and situations being featured, and it was only interrupted at the end of each spot by the voice of Robert Redford intoning, "Where you go in life is up to you. There's an airline that can take you there—United. It's time to fly."

Print ads similarly employed illustrations, some of which had been conceived as original artwork for the *New Yorker* magazine, and again the intent was to show business travelers that United understood them and the role that flying played in their lives. In one, a man ascending at a subway stop found himself emerging into a literal jungle. The accompanying copy read, "You didn't get where you were going by finding the most comfortable spot in the office." Other print ads communicated United's role in the business traveler's lifestyle with messages such as "Let's face it. It's hard to climb the corporate ladder without going up 30,000 feet" and "Business is a series of battles. We make the chariots."

HOW DID THEY DO THAT?

To create the United spot "Interview," Academy Award–nominated animation partners Wendy Tilby and Amanda Forbis used the same process they had used in their acclaimed short film, "When the Day Breaks." First they shot digital-camera footage of their friends and neighbors realistically performing the roles in the film, and then they edited the story using the software programs iMovie and After Effects. Using the animation program Flash, they made computer drawings on top of the real-life scenes before printing out the images and painting them by hand. Among Tilby and Forbis's chief worries during this process was the possibility that the main character looked too much like the actor Ben Affleck. To correct this potential pitfall the animators altered and exaggerated the main character's features.

COMPETITION

United was number two among air carriers during the "It's Time to Fly" campaign. American Airlines, owned by AMR Corporation of Fort Worth, Texas, was the world's number one airline, and Atlanta-based Delta Air Lines was number three. Like United, both of these companies had been posting heavy losses and had been advertising only minimally in the years since the terrorist attacks of September 11. Both, likewise, had flirted with bankruptcy and were in the process of downsizing as a means of moving back toward profitability.

In 2004 American, like United, launched a branding campaign for the first time in several years. American's "Something Special in the Air" commercials had stopped airing in the late 1990s, and a brand campaign had been in development when American lost two of its planes in the September 11 attacks. (American then lost a third plane in a November 2001 crash.) Following on the heels of near-bankruptcy, layoffs, and restructuring, the 2004 campaign, called "Tickets to Life," attempted to show that American was the carrier with the best understanding of its customers. Each of the campaign's four TV spots featured a passenger heading to or from an important event, the significance of which an American Airlines employee clairvoyantly understood, and each ended with the tagline, "We know why you fly." The branding effort's estimated 18-month price tag was $60 million.

Delta Air Lines remained on the brink of bankruptcy through 2004, with high fuel prices and labor costs prolonging its difficulties and forcing it to cut jobs and reduce expenses. Its plan to stay aloft in the coming years included expanding its presence at several airports and expanding its low-fare subsidiary, Song, launched in 2003. In 2004 Delta ran an integrated campaign on behalf of its flagship brand, featuring an emphasis on its recently expanded operations at New York's JFK Airport. As part of the New York effort Delta unveiled a 30-story mural designed by artist Bruce McCall, best known for his contributions to the *New Yorker*. It also decorated Mini Coopers like Delta jets and employed drivers and street crews to engage passersby with a range of promotional offers.

Dallas-based Southwest Airlines was the only major airline in America to maintain its full flight schedule and to avoid employee layoffs in the aftermath of September 11. Its straightforward business strategy allowed it to remain profitable despite the overwhelming problems plaguing the rest of the industry. Southwest kept costs to a minimum through its exclusive use of one type of aircraft, the Boeing 737, its focus on short flights and small airports, and its no-assigned-seats policy. The airline, which had begun as a regional carrier, took advantage of its competitors' cutbacks by expanding during the industry downturn, adding direct international flights and adding to its East-Coast presence with service to Philadelphia and Pittsburgh.

MARKETING STRATEGY

"It's Time to Fly" was launched on February 18, 2004, with a print ad in the *Wall Street Journal*. The print ads, numbering 10 in all, used illustrations by *New Yorker* contributors such as Carter Goodrich, Rea Irvin, and Charles Martin. Other publications selected for the print run, which continued throughout 2004, were the *New York Times Magazine, Time, Newsweek, BusinessWeek, Fortune,* and *Fast Company*.

A total of four TV spots headlined the campaign. The first, "Interview," broke in United's hub markets during the Academy Awards telecast on February 29, 2004. The TV spots, each of which was scripted by Fallon and paired with a version of *Rhapsody in Blue,* were crafted by award-winning animators, who were given a choice of scripts and allowed substantial creative freedom. Academy Award–winning animators Aleksandr Petrov and Michael Dudok de Wit designed "A Life" and "Rose," respectively; while Academy Award–nominees Wendy Tilby and Amanda Forbis animated "Interview," and two-time Academy Award–nominee Joanna Quinn animated "Lightbulb." Each spot was dialogue-free, with the on-screen action tied to the ebb and flow of the Gershwin song, and each included the closing voice-over by Robert Redford. TV placements beyond the Oscar-night launch included hub-market buys during national events, including the U.S. Open golf tournament and national cable programming that tended to interest business travelers, such as *CNN Headline News,* CNBC's *Squawk Box,* and A&E's *Biography*.

Outdoor ads ran on billboards in Chicago and Los Angeles, featuring similarly distinctive illustrations that supported the overall look of the campaign. An online campaign—United's first—focused on British business travelers, targeting U.K.-based websites with a high concentration of business traffic. United and Fallon targeted London commuters in the Bank Underground station, inserting panels down a 160-yard length of station corridor to duplicate the appearance of a plane's interior. Views of scenery en route to New York or San Francisco from London were visible beyond the make-believe windows. United and Fallon likewise utilized Hong Kong's MTR underground system, installing backlit images along 300 yards of wall space between subway stations to create an effect comparable to that of a cartoon flip book. The resulting 20-second "movie" simulated a flight from Hong Kong to Chicago, showing views of both cities and both airports along with views visible along the way.

The global media campaign was also synchronized with in-house efforts aimed at bringing United's various operations together under a strengthened brand image. These efforts included a new look for the planes' exteriors. A blue-and-white paint job replaced United's predominantly gray livery and complemented the look of the company's just-commissioned Ted planes.

OUTCOME

"It's Time to Fly" attracted admiring press coverage and made United, according to *Advertising Age*'s Bob Garfield, "the most elegantly advertised" airline of the time period. The TV commercial "Interview" was named a *Shoot* magazine "Top Spot" in April 2004, was one of five nominees for an Emmy Award for best prime-time commercial, and was one of five spots nominated in the advertising category of the International Animated Film Society's Annie Awards.

The favorable attention did not translate into profitability for the airline, however. UAL kept struggling through 2004. In 2005 the company continued to trim expenses, winning permission to default on its employee pension plans and announcing that some among its senior management team would take a 15 percent salary cut. Pilots saw increased flying time and other benefit reductions, as the company considered another round of major layoffs.

FURTHER READING

Beirne, Mike. "Ailing Delta Draws Attention to NY Hub." *Brandweek,* July 12, 2004.

"Campaign: United 'It's Time To Fly.' " *Creativity,* April 2005.

Carey, Susan. "United Airlines Paints New Image with Ads, Its Jets." *Wall Street Journal,* February 18, 2004.

Carpenter, Dave. "United Airlines Flies New Advertising Campaign, New Colors." *Marketing News,* March 15, 2004.

Champagne, Christine. "United Airlines Ad Illustrates the Benefits of Flying." *Shoot,* April 2, 2004.

DeSalvo, Kathy. "Top of the Crop." *Shoot,* August 20, 2004.

Garfield, Bob. "Beleaguered United May Find Relief with Simple, Artful Ads." *Advertising Age,* March 8, 2004.

———, "Ten Ads I Loved." *Advertising Age,* December 20, 2004.

Goldrich, Robert. "Six Appeal." *Shoot,* August 20, 2004.

Janoff, Barry. "Flying Faster than the Speed of Light (Bulbs)." *Brandweek,* March 22, 2004.

Madden, Normandy, and Laurel Wentz. "Spotlight." *Advertising Age,* May 10, 2004.

Sudhaman, Arun. "United Campaign Ahead of Pack on Tracks." *Media Asia,* May 7, 2004.

Takaki, Millie. "Annie, You're Your TV Spot Nominations." *Shoot,* December 17, 2004.

Trottman, Melanie. "American Air Plans 'Tickets to Life' Ad Pitch." *Wall Street Journal,* September 10, 2004.

"UA Targets Business Travellers via Online Fallon Ad Campaign." *Campaign,* June 4, 2004.

Mark Lane

RISING CAMPAIGN

OVERVIEW

"Fly the Friendly Skies" had been a stalwart slogan for United Airlines since 1966, but as legions of business travelers could attest, the skies became increasingly unfriendly in the 1990s. The airline industry developed a decidedly negative public image because of deregulation, delayed takeoffs, lost baggage, cramped seating, and unsatisfactory customer service. A subsidiary of the UAL Corporation, United Airlines was the world's largest carrier, and its executives felt compelled to turn a new face toward fed-up consumers. After an exhaustive consumer research study, the airline began to revamp its positioning. United released "Rising," a campaign that acknowledged the lack of quality in the industry with a message promising to make things better. The airline hoped that such an honest approach would gain it consumers' trust and increase business.

Created by the ad agency Fallon McElligott, the $140 million print and television campaign debuted on May 22, 1997. Marketing experts initially called the campaign bold because it was the first in the airline industry to acknowledge the "rising" dissatisfaction flyers felt with all carriers. Instead of saturating viewers with the industry's advertising stereotypes—images of contented passengers headed (on time) for exotic locales while enjoying gourmet in-flight meals—the United campaign admitted that customers had a right to resent poor service and vowed to do whatever it took to satisfy the customer. The voice-over for one spot remarked, "If Orville and Wilbur had to go through what you do just to fly, they would have stayed in the bicycle business." After United employees and ad critics later criticized the campaign's condescension, the strategy shifted to a more ambiguous, uplifting message. The campaign concluded in late 1999.

During the later half of "Rising," the net income for United dipped to $187 million in 1999 from $218 million the year before. At first the campaign fared well, even garnering a few ad-industry awards. During its last year, however, ad critics ruthlessly discredited the campaign for promising something that United ultimately never delivered.

HISTORICAL CONTEXT

The world's leading passenger air carrier, United was also one of the oldest major airlines. In 1929 United Aircraft and Transport was formed by the partnership of aircraft designer William Boeing and engine designer Fred Rentschler. Then based in New York, the startup company—renamed United Airlines in 1931—was the first carrier to offer coast-to-coast services. By 1934 a reorganization brought United's transportation headquarters to Chicago, where it remained.

United was the largest business under the umbrella of parent company UAL Corporation, which also operated subsidiaries that included Apollo Travel Services, Galileo International Partnership, Shuttle by United, and United Express. In 1997 UAL formed the Star Alliance partnership with international airlines including Germany's Lufthansa, Scandinavian Airlines System (SAS), Air Canada, and Thai Airways to further increase international business. With hubs in Chicago, Denver, San Francisco, Tokyo, and Washington, D.C., United delivered passengers to 140 destinations worldwide; its fleet of 50 jumbo jets was among the industry's largest.

Though not known for technical innovation (United's first foray into jet service in 1959 trailed that of competitor American Airlines), the company parlayed partnerships, acquisitions, and a reputation for customer service to grow into the world's leading air carrier. During the 1960s and 1970s new management brought related industries into the fold. Hotels, car rental services, and a computer reservation company at one time were part of the company briefly known as the Allegis Corporation, whose goal was to become a travel conglomerate. But with the 1987 resignation of CEO Richard Ferris, the revamped UAL sold off the non-core acquisitions to focus on the core business of delivering "the friendly skies."

By the 1990s changes in the airline industry brought a proliferation of new names to airports across the United States, cutting into United's profits. In addition, skyrocketing fuel oil prices and a recession brought fierce cost-cutting measures from large and small carriers. Seeking a new way of doing business, United sought a union buyout in 1993. Losing almost $800 million a year, the company was forced to lay off thousands of employees and cut management salaries. Conflicts with pilots, machinists, and flight attendants continued to threaten UAL's operations until 1994, when stockholders approved an employee purchase of the company in exchange for almost $5 billion in wage concessions. With United employees holding 55 percent of the stock, the air carrier was among the world's largest employee-owned publicly traded companies.

But growth came at a cost. Deregulation and "fare wars" were bringing more people into airports, resulting in overbooked flights and crowded runways. Something had to give, and for the typical high-volume business traveler—United's target customer—that something was reliable service. Research revealed that United's passengers considered the airline no more capable of delivering "friendly skies" than its competition. So in 1997 UAL retired its venerable slogan (and its longtime ad agency) to establish a new image. The Minneapolis agency Fallon McElligott was charged with creating a campaign that would speak to U.S. business travelers on their own terms.

TARGET MARKET

United's core customer was the business traveler; such customers constituted 9 percent of United's passengers yet provided 44 percent of the airline's revenue. With its large fleet and service to major business centers, United had a great investment in this customer category and could not afford to alienate the frequent flyer, who also tended to be among United's most vocal critics. These travelers valued reliable takeoffs, comfortable travel, and easy access, all of which the airline industry was hard-pressed to deliver during the 1990s.

> **INTERNATIONAL ENDORSERS**
>
> Marlon Brando's voice-over in United Airline's international commercials represented a trend among high-profile actors. These celebrities, who may not otherwise have compromised their A-list integrity by making American commercials, appeared in or provided voice-over work for advertising spots screened exclusively overseas. Some of the more notable commercial stars included Woody Allen, Jodie Foster, and Leonardo DiCaprio.

The recreational traveler was not ignored; print ads highlighted pleasurable upgrades such as improved meals and the addition of Starbucks coffee to in-flight service. An *Advertising Age* report also noted that United had "become the first major airline to advertise specifically to the 'gay market' by adding a gay-oriented magazine to its 'Rising' print media plan."

COMPETITION

In the growing universe of passenger carriers, United had to compete not only with major names like Delta, Trans World Airline (TWA), Continental, and Northwest but also with smaller or regional/international names such as America West, Virgin Group, Japan Air Lines, Italy's Alitalia, British Airways, and New Zealand's Kiwi Air Lines. United's major competitor, Delta Airlines, introduced its own new advertising slogan in 1997. Delta's "On top of the world," meant to reinforce good impressions of flying, was more in keeping with the kind of advertising traditional to the airlines market. In a 1997 J.D. Power & Associates survey, United finished with a "below average" rating among commercial airlines for flights under 500 miles. For flights longer than 500 miles, the company landed in third place behind Continental and TWA.

Competition outside of the airline industry included regional and national rail and bus lines, such as Amtrak and Greyhound. Some people chose to travel by train or bus because they were put off by the cost or inconvenience of airlines or because of fear of flying.

MARKETING STRATEGY

Prior to the "Rising" campaign United invested hundreds of millions in improving and upgrading its equipment, from ordering more wide-bodied Boeing 777s to redesigning each airline seat for the comfort of the passenger. In early 1997 the ad agency Fallon McElligott began talking to United's target customers. The answers they received were eye-opening, said Fallon planning director Rob White in a *Chicago Tribune* article. According to frequent business flyers—"road warriors," as they were dubbed—the idea of an airline turning around its service overnight was unfathomable. "They were telling us that we have to spend time in purgatory first," White said. "You can't just go from hell to heaven without a stop in between." A proposed campaign based on sarcastic humor did not go over well. Other storyboards showing superior customer service were dismissed as containing undeliverable claims.

"Then," reported the *Tribune* article, "the agency struck gold." A focus-group meeting of frequent flyers of all airlines revealed layers of resentment and frustration over poor customer service. What if United, instead of trying to counter those opinions, agreed with them? That idea "just resonated with people," said White, and the $140 million "Rising" campaign was born.

With "Rising" United took the unorthodox step of acknowledging that air travel had become more stressful of late. One commercial reenacted the Wright Brothers' historic first flight of 1912—except that the brothers were now plagued with modern-day delays. Meanwhile, a voice-over remarked, "If Orville and Wilbur had to go through what you do just to fly, they would have stayed in the bicycle business." In another commercial less-than-appetizing airline food was the focus. And in a third spot United employees who had assembled for the start of a six a.m. meeting were left waiting—chagrined and confused—when the meeting leader intentionally showed up late. The purpose was to remind the staff how their passengers felt during delays and other travel-related frustrations. "Air travel needs to be easier, more professional, especially for the people who do it most," noted the voice-over in one spot. "Now it will be, because, compared to the rest of the industry, United Airlines is headed in a different direction." Each commercial ended with the tagline "United Airlines. Rising."

The theme was taken up not only in broadcast spots but also in print ads. One ad touted United as "a better way for cynics to travel," while another mocked traditional airline advertising by asking, "Wouldn't it be great if we could all fly commercials?" Even United's 1997 annual report replaced corporate "silver linings" with featured letters from unsatisfied customers, along with replies from the company on its plans for improving poor service.

Internationally "Rising" broke in United's Latin American, Asian, and European markets in October 1997. Notable in these spots was the voice-over of actor Marlon Brando in his first television commercials. The strategy was to "tackle perceived low-brand awareness overseas, where our image is either confused or nonexistent," said the company's international advertising manager in an *Advertising Age* piece. He added that, outside the United States, American-based airlines "tend to be lumped together. We're seeking to stand out."

The international campaign was produced by the global ad agency Young & Rubicam, with creative treatments centered less on acknowledging customer dissatisfaction than on showing the history and resources of this major air carrier. One television spot began with a little boy playing with a model airplane while behind him rose images of vintage aircraft through the years, culminating in a new Boeing 777. As *Advertising Age* continued, "Print ads focus on the particulars of the airline, such as the one that shows a hand-written pie chart explaining, 'You've got $710 million to improve the life of the business traveler. How do you spend it?'"

Near the end of 1998 the campaign's creators changed strategies after months of criticism. Ad critics attacked "Rising" for advertising the faults of an industry that United dominated and then for never setting a high-water mark for service after promising improvement. On January 2, 1999, the "Rising" campaign was modified to advertise United's advantages instead of industry shortcomings. One spot, titled "Dreamer," featured a United jetliner taking off and magically transforming into a child's toy. Similar spots followed. In one a United jet was shown integrating into a flying flock of geese; in another commercial, titled "Circus," the United aircraft blended into a Cirque du Soleil dance troupe. Despite Fallon's attempt to improve the campaign, the 1999 spots were accused of being vague and not adding to United's brand. One print ad featured the text "Rising is astonishing. Rising is imagination. Rising is borderless and big. Rising is go. Rising is unstoppable. Rising is performance. Rising is leading the way."

OUTCOME

United executives were initially pleased with the campaign. In a press release United senior vice president David Coltman announced, "Our TravelTrak scores rating 'customer preference' have risen over the past year. Similarly, our high-yield revenue numbers have steadily improved, so it appears the Rising campaign is having the desired impact on our target audience." United's sales were up 6 percent in 1997. The campaign collected a Gold EFFIE Award for most effective campaign in the transportation category. The Chicago American Marketing Association gave "Rising" its Champs Gold Medal Award for marketplace effectiveness. The campaign also earned two certificates of excellence for creativity in public relations.

Among the advertising community, reaction to the unconventional "Rising" ranged from admiring to skeptical. "Inspired and inspiring—in addition to being risky bordering on reckless" is how an *Advertising Age* reviewer characterized the campaign. "It's easy enough to identify the problems," the article continued. "With clever advertising such as this, it's also easy to persuade viewers you're solving them . . . The trick—not on the airwaves but in the air—is to prove that you weren't lying. Every testy gate agent or ill-explained cancellation will turn 'Rising' into an ugly joke that rebounds on United."

Unfortunately for United, sales dipped from $218 million in 1998 to $187 million in 1999. During the campaign's final year, ad critics united against it. In June the ad critic David Snyder wrote in *Crain's Chicago Business,* ". . . the whole 'Rising' theme is flawed. Saying you're rising implies that you were schlock before, but now are really trying to make things better. Hardly a leadership position for the world's largest airline."

Despite dropping sales and a lack of fanfare, United executives stood by the campaign. John Kiker, United's vice president for advertising and communications, said in *Adweek* (Midwest edition), "We don't regret [the campaign] at all. It did us a lot of good and helped us learn what we needed to improve on." The executive admitted in the same January 10, 2000, publication that the message behind the campaign was too lofty for most consumers. A few days earlier, in an interview with the *New York Times,* Kiker said, "In all honesty, senior management's opinion is that 'Rising' did us a lot of good. . . . It was interesting, intriguing and made us focus on what we had to fix. But employees felt it laid a lot of blame on them and that was unfortunate." Fallon released a new campaign for United in January 2000.

FURTHER READING

"Ad Agencies Rise to United's Challenge." *Chicago Tribune,* June 15, 1997.

Baar, Aaron. "How Fallon Got United's Blessing." *Adweek* (New England ed.), January 29, 2001, p. 6.

"Candid Ads Acknowledge Consumers Are Dissatisfied with Air Travel." *M2 Presswire,* May 23, 1997.

Comerford, Mike. "Red Ink, Blue Skies." *Arlington Heights (IL) Daily Herald,* February 19, 2004, p. 1.

"Curtain to Rise on United Airlines' New 'Rising' Ad Campaign." *PR Newswire,* May 22, 1997.

Garcia, Sandra. "Rising to the Occasion." *Shoot,* December 7, 2001, p. 32.

Garfield, Bob. "Beleaguered United May Find Relief with Simple, Artful Ads." *Advertising Age,* March 8, 2004, p. 53.

"New Delta Ads Can't Stay Afloat; United 'Rising' Hinges on Service." *Advertising Age,* May 26, 1997.

"United Ads Mark a Bold Departure." *Houston Chronicle,* May 25, 1997.

"United Is 1st Major Airline to Target Gays." *Advertising Age,* June 2, 1997.

"United's 'Rising' Theme Expands to International Campaign." *Advertising Age,* September 15, 1997.

"When Ads Get Creative, Some Click, Some Bomb." *USA Today,* December 15, 1997.

Susan Salter
Kevin Teague

TED LAUNCH CAMPAIGN

OVERVIEW

In 2002 UAL Corp.'s United Airlines was forced into bankruptcy by years of dwindling profits compounded by the terrorist attacks of September 11, 2001, which left the airline industry in disarray. Though United remained the world's number two carrier, it faced particularly daunting challenges as a full-service airline, given the growing consumer shift to low-fare, one-class airlines. A critical part of the company's strategy for exiting bankruptcy, then, was the launch of a low-fare subbrand called Ted, whose name was derived from the last three letters of the flagship brand. Rather than advertising the new brand with a costly, full-scale traditional campaign, UAL and its agency of record, Fallon Worldwide of Minneapolis, targeted Ted's future home base of Denver, Colorado, in a self-described guerrilla campaign revolving around the Ted name.

The teaser campaign, which was launched on October 29, 2003, was meant to introduce the Ted personality even as Denver and the wider world were kept in the dark as to Ted's identity, and United successfully kept its secret through most of the two weeks between the marketing launch and the new carrier's official unveiling. Ted claimed responsibility for random acts of kindness, such as the delivery of flowers to a Denver hospital, and actors on Segway scooters wore signs reading, "I'm not Ted." A website featuring cryptic messages from Ted was established, and Ted was spelled out in enormous sod letters in a farmer's field near Denver. After the launch the offbeat tone of the Ted personality was extended to a radio campaign purporting to chronicle the search for a Ted spokesperson. This campaign moved to television in 2005.

The guerrilla campaign effectively attracted media attention, and Ted grew according to schedule in its first year. United claimed, at the one-year anniversary of

Ted's first flight, that the brand had exceeded company expectations, and Ted's flight schedule continued to grow as United struggled to exit bankruptcy protection.

HISTORICAL CONTEXT

In the late 1990s Dallas-based Southwest Airlines Company expanded into a national industry force, attracting passengers with its consistently low fares and on-time departures and arrivals. Southwest was able to keep prices low thanks largely to a straightforward business strategy calling for the exclusive use of one type of aircraft (the Boeing 737), a focus on short flights and small airports, one-class service, and a no-assigned-seats policy. A host of new airlines copied and modified Southwest's business model even as the original low-fare airline expanded. By the turn of the millennium, traditional full-service carriers, unable to match the fares of these new competitors, were struggling to remain profitable. United, which had a 70 percent route overlap with low-fare carriers, was particularly vulnerable in the evolving airline marketplace.

Airlines experienced unprecedented challenges in 2001, and United had it tougher than most. A proposed merger with U.S. Airways was blocked by antitrust regulators, and then two United jets were involved in the terrorist attacks of September 11, 2001, which, while changing global politics, left the airline industry in shambles. During the decline in air travel that followed the attacks, United had to lay off more than 20 percent of its employees and eliminate a substantial number of its flights. The airline lost $2.1 billion in 2001 and filed for Chapter 11 bankruptcy protection in late 2002. UAL progressively cut its workforce and instituted pay and benefit decreases during bankruptcy reorganization.

In the fall of 2003 United prepared to launch a low-fare carrier called Ted (a shortened version of the brand name United), to begin flying in February 2004. Based in Denver and primarily servicing leisure destinations, Ted was a critical component of United's strategy for the future. Though skeptics pointed to UAL's own previous unsuccessful attempt to launch a low-fare subbrand, the Shuttle by United, as well as to a similar failed attempt by Continental Airlines, UAL planned to expand Ted's fleet from an initial 4 aircraft to 45 within a year. Ultimately UAL projected a Ted fleet of 156 planes.

TARGET MARKET

UAL and its primary advertising agency, Fallon Worldwide, set out to establish a unique personality for the Ted brand while acknowledging, through the very name of the discount carrier, its connection to parent airline United. With a promise to keep last-minute one-way fares below $299, Ted appealed to business travelers, who buy the majority of plane tickets on short notice, but the Denver-based carrier's primary focus was on markets with a large percentage of leisure travelers (such as Orlando, New Orleans, Las Vegas, Phoenix, San Francisco, and Los Angeles). Ted therefore sought to establish an image of friendliness and approachability. As Fallon creative director Bruce Bildsten told *Brandweek.com,* "When people fly on leisure the flight is actually part of the vacation experience. They want to have a fun time on the flight so the experience on Ted is going to be in line with the mentality of the people taking the trip."

The advertising supporting the Ted launch was, accordingly, offbeat and untraditional. Two weeks prior to the announcement of the carrier's launch, Fallon enlisted guerilla-marketing specialists in Ted's hometown of Denver, allowing United to conceal its role in an unbranded teaser campaign meant to introduce the Ted personality. The teaser campaign, which, according to Bildsten, was "about being friendly and doing good things in the community in a way that endear [sic] the airline to the community rather than imposing on it," featured stealthy acts of kindness supposedly committed by someone named Ted as well as numerous mysterious appearances of the Ted name. Throughout the teaser campaign United kept its connection to Ted secret, leaving Denver residents to guess the identity and significance of the Ted personality.

COMPETITION

Though United was the number two airline in the world, the creation of Ted was a response not to its traditional rivals but to smaller low-fare carriers, whose robust growth had been achieved at the expense of the major full-service airlines, all of which were struggling. Southwest was America's low-fare leader, and JetBlue Airways Corp. (based in Forest Hills, New York) was a rising star in the expanding subsector. Among the leading traditional airlines, only Atlanta's Delta Air Lines, Inc., had an existing low-fare subsidiary.

Southwest was the only major airline in America to maintain its full flight schedule and to avoid employee layoffs in the aftermath of the terrorist attacks of September 11, 2001. The airline took advantage of its competitors' cutbacks by expanding during the industry downturn, adding direct international flights and adding to its East Coast presence with service to Philadelphia and Pittsburgh. Southwest was also the airline industry's biggest advertiser, supplementing local fare-oriented advertising with national branding work. The airline ran branding campaigns focused on its NFL and NHL sponsorships, while also continuing to update its long-running "Wanna Get Away?" campaign. In keeping with Southwest's friendly, fun-loving image, "Wanna Get

NEW CARRIER, OLD PROBLEMS

United Airlines had a history of labor-relations difficulties prior to the Ted launch, and a new chapter in that history threatened to tarnish Ted's introductory flights. Having laid off a substantial portion of its workforce as a part of bankruptcy reorganization, United enticed 2,500 flight attendants into early retirement in the summer of 2003. When, about a month before Ted was scheduled to begin flying in February 2004, the company announced that it needed retirees to pay higher premiums for health care than had been agreed upon months earlier, the retirees claimed that they had been induced to retire under the assumption that their health-care benefits would not be changed. The Association of Flight Attendants organized picketing at airports and public events and ran advertisements that lampooned the new United subbrand, such as "UniTED cheaTED its Retirees."

Away?" featured individuals who, after becoming involved in extremely embarrassing situations, had a clear, humorous motivation for wanting to get away. In 2003 Southwest expanded its sports branding work with a campaign surrounding its newly minted sponsorship of the NBA.

JetBlue, operating out of New York's JFK airport, adapted the one-class ticketing and short-haul model introduced by Southwest and achieved profitability soon after its February 2000 launch. Modifying the Southwest model by offering assigned seats as well as seatback satellite television and by flying more than one type of plane in order to serve smaller markets more efficiently, JetBlue, like Southwest, capitalized on the industry behemoths' troubles by expanding each year following its launch. Among JetBlue's advertising was a campaign of "mockumentaries" satirizing traditional airline advertising. For instance, a pilot being interviewed said, in one commercial, "The whole plane wanted to go to California." The documentary interviewer asked, "What did you do?" and the pilot answered, with mock earnestness, "We took 'em." Similarly, in another scene, a flight attendant proclaimed, "A woman asked me for a soda, so I gave it to her. With ice." JetBlue thereby positioned itself as a new alternative to an airline culture in which competitors congratulated themselves for doing jobs that should be taken for granted.

Delta, meanwhile, remained on the brink of bankruptcy through 2004, with high fuel prices and labor costs prolonging its difficulties and forcing it to cut jobs and reduce expenses. Its plan to stay aloft in the coming years included expanding its presence at several airports and expanding its low-fare subsidiary, Song, launched in 2003. Song did only minimal marketing during its roll-out. Delta planned to wait until Song reached its first-year goal of 144 flights daily before choosing a full-time advertising agency for the account.

MARKETING STRATEGY

On September 30, 2003, UAL notified Fallon executives about its plans to launch Ted and asked the agency to begin work on a buzz marketing campaign preparatory to the November announcement of the new carrier's launch. As Fallon's account director for United, Alex Leikh, told *Advertising Age,* "A week later we had 60 to 65 pieces of creative on the table, from teaser print ads to outdoor boards, and a week after that we came back with another 150 pieces." Fallon contracted with a guerilla-marketing firm in Denver and made sure to keep its fingerprints off the campaign in order to preserve the mystery of Ted's identity. "There's been a lot of cynicism about low-cost airlines," Leikh said, "so United decided to introduce it directly to the consumer." The teaser campaign was launched on October 29 in Denver, Ted's home base.

The campaign attempted to generate as much interest as possible with what was clearly a small budget. Actors, sometimes riding Segway scooters, carried signs reading "I'm not Ted" on Denver streets, while flowers were sent to hospital patients and a restaurant full of diners were treated to dessert, both courtesy of Ted. At sporting events Ted was wished happy birthday, and Ted was spelled out with gigantic sod letters in a field near Denver. A website, www.meetted.com, accompanied the campaign, offering mysterious messages including, "Here's to friends who answer the phone at 3 a.m." and "Here's to movies with orangutans." The campaign ran for two weeks, and on November 12 United confirmed the gradually building suspicions of media outlets like the *Denver Post,* announcing details of Ted's business strategy as well as setting February 12, 2004, as the date for its first flights.

As Ted began flying, United and Fallon added a radio campaign touting a fictional search for a Ted spokesperson. In addition to Denver the radio campaign ran in Chicago and Washington, D.C., United hub cities added to Ted's service roster following the carrier's successful launch. In 2005 the spokesperson search moved to television, with nine 30-second spots filmed on location in Las Vegas and Miami and featuring real people selected on the street by Fallon's creative team. The supposed aspiring spokespersons were shown on camera responding to cues given by improvisational comedian

Jonathan Mangum. In one a man with a metal detector said, "If you don't want to keep hunting for fares, go to flyted.com." In another, Mangum asked a self-described ventriloquist to explain, in a British accent, that Ted does not charge booking fees. The TV spots ran on cable and network stations in Denver.

OUTCOME

The teaser campaign on behalf of Ted achieved its goal of attracting the attention of consumers and the media prior to the Ted launch. United announced the successful rollout of its initial 196 daily flights on August 11, 2004. Sean Donohue, vice president of Ted, said, "We've received strong endorsements from customers, outpaced our goals for on-time departures and arrivals, had positive financial performance and made significant competitive inroads in the markets we serve." By Ted's first anniversary the airline's number of daily flights had grown to 208, and United claimed solid market share gains, which it attributed to the addition of its low-fare carrier. As Donohue said in a company press release, "Ted has met or exceeded all of our expectations… Financially Ted delivered strong year-over-year margin improvement driven by an increase in both United elite customers as well as new customers to the airline." Ted continued to expand through 2005, though United had not yet found its way out of bankruptcy.

FURTHER READING

Allison, Melissa, and Susan Chandler. "United's Future Flies with Ted: Discount Airline Begins Operations on Thursday." *Chicago Tribune,* February 8, 2004.

Baar, Aaron. "Fallon, Ted Move Talent Search to TV." *Adweek.com,* May 20, 2005.

———. "United Sets Offbeat Intro for Low-Cost Carrier." *Adweek.com,* November 10, 2003.

Beirne, Mike. "Southwest Airlines Flies Campaign, Profits as Competition Hits Turbulence." *Brandweek,* April 28, 2003.

Cameron, Doug. "United Denies 'Ted' Reports." *Financial Times* (London), November 11, 2003.

Carey, Susan. "The Importance of Not Being Earnest—JetBlue Spoofs Commercials of Rivals, but Airline Says Spots Aren't Mean-Spirited." *Wall Street Journal,* June 5, 2003.

———. "Meet Ted, United's Low-Fare Carrier." *Wall Street Journal,* November 12, 2003.

Griffin, Greg. "United Airlines Likely behind Quirky 'Ted' Marketing Ploy in Denver." *Denver Post,* November 7, 2003.

Lewis, Al. "The Denver Post Al Lewis Column." *Denver Post,* November 16, 2003.

Thomaselli, Rich. "Delta Takes Low-Key Ad Approach to Low-Cost Carrier." *Advertising Age,* May 5, 2003.

———. "United, Fallon Go Stealthy to Intro Low-Cost Carrier." *Advertising Age,* November 17, 2003.

"United Airlines Says Ted Is Good to Go." *Brandweek.com,* November 18, 2003.

"United Battles Attendants Union." *Wall Street Journal,* February 3, 2004.

"United's Low-Cost Ted Completes Rollout." *Airports,* August 17, 2004.

Wilcha, Kristin. "Ted Searches for New Spokesperson among Real People." *Shoot,* June 3, 2005.

Mark Lane

United Distillers and Vintners of North America

750 E. Main Street
Stamford, Connecticut 06902-3845
USA
Telephone: (203) 602-5000
Web site: www.stoli.com

RUSSIAN ART CAMPAIGN

OVERVIEW

Non-Russian drinkers of vodka might not have been familiar with the names of artists such as Kamalova, Shakirov, or Volcov, but most people would recognize the name Gorbachev. Besides belonging to the former president of the Soviet Union, the name also belonged to a Russian artist, Mikhail's nephew Yuri, who was nicknamed the "Russian Rousseau." Hoping to translate name recognition into sales, the Russian distiller Stolichnaya commissioned the artist to produce a work combining references to its vodka (nicknamed Stoli) with a Christmas theme for the holiday installment of its "Russian Art" advertising campaign.

Yuri Gorbachev responded with a painting titled "The Russian Country," which featured a Stolichnaya bottle riding in a sleigh. The "Russian Art" campaign, introduced in 1997, was created by Stolichnaya's advertising agency, Margeotes/Fertitta & Partners of New York. It played off an ongoing ad campaign launched in 1980 by rival vodka Absolut, a Swedish product, that featured the instantly recognizable shape of an Absolut bottle as rendered by famous artists like Andy Warhol and Keith Haring. But the objective of the Stolichnaya campaign differed significantly from Absolut's goal. Whereas Absolut sought to extend its reputation for sophistication by depicting its bottle as a work of art, Stolichnaya sought to ground its own brand in its Russian roots through the work of contemporary Russian artists. Further accentuating its Russian heritage, Stolichnaya sponsored the maintenance of four Russian-made Mikoyan-Gurevich (MiG) fighter jets in 1999. Adorned with Stolichnaya's logo, the Cold War jets appeared in air shows across America. The campaign ended in early 2001.

"Russian Art" helped Stolichnaya stop a sales decline that had begun in the early 1990s. In 1999 sales of Stolichnaya increased to 1.3 million cases, which was significantly greater than the 1.1 million posted in 1996. At the campaign's conclusion Stolichnaya reigned as the number one vodka brand worldwide and second in America only to Absolut.

HISTORICAL CONTEXT

According to Russians, vodka, whose name was a Russian diminutive that might be translated as "little water" or "water of life," originated in the twelfth century. Distilled from grain, beets, or potatoes, vodka was described by the U.S. Code of Federal Regulations as "neutral spirits so distilled . . . as to be without distinctive character, aroma, taste or color." Rival brand Smirnoff took advantage of this designation in its first advertising campaign in 1946 with the tagline "It leaves you breathless," highlighting the "no taste, no smell" advantage of vodka over other spirits that left their mark on the breath of the drinker. There were a number of quality gradations in the vodka market, and Stolichnaya, produced in five distilleries in Russia for export, asserted its superior quality by stressing its Russian status.

Stolichnaya's ad agency, Margeotes/Fertitta & Partners, introduced the "Freedom of Vodka" campaign, which featured contemporary Russian art, in September 1994. In 1997 this campaign evolved seamlessly into the "Russian Art" campaign, with the style of artwork remaining the same and only the "Freedom of Vodka" tagline eliminated. In 1995 Stolichnaya became the first distilled-spirits marketer to establish its presence on the World Wide Web when Margeotes, in conjunction with CyberSight, developed the website "Stoli Central." The initiative broke the voluntary ban on advertising in the electronic media by spirits distillers in the United States. Stolichnaya thus took advantage of the graphic sophistication of the Web to extend its "Freedom of Vodka"/ "Russian Art" campaigns beyond the confines of print advertising. The Stoli website gathered more than a dozen of the artistic images from the "Freedom of Vodka"/"Russian Art" campaigns for display. Patricia Barroll, vice president of marketing communications for Carillon Importers, which marketed Stoli in the United States at the time, was unrepentant about the decision to establish a presence on the Web. In keeping with its existing print advertising and its tradition for responsible marketing, the company maintained strict quality standards with respect to the content of the website. Barroll stated in a 1998 *Brandweek* article, "It was not a problem for us because we've always taken the high road... We always strived to make [the website] sophisticated, not sophomoric. Just like our print campaign."

TARGET MARKET

"Stoli Central" allowed the brand to reach a broader audience while maintaining its reputation for sophistication. In its Web advertising Stolichnaya targeted the 21-to 45-year-old demographic group by hiring MXNT's entertainment division, MaxPlanet Media, to produce a separate site, the "Virtual www.Stoli2000.com Millennium Tour," in late 1998. The site broadcast so-called Virtual Parties, with MTV-style concert footage geared specifically to Stoli's target audience. According to Keith Benjamin, an analyst with BancBoston Robertson Stephens, one strength of the medium over television, radio, magazines, and newspapers was its accountability, since all activity on the MaxPlanet Media website could be digitally monitored. "We believe [the Web] is the first widespread consumer medium that has the capability to deliver measurable [return-on-investment] data to advertisers," Benjamin stated in a *PR Newswire* press release. Another strength was the inherently global reach of the Web, allowing Stolichnaya to tap into its international brand awareness.

LEMON RUSKI WINE COOLER?

United Distillers Australia (UDA) introduced Stolichnaya Lemon Ruski alcoholic soda in late 1997, and when the demand created by television advertising outpaced the supply in January 1998, UDA had to suspend the ads. UDA ascribed the success of the launch to the combination of wine, vodka, and lemon flavoring as well as to the brand recognition of Stolichnaya. In March 1998, however, Independent Liquor filed a lawsuit against UDA for misleading advertising. Independent Liquor's managing director, Michael Erceg, explained that the advertising portrayed Lemon Ruski as a vodka drink, while in reality its vodka content was quite low, with wine contributing the majority of the alcoholic punch to the drink. In that sense the drink was more of a wine cooler than a vodka soda. The Australian Federal Court heard the case on March 27, 1998.

It was Russia, however, that had the largest vodka market in the world. According to beverage-industry journal *Impact International,* 80 percent of Russians drank vodka on a regular basis. This translated into astronomical sales: in 1996, for example, an estimated 250 million cases of vodka were sold on the Russian market, compared to 33.4 million cases sold in the United States. The maturation and opening up of the Russian market sent international vodka distillers scurrying to the motherland. Expatriate brand Smirnoff highlighted the double *f* in its name, reminding Russians of its connection to the imperial Romanoff family, which had appointed the Pierre Smirnoff Company as its sole purveyor of vodka from 1886 until the Russian Revolution of 1917, when Vladimir Smirnoff fled across Europe to the United States to reestablish his family's brand. Such intense interest in the vast Russian market reinforced Stoli's authenticity and boosted its status as an export.

COMPETITION

Poland backed up its claim to be vodka's country of origin with an onslaught of products in the "ultrapremium" category, also known as "Polish luxury vodka," which chipped away at Stoli's market share. Belvedere and Chopin spearheaded this development. Both were imported exclusively by Millennium Import Co. of Minnesota, a subsidiary of Phillips Beverage Co., which spent $15 million on advertising for the two brands from their 1996 launch until 1998. Belvedere was bottled in satin glass with an etched "window" engraved with the likeness of the Belvedere Palace in Warsaw. Millennium pushed both brands by sending gift boxes to celebrities such as Robert DeNiro, Robert Redford, and Michael Jordan and his Chicago Bulls teammates, as well as to the managers of General Motors, a strategy that earned Belvedere a 1998 Gold EFFIE from the American Marketing Association. Belvedere alone had exports totaling $1.6 million in 1996, $3.7 million in 1997, and an estimated $7 million in 1998.

The brand ran into trouble, however, when the French producer of the distinctive bottle, which held the rights to the Belvedere trademark, stopped shipment because of lack of payment from the Polish distiller, the state-run Polmos Uyrard-w. This produced a backlog in exports to the United States, hampering the growth of the brand. But Belvedere and Chopin were not the only brands in the Polish luxury vodka category. The Original brand underlined its heritage with its name. *Wall Street Journal* reporters Ernest Beck and Daniel Michaels interviewed 52-year-old New York City property developer Bob Shapiro, who had switched from Stoli after taste-testing Original, which he described as "viscous, and well-refined. . .a cut above." Descriptions such as this, as well as fancy bottles, led Smirnoff to run a campaign that parodied the Original advertising. The Smirnoff ads featured cartoon characters boasting that their vodka of choice "comes in a bottle designed by albino monks from Tibet," and Smirnoff's tagline read, "All vodka. No pretense."

Finlandia, the number three imported vodka behind Absolut and Stoli in the U.S. market, added fuel to Smirnoff's mockery with its own bottle redesign. Louisville-based Brown-Forman Corp., which also marketed Jack Daniel's and Southern Comfort, ordered the new design from Philadelphia-based Hanson Associates, which created a bottle in smooth, carved glass, as if it were the melting ice of a Finnish glacier, the source of the water for the vodka. The label was printed in organic inks directly onto the bottle. A new advertising campaign, the first in 18 months, was unveiled in 1997 in anticipation of the introduction of the new bottle in May 1998. The campaign created sales spikes, with sales in December 1997 increasing 22 percent over the same period the previous year.

Even with such increases, however, Finlandia would be hard-pressed to catch the leaders of the $1.2 billion premium-vodka market in the United States, for it maintained a mere 4 percent share, compared to Absolut's 55 percent and Stoli's 16 percent. What was more, Absolut was on an upward sales trend. Global sales of Absolut in 1997 amounted to 3.5 million cases, an increase of 5.9 percent over 1996, according to *Impact Databank.* Some of Absolut's success resulted from its line extensions into flavored vodkas such as lemon and pepper. The appeal of flavored vodkas resided in their mixability. Citrus-based drinks such as the screwdriver could be given an increased bite with lemon-flavored vodka, and spicy drinks such as the Bloody Mary got more fire with use of the pepper-flavored vodka. In January 1998 Stolichnaya followed in its rivals' footsteps by introducing six flavored vodkas: Razberi (raspberry), Strazberi (strawberry), Persik (peach), Vanil (vanilla), Zinamon (cinnamon), and Kafya (coffee). Stolichnaya later added four more flavors: Ohranj (orange), Limonnaya (lemon), Pertsovka (pepper), and Okhotnichya (herb and spice).

MARKETING STRATEGY

In order to underline the authentic Russian heritage of Stoli, the talents of contemporary Russian artists were enlisted to incorporate the Stolichnaya bottle or logo into works to be used as print advertisements. The ad titles from the "Freedom of Vodka" and "Russian Art" campaigns were broad and included "Accordion," "Ballet," and "Business," with artwork by Serguei Volcov; "Boat" and "Planes" by Eugeni Mitta; "Dance" and "Dining" by Fathulla Shakirov; "Epicurean" by Guram Abramischvili; "Fashion" by Irina Raevskaja; "Film" by Aidan Salakhova; "Kosolopov" by Alexander Kosolopov; "Orange" and "Shout" by Khurshida Kamalova; and "Tower" by Konstantine Jouravlev. The ads included text in Russian, translated on the "Stoli Central" Web page. Volcov's "Business," for example, was accompanied by the text "After work, Stolichnaya Vodka," and his "Accordion" had text that read, "In Russia, in America, in Europe, in restaurant, in cafe, in bar, at home, with beloved, with good people, with a friend, in nice company or just in a crowd of friends."

The "Stoli Central" website also featured an encyclopedic list of recipes for vodka cocktails, including lesser-known drinks such as one called To Russia with Love, which was made with vodka, cherry liqueur, half-and-half, coconut rum, and egg whites; and the Muscovy Martini, concocted from two different kinds of vodka along with triple sec, orange juice, and cinnamon. Some cocktails were exclusive to the list, such as the Pertsovka Angelic Ruble, the Preferred Chekhov Libation, Aunt Olga's Slick Cosmonaut, and Das Chartreuse Bolshoi. Besides drinks, the site featured two games, Stoli Cipher and Stoli Says. The former challenged its players to reconfigure a picture from jumbled mosaic squares, and the latter tested its players' memory. In early 1998 Stolichnaya upgraded its website to version 2.1 to include Quicktime video. MaxPlanet Media integrated Real

Audio and Real Video into www.Stoli2000.com, its website dedicated to Stolichnaya.

In 1999 the American pilots Randy Howell and Jerry Gallud were looking for sponsors to fund U.S. air-show appearances for their four MiG-17s, fighter jets used by the former Soviet Union. The open-nosed jets consumed about 1,000 gallons of jet fuel an hour, an exorbitant expense compared to the 12 to 15 gallons used by small stunt planes. Peter Heyworth, an executive for United Distillers, jumped at the opportunity for the sponsorship. "The MiG is an icon of Russia, and Stolichnaya is an authentic Russian product with a lot of heritage," Heyworth was quoted in the *San Francisco Chronicle.* "It's not often in marketing that you get such a close fit." Stolichnaya covered the pilots' fuel costs. In return the jets were painted bright red and renamed "Stoli MiGs." The jets made their first air-show appearance at the Paso Robles Air Show in California. An executive from Stolichnaya stated that, even though they were using MiGs for an art-themed campaign, the jets themselves also celebrated Russia's heritage. Both were "as authentic as the soul of Russia herself," according to the *San Francisco Chronicle.*

OUTCOME

David Proffitt of the *Arizona Republic* applauded the "Stoli Central" website for its diversity of cocktail recipes. Otherwise he panned the site: "Its entertainment value is about as low as the temperature during a Moscow winter." The goal of advertising campaigns was to increase sales, however, not to please reviewers. When Margeotes launched the "Freedom of Vodka" campaign in 1994, sales of Stolichnaya vodka had fallen to 900,000 cases from 1.1 million cases in 1991, a decline of 18 percent. By 1996 sales had gone back to 1.1 million cases. Turnarounds were rare in the highly competitive distilled-spirits market, and this represented one of the few instances when a major brand of spirits had reversed a downward trend in sales.

Yuri Gorbachev's business manager, Beatrice Booth, was quoted in *Art Business News* as saying that executives from Stolichnaya liked Gorbachev's painting for "Russian Art" so much that they asked him to contribute a new piece every holiday season for the campaign. "Yuri's Stoli ads made the product very successful," said Booth, "and the ads gave Yuri's career a tremendous boost. Collectors tell us all the time that they cut them out of magazines and frame them."

"When fine art is used in advertising," Gorbachev explained to *Art Business News,* "the quality, strength and feeling of the art transfers to the product, enhances it. And when an artist is unique, he gives a uniqueness to the product as well. Art connects emotionally with people. It is less artificial and has a stronger impact." The campaign helped Stolichnaya increase its U.S. sales from 1.1 million cases in 1996 to 1.3 million cases in 1999. Stolichnaya was the second-largest vodka brand in America and the largest vodka brand worldwide. In 1998 one in every three Russians drank it. Stolichnaya executives eventually awarded the brand's advertising account to BBDO Chicago, which in 2001 released a new campaign with the tagline "See what unfolds."

FURTHER READING

Beck, Ernest. "Absolut Frustration: Why Foreign Distillers Find It So Hard to Sell Vodka to the Russians." *Wall Street Journal,* January 15, 1998.

Beck, Ernest, and Daniel Michaels. "Marketing: A Simple Spirit, Vodka, Rises to Fashion Icon." *Wall Street Journal Europe,* May 7, 1998.

Gehman, Geoff. "Yuri Gorbachev Fills Bixler with Something for Everyone." *Allentown Morning Call,* December 26, 1998.

Ho, Dorothy. "Stoli's Hyperreality." *Photo District News,* June 1, 2002, p. 24.

Oljasz, Tomasz. "Belvedere Bottle Battle Relations Turn Frosty between Makers of a Frosted-Glass Vodka Bottle and Polmos Uyrard-w, which Fills the Bottles with Its Super-Premium Spirit." *Warsaw Voice,* August 23, 1998.

Proffitt, David. "Russian Secrets." *Arizona Republic,* May 28, 1998.

Smith, Rebecca. "War Birds without Talons." *San Francisco Chronicle,* June 19, 1999, p. D1.

William D.Baue
Kevin Teague

United Parcel Service, Inc.

55 Glenlake Parkway NE
Atlanta, Georgia 30328
USA
Telephone: (404) 828-6000
Fax: (404) 828-6562
Web site: www.ups.com

MOVING AT THE SPEED OF BUSINESS CAMPAIGN

OVERVIEW

The "Moving at the Speed of Business" campaign was designed to modernize the image of the world's largest package-delivery company, United Parcel Service of America, Inc., commonly known as UPS. Over the years the corporation's advertising had helped it build a solid reputation for the efficient delivery of small parcels and documents, but many consumers were not aware that the company had changed significantly and offered a diverse mix of services and state-of-the-art technology.

The slogan "Moving at the speed of business" referred to the swift delivery of packages but also described the rapid manner in which UPS continually adapted to the changing needs of its business customers. One advertisement in *BusinessWeek* featured a photograph of a UPS truck parked at the Vatican in Rome, Italy. The headline read, "Fortunately, there's a global delivery service as good as UPS." Some spots in the campaign used humor to show UPS solving problems for its customers. In a television commercial that aired in December 1998, a rebellious elf took Santa's sleigh for a joyride and wrecked it in a snowbank. Stranded at the North Pole, Santa enlisted UPS to save Christmas by delivering presents for him.

"Moving at the Speed of Business" was handled by the New York office of Ammirati Puris Lintas (later renamed Lowe Lintas). It ran in print and broadcast media from 1995 through 2002. But as other shippers, such as FedEx, increased their market share, UPS felt that it was time to highlight what it could do beyond package delivery: supply-chain management, customhouse brokerage, and logistics-technology services. For a number of months UPS went without a tagline before unveiling the "What Can Brown Do for You?" campaign in 2002.

HISTORICAL CONTEXT

The firm that became United Parcel Service (UPS) was founded in Seattle, Washington, in 1907—an era before the widespread use of telephones and parcel post—when a teenager named James E. Casey established the American Messenger Company to deliver personal messages, luggage, and packages. Casey enlisted a crew of teenage helpers, including his brother George Casey, and funded the operation with $100 borrowed from a friend. The company's first promotional slogan, "Best service and lowest rates," summarized a business philosophy that ensured steady growth. In 1913 the enterprise merged with a competing company operated by Evert McCabe to form Merchants Parcel Delivery, which served many of the area's retail stores. The operation expanded to California and in 1929 launched an air delivery service called United Air Express, but that endeavor was discontinued at the onset of the Great Depression. During the 1930s the company expanded its territory to other states, changed its name to United Parcel Service, and painted its trucks brown to project a professional, dignified image.

In the 1950s UPS began pressing for common carrier rights, which would authorize it to make deliveries for any private or commercial customer in all 48 contiguous states. The company was finally granted that right in 1975, a development that placed it in direct competition with the United States Postal Service, the federal agency that handled most of the nation's mail and parcels. Since 1953 UPS had been offering two-day delivery service to large cities by sending packages in the cargo holds of regularly scheduled airlines and then completing the deliveries by truck, but during the 1980s the company began operating its own fleet of jets and could offer overnight air delivery. By 1998 UPS Airline was one of the 10 largest airlines in the nation, and UPS was the largest express carrier and package-delivery company in the world, delivering small parcels and documents to more than 200 countries and territories.

The industry and the corporation had changed dramatically over the years, but many consumers still perceived UPS as the company with delivery personnel in brown suits driving brown trucks, not a modern enterprise with innovative technology and a broad range of services. The company's advertising slogans had focused on the swift delivery of packages, evolving from "Best service, lowest rates" during the 1970s to "The tightest ship in the shipping business" during the 1980s and "The package delivery company more companies count on" during the early 1990s. In the mid-1990s UPS released a new campaign, "Moving at the Speed of Business," to modernize its image and publicize some of the other services it provided.

TARGET MARKET

The "Moving at the Speed of Business" campaign was designed to explain the company's diverse products and services primarily for business customers. UPS continually invested in sophisticated technology to operate efficiently, maintain competitive prices, and provide state-of-the-art services. For example, by 1998 it was delivering 12.4 million packages and documents every day and had developed a system that could track the progress of each item. Its site on the World Wide Web was the first in the industry to record more than a million tracking requests in one day from consumers inquiring about the status of items they had shipped. One study found that the company transported more than half of the merchandise that consumers ordered over the Internet during the holiday shopping season at the end of 1998. That year 6 of the top 10 merchants selling goods over the Internet shipped their wares via UPS.

The company had expanded into logistics management, which involved the warehousing, distribution, and tracking of merchandise for its customers. These services were useful for businesses that preferred to have merchandise delivered only when it was needed instead of keeping large inventories on hand. UPS also offered professional consulting and financial services. In addition, its Document Exchange product could deliver financial records, medical records, and other documents electronically with a password to protect their security and a certificate to show who received them. In a fast-paced era of expanding Internet commerce, electronic transmissions, and express delivery of packages, companies were changing the way they did business. The "Moving at the Speed of Business" campaign assured consumers that UPS understood those changes and was adapting to meet the needs of its customers.

ROAD SHOW

Near the end of 1998 United Parcel Service was considering a second traveling seminar to follow a successful road show it had conducted two years earlier. Over a period of five months the company had hosted 50 seminars in 34 cities to explain its technology and services directly to some of its most loyal customers. The road show included workshops, face-to-face interaction with customers, and the opportunity for people to try some of the company's equipment. The traveling exhibit cost a few hundred thousand dollars and generated enough sales to recoup that expense within six months. About 90 percent of those who attended said they would recommend the road show to an associate.

COMPETITION

The two main competitors for UPS were the United States Postal Service—an independent government agency that monopolized the delivery of first-class mail—and Federal Express Corporation, commonly known as FedEx. In 1997 FedEx had about 43 percent of the market for express delivery services, UPS had 27 percent, Airborne Freight Corporation (commonly known as Airborne Express) had 15 percent, and the Postal Service had 5 percent, according to *Fortune* magazine. UPS delivered more than express packages, however. Its total sales were about twice as large as FedEx's and a third as large as the Postal Service's. In 1998 the Postal Service had sales of $60.0 billion, UPS had $25.0 billion, and FedEx had $13.3 billion.

During 1998 the Postal Service continued the controversial "What's Your Priority?" advertising campaign, in which it compared its prices with those of UPS and FedEx. One print advertisement featured a graphic depiction of Earth above the headline "Sure, FedEx and UPS may promise you the world. But not for seven bucks." Pictures of the companies' distinctive mailing envelopes were aligned above flat rates for international deliveries. The Postal Service's price was $7, compared with $26 for FedEx and $28 for UPS. An arrow led from the Postal Service's envelope to the slogan "What's your global priority?" The text said that the Postal Service's Global Priority Mail might take a few days longer than delivery by the other two carriers, but it could save the customer up to 70 percent.

FedEx in 1996 had responded to the Postal Service's campaign by launching a series of negative radio advertisements and by filing a lawsuit and complaining to the National Advertising Division of the Council of Better Business Bureaus. UPS also criticized the campaign and in 1998 accused the Postal Service of using unfair operating practices and abusing its status as a government agency to undermine competition from the private sector. The Postal Service discontinued the advertising campaign at about the end of 1998 after negotiating an agreement to end the lawsuit filed by FedEx.

In 1997 FedEx had revenues of $11.5 billion and shipped about 3 million items every day. UPS shipped 10 times that number and had sales of $22.5 billion. In the fall of 1997 FedEx announced that it would merge with Caliber Systems, Inc., a trucking company with sales of $2.7 billion that year. Both firms became subsidiaries of a new holding company, FDX Corporation, but they continued to operate independently during 1998, with FedEx making express deliveries and Caliber Systems carrying nonexpress packages. During the 1970s FedEx had been one of the first companies to offer express shipping, a service that it promoted with the slogan "When it absolutely, positively has to be there overnight." In the late 1990s FedEx used the taglines "The world on time" and "The way the world works" to emphasize that express delivery had become an important part of the way modern companies conducted business. During 1998 the company's slogan was "Be absolutely sure." According to *Advertising Age,* FedEx spent about $57.4 million on advertising in 1997.

MARKETING STRATEGY

The New York office of Ammirati Puris Lintas developed the "Moving at the Speed of Business" campaign in 1995 to emphasize the information-technology and global services of UPS and to demonstrate that the corporation had changed significantly. UPS had progressed beyond the rapid delivery of packages and could help solve a variety of business problems. "Speed and reliability are now taken for granted in our industry," Peter Fredo, UPS vice president for advertising, said in a press release. "The challenge is to be innovative and flexible enough to bring new solutions and increased information to our customers. Our new tagline reflects the efforts UPS is making in these areas." The first television commercials in the campaign commented that the business environment was changing so rapidly that "the American business day has no beginning, middle, or end" and "business as usual can put you out of business." The spots called attention to the fact that UPS offered guaranteed delivery by 8 a.m. in addition to bar coding, inventory management, and tracking of packages.

A 1998 television commercial named "Ozone Monday" parodied Hollywood action films by showing a UPS deliveryman saving the day for a motion-picture crew frantically trying to work despite overwhelming difficulties. The spot opened with an explosion and a fireball roaring out of the roof of a building. A director shouted orders at the movie's star—an actress with voluminous hair and a bizarre superheroine costume—while the film's harried producer made calls on his cellular telephone. Several scenes followed in quick succession. The heroine clung to a rail, horizontally airborne in a howling wind full of rain and snow. The scene shifted to show her in a futuristic wedding dress, then shifted again to a group of mechanical pigs on wobbling wheels, their spring-loaded heads bobbing and their eyes spinning. Then the actress was shown in her dressing room amid a clutter of New Age paraphernalia, upset because she had not received her shipment of psychic healing tapes. The crisis was solved by the arrival of the UPS deliveryman, package in hand. A female narrator said, "Ozone Monday is going to be big, and you're the producer. But the director, first he wants a monsoon, then a blizzard, so you call UPS. You need the gowns for the wedding in three days; the metal pigs, second day by noon; and the star's psychic healing tapes—thank you—8 a.m.! Is there a happy ending? Two words—acceptance speech." The commercial concluded with a shot of the producer receiving an award for the film.

An advertisement that ran in *Fortune* magazine in August 1998 featured a large photograph of a two-lane highway running across open, rolling hills and past a distant city. The headline said, "Route 66. The Pacific Coast Highway. I-95. All freshly paved with the same guarantee. Introducing Guaranteed Ground. Only from UPS." The text explained that UPS guaranteed it would deliver packages to any business address nationwide by the day it was promised. The ad concluded with the slogan "Moving at the speed of business" and the company's logo, Internet address, and toll-free telephone number.

Some of the first television spots in the campaign aired during coverage of the 1996 Olympic Summer Games, professional basketball and golf competitions, and network television programs such as *60 Minutes* and the *NBC Sunday Movie.* Print advertisements appeared in the *Wall Street Journal, BusinessWeek, Newsweek, USA Today,* and other publications. *Advertising Age* reported that UPS spent $85.2 million on advertising in 1998, up 30.4 percent from $65.3 million in 1997. Of that amount, $65.4 million went for television commercials (a 52.4 percent increase) and $17.9 million for print advertisements.

The "Moving at the Speed of Business" campaign featured new executions in 1999. In a television spot called "Printer" a narrator said, "Imagine if people could just order things online and out they came." The spot showed scuba-diving equipment, a trombone, a watercooler, and a football being delivered through a computer printer. It ended with the conclusion that, in the real world, "The best way to get stuff off the Web is UPS." The tagline featured a new twist on the old slogan: "Moving at the speed of e-business."

UPS began in the new century to pivot away from the "Moving at the Speed of Business" theme, which pigeonholed the company as nothing more than a fast shipper. In reality, UPS now offered a wide range of logistical services to customers that many were simply not aware of. In 2000 UPS aired a spot called "Consultants," which featured a pair of slick consultants offering several business nostrums: integrate your global supply chain, move assembly overseas, accelerate inventory velocity. But when the client told them, "Do it," one consultant had to admit, "We don't actually do what we propose," and the other added, "We just propose it." A voice-over then delivered the new message: "UPS can help redesign your supply chain.... We deliver more than just packages." At the time UPS went without a tagline, as the television spots shown during the 2000 Olympics in Sydney focused on nondelivery services. The company also changed its advertising agency of record, dropping Lowe Lintas after 17 years in favor of the Martin Agency of Richmond, Virginia.

OUTCOME

In October 1998 a *Fortune* survey named UPS as the most admired delivery company in the world. In February 1999 another survey by *Fortune* cited UPS as America's most admired mail, package, and freight company. It was the 16th time the firm had received the honor. In a press release Jim Kelly, the chairman and chief executive officer of UPS, commented, "You don't earn that distinction for 16 consecutive years by resting on your laurels. UPS is working every day to help its customers stay ahead of the absolutely stunning pace of change in today's business world, especially in areas such as electronic commerce. That's why, for example, we spend more than a billion dollars a year on information technology." UPS reported revenues of $24.8 billion in 1998, up from $22.5 billion in 1997 and $19.6 billion in 1994. The company delivered 3.14 billion packages and documents in 1998 compared with 3.04 billion in 1997 and 3.03 billion in 1994.

Aided by a UPS strike in 1997, the competition was beginning to nip at the heels of UPS by the turn of the millennium, prompting a change in marketing strategy and a repositioning of the brand. No longer did it make sense to promote UPS as a shipper; it needed to be seen as a solutions provider, with shipping being just one service it offered. After several months of development UPS unveiled a new campaign and tagline in early 2002: "What Can Brown Do for You?" The new effort took advantage of the signature brown color of its trucks and drivers' uniforms to promote all that UPS had to offer customers beyond package delivery. The "Moving at the Speed of Business" campaign had adequately served its purpose, but, in a sense, the speed of business now dictated a change of course for a UPS looking to remain ahead of the pack.

FURTHER READING

Bradley, Sam. "One World, One UPS." *Brandweek,* February 5, 1996, p. 20.

Brownlee, Lisa. "UPS Launches a New Campaign to Regain Customers' Confidence." *Wall Street Journal* (Marketing & Media, Advertising), August 21, 1997.

Callahan, Sean. "Television. (United Parcel Service of America Inc., Lowe, Lintas & Partners." *B to B,* December 4, 2000, p. 42.

De Marco, Donna. "UPS Celebrates Brown in Biggest Ad Campaign." *Washington (DC) Times,* February 8, 2002, p. C09.

"Driving the UPS Brand." *Sales & Marketing Management,* December 1998, p. 47.

Hall, Carol. "High Fliers." *Marketing & Media Decisions,* August 1986, p. 137.

Leith, Scott. "UPS Foes with New Advertising Agency." *Atlanta Journal-Constitution,* April 24, 2001, p. D3.

Oberlag, Reginald. "Sonzero Spoofs Action Flicks for United Parcel Service." *Shoot,* March 6, 1998, p. 12.

Teinowitz, Ira, and Sean Callahan. "Post Office Axes Ads Rapping Its Rivals." *Advertising Age,* December 7, 1998, p. 1.

"Today's Businesses Stretching the Limits of Brand Elasticity, UPS Executive Says." *PR Newswire,* February 12, 1999.

Susan Risland
Ed Dinger

WHAT CAN BROWN DO FOR YOU? CAMPAIGN

OVERVIEW

In January 2002 United Parcel Service, Inc. (UPS), enjoyed a clear lead over FedEx, its major competitor, in the ground delivery business. At the same time, as part of a major rebranding campaign, UPS wanted to move beyond package delivery to include a variety of related services. To prepare for the impending rebranding, UPS launched the biggest U.S. advertising endeavor in its history. The high-priced, multilevel "What Can Brown Do for You?" campaign was intended to reveal fully what the company's growing capabilities were for just about anyone in nearly every aspect of the delivery business. In this way the campaign asked customers to look to the future. At the same time, with the focus on brown, the color the company had been associated with since its beginning in 1907, UPS was also reminding customers of its long heritage.

The "What Can Brown Do for You?" campaign, developed by the Martin Agency, debuted in January 2002 with such television spots as "Mailroom Guy," "Logistics Manager," "Shipping Manager," and "CEO." The first ads reflected the all-inclusive approach UPS wanted to convey. According to the spots, no matter where somebody fell on the managerial ladder, UPS could help that person. Later, in August 2002, the campaign shifted direction with the introduction of a new line of spots that focused on UPS employees. The emphasis in this later advertising varied from the recruitment of new employees to the commitment of UPS and its employees to the community. In "Keith Jones," for example, UPS outlined a worker's eventual advancement from part-time employee to corporate health and safety manager. In another spot, "Scholarship," a high school graduate explained how the company, through a tuition and assistance program called "Earn and Learn," had helped her realize her dream of attending college. The "What Can Brown Do for You?" campaign had its debut during the telecast of the opening ceremony of the 2002 Olympic Winter Games and appeared later that year during the Academy Awards. The spots were also broadcast on other sports, news, and entertainment programs during prime time. During 2002 alone more than 10 television commercials were released, and there was a national print promotion, all of which cost UPS $45 million.

The "What Can Brown Do for You?" campaign successfully set the stage for the rebranding efforts that followed. The campaign's television spots spoke directly to potential customers, and the customer base grew, as did sales. By the end of fiscal 2003 domestic revenue for UPS had increased by more than $1 billion, while international revenue had increased by just under $1 billion, or 25 percent. The "Synchronizing the World of Commerce" campaign that followed in 2003 further aided UPS in achieving its financial goals, but it was "What Can Brown Do for You?" that prepared the way for the global campaign.

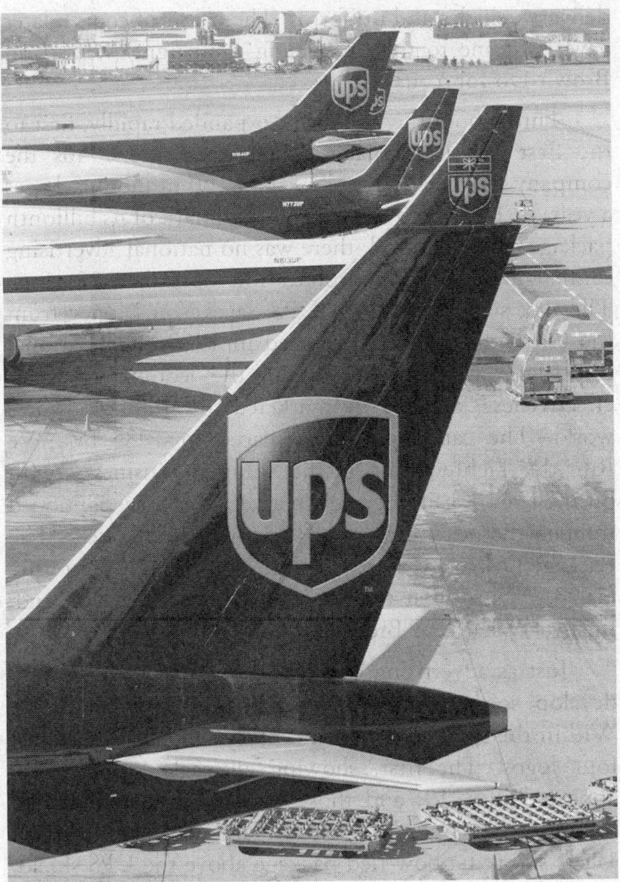

© JOHN SOMMERS II/REUTERS/CORBIS.

HISTORICAL CONTEXT

UPS traced its origins to the American Messenger Company, which was founded in Seattle in 1907. The company ran errands, delivered packages, and carried notes, baggage, and trays of restaurant food, mostly to local businesses. The American Messenger Company thrived, even without major advertising efforts. In 1913 the company bought its first delivery car, a Model T Ford, and inscribed its new name, Merchants Parcel Delivery, on the side. The inscription represented one of the company's few early advertising endeavors. In 1919 the company took its third name, United Parcel Service, or UPS, and moved beyond Seattle, to California. By this time UPS had chosen brown as the color for its delivery vehicles and uniforms. The color, of course, later gave its name to the advertising campaign "What Can Brown Do for You?"

Throughout the years UPS expanded rapidly, first to the East Coast and later overseas. By the 1940s the company was delivering more than 100 million packages a year. In 1946 UPS reached the landmark of its billionth package delivered. Still, there was no national advertising campaign in the United States for more than 35 years. The first such campaign, "UPS Saves You Money from the Ground Up," was launched in 1982. This national campaign, which focused on the company's cost-effectiveness, was heavily marketed toward the business world. The campaign was replaced in 1985 by "We Run the Tightest Ship in the Shipping Business," with business once again the target market. This focus continued through the next three campaigns, which included "The Package Delivery Company More Companies Count On" (1993), "Moving at the Speed of Business" (1995), and, finally, "What Can Brown Do for You?" (2002).

Just as advertising campaigns for UPS were slow to develop, so the company's logos changed only gradually. Within the span of almost a century, UPS had used just four logos. The first, showing an eagle on a shield, appeared in 1919, and those that followed represented minor changes on this. The third logo, which appeared in 1961, showed a bow-tied package above the UPS shield. Following the launching of the "What Can Brown Do for You?" campaign in 2002, UPS abandoned the package, which had been used for more than 40 years. The new logo, like those that had preceded it, continued to use brown as the trademark color.

TARGET MARKET

With more than 8 million people using its services every day, the UPS customer base was wide ranging. While individual consumers made up a portion of the base, businesses were a clear majority. Because businesses, the people who worked in them, and the jobs they did were diverse, the company's advertising aimed for a wide appeal. Thus, the "What Can Brown Do for You?" campaign was used to remind people at all levels of a business how UPS could be of help to them. In addition, the employee-centered ads, which touted the benefits of working for UPS, served as an attempt to recruit part-time workers.

Although UPS aimed for diversity in its approach, research on the campaign concluded that the advertisements were most effective with those in senior management positions. When, therefore, UPS created a new corporate tagline for use in a global rebranding effort, it focused on this group. The result was "Synchronizing the World of Commerce," a large-scale international print and television campaign that succeeded "What Can Brown Do for You?" Directed toward senior management, the print ads in this later campaign ran throughout the world, with television spots airing in a total of 144 countries.

WHAT CAN BROWN DO FOR YOU TODAY?

The website captionmachine.com asked people to submit captions for various humorous photos. One photo, entitled "UPS and FedEx Crash," captured an accident between the two companies' trucks. A total of 158 people submitted captions for the photo, including "FedEx + UPS = Fedup," "There can be only one," and "What can Brown do for you today?"

COMPETITION

The competition between UPS and FedEx was well known in the business world. In 2003, in response to UPS advertising, FedEx responded with a major marketing effort of its own. Its campaign, "Relax, It's FedEx," was launched during the season-opening telecast of ABC's *Monday Night Football.* The campaign included eight television spots that highlighted various FedEx services, including air, ground, freight, and international shipping. Its message to customers was that, if they were using FedEx, as opposed to, say, UPS, they would have peace of mind.

FedEx had earlier begun to encroach on UPS's prime market, especially when it purchased Caliber Systems, a major competitor in ground delivery. In addition, in what was labeled a "copy-cat move," FedEx purchased Kinko's soon after UPS had acquired Mail Boxes Etc. Still, UPS maintained a significant lead in the ground delivery business and, at the same time, proved more than competitive in other ways. Between 2002 and 2004, for example, total revenue for UPS ranged from $31 to $36.5 billion. This far exceeded revenue for FedEx, which during the same years never broke out of the $20 billion range.

Other UPS competitors included the United States Postal Service (USPS), the independent government agency that had nearly $70 billion in revenue in 2004. Still, much of the USPS's revenue was derived from the mailing of nonurgent mail, such as cards and letters, a service on which it held a monopoly. Its package delivery service, on the other hand, faced fierce competition from UPS and FedEx, as well as from the fast-growing DHL, the world's leader in cross-border express deliveries. DHL's overall revenue growth of nearly 8 percent in 2004, along with $30 billion in sales, made it a serious competitor. With its large-scale print and online advertising and a broadcast campaign that ran during the 2004 Olympic Games—in which the company promoted its Express Delivery Service in the United States—DHL created increasing competition for UPS.

MARKETING STRATEGY

The century-long heritage of UPS, embodied in the color brown, was something that could itself be marketed. The company's brown trucks and uniforms had long ago become an American icon, comparable to the Coca-Cola script or the Nike swoosh. Thus, in February 2002 UPS, under the guidance of the Martin Agency in Virginia, launched the "What Can Brown Do for You?" campaign. It was the largest and the most expensive U.S. advertising campaign in the company's history, yet only its fifth ever. The campaign debuted during the telecast of the opening ceremony of the 2002 Olympic Winter Games and later appeared during another high-profile event, the Academy Awards. In addition, the spots ran during prime-time sports, news, and entertainment programming, and print ads were also used. UPS spent a total of $45 million on the campaign.

The television spots in the "What Can Brown Do for You?" campaign were designed to work on different levels. The initial spots emphasized diversity, with titles such as "Small Business," "My Business," "CEO," "CFO," "Logistics Manager," "Shipping Manager," and "Mailroom Guy." The spots represented UPS's desire to convey to everyone, from CEOs to mailroom employees, what the company could do for them. In essence UPS wanted to assure people that, no matter what their position within a company, it could make their lives easier and help them do their work and achieve their professional goals. Later in 2002 UPS launched an extension of the "What Can Brown Do for You?" campaign. These later spots highlighted the experiences of representative employees, with the intent being to recruit part-time workers and to tout UPS's commitment to the community. In one such spot, "Road Trip," a 20-something employee explained how the company's generous starting wage and weekends-off policy allowed him to attend concerts with friends. Meanwhile, a more community-focused spot portrayed a UPS regional manager who had completed four weeks in the company's Community Internship Program, which benefited struggling communities throughout the United States. Thus, the campaign as a whole aimed to connect customers with UPS's longstanding commitment to the business world, to individual employees, and to communities.

While the "What Can Brown Do for You?" campaign worked to help customers make a connection with the company's past, it also directed them to look forward. By emphasizing the company's ever-growing capabilities, the campaign served as a springboard for an aggressive rebranding of UPS. The company wanted to move beyond package delivery to include services in logistics, freight forwarding, customs clearance, technology, and finance. As a result, between 1998 and 2004 UPS had made 28 acquisitions, including the purchase of Mail Boxes Etc. To highlight its rebranding, UPS introduced a new logo in 2003, abandoning the brown-and-white bow-tied package that had been used for 40 years. While the new logo kept the signature brown shield, it dropped the package, thus symbolizing the company's growth into areas other than delivery services. The transformation was to continue through 2009, by which time UPS would have changed every existing logo, something that involved thousands of vehicles, 250 aircraft, 1,700 facilities, 70,000 drop-off and retail boxes, and more than 1 million uniforms.

OUTCOME

"What we found was that not even we—brown-bleeding UPS'ers—had completely understood the power of 'brown' and the connection audiences have with it," said a company spokesperson. Thus, one indication of the success of the "What Can Brown Do for You?" campaign was that the unspoken message, centering on the color brown, was perhaps as significant than the spoken one. Still, the advertisements served as a means of getting the UPS message across.

The "What Can Brown Do for You?" campaign appeared to be successful in setting the stage for the rebranding campaign that followed in 2003. By portraying the diverse customer base of UPS, the television spots in the campaign helped to draw in new customers. The global "Synchronizing the World of Commerce" campaign that followed used research derived from the effectiveness of the "What Can Brown Do for You?" campaign, allowing UPS to determine that its new international advertising would be most effective if targeted toward those in senior management positions. Further, the early success of the UPS rebranding prompted another global advertising campaign, "Deliver More," which was launched in 2005. This campaign focused on the company's international package delivery services and, in the spirit of the rebranding efforts, highlighted the ability of UPS to use its wide range of capabilities to make it easier to conduct business internationally.

The "What Can Brown Do for You?" campaign was accompanied by improvements in UPS finances. At the end of fiscal year 2002, UPS's domestic revenue was virtually stagnant. By the end of fiscal year 2003, however, U.S. revenue had increased by more than $1 billion, from $23.9 to more than $25 billion. Further, international revenue for UPS increased by approximately 25 percent in 2003, from $4.6 to $5.5 billion. Overall 2003 revenue for the company increased more than $2 billion compared to the previous year. This success was seen as being largely a product of the rebranding efforts. UPS needed to lay the groundwork, which including reminding customers of its heritage, before it could effectively spread its rebranding message, however, and it was the "What Can Brown Do for You?" campaign that succeeding in doing this.

FURTHER READING

"Brown and a Better Life." August 21, 2002. Available from <http://www.pressroom.ups.com>

Callahan, Sean. "Look What Brown Has Done for UPS." *B to B,* October 25, 2004.

Carnegie, Jim. "UPS Kicks Off International Advertising Initiative." *Radio Business Report* 22, no. 37 (February 22, 2005).

"FedEx Companies Star in New Advertising Campaign: Ads Reinforce Reliability, Peace of Mind; 'Relax, It's FedEx.'" *FedEx Archives,* 2003.

"FedEx Taps BBDO for Kinko's Advertising Campaign." *Memphis Business Journal,* July 6, 2004.

Griswold, Alicia. "Martin Presents New Look: UPS." *Adweek,* March 25, 2003.

Lazare, Lewis. "One Place UPS Doesn't Deliver: Latest TV Campaign." *Chicago Sun-Times,* March 14, 2005.

Manning-Schaffel, Vivian. "UPS & FedEx Compete to Deliver." *brandhome,* May 17, 2004.

"UPS Delivers International Ad Campaign." *Business First,* March 3, 2005.

"UPS 'Delivers More' in New Advertising Campaign." *Strategy,* February 23, 2005.

"UPS Launches Biggest, 'Brownest' Ad Campaign Ever." February 7, 2002. Available from <http://www.pressroom.ups.com>

"UPS Unveils 'What Can Brown Do for You?' Ad Campaign." *Business First,* February 7, 2002.

Candice Mancini

United States Postal Service

475 L'Enfant Plaza SW
Washington, DC 20260
USA
Telephone: (202) 268-2000
Fax: (202) 268-2000
Web site: www.usps.gov

FLY LIKE AN EAGLE CAMPAIGN

OVERVIEW

Even though the United States Postal Service (USPS) was made an independent agency in the 1970s, it was not until Loren Smith became the chief of postal marketing for USPS in 1994 that the organization aggressively competed in the private sector. The two largest competitors of USPS, the FedEx Corporation and United Parcel Service, Inc. (UPS), both dominated the global market for overnight and two- to three-day deliveries. Before Smith approved several of USPS's successful marketing campaigns, public perception was that the Postal Service was slow and unreliable. Even though Smith resigned from USPS in 1996, his marketing prowess remained. USPS released its "Fly Like an Eagle" campaign two years later to further elevate its stodgy image and publicize its products and services.

The $15 million television and print campaign was created by the New York branch of the advertising agency Foote Cone & Belding. "Fly Like an Eagle" began on October 19, 1998, and extended through the holiday season—the USPS's busiest time of year—to assure Americans that the Postal Service was poised to handle the holiday rush. The three debut television spots were set to the Steve Miller Band song "Fly Like an Eagle," which had been popular in the 1970s. Print ads adopted "Fly Like an Eagle" as the tagline as well. Though the campaign was scheduled to run for only three months, its success was such that subsequent campaigns in 1999 continued to employ the "Fly Like an Eagle" theme. In February 2000 the song and tagline resurfaced for a spot titled "Robot" that advertised the USPS's holiday return services. The campaign ended shortly after the September 11, 2001, terrorist attacks.

"Fly Like an Eagle" yielded a positive net income for USPS during its first year. The spot "Robot" was awarded *Shoot* magazine's Top Spot of the Week honor; and the campaign helped increase the number of monthly visitors to the website www.USPS.com. Larry Speakes, the USPS advertising manager, would later criticize the campaign in a February 25, 2002, *Advertising Age* article, explaining that it "didn't test well, while the [subsequent campaign that began in 2002] can translate into a variety of more targeted efforts."

HISTORICAL CONTEXT

Established in 1775 as the Post Office Department, the agency was tied closely to the federal government until the early 1970s, when it became an independent agency. This freed the agency, which operated within the federal government's executive branch, to compete within the business sector while continuing to receive government subsidies. A major competitive thrust came in 1994 when Loren Smith became the chief of postal marketing. Smith implemented a number of new programs and services, including the marketing of postal paraphernalia, such as T-shirts and games, and the creation of phone cards. Smith also added new agencies to the marketing roster—the USPS's longtime primary agency, Young & Rubicam (Y&R), New York, was joined by Foote Cone & Belding (FCB), Chicago's Draft Worldwide, and Chicago's Frankel & Co. While Y&R handled advertising for Global Priority Mail and all media buying, FCB took charge of U.S. Priority Mail and stamp advertising, two areas Smith planned to boost. Smith, in fact, took $80 million allocated to other marketing purposes and spent it on Priority Mail advertising in the mid-1990s without the approval or permission of the Postal Service Board of Governors. By 1996 Smith had exceeded the USPS's annual advertising budget by 62 percent, spending $87 million more than the allotted $140 million. As a result he left the agency in late 1996.

Though Smith's attempts at diversification met with negative reactions from some in the administration, his efforts succeeded in making U.S. Priority Mail a hit and provided the USPS with a significant increase in revenue. The "What's Your Priority?" campaign, launched in 1996 and developed by FCB, compared the cost of sending a package using Priority Mail versus mailing the package through a competing vendor's similar service, such as Federal Express Corporation's (FedEx) Two-Day Service or United Parcel Service of America's (UPS) Second-Day Air. The campaign continued through 1997 and 1998, and Priority Mail quickly became the USPS's fastest-growing service. In the 1996–97 fiscal year, according to *Traffic World,* Priority Mail accounted for more than $3.4 billion in revenue. Despite the campaign's achievements, however, a number of factors—including outcry from rivals claiming the comparative ads were unfair, the USPS's desire to make known its myriad of services, and the agency's wish to enhance its image—led the Postal Service to introduce the "Fly Like an Eagle" image campaign. The USPS's Roxanne Symko, manager of advertising and promotion, explained in *Advertising Age*: "People are familiar with the postal service, but to know us on the surface doesn't mean they know the kind of progress we have made in recent past. ... We want to position ourselves in a new light, as innovative and looking forward."

YOU CAN'T HAVE IT ALL

Not only did the USPS face competition from UPS, FedEx, and other large shipping vendors, but it also met with challenges from small companies such as Mail Boxes Etc. and from technological advances, such as E-mail and computerized banking services, that enabled consumers to pay bills through the Internet or by telephone. Shopping via the Internet, known as e-commerce, was a growing arena as well, predicted by Forrester Research of Cambridge, Massachusetts, to increase to more than $100 billion by 2003, up from $8 billion in 1998. Although a survey of Internet shoppers conducted by Zona Research Inc. found that 32 percent received their merchandise from the USPS, 55 percent got their wares via UPS.

TARGET MARKET

Although the USPS developed different campaigns targeted toward specific audiences, the agency introduced a number of campaigns in the 1980s and 1990s designed to attract the general public. A major hurdle faced by the Postal Service was its poor image. Roxanne Symko told Sloane Lucas of *Advertising Age,* "Our delivery standards are high, and we are a changing, progressive company but our research showed that people see us as old and stodgy." Many customers also considered the Postal Service to be somewhat unreliable, and the agency addressed this in a 1997 advertising campaign created by Y&R. Continuing with the "We Deliver" theme and tagline, the "If I Ran the Post Office" campaign focused on the postal customer and included television spots featuring customers presenting their suggestions for improving mail service and delivery. The campaign failed to garner much enthusiasm from the public, however, and it was abandoned.

Despite the Postal Service's image problem, the public appeared to be satisfied with the overall service provided by the USPS. A study conducted by the Pew Research Center for the People & the Press revealed that the USPS was the top-ranked federal agency in 1997, earning a favorability rating of 89 percent. A decade earlier the Postal Service's rating was 76 percent. Similarly, members of a panel of catalog marketers assembled by the USPS in June 1998 agreed that they were generally satisfied with the agency's delivery service but that customers continued to look upon the USPS with disfavor. In order to enhance its image, the USPS needed to promote its many services with a new, updated approach, such as the "Fly Like an Eagle" campaign.

COMPETITION

The Postal Service's most visible and energetic competitors were shipping-service providers FedEx and UPS. For the Postal Service, competition was a tricky matter;

the Postal Service was a government-subsidized entity with many advantages. Its rivals frequently maintained that the USPS used revenues generated from its monopoly on mail delivery to fund services designed to compete against private companies. The USPS, exempt from most taxes, including federal and state, free from parking fines, and able to clear foreign customs more easily than its competitors, seemed to hold the upper hand in the marketplace. In addition, postal laws required that private companies charge twice as much for services also offered by the USPS, allowing the agency to significantly undercut competing prices. UPS chairman and CEO Jim Kelly spoke out against such policies in a speech given to the National Press Club in 1998 and declared, "I'm hard pressed to think of a better example of anti-competitive practices than setting your competitors' rates." The Postal Service defended the postal rules and pointed out that UPS and FedEx charged more than double the USPS's $3.20 Priority Mail charge for two-day delivery services. USPS spokesperson Norm Scherstrom said in the *Journal of Commerce,* "If I recall, when we started our Priority Mail ads, UPS was charging about $8 and FedEx was charging about $12.... If the requirement was a double postage rule why were they way above that?"

As powerful as the Postal Service was, it faced substantial competition from many challengers and did not command all delivery categories. In the express-delivery service segment, FedEx was the largest express shipping company in the world and the market leader with a 43 percent share in 1997. UPS took the second place spot with 27 percent, followed by Airborne Express at 15 percent, other services with 8 percent, and the Postal Service with 5 percent, according to the Colography Group. For two-day deliveries, however, the USPS's Priority Mail held a strong market share of 45 percent in 1997, thanks in part to the aggressive "What's Your Priority?" campaign. The campaign displeased the Postal Service's rivals considerably, with FedEx filing a lawsuit for false advertising and lodging a complaint with the National Advertising Division of the Council of Better Business Bureaus. UPS openly criticized the campaign as well.

MARKETING STRATEGY

The "Fly Like an Eagle" campaign marked a discernible and intentional change in the Postal Service's advertising. The Postal Service chose to focus on the agency as a whole rather than concentrating on a specific service or product. Symko explained in the November/December 1998 issue of the USPS publication *Postal Life,* "The 'Fly Like an Eagle' campaign tells customers that the Postal Service is one organization with many products... with one unified advertising message. This campaign will serve as a touchstone for everything the Postal Service does, and it will reinforce our promotional message to our customers."

THE SONGS THAT WOULDN'T DIE

Songs popular in the 1960s and 1970s continually seeped into advertising campaigns during the late 1990s. In addition to the Steve Miller Band's "Fly Like an Eagle," other old songs were featured in a diverse array of advertising campaigns. Burger King Corporation produced a series of commercials including different tunes, including the Trammps's "Disco Inferno." Ameritech used an adaptation of Don McLean's "Bye, Bye, Miss American Pie," Toyota Motor Sales USA Inc. used Sly Stone's "Everyday People," and AT&T ads featured Elton John's "Rocket Man."

The Postal Service regularly created holiday campaigns to inform customers of its ability to handle the holiday rush—during the Christmas season, the USPS delivered more than 5 billion letters and cards and 100 million packages—but they generally aired only during the holiday season. With "Fly Like an Eagle" the Postal Service planned to extend the duration of the campaign and adopted the new tagline and theme for all its promotions and advertising. The song was also used in all advertising. Symko explained in *Postal Life,* "We selected this song because besides being universally recognizable, likable and memorable, the music was an ideal fit for our message."

The "Fly Like an Eagle" campaign began airing on major networks and cable channels in mid-October and consisted of three commercials—the first presented the USPS's ability and willingness to help, the second focused on various USPS services designed to accommodate busy customers, and the third, which aired after Christmas, expressed thanks to the hardworking postal employees. The spots included montage sequences of smiling postal workers, employees loading airplanes and trucks, and delivery workers walking through the snow and empty streets to make sure customers received their mail on time. Intercut with these scenes were shots of the Postal Service's various products and services. One scene showed a woman looking out her window, anxiously waiting for her holiday packages to arrive. When the postal employee arrived, the woman rushed to the door to greet the delivery person. Another scene featured a child opening a gift—a gift that arrived just in time for Christmas, thanks to the Postal Service. Copy appeared on the screen and asked: "We've added a fleet of planes ... an army of trucks.... 40,000 more employees. We're ready for the holidays. Are you?" Symko stated, "The ads evoke images of speed, strength, integrity and dependability, all images associated with the Postal Service.... This campaign portrays the Postal Service as a customer-friendly, hard-working organization that is dedicated to meeting our customers' needs."

In 2000 FCB created a spot titled "Robot" to tout a USPS service that allowed customers of online retailers to print their own return labels via the Internet. In the 30-second spot a woman was featured talking on the phone. An unopened box was sitting on her coffee table. "Oh, he already has Zogatron," she said. "I'll exchange it." Inside the box, a robot's eyes opened. It then kicked its way out of the packaging, leapt up to the family's computer thanks to computer-generated special effects, and printed its own return label. The robot reinserted itself into the now-labeled package before the woman even noticed. The spot ended with Steve Miller's song and the text "Fly Like an Eagle." The USPS advertising budget was reduced in 2000. The campaign officially ended after the terrorist attacks of September 11, 2001.

OUTCOME

The Postal Service enjoyed revenues of $60.1 billion and a surplus of $550 million in 1998. It was the first time the agency had experienced four consecutive years of positive net income. Though the successful "What's Your Priority?" campaign was discontinued at the end of 1998, the "Fly Like an Eagle" campaign was so well received that the Postal Service continued to employ the theme and tagline in promotions and advertising campaigns into 2001. Even musician Steve Miller approved of the campaign. In a letter in the January/February 1999 issue of *Postal Life,* Miller wrote: "I've been turning down commercial appeals to use this song for over 20 years and it wasn't until your request that I felt the full potential of this song could be reached . . . I look forward to continuing to make sure that the Postal Service continues to have the smartest and most meaningful promotions in the country and that the integrity of this message is maintained."

In 1999 the USPS continued to implement new programs and services to keep consumers satisfied and enhance the brand. Postal Service packaging boldly displayed the eagle symbol, new uniforms were planned for postal employees by the end of 1999, and packaging of products sold in post offices was revamped and updated. The Postal Service formed an alliance with private delivery service DHL Worldwide Express Inc. in early 1999 for its Priority Mail Global Guaranteed program, a service for two-day delivery of mail to Europe. The USPS's most significant new program in 1999, however, was delivery confirmation, and it was supported by the Postal Service's largest marketing program of the year. Delivery confirmation allowed the agency to compete more effectively with FedEx and UPS, which had long offered shipment tracking and delivery confirmation. The estimated $50 million campaign, which began in March, was developed by FCB, which seemed to be supplanting 20-year USPS advertising veteran Y&R as the organization's key agency. The Postal Service's Ron Landis explained in *Postal Life* that the agency was taking progressive measures to fly like an eagle into the future. Landis stated: "[W]e are taking a major step into the future and grooming ourselves to be contenders on a global scale.... We are showing the world who we are and what we can do, and we are doing it with flair."

The campaign was not appreciated by all USPS executives. In 2002 Larry Speakes suggested that the campaign's target audience was not effectively reached and that the campaign did not convey enough emotion. Nonetheless, six months after the campaign began, the website www.USPS.com reported a rise in monthly traffic. The spot "Robot" also collected *Shoot* magazine's Top Spot of the Week honor.

FURTHER READING

Bremner, Faith. "Postal Service Ad: Fly Right." *USA Today,* October 19, 1998, p. B8.

Lucas, Sloane. "FCB Breaks New USPS Image Work." *Adweek,* October 19, 1998.

Teinowitz, Ira. "Changing Themes." *Advertising Age,* February 25, 2002, p. 8.

———. "Postal Service Tries Image of Innovation: Steve Miller Song 'Fly Like an Eagle' Sets Tone of New FCB Campaign." *Advertising Age,* October 19, 1998, p. 6.

———. "USPS Confirms Delivery of $50 Mil Campaign." *Advertising Age,* February 22, 1999, p. 1.

Teinowitz, Ira, and Sean Callahan. "Post Office Axes Ads Rapping Its Rivals." *Advertising Age,* December 7, 1998, p. 1.

Teinowitz, Ira, and Beth Snyder. "USPS Plans $200 Mil-plus Review." *Advertising Age,* April 19, 1999.

Williamson, Debra Aho. "USPS Stats." *Advertising Age,* August 2, 1999, p. 36.

Woodward, Sarah. "Toy Robot Brings Many Happy Returns to USPS." *Shoot,* March 3, 2000, p. 12.

Mariko Fujinaka
Kevin Teague

United States Tennis Association

70 West Red Oak Lane
White Plains, New York 10604
USA
Telephone: (914) 696-7000
Fax: (914) 696-7019
Web site: www.usta.com

■■■

US OPEN EXCITEMENT CAMPAIGN

OVERVIEW

The United States Tennis Association (USTA) was the official governing body of American tennis and the owner of the US Open, the only Grand Slam tournament held in the United States. But the USTA membership, while holding at 500,000 individuals and 6,000 organizations, was not growing, and Nielsen ratings for telecasts of the US Open had dropped from a high of 5.8 in 1981 to 2.8 in 1998. The organization had earned a reputation as a group for professionals rather than the average tennis player, and the US Open had come to be viewed as a slow-paced, unexciting event, entertaining only to older audiences.

In 1999 the USTA launched a $2 million, two-phase marketing campaign created by ad agency Fallon McElligott New York. Phase one was intended to build interest in and to help boost ticket sales and television viewership for the US Open, held at the National Tennis Center in Queens, New York, and phase two was aimed at increasing membership in the USTA. The first phase, titled "US Open Excitement," included television spots that ran on cable, network, and local New York channels and print ads that appeared in publications like the *New York Times* and *USA Today.* The second phase, called "Direct Response TV," consisted of two television spots that ran during the airing of the US Open.

Both phases of the campaign far exceeded their goals of increasing ticket sales and television viewership by 10 percent each and of adding 10,000 new members to the USTA. The "US Open Excitement" campaign helped increase television ratings 100 percent over 1998, and ticket sales for the event were up 16 percent. Following the "Direct Response TV" campaign, memberships in the USTA jumped 69 percent, with the organization adding more than 16,000 new members. In addition, both campaigns were recognized with EFFIE, CLIO, and Athena awards.

HISTORICAL CONTEXT

The United States National Lawn Tennis Association was founded in 1881 as the governing organization for the sport. By 1999 the organization's name had been changed to the United States Tennis Association, and its purpose had grown to include promoting both community and professional tennis, developing world-class American tennis players by helping to provide the best coaches and training facilities, and encouraging cultural diversity in the sport. The organization also owned the US Open, one of four worldwide Grand Slam tennis tournaments.

Despite its long history and its appeal as a sport people could play throughout their lives, tennis was in a decline that had begun in the 1980s. In 1995 the USTA replaced its New York agency, Ammirati & Puris/Lintas, and launched a marketing campaign created by Grybauskas Beatrice, also based in New York. The campaign, which was designed to attract new players to the sport, was titled "Get in the Game" and featured tennis players like Pete Sampras and Andre Agassi. But interest in the sport continued to slip. According to the USTA, in 1999 the number of tennis players overall had dropped by 50 percent since the early 1980s. The number of players younger than 25 had dropped 15 percent during the same period. Further evidence of the declining participation in tennis was seen in the sales of such equipment as tennis racquets, which fell 40 percent in the 1990s. Although interest in the US Open was strong, ticket sales were down, and while individual memberships in the USTA were at 500,000, growth was stagnant, with only a reported 3 of every 100 tennis players signing on as members in 1999.

With the goal of increasing ticket sales for the US Open as well as television viewership for the tournament, the USTA reviewed a list of agencies, including Lowe & Partners, NW Ayer, and the Lord Group. The organization finally selected Fallon McElligott to create a multimedia campaign to promote the US Open and to increase membership in the USTA.

WEBSITE ENCOURAGES KIDS TO PLAY TENNIS

The United States Tennis Association created a website targeting kids who wanted to play tennis, along with their parents. The site, littletennis.com, included games and contests as well as information for parents, such as how to locate Little Tennis programs for kids, an online magazine with tennis-related articles, and a calendar of tennis and Little Tennis events.

TARGET MARKET

The USTA's 1999 marketing campaign was two pronged, and it was aimed at two distinct target audiences. Phase one of the campaign, "US Open Excitement," was directed at younger audiences as well as a wider group of sports enthusiasts who had lost interest in watching the USTA's flagship event, the annual US Open. Phase two, "Direct Response TV," targeted tennis players who enjoyed participating in the sport but who had never become members of the USTA.

Over the years tennis had gradually earned the reputation of being slow moving and boring to watch. By the mid-1990s the typical audience attending the US Open was skewed toward older, well-educated, affluent, conservative fans. The goal of the "US Open Excitement" campaign was to win back younger enthusiasts, those between the ages of 18 and 25, along with other fans who had tuned out tennis in favor of such high-octane sports as the X Games, the events shown on ESPN's SportsCenter, and college or professional football and hockey.

Although baby boomers were playing tennis, the number of players under the age of 25 had begun to decline in the 1980s. In addition, players of all ages were going on their own rather than joining the USTA and taking advantage of the benefits it offered. According to the organization, only 3 of every 100 tennis players were members in 1999. The goal of "Direct Response TV" was to build interest in the sport and attract younger players to the game. It also was designed to build awareness of the USTA with active tennis players of all ages and to change the perception that membership in the organization was only for advanced players or for tennis professionals.

COMPETITION

Two professional sports that were winning ticket-buying fans away from the US Open, which in 1999 attracted 584,490 people during its two-week run, were baseball and football. With New York the home to two Major League Baseball and two National Football League teams, among many other diversions, the US Open thus had strong competition for local audience dollars and ticket sales as well as for television viewers. In addition, the US Open was played during the end of the professional baseball and the beginning of the professional football seasons.

Traditionally known as America's pastime, Major League Baseball in 1999 had an average attendance of 28,888 fans per game, for a season total of more than 70 million. New York's baseball teams—the Yankees and the Mets—reported per-game attendances higher than the national average, with 40,651 and 33,650, respectively, and 1999 season totals of 3.2 million fans for the Yankees and 2.7 million for the Mets. Both teams worked with their ad agencies in 1999 to create marketing campaigns designed to boost ticket sales. The Yankees choose BBDO New York to create a series of newspaper, radio, and billboard ads that emphasized the team's successful past, including 24 World Series championships. Working with its longtime agency, Della Femina/Jeary and Partners, the Mets focused on the present and the team's up-and-coming status with a campaign that used the tagline "Are you ready? New year. New team. New magic."

The National Football League's pregame battle cry was "Are you ready for some football?" For fans the answer was typically yes. In 1999 the average per-game attendance nationally was 65,349, with the total attendance for the season at 16.2 million. In New York, fans of the Jets and the Giants were equally enthusiastic. For both teams home attendance averaged about 78,000 per game in 1999. The season totals were also about the same for both, with a total of 624,847 fans attending Jets games and 623,777 attending Giants games. Traditionally seen as a blue-collar game, football was going through a transition by 1999, attracting fans who arrived at games in Range Rovers and who preferred snacking on wine and aged cheese rather than on beer and peanuts. As the crowd morphed into a wealthier, more educated demographic, it was also getting older. According to a report in the *Tribune Business News,* Russ Hawley, the vice president of marketing for the New York Giants, explained the reason for the changing fan base: "The fan who first bought tickets in 1970 at age 29 is now 58 and, most likely, making better money."

MARKETING STRATEGY

In 1999 the USTA was confronted with two challenges: turning around steadily dropping tickets sales for its main event, the US Open, and bolstering the number of people actually participating in the sport of tennis and in the USTA, whose membership had also been on a steady decline. To reverse the slide in both areas, the USTA joined with Fallon McElligott to create two separate marketing campaigns. The cost of the campaigns was estimated at $2 million.

To promote interest in the annual US Open and to increase ticket sales as well as television viewership among people unable to attend the tournament in person, Fallon McElligott created the "US Open Excitement" campaign. Besides stirring interest in the event, the campaign was designed to change the perception that watching tennis was boring and appealed only to an older, country-club set. The multimedia campaign included television spots that were aired on national networks to encourage viewers to tune in to the US Open and on channels in the New York City area to convince local residents to buy a ticket and see the action in person.

The cable, national network, and New York television spots all used humor to appeal to a younger audience. They featured an eccentric spokesman who compared tennis to such exciting-to-watch sports as basketball and figure skating, with each spot portraying what might happen if those sports took place on a tennis court. In one spot, for example, a pair of figure skaters attempted unsuccessfully to execute a difficult routine on a hard-surface tennis court rather than in an ice rink. At the end of each spot the claim was made that nothing beats "the excitement of U.S. Open tennis."

The print ads were aimed at sports fans in New York. Running in such publications as the *New York Times* and *USA Today,* they featured tennis star Andre Agassi poking good-natured fun at people skeptical of his abilities. In the ads Agassi's tournament opponents consisted of the criticisms he had faced during his career, including "Can't win the big ones" and "Doesn't train hard." He advanced through the brackets and ultimately won by defeating each charge. Other ads, which appeared on New York City buses, pictured rows of people sitting in stadium seats, with Upper East Side society women wearing hats and holding small dogs on one side and East Village punk rockers on the other. The text stated that all were "going to the U.S. Open. Are you?" Ads that appeared in New York metropolitan area commuter trains had a similar theme. In one an out-of-shape man was leading a step aerobics class. The text read that the regular instructor "will be out at the U.S. open next Thursday. You may want to do the treadmill that day. Almost everyone's going to the U.S. Open. Are you?"

The second phase of Fallon McElligott's effort, to build enthusiasm for participation in the game of tennis and to increase membership in the USTA, resulted in the creation of the "Direct Response TV" campaign. To dispel the perception that membership in the USTA was only for serious tennis players and to convince people that the organization offered something for every level of player, from beginners to professionals, Fallon McElligott developed two television spots with the tagline "Help us grow the game we all love." The spots were aired on CBS and the USA Network during the US Open. One ad, titled "Anthem," portrayed the emotional aspect of tennis, with players both winning and losing competitions. A second ad, "Benefits," took a more reasoned approach in trying to motivate people to join the USTA. The commercials included the organization's phone number and listed some of the benefits of membership, such as a free subscription to *Tennis Magazine.*

OUTCOME

Turning to Fallon McElligott for its two-part marketing campaign produced the results that the USTA wanted. The 1999 "US Open Excitement" campaign led to increased ticket sales, and it increased television viewership for the finals as well, with ratings up an astounding 100 percent compared to the previous year. The campaign to increase USTA membership, "Direct Response TV," had similarly positive results. According to the USTA, following the campaign's launch the organization added almost 17,000 new members in a two-week period, the single largest increase in its history.

Fallon McElligott's 1999 creative efforts for the USTA did not go unnoticed by the advertising trade. Both campaigns were awarded 2000 EFFIEs. The "US Open Excitement" campaign received a Bronze EFFIE for helping to shatter the myth that tennis matches were stuffy and boring and for increasing interest in the sport. The "Direct Response TV" campaign was recognized with a Silver EFFIE for helping to change the perception that the USTA was only for professionals or serious tennis players. Further, two of the print ads featuring Agassi were recognized with 2000 CLIO awards. The "Fed Cup Congrats" ad was included on the award short list, and the "Agassi" ad received a Bronze CLIO. The Newspaper Association of American also awarded the "Agassi" ad a grand prize in its 2000 ATHENA awards for outstanding creativity. Fallon McElligott shared the top honor, and the $100,000 prize, with Ogilvy & Mather.

FURTHER READING

Adams, Jodie. "A Perfect Match—Plan to Increase Number of Tennis Players." *Parks & Recreation,* October 1, 1998.

Collins, Glenn. "Tennis Association Picks a New Agency." *New York Times,* July 27, 1995, p. 9.

Ebenkamp, Becky. "Full Contact Tennis." *Brandweek,* August 23, 1999.

Goldstein, Matthew. "Yankees and Mets Pitch Hot Teams to Bring in Fans: Nostalgia in the Bronx; Pizzazz in Queens." *Crain's New York Business,* August 16, 1999.

Hanover, Dan. "US Open Sponsors Take Their Games off the Court with Activation Strategies Worthy of a Grand Slam Event." *Promo,* September 1, 2000.

Hlotyak, Elizabeth. "USTA Planning a Major Tennis Marketing Effort." *Westchester County (NY) Business Journal,* August 14, 2000.

Kirkpatrick, David D. "Fallon and Ogilvy Share Top Award." *New York Times,* September 22, 2000, p. 17.

Levere, Jane. "Tennis Group Aims Campaign at Diverse Audience to Reverse Slide in U.S. Open TV Viewing." *New York Times,* August 30, 1999.

"Ogilvy & Mather, Fallon Share $100,000 Grand Prize in NAA 2000 Athena Awards for Creative Newspaper Advertising; $5,000 Student Prize to the Art Center College of Design in Pasadena, Calif." *PR Newswire,* September 22, 2000.

Simon, Ellen. "Football Draws a More Upscale Crowd." *Knight Ridder/Tribune Business News,* September 14, 1999.

"TENNIS.COM—www.LittleTennis.com Site for Kid's Programs." *Parks & Recreation,* November 1, 1999.

"Tennis Growth." *Parks & Recreation,* June 1, 1999.

"United States Tennis Association Selects Fallon McElligott New York City to Produce US OPEN and USTA Advertising Campaigns." *Business Wire,* May 3, 1999.

"USTA and NRPA: A Logical Partnership." *Parks & Recreation,* July 1, 2000.

Rayna Bailey

UnitedHealth Group, Inc.

UnitedHealth Group Center
9900 Bren Road East
Minnetonka, Minnesota 55343
USA
Telephone: (952) 936-1300
Fax: (952) 936-7430
Web site: www.unitedhealthgroup.com

IT JUST MAKES SENSE CAMPAIGN

OVERVIEW

UnitedHealth Group, Inc., founded in 1974 as Charter Med Inc., was at the top of the health-insurance business in 2003, providing to 40 million consumers services that included a health maintenance organization (HMO), administrative support for companies providing their own insurance, and specialized services for Medicare beneficiaries. Financially the company was also at a high point, with revenues increasing from $11.8 billion in 1997 to an estimated $29 billion in 2003. But UnitedHealthcare, the company's business segment that served as an HMO, was suffering an identity crisis. Although UnitedHealthcare counted nearly eight million members, it believed that it had low brand awareness, no brand equity, and little brand definition among consumers. The HMO provider was also concerned about consumers' negative perceptions of health maintenance organizations.

To build brand awareness and brand identity as well as to reverse consumers' opinions that HMOs were more concerned about rate increases and benefits reductions than patient care, UnitedHealthcare released a marketing campaign in 2003. A pilot campaign with the theme and tagline "It Just Makes Sense" was introduced in three target markets. Created by Austin, Texas–based GSD&M, which had been UnitedHealthcare's agency since 2000, the campaign included television and radio spots and newspaper print ads. Budget information specific to the campaign was unavailable, but *Adweek* reported that the account was estimated at $25 to $30 million when GSD&M won it.

The humorous advertisements, which featured people caught in different situations that guaranteed they would need an HMO in the end, were a success. Not only did the campaign achieve its goals of increasing brand awareness and strengthening brand identity, but in 2004 "It Just Makes Sense" was broadened into UnitedHealthcare's first national campaign. The campaign was also awarded a Silver EFFIE in 2005 for helping to position UnitedHealthcare as an "innovative leader in health care coverage."

HISTORICAL CONTEXT

Charter Med Inc. was founded in 1974; three years later United Healthcare Corp. was created and acquired Charter Med. The company's name was changed in 1998 to UnitedHealth Group, and through a strategic realignment UnitedHealthcare became one of six independent but linked businesses operating under the UnitedHealth Group banner, which also included Americhoice, Ovations, Uniprise, Ingenix, and Specialized Care Services. Each business segment provided its own unique services: Americhoice focused on consumers enrolled in Medicare and other government-sponsored programs; Ovations provided services to Americans 50 years and older; Uniprise offered administrative services to self-insured companies; Ingenix provided software and information services to doctors and other health-care professionals; and Specialized Care Services was a collection of specialty business subsidiaries offering specific health and wellness benefits, such as chiropractic, dental, vision, life, accident, and critical illness plans. UnitedHealthcare was an HMO with almost eight million individual, small business, and midsize business members.

In 2002 UnitedHealth Group's net income climbed 48 percent to $1.35 billion on a revenue increase of 6.7 percent to $25 billion. By 2003 the company had grown to become the largest health insurer in the United States, providing services, coverage, and products that affected more than 40 million consumers. Despite its business diversification and solid financial standing, some analysts were questioning the quality of the company's earnings—which were partly based on double-digit premium increases—and the sustainability of its growth in a health-care environment that some Wall Street insiders believed was heading toward a fall.

ADVERTISING CAMPAIGN PROMOTES MAKING INFORMED HEALTH CHOICES

UnitedHealthcare's United Health Foundation released a print advertising campaign designed to help educate consumers about the health-care system and how to make better decisions related to their own health care. The campaign, which ran from October 2003 through February 2004, featured ads in consumer magazines, including *People, Better Homes and Gardens,* and *TV Guide.* Related ads appeared on the websites ABCNews.com and Parents.com, among others. The ads focused on three topic areas important to helping consumers make wise health-care decisions: "Getting the most out of a visit to the doctor's office," "Taking charge of your care," and "Using antibiotics appropriately."

TARGET MARKET

Typically the female head of household oversaw her family's health-care needs, from taking care of family members when they were ill to making decisions about when a doctor should be contacted. Women were also often responsible for the household budget. With those facts in mind, GSD&M aimed UnitedHealthcare's marketing campaign at adults 25 to 54 years old but with an emphasis on women in that age demographic. GSD&M noted in its brief submitted for the 2004 EFFIE Awards competition that the skew ratio of the campaign was 7 women for every 3 men. It stated further that women in particular were frustrated with the health-care industry and were concerned about whether their family's health-care plan would provide the best coverage for the money. These female heads of household considered it necessary that a health-care insurance provider include prescription coverage, preventive care, a large network of doctors, and products and services that were easy to understand and use.

COMPETITION

Blue Cross and Blue Shield (BCBS) provided health-care coverage to more than 85 million Americans through a variety of services, including indemnity insurance, HMOs, preferred provider organizations (PPOs), point-of-service plans, and fee-for-service plans. The company was also perhaps one of the most recognizable names in the health-care industry, due in part to its advertising efforts over the years. In 2003 increases in the price of health care were hitting consumers hard, and HealthNow, a Blue Cross Blue Shield plan provider in upstate New York, was experiencing even higher rate increases than its closest competitor. To give consumers in that market a convincing reason to pay more for BCBS, the company released an advertising campaign targeted to that specific market. The "Big Blue Arm" campaign, created by ad agency Arnold Worldwide of McLean, Virginia, was designed to present BCBS as an advocate for its members and as worth more than other insurance companies. One TV spot showed a man sitting in a restaurant ready to enjoy a meal of two big cheeseburgers. When he looked away for a moment the Big Blue Arm swooped down and knocked one of the burgers off the plate. When the man turned to see what had swept his burger away, the arm came from another angle and swiped the second burger off the plate. Additional advertisements targeted smoking, inactivity, and other health concerns, all with the Big Blue Arm intervening to help people make healthy choices. Although some consumers were offended by the ads, overall the campaign was a success. Following its 16-week run BCBS reported that membership had grown 8 percent, an all-time company high. In addition, the campaign received top honors in 2004 during the Buffalo News Creative Advertising Awards, and it earned a 2005 Bronze EFFIE Award.

Aetna, Inc., was struggling in 2003. The insurer, which had been one of the nation's largest, was facing charges by doctors claiming the company used unfair billing practices and patient-care interference. And Aetna was in trouble financially, a problem blamed in part on overpriced acquisitions, such as the $1 billion purchase in 1999 of Prudential Healthcare. By 2001 Aetna's problems had resulted in a net loss of $279.6 million. To rein in costs and get the company back on stable ground, chairman and chief operating officer John W. Rowe increased annual rates 16 percent, cut 15,000 jobs, and reduced Aetna's customer base from 21 million in 2000 to 13 million in 2003. He also eliminated from the company's rosters about half of the U.S. counties in which Aetna had provided Medicare services. As things began to stabilize, Aetna rebuilt. In 2004 the company launched a national marketing campaign designed to reinforce the brand's value and relevance to consumers. Themed "We Want You to Know," the campaign targeted benefits consultants and brokers and the employee-benefits decision makers for companies. Print ads appeared in publications such as the *Wall Street Journal, Forbes, Fortune,* and *BusinessWeek.*

MARKETING STRATEGY

When GSD&M began work on UnitedHealthcare's "It Just Makes Sense" campaign, it was faced with the challenge of building awareness of and familiarity with the brand in a health-care environment that was increasingly leaning toward consumer-directed health care, which placed more choices and financial responsibility on the patient. The pilot campaign was designed for three test markets based on specific population criteria, including levels of consumer awareness of UnitedHealthcare (from emerging to established to heritage, or longstanding, customers). Working from the assumption that most consumers believed that the health-care process was confusing and irrational, GSD&M developed a campaign that used humor to point out the lack of common sense in both the industry and consumers. It further noted UnitedHealthcare's practical approach to health care and how it helped confused consumers to achieve healthier outcomes. The campaign, which first ran for a week in April 2003, included television and radio spots and newspaper ads in the target markets. That was followed by a second wave of advertising from November 10 to December 3.

Television spots included three that showed people making decisions with final results that made access to an HMO such as UnitedHealthcare seem like a good idea. In the first spot, titled "Bridesmaids," a wedding party was gathered in a beautiful meadow. Viewers did not realize that the meadow was at the top of a hill until the bride followed tradition and tossed her bouquet. It sailed through a pristine blue sky. As the bridesmaids raced to catch the flowers, the hapless young women went tumbling off the side of a cliff, bouncing and rolling across rocks and cacti into a lake below, to the surprise of an unsuspecting fisherman sitting in a boat on the lake. A second commercial, "Lions," featured a film crew in Africa making a documentary about lions. As a man wearing a giant lion's head approached a group of the beasts, the director said to him, "Just as I suspected, the lions are getting alarmed. Whatever happens, hold your ground. Now, initiate agitation phase." Following the instructions, the man wearing the lion's head started waving his arms and roaring. The final spot, "Hornet's Nest," showed a man on a ladder wearing gloves and goggles and facing a huge hornet's nest hanging from a branch of a tree. He said to his friend, who was waiting below with a garbage can, "Now when it drops make sure you get that lid on fast." When the man reached with clippers to cut off the branch, however, the ladder fell over, sending the man and the nest crashing to the ground and causing the angry, stinging wasps to surround both men. A voice-over at the end of each spot said, "People don't always use common sense. Fortunately, there's a health-care company that does."

The print ads and a spot that was aired on the radio reinforced the message delivered in the TV commercials. The radio spot had a woman thanking a man for helping her move some boxes and warning him to be careful on the stairs. Once the man was laden with piles of boxes, the woman asked him if he could see. The man answered that he could, which was followed by crashing and thumping sounds as he fell down a flight of stairs. When the sounds stopped, indicating that the man's fall had ended, the woman asked him, "Are you okay, can you stand?" The man responded that he was okay. He apparently tried to stand, and suddenly there were the crashing sounds of the man falling down more stairs. The same tagline used in the television spots followed. Newspaper ads included a variation of the "Hornet's Nest" TV spot: a man was depicted trying to remove a hornet's nest from the second-story eaves of his house with a rapidly spinning weed-whacker. Another print ad, "Lawnmower," pictured a man lifting a buzzing power lawnmower over his head in an attempt to trim a towering hedge surrounding his lawn.

OUTCOME

"It Just Makes Sense" was so successful at achieving its goals of increasing UnitedHealthcare brand awareness and building a positive perception of the brand among consumers in test markets that, rather than proceed with a planned final media wave in the test areas, the campaign was expanded into a national promotion in 2004. It was the company's first national marketing campaign.

Following the initial release of the campaign, *Adweek* included the television spot "Hornet's Nest" on its June 2003 Best Spots list, describing the campaign as turning good sense into an art form. The campaign was awarded a Silver EFFIE by the New York American Marketing Association in 2005. In addition, the company reported that the campaign resulted in significant increases in brand awareness among consumers; awareness jumped from 65 percent prior to the April 2003 launch to 79 percent afterward. Consumers' perceptions of the UnitedHealthcare brand's key attributes also showed positive increases. Research based on a seven-point scale showed one-point increases, or slightly less, in most areas, including perceptions that UnitedHealthcare was a strong and stable company (4.6 to 5.6), that it provided a practical approach to health care (4.3 to 5.3), that it was a health-care company that made sense (4.3 to 5.3), and that it was a leader in the health-care industry (5.4 to 5.4).

FURTHER READING

"Aetna Launches New National Advertising Campaign." *Business Wire,* February 16, 2004.

"Aetna's Painful Recovery. Jack Rowe Fixed the Insurer's Finances—But Are His Methods Good for Health Care?" *BusinessWeek Online,* December 8, 2003. Available from <http://businessweek.com/magazine/content/03_49/b3861097.htm>

"Buffalo, N.Y., Newspaper Presents Awards for Creativity in Advertising." *Buffalo (NY) News,* June 29, 2004.

Chura, Hillary. "Sharing Strategies: GSD&M Clients Hit Austin City Limits." *Advertising Age,* February 18, 2002.

Desloge, Rick. "Walli to Replace Turvey as Head of United Healthcare." *St. Louis (MO) Business Journal,* September 19, 2003.

Lang, Mark. "Best Spots of June: United Healthcare Tickles the Funny Bone." *Adweek,* July 14, 2003.

"Quiet Giant." *HealthLeaders Magazine,* April 1, 2003.

"UnitedHealth Group Reports Record First Quarter Earnings of $1.29 Per Share." *Business Wire,* April 16, 2003.

Wasserman, Todd. "Advertising: UHC Looks on Light Side of Pain, Injuries." *Adweek,* July 14, 2003.

Rayna Bailey

V & S Vin & Sprit AB

Box 47319
Stockholm, SE 117 97
Sweden
Telephone: 46 8 7447000
Web site: www.vinsprit.se

■■■

ABSOLUT DIRECTOR CAMPAIGN

OVERVIEW

Absolut Vodka, owned by the Swedish government monopoly V & S Vin & Sprit AB, was a brand built entirely on image. The famous Absolut print campaign, created by ad agency TBWA\Chiat\Day and launched in 1981, featured endless permutations of a single formula: an image of the iconic bottle along with minimal copy pairing the brand name with a single proper or common noun. By its 20th year the print campaign could claim not only to have almost single-handedly led Absolut from obscurity to monumental success but also to have engineered a distinct Absolut personality, one of the most recognizable consumer-product images in the world. Often described as witty, stylish, smart, and trendsetting, the Absolut brand was, then, a natural candidate to experiment with the implementation of new technologies on its consumer website. Having already established a commitment to interactivity on its website, Absolut in 2001 unveiled "Absolut Director," an application that allowed online visitors to make their own short films.

"Absolut Director" provided more than 35 clips from an old Japanese monster movie, which users could rearrange as they pleased, while writing their own dialogue and building a soundtrack from a range of speaking voices and musical accompaniment. The final products created ranged in length from 30 seconds to four minutes, and the site encouraged the amateur filmmakers to E-mail a link allowing friends to view their handiwork, thereby increasing the number of visitors to "Absolut Director." A print ad carrying the same tagline likewise raised awareness of the site in an attempt to generate more online visits.

Linking such online promotions to actual sales was extremely difficult, and industry observers were split on the question of whether or not platforms like "Absolut Director" did any useful branding work. Absolut continued to experiment with interactive online marketing, however. Though the brand continued to be the top imported vodka in America, its sales remained flat amid increasing competition from higher-priced brands and an overall vodka-industry boom.

HISTORICAL CONTEXT

Owned by V & S Vin & Sprit AB, which was backed by the Swedish government, Absolut Vodka nominally traced its history to 1879, when a brand of vodka carrying the Absolut name was first brewed near Ahus in southern Sweden. That original brand ultimately dropped the Absolut from its name, and in the late 1970s an entrepreneur named Gunnar Broman decided to use the name, while claiming the older product's historical and geographical roots, for a new brand of vodka he planned on exporting from Sweden to America. Absolut Vodka did not yet exist as a product—there was no formula for

A print ad from the "Absolut Director" campaign. PHOTO COURTESY OF THE ABSOLUT SPIRITS COMPANY, INC. REPRODUCED BY PERMISSION.

the beverage, nor was there any distribution network in place—when Broman arrived in New York with prototypes of the distinctive bottle that would ultimately define the brand, trying to enlist an advertising agency to his cause. After a slow start following the product's 1979 launch, Absolut was dropped by its first ad agency, but then the account moved to TBWA\Chiat\Day, which built the Absolut brand virtually from scratch.

The Absolut print campaign's multiple-decade run began in 1981. It featured hundreds of variations on the same format: an image in the shape of the product's bottle ran with a two-word tag line that always began with "Absolut." The campaign's first execution, tagged "Absolut Perfection," featured a simple image of the bottle topped by a halo. Absolut-bottle-shaped images designed by famous artists, beginning with Andy Warhol in 1985, lent the brand a cutting-edge reputation, as did a focus on individuals from the world of high fashion, but the concept was infinitely mutable. It was applied, for example, to cities, countries, writers, photographers, holidays, seasons, topographical features, states of mind, and abstract concepts. Each twist on the format was meant to represent an interpretation of the world from an "Absolut perspective," and together the different executions amounted to a brand personality often described as elegant, hip, sophisticated, creative, and intelligent. In 1999 *Advertising Age* ranked the still-running Absolut campaign in the top 10 twentieth-century advertising campaigns.

With the rise of the Internet, distilled-spirits brands in particular saw a new avenue for marketing. Largely locked out of the image-building possibilities offered by television advertising, Absolut and other liquor brands established an early and often elaborate cyberspace presence, despite the fact that they could not sell their products online. Absolut first experimented with a website catering to early users of the Internet in 1996. In October 2000 the brand launched its well-regarded Absolut.com site, meant to appeal to the entire range of the Absolut target market. Among the initial features offered to visitors to www.Absolut.com was an interactive component called "Absolut DJ," which allowed Web surfers to mix dance songs and samples into new musical concoctions of their own.

ABSOLUT ONLINE

Though its print campaign was one of the longest running in advertising history, Absolut was hardly complacent when it came to investigating new ways of communicating with consumers. Absolut had been exploring ways to make creative use of its website since the early days of the Internet. In 1996, as competitors launched websites for general audiences, Absolut understood that its online audience at that time must necessarily be a technology-savvy group seeking out cutting-edge Web experiences. Early versions of the site therefore focused on the art and design elements behind the long-running print campaign. Then, as the Internet became populated by a broader range of the Absolut target market, the brand adapted its website accordingly. The result was a site that many pointed to as one of the alcohol industry's best, balancing creativity and sophistication with accessibility, all aimed at reinforcing the clear product image for which the brand was renowned.

TARGET MARKET

Though Absolut, in its print campaign, had long been able to tailor individual executions of its bottle concept to specific subsets of its target market, its branded online content was intended for the entire range of young people in its target group: 21- to 40-year-old drinkers of premium-priced liquors who were, according to V & S, "youthful in mind, active, outgoing, sociable, somewhat trend-conscious and fashionable."

"Absolut Director," moreover, built on the brand's 20-year heritage of creativity, as established in its print campaign. Having consistently used figures from the art and fashion worlds to communicate with those who appreciated creativity, Absolut was a natural fit for the marketing profile that an interactive movie-making platform offered. By allowing members of its target market to exercise their own creativity, the brand underscored its well-established commitment to creativity. In showing its adeptness with new technologies well in advance of most consumer products, Absolut likewise reaffirmed its reputation for cutting-edge sophistication.

COMPETITION

Though Absolut was America's top imported vodka, its sales fell well short of those of the total vodka-market leader, the more affordable domestic brand Smirnoff. Absolut, which was categorized as a premium vodka, was likewise being threatened, during this time, by a range of higher-priced imports, so-called super-premium competitors, such as Grey Goose and Belvedere. Vodka was the leading growth category among spirits in the U.S. during the early years of the new millennium, with much of that growth attributable to the explosive market gains made by these super-premium brands.

Smirnoff, whose sales had declined significantly from a 1990 peak, was attempting to increase awareness of the brand through various channels in the early 2000s. The brand became the first liquor to be advertised on network TV when, in 2001, NBC announced that it was rescinding the voluntary ban on hard alcohol ads that the three major networks had observed since the 1950s. In keeping with a list of 19 restrictions imposed by NBC, Smirnoff began running branded public-service spots warning against drunk driving, before NBC reversed itself, a few months later, under pressure from advocacy groups. But the Smirnoff name was, at the same time, reaching consumers via network and cable television in another way. Its British parent company, Diageo, had recently unveiled an entry in the category of "malternatives"—sweet, lightly carbonated beverages brewed like beer and thus not subject to the marketing restrictions imposed on hard liquor—under the Smirnoff name. Smirnoff Ice, as this product was called, became the top seller in a category whose target market largely consisted of entry-age drinkers. Industry observers noted that Smirnoff vodka, which otherwise had been unsuccessful in appealing to young people, benefited from its sibling brand's popularity and comparatively unrestricted ability to advertise on television. Smirnoff vodka's sales volume rose 25 percent between 2000 and 2003.

Super-premium vodka brands, meanwhile, began cutting into Absolut's market share from above, challenging its long-established near-monopoly among stylish high-end vodka drinkers. Brands such as Grey Goose and Belvedere, which cost approximately $30, compared with Absolut's $20 per bottle, emphasized such product attributes as the types of grain and distillation processes used to manufacture their vodkas. Grey Goose, the leading super-premium brand, found particular success in touting taste-test results supposedly indicating that it was the "World's best tasting vodka." In building its brand, Absolut had typically eschewed any reference to the product itself, focusing almost exclusively on image and style as embodied by its iconic bottle. As specialty-cocktail drinkers in hip urban nightclubs began claiming they could taste the difference between Grey Goose and Absolut—even when the seasoned bartenders who made those cocktails, as *Forbes* reported, could not—Absolut began running print ads emphasizing the grain and water from which its vodka was made. Grey Goose sales grew by 410 percent between 2000 and 2004.

MARKETING STRATEGY

"Absolut Director" was created by the New York–based branding and entertainment studio Submarine, together with agency of record TBWA\Chiat\Day, the interactive design and direction firm Zendo Studios, and system architects Pillar Applications. The website, part of the larger Absolut.com home page, was meant to support the brand's wider marketing profile as maintained in the vaunted Absolut print campaign, while also raising awareness of the product's online presence. Although Absolut marketing executives acknowledged the difficulty of linking sales figures to branded content on a product's Internet home page, they believed that a dynamic online presence helped to establish or augment the consumer-to-brand relationship. Absolut's strategy for initiating this process hinged on the inclusion of interactive features on its website. "Absolut Director," like its online predecessor "Absolut DJ," maximized website visitors' interaction with the brand.

The application allowed visitors to select and arrange to their own liking more than 35 snippets of a 1960s Japanese science-fiction film, which they could then enhance with their own dialogue, speaking voices of their choice, and a variety of music options. This format was, according to Submarine's creative team, inspired by the Woody Allen movie *What's Up Tiger Lily,* which paired a preexisting Japanese spy movie with a new, tongue-in-cheek script. The finalized "Absolut Director" movies varied from 30 seconds and four minutes in length, and the creators were given the option of inviting family and friends to watch their movies. Such invitations, delivered in E-mail messages providing a Web link, drove further traffic to the "Absolut Director" site. Participants also had the option of entering their movies as "must see" picks to be showcased, if chosen, in a prominent position on the site.

Absolut enlisted high-profile feature-film directors to create the first movies using the "Absolut Director" application, thus stoking interest in the site while providing examples for the creative utilization of the supplied materials. Spike Lee was the first director to make a movie using the "Absolut Director" materials, and his effort was followed by films from directors Mary Harron, Chris Smith, John C. Walsh, and Mary Gillen. Simultaneously, TBWA\Chiat\Day crafted an "Absolut Director" ad following the classic print campaign format. It ran in magazines as a means of publicizing the site.

A Submarine-developed technology called H.I.L.D.E. (Highly Interactive Language-Enabled Director Experiment) was at the center of the "Absolut Director" experience. H.I.L.D.E. appeared as a female on-screen icon who guided website visitors through the process of making their movies. The technology also enabled the translation of typed dialogue into a voice file so that the onscreen actors actually spoke the words devised by movie makers.

OUTCOME

Industry analysts were divided on the efficacy of the branding accomplished via platforms such as "Absolut Director." Some argued that consumers visited product websites in search of practical information and promotional offers, not to interact with the brand. Supporters of the marketing approach, by contrast, believed that interactive online sites encouraged intimacy with the essence of a brand, which was the ultimate goal of conventional advertising and supposedly a primary driver of consumer choice. The difficulty of correlating Web visits to sales meant that no clear answer to the debate was likely to emerge.

Absolut continued to take a clear position on such issues, however. The brand remained committed to an interactive online presence and followed up "Absolut Director" with its first online campaign beyond its own homepage. The ads, placed on such websites as Yahoo!, E! Online, and CBS Marketwatch, featured the trademark format of a bottle and a two-word tagline from the print campaign, but they allowed Web visitors to rearrange the image, text, and other elements. As they did so, the elements of the ad underwent intriguing graphic and textual transformations. Absolut.com, moreover, remained one of the alcohol industry's most elaborate interactive websites.

Absolut's struggle to maintain its market share in the face of vigorous growth among super-premium vodkas was further complicated when its U.S. distributor, Seagram, divested itself of its alcohol holdings as part of a merger with French conglomerate Vivendi. Though V&S eventually partnered with Jim Beam Brands for the U.S. distribution of Absolut, the shakeup was partly blamed for what became an extended period of lackluster sales. Between 2000 and 2004 Absolut sales remained flat at about 4.5 million cases per year, whereas total vodka sales in the United States increased by 17 percent during the same period.

FURTHER READING

Branch, Shelly. "Absolut's Latest Ad Leaves Bottle Behind." *Wall Street Journal,* May 3, 2001.

Chura, Hillary. "Drinking In the Internet." *Advertising Age,* September 3, 2001.

Cocoran, Ian. "Absolut Brilliance." *Brandchannel.com,* March 11, 2002. Available from <http://www.brandchannel.com/features_profile.asp?pr_id=60>

Hein, Kenneth. "Grey Goose Builds Nest with Drinks, Dollars." *Brandweek,* March 11, 2002.

Kaplan, David. "NBC Falls off the Wagon." *Adweek,* December 17, 2001.

Korolishin, Jennifer. "Click to Quench." *Beverage Industry,* September 2004.

Lewis, Richard. *Absolut Book: The Absolut Vodka Advertising Story.* Boston: Journey Editions, 1996.

Mack, Ann M. "Absolut Launches Net Campaign." *Adweek,* August 6, 2001.

Miller, Matthew. "Absolut Chaos." *Forbes,* December 13, 2004.

Saunders, Christopher. "Absolut Unveils 'Director' Web Promotion." *ClickZ News,* May 22, 2001. Available from <www.clickz.com/news/article.php/771201>

Mark Lane

ABSOLUT PRINT CAMPAIGN

OVERVIEW

In 1981 Carillon Importers released an advertising campaign to establish an identity for Absolut Vodka, a premium vodka made in Sweden and owned by that country's government-backed monopoly V&S Vin & Sprit. At the time Absolut was unknown in the United States, and Americans were not accustomed to paying a premium for vodka. Experts in the distilled-spirits market predicted a quick death for the higher-priced product. But largely because of Absolut's innovative and tremendously popular print ad campaign, Absolut rapidly became the best-selling imported vodka in the United States and captured a sizable portion of total vodka sales.

Created by the ad agency TBWA (which later became TBWA\Chiat\Day), the campaign was one of the longest running in advertising history. It consisted of hundreds of print ads that appeared in magazines ranging from the mainstream *Sports Illustrated* to the limited-circulation *I.D.* Each ad featured the Absolut bottle, or a representation of it, in a humorous or clever situation. Accompanying the bottle was a two-word tagline, the first word of which was always "Absolut." One early ad, for example, consisted of an Absolut bottle surrounded by fish and coral with the tagline "Absolut Treasure." Over the years TBWA broadened the concept of the campaign to include original artwork incorporating the Absolut bottle, with the first of these crafted by pop artist Andy Warhol. Moreover, TBWA oversaw the creation of new categories: Absolut fashion ads, which displayed the clothes of designers; so-called spectaculars, onetime ads that often included a gift for the consumer; and ads on cities, which paid homage to both particular cities and the Absolut bottle.

The "Absolut Print" campaign was one of the most lauded and successful in advertising history. It won every major advertising award and was widely viewed as being almost single-handedly responsible for Absolut's 20 years of explosive growth. From the campaign's inception in 1981 to 1995, sales increased 14,900 percent. Collectors of Absolut ads abounded, and hundreds of websites devoted to the ads sprang up on the Internet. Absolut continued to see consistent growth through 2000, but flattening sales thereafter led some to predict that the brand's heyday had passed.

HISTORICAL CONTEXT

Absolut Vodka had been produced since the 1870s. By 1970, however, Absolut's brand owners, V&S Vin & Sprit, realized that the company's distillery in Aarhus, Sweden, could remain viable only by increasing sales volume through exports. During the 1970s the United States accounted for 60 percent of the vodka consumed in the world. Thus, it was natural that the Swedish vodka would target Americans, but entry into the U.S. market posed a challenge. Almost all of the vodka consumed in the United States was domestically made, and the niche for imported vodka was dominated by Russian brands, especially Stolichnaya. Moreover, most Americans were not willing to spend more to purchase a "luxury" imported vodka, which was generally valued for its relative tastelessness rather than for any qualities that connoisseurs might appreciate.

Vin & Sprit set out to secure an importer for Absolut and in 1978 settled on Carillon Importers, which also imported the high-end liquor Grand Marnier. Carillon sought to create a unique look and feel for Absolut. In order to distinguish the product from other vodkas, Carillon designed a short-necked, rounded bottle inspired by Swedish medicine decanters and printed the product information directly on the bottle rather than on the standard paper labels. When TBWA landed the Carillon account in 1980, it faced a daunting task. The agency "had to establish that Absolut was the best vodka on the market without actually saying that in the ad," Richard Lewis, TBWA\Chiat\Day's worldwide account director for the brand, wrote in *Absolut Book: The Absolut Vodka Advertising Story.*

In attempting to craft an ad campaign that reflected positively on both the product and the person consuming it, the TBWA creative team of Geoff Hayes and Graham Turner decided to focus on the architecture of the Absolut bottle. In a burst of inspiration Hayes hit upon the idea of "Absolut Perfection," which featured a slick photo of the Absolut bottle topped with a halo. The hallmark of the ad was its utter simplicity and a good measure of humor, characteristics TBWA sought for the entire campaign. "Absolut Bravo," which followed shortly afterward, was the first of the ads to be designed for a specific magazine. In this ad, roses were being flung at the Absolut bottle, as if after a bravura performance. The shot was constructed to appear in *Playbill,* and the theme targeted the magazine's audience. "We wanted to get into the reader's head, wherever he or she was at that very moment," said Lewis. The ad was both a salute to the product and to the actual performance taking place. "Absolut Phenomenon," which covered two pages and showed a rainbow emanating from an Absolut bottle and arcing into a glass of ice, was the first in which Carillon and TBWA experimented with an ad's placement in a magazine.

All of these were what Lewis termed "product ads," in that they featured the Absolut bottle. As the product and the campaign became more recognizable, Carillon and TBWA branched out. "Absolut Stardom," which appeared in 1984, was the first in which the image presented in the ad was not the actual glass bottle. Instead, the bottle image—depicted as a Broadway marquee—was made up of nearly 5,000 individual lights. Although "Absolut Stardom" marked a shift away from literal representations of the Absolut bottle, the trademark remained the distinctive image of the round-shouldered bottle with the perky lid.

In 1985 the Absolut campaign expanded in another innovative direction. Michel Roux, CEO of Carillon, wanted to shore up the vodka's fashionable identity. He commissioned Warhol to produce an original artwork that contained a representation of the Absolut bottle. It was the first time a company had employed art as a marketing strategy. "Absolut Warhol" was a success, and Absolut then commissioned original works from a diverse group of artists. Later collections of works by African-American, Russian, and gay artists were released. A similar venture was the "Absolut Fashion" collection, which began in 1987. After commissioning original designs from top fashion designers featuring representations of the Absolut bottle, TBWA and Carillon photographed models wearing the clothes. Not surprisingly, these ads generally ran in fashion-oriented magazines such as *Cosmopolitan* and *GQ.* Another subgenre of the campaign was dubbed "Absolut Spectaculars." These were onetime advertising extravaganzas that often involved a prize for consumers. On Father's Day in 1997, for example, Absolut inserted ties into copies of the *New York Times* delivered in 12 major cities. The ties, a nod to the stereotypical Father's Day present, were emblazoned with Absolut bottle-shaped sperm.

TARGET MARKET

As a high-end imported vodka, Absolut first sought to reach consumers with a college degree who were working at either their first or second job and who enjoyed the arts and nightlife. According to Lewis, however, the Absolut strategy had always been one of inclusiveness. "We really are interested in men and women of the legal drinking age and over," he said. "Our campaign has an open-door policy. It welcomes all consumers." He stressed that, by rarely featuring people in the ads, the campaign did not limit its appeal to different groups of people. "The brand remains interesting to the ever-new waves of consumers because we fit inside the consumer's imagination about the role the brand plays with them."

One group that the "Absolut Print" campaign consistently targeted was the arts community. The sophistication of the arts ads, especially the "Absolut Artists" and "Absolut Fashion" series, was intended both to appeal to a more urbane audience and to shore up the brand's chic image. After an artist's commissioned work for Absolut was completed, the company hosted an opening that served to publicize the product in the art world. Similarly, some of the "Absolut Fashion" ads ran as multipage inserts in fashion magazines. As a matter of strict policy, Absolut ads portrayed only items or locations that were classy or prestigious. "We perennially strove to maintain Absolut's premium image," Lewis wrote in *Absolut Book.*

TBWA and Absolut also attempted to reach an audience beyond those who actually encountered the ads in magazines. "Absolut Spectaculars" were designed to attract media attention and enhance the brand's presence in the public consciousness. The first such effort was made in 1987, when Absolut embedded a musical chip that played Christmas carols into a card inserted in *New York* magazine. Not only were individual consumers enchanted with what was at the time a high-tech trick, but newscasters demonstrated the card on the air, giving Absolut a bonanza of free publicity. Even a *New Yorker* cartoon was devoted to the subject. In later years Absolut gave away Nicole Miller ties, Donna Karan gloves, and the 1997 Father's Day tie, all inside magazines or newspapers and all designed to bring the product to the attention of a large segment of the population.

Absolut did seek to appeal to specific demographic groups, however. The "Absolut Cities" series, using the Absolut bottle in ways that played off familiar landmarks or perceptions of cities, originated as a way of increasing the brand's visibility in specific markets. The first of the series, "Absolut L.A.," featuring a swimming pool shaped like an Absolut bottle, appeared in 1987 as the brand sought to reach more southern California consumers. The ad first ran in regional publications before being incorporated into the national campaign. Absolut repeated the strategy with cities such as Miami, Pittsburgh, Saint Louis, Chicago, and San Francisco. The company also reached out to the gay community by advertising in the gay press and to African-Americans by commissioning original artworks by well-known black artists.

COMPETITION

Absolut's print campaign revolutionized advertising for alcoholic beverages. While traditional alcohol ads portrayed party scenes, happy-go-lucky couples imbibing the product, or a simple close-up of a bottle, Absolut focused on image. "We made alcohol advertising interesting, funny, and challenging," said Lewis. Absolut's efforts paid off. By 1987 Absolut's sales were soaring and had surpassed Stolichnaya, formerly the leading imported vodka. But Absolut's success served as an example for other vodka and spirits makers, and the import business grew quickly. Absolut faced competition not only from its old rival Stolichnaya but also from Brown-Forman's Finlandia, Skyy Spirits' Skyy Blue, Sidney Frank Importing's Grey Goose, and Millennium Import's Belvedere. Although vodka sales in general were flat, sales of premium brands continued to grow.

According to *Advertising Age,* many of the premium vodka brands "rely more on word-of-mouth and offbeat marketing techniques than paid media advertising to drive sales." Nevertheless, many of Absolut's competitors learned the lesson summarized by an analyst for the *Buffalo News*: "Well-advertised brands, such as Absolut Vodka, are doing well." In 1998 Finlandia, which controlled 4 percent of the market in imported premium vodka, launched a redesigned bottle. At the same time Finlandia embarked on a new print campaign that stressed the brand's "purity." According to the *St. Louis Courier-Journal,* the goal was to "create a more sophisticated image for the brand." In addition to adopting a more hands-on advertising approach, Sidney Frank Importing began an upscale ad campaign for its Grey Goose vodka in 1997. Skyy Blue vodka likewise relied on chic print ads that played off the architecture of the Skyy bottle. Stolichnaya's print campaign featured illustrations done in the Soviet socialist realist style.

Another challenge for Absolut was that in about 1998 the imported-vodka market in the United States began to change. Absolut had virtually created the U.S. market for expensive imported vodka, but superpremium vodkas, led by Grey Goose, effectively created an even more rarified vodka category. Whereas Absolut had in essence dodged the question of product quality and sold itself strictly based on a distinct brand image, Grey Goose found success with a product-quality pitch communicated both through print advertising and by word-of-mouth work with bartenders. Grey Goose grew 410 percent between 2000 and 2004, and a host of superpremiums jumped on the product-quality bandwagon. The rapid growth of the superpremium category came mainly at the expense of Absolut, whose sales began flattening in 2000.

THE JOKE'S ON YOU

An Absolut ad appeared in the *New York Times* on April 1, 1997, that raised the hackles of readers, with thousands calling the company to complain. "You are now reading the first ad in the new Absolut Vodka campaign," the ad copy proclaimed. "The first in a series of messages from a company that has a lot to say about vodka." The ad then recounted the delightful aspects of Absolut—the tiny Swedish hamlet in which the vodka was distilled and the grain from Sweden that was the vodka's "secret ingredient." The ad listed a phone number for readers to call with comments. Those who telephoned heard a recording that ended with the following statement: "As for that bit about the demise of the advertising campaign as you know it, well, Absolut April Fools. Cheers."

MARKETING STRATEGY

Absolut employed a two-pronged strategy in its efforts to break into and then increase its share of the U.S. vodka market. It strove to craft ads that had broad appeal because of both their content and the mainstream magazines in which they ran. In addition, by creating tailor-made ads, the brand targeted many narrower consumer segments simultaneously. Absolut commissioned ads from a Chicago group called Thirst specifically to appear in the international design magazine *I.D.* Digital artists made ads for the back cover of *Wired* magazine. In 1997 Absolut joined forces with fashion designer Gianni Versace and photographer Herb Ritts for an ad exclusively for *Vogue,* the preeminent fashion magazine. Gay artists were commissioned to produce ads for publications such as the *Advocate.* Matching ads to magazines meant that the campaign was able to target groups with precision and build its customer base.

TBWA and Absolut sought advice from the magazines themselves in creating these tailor-made ads. By doing so, they redefined the relationship of advertisers and the magazines paid to carry their messages. Moreover, because Absolut spent almost its entire budget on the print campaign (between 1997 and 2005 the annual budget varied, ranging from $25 million to $35 million), the brand was an important source of revenue for the publications in which it advertised. The campaign's success created what Lewis termed the "Pied Piper effect." Magazines clamored for Absolut's advertising because the presence of its ads attracted other advertisers to the publications. Absolut thus developed a nearly symbiotic relationship with its chosen medium.

The "Absolut Print" ads appeared in more than 200 magazines. The Absolut brand team's primary concern in selecting a publication in which to advertise was to ensure that the magazine reflected the brand's image of status and quality. "It has to be a magazine that has good editorials and that is good-looking," said Lewis. "We are careful with whom we associate the brand." Absolut ads appeared in mainstream publications such as the *New Yorker, Rolling Stone,* and *Vanity Fair* as well as in magazines with a more specialized focus and smaller circulation, including *Art and Antiques, Spy Magazine,* and *BOMB.*

OUTCOME

The "Absolut Print" campaign was wildly popular among consumers. Collectors scanned magazines, clipped ads, and traded with other devotees, and more than 200 websites were established by people who wanted to post their collections. Richard Lewis of TBWA\Chiat\Day wrote a glossy book about the campaign, *Absolut Book: The Absolut Vodka Advertising Story,* which became one of the best-selling business books in recent decades. The campaign transcended advertising to become an icon of pop culture, but it did more than appeal to the artistic sensibilities of magazine readers. "The Absolut campaign is one of the very lasting campaigns that has really made its mark, which is very hard to do these days," an analyst told the *Star-Ledger.* "It's taken Absolut from a brand that no one ever heard of and made it the leader in its category."

Despite increasing competition, Absolut maintained a 70 percent share of the premium-vodka category through the end of the twentieth century, well ahead of its closest competitor, Stolichnaya. In 1994 V&S terminated its relationship with Carillon, opting instead for the international marketing muscle of the House of Seagram. The marketing campaign continued unchanged. By 1995 sales had increased 14,900 percent since the campaign's inception. As "Absolut Print" approached its 20th year, and despite a late-1990s decline in the sales of distilled spirits, Absolut regularly posted annual sales growth of 5 percent. All analysts concurred that the Absolut campaign was an integral part of the brand's continuing strong performance. *USA Today* termed the campaign "a textbook case for creating successful print advertising." The campaign won virtually every advertising award in existence (over 350 total), including two Stephen E. Kelly Awards for the best magazine campaign in America. In 1999 *Advertising Age* named "Absolut Print" one of the 10 best advertising campaigns of the twentieth century.

It was the case, however, that the brand benefited from social and economic trends. *Brandweek* credited some of Absolut's success in the 1990s to "connoisseur consumerism," whereby "retro-minded consumers ... [were] experimenting with '90s versions of classic cocktails mixed with premium and luxury-priced spirits." According to the *Buffalo News,* the booming economy of the 1990s empowered consumers to drink higher-priced wines and spirits such as Absolut.

Although the economy slowed in the early years of the new century, vodka sales flourished, rising by 17 percent between 2000 and 2004, primarily on the strength of explosive growth in the superpremium category. Absolut, meanwhile, saw its sales peak in 2000 and remain flat in subsequent years. This fall-off in performance was, of course, partly a result of the superpremiums' success—they had directly targeted a niche that had been Absolut's stronghold—but a portion of Absolut's struggles were also attributed to distribution miscues stemming from a 2001 split with Seagram's.

The "Absolut Print" campaign continued to run, but the brand also began to experiment more seriously with other advertising formats. One of the first consumer brands to have devoted substantial resources to its website, Absolut used interactive branding vehicles such as

Absolut DJ and Absolut Director, online applications that, respectively, enabled consumers to compose their own music and make their own short films, and the brand unveiled its first full-scale online campaign in 2001. Absolut also debuted its first-ever U.S. TV spot on cable in 2004, a commercial for the newly launched Absolut Rasberri flavor that was notably consistent with the print campaign: it showed time-lapse footage of an artists' collective painting 12-foot-tall Absolut bottles. Television was also used the following year for the launch of Absolut Apeach. The most significant indicator that Absolut might be plotting a long-term change of direction, however, came in late 2005 when V&S announced that online would thereafter be Absolut's media of choice. "Print is not the key media anymore," Absolut's communications manager for new media told *Brandweek.* "Our consumer is more focused on the Internet and mobile communication so we're shifting also."

FURTHER READING

Allan, Terri. "Sizzle in the Swizzle." *Brandweek,* October 27, 1997.

Arndorfer, James. "Models to Troll Taverns for Pricey French Vodka." *Advertising Age,* May 5, 1997.

Enrico, Dottie. "Absolut Vodka's Ad Spots Withstand the Test of Time." *USA Today,* September 15, 1997.

Fitzgerald, Beth. "The Garden State Seen through an Absolut Filter." *Newark (NJ) Star-Ledger,* March 19, 1998.

Goetz, David. "Brown-Forman Set to Push Finlandia: Distributor Hopes Finnish Vodka Can Challenge Absolut." *St. Louis Courier-Journal,* March 26, 1998.

Hein, Kenneth. "Print Ad Pioneer Absolut Shifts Its Focus to the Web." *Brandweek,* November 21, 2005.

Lewis, Richard W.. *Absolut Book: The Absolut Vodka Advertising Story,* Boston: Journey Editions, 1996.

Mack, Ann M.. "Absolut Launches Net Campaign." *Adweek,* August 6, 2001.

Mathews, Jay. "Sales Raising Spirits in the Beverage Industry, but Caution Advised on Their Stocks." *Buffalo (NY) News,* January 20, 1997.

Miller, Matthew. "Absolut Chaos." *Forbes,* December 13, 2004.

Parpis, Eleftheria. "Message on a Bottle." *Adweek,* September 6, 2004.

Rebecca Stanfel
Mark Lane

Jesse Ventura for Governor

Minneapolis, Minnesota
USA

RETALIATE IN '98 CAMPAIGN

OVERVIEW

One of the most noteworthy surprises to emerge from the nationwide elections of November 3, 1998, was the election of Jesse "The Body" Ventura as governor of Minnesota. A former professional wrestler who had appeared alongside Arnold Schwarzenegger and others in a number of action movies, Ventura had served as a Navy SEAL and in 1990 had become mayor of Brooklyn Park, Minnesota. His showmanlike antics, his outspoken nature, and his appearance—Ventura had an impressive physique and a shaved head—had certainly attracted notice; but much of the credit for his electoral success went to Bill Hillsman, president of North Woods Advertising of Minneapolis. With a budget of just $500,000—as opposed to some $13 million in combined spending by Democratic opponent Hubert H. "Skip" Humphrey and Republican Norman Coleman—Hillsman and North Woods managed to craft some of the most memorable ads of the 1998 elections. The overall Ventura theme was "Retaliate in '98," and prominent television spots included "Action Figure" and "Jesse the Mind."

Ventura ran as a Reform Party candidate, distancing himself from the two traditional parties with a platform that emphasized fiscal conservatism on the one hand and social libertarianism on the other. The Ventura campaign appealed to voters disaffected with the Democrats' reputation for making government ever larger and more intrusive and the Republicans' reputation for supporting measures to limit personal freedom. Advertising took a tongue-in-cheek approach while stressing issues such as lowering property and income taxes. "Jesse hit a nerve with people," Hillsman told Kate Fitzgerald of *Advertising Age.* "The grass roots nature of the campaign and the basic values we were communicating got across—proving it's not about media tonnage but about impact."

HISTORICAL CONTEXT

Minnesota had a history of supporting candidates outside the "political establishment," according to Steven E. Schier in *Washington Monthly.* Thus in 1990 and 1996, Democrat "Paul Wellstone's tie-dyed leftist insurgency" for the Senate "carried him to victory over establishment Republican Rudy Boschwitz." Hillsman and North Woods also worked on the Wellstone campaign. And "Rod Grams, as emphatically to the right as Wellstone is to the left, won a Senate seat during the 1994 nationwide Republican insurgency, defeating Ann Wynia, a conventional liberal well-known and widely respected among Minnesota's political establishment."

The tradition of dissent in Minnesota and neighboring Wisconsin, whose Governor Robert La Follette was an outstanding figure of the Progressive Party during the mid-twentieth century, went back a long way. In the 1990s this came into alignment with a larger nationwide trend that had political stargazers scratching their heads. Voters had thrown out President George Bush despite

Jesse Venture posed as Rodin's "The Thinker", in a still from a television ad that ran during his campaign for governor of Minnesota. **BILLSMAN, NORTH WOODS ADVERTISING. REPRODUCED BY PERMISSION.**

the latter's popularity following the Gulf War of 1991, and Democrat Bill Clinton had won the 1992 presidential election in part because conservative voters deserted Bush for third-party candidate Ross Perot. Democrats who considered Clinton's victory a mandate for larger government were shocked by the 1994 Congressional elections, which returned Republican control to both houses of Congress after a hiatus of four decades. But in 1996 Republicans had more shocks of their own when Clinton was reelected, and Republican control of Congress began to erode.

Enter Ventura, a candidate for Minnesota governor representing the Reform Party, which Perot had established. Born in 1951, Ventura had served with the Navy SEALs, an ultra-elite special operations force, before going on to a career as a professional wrestler in 1975. He competed in the World Wrestling Federation and the American Wrestling Association and displayed the sort of antics typical of wrestlers. A skeptical writer in *Time,* on the eve of the November 1998 elections, described Ventura's early career thus: "When Jesse ('The Body') Ventura starred on the professional wrestling circuit in the 1970s and '80s, he was usually cast as the bad guy. Decked out in a feather boa, sequins, and the kind of oversize glasses Elton John made famous, the 6-ft. 4-in. Ventura would flex his muscles, glower at opponents, and spit out such gems of wrestling wisdom as, 'Win if you can, lose if you must, but ALWAYS cheat!'."

In the 1998 campaign Ventura produced more priceless wisdom, such as this *bon mot* quoted by Debra Goldman in *Adweek:* "I believe Minnesota should return the entire $4 billion tax surplus to the hardworking people who paid it. I believe Led Zeppelin and the Rolling Stones are two of the greatest rock bands ever." Yet all clowning aside, Ventura—who in the 1980s appeared in movies such as *Predator*—did a creditable job as mayor of Brooklyn Park from 1990 to 1994. With the launch of the 1998 campaign he positioned himself as a fiscal conservative and a social liberal.

TARGET MARKET

David Kirby of the *Advocate,* a national gay and lesbian news magazine, described Ventura as "A straight-talking macho man and former Navy SEAL [who] . . . was the darling of fraternity boys, construction men, and other stereotypically red-blooded males. But with his libertarian views, belief in social tolerance, and friendships with gay men, Governor Ventura has turned out to be something of a gay ally, even if some of his views put him squarely opposite most gays and lesbians."

The latter was probably a reference to the fact that many gay voters favored Democratic candidates who, along with social views that were more tolerant than those of many Republicans, offered an agenda of increased government spending which was anathema to Ventura. But the fact that Ventura sat for an interview with the *Advocate* appeared to refute assertions that he was a right-wing extremist. His comments included this remark: "I believe everybody's a human being and should be treated with the dignity accorded to every human being."

Time listed some of Ventura's "favorite targets: a corrupt campaign-finance system, the sensationalist media, and most of all, career politicians." The article went on to note his strong appeal among young voters, but as Ventura told Kirby: "We didn't do outreach to any groups at all. Our campaign was based on no groups at all, only individuals." Certainly his appeal was strong among voters who favored greater power for the individual and less power for government.

Nick Gillespie in *Reason* addressed the complaint of American University historian Michael Kazin that Ventura was not a true populist because he did not attack the "ungodly 'money power'" that the Populist movement of the 1890s opposed: "at the end of the 20th century, 'money power'—indeed, power in general—is far more concentrated in government hands than in corporate ones. If populism is at all about articulating fears of 'hard-working, productive Americans,' then Ventura is a fitting spokesman. The people of Minnesota—and the rest of the United States—have far fewer reasons to resent, say, Maplewood-based 3M or the owners of Bloomington's Mall of America than they do the local, state, and federal governments that levy all sorts of regulations on them and combine to take one-third to two-fifths of their income in the form of taxes."

COMPETITION

Gillespie made these comments as part of a larger discussion that centered around famed consumer advocate Ralph Nader, one of Ventura's most outspoken critics. As Gillespie noted, on the surface one might have supposed that Nader, who had long spoken of giving power back to the "people," would have taken encouragement from Ventura's candidacy; in fact quite the opposite was true. Nader supported the idea of more government control, not less, and this put him squarely at odds with Ventura.

Likewise Ventura managed to position himself in such a way as to present both his Democratic and Republican opponents as two peas in a big-government pod. On the one side was Humphrey, son of the late Vice President Hubert H. Humphrey, a Democrat who enjoyed popularity during his tenure as the state's U.S. Senator; on the other was Coleman, the Republican mayor of St. Paul. Both, as Schier noted, were "life-long government employees and officeholders. Each was personally cautious and 'button-down' in demeanor. They provided a nice gray background for Jesse's campaign antics. Every act needs a straight man, and Jesse had two of them."

ON TO 2000

With the 1998 congressional and gubernatorial races behind them, ad agencies in early 1999 began to align themselves with political candidates intent on gaining the White House. North Woods Advertising of Minneapolis, whose president Bill Hillsman was widely acclaimed as a major force behind Jesse Ventura's victory in the Minnesota governor's race, threw its lot in with Rep. John Kasich in the Ohio Republican's bid for the presidency in 2000.

Republican front-runner George W. Bush, governor of Texas and son of former President George Bush, had assembled a team that included representatives from a number of agencies, including Public Strategies in Austin, Garcia LKS in San Antonio, and Alexandria, Virginia's Stevens Schriefer Group. Alex Kroll, Young & Rubicam's chairman emeritus, was leaning toward Senator Bill Bradley in his push for the Democratic nomination over Vice President Al Gore, according to Justin Dini in *Adweek.* Arizona Republican Sen. John McCain was working with a media consultant from Stevens, Reed & Curcio of Alexandria.

And what about the other most talked-about race of 2000, which would potentially place Hillary Rodham Clinton against New York's Republican Mayor Rudolph Giuliani for the New York Senate seat left open by retiring Sen. Daniel Patrick Moynihan? According to Dini's sources, Giuliani was likely to work with Doner Public Affairs of Tampa, Florida. Clinton's team would include White House consultant Mandy Grunwald and others.

In the end Ventura dealt a sound blow to both candidates, in part by bringing out disaffected voters who might not have come to the polls had the election been a straight two-party split. But Ventura still had to deal with his many critics, in particular among the intellectual elite, who dismissed him as an intellectual lightweight made up more of style than substance. Playing on the theme of a prominent North Woods spot, some of his detractors referred to him as a mere "action figure."

MARKETING STRATEGY

The latter reference was drawn from a 30-second spot that followed "Flag" in the buildup to the November elections. The "Flag" spot showed a split screen, one side red and the other white. These were respectively labeled

"Democrat" and "Republican," and the camera pulled back to show that the red and white were part of an American flag. As the pullback continued to reveal the flag's blue canton, a voice-over explained the need to have a choice between the first two alternatives.

"Action Figure" and "Drive to Victory" followed. The first of these showed two young boys playing with a Jesse Ventura action figure resembling a popular variety of toy. The Ventura action figure faced an enemy called "Evil Special Interest Man," who announced "We politicians have powers the average man can't comprehend!" The boy holding the Ventura doll responded, "I don't want your stupid money!" After a voice-over message, the Ventura doll pounded its fist on a desk with the help of one of the boys, who shouted: "This bill wastes taxpayers' money. Redraft it!" The spot concluded with a voice-over warning, "Don't waste your vote on politics as usual." The "Drive to Victory" spot also used the action figure, this time riding in a recreational vehicle—a promotion of Ventura's 72-hour marathon driving tour of the state during the last days of the electoral campaign.

Then there was "Jesse the Mind," which Kathy DeSalvo described in *SHOOT:* "Sepia-toned visuals picture Ventura, wearing briefs, sitting in the pose of [Auguste] Rodin's 'The Thinker.' Through dissolves and soft-panning camera moves, the POV [point of view] drifts around Ventura. Over operatic needledrop music, a voiceover relates the candidate's qualifications: 'Navy Seal. Union member. Volunteer high school football coach. Outdoorsman. Husband of 23 years. Father of two. A man who will fight to return Minnesota's budget surplus to the taxpayers. He will fight to lower property and income taxes. He does not accept money from special interest groups and will work to improve public schools by reducing class sizes.' At spot's end the camera comes to rest on the face of Ventura, who winks."

OUTCOME

By winning the November election, Ventura instantly became the nation's most recognizable new governor. In January 1999 Schier reported that "he has signed a book contract in the mid-six figures with a major publishing house, and is in negotiation with NBC for a possible TV bio-pic. Stores in Minnesota feature T-shirts proclaiming 'My Governor Can Kick Your Governor's Ass' and, more tamely, 'My Governor Can Beat Up Your Governor.'"

Also in January the new governor appeared in a public service announcement conceptualized by North Woods—and directed by Tyrel Ventura, his 19-year-old son. The spot, which he made for the Minnesota State Colleges and Universities, encouraged students to go straight to college from high school rather than taking time off.

In June 1999 Nevada personal injury attorney Edward Bernstein announced that he was exploring the possibility of a run for his state's senate seat, a move that, according to Bernstein, Ventura's success had inspired him to make. June also saw the NBC television movie, but as Michael McCarthy and others reported in *Adweek,* the film proved that "Ad agencies don't get much respect—particularly in the make-believe world of Hollywood." In the film's version of the Ventura story, wife Terry comes up with the idea of the campaign commercials while going through a trunk in the family's attic. Hillsman and other creative forces were incensed by the portrayal of events in the movie, which Ventura himself had neither authorized nor endorsed.

The elimination of Hillsman from the picture was certainly a gross omission; by contrast, *Washington Monthly* called him "The Man Behind Ventura." His spots for Ventura won praise from *Adweek,* which listed them among the best ads of 1998, and *Advertising Age* also listed these among the year's notable advertising. "If you don't do something out of the ordinary," Hillsman told Alexandra Starr of *Washington Monthly,* "it's going to be expensive and ineffective." In a day and age when it cost $20 million even to become a serious candidate for president, Hillsman had managed to get a man elected as governor of the nation's 20th largest state on a budget of just half a million dollars. "There is no reason why a presidential campaign should cost $20 million," he said. "It's ineffective communication that drives the price that high."

FURTHER READING

Baar, Aaron. "'Body' Politic." *Adweek* (Eastern edition), November 9, 1998, p. 3.

"Body-Slam Politics." *Time,* November 2, 1998, p. 50.

DeSalvo, Kathy. "Ventura for Governor—Yes! The Body's Quirky Ads Help Win Minnesota Race." *SHOOT,* November 20, 1998, pp. 7–9.

———. "Tyrel Ventura Directs Dad/Governor Jesse in PSA." *SHOOT,* January 18, 1999, pp. 7–8.

Dini, Justin. "Ad Figures Picking Sides for 2000" *Adweek* (Eastern edition), June 14, 1999, p. 7.

Fitzgerald, Kate. "Gov. Jesse Ventura: Bill Hillsman." *Advertising Age,* June 28, 1999, p. S-14.

Gillespie, Nick. "Populist Psychology: Why Ralph Nader Hates Jesse Ventura." *Reason,* March 1999, pp. 6–7.

Goldman, Debra. "Think Negative." *Adweek* (Eastern edition), November 2, 1998, p. 58.

Kirby, David. "The Body Speaks." *Advocate,* May 25, 1999, p. 25.

McCarthy, Michael, et al. "Director's Cut." *Adweek,* June 28, 1999, p. 46.

Schier, Steven E. "Jesse's Victory: It Was No Fluke." *Washington Monthly,* January 1999, p. 8.

Starr, Alexandra. "The Man Behind Ventura." *Washington Monthly,* June 1999, p. 25.

Judson Knight

VF Corporation

105 Corporate Center Blvd.
Greensboro, North Carolina 27408
USA
Telephone: (336) 424-6000
Fax: (336) 424-7631
Web site: www.leejeans.com

CUT TO BE NOTICED CAMPAIGN

OVERVIEW

The Lee Apparel Company, a division of VF Corporation, piloted an image-altering advertising campaign that began in the autumn of 1995 and continued through 1997. Lee hoped to update its brand image in the increasingly cutthroat denim market to become relevant to a younger, hipper consumer group. Lee brand jeans had long been the favorite among female adults, and the company's marketing campaigns revolved around the message that Lee jeans were comfortable and fit well. In the 1990s, however, competition in the jeans market grew, and comfort was no longer a strong selling factor for consumers faced with numerous choices.

Fashion-conscious youths and young adults, who accounted for a large portion of denim sales, desired jeans that made them look "cool," that conveyed an attitude and a hip image. To attract this consumer group, Lee and its advertising agency, Minneapolis-based Fallon McElligott, produced a series of television spots that marked a departure from past Lee ads that relied primarily on humor to promote its jeanswear. The new ads, filmed in black and white, featured attractive, young, Lee-jeans-wearing men and women in search of romance. In the spots the desired party wore Lee jeans, which suggested that those who wore Lee jeans looked enticing. Ellen Rohde, Lee's vice president of strategic planning and advertising at the time of the campaign launch, explained, "Our goal is to get young adults thinking about Lee in an entirely different way." She added, "Now that they know us as the brand that fits, we'll be working hard to promote our new products and updated image to develop an emotional connection with them."

HISTORICAL CONTEXT

VF Corporation, one of the world's largest publicly held clothing manufacturers, had the apparel industry covered from head to toe. In the 1980s and 1990s, VF acquired a number of companies to stay competitive in the increasingly crowded clothing market. VF owned businesses that manufactured intimate apparel and lingerie, swimwear, sports apparel, children's clothing, and outdoor gear, such as daypacks. The company's jeanswear division, the largest portion of the company, included the Wrangler, Rustler, and Riders brands along with Lee.

Though the denim market continued to grow through the 1990s, the apparel industry overall hit a snag in the mid-1990s as consumers tightened their pocketbooks. Many in the industry felt the pinch, including VF, which saw profits decline nearly 20 percent in 1995. VF reevaluated its business strategies and decided it needed to create demand and coax consumers to buy, and to that end VF chose to create products geared toward specific consumer groups and to freshen the images of its many brands.

For previous marketing campaigns, Lee had relied on humor to send the intended message that Lee jeans were comfortable, and many spots promoted the tag line "The brand that fits." Many television ads featured women attempting to squeeze into ill-fitting jeans. One spot starred a man singing in the shower in a baritone voice. As he got dressed and put on his non-Lee jeans, he suddenly became a soprano, indicating that the jeans were too tight. Although these ads successfully educated viewers about the comfortable fit of Lee jeans, they did not provide any other compelling reasons for purchasing Lee jeans, least of all that they were "cool."

TARGET MARKET

Lee traditionally targeted adult women and had enjoyed success with this audience. For many years, including 1996, Lee was the top-selling women's jeans brand. Lee decided to shift its aim toward younger consumers in the mid-1990s as Lee introduced trendier styles, such as the Lee Riveted jeans line featured in the "Cut to Be Noticed" campaign. According to *Adweek,* Lee Riveted jeans were geared toward style- and image-conscious young adults who wished to be viewed as fashionable and attractive. The youth market, particularly teens, accounted for a large portion of denim sales, and many jeans manufacturers clamored to win their approval. Lee vice president Gordon Harton emphasized the importance of attracting youths in *Business Week* and noted, "By the time they're 24, they've adopted brands that they will use for the rest of their lives." Lee believed its Lee Riveted line would appeal to young adults as well as teens, and thus the "Cut to Be Noticed" campaign was geared to those aged 18 to 34.

When young adults shopped for jeans, the status and stylishness of the jeans played heavily into their decisions, so Lee decided to veer away from their traditional ads that focused on comfort and fit. Ellen Rohde told *USA Today* that consumers felt Lee's old ads were out-of-date. The old ads were humorous in a slightly embarrassing manner, which grated against the target audience's intent of looking "cool." By producing stylish spots filled with good-looking young men and women wearing Lee jeans, Lee hoped to successfully energize its brand image and generate sales. According to the Associated Press, Mackey McDonald, VF's CEO, declared, "We will be emphasizing not only that Lee jeans are comfortable, but that they're flattering, they make you look good and feel good."

COMPETITION

The jeans industry grew dramatically in the 1990s, and everyone scrambled to get a piece of the pie. According to market research firm NPD Group, U.S. jean sales hit $10.65 billion in 1996. Although VF Corp., with about 27 percent of the jeans market, continued to dominate the denim arena, the company finished second to competitor Levi Strauss & Company as the world's largest apparel manufacturer. *USA Today* also indicated that in 1996 Lee placed second, with 12 percent of the market, in terms of denim sales in department and specialty stores, which sold about 280 million pairs of jeans annually. Levi's commanded 28 percent.

VF's jean brands overall, however, enjoyed increasing sales in the denim market. According to figures from research firm Tactical Retail Solutions, Levi's held a market share of 48.2 percent in the men's denim market in 1990, while VF followed with 22.1 percent. Levi's share shrunk to 26.2 percent by 1997, whereas VF's grew to 31 percent. In the women's market, VF had a 14 percent share in 1990, and Levi's held 8.5 percent. VF's share increased to 16.2 percent in 1997, but Levi's share rose as well, to 9.3 percent.

VF had to contend not only with Levi's competition, but also with a market increasingly crowded with private-label jeans manufacturers and designer labels. Tommy Hilfiger, Ralph Lauren, Donna Karan, and Calvin Klein were among the designers producing high-end jeans. In 1997 designer labels accounted for about 4 percent of the market in both the men's and women's markets. Private-label jeans posed a stronger threat: In the men's market, the share held by private-label manufacturers rose from 3.2 percent in 1990 to 19.1 percent in 1997. In the women's market, the share rose from 3.1 percent to 30.1 percent. According to the *Los Angeles Times,* J.C. Penney's Arizona Jeans line grew into a $1 billion line in a mere six years, and Sears, Roebuck's Canyon River Blues line, only two years old in 1996, enjoyed more than $200 million in sales and blossomed into the company's largest private-label clothing line.

DENIM DIFFERENCES?

Curiously, many jeans manufacturers produced oddly similar advertising campaigns in the 1990s. Levi's, Lee, and even J.C. Penney rolled out stylized, image-conscious vignettes starring handsome young men and women in various styles of jeans. Were these companies trying to differentiate their brands from others, or were they hoping to be mistaken for another line? Marketing consultant Jack Trout told *USA Today,* "One of the risks Lee may be running with its new hip ads is consumers might think they're trying to be more like Levi's and less like themselves."

MARKETING STRATEGY

In an increasingly competitive denim market, Lee needed to make an impact on or connection with consumers. Fallon McElligott's Harvey Marco told *Adweek,* "Lee wanted to rebrand itself.... They felt they weren't being taken seriously as a fashion brand." The "Cut to Be Noticed" campaign was Lee's vehicle for ensuring its jeans would be noticed and the brand's image updated. To appeal to the target market, the stylized, black-and-white television spots emphasized relevant issues for the 18-to-34 age group, such as taking risks with romance, the awkwardness of meeting someone new, and feeling attractive and confident thanks to fashion. Lee did not dispense with humor completely, but the "Cut to Be Noticed" spots involved humor meant to be endearing and touching rather than campy.

To specifically reach the target audience, Lee relied heavily on cable television. In the past, Lee opted for mass-market appeal and televised spots on network television. Jamie Lockard, Lee's director of advertising, explained the advantages of buying time on cable television to *Adweek* and said, "There is an extremely high likelihood that you can find a specific outlet for your message on cable, one that closely matches up your merchandise with the people whose attitude and lifestyle make them the best possible target for your product." Because of this strategy, the "Cut to Be Noticed" spots appeared on MTV, Comedy Central, and also on Fox.

The campaign first launched in September 1995 with "Ferry Boat" and "Dandelion." "Ferry Boat" continued to air through 1997 because of its popularity. Initially intended to lure female consumers ("Dandelion" targeted males), the spot starred a Lee-jeans-wearing young woman on a ferryboat. Her car boasted an Ohio license plate, and suitcases rested atop the roof. As the ferryboat prepared to leave the dock, a truck screeched into the parking lot, and a young man sprinted onto the boat. He found the woman on the deck, cautiously handed her a necklace, and said, "Excuse me, but you dropped this back there." When she asked, "Where?" he replied, "In Nebraska." The spot ended with the tag line, "Cut to fit."

Two new spots, "Coffee Shop" and "Laundry Room," began airing in 1996 and were televised through 1997. These ads also played on the theme of taking extreme measures to meet the desired person in Lee jeans. In "Coffee Shop" a young man sat in a coffee shop, drinking cup after cup of coffee. His waitress wore Lee jeans, and it was clear he hoped to meet her. The hours passed, and the waitress placed the "Closed" sign on the door. She asked the young man if he wanted anything else, and he nervously suggested, "Well, ummm, maybe if you're not busy... maybe we can go... get a cup of coffee?" He then looked defeated by his comment, and the screen cut to the Lee Riveted logo and a final shot with the tag line, "Cut to be noticed."

In "Laundry Room," a male in Lee jeans was the target of affection. A young woman in the laundry room of an apartment building pushed dollar after dollar into the change machine until the "out of change" light began to flash. As she sat down, a young man entered the room with his laundry. He approached the change machine, but, to his dismay, it was empty. He looked around, spotted the young woman, and walked up to her. "Excuse me. Do you have any change?" he asked. She nonchalantly replied, "Ummm... let me check," and slid her purse full of quarters under her chair with her foot. The implication was that Lee jeans made one irresistible. Fallon McElligott's Dean Buckhorn, a copywriter who worked on the campaign, told *Adweek,* "There's someone going to great lengths to meet the hero wearing Lee jeans." Though some of the scenarios may have seemed far-fetched, Buckhorn explained that they were based in reality. "We were trying to go for a situation we've all been in."

OUTCOME

Consumers responded positively to the "Cut to Be Noticed" campaign. Company research indicated that the initial spots were on target with the intended audience and that both men and women enjoyed the ads. Gordon Harton noted, "[The consumers] seem to relate to the product benefit in the spots—being attractive to the opposite sex because you look and feel great in Lee jeans." According to a poll conducted by *USA Today* that determined the popularity of all the spots that aired during the 1996 Olympic Games, "Laundry Room" ranked fifth with the under-35 age group. The survey also found that "Laundry Room" was the ninth most popular overall. "Coffee Shop" was voted one of the best ads of July 1996 by *Adweek,* and the campaign did relatively well with Ad Track, *USA Today*'s poll that measured the popularity and effectiveness of an advertising campaign. Of those surveyed, 22 percent said they enjoyed the ads a lot and 19 percent felt they were effective. With the younger crowd, those aged 18 to 24, the campaign was more successful—28 percent really liked the spots, and 24 percent found them effective.

The jeanswear division of VF Corp. accounted for nearly 54 percent of the company's total revenues in 1996, and despite increased competition in the denim market, VF enjoyed increased sales through 1997. The jeans market swelled to a $12.5 billion market, and VF continued to grow. Lee president Terry Lay spoke with CNN's *Biz Buzz* and noted that NPD Group figures indicated that Lee's market share grew 16 percent in the first half of 1998. *Adweek* reported NPD Group data that showed a 2 percent increase in Lee's market share with women in the 20-to-34 age group in 1996, as well as a 13 percent rise among males aged 14 to 19. In early 1998 Standard & Poor upgraded its ratings outlook on VF Corp. from stable to positive, and VF appeared on track to reach its goal of generating $7 billion in revenues by the year 2000.

FURTHER READING

Enrico, Dottie. "Lee Jeans' 'Hip' Visuals Fit Young, Affluent Consumers." *USA Today,* July 8, 1996.

Garfield, Bob. "Lusty Jeans Watchers Provide Pants for Lee." *Advertising Age,* July 22, 1996.

Haley, Kathy. "Lee Zeroes in on Younger Customers." *Adweek,* March 24, 1997.

Martin, Ellen Rooney. "Fallon McElligott's Black-and-White Television Campaign for Lee Apparel Co." *Adweek,* December 16, 1996.

———. "True Believers." *Adweek,* December 16, 1996.

Rosenberg, Joyce M. "There's a War out There, and VF Boss Knows It." *Associated Press,* February 7, 1996.

Mariko Fujinaka

FIND YOUR ONE TRUE FIT CAMPAIGN

OVERVIEW

In 2003, Lee Jeans, a division of VF Corporation, was a 114-year-old company whose brand of women's jeans, Lady Lee Riders, had been a staple of closets for more than 50 years. But Lee was losing young women customers to trendier brands that were tailored and marketed directly to them. Lee's challenge was to shake off the perception of young women that the brand was unfashionable, uncool, and a style their mothers wore, not a pair of jeans a hip young woman would buy.

To change this perception and to convince young women between the ages of 18 and 34 to come back to the brand, Lee introduced the One True Fit jeans. The introduction was supported by a marketing campaign, "Find Your One True Fit," developed by the company's longtime agency, Minneapolis-based Fallon Worldwide. Although the exact cost of the campaign was not revealed, according to *Adweek,* Lee spent $6 million and $7 million on advertising in 2001 and 2002, respectively. For the initial launch in 2003, Fallon focused exclusively on television spots that ran on the major broadcast and cable networks, including ABC, CBS, NBC, Fox, MTV, and E! Entertainment Television. In 2005 the campaign shifted to print media and was broadened to include older women who also wanted better fitting jeans. Ads appeared in such national magazines as *People, More,* and *Marie Claire.*

The "Find Your One True Fit" campaign was well received both by the consumers it targeted and by the media. Shortly after the campaign's launch, Lee reported a 20 percent overall sales increase compared with the same period in 2002. Further, consumers' positive perception of the brand jumped from 25 percent prior to the campaign to 47 percent after it had begun. In 2003 *Marie Claire* named One True Fit an "Editor's Pick," and in 2004 *Health Magazine* named the brand "Dream Jeans." In 2005 the campaign won a Silver EFFIE.

HISTORICAL CONTEXT

Lee Jeans was founded in 1889 as a dry goods company. The firm began manufacturing its own brand of work clothes in 1911 when the founder, Henry David Lee, became dissatisfied with the quality of merchandise his suppliers were providing. From work clothes the brand grew to include a variety of product lines that ranged from western to casual wear. In 1949 Lee introduced Lady Lee Riders, the first line of women's jeans. Lee became the first brand to offer women's jeans with multiple fits, which were introduced in 1983. But as niche brands offering fashion jeans, such as Gap, Mudd, American Eagle, and Express, went after women under the age of 30, Lee's sales began to suffer. To reverse its sales decline and attract younger consumers, Lee developed a spin-off of its women's brand, described by the company as "The brand that fits for her mother," and introduced One True Fit jeans. The new style was based on its popular five-pocket jeans worn by generations of women, but it had a contemporary flair that met four criteria young women said they wanted: style, comfort, looks, and a construction that made women's derrieres look good as they walked away.

TARGET MARKET

Throughout the 1980s and into the early 1990s Lee consistently held the number one share in the women's denim jeans category. But the brand's customers were aging, and Lee jeans began to develop the reputation of not being the type of jeans worn by hip, younger women. Thus, attracting under-30 women was the challenge facing Lee in 2003. The "Find Your One True Fit" campaign was designed to reach young women who were no longer shopping in the junior department but who were not yet ready for the missy department. Lee's target audience was 18- to 34-year-old women who were recent college graduates starting new careers, getting married and having children, buying homes, and facing other transitions. Despite the changes that were occurring in their lives, these women still cared about looking good

NATIONAL DENIM DAY RAISES MONEY FOR BREAST CANCER RESEARCH

For the 2003 National Denim Day, Lee Jeans signed actress Christina Applegate as its spokeswoman. Since its inception the annual event, which was introduced by Lee Jeans in 1996, has raised millions of dollars for the Susan G. Komen Breast Cancer Foundation. National Denim Day encourages employers to let staff members make a $5 donation in exchange for wearing jeans to work on a specific day each October. In 2003 the wear-jeans-to-work day was October 10. Applegate, best known for her role as Kelly Bundy in the 1990s hit television show *Married with Children,* was chosen by Lee Jeans to promote the event because her mother was a breast cancer survivor. Applegate also fell into the target consumer demographic for Lee Jeans, contemporary women shoppers in their mid-30s.

and dressing in style. For them getting older did not mean giving up sexy clothes and dressing like their mothers. Liz Cahill, Lee's director of advertising, told *Adweek* that One True Fit jeans had evolved from research indicating that young women liked the Lee jeans style but wanted jeans with a new fit. "She is no longer a junior and not quite a missy. We did fit try-ons like crazy. Luckily, she is still willing to try new things," Cahill said of the target consumer.

COMPETITION

Levi Strauss & Company had invented denim jeans in 1853. By 2003, although Levi's had been in a five-year sales slump, it was still the most recognized brand in the denim category. Taking credit for inventing jeans, Levi Strauss also took credit for reinventing jeans when, in February 2003, it introduced a new brand—Typ. 1 Jeans—and supported it with a marketing campaign using print ads. The initial ads, one of which appeared in the swimsuit issue of *Sports Illustrated,* were described as bold and sexy, like the new jeans being promoted. The ad that appeared in *Sports Illustrated* featured model Liliana Domínguez wearing Typ. 1 Jeans and a denim jacket and standing near a hubcap. After the initial launch, ads ran in other national magazines, including *Allure, Teen People, GQ,* and *Spin.* Outdoor advertising featuring Typ. 1 Jeans appeared in New York's Times Square and in Los Angeles on the Hyatt Regency Hotel on Sunset Boulevard. Television spots for the campaign began running in June 2003. Also in 2003, to increase its reach with consumers, Levi introduced a spin-off jeans line—Levi Strauss Signature—that was offered for sale in Wal-Mart stores.

Like Levi Strauss, Gap was on a downward spiral in the denim jeans category. In 2000, after shifting the focus of its marketing and product branding away from its core customers, baby boomers, and toward the teen market, Gap went into a 22-month sales decline. The chain reported a 24 percent drop in sales in April 2002 at stores open one year or more. To win back its customers and reverse its sales decline, Gap revamped its product offerings, shaking off glitzy, trendy merchandise and bringing back the staples that customers had come to expect, including basic T-shirts, khakis, and denim jeans. Supporting Gap's effort was a marketing campaign titled "For Every Generation." The new campaign included television spots and print ads with a full roster of celebrities wearing Gap jeans and other items of clothing from the brand. Print ads included a 12-page insert that ran in *Vogue, GQ, InStyle,* and *Rolling Stone.* Television spots, which focused on Gap jeans and their fit, featured appearances by such stars as comedian Whoopie Goldberg, country singer Willie Nelson, and actresses Gena Rowlands and Sissy Spacek.

MARKETING STRATEGY

Fallon Worldwide had worked as the creative agency for Lee Jeans since 1986. The agency's "Coincidences" campaign, launched in 2002, helped revive the Lee Dungarees brand after it had slipped among its target market of young men between the ages of 17 and 24. The campaign was successful in achieving its goals of restoring the cool image of the brand among young men and improving sales, and it won a Silver EFFIE in 2004. Thus it was that in 2003 Fallon developed the campaign to rejuvenate another of Lee's fading brands, this time women's jeans. The "Find Your One True Fit" campaign tackled the challenges of convincing young women that Lee jeans were not just for their mothers, and like the campaign for Lee Dungarees, it was designed to restore the image of the brand as cool. To assure that the campaign for One True Fit jeans reached its target audience, it was developed through the efforts of an all-female team whose members were in the same demographic.

Because women were often bombarded with print fashion ads, the "Find Your One True Fit" campaign was initially limited to television spots that had their debuts during the telecast of the 2003 Emmy Awards. This was followed with spots that aired on the major national networks—ABC, CBS, NBC, and Fox—and cable networks, including MTV and E! Entertainment Television.

The initial spots, titled "Find Your Edge" and "Find Yourself," were described as a tribute to young women and how they felt when they thought they looked good. Harvey Marco, the Fallon's group creative director, explained in an interview with *Business Wire* that, although they were uncomplicated, the spots were meant to connect with women on several different levels. "This campaign is sexy, cool and relevant to the target audience," he said.

Additional television spots were developed for subsequent use and were aired throughout 2004. One spot, titled "Happy Place A," featured the seductive music of the French singer Pierre Avia performing "Why Should I Cry." The spot opened with a close-up of an attractive 20-something woman and then followed her through a variety of situations, all starting with the advice "Find your . . ." Included were shots of the woman in the bathtub, with "Find your sanctuary;" pulling on and zipping up a well-fitting pair of Lee jeans, with "Find your center;" playing a guitar, with "Find your voice;" jumping off a balcony into a swimming pool, with "Find your fear;" and speeding away in a white Porsche, with "Find your escape." The spot concluded with a rear view of the woman walking down a hall dressed in her Lee jeans and the text "Find your one true fit. Lee Jeans." Another spot, "Happy Place B," was an abbreviated version of the first.

The television spots in the "Find Your One True Fit" campaign ended in 2005, and the focus then shifted to print advertising. Ads ran in national fashion and women's magazines, including *Glamour, InStyle, People, Redbook, More* and *Marie Claire.* One print ad showed a woman standing on a beach dressed in Lee jeans and holding a puppy on her shoulder. The text read, "Write your own fashion statement. Have you found your perfect fit? Lee." Cahill said that the campaign was also broadened in 2005 to appeal to the mothers of the young women in the original target demographic. In a company press release she stated that the One True Fit brand was able to satisfy the needs of many women: "Women want to look good no matter what life stage they are in or title they carry."

OUTCOME

The "Find Your One True Fit" campaign for Lee Jeans achieved its goals of reversing the perception of younger shoppers that the brand was not fashionable or cool and that it was the jeans of choice only of their grandmothers. The company reported that within two months after it was launched the campaign had succeeded in increasing the positive perception of the product among consumers. A 2003 tracking study by Lee Jeans found that prior to the campaign, 25 percent of consumers surveyed thought its jeans were fashionable, compared to 47 percent who felt they were fashionable after the campaign had been introduced. In addition, one week after the launch of the campaign, Lee Jeans reported that One True Fit jeans had increased the company's overall sales volume by 20 percent compared to the same period in 2002.

In 2003 *Marie Claire* magazine named One True Fit jeans its "Editor's Pick" as the most flattering jeans for women with all figure types. In 2004 *Health Magazine* named them "Dream Jeans" for their ability to please all of the women on the publication's editorial staff. Further accolades for the "Find Your One True Fit" campaign included a Silver EFFIE in 2005 for achieving "significant gains in Lee's fashion imagery, coolness and purchase consideration."

FURTHER READING

Burrows, Dan. "Denim Dish: Lee Jeans to Debut High-End Jeans Called Lee Authentics, Developed in Europe." *WWD,* August 7, 2003.

"Curve Appeal." *Mommy Too! Magazine,* January–February 2005, p. 4.

DeMarco, Donna. "Gap Goes Back to Basics to Stop Sales Slouch: Retailer Returns to Less Flashy Clothes." *Washington Times,* May 10, 2002.

"Lee Jeans Helps Women Find Their One True Fit: Denim Powerhouse Introduces New Line, a New Ad Campaign." *Business Wire,* June 11, 2003.

"From Packs to Jeans, VF Meets Back-to-School Needs with High-Value, High-Style Innovations." *Business Wire,* August 1, 2003.

Kleinman, Rebecca. "Lee Denim Taps Applegate." *WWD,* June 5, 2003.

"Lee Serves Up Mid-Tier Missy." *DSN Retailing Today,* March 22, 2004.

"Levi's Typ. 1 Jeans Print Campaign to Break in Sports Illustrated Swimsuit Issue: Levi's to Co-Host Live Webcast at Exclusive Sports Illustrated Swimsuit Event to Mark the Unveiling." *Business Wire,* February 13, 2003.

Lockwood, Lisa. "Jeans Advertising: In Search of Steam." *WWD,* July 17, 2003.

MacMillan, Carrie. "Majoring in the Classics." *Promo,* May 1, 2003.

Malone, Scott. "True Blue. Jeans Marketing." *WWD,* June 23, 2003.

"Moms Are Getting Hip and Hot: Historic Jeans Maker Is Primed; Lee Jeans Touts Its One True Fit Jean the Choice of Hot Moms." *PR Newswire,* February 1, 2005.

O'Loughlin, Sandra. "Strategy: Lee Jeans Launching One True Fit in Move to Extend Market." *Adweek,* January 13, 2005.

Seckler, Valerie. "Levi Makes Advertising Return to Times Square: Levi Strauss & Co. Has Leased a 45-by-45-Foot Billboard on Times Square." *WWD,* February 3, 2003.

"Type 1 Gets Makeover." *Advertising Age,* June 30, 2003.

Rayna Bailey

RUGGED WEAR CAMPAIGN

OVERVIEW

Wrangler, Inc., a division of VF Corporation, launched a new line of clothing in 1993. The Rugged Wear line featured sturdy fabrics, camouflage patterns, and layers of warmth to appeal to those who enjoyed hunting, fishing, and other outdoor activities. Already a major player in the western wear and blue jeans segments of the apparel industry, Wrangler intended for Rugged Wear to complement the company's existing market niches. In the fiercely competitive clothing industry, image was often a substantial factor in an item's sales. Like cars, clothes conveyed a definite message about the consumer who chose them.

In order to craft such an image for its Rugged Wear line, Wrangler turned to its advertising shop, the Martin Agency, in 1997. The resulting "Rugged Wear" campaign relied on striking visual scenes and clever copy to distinguish Wrangler's outdoor line from those of its competitors. Consisting of three print ads, the "Rugged Wear" campaign appeared in magazines, on billboards, and in stores where the clothes were sold. One ad was for Wrangler Fishing Pants and pictured a laden clothesline. Four cats climbed up the legs of a pair of khaki pants hanging on the line. The text asserted, "Experts agree. Wrangler Anglers are true fishing pants" and concluded with a witty aside, "Sorry, fish smell not included." A chameleon sporting a pair of Wrangler Camouflage Jeans provided a humorous focus for a second ad: "Wrangler Rugged Wear. The #1 choice of incognito hunters." The third ad, for the brand's briar-resistant Teflon-coated field pants, did not show the actual product. Instead, it showed a vast briar field with a leg-shaped clearing in it. The implication was that the Wrangler wearer had been able to slice easily through the thicket thanks to his pants. Each ad was bordered by stitched leather and displayed the line's logo, which appeared to be branded into leather: "Wrangler Rugged Wear. Geared for the Outdoors."

Wrangler was pleased with the results of the campaign. Its new line proved to be a good bridge to Wrangler's traditional western wear line, and the campaign itself was quite well received by consumers. Some went so far as to contact the company for copies of the ads to hang in their homes. The advertising community praised the ads as well, bestowing several awards on the campaign, including the prestigious Addy Award.

HISTORICAL CONTEXT

Blue jeans were invented in the 1850s as sturdy work clothes for cowboys, ranchers, and miners in the American West. In the 1950s film stars James Dean and Marlon Brando popularized the denim pants as the clothing of choice for rebellious and trendy youth. By the 1970s, when "designer" brands such as Jordache, Gloria Vanderbilt, and Sergio Valente became popular, jeans had become as much about fashion, style, and image as they had about comfort and durability. "Jeans are a badge," Angelo Lagrega, a Wrangler executive, told the *Greensboro News and Record.* "When you wear a jean, you are making a statement."

Wrangler, a division of VF Corporation, had forged a specialized image for its own products that was distinct from the mainstream appeal of rival Levi's or ultra-fashionable designer brands popular with a younger urban generation, such as Calvin Klein, Nautica, and Tommy Hilfiger. Wrangler had instead staked its claim in the Western wear segment of the market. Fifty-five percent of the brand's sales came from its Western products, which clothed America's real and aspirational cowboys. Western wear was "the crown jewel and the real heritage of the company," Lagrega said in the *Daily News Record.* "We dominate that business." The company also produced Wrangler Hero, a less expensive mainstream line of clothing intended to be sold at nationwide chain stores like Wal-Mart and Kmart.

In the course of its long-term business relationship with the Martin Agency, Wrangler had learned the value of niche marketing to sell its products. A director of media planning at Martin related to *Brandweek* the strategy the agency devised for its client: "We told Wrangler, 'You don't need to be in New York, and you don't need to be in San Francisco.'" In other words, Wrangler placed its primary emphasis on people who would use its products for work and play, rather than as fashion accessories. Thus, instead of buying air time during mainstream television shows, Wrangler diligently pursued its cowboy aficionados. To raise its profile in this market, the company became an exclusive sponsor of the 1996 Country Music Awards and used country music star George Strait as a celebrity endorser. In addition, Wrangler sponsored rodeo events and rodeo stars Ty Murray and Joe Beavers. This focus on real cowboys paid dividends in the broader market as well. Because of its authenticity, the company came to have a strong appeal for yuppie cowboy-wannabes—who were attracted to the brand's cachet and image—without having to advertise heavily in the urban markets where these consumers lived. Lagrega succinctly encapsulated Wrangler's tactics to the *Daily News Record:* "We're using a rifle approach, not a shotgun approach . . . . We find large niches to attack, and then advertise to our consumer." The quest for new market niches led to the introduction of the Rugged Wear collection.

TARGET MARKET

The launch of Wrangler's Rugged Wear marked a point of departure for the company. The line's distinctive items such as camouflage-patterned jeans, jackets, and hats, thermal jeans, and Teflon-coated field pants did not at first glance neatly conform to the company's two target markets: Western admirers (and Westerners) and mainstream consumers shopping at mass market stores. The Rugged Wear line was designed for fishing and hunting, for hacking through a thicket or waiting for ducks on a chilly, pre-dawn pond—not for the rodeo and country music scene embraced by Wrangler's Western wear. According to the *Daily News Record,* however, Wrangler and other Western wear manufacturers and retailers had found that "the traditional Western consumer tends to be a rancher, hunter, fisherman, or hiker anyway."

According to John Boone and David Oakley, the creative team at Martin who crafted the "Rugged Wear" campaign, the ads targeted consumers who had relied on Wrangler for Western wear and who would be pleased to realize that their favorite brand also made tough clothes for outdoor activities. The campaign specifically sought to appeal to men aged 25 to 49 who fished, hunted, and enjoyed the outdoors lifestyle.

Unlike many of its competitors' campaigns, the "Rugged Wear" campaign attempted to use striking images and humor to reach its target audience. The subtle wit of the campaign was meant to show respect to the consumer. Instead of "talking down" to its intended audience, the ads attempted, in the words of Oakley, to "give the audience credit to understand a joke."

COMPETITION

According to *Adweek,* "even powerful jeans marketers are finding that snaring—and retaining—consumer loyalty is an increasingly slippery endeavor." With its traditional emphasis on Western wear, Wrangler had done quite well in building consumer allegiance to its products. By 1997 the company had seized 27 percent of the jeans market in the United States, selling 100 million pairs of jeans annually. One out of every five pairs of jeans sold in the United States each year carried the Wrangler logo. The company was well poised to remain in its leadership position in this area, though always mindful of other jeans giants such as Levi's and Lee.

When it entered the outdoors wear sector, however, Wrangler encountered a new group of competitors, all of whom were poised to capitalize on the rapidly increasing popularity of wilderness activities such as backpacking and fly fishing. L. L. Bean, the well-known outdoor clothing company, reached consumers through its catalogues that featured clothing such as waterproof jackets and flannel-lined jeans, and which had a broad appeal with more affluent customers. Bass Pro Shops represented another challenge for Wrangler's Rugged Wear, as did Cabela's.

A MISUNDERSTOOD ATTEMPT AT DO-GOODING

In a preceding campaign for the Rugged Wear line, Wrangler marketed the outdoors clothes as being ecologically correct. Touting the use of biodegradable enzymes and eco-friendly dyes, Wrangler expected a positive response to its "Earth Wash" concept. The company's extensive research had revealed that half of Rugged Wear's target market expressed concerns about environmental issues. In stores, however, shoppers were not willing to manifest this zeal. Not only did customers dislike the softer colors that resulted from the use of biodegradable dyes, they also were wary that they were being charged more for "green" clothes. In response, Wrangler brightened the colors. But while it stopped emphasizing the environmental benefits of the apparel, it continued to use most of the eco-friendly manufacturing innovations in the Rugged Wear line.

In order to favorably distinguish Rugged Wear from its competitors, Martin sought to create a campaign that was memorable. Instead of relying on the generic outdoors-wear advertising tactic of portraying a forest tableau with a man in hunting pants holding a gun, Martin focused on a certain lightheartedness in the "Rugged Wear" campaign. The use of animals—the chameleon in camouflage attire and the pants-climbing cats—was meant to distinguish Wrangler from other companies' advertising efforts, as was the playful tone. By excluding actual people from the prints, the "Rugged Wear" campaign served to emphasize a connection with nature and the wilderness. In essence, Wrangler's ads, unlike those of its competitors, suggested that the clothes could take the consumer to the land of open sky, where the only "person" visible would be one's own silhouette cutting through an underbrush of briars. Moreover, the three component Rugged Wear print ads were not merely function-oriented presentations of the product line. Instead, the leather-stitched border and the burnt and branded look of the Wrangler logo in each ad served to convey more than the "nuts and bolts" of the products. Martin strove to give the Rugged Wear line an indelible image.

MARKETING STRATEGY

Wrangler had already mastered niche marketing for its Western wear products, and it applied the same strategy in the "Rugged Wear" campaign. By using only print media, Wrangler was able to hone its message to reach the narrow target audience it desired. The ads appeared in magazines such as *Field and Stream, Hunting, American Hunter, Outdoor Life,* and *Bassmaster.* As the campaign's popularity became evident, Wrangler expanded its scope to include outdoor billboards. Once more, the company did not seek upscale urban consumers. Instead, it chose rural locations for the billboards. The posters were also enlarged to be used as "point of sale" ads, located in specialty stores where the Rugged Wear line was carried. Just as the company had sponsored rodeo events and riders, Wrangler attempted visibly to bring its message to its desired consumers. For this reason, Wrangler entered the growing sport of bass fishing in high profile by sponsoring the "Wrangler Anglers." This training program for amateur fishermen was a huge hit. "We realized that our consumers for outdoor products were grass-roots guys out there in the ranks of the Bass Anglers Sportsman Society Federation, and we wanted to do something to support them while introducing our products," a Wrangler public relations director told the *Greensboro News and Record.*

As part of its marketing tactics, Wrangler was careful to never completely sever the association of Rugged Wear with its popular and well-known Western clothes. The Western-style border and brand on each of the posters served to assert Rugged Wear's claim to the Wrangler heritage. Since the target markets for the two sectors showed some overlap, this strategy served to span the distance between Wrangler's broad Western wear consumer base and its outdoors sportspeople.

Indeed, this strategy conformed perfectly to an emerging trend in the Western wear category. According to the *Daily News Record,* Western wear shoppers began to seek out more "rugged, outdoors-inspired merchandise." Bill Koronis, vice-president and general manager of VF's Western wear discussed the shift with that newspaper. "Up until now we were selling [Rugged Wear] primarily to sporting goods and farm stores, but in the past couple of years, Western wear retailers have been looking for something else to sell to their consumer."

In order to capitalize on this shift more fully, Wrangler joined with traditional Western wear stores such as Sheplers to launch in-store shops for the Rugged Wear line. These shops displayed canoes, tents, and outdoor motifs to illustrate the underlying purpose of the Rugged Wear line. "If you just stick these items on a rack, they fail," said Koronis in the *Daily News Record.* "But if you make the investment in presentation, it's very successful."

OUTCOME

Banking on the bridge between Western wear and outdoors wear was a risk for Wrangler. "It was a big step for the company," said Martin copywriter Oakley about the "Rugged Wear" campaign. But the plunge served Wrangler well. On an anecdotal level, the campaign gained the admiration of consumers. Hunters and fishermen so liked the prints that they contacted the company and requested copies of the component ads to hang in their homes. Wrangler was so pleased with the response that it expanded the campaign into 1998. The "Rugged Wear" campaign was also lauded within the advertising industry. Most noteworthy was the Addy Award garnered by the "Chameleon" ad. The Rugged Wear campaign and product line were widely praised by publications as diverse as the conservative political paper the *Washington Times* and the industry-standard *Advertising Age.*

Despite slumps in its mainstay Western wear and discount markets, Wrangler continued to see steadily rising sales. A Wrangler executive told the *Daily News Record* that the Rugged Wear line was "showing good growth."

FURTHER READING

Casada, Jim. "Amateurs Fight Long Odds." *Greensboro News and Record,* August 2, 1995.

Krouse, Peter. "Jeans: Life's Little Labels." *Greensboro News and Record,* November 2, 1997.

Mundy, Alicia. "She Works for a Conventional Agency, But She Has a Decidedly Unconventional Approach to Media." *Brandweek,* December 8, 1997.

Palmieri, Jean. "The New and Improved Wrangler." *Daily News Record,* March 2, 1998.

Parpis, Eleftheria. "Searching for the Perfect Fit." *Adweek,* September 15, 1997.

Rebecca Stanfel

Village Voice LLC

36 Cooper Sq.
New York, New York 10003
USA
Telephone: (212) 475-3333
Web site: www.villagevoice.com

■■■

NOT AMERICA'S FAVORITE PAPER CAMPAIGN

OVERVIEW

Beginning April 10, 1996, *The Village Voice* —a liberal New York newspaper expressing the concerns of intellectual and political freedom—was distributed free throughout Manhattan in an attempt to boost its circulation and advertising. In anticipation of this change, the *Voice* commissioned a new advertising campaign from its agency, New York City's Mad Dogs and Englishmen. Mad Dogs responded with a campaign that maintained a tone consistent with its previous work for the *Voice* but capitalized more profoundly on the paper's truculent reputation to bolster the risky move to free circulation in Manhattan (readers in the other four boroughs and outside New York City still had to pay the $1.25 cover price). Mad Dogs created the tag line "Not America's Favorite Paper" as an ironic appeal to the *Voice* 's readership, who prided themselves on living outside the mainstream. The strategy was to regain the *Voice* 's position as the favorite paper of New York City's subcultures.

The print ads appeared mainly in the *Voice* itself but also appeared in other New York City newspapers (the *Voice* bartered ad space with other papers on an even trade) and on walls around the city. The ads relied on the stereotyping of the *Voice*'s nonreaders, the types against whom *Voice* editorials ranted. One ad showed a member of the National Rifle Association (NRA) at a shooting range; with the choice of targeting a bull's-eye or a copy of the *Village Voice,* his rifle was pointed squarely at the newspaper. Another depicted two older upper-class women sitting together with crossed legs commenting demurely, "It's so nice that homosexuals, Jews, and terrorists have a newspaper to read." Yet another simply showed a copy of the *Voice* strapped into an electric chair.

The ads helped smooth the transition to free circulation, doubling both circulation and advertising. The campaign, which ran throughout the circulation transition and into the spring of 1997, reached audiences as far away as Israel and Japan, where critics appreciated the ads as examples of America's freedom of expression. Most importantly, though, the campaign maintained the radical tone of the paper to insure its readers that the move to free circulation, which ran the risk of appearing as a transformation from a hard news journal to a soft "shopper" —a mere advertising medium—did not represent a sellout but rather represented a means of spreading the liberal word further afield. Publisher David Schneiderman affirmed that "the *Voice* will remain the *Voice*."

HISTORICAL CONTEXT

The *Village Voice* was founded in 1955 to capture the nonconformist political ideology and social currents of the Beatnik movement emanating from Manhattan's Greenwich Village. Norman Mailer, a controversial

American novelist, was one of the newspaper's first writers. In the 1990s, however, writers and editors at the *Voice* began to sense that the weekly was losing its voice of influence over New York City's political and cultural scenes. The paper was also losing readership, falling from 136,000 in 1994 to 121,000 in November 1995. This circulation decrease coincided with a price increase from $1.00 to $1.25 in 1994.

The decision to go free was devised to reverse all of these trends; more people were likely to pick up a paper that was free than one they had to pay for, which would boost circulation and thus increase the influence the paper held in the city. Most alternative weeklies were free, including the *LA Weekly,* the West-coast equivalent of the *Voice* owned by the same parent company, Stern Publishing. What these papers might have lost in subscriptions and newsstand sales was recouped by increased advertising because the ads reached more readers. When the *Voice* went free, it lost approximately $3 million in circulation revenues. Making up that amount might take two to three years, Schneiderman predicted, but it was a short-term sacrifice to secure more long-range goals. "For us it is a preemptive strike into the future," said Schneiderman. "We don't think there is much future for newsstands in New York."

Mad Dogs and Englishmen had become the ad agency for the *Voice* in 1991 to help build up subscriptions. The marketing strategy came naturally to creative director Michael Reich since he considered himself a member of the counterculture that the paper targeted. The *Voice* and its readership positioned themselves as distinct from the rest of the world; their opinions railed against the opinions held by the majority of mainstream culture.

Mad Dogs' ads took advantage of the *Voice* 's often extreme leftist editorial position by dramatizing the extreme political right's revilement of all that the *Voice* represented. *Voice* readers loved to be hated, so Mad Dogs invoked the ire of the *Voice* 's political enemies. The ads relied on tongue-in-cheek exaggeration. One ad presented itself as a *Village Voice* subscription coupon that took up an entire page, complete with huge "Yes" and "No" boxes. The "No" box was checked, and below it was scrawled a diatribe against the left by a radical right-winger. The success of the ads derived from a kind of reverse snobbery, tacitly looking down on those who looked down on the *Voice.*

TARGET MARKET

The *Village Voice* 's promotions manager Tony Cima to described the paper's readership succinctly as "young, hip, and affluent." Since the *Voice* was distributed in the New York City metropolitan area, the readership consisted primarily of urban New Yorkers as well as New Jersey and Connecticut residents. Mad Dogs' Reich considered himself a quintessential *Voice* reader; he thus had a more developed conception of the target market. Reich, like many *Voice* readers, had moved to the city to get away from the suburbs. Reich and others believed New York City offered limitless opportunity for artistic and political expression.

The *Voice* and its readership had a complementary relationship in that both had strong personalities. *Voice* readers had their own distinctive identity, but the paper gave them a collective voice that Reich called "the unchartered minority of America." The subculture that the *Voice* appealed to included those ostracized almost everywhere else: gays, feminists, pacifists, ethnic minorities, and underground artists. *Voice* readers generally defined themselves in opposition to more predominant ideologies; thus Reich hit upon the idea of harnessing that opposition by advertising it. The *Voice* had a clear understanding of who its readers were and an even clearer understanding of who its readers were not. The irony that the ads played upon was the fact that certain people would never under any circumstances read the *Voice.* The *Voice* preached to the converted, so Mad Dogs advertised to the converted.

COMPETITION

When the *Village Voice* eliminated its cover price, the *New York Observer* took over its newsstand space and consequently doubled its newsstand distribution. But the *Voice* was less concerned with the *Observer* 's success than with the highly combative competitive strategies of its main rivals, the alternative weeklies *TimeOut New York* and the *New York Press. TimeOut* ran billboards claiming that its listings were "enough to make you lose your voice." The *Press* changed its distribution day in order to preempt the *Voice*'s distribution, shifting from Wednesday (the day the *Voice* was distributed) to Tuesday. The *Press* also increased its editorial features space and its staff, adding a Washington correspondent.

Press publisher Ron Mann called the *Voice*'s switch to free circulation disastrous, claiming that the *Voice* had not picked up any new business (a point refuted by the *Voice*) because it had priced its ad space above the market. A quarter-page, four-time ad in the *Press* went for $600; the same ad space in the *Voice* ran $1,800, Mann pointed out. The Voice commissioned a consultant to assess whether its ad rates were out of line with the market. The issue boiled down to the results ads could produce: *TimeOut* ads were seen by 50,000 readers, *Press* ads by twice as many, while *Voice* ads reached three times as many readers, even before the circulation switch.

THE VOICE OF LONG ISLAND

Mad Dogs and Englishmen's creative director Michael Reich claimed that he fled Long Island, where he grew up, to find his own kind of people in New York City—namely, the types who would read the *Village Voice.* Ironically, *Voice* circulation spread to the suburbs in April 1997 with the launching of the Long Island *Voice,* following the national trend toward suburbanizing urban alternative weeklies. The *Voice,* however, did not export all of its attitude. For example, while the *Village Voice*'s sex columnist was openly gay, the Long Island *Voice*'s was straight. *Village Voice* publisher David Schneiderman, a Long Island native, defended the move as a means of asserting that his hometown was not as vacuous as its reputation—there was more to Long Island than underage sex scandals involving Joey Buttafuoco and Amy Fisher, Schneiderman attested.

MARKETING STRATEGY

The *Voice*'s decision to concentrate most of the "Not America's Favorite Paper" campaign in its own pages was driven by two main factors: first, one of the main goals of the campaign was to retain readers through the price elimination, so the *Voice* devoted itself to reassuring it readers that the attitude of the paper would not disappear with the price; second, the *Voice* could scarcely afford an expensive ad campaign, so its own pages represented a much cheaper medium than other outlets. The "bargain basement" approach to advertising was also consistent with the anticapitalistic tenets of the countercultural movement. Bartering, a mainstay of leftist economics, represented a way to avoid the transaction of money, transacting services instead. In this case the *Voice* bartered advertising space in its own pages in exchange for ad space in its rivals' pages, thus accessing its rivals' readers.

The *Voice* used another tactic invented by the counterculture: "sniping," or what Mad Dogs' Reich called "unofficial media buys." The term comes from the military practice of shooting at unsuspecting targets, except in this instance the *Voice* "attacked" unsuspecting passersby with its ads. This urban guerilla tactic involved plastering its poster ads on open spaces such as the sides of abandoned buildings or the plywood fences surrounding construction sites. The act had an illicit feel to it, even if it wasn't technically illegal. The efficacy of sniping was slightly diluted by the corporate co-opting of this underground tactic, with Calvin Klein and other corporate ads plastered all over New York City. Nevertheless, the strategy managed to raise the visibility of the *Voice* in a way that cost much less than buying official ad space on billboards or on the sides of city buses while also allowing the *Voice* to maintain its integrity.

The final advertising mode that the "Not America's Favorite Paper" campaign employed was a direct mailing of postcards. This tactic directly confronted the recipients of the postcards with a choice: either they were or they were not thinkers who sympathized with the *Voice*'s perspective, with no middle ground. The brilliance of the "Not America's Favorite Paper" campaign was that it forced the people viewing the ads to take a stand either way. While the text of the ads disparaged the *Voice,* the subtext of the ads disparaged those who disparaged the *Voice* by implied mockery of their political or social views. The campaign alluded that only those hip to the message got the message.

OUTCOME

The *Village Voice*'s "Not America's Favorite Paper" campaign achieved its main objectives of increasing circulation and advertising. Circulation increases surpassed their goals both in Manhattan (more than doubling from 71,000 to 185,000) and in total circulation (increasing from 150,000 to 235,000), making the *Voice* the most distributed weekly in the country. As a result, advertising almost doubled.

The circulation transition was marred by a few glitches. Since newsstands no longer sold the paper, some readers had trouble finding one of the 2,000 retail outlets in Manhattan where copies were distributed; those who could find the bright red distribution boxes often found them empty or vandalized. Some homeless entrepreneurs exported stacks from Manhattan (where the paper was free) to Brooklyn (where they undersold the official $1.25 rate). Additionally, vendors within certain Manhattan commuter points, such as Grand Central and Penn Stations, as well as the Port Authority Bus Terminal, continued the full-price policy of their distributor, Hudson News. *Voice* publisher Schneiderman dismissed the story of the homeless peddlers as untrue and expressed faith in commuters' ability to find readily available free copies. While he promised to restock the distribution boxes more frequently, he admitted that it would be impossible to keep them full; the only problem, according to Schneiderman, was that the paper was simply too popular. Public perception was critical of the *Voice*'s decision to go free. Robert Farrell, a business owner who had advertised in the *Voice* before switching to the *Press* a few years before the circulation change, commented that "when a business goes free, that shows weakness." Other critics echoed this sentiment, suggesting that the *Voice*'s transformation into a free paper signaled a move away from journalistic integrity and toward advertisement-driven decisions. "It's a sad day for the *Voice*," lamented former *Voice* editor Jonathan Larsen. "Now it's become just another shopper," he added, suggesting that the paper's free pricetag would mean a predominance of advertising and listings over its former journalistic innovation. Soon after the paper went free, it reduced the number of issues of the *Voice Literary Supplement* from 10 per year to just four, a fact many believed seemed to support Larsen's charge.

Publisher Schneiderman countered the cynical charges of selling out with a more balanced response, pointing out that the increased market penetration for readers and advertisers would allow the *Voice* "to deliver the best in journalism," a pledge that was harder to uphold when the $1.25 price decreased sales. The *Voice* could continue its commitment to journalistic excellence only if it could afford to remain in business. In order to compete against other alternative free papers, the *Voice* had to join their ranks. However, the *Voice* held a trump card: while none of the alternative papers could be considered America's favorite newspaper, only the *Village Voice* held the distinction of being America's least favorite paper.

FURTHER READING

Case, Tony. "Moving to Free: Success or Disaster?" *Editor and Publisher*, July 27, 1996.

Wulfhorst, Ellen. "*Village Voice* to be Distributed Free in Manhattan." *Reuters*, February 7, 1996.

William D. Baue

Virgin Atlantic Airways Limited

The Office
Manor Royal
Crawley, West Sussex RH10 2NU
United Kingdom
Telephone: 44 1293 616161
Fax: 44 1293 561721
Web site: www.virgin-atlantic.com

■■■

GO, JET SET, GO! CAMPAIGN

OVERVIEW

Helmed by the British entrepreneur Sir Richard Branson, Virgin Atlantic Airways Limited hoped to attract the posh jet-setters abandoned by Concorde, a line of supersonic jets owned by British Airways. The Concorde flew twice the speed of most commercial jets, but on October 24, 2003, British Airways discontinued its service because of economic factors and a marred image after a Concorde crashed in France. Even though the Concorde disaster claimed 113 lives, British Airways in 2002 still dominated the U.K. airline industry with $11.8 billion in sales, overshadowing Virgin's $2 billion.

Branson, famous for his playboy antics and shrewd business instincts, was disappointed by Virgin's "Serious Fun" campaign, which had begun in the late 1990s. In 2003 Virgin awarded its advertising budget, estimated at $12 to $15 million, to Miami-based agency Crispin Porter + Bogusky. The agency created a campaign dubbed "Go, Jet Set, Go!" It began in late 2003 with advertising appearing across print, outdoor, online, television, movie product placement, television product placement, and alternative advertising. Chris Rossi, vice president of sales and marketing at Virgin Atlantic, said to the *PR Newswire,* "The goal of this campaign is to communicate the style and glamour of our Upper Class cabin and the new Upper Class Suite product features in a way that will captivate and entertain business flyers." The campaign coincided with Virgin embellishing its Upper Class service by adding features such as in-flight massages, larger sleeping areas, in-flight beauty therapists, and a stand-up bar, similar to minibars located in shopping malls.

"Go, Jet Set, Go!" earned Crispin Porter + Bogusky a silver EFFIE along with other awards, and it helped Virgin increase sales from $2 billion in 2002 to $8.1 billion in 2004. Alex Bogusky, a partner at Crispin Porter + Bogusky, told *Advertising Age,* "As Virgin Atlantic has grown up, the pressure has been on to be a more grown-up company and less fun. But we're embracing fun to make the product less of a commodity and more about the experience."

HISTORICAL CONTEXT

As a young man, Richard Branson founded a London-based recording studio called Virgin in the early 1970s, his first of many Virgin-branded companies. Branson's empire eventually grew to include magazines, cola, a music retail chain, trains, a mobile-phone service provider, and his most ambitious project, Virgin Atlantic Airways, which was founded in 1984. Virgin's maiden flight was made between London's Gatwick Airport and Newark, New Jersey, with the airline's only plane, a used Boeing 747, filled with pop stars and journalists. The airline continued targeting the wealthy, celebrities, and fashionistas into the late 1990s.

Virgin's "Serious Fun" campaign exploited the success of the *Austin Powers* movies. Billboards for the campaign displayed actor Mike Myers, outfitted as Mr. Powers, beneath the tagline: "Five times a day. Yeah, baby." The ad referred to Virgin's addition of a fifth daily flight between New York and London. Barbara Lippert, writer for *Adweek,* stated, "The whole thing is aimed at the sensibility of a 12-year-old boy and that's who advertisers want to reach, even if that 12-year-old is 24." After the campaign ended, Virgin representatives discredited it as "moronic" and a "cop-out." In 2003 the airline shopped a plethora of agencies in search of a more sophisticated advertising approach.

In 2003 Crispin Porter + Bogusky pitched a new image for Virgin flights as the "party on the way to London." John Riordan, Virgin's vice president for customer services, told *Newsweek* that Virgin was hesitant about the concept at first. Eventually, however, the company embraced Crispin Porter + Bogusky's vision, with the caveat that the word "party" was not to appear in any ad. Crispin Porter + Bogusky creatives in August 2003 toyed with campaign taglines such as "Jet swanky" and "Going up?" before they settled on "Go, Jet Set, Go!" The tagline played on the appellation "jet-setter," defined as a wealthy traveler who jets from one fashionable location to the next. "We're thinking of it as the 'Just do it' of travel," Bogusky told *Newsweek.* "It's a call to action to get out there and do great things."

TARGET MARKET

"Go, Jet Set, Go!" targeted affluent, international flyers who did not classify as the typical business traveler. This included rock stars, supermodels, financiers, rap stars, and electronica DJs. Bogusky told the *New York Times* that Crispin Porter + Bogusky wanted to "appeal to the kind of people who appreciate the idea that though they're working hard, they deserve to have a good time." The firm, aware that their target was typically too busy to be exposed to network television spots or direct mail, used alternative advertising to increase visibility. Upper Class Virgin Atlantic beds were placed inside swanky department stores for people to try out. In order to target passengers descending in their competitor's aircraft, Virgin fixed massive advertisements to the rooftops of airport buildings.

One of the campaign's boldest moves involved creating a short pornography-spoof titled "Suite and Innocent." Crispin Porter + Bogusky felt the film was an effective way to attract the 78 percent of the target market that stayed at hotels equipped with LodgeNet, the pay-per-view channels that the film played on. "We were trying to figure out the best way to reach these highly elusive business travelers and this is where they're spending their time," Chris Rossi, vice president for North American sales and marketing, told the *New York Times.*

> ### SIR RICHARD BRANSON'S SPACE TRAVEL
>
> Sir Richard Branson, the entrepreneur that the British, in a poll, voted as the third most qualified Brit to rewrite the Ten Commandments, became one of the world's best-known "rebel billionaires." Some of his commercial exploits involved helming the first commercial rock station in the U.K. as well as launching a commercial music retail chain, a commercial train service, and a pay-as-you-go mobile phone service. In 1999 Branson conceived Virgin Galactic, an airline that promised commercial space travel. By leaving the earth's atmosphere, the service would reduce the flight between London and Sydney to a mere three hours. Virgin hoped to have the service operating by 2010.

COMPETITION

British Airways, the fifth-largest airline in the world and the largest in the United Kingdom, pitted itself fiercely against Virgin in the early 1990s. In 1993 Branson took British Airways to court after it inflated rumors about Virgin's debt and Branson's drug addiction. In the libel settlement Branson won $5 million, which he distributed amongst his employees. One of the most galvanizing decisions British Airways made to ensure its position in the United Kingdom was partnering with American Airlines, the world's largest airline in 2003. Branson described competing against the two giants as comparable to "having a bleeding contest with a blood bank." British Airways posted sales at $14 billion in 2000, a figure which had slipped slightly below $14 billion by 2004. The slippage was attributed to the terrorist attacks of September 11, 2001, the surfacing of cheaper no-frills airlines, and the emergence of international European airlines such as Deutsche Lufthansa, British Midland Airways, and Virgin.

To keep its grip on the U.K. market, British Airways spent an estimated $100 million on marketing in 2005. P.J. O'Rourke, the biting American satirist, became the airline's new spokesperson. British Airways began

GOD SAVE THE KNIGHT

"God Save the Queen," a Sex Pistols hit that bashed the queen of England, was recorded at Richard Branson's Virgin recording studio during the mid-1970s. The band later played the song on a boat upon the Thames during Britain's 1977 Jubilee. The band was quickly stopped and arrested. Ironically, Branson was later knighted by the queen. "It's strange," Branson said regarding the ceremony, "… I was wondering whether the sword, instead of touching [my shoulders], was going to [chop off my head]!"

announcing bargain flight deals, such as "only £69 to go to Paris," on the back of ATM receipts. In a live-theater advertisement that took place throughout Heathrow Airport, actors were hired to perform scripts that boasted of British Airway's services. Employees also posted pro-British Airways content in Internet chat rooms. Jayne O'Brien, British Airways' marketing chief, told the *Independent,* "People see about 3,000 advertising statements a day. The challenge to the marketer is how you are going to get your message heard, engaged with and understood by the market."

MARKETING STRATEGY

Early ads for "Go, Jet Set, Go!" were launched in late 2003, during the final days of British Airways' Concorde. Virgin ads toasted the Concorde's final flight and offered its abandoned clientele their services. Complimentary copies of a short book titled "Night-Night Jet Set," mimicking the children's book format, began appearing in Virgin's upper-class suites. It featured text such as, "Night-Night rap superstar lounging in 7F. When finished signing contracts your massage waits to the left," and "Night-Night fashion goddess reading in 5D. Where did you get those shoes? We really must see." Airsickness bags doubled as origami 747s and planting pots. Virgin began product placement in movies such as *Love Actually* and *Calendar Girls,* both British-made. Virgin branding also appeared on NBC's reality-TV show *American Princess.* Ralph Bershefsky, a manager of advertising for Virgin in the United States, told *Advertising Age,* "We receive between 100 to 200 requests for sponsorship a week, so we have a tough time deciding what to do."

At the time of the campaign's launch, Virgin furnished its upper-class suites with a flat bed, table, and chair that could be enclosed with a temporary wall. The beds were the longest in the airline industry. Models of upper-class suites were placed inside posh department stores so that shoppers could see Virgin's improved features. Andrew Keller, Crispin Porter + Bogusky's creative director, told *Advertising Age,* "We're going to have events in the sky, such as business summits. We want to change the culture of flying so that it's not all about the destination. We want to change the game and make people want the experience." Virgin handed out destination luggage labels, similar to ones that were popularized in the late nineteenth century. As Christine Bittar wrote in *Brandweek,* "Experience is more meaningful than size for the Richard Branson airline. Making the Upper Class Suite flight more than just a trip means clients can eat meals whenever they want, enjoy a scalp and shoulder massage at the salon area, or mingle at the bar."

Print ads that appeared in magazines mimicked the laminated safety-information sheets found in airplane seat-pockets. Text stating, "No bouncing on the largest fully flat bed in business class," appeared above a diagram of a man jumping on his bed. Crispin Porter + Bogusky placed a 120-by-520-foot "Go, Jet Set, Go!" billboard on a rooftop near Los Angeles International Airport to target flyers looking out their windows as they landed. A similar ad was placed near New York's JFK airport. Crispin Porter + Bogusky used such innovative mediums to overcome one of the campaign's greatest challenges: reaching international travelers who were unlikely to take heed of traditional advertising. In October 2004 Virgin launched its nine-and-a-half-minute pornography parody, "Suite and Innocent", which cost $1 million and ran on pay-per-view channels in hotels until the end of 2004. Although the spoof was without nudity or profanity, it was riddled with double entendres and featured characters with such names as Miles High, Big Ben, and Summer Turbulence. "Virgin is a brand that likes to push the edge," Chris Rossi, one of Virgin's vice presidents, told *Fast Company* magazine. "Even so, I would never have given the green light for the LodgeNet piece if the agency didn't have the strategic thinking and research to back it up."

OUTCOME

"Go, Jet Set, Go!" ran during a time of increased sales growth for Virgin, whose $2 billion in sales for 2002 had risen to $8.1 billion by 2004. The percentage increase was significantly higher than that of Virgin's largest domestic competitor, British Airways, which improved from $11.8 billion in 2002 to just below $14 billion in 2004. Ad industry success ensued as well. In 2005 the campaign won a silver EFFIE Award along with a gold Clio Award for Contact and Content (a category that recognized innovation in reaching customers).

Many sources also noted the mutual admiration between Crispin Porter + Bogusky and Virgin. Of working with Virgin, Crispin Porter + Bogusky, well known for its MINI Cooper "Let's Motor" campaign and Burger King "Subservient Chicken" campaign, said: "The opportunity to work for one of the coolest brands in the world was something we found very appealing. When we learned more about it and found that it truly did reflect the maverick spirit and entrepreneurial drive of founder Richard Branson, we got even more fired up." Virgin also seemed happy to end its previous "Serious Fun" campaign and doted on Crispin Porter + Bogusky.

FURTHER READING

Anderson, Mae. "A New Playing Field: Some of the Smartest Creative Ideas Are Right Outside Your Window." *Adweek,* April 19, 2004, p. 28.

Atkinson, Claire. "Virgin Airlines Promo Targets 'Jetrosexuals'; Movie and TV Tie-Ins Also Part of Major Push." *Advertising Age,* November 3, 2003, p. 58.

Bittar, Christine. "Tools of the Trade." *Brandweek,* February 23, 2004.

Burrell, Ian. "In It for the Long Haul: Marketing: British Airways." *Independent* (London), June 20, 2005, p. 12.

Campo-Flores, Arian. "Virgin's New Flight of Fancy." *Newsweek,* November 10, 2003, p. 42.

Elliot, Stuart. "Sir Richard's Airline, Always Irreverent, Moves to the Next Plateau with a Spoof of Pornography." *New York Times,* October 4, 2004, p. 10.

Ives, Nat. "Tongue-in-Cheek Ads from Virgin Atlantic." *New York Times,* October 27, 2003, p. 8.

Lauro, Patricia Winters. "Big Marketers Are Betting on 'Austin Powers' to Endear Them to Young People." *New York Times,* June 14, 1999, p. 17.

Lazare, Lewis. "Diageo Ads Tout No-Carb Brands." *Chicago Sun-Times,* April 21, 2004, p. 83.

Mack, Ann. "CP+B Takes Flash Ads into Virgin Territory." *Adweek,* April 26, 2004, p. 12.

Waples, John. "Branson's Biggest Battle." *Sunday Times* (London), November 18, 2001.

Kevin Teague

Virginia Tourism Corporation

901 East Byrd Street
Richmond, Virginia 23219-4048
USA
Telephone: (804) 786-2052
Fax: (804) 786-1919
Web site: www.vatc.org

MEET VIRGINIA CAMPAIGN

OVERVIEW

Despite a limited budget, the Virginia Tourism Corporation (VTC) had been a model promoter of state tourism for most of the second half of the twentieth century. In the late 1960s it began using the slogan "Virginia Is for Lovers," a phrase that became well known and served as the foundation for all VTC marketing campaigns that followed. It was still deemed relevant at the start of the new century. Virginia's tourism industry, like that of the rest of America, received a major blow when terrorists attacked New York and Washington, D.C., on September 11, 2001, leading to a severe decline in travel. People looked to take shorter trips closer to home, and state tourism boards aggressively courted this business with a bevy of new slogans and increased ad spending. Virginia, on the other hand, cut its marketing budget for tourism and instead looked to make do with less by freshening up it venerable "Virginia Is for Lovers" slogan. The result was the "Meet Virginia" campaign, which sought to personify the state as a family friend. It began in February 2004.

"Meet Virginia," created by Virginia ad agency White & Baldacci (later renamed White & Partners) with a budget of about $2.5 million, primarily targeted mothers, who were the key decision makers in determining the destination of family vacations. Most of the campaign resources were devoted to print ads, which ran in more than a dozen national magazines. The ads portrayed different aspects of Virginia's personality. One execution said that "she" was "a breath of fresh air," accompanied by a picture of a woman standing atop a mountain. On the side were listed a number of destinations and outdoor activities in keeping with that ad's theme. The "Virginia Is for Lovers" slogan and logo were retained, anchoring a bottom corner of the full-page ads.

The "Meet Virginia" campaign succeeded in nearly tripling the number of requests for the state's official Virginia travel brochure. In addition, hotel bookings surged. The "Meet Virginia" theme was retained by the VTC, and the campaign was continued in 2005 and beyond. It also garnered national recognition, including an EFFIE Award, one of the top honors in the advertising industry.

HISTORICAL CONTEXT

Since the introduction of the slogan "Virginia Is for Lovers" in 1969, the Virginia Tourism Corporation was one of the most aggressive promoters of state tourism in the United States. Despite lacking the budgets of other locales, the VTC brought Virginia's tourist attractions to the attention of travelers around the world. It also benefited from its geographical location: about 55 percent of the U.S. population lived within 500 miles of the state.

Travelers spent some $14 billion each year in Virginia and paid more than $1.8 billion in local and state taxes. Furthermore, well over 260,000 jobs in Virginia were tourism related.

Over the years the competition for travel dollars grew steadily, and then the terrorist attacks of September 11, 2001, caused a significant drop in international air travel, leading to more domestic trips. In addition, people were looking for trips that were shorter and closer to home. In the Northeast this led to even fiercer competition between tourism boards intent on capturing their share of this business. Many states increased advertising, leading to a blizzard of similar messages promoting sites of interests.

The VTC had the most recognizable travel slogan in the United States, but in the post–September 11 landscape it decided that "Virginia Is for Lovers" needed a little freshening up. In 2002 the VTC unveiled a series of three television spots offering an irreverent and somewhat literal spin on the venerable slogan. Each spot opened with the question "What comes to mind when you hear the slogan 'Virginia is for lovers?'" In the "Hotel" spot a bellhop introduced a puzzled family to a gaudy hotel love nest, complete with a heart-shaped bed and a neon lips sculpture. Also using a hotel setting, "Maids" showed a cleaning staff waiting in a hotel corridor, unable to work because from every door hung a "Do Not Disturb" placard. In the spot entitled "Beaches" a lover said, "I feel as if I've found my soul mate and best friend." The phrase was then echoed by countless other couples on the beach. The spots closed with a voice-over that stated, "It's easy to get the wrong impression." Viewers were then directed to a website, www.virginiaisforlovers.com, where they could learn about Virginia tourist sites and "more than 100 ways to love Virginia."

In 2003 the state cut the tourism advertising budget by 40 percent and mandated that the VTC review the ideas of new advertising agencies and reassign the account. Moreover, the state developed a strategic plan that called for less emphasis on radio and television commercials and more on print ads in niche publications. Northern Virginia ad agency White & Baldacci (subsequently renamed White & Partners) won the VTC account in September 2003. It developed its own twist on the "Virginia Is for Lovers" theme with the "Meet Virginia" campaign, which was released in February 2004.

"VIRGINIA IS FOR LOVERS"

The Virginia Tourism Corporation's longtime slogan, "Virginia Is for Lovers," was created in 1969 by Robin McLaughlin, a copywriter for the Martin Agency of Richmond, Virginia. It was first used, appropriately enough, in an ad that appeared in the March 1969 issue of *Modern Bride.*

TARGET MARKET

Surveys conducted by the VTC revealed a profile of Virginia tourists: 60 percent were college educated, more than half had household incomes in excess of $60,000, and their average household head was 54 years of age. The largest numbers came from nearby Washington, D.C. (11.5 percent), followed by New York City (7.8 percent), Baltimore (5.4 percent), Raleigh-Durham, North Carolina (5 percent), and Philadelphia (4.9 percent). Residents of Virginia itself were also a main source of visitors, and to a lesser degree the state attracted tourists from Atlanta; Pittsburgh; Charlotte, North Carolina; and Boston. To attract the family business in these markets, the "Meet Virginia" campaign specifically targeted the one person in the family most responsible for planning vacations: the mother. Hence, the target audience consisted of college-educated women between the ages of 25 and 54 who had at least one child under 18 years old. In addition, the family's household annual income would total at least $70,000. This composite person was kept in mind as the advertisements were crafted and the decisions were made about the most appropriate places to run them. White & Partners also made sure that the campaign did not neglect the interests of the rest of the family. While a woman was generally highlighted in an ad, family members were usually included in the background, and to attract the attention of husbands and children a variety of destinations and activities were featured.

COMPETITION

Because so many families were taking shorter trips to nearby locations, Virginia competed against surrounding states. New York City was rebuilding its tourism business after experiencing a serious downturn in 2001, and the state of New York had been successfully exploiting its own well-known slogan, "I Love New York," since the 1970s. New Yorkers who might pay visits to Virginia were also tempted by the Native American casinos Foxwoods and Mohegan Sun in Connecticut. Casinos in Atlantic City, New Jersey, also competed for tourists from New York and Philadelphia. The state of Pennsylvania, which for years had exploited its slogan, "You've got a friend in Pennsylvania," also vied aggressively for travel business. With its historic sites, Philadelphia was a perennial tourist attraction, as was

Lancaster County, 50 miles to the west, which offered Amish and Pennsylvania Dutch tourist attractions that were well marketed. Even Maryland, which had long neglected its tourism trade, was becoming more aggressive in promoting itself.

Closer to home was Washington, D.C., an international tourist attraction, but the capital served more as a compliment to Virginia tourism than competition, drawing tourists from around the world who might choose to spend some time and money in nearby Virginia. To the south Virginia had a rival in North Carolina, which offered mountain activities as well as coastal attractions. In addition, Orlando, Florida, home to Disney World and a number of other attractions, was only a short flight from Virginia's core markets, and Orlando commanded a larger tourism budget. Virginia's tourism budget was less than half of the $12 million that other states spent on average and a small fraction of the $550 million that 46 reporting states spent in 2003, according to the Travel Industry Association of America.

MARKETING STRATEGY

The underlying concept of the "Meet Virginia" campaign was to personify the state as a woman, someone that other women in particular would find appealing and want to know better. Within this framework Virginia's tourist attractions were portrayed as aspects of the character's personality. Media elements included a limited amount of television and radio advertising as well as some out-of-home ads (such as signage) and Internet advertising, but the anchor of the campaign was print advertising. Print ads ran in 15 national magazines, including *National Geographic, Smithsonian, Southern Living, Better Homes & Gardens, Good Housekeeping,* the *New Yorker, Audubon, Bon Appétit, Reader's Digest, Travel & Leisure,* and *O: The Oprah Magazine.* Specialty print ads were also produced for trade publications: ads aimed at groups were placed in such niche magazines as *Group Tour Magazine* and *Leisure Group Travel*; and an ad focusing on meetings ran in periodicals that included *Association Management Magazine, Convene,* and *Convention South.*

Each full-page print ad attempted to offer a different side of Virginia's personality, accompanied by a list of relevant tourist attractions and destinations. In one execution a female hiker was shown standing at the top of a mountain and taking in a glorious view. Superimposed in script over the large "Meet Virginia" headline was "She's a breath of fresh air." Addition text read, "With miles of awe-inspiring mountains and valleys to explore, the fresh air does more than fill your lungs. It also clears your mind." In the margin was a list of outdoor activities to consider, such as visiting Busch Gardens, Civil War Battlefields, and Shenandoah National Park. In a lower corner of the ad was the "Virginia Is for Lovers" slogan and a variation on its heart logo, thereby providing continuity with the state's long-term campaign theme.

Another print ad showed a female golfer celebrating a successful putt. The headline read, "She brings out the tiger in you." A number of golf courses and related attractions, such as the Virginia State Golf Association Museum, were highlighted in a sidebar. In another execution a family was shown buried in sand up to their heads, the headline reading, "She'll help you escape." Virginia Beach and other outdoor venues were highlighted to the side. Winter activities were addressed in an ad that featured a woman snowboarder, accompanied by the headline, "She doesn't believe in spectator sports." Yet another ad promoted the state's historic sites. It showed a picture from the American Revolution battlefield of Yorktown, with a family watching a colonial soldier firing a musket. The headline was "Kids think she's a blast."

OUTCOME

The "Meet Virginia" campaign was so successful that the VTC continued it beyond 2004. The VTC's goal for the campaign was to generate about 100,000 requests for its annual "Virginia Travel Guide" vacation-planning brochure, but after just seven months it more than doubled that target, receiving 220,000 unique requests for the material. Another indicator of the campaign's effectiveness could be found in the state's hotel sector. According to "Virginia Tourism Monitor," a monthly research publication compiled by the VTC, during the first quarter of 2004 occupancy rates in the state were 8.7 percent higher than they had been during the first quarter of 2003. Moreover, this was nearly twice the national average increase of 4.4 percent, as tabulated by the Travel Industry Association of America.

The work done by White & Partners was also recognized by the advertising industry. "Meet Virginia" won a Bronze in the Travel/Tourism/Destination category of the 2005 EFFIE Awards, a highly prestigious competition produced by the New York American Marketing Association, a trade organization for marketing professionals. In addition, "Meet Virginia" was named the Best Overall Advertising Campaign at the 2004 Educational Seminar for Tourism Organization, an annual event hosted by the Travel Industry Association of America.

FURTHER READING

Coppola, Vincent. "Lighter Love Stories for Virginia." *Adweek* (southwest ed.), May 6, 2002, p. 7.

Dunham, Linda. "Virginia Tourism Official Enjoys Chance to Merge Passions: State, Literature." *Richmond (VA) Times-Dispatch,* May 18, 2004.

Griswold, Alicia. "There's Less of Virginia Tourism to Love." *Adweek* (southeast ed.), June 10, 2003.

———. "Virginia Tourism Goes to White & Baldacci." *Adweek* (southeast ed.), September 16, 2003.

Scutt, Caroline. "State to Mark 25th Anniversary of 'Lovers' Tourism Theme." *Travel Weekly,* November 22, 1993, p. T23.

Ed Dinger

Visa U.S.A., Inc.

900 Metro Center Boulevard
Foster City, California 94404
USA
Telephone: (650) 432-3200
Web site: www.visa.com

VISA. IT'S EVERYWHERE YOU WANT TO BE CAMPAIGN

OVERVIEW

In 1985 Visa U.S.A. was the world's largest credit card company, but it lacked a specific brand image. The American Express Company advertised its cards as the best way to pay for travel and entertainment expenses. MasterCard International positioned its brand for middle- and lower-income consumers. Visa, however, aimed for both American Express's and MasterCard's target markets as well as for more traditional consumers who paid with cash and checks. Visa realized that one advantage it had over its competition was that merchants worldwide accepted Visa more than any other credit card. Hoping to gain more customers, the company released its "Visa. It's Everywhere You Want to Be" campaign to brand Visa as the most widely accepted credit card in the world.

The campaign, created by the ad agency BBDO New York, debuted on October 1, 1985. Its budget began at $20 million. At the end of its 20-year lifespan the campaign consumed a budget of $335 million. Always lauding Visa as the most widely accepted credit card, "Visa. It's Everywhere You Want to Be" targeted a broad market and employed television, radio, print, Internet, and billboard advertisements. The original advertisements featured unique and upscale businesses that accepted Visa but not American Express. Later spots advertised the advantages of Visa Check Cards over paper checks. In 2000 the campaign heralded the "smart Visa card," a card with a security chip. Four years later the spots promoted the Visa Signature card, the company's first limitless credit card. The campaign became a mainstay of Super Bowl and Olympics advertising. The campaign ended just before the 2006 Winter Olympics.

Advertising critics praised the campaign throughout its 20-year run. It collected may of the ad industry's most prestigious awards, including EFFIEs, Clios, and Cannes Lions. Visa's credit card market share expanded from 43.8 percent in 1985 to 52 percent in 2004, an increase the company attributed to the campaign.

HISTORICAL CONTEXT

Although Visa had been steadily capturing American consumers since its inception in 1958, the company suffered from a lackluster image. Rival American Express "projected status and prestige," explained the *Wall Street Journal,* by airing commercials featuring glamorous celebrities who used the charge card. Visa, on the other hand, lacked a coherent brand message and was often confused with MasterCard, another bank card competitor. An in-house marketing shop produced all of Visa's advertising, which, according to the September 9, 1994, *American Banker,* was "quite similar" to MasterCard's, with both companies "hammering the point that a single card could be used anywhere for anything, with the ability to spread payments or assist in budgeting."

In 1984, however, Visa brought in renowned ad agency BBDO in hopes of revitalizing its image. Visa and BBDO approached the crafting of a new campaign with two goals: to differentiate Visa from MasterCard, which was increasingly encroaching on Visa's market share, and to "reinforce [Visa's] upscale image and remind consumers that it [w]as . . . the most widely accepted payment card in the world." The company decided that the best way to achieve both aims was to take on American Express. At the time AmEx dominated the lucrative travel and entertainment sector of the market. Visa sought "to piggyback on American Express' image as the premier travel and entertainment card," explained an article in the September 27, 1985, issue of *American Banker.* Thus, in ad after ad Visa drove home the point that elite and trendy restaurants, hotels, and shops—the sorts of establishments most consumers associated with American Express—emphatically did not accept that card.

TARGET MARKET

"It's Everywhere You Want to Be" initially pursued adults who were American Express's core customers. Although the Visa card was carried by more American consumers and was accepted at more merchants than AmEx, market research at the time revealed that "people tend[ed] to spend more on their American Express cards," according to the November 27, 1989, edition of the *Wall Street Journal.* The original target audience of the "It's Everywhere" campaign was adults aged 25 to 54 who lived in major metropolitan areas and had an annual income of more than $20,000. In order to tout its acceptance in the travel and entertainment sector, Visa's early commercials focused exclusively on such businesses, especially restaurants, hotels, and leisure activities. For instance, the three launch commercials portrayed Rosalie's Restaurant, Captain John's Boatyard in Mangrove Bay, Bermuda, and a fishing tackle store in Texas. Later spots featured the exclusive Telluride Ski Resort, the Jack Nicklaus/Flick Golf Schools, and Granita, a chic eatery in Malibu, California.

To reach this audience of older, more affluent Americans, Visa also took care to form advertising alliances with celebrities who appealed to these baby boomers. In 1989 the company teamed up with Paul McCartney. Visa sponsored the ex-Beatle's solo U.S. concert tour in exchange for billing as the only credit card accepted at the event. McCartney's allure was evident, as a BBDO spokesperson explained to the *Wall Street Journal*: "He spans generations; he has an international image, and he has a family image."

As the "It's Everywhere" campaign flourished, Visa expanded its target market. Generation Xers, those Americans born after 1964, accounted for 30 percent of all credit card purchases. Visa crafted television commercials and print ads that were designed to capture the allegiance of this demographic group. "The Attic," for example, targeted 20- and 30-year-olds with its "fast-paced montage of live fashion shots [that] could easily be part of a music video," according to a Visa press release. Indeed, the commercial's "funky music, hip Gen Xers, and popular vintage clothing" were carefully selected to reach this more youthful audience. "The only thing that's out of style," quipped the commercial, "is using American Express." In a similar vein, Visa also crafted a group of spots to attract owners of small businesses.

In 1996 the campaign targeted consumers accustomed to using paper checks, encouraging them to switch to its Visa Check Card with advertisements that carried the tagline "Works Like a Check." Four years later spots for the new "smart Visa card" targeted what BBDO called "alpha consumers," or technologically minded Americans between 18 and 34 years old. In 2004, with commercials that advertised Visa's Signature card, a limitless credit card aimed at wealthy consumers, the campaign's target shifted toward professionals aged 35 to 54 who earned at least $125,000 per year.

COMPETITION

When Visa set out to garner a more prosperous consumer base, especially in the travel and entertainment sector, it faced fierce competition from both American Express and MasterCard. Indeed, the *Chicago Sun-Times* succinctly concluded that AmEx "owned" the travel and entertainment category at the time of the 1985 launch of the "It's Everywhere" campaign. For years American Express had cultivated an elite image through its "Portraits" campaign and its series of "Don't Leave Home without It" advertisements. "We have always directed all our efforts toward the upscale market in the United States," an AmEx executive told *Gannett News Service.* When Visa began its barrage of comparative advertising against its competitor, AmEx first sought to remain above the fray. By 1992, however, with its market share in a tailspin, American Express struck back with a counterattack to Visa's Olympic Games advertising. Working with a new agency, Chiat/Day/Mojo, American Express released two spots that were set in Barcelona, the location of the 1992 Olympic Games. The copy in the spots slyly sniped at Visa with slogans such as "And remember, to visit Spain, you don't need a visa" and

TAKING THE GLOVES OFF

Ad agency BBDO was quite clear in an interview with *Adweek* that its explicit strategy for the "Visa. It's Everywhere You Want to Be" campaign was to "attack American Express." Stung by Visa's success, American Express (or AmEx) often vociferously complained that Visa's much-vaunted universal acceptance was the result of "buying off" the merchants who appeared in its highly publicized commercials. But the "Telluride" commercial generated particular controversy. The spot—which proclaimed, "at Telluride Ski Resort, they'll let you take the plunge, but they won't take American Express. Visa. It's Everywhere You Want to Be" —also showed 13 shops on Telluride's main street, 10 of which accepted American Express, and also showed a hotel in town that took AmEx. American Express cried foul and sought an injunction to prevent Visa from running the spot. Visa agreed to pull the spot until it had removed the scenes of merchants that accepted American Express. But this did not end the bitterness between the rivals. According to *Corporate Legal Times,* in a court document American Express claimed that Visa "singled out high-visibility American Express clients and persuaded them to cancel their AmEx contracts in return for television advertising."

"Obviously, we're here for more than just fun and games." Nevertheless, AmEx's market share continued to decline, dropping that year from 20.4 to 19.6 percent, while Visa's remained strong, at 45.4 percent. Still striving to rebound, American Express initiated a national print and television campaign in 1997 that openly criticized Visa. "Visa says they're everywhere, but isn't it more important to have a card that helps you with just about everything?" queried one such commercial. AmEx also signed comedian Jerry Seinfeld as a spokesperson to appear in a variety of witty ads. American Express's era of decline ended when in 1997 the company's market share rose to 17 percent, up from 16.4 percent in 1996.

While Visa wrested control of the upscale market from American Express, MasterCard strove to reach middle-class consumers. In 1993, MasterCard abandoned its long-standing "Master the Moment" campaign, which relied on scenes of celebrities and carefree spending, in favor of "It's More Than a Credit Card. It's Smart Money." Component spots showed regular people using MasterCard in their daily lives, for example, while shopping at the supermarket. Instead of emphasizing prestige, MasterCard hammered home the value of its card and its practicality. In 1997, however, MasterCard switched strategies once more with the debut of the "Priceless" campaign from its new ad agency, McCann-Erickson. After boosting its ad budget 8 percent, to $106.2 million, in that year and honing its message to reach more affluent consumers, MasterCard saw its market share rise to 27.8 percent.

MARKETING STRATEGY

The $20 million campaign's initial goal was to reinforce its upscale image and establish itself as the most widely accepted payment card in the lucrative sector of travel and entertainment. "Just a little north of Boston, in the old town of Marblehead, is a place where only the local people used to eat," declared the inaugural spot of the campaign. "Where the scaloppini and the scampi were so good that word soon got out that a night at Rosalie's was like a night in Milan. But if you go there, remember, bring a big appetite and bring your Visa card. Because at Rosalie's they don't take no for an answer and they don't take American Express. Visa. It's everywhere you want to be."

Eighty percent of the campaign's budget was spent on commercials aired during programming such as the *Today Show* and *Good Morning America,* both popular with the initial target audience; the NFL's Super Bowl, which annually drew the largest television viewership of any single event; *Monday Night Football*; and the final episode of the popular situation comedy *Seinfeld.* As a company spokesperson explained in a press release, Visa often selected venues such as *Seinfeld* to carry the "It's Everywhere" message because spots broadcast on such shows were "in the position to reach millions of current and potential cardholders in numerous market segments." Visa and BBDO also crafted print ads and radio spots that furthered the "It's Everywhere" theme.

In addition to airing television spots, the campaign built alliances with high-profile events. In 1986 Visa teamed up with the Olympic Games as an official sponsor, a relationship that would continue for the breadth of the campaign. Visa subsequently forged exclusive contracts with the National Football League, Paul McCartney's Concert Tour, and the Ringling Brothers and Barnum & Bailey Circus. In addition to using these relationships in its advertising to hype that the organizations did not take American Express, Visa was able to capitalize on the cachet that events such as the Olympics possessed.

To target people between 18 and 34 years old, one spot in 1999 featured young people salsa dancing. The voice-over, provided by the actor Ed Grover, explained that the Salsa Lovers Dance Studio in Miami did not accept American Express, only Visa. The spot was one of many Visa advertisements that used Latin culture to attract consumers. "I think Latin culture used to be for Latins, but not anymore," Jimmy Siegel, a BBDO senior creative director, said to the *New York Times.* "Latin culture has become hip, and it's sort of on the edge of becoming more popular in the mainstream. I would expect more commercials with some sort of Latin influence." The campaign targeted tech-savvy "alpha consumers" the next year by advertising the new smart Visa card, a card that interacted with the Internet via a security chip. One Internet ad on www.NFL.com, the official site of the National Football League, read, "They don't take American Express—not even Blue." (The Blue Card was AmEx's version of the smart Visa card.) The copy referenced Visa's exclusive relationship with the NFL.

In 2003 the campaign focused more on business credit card advertisements. One spot that aired on ABC, CBS, CNN, Fox, MSNBC, ESPN, and other networks featured a clothing-store owner using her business credit card to make purchases, track expenses, and accept deliveries. Print ads and more television spots targeted larger businesses the next year. One 2004 print ad showed a business executive sitting in a swan chair (an office chair that was an icon of midcentury furniture design) beside stacks of paper. The ad's copy stated, "I want to be surrounded by intelligence, not information." Other ads used the "I want to be . . ." tagline and featured executives reposed in the same chair. "The swan chair is a platform to speak from, for business executives to voice their aspirations," Dawn Volan, director of advertising at Visa, said in *B to B.* "We want to use the chair as an identifier that Visa and Visa Commercial Solutions can help you reach those aspirations." The ads featured the modified tagline "It's everywhere you want your company to be."

One of the campaign's last efforts was promoting the Visa Signature card. Spots linked the no-limit credit card to other "signature" icons. Part of Visa's $335 million ad budget was used to create a spot that compared the Signature card to Marilyn Monroe, "the signature blonde," Frank Sinatra, "the signature voice," and the classic Ford Thunderbird, "the signature sports car." The spot ended with a voice-over explaining, "It's not just everywhere you want to be, it's everything you've ever wanted." The campaign ended in early 2006.

OUTCOME

"It's Everywhere You Want to Be" was heralded by both Visa executives and advertising analysts as an unequivocal success. From 1989 to 1993 Visa doubled its sales in the travel and entertainment sector. The company's share of the total credit card market increased from 43.8 percent in 1985 to 52 percent in 2004. "The ad campaign has succeeded beyond anybody's wildest imagination," a Visa spokesperson told the September 23, 1993, issue of *American Banker.* "It's Everywhere" collected many advertising awards, including a Gold Lion at the prestigious International Advertising Festival in Cannes, France, and numerous EFFIEs, Clios, and ADDYs.

Even though the campaign jabbed at American Express for nearly 20 years, Elizabeth Silver, the senior vice president of advertising at Visa, said in an interview with *Advertising Age,* "American Express was a foil. Our real aim was MasterCard." When the campaign started, there was not much brand discernment between MasterCard and Visa. According to Visa, the company split the market nearly two to one with MasterCard. By the campaign's end Visa completely outpaced MasterCard with more than 50 percent of the entire credit card market.

Unfortunately for BBDO, by a few years into the new millennium Visa was viewing the campaign's message as outdated. In 2005 most merchants accepted American Express, Visa, and MasterCard. Consumers were not worrying about their American Express cards being denied. "We've had a very successful campaign with 'It's Everywhere You Want to Be,'" Visa's chief marketing officer, Susanne Lyons, said to the *New York Times.* "Acceptance was a great differentiator 20 years ago. But it's not so important now as qualities like security and convenience." Just before the 2006 Winter Olympics, Visa awarded its $335 million ad account to the agency TBWA\Chiat\Day Los Angeles. The 20-year campaign was replaced with the new agency's "Life Takes Visa" campaign.

FURTHER READING

Barge, Jeff. "Fantastic Plastic Commercial Squelched as Too Misleading." *Corporate Legal Times,* December 1993.

Bird, Laura. "Race for MasterCard's Account Narrows." *Wall Street Journal,* August 7, 1992.

Dash, Eric. "To Make the Card Special, Try the Warm and Familiar." *New York Times,* February 8, 2006, p. 4.

Elliott, Stuart. "VISA USA Decides It Wasn't Where It Wanted to Be." *New York Times,* November 15, 2005, p. 13.

Garfield, Bob. "Not Catchy, Not Creative, but Visa Found a Keeper." *Advertising Age,* February 27, 2006, p. 59.

Gross, Laura. "30 Years of Bank Credit Cards." *American Banker,* September 9, 1994.

Gross, Laura, and David Tyson. "Visa Ad Campaign Emphasizes Wide Acceptance." *American Banker,* September 27, 1985.

Lipman, Joanne. "McCartney: Madison Avenue's Newest Pitchman." *Wall Street Journal,* November 27, 1989.

Maddox, Kate. "Visa Effort Aims to Raise B-to-B Profile." *B to B,* July 19, 2004, p. 4.

Meece, Mickey. "Credit Cards Increase Market Share." *American Banker,* September 23, 1993.

Millman, Nancy. "DDB Needham Management Shaken by Defections." *Chicago Sun-Times,* February 11, 1987.

———. "Visa Charges Ahead with Successful Ads." *Chicago Tribune,* January 30, 1994.

Voight, Joan, and Andrew McMains. "Storming the Citadel." *Adweek,* October 5, 1998.

Woller, Barbara. "Credit Cards Fight to Get Into, and Out of, Consumers' Wallets." *Gannett News Service,* July 26, 1990.

Rebecca Stanfel
Kevin Teague

WORKS LIKE A CHECK CAMPAIGN

OVERVIEW

With little fanfare and virtually no advertising support, Visa U.S.A. introduced the Visa Check Card in 1979. This off-line debit card, which resembled a traditional credit card except that it deducted funds from a user's bank account like a check, was accepted by a wide range of businesses. It was not until the mid-1990s, however, when technology played a stronger role in American culture, that Visa executives decided that there was a vast market for its Check Card. Banks favored the card system because it reduced the amount of transaction fees they had to pay in comparison to covering checks. Merchants welcomed Check Cards because a transaction was approved only if the user had sufficient funds to cover the cost. Hoping to increase consumer awareness, acceptance, and use of the Visa Check Card, Visa released its "Works Like a Check" campaign.

Created by the ad agency BBDO New York, the estimated $45 million television campaign debuted during coverage of the 1996 Summer Olympics. Its emphasis was that using the Check Card was a significantly more convenient way to pay for a purchase than writing a conventional paper check. The first six commercials featured a wide range of celebrities, including 1996 U.S. presidential candidate Bob Dole, professional football player Deion Sanders, and actor Pierce Brosnan. Despite their fame, all the featured celebrities were unable to pay by check without their photo identification. Early spots ended with a voice-over explaining Visa's Check Card: "It works like a check . . . only better." Later spots featured a voice-over that stated, "Get in, get out, get on with life," which was followed by Visa's long-standing tagline, "Visa. It's everywhere you want to be." Visa simultaneously ended the campaign and its longtime relationship with BBDO just before the 2006 Winter Olympics.

Visa was delighted with the campaign's results. According to the Nilson Report, a publication for the credit card industry, charges made on Visa Check Cards skyrocketed from $20.2 billion in 1995 up to $467 billion in 2004. The campaign was critically acclaimed as well; it garnered a plethora of advertising awards, including a coveted Gold Lion at the Cannes International Advertising Festival.

HISTORICAL CONTEXT

Visa U.S.A. first introduced its debit card in 1979, when it issued 917,000 Check Cards. The cards, which were released by banks and credit unions, carried the Visa logo and looked almost identical to the already familiar credit cards. But unlike credit cards, the off-line debit cards deducted the funds used to make the purchase directly from the cardholder's bank account. Off-line debit cards also differed from ATM cards issued by banks in that the check cards did not require the cardholder to use any sort of personal identification number (PIN) or password. Banks found the Check Cards to be quite a boon to their operations. When their customers chose to pay for purchases with debit cards, the bank only paid around 30 cents in transaction fees, as opposed to the 65-cent cost it incurred when a customer paid with a check. Customers did not embrace the concept immediately, however. Many who received the new cards in the mail did not distinguish them from credit cards. Nor were the off-line debit cards "well entrenched in the marketplace," according to *Credit Card Management.*

Visa had never devoted an extensive advertising campaign to promoting its Check Card, although the number of cardholders had climbed slowly to 9.2 million by 1991. But Visa recognized the growth potential of the Check Card. Not only would banks prefer the lower transaction costs of the debit card but merchants would also benefit from the guaranteed payment of the Check Card. In Gallup polls American adults expressed interest in a payment method at checkout counters that was easier to use than a personal check. Moreover, people were increasingly reluctant to carry large amounts of cash, a concern that the Check Card could address.

TARGET MARKET

Because of the ubiquity of personal checks, Visa was interested in reaching virtually every American consumer. The company decided that celebrity spokespeople would be the best way to convey its message to its desired audience. Using a famous face to pitch a product was a tried-and-true advertising strategy. But Visa did not want generic "stars"; it wanted "unmistakable personalities" to deliver its key message—that even the "unmistakable" can be hassled to prove their identity. The next step was to use care and select as its spokespeople those whose appeal was broad enough to cross demographic lines. For instance, Tony Bennett, who appeared in the sixth installment of the campaign, was not only well liked by his retirement-age contemporaries but was also growing increasingly popular among a younger audience of baby boomers and Generation Xers. "His renditions of timeless classics have struck a chord with an entirely new generation of music lovers in their twenties and thirties," said Liz Silver, Visa's senior vice president of advertising.

Visa and BBDO were also sensitive to consumers' potential apprehensions about a new product—especially one that dealt with their finances. Featuring Bob Dole, a retired senator with a reputation for honesty and service, as well as cantankerousness, enhanced the product's credibility in a relaxed and entertaining way. "By having this very conservative, rather traditional, non-techie person use a newfangled way of doing business, you eliminate the objections of a lot of people who were uncomfortable with the product," Alvin Schechter, chairman of the brand-consulting firm Interbrand-Schechter, told *American Banker.*

The campaign's primary appeal, though, was its use of humor, which was intended to make the commercials—and Visa's Check Card—unforgettable to viewers. "Our philosophy is that the commercials need to entertain," Matthew Brispiel, Visa's director of advertising, told *Credit Card Management.* "If it doesn't entertain, it becomes wallpaper, and no one pays attention." Moreover, the campaign's comic elements were designed to put viewers at ease and to allow them to relate to the situations depicted. According to Visa's Silver, each scenario portrayed in the campaign served "to illustrate the frustration felt when paying by check in a light-hearted way. The punch line is that we're not alone—celebrities as recognizable as Tony Bennett can't avoid I.D. hassles."

COMPETITION

The "Works Like a Check" campaign's use of ironic humor and quirky celebrities distinguished Visa from the marketing efforts of its primary competitor, MasterCard. In launching a 1997 campaign for its own debit card, MasterMoney, MasterCard eschewed many of Visa's strategies for reaching its target market. MasterCard's "Priceless" campaign centered on the speed of making purchases with a debit card. One of the spots in that series, called "Paint," related the plight of a man waiting to buy a can of paint in a long hardware-store line while another customer paid with a check. "Al," the slow-moving manager, first had to approve the check. The man finally escaped when another register opened, and he was able to use his debit card quickly. The on-screen caption read: "Knowing you will never have to wait for Al—Priceless." Another spot portrayed the experiences of two women, one who successfully caught her train because she shopped quickly using a MasterMoney card, and the other who missed hers because she made her purchases by check.

Visa spent significantly more on advertising than its rival. In 1997 Visa devoted $46.7 million to promoting its Check Card, compared with the $10.9 million spent to market MasterMoney. Not surprisingly, Visa had issued over 50 million Check Cards by the end of 1997, while only 15.6 million MasterMoney cards had been issued to consumers. MasterCard, however, remained optimistic that its promotional strategy would close this gap at less cost to MasterCard. Instead of running a blitz of high-profile commercials during prime-time television slots, the company tried to win over viewers in other ways. For example, MasterCard took part in a 1997 contest on the television show *Live with Regis and Kathy Lee,* seen by more than 27.6 million consumers. Contestants had the chance to win a MasterMoney card with $5,000 or more on it. "While we may get 30 seconds to promote MasterMoney on a commercial, we'll be getting considerably more exposure through this promotion," MasterCard vice president Irene Katen told *Credit Card Management.*

Analysts noted that in 1996 and 1997 Visa and MasterCard's true competitors were not each other. According to *Credit Card Management,* "the goal for both . . . was persuading Americans to stop using cash and checks and to use debit cards instead." Although Visa held a far larger share of the debit card market, neither its ads nor MasterCard's were intended simply to outdo the other. Rather, both companies sought to build market acceptance for debit cards. Key competition for both Visa Check Card and MasterMoney was checks and the force of habit that kept consumers using them to make purchases. In essence, the campaigns for the only two off-line debit cards were mutually reinforcing. Neither company, however, lost sight of its ultimate goal of dominating the debit card market.

A PROMOTIONAL ALLIANCE

The 60-second James Bond commercial that appeared in 1997 marked a new step for the "Works Like a Check" campaign. Visa forged a promotional alliance with MGM Pictures that was intended both to aid Visa's overall strategy and to hype the MGM-produced James Bond film *Tomorrow Never Dies* that was released at almost the same time that the campaign debuted.

MARKETING STRATEGY

Visa's goal was to increase the profile of its Check Card. In an effort to reach as broad an audience as possible, it opted for a strategy of "," which entailed running the commercials during some of television's highest-rated shows. According to *Credit Card Management,* Visa's commercials reached more viewers than MasterCard's "because of the types of programs on which they appear." The first spot of the campaign, featuring all-world athlete Deion Sanders, premiered during NBC's broadcast of the 1996 Summer Olympics. The best-known commercial of the series, which debuted during the 1997 Super Bowl (at an estimated cost to Visa of $40,000 per second simply for the airtime), featured the recently defeated presidential candidate Bob Dole returning to his hometown of Russell, Kansas. The 60-second spot cut between scenes of Dole's homecoming speech to the residents of Russell, a parade held in his honor, and tributes from local residents who had long-standing relationships with him. A sign in front of a grain silo declared, "Welcome to Russell, Kansas. Home of Bob Dole." After Dole finished lunch at the town diner, he asked the waitress, "Take a check?" "Of course," she replied, and then added with the first stern look in the commercial, "Can I see some I.D.? Driver's license, passport, military I.D., voter..." A voice-over interjected, "Maybe it's time you tried the Visa Check Card. It automatically deducts from your checking account everywhere Visa is accepted. No questions asked. No I.D. needed." The final image was of Dole: "I just can't win," he quipped. The voice-over that closed the spot stated, "The Visa Check Card. It works like a check, only better."

Another commercial, starring Pierce Brosnan, debuted during ABC's *Monday Night Football* telecasts during the fall of 1997. When Brosnan as James Bond tried to write a check to cover his caviar at a Secret Service snack bar, he was asked for I.D. even though he had already successfully passed through a building security system that confirmed his identity by scanning his voice, handprint, and even his retina. According to Matthew Brispiel, Visa's director of advertising, the celebrity in each spot was used as a foil. It was the product that was "held up as the hero."

Despite the overwhelming popularity of the "Works Like a Check" campaign, Visa did have to overcome some negative publicity regarding the possibility that off-line debit cards made consumers easy targets for fraud. Because the card did not require a consumer to enter a PIN at the time of a purchase, some contended that the card was unsafe. The Consumers Union emphasized that, in cases of fraud, it often took banks weeks to reinstate the stolen funds. In response, Visa announced a new cardholder protection policy to alleviate this concern.

In midcampaign Visa adjusted the commercials' voice-over endings. Visa's brand-management team believed that they no longer needed to explain that a Check Card "Works Like a Check." In TV spots released in 1999 the voice-overs touted the convenience of the Check Card with the phrase "Get in, get out, get on with life." Liz Silver, senior vice president of brand management and advertising for Visa, explained the shift in *Brandweek.* "We were moving up that ladder of consumer benefit... to the ability to get on with the things that are truly important to you and enabling your lifestyle," she said.

One spot that aired during the 2002 Super Bowl featured the actor Kevin Bacon struggling to make a purchase with a paper check. Referencing a trivia game called "Six Degrees of Kevin Bacon," in which players linked any actor to Bacon by referencing other actors who had worked with him (the idea being that he could be connected to any film actor in six steps or less), Kevin Bacon was humorously featured trying to prove his own identity to a convenience-store clerk. When denied purchase, Bacon tracked down six people who, through a series of relationships, ultimately linked him to the clerk. For a subsequent Super Bowl commercial the Chinese basketball star Yao Ming and baseball legend Yogi Berra grew frustrated with a clerk who would not accept their checks. The campaign ended in early 2006.

OUTCOME

Early on in the campaign Visa declared its "Works Like a Check" campaign to be an unequivocal success. The number of Check Cards issued rose from 46 million in 1996 to 58 million in 1997. These figures validated Visa's assertion that its advertising campaign had achieved its primary goal of promoting awareness of its debit card. According to the *Business Wire,* Visa attributed the card's growing popularity in large part to its "consistent and high profile advertising." Testing done throughout the campaign revealed that consumers became increasingly more conscious of the option of using Visa's debit card. According to *American Banker,* Visa's tracking index indicated that by July 1997, 80 percent of consumers knew what a debit card was.

The advertising industry lauded the campaign as well. In June 1998 BBDO took top honors in the financial services category at the EFFIE Awards for the "Works Like a Check" commercials. The same year Visa won three Clio Awards for individual ads in the campaign. Moreover, the Bob Dole spot was honored with a Gold Lion at the International Advertising Festival in Cannes, France. The campaign also collected the prestigious 2004 Bronze EFFIE in the Sustained Success category, which honored campaigns over five years old.

The campaign was probably best measured by the increase in Visa Check Card use over the campaign's lifetime. The annual charges to Visa Check Cards surged from $20.2 billion in 1995 to $537 billion in 2004. Unfortunately for BBDO, Visa executives decided to end the campaign just before the 2006 Winter Olympics. Susanne Lyons, Visa's chief marketing officer, explained the campaign's later weaknesses to *USA Today*: "After the ads run for a long time, they become formulaic, and you become wallpaper . . . You have the same comic twist and you get a little predictable." Visa awarded its advertising account to the ad agency TBWA\Chiat\Day.

FURTHER READING

Arndorfer, James. "The Marketing 100: Visa Check Card: Liz Silver." *Advertising Age,* June 30, 1997.

Bloom, Jennifer Kingson. "MasterCard's 'Priceless' Ads Win Top Honors." *American Banker,* June 15, 1999, p. 16.

Coulton, Antoinette. "MasterCard Adds Debit to 'Priceless' Ad Campaign." *American Banker,* June 25, 1998.

Green, Jeffrey. "Take 2 for Debit Commercials" *Credit Card Management,* November 1, 1997.

Howard, Theresa. "Visa to Change Strategies in Upcoming Ads." *USA Today,* January 22, 2006.

Meece, Mickey. "Financial Firms Look to Score with Super Bowl Ads." *American Banker,* January 24, 1997.

"Shifting Gears." *CardFAX,* April 13, 1998.

"Visa Bonds with 007 in Its Latest Check Card Commercial." *PR Newswire,* November 10, 1997.

"Visa Check Card Experiences Double-Digit Growth." *Business Wire,* April 21, 1998.

Wallenstein, Andy. "A Lot of Famous Agencies Are Not Named after Agency Producers." *Shoot,* August 21, 1998, p. 51.

Rebecca Stanfel
Kevin Teague

Volkswagen of America, Inc.

3800 Hamlin Road
Auburn Hills, Michigan 48326
USA
Telephone: (248) 340-5000
Fax: (248) 754-4930
Web site: www.vw.com

■■■

ALL GROWN UP. SORT OF. CAMPAIGN

OVERVIEW

Volkswagen of America, Inc. (VWoA), the U.S. extension of Europe's largest automaker, Volkswagen AG, released its fourth-generation Jetta sedan in 1999. The Jetta's exterior resonated so well with 20-somethings that it outsold all other VWoA models, including the Golf, the GTI, the Passat, the New Beetle, and the EuroVan Camper. In 2004 the Jetta accounted for 40 percent of VWoA's total sales, but company executives feared that Volkswagen was losing customers to competing brands with more power and greater features. In 2005 VWoA released an all-new, fifth-generation Jetta called the A5 Jetta. Automotive critics raved about its upgraded interior and engineering but criticized its bland exterior. To attract consumers who had favored the 1999 Jetta but now wanted more from a car, VWoA released a campaign titled "All Grown Up. Sort Of."

The campaign was created by VWoA's longtime ad agency Arnold Worldwide of Boston. It included print ads, radio spots, television spots, and alternative mediums such as wooden puzzles, coloring books, and a six-minute film titled *The Check Up.* The campaign debuted on March 19, 2005. The first commercial, "Airport," featured a young businessman using his A5 Jetta to shuttle an older, conservative executive from the airport. When the stodgy executive turned on the Jetta's radio to "check the scores," the speakers blared out heavy-metal music. The spot ended with the tagline "The new Jetta. It's all grown up. Sort of." Although the campaign's cost was undisclosed, Volkswagen spent an estimated $30 million on Jetta advertising in 2004, according to the media researcher Nielsen Monitor-Plus. VWoA ended its relationship with Arnold in September 2005.

The campaign earned Best of Show honors at the 2005 Francis W. Hatch Awards, which recognized creative excellence within New England's advertising community. Some VWoA car dealers criticized the campaign for not informing customers about the A5 Jetta's features. Nevertheless, the campaign helped Jetta sales increase 25 percent in the first three months of 2005 compared to the same period the previous year.

HISTORICAL CONTEXT

When the ad agency Doyle Dane Bernbach of New York released VWoA's "Think Small" campaign in the 1950s, automotive advertising in America changed forever. Before "Think Small," print ads for automotive brands typically depicted large, showy cars against imposing backdrops. In contrast, "Think Small" featured one small image of a Volkswagen Beetle juxtaposed on a stark white background. "It was one of the first advertising campaigns to treat audiences like they had some intelligence.

It was tongue-in-cheek and unexpected," Linda Scott, associate professor of advertising, art, and design at the University of Illinois, said to *Automotive News.*

In 1986 Doyle Dane Bernbach merged with the ad agency Needham Harper & Steers of Chicago to become DDB Needham Worldwide. During the latter half of the 1980s the expanded agency created campaigns that touted Volkswagen's German engineering. Spots featured Volkswagens speeding around test tracks. In 1990 DDB Needham Worldwide crafted a campaign around the German word for driving pleasure, "Fahrvergnugen," which was paired with a small stick figure. After experiencing waning sales VWoA briefly awarded its advertising account to Berlin Cameron Doyle and finally to Arnold in March 1995. Arnold's first executions featured the tagline "Drivers Wanted," which Arnold used for 10 years. Because VWoA did not release a new model during Arnold's first two years, the ad agency cross-promoted Volkswagen with Trek mountain bikes and K2 skis.

The 1999 Jetta resonated so well with younger customers that VWoA claimed to have the automotive industry's lowest average customer age: 33 years old. Over the next three years, however, the Jetta lost ground to competing brands, such as the Audi A4 and the MINI Cooper. Although its exterior remained popular, the fourth-generation Jetta's lack of power and limited features were cited for decreasing sales. To inject juvenescence into the brand Volkswagen engineers upgraded the fifth-generation Jetta, called the A5 Jetta, in size and features. According to automotive critics, the Jetta's popular exterior was lost in the upgrade. To suggest that the larger, more expensive A5 Jetta still exhibited the youthful uniqueness of its 1999 predecessor, Arnold released the "All Grown Up. Sort Of" campaign.

TARGET MARKET

The campaign targeted college graduates who were beginning to make their first adult life changes, including purchasing a home, starting lifelong careers, or committing to long-term personal relationships. Both of the campaign's TV spots featured 20-somethings performing notably adult activities, while still listening to hard-rock music. The campaign reached for "that person in the in-between stage in life," David Weist, Arnold's creative director for the campaign, told *Adweek.* "Where they're half grown up and still half a kid. They have a better job, they might have a steady relationship with someone, but they still can't quite throw that futon away or the monkey lamp. That's where the car is."

Volkswagen dealers criticized the spots for not providing enough imagery or information about the newly engineered Jetta. Ad critics, however, remarked that a strategy focusing more on image than on information was effective. If the tech-savvy target connected with the content, according to Arnold, the target would later research the Jetta themselves. "For the younger consumer, it's all about image and about wanting to feel good about yourself," Wes Brown, a partner in the Los Angeles marketing firm Iceology, explained to *Automotive News.* "If you've got a good image, they'll come in, and the product will speak for itself."

The fifth-generation Jetta was designed for a more affluent target than the previous Jetta. The A5 Jetta's baseline price of $20,390 was nearly $4,000 above that of the 1999 model. The A5 was also 17 centimeters longer, loaded with more features, and outfitted with a larger engine. In addition, according to automotive critics, it resembled the Toyota Corolla, a car popular with 30-something drivers. One of the campaign's spots, "Independence Day," featured a man and a woman in their late 20s who used an A5 Jetta to tote large speakers off to a newly purchased home. The spot implied that the fun-loving couple had moved from an apartment to a house just so that they could dance to loud rock music.

JETTA: IT'S A BREEZE

After Volkswagen's marketing team noticed that North Americans preferred sedans and coupes over hatchback-shaped automobiles, Volkswagen released its first Jetta, a larger version of the Golf hatchback. The first Jetta was released worldwide in 1980. Later generations emerged in 1984, 1991, 1998, and 2005. The original version's name came from the jet stream—the swift air currents that circle the earth. Although Canada, the United States, and South Africa retained the Jetta name across all five generations, the 1991 model in Europe was called Vento after the Italian word for "wind." Continuing its tempestuous naming convention, Europe's fourth generation model was titled Bora, the name of an air current above the Adriatic Sea. The 2005 version was once again called the Jetta in Europe but not across the globe. It took the name Sagitar in China, Bora in Mexico, and Vento in regions of South America.

COMPETITION

While automotive critics compared the new Jetta's exterior to that of the Toyota Corolla, they likened its interior to that of an Audi—a brand partially owned by Volkswagen AG. Although the baseline Audi A4 and

Audi A3 were slightly pricier than the A5 Jetta, Audi's advertising targeted a similar market. In March 2005 Audi of America, the North American branch of Audi, released its "Never Follow" campaign to herald the release of its seventh-generation A4 sedan. One campaign promotion asked consumers to locate nine Internet banner ads that highlighted new A4 features. Participants in the contest were eligible for a two-year lease on a new A4. Other prizes included PalmOne and Bose products. The campaign targeted 25- to 39-year-old men and was developed by ad agency McKinney + Silver of Raleigh, North Carolina. "We decided to engage the user, let them interact with the brand and let them see what's changed," Erin Bredemann, interactive strategist at McKinney + Silver, said to *Adweek*. "You collect these parts and also learn about the car through the game."

In June 2005 McKinney + Silver released its "The Art of the Heist" campaign to announce the all-new Audi A3, with a suggested retail price of more than $26,000. The campaign told the story of two hit men chasing the fictional Ian Yarbrough, who had recovered a stolen Audi A3 containing valuable computer files, across America. A plethora of media were used to tell the campaign's narrative, including one 30-second television commercial, print ads, outdoor ads, online banners, and the website www.AudiUsa.com/A3. According to Audi, more than 200,000 people interacted with the Audi website in a single day of the campaign.

MARKETING STRATEGY

The campaign's two television spots, "Airport" and "Independence Day," debuted on March 19, 2005. "Airport" showed a 20-something man picking up his older, more conservative colleagues at the airport. At the spot's beginning the 20-something impressed the older men with a well-articulated business conversation. The mood inside the A5 Jetta deteriorated, however, when the man seated next to him stated that he wanted to "check the scores" and turned on the car stereo. Rock music blasted out of the speakers. The spot "Independence Day" featured a young couple dancing in their apartment to the Kings of Leon rock song "Molly's Chambers." After a downstairs neighbor complained, the couple used their A5 Jetta to transport larger speakers to what the spot later revealed was their new house. The commercial ended with the two dancing inside their new living room. Both spots concluded with the copy "The new Jetta. It's all grown up. Sort of."

To the dismay of Volkswagen dealers, neither spot explained the new Jetta's features. Also, the commercials rarely aired images of the A5's revamped design. Defending the campaign strategy in *Automotive News,* VWoA vice president Len Hunt said, "Everybody reaches for the obvious, 'I'm going to spend $20 million, so I better show what the car's got.' . . . We know our audience loves our brand, and we've made a name for ourselves with our ads, and we're sticking to that. We desperately try to keep this VW character in our ads."

For a less traditional effort of the campaign, Arnold hired uniformed 20-somethings to disperse coloring books and wooden puzzles with the "All grown up. Sort of" theme within Boston, Chicago, San Francisco, Miami, Washington, D.C., and Seattle. The coloring books featured adults performing mundane tasks, such as washing dishes, computing taxes, and engaging in boring conversations, until being "rescued" by A5 Jettas.

Two-page foldout print ads were published in national magazines. Before the ads were unfolded, new Jettas appeared in serene settings such as in front of an upscale restaurant. Once the ads were opened, images showed much rowdier Jettas performing stunts such as driving in tight circles ("doing doughnuts") in the snow. One ad featured two nude owners running along the beach. "It's a different walk to take," Brown said in *Automotive News.* "Do you talk about all these features that are new to you and your buyer, or do you do it more abstract[ly] and say, 'If this is the way you lead your life, this is the brand for you.' European brands tend to go the more abstract way."

Arnold also created for the campaign a six-minute film titled *The Check Up,* starring Joe Pantoliano, formerly of the mob-family TV drama *The Sopranos.* Two million DVDs were inserted in *Entertainment Weekly.* Another 1.5 million were made available at Volkswagen dealerships. The film's narrative featured a 31-year-old man being investigated by a case officer for something called the "Federal Commission of Adulthood." The investigator, played by Pantoliano, monitored the maturation of young adults and made sure that the 31-year-old was accruing responsibilities. In addition to *The Check Up,* the DVD contained interviews with Volkswagen designers and driving footage of the new Jetta.

OUTCOME

Although the campaign helped A5 Jetta sales for the first three months of 2005 increase 25 percent over Jetta sales for the same period in 2004, other Volkswagen brands were underselling. Comprehensive sales for VWoA's first seven months of 2005 were 22 percent below the previous year. Volkswagen eventually severed its 10-year relationship with Arnold in September 2005 and awarded the account to Crispin Porter + Bogusky without a repitch from Arnold. Arnold executives blamed their loss on Kerri Martin, the new director for brand innovation at VWoA, who had previously served as the marketing communications manager for BMW of North America. Martin had worked closely with Crispin Porter + Bogusky to relaunch BMW's MINI Cooper in 2001.

"All Grown Up. Sort Of" earned Best of Show honors at the 2005 Hatch Awards, an annual event organized by the Ad Club of New England. Arnold executives readily defended their work after their campaign collected the award. "Certainly [the win is] bittersweet because VW was so much a part of the agency," Ron Lawner, chief creative officer at Arnold, said to *Adweek*. "But I think [the awards] speak very loudly about how modern and integrated this agency really is. We won for a body of fully integrated campaigns, and to be slapped for not thinking outside the box when we in fact live outside the box [is frustrating.]" Lawner was speaking only a few days after VWoA announced that it would use Crispin Porter + Bogusky.

FURTHER READING

Crain, Rance. "Integrated Ideas Are Not King at Frat-Boy Jokester Crispin Porter." *Advertising Age,* November 14, 2005, p. 22.

Creamer, Matthew, and Jean Halliday. "How Crispin Drove Off with VW." *Advertising Age,* September 12, 2005, p. 1.

Dutka, Elaine. "Volkswagen Commercial Now Available on DVD." *Los Angeles Times,* March 27, 2005, p. G7.

Elliott, Stuart. "With Sales Slumping, VW Switches Agencies." *New York Times,* September 7, 2005, p. 2.

Geist, Laura Clark. "Humor Is Hallmark of VW Ads." *Automotive News,* October 17, 2005, p. 36.

———. "New VW Passat Advertising Highlights Features, Safety." *Automotive News,* September 19, 2005, p. 16.

Harper, Brian. "Grown Up, but Will Anyone Notice?" *Montreal (Quebec) Gazette,* April 13, 2005, p. E5.

———. "Volkswagen Has a Lot Riding on Its New Jetta." *Edmonton (Alberta) Journal,* April 15, 2005, p. 13.

Joyce, Kathleen M. "Talking Shop." *Promo,* October 1, 2005, p. 24.

LaReau, Jamie. "VW Pushes Lifestyle over Product in Ads." *Automotive News,* April 4, 2005, p. 28D.

Lazare, Lewis. "It's No Secret that Volkswagen Needs the New Jetta to Be a Certified Hit in the North American Market." *Chicago Sun-Times,* March 22, 2005, p. 51.

Sabatini, Jeff. "Once a Standout, Now Lost in the Crowd." *New York Times,* September 18, 2005, p. 1.

Scanlan, Dan. "The Redesigned 2005 Jetta: 'All Grown Up.'" *Jacksonville Florida Times-Union,* July 9, 2005, p. G-1.

Kevin Teague

DRIVERS WANTED CAMPAIGN

OVERVIEW

While Volkswagen had been the leading import car company in the United States during the 1960s and early '70s, by the late 1970s it had begun to lose its base of American consumers to emerging imports produced by companies such as Honda Motor Co. and Toyota Motor Corporation. In the early 1990s Volkswagen's sales hit a low of 49,533 units from a peak of 569,696 units in 1970. In addition to the low sales, the quality of cars being produced at Volkswagen's Mexico plant had become notoriously poor. The Germany-based automaker began considering a complete withdrawal from the North American market. In an attempt to inject the joy of driving back into its brand and improve its U.S. sales, Volkswagen released a campaign called "Drivers Wanted."

Created by the ad agency Arnold Fortuna Lawner & Cabot, which was soon renamed Arnold Worldwide, the television, billboard, Internet, and print campaign first surfaced in July 1995. It was created with Volkswagen's estimated $110 million North American advertising budget. Initial TV spots featured quirky and fast-paced content that was intended to target all consumers younger than 45, but the company particularly wanted to attract those between the ages of 18 and 34. Set to rock music and filmed in a quick-cutting style reminiscent of MTV videos, the campaign debuted with eight television spots suggesting that the Volkswagen Golf, a compact hatchback, helped drivers engage more fully with life. The spots' voice-over explained, "On the road of life, there are passengers and there are drivers. Drivers Wanted." The "Drivers Wanted" slogan would be used in almost every Volkswagen vehicle launch for the next 10 years. Volkswagen ended its relationship with Arnold on December 5, 2005, which served as the official end date of the "Drivers Wanted" campaign.

During Arnold's 10-year stint with Volkswagen, "Drivers Wanted" reversed the automaker's sales decline and eventually tripled its North American sales. Besides collecting a plethora of ad-industry awards, the campaign was considered by automotive critics to feature one of the most recognizable ad slogans in automotive history.

HISTORICAL CONTEXT

Volkswagen entered the U.S. new-car market in 1949 with the introduction of the Beetle. The company joined forces with agency Doyle Dane Bernbach in 1959, and this partnership led to what *Advertising Age* named "some of the most celebrated advertising ever done." These simple, yet tremendously effective, print pieces helped make the Beetle one of the most successful cars in U.S. history. A generation of young Americans—the baby boomers—embraced the Beetle for its low price, its fuel efficiency, and its cute appearance. By 1970 the Beetle "was an emblem of the time," according to the *Boston Globe.* At its peak Volkswagen sold a stunning 569,696 Beetles in the United States alone. In the 1970s, however,

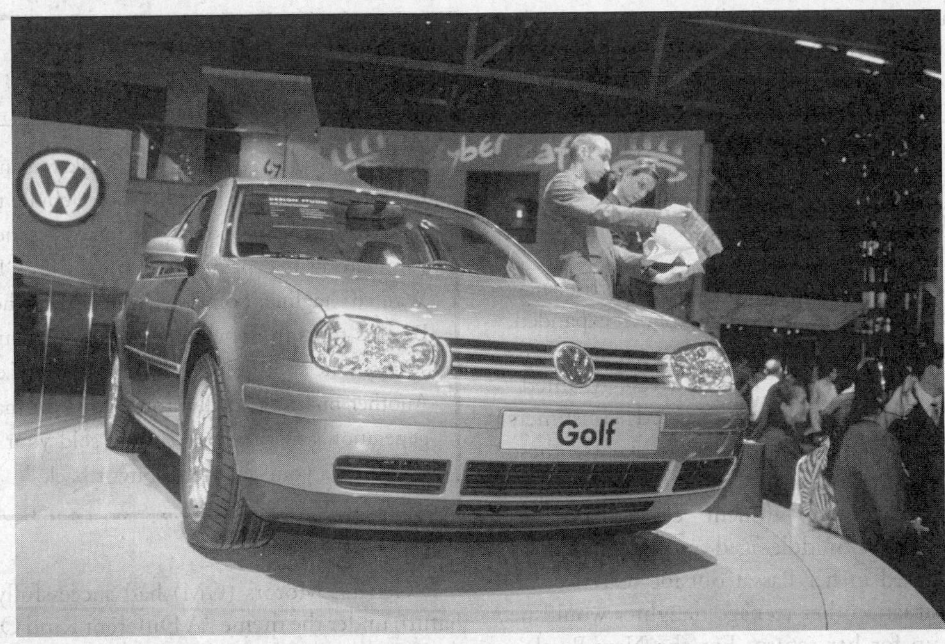

Volkswagen's Golf. © RÉGIS BOSSU/SYGMA/CORBIS.

Volkswagen faced new competition from Japanese automakers such as Toyota and Honda that followed Volkswagen's formula of providing both quality and value. By 1979 Japanese cars had begun to dominate the market, and Volkswagen struggled to redefine itself. The company lurched from one marketing effort to another with an array of agencies at the helm, never effectively conveying a post-Beetle identity. During the 1990s "Fahrvergnügen," which was the German word for "driving pleasure," became one of Volkswagen's largest campaigns. The effort was created by the ad agency DDB Needham and featured a simple stick figure with the Volkswagen logo. Despite the campaign's attempt to reinvigorate Volkswagen's brand, sales still dropped. DDB Needham was eventually relieved from the account.

"There was a time when people throughout the country knew Volkswagen," a senior executive told the *Wall Street Journal.* "Somewhere along the way, we lost our sense of direction. The public forgot who we were." U.S. sales fell to an all-time low of 49,533 cars in 1993. Some analysts speculated that Volkswagen—still a European powerhouse—would abandon its American market.

TARGET MARKET

In April 1995 Volkswagen chose Boston-based agency Arnold Communications (then Arnold Fortuna Lawner & Cabot) to forge a new image for the company. Arnold "determined that young people were the core market," according to *Advertising Age,* and then crafted "Drivers Wanted" around the values, needs, and desires of this group. Although its target audience was adults aged 21 to 44, the initial ads "skewed towards twenty-somethings looking for something beyond a boring econo-box," said *USA Today.* Instead of setting its sights on a mass market, as it had done in the past, Volkswagen sought to appeal to this narrow segment. Successfully pitching a product to Generation Xers was no easy task, however. Raised in the era of cable, and therefore used to dozens of television channels and their incessant commercials, Xers were more accustomed to advertising than their forebears—and also more impatient. If a commercial bored them, they changed the channel. Xers were also renowned cynics, inured and unreceptive to traditional advertising techniques.

"Drivers Wanted" tried to connect with this audience. Humor and an aggressive "anti-advertising" stance were both essential to the campaign. Unlike traditional car advertising, which was heavy on lists of attributes and footage of cars whizzing around curves, "Drivers Wanted" recognized that this hard sell was rather ineffective with Xers. Instead the Volkswagen campaign used clever narratives to convey the intangible essence of the brand. In a commercial titled "Sunday Afternoon," two young men tooled about in their Jetta with no particular place to go. They found a chair by the side of the road and loaded it into their hatchback. When its malodorous qualities became evident, they abandoned it on the street once more. "It's the commercial about nothing," a

Volkswagen employee told the *Wall Street Journal.* The spot humorously depicted the "slacker" mentality for which Generation X was criticized. The voice-over ("It fits your life. Or complete lack thereof.") wittily conveyed, as one Arnold executive said in a press release, that "we aren't always doing cool, active things." "Sunday Afternoon" also featured a sound track popular among college students.

As "Drivers Wanted" continued to advertise new Volkswagen models, the campaign's target market expanded. When Volkswagen introduced an updated version of its more upscale Passat in 1997, the "Drivers Wanted" target included commercials that targeted consumers above the age of 30. Like the previous spots, these commercials relied on slice-of-life vignettes and humor to reach older and more affluent consumers. For instance, in one spot a middle-aged mother embarked on a date. She paused in her Passat outside to reflect on the irony of the situation: her teenage daughter would be the one waiting up for her return. For the New Beetle's 1998 debut, "Drivers Wanted" first targeted baby boomers, or Americans born between 1946 and 1964. After the New Beetle proved unexpectedly popular with members of Generation X, the campaign was directed at two audiences, targeting baby boomers with spots that referenced the 1960s and Generation Xers with content that was more contemporary. The target for "Drivers Wanted" would be adjusted throughout its 10-year lifespan according to what car model was being advertised.

COMPETITION

Volkswagen's line of small cars faced competition from a bevy of American and Japanese companies that strove to attract the same youthful audience as "Drivers Wanted." In 1994 the Chrysler Corporation introduced the Neon, a compact auto offered under both its Dodge and Plymouth labels. With ad agency BBDO Worldwide, Chrysler created the $85 million "Hi" campaign, directed at consumers aged 18 to 29. This print, outdoor, and television effort ran during high-profile events, such as the Super Bowl, and gained a great deal of attention as a result. The spots attempted to imbue the Neon with a likable, distinctly human personality. Commercials showed the little car driving through unusual landscapes, and at the end of each spot the Neon stopped facing the camera and delivered the campaign's tagline: "Hi" (which was written above the car). One print piece declared, "Hi. What could be friendlier than Neon's spacious cab-forward interior?" and answered itself, "It's friendly right down to the sticker. Gotta run." Chrysler continued "Hi" until 1997, when it incorporated Neon's advertising under an umbrella brand campaign.

> ### DÉJÀ VU
>
> Buoyed by its revived fortunes, Volkswagen resurrected the legendary Beetle in 1998. To celebrate the debut of the New Beetle, Volkswagen created a series of commercials and print ads that used the "Drivers Wanted" tagline. Some slyly referred to the original Beetle's roots in the counterculture movement of the 1960s. One spot quipped "More Power. Less Flower." Another put a decidedly ironic twist on that generation's maturation: "If you sold your soul in the '80s, here's your chance to buy it back."

General Motors (GM) had successfully marketed its Saturn under the theme "A Different Kind Of Company, A Different Kind Of Car" since the brand's introduction in 1990. An analyst for the *Tennessean* praised the campaign as "the most brilliant marketing campaign of any car in the last decade." Saturn's commercials, like those in "Drivers Wanted," favored vignettes about its drivers over traditional car-advertising tactics. In 1994 GM spent $141 million on advertising Saturn. Commercials included the depiction of a security guard who logged 100,000 miles on his Saturn without ever leaving his small community.

In 2002 German automaker Bayerische Motoren-Werke AG (BMW) reintroduced the MINI Cooper, which many automobile analysts considered a direct competitor with the New Beetle. BMW hired the agency Crispin Porter + Bogusky to handle advertising for the brand. To promote the car's recreational qualities, the agency famously strapped MINI Coopers to the roofs of SUVs and drove them across America. MINI Coopers were also parked in the bleachers of sporting venues. *Playboy* even allowed a MINI Cooper to be featured as a 2002 centerfold.

One of Volkswagen's later competitors was the Toyota Scion, which debuted in 2004. Scion was a brand created by Toyota to target Generation Y consumers, people born between 1978 and 2000. Seventy percent of Scion's marketing budget was spent on lifestyle events, including small-venue concerts. Because Generation Y was considerably more savvy about technology than older generations, Scion allowed its customers to accessorize their cars via the Internet before even stepping foot on a lot.

MARKETING STRATEGY

Volkswagen employed a variety of traditional and innovative marketing strategies to outmaneuver its competitors.

The company aired its "Drivers Wanted" spots during television programming that was popular with its target audience. The campaign debuted on *Seinfeld* and *ER,* and later installments of the campaign ran during Generation Xer favorites *Melrose Place, Mad about You, Saturday Night Live,* and *The Late Show with David Letterman,* as well as during NFL games. In 1997 commercials appeared during *The X-Files* and *Millennium* and on a controversial episode of the sitcom *Ellen,* in which the eponymous main character revealed that she was gay. While controversy-fearing car companies chose not to advertise during this particular episode, Volkswagen "figur[ed] that the subject matter [was] in keeping with its own slightly edgy pitch to young adults," according to the *Wall Street Journal.* "Volkswagen is a very cool, progressive company and isn't into prejudice," an Arnold representative told the *Journal.* "People who have alternative lifestyles also make money and buy cars." Volkswagen sought to place its print ads in publications that were read by its desired audience, including *Rolling Stone, Shape, Outdoor,* and *Men's Health.*

Volkswagen also pursued unique avenues to widen the reach of "Drivers Wanted." Volkswagen entered into a partnership with Trek bicycles and K2 Ski equipment and offered its Jetta with a special car rack and a mountain bike, skis, or a snowboard. Special commercials touted the arrangement. A spokesperson explained the strategy in a 1996 press release: "'Drivers Wanted' is all about connecting to life. The activity of mountain biking, like driving a Volkswagen, is also about connecting back to life and the outside world." The slogan would outlive its original 1995 campaign and be used for the remainder of Arnold's relationship with Volkswagen, serving to introduce models such as the New Beetle, the Touareg SUV, and the Phaeton.

In 1998 "Drivers Wanted" was the slogan for the "New Beetle" campaign, which used copy such as "Less Flower. More Power" and "If you sold your soul in the '80s, here's your chance to buy it back." Later "New Beetle" advertisements featured the copy "Hellooo rich hippies!" to target baby boomers nostalgic for the 1960s. "Drivers Wanted" surfaced again to advertise the fourth-generation Jetta and the redesigned Golf, both of which were made available in 1999. That same year Volkswagen executives claimed that the average Volkswagen buyer was 33 years old, the youngest average age in the North American automobile industry.

In 2002 Volkswagen's U.S. sales began to decline. "We didn't have the product strength, and the brand was sort of feeling its way at the same time," Karen Marderosian, director of marketing for Volkswagen of America, explained to *Automotive News.* "I do think that the advertising had become watered down mainly by...what was going on with the brand overall." Between 2002 and 2004 Volkswagen sales dropped nearly 20 percent. A decrease in Volkswagen's quality exacerbated the problem. According to a "Vehicle Dependability Survey" conducted by marketing-information firm J.D. Power and Associates in 2004, Volkswagens reportedly exhibited 40 percent more problems than the industry average.

During the final year of the "Drivers Wanted" slogan, Arnold released an integrated campaign for the New Beetle that touted the bubble-shaped car as a "Force of Good." The agency hired "ambassadors of good" to feed parking meters and hand out refreshments. In 2005 Arnold advertised the fifth-generation Volkswagen Jetta with a campaign titled "All grown up. Sort of," which also retained the "Drivers Wanted" slogan. On December 5, 2005, Volkswagen officially awarded its $340 million advertising budget to Crispin Porter + Bogusky. That date marked the end of the "Drivers Wanted" campaign.

OUTCOME

Volkswagen directly correlated its rising sales and brand recognition in the American car market with "Drivers Wanted." Sales in 1995 rose 18.5 percent from the previous year, to reach 115,114 cars, and Volkswagen noted in a press release that "consumers and dealers are responding positively to our marketing message." In 1996 Volkswagen's sales increased 18.1 percent, while the overall market grew a mere 1.8 percent. An Arnold executive told the *Boston Globe* that Volkswagen had "seen positive sales results from the first day 'Drivers Wanted' ads went on the air." The advertising industry also deemed the campaign a success. At the 1997 Best of Broadcasting Awards, "Drivers Wanted" took home the top honors, and the campaign won an EFFIE Award in 1998.

The campaign helped Volkswagen triple its North American sales. By 2005 "Drivers Wanted" was not just an advertising campaign but the foundation of all Volkswagen marketing. Unfortunately for Arnold, the automaker's sales had begun to decline in 2002. Executives at Volkswagen blamed the sales loss on lackluster advertising and on the poor quality of vehicles made at the company's main Mexico plant. After Volkswagen hired MINI Cooper's marketing and communications manager, Kerri Martin, to lead Volkswagen's North American marketing, Arnold was replaced by Crispin Porter + Bogusky, the agency credited for MINI's successful reappearance in 2002. During its heyday "Drivers Wanted" was considered the most recognizable tagline in the automotive industry, according to the global market-research firm NOP World.

FURTHER READING

Beatty, Sally Goll. "Volkswagen Isn't Steering Clear of Controversial 'Ellen' Episode." *Wall Street Journal,* April 25, 1997.

Bosman, Julie. "VW's Quirky Campaign to Revive U.S. Sales." *New York Times,* February 17, 2006, p. 2.

Box, Terry. "Drivers Wanted for VW Reversal." *Albany (NY) Times Union,* July 17, 2005, p. B1.

Enrico, Dottie. "VW Isn't Bugged by Consumer Response." *USA Today,* December 16, 1995.

Garfield, Bob. "Bob Garfield's Ad Review." *Advertising Age,* December 8, 1997.

Gatlin, Greg. "Bugged about Sales, VW Dumps Ad Agency." *Boston Herald,* September 7, 2005, p. 25.

Newman, Heather. "Saturn on the Line." *Tennessean,* May 28, 1985.

Noyes, Jesse. "In Your Face." *Boston Herald,* September 16, 2005, p. 29.

Parpis, Eleftheria. "New Directions." *Adweek,* January 27, 1997.

Reidy, Chris. "Shifting into High Gear." *Boston Globe,* July 19, 1995.

———. "Volkswagen Campaign Found Its Drivers." *Boston Globe,* January 4, 1997.

Sante, Mike. "Wanted: Serious Drivers." *Orlando Sentinel,* December 14, 1995.

Serafin, Raymond. "It Was Billed as a Historic Moment." *Advertising Age,* September 13, 1993.

Wollenberg, Skip. "Get In. Be Moved. Mazda's New Ads Court People Who Like to Drive." Associated Press, March 2, 1998.

Rebecca Stanfel
Kevin Teague

LIVE LARGE CAMPAIGN

OVERVIEW

In November 1997 Volkswagen of America introduced an advertising campaign for its redesigned Passat. Arnold Communications, the Boston-based ad agency that won the lucrative $110 million North American Volkswagen advertising account in 1995, had created much momentum with its "Drivers Wanted" campaign, marketing the Golf and the Jetta to a target audience between the ages of 18 and 34. Arnold hoped to carry that momentum into the new Passat campaign. Since the Passat was a larger automobile than either the Golf or the Jetta, Arnold highlighted this feature with the tag line that urged customers to "Live Large."

Marketing the Passat represented a distinct challenge for VW and Arnold on several different levels: first, the redesigned Passat was geared toward an older, more affluent market than VW traditionally targeted; second, the new Passat was positioned to compete with Mercedes and BMW, a departure from VW's traditional competitors, the Japanese quartet of Honda, Toyota, Nissan, and Mazda; and third, this Passat represented a major status shift for Volkswagen from the image of the "people's car," exemplified by the original Beetle, to that of a higher-end car of prestige. Transforming Volkswagen's reputation to promote the Passat as a luxury car promised to be difficult if not impossible, some critics suggested, but other observers noted Volkswagen's wisdom in expanding its market.

Since the "Live Large" campaign represented only the first step in VW's long-term diversification project, the three commercials did not necessarily confront all three of these challenges simultaneously. Instead, the "Live Large" spots depicted characters forced to make choices. One spot showed a man at an intersection where he had to choose not which direction to go but between sowing more wild oats or getting married; in another spot a man in his forties visited a diner and tried rhubarb pie for the first time, prompting him to try other new experiences; and the last spot contrasted a middle-aged single mother's anxiety about driving to a date with her teenage daughter's higher anxiety about mom's timely arrival home that evening. Whereas the "Drivers Wanted" campaign had focused on less-consequential choices, such as whether to keep a scavenged easy chair that smelled bad, the "Live Large" campaign specifically addressed more mature decisions and episodes. While critics wondered what relevance these ads had to the car, the "Live Large" campaign set the foundation for Volkswagen's change of image.

HISTORICAL CONTEXT

In the late 1950s Volkswagen established itself in the U.S. automobile market with a counterintuitive marketing strategy based on honesty, humor, and humility rather than hyperbole. Bill Bernbach had founded DDB New York, Volkswagen's ad agency for its first 40 years in the United States, on the assumption that advertising was not an exact science determined by data but rather a creative art appealing to intelligence and emotion. Bernbach's Beetle ads set a precedent in car marketing by creating a "personality" for the car. Paul McCann of the London *Independent* pointed out Bernbach's savvy in realizing that "being ironic about selling to the public was a really successful way to sell to the public."

"This insight has become the basis of many subsequent advertising campaigns," said Tony Cox, creative director of DDB New York. "Indeed, you can hear papers about it delivered at every advertising convention you go to—nowadays its usually called post-modernism." Arnold Communications overhauled the faltering image of Volkswagen (sales had reached their lowest point in

1993) with its decidedly post-modern "Drivers Wanted" campaign. The outstanding spot of that campaign, "Sunday Afternoon," which featured two slackers with nothing better to do than tool around in their Volkswagen, struck a chord with its Generation X target market. Lance Jensen, Arnold's creative director who wrote the commercial, spoke with *The Boston Globe*'s John Koch in words that echoed Bernbach's philosophies: Jensen called advertising the "unholy alliance of art and commerce," but he also explained that the "unfortunate thing about advertising, and the wonderful thing, is that it's subjective. It's not math; you can't go to business school and find out how to make great advertising. That's frustrating for clients and people who have budgets. It's a tough gamble."

After the success of the "Drivers Wanted" campaign, Arnold was challenged to produce a similarly successful but very different campaign for the larger, more luxurious Passat. But Arnold had managed to maintain consistency with Volkswagen's history of outstanding advertising by following the same technique established by DDB New York under Bernbach: the coupling of honesty with irony. Arnold's campaign for Passat extended the trajectory of VW advertising by fusing the Beetle marketing strategy of creating personality for the car with the "Drivers Wanted" technique of focusing on the driver, resulting in a hybrid that simultaneously described the car and the driver with its tag line "Live Large."

DON'T SWEAT IT

In England advertising for the Passat raised quite a stink. Volkswagen ran ads depicting the sweat-stained backs of naked models to promote air-conditioning in the cabins of its cars. Within days Citroen launched almost-identical ads—by coincidence both companies worked up the same idea simultaneously, Citroen claimed. VW elected not to pursue any legal action against Citroen, since both carmakers were imitating a previous Sure anti-perspirant campaign. Subsequently, however, Citroen ran ads pointing out that VW charged 500 pounds more than Citroen for air-conditioning. Nigel Brotherton, VW's advertising manager, countered that Citroen's claim was "unethical and erroneous" since it cited incomparable car models: a direct comparison would have revealed that Citroen's comparable models—the AX and the ZX, equivalents of VW's Polo and Golf—didn't even offer air-conditioning. VW's comparable model, the Passat, offered air-conditioning as a standard feature. Brotherton stated, "We were prepared to be gentlemanly about Citroen using the same ads. It now seems that was the wrong course of action."

TARGET MARKET

The success of the "Drivers Wanted" campaign helped strengthen VW's loyal base of customers under age 35, who represented more than half of its sales. Looking toward the future, though, VW realized that its current customers would not remain under 35 forever, so it devised a means of retaining its following through their middle years. As people grow, so do their incomes, the sizes of their families, and their expectations of comfort and status, VW reasoned. In response to these trends VW designed a larger, more luxurious, and more expensive car. The Passat specifically targeted those between 30 and 50 years of age with a household income of more than $80,000. Most of the target market would be married, hold college degrees, and one-third would have children living under their roofs.

Some questioned Volkswagen's logic. Wes Brown of Nextrend, an auto consulting firm, suggested that VW should maintain its strategic status quo instead of attempting to evolve. "I mean, this is VW—people's car. It'll be amazing if they can pull it off," he said. "They've got a lock in gen X with Golf and Jetta. The numbers show that the only thing close is the Honda Civic. Now it sounds as if they're about to move away from gen X in price." Brown assumed, however, that this generation was a static entity, while VW realized that Generation X would eventually grow out of its labels and stereotypes and forge its own future.

The transition from targeting one market to targeting another proved to be a slower process than expected. An *Ad Track* survey reported by *USA Today* revealed that Arnold's advertising still appealed more to the "Drivers Wanted" target market than to the "Live Large" target market. Of the consumers asked who were between the ages of 18 and 29, 14 percent liked the ads a lot while only 8 percent of those between 30 and 49 said they liked the spots a lot. However, the goal of the advertising was not to poll well but rather to sell more cars, which happened after the "Live Large" campaign.

COMPETITION

Volkswagen intended the Passat to attract drivers from traditional competitors—makers of Japanese and European mid-sized sedans—as well as "hip Americans who own a Chrysler Cirrus or Dodge Stratus, for example, but want a more active and enthusiastic driving experience," according to senior marketing executive Steve Wilhite. More significantly, Volkswagen AG chairman Ferdinand Piech declared at a press conference at the international headquarters in Wolfsburg, Germany, that he planned to pit the Passat against entry-level models from BMW and Mercedes in head-to-head competition in the United States. The main obstacle to this strategy was overcoming the pervasive association of VW with the Beetle. The legacy of the Beetle's success in the United States haunted these efforts to redefine the image and reputation of VW.

Japanese carmakers overcame a similar obstacle by diversifying brand names, with each major company spinning off an upscale brand: Honda created Acura, Toyota created Lexus, and Nissan created Infiniti. Volkswagen was structured to do the same, with its own upscale brand, Audi. However, VW wanted each of its brands to be its own premium marque, with overlapping instead of graduated markets. Volkswagen would thus compete not only with Honda, Nissan, and Toyota, as it traditionally had, but also with their upscale counterparts as well. "We want to be in the group of Lexus and Infiniti as soon as possible," vowed Piech.

Volkswagen attempted to achieve its goal of competing with BMW, Mercedes, Lexus, and Infiniti by equaling its rivals' quality while underbidding its competitors' prices. According to Piech, "We are working on a car a little bigger in size than Passat for early next century, equal to Mercedes-Benz at 20 percent lower price."

"People are sensible," Piech continued, suggesting that no one would pay $10,000 extra for a comparable car just because of its brand name. While Piech sounded urgent about competing with Lexus and Infiniti, in reality the deadline for moving into this accelerated class was more fluid. "It's a directional thing," VW of America's director of communications Maria Leonhauser pointed out. "There's no time frame in which we want to do this."

MARKETING STRATEGY

The "Live Large" campaign maintained common threads with the "Drivers Wanted" campaign; both were based in reality, portraying scenarios that really could happen. The "Live Large" campaign simply shifted the reality by a couple of decades, depicting life situations that 40-somethings, not 20-somethings, faced. So the main difference between the campaigns was the age of the people cast for the commercials. One constant remained: after doing market research, Arnold realized that they were pitching the Passat not to a new market, but to an older, perhaps wiser, segment of the same market. "They're still VW people," commented Arnold's Jensen, who worked on both the "Drivers Wanted" and the "Live Large" campaigns. "They're still cool, still young in spirit."

Volkswagen had created an image that defied convention; naturally, its customers would defy convention as well. "A car is like a piece of jewelry," Jensen philosophized—jewelry not only adorns its owner, but it also says a lot about the personality of its owner. VW people would never wear a gem larger than one karat, if that, because it would be pretentious. Similarly, VW people wouldn't want to drive a Mercedes—"they wouldn't need the badge, and they wouldn't need the baggage," Jensen stated, suggesting that upscale brands carry symbolic weight signifying social status for their owners. VW didn't want to be associated with "snob appeal."

However, there was a growing market of loyal Volkswagen owners who could afford more but wanted to retain the funky VW image. Jensen imagined how they got where they were: "As you grow up, you're forced to make decisions that aren't always fun—maybe you're stuck in suburbia, maybe you're 45 and having a midlife crisis, maybe you're divorced, maybe your life is just in a rut. This is true—people deal with these things, but that doesn't define them." A car represented a highly visible means of redefining one's reality. The "Live Large" ads, with their divorced mother and aging bachelor, depicted people making decisions that help them define themselves. One of those decisions, the ads suggested, was to drive a Passat, a good decision that might compensate for some of the more difficult issues they've faced.

OUTCOME

The results of the *Ad Track* survey could be deceptive, Jensen suggested, since *USA Today* 's readership tended to be much more mainstream than Passat's target market. The ads spoke to a very specific cross-section, and the message got through to its audience, VW spokesperson Tony Fouladpour reported. VW sold 2,563 Passats in the United States in January 1998, a 114 percent increase compared to sales for the month of January 1997. *USA Today* 's Dottie Enrico reported that VW officials were happy with the "Live Large" campaign and that sales had "skyrocketed since the ads began in November." Chris Cedergren of Nextrend assessed the campaign as follows: "All in all, the Passat has been a success story for VW, so I don't imagine they're going to question their ad strategy even if the campaign doesn't perform well in the popularity polls."

Ad Age 's reviewer Bob Garfield called the "Live Large" commercials "neither very good nor very bad." He complained that the spots promoted an emotional connection to the people in the commercials but failed to promote the Passat. The commercials, however, weren't intended to sell Volkswagen—the target market was already sold on the brand. They simply needed to be informed that the Passat represented an automobile option appropriate for their lifestyle.

The most outspoken opponent of VW's marketing strategy for the Passat was Jack Trout, a long-time marketing strategist and president Trout & Partners in Connecticut. He proclaimed that pitting the VW brand against Mercedes "Makes no sense. It ain't gonna work, trust me. You can bet a lot of money on that." There were probably many people who made similar proclamations upon first sight of the Beetle in 1938. But given that the Beetle went on to become the most-produced car in history, betting against VW's overwhelming brand loyalty would make no sense.

FURTHER READING

Healey, James R. "VW Longs for Life in Luxury Lane; Will USA Pay the Premium?" *USA Today,* July 11, 1997.

Koch, Paul. "Lance Jensen." *The Boston Globe Sunday Magazine,* January 11, 1998.

McCann, Paul, "The Ads that Broke the Mould: When a Boy from the Bronx Got Together with VW, Advertising Became Art with Creativity at its Heart." *The Independent* (London), June 1, 1998.

William D. Baue

NEW BEETLE CAMPAIGN

OVERVIEW

To herald the arrival of its newest car, Volkswagen of America Inc. launched a high-profile television, print, and outdoor advertising campaign in March 1998. The company had stopped selling its most famous car, the Beetle, in the United States in 1979, but the little car remained a cultural icon for many. Baby boomers fondly recalled tooling about in the 1960s and 1970s in their humpbacked Beetles. The car conjured up images of the counterculture, flower power, and nonconformity. In 1998, to further the company's revival, Volkswagen (VW) brought back the Beetle. While the New Beetle, as it was called, shared the rounded shape of its progenitor, the updated version had a more powerful engine, a roomier interior, and excellent safety features. It also had some quirky touches, such as a dashboard bud vase. Although the New Beetle caused quite a stir when Volkswagen first displayed it at auto shows, the company wanted an ad campaign that could bring a legend from the past into the landscape of the present.

With its Boston-based ad agency, Arnold Communications, Volkswagen conceived a series of ads for the New Beetle that were stunningly basic. "We wanted to keep the ads as simple as they can be," the chief creative director of the New Beetle campaign told the Associated Press. "This car is really about the way it makes you feel." The initial six New Beetle television commercials presented the car against a white background. The spots contained no voice-over or spokesperson and presented no specific details about the car. Instead, they showcased the New Beetle itself to sound tracks of alternative rock music. Each commercial displayed a single written tag line that matched the music and the images in the ad. One spot, for instance, showed seven yellow New Beetles together so that they formed a bright daisy. The copy declared, "Less flower. More power." Other television ads employed tag lines such as "If you sold your soul in the '80s, here's your chance to buy it back"; "A work of art with airbags and a budvase"; and "Suddenly the world is half-full again." Print ads followed a similar format: a single photo of the New Beetle accompanied by snappy copy.

The challenges confronting Volkswagen and Arnold in the New Beetle campaign were manifold. Obviously, baby boomers would have fond memories of the original Beetle and a likely affinity for the new version. But since 1995 Volkswagen had been assiduously building its brand to appeal to younger consumers, and it wanted the ads for the New Beetle to reach this group as well. To do so, Volkswagen strove to create ads that could "evoke memories from consumers old enough to remember the original car while being humorous enough to appeal to a younger crowd," according to *Adweek.* The New Beetle campaign achieved this by, in part, using tag lines in each ad that appealed to specific groups. While the copy in one print ad, "Comes with wonderful new features like heat," resonated particularly with older consumers who had endured the original Beetle's often faulty heating system, the tag line "Reverse-engineered from UFOs" appealed to younger drivers, specifically Generation X consumers who watched science fiction programs such as *The X-Files.*

The New Beetle campaign was a smashing success. It won several prestigious advertising awards and was praised by commentators in publications ranging from *Advertising Age* to *USA Today.* The goal Volkswagen set for itself was a lofty one, however. Company officials revealed that they hoped the New Beetle and its catchy campaign would bolster sales in the entire Volkswagen division. "Its success would not only be measured in sales of new Beetles, but in the overall growth of the brand and increased sales of VW's other models," a spokesperson from Arnold Communications told *Adweek.*

HISTORICAL CONTEXT

Between its arrival in the United States in 1949 and its discontinuation in 1979, the Volkswagen Beetle claimed a place for itself in American history. It surpassed the Model T Ford to become the best-selling car of all time.

Volkswagen's new Beetle. GETTY IMAGES.

Its original appeal lay in its uniqueness. While most American cars of the 1960s and 1970s were giant gas-guzzlers, the Beetle was a small fuel-efficient vehicle that offered an alternative to a generation of young consumers who strove to define themselves as living outside the mainstream world of their parents. As a reporter explained in *World News Sunday,* "The Beetle became a symbol of flower power." Pop artist Andy Warhol depicted the Beetle in a series of prints, and actor Woody Allen included a reference to the car in his 1973 hit movie *Sleeper.*

Part of the Beetle's allure originated in the groundbreaking advertising created by Doyle Dane Bernbach. *Advertising Age's Creativity* described the marketing of the original Beetle as "the benchmark for great consumer product advertising." Like the Beetle itself, the ads were understated, with their impact coming through offbeat humor. While traditional car advertising of the era played up the size and shininess of American sedans, the original Beetle spots used the car's smallness and homeliness as selling points.

By the 1970s the Beetle faced increasing competition from, and was losing market share to, the Japanese imports that were flooding the American market. Like the Beetle, the Japanese cars were inexpensive, reliable, and fuel-efficient. In an attempt to halt its decline, Volkswagen discontinued the Beetle in 1979 and introduced the Rabbit in its place. But the Rabbit never gained the same sort of cachet. The company struggled in United States during the 1980s and early 1990s. While Volkswagen sales boomed in Europe, Americans opted for Japanese or domestic autos. Volkswagen was "a nearly moribund brand in this country," declared the *Washington Post.* In 1995, however, the company's fortunes began to change. With an updated roster of sporty cars and an energized new ad campaign—"Drivers Wanted"—from Arnold, Volkswagen's sales began to climb once more. After introducing a concept car with a shape similar to the beloved original Beetle at a 1995 auto show, Volkswagen was inundated with letters from customers beseeching the company to bring back the Beetle.

TARGET MARKET

With the Beetle's rich American legacy, Volkswagen could not disassociate its New Beetle from the original car. While some analysts had speculated that the New

Beetle would mainly attract baby boomers who had owned the original, Volkswagen quickly realized that the New Beetle's appeal "cut across traditional automotive demographic boundaries," according to a company press release. A spokesperson emphasized that early marketing studies had indicated that "people of all ages, young and old, and from different backgrounds responded in exactly the same way—with a big smile." Armed with this insight, Volkswagen instructed Arnold to craft a campaign for the New Beetle that would target a diverse audience.

Baby boomers who had come of age during the era of the first Beetle were an important population to reach with the New Beetle campaign. "We have this... tremendous heritage with the baby boomers," Volkswagen's marketing director told the *Washington Post.* Many aspects of the New Beetle ads were designed to remind the children of the 1960s about the car of their youth. The essence of the New Beetle campaign was similar to the legendary Doyle Dane Bernbach print pieces. Both campaigns made the car the "hero" of the ads; both used a stark white background, from which the Beetle boldly emerged; both shared the same typeface and understated sensibility. Several of the New Beetle ads deliberately hearkened back to the original car. One print ad proclaimed, "A car like this comes along only twice a lifetime," while one of the television commercials spoofed the original Beetle's notorious lack of acceleration with the wry tag line "0 to 60? Yes." One print piece even used a former Doyle Dane Bernbach ad as a reference point. In "Lemon" an original Beetle had been declared defective because the chrome was slightly marred. The New Beetle installment arrayed a vibrantly green New Beetle beneath the word "Lime."

The New Beetle ads walked a fine line, however. As much as Volkswagen sought to tap into baby boomers' nostalgia—and thus propel them to their nearest Volkswagen dealer—their tastes had changed in 19 years. The original Beetle's safety record was poor, and as baby boomers became parents, and even grandparents, they would not tolerate such flaws. Moreover, baby boomers had become comfortable living in suburban homes and driving sport utility vehicles or BMWs. A rattling car with little heat would not be desirable. Thus, Arnold Communications took care to present the spirit of the original Beetle in the new campaign, but it used copy that stressed the changes and the improvements in the New Beetle.

The New Beetle campaign also sought to reach consumers under the age of 35, who had few memories of the original. This demographic group was essential to Volkswagen. Priced beginning at about $16,000, the New Beetle aimed to draw first-time car buyers to the Volkswagen brand. Consumer studies had revealed that allegiances to brands were forged early in life, and the company hoped that engendering brand loyalty would eventually keep these younger buyers within the "chain" of Volkswagen vehicles as they aged and saw their incomes rise. This audience would not respond to the same pitch as baby boomers, however. "Nostalgia wasn't going to be enough to sell this car to the youth market," an Arnold executive told *Advertising Age's Creativity.* "We had to bring the Beetle into the present."

To accomplish this goal, the New Beetle spots employed cutting-edge music. Songs from fringe bands such as Spiritualized, Hurricane #1, and Fluke—all popular among college students—were used to back the commercials. Furthermore, specific ads targeted a younger audience. For example, in the style of updated versions of computer software, one print ad coyly labeled the car "Beetle 2.0." Arnold was confident that younger consumers—particularly retro-crazed Generation Xers—would understand the tongue-in-cheek allusions to the original Beetle. While "everyone knows about the Beetle and what it represented," an Arnold spokesperson explained to *Advertising Age's Creativity,* the New Beetle campaign made it clear that the most recent incarnation of the Beetle "is different—so the idea is, it's back, but this time it's for you, not your parents."

COMPETITION

The New Beetle was not the only small car vying for the competitive U.S. car market, however. DaimlerChrysler's Neon, which was introduced in 1994 and which was sold under both the Dodge and Plymouth brands, launched a new $40 million campaign on March 15, 1999. While Neon had been imbued with an endearing personality thanks to the "Hi" campaign that attended its introduction, the company hoped to update the Neon's image. "We tried to get away from cute, so the ads are more sophisticated in keeping with the changes of the car," a DaimlerChrysler spokesperson told *Advertising Age.* The campaign, created by BBDO Worldwide, had television, magazine, newspaper, and outdoor components, as well as Internet ads that appeared on prominent websites. Like the New Beetle, Neon attempted to capture a younger audience of consumers aged 20 to 34. To do so, BBDO employed what *Advertising Age* termed a "purposefully soft sell approach." The initial three television ads featured a voice-over by comedian George Carlin, who read BBDO-created lyrics to three songs: Dean Martin's "Amore," the Lovin' Spoonfuls' "You Didn't Have to Be So Nice," and the Mamas & the Papas' "Dream a Little Dream of Me."

In 1998 Oldsmobile introduced its Alero, which it aimed at "younger, more-forward thinking consumers,"

NOT SO POPULAR AT HOME

Despite the New Beetle's warm reception in the United States, the car did not fare as well in Germany, the company's headquarters and home country. The Beetle, which was known there as the Kaefer—the German word for "beetle"—was deemed too expensive. Rumors circulated that Volkswagen would offer a no-frills, stripped-down version of the car in Germany.

according to *Adweek.* In its $80 million "Start Something" campaign, Oldsmobile and its agency, Leo Burnett, used fast-paced footage of real families set to electronic music. "The spots are trying to communicate a certain way of thinking and living," an Oldsmobile representative told *Adweek.* In March 1999, Mazda broke a new campaign for its sporty Miata. These ads, which used the tag line "Get in. Be moved," were executed by W.B. Doner & Company and attempted to strengthen the Mazda brand.

MARKETING STRATEGY

Even before the car went on sale, the New Beetle received a marketing boost over its competitors. Newspapers breathlessly anticipated its introduction, and several columnists wrote paeans to their first Beetles. An industry analyst noted to the Associated Press that "Volkswagen really won't have to do much in marketing." But to meet its goals of selling 50,000 New Beetles in the United States in 1998 and bolstering Volkswagen's overall sales, the company chose not to rely on hype and instead spent an estimated $40 million during the first eight months of the campaign. While some rival car companies released narrative campaigns that portrayed quirky characters or elaborate story lines, Volkswagen's strategy for the New Beetle was to focus solely on the car. *Advertising Age* noted that the spots were a kind of "Rorschach ink blot [that allowed] each consumer [to] process the imagery and respond according to his own values, background, and personality."

To take the campaign to the diverse audiences it wanted to reach, Volkswagen aired the ads during mainstream television shows and in publications that reached large numbers of consumers. But television shows that were popular with consumers under 30, such as *The X-Files, Melrose Place, Seinfeld,* and *Suddenly Susan,* were targeted as well in order to attract a Generation X audience. Print pieces ran in popular consumers magazines such as *Vanity Fair,* as well as in more cutting-edge, niche publications like *Wired.* Volkswagen also displayed New Beetle ads on Yahoo!'s home page. With its billboards Volkswagen opted for a city-specific strategy. For instance, a New York outdoor ad offered a picture of the New Beetle with the wry comment "Just what New York needs, a car that stops traffic." In a further effort to gain the attention of Generation Xers, Volkswagen signed the New Beetle on as an official sponsor of the Lilith Fair musical tour, which, according to *Shoot,* was an event that "appeal[ed] to one of the Beetle's target markets, young men and women."

OUTCOME

The New Beetle's introduction was a triumph. Demand quickly outstripped the limited number of the cars at dealerships. Indeed, some consumers were so eager to own New Beetles that they paid thousands of dollars above the retail sticker price for used ones. By August 1998, Volkswagen had sold 32,450 New Beetles, and by October it had surpassed its goal of 50,000 for the year. As the company had hoped, the excitement surrounding the New Beetle appeared to lift the entire Volkswagen brand. "The New Beetle is fulfilling its role as a magnet for the VW brand," an Arnold executive told *Adweek.* Sales for the Jetta, Cabriolet, and Passat increased after the New Beetle's arrival.

Industry critics showered the New Beetle campaign with plaudits as well. It won the highest honors (Grand Prix Award) for the best print ad at the illustrious International Advertising Festival in Cannes, France. According to *USA Today,* a judge at the show declared that the ads "made me want to buy the car." Furthermore, at the MPA Kelly Awards the campaign took home the prize for the best campaign appearing in magazines. Commentators in *USA Today* and *Advertising Age* named the New Beetle ads as among the best of the year. Although it was difficult to correlate ad campaigns with sales figures, 1998 was certainly Volkswagen's best sales year in the United States since 1981. In 1999 Volkswagen introduced a high-powered version of the New Beetle, the 1.8 T, and Arnold oversaw the creation of "Turbonium," a commercial vaunting the car's turbocharged capacity.

FURTHER READING

"Alero Begins Olds' Minority Push." *Adweek,* July 17, 1998.

Berger, Warren. "Nothing to Be Bugged About." *Advertising Age's Creativity,* April 1, 1998.

Garfield, Bob. "Flower Power." *Advertising Age,* May 31, 1999.

Halliday, Jean. "Campaign Urges Drivers to Say Hello to New Neon." *Advertising Age,* March 8, 1999.

Kaufman, David. "New Beetle Campaign Gets the Bugs Out for Volkswagen." *Shoot,* March 20, 1998.

Span, Paula. "Return of the Beetle." *Washington Post,* March 13, 1998.

Suhr, Jim. "Months from Reaching Showrooms, Beetle Already Creates Stir." Associated Press, January 9, 1998.

Takaki, Millie. "Meet the Beetle: Ad Lineage Makes Intro of New VW Bug a Daunting Creative Challenge." *Shoot,* March 6, 1998.

Waner, Judy, and Gazdik, Tanya. "Arnold Readies Ads for New VW Bug." *Adweek,* January 12, 1998.

Wells, Melanie. "Likeable Beetle Ads Win Print Division." *USA Today,* June 24, 1998.

"With a Simple, Well-Rounded Strategy for the New Bug, VW Recaptures Its Lost Youth." *Adweek,* July 13, 1998.

Wollenberg, Skip. "Volkswagen Relies on Beetle's Distinctive Shape, Fond Memories in New Ads." Associated Press, March 12, 1998.

Rebecca Stanfel

Wachovia Corporation

1 Wachovia Center
Charlotte, North Carolina 28288
USA
Telephone: (704) 374-6565
Fax: (704) 374-3425
Web site: www.wachovia.com

■■■

FINANCIAL WORLD CAMPAIGN

OVERVIEW

NOTE: Since the initial appearance of this essay in the 1999 edition of *Major Marketing Campaigns Annual,* First Union Corporation became Wachovia. The essay continues to refer to the company's former name, as that was the official name of the organization when the campaign was launched.

On September 27, 1998, First Union Corporation debuted a commercial unlike any other in the financial services industry. In this spot the company avoided the stock images of financial services advertising—smiling customers, affluent retirees, and happy families. Instead, First Union depicted a chaotic and disturbing landscape—the "Financial World"—that was filled with symbolic representations. In "Launch," the initial execution, faceless people clad in black coats and bowler hats walk a city of garish neon. When one falls to the ground, his face shatters. Mutual funds are hawked by a fellow carrying a cigarette tray, and a fire-breather comes into view. A voice-over explains this dark scene: "This is a world only a few know well, a world of risk and uncertainty, where the roads can take you to success or prosperity—or sometimes to no place at all. This is the financial world." The images suddenly shift as the camera focuses on a towering edifice of steel and glass, shining in the sun and looming over the sordid scene beneath it. The voice-over concludes: "Yet high above the horizon, another mountain has risen—a mountain called First Union, with 16 million customers, the nation's eighth-largest brokerage and sixth-largest bank. For a new perspective of the financial world come to a mountain called First Union. Or, if you prefer, the mountain will come to you."

Created by the San Francisco-based ad agency Publicis & Hal Riney, "Financial World" was First Union's first national advertising campaign and was intended to introduce First Union to the world. Although a series of acquisitions had made First Union one of the largest financial-services corporations in the nation, few people were aware of the company's scale and range of offerings. "We want people to know that we're a substantial institution—a major player in the financial services world that can meet any financial need," Jim Garrity, First Union's vice president of advertising, told *Adweek.* With the stated goal of "breaking through the clutter of advertising," Publicis & Hal Riney turned to *Star Wars* creator George Lucas's company, Industrial Light and Magic (ILM), for cutting-edge special effects. Although some critics blasted the campaign as bleak and intimidating, Garrity averred that "the financial world is not always a warm and fuzzy place.... [W]e wanted to acknowledge what the real world is like and show how our expertise can help customers succeed in it." Each of the five commercials that comprised "Financial World" closed with an explanation of how First Union could assist consumers and with the same tag line: "Come to the mountain called First Union. Or, if you prefer, the mountain will come to you."

HISTORICAL CONTEXT

First Union's growth had been rapid. Beginning in the early 1980s, the Charlotte-based bank, headed by Edward Crutchfield, took over nearly 85 banks to become the sixth-largest bank in the United States. Its retail presence eventually stretched along the East Coast from Connecticut to Florida. In 1994 First Union started to expand into the arena of mutual funds and brokering. Two years later it bought Boston-based Keystone Investments Inc., a large manager of stock, bond, and money market funds. At the time, Crutchfield explained to an interviewer that the company was "trying to build a business that is about 50 percent traditional bank while the other [half] needs to look like [brokerages] Merrill Lynch, Fidelity, and Charles Schwab," according to the *Boston Globe*.

In 1997 First Union ran a branding campaign on the East Coast, where its retail presence was most strongly concentrated. That effort, which First Union credited with tripling awareness of the company in the area, focused on how the brand provided "smart, straightforward financial solutions in the customer's best interest." But First Union had its sights set higher than being simply a regional power. It believed it could purvey its services to consumers across the country and therefore decided to initiate a national advertising campaign. "We want to build upon that momentum [of the 1997 campaign] so that First Union is on the short list of top financial providers in the mind of every potential customer," Garrity said.

TARGET MARKET

Though many of its competitors aired commercials that targeted a mass market, First Union aimed "Financial World" at a more narrow audience. "We wanted to target the top 5 percent," is how Publicis & Hal Riney's Brad Fogel explained it. In other words, First Union sought to appeal to two major groups—major corporations' chief financial officers (CFOs) and chief executive officers (CEOs) on the one hand, and the most sophisticated of individual investors—those who controlled over one million dollars of investable assets—on the other. "[W]e're reaching a point where we need to attract customers not just by buying institutions but by attracting prospects from around the country to do business with us," Garrity told *American Banker*.

In its effort to court an audience described by *American Banker* as "corporate leaders and wealthy people," First Union eschewed typical financial services marketing in favor of the edgy "Financial World" spots. The scenes of chaos and danger were chosen for a reason. "That's the reality," Fogel said. "That's the way [this demographic] see[s] the financial world. We had to speak with credibility." For instance, in "Change," First Union painted a depressing portrait of a system in flux. "In the financial world, banking as we know it has become a thing of the past," the voice-over intoned while images of collapsed neoclassical buildings, broken statuary, and currency drifting haphazardly in the wind flickered across the screen. "Teller windows have become electronic gateways," the narrator continues, and then proceeds to detail the various upheavals wracking the banking industry. By acknowledging the "real world," First Union hoped to earn the respect of experienced individual and corporate investors, those who had both gained and, inevitably, lost money in the course of investing.

"Financial World" also directly addressed corporate investors by discussing the problems specifically confronting corporate investments (and the solutions First Union could provide). "Sharks," for example, depicted a frog attempting to navigate its way across a body of water teeming with sharks and alligators. "Sometimes to defend against larger, fiercer competitors, your best choice is merger or acquisition," the narrator said. "But beware, lest your careful, well-planned strategy should result in failure. In these troubled waters, experience, knowledge, and size are your best allies." As the frog safely reaches a serene pond in the shadow of First Union's magnificent building, the voice-over concludes: "If you're considering strengthening your company through mergers or acquisition, think first of First Union. Wherever you plan to go, we have been there before."

COMPETITION

The financial services sector that First Union was entering had become intensely competitive. In addition to First Union, several other large banks were in the process of staging massive branding efforts. "Historically, they haven't been savvy marketers because they worked in defined territories with a limited set of products," noted *Advertising Age.* "But as they enter new markets and add products and services, creating a strong brand image is essential." In May 1998 Chase Manhattan Corp., the largest bank in the United States, teamed up with San Francisco-based advertising firm Foote Cone & Belding to "forge a more distinct image for the bank," according to *Advertising Age.* Dissatisfied with its long-standing tag line, "The Right Relationship Is Everything," Chase opted to build its brand through clever credit card ads in which it showed what people could buy with a Chase card in a weekend.

FINANCIAL INNOVATIONS

Several aspects of First Union's "Financial World" campaign were unique from an advertising perspective. One was the unusual degree of involvement by the founder of Publicis & Hal Riney, the agency that worked on the campaign. Not only did Hal Riney play a large part but he also provided the voice-over in each commercial. Moreover, because special effects were central to the vision of "Financial World," many of the specific details of the commercials were left to the discretion of Industrial Light & Magic (ILM), which created the effects. Riney would provide a conceptual framework, and ILM would draft the script. First Union was the ideal client for an ad agency, Riney's Brad Fogel said. Its only desire was that the campaign be unique and that it help First Union stand out. Everyone involved with "Financial World" was therefore given considerable creative freedom.

Bank One Corp. was also seeking to revitalize its advertising. After acquiring First Chicago NBD Corp. in 1998 Bank One ended its decade-long relationship with the Martin Agency. "They're looking for someone that can help them transcend their regional bank image," an analyst told the January 11, 1999, *Advertising Age.* With its ad account in review, Bank One planned to make its next agency one that could "help it build its image as a major national player in the financial services arena."

In addition to the bevy of emerging mega-banks, First Union's rivals included major brokerages. Foremost among these firms was Merrill Lynch & Company, which—despite its position as the nation's largest brokerage business—met with increasingly stiff competition in the consolidating sector. After ending its partnership of 12 years with Bozell Worldwide in February 1998, Merrill Lynch selected J. Walter Thompson to craft a new campaign. "It's not a problem of people recognizing Merrill Lynch," a company spokesperson told the July 6, 1998, *Advertising Age.* "But we do need to be more completely understood." In March 1999 Merrill Lynch launched its "Human Achievement" campaign, which was designed to stress the importance of human experience and knowledge in the investing world. One print ad proclaimed, for instance: "We love technology. It's new and it inspires a certain awe. Technology is good at heavy lifting. People are good at heavy thinking. . . . Computers are plastic and metal and sand. People are brilliance and discernment and vision." Other ads used legendary blues musician B.B. King to convey a similar message.

MARKETING STRATEGY

First Union realized that winning over its elite target audience from established competitors like Chase or Merrill Lynch would be no easy task. Therefore, the company's goal for "Financial World" was simply to encourage the investors it wished to reach to consider First Union when planning their financial transactions. To accomplish this aim, the campaign had to get these people's attention. The stunning visual imagery ILM created for the commercials was an important part of this effort. The campaign "keeps hitting you with images and it stops you and it makes you want to look," Steve Beck, the commercials' director, told the *San Francisco Examiner.* Beck later explained to *Bank Marketing* that "[w]e've created these 60-second miniature films that will make you want to watch them over and over again." "Financial World" was deliberately different from the marketing of its competitors to ensure that the campaign stood out. It "will not be mistaken for anyone else's," Hal Riney, the chairman of Publicis & Hal Riney, said. Garrity echoed this sentiment. "One of our biggest goals was to break through the clutter of financial services advertising where you typically see smiling people shaking hands."

Just as the First Union building towered over the urban landscape in the commercials, so too did "First Union want to be perceived differently from other financial institutions," a Riney executive told *Brandweek.* Although "the conventional wisdom for financial institutions was to use business print and direct mail to target high-end investors," he continued, First Union wanted "a high impact environment." Following the lead of other successful brand builders such as the Coca-Cola Company, First Union turned to television to carry the bulk of its message. After the campaign's launch during National Football League (NFL) games, "Financial World" appeared frequently on sports programming including regular-season NFL and Major League Baseball games, and especially during what *Brandweek* called "must-see" events—such as the 1999 Super Bowl, baseball's World Series, the NCAA basketball tournament's Final Four games, and Wimbledon tennis. News programs were another important venue—"Financial World" aired during *60 Minutes, Dateline,* and *20/20.* But cable television was perhaps the most significant part of First Union's advertising efforts. Instead of focusing only on prime-time cable news shoes First Union aimed to hit a "variety of different programs to catch investors at different points in their day," said *Brandweek.* Some of the shows selected by First Union included CNBC's

Today's Business, Power Lunch, and *Market Wrap,* as well as MSNBC's *Morning Line* and Fox News Channel's *Financial World,* which also aired during telecasts of the Academy Awards and Tony Awards because of the more affluent audience those events garnered.

The appearance of "Financial World" during the Super Bowl also reflected a key facet of First Union's strategy. Although the Super Bowl was famous for its ability to capture a mass audience, a Super Bowl ad also represented a prestige decision, since companies that could afford the astronomical cost of airtime during the game received a considerable amount of free media attention in the ubiquitous Super Bowl ad previews and recaps in newspapers such as *USA Today* and the *New York Times.* As the *Oklahoma City Journal Record* explained, the Super Bowl afforded companies "a once-a-year opportunity . . . to create reputations and flaunt their best." Moreover, because of the game's cachet those businesses that did advertise during the Super Bowl were widely regarded as leaders in their fields—exactly the message First Union sought to convey with the "Financial World" ads themselves. The Super Bowl was part of what Fogel termed First Union's "big dog media campaign." By appearing there First Union demonstrated that it was at least on a par with its more established competitors.

OUTCOME

First Union expressed complete satisfaction with "Financial World." According to *Brandweek,* national awareness of First Union tripled in the first few months of the campaign. "The feedback from the ads has just been unreal," company spokesperson Sandy Deem told the *Washington Times.* "It has turned into revenue." On average First Union received about 100 calls a day to the phone number listed in the ads. The company also conducted tracking studies after the commercials aired and found that its target audience understood and was enthusiastic about the message conveyed in "Financial World." Even more interesting was the fact that the mass market outside the company's targeted groups responded well to the campaign and was able to articulate the commercials' premise that First Union was a haven in a turbulent financial world.

The campaign won several awards, including four Clios. But while many commentators applauded the campaign's bold images and innovative strategy, others did not. *Advertising Age* lambasted "Financial World" as "suicide" on First Union's part and concluded that the campaign presented the bank as "the prince of financial darkness." The *New York Times* called the commercials a "low point" of 1998 and characterized the campaign as "overblown, overbusy."

Other events made it difficult to gauge the effect "Financial World" had on First Union's bottom line. The company's fiscal earnings during the campaign's run proved lower than had been forecast as a result of the effects of First Union's numerous acquisitions. Consequently, the company's share price plummeted in the face of Wall Street's concern about the firm's future profitability. In this environment focus on the innovative ad campaign quickly gave way to speculation that First Union's merger mania might lead to the company being taken over itself.

FURTHER READING

Arndorfer, James (with Beth Snyder). "Bank One $60 Million Review Set." *Advertising Age,* January 11, 1999.

Arndorfer, James (with Mercedes Cardona). "Chase Asks FCB To Hone Bank's Brand Perception." *Advertising Age,* May 18, 1998.

Arndorfer, James. "JWT's Vision of Merrill Lynch Earns $90 Million." *Advertising Age,* July 6, 1998.

"Banking on Business." *Brandweek,* April 12, 1999.

Campbell, Mike. "Bank Wars." *Bank Marketing,* March 1, 1999.

Kopecki, Dawn. "First Union Ad Gets Boos, Rave Review." *Boston Globe,* January 26, 1999.

Nucifora, Alf. "Below Average Ads." *Oklahoma City Journal Record,* February 8, 1999.

Raine, George. "To Experience and Describe the Chaos and Uncertainty Of . . . ." *San Francisco Examiner,* October 4, 1998.

"Shop Builds Dark 'Financial World' for First Union." *Adweek,* September 28, 1998.

Warsh, David. "Meet Fast Eddie." *Washington Times,* January 27, 1999.

Rebecca Stanfel

UNCOMMON WISDOM CAMPAIGN

OVERVIEW

In 2001 First Union Corporation, based in Charlotte, North Carolina, acquired its smaller in-state rival, Wachovia Corporation, and the new entity took the Wachovia name. The merger, which made Wachovia the nation's fourth-largest bank, was followed by a large, multi-year branding effort. Conceived by the Winston-Salem, North Carolina, office of Mullen Advertising, the "Uncommon Wisdom" campaign broke in the summer of 2002 with the intent of raising the brand's profile and introducing, in stages, the various capabilities that Wachovia, a company composed of a range of corporate and retail financial-services divisions, offered as a result of the merger.

Employing both print and television advertising, the campaign used common occurrences and objects—motorcycle handlebars and haircuts, for instance—as metaphors to communicate the idea that wisdom could be found everywhere but that Wachovia had the unique ability to identify and use its wisdom on behalf of its customers. This concept was applied to individual company divisions in turn, beginning in July 2002 with spots supporting Wachovia Securities, the conglomerate's brokerage arm. That winter a portion of the campaign devoted to Wachovia's retail businesses was launched to coincide with the gradual conversion of First Union branches, beginning with Florida and moving north. In early 2003 Wachovia Wealth Management ads, aimed at investors, began appearing in national print publications and markets along the East Coast. Wachovia further supported its branding campaign with high-profile sports sponsorships in individual markets. The campaign cost an estimated $60 to $75 million in its first year and approximately $160 million in its second.

During the time that "Uncommon Wisdom" ran, Wachovia continued to expand, primarily through mergers and acquisitions, and the newly branded company was well positioned to compete with other banks that were steadily consolidating. In 2005 Wachovia executives claimed that the company profits had grown at an annual rate of 13 percent over the four-year period after the merger with First Union.

HISTORICAL CONTEXT

Wachovia Corporation had been expanding its banking operations regionally throughout the late 1980s and 1990s, and in the late 1990s it entered global banking, underwriting, and capital-formation markets. Prior to the 2001 merger with First Union Corporation, it had also expanded into New York and Florida.

Meanwhile, as a result of its policy of aggressive acquisition, First Union Corporation had become a major financial-services force. During Edward Crutchfield's 1988–2000 tenure as CEO, First Union absorbed more than a dozen separate banks and assorted financial services companies, including CoreStates Financial in 1998, an acquisition that, at the time, was the largest bank merger in history. After Crutchfield stepped down, and while First Union was still recovering from complications related to the cumbersome CoreStates merger, the new CEO, G. Kennedy Thompson, surprised analysts by bidding for Wachovia. First Union competed against SunTrust Banks for the purchase of Wachovia, acquiring the smaller company in a 2001 shareholder vote. The new entity, which chose Wachovia Corporation as its name, covered the East Coast from Florida to Connecticut.

After the merger Wachovia was the nation's fourth-largest bank, with operations spanning private banking, asset management, and brokerage, but its brand name was little known outside the southeastern United States. Wachovia's competitors, too, had been consolidating, so that the industry as a whole was perceived as increasingly faceless and corporate. At the same time the public's view of financial-services firms was distinctly colored by the 2001 stock-market crash and the waves of corporate scandals that followed. Though Wachovia, in its branding effort, had to operate amidst this climate of widespread public skepticism of financial institutions, it had not been involved in any of the scandals, and its banking heritage distinguished it from competitors, many of whom were identified with Wall Street.

TARGET MARKET

The first "Uncommon Wisdom" advertisements centered on Wachovia Securities, the company's brokerage division, and used noticeably high production values and metaphors meant to appeal to the sensibilities of the wealthy. Examples included a TV commercial depicting a middle-aged couple in a canoe, a metaphor for maintaining balance in one's investments, and a spot called "Handlebars," featuring a Harley Davidson and illustrating what handlebars could teach people about financial relationships (the answer was "You have to reach out to make them work"). The message of everyday wisdom and stability positioned Wachovia to appeal to investors anxious about market conditions. Furthermore, the products featured, such as expensive motorcycles, were obviously intended to appeal to the wealthy. Beyond this initial targeted appeal, the first phase of the campaign functioned, according to Wachovia's Jim Garrity, as "a big coming-out party" meant to create awareness and prepare the way for the ensuing mass-market push.

The retail-focused portion of "Uncommon Wisdom," which broke in Florida and migrated north along the East Coast as branches were converted to the Wachovia name, continued to use metaphors that signified strategies for achieving financial well-being, but this phase primarily emphasized brand recognition—especially in markets where the bank had no prior presence—through the simple act of teaching consumers how to pronounce Wachovia. Additionally, the metaphor concept was given a more down-to-earth spin and broader potential appeal. The TV spot "Salon" used the act of getting a haircut to explain Wachovia's principles for working with small businesses, such as its commitment to careful listening. Other spots illustrated financial knowledge through images of children in a school play and on carnival rides. For the Florida portion of the campaign, Wachovia employed Hispanic agency Zubi Advertising of Coral

Gables to "transcreate" ads whose metaphors appealed specifically to Spanish-speaking residents of that state.

Ads supporting Wachovia Wealth Management, which followed on the heels of the retail push, used the ongoing "Uncommon Wisdom" message to target investors "who are looking for financial advice, have $1 million of investable assets, and have $2.5 million or more of assets in all," according to *American Banker*. Wachovia marketing officer Raj Madan posited that such individuals placed a premium on access and advice, concerns that were answered with advertising such as a print ad that appeared in 2003. It featured a stained-glass window and the question, "What can a stained-glass window teach us about managing assets?" The answer was, "Sometimes you have to step back to see the whole picture." The copy elaborated, "If you were asked where you stood financially, how many calls would it take to answer? Accountant. Attorney. Broker. Banker." Because of the merger and the ensuing evolution of the company, Wachovia was able to offer wealthy individuals exactly such a big-picture view of their finances, and it had wealth management teams in close proximity to all the major markets this portion of the campaign targeted: Florida, New Jersey, Connecticut, the New York City suburbs, Philadelphia, and Washington, D.C. Additionally, the continuing emphasis on brand awareness was meant to let high-net-worth individuals know that they were doing business with a major player in the financial-services world.

COMPETITION

Citigroup Inc. was the largest company of its kind in the world, and—like most of the major financial-services companies at the time—it continued to grow as a result of large-scale mergers and acquisitions. Though its purchases were not as flashy as those of its top competitors, Citigroup understood the need to maintain a human face in this era of consolidation. Likewise, a weak market for investment banking encouraged Citigroup, like other banks, to renew its focus on retail customers. The marketing results of this banking milieu were popular and critically acclaimed Citibank advertising campaigns, such as "Live Richly" and "Identity Theft Solutions." "Live Richly" focused on the idea that there was more to life than money, and "Identity Theft Solutions" comically dramatized the idea of identity theft by showing victims speaking in the lip-synched voices of those who had stolen their identities. Both campaigns tried to assure consumers that Citibank cared about their interests and understood what was important to them.

America's second-largest bank, JP Morgan Chase & Co., was a product of the 2001 merger of retail-banking giant Chase Manhattan and investment-banking stalwart JP Morgan. In 2002 the company, in line with industry-wide trends toward customer-centered advertising, launched a TV campaign that used the tagline "The right relationship is everything" and that focused on customer relationships rather than on specific products or services. The campaign was adapted in 2003 for ads aimed at African-Americans, Hispanics, and Asian-Americans. In 2004 JP Morgan Chase swallowed up the country's sixth-biggest bank, Bank One, extending its reach into the South and the Midwest, and initiated a media review process for selecting agencies to handle post-merger advertising.

> **BUT WHAT DOES IT MEAN?**
>
> "Wachovia" (wah-KO-vee-yah) refers to an area of North Carolina settled by Moravian religious dissenters in 1753. The land, given to them by the English nobleman and North Carolina landowner Lord Granville, reminded them of a German river valley called Der Wachau. Wachovia is the Latinized form of the German word.

Wachovia's hometown rival, Bank of America, was the third-largest bank in the United States and, with approximately 5,800 locations in 30 states and the District of Columbia, the leader among retail banks. A 2004 merger with FleetBoston set the stage for a massive rebranding push. In light of the challenges posed by the blockbuster acquisition, Bank of America—which had more than 15 separate advertising agencies on its roster—hired a third-party consultant to help maximize its estimated $180 million marketing budget.

MARKETING STRATEGY

The idea behind the "Uncommon Wisdom" campaign came from Mullen's successful 2001 pitch for the post-merger Wachovia account. The campaign's first spots, supporting Wachovia Securities, appeared in May 2002 and ran in financial magazines such as *Fortune* and *Forbes* and in newspapers such as the *Wall Street Journal* and *USA Today*. The television portion of the campaign began on July 20 of that year, during the British Open golf tournament, and the series of six initial spots subsequently appeared primarily on weekend sports, financial, and public-affairs programs. Spending during the campaign's first year was estimated at $60 to $75 million.

The fallout from the numerous reports of corporate malfeasance during this period made it "a tricky time to be marketing wealth management services," according to

U.S. Banker, but Wachovia Securities—a bank brokerage able to distance itself from Wall Street and accounting firms—was positioned to offer itself as a trustworthy alternative to some of its larger competitors. The campaign thus emphasized everyday life as a source of wisdom and cast Wachovia as a steady presence intent on gleaning that wisdom for the sake of its customers. As Wachovia's Kirt Hibbits told *American Banker,* "This new campaign shows Wachovia as a company that cares about its customers and wants to take all that they know and all that we have learned to create shared success."

At the outset of the campaign another challenge facing Wachovia and Mullen was the disparity between Wachovia's new size and the relative obscurity of the brand name. The campaign's launch, therefore, rolled out the company's brokerage services while serving the ongoing goal of establishing Wachovia as a known quantity in the banking world. That goal took center stage in the retail phase of the campaign, which included advertising teaching customers in new markets how to pronounce the company name. Eight TV spots, some of which were in Spanish for the Florida market, led the retail portion of the campaign and were supported by print, radio, and outdoor ads.

In the campaign's second year, ad spending roughly doubled, reaching an estimated $160 million. The retail push gradually reached local markets, from Florida to Connecticut, and the company introduced another series of ads in support of Wachovia Wealth Management. The Wachovia Wealth Management phase of the campaign consisted of print ads in regional publications and in national magazines such as *Forbes, Fortune,* and *Fast Company,* and it also featured PBS and NPR sponsorships. In the summer of 2003 Wachovia sponsored the Wachovia Championship, a professional golf tournament in Charlotte, and continued to enhance its name recognition in key markets by sponsoring sports teams, including the Miami Dolphins and the New York Giants.

OUTCOME

During and after the "Uncommon Wisdom" campaign, Wachovia remained the fourth-largest bank in the United States, keeping pace with competitors. Maintaining this position was more than a matter of simply holding on, however. Wachovia's continued growth—like that of Citigroup, JP Morgan Chase, and Bank of America—was primarily the result of a constant diet of mergers and acquisitions, the most prominent being the takeover of SouthTrust, a bank based in Birmingham, Alabama, in late 2004. Wachovia's profits grew at a 13 percent compound annual rate between 2001 and 2005, and the company was prepared to meet the challenges of a merger-heavy banking market. In a 2005 *Forbes* story on the company's positioning and outlook, CEO G. Kennedy Thompson, architect of post-merger Wachovia's rebranding and growth, offered the following prediction about the future of the banking industry: "I think there will be a handful of universal banks, and I think Wachovia will be one."

FURTHER READING

Boraks, David. "Wachovia Plans Big Brand Campaign." *American Banker,* January 6, 2003.

———. "Wachovia Renews Dolphin Pact." *American Banker,* August 29, 2003.

———. "Wachovia's Post-Merger Blitz Doubled Up in Second Year." *American Banker,* March 12, 2004.

Cardona, Mercedes. "Wachovia." *Advertising Age,* October 1, 2004.

———. "Wachovia Debuts Effort after First Union Merger." *Advertising Age,* July 15, 2002.

Chapelle, Tony. "Brokerage Ad Spending Increases." *On Wall Street,* December 1, 2003.

DePaula, Matthew. "Wachovia Waxes Metaphoric." *U.S. Banker,* September 2002.

Gjertsen, Lee Ann. "Wachovia's Wealth Unit in Post-Merger Rebranding." *American Banker,* February 27, 2003.

Griswold, Alicia. "Mullen Breaks Wachovia TV Ads." *Adweek,* January 6, 2003.

"Hotline." *Adweek,* July 22, 2002.

Julavitz, Robert. "Ad Spending's Up, Reflecting Bigger Emphasis on Retail." *American Banker,* July 25, 2003.

Kresbach, Karen. "Wachovia Aids Its Brand." *Bank Investment Consultant,* May 2003.

"Mullen, HH Get Wachovia Wisdom." *Shoot,* November 29, 2002.

"Wachovia Wealth Management." *Sales & Marketing Management,* June 2003.

Mark Lane

Walgreen Company

200 Wilmot Road
Deerfield, Illinois 60015
USA
Telephone: (847) 914-2500
Fax: (847) 914-2804
Web site: www.walgreens.com

PERFECT CAMPAIGN

OVERVIEW

In 2002 the 101-year-old Walgreens, owned by Walgreen Company, was the number one drugstore chain in the United States with annual sales hitting $28.68 billion. That year it filled more than 361 million prescriptions at its nearly 4,000 pharmacies. But rapidly growing drug chains CVS Corporation and Rite Aid Corporation were encroaching on Walgreens' business. Further, while filling prescriptions accounted for the lion's share—some 64 percent—of Walgreens' sales, encouraging customers to shop the stores' front ends for nonprescription items was critical for the chain to maintain and increase its market share. Walgreens' senior vice president of marketing, George Riedl, told *Drug Store News* that increasing front-end sales could be accomplished only by getting more customers into the stores.

In order to accomplish this goal, Walgreens in 2002 partnered with Euro RSCG Tatham Partners/Chicago to create a new advertising campaign. The campaign, "Perfect," was designed to reinforce the drugstore chain's image and brand while pointing out that it was the perfect place for busy consumers to shop and not just get prescriptions filled. No budget for the campaign, which was a series of television spots set in the mythical village of Perfect, was available, but the company typically spent $25 million to $30 million on all advertising each year.

The campaign was well received by consumers, industry insiders, and the media. According to a Walgreens spokeswoman, after the 2002 launch of the campaign, the company began receiving phone calls from people who had seen the spots and wanted to buy copies of their own. Praise for the campaign ranged from *Adweek* magazine calling it an "exceptionally eye-pleasing campaign" to the *Chicago Sun-Times* comment that the spots were standouts because "the ad copy is as strong as the visuals." In addition, the "Perfect" campaign was recognized by the *Chicago Sun-Times* as one of the top efforts produced by a Chicago-based advertising agency in 2002. The campaign continued in following years with the addition of new spots centered around holidays and special occasions.

HISTORICAL CONTEXT

When pharmacist Charles R. Walgreen, Sr., spent $6,000 to purchase the drugstore on the south side of Chicago where he was employed in 1901, he founded what would eventually become the Walgreens drugstore chain. From those beginnings Walgreens added stores, growing to nearly 4,000 stores nationwide by the end of 2002. The forward-thinking Walgreen also wanted to do more for customers than fill prescriptions. From that idea the store's front end evolved. Walgreens began adding a variety of nonpharmacy products to its merchandise mix, from hot food at the store's soda fountain to pots and pans and other household items stocked on the shelves lining its aisles. Despite offering in its front end a broad selection of personal items, household gadgets, gifts, toys, and over-the-counter health-care products, Walgreens' primary business remained its pharmacies, which accounted for 64 percent of its overall sales in 2002. It continued to advertise its pharmacies, launching in 2002 a new marketing campaign called "Rx Safety Net" that focused on pharmacy services. Simultaneously, however, Walgreens shifted some of its marketing focus to its front end and released a new national advertising campaign specifically designed to inform consumers about what was available in the stores beyond prescription drugs. The new campaign, titled "Perfect," was designed to send the message that whatever someone wanted, and whenever they wanted it, Walgreens was there to meet their needs.

WALGREENS HEALTH ADVICE ON TV

Walgreens drugstores, known for providing in-store pharmacy customers with advice about their health and medications, expanded its services to reach consumers outside of the store with the release of a television series, *Walgreens Health Corner.* The 30-minute program hit the air on Chicago's WGN-TV on January 3, 2004. *Walgreens Health Corner* was expected to reach a national audience through Superstation WGN. Working with a news-magazine format, the program ran on Saturday mornings and discussed a variety of health-related topics each week, including headaches, eating for optimum health, living through cancer, and cold and flu prevention.

TARGET MARKET

In 2002 busy consumers were already familiar with the pharmacy services available at Walgreens drugstores and took advantage of them. According to the company, it received 14,500 prescriptions to be filled each day through its website and filled more than 361 million total prescriptions in its stores in 2002. But the goal of the "Perfect" campaign was to drive consumers (both men and women) of all ages and ethnic demographics to shop the chains' front end. It stressed to all shoppers that, beyond its pharmacy, the chain could fulfill everyday nonprescription needs and was the ideal place for busy, time-strapped consumers to shop. The campaign touted the convenience of shopping in Walgreens stores and promoted the idea that everyone could find what they needed in its product mix, from cosmetics and greeting cards to exercise equipment and home health-care items such as wheelchairs. "You need to attract that customer into your store who will add to the market-basket," Walgreens' George Reidl said in an interview with *Drug Store News.*

COMPETITION

The CVS drugstore chain was founded in 1963 in Lowell, Massachusetts, as a shop selling a variety of beauty products and over-the-counter health aids. In 1967 CVS added pharmacies to its stores and began expanding. By 2001 the CVS chain boasted 4,000 stores and sales in excess of $22 billion, and it was the number two drugstore chain based on sales behind the granddaddy in the category, Walgreens. To keep its momentum going and encourage busy women in all age groups to go to a CVS store for more than just filling a prescription, in October 2002 the chain began a multimedia marketing campaign that included television spots and print ads with the tagline "Life to the Fullest." The campaign was created by Boston-based agency Hill, Holliday, Connors, Cosmopulos. Each ad or spot featured a CVS store aisle marker paired with a contemporary image of a shopper somewhere other than a drugstore. The aisle markers contained text that, rather than directing shoppers to a specific product or merchandise category, related to an individual CVS shopper's experience. One spot portrayed a young woman sitting in a bright orange chair under a CVS aisle marker in the middle of a stark white room. The marker read: "Great Pharmacists, Expert Advice, Rapid Refill, A Prescription for Living Well."

Rite Aid Corporation, the number three drugstore chain in the United States based on sales (in 2002 annual sales totaled $15 billion, and the company had 3,500 stores), opened the doors of its first store in 1962 in Scranton, Pennsylvania. While Rite Aid had a busy front-end section with a variety of over-the-counter health aids, beauty products, and more, 63 percent of the chain's sales were in its pharmacy departments. Given Rite Aid's ongoing efforts to save consumers money by filling prescriptions with generic drugs rather than the higher-priced brand-name products, in 2002 the chain was featured in an advertising campaign for the health-insurance carrier Michigan Blue Cross Blue Shield. In the $1 million campaign, which was limited to print media, a Rite Aid pharmacist was quoted about the benefits of generic drugs. The tagline asked the question "Want the truth about generic drugs?" Reversing its competitors' trend of driving consumers to shop their stores' front ends in addition to their pharmacies, in 2003 Rite Aid launched an effort to encourage its front-end shoppers to use Rite Aid pharmacies to have prescriptions filled. A company spokesman noted in a *Chain Drug Review* article that Rite Aid's brand "starts with the pharmacy. It's the heart and soul of what we do." The effort included print ads and promotional mailings sans tagline with plans to add television and radio spots in the future.

MARKETING STRATEGY

When Euro RSCG planned its new marketing campaign for Walgreens drugstores, the challenge was to shift the chain retailer's advertising focus away from its core business, pharmacy services, and toward the front end of the stores, the area where everything else was sold. Additionally, Euro RSCG wanted to create a campaign that was a break from traditional drugstore advertising, which often featured a serious pharmacist standing behind a counter backed by shelves of pill bottles. The campaign, which was released in February 2002, was designed to change consumers' perception that a drugstore was only a place to pick up prescriptions by showing that shoppers could make other purchases at Walgreens, from cosmetics and greeting cards to gift items. It included six television spots set in the mythical town of Perfect, located "in a valley, near a river." No budget was available for the campaign, but Walgreen's annual advertising budget was typically between $25 million and $30 million, according to a report in the *Chicago Tribune.*

Because Valentine's Day was the big holiday in February, one of the initial spots showed what life in Perfect was like as its lucky citizens prepared for the special day. During the spot the camera showed scenes of an idyllic village while a voice-over said that Perfect was a place "where every day is filled with love, especially February 14. Valentines are handmade, and every man brings home roses. In Perfect, the only one in the doghouse is the dog." As the spot continued, the voice-over reminded viewers that they did not live in Perfect, "so we have Walgreens, where we can get what's needed for the real world." A subsequent spot that was released for the Christmas holiday had the snow-blanketed village decorated with twinkling lights and resembling a Currier & Ives Christmas card. As the camera scanned the village, there was a shot of a car carrying a Christmas tree, a happy couple on a ladder decorating the town hall, and a little girl catching snowflakes in her mouth. The voice-over said, "In Perfect snowflakes are caught more often than colds." Another spot, referring to the rush by some people to exchange unwanted Christmas gifts, showed the little girl running through the snow to the mailbox in front of her house while the voice-over noted that in Perfect the only thing exchanged was thank-you notes. Each spot ended with the tagline "That's life. This is Walgreens."

As the campaign continued through 2004, new spots were added. In 2005 the campaign received an update with new spots that presented a more realistic image of the town of Perfect and typical shoppers. In one spot, titled "Last Minute," the residents of the town, which was still blanketed with snow, were shown watching their clocks as they ticked toward midnight Christmas Eve. When the fated hour chimed, people dashed from homes and offices for gift shopping at the nearby Walgreens while the voice-over noted that the chain was always ready to accommodate those who waited until the last minute to shop.

OUTCOME

Following the introduction of the Walgreens "Perfect" campaign, industry insiders complimented the effort for helping the drugstore chain strengthen its brand identity and for driving home the message that Walgreens stores were the perfect place for busy consumers to shop. *Adweek* described the campaign's spots as "exceptionally eye-pleasing." The campaign also was well received by the media. In 2003 *Chicago Sun-Times* columnist Lewis Lazare included the campaign as one of the top 10 memorable television commercial efforts by Chicago-based advertising agencies. Lazare wrote, "This campaign transported us about as far as you can get from the dreary pharmacy department that is the epicenter of most drug stores." Based on the campaign's success, in 2003 and 2004 a new series of spots was introduced that were tied to different holidays throughout the year, such as Valentine's Day and Christmas. Other spots focused on specific services that Walgreens offered—such as its drive-through pharmacies—that helped consumers deal with life's daily problems. When Euro RSCG creative officer and developer of the "Perfect" campaign Jim Schmidt left the agency and joined Downtown Partners Chicago, an affiliate of Omnicom Group's DDB, in 2004 Walgreens followed, shifting its advertising business to the new agency. Downtown Partners modified the campaign and launched a series of new spots in 2005.

FURTHER READING

"Ads Tout Belief in Customer Service (CVS Corp. Advertising Strategy)." *Chain Drug Review,* December 11, 2000.

Alexander, Antoinette. "Customer Loyalty Is in This Contender's Corner." *Drug Store News,* March 21, 2005.

Baar, Aaron, and Trevor Johnson. "Walgreens Set for Shift to DDB Unit." *Adweek,* June 9, 2004.

"Conveying the Retailer's Message (Walgreens: The Jorndt Years)." *Chain Drug Review,* December 16, 2002.

Eder, Rob. "Challenge for Walgreens Is Not to Act Its Age." *Drug Store News,* March 21, 2005.

———. "CVS Breaks New Lifestyle-Oriented Ads." *Drug Store News,* October 21, 2002.

Gatlin, Greg. "CVS Aims Ads at Busy Women." *Boston Herald,* October 10, 2002.

Johnsen, Michael. "'Perfect' Campaign Steers Top-Line Growth—Walgreens Destined to Dominate: Marketing." *Drug Store News,* March 23, 2003.

Kirk, Jim. "Chicago Tribune Marketing Column." *Chicago Tribune,* January 10, 2002.

Lazare, Lewis. "New Walgreens Holiday Spots Still 'Perfect.'" *Chicago Sun-Times,* November 22, 2005.

———. "Our Vote for Top Chicago Commercial Efforts." *Chicago Sun-Times,* January 6, 2003.

———. "Walgreen Spots Improve on 'Perfect.'" *Chicago Sun-Times,* November 27, 2002.

"Rite Aid Aims to Break Out from the Pack (Building a New Rite Aid)." *Chain Drug Review,* October 27, 2003.

"Rite Aid Featured in Ad Campaign Touting Generics." *Chain Drug Review,* June 10, 2002.

"'Walgreens Health Corner' TV Show Debuts Nationally on Jan. 3." *PR Newswire,* December 22, 2003.

Rayna Bailey

Washington Mutual, Inc.

1201 3rd Avenue
Seattle, Washington 98101
USA
Telephone: (206) 461-2000
Web site: www.wamu.com

■■■

FEAR NOT CAMPAIGN

OVERVIEW

In just 13 years Washington Mutual, Inc., a thrift lender that offered commercial and residential banking services, soared from being a Pacific Northwest regional bank to reigning as America's largest home lender with $268 billion in assets at the start of 2003. Part of the bank's success, according to analysts, stemmed from its CEO and president Kerry Killinger's unyielding ambition to acquire as many other American thrift lenders as possible. The flexible mortgages Washington Mutual offered also helped the bank excel. While its competition grappled for higher-earning customers, Washington Mutual tailored its advertising to customers within lower income brackets. To continue targeting people who had been denied by other lenders, Washington Mutual released its "Fear Not" campaign.

Created by the ad agency Sedgwick Rd., commercials for "Fear Not" first aired on ABC during the March 10, 2003, Academy Awards ceremony. The budget of the campaign's eight television spots and other radio, newspaper, and billboard advertising was not disclosed, but *Brandweek* magazine's Todd Wasserman noted that a similar campaign had cost Washington Mutual $25 million the previous year. The "Fear Not" campaign featured pitiable characters who, after being approved for a mortgage through Washington Mutual, experienced a newfound joy for life. In the spot "Paul" an irritable office worker named Paul applied at Washington Mutual for a home loan. After being approved, the thankful homeowner laughed off such calamities as being scalded with hot coffee and a drilling mishap at the dentist office. The campaign ended in the summer of 2003.

Other Washington Mutual advertising campaigns that were appearing simultaneously with "Fear Not" did not overshadow its ad-industry success. It collected a Silver Lion for Banking at the 2003 Cannes Lions International Advertising Festival. "Fear Not" also earned a Bronze award at the 2004 International ANDY Awards and collected a Gold EFFIE Award for Financial Services/Products in 2004.

HISTORICAL CONTEXT

Seattle's city officials formed Washington National Building Loan and Investment Association to help rebuild the city's business district after it was destroyed by a fire in 1889. By 1908 the bank had established principles that would define the institution for decades, such as reduced fees, relaxed withdrawal policies, and a focus on public relations. After making more than 20 acquisitions throughout the 1990s, Washington Mutual became America's leading lender.

The agency Sedgwick Rd., formerly known as McCann-Erickson Seattle, had created advertising for Washington Mutual since 1991. The bank's tagline

"The Power of Yes," which had been used since 1998, epitomized the lender's dedication to providing mortgages for consumers who were denied mortgages by other institutions. Ad-industry research firm Taylor Nelson Sofres' CMR estimated that Washington Mutual spent $72 million on advertising in 2002. One television spot, which Washington Mutual aired during the 2002 Academy Awards ceremony, featured a man searching for his old pay stub inside a mountain of garbage. He needed the stub to prove his creditworthiness to his bank. Another spot featured a man undergoing a torturous interrogation by a bank that was approving his mortgage. The voice-overs for both spots explained that getting mortgages with Washington Mutual was easier with "the power of yes."

In an attempt to establish Washington Mutual as the foremost lender in Chicago, in fall of 2002 Sedgwick Rd. erected a 24-by-25-foot cave, referencing a prehistoric dwelling, on a plaza in a Chicago business district. Chiseled into the cave's entrance was advertisement copy that read, "We've been getting people into their dream homes for years." It also featured Washington Mutual's logo and the tagline "The Power of Yes." The cave remained in place into 2003. In Manhattan's Times Square, Sedgwick Rd. placed billboard advertisements with life-sized cutouts of homes that promised, "Whatever your dream home is, we have your loan." Similar billboards appeared around Yankee Stadium in the Bronx.

TARGET MARKET

Washington Mutual's "Fear Not" campaign specifically targeted first-time home buyers who had been denied mortgages from other banks. Because Washington Mutual offered a wide selection of products, including both fixed-rate and variable-rate loans, it could offer mortgages to a variety of different homeowners. While most banks targeted consumers who were within a higher income bracket, Washington Mutual's average customer earned $30,000 to $50,000 per year. The average balance for a Washington Mutual bank account was $1,000, while most banks averaged $3,500 per account balance. According to *Institutional Investor,* Richard Hartnack, the vice chairman for Union Bank of California, explained, "[Washington Mutual is] a bigger competitor for the smaller-balance accounts, those under $1,000, but I don't want an $800 account that doesn't pay me anything, anytime, anywhere." To compensate for accounts with smaller balances, Washington Mutual charged $20 per bounced check. Washington Mutual customers bounced an average of six checks a year.

The campaign's eight television spots featured characters such as office workers, supermarket checkers, and other middle-class employees that typically earned $30,000 to $50,000 per year. In each spot the main character or characters, disheartened by being denied mortgages from other institutions, were elated after being approved by Washington Mutual. "We take a fresh approach to our advertising and to the way we do business," Dave King, senior vice president of advertising and brand management for Washington Mutual's Home Loans and Insurance Services Group, was quoted by *Business Wire.* "Consumers who may have been anxious or confused about the home buying process in the past will find that we simplify the experience and help them find the best loan to meet their needs."

THRIFT LENDERS

Washington Mutual, which was classified as a thrift lender, reigned as America's top financer of home mortgages in 2003. Banks such as Washington Mutual qualified as thrift lenders if a certain percentage of their assets were housing-related investments. Once this percentage was met, one of America's 12 Federal Home Loan Banks would offer the thrift lender low-cost advances.

COMPETITION

In February 2003 the consumer bank with the greatest amount of deposits, Bank of America Corp., launched a $100 million campaign titled "Higher Standards." Created by several ad agencies belonging to the Interpublic Group of Companies, the new campaign distanced the Bank of America brand from any semblance of riskier businesses such as the scandal-ridden Enron Corp. Bank of America's previous tagline was "Embracing ingenuity." According to the *New York Times,* Timothy R.V. Foster, founder of the marketing company AdSlogans Unlimited in London, stated, "Given the current state of play in financial services, the last skill I want my bank to embrace is ingenuity. My bank should embrace compliance." Most "Higher Standards" commercials touted Bank of America's free online checking services. One television spot portrayed the paper checkbook as an antiquated tool for banking. Another spot demonstrated the reduced paperwork afforded by online banking.

In January 2003 Wachovia Corp., America's fourth-largest bank, released a campaign featuring the tagline "Uncommon Wisdom." Created by Mullen, an ad agency within the Interpublic Group, the campaign advertised Wachovia's dedication to money management,

WASHINGTON MUTUAL AND THE BEANSTALK

In October 2003 the financial institution Washington Mutual unveiled an 80-foot-tall advertisement that appeared to be growing outside of the Five Times Square building in New York City. The three-dimensional structure resembled an illustration from the children's story *Jack and the Beanstalk.* Copy for the advertisement read, "Whatever your dream home is, we have your loan."

financial relationships, and small-business management. "Uncommon Wisdom" included seven television spots along with print, outdoor, and radio advertisements. "Consumers are looking for a fresh voice in the financial services industry," Denzil Strickland, executive vice president and creative director at Mullen, explained to the *PR Newswire.* "They are looking for relevance. The Uncommon Wisdom campaign is about living in this world. By learning from the real world, and by applying that knowledge to financial issues, Wachovia stands apart from other financial institutions."

MARKETING STRATEGY

Television spots for "Fear Not" first aired on ABC in March 2003, during the Academy Awards ceremony. "Marketers recognize that the Academy Awards is one of the prime branding opportunities of the year," Dave King, Washington Mutual's national advertising manager, told *Business Wire.* Besides radio, newspaper, and billboard advertising, the campaign consisted of eight television spots titled after the names of their leading characters. In "Roy" the commercial's protagonist was presented as a fainthearted man who, after being approved for a mortgage through Washington Mutual, became overly courageous. Soon after hearing of his new home loan, he tried to shatter cement blocks with a martial-arts head-butt. Then he ordered a serving of day-old sushi, and finally he rode his dirt bike off a cliff.

Each of the television spots featured similar storylines about middle-class consumers who were able to overcome their personal hang-ups after being approved for a Washington Mutual mortgage. " 'The power of yes' is a brand statement that underscores our commitment to put people in homes," Genevieve Smith, vice president of e-commerce at Washington Mutual, told *Brandweek.* "While many of our competitors target the high-income customer, we've made our name by having great financial services for everyone. We've developed our brand as being inviting and approachable."

In the 30-second commercial "Paul," the spot's irritable main character was first shown popping a child's balloon because it drifted too close to his newspaper. After being approved for a mortgage with Washington Mutual, Paul's temperament improved. When his dentist admitted to drilling the wrong side of Paul's mouth, Paul calmly replied, "No problem." When a coworker knocked an entire urn of scalding coffee across Paul's back, he jokingly responded, "I guess I'm having tea." He merely chuckled after discovering a parking ticket on his windshield. The spot ended with the Washington Mutual logo and the tagline "The Power of Yes." The campaign included similarly titled spots such as "Debra," "Rick," "Jim & Karen," "Jen," "Tom," and "Julie." Some commercials ended with Washington Mutual's logo followed by the tagline "Home Loans. More Human Interest." Print and outdoor advertisements featured the same copy on white backgrounds.

Washington Mutual had been using humor to advertise its "The Power of Yes" message since the 1990s. According to advertising critics, humor made the brand appear more accessible and distinguished it from its competitors. Sedgwick Rd.'s creative director, Steve Johnston, explained in *Advertising Age's Creativity* that the campaign's "point is to differentiate Washington Mutual in a relevant way that makes people laugh."

OUTCOME

"Fear Not" was one of many Sedgwick Rd. campaigns in 2003 that helped Washington Mutual secure its position as the largest home financer in America. "Fear Not" collected a Silver Lion for Banking at the 2003 Cannes Lions International Advertising Festival. It also won a Gold EFFIE for Financial Services / Products at the 2004 EFFIE Awards, given out by the New York American Marketing Association, and it earned a Bronze award at the New York Advertising Club's 2004 International ANDY Awards (Financial Products & Services category).

Three of Sedgwick Rd.'s Washington Mutual campaigns, including "Fear Not," won top honors at the Midas Awards, an annual competition dedicated to advertising and marketing achievements in the financial-services industry. According to *Business Wire,* during the Midas Awards ceremony Jim Walker, the president of Sedgwick Rd., noted that it was a difficult challenge to reach the "ever-skeptical financial services audience." He continued, "Winning the grand prize is a testament to what a little humor and humanity can do to differentiate a brand." The commercial "Paul" scored as the best television commercial at the Midas Awards. Overall the campaign helped Washington Mutual generate an income of $12.2 billion from loan interest during 2003, one of the most profitable years in the bank's history.

FURTHER READING

Bergquist, Erick. "Wamu Targets Chicago for Affordable-Loan Push." *American Banker,* September 19, 2002, p. 10.

Cardona, Mercedes M. "Mortgages on the Rise: Smaller Players Give Financial Ads a Boost." *Advertising Age,* September 30, 2002, p. 4.

Cisterna, Fred. "Friendly Banking: La Agencia De Orci Introduces Washington Mutual to New York." *Shoot,* September 27, 2002, p. 17.

Cuneo, Alice Z. "Washington Mutual: Brad Davis." *Advertising Age,* October 8, 2001, p. S18.

Deeken, Aimee. "Sedgwick Rd.: Best Use of Out-of-Home." *Adweek,* June 23, 2003, p. SR26.

Flass, Rebecca. "Washing-Stone Mutual." *Adweek* (western ed.), September 23, 2002, p. 3.

Heim, Sarah J. "Sedgwick Rd. Embraces Change: McCann-Erickson Outpost Expands Business, Hires Key Staffers." *Adweek* (western ed.), December 17, 2001, p. 5.

Kattleman, Terry. "Paul Elledge: The Man Behind the Lens on the Nutty Washington Mutual Campaign Also Shoots Kids for Cereal Ads and, Strange but True, Album Covers Like Ministry's Filth Pig." *Advertising Age's Creativity,* June 1, 2003, p. 66.

Kuykendall, Lavonne. "Financial Firms Take Hard Look at Ad Spending as Biggest Banks Pull Back, Regionals and Insurers See Opportunity to Gain Market Share." *American Banker,* November 13, 2002, p. 3A.

Mandaro, Laura. "To Jump-Start Its Shares, Wamu Tries a Direct Pitch." *American Banker,* August 28, 2003, p. 2.

Sisk, Michael. "Ad Beat: Jack and the Beanstalk Hit the Big City." *U.S. Banker,* December 1, 2003, p. 28.

Stewart, Al. "Wamu Debuts N.Y Ads." *Adweek* (eastern ed.), July 22, 2002, p. 6.

Wilcha, Kristin. "Ikea's 'Lamp' Shines at Cannes Advertising Festival." *Shoot,* June 27, 2003, p. 1.

Kevin Teague

The Weather Channel Companies

300 N Interstate Pkwy.
Atlanta, Georgia 30339-2404
USA
Telephone: (770) 226-0000
Fax: (770) 226-2390
Web site: www.weather.com

PAINTED FACES CAMPAIGN

OVERVIEW

When it was launched in 1982 by the privately held media conglomerate Landmark Communications, The Weather Channel (TWC) represented a new concept—around-the-clock weather programming on television. Available on cable stations throughout the United States, TWC provided five-day national forecasts, warnings of dangerous weather, and reports on weather in Europe. Approximately every 10 minutes there was a brief rundown of local weather. There also were occasional specials, for example, a program on the effects of weather conditions on airplane crashes, and special updates on things such as skiing conditions. TWC employed some 60 meteorologists to analyze National Weather Service data and to prepare the thousands of customized weather forecasts that were beamed by satellite to individual cable stations. Other services provided by TWC included an award-winning Internet website, syndicated products such as maps and satellite images, a toll-free phone number for weather information, and radio and newspaper partnerships.

Until the "Painted Faces" campaign in 1997, TWC had not directly addressed its "geeky" image or the impact on viewers. The image arose in part from the program visuals: announcers who did not pretend to charm and sparkle, no-frills studios and weather maps, and matter-of-fact presentations. In contrast, broadcast weather announcers tried to lure viewers and keep them entertained. TWC was the undisputed leader in accurate information on weather, but most viewers tuned in only when they had a need for specific information.

With its European venture faltering and competition in the United States intensifying, TWC recognized the need to reconstruct its brand identify and its relationship with viewers. Steve Clapp, TWC's vice president of strategic marketing, sought a new agency and a new approach. This led to the television campaign "Painted Faces," which was launched in the spring of 1997 and was scheduled to run through 1998. According to the advertising agency, TBWA Chiat/Day of Venice, California, the principal goals of the campaign were to increase the awareness of TWC and to create a brand image for the channel.

Chiat/Day's research revealed a core of viewers who were obsessed with weather and watched TWC regularly. The agency studied this group to understand the source of the people's interest and to use it to stimulate interest in other viewers. The result was a series of ad spots set in a weather bar called The Front that mimicked a sports bar not just in looks but also in its role as a refuge for the obsessed. Drinks were named the "monsoon," walls held photos of legendary weather announcers, and patrons discussed weather statistics. The "Painted Faces" spot focused on two men who were "Weekend Update" fans.

Their faces were painted, one red as a warm-weather front and the other blue as a cool-weather front. As they heard the update, one was thrilled and the other dejected. The "winner" gloated, "Who looks ridiculous now?" The tag line of the ad wrapped it up: "Weather fans, you're not alone." An accompanying print campaign, which began in February 1997 and ran for 52 weeks as banner ads at the bottom of the *USA Today* weather page, also incorporated humor, joking about TWC's obsession with weather: "If you've never watched The Weather Channel, we have one thing say to you: Get a life!"

HISTORICAL CONTEXT

TWC lost $10.6 million in 1982, its first year of operation, and it did not turn a profit until 1985. Yet Landmark's president and CEO, John O. "Dubby" Wynne, felt that the company "had a winner." Indeed, by 1998 TWC was available in about 70 million U.S. homes, or 98 percent of those with cable. The number rose to 85 million if overseas customers were included. TWC also maintained operations in Latin America and had a 50 percent stake in its Canadian counterpart, Pelmorex. But a 1995 initiative to expand into Europe faced significant obstacles and was halted in late 1997.

TWC launched its first national advertising campaign in 1996, giving the account to Bozell Worldwide in New York. The $6 million campaign aired spots on other cable networks, including ESPN and TBS, and print ads appeared in *Time, TV Guide,* and *People.* The pitch was intended to be humorous. Print ads proclaimed, "No place on earth has better weather," and one television spot showed a woman hanging onto a post in high winds until a gust blew her down the street. Commenting on the Bozell campaign in *Marketing News,* Clapp noted, "Last year [1996] was a landmark because we really stepped up and made a significant investment behind branding activities." At the same time TWC reporters began doing on-the-scene coverage, which provided a change from the no-frills approach.

By early 1997 TWC was becoming a more powerful brand name. As Clapp noted, "Viewers perceive us as being very professional. They know they can turn to us for quality forecasts and weather expertise." What he sought, however, was to go a step further and "emotionally bond with the viewer." Hayes Roth, executive director for corporate identity of Landor Associates in New York and an expert on branding, commented, "Right now, [TWC's] advertisers are not always top-tier." He noted that the brand needed to become or be seen as "hipper or cooler." "Boring as toast," he said regarding TWC's brand name, even while acknowledging its loyal base of viewers. "They're doing a mediocre job of on-air branding." Roth claimed that TWC should build stronger ties to viewers and advertisers, and Clapp apparently had similar sentiments when he chose TBWA Chiat/Day over two other finalists for a new $10 million campaign.

TARGET MARKET

Understanding that TWC viewers encompassed a wide range of demographic and lifestyle characteristics was the first step in defining the market. Speaking to David Bauder of the *Chicago Tribune,* Michael Eckert, TWC's CEO, said, "Many viewers . . . stop briefly on the channel during a remote control surf. As expected, the channel's ratings zoom when a hurricane or big snowstorm is bearing down on a population center. They also jump each day in the early morning, when people who work outside tune in to find out what the day will be like. Gamblers are heavy watchers; they want to see if horses will be running on a fast or muddy track." He concluded, "As you put all these lifestyles together who are using us for different reasons, you start to build a mass."

Chiat/Day divided the viewers into two main groups. The first consisted of functional viewers, those who "get the information they needed, and tune out," for example, a person who might watch for comprehensive coverage at a given time or check the station when the weather affects a family member. The second group consisted of core viewers, "devoted TWC junkies, who religiously watched the channel" from between three and five hours at a time. They made up about one-fifth of all viewers. The first group represented the area of potential growth and became the primary target of the campaign. The key was to get them to see TWC the way the core viewers saw it.

COMPETITION

Although there was no other 24-hour weather channel, there were numerous sources of information on weather, and each presented a competitive challenge to TWC. As Chiat/Day noted, while people respected TWC, "they seemed to *like* their local weather guy, and he was the one they were turning to for their daily weather needs." TWC drew viewers in special situations, but for the most part it did not serve as their day-to-day source. For that people turned elsewhere, including broadcast stations, where weather announcers maintained viewers' loyalty by entertaining them. Nonetheless, for the most part TWC had no major rivals for its 24-hour coverage.

In 1997, however, there arose a new threat to TWC, a partnership between MSNBC's on-line Weather by INTELLICAST and Primestar Satellite Service, a provider of direct broadcast satellite (DBS) programming. MSNBC created a video version of its INTELLICAST service, with the focus on local forecasts. MSNBC's strategic goals were far-reaching, however, and included

AWARDS

The "Painted Faces" campaign met with critical acclaim. It appeared on a number of top 10 and best advertising lists of 1997, including those of *Adweek, Time, TV Guide,* and *Entertainment Weekly.* It also won a number of industry awards. These included three Belding Awards and a Communication Arts Award.

the addition of INTELLICAST to the digital tiers being developed by cable TV operators. *Advertising Age* quoted an executive at INTELLICAST as saying that these developments made TWC "vulnerable to something more locally oriented." It was at this time that TWC's new advertising push occurred.

MARKETING STRATEGY

In order to transform so-called functional viewers into "weather-engaged" viewers, Chiat/Day recognized the need to define the essence of the latter group's passion for TWC. The agency thus performed in-depth customer research before developing its campaign. Brand personification exercises, for example, generated drawings of TWC as "men in gray suits, 100-year-old robots and nerds named Eugene with bottle-cap glasses ... The Weather Channel and its meteorologists were seen as a bunch of weather geeks." It was found that TWC had the respect of viewers, so that when people needed critical weather information, they tuned in. Otherwise they likely watched the weather on broadcast stations, which they saw as more entertaining but less serious and substantial. The challenge for Chiat/Day was to develop a stronger brand image and sense of personality for TWC while at the same time maintaining emphasis on the channel's expertise.

When the agency asked those identified as weather-engaged to keep journals, it appeared that they were somewhat embarrassed about the extent of their viewing. As they described their habit of keeping TWC on all day, for example, they sometimes qualified their statement with a comment like "this is going to sound ridiculous ..." Chiat/Day's research revealed "a relationship to weather that was deeper than the rational need for accurate forecasting and the emotional need to feel in control." To find out what was at the root of this relationship, Chiat/Day had the subjects draw a single image of what they liked about the weather. Among the many drawings of the sun, one stood out, a zigzagging line underscored with the word "unpredictability." The image seemed to represent the opposite of the oft-expressed wish for accuracy in forecasts.

Chiat/Day explored this contradiction for clues to TWC's appeal among the weather-engaged. When the agency prepared a mock newspaper article proclaiming an imminent breakthrough in weather prediction that was 100 percent accurate, respondents hated the idea. Chiat/Day concluded, "The unconscious, instinctual relationship turned out to be about a fascination with the awe, mystery and wonder of Mother Nature." This seemed to be at odds with the image of TWC's meteorologists, for whom accuracy signified success. Research with the meteorologists, however, showed that they themselves had a passion and respect for the ultimate unpredictability of weather. In fact, it was this that had led many of them into the field in the first place. Further, they had no illusion about 100 percent accuracy. This information produced a new challenge for Chiat/Day: "How could we reconcile what was interesting about weather (mystery) with what was necessary about it (accuracy)?" The decision was made to accept the paradox and to allow the two poles to "co-exist in a yin-yang relationship."

One element of this approach was to encourage the TWC meteorologists to reveal their passion for the weather in the belief that their feelings would become contagious. It was thought that the passion of people who devoted their lives to learning and communicating about weather could be used as an energizing force. Showing the brand presentation and the ads to the meteorologists inspired them to voice their enthusiasm and wonder for weather. New on-air promotions and identity spots also were developed, and everything from set design to the meteorologists' style of presentation was revamped to align with this approach.

Chiat/Day thus attempted to control the image of TWC and craft an effective brand personality. The elements the agency had to work with were a bundle of contradictions: mystery, accuracy, geekiness, seriousness, passion. The journals of the weather-engaged had shown that these people recognized it to be a bit odd to be so "into weather." Working with this reality, Chiat/Day devised a brand personality—endearingly quirky—that was absolutely true to the character of TWC in all of its contradictions.

This brand personality allowed for the type of self-deprecating humor that evolved into the "Painted Faces" campaign. According to Chiat/Day, both the ad itself, which was directed by David Ramser, and the bar in which it was set gave "weather junkies a sense of acceptance and belonging and ... permission to be into the weather. It's a place that also invites others to join in on the fun." Chiat/Day sought nothing less than to make TWC a part of pop culture. The ad ran on a number of cable channels, including the Discovery Channel, CNN, and A&E Network, on broadcast shows such as *The Tonight Show,* and on popular reruns and syndicated shows like *Seinfeld* and *Wheel of Fortune.*

OUTCOME

Chiat/Day's follow-up research, including both before-and-after drawings of brand personification, indicated that the campaign was successful in more deeply engaging functional viewers. This conclusion was supported by a Millard Brown Tracking Study showing that the brand image "passionate about the weather" was associated with TWC by 73 percent of those who recognized the "Painted Faces" ad as compared to 38 percent who did not. Furthermore, following two months of advertising in New York and Chicago, advertising awareness in these markets increased 13 percent as against 3 percent in a national control group. Of those aware of the ads, 63 percent linked the ads to TWC, more than doubling the average brand linkage of 31 percent.

Anecdotal evidence confirmed these positive results. Chiat/Day reported that TWC was flooded with fan mail and received requests for posters of "Painted Faces." A 1997 survey by Young and Rubicam indicated that, along with the Discovery Network, TWC was one of the three most recognized names on cable.

FURTHER READING

Bauder, David. "Rain or Shine, Weather Channel Is Becoming a Habit with Viewers." *Chicago Tribune,* April 12, 1997.

Garfield, Bob. "Clouds of Geekiness Part for Weather Fans." *Advertising Age,* September 1997.

Haddad, Charles. "The Weather Channel Yields to Poor Climate in European TV." *Atlanta Constitution Journal,* January 30, 1998.

McCarthy, Michael. "A Channel Switch." *Adweek* (Western Edition), February 3, 1997.

Miller, Cyndee. "Big Audience Has Weather Channel Singin' in the Rain." *Marketing News,* February 17, 1997, p. 2.

Osterman, Jim. "Sun Shines on 3 Finalists for the Weather Channel." *Adweek,* December 9, 1996.

Ross, Chuck. "Video Version of Online Intellicast Set for Primestar Satellite Service." *Advertising Age,* February 17, 1997.

"$6 Million TV, Print Campaign Touts Weather Channel." *Brandweek,* February 26, 1996.

"The Weather Channel Has Become Part of America's Television Climate." *Roanoke Times* & *World News,* January 21, 1998.

Wolverton, Brad. "Cable's Storm King Reinvents Itself." *Business Week,* August 11, 1997, p. 6.

Cynthia Tokumitsu

Wendy's International, Inc.

One Dave Thomas Blvd.
Dublin, Ohio 43017-0256
USA
Telephone: (614) 764-3100
Fax: (614) 764-3330
Web site: www.wendys.com

FRESH STUFFED PITA CAMPAIGN

OVERVIEW

In a fast-food universe dominated by industry giant McDonald's, the task for the challengers has always been to devise a competitive posture that emphasizes differences that resonate with consumers. As customers began to assert their preference for fresh ingredients and made-to-order products, aggressive smaller chains moved to fill this demand. One of the first and most successful to do so was Wendy's International Inc.

Founded by R. Dave Thomas in 1969, the chain began by offering the kind of "fresh" burgers and shakes customers remembered from the days of the corner diner, a far cry from the processed patties that studded the menus of Wendy's big-name competitors. A series of quirky ad campaigns reinforced the company's image as a friendly, customer-oriented purveyor of simple comfort staples. Having established its niche, Wendy's continued to innovate, using menu flexibility to reflect the changing tastes of fast-food consumers. As tastes veered away from burgers and toward more healthful alternatives, Wendy's was thus in an ideal position to cater to this emerging market.

Consumers went through burger wars and price wars. Increasingly, however, they began to demand light but filling sandwiches that were more healthful than the traditional combinations of ground beef and cheese. By the late 1990s the demand for healthful fast-food items seemed to reach its peak.

Wendy's menu had long featured unconventional fast-food fare, including baked potatoes and chili. In response to the demands of health-conscious consumers, in 1979 it became one of the first chains to introduce a salad bar, which it did over the initial objections of Thomas. On the other hand, when McDonald's tried to introduce McPizza, consumers rejected it as bizarre and unappetizing. This was partly because McDonald's strong association with hamburgers left it ill-prepared for such a change in its menu. Wendy's, which was not encumbered by such associations, could and did respond more easily to the wishes of its customers.

One of the results was the introduction of the Fresh Stuffed Pita line in 1997. Inspired in part by the growing popularity of wrap sandwiches on restaurant menus, the four-sandwich line was designed to offer consumers the healthful benefits of a salad with a sandwich's portability. The common ingredient shared by all four sandwiches was the heated flatbread used to envelop the chilled ingredients. Two of the sandwiches incorporated chicken chunks, one with salad greens and a Caesar vinaigrette dressing and one with fresh vegetables and ranch dressing. A third, called Classic Greek, blended feta cheese into the mix, while the Garden Veggie Pita, which did not have meat or cheese, was the lightest option.

Using a massive promotional campaign, Wendy's sought to sell the new line to its existing customers while enticing salad lovers to its restaurants for the first time. The continuity of the new campaign with the chain's existing philosophy made the undertaking especially favorable. As John Barker, Wendy's vice president of investor relations, told *Nation's Restaurant News,* the Fresh Stuffed Pita line "reinforces Wendy's unique position in the market in that it's fresh and made-to-order."

HISTORICAL CONTEXT

The story of Wendy's marketing success was, in many ways, the story of founder Thomas. His blend of folksy charm and down-home homilies gave Wendy's campaigns their unique appeal and made him one of advertising's icons. "More than anything, I'm a marketer," Thomas confessed in his 1991 memoir, *Dave's Way.* His nose for promotion served as one of the pillars of Wendy's success.

The adopted son of an itinerant handyman, Thomas developed his love for the restaurant business early in life. In 1948 he dropped out of high school to work full-time in the industry. His big break occurred when he became a Kentucky Fried Chicken franchisee. Thomas was schooled at the knee of Colonel Harland Sanders, the founder of the chain of fast-food restaurants. Sanders's dedication to promoting his business became the template for Thomas's own marketing approach.

Using money he earned from turning around failing Kentucky Fried Chicken franchises, Thomas opened his first Wendy's in 1969. Named for one of his daughters, the burger-and-fries operation rapidly expanded from its Midwestern base. Advertising, along with shrewd menu innovations, were integral to the company's early growth. For the first eight years of its existence, however, Wendy's had no national advertising. Its commercials appeared only on local television and radio. The company's first nationally televised commercial, titled "Hot 'n Juicy," aired in April 1977. The $4 million inaugural campaign ran from 1977 to 1980, won a Clio Award for creativity, and established national name recognition for the fledgling company.

In 1981 the newly assertive company switched gears, debuting a glitzy Hollywood-style campaign that had employees and customers singing the jingle "Wendy's Has the Taste." A salad bar and chicken sandwich were featured in the advertising. Thomas also made his first appearance in a commercial. In each ad he related one of his basic business maxims. "Now given that," went the tag line, "why would anyone go anyplace else?" The camera then moved to one of several dining room scenes, where customers explained that there "Ain't No Reason" to go anyplace else. The use of the colloquial "ain't no" created substantial national and local publicity. The company's next campaign, "Wendy's Kind of People," debuted in June 1982. Its folksy theme was used in many later advertising, public relations, and sales promotion projects. In that same year Thomas became senior chairman of the company and gave up running the day-to-day operations. He would not appear in a Wendy's ad for the next seven years.

In the summer of 1983 Wendy's entered what were called the burger wars with a series of biting ads depicting the customer as a victim of "those other hamburger places." Hapless consumers were ordered to "step aside" or "park it" and wait for "frozen stiff" hamburgers. In January 1984 Wendy's unveiled its most famous campaign, indeed one of the singular campaigns in advertising history. The aim was to attack the misconception that Wendy's single hamburger was smaller than competitors' "big-name" hamburgers. Created by Dancer Fitzgerald Sample and the director Josef Sedelmaier, the man behind the FedEx famous fast talker, the "Where's the Beef?" campaign consisted at first of four commercials featuring 70-something actress Clara Peller and sidekicks Mildred Lane and Elizabeth Shaw.

Few marketing campaigns have hammered home the concept of bang-for-the-buck as effectively as "Where's the Beef?" The ads made a national folk heroine out of the feisty, diminutive Peller and spawned a catchphrase that ranked with the most memorable in advertising history. Before Peller brayed her way into the nation's consciousness, only 37 percent of American consumers were familiar with Wendy's advertising. After the debut of "Where's the Beef?" the figure jumped to 60 percent. But the impact of "Where's the Beef?" transcended the fast-food industry. The phrase was soon appearing everywhere, from bumper stickers to Sunday morning sermons. The tag line even appeared in the 1984 presidential campaign, when Democratic aspirant Walter Mondale used it to tweak rival Gary Hartin a televised debate. "I'm happy to say the slogan worked better for us than it did for Mr. Mondale," cracked Thomas in his memoir.

Wendy's did not rest on its "Where's the Beef?" laurels, however. It continued to produce unique, quirky ads that garnered industry accolades. In December 1984 Wendy's rolled out a series of humorous spots for chicken sandwiches under the banner "Parts Is Parts." It was another Clio winner. In 1985 Wendy's even managed to incorporate political humor into its advertising. Its commercial "Russian Fashion Show" lampooned the dreary monotony of life under the Soviet jackboot. This spot also won a Clio.

In June 1987 Wendy's introduced the "Hamburger A, Hamburger B" campaign, in which an interviewer asked people to choose between a fresh Wendy's hamburger and an unappealing hamburger made from frozen beef, presumably produced by one of the chain's rivals. With the burger wars having subsided, however, Wendy's returned to its folksy approach. In April 1989 Thomas returned in a series of ads in which he offered a money-back guarantee if consumers did not agree that Wendy's had the best tasting hamburgers in the business. Nearly 400 consumers nationwide took part in the accompanying testimonial campaign, one of the largest such campaigns in television history.

Wendy's next campaign, "Old Fashioned Guy," continued along the same line. The ads placed Thomas in a Wendy's restaurant expounding on his "old-fashioned philosophy" of making hamburgers. After asking people to "come on in" for an old-fashioned hamburger, Thomas concluded the ads by saying, "Our hamburgers are the best in the business, or I wouldn't have named the place after my daughter." Thomas's return could not have come at a better time for Wendy's. Sales throughout the fast-food sector had slowed, and it was believed that the burger war ads had taken Wendy's too far afield from its traditional strengths. With Thomas's return—and an aggressive quality control initiative that saw him spending 35 weeks a year schmoozing with franchisees—systemwide sales jumped to more than $3 billion in 1990, a 29 percent increase from the year before. Competitors' sales remained flat.

In the 1990s, despite suffering a serious heart attack, the genial Thomas continued to star in Wendy's ads. The founder's credibility as a spokesperson helped Wendy's to consistently increase its advertising awareness figures, surpassing even the "Where's the Beef?" campaign. As the decade wore on, the commercials began to emphasize the wide variety of Wendy's menu items, from specialty sandwiches such as Monterey Ranch Chicken to the Super Value Menu to the highly touted launch of stuffed pita sandwiches in 1997.

TARGET MARKET

In the 1990s Wendy's was among the leaders in fast-food franchises in responding to the needs of health-conscious consumers. As consumer tastes turned away from beef—and in the face of threats of increases in the price of beef—the company began to incorporate more chicken into its menu items. The marriage of chicken with salad on a light flatbread in the Fresh Stuffed Pita seemed tailor-made for a market that wanted a low-fat, low-cholesterol sandwich. "Fresh Stuffed Pitas provide Wendy's with a very attractive alternative to the typical fast food hamburger fare," observed Mitchell B. Pinheiro, an analyst with Janney Montgomery Scott, in a 1997 report on the company.

Early consumer tracking showed that the sandwiches were most in favor among young women, who had traditionally gravitated toward low-fat, salad-based products. Salad lovers who would not normally patronize fast-food restaurants soon became a valuable segment of the market as well. In an all-things-to-everyone approach, Wendy's spokespeople positioned Fresh Stuffed Pitas as the perfect choice for those who wanted a filling sandwich that was also light and easy to eat.

VEGETARIAN OR NOT?

The public expected a product called Garden Veggie Pita and designated as "vegetarian" on a brochure not to contain meat. Wendy's faced a public relations firestorm when it was revealed that this particular pita contained a gelatin additive made from animal by-products. Some consumers had complained when they noticed that the dressing on the sandwich wraps seemed thicker and more saucelike than customary vegetarian toppings. After fielding numerous complaints, Wendy's admitted that the dressing was derived from hide, beaks, and connective tissue, ingredients usually earmarked for pet food. The company agreed to retire the gelatin-based dressing once existing stocks ran out, and competing chains that also used animal extracts in vegetarian entrees rushed to change their practices as well.

COMPETITION

As the 1990s wore on, McDonald's embarked on a series of aggressive marketing campaigns that threatened to cut into Wendy's profit margins. Wendy's response to the threat was to diversify its menu even further. This strategy represented a counterattack against McDonald's, which in the eyes of many industry observers had for too long failed to innovate in the development of products.

A report by Everen Securities analyst Dean T. Haskell in the spring of 1997 found that McDonald's domestic operations were under intense competitive pressure from other major fast-food chains. "Competitive pressure in the United States persists because of a continuing proliferation of chain restaurants and weak consumer spending," Haskell observed. "Competitors of McDonald's are also building aggressively, using traditional and nontraditional units to penetrate markets." While McDonald's own growth remained solid, it found its competitive position jeopardized by such innovations as value pricing and menu diversification. Wendy's introduction of the Fresh Stuffed Pita in 1997 was only the latest in a series of product rollouts designed to take advantage of this competitive atmosphere.

MARKETING STRATEGY

Fresh Stuffed Pitas were initially test-marketed in Norfolk, Virginia, and Omaha, Nebraska, in January 1996. After receiving a favorable response, they were added to the menus of Wendy's franchises in eight other markets in the fall of 1996. They were priced from $1.99 to $2.99 and carried a low food cost, meaning that there would be relatively high margins if the line sold at all. Wendy's officials hoped to have the sandwiches replace the higher-cost salad bars still in place in many franchises.

By April 1997 Wendy's entire 4,400-unit U.S. system was in the training stage for the rollout. While there was initial reluctance on the part of some franchisees regarding the adjustments in operations required for the new product, strong, incremental sales gains based only on point-of-purchase advertising soon eased their reservations. "What we're doing is gradually increasing demand for the pita as stores gradually get used to carrying it, so the operations don't suffer," explained Wendy's Barker.

Promotional materials provided to franchisees stressed the fun of eating the sandwich. One promotion showed a cartoon Thomas dryly instructing consumers "how to eat a pita." Dummy press releases were designed to announce the launch of Fresh Stuffed Pitas in each market, while the entire press package was festooned with the legend "Fresh Like a Salad, Filling Like a Sandwich."

Once the entire Wendy's system became accustomed to assembling the pitas, the company launched television advertising. The New York-based agency Bates Worldwide designed the ads, which debuted in the spring of 1997. The initial spot featured Thomas explaining the concept of "a salad in a sandwich." A subsequent ad had him settling an argument between a young couple over whether the new product was a salad or a sandwich. "It's both," says a reassuring Thomas. Other spots in the national campaign showed Thomas donning a series of disguises and making a big announcement about the pita line to a gathering of Wendy's employees.

OUTCOME

Given the high-profile rollout of the ads, public response to the "Fresh Stuffed Pita" campaign was something of a disappointment. *USA Today*'s Ad Track measured the popularity and effectiveness of the new ads. Its initial findings indicated that only 16 percent of respondents liked the commercials a great deal, while 26 percent found them effective. Older consumers responded more favorably than did younger consumers, with 24 percent of those over age 50 saying they liked the ads a lot.

Analysts differed over whether the product or the pitch was responsible for the lukewarm response to the ads. Carlie Rath, Wendy's executive vice president of marketing, told *USA Today,* "We realize the pita is a product that isn't going to appeal to all of our customers." While conceding that Thomas was one of the most recognizable chief executives in America, marketing consultant Lynn Upshaw felt that Wendy's "may need to reexamine how they can best use his image. That's one of the pitfalls of any long-running campaign."

Nevertheless, Wendy's declared the campaign a sales success. Certainly the early sales returns were favorable. A report by analyst Pinheiro found that Wendy's same-store sales had increased 9.1 percent in the first quarter of 1997. The growth was accompanied by a 6.6 percent increase in transactions. "Even more interesting is that the company has achieved these transaction gains while initiating some price increases," Pinheiro noted. "We cannot name another quick-serve restaurant chain that has been able to raise prices, a testament to the underlying strength of the concept." While declining to issue specific numbers, Wendy's acknowledged that, as of November 1997, pita sales were meeting or exceeding its own projections.

FURTHER READING

Enrico, Dottie. "Consumers Bought Into Real-World Ads in '97." *USA Today,* December 29, 1997.

———. "Dave Comes Up Flat as Wendy's Pita Pusher." *USA Today,* November 3, 1997.

Hamstra, Mark. "Wendy's Blends Elements of Salad and Sandwich in New Pita Promo." *Nation's Restaurant News,* March 31, 1997.

Killian, Linda. "Hamburger Helper." *Forbes,* August 5, 1991, p. 106.

Mulrine, Anna. "Psst. About That Veggie Pita." *U.S. News & World Report,* July 8, 1997.

Pollack, Judann, and Mark Gleason. "Wendy's, McDonald's Seek New Menu Sizzle." *Advertising Age,* March 5, 1997, p. 12.

Ross, Chuck. "Wendy's Shifts National Media Back to Bates." *Advertising Age,* March 5, 1997, p. 1.

Robert Schnakenberg

GOOD TO BE SQUARE CAMPAIGN

OVERVIEW

Wendy's International, Inc., was the United States' third-largest burger chain in the early 2000s, and it had a reputation for high-quality food that was the envy of the industry. The public face of the Wendy's brand was company founder Dave Thomas, who, with his folksy persona and rags-to-riches success story, had become an icon inseparable from the Wendy's brand, thanks to his starring role in a 12-year advertising campaign. Thomas's death in 2002 thus left Wendy's without a clear voice or direction in its marketing, a problem that was compounded by the growing marketing effectiveness of competitors McDonald's and Burger King. In 2005, as a means of updating the Wendy's image, the company and its agency, the New York office of McCann-Erickson Worldwide, introduced a comprehensive advertising platform under the tagline "Do What Tastes Right." Designed to speak in different ways to different target groups, it was particularly noteworthy for its inclusion of an online, viral (designed to be passed around by consumers via E-mail and other means), and TV campaign called "Good to Be Square."

"Good to Be Square" targeted young adults, especially males, prime consumers of fast food whom Wendy's had not effectively reached with preceding campaigns. All elements of the campaign were built around a central conceit in which an animated character called Smart Square (modeled after the square hamburger patties characteristic of Wendy's) demonstrated his superiority to throngs of round "Beadicons" (circular figures meant to evoke competitors' hamburgers). "Good to Be Square" began as an unbranded website featuring a short film and other elements that could be transmitted to other Internet users via E-mail. Soon after the site's launch in mid-May 2005, TV spots featuring Smart Square and the Beadicons began appearing, and the website became a branded one linked to the main Wendy's site.

Although "Good to Be Square" and the larger shift in Wendy's marketing strategy were seen as promising steps toward the goal of establishing a clear and updated brand identity, Wendy's in 2005 experienced its first full-year sales decline since 1987. This outcome was at least partly explained, however, by strengthened competition from McDonald's and Burger King as well as by a hoax that had damaged the chain's reputation among consumers in the spring of that year.

HISTORICAL CONTEXT

Wendy's became America's third-biggest fast-food chain thanks in large part to its founder, Dave Thomas. Thomas began working in inexpensive restaurants at age 12 and did not finish high school. In 1969, after years of restaurant toil, he opened his own establishment, the original Wendy's, in Columbus, Ohio. Although the restaurant chain's extreme growth in subsequent decades

© MIKE CASSESE/REUTERS/CORBIS.

lifted Thomas far above his roots, his humble background and no-nonsense personality continued to infuse the corporate culture, and arguably the food, at Wendy's.

The chain was known as a higher-quality alternative to competitors Burger King and McDonald's, a perception reinforced by the classic advertising campaign "Where's the Beef?" which used humor to posit that competitors' hamburgers fell far short of the standard set by Wendy's. Wendy's likewise augmented the industry-standard burger-and-fries offerings with a focus on chicken sandwiches and such items as chili, baked potatoes, and salads, which strengthened its image as an upscale fast-food chain and contributed to a corresponding impression that its food was healthier than that on offer at McDonald's or Burger King. Beginning in 1989 Wendy's and its advertising agency, the New York office of Bates Worldwide, linked this reputation for food quality with the personality of founder Thomas, who became the public face of the brand in its TV commercials. The spots depicted Thomas in a variety of humorous scenarios that demonstrated his honesty, commitment to quality, and lack of pretension, attributes that were successfully integrated into the Wendy's identity over the 12-year course of the campaign's run.

Thomas's death in 2002 therefore left Wendy's at a marketing crossroads. Because he served as the Wendy's spokesman, Thomas had become virtually synonymous with the chain itself, and there was no clear way to extend his legacy in future advertising campaigns or to promote an identity apart from his personality, at least in the years immediately following his death. Although the chain continued to perform well in 2002 and 2003, it struggled to find a consistent advertising strategy. In 2004 Wendy's settled on a new campaign featuring an "unofficial" spokesman, the fictional Mr. Wendy, who proselytized on behalf of the chain's food despite having been issued a cease-and-desist order from the corporate office. In TV, print, and online components crafted by the New York office of McCann-Erickson Worldwide for a family audience, Mr. Wendy was shown zealously encouraging people to try Wendy's against backdrops ranging from a Little League game to a Hollywood party. The Mr. Wendy concept was intended to provide a long-running framework for a variety of product pitches, as the commercials featuring Thomas had done. The campaign corresponded with surprisingly sharp sales declines, however, and many observers complained that Mr. Wendy represented a feeble and less-than-subtle attempt to replace Thomas. The campaign was pulled within a year of its introduction.

Wendy's faced additional problems during this time. McDonald's and Burger King had both found effective marketing messages at the same time that they were closing the perceived gap in menu quality that had historically set Wendy's apart from them. A March 2005 hoax in which a woman claimed to have found a severed finger in a bowl of Wendy's chili further damaged Wendy's brand image and proved temporarily devastating to sales chainwide. In May 2005 Wendy's and McCann-Erickson unveiled a new umbrella campaign called "Do What Tastes Right." In addition to marking a substantial break in tone from past advertising, "Do What Tastes Right" was projected to provide flexibility for speaking to different target groups with different creative strategies.

DAVE THOMAS, 1932–2002

A portly older man in an unstylish short-sleeved dress shirt and tie, Dave Thomas, as the longtime TV spokesman for his burger chain Wendy's, came across as a straight-talking everyman. His unassuming exterior was all the more appealing for being paired with one of the most compelling rags-to-riches stories in corporate America. An orphan whose adoptive mother died when he was five, Thomas lived in a succession of Midwestern towns as his father struggled to hold a steady job, and the two ate dinner at inexpensive diners and family restaurants every night. This gave the boy a sense of being at home in such establishments, and he began working in the restaurant industry at age 12, dropping out of school in the 10th grade to support himself by working in a restaurant. Even once Thomas had become one of America's most successful entrepreneurs, he exuded humility and authenticity. *Adweek* magazine critic Barbara Lippert said of the Wendy's commercials in which Thomas starred, "Even though the spots were only mildly smile-producing, that aggregate of genuine Daveness is what resonated: It made the commercials feel like home, like what Dave was looking for all his life."

TARGET MARKET

Although "Do What Tastes Right" featured a variety of creative executions and placements for different target markets, one of the overall goals of the campaign was to reach males aged 18 to 34. Wendy's recognized that it had not effectively targeted this younger market with the folksy, family-oriented advertising of the Thomas era and of the Mr. Wendy campaign, and "Good to Be Square" represented the chain's most daring and offbeat attempt to reach this younger audience. A combined Internet, TV, and viral campaign, "Good to Be Square" showed that Wendy's was cognizant of this target group's growing preference for online entertainment over watching television. Young adults were also among the most finicky of American consumers, in part, it was believed, because they were suspicious of traditional marketing techniques. The online portion of the campaign, accessible at www.goodtobesquare.com, thus offered entertainment—a short animated film as well as interactive functions featuring the character Smart Square and the hapless round "Beadicons" surrounding him—rather than overt branding.

COMPETITION

Although McDonald's was the U.S. fast-food-industry leader with more than double the estimated market share of Burger King and more than three times that of Wendy's in 2003 (43.1 percent versus 18.5 percent and 13.2 percent, respectively), it had seen sales flag in recent years at least partly because of a wider consumer backlash against fast foods that were perceived as unhealthy. Wendy's had been well positioned, thanks to its salads and other comparatively healthy menu options, to cope with changing consumer tastes, but in 2003 McDonald's began to engineer a sales turnaround that surprised analysts and threatened Wendy's positioning. A key part of the McDonald's resurgence was an updating of its menu: notably, the chain introduced a line of premium salads, reformulated its Chicken McNuggets to consist exclusively of white meat, and introduced sandwiches featuring whole-breast chicken fillets. This menu overhaul allowed the burger giant to claim many of the product-quality and health attributes that had long set Wendy's apart in the category. A well-received advertising campaign tagged "I'm Lovin' It" drew attention to the product innovations with help from celebrities including tennis stars Venus and Serena Williams and basketball star Yao Ming. McDonald's posted sales gains of $2 billion in 2004, for a sales total of $24.4 billion, larger than sales totals of its three top challengers—Burger King, Wendy's, and Subway—combined. McDonald's continued to post consistent sales growth in 2005 and was almost universally believed to be well positioned for future category dominance.

After experiencing sales declines in 2003 that left total revenues at $7.9 billion compared with $8.3 billion for 2002, Burger King was, like Wendy's, attempting to find a new direction for its marketing in 2004. It moved its advertising account from Chicago's Young & Rubicam to Miami's Crispin Porter + Bogusky. Then the company revived a long-running tagline from previous years, "Have It Your Way," and used it to promote the chain's chicken-based menu items with a much-publicized online and viral campaign aimed at young adults. Called "Subservient Chicken," the campaign featured a website, www.subservientchicken.com, where users could manipulate visuals of a human in a chicken suit. Web surfers could command the chicken to perform a number of actions, including dancing, watching television, and doing push-ups. The site's designers had programmed the chicken to respond to lewd or inappropriate commands with a disapproving wag of his wing, and a webcam frame made the chicken appear to be conscious of the Web surfers who gave him commands. Within eight days of the website's launch on April 7, 2004, it had attracted 15 to 20 million hits. The campaign was credited with helping the Burger King brand connect to young males and with sparking sustained growth over the next year. "Subservient Chicken" also won numerous advertising awards and was an obvious influence on Wendy's' entry into the world of viral marketing the following year.

MARKETING STRATEGY

In keeping with the larger "Do What Tastes Right" directive to focus on the chain's food, the "Good to Be Square" concept was rooted in the trademark square shape of Wendy's burgers. Online and TV executions were centered on the character Smart Square, a simple animated, square-shaped figure with arms, legs, an impassive facial expression, and a self-assured baritone voice. Smart Square was surrounded by Beadicons, circle-shaped characters evocative of other burger patties. The Beadicons were anxiety-ridden and ineffectual and could communicate only via tiny chirps and squeals.

"Good to Be Square" was launched simultaneously with the larger "Do What Tastes Right" effort in mid-May of 2005. Originally website banners featuring a visual of Smart Square against a red background encouraged users to link to the "Good to Be Square" website, which at that point was unbranded. The 60-second film available for viewing there likewise contained no references to Wendy's, instead following Smart Square as he helped the hapless Beadicons solve a variety of problems: he effortlessly found a needle in a haystack for them, saved a group of Beadicons stranded in a boat by kicking an oar to them in one swift motion, and opened a gate that had been stymieing a bunch of Beadicons. Once he had opened the gate, a crowd of Beadicons slavishly followed him into a flowering meadow. As they gathered around him, a rainbow emerged in the background, and Smart Square coolly asked, "Why? Why are they following me?" The film's soundtrack was the upbeat 1970s song "Ooh Child," by the Five Stairsteps, whose reassuring message that "things are gonna get easier" corresponded with Smart Square's problem-solving efforts. The website's viral components included a feature enabling viewers to E-mail the website link to friends as well as downloadable images of Smart Square and the Beadicons making a variety of expressions.

"Good to Be Square" content later moved to branded TV spots. Like the online film, the TV spots showed Smart Square surrounded by squeaking circular Beadicons and demonstrating that he was far more self-assured and capable than they were, but in ways that more overtly pushed a Wendy's food-quality message. One spot featured Smart Square singing, "It takes flair to be a square . . . it's better than being round or being a king or a clown" ("king" and "clown" being references, respectively, to Burger King and the McDonald's mascot, Ronald McDonald). Smart Square's song closed with images of actual Wendy's burgers and the casually intoned command "Eat me." Another TV spot showed the circular Beadicons sweating and worrying under heat lamps before Smart Square appeared, saying, "If heat lamps have this much power over little animated circle people, you can just imagine what they do to your hamburger." This was a reference to new grilling equipment that Wendy's had installed in its restaurants, allowing for faster food preparation and making heat lamps unnecessary. The TV spots ran under the "Do What Tastes Right" tagline and directed viewers to the website www.goodtobesquare.com. The "Good to Be Square" website thus became branded with the Wendy's name and was linked to the main company site. The TV spots were made available for viewing on www.goodtobesquare.com, and the initial film was still available but with branded Wendy's elements added at its conclusion.

Wendy's did not disclose budget figures for "Good to Be Square" or "Do What Tastes Right," suggesting only that the new umbrella campaign marked an increase over the brand's typical yearly ad spend of between $350 and $400 million. "Good to Be Square" was, however, certainly a more cost-effective campaign than a traditional media effort would have been, because its online components required no purchasing of broadcast time and its viral components relied on Web users themselves to spread the word about the campaign.

OUTCOME

Although "Good to Be Square" and the larger shift in the tone of Wendy's advertising were generally well received, in 2005 the chain posted its first full-year sales loss—a decline of 3.7 percent—in 18 years. Wendy's cited the increased competition from McDonald's and Burger King as well as the ruse about the human finger in Wendy's chili as the reasons for the losses, and the company continued to develop its "Do What Tastes Right" marketing platform.

FURTHER READING

Cebrzynski, Gregg. "Wendy's Revamps Ad, Media Strategies to Zero in on Diverse Targets." *Nation's Restaurant News,* May 30, 2005.

Garfield, Bob. "Seven Things Wendy's Commercials Do Right." *Advertising Age,* May 23, 2005.

Gibson, Richard. "Wendy's Faces Advertising Dilemma." *Wall Street Journal,* November 10, 2004.

Hein, Kenneth. "Big Boys (and Bigger Burgers) Are Back!" *Brandweek,* June 20, 2005.

———. "Fast Food." *Brandweek,* April 25, 2005.

Howard, Theresa. "'Viral' Ads Are So Fun You Pass 'Em Along." *USA Today,* May 19, 2005.

Lippert, Barbara. "The Natural." *Adweek,* January 14, 2002.

MacArthur, Kate. "As Sales Slip, Wendy's Revamps Brand Team." *Advertising Age,* October 31, 2005.

———. "Rowden Grabs Wendy's Collar, Yanks It Forward." *Advertising Age,* June 27, 2005.

———. "Salad Days at McDonald's." *Advertising Age,* December 13, 2004.

———. "Wendy's Struggles to Serve Up Success." *Advertising Age,* February 21, 2005.

Steinberg, Brian, and Suzanne Vranica. "Burger King Seeks Some Web Heat; Interactive Site Is Created to Promote Chicken Items to Young-Adult Market." *Wall Street Journal,* April 15, 2004.

Mark Lane

Wholesome & Hearty Foods Company

15615 Alton Pkwy., Ste. 350
Irvine, California 92618
USA
Telephone: (949) 255-2000
Fax: (949) 255-2010
Web site: www.gardenburger.com

EATING GOOD JUST GOT GREAT CAMPAIGN

OVERVIEW

NOTE: Since the initial appearance of this essay in the 1999 edition of *Major Marketing Campaigns Annual*, Gardenburger Inc. changed its name to Wholesome & Hearty Foods. The essay continues to refer to the company's former name, as that was the official name of the organization when the campaign was launched.

Gardenburger, Inc., a manufacturer and distributor of meatless food products, launched its first television advertising campaign in 1998 and took a heady gamble by investing approximately $1.5 million, a sizable portion of Gardenburger's annual advertising budget of about $14 million, on one 30-second advertising slot on the final episode of the popular television program *Seinfeld.* The program, which aired on NBC, had generated a dedicated following of viewers, and the show's finale was purported to have the most expensive commercial advertising time in television history, outdoing even the much-watched Super Bowl. Despite skepticism among competitors and industry analysts regarding Gardenburger's decision to invest more than 10 percent of its modest advertising budget on 30 seconds, Lyle G. Hubbard, Gardenburger's CEO and president, spoke enthusiastically about the *Seinfeld* slot in a company news release. "The purpose of Gardenburger's advertising campaign is to take the brand from niche to mainstream, and what better way to do it than on one of America's favorite television shows," Hubbard stated. "There is huge consumer demand right now for low fat products that taste great, so the last episode of *Seinfeld* is a once-in-a-lifetime opportunity for Gardenburger."

The television campaign, developed by agency Publicis/Hal Riney & Partners, consisted of three animated spots. The whimsical commercials promoted the convenience, wholesomeness, and good taste of Gardenburger veggie patties. Narrated by actor Samuel L. Jackson, each ad used the tag line, "Eating Good Just Got Great" and focused on the motto, "Surprising Great Taste." The campaign began on May 4, 1998, the start of the company's peak sales season, with the second of the three ads airing on the last episode of *Seinfeld* on May 14, 1998. Even before the campaign commenced, however, the small, relatively unknown Gardenburger received a substantial amount of media publicity for its *Seinfeld* gamble. "Eating Good Just Got Great" continued through the summer, though it was initially scheduled for a five-week run due to the company's limited budget. The campaign also included a print effort in consumer magazines and was supported by a public relations plan implemented by public relations agency Publicis Dialog (formerly EvansGroup Public Relations). Publicis/Hal Riney's Paul Janus discussed Gardenburger's goal of attracting a mainstream audience and the logic behind its aggressive, albeit risky, advertising strategy in the *Wall Street Journal* and said: "If this is truly going to be a big category [meatless food products], somebody's got to be there first.... This is where we stick our flag in the ground."

HISTORICAL CONTEXT

In the early 1990s the public began to grow increasingly conscious of health and nutrition matters, sparking a trend in the consumption of meat alternatives among nonvegetarians. According to market research firm FIND/SVP, sales of meat-substitute and dairy-alternative products more than doubled from 1989 to 1994, increasing from $138 million to $286 million, and were projected to continue growing to reach an estimated $662 million by 1999. Many were buying these products not in health food stores but in supermarkets, which in 1996 accounted for 52 percent of meat-substitute sales, according to FIND/SVP. Founded in 1985, Gardenburger had made its mark in the niche category that consisted of natural and health foods. The company, which had traditionally geared its advertising efforts to the health food shopper with ads that urged consumers to help save the planet, and the cows, by avoiding meat, hoped to capitalize on this nationwide healthful eating movement. By the mid-1990s, however, the company found itself in a rather unpleasant situation—though revenues were increasing, earnings were flat.

Gardenburger's fate changed in 1996 when it hired Hubbard, a former executive at Quaker Oats who had been responsible for turning the sagging rice cake business into a $200 million division in three years. Hubbard implemented a new growth strategy designed to mainstream the meatless food product category and transform Gardenburger into the market leader. Revenues quickly began to rise, increasing 10 percent in 1996 and 45 percent in 1997. In 1997 Gardenburger products became available in retail stores nationwide, up from 20 percent availability when Hubbard joined the company, and continued its push in the food service and restaurant arena. The company also began to broaden its marketing efforts to increase the brand's visibility—in 1997 Gardenburger launched a national print campaign that included ads in such mainstream publications as *People, Rolling Stone,* and *USA Today.*

TARGET MARKET

The traditional audience for Gardenburger veggie patties included strict vegetarians, a group that made up only 1 percent to 2 percent of the population. Other likely consumers were semivegetarians and those required by their physicians to change their eating habits because of medical conditions. These consumers represented a limited portion of the population, but a growing number of people began to focus on eating more healthily, and Gardenburger was able to expand its target audience. By 1998 most shoppers were aware of the healthfulness of various food products and had committed themselves to improving their diets, but most had still not tried many meat alternatives. Gardenburger's research had found, however, that about six out of 10 U.S. households unfamiliar with Gardenburger veggie patties were not only willing to try them but were also apt to consume them on a regular basis if they were easy to prepare, flavorsome, and good for their health.

For the "Eating Good Just Got Great" campaign Gardenburger hoped to appeal to a wide audience that included the 33 million college-educated American adults who attempted to eat healthily and maintain relatively active lifestyles. *Seinfeld* was a popular program with this group, and *Seinfeld* particularly appealed to women between the ages of 25 and 54, a key audience for Gardenburger's veggie patties. Publicis/Hal Riney's Douglas Seay stated in a Gardenburger news release: "*Seinfeld* has owned the number-one or -two position with women every Thursday night at 9 p.m. for several years now.... The show's audience is a solid match with the demographic profile of Gardenburger's target market." It was up to Gardenburger and Publicis/Hal Riney to convince these loyal *Seinfeld* fans that Gardenburger products were worth trying—in 30 seconds.

COMPETITION

When Gardenburger embarked upon its ambitious growth endeavor, it was not the leader of the meat-alternative category; rather, that honor went to Worthington Foods Inc. of Ohio, the maker of such brands as Morningstar Farms, Natural Touch, and Worthington. According to "Business First-Columbus", Worthington's Morningstar Farms brand enjoyed a market share of 60 percent in the meatless food segment in 1995. Another rival, Pillsbury Company and Archer Daniels Midland Company's Harvest Burger brand, had a 23 percent share in 1995. Before Harvest Burger entered the meatless product category in 1993, Morningstar Farms' market share was a commanding 95 percent. Gardenburger trailed behind until 1997, when it began expanding its distribution channels and advertising with a national print campaign. At the beginning of that year Gardenburger's market share was 12 percent, but, the company reported, by the end of August its share had climbed significantly to 32 percent. Worthington Foods' share, meanwhile, hovered around 36 percent. Demand for veggie patties increased as well, growing 37 percent in the year ending May 1998, according to A.C. Nielsen Company.

A BURGER BY ANY OTHER NAME

Meatless patties found themselves divided into two overall categories—those that were intended to simulate meat both in taste and appearance, and those that were not. The meat-like products were generally composed of soy products, while the veggie patties tended to consist of vegetables and grains. Gardenburger veggie patties, for instance, were made of brown rice, bulgur wheat, onions, mushrooms, egg whites, and low-fat cheese.

Gardenburger was the first to take the high-visibility plunge into national television advertising. Though Worthington invested in advertising—the company spent about $1 million in 1995—it chose a slower strategy and promoted its products through print ads, coupons, and other promotions targeted to a more tailored audience. Worthington CEO Dale Twomley voiced his skepticism regarding Gardenburger's aggressive mainstreaming approach in the *Columbus Dispatch* and said: "It's way too broad of an approach. We're not selling waffles, orange juice or Twinkies. It's much more of a niche market. Our dollars are targeted on consumers who have an interest or are likely to have an interest."

MARKETING STRATEGY

As 1998 began, the management at Gardenburger had little intent of launching a national television campaign. CEO Hubbard planned to allot about $4 million on a print campaign, which was reasonable for a company with sales of $58 million in 1997. Gardenburger's ad agency, however, convinced Hubbard in January 1998 that a television effort would reach the widest audience. It would also give the company the best chance of branding the category and changing the perception of the veggie patty as a health-food item to a mainstream consumer product. Gardenburger also hoped to become a household name, much like Kleenexor Xerox, so it was imperative that Gardenburger get to the starting line before its rivals and that the advertising be memorable. Hubbard explained in *Prepared Foods,* "The thinking was 'let's just market veggie burgers and market them well enough so we can own the category in the mind of the consumer,' just like Gatorade did when it became the beverage for fluid replacement."

In order to finance the ambitious campaign and the *Seinfeld* slot, Gardenburger used $15 million of privately placed debt. The budget for the "Eating Good Just Got Great" campaign, which was Gardenburger's sole advertising effort in 1998, was three times as much as the company's 1997 ad budget. The slogan, "Surprising Great Taste," conveyed Gardenburger's understanding that many consumers believed meatless food products would not taste good, and it also prompted shoppers to give the veggie patty a try through the implication that they would be pleasantly surprised with the taste. The television spots were adapted from the print ads, which featured cartoon characters such as Lucy the Lion Tamer, who ate Gardenburger veggie patties so the lions would not smell meat on her breath. In addition to the *Seinfeld* finale, the spots were planned to air on major broadcast and cable networks during popular shows, including *Ellen, Third Rock from the Sun, ER, Home Improvement,* and the *Oprah Winfrey Show,* for a total of more than 1,500 instances.

All three of the television ads promoted the convenience, healthfulness, and good taste of Gardenburger patties. The second of three ads, "Vern," debuted on the *Seinfeld* final alongside spots from such advertising giants as Anheuser-Busch Company, Visa USA, and Wendy's International Inc. The spot, enthusiastically narrated by Jackson, featured the animated characters Vern and Edna. The generously proportioned Vern took hula lessons and invited Edna to a luau, hoping to impress her. When he attempted to serve her the traditional luau fare of roast pig, Edna frowned, requesting something "tasty and healthy" instead. Vern then saved the day by serving Gardenburgers, but then he donned a grass skirt and demonstrated his hula skills, leaving Edna to wonder when the other guests would arrive. The narrator asserted, "Discover Gardenburger—all natural, really tasty, end of story, because eating good just got great." Another spot featured Polly, who jumped on a pogo stick to catch a glimpse of the desirable Ned in his second-story apartment. She spied him eating a Gardenburger patty then continued jumping higher and higher, observing a man on an airplane eating a Gardenburger and cosmonauts munching on the veggie patties in a spaceship. Polly then reached heaven, where she saw her grandmother eating one. The narrator explained that "they are healthy and tasty and good!" The third spot, "Paul," gave the story of chef and Gardenburger creator Paul Wenner. Paul invented a patty with no meat, which he nervously tested on looming construction workers and truck drivers. Much to his delight and relief, the workers enjoyed the veggie patties, and Paul became a famous chef, worshipped by cows.

OUTCOME

The "Eating Good Just Got Great" campaign was a wild success, and the company's decision to advertise on

Seinfeld generated more than 1,000 news reports even before the ads aired, including stories on CNN Headline News and NBC and reports in the *Wall Street Journal, USA Today,* and the *New York Times.* One week after the *Seinfeld* episode, which reached more than 100 million viewers according to NBC, Nielsen scanner data indicated that Gardenburger sales skyrocketed—the company sold more veggie patties in that one-week period than it had in all of 1997, amounting to an increase of 411 percent and a total of $2 million in sales. Gardenburger also became the top-selling brand in the veggie patty segment, its market share jumping up to 50 percent. The company managed to hang onto its leading position even after the *Seinfeld* hype died down—in early 1999 Nielsen scanner data indicated that Gardenburger's share of the veggie patty category was 55 percent, significantly ahead of second-place Worthington, which had a share of 22 percent. Harvest Burger, acquired by Worthington in September 1998, held a 7 percent share. The overall meatless burger category was boosted by Gardenburger's advertising as well, and retail sales of veggie patties increased 57 percent in 1998.

Not only did Gardenburger's sales and recognition increase, but its ads were well-received by the viewing audience. The NPD Group, a research firm, conducted a survey following the *Seinfeld* finale and found that the Gardenburger spot demonstrated the second highest recall among the total of 28 commercials that aired during the program. The same poll rated "Vern" as the third favorite of the *Seinfeld* ads. The campaign won a gold EFFIE Award and a Genesis Award, given to organizations focused on animal issues. Because of the popularity and effectiveness of the "Eating Good Just Got Great" campaign, Gardenburger launched a second television campaign in April 1999 with a budget of $15 million. The 1999 campaign, developed by Chicago agency Rubin Postaer & Associates, featured the television spots from 1998 and was scheduled to run through the spring and summer in a continued effort to mainstream the veggie patty.

FURTHER READING

Hill, Jim. "*Seinfeld* Finale Will Serve as Gardenburger's Entree." *Portland Oregonian,* March 3, 1998, p. A1.

Leeson, Fred. "Gardenburger Eats Up Fame," *Portland Oregonian,* May 15, 1998, p. B1.

Richards, Bill. "Gardenburger Bets The (Soybean) Farm On the Last 'Seinfeld,'" *Wall Street Journal,* April 13, 1998.

Rose, Michael. "Rice-caking Gardenburger Marketing Whiz Hubbard is Transforming the Veggie Vendor," *The Business Journal-Portland,* April 10, 1998, p. 23.

Stapankowsky, Paula L. "Gardenburger Ad Campaign Has Fast Results." *Wall Street Journal,* May 4, 1999, p. B13.

Mariko Fujinaka

Wm. Wrigley Jr. Company

410 N. Michigan Ave.
Chicago, Illinois 60611
USA
Telephone: (312) 644-2121
Fax: (312) 644-0097
Web site: www.wrigley.com

ALTOIDS CAMPAIGN

OVERVIEW

A British brand of breath mints dating from the eighteenth century and described as "curiously strong," Altoids was purchased in 1993 by Kraft Foods, Inc. Having discovered that Altoids had a cult following among young Seattle sophisticates in the mid-1990s, Kraft tapped the advertising agency Leo Burnett for a 1995 outdoor and print campaign meant to build brand awareness beyond the Pacific Northwest.

The initially modest campaign targeted hip young adults in select American cities, and it gained momentum thanks to a mix of unconventional outdoor placements, ironic humor, and provocative images and text, all of which worked to promote the idea of Altoids' "curious" strength. The success of the outdoor campaign led Kraft and Leo Burnett to take the campaign to print media that included alternative newsweeklies and, later, national publications closely associated with the target audience. The print and outdoor ads used the same images and copy; the campaign's initial ad, featuring a male bodybuilder and copy reading, "Nice Altoids," established the retro look and knowing humor that would remain the long-running campaign's hallmark attributes.

The Altoids campaign was, from 1995 to 1999, one of the most successful in advertising history. During those years Altoids went from being a little-known niche brand with 2 percent of the breath-mint category to being the best-selling mint in America, independent of any product innovations or corporate intervention beyond the marketing campaign. The campaign won numerous awards and was adapted to the needs of new Altoids products in later years. Altoids' sales began to level off in 2002, and the brand pursued further growth through the introduction of still more product lines. In 2004 the brand was purchased, along with other Kraft-owned brands, by Chicago's Wm. Wrigley Jr. Company.

HISTORICAL CONTEXT

Altoids Mints dated to eighteenth-century London, where the William Smith Co. first sold the white candies as an "antidote to poisons in the stomach." It is legend that, when George III learned that he had lost the American colonies, he first reached for an Altoid. Although Altoids entered the American market in the 1950s, the brand languished in a gum and mint industry dominated by brands such as Certs, Tic Tac, and Breath Savers. Seattle was the sole exception to this trend. The city that embraced grunge music, dark-roasted coffee, and microbrewed beer also consumed a great many tins of Altoids each year.

After Kraft Foods acquired Callard & Bowser-Suchard, it set out to revamp the marketing efforts of the British company. Although Callard had run radio advertising that featured former Monty Python comic John Cleese spoofing the mints' British heritage, there had been no concerted effort to promote the brand. According to Steffan Postaer, one of the two Leo Burnett creative directors responsible for the Altoids campaign, "Altoids had always been considered a unique item, but no one had ever put much marketing behind it." Kraft believed that, if consumers were made aware of the Altoids brand and its unique qualities, they would try and enjoy the product. Leo Burnett was given the task of constructing a campaign that would fuel demand by elevating consumer awareness.

TARGET MARKET

The offbeat and laconic humor of the campaign was intended to appeal to a sophisticated, largely urban audience. Both Kraft and Leo Burnett were aware of Altoids' success in the Seattle area, and their market research revealed that the city's progressive, hip, and educated residents were the primary consumers of Altoids. "We knew we were talking to people in the arts; people in show business; executives; people with a college education; people who had made money, people who wanted to make some money, or people who thought making money was crude," said Postaer. "We were looking to reach people who think . . . not just the random middle section of the culture." Moreover, age was a factor in the original target market. The campaign specifically sought to captivate those between the ages of 20 and 40.

This demographic group was most likely to prefer the stronger flavors of a more potent mint. Kitty Kevin, a food-industry analyst, explained to *Minneapolis-St. Paul City Business* that "the stronger mint flavor is becoming more popular because stronger flavors in food are becoming popular." As ethnic foods, with their abundant use of garlic, onion, and spices, became more prevalent, a more powerful breath-freshening mint became more desirable. Moreover, as Americans became more accustomed to new food tastes, they wanted more robust flavors in all things, including mints. "Americans have an openness toward food now," said Susan Smith, a spokesperson for the National Confectioners Association, to *Tulsa World.* "They like ethnic food, spicy food, and lots of high flavors." Furthermore, for a generation obsessed with its weight, three Altoids tablets had only 10 calories and no fat.

Leo Burnett strove to appeal to its target market by capitalizing on the "adult" feel of Altoids. "We have exploited the adult nature of the product," said Postaer. "Altoids are more expensive than other mints, sold where you buy cigarettes, and they look powerful—more like medicine than candy." The explicit humor and the almost stark feel of the ads were purposefully designed to emphasize this aspect of Altoids. Indeed, one ad featured the photo of a leather-clad dominatrix brandishing a Whip alongside copy reading, "Pleasure in Pain." Postaer explained, "We reached our target through the look and feel of our ads."

ITS OWN WEBSITE

Kraft Foods dedicated a website to Altoids (www.altoids.com), at which it offered, among other interactive features, free T-shirts to consumers who posted innovative uses for empty Altoids tins. Some of the more creative suggestions included pressing the tin into service as a goldfish coffin, a place to keep a nose ring or guitar picks, or a condom container. As the Altoids campaign matured, one of the website's defining features became an "Ad Gallery" devoted to some of the campaign's most memorable ads.

COMPETITION

The breath-freshener category to which Altoids belonged was a $238 million a year industry in 1997. An analyst reported to *Gannett News Service* that, although the mint market was substantial, its growth for the most part was "flat and slow." Altoids, however, saw its sales soar. Indeed, according to *Brandweek,* Altoids "raised the bar for manufacturers . . . in the breath-freshener category." In 1996 Altoids saw its sales rise 27 percent to reach $23.2 million for the year, and it became the fourth-best-selling brand of mint in America, behind Breath Savers, Tic Tac, and Certs. The *Hartford Courant* declared that Altoids were "eating into the profits generated by bad-breath-beating titans."

Needless to say, the industry took notice of Altoids' success and of the concept of "curiously strong mints" that proved to be so lucrative. A flood of potent, premium-priced mints streamed onto the market, all of which, according to *Brandweek,* owed a debt to Altoids. Not only did Certs, Tic Tac, and Breath Savers infuse their mints with "more flavor," but also, Warner-Lambert—the brand owner of third-ranked Certs—also introduced Certs Powerful Mints with retsyn in 1997. These more concentrated candies were packaged in a horizontal container reminiscent of the Altoids tin and cost 40 percent more than previous Certs products. Warner-Lambert devoted $10 million to advertising its new product, on top of the $20 million already used to promote other Certs offerings. Similarly, the Minneapolis-based Dayton Hudson Corp. released a new line of its well-known Frango Mints in 1997. The Frango Purely Powerful Peppermints were small white circular tablets like Altoids, and they came in pocket-sized metal tins very similar to the container so closely associated with the Altoids brand. Also in 1997, Velamints began making Intense Velamints, likewise packaged in small metal tins. Chupa Chups U.S.A. launched a new Smints product accompanied by an advertising campaign that flatly pronounced, "No Smint. No Kiss." Starbucks Coffee and the upscale department store Neiman Marcus also came out with stronger mint lines in 1997 and 1998. Overall, sales of power mints climbed 11.5 percent in the first three months of 1998 alone.

Not only did Altoids face new competition from other mint brands, but it was also challenged by chewing-gum manufacturers, who introduced so-called power gums. American Chicle added Dentyne Ice, a stronger-flavored gum, to its product line. The gum was packaged in flat cardboard boxes that resembled a pack of cigarettes more than the standard foil-and-paper chewing gum ensemble. Fleer Confections came out with small, chewable mint squares dubbed Arctic Chews. The marketing manager of the company explained the new item to *National Petroleum News*: "We recognized that there was a not a lot of growth in the gum market, but there was a lot of growth in the fresh breath market."

Both Leo Burnett and Kraft Foods were faced with their competitors' efforts to capitalize on Altoids' achievements. Postaer noted that when Altoids' campaign was initiated in 1995 the British mint did not have anything resembling the sort of competition it faced two years later. "When we started out, we competed against chewing gum and candy," he said. "No mints advertised themselves as superpowerful. They had always couched their campaigns in terms of breath-freshening capacity or some other benefit. We put an interstate right through that."

MARKETING STRATEGY

Postaer and Mark Faulkner, the other creative director responsible for the campaign, were simultaneously restricted and liberated by the nominal budget Kraft allotted to the initially modest effort. For the most part the ad agency was unconstrained by corporate strategies or planners. Postaer and Faulkner proposed four possible campaigns: one that played off Altoids' British heritage; another that was "competitive," comparing Altoids to other available mints; a third that was similar to the one ultimately chosen; and, finally, the campaign that was selected, which dramatized the "curious" strength of Altoids. Since the phrase "curiously strong" had been inscribed on the Altoids box for the better than 200-year history of the mint, Postaer and Faulkner decided to base their campaign on the slogan. "Those words conveyed the exact balance of quirky charm and ownable essence that the brand represents," Postaer said.

Rather than quickly expend the campaign's budget on television spots, Kraft and Leo Burnett opted to spread the message of Altoids' curious strength through an outdoor print campaign. Because both Kraft and Leo Burnett had an accurate sense of Altoids' target market—the hip, educated, and affluent crowd that had already made the mints a success among Seattle's "alternative" population—they wanted to reach the same kinds of people in other cities. For this reason they set out to bring their message into the lives of their target market. Instead of targeting at the level of regions, states, or even cities, the advertisements were matched with specific neighborhoods in order to "reach our very definable target where they lived, worked, and played," as Postaer explained.

After the campaign's launch in Chicago in April 1995, Altoids billboards quickly went up in San Francisco and in Portland, Oregon. Particular billboards and walls in key neighborhoods were adorned with the ads. Minneapolis, Los Angeles, and New York were also among the early cities whose hippest neighborhoods were targeted. Kraft bought ad spaces on the sides of buses that traveled specific routes in order to increase the campaign's visibility in theater districts and along streets with trendy cafes and restaurants. When the campaign showed success, the ads were also placed in magazines. Alternative newspapers such as the *Reader* were chosen, as well as 47 more mainstream publications, including *Sports Illustrated, People, Bikini, Spin, Men's Journal,* and *Rolling Stone.* Each of the ads—with the magazine versions simply smaller copies of the billboards—featured the tongue-in-cheek humor of the first ad of the campaign: a photograph of a flexing male bodybuilder was paired with the text "Nice Altoids." Each subsequent ad also used the notion of "curious strength" as its jumping-off point. Early taglines included "Luckily Not Available in Extra Strength," "Are You a Mint or a Mouse?" "Go Medieval on Your Mouth," "Mints with a Kung Fu Grip," and "Mints So Strong They Come in a Metal Box." The campaign focused on print ads in national magazines in subsequent years, although unconventional outdoor placements remained part of the Leo Burnett arsenal even after the brand had become almost universally known. A 1999 effort, for instance, featured a poster affixed to the roof of a building near Chicago's O'Hare International Airport. The ad, visible only to airborne passengers, included the Altoids brand name as well as a message that perhaps implicitly addressed the mint's meteoric rise to the top of its category: "Look Out Below."

The campaign's controlling theme of "curious strength" was given a twist in ads touting a new Altoids flavor, Wintergreen, which was introduced in 1997. One ad, for instance, showed a young boy in a winter coat and hat, with his tongue stuck to an Altoids Wintergreen tin; others featured copy such as "Uncommon Cold," "Nuclear Wintergreen," and "Baby, That's Cold!" The fact that Altoids now boasted two flavors provided the concept for another memorable ad tailored to the brand's progressive target group: an image of the two tins was paired with copy reading "Bi-Curious?" 1999 saw Altoids' introduction of a Cinnamon flavor, and the ongoing print campaign was again modified, this time to pitch the new product's heat-generating properties. The Cinnamon launch also included a Web film element, Altoids' first flirtation with that medium. Later brand extensions—including a sour hard-candy line, a breath-strips line, a line of miniature-sized Altoids, and a gum line, in addition to Spearmint, Ginger, and Liquorice flavors of the original mint tablet—typically used the classic Altoids print format at least occasionally, though the Altoids Sours line in particular diverged from this model after its 2002 introduction. Even so, those Altoids Sours efforts that deviated from the archetypal print campaign's tactics—"Altoids Gone Sour" and "Altoidia"—continued to employ a markedly similar brand of humor while also remaining true to the "curiously strong" brand positioning first outlined by Leo Burnett in 1995.

OUTCOME

Kraft and Leo Burnett watched with glee as their campaign gained momentum. Not only did the witty print ads gain Altoids adherents among the campaign's selected target market, but the mints also became the epitome of chic for the culture at large. Rosie O'Donnell, the television talk show diva of the 1990s, conspicuously chewed Altoids during her program. Comedian Joan Rivers and actress Mariel Hemingway also lauded the mints to the *Greensboro News and Record.* Gannett News Service interviewed a businesswoman who succinctly described Altoids' crossover into the wider public: "It's a lot cooler than carrying around a roll of Mentos." Leo Burnett's campaign was credited with achieving its goal of driving up sales by making the product better known. At the time of the launch of the Altoids campaign in 1995, the mint's U.S. market share stood at 2 percent. By the end of 1999 the brand's market share was approaching 50 percent, and Altoids had outsold Tic Tac to become America's most popular mint.

Leo Burnett and Altoids became darlings on the ad-industry awards circuit as well. In 1996 the agency took home the Best of Show trophy at the Outdoor Advertisers Association of America's Obie Awards. The campaign was also recognized by the Chicago ADDY Awards as Best of Show. Most prestigious, however, was the honor of winning the Magazine Publishers of America's Kelly Award for the best magazine advertising campaign of 1997. Postaer gave credit to Altoids. "It was incumbent upon us to do superior advertising for this product because the product deserved it."

The intense competition created by the numerous Altoids copycat brands in the late 1990s, however, eventually took its toll. By 2002 sales had begun to plateau, and the brand pinned its hopes for future growth largely on new products such as the Altoids Sours line. In subsequent years Altoids Sours advertising eclipsed the ongoing, now-classic print campaign. In 2004, as part of a streamlining of its operations, Kraft sold the Altoids brand, along with LifeSavers and other confectionery units, to the Wm. Wrigley Jr. Company.

FURTHER READING

Baar, Aaron, and Mike Beirne. "Altoids Seeks to Stay Fresh." *Adweek* (midwest ed.), December 9, 2002.

Berman, Laura. "Candy Is on a Power Trip, with Breathtaking Results." *Gannett News Service,* February 24, 1997.

Bundy, Beverly. "Americans Showing an Intense Taste for Growing Variety of Power Mints." *Tulsa World,* April 26, 1998.

Clapp, Kevin. "Altoids' Kick Extends beyond Your Breath." *Hartford (CT) Courant,* July 24, 1997.

Dean, Paul. "Altoids Peppermints: A Breath of Fresh Air." *Greensboro (NC) News & Record,* February 26, 1997.

De Stephen, Nicole. "High Intensity." *National Petroleum News,* September 1, 1997.

Jensen, Trevor. "Burnett's Altoids Work Extends Awards Streak at Chicago Addys." *Adweek,* May 25, 1998.

Mehegan, Sean. "Van Melle to Make Big-Buck Push into Altoids' Power Mint Turf." *Brandweek,* June 16, 1997.

Parpis, Eleftheria. "Printed Matter." *Brandweek,* March 8, 1999.

Richard, Diane. "Dayton Introduces Curiously New Mint." *Minneapolis-St. Paul City Business,* August 1, 1997.

Thompson, Stephanie. "Brands in Trouble—in Demand." *Advertising Age,* December 13, 1999.

Rebecca Stanfel
Mark Lane

ALTOIDS GONE SOUR CAMPAIGN

OVERVIEW

NOTE: Since the writing of this essay, William Wrigley Jr. Co. bought the Altoids brand from Kraft. The essay continues to refer to Kraft, as they were the initiators of the campaign when it was first launched.

Altoids peppermints were not advertised in the United States until 1993, when Kraft Foods bought the product's manufacturer and launched a campaign meant to build on Altoids' popularity among upscale, hip Seattle residents. The ad agency Leo Burnett USA's Chicago office helmed the niche-marketing, print, and outdoor campaign, which targeted in-crowd urbanites in other major cities by using offbeat, ironic humor. The campaign touched off explosive brand growth and led Altoids to the top of the breath-mint heap, but by 2002 increased competition had begun to erode Altoids' sales. In an attempt to build the brand in a new category, Kraft introduced a hard fruit candy called Altoids Sours and again pinned its brand-building hopes on Leo Burnett.

"Altoids Gone Sour" was a combined print, outdoor, television, and online push meant to convey the idea "Your Altoids are changing." In keeping with the Altoids heritage of ironic, in-crowd appeals, the campaign used the awkwardness of adolescence as a metaphor for the idea of changing Altoids. The TV spots, Altoids' first-ever venture in the medium, ran during the summer of 2002 and mimicked old-style educational videos, while the print and outdoor ads were reproductions of 1970s yearbook photos. Together these advertisements drove traffic to an Altoids Sours website (www.gonesour.com), the layout of which resembled a school yearbook. There consumers could find out more about the change Altoids was undergoing and watch longer versions of the TV commercials.

Leo Burnett claimed that the campaign had to be discontinued because Altoids Sours sold out after the summer 2002 launch. The print portion of the campaign won numerous top honors on the 2003 ad-industry awards circuit. Altoids Sours effectively created a new candy market—hard sours for adults—and subsequent Sours advertising remained true to the Altoids heritage. In 2004 the Altoids brand was purchased by the Wm. Wrigley Jr. Company.

HISTORICAL CONTEXT

First manufactured in the United Kingdom in the 18th century, Altoids peppermints were originally marketed as a cure for intestinal discomfort. They came to America via Seattle, and for most of the twentieth century their distribution network did not reach beyond the Pacific Northwest. By the late 1980s Altoids had, thanks to its slogan "curious strength" and distinctive tin-box packaging, attracted a cult-like, word-of-mouth following among the denizens of Seattle's upscale coffee shops and nightclubs, despite the fact that British confectioners Callard and Bowser-Suchard, the makers of Altoids, did virtually no U.S. advertising behind the brand. In 1993 Callard and Bowser-Suchard was bought by Kraft Foods, and Kraft hired Leo Burnett to produce a small-scale campaign that would leverage Altoids' chic image and devoted word-of-mouth following. The campaign broke in 1995.

Kraft and Leo Burnett initially ruled out any attempt to create mainstream national awareness of the Altoids brand. Instead, they focused strictly on major American cities, such as Minneapolis, New York, Chicago, and Los Angeles, and within those cities they pinpointed neighborhoods frequented by successful, savvy young adults. Altoids posters, touting the mints' "curiously strong" flavor, were placed in bus shelters, subways, and alternative weeklies, and used ironic humor, a retro look, and offbeat, sometimes provocative imagery to appeal to their in-crowd target. For instance, a bodybuilder squeezing an Altoids tin was paired with the copy, "Nice Altoids." A dominatrix was featured in one poster along with the phrase "Pleasure in Pain." The copy that ran with some ads, "Mints so strong they come in a metal box," was adapted to fit the exterior of a Chicago El train and also ran on the backs of fare cards: "Mints for people who ride in a metal box." Other unique ad placements included a tugboat that circumnavigated New York harbor and rickshaws that traversed targeted Manhattan neighborhoods. Later ads were placed in magazines with national circulations.

The Altoids print and outdoor launch campaign was one of the most successful of its time. It won numerous ad-industry awards and triggered a period of extreme growth for the Altoids brand. Between 1995 and 1999 Altoids went from a 2 percent market share in the breath-freshener market to the category leader, besting longtime top mint Tic Tac on the way to transforming the category. Extra-strength imitators flooded the market, and Altoids itself introduced new flavors Wintergreen and Cinnamon. By 2002, however, sales had begun to slump, partly as a result of the newly saturated market. That year Kraft introduced several additional Altoids product lines, including a hard candy in sour fruit flavors meant to grow the brand in a new direction.

TARGET MARKET

The "Altoids Gone Sour" campaign, like the Altoids advertising that preceded it, targeted trendsetting urbanites. Kraft and Leo Burnett expected the brand's heritage of "curious strength" and hipness to resonate with members of this group, whether or not those individuals were already Altoids consumers. Altoids maintained a strong hold on young adults, but the "Altoids Gone Sour" spots appealed more to a mindset than a particular age or income group. The campaign was overtly geared toward media-savvy individuals with a postmodern sense of irony, people who placed a premium on being "in the know."

THE FLAVORS

Altoids built its brand on a single, centuries-old, extra-strength peppermint flavor, but with increasing competition after its hugely successful late-1990s marketing campaign, the brand began diversifying into other "curiously strong" flavors as a way of building and maintaining market share. The Altoids mints line was enlarged to include wintergreen, cinnamon, and spearmint; the Altoids Sours line expanded beyond its initial offering of citrus and tangerine to include apple and raspberry; a line of Altoids breath strips was launched and then discontinued; and Altoids branched out into gum, with peppermint and cinnamon flavors as well as Sours gum in apple and cherry flavors. A tiny version of the original Altoids mints was launched, complete with its own tiny tin, and a Specialty line, featuring ginger and licorice flavors, rounded out the Altoids family of products.

The print and outdoor portions of the campaign featured humorously awkward, 1970s-style high-school yearbook photos, using the changes experienced during adolescence to introduce the idea "Your Altoids are changing." For the first time Altoids ran television commercials, airing parodies of old-style educational films that supported the adolescent theme. While the move to TV risked making the brand seem more mainstream, the spots appeared only on cable stations, and the increasingly specialized cable-TV marketplace allowed Kraft and Leo Burnett to select specific audiences with a degree of precision comparable to its established model of highly targeted print and outdoor placements. Print, outdoor, and TV advertisements all directed consumers to an Altoids Sours website, where longer versions of the TV spots were integrated, along with the print and outdoor imagery, into a school-yearbook format.

COMPETITION

One measure of Altoids' success in the late 1990s was the number of competitors who attempted to copy the brand's extra-strength product and distinctive packaging. Life Savers unveiled its Ice Breakers line, and Certs (previously number two in the category) launched Powerful Mints. Department store Neiman Marcus, discount store Target, and coffee-retailing giant Starbucks, among many others, each introduced extra-strength mints packaged in tin boxes. The proliferation of such super-mint copycats and the resultant erosion of Altoids sales was one of the reasons the brand began turning to new product lines such as Altoids Sours.

Former category leader Tic Tac, owned by Ferrero S.p.A., was virtually alone in the breath-freshener category in remaining true to its original product during the super-mint onslaught of the late 1990s. "We had the same Tic Tac strategy in 1980 as there is today," Ferrero's U.S. director of marketing told *Candy Industry* in 2002. Tic Tacs, like Altoids, boasted their own distinctive product and packaging, small colored pellets that rattled when shaken in their trademark plastic dispenser, and though Ferrero lost market share as well as its industry-leading position to Altoids in the late 1990s, the Tic Tac formula continued to prove successful. As the breath-mint category showed signs of waning in 2002 and Altoids turned to fruity flavors, Tic Tac likewise began to emphasize fruit. Having noticed more sales consistency from its orange flavor during the mint downturn, Ferrero accordingly made its seasonal lime flavor a permanent part of the Tic Tac stable.

Meanwhile, Vitech America, Inc., was one of the only confections manufacturers to have a preexisting product positioned to compete with Altoids Sours. Vitech's Squyntz! were, like Altoids Sours, one of the few fruit candies targeting adults. Vitech, which also boasted an Altoids competitor called Myntz!, began developing a marketing push in 2002 to position its candies, in the Altoids manner, as fashion accessories for discerning consumers.

MARKETING STRATEGY

Altoids Sours applied the principle of extra-strength flavor to a sour fruit candy for adults. At the time the hard-candy market was primarily focused on children, so Kraft and Leo Burnett saw themselves as creating a new product category, as they had done with the original Altoids campaign in the 1990s. The Altoids strategy of using irony and a retro look to speak to knowing, cutting-edge hipsters remained in place, but the "Altoids Sours" campaign had its own distinctive look and trajectory. As Altoids' senior brand manager Andrew Burke told *Advertising Age,* "[Moving into hard candy] is a big change, and we thought, 'How do we take the next step?' "

That next step included, significantly, television advertising. The Altoids brand had been built on its cutting-edge, alternative image, so television represented a calculated risk. As Leo Burnett's Steffan Postaer said, "The biggest reason not to [use TV] was the fear of going mainstream." A changing cable marketplace, however, meant that the Sours commercials could be programmed to reach Altoids' core audience of culturally aware, trend-setting types.

Airing during the summer of 2002 on cable networks that included MTV, VH1, E! Entertainment, and Bravo, the Sours TV spots were 15-second versions of 60-second Web films. The TV commercials were meant to spark interest in the new product and drive traffic to an Altoids Sours website (www.gonesour.com), whose layout mimicked a school yearbook and where, among other features, the full films were available for viewing. Parodying educational videos aimed at schoolchildren of an earlier era, the Web films reproduced the grainy look of old film reels and their accompanying cautionary voice-over, while weaving Altoids Sours into their storylines. In "Making Friends with Fruit," for instance, a boy in early adolescence was shown arriving at a pool party with actual citrus fruit in a metal lunchbox. When another boy attracted the attention of numerous girls with his circular tin of Altoids Sours, the voice-over proclaimed the film's message: "When making friends, not just any fruit in a metal box will do." Another Web film, "Healthy Curiosity," featured a boy performing science experiments in a school laboratory. During the course of an experiment designed to determine "what makes sour things sour," the boy fed an Altoids Sour to the class's pet guinea pig. The guinea pig exploded, providing "scientific evidence of curiously strong citrus sour flavor."

The print and outdoor portions of the "Altoids Gone Sour" campaign, which communicated the idea "Your Altoids are changing," without providing any full explanation of that change, likewise drove traffic to the campaign's website. In keeping with the TV spots and the website format, the print ads and outdoor posters were reproductions of 1970s yearbook photos featuring humorously awkward adolescents. A teenage girl was shown above copy that read, "Soon your Altoids will blossom." The other three school portraits were of boys. One photograph ran with copy advising, "Don't be afraid to explore your Altoids"; another declared, "It's normal for your Altoids to change"; and a third informed consumers, "My Altoids are changing, and I'm OK with that." Each of the print spots included the www.gonesour.com website address.

OUTCOME

Within the first four weeks of the product launch, the "Altoids Gone Sour" push resulted in more than 500,000 visits to the brand's interactive website. Sales of Altoids Sours exceeded expectations. According to Leo Burnett, the campaign was so successful that it had to be discontinued: Altoids Sours sold out after the launch. The print component of the campaign was a star on the 2003 advertising-awards circuit, winning a Clio, an Andy, and a Gold EFFIE.

Subsequent Altoids Sours advertising remained true to the brand's trademark ironic humor and retro imagery and helped the Altoids brand stake out another new category in the candy industry. A print and outdoor campaign similar to classic Altoids posters used copy such as "Fruity Yet Strong" and "One Bad Motherpucker" in 2003. In 2004 the Altoids brand was purchased, along with LifeSavers and other Kraft confectionery divisions, by the Wm. Wrigley Jr. Company. Altoids' second-ever TV campaign followed. Also featuring print and online components, the TV spots starred a fictional British anthropologist and explorer, Sir Gerald Pines, who reported, in mock-documentary format, on the Altoidians, an aboriginal tribe whose "constant exposure to curiously strong sour has rendered them immune to pain." The Sir Pines spots helped Leo Burnett and new Altoids owners Wrigley to win a 2005 Gold Lion at the International Advertising Festival in Cannes, France.

FURTHER READING

Beirne, Mike. "Altoids Seeks to Stay Fresh." *Adweek,* December 9, 2002.

———. "Mint Condition." *Brandweek,* March 25, 2002.

Cox, Beth. "A Curiously Quirky Ad Campaign." *ClickZ,* August 16, 2002.

Embry, Liz. "Altoids: 'Curiously Strong' . . . And Now Sour, Too." *Houston Chronicle,* September 22, 2004.

Kanner, Bernice. "Altoids Comes on Strong with Launch of New Flavor." *Denver Rocky Mountain News,* September 22, 1997.

Sectzer, Jessie Ray. "Shakeout Leaves Classic, Creative Mints on Top." *Candy Industry,* January 2002.

Thompson, Stephanie. "Altoids Takes to TV with Spots for Sours." *Advertising Age,* July 15, 2002.

———. "Curiously Strong Altoids Moves Up Closer to No. 1." *Advertising Age,* December 13, 1999.

Wechsler, Pat. "A Curiously Strong Campaign." *BusinessWeek,* April 21, 1997.

"Wrigley to Buy Altoids and Life Savers from Kraft." *Candy Industry,* November 2004.

Mark Lane

GOTTA HAVE TWISTED SWEET CAMPAIGN

OVERVIEW

Soon after its introduction in 1893, the Wm. Wrigley Jr. Company's Juicy Fruit chewing gum became the best-selling gum in the United States. Although Juicy Fruit was still number one in the early 2000s, with a 31 percent market share worldwide, the brand was losing ground to other gum brands, including Cadbury Schweppes' Trident, Dentyne, and Chiclets brands, which together claimed a 26 percent share of the worldwide chewing-gum market.

To reconnect with its key consumers—kids ages 12 to 17—in 2002 Wrigley launched an effort to reposition its Juicy Fruit brand. The company updated the product's packaging, and its longtime agency, BBDO Chicago, created edgy new television spots as part of its ongoing "Gotta Have Sweet" campaign. In 2003 Wrigley introduced two new Juicy Fruit flavors, Grapermelon and Strappleberry, each of which twisted together two different fruits. To support the new products' launch, BBDO revamped the "Gotta Have Sweet" campaign as "Gotta Have Twisted Sweet" and created new television spots, print ads, and a print-to-Web effort, which used print ads to direct consumers to a Juicy Fruit website.

The "Gotta Have Twisted Sweet" campaign had mixed results. Two television spots, "Piñata" and "No Dummy," were named Best Spots by *Adweek* in 2003 and 2004, respectively. Also in 2004, at the Chicago Creative Club's annual award ceremony, the Juicy Fruit television spot "Officeflage" earned both the People's Choice award, which was voted on by the public, and the Best of Show award, which was determined by a panel of judges. In 2005, however, the campaign's print-to-Web segment was cited by the Children's Advertising Review Unit for being potentially misleading to the young consumers it targeted. Following the ruling Wrigley ended the print-to-Web advertising, but the television spots and other print ads were continued in 2005.

HISTORICAL CONTEXT

The Wm. Wrigley Jr. Company got its start in 1891 selling soap, a product that William Wrigley, Jr.'s father manufactured. To boost sales the younger Wrigley offered customers free premiums, including baking powder, with each purchase. Realizing that baking powder was more popular with customers than the soap, Wrigley began selling baking powder and offering packages of chewing gum as the free premium. The gum was an even bigger hit with customers, and in 1892 Wrigley began to sell chewing gum under his own name. Wrigley's first gum brands were Lotta and Vassar. Juicy Fruit was introduced in 1893 and quickly became the number one gum brand in the United States. Its flavor, though fruity, was never associated with any particular fruit.

During World War II Wrigley stopped selling Juicy Fruit and its other gum brands to American consumers, dedicating the entire available product to the country's military troops. To ensure that consumers did not forget the brand while it was unavailable, Wrigley launched an unusual marketing campaign in 1944 that consisted of print ads with a picture of the gum wrapper and the tagline "Remember this wrapper!" When the brand was reintroduced to American consumers in 1946, its ads had the tagline "For a refreshing change enjoy this completely different flavour."

One of Juicy Fruit's most notable taglines, "Taste is gonna move you," was introduced in 1983. By 1998 the slogan had lost its appeal with consumers, especially teens, Juicy Fruit's key market. Confronted with dropping sales, the company and its ad agency, BBDO Chicago, conducted extensive research among kids who chewed Juicy Fruit gum to learn what they liked about the product. The answer was that they chewed the gum because it was sweet. Based on the research the "Gotta Have Sweet" campaign was released in August 1998.

When William Wrigley, Jr., great-grandson of the company's founder, took over as chief executive officer in 1999 following the death of his father, the 35-year-old became the fourth generation of the family to head up Wrigley. In 2001 he revamped the company's marketing department and began looking past BBDO Chicago, which had worked with Wrigley for more than 70 years, for new ideas for marketing Wrigley products. BBDO heeded the warning and updated the agency's campaign efforts for Wrigley's gum brands. In addition, Juicy Fruit's packaging was redesigned for the first time since the 1980s, and to promote its two new flavors, in 2003 the "Gotta Have Sweet" campaign was modified as "Gotta Have Twisted Sweet."

TARGET MARKET

Besides being the number one fruit-flavored brand of gum in the United States among all consumers, Juicy Fruit also was the best-selling gum among kids 12 to 17 years old. Juicy Fruit had always been considered a bridge between kid-favored bubble gum and more adult gum choices such as Wrigley's Spearmint, and the two new flavors added to the Juicy Fruit family—Grapermelon and Strappleberry—were designed specifically for teens moving beyond bubble gum. Consumers in the company's target audience were described by the *Chicago Sun-Times* as "Skippies," schoolkids with income and purchasing power. According to Teenage Research Unlimited, a Chicago-based company that tracked trends among youths, Skippies spent $170 billion on products for themselves or their families in 2002, up from $155 billion in 2000. Reaching this key demographic was the goal of Wrigley's edgy new campaign, "Gotta Have Twisted Fruit." As the popularity of the new flavors became evident, Wrigley shifted its focus to even younger consumers, targeting children 8 to 11 years old.

COMPETITION

Cadbury Schweppes, based in London, England, was best known as the number three producer of soft drinks,

JUICY FRUIT FASHION FOR BRITISH FANS

Beginning in 2002 girls and young women in England could do more than chew Juicy Fruit gum. They could also head to a nearby Top Shop or Debenhams department store to buy Juicy Fruit–branded clothes. The new line, available only in select U.K. stores, included four styles of tops, hats, belts, and bags. According to a Wrigley spokeswoman, the new apparel targeted girls and women ages 11 to 24 years old.

behind the Coca-Cola Company and PepsiCo. Its beverage brands included 7 Up, A&W Root Beer, Dr Pepper, and Hawaiian Punch. In 2003 Cadbury completed a $4.2 billion deal with New York–based Pfizer, Inc., and purchased the pharmaceutical giant's Adams candy division. Included in the purchase were the Adams gum brands Trident, Dentyne, and Bubbas. Adding the Adams gum brands to its product offerings pushed Cadbury into the number two spot in the chewing-gum market, with a 26 percent worldwide share (behind Wrigley, which had a 31 percent share). Cadbury also claimed one-third of the sugarless-gum market in the United States. In 2004 Cadbury announced plans to expand its Trident brand to include fruit flavors; these would directly compete with Wrigley's fruit-flavored Juicy Fruit.

For more than 50 years the Topps Company of New York had given bubble-gum lovers and collectors of sports memorabilia a combination of their two favorite things: packs of Bazooka bubble gum and sports trading cards. Since its introduction in the 1940s Topps had used a variety of marketing techniques to increase its Bazooka brand's appeal to kids, including introducing *Bazooka Joe* comics in 1953 and adding new flavors, such as grape, strawberry, and a sugarless variety, to the original gum. The company also increased the variety of sports trading cards that were packaged with the gum; from the original cards, introduced in 1951, that featured pictures of baseball stars, the offerings were expanded to include popular hockey players beginning in 1954, football players in 1955, and basketball players in 1957. In 1967 Topps introduced Wacky Packages trading cards, which were sold with Bazooka bubble gum. The cards spoofed everything from Jell-O (tagged Jail-O and called the favorite dessert of Sing Sing inmates) to Minute Rice (Minute Lice) and were a hit with junior high school students. The 1985 introduction of Garbage Pail Kids trading cards, a parody of Cabbage Patch Kids dolls, helped fuel sales of Bazooka bubble gum despite complaints from parents that the gross-out humor of the cards was in poor taste. The Wacky Packages were discontinued in 1976, and the Garbage Pail Kids were canceled in 1988, but Topps reintroduced the trading cards to a new audience of young consumers in 2003 (Garbage Pail Kids) and 2004 (Wacky Packs).

MARKETING STRATEGY

In 2003 Wrigley added to its 100-year-old brand Juicy Fruit two new flavors, Grapermelon and Strappleberry, that each combined, or twisted together, two fruit flavors. The company turned to its longtime agency, BBDO Chicago, for an advertising campaign that would support the 2003 launch of the product. The new campaign, themed "Gotta Have Twisted Sweet," was a variation on the brand's "Gotta Have Sweet" campaign, which had begun in 1998. Staying with the original campaign's humorous theme, the new one put a unique edge on seemingly ordinary situations to promote the new gum flavors. Included were television spots that targeted teens and 20-somethings, print ads aimed at middle school kids, and a print-to-Web effort that was developed for kids as young as eight years old.

The initial television spot, "Piñata," aired in October 2003 and depicted a children's birthday party. The center of attention, however, was not the birthday girl but a donkey-shaped piñata full of goodies and suspended from the ceiling. The celebrants took turns whacking the piñata in an effort to break it and get the treats inside. When it was finally broken, it dropped from the ceiling and began chasing one of the children who had grabbed the package of Grapermelon Juicy Fruit. After retrieving the prized gum from the terrified child, the piñata made its escape through a dog door. Another spot, "Officeflage," featured office workers camouflaging themselves as office furniture and equipment in order to grab a pack of the new Juicy Fruit gum from their unsuspecting coworkers. The first worker bought a pack of Strappleberry from an office vending machine. As he walked down the hall preparing to pop a piece of the gum into his mouth, a coworker disguised as a file cabinet swiped the pack of gum, shook off the disguise, and ran down the hall. As the second coworker stopped to retrieve a piece of gum, a third person, who had been lurking on a windowsill disguised as miniblinds, jumped from the window, snatched the gum, and ran into the office lunchroom. As he sat on the floor opening the treasured pack of gum, he noticed another coworker disguised as a water cooler poised to grab the Juicy Fruit.

The campaign continued in 2004 with a third television spot. As with "Piñata," the new spot involved an inanimate object coming to life. In "No Dummy" a class of high school students were shown beside a swimming pool learning CPR. As a teenage boy was practicing mouth-to-mouth resuscitation on a dummy, it came to life and stole the Juicy Fruit gum from his mouth. With the gum in its own mouth, the dummy made its escape, losing an arm and a leg in the process. When the dummy crashed its getaway vehicle—a bicycle—into a car and was knocked unconscious, the boy caught up, retrieved his gum, and continued performing CPR on the dummy. The television spots aired on national network and cable channels, such as MTV, that ran programming that appealed to teens.

Print-to-Web ads, which appeared in *Disney Adventures* magazine and targeted younger kids, also adopted a unique approach. Described as "mock ads" by the Promotions Marketing Industry, the two separate ads listed websites that appeared to promote a new boy band (www.luvboiseboys.com) and a movie (www.lambzilla.com) by directing readers to the Internet sites. When readers visited either website, however, rather than images of the band or scenes from the movie, they reached a Juicy Fruit webpage that played the "Gotta Have Twisted Sweet" television spot "No Dummy." Other print ads, aimed at preteens and tagged "Gotta Have Twisted Comics," ran in *Nickelodeon* magazine. The ads, which employed a comic-strip format, followed the ongoing adventures of students at the fictitious Dewey Needit Junior High School and eventually answered the question, "Who gets the Juicy Fruit in the end?"

OUTCOME

The "Gotta Have Twisted Sweet" campaign's television spots were included in *Adweek* 's Best Spots list in both 2003 and 2004; the "Piñata" spot was recognized in 2003, and the "No Dummy" spot was recognized the following year. Also in 2004, the Chicago Creative Club, an organization of Chicago-based advertising and design leaders that each year recognized the high standards of the Chicago creative community, presented its annual People's Choice honors to the "Officeflage" spot. "Officeflage" was named the Best of Show in the TV Commercial category as well.

Although the "Twisted Sweet" television spots were well received, the print ads that appeared in *Disney Adventures* magazine were criticized by the Children's Advertising Review Unit (CARU), a division of the Council of Better Business Bureaus and the self-regulatory forum of the children's-advertising industry. CARU cited that portion of the campaign for using mock ads that supposedly led children to websites for either a new band or a new movie but that actually directed Internet users to a Juicy Fruit ad. According to a report in *Advertising Age,* CARU stated that the overall print-to-Web campaign was "potentially misleading" and misinformed youngsters about the source of the ads. Further, CARU noted that, while older children might understand the humor of the commercial featuring a CPR dummy that came to life, stole a boy's gum, and was ultimately chased down by the boy, the commercial "could be too disturbing for younger children." Wrigley agreed to pull the online commercial. The websites were also discontinued.

FURTHER READING

Alpert, Lukas I. "Garbage Pail Kids Stickers Set to Return." *Salt Lake City Deseret News,* July 12, 2003.

———. "'Wacky Packages' to Return." *Chicago Sun-Times,* March 10, 2004.

Armitage, Jim. "Cadbury Outstrips Rivals after Adams Gum Buy." *Evening Standard* (London), February 23, 2005.

Boorstin, Julia. "Why Is Wrigley So Wrapped Up? Because It's in the Company's DNA." *Fortune,* March 3, 2003.

"Chewing-Gum Ads Sport New Flavor. Candy Makers' Sales Climb as Conservative Pitches Get Stuck under the Desk." *Wall Street Journal,* December 31, 2004.

"Confectioner and Beverage Maker Cadbury Schweppes PLC Said It Plans to Sell Its European Beverages Business as It Focuses on More Profitable Lines, Including Operations in the United States." *Food & Drink Weekly,* September 12, 2005.

"'Double Your Pleasure' Duds and Accessories." *Candy Industry,* June 1, 2002.

"Genius Products Secures Rights to Bazooka Brand for New Line of All-Family DVDs Hosted by Bazooka Joe." *Business Wire,* December 24, 2004.

Guy, Sandra. "Wrigley Eyes New Products to Fend Off Revived Rival." *Chicago Sun-Times,* March 12, 2003.

Irvine, Martha. "To Freshen Old Brands, Firms Ask 'Skippies.'" *Chicago Sun-Times,* July 4, 2003.

Lazare, Lewis. "Wrigley Ad Is the People's Choice." *Chicago Sun-Times,* September 30, 2004.

Platt, Gordon. "The Americas: Cadbury Schweppes Buys Pfizer Unit." *Global Finance,* February 2003.

Podmolik, Mary Ellen. "Juicy Fruit; Jennifer Crotty." *Advertising Age,* June 26, 2000.

Teinowitz, Ira. "Food Advertising Pushed into Harsh Spotlight." *Advertising Age,* March 15, 2005.

"Wrigley Extends Juicy Fruit to Pellet Gum." *Professional Candy Buyer,* May 1, 2003.

Rayna Bailey

NO MATTER WHAT CAMPAIGN

OVERVIEW

In 2001, supported by a campaign titled "No Matter What," the Wm. Wrigley Jr. Company introduced its Orbit gum, long available in Europe, to the United

States. Orbit was different from such Wrigley brands as Doublemint and Juicy Fruit in that it was sugar-free, and the introduction of Orbit in the United States occurred at a time of increasing emphasis on dental health. Wrigley, however, was not the first U.S. company to offer sugar-free gum, for competitor Trident had been sugar-free since the 1960s. In fact, Orbit was not the first sugarless Wrigley product available in the United States; the company's Extra had been introduced in 1984 and Eclipse in 1999. Still, Wrigley wanted another alternative in its sugar-free lineup, especially since U.S. sales of chewing gum had been lagging for a decade. The timing turned out to be perfect, for in 2002 Wrigley's top two U.S. competitors—Trident and Dentyne—were purchased by Cadbury Schweppes. Thus, the competition in the chewing gum market intensified, and Wrigley, with a wider selection, was in a better position to compete.

The "No Matter What" campaign, led by the Chicago advertising agency Energy BBDO, sought to target a market of working people and their families between the ages of 18 and 49. The ads featured the actress Vanessa Branch, usually referred to simply as Vanessa, as a vivacious researcher at the so-called Orbit Institute, showing how the gum could help people feel neater and more "put together." They were also used as a way to introduce new flavors of Orbit gum. Television spots, which accounted for most of the total costs of the campaign, were aimed at showing how Orbit could leave a mouth clean "no matter what." In a variety of humorous scenarios the *New York Times* pegged as "seemingly inspired by Austin Powers movies," including one in which a tourist was nearly eaten by an enormous Venus flytrap, Vanessa was able to keep any mouth clean she happened to stumble across. The television spots were supported by other marketing efforts, including print ads and point-of-relevance posters that appeared in such places as taxicabs.

The "No Matter What" campaign was a success on several levels. First, studies measuring both advertising awareness and brand linkage among viewers of the television spots showed that the campaign had indeed reached its intended audience. The campaign won advertising honors, including a prestigious EFFIE Award, for its achievements. In addition, financial results seemed to confirm the success of the campaign. In 2004, just three years after Orbit had been introduced, the gross sales of all Orbit products in the United States exceeded $90 million, and the gum was outselling second-place Trident. Further, Orbit was accounting for one-third of Wrigley's profits.

HISTORICAL CONTEXT

William Wrigley, Jr., founded the Wm. Wrigley Jr. Company in Chicago in 1891. At first he sold soap, but he soon replaced soap with baking soda. In a move that demonstrated his flair for marketing, Wrigley offered customers a bonus with every purchase of Wrigley's Baking Powder: two packages of chewing gum. By 1892 Wrigley had begun selling packs of chewing gum independently, marketing the product under his own name. The first two brands were Vassar and Lotta, followed in 1893 by Juicy Fruit and Wrigley's Spearmint.

Wrigley was a true salesman, believing in his products and enthusiastically spreading the word about them. As he put it, to be successful a businessman had to "make a good product at a fair price—then tell the world." But Wrigley did not simply send salesmen onto the streets to sell his products directly, which at the time was the common marketing strategy. Instead, he became one of the first entrepreneurs to use large-scale advertising to promote sales. In the early 1900s Wrigley began to advertise his chewing gum in newspapers and magazines, as well as on outdoor posters. The ads promoted the gum's ability to provide relief for indigestion and stress. They were intended to reach the general population of consumers, who would then request that their local stores carry Wrigley chewing gum. Wrigley understood that retail stores could reach far more potential customers than could a sales force. Although it was not widely used at the time, this marketing strategy was simple.

In the 1930s Wrigley introduced the "Doublemint Twins" campaign, which became one of the most successful advertising efforts ever developed in the United States. Playing on the "Doublemint" name, the campaign portrayed the double-image concept in various ways. The earliest ads in the campaign were radio spots that featured, among others, two piano players, two comedians, and two violinists. Billboard ads featured air-brushed images of innocent-looking twins chewing the gum. From 1959 through 1963 Jayne and Joan Boyd appeared as the Doublemint twins. Projecting a tone of innocence, they appeared in a series of 12 commercials in which they portrayed the fun of being double as they sang the jingle "Double your pleasure, double your fun with Doublemint gum." The jingle, as well as the twins concept, was used through the 1980s. The company then tried a series of new campaigns, although all remained true to the theme of innocence. These later campaigns included "Small-Town America" in the 1980s and "Healthy Gums" in the 1990s. In 2005 the company reintroduced the "Doublemint Twins" campaign. Meanwhile, however, the company had launched the "No Matter What" campaign to promote the Orbit brand. With sugar-free Orbit, which had long been popular in Europe, the company hoped to gain a new wave of customers in the United States.

TARGET MARKET

Wrigley's sugar-free Orbit was introduced in the United States in 2001 as an aid to dental health. Its first national advertising campaign claimed that "regular chewing helps knock tooth decay into orbit." The tagline reinforced the point by maintaining that the gum would convey a "just brushed clean feeling." Orbit White, which contained sodium bicarbonate, a tooth-whitening agent, was introduced in January 2002. This newest product followed a three-year trend that had made whitening products the fastest-growing group in oral care.

The "No Matter What" campaign targeted people between the ages of 18 and 49, who accounted for more than half of all gum purchases in the United States. Research indicated that, of potential consumers, those most likely to use the product were people who lived busy lives involving work and a family. These were the people for whom the feeling of a clean mouth was most important. Research also showed that this customer base wanted a variety of gum flavors, not simply mint. Thus, by 2005 a total of seven flavors of Orbit were available in the United States, all of them promoted through the "No Matter What" campaign.

COMPETITION

The year after Orbit was introduced in the United States, its top two competitors, Trident and Dentyne, had a new owner. In December 2002 the British food giant Cadbury Schweppes purchased Adams, the maker of both gums, from the U.S. pharmaceutical company Pfizer as a result of the $4.2 billion deal, Cadbury Adams USA LLC was created. But Trident and Dentyne had both established their names in the chewing gum business much earlier.

In the 1960s Trident became the first national brand of sugar-free chewing gum to be sold in the United States. Its 1964 advertising slogan, "The Great Taste That Is Good for Your Teeth," promoted the fact that the gum used saccharin instead of sugar. When the advertising changed with the claim that "4 out of 5 dentists surveyed would recommend sugarless gum to their patients who chew gum," Trident immediately became associated with dental health. The "4 out of 5" pitch continued through the following decades, reinforcing the association. In 2001 Trident introduced a tooth-whitening gum, Trident White, which competed directly with Orbit White. Within a mere nine months Trident White had gained more than 60 percent of all whitening gum sales. Cadbury Adams undertook large-scale advertising efforts for Trident. In 2004, largely to compete against Wrigley, the company spent an astonishing $60 million on Trident advertising. The new campaign featured the adventures of Little Mouth, an animated wind-up, chattering mouth. At the same time Trident continued to expand the flavors offered, a necessity in a market that demanded variety. New flavors introduced by the Little Mouth character included Watermelon Twist, Trident Splash Strawberry with Lime, and Trident Splash Peppermint with Vanilla.

> ### THE WAR ON GUM
>
> In 2004, when the William Wrigley Jr. Company won licenses to sell Orbit in Singapore, that country lifted a 12-year ban on the sale and use of chewing gum. The ban had been imposed after someone stuck a wad of chewing gum in the door of a high-speed commuter train, causing serious delays in service. But the lifting of the ban did not come without conditions. Orbit could be sold over the counter only by pharmacists, who were required to record the names of those who bought the product.

While advertising for Orbit and Trident focused on the dental health of the general population, that for sugar-free Dentyne focused on the youth market. Dentyne's target market was 15- to 24-year-old daters in search of fresh breath. The Dentyne Ice brand, introduced in 1996, illustrated this focus, with its advertising most often featuring young couples kissing. In one such ad, as a young man attempted to kiss his attractive date, he imagined himself surrounded by every guy she had ever kissed, which made him feel insecure. Dentyne Ice served as a quick confidence booster, however, and he carried on with the kiss. After Cadbury Adams bought the company, advertising for Dentyne was skewed toward an even younger target market. For example, a 2004 digital campaign with the tagline "Go bold!" was aimed at 13- to 17-year-olds, with ads running on Yahoo!'s instant-messenger and Launch music platforms.

MARKETING STRATEGY

Wrigley's "No Matter What" campaign was launched following a decade-long lag in sales of chewing gum in the United States. At the same time other breath-freshening products, such as mints and breath strips, were experiencing sales increases. In response Wrigley introduced sugar-free Orbit, with the large-scale advertising campaign led by Energy BBDO, an agency based in Chicago. The ads featured the actress Vanessa as the spokesperson, demonstrating how Orbit could transform any "dirty" mouth into one that felt clean. As such, the ads directly targeted Orbit's market, reinforcing the link between a clean mouth and a well-organized life. In the ads Vanessa found herself in a variety of "scenes of the grime," seeking to prove that "no matter what" Orbit left all sorts of mouths feeling clean.

The "No Matter What" campaign, which cost an average of $5 to $10 million a year between 2001 and 2005, included television and magazine advertising, as well as point-of-relevance posters. The latter were displayed in areas likely to reach Orbit's target audience: taxicabs, which were used by busy American workers; nail salons and health clubs, to reinforce the idea that the gum could help a person look and feel good; and dental offices, which supported the idea of a mouth that felt clean. In addition, new gum flavors introduced during the campaign were displayed in stores on shelf danglers, which helped highlight the new flavors and entice customers to try them. It was the television commercials, however, that accounted for the bulk of the advertising budget, on average 87 percent of all spending. From 2001 through 2005 several commercials were aired, largely on prime-time and late-night shows in an effort to reach the target audience. Each time a new commercial was introduced, it ran frequently in order to create brand presence before it then tapered off.

Each of the "No Matter What" television spots portrayed dirty mouths turned clean by Orbit. The mouths included those of a teacher, a school bus driver, a mailman, a biker, lovers at a picnic, clowns, and even a Venus flytrap. Although the initial emphasis was on introducing the Orbit brand in the United States, as new flavors became available, the focus of the campaign shifted. In 2003, for instance, the two television spots "Clowns" and "Equestrian" were used to introduce the new flavors Cinnamint and Bubblement. In the spirit of the campaign, one commercial showed Vanessa improving the dirty mouths of clowns and the other of a female rider. In 2005, in the hilarious "Fly Trap," in which a visitor to a botanical garden was swallowed by the world's largest Venus flytrap, Vanessa improved the dirty mouth of the plant while introducing Orbit's newest flavor, Citrus Mint. During the campaign other, more unconventional ways were used to promote Orbit. In 2003, for example, Wrigley sponsored the Chews Wisely Challenge, in which assistants of Vanessa, dressed in lab coats, appeared in such areas as Pike Place Market in Seattle to ask people to compare the taste of Orbit to that of Trident.

OUTCOME

The "No Matter What" campaign was successful in introducing Orbit in the United States. In 2004, the gross U.S. sales of all Orbit products exceeded $90 million, beating competitor Trident by nearly $8 million. According to Wrigley, by this point Orbit was accounting for a third of its total domestic profits. Further, Orbit had become the third best-selling gum in the United States, behind two other Wrigley products, Extra ($146 million in sales) and Eclipse ($93.3 million).

The "No Matter What" television commercials were given much of the credit, by both Wrigley and by advertising critics, for the campaign's success. As the *New York Times* put it, "The cheeky commercials, which also took occasional swipes at a not-so-mysterious 'Brand T,' quickly propelled most Orbit products to the top of the sales charts." As a result of the success of the campaign, new flavors were quickly added to the Orbit brand, and by 2005 seven were available: Original Peppermint, Spearmint, Wintermint, Bubblemint, Cinnamint, Citrusmint, and Sweet Mint.

The campaign also won awards from the advertising industry. The 2005 "Fly Trap" commercial earned recognition from *Adweek* as one of its Best Spots. The 2003 commercials "Clowns" and "Equestrian," which promoted the new flavors Cinnamint and Bubblemint, won an EFFIE Award. Created by the New York American Marketing Association in 1968, the EFFIE focused on the results of advertising campaigns, and the results of the 2003 spots were impressive. As indicated by a 2004 Communicus Advertising Effectiveness Study, the commercials succeeded in reaching customers. The study revealed that among viewers "Clowns" resulted in an advertising awareness of 46 percent and a brand linkage of 23 percent, with the numbers for "Equestrian" being 61 percent and 26 percent, respectively. These results were well above the norms of 37 percent for advertising awareness and 13 percent for brand linkage. Supported by their award-winning advertising, the new Cinnamint and Bubblemint flavors came to account for two-thirds of the overall growth of Orbit.

FURTHER READING

Barr, Aaron. "BBDO Casts Wrigley's Doublemint Twins." *Adweek,* March 9, 2005. Available from <http://www.adweek.com>.

Beirne, Mike. "Category Wars: Wrigley Returns to Orbit in Whitening Showdown." *Brandweek,* May 17, 2004. Available from <http://www.brandweek.com>.

———. "Strategy: Wrigley Rebounds with $70M for 3 Brands." *Brandweek,* April 21, 2003. Available from <http://www.brandweek.com>.

"Cadbury Takes $4.2 Billion Gulp: Adams' Brands of Chewing Gum May Be a Treat." *Houston Chronicle,* December 18, 2002, p. 1.

"Dentyne Breaks Digital Ad Effort." *Adweek,* October 18, 2004. Available from <http://www.adweek.com>.

Koerner, Brendan I. "Wrigley's Second Chance to Smile." *New York Times,* June 20, 2004, p. 2.

Kruger, Renee Marisa. "Chewing Power: Loaded with Innovation, Chewing Gum Is Giving the Confection Industry a Lot More to Chomp On." *Business and Industry,* October 2002, p. 60.

Prystay, Cris. "At Long Last, Gum Is Legal in Singapore, but There Are Strings." *Wall Street Journal,* June 4, 2004, p. A1.

Todd, David. "Dentyne Ice Locks Lips with Youth Target." *Strategy Magazine,* May 8, 2000, p. B14.

Tylee, John. "AMV Launches Wrigley's Orbit Ads." *Campaign,* April 20, 2001, p. 7.

Candice Mancini

Working Assets Long Distance

101 Market St., Ste. 700
San Francisco, California 94105
USA
Telephone: (415) 369-2000
Fax: (415) 369-2000
Web site: www.workingassets.com

■■■

DIRECT MARKETING CAMPAIGN

OVERVIEW

Founded in 1989, Working Assets Long Distance was the only enterprise offering a long-distance phone service and regularly donating to nonprofit organizations. It was a subsidiary of Working Assets Funding Service, Inc., which had been established four year earlier by Laura Scher, Michael Kieschnick, and Peter Barnes. Compared with the telecommunications giants AT&T, Sprint Corp., and MCI Communications Corp., Working Assets was a minuscule player. Nevertheless, it had succeeded in rapidly developing a base of customers and in generating considerable annual profits. Hoping to instill loyalty in its subscribers by sending them mailers that addressed social issues and its philanthropic work, Working Assets created an inexpensive direct-marketing campaign.

Every month Working Assets enclosed a letter with its subscribers' long-distance phone bill. The letters, which were printed with soy ink on recycled paper, informed customers about political issues and encouraged them to phone their Congressional representatives to register their opinions. Ten minutes of free long distance were allotted for every customer to call representatives in Washington, D.C., once a month. Without the burden of a large marketing budget, Working Assets was able to charge fees that were actually lower than those of most other companies. The company also donated 1 percent of its gross revenues (as opposed to profits) to an array of progressive nonprofit organizations. The subscribers voted annually on which organization should receive the funds.

Working Assets' political agenda and generosity brought the company a degree of publicity transcending that which it could have obtained from a more conventional marketing effort. Between 1985 and 2005 the Working Assets companies donated more than $50 million to nonprofit organizations. Although its direct-marketing campaign was responsible for spurring the bulk of the company's new subscribers to sign up, it was Working Assets' fundamental principles that ensured it a loyal base of consumers.

HISTORICAL CONTEXT

Working Assets Long Distance was the brainchild of Peter Barnes, who had established the Working Assets Money Fund in 1983. This mutual fund refused to invest in the stocks of companies that were involved in defense contracting, had poor environmental practices, or did business with oppressive political regimes. Once the viability of the Working Assets Money Fund was assured, Barnes diversified his interests and introduced the Working Assets credit card, which donated 5 percent of the value of all purchases charged to the card to various progressive charities.

When contemplating his next business venture, Barnes hit upon the idea of offering long-distance service. He determined that such an enterprise would satisfy the criteria he had laid down for all of his forays into the consumer market. As Barnes explained to the *Chicago Sun-Times,* he was only willing to get involved with a product that could offer "a basic service, could be marketed nationwide, and could be donation linked." From these principles Working Assets was born in 1989. Operating as a long-distance re-seller (that is, as a company that bought phone-line capacity from other providers rather than owning its own), Working Assets purchased service in bulk from Sprint (and later MCI), which it then sold to its own customers. After starting small the company began to market itself to a national audience with a direct-mail blitz in 1992. Between 1992 and 1997 its roster of subscribers grew from 50,000 to 250,000.

TARGET MARKET

This dramatic expansion was a result in part of the receptive market the company had discovered. According to *Marketing News,* Barnes's venture tapped into "a growing niche [of] people who want to change the world, but don't want to go to too much trouble about it." Working Assets estimated that 20 million Americans were "societally conscious" and open to discovering new ways to support their beliefs. As a result, its potential audience was quite broad. The company focused primarily on residential long-distance consumers who subscribed to another carrier (generally perceived as a large and impersonal bureaucracy) and who often felt marginalized and disrespected by politicians and corporations. Characterized by their commitment to liberal social and political causes, this group spanned divisions of age, race, and income. "The demographics of an average [Working Assets] subscriber are hard to define, since they range in age from 20 to 75," Robin Greiner, a company manager, told *Marketing News.* "It's more of a psychographic," she added, a shared mindset as opposed to the sorts of commonalities that more traditionally defined targeted audiences. What potential Working Assets customers had in common was a dedication to causes such as abortion rights, civil liberties, and economic justice. They tended to live in major urban areas (particularly San Francisco, Chicago, and Boston) and were a highly educated lot. As the *San Francisco Examiner* noted, a full one-third of Working Assets' customers had postgraduate degrees. They were "take action" people, Greiner emphasized, the sorts who would write letters to the editor and wanted to be involved in effecting political and social change.

The primary way Working Assets sought to connect with this audience was through its corporate policies. The organizations and ideals the company supported matched those of the group it hoped to reach. The direct-mail campaign was essential in driving home this convergence of interests to potential consumers. Because these ads were in a letter format, Working Assets could explain its policy positions and its unique place within the telecommunications industry in a clear and detailed manner. This medium allowed the company to elaborate its goals without having to resort to the generalizations and oversimplifications that so often pervaded 30-second television commercials. Moreover, for Working Assets' highly educated target audience, the low-tech and traditional format of a letter carried more credibility than flashy television advertising.

In its direct-mail missives Working Assets positioned itself as an altruistic organization, more like a selfless political crusader than a profitable telecommunications company. Although it always noted that its rates were at least competitive with (if not better than) other long-distance service providers, Working Assets devoted most of its direct mail ads to informing consumers about its substantial charitable donations and its endeavors to mobilize the public in support of various causes. The ads touted the range of "Citizen Actions" the company had supported as another way in which Working Assets was more than just another corporate player. Special programs were highlighted as well, such as different phone-card giveaways Working Assets had run to encourage people to contact their elected representatives (at the company's expense). In 1995, for example, Working Assets distributed a bevy of "Stop Newt" calling cards (and not exclusively to Working Assets customers) in an effort to mobilize opposition to Republican Speaker of the House Newt Gingrich's action plan, the "Contract with America."

COMPETITION

With its corporate objective of "build[ing] a world that is more just, humane, and environmentally sustainable," Working Assets had a strong platform from which to differentiate itself from other long-distance service providers. For the most part its three largest competitors—AT&T, MCI, and Sprint—used price and convenient calling plans to attract residential long-distance customers. The market was fiercely competitive, constantly shifting, and saturated with advertising. The "Big Three" (as AT&T, MCI, and Sprint were collectively dubbed) flooded television, radio, and print media with a steady stream of commercials (both product-specific as well as image-oriented). Telemarketers from all of these companies also frequently contacted consumers at home (often in the evenings around dinnertime), promising cheaper rates and better services than their rivals. AT&T was the

A SWEET DEAL

In another effort to draw people to its long-distance services, Working Assets entered into an arrangement with the famously progressive Ben & Jerry's ice cream company whereby new subscribers to Working Assets phone services would receive coupons good for one free pint a month of the Vermont-based firm's delectable dairy offerings for their first year as Working Assets customers.

largest of the three and had an annual marketing budget of about $300 million. Employing these resources the company aired a slew of commercials that played up its status as the oldest long-distance provider in the country. Beginning in 1996 AT&T used actor Paul Reiser (from the television show *Mad About You*) in television spots that patiently explained how AT&T's calling plans were a simple alternative to the often gimmicky offerings from Sprint and MCI. These commercials, conceived by ad agency Foote Cone & Belding, were updated in 1997 and 1998. In May 1998 Reiser was portrayed on top of a mountain promoting AT&T's updated One Rate Plus calling plan.

Both MCI and Sprint incorporated celebrity endorsers into their marketing strategies as well. Like AT&T they went "tit-for-tat [in] lowering per price minutes and offering package details," noted an article in the September 8, 1997, *Advertising Age.* In September 1998 MCI, the country's second-largest telecommunications company, used National Basketball Association icon Michael Jordan in partially animated spots that featured a cast of Warner Brothers cartoon characters such as Bugs Bunny. In August 1998 the company brought back Jordan and his cartoon companions to herald MCI's new Five Cents Everyday calling plan in spots created by ad agency Messner Vetere Berger McNamee Schmetterer/Euro RSCG. In addition to its Jordan-centered spots, MCI used actor John Lithgow in Messner-produced advertising designed to promote its 10-321 (later 10-10-321) service, which was provided by MCI's wholly owned subsidiary Telecom USA. The digits were actually an access code that, when entered prior to dialing a number, would route a customer's call through MCI's telephony facilities irrespective of which company putatively provided long-distance service to the residence where the call originated. The 10-321 service was "the fastest-growing product MCI ha[d] ever introduced," the company told *Advertising Age* in 1997. MCI particularly hoped to win consumers away from AT&T with this effort.

Sprint opted for Candice Bergen to represent its telephone service. In 1997 the company dropped her long-standing "Dime Lady" persona (which focused on Sprint's offering of long-distance service at the rate of a dime a minute) and opted instead for commercials that looked more broadly at the company's low 10-cent rates and its calling plans. In three spots produced by ad agency J. Walter Thompson, Sprint "stress[ed] the power of a dime to bring simplicity and control to consumers' lives," according to the January 13, 1997, *Advertising Age.* Sprint severed its relationship with J. Walter Thompson in May 1997 in favor of Grey Advertising, which it commissioned to create a corporate-branding campaign.

Furthermore, Working Assets was not the only long-distance provider that strove to distinguish itself from the three telecommunications titans. An upstart phone company, Qwest Communications, launched a $50 million advertising campaign in February 1998. As *Advertising Age* revealed on February 23, 1998, the commercials, by Omnicom Group's Focus Agency, "toss[ed] humorous barbs at the entrenched long-distance telephone companies." The clever spots related the misadventures of "Bob," an employee of a "big long distance company." In one commercial Bob was beaten by a priest and a nurse in a hospital when they discovered his occupation. Working Assets also had a rival from a long-distance reseller at the opposite end of the political spectrum. Lifeline, owned by AmeriVision Communication, donated a portion of its proceeds to conservative organizations such as the Christian Coalition, Operation Rescue, and the Moore Foundation for Home Schooling.

MARKETING STRATEGY

Working Assets concentrated its marketing efforts on the features that distinguished it from other phone companies (indeed from most other corporations). As the newsletter *Report on AT&T* noted, "knocking on customers' doors and getting involved with their causes is a good way to steal away part of the . . . long distance market from the likes of AT&T." An industry analyst concurred with this assessment in *Telephony.* "They're selling brand differentiality in a way that a large carrier could not." Ironically, irrespective of the (progressive) personal convictions of Barnes and his company's employees, positioning Workings Assets as a socially responsible company made good business sense. Recognizing this fact, Working Assets took every opportunity to trumpet its generous donations, its activism, and its liberal pedigree.

The company encouraged its customers to get involved in national political debates in other ways as well. Each phone bill contained two "Citizen Actions." These consisted of briefs on particular issues coupled with pleas from the company for its customers to take stands concerning these topics. In 1993 the company launched "Have a Heart," in which it advocated aggressive lobbying on behalf of a smaller defense budget. "We are trying to increase the number of ways that people can make a positive social impact from money that they spend in their daily lives," Working Assets' founder told the *San Francisco Chronicle.*

Direct-mail letters lay at the heart of Working Assets' efforts to grow its business. According to *Telephony,* direct mail was the company's "largest source of acquiring new customers." To aim the letters at consumers most likely to respond to them, Working Assets obtained mailing lists from various like-minded political organizations and publications (such as The *Nation, Utne Reader,* and *Mother Jones*) who shared information about customers and subscribers. In the mid-1990s the company added small perks to encourage consumers to switch over to Working Assets. The company offered 60 free minutes of long-distance services in an initial bonus for becoming a customer. Beyond such tactics (and the occasional print ad placed in progressive publications such as the *Nation*) Working Assets relied on word of mouth to raise consumers' awareness of its services and products. *Report on AT&T* concluded that the company's "most successful marketing channel is its own customers," from whom it generated nearly 25 percent of its business. While its large competitors offered rebates, frequent-flyer miles, and other incentive programs to capture new customers, Working Assets depended predominantly on its community values and the goodwill of its subscribers.

OUTCOME

Working Assets' marketing strategies were a success. "We've proven it's possible to do good and do well at the same time," Barnes announced to the *San Francisco Chronicle.* By 1998 the company could claim 320,000 subscribers, and future prospects looked promising. Although Working Assets had only a small fraction of the customer bases of AT&T, MCI, and Sprint, it found that its subscribers were ideal consumers. The massive telecommunications giants were plagued by fickle customers who hopped from provider to provider in search of the latest deal. Working Assets subscribers, because they joined for political as well as economic reasons, tended to be more loyal. Moreover, because they believed in the company's mission, they were more responsible and timely in paying their phone bills. In 1997 Working Assets expanded its enterprise and began offering both pager and Internet services.

Working Assets evaluated its success partly in terms of the activism it had engendered. In 1998 alone Working Assets consumers generated more than 1 million calls and letters to Congress and the White House. That same year the company succeeded in advancing political causes ranging from safeguarding the integrity of the organic food label to securing higher levels of government funding for civil rights enforcement and family planning. In 2005 all of the Working Assets companies donated more than $4 to progressive organizations, bringing the cumulative total since 1985 to $50 million. The campaign continued into 2006.

FURTHER READING

Barbagallo, Paul. "Shared Vision, Shared Trust." *Target Marketing,* June 1, 2003.

Cleland, Kim. "Bergen Leaves Spotlight in Sprint's New 'Dime' Ads." *Advertising Age,* January 13, 1997.

Eckhouse, John. "Make a Call, Save a Whale." *San Francisco Chronicle,* September 25, 1993.

Goerne, Carrie. "Reach Out and Change the World." *Marketing News,* March 16, 1992.

"Little Guys Set Sights Low to Compete with AT&T." *Report on AT&T,* February 12, 1996.

Peregrin, Tony. "A Win-Win Situation." *Telephony,* May 13, 1999.

Rosenspan, Alan. "Improve Your Response." *Direct Marketing,* September 1, 2001, p. 34.

Rumbler, Bill. "Long-Distance Firm Profits from Dial-A-Conscience." *Chicago Sun-Times,* January 6, 1992.

Snyder, Beth. "Long-Distance Upstarts Aim Ads at Category's Big 3." *Advertising Age,* February 23, 1998.

———. "MCI Touts Success of 10-321 Service." *Advertising Age,* November 10, 1997.

———. "Phone Foes Open New Big-Bucks Marketing War."

Spencer, Jane. "The Worst Phone Service in America." *Wall Street Journal,* October 3, 2002, p. D1.

Tuller, David. "Phone Service to Give Part of Income Away." *San Francisco Chronicle,* February 18, 1989.

Rebecca Stanfel
Kevin Teague

Wyeth

5 Giralda Farms
Madison, New Jersey 07940-0874
USA
Telephone: (973) 660-5000
Fax: (973) 660-7026
Web site: www.wyeth.com

■■■

LIQUI-GELS CAMPAIGN

OVERVIEW

NOTE: Since the initial appearance of this essay in the 1999 edition of *Major Marketing Campaigns Annual,* American Home Products became a part of the Wyeth organization. The essay continues to refer to the company's former name, as that was the official name of the organization when the campaign was launched.

Through its Whitehall-Robins Healthcare subsidiary, American Home Products (AHP) had been producing an ibuprofen-based analgesic under the brand name Advil for 14 years when in August 1998 it introduced Advil Liqui-Gel caplets, coated with gelatin for easy swallowing. AHP accompanied the brand-extension launch with a print and television campaign overseen by Young & Rubicam of New York City. As was typical of most advertising in the highly competitive analgesics category, spots targeted competitor Tylenol, a Johnson & Johnson brand marketed through its McNeil Pharmaceuticals subsidiary. AHP spent a sizeable portion of its $320 million advertising budget in 1998 on Liqui-Gels—$30 million. One particularly memorable commercial, though it was not specifically for Liqui-Gels, aired on the May 14 final episode of the enormously popular NBC sitcom *Seinfeld.* The 30-second spot cost an estimated $1.7 million to run.

Introduced in 1984, Advil became the first nonprescription pain reliever to contain ibuprofen, first developed in the 1960s. Like aspirin, ibuprofen inhibited the body's production of prostaglandins, chemicals that scientists believed provoked neural pain receptors. This came at a fortuitous time, as more and more Americans turned against aspirin in response to reports concerning gastrointestinal side effects, but if Advil's makers had little to fear from aspirin, they faced plenty of competition in the form of Tylenol, and the two brands waged a lengthy battle of attrition during the 1980s and 1990s. Advil Liqui-Gels, launched at about the same time as Tylenol Arthritis, went head to head with Extra Strength Tylenol. By the end of 1998, however, the two brands' relative positions remained the same, with Tylenol in first place and Advil in second.

HISTORICAL CONTEXT

Incorporated in 1926, American Home Products grew through consolidation and acquisition. Among the significant products it added in its early years was an oil for the treatment of sunburns, acquired in 1935; this it marketed under the brand name Preparation Has a product intended for the treatment of hemorrhoids. Also in the 1930s AHP bought the aspirin brand Anacin, which would prove enormously popular during the 1950s, thanks in part to a celebrated advertising campaign. Anacin's commercials, created by legendary adman Rosser Reeves, promised "Fast-fast-fast relief!" If some television viewers complained that the strident commercial was enough to cause headaches, it certainly proved effective, and Anacin became one of the leading brands during the decade and for some time thereafter.

But changes were afoot in the world of analgesic relief medications. In the 1960s chemists for the Boots Pharmaceutical Company, a British corporation, began developing a carboxylic acid derivative called ibuprofen. Boots introduced the drug as a prescription medication in 1964 and held the worldwide patent until 1985. Doctors prescribed ibuprofen for pain and inflammation associated with arthritis, menstrual cramps, and other conditions.

The first U.S. company to gain marketing rights for ibuprofen was the Upjohn Company, which sold it under the brand name Motrin. After AHP's Whitehall Laboratories gained approval from the U.S. Food and Drug Administration (FDA) to market a nonprescription form of ibuprofen, Upjohn chose not to compete with it but rather sold Motrin's rights to Bristol-Myers, who marketed it under the brand name Nuprin. Meanwhile AHP in 1988 bought out A.H. Robins, a pharmaceutical company that had gone bankrupt as a result of lawsuits over its Dalkon Shield contraceptives. It later merged A. H. Robins with Whitehall Laboratories to create Whitehall-Robins Healthcare.

Advil appeared on the market in 1984 with the slogan "Advanced medicine for pain" and was well-poised to take the lead over Nuprin. By 1987 ibuprofen had emerged as the fastest-growing segment of an analgesics market estimated at more than $1.5 billion. Nuprin stood little chance against Advil, thanks to AHP's large direct-sales force, who helped gain prime grocery and pharmacy shelf space for their product. By the early 1990s, despite the appearance of numerous generic brands, Advil accounted for about half of all ibuprofen sales in the United States.

TARGET MARKET

By the mid-1980s statistics showed that about 80 percent of all adults in the United States used some variety of pain reliever. More and more Americans had begun to accept the idea of medication for pain, and with OTC drugs offering relief for a variety of symptoms beyond mere headaches, consumption of analgesics had increased noticeably. Whereas a study in 1984, the year of Advil's introduction, showed that some 80 percent of all Americans used one variety of pain reliever or another, by 1990 the figure had risen to more than 87 percent. This was a good sign for Advil, and an even better one appeared with the evidence of declining aspirin consumption. The latter resulted from the release of several studies showing negative effects on the gastrointestinal systems of persons who took aspirin.

Ibuprofen users tended to use the drug over long periods of time, often to treat arthritis, and this long-term use posed further benefits to the makers of Advil. According to a 1992 study published in *BrandAdvantage* magazine, some 45 percent of Advil users were in the 18-to-34-years-old category, suggesting that the medication was particularly popular with the young. Persons in the 35-to-54 category made up almost 37 percent of Advil users, and those 55 years of age or older accounted for the other 18 percent. Ibuprofen advertising in general, and that of Advil in particular, targeted the young: thus in 1993 Advil ran a commercial featuring major-league baseball pitcher Nolan Ryan, a symbol of physical fitness and robust activity.

Advil also had a strong female buying public, with more than 57 percent of its customer base being women. This placed it in a better position, relative to female buyers, than either Tylenol or Bayer, whose customers were 55 and 49 percent female respectively. In the late 1980s and early 1990s Advil had gone after a market it had previously left untouched: children. Thus in 1989 it introduced Children's Advil Suspension, a sweet liquid for the reduction of fever.

By the time Advil launched Liqui-Gels in the late 1990s ibuprofen had come under the same sorts of attacks that aspirin had previously encountered, with studies showing that the drug caused stomach pains and possibly even ulceration and bleeding. AHP fought a successful battle to avoid having to list possible side effects on the label. The FDA did, however, require a warning suggesting that consumers consult their doctors if they experienced unusual side effects after taking the drug. With the introduction of Liqui-Gels, however, Advil included a warning with language proposed by the FDA: "If you generally consume three or more alcohol-containing drinks a day, you should consult your physician for advice on when and how you should take Advil Liqui-Gels or other pain relievers."

COMPETITION

The fact that Advil was required to include the alcohol warning was ironic, not simply because AHP had long fought the requirement to include such a warning, but because the topic of combined alcohol and analgesic use had been the basis of a heated dispute with its leading competitor. So fierce had this battle become, in fact, that in March 1996 NBC, ABC, CBS, and CNN took an almost unprecedented step, refusing to run commercials for analgesics that made safety claims regarding competitors.

The cause of this highly unusual measure was an Advil commercial created by Young & Rubicam and first broadcast in February of that year. The spot featured a close-up of an alcohol warning label on a bottle of

A SHOW ABOUT NOTHING

On Thursday, May 14, 1998, the ultra-popular situation comedy *Seinfeld* broadcast its final episode on NBC, and advertisers were eager to get on the bandwagon. Many critics proved less than enthusiastic over the final show's plot, and Bob Garfield of *Advertising Age* was similarly negative about the commercials themselves—including one for Advil, which he dubbed "a waste of money."

In fact Garfield dismissed almost all the spots in such a manner. He called a commercial for Apple Computers, part of its "Think Different" campaign by TBWA Chiat/Day, "a bit excessive." Yet "it was all somehow apropos," in Garfield's opinion. "In this series putatively about nothing"—*Seinfeld* was famous for its loose plot lines—"taking its leave amid the biggest ad rates in history—$3.4 million per minute, give or take—a whole lot of expensive nothing is exactly what was delivered."

USA Today invited a panel of advertising experts to rate the ads in the 75-minute episode. They gave the highest score, 9.21 on a scale of 1 to 10, for Coors' Zima "Dog Bites Man" spot. The lowest rating went to Nissan's Altima commercial, which received a 3.25. Advil's "The Pain of Separation" fell almost exactly in the middle of the 29 ads, with a 5.44 rating.

Tylenol, with a voice-over suggesting that persons who drank three or more glasses of wine, beer, or mixed drinks a day should ask their doctors whether it might be safer to use Advil instead of Extra Strength Tylenol. According to *OTC Business News,* "An actor draws attention to the Tylenol warning label, pointing out the potential for liver damage if the product is taken in combination with alcohol."

The same report noted that the makers of Tylenol "reacted sharply to the Advil commercial, launching a public information campaign and taking 'concerns' about the advertising to the Food and Drug Administration and television networks." The campaign by McNeil, producers of Tylenol, included information statements on television and in newspapers and magazines, a nationwide direct-mail campaign aimed at doctors and pharmacists, and a toll-free information line.

According to *OTC Business News:* "Whitehall-Robins defended the Advil commercial, insisting that it was not 'deceptive in any way. The advertisement is meant to alert consumers to the risk of liver damage for those people who regularly consume alcoholic beverages and take Extra Strength Tylenol.... Nevertheless, Whitehall-Robins applauds ABC television network's decision to cease airing all commercials that make negative safety claims about competing analgesics.... We are especially pleased that ABC has decided to stop airing several recent Tylenol advertisements that make false claims about the safety of Advil.'"

At that point, the lead positions in the analgesics market were as they had been for some time and would remain through 1998, with Tylenol in first place and Advil in second. By the end of 1998 only the combined total of all generic brands, with $630.3 million in sales, held a higher market position than Tylenol's total sales of $567 million. Advil formed a distant second with $355.8 million, and third-place Aleve, a Bayer product, was even further down the line with $141 million. In fourth place was Excedrin, produced by Bristol-Myers Squibb—who had sold the Motrin brand to McNeil—with $114 million in sales. Thus by far the most serious competition for Advil came from Tylenol, and therefore most of its advertising was directed toward the market leader.

MARKETING STRATEGY

Compared to the 1996 ads concerning Tylenol and alcohol use, Advil's 1998 advertising was relatively tame. In fact it gained very little press—certainly far less, for instance, than Aleve's "Real relief is all day relief," created by BBDO Chicago and launched in April. The only Advil commercial that received much attention from journalists was not even a Liqui-Gels commercial, but a spot called "The Pain of Separation" that ran on the final episode of *Seinfeld.* The commercial played on viewers' feelings of separation anxiety with the end of the popular show and made a tongue-in-cheek recommendation of Advil as a cure for that pain.

Part of the lack of attention to Liqui-Gels in 1998 came from the fact that their launch occurred at the end of summer, well into the year. In August *Health News Daily* reported that the company had begun retail shipments of its brand extension on August 3, and that in September it would begin running print and television advertising created by Young & Rubicam. As for the actual content of those ads, one of the only places this even received mention was in a September 7 *Advertising Age* story by Michael Wilke, who wrote that "AHP last week launched an estimated $30 million TV and print campaign from Y&R Advertising, New York, for Advil Liqui-Gels, with ads emphasizing faster action than Extra Strength Tylenol."

Advil supplemented its television and print advertising with point-of-sale brochures to be distributed at retail buying centers. It backed up its advertising with a news release on September 25, following the annual meeting of the American College of Clinical Pharmacology. The news release reported that a study presented at the conference provided evidence that "Patients who were treated with Advil Liqui-Gels reported a faster onset of analgesic relief on tough headache pain, both for confirmed first perceptible relief and meaningful relief, than those who received Extra Strength Tylenol."

OUTCOME

In January 1999 Bayer's Aleve launched a $28 million advertising campaign for its own gelcaps, complete with television spots featuring the tag line "All day strong, all day long." This would be supplemented with print ads in a variety of magazines, including *People, Better Homes & Gardens, Ebony, Readers Digest,* and *Prevention.* Advil, by contrast, began a much more low-key campaign for Advil original, Advil 400 Extra Strength, and Advil Cold & Sinus, which would run from February to September. Meanwhile, Bob Garfield in *Advertising Age* attacked Tylenol's Allergy Sinus commercials, comparing them to political ads.

At least the Tylenol spots got attention, however, whereas the response to Advil's Liqui-Gels was muted. AHP had enjoyed a good year in 1998, with its stock rising from $43.93 to $70.25 per share, but as Justin Dini and Andrew McMains reported in *Adweek* in May 1999, it had begun "talking to six or seven agencies regarding a $15-25 million corporate-image assessment, sources said." Company leadership, according to Dini's and McMains's sources, "hop[ed] a corporate campaign might increase [AHP's] visibility on Wall Street."

FURTHER READING

"Advil Liqui-Gels Advertising to Begin in September; Latest Formulation of 14-Year-Old Whitehall-Robins OTC Analgesic Began Retail Shipments Aug. 3." *Health News Daily,* August 27, 1998.

"Advil Offers Proof." *Community Pharmacy,* May 1999, p. 40.

"Bayer Ad Campaign for Aleve Focuses on 'All Day Relief,'" *Tan Sheet,* April 20, 1998.

"Bayer Aleve Gelcaps Backed with $28 Mil. in Ad/Promo Spread" *Tan Sheet,* January 4, 1999.

Dini, Justin (with Andrew McMains). "AHP Seeking an Image Groomer" *Adweek* (Eastern edition), May 17, 1999.

Garfield, Bob. "Yech and Yada in 'Seinfeld' Ads." *Advertising Age,* May 18, 1998, p. 63.

———. "Tylenol Allergy Sinus Redefines Ad Sleaze." *Advertising Age,* May 10, 1999, p. 65.

"How the Ads Rank." *USA Today,* May 15, 1998.

"McNeil's Motrin IB Sales Up 19 Percent Through Mid-September." *Tan Sheet,* October 19, 1998.

"New Study Demonstrates That Advil Liqui-Gels Provide Faster Relief of Headache Pain Than Extra Strength Tylenol." *Business Wire,* September 25, 1998.

"TV Networks Wash Hands of Tylenol/Advil Battle." *OTC Business News,* March 21, 1996, p. 1.

Wilke, Michael. "Tylenol's $50 Million Intro Aims at Rx Rivals: Arthritis Brand is Crucial Launch." *Advertising Age,* September 7, 1998, p. 1.

Judson Knight

Xerox Corporation

800 Long Ridge Rd.
Stamford, Connecticut 06904
USA
Telephone: (203) 968-3000
Fax: (203) 968-3218
Web site: www.xerox.com

KEEP THE CONVERSATION GOING, SHARE THE KNOWLEDGE CAMPAIGN

OVERVIEW

In October 1998 the Xerox Corporation launched a $10 million advertising campaign in an effort to change people's perception of the Xerox brand. Although long known simply as a photocopy-machine company, Xerox had been diversifying its offerings to include an array of digital products, such as high speed digital copiers (copiers connected to computer networks), laser and ink jet printers, and multifunction devices that combined faxing, scanning, and printing capabilities. In fact, the company had generated 36 percent of its $18.2 billion sales revenue in 1997 from these high-tech items. But, as the *Wall Street Journal* recognized, "that means that Xerox is competing less with traditional copier rivals such as Canon Corp., Konica Corp., and Ricoh, Inc. and more with printer giants such as Hewlett Packard. As a result, according to the *Wall Street Journal*, Xerox faces competitive threats from printer companies, which are vying for the same corporate customers" Xerox wanted to reach. Moreover, many of Xerox's potential customers were unaware of these shifts in the company's focus. To address this situation, Xerox turned to advertising agency Young & Rubicam, which created "Keep the Conversation Going, Share the Knowledge" to promote the full range of Xerox's goods.

Xerox hoped this campaign would serve the dual purpose of helping the company break into the lucrative small business, home office, and retail equipment markets and of bringing Xerox's traditional group of customers—large businesses—into its digital fold. Seeking to stress its creativity and to reach a broad base of viewers, Xerox opted for a rather unconventional campaign. The campaign initially consisted of four television spots that discussed Xerox's role in offices ever more dominated by computer technology. The commercials' lighthearted vignettes demonstrated how Xerox made creating, transmitting, and sharing documents an easier task, but it was the fact that "Keep the Conversation Going" was structured around a classical Greek chorus led by a toga-wearing sage (played by actor John O'Hurley who was well-known for his role on the hit television show *Seinfeld*) that truly made the effort stand out. The chorus, which was shown standing in a white amphitheater complete with massive columns, sculpture, and giant pools of water, dispensed advice to businesses confronted with information-age dilemmas. In one ad, for instance, business associates congregate at the funeral of a colleague who had died suddenly without telling them the details of a lucrative contract he had won. "Now they're really consumed with grief," the

A still featuring John O'Hurley, from Xerox's "Keep the Conversation Going" television campaign. XEROX CORPORATION. REPRODUCED BY PERMISSION.

Greek chorus chimed in unison. "If only they knew that John scanned all his contracts into the Xerox Information Center."

Although advertising pundits lambasted the campaign for being "overly ambitious," as the *Fort Worth Star-Telegram* sniped, for example, consumers themselves responded well to "Keep the Conversation Going." Xerox continued the campaign into 1999 because "people get the message," Nancy Wiese, Xerox's director of worldwide marketing, told *USA Today.*

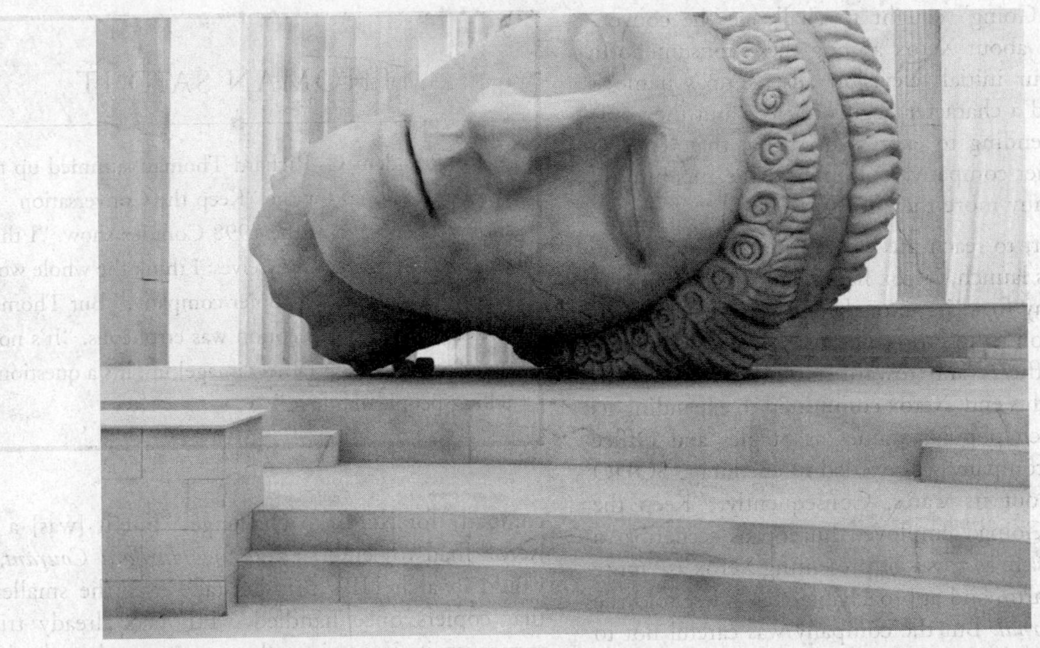

A still from Xerox's "Keep the Conversation Going" television campaign. XEROX CORPORATION. REPRODUCED BY PERMISSION.

HISTORICAL CONTEXT

Xerox had good reason to strive to keep up with the digital revolution of the 1990s—it had paid a high price for failing to do so in the 1970s. Then, Xerox's research labs invented what proved to be many integral parts of the personal computer, including the mouse and Windows-style icons. Convinced that, as a copier company, it had no need for these technologies (which, of course, would soon change the world), Xerox chose not to exploit them, essentially giving them away to others. "That episode has gone down in history as a textbook example of corporate myopia," opined the *Sunday Times of London.* At least as problematic was that Xerox was unprepared for the onslaught of Japanese competitors, such as the Canon Corp. that stormed the U.S. copier market in the 1970s and 1980s. During that period, Xerox's market share plummeted from a high of nearly 80 percent to a low of 7 percent. The company did fight its way back, however, attaining 18 percent of the market by 1992. In fact, after "focus[ing] on its core copier business," especially high-end machines, Xerox eventually surpassed archnemesis Canon and maintained a 27 percent share of the market in 1997.

Xerox's newfound success was threatened, however, by the changing nature of business itself. The rise of the personal computer and the Internet in the 1990s meant that paper documents no longer were the sole means of creating and disseminating information. "Ultimately, the paperless office will probably happen," a Xerox official told the *Sunday Times of London.* Computer printers, networks, and fax machines all diminished the centrality of the copier to business. In response to this tectonic shift, Xerox rapidly began to expand into this new class of machines. Instead of simply producing equipment to photocopy paper, Xerox created machines that were "portals... for easily moving documents between the physical and virtual worlds," according to the *Hartford Courant.* In September 1998 the company proudly announced its new combination digital copier/printer and committed to launching a bevy of printers, small copiers, and other personal products.

TARGET MARKET

Despite these changes, Xerox was still pigeonholed by many as a one-product firm. "It's the downside of having a strong brand," Anne Mulcahy, Xerox's chief staff officer, told the *Wall Street Journal.* "Sometimes it is hard to move away from things you have been successful with." With "Keep the Conversation Going," Xerox hoped to reposition itself, particularly in the eyes of two important groups: the large corporations to whom it had long sold its copiers; and the fast-growing sector the company referred to as the "SOHO" market, which consisted of small business people with home offices and other technologically savvy users interested in the kinds of digital products Xerox had come to offer. "Keep the

Conversation Going" sought to challenge the conventional wisdom about Xerox among these consumers. In one of the four initial television ads, Xerox's name is mentioned and a character begins to say, "but they only make . . .," intending to express his belief that Xerox is still just a copier company. O'Hurley's sage cuts him off sharply: "not any more they don't."

In an effort to reach the SOHO market even before the campaign's launch, Xerox had begun to shift its sales techniques away from its trained staff who generally had pitched the company's products directly to corporate information officers and toward a more retail-oriented approach. To this end, Xerox committed to expanding its presence at such popular venues as Staples and Office Max. But the company still needed to encourage SOHO users to seek out its wares. Consequently, "Keep the Conversation Going" employed humorous scenarios to convey its message as a way of presenting Xerox as "more human, and warm, and approachable," as Wiese told the *Wall Street Journal.* But the company was careful not to undersell the range of products and services it could provide. Many of the offerings touted by Xerox in "Keep the Conversation Going" (such as networked copiers and document-sharing software) transcended the needs of most SOHO consumers. But by overselling itself this way, the company hoped to reinforce the notion that it was a technological leader, and not "just" a copier business.

This focus on higher-end products also helped ensure that Xerox would continue to reach large businesses. To buttress this effort, the campaign's commercials were studded with trendy management buzzwords such as "knowledge management" and "knowledge sharing." Moreover, the stories portrayed in some of the spots reflected the dilemmas faced by corporate personnel working in large offices. In one commercial, bickering team members complain to their leader, Wanda, about her decision to hire an outside consultant. "He doesn't think the way we do! He doesn't even use the same systems," an underling tells her. The Greek chorus intercedes and tells Wanda everything will be fine. Because the group has Xerox's Docushare, everyone can access and share documents easily. Each of the four commercials illustrated how Xerox "united people through documents," said Wiese, and the Greek chorus, which spoke in unison, "represent[ed] [the] collaboration" Xerox enabled.

THOMAN SAID IT

Xerox President G. Richard Thoman summed up the company's hopes for the "Keep the Conversation Going" campaign at the 1998 Comdex show. "I think we have to legitimize ourselves; I think the whole world views us as an analog copier company." But Thoman stressed that this perception was erroneous. "It's not a question of making [a new image] up; it's a question of telling people about it."

COMPETITION

By expanding into the retail office equipment market—and especially by making high-capacity printers—Xerox put itself in direct competition with the industry leading Hewlett Packard Company (HP). HP was a difficult company for Xerox to challenge, "but it [was] a battle Xerox [had to] enter," said the *Hartford Courant,* or it would "watch HP's printers take over the smaller jobs that copiers once handled." HP had already tried to spruce up its image in order to garner a broader base of consumers. In November 1997 the company began packaging its printers and computers in boldly colored boxes that would be more "exciting or enticing," as an HP spokesperson told the *Wall Street Journal.* HP also inaugurated its "Expanding Possibilities" campaign, a branding effort for its entire product line. As Xerox would do in "Keep the Conversation Going," HP's campaign stressed that company's changing face. In a press release, HP noted that marketing studies had revealed that "it was not perceived as innovative or inspirational." To counteract these impressions, one of the campaign's component commercials featured a former Negro League baseball player using the company's computers, scanners, and printers to make and sell Negro League baseball cards on-line.

HP recognized the threat Xerox's move into its territory could pose and was "watching Xerox at every turn . . . not about to give an inch to the copier interloper," noted the *Wall Street Journal.* HP quickly introduced its own multifunction device, the Mopier, which—like some of Xerox's newest equipment—combined scanning, printing, and networking. In October 1998 HP launched a $125 million print, radio, and on-line campaign, the largest advertising campaign ever for its color printers. "Even with a strong brand, and a strong market share, the company doesn't want to just sit on its laurels," an HP executive told the *Business Journal.* "We intend to be everywhere with our ads," he said. Part of the overarching "Expanding Possibilities" campaign, the new offerings—conceived by Goodby, Silverstein & Partners—claimed that HP's printers created the best color documents, "no matter what you're printing." The campaign had a broad target audience of corporate customers, home users, students, and small businesses, and the print components ran in the *New York Times, Wall Street Journal,* and *USA Today,* as well as in publications such as *PC World, People,* and *Golf Digest.*

Xerox also faced competition from its traditional copier rival, Canon. Like Xerox, Canon undertook a big-budget repositioning to signal that it was more than just a copier company, according to the *Wall Street Journal.* In 1997 Canon debuted a $9 million campaign devised by Devito/Verdi that strove to "elevate top-of-mind awareness that Canon is number 1 in the market," a company spokesperson told *Advertising Age.* These print, television, outdoor, and direct marketing ads used catchy slogans like "Business is War. Choose your weapons wisely" to promote Canon's business equipment. In June 1998 Canon began a new print and outdoor campaign that used the tag line "If it were that easy, you wouldn't need us." This effort used humor to stress the necessity of reliable business equipment. In one spot, a secretary tells her boss that the fax machine is down, to which he responds: "That's OK, I'll run it over there myself."

MARKETING STRATEGY

For the initial 10 week run of the campaign, Xerox relied exclusively on television advertising. (The company added print pieces as well when it continued to run "Keep the Conversation Going" ads in 1999.) To drive its message home to its audience, Xerox opted for 60-second spots instead of the more conventional 30-second ones. These longer installments not only allowed the company to convey a significant amount of information about its newest products, but also helped the company better connect with consumers. As one marketing analyst told the *Wall Street Journal,* "by the time I come back to my TV from the refrigerator, at least I'll remember what company was behind the ad." Furthermore, Xerox unleashed the "Keep the Conversation Going" commercials during a Major League Baseball playoff game and then ran them in what Wiese termed a blitz on a slew of broadcast and cable channels in hopes of reaching the greatest number of consumers possible—particularly those in the SOHO market.

Xerox also wanted to be sure to inform the corporate world of its diversification. To this end, the company arranged to make a high-profile appearance at the 1998 Comdex show, a computer industry exposition. At Comdex, Xerox actually re-created the set from its ads, building a coliseum two stories high and half the size of a football field. In keeping with this distinctive approach, the company chose not to deliver a keynote address at the gathering, but rather brought O'Hurley (dressed in a tunic) to conduct a mock Socratic dialogue with Xerox President G. Richard Thoman. Thoman used this platform to take the assembled industry representatives through the message of "Keep the Conversation Going." As *Interactive Week Online* explained, Thoman "showcase[d] [Xerox's] transition from a box-based analog copier manufacturer to a vested player in the realm of information technology."

The sensation Xerox created at Comdex (*Interactive Weekly Online* later described it as "this digital debutante's coming-out party") mirrored an underlying strategy of much of the campaign. No longer content to be perceived as a staid provider of copier machines to businesses, Xerox devised "Keep the Conversation Going" to attract attention. All aspects of the campaign were meant to mirror the changes occurring within the company. Xerox hired a big-budget film director, Gore Verbinski, to direct the campaign; it aimed to be "the most impressive display" at Comdex, as a company press release announced. In short, much of Xerox's motivation in executing "Keep the Conversation Going"—from pitching technology with a multicultural Greek chorus to assembling a coliseum for Comdex with pillars the size of redwoods—was make viewers look anew at Xerox and, in the words of a company press release, muse "And who would have thought this was from Xerox?"

OUTCOME

With a goal as difficult to quantify as repositioning itself and changing the way consumers viewed the company, it was complicated to gauge the outcome of "Keeping the Conversation Going." Xerox's hyperbolic ploys certainly did not win rave reviews from ad industry insiders. Both *Adweek* and *Advertising Age* criticized the campaign for using the Greek chorus as a motif—"Other than Woody Allen employing it as a device in 'Mighty Aphrodite,' you don't see it much after the second century B.C.," *Adweek's* commentator wryly noted. Both *USA Today* and the *New York Times* included "Keep the Conversation Going" among their "worst of 1998" ad compilations.

Nevertheless, consumers liked the campaign. A *USA Today* AdTrack survey revealed that baby boomers in particular found the campaign entertaining and effective. Wiese asserted that the commercials had scored well in postrun marketing surveys. "People get the message. They say, 'You're getting your sense of humor back,'" she told *USA Today.* Xerox dedicated $200 million to expanding the campaign in 1999 to include more television spots, as well as the introduction of print ads.

FURTHER READING

Beatty, Sally Goll. "HP to Get Marketing Makeover." *Wall Street Journal,* November 11, 1997.

Elliott, Stuart. "The Adept and the Inept." *Fort Worth Star-Telegram,* January 1, 1999. Reviews the "Keep the Conversation Going" campaign.

Goldfisher, Alastair. "HP to Spend $125 M on Ad Campaign." *Business Journal,* November 2, 1998.

Klein, Alec. "Xerox Posts Operating Gain but Issues Warning." *Wall Street Journal,* July 23, 1999.

Krol, Carol. "Canon Devotes $9 Million to Biz Equipment Ads." *Advertising Age,* July 21, 1997.

Lynn, Matthew. "Xerox Chief Aims to Copy Past Triumph." *Sunday Times of London,* June 15, 1997.

Moran, John. "Not Copying the Original Market Plan." *Hartford Courant,* November 19, 1998.

Narisetti, Raju. "Xerox Aims to Imprint High-Tech Image." *Wall Street Journal,* October 6, 1998.

Wells, Melanie. "Quirky Xerox Ads Appeal to Boomers." *USA Today,* February 8, 1999.

Rebecca Stanfel

Yahoo! Inc.

701 First Avenue
Sunnyvale, California 94089
USA
Telephone: (408) 349-3300
Fax: (408) 349-3301
Web site: www.yahoo.com

DO YOU YAHOO!? CAMPAIGN

OVERVIEW

Yahoo!, one of the early stars of the Internet, was launched in 1993 as Jerry's Guide to the World Wide Web, offering early users of the Web a way to navigate the quickly expanding Internet—in effect a table of contents. The company's founders soon dropped the name "Jerry's Guide" in favor of something more memorable, Yahoo!, an acronym for Yet Another Hierarchical Officious Oracle. To build the fledgling brand, in April 1996 the company released the "Do You Yahoo!?" marketing campaign.

The $5 million effort included television, radio, and print elements. One of the most memorable of the television spots, which aired in 1997, featured a balding young man using Yahoo! to search for a cure for his thinning hair. The final shot of the spot showed him strutting down the street with a huge, bushy Afro, turning the heads of his fellow pedestrians.

The "Do You Yahoo!?" campaign succeeded in raising the brand recognition of Yahoo! and attracting more visitors to the Web portal. In the late 1990s Yahoo! was far and away the most valuable Internet business, with a market value exceeding $4.3 billion. Yahoo! stumbled when the Internet sector crashed in the first few years of the new millennium, and its search-engine business was surpassed by a new rival, Google. But Yahoo! was able to rebound and continued to market its portal with the "Do You Yahoo!?" campaign until 2004.

HISTORICAL CONTEXT

In 1993 Stanford engineering student Dave Filo's personal list of favorite websites had grown beyond 200 "bookmarks." He and fellow engineering student Jerry Yang wrote software that grouped their favorites sites into convenient on-screen folders. When they posted their list on the Web under the title "Jerry's Guide to the World Wide Web," people all over the world contacted them to say thanks. It was the Web's first table of contents.

Filo and Yang then planned to visit and categorize 1,000 websites a day. They decided to avoid the engineer's natural impulse to automate the process, instead throwing tremendous hours of human labor into the project. Yang hated the name "Jerry's Guide," so he and Filo followed the technology community's affinity for acronyms and came up with Yahoo! which stood for "Yet Another Hierarchical Officious Oracle."

Yahoo!'s distinguishing founding idea was using a cadre of professional Web surfers to organize a directory of websites into coherent categories. This approach differed from competitors like Excite (then called Architex), which relied on Web-scouring software to view and catalog. According to *Fortune* magazine, "Yahoo! had the best name, the worst technology, and a quaint belief

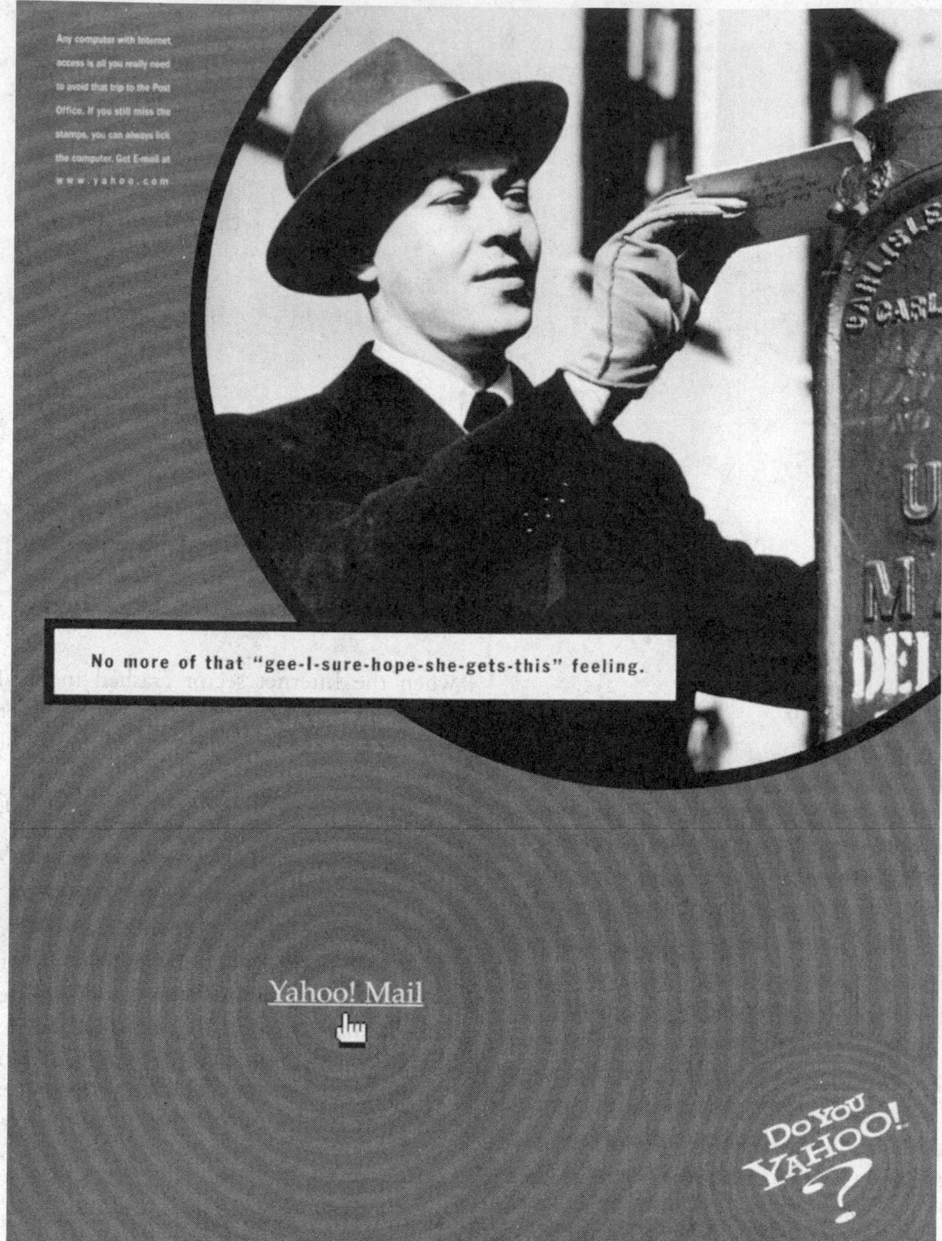
Any computer with Internet
access is all you really need
to avoid that trip to the Post
Office. If you still miss the
stamps, you can always lick
the computer. Get E-mail at
www.yahoo.com
No more of that "gee-I-sure-hope-she-gets-this" feeling.
Yahoo! Mail
Do You Yahoo!?

A print advertisement from the "Do You Yahoo?" campaign. BLACK ROCKET. REPRODUCED BY PERMISSION.

that while other companies' machines were able to survey website addresses by the thousands every second, the human touch could somehow win out."

In 1995 Netscape and America Online both offered to absorb Yahoo! Yang and Filo declined but later signed with Sequoia Capital. Sequoia put up $1 million, which grew to $560 million by the end of 1997. Among the strong competitors that emerged were Excite, developed by another group of Stanford graduate students, and Lycos, which was developed at Carnegie Mellon.

But while human intelligence gave Yahoo! the early lead among Web search engines, what enabled Yahoo! to far outdistance the pack was a rapid rollout of E-mail, financial services, and a strong marketing effort. According to *Fortune,* in the first quarter of 1996 Yahoo!, Lycos, Excite, and Infoseek all delivered roughly the same number of pages. By the end of 1996, however, Yahoo! delivered twice as many pages as second-place Excite. By the third quarter of 1997 Yahoo! visitors looked at 50 million pages a day—more than the other three search engines combined.

Up to the minute financial news. Stock quotes. Market research. 24 hours a day. So you'll know right away if you'll be rolling in cash, or wallowing in self pity.
www.yahoo.com
Get that "I got out before the market crashed" feeling.
Yahoo! Finance
DO YOU YAHOO!?

A print ad from the "Do You Yahoo?" campaign. BLACK ROCKET. REPRODUCED BY PERMISSION.

TARGET MARKET

"Do You Yahoo!?" aimed to attract those people who intended to go online, an estimated 18 million people in 1998, according to IntelliQuest. Karen Edwards, Yahoo!'s director of brand management, referred to the company's target market as Internet intenders or near-surfers. This market's demographics skewed toward educated, affluent males, generally in the 25–54 age range. As time went on and women gained more interest in the Internet, the target group broadened to include them, and in the 2000s the ongoing campaign targeted a mass audience, touting Yahoo!'s wide range of services. Moreover, as Yahoo!'s overseas traffic increased, the campaign had to be adopted to different cultures and translated into various languages, although "Do you Yahoo!?" tested much better in English than translated.

In 1997 Yahoo! and other high-tech advertisers were counting on television to expand their markets. In May of that year *BusinessWeek* reported that 40 percent of U.S. homes had computers, but annual growth was down

INTERESTING YAHOO! FACTS

- In 1999 Yahoo! was an $11 billion company that did not own a building
- Although a billionaire, company cofounder David Filo put in 100-hour workweeks
- Cofounder Jerry Yang was so popular in his parents' home country of Taiwan that he registered in hotels under an assumed name
- Yahoo!'s grassroots marketing included a "Yahoo! for Barry Bonds" sign that flashed on the screen at the San Francisco baseball player's home stadium every time he hit a home run
- In 1998 Yahoo! was the most popular website in Japan, where 10 million people were online

from the 20–30 percent clip of the past few years to about 13 percent. Yahoo! and others used advertising to show the ease and advantages of going online, in hopes of drawing more and more people into the Internet services market.

COMPETITION

Yahoo!'s strengths against its competition included a huge lead in market capitalization and its reputation as being tops in the search, finance, and news areas. Lycos was more aggressive than Yahoo! in pursuing acquisitions that added new services and broadened its market appeal. Lycos also chose to link separately branded sites to serve different demographic segments. Infoseek and Altavista benefited from the massive shadows of their owners, Disney and Compaq respectively.

Excite had strong health and search features and was the Web page for Dell's PC buyers. In October 1996 Excite introduced a $10 million campaign from Foote Cone & Belding featuring the Jimi Hendrix song "Are You Experienced?" On December 7, 1998, Excite premiered a new network and cable television campaign. Six 30-second commercials showed people botching common activities in embarrassing, humorous ways. One spot told viewers that the woman pictured could send photographs to friends around the world using Excite. She then walked through a screen door she had just closed. In another spot a man was all thumbs as he installed an air conditioner only to watch it plummet from his window. The spots ended with the suggestion that if this person could use Excite "you can too."

By 1998 Yahoo!'s growth and success had moved it into the domain of a new set of competitors. The company was being viewed as a key part of the computing establishment and a great destination for Web users. It felt less like a search engine and more like an online service. The competition grew to include Microsoft and America Online (AOL). Microsoft was spending $61 million on television spots built around its theme "Where do you want to go today?" Trying to outduel Microsoft, AOL spent about $66 million on television advertising. AOL's advantages included billions in monthly Internet user fees and the longest track record as a content aggregator.

In 1998 NBC launched a television campaign for its Web portal company Snap!. The commercials used the tagline "Don't Suffer from Information Overload. Snap! Out of It." A 1996 multimillion dollar campaign from Infoseek appeared regularly in full-page ads in the *Wall Street Journal.* All told, at one point in the 1990s Yahoo! had to contend with nearly 60 different competitors, yet its chief rival had yet to emerge: Google, the search engine that turned itself into a verb, something Yahoo! had failed to achieve. Yahoo! would be forced to reengineer its search capabilities to compete with Google, but more importantly Yahoo! retooled its business model, so that shopping and entertainment and other ventures overshadowed its search-engine business.

MARKETING STRATEGY

Yang believed that success depended upon giving Web users what they wanted and publicizing the brand voraciously. He recruited Karen Edwards to promote the brand. Edwards, who came from BBDO, where she had worked on the Apple account, wasted little time before putting Yahoo! on television with the $5 million ad campaign.

By 1997 advertising of Internet services had grown dramatically. High-tech products like personal computers, printers, and Internet service providers were becoming commodities. Yahoo! and its competitors offered the same access for the same price. As Edwards observed, "It's just like beer or cars. The products are similar enough that image has a lot to do with why people buy one instead of the other."

Chris Charron, an analyst with Forrester Research in Boston, noted, "Users find what they're looking for at Yahoo! While many competitors load their sites with elaborate graphics that can confuse users and delay them, Yahoo!'s site is clear, uncluttered, and fast." A search on competitor Alta Vista might return millions of matches, while the same search on Yahoo! would return a more manageable number of matches arranged in categories.

Edwards also led a so-called guerrilla marketing approach that saw Yahoo! popping up seemingly everywhere, including in magazines and at rock concerts, sports contests, and some unconventional venues. She gave a free auto paint job to any employee who would agree to having the Yahoo! logo displayed on his or her car. The company had a barter deal with the National Football League's 49ers in which the fans shouted, "Yahoo!" to cheer their team as the portal's purple logo burst onto the football stadium screen. Millions saw the Yahoo! Zamboni from the San Jose hockey arena in a scene from the movie *EdTV.* The Yahoo! logo appeared on a wide array of products, including backpacks, sunglasses, baseballs, computer glasses, skateboards, Slinkys, surfboards, yo-yos, and school stationery.

Some analysts, like those at *Fortune,* said that these early and inexpensive grassroots promotions were critical in getting Yahoo! far in front of the competition. With little advertising money, Yahoo! often bartered services to expand its reach. And it launched national advertising before nearly all of its competitors. *Fortune* also lauded Yahoo!'s cobranding of products, services, and contests with well-regarded brands, such as Ben & Jerry's, Visa, and MCI, and with community outreach to 75 nonprofit organizations. All the advertising and marketing would not have helped if Yahoo! did not also evolve and add new services. Users grew accustomed to finding something new at Yahoo! continually. Stock quotes, maps, chat rooms, news, weather, sports, Yellow Pages, and classifieds all broadened the site's appeal and kept its image of being fresh and cool.

Black Rocket's advertising strategy meshed well with Yang's vision of the company. The agency treated Yahoo! not like a technology company but as a consumer brand. "By conjuring up a cool California image—hip but not rad, easy-to-use but not simplistic—it managed to create a cult-like following not unlike that of Apple Computer Inc.'s Macintosh," said *BusinessWeek.* As it expanded, Yahoo! kept promoting new services under its single brand name. Competitor Lycos took the opposite strategy and built separately branded sites, including Tripod and WhoWhere.

The Yahoo! name itself paid dividends. The memorable and fun name gained wide credit for helping to attract investor attention and build a following. Black Rocket convinced Yahoo! to use the company name in the advertising slogan because it was unusual, irreverent, and memorable. "The name contains the promise of the product," said Owen Shapiro, senior analyst at market and brand research firm Leo J. Shapiro & Associates in *BusinessWeek.* "It reinforces the idea that when I go to Yahoo!, I'll be so pleased I'll be Yahooing afterwards." The name also implied that everyone knew what Yahoo! was.

While the early ads in the campaign emphasized Yahoo!'s search engine, by 1998 the company was emphasizing its shopping capabilities with spots showing an Arctic fisherman using Yahoo! to buy a hot tub and an overweight superhero buying handbags through Yahoo! to give to crime victims because he could no longer run down purse snatchers.

As the new century dawned, the idea of "Yahooing" did not catch on with Internet users as the company had hoped. Instead, users began to use the term "Googling" to mean "performing an online search." Nevertheless, Yahoo's brand recognition was still strong, and the company found its own lucrative niche on the Web, supported by new executions of the "Do You Yahoo!?" campaign that promoted Yahoo!'s varied product offerings. For example, one 30-second television spot, which premiered during the 2002 Super Bowl, took place on the island of Palau in Micronesia and featured a tourist and dolphin who both realized that they had settled on their vacation destination by using Yahoo! Campaign spots were also translated into other languages to reach an increasingly global market.

OUTCOME

A rapid rise in its stock price gave Yahoo! a market value of $4.3 billion in early 1998—by far the highest of any Internet company. More people accessed Yahoo! at work than any other website, and it ranked second only to America Online in traffic from home. In February 1998 Yahoo! attracted 31.2 million users to its site, 8 million more than second-place finisher Netscape and 13 million more than third-place finisher Microsoft. In May 1999 *Advertising Age* named Yahoo! its top marketer in the portal category. The company also regularly ranked among the top five sites in average minutes a user spent online a month, according to Media Metrix. And, unlike many early Internet giants, Yahoo! was profitable.

Yahoo! was not, however, immune to the effects of the dot-com crash that occurred at the start of the twenty-first century. Chief executive Timothy Koogle stepped down in the spring of 2001, and a few months later Karen Edwards, part of the team that had developed the "Do You Yahoo!?" tagline, quit "to spend more time with her family." The company continued to use the tagline for nearly two more years. Black Rocket lost the Yahoo! account in August 2003, and the company's new ad agency developed a marketing campaign anchored by the tagline "Life engine."

FURTHER READING

Armstrong, Larry. "Cars, Beer, and Web Browsers." *BusinessWeek,* May 12, 1997.

Himelstein, Linda. "Yahoo! The Company, the Strategy, the Stock." *BusinessWeek,* September 7, 1998, p. 66.

Mack, Ann. "No More Funny Stuff." *Adweek* (western ed.), March 4, 2002, p. 23.

———. "Yahoo!'s New Tune." *Adweek,* April 5, 2004, p. 10.

Nakache, Patricia. "Secrets of the New Brand Builders: AOL, Yahoo, Palm Computing." *Fortune,* June 22, 1998.

Piller, Charles. "The Cutting Edge; Sitting on Top of the World; Internet: Yahoo's Lean, Nimble Approach Has Made It the Richest of Web Portals." *Los Angeles Times,* October 12, 1998, p. C1.

Riedman, Patricia. "Yahoo! Forges Strong Brand while Adding Meaty Content." *Advertising Age,* May 3, 1999, p. S4.

Saunders, Christopher. "Yahoo! Launches TV, Radio Campaign." *Internetnews.com,* November 21, 2001. Available from <http://siliconvalley.internet.com/news/print.php/92791>

Stross, Randall E.. "How Yahoo! Won the Search Wars." *Fortune,* March 2, 1998, p. 148.

Voight, Joan, and Becky Ebenkamp. "Yahoo! TV Spot Is Aimed at Educated, Affluent Men." *Adweek* (eastern ed.), April 21, 1997, p. 2.

Chris JohnAmorosino
Ed Dinger

LIVE BILLBOARD DATING CAMPAIGN

OVERVIEW

Shortly after its launch in 1994 Yahoo! Inc. became one of the Internet's top search engines. Although the company remained primarily associated with its search engine in subsequent years, it also expanded its business operations to include a range of integrated online products and services, including Yahoo! Personals, America's second-most-popular forum for online dating. In 2004 Yahoo! Personals set out to differentiate itself from competitors by using select members of its paid subscription base as the stars of its online advertising. This effort, dubbed "Project: Real People," was not particularly newsworthy on its own, and Yahoo! Personals did not have a media budget sufficient to achieve saturation among its target market of professional singles. A three-day launch event, the "Live Billboard Dating Campaign," sought to rectify this situation.

The "Live Billboard Dating Campaign" was a $140,000 attempt to generate widespread media coverage of the Yahoo! Personals brand. The campaign, which began on January 7, 2004, centered on the efforts of one Yahoo! Personals subscriber, Julie Koehnen, to find an eligible bachelor using the online service. What made the campaign so noteworthy, however, was the fact that Koehnen conducted this search for a date while living, over the course of three days, on a platform erected along the bottom of a highly visible billboard on the Sunset Strip in Los Angeles. The billboard featured Koehnen's Yahoo! Personals photo and text stating, "Julie is looking for a few good dates. (And she's not coming down until she gets them!)" The attached platform offered the amenities necessary for Koehnen to search for dates using Yahoo! Personals and to host romantic prospects live at the billboard before choosing one among the group for further dates. Koehnen's life atop the billboard platform was broadcast, unedited, on the Yahoo! Personals website.

The campaign generated hundreds of stories in the local and national media, including live interviews of Koehnen on such programs as *Good Morning America,* and it spurred substantial increases in online traffic to the Yahoo! Personals site. Yahoo! Personals overtook Match.com during the first quarter of 2004 to become the nation's leading online dating service. The "Live Billboard Dating Campaign" won a Gold EFFIE Award in 2005.

HISTORICAL CONTEXT

Yahoo! was founded in 1994 by Stanford University Ph.D. students David Filo and Jerry Yang, and it quickly became one of the Internet's leading search engines. In the late 1990s and early 2000s the company expanded into a broad range of online communications, content, and shopping products and services, including the dating website Yahoo! Personals, which debuted in 1997.

Yahoo! Personals served as a forum for singles to search for and communicate with prospective romantic partners. A user created his or her own personal profile, including a photo, and could search the profiles of all other users for potential dates. Yahoo! Personals introduced a subscription model into its service in 2001. Users could still search listings for free, but to interact fully with other singles and post one's own profile, a monthly subscription fee was required. Subscription fees discouraged frivolous use, thereby allowing the larger community of users to take the site more seriously. As Yahoo! Personals and its competitors refined their services—the subscription model became the industry standard—more and more Internet-savvy singles turned to such online dating forums. By 2003 the personals category was outperforming all other online revenue sources (excluding gambling and pornography), and Yahoo! Personals was the number two dating service in cyberspace.

Among the primary marketing challenges facing Yahoo! Personals in this rapidly expanding market was the difficulty of differentiating itself from its competitors.

Most online dating sites offered roughly the same services at roughly the same prices, and there were limited possibilities for cultivating brand allegiance. Another primary challenge was the still-prevalent, if declining, stigma attached to online dating. Many potential users feared the idea that individuals would misrepresent themselves online; others were worried about the embarrassment connected with telling friends and family that a romantic partner had been located via the Internet.

A 2003 Yahoo! Personals campaign called "Believe," crafted by the advertising agency Black Rocket Euro RSCG, sought to position the company as a source of hope in a bleak world, eschewing sexual messages in print and TV work that focused on the common fears and anxieties, as well as the fundamental optimism, of the dating experience. In 2004 Yahoo! Personals attempted to meet these challenges in a new way by focusing on real people in its advertising. The "Project: Real People" campaign, which was introduced with the "Live Billboard Dating Campaign," was built on a strategy of using actual Yahoo! Personals customers as models in online and print ads. This not only served the purpose of differentiating the brand's communications from those of competitors who employed professional models, but also spoke to the issue of stigmatization by showcasing the attributes of actual users of the service.

TARGET MARKET

The "Live Billboard Dating Campaign" had a primary target group of women and a secondary, complementary target group of men. Both groups fit the same profile: 25- to 49-year-old professionals who had never been married, who lived in one of the top 10 Yahoo! Personals urban markets, who were curious but unsure about online dating, and who were interested in an alternative to the dating environment offered by nightclubs and bars.

Like the broader "Project: Real People" effort, the "Live Billboard Dating Campaign" counted among its primary goals the destigmatization of online dating as well as the communication of the idea that real people found real romance via the service. The selection of Julie Koehnen as the subject of the campaign was thus calibrated to perform these functions vis-à-vis both target groups. As an attractive, well-spoken 39-year-old screenwriter, she was meant to show the female target group that Yahoo! Personals was an appropriate forum for impressive, interesting women to meet men. Meanwhile, Koehnen was intended to show men that they might meet someone as desirable as her by using Yahoo! Personals. Koehnen selected and conducted her dates live at the billboard site, effectively showcasing the Yahoo! Personals process.

LOCATION, LOCATION, LOCATION

The location for the "Live Billboard Dating Campaign"—the Sunset Strip in Hollywood—was ideal for a number of reasons. First, a warm climate was essential to the event, as the campaign's star, Julie Koehnen, would be living outdoors for three days in midwinter. Also, Los Angeles was one of the top markets for Yahoo! Personals, and within Los Angeles the Sunset Strip had a particularly high concentration of vehicle and foot traffic as well as a trendy reputation that would resonate with the campaign target of single professionals. But other, less obvious factors were also crucial to the selection of this location. The outdoor-advertising company that owned the billboard was able to fit the three-day Yahoo! Personals campaign in between two other, longer-term advertisers—not necessarily an easy scheduling feat—and the prevalence of movie filming in the area made it possible for Yahoo! to acquire the appropriate permits for the live webcast in spite of the unusual filming setup. The various elements of the campaign thus fell into place.

Local and national media outlets were also a crucial target for the hybrid event. The "Live Billboard Dating Campaign" sought to make an impression across America with a limited budget, and it could only do so if print publications and TV programs became convinced that it was a newsworthy event. The project was designed specifically to generate media coverage—i.e., free airtime and print space for Yahoo! Personals—and a variety of media outlets were contacted in advance of the January 7 launch so that they would arrive to cover Koehnen's activities live.

COMPETITION

The leading online dating site prior to the "Live Billboard Dating Campaign" was Match.com, which offered a $25 monthly subscription service similar to Yahoo! Personals' $20 service. Match.com, like Yahoo! Personals, built an advertising campaign influenced by reality TV. Helmed by Bartle Bogle Hegarty and debuting in July 2003 on the reality program *Cupid,* the campaign spots attempted to mimic the spirited bickering characteristic of reality TV, which was often structured around head-to-head competition between participants. The spots opened with the personal-ad photos of two supposed Match.com users, and then the photos morphed into characters who competitively berated one another. For instance, one female addressed a competing Match.com user, pictured alongside a palm tree, with this over-the-top diagnosis of her personality: "You're insane, and I hope you never leave that little island you're stuck on."

Though not among the Internet's most popular dating sites, eHarmony, introduced in 2000, offered a matchmaking formula that distinguished it from most of Yahoo! Personals' competitors, and a correspondingly higher subscription fee made it one of the more lucrative of competing services. Priced at $50 a month, more than twice the cost of Yahoo! Personals, eHarmony claimed to use scientifically sound psychological profiling to match its subscribers with one another. Rather than simply submitting a personal profile and making contacts with prospective dates of their own volition, eHarmony subscribers submitted to a psychological evaluation consisting of 436 questions, and the service used the results to generate a list of compatible fellow subscribers. EHarmony grew from a base of 20,000 subscribers in December 2000 to more than 4.5 million by the end of 2004.

MARKETING STRATEGY

"Project: Real People," a projected yearlong campaign, was built around 50 Yahoo! Personals members chosen from a pool of 38,000 who had responded to a casting call in the months leading up to the launch. The 50 "Project: Real People" participants, representing a diverse cross-section of the online dating community, were photographed for print and online ads that were slated to run in the weeks and months following the "Live Billboard Dating Campaign." Though the idea of using real people to pitch the dating service was unique in the industry, it was of limited news value, and Yahoo! Personals did not have budgetary resources sufficient to achieve saturation via a traditional media campaign.

The "Live Billboard Dating Campaign," largely conceived and implemented by Yahoo! in-house marketers working within a $140,000 budget, was designed to address these issues. Both a three-day launch event for the larger "Project: Real People" campaign and an innovative marketing campaign in its own right, the "Live Billboard" effort was a hybrid of outdoor advertisement, buzz-marketing stunt, and reality TV show starring an actual Yahoo! Personals subscriber. Beyond announcing the "Project: Real People" campaign, the "Live Billboard Dating Campaign" was intended to drive traffic to the Yahoo! Personals website, to spur subscriptions, and to build awareness of the process by which singles met one another using the service.

A billboard on a high-traffic area of the famous Sunset Strip in Hollywood was outfitted with a living room, dining room, and office featuring wireless Internet capability. Julie Koehnen, one of the 50 "Project: Real People" finalists, was singled out for her ability to represent the dynamism, attractiveness, and charm that Yahoo! wanted consumers to associate with users of its online dating service. She was asked to live on the billboard for approximately 12 hours a day from January 7 to January 9, 2004, while conducting a search for dates using Yahoo! Personals.

The focus of Koehnen's days on the billboard was the conducting of this search, made possible by her wireless-equipped office, but she was also treated to a variety of wellness and entertainment services, including yoga sessions and visits from a fortune-teller and a comedian, and she made time for the numerous media interviews that the campaign was intended to generate. Over the course of the three days Koehnen interviewed, in person, three men per day at the billboard. At the end of this process she selected one bachelor to invite back for a date on the final evening of her billboard residency. From 8 a.m. to 6 p.m. each day Koehnen's activities were aired, uncut and unedited, on the Yahoo! Personals website, as "Live Julie TV." The billboard above Koehnen's living space featured her photograph and copy reading, "Julie is looking for a few good dates. (And she's not coming down until she gets them!)" The Yahoo! Personals logo as well as the Web address where users could go to view Koehnen's profile were also prominently showcased.

OUTCOME

The three-day campaign generated 347 television and radio stories in more than 100 American markets, including coverage on every major Los Angeles network affiliate, more than 50 stories on Los Angeles TV stations alone, and live interviews or stories on such national shows as *CNN Headline News, Good Morning America, Good Day Live, ABC News Live,* and ESPN2's *Cold Pizza.* Traffic to the Yahoo! Personals website spiked significantly: unique visits increased 19 percent from the two-week period preceding the campaign and increased 44 percent compared to the same period the previous year. More than half a million viewers watched "Live Julie TV" over the course of its three-day run, and Koehnen received more than 1,000 E-mails from Yahoo! Personals subscribers as a result of her billboard residency.

Yahoo! Personals subscriptions increased 199 percent compared with the same period the previous year and 27 percent compared with the two weeks prior to the campaign, and the creation of individual profiles on the site increased by 250 percent and 14 percent respectively, by those same measures. During the first quarter of 2004 Yahoo! Personals overtook Match.com as the most popular online dating service, with an average of 6.4 million visitors per month, compared to Match.com's 5.2 million. The "Live Billboard Dating Campaign" won a Gold EFFIE Award in 2005; hosted by the New York American Marketing association, this annual awards event was one of the most prestigious in the advertising industry. "Project: Real People" ran through 2004 and was extended, featuring new batches of Yahoo! Personals subscribers, in subsequent years.

FURTHER READING

Arnold, Catherine. "Web of Love: How Marketers Capitalize on E-motions." *Marketing News,* November 10, 2003.

Deeken, Aimee. "MindShare." *Mediaweek,* June 21, 2004.

Lauro, Patricia Winters. "Online Dating, a Hushed Subject but a Roaring Business, Goes Very Public in a Marketing Battle." *New York Times,* January 27, 2003, p. C9.

Lippert, Barbara. "True Romance." *Adweek,* April 14, 2003.

Richmond, Riva. "Web Firms Find Bliss in Personals." *Wall Street Journal,* February 11, 2003.

———. "Yahoo Plays Cupid to Millions and Finds He Is Very Well-Paid." *Wall Street Journal,* February 11, 2004.

Walker, Leslie. "Yahoo's 1st-Quarter Profit, Revenue Rise; Internet Advertising Drives Rebound." *Washington (D.C.) Post,* April 8, 2004, p. E05.

Mark Lane

Yard Strength, Inc.

1106 Hermosa Avenue
Hermosa Beach, California 90254
USA
Telephone: (310) 376-4011
Fax: (310) 376-1341
Web site: www.yardstrength.com

YARD FITNESS CENTER CAMPAIGN

OVERVIEW

Despite rising cases of obesity and gestational diabetes in the United States, one of the fastest-growing American business sectors during the late 1990s was the health and fitness industry. Between 1988 and 2002 memberships at health clubs in the United States rose 95 percent and yielded more than $12 billion in annual sales. An estimated 58 million individuals attended the 18,000 gyms nationwide during 2001. To gain ground on its Los Angeles–area competition, which included the much-larger Sports Club Company chain, Yard Strength, Inc., released a campaign titled after its only gym, Yard Fitness Center, in 2001.

Created by Los Angeles–based agency JC Advertising, the "Yard Fitness Center" campaign, which cost $12,000, consisted of only two television spots that appeared on local ESPN, Fox, and TBS stations. The Yard Fitness Center was located in Hermosa Beach, 22 miles southwest of downtown Los Angeles. Differentiating it from nearby gyms that advertised with in-club events and print ads, the August 2001 campaign's television spots suggested that gym members did not necessarily exercise for health reasons but simply to look better without clothes on. The television spot "Coverage" humorously began with a group of men playing basketball on public courts. Much to the unease of everyone playing, one of the more obnoxious players wore nothing but socks, sneakers, eyeglasses, and a headband. The spots ended with the tagline "Feel comfortable in your own skin" and the Yard Fitness Center logo.

Despite the fitness center's meager budget and single 4,500-square-foot facility, "Yard Fitness Center" achieved ad-industry success usually reserved for larger corporations. It won an award for Low Budget Campaign at the London International Advertising Awards and a Bronze Lion at the Cannes International Advertising Festival. "Yard Fitness Center" also increased awareness of the gym in Los Angeles. For the year following the campaign, Yard Fitness Center received thousands of E-mails from consumers who had enjoyed the commercials.

HISTORICAL CONTEXT

Located in Hermosa Beach, California, the Yard Fitness Center expanded between 1994 and 2005 to become a reputable high-end gymnasium within the Los Angeles coastal community. With one 4,500-square-foot facility, cutting-edge fitness machines, more than 10,000 pounds of free weights, and a boxing center, the gym appealed to some of the world's best professional athletes and Olympians. Much of the center's early publicity arose from magazines—such as *Benningan's Health & Fitness, HEAT Volleyball Magazine,* and *Muscle Media*—publishing articles about the gym's charismatic owner, Jeremy

"Troll" Subin. Subin was a former National Championship powerlifter whose career highlights included competing for the United States at competitions in the Soviet Union. While overseeing the Yard Fitness Center he began training professional athletes such as the Dodgers' MVP catcher Mike Piazza; Rookie of the Year Eric Karros, also a Dodger; and three-time Olympic volleyball medalist Steve Timmons. In the *South Bay Weekly,* Jason Kendall, catcher for the Pittsburgh Pirates, stated, "Troll helps me stay strong for 162 games without losing my flexibility. I'm different from Karros, and I'm different from Piazza. I'm a guy who has to use my flexibility, and that's what Troll focuses on."

Outside of the favorable press coverage and word-of-mouth praise, the Yard Fitness Center did little to advertise. Subin occasionally used his personal success to endorse the fitness center. In an issue of *Benningan's Health & Fitness,* he stated, "If you really want to improve your performance and prevent injuries, you need to train like an athlete, regardless of your level. At The Yard, we've carefully selected high-end equipment to help both professional athletes and 'civilians' maximize their physical potential." A few ads appeared in local publications with photographs of Mike Piazza or Eric Karros beside the gym's logo. Taglines for the ads read, "Where the good people are," or "Where preparation meets opportunity."

TARGET MARKET

The campaign's first spot, "Coverage," targeted 20- to 40-year-old male sports enthusiasts, and the second spot, "Dressed For Dinner," featuring an easygoing naked couple going to dinner with another couple, who wore clothes, targeted 20- to 40-year-old women. Both groups of consumers differed from the Yard Fitness Center's previous target: athletes. "For this campaign, we targeted sports enthusiasts that enjoyed sports. Even though we previously targeted athletes, they only made up 2 percent of our clientele," Subin said. "We knew athletes would keep coming in because of our reputation, but this campaign was going to target the masses." Between 1988 and 2002 memberships at U.S. health clubs rose 95 percent. The average gym member had changed during that period as well. In 1987 Americans 55 years old and up constituted only 9 percent of gym members, but the number had jumped to 17 percent by 2002.

COMPETITION

The Sports Club Company, Inc., one of the most elite high-end fitness organizations in Los Angeles, carried memberships with some of America's best-known celebrities, such as Michael Jordan and Tom Cruise. Branded as the Sports Club, the Los Angeles–based gym prided itself as being the "Ritz-Carlton of gyms" and limited its advertising to on-site promotions, a newsletter, and cross-promotions with brands such as Giorgio Armani, American Airlines, and luxury watch manufacturer Audemars Piguet. In 2001 the Sports Club did not release print, television, or other traditional forms of advertisement. The club's cofounder, Nanette Pattee Francini, said in *American Demographics* that the Sports Club positioned itself as "a sanctuary from daily life. We don't do really blatant advertising." The chain of nine clubs, two of which were in the Los Angeles area, posted $102 million in sales for 2001, a 33 percent increase from 2000.

America's largest fitness chain, Bally Total Fitness Holding Corp., boasted 415 gyms and posted $852 million in sales for 2001. The corporation's flagship club, Bally Total Fitness, allowed outside brands to dispense free samples to members inside their gym. According to the trade group Promotion Marketing Association's Product Sampling and Demonstration Council, 68 percent of gym members were excited about receiving free samples. In 2001 Bally allowed consumer-product giant Unilever, which owned brands such as Dove, Bird's Eye, and Hellman's, to sponsor "Dove Days." This promotion, for which club staffers wore Dove apparel, included free fitness classes for Bally members. Female members were handed Dove Body Refreshers upon entering the gyms. To target calorie-conscious consumers, Kraft Foods placed coupons for its low-fat cheese products in Bally gyms during 2001. The coupons could be redeemed for a complimentary, 14-day Bally membership or $75 towards a future membership. The promotion was advertised in consumer magazines such as *People, Shape,* and *Reader's Digest.* Bally allowed similar promotions with Sunkist Growers, the Kellogg Company, and Eastman Kodak Company.

MARKETING STRATEGY

The "Yard Fitness Center" campaign's two spots, "Coverage" and "Dressed For Dinner," were written by

SHOOTING LOCATION

One of "Yard Fitness Center" campaign's two commercials, "Coverage," was filmed in six hours and featured a group of clothed, uncomfortable men trying to play basketball with one naked player. Even though the main actor wore nothing but a "small device" to cover his genitalia, the spot was filmed in a public park next to a daycare center.

"TROLL"

Jeremy Subin, owner of the Yard Fitness Center, preferred to be called "Troll" by gym members and colleagues. The 5'2', 175-lb fitness expert trained a plethora of Los Angeles–based athletes, including baseball's 1993 Rookie of the Year, Mike Piazza, and Eric Karros, the 1992 Rookie of the Year. Subin monitored the athletes' diets and heart rates and also changed their training regimens to involve medicine-ball tosses, baseball drills, and Olympic weight-lifting drills.

JC Advertising's Josh Caplan and directed by Backyard Production's Kevin Smith. A writer for the *Creative Review* commented that the campaign "proposes that people go to the gym not to feel healthy, but to look good naked." The first 30-second spot, "Coverage," began with a close-up of three basketball players whispering at the edge of a public basketball court. "I can't cover this guy, man," one said. Another pleaded, "I don't wanna cover him." The third implored, "What're we gonna do?" The camera then showed the player no one wanted to cover: a trash-talking, frizzy-haired player wearing nothing but shoes, socks, glasses, and a headband. The naked player shouted to the three whispering, "OK, ladies. Let's go. Time-out's over."

The spot then showed the naked man, with his genitalia blurred, frightening off opponents with full-body presses and other physical contact that, had he been wearing clothes, would be considered appropriate during a basketball game. At one point the naked man jumped for a slam dunk and, much to the dismay of an opponent, pressed his groin into the opponent's face. Unapologetic, the naked man shouted, "You want a piece of me?" The commercial continued with the nudist scoring and trash-talking opponents until the spot faded blue and the tagline, "Feel comfortable in your own skin," appeared. The logo for Yard Fitness and its Hermosa Beach address followed. Director Kevin Smith told *Advertising Age's Creativity,* "It seemed doable and it seemed like it might be pretty funny. But it would be very easy to take it over the top." As for encouraging the actors' disgust towards the nearly naked antagonist, Smith continued, "That's pretty much the natural reaction someone would have playing basketball with a naked guy."

The second spot, "Dressed For Dinner," began when a naked, 30-something woman opened the door to a clothed man and woman who were immediately dumbstruck by her lack of attire. They couple was obviously meeting the naked woman for dinner at a restaurant. "Oh, hi guys," greeted the naked woman, sounding cheerful. The spot became more absurd when the woman's husband appeared wearing only a tie, black socks, and black shoes. "Rog isn't wearing a tie," the naked man pleaded with his wife. "No," she said, grinning at his tie. "You're wearing it."

Conceptually, the 30-second spot followed "Coverage" by featuring individuals, who after apparently joining the Yard Fitness Center, felt extremely comfortable without their clothes on. "Dressed For Dinner" ended the same way the other spot had, with the tagline and the Yard logo. The final shot featured the naked man looking completely content and settling into the front seat of the clothed man's minivan. "Wow," he said as his naked body squeaked over the leather seats, "leather—I like it." The clothed man's eyes opened wide with revulsion.

OUTCOME

According to Yard Fitness Center president, Jeremy "Troll" Subin, the campaign "Caused quite a disturbance. Some people thought we were crazy." Commercial Closet, an organization dedicated to improving public sensibilities toward lesbian, gay, bisexual, and transgender issues within advertisement, attacked "Coverage" for using "fear of same-sex attraction (homophobia) or 'inappropriate' gender behavior (transphobia)—accompanied by a horrific reaction by someone straight—as their source of humor." The spot "Coverage" was placed into a category of commercials that "[did] not meet Commercial Closet's Best Practices."

For the months following the campaign, the Yard Fitness Center did not record a significant rise in gym memberships. A year later, however, its brand awareness began to grow. The campaign's blend of absurdity and nudity was smiled upon at some of the largest advertising award shows of 2002. Even though the campaign's budget was a mere $12,000, "Coverage" won a Bronze Lion at the 2002 Cannes International Advertising Festival. The "Yard Fitness Center" campaign also won Low Budget Campaign of the year at the 2002 London International Advertising Awards. "Coverage" made the shortlist for the western United States region of *AdForum* magazine's first Creative Hits awards, which allowed *AdForum* website visitors to rate commercials online. By mid-2002, after the commercials were repeated on several network shows showcasing America's funniest commercials, Yard Fitness Center received thousands of E-mails and phone calls from people who had enjoyed the spots.

FURTHER READING

Champagne, Christine. "'Tag' Is It at London Int'l Ad Awards." *Shoot,* November 15, 2002, p. 1.

Fass, Allison, and Jonathan D. Glater. "Bally Fitness Selects Foote, Cone." *New York Times,* August 14, 2002, p. 3.

Frank, John. "MWW Creates Nutrition and Supplements Practice." *PR Week US,* June 24, 2002, p. 5.

Hanas, Jim. "Production Notes." *Advertising Age's Creativity,* September 1, 2001, p. 51.

Lazare, Lewis. "Ad Notes." *Chicago Sun-Times,* September 30, 2002, p. 53.

———. "FCB Chief Survives Grueling Year." *Chicago Sun-Times,* September 9, 2002, p. 49.

Lockwood, Lisa. "Mags Brace for Challenging '03." *Women's Wear Daily,* November 8, 2002, p. 30.

McDermott, Maura. "With Some of These Deals, What You Lose Is Your Money." *Newark (NJ) Star-Ledger,* August 11, 2002, p. 2.

Paul, Pamela. "Locker Room Advertising." *American Demographics,* December 1, 2002, p. 28.

Singh, Rashmi Uday. "A Bloody Good Restaurant." *India Today Plus,* October 1, 2002, p. 58.

Takaki, Millie. "'In Your Face': An Unguardable Player." *Shoot,* August 24, 2001, p. 13.

Ward, Alyson. "Marketers Finding Sneaky New Ways to Pitch." *Seattle Post-Intelligencer,* September 17, 2002, p. E1.

Woodward, Sarah. "Avenue Grows Roster." *Shoot,* June 28, 2002, p. 8.

———. "Editor Mori Joins CO-OP." *Shoot,* August 23, 2002, p. 7.

Kevin Teague

Index

Bold page numbers refer to the main entries for companies or organizations profiled in EMMC. *Page numbers in* italics *refer to photos. Cross references are included for user reference.*

A

A & E Television Networks, **1–3**
Airline, 44
Discovery Communications, as competitor of, 453
Public Broadcasting Service, as competitor of, 1411
TBS, as competitor of, 1663–1664
Turner Classic Movies, as competitor of, 1661
"A & F Quarterly" campaign, 9–12, 580–581
AAAA. *See* American Association of Advertising Agencies
AAdvantage program, 7
AAF. *See* American Advertising Federation
Aaker, David, 21, 841
Aardman Animations, 1501, 1503
Aaron, Hank, 1107
Aaron, Marcia, 1229
"Aaron Burr" spot, 183, 257, 259
AARP, 1263
"Abandoned Mr. S" spot, 28
Abbott Mead Vickers, 429
"Abbreviated" campaign, 493–496
ABC, Inc., **5–8**
ESPN, partnership with, 514
Game Show Network, as competitor of, 593
PowerAde, partnership with, 342
TBS, as competitor of, 1663–1664
Aber Diamond Corp., 444
Abercrombie & Fitch, **9–13**, *10*
French Connection, as competitor of, 580–581
Gap, as competitor of, 596–597, 599, 603
Abramischvili, Guram, 1707
Absolut
"Absolut Director" campaign, 1729–1733, *1730*
"American Apparel" campaign compared to campaign of, 74
Johnnie Walker, as competitor of, 425
Stolichnaya, as competitor of, 1707
"Absolutely, Positively Overnight" campaign, 540
Academy Awards
"The Joy of Pepsi" campaign, 1280, 1282
Lipton Brisk "That's Brisk Baby!" campaign, 1301
Mercedes "Unlike Any Other" campaign, 994, 996
Washington Mutual "Fear Not" campaign, 1801, 1803
The Academy Awards Movie, 140
Accenture, Ltd., **15–18**
Access Codes for dial-around services, 976
Accident/liability insurance. *See* Insurance
Accord, Honda
Galant, as competitor of, 1033
"Grrr" campaign, 745–748
Oldsmobile Alero, as competitor of, 654
Ace K, 1304, 1305
Acesulfame potassium, 1304, 1305
Ackerman McQueen, 879–881, 955
Acquisitions. *See* Mergers and acquisitions
"Action Figure" spot (Ventura for Governor), 1742
"Action Figures" spot (FedEx), 537, 540
"Action Figures" spot (Geico), 615
"Action" spot, 735
Acura, 95
Ad Store
"Godaddy.com Super Bowl Commercial" campaign, 675–678
"JetBlue Launch" campaign, 819–822
Adams, Dick, 960
Adams, Joey Lauren, 1426
Adams gum, 1828–1829
Adamson, Allen, 60, 228
Adamson, James B., 226
Adbusters (magazine), 72
ADDY Awards
A & E "In Case You Missed It" campaign, 3
"Altoids" campaign, 1824
Ameritech "Privacy Manager" campaign, 156
Anheuser-Busch "Real American Heroes/Real Men of Genius" campaign, 126

ADDY Awards, *continued*
AT&T "It's All Within Your Reach" campaign, 153
California Milk Processor Board "Got Milk?" campaign, 260
Cheerios "Stories" campaign, 627, 629
Discover Brokerage "Tow Truck" campaign, 1059
ESPN "This Is SportsCenter" campaign, 517, 519–520
Hollywood Video "Welcome to Hollywood" campaign, 736
H&R Block, "Worried About Bill" campaign, 687, 689
"The Joy of Pepsi" campaign, 1282
Lipton Brisk "That's Brisk Baby!" campaign, 1302
Little Caesar "Grand Canyon" campaign, 903
Little Caesar "Safety Video" campaign, 906
Lubriderm "See You Later, Alligator" campaign, 1321
Maryland State Lottery campaign, 948
Mercedes "Passion" campaign, 990
"Miller High Life Man" campaign, 1021
"NFL Playoffs" campaign, 1101
Pabst "Remember Rainier" campaign, 1245, 1248
Polaroid "I-Zone/Joycam/Sticky Film Teen" campaign, 1359
"Relax, It's FedEx" campaign, 544
"Rolling Rock Ads" campaign, 870
Sims Sports "Be Free" campaign, 1516
Sony "What's Next?" campaign, 1534
"Sprint PCS" campaign, 1554, 1556
Staples "Yeah, We've Got That" campaign, 1569
Tabasco "Mosquito" campaign, 981
Time "The World's Most Interesting Magazine" campaign, 1617
"Visa. It's Everywhere You Want to Be" campaign, 1765, 1768
Wrangler "Rugged Wear" campaign, 1749, 1751
AdForum Creative Hits award, 996
adidas America, Inc., **19–22**
Fila, as competitor of, 553
logo, *24*
New Balance, as competitor of, 1124
Nike, as competitor of, 1140, 1146, 1152–1153
adidas-Salomon AG, **23–29**
Adiemus (song), 413, 414
"Adios, Amigos" spot, 1021
Adkins, Trace, 841
"Adoption" spot, 629
"Ads by Dick" campaign, 115, 125, 128
Advanced Micro Devices Inc., 769–770, 773–774
Advanced Photo System, 479–481, 1164
Advantage Razor, 1191
Advantix campaign, 479–482, 485–488
Advent Rising (video game), 1003
Advertising Age
ACLU "Racial Profiling" campaign, recognition of, 75, 78
Anheuser-Busch "Louie the Lizard" campaign recognition, 119
CVS "Life to the Fullest" campaign recognition, 375
Electronic Data Systems "Cat Herders" campaign recognition, 503
FedEx "Be Absolutely Sure" campaign recognition, 540
Gap campaign recognition, 602
"It's Not T.V. It's HBO" campaign recognition, 740
Little Caesar "Safety Video" campaign recognition, 906
McDonald's "I'm Lovin' It" campaign recognition, 964, 966
Nissan "Enjoy the Ride" campaign recognition, 1173
SBC Communications "Laurel Lane" campaign recognition, 1473, 1475
Advertising agencies. *See* Specific agencies
The Advertising Council, Inc., **31–34**
"Art. Ask for More" campaign, 101–103
ConAgra Foods' Feeding Children Better "Child Hunger" campaign, 363–366
Advertising Standards Authority (United Kingdom), 1038
Advertising Walk of Fame, 35, 37, 39
Advertising Women of New York "Good" Award
MasterCard "Priceless" campaign, 952
"Nordstrom "Reinvent Yourself" campaign, 1187
Advil "Liqui-Gels" campaign, 1839–1842
Adweek
adidas "Yankee Fans" campaign recognition, 29
Allstate "Our Stand" campaign recognition, 53
American Legacy Foundation "Truth" campaign recognition, 100
Apple Computer "Silhouette" campaign recognition, 138
Apple Computer "Switchers" campaign recognition, 139, 140, 141
Burger King "Lunch Break" campaign recognition, 222
CareerBuilder "Time to Move On" campaign recognition, 281
Cheerios "Stories" campaign recognition, 627, 629
Citibank "Identity Theft Solutions" campaign recognition, 325, 328
CVS "Life to the Fullest" campaign recognition, 375
"Echo" spot, 250
FedEx "Be Absolutely Sure" campaign recognition, 540
Game Show Network "You Know You Know" campaign recognition, 593
Gatorade "Origins" campaign recognition, 1286, 1289
Hewlett-Packard "You + HP" campaign recognition, 726
Kinko's "Our Office Is Your Office" campaign recognition, 543
Lipton Sizzle & Stir "Real Cooking" campaign recognition, 1687, 1689
Little Caesar "Safety Video" campaign recognition, 906
MasterCard "Priceless" campaign recognition, 952
"Minnesota Partnership for Action against Tobacco" campaign recognition, 1027, 1030
New Balance "Thunderstorm, Stairs" campaign, 1123
"On the Wings of Goodyear" campaign recognition, 681, 682
PowerAde "Keep Playing" campaign recognition, 341, 343
priceline.com "Troubadour" campaign recognition, 1369, 1372
Reebok "Terry Tate, Office Linebacker" campaign recognition, 1417, 1420
Snapple "Bottles Personified" campaign, 239
Staples "That Was Easy" campaign recognition, 1563, 1566
Aerosmith, 1285
Aetna, 1726–1727
AFC Enterprises, 317, 318
Affleck, Ben, 209
Aflac, Inc., **35–41**

Aflac Cancer Center, 37, 39
"The Aflac Duck" campaign, 35–38
African-American history, 1202
Negro Leagues Baseball Museum "1998 Print" campaign, 1107–1109
African-American market
Chevrolet "An American Revolution" campaign, 632
Ford "Storytelling" campaign, 562
Miles Thirst as stereotype, 349
Oldsmobile Alero "Start Something" campaign, 653–654, 655
Popeyes "Stand Up for Flavor" campaign, 841
Sears campaign, 1489
Sprite "Obey Your Thirst" campaign, 346–347
Texaco "A World of Energy" campaign, 308
Toyota "A Car to Be Proud of Campaign," 1633
Tyson Foods "Powered by Tyson" campaign, 1673, 1674
African-Americans
Hilton campaign, 730
in Tommy Hilfiger ads, 1628
Agadi, Harsha V., 318
Agassi, Andre
annual endorsement income, 552
Canon camera spots, 346
"Do the Dew" campaign, 1271
Nike campaign, 1132
"U.S. Open Excitement" campaign, 1722, 1723, 1724
Agency.com, 998
Agent Orange (film), 61
Ages of Myst (computer game), 380
Agri-Mark, Inc., 255
Aguilera, Christina, 129, 1479
Aguirre, Luis, 93
AICP Show, 1409, 1412
AIDS prevention, 312
Air France, 415
Air Jordan shoes, 1131–1132
Air Max shoe, 1149
Airborne Express, 420
Airline (television show), 44
Airlines
AirTran "Go. There's Nothing Stopping You" campaign, 43–46
Amtrak, as competitors of, 1105
Delta Air Lines "On Top of the World" campaign, 411–414, 415
Delta Air Lines "The Passenger's Airline" campaign, 414–417
"JetBlue Launch" campaign, 819–822
Northwest Airlines "E-Ticket" campaign, 1205–1208
Song Airlines "Let Yourself Fly" campaign, 407–410
Southwest Airlines "Must Be Football Season" campaign, 1535–1538
"Ted Launch" campaign, 1701–1704
United Airlines "It's Time to Fly" campaign, 1695–1698
United Airlines "Rising" campaign, 1698–1701
Virgin Atlantic Airways "Go, Jet Set, Go!" campaign, 1757–1760
Airplane! (film), 805
"Airplane" spot, 503
"Airport" spot, 158–159, 1773, 1775
AirTran Holdings, Inc., **43–46**
Airwair. *See* Dr. Martens Airwair USA LLC
Airwalk, 1152
"Al" spot, 1770
Alaska, 1444
Alba, Jessica, 600
Albers, Tom, 1251
Albert, Michael, 1062
Albertsons grocery stores, 1688
Alcoholic beverages
"Absolut Director" campaign, 1729–1733
"Absolut Print" campaign, 1733–1737
Glenfiddich "Single Malt" campaign, 683–686
Johnnie Walker "Keep Walking" campaign, 423–426
Mike's Hard Lemonade "Hard Day" campaign, 1013
Stolichnaya "Russian Art" campaign, 1705–1708
Alden, Gary, 452
Aldrich, Jay, 1084
Alero
New Beetle, as competitor of, 1785–1786
"Start Something" campaign, 652–656
Alex, as competitor of Crayon, 188
Alexander, Greg, 1043
Alexander, Jason, 319, 385, 767, 770
ALF. *See* American Legacy Foundation
"Alguien digo McDonald's?" campaign, 962
Ali, Laila, 23, *25*, 26
Ali, Muhammad
adidas campaign, 23–25, *25*
Apple Computer "Think Different" campaign, 142
IBM "Linux" campaign, 795, 796–797
All-American Soccer Stars Victory Tour, 1274
"All Grown Up. Sort Of." campaign, 158–159, 1773–1776
All Japan CM Festival awards, 1134
All Sport, 1288
All-Star Benefit Concert, 1274
Allan, Beth, 1049
Allard, J., *1002*
Allard, Wayne, 657
Allegra
Freedom Forecast, 1462
"Spirit of Freedom" campaign, 1461–1464
Zyrtec, as competitor of, 1313
Allen, Gracie, 832
Allen, Marcus, 1549
Allen, Paul, 1241
Allen, Rick, 452
Allen, Steve, 1358
Allen, Tim, 650
Allergen counts, 1462
Alley, Kirstie, 815–818, *816*
Allied Domecq PLC, **47–50**
Allison, Donnie, 1094
The Allstate Corporation, **51–54**, 617, 620
Ally & Gargano
Dunkin' Donuts "Fred the baker" campaign, 48
FedEx "Fast-Paced World" spot, 538
Alpert, Herb, 608
Alpha-Bits, 628–629
Alpha Kappa Alpha Sorority, 1674
Alter, Stewart, 611
Alternate reality games, 157–160
Alternative music
Dr. Martens Airwair "Beliefs" campaign, 459, 460, 461
Fusion Flash Concerts, 560
Altmann, Olivier, 1609
"Altoids" campaign, 1821–1824, 1825
"Altoids Gone Sour" campaign, 1824–1827
Altria Group Inc., **55–58**, 249
See also Philip Morris Companies Inc.
"Always Coca-Cola" campaign, 351
"Always Out There" campaign, 431–434
Amacher, Jacquie, 1070
"Amazing Sprint Sense Dime Find" contest, 1546
"Amazon Theater" campaign, 59–62

Amazon.com, Inc., **59–62**
Borders, as competitor of, 197
eBay, as competitor of, 497
Ambrosio, Chris, 1069
Ambush (film), 177–178
AMC. *See* American Movie Classics
AMD. *See* Advanced Micro Devices Inc.
Amelie (film), 1652
America Online, Inc., **63–69**
American Greetings, partnership with, 693
Lycos, as competitor of, 917
TelSave, partnership with, 151
Yahoo!, as competitor of, 1852
American Advertising Awards. *See* ADDY Awards
American Advertising Federation
adidas "Yankee Fans" campaign, 29
"Campaign for Freedom" campaign, 32
American Advertising Foundation Center on Multiculturalism, Corporate Mosaic Award, 1282
American Airlines
AAdvantage program, 7
Delta Air Lines, as competitor of, 413, 415–416
national monuments in advertising, 1604
Northwest Airlines, as competitor of, 1206–1207
Southwest Airlines, as competitor of, 1537
United Airlines, as competitor of, 1696–1697
American Apparel Inc., **71–74**, 581
American Association of Advertising Agencies, 32
American Cancer Society, 97, 664
American Chicle Group, 233–234
American Civil Liberties Union, **75–78**
American Eagle Outfitters, 11, 598, 599
American Express Company, **79–90**
Amazon.com partnership with, 62
"Charge against Hunger" campaign, 364–365
Citibank, as competitor of, 327
Discover, as competitor of, 1051–1052, 1054–1055
MasterCard, as competitor of, 951
"Seinfeld" campaign, 1056
Visa, as competitor of, 1766
American Greetings Corporation, 693
American Home Products, 1839–1842
American Honda Motor Company, **91–95**, *92, 93*
American Idol (television show), 48
American Legacy Foundation, **97–100**, 249–250, 1029
American Medical Women's Association, 1329, 1331, 1332
American Movie Classics, 1659, 1660–1661
American Movie (film), 1642
"An American Revolution" campaign, 631–634
"American Tartans" campaign, 1627–1630
American Telemarketing Association, 156
American Tobacco Company, 55
Americans for the Arts, **101–104**
"America's Adventure Place" campaign, 873
"America's Best Classroom" program, 1688
America's Second Harvest, 364, 365
Ameritech. *See* AT&T Inc.
Ameritrade, 529
Ammirati Puris Lintas
Ameritech "Privacy Manager" campaign, 153–156
Burger King "When You Have It Your Way, It Just Tastes Better" campaign, 225–228
Compaq "Has It Changed Your Life Yet?" campaign, 134
"Rolling Rock Ads" campaign, 867–870
UPS "Moving at the Speed of Business" campaign, 1709–1712
Amos, James, 920
Amos, John, Paul, and Bill, 35, 38
Amtrak "Life on Acela" campaign, 1103–1106, *1104*
AMWA. *See* American Medical Women's Association
Amway, 1685
ANA. *See* Association of National Advertisers
ANA/AICP Battle of the Brands, 1248
Andersen Consulting. *See* Accenture, Ltd.
Anderson, Fred, 142
Anderson, Lonnie, 1689
Anderson, Richard Dean, 952
Anderson, Scott, 213
Anderson, Wes, 757
Andrew, Kyle, 596
Andrews, Jim, 554
Andrews, William, 1111
Androgyny, 262
ANDY Awards
"Altoids Gone Sour" campaign, 1827
Anheuser-Busch "Real American Heroes/Real Men of Genius" campaign, 126
AT&T "It's All Within Your Reach" campaign, 153
ESPN NFL 2K5 "Beta-7" campaign, 1499
E*TRADE "Monkey Trilogy" campaign, 525, 528
Honda "Grrr" campaign, 745
Kinko's "Our Office Is Your Office" campaign, 543
Little Caesar "Grand Canyon" campaign, 903
Little Caesar "Safety Video" campaign, 906
Marriott International "Never Underestimate the Importance of a Good Night's Rest" campaign, 930
MTV "Watch and Learn" campaign, 1079
Museum of Contemporary Art "Labels" campaign, 1081, 1084
Rock the Vote "Yes/No Ballot Box" campaign, 1427
Seattle SuperSonics "In Your Home" campaign, 168
Sony "What's Next?" campaign, 1534
Washington Mutual "Fear Not" campaign, 1801, 1803
Andy Head Award, 544
Anelka, Nicolas, 25
Angelo, David, 1298
Angona, Bob, 908
Angotti, Thomas, Hedge, 569–573
Angry Leprechaun web site, 441
"Angst Band" spot, 205
Anheuser, Eberhard, 105, 109
Anheuser-Busch Companies, Inc., **105–130**, *124, 127*
Miller Brewing Company, as competitor of, 1019–1020
SABMiller, as competitor of, 1449–1451, 1454
Samuel Adams labeling practices, 201
Animal mascots
Aflac duck, 35–40
Bud Ice penguins, 120–122
Budweiser frogs, 108–112
Budweiser Louie the Lizard, 116–120
Cadillac Catera duck, 639
Dinky (Taco Bell dog), 1594–1597
GEICO "Gecko" campaign, 613–616
Serta sheep, 1501–1503

Animal Planet, 451
Animal testing, 191, 192
Animatronics
  Anheuser-Busch "Frogs" campaign, 108–112
  Anheuser-Busch "Louie the Lizard" campaign, 116–120
Annie Awards, 1695, 1697
Ansell Consumer Products, 312, 313
"ANSKY guys," 28–29
Antacids, 1322–1325
"Anthem" spot (Campbell's soup), 271
"Anthem" spot (Dr. Pepper), 466
"Anthem" spot (Fila), 553
"Anthem" spot (Häagen-Dazs), 1119, 1121
"Anthem" spot (Hewlett-Packard), 724
"Anthem" spot (T-Mobile), 1625
"Anthem" spot (United States Tennis Association), 1723
Anti-brands, 72–73
Anti-impotency drugs, 1325–1328
Anti-Money Laundering Act, 322
Antidepressants
  Paxil "Social Anxiety Disorder" campaign, 665–668
  Prozac print campaign, 505–508
Antiestablishment campaigns, 1086
Antiperspirants. *See* Deodorants and antiperspirants
Antismoking campaigns
  California Department of Health, Tobacco Control Section campaigns, 243–247, *244, 245,* 248–251
  "Minnesota Partnership for Action against Tobacco" campaign, 1027–1030
  "Truth" campaign, 97–100
Antitrust trial of Microsoft, 1005
Antonini, Joseph, 851
"Anything Else Would Be Uncivilized" campaign, 669–673
"AOL Latino" campaign, 63–66
AOL Time Warner, 1241, 1242, 1244
  See also America Online, Inc.
"Apartment 10G" spot, 1296, 1303
"Apartment" spot, 611
"APB" spot, 652
Apicella, David, 88
"Apology" spot, 537, 539
Apple Computer, Inc., **131–145**, *132, 133*
  Hewlett-Packard, as competitor of, 722
  Hewlett-Packard, partnership with, 726
  Intel, as competitor of, 770, 774
  iPod, *136*
  Microsoft, as competitor of, 1006
Apple stores, 139
Applegate, Christina, 1747
The Apprentice (television show), 221, 1041
APS. *See* Advanced Photo System
Aquafina "Drink More Water" campaign, 1274–1277
Aquos televisions, 1505, 1506, 1507
Arch Deluxe, 957, 961
Archer Daniels Midland Company, 287, 1036
"The Architect" spot, 1362
"Arctic Ground Squirrel" spot, 431, 433
Are You Experienced? (song), 1852
Ariel, 1378
Arison, Micky, 294
Arison, Ted, 293, 294
Arliss (television show), 951
Arm & Hammer laundry detergent, 1396
  See also Church & Dwight Company, Inc.
Armageddon (film), 633, 1590
Armstrong, C. Michael, 977
Armstrong, Lance
  adidas "Impossible Is Nothing" campaign, 24
  Coca-Cola "Real" campaign, 352
  Nike campaign, 1145
Armstrong, Louis, 103
Armstrong, Neil, 3
"Army of One" campaign, 1263
Arnell, Peter, 1230, 1418
Arnell Group
  Fila "Grant Hill 4" campaign, 553
  Reebok "Terry Tate, Office Linebacker" campaign, 1417
Arnold, Tim, 677
Arnold Communications
  JetBlue campaign, 408–409, 820, 821
  McDonald's "Donna Summer" spot, 963
  Volkswagen "New Beetle" campaign, 1783–1786
Arnold Worldwide
  American Legacy Foundation "Truth" campaign, 97–100
  Antismoking campaign, 249–250
  FootJoy "Sign Boy" campaign, 565–568
  "On the Wings of Goodyear" campaign, 679
  Royal Caribbean "Get Out There" campaign, 1441–1444
  Tyson Foods "Powered by Tyson" campaign, 1671–1674
  Volkswagen "Drivers Wanted" campaign, 1776–1779
  Volkswagen Jetta "All Grown Up. Sort Of." campaign, 1773–1776
  Volkswagen New Beetle "Drivers Wanted" campaign, 170–171
  Volkswagen Passat "Live Large" campaign, 1780–1783
Arquette, David
  AT&T "It's All Within Your Reach" campaign, 153
  Coca-Cola "Real" campaign, *350,* 352
  Gap campaign, 602, 607
Arquette, Rosanna, 496, 498
"The Arquettes" spot, 352
"Arrest" spot, 33
Arrow Trading Company, 1588
Art
  "Absolut Print" campaign, 1730, 1733–1737
  "Art. Ask for More" campaign, 101–104
  Museum of Contemporary Art "Labels" campaign, 1081–1084
  Stolichnaya "Russian Art" campaign, 1705–1708
"Art. Ask for More" campaign, 101–104
Art Directors Club Awards
  "Miller High Life" campaign, 1455
  Napster "It's Coming Back" campaign, 1088
  Negro Leagues Baseball Museum "1998 Print Campaign," 1109
"The Art of the Heist" campaign, 157–160, 1775
Arthritis Foundation, 1438, 1439, 1440
Arthur Andersen, 15–16
Arts-and-crafts toys, 189
Arts and Entertainment Television Networks. *See* A & E Television Networks
Ashby, Deanna, 873
Ashe, Arthur, 1137
Asher & Partners, 243–247
Asher/Gould, 248–251
Asherton-Pickett, M.D., 928
Asian-Americans
  in Tommy Hilfiger ads, 1628
  Toyota "Kids Rule" campaign, 1644
"AsiaOne" campaign, 549
ASIMO (robot), 741, 743
"Ask-a-Tech" sessions, 609, 611
"Ask Iris" web site, 1387
Aspartame, 241, 1304

Association of National Advertisers, 32
Association of Volleyball Professionals, 1275
Astaire, Fred, 1437–1439, *1438*
Astaire, Robyn, 1438, 1439, 1440
Astin, Sean, 1235, 1236
Aston, Lottie, 1143
"At Your Side" campaign, 1047–1050
ATHENA Awards
  Americans for the Arts "Art. Ask for More" campaign, 101, 103
  Borders "This Season, It's the Original Thought That Counts" campaign, 195, 197
  "US Open Excitement" campaign, 1721, 1724
Athletes
  Breathe Right Strips, 338
  Charles Schwab "Smarter Investors" campaign, 303–304
  Fila "Grant Hill 4" campaign, 551–554
  Gillette "Anything Else Would Be Uncivilized" campaign, 672
  Nike campaigns, 1132, 1139, 1145
  Nike "Move" campaign, 1142, 1144
  Nike "Product Assault" campaign, 1149
  PowerAde "Keep Playing" campaign, 343
  Rolex "Celebrity Endorsement" campaign, 1043, 1046
  shoe company endorsements, 751
  Sports-fantasy promotions, 47, 48, 49
  Yard Fitness Center, 1860
  See also Specific athletes
Athletic apparel
  Nike "Move" campaign, 1141–1144
  Nike "Play" campaign, 1144–1147
  Nike "What If We Treated All Athletes the Way We Treat Skateboarders?" campaign, 1150–1154
  Nike "Women's" campaign, 1154–1157
Athletic footwear
  adidas America, Inc., 19–22
  adidas-Salomon AG, 23–26
  Fila USA "Grant Hill 4" campaign, 551–554
  FootJoy "Sign Boy" campaign, 565–568
  New Balance "Thunderstorm, Stairs" campaigns, 1123–1125
  Nike "Hello World" and "I Am Tiger Woods" campaigns, 1134–1138
  Nike "Meet the LeBrons" campaign, 1138–1141
  Nike "Move" campaign, 1141–1144
  Nike "9,000 Shots" campaign, 1131–1134
  Nike "Play" campaign, 1144–1147
  Nike "Product Assault" campaign, 1147–1150
  Nike "What If We Treated All Athletes the Way We Treat Skateboarders?" campaign, 1150–1154
  Nike "Women's" campaign, 1154–1157
  Reebok "Terry Tate, Office Linebacker" campaign, 1417–1420
Atkins Diet
  Advantage bars, 933
  Diamond Foods "Emerald Nuts marketing campaign," 440
  Diet Rite and, 240, 242
  Tyson Foods "Powered by Tyson" campaign, 1672–1673
Atlas, Jacoba, 1410
AT&T Inc., **147–156**, 1625
  MCI, as competitor of, 972–973, 976–977
  SBC Communications, as competitor of, 1474–1475
  Sprint, as competitor of, 1544–1545, 1548
  Sprint PCS, as competitor of, 1555
  Working Assets Long Distance, as competitor of, 1836–1837
"The Attic" spot, 84
Aubrey, Stever, 231
Auctions, online
  eBay 2004 television campaign, 496–499
  eBay "Abbreviated" campaign, 493–496
Audi of America, Inc., **157–160**
  Honda, as competitor of, 747
  Mercedes-Benz, as competitor of, 995
  Volkswagen, as competitor of, 1774–1775
Augustsson, Peter, 1446
"Aunt Rosalina" spot, 355, 356
Aurius, 445
Austin, Debi, 246
Austin Powers (film), 707, 1335
Ausubel, Lawrence, 88
Auto racing, 1093–1096
"AUTOgraphs for Education" program, 1459
Automobiles
  American Honda Motor Company "What About Now?" campaign, 91–95
  Audi "Art of the Heist" campaign, 157–160
  BMW "The Hire" campaign, 175–179
  "The Caddy That Zigs" campaign, 638–641
  Cadillac "Break Through" campaign, 634–637
  Chevrolet "An American Revolution" campaign, 631–634
  Chrysler "Engineered to be Great Cars" campaign, 386–389
  Chrysler Group "Employee Pricing Plan Plus" campaign, 383–386
  Ford "Driving American Innovation" campaign, 555–558
  Ford "Life In Drive" campaign, 558–561
  Ford "Storytelling" campaign, 561–564
  General Motors "EV1 Introduction" campaign, 641–645
  General Motors "Hummer" campaign, 645–648
  Honda "Grrr" campaign, 745–748
  Honda "The Power of Dreams" campaign, 741–744
  Infiniti "Own One and You'll Understand" campaign, 1177–1180
  Isuzu "The Call" campaign, 803–806
  "Jeep" campaign, 389–392
  Jeep "There's Only One" campaign, 392–394
  Lexus "The Road Is Calling" campaign, 1646–1649
  "Mercedes-Benz Corporate Branding" campaign, 983–987
  Mercedes M-Class "Smooth Ride" campaign, 990–994
  Mercedes "Passion" campaign, 987–990
  Mercedes "Smooth Ride" campaign, 990–994
  Mercedes "Unlike Any Other" campaign, 994–996
  MINI Cooper "Counterfeit" campaign, 169–172
  MINI Cooper "MINI Robots" campaign, 172–175
  Mitsubishi "Wake Up and Drive" campaign, 1031–1034
  Nissan "Do You Speak Micra?" campaign, 1167–1170
  Nissan "Enjoy the Ride" campaign, 1171–1174

Nissan "Quest Minivan Launch" campaign, 1174–1177
Oldsmobile Alero "Start Something" campaign, 652–656
Porsche "Cayenne Launch" campaign, 1365–1368
Saab "Life Is Not a Spectator Sport" campaign, 1445–1447
"Saturn Relaunch" campaign, 1465–1467
Saturn "Why Didn't Anyone Think of This Before?" campaign, 1468–1472
Sierra Club "Hybrid Evolution" campaign, 1509–1512
Stanley Steamer, 1560
Suburban Auto Group "Trunk Monkey" campaign, 1579–1582
Toyota Celica "Get the Feeling" campaign, 1641–1643
Toyota Corolla "A Car to Be Proud Of" campaign, 1631–1634
Toyota "Everyday" campaign, 1634–1637
Toyota "Fuel for Thought" campaign, 1638–1640
Toyota Sienna "Kids Rule" campaign, 1643–1646
Volkswagen "Drivers Wanted" campaign, 1776–1779
Volkswagen Jetta "All Grown Up. Sort Of." campaign, 1773–1776
Volkswagen "New Beetle" campaign, 1783–1786
Volkswagen Passat "Live Large" campaign, 1780–1783
Automotive service centers
General Motors "Looking for Mr. Goodwrench" campaign, 648–652
"Trust the Midas Touch" campaign, 1009–1012
Autry, Gene, 986
Aveda
The Body Shop, as competitor of, 192
Herbal Essences, as competitor of, 334
Avedon, Richard, 261
Avery Dennison, 1458
Avia, Pierre, 1748
AXA Financial, 764–765
Axtman, Melanie, 1083

B

Babb, Stuart, 1125
"The Babe" spot, 1300, 1301
"Baby Bob" campaign, 1413–1415
Baby boomers
Burger King "Lunch Break" campaign, 220
Cadillac "Break Through" campaign, 635–636, 636–637
Carnival Corporation "Fun Ships" campaign, 294
Chrysler "Engineered to Be Great Cars" campaign, 387
Crate & Barrel 1998 print ads campaign, 533–536
Dirt Devil "Fred Astaire" campaign, 1439
Ford Explorer campaign, 993
Gap "For Every Generation" campaign, 596
Gap "Khakis" campaign, 602
Gap stores, redesigned, 599
Infiniti "Own One and You'll Understand" campaign, 1179
Intel "Bunny People" campaign, 769
Lincoln National "Hello Future" campaign, 894
MasterCard "Priceless" campaign, 950
Mercedes "Corporate Branding" campaign, 984, 985, 986
Mercedes M-Class "Smooth Ride" campaign, 993
"Miller High Life" campaign, 1453
Nature Made "Trusted By the Ones You Trust" campaign, 1330
priceline.com "Troubadour" campaign, 1370
Round Table Pizza "The Last Honest Pizza" campaign, 1430
Royal Caribbean "Get Out There" campaign, 1441, 1442
1960s and 1970s songs in advertisements, 637
Toyota "Everyday" campaign, 1634–1635
Volkswagen "New Beetle" campaign, 1785
Volkswagen New Beetle "Drivers Wanted" campaign, 170
"Baby Smokers" spot, 247
"Baby" spot, 996
"Baby-sitter" spot, 719, 720
"Babysitters" spot, 45
Bacardi Silver, 1015
Bach, Robbie, 1001, 1002
Bachman-Turner Overdrive, 1214
"Back in the Sack" campaign, 337–340
Back-to-school campaigns
Kmart "Joe Boxer Launch" campaign, 847
Staples "That Was Easy" campaign, 1565–1566
Staples "Yeah, We've Got That" campaign, 1567–1569
"Backstage" spot, 1301
Bacon, Kevin
E*TRADE "Why Wouldn't You?" campaign, 531
Visa Check Card "Works Like a Check" campaign, 1771
Bad Boys (film), 633
"Badge" spot, 388
"Badminton" spot, 1096
Baegte, Jim, 1354
"Bag Boy Fantasy" spot, 890, 891
Bagley, Stan, 1105
Bagni, Gregg, 1252
Bagotronics (fictitious company), 792–794
Baird, Lisa, 785
Baker, Brian, 1553
Baker, Matt, 1071
Baker, Vin, 166
Balance Bar, 932
Balch, John, 1435
Baldwin, Alec, 103
Ballmer, Steve, 1089, 1091
"Balloon" spot, 787
"Balls" spot, 1526, 1528–1529
Bally Total Fitness, 1860
Balzer, Harry, 698
Ban antiperspirant, 1402
Banaag, Ricky, 771
Banana Republic, 596
Bank of America
Citigroup, as competitor of, 331
Wachovia, as competitor of, 1794
Washington Mutual, as competitor of, 1802
Bank One Corp., 1791
Banking
Citigroup "Live Richly" campaign, 329–332
First Union "Financial World" campaign, 1789–1792
Wachovia "Uncommon Wisdom" campaign, 1792–1795
Washington Mutual "Fear Not" campaign, 1801–1804
Bankruptcy
Kmart Corp., 847, 848, 850, 854
Malden Mills Industries, Inc., 923, 924
Schwinn/GT Cicycles, 1251
United Airlines, 1695
Banks, Ernie, 1107
Banks, Tyra, 1045, 1277
"Bar" ad, 1607, 1608, 1609
"Barbecue" spot, 761
Barclays Global Investors, 161–164
Barcome, Don, 1215

Barenaked Ladies, 1034, 1128, 1129
Barker, John, 1810, 1812
Barkley, Charles
Gillette "Anything Else Would Be Uncivilized" campaign, 672
Nike campaign, 1132, 1152
Nike promotional show, 1143
Barnard, Kurt, 851, 1229, 1566
Barnes, Derek, 1580, 1581
Barnes, Peter, 1835–1836, 1838
Barnes and Noble
Amazon.com, as competitor of, 60–61
Borders, as competitor of, 196–197
Barnett, Alan, 999
Barrabee, Linda, 300
Barracuda Networks, Inc., 323
Barrett, Craig, 1091
Barrett, Dean, 967
Barrett, Jamie, 1132, 1467
Bartle Bogle Hegarty
ConAgra Foods' Feeding Children Better "Child Hunger" campaign, 363–366
Johnnie Walker "Keep Walking" campaign, 423–426
"Levi's Type 1 Jeans" campaign, 886–889
Lipton Sizzle & Stir "Real Cooking" campaign, 1687–1690
"Monsanto Image" campaign, 1035, 1037
"Rolling Rock Ads" campaign, 869
Baryshnikov, Mikhail, 83
Baseball (documentary), 1109
Basich, Tina, 1515
Basinger, Kim, 602
Basketball
Detroit Pistons "Goin' to Work. Every Night." campaign, 1257–1260
Seattle SuperSonics "In Your Home" campaign, 165–168
Basketball Club of Seattle, LLC, **165–168**
Baskin-Robbins, 48
Bass fishing, 1751
BASS PLC. *See* Intercontinental Hotels Group PLC
Basserman, Michael, 986, 990
Bassett, Steve, 615
Bates, Jack, 1560
Bates Worldwide, 314
Bath & Body Works, 192
Batteries, 509–512
Baum, Herb, 436
Bay, Michael, 88, 633
Bayer AG, 1327
Bayerische Motoren Werke AG, **169–179**, *176*
Bayless Cronin, 317–319
Bays, Joe, 1295
Bazooka gum, 1829
BBDO
AOL "Welcome to the World Wide Wow" campaign, 66–69
Aquafina "Drink More Water" campaign, 1274–1277
Campbell Soup Company "Make It Campbell's Instead" campaign, 268–271
Charles Schwab "Smarter Investor" campaign, 301–304
Chrysler Group "Employee Pricing Plan Plus" campaign, 383–386
Delta Air Lines campaigns, 414–415
eBay account, 495
Fédération des producteurs de lait du Québec milk campaign, 183
FedEx "Be Absolutely Sure" campaign, 539–540
FedEx "The Way the World Works" campaign, 547–550
Frito-Lay "The Loudest Taste on Earth" campaign, 583–586
General Electric "Imagination At Work" campaign, 623–626
Icehouse Beer campaign, 121
"It's Not T.V. It's HBO" campaign, 737–740
"JetBlue Launch" campaign, 819–822
"The Joy of Pepsi" campaign, 1280–1283
Juicy Fruit "Gotta Have Twisted Sweet" campaign, 1828–1830
Kinko's "Our Office Is Your Office" campaign, 541–543
Mountain Dew campaign, 465
Mountain Dew "Code Red" campaign, 1267–1270
Office Depot "What You Need. What You Need to Know." campaign, 1213–1216
Orbit gum "No Matter What" campaign, 1831–1833
Peace Corps "Life Is Calling. How Far Will You Go?" campaign, 1261–1265
"Pepsi, It's the Cola" campaign, 1289–1292
Pepsi Edge campaign, 241
Pepsi "Generation Next" campaign, 1277–1280
Pepsi "Security Camera" campaign, 1295–1298
Pepsi Vanilla "The Not-So-Vanilla Vanilla" campaign, 1283–1286
Pizza Hut "Big New Yorker Pizza" campaign., 1345–1348
"Relax, It's FedEx" campaign, 544–547
"Snickers Cruncher" campaign, 941–943, 942–943
Snickers Marathon bars "The Energy You Crave" campaign, 931–934
Texaco "A World of Energy" campaign, 305–309
"Visa. It's Everywhere You Want to Be" campaign, 1765–1768
Visa Check Card "Works Like a Check" campaign, 1769–1772
BC Dairy Foundation, **181–185**
"Be a DiGiorno Delivery Guy" promotion, 865
"Be Bullish" campaign, 526–527
"Be Direct" campaign, 143
"Be Like Mike" campaign, 343, 1287
"Be More" campaign, 1409–1412
"Be Your Own Rock" campaign, 1405–1408
"Be yourself again" tagline, 1211
"Beach" ad, 1607, 1608, 1609
"Beach Chairs & Umbrellas" spot, 295
"Beaches" spot, 152, 153, 1762
"Beadicons," 1813, 1814, 1815
Beam, 174
"Bears" spot, 1277
Beatles, 174, 1139
Beattie, Richard, 1635
Beattie, Trevor, 580, 1525
Beauty
Body Shop "Ruby" campaign, 191–194
Dove "Campaign for Real Beauty" campaign, 1679–1683
"Beaver España" campaign, 1607, 1608
Beavers, Joe, 1749
Bebear, Claude, 764
Bécaud, Gilbert, 183
"Because Life Is Not a Spectator Sport" campaign, 25
Becker, Boris, 1589
Beckett, Alec, 924
Beckham, David, 23
Beckstead, June, 605
Bed Bath and Beyond, 756
"Bed-in for Peace," 729
Bedding
Dial-A-Mattress "Always Out There" campaign, 431–434
Serta "Counting Sheep" campaign, 1501–1503
Beebe, Dion, 1412

"Beer . . . or Michelob?" campaign, 105–108
Beer commercials
Anheuser-Busch "Beer . . . or Michelob?" campaign, 105–108
Anheuser-Busch "Louie the Lizard" campaign, 116–120
Bud Ice "Oh, and Beware of the Penguins" campaign, 120–123
Bud Light "I Love You, Man" campaign, 112–116
Bud Light "Real American Heroes/ Real Men of Genius" campaign, 123–126
Budweiser "Whassup?!" campaign, 126–130, *127*
Foster's "How to Speak Australian" campaign, 569–573
"Frogs" campaign, 108–112
Guinness "Not Everything in Black and White Makes Sense" campaign, 426–429
Heineken "It's All About the Beer" campaign, 705–708
"Miller High Life" campaign, 1452–1455
"Miller High Life Man" campaign, 1017–1021
Miller Lite "Low Carb" campaign, 1449–1452
Miller Lite "Miller Time" campaign, 1021–1025
Pabst "Remember Rainier" campaign, 1245–1248
"Rheingold Beer" campaign, 1421–1424
"Rolling Rock Ads" campaign, 867–870
Rolling Rock "Grab a Rock" campaign, 759–762
Samuel Adams, 199–202
"Beer Man" campaign, 129
Beetle, Volkswagen, 1776–1777, 1783–1784
Being John Malkovich (film), 757, 758
Belatti, Frank, 318, 319
Belding Awards
ESPN "The Rick" campaign, 516
Jack in the Box "Jack's Back" campaign, 814
Weather Channel "Painted Faces" campaign, 1807
Bell, Cathy, 963
Bell, Charlie, 965
Bell, Glen, 1591–1592
Bell, James, 370
Bell, James "Cool Papa," 1107
Bell, Nicola, 484
Bell Atlantic, 155
Bella (chimpanzee), 1581
Bellas, Michael, 114, 1272
Belsh, Kim, 243, 244, 247
Belvedere
Absolut, as competitor of, 1731, 1732
Stolichnaya, as competitor of, 1706–1707
Ben & Jerry's Ice Cream
Brigham's, as competitor of, 208
Häagen-Dazs, as competitor of, 1119, 1120–1121
Working Assets Long Distance, partnership with, 1837
Yahoo!, partnership with, 1853
Ben Folds Five, 1370
Ben-Hur (film), 1661
"Ben-Hur" spot, 1661, 1662
"Benefits" spot, 1722
Beninati, Marie Drum, 890
Benjamin, Jeff, 224
Benjamin, Keith, 1706
Bennett, Chuck, 1595, 1596
Bennett, Kuhn & Varner, 1433–1436
Bennett, Lisa, 415, 416
Bennett, Tony, 1770
Benz, Carl, 987
Berdusco, Roger, 586
Berg, Peter, 607
Berg, Scott, 725, 726
Bergen, Candice
"Dime Lady" campaign, 1547
"Dime Zone" campaign, 1545
"Speak Freely on Monday Nights" campaign, 1549
Sprint campaign, 152, 973, 1837
"Sprint Sense" campaign, 1543
Berger, Charles, 1484, 1485
Berger, Dennis, 228
Berger, Matthew, 228
Berkeley, Joe, 229, 231
Berkenfield, Andy, 891
Berkov, Stephen, 157, 158, 160
Berle, Milton, 306
Berlin, Andy, 368
Berlin Cameron & Partners, 1114–1117
Berlin Cameron/Red Cell
C2 campaign, 241
Coca-Cola "Real" campaign, 352
Berman, Chris, 517, 520
Bernard, Harry, 891
Bernbach, Bill, 1780, 1781
Bernstein, Edward, 1742
Berra, Yogi, 37, 39, 1771
Berry, Halle, 446, 938
Bershefsky, Ralph, 1759
Bertelsmann AG, 196
Bertini, Bob, 356
Bertino, Fred, 826
Besson, Luc, 1446
Best Buy, 1494
"The Best Part of Photography Is the Prints" campaign, *482*, 482–485
"The Best Part of Wakin' Up Is Folgers In Your Cup" campaign, 1373–1376
"The Best Stuff Is Here" tagline, 1658
"Beta-7" campaign, 1497–1500
"Better Beef" spot, 287
Better Business Bureau, 80, 82
"Better Place" spot, 1234
Betty Crocker, 1688
Bevan, Michael, 1637
Beverages
Aquafina "Drink More Water" campaign, 1274–1277
DoubleShot "Bring on the Day" campaign, 1197–1200
"Return of the Snapple Lady" campaign, 1655–1658
Snapple "Bottles Personified" campaign, 237–240
See also Alcoholic beverages; Milk; Soft drinks
Bewkes, Jeffrey, 738
Bezos, Jeff, 59, 60, 61, 1591
BHP Billiton, 444–445
Bibendum, 681
BIC, 1458, 1479
Bickler, David, 125
"Bicycle" spot, 426
Bicycles
Schwinn/GT "Fast. It's Corporate Policy." campaign, 1249–1252
Schwinn "What a Ride" campaign, 1252–1256
"Specialized" campaign, 1539–1542
Bierbaum, Tom, 864
"Big Blue Arm" campaign, 1726
Big-box stores, 1494
"Big Daddy" spot, 993
"Big Dig" flavor, 207, 208
"Big Drop" spot, 1321
"Big Match" spot, 1446, 1447
"Big New Yorker Pizza" campaign, 1345–1348
"Big News" spot, 613
"Big Pieces, Little Pieces" campaign, 318
"Big Show" spot, 987, 993
"Big Wrestlers" spot, 356
Bigley, Deirdre, 797
Bijur, Arthur, 734, 735
Bijur, Peter I., 307
Bildsten, Bruce, 176, 178, 1161, 1702

"Bill of Rights" campaign, 1432
Billboards
  "Altoids" campaign, 1823
  Aquafina "Drink More Water" campaign, 1276
  Dove "Campaign for Real Beauty" campaign, 1681–1682
  General Motors "EV1 Introduction" campaign, 643, 644
  Kellogg "Special K Kick-Start Diet Plan" campaign, 834
  Museum of Contemporary Art "Labels" campaign, 1081–1084
  Nike "Product Assault" campaign, 1148
  "Special K Kick-Start Diet Plan" campaign, 836
  United Airlines "It's Time to Fly" campaign, 1697
  Wrangler "Rugged Wear" campaign, 1751
  Yahoo! "Live Billboard Dating" campaign, 1854–1857
"Billiards" spot, 577
Bilxseth, Sean, 1580
Bindbeutel, Henry, 1426
Bingman, Pam, 1062
Binney, Alice, 189
Binney & Smith, **187–190**
Bioré, 1691–1692
Bird, Larry, 1552
"Birds" spot, 735, 1411
Bitterman, Larry, 1573
Black, Bryan, 1040
Black, Jack, 60
Black, Lee, 1088
Black & Decker, 1436
Black Entertainment Television, 347
Black Eyed Peas, 137
Black Label Johnnie Walker, 425
Black Rocket
  Discover Brokerage "Tow Truck" campaign, 1056–1059
  "Do You Yahoo!?" campaign, 1853
  Yahoo! "Live Billboard Dating" campaign, 1855–1857
Blackspot Anticorporation, 72
Blackwell, Mark, 1352
Blades, Joan, *1074*
Blair Witch Project (film), 1507
Blanks, Billy, 457
Blaskey, Rick, 460
Blass, Bill, 984
Bledsoe, Drew, 519
Blige, Mary J.
  National Football League Kickoff festival, 1285
  "National Youth Anti-Drug Media" campaign, 1217
Blimpie International
  Quiznos, as competitor of, 1415
  Subway, as competitor of, 456–457
"Blind Date" spot, 770
"Blizzard" spot, 355–356
Bloch, Henry and Richard, 687
"Block Air" spot, 689
Blockbuster, 734–735
Blogs, 211–214
Bloom Agency, 1343
Bloomberg, Michael, 1424
Blue Card, 86, 89
Blue Cross and Blue Shield, 1726
Blue Man Group, 1041
"Blue Skies" campaign, 1313
Blue (song), 397
Bluestein, Bill, 798
Bluetooth wireless technology, 1066
Blum, Brad, 221
Blur, 460
BMW
  Lexus, as competitor of, 1647–1648
  Mercedes-Benz, as competitor of, 985–986, 988–989, 995
BMX bikes, 1249–1252
Boardman, Robyn, 178
Boards Magazine, 45
"Boat" spot, 1020, 1455
"Bob" campaign, 1837
Bobby Award, 1282
Bock, Gayle, 413
Bodett, Tom, 778, 782
Body Geometry bicycle saddle, 1540, 1541
The Body Shop International PLC, **191–194**, 334
Body size, 1682
Boeing, William, 1698
Bogusky, Alex
  American Legacy Foundation "Truth" campaign, 98
  Burger King "Subservient Chicken" campaign, 223, 225
  IKEA "Unböring" campaign, 756
  MINI Cooper "Counterfeit" campaign, 171, 172
  Virgin Atlantic Airways "Go, Jet Set, Go!" campaign, 1758
"Boiling Turkey" spot, 53
Boise Cascade, 1565
Bologna, Anne, 326, 330
Bombardier, 1355
Bonaparte, Andy, 225, 228, 959
Bond, Richard L., 1672
Bonds, Barry, 304, 1852
Bonham, Bill, 1431
Bonham, John, 636
Bono, 135
The Book of Days Engagement Calendar, 56
The Book of Dreams, 743
"The Book of Harley-Davidson" campaign, 701–704
"Book with Travelocity. Don't Forget Your Hat" tagline, 1653
Booksellers, 195–198
Boomerang, 1612
Boone, John, 1750
Booth, Beatrice, 1708
Borchardt, Mark, 1474, 1642
Borders Group, Inc., **195–198**
Borders Perrin Norrander, 359–362
Borel, Daniel, 911
Boston Beer Company, Inc., **199–202**, *200*
Boston Chicken, **203–206**
Boston Idea Group, 100
Boston Marathon, 1419
Boston Market Corp., **203–206**
Boston Red Sox, 207–210
Bosworth, Brian, 672
Bottled water, 1274–1277
"Bottles Personified" campaign, 237–240
"Botulism" spot, 593
Bouchez & Kent, 1041
Boudreau, Walter, 1411
"Bouncing Balls" spot, 681, 682
"Bouncing Car" spot, 239
Bousquette, Matt, 956
Bovine growth hormones, 1035, 1037
Bow Wow, 271
Bowerman, Bill, 1138, 1140
"Bowling" spot, 577
"Boxer" spot, 369
"Boxing" spot, 3
Boxster, 1365, 1366, 1367
"Boy" spot, 585
"Boy Band" spot, 239
Boyd, Carol, 56
Boyd, Jayne and Joan, 1831
Boyd, Wes, *1074,* 1075
Boyle, Gert, 359–362
Boyle, Tim, 359–362
Boylson, Michael, 808
Boys and Girls Clubs, 1688
Bozell
  celebrity milk mustache campaign, 183

Chrysler "Engineered to be Great Cars" campaign, 386–389
"It Happens At the Hilton" campaign, 729–732
"Jeep" campaign, 389–392
Little Caesar "Talking Pizzas" campaign, 906–910
Lycos "Go Get It" campaign, 915–918
Verizon Wireless "Can You Hear Me Now?" campaign, 297–300
Brabeck, Peter, 932
Bradham, Caleb, 1280, 1284, 1295
Bradley, Bill, 1741
Brady, Tom, 598, 600
The Brady Bunch (television show), 1225, 1227
Brancheau, Jon, 650
Brand, Barry, 666
Brand Buzz, 240–242
Brand Content, 1042
Brand-name CDs
Dr. Martens *Unlaced*, 460
The White Album (Fédération des producteurs de lait du Québec), 183
Woman Thing Music, 57–58
Brand placement. *See* Product placement
Branded entertainment, 59–62
Brando, Marlon
Harley-Davidson, 1350
iPods, 136
jeans, 1749
Levi's jeans, 883
Pepsi "The Joy of Cola" campaign, 1281
United Airlines "Rising" campaign, 1700
Brandvik, Erika, 871
Brandweek awards, 871
Branson, Richard, 1235, 1757–1760
Brant, Ryan, 1498
Braun, 1190
"BRAVIA" campaign, 1526–1529
Bravo Network, 592
"Break Through" campaign, 634–637
"Break Up" spot, 163
"Breakdance" spot, 239
"Breakfast in Bed" spot, 629
Breast cancer, 1747
Breath mints, 1821–1824
Breathe Right strips, 337–340, *338*
Breeders, 460
Breen, Howard, 689
Breitenbach, Paul, 1370
Brenneman, Greg, 221
Brenner, Sean, 553
Brentjens, Bart, 1541
Brew, Alan, 1657
Breyers ice cream, 468
Bricken, Knox, 1624
"Bridesmaids" spot, 1727
Bridgestone/Firestone, 680–681
Brigham's, Inc., **207–210**
BrightHouseLive, 265–268
Brimley, Wilford, 1293
Brinegar, Brad, 1653
"Bring on the Day" campaign, 1197–1200
Brinkley, David, 1326, 1327
Brispiel, Matthew, 1771
British Airways, 1758–1759
British Open golf tournament, 1794
British Television Advertising Awards
Honda "Grrr" campaign, 745
Honda "The Power of Dreams" campaign, 741
Orange "Goldspot" campaign, 1236
"Britney Rooftop" spot, 1280, 1282
Brittin, Lewis, 1205
Broadband, AOL, 66–69
"Broadcast News" spot, 519
Broadcast promotions
A & E Television Networks, 1–3
ABC "TV Is Good" campaign, 5–8
"Cartoon Network Promotional and Branding" campaign, 1611–1615
ESPN "The Rick" campaign, 513–516
ESPN "This Is SportsCenter" campaign, 517–520
ESPN "Without Sports" campaign, 520–523
Game Show Network "You Know You Know" campaign, 591–594
"It's Not T.V. It's HBO" campaign, 737–740
MTV "Watch and Learn" campaign, 1077–1080
"NHL on Fox" campaign, 575–578
Oxygen Media "Fresh Television for Women" campaign, 1241–1244
PBS "Be More" campaign, 1409–1412
Turner Broadcasting System "TBS Very Funny" campaign, 1662–1665
Turner Classic Movies "31 Days of Oscar" campaign, 1659–1662
Weather Channel "Painted Faces" campaign, 1805–1808
Broce, Alan, 518
Brøderbund, 379, 381, 382
Brokaw, Tom, 60, 1230, 1238
"The Broken Leg" campaign, 38–41
Brolick, Emil, 1592
Broman, Gunnar, 1729
Bronze Lion. *See* Lion Awards
Bronze Pencil Awards. *See* One Show Awards
Brooker, Brian, 1537, 1538
Brooks, Baba, 1406
Brookter, Carolyn, 1604
Brosnan, Pierce, 986, 1549, 1769, 1771
Brothers, Dr. Joyce, 1230, 1548
Brotherton, Nigel, 1781
Brown, Billy, 603
Brown, Cleyson, 1544
Brown, Garrett, 929
Brown, James, 178
Brown, James (basketball player), 576
Brown, James (singer), 1298, 1302
Brown, Junior and Tanya Rae, 607
Brown, Karen, 1149
Brown, Larry, 1259
Brown, Margy, 1004, 1007
Brown, Richard, 502
Brown, Rob, 1003
Brown, Wendy, 151
Brown, Wes, 1774
Brown & Williamson Tobacco Company, 246, 1294
Browne, Liz, 1525
Brownstein, Carrie, 1371
Brubeck, Dave, 1178
Bruce, Bill, 1272
Bruce, Bruce, 841
Brundage, Damon, 960
Brunswick, 1355
Bruyn, Steven, 387, 388
Bryant, Kobe, 346, 347–348
Bryce, Michael, 448
Buchanan, Bob, 608
Buchner, Rob, 60
Buck, Peter, 455
"Buck" spot, 718, 721, 723
Buckhorn, Dean, 1745
Buckley, Bryan
Dial-a-Mattress "Always Out There" campaign, 432
E*TRADE "Monkey Trilogy" campaign, 527
MINI Cooper "Counterfeit" campaign, 171
"On the Wings of Goodyear" campaign, 680, 681
"Vegas Stories" campaign, 873
Bud Ice, 120–122
Bud Light
"I Love You, Man" campaign, 112–116

Bud Light, ***continued***
Miller Lite, as competitor of, 1023, 1449–1451
Budgen, Frank, 1145
Budget Rent A Car System, Inc., **211–214**
Budweiser
"Frogs" campaign, 109–112, 539
Heineken, as competitor of, 706
"Louie the Lizard" campaign, 539
Miller High Life, as competitor of, 1454
Rolling Rock, as competitor of, 761–762
Buechert, Courtney, 29
"Buffalo" spot, 936
Buffett, Warren, 614, 616, 619
Bugaboo jacket, 360
"Built By Engineers, Used By Ordinary People" campaign, 717–720
"Bull's-eye" logo, 1599, 1601
Bunge Ltd., 287
"Bunker Shot" spot, 1136
"Bunny Chasers" campaign, 509–512
"Bunny People" campaign, 144, 767–771, *768, 769,* 772
Burch, Howe, 554, 1149
Bureau of Engraving and Printing, **215–218,** *216*
Burgay, Steve, 827
Burger King Corp., **219–228,** *220*
Carl's Jr., as competitor of, 291
Hardee's, as competitor of, 698
McDonald's, as competitor of, 959, 962, 965, 968–969
Wendy's, as competitor of, 1815
"Burger" spot, 1020
Burke, Andrew, 1826
Burke, Bill, 1486
Burke, Kevin, 1394
Burlington Industries, 925
Burnard, Alex, 1251
Burns, Brad, 975, 976
Burns, Clare, 1608
Burns, Curt, 684
Burns, George, 832
Burns, Ken, 1109
Burrell Communications Group
Toyota "A Car to Be Proud of Campaign," 1631, 1633
Verizon Wireless "Can You Hear Me Now?" campaign, 298
Burrier, Dan, 1068
Burson-Marsteller, 215–218
Burton, Jake, 84, 1514
Burton, LeVar, 129
Burton, Rick, 1143
Burton Snowboards, 1514–1515
Burwick, Dave, 1270, 1272, 1291
"Bus Ride" spot, 341, 343
"Bus" spot, 184, 1596
Busch, Adolphus, 105, 106, 109
Busch, August, III, 110
Busch, August A., IV, 109, 123, 127, 130
Bush, George H. W., 76, 1426
Bush, George W., 1073–1076
defense spending, 229, 232
gay rights, 658
iPods, 136, 138
Kyoto Protocol, withdrawal from the, 1510, 1511
Peace Corps, 1263, 1265
political campaign, 1741
Sierra Club "Hybrid Evolution" campaign, 1509–1512
"Swift Boat Veterans for Truth" campaign, 1583
Business Leaders for Sensible Priorities, **229–232**
Business services, 919–922
Business travelers
Amtrak "Life on Acela" campaign, 1104
Delta Air Lines "On Top of the World" campaign, 411–412
Delta Air Lines "The Passenger's Airline" campaign, 415
Holiday Inn Express "Stay Smart" campaign, 780, 781
Marriott International "Never Underestimate the Importance of a Good Night's Rest" campaign, 927–930
United Airlines "It's Time to Fly" campaign, 1696
United Airlines "Rising" campaign, 1699
BuSpar, 667
Butler, John, 1431
Butler, Shine & Stern
Round House Pizza "The Last Honest Pizza" campaign, 1429–1432
"Specialized" campaign, 1539–1542
Butler, Thomas R., 1054
Buttonwood Agreement, 1091
Byers, David, 688, 689
Byrd, Richard, 1113
Byrne, Martha, 57
Byrne, Mike, 1146

C

C2, 241
Cable & Telecommunications Association for Marketing Hall of Fame
ESPN "This Is SportsCenter" campaign, 517, 520
"It's Not T.V. It's HBO" campaign, 740
Cable Car Awards, 1059
Cable television
branding, 6–7
Cargill
"Collaborate>Create>Succeed" campaign, 288
"Cartoon Network Promotional and Branding" campaign, 1611–1615
Court TV "Linda Lo-Cal" vignette, 836
Discovery Communications "Two Guys" campaign, 451–453
ESPN "The Rick" campaign, 513–516
ESPN "This Is SportsCenter" campaign, 517–520
ESPN "Without Sports" campaign, 520–523
Game Show Network "You Know You Know" campaign, 591–594
"It's Not T.V. It's HBO" campaign, 737–740
Lee jeans "Cut to Be Noticed" campaign, 1745
MINI Cooper "Counterfeit" campaign, 170, 171
MTV "Watch and Learn" campaign, 1077–1080
Old Navy "Destination" campaign, 1229
Oxygen Media "Fresh Television for Women" campaign, 1241–1244
Saab "Life Is Not a Spectator Sport" campaign, 1447
Turner Broadcasting System "TBS Very Funny" campaign, 1662–1665
Turner Classic Movies "31 Days of Oscar" campaign, 1659–1662
Victory Motorcycles "The New American Motorcycle" campaign, 1351
Cable *vs.* DSL Internet service, 1475
Cadbury Adams USA LLC, **233–236,** 1828–1829
Cadbury Schweppes Americas Beverages, **237–242**
Coca-Cola Company, as competitor of, 351–352
PepsiCo, as competitor of, 1282, 1284, 1291

"The Caddy That Zigs" campaign, 638–641
Cade, Robert, 1286
Cadillac
"Break Through" campaign, 634–637, *635*
"The Caddy That Zigs" campaign, 638–641
Caffeine, 1268
Caffrey's, 428
Cage, Nicolas, 633
Cahill, Liz, 1747, 1748
Cajun Holding Company, 318
Calderin, Rob, 227, 228, 841
Calderwood, Graham, 792
Calhoun, Steve, 658–659
California
antismoking campaigns, 1028
emissions mandates, 641
California Department of Health Services, Tobacco Control Section, **243–251**, 1028–1029
California Milk Advisory Board, **253–256**, *254*
California Milk Processor Board, 183, **257–260**
"California" spot, 828
California Tobacco Health Protection Act, 248
"The Call" campaign, 803–806
"Call to action" campaigns, 170, 171
Callihan, Barbara, 1370
Calloway, Wayne, 1299
Calthey, Robert, 880
Calvin Klein Cosmetics Company, **261–264**
Cameras. *See* Photography
Cameron, Evan, 553
Cameron, Kirk, 1281
"Campaign for Freedom" campaign, 31–34
"Campaign for Real Beauty" campaign, 1679–1683, *1680*
Campanella, Roy, 1107
Campbell, Lori, 432
Campbell, Naomi, 729, 730, 731
Campbell Doyle Dye, 177
Campbell-Ewald
Borders "Find Out" campaign, 195
Chevrolet "An American Revolution" campaign, 631–634
Campbell Mithun Esty, 854–857
Campbell Soup Company, **265–271**, *266*
Camry, Toyota
Ford Fusion, as competitor of, 559
Galant, as competitor of, 1033
Mitsubishi Galant, as competitor of, 1033
Oldsmobile Alero, as competitor of, 654
overview, 1639
"Can You Hear Me Now?" campaign, 297–300, *298*
"Can You See It?" campaign, 785–788
"Can You Wait?" campaign, 371–374
"Can Your Camera Do This?" spot, 481
Canadian Film Centre, **273–276**, *274*
"Cancer by Carton" article, 97–98
Cancer-expense insurance, 35–40
Candido, Jeff, 872, 873
Candie's Foundation, 752
Candy
"Altoids Gone Sour" campaign, 1824–1827
Hershey ReeseSticks "The Crisp You Can't Resist!" campaign, 709–712
Hershey "There's No Wrong Way to Eat a Reese's" campaign, 712–715
M&M's "New Millennium" campaigns, 937–940
"Snickers Cruncher" campaign, 940–943
Cannondale, 1251, 1540
Canon U.S.A., Inc., **277–280**
Hewlett-Packard, as competitor of, 718
Kodak, as competitor of, 480, 487
Nikon, as competitor of, 1164
Xerox, as competitor of, 1847
Cantalupo, James, 965
"Canterbury" spot, 1648
Cantone, Mario, 1664
Canyon Gang, 1250
Capital Cities Inc., 514
Capital One, 327
Capitol Records, 263–264
Caplan, Josh, 1861
Cappelli, Paul, 526, 797
Caputo, Gerard, 1410
"Car Alarm" spot, 941, 942
"Car Carrier" spot, 633
"Car Chase" spot, 891
Car rental companies, 211–214
"Car" spot, 888
"A Car to Be Proud Of" campaign, 1631–1634
"Car Wash" spot, 891
Caraccioli, Laura, 1411
Card Photo Printers, 277–279
CareerBuilder Inc., **281–284**, 1040
Careful What You Wish For (film), 61
Carerre, Tia, 713
Cargill, Inc., **285–288**, *286*
Cargill, William Wallace, 287
Carillon Importers, 1734
Carlesimo, P.J., 166
Carlin, George, 1471, 1785
Carl's Jr., **289–292**, *290*
Hardee's, and, 698, 699
Jack in the Box, as competitor of, 813
Carlson, Charles, 1256
Carlston, Doug and Gary, 379
Carmichael Lynch
Polaris campaign, 1355
Porsche "Cayenne Launch" campaign, 1365–1368
Rapala "Custom Lures" campaign, 1193–1196
Schwinn/GT "Fast. It's Corporate Policy." campaign, 1249–1252
Schwinn "What a Ride" campaign, 1252–1256
Carmichael Lynch Spong, 702–704
Carnahan, Joe, 178
Carney, Frank and Dan, 1345
Carnival Corporation, **293–296**
Cunard Line, as competitor of, 373
Royal Caribbean Cruises, as competitor of, 1443
Carol H. Williams Advertising, 243
Carolson, Pete, 1579
Carpet-cleaning services, 1557–1561
"Carpooling" spot, 681
Carr-Locke, Robin, 1136, 1137
Carrey, Jim, 39, 617
Carroll, Chris, 457
Carroll, John, 348
Carrot Top
AT&T "Carrot Top" campaign, 147–150, *148*
ESPN "This Is SportsCenter" campaign, 519
Carson, Johnny, 1458
Carter, Caroline, 1067, 1070
Carter, David, 176
Carter, Dennis, 770
Carter, Jimmy, 1238
Carter, Vince, 1095, 1100, 1144
Carter-Miller, Jocelyn, 1066
Carter Products "Trojan Man" campaign, 311–315
"Cartoon Crisis Center" spot, 1613
"Cartoon Network Promotional and Branding" campaign, 1611–1615
CARU. *See* Children's Advertising Review Unit (CARU)
Casanova Pendrill Publicidad, 64
Case, Paula, 1427

Case, Stephen M., 64
Casey, George, 1709
Casey, James E., 1709
Casey, Kerry, 703
"Cash in Hand" campaign, 945–948
"Cashback Bonus" program, 1050, 1051, 1052
Cashen, Jon, 835
"Cat Herders" campaign, 501–504
"The Catch" spot, 1101
Catera, Cadillac, 638–640
"Catfight" campaign, 1450
Cats, 934
Cattrall, Kim, 336, 1161
"Cayenne Launch" campaign, 1365–1368, *1366*
CBS
"Network Executive" spot, 1621
"Welcome Home" campaign, 6
CDC. *See* Centers for Disease Control and Prevention
CDs
AOL "Welcome to the World Wide Wow" campaign, 65, 66–69, *67*
Dr. Martens *Unlaced*, 460
The White Album (Fédération des producteurs de lait du Québec), 183
Woman Thing Music, 57–58
Cedar, Larry, 1059
Cedergren, Christopher, 644, 1782
Celebrex campaign, 667
Celebrities
Aflac "Duck" spots, 37, 39
Amazon.com branded entertainment, 59–62
American Express "Do More" campaign, 82–86
Apple Computer "Switchers" campaign, 140
"Celebrities Read Fan Mail to DirecTV (Become a DirecTV Fan Now)" campaign, 447–450
dead, 1439
dial-around numbers, 976, 977
Discover "Make a Statement" campaign, 1055
Gap campaign, 887–888
Gap "For Every Generation" campaign, 597
Gap "How Do You Wear It?" campaign, 598, 600
Gap "Who Wore Khakis?" campaign, 602
Levi's "They Go On" campaign, 890
MCI "1-800-Collect" campaign, 971
MINI Cooper drivers, 174
prescription drug campaigns, 667
Rolex "Celebrity Endorsement" campaign, 1043–1046
Visa Check Card "Works Like a Check" campaign, 1770–1771
"Celebrities Read Fan Mail to DirecTV (Become a DirecTV Fan Now)" campaign, 447–450
Celebrity voice-overs
Arquette, Rosanna (eBay 2004 television campaign), 496, 498
Bacon, Kevin (E*Trade "Why Wouldn't You?" campaign), 531
Baldwin, Alec ("Art. Ask for More" campaign), 103
Brando, Marlon (United Airlines "Rising" campaign), 1700
Carlin, George (Saturn "Why Didn't Anyone Think of This Before?" campaign), 1471
Carlin, George (Volkswagen "New Beetle" campaign), 1785
Cattrall, Kim (Herbal Essences campaign), 336
Cleese, John (Lexus "The Road Is Calling" campaign), 1646, 1648
Collins, Jackie (Charles Schwab "Smarter Investor" campaign), 304
Daniels, Jeff (Microsoft "Where Do You Want to Go Today?" campaign), 1004
Dreyfuss, Richard (Apple "Think Different" campaign), 142, 143, 774
Gifford, Kathie Lee (Carnival "Fun Ships" campaign), 294, 295
Grammer, Kelsey (Lexus "The Road Is Calling" campaign), 1648
Irons, Jeremy (Lexus "The Road Is Calling" campaign), 1648
Jackson, Samuel L. (Gardenburger "Eating Good Just Got Great" campaign), 1817
Jones, James Earl (Ameritech "Privacy Manager campaign), 155
Keillor, Garrison (Honda Motor Company "The Power of Dreams" campaign), 743
Keillor, Garrison (Honda UK "Grrr" campaign), 745
Lahti, Christine (Delta Air Lines "On Top of the World" campaign), 413
McConaughey, Matthew (Peace Corps "Life is Calling. How Far Will You Go?" campaign), 1261, 1264
Moore, Demi (Lexus "The Road Is Calling" campaign), 1646, 1648
Newman, Paul ("A World of Energy") campaign, 305, 308
Pesci, Joe (Lexus "The Road Is Calling" campaign), 1648
Redford, Robert (United Airlines "It's Time To Fly" campaign), 1697
Sinise, Gary (Cadillac "Break Through" campaign), 637
Turner, Kathleen (McDonald's "Got the Urge?" campaign), 968
Weaver, Sigourney (John Hancock "Insurance for the Unexpected. Investments for the Opportunities" campaign 1996), 823
Weaver, Sigourney (Sarajevo Olympic Children's Fund), 107
Celica "Get the Feeling" campaign, 1641–1643
Cellco Partnership, 297–300, *298*
Cellular phones. *See* Mobile phones; Wireless services
Cendant Car Rental Group, 211
Censorship
"Censorship is UnAmerican" tagline, 1425–1426
"Godaddy.com Super Bowl Commercial" campaign, 675–678
Center for Science in the Public Interest (CSPI)
Aspartame, 241
Olean, 1399
"Quaker-Warms You, Heart and Soul" campaign, 1292, 1293, 1294, 1295
Sprint "Monday Nights Free and Clear" campaign, 1550
Centers for Disease Control and Prevention, 312
Centrum Silver, 1331
Cereal
Cheerios "Stories" campaign, 627–630
Kellogg "Gotta Have My Pops" campaign, 831–834
Kellogg "Special K Kick-Start Diet Plan" campaign, 834–837
"Quaker-Warms You, Heart and Soul" campaign, 1292–1295
Cereda, Flavio, 554
Certs, 1822–1823
Cezares, Gabriel, 1595
"Chair" spot, 1173
"The Chamber of Fear" campaign, 1139, 1140
Chambers, John, 1091
"Champagne of Beers" slogan, 1453

Champine, Laura, 876
"A Championship Season" spot, 1156
Champs Gold Medal Award, 1700
Chan, Jackie, 1273
Chance 2 Motorsports team, 839
Chang, Michael, 1055, 1133
Change, 1509–1512
"Change + HP" campaign, 726
"Change" spot, 33, 1790
"Changes" campaign, 966
"Channel Surfing" spot, 385
Chapelle, Dave, 1289, 1291
"Chaperone" spot, 1581
"Charade" spot, 589
Charities
  drugstore.com Foundation, 472
  Lee jeans "National Denim Day" campaign, 1747
  Target "Take Charge of Education" campaign, 1603–1606
Charles, Prince, 1035, 1037
Charles, Ray, 1304, 1552
The Charles Schwab Corporation, **301–304**, *302*, 527
"Charlie's Parents" spot, 563
Charney, Dov, 71–74
Charron, Chris, 1852
Chase, Chevy, 37, 39
Chase Manhattan
  Citigroup, as competitor of, 331
  First Union, as competitor of, 1790
  Wachovia, as competitor of, 1794
"Chase" spot, 1296
Chastain, Brandi, 1156
Cheadle, Don, 178, 1099, 1100, 1101
The Check Up (short film), 159, 1775
"Checkerboard" logo, 1113
Cheerios "Stories" campaign, 627–630
Cheese
  California Milk Advisory Board "Happy Cows" campaign, 253–256
  on Kraft DiGiorno Rising Crust Pizza, 863
Cheez-It crackers, 267
"Chef Jimmy" campaign, 456, 1414
Chelsea Pictures/ Campfire, 157–160
Cheltenham festival, 429
Chem-Dry Cleaning, 1559
Chemistri, 650–652
Chenault, Kenneth, 80
Chesebrough-Pond, 1320
Chevrolet, Louis, 631
Chevrolet "An American Revolution" campaign, 631–634
Chevron Corporation, **305–309**
Chevy Cavalier, 94
Chewing gum
  Juicy Fruit "Gotta Have Twisted Sweet" campaign, 1827–1830
  Orbit gum "No Matter What" campaign, 1830–1833
  Trident "Four Out of Five Dentists" campaign, 233–236
Chiat\Day
  Body Shop "Ruby" campaign, 193
  Honda advertising, 92
Chicago Creative Club, 1830
Chicago Region Toyota Dealer Association, 1638–1639
Chicago Windy Awards, 1359
Chick-fil-A
  Church's Chicken, as competitor of, 318–319
  KFC, as competitor of, 840–841
"Chicken Pox" spot, 365
Chicvara, Jerome, 201
"Child Hunger" campaign, 363–366
Children
  Anheuser-Busch "Frogs" campaign, 111, 112, 117
  Anheuser-Busch ""Spuds McKenzie" campaign, 113–114
  Burger King "When You Have It Your Way, It Just Tastes Better" campaign, 228
  Cheerios "Spoonfuls of Stories" literacy project, 628
  Juicy Fruit "Gotta Have Twisted Sweet" campaign, 1828
  LeapFrog "Learn Something New Every Day!" campaign, 879–882
  obesity, 457
  Post Cereals partnership with Reach Out and Read program, 628–629
  Secret Sparkle Body Spray, 1401, 1403
  Subway "F.R.E.S.H. Steps" campaign, 457
  Target/Golden Books Entertainment partnership, 1605
Children's Advertising Review Unit (CARU), 1403, 1828, 1830
Children's Books & Toys, Inc., 196
Children's Healthcare of Atlanta, 37, 39
"Child's Play" spot, 1074
"Chimps" spot, 737–740
China, 546, 547
Chinese-Americans, 1644
"Chinese Office" spot, 544
Chipotle, 1593
"The Chivas Life" campaign, 424–425
Chivas Regal, 424–425
Chodosh, Joe, 1095
"Choice" spot, 33
"Chop Shop" spot, 53
Christine, Virginia, 1374
Christopher, Douglas, 1592
Chrysler. *See* DaimlerChrysler Corp.
Chrysler, Walter P., 384, 386
Chuck D, 103
Chunky soups, 270
Church & Dwight Company, Inc., **311–315**
  Procter & Gamble, as competitor of, 1396
  Super Scoop, 1116
Churchill, Winston, 729, 730
Church's Chicken, **317–320**
Chux, 1381
Cialis, 1327
Ciara, 752
Cigarettes
  Altria Group Inc., 55–58
  California Department of Health Services "Antitobacco" campaign, 243–247, *244*
  Six Flags theme parks smoking ban, 1520
  "Tobacco Control Section" media campaign, 248–251
  "Truth" campaign, 97–100
Cigars, 246–247
Cima, Tony, 1754
"Cinderella" spot, 523
Cingular
  T-Mobile, as competitor of, 1625
  Verizon Wireless, as competitor of, 298–299
Cisco Systems, Inc., **321–324**
Citibank, **325–328**, *326*
Citigroup Inc., **329–332**
  ING, as competitor of, 764
  Wachovia, as competitor of, 1794
"Citizen Actions," 1836, 1837
Citroen, 1781
"The City Never Sleeps" campaign, 330
Civic "What About Now?" campaign, 91–95, *92*, *93*
Civil rights movement, 1201
"cK be" campaign, 261–264
CKE Restaurants, 698
Clairol, Inc., **333–336**
Clairty Coverdale Fury, 1027–1030
Clapp, Gordon, 1201–1204, 1669
Clapp, Steve, 1805, 1806
Clapton, Eric, 989
Claritin
  Allegra, as competitor of, 1463
  Zyrtec, as competitor of, 1312–1313
Clark, Allan, 1515

Clark, Dick, 308, 937, 940
Clarke, John, 464, 465
Clarke, Tom, 1146
Clarkson, Kelly, 749, 752
Clay, Peter, 672
Claymation
  Maryland State Lottery "Cash in Hand" campaign, 947
  Serta “Counting Sheep” campaign, 1501, 1503
Clayton, Joseph, 1334
Clayton, Paul, 226, 227
Clean Air Act, 94
“Clean Slate” spot, 163
“Cleaner Close” campaign, 1377–1379
“Clear solutions in a complex world” tagline, 893
Cleese, John, 1646, 1648, 1822
Clelland, John, 1624
Clement, Ruth, 954
Clendenin, Tom, 517
Cleverly, Bruce, 1315
“Click, Instantly” tagline, 1359
Click Em On Markers, 189, 190
“Client Dinner” spot, 45
Cliff Freeman & Partners
  Hollywood Video “Welcome to Hollywood” campaign, 733–736
  Little Caesar “Cloning” campaign, 897–900
  Little Caesar “Grand Canyon” campaign, 900–903
  Little Caesar “Safety Video” campaign, 903–906
  Midas campaign, 1010
  Mike’s Hard Lemonade “Hard Day” campaign, 1013–1016
  “NHL on Fox” campaign, 575–578
  Snapple campaign, 239
  Staples “Yeah, We’ve Got That” campaign, 1567–1569
Cline, Davis & Mann, 1326–1328
Cline, Patsy, 1397, 1548
Clinton, Bill
  1992 election, 1740
  Biography spot, 1661
  “Cat Herders” spot, reference to, 503
  Joe Boxer campaign, 847
  “Motor Voter Bill,” 1426
  National and Community Service Trust Act, 1426
  Specialized bicycle ad, 1540
  Time “The World’s Most Interesting Magazine” campaign, 1615
  youth vote, 1425
Clinton, Hillary Rodham, 60, 246, 1741
Clio Awards
  adidas “Yankee Fans” campaign, 27, 29
  “Altoids Gone Sour” campaign, 1827
  Anheuser-Busch “Frogs” campaign, 112
  Anheuser-Busch “Louie the Lizard” campaign, 119
  Anheuser-Busch “Real American Heroes/Real Men of Genius” campaign, 126
  Anheuser-Busch “Whassup?!” campaign, 128, 129
  Bay, Michael, spots by, 633
  BC Dairy Foundation “Don’t Take Your Body for Granted” campaign, 184
  BMW “The Hire” campaign, 178
  Borders “This Season, It’s the Original Thought That Counts” campaign, 197
  Burger King campaign, 965
  Burger King “Lunch Break” campaign, 219
  Burger King “Subservient Chicken” campaign, 223, 225
  Business Leaders for Sensible Priorities “Move Our Money” campaign, 232
  California Milk Processor Board “Got Milk?” campaign, 257, 260
  Canadian Film Centre “2004 Toronto Worldwide Short Film Festival” campaign, 273, 276
  Columbia Sportswear “Mother Boyle” campaign, 361
  Dial-A-Mattress “Always Out There” campaign, 434
  eBay “Abbreviated” campaign, 493, 495
  Electronic Data Systems “Cat Herders” campaign, 503
  ESPN NFL 2K5 “Beta-7” campaign, 1498, 1499
  First Union “Financial World” campaign, 1792
  Game Show Network “You Know You Know” campaign, 591, 593
  Gill Foundation “TurnOut” campaign, 657, 659
  Häagen-Dazs “Made Like No Other” campaign, 1119, 1121
  Hewlett-Packard “Built By Engineers, Used By Ordinary People” campaign, 720
  Hewlett-Packard “Expanding Possibilities” campaign, 723
  Hollywood Video “Welcome to Hollywood” campaign, 736
  Honda “Grrr” campaign, 745
  IBM “Solutions for a Small Planet” campaign, 800
  IKEA “Unböring” campaign, 755, 758
  “It’s Not T.V. It’s HBO” campaign, 737, 740
  Jeep “There’s Only One” campaign, 392, 394
  John Hancock “Insurance for the Unexpected. Investments for the Opportunities” campaign, 826
  Lipton Brisk “That’s Brisk Baby!” campaign, 1302
  Little Caesar “Cloning” campaign, 900
  Little Caesar “Grand Canyon” campaign, 903
  Little Caesar “Safety Video” campaign, 906
  MADD “Drunk Driving’s a Serious Crime. Let’s Treat It That Way.” campaign, 1063
  Maryland State Lottery “Cash in Hand” campaign, 948
  “NHL on Fox” campaign, 578
  Nike “Move” campaign, 1144
  Nike “Play” campaign, 1147
  Nordstrom “Make Room for Shoes” campaign, 1181, 1183
  Pabst “Remember Rainier” campaign, 1245, 1248
  PBS “Be More” campaign, 1409, 1412
  Pepsi “Security Camera” campaign, 1298
  Schwinn/GT “Fast. It’s Corporate Policy.” campaign, 1249, 1251
  Seattle SuperSonics “In Your Home” campaign, 168
  Sharp “More to See” campaign, 1505, 1507
  Staples “Yeah, We’ve Got That” campaign, 1569
  Toyota Celica “Get the Feeling” campaign, 1643
  Toyota Corolla “A Car to Be Proud Of” campaign, 1631, 1633
  Turner Broadcasting System “TBS Very Funny” campaign, 1665
  “US Open Excitement” campaign, 1721, 1724
  Virgin Atlantic Airways “Go, Jet Set, Go!” campaign, 1759
  “Visa. It’s Everywhere You Want to Be” campaign, 1765, 1768
“Cloning” campaign, 897–900
Clooney, Rosemary, 1605
Clorox Company
  Fresh Step, 1116
  Procter & Gamble, as competitor of, 1383

Clothing
Abercrombie & Fitch, 9–12
American Apparel Inc., 71–74
Columbia Sportswear "Mother Boyle" campaign, 359–362
"Come See the Softer Side of Sears" campaign, 1490
Gap "For Every Generation" campaign, 595–598
Gap "How Do You Wear It?" campaign, 598–601
Gap "Khakis" campaign, 601–604
Gap "This Is Easy" campaign, 605–608
Kmart "Joe Boxer Launch" campaign, 847–850
Lee jeans "Cut to Be Noticed" campaign, 1743–1746
Lee jeans "Find Your One True Fit" campaign, 1746–1748
Levi's "It's Wide Open" campaign, 883–886
Levi's "They Go On" campaign, 889–892
"Levi's Type 1 Jeans" campaign, 886–889
Nordstrom "Reinvent Yourself" campaign, 1184–1187
Old Navy "Destination" campaign, 1228–1231
Old Navy "'70s Retro TV" campaign, 1225–1228
Tommy Hilfiger "American Tartans" campaign, 1627–1630
Virginia Slims V-Wear, 56
Wrangler "Rugged Wear" campaign, 1749–1751
"Cloud" spot, 255
Clouser, Chris, 699
Clow, Lee
ABC "TV Is Good" campaign, 7
Apple "Silhouette" campaign, 136
Apple "Think Different" campaign, 142, 143
Infiniti "Own One and You'll Understand" campaign, 1177, 1179
Mercedes "Falling in Love" spot, 987
Taco Bell "Want Some?" campaign, 1595
"Clowns" spot, 1833
Clydesdale horses, 106, 109
CME. *See* Campbell Mithun Esty
CMJ Music Marathon, 1423
CNBC, 37
CNN-SI, 515, 518
CNS, Inc., **337–340**
Co-op marketing, 770–771, 772
"Coach" spot, 521, 522
Coad, R. B., 411
"Coaster 2 Coaster" campaign, 1611, 1614
Coate, Brian, 495
Cobranded credit cards, 1054
The Coca-Cola Company, **341–357**, *350*
Dasani, 1275
Diet Rite, C2 as competitor of, 241
Nestea Cool, 1300–1301
PepsiCo, as competitor of, 1278, 1281–1282, 1290–1291, 1296–1297
PowerAde, 1288
Snapple, as competitor of, 1657
Surge, 1268–1269, 1271–1272
Vanilla Coke, 1284–1285
Coca-Cola Zero, 352
Cocciolo, Harry, 681
Cochrane, Lisa, 53
"Code Red" campaign, 1267–1270, 1273
"Coffe Shop" spot, 1745
Coffee
Folgers "The Best Part of Wakin' Up Is Folgers In Your Cup" campaign, 1373–1376
General Foods International Coffees "It's How to Unplug" campaign, 859–862
"Coffee Cup" spot, 913
"Cog" spot, 741, 743, 746, 747
Cohen, Alan, 6, 7, 8
Cohen, Ben, 72, 229–231, *230*
Cohen, Betty, 1612
Cohen, Dr. Dan, 340
Cohen, Ian, 1513, 1514, 1516
Cohen, Margaret Kirch, 1295
Cohn, Linda, 519
Cohn & Wolfe
Diet Rite "Go for Zero" campaign, 240–242
Paxil "Social Anxiety Disorder" campaign, 665–668
Colbert, Stephen, 648–652, *649*
Cold and allergy products
Allegra "Spirit of Freedom" campaign, 1461–1464
Breathe Right Strips "Back in the Sack" campaign, 337–340
Kimberly-Clark "Kleenex Anti-Viral" campaign, 843–846
"The Power of Zyrtec" campaign, 1311–1314
Cole, Charles, 749, 750
Cole, Frank, 863
Cole, Kenneth, 749–750
Cole, Neil, 749, 750, 751, 752, 753
Cole & Weber/Red Cell, 1245–1248
Cole Henderson Drake, 399–402
Coleman, Jay, 242
Coleman, Norman, 1739, 1741
Colette, DJ, 1071
Colgate-Palmolive European detergents, 1396
Collaborate
Logitech "What Will You Do With All That Freedom?" campaign, 911–914
Rock the Vote "Yes/No Ballot Box" campaign, 1425–1428
"Collaborate>Create>Succeed" campaign, 285–288, *286*
Collect calls
AT&T "Carrot Top" campaign, 147–150
MCI "1-800-COLLECT" campaign, 971–974
Collective Soul, 560
College Bowl Championship Series, 1039, 1041
Collins, Jackie, 304
Collins, Jerry, 841
Collins, Joan, 1228
Collins, Kim, 25
Collins, Michael, 1393
"Collisions" spot, 713
Collopy, Mary, 1129, 1130
Colorado, 657–660
"Colour like.no.other" tagline, 1528
Coltman, David, 1700
Columbia Sportswear Company, **359–362**
Columbia TriStar Television Distribution (CTTD), 1605
Comaneci, Nadia, 25
Combs, Roberta, 581
Combs, Sean "Puffy," 1001, 1003
Comdex show, 1846, 1847
"Come Home" spot, 129
Come On-a My House (song), 1605
"Come See the Softer Side of Sears" campaign, 1487–1491, 1493
"Comedy Cure II," 664
Comfort foods, 203
Commercial Closet, 1861
Commission for Racial Equality, 730
"Commitment 2000: Raising a Better Tomorrow" initiative, 102
Commodore personal computers, 68
Common, 350, 352
Communication Arts Awards
Little Caesar "Cloning" campaign recognition, 900

Communication Arts Awards, ***continued***
Weather Channel "Painted Faces" campaign, 1807
Community Nutrition Institute, 241
Community service. *See* Social responsibility
"Community" spots, 1004–1007
Community Trade Programme, 192
Compaq
Hewlett-Packard, as competitor of, 722
Hewlett-Packard acquisition of, 724
iMac, as competitor of, 133–134
"Competition. Bad for Them. Great for You." campaign, 419–422
"Competitive" campaign, 79–82
Computer games, 379–382
Computer mice and keyboards. *See* Computer peripherals
Computer operating systems, 794–797
Computer peripherals, 911–914
Computer worms, trojans, and viruses, 322
Comstock, Beth, 624, 626
ConAgra, 1036
ConAgra Foods' Feeding Children Better Foundation, **363–366**
Concept Farm, 1–3
Concord watches, 1045
Conde Nast Publications
General Motors partnership with, 94
Mercedes partnership with, 989
Condoms, 311–315
Cone, David, 28
Conill Advertising, 1631, 1633
Conlon, Peggy, 32, 34
Conn, David, 751, 752
Conner, Bart, 667
Connery, Sean, 633
Connors, Jimmy, 1145
"Conquer the Highlands" project, 424
Conseco, Inc., **367–370**
"Consultants" spot, 1712
Consumer electronics
Hewlett-Packard "Built By Engineers, Used By Ordinary People" campaign, 717–720
Hewlett-Packard "Expanding Possibilities" campaign, 720–723
Philips Electronics "Getting Better" campaign, 1333–1336
Sharp "More to See" campaign, 1505–1508
"Sony Bravia" campaign, 1526–1529
Sony "What's Next?" campaign, 1531–1534
Contests
"Amazing Sprint Sense Dime Find," 1546
Audi "Art of the Heist" campaign, 158
Brigham's "Reverse the Curse" campaign, 207–210
Kraft "Be a DiGiorno Delivery Guy" promotion, 865
Mail Boxes Etc. scratch-off game, 920
Mail Boxes Etc. "See Your Small Business on the Super Bowl" campaign, 919–922
M&M's "Help us find our colors" contest, 937, 940
Nordstrom "Win Shoes for Life," 1182
Purina "Incredible Dog Challenge," 1113–1114
Royal Appliance "Scratch & Win-Match & Win" contest, 1440
Sharp "More to See" campaign, 1507
Continental Airlines, 412
Controversies
Abercrombie & Fitch, 9, 11–12
Abercrombie & Fitch "XXX" campaign, 596–597, 599–600
ACLU ads, 76, 77
adidas sponsorship of the New York Yankees, 26–29
Diet Coke "Aunt Rosalina" spot, 356
FCUK brand, 579–582
"Godaddy.com Super Bowl Commercial" campaign, 675–678
Honda "Mr. Clean" campaign, 94
"Jenny McCarthy for Candie's" campaign, 749, 751
John Hancock "Immigration" spot, 829
MoveOn.org "Child's Play" spot, 1074
Nike's international labor practices, 1134, 1142, 1151, 1155
Super Bowl "wardrobe malfunction" incident, 675, 676
"Vegas Stories" campaign, 871, 873
Cook, Dave, 158
Coolio, 1298, 1302
Coolpix cameras, 1159–1161
Cooper, Ric, 1443
Coors Brewing Company
Anheuser-Busch, as competitor of, 118, 125, 129
Bud Light, as competitor of, 114–115
Miller High Life, as competitor of, 1454
Miller Lite, as competitor of, 1451
Negro Leagues Baseball Museum sponsorship, 1108
Rolling Rock, as competitor of, 868
Coppola, Julia, 1061
Coppola, Sophia, 758
Cor Boonstra, 1334
Corbett, John, 561, *562*, 563, 1033
Cordner, Tom, 1647
Corlett, Candace, 197
Corn Pops "Gotta Have My Pops" campaign, 831–834
Cornelius, Don, 346
Corolla "A Car to Be Proud Of" campaign, 1631–1634
Corona
Foster's, as competitor of, 571
Heineken, as competitor of, 707
Rolling Rock, as competitor of, 762
"Coronation" spot, 3
Corporate Mosaic Award, 1282
Corpus, Vizhier, 1155
Corra, Henry, 611
Cortese, Dan, 962
Corwin, Hank, 1041
Cosby, Bill, 1617
Cosmetics and fragrances
Body Shop "Ruby" campaign, 191–194
Calvin Klein "cK be" campaign, 261–264
French Connection "Scent to Bed" campaign, 579–582
See also Skin care products
Cossette Communication-Marketing, 183
Costello, John H., 1488
Cotsakos, Christos, 526, 528, 530
"Counterfeit" campaign, 159, 169–172
Counterfeiting, 215–218, 1044
"Counting Sheep" campaign, 1501–1503
Country Music Awards, 1749
Couric, Katie, 218, 1223
Court cases, 76
Court TV, 836
Courtyard by Marriott, 927–930
"Coverage" spot, 1859, 1860, 1861
Coverdale, Jac, 1028
Cowen, Tyler, 1132
Cowens, Dave, 209
Cowher, Bill, 464
Cows and Gateway, 610
Cox, Tony, 1780

Cox Arquette, Courtney, *350,* 350–352, 1282
Coyle, Walter, 1230
Coza, Dave, 434
Crabtree & Evelyn, 192
Craft brews
  "Rolling Rock Ads" campaign, 867–870
  Samuel Adams "It's What's Inside" campaign, 199–202
Craig, Sid, 815
Cramer-Krasselt
  AirTran "Go. There's Nothing Stopping You" campaign, 43–45
  CareerBuilder campaign, 281–284, 1040
  Hyatt Hotels campaign, 731
Crandall, Court, 515
Crate & Barrel 1998 print ads campaign, 533–536
Craven, Sheila, 771
Crawford, Cindy
  adidas apparel, 20
  Cadillac "The Caddy That Zigs" campaign, 639
  Pepsi campaign, 1277, 1279, 1284
Crawford, Steve, 415
Crayola, 187–190, *188,* 189
Crayons, 187, *188,* 189
Crazy (song), 1397
"Crazy" spot, 1101
"Creating a world of smarter investors" tagline, 301
Creative Excellence in Business Advertising award, 285, 288
Creative Response Concepts, 1585
Creativity Awards, 1081, 1084
Credit cards
  American Express, 79–90
  Citibank "Identity Theft Solutions" campaign, 325–328
  Discover card "It Pays to Discover Revisited" campaign, 1050–1053
  Discover "Make a Statement" campaign, 1053–1056
  Marriott cobrands, 930
  MasterCard "Priceless" campaign, 949–952
  Target Guest Card, 1603–1606
  "Visa. It's Everywhere You Want to Be" campaign, 1765–1768
"Credits" spot, 735
Creed, Greg, 1593
Creidenberg, Jan, 1463
Crew Chief Club, 1674
"Crew Morning" spot, 1376
Crisp, Quentin, 890
"The Crisp You Can't Resist!" campaign, 709–712
Crispin Porter + Bogusky
  American Legacy Foundation "Truth" campaign, 97–100
  antismoking campaign, 249–250
  Borders "This Season, It's the Original Thought That Counts" campaign, 195–198
  Burger King "Lunch Break" campaign, 219–222
  Burger King "Subservient Chicken" campaign, 222–225
  "Counterfeit" campaign, 159
  IKEA "Unböring" campaign, 755–758
  MINI Cooper "Counterfeit" campaign, 169–172
  MINI Cooper "MINI Robots" campaign, 172–175
  Schwinn/GT "Fast. It's Corporate Policy." campaign, 1249–1252
  Virgin Atlantic Airways "Go, Jet Set, Go!" campaign, 1757–1760
CRK Advertising, 261–264
Cronin, Jay, 1263
Cronin, Joe, 1636
Crosby, David, 153
Crosby, Stills, and Nash, 153
Cross-promotions. *See* Partnerships and cross-promotions
"Crossing" spot, 1247
Crouching Tiger, Hidden Dragon (film), 275
Crowne Plaza, 731
CRT TVs, 1506
Cruise, Tom, 1860
Cruise lines
  Carnival Corporation "Fun Ships" campaign, 293–296
  Cunard Line "Can You Wait?" campaign, 371–374
  Royal Caribbean "Get Out There" campaign, 1441–1444
"Crush" spot, 1183
Crutchfield, Edward, 1790, 1793
Cruz, Irma, 890
Cruz, Penelope, 350, 351, 352, 1281
Crystal, Billy, 1304
Crystal, Scott, 1668
Crystal Method, 601, 602
CSPI. *See* Center for Science in the Public Interest (CSPI)
CTS, Cadillac, 634–637, *635*
CTTD. *See* Columbia TriStar Television Distribution (CTTD)
Cuarón, Alfonso, 1409, 1411
Cude, Jonathan, 159
Cuffe, Alison, 1384
Cullinan, Joseph "Buckskin," 305
Cumming, Alan, 1235, 1236
Cunard Line Limited, 371–374
Cure, 724, 726
"Curse of the Bambino," 208
"Curse Reversed" ice-cream flavor, 209
Curtis, Benjamin, *404,* 405, 406
Curtis, Hal, 1144, 1147
Curtis, Jamie Lee, 888, 1623, 1624
Cusack, Joan, 447, 449
Custom Cleaner, 1383–1384
"Custom Lures" campaign, 1193–1196
"Cut to Be Noticed" campaign, 1743–1746
Cutter, John, 470
CVS Corporation, 375–378
  drugstore.com, as competitor of, 473
  Walgreen, as competitor of, 1798
Cyan Worlds Inc., 379–382
"CyberSavers" program, 1206
Cyrix, 769, 774
"Czech" spot, 1625
Czerkinsky, Gregory, 1467

D

"Dad, Can I Have Some Money—Tax Day 6" spot, 689
Daffy's, 76
Dahlin, John, 771
Dahlin Smith White, 772
Daiberl, Stefan, 1069
Daily Defense hair care products, 335
The Daily Show (television show), 651
Daimler, Gottlieb, 987
DaimlerChrysler Corp., 383–394, *392*
  "Employee Pricing Plan Plus" campaign, 383–386
  "Engineered to be Great Cars" campaign, 386–389
  Ford, as competitor of, 562–563
  Saturn, as competitor of, 1470–1471
  Volkswagen, as competitor of, 1778, 1785
Dairy Farmers of Ontario, 182
Dairy Management, Inc., 259
Dairy products
  BC Dairy Foundation "Don't Take Your Body for Granted" campaign, 181–185
  California Milk Processor Board "Got Milk?" campaign, 257–260
  Posilac and, 1035–1038
Dale, Jeremy, 1234, 1235
D'Alessandro, David, 825
Dalhoon, Don, 969

Dali, Salvador, 274
Dallas, Eugenia, 33
Dalsey, Adrian, 419
Dalton, Tony, 1677
Daly, John, 566
Daly, Lee Ann, 523
Damon, Johnny, 422
Damon, Matt, 209
"Dan the installer" campaign, 447–448
Dan the Product Guy (character), 1592–1593
"Dance Party" spot, 1550, 1552, 1553
"Dancing Fish" spots, 295
"Dandelion" spot, 1745
Daneyko, Ken, 519
Danforth, William H., 1111, 1113
Dangerfield, Rodney, 664
Daniels, Jeff, 1004
Daniels, Preston, 230
"Dante Hall" spot, 1101
Dante's Peak (film), 1549
Danza, Tony, 975, 976
D'Arcy Masius Benton & Bowles
  Anheuser-Busch "This Bud's for You" campaign, 109, 117
  Cadillac "Break Through" campaign, 634–637
  Norelco "Reflex Action Razor" campaign, 1189–1192
  Whiskas campaign, 934–935
Darden restaurants, Inc., **395–398**
Dare, Virginia, 1201
"Darin'" campaign, 1433–1436, *1434*
DarkGrey, 322
"Dart" spot, 361
Dasani, 1275
Daschle, Tom, 659
Dassler, Adolf (Adi), 19–20, 23–24
Dassler, Horst, 20, 24
Dassler, Rudi, 23–24
"Date" spot, 589, 590
Dave Matthews Band, 1120
Davenport, Lindsay, 1144
Davey, Charles, 921
David Ogilvy Research Award, 260
Davidson, John "J.D.", 577
Davidson Development Inc., **399–402**
Davie-Brown Entertainment, 216–217
Davies, Steve, 1234
Davino, Flavio, 343
Davis, Ann, 1125
Davis, Bob, 917, 918
Davis, Catherine, 1051
Davis, Dale, 167
Davis, Gary, 1427
Davis, Jim, 1124, 1125
Davis, Larry, 856
Davis, Mark, 542
Davis, Marvin, 298
Davis, Mike, 1230
Davis, Miles, 1230
Davis, Paula, 1488, 1489, 1490
Davis, Steve, 706, 708
Davis, Thornetta, 1259
Day, Janet, 852
Dayton, George Draper, 1603
Dayton, Jonathan, 238
Dayton Company, 1599, 1603
Dayton Foundation, 1603
Daz "Cleaner Close" campaign, 1377–1379
DC Comics, 1614
DCA Advertising, 277–279
DDB
  Anheuser-Busch "Real American Heroes/Real Men of Genius" campaign, 124–126
  Anheuser-Busch "Whassup?!" campaign, 127–130
  Dell "Dude, You're Getting a Dell" campaign, 405–406
  Dial "Doesn't That Feel Better" campaign, 436
  Gill Foundation "TurnOut" campaign, 657–660
  Golf GTI commercial, 170
  J.C. Penney "It's All Inside" campaign, 807–810
  McDonald's "I'm Lovin' It" campaign, 964–967
  McDonald's "We Love to See You Smile" campaign, 967–970
  New York State Lottery "If I Had a Million Dollars" campaign, 1127–1130
  OfficeMax "What's Your Thing?" campaign, 1221–1224
  State Farm "True Stories" campaign, 1571–1573
  "Trust the Midas Touch" campaign, 1009–1012
DDB Needham
  Amtrak "Life on Acela" campaign, 1103–1106
  Anheuser-Busch "Frogs" campaign, 109–112
  Anheuser-Busch "I Love You, Man" campaign, 113–116
  "Did Somebody Say McDonald's?" campaign, 961–963
  Discover "Make a Statement" campaign, 1055–1056
  Tabasco "Mosquito" campaign, 979–982
De Beers SA, 443–444
De Luca, Geurrino, 912
De Wit, Michael Dudok, 1697
Dead celebrities, 1439
Dean, Howard, 1037
Dean, James, 883, 1230, 1749
Dean Witter, 1047, 1048, 1051
Deaver, Scott, 212, 213, 214
Debit cards
  MasterCard, 951, 952
  Visa, 84, 951, 1769–1772
DeCecco, Dave, 1290
"Decisions" spot, 388
Decker, Bill, 335
Dedrick, Gregg, 840
Deem, Sandy, 368, 1792
"Deeper" campaign, 16–17
Defense spending, 229–232
DeGeneres, Ellen, 1617
DEKALB Genetics, 1036
Del Rivero Messianu, 962
Del Russo, Mark, 93
Del Taco, 1592
Delaney, Greg, 731
Delaney, Kathy, 1040
Delivery services
  DHL "Competition. Bad for Them. Great for You." campaign, 419–422
  FedEx "Be Absolutely Sure" campaign, 537–541
  FedEx "The Way the World Works" campaign, 547–550
  "Relax, It's FedEx" campaign, 544–547
  United States Postal Service "Fly Like an Eagle" campaign, 1717–1720
  UPS "Moving at the Speed of Business" campaign, 1709–1712
  UPS "What Can Brown Do for You?" campaign, 1713–1716
Dell, Michael, 140, 403, 1091
Dell Inc., **403–406**, *404*
  Apple Computer, as competitor of, 140, 143
  Gateway, as competitor of, 610
  Hewlett-Packard, as competitor of, 722
Della Femina, Fravisano, and Partners, 804
Della Monica, Joe, 962
Delta Air Lines, Inc., **407–417**, *408*
  American Express partnership with, 83
  Northwest Airlines, as competitor of, 1206–1207
  Southwest Airlines, as competitor of, 1537
  United Airlines, as competitor of, 1697

"Delta Marathon" campaign, 411, 415
DeLuca, Fred, 455
"Dennis Miller Ads" campaign, 974–978
Dentyne Ice, 1832
Deodorants and antiperspirants
  Gillette "Anything Else Would Be Uncivilized" campaign, 669–673
  Secret Sparkle "When You're Strong, You Sparkle" campaign, 1401–1403
Department stores
  "Come See the Softer Side of Sears" campaign, 1487–1491
  J.C. Penney "It's All Inside" campaign, 807–810
  Kmart "Joe Boxer Launch" campaign, 847–850
  Kmart "Rosie O'Donnell and Penny Marshall" campaign, 854–858
  "Martha Stewart Everyday" campaign, 850–854
  "Sears. Where Else?" campaign, 1491–1495
  Target "*New Yorker* Magazine Sponsorship" campaign, 1599–1602
  Target "Take Charge of Education" campaign, 1603–1606
Dermar, David, 115
Dershin, Sharon, 156
DeShannon, Jackie, 821
Design & Art Direction Awards
  Honda "Grrr" campaign, 745
  "Nextel. Done." campaign, 1550, 1553
  "Sprint PCS" campaign, 1554, 1556
Designer jeans, 1744
DeSio, Anthony, 919
"Desk" spot, 385
Desmond, Paul, 1178
Desreux, Michele, 295
Desrozier, James, 79
"Destination" campaign, 1228–1231
Destino (film), 274, 275
"Destiny" spot, 202
Destiny's Child, 752
Detroit Lions, 557
Detroit Pistons "Goin' to Work. Every Night." campaign, 1257–1260
Detroit Red Wings, 1258–1259
Detroit Shock, 1259
Detz, Rudy, 262
Deutsch
  California Milk Advisory Board "Happy Cows" campaign, 253–256
  DirecTV "Celebrities Read Fan Mail to DirecTV (Become a DirecTV Fan Now)" campaign, 447–450
  Mitsubishi "Wake Up and Drive" campaign, 1031–1034
  Monster "Today's the Day" campaign, 1040–1042
  Novartis Zelnorm "Tummies" campaign, 1209–1212
  Old Navy "Destination" campaign, 1229–1230
  Old Navy "'70s Retro TV" campaign, 1226–1228
  Snapple "Bottles Personified" campaign, 237–240
Deutsche Post World Net, 419–420, 421
Deutsche Telekom, 1624
"Deviled Egg" spot, 1020
DeVito, Danny, 447, 449, 1302
DeVito/Verdi
  ACLU "Racial Profiling" campaign, 75–78
  "Campaign for Freedom" campaign, 33
Dewar's, 424
Dexter's Laboratory (television show), 1613–1614
DeYoung, William, 312
DHL Holdings (USA), Inc., **419–422**, *420*
  United Parcel Service, as competitor of, 1714–1715
  United States Postal Service, partnership with, 1720
Di Caprio, Leonardo, 294, 1147
Diageo plc, **423–429**
Dial-A-Mattress, **431–434**
Dial-arounds, 975–978
The Dial Corporation, **435–438**, 1383–1384
Diallo, Amadou, 7
Diamond, Lynn, 444
Diamond Foods, Inc., **439–442**, *440*
The Diamond Trading Company, **443–446**
Diana, Princess, 1062
Diaz, Cameron, 446
Dick, Andy, 12
"Dick" campaign, 1021–1024
Dick Clark's New Year's Rockin' Eve (television show), 631, 633, 937, 940
"Did Somebody Say McDonald's?" campaign, 960–964
Diesel, Rudolf, 747
Diesel engine, 747
Dieste, Stephanie, 980, 981
Diet Coke
  Diet Pepsi, as competitor of, 1304–1305
  "Untapped" promotion, 354
  "You Are What You Drink" campaign, 353–357
Diet Debbie doll, 835
Diet Pepsi
  Diet Coke, as competitor of, 353, 355
  "This Is Diet?" campaign, 1303–1305
  "Uh-huh" campaign, 1552
Diet programs. *See* Weight loss
Diet Rite, 240–242
Diet soft drinks. *See* Soft drinks
Dietary supplements, 1329–1332
Dietrich, Marlene, 986, 987
Digital Domain, 242
Digital imaging technology
  Advantix "Take Pictures. Further" campaign, 485
  Canon "85 Second Photo Lab" campaign, 277–280
  Fuji Photo Film "Meet the Greens" campaign, 587–590
  Hewlett-Packard "You + HP" campaign, 723–727
  Kodak "The Best Part of Photography Is the Prints" campaign, 482–485
  Nikon "Mass Market Initiative" campaign, 1159–1162
  Xerox "Keep the Conversation Going, hare the Knowledge" campaign, 1845, 1846
Digital music
  Apple Computer "Silhouette" campaign, 135–138
  Echo, 196
Digital video recorders, 1619–1622
Dilbert, 1568
Dilbert (comic strip), 1576
Dillard's, 1186
Dillon, Nan, 666
Dillon, Thomas, 290
"Dime Lady" campaign, 973, 1547, 1837
"Dime Zone" campaign, 1543–1546, 1547
"Diner" spot, 947, 1096
"Ding Dong" spot, 253, 1605
Dinky (Taco Bell dog), *1594*, 1594–1597
Dinley, Pat, 1190
"Dinner" spot, 103
"Dinosaur" spot, 915

Direct mail advertising
  "AOL Latino" campaign, 65
  AOL "Welcome to the World Wide Wow" campaign, 66–69
  Barclays Global Investors "New School" campaign, 163
  Little Caesar "Talking Pizzas" campaign, 906–907, 909
  Mercedes "Smooth Ride" campaign, 991–992
  Village Voice "Not America's Favorite Paper" campaign, 1755
  Working Assets Long Distance "Direct Marketing" campaign, 1835–1838
"Direct Response TV" campaign, 1721–1724
Direct-to-consumer advertising
  Novartis Zelnorm "Tummies" campaign, 1209–1212
  Paxil "Social Anxiety Disorder" campaign, 665–668
  "The Power of Zyrtec" campaign, 1311–1314
  prescription drugs, 1461, 1462, 1464
  Prozac print campaign, 505–508
  "Viagra Launch" campaign, 1325–1328
"Director" spot, 276
Directors Guild of America Awards, 498
DirecTV Group, Inc., 447–450
Dirks, Robert, 729, 731
Dirt Devil
  "Darin'" campaign, 1433–1436, *1434*
  "Fred Astaire" campaign, 1437–1440
The Dirty Dozen (film), 1661
"Dirty Dozen on Ice" spot, 1661, 1662
Discover card "Make a Statement" campaign, 1053–1056
"Discover the Better Taste of Progresso" campaign, 270
Discovery Communications, Inc., 451–453
  drugstore.com, alliance with, 473
  Game Show Network, as competitor of, 593
  Public Broadcasting Service, as competitor of, 1411
Discovery Health Media, 473
Dish Network, 448
Disney, Walt, 274
Disney Channel, 1664
Disposable diapers, 1380–1382
Distilled spirits
  "Absolut Director" campaign, 1729–1733
  "Absolut Print" campaign, 1733–1737
  Glenfiddich "Single Malt" campaign, 683–686
  Johnnie Walker "Keep Walking" campaign, 423–426
  Stolichnaya "Russian Art" campaign, 1705–1708
Ditka, Mike, 973, 1327
DiVencenzo, Joseph T., 1106
Diveny, Larry, 1323
"Diver" spot, 1573
Diversity, 1628
Dixie Chicks, 752, 1217
Dixon, Chris, 1677
DMB&B
  Allegra "Spirit of Freedom" campaign, 1461–1464
  Cadillac "The Caddy That Zigs" campaign, 639–641
DMs. *See* Dr. Martens Airwair USA LLC
"Do Geese See God" (film), 60, 61
"Do It Once. Do It Right." campaign, 1683–1686
Do-it-yourself digital-photo kiosks, 483, 484
"Do More" campaign, 81, 82–86, 86–89, 951
"Do the Dew" campaign, 1268, 1270–1274
"Do What Tastes Right" campaign, 221
"Do You Have a Honda?" campaign, 742
"Do You Know Me?" campaign, 83, 84, 87
"Do you smell smoke" tagline, 250
"Do you speak Fuji?" tagline, 589
"Do You Yahoo!?" campaign, 917, 1849–1853, *1850, 1851*
Dobalo, Laurel, 314
Dobson, James, 658
Doc Martens. *See* Dr. Martens Airwair USA LLC
Dockers, 603
Doctor's Associates Inc., 455–458
"Doctors" spot, 883, 884, 885
"Doesn't Lose Suction" campaign, 475–478
"Doesn't That Feel Better" campaign, 436
"Dog and Cat" spot, 1362
Dog Chow, 1111–1114
"Dog Door" spot, *1558*, 1560
"Dog" spot, 1643
"Dog Trilogy" spot, 952
"Dog Walker" spot, *182*, 184
Dogbert, 1214
"Doggie Mind Control" spot, 1173
"Doggie" spot, 560
"Dogs love trucks" tagline, 1173
Dole, Bob
  "The Joy of Pepsi" campaign, 1280, 1281, 1282
  Purina Dog Chow Search for America's Most Incredible Dog, 1114
  "Viagra Launch" campaign, 1325–1328
  Visa Check Card "Works Like a Check" campaign, 951, 1769, 1770, 1771
Dollar Thrifty Automotive Group, 213
Dolls
  Bunny People dolls, 770
  Diet Debbie, 835
  "Rosie O'Doll," 856
Domain name registration, 675–678
Domino's
  Little Caesar, as competitor of, 898, 899, 902, 904–905, 907–908
  Pizza Hut, as competitor of, 1347
"Don" spot, 735
Donaghy, Mary Ann, 64
Dondero, Rob, 873
Doner
  La-Z-Boy "The New Look of Comfort" campaign, 875–878
  Serta "Counting Sheep" campaign, 1501–1503
  Six Flags "It's Playtime" campaign, 1517–1520
Donlay, Chris, 738
The Donnas, 1403
Donny & Marie (television show), 1605
Donohue, Marty, 48, 50
Donohue, Sean, 1704
Donovan, Carrie, 1226, 1228, 1230
Donovan, John, 1123
Donovan, Landon, 1144
"Don't Fence Me In" spot, 986
"Don't Leave Home Without It" campaign, 87
"Don't Mess with Dinner" campaign, 204
"Don't Take Your Body for Granted" campaign, 181–185
Doom (computer game), 381
"Doorstep Challenge" campaign, 1377
"Doorstep" spot, 1183
"Doorway" spot, 1186

Doris Duke Charitable Foundation, 102
Doritos, 583–586
Doston, Robert, 1625
Doswell, Raymond, 1108
"Doublemint Twins" campaign, 1831
DoubleShot "Bring on the Day" campaign, 1197–1200
"Doug" spot, 550
"Doughnut" spot, 1020
Douglass, John W., 231
Dove
  "Campaign for Real Beauty" campaign, 1679–1683, *1680*
  Dial, as competitor of, 436
  "Dove Days" promotion, 1860
  Dove Self-Esteem Fund, 1682
  Secret Sparkle, as competitor of, 1402
Dr. Dre, 1022
Dr. Martens Airwair USA LLC, **459–462**
Dr Pepper/Seven Up, Inc., **463–466**
  lemon-lime beverage competition, 1290
  Pepsi, as competitor of, 1282, 1291
  Pepsi Vanilla, as competitor of, 1284
  Sprite, as competitor of, 345, 348
Drako, Dean, 323
"Dream Garage" spot, 1172
"Dream Team," 1133, 1142
"Dreams found faster" tagline, 283
"Dreams/Yume No Chikara" spot, 742, 743
Drees, Stephen, 1055
Drescher, Fran, 1226, 1345, 1348
"Dressed for Dinner" spot, 1861
Drexler, Mickey, 602, 1229
Drexler, Millard, 596, 605, 607
Dreyer, William, 1121
Dreyer's Grand Ice Cream Holdings, Inc., **467–470**, 1119
Dreyfuss, Richard, 142, 143, 774
Driggs, Steve, 327
"Drink More Water" campaign, 1274–1277
"Drink Up" spot, 1274, 1276
"Drinking 101" piece, 12
"The Drive/Revised" spot, 1136
"Drive to Victory" spot, 1742
Driver, Minnie, 61
"Drivers Wanted" campaign, 170–171, 173, 1776–1779
"Driving American Innovation" campaign, 555–558
"Driving while black." *See* "Racial Profiling" campaign
Drug abuse prevention, 1217–1219
Drug Induced Nutritional Deficiency Program, 1332
drugstore.com, inc., **471–474**
Drugstores
  CVS Corporation "Life to the Fullest" campaign, 375–378
  drugstore.com "A Very Healthy Way to Shop" campaign, 471–474
  Walgreen "Perfect" campaign, 1797–1799
"Drunk Driving's a Serious Crime. Let's Treat It That Way." campaign, 1061–1063
Dry Cleaner's Secret, 1384
Dryel "Habits" campaign, 1382–1385
DSL Internet services, 1473–1476
Dubois, Andre, 1601
"Duck *vs.* Rabbit" spot, 1614
Ducks
  Aflac, 35–37, 38–40
  Cadillac Catera, 639, 640
"Duct Tape" spot, 1020, 1455
"Dude, You're Getting a Dell" campaign, 403–406, *404*
Dudrek, Tom, 111
"Dueling Disorders" spot, 522
Duff, Hillary, 652
Dufour, Gérard, 1335, 1336
Duhamel, Josh, 600
Dukakis, Michael, 76
Dumars, Joe, 1258, 1259
Dun, Andrew, 396
Duncan, Tim, 23, 346, 1095, 1100
Dundore, Bruce, 246
Dunkin' Donuts
  "Fred the baker" campaign, 48
  "Just the Thing" campaign, 49–50
  "Loosen Up a Little" campaign, 47–50
Dunlap, Angela, 973
Dunlap, Bill, 856
Dunlap, John, III, 641
Dunlop, Kerry, 1061
Dupont, Stephen, 1355
Dupri, Jermaine, 560
Duracell, 510
Durant, William, 631
Durex Consumer Products, 313, 315
Dusenberry, Philip B., 32
DustBuster, 1436
Duval, David, 566
Duvall, Robert, 447, 448
DVDs
  MINI Cooper "Counterfeit" campaign, 171
  TV Guide, 1668
Dweck, Michael, 431, 433, 434
Dweck & Campbell, 431–434
"Dye Hard Snapple Tour," 239
Dylan, Bob, 142Einstein, Albert
Dyson, James, 475, 476, 477
Dyson Ltd., **475–478**

E

E. Morris Communications, 1673
E-commerce
  Amazon.com "Amazon Theater" campaign, 59–62
  drugstore.com "A Very Healthy Way to Shop" campaign, 471–474
  "E-Business" campaign, 792
  IBM "Can You See It?" campaign, 785–788
  IBM "E-Business" campaign, 788–791
  IBM "Gizmo" campaign, 791–794
  Lycos store, 918
  Nordstrom "Make Room for Shoes" campaign, 1181–1184
"E-Ticket" campaign, 1205–1208
Earhart, Amelia, 10, 55
"Early A.M." campaign, 549
"Early Intervention Youth" campaign, 1217–1219
Earnhardt, Dale, Jr., 839, 841, 1095
"Earth Wash" concept, 1750
"Earthquake" spot, 915
Easley, Robert, 1190
Eastman, George, 482, 483, 485, 489
Eastman Kodak Company, **479–491**, *482*
  Fuji Photo Film, as competitor of, 588–589
  Hewlett-Packard, as competitor of, 725
  Nikon, as competitor of, 1164
  Polaroid, as competitor of, 1358, 1361
Eastwood, Clint, 1409
EasyShare system, 483
"Eat fresh" tagline, 457
"Eat Mor Chikin" campaign, 841
"Eat Something" campaign, 203–206
"Eating Good Just Got Great" campaign, 1817–1820
Eatzi's Market and Bakery, 205
Ebaugh, Susan, 1503
eBay Inc., **493–499**, *497*
  Amazon.com, as competitor of, 61
  "Listed on Nasdaq" campaign, 1091
Eberhard Faber, 1458
Eberle, John, 554

Ebert, Roger, 275
Echo, 196
Echo-boomers. *See* Generation Y
"Echo" spot, 250
Eckert, Bob, 863
Eckert, Michael, 1806
Eckstein, David, 1057
Eclipse, Mitsubishi, 1033–1034
"Ecomagination," 625
Edgerly, Albert Wester, 1111
Edgerton, David, 226
eDiets.com, 817
Edison, Thomas, 624
Edmondson-Jones, Gareth, 822
EDS. *See* Electronic Data Systems
Education funding, 229–232
Educational toys
  Fisher-Price "Play. Laugh. Grow." campaign, 953–956
  LeapFrog "Learn Something New Every Day!" campaign, 879–882
Edwards, Karen, 1851, 1852, 1853
Edy, Joseph, 1121
EFFIE Awards
  Accenture "I Am Your Idea" campaign, 18
  adidas "Impossible Is Nothing" campaign, 25
  AirTran "Go. There's Nothing Stopping You" campaign, 45
  "Altoids Gone Sour" campaign, 1827
  American Legacy Foundation "Truth" campaign, 100
  Apple Computer "Silhouette" campaign, 136, 138
  AT&T "Carrot Top" campaign, 147–150
  AT&T "It's All Within Your Reach" campaign, 151, 153
  Barclays Global Investors "New School" campaign, 161, 163
  Binney & Smith "Make Play" campaign, 187, 189
  Blue Cross and Blue Shield "Big Blue Arm" campaign, 1726
  Breathe Right Strips "Back in the Sack" campaign, 337, 340
  Breathe Right Strips "On the Nose" campaign, 338
  California Milk Processor Board "Got Milk?" campaign, 257, 260
  Canon "85 Second Photo Lab" campaign, 277, 279
  CareerBuilder "Time to Move On" campaign, 281–284
  Carl's Jr. "Six Dollar Burger" campaign, 289, 291
  Cheerios "Stories" campaign, 627, 629
  Cisco Systems "The Self-Defending Network" campaign, 321, 324
  Citigroup "Live Richly" campaign, 332
  "Come See the Softer Side of Sears" campaign, 1490
  ConAgra Foods' Feeding Children Better Foundation "Child Hunger" campaign, 365
  Cunard Line "Can You Wait?" campaign, 371, 374
  Davidson Development "Repositioning" campaign, 399, 402
  Daz "Cleaner Close" campaign, 1377, 1379
  Delta Air Lines "The Passenger's Airline" campaign, 414, 416
  Detroit Pistons "Goin' to Work. Every Night." campaign, 1257, 1259, 1260
  Diamond Foods "Emerald Nuts marketing campaign," 439
  Diamond Trading Company "Raise Your Right Hand" campaign, 443, 446
  Diet Rite "Go for Zero" campaign, 242
  DoubleShot "Bring on the Day" campaign, 1197, 1198, 1199
  Dove "Campaign for Real Beauty" campaign, 1683
  Dreyer's Grand Light "Unbelievable" campaign, 467, 470
  drugstore.com "A Very Healthy Way to Shop" campaign, 471, 474
  Dryel "Habits" campaign, 1383, 1385
  Dyson "Doesn't Lose Suction" campaign, 475–478, 477
  Ebay television campaign, 496
  Electronic Data Systems "Cat Herders" campaign, 503
  Febreze "Sharing and Connecting" campaign, 1389, 1390
  FedEx "Absolutely, Positively Overnight" campaign, 540
  Fisher-Price "Play. Laugh. Grow." campaign, 953, 956
  Fisher-Price PowerTouch "Play. Laugh. Grow." campaign, 881
  FootJoy "Sign Boy" campaign, 565, 567
  Foster's "How to Speak Australian" campaign, 569, 572
  Gain "Strange But True" campaign, 1395, 1397
  Gardenburger "Eating Good Just Got Great" campaign, 1820
  General Motors "Looking for Mr. Goodwrench" campaign, 652
  Häagen-Dazs "Made Like No Other" campaign, 1119, 1121
  Hallmark Cards "Sneak a Peak" campaign, 691–695
  Hardee's "Revolution" campaign, 697, 699
  Holiday Inn Express "Stay Smart" campaign, 780, 783
  IBM "E-Business" campaign, 791
  IBM "Gizmo" campaign, 792, 794
  IBM "Linux" campaign, 795, 797
  Jack in the Box "Jack's Back" campaign, 811, 814
  Johnnie Walker "Keep Walking" campaign, 423, 426
  "The Joy of Pepsi" campaign, 1282
  Kellogg "Special K Kick-Start Diet Plan" campaign, 834, 837
  Kodak "The Best Part of Photography Is the Prints" campaign, 482, 484
  Kodak "Tall Tales" campaign, 489, 491
  LeapFrog "Learn Something New Every Day!" campaign, 879, 881, 955
  Lee jeans "Find Your One True Fit" campaign, 1746, 1748
  "Listed on Nasdaq" campaign, 1089, 1091
  MasterCard "Priceless" campaign, 952
  "Mello Yello: It's Smooth" campaign, 1269
  Millennium campaign, 1707
  Miller Lite "Low Carb" campaign, 1452
  Morgan Stanley "At Your Side" campaign, 1050
  Mountain Dew "Code Red" campaign, 1267, 1270
  NASCAR "How Bad Have You Got It?" campaign, 1093, 1096
  "NFL Playoffs" campaign, 1099, 1101
  Nissan "Do You Speak Micra?" campaign, 1167, 1169
  Nissan "Quest Minivan Launch" campaign, 1174, 1176
  Novartis Zelnorm "Tummies" campaign, 1209, 1212
  Orbit gum "No Matter What" campaign, 1831, 1833
  Pampers "Got the Power" campaign, 1380, 1382
  Peace Corps "Life Is Calling. How Far Will You Go?" campaign, 1261–1265

Pepsi Vanilla "The Not-So-Vanilla Vanilla" campaign, 1283, 1286
Piedmont Federal "It's Your Mortgage. Keep It Here." campaign, 1341, 1343–1344
Polaroid "I-Zone/Joycam/Sticky Film Teen" campaign, 1359
Polaroid "See What Develops" campaign, 1362
"Purina Dog Chow Every Day" campaign, 1112
"Rheingold Beer" campaign, 1421, 1424
Rock the Vote "Yes/No Ballot Box" campaign, 1427
Royal Caribbean "Get Out There" campaign, 1441, 1444
SBC Communications "Laurel Lane" campaign, 1475
Schick Intuition "Shaving Made Simple" campaign, 1477–1480, 1479
Scotts Miracle-Gro "Neighbor to Neighbor" campaign, 1486
Seattle SuperSonics "In Your Home" campaign, 168
Secret Sparkle "When You're Strong, You Sparkle" campaign, 1401, 1403
Serta "Counting Sheep" campaign, 1501, 1503
Snickers Marathon bars "The Energy You Crave" campaign, 931, 933
Sprint "Dime Zone" campaign, 1546
Stanley Steemer "Living Brings It In. We Take It Out." campaign, 1557, 1560
Staples "Yeah, We've Got That" campaign, 1569
T-Mobile "Get More" campaign, 1623, 1625
Tampax Pearl "Ingenious Protection for Ingenious Women" campaign, 1386, 1388
Toyota Celica "Get the Feeling" campaign, 1643
Toyota "Fuel for Thought" campaign, 1638, 1640
Toyota Sienna "Kids Rule" campaign, 1644, 1646
Travelocity "Roaming Gnome" campaign, 1651, 1654
Turner Broadcasting System "TBS Very Funny" campaign, 1665
TV Guide "On the Inside" campaign, 1667, 1669
United Airlines "Rising" campaign, 1700
UnitedHealth Group "It Just Makes Sense" campaign, 1725, 1728
"US Open Excitement" campaign, 1721, 1724
Virgin Atlantic Airways "Go, Jet Set, Go!" campaign, 1757, 1759
Virginia Tourism Corporation "Meet Virginia" campaign, 1761, 1763
"Visa. It's Everywhere You Want to Be" campaign, 1765, 1768
Visa Check Card "Works Like a Check" campaign, 1771
Volkswagen "Drivers Wanted" campaign, 1779
Washington Mutual "Fear Not" campaign, 1801, 1803
Xbox "It's Good to Play Together" campaign, 1001, 1003
Yahoo! "Live Billboard Dating" campaign, 1854, 1857
Egger, Brian, 295
eHarmony, 1856
Ehringer, Sean, 19, 21
"85 Second Photo Lab" campaign, 277–280
Einhorn, Eric, 138
Einstein, Albert, 142
Eisen, Rich, 241
Eisner & Associates, Inc., 945–948
"EKG" spot, 1087
El Pollo Loco, 1596
"El Toro" spot, 389, 390, 391
Elder, Lee, 1137
Electric cars, 641–644
Electric shavers, 1189–1192
Electronic Arts (EA), 1497, 1498, 1499
Electronic communications networks (ECNs), 1089, 1090
Electronic Data Systems, 17, **501–504**
"Elevator Fantasy" spot, 883, 885
Elfman, Bodhi, 890
Elfman, Danny, 890
Eli Lilly and Company, **505–508**, 1327
Elias, Jonathan, 1144
Elizabeth II
"Coronation" spot, 3
iPods, 136
Ellen (television show), 1779
Elliott, Chris, 584
Elliott, Gordon, 269–271
Elliott, Missy, 600, 608, 888, 1146
Ellis, Davis W., 52
Email, 1148–1150
"Embarassment" spot, 1388
Emerald Nuts, 439–442, *440*
Emissions, automobile, 94
Emmy Awards
Citibank "Identity Theft Solutions" campaign, 325, 328
"It's Not T.V. It's HBO" campaign, 737, 740
J.C. Penney "It's All Inside" campaign, 809
Levi's "It's Wide Open" campaign, 885
Nike "Move" campaign, 1142, 1144
PBS "Be More" campaign, 1409, 1412
United Airlines "It's Time to Fly" campaign, 1695, 1697
The Emperors of Chocolate: Inside the Secret World of Hershey and Mars (Brenner), 941, 942
"Employee Pricing Plan Plus" campaign, 383–386
Employment web sites
CareerBuilder "Time to Move On" campaign, 281–284
Monster "Today's the Day" campaign, 1039–1042
"Empowering the Internet Generation" campaign, 321–322
Empty Nest (television show), 805
Enderle, Rob, 725
Energizer Holdings, Inc., **509–512**
Energy bars, 931–934
Energy issues, 1509–1512
"The Energy You Crave" campaign, 931–934
Engelbart, Douglas C., 913
English, David, 106
Ennis, Tom, 437
Enos, Joe, 1228
Enrico, Dottie, 1134
Enrico, Roger, 1278
"Envious Nomads" spot, 441
Environmental issues
Body Shop, 192
Citibank, 330
Clairol Employee Commuter Program, 335
Ford, William "Bill," 557
Ford hybrid cars, 558
General Electric "Ecomagination," 625
General Motors "EV1 Introduction" campaign, 641–645
"Monsanto Image" campaign, 1038
personal watercraft, 1354
Sierra Club "Hybrid Evolution" campaign, 1509–1512
Texaco "A World of Energy" campaign, 306
Wrangler "Earth Wash" concept, 1750
"The Envy" spot, 707
Epica Awards, 745

Episodic advertising
Daz "Cleaner Close" campaign, 1377–1379
Levi's "They Go On" campaign, 890–891
Epperson, Jerry, 756
"Equestrian" spot, 1833
Erbor, Stan, 1433, 1435
Erceg, Michael, 1706
Erhart, Charles, 1325
Erickson, Paul, 973
Erickson, Ryan, 20
Ernst, Mark, 688
ES 300, Lexus, 1646–1649
ESPN, Inc., 513–523
MTV, as competitor of, 1078–1079
PowerAde, partnership with, 342
Rolling Rock, partnership with, 761–762
ESPN NFL 2K5 "Beta-7" campaign, 1497–1500
ESPNews, 513–516
Esrey, William, 1544
"Essentials" campaign, 94
Estates of World Golf Village "Repositioning" campaign, 399–402
Estefan, Gloria, 1281, 1296, 1488
Ethan Allen, 876–877
Etonic Athletic Worldwide, 566
"eToys" spot, 84
E*TRADE Financial Corp., 303, 525–531
Eubanks, Kevin, 849
EURO RSCG DSW Partners, 767–771
Euro RSCG Tatham
ConAgra Foods' Feeding Children Better "Child Hunger" campaign, 363–366
Red Lobster "Life on Land Is Dry" campaign, 395–398
Walgreen "Perfect" campaign, 1797–1799
Eurobest Awards, 3
Euromarket Design, Inc., 533–536
Europe
Club 18-30 "Perspectives" campaign, 1607–1609
"Levi's Type 1 Jeans" campaign, 887
"EV1 Introduction" campaign, 641–645, *642*
Evans, Daryl, 298
Evans, Katherine, 1660
Evans, Romer v., 76
Eveready, 509–512
Everhart, Angie, 149
Evers, Reinier, 158
Eversen, Carol, 149
"Everybody Chill" campaign, 352
"Everyday" campaign, 1471, 1634–1637
Everyday People (song), 1634, 1636
"Everything Fits" spot, 1335
"Everything Is Possible" campaign, 405
"Evolution" spot, 870
Excite
Lycos, as competitor of, 917
MasterCard partnership with, 952
Yahoo!, as competitor of, 1852
"Expanding Possibilities" campaign, 134, 718, 720–723, 1846–1847
Expedia, 1652–1653
"Experiment" spot, 40
Explorer, Ford, 680, 993
Express delivery services
DHL "Competition. Bad for Them. Great for You." campaign, 419–422
FedEx "Be Absolutely Sure" campaign, 537–541
FedEx "The Way the World Works" campaign, 547–550
"Relax, It's FedEx" campaign, 544–547
United States Postal Service "Fly Like an Eagle" campaign, 1717–1720
UPS "Moving at the Speed of Business" campaign, 1709–1712
UPS "What Can Brown Do for You?" campaign, 1713–1716
Extra gum, 234
ExtraCare program, 376
Extreme Carver sandwiches, 203, 204, 205
Extreme sports
athletic footwear manufacturers' campaigns, 1152–1153
Harris, Rob, 1272
Exxon Mobil Corporation, 307
Eye of the Tiger (song), 125, 805, 1197, 1199

F

F-Series trucks, 564
Faber Castell, 188
Fabric sprays, 1388–1391
Fabrics, 923–926
Facial tissue, 843–846
Factor, Davis, 751
"Factory" spot, 322
The Faculty (film), 603
Fadner, Hilary, 1427
Failed products, 1399
Fairchild, Morgan, 1225, *1226*, 1227, 1228
Falk, David, 1131
"Falling in Love Again" spot, 987, 989, 990
Fallon, Pat, 778, 1408
Fallon McElligott
Conseco "Protect/Create Wealth" campaign, 367–370
drugstore.com "A Very Healthy Way to Shop" campaign, 471–474
Electronic Data Systems "Cat Herders" campaign, 501–504
"Holiday Inn Brand Rejuvenation" campaign, 777–780
Holiday Inn campaign, 929
Holiday Inn Express campaign, 929
Holiday Inn Express "Stay Smart" campaign, 780–783
Lee jeans "Cut to Be Noticed" campaign, 1743–1746
Miller Brewing Company "Ads by Dick" campaign, 115
Miller Lite "Miller Time" campaign, 1021–1025
Nikon "Mass Market Initiative" campaign, 1159–1162
"The Nikon School" campaign, 1162–1165
Nordstrom "Make Room for Shoes" campaign, 1181–1184
Nordstrom "Reinvent Yourself" campaign, 1185–1187
Prudential "Be Your Own Rock" campaign, 1405–1408
Purina "Incredible Dogs" campaign, 1111–1114
Time "The World's Most Interesting Magazine" campaign, 1615–1617
United Airlines "Rising" campaign, 1698–1701
"US Open Excitement" campaign, 1721–1724
Fallon Worldwide
"Amazon Theater" campaign, 59–62
BMW "The Hire" campaign, 175–179
Citibank "Identity Theft Solutions" campaign, 325–328
Citigroup "Live Richly" campaign, 329–332
DoubleShot "Bring on the Day" campaign, 1197–1200
Dyson "Doesn't Lose Suction" campaign, 475–478
Electronic Data Systems (EDS) ad, 17
Lee jeans "Find Your One True Fit" campaign, 1746–1747

PBS "Be More" campaign, 1409–1412
"Sony BRAVIA" campaign, 1526–1529
"Ted Launch" campaign, 1701–1704
United Airlines "It's Time to Fly" campaign, 1695–1698
False claims, 688
"Family Dinner" radio spot, 905
"Family Vacations" spot, 680
Fanning, Shawn, 1085, 1086
Fantappie, Giancarlo, 1339
Fantasy sports promotions, 1279
Farley, Chris, 1323
Farley, Jim, 174
"Farmer" spot, 1173
Farrell, Robert, 1755
Farrell, Sean, 1475
Fashion designers, 878
"Fashion Models" spot, 800
"Fast. It's Corporate Policy." campaign, 1249–1252
Fast food restaurants
Carl's Jr. "Six Dollar Burger" campaign, 289–292
Church's Chicken "Full Flavor, Full Pockets, Full Life" campaign, 317–320
"Did Somebody Say McDonald's?" campaign, 960–964
Hardee's "Revolution" campaign, 697–699
Jack in the Box "Jack's Back" campaign, 811–814
KFC "Chicken Capital USA" campaign, 839–842
McDonald's "Campaign 55" campaign, 957–960
McDonald's "I'm Lovin' It" campaign, 964–967
McDonald's "We Love to See You Smile" campaign, 967–970
Quiznos "Baby Bob" campaign, 1413–1415
Subway "Jared Fogle" campaign, 455–458
Taco Bell "Think Outside the Bun" campaign, 1591–1594
Taco Bell "Want Some?" campaign, 1594–1597
Wendy's "Fresh Stuffed Pita" campaign, 1809–1812
Wendy's "Good to Be Square" campaign, 1812–1816
"Fast-Paced World" spot, 538
"Fast-Talking Man" ads, 538, 546
Fat-Free Pringles "Tasting Is Believing" campaign, 1398–1400
Fat Joe, 560
"Father and Son" spot (AT&T), 153
"Father/Son" spot (Mastercard), 949
Faulkner, Mark, 1823
Favat, Pete, 1442
Favre, Brett, 1273
Fawcett, Mark, 1515
FCUK Him and FCUK Her fragrances, 579–582
FDA. *See* Food and Drug Administration (FDA)
"Fear Not" campaign, 1801–1804
Fearing, Judy, 517, 519, 520, 1273
Febreze "Sharing and Connecting" campaign, 1388–1391
Federal Communications Commission, 1410
Federal Open Market Committee Meetings, 163
Federal Trade Commission, 1295
Federated Department Stores, Inc., 1185–1186
Fédération des producteurs de lait du Québec, 183
FedEx Corp., **537–550**, *545*
DHL, as competitor of, 420–421
name change to FedEx, 548
Staples, partnership with, 1568
United Parcel Service, as competitor of, 1711, 1714
FedEx Field, 545
Feeding Children Better Foundation, ConAgra Foods', **363–366**
"Feel All Right" tagline, 240
"Feel comfortable in your own skin" tagline, 1859
Feel 'n Learn Advanced Trainers, 1380–1382
Feiss, Ellen, 140
Feldman, Alan, 1009, 1010, 1012
Felix da Housecat, 1069, 1071
Fellows, John, 420
Feminine hygiene products
"Ingenious Protection for Ingenious Women" campaign, 1385–1388
Kotex feminine pads, 845
Feminism
Calvin Klein "cK be" campaign, 262–263
Nike, accusations of exploitation of women by, 1155
Ferguson, Sarah, 816
Fernandez, Mary Joe, 303
Ferraro, Geraldine, 1303
Ferrell, Will, 140, 887
Ferrero S.p.A., 1826
Ferris, Richard, 1699
Ferroni, Cameron, 1003
"Ferry Boat" spot, 1745
Fertman, Don, 456
Feuerstein, Henry, 923
Feuling, Steven, 849
Fidelity Investments
Charles Schwab, as competitor of, 303
E*TRADE, as competitor of, 530
iShares, as competitor of, 162
Paine Webber, as competitor of, 1676
Fields, Bill, 1252
Fifth Third Bank, 1091
50-Plus Communications Consulting, 1342
Figliulo, Mark, 1494
Fila USA, **551–554**, 1149
File-sharing industry, 1085–1088
Filo, David, 1849, 1850, 1852, 1854
"Fin" spot, 187, 189
Financial Advisers, 161–163
Financial Communications Society Portfolio Awards, 1050
Financial services
Charles Schwab "Smarter Investor" campaign, 301–304
Conseco "Protect/Create Wealth" campaign, 367–370
Discover Brokerage "Tow Truck" campaign, 1056–1059
E*TRADE "Monkey Trilogy" campaign, 525–528
E*TRADE "Why Wouldn't You?" campaign, 528–531
H&R Block "Worried About Bill" campaign, 688
"ING Launch" campaign, 763–766
"It's Your Mortgage. Keep It Here." campaign, 1341–1344
John Hancock "Insurance for the Unexpected. Investments for the Opportunities" campaign (1996), 823–826
Lincoln National "Hello Future" campaign, 893–896
"Listed on Nasdaq" campaign, 1089–1092
Morgan Stanley "At Your Side" campaign, 1047–1050
sports sponsorships, 369
"Thank You, Paine Webber" campaign, 1675–1678
"Financial World" campaign, 1789–1792
Fincher, David, 175
"Find Out" campaign, 195
"Find Your One True Fit" campaign, 1746–1748

Fingerman, Jeremy, 269
Finlandia, 1707
"Finn" the Goldfish, 265–268
Finver, Jody, 156
Fiorina, Carly, 723–726, *724*, 793
FireBlocker mattresses, 1502
"Fired" spot, 163
Firefly, 693
Fireman, Paul, 1417, 1418
Firestone, 680–681
First Boards Award, 503
First Choice, 1609
"First Date" spot, 1052
"First" spot, 543
First Union, 1789–1792, 1793
FIRST USA credit card, 1294
Fischer, Cathryn, 679, 680
"Fish" spot, 1409, 1411
Fishbone, 1370
Fishburne, Laurence, 447, 449
Fisher, Carrie, 1234, 1235
Fisher, Dana, 1130
Fisher, Donald, 605, 608
Fisher, Doris and Don, 595, 598, 601–602, 1225, 1228
Fisher, Eddie, 1234
Fisher, George, 489
Fisher-Price
  "Play. Laugh. Grow." campaign, 953–956
  PowerTouch Learning System, 880–881
Fishing, 1751
Fishing lures, 1193–1196
Fitness centers, 1859–1861
FitzGerald, Niall, 1685
Fitzgerald, Rob, 113, 116
Fitzpatric, Robert, 1083
Five Stairsteps, 1815
527 groups, 1075, 1584–1585
"Flag" spot, 1741
Flaherty, Patrick, 1532
Flake-Wilkerson Market Insights, 880
Flanagan, John, 891
Flanagan, Lawrence, 949
Flanders, Steven, 1087
"Flaps" spot, 327
Flash mobs, 560
Flavored creamers, 861
Fleadh Irish Music Festival, 429
Fleming, Michael, 592
Fletcher, Jim, 1430
Flickinger, Burt, 1121
"Floating Man" spot, 1000
Florida
  Anheuser-Busch "Oh, and Beware of the Penguins" campaign, 122
  antismoking campaign, 249
  "Truth" campaign, 97–100, 1029
Florida Atlantic University, Small Business Development Center, 1214, 1215
Floris, Gus, 884
Floss, Ken, 1507
Fluke, 1785
Flutie, Doug, 209, 976, 977
FLW Outdoors, 932
"Fly Like an Eagle" campaign, 1717–1720
Fly Like an Eagle (song), 1717, 1719, 1720
"Fly" spot, 235
"Fly Trap" spot, 1831, 1833
"Fly Your Own Song" campaign, 410
FMR Corp., 303
Focus on the Family Action, 657, 658
The Fog of War (film), 140, 1454
Fogel, Brad, 1790
Fogle, Jared, 455–458
Foley, Tim, 48
Folger, James A., 1373
Folgers, 861
Food and Drug Administration (FDA)
  advertising guidelines, 1313, 1326
  Advil warning labels, 1840
  dietary supplement claims, 1330
  Lotronex, 1211
  Novartis Zelnorm, 1210
  Posilac, 1036
  prescription drug advertising regulations, 1461
  product health claims, 1293
Food delivery services, 817
Food products
  California Milk Advisory Board "Happy Cows" campaign, 253–256
  Campbell Soup Company "Make It Campbell's Instead" campaign, 268–271
  Cargill
    "Collaborate>Create>Succeed" campaign, 285–288
  Diamond Foods "Emerald Nuts marketing campaign," 439–442
  Dunkin' Donuts "Loosen Up a Little" campaign, 47–50
  Gardenburger "Eating Good Just Got Great" campaign, 1817–1820
  General Mills "Stories" campaign, 627–630
  Lipton Sizzle & Stir "Real Cooking" campaign, 1687–1690
  Pepperidge Farm "Goldfish Crackers" campaign, 265–268
  Perdue "Now Arriving" campaign, 1307–1310
  Tabasco "Mosquito" campaign, 979–982
  Tyson Foods "Powered by Tyson" campaign, 1671–1674
Food Research and Action Center (FRAC), 364
Food safety, 1308–1309
Food Sightings Museum, 1592
Foodmaker, Inc. *See* Jack in the Box, Inc.
Foote Cone & Belding
  Citibank "The City Never Sleeps" campaign, 330
  Dockers "One Leg At a Time" campaign, 603
  Jeep "There's Only One" campaign, 392–394
  KFC "Chicken Capital USA" campaign, 839–842
  Kraft Foods "It's Not Delivery, It's DiGiorno" campaign, 862–866
  Levi's "It's Wide Open" campaign, 885–886
  Levi's "They Go On" campaign, 889–892
  "Quaker-Warms You, Heart and Soul" campaign, 1292–1295
  Snapple "Return of the Snapple Lady" campaign, 1658
  Taco Bell "Think Outside the Bun" campaign, 1591–1594
  United States Postal Service "Fly Like an Eagle" campaign, 1717–1720
FootJoy "Sign Boy" campaign, 565–568
Footwear News, 25
"Footy," 572
"For Every Generation" campaign, 595–598, 599, 600, 1747
Forbes, Malcolm, 702
Forbis, Amanda, 1696, 1697
Ford, Chris, 1621
Ford, Gerald, 1073–1074
Ford, Henry, 555, 559, 561
Ford, Neal, 1642
Ford, Richard, 1366
Ford, William "Bill," Jr., 555, *556*, 557
Ford Motor Company, 555–564
  Chevrolet, as competitor of, 632–633
  Explorer, 680, 993
  General Motors, as competitor of, 643
  Iacocca, Lee, 384

Nissan Quest, collaboration on the, 1175
Saturn, as competitor of, 1471
Taurus, 107, 1033
Toyota, as competitor of, 1642
Foreman, George, 650
Formula One racing, 93
Forschner, Charles, 1587
Forth & Towne, 1227
Fortune Brands, Inc., **565–568**
Foster, Rube, 1107
Foster's Group Limited, **569–573**
Foster's "How to Speak Australian" campaign, *570, 571*
FOTFA. *See* Focus on the Family Action
"Foul Me" spot, 523
Fouladpour, Tony, 1782
"Found" spot, 1223
"Four Out of Five Dentists" campaign, 233–236
Fox, Michael J.
Diet Pepsi campaign, 1303, 1304
Gateway "People Rule" campaign, 609, 611
Pepsi campaign, 1284, 1296
Fox, Robert, 977
Fox Entertainment Group, Inc., **575–578**
Fox Sports Network, 515, 518, 522
"Godaddy.com Super Bowl Commercial" campaign, 675, 677
FRAC (Food Research and Action Center), 364
Fragrances. *See* Cosmetics and fragrances
France, William, Sr., 1093
Franchino, Joey, 48
Francis, Karen, 655
Francis W. Hatch Awards
Dunkin' Donuts "Loosen Up a Little" campaign, 47
"Swiss Army Equipped" campaign, 1590
Franck, Daniel, 1152
Frank, Sidney, 1735
Frankenheimer, John, 60, 175
Frankie J., 560
Franklin, Aretha
Folgers campaign, 1376
National Football League Kickoff festival, 1285
Pepsi "The Joy of Cola" campaign, 1281
Franklin, Rachelle, 1067
Franz, Dennis, 1305
Frappuccino, 1197
Frazee, Emily, 327, 328
Frazee, Harry, 208
"Fred Astaire" campaign, 1437–1440
"Fred the baker" campaign, 48
Frederick Brewing Company, 201–202
Fredo, Peter, 1711
Free trials, 66–69, *67*
Freed, Vicki, 293
"Freedom. Appreciate it. Cherish it. Protect it." tagline, 33
"Freedom Party" campaign, 872
Freeman, Cliff, 577
French, Susan, 566
French Connection Group PLC, **579–582**
Frenette, Charles S., 357
Frequent-flier programs, 83
Freschetta, 864
Fresh Care, 1389
Fresh Start, 1685
Fresh Step, 1116
"Fresh Stuffed Pita" campaign, 1809–1812
"Fresh Television for Women" campaign, 1241–1244
FreshCare, 1383
Frey, Larry, 517
"The Friday Scotch" campaign, 683, 685
Friedman, Eli, 1003
Friestad, Marian, 1581
Frisch, Amy, 1617
Frito-Lay Inc., **583–586**
Diet Pepsi, co-promotion with, 1305
PepsiCo control, 1278
Procter & Gamble, as competitor of, 1399
See also PepsiCo
"Frogs" campaign, 108–112, 117, 539
Frost, Geoffrey, 1066, 1069, 1070, 1071
"Frozen Moment" spot, 1132
Frozen pizza, 862–865
Fry Multimedia, 535
Fudo, Frank, 554
"Fuel for Thought" campaign, 1638–1640
Fuji Photo Film U.S.A., Inc., **587–590**
Kodak, as competitor of, 481, 487, 490
Nikon, as competitor of, 1163
"Full Flavor, Full Pockets, Full Life" campaign, 317–320
Full Sail Brewing Company, 201
Full Voice (magazine), 194
"Fun, Anyone?" campaign, 1523–1526
"Fun Ships" campaign, 293–296
Funicular, Jeff, 335
Funk, Dr. Herbert, 459
Furniture, 875–878
Fuse TV, 137
Fusion Flash Concerts, 560
Fusion "Life in Drive" campaign, 558–561

G

Gable, Clark, 10
Gagnon, Pierre, 1032, 1033, 1034
Gain "Strange But True" campaign, 1395–1397
"Gala Event" spot, *245*, 246, 247
Galant "Wake Up and Drive" campaign, 1031–1034
Galbin, Paul, 1065
Galia, Julia, 94
Gall, Joanne, 1648
Gallagher, Daniel, 1544, 1545
Gallo, Vincent, 262
Gallud, Jerry, 1708
Gamble, James, 1377, 1380, 1398
Game Show Network, **591–594**
Game shows, 217
GameCube, 1003
Gamgort, Bob, 939, 943
Gammons, Peter, 514
Gannon, Laura, 1594–1597
Ganot, Harvey, 1323
Gap Inc., **595–608**
Lee jeans, as competitor of, 1747
Levi's jeans, as competitor of, 887–888
Old Navy, as competitor of, 1230
Sears, as competitor of, 1489
Garbage Pail Kids, 1829
Garbo, Greta, 10
Garcia, Andy, 447, 449
Garcia, Bonnie, 954
Garciaparra, Nomar, 48
Garden-care products, 1481–1486, *1482–1483*
Gardenburger "Eating Good Just Got Great" campaign, 1817–1820
Gardiner, Dave, 229, 231
Garfield, Bob, 539
Garfinkel, Lee, 344, 706, 708
Garland, Dwight, 1567
Garland, Eric, 136–137
Garland, Judy, 1661
"Garlic" spot, 343
Garner, Art, 94
Garner, James, 174, 1358
Garnett, Kevin, 1140

Garr, Jennifer, 588
Garrity, Jim, 1789, 1790, 1793
Garson, Willie, 1664
Gartner, Jim, 770
Gary Garlic (character), 1431
"Gas Station" spot, 86–87, 89
Gates, Bill, 752, 1005, 1007
Gates, Henry Louis, 795
Gateway, Inc., 405, **609–612**
Gatorade
"Origins" campaign, 1286–1289
PowerAde, as competitor of, 342–343
Gault, Stanley, 679
Gay market
"Absolut Print" campaign, 1735
Jesse Ventura "Retaliate in '98" campaign, 1740–1741
United Airlines "Rising" campaign, 1699
Volkswagen "Drivers Wanted" campaign, 1779
"Yard Fitness Center" campaign, 1861
Gay rights, 657–660
"Gay/Straight" spot, 1079
Gayles, Valencia, 1648
Gays and lesbians
A & F Quarterly campaign, 11
Gill Foundation "TurnOut" campaign, 657–660
Guinness ad (unreleased), 428, 429
John Hancock "Insurance for the Unexpected. Investments for the Opportunities" campaign (2000), 826–827, 829
"Gecko" campaign, 613–616, 619
Gecko Motion, 317, 319
GEICO, **613–621**
Allstate, as competitor of, 51, 52
State Farm, as competitor of, 1571, 1572
Geier, P. A., 1433, 1438
Geldenhuys, Kim, 1161
General Electric Co., **623–626**, 1053
General Foods International Coffees "It's How to Unplug" campaign, 859–862
General Mills, Inc., **627–630**
Kellogg Company, as competitor of, 832, 836
Unilever, as competitor of, 1688–1689
General Motors Corporation, **631–656**
Chrysler Group, as competitor of, 384
Ford, as competitor of, 557, 562–563
Honda, as competitor of, 94
Saab Cars USA, Inc., 1445–1446
Volkswagen, as competitor of, 1778
General Nutrition Center, 471, 472
Generation C, 158
"Generation Next" campaign, 259, 1277–1280
Generation To Generation (music CD), 461
Generation X
Anheuser-Busch "Frogs" campaign, 110, 117
Anheuser-Busch "I Love You, Man" campaign, 115
Boston Market "Eat Something" campaign, 204
Burger King "Lunch Break" campaign, 220
Calvin Klein "cK be" campaign, 262
Citigroup "Live Richly" campaign, 330
Diet Coke "You Are What You Drink" campaign, 354
Energizer "Bunny Chasers" campaign, 510
Fisher-Price "Play. Laugh. Grow." campaign, 953, 954, 955, 956
Fisher-Price PowerTouch "Play. Laugh. Grow." campaign, 881
Frito-Lay "The Loudest Taste on Earth" campaign, 584
Gap "Khakis" campaign, 602, 603
Jack in the Box "Jack's Back" campaign, 812
Miller Lite "Miller Time" campaign, 1022
Mountain Dew "Do the Dew" campaign, 1273
Piedmont Federal "It's Your Mortgage. Keep It Here." campaign, 1342
Royal Caribbean "Get Out There" campaign, 1441, 1442
Sprint "Obey Your Thirst" campaign (1998), 344, 345
"Visa. It's Everywhere You Want to Be" campaign, 1766
Visa ads, 84
Volkswagen "Drivers Wanted" campaign, 1777–1778
Volkswagen "New Beetle" campaign, 1785, 1786
Generation Y
Burger King "Lunch Break" campaign, 220
Dr Pepper "This Is the Taste" campaign, 464
Gap "Khakis" campaign, 602, 603
Honda "What About Now?" campaign, 93
Ice Breaker gum, 235
Nike "Skateboarders" campaign, 1151–1152
Snapple "Bottles Personified" campaign, 238
Toyota Scion, 174, 1778
Generic brands, 831
Genesis Award, 1820
Genesis Team, Toyota, 93
Genetically modified foods, 1035, 1036
Gennaro, Mary Jo, 57
Gentle Glide tampons, 1385–1387
Genuine Swiss Army Knives, 1588–1589
George, Eddie, 1095
Georgescu, Peter, 999
Gerald Pines (character), 1827
Gerard de Thame Films, 394
Gerbrandt, Larry, 740
Germany, 964
Gerstner, Louis V., Jr., 788, 789, 798
"Get a piece of the rock" tagline, 1406
"Get More" campaign, 1623–1626
Get on Board, Lil' Children (song), 1523, 1525
"Get Out There" campaign, 1441–1444
"Get the Facts" campaign, 796
"Get the Feeling" campaign, 1641–1643
"Get Tooned" campaign, 1611, 1613
"Getting Better" campaign, 1333–1336
Getting Better (song), 1333
Gevorigian, Yuri, 33
Ghosn, Carlos, 1167–1168, 1175
Giancamilli, Andy, 853
"Giant Antenna" spot, 1551
Giant Caesar pizza, 900–903
Gibbs, Mike, 477
Gibson, Josh, 1107
Gibson, Kirk, 672
Gibson Greetings, Inc., 693
Gier, Randy, 239, 242
Gies, Brian, 221, 222
Gifford, Kathie Lee, 293, 294, 295
"The Gift" spot, 1335
Gilda's Club, 1488
Gill, Tim, 658
Gill Foundation, **657–660**
Gillen, Mary, 1732
Gillespie, Dizzy, 602, 1230
Gillette
"Anything Else Would Be Uncivilized" campaign, 669–673, *670, 671*
Norelco, as competitor of, 1190–1191

Schick, as competitor of, 1316, 1478–1479
Sensor razors, 1315
Gillette, King C., 669
Gillette, Ray, 1055
"Gimme a Light" campaign, 114
Gingrich, Newt, 1836
Giraldi, Bob, 155–156
Girard, François, 1409, 1411
Girl Scouts of America, 1682
"Girl" spot, 103
"Girl's Trend" spot, 849
"Girlwatchers" campaign, 1303
Giuliani, Rudolph, 76, 1348, 1741
Givaudan-Roure, 262
"Gizmo" campaign, 786, 787, 791–794
Gladman, Julie, 1464
Glaser, Milton, 1602
Glasser, Ira, 76
Glastonbury Festival, 460
GlaxoSmithKline plc, **661–668**, 1210–1211, 1324, 1327
"Glee Club" spot, 739
"Glen" spot, 1197, 1199
Glendening, Parris N., 945
Glenfiddich "Single Malt" campaign, 683–686
Glennon Company, 107
"Global Color Vote" promotion, 937, 939–940
Global Gillette, **669–673**
Glowing puck, 577
Glueck, Jeff, 1653
Gnome Liberation Front, 1653
"Go, Jet Set, Go!" campaign, 1757–1760
"Go. There's Nothing Stopping You" campaign, 43–45
"Go Back in Time" campaign, 2
Go Daddy Software, Inc., **675–678**
"Go for Zero" campaign, 240–242
"Go Get It" campaign, 915–918, *916*
God Save the Queen (song), 1759
"Godaddy.com Super Bowl Commercial" campaign, 675–678
Godin, Seth, 136
Godzilla (film), 711
"Goin' to Work. Every Night." campaign, 1257–1260
Gold Label Johnnie Walker, 425
Gold Lion. *See* Lion Awards
Gold Pencil Awards. *See* One Show Awards
"Gold Rush" promotion, 886, 888
Goldberg, Whoopi, 597, 598, 1747
Goldblum, Jeff, 133, 134
Golden, Hyman, 1657
Golden Award of Montreux, 1611, 1614
Golden Books Entertainment, 1605
Golden Kompass Award, 413
Golden Marble Awards, 1614
Golden Pencil Awards. *See* One Show Awards
Goldeneye (film), 986, 989
"Goldfish Crackers" campaign, 265–268, *266*
Goldman, Gary, 178
Goldman, Manny, 354
Goldner, Brian, 954
Goldsmith, Gary, 1532, 1534, 1637
"Goldspot" campaign, 1233–1236
Goldstein, Adam, 295, 1215
Goldstein, Stanley and Sidney, 375
Goldstein, Steve, 884, 885, 890
Golf, Volkswagen, 170, 1169, *1777*
Golf footwear and apparel
FootJoy "Sign Boy" campaign, 565–568
Nike "Hello World" and "I Am Tiger Woods" campaigns, 1134–1137
"Golf Gods" campaign, 567
Golf sponsorship, 108
"Golf" spot, 577, 1153
"Golf Swing" spot, 1136
"Golfing Buddies" spot, 385
"Golf's Not Hard, with Tiger Woods" campaign, 1136
Golin, Steve, 177
Golub, Harvey, 87
Golvin, Charles, 1624
Gomez, 1335
González, Alejandro, 177
González, José, 1528, 1529
"The Good, the Bad, and the Ugly" awards, 1187
"Good Cop, Bad Cop" spot, 276
Good Housekeeping Seal of Approval, 1390
"Good News" campaign, 615, 616–618, 619
"Good to Be Square" campaign, 1812–1816
"Good to the last drop." slogan, 859
Good Will Hunting (film), 735–736
Goodall, Jane, 738, 739
Goodby, Jeff
California Milk Processor Board "Got Milk?" campaign, 258
Diamond Foods "Emerald Nuts marketing campaign," 441
founding of Goodby, Silverstein & Partners, 494
Häagen-Dazs "Made Like No Other" campaign, 1121
Nike "Skateboarders" campaign, 1153
on "Tag" spot, 1147
Goodby, Silverstein & Partners
Anheuser-Busch "Nice Finish" campaign, 108
Anheuser-Busch "Oh, and Beware of the Penguins" campaign, 120–123
California Milk Processor Board "Got Milk?" campaign, 183, 257–260
Diamond Foods "Emerald Nuts marketing campaign," 439–442
Discover card "It Pays to Discover Revisited" campaign, 1050–1053
Dreyer's Grand Light "Unbelievable" campaign, 467–470
Ebay 2004 television campaign, 496–499
eBay "Abbreviated" campaign, 493–496
E*TRADE "Monkey Trilogy" campaign, 525–528
Häagen-Dazs "Made Like No Other" campaign, 1119–1122
Hewlett-Packard "Built By Engineers, Used By Ordinary People" campaign, 719–720
Hewlett-Packard "Expanding Possibilities" campaign, 134, 721–723
Hewlett-Packard "You + HP" campaign, 723–727
Isuzu Axiom "The Call" campaign, 805–806
Nike "What If We Treated All Athletes the Way We Treat Skateboarders?" campaign, 1150–1154
Nike "Women's" campaign, 1156
"On the Wings of Goodyear" campaign, 679–682
Polaroid "See What Develops" campaign, 1360–1363
"Saturn Relaunch" campaign, 1465–1467
SBC Communications "Laurel Lane" campaign, 1473–1476
"TiVo TV Your Way" campaign, 1619–1622
Gooding, Cuba, Jr., 1426
Goodman, John, 449
Goodman, Larry, 514
Goodwin, Leo and Lillian, 620

The Goodyear Tire & Rubber Company, **679–682**
Google
eBay, as competitor of, 494, 497
Yahoo!, as competitor of, 1852
Gorbachev, Mikhail, 540
Gorbachev, Yuri, 1705, 1708
Gordeeva, Ekaterina, 1046
Gordon, Grant, 684
Gordon, Russ, 1062
Gordon, Stephen, 535
Gore, Al, 783
Gore & Associates, 924–925
Gore-Tex, 924–925
Goren, Ed, 576, 577, 578
Gorman, James, 527, 689
Gorme, Eydie, 81
Gossamer Condor (plane), 643
"Got Milk?" campaign, 181–182, 183, 257–260
"Got the Power" campaign, 1380–1382
"Gotta Have My Pops" campaign, 831–834
"Gotta Have Twisted Sweet" campaign, 1827–1830
Gottesman, Blake, 138
Gottfried, Gilbert, 35–37, 38–40
Gottliebas, Ann, 262
Goudge, Dave, 1565
Goulet, Robert, 517, 987
"Grab Your Own Style" campaign, 535
Graf, Gerry, 527
Graham, Heather, 685
Graham, Jamie, 566, 567
Graham, Martha, 144
Graham, Nick, 849
Gramaglia, Jerry, 1549
Grammer, Kelsey, 614, 1648
Grammy Awards, 354
Grams, Rod, 1739
Granato, Cammi, 107
"Grand Canyon" campaign (Little Caesar), 900–903
"Grand Canyon" spot (American Express), 81
Grand CEBA awards, 1575, 1578
Grand Cherokee, 389–391, 392–394, 992–993
Grand Prix Award
Club 18-30 "Perspectives" campaign, 1607, 1609
Dove "Campaign for Real Beauty" campaign, 1683
Nike "Play" campaign, 1145, 1147
Nike "Skateboarders" campaign, 1153
Sony PlayStation 2 "Fun, Anyone?" campaign, 1524
Toyota Celica "Get the Feeling" campaign, 1643
Volkswagen "New Beetle" campaign, 1786
Grand Turismo, 1339–1340
"The Grandfather" spot, 1406
Grano, Joseph J., 1676
Grant & Sons Ltd., **683–686**
"Grant Hill 4" campaign, 551–554
Grasse, Steven, 1019
"Grave" spot, 163
Graves, Leon, 1037
Graves, Michael, 535, 852, 1600, 1604
Graves, Tom, 491
Gray, Dave, 526, 527
Gray, Macy, 137, 1267, 1269
Gray, Mike, 1355
Green, John, 1239
Green, Maurice, 343
Green, Simon, 194
"Green Acres" spot, 1225, 1226
Green Acres (television show), 1225, 1226, 1227
Greenberg, Arnold, 1657
Greenberg, Jack, 958, 965
Greenblatt, Andrew, 230
Greene, Mike, 835
Greenpeace, 1037
Greenspan, Alan, 163
Greenwood, Galen, 981
Greeting cards, 691–694
Greiner, Robin, 1836
Gretemeyer, Janice, 312
Grey Goose, 1731, 1732, 1735
Grey Worldwide
"call to action" campaigns, 171
Fat-Free Pringles "Tasting Is Believing" campaign, 1398–1400
Febreze "Sharing and Connecting" campaign, 1388–1391
Red Lobster, 395–396
Griesser, Matt, 565, 566
Griffey, Ken, Jr., 552
Griffin, Kathy, 1669
Griffiths, James, 1608, 1609
Griggs, Stephen, 460, 461
"Grim Reaper" spot, 369
Grinkov, Sergei, 1046
Grinstein, Gerald, 410
Grossman, Jeff, 974
Grossman, Mike, 506, 508
Grotz, Beth, 651, 652
Ground Zero
California Department of Health "Tobacco Control Section" media campaign, 248
ESPN "The Rick" campaign, 513–516
"JetBlue Launch" campaign, 819–822
Grove, Dr. Andrew S., 768
Grover, Ed, 1767
"Grow" campaign, 331
Growney, Bob, 1067
"Growth" spot, 250
"Grrr" campaign, 745–748, *746*
Grunwald, Mandy, 1741
Gruss, Joe, 870
GSD&M
Advertising Council "Campaign for Freedom" campaign, 31–32
Americans for the Arts "Art. Ask for More" campaign, 101–104
Dial "You're Not As Clean As You Think" campaign, 435–438
Southwest Airlines campaign, 416
Southwest Airlines "Must Be Football Season" campaign, 1535–1538
UnitedHealth Group "It Just Makes Sense" campaign, 1725–1728
GT Bicycles, 1249–1252, 1540
"Guardian Angels" spot, 681
"Guardrail" spot, 53
Guest, Annie, 888
Guest, Christopher, 515, 575
"Guests" spot, 833
"Guidance Counselor" spot, 893, *894*, 896
Guinn, Kenny, 874
Guinness, Arthur, 427
Guinness "Not Everything in Black and White Makes Sense" campaign, 426–429, *427*
Gunbaum, Eric, 137
Gunn, Donald, 1609
Gunshanan, Jim, 1499
"Guppy" spot, *570*, 572
Gupta, Sanjay, 845
"Guru" spot, 843, 845
Gustin, Carl, 483, 489, 490
Guth, Charles, 1281, 1284
Gutierrez, Eric, 658, 659
Gutwillig, Ken, 1023
"Guy's Trend" spot, 849
Gyorgy, Christopher, 1107, 1109
Gyro Worldwide, 683, 685–686

H

H2 blockers, 1322, 1324, 1325
Häagen-Dazs "Made Like No Other" campaign, 1119–1122

Haas, Bob, 889
Haas, Jay and Bill, 567
Haas, Lukas, 607
Haas, Robert, 884
Habitrol, 663
"Habits" campaign, 1382–1385
Hacker, George, 1014
Hacking, 1624
Hacohen, Dean, 1532
Hadlock, Carolyn, 150
Hafitz, Robin, 300
Hagerdon, Horace, 1481, 1484
Haggar Clothing Company, 603
Hagler, Marvin, 672
Haglund, Margaretha, 57
Hahn, Kurt, 1237
Hainer, Herbert, 24
Hair care products
  Clairol "Totally Organic" campaign, 333–336
  Pert Plus "Sink Boy" campaign, 1391–1394
"Haircuts" spot, 739
Hal Riney & Partners
  General Motors "EV1 Introduction" campaign, 641–645
  Saturn campaign, 1465–1466
  Sprint "Monday Nights Free and Clear" campaign, 1549
Hale, Marcia, 1037
Haley, Brad, 698, 811–813
"Half Pipe" spot, 279
"Half" spot, 1177, 1180
"Halftime" spot, 466
Hall, Anthony Michael, 522
Hall, Arsenio, 971, 974
Hall, Bridget, 1277
Hall, Christy, 1536
Hall, Dante, 1101
Hall, David, 1652
Hall, Don, 1002
Hall, Floyd, 850, 851
Hall, Jerry, 1230
Hall, Joyce, 691, 692
Hall, Steve, 212
Hall, Tina, 1149
Hall, Trey, 205, 1414
Hallmark Cards, Inc., **691–695**, *692*
"Hallmark Hall of Fame" series, 692
Halloween, 694
Halo 2 (video game), 1499
Halvoline motor oil, 308
"Hamburger" spot, 1455
Hamill, Dorothy, 667
Hamilton, George, 1689
Hamilton, Linda, 1549
Hamilton, Rhona, 142, 144
Hamilton, Richard, *1258*
Hamlin, Pam, 1442
Hamm, Mia, 1154, 1156, 1289
Hammerquist & Halverson, 1513–1516
Hampton Inn, 929
Hancock, George, 201
"Handlebars" spot, 1793
"Hands" spot, 562, 563
Hanks, Tom, 1661
Hanna-Barbera cartoons, 1611–1613
Hannah, Darryl, 61
Hannen, Geoff, 1251
Hannum, Marshall, 1250
Hanson, Dan, 1004
"Happy Cows" campaign, 253–256, *254*
"Happy Place" spots, 1748
Harbaugh, Jim, 515
"Hard Day" campaign, 1013–1016
Hardee's Food Systems, Inc., **697–699**
Harlan Page Hubbard Lemon Awards, 1294
Harley-Davidson Motor Company, **701–704**, *702*
  Dr. Martens, similarity with, 461
  Victory Motorcycles, as competitor of, 1349, 1350–1351
Harlow, Shalom, 597
Harousseau, Philippe, 1679, 1682
Harper, Ron, 566
Harrelson, Woody, 1426
Harris, Estelle, 1664
Harris, Jon, 1299, 1300, 1302
Harris, Ken, 1058
Harris, Mary Ann, 370
Harris, Rob, 1272
Harrison, Mark, 1203
Harrison Carloss, 459, 461
Harron, Mary, 1732
Hart, Michael, 477
Harteveldt, Henry, 1652
Hartford Wolfpack, 1189, 1190, 1191
Hartin, Gary, 1810
Hartley, Gregg, 553
Hartley, Mariette, 1358
Hartman, A. A. "Ollie," 1271
Hartnack, Richard, 1802
Harton, Gordon, 884, 1744, 1745
Harvick, Kevin, 651
"Has It Changed Your Life Yet?" campaign, 134
Hashagen, Warren, 605, 606, 608
Haskell, Dean T., 1811
Hatch, Orrin, 75
Hatch Awards
  John Hancock "Insurance for the Unexpected. Investments for the Opportunities" campaign, 826
  MADD "Drunk Driving's a Serious Crime. Let's Treat It That Way." campaign, 1063
  Volkswagen Jetta "All Grown Up. Sort Of." campaign, 1773, 1776
"Have a Heart" campaign, 1838
"Have It Your Way" campaign, 219, 220, 223, 226–228, 291
Havers, Nigel, 411
Haviland, Lyndon, 98
Hawk, Tony, 140
Hawkins, Hersey, 552
Hawkins, Sherry, 1642
Hawley, Russ, 1723
Haworth, 1576–1577
Haxan Films, 1507
Hayden, Steve, 790
Hayek, Salma, 597
Hayes, Geoff, 1734
Hayes, John, 79, 81–84
Haysbert, Dennis, 51–53
HBO. *See* Home Box Office, Inc.
Health centers, 1859–1861
Health claims, 1292, 1293
Health insurance. *See* Insurance
Health issues
  Subway "F.R.E.S.H. Steps" campaign, 457
  Walgreens Health Corner, 1798
Health maintenance organizations, 1725–1728
Health Medical Consumer Advertising & Marketing, 1311–1314
Healthy Curiosity (short film), 1827
Heard, David, 1607
Heard, Dennis, 584
Heartbeat (song), 1528
"Heartbeat" spot, 629
"Heat or Food" spot, 363
Heater, Bill, 1369, 1370
Hecker, Gordon, 1481, 1485
Heffernan, Paul, 1124
Hefner, Hugh, 290
Heggie, Janice, 1062
Heidegger, Ian (character), 273, *274*, 275–276
Heim, Scott, 1384
Heimdichner, Brad, 610
Hein, Sheila, 659

Heineken USA Inc., **705–708**, *706*
Foster's, as competitor of, 571
Rolling Rock, as competitor of, 762
Helfant, Adam, 1146
Heller, Jeffrey M., 502
"Hello Future" campaign, 893–896, *894*
"Hello World" campaign, 1134–1138
"Hellooo Federal" tagline, 546
"Help us find our colors" contest, 937, 940
"Helping Hand" spokescharacter, 1689
Hemingway, Ernest
Abercrombie & Fitch, 10, 596, 599
Gap "Who wore khakis?" campaign, 602, 1230
Hemingway, Mariel, 1824
Hemsley, Sherman, 1227, 1230
Henderek, Weston, 1624–1625
Henderson, Alan C., 244
Henderson, Susan, 868
Hendra, Carla, 791, 792
Hendricks, John, 452, 1411
Hendrix, Jimi, 1852
Henin-Hardenne, Justine, 23
Henrich, Emo, 1514
Henson, Jim, 83
Hepburn, Audrey, 1337
Hepburn, Katharine, 10
Herbal Essences, 333–336, 1393
"Heritage" campaign, 1201–1204
Heritage trails program, 1203, 1204
Herman Miller, 1576
Herrera, Lisa, 658, 659
Hershey, Milton S., 709
The Hershey Company, **709–715**
Ice Breaker gum, 235
Mars, as competitor of, 939, 941–942
SmartZone bar, 932–933
"Herta" spot, 721
Heston, Charlton, 113, 115, 124
Heston, William, 1292
Hetteen, Allan, 1353
Hetteen, Edgar, 1353
Hewitt, Dan, 1498
Hewlet, William, 717
Hewlett, Walter, 725
Hewlett, William, 721
Hewlett-Packard Company, 717–727, *721*
Apple Computer, as competitor of, 140
Apple iPod, 136
Dell, as competitor of, 405
IBM, as competitor of, 793
iMac, as competitor of, 134
Xerox, as competitor of, 1846–1847
Hey, Mama (song), 137
Heye & Partner, 220, 964–967
Heyes, John, 1608
Heyworth, Peter, 1708
"Hi" campaign, 1470–1471, 1778, 1785
Hicks, Jeff, 223
Hicks, Scott, 1410, 1412
High-definition cameras, 149
High School Reunion (television show), 48
"Higher Standards" campaign, 1802
Hilbert, Daniel R., 761, 762
Hilbert, Stephen C., 367
Hilfiger, Tommy, 1629, 1630
Hill, Grant
ESPN "This Is SportsCenter" campaign, 518
Fila campaign, 751, 1149
Fila "Grant Hill 4" campaign, 551–554
Orlando Magic, 167
Sprite "Obey Your Thirst" campaign, 344, 346, 347, 465
Hill, Holliday, Connors, Cosmopulous, Inc.
Business Leaders for Sensible Priorities "Move Our Money" campaign, 229–232
Cisco Systems "Empowering the Internet Generation" campaign, 321–322
CVS "Life to the Fullest" campaign, 375–378
Dunkin' Donuts "Loosen Up a Little" campaign, 47–50
John Hancock "Insurance for the Unexpected. Investments for the Opportunities" campaign (1996), 823–826
John Hancock "Insurance for the Unexpected. Investments for the Opportunities" campaign (2000), 826–829
priceline.com "Troubadour" campaign, 1369–1372
Hill, Vada, 1595, 1597
Hillblom, Larry, 419
Hills Bros. Coffee, 861
Hillsman, Bill, 1739, 1741, 1742
Hilton, Chip, 1288
Hilton, Conrad, 730
Hilton, Paris, 698, 1624
Hilton Hotels Corporation, **729–732**
Hines, Gregory, 1055
Hintermeister, Stacy, 896
Hip-hop
Chevrolet "An American Revolution" campaign, 634
Fusion Flash Concerts, 560
Gap "This Is Easy" campaign, 607
Sprite "Obey Your Thirst" campaign (2004), 348
Tommy Hilfiger clothing, 1629
"The Hire" campaign, 175–179, 995
Hirsch, Andy, 989
Hirshberg, Eric, 450, 1033, 1653
Hispanic Americans
Taco Bell "Want Some?" campaign, 1595
in Tommy Hilfiger ads, 1628
Hispanic market
Allstate insurance, 53
"AOL Latino" campaign, 63–66
Chevrolet "An American Revolution" campaign, 632
Dunkin' Donut "Loosen Up a Little" campaign, 48, 49
Fisher-Price "Play. Laugh. Grow." campaign, 954, 955, 956
Ford "Storytelling" campaign, 562
Gain "Strange But True" campaign, 1395–1396
J.C. Penney, 809
McDonald's "Did Somebody Say McDonald's?" campaign, 962
McDonald's "We Love to See You Smile" campaign, 970
Oldsmobile Alero "Start Something" campaign, 653–654, 655
Peace Corps "Life Is Calling. How Far Will You Go?" campaign, 1263
Pizza Hut campaign, 1347
Sears "Todo para ti (Everything for you)" campaign, 1489
Texaco "A World of Energy" campaign, 308
Toyota "A Car to Be Proud of Campaign," 1633
"Trust the Midas Touch" campaign, 1012
Tyson Foods "Powered by Tyson" campaign, 1673
Wachovia "Uncommon Wisdom" campaign, 1793–1794
Hispanic Serving Institutions, 1263
Historically Black Colleges and Universities, 1263
History Channel International, 1–3
"History" spot, 870
Hitler, Adolf, 1367
Hittle, Brad, 870
HIV/AIDS, 1411
Hladecek, Joel, 719

HMS Partners, 293–296
Hoagland, Ralph, 375
"Hockey" spot, 1189, 1190, 1191
Hodge, Lynda, 1668
Hodges, William, 1053, 1055
Hodgetts, Phil, 644
Hoechst, 1313
Hoechst Marion Roussel. *See* Sanofi-Aventis
Hoff, Jason, 872
Hogan, Paul, 570
Hogan, Terry "Hulk," 672
Hogue, Benoit, 576
Holcomb, Jim, 1437, 1439
"Hold Up" spot, 1234
Holiday Inn
  "Brand Rejuvenation" campaign, 777–780
  Hilton Hotels, as competitor of, 731
Holiday Inn Express
  Courtyard by Marriott, as competitor of, 929
  "Stay Smart" campaign, 780–783
"Holiday Magic" spot, 856–857
"Holidays your mother wouldn't like." tagline, 1607
Hollywood Entertainment Corporation, 733–736
Holmes, Katie, 888
Holtkamp, Deborah, 1436
Holubiak, Myron, 508
Holyfield, Evander, 518, 519
Home Box Office, Inc., 737–740, 951
Home Depot, 1494
Home dry cleaning products, 1382–1385
Home furnishings, 755–758
Home meal replacements, 203–206
"Home Movie" spot, 908, 909
Honda, Soichiro, 741
Honda Motor Company, 741–744
  General Motors, as competitor of, 643
  Mitsubishi, as competitor of, 1033
  Nissan, as competitor of, 1168, 1172, 1176
  Oldsmobile, as competitor of, 654
  Piaggio, as competitor of, 1338–1339
  Saturn, as competitor of, 1471
  Toyota, as competitor of, 1632–1633, 1635, 1639, 1641–1642, 1645
  "What About Now?" campaign, 91–95, *92, 93*
Honda UK, 745–748
Honey, Stan, 577
Honored Guest Awards program, 930
Hood ice cream, 208
Hooper's Hooch, 1013, 1016
"Hoops" spot, 1269
Hoover, 476–477
Hoover, Harry, 1202
Hope, Bob, 306
Hopper, Dennis, 447, 449
Horizons line of furniture, 876–877
Horne, Lena, 602
"Hornet's Nest" spot, 1727
Hornsby, Andre, 880
Horowitz, Alexandre, 1189
Horowitz, David, 77
"Horse" spot, 888
Horsfall, Jan Robert, 915–916
Horton, Sherry, 998
Host, Theodore J., 1481, 1484
"Hot and Fresh" campaign, 319
Hot Legs (song), 397
"Hot News for Burger Lovers" campaign, 456
"Hotel" spot, 940, 1762
Hotels
  "Holiday Inn Brand Rejuvenation" campaign, 777–780
  Holiday Inn Express "Stay Smart" campaign, 780–783
  "It Happens At the Hilton" campaign, 729–732
  Marriott International "Never Underestimate the Importance of a Good Night's Rest" campaign, 927–930
HotJobs.com Ltd.
  CareerBuilder Inc., as competitor of, 283
  Monster, as competitor of, 1040–1041
House, Andrew, 1524
"House Party" spot, 237, 239
"Housekeeper" spot, 65
Houseman, John, 1047
Housewares
  Crate & Barrel 1998 print ads campaign, 533–536
  Kmart "Martha Stewart Everyday" campaign, 850–854
Houston Herstek Favat, 249
"How Bad Have You Got It?" campaign, 1093–1097
"How Do You Wear It?" campaign, 598–601
"How to Speak Australian" campaign, 569–573, *570, 571*
"How to Speak 'Footy'" campaign, 572
Howard, Juwan, 346
Howell, Randy, 1708
H&R Block, Inc., **687–690**
Hu, Judy, 624–625
Hubbard, Lyle G., 1817, 1818
Hubbe, Nikolaj, 607
Hubbert, Juergen, 989
Hudler, Scott, 940
Huff Daland Dusters, 411, 414
Huffington, Arianna, 507
Huggies, 1381
Hughes, Marli Brianna, 833
Hughes, Mike, 1609
"Human Achievement" campaign, 303, 1791
Hume, Amy, 836
"Hummer" campaign, 645–648, *646*
Humphrey, Hubert H. "Skip," 1739, 1741
Hunger prevention programs, 363–366
"Hungry? Crunch this" tagline, 941, 942
Hunt, John, 1552
Hunt, Len, 1775
Hunt Adkins, 1205, 1207
"Hunt for 33" contest, 761–762
Hurley, Bill, 990
Hurricane #1, 1785
The Hurricane (film), 275
Hurricane Katrina, 1673
Huschle, Cynthia, 1211
Hutcheson, Tad, 44, 45
Hutchinson, Lisa, 1468
Hutt, Harry, 168
Hutton, Lauren, 597, 1331
Hyatt Hotels, 731
Hybrid cars
  Ford, 556, 558
  Sierra Club "Hybrid Evolution" campaign, 1509–1512
Hyde, Andrea, 581
"Hype" spot, 790

I

"I Am an American" spot, 32
"I Am Tiger Woods" campaign, 1134–1138
"I Am Your Idea" campaign, 15–18
"I Feel Love" spot, 1041
"I Love You, Man" campaign, 112–116, 1023
"I think therefore iMac" tag line, 132
I Will Evolve website, 1512
"I-Zone/Joycam/Sticky Film Teen" campaign, 1357–1360
Iacocca, Lee, 383, 384, 385, 386, 387
Iacocca Foundation, 385
Iams, 935

IBM
  Apple Computer, as competitor of, 143
  "Deeper" campaign, 16–17
  Dell, as competitor of, 405
  Electronic Data Systems, as competitor of, 502
  iMac, as competitor of, 134
Ibuka, Masaru, 1526, 1532
Ibuprofen, 1839–1842
Ice Breaker gum, 235
Ice cream
  Brigham's "Reverse the Curse" campaign, 207–210
  Dreyer's Grand Light "Unbelievable" campaign, 467–470
  Häagen-Dazs "Made Like No Other" campaign, 1119–1122
"Ice Cream Man" spot, 891
Ice-T, 1022
Icehouse Beer campaign, 121
Iceland supermarket chain, 1038
Icon Awards
  Hewlett-Packard "Built By Engineers, Used By Ordinary People" campaign, 720
  Hewlett-Packard "Expanding Possibilities" campaign, 723
  IBM "Can You See It?" campaign, 785, 787
Iconix Brand Group, Inc., **749–753**
"Icons" ads, 425, 426
"I'd like to buy the world a Coke" campaign, 351
Idei, Nobuyuki, 1532, 1533
"Identity Theft Solutions" campaign, 325–328, 332, 1794
IDEO, 1105
iExplore.com, 453
"If I Had a Million Dollars" campaign, 1127–1130
"If You Let Me Play" spot, 1155
"Ignition" spot, 560
IKEA International A/S, **755–758,** *756*
  Crate & Barrel, as competitor of, 535
  La-Z-Boy, as competitor of, 877
Ilitch, Denise, 909
Ilitch, Michael and Marina, 897, 901, 904, 907
Illingworth, Dave, 1636
I'm a Believer (song), 1173
"I'm Lovin' It" campaign, 291, *964,* 964–967
"iMac" campaign, 131–135, *132, 133*
Imada Wong Communications Group Inc., 243
"Image is nothing. Thirst is everything. Obey your thirst." tagline, 344
"Imagination At Work" campaign, 623–626
Immelt, Jeffrey R., 623, 624
Immigrants, 33
"Immigration" spot, 829
"Impala Man" spot, 891
"Impala" spot, 936
Impax Marketing Group, 212
"Impossible Is Nothing" campaign, 23–26
Impotence and smoking, 246, 247
Imus, Don, 1191
"In a World of Technology, People Make the Difference" tag line, 154
"In Case You Missed It" campaign, 1–3
In the Heat of the Night (film), 275
"In Your Home" campaign, 165–168
Iñárritu, 177
InBev USA, **759–762**
"Incredible Dogs" campaign, 1111–1114
"Independence Day" spot, 1774, 1775
Independent Media, 1642–1643
India, 684
"India" spot, 950, 951
Indiana Baseball Hall of Fame, 1109
"Individuals of Style" campaign, 600
Indriago, Carolina, 1347
Industrial Light and Magic, 643, 1461, 1789, 1791
"Industrial Strength Investment Tools" tag line, 162
"Infect Truth" viral kits, 99, 100
Infiniti "Own One and You'll Understand" campaign, 1177–1180
Information technology services, 501–504
ING Groep N.V., **763–766**
Ingels, Marty, 1297
"Ingenious Protection for Ingenious Women" campaign, 1385–1388
Ink, Stephen, 1293
"Ink Cartridge Bingo" spot, 1563, 1564, 1565
InMarketing, Inc., 749–753
Inner Actives, Nike, 1156
"Inner Beast" campaign, 934–937
"Innovation Delivered" tagline, 15, 17
"Innovation" spot, 557–558
Insale awards, 126
Inserts
  "Absolut Print" campaign, 1735
  Borders "This Season, It's the Original Thought That Counts" campaign, 195–198, 197
  Breathe Right Strips "Back in the Sack" campaign, 339
  Chevrolet "An American Revolution" campaign, 634
  cK fragrance strips, 263
  Fuji Photo Film "Meet the Greens" campaign, 590
  General Electric "Ecomagination," 625
  Hewlett-Packard "You + HP" campaign, 723–724, 725–726
  Lincoln National "Hello Future" campaign, 896
"Inside Job" spot, 323
"Inside Microsoft Anthem" spot, 1004
"Instructoart," 1077–1080
"Insult" spot, 620
Insurance
  Aflac, Inc., 35–40
  The Allstate Corporation, 51–54
  Conseco "Protect/Create Wealth" campaign, 367–370
  GEICO "Gecko" campaign, 613–616
  GEICO "Good News" campaign, 616–618
  GEICO "Mini-Campaigns," 618–621
  John Hancock "Insurance for the Unexpected. Investments for the Opportunities" campaign (1996), 823–826
  John Hancock "Insurance for the Unexpected. Investments for the Opportunities" campaign (2000), 826–829
  "MetLife Helps You Make Sense of It All" campaign, 997–1000
  Prudential "Be Your Own Rock" campaign, 1405–1408
  State Farm "True Stories" campaign, 1571–1573
  UnitedHealth Group "It Just Makes Sense" campaign, 1725–1728
"Insurance for the Unexpected. Investments for the Opportunities" campaign (1996), 823–826, 827
"Insurance for the Unexpected. Investments for the Opportunities" campaign (2000), 826–829
Intel Corporation, 144, 767–775
INTELLICAST, 1806–1807
"Intelligence Everywhere" campaign, 1065–1068, 1069
"Intensity Hunter" market, 1198
Interactive advertising
  Nike "Product Assault" campaign, 1147–1150
  Sharp "More to See" campaign, 1507

Intercontinental Hotels Group PLC, 777–783

"Intern" spot, 1568, 1569

International Advertising Festival in Cannes
- American Express "Paris" spot, 82
- Anheuser-Busch "Whassup?!" campaign, 128, 129–130
- Hollywood Video "Welcome to Hollywood" campaign honors, 736
- Honda "Grrr" campaign, 745
- IBM "E-Business" campaign, 791
- IBM "Solutions for a Small Planet" campaign, 800
- IKEA "Unböring" campaign, 755, 758
- "The Joy of Pepsi" campaign, 1282
- Napster "It's Coming Back" campaign, 1085, 1088
- Nike "Play" campaign, 1145, 1147
- Nike "Skateboarders" campaign, 1153
- Sony PlayStation 2 "Fun, Anyone?" campaign, 1524
- Volkswagen "New Beetle" campaign, 1786

International ANDY Awards
- Business Leaders for Sensible Priorities "Move Our Money" campaign, 229
- ConAgra Foods' Feeding Children Better Foundation "Child Hunger" campaign, 365

International Automotive Advertising Awards, 1649

International Business Machines Corp., 785–801

International campaigns
- American Express "Do More" campaign, 84
- Delta Air Lines "On Top of the World" campaign, 413–414
- Dove "Campaign for Real Beauty" campaign, 1681
- Dr Petter "This Is the Taste" campaign, 465
- General Electric "Imagination At Work" campaign, 625
- IBM "Solutions for a Small Planet" campaign, 797–801
- "It Happens At the Hilton" campaign, 732
- McDonald's campaign, 964, 966–967
- Nissan "Do You Speak Micra?" campaign, 1167–1170
- Sharp "More to See" campaign, 1507
- "Sony BRAVIA" campaign, 1526–1529
- Sony PlayStation 2 "Fun, Anyone?" campaign, 1525
- United Airlines "Rising" campaign, 1700

International Coffees ""It's How to Unplug" campaign, 859–862

International Dairy Foods Association, 210

International labor issues, 1134, 1142, 1151, 1155

International Modern Pentathlon, 1124

International Mountain Biking Association, 1541

Internet
- "Absolut Director" campaign, 1729–1733
- adidas "Impossible Is Nothing" campaign, 25, 26
- "Altoids" campaign, 1822
- "Altoids Gone Sour" campaign, 1825, 1827
- Amazon.com, Inc., 59–62
- America Online, Inc., 63–69
- American Express "Seinfeld" campaign, 89
- American Greetings/America Online partnership, 693
- Anheuser-Busch "Oh, and Beware of the Penguins" campaign, 122
- Audi "Art of the Heist" campaign, 157–160
- Barnes & Noble web site, 196
- BC Dairy Foundation "Don't Take Your Body for Granted" campaign, 184
- BMW "The Hire" campaign, 175–179
- Breathe Right Strips "Back in the Sack" campaign, 339
- Budget Rent A Car "Up Your Budget" campaign, 211–214
- Bureau of Engraving and Printing "The New Color of Money" campaign, 217
- cable *vs.* DSL, 1475
- "Campaign for Freedom" website, 33
- captionmachine.com, 1714
- CareerBuilder "Time to Move On" campaign, 281–284
- Cheerios "Stories" campaign, 629
- Church's Chicken "Full Flavor, Full Pockets, Full Life" campaign, 319
- Cisco Systems "The Self-Defending Network" campaign, 321–324
- computer worms, trojans, and viruses, 322
- Crate & Barrel website, 535
- Diamond Foods "Emerald Nuts marketing campaign," 441, 442
- Discover Brokerage "Tow Truck" campaign, 1056–1059
- Discovery Communications "Two Guys" campaign, 451–453
- Discovery.com campaign, 593
- "Do You Yahoo!?" campaign, 1849–1853
- drugstore.com "A Very Healthy Way to Shop" campaign, 471–474
- e-commerce, 1718
- eBay 2004 television campaign, 496–499
- eBay "Abbreviated" campaign, 493–496
- eDiets.com, 817
- *ESPN NFL 2K5* "Beta-7" campaign, 1497–1500
- "ESPNet SportsZone," 514
- E*TRADE "Monkey Trilogy" campaign, 525–528
- E*TRADE "Why Wouldn't You?" campaign, 528–531
- Food Sightings Museum, 1592
- Ford Fusion "Life in Drive" campaign, 559, 560–561
- Game Show Network website, 592
- General Electric "Pen" subcampaign, 625
- "Godaddy.com Super Bowl Commercial" campaign, 675–678
- Hewlett-Packard "Built By Engineers, Used By Ordinary People" campaign, 719–720
- IBM "Can You See It?" campaign, 785–788
- IBM "E-Business" campaign, 788
- IBM "Solutions for a Small Planet" campaign, 797–801
- "iMac" campaign, 133
- "ING Launch" campaign, 765
- "Instructoart," 1079
- Jack in the Box "Jack's Back" campaign, 812
- J.C. Penney "It's All Inside" campaign, 810
- Juicy Fruit "Gotta Have Twisted Sweet" campaign, 1830
- Kinko's, 921
- Kodak "Tall Tales" campaign, 490–491
- Kodak.com, 486
- Levi's "They Go On" campaign, 889, 891
- Lincoln National "Hello Future" campaign, 896
- Lycos "Go Get It" campaign, 915–918
- MasterCard/Excite partnership, 952
- MetLife, 998

Internet, *continued*
MINI Cooper "Counterfeit" campaign, 169–172
MINI Cooper "MINI Robots" campaign, 172–175
Monster "Today's the Day" campaign, 1039–1042
MoveOn.org "Real People" campaign, 1073–1076
Napster "It's Coming Back" campaign, 1085–1088
Nike "Meet the LeBrons" campaign, 1141
Nike "Product Assault" campaign, 1148–1150
Nissan "Do You Speak Micra?" campaign, 1169
Nordstrom "Make Room for Shoes" campaign, 1181–1184
Northwest Airlines "E-Ticket" campaign, 1205–1208
Oldsmobile Alero "Start Something" campaign, 654–656
Oxygen Media, 1241
Peace Corps "Life Is Calling. How Far Will You Go?" campaign, 1264
Pepperidge Farm "Goldfish" web site, 266, 268
Polartec "Forward Fabric" campaign, 925
Procter & Gamble feminine hygiene websites, 1387
Rock the Vote "Yes/No Ballot Box" campaign, 1427
Royal Caribbean "Get Out There" campaign, 1444
SBC Communications "Laurel Lane" campaign, 1473–1476
Secret Sparkle "When You're Strong, You Sparkle" campaign, 1402–1403
Sharp "More to See" campaign, 1507–1508
The Sidekick, 1624
Sierra Club "Hybrid Evolution" campaign, 1511–1512
Sprint PCS, 1554, 1555
Stolichnaya "Russian Art" campaign, 1706, 1707–1708
"Subservient Chicken" campaign, 222–225
Toyota Chinese-language website, 1644
Toyota Sienna "Kids Rule" campaign, 1645
Travelocity "Roaming Gnome" campaign, 1651, 1653–1654
Turner Broadcasting System "TBS Very Funny" campaign, 1664
United States Tennis Association, 1722
Wendy's "Good to Be Square" campaign, 1813, 1815
Xbox Live, 1001–1003
Yahoo! "Live Billboard Dating" campaign, 1854–1857
Internet Explorer, 1005
"Interrogation" spot, 1305
"Interview" spot, 1696, 1697
Intuition "Shaving Made Simple" campaign, 1477–1480
Intuition (song), 1477, 1479
Inventions, 624
Investment companies
Barclays Global Investors "New School" campaign, 161–164
Charles Schwab "Smarter Investor" campaign, 301–304
Discover Brokerage "Tow Truck" campaign, 1056–1059
John Hancock "Insurance for the Unexpected. Investments for the Opportunities" campaign (1996), 823–826
John Hancock "Insurance for the Unexpected. Investments for the Opportunities" campaign (2000), 826–829
Morgan Stanley "At Your Side" campaign, 1047–1050
"Thank You, Paine Webber" campaign, 1675–1678
IPA Advertising Effectiveness awards, 741
iPod, *136*
Ford Fusion "Particle" spot, 560
Hewlett-Packard branded, 726
"Silhouette" campaign, 135–138, 1086–1087
Ireland, Kathy, 1502
"Ireland" spot, 950, 951
Irish stout, 426–429
"Ironic Quotes" spot, 247
Irons, Jeremy, 1648
Irritable Bowel Syndrome, 1209–1212
Isaacson, Walter, 1616–1617
iShares, 161–163
"iShares. This is the new school of investing" tag line, 163
Israel, 584
Isuzu Motors America, Inc., **803–806**
Isuzu Trooper commercials, 563
"It Happens At the Hilton" campaign, 729–732
IT industry. *See* Information technology services
"It Just Makes Sense" campaign, 1725–1728
"It Pays to Discover Revisited" campaign, 1050–1053
"It pays to Discover" tagline, 1050, 1051
"It stirs the soul" tagline, 862
"Italian Woman" spot, 279, 369
"It's a Woman Thing" campaign, 55–58
"It's All About the Beer" campaign, 705–708
"It's All Within Your Reach" campaign, 150–153, 1548
"It's Always Been Survival of the Fittest. Drink Milk." campaign, 183
"It's Coming Back" campaign, 1085–1088
"It's Everywhere You Want to Be" campaign, 84, 951
"It's Good to Play Together" campaign, 1001–1004
"It's Him" spot, 356
"It's How to Unplug" campaign, 859–862
"It's not an ending, it's a beginning." tagline, 763
"It's Not Delivery, It's DiGiorno" campaign, 862–866
"It's Playtime" campaign, 1517–1520
"It's Something Else" campaign, 43, 44
"It's the Cheese" tagline, 253
"It's Time to Drink Beer" campaign, 117–118
"It's Time to Fly" campaign, 1695–1698
"It's What's Inside" campaign, 199–202
"It's Wide Open" campaign, 883–886
"It's Your Mortgage. Keep It Here." campaign, 1341–1344
iTunes
Hewlett-Packard personal computers, 726
iPod "Silhouette" campaign, 137, 138
Motorola partnership with, 1071
Napster, as competitor of, 1086–1087
Iverson, Allen, 1146, 1418

J

J. W. Foster Company, 25
J. Walter Thompson
Citibank campaign, 330
Diamond Trading Company "Raise Your Right Hand" campaign, 443–446
Ford Fusion "Life in Drive" campaign, 558–561
Ford "Storytelling" campaign, 561–564

Jenny Craig "Kirstie Alley" campaign, 815–818
"Kleenex Anti-Viral" campaign, 843–846
Lipton Brisk "That's Brisk, Baby!" campaign, 1298–1303
Lubriderm "See You Later, Alligator" campaign, 1317–1322
Rolaids "Super Fans" campaign, 1322–1325
Schick Intuition "Shaving Made Simple" campaign, 1478–1480
"Schick Tracer FX Ads" campaign, 1315–1317
Sprint "Dime Zone" campaign, 1544–1546
Sprint "Speak Freely on Monday Nights" campaign, 1549
Trident "Four Out of Five Dentists" campaign, 233–236
U.S. Marines campaign, 1263–1264
Wisk "Do It Once. Do It Right." campaign, 1683–1686
Jack in the Box, Inc., **811–814**
"Jackie Collins" spot, 304
Jackobson, Michael, 1399
"Jack's Back" campaign, 811–814
Jack's Pizza, 864
Jackson, Alan, 561
Jackson, Bo, 1139, 1142
Jackson, Janet, 440, 675, 676
Jackson, Jesse, 1134
Jackson, Keith, 1288
Jackson, Michael (Mercedes-Benz executive), 983, 986, 989, 990, 991
Jackson, Michael (performer), 1278, 1281, 1284, 1296
Jackson, Michael (Scotch authority), 684
Jackson, Peter, 1069
Jackson, Reggie, *1300,* 1301
Jackson, Richard J., 251
Jackson, Samuel L., 1817
Jackson, Sheldon, 343
Jacobs, Chris, 1107
Jacobs, Irwin, 1354–1355
Jacobs, Susan, 986
Jacobs, Tony, 241
Jacobs' Pharmacy, 350
Jacobson, Peter, 1135
Jadakiss, 1146
Jaffe, Richard E., 12
Jail House Rock (song), 1302
"Jailbreak" spot, 1087
Jaksich, Nancy and Jerry, 1579–1580
"Jamais sans mon lait" tag line, 183
Jamar, Stacy, 398, 960
James, Harry, 844
James, LeBron, 24, 347–349, 1138–1140, *1139*
James, Rick, 1140
Jameson, Jenna, 12, 137
Jamieson, Paul, 332
Janus, Paul, 1817
Jaoume, Leon, 1235
Japan, 490
"Japanese Surgeons" spot, 800
"Jared Fogle" campaign, 455–458, 813, 814
"Jargon" spot, 1000
Jarmon, Steve, 238
Java software, 786
Jay, John, 1149
Jay-Z, 1418
Jayne, Billy, 149
Jazz, Honda, 1168–1169
J.C. Penney Company, Inc., **807–810,** *808,* 1489, 1493
JC Advertising, 1661
Jean, Wyclef, 1235
Jeans
Gap "This Is Easy" campaign, 605–608
Lee jeans "Cut to Be Noticed" campaign, 1743–1746
Lee jeans "Find Your One True Fit" campaign, 1746–1748
Levi's "It's Wide Open" campaign, 883–886
Levi's "They Go On" campaign, 889–892
"Levi's Type 1 Jeans" campaign, 886–889
Jeep, *392*
Grand Cherokee, 992–993
Hummer, as competitor of, 646, 647
"Jeep" campaign, 389–392
"There's Only One" campaign, 392–394
The Jeffersons (television show), 1301
Jeffries, Michael, 10, 600
Jenkins, Jim, 1552, 1659
Jenner, Bruce, 667
Jenny Craig, Inc., **815–818**
"Jenny McCarthy for Candie's" campaign, 749–753, *750*
Jensen, Jeff, 107
Jensen, Lance, 645, 646, 648, 1781, 1782
Jensen, Mike, 1390
Jeopardy (television show), 299
Jeremy's MicroBatch Ice Creams, 922
Jergens
Lubriderm, as competitor of, 1320
Procter & Gamble, as competitor of, 1402
"Jerry's Guide to the World Wide Web," 1849
"Jesse the Mind" spot, 1742
Jesse Ventura for Governor, **1739–1742**
JetBlue Airways Corporation, **819–822,** *820*
Song Airlines, as competitor of, 408–409
Ted, as competitor of, 1702, 1703
"JetBlue Launch" campaign, 819–822
Jeter, Derek, 1279, 1289
Jetskis, 1352–1356
Jetsons, 1548
Jetta "All Grown Up. Sort Of." campaign, 1773–1776
Jewel, 1479
Jewelry, 443–446
Jewison, Norman, 275
JibJab, 119
"Jingle for Goldfish" campaign, 266
Jingles
"The Best Part of Wakin' Up Is Folgers In Your Cup," 1373–1376
"Have It Your Way," 228
"Pepsi-Cola Hits the Spot," 1284, 1290
Texaco, 306
"JoAnn" spot, 1215
Job sites
CareerBuilder ""Time to Move On" campaign, 281–284
Monster "Today's the Day" campaign, 1039–1042
Jobs, Steve
APPLE "Silhouette" campaign, 136
APPLE "Switchers" campaign, 139, 140
APPLE "Think Different" campaign, 132, 141, 142
"Joe Boxer Launch" campaign, 847–850
Joe Isuzu (character), 803–806
"Joe" spot, 1101
John, Elton, 1548, 1719
John Hancock Financial Services Inc., 107, **823–829**
Johnnie Walker "Keep Walking" campaign, 423–426
Johnson, Allison, 724
Johnson, Betsey, 446, 750
Johnson, Bruce, 339, 340
Johnson, Carole, 672
Johnson, David, 1353

Johnson, Earvin "Magic"
  AIDS awareness, 312
  American Express ads, 84, 85
  American Express campaign, 951
Johnson, Lyndon, 1073–1074
Johnson, Mark, 114
Johnson, Michael, 1273
Johnson, Mike, 115, 1019, 1021, 1024
Johnson, Ted, 47, 48
Johnson & Johnson
  Chesebrough-Pond's, as competitor of, 1692
  Nicotrol, 661–662
  Procter & Gamble, as competitor of, 1381
Johnston, Kristen, 334
Johnston, Paul, 1514
Jonah (chimpanzee), 1580, 1581
Jones, Andy, 567
Jones, James Earl, 155
Jones, John Paul, 636
Jones, Karen, 422
Jones, Marion, 1143
Jones, Orlando, 1282
Jones, Timothy, 364
Jones, Tommy Lee, 1549
Jonze, Spike, 757, 758
Joplin, Janis, 984, 989, 994
Jordan, J. J., 1317, 1684
Jordan, James, 1684
Jordan, McGrath, Case, Taylor, New York, 661–665
Jordan, McGrath, Case & Partners, 763–766
Jordan, Michael
  annual endorsement income, 552
  endorsements, 553
  Gatorade campaign, 343, 1286, 1287, 1288, 1289
  McDonald's campaign, 1552
  MCI campaign, 971, 974, 1837
  National Basketball Association, 1095, 1100–1101
  Nike campaign, 28, 1131–1134, 1139, 1142, 1145
  Rayovac campaign, 511
  Sports Club Company, Inc., 1860
Jordon, J. J., 1302
Jouravlev, Konstantine, 1707
"Journeys" ads, 425
"The Joy of Pepsi" campaign, 1280–1283
JoyCam cameras, 1357–1360
JP Morgan Chase & Co.
  "Amazon Theater" campaign, 59, 61
  Citigroup, as competitor of, 331
Jr. Fire Ridge Parka, 360
Judd, Naomi and Wynonna, 857
Juicy Fruit "Gotta Have Twisted Sweet" campaign, 1827–1830
"Jukka Brothers" campaign, 1077, 1078
Julian, Peter, 21
"Julie" ad, 365
Jung, Andy, 836–837
"Jungle" spot, 120
"Just Do It" campaign, 21, 28, 1139, 1152
"Just for the taste of it" tagline, 353
"Just Screw It" tagline, 749, 752
"Just the Thing" campaign, 49–50

K

Kaehler, Kathy, 1692
Kagan, Jeff, 152, 1626
Kahn, Bette, 535
Kahn, Joseph, 560
Kalember, Patricia, 663
Kamalova, Khurshida, 1707
Kamber, Victor, 76
Kamen, Harry P., 999
Kaminsky, Alex, 516
Kanawa, Kiri Te, 1044
"Kandoo" launch campaign, 1381
Kane, Tim, 156
Kanefsky, Jason, 521
Kansas City, Missouri, 1107–1109
Kansas State University, College of Education, 1108
Kaplan, Dena, 594
Kaplan Thaler, Linda, 36, 38, 335
Kaplan Thaler Group
  Aflac "Broken Leg" campaign, 38–41
  "The Aflac Duck" campaign, 35–38
  Church & Dwight "Trojan Man" campaign, 314
  Herbal Essences account, 335–336
Kar-wai, Wong, 177
Karan, Donna, 984
Karcher, Carl, 289
Karl, George, 166
Karlson, John, 1215, 1565
Karlsson, Linus, 1022
Karros, Eric, 1860, 1861
Karsch, Tom, 1660, 1661
Kasich John, 1741
Katayama, Yutaka, 1171
Katen, Irene, 1770
Katz, Francine, 201
Kaufman, Wendy, 1655–1658
Kay, Woody, 1062, 1063
Kaye, Tony, 426, 823
Kazin, Michael, 1741
Keast, Brodie, 1621
Keebler Sunshine Cheez-It crackers, 267
Keener, Ray, 1250
"Keep Playing" campaign, 341–344
"Keep the Conversation Going, Share the Knowledge" campaign, 1843–1847, *1844, 1845*
"Keep Walking" campaign, 423–426
Keeter, Phil, 1355
Keillor, Garrison, 743, 745, 747
Keister, Paul, 758
Keitel, Harvey, 424
Kellam, Doug, 475
Kelleher, Herb, 1535
Kelleher, John, 1678
Keller, Andrew, 173, 221, 1759
Keller, Casey, 1400
Keller, Kevin, 219
Keller, Mary Ann, 648
Kelley, Brian, 947
Kellogg, Dr. John Harvey, 834
Kellogg Company, **831–837**, *835*
  General Mills, as competitor of, 628
  Keebler Sunshine Cheez-It crackers, 267
Kelly, Albert, 1120
Kelly, Gene, 170
Kelly, Jim, 1712, 1719
Kelly, Paul, 1324
Kelly, R., 1146
Kelly Awards
  "Absolut Print" campaign, 1736
  "Altoids" campaign, 1824
  Apple Computer "Silhouette" campaign, 136, 138
  Citibank "Identity Theft Solutions" campaign, 328
  General Motors "EV1 Introduction" campaign, 644
  Nordstrom "Make Room for Shoes" campaign, 1181
  Polaroid "I-Zone/Joycam/Sticky Film Teen" campaign, 1359
  "Specialized" campaign, 1542
  Volkswagen "New Beetle" campaign, 1786
Kendall, Jason, 1860
Kennedy, John F., 1261–1262
Kennedy, Joseph, 642, 643
Kenneth C. Smith Advertising, 919–922
Kerkorian, Kirk, 384
Kerouac, Jack, 599
Kerry, John, 1073–1076, 1583–1585
Kerstetter, Bob, 1058
Ketchum, John, 1203

Kevin, Kitty, 1822
"Key Party" spot, 1631, 1633
"The Key" spot, 1507
Keyes, Susan, 868
KFC Corp., **839–842**
  Church's Chicken, as competitor of, 318–319
  reimaging campaign, 397
"Khakis" campaign, 601–604
"Kick-Start Diet" campaign, 834–837
"Kids Rule" campaign, 1643–1646
"KidsCenter" spot, 518, 519
Kieschnick, Michael, 1835
Kiker, John, 1701
Kilborn, Craig, 352
Kilcoyne, Jill, 751
Kilduff, Jack, 464
Kilmer, Val, 1161
Kimball, Alayna, 402
Kimball, John E., 197
Kimball Tobacco Company, 55
Kimberly-Clark Corporation, **843–846,** *844,* 1381
Kimble, Victor, 370
Kimmel, Ken, 48
King, Arlene, 719
King, B. B., 713, 1791
King, Dave, 1802
King, Larry, 729
King, Martin Luther, Jr.
  ACLU "Racial Profiling" campaign, 75, 77
  Apple Computer "Think Different" campaign, 144
King, Rick, 1120
King, Rollin, 1535
King & Bear golf course, 400, 401
Kings of Leon, 1775
Kinko's
  Mail Boxes Etc. as competitor of, 921
  "Our Office Is Your Office" campaign, 541–544
Kinks, 724, 726
Kiosks
  do-it-yourself digital-photo kiosks, 483, 484
  General Foods International Coffees "It's How to Unplug" campaign, 860
Kirshenbaum Bond + Partners
  Netscape Navigator campaign, 1006
  Song Airlines "Let Yourself Fly" campaign, 407–410
  "Vespa reintroduction" campaign, 1339
"Kirstie Alley" campaign, 815–818
KISS, 1281
Kissmobile, 714
"Kitchen" spot, 757
Kitty litter, 1114–1117
Klacking, John, 1430–1431
"Kleenex Anti-Viral" campaign, 843–846, *844*
Klein, Calvin, 1629
Klein, Kelly, 597
Klein, Rochelle, 765
Klein, Russ, 220, 221, 222, 223
Kleinman, Ronald E., 1036
Kline, Richard, 313, 314
Kling, Jeff, 1453, 1454
Klug, Jan, 562, 563, 564
Kmart Corp., **847–858,** *851*
  Little Caesar, partnership with, 901
  Sears, acquisition of, 1495
  Sears, as competitor of, 1489
Knabusch, Edward, 875
"Knicks Tickets" spot, 88
Knight, Philip, 1131, 1132, 1138, 1140, 1151
Knight, Wayne, 973
Knives, 1587–1590
Knopfler, Mark, 823, 824
Knowles, Beyoncé
  "The Joy of Pepsi" campaign, 1280, 1281, 1282
  Pepsi Vanilla "The Not-So-Vanilla Vanilla" campaign, 1285
Knox, Dave, 1401
Koch, James, 199
Koch, Jim, 201, 202
Kodak. *See* Eastman Kodak Company
Koehnen, Julie, 1850, 1854, 1855
Koelker, Mike, 889
Koenig, Joe, 107
Koepke, Gary, 1121, 1149
Kogan, Theo, 261
Kohl's, 809
Koivisto, Eric, 790, 1004
Kolodny, Abigail, 1105
Koogle, Timothy, 1853
Koonin, Steven, 1663, 1665
Kopald, Larry, 94
Korey, Kay & Partners, 295
Kornhauser, Henry, 234
Koronis, Bill, 1751
Kosolopov, Alexander, 1707
Kotex, 845, 1387
Kournikova, Anna, 303–304, 527, 1152, 1624
Koval, Robin, 36, 38
Kowloon Wholesale Seafood Company, 811
Kraft, J. L., 862
Kraft, Robert and Kim, 1250
Kraft Foods, Inc., **859–866**
  "Altoids" campaign, 1821–1824
  "Altoids Gone Sour" campaign, 1824–1827
  Balance Bar, 932
  Cartoon Network, partnership with, 1611, 1613
  Unilever, as competitor of, 1688
Kramer, Jill, 723
Kraus, Jeremy, 922
Krauss, Jurgen, 220
Kravitz, Lenny
  Gap "How Do You Wear It?" campaign, 598, 599, 600
  Levi's "They Go On" campaign, 890
Kricfalusi, John, 1041
Krivkovich, Peter, 44
Kroc, Ray, 961, 967
Kroger, Fred, 312
Kroha, Sally, 1292
Kroll, Alex, 1741
Kronmuller, Lisa, 710
Kruger, Barbara, 1082
Krugman, Scott, 933
Krupnick, Elizabeth, 1405–1408
Krutick, Jill, 1355
Kuenheim, Eberhard von, 985
Kuhn, Barbara, 663
Kuhnie, Jay, 388
Kusin, Gary, 542
Kusnetzky, Dan, 795, 796
Kyoto Protocol, 1510, 1511

L

L. L. Cool J., 602
La Agencia de Orcí & Asociados, 298
La Broad, Michael, 121
La-Z-Boy Inc., **875–878**
Labadie, Peter, 507
Labatt USA, **867–870**
  See also InBev USA
Labels
  Advil, 1840
  Rolling Rock 33 mystery, 760, 869
  Samuel Adams beer, 201
"Labels" campaign, 1081–1084
Labor issues
  Nike, 1134, 1142, 1151, 1155
  United Airlines, 1703
  UPS strike, 538–539
Labrador retriever, Lycos, *916,* 918
LaBroad, Michael, 118
Lacey, Katie, 1290

Lachky, Bob
  Anheuser-Busch "Frogs" campaign, 111, 112
  Anheuser-Busch "I Love You, Man" campaign, 115
  Anheuser-Busch "Oh, and Beware of the Penguins" campaign, 121
  Anheuser-Busch "Real American Heroes/Real Men of Genius" campaign, 123, 125, 126
  Anheuser-Busch "Whassup?!" campaign, 128
  "Charlton Heston" spots, 124
LaCivita, Chris, 1585
Lady Lee Riders "Find Your One True Fit" campaign, 1746–1748
Lafavore, Michael, 1667, 1668
Lafayette, Colorado, 1294–1295
LaFontaine, Don, 734, 735
Lagrega, Angelo, 1749
Lahde, Scott, 1040
Lahti, Christine, 413
Lai, Ann, 52
Laimbeer, Bill, 1259
Laird, Trey, 597
Laird + Partners
  Gap "For Every Generation" campaign, 595–598
  Gap "How Do You Wear It?" campaign, 598–601
Lake, Charlene, 1475
"Lake" spot, 1219
Lake Tahoe, Nevada, 1354
Lambatos, Jimmy, 456, 1414
Lambert, Jordan, 1320
Lambie, Jim, 1342
Lambrettas, 461
Lamfrom, Paul and Marie, 359
"Lamp" spot, 755, 757
Lancer, Mitsubishi, 1034
Land, Edwin, 1357, 1360
Land of Point, 382
Land Rover, 680
Landis, Ron, 1720
Landsberg, Steven, 1105
Landsberger, Gidi, 584
Lane, Ken, 250
Langbo, Arnold, 832
Lange, Robert, 921
"Language Tape" spot, 129
Larkins, Sean, 194
Larsen, Jonathan, 1756
Larsen, Mark, 511
Larson, Dave, 1146
Larson, William, 1429
Las Vegas, Nevada, *872*
Las Vegas Convention & Visitors Authority, **871–874**
"Las Vegas—It's anything and everything" campaign, 872
Lasorda, Tommy, 1324
Lasser, Stuart, 1471
"The Last Honest Pizza" campaign, 1429–1432
"Last Minute" spot, 1799
Late Show (television show), 959
Latin America, 1347
"Latin" spot, 466
LaTorre, Lou, 1323
Latrobe Brewing Company, 759–762, 867–870
Lauer, Matt, 1223
"Laughing Mouths" spot, 1525
Launch campaigns
  "Cayenne Launch" campaign, 1365–1368
  First Union "Launch" spot, 1789
  "ING Launch" campaign, 763–766
  "JetBlue Launch" campaign, 819–822
  "Joe Boxer Launch" campaign, 847–850
  "Kandoo," 1381
  Nissan "Quest Minivan Launch" campaign, 1174–1177
  "Sony BRAVIA" campaign, 1526–1529
  "Ted Launch" campaign, 1701–1704
  "Viagra Launch" campaign, 1325–1328
Laundry products
  Daz "Cleaner Close" campaign, 1377–1379
  Dryel "Habits" campaign, 1383–1385
  Gain "Strange But True" campaign, 1395–1397
  Wisk "Do It Once. Do It Right." campaign, 1683–1686
"Laundry Room" spot, 1745
"Laundry Spa" service, 1384
"Laurel Lane" campaign, 1473–1476
Lauterborn, Robert, 625
Lawn care, 1481–1486
Lawner, Ron, 1776
Lawrence, Carol, 860
Lawrence, Steve, 81
Lawson, Roger, 1405
Lawsuits
  Boise Cascade lawsuit against Staples, 1565
  Gillette lawsuit against Norelco, 1191
  Hoeschst lawsuit over Schering-Plough ad, 1463
  MasterCard International's Home Box Office lawsuit, 951
  MetLife, 998
  Microsoft antitrust trial, 1005
  Playtex lawsuits against Procter & Gamble, 1385–1386
  Prudential Insurance Company, 1406
  SABMiller lawsuit over Anheuser-Busch ads, 1450
  "Swiss Army knife" term, 1588
"Lawyer" spot, 617
Lay, Terry, 1745
Laybourne, Geraldine, 1241
Lazare, Lewis, 1602
LCD technology, 1505–1507, 1526–1529
Leagas Delaney
  adidas "Runners, Yeah, We're Different" campaign, 19–22
  adidas "Yankee Fans" campaign, 26–29
League of United Latin American Citizens (LULAC), 1595
"Leak" spot, 1387–1388
Leap Partnership of Chicago, 105–108
LeapFrog Enterprises, Inc., **879–882**, 954–955
Learish, John, 377
"Learn Something New Every Day!" campaign, 879–882, 955
Learning Channel, 451
The Learning Company. *See* Cyan Worlds Inc.
Leary, Denis, 209, 1078
Leatherman, 1588
"Leave It to Beezer" spot, 576
"Leaving Early" spot, 91
Lebda, Doug, 1343
"LeBron" spot, 347, 349
Led Zeppelin, 635, 636–637
"Ledge" spot, 1613, 1614
Lee, Ang, 60, 177
Lee, Dylan, 1063
Lee, Harmon, 603
Lee, Joe R., 398
Lee, Sandra, 271
Lee, Spike
  "Absolut Director" campaign, 1732
  "Knicks Tickets" spot, 88
  Nike "9,000 Shots" campaign, 1131, 1133
  Orange "Goldspot" campaign, 1233, 1235, 1236
  Pizza Hut "Big New Yorker Pizza" campaign, 1345, 1348

Snapple campaign, 1656
Spike DDB, 576
Lee jeans
"Cut to Be Noticed" campaign, 1743–1746
Levi's jeans, as competitor of, 887
Leggett, Dennis, 1226, 1227
Legh, Chris, 1286, 1288
Legislation
National and Community Service trust Act, 1426
National Voter Registration Reform Act, 1426
Leibovitz, Annie, 87
Leikauskas, Darryln, 208, 209, 210
Leikh, Alex, 1703
Leisure, David, 803, 804, 805
Lemon Awards, 1294, 1550
Lemon Ruski, 1706
Lemony Snicket's A Series of Unfortunate Events (movie), 39
LendingTree, 1343
Lennon, John, 729, 730, 1333
Leno, Jay, 209, 702
Lenza, Al, 1208
Leo Burnett
"Altoids" campaign, 1821–1824
"Altoids Gone Sour" campaign, 1824–1827
Altria Group "It's a Woman Thing" campaign, 55–58
"Army of One" campaign, 1263
Binney & Smith "Make Play" campaign, 187–190
Daz "Cleaner Close" campaign, 1377–1379
Delta Air Lines "The Passenger's Airline" campaign, 414–417
Dryel "Habits" campaign, 1383–1385
Fila "Grant Hill 4" campaign, 551–554
Gain "Strange But True" campaign, 1395–1397
Hallmark Cards "Sneak a Peek" campaign, 694
Kellogg "Gotta Have My Pops" campaign, 833–834
Kellogg "Special K Kick-Start Diet Plan" campaign, 834–837
"Marlboro Man" campaign, 99
McDonald's "Campaign 55" campaign, 957–960
Morgan Stanley "At Your Side" campaign, 1047–1050
Nature Made "Trusted By the Ones You Trust" campaign, 1329–1332
Oldsmobile Alero "Start Something" campaign, 652–656
Pert Plus "Sink Boy" campaign, 1391–1394
Polaroid "I-Zone/Joycam/Sticky Film Teen" campaign, 1357–1360
product characters, 1049
Prozac print campaign, 505–508
Secret Sparkle "When You're Strong, You Sparkle" campaign, 1401–1403
Tampax Pearl "Ingenious Protection for Ingenious Women" campaign, 1385–1388
Leonard, Buck, 1107
Leonard, Sugar Ray, 976
Leonhauser, Maria, 1782
Lesbians. *See* Gays and lesbians
Leslie, Lisa, 1154
"Less flower. More power" tagline, 1783
"Let the Dance Begin" tagline, 1325
"Let Yourself Fly" campaign, 407–410
"Let's Motor" tagline, 169
Letterman, David
McDonald's "Campaign 55," 959
on the new twenty dollar bill, 217
Lever Brothers. *See* Unilever PLC
Levi Strauss & Co., **883–892**
Dockers "One Leg At a Time" campaign, 603
Gap, as competitor of, 606
Gap and Old Navy history, 1229, 1230
Lee jeans, as competitor of, 1744, 1747
Levine, Chuck, 1549
Levine, Marty, 388
Levine, Ned, 1020
"Levi's Type 1 Jeans" campaign, 886–889
Levitra, 1327
Levitt, Arthur, 1057
Lewinsky, Monica, 750
Lewis, Richard, 1734, 1735, 1736
Lewnes, Ann, 767
Lexmark, 718–719
Lexus
BMW, as competitor of, 177
Cadillac, as competitor of, 636, 638
Infiniti, as competitor of, 1179
Mercedes, as competitor of, 989, 995
"The Road Is Calling" campaign, 1646–1649
Liberty Bowl, 540
Liberty Tax Service, 688
Lieberman, Joe, 1426
Liebler, Arthur, 1471
Liebman, Bonnie, 1294
Liebman, Joseph, Henry, and Charles, 1421
Liebmann, Wendy, 600
Liewald, Bob, 552
Life Cereal, 833
"Life in Drive" campaign, 558–561
"Life is a journey. Enjoy the Ride" tagline, 1172
"Life Is Calling. How Far Will You Go?" campaign, 1261–1265, *1262*
"Life Is Not a Spectator Sport" campaign, 1445–1447
"Life Is Short, Play Hard" campaign, 25
"Life Is Short, Play More" campaign, 1002
Life (magazine), 1195
"Life on Acela" campaign, 1103–1106, *1104*
"Life on Land Is Dry" campaign, 395–398
"Life Raft" spot, 53
"A Life" spot, 1696
"Life Tastes Good" campaign, 351
"Life to the Fullest" campaign, 375–378
Lifeline, 1837
LifeStyles condoms, 312, 313
Lifetime, 1243
Light, Larry, 966
Lightner, Candy, 1062
"Lights" spot, 250
Lil' Kim, 1226
Lilith Fair, 1692
Lilly, Kristine, 49
The Limited, Inc., 10
Lincoln, 636
Lincoln, Abraham, 424, 895
Lincoln, Robert, 895
Lincoln National Corp., **893–896**
"Linda Lo-Cal" vignette, 836
Lindbergh, Charles, 9–10
Linder, Rolf, 1239
Lindros, Eric, 515
Linens 'n Things, 756–757
Linton, Doug, 1148
"Linux" campaign, 794–797
Lion Awards
adidas "Impossible Is Nothing" campaign, 25
adidas "Yankee Fans" campaign, 27, 29
Anheuser-Busch "Frogs" campaign, 112
Anheuser-Busch "Louie the Lizard" campaign, 119

Lion Awards, ***continued***
- Anheuser-Busch "Real American Heroes/Real Men of Genius" campaign, 126
- Bay, Michael, spots by, 633
- BC Dairy Foundation "Don't Take Your Body for Granted" campaign, 184
- BMW "The Hire" campaign, 178
- Borders "This Season, It's the Original Thought That Counts" campaign, 197
- Burger King campaign, 965
- Burger King "Lunch Break" campaign, 219
- Business Leaders for Sensible Priorities "Move Our Money" campaign, 232
- California Milk Processor Board "Got Milk?" campaign, 257, 260
- Club 18-30 "Perspectives" campaign, 1607
- Conseco "Protect/Create Wealth" campaign, 370
- Dial-A-Mattress "Always Out There" campaign, 434
- eBay "Abbreviated" campaign, 493, 495
- Electronic Data Systems "Cat Herders" campaign, 503
- ESPN "This Is SportsCenter" campaign, 520
- ESPN "Without Sports" campaign, 521, 523
- E*TRADE "Monkey Trilogy" campaign, 525, 528
- Game Show Network "You Know You Know" campaign, 591, 593
- "Gas Station" spot, 86, 89
- Gill Foundation "TurnOut" campaign, 657, 659
- Harley campaign, 704
- Hewlett-Packard "Built By Engineers, Used By Ordinary People" campaign, 720
- Honda "Grrr" campaign, 745
- Honda "The Power of Dreams" campaign, 741, 744
- Jack in the Box "Jack's Back" campaign, 811, 814
- John Hancock "Insurance for the Unexpected. Investments for the Opportunities" campaign, 826
- Levi's "It's Wide Open" campaign, 885
- "Levi's Type 1 Jeans" campaign, 888
- Marriott International "Never Underestimate the Importance of a Good Night's Rest" campaign, 930
- MasterCard "Priceless" campaign, 952
- MINI Cooper "Counterfeit" campaign, 169, 171–172
- Napster "It's Coming Back" campaign, 1085, 1088
- NASCAR "How Bad Have You Got It?" campaign, 1093, 1096
- "Nextel. Done." campaign, 1550, 1553
- "NFL Playoffs" campaign, 1099, 1101
- "NHL on Fox" campaign, 578
- Nike "Move" campaign, 1144
- Nike "Play" campaign, 1145, 1147
- Nordstrom "Make Room for Shoes" campaign, 1181
- Orange "Goldspot" campaign, 1233, 1236
- Reebok "Terry Tate, Office Linebacker" campaign, 1417, 1420
- "Saturn Relaunch" campaign, 1467
- SBC Communications "Laurel Lane" campaign, 1473, 1475
- Schwinn/GT "Fast. It's Corporate Policy." campaign, 1249, 1251
- Sony PlayStation 2 "Fun, Anyone?" campaign, 1524
- Tabasco "Mosquito" campaign, 981
- Toyota Celica "Get the Feeling" campaign, 1641, 1643
- Toyota Corolla "A Car to Be Proud Of" campaign, 1631, 1633
- Turner Classic Movies "31 Days of Oscar" campaign, 1659, 1662
- "Visa. It's Everywhere You Want to Be" campaign, 1768
- Visa Check Card "Works Like a Check" campaign, 1769, 1771
- Washington Mutual "Fear Not" campaign, 1801, 1803
- "Yard Fitness Center" campaign, 1859, 1861

"Lions" spot, 1727
Liotta, Ray, 178, 888
Lippert, Barbara, 26
Lippitt, Scott, 206
Lipson, David, 880
Lipton Brisk "That's Brisk, Baby!" campaign, 1298–1303, *1299, 1300*
Lipton Sizzle & Stir "Real Cooking" campaign, 1687–1690
Lira, Mananita, 74
"Listed on Nasdaq" campaign, 1089–1092
Listerine Antiseptic mouthwash, 1320
Literacy
- Cheerios "Spoonfuls of Stories" project, 628
- Post Cereals partnership with Reach Out and Read program, 628–629
- Target/Golden Books Entertainment partnership, 1605

Lithgow, John, 975, 976, 1055, 1837
Lithia Motors, Inc., 1581
Little, Tony, 618
Little Caesar Enterprises, Inc., **897–910**
Little Children (Perrotta), 267
"Little Fruits" campaign, 237
"Little Girl" ad, 323
Little Richard, 1689
Littlewood, Peter, 937, 939
Liukin, Nastia, 25
"Live Billboard Dating" campaign, 1854–1857
"Live Large" campaign, 1780–1783
"Live Richly" campaign, 325, 326, 327, 328, 329–332, 764, 1794
"Live Your Best Life" tour, 1645
Living and Learning Centres Inc., 204
Living billboard, Delta's, 412
"Living Brings It In. We Take It Out." campaign, 1557–1561, *1558, 1559*
"Living Room" spot, 757
LL Cool J, 607
Lockard, Jamie, 1745
Lockhart, H. Eugene, 80
Loeb, Lisa, 1370
Loeffler Ketchum Mountjoy, 1201–1204
Loft Candy Company, 1282, 1284, 1296
Logan, Judy, 1006
Logical Progression III, 460
Logitech International S.A., **911–914**
Logos
- adidas, *24*
- Burger King, *220*
- Chrysler, 388
- Mercedes, 986, *988*
- Nike swoosh, 28
- Purina "checkerboard," 1113
- "Striding Man," 423, 424, 425, 426
- Target "bull's-eye," 1599, 1601

Lohan, Lindsay, 1624
Lollapalooza, 460
Lombard Brokerage, 1056, 1057
London International Advertising and Design Awards
- MTV "Watch and Learn" campaign, 1080
- "Relax, It's FedEx" campaign, 544
- "Yard Fitness Center" campaign, 1861

The Lone Ranger (radio and television show), 627
Long, Howie, 634

Long, Robert, 1251
Long distance service
  AT&T "Carrot Top" campaign, 147–150
  AT&T "It's All Within Your Reach" campaign, 150–153
  MCI "1-800-COLLECT" campaign, 971–974
  MCI "Dennis Miller Ads" campaign, 974–978
  Sprint "Dime Zone" campaign, 1543–1546
  Sprint "Monday Nights Free and Clear" campaign, 1546–1550
  Working Assets Long Distance "Direct Marketing" campaign, 1835–1838
"Long Time Gone" spot, 153
Longneck bottles, 869–870
"Looking for Mr. Goodwrench" campaign, 648–652, *649*
"Looks Fast" tagline, 1643
"Loosen Up a Little" campaign, 47–50
Loraine, Martin, 170
Lord Group
  Verizon Wireless "Can You Hear Me Now?" campaign, 298
  "Wild Things Are Happening" campaign, 155
L'Oreal's Plenitude, 1320
Loren-Snyder, Barbara, 850
Lorillard, 250
"Lost" spot, 1223
The Lost World: Jurassic Park (film), 959, 989, 993
Lotronex, 1210–1211
Lott, Ronnie, 1619, 1620
Lott, Trent, 212
Lotteries
  Maryland State Lottery "Cash in Hand" campaign, 945–948
  New York State Lottery "If I Had a Million Dollars" campaign, 1127–1130, *1128*
Lotus software, 799
"The Loudest Taste on Earth" campaign, 583–586
Loughlin, John, 1668, 1669
"Louie the Lizard" campaign, 116–120
Louis, Joe, 2, 3
Louis-Dreyfus, Robert, 20, 24, 27
"Louis the Lizard" campaign, 539
"Lounge Chair" spot, 913
Louvre, Nancy, 664
"Love Scene" spot, 275–276
"Love Your Body" campaign, 193
Loverde, Loren, 140
"Low Carb" campaign, 1449–1452
Low carb diets
  Carl's Jr., 291
  Miller Lite "Low Carb" campaign, 1449–1452
  Snickers Marathon Low Carb Lifestyle Energy Bar, 933
Low-fat foods
  Fat-Free Pringles "Tasting Is Believing" campaign, 1398–1400
  Frito-Lay, 584
Low Rider (song), 1173
Lowe & Partners
  "Campaign for Freedom" campaign, 32
  Diet Coke "You Are What You Drink" campaign, 353–357
  Heineken "It's All About the Beer" campaign, 705–708
  Marriott International "Never Underestimate the Importance of a Good Night's Rest" campaign, 927–930
  "Mercedes-Benz Corporate Branding" campaign, 983–987
  Mercedes M-Class "Smooth Ride" campaign, 990–994
  Mercedes "Passion" campaign, 987–990
  Perdue "Now Arriving" campaign, 1307–1310
  Saab "Life Is Not a Spectator Sport" campaign, 1445–1447
  Sony "What's Next?" campaign, 1531–1534
  Sprite "Obey Your Thirst" campaign (1998), 344–347, 464–465
Lowell, Christopher, 1215
Lowery, Vaughn, 847, 848, 849
Lubars, David
  Citibank "Live Richly" campaign, 330
  drugstore.com "A Very Healthy Way to Shop" campaign, 472
  Dyson "Doesn't Lose Suction" campaign, 477
  Electronic Data Systems "Cat Herders" and "Airplane" spots, 503
Lubriderm "See You Later, Alligator" campaign, 1317–1322, *1318*, *1319*
Lucky Dog, 976, 977
Lucky Star (film), 177
Lucky Strike cigarettes, 55
Lucy, John, 797
Ludwig, Saul, 680
Luechtefeld, Monica, 1214
"Luggage" spot, 543
LULAC (League of United Latin American Citizens), 1595
"Lunch Break" campaign, 219–222, 291
Lunden, Joan, 1313
Luscious Jackson, 20
Lush, 460
Lusk, Wyoming, 1006, 1007
"Lust for Life" campaign, 373
Lust for Life (song), 1441, 1443, 1444
LVCVA. *See* Las Vegas Convention & Visitors Authority
Lycos, Inc., **915–918**, *916*, 1852
Lynch, David, 1169
Lynch, Jill, 884
Lynch, Joe, 1478
Lynch, Peter, 1058
Lynch, Tom, 1066
Lynn, Robert, 419
Lyons, Susanne, 1768, 1772
Lyons Lavey Nickel Swift, 1311–1314

M

M-Class SUV, 990–993, *991*
Ma, Yo-Yo, 140, 1044, 1046
Mabius, Eric, 607
Macchiarulo, Lynne, 1478
MacCready, Paul, 643
Macdonald, R. Fulton, 855
MacDonough, Jack, 1022, 1024
MacGowan, Shane, 429
Machida, Katsuhiko, 1505
Mack, Walter, 1284
Mackin, Tom, 1195
MacLaine, Shirley, 951
MacLennan, Moray, 1607
Macleod, Hugh, 213
Macy, William H., 607
"Macy" spot, 1269
Macy's department stores, 94
Mad Dogs and Englishmen, 1753–1756
Madan, Raj, 1794
MADD "Drunk Driving's a Serious Crime. Let's Treat It That Way." campaign, 1061–1063
Madden, John, 463, 464
Madden NFL 2005, 1498
"Made Like No Other" campaign, 1119–1122
Madonna
  adidas apparel, 20
  BMW "The Hire" campaign, 175, 178
  Dr. Martens, 460
  Gap campaign, 600, 888
  Pepsi endorsement, 1278
  youth vote, 1426
Maertens, Dr. Klaus, 459

Magali, 1315, 1316
Magalogs, 9–12, 580–581
Magazines
  Time "The World's Most Interesting Magazine" campaign, 1615–1617
  TV Guide "On the Inside" campaign, 1667–1670
Magerman, Michael, 731
Magic the Dog, 1226, 1228, 1230
"Magician" spot, 1021
Maguire, Tobey, 1147
"Maids" spot, 1762
Mail Boxes Etc., Inc., 539, 542, **919–922**
Mailer, Norman, 1753
"Main Street USA" spot, 33
Major, John, 429
Major League Baseball
  adidas sponsorship of the New York Yankees, 27, 28
  Anheuser-Busch sponsorship, 118
  Aquafina "Drink More Water" campaign, 1274, 1276
  DHL sponsorship, 422
  MasterCard sponsorship, 951
  Pepsi, alliance with, 1277–1278, 1279
  Pepsi participation at the All-Star Fanfest, 1279
  United States Tennis Association, as competitor of, 1722
"Make a Difference" campaign, 314
"Make a Statement" campaign, 1053–1056
"Make It Campbell's Instead" campaign, 268–271
"Make It With MD" campaign, 1533
"Make Life Rewarding" tagline, 86
"Make Play" campaign, 187–190
"Make Room" campaign, 883, 884
"Make Room for Shoes" campaign, 1181–1184, 1185
"Make Up Artist" spot, 1669
"Makeshift" spot, 523
Malden, Karl, 87
Malden Mills Industries, Inc., **923–926**
"The Male Bonding Incident" spot, 707
Maleeny, Tim, 453
Maloney, Dave, 576
"Malternatives," 1013–1016
Mambro, Jamie, 825
Mamorsky, Leo J., 1129
"Man in the Field" spot, 1021
"Man with the Guinness" campaign, 427
Mancuso, Paulanne, 261, 263
Mandela, Nelson, 729, 730
Mangum, Jonathan, 1704
Mann, Michael, 177
Mann, Ron, 1754
"Mannequin" spot, 1470
Manning, Jeff, 258, 260
Manning, Taryn, 597
Mannion, Bill, 1335
Manson, Charles, 75, 77, 685
Mansur, Bernadette, 576
Mantle, Mickey, 1301
Mapes, Tim, 408, 410
MapQuest, 64
Marathon bars "The Energy You Crave" campaign, 931–934
"Marathon" spot, 1474–1475
Marcarelli, Paul, 297, 298, 299
Marchington, Philip, 1653
Marco, Harvey, 1745, 1748
Marcus, Pam, 1229
Marderosian, Karen, 1779
Margeotes/Fertitta & Partners, 1705–1708
Margulies, Sherri, 739
Marineau, Philip, 886, 887, 888
Marino, Dan, 1296
Marino, Mary Ann, 156
Marjoram, Gary, 1003
"Mark" campaign, 777–780, 781
Mark-It, 1458
Markowitz, Michael, 526
Marks, Stephen, 579, 580, 582
Marks-A-Lot, 1458
Marlboro 500 auto race, 663
Marlboro Man, 99
"Marlboro Man" antismoking campaign, 248, 1028–1029
"Marriage Counselor" spot, 572
Marriott International, **927–930**
Mars, Forrest, 937, 939, 940, 941
Mars, Frank, 931, 937, 941
Mars, Inc., **931–943**
  Hershey, as competitor of, 710–711, 713–714
  Purina, as competitor of, 1112–1113
Marsh, Leonard, 1657
Marshall, Penny, 795, 849, 854–857, 1489
"Marsupial" spot, 593
Martha Stewart brand, 847, 848
"Martha Stewart Everyday" campaign, 850–854, *851*, 1489
Martha Stewart Living Omnimedia, 850, 851
Martin, Billy, 1301
Martin, Joe, 662
Martin, Kerri, 173, 174, 1775
Martin, Mark, 1328
Martin, Paul, 1107
Martin Agency
  GEICO "Gecko" campaign, 613–616
  GEICO "Good News" campaign, 616–618
  GEICO "Mini-Campaigns," 618–621
  Negro Leagues Baseball Museum "1998 Print Campaign," 1107–1109
  UPS "What Can Brown Do for You?" campaign, 1713–1716
  Wrangler "Rugged Wear" campaign, 1749–1751
Martin/Williams
  E*TRADE "Why Wouldn't You?" campaign, 528–531
  Lincoln National "Hello Future" campaign, 893–896
  Polaris "Ride the Best" campaign, 1352–1356
  Staples "That Was Easy" campaign, 1214–1215, 1563–1566
  Steelcase "Work Effectiveness" campaign, 1575–1578
  Victory Motorcycles "The New American Motorcycle" campaign, 1349–1352
Martinez, Arthur C., 1487, 1488, 1489
Marting, Merle, 1137
Marx, Louis, Jr., 1587
Maryland State Lottery Agency, **945–948**
Mascots
  Miles Thirst, 347, 348, 349
  Trump, 1041
Mashburn, Jamal, 552
Mason, Bill, 601
"Mason" spot, 721
"Mass Market Initiative" campaign, Nikon, 1159–1162
Massachusetts, 246, 249
MasterCard International, **949–952**, *950*
  American Express, as competitor of, 80, 81, 84, 88, 89
  Discover, as competitor of, 1051–1052, 1054–1055
  Visa, as competitor of, 1767, 1770
Masterfoods USA, 931, 932, 934–937
Mastromonaco, John, 205
Match.com, 1855–1856
Matejczyk, John, 689
Mathieu, Christian, 756
The Matrix Reloaded (film), 636

Matrix, Toyota, 1632
Matsunaka, Stan, 658
Mattel, Inc., **953–956**
Mattes, Richard, 835
Mattresses
Dial-A-Mattress, 431–434
Serta "Counting Sheep" campaign, 1501–1503
Mattus, Reuben, 1119
MaxPlanet Media, 1706, 1707
Maxwell, Jack, 1019
May, Barbara, 1195
May, Kenneth A., 542
May, Peter, 1656
"Maybe It's Your Cooking" campaign, 317
Mayday, Charlie, 2
"Mayday for Marriage" rally, 659
Mayer, Oscar, 862
Mayo, Pat, 751
Mays, Willie, 1107
Mazda
Oldsmobile, as competitor of, 654
Toyota, as competitor of, 1635–3636
Mazza, Mike, 1554
MBI. *See* Millward Brown International
McAnsh, Craig, 1613, 1614
McAteer, Seamus, 1625
McBride, Chuck, 885, 891
McBride, Sandra, 439, 440
McCabe, Evert, 1709
McCadden, Michael, 606
McCaffery, Paisley, 149
McCain, John, 230, 1741
McCammon, Lou "Mack," 1113
McCann-Erickson
California Milk Advisory Board "Milk. It Does a Body Good" campaign, 258
Coca-Cola "Real" campaign, 352
drugstore.com campaign, 471, 472
Gateway "People Rule" campaign, 609–612
Glenfiddich "The Friday Scotch" campaign, 683, 685
MasterCard "Priceless" campaign, 85, 949–952
Microsoft "Where Do You Want to Go Today?" campaign, 1005, 1007
PowerAde "Keep Playing" campaign, 341–344
Rolling Rock "Grab a Rock" campaign, 760–762
Samuel Adams "It's What's Inside" campaign, 199–202
Sharpie "Write Out Loud" campaign, 1457–1459
Xbox "It's Good to Play Together" campaign, 1001–1004
McCarter, Guy, 1410
McCarthy, Jenny, 749–753
McCartney, Paul, 1333, 1766, 1767
McCarvillean, Bridget, 94
McClure, Michael, 995
McConaughey, Matthew, 1261, 1264
McConnaughy Stein Schmidt Brown, 533–536
McCook, Jacqueline, 227
McCormick, Carolyn, 661
McCormick, Fritz, 1474
McCourt, Rob, 1431
McCurrach, Jeff, 1691
McDonagh, Joe, 1634, 1636
McDonald, Bill, 205
McDonald, Dan, 421
McDonald, Dick and Mac, 961
McDonald, Mackey, 1744
McDonald's Corporation, **957–970**, *964, 968*
Burger King, as competitor of, 220, 224, 227
Carl's Jr., as competitor of, 290–291
Hardee's, as competitor of, 698
"Nothing But Net" campaign, 1552
size, 225
Taco Bell, as competitor of, 1593
Wendy's, as competitor of, 1811–1812, 1814–1815
McDowell, Jim, 176
McEnery, Tom, 1163, 1165
McEnroe, John, 1132, 1139
McEnroe, Kate, 1660
McFarlane, Rodger, 658
McGinnis, Marjorie A., 202
McGrady, Tracy
adidas "Nothing Is Impossible" campaign, 23
adidas T-MAC shoe, 1124
"Code Red" campaign, 1267, 1269
Seattle SuperSonics, 167
McGwire, Mark, 950, 951
McHugh, Peter, 1183
MCI LLC, **971–978**
American Greetings partnership with, 693
AT&T, as competitor of, 148, 151, 152
Sprint, as competitor of, 1545, 1548
Working Assets Long Distance, as competitor of, 1837
Yahoo!, partnership with, 1853
McIlhenny, Edmund, 979–980
McIlhenny Company, **979–982**
McKee, Bonnie, 1403
McKee, Elizabeth, 151
McKeever, Ellen, 692
McKellar, Tyler, 495
McKelvey, Andrew J., 1039, 1040
McKenna, Travis, 1059
McKenzie, Stacey, 261
McKinney & Silver
Audi "Art of the Heist" campaign, 157–160
"Listed on Nasdaq" campaign, 1089–1092
Travelocity "Roaming Gnome" campaign, 1651–1654
McLamore, James, 226
McLaren, Wayne, 99
McLaughlin, Robin, 1762
McLaughlin, Susan, 1652
McLean, Brian, 1148
McLean, David, 99
McLean, Don, 1719
McMahon, Ed, 985, 989
McMillan, Nate, 167
McMillin, John M., 1672
McNally, Howard, 977
McNamara, Robert S., 140
McNeil Consumer Products Company, 661–662, 663–665
McQueen, Steve, 174, 275
McWilliams, Larry, 269, 270
"The Meadow" spot, 613, 615
Mears, Mark, 457
Meatpacking District Initiative, 409
Media Kitchen, 410
Medical Marketing & Media Awards, 1209, 1212
"Medicine or Food" spot, 363
Medicus, 1461–1464
Meehan, Emily, 452
"Meet the Greens" campaign, 587–590
"Meet the LeBrons" campaign, 1138–1141
"Meet Virginia" campaign, 1761–1764
"Meeting Paper Shuffle" spot, 1565
"Meeting" spot, 1552
"Megaphone" radio spot, 905
Meineke Car Care Centers, 650
Meisels, Blair, 628
Meldrum & Fewsmith Communications, 1438–1440
Melendez, Bill, 999
Mello Yello, 1268–1269
Mellors, Tim, 171
The Melting Pot, 397
"Membership has its privileges" tagline, 80

Membership Rewards program, American Express, 80–83
Men
Body Shop cosmetics, 193
herbal and vitamin remedies, 1331
Subway Steakburger, 456
"Men don't obsess over these things. Why do we?" tagline, 835
Men in Black (film), 1549
Men in Black II (film), 1553, 1555–1556
Men of Metal (novelette), 172, 173
Mendelsohn, Jordin, 813
Mendelsohn/Zein Advertising
Carl's Jr. "Six Dollar Burger" campaign, 289–292
Hardee's "Revolution" campaign, 697–699
Mendes, Michael J., 440
Mendes, Sam, 53
Mennen Speed Stick, 672
Men's Journal, 424
"Mentorship" program, 425
Meow Mix, 935
Mercedes Benz (song), 984, 989, 995
Mercedes-Benz USA, LLC, **983–996,** *984, 988*
BMW, as competitor of, 177
Lexus, as competitor of, 1647–1648
middle-class market, 1044
Merchandising
Bunny People dolls, 770
Serta sheep, 1503
Taco Bell "Dinky" merchandise, 1597
Merck, Mandy, 56
Mercury Award, 1569
"Mercury" spot, 986
Mercury Villager minivan, 1174–1175
Mergers and acquisitions
Capital Cities Inc. acquisition of ABC and ESPN, 514
CKE Restaurants acquisition of Hardee's, 698
Hewlett-Packard acquisition of Compaq, 724
Kleenex merger with Scott Paper, 844, 845
Kmart acquisition of Sears, 850, 1495
Morgan Stanley/Dean Witter merger, 1047, 1048, 1051
PepsiCo acquisition of Taco Bell, 1592
Philip Morris Company acquisition of Miller Brewing Company, 1017
Quaker Oats acquisition of Gatorade, 1287
Quaker Oats acquisition of Snapple, 259, 1655, 1656–1657
SBC acquisition of AT&T, 150
Walt Disney Company acquisition of ESPN, 514
Warren Buffett acquisition of GEICO, 614
Wolf Group acquisition of Meldrum & Fewsmith, 1439
Merkley Newman Harty & Partners
JetBlue "Unbelievable" campaign, 818–822
Mercedes "Unlike Any Other" campaign, 994–996
Merlo, Ellen, 56
Merrill Lynch & Co.
Charles Schwab, as competitor of, 303
E*TRADE, as competitor of, 526–527
First Union, as competitor of, 1791
H&R Block, as competitor of, 689
Paine Webber, as competitor of, 1676
Merriman, Michael, 1440
Merritt, Necole, 642
Mersereau, Marilyn, 322
"The Message" spot, 1473–1474
Messner Vetere Berger McNamee & Schmetterer
MCI "1-800-Collect" campaign, 971
New Balance "Thunderstorm, Stairs" campaigns, 1123–1125
Messner Vetere Berger McNamee Schmetterer/Euro RSCG
Intel "Time for a Pentium II Processor?" campaign, 771–775
MCI "Dennis Miller Ads" campaign, 975–978
Philips Electronics "Getting Better" campaign, 1333–1336
Metal Gear Solid, 1533
MetLife, Inc., **997–1000**
John Hancock, as competitor of, 827–828
Prudential, as competitor of, 1406–1407
Mettler, Robert L., 1488
Metzler, Richard, 421
MGM cartoons, 1611
MGM Pictures, 1770
"MIBII" spot, 1556
Michalski, Jerry, 788
Michelin, 681
Michelle, Candice, 678
Michelob, 105–108
Mickelson, Phil, 565
Micra, Nissan, 1167
Microprocessing chips
Intel "Bunny People" campaign, 767–771
Intel "Time for a Pentium II Processor?" campaign, 771–775
Microsoft Corp., **1001–1007,** *1005*
Apple Computer, as competitor of, 139–140, 143
IBM, as competitor of, 796, 799
Logitech, as competitor of, 912
Lycos, as competitor of, 917
Sega and Take-Two, as competitor of, 1499
Sony, as competitor of, 1524–1525
Taco Bell, partnership with, 1593
Yahoo!, as competitor of, 1852
MicroStrategy, 1067
Midas, Inc., **1009–1012**
Midas Awards
Barclays Global Investors "New School" campaign, 161, 163
Washington Mutual "Fear Not" campaign, 1803
Miesmer, Charlie, 303
"The Mighty Jeep: A Legend Turns 60" (exhibit), 393
Mike's Hard Lemonade Company, **1013–1016**
"Mikey" spot, 833
Milano, Alyssa, 971, 974
Milbrett, Tiffney, 1156
Miles Thirst (mascot), 347, 348, 349
Military, 924
Milk
BC Dairy Foundation "Don't Take Your Body for Granted" campaign, 181–185
California Milk Processor Board "Got Milk?" campaign, 257–260
Posilac, 1035, 1036
"Milk, It Does a Body Good" campaign, 258
Milk Calendar, 182
"The Milk Chocolate Melts in Your Mouth—Not in Your Hand" slogan, 937
Milk Processor Education Program, 183
Millar, Kevin, 209
Millar, Ronny, 685
Millennium, 1706–1707
Miller, Dennis, *975*
DirecTV radio spots, 447
MCI campaign, 974–978
M&M's campaign, 713, 938
Monday Night Football, 519
Miller, Mark Crispin, 33, 334
Miller, Mike, 167
Miller, Nicole, 750

Miller, Reggie, 167, 1149
Miller, Robyn, 382
Miller, Steve, 1720
Miller Brewing Company, **1017–1025**
Anheuser-Busch, as competitor of, 110, 117–118, 121, 125, 128
Foster's "How to Speak Australian" campaign, 569–573
Lemon Awards candidacy, 1294
Rainier and, 1246
Rolling Rock, as competitor of, 868
See also SABMiller plc
Miller High Life, *1018*
Rainier, as competitor of, 1246–1247
Rheingold Beer, as competitor of, 1422–1423
"Miller High Life" campaign, 1452–1455, *1453*
"Miller High Life Man" campaign, 1017–1021, *1019*
"Miller High Life Manifesto" spot, 1453
Miller Lite
"Ads by Dick" campaign, 125, 128
Bud Light, as competitor of, 113–114
"Miller Time" campaign, 1021–1025, *1023*
Milligan, Stephen, 429
Mills, Simon, 461
Millstein, Alan, 608, 884, 885, 890
Millward Brown International, 491
Milner, Duncan, 137
Ming, Jenny, 1226, 1229
"Mini-Campaigns," 618–621
MINI Cooper
Audi, as competitor of, 159
"Counterfeit" campaign, 169–172, *170*
"MINI Robots" campaign, 170, 172–175
Volkswagen, as competitor of, 1778
MiniDisc, 1533
Minnesota Partnership for Action against Tobacco, **1027–1030**
Minolta, 481
Minorities. *See* Race/ethnicity
Mintz, Richard I., 217
Miracle-Gro "Neighbor to Neighbor" campaign, 1481–1486, *1482–1483*
"Miracle" spot, 587, 589
Mirren, Helen, 1069
Misdom, Janine, 119, 1019
Misleading advertising, 1294
"Miss Rheingold" pageant, 1421, 1423
"Missed Cue" spot, 927
"Missed It" spot, 947
Mitchell, Bill, 947
Mitchell, Gary, 508
Mitchell, Grace, 204
Mitchell, Nick, Jr., 1342
Mitchell, Pat, 1409, 1410, 1412
Mitchell Gold, 877
"Mitre Saw" spot, 651
Mitsubishi Consumer Electronics America, 1335
Mitsubishi Motors North America, Inc., **1031–1034**, 1635
Mitta, Eugeni, 1707
MIXX Awards, 157, 160
Mizrahi, Isaac, 985, 1242
"M'm! M'm! Good! To Go!" campaign, 270
"Mmmm ... Toasty." tagline, 1413, 1414, 1415
M&M's
"New Millennium" campaigns, 937–940
Reese's, as competitor of, 713–714
MMX technology, 767–771
Mobile phones
Motorola "Intelligence Everywhere" campaign, 1065–1068
Motorola "Moto" campaign, 1068–1071
See also Wireless services
Moddelmog, Hala, 318, 319
Model Magic, 189–190
Modernista!, 645–648
Molly's Chambers (song), 1775
"Moments of Truth" campaign, 85
Mondale, Walter, 1810
Monday Night Football
Anheuser-Busch "Frogs" campaign, 109
Electronic Data Systems "Cat Herders" campaign, 503
FedEx "Be Absolutely Sure" campaign, 539
"It's Not T.V. It's HBO" campaign, 739
Logitech "What Will You Do With All That Freedom?" campaign, 913
Nike "Hello World" campaigns, 1134
Nike "Tiger Woods" spot, 567
"Visa. It's Everywhere You Want to Be" campaign, 1767
Visa Check Card "Works Like a Check" campaign, 1771
Monday Night Madness Mobile, 1547
"Monday Nights Free and Clear" campaign, 1546–1550
The Monkees, 1173
"Monkey Trilogy" campaign, 525–528
Monroe, Marilyn
beauty standards, 1682
Gap "Who Wore Khakis?" campaign, 602
Levi's campaign, 1230
Visa Signature card campaign, 1768
Monroe, Steve, 981
Monsanto Company, **1035–1038**
"Monsanto Image" campaign, 1035–1038
Monsarrat, Nancy, 24
Monster, 282–283, **1039–1042**
Montague, Ty, 845, 1498, 1499
Montana, Joe
Allstate campaign, 52
annual endorsement income, 552
Pepsi campaign, 1296
"TiVo TV Your Way" campaign, 1619, 1621
Montero, Mitsubishi, 1033
Montgomery Ward, 1488–1489
Montres Rolex SA, **1043–1046**, *1045*, 1589
"Moo Cow" spot, 756, 757
"Mood Swing" spot, 707
"Moon Landing" spot, 3
Mooney, Carla, 1063
Moore, Demi, 1646, 1648
Moore, Jacques J., 640
Moore, Peter, 1001
Morales, Esai, 53
Moran, Jeffrey, 932, 933
Morden, Bill, 389, 390, 391
Morel, Paul, 564
Morfitt, Marti, 338
Morgan, Alan James, 1603, 1605
Morgan, J. P., 1048
Morgan, Tracy, 1499
Morgan Stanley, 327, **1047–1059**
Morita, Akio, 1526
Morita, Pat, 1689
"Morning Again in America" spot, 1467
"Morning Break" spot, 661
"Morning Commute" spot, 681
Morningstar Farms, 1818–1819
Morris, Errol
Apple "Switchers" spot, 140
Citigroup "Live Richly" campaign, 331
"Miller High Life" campaign, 1452, 1454–1455
"Miller High Life Man" campaign, 1020
MoveOn.org "Real People" campaign, 1073–1076

Morris, Errol, ***continued***
Sharp "More to See" campaign, 1507
State Farm "True Stories" campaign, 1572
Morrison, Phil, 509, 511, 1371
Morrison, Van, 429
Morrow, Ronald, 1375
Mortenson, Chris, 514
Moschitta, John, 538
Moser, Mark, 998
Moses, Elissa, 1334, 1335
"Mosquito" campaign, 979–982
"Mosquito" spot, 1608
Moss, Tara, 244
"The Most popular cruise line in the world" tagline, 296
Motel 6
Holiday Inn, as competitor of, 778–779
Holiday Inn Express, as competitor of, 782
"Mother Boyle" campaign, 359–362
Mother Ltd., 1233–1236
Mothers Against Drunk Driving, Connecticut Chapter, **1061–1063**
Motley, Don, 1109
"Moto" campaign, 1068–1071
"Motor Voter Bill," 1426
"Motorcycle Cop" spot, 1643
Motorcycles and motor scooters
"The Book of Harley-Davidson" campaign, 701–704
"Vespa Reintroduction" campaign, 1337–1340
Victory Motorcycles "The New American Motorcycle" campaign, 1349–1352
Motorola, **1065–1071,** *1066*
Motown Live (television show), 1335
Mottolese, Maura, 238, 239
Moudry, Tom, 981
Mountain bikes
Schwinn "What a Ride" campaign, 1252–1256
"Specialized" campaign, 1539–1542
Mountain Dew
"Code Red" campaign, 1267–1270, 1273
Dr Pepper, as competitor of, 464, 465
"Mountain" spot, 1523, 1524, 1525
Mountjoy, Jim, 1201
Mourning, Alonzo, 1149
"Mouthwash" spot, 45
Movado Group, 1045
"Move" campaign, 1141–1144
"Move Our Money" campaign, 229–231
"Move Over" spot, 1279
MoveOn.org, **1073–1076,** 1584–1585
Movie theater spots
Amtrak "Life on Acela" campaign, 1103–1106
Orange "Goldspot" campaign, 1233–1236
MovieFone, 64
"Moving at the Speed of Business" campaign, 1709–1712
"Moving Day" spot, 1459
"Moving Van" spot, 1183
"Mower" spot, 719, 720
Moyer, Greg, 451
MP3 players
Apple Computer "Silhouette" campaign, 135–138
Hewlett Packard-Apple partnership, 726
technology, 1087
"Mr. Clean" campaign, 94
Mr. Goodwrench, 648–652
Mr. K. (character), 1171, 1173
Mr. Peanut, 441
"Mr. Really Bad Toupe Wearer" spot, *124*
Mr. Six (character), 1517, 1519–1520
Mr. T, 1689
"Mr. Wendy" campaign, 1813, 1814
"Mrs. Olson" spots, 1375
MSN Music, 1087
MSNBC, 1806–1807
MSN.com, 473
MTV Networks Company, **1077–1080**
MTV Video Music Awards
MTV "Watch and Learn" campaign, 1077
Pepsi Vanilla "The Not-So-Vanilla Vanilla" campaign, 1285
"Muhammad Ali" spot, 797
Muir, John, 1509
Mulcahy, Anne, 1845
Mullahy, Jim, 572
Mullen Advertising
Oxygen Media "Fresh Television for Women" campaign, 1241–1244
"Swiss Army Equipped" campaign, 1587–1590
"Vespa reintroduction" campaign, 1337, 1339, 1340
Wachovia "Uncommon Wisdom" campaign, 1792–1795, 1802–1803
Mulligan, Richard, 805
Mullin, Clare, 476, 477
"Multi-Tasker" spot, 913
"Multiple Strength for Multiple Cats" campaign, 1114–1117
Murphy, Tim, 566
Murphy, Victoria, 506
Murphy's "Vincent Murphy" campaign, 428
Murray, Ralph, 1253
Murray, Ty, 1749
Murro, Noam, 496, 498, 1467
Musachio, Heidi, 533
Musco, Tre, 840
Muse, 1326
The Museum of Contemporary Art, Los Angeles, **1081–1084,** *1082*
"Museum" spot, 785
Museums
The Museum of Contemporary Art "Labels" campaign, 1081–1084
Negro Leagues Baseball Museum "1998 Print Campaign," 1107–1109
Musgrave, Marilyn, 657
Music
Apple Computer "Silhouette" campaign, 135–138
Calvin Klein Cosmetics/ Ticketmaster cross-promotion, 263–264
Dr. Martens Airwair "Beliefs" campaign, 459, 460, 461
Fusion Flash Concerts, 560
Lilith Fair, 1692
Motorola technology, 1068
Napster "It's Coming Back" campaign, 1085–1088
Pepsi sponsorship, 1279
Woman Thing Music, 57–58
Music & Media Partnership, 460
Music Mixer, 1002
"Musical Instruments" spot, 1079
"Musical" spot, 735
Musicmatch, 1087
"Must Be Football Season" campaign, 1535–1538, *1536*
Mustang, 1642
"Mustang" spot, 1304
Musto, Mark, 448
Mutombo, Kidembe, 303
"Mutual Admiration" spot, 908, 909
Mutual funds, 161–163
My Best Friend's Wedding (movie), 246
"My McDonald's" campaign, 959
"My Pleasure" spot, 314
Mya, 350, 352
Myers, Dave, 137
Myers, Mike, 707, 1758

MySpace.com, 1402–1403
Myst (computer game), 379, 380, 382

N

Nabisco, 267
Nacmias, Andrea, 553
Naddaff, George, 204
Nader, Ralph, 171
Nagahiro, Kenichi, 745–746, 747
Nail Communications, 923–926
Nakamura, Shiro, 1177
"Naked Emperor" spot, 1411
Namath, Joe, 1101
Nano-Dry, 925
NanoTex LLC, 925
Napster, Inc., **1085–1088**
Nasalcrom, 1313
NASCAR, **1093–1097**, *1094*
  Anheuser-Busch sponsorship, 118
  AT&T "Carrot Top" campaign, 149–150
  Coca-Cola "Real" campaign, 352
  Discover card sponsorship, 1050, 1052
  Dr Pepper car sponsorship, 465–466
  Ford Fusion, 559
  KFC team sponsorship, 839, 841
  National Football League, as competitor of, 1101
  Philips Electronics sponsorship, 1335
  PowerAde sponsorship, 1288
  Sharpie, partnership with, 1458
  Tabasco sponsorship, 982
  Viagra sponsorship, 1328
  Visa sponsorship, 84
"NASCAR Garage" spot, 651
The Nasdaq Stock Market, Inc., **1089–1092**
National Advertising Division, Better Business Bureau, 80, 82
National and Community Service Trust Act, 1426
National Association for Stock Car Auto Racing. *See* NASCAR
National Baseball Hall of Fame and Museum, 1109
National Basketball Association
  NASCAR, as competitor of, 1095
  National Football Association, as competitor of, 1100–1101
  Reebok apparel contract, 1146
  Schick sponsorship, 1315, 1317
  Sprite cross-promotion, 344, 346, 347–349
National Comstock Law, 311
National Consumers League, 1014
National Denim Day, 1747
National Football League, **1099–1102**
  Heineken "It's All About the Beer" campaign, 707
  Hershey "$1 Million Kick" promotion, 711
  IBM, partnership with, 795
  Kickoff festival, 1285
  NASCAR, as competitor of, 1095
  Southwest Airlines sponsorship, 1535–1538
  Sprint sponsorship, 1546–1549
  United States Tennis Association, as competitor of, 1723
  Visa sponsorship, 1767, 1768
National Geographic Channel, 452–453
National Geographic (magazine), 792
National Geographic Society website, 792
National Hockey League
  Anheuser-Busch sponsorship, 120, 122
  "NHL on Fox" campaign, 575–578
  Norelco sponsorship, 1191
  Southwest Airlines sponsorship, 44, 416, 1535, 1537
National monuments, 1604
National Outdoor Leadership School, 1238, 1239
National Park Foundation, 1604, 1688
National Public Radio, 1447, 1599
National Railroad Passenger Corporation, **1103–1106**
National Tobacco Control Foundation, 247
National Voter Registration Reform Act, 1426
"National Youth Anti-Drug Media" campaign, 1217–1218
Natural products
  Body Shop, 191–194
  Clairol "Totally Organic" campaign, 333–336
  Nature Made "Trusted By the Ones You Trust" campaign, 1329–1332
Natural Resources Defense Council (NRDC), 1275
Nature Made "Trusted By the Ones You Trust" campaign, 1329–1332
Nauser, Debbie, 1520
Nautica, 1628
Navigator browser, 1006
NBA Jam Session, 346
NBC
  DHL sponsorship, 422
  Game Show Network, as competitor of, 593
  mock promotions of ABC's campaign, 6
  "Must-see TV" campaign, 6
NCAA basketball
  Coca-Cola "Real" campaign, 352
  Conseco "Protect/Create Wealth" campaign, 368
  Delta Air Lines "The Passenger's Airline" campaign, 416
  FedEx "Be Absolutely Sure" campaign, 540
  Mercedes "Unlike Any Other" campaign, 994, 996
  Oldsmobile Bravada campaign, 655
Needham Harper Steers, 92
Neeleman, David, 819–820
Neff, Peggy, 659
Negro Leagues Baseball Museum, **1107–1109**
"Neighbor" spot, 1096
"Neighbor to Neighbor" campaign, 1481–1486
"Neighborhood" spot, 1475
Neiman, Adam, 72–73
Nelly, 522
Nelson, Bruce, 1214, 1215
Nelson, Dave, 939
Nelson, Jim, 703
Nelson, Ozzie and Harriet, 482
Nelson, Willie
  Gap "For Every Generation" campaign, 597, 598, 599, 1747
  Lipton Brisk "That's Brisk, Baby!" campaign, 1298, 1302
Neon
  "Hi" campaign, 1470–1471, 1778
  New Beetle, as competitor of, 1785
Ness, Ann, 287
Nestea Cool, 1300
Nestlé, Henri, 939
Nestlé Purina PetCare Co., 935–936, **1111–1117**
Nestlé S.A., **1119–1122**
  The Coca-Cola Company, as competitor of, 352
  General Foods International Coffees, as competitor of, 861
  The Hershey Company, as competitor of, 711
  Mars, as competitor of, 939, 942
  PepsiCo, as competitor of, 1275–1276
  PowerBar, 932
Netscape Communications Corp., 64, 1006
"Network Executive" spot, 1621
Network Solutions, 676
Network Walkman, 137
Neuberger, Karen, 1502

Neufville, Richard de, 644
Neupert, Peter, 472
Neutrogena, 1692
"Never Follow" tag line, 158
"Never Miss a Genuine Opportunity" campaign, 128
"Never Stop Milk." tag line, 183
"Never without my milk" tag line, 183
"The New American Motorcycle" campaign, 1349–1352
New Balance Athletic Shoe, Inc., **1123–1125**
Nike, as competitor of, 1146
Reebok, as competitor of, 1418
New Beetle, 170–171, 173–174, 1020, 1778, 1779
"New Beetle" campaign, 1783–1786, *1784*
"The New Color of Money" campaign, 215–218, *216*
"New Driver" spot, 1573
New England Broadcasting Association awards, 826
"The New Look of Comfort" campaign, 875–878
"New Millennium" campaigns, 937–940
"New Neighbors" spot, 531
New Order, 460
"New School" campaign, 161–164
"New Shoes" spot, 1140
New York American Marketing Association, 914
New York Art Director's Club Awards, 981
New York Giants, 1723
New York Institute of Photography, 1164
New York Life
MetLife, as competitor of, 998–999
Prudential, as competitor of, 1406–1407
New York Mets, 1722
"New York Miracle" spot, 822
New York Press, 1754
New York State Lottery, **1127–1130,** *1128*
New York Stock Exchange, 1090, 1091
New York Times, 49
New York World's Fair, 1358
New York Yankees, 1722
adidas, 26–29
Ruth, Babe, 208
"*New Yorker* Magazine Sponsorship" campaign, 1599–1602
Newell Rubbermaid, 188–189
Newman, Lee, 159
Newman, Paul
Business Leaders for Sensible Priorities "Move Our Money" campaign, 231
Texaco "A World of Energy" campaign voice-over, 305, 308
"News" spot, 617
Newsom, Gavin, 657
Newspapers, 1753–1756
Newsweek, 1616
Newton, Wayne, 37
Newton-John, Olivia, 750
"The Next Shift" spot, 724
Nextel
"Nextel. Done." campaign, 1550–1553
Sprint PCS, as competitor of, 1555
NFL Fever 2004 (video game), 1001, 1003
"NFL Playoffs" campaign, 1099–1102
"NHL on Fox" campaign, 575–578
"Nice Finish" campaign, 108
Nice 'n Easy hair coloring, 334
Nickelodeon
Cartoon Network, as competitor of, 1612–1613
Holiday Inn, partnership with, 779
Nickerson, Thomas, 1263
Nicklaus, Jack, 84, 399, 400, *400,* 552
NicoDerm CQ "Power to Quit" campaign, 661–665
Nicotine replacement therapies, 661–665
Nicotrol, 661, 663
Nielsen, Karl, 460
"Night" spot, 187, 189"
Nike, Inc., **1131–1157,** *1135*
adidas, as competitor of, 20–21, 24–25, 27–28
Candie's, as competitor of, 751
Fila, as competitor of, 553
FootJoy, as competitor of, 566
"Hello World" campaign, 1134–1138
"I Am Tiger Woods" campaign, 1134–1138
New Balance, as competitor of, 1124
Olympics sponsorship, 23
real women in ads, 1683
Reebok, as competitor of, 1418
Nikon Corporation, 481, **1159–1165**
"Nimrods" spot, 522, 523
"9,000 Shots" campaign, 1131–1134
Nine West, 751
"1998 Negro Leagues Baseball Museum Print Campaign," 1107–1109
Nintendo
GameCube, 1003
Sega and Take-Two, as competitor of, 1499
Sony, as competitor of, 1524–1525
Nissan, Colin, 1475
Nissan Motor Company, Ltd., **1167–1170**
Nissan North America, Inc., **1171–1180**
Honda, as competitor of, 743
Oldsmobile, as competitor of, 654
Toyota, as competitor of, 1632–1633, 1635, 1639, 1645
Nivea
Dove, as competitor of, 1681
Lubriderm, as competitor of, 1320
"No Dummy" spot, 1829–1830
"No-Hassle Card" campaign, 327
"No Matter What" campaign, 1830–1833
No Sweat, 72–73
Noble, Eric, 93
Nokia, 1067, 1069–1070
Nonconformism
Dr. Martens Airwair "Beliefs" campaign, 459–462
Harley-Davidson, 461
Nordhielm, Kristie, 299–300
Nordstrom, Dan, 1182
Nordstrom, Inc., **1181–1187,** *1185*
Nordstrom, John W., 1181
Norelco Consumer Products Company, **1189–1192**
Norman, Greg, 553, 1136
Norman, Richard, 1464
Normark Corporation, **1193–1196**
Norono, David, 1347
North American Coffee Partnership, 49, **1197–1200**
North Carolina Division of Tourism Film and Sports Development, **1201–1204**
North Face, 361
North Woods Advertising, 1739–1742
Northern Exposure (television show), 561, 563
Northwest Airlines Corporation, 412–413, **1205–1208**
Norton, Nancy, 1210
"Nose" ad, *1253,* 1255
Nostalgia
brand revivals, 1020
Gap "Khakis Swing" spot, 602, 603
"Miller High Life Man" campaign, 1018
"Not America's Favorite Paper" campaign, 1753–1756

"Not Everything in Black and White Makes Sense" campaign, 426–429
"The Not-So-Vanilla Vanilla" campaign, 1283–1286
Notebaert, Richard, 154
Noth, Chris, 61
"Nothing But Net" campaign, 1552
NOTICEables, 1391
Nottoli, David, 638, 640
Novak, David, 841
Novartis AG, **1209–1212**
Novica, 452–453
Novick, Chip, 1554, 1556
Novus Services, 1054
"Now & Then" spot, 1282
"Now It Gets Interesting" campaign, 16
NRDC. *See* Natural Resources Defense Council (NRDC)
Nuchow, Leslie, 57
Nuclear weapons, 231, 232
Nugent, Robert, 812
Nullsoft, 64
"Nuns" spot, 800
NutraSweet, 1035
NW Ayer, 1374
NW Ayer & Partners, 670–673
Nye, Bill, 1055
N'Yeurt, Felix, 262

O

Oakley, David, 1750, 1751
Obesity
  Jenny Craig, Inc., 816
  Subway "F.R.E.S.H. Steps" campaign, 457
  Subway "Jared Fogle" campaign, 455, 456
  Trident gum, 234
"Obey Your Thirst" campaign (1998), 205, 344–347, 464–465
"Obey Your Thirst" campaign (2004), 347–350
O'Brien, Conan, 617
O'Brien, Don, 1149
O'Brien, Jayne, 1759
O'Brien, Joanne, 774
O'Brien, Steve, 515–516
Obsession cologne ad campaign, 9, 10
Occidental Studios, 238
"Oceans, Mountains, Forests, Fear. Which Do You Conquer First?" campaign, 1237–1240
Ochman, B. L., 212
O'Connell, Tom, 1058
O'Connor, Sinead, 429
O'Donnell, Rosie, 465, 849, 854–858, 1489, 1824
Odor eliminators, 1388–1391
OdorFree, 1389
Odyssey, Honda
  Nissan Quest, as competitor of, 1176
  Sienna, as competitor of, 1645
Oetting, Rudy, 156
Office and print services, 541–543
Office cubicles, 1575, 1576
Office Depot, Inc., **1213–1216**
  OfficeMax, as competitor of, 1222
  Staples, as competitor of, 1568
Office furniture, 1575–1578
Office machines, 1843–1847
Office of National Drug Control Policy, **1217–1219**
Office supplies
  Kinko's online outlet, 542
  Office Depot "What You Need. What You Need to Know." campaign, 1213–1216
  OfficeMax Inc. "What's Your Thing?" campaign, 1221–1224
  Staples "That Was Easy" campaign, 1563–1566
  Staples "Yeah, We've Got That" campaign, 1567–1569
"Officeflage" spot, 1828, 1830
OfficeMax Inc., **1221–1224**, 1565, 1568
Ogilvy & Mather
  American Express "Do More" campaign, 82–86, 951
  "Campaign for Freedom" campaign, 33
  Chesebrough-Pond's "Soothing Cucumber Eye Treatments Ads" campaign, 1690–1693
  Cisco Systems "The Self-Defending Network" campaign, 321–324
  Dove "Campaign for Real Beauty" campaign, 1679–1683
  Ford "Driving American Innovation" campaign, 555–558
  Foster's account, 573
  Guiness "Not Everything in Black and White Makes Sense" campaign, 426–429
  Hershey "There's No Wrong Way to Eat a Reese's" campaign, 712–715
  IBM "Can You See It?" campaign, 785–788
  IBM "E-Business" campaign, 788–791
  IBM "Gizmo" campaign, 792–794
  IBM "Linux" campaign, 794–797
  IBM "Solutions for a Small Planet" campaign, 134, 798–801
  Kodak "Advantix" campaign, 479–482
  Kodak "The Best Part of Photography Is the Prints" campaign, 482–485
  Kodak "Take Pictures. Further" campaign, 485–488
  Kodak "Tall Tales" campaign, 488–491
  Kotex "Red Dot" campaign, 1387
  Miller Lite "Low Carb" campaign, 1449–1452
  Motorola "Intelligence Everywhere" campaign, 1065–1068
  Motorola "Moto" campaign, 1068–1071
  Office of National Drug Control Policy "Early Intervention Youth" campaign, 1217–1219
  Outward Bound "Oceans, Mountains, Forests, Fear. Which Do You Conquer First?" campaign, 1237–1240
  Sprite "Obey Your Thirst" campaign (2004), 347–350
  "Wear a Moustache" campaign, 182
Ogilvy Award, 1490
"Oh, and Beware of the Penguins" campaign, 120–123
O'Hagan, John, 431, 432, 433
O'Hurley, John, 1843, *1844,* 1846, 1847
Oil companies, 305
Oil of Olay, 1320–1321
OK Soda, 345
Olajuwon, Hakeem, 1056
Olbermann, Keith
  Boston Market "Eat Something" campaign, 203–206
  ESPN "This Is SportsCenter" campaign, 515, 520
  SportsCenter, 517
"Old Fashioned Guy" campaign, 1811
"Old Man" spot, 426–427, 1643
Old Navy, Inc., 596, **1225–1231**
"Old School" spot, 1087
Old Spice, 1402
Oldham, Todd, 875, 876, 878
Oldsmobile
  Alero "Start Something" campaign, 652–656
  Volkswagen, as competitor of, 1785–1786
Olean, 1398–1399
Olestra, 584
Olive, Jason, 261
"Olive" spot, 322
Olivio, Allen, 771
Olson, John, 1259

Olson & Company
Breathe Right Strips "Back in the Sack" campaign, 337–340
Detroit Pistons "Goin' to Work. Every Night." campaign, 1257–1260
Olympics
A & E "Go Back in Time" campaign, 2
adidas "Impossible Is Nothing" campaign, 25
American Legacy Foundation "Truth" campaign, 99
Anheuser-Busch "Beer . . . or Michelob?" campaign, 105, 106, 107
Chevrolet "An American Revolution" campaign, 633
"Delta Marathon" campaign, 411, 415
DHL sponsorship, 421–422
Diamond Foods "Emerald Nuts marketing campaign," 440, 441
Fat-Free Pringles "Tasting Is Believing" campaign, 1399
Ford "Storytelling" campaign, 561, 563
IBM "Solutions for a Small Planet" campaign, 799, 800
IBM sponsorship, 790
"Jeep" campaign, 391
John Hancock "Insurance for the Unexpected. Investments for the Opportunities" campaign (1996), 823
John Hancock "Insurance for the Unexpected. Investments for the Opportunities" campaign (2000), 826, 828
Kodak "Take Pictures. Further" campaign, 487
Kodak "Tall Tales" campaign, 490
Lee jeans "Cut to Be Noticed" campaign, 1745
M&M's sponsorship, 938
Monster sponsorship, 1040
Nike "Move" campaign, 1141–1144
Nike "Women's" campaign, 1156, 1157
Office Depot "What You Need. What You Need to Know." campaign, 1215
Owens, Jesse, 19–20, 23
Reebok sponsorship of the "Dream Team," 1133, 1142
snowboarding, 1514
sponsorship, 23
Texaco sponsorship of the U.S. Olympic Team, 307
UPS "Moving at the Speed of Business" campaign, 1712
UPS "What Can Brown Do for You?" campaign, 1715
Visa/American Express competition, 79–80, 1766–1767
Visa sponsorship, 84, 1767
women athletes, 1154
O'Malley, Mike, 515, 516
Omnicom Group, 32
"On the Nose" campaign, 338
"On the One Twos" radio spot, 1269
"On the Street" spot, 651
"On the Wings of Goodyear" campaign, 679–682
"On Top of the World" campaign, 411–414, 415, 1207, 1537
Onak, Dave, 155
ONDCP *See* Office of National Drug Control Policy
One-A-Day, 1331
"The One and Only" tagline, 628
"One client at a time" tagline, 1048
"1-800-COLLECT" campaign, 971–974
180 (ad agency), 23–26
"One Leg At a Time" campaign, 603
One Show Awards
A & E "In Case You Missed It" campaign, 3
adidas "Yankee Fans" campaign, 29
Advertising Council "Campaign for Freedom" campaign, 31, 33
Borders "This Season, It's the Original Thought That Counts" campaign, 197
Burger King "Subservient Chicken" campaign, 223, 225
Business Leaders for Sensible Priorities "Move Our Money" campaign, 232
"Cartoon Network Promotional and Branding" campaign, 1611, 1614
ESPN NFL 2K5 "Beta-7" campaign, 1499
"Father and Son" spot, 153
Hewlett-Packard "Built By Engineers, Used By Ordinary People" campaign, 720
Honda "Grrr" campaign, 745
Little Caesar "Safety Video" campaign, 906
MADD "Drunk Driving's a Serious Crime. Let's Treat It That Way." campaign, 1063
"Miller High Life Man" campaign, 1021
Motorola "Intelligence Everywhere" campaign, 1068
MTV "Watch and Learn" campaign, 1079
Napster "It's Coming Back" campaign, 1085, 1088
Sims Sports "Be Free" campaign, 1516
Sony "What's Next?" campaign, 1534
"Specialized" campaign, 1542
Sprite "Obey Your Thirst" campaign, 347
Sprite "Obey Your Thirst" campaign (2004), 349
Suburban Auto Group "Trunk Monkey" campaign, 1579, 1582
"Swiss Army Equipped" campaign, 1590
"Vespa reintroduction" campaign, 1337, 1340
One Tough Mother: Success in Life, Business, and Apple Pies (Boyle), 359, 361
O'Neal, Shaquille
All Sport campaign, 1287
annual endorsement income, 552
music video, 1596
National Basketball Association, 1095, 1100
Pepsi campaign, 1296
Pepsi "Generation Next" campaign, 129, 1277
Reebok campaign, 28
Reebok endorsements, 1133
O'Neil, Buck, 718, 721, 1107
O'Neill, Ed, 973
O'Neill, John, 1583–1584, 1585
O'Neill, Patrick, 849
Oneworld Alliance, 415
Online auctions
eBay "Abbreviated" campaign, 493–496
eBay 2004 television campaign, 496–499
Onlineshoes.com, 1182–1183
"Only in New York" tagline, 28
Ono, Apolo Anton, 1141, *1142*
Ono, Yoko, 729
Ontario Milk Marketing Board, 182
Oobeya, 1632
Ooh Child (song), 1815
Oppenheimer, Brent, 1105
"Opportunity Knocks" spot, 539, 540
The Oprah Winfrey Show, 815, 818, 1242, 1243
Optima credit card, 80, 83
Orange S. A., 1233–1236
Orbe, Tom, 1171, 1172, 1173, 1178
Orbit gum, 234, 1830–1833
Orbitz, 1652–1653

"Orchestra" spot, 1411
Oreck, David, 477–478
Oreck Company, 477
"Origins" campaign, 1286–1289
Orloff, Glennis, 1477–1478
O'Rourke, P. J., 1758
Ortega, Daniel, 804
Osborn, John, 933
Osburn, Melissa, 1114
Osmond, Donny, 667
Ostrom, Ray, 1194
Otsuka Pharmaceutical Company, Ltd., 1330
Otto, Ed, 1093
"Our Office Is Your Office" campaign, 541–544
"Our Stand" campaign, 51–54
Out of Order: Rock the Vote Targets Health (short film), 1426
Outboard Marine, 1355
Outbreak Tour, 99–100
Outdoor Systems Inc., 1148
Outdoor wilderness education, 1237–1240
"Outfit" spot, 328
"Outperform" campaign, 25
Outward Bound USA, **1237–1240**
Ouweleen, Michael, 1611, 1613
Overbeck, Carla, 554
Overend, Ned, 1541
Owen, Clive, 175–178, 995
Owen, Jane, 334
Owens, Jesse
  adidas "Impossible Is Nothing" campaign, 25
  adidas shoes, 19–20, 23
  History Channel "Go Back in Time" campaign, 2
Owens, Terrell, 1459
"Own One and You'll Understand" campaign, 1177–1180
Oxygen Media, **1241–1244**
"Ozone Monday" spot, 1711

P

Paar, Jack, 1358
Pabst Brewing Company, **1245–1248**
  Rainier, as competitor of, 1247
  Rheingold Beer, as competitor of, 1423
Pace, Grant, 442
Pacheco, Steve, 548, 549, 550
Pacific Bell DSL "Laurel Lane" campaign, 1473–1476
Pacific Cycle, Inc., **1249–1256**
Package delivery. *See* Delivery services
Packaging
  Altoids tins, 1822
  Foster's beer, 573
  General Foods International Coffee tins, 861
  Hewlett-Packard "Expanding Possibilities" campaign, 718
  Miller High Life, 1017
  Rolling Rock longneck bottles, 869–870
Packard, David, 717, 721
Pagano Schenck & Kay, 1061–1063
Page, Jimmy, 636
Paige, Satchel, 1107
"The Pain of Separation" spot, 1841
Pain relievers, 1839–1842
"Paint" spot, 1770
"Painted Faces" campaign, 1805–1808
PAL program, 26
Palace Sports & Entertainment, **1257–1260**
Palmer, Arnold, *400*
  annual endorsement income, 552
  Estates of World Golf Village, 399, 400
  Rolex "Celebrity Endorsement" campaign, 1043
Palmer, Shawn, 1541
Palmer Jarvis DDB, 181–184
Palminteri, Chazz, 1284–1285
Palmisano, Samuel J., 769, 786, 792
Pampers "Got the Power" campaign, 1380–1382
"Pamplona" spot, 239
Panasonic, 1335
Pantoliano, Joe, 1775
Papa John's
  Little Caesar, as competitor of, 898–899, 902, 904–905, 907–908
  Pizza Hut, as competitor of, 1347
  Round Table Pizza, as competitor of, 1431
"Parasailing" spot, 1673
"Parents" spot, 873
"Paris" spot, 80, 81, 82
"Park Bench" spot, 37, 38–39
Parker, Sarah Jessica, 598–601
Parks, Rosa, 144
Parmar, Belinda, 488
Parmet, Nancy, 738, 739
Parody advertising
  "Altoids Gone Sour" campaign, 1827
  Boston Market "Eat Something" campaign, 205
  Daz "Cleaner Close" campaign, 1377–1379
  Levi's "Doctors" spot, 883, 884, 885
  of MasterCard "Priceless" campaign, 951, 952
  Mike's Hard Lemonade "Hard Day" campaign, 1015
  Old Navy "'70s Retro TV" campaign, 1225–1228
  Pepsi "Bob Dole" spot, 1326
  Sims Sports mock product offers, 1515
  "Tiny House" spot, 620–621
  Turner Classic Movies "31 Days of Oscar" campaign, 1659
  UPS "Moving at the Speed of Business" campaign, 1711
  Virgin Atlantic Airways "Go, Jet Set, Go!" campaign, 1759
Parr, Jack, 1458
Parsey, Tim, 1068–1071
Parsons, Bob, 675–676, 678
"Particle" spot, 560
Partners & Shevack, 1481–1486
Partnership for a Drug-Free America, 1218
Partnerships and cross-promotions
  ABC/American Airlines, 7
  American Express/Delta Airlines, 83
  American Greetings/America Online, 693
  Bally Total Fitness/Unilever, 1860
  Borders/Children's Books & Toys, 196
  Burger King/*The Apprentice,* 221
  Calvin Klein Cosmetics Company/Ticketmaster, 263–264
  Cartoon Network/Kraft Foods, 1611, 1613
  Cartoon Network/Pepperidge Farms, 1611, 1614
  Cartoon Network/Six Flags theme parks, 1611, 1613–1614
  CVS/MSN.com, 473
  Dewar's/*Men's Journal,* 424
  Dexter/Discovery Zone partnership, 1613
  Dial/*Shrek 2,* 435, 436, 437
  Diet Rite/Zero Gravity Corporation, 240, 242
  Discover/General Electric Consumer Finance, 1053
  Discover/Wal-Mart, 1053
  drugstore.com/Discovery Health Media, 473
  drugstore.com/General Nutrition Center/Rite Aid, 471, 472
  General Motors/Macy's/Conde Nast Publications, 94
  Häagen-Sazs/Showtime, 1120
  Hewlett-Packard/Apple, 726
  Holiday Inn/Nickelodeon, 779
  IBM/National Football League, 795
  Isuzu/General Motors, 803–804

Partnerships and cross-promotions, *continued*
Little Caesar/Kmart, 901
MasterCard/Excite, 952
McDonalds/Walt Disney Studio Entertainment, 224
Mercedes/Conde Nast, 989
Monster/WeightWatchers.com, 1040
Motorola/iTunes, 1071
National Park Foundation/corporate advertisers, 1604
Nissan/Ford, 1174–1175
Nissan/Yahoo!, 1169
Nordstrom/*Teen People,* 1186
Oldsmobile/ABC "Start Something Tuesdays on ABC Sweepstakes," 655
Oxygen Media/AOL Time Warner, 1241, 1242, 1244
Peace Corps partnerships, 1263
Pepsi/Lipton, 1298–1302
Pepsi/Major League Baseball, 1277–1278, 1279
PowerAde-ESPN/ABC, 342
Rolling Rock/ESPN, 761–762
Secret Sparkle/MySpace.com, 1402–1403
Sega/Take-Two partnership, 1497–1500
Sharpie/NASCAR, 1458
Snapple/Viacom, 238
Song Airlines/Meatpacking District, 409
Sony/Samsung, 1526–1528
Spring/*Men in Black II,* 1553, 1555–1556
Sprite/National Basketball Association, 344, 346
Staples/Federal Express, 1568
Starbucks/*New York Times,* 49
Starbucks/PepsiCo, 49, 1197–1198
Swiss Army Brands/*Armageddon,* 1590
Taco Bell/Microsoft, 1593
Target/Golden Books Entertainment, 1605
Target/Revlon, 1605
Unilever/National Park Foundation, 1688
United States Postal Service/DHL, 1720
Visa/MGM Pictures, 1770
Volkswagen/Trek, 1779
Working Assets Long Distance/Ben & Jerry's, 1837
Xbox/Showtime Networks, 1002
Yahoo!/Ben & Jerry's/Visa/MCI, 1853
See also Sponsorships
"Party Cup" spot, 1459
"Party Dress" spot, 1633
"The Party's Over" sot, 1223
Pascarella, Carl, 81
Pascoe, Gary, 935, 936
"The Passenger's Airline" campaign, 414–417
"Passion" campaign, 986, 987–990
Pastore, Lorraine, 1462
Pataki, George E., 1128
Patrick, Dan, 515, 517, 518, 520
Patrick, Sharon, 852
Patterson, Thomas, 1427
Patti, Michael, 1297
Patton, David, 1527, 1529
Patton, Erin, 1133
Patton (movie), 231
Paul, Ron, 396, 960
"Paul" spot, 1803, 1819
Paxil
Prozac, as competitor of, 507
"Social Anxiety Disorder" campaign, 665–668
Paxton, Mickey, 1300
"Pay Phone" spot, 53
Payne, John, 935, 936
Payne, William, 1675
Payton, Gary, 166, 167, 1149, 1150
PBS. *See* Public Broadcasting Service
PCs. *See* Personal computers
Peabody, Bo, 917
Peace Corps, **1261–1265**, *1262*
Pearl Harbor attack, 32
Pearl tampons, 1385–1388
Pearlstine, Norman, 1617
Pediatric AIDS Foundation, 1274
"Pediatric Edition" spot, 1581
Pelé, 1661
Peller, Clara, 224, 406, 1810
Pelliccioni, David, 1637
Peltz, Nelson, 1656
Pemberton, John, 350
Pen Pals program, 1203
Pen Schoen & Berland, 555–558
"Pen" subcampaign, 625
"Penelope" spot, 352
Penney, James Cash, 807
Penney's. *See* J.C. Penney Company, Inc.
Pennington, Ty, 1494
Pentium II processors, 771–775
"People Are Good" campaign, 61
"People first" tagline, 1465
People for the Ethical Treatment of Animals (PETA), 255
"People Rule" campaign, 609–612
Pepcid AC, 1324
Pepper, Dan, 812
Pepper, John E., 1400
Pepperidge Farm, Inc.
Cartoon Network, partnership with, 1611, 1614
"Goldfish Crackers" campaign, 265–268, *266*
Peppermint Prozac, 507
"Pepsi, It's the Cola" campaign, 1289–1292
Pepsi Blue, 1285
"The Pepsi Challenge" campaign, 1296
Pepsi Stuff, 1279
PepsiCo, Inc., **1267–1305**
The Coca-Cola Company, as competitor of, 351, 352
Gatorade, 342–343
"Generation Next" campaign, 259
Pepsi Edge, 241
Slice revival, 1020
Snapple, as competitor of, 1657
Starbucks, partnership with, 49, 1197–1198
Taco Bell, acquisition of, 1592
See also Frito-Lay Inc.
Perdue, Arthur W., 1307–1308
Perdue, Frank, 1307, 1308, 1309
Perdue, Jim, 1307–1308, 1309, 1310
Perdue Farms Inc., **1307–1310**
Pereira, Frank, 642
Perez, Antonio, 722–723
Perez, William, 1140
"Perfect" campaign, 376–377, 1797–1799
Periera, Frank, 644
Peripherals, computer, 911–914
Perkins, Sam, 167
Perlman, Hank, 518–519
Perot, H. Ross, 501, 502
Perry, Luke, 485
Persil, 1378, 1685
"Person to Person" campaign, 414, 416–417
Personal computers
AOL Optimized PC, 65
Apple Computer "Switchers" campaign, 138–141
Apple Computer "Think Different" campaign, 141–145
Dell "Dude, You're Getting a Dell" campaign, 403–406
Gateway "People Rule" campaign, 609–612
Hewlett-Packard "Expanding Possibilities" campaign, 721–723
IBM, 789
IBM "Solutions for a Small Planet" campaign, 797–801
"iMac" campaign, 131–135

Intel microprocessors, 767–771, 771–775
peripherals, 911–914
Personal watercraft, 1352–1356
"Personally Invested" campaign, 162
Personals ads, 1854–1857
"Perspectives" campaign, 1607–1609
Pert Plus "Sink Boy" campaign, 1391–1394
Pesci, Joe, 1648
Pestridge, Simon, 1142
Pet food
Mars, Forrest, canned pet-food invention by, 939
Purina "Incredible Dogs" campaign, 1111–1114
Whiskas "Inner Beast" campaign, 934–937
"Pet Store" spot, 40
Peter Pan syndrome, 1627–1628
Peterman, Dan, 1083
Peters, Erich, 1298
Peterson, Bob, 1513
Peterson, Duane, 230, 231
Peterson, George, 522
Peterson, Jack, 361
Peterson, Kim, 16
Peterson, Matt, 1513
Peterson, Robert, 811
Peterson Milla Hooks, 1599–1602
Pete's Brewing Company, 201
Petro, Aleksandr, 1697
Petty, Kyle, 841
Petty, Richard, 1094
Petty, Tom, 136
Pfizer, Charles, 1311, 1325
Pfizer Inc., **1311–1328**
PGA Tour, 399–401
Pharmaceuticals
Advil "Liqui-Gels" campaign, 1839–1842
Novartis Zelnorm "Tummies" campaign, 1209–1212
Paxil "Social Anxiety Disorder" campaign, 665–668
"The Power of Zyrtec" campaign, 1311–1314
Prozac print campaign, 505–508
Rolaids "Super Fans" campaign, 1322–1325
"Viagra Launch" campaign, 1325–1328
Pharmacia & Upjohn, Inc., 1313
Pharmacies. *See* Drugstores
"Pharmacy" spot, 661
Pharmavite LLC, **1329–1332**
Phelan, Patricia, 515
Philadelphia Eagles, 894
Philip Morris Companies Inc.
"Antitobacco" campaign and, 246
"Marlboro Man" campaign, 99
Miller Brewing Company, acquisition of, 1017
name change, 249
"Think. Don't Smoke" campaign, 98
See also Altria Group Inc.
Philips, Anton, 189
Philips, Brian, 546
Philips, Gerard, 1189
Philips Company, 1189
Philips Electronics North America Corp., **1333–1336**, 1528
Phillips, Paul, 793
Phillips Petroleum Company, 307
Phoenix, Lauren, 74
Phoenix Companies, 688–689
"Photo Fusion" feature, 559, 560–561
Photography
Canon "85 Second Photo Lab" campaign, 277–280
Fuji Photo Film "Meet the Greens" campaign, 587–590
Hewlett-Packard "You + HP" campaign, 723–727
Kodak "Advantix" campaign, 479–482
Kodak "The Best Part of Photography Is the Prints" campaign, 482–485
Kodak "Tall Tales" campaign, 488–491
Nikon "Mass Market Initiative" campaign, 1159–1162
"The Nikon School" campaign, 1162–1165
Polaroid "I-Zone/Joycam/Sticky Film Teen" campaign, 1357–1360
Polaroid "See What Develops" campaign, 1360–1363
"Take Pictures. Further" campaign, 485–488
Piaf, Edith, 183
Piaggio, Enrico, 1338
Piaggio USA, Inc., **1337–1340**
Piazza, Mike, 1860, 1861
Picasso, Pablo, 602, 1230
"Picture Book" spot, 726
Piech, Ferdinand, 1782
Piedmont Federal Savings and Loan Association, **1341–1344**
"Pigeons" spot, 1173
Pilgrim, Lonnie "Bo," 1673
Pilgrim's Pride, 1673
"Piñata" spot, 1828, 1829
Pinheiro, Mitchell B., 1811, 1812
"Pink Room" spots, 1594, 1596
Pinkett Smith, Jada, 598, 600
Pippen, Scottie, *671*, 672–673, 1056
Pirko, Tom, 241, 347, 1297
Piscopo, Joe, 1301
"Pitcher" spot, 617
Pitney, Jack, 170, 172, 173
Pitt, Brad, 1617
Pizza, frozen, 862–865
Pizza chains
Little Caesar "Cloning" campaign, 897–900
Little Caesar "Grand Canyon" campaign, 900–903
Little Caesar "Safety Video" campaign, 903–906
Little Caesar "Talking Pizzas" campaign, 906–910
Pizza Hut "Big New Yorker Pizza" campaign., 1345–1348
Round Table Pizza "The Last Honest Pizza" campaign, 1429–1432
Pizza Hut, Inc., **1345–1348**, *1346*
Little Caesar, as competitor of, 898, 899, 902, 904–905
Round Table Pizza, as competitor of, 1431
"Pizza! Pizza!" tagline, 898, 905
"Plan B" ad, 1207
"Planet Zortron" ad, 1207
Plansker, Jeffery, 1407
Plant, Robert, 636
Planters Nuts, 441
Platt, Lewis, 721, 722
"Play" campaign, 1144–1147
PLAY Foundation, 1137
"Play. Laugh. Grow." campaign, 881, 953–956
Play That Funky Music (song), 769, 771
Playboy magazine, 170, 173
PlayStation 2
"Fun, Anyone?" campaign, 1523–1526
Xbox, as competitor of, 1001, 1002–1003
Playtex, 1385–1387
"Please Be Quiet—Tax Day 20" spot, 689
"The Poachers" spot, 707
Pocket Pumps, 921, 922
Pocketknives, 1587–1590
Pogany, Don, 127, 1223
Poh, Jim, 170
"Point of View" spot, 962
Poitier, Sidney, 275
Poland Spring, 1275–1276

Polaris Industries, Inc., **1349–1356**, *1350, 1353*
Polaroid Corporation, **1357–1363**
Polartec "Forward Fabric" campaign, 923–926
Polhemus, John, 681
Police Athletic League (PAL) program, 26
Political advertising
  Jesse Ventura "Retaliate in '98" campaign, 1739–1742
  "Morning Again in America" spot, 1467
  MoveOn.org "Real People" campaign, 1073–1076
  "Swift Boat Veterans for Truth" campaign, 1583–1585
Polk Automotive Loyalty Awards, 394
Polo, 1628
"Polygraph Backrub" spot, 1012
Polynice, Olden, 166
Polzin, Michael, 511
Pond's "Soothing Cucumber Eye Treatments Ads" campaign, 1690–1693
"Poodle" spot, 588
"Pool" ad, 1607, 1608, 1609
"The Pool" spot, 1507
Pop, Iggy, 1426, 1441, 1443
Popeyes Chicken & Biscuits, 318, 841
Popkowski, John, 1323
Poppen, Sherman, 1514
Popular Photography (magazine), 1163, 1164
Populism, 1741
Pore Perfect strips, 1691–1692
Porges, Shelly, 1054
Porizkova, Paulina, 985
Porsche, Ferdinand, 1367
Porsche Cars North America Inc., **1365–1368**, *1366*
Porter, Chuck, 171
Porter, Emily, 82
Portfolio Awards, 1059
Portland Trailblazers, 168
Portrait (film), 61
"Portraits" campaign, 83, 84, 1041
Posehn, Brian, 651
Posen, Zac, 446
Posilac, 1035–1038
Posner, Victor, 1656
Post, Charles William "C. W.", 859, 862
Post, George, 411
Post Cereals
  General Mills, as competitor of, 628–629
  Kellogg Company, as competitor of, 832–833, 836
Postaer, Larry, 92
Postaer, Steffan, 1822, 1823, 1824
Poster campaigns
  Amtrak "Life on Acela" campaign, 1103, 1105
  Glenfiddich "Single Malt" campaign, 685
  MADD "Drunk Driving's a Serious Crime. Let's Treat It That Way." campaign, 1061–1062, 1063
  Travelocity "Roaming Gnome" campaign, 1651–1654
  Village Voice "Not America's Favorite Paper" campaign, 1755
  Wrangler "Rugged Wear" campaign, 1751
Pottery Barn, 535
Potts, Annie, 1331
Potty Training Kelly, 751
Poundstone, Paula, 1055
Powell, Matt, 1125
Powell of New York, 1421–1424
Power Lunch (television show), 37
"The Power of All of Us" tagline, 495, 498
"The Power of Dreams" campaign, 741–744
"The Power of Yes" campaign, 1802
"The Power of Zyrtec" campaign, 1311–1314
The Power (song), 1380
"Power to Quit" campaign, 661–665
PowerAde, 341–343, 1288, 1289
PowerBar, 932
"Powered by Tyson" campaign, 1671–1674
Powerpuff Girls (television show), 1614
PowerTouch Learning System
  LeapFrog, as competitor of, 880–881
  "Play. Laugh. Grow." campaign, 953–956
Prager, Iris, 1387
Pray, Doug, 659
Prefontaine, Steve, 1132, 1139
Preiss, Jeff, 1041
"Premature Pour" spot, 707
"Prepared so fresh you can taste it" campaign, 396
Prescription drugs. *See* Pharmaceuticals
"President of Beers" ad, 1450, 1452
Presidential campaigns. *See* Political advertising
Presley, Elvis, 1298, 1302
"Press Conference" spot, 986
Pressler, Paul, 887
Price, Greg, 780
Price, Nick, 1135
Price, Tim, 975
"Priceless" campaign, 84–85, 949–952, *950*, 1767, 1770
Priceline.com Incorporated, **1369–1372**
Pricing, 957–960
"A Priest, a Rabbi, and an Imam Are Walking Down the Street" spot, 33
Prima, Louis, 601
"Prime-time roadblock" strategy, 37
Prince George's County Public School, 880
Princess Cruise Lines, 1443
Pringles, 1398–1400
Print advertising
  A & F Quarterly campaign, 9–12
  "Absolut Print" campaign, 1729, 1730–1731, 1733–1737
  ACLU "Racial Profiling" campaign, 77
  Allegra "Spirit of Freedom" campaign, 1462
  "Altoids" campaign, 1823, 1825
  "American Apparel" campaign, 71–74
  American Express, 81
  American Express "Do More" campaign, 85
  Americans for the Arts "Art. Ask for More" campaign, 103
  Apple Computer "Think Different" campaign, 144
  Aquafina "Drink More Water" campaign, 1276
  BC Dairy Foundation "Don't Take Your Body for Granted" campaign, 184
  "The Book of Harley-Davidson" campaign, 701–704
  Borders "This Season, It's the Original Thought That Counts" campaign, 195–198
  Brigham's "Reverse the Curse" campaign, 207–210
  Business Leaders for Sensible Priorities "Move Our Money" campaign, 229–232
  "Campaign for Freedom" campaign, 33
  CareerBuilder "Time to Move On" campaign, 283
  Cargill
    "Collaborate>Create>Succeed" campaign, 287, 288
  Charles Schwab "Smarter Investors" campaign, 304

Chesebrough-Pond's "Soothing Cucumber Eye Treatments Ads" campaign, 1690–1693
Chevrolet "An American Revolution" campaign, 634
Chrysler "Engineered to Be Great Cars" campaign, 387
Cisco Systems "The Self-Defending Network" campaign, 323
Citigroup "Live Richly" campaign, 331
Club 18-30 "Perspectives" campaign, 1607–1609
Columbia Sportswear "Mother Boyle" campaign, 359–362
"Come See the Softer Side of Sears" campaign, 1487
Crate & Barrel 1998 campaign, 533–536
Cunard Line "Can you Wait?" campaign, 373–374
CVS "Life to the Fullest" campaign, 377
DHL "Competition. Bad for Them. Great for You." campaign, 421
Diamond Trading Company "Raise Your Right Hand" campaign, 443–446
Discover Brokerage campaign, 1058
Discover "Make a Statement" campaign, 1055
Dr. Martens Airwair "Beliefs" campaign, 459, 461
Dreyer's Grand Light "Unbelievable" campaign, 469–470
Estates of World Golf Village "Repositioning" campaign, 400–402
Ford "Driving American Innovation" campaign, 558
French Connection "Scent to Bed" campaign, 579–582
Fuji Photo Film "Meet the Greens" campaign, 589–590
Gap "For Every Generation" campaign, 597
Gap "How Do You Wear It?" campaign, 600
Gap "This Is Easy" campaign, 607
Gateway "People Rule" campaign, 611
General Electric "Imagination At Work" campaign, 625
General Foods International Coffees "It's How to Unplug" campaign, 862
General Motors "EV1 Introduction" campaign, 643–644
General Motors "Hummer" campaign, 647
General Motors "Looking for Mr. Goodwrench" campaign, 651
Hallmark Cards "Sneak a Peek" campaign, 694
Hershey Reese's "There's No Wrong Way to Eat a Reese's" campaign, 712, 714
Hewlett-Packard "You + HP" campaign, 723–724
Honda "The Power of Dreams" campaign, 743
Honda "What About Now?" campaign, 91, *92, 93*
IBM "Can You See It?" campaign, 787
IBM "Linux" campaign, 796
"iMac" campaign, 134
"ING Launch" campaign, 765
"It Happens At the Hilton" campaign, 731–732
"Jenny McCarthy for Candie's" campaign, 749–753
JetBlue "Unbelievable" campaign, 818–822
Johnnie Walker "Keep Walking" campaign, 425
Kraft "It's Not Delivery, It's DiGiorno" campaign, 865
La-Z-Boy "The New Look of Comfort" campaign, 877
LeapFrog "Learn Something New Every Day!" campaign, 881
Lee jeans "Find Your One True Fit" campaign, 1748
Levi's "They Go On" campaign, 890
"Levi's Type 1 Jeans" campaign, 888
Lincoln National "Hello Future" campaign, 896
Little Caesar Unlimited Pizzas campaign, 899
Logitech "What Will You Do With All That Freedom?" campaign, 913
Lubriderm "See You Later, Alligator," 1322
Lycos "Go Get It" campaign, 915, *916*
MCI "1-800-COLLECT" campaign, 973
Motorola "Intelligence Everywhere" campaign, 1065–1068
Mountain Dew "Code Red" campaign, 1269
NASCAR "How Bad Have You Got It?" campaign, 1096
Negro Leagues Baseball Museum "1998 Print Campaign," 1107–1109
New York State Lottery "If I Had a Million Dollars" campaign, 1129
"Nextel. Done." campaign, 1552
Nike "Product Assault" campaign, 1147–1150
"The Nikon School" campaign, 1162–1165
Nissan "Quest Minivan Launch" campaign, 1176
Nordstrom "Make Room for Shoes" campaign, 1183
Nordstrom "Reinvent Yourself" campaign, 1184, 1186–1187
North Carolina "Heritage" campaign, 1201, 1203–1204
Northwest Airlines "E-Ticket" campaign, 1205–1208
Novartis Zelnorm "Tummies" campaign, 1211
Outward Bound "Oceans, Mountains, Forests, Fear. Which Do You Conquer First?" campaign, 1237–1240
Peace Corps "Life Is Calling. How Far Will You Go?" campaign, 1264
Perdue "Now Arriving" campaign, 1310
Philips Electronics "Getting Better" campaign, 1335
Piedmont Federal "It's Your Mortgage. Keep It Here." campaign, 1343
Polaroid "I-Zone/Joycam/Sticky Film Teen" campaign, 1359
Polaroid "See What Develops" campaign, 1361
Polartec "Forward Fabric" campaign, 925
Prozac print campaign, 505–508
Purina "Incredible Dogs" campaign, 1111, 1113
Rolex "Celebrity Endorsement" campaign, 1043–1046
"Rolling Rock Ads" campaign, 869
Royal Caribbean "Get Out There" campaign, 1443
Saab "Life Is Not a Spectator Sport" campaign, 1447
Schwinn/GT "Fast. It's Corporate Policy." campaign, 1249–1252
Schwinn "What a Ride" campaign, 1252–1256
Sears "Todo para ti (Everything for you)" campaign, 1489
Seattle SuperSonics "In Your Home" campaign, 167
Secret Sparkle "When You're Strong, You Sparkle" campaign, 1402
Sierra Club "Hybrid Evolution" campaign, 1509
Sims Sports "Be Free" campaign, 1513–1516

Print advertising, ***continued***
Snickers Marathon bar "The Energy You Crave" campaign, 933
Song Airlines "Let Yourself Fly" campaign, 409–410
Sony "What's Next?" campaign, 1531–1534
"Specialized" campaign, 1539–1542
Stanley Steemer "Living Brings It In. We Take It Out." campaign, 1560
Steelcase "Work Effectiveness" campaign, 1575–1578
Stolichnaya "Russian Art" campaign, 1705–1708
"Swiss Army Equipped" campaign, 1587–1590
Tampax Pearl "Ingenious Protection for Ingenious Women" campaign, 1388
Target "*New Yorker* Magazine Sponsorship" campaign, 1599–1602
Texaco "A World of Energy" campaign, 308
Time "The World's Most Interesting Magazine" campaign, 1615–1617
Tommy Hilfiger "American Tartans" campaign, 1627–1630
TV Guide "On the Inside" campaign, 1669
Tyson Foods "Powered by Tyson" campaign, 1674
United Airlines "It's Time to Fly" campaign, 1696, 1697
United Airlines "Rising" campaign, 1700
UnitedHealth Group "It Just Makes Sense" campaign, 1727
UPS "Moving at the Speed of Business" campaign, 1711–1712
"US Open Excitement" campaign, 1723
Verizon Wireless "Can You Hear Me Now?" campaign, 299
Victory Motorcycles "The New American Motorcycle" campaign, 1349–1352
Village Voice "Not America's Favorite Paper" campaign, 1753–1756
Virgin Atlantic Airways "Go, Jet Set, Go!" campaign, 1759
Virginia Tourism Corporation "Meet Virginia" campaign, 1763
"Visa. It's Everywhere You Want to Be" campaign, 1768
Wrangler "Rugged Wear" campaign, 1749–1751
Xbox "It's Good to Play Together" campaign, 1001, 1002

"Printer" spot, 1712
Printers
Hewlett-Packard "Built By Engineers, Used By Ordinary People" campaign, 717–720
Xerox "Keep the Conversation Going, Share the Knowledge" campaign, 1843–1847
Priority Mail, 1718, 1720
"Privacy Manager" campaign, 153–156
Private-label jeans
Lee jeans, as competitor of, 1744
Levi's jeans, as competitors of, 884–885
Private label vitamins and herbal supplements, 1329, 1331
Procter, William, 1377, 1380, 1398
The Procter & Gamble Company, **1373–1403**
cat food, 935
Clairol, purchase of, 336
Frito-Lay, as competitor of, 585
Kimberly-Clark, as competitor of, 844–855
Pfizer, as competitor of, 1320–1321
Unilever, as competitor of, 1684–1685
See also Global Gillette
Proctor, Mike, 1513
"Proctor" radio spot, 688
"Prodigy" spot, 795, 796–797
"Product Assault" campaign, 1147–1150
Product placement
BMW motorcycle in *Tomorrow Never Dies,* 986, 989
BMW Z3 in *Goldeneye,* 986, 989
Dunkin' Donuts, 48
HotJobs.com on *The Apprentice,* 1041
Mercedes ML320 in *Lost World: Jurassic Park,* 989, 993
new twenty dollar bill, 217–218
Swiss Army Brands in *Armageddon,* 1590
Tyson Foods on Viacom shows, 1674
"Product Tester" spot, 1021
Production Farm, 3
Proferes, Patricia, 973
Professional Golfers' Association, 1275
Progressive Insurance
Allstate, as competitor of, 52
Geico, as competitor of, 614, 620
State Farm, as competitor of, 1571, 1572
Progresso soups, 270
Prohibition, 106

"Project: Real People" campaign, 1855, 1856
Promax Judge's Choice award, 593
Promotions
"Diet Coke Untapped," 354
Diet Rite/Zero Gravity Corporation promotion, 240, 242
Kraft "Be a DiGiorno Delivery Guy" promotion, 865
Levi's "Gold Rush" promotion, 886, 888
M&M's "Global Color Vote" promotion, 937, 939–940
Purina "Incredible Dog Challenge," 1113–1114
Propaganda
"Campaign for Freedom" campaign as, 33–34
"It's a Woman Thing" campaign as, 57
Propaganda Films, 88
Proposition 99 (California), 244
"Protect/Create Wealth" campaign, 367–370
Proudfoot, Kevin, 522
Proulx, Erik, 1251
Prozac, 505–508, *506,* 665–666
The Prudential Insurance Company of America, **1405–1408**
John Hancock, as competitor of, 825, 827–828
MetLife, as competitor of, 998–999
Pruismann, Jason, 1371
Pryce, Jonathan, 1178, 1179
PT Cruiser, 387, 388
Public Broadcasting Service, **1409–1412**
Public service campaigns
American Legacy Foundation "Truth" campaign, 97–100
Americans for the Arts "Art. Ask for More" campaign, 101–104
"Campaign for Freedom" campaign, 31–32
ConAgra Foods' Feeding Children Better "Child Hunger" campaign, 363–366
MADD "Drunk Driving's a Serious Crime. Let's Treat It That Way." campaign, 1061–1063
Rock the Vote "Yes/No Ballot Box" campaign, 1425–1428
Publicis
Fuji Photo Film "Meet the Greens" campaign, 587–590
T-Mobile "Get More" campaign, 1623–1626
TBS campaign, 522

Turner Broadcasting System "TBS Very Funny" campaign, 1662–1665
Publicis & Hal Riney
Discovery Communications "Two Guys" campaign, 451
First Union "Financial World" campaign, 1789–1792
Gardenburger "Eating Good Just Got Great" campaign, 1817–1820
Saturn "Why Didn't Anyone Think of This Before?" campaign, 1468–1472
"Sprint PCS" campaign, 1553–1556
Puentes, Bill, 437
Puffs, 844–845
Puppies, 1435
Purcell, Philip, 1050
Purina
"Incredible Dogs" campaign, 1111–1114
"Purina Dog Chow Every Day" campaign, 1112
Whiskas, as competitor of, 935–936
"Purse" spot, 530–531
Pursell, 1485
Push-to-talk technology, 1551, 1552
"Putting You Back in the Picture" campaign, 415
Puzder, Andrew, 290, 697, 699
PWC. *See* Personal watercraft
Pyne, Ben, 1664
Pyro, 459–462
Pytka, Joe, 365, 1180, 1298, 1552

Q

Q45, Infiniti, 1177–1180
Q-Link, 63, 64, 68
Quake (computer game), 381
Quaker Oats Company
Gatorade, 342, 343, 1287
Kellogg Company, as competitor of, 833
"Quaker-Warms You, Heart and Soul" campaign, 1292–1295
Snapple, acquisition of, 259, 1655, 1656–1657
Qualcomm phones spot, 539
Quality Care service centers, 650
Qualls, Roxanne, 1400
Quantum Computer Services, Inc., 63, 68
Quark, Inc., 658
Queen, 599
Queen Mary 2 (ship), 371–374
"Queen of Carbs" ad, 1450, 1452
"Queen" spot, 355, 356
Queeny, John, 1035
Quesnelle, George, 662, 664
Quest
"Launch" campaign, 1174–1177
Sienna, as competitor of, 1645
Questrom, Allen, 807, 808
"Quick and Easy" spot, 915
"Quicksand" spot, 389, 390, 391
Quinlan, Michael, 963
Quinn, Joanna, 1697
The Quiznos Master LLC, 456, **1413–1416**
Qwest Communications, 1837

R

R. C. Auletta & Company, 1339
R. Griggs Group, 459, 460
R. J. Reynolds, 1094
R/West, 1580–1582
Raab, Steve, 1499
"Race-car" campaign, 1684
Race/ethnicity
Abercrombie & Fitch, 12
ACLU "Racial Profiling" campaign, 75–78
California Department of Health Services "Antismoking" campaign, 243
Nike "Hello World" and "I Am Tiger Woods" campaigns, 1136–1137
smoking, 56
"Race" spot, 255
"Racial Profiling" campaign, 75–78
Radcliffe, Ted "Double Duty," 1107
Radiant Silk, 1402
Radio, 580
Radio advertising
Americans for the Arts "Art. Ask for More" campaign, 103
Anheuser-Busch "Louie the Lizard" campaign, 118
Anheuser-Busch "Real American Heroes" campaign, 123–126
"AOL Latino" campaign, 65
Breathe Right Strips "Back in the Sack" campaign, 339
Brigham's "Reverse the Curse" campaign, 207
Business Leaders for Sensible Priorities "Move Our Money" campaign, 231
Carter Products "Trojan Man" campaign, 314
Coca-Cola "Real" campaign, 352
DirecTV "Celebrities Read Fan Mail to DirecTV (Become a DirecTV Fan Now)" campaign, 449
drugstore.com "A Very Healthy Way to Shop" campaign, 473
eBay "Abbreviated" campaign, 493–496
Hollywood Video "Welcome to Hollywood" campaign, 735–736
"iMac" campaign, 134–135
Lincoln National "Hello Future" campaign, 896
Little Caesar "Pizza by the Foot" campaign, 905
Mountain Dew "Code Red" campaign, 1269
priceline.com, 1370
Red Lobster "Life on Land Is Dry" campaign, 397
Scotts Miracle-Gro "Neighbor to Neighbor" campaign, 1485
"Ted Launch" campaign, 1703
Radio Mercury Awards
Anheuser-Busch "Real American Heroes/Real Men of Genius" campaign, 126
eBay "Abbreviated" campaign, 493, 495
RadioShack, 1548
Radner, Gilda, 1488
Raevskaja, Irina, 1707
Rafferty, Bill, 865
"Rainbow Connection" campaign, 283
Rainbow/Push Coalition, 349
Rainey Kelly Campbell Roalfe/Y&R, 1235
Rainforest Action Network, 330
RainierVision, 1245, 1246, 1247
"Raise Your Right Hand" campaign, 443–446
"Raising the Bar" campaign, 299
Raj, Robin, 1426, 1427
Ralenkotter, Rossi, 873
Ralston Purina. *See* Nestlé Purina PetCare Co.
Ramsay, Michael, 1620, *1620*
Randee of the Redwoods, 1078
Rao, Maya, 1083
Rap. *See* Hip-hop
Rapaille, G. Clotaire, 387, 388, 1375
Rapala "Custom Lures" campaign, 1193–1196
Raphael, Sally Jesse, 1689
Rasmussen, Bill, 517, 521
Rasmussen, Robert, 1499
Rasmussen, William F., 513
Rath, Carlie, 1812
Ratings, television, 5, 8
Rattin, Mark, 1394

"Ravaged" spot, 1585
Raven, Abbe, 1663
Ravenhall, Kitty, 315
Rawlings, Mike, 1346, 1348
Rayovac, 510–511
Razors
 Schick Intuition "Shaving Made Simple" campaign, 1477–1480
 "Tracer FX Ads" campaign, 1314–1317
3rd Rock from the Sun (television show), 6
"Read-In" literacy program, 1605
Reader's Digest, 97–98, 1677
Ready-to-drink coffees, 1197–1198
Ready-to-drink teas, 1298–1302
"Ready to Move Up?" tagline, 303
Reagan, Ronald, 804, 1467, 1661
"Real American Heroes/Real Men of Genius" campaign, 123–126, *124*
"Real California Cheese" campaign, 253, 254, 255
"Real" campaign, 350–353
"Real Compared to What" spot, 352
"Real Cooking" campaign, 1687–1690
Real estate, 399–402
"Real Experiences" campaign. *See* "Bottles Personified" campaign
"Real Life, Real Answers" campaign, 823, 824, 827
"Real People" campaign, 1073–1076
Reality-based television commercials, 269
Reality Bites (movie), 246
Reality shows
 Airline, 44
 Burger King/*The Apprentice* partnership, 221
 "Tiny House" spot, 620–621
RealPlayer, 1087
Reames, Scott, 1143
Rebates, 1050
"Red Dot" campaign, 1387
Red Hot Chili Peppers, 1426
Red Label Johnnie Walker, 425
Red Lobster, 395–398
Red Orb Entertainment, 379–380, 381, 382
Red Sky, 719–720
"Red X" campaign, 768, 772
Red Zone, 1402
Redenbacher, Orville, 1309
Redford, Robert, 1409, 1410, 1697
Redington, Frederick W., 1457
Reebok International Ltd., 1417–1420
 adidas, as competitor of, 21, 25
 Fila, as competitor of, 553
 Nike, as competitor of, 1133, 1136, 1140, 1146, 1149, 1155
Reed, Rick, 1585
Reene, Michael, 790
Reese, Harry Burnett, 710, 712
ReeseSticks "The Crisp You Can't Resist!" campaign, 709–712
Reeves, Rosser, 1839
"Reflex Action Razor" campaign, 1189–1192
Reform Party, 1739–1741
Refund Rewards ad, 688
Register.com, 676–677
Reich, Michael, 1754, 1755
Reid, Peter, 116
Reidl, George, 1798
ReignCom Ltd., 137
Reilly, Anne-Michelle, 1264
Reimaging
 KFC, 397
 The Melting Pot, 397
 Red Lobster, 398
"Reincarnation" spot, 994, 996
Reingold, Arthur, 863, 864
Reinman, Sally, 1635
"Reinvent Yourself" campaign, 1184–1187
Reiser, Paul, 153, 1545, 1548, 1837
Reith, Kathryn, 1154
"Relax, It's FedEx" campaign, 544–547
"Relay" spot, 726
"Remember Rainier" campaign, 1245–1248
Remington, 1190
Remodeling
 CVS, 376
 Holiday Inn, 779
 KFC restaurants, 840
 Little Caesar's stores, 908
 Office Depot, 1214, 1216
Renaissance, 1037
Renault, 1167, 1168, 1175
Reno, Nevada, 872–873
Renovation. *See* Remodeling
"Rent or Food" spot, 363
Rentschler, Fred, 1698
ReplayTV, 1620, 1621–1622
"Report on Sustainable Development" (Monsanto), 1038
"Repositioning" campaign, 399–402
"Reshape Your Attitude" campaign, 835
Resolve Fabric Freshener, 1389
"Restaurant" spot, 790
Restaurants
 Boston Market "Eat Something" campaign, 203–206
 Burger King "Lunch Break" campaign, 219–222
 Burger King "Subservient Chicken" campaign, 222–225
 Burger King "When You Have It Your Way, It Just Tastes Better" campaign, 225–228
 Carl's Jr. "Six Dollar Burger" campaign, 289–292
 Church's Chicken "Full Flavor, Full Pockets, Full Life" campaign, 317–320
 "Did Somebody Say McDonald's?" campaign, 960–964
 Hardee's "Revolution" campaign, 697–699
 Jack in the Box "Jack's Back" campaign, 811–814
 KFC "Chicken Capital USA" campaign, 839–842
 McDonald's "Campaign 55" campaign, 957–960
 McDonald's "I'm Lovin' It" campaign, 964–967
 McDonald's "We Love to See You Smile" campaign, 967–970
 Quiznos "Baby Bob" campaign, 1413–1415
 Red Lobster "Life on Land Is Dry" campaign, 395–398
 Subway "Jared Fogle" campaign, 455–458
 Taco Bell "Think Outside the Bun" campaign, 1591–1594
 Taco Bell "Want Some?" campaign, 1594–1597
 Wendy's "Fresh Stuffed Pita" campaign, 1809–1812
 Wendy's "Good to Be Square" campaign, 1812–1816
Restoration Hardware, 535
"Restore" spot, 724
Retail stores
 "Gateway Country," 611
 Negro Leagues Baseball Museum gift shop, 1108
 Song Airlines, 45, 410
 See also Department stores
"Retaliate in '98" campaign, 1739–1742, *1740*
Retired Teachers Association, 1263
"Retirement Home" spot, 304, 1520
Retton, Mary Lou, 1689
"Return of the Snapple Lady" campaign, 1655–1658
"Reunion" spot, 1087
Reuter, Edzard, 984
"Reverse the Curse" campaign, 207–210

Revlon
real women in ads, 1683
Target/Revlon advertising supplement, 1605
"Revolution" campaign (Hardee's), 697–699
"Revolution" spot (Nike), 1139
Rewards programs
American Express, 80–83
Marriott Rewards program, 930
Rexer, William, 177
Reynolds, Debbie, 1234
Reynolds, Patrick, 249, 1029
Rhapsody in Blue (song), 1695
The Rheingold Brewing Company, 1247, **1421–1424**
Rhymes, Busta, 1269, 1273
Ribisi, Giovanni, 1426
Ricci, Christina, 598, 599
Ricciardi, Joe, 644
Rice, Donna, 750
Rice, Jerry, 52, 338
Richards, Michael, 985, 989
Richards Group, 1667–1670
Richie, Lionel, 1278, 1296
Richino, Nick, 1125
Richmond Show, 1109
"The Rick" campaign, 513–516
Rickles, Don, 1058
Riddler, Sarah, 1422
"The Ride" spot (Schwinn), 1250
"Ride" spot (Trident gum), 233, 235
"Ride the Best" campaign, 1352–1356, *1353*
Riedl, George, 1797
Ries, Al, 330
Rigali, Monica, 1146
Right Guard "Anything Else Would Be Uncivilized" campaign, 669–673
"Right Hands" campaign, 52
"Rikkia" spot, 348
Riklis, Meshulam, 293
Rimes, LeAnn, 397
Riney, Hal, 1467
"Ring-around-the-Collar" campaign, 1683
Ringer, Randy, 150
Ringling Brothers and Barnum & Bailey Circus, 1767
"Ringo" spot, 527
Riordan, John, 1758
Ripken, Cal, Jr., 1396
"Rising" campaign, 1206–1207, 1537, 1695, 1698–1701
Risko, Robert, 1602
Riswold, Jim, 1133, 1136
Ritchie, Ashton, 1486
Ritchie, Guy, 60, 175, 177, 178, 995
Rite Aid
CVS, as competitor of, 377
drugstore.com partnership with, 471, 472
Walgreen, as competitor of, 1798
Ritts, Herb, 1736
Ritz crackers, 267
"Riven" campaign, 379–382
"River" spot, 1000
Rivers, Joan, 1824
R.J. Reynolds Tobacco Company
"Antitobacco" campaign, 246
lawsuit concerning antismoking spots, 250
"Roach Motel" spot, 739
"The Road Is Calling" campaign, 1646–1649
"Road Rage" spot, 1579, 1580, 1581
Road Runner, 1474
"Road Trip" spot, 770, 1715
"Roaming Gnome" campaign, 1651–1654
Roan, Tim, 1484, 1485
Robert Falls and Company, 1440
Roberts, Julia, 246
Roberts, Mike, 966
Roberts, Wyman, 396, 397
Robinson, George, 1111
Robinson, Jackie, 1107, 1137, 1233, 1235
Robinson, James, III, 87
"Robot" spot, 1717, 1720
"Rock Climber" spot, 999–1000
The Rock (film), 633
Rock n' Roll (song), 635, 636, 637
Rock the Vote, 1120, **1425–1428**
Rockapella, 1376
"Rocket Man" spot, 153
Rocky (film), 1659, 1661
Rocky Road ice cream, 1121
"Rocky" spot, 1659, 1661–1662
Roddick, Anita, 191, 192
Rode, Ellen, 1743
Rodeo, 1749
Rodkin, Gary, 1268
Rodman, Dennis
Converse campaign, 751
ESPN "This Is SportsCenter" campaign, 520
Roffman, Marvin, 734
Roger, Bob, 388
Rogers, Gary, 468, 470
Rogers, Mike, 1486
Rogers, Roy, 1293
Rogge, Joyce, 1537
Rohde, Ellen, 1744
Roisum, Joan, 1573
Rolaids "Super Fans" campaign, 1322–1325
Rolex
"Celebrity Endorsement" campaign, 1043–1046
Swiss Army Brands, as competitor of, 1589
Rolling Rock
"Grab a Rock" campaign, 759–762
"Rolling Rock Ads" campaign, 867–870
Rolling Stone magazine, 263
Rolling Stones, 1005
Rolston, Matthew, 1227
Roman Holiday (film), 1337
"Romeo and Juliet" spot, 1552
Romer v. Evans, 76
Ron Felcher (character), 1417, 1419
Ronald McDonald (character), 967–968, 969
Roogow, Buddy, 945, 946, 948
"Room Service" spot, 569
"Room" spot, 719, 720
Roosevelt, Franklin and Eleanor, 144
Roosevelt, Franklin D., 106
Roosevelt, Theodore
Abercrombie & Fitch, 9, 596, 599
"Good to the last drop." slogan, 859
Roper, Tim, 196, 197
Rose, Claudia, 445
Rose, John W., 1727
Rose Art, 188
Rosen, David, 238
Rosen, Rob, 279
Rosendahl, Tim, 398
Rosensteele, Jim, 367
Rosenthal, Amy, 890
"Rosie O'Doll," 856
"Rosie O'Donnell and Penny Marshall" campaign, 849, 854–858, 1489
Ross, Matt, 800
Ross, Rich, 1664
Ross & Company, 925
Rossi, Chris, 1757, 1758, 1759
Roth, Hayes, 1806
Rothman, Sam, 27, 28
Round Table Pizza, **1429–1432**
Roundtree, Richard, 1277
Roundup, 1035
Rourke, Mickey, 175, 702
Routenberg, Eric, 1359
Roux, Michel, 1734
Rowden, Ian, 221
Rowlands, Gena, 1747
Rowley, Craig, 703, 704

Roxio, 1085–1088
Royal Appliance Manufacturing Company, **1433–1440**
Royal Caribbean Cruises Ltd., **1441–1444**, *1442*
  Carnival Corporation, as competitor of, 295
  Cunard Line, as competitor of, 373
Rozenich, Anna, 959
R&R Partners, 871–874
RSA USA, 61
"Rubber Ducky" spot, 156
"Rubberband Man" spot, 1221, 1222–1223, 1565
Rubin, Gerry, 92
Rubin Postaer, 92–95
"Ruby" campaign, 191–194
Rudkin, Margaret, 265, 266
Rudolph, Steve, 531
Rudy, Frank, 1138
"The Rugby Bunch" spot, 1225, 1227
"Rugged Wear" campaign, 1749–1751
Rukeyser, Louis, 1410
Run-DMC, 608
"Run" spot, 744
"Runners, Yeah, We're Different" campaign, 19–22
"Running Man" icon, 65, *67*, 68–69
"Running Man" spot, 1648
Running shoes. *See* Athletic footwear
"Running" spot, 1153
"Running with the Squirrels" spot, 503, 504
Rusen, Hart, 1580
Rush, Marvin, 644
Ruskin, Gary, 199, 242
Russ, Peter, 553
Russell, Alan, 184
Russell, Tom, 1222
Russell Stover Candies, 711
"Russian Art" campaign, 1705–1708
Rust, Edward B., Jr., 1573
Ruth, Alice, 606
Ruth, Babe, 208, 1293
Rutherford, Joan C., 588
Ryan, Nolan, 515
Ryder, Tom, 1677
Ryder, Winona, 246
Ryman, Steve, 852, 853

S

Saab Cars USA, Inc., **1445–1448**
Saarinen, Eric, 999
Saarinen, Lauri, 1193–1194, 1195
Saatchi & Saatchi Advertising
  Cheerios "Stories" campaign, 627–630
  Club 18-30 "Perspectives" campaign, 1607–1609
  Delta Air Lines "On Top of the World" campaign, 411–414, 415
  Gillette "Anything Else Would Be Uncivilized" campaign, 673
  "Riven" campaign, 379–382
  "Smiley" the Goldfish, 266
  "Thank You, Paine Webber" campaign, 1675–1678
  Toyota Corolla "A Car to Be Proud Of" campaign, 1631–1634
  Toyota "Everyday" campaign, 1634–1637
  Toyota "Fuel for Thought" campaign, 1638–1640
  Toyota Sienna "Kids Rule" campaign, 1645–1646
SABMiller plc, **1449–1455**
  See also Miller Brewing Company
Sabre Holdings, 1651
Sachs, Becky, 977, 1294
Sack, Mary Lou, 1406
"Safety Video" campaign, 903–906
"Sailor" spot, 314
Salakhova, Aidan, 1707
Salasnek, Noah, 1515
Salon Selectives, 1393
"Salon" spot, 1793
Salt-N-Pepa, 1552
Salzman, Marian, 136
Same-sex marriage, 657–660
Sample, Fitzgerald, 1810
Samples, 864
Sampras, Pete, 1722
Samsung
  Motorola, as competitor of, 1070
  Sony, partnership with, 1526–1528
Samuel Adams beer, 199–202, *200*
San Francisco Ad Club awards, 885
Sanders, Barry, 1149
Sanders, Deion
  annual endorsement income, 552
  Visa Check Card "Works Like a Check" campaign, 1769, 1771
Sanders, Harland, 397
Sandor, David, 82
Sands, Mike, 653, 655
Sanford, Isabelle, 1230
Sanford, L.P., **1457–1460**
Sanford, William H., Jr., 1457
Sann, Ted, 303, 527, 1297
Sanofi-Aventis, **1461–1464**
Sapka, Steve, 220, 221
Sappi Print Media Efficiency Award, 18
"Sarah's Escapade" spot, 321
Sarajevo Olympic Children's Fund, 107
Sarandon, Susan, 1683
"Sara's Escapade" spot, 323
Sargent, Ron, 1215, 1563, 1564, 1566
Satellite television, 447–450
"Saturday Night" spot, 828–829
"Saturday" spot, 491
Saturn Corporation, **1465–1472**
  "Saturn Relaunch" campaign, 1465–1467
  "Why Didn't Anyone Think of This Before?" campaign, *1470*
Savage, Terry, 1308, 1524
Sawyer, Linda, 756
Sayers, Tyrone, 1627, 1629, 1630
SBC Communications Inc., 150, **1473–1476**
Scaglione, Bob, 1508
Scaly, Sam, 1309
Scandal Music, 125
Scandals
  insurance companies, 1406, 1407
  LeapFrog, 880
Scaros & Casselman, 731
Scarpelli, Bob
  Bud Light campaign, 116, 1023
  Ikea campaign, 755
  J. C. Penney "It's All Inside" campaign, 807, 810
"Scent to Bed" campaign, 579–582
Schaden, Rick, 456
Schaefer, Audrey, 1551
Schaefer, George, 1091
Schaeffer, Pierre, 484
Schechter, Alvin, 1770
Scheider, Roy, 1235
Schenck, Ernie, 825
Schenkenburg, Markus, 1230
Scher, Laura, 1835
Scherck, Ted, 546
Schering-Plough
  Hoescht, as competitor of, 1463
  Pfizer, as competitor of, 1312–1313
Scherstrom, Norm, 1719
Schettini, William, 457
Schick, Jack, 1478
Schick, Jacob, 1189
"Schick Tracer FX Ads" campaign, 1314–1317
Schick-Wilkinson Sword, **1477–1480**
Schiffer, Claudia, 888
Schiller, Derek, 27
Schindler, Scott, 1041
Schlaet, Arnold, 305–306
Schmeling, Max, 2, 3

Schmid, Ron, 663
Schmidt, Jim, 534, 535, 1799
Schneider, Don, 1297
Schneider, George, 105
Schneiderman, David, 1753, 1754, 1755, 1756
Schoen, Kim, 521
Schofield, Stan, 672
"School" spot, 65
School supplies
  Staples "That Was Easy" campaign, 1565–1566
  Staples "Yeah, We've Got That" campaign, 1567–1569
Schroer, Jim, 564
Schulman, Dan, 151
Schulman, Jessica, 142, 143
Schultz, Howard, 1089, 1091
Schumacker, Jim, 114, 122
Schwab, Bill, 370
Schwab, Charles, 301
Schwab, Mark J., 693
Schwan's Sales Enterprises, 864
Schwarzenegger, Arnold, 645
Schweitzer, Mark, 1551, 1552
Schwinn/GT "Fast. It's Corporate Policy." campaign, 1249–1252
Schwinn "What a Ride" campaign, *1253, 1254*
Sciarra, Pina, 346
Scient Corp., 502
Scion, 174, 1778
Scooby-Doo (television show), 1612, 1614
Scoop, Fatman, 1269, 1273
"Score" spot, 276
Scorsese, Martin, 1409, 1410
Scotch whiskey, 683–686
Scothon, Chuck, 954
Scott, George C., 231, 739
Scott, Jake, 1143
Scott, Kirk, 282
Scott, O. M., 1481
Scott, Ridley, 178, 1234
Scott, Ridley and Tony, 61
Scott, Tony, 178
Scott, Willard, 295
Scott Paper, 844, 845
Scotts Miracle-Gro Company, **1481–1486**
"Scratch & Win-Match & Win" contest, 1440
"Screw" spot, 681
"Screwy, Ain't It?" tagline, 1611, 1613
Scrubs (television show), 849
Scully, Kevin, 1240
Scurry, Briana, 1156
Sea-Doo, 1355
"Sea Monster" spot, 279
Seacrist, Kelly, 977
Seade, Liz, 1057, 1059
Sealy, 1502
"Seamless" spot, 1648
Search engines
  "Do You Yahoo!?" campaign, 1849–1853
  Lycos "Go Get It" campaign, 915–918
"Search for America's Most Incredible Dog" contest, 1114
"The Search" spot, 1159, 1161
"Searchlight" spot, 204
Sears, Barry, 932
Sears, Roebuck & Co., **1487–1495**, *1492*
  Discover card, 1050, 1051, 1054
  J.C. Penney, as competitor of, 809
  Kmart, as competitor of, 855–856
  Kmart merger with, 850
  Target, as competitor of, 1604
"Sears. Where Else?" campaign, 1491–1495
Sears Tower, 1493
Seattle SuperSonics, 165
Seay, Douglas, 1818
SEC. *See* Securities and Exchange Commission (SEC)
Second City, 566
Secondhand smoke, 246, 247, 250
Secret Sparkle "When You're Strong, You Sparkle" campaign, 1401–1403
Securities and Exchange Commission (SEC), 1057
"Security Camera" campaign, 1295–1298
Sedelmaier, Josef, 1810
Sedgwick Rd., 1801–1804
"See What Develops" campaign, 1360–1363
"See You Later, Alligator" campaign, 1317–1322, *1318, 1319*
"See Your Small Business on the Super Bowl" campaign, 919–922
"See Yourself Succeeding" campaign, 303
Seergy, Michael, 1174
Seese, Guy, 1247
Sega of America, Inc., **1497–1500**, 1524–1525
Segal, Gordon and Carole, 534, 536
Seger, Bob, 564
Sehorn, Jason, 303, 304
Seibert, Fred, 1612
Seinfeld, Jerry
  A&E profiles, 1661
  American Express campaign, 951
  American Express "Do More" campaign, 82–86
  "Seinfeld" campaign, 86–90, 327, 1056
Seinfeld (television show), 87, 88
  advertisers, 1841
  Advil "Liqui-Gels" campaign, 1841
  Gardenburger "Eating Good Just Got Great" campaign, 1817, 1818, 1819, 1820
  mock promotion of ABC's campaign, 6
  Nice 'n Easy hair coloring ad, 334
  Old Navy "Woof" spot, 1228
  "Visa. It's Everywhere You Want to Be" campaign, 1767
Selassie, Haile, 25
Seldane, 1313, 1462, 1463
"The Self-Defending Network" campaign, 321–324
Self-service digital-photo kiosks, 483, 484
Selig, Allan H. "Bud," 1278
Selleck, Tom, 857
Sellers, Peter, 174
Seminars, 1710
Senate Foreign Relations Committee, 1584
Sendak, Maurice, 155
Senior citizens, 1342
Sensor razors, 1315, 1316
Seomin, Scott, 829
September 11th terrorist attacks
  A & F Quarterly campaign, 12
  ACLU ads, 77
  Advertising Council "Campaign for Freedom" campaign, 31–34
  airline industry, 1695, 1702
  American Express advertising, 86
  Americans and their finances, 330
  Amtrak ridership, 1106
  Anheuser-Busch "Real American Heroes/Real Men of Genius" campaign, 126
  antidepressants and antianxiety drugs, 668
  Cartoon Network ratings, 1615
  Charles Schwab Corporation, 304
  Coca-Cola "Life Tastes Good" campaign, 351
  defense spending, 232
  Delta Air Lines "Person to Person" campaign, 414, 416–417
  Diamond Trading Company campaign, 444
  Dunkin' Donuts "Loosen Up a Little" campaign, 47, 49

September 11th terrorist attacks, *continued*
fast food restaurants, 318
"Holiday Inn Brand Rejuvenation" campaign, 777
IBM "Leaning Tower of Pisa" spot, 793
JetBlue campaign, 821–822
Johnnie Walker "Keep Walking" campaign, 424
Jordan, Michael, donation of, 1100–1101
museum attendance, 1084
New York State Lottery "If I Had a Million Dollars" campaign, 1129
Royal Caribbean "Get Out There" campaign, 1444
Southwest Airlines profitability, 1538
tourism slump, 871
travel and tourism, 296, 1762
United States Postal Service "Fly Like an Eagle" campaign, 1720
Sequoia Capital, 1850
"Serious Fun" campaign, 1758
Serta International, **1501–1504**
"Service Bay" spot, 651
ServiceMaster Clean, 1559
Sesame Street (television show), 1411
"Set Yourself Free" campaign, 315
Seven Up. *See* Dr Pepper/Seven Up, Inc.
Seward, Lisa, 331
Sex and the City (television show), 446, 598, 599, 600, 1664
"Sex Bicycles" ad, 1249, 1251
Sex Pistols, 1759
Sexual harassment, 73
Sexuality
A & F Quarterly campaign, 9–12
Abercrombie & Fitch "XXX" campaign, 596–597, 599–600
"American Apparel" campaign, 71–74
Carl's Jr. "Six Dollar Burger" campaign, 290
Clairol "Totally Organic" campaign, 333–336
Club 18-30 "Perspectives" campaign, 1607–1609
French Connection "Scent to Bed" campaign, 579–582
Hardee's Paris Hilton spot, 698
"Jenny McCarthy for Candie's" campaign, 749–753
"Vegas Stories" campaign, 873
Virgin Atlantic Airways "Go, Jet Set, Go!" campaign, 1759
Vodafone campaign, 1234–1235
"Sexy Moms," targeting of, 1174–1176
Seymour, Henry O., 1292
Seymour, Stephanie, 354
"Shade Running" spot, 1146
Shaffer, Gina, 1022, 1023, 1024
Shaggy, 1279
Shahid, Sam, 9, 10, 11
"Shake" spot, 392, 394
Shakira, 25, 1280, 1282
Shakirov, Fathulla, 1707
Shalhoub, Tony, 522
Shampoo. *See* Hair care products
Shanahan, Jack, 229, 231, 232
Shanet, Larry, 431
Shanks, Gordon, 891, 892
Shapiro, Bob, 1707
Shapiro, Owen, 1853
Shapiro, Robert, 1036
"Shaq/Shaft" spot, 1277
Share Our Strength (SOS), 364–365
"Shared Food" spot, 363, 365
"Sharing and Connecting" campaign, 1388–1391
"Sharks" spot, 1790
Sharp Corp., **1505–1508**
Sharpe, Shannon, 303, 304, 527
Sharpie "Write Out Loud" campaign, 1457–1459
Shatner, William, 1369–1372
Shaum, Lucy, 201
ShaveMyYeti.com, 925
"Shaving Follies" spot, 1479
"Shaving Made Simple" campaign, 1477–1480
Shaving razors. *See* Razors
Shea, Maggie, 331
Sheehan, Mike, 825
Sheep, Serta, 1501–1503
SheepAreEvil.com, 925
"Sheet Metal" spot, 1467
Sheik condoms, 313
"Sheldon" spot, 343
Shell Oil, 307, 308
Shelmerdine, Guy, 515
Shepardson Stern & Kaminstky, 410
Shepherd, Kenny Wayne, 607–608
Sherbow, Sue, 902, 907
Sheriff, Karen, 154
Sherman, Nate, 1009
Shields, Brooke, 262
Shimotakahara, Lisa, 1653
Shipping companies. *See* Delivery services
"Shipping" spot, 45
"Ships" spot, 800
Shoe Pie (music CD), 460
Shoes
Dr. Martens Airwair "Beliefs" campaign, 459–462
"Jenny McCarthy for Candie's" campaign, 749–753
Nordstrom "Make Room for Shoes" campaign, 1181–1184
See also Athletic footwear
Short, Len, 66–69
Short films
"2004 Toronto Worldwide Short Film Festival" campaign, 273–276
"Absolut Director" campaign, 1729–1733
Amazon Theater, 59–62
BMW "The Hire" campaign, 175–179
The Check Up, 159, 1775
Healthy Curiosity (short film), 1827
Napster "It's Coming Back" campaign, 1087
"Out of Order: Rock the Vote Targets Health," 1426
Wendy's "Good to Be Square" campaign, 1815
"Shower" ad (Schwinn), 1255
"Shower" spot (Snapple), 239
Showtime Networks
Häagen-Sazs, partnership with, 1120
Xbox, partnership with, 1002
Shrek 2 (film), 435, 436, 437
Shue, Andrew, 515
Shuldman, Ken, 1105
Shulman, Bruce, 1179
"Shuttle" spot, 681
Sicher, John, 347, 348, 1273, 1290, 1305
Sick, Fritz, 1245
The Sidekick, 1624
Siegel, Jimmy, 302
Sienna "Kids Rule" campaign, 1643–1646
Sierra Club, **1509–1512**
Sierra Mist, 1290
Sifford, Charlie, 1137
Sight Effects, 999
Sigma Corporation of America, 1163
"Sign Boy" campaign, 565–568
"Sign On a Friend" promotion, AOL, 65
Signature jeans, Levi Strauss, 886, 887
"Silent Car" spot, 873
"Silent Hero" spot, 323
"Silhouette" campaign, 135–138, 1086–1087
Siltanen, Rob, 1171, 1172, 1174

Siltanen & Partners, 1413–1415
Silver, Elizabeth, 1768
Silver, Eric, 450
Silver Lion. *See* Lion Awards
Silver Pencil Awards. *See* One Show Awards
Silver Skillet award, 289, 291
Silverglade, Bruce, 1293
Silverstein, Rich
  E*TRADE "Monkey Trilogy" campaign, 526
  founding of Goodby, Silverstein & Partners, 494
  Nike "Women's campaign," 1156
Simmonds, Richard, 295
Simmons, 1502–1503
Simmons, Chet, 521
Simmons, Nate, 924, 926
Simon, Julian, 947
Simoncelli, Peter, 684
"Simplicity Shootout" spot, 133, 134
The Simpsons (television show), 773
Sims, Tom, 1513
Sims Sports, Inc., **1513–1516**
Sinatra, Frank
  Lipton Brisk "That's Brisk, Baby!" campaign, 1298, 1301
  Visa Signature card campaign, 1768
Singh, Tarsem, 1625
"Single Malt" campaign, 683–686
Sinise, Gary, 637
"Sink Boy" campaign, 1391–1394
Sinyard, Mike, 1539
"Sir Pines" spots, 1827
Sisson, Alan, 552
Sitley, Mark, 1411
Sittig, Dick, 811
"Six Dollar Burger" campaign, 289–292
Six Flags, Inc., **1517–1521**, *1518, 1519,* 1611, 1613–1614
"Six Million Dollar Man" spot, 68
60 Minutes (television show), 1186
Size, body, 1682
"Skateboard" spot, 239
"Skateboarders" campaign, 1150–1154
Skin care products
  Chesebrough-Pond's "Soothing Cucumber Eye Treatments Ads" campaign, 1690–1693
  Dial "You're Not As Clean As You Think" campaign, 435–438
  Dove "Campaign for Real Beauty" campaign, 1679–1683
  Lubriderm "See You Later, Alligator" campaign, 1317–1322
  See also Cosmetics and fragrances
Skinner, David, 689
Skrzypczak, Milosz, 1066
SkyTeam Alliance, 415
Slade, David, 60
Slater, Christian, 597
Slater, Kelly, 140
"Sled Dogs" spot, 361
"Sleight of Hand" spot, 218
Slice, 1020
Slifka, Tom, 1250
"Slive" spot, 1136
Slum Village, 634
Sly and the Family Stone, 1634, 1636, 1719
"Smackdown Your Vote" campaign, 1427
Small Business Development Center, Florida Atlantic University, 1214, 1215
Smart, Amy, 1426
"Smart Heart Challenge," 1292, 1294
SmarTalk, 793
"Smarter Bombs" ad, 232
"Smarter Investors" campaign, 301–304, 527
SmartZone bar, 932–933
"Smile" spot, 49
"Smiley" the Goldfish, 266
Smirnoff
  Absolut, as competitor of, 1731–1732
  Smirnoff Ice, 1014
  Stolichnaya, as competitor of, 1707
Smith, Allan, 1576
Smith, B., 269, 271
Smith, Baker, 449
Smith, Bill, 1250
Smith, Chip, 1540
Smith, Chris
  "Absolut Director" campaign, 1732
  SBC Pacific Bell "Laurel Lane" campaign, 1474, 1475
  Toyota "Get the Feeling" campaign, 1642, 1643
Smith, Emmitt, 673, 1133
Smith, Frederick, 537, 541, 549
Smith, Genevieve, 1803
Smith, Jaclyn, 855
Smith, Jimmy, 1147, 1149
Smith, Jud, 702
Smith, Kevin, 1861
Smith, Loren, 1717–1718
Smith, Nadine, 660
Smith, Ray, 155
Smith, Robert, 1041
Smith, Susan, 1822
Smith, Will, 633, 1549
SmithKline. *See* GlaxoSmithKline plc
Smoking and Health (report), 98
Smoking cessation products, 661–665
Smoley, Sandra, 245
"Smooth Move" campaign, 1014
Smothers Brothers, 1230
Snack foods
  Diamond Foods "Emerald Nuts marketing campaign," 439–442
  Fat-Free Pringles "Tasting Is Believing" campaign, 1398–1400
  Frito-Lay "The Loudest Taste on Earth" campaign, 583–586
  Pepperidge Farm "Goldfish Crackers" campaign, 265–268
  Snickers Marathon bars "The Energy You Crave" campaign, 931–934
Snap!
  Lycos, as competitor of, 917
  Yahoo!, as competitor of, 1852
Snap advertising, 1380
Snapple
  "Bottles Personified" campaign, 237–240
  milk, as competitor of, 259
  "Return of the Snapple Lady" campaign, 1655–1658
"Sneak a Peek" campaign, 691–695
Snickers, 714, 931–934
Snoop Dogg, 383, 385, 1147, 1629
Snoopy, 828, 997–1000
"Snooze" spot, 156
Snoring, 337–340
"Snorkeling" spot, 91
"Snow Covered" spot, 389, 390, 391
Snowboards, 1513–1516
Snowden, 1605
Snowden on Ice (television show), 1605
Snowmobiles, 1353
Snurfers, 1514
Snyder, Daniel, 1520
Soap. *See* Skin care products
Soap operas, 1377–1379
"Soap Slip" spot, 1479
"Soap" spot, 633
Soccer, 1156
"Social Anxiety Disorder" campaign, 665–668
Social responsibility
  American Apparel Inc., 72–73
  Body Shop, 191–192
  Round Table Pizza franchisees, 1430
  Working Assets Long Distance "Direct Marketing" campaign, 1835–1838

"Sock" ad, *1254,* 1255
Soft drinks
Coca-Cola "Real" campaign, 350–353
Diet Coke "You Are What You Drink" campaign, 353–357
Diet Pepsi "This Is Diet?" campaign, 1303–1305
Diet Rite "Go for Zero" campaign, 240–242
Dr Pepper "This Is the Taste" campaign, 463–466
"The Joy of Pepsi" campaign, 1280–1283
Mountain Dew "Code Red" campaign, 1267–1270
Mountain Dew "Do the Dew" campaign, 1270–1274
"Pepsi, It's the Cola" campaign, 1289–1292
Pepsi "Generation Next" campaign, 1277–1280
Pepsi "Security Camera" campaign, 1295–1298
Pepsi Vanilla "The Not-So-Vanilla Vanilla" campaign, 1283–1286
"Return of the Snapple Lady" campaign, 1655–1658
Snapple "Bottles Personified" campaign, 237–240
Sprite "Obey Your Thirst" campaign (1998), 344–347
Sprite "Obey Your Thirst" campaign (2004), 347–350
Software
"Godaddy.com Super Bowl Commercial" campaign, 675–678
Microsoft "Where Do You Want to Go Today?" campaign, 1004–1007
Sogard, Harold, 680
"SOHO" market, 1845–1846, 1847
"Solutions for a Small Planet" campaign, 134, 143, 788–789, 797–801
"Somebody Up There Likes You" campaign, 821
Song Airlines
AirTran, as competitor of, 45
"Let Yourself Fly" campaign, 407–410
Ted, as competitor of, 1703
Sony Corporation, **1523–1529, 1531–1534**
Apple iPods, as competitor of, 137
Hewlett-Packard, as competitor of, 725
PlayStation 2, 1001, 1002–1003
Sony Pictures Digital, 560
Sony Pictures Entertainment, 1553
"The Sooner you believe it, the sooner we can end it" tagline, 363, 365
"Soothing Cucumber Eye Treatments Ads" campaign, 1690–1693
SOS (Share Our Strength), 364–365
Sosa, Omar, 603
Sosa, Sammy, 554, 950, 951
Souder, Kirk, 515
Soul Coughing, 460
"Soulmates" spot, 1041
Soups, 268–271
Southern Community Financial, 1342–1343
Southwest Airlines Company, **1535–1538**
AirTran Holdings, Inc., as competitor of, 44
Delta Air Lines, as competitor of, 416
JetBlue, as competitor of, 820
Ted, as competitor of, 1702
United Airlines, as competitor of, 1697
Sowle, Erinn, 1581
Spacek, Sissy, 597, 1747
Spade, Andy, 407, 409, 410
Spade, David, 971, 974
Spade, Kate, 407, 409
Spahn, Gerry, 1173
Spanish-language television
Chevrolet "An American Revolution" campaign, 632
Fisher-Price "Play. Laugh. Grow." campaign, 954, 955
"Trust the Midas Touch" campaign, 1012
"Speak Freely on Monday Nights" campaign, 1549
Speakes, Larry, 1717, 1720
Speakman, Lisa, 349
Spears, Britney
Herbal Essences campaign, 333, 334, 336
"The Joy of Pepsi" campaign, 1280, 1282
National Football League Kickoff festival, 1285
Pepsi campaign, 1284
Specht, Ilon, 662
"Special FX" spot, 273, 275, 276
"Special K Kick-Start Diet Plan" campaign, 834–837, *835*
Specialized Bicycle Components Inc., **1539–1542**
"Speed Racer" spot, 618
"Speeding Tickets Bicycles" ad, 1251
Speight, Lester, 1417, 1418, 1419
Speiser, Mitchell, 398
"Spelling Trouble" spot, 28
Spence, Mitch and Tracey, 920
Spice Girls, 1277, 1278, 1279
"Spicy Crispy chicks" spot, 813
Spiegel, Brennan M. R., 1210
Spielberg, Steven, 1617
Spike DDB, 576
Spinella, Art, 563, 564
Spinks, Leon, 355
Spinner Networks, 64
Spinners, 1221
Spinozzi, Mike, 196
"Spirit of Freedom" campaign, 1461–1464
Spiritualized, 1785
Splenda, 241
Spokescandies, 937, *938,* 939, 940
"Spongemonkeys" campaign, 1414, 1415
Sponsorships
adidas sponsorship of the New York Yankees, 27
adidas sponsorship of the X Games, 1153
Anheuser-Busch sponsorship of NASCAR, 118
Anheuser-Busch sponsorship of the National Hockey League, 120, 122
Anheuser-Busch sponsorship of women's professional sports, 108
Aquafina sponsorship of the All-American Soccer Stars Victory Tour, 1274
Aquafina sponsorship of the All-Star Benefit Concert, 1274
Aquafina sports sponsorships, 1275
Biore sponsorship of Lilith Fair, 1692
Cheerios sponsorship of *The Lone Ranger,* 627
Coors Brewing Company sponsorship of the Negro Leagues Baseball Museum, 1108
DHL sponsorship of Major League Baseball, 422
DHL sponsorship of the Olympics, 421–422
Diet Coke sponsorship of the Grammy Awards, 354
Diet Rite and Oprah Winfrey's *Live Your Best Life Tour,* 241
Discover card sponsorship of NASCAR, 1050, 1052
Dr. Martens sponsorship of alternative music bands, 460
FedEx sports sponsorships, 545
Glenfiddich sponsorship of the Triangular Cricket Tournament, 684

Guiness music festivals sponsorship, 429
Hallmark Hall of Fame series, 692
IBM sponsorship of the Olympics, 790
KFC sponsorship of NASCAR Chance 2 Motorsports team, 839, 841
Lincoln Financial Field, 894
MasterCard sponsorship of Major League Baseball, 951
M&M's sponsorship of the Olympics, 938
Monster sponsorship of the Olympics, 1040
Mountain Dew sponsorship of the X Games, 465, 1270, 1273
New Balance sponsorship of the International Modern Pentathlon, 1124
New Balance sponsorship of the Susan G. Komen Race for the Cure, 1124
NicoDerm sponsorship of a Marlboro 500 auto race car, 663
NicoDerm sponsorship of the American Cancer Society, 664
Norelco sponsorship of the National Hockey League, 1191
Olympics, 23
Philips Electronics, 1335
PowerAde sponsorship of NASCAR, 1288
Purina's sponsorship of the McCammon's traveling animal act, 1113
R. J. Reynolds sponsorship of the Winston Cup, 1094
Reebok sponsorship of the "Dream Team," 1133, 1142
Saab sponsorship of National Public Radio, 1447
Schick sponsorship of the National Basketball Association, 1315, 1317
Sears, 1488
single-sponsor advertising, 1601
Snickers Marathon bars sponsorship of FLW Outdoors fishing tournaments, 932
Southwest Airlines' National Hockey League sponsorship, 44
Southwest Airlines sponsorship of the National Football League, 1535–1538
Southwest Airlines sponsorship of the National Hockey League, 416, 1535, 1537
Sprint sponsorship of the National Football League, 1546–1549
Sprite sponsorship of the *Soul Train Music Awards* show, 346–347
Stolichnaya sponsorship of MiG-17s, 1708
Tabasco sponsorship of NASCAR, 982
Target "*New Yorker* Magazine Sponsorship" campaign, 1599–1602
Texaco sponsorship of the U.S. Olympic Team, 307
Toyota sponsorship of the "Live Your Best Life" tour, 1645
Viagra sponsorship of NASCAR, 1328
Visa, 84
Visa exclusive contracts, 1767
Visa sponsorship of Paul McCartney tour, 1766, 1767
Wachovia sports sponsorships, 1795
"Wrangler Anglers," 1751
Wrangler sponsorship of the Country Music Awards, 1749
See also Partnerships and cross-promotions
"Sport Life Fila" tagline, 554
Sporting goods
  Rapala "Custom Lures" campaign, 1193–1196
  Sims Sports "Be Free" campaign, 1513–1516
"Sporting Goods" spot, 1052
Sports
  financial services company sponsorships, 369
  Lincoln National sponsorship, 894
  NASCAR "How Bad Have You Got It?" campaign, 1093–1097
  Negro Leagues Baseball Museum "1998 Print Campaign," 1107–1109
  "NFL Playoffs" campaign, 1099–1102
  "NHL on Fox" campaign, 575–578
  Nike "Move" campaign, 1141–1144
  Samuel Adams "It's What's Inside" campaign, 200–201
Sports Club Company, Inc., 1860
Sports drinks
  Gatorade "Origins" campaign, 1286–1289
  PowerAde "Keep Playing" campaign, 341–344
Sports-fantasy promotions, 47, 48, 49
SportsCenter (television show)
  "PowerAde Break" segments, 342
  Rolling Rock/ESPN partnership, 761–762
  "This Is SportsCenter" campaign, 517–520
Sportswear. *See* Clothing
Sprewell, Latrell, 166, 672
Springsteen, Bruce, 60
"Sprint Guy," 1553, 1554
Sprint Nextel Corporation, **1543–1556**
  AT&T, as competitor of, 151, 152
  MCI, as competitor of, 973
  T-Mobile, as competitor of, 1624
  Verizon Wireless, as competitor of, 299
  Working Assets Long Distance, as competitor of, 1837
Sprite
  Dr Pepper, as competitor of, 464–465
  "Obey Your Thirst" campaign (1998), 205, 344–347, 464–465
  "Obey Your Thirst" campaign (2004), 347–350
  Sprite Remix, 1269, 1290
Spry, Scott, 1049
"Spuds McKenzie" campaign, 113–114
"Sputnik" spot, 593
"Squash" spot, 577–578
"Squirrel" spot, 233, 235
Squyntz!, 1826
SSR. *See* Super Sports Roadster (SSR)
SSRIs. *See* Antidepressants
St. Jude Children's Research Hospital, 1605
Stack, Peter, 1595, 1596–1597
Stacker, Pete, 125
Stackhouse, Jerry, 519, 552
"Stacy" spot, 491
Stadler, Craig, 567
Staffen, John, 1128, 1129
Staind event, 560
"Stairs" campaign, 1123–1125
Stallone, Sylvester, 1301, 1302
"Stampede" spot, 886, 888
"Stand Up for Flavor" campaign, 841
Stanley, Francis Edgar, 1560
Stanley Cup Finals, 576
Stanley Steemer International, Inc., **1557–1561**
Stanton, John, 240, 1626
Staples, Inc., **1563–1569**
  Mail Boxes Etc., as competitor of, 921
  Office Depot, as competitor of, 1214–1215
  OfficeMax, as competitor of, 1222
  "That Was Easy" campaign, *1564*
Staples, J. Fred, 1426
Star Alliance, 415
Star (film), 178
"Star of the American Road" campaign, 306

Starbucks Corp., **1197–1200**
Dunkin' Donuts, as competitor of, 48–49
General Foods International Coffees, as competitor of, 861
"Listed on Nasdaq" campaign, 1091
Starcom, 834–837
"Starfish" spot, 295
Starr, Ringo, 304, 527
"Start Something" campaign, 652–656
State Farm Mutual Automobile Insurance Company, **1571–1574**
Allstate, as competitor of, 52
GEICO, as competitor of, 614, 617, 620
"Statue" spot, 726
Status symbols, 1044, 1045
"Stay Curious" campaign, 1410
"Stay Smart" campaign, 780–783
Steelcase, Inc., **1575–1578**
Steeples, Eddie, 1223, 1565
Steiger, Rod, 275
Steinberg, David, 854, 856
Steinberg, Scott, 1086, 1087
Steinbrenner, George, 1301
Steiner, Charley, 515, 517, 518
Steinhour, Jeff, 224, 1251
Steinke, David, 197
Stemberg, Thomas, 1563, 1564
Stendahl, Tom, 1254
Stenger, Griffin, 1, 3
Stereotypes, 349
Stern, Charlene, 1059
Stern, Greg, 1541
Stern, Howard, 125
Stern, Jackie, 1371
Stern, Peter, 1140
Sternberg, Chris, 908, 1347
Sternberg, Tom, 1089, 1091
Steve Miller Band, 1717, 1719, 1720
Steven (character), 403–406
Stevens Reed Curcio & Potholm, 1583–1585
Stever, Dave, 1120
Stewart, Martha, 847, 850–854, 1489
Stewart, Rod, 397
Steyer, Robert, 1036
Stibel, Gary, 1556
Stick film cameras, 1357–1360
"Stick-Up" spot, 1470
Stimson, Drake, 1390
Stires, Denise Benou, 190
Stites, Tom, 770
Stock car races. *See* NASCAR
Stokely-Van Camp, 343, 1287
"Stoli Central" website, 1706
Stolichnaya "Russian Art" campaign, 1705–1708
Stone, Charles, III, 128, 129
Stone, Joss, 598, 601
Stone, Oliver, 1133
Stone, Sharon, 66, 68–69
Stoner, Michael, 572
"Stop Newt" calling cards, 1836
"Stop the Waste?" campaign, 364
"Stories" campaign, 627–630
"Storytelling" campaign, 561–564
Stout, 426–428
Strange, Curtis, 1135
"Strange But True" campaign, 1395–1397
"Strange Fruit" spot, 1664
Stranger, Peter, 1595
Strauss, Levi, 886
"Strawberry" spot, 1119, 1121
Street, Picabo, *1044*
Charles Schwab "Smarter Investor" campaign, 303
Nike "Move" campaign, 107, 1141, 1144
Rolex "Celebrity Endorsement" campaign, 1043, 1046
Strick, Jeremy, 183, 1081, 1082
Strickland, Denzil, 1803
"Striding Man" logo, 423, 424, 425, 426
Strong, Henry, 485
Stuart, Don, 663
Studies and reports
"Report on Sustainable Development" (Monsanto), 1038
Smoking and Health, 98
Sturm, Steve, 1647, 1649
Style Holidays, 1608–1609
StyleWar, 757
Subin, Jeremy "Troll," 1859–1860, 1861
Submarine (studio), 1732
"Subservient Chicken" campaign, 222–225, 1815
"Subtitles" campaign, 502
Suburban Auto Group, **1579–1582**
Subway
"Jared Fogle" campaign, 455–458
Quiznos, as competitor of, 1414–1415
"Subway" spot, 824
Suede, 460
"Sugar-Free Chocolate" spot, 287
Sugarless gum
Orbit gum "No Matter What" campaign, 1830–1833
Trident "Four Out of Five Dentists" campaign, 233–236
Suh, Chan, 998
Sui, Anna, 750
Suissa Miller
Acura advertising, 95
Boston Market "Eat Something" campaign, 203–206
Sullivan, Ed, 482, 987, 993
Sullivan, Michael, 1342
"Sum of All Parts Challenge" campaign, 158
Summer, Donna, 961, 963
"Summer Job" spot, 1291
"Summer of Play" party, 1147
Sun Microsystems
Dell, as competitor of, 405
IBM, as competitor of, 786–787, 793
"Sunbeam" spot, 388
"Sunday Afternoon" spot, 1781
Sunglasses, 1589
"Sunshine" spot, 1029–1030
Super Bowl advertising
Accenture, Ltd., 16
American Express "Do More" campaign, 83
American Express "Seinfeld" campaign, 89
Anheuser-Busch "Frogs" campaign, 111
Anheuser-Busch "Louie the Lizard" campaign,118
Anheuser-Busch "Oh, and Beware of the Penguins" campaign, 120–123
Anheuser-Busch "Real American Heroes/Real Men of Genius" campaign, 126
Anheuser-Busch ""Spuds McKenzie" campaign, 113
Anheuser-Busch "Whassup?!" campaign, 129
AT&T "It's All Within Your Reach" campaign, 152
Cadbury Adams "Four Out of Five Dentists" campaign, 235
Cadillac "Break Through" campaign, 635, 637
Cadillac "The Caddy That Zigs" campaign, 639
CareerBuilder "Time to Move On" campaign, 282
Charles Schwab "Smarter Investors" campaign, 304, 527
"Child's Play" spot controversy, 1074
Diamond Foods "Emerald Nuts marketing campaign," 439, 440, 441, 442

Dirt Devil "Fred Astaire" campaign, 1437, 1439, 1440
"Do You Yahoo!?" campaign, 1853
Dove "Campaign for Real Beauty" campaign, 1679
Dove Self-Esteem Fund, 1682
Electronic Data Systems "Cat Herders" campaign, 503
Electronic Data Systems (EDS), 17
E*TRADE "Monkey Trilogy" campaign, 525–528
FedEx "Be Absolutely Sure" campaign, 539
FedEx "Relax, It's FedEx" campaign, 546
First Union "Financial World" campaign, 1791, 1792
Frito-Lay "The Loudest Taste on Earth" campaign, 586
"Frogs" campaign, 109
Garfield, Bob, favorites of, 539
"Godaddy.com Super Bowl Commercial" campaign, 675–678
Heineken "It's All About the Beer" campaign, 707
"Holiday Inn Brand Rejuvenation" campaign, 777, 778
IBM "Linux" campaign, 795, 796–797
Intel "Bunny People" campaign, 770
Isuzu "Joe Isuzu" spots, 804
"The Joy of Pepsi" campaign, 1280, 1282
"Levi's Type 1 Jeans" campaign, 886, 888
Lipton Brisk "That's Brisk Baby!" campaign, 1302
Mail boxes Etc. "See Your Small Business on the Super Bowl" campaign, 919–922
MasterCard "Priceless" campaign, 951–952
M&M's "Hotel" spot, 940
Monster "Today's the Day" campaign, 1039, 1041–1042
Monster "When I Grow Up" campaign, 1040
Mountain Dew "Do the Dew" campaign, 1272
Nissan "Enjoy the Ride" campaign, 1173
Oldsmobile Alera "Start Something" campaign, 655
Oxygen Media "Fresh Television for Women" campaign, 1241
Pepsi "Generation Next" campaign, 1277, 1280
Pepsi "Security Camera" campaign, 1295, 1296, 1297
Philips Electronics "Getting Better" campaign, 1336
Pizza Hut "Big New Yorker Pizza" campaign, 1345, 1348
Prudential "Be Your Own Rock" campaign, 1405, 1408
Reebok "Terry Tate, Office Linebacker" campaign, 1417, 1418, 1419, 1420
Staples "That Was Easy" campaign, 1566
Suburban Auto Group "Trunk Monkey" campaign, 1579
Tabasco "Mosquito" campaign, 981
"Visa. It's Everywhere You Want to Be" campaign, 1767
"Super Fans" campaign, 1322–1325
Super Scoop, 1116
Super Sports Roadster (SSR), *632*
"Superman" spot, 85, 89
SuperSonics. *See* Seattle SuperSonics
Supple, Jack, 703, 1194
Supplemental insurance, 35–40
"Support the ACLU" tagline, 76
Surge, 1272
Surgeon General, U.S., 98
"Surprise" spot, 107
"Surprisingly Real" tagline, 1687
Survivor, 1197, 1199
Survivor benefits, 659
Survivor (television show)
Snickers sponsorship of, 943
Susan G. Komen Breast Cancer Foundation, 1747
Susan G. Komen Race for the Cure, 1124
Susetka, Bill, 336
Sutton, Mark B., 1676
SUVs
General Motors "Hummer" campaign, 645–648
Isuzu Axiom "The Call" campaign, 803–806
"Jeep" campaign, 389–392
Jeep "There's Only One" campaign, 392–394
Mercedes, 989
Mercedes M-Class "Smooth Ride" campaign, 990–994
Porsche "Cayenne Launch" campaign, 1365–1368
Suzuki, 1339
Swan, John, 463, 841
Swangard, Paul, 24, 361
Swearingen, Amy, 1063
Sweatshop-free clothing, 71–74
SweatX, 72
Sweepstakes
Fuji Photo Film "Meet the Greens" campaign, 590
"Start Something Tuesdays on ABC Sweepstakes," 655
Sweet, Joe, 176
Sweetwood, John, 779
Swette, Brian, 1278, 1279
Swift Boat Veterans for Truth, 1075, **1583–1586**
Swing dancing, 603
Swiss Army Brands, Inc., **1587–1590**
"Switchers" campaign, 1075
Swoopes, Sheryl, 1055
Swoosh logo, 28
"Symbols" spot, 986
Symko, Roxanne, 1718, 1719, 1720
"Synchronized Flying" spot, 413–414
Syndication, 1581–1582
Synia, Ann, 1739

T

T. Rowe Price Group, 162
T-MAC basketball shoe, 1124
T-Mobile International AG & Company KG, **1623–1626**
Tabasco "Mosquito" campaign, 979–982, *980*
Taco Bell Corp., **1591–1597**
Tae Bo, 457
TAG Heuer, 1045, 1589
"Tag" spot, 1145
Tagamet, 1324
Taggert, Adam, 134
Taglines
"Acértate a tu mundo," 65
"Be yourself again," 1211
"The Best Stuff Is Here," 1658
"Book with Travelocity. Don't Forget Your Hat," 1653
"Censorship is UnAmerican," 1425–1426
"Cingular fits you best," 298
"Clear solutions in a complex world," 893
"Click, Instantly," 1359
"Colour like.no.other," 1526, 1528, 1529
"Creating a world of smarter investors," 301
Diet Coke, 355
"Do you smell smoke," 250
"Do you speak Fuji?", 589
"Dogs love trucks," 1173
"Dreams found faster," 283
"Eat fresh," 457
FedEx spots, 546
"Feel All Right," 240

Taglines, ***continued***
"Feel comfortable in your own skin," 1859
"Freedom. Appreciate it. Cherish it. Protect it.", 33
"Get a piece of the rock," 1406
"Get closer to your world," 65
"Have it your way," 223, 226–228
"Holidays your mother wouldn't like.", 1607
"Hungry? Crunch this," 941, 942
"I think therefore iMac," 132
"Image is nothing. Thirst is everything. Obey your thirst.", 344
"In a World of Technology, People Make the Difference," 154
"Industrial Strength Investment Tools," 162
"Innovation Delivered," 15, 17
"iShares. This is the new school of investing," 163
"It pays to Discover," 1050, 1051
"It stirs the soul," 862
"It's not an ending, it's a beginning.", 763
"It's the Cheese," 253
"Jamais sans mon lait" tag line, 183
"Just Do It," 21
"Just for the taste of it," 353
"Just Screw It," 749, 752
"Less flower. More power," 1783
"Let the Dance Begin," 1325
"Let's Motor," 169
"Life is a journey. Enjoy the Ride," 1172
"Looks Fast," 1643
"Make Life Rewarding" tagline, 86
"Membership has its privileges," 80
"Men don't obsess over these things. Why do we?", 835
"Mmmm ... Toasty.", 1413, 1414, 1415
"The Most popular cruise line in the world," 296
"Never Follow," 158
"Never Stop Milk.", 183
"Never without my milk," 183
"The One and Only," 628
"One client at a time," 1048
"Only in New York," 28
"People first," 1465
"Pizza! Pizza!", 898, 905
"The Power of All of Us," 495, 498
"Ready to Move Up?", 303
"Red Lobster for the Seafood Lover in You," 395
"Screwy, Ain't It?", 1611, 1613
"The Sooner you believe it, the sooner we can end it," 363, 365
"Sport Life Fila," 554
"Support the ACLU," 76
"Surprisingly Real," 1687
"There Are Some Things Money Can't Buy. For Everything Else There's MasterCard," 85
"Thinking of You," 1178
"This Is What It's All About," 1099, 1101
"True," 129
"Trust Your Intuition," 1479
"Two great tastes that taste great together," 710, 712
"Very real power" tagline, 341, 343
"We Take the World's Greatest Pictures. Yours," 1163, 1164
"We'll leave the light on for you," 778, 782
"What Cats Want," 936
"What happens here, stays here.", 871, 873
"What's my thirst?", 347, 348
"When you cook, you're a family," 1689
"Where's your Mustache?", 183
"The World On Time," 548
"Your Link to Better Communication," 154
"You're in Good Hands with Allstate," 51, 52
Tahoe Regional Planning Agency (TRPA), 1354
"Tailgating" spot, 1146
"Take Charge of Education" campaign, 1603–1606
Take Five (song), 1178
"Take Pictures. Further" campaign, 485–488
Take-Two Interactive Software, Inc., **1497–1500**
Talese, Gay, 989
"The Talk" spot, 65
"Talk value" concept, 129
"Talking Pizzas" campaign, 906–910
"Tall Tales" campaign, 480, 487, 488–491
Tam, Vivienne, 750
Tampax Pearl "Ingenious Protection for Ingenious Women" campaign, 1385–1388
"Tango" spot, 1282
Tapie, Bernard, 20, 24
Target Corporation, **1599–1606**, *1600*
Crate & Barrel, as competitor of, 535
J.C. Penney, as competitor of, 809
Kmart, as competitor of, 852
Tarses, Jamie, 7
Tasone, Don, 1375
Taster's Choice
Folgers, as competitor of, 1374
General Foods International Coffees, as competitor of, 861
"Tasting Is Believing" campaign, 1398–1400
"Tattoo" spot, 488, 491
Taurus, Ford, 107, 559, 1033
Tauzin, Billy, 1411
Tax-preparation companies, 687–689
Taxi, 273–276
Taylor, Elizabeth, 1234, 1660
Taylor, Jeff, 1039, 1040
Taylor, Martin, 76
Taylor-Hines, Charlee, 1290
TBS Superstation
ESPN, as competitor of, 522
MTV, as competitor of, 1078–1079
"TBS Very Funny" campaign, 1662–1665
TBWA GGT Simons Palmer, 462
TBWA\Chiat\Day
ABC "TV Is Good" campaign, 5–8
"Absolut Director" campaign, 1729–1733
"Absolut Print" campaign, 1733–1737
adidas "Impossible Is Nothing" campaign, 23–26
Apple Computer "Silhouette" campaign, 135–138
Apple Computer "Switchers" campaign, 139–141
Apple Computer "Think Different" campaign, 142
"Campaign for Freedom" campaign, 32, 33
Cunard Line "Can You Wait?" campaign, 371–374
Energizer "Bunny Chasers" campaign, 509–512
Game Show Network "You Know You Know" campaign, 591–594
"iMac" campaign, 131–135
Infiniti "Own One and You'll Understand" campaign, 1177–1180
Jack in the Box "Jack's Back" campaign, 811–814
Kmart "Joe Boxer Launch" campaign, 847–850
Kmart "Martha Stewart Everyday" campaign, 850–854
Museum of Contemporary Art "Labels" campaign, 1081–1084
"Nextel. Done." campaign, 1550–1553
Nissan "Enjoy the Ride" campaign, 1171–1174
Nissan "Quest Minivan Launch" campaign, 1174–1177

Taco Bell "Want Some?" campaign, 1594–1597
Weather Channel "Painted Faces" campaign, 1805–1808
Whiskas "Inner Beast" campaign, 934–937
TBWA\G1 Europe, 1167–1170
TBWA\London
French Connection "Scent to Bed" campaign, 579–582
Sony "Fun, Anyone?" campaign, 1523–1526
Tea, 1298–1302
Teachers, 764
Team One Advertising, 177, 1646–1649
"Team Prayer" spot, 714
Teamsters, 538–539
TeamX, 72
Teasdale, Mark, 685
Ted airlines, 409
"Ted Launch" campaign, 1701–1704
Teen antismoking campaign, 97–100
"Teen Date" spot, 152, 153
Teen People (magazine), 1186
Teen pregnancy prevention, 313
Teenage Ska (song), 1406
"Teenager" spot, 1059
Tel-Save, 151
Telecom, USA, 1294
Telecommunications
Ameritech "Privacy Manger" campaign, 153–156
AT&T "Carrot Top" campaign, 147–150
AT&T "It's All Within Your Reach" campaign, 150–153
MCI "1-800-COLLECT" campaign, 971–974
MCI "Dennis Miller Ads" campaign, 974–978
Motorola "Intelligence Everywhere" campaign, 1065–1068
Motorola "Moto" campaign, 1068–1071
"Nextel. Done." campaign, 1550–1553
Orange "Goldspot" campaign, 1233–1236
Sprint "Dime Zone" campaign, 1543–1546
Sprint "Monday Nights Free and Clear" campaign, 1546–1550
"Sprint PCS" campaign, 1553–1556
T-Mobile "Get More" campaign, 1623–1626
Verizon Wireless "Can You Hear Me Now?" campaign, 297–300
Working Assets Long Distance "Direct Marketing" campaign, 1835–1838
Telemarketing, 153–156
Television
Burger King/*The Apprentice* partnership, 221
on JetBlue Airways, 821
Television commercials
A & E "In Case You Missed It" campaign, 1–3
ABC "TV Is Good" campaign, 5–8
Absolut campaign, 1737
ACLU "Racial Profiling" campaign, 77
Advertising Council "Campaign for Freedom" campaign, 31–34
Advil "Liqui-Gels" campaign, 1839–1842
Aflac "Broken Leg" campaign, 38–41
"Aflac Duck" campaign, 35–38
"Altoids Gone Sour" campaign, 1825–1827
Americans for the Arts "Art. Ask for More" campaign, 103
Anheuser-Busch "Frogs" campaign, 109–112
Anheuser-Busch "Louie the Lizard" campaign, 116–120
Anheuser-Busch "Real American Heroes/Real Men of Genius" campaign, 126
"AOL Latino" campaign, 65
AOL "Welcome to the World Wide Wow" campaign, 66, 68–69
Apple Computer "Think Different" campaign, 144
Aquafina "Drink More Water" campaign, 1274, 1276
AT&T "Carrot Top" campaign, 147–150
Barclays Global Investors "New School" campaign, 161–164
BC Dairy Foundation "Don't Take Your Body for Granted" campaign, *182*, 184
Binney & Smith "Make Play" campaign, 187–190
Boston Market "Eat Something" campaign, 203–206
Breathe Right Strips "Back in the Sack" campaign, 339
Bureau of Engraving and Printing "The New Color of Money" campaign, 218
Burger King "When You Have It Your Way, It Just Tastes Better" campaign, 228
Business Leaders for Sensible Priorities "Move Our Money" campaign, 231–232
Cadillac "Break Through" campaign, 634–637
Cadillac "The Caddy That Zigs" campaign, 638–641
California Milk Advisory Board "Happy Cows" campaign, 253–256
Campbell Soup Company "Make It Campbell's Instead" campaign, 268–271
Canadian Film Centre "2004 Toronto Worldwide Short Film Festival" campaign, 273–276
Canon "85 Second Photo Lab" campaign, 279
CareerBuilder "Time to Move On" campaign, 282, 283
Cargill "Collaborate>Create>Succeed" campaign, 287
Carnival Corporation "Fun Ships" campaign, 295
Carter Products "Trojan Man" campaign, 311–315, 314
"Cartoon Network Promotional and Branding" campaign, 1611–1615
Charles Schwab "Smarter Investors" campaign, 303–304
Cheerios "Stories" campaign, 627–629
Chrysler "Engineered to Be Great Cars" campaign, 387–389
Chrysler Group "Employee Pricing Plan Plus" campaign, 383–386
Church's Chicken "Full Flavor, Full Pockets, Full Life" campaign, 319
Cisco Systems "The Self-Defending Network" campaign, 321–324
Citibank "Identity Theft Solutions" campaign, 325–328
Citigroup "Live Richly" campaign, 329–332, 331, 332
Clairol "Totally Organic" campaign, 333–336
Coca-Cola "Real" campaign, 350–352
Columbia Sportswear "Mother Boyle" campaign, 359–362
"Come See the Softer Side of Sears" campaign, 1489–1490
ConAgra Foods' Feeding, 363–366
Conseco "Protect/Create Wealth" campaign, 367–370
CVS "Life to the Fullest" campaign, 377
Dell "Dude, You're Getting a Dell" campaign, 403–406

Television commercials, ***continued***
Detroit Pistons "Goin' to Work. Every Night." campaign, 1257–1260
DHL "Competition. Bad for Them. Great for You." campaign, 421, 422
Dial "You're Not As Clean As You Think" campaign, 435–438
Diamond Foods "Emerald Nuts marketing campaign," 439–442
"Did Somebody Say McDonald's?" campaign, 961–963
Diet Rite "Go for Zero" campaign, 240–242
DirecTV "Celebrities Read Fan Mail to DirecTV (Become a DirecTV Fan Now)" campaign, 447–450
Dirt Devil "Darin'" campaign, 1433–1436
Discover Brokerage "Tow Truck" campaign, 1056–1059
Discover "Make a Statement" campaign, 1055–1056
"Do You Yahoo!?" campaign, 1853
DoubleShot "Bring on the Day" campaign, 1197–1199
Dr. Martens Airwair "Beliefs" campaign, 461
Dr Pepper "This Is the Taste" campaign, 463–466
Dreyer's Grand Light "Unbelievable" campaign, 469
drugstore.com "A Very Healthy Way to Shop" campaign, 473
Dryel "Habits" campaign, 1384–1385
Dunkin' Donuts "Loosen Up a Little" campaign, 47–50
Dyson "Doesn't Lose Suction" campaign, 475–478
Ebay 2004 television campaign, 496–499
Electronic Data Systems "Cat Herders" campaign, 501–504
Energizer "Bunny Chasers" campaign, 509–512
ESPN "The Rick" campaign, 513–516
ESPN "This Is SportsCenter" campaign, 517–520
ESPN "Without Sports" campaign, 520–523
E*TRADE "Monkey Trilogy" campaign, 525–528
E*TRADE "Why Wouldn't You?" campaign, 528–531
FedEx "Be Absolutely Sure" campaign, 537–541
FedEx "The Way the World Works" campaign, 547–550
Fisher-Price "Play. Laugh. Grow." campaign, 953–956
Folgers "The Best Part of Wakin' Up Is Folgers In Your Cup" campaign, 1373–1376
FootJoy "Sign Boy" campaign, 565–568
Ford "Driving American Innovation" campaign, 555–558
Ford "Storytelling" campaign, 561–564
Foster's "How to Speak Australian" campaign, 569–573
Frito-Lay "The Loudest Taste on Earth" campaign, 583–586
Fuji Photo Film "Meet the Greens" campaign, 587–590
Gap "How Do You Wear It?" campaign, 600
Gap "Khakis" campaign, 601–604
Gap "This Is Easy" campaign, 605–608
Gateway "People Rule" campaign, 611
GEICO "Gecko" campaign, 613–616
GEICO "Good News" campaign, 616–618
GEICO "Mini-Campaigns," 618–621
General Electric "Imagination At Work" campaign, 623–626
General Motors "EV1 Introduction" campaign, 643
General Motors "Hummer" campaign, 647–648
Gill Foundation "TurnOut" campaign, 657–660
Gillette "Anything Else Would Be Uncivilized" campaign, 670–673
"Godaddy.com Super Bowl Commercial" campaign, 675–678
Häagen-Dazs "Made Like No Other" campaign, 1121
Hallmark Cards "Sneak a Peak" campaign, 691–695
Hardee's "Revolution" campaign, 697–699
Heineken "It's All About the Beer" campaign, 705–708
Hershey Reese's "There's No Wrong Way to Eat a Reese's" campaign, 712–715
Hewlett-Packard "Built By Engineers, Used By Ordinary People" campaign, 719
Hewlett-Packard "Expanding Possibilities" campaign, 720–723
Hewlett-Packard "You + HP" campaign, 726
"Holiday Inn Brand Rejuvenation" campaign, 777–780
Holiday Inn Express "Stay Smart" campaign, 780–783
Hollywood Video "Welcome to Hollywood" campaign, 735
Honda "Grrr" campaign, 745–748
Honda "What About Now?" campaign, 91–95
H&R Block "Worried About Bill" campaign, 687–690
IBM "Can You See It?" campaign, 785–788
IBM "E-Business" campaign, 790
IBM "Linux" campaign, 794–797
IBM "Solutions for a Small Planet" campaign, 797–801
IKEA "Unböring" campaign, 755–758
"iMac" campaign, 133, 134
Infiniti "Own One and You'll Understand" campaign, 1177
"ING Launch" campaign, 765
Intel "Time for a Pentium II Processor?" campaign, 771–775
Isuzu Axiom "The Call" campaign, 803–806
"It's Not T.V. It's HBO" campaign, 737–740
Jack in the Box "Jack's Back" campaign, 811–814
J.C. Penney "It's All Inside" campaign, 807–810
"Jeep" campaign, 389–392
Jenny Craig "Kirstie Alley" campaign, 815–818
Jesse Ventura "Retaliate in '98" campaign, 1739–1742
"JetBlue Launch" campaign, 821–822
John Hancock "Insurance for the Unexpected. Investments for the Opportunities" campaign (1996), 823–826
John Hancock "Insurance for the Unexpected. Investments for the Opportunities" campaign (2000), 826–829
Juicy Fruit "Gotta Have Twisted Sweet" campaign, 1828–1830
Kellogg "Gotta Have My Pops" campaign, 831–834
Kellogg "Special K Kick-Start Diet Plan" campaign, 834–837
KFC "Chicken Capital USA" campaign, 839–842
"Kleenex Anti-Viral" campaign, 843–846
Kmart "Joe Boxer Launch" campaign, 847–850
Kmart "Rosie O'Donnell and Penny Marshall" campaign, 854–858

Kodak "Advantix" campaign, 479–482
Kodak "The Best Part of Photography Is the Prints" campaign, 482–485
Kodak "Tall Tales" campaign, 491
Kraft "It's Not Delivery, It's DiGiorno" campaign, 864–866
La-Z-Boy "The New Look of Comfort" campaign, 877
LeapFrog "Learn Something New Every Day!" campaign, 881
Lee jeans "Cut to Be Noticed" campaign, 1743–1746
Lee jeans "Find Your One True Fit" campaign, 1746–1747
Levi's "It's Wide Open" campaign, 885–886
Levi's "They Go On" campaign, 889–892
"Levi's Type 1 Jeans" campaign, 886–889
Lexus "The Road Is Calling" campaign, 1646–1649
Lincoln National "Hello Future" campaign, 895–896
Lipton Brisk "That's Brisk, Baby!" campaign, 1298–1303
Lipton Sizzle & Stir "Real Cooking" campaign, 1687–1690
"Listed on Nasdaq" campaign, 1090–1092
Little Caesar "Cloning" campaign, 897–900
Little Caesar "Grand Canyon" campaign, 900–903
Little Caesar "Safety Video" campaign, 903–906
Little Caesar "Talking Pizzas" campaign, 906–910
Logitech "What Will You Do With All That Freedom?" campaign, 911–914
Lubriderm "See You Later, Alligator," 1321–1322
Lycos "Go Get It" campaign, 915–918
MADD "Drunk Driving's a Serious Crime. Let's Treat It That Way." campaign, 1061–1063
Marriott International "Never Underestimate the Importance of a Good Night's Rest" campaign, 927–930
Maryland State Lottery "Cash in Hand" campaign, 945–948
MasterCard "Priceless" campaign, 949–952
McDonald's "I'm Lovin' It" campaign, 964–967
McDonald's "We Love to See You Smile" campaign, 967–970
MCI "1-800-Collect" campaign, 971
Mercedes "Corporate Branding" campaign, 986
Mercedes "Passion" campaign, 987–990
Mercedes "Unlike Any Other" campaign, 994–996
Microsoft "Where Do You Want to Go Today?" campaign, 1004–1007
Mike's Hard Lemonade "Hard Day" campaign, 1013–1016
"Miller High Life" campaign, 1452–1455
"Miller High Life Man" campaign, 1017–1021
Miller Lite "Low Carb" campaign, 1452–1453
Miller Lite "Miller Time" campaign, 1021–1025
"Minnesota Partnership for Action against Tobacco" campaign, 1027–1030
Mitsubishi "Wake Up and Drive" campaign, 1031–1034
Monster "Today's the Day" campaign, 1039–1042
Morgan Stanley "At Your Side" campaign, 1047–1050
Mountain Dew "Code Red" campaign, 1267–1270
MoveOn.org "Real People" campaign, 1073–1076
MTV "Watch and Learn" campaign, 1077–1080
NASCAR "How Bad Have You Got It?" campaign, 1093–1097
Nature Made "Trusted By the Ones You Trust" campaign, 1331–1332
New Balance "Thunderstorm, Stairs" campaigns, 1123–1125
"NFL Playoffs" campaign, 1099–1102
"NHL on Fox" campaign, 575–578
NicoDerm CQ "Power to Quit" campaign, 661–665
Nike "Hello World" and "I Am Tiger Woods" campaigns, 1134–1138
Nike "9,000 Shots" campaign, 1131–1134
Nike "Play" campaign, 1144–1147
Nike "Product Assault" campaign, 1150
Nike "What If We Treated All Athletes the Way We Treat Skateboarders?" campaign, 1150–1154
Nike "Women's" campaign, 1154–1157
Nikon "Mass Market Initiative" campaign, 1159–1162
Nissan "Do You Speak Micra?" campaign, 1169
Nissan "Enjoy the Ride" campaign, 1171–1174
Nissan "Quest Minivan Launch" campaign, 1176
Nordstrom "Make Room for Shoes" campaign, 1181–1184
Novartis Zelnorm "Tummies" campaign, 1211
Office Depot "What You Need. What You Need to Know." campaign, 1215
OfficeMax "What's Your Thing?" campaign, 1221–1224
Old Navy "Destination" campaign, 1228–1231
Old Navy "'70s Retro TV" campaign, 1225–1228
"On the Wings of Goodyear" campaign, 679–682
Orbit gum "No Matter What" campaign, 1830–1833
Oxygen Media "Fresh Television for Women" campaign, 1241–1244
Paxil "Social Anxiety Disorder" campaign, 665–668
PBS "Be More" campaign, 1409–1412
Peace Corps "Life Is Calling. How Far Will You Go?" campaign, 1261–1265
Pepperidge Farms "Goldfish Crackers" campaign, 265–268
Pepsi "Generation Next" campaign, 1277–1280
Pepsi Vanilla "The Not-So-Vanilla Vanilla" campaign, 1283–1286
Perdue "Now Arriving" campaign, 1310
Pert Plus "Sink Boy" campaign, 1391–1394
Philips Electronics "Getting Better" campaign, 1335–1336
Polaroid "I-Zone/Joycam/Sticky Film Teen" campaign, 1357–1360
Polaroid "See What Develops" campaign, 1360–1363
Polartec "Forward Fabric" campaign, 925
"The Power of Zyrtec" campaign, 1313–1314
PowerAde "Keep Playing" campaign, 341–344
Prudential "Be Your Own Rock" campaign, 1405–1408
Quiznos "Baby Bob" campaign, 1413–1415

Television commercials, *continued*
Red Lobster "Life on Land Is Dry" campaign, 397
"Relax, It's FedEx" campaign, 544–547
"Return of the Snapple Lady" campaign, 1655–1658
"Riven" campaign, 381–382
"Rolling Rock Ads" campaign, 867–870
Rolling Rock "Grab a Rock" campaign, 759–762
Royal Caribbean "Get Out There" campaign, 1443, 1444
"Saturn Relaunch" campaign, 1467
SBC Communications "Laurel Lane" campaign, 1473–1476
Scotts Miracle-Gro "Neighbor to Neighbor" campaign, 1485–1486
"Sears. Where Else?" campaign, 1491–1495
Seattle SuperSonics "In Your Home" campaign, 165–168
Serta "Counting Sheep" campaign, 1501–1503
Sharpie "Write Out Loud" campaign, 1457–1459
Sims Sports "Be Free" campaign, 1515–1516
Six Flags "It's Playtime" campaign, 1517–1520
"Snickers Cruncher" campaign, 940–943
Snickers Marathon bar "The Energy You Crave" campaign, 933–934
Song Airlines "Let Yourself Fly" campaign, 410
"Sony BRAVIA" campaign, 1526–1529
Southwest Airlines "Must Be Football Season" campaign, *1536*
Sprint "Dime Zone" campaign, 1545–1546
Sprite "Obey Your Thirst" campaign (2004), 347–350
Stanley Steemer "Living Brings It In. We Take It Out." campaign, 1557–1561
Staples "Yeah, We've Got That" campaign, 1567–1569
State Farm "True Stories" campaign, 1571–1573
Suburban Auto Group "Trunk Monkey" campaign, 1579–1582
"Swift Boat Veterans for Truth" campaign, 1583–1585
T-Mobile "Get More" campaign, 1623–1626
Tabasco "Mosquito" campaign, 979–982
Taco Bell "Think Outside the Bun" campaign, 1593
Taco Bell "Want Some?" campaign, 1594–1597
"Ted Launch" campaign, 1703–1704
Texaco "A World of Energy" campaign, 308
"Thank You, Paine Webber" campaign, 1677–1678
Tidy Cat "Multiple Strength for Multiple Cats" campaign, 1115–1117
"TiVo TV Your Way" campaign, 1619–1622
Toyota "A Car to Be Proud of Campaign," 1631–1634
Travelocity "Roaming Gnome" campaign, 1651–1654
Trident "Four Out of Five Dentists" campaign, 233–236
"Trust the Midas Touch" campaign, 1011–1012
Turner Broadcasting System "TBS Very Funny" campaign, 1662–1665
Turner Classic Movies "31 Days of Oscar" campaign, 1659–1662
TV Guide "On the Inside" campaign, 1669
United Airlines "It's Time to Fly" campaign, 1695–1698
United Airlines "Rising" campaign, 1700
UnitedHealth Group "It Just Makes Sense" campaign, 1727–1728
UPS "Moving at the Speed of Business" campaign, 1711–1712
UPS "What Can Brown Do for You?" campaign, 1713–1716
"US Open Excitement" campaign, 1721–1724
"Vegas Stories" campaign, 871–874
Verizon Wireless "Can You Hear Me Now?" campaign, 297–300
"Viagra Launch" campaign, 1325
Victory Motorcycles "The New American Motorcycle" campaign, 1351
"Visa. It's Everywhere You Want to Be" campaign, 1765–1768
Volkswagen "Drivers Wanted" campaign, 1776–1779
Volkswagen Jetta "All Grown Up. Sort Of." campaign, 1773–1776
Volkswagen Passat "Live Large" campaign, 1780–1783
Wachovia "Uncommon Wisdom" campaign, 1792–1795
Walgreen "Perfect" campaign, 1797–1799
Washington Mutual "Fear Not" campaign, 1801–1804
Wendy's "Good to Be Square" campaign, 1815
Whiskas "Inner Beast" campaign, 934–937
Wisk "Do It Once. Do It Right" campaign, 1685–1689
Xbox "IT's Good to Play Together" campaign, 1001, 1003
Xerox "Keep the Conversation Going, Share the Knowledge" campaign, 1843–1847
"Yard Fitness Center" campaign, 1859–1862
Televisions
Sharp "More to See" campaign, 1505–1508
"Sony BRAVIA" campaign, 1526–1529
"Telluride" spot, 1767
Temerlin McClain, 298
Temple, Shirley, 1523, 1525
Tempo awards, 284
Temujin (computer game), 381
"10" spot, 1052
Tench, Diane Cook, 1435
Tendercrisp Chicken Sandwich, 222–225
Tennis
Anheuser-Busch sponsorship, 108
"US Open Excitement" campaign, 1721–1724
Virginia Slims tour, 56
"Tennis Player" spot, 303–304
"Tennis" spot, 1153
Terminology, 789
Terry, Luther, 98
"Terry Tate, Office Linebacker" campaign, 1417–1420
Tesh, John, 520
Teske, Naomi, 1355
"Test Drive" spot, 891
"Testimonial" spot, 1280, 1281, 1282
"Testman" campaign, 297–300, 1552
Texaco Star Theater (television show), 306
Texaco "A World of Energy" campaign, 305–309
Textiles, 923–926
Textron, 1353
T.G.I. Friday's, 292
Thacker, Robert, 1604
Thale, Karyn, 22
Thame, Gerard de, 394
"That Jazz" spot, 1178
"That Was Easy" campaign, 1214–1215, 1563–1566, *1564*

"That's Brisk, Baby!" campaign, 1298–1303, *1299, 1300*
"That's Entertainment" spot, 857
Theme parks, 1517–1520
"There Are Some Things Money Can't Buy. For Everything Else There's MasterCard" tagline, 85
"There's No Wrong Way to Eat a Reese's" campaign, 712–715
"There's Only One" campaign, 392–394
Theriault, Roger, 207
Theron, Charlize, 446
"They Go On" campaign, 889–892
"Think. Don't Smoke" campaign, 98
"Think Different" campaign, 132, 138, 139, 141–145, 1006
"Think Outside the Bun" campaign, 1591–1594
"Thinking of You" tagline, 1178
"Thirsty" spot, 870
"31 Days of Oscar" campaign, 1659–1662
"33" on Rolling Rock labels, 760, 869
"This Bud's for You" campaign, 109, 117
"This Is Diet?" campaign, 1303–1305
"This Is Easy" campaign, 605–608
This Is Spinal Tap (film), 799
"This Is SportsCenter" campaign, 515, 517–520
"This is the Power of the Network. Now" campaign, 322
"This Is the Taste" campaign, 463–466
"This Is What It's All About" tagline, 1099, 1101
"This Season, It's the Original Thought That Counts" campaign, 195–198
Thoman, G. Richard, 800, 1846, 1847
Thomas, Bill, 1511
Thomas, Dave, 220, 224, 969, 1809–1814
Thomas, Frank, 1133
Thomas, Joyce King, 952
Thomas Cook Tour Operations Ltd., **1607–1610**
Thomason, Scott, 1580
Thomason Auto Group, 1580
Thompson, Geoffrey, 885
Thompson, Robert, 1663
Thompson, Sean, 747
Thorne-Smith, Courtney, 877
Thornton, Joe, 49
"Three Amigos" spot, 1485
"Three Reasons to Own a Good Pair of Boots" ad, 361
"Three-Second rule" spot, 1079
Three-stone-jewelry campaign, 444
Threespot Media, 1264
3T, 1279
Thrifty car rental, 213
"Thrill Ride" spot, 1433, *1434*
"Throwing Eggs" spot, 1581
Throwing Muses, 460
"Thugs" spot, 757
"Thunderstorm" campaign, 1123–1125
Thurber, Rawson, 1418, 1419
Tic Tac, 1826
Ticketmaster, 263–264
Tide, 1685
Tidmarsh, David, 519
Tidy Cat "Multiple Strength for Multiple Cats" campaign, 1114–1117
Tie-ins
  Burger King movie tie-ins, 959
  Dr. Martens tie in to World Cup soccer tournament, 459, 461
  McDonald's/Walt Disney Corporation tie-ins, 959
  Spring/*Men in Black II* cross-promotion, 1553, 1555–1556
  Sprint/Monday Night Football tie-ins, 1546, 1547, 1548
  Sprint movie tie-ins, 1549
  Taco Bell/Xbox partnership, 1593
  Target tie-ins to the *Donny & Marie* show, 1605
Tiger Power, 628
"Tiger" spot, 999
Tiger Woods Foundation, 1137
Tilby, Wendy, 1696, 1697
Tiles, Neal, 450, 576, 577
Tilford, Todd, 461
Tillamook County Creamery Association, 255
"Tim and Chuck," 1245–1248
Timberlake, Justin, 964, 966
Timberland, 360–361
"Time for a Pentium II Processor?" campaign, 771–775
"Time to Move On" campaign, 281–284
Time Warner, Inc., 64, 66, 67, **1611–1617**
Time "The World's Most Interesting Magazine" campaign, 1615–1617
"Timeless Ride" spot, 996
TimeOut New York, 1754
Timex Expedition watch, 1589
Timmons, Steve, 1860
"Timmy" radio spot, 905
Timon, Clay, 94
Timony, Mary, 1371
"Tiny House" spot, 620–621
Tip Corporation, 1271
"Tire Swing" spot, 332, 1096
Tires, 679–682
Titanic (film), 294
Titanium Lions. *See* Lion Awards
Title IX, 1154, 1155
Tito, James, 869
Tito family, 759
TiVo Inc., **1619–1622**
"TiVo TV Your Way" campaign, 1619–1622
TLP-Dallas, 416
TNT, 1612
"Toasted Bunny" spot, 770
Tobacco Industry Research Council, 98
Tobacco industry settlement agreement, 97, 98, 249, 1028
Tobak, Steve, 769
Tobin, Clare, 1609
Today Show
  Dreyer's Grand Light taste test, 470
  new twenty dollar bill, 218
"Today" spot, 1041
Togo's Eateries, 48
Toilet training, 1380–1382
Toledo, Elizabeth, 1155
Tom, Glenn, 1057
"Tom" spot, 33, 546
Tomb Raider (computer game), 381
Tombstone pizza, 864
Tomlin, Lily, 1058
Tommy Hilfiger U.S.A., Inc., 603, **1627–1630**
Tomorrow Never Dies (film), 986, 989, 1770
Toms, David, 565
The Tonight Show
  Kmart "Vaughn" spot, 849
  Stallone, Sylvester, appearance by, 1302
Tooker, Steve, 436
Tools, 1590
Tooth Fairy (film), 61
"The Tooth" spot, 1507
Topolewski, Gary, 391, 908, 909
Topps Company, 1829
Tor, Tom, 33
Tormé, Mel, 1271, 1272
Toronto Worldwide Short Film Festival, 273–276
Torres, Liz, 1055
Torvalds, Linus, 795
"Totally Organic" campaign, 333–336, 1393

Toth, Michael, 1628
Toth Design and Advertising, 1627–1630
"Tour Guide" spot, 1653
"Tour" spot, 828
Tours
  hybrid car, 1511
  "Swiss Army Equipped" campaign, 1590
  United Parcel Service seminars, 1710
"Tow Truck" campaign, 1056–1059
Tower Records, 263
Townley, Jay, 1251
Townshend, Pete, 426, 459–460
"Toy Boat" spot, 496, 498
"Toy Mania" spot, 856
A Toy Story (movie), 143
Toyoda, Eiji, 1646
Toyota Motor Sales, U.S.A., Inc., **1631–1650**
  Chevrolet, as competitor of, 632
  Ford, as competitor of, 557, 559
  General Motors, as competitor of, 643
  Generation Y marketing, 93
  Honda, as competitor of, 742–743
  MINI Cooper, as competitor of, 174
  Mitsubishi, as competitor of, 1033
  Nissan, as competitor of, 1168, 1172, 1179
  Oldsmobile, as competitor of, 654
  Saturn, as competitor of, 1471
Toys
  Fisher-Price "Play. Laugh. Grow." campaign, 953–956
  LeapFrog "Learn Something New Every Day!" campaign, 879–882
"Toys" spot, 1172
"Tracer FX Ads" campaign, 1314–1317
Trademark disputes, 1588
Trading cards, 1829
Train service, 1103–1106
"Training Camp" spot, 1419
Trammps, 1719
"Translation" spot, 719
Transportation. *See* Travel and tourism
"Trash Day" spot, 560
"Trash Talk" spot, 304
Travel and tourism
  Amtrak "Life on Acela" campaign, 1103–1106
  Carnival Corporation "Fun Ships" campaign, 293–296
  Clairol Employee Commuter Program, 335
  Club 18-30 "Perspectives" campaign, 1607–1609
  Cunard Line "Can You Wait?" campaign, 371–374
  Delta Air Lines "On Top of the World" campaign, 411–414
  Delta Air Lines "The Passenger's Airline" campaign, 414–417
  Marriott International "Never Underestimate the Importance of a Good Night's Rest" campaign, 927–930
  North Carolina "Heritage" campaign, 1201–1204
  Northwest Airlines "E-Ticket" campaign, 1205–1208
  priceline.com "Troubadour" campaign, 1369–1372
  Royal Caribbean "Get Out There" campaign, 1441–1444
  Six Flags "It's Playtime" campaign, 1517–1520
  Song Airlines "Let Yourself Fly" campaign, 408–410
  Southwest Airlines "Must Be Football Season" campaign, 1535–1538
  "Ted Launch" campaign, 1701–1704
  Travelocity "Roaming Gnome" campaign, 1651–1654
  United Airlines "It's Time to Fly" campaign, 1695–1698
  United Airlines "Rising" campaign, 1698–1701
  "Vegas Stories" campaign, 871–874
  Virgin Atlantic Airways "Go, Jet Set, Go!" campaign, 1757–1760
  Virginia Tourism Corporation "Meet Virginia" campaign, 1761–1764
Travel South Marketplace, 1203
Travelers Group, 329
Travelocity, 1370–1371, **1651–1654**
Treasure hunt, 211–214
Tree, David, 855, 857
Trees, Wendy, 1321
Trek
  Schwinn, as competitor of, 1250–1251, 1254
  Specialized, as competitor of, 1540
  Volkswagen, partnership with, 1779
Trenet, Charles, 183
Trevino, Lee, 566
Triangular Cricket Tournament, 684
Triarc Companies, Inc., **1655–1658**
Tribeca Film Festival, 59, 62
Trident, 233–235, 1832
"Trim-A-Home" spot, 856
Trimpa, Ted, 658
Triple Crown races, 84
"Triple Squeeze" spot, 823–824
TRM Copy Centers, 921
Troggs, 962
"Trojan Man" campaign, 311–315
"Troubadour" campaign, 1369–1372
Trout, Jack, 744, 1783
Troyer, Verne, 974, 1235, 1236
TRPA. *See* Tahoe Regional Planning Agency (TRPA)
Truckee River Whitewater Park, 873
Trucks
  Chevrolet "An American Revolution" campaign, 631–634
  Ford, 564
"Trucks" spot, 1283, 1285
True (film), 128, 129
"True Stories" campaign, 1571–1573
"True" tagline, 129
Trump, Donald, 221, 1345, 1348
Trump, Melania, 40
Trump (mascot), 1041
"Trunk Monkey" campaign, 1579–1582
"Trust the Midas Touch" campaign, 1009–1012
"Trust Your Intuition" tagline, 1479
"Trusted By the Ones You Trust" campaign, 1329–1332
"Truth" campaign, 97–100, 249–250, 1029
"Truth *vs.* Advertising" ad, 247
Trzaskoma, Greg, 1259
"The Ts" spot, 1689
"Tuba" spot, 1468, 1471
Tucker, Chris, 1446
Tucker, Laurie A., 544
Tucker Tapia, 533, 536
Tudor line, Rolex, 1043–1047
Tull, Jodi, 1613
Tully, Patrick, 685
"Tummies" campaign, 1209–1212
Tums, 1324
"Turbulence" spot, 637
Turlington, Christie, 262
Turnbull, Craig, 1259
Turner, Cathy, 1384
Turner, Gary, 1251
Turner, Graham, 1734
Turner, Kathleen, 968
Turner, Ted, 1323, 1663
Turner, Tina, 1278, 1296
Turner Broadcasting System, Inc., 1323, 1611–1613, **1659–1665**
Turner Classic Movies, 1612
Turner Field, 487

"TurnOut" campaign, 657–660
Turow, Joseph, 6
TV Guide, Inc., **1667–1670**
ESPN "This Is SportsCenter" campaign recognition, 517
Hewlett-Packard "You + HP" campaign recognition, 726
"TV Is Good" campaign, 5–8
"TV" spot, 620
TWC. *See* The Weather Channel Companies
Twenty dollar bill, *216*
"Twice as Nice for Your School" promotion, 1605
Twiggy, 174, 1682
Twister (film), 509, 510, 511
Twitchell, James, 891
"Two great tastes that taste great together" tagline, 710, 712
"Two Guys" campaign, 451–453, 593
"Two Sprites" spot, 349
"2004 Toronto Worldwide Short Film Festival" campaign, 273–276, *274*
2GO card, Discover, 1050, 1051, 1052
Twomley, Dale, 1819
2wentys, 1609
Tylenol, 1841
"Type 1 jeans" campaign, 886–889
Tyson, John, 1671, 1674
Tyson, Mike, 355, 518, 519
Tyson Foods, Inc., 1309, **1671–1674**, *1672*

U

U2 (rock band), 135–138
"U Slice the Pie" campaign, 230
UBS Financial Services Inc., **1675–1678**
"Uh-huh" campaign, 1552
Ulene, Art, 1331
Ullman, Tracey, 1242
"Un Testimonials" campaign. *See* "Special K Kick-Start Diet Plan" campaign
"Unbelievable" campaign (Dreyer's Grand Light), 467–470
"Unbelievable" campaign (JetBlue), 818–822
"Unclaimed Luggage" spot, 873
"Uncommon Wisdom" campaign, 1792–1795, 1802–1803
"Under the Cap 'Obey Your Thirst' Promotion," 346
Under the Influence (television show), 1660
Underhill, Rod, 1669
"Understanding Comes with *Time*" campaign, 1616
Underwear, 847–850
Underwood, Blair, 60, 61
"Undo" campaign, 250
"Unfulfilled Idealists" market, 1261, 1263, 1264
Unilever PLC, **1679–1686**
Unilever United States, **1687–1693**
Bally Total Fitness, partnership with, 1860
Procter & Gamble, as competitor of, 1396, 1402
Unions, 72–73
United Airlines Corp., **1695–1704**
Delta Air Lines, as competitor of, 412
Northwest Airlines, as competitor of, 1206–1207
Southwest Airlines, as competitor of, 1537
United Distillers and Vintners of North America, **1705–1708**
United Kingdom
"Cleaner Close" campaign, 1377–1379
Club 18-30 "Perspectives" campaign, 1607–1609
Honda "Grrr" campaign, 745–748
Honda "The Power of Dreams" campaign, 741–744
"Jeep" campaign, 391
McDonald's "Changes" campaign, 966
"Monsanto Image" campaign, 1035, 1037
Orange "Goldspot" campaign, 1233–1236
United Airlines "It's Time to Fly" campaign, 1697
Whiskas spot for cats, 934
United Media, 998
United Parcel Service, Inc., **1709–1716**, *1713*
DHL, as competitor of, 420–421
FedEx, as competitor of, 538–539, 545, 548–549
Kinko's, as competitor of, 542
United States Postal Service, as competitor of, 1719
United States Postal Service, **1717–1720**
FedEx, as competitor of, 538, 545, 549
United Parcel Service, as competitor of, 1710–1711, 1714
United States Tennis Association, **1721–1724**
United Telecommunications, 1544
United Way, 1100
UnitedHealth group, Inc., **1725–1728**
Universal Parks and Resorts, 1518–1519
University of Florida, 1286
Univision Radio, 65
Uniworld, 562
Unlaced (music CD), 460
"Unlike Any Other" campaign, 994–996
Unlimited Pizza, Little Caesar's, 897–899
Unsung Heroes Awards, 764
Untouchables, 461
"Unwind" spot, 1103
Urlacher, Brian, 1402
Uronis, Will, 646
U.S. Army, 1263
U.S. Department of Agriculture, 366
U.S. Department of Defense, 924
U.S. Department of Justice, 1005
U.S. Government
Bureau of Engraving and Printing "The New Color of Money" campaign, 215–218
Business Leaders for Sensible Priorities "Move Our Money" campaign, 229–232
U.S. House of Representatives, 1354
U.S. Marine Corps, 1263–1264
U.S. News & World Report, 1616
U.S. Soccer, 1275
U.S. Surgeon General, 98
"US Open Excitement" campaign, 1721–1724
Us Weekly, 1668–1669
USA Gymnastics, 1674
USA Network, 522
USA Today, 1134
USA Weekend, 1668
USPS. *See* United States Postal Service
Utton, Nicholas, 531
Uva, Joe, 1613
Uzzie, Don, 502, 503

V

V & S Vin & Sprit AB, **1729–1737**
V-Wear, 56
Vacuum cleaners
Dirt Devil "Darin'" campaign, 1433–1436
Dyson "Doesn't Lose Suction" campaign, 475–478
Vadervalk, Melanie, 299
Valdes Zacky and Associates Inc., 243
Vale, Michael, 48
Valentine McCormick, 1207–1208
Valkonen, Stefani, 1394

ValuJet, 43–44
Van Andel, Doug, 1642
Van Auken, Brad, 691, 694
Van der Merwe, Robert P., 844
Van Dyke, Dick, 482
Van Dyke, Paul, 1069, 1071
Van Eden, Steven, 343
Van Halen, 1172
Van Munching, Philip, 868
Van Pelt, Scott, 519
Van Wees, David, 760
Vanbiesbrouck, John, 576
Vandersnick, Roger, 1096
Vanessa, 1831, 1832, 1833
Vanilla Coke, 1284–1285
"Vanilla" spot, 1119, 1121
Vans, 1152
Vanzura, Liz, 645, 646
Vartan, Michael, 600
Vaseline Intensive Care, 1320
Vasquez, Gaddi, 1263
Vassiliadis, Billy, 874
Vaughan, Brian, 890
"Vaughn" spot, 847, 849
"Vegas Stories" campaign, 871–874
Vegetarian fare, 1811, 1817–1820
Veggie burgers, 1817–1820
Velasquez, Mario, 1425
Venables, Bell & Partners
  Barclays Global Investors "New School" campaign, 162–163
  Napster "It's Coming Back" campaign, 1085–1088
Venables, Paul, 1086, 1087
Vengaboys, 1519
Ventura, Tyrel, 1742
Ventura for Governor, **1739–1742**
Venturini, Tisha, 1156
Venus, 1478–1479
Verástegui, Eduardo, 1261, 1262
Verbinki, Gore, 1847
Verdi, Ellis, 76
Vergrugge, Moe, 1083
Verizon
  "Can You Hear Me Now?" campaign, 297–300, *298*
  Nextel, as competitor of, 1551–1552
  Sprint PCS, as competitor of, 1555
  T-Mobile, as competitor of, 1624–1625
"Vern" spot, 1819
Versace, Gianni, 1736
Vertigo (song), 137, 138
"A Very Healthy Way to Shop" campaign, 471–474
"Very real power" tagline, 341
Vescovo, Matt, 225, 735, 1077, 1078–1080
"Vespa Reintroduction" campaign, 1337–1340
Veterinary Medicine Advisory Committee (VMAC), 1036
VF Corporation, 909, **1743–1751**
Viacom, 238
"Viagra Launch" campaign, 1325–1328
Viant Corp., 502
Vick, Edward H., 153
Vick, Michael, 341
Victorinox, 1587, 1588, 1590
Victory Motorcycles "The New American Motorcycle" campaign, 1349–1352, *1350*
Video games
  ESPN NFL 2K5 "Beta-7" campaign, 1497–1500
  Sony PlayStation 2 "Fun, Anyone?" campaign, 1523–1526
  Xbox "It's Good to Play Together" campaign, 1001–1004
Video stores, 733–736
Videotape, 589
"Videotape" spot, 1457, 1459
Viesturs, Ed, 1043
Vietnam Veterans for a Just Peace, 1584
Vietnam War, 1075, 1583–1585
Viewpoint Studios, 1339
Vigoro, 1484–1485
Village Voice LLC, **1753–1756**
Villante, Christina, 1322
"Vincent Murphy" campaign, 428
Vino Classic, 1339
Vioxx, 667
Viral Awards
  Burger King "Subservient Chicken" campaign, 225
  MTV "Watch and Learn" campaign, 1080
Viral marketing
  Budget Rent a Car "Up Your Budget" campaign, 211–214
  Burger King "Subservient Chicken" campaign, 222–225
  MINI Cooper "MINI Robots" campaign, 172–175
  Suburban Auto Group "Trunk Monkey" campaign, 1582
Virgin Atlantic Airways Limited, **1757–1760**
Virgin Mobile Telecoms, 1235
Virgin Records, 380
"Virginia Is for Lovers" campaign, 1761, 1762
Virginia Military Institute (VMI), 1191–1192
Virginia Slims cigarettes, 55–58
Virginia Tourism Corporation, 1202, **1761–1764**
Virginia Victims of Crime Act, 659
"Virtual Reality" spot, 81–82, 82
"Virus" spot, 790, 791
Visa U.S.A., Inc., **1765–1772**
  American Express, as competitor of, 84, 88, 89
  American Express "Competitive" campaign, 79–82
  Discover, as competitor of, 1051–1052, 1054–1055
  MasterCard, as competitor of, 950–951
  Yahoo!, partnership with, 1853
"Visit Planet Earth" campaign, 1653
"The Visit" spot, 811, 814
Vitale, Dick, 865
Vitamins, 1329–1332
Vitech America, 1826
Vitolo, Danny, 663
VIVUS, Inc., 1326
VMAC. *See* Veterinary Medicine Advisory Committee (VMAC)
VMI. *See* Virginia Military Institute (VMI)
Vodafone, 1234–1235
Vodka
  "Absolut Director" campaign, 1729–1733
  "Absolut Print" campaign, 1733–1737
  Johnnie Walker "Keep Walking" campaign, 423–426
  Stolichnaya "Russian Art" campaign, 1705–1708
Vogel, François, 723, 726
Vogel, Mark, 1143
Voice-overs. *See* Celebrity voice-overs
"Voicebox Smoker" spot, 246
VoiceStream, 1623–1624
Voit, Fred, 156, 976, 978
Volan, Dawn, 1768
Volcov, Serguei, 1707
Volkswagen of America, Inc., **1773–1787**
  Audi, as competitor of, 158–159
  Golf, *1777*
  Honda, as competitor of, 94
  MINI Cooper, as competitor of, 170–171, 173–174
  New Beetle, 1020
  Nissan, as competitor of, 1169
  Saturn, as competitor of, 1471

Volkwein, Ed, 1333, 1334, 1336
Volunteerism
  National and Community Service Trust Act, 1426
  Peace Corps "Life Is Calling. How Far Will You Go?" campaign, 1261–1265
Von Bismarck, Otto, 109
Vonckx, Ginny, 855, 857
Vonk, Nancy, 1607, 1609
Vonnegut, Kurt, 1055
VOOM, 448
Voting, 1120, 1425–1428

W

W. B. Doner & Company
  Serta "Counting Sheep" campaign, 1501–1503
  Six Flags "It's Playtime" campaign, 1517–1520
"W-2—Tax Day 5" spot, 689
Waalkes, Jeff, 1019
Wachovia Corporation, **1789–1795**, 1802–1803
Wacker, Watts, 1132
Wagner, Lindsay, 1502
Waitkus, Diane, 1430, 1431
"Waitresses" spot, 247
Waitt, Ted, 609–612
"Wake Up and Drive" campaign, 1031–1034
"Wake-Up Call" spot, 572
Wal-Mart
  Amazon.com, as competitor of, 61
  Discover, partnership with, 1053
  J.C. Penney, as competitor of, 809
  Kmart, as competitor of, 852, 855–856
  Sears, as competitor of, 1493–1494
  Target, as competitor of, 1601, 1604
Walchli, Suzanne, 440
Waldenbooks, 197
Walgreen, Charles R., Sr., 1797
Walgreen Company, **1797–1800**
  CVS, as competitor of, 376–377
  drugstore.com, as competitor of, 472–473
Walgreens Health Corner (television show), 1798
Walker, Alice, 1155
Walker, Herschel, 338
Walker, Jay, 1369
Walker, Jim, 1803
Walker, Joan, 154, 155
Walkie-talkie service, 1551
Wall, Chris, 786, 794, 1068
Wallace, Rusty, 149
Wallace, William, 109
Wallboards
  Kellogg "Special K Kick-Start Diet Plan" campaign, 834
  "Special K Kick-Start Diet Plan" campaign, 836
Waller, Peter, 1594, 1597
Wallflowers, 560
Walsh, John, 517
Walsh, John C., 1732
Walt Disney Company
  ESPN, acquisition of, 514
  McDonald's tie-ins, 959
  Six Flags, as competitor of, 1518
Walter, Tiffany, 56
Walter P. Chrysler Museum, 393
Walters, Brian, 177
Walters, John P., 1218
Walton, Jim, 515
"Wanna Get Away?" campaign, 1702–1703
"Wannabe" spot, 431, 433
"Want Some?" campaign, 1592, *1594*, 1594–1597
Warbreeds (computer game), 382
Ward, Edward, 614, 615, 618
Warhol, Andy, 1730, 1733–1737
Warner, William R., 1320
Warner Brothers cartoons, 1612, 1613
Warner-Lambert. *See* Pfizer Inc.
"Warning" spot, 1061
Warschauer, Bonnie, 840
Wasch, Ken, 1005
Washing machines, 476
Washington, Denzel, 275
Washington Monument, 1604
Washington Mutual, Inc., **1801–1804**
Washington Redskins, 545
Wasiak, Greg, 1–2
Wasserman, Gail, 1054
Watches
  Rolex "Celebrity Endorsement" campaign, 1043–1046
  "Swiss Army Equipped" campaign, 1589
Waterfield, Phebe, 324
Waters, Maxine, 1155
Waters, Robyn, 606
Watersmeet High school Nimrods, 522, 523
Watkins, James, 225
Watson, Thomas, 787
Wattles, Mark J., 733, 734, 735
"The Way the World Works" campaign, 547–550
WCRS Group, 1234
WE, 1243
"We Got the Crunch" campaign, 317
"We Gotta Get Out of This Place" spot, 1369, 1372
"We Love to See You Smile" campaign, 967–970
"We Love TV" campaign, 5
"We Take the World's Greatest Pictures. Yours" tagline, 1163, 1164
We Will Rock You (song), 599
"Wear a Moustache" campaign, 181–182
"The Weasel" spot, 707
The Weather Channel Companies, 68, **1805–1808**
Weaver, Jill, 52
Weaver, Sigourney, 107, 823
"Web Jam" spot, 790
Web portals, 1849–1853, 1854–1857
Webb, David F., 1685
Webber, Chris, 1267, 1269
Webber, Wallace, 1675
Weber, Bruce, 9, 10
Weber, Ron, 1194
Webisodes, 812
Weblogs. *See* Blogs
Wedding anniversaries, 445
Wedding gift registry, 534
"Wedding Rock" spot, 761
"Wedding" spot (Diet Pepsi), 1305
"Wedding" spot (MetLife), 1000
"Wedding" spot (Nextel), 1552
Weedfald, Peter, 1070
Weight loss
  Fogle, Jared, 455–458
  Jenny Craig "Kirstie Alley" campaign, 815–818
  Kellogg "Special K Kick-Start Diet Plan" campaign, 834–837
Weight Watchers, 816–817, 1040
Weigman, Tom, 1548
Weinstein, Alice, 159
Weinstein, Jerry, 1464
Weinstein, Mike, 1655, 1657, 1658
Weisbaum, Herb, 1385
Weiss, Albert, 985, 989–990
Weist, David, 1774
Weitzen, Jeffrey, 609, 610, 611
Wek, Alek, 597
Welch, John F. "Jack," 623–624
"Welcome Aboard" spot, 543
"Welcome to the State of Independence" spots, 1447
"Welcome to the World Wide Wow" campaign, 66–69

"We'll leave the light on for you" tagline, 778, 782
Wellington, Bruce, 1406
Wells, Mary, 1011
Wells Rich Greene, 333–336, 1011
Wellstone, Paul, 1739
Wendel, Hal, 1354
Wendy the Snapple Lady, 237, 259
Wendy's International, Inc., **1809–1816,** *1813*
  Burger King, as competitor of, 220–221, 224
  McDonald's, as competitor of, 962, 965, 969
Wenger, 1588–1589
Werme, Judith, 334, 335
Werner, Helmut, 985
Westbrook, Bill, 779, 1405, 1407
Westerman, Mark, 553
Western wear, 1749–1751
Westheimer, Dr. Ruth, 335, 1393
"Whassup?!" campaign, 126–130, *127*
"What a Ride" campaign, 1252–1256, *1253, 1254*
"What About Now?" campaign, 91–95, *92, 93*
"What Can Brown Do for You?" campaign, 1713–1716
"What Cats Want" tagline, 936
"What Do We Have Here?" campaign, 1023–1024
"What happens here, stays here." tagline, 871, 873
"What If?" campaign, 24
"What If We Treated All Athletes the Way We Treat Skateboarders?" campaign, 1150–1154
"What Matters Most" campaign, 779
"What You Need. What You Need to Know." campaign, 1213–1216
"What's in Your Wallet?" campaign, 327
"What's my thirst?" tagline, 347, 348
"What's Next?" campaign, 1531–1534
"What's Your Priority?" campaign, 1718
"What's Your Story?" contest, 239
"What's Your Thing?" campaign, 1221–1224
"Wheat-surfer" spot, 1461, 1463, 1464
"When I Grow Up" campaign, 1039, 1040
When the Day Breaks (short film), 1696
"When You Are as Old as the Hills" ad, 361
"When you cook, you're a family" tagline, 1689
"When You Have It Your Way, It Just Tastes Better" campaign, 225–228
"When You're Strong, You Sparkle" campaign, 1401–1403
"Where Do You Want to Go Today?" campaign, 1004–1007
"Where's the Beef?" campaign, 1810
"Where's Your Mustache?" campaign, 183
Whiskas "Inner Beast" campaign, 934–937
Whitacer, Jack, 1187
White, Reggie, 1149
White, Rob, 1024
White, Steve, 421
White & Baldacci, 1761–1763
White House Office of National Drug Control Policy, **1217–1219**
Whittaker, Forrest, 175
"Whizzy Website" spot, 790, 791
Wholesome & Hearty Foods Company, **1817–1820**
Whopper, 226
"Why" campaign, 331
"Why Didn't Anyone Think of This Before?" campaign, 1468–1472, *1470*
"Why Wouldn't You?" campaign, 528–531
Wiborg, Jack, 328
Wide Leg jeans, 883–886
Wieden, Dan, 1145, 1149
Wieden+Kennedy
  Diet Coke campaign, 356
  ESPN NFL 2K5 "Beta-7" campaign, 1497–1500
  ESPN "This Is SportsCenter" campaign, 515, 517–520
  ESPN "Without Sports" campaign, 520–523
  Foster's account, 573
  Microsoft "Where Do You Want to Go Today?" campaign, 1005–1007
  Miller Brewing Company campaigns, 110–111, 117–118
  "Miller High Life" campaign, 1452–1455
  "Miller High Life Man" campaign, 1017–1021
  Nike "Hello World" and "I Am Tiger Woods" campaigns, 1134–1138
  Nike "Meet the LeBrons" campaign, 1138–1141
  Nike "Move" campaign, 1141–1144
  Nike "9,000 Shots" campaign, 1131–1134
  Nike "Play" campaign, 1145–1147
  Nike "Product Assault" campaign, 1147–1150
  Nike "Women's" campaign, 1154–1157
  OK soda campaign, 345
  PowerAde "Very Real Power" campaign, 341, 343
  Round Table Pizza campaign, 1429, 1432
  Sharp "More to See" campaign, 1506–1508
Wieden+Kennedy London
  Honda "Grrr" campaign, 745–748
  Honda "The Power of Dreams" campaign, 741–744
Wiese, Nancy, 1844, 1846
Wilcoxon, Cleve, 1094
Wild, Scott, 28
Wild Cherry, 769, 771
The Wild One (film), 1350
"Wild things are happening" campaign, 155
Wilderness survival, 1238
Wilinsky, Dan, 1554
Wilke, Mike, 829
Wm. Wrigley Jr. Company, **1821–1834**
William Grant & Sons Ltd., **683–686**
William Morris Agency, 216–217
Williams, Brad, 889
Williams, Christopher, 795, 796, 1003
Williams, Clay, 511, 1595, 1596
Williams, Hank, 1295, 1298
Williams, Jeff, 1454
Williams, Michael, 140
Williams, Scott, 1221
Williams, Serena, 24, 1815
Williams, Todd, 22
Williams, Venus, 1146, 1815
Williamson, Jeff, 1486
Williamson, Randy, 191
Willis, Bruce
  Armageddon (film), 633, 1590
  The Fifth Element, 1446
  Lipton Brisk "That's Brisk, Baby!" campaign, 1298, 1301
Wilsdorf, Hans, 1043
Wilson, Hank, 607
Wilson, John, 1410
Wilson, Jon, 836
Wilson, Kemmons, 777–778
Wilson, Nancy, 1178
Wilson, Pete, 244
Wilson, Tom, 1259, 1260
WIN Award. *See* Women's Image Network (WIN) Ad Award

"Win Shoes for Life" contest, 1182
Window Writers, 187–188
Windows, 796
Windy Awards, 1492
Winfrey, Oprah, *1242*
  "Live Your Best Life" tour, 241, 1645
  Oxygen Media, 1241, 1243
Wingate Inn, 929
"Wings" spot, 387, 388
"Wingtips" spot, 397
Winn, Anne, 929
Winner, Michael, 1235
Winston, Stan, 224
Winston Cup, 1094
Winter, Bob, 126
Winterton, Bruce, 1018, 1020
Wireless services
  "Nextel. Done." campaign, 1550–1553
  Orange "Goldspot" campaign, 1233–1236
  "Sprint PCS" campaign, 1553–1556
  T-Mobile "Get More" campaign, 1623–1626
  Verizon Wireless "Can You Hear Me Now?" campaign, 297–300
  See also Mobile phones
Wisconsin dairy industry, 255
Wisely, Robert, 813
Wish Book catalog, 1489
Wisk "Do It Once. Do It Right." campaign, 1683–1686
"Without Sports" campaign, 520–523
"Witness Protection Program" spot, 572
Wladawsky-Berger, Irving, 789, 791
Wm. Wrigley Jr. Company, 234
WNBA. *See* Women's National Basketball Association (WNBA)
"Wobbler" spot, 1479
Wolf, Darin, 869, 870
Wolf Group
  Dirt Devil "Darin" campaign, 1433–1436
  Meldrum & Fewsmith, acquisition of, 1439
  Scotts Miracle-Gro "Neighbor to Neighbor" campaign, 1481–1486
Wolfe, Sidney, 1211
Wolfe, Thomas, 1201
Wolzien, Tom, 69, 734
"Woman on Pillow" ad, 323
"Woman" spot, 996
Woman Thing Music, 57–58
Women
  Anheuser-Busch sponsorship of women's professional sports, 108
  Body Shop "Ruby" campaign, 191–194
  brand popularity among, 955
  "Come See the Softer Side of Sears" campaign, 1488, 1489–1490
  CVS makeover, 376
  Dial "You're Not As Clean As You Think" campaign, 436, 437
  Diamond Trading Company "Raise Your Right Hand" campaign, 443–446
  Dove "Campaign for Real Beauty" campaign, 1680
  drugstore.com "A Very Healthy Way to Shop" campaign, 471, 472
  Estates of World Golf Village "Repositioning" campaign, 400
  Fuji Photo Film "Meet the Greens" campaign, 588
  General Foods International Coffees "It's How to Unplug" campaign, 860
  Kodak "The Best Part of Photography Is the Prints" campaign, 483
  La-Z-Boy "The New Look of Comfort" campaign, 876
  Nature Made "Trusted By the Ones You Trust" campaign, 1330–1331
  New Balance "Thunderstorm, Stairs" campaigns, 1123–1125
  Nike, accusations of exploitation by, 1155
  Nike "Women's" campaign, 1154–1157
  Novartis Zelnorm "Tummies" campaign, 1210
  Office Depot store interiors, 1214, 1216
  Olympics advertisements, 107
  Samuel Adams "It's What's Inside" campaign, 200–201
  Schick Intuition "Shaving Made Simple" campaign, 1477–1480
  "Sears. Where Else?" campaign, 1492, 1493
  Serta "Counting Sheep" campaign, 1502
  Song Airlines "Let Yourself Fly" campaign, 408
  "Special K Kick-Start Diet Plan" campaign, 834–837
  Tampax Pearl "Ingenious Protection for Ingenious Women" campaign, 1385–1388
  Virginia Slims advertising, 55–58
"Women's" campaign, Nike, 1154–1157
Women's Image Network (WIN) Ad Award, 1274, 1276
Women's National Basketball Association (WNBA), 1259
Women's NCAA basketball tournament, 200–201
WongDoody, 165–168
Woo, John, 178, 995
Wood, Ben, 1067
Wood, Elijah, 1003
Wood, Mary, 585
Wood, Michael, 580
Wood, Mike, 879, 955
Wood, Robert E., II, 1054
Woodall, Rob, 441
Woodard, Thad, 1342
Woodbine Agency, 1341–1344
Woods, Tiger, *1135*
  Accenture, Ltd., 18
  American Express "Do More" campaign, 82, 83, 84, 85, 87–88, 951
  annual endorsement income, 552
  endorsements, 553
  ESPN "This Is SportsCenter" campaign, 520
  Lincoln Financial Battle at the Bridges, 894
  Nike campaign, 71, 565, 566, 567, 1145
  Nike "Hello World" and "I Am Tiger Woods" campaigns, 1134–1138
  Rolex "Celebrity Endorsement" campaign, 1043, 1044, 1045–1046
"Woof" spot, 1228
Woolery, Chuck, 1689
"The Woolerys" spot, 1689
Woolman, C. E., 411
Word-of-mouth marketing, 192
"Work Effectiveness" campaign, 1575–1578
Working Assets Long Distance, 1835–1838
"Works Like a Check" campaign, 951, 1769–1772
World Cup Soccer Team, Women's, 1156
World Cup soccer tournament
  Dr. Martens tie in, 459, 461
  Saab "Life Is Not a Spectator Sport" campaign, 1445, 1447
World Financial Center, 86
World Golf Village "Repositioning" campaign, 399–402

"A World of Energy" campaign, 305–309
"The World On Time" tagline, 548
World Series
Anheuser-Busch ""Spuds McKenzie" campaign, 113
Brigham's "Reverse the Curse" campaign, 207–210
John Hancock "Insurance for the Unexpected. Investments for the Opportunities" campaign (2000), 828
Pepsi/Major League Baseball alliance, 1279
World Trade Center, 304
World Trade Organization (WTO), 490
World War II
The Advertising Council, 32
Cunard Line Limited, 372
Jeep, 389–390, 392
World Wrestling Federation, 1427
WorldCom, 1545
"The World's Most Interesting Magazine" campaign, 1615–1617
"Worried About Bill" campaign, 687–690
Worthington Foods, 1818–1819
WPP Group, 555, 557
Wrangler, Jeep, 389–392, 393, 646
"Wrangler Anglers" program, 1751
Wrangler (clothes)
Levi's jeans, as competitor of, 887
"Rugged Wear" campaign, 1749–1751
Wrapping paper, 195, 196, 197
Wreaks, Bill, 1049
"Wrestler" spot (PowerAde), 343
"Wrestlers" spot (Dial-a-Mattress), 431
Wright, Frank Lloyd, 144
Wrigley, William, Jr., 1828, 1831
"Write Out Loud" campaign, 1457–1459
"Wrong" spot, 546
Wunderman, 955
Wyeth, **1839–1842**
Wynant, Wilbur, 895
Wynne, Angus, 1517
Wynne, John O. "Dubby," 1806
Wynne, Steve, 20
Wyville, Jon, 1095

X

X Games
adidas sponsorship, 1153
Mountain Dew "Code Red" campaign, 1269
Mountain Dew "Do the Dew" campaign, 1270
Mountain Dew sponsorship, 465, 1270, 1273
Nike "Skateboarders" campaign, 1153
Time "The World's Most Interesting Magazine" campaign, 1615
Xbox
"It's Good to Play Together" campaign, 1001–1004
Taco bell tie-ins, 1593
Xerox Corporation, 718, **1843–1848**
XM radio, 637

Y

Yahoo! Big Idea Chair Awards
Burger King "Subservient Chicken" campaign, 225
ESPN NFL 2K5 "Beta-7" campaign, 1499
Pabst "Remember Rainier" campaign, 1248
Yahoo! Inc., **1849–1857**
adidas search term, 26
eBay, as competitor of, 494
Lycos, as competitor of, 917
Musicmatch, 1087
Nissan, partnership with, 1169
Yamaha, 1338–1339
Yang, Jerry, 1849, 1850, 1852, 1854
"Yankee Fans" campaign, 26–29
Yao Ming, 24, 1771, 1815
Yapp, Jeff, 733
Yarborough, Cale, 1094
"Yard Fitness Center" campaign, 1859–1862
"Yard Sale" spot, 239
Yard Strength, Inc., **1859–1862**
Yaris, Toyota, 1168–1169
Yates, Liam, 137
"Yeah, We've Got That" campaign, 1567–1569
Yearwood, Trisha, 1055
Yellowcard, 560
"Yes/No Ballot Box" campaign, 1425–1428
"YMCA" spot, 1277
"Yo Quiero Taco Bell" campaign. *See* "Want Some?" campaign
Yokum, Dwight, 601
York, John, 1250
Yorn, Pete, 560
Yost, John, 1057
"You + HP" campaign, 405, 723–727
"You Are What You Drink" campaign, 353–357
"You Can Trust Your Car to the Man Who Wears the Star" campaign, 306
"You Know You Know" campaign, 591–594
"You" spot, 726
Young, Donald, 642
Young & Laramore, 1557–1561
Young & Rubicam
Accenture "I Am Your Idea" campaign, 15–18
Advil "Liqui-Ges" campaign, 1839–1842
AT&T "Carrot Top" campaign, 147–150
AT&T "It's All Within Your Reach" campaign, 152–153
Citibank campaign, 330
"Come See the Softer Side of Sears" campaign, 1487
Dr Pepper "This Is the Taste" campaign, 463–466
Fisher-Price "Play. Laugh. Grow." campaign, 953–956
Fisher-Price PowerTouch "Play. Laugh. Grow." campaign, 881
General Foods International Coffees ""It's How to Unplug" campaign, 859–862
H&R Block, "Worried About Bill" campaign, 687–690
"Jingle for Goldfish" campaign, 266
"MetLife Helps You Make Sense of It All" campaign, 997–1000
NASCAR "How Bad Have You Got It?" campaign, 1093–1097
National Football League campaign, 1095
Network Walkman campaign, 137
"NFL Playoffs" campaign, 1099–1102
"Sears. Where Else?" campaign, 1491–1495
Seven Up campaign, 348
United Airlines "Rising" campaign, 1700
Xerox "Keep the Conversation Going, Share the Knowledge" campaign, 1843–1847
"Young Voyagers" spot, 1012
Younger, Ben, 177
"Your Airline Has Arrived" campaign, 43, 44
Your Cheatin' Heart (song), 1295, 1298
"Your Link to Better Communication" tag line, 154
"You're in Good Hands" campaign, 51
"You're Not As Clean As You Think" campaign, 435–438
"You're Virtually There" ad, 1207–1208

YourStyle weight management program, 816–817
Youth market
- Abercrombie & Fitch, 9–12
- "Antitobacco" campaign, 245–246
- Dr. Martens Airwair "Beliefs" campaign, 459–462
- "Jenny McCarthy for Candie's" campaign, 751
- Lee jeans "Cut to Be Noticed" campaign, 1744
- Lee jeans "Find Your One True Fit" campaign, 1746–1747
- Levi's "It's Wide Open" campaign, 883–886
- "malternatives," 1014
- Nordstrom campaign, 1186
- Office of National Drug Control Policy "Early Intervention Youth" campaign, 1217–1219
- Polaroid "I-Zone/Joycam/Sticky Film Teen" campaign, 1357–1360
- Rock the Vote "Yes/No Ballot Box" campaign, 1426
- Secret Sparkle "When You're Strong, You Sparkle" campaign, 1401
- smoking, 56
- "Truth" campaign, 97–100

"Youth Vote 2000" campaign, 1426–1427
"You've Come a Long Way, Baby" campaign, 55–56
Yuen, Henry, 1668

Z

Z3 roadster, 986
Z4 roadster, 175, *176,* 177
Zambow, 1376
Zander, Ed, 1067
Zandl, Irma, 756
Zantac, 1324
ZapMail, 538
Zappacosta, Pierluigi, 911
Zappos.com, 1182
"Zebra" spot, 936
Zelnorm "Tummies" campaign, 1209–1212
Zero Gravity Corporation, 240, 242
Zeta-Jones, Catherine, 1623–1626
Zima, 1014, 1016
Zimmerman, Chris
- Nike "9000 Shots" campaign, 1134
- Nike "Product Assault" campaign, 1147, 1148, 1149, 1150
- Nike target markets, 1135

Zimmerman, Eric, 1061
"Zipper" spot, 950, 951
Zoic Studios, 174
Zoloft
- Paxil, as competitor of, 666
- Prozac, as competitor of, 507

Zoom LeBron basketball shoe, 1138–1140
Zubi Advertising, 562, 1793–1794
Zyban, 663
Zyman, Sergio
- on the Gap campaign, 608
- "Obey Your Thirst" campaign, 344, 345
- "You Are What You Drink" campaign, 354, 356, 357

Zyman Group, 196